MW01255821

The Celebrity Black Book 2019: Over 56,000+ Verified Celebrity Addresses for Autographs & Memorabilia, Nonprofit Fundraising, Celebrity Endorsements, Free Publicity, PR/Public Relations, Small Business Sales/Marketing & More!

Contact Any Celebrity
8721 Santa Monica Boulevard, #431
West Hollywood, CA 90069-4507
310-691-5466 (Phone) | 310-388-6084 (Fax)
ContactAnyCelebrity.com
support@contactanycelebrity.com

Printed in the United States of America.

All addresses verified by the U.S. Postal Service NCOA (National Change of Address) System.

Please visit ContactAnyCelebrity.com for more information on our products and services.

ISBN-16: 978-1-60487-017-6

Library of Congress Control Number: 2004115012

Edited by Jordan McAuley, Founder – ContactAnyCelebrity.com
Cover Design by Matt Burkhalter – MattBurkhalter.com
Directory Design by Data Management, Inc. – DBMan.com

STAY UP-TO-DATE:
FREE 30-DAY TEST DRIVE!

Get Celebrity Address Updates, Free Research Requests,
Postage Refunds, Insider Expert Webinars & More
FREE For 30 Days Using This Activation Link:

ContactAnyCelebrity.com/activate

ALSO BY THE AUTHOR:

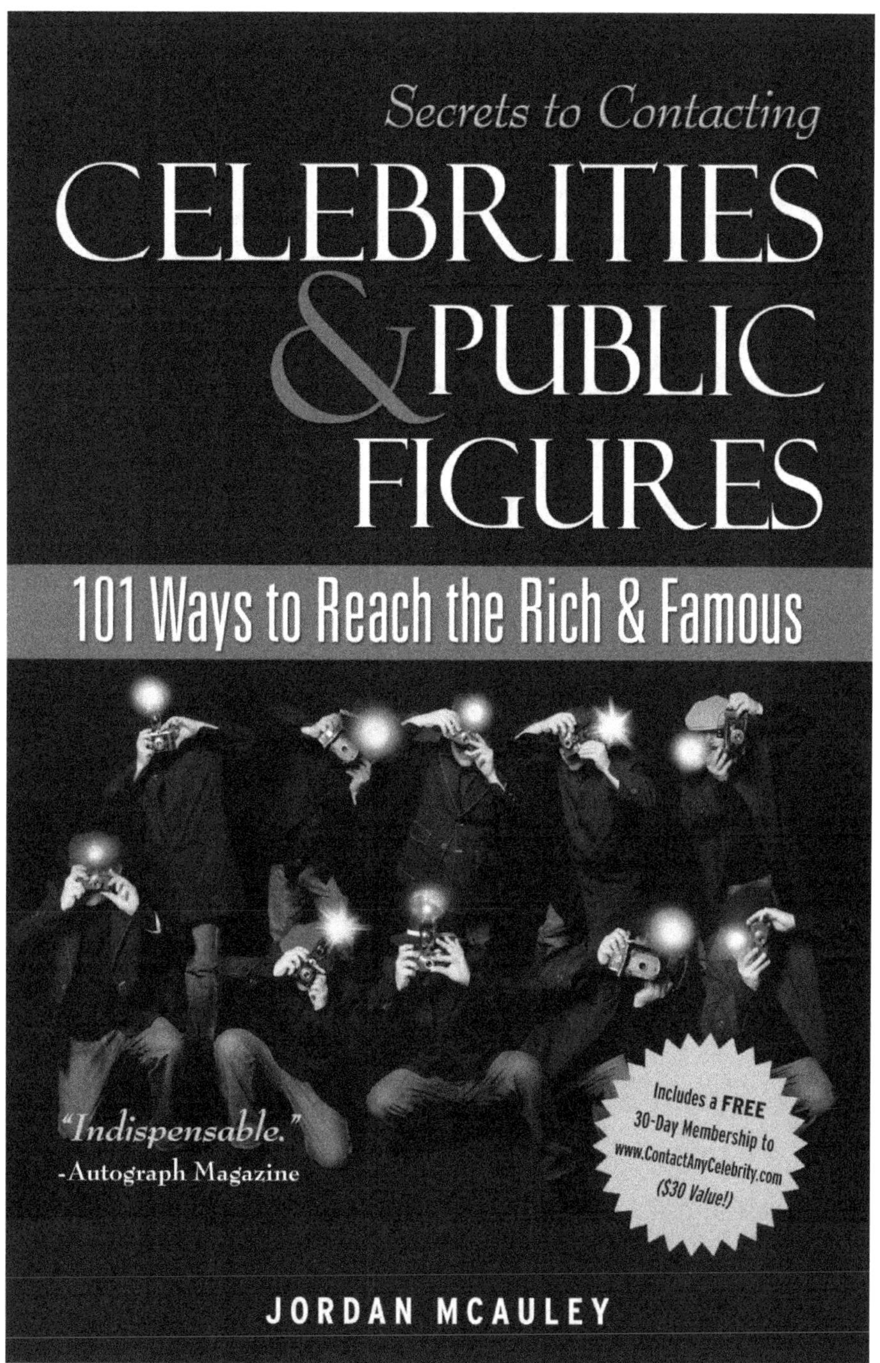

Secrets to Contacting Celebrities:
101 Ways to Reach the Rich & Famous

Available on Amazon.com

ALSO BY THE AUTHOR:

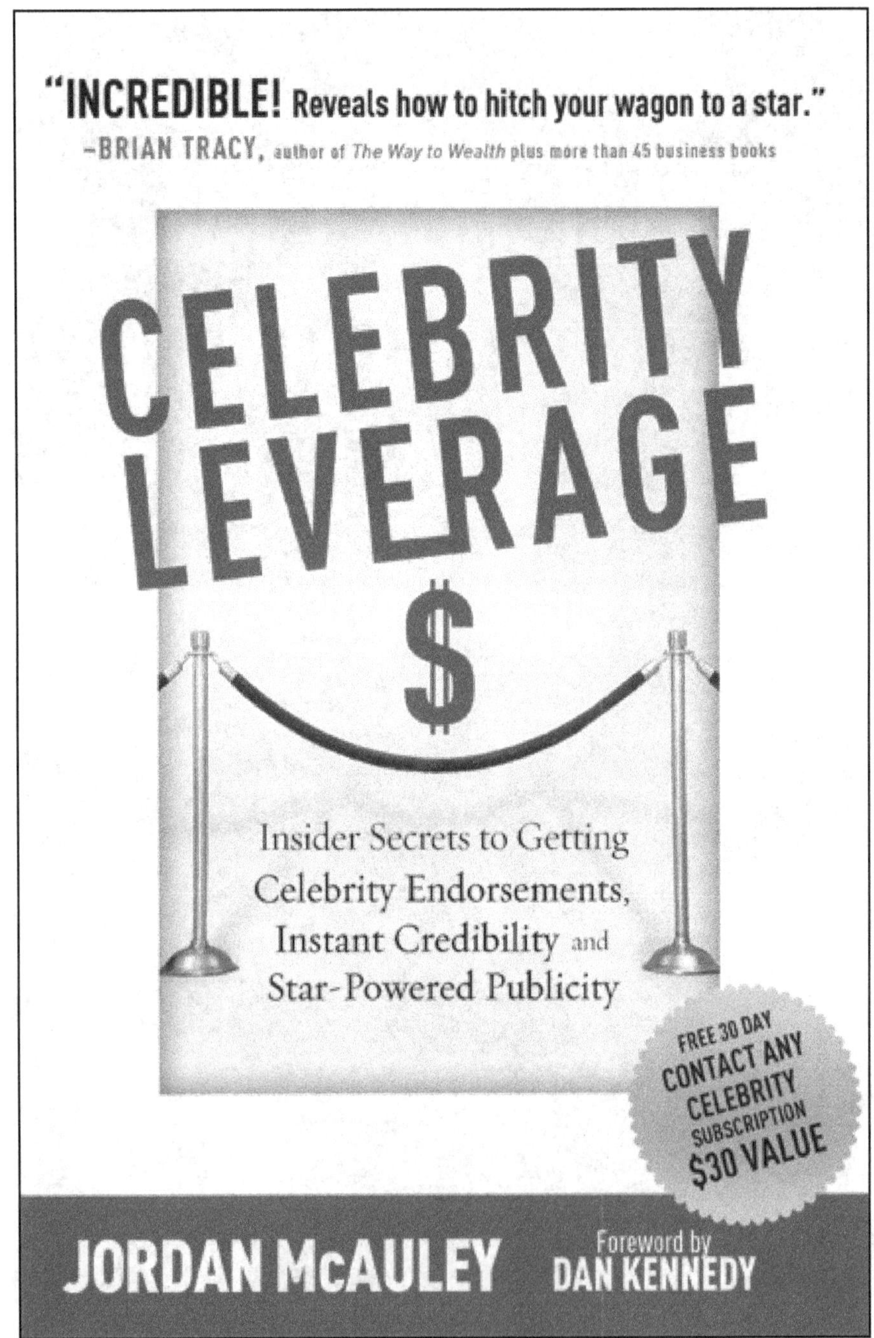

Celebrity Leverage:
Insider Secrets to Getting Celebrity Endorsements,
Instant Credibility & Star-Powered Publicity

Available on Amazon.com

ALSO BY THE AUTHOR:

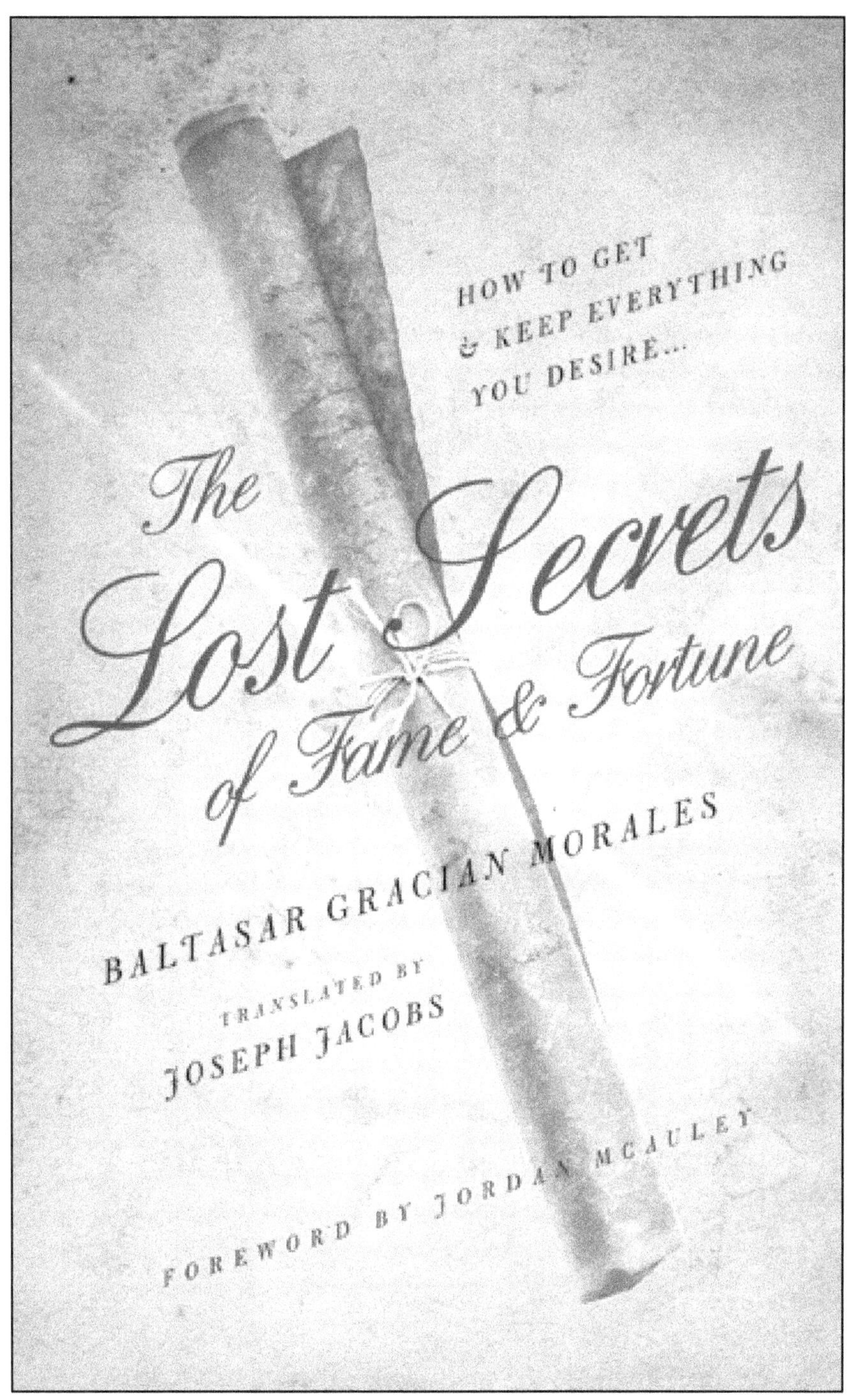

The Lost Secrets of Fame & Fortune:
How to Get – And Keep – Everything You Desire!

Available on Amazon.com

Additional Resources

Books:

(Available as free downloads when you join ContactAnyCelebrity.com or on Amazon.com).

Celebrity Leverage: Insider Secrets to Getting Celebrity Endorsements by Jordan McAuley

Secrets to Contacting Celebrities: 101 Ways to Reach the Rich & Famous by Jordan McAuley

The Lost Secrets of Fame & Fortune by Baltasar Gracian Morales & Jordan McAuley

Services:

Contact Any Celebrity - ContactAnyCelebrity.com

Get the best mailing address, agent, manager, publicist, and production company for over 59,000+ celebrities, influencers & public figures with phone, fax and email addresses.

The National Publicity Summit – CelebrityPRSummit.com

Get big-time publicity for your business, book, product, cause or yourself! Meet national TV producers and print/online editors one-on-one, face-to-face. Spaces are limited. Apply now!

STAY UP-TO-DATE:
FREE 30-DAY TEST DRIVE!

Get Celebrity Address Updates, Free Research Requests,
Postage Refunds, Insider Expert Webinars & More
FREE For 30 Days Using This Activation Link:

ContactAnyCelebrity.com/activate

About The Editor

"Contact Any Celebrity can help you get in contact with someone you've always dreamed of. This online directory and its helpful staff will help you find any celebrity in the world."
- Tim Ferriss, #1 New York Times Bestselling Author, The 4-Hour Workweek

Jordan McAuley is the founder of ContactAnyCelebrity.com, an online service that helps fans, authors, businesses, the media, and nonprofits contact 59,000+ celebrities, influencers, and public figures worldwide.

He is the editor of the best-selling annual directory, *The Celebrity Black Book*, and the author of *Secrets to Contacting Celebrities: 101 Ways to Reach the Rich & Famous* plus *Celebrity Leverage: Insider Secrets to Getting Celebrity Endorsements, Instant Credibility, and Star-Powered Publicity*.

Jordan's books and services have been featured by ABC News, American Express OPEN, The Associated Press, CBS News, CNN, E! News, Entrepreneur Magazine, Forbes, Fox News, Investor's Business Daily, New York Daily News, Out Magazine, Publisher's Weekly, Sirius/XM Satellite Radio, The 4-Hour Workweek, The Guardian UK, Tim Ferriss, USA Today and more.

McAuley got his start as an intern in the public relations departments of CNN and Turner Entertainment. He later worked at a prominent modeling agency in Miami Beach; a film production company in Hollywood, and a top talent agency in Beverly Hills before founding ContactAnyCelebrity.com.

Contact Any Celebrity is recommended in several best-selling books including Tim Ferris's *The 4-Hour Workweek*, Dan Kennedy's *No B.S. Marketing to the Affluent*, Dan Poynter's *Publishing Encyclopedia*, John Kremer's *1001 Ways to Market Your Books*, Robin Blakely's *Get PR Therapy*, and Tsufit's *Step Into the Spotlight: A Guide to Getting Noticed*.

Jordan is a member of the Association of Fundraising Professionals (AFP), the Independent Book Publishers Association (IBPA), the Information Marketing Association (IMA), the GLAAD Media Circle, the Public Relations Society of America (PRSA) and The Trevor Project Game Changers.

Look What People Are Saying...

"The range is amazing – this thing is huge!"
- *CNN*

"Similar titles do not boast as many entries. If your library needs a current celebrity address book, this would be good. Recommended for all libraries."
- *Library Journal*

"Many small businesses, publicists, and marketers want to get their products into celebrities' hands. This book is the solution."
- *Entrepreneur Magazine*

"Of all the resources for celebrity addresses, this book is far and away the most useful. It is essential for any serious autograph collector. Indispensable!"
- *Autograph Magazine*

"A superb, quick and easy-to-use reference for entertainment professionals and fans alike."
- *Midwest Book Review*

"This guide offers priceless information that would otherwise take hours to research. Owning this book is like cutting six degrees of separation down to one simple degree."
- *Curled Up With A Good Book*

"The time saved by already having the celebrity's contact information rather than Googling and cold-calling will certainly pay for this book in the long run."
- *Absolute Write*

"Some of the best money you'll ever spend. This book is an excellent value and provides you (and me) with great publicity opportunities."
- *Paul Hartunian, Free Publicity Information Center*

"The most helpful book I have ever owned. Worth every penny."
- *Jill Jackson, Syndicated Columnist, Jill Jackson's Hollywood*

"If you opt to pursue a celebrity or celebrities on your own or to use in your advertising, or to get a 'blurb' from for your book, this is the place to get contact information."
- *Dan Kennedy, No B.S. Guide to Marketing to the Affluent*

*** Visit ContactAnyCelebrity.com for more testimonials and success stories!**

Introduction

Welcome to the Celebrity Black Book 2019!

Whether you're a fan/autograph seeker, fundraiser/nonprofit, author/publisher, journalist/media or marketer/small business, you're bound to find this book useful. Inside you'll discover mailing addresses for over 56,000+ celebrities, influencers and public figures worldwide.

All of these celebrity addresses were verified by ContactAnyCelebrity.com and the U.S. Postal Service's NCOA (National Change of Address) System in January, 2019.

Everyone who is anyone inside: actors, athletes, musicians, politicians, world leaders, authors, reality TV stars and more. The list goes on and on as you'll see once you begin browsing the following pages.

The Celebrity Black Book is a staple for fans who want autographs; charities and nonprofits who want to raise money for their cause; entrepreneurs and marketers who want celebrity endorsements and free publicity for their producers/services; authors who want blurbs for their books; and journalists/media who want quotes and interviews.

There are so many uses, the possibilities are endless!

Of course, with over 56,000+ celebrities who move and change addresses on a daily basis, this book cannot possibly be 100% accurate. This is why you also get a **FREE 30-Day Membership** to ContactAnyCelebrity.com's Private Online Database so you can get real-time updates.

This Private Online Database contains the best mailing address, agent, manager, publicist, production company and charitable cause for each celebrity, plus contact information for over 7,000 personal representatives and 5,000 entertainment companies with phone, fax and email addresses.

Activate your FREE 30-Day Membership here: ContactAnyCelebrity.com/activate

You may be wondering how to write a fan letter, request an autograph, or get your product and service in the hands of celebrities. To find out, check out our other books (available on Amazon):

Secrets to Contacting Celebrities: 101 Ways to Reach the Rich & Famous

Celebrity Leverage: Insider Secrets to Getting Celebrity Endorsements, Instant Credibility & Star-Powered Publicity

Enjoy your *Celebrity Black Book 2019* -- please let me know your success stories!

Reach for the stars,

Jordan

Jordan McAuley, Founder
ContactAnyCelebrity.com

You may be wondering how to write a fan letter, request an autograph, or get your product or service in the hands of celebrities. If so, check out our other books on Amazon:

- Secrets to Contacting Celebrities: 101 Ways to Reach the Rich & Famous
- Celebrity Leverage: Insider Secrets to Getting Celebrity Endorsements, Instant Credibility & Star-Powered Publicity
- The Lost Secrets of Fame & Fortune: How to Get – and Keep – Everything You Desire!

Enjoy your new *Celebrity Black Book 2019*, and let me know your success stories!

Reach for the stars,

Jordan McAuley, Founder
Contact Any Celebrity
8721 Santa Monica Blvd. #431
West Hollywood, CA 90069-4507
310-691-5466 (Phone)
support@contactanycelebrity.com
ContactAnyCelebrity.com

2 Chainz (Musician)
c/o Peter Kadin *The Chamber Group*
75 Broad St Rm 708
New York, NY 10004-3244, USA

30 Seconds to Mars (Music Group)
c/o Irving Azoff *Azoff Music Management*
1100 Glendon Ave Ste 2000
Los Angeles, CA 90024-3524, USA

5 Seconds of Summer (Musician)
c/o Matt Emsell *Wonder Management*
10-16 Scrutton St
Level 4
London EC2A 4RU, UNITED KINGDOM

A3 (Music Group)
c/o Staff Member *Progressive Global Agency*
PO Box 50294
Nashville, TN 37205-0294, USA

Aaker, Lee (Actor)
PO Box 1386
Mammoth Lakes, CA 93546-1386, USA

Aames, Willie (Actor)
c/o Tyman Stewart *Characters Talent Agency*
200-1505 2nd Ave W
Vancouver, BC V6H 3Y4, CANADA

Aardsma, David (Athlete, Baseball Player)
6009 E Turquoise Ave
Paradise Valley, AZ 85253-1234, USA

Aaron, Caroline (Actor)
Mindel/Donigan
9057-C Nemo St
W Hollywood, CA 90069, USA

Aaron, Hank (Athlete, Baseball Player)
1611 Adams Dr SW
Atlanta, GA 30311-3625, USA

Aaron, Lee (Musician)
c/o Staff Member *Paquin Entertainment Agency (Winnipeg)*
468 Stradbrook Ave
Winnipeg MB M6K 3J1, CANADA

Aaron, Quinton (Actor)
c/o Sandra Kaye *NuVision Entertainment Media PR*
6520 Platt Ave Ste 366
West Hills, CA 91307-3218, USA

Aaron, Tommy (Athlete, Golfer)
440 E Lake Dr
Gainesville, GA 30506-1740, USA

Aarons, Bonnie (Actor)
c/o Alan Mills *Mills Kaplan Entertainment*
5225 Wilshire Blvd Ste 500
Los Angeles, CA 90036-5194, USA

Aase, Don (Athlete, Baseball Player)
4590 Avenida Del Este
Yorba Linda, CA 92886-3003, USA

Abad, Andy (Athlete, Baseball Player)
1092 Chickasaw St
Jupiter, FL 33458-5610, USA

Abagnale Jr, Frank (Writer)
Abagnale Associates
601 Pennsylvania Ave NW
900 S Bldg
Washington, DC 20004-2601, USA

Abair, Mindi (Musician)
c/o Bud Harner *Chapman Management*
14011 Ventura Blvd Ste 405
Sherman Oaks, CA 91423-5230, USA

Abatantuono, Diego (Actor)
c/o Staff Member *Moviement*
Via P Cavallini 24
Rome 00193, ITALY

Abbass, Hiam (Actor)
c/o Michael Lazo *Untitled Entertainment*
350 S Beverly Dr Ste 200
Beverly Hills, CA 90212-4819, USA

Abbatiello, Carmine (Horse Racer)
7 Whirlaway Rd
Manalapan, NJ 07726-9566, USA

Abbatiello, Tony (Horse Racer)
176 Stone Hill Rd
Colts Neck, NJ 07722-1730, USA

Abbington, Amanda (Actor)
c/o Staff Member *Lip Service Casting Ltd*
60-66 Wardour St
London W1F 0TA, UK

Abbot, Russ (Actor, Comedian)
c/o Staff Member *Harvey Voices*
54-55 Margaret St Fl 4
London W1W 8SH, UNITED KINGDOM

Abbott, Christopher (Actor)
c/o Eric Kranzler *Management 360*
9111 Wilshire Blvd
Beverly Hills, CA 90210-5508, USA

Abbott, Diahnne (Actor)
460 W Avenue 46
Los Angeles, CA 90065-5006, USA

Abbott, Glenn (Athlete, Baseball Player)
4413 Dawson Dr
North Little Rock, AR 72116-7037, USA

Abbott, Gregory (Musician)
PO Box 68
Bergenfield, NJ 07621-0068, USA

Abbott, Jeff (Athlete, Baseball Player)
1095 Stonegate Ct
Roswell, GA 30075-2265, USA

Abbott, Jim (Athlete, Baseball Player, Olympic Athlete)
3449 Quiet Cv
Corona Del Mar, CA 92625-1637, USA

Abbott, Josh (Musician)
c/o Henry Glascock *WME (Nashville)*
1201 Demonbreun St
Nashville, TN 37203-3140, USA

Abbott, Kurt (Athlete, Baseball Player)
1704 NW Spruce Ridge Dr
Stuart, FL 34994-9528, USA

Abbott, Kyle (Athlete, Baseball Player)
10 Christi Ln
Krum, TX 76249-5327, USA

Abbott, Norman (Director)
24359 Vista Hills Dr
Valencia, CA 91355-3100, USA

Abbott, Paul (Athlete, Baseball Player)
330 E Rosslynn Ave
Fullerton, CA 92832-2525, USA

Abbott, Reg (Athlete, Hockey Player)
203-738 Sayward Hill Terr
Victoria, BC V8Y 3K1, CANADA

Abboud, A Robert (Business Person)
A Robert Abboud Co
960 Route 22
#212
Fox River Grove, IL 60021, USA

Abboud, Joseph M (Designer, Fashion Designer)
650 5th Ave Ste 2700
New York, NY 10019-6108, USA

Abbrederis, Jared (Athlete, Football Player)
c/o Michael McCartney *Priority Sports & Entertainment (Chicago)*
325 N La Salle Dr Ste 650
Chicago, IL 60654-8182, USA

Abdelkader, Justin (Athlete, Hockey Player)
1080 Edinborough Dr
Norton Shores, MI 49441-5371, USA

Abdi, Barkhad (Actor)
c/o Staff Member *SMS Talent*
8383 Wilshire Blvd Ste 230
Beverly Hills, CA 90211-2436, USA

Abdoo, Rose (Actor)
c/o Judy Orbach *Judy O Productions*
6136 Glen Holly St
Hollywood, CA 90068-2338, USA

Abdul, Paula (Dancer, Musician)
c/o Brett Ruttenberg *Imprint PR*
6121 W Sunset Blvd
Neuehouse
Los Angeles, CA 90028-6442, USA

Abdul-Aziz, Zaid (Athlete, Basketball Player)
Sunlight Inc
PO Box 75184
Seattle, WA 98175-0184, USA

Abdul-Jabbar, Kareem (Athlete, Basketball Player, Coach)
c/o Deborah Morales *Iconomy*
20434 S Santa Fe Ave # 194
Long Beach, CA 90810-1121, USA

Abdul-Jabbar, Karim (Athlete, Football Player)
17044 Downing St
Gaithersburg, MD 20877-3602, USA

Abdullah, Husain (Athlete, Football Player)

Abdullah, Khalid (Athlete, Football Player)
7634 Wexford Club Dr E
Jacksonville, FL 32256-2330, USA

Abdullah, Rabih (Athlete, Football Player)
12810 Wallingford Dr
Tampa, FL 33624-6354, USA

Abdullah, Rahim (Athlete, Football Player)
7634 Wexford Club Dr E
Jacksonville, FL 32256-2330, USA

Abdul-Mateen II, Yahya (Actor)
c/o Dara Gordon *Anonymous Content*
155 Spring St Frnt 3
New York, NY 10012-5208, USA

Abdulov, Aleksandr G (Actor)
Peschanaya Str 4 #3
Moscow 125252, RUSSIA

Abdul-Quddus, Isa (Athlete, Football Player)
c/o Alan Herman *Sportstars Inc*
1370 Avenue of the Americas Fl 19
New York, NY 10019-4602, USA

Abdul-Saboor, Mikal (Athlete, Football Player)
400 17th St NW Unit 2307
Atlanta, GA 30363-1056, USA

Abdur-Rahim, Shareef (Athlete, Basketball Player)
c/o Staff Member *Atlanta Hawks*
190 Marietta St NW Ste 405
Atlanta, GA 30303-2717, USA

Abdus-Salaam, Sultan (Athlete, Football Player)
12715 Joust St
North Las Vegas, NV 89030, USA

Abed, Rodrigo (Actor)
c/o Gabriel Blanco *Gabriel Blanco Iglesias (Mexico)*
Rio Balsas 35-32
Colonia Cuauhtemoc
DF 06500, Mexico

Abel, Gerry (Athlete, Hockey Player)
464 Allard Ave
Grosse Pointe Farms, MI 48236-2812, USA

Abel, Jake (Actor)
c/o Annie Schmidt *Untitled Entertainment (NY)*
215 Park Ave S Fl 8
New York, NY 10003-1622, USA

Abel, Jessica (Artist)
c/o Staff Member *Fantagraphics Books*
7563 Lake City Way NE
Seattle, WA 98115-4218, USA

Abell, Bud (Athlete, Football Player)
919 E 25th Plz
Panama City, FL 32405-5255, USA

Abell, Tim (Actor)
c/o Staff Member *Tactical Media Productions*
578 Washington Blvd # 346
Marina Del Rey, CA 90292-5442, USA

Abendschan, Jack (Athlete, Football Player)
5626 Legacy Dr
Abilene, TX 79606-4387, USA

Abercrombie, Neil (Congressman, Politician)
300 Ala Moana Blvd Rm 4104
Prince Kuhio Federal Building
Honolulu, HI 96850-4104, USA

Abercrombie, Reggie (Athlete, Baseball Player)
5920 Buxton Dr
Columbus, GA 31907-3635, USA

Abercrombie, Walter (Athlete, Coach, Football Coach, Football Player)
217 Westlane Cir
Woodway, TX 76712-3186, USA

Abernathy, Brent (Athlete, Baseball Player, Olympic Athlete)
212 Crewilla Dr NW
Fort Walton Beach, FL 32548-3906, USA

Abernathy, Robert (Athlete, Baseball Player)
2491 Walker Ln
Nashville, TN 37207-4213, USA

Abernethy, Tom (Athlete, Basketball Player)
5268 Woodfield Dr N
Carmel, IN 46033-8794, USA

Abgrall, Dennis (Athlete, Hockey Player)
16607 S 12th Pl
Phoenix, AZ 85048-4703, USA

Abigail (Musician)
c/o Staff Member *T-Best Talent Agency*
508 Honey Lake Ct
Danville, CA 94506-1237, USA

Abiodun, Oyewole (Musician)
c/o Staff Member *UTA Music/The Agency Group (UK)*
361-373 City Rd
London EC1V 1PQ, UNITED KINGDOM

Abkarian, Simon (Actor)
c/o Staff Member *Cineart*
28 Rue Mogador
Paris F-75009, FRANCE

Able, Forest (Athlete, Basketball Player)
11102 Mitchell Hill Rd
Fairdale, KY 40118-9425, USA

Able, Whitney (Actor)
c/o Lisa Gallant *Gallant Management*
1112 Montana Ave # 454
Santa Monica, CA 90403-1652, USA

Ableson, Andrew (Actor)
c/o Stephanie Blume *Imperium 7 Talent Agency*
5455 Wilshire Blvd Ste 1706
Los Angeles, CA 90036-4217, USA

Abner, Shawn (Athlete, Baseball Player)
1443 Olde Oak Ct
Mechanicsburg, PA 17050-9198, USA

Abney Culberson, John (Congressman, Politician)
2352 Rayburn Hob
Washington, DC 20515-2201, USA

Aboulhosn, Hassan (Athlete, Football Player)
2703 Oaklawn Blvd
Hopewell, VA 23860-4934, USA

Abourezk, James G (Politician)
1509 E Cedar Ln
Sioux Falls, SD 57103-4516, USA

Abraham, Clifton (Athlete, Football Player)
1413 Dutchman Creek Dr
Desoto, TX 75115-3659, USA

Abraham, Donnie (Athlete, Football Player)
3038 Wentworth Way
Tarpon Springs, FL 34688-8445, USA

Abraham, F Murray (Actor)
c/o Johnnie Planco *Parseghian Planco LLC*
920 Broadway Fl 16
New York, NY 10010-8004, USA

Abraham, John (Actor)
c/o Staff Member *Filmi Geeks Entertainment*
Suite 608 Northway House
1379 High Road, Whetstone
London N20 9LP, UK

Abraham, John (Athlete, Football Player)
c/o Amanda Mitchell *Southern Hospitality Marketing & PR*
122 W 26th St
New York, NY 10001-6804, USA

Abraham, Nate (Athlete, Football Player)
3038 Wentworth Way
Tarpon Springs, FL 34688-8445, USA

Abraham, Robert (Athlete, Football Player)
831 Canal St
Myrtle Beach, SC 29577-3455, USA

Abraham, Spencer E (Politician)
Energy Dept
8016 Greenwich Woods Dr
Mc Lean, VA 22102-1332, USA

Abraham, Vader (Musician)
c/o Staff Member *Piet Roelen Talent Agency*
Antwerpsesteenweg 16
Vosselaar BE 02350, Belgium

Abrahamian, Emil (Cartoonist)
147 Woodleaf Dr
Winter Springs, FL 32708-6159, USA

Abrahams, Jim S (Director)
c/o Staff Member *ICM Partners*
10250 Constellation Blvd Fl 7
Los Angeles, CA 90067-6207, USA

Abrahams, Jon (Actor)
c/o Staff Member *Management Production Entertainment (MPE)*
9229 W Sunset Blvd Ste 301
W Hollywood, CA 90069-3417, USA

Abrahamse, Taylor (Musician)
Rockyz Kidz
146 Shuter St
Studio B
Toronto, ON M5A 1V9, Canada

Abrahamson, James A (Astronaut)
2300 N Scenic Hwy
Lake Wales, FL 33898-6626, USA

Abrahamson, Lenny (Director)
c/o Bumble Ward *Hive Communications*
Prefers to be contacted by email or phone.
Los Angeles, CA NA, USA

Abrahamsson, Thommy (Athlete, Hockey Player)
Bjorkgatan 7
Kunghamm 45632, Sweden

Abram, Norm (Television Host)
This Old House Show
PO Box 130
Concord, MA 01742-0130, USA

Abramoff, Jack (Business Person, Producer)
c/o Monique Moss *Integrated PR*
9025 Wilshire Blvd Ste 400
Beverly Hills, CA 90211-1828, USA

Abramovich, Roman (Business Person)
Governor's Office
Beringa Str 20
Abadyr, Chukotka 689000, RUSSIA

Abramowicz, Daniel (Danny) (Athlete, Football Player)
479 N Harlem Ave Apt 801
Oak Park, IL 60301-6409, USA

Abrams, Austin (Actor)
c/o Michael Hepburn *Industry Entertainment Partners*
955 Carrillo Dr Ste 300
Los Angeles, CA 90048-5400, USA

Abrams, Bobby (Athlete, Football Player)
PO Box 240822
Montgomery, AL 36124-0822, USA

Abrams, Casey (Musician)
c/o Simon Fuller *XIX Entertainment (UK)*
32/33 Ransomes Dock
London SW11 4NP, UNITED KINGDOM (UK)

Abrams, Dan (Television Host)
148 Waverly Pl Apt C
New York, NY 10014-6836, USA

Abrams, Elliott (Politician)
10607 Dogwood Farm Ln
Great Falls, VA 22066-2937, USA

Abrams, JJ (Actor, Producer, Writer)
c/o Staff Member *Bad Robot*
1221 Olympic Blvd
Santa Monica, CA 90404-3721, USA

Abrams, Kevin (Athlete, Football Player)
1314 E Wilder Ave
Tampa, FL 33603-2433, USA

Abrams, Robert (Politician)
531 Weaver St
Larchmont, NY 10538-1013, USA

Abrams, Stephanie (Television Host)
c/o Rick Ramage *United Talent Agency (UTA)*
888 7th Ave Fl 7
New York, NY 10106-0700, USA

Abramson, Leslie (Actor)
122A E Foothill Blvd # 4
Arcadia, CA 91006-2505, USA

Abramson, Neil (Director, Writer)
c/o Staff Member *United Talent Agency (UTA)*
9336 Civic Center Dr
Beverly Hills, CA 90210-3604, USA

Abrego, Johnny (Athlete, Baseball Player)
PO Box 681144
San Antonio, TX 78268-1144, USA

Abreu, Aldo (Musician)
Concert Artists Guild
850 7th Ave # 1205
New York, NY 10019-5230, USA

Abreu, Bobby (Athlete, Baseball Player)
5 Rockledge Ct
Marlton, NJ 08053-9774, USA

Abreu, Irina (Actor)
c/o Staff Member *Televisa*
Blvd Adolfo Lopez Mateos 232
Colonia San Angel INN
DF CP 01060, MEXICO

Abril, Victoria (Actor)
c/o Stephane Zitzerman
1 Rue du Louvre
Paris 75001, FRANCE

Abronzino, Umberto (Soccer Player)
1336 Settle Ave
San Jose, CA 95125-2363, USA

Abrue, Bobby (Athlete, Baseball Player)
c/o Staff Member *Los Angeles Dodgers*
1000 Elysian Park Ave
Los Angeles, CA 90012, USA

Abrunhosa, Pedro (Musician)
Polygram Records
825 8th Ave
Worldwide Plaza
New York, NY 10019-7416, USA

Abruzzo, Ray (Actor)
c/o Staff Member *Peter Strain & Associates Inc (LA)*
10901 Whipple St Apt 322
N Hollywood, CA 91602-3245, USA

Absher, Dick (Athlete, Football Player)
353 Tavistock Dr
Saint Augustine, FL 32095-8401, USA

Acaba, Joseph M (Astronaut)
2620 Loganberry Cir
Seabrook, TX 77586-1525, USA

Accardo, Jeremy (Athlete, Baseball Player)
1543 S Gibson St
Gilbert, AZ 85296-4290, USA

Accola, Candice (Actor)
c/o CeCe Yorke *True Public Relations*
3575 Cahuenga Blvd W Ste 360
Los Angeles, CA 90068-1361, USA

Accola, Paul (Skier)
Bolgenstr 17
Davos Platz 07270, SWITZERLAND

AC/DC (Music Group)
c/o Christopher Dalston *Creative Artists Agency (CAA)*
2000 Avenue of the Stars Ste 100
Los Angeles, CA 90067-4705, USA

Ace, Buddy (Musician)
Rodgers Redding
1048 Tattnall St
Macon, GA 31201-1537

Ace of Base (Music Group, Musician)
c/o John Orlando *Urbania Group (Sweden)*
Box 3184
Stockholm 103 63, Stockholm

Acevedo, Juan (Athlete, Baseball Player)
143 Madera Cir
Carpentersville, IL 60110-1110, USA

Acevedo, Kirk (Actor)
c/o Stacy Abrams *Abrams Entertainment*
5225 Wilshire Blvd Ste 515
Los Angeles, CA 90036-4349, USA

Ache, Steve (Athlete, Football Player)
22 Lashley Estates Dr
Swansea, IL 62226-2502, USA

Achica, George (Athlete, Football Player)
3165 Lone Bluff Way
San Jose, CA 95111-1264, USA

Acho, Sam (Athlete, Football Player)
c/o Pat Dye Jr *SportsTrust Advisors*
3340 Peachtree Rd NE Fl 16
Atlanta, GA 30326-1000, USA

Achtymichuk, Gene (Athlete, Hockey Player)
305-9985 93 Ave
Fort Saskatchewan, AB T8L 1N5, Canada

Acid Test (Music Group)
83 Riverside Dr
New York, NY 10024-5713, USA

Acker, Amy (Actor)
3721 Blue Canyon Dr
Studio City, CA 91604-3802, USA

Acker, Bill (Athlete, Football Player)
1809 Walker Dr
Alice, TX 78332-4126, USA

Acker, Jim (Athlete, Baseball Player)
PO Box AA
Freer, TX 78357-2027, USA

Acker, Tom (Athlete, Baseball Player)
2502 School House Ln
Narvon, PA 17555-9009, USA

Ackeren, Robert V (Director)
Kurfurstendamm 132A
Berlin 10711, GERMANY

Acker-Macosko, Anna (Athlete, Golfer)
304 Earl Dr
Kerrville, TX 78028-7019, USA

Ackerman, Doug (Horse Racer)
530 Lighthorse Cir
Aberdeen, NC 28315-3770, USA

Ackerman, Gary (Congressman, Politician)
2111 Rayburn Hob
Washington, DC 20515-0201, USA

Ackerman, Joshua (Actor)
c/o Joannie Burstein *Burstein Company*
15304 W Sunset Blvd Ste 208
Pacific Palisades, CA 90272-3656, USA

Ackerman, Leslie (Actor)
5065 Calvin Ave
Tarzana, CA 91356-4419, USA

Ackerman, Rick (Athlete, Football Player)
125 Zog Ln
Laramie, WY 82072-9546, USA

Ackerman, Tom (Athlete, Football Player)
c/o Allain Roy *RSG Hockey, LLC*
16476 Wild Horse Creek Rd Fl 2
Chesterfield, MO 63017-1402, USA

Ackermann, Rosemarie (Athlete, Track Athlete)
Str der Jugend 72
Cottbus 03050, GERMANY

Ackland, Joss (Actor)
c/o Staff Member *Jonathan Altaras Assoc Ltd*
11 Garrick Street
Covent Garden
London WC2E 9AT, UNITED KINGDOM (UK)

Ackland, Oliver (Actor)
c/o Tory Howard *Atlas Artists*
9220 W Sunset Blvd Ste 225
Los Angeles, CA 90069-3513, USA

Ackles, Danneel (Actor)
c/o Jason Newman *Untitled Entertainment*
350 S Beverly Dr Ste 200
Beverly Hills, CA 90212-4819, USA

Ackles, Jensen (Actor)
PO Box 850812
Richardson, TX 75085-0812, USA

Ackroyd, David (Actor)
273 N Many Lakes Dr
Kalispell, MT 59901-8344, USA

Ackroyd, Peter (Writer)
Anthony Shell Assoc
43 Doughty St
London WC1N 2LF, UNITED KINGDOM (UK)

Acks, Ron (Athlete, Football Player)
563 Licklog Rdg
Hayesville, NC 28904-4879, USA

Acomb, Doug (Athlete, Hockey Player)
18 Millstone Crt
Markham, ON L3R 7M4, Canada

Acorah, Derek (Actor)
PO Box 32
Ormskirk
Lancashire L40 9SN, UNITED KINGDOM

Acosta, Cy (Athlete, Baseball Player)
Aug Ramirez 1420 Col
Gab Levva Culiacan
Sinaloa, Mexico, USA

Acosta, Eduardo (Ed) (Athlete, Baseball Player)
22822 Boltana
Mission Viejo, CA 92691-1717, USA

Acosta, Jim (Journalist, Television Host)
c/o Staff Member *CNN (NY)*
10 Columbus Cir
Time Warner Center
New York, NY 10019-1158, USA

Acovone, Jay (Actor)
c/o Geneva Bray *GVA Talent Agency Inc*
193 N Robertson Blvd
Beverly Hills, CA 90211-2103, USA

Acre, Mark (Athlete, Baseball Player)
840 E Riviera Pl
Chandler, AZ 85249-6970, USA

Acres, Mark (Athlete, Basketball Player)
26357 Silver Spur Rd
Rolling Hills Estates, CA 90275-2313, USA

Acta, Manny (Athlete, Baseball Player, Coach)
6427 Shoreline Dr
Saint Cloud, FL 34771-8786, USA

Acton, Bud (Athlete, Basketball Player)
PO Box 87
Empire, MI 49630-0087, USA

Acton, Keith (Athlete, Coach, Hockey Player)
Toronto Maple Leafs
82 Mill St
Stouffville, ON L4A 1C6, Canada

Acton, Loren W Dr (Astronaut)
8490 Overlook Ln
Bozeman, MT 59715-7753, USA

Acuff, Amy (Athlete, Olympic Athlete, Track Athlete)
4102 Bobwhite
Robstown, TX 78380-6060, USA

Acuna, Jason (Actor)
1523 Manhattan Ave
Hermosa Beach, CA 90254-3637, USA

Acuna, Ronald (Athlete, Baseball Player)
c/o Peter Greenberg *TLA Worldwide (The Legacy Agency)*
1500 Broadway Ste 2501
New York, NY 10036-4082, USA

Adair, Deborah (Actor)
1605 Lindamere Pl
Los Angeles, CA 90077-1905, USA

Adair, Tatum (Actor)
Mission Talent Agency
10929 Vanowen St Ste 138
Atten: Goro Hamasaki
North Hollywood, CA 91605-6435, USA

Adam, Ken (Designer)
c/o Staff Member *Mirisch Agency*
8840 Wilshire Blvd Ste 100
Beverly Hills, CA 90211-2606, USA

Adam, Russ (Athlete, Hockey Player)
69 Old Petty Harbour Rd
St. John's, NL A1G 1H6, Canada

Adamchik, Ed (Athlete, Football Player)
234 Princeton Ave
Pittsburgh, PA 15229-1516, USA

Adamkus, Valdas (Politician, President)
President's Office
Gediminas 53
Vilnius 232026, LITHUANIA

Adamle, Mike (Sportscaster)
826 Lincoln St
Evanston, IL 60201-2405, USA

Adamowicz, Tony (Race Car Driver)
633 Skyview Ln
Costa Mesa, CA 92626-3134, USA

Adams, Alvan (Athlete, Basketball Player)
5617 N Palo Cristi Rd
Paradise Valley, AZ 85253-7544, USA

Adams, Amy (Actor)
c/o Stacy O'Neil *Brillstein Entertainment Partners*
9150 Wilshire Blvd Ste 350
Beverly Hills, CA 90212-3453, USA

Adams, Beverly Sassoon (Model)
2533 Benedict Canyon Dr
Beverly Hills, CA 90210-1020, USA

Adams, Bob (Athlete, Baseball Player)
31713 157th St E
Llano, CA 93544-1222, USA

Adams, Brent (Athlete, Football Player)
3615 Parkmont Ct
Norcross, GA 30092-4521, USA

Adams, Brooke (Actor)
248 S Van Ness Ave
Los Angeles, CA 90004-3921, USA

Adams, Bryan (Athlete, Hockey Player)
c/o Staff Member *Sports Personnel Services*
125 Lake St W Ste 200
Wayzata, MN 55391-1573, USA

Adams, Bryan (Musician)
c/o Bruce Allen *Bruce Allen Talent*
425 Carrall St
Suite 400
Vancouver, BC V6B 6E3, CANADA

Adams, Chante (Actor)
c/o Jared Sheer *WME|IMG (NY)*
11 Madison Ave Fl 18
New York, NY 10010-3669, USA

Adams, Charles (Athlete, Baseball Player)
6058 Puerto Dr
Rancho Murieta, CA 95683-9314, USA

Adams, Charles J (Religious Leader)
Progressive National Baptist Convention
601 50th St NE
Washington, DC 20019-5498

Adams, Corin (Athlete, Basketball Player)
c/o Gigi Rock *Heraea Marketing*
10905 E Pear Tree Dr
Cornville, AZ 86325-5523, USA

Adams, Craig (Athlete, Hockey Player)
122 Grosvenor Rd
Needham, MA 02492-4445, USA

Adams, Curtis (Athlete, Football Player)
258 W Towering Oaks Cir
Muskegon, MI 49442-8442, USA

Adams, Danny (Athlete, Basketball Player)
7832 Surreywood Dr
North Bend, OH 45052-9616, USA

Adams, Davante (Athlete, Football Player)
c/o Frank Bauer *Sun West Sports*
7883 N Pershing Ave
Stockton, CA 95207-1749, USA

Adams, Dave (Athlete, Football Player)
2780 N La Cienega Dr
Tucson, AZ 85715-3504, us

Adams, Dick (Athlete, Baseball Player)
300 Hohokam Dr
Sedona, AZ 86336-4326, USA

Adams, Doug (Athlete, Baseball Player)
1129 Harmony Cir NE
Janesville, WI 53545-2072, USA

Adams, Earnest (Athlete, Football Player)
1061 NW 25th Way
Ft Lauderdale, FL 33311-5710, USA

Adams, Evan (Actor)
c/o Staff Member *Characters Talent Agency*
200-1505 2nd Ave W
Vancouver, BC V6H 3Y4, CANADA

Adams, Flozell (Athlete, Football Player)
5201 Reflection Ct
Flower Mound, TX 75022-8144, USA

Adams, George (Athlete, Basketball Player)
508 Watergate Cir
Gastonia, NC 28052-7718, USA

Adams, George (Athlete, Football Player)
2410 Damsel Katie Dr
Lewisville, TX 75056-5801, USA

Adams, Gerard (Gerry) (Politician)
Sinn Fein/IRA
51/55 Falls Road
Belfast, Northern Ireland BT 12, USA

Adams, Glenn (Athlete, Baseball Player)
12333 E Tecumseh Rd
Norman, OK 73026-8640, USA

Adams, Greg (Athlete, Hockey Player)
19864 N 83rd Pl # Pi
Scottsdale, AZ 85255-3915, USA

Adams, Greg (Athlete, Hockey Player)
c/o Staff Member *Cowichan Valley Capitals*
2687 James St
Duncan, BC V9L 2X5, Canada

Adams, Hank (Athlete, Football Player)
53 4th St
California, PA 15419-1109, USA

Adams, Jane (Actor)
c/o Staff Member *Framework Entertainment*
9057 Nemo St # C
W Hollywood, CA 90069-5511, USA

Adams, Jeb Stuart (Actor)
1163 Calle Vista Dr
Beverly Hills, CA 90210-2507, USA

Adams, Jeff (Athlete, Football Player)
c/o Alan Herman *Sportstars Inc*
1370 Avenue of the Americas Fl 19
New York, NY 10019-4602, USA

Adams, Joey Lauren (Actor)
c/o Jack Kingsrud *Zero Gravity Management*
11110 Ohio Ave Ste 100
Los Angeles, CA 90025-3329, USA

Adams, John (Athlete, Golfer)
5135 Amherst Ct
Paris, TX 75462-1304, USA

Adams, John (Athlete, Hockey Player)
109 Nottingham Cres
Thunder Bay, ON P7G 1B4, Canada

Adams, John C (Musician)
c/o Staff Member *Elektra Records*
75 Rockefeller Plz Fl 17
New York, NY 10019-6927, USA

Adams, John H (Religious Leader)
African Methodist Church
1134 11th St NW
Washington, DC 20001-4316

Adams, Julius (Athlete, Football Player)
2135 Jefferson Davis St
MacOn, GA 31201, USA

Adams, Kev (Actor)
c/o Staff Member *United Talent Agency (UTA)*
9336 Civic Center Dr
Beverly Hills, CA 90210-3604, USA

Adams, Kevyn (Athlete, Hockey Player)
Buffalo Sabres 1 Seymour H Knox Ill Plz Ste 1
Buffalo, NY 14203-3096

Adams, Lindsey (Race Car Driver)
819 W Arapaho Rd Ste 24B PMB 188
Richardson, TX 75080-5040, USA

Adams, Lorraine (Journalist)
Washington Post - Editorial Dept
1150 15th St
Washington, DC 20071-0002

Adams, Mary Kay (Actor)
Roe Enterprises
PO Box 2023
Fairfield, IA 52556-0034, USA

Adams, Maud (Actor)
9420 Eden Dr
Beverly Hills, CA 90210-1309, USA

Adams, Mike (Athlete, Football Player)
228 Flinn St
Hutto, TX 78634-3298, USA

Adams, Mike (Athlete, Baseball Player)
13205 Jo Ln NE
Albuquerque, NM 87111-7112, USA

Adams, Mike (Athlete, Baseball Player)
800 Booty St
Sinton, TX 78387-3210, USA

Adams, Mike (Athlete, Football Player)
70 Graham Ave Apt 1
Paterson, NJ 07524-2423, USA

Adams, Mike (Football Player)
228 Flinn St
Hutto, TX 78634-3298, us

Adams, Neal (Producer)
Continuity Studios
15 W 39th St Fl 9
New York, NY 10018-0631, USA

Adams, Nicola (Athlete, Boxer)
Haringey Amateur Boxing Club
701 High Rd
Tottenham
Greater London N17 8AD, UNITED KINGDOM

Adams, Noah (Correspondent)
National Public Radio
635 Massachusetts Ave NW
Washington, DC 20001-3740, USA

Adams, Oleta (Music Group)
c/o Tom Estey *Tom Estey Publicity*
144 E 22nd St Apt 1B
New York, NY 10010-6333, USA

Adams, Pat (Artist)
370 Elm St
Bennington, VT 05201-2214, USA

Adams, Patch (Doctor)
Gesundheit Institute
PO Box 288
Hillsboro, WV 24946-0288, USA

Adams, Patrick (Actor)
c/o Andy Corren *Andy Corren Management*
PO Box 5955
Sherman Oaks, CA 91413-5955, USA

Adams, Pete (Athlete, Football Player)
1443 Hygeia Ave
Encinitas, CA 92024-1624, USA

Adams, Red (Athlete, Baseball Player)
6058 Puerto Dr
Rancho Murieta, CA 95683-9314, USA

Adams, Russ (Athlete, Baseball Player)
7940 Scotch Meadows Dr
Laurinburg, NC 28352-2162, USA

Adams, Ryan (Musician, Songwriter)
c/o Michele Hug *Nasty Little Man*
285 W Broadway Rm 310
New York, NY 10013-2257, USA

Adams, Sam (Athlete, Football Player)
8507 NE Juanita Dr
Kirkland, WA 98034-3524, USA

Adams, Sam E (Athlete, Football Player)
12010 Holly Stone Dr
Houston, TX 77070-5420, USA

Adams, Sandy (Congressman, Politician)
216 Cannon Hob
Washington, DC 20515-4325, USA

Adams, Scott (Football Player)
1171 Middlebrooks Rd
Watkinsville, GA 30677-3820, us

Adams, Scott (Athlete, Football Player)
1171 Middlebrooks Rd
Watkinsville, GA 30677-3820, USA

Adams, Scott (Cartoonist)
Harper Business Publishers
2751 Crellin Rd
Pleasanton, CA 94566-6914, USA

Adams, Stan (Athlete, Football Player)
502 S Highland Dr
Cedar Hill, TX 75104-2873, USA

Adams, Stefon (Athlete)
1734 Trotters Ln
Stone Mountain, GA 30087-2337, USA

Adams, Stefon (Athlete, Football Player)
937 Bingham Ln
Stone Mountain, GA 30083-2424, us

Adams, Sunrise (Adult Film Star)
c/o Staff Member *Vivid Entertainment*
1933 N Bronson Ave Apt 209
Los Angeles, CA 90068-5632, USA

Adams, Tag (Adult Film Star)
c/o Staff Member *Diva Central Inc*
7510 W Sunset Blvd # 1445
Los Angeles, CA 90046-3408, USA

Adams, Terry (Athlete, Baseball Player)
11315 Howells Ferry Rd
Semmes, AL 36575-6655, USA

Adams, Theo (Athlete, Football Player)
9555 Highland Park Dr
Roseville, CA 95678-2911, USA

Adams, Tom (Athlete, Football Player)
20606 Crystal Springs Loop
Grand Rapids, MN 55744-5183, USA

Adams, Tony (Athlete, Football Player)
15919 Fontana St Apt 230
Stilwell, KS 66085-8454, USA

Adams, Valerie (Athlete, Track Athlete)
1155 Union Cir
Denton, TX 76203-5017, USA

Adams, Vashone (Athlete, Football Player)
2940 S Parker Ct
Aurora, CO 80014-3018, USA

Adams, William J (Athlete, Football Player)
12 Willowby Way
Lynnfield, MA 01940-1022, USA

Adams, Willie (Athlete, Baseball Player)
11903 Kibbee Ave
La Mirada, CA 90638-1518, USA

Adams, Willie J (Athlete, Football Player)
2513 Forest Creek Dr
Fort Worth, TX 76123-1145, USA

Adams, Willis (Athlete, Football Player)
7831 Quail Meadow Dr
Houston, TX 77071-2337, USA

Adams, Yolanda (Musician)
c/o Lynn Jeter *Lynn Jeter & Associates*
3699 Wilshire Blvd Ste 850
Los Angeles, CA 90010-2737, USA

Adamson, Andrew (Director)
c/o Jeremy Zimmer *United Talent Agency (UTA)*
9336 Civic Center Dr
Beverly Hills, CA 90210-3604, USA

Adamson, James C Colonel (Astronaut)
25 Tradewind Cir
Fishersville, VA 22939-2141, USA

Adamson, Joel (Athlete, Baseball Player)
14832 S 46th Pl
Phoenix, AZ 85044-6872, USA

Adamson, Ken (Athlete, Football Player)
5061 Jardin Ln
Carmichael, CA 95608-6070, USA

Adamson, Mike (Athlete, Baseball Player)
17610 Canterbury Dr
Monument, CO 80132-8310, USA

Adamson, Robert (Actor)
c/o Theo Swerissen *Theo Swerissen Management*
Prefers to be contacted via telephone or email
Los Angeles, CA, USA

Addae, Jahleel (Athlete, Football Player)
c/o Sean Kiernan *Impact Sports (LA)*
12429 Ventura Ct
Studio City, CA 91604-2417, USA

Addai, Joseph (Athlete, Football Player)
7521 Dubonnet Way
Indianapolis, IN 46278-1591, USA

Addai-Robinson, Cynthia (Actor)
c/o Cory Richman *Liebman Entertainment*
29 W 46th St Fl 5
New York, NY 10036-4104, USA

Addams, Abe (Athlete, Football Player)
9225 River Trail Dr
Louisville, KY 40229-5249, USA

Addams, Calpernia (Actor, Reality Star)
c/o Staff Member *Deep Stealth Productions*
5419 Hollywood Blvd Ste C PMB 142
Los Angeles, CA 90027-3478, USA

Addazio, Steve (Athlete, Football Coach, Football Player)
Boston College
Athletic Dept
Chestnut Hill, MA 02467, USA

Adderley, Herb (Athlete, Football Player)
1058 Tristram Cir
Mantua, NJ 08051-2204, us

Addica, Milo (Director)
c/o Adam Perry *Agency for the Performing Arts (APA)*
405 S Beverly Dr Ste 500
Beverly Hills, CA 90212-4425, USA

Addis, Bob (Athlete, Baseball Player)
7466 Hollycroft Ln
Mentor, OH 44060-5611, USA

Addison, Rafael (Athlete, Basketball Player)
6 Bernadette Ct
East Hanover, NJ 07936-3425, USA

Addonizio, Kim (Writer)
3749 Park Boulevard Way
Oakland, CA 94610-2837, USA

Addotta, Kip (Actor, Comedian)

Adduci, Jim (Athlete, Baseball Player)
9529 S Sawyer Ave
Evergreen Park, IL 60805-2343, USA

Adduono, Ray (Athlete, Hockey Player)
108A Spruce Crt
Thunder Bay, ON P7C 1X6, Canada

Adduono, Rick (Athlete, Hockey Player)
153 Donald St W
Thunder Bay, ON P7E 5X8, Canada

Addy, Mark (Actor)
c/o Jane Epstein *Independent Talent Group*
40 Whitfield St
London W1T 2RH, UNITED KINGDOM

Ade, King Sunny (Music Group)
Monterey International
72 W Adams St # 1000
Chicago, IL 60603-5107, USA

Adebayor, Emmanuel (Athlete, Soccer Player)
c/o Staff Member *Manchester City FC*
City of Manchester Stadium
SportCity
Manchester M11 3FF, UK

Adedapo, Naima (Musician)
c/o Simon Fuller *XIX Entertainment (UK)*
32/33 Ransomes Dock
London SW11 4NP, UNITED KINGDOM (UK)

Adele (Musician)
5 Western Esplanade
Portslade
Brighton, East Sussex BN41 1WE, UNITED KINGDOM

Adelman, Jason (Actor)
11 Marine Ter Unit 5
Santa Monica, CA 90401-3115, USA

Adelman, Rick (Athlete, Basketball Player, Coach)
11919 SW Breyman Ave
Portland, OR 97219-8412, USA

Adelson, Sheldon (Business Person)
Venetian Resort Hotel Casino
3355 Las Vegas Blvd S
Las Vegas, NV 89109-8931, USA

Adelstein, Paul (Actor)
c/o Marsha McManus *Principal Entertainment*
9255 W Sunset Blvd Ste 500
Los Angeles, CA 90069-3301, USA

Adem (Music Group)
c/o Staff Member *Paradigm (Monterey)*
404 W Franklin St
Monterey, CA 93940-2303, USA

Aderholt, Robert (Congressman, Politician)
205 4th Ave NE Ste 104
Cullman, AL 35055-1965, USA

Adeyamju, Victor (Athlete, Football Player)
5375 S Maplewood Ave
Chicago, IL 60632-1537, USA

Adeyanju, Victor (Athlete, Football Player)
5218 W Cavedale Dr
Phoenix, AZ 85083-1270, us

Adickes, John M (Athlete, Football Player)
205 W Fair Oaks Pl
San Antonio, TX 78209-3710, USA

Adickes, Mark (Athlete, Football Player)
7200 Cambridge St
Houston, TX 77030-4202, USA

Adie, Kate (Journalist)
c/o Staff Member *Peller Artistes Limited*
39 Princes Ave
London N3 2DA, UK

Adiga, Aravind (Writer)
c/o Staff Member *Penguin Group (Australia)*
P.O. Box 701
Hawthorn VIC 3122, Australia

Adjani, Isabelle (Actor)
c/o Roberto Almagia *Media Vision Artists (Italy)*
Via Luigi Calamatta 16
Rome 00193, ITALY

Adkins, Derrick (Athlete, Olympic Athlete, Track Athlete)
909 Derrick Adkins Ln
W Hempstead, NY 11552-3915, USA

Adkins, James (Athlete, Baseball Player)
185 Cedar Ridge Ct
Coppell, TX 75019-2981, USA

Adkins, Jim (Musician)
c/o John Silva *SAM*
722 Seward St
Los Angeles, CA 90038-3504, USA

Adkins, Jon (Athlete, Baseball Player)
5322 Fisher Bowen Branch Rd
Wayne, WV 25570-5946, USA

Adkins, Kevin (Athlete, Football Player)
209 Redwood Dr
Coppell, TX 75019-5422, USA

Adkins, Margene (Athlete, Football Player)
2312 Donnyville Ct
Fort Worth, TX 76119-3111, USA

Adkins, Sam (Athlete, Football Player)
15912 NE 160th St
Woodinville, WA 98072-8910, USA

Adkins, Seth (Actor)
c/o Alisa Adler *Paradigm*
8942 Wilshire Blvd
Beverly Hills, CA 90211-1908, USA

Adkins, Trace (Musician)
c/o Ken Levitan *Vector Management*
PO Box 120479
Nashville, TN 37212-0479, USA

Adler, Charlie (Actor)
c/o Neil Dickens *WTD PR*
200 N Larchmont Blvd
Los Angeles, CA 90004-3707, USA

Adler, Cisco (Musician)
21653 Rambla Vis
Malibu, CA 90265-5125, USA

Adler, Gilbert (Director, Producer)
2711 Bowmont Dr
Beverly Hills, CA 90210-1816, USA

Adler, Jerry (Actor)
c/o Alisa Adler *Paradigm*
8942 Wilshire Blvd
Beverly Hills, CA 90211-1908, USA

Adler, Jonathan (Designer)
74 Gardiners Bay Dr
Shelter Island, NY 11964, USA

Adler, Lee (Artist)
Lime Kiln Farm
Climax, NY 12042, USA

Adler, Max (Actor)
c/o Rodney Ponder *Justice & Ponder*
PO Box 480033
Los Angeles, CA 90048-1033, USA

Adler, Steven (Music Group)
Big FD Entertainment
301 Arizona Ave Ste 200
Santa Monica, CA 90401-1364, USA

Adlesh, Dave (Athlete, Baseball Player)
9770 Avenida Monterey
Cypress, CA 90630-3446, USA

Adlon, Pamela (Actor, Producer)
c/o Court Barrett *ID Public Relations*
7060 Hollywood Blvd Fl 8th
Los Angeles, CA 90028-6021, USA

Adni, Daniel (Musician)
64A Menelik Road
London NW2 3RH, UNITED KINGDOM (UK)

Adorf, Mario (Actor)
Perlacher Str 28
Grunwald D-82031, GERMANY

Adoti, Rasaaq (Actor)
c/o Staff Member *Coast to Coast Talent Group*
3350 Barham Blvd
Los Angeles, CA 90068-1404, USA

Adoti, Razaaq (Actor, Producer)
c/o Staff Member *Coast II Coast Entertainment*
3350 Wilshire Blvd Apt 1200
Los Angeles, CA 90010-4211, USA

Adria, Ferran (Chef)
El Bulli
En Cala Montjoi Roses
Girona 17480, SPAIN

Adrian, Nathan (Athlete, Swimmer)
152 Sheridan Rd
Bremerton, WA 98310-2088, USA

Adsit, Scott (Actor)
c/o Melanie Truhett *Truhett / Garcia Management*
8033 W Sunset Blvd
West Hollywood, CA 90046-2401, USA

Adu, Helen Folasade (Sade) (Actor, Musician)
c/o Staff Member *RCA Records (UK)*
9 Derry St
London W8 5HY, UNITED KINGDOM (UK)

Adu, Sade (Musician)
c/o Steven Manzano *RDWM America*
1158 26th St Ste 564
Santa Monica, CA 90403-4698, USA

Aduba, Uzo (Actor)
c/o Kelly Bush Novak *ID Public Relations*
7060 Hollywood Blvd Fl 8th
Los Angeles, CA 90028-6021, USA

Adubato, Richie (Basketball Coach, Coach)
290 Chiswell Pl
Lake Mary, FL 32746-4123, USA

Adway, Dwayne (Actor)
c/o Staff Member *Diverse Talent Group*
1875 Century Park E Ste 2250
Los Angeles, CA 90067-2563, USA

Aebischer, David (Athlete, Hockey Player)
365 Jackson St
Denver, CO 80206-4538, USA

Aedo, Daniela (Actor)
c/o Staff Member *Televisa*
Blvd Adolfo Lopez Mateos 232
Colonia San Angel INN
DF CP 01060, MEXICO

Aerosmith (Music Group)
c/o Trudy Green *Azoff Music Management*
1100 Glendon Ave Ste 2000
Los Angeles, CA 90024-3524, USA

Afenir, Troy (Athlete, Baseball Player)
459 Old Via Rancho Dr
Escondido, CA 92029-7959, USA

Affeldt, Jeremy (Athlete, Baseball Player)
10111 S Green Gate Ln
Medical Lake, WA 99022-8531, USA

Affholter, Erik (Athlete, Football Player)
41734 N Maidstone Ct
Anthem, AZ 85086-1187, USA

Afflalo, Arron (Athlete, Basketball Player)
1221 Ocean Ave Apt 1603
Santa Monica, CA 90401-1049, USA

Affleck, Ben (Actor, Director, Producer)
c/o Staff Member *Spanky Taylor*
3010 Adornos Way
Burbank, CA 91504-1609, USA

Affleck, Bruce (Athlete, Hockey Player)
1847 Oxborough Ct
Chesterfield, MO 63017-8037, USA

Affleck, Bruce (Athlete, Hockey Player)
StLouis Blues 1401
Saint Louis, MO 63103-2700

Affleck, Casey (Actor, Producer)
c/o Staff Member *The Affleck/Middleton Project*
25 Valley St
Pasadena, CA 91105-2015, USA

Affleck, James G (Business Person)
American Cyanamid
5 Giralda Farms
Madison, NJ 07940-1027, USA

Afghan Raiders (Music Group)
c/o David Benveniste *Velvet Hammer*
9014 Melrose Ave
Los Angeles, CA 90069-5610, USA

AFI (Music Group)
c/o John Silva *SAM*
722 Seward St
Los Angeles, CA 90038-3504, USA

Afinogenov, Maxim (Athlete, Hockey Player)
3700 S Ocean Blvd Apt 1502
Highland Beach, FL 33487-3376, USA

Afrika, Bambaataa (Artist, Musician)
KLB Productions
70A Greenwich Ave # 441
New York, NY 10011-8300, USA

Afrojack (DJ, Musician)
c/o Joel Zimmerman *WME/IMG (NY)*
11 Madison Ave Fl 18
New York, NY 10010-3669, USA

Afroman (Musician)
c/o Zack Johnson *Union Artists Group*
Prefers to be contacted by phone.
Los Angeles, CA NA, USA

Agajanian, Ben (Athlete, Football Player)
27950 Avenida Terrazo
Cathedral City, CA 92234-9401, us

Agajanian, Benjamin (Ben) (Athlete, Football Player)
4471 Farquhar Ave
Los Alamitos, CA 90720-3719, USA

Aga Khan IV, Prince Karim (Religious Leader)
Aiglemont
Gouvieux 60270, FRANCE

Agam, Yaacov (Artist)
26 Rue Boulard
Paris 75014, FRANCE

Agassi, Andre (Athlete, Olympic Athlete, Tennis Player)
9709 Winter Palace Dr
Las Vegas, NV 89145-8637, USA

Agbayani, Benny (Athlete, Baseball Player)
66-948 Kolu Pl
Waialua, HI 96791-9743, USA

Age, Louis (Athlete, Football Player)
7517 Park Ave
Houma, LA 70364-3631, USA

Agee, Tommie (Athlete, Football Player)
1004 Lenora Ln
Andalusia, AL 36421-2324, USA

Agena, Keiko (Actor)
c/o Staff Member *Fenton Kritzer Entertainment*
8840 Wilshire Blvd Fl 3
Beverly Hills, CA 90211-2606, USA

Ager, Nikita (Actor)
c/o Kim Byrd *Innovative Artists*
1505 10th St
Santa Monica, CA 90401-2805, USA

Aghdashloo, Shohreh (Actor)
c/o Tamara Houston *Round Table Entertainment*
509 N Fairfax Ave Ste 200
Los Angeles, CA 90036-1733, USA

Agholor, Nelson (Athlete, Football Player)
c/o Tory Dandy *Independent Sports & Entertainment (ISE-IN)*
6435 W Jefferson Blvd # 197
Fort Wayne, IN 46804-6203, USA

Agliotti, Marilyn (Athlete, Track Athlete)
c/o Staff Member *Oranje-Zwart MHC*
Charles Roelstaan 13
Eindhoven 05644, NETHERLANDS

Agna, Tom (Actor, Producer, Writer)
c/o Lisa Harrison *WME/IMG*
9601 Wilshire Blvd
Beverly Hills, CA 90210-5213, USA

Agnel, Yannick (Athlete, Swimmer)
30 Boul General Louis Delfino
Nice 06300, FRANCE

Agnelo, Geraldo Majella Cardinal (Religious Leader)
Rue Martin Alfanso de Souza 270
Salvador, BA 40100-050, BRAZIL

Agnew, Jim (Athlete, Hockey Player)
2747 Ancabide Ln
Missoula, MT 59803-2904, USA

Agnew, Ray (Athlete, Football Player)
2215 Cline St
Winston Salem, NC 27107-2411, USA

Agnus, Michael (Business Person)
Whitbread PLC
Chiswell St
London EC1Y 4SD, UNITED KINGDOM (UK)

Agoos, Jeff (Athlete, Soccer Player)
235 Pascack Rd
Park Ridge, NJ 07656-1125, USA

Agostini, Didier (Actor)
Cineart
36 Rue de Ponthieu
Paris 75008, FRANCE

Agosto, Ben (Athlete, Figure Skater, Olympic Athlete)
529 Kingsmoor Dr
Simpsonville, SC 29681-3500, USA

Agosto, Juan (Athlete, Baseball Player)
3815 65th St E
Bradenton, FL 34208-6613, USA

Agre, Bernard Cardinal (Religious Leader)
Archeveche
Ave Jean-Paul II
Abidjan 01 BP 1287, IVORY COAST

Agron, Dianna (Actor, Musician)
c/o Jessica Kolstad *Relevant*
400 S Beverly Dr Ste 220
Beverly Hills, CA 90212-4404, USA

Aguayo, Luis (Athlete, Baseball Player)
501 Calle Julio Andino
San Juan, PR 00924-2106, USA

Aguiar, Louie (Athlete, Football Player)
1411 Palmer Creek Dr
Columbia, IL 62236-2747, USA

Aguila, Chris (Athlete, Baseball Player)
2011 Brittany Meadows Dr
Reno, NV 89521-5272, USA

Aguilar, Macarena (Athlete)
c/o Staff Member *Randers HK*
Sjaellandsgade 57
Randers 08900, SPAIN

Aguilar, Pepe (Musician)
c/o Eric Rovner *WME|IMG*
9601 Wilshire Blvd
Beverly Hills, CA 90210-5213, USA

Aguilera, Christina (Musician)
c/o Brett Ruttenberg *Imprint PR*
6121 W Sunset Blvd
Neuehouse
Los Angeles, CA 90028-6442, USA

Aguilera, Hellweg Max (Artist, Photographer)
PO Box 289
White Plains, NY 10605-0289, USA

Aguilera, Marian (Actor)
c/o Staff Member *Kuranda Management*
Isla De Oza, 30
Madrid 28035, SPAIN

Aguilera, Richard W (Rick) (Athlete, Baseball Player)
PO Box 174
Rancho Santa Fe, CA 92067-0174, USA

Aguirre, Beatriz (Actor)
c/o Staff Member *Televisa*
Blvd Adolfo Lopez Mateos 232
Colonia San Angel INN
DF CP 01060, MEXICO

Aguirre, Mark (Basketball Player, Olympic Athlete)
10281 Highland Ct
Frisco, TX 75033-2415, USA

Agustoni, Gilberto Cardinal (Religious Leader)
Piazzi della Citla Leorina 9
Rome 00193, ITALY

Agutter, Jenny (Actor)
c/o Gilly Sanquinetti *The Artists Partnership*
101 Finsbury Pavement
London EC2A 1RS, UNITED KINGDOM

Agyeman, Freema (Actor)
c/o Sarah Camlett *Independent Talent Group*
40 Whitfield St
London W1T 2RH, UNITED KINGDOM

Ahanotu, Chidi (Athlete, Football Player)
301 W Platt St
Tampa, FL 33606-2292, USA

Ahdout, Jonathan (Actor)
c/o Staff Member *Paradigm*
8942 Wilshire Blvd
Beverly Hills, CA 90211-1908, USA

Aheam, Kevin (Athlete, Hockey Player)
174 Marlborough St
Boston, MA 02116-1822, USA

Ahearn, Kevin (Athlete, Hockey Player, Olympic Athlete)
174 Marlborough St
Boston, MA 02116-1822, USA

Ahearne, Pat (Athlete, Baseball Player)
3354 S Flower St Apt 60
Lakewood, CO 80227-4661, USA

Ahem, Jim (Golfer)
314 E Wagon Wheel Dr
Phoenix, AZ 85020-4066, USA

Ahern, Cecelia (Writer)
c/o Staff Member *Bazar Forlag*
Hammarby Fabriksvag 25
Stockholm 12033, Sweden

Ahern, Fred (Athlete, Hockey Player)
807 E 5th St
Boston, MA 02127-3217, USA

Ahern, Jim (Athlete, Golfer)
8216 N 3rd Ave
Phoenix, AZ 85021-5505, USA

Ahmed, Riz (Actor, Musician)
c/o Kate Bryden *Gordon and French*
12-13 Poland St
London W1F 8QB, UNITED KINGDOM (UK)

Ahola, Peter (Athlete, Hockey Player)
Hiiralantie 11a
Espoo 02160, Finland

Ahrens, Chris (Athlete, Hockey Player)
1412 Linstock Dr
Holiday, FL 34690-6634, USA

Ahrens, Dave (Athlete, Football Player)
10224 Stillwell Dr
Avon, IN 46123-1121, us

Ahrens, David (Dave) (Athlete, Football Player)
5864 Manchester Ct
Pittsboro, IN 46167-9064, USA

Ahrens, Lynn (Musician)
c/o Staff Member *Gersh*
9465 Wilshire Blvd Ste 600
Beverly Hills, CA 90212-2605, USA

Ahtisaari, Martti (Politician)
H E The President of Finland
Tasavallan Presidentin
Kanslia, Helsinki SF-00170, Finland

Ah You, Junior (Athlete, Football Player)
55-690 Wahinepee St
Laie, NV 89129-7657, USA

Aicardi, Matteo (Athlete, Olympic Athlete, Water Polo Player)
c/o Staff Member *ASD Pro Recco*
Via Biagio Assereto 10/A
Recco (GE) 16036, ITALY

Aiello, Anthony (Athlete, Football Player)
9 Taylor Ave
Norwalk, OH 44857-1645, USA

Aiello, Danny (Actor, Director, Producer)
c/o Tracey Miller *Tracey Miller & Associates*
2610 Fire Rd
Egg Harbor Township, NJ 08234-9551, USA

Aiken, Blair (Race Car Driver)
4855 Highland Springs Rd
Lakeport, CA 95453-9346, USA

Aiken, Clay (Musician)
c/o Erica Gerard *PMK/BNC Public Relations*
622 3rd Ave Fl 8
New York, NY 10017-6707, USA

Aiken, John (Athlete, Hockey Player)
18 Pinetree Rd
Billerica, MA 01821-3446, USA

Aiken, Johnny (Athlete, Hockey Player)
18 Pinetree Rd
Billerica, MA 01821-3446, USA

AIken, Liam (Actor)
c/o JoAnne Colonna *Brillstein Entertainment Partners*
9150 Wilshire Blvd Ste 350
Beverly Hills, CA 90212-3453, USA

Aiken, Sam (Athlete, Football Player)
103 New Bingham Ct
Cary, NC 27513-4093, USA

Aiken, Sam (Athlete, Football Player)
PO Box 32
Wake Forest, NC 27588, us

Aikens, Carl (Athlete, Football Player)
931 W Arquilla Dr Apt 114
Glenwood, IL 60425-1143, USA

Aikens, Carl (Athlete, Football Player)
931 W Arquilla Dr Apt 114S
Glenwood, IL 60425-1179, s

Aikens, Curtis (Chef)
68 Baca Vis
Novato, CA 94947-2102, USA

Aikens, Willie (Athlete, Baseball Player)
10206 Locust St
Kansas City, MO 64131-4214, USA

Aikman, Laura Holly (Actor)
551 Green Lanes
Palmers Green
London N13 3DR, UNITED KINGDOM (UK)

Aikman, Troy (Athlete, Football Player, Sportscaster)
Aikman Enterprises
PO Box 192309
Dallas, TX 75219-8517, USA

Aiko, Jhene (Musician)
c/o Tammy Brook *FYI Public Relations*
174 5th Ave Ste 404
New York, NY 10010-5964, USA

Aimee, Anouk (Actor)
c/o Staff Member *ArtMedia*
8 rue Danielle Casanova
Paris 75002, FRANCE

Aimi, Milton (Athlete, Soccer Player)
19927 Stonelodge Dr
Katy, TX 77450-5201, USA

Ainge, Erik (Athlete, Football Player)
634 NE Kathleen Ct
Hillsboro, OR 97124-4029, USA

Ainsleigh, H Gordon (Athlete, Track Athlete)
17119 Placer Hills Rd
Meadow Vista, CA 95722-9508, USA

Ainsworth, Kurt (Athlete, Baseball Player, Olympic Athlete)
14909 Purple Martin Ct
Baton Rouge, LA 70810-8420, USA

Air, Donna (Model, Television Host)
c/o Staff Member *The Richard Stone Partnership*
3 De Walden Ct
85 New Cavendish Street
London W1W 6XD, UNITED KINGDOM

Airborne Toxic Event, The (Music Group)
c/o Staff Member *Paradigm (Monterey)*
404 W Franklin St
Monterey, CA 93940-2303, USA

Airpushers (Music Group)
c/o Staff Member *Paradigm (Monterey)*
404 W Franklin St
Monterey, CA 93940-2303, USA

Air Supply (Music Group, Musician)
c/o Staff Member *Agency for the Performing Arts (APA)*
405 S Beverly Dr Ste 500
Beverly Hills, CA 90212-4425, USA

Air Traffic (Music Group, Musician)
c/o Staff Member *SuperVision Management Group*
Zeppelin Building
59-61 Farringdon Rd
London EC1M 3JB, UK

Al-Saud, Salman Sultan (Astronaut)
PO Box 18368
Riyadh 11415, SAUDI ARABIA

Aislin (Artist, Cartoonist)
Gazette
200-1010 Sainte-Catherine Rue O
Montreal, QC H3B 5L1, CANADA

Aitay, Victor (Musician)
800 Deerfield Rd Apt 203
Highland Park, IL 60035-3548, USA

Aitch, Matt (Athlete, Basketball Player)
1525 Bentbrook Cir
Lansing, MI 48917-1402, USA

Aitken, Brad (Athlete, Hockey Player)
825 Royal Orchard Dr
Oshawa, ON L1K 1Z8, Canada

Aitken, John (Artist)
University College
Slade Art School
London WC1E 6BT, UNITED KINGDOM (UK)

Aivazoff, Micah (Athlete, Hockey Player)
6916 Hammond St
Powell River, BC V8A 1R4, Canada

Aizley, Carrie (Actor)
c/o Staff Member *Much and House Public Relations*
8075 W 3rd St Ste 500
Los Angeles, CA 90048-4325, USA

Aja, Alexandre (Director)
c/o Sara Bottfeld *Industry Entertainment Partners*
955 Carrillo Dr Ste 300
Los Angeles, CA 90048-5400, USA

Ajae, Franklyn (Comedian)
1312 S Orange Dr
Los Angeles, CA 90019-2901, USA

Ajala, David (Actor)
c/o Gertie Lowe *Public Eye Communications*
535 Kings Rd
#313 Plaza
London SW10 0SZ, UNITED KINGDOM

Ajirotutu, Seyi (Athlete, Football Player)
c/o Frank Bauer *Sun West Sports*
7883 N Pershing Ave
Stockton, CA 95207-1749, USA

Akana, Anna (Actor)
c/o Samantha Hill *Wolf-Kasteler Public Relations*
6255 W Sunset Blvd Ste 1111
Los Angeles, CA 90028-7426, USA

Akayev, Askar (President)
President's Office
Government House
Bishkek 720003, KYRGYZSTAN

Akbar, Hakim (Athlete, Football Player)
300 W Ocean Blvd Apt 6510
Long Beach, CA 90802-7959, us

Akbar, Hakim (Athlete, Football Player)
29869 Vanderbilt St Apt 4
Hayward, CA 94544-6873, USA

Akbar, Taufik (Astronaut)
Jalan Simp
Pahlawan III/24
Bandung 40124, INDONESIA

Akebono (Wrestler)
Azumazeki Stable
4-6-4 Higashi Komagala
Ryogoku
Tokyo, JAPAN

Aker, Jack (Athlete, Baseball Player)
5911 E Bloomfield Rd
Scottsdale, AZ 85254-4338, USA

Akerlund, Jonas (Director)
c/o Staff Member *ICM Partners*
10250 Constellation Blvd Fl 7
Los Angeles, CA 90067-6207, USA

Akerman, Malin (Actor)
c/o Keleigh Thomas Morgan *Sunshine Sachs*
720 Cole Ave
Los Angeles, CA 90038-3606, USA

Akers, David (Athlete, Football Player)
c/o Jerrold C Colton *CS Sports Management*
1103 Laurel Oak Rd
Voorhees, NJ 08043-4318, USA

Akers, Michelle (Athlete, Olympic Athlete, Soccer Player)
c/o Staff Member *US Soccer Federation*
1801 S Prairie Ave
Chicago, IL 60616-1356, USA

Akers, Thomas D Colonel (Astronaut)
14930 State Rte E
Eminence, MO 65466, USA

Akihito, Emperor (Politician)
Imperial Palace
1-1 Chiyoda-Chiyoda-Ku, Tokyo 00100, Japan

Akil, Mara Brock (Producer)
c/o Joy Fehily *PMK/BNC Public Relations*
1840 Century Park E Ste 1400
Los Angeles, CA 90067-2115, USA

Akil, Salim (Director)
c/o Joy Fehily *PMK/BNC Public Relations*
1840 Century Park E Ste 1400
Los Angeles, CA 90067-2115, USA

Akili, Samaji (Athlete, Football Player)
10605 Caminito Cascara
San Diego, CA 92108-2601, USA

Akin, Harold (Athlete, Football Player)
13116 Carriage Way
Oklahoma City, OK 73142-3308, us

Akin, Harold (Athlete, Football Player)
13116 Carriage Way
Oklahoma City, OK 73142-3308, USA

Akin, Henry (Athlete, Basketball Player)
2012 Mill Pointe Dr SE
Mill Creek, WA 98012-4800, USA

Akin, W. Todd (Congressman, Politician)
117 Cannon Hob
Washington, DC 20515-2502, USA

Akinnuoye-Agbaje, Adewale (Actor)
c/o Michael Lazo *Untitled Entertainment*
350 S Beverly Dr Ste 200
Beverly Hills, CA 90212-4819, USA

Akinradewo, Foluke (Athlete, Volleyball Player)
1181 NW 101st Way
Plantation, FL 33322-6556, USA

Akins, Chris (Athlete, Football Player)
60 Gold Mine Springs Rd
Conway, AR 72032-8204, USA

Akins, Chris (Athlete, Football Player)
11 McClure Acres Rd Apt 6
Conway, AR 72032-9252, us

Akins, Rhett (Musician, Songwriter)
108 Cumberland Blue Trl
Hendersonville, TN 37075-7703, USA

Akins, Sid (Athlete, Baseball Player, Olympic Athlete)
1655 W Sandtown Rd SW
Marietta, GA 30064-3744, USA

Akiu, Mike (Athlete, Football Player)
PO Box 1845
Kailua, HI 96734-8845, USA

Akiu, Mike (Athlete, Football Player)
297 Kakahiaka St
Kailua, HI 96734-3461, us

Akiyama, Toyohiro (Astronaut, Journalist)
Tokyo Broadcasting Systems
3-6-5 Akasaka
Minaloku
Tokyo 00107, JAPAN

Akon (Musician)
c/o Jaime Cassavechia *EJ Media Group*
349 5th Ave Fl 3
New York, NY 10016-5021, USA

Akoshino (Royalty)
Imperial Palace
Tokyo, JAPAN

Akroyd, Dan (Actor, Musician, Producer, Writer)
c/o Fred Specktor *Creative Artists Agency (CAA)*
2000 Avenue of the Stars Ste 100
Los Angeles, CA 90067-4705, USA

Aksyonov, Vassily P (Writer)
Random House
1745 Broadway Frnt 3 # B1
New York, NY 10019-4343, USA

Alabama (Music Group)
c/o Staff Member *Conway Entertainment Group*
1625 Broadway Ste 500
Nashville, TN 37203-3166, USA

Alagia, John (Producer)
c/o Sandy Robertson *World's End Inc*
183 N Martel Ave Ste 270
Los Angeles, CA 90036-2755, USA

Alaia, Azzeddine (Designer, Fashion Designer)
18 Rue de la Verrerie
Paris 75008, FRANCE

Alaimo, Marc (Actor)
1936 Seminole Dr
Agoura Hills, CA 91301-2942, USA

Alaina, Lauren (Musician)
c/o Michelle Young *19 Entertainment*
401 Wilshire Blvd Ste 1070
Santa Monica, CA 90401-1428, USA

Alam, Natasha (Actor, Model)
c/o Mike Baldridge *Momentum Talent and Literary Agency*
3500 W Olive Ave Ste 300
Burbank, CA 91505-4647, USA

Alan, Buddy (Musician)
600 E Gilbert Dr
Tempe, AZ 85281-2021, USA

Alan, Reuber (Athlete, Football Player)
1202 Crosswind Dr
Murphy, TX 75094-4110, USA

Al and the Transamericans (Music Group)
c/o Staff Member *Paradigm (Monterey)*
404 W Franklin St
Monterey, CA 93940-2303, USA

Alapa, Clifton (Athlete, Football Player)
3928 Country Lights St
Las Vegas, NV 89129-7657, USA

Alarie, Mark (Athlete, Basketball Player)
8514 Country Club Dr
Bethesda, MD 20817-4581, USA

Al-Assad, Bashar (Politician, President)
c/o Staff Member *Presidential Office (Syria)*
Muharreem Abu Rumanch
Al-Rashid Street
Damascas, Syria

Alatorre, Javier (Actor)
c/o Staff Member *TV Azteca*
Periferico Sur 4121
Colonia Fuentes del Pedregal
DF CP 14141, Mexico

Alazraqui, Carlos (Actor)
4934 Cartwright Ave
North Hollywood, CA 91601-4727, USA

Alba, Gibson (Athlete, Baseball Player)
71 Orchard St
Elmwood Park, NJ 07407-2112, USA

Alba, Jessica (Actor)
c/o Brad Cafarelli *PMK/BNC Public Relations*
1840 Century Park E Ste 1400
Los Angeles, CA 90067-2115, USA

Albaladejo, Jonathan (Athlete, Baseball Player)
12517 River Birch Dr
Riverview, FL 33569-8206, USA

Alban, Carlo (Actor)
c/o Gloria Bonelli *Gloria Bonelli & Associates*
11 Victoria Ter
Goshen, NY 10924-2205, USA

Alban, Richard (Dick) (Athlete, Football Player)
PO Box 87
Berwyn, PA 19312-0087, USA

Albarn, Damon (Musician, Songwriter, Writer)
CMO Mgmt
Ransomes Dock
35 Parkgale Road #32
London SW11 4NP, UNITED KINGDOM (UK)

Albea, Troy (Athlete, Football Player)
1070 L and N Rd
Lincolnton, GA 30817-4724, USA

Albeck, Stan (Basketball Coach, Coach)
130 Tall Oak Dr
San Antonio, TX 78232-1316, USA

Albelin, Tommy (Athlete, Coach, Hockey Player)
c/o Staff Member *New Jersey Devils*
165 Mulberry St
Continental Arena
Newark, NJ 07102-3607, USA

Albelin, Tommy (Athlete, Hockey Player)
51 S Pearl St Ste 14
Attn: Coaching Staff
Albany, NY 12207-1500, USA

Alberghetti, Anna Maria (Actor, Musician)
10333 Chrysanthemum Ln
Los Angeles, CA 90077-2812, USA

Alberoni, Sherry (Actor)
PO Box 161936
Altamonte Springs, FL 32716-1936, USA

Albers, Chantelle (Actor)
c/o Jessica Katz *Katz Public Relations*
14527 Dickens St
Sherman Oaks, CA 91403-3756, USA

Albers, Hans (Business Person)
BASF AG
Carl-Bosch-Str 38
Ludwigshafen 78351, GERMANY

Albers, Kristi (Athlete, Golfer)
5872 Via Cuesta Dr
El Paso, TX 79912-6608, USA

Albers, Matthew James (Athlete, Baseball Player)
15 S Swanwick Pl
Tomball, TX 77375-4478, USA

Alberstein, Chava (Musician)
Aviv Productions Inc
10418 E Meadowhill Dr
Scottsdale, AZ 85255-1747, USA

Albert, Branden (Athlete, Football Player)
c/o Staff Member *Kansas City Chiefs*
1 Arrowhead Dr
Kansas City, MO 64129-1651, USA

Albert, Calvin (Artist)
6525 Brandywine Dr S
Margate, FL 33063-5538, USA

Albert, Kenny (Commentator, Sportscaster)
c/o Staff Member *Fox Sports (NY)*
1211 Avenue of the Americas Ste 302
New York, NY 10036-8799, USA

Albert, Lewis (Athlete, Football Player)
3532 Macedonia Rd
Centreville, MS 39631-3634, USA

Albert, Marv (Sportscaster)

Alberti, Micah (Actor)
c/o Ryan Daly *Zero Gravity Management*
11110 Ohio Ave Ste 100
Los Angeles, CA 90025-3329, USA

Alberto, Padre (Actor)
c/o Staff Member *Telemundo*
2470 W 8th Ave
Hialeah, FL 33010-2000, USA

Albert (Prince) (Royalty)
Palais de Monaco
Boite Postale 518
Monacode Cedex 98015, MONACO

Alberts, Andrew (Athlete, Hockey Player)
205 Mill St Apt 302
Excelsior, MN 55331-2105, USA

Alberts, Francis (Butch) (Athlete, Baseball Player)
3063 Amberlea Ln
Baldwinsville, NY 13027-1613, USA

Alberts, Trev (Athlete, Football Player)
10430 E Hickory Ridge Dr
Rochelle, IL 61068-9790, USA

Albita (Musician)
Estefan Enterprises
6205 Bird Rd
Miami, FL 33155-4823, USA

Albom, Mitch (Writer)
25600 Franklin Park Dr
Franklin, MI 48025-1211, USA

Alborn, Alan (Athlete, Olympic Athlete, Skier)

Alborzian, Cameron (Model)
c/o Staff Member *Storm Model Management*
5 Jubilee Pl
1st Floor
London SW3 3TD, UK

Albrecht, A Chim (Wrestler)
Physique Promotions
9668 Moss Glen Ave
Fountain Valley, CA 92708-1053, USA

Albrecht, Alex (Actor)
c/o Mieke Gotha *Agentur Gotha*
Elisabethstrasse 19
München 80796, Germany

Albrecht, Daniel (Athlete, Skier)
Hotel Des Alpes
3984 Fiesch
SWITZERLAND

Albrecht, Kate (Actor)
c/o Brad Petrigala *Brillstein Entertainment Partners*
9150 Wilshire Blvd Ste 350
Beverly Hills, CA 90212-3453, USA

Albright, Ethan (Athlete, Football Player)
19181 Ferry Field Ter
Leesburg, VA 20176-1276, USA

Albright, Ethan (Athlete, Football Player)
PO Box 38337
Greensboro, NC 27438-8337, us

Albright, Gerald (Musician)
c/o Ron Moss *Chapman Management*
14011 Ventura Blvd Ste 405
Sherman Oaks, CA 91423-5230, USA

Albright, Ira (Athlete, Football Player)
4019 Wind River Dr
Dallas, TX 75216-6064, USA

Albright, Madeleine (Politician)
1318 34th St NW
Washington, DC 20007-2801, USA

Albright, Tenley (Athlete, Figure Skater, Olympic Athlete)
70 Suffolk Rd
Chestnut Hill, MA 02467-1218, USA

Albright, William (Bill) (Athlete, Football Player)
315 Bolands Private Dr
Shell Lake, WI 54871-8723, USA

Albritton, Vince (Athlete, Football Player)

Albuquerque, Lita (Artist)
305 Boyd St
Los Angeles, CA 90013-1509, USA

Albury, Victor (Vic) (Athlete, Baseball Player)
2109 E Bougainvillea Ave
Tampa, FL 33612-7035, USA

Albus, Jim (Athlete, Golfer)
3972 Somerset Dr Unit 1
Sarasota, FL 34242-1110, USA

Alcala, Santo (Athlete, Baseball Player)
Ramon Mota #18
San Pedro de Macoris, Dominican Republic, USA

Alcantara, Izzy (Athlete, Baseball Player)
4059 240th Pl SE
Sammamish, WA 98029-6304, USA

Alcaraz, Luis (Athlete, Baseball Player)
679 Calle Chihuahua
Urb Venus Gdns Norte
San Juan, PR 00926-4614, USA

Alcivar, Patricia (Athlete, Boxer)
c/o Gigi Rock *Heraea Marketing*
10905 E Pear Tree Dr
Cornville, AZ 86325-5523, USA

Alcorn, Gary (Athlete, Basketball Player)
2552 Trenton Ave
Clovis, CA 93619-4249, USA

Alcott, Amy S (Athlete, Golfer)
323 Amalfi Dr
Santa Monica, CA 90402-1127, USA

Alda, Alan (Actor)
PO Box 360
Water Mill, NY 11976-0360, USA

Alda, Rutanya (Actor)
c/o Randi Ross *Phoenix Artists*
330 W 38th St Rm 607
New York, NY 10018-2908, USA

Aldcorn, Gary (Athlete, Hockey Player)
24 Bendamere Cres
Markham, ON L3P 6Y2, CANADA

Aldean, Jason (Musician)
c/o Kevin Neal *WME (Nashville)*
1201 Demonbreun St
Nashville, TN 37203-3140, USA

Alden, Bruce (Producer)
c/o Staff Member *Vision Art Management*
750 N San Vicente Blvd Ste RE800
West Hollywood, CA 90069-5778, USA

Alden, Ginger (Actor, Model, Musician)
25 Rolling Hill Ct W
Sag Harbor, NY 11963-2012, USA

Alden Robinson, Phil (Director, Producer, Writer)
Writers Co-op
4000 Warner Blvd Bldg 1
Burbank, CA 91522-0001, USA

Alderete, Loretta (Athlete, Golfer)
PO Box 6882
La Quinta, CA 92248-6882, USA

Alderfer-Benner, Gertrude (Athlete, Baseball Player)
2191 County Line Rd
East Greenville, PA 18041-2700, USA

Alderman, Darrell (Race Car Driver)
DA Construction Co
8130 Flemingsburg Rd
Morehead, KY 40351, USA

Alderman, Grady (Athlete, Football Player)
62 Elk Valley Way
Evergreen, CO 80439-4951, USA

Alderman, Grady (Athlete, Football Player)
62 Elk Valley Way
Evergreen, CO 80439-4951, us

Alderson, Kristen (Actor)

Alderson, Richard Sandy (Commentator)
305 E 85th St PH B
New York, NY 10028-4672, USA

Alderton, John (Athlete, Football Player)
12314 Williams Rd SE
Cumberland, MD 21502-7961, USA

Aldiss, Brian (Writer)
Woodlands, Foxcombe Road
Boars Hill
Oxfordshire, OX1 5DL, England

Aldiss, Brian W (Writer)
Hambledon
39 Saint Andrews Road
Old Headington
Oxford OX3 9DL, UNITED KINGDOM (UK)

Aldo, Jose (Athlete, Mixed Martial Arts)
c/o Staff Member *UFC*
PO Box 26959
Las Vegas, NV 89126-0959, USA

Aldred, Scott (Athlete, Baseball Player)
13435 Lakebrook Dr
Fenton, MI 48430-8420, USA

Aldred, Sophie (Actor)
1 Duchess St
#1
London S1N 3EE, UNITED KINGDOM (UK)

Aldrete, Mike (Athlete, Baseball Player)
22160 Toro Hills Dr
Salinas, CA 93908-1131, USA

Aldrich, Cole (Athlete, Basketball Player)
c/o Jeff Schwartz *Excel Sports Management*
1700 Broadway Fl 29
New York, NY 10019-6559, USA

Aldrich, Jay (Athlete, Baseball Player)
9209 S 51st St
Franklin, WI 53132-9275, USA

Aldridge, Allen (Athlete, Football Player)
1702 Mossback Cir
Fresno, TX 77545-9226, us

Aldridge, Cory (Athlete, Baseball Player)
417 Penrose Dr
Abilene, TX 79601-6228, USA

Aldridge, Jerry (Athlete, Football Player)
297 Ellis
Jacksonville, TX 75766, USA

Aldridge, Keith (Athlete, Hockey Player)
80 Joslyn Rd
Lake Orion, MI 48362-2215, USA

Aldridge, Kevin (Athlete, Football Player)
2820 McKinnon St Apt 3009
Dallas, TX 75201-1025, USA

Aldridge, Kevin (Athlete, Football Player)
3130 Brookhaven Club Dr
Dallas, TX 75234, us

Aldridge, Lamarcus (Athlete, Basketball Player)
409 Saint Tropez Dr
Southlake, TX 76092-1189, USA

Aldridge, Lily (Model)
c/o Lisa Benson *IMG Models (NY)*
304 Park Ave S PH N
New York, NY 10010-4303, USA

Aldridge, Melvin (Athlete, Football Player)
14618 Braden Dr E
Houston, TX 77047-6752, USA

Aldridge, Sabrina (Actor, Model)
c/o Staff Member *Directions USA*
3922 W Market St
Greensboro, NC 27407-1304, USA

Aldridge Jr, Allen (Athlete, Football Player)
2111 Hammerwood Dr
Missouri City, TX 77489-4137, USA

Aldridge Sr, Allen (Athlete, Football Player)
2111 Hammerwood Dr
Missouri City, TX 77489-4137, USA

Aldrin Jr, Edwin (Buzz) (Astronaut)
c/o Dick Guttman *Guttman Associates Public Relations*
118 S Beverly Dr Ste 201
Beverly Hills, CA 90212-3016, USA

Al Duhami, Ramzi (Athlete, Horse Racer)
Haras de Wisbecq
Rue du Bierghes
Rebecq 41430, BELGIUM

Ale, Arnold (Athlete, Football Player)
308 E Desford St
Carson, CA 90745-2111, USA

Aleaga, Ink (Athlete, Football Player)
14612 22nd Ave SW
Burien, WA 98166-1610, USA

Aleandro, Norma (Actor)
Blanco Encalada 1150
Buenos Aires 01428, ARGENTINA

Alechinsky, Pierre (Artist)
2 Bis Rue Henri Barbusse
Bougival 78380, FRANCE

Alejandro, Kevin (Actor)
c/o Pamela Sharp *Sharp & Associates*
1516 N Fairfax Ave
Los Angeles, CA 90046-2608, USA

Alejandro, Raphael (Actor)

Alekperov, Vagit (Business Person)
Lukoil
11, Sretensky Blvd
Moscow 101000, Russia

Aleksander, Grant (Actor)
66 Crow Hill Rd
Freehold, NJ 07728-8404, USA

Aleksinas, Charles (Chuck) (Athlete, Basketball Player)
16 Litchfield Rd
Morris, CT 06763-1522, USA

Aleksiy II (Religious Leader)
Moscow Patriarchy
Chisty Per 5
Moscow 119034, RUSSIA

Aleno, Charles (Athlete, Baseball Player)
601 Marion Ct
Deland, FL 32720-3217, USA

Alesi, Jean (Race Car Driver)
HWA GmbH
Benzstr 8
Affalterbach 71563, GERMANY

Alessi, Raquel (Actor)
c/o Rhonda Price *Gersh*
41 Madison Ave Ste 3301
New York, NY 10010-2210, USA

Alesso (Musician)
c/o Staff Member *WME/IMG*
9601 Wilshire Blvd
Beverly Hills, CA 90210-5213, USA

Alex (Actor)
2 Rajaji North Street
Pushpa Nagar Nungambakkam
Chennai, TN 600 034, USA

Alex, Keith (Athlete, Football Player)
6985 Reno Cir
Beaumont, TX 77708-3594, USA

Alexakis, Art (Musician)
Pinnacle Entertainment
30 Glenn St
White Plains, NY 10603-3254, USA

Alexakos, Steve (Athlete, Football Player)
306 W Linden St
Boise, ID 83706-4830, USA

Alexakos, Steve (Athlete, Football Player)
22300 Hathaway Ave Unit A
Hayward, CA 94541-4896, us

Alexander, Andrew (Producer)
1569 Lindacrest Dr
Beverly Hills, CA 90210-2521, USA

Alexander, Brent (Athlete, Football Player)
349 Remington Ave
Gallatin, TN 37066-7536, USA

Alexander, Brooke (Actor)
c/o Staff Member *Abrams Artists Agency*
750 N San Vicente Blvd
E Tower Fl 11
Los Angeles, CA 90069-5788, USA

Alexander, Bruce (Athlete, Football Player)
508 Englewood Dr
Lufkin, TX 75901-5844, USA

Alexander, Caroline (Writer)
c/o Staff Member *Random House Publicity (Toronto)*
1 Toronto St Suite 300
Toronto, ON M5C 2V6, Canada

Alexander, Charles (Athlete, Football Player)
5003 Lockridge Sky Ln
Sugar Land, TX 77479-6805, USA

Alexander, Claire (Athlete, Hockey Player)
11 Tammy Cir
St Catharines, ON L2N 1R2, Canada

Alexander, Corey (Athlete, Basketball Player)
440 Alpha St
Waynesboro, VA 22980-3904, USA

Alexander, Cory (Athlete, Basketball Player)
1226 Cardwell Rd
Crozier, VA 23039-2402, USA

Alexander, Dan (Athlete, Football Player)
58520 Saint Clement Ave
Plaquemine, LA 70764-3532, USA

Alexander, Dan (Athlete, Football Player)
3846 Somers Ln
Thompsons Station, TN 37179-9617, USA

Alexander, David (Athlete, Football Player)
3328 W Delmar St
Broken Arrow, OK 74012-7763, USA

Alexander, Denise (Actor)
270 N Canon Dr Ste 1919
Beverly Hills, CA 90210-5300, USA

Alexander, Derrick (Athlete, Football Player)
5301 Gulf Blvd Apt E303
St Pete Beach, FL 33706-2381, USA

Alexander, Doyle (Athlete, Baseball Player)
5416 Hunter Park Ct
Arlington, TX 76017-3557, USA

Alexander, Eric (Musician)
Joel Chriss
300 Mercer St Apt 3J
New York, NY 10003-6732, USA

Alexander, Erika (Actor)
c/o Staff Member *Untitled Entertainment*
350 S Beverly Dr Ste 200
Beverly Hills, CA 90212-4819, USA

Alexander, Flex (Actor)
c/o April Lim *Global Artists Agency*
6253 Hollywood Blvd Apt 508
Los Angeles, CA 90028-8251, USA

Alexander, Frank (Athlete, Football Player)

Alexander, Gary (Athlete, Baseball Player)
5420 Senford Ave
Los Angeles, CA 90056-1029, USA

Alexander, Gerald (Athlete, Baseball Player)
307 Woodland Dr
Donaldsonville, LA 70346-9752, USA

Alexander, Gwen Cheeseman (Athlete, Hockey Player, Olympic Athlete)
45 Holly Park Ln APT 232
Lexington, VA 24450-3755, USA

Alexander, Harold (Athlete, Football Player)
590 J D Dr
Pickens, SC 29671-9035, USA

Alexander, J (Reality Star, Television Host)
c/o Staff Member *Bankable Productions*
226 W 26th St Fl 4
New York, NY 10001-6700, USA

Alexander, Jaimie (Actor)
c/o Kate Rosen *The Lede Company*
401 Broadway Ste 206
New York, NY 10013-3033, USA

Alexander, Jane (Actor)
c/o Scott Henderson *WME/IMG*
9601 Wilshire Blvd
Beverly Hills, CA 90210-5213, USA

Alexander, Jason (Actor, Comedian, Producer)
355 S June St
Los Angeles, CA 90020-4809, USA

Alexander, Jeff (Athlete, Football Player)
4333 Deephaven Ct
Denver, CO 80239-5069, USA

Alexander, John (Athlete, Football Player)
312 Lee Pl
Plainfield, NJ 07063-1337, USA

Alexander, Jules (Musician)
Variety Artists
1111 Riverside Ave Ste 501
Paso Robles, CA 93446-2683, USA

Alexander, Keith (Actor)
c/o Staff Member *Cunningham Escott Slevin & Doherty (CESD)*
10635 Santa Monica Blvd Ste 130
Los Angeles, CA 90025-8306, USA

Alexander, Kenneth (Cartoonist)
1182 Glen Rd
Lafayette, CA 94549-3044, USA

Alexander, Kermit (Athlete, Football Player)
16651 Stallion Pl
Riverside, CA 92504-5872, USA

Alexander, Khandi (Actor)
8262 Woodshill Trl
Los Angeles, CA 90069-1636, USA

Alexander, Lamar (Politician)
565 Pennsylvania Ave NW Apt 1208
Washington, DC 20001-4945, USA

Alexander, Lorenzo (Athlete, Football Player)

Alexander, Manny (Athlete, Baseball Player)
3660 N Lake Dr
Apt 2664
Chicago, IL 60613, USA

Alexander, Matt (Athlete, Baseball Player)
2419 Stonewall St
Shreveport, LA 71103-3451, USA

Alexander, Michelle (Writer)
c/o Julie McCarroll *The New Press*
120 Wall St Fl 31
New York, NY 10005-4007, USA

Alexander, Mike (Athlete, Football Player)

Alexander, Millette (Actor)
157 Roseville Rd
Westport, CT 06880-2615, USA

Alexander, Monty (Musician)
Bennett Morgan
1282 RR 376
Wappingers Falls, NY 12590, USA

Alexander, Newell (Actor)
5830 Morella Ave
N Hollywood, CA 91607-1322, USA

Alexander, Nicholas (Actor)
c/o Chris Fioto *WME/IMG*
9601 Wilshire Blvd
Beverly Hills, CA 90210-5213, USA

Alexander, Olly (Musician)
c/o Ed Smith *Sherpa Management*
Valiant House
Vicarage Crescent
London SW11 3LX, UNITED KINGDOM

Alexander, Patrise (Athlete, Football Player)
15035 Westpark Dr Apt 514
Houston, TX 77082-3942, USA

Alexander, Ray (Athlete, Football Player)
119 Deer Lake Cir
Ormond Beach, FL 32174-4266, USA

Alexander, Robert (Athlete, Football Player)
2704 Morrell Ave
Saint Albans, WV 25177-2135, USA

Alexander, Roc (Athlete, Football Player)

Alexander, Rodney (Congressman, Politician)
316 Cannon Hob
Washington, DC 20515-1805, USA

Alexander, Rogers (Athlete, Football Player)
8182 Rainwater Cir
Manassas, VA 20111-5231, USA

Alexander, Sarah (Actor)
c/o Jane Brand *Independent Talent Group*
40 Whitfield St
London W1T 2RH, UNITED KINGDOM

Alexander, Sasha (Actor, Producer)
c/o Meredith O'Sullivan Wasson *The Lede Company*
9701 Wilshire Blvd # 930
Beverly Hills, CA 90212-2020, USA

Alexander, Scott (Director, Producer)
c/o Joe Cohen *Creative Artists Agency (CAA)*
2000 Avenue of the Stars Ste 100
Los Angeles, CA 90067-4705, USA

Alexander, Shaun (Athlete, Football Player)
4314 E Madison St
Seattle, WA 98112-2797, USA

Alexander, Stephen (Athlete, Football Player)
4700 Flint Ridge Cir
Norman, OK 73072-4463, USA

Alexander, Susana (Actor)
c/o Staff Member *TV Azteca*
Periferico Sur 4121
Colonia Fuentes del Pedregal
DF CP 14141, Mexico

Alexander, Victor (Athlete, Basketball Player)
3450 Holly Trail Ln
Alpharetta, GA 30022-5943, USA

Alexander, Vincent (Athlete, Football Player)
622 W 30th Ave
Covington, LA 70433-2012, USA

Alexander, Willie (Athlete, Football Player)
7219 Holder Forest Cir
Houston, TX 77088-7431, USA

Alexander, Willie (Musician)
Tournmaline Music Group
894 Mayville Rd
Bethel, ME 04217-4605, USA

Alexeev, Nikita (Athlete, Hockey Player)
PO Box 3342
Riverview, FL 33568-3342, USA

Alexie, Sherman (Writer)
PO Box 376
Wellpinit, WA 99040-0376, USA

Alexis, Alton (Athlete, Football Player)
7020 Shadow Creek Ct
Fort Worth, TX 76132-4550, USA

Alexis, Kim (Athlete, Hockey Player)
982 Ponte Vedra Blvd
Ponte Vedra Beach, FL 32082-4068, USA

Alexus, Ajiona (Actor)
c/o Liza Anderson *Anderson Group Public Relations*
8060 Melrose Ave Fl 4
Los Angeles, CA 90046-7038, USA

Alfaro, Jason (Athlete, Baseball Player)
5912 Oak Hill Rd
Watauga, TX 76148-1652, USA

Al-Fayed, Mohamed (Business Person)
Craven Cottage Stevenage Road
Fulham
London SW6 6HH, UNITED KINGDOM (UK)

Alfieri, Janet (Cartoonist)
15 Bumpus Rd
Plymouth, MA 02360-3511, USA

Alflen, Ted (Athlete, Football Player)
960 NE 27th Ave
Pompano Beach, FL 33062-4214, USA

Alfonseca, Antonio (Athlete, Baseball Player)
3020 SW 189th Ter
Miramar, FL 33029-5861, USA

Alfonsi, Sharyn (Correspondent)
c/o Staff Member *ABC News*
77 W 66th St Fl 3
New York, NY 10023-6201, USA

Alfonso, Carlos (Athlete, Baseball Player, Coach)

Alfonso, Kristian (Actor)
7577 Mulholland Dr
Los Angeles, CA 90046-1238, USA

Alfonzo, Edgar (Athlete, Baseball Player)
9019 Cormorant Ct
Tampa, FL 33647-2980, USA

Alfonzo, Edgardo (Athlete, Baseball Player)
8035 Spendthrift Ln
Port Saint Lucie, FL 34986-3122, USA

Alford, Brian (Athlete, Football Player)
31230 Huntley Sq W
Beverly Hills, MI 48025-5326, USA

Alford, Darnell (Athlete, Football Player)
8629 W 84th Ter
Overland Park, KS 66212-2708, USA

Alford, David (Actor)
c/o Robert Attermann *Abrams Artists Agency*
275 7th Ave Fl 26
New York, NY 10001-6708, USA

Alford, Jay (Athlete, Football Player)
c/o Peter Schaffer *Authentic Athletix*
400 S Steele St Unit 47
Denver, CO 80209-3535, USA

Alford, Lynwood (Athlete, Football Player)
355 Moon Clinton Rd Apt 2
Coraopolis, PA 15108-2486, USA

Alford, Mike (Athlete, Football Player)
801 Valparaiso Blvd
Niceville, FL 32578-3406, USA

Alford, Robert (Athlete, Football Player)

Alford, Steve (Basketball Player, Olympic Athlete)
5425 Collingwood Cir
Calabasas, CA 91302-3141, USA

Alfredsson, Daniel (Athlete, Hockey Player)
c/o Staff Member *CAA Hockey*
Prefers to be contacted by email or phone.
Los Angeles, CA NA, USA

Alfredsson, Helen (Athlete, Golfer)
6043 Jamestown Park
Orlando, FL 32819-4435, USA

Algabid, Hamid (President)
National Assembly
Vice President's Office
Niamey, NIGER

Alger, Brittney (Actor)
c/o Siri Garber *Platform PR*
2666 N Beachwood Dr
Los Angeles, CA 90068-2308, USA

Ali, Laila (Athlete, Boxer)
She Bee Stingin', Inc.
26500 Agoura Rd
Suite 102-715, Calabasas CA, USA

Ali, Mahershala (Actor)
c/o Carolyn Govers *Anonymous Content*
3532 Hayden Ave
Culver City, CA 90232-2413, USA

Ali, May May (Actor)
c/o Kristene Wallis *Wallis Agency*
210 N Pass Ave Ste 205
Burbank, CA 91505-3936, USA

Ali, Sophia Taylor (Actor)
c/o Staff Member *Industry Entertainment Partners*
955 Carrillo Dr Ste 300
Los Angeles, CA 90048-5400, USA

Ali, Tariq (Writer)
c/o Anthony Arnove *Roam Agency*
45 Main St Ste 727
Brooklyn, NY 11201-1076

Ali, Tatyana (Actor)
c/o Jennifer Shoucair Weaver *S/W PR Shop*
584 N Larchmont Blvd # B
Los Angeles, CA 90004-1306, USA

Alibar, Lucy (Writer)
c/o David Gersh *Gersh*
9465 Wilshire Blvd Ste 600
Beverly Hills, CA 90212-2605, USA

Alicea, Luis (Athlete, Baseball Player)
2140 C Rd
Loxahatchee, FL 33470-3837, USA

Alicea, Wilmer (Baby Rasta) (Musician)
c/o Staff Member *Universal Music Publishing Group*
2440 S Sepulveda Blvd Ste 100
Los Angeles, CA 90064-1744, USA

Alice In Chains (Music Group)
c/o David Benveniste *Velvet Hammer*
9014 Melrose Ave
Los Angeles, CA 90069-5610, USA

Alicia, Ana (Actor)
3446 Longridge Ave
Sherman Oaks, CA 91423-4914, USA

Alien Ant Farm (Music Group)
c/o David Gibson *New Ocean Media*
270 Doug Baker Blvd Ste 700
Birmingham, AL 35242-8300, USA

Aliens, The (Music Group)
c/o Staff Member *Paradigm (Monterey)*
404 W Franklin St
Monterey, CA 93940-2303, USA

Alipate, Tuineau (Athlete, Football Player)
801 E 101st St
Minneapolis, MN 55420-5121, USA

Alisha (Musician)
Famous Artists Agency
250 W 57th St
New York, NY 10107-0001, USA

Alison, Jane (Writer)
FarrarStraus Giroux
19 Union Sq W
New York, NY 10003-3304, USA

Aliyev, Ilham (President)
President's Office
Baku 370066, AZERBAIJAN

Alkan, Erol (Musician)
c/o Joel Zimmerman *WME/IMG (NY)*
11 Madison Ave Fl 18
New York, NY 10010-3669, USA

Al-Kharafi, Nasser (Business Person)
M A Kharafi Group Building
Shuwaikh Industrial Area
P.O. Box 886
Kuwait Safat 13009, Kuwait

Allam, Roger (Actor)
Richard Stone Partnership
2 Henrietta St
London WC2E 8PS, UNITED KINGDOM

All American Rejects (Music Group)
c/o Staff Member *Interscope Records*
1755 Broadway Fl 6
New York, NY 10019-3768, USA

Allan, Gabrielle (Producer)
c/o Staff Member *United Talent Agency (UTA)*
9336 Civic Center Dr
Beverly Hills, CA 90210-3604, USA

Allan, Gary (Musician)
114 Walnut Dr
Hendersonville, TN 37075-5030, USA

Allan, Stephen (Athlete, Golfer)
c/o Jens Beck *Pro-Sport Management*
6157 E Indian School Rd
Scottsdale, AZ 85251-5441, USA

Allanson, Andy (Athlete, Baseball Player)
38713 Tierra Subida Ave # 102
Palmdale, CA 93551-4562, USA

Allard, Brian (Athlete, Baseball Player)
22102 N Perry Rd
Colbert, WA 99005-9488, USA

Allard, Wayne (Politician)
5328 Lighthouse Point Ct
Loveland, CO 80537-7915, USA

Allegre, Raul (Athlete, Football Player)
6500 Rain Creek Pkwy
Austin, TX 78759-6147, USA

Allem, Fulton (Athlete, Golfer)
2397 Northumbria Dr
Sanford, FL 32771-6491, USA

Allen, Aleisha (Actor)
c/o Jan Jarrett *Jordan Gill & Dornbaum*
150 5th Ave Ste 308
New York, NY 10011-4311, USA

Allen, Alfie (Actor)
c/o Romilly Bowlby *DDA Public Relations*
192-198 Vauxhall Bridge Rd
London SW1V 1DX, UNITED KINGDOM

Allen, Andrew (Astronaut)
205 Highland Woods Dr
Safety Harbor, FL 34695-5437, USA

Allen, Andrew M Lt Colonel (Astronaut)
205 Highland Woods Dr
Safety Harbor, FL 34695-5437, USA

Allen, Anthony (Athlete, Football Player)
1213 Dayton Pl NE
Renton, WA 98056-2798, USA

Allen, Antonio (Athlete, Football Player)
c/o Joel Segal *Lagardere Unlimited (NY)*
456 Washington St Apt 9L
New York, NY 10013-1555, USA

Allen, Beau (Athlete, Football Player)
c/o Scott Smith *XAM Sports*
3509 Ice Age Dr
Madison, WI 53719-5409, USA

Allen, Bernie (Athlete, Baseball Player)
3725 Coventry Way
Carmel, IN 46033-3026, USA

Allen, Beth (Athlete, Golfer)
1602 Peacock Ave
Sunnyvale, CA 94087-4917, USA

Allen, Bob (Athlete, Baseball Player)
PO Box 677
Tatum, TX 75691-0677, USA

Allen, Bob (Athlete, Basketball Player)
117 Quarter Mile Way
Nicholasville, KY 40356-8220, USA

Allen, Bruce (Race Car Driver)
Reher Morrison Motorsports
1120 Enterprise Pl
Arlington, TX 76001-7138, USA

Allen, Bryan (Athlete, Hockey Player)
Octagon Sports Management
66 Slater St 23rd Fl
Attn Larry Kelly
Ottawa, ON K1P 5H1, Canada

Allen, Buddy (Athlete, Football Player)
3689 Westmoreland Dr
Mays Landing, NJ 08330-3240, USA

Allen, Byron (Comedian)
c/o Staff Member *Entertainment Studios*
1925 Century Park E Ste 1025
Los Angeles, CA 90067-2729, USA

Allen, Carl (Athlete, Football Player)
1614 Hornsby Ave
Saint Louis, MO 63147-1410, USA

Allen, Chad (Actor)
c/o Thomas DeLorenzo *SmartPR*
8033 W Sunset Blvd Ste 1033
Los Angeles, CA 90046-2401, USA

Allen, Chad (Athlete, Baseball Player, Olympic Athlete)
7152 Blackwood Dr
Dallas, TX 75231-5604, USA

Allen, Christa B (Actor)
c/o Brett Ruttenberg *Imprint PR*
6121 W Sunset Blvd
Neuehouse
Los Angeles, CA 90028-6442, USA

Allen, Cortez (Athlete, Football Player)
c/o Scott Smith *XAM Sports*
3509 Ice Age Dr
Madison, WI 53719-5409, USA

Allen, Dalva (Athlete, Football Player)
411 County Road 1925
Mt Pleasant, TX 75455, USA

Allen, Damon (Athlete, Football Player)
26-111 Zenway Blvd
Damon Allen Quarterback Academy
Vaughan, ON L4H 3H9, Canada

Allen, Danielle Sherie (Actor)
c/o Staff Member *Privilege Talent Agency*
PO Box 260860
Encino, CA 91426-0860, USA

Allen, Debbie (Actor, Dancer)
c/o Staff Member *Red Bird Productions*
3791 Santa Rosalia Dr
Los Angeles, CA 90008-3603, USA

Allen, Dennis (Football Coach)
c/o Jimmy Sexton *CAA (Memphis)*
6060 Poplar Ave Ste 470
Memphis, TN 38119-0910, USA

Allen, Derek (Athlete, Football Player)
6206 Woodward Ln
Milton, FL 32570-4577, USA

Allen, Dick (Athlete, Baseball Player)
983 Possum Hollow Rd
Wampum, PA 16157-2817, USA

Allen, Dick (Athlete, Baseball Player)
PO Box 254
Wampum, PA 16157-0254, USA

Allen, Don (Athlete, Football Player)
17303 Kermier Rd
Hockley, TX 77447-9100, USA

Allen, Doug (Artist)
c/o Staff Member *Fantagraphics Books*
7563 Lake City Way NE
Seattle, WA 98115-4218, USA

Allen, Doug (Athlete, Football Player)
10245 Collins Ave Apt 8A
Bal Harbour, FL 33154-1406, USA

Allen, Duane (Actor)
216 Spring Valley Rd
Hendersonville, TN 37075-9657, USA

Allen, Dusty (Athlete, Baseball Player)
913 Estrella Vista St
Las Vegas, NV 89138-7578, USA

Allen, Dwayne (Athlete, Football Player)
c/o Michael Perrett *Element Sports Group*
3340 Peachtree Rd NE Fl 16
Atlanta, GA 30326-1000, USA

Allen, Earl (Athlete, Football Player)
8015 Duffield Ln
Houston, TX 77071-2016, USA

Allen, Eddie (Athlete, Football Player)
3321 W Fisher St
Pensacola, FL 32505-4909, USA

Allen, Egypt (Athlete, Football Player)
2115 Rubens Dr
Dallas, TX 75224-4146, USA

Allen, Eric (Athlete, Football Player)
484 San Elijo St
San Diego, CA 92106-3463, USA

Allen, George (Politician)
4296 Neitzey Pl
Alexandria, VA 22309-3069, USA

Allen, Grady (Athlete, Football Player)
317 Circleview Dr N
Hurst, TX 76054-3518, USA

Allen, Greg (Athlete, Football Player)
5006 Persimmon Hollow Rd
Milton, FL 32583-2739, USA

Allen, Hank (Athlete, Baseball Player)
PO Box 4612
Upper Marlboro, MD 20775-0612, USA

Allen, Herb (Business Person)
Allen & Co
711 5th Ave Fl 9
New York, NY 10022-3168, USA

Allen, Jackie (Athlete, Football Player)
7152 Blackwood Dr
Dallas, TX 75231-5604, USA

Allen, Jamie (Athlete, Baseball Player)
2168 E Glacier Pl
Chandler, AZ 85249-3494, USA

Allen, Jared (Athlete, Football Player)
c/o Ken Harris *Optimum Sports Management*
3225 S Macdill Ave Ste 330
Tampa, FL 33629-8171, USA

Allen, Jared (Athlete, Football Player)
c/o Denise White *EAG Sports Management*
909 N Pacific Coast Hwy Ste 360
El Segundo, CA 90245-3864, USA

Allen, Jason (Athlete, Football Player)
2002 Edwards Ave
Muscle Shoals, AL 35661-1918, USA

Allen, Jeff (Athlete, Football Player)
902 Warren Dr
Centerville, IN 47330-9533, USA

Allen, Jerry (Athlete, Football Player)
14 Washington Valley Rd
Morristown, NJ 07960-3412, USA

Allen, Jimmy (Athlete, Football Player)
13832 Iron Rock Pl
Victorville, CA 92395-4816, USA

Allen, Joan (Actor)
250 W 94th St # 15G
New York, NY 10025-6954, USA

Allen, Johnny (Race Car Driver)
301 Rockmont Rd
Greenville, SC 29615-1862, USA

Allen, Jonelle (Actor)
c/o Staff Member *SMS Talent*
8383 Wilshire Blvd Ste 230
Beverly Hills, CA 90211-2436, USA

Allen, Joseph P (Astronaut)
LBJ Space Center
2101 Nasa Pkwy # 1
C/O Astronaut Office
Houston, TX 77058-3607, USA

Allen, Joseph P Dr (Astronaut)
4051 Mansion Dr NW
Washington, DC 20007-2135, USA

Allen, Josh (Athlete, Football Player)
c/o Tom Condon *Creative Artists Agency (CAA)*
401 Commerce St PH
Nashville, TN 37219-2516, USA

Allen, Karen (Actor)
Karen Allen Fiber Arts
8 Railroad St
Great Barrington, MA 01230-1521, USA

Allen, Keegan (Actor)
c/o Konrad Leh *Creative Talent Group*
1900 Avenue of the Stars Ste 2475
Los Angeles, CA 90067-4512, USA

Allen, Keenan (Athlete, Football Player)
c/o David Dunn *Athletes First*
23091 Mill Creek Dr
Laguna Hills, CA 92653-1258, USA

Allen, Keith (Athlete, Hockey Player)
10000 Highland Ave
Long Beach Township, NJ 08008-3166, USA

Allen, Kenderick (Athlete, Football Player)
5214 Lost Cove Ln
Spring, TX 77373-7978, USA

Allen, Kevin (Athlete, Football Player)
2422 Hazelcrest Ln
Cincinnati, OH 45231-1132, USA

Allen, Kevin (Director)
William Morris Agency
52/53 Poland Place
London W1F 7LX, UNITED KINGDOM (UK)

Allen, Kim (Athlete, Baseball Player)
2705 La Praix St
Highland, CA 92346-1928, USA

Allen, Kris (Musician)
c/o Staff Member *19 Entertainment*
35-37 Parkgate Rd #32/33
#32/33 Ransomes Dock
London SW11 4NP, UNITED KINGDOM

Allen, Krista (Actor)
137 S Robertson Blvd # 219
Beverly Hills, CA 90211-2801, USA

Allen, Kyle (Actor)
c/o Brett Ruttenberg *Imprint PR*
6121 W Sunset Blvd
Neuehouse
Los Angeles, CA 90028-6442, USA

Allen, Larry C (Athlete, Football Player)
401 Kingswood Ln
Danville, CA 94506-6066, USA

Allen, Leo (Writer)

Allen, Lily (Musician)
c/o Brad Petrigala *Brillstein Entertainment Partners*
9150 Wilshire Blvd Ste 350
Beverly Hills, CA 90212-3453, USA

Allen, Lloyd (Athlete, Baseball Player)
2340 Castlewood Dr
Toledo, OH 43613-3923, USA

Allen, Loy Jr (Race Car Driver)
3197 Steamboat Ridge Rd
Port Orange, FL 32128-6917, USA

Allen, Lucius (Athlete, Basketball Player)
1915 Buckingham Rd
Los Angeles, CA 90016-1701, USA

Allen, Luke (Athlete, Baseball Player)
282 Cooper Rd
Social Circle, GA 30025-5119, USA

Allen, Marcus (Athlete, Football Player)
5301 Forecastle Ct
Carlsbad, CA 92008-3826, USA

Allen, Marvin (Athlete, Football Player)
1806 Las Cruces Ln
Wichita Falls, TX 76306-5205, USA

Allen, Michael (Athlete, Football Player)
8839 NE 147th St
Kenmore, WA 98028-4727, USA

Allen, Michael (Athlete, Golfer)
5827 E Anderson Dr
Scottsdale, AZ 85254-5941, USA

Allen, Mike (Athlete, Hockey Player)
PO Box 1416
International Falls, MN 56649-1416, USA

Allen, Nancy (Actor)
weSPARK
13520 Ventura Blvd
Sherman Oaks, CA 91423-3802, USA

Allen, Natalie (Correspondent)
Cable News Network
1050 Techwood Dr NW
News Dept
Atlanta, GA 30318-5695, USA

Allen, Nate (Athlete, Football Player)
8239 Queen Ave N
Minneapolis, MN 55444-1513, USA

Allen, Neil (Athlete, Baseball Player)
3619 Torrey Pines Blvd
Sarasota, FL 34238-2828, USA

Allen, Pam (Athlete, Golfer)
809 Delphinium Dr
Billings, MT 59102-3409, USA

Allen, Patrick (Athlete, Football Player)
427 20th Ave E
Seattle, WA 98112-5313, USA

Allen, Rae (Actor)
c/o Staff Member *Kyle Fritz Management*
6325 Heather Dr
Los Angeles, CA 90068-1633, USA

Allen, Randy (Athlete, Basketball Player)
10185 Nichols Lake Rd
Milton, FL 32583-9267, USA

Allen, Rax Jr (Music Group)
209 10th Ave S Ste 527
Nashville, TN 37203-7103, USA

Allen, Ray (Actor, Athlete, Basketball Player)
5 Tahiti Beach Island Rd
Miami, FL 33143-6550, USA

Allen, Ricardo (Athlete, Football Player)
c/o Eugene Parker *Independent Sports & Entertainment (ISE-IN)*
6435 W Jefferson Blvd # 197
Fort Wayne, IN 46804-6203, USA

Allen, Rice (Athlete, Football Player)
4906 Laurel Hill Ct
Sugar Land, TX 77478-5424, USA

Allen, Richard (Actor)
89 Saltergate
Chesterfield S40 IUS, UNITED KINGDOM (UK)

Allen, Richard A (Richie) (Athlete, Baseball Player)
RR2
Possum Hollow Rd
Wampum, PA 16157, USA

Allen, Rick (Musician)
c/o Rod MacSween *International Talent Booking*
9 Kingsway
Fl 6
London WC2B 6XF, UNITED KINGDOM

Allen, Rod (Athlete, Baseball Player)
3150 E Woodland Dr
Phoenix, AZ 85048-7702, USA

Allen, Ron (Athlete, Baseball Player)
917 Winona Dr
Youngstown, OH 44511-1404, USA

Allen, Rosalind (Actor)
c/o John Carrabino *John Carrabino Management*
5900 Wilshire Blvd Ste 740
Los Angeles, CA 90036-5032, USA

Allen, Ryan (Athlete, Football Player)
c/o Ryan Morgan *MAG Sports Agency*
8222 Melrose Ave Fl 2
Los Angeles, CA 90046-6825, USA

Allen, Sam (Athlete, Baseball Player)
2734 Gate House Rd Apt 108
Norfolk, VA 23504-4057, USA

Allen, Sian Barbara (Actor, Writer)
1411 N Alberta St Apt 7
Portland, OR 97217-3761, USA

Allen, Taje (Athlete, Football Player)
1209 Valorie Ct
Cedar Park, TX 78613-4023, USA

Allen, Ted (Chef, Television Host)
c/o Lisa Shotland *CAA (London)*
3 Shortlands, Hammersmith
Fl 5
London W6 8DA, UNITED KINGDOM

Allen, Terry (Athlete, Football Player)
3176 Sable Ridge Dr
Buford, GA 30519-7681, USA

Allen, Tessa (Actor)
c/o Staff Member *Bobby Ball Talent Agency*
4342 Lankershim Blvd
Universal City, CA 91602, USA

Allen, Tim (Actor, Comedian, Producer)
c/o Staff Member *Boxing Cat Productions*
11500 Hart St
N Hollywood, CA 91605-6203, USA

Allen, Todd (Actor, Producer)
c/o David (Dave) Fleming *Atlas Artists*
9220 W Sunset Blvd Ste 225
Los Angeles, CA 90069-3513, USA

Allen, Tony (Athlete, Basketball Player)
c/o Raymond Brothers *International Athlete Management, Inc*
433 N Camden Dr Ste 600
Beverly Hills, CA 90210-4416, USA

Allen, Tremayne (Athlete, Football Player)
2910 Girvan Dr
Land O Lakes, FL 34638-7877, USA

Allen, Will (Athlete, Football Player)
15 Fox Hill Dr
Wayne, NJ 07470-2539, USA

Allen, Will (Athlete, Football Player)
3020 E Signature Dr Apt 1006
Davie, FL 33314-6445, USA

Allen, Will (Athlete, Football Player)
12721 Tar Flower Dr
Tampa, FL 33626-2341, USA

Allen, Woody (Actor, Comedian, Director)
c/o Leslee Dart *42West*
600 3rd Ave Fl 23
New York, NY 10016-1914, USA

Allenby, Robert (Athlete, Golfer)
105 Quayside Dr
Jupiter, FL 33477-4020, USA

Allende, Fernando (Actor)
c/o Staff Member *El Dorado Pictures*
725 Arizona Ave Ste 100
Santa Monica, CA 90401-1734, USA

Allende, Isabel (Writer)
24 Windward Rd
Belvedere Tiburon, CA 94920-2341, USA

Allende, Isabel (Writer)
116 Caledonia St
Sausalito, CA 94965-1925, USA

Allen Jr, Glenn (Race Car Driver)
7280 Jerry Dr
West Chester, OH 45069-4216, USA

Allen Jr, Rex (Musician)
PO Box 13086
Wichita, KS 67213-0086, USA

Allenson, Gary (Athlete, Baseball Player)
711 SE 34th St
Cape Coral, FL 33904-4900, USA

Allensworth, Jermaine (Athlete, Baseball Player)
1824 Euclid Dr
Anderson, IN 46011-3937, USA

Allerman, Kurt (Athlete, Football Player)
2511 Blue Heron Dr
Hudson, OH 44236-1866, USA

Allernan, Kurt (Athlete, Football Player)
2511 Blue Heron Dr
Hudson, OH 44236-1866, USA

Allert, Ty (Athlete, Football Player)
1504 County Road 308
Lexington, TX 78947-4113, USA

Alley, Alphonse (President)
Carre 181-182
BP 48
Cotonou, BENIN

Alley, Donald (Athlete, Football Player)
3258 W Parade Cir
Colorado Springs, CO 80917-2931, USA

Alley, Gene (Athlete, Baseball Player)
10236 Steuben Dr
Glen Allen, VA 23060-3072, USA

Alley, Kirstie (Actor, Producer)
c/o Jason Weinberg *Untitled Entertainment*
350 S Beverly Dr Ste 200
Beverly Hills, CA 90212-4819, USA

Alley, Steve (Athlete, Hockey Player)
545 College Rd
Lake Forest, IL 60045-2319, USA

Alley Cats, The (Music Group, Musician)
c/o Staff Member *Harmony Artists*
8455 Beverly Blvd Ste 400
Los Angeles, CA 90048-3437, USA

All For One / All-4-One (Music Group)
c/o Michael Pick *MPI Talent Agency*
9255 W Sunset Blvd Ste 407
Los Angeles, CA 90069-3302, USA

Allgaier, Justin (Race Car Driver)
c/o Staff Member *Penske Racing South*
200 Penske Way
Mooresville, NC 28115-8022, USA

Allgood, Lonnie (Athlete, Football Player)
12 Drake Rd
Somerset, NJ 08873-2369, USA

Allie, Gair (Athlete, Baseball Player)
11818 Button Willow Cv
San Antonio, TX 78213-1220, USA

Allinson, Michael (Actor)
112 Knollwood Dr
Larchmont, NY 10538, USA

Allione, Tsultrim (Religious Leader)
Tara Mandala Retreat Center
PO Box 3040
Pagosa Springs, CO 81147-3040, USA

Allison, Aundrae (Athlete, Football Player)
2024 Summit Ridge Ln
Kannapolis, NC 28083-6284

Allison, Bobby (Race Car Driver)
PO Box 3696
Mooresville, NC 28117-3696, USA

Allison, Dana (Athlete, Baseball Player)
322 Thomas Dr
Middletown, VA 22645-3992, USA

Allison, Dave (Athlete, Coach, Hockey Player)
c/o Staff Member *Iowa Stars*
833 5th Ave
Des Moines, IA 50309-1399, USA

Allison, Donnie (Race Car Driver)
355 Quail Dr
Salisbury, NC 28147-8860, USA

Allison, Henry (Hank) (Athlete, Football Player)
458 W Ellis Ave
Inglewood, CA 90302-1109, USA

Allison, Jason (Athlete, Hockey Player)
4965 16th Sideroad
Schomberg, ON L0G 1T0, Canada

Allison, Jeff (Athlete, Baseball Player)

Allison, Jerry (Musician, Songwriter, Writer)
8455 New Bethel Rd
Lyles, TN 37098-1909, USA

Allison, Jim (Athlete, Football Player)
5706 Laramie Way
San Diego, CA 92120-1426, USA

Allison, Kate (Athlete, Golfer)
349 Canterbury Ln
Wyckoff, NJ 07481-2305, USA

Allison, Mike (Athlete, Hockey Player)
PO Box 1416
International Falls, MN 56649-1416, USA

Allison, Odis (Athlete, Basketball Player)
2945 20th St
San Pablo, CA 94806-2431, USA

Allison, Ray (Athlete, Hockey Player)
106 N Valleybrook Rd
Cherry Hill, NJ 08034-3809, USA

Alliss, Peter (Sportscaster)
Peter Alliss Golf Ltd
PO Box 224
Surrey GU26 6WQ, UNITED KINGDOM

Alliston, Vaughn (Buddy) (Athlete, Football Player)
7493 Apple Yard Ln
Cordova, TN 38016-8770, USA

Allman, Jamie Anne (Actor)
c/o Michael Greene *Greene & Associates*
1901 Avenue of the Stars Ste 130
Los Angeles, CA 90067-6030, USA

Allman, Marshall (Actor)
c/o Nate Steadman *Gersh*
9465 Wilshire Blvd Ste 600
Beverly Hills, CA 90212-2605, USA

Allmendinger, AJ (Race Car Driver)
Richard Petty Motorsports
1120 Enterprise Pl
Arlington, TX 76001-7138, USA

Allo, Andy (Musician)
c/o Siri Garber *Platform PR*
2666 N Beachwood Dr
Los Angeles, CA 90068-2308, USA

Allouache, Merzak (Director)
Cite des Asphodeles Bt D15
183 Ben Aknoun
Algiers, ALGERIA

Allport, Chris M (Actor)
1324 Pine St
Santa Monica, CA 90405-2612, USA

Allport, Christopher (Actor)
c/o Staff Member *Pakula/King & Associates*
9229 W Sunset Blvd Ste 315
Los Angeles, CA 90069-3403, USA

Allred, Beau (Athlete, Baseball Player)
2094 S Shannon Rd
Safford, AZ 85546-9344, USA

Allred, Brian (Athlete, Football Player)
16470 Ed Warfield Rd
Woodbine, MD 21797-7806, USA

Allred, Corbin (Actor)
c/o Staff Member *Aquarius Public Relations*
5320 Sylmar Ave
Sherman Oaks, CA 91401-5612, USA

Allred, Gloria (Attorney)
6300 Wilshire Blvd Ste 1500
Los Angeles, CA 90048-5217, USA

Allred, Jason (Athlete, Golfer)
1809 153rd Street Ct NW
Gig Harbor, WA 98332-9765, USA

Allred, John (Athlete, Football Player)
PO Box 748
Del Mar, CA 92014-0748, USA

All Saints (Music Group)
72 Chancellors Rd
London W6 9SG, UNITED KINGDOM (UK)

Allsopp, Kirstie (Actor)
c/o Staff Member *Arlington Enterprises Ltd*
1-3 Charlotte St
London W1P 1HD, UNITED KINGDOM (UK)

Allstar Weekend (Music Group, Musician)
c/o Staff Member *Hollywood Records*
500 S Buena Vista St
Burbank, CA 91521-0002, USA

Allsup, Mike (Music Group, Musician)
Mckenzie Accountancy
5171 Caliente St Unit 134
Las Vegas, NV 89119-2198, USA

All Time Low (Music Group)
Hopeless Records
PO Box 7495
Van Nuys, CA 91409-7495, USA

Allums, Darrell (Athlete, Basketball Player)
3584 Brenton Ave Apt B
Lynwood, CA 90262-2054, USA

Ally, Usman (Actor)
c/o Jordyn Palos *Persona Public Relations*
6255 W Sunset Blvd Ste 705
Hollywood, CA 90028-7408, USA

Almanza, Armando (Athlete, Baseball Player)
1717 Villa Santos Cir
El Paso, TX 79935-3506, USA

Almanzar, Carlos (Athlete, Baseball Player)
c/o Staff Member *San Diego Padres*
100 Park Blvd
San Diego, CA 92101-7405, USA

Almee, Anouk (Actor)
ICM France
37 Rue de Acacias
Paris 75017, FRANCE

Almen, Lowell G (Religious Leader)
Evangelical Lutheran Church
8765 W Higgins Rd Ste 600
Chicago, IL 60631-4100, USA

Almirola, Aric (Race Car Driver)
Aric Almirola Inc
215 Overhill Dr Ste A
Mooresville, NC 28117-7037, USA

Almodovar, Pedro (Director)
c/o Staff Member *El Deseo*
Francisco Navacerrada 24
Madrid 28028, SPAIN

Almon, Bill (Athlete, Baseball Player)
42 Channel Vw Unit 4
Warwick, RI 02889-6544, USA

Almond, David (Writer)
c/o Staff Member *Doubleday/ RandomHouse*
1745 Broadway
New York, NY 10019-4640, USA

Almond, Marc (Musician)
105 Shad Row Ste B
Piermont, NY 10968-3001, USA

Almonte, Edwin (Athlete, Baseball Player)
3078 Clairmont Rd NE
NE Act 231
Brookhaven, GA 30329-1656, USA

Almonte, Erick (Athlete, Baseball Player)
13505 Thicket Ct
Charlotte, NC 28273-6749, USA

Almonte, Hector (Athlete, Baseball Player)
16742 SW 12th St
Pembroke Pines, FL 33027-1408, USA

Almy, Brook (Actor)
c/o Nyle Brenner *Brenner Management*
9171 Wilshire Blvd Ste 441
Beverly Hills, CA 90210-5516, USA

Al Nahyan, Mansour bin Zayed (Business Person)
First Gulf Bank
P.O. Box 6316
Abu Dhabi, United Arab Emirates

Al Nahyan, Sheikh Khalifa Bin Zayed (Royalty)
President°s Office
Manhal Palace
Abu Dhabi, United Arab Emirates

Alomar, Roberto (Athlete, Baseball Player)
901 Palacio De Avila
Tampa, FL 33613-5224, USA

Alomar Jr, Sandy (Athlete, Baseball Player)
2725 Stanford Ave
Dallas, TX 75225-7915, USA

Alomar Sr, Sandy (Athlete, Baseball Player)
PO Box 367
Salinas, PR 00751-0367, USA

Alonso, Adrian (Actor)
c/o Staff Member *Featured Artists Agency*
1880 Century Park E Ste 1402
Los Angeles, CA 90067-1630, USA

Alonso, Anabel (Actor)
GRPC SL
Calles Fuencarral 17
Madrid 28004, SPAIN

Alonso, Daniella (Actor)
c/o Staff Member *Gersh*
9465 Wilshire Blvd Ste 600
Beverly Hills, CA 90212-2605, USA

Alonso, Fernando (Race Car Driver)
Villamiana, 67
Miami, FL 33199-0001, SPAIN

Alonso, Kiko (Athlete, Football Player)

Alonso, Laz (Actor)
c/o Ron West *Thruline Entertainment*
9250 Wilshire Blvd Fl Ground
Beverly Hills, CA 90212-3352, USA

Alonso, Maria Conchita (Actor, Musician)
c/o Rona Menashe *Guttman Associates Public Relations*
118 S Beverly Dr Ste 201
Beverly Hills, CA 90212-3016, USA

Alonzo, Cristela (Actor, Comedian, Talk Show Host)
c/o Jennifer Sims *Imprint PR*
375 Hudson St
New York, NY 10014-3658, USA

Alosio, Ryan (Actor)
c/o Alexander Shekarchian *ASManagement*
9440 Santa Monica Blvd Ste 700
Beverly Hills, CA 90210-4609, USA

Alou, Felipe (Athlete, Baseball Player)
6891 Cobia Cir
Boynton Beach, FL 33437-3639, USA

Alou, Jesus (Athlete, Baseball Player)
Apartado Postal 539/2
Lafaria
Santo Domingo, Dominican Republic, USA

Alou, Moises (Athlete, Baseball Player)
13521 Old Sheridan St
Southwest Ranches, FL 33330-3753, USA

Alpay, David (Actor)
c/o Brian Wilkins *LINK Entertainment*
11872 La Grange Ave
Los Angeles, CA 90025-5282, USA

Alpert, Herb (Musician)
31930 Pacific Coast Hwy
Malibu, CA 90265-2524, USA

Alphand, Luc (Skier)
Chalet Le Balme Chantemarie
Sierra Chavalier 05330, FRANCE

Alphin, Big Kenny (Musician)
2325 Golf Club Ln
Nashville, TN 37215-1107, USA

Alphin, Gerald (Athlete, Football Player)
4760 Lorient Ct
Snellville, GA 30039-8721, USA

Al Saud, HRH Crown Prince Emir Bandar Ibn Sultan (Royalty)
Council of Minister
Murabba, Riyadh 11121, Saudi Arabia

Alsgaard, Thomas (Skier)
Cathinka Guldbergsveg 16
Holter 02034, NORWAY

Alsina, August (Musician)
c/o Staff Member *WME|IMG*
9601 Wilshire Blvd
Beverly Hills, CA 90210-5213, USA

Alsop, Marin (Musician)
c/o Staff Member *ICM Partners*
10250 Constellation Blvd Fl 7
Los Angeles, CA 90067-6207, USA

Alston, Barbara (Music Group)
Superstars Unlimited
PO Box 371371
Las Vegas, NV 89137-1371, USA

Alston, Dell (Athlete, Baseball Player)
101 Enchanted Hills Rd Apt 103
Owings Mills, MD 21117-2793, USA

Alston, Garvin (Athlete, Baseball Player)
4705 E Thunderhill Pl
Phoenix, AZ 85044-4905, USA

Alston, Gerald (Musician)
c/o Staff Member *Wenig-LaMonica Associates*
303 S Broadway Ste 221
Tarrytown, NY 10591-5410, USA

Alston, Lyneal (Athlete, Football Player)
1318 Morning Sun Cir
Birmingham, AL 35242-2907, USA

Alston, Mack (Athlete, Football Player)
5421 Echols Ave
Alexandria, VA 22311-1344, USA

Alston, Rafer (Athlete, Basketball Player)
c/o Staff Member *Toronto Raptors*
400-40 Bay St
Toronto, ON M5J 2X2, CANADA

Alstott, Mike (Athlete, Football Player)
Mike Alstott Family Foundation
PO Box 40055
St Petersburg, FL 33743-0055, USA

Alsup, Bill (Race Car Driver)
93 Rio Grande Dr
Durango, CO 81301-7113, USA

Alt, Carol (Actor)
c/o Scott Hart *Scott Hart Entertainment*
14622 Ventura Blvd # 746
Sherman Oaks, CA 91403-3600, USA

Alt, John M (Athlete, Football Player)
1 Scotch Pine Rd
Saint Paul, MN 55127-2033, USA

Altamirano, Porfi (Athlete, Baseball Player)
15445 SW 138th Ter
Miami, FL 33196-6001, USA

Altberg, Jonas Erik (Basshunter) (Musician)
c/o Staff Member *Hackford Jones PR*
19 Nassau St
London W1W 7AF, UK

Alther, Lisa (Writer)
1086 Silver St
Hinesburg, VT 05461-9450, USA

Althoff, James (Jim) (Athlete, Football Player)
150 Red Top Dr Apt 302
Libertyville, IL 60048-5237, USA

Altidore, Jozy (Athlete, Soccer Player)
c/o Richard Motzkin *Wasserman Media Group*
10960 Wilshire Blvd Ste 1200
Los Angeles, CA 90024-3714, USA

alt-J (Music Group)
c/o Staff Member *Paradigm (Chicago)*
2209 W North Ave
Chicago, IL 60647-6084, USA

Altman, Chelsea (Actor)
c/o Matthew Sullivan *Sullivan Talent Group*
305 W 105th St Apt 3B
New York, NY 10025-9116, USA

Altman, George (Athlete, Baseball Player)
6 Emerson Ct
O Fallon, MO 63366-7444, USA

Altman, Jeff (Actor)
c/o Staff Member *Richard De La Font Agency*
3808 W South Park Blvd
Broken Arrow, OK 74011-1261, USA

Altman, Josh (Business Person, Reality Star)
The Altman Brothers Realty
250 N Canon Dr
Beverly Hills, CA 90210-5322, USA

Altman, Scott D (Astronaut)
3011 Harvest Hill Dr
Friendswood, TX 77546-5047, USA

Altman, Scott D Cdr (Astronaut)
1247 33rd St NW
Washington, DC 20007-3228, USA

Altmire, Jason (Congressman, Politician)
332 Cannon Hob
Washington, DC 20515-3226, USA

Altobelli, Joe (Athlete, Baseball Player, Coach)
444 1/2 Lake Rd
Webster, NY 14580-1051, USA

Altucher, James (Writer)
47 South Ave
Beacon, NY 12508-3136, USA

Altuve, Jose (Athlete, Baseball Player)
c/o Scott Pucino *Octagon (Chicago)*
875 N Michigan Ave Ste 2700
Chicago, IL 60611-1822, USA

Alualu, Tyson (Athlete, Football Player)
c/o Ken Zuckerman *Priority Sports & Entertainment - (LA)*
15233 Ventura Blvd Ste 718
Sherman Oaks, CA 91403-2237, USA

Alusik, George (Athlete, Baseball Player)
581 Garden Ave
Woodbridge, NJ 07095-3850, USA

Alvarado, Allen (Actor)
c/o Scott Appel *Scott Appel Public Relations*
13547 Ventura Blvd # 203
Sherman Oaks, CA 91423-3825, USA

Alvarez, Barry (Coach, Football Coach)
University of Wisconsin
Athletic Dept
Medison, WI 53711, USA

Alvarez, Brian Jordan (Actor)
c/o Shepard Smith *Luber Roklin Management*
5815 W Sunset Blvd Ste 208
Los Angeles, CA 90028-6481, USA

Alvarez, Fede (Actor)
c/o Heidi Lopata *Narrative*
1601 Vine St Fl 6
Los Angeles, CA 90028-8802, USA

Alvarez, Frankie J (Actor)
c/o Staff Member *Buchwald (NY)*
10 E 44th St
New York, NY 10017-3601, USA

Alvarez, Gabe (Athlete, Baseball Player)
4401 La Madera Ave
El Monte, CA 91732-2009, USA

Alvarez, Isabel (Athlete, Baseball Player)
2402 Monmouth Ave
Fort Wayne, IN 46809-1732, USA

Alvarez, Jose (Athlete, Baseball Player)
210 Murphy Ln
Greenville, SC 29607-4934, USA

Alvarez, Juan (Athlete, Baseball Player)
10995 SW 107th Ave
Miami, FL 33176-3444, USA

Alvarez, Orlando (Athlete, Baseball Player)
Cummunidad Dolores 37
Rio Grande, PR 00745, USA

Alvarez, Rogelio (Athlete, Baseball Player)
5010 NW 183rd St
Miami Gardens, FL 33055-2929, USA

Alvarez, Victor (Athlete, Baseball Player)
c/o Staff Member *Los Angeles Dodgers*
1000 Elysian Park Ave
Los Angeles, CA 90012, USA

Alvarez, Wilson (Athlete, Baseball Player)
State College Spikes
1204 Suncast Ln Ste 2
El Dorado Hills, CA 95762-9665, USA

Alvarez Martinez, Francisco Cardinal (Religious Leader)
Arco de Palacio 3
Toledo 45002, SPAIN

Alvers, Steve (Athlete, Football Player)
9751 SW 115th Ave
Miami, FL 33176-2553, USA

Alverson, Tommy (Musician)
c/o Staff Member *Ken-Ran Entertainment*
418 S Barton St
Grapevine, TX 76051-5344, USA

Alves, Camila (Model, Television Host)
c/o Diandra Escamilla *PMK/BNC Public Relations*
1840 Century Park E Ste 1400
Los Angeles, CA 90067-2115, USA

Alves, Joe (Director)
4176 Rosario Rd
Woodland Hills, CA 91364-6025, USA

Alvim, Anna (Actor)
c/o Michael Lewis Goldberg *Element Talent Agency*
2029 Verdugo Blvd # 203
Montrose, CA 91020-1626, USA

Alvin, Dave (Musician, Songwriter, Writer)
Mark Pucci
5000 Oak Bluff Ct
Atlanta, GA 30350-1069, USA

Alvina, Anicee (Actor)
41 Rue de l'Echese
Le Visinet 75008, FRANCE

Alvis, Max (Athlete, Baseball Player)
4106 College Dr Apt 215
Lufkin, TX 75901-7371, USA

Alvord, Steve (Athlete, Football Player)
3624 Westridge Pl
Bellingham, WA 98226, USA

Alward, Tom (Athlete, Football Player)
5051 Bensett Trl
Davison, MI 48423-8781, USA

Alworth, Lance (Athlete, Football Player)
990 Highland Dr Ste 300
Solana Beach, CA 92075-2438, USA

Alwyn, Joe (Actor)
c/o Lizzie Newell *Independent Talent Group*
40 Whitfield St
London W1T 2RH, UNITED KINGDOM

Al-Yawer, Sheik Ghazi Mashal Ajll (President)
President's Office
Al-Sijound Majalis
Karradat Mariam
Baghdad, IRAQ

Alyea, Brant (Athlete, Baseball Player)
3323 Manor Rd
Huntingdon Valley, PA 19006-4147, USA

Alyson, Jocelyn E (Musician)
c/o Staff Member *Diva Central Inc*
7510 W Sunset Blvd # 1445
Los Angeles, CA 90046-3408, USA

Alzate, Natalie (Internet Star)
c/o Staff Member *Brillstein Entertainment Partners*
9150 Wilshire Blvd Ste 350
Beverly Hills, CA 90212-3453, USA

Alzner, Karl (Athlete, Hockey Player)
c/o J P Barry *CAA Hockey*
Prefers to be contacted by email or phone.
Los Angeles, CA NA, USA

Ama, Shola (Musician)
12 One Mgmt
Executive Suite
20 Damien St
London E1 2HX, UNITED KINGDOM (UK)

Amaechi, John (Athlete, Basketball Player)
5747 E Aire Libre Ave
Scottsdale, AZ 85254-1206, USA

Amaker, Tommy (Athlete, Basketball Player, Coach)
University of Michigan
Athletic Dept
Ann Arbor, MI 48109, USA

Amalfitano, J Joseph (Joey) (Athlete, Baseball Player, Coach)
265 Bowstring Dr
Sedona, AZ 86336-6523, USA

amalfitano, joe (Athlete, Baseball Player)
60 Sheath Dr
Sedona, AZ 86336-6510, USA

Amalou, J K (Director)
William Morris Agency
52/53 Poland Place
London W1F 7LX, UNITED KINGDOM (UK)

Amanar, Simona (Gymnast)
Gymnastic Federation
Str Vasile Conta 16
Budapest 70139, ROMANIA

Amandes, Tom (Actor)
2751 Pelham Pl
Los Angeles, CA 90068-2326, USA

Amano, Eugene (Athlete, Football Player)
8354 Lochinver Park Ln
Brentwood, TN 37027-9121, USA

Amanpour, Christiane (Correspondent, Journalist)
c/o Staff Member *CNN (NY)*
10 Columbus Cir
Time Warner Center
New York, NY 10019-1158, USA

Amante, Tony (Athlete, Hockey Player)
58 Turners Way
Norwell, MA 02061-2339, USA

Amaral, Bob (Actor)
c/o Staff Member *Professional Artists Agency*
630 9th Ave Ste 207
New York, NY 10036-4752, USA

Amaral, Rich (Athlete, Baseball Player)
3122 Country Club Dr
Costa Mesa, CA 92626-2344, USA

Amaro, Jace (Athlete, Football Player)
c/o Erik Burkhardt *Select Sports Group*
2700 Post Oak Blvd Ste 1450
Houston, TX 77056-5785, USA

Amaro, Melanie (Musician)
6441 NW 24th Pl
Sunrise, FL 33313-2162, USA

Amaro Jr, Ruben (Athlete, Baseball Player, Commentator)
Philadelphia Phillies
1063 Country Hills Rd
Yardley, PA 19067-6024, USA

Amaro Sr, Ruben (Athlete, Baseball Player)
4098 Cinnamon Way
Weston, FL 33331-3810, USA

Amash, Justin (Congressman, Politician)
114 Cannon Hob
Washington, DC 20515-3601, USA

Amato, Bruno (Actor)
c/o Wendy Peldon *Caviar Entertainment*
2934 N Beverly Glen Cir # 115
Los Angeles, CA 90077-1724, USA

Amato, Joe (Race Car Driver)
Amato Racing
44 Tunkhannock Ave
Exeter, PA 18643-1221, USA

Amato, Ken (Athlete, Football Player)
641 Old Hickory Blvd Unit 305
Brentwood, TN 37027-3949, USA

Amatrudo, Ed (Actor)
c/o Harold Augenstein *Kazarian, Measures, Ruskin & Associates*
5200 Lankershim Blvd Ste 820
N Hollywood, CA 91601-3194, USA

Amavia, Daniela (Actor, Model)
c/o Tom Greenberg *Del Shaw Moonves Tanaka Finkelstein & Lezcano*
2029 Century Park E Ste 1750
Los Angeles, CA 90067-3036, USA

Amaya, Armando (Artist)
Lopex 137
Depto 1
Mexico City 06070 CP, MEXICO

Amaya, Rafael (Actor, Model, Musician)
c/o Liza Anderson *Anderson Group Public Relations*
8060 Melrose Ave Fl 4
Los Angeles, CA 90046-7038, USA

Amays, Ashraf (Athlete, Basketball Player)
25030 Round Barn Rd
Plainfield, IL 60585-7490

Amazing Jonathan, The (Actor)
c/o Staff Member *ICM Partners*
10250 Constellation Blvd Fl 7
Los Angeles, CA 90067-6207, USA

Amazing Rhythm Aces (Music Group)
c/o Staff Member *Fat City Artists*
1906 Chet Atkins Pl Apt 502
Nashville, TN 37212-2122, USA

Amber (Musician)
Artists & Audience Entertainment
PO Box 35
Pawling, NY 12564-0035, USA

Ambinder, Marc (Writer)
c/o Staff Member *Cohen & Gardner*
345 N Maple Dr Ste 181
Beverly Hills, CA 90210-5185, USA

Ambres, Chip (Athlete, Baseball Player)
4460 Beale St
Beaumont, TX 77705-4705, USA

Ambros, Wolfgang (Musician)
c/o Staff Member *Sony Music Entertainment Germany*
Neumarkter Str. 28
Muenchen 81673, Germany

Ambrose, Ashley (Athlete, Football Player)
1590 Briergate Dr
Duluth, GA 30097-4320, USA

Ambrose, Dean (Wrestler)
c/o Staff Member *World Wrestling Entertainment (WWE)*
1241 E Main St
Stamford, CT 06902-3520, USA

Ambrose, Lauren (Actor)
c/o Jennifer Sims *Imprint PR*
375 Hudson St
New York, NY 10014-3658, USA

Ambrose, Marcos (Race Car Driver)

Ambrose, Richard (Dick) (Athlete, Football Player)
24049 Stonehedge Dr
Cleveland, OH 44145-4864, USA

Ambrosio, Alessandra (Model)
2314 La Mesa Dr
Santa Monica, CA 90402-2331, USA

Ambrosius, Marsha (Musician)
c/o Dana Sims *ICM Partners*
10250 Constellation Blvd Fl 7
Los Angeles, CA 90067-6207, USA

Ambroziak, Peter (Athlete, Hockey Player)
6052 Crownpoint Dr NE
Rio Rancho, NM 87144-8714, USA

Ambudkar, Utkarsh (Actor)
1586 York Ave Apt 3
New York, NY 10028-6026, USA

Ambuehl, Clindy (Actor)
Paul Kohner
9300 Wilshire Blvd Ste 555
Beverly Hills, CA 90212-3211, USA

Ambulance Ltd (Music Group)
c/o Staff Member *Paradigm (Monterey)*
404 W Franklin St
Monterey, CA 93940-2303, USA

Amedori, John Patrick (Actor)
c/o Anne Woodward *Authentic Talent & Literary Management*
3615 Eastham Dr # 650
Culver City, CA 90232-2410, USA

Ameen, Aml (Actor)
c/o Jamie Harhay Skinner *Baker Winokur Ryder Public Relations*
9100 Wilshire Blvd
W Tower #500
Beverly Hills, CA 90212-3415, USA

Ameling, Elly (Music Group, Musician)
Hubstein Artist Services
65 W 90th St Apt 13F
New York, NY 10024-1510, USA

Amelio, Gilbert F (Business Person)
InterDigital
1001 E Hector St Ste 300
Conshohocken, PA 19428-2395, USA

Amell, Cassandra Jean (Actor, Model)
c/o Kalee Harris *Play Management*
220-807 Powell St
Vancouver, BC V6A 1H7, CANADA

Amell, Robbie (Actor)
c/o David Eisenberg *Protege Entertainment*
710 E Angeleno Ave
Burbank, CA 91501-2213, USA

Amell, Stephen (Actor)
c/o Michael Garnett *Leverage Management*
3030 Pennsylvania Ave
Santa Monica, CA 90404-4112, USA

Amelung, Ed (Athlete, Baseball Player)
11591 Elderberry Ln
Corona, CA 92883-4717, USA

Amen, Irving (Artist)
PO Box 812365
Boca Raton, FL 33481-2365, USA

Amenabar, Alejandro (Director, Musician, Writer)
c/o Sunmin Park *Maxmedia*
1620 Broadway Ste C
Santa Monica, CA 90404-2777, USA

Amend, Bill (Cartoonist)
721 W 16th St
Kansas City, MO 64108-1189, USA

Amendola, Danny (Athlete, Football Player)
c/o Erik Burkhardt *Select Sports Group*
2700 Post Oak Blvd Ste 1450
Houston, TX 77056-5785, USA

Amendola, Tony (Actor)
c/o Staff Member *Beacon Talent Agency*
170 Apple Ridge Rd
Woodcliff Lk, NJ 07677-8149, USA

Ament, Jeff (Musician)
5702 SW Andover St
Seattle, WA 98116-3555, USA

Amer, Nicolas (Actor)
14 Great Russell St
Flat 1
London WC1B 3NH, UK

American Gladiators (Reality Star)
MGM Television
10250 Constellation Blvd
Los Angeles, CA 90067-6200, USA

American Pickers (Music Group)
c/o Jonathan Adelman *Paradigm*
140 Broadway Ste 2600
New York, NY 10005-1011, USA

American Young (Music Group)
c/o Todd Thomas *Caption Management*
47 Music Sq E
Nashville, TN 37203-4324, USA

Amerie (Musician)
c/o Len Nicholson *Feenix Entertainment & Management*
1360 Clifton Ave Ste 318
Clifton, NJ 07012-1453, USA

Amerson, David (Athlete, Football Player)

Amerson, Glenn (Athlete, Football Player)
4857 Mustang Rd
Brenham, TX 77833-8746, USA

Ames, David (Athlete, Football Player)
7909 Alvarado Rd
Richmond, VA 23229-4208, USA

Ames, Denise (Actor)
Studio Talent Group
1328 12th St
Santa Monica, CA 90401-2051, USA

Ames, Ed (Actor, Musician)
c/o Staff Member *Paradise Artists*
108 E Matilija St
Ojai, CA 93023-2639, USA

Ames, Frank Anthony (Musician)
721 E Foothill Blvd
Monrovia, CA 91016-2405, USA

Ames, Rachel (Actor)
Atkins Assoc
8040 Ventura Canyon Ave
Panorama City, CA 91402-6313, USA

Amey, VInce (Athlete, Football Player)
4433 Callecita Ct
Union City, CA 94587-3829, USA

Amezaga, Alfredo (Athlete, Baseball Player)
12887 W Virginia Ave
Avondale, AZ 85392-7123, USA

Amft, Diana (Actor)
c/o Staff Member *Agentur Britta Imdahl*
Paddenbett 6
Bochum 44803, GERMANY

Amge, Jyoti (Actor)
c/o Drew Elliot *Artist International*
333 E 43rd St Apt 115
New York, NY 10017-4822, USA

Amick, Madchen (Actor)
c/o Kesha Williams *KW Entertainment*
425 N Robertson Blvd
West Hollywood, CA 90048-1735, USA

Amiel, Jon (Director)
c/o Dave Brown *Echo Lake Management*
421 S Beverly Dr Fl 8
Beverly Hills, CA 90212-4408, USA

Amiez, Sebastien (Athlete, Skier)
Ave Chasse-Foret
Pralognan 73710, FRANCE

Amigo Vallejo, Carlos Cardinal (Religious Leader)
Archdiocese
Piaza Virgin de los Reyes S/N
Seville 41004, SPAIN

Amiina (Musician)
c/o Staff Member *Paradigm (Monterey)*
404 W Franklin St
Monterey, CA 93940-2303, USA

Amis, Martin (Journalist, Writer)
P F D
Drury House
34-43 Russell St
London WC2B 5HA, UNITED KINGDOM (UK)

Amis, Suzy (Actor, Model)
Amis Construction Co
1647 Exchange Ave
Oklahoma City, OK 73108-3027, USA

Amlee, Jessica (Actor)
c/o Kalee Harris *Play Management*
220-807 Powell St
Vancouver, BC V6A 1H7, CANADA

Amlong, Thomas (Athlete)
166 Four Mile River Rd
Old Lyme, CT 06371-1325, USA

Ammaccapane, Danielle (Athlete, Golfer)
13214 N 13th St
Phoenix, AZ 85022-4936, USA

Ammaccapane, Dina (Athlete, Golfer)
4407 E Blanche Dr
Phoenix, AZ 85032-4881, USA

Amman, Dick (Athlete, Football Player)
2907 Lake Joanna Dr
Eustis, FL 32726-7824, USA

Amman, Richard (Athlete, Football Player)
2907 Lake Joanna Dr
Eustis, FL 32726-7824, USA

Ammann, Alberto (Actor)
c/o Katrina Bayonas *Kuranda Management*
Isla De Oza, 30
Madrid 28035, SPAIN

Ammann, Simon (Athlete, Speed Skater)
Ski Verband
Worbstr 52
Muri 03074, SWITZERLAND

Amodeo, Mike (Athlete, Hockey Player)
556 Fralicks Beach Rd RR 5
Port Perry, ON L9L 1B6, Canada

Among the Oak & Ash (Music Group, Musician)
c/o Staff Member *MCT Management*
520 8th Ave Rm 2205
New York, NY 10018-4160, USA

Amons, Mary Schmidt (Reality Star)
c/o Staff Member *Bravo TV (NY)*
30 Rockefeller Plz
New York, NY 10112-0015, USA

Amonte, Tony (Athlete, Hockey Player, Olympic Athlete)
58 Turners Way
Norwell, MA 02061-2339, USA

Amor, Vicente (Athlete, Baseball Player)
13871 SW 52nd St
Miramar, FL 33027-5945, USA

Amor, Vincente (Athlete, Baseball Player)
13871 SW 52nd St
Miramar, FL 33027-5945, USA

Amorosi, Vanessa (Musician)
Mar Jac Productions
PO Box 51
Caulfield South, VIC, AUSTRALIA

Amoruso, Sophia (Business Person)
c/o Brett Ruttenberg *Imprint PR*
6121 W Sunset Blvd
Neuehouse
Los Angeles, CA 90028-6442, USA

Amos, John (Actor)
c/o Staff Member *AWJ Platinum PR*
8350 Wilshire Blvd
#200
Los Angeles, CA 90048, USA

Amos, Tori (Musician)
c/o Carole Kinzel *Creative Artists Agency (CAA)*
2000 Avenue of the Stars Ste 100
Los Angeles, CA 90067-4705, USA

Amos, Wally (Famous) (Business Person)
9209 Palmetto Pl
Fort Mill, SC 29708-6473, USA

Amoyal, Pierre A W (Musician)
Jacques Thelen
252 Rue de Faubourg Saint-Honore
Paris 75008, FRANCE

Amplas, John (Actor)
443 Meridian Dr
Pittsburgh, PA 15228-2613, USA

Amsler, Marty (Athlete, Football Player)
4009 Fairfax Rd
Evansville, IN 47710-3718, USA

Amstrong, Otis (Athlete, Football Player)
7183 S Newport Way
Centennial, CO 80112-1613, USA

Amstutz, Joe (Athlete, Football Player)
24840 Arrow Ct Apt 29
Tehachapi, CA 93561-7124, USA

Amukamara, Prince (Athlete, Football Player)
c/o Todd France *Creative Artists Agency (CAA) Sports*
3500 Lenox Rd NE
Atlanta, GA 30326-4228, USA

Amukamura, Prince (Football Player)
c/o Todd France *Creative Artists Agency (CAA) Sports*
3500 Lenox Rd NE
Atlanta, GA 30326-4228, USA

Amundsen, Norman (Athlete, Football Player)
3901 Hemlock Dr
Valparaiso, IN 46383-1813, USA

Amurri, Eva (Actor)
c/o Steve Small *aTa Management (LA)*
2508 N Vermont Ave # 702
Los Angeles, CA 90027-1243, USA

Amy, Susie (Actor, Model)
c/o Martin (Marty) Berneman *Precision Entertainment*
6338 Wilshire Blvd
Los Angeles, CA 90048-5002, USA

An, Yoson (Actor)
c/o Grahame Dunster *Auckland Actors*
PO Box 56-460
Dominion Road
Auckland 00003, NEW ZEALAND

Anae, Tumua (Athlete, Olympic Athlete, Water Polo Player)
Allen F Anae
1800 Kaioo Dr Apt C504
Honolulu, HI 96815-5830, USA

Anahi (Actor)
c/o Staff Member *Televisa*
Blvd Adolfo Lopez Mateos 232
Colonia San Angel INN
DF CP 01060, MEXICO

Anakin, Douglas (Athlete)
PO Box 27
Windermere, BC V0B 2L, CANADA

Anapau, Kristina (Actor)

Anastacia (Musician)
c/o Lisa Braude *Braude Management Inc*
PO Box 7249
San Diego, CA 92167-0249, USA

Anastasio, Trey (Musician)
40 Lawrence Ln
Palisades, NY 10964-1604, USA

Anaya, Rudolfo (Writer)
5324 Canada Vista Pl NW
Albuquerque, NM 87120-2412, USA

Anaya, Toney (Politician)
Maldef
634 S Spring St Ste 802
Los Angeles, CA 90014-3905, USA

Ancelotti, Carlo (Athlete, Soccer Player)
FC Milan
Via Filippo
Turati 3
Milan 20121, ITALY

Ancheta, Bernie (Director, Writer)
c/o Staff Member *Lenhoff & Lenhoff*
324 S Beverly Dr
Beverly Hills, CA 90212-4801

Ancona, Bill (Race Car Driver)
260 Nelson Wyatt Rd
Mansfield, TX 76063-6031, USA

Andabaker, Rudy (Athlete, Football Player)
450 8th St
Donora, PA 15033-2108, USA

Anden, Mini (Actor, Model)
c/o Ashley Franklin *Thruline Entertainment*
9250 Wilshire Blvd Fl Ground
Beverly Hills, CA 90212-3352, USA

Andere, Jacqueline (Actor)
c/o Staff Member *Televisa*
Blvd Adolfo Lopez Mateos 232
Colonia San Angel INN
DF CP 01060, MEXICO

Anderegg, Bob (Athlete, Basketball Player)
11708 E Onyx Ave
Scottsdale, AZ 85259-5017, USA

Anders, Andrea (Actor)
3615 Dixie Canyon Ave
Sherman Oaks, CA 91423-4823, USA

Anders, Beth (Athlete, Hockey Player, Olympic Athlete)
9727 Bay Point Dr
Norfolk, VA 23518-2019, USA

Anders, David (Actor)
c/o Ashton Lunceford *Portrait PR*
5320 Sylmar Ave
Sherman Oaks, CA 91401-5612, USA

Anders, Kimble (Athlete, Football Player)
801 Landing Blvd
League City, TX 77573-3315, USA

Anders, Sean (Director, Producer, Writer)
c/o John Elliott *Mosaic Media Group*
407 N Maple Dr # 100
Beverly Hills, CA 90210-3818, USA

Anders, William A Maj Gen (Astronaut)
1156 Brighton Crest Dr
Bellingham, WA 98229-6905, USA

Andersen, Anthony (Actor)
1619 Broadway # 900
New York, NY 10019-7412, USA

Andersen, Barbara (Actor)
PO Box 10118
Santa Fe, NM 87504, USA

Andersen, Chris (Birdman) (Athlete, Basketball Player)
c/o Leon Rose *CAA Basketball*
308 Harper Dr Ste 210
Moorestown, NJ 08057-3245, USA

Andersen, Elmer (Politician)
1483 Bussard Ct
Saint Paul, MN 55112-3628, USA

Andersen, Gary (Football Coach)
University of Wisconsin
Athletic Dept
Madison, WI 53706, USA

Andersen, Greta (Athlete, Olympic Athlete, Swimmer)
16222 Monterey Ln Spc 264
Huntington Beach, CA 92649-2248, USA

Andersen, Jason (Athlete, Football Player)
4530 County Road 16 Apt 410
Canandaigua, NY 14424-8316, USA

Andersen, Larry (Athlete, Baseball Player)
120 Dickinson St Rear A
Philadelphia, PA 19147-6100, USA

Andersen, Mogens (Athlete, Football Player)
Strandagervej 28
Hellerup, Copenhagen 02900, Denmark

Andersen, Morten (Athlete, Football Player)
6501 Old Shadburn Ferry Rd
Buford, GA 30518-1137, USA

Andersen, Pip (Actor)
c/o Shani Rosenzweig *United Talent Agency (UTA)*
9336 Civic Center Dr
Beverly Hills, CA 90210-3604, USA

Andersen, Reidar (Skier)
National Ski Hall of Fame
PO Box 191
Ishpeming, MI 49849-0191, USA

Andersen, Thomas (Actor, Musician)
c/o Staff Member *Allendorf-Bremm Management*
Cologne Alpener Stra 16
Cologne 50825, GERMANY

Andersen, Watts Teresa (Swimmer)
2582 Marsha Way
San Jose, CA 95125-4029, USA

Andersion, Robert P (Athlete, Football Player)
244 Carmel Dr
Melbourne, FL 32940-7782, USA

Anderson, Alfred (Athlete, Football Player)
2805 Chesterwood Ct
Mansfield, TX 76063-8809, USA

Anderson, Allan (Athlete, Baseball Player)
1491 Lancaster Kirkersville Rd NW
Lancaster, OH 43130-8969, USA

Anderson, Alyssa (Athlete, Swimmer)
Randy Anderson
1802 California Ave
Santa Monica, CA 90403-4411, USA

Anderson, Anthony (Actor, Television Host)
c/o Cindy Guagenti *Baker Winokur Ryder Public Relations*
9100 Wilshire Blvd
W Tower #500
Beverly Hills, CA 90212-3415, USA

Anderson, Anthony (Athlete, Football Player)
4001 Kennett Pike Ste 134
Wilmington, DE 19807-2000, USA

Anderson, Antonio (Athlete, Football Player)
463 Lexington Ave
Brooklyn, NY 11221-1203, USA

Anderson, Aric (Athlete, Football Player)
16306 Rolling View Trl
Cypress, TX 77433-5856, USA

Anderson, Aric (Athlete, Football Player)
528 Halifax Ln
Coppell, TX 75019-2448, USA

Anderson, Audrey Marie (Actor)
c/o Staff Member *Untitled Entertainment (NY)*
215 Park Ave S Fl 8
New York, NY 10003-1622, USA

Anderson, Bennie (Athlete, Football Player)
6450 Virginia Ave
Saint Louis, MO 63111-2705, USA

Anderson, Bill (Athlete, Football Player)
6924 Lark Ln
Knoxville, TN 37919-5928, USA

Anderson, Bill (Whispering) (Musician, Songwriter)
PO Box 888
Hermitage, TN 37076-0888, USA

Anderson, Blake (Actor, Comedian)
c/o Lewis Kay *Kovert Creative*
506 Santa Monica Blvd Ste 400
Santa Monica, CA 90401-2412, USA

Anderson, Bob (Athlete, Football Player)
244 Carmel Dr
Melbourne, FL 32940-7782, USA

Anderson, Bob (Athlete, Baseball Player)
8417 S 84th East Pl
Tulsa, OK 74133-8028, USA

Anderson, Bobby (Athlete, Football Player)
79125 Big Horn Trl
La Quinta, CA 92253-4523, USA

Anderson, Brad (Athlete, Football Player)
13730 E Gary Rd
Scottsdale, AZ 85259-4644, USA

Anderson, Brad (Race Car Driver)
1240 S Cucamonga Ave
Ontario, CA 91761-4505, USA

Anderson, Bradford (Actor)

Anderson, Brady (Athlete, Baseball Player, Television Host)
2205 Warwick Way Ste 200
Marriottsville, MD 21104-1632, USA

Anderson, Brain (Athlete, Baseball Player)
W275N9303 Lake Five Rd
Hartland, WI 53029-9016, USA

Anderson, Brett (Musician)
c/o Staff Member *13 Artists (UK)*
11-14 Kensington St
Brighton BN1 4AJ, UNITED KINGDOM

Anderson, Brian (Commentator)
W275N9303 Lake Five Rd
Hartland, WI 53029-9016, USA

Anderson, Brian (Athlete, Baseball Player)
c/o Staff Member *Miami Marlins*
501 Marlins Way
Miami, FL 33125-1121, USA

Anderson, Brian (Athlete, Baseball Player)
660 Saxony Blvd
St Petersburg, FL 33716-1284, USA

Anderson, Brian (Athlete, Baseball Player)
9553 N Corte Roca De Plata
Tucson, AZ 85704-8609, USA

Anderson, Brooke (Television Host)
c/o Staff Member *ABC Television (LA)*
500 S Buena Vista St
Burbank, CA 91521-0001, USA

Anderson, Bruce A (Athlete, Football Player)
910 NE Parkview Ct
Roseburg, OR 97470-2136, USA

Anderson, Bud (Athlete, Baseball Player)
240 Twin Ln E
Wantagh, NY 11793-1963, USA

Anderson, Camille (Actor)
c/o Steven Neibert *Imperium 7 Talent Agency*
5455 Wilshire Blvd Ste 1706
Los Angeles, CA 90036-4217, USA

Anderson, Chantelle (Athlete, Basketball Player)
Cleveland Rockers
1 Center Ct
Gund Arena
Cleveland, OH 44115-4001, USA

Anderson, Charlie (Athlete, Football Player)
318 Greenacres Blvd
Bossier City, LA 71111-6052, USA

Anderson, Chris (Business Person, Writer)
The Long Tail
1165 Miller Ave
Berkeley, CA 94708-1754, USA

Anderson, C.J. (Athlete, Football Player)
c/o Peter Schaffer *Authentic Athletix*
400 S Steele St Unit 47
Denver, CO 80209-3535, USA

Anderson, Clayton (Astronaut)
2883 Carrera Ct
League City, TX 77573-2291, USA

Anderson, Clifford (Athlete, Basketball Player)
2096A S John Russell Cir
Elkins Park, PA 19027-1017, USA

Anderson, Colt (Athlete, Football Player)

Anderson, Courtney (Athlete, Football Player)
340 34th St
Richmond, CA 94805-2168, USA

Anderson, Craig (Athlete, Baseball Player)
19217 SW 96th Loop
Dunnellon, FL 34432-4201, USA

Anderson, Craig (Athlete, Hockey Player)
12120 Summer Ridge Ln
Huntley, IL 60142-7731, USA

Anderson, Curtis (Athlete, Football Player)
967 Kemper Meadow Dr
Cincinnati, OH 45240-1463, USA

Anderson, Dale (Athlete, Hockey Player)
2217 Haultain Ave
Saskatoon, SK S7J 1P7, Canada

Anderson, Dale (Athlete, Hockey Player)
2217 Av Haultain
Saskatoon, SK S7J 1P7, CANADA

Anderson, Damien (Athlete, Football Player)
3563 S Cox Ct
Chandler, AZ 85248-4436, USA

Anderson, Dan (Athlete, Basketball Player)
2230 SW Winchester Ave
Portland, OR 97225-4460, USA

Anderson, Dan (Athlete, Basketball Player)
100 3rd Ave S Unit 2002
Minneapolis, MN 55401-2716, USA

Anderson, Darren (Athlete, Football Player)
7328 Overland Park Ct
West Chester, OH 45069-5560, USA

Anderson, Daryl (Actor)
24136 Friar St
Woodland Hills, CA 91367-1240, USA

Anderson, Dave (Athlete, Baseball Player)
21 Quinn Way
Mission Viejo, CA 92691-5651, USA

Anderson, David (Athlete, Baseball Player)
207 Athletic Office Bldg
Memphis, TN 38152-3730, USA

Anderson, Dennis (Race Car Driver)
Clear Channel Entertainment
495 N Commons Dr Ste 200
Aurora, IL 60504-8295, USA

Anderson, Derek (Athlete, Football Player)
c/o David Dunn *Athletes First*
23091 Mill Creek Dr
Laguna Hills, CA 92653-1258, USA

Anderson, Derek (Athlete, Basketball Player)
5562 Werburgh St
Charlotte, NC 28209-3693, USA

Anderson, Dick (Athlete, Football Player)
4603 Santa Maria St
Miami, FL 33146-1132, USA

Anderson, Dion (Actor)
S D B Partners
1801 Ave of Stars
#902
Los Angeles, CA 90067, USA

Anderson, Don (Athlete, Football Player)
10090 Beechdale St
Detroit, MI 48204-2567, USA

Anderson, Drew (Athlete, Baseball Player)
411 N 10th St
Brainerd, MN 56401-3027, USA

Anderson, Dwain (Athlete, Baseball Player)
1807 Fallbrook Dr
Alamo, CA 94507-2810, USA

Anderson, Earl (Athlete, Hockey Player)
602 3rd Ave NE
Roseau, MN 56751-1809, USA

Anderson, Eddie Lee (Athlete, Football Player)
209 Shenandoah Trl
Warner Robins, GA 31088-6284, USA

Anderson, Ella (Actor)
c/o Elizabeth Much *East 2 West Collective*
11022 Santa Monica Blvd Ste 350
Los Angeles, CA 90025-7532, USA

Anderson, Erich (Actor)
Paradigm Agency
10100 Santa Monica Blvd Ste 2500
Los Angeles, CA 90067-4116, USA

Anderson, Erick (Athlete, Football Player)
25483 Bryden Rd
Beachwood, OH 44122-4161, USA

Anderson, Erika (Actor)
c/o Staff Member *Flick Commercials*
9057 Nemo St # A
W Hollywood, CA 90069-5511, USA

Anderson, Erriestine I (Musician)
Thomas Cassidy
11761 E Speedway Blvd
Tucson, AZ 85748-2017, USA

Anderson, Flipper (Athlete, Football Player)
190 Abbey Hill Rd
Suwanee, GA 30024-1976, USA

Anderson, Fred (Athlete, Football Player)
11810 NE 48th Pl
Kirkland, WA 98033-8750, USA

Anderson, Garret (Athlete, Baseball Player)
1 Linda Isle
Newport Beach, CA 92660-7205, USA

Anderson, Gary W (Athlete, Football Player)
1 Ridgefield Ct
Little Rock, AR 72223-4608, USA

Anderson, Gayle (Correspondent)
KTLA-TV
5800 W Sunset Blvd
Los Angeles, CA 90028-6607, USA

Anderson, Gillian (Actor)
c/o Ciara Parkes *Public Eye Communications*
535 Kings Rd
#313 Plaza
London SW10 0SZ, UNITED KINGDOM

Anderson, Glenn (Athlete, Hockey Player)
42 W 69th St Apt 2A
New York, NY 10023-5265, USA

Anderson, Haley (Athlete, Swimmer)
Randy Anderson
9620 Oak Leaf Way
Granite Bay, CA 95746-8919, USA

Anderson, Hannah Emily (Actor)
c/o Emma Laird *GGA Agency*
149 Church St
Fl 2
Toronto ON CANADA, M5B 1Y4

Anderson, H George (Religious Leader)
Evangelical Lutheran Church
8765 W Higgins Rd Ste 600
Chicago, IL 60631-4100, USA

Anderson, Ho Che (Artist)
c/o Staff Member *Fantagraphics Books*
7563 Lake City Way NE
Seattle, WA 98115-4218, USA

Anderson, Howard A (Actor)
PO Box 2230
Los Angeles, CA 90051-0230, USA

Anderson, Ian (Musician, Songwriter)
43 Brook Green
London W6 7ER, UNITED KINGDOM (UK)

Anderson, Jacob (Actor)
c/o Mike Smith *Principal Entertainment*
9255 W Sunset Blvd Ste 500
Los Angeles, CA 90069-3301, USA

Anderson, Jamal (Athlete, Football Player)
10540 Montclair Way
Duluth, GA 30097-1840, USA

Anderson, James (Athlete, Football Player)
1544 Taylor Point Dr
Chesapeake, VA 23321-0181, USA

Anderson, James F (Religious Leader)
12 Surf Ave
Ocean Grove, NJ 07756-1629, USA

Anderson, Jamie (Actor)
c/o JoAnn Smolen *Rage Talent Agency (RTA)*
23679 Calabasas Rd Ste 501
Calabasas, CA 91302-1502, USA

Anderson, Janet (Athlete, Golfer)
4311 W Ardmore Rd
Laveen, AZ 85339-2112, USA

Anderson, Jason (Athlete, Baseball Player)
2022 Hidden Lake Dr Apt F
Stow, OH 44224-5321, USA

Anderson, J C (Athlete, Golfer)
1418 S 39th St
Quincy, IL 62305-6104, USA

Anderson, Jeff (Actor, Director)
c/o Staff Member *Imperium 7 Talent Agency*
5455 Wilshire Blvd Ste 1706
Los Angeles, CA 90036-4217, USA

Anderson, Jesse (Athlete, Football Player)
4374 Redwood Cir
Jackson, MS 39212-3645, USA

Anderson, Jim (Athlete, Baseball Player)
2111 Bennington Ct
Thousand Oaks, CA 91360-1977, USA

Anderson, Jimmy (Athlete, Baseball Player)
148 Yorkshire Ct
Portsmouth, VA 23701-2140, USA

Anderson, Jimmy (Athlete, Hockey Player)
4H Castle Hill Rd # H
Agawam, MA 01001-2460, USA

Anderson, Jo (Actor)
c/o Staff Member *Innovative Artists*
1505 10th St
Santa Monica, CA 90401-2805, USA

Anderson, Joe (Actor)
c/o Lindy King *United Agents*
12-26 Lexington St
London W1F OLE, UNITED KINGDOM

Anderson, John (Athlete, Football Player)
14730 Crestwood Ct
Elm Grove, WI 53122-1603, USA

Anderson, John (Athlete, Hockey Player)
6751 N Sunset Blvd Ste 200
Glendale, AZ 85305-3162, USA

Anderson, John (Musician)
1009 16th Ave S
Nashville, TN 37212-2302, USA

Anderson, Jon (Musician)
Sun Artists
9 Hillgate St
London W8 7SP, UNITED KINGDOM (UK)

Anderson, Josh (Athlete, Baseball Player)
3780 E Highway 452
Eubank, KY 42567-9731, USA

Anderson, Kalen (Athlete, Golfer)
c/o Jim Lehrman *Medalist Management Inc*
36855 W Main St Ste 200
Purcellville, VA 20132-3561, USA

Anderson, Keith (Musician)
c/o Staff Member *Fitzgerald-Hartley Co (Ventura)*
34 N Palm St Ste 100
Ventura, CA 93001-2610, USA

Anderson, Ken (Athlete, Football Player)
41 Sedge Fern Dr
Hilton Head Island, SC 29926-2782, USA

Anderson, Kenny (Athlete, Basketball Player)
18145 SW 5th Ct
Pembroke Pines, FL 33029-4352, USA

Anderson, Kent (Athlete, Baseball Player)
925 E Twin Church Rd
Timmonsville, SC 29161-8528, USA

Anderson, Kevin (Actor)
c/o Staff Member *ICM Partners*
10250 Constellation Blvd Fl 7
Los Angeles, CA 90067-6207, USA

Anderson, Kevin J (Writer)
Tom Doherty Associates, LLC
175 5th Ave Ste 810
New York, NY 10010-7711, USA

Anderson, Kim (Athlete, Basketball Player)
1210 Shady Bank Ln
Columbia, MO 65201-2889, USA

Anderson, Kim S (Athlete, Football Player)
464 E Mariposa St
Altadena, CA 91001-2207, USA

Anderson, Larry (Athlete, Baseball Player)
1135 Saratoga Ave
Grover Beach, CA 93433-1723, USA

Anderson, Lars (Athlete, Baseball Player)
3948 Bannister Rd
Fair Oaks, CA 95628-6806, USA

Anderson, Laurie (Musician)
195 Chrystie St # 501F
New York, NY 10002-1214, USA

Anderson, Lawrence A (Larry) (Athlete, Football Player)
3170 Blanchard Rd
Shreveport, LA 71103-2142, USA

Anderson, Lloyd L (Astronaut)
1939 Live Oak Cemetery Rd
Killeen, TX 76542-5100, USA

Anderson, Loni (Actor)
Sandy Hook Productions
20652 Lassen St Spc 98
Chatsworth, CA 91311-0698, USA

Anderson, Louie (Actor, Comedian, Producer)
c/o Staff Member *Buried Treasure Entertainment*
287 S Robertson Blvd Ste 543
Beverly Hills, CA 90211-2810, USA

Anderson, Loule (Actor, Comedian)
8033 W Sunset Blvd # 605
West Hollywood, CA 90046-2401, USA

Anderson, Marina (Actor)
c/o Nancy Harding *Powerhouse Talent*
PO Box 261939
Encino, CA 91426-1939, USA

Anderson, Mark (Athlete, Football Player)
9725 Woods Dr Unit 1617
Skokie, IL 60077-4456, USA

Anderson, Marlon (Athlete, Baseball Player)
1603 Turning Leaf Ct
Sugar Land, TX 77479-6489, USA

Anderson, Marques (Athlete, Football Player)
213 W Gardner St
Long Beach, CA 90805-2034, USA

Anderson, Mary (Actor)
1127 N Norman Pl
Los Angeles, CA 90049-1538, USA

Anderson, Matt (Athlete, Golfer)
c/o Jim Lehrman *Medalist Management Inc*
36855 W Main St Ste 200
Purcellville, VA 20132-3561, USA

Anderson, Matt (Athlete, Baseball Player)
4115 Woodmont Park Ln
Louisville, KY 40245-8431, USA

Anderson, Melissa Sue (Actor, Producer)
c/o Staff Member *Globe Pequot Press*
246 Goose Ln Ste 200
PO Box 480
Guilford, CT 06437-2186, USA

Anderson, Melody (Actor)
PO Box 24483
Los Angeles, CA 90024-0483, USA

Anderson, Michael (Musician, Songwriter, Writer)
Brock Assoc
7106 Moores Ln # 200
Brentwood, TN 37027-2903, USA

Anderson, Mike (Athlete, Baseball Player)
1702 E Juniper Way
Hartland, WI 53029-8669, USA

Anderson, Mike (Athlete, Coach, Football Player)
PO Box 12753
Chandler, AZ 85248-0030, USA

Anderson, Mitchell (Actor)
MetroFresh
931 Monroe Dr NE Ste A106
Atlanta, GA 30308-1795, USA

Anderson, Murray (Athlete, Hockey Player)
38 Head Ave
PO Box 38 Stn Main
The Pas, MB R9A 1K3, Canada

Anderson, Neal (Athlete, Football Player)
10626 SW 41st Pl
Gainesville, FL 32608-7126, USA

Anderson, Neilson (Athlete, Basketball Player)
163 Harbor Isle Cir N
Memphis, TN 38103-0841, USA

Anderson, Neil T. (Writer)
Freedom in Christ Ministries
9051 Executive Park Dr Ste 503
Knoxville, TN 37923-4632, USA

Anderson, Nick (Athlete, Basketball Player)
6672 Cherry Grove Cir
Orlando, FL 32809-6658, USA

Anderson, Nicole (Actor)
c/o Todd Justice *Justice & Ponder*
PO Box 480033
Los Angeles, CA 90048-1033, USA

Anderson, Ottis (OJ) (Athlete, Football Player)
74 Park Ter
Caldwell, NJ 07006-5548, USA

Anderson, Pamela (Actor)
c/o Ann Gurrola *Marleah Leslie & Associates*
1645 Vine St Apt 712
Los Angeles, CA 90028-8812, USA

Anderson, Paul (Actor)
c/o Kate Buckley *42 Management (UK)*
8 Flitcroft St
London WC2H 8DL, UNITED KINGDOM

Anderson, Paul Thomas (Director, Writer)
Ghoulardi Film Company
13351D Riverside Dr # 245
Sherman Oaks, CA 91423-2508, USA

Anderson, Paul W S (Director)
c/o Ken Kamins *Key Creatives*
1800 N Highland Ave Fl 5
Los Angeles, CA 90028-4523, USA

Anderson, Perry (Athlete, Hockey Player)
8113 E Palm Ln
Scottsdale, AZ 85257-3003, USA

Anderson, Ralph (Athlete, Football Player)
908 Hilltop Dr Apt C
Irving, TX 75060-3925, USA

Anderson, Randy (Race Car Driver)
Anderson Racing
1240 S Cucamonga Ave
Ontario, CA 91761-4505, USA

Anderson, Rashard (Athlete, Football Player)
676 N First Ave
Forest, MS 39074-3637, USA

Anderson, Ray (Musician)
James faith Entertainment
318 Wynn Ln Ste 14
Port Jefferson, NY 11777-1699, USA

Anderson, Reid B (Dancer, Director)
Stuttgart Ballet
Ober Schlossgarten 6
Stuttgart 70173, GERMANY

Anderson, Renee (Actor)
2818 Laurel Canyon Blvd
Los Angeles, CA 90046, USA

Anderson, Richard Dean (Actor)
Gekko Film Corp
2400 Boundary Rd
Burnaby, BC V5M 3Z3, CANADA

Anderson, Richard (Dick) J (Athlete, Football Player)
206 Baker Ave
Lodi, OH 44254-1407, USA

Anderson, Richard P (Dick) (Athlete, Football Player)
4603 Santa Maria St
Coral Gables, FL 33146-1132, USA

Anderson, Richie (Athlete, Football Player)
6311 Meandering Woods Ct
Frederick, MD 21701-4955, USA

Anderson, Rick (Athlete, Baseball Player)
3929 Benjamin Dr
Saint Paul, MN 55125-3396, USA

Anderson, Rick (Athlete, Baseball Player)
Minnesota Twins
1 Twins Way
Minneapolis, MN 55403-1418, USA

Anderson, Robert (Writer)
William Morris Agency
1325 Avenue of the Americas Bsmt 2
New York, NY 10019-6047, USA

Anderson, Ron (Athlete, Hockey Player)
4470 Meadowvale Dr
Niagara Falls, ON L2E 5W9, Canada

Anderson, Ron (Athlete, Hockey Player)
72 Woodside Close NW
Airdrie, AB T4B 2C7, Canada

Anderson, Ross (Journalist)
Seattle Times
1120 John St
Editorial Dept
Seattle, WA 98109-5321, USA

Anderson, Russ (Athlete, Hockey Player)
76 Fern Dr
Plantsville, CT 06479-1810, USA

Anderson, Ryan (Athlete, Basketball Player)
c/o Staff Member *New Orleans Pelicans*
1250 Poydras St Ste 101
New Orleans, LA 70113-1804, USA

Anderson, Sam (Actor)
c/o Staff Member *TalentWorks*
3500 W Olive Ave Ste 1400
Burbank, CA 91505-5512, USA

Anderson, Scot (Writer)
c/o Staff Member *Premiere Speakers Bureau*
109 International Dr Ste 300
Franklin, TN 37067-1764, USA

Anderson, Scott (Athlete, Baseball Player)
13061 Amber Pl
Lake Oswego, OR 97034-1524, United States

Anderson, Scott (Athlete, Baseball Player)
13061 Amber Pl
Lake Oswego, OR 97034-1524, USA

Anderson, Scott (Athlete, Football Player)
2836 Queen Bee Ln
Saint Louis, MO 63129-5644, USA

Anderson, Scotty (Athlete, Football Player)
1405 Leon Dr
Jonesboro, LA 71251-2213, USA

Anderson, Shamier (Actor)
c/o Paul Nelson *Mosaic Media Group*
407 N Maple Dr # 100
Beverly Hills, CA 90210-3818, USA

Anderson, Shandon (Athlete, Basketball Player)
1257 Weston Dr
Decatur, GA 30032-2550, USA

Anderson, Shawn (Athlete, Hockey Player)
Hockey Specific Training
274 Boul Pincourt
Pincourt, QC J7W 9X9, Canada

Anderson, Shelly (Race Car Driver)
1240 S Cucamonga Ave
Ontario, CA 91761-4505, USA

Anderson, Sterling (Producer)
c/o Jared Bloch *Reed Smith*
599 Lexington Ave Fl 26
New York, NY 10022-7684, USA

Anderson, Stevie (Athlete, Football Player)
1405 Leon Dr
Jonesboro, LA 71251-2213, USA

Anderson, Stuart (Athlete, Football Player)
100 Careys Ln
Cardinal, VA 23025-2006, USA

Anderson, Sunny (Chef)
c/o Jonathan Rosen *WME|IMG (NY)*
11 Madison Ave Fl 18
New York, NY 10010-3669, USA

Anderson, Sylvia (Actor)
c/o Staff Member *Hermes Press*
2100 Wilmington Rd
New Castle, PA 16105-1931, USA

Anderson, Taz (Athlete, Football Player)
2931 Paces Ferry Rd SE Ste 150
Atlanta, GA 30339-3735, USA

Anderson, Taz (Athlete, Football Player)
Taz Anderson Realty
2931 Paces Ferry Rd SE Ste 150
Atlanta, GA 30339-5727, USA

Anderson, Terence (Politician)
668 Oak Tree Rd
Palisades, NY 10964-1532, USA

Anderson, Terence (Terry) (Journalist)
17 Sunlight Hl
Yonkers, NY 10704-2903, USA

Anderson, Terry (Producer)
Pinewood Studios
Iverheath
Iver
Bucks SL0 0NH, UNITED KINGDOM (UK)

Anderson, Tom (Actor, Producer, Writer)
c/o Staff Member *Gersh*
9465 Wilshire Blvd Ste 600
Beverly Hills, CA 90212-2605, USA

Anderson, Tom (Business Person)
c/o MySpace, Inc
6060 Center Dr Ste 300
Los Angeles, CA 90045-8842, USA

Anderson, Tori (Actor, Producer)
c/o Darren Boidman *Carrier Talent Management*
705-1080 Howe St
Vancouver, BC V6Z 2T1, CANADA

Anderson, Tracy (Fitness Expert)
Tracy Anderson Studios
408 Greenwich St Fl 3
New York, NY 10013-2077, USA

Anderson, Vickey Ray (Athlete, Football Player)
4036 Neptune Dr
Oklahoma City, OK 73116-1658, USA

Anderson, Wayne (Race Car Driver)
Liberty Racing
3086 N US Highway 301
Wildwood, FL 34785-8371, USA

Anderson, Wes (Director, Producer)
c/o Staff Member *Moxie Pictures*
2644 30th St Ste 100
Santa Monica, CA 90405-3051, USA

Anderson, Wessell (Musician)
Fat City Artists
1906 Chet Atkins Pl Apt 502
Nashville, TN 37212-2122, USA

Anderson, Willie (Athlete, Basketball Player)
Toronto Raptors
40 Bay St
Air Canada Center
Toronto, ON M5J 2X2, Canada

Anderson, Willie (Athlete, Football Player)
1490 Meadowcreek Ct
Atlanta, GA 30338-3803, USA

Anderson, W William (Athlete, Football Player)
6924 Lark Ln
Knoxville, TN 37919-5928, USA

Anderson-Emmons, Aubrey (Actor)
c/o Carlyne Grager *Dramatic Artists Agency*
103 W Alameda Ave Ste 139
Burbank, CA 91502-2253, USA

Anderson III, Shedrack (Actor)
c/o Staff Member *Rogers Orion Talent Agency*
3500 W Olive Ave Ste 300
Burbank, CA 91505-4647, USA

Andersson, Bibi (Actor)
Agents Associes Beaume
201 Faubourg Saint Honore
Paris 75008, FRANCE

Andersson, Erik (Athlete, Hockey Player)
Persilijav 9
Karlstad S-65351, Sweden

Andersson, Harriet (Actor)
Roslagsgatan 14/6
Stockholm 113 55, Sweden

Andersson, Henrik (Musician)
MOB Agency
6404 Wilshire Blvd Ste 505
Los Angeles, CA 90048-5507, USA

Andersson, Kent-Erik (Athlete, Hockey Player)
Babordsg 11 7Tr
Karlstad S-65351, Sweden

Andersson, Mikael (Athlete, Hockey Player)
c/o Staff Member *Tampa Bay Lightning*
401 Channelside Dr
Ice Palace
Tampa, FL 33602-5400, USA

Andersson, Peter (Athlete, Hockey Player)
Sultronvagen 35
Umea 904 35, Sweden

Anderton, Sophie (Actor, Model)
c/o Staff Member *Premier Model Management*
40-42 Parker St
London WC2B 5PQ, UK

Andino, Robert (Athlete, Baseball Player)
645 Santa Clara Trl
Wellington, FL 33414-3921, USA

And One (Music Group, Musician)
c/o Gero Herrde *SPV Schallplatten, Produktion und Vertrieb GmbH*
Boulevard der EU 8
Hannover 30539, Germany

Andov, Stojan (President)
Sobranje
11 Oktombri Blvd
Skopje 91000, MACEDONIA

Andrade, Fernanda (Actor)
c/o Priya Satiani *Grandview*
7122 Beverly Blvd Ste F
Los Angeles, CA 90036-2572, USA

Andrade, Sergio (Musician)
DreamWorks Records
9268 W 3rd St
Beverly Hills, CA 90210-3713, USA

Andrade, William T (Billy) (Athlete, Golfer)
4439 E Brookhaven Dr NE
Atlanta, GA 30319-1007, USA

Andrascik, Steve (Athlete, Hockey Player)
11204 Coastal Hwy # 12
Ocean City, MD 21842-2555, USA

Andre, Carl (Artist)
689 Crown St
Brooklyn, NY 11213-5303, USA

Andre, Peter (Musician, Television Host)
c/o Staff Member *Can Associates Lir*
P.O. Box 602
Horsham
West Sussex RH13 8WE, UK

Andrea, Paul (Athlete, Hockey Player)
136 Regent St
North Sydney, NS B2A 2G5, Canada

Andreachuk, Randy (Athlete, Hockey Player)
17294 2 Ave
Surrey, BC V3Z 9P9, Canada

Andreas, G Allen (Business Person)
Archer-Daniels-Midland
4666 E Faries Pkwy Ste 1
Decatur, IL 62526-5632, USA

Andreeff, Starr (Actor)
C N A Assoc
1875 Century Park E Ste 2250
Los Angeles, CA 90067-2563, USA

Andreessen, Marc (Business Person)
23910 Malibu Rd
Malibu, CA 90265-4606, USA

Andrei, Alessandro (Athlete, Track Athlete)
Via V Bellini 1
Scandicci, Firenze 50018, ITALY

Andress, Ursula (Actor)
5329 Captains Pl
Agoura Hills, CA 91301-1923, USA

Andretti, Jeff (Race Car Driver)
Andretti Racing Group
7615 Zionsville Rd
Indianapolis, IN 46268-2174, USA

Andretti, John (Race Car Driver)
Andretti Autosport
7615 Zionsville Rd
Indianapolis, IN 46268-2174, USA

Andretti, Marco (Race Car Driver)
c/o John Caponigro *Sports Management Network*
1301 W Long Lake Rd Ste 250
Troy, MI 48098-6326, USA

Andretti, Mario (Race Car Driver)
457 Rose Inn Ave
Nazareth, PA 18064-9234, USA

Andretti, Michael (Athlete, Race Car Driver)
471 Rose Inn Ave
Nazareth, PA 18064-9234, USA

Andrew, Kim (Athlete, Baseball Player)
10052 Densmore Ave
North Hills, CA 91343-1454, USA

Andrew, Phillip (Actor)
c/o Bonnie Liedtke *Authentic Talent & Literary Management*
3615 Eastham Dr # 650
Culver City, CA 90232-2410, USA

Andrew, Prince (Royalty)
Buckingham Palace
London SW1A 1AA, UNITED KINGDOM (UK)

Andrew, Troy (Athlete, Football Player)
James Crystal Radio Inc
206 Johnstone Ct
Durham, NC 27712-9454, USA

Andrews, Al (Athlete, Boxer)
1119 River St
Rhinelander, WI 54501-2404, USA

Andrews, Al (Athlete, Football Player)
PO Box 82256
Atlanta, GA 30354-0256, USA

Andrews, Amy Leigh (Model)

Andrews, Andy (Actor, Comedian)
PO Box 17321
Nashville, TN 37217-0321, USA

Andrews, Anthony (Actor)
13 Manor Place
Oxford, Oxon, UNITED KINGDOM (UK)

Andrews, Ariel (Race Car Driver)
PO Box 374
Newburgh, IN 47629-0374, USA

Andrews, Billy (Athlete, Football Player)
PO Box 703
17164 HIGHWAY 10 E
Clinton, LA 70722-0703, USA

Andrews, Clayton (Athlete, Baseball Player)
1906 Westley St
Safety Harbor, FL 34695-2147, USA

Andrews, Donna (Athlete, Golfer)
2301 Hawthorne Rd
Lynchburg, VA 24503-2903, USA

Andrews, Erin (Journalist, Sportscaster, Television Host)
c/o Staff Member *Fox Sports (LA)*
10201 W Pico Blvd Bldg 101
Los Angeles, CA 90064-2606, USA

Andrews, Fred (Athlete, Baseball Player)
PO Box 898
Wedowee, AL 36278-0898, USA

Andrews, Giuseppe (Actor)
PO Box 24561
Ventura, CA 93002-4561, USA

Andrews, Jeff (Baseball Player)
2613 NW 162nd Ter
Edmond, OK 73013-1257

Andrews, Jessica (Musician)
6535 Melinda Dr
Nashville, TN 37205-3934, USA

Andrews, John (Athlete, Baseball Player)
6348 Jasper St
Rancho Cucamonga, CA 91701-3226, USA

Andrews, Julie (Actor, Musician)
c/o Steve Sauer *Media Four*
10100 Santa Monica Blvd Ste 2300
Los Angeles, CA 90067-4135, USA

Andrews, Ken (Musician)
c/o Staff Member *Paradigm (Monterey)*
404 W Franklin St
Monterey, CA 93940-2303, USA

Andrews, Lee (Musician)
Mars Talent
27 L Ambiance Ct
Bardonia, NY 10954-1421, USA

Andrews, Mark (Politician)
4255 30th Ave S Apt 3015
Fargo, ND 58104-9036, USA

Andrews, Mike (Athlete, Baseball Player)
5 Patriot Ln Unit 10
Georgetown, MA 01833-2246, USA

Andrews, Mitch (Athlete, Football Player)
129 Grand Ave
Lafayette, LA 70503-4636, USA

Andrews, Naveen (Actor)
c/o Ellen Meyer *Ellen Meyer Management*
315 S Beverly Dr Ste 202
Beverly Hills, CA 90212-4310, USA

Andrews, Rob (Athlete, Baseball Player)
1280 Mountbatten Ct
Concord, CA 94518-3927, USA

Andrews, Robert (Writer)
G P Putnam's Sons
375 Hudson St
New York, NY 10014-3658, USA

Andrews, Robert E (Congressman, Politician)
2265 Rayburn Hob
Washington, DC 20515-0552, USA

Andrews, Shane (Athlete, Baseball Player)
1816 N Guadalupe St
Carlsbad, NM 88220-8813, USA

Andrews, Shawn (Actor)
c/o Laura Berwick *Berwick & Kovacik*
9465 Wilshire Blvd Ste 420
Beverly Hills, CA 90212-2603, USA

Andrews, Shawn (Athlete, Football Player)
204 Deauville Pl
Little Rock, AR 72223-5508, USA

Andrews, Stacy (Athlete, Football Player)
7 Deauville Cir
Little Rock, AR 72223-5532, USA

Andrews, Theresa (Athlete, Olympic Athlete, Swimmer)
2004 Homewood Rd
Annapolis, MD 21409-5970, USA

Andrews, Thomas (Tom) (Athlete, Football Player)
1918 Wickham Way
Louisville, KY 40223-1059, USA

Andrews, Tina (Actor)
c/o Staff Member *Sharp & Associates*
1516 N Fairfax Ave
Los Angeles, CA 90046-2608, USA

Andrews, William D (Athlete, Football Player)
PO Box 703
Clinton, LA 70722-0703, USA

Andrews, William L (Athlete, Football Player)
3916 Toccoa Falls Dr
Duluth, GA 30097-8104, USA

Andrews II, George E (Athlete, Football Player)
10195 Overhill Dr
Santa Ana, CA 92705-1515, USA

Andreychuk, Dave (Athlete, Hockey Player)
401 Channelside Dr
Tampa, FL 33602-5400, USA

Andreychuk, Dave (Athlete, Hockey Player)
107 Sable Park
East Amherst, NY 14051-2209, USA

Andrieu, Sebastien (Actor, Model)

Androsky, Carol (Actor)
Henderson/Hogan
8285 W Sunset Blvd Ste 1
West Hollywood, CA 90046-2420, USA

Andruff, Ron (Athlete, Hockey Player)
72 1/2 Irving Pl Apt 1F
New York, NY 10003-2223, USA

Andrulis, Greg (Coach, Football Coach)
Columbus Crew
2121 Velma Ave
Columbus, OH 43211-2085, USA

Andrus, Lou (Athlete, Football Player)
739 W 550 S
Orem, UT 84058-6070, USA

Andrus, Sheldon (Athlete, Football Player)
210 Belle Meade Blvd
Thibodaux, LA 70301-4908, USA

Andrusak, Greg (Athlete, Hockey Player)
5240 3A Hwy
Nelson, BC V1L 6N6, Canada

Andruski, Frank (Athlete, Football Player)
8219 E Mulberry Ln
Scottsdale, AZ 85251-5862, United States

Andrusyshsyn, Zenon (Athlete, Football Player)
2823 Lake Saxon Dr
Land O Lakes, FL 34639-6620, USA

Andruzzi, Joe (Athlete, Football Player)
130 Brown Ave
Mansfield, MA 02048-1046, USA

Anduiar, Joaauin (Baseball Player)
Ave L. Amiama Tio #47
San Pedro de Macoris Dominican Rep_ublic, USA

Andy, Dorris (Athlete, Football Player)
12391 Ike White Rd
Conroe, TX 77303-3044, USA

Andy, Ekern (Athlete, Football Player)
2041 W Bradley Pl
Chicago, IL 60618-4907, USA

Ane, Charles T (Charlie) III (Athlete, Football Player)
749 16th Ave
Honolulu, HI 96816-4121, USA

Anemone (Actor)
82 rue Bonaparte
Paris 75006, France

Ang, Michelle (Actor)
c/o Karen Kay *Karen Kay Management*
2/25 Sale St
Freemans Bay, Auckland 01010, New Zealand

Angarano, Michael (Actor)
c/o Jacob Fenton *United Talent Agency (UTA)*
9336 Civic Center Dr
Beverly Hills, CA 90210-3604, USA

Angel, Asher (Actor)
c/o Brett Ruttenberg *Imprint PR*
6121 W Sunset Blvd
Neuehouse
Los Angeles, CA 90028-6442, USA

Angel, Ashley Parker (Musician)
c/o Robert Klebanoff *Studio XIV*
9107 Wilshire Blvd Ste 450
Beverly Hills, CA 90210-5535, USA

Angel, Criss (Magician, Musician)
1 Club Point Ct
Henderson, NV 89052-6641, USA

Angel, Joanna (Actor, Adult Film Star, Model)
c/o David Rudy *Armada Partners*
815 Moraga Dr
Los Angeles, CA 90049-1633, USA

Angel, Joe (Commentator)
209 S Temelec Cir
Sonoma, CA 95476-8329, USA

Angel, Juan Pablo (Athlete, Soccer Player)
c/o Patrick Tully *PR/PR*
1515 Broadway Ste 73
New York, NY 10036-8901, USA

Angel, Ryland (Musician)
c/o Staff Member *Paradigm (Monterey)*
404 W Franklin St
Monterey, CA 93940-2303, USA

Angel, Vanessa (Actor, Model)
c/o Joseph Le *Joseph Le Talent Agency*
3500 W Olive Ave Ste 300
Burbank, CA 91505-4647, USA

Angelil, Rene (Actor, Writer)
c/o Staff Member *United Talent Agency (UTA)*
9336 Civic Center Dr
Beverly Hills, CA 90210-3604, USA

Angelini, Norm (Athlete, Baseball Player)
15063 E Chenango Pl
Aurora, CO 80015-2136, USA

Angelis, Alix (Actor, Reality Star)
c/o Fiona Turner *LTA*
PO Box 19599
New Orleans, LA 70179-0599, USA

Angello, Steve (DJ, Musician)
c/o Jules Ferree *Scooter Braun Projects*
1755 Broadway
New York, NY 10019-3743, USA

Angelos, Peter (Commentator)
Baltimore Orioles
100 N Charles St
Baltimore, MD 21201-3805, USA

Angels & Airwaves (Music Group)
c/o Staff Member *Geffen Records*
9126 Sunset Blvd
West Hollywood, CA 90069, USA

Angelson, Genevieve (Actor)
c/o Jeffrey Chassen *Imprint PR*
6121 W Sunset Blvd
Neuehouse
Los Angeles, CA 90028-6442, USA

Angelstad, Mel (Athlete, Hockey Player)
224-910 Main St RR 1
Humboldt, SK S0K 2A1, Canada

Angelycal Musical (Music Group)
c/o Staff Member *Sony Music (Miami)*
404 Washington Ave Ste 700
Miami Beach, FL 33139-6615, USA

Angelyne (Actor, Model)
PO Box 3864
Beverly Hills, CA 90212-0864, USA

Anger, Bryan (Athlete, Football Player)
c/o Frank Bauer *Sun West Sports*
7883 N Pershing Ave
Stockton, CA 95207-1749, USA

Angerer, Pat (Athlete, Football Player)

Angerer, Peter (Athlete)
Wagenau 2
Hammer 17326, GERMANY

Angle, Kurt (Athlete, Olympic Athlete, Wrestler)
5032 Stags Leap Ln
Coraopolis, PA 15108-9481, USA

Anglim, Philip (Actor)
2404 Grand Canal
Venice, CA 90291-4508, USA

Anglin, Jennifer (Actor)
651 N Kilkea Dr
Los Angeles, CA 90048-2213, USA

Angotti, Lou (Athlete, Hockey Player)
2850 NE 14th Street Cswy Apt 401B
Pompano Beach, FL 33062-3640, USA

Anguiano, Raul (Artist)
Anaxagoras 1326
Colonia Narvate
Mexico City 13 DF, MEXICO

Angullo, Richard (Athlete, Football Player)
3015 Val Verde Dr NE
Albuquerque, NM 87110-1628, USA

Angus & Julia Stone (Music Group, Musician)
c/o Dan Efram *The Muse Box - NY*
205 Lexington Ave Fl 2
New York, NY 10016-6053, USA

Anhalt, Darrell (Athlete, Hockey Player)
4935-49th St
Hughenden, AB TOB 2EO, Canada

Anholt, Christien (Actor)
Covington International
4237 Morro Dr
Woodland Hills, CA 91364-5521, USA

Anholt, Darrell (Athlete, Hockey Player)
4935 49th St
Hughenden, AB T0B 2E0, Canada

Anikulap-Kuti, Femi (Musician, Songwriter, Writer)
MCA Records
70 Universal City Plz
Universal City, CA 91608-1011, USA

Animal Collective (Music Group)
c/o Tom Windish *Paradigm (Chicago)*
2209 W North Ave
Chicago, IL 60647-6084, USA

Animals, The (Music Group)
PO Box 1821
Ojai, CA 93024-1821, USA

Anissina, Marina (Figure Skater)
c/o Staff Member *Champions on Ice*
3500 American Blvd W Ste 190
Minneapolis, MN 55431-4431, USA

Aniston, Jennifer (Actor)
c/o Stephen Huvane *Slate PR*
901 N Highland Ave
W Hollywood, CA 90038-2412, USA

Aniston, John (Actor)
c/o Richard Lewis *Richard Lewis Management*
1120 N Clark St
Los Angeles, CA 90069-2022, USA

Anitta (Musician)
c/o Rob Markus *WME/IMG*
9601 Wilshire Blvd
Beverly Hills, CA 90210-5213, USA

Anka, Paul (Actor, Musician)
c/o Maureen O'Connor *Rogers & Cowan*
1840 Century Park E Fl 18
Los Angeles, CA 90067-2101, USA

Ankiel, Rick (Athlete, Baseball Player)
126 Sandpiper Cir
Jupiter, FL 33477-8433, USA

Ankrom, Scott (Athlete, Football Player)
1206 Harvest Cyn
San Antonio, TX 78258-3836, USA

Annable, Dave (Actor)
c/o Melissa Kates *Viewpoint Inc*
8820 Wilshire Blvd Ste 220
Beverly Hills, CA 90211-2622, USA

Annable, Odette (Actor)
c/o Ruth Bernstein *Viewpoint Inc*
8820 Wilshire Blvd Ste 220
Beverly Hills, CA 90211-2622, USA

Annaud, Jean-Jacques (Director)
Reperage
16 Rue Saint-Vincent
Paris 75018, FRANCE

Anne (Royalty)
Gatecombe Park
Gloucestershire, UNITED KINGDOM (UK)

Anne of Bourbon-Palma (Royalty)
Villa Serena
77 Chemin Louis-Degallier
Versoix-Geneva 01290, SWITZERLAND

Annett, Chloe (Actor)
c/o Staff Member *Innovative Artists*
1505 10th St
Santa Monica, CA 90401-2805, USA

Annett, Michael (Race Car Driver)
Germain Racing
PO Box 3774
Mooresville, NC 28117-3774, USA

Annis, Francesca (Actor)
c/o Paul Lyon-Maris *Independent Talent Group*
40 Whitfield St
London W1T 2RH, UNITED KINGDOM

Anno, Sam (Athlete, Football Player)
12934 Ferndale Ave
Los Angeles, CA 90066-3520, USA

Annunziata, Robert (Business Person)
Global Crossing Ltd
Wessex House
45 Reid St
Hamilton, HM 00012, BERMUDA

Anoa, Leati Joe (Roman Reigns) (Athlete, Wrestler)
c/o Staff Member *World Wrestling Entertainment (WWE)*
1241 E Main St
Stamford, CT 06902-3520, USA

Ansah, Ezekiel (Athlete, Football Player)
c/o Frank Bauer *Sun West Sports*
7883 N Pershing Ave
Stockton, CA 95207-1749, USA

Ansara, Edward (Actor)
Jack Scagnetti
5118 Vineland Ave # 102
North Hollywood, CA 91601-3814, USA

Ansari, Anousheh (Astronaut)
6101 W Plano Pkwy # 210
Plano, TX 75093-8201, USA

Ansari, Aziz (Comedian)
c/o David Miner *3 Arts Entertainment*
9460 Wilshire Blvd Fl 7
Beverly Hills, CA 90212-2713, USA

Anschutz, Jody (Athlete, Golfer)
27307 N Palo Fierro Rd
Rio Verde, AZ 85263-5087, USA

Anschutz, Philip F (Business Person)
c/o Staff Member *Anschutz Film Group*
1888 Century Park E Ste 1400
Century City, CA 90067-1718, USA

Anschutz, Philip F. (Business Person)
Anschutz Company
555 17th St Ste 2400
Denver, CO 80202-3941, USA

Anselmo, Philip (Musician)
Concrete Mgmt
361 W Broadway # 200
New York, NY 10013-2209, USA

Ansley, Michael (Athlete, Basketball Player)
1809 Wood Violet Dr
Orlando, FL 32824-6411, USA

Anspaugh, David (Director, Producer)
c/o John Burnham *ICM Partners*
10250 Constellation Blvd Fl 7
Los Angeles, CA 90067-6207, USA

Ant, Adam (Musician)
c/o Lee Runchey *Chrome PR*
9107 Wilshire Blvd Ste 450
Beverly Hills, CA 90210-5535, USA

Antal, Nimrod (Director)
c/o Scott Greenberg *Creative Artists Agency (CAA)*
2000 Avenue of the Stars Ste 100
Los Angeles, CA 90067-4705, USA

Antes, Horst (Artist)
Hohenbergstr 11
Karlsruhe (Wolfartsweier 76228, GERMANY

Anthony, Carmelo (Athlete, Basketball Player)
508 W 24th St # 5NS
New York, NY 10011-1161, USA

Anthony, Charles (Athlete, Football Player)
38709 Farwell Dr
Fremont, CA 94536-7218, USA

Anthony, Denman (Athlete, Football Player)
PO Box 2733
Spring, TX 77383-2733, USA

Anthony, Edward (Athlete, Football Player)
PO Box 363
Pfafftown, NC 27040-0363, USA

Anthony, Eric (Athlete, Baseball Player)
42 Fosters Ct
Sugar Land, TX 77479-5866, USA

Anthony, Gethin (Actor)
c/o Dallas Smith *United Agents*
12-26 Lexington St
London W1F OLE, UNITED KINGDOM

Anthony, Greg (Athlete, Basketball Player)
901 Wiggin Rd
Delray Beach, FL 33444-2851, USA

Anthony, Jasmine Jessica (Actor)
c/o Adam Griffin *LINK Entertainment*
11872 La Grange Ave
Los Angeles, CA 90025-5282, USA

Anthony, La La (Actor, Musician)
c/o Stephanie Simon *Untitled Entertainment*
350 S Beverly Dr Ste 200
Beverly Hills, CA 90212-4819, USA

Anthony, Lysette (Actor)
c/o Philip Belfield *Belfield & Ward*
26 - 28 Neal St
London WC2H 9QQ, UNITED KINGDOM

Anthony, Marc (Musician, Songwriter)
c/o Michel Vega *WME|IMG (Miami)*
119 Washington Ave Ste 400
Miami Beach, FL 33139-7202, USA

Anthony, Michael (Musician)
c/o Staff Member *Gray Talent Group (IL)*
727 S Dearborn St Apt 312
Chicago, IL 60605-3822, USA

Anthony, Piers (Writer)
PO Box 2289
Inverness, FL 34451-2289

Anthony, Plers (Writer)
PO Box 2289
Inverness, FL 34451-2289, USA

Anthony, Ray (Musician)
9288 Kinglet Dr
Los Angeles, CA 90069-1114, USA

Anthony, Reidel (Athlete, Football Player)
PO Box 389
South Bay, FL 33493-0389, USA

Anthony, Stephone (Athlete, Football Player)

Anthony, Terry (Athlete, Football Player)
1200 Beville Rd Apt 91
Daytona Beach, FL 32114-5778, USA

Anthrax (Music Group)
c/o Dan Devita *The Kirby Organization (TKO-UK)*
6 Walter Ln
Camden
London NW1 8NZ, UNITED KINGDOM

Antin, Robin (Actor, Dancer)
c/o Cheryl McLean *Creative Public Relations*
3385 Oak Glen Dr
Los Angeles, CA 90068-1311, USA

Antin, Steve (Actor, Writer)
c/o Doug MacLaren *ICM Partners*
10250 Constellation Blvd Fl 7
Los Angeles, CA 90067-6207, USA

Antistia, Azlea (Adult Film Star)
29 Harley St
Suite B
London W1G 9QR, UK

Antoine, Lionel (Athlete, Football Player)
1455 Glencliff Dr
Dallas, TX 75217-2686, USA

Antoine, Tamlin (Athlete, Football Player)
5452 New Grange Garth
Columbia, MD 21045-2422, USA

Anton, Alan (Musician)
c/o Staff Member *Feldman Agency (Toronto)*
200-1505 2nd Ave W
Vancouver, BC V6H 3Y4, CANADA

Anton, Craig (Actor)
c/o Staff Member *United Talent Agency (UTA)*
9336 Civic Center Dr
Beverly Hills, CA 90210-3604, USA

Anton, Susan (Actor, Producer)
c/o Bette Smith *Bette Smith Management*
499 N Canon Dr
Beverly Hills, CA 90210-4887, USA

Antonelli, Dominic A (Astronaut)
4106 Oak Blossom Ct
Houston, TX 77059-3264, USA

Antonelli, Dominic A Lt Cmdr (Astronaut)
4106 Oak Blossom Ct
Houston, TX 77059-3264, USA

Antonelli, Ennio Cardinal (Religious Leader)
Archdiocese
Piazza S Giovanni 3
Florence 50129, ITALY

Antonelli, Johnny (Athlete, Baseball Player)
18 Tobey Ct
Pittsford, NY 14534-1854, USA

Antonelli, matt (Baseball Player)
1 Antonelli Way # Y
Peabody, MA 01960-3772, USA

Antonetti, Chris (Commentator)
19500 Frazier Dr
Rocky River, OH 44116-1631, USA

Antonio (Dancer)
Caslada 7
Madrid, SPAIN

Antonio, Lou (Actor)
530 S Gaylord Dr
Burbank, CA 91505-4714, USA

Antonoff, Jack (Musician)
c/o Inge Coleson *Girlie Action*
243 W 30th St Fl 12
New York, NY 10001-2812, USA

Antonovich, Mike (Athlete, Hockey Player)
PO Box 224
Coleraine, MN 55722-0224, USA

Antony and the Johnsons (Music Group, Musician)
c/o Staff Member *Alias Production*
22, Rue Douai
Paris F-75009, France

Antoski, Shawn (Athlete, Hockey Player)
285 Tannery Rd RR 2
Madoc, ON K0K 2K0, Canada

Antoun (Khouri), Bishop (Religious Leader)
Antiochian Orthodox Christian Archdiocese
358 Mountain Rd
Englewood, NJ 07631-3798, USA

Antropov, Nikolai (Athlete, Hockey Player)
Newport Sports Management
400-201 City Centre Dr
Attn Don Meehan
Mississauga, ON L5B 2T4, Canada

Antuofermo, Vito (Boxer)
16019 81st St
Howard Beach, NY 11414-2924, USA

Anu, Christine (Musician)
Robert Bamham Mgmt
432 Tyagarah Road
Myocum, NSW 02481, AUSTRALIA

Anuszkiewicz, Richard J (Artist)
76 Chestnut St
Englewood, NJ 07631-3045, USA

Anwar, Gabrielle (Actor)
432 W 41st St
Miami Beach, FL 33140-3504, USA

Anzulot, Cynthia (Athlete, Golfer)
21 Spring Creek Mnr
Hershey, PA 17033-1327, USA

Aoki, Devon (Actor, Model)
229 Oceano Dr
Los Angeles, CA 90049-4123, USA

Aoki, Isao (Athlete, Golfer)
I M G
1360 E 9th St Ste 100
Cleveland, OH 44114-1730, USA

Aoki, Rocky (Athlete, Business Person)
Benihana of Tokyo
8685 NW 53rd Terr
#201
Miami, FL 33166, USA

Aoki, Steve (DJ, Musician)
c/o Kirk Sommer *WME|IMG*
9601 Wilshire Blvd
Beverly Hills, CA 90210-5213, USA

Aoloo Sunshine (Music Group)
c/o Staff Member *Paradigm (Monterey)*
404 W Franklin St
Monterey, CA 93940-2303, USA

Aouita, Said (Athlete, Track Athlete)
Abdejil Bencheikh
9 Rue Soivissi
Loubira
Rabat, MOROCCO

Apa, KJ (Actor)
c/o Lena Roklin *Luber Roklin Management*
2300 W Empire Ave Unit 450
Burbank, CA 91504-5399, USA

Apap, Gilles (Musician)
Columbia Artists Mgmt Inc
165 W 57th St
New York, NY 10019-2201, USA

Aparicio, Luis (Athlete, Baseball Player)
Baltimore Orioles
333 W Camden St Ste 1
Baltimore, MD 21201-2476, USA

Apatow, Judd (Director, Producer, Writer)
c/o Staff Member *Apatow Productions*
11788 W Pico Blvd
Los Angeles, CA 90064-1309, USA

Apel, Katrin (Athlete)
Suedlung 9
Grafenroda 99330, GERMANY

Apfel, Iris (Designer, Writer)
c/o Emerson Bruns *Bruns Brennan Berry*
99 Madison Ave Fl 5
New York, NY 10016-7419, USA

Apice, Robert (Horse Racer)
69 Alissa Ter
Jackson, NJ 08527-3116, USA

Apke, Steve (Athlete, Football Player)
427 Kenmont Ave
Pittsburgh, PA 15228-1405, USA

Aplin, Gabrielle (Musician)
c/o Staff Member *James Barnes Music*
118-120 Great Titchfield Street
3rd Floor
London W1W 6SS, UK

Apodaca, Bob (Athlete, Baseball Player)
2001 Blake St
Denver, CO 80205-2060, USA

Apodaca, Jerry (Politician)
6223 Utah Ave NW
Washington, DC 20015-2431, USA

Appel, Deena (Designer)
c/o Jon Furie *Montana Artists Agency*
9150 Wilshire Blvd Ste 100
Beverly Hills, CA 90212-3459, USA

Appetite for Destruction (Music Group, Musician)

Appice, Carmine (Musician)
Long Distance Entertainment
568 E Woolbright Rd # 234
Boynton Beach, FL 33435-6033, USA

Appier, Kevin (Athlete, Baseball Player)
30743 Victory Rd
Paola, KS 66071-9477, USA

Apple, Fiona (Musician)
2212 Meade Pl
Venica, CA 90291, USA

Appleby, Shiri (Actor)
c/o Ruth Bernstein *Viewpoint Inc*
8820 Wilshire Blvd Ste 220
Beverly Hills, CA 90211-2622, USA

Appleby, Stuart (Athlete, Golfer)
9724 Chestnut Ridge Dr
Windermere, FL 34786-8943, USA

Applegate, Christina (Actor)
c/o Ame VanIden *VanIden Public Relations*
4070 Wilson Pike
Franklin, TN 37067-8126, USA

Applegate, Fred (Actor)
811 E Olive Ave
Burbank, CA 91501-1425, USA

Applegate, Gideon (Athlete, Baseball Player)
7 Jenness Dr
South Newfanc, VT 05351-9753, USA

Applegate, Jodi (Correspondent)
WNYW
205 E 67th St
New York, NY 10065-6089, USA

Applewhite, Major (Athlete, Football Player)

Appolonia (Kotero) (Actor)
c/o Staff Member *TalentWorks*
3500 W Olive Ave Ste 1400
Burbank, CA 91505-5512, USA

Aprea, John (Actor)
727 N Martel Ave
Los Angeles, CA 90046-7506, USA

April, Johnny (Musician)
c/o Staff Member *Mitch Schneider Organization (MSO)*
14724 Ventura Blvd Ste 410
Sherman Oaks, CA 91403-3537, USA

Apt, Jerome (Jay) (Astronaut)
201 Gladstone Rd
Pittsburgh, PA 15217-1111, USA

Apted, Michael (Director)
12857 Via Grimaldi
Del Mar, CA 92014-3839, USA

Apuna, Ben (Athlete, Football Player)
950 Lehua Ave Apt 804
Pearl City, HI 96782-3339, USA

Aqualung (Music Group)
c/o Staff Member *Paradigm (Monterey)*
404 W Franklin St
Monterey, CA 93940-2303, USA

Aquarium Rescue Unit (Music Group, Musician)
c/o Staff Member *Skyline Music*
28 Union St
Whitefield, NH 03598-3503, USA

Aquino, Amy (Actor)
c/o Mona Loring *Status PR*
PO Box 6191
Westlake Village, CA 91359-6191, USA

Aquino, Corazon C (Politician)
119 de la Rosa Corner
Castro Street
Makati City, Manila, The Phillipines

Aquino, Ivory (Actor)
c/o Danielle Delawder *Abrams Artists Agency*
275 7th Ave Fl 26
New York, NY 10001-6708, USA

Aquino, Kris (Actor)
c/o Chris Lee *Authentic Talent & Literary Management*
3615 Eastham Dr # 650
Culver City, CA 90232-2410, USA

Aquino, Luis (Athlete, Baseball Player)
17201 Collins Ave Apt 606
Apt 606
Sunny Isles Beach, FL 33160-3476, USA

Aquino III, Benigno (President)
Malacanang Palaces
J P Laurel St. Metro
Manila 00100, Philippines

Arad, Avi (Producer)
29 Beverly Park Ter
Beverly Hills, CA 90210-1563, USA

Aragon, Art (Boxer)
19050 Wells Dr
Tarzana, CA 91356-3937, USA

Aragon, Francisco (Frank) (Director)
99 W California Blvd # 50992
Pasadena, CA 91105-3026, USA

Aragones, Sergio (Cartoonist)
PO Box 696
Ojai, CA 93024-0696, USA

Araguz, Leo (Athlete, Football Player)
3201 Leo Araguz St
Harlingen, TX 78552-7835, USA

Arakawa, Toyozo (Artist)
4-101 O-Hatacho
Tokyo, JAPAN

Araki, Gregg (Director)
c/o Brian Young *Three Six Zero (LA)*
7175 Willoughby Ave Fl 2
Los Angeles, CA 90046-6711, USA

Aramburu, Juan Carlos Cardinal (Religious Leader)
Arzobispado
Suipacha 1034
Buenos Aires 01008, ARGENTINA

Arana, Facundo (Actor)
c/o Staff Member *Telefe (Argentina)*
Pavon 2444
Buenos Aires C1248AAT, ARGENTINA

Arana, Tomas (Actor)
c/o Kesha Williams *KW Entertainment*
425 N Robertson Blvd
West Hollywood, CA 90048-1735, USA

Arango, Juan Carlos (Actor)
c/o Gabriel Blanco *Gabriel Blanco Iglesias (Mexico)*
Rio Balsas 35-32
Colonia Cuauhtemoc
DF 06500, Mexico

Arapostathis, Evan (Athlete, Football Player)
5353 W Falls View Dr
San Diego, CA 92115-1427, USA

Arau, Alfonso (Director)
Productions AA
Privada Rafael Oliva 8
Coyoacan 04120, MEXICO

Arau, Fernando (Actor)
c/o Staff Member *Sanctuary Artist Management (UK)*
Sanctuary House
45-53 Sinclair Road
London W14 0NS, UNITED KINGDOM

Araujo, Serafim Fernandes de Cardinal (Religious Leader)
Curia Metropolitana
Av Brasil 2079
Belo Horizonte, MG 30240-002, Brazil

Araya, Zeudy (Actor)
Carol Levi Co
Via Giuseppe Pisanelli
Rome 00196, ITALY

Arbanas, Frederick V (Fred) (Athlete, Football Player)
3350 SW Hook Rd
Lees Summit, MO 64082-1524, USA

Arbour, John (Athlete, Hockey Player)
125 Waterloo St
Fort Erie, ON L2A 3K1, Canada

Arbour-Parrott, Beatrice (Athlete, Baseball Player)
691 Elm St
Somerset, MA 02726-4034, USA

Arbubakrr, Hasson (Athlete, Football Player)
76 Custer Ave
Newark, NJ 07112-2510, USA

Arbuckle, Charles (Athlete, Football Player)
805 Oak Park Dr
Round Rock, TX 78681-4077, USA

Arbus, Loreen (Producer)
Loreen Arbus Productions
8075 W 3rd St Ste 410
Los Angeles, CA 90048-4319, USA

Arcade Fire (Music Group)
c/o Perri Cohen *Nasty Little Man*
285 W Broadway Rm 310
New York, NY 10013-2257, USA

Arcelus, Sebastian (Actor)
c/o Tim Sage *Paradigm*
140 Broadway Ste 2600
New York, NY 10005-1011, USA

Arch, Lisa (Actor)
c/o Staff Member *The Paradise Group*
PO Box 69451
West Hollywood, CA 90069-0451, USA

Archambault, Lee J (Astronaut)
4318 Sweet Cicely Ct
Houston, TX 77059-3126, USA

Archambault, Lee J Lt Colonel (Astronaut)
4318 Sweet Cicely Ct
Houston, TX 77059-3126, USA

Archambault, Yves (Athlete, Hockey Player)
Promotion Archie Sports Inc 7418 Av Baldwin
Aniou, QC HlK 3C8, Canada

Archambeau, Lester (Athlete, Football Player)
10520 Montclair Way
Duluth, GA 30097-1840, USA

Archer, Anne (Actor)
PO Box 57593
Sherman Oaks, CA 91413-2593, USA

Archer, Beverly (Actor)
811 Adelaine Ave
S Pasadena, CA 91030-2403, USA

Archer, Dan (Athlete, Football Player)
65 Sunnyside Ave
Mill Valley, CA 94941-1924, USA

Archer, Dave (Artist)
1541 Buckhorn Rd
Roseburg, OR 97470-8461, USA

Archer, David (Athlete, Football Player)
3831 Upland Dr
Marietta, GA 30066-3064, USA

Archer, Dri (Athlete, Football Player)
c/o Joel Segal *Lagardere Unlimited (NY)*
456 Washington St Apt 9L
New York, NY 10013-1555, USA

Archer, Jeffrey (Actor, Writer)
c/o Staff Member *Curtis Brown Ltd*
28-29 Hay Market
Hay Market House
London SW1Y 4SP, UNITED KINGDOM

Archer, Jeffrey H (Writer)
93 Albert Embankment
London SE1, England

Archer, Jim (Athlete, Baseball Player)
1012 Lake Avoca Ct
Tarpon Springs, FL 34689-7103, USA

Archer, John (Writer)
10901 176th Cir NE # 3601
Redmond, WA 98052-7218, USA

Archer, Tasmin (Musician)
c/o Staff Member *Mushroom Music Publishing*
9 Dundas Ln
P.O. Box 158
Albert Park VIC 3206, Australia

Archer, Tommy (Race Car Driver)
Archer Motorsports
4415 Venture Ave
Duluth, MN 55811-5705, USA

Archibaid, Nathaniel (Nate) (Athlete, Basketball Player)
2920 Holland Ave
Bronx, NY 10467-8304, USA

Archibald, Dave (Athlete, Hockey Player)
6792 Henry St
Chilliwack, BC V2R 2W1, Canada

Archibald, Nate (Tiny) (Athlete, Basketball Player)
2920 Holland Ave
Bronx, NY 10467-8304, USA

Archibald, Nolan D (Business Person)
Black & Decker Corp
701 E Joppa Rd
Towson, MD 21286-5502, USA

Archie, Mike (Athlete, Football Player)
1178 Old Hickory Blvd
Brentwood, TN 37027-4221, USA

Archila, Hunter Tylo (Actor)
11684 Ventura Blvd # 910
Studio City, CA 91604-2699, USA

Archipoeski, Ken (Musician)
PO Box 656507
Fresh Meadows, NY 11365-6507, USA

Architecture in Helsinki (Music Group)
c/o Staff Member *Paradigm (Monterey)*
404 W Franklin St
Monterey, CA 93940-2303, USA

Archuleta, Adam (Athlete, Football Player)
1237 W Galveston St
Chandler, AZ 85224-4335, USA

Archuleta, David (Musician)
c/o Roger Widynowski *19 Entertainment*
401 Wilshire Blvd Ste 1070
Santa Monica, CA 90401-1428, USA

Arcia, Jose (Athlete, Baseball Player)
7325 NW 3rd St
Miami, FL 33126-4211, USA

Arcieri, Leila (Actor)
c/o Staff Member *Paradigm*
8942 Wilshire Blvd
Beverly Hills, CA 90211-1908, USA

Arcila, Stephanie (Actor)
c/o Wendy Pineda *Supersonix Media*
560 W Main St Ste C PMB 337
Alhambra, CA 91801-3376, USA

Arctic Monkeys (Music Group)
c/o Chloe Walsh *Grandstand Media*
39 W 32nd St Rm 1603
New York, NY 10001-3839, USA

Arcuri, Mike (Congressman, Politician)
10 Broad St Rm 330
Utica, NY 13501-1233, USA

Ard, Jim (Athlete, Baseball Player)
2325 Wayfarer Dr
Discovery Bay, CA 94505-9225, USA

Ard, Johnny (Athlete, Baseball Player)
605 Georgia Ave
Valdosta, GA 31602-2430, USA

Ard, William D (Bill) (Athlete, Football Player)
166 State St Apt 1
Brooklyn, NY 11201-5611, USA

Ardant, Fanny (Actor)
c/o Staff Member *ArtMedia*
8 rue Danielle Casanova
Paris 75002, FRANCE

Ardell, Dan (Athlete, Baseball Player)
910 Meadowlark Dr
Laguna Beach, CA 92651-2806, USA

Arden, Alicia (Actor)
c/o Vance Payton *Advance LA*
7904 Santa Monica Blvd Ste 200
West Hollywood, CA 90046-5170

Arden, Jann (Musician, Songwriter, Writer)
Macklam Feldman Mgmt
200-1505 2nd Ave W
Vancouver, BC V6H 3Y4, CANADA

Arden, Michael (Actor)
3826 Sunset Dr
Los Angeles, CA 90027-4750, USA

Arden, Toni (Musician)
1 N Golfview Rd Apt 300
Lake Worth, FL 33460-3948, USA

Arditi, Pierre (Actor)
c/o Staff Member *VMA*
20 Avenue Rapp
Paris 75007, FRANCE

Ardito, Doug (Musician)
7820 Caverna Dr
Los Angeles, CA 90068, USA

Ardito Barletta, Nicolas (President)
PO Box 7737
Panama City 00009, PANAMA

Arditti, Irvine (Musician)
Lattidue Arts
109 Boul Saint-Joseph O
Montreal, QC H2T 2P7, CANADA

Ardizoia, Rinaldo (Athlete, Baseball Player)
130 Santa Rosa Ave
San Francisco, CA 94112-1930, USA

Ardizzone, Anthony (Tony) (Athlete, Football Player)
27 S Farview Ave
Paramus, NJ 07652-2629, USA

Ardoin, Danny (Athlete, Baseball Player)
1524 Lee St
Ville Platte, LA 70586-6364, USA

Ardolino, Todd (Director)
c/o Staff Member *Creative Artists Agency (CAA)*
2000 Avenue of the Stars Ste 100
Los Angeles, CA 90067-4705, USA

Aregood, Richards L (Journalist)
Philadelphia Daily News
400 N Broad St
Editorial Dept
Philadelphia, PA 19130-4015, USA

Arellano, Stephanie (Actor)
c/o Ken Jacobson *Ken Jacobson Management*
Preferred to be contacted by phone or email
Los Angeles, CA 91367, USA

Arena, Tina (Musician)
Magnus Entertainment
5 Darley St
Neutral Bay, NSW 02089, AUSTRALIA

Arenas, Gilbert (Athlete, Basketball Player)
4550 Gable Dr
Encino, CA 91316-4354, USA

Arenas, Javier (Athlete, Football Player)
c/o Hadley Engelhard *Enter-Sports Management*
6000 Lake Forrest Dr Ste 370
Atlanta, GA 30328-5902, USA

Arenas, Joe (Athlete, Football Player)
780 W Bay Area Blvd Apt 1215
Webster, TX 77598-4057, USA

Arenberg, Lee (Actor)
c/o Rick Ax *Gold Coast Management*
935 Victoria Ave Frnt
Venice, CA 90291-3933, USA

Arend, Geoffrey (Actor)
c/o Jill McGrath *Door24*
115 W 29th St Rm 1102
New York, NY 10001-5106, USA

Arend, Jeff (Race Car Driver)
888 De Anza Heights Dr
La Verne, CA 91750-5702, USA

Aresco, Joey (Actor)
Northern Exposure Talent Management Group
2888 Birch St Unit 1
C/O Lisa King
Vancouver, BC V6H 2T6, CANADA

Areshenkoff, Ron (Athlete, Hockey Player)
329 12th Ave
Estevan, SK S4A 1E3, Canada

Aretsky, Ken (Business Person)
21 Club
21 W 52nd St
New York, NY 10019-6181, USA

Arfons, Arthur E (Art) (Race Car Driver)
PO Box 1409
Saint Charles, MO 63302-1409, USA

Argento, Asia (Actor)
Two Be Consulting
Via Moscova 51
Milano 20121, ITALY

Argento, Dario (Director)
ADC
Via Balemonti 2
Rome, ITALY

Argenziano, Carmen (Actor)
824 S Bel Aire Dr
Burbank, CA 91501-1558, USA

Argerich, Martha (Musician)
c/o Staff Member *Agence Artistique Jacques Thelen*
15 Avenue Montaigne
Paris 75008, France

Argota, Ashley (Actor)
c/o Monique Moss *Integrated PR*
9025 Wilshire Blvd Ste 400
Beverly Hills, CA 90211-1828, USA

Argott, Don (Director, Producer)
c/o David Gersh *Gersh*
9465 Wilshire Blvd Ste 600
Beverly Hills, CA 90212-2605, USA

Argov, Sherry (Writer)
PO Box 91298
Los Angeles, CA 90009-1298, USA

Arianda, Nina (Actor)
c/o Adam Schweitzer *ICM Partners (NY)*
730 5th Ave
New York, NY 10019-4105, USA

Arias, Alex (Athlete, Baseball Player)
37 Edmund Rd
West Park, FL 33023-5231, USA

Arias, George (Athlete, Baseball Player)
4343 W Tellurite Dr
Tucson, AZ 85745-4193, USA

Arias, Mariana (Actor)
c/o Staff Member *Telefe (Argentina)*
Pavon 2444
Buenos Aires C1248AAT, ARGENTINA

Arias, Moises (Actor)
c/o Matt Fletcher *TalentWorks*
3500 W Olive Ave Ste 1400
Burbank, CA 91505-5512, USA

Arias, Ricardo M (President)
Apdo 4549
Panama City, PANAMA

Arias, Rudy (Athlete, Baseball Player)
2681 S Parkview Dr
Hallandale Beach, FL 33009-2922, USA

Arias, Silvana (Actor)
Diane Perez Entertainment
838 N Fairfax Ave
Los Angeles, CA 90046-7208, USA

Arias, Yancey (Actor)
c/o Chris Henze *Thruline Entertainment*
9250 Wilshire Blvd Fl Ground
Beverly Hills, CA 90212-3352, USA

Arie, India (Musician, Songwriter)
5666 Stonehaven Dr
Stone Mountain, GA 30087-5766, USA

Ariey, Mike (Athlete, Football Player)
PO Box 708
Bakersfield, CA 93302-0708, USA

Arinze, Cardinal Francis (Religious Leader)
Pontifical Council for Inter-Religious Dialogue
Vatican City 00193

Arison, Amair (Actor)
c/o Lillian LaSalle *Sweet 180*
141 W 28th St Rm 300
New York, NY 10001-6187, USA

Arison, Amir (Actor)
c/o Christina Papadopoulos *Baker Winokur Ryder Public Relations*
200 5th Ave Fl 5
New York, NY 10010-3307, USA

Arison, Micky (Business Person)
Carnival Cruise Lines
3655 NW 87th Ave
Doral, FL 33178-2428, USA

Aristide, Jean-Bertrand (President)
President's Office
Palace du Gouvernement
Port-Au-Prince, HAITI

Ariyoshi, George R (Politician)
745 Fort Street Mall Ste 500
Honolulu, HI 96813-3805, USA

Ariza, Trevor (Athlete, Basketball Player)
5848 Tampa Ave
Tarzana, CA 91356-3134, USA

Arjona, Adria (Actor)
c/o Kate Rosen *The Lede Company*
401 Broadway Ste 206
New York, NY 10013-3033, USA

Arkadius (Designer, Fashion Designer)
c/o Staff Member *Arkadius*
41 Brondesbury Road
London, England NW6 6BP, United Kingdom

Arkangel R-15 (Music Group)
c/o Staff Member *Sony Music (Miami)*
404 Washington Ave Ste 700
Miami Beach, FL 33139-6615, USA

Arkhipov, Denis (Athlete, Hockey Player)
716 Sweet Cherry Ct
Nashville, TN 37215-6174, USA

Arkin, Adam (Actor)
3531 Coldwater Canyon Ave
Studio City, CA 91604-4060, USA

Arkin, Alan (Actor)
c/o Estelle Lasher *Lasher Group*
1133 Avenue of the Americas Fl 27
New York, NY 10036-6710, USA

Ark, The (Music Group)
c/o Staff Member *Paradigm (Monterey)*
404 W Franklin St
Monterey, CA 93940-2303, USA

Arlauckas, Joe (Athlete, Basketball Player)
8 Brimley Mnr
Rochester, NY 14612-4414, USA

Arlich, Don (Athlete, Baseball Player)
7877 73rd St S
Cottage Grove, MN 55016-1919, USA

Arlin, Steve (Athlete, Baseball Player)
6819 Claremore Ave
San Diego, CA 92120-3125, USA

Arlovski, Andrei (Athlete, Boxer)
c/o Staff Member *John Lewis Entertainment Group*
3071 S Valley View Blvd
Las Vegas, NV 89102-7889, USA

Arm, Allisyn Ashley (Actor)
c/o Tess Luthman *Red Walk Talent PR*
5900 Wilshire Blvd Ste 2600
Los Angeles, CA 90036-5028, USA

Arm, Mark (Musician)
Legends of 21st Century
7 Trinity Row
Florence, MA 01062-1931, USA

Arman (Artist)
Arman Studios
430 Washington St
New York, NY 10013-1721, USA

Armani, Giorgio (Designer, Fashion Designer)
Giorgio Armani Cor
114 5th Ave # 1700
New York, NY 10011-5604, ITALY

Armaou, Lindsay (Musician)
Clintons
55 Drury Lane
Covent Garden
London WC2B 5SQ, UNITED KINGDOM (UK)

Armas, Antonio R (Tony) (Athlete, Baseball Player)
Los Mercedes #37
P Piruto-Edo
Anzoatequi, VENEZUELA

Armas, Chris (Soccer Player)
Chicago Fire
980 N Michigan Ave Ste 1998
Chicago, IL 60611-7504, USA

Armas, Marcos (Athlete, Baseball Player)
Calle Las Mercedes #37
Puerto Piritu, VENEZUELA

Armas, Tony (Athlete, Baseball Player)
c/o Staff Member *Washington Nationals*
1500 S Capitol St SE
Washington, DC 20003-3599, USA

Armato, Ange (Athlete, Baseball Player)
5082 Valley Pines Dr
Rockford, IL 61109-3774, USA

Armatrading, Joan (Musician, Songwriter, Writer)
21 Ramilles St
London W1V 1DF, UNITED KINGDOM (UK)

Armbrister, Ed (Athlete, Baseball Player)
McQuay St
Box 2003
Nassau, Bahamas, WEST INDIES

Armdt-Proefrock, Ellen (Athlete, Baseball Player)
905 Alpine St
Brodhead, WI 53520-1052, USA

Armenante, Jillian (Actor)
574 N Irving Blvd
Los Angeles, CA 90004-1407, USA

Armisen, Fred (Actor, Comedian)
c/o Tim Sarkes *Brillstein Entertainment Partners*
9150 Wilshire Blvd Ste 350
Beverly Hills, CA 90212-3453, USA

Armitage, Alison (Actor, Model)
9220 W Sunset Blvd Ste 305
West Hollywood, CA 90069-3503, USA

Armitage, Richard (Actor)
c/o Ruth Bernstein *Viewpoint Inc*
8820 Wilshire Blvd Ste 220
Beverly Hills, CA 90211-2622, USA

Armor, James Majgen (Astronaut)
9120 Maria Ave
Great Falls, VA 22066-4008, USA

Armour, Jojuan (Athlete, Football Player)
1436 Rollins Rd
Toledo, OH 43612-1633, USA

Armour, Justin (Athlete, Football Player)
765 Mays Hollow Ln
Encinitas, CA 92024-2734, USA

Armour, Justin (Athlete, Football Player)
8 Crystal Park Pl Unit B
Manitou Springs, CO 80829-2654, us

Armour, Tommy (Athlete, Golfer)
3700 Cole Ave APT 211
Dallas, TX 75204-4544, USA

Armstead, Arik (Athlete, Football Player)
c/o Joel Segal *Lagardere Unlimited (NY)*
456 Washington St Apt 9L
New York, NY 10013-1555, USA

Armstead, Jessie (Athlete, Football Player)
1316 Mill Stream Dr
Dallas, TX 75232-4604, USA

Armstead, Ray (Athlete, Olympic Athlete, Track Athlete)
7953 Bloom Dr
Saint Louis, MO 63133-1109, USA

Armstead, Terron (Athlete, Football Player)
c/o Dave Butz *Sportstars Inc*
1370 Avenue of the Americas Fl 19
New York, NY 10019-4602, USA

Armstrong, Adger (Athlete, Football Player)
6403 Paddington St
Houston, TX 77085-3000, USA

Armstrong, Alan (Actor)
Markham & Froggatt
Julian House
4 Windmill St
London W1P 1HF, UNITED KINGDOM (UK)

Armstrong, Antonio (Athlete, Football Player)
11487 Brook Meadow Dr
Houston, TX 77089-5321, USA

Armstrong, Bess (Actor)
PO Box 69279
Los Angeles, CA 90069-0279, USA

Armstrong, Bill (Athlete, Hockey Player)
21-420 York St
CENTURY
London, ON N6B 1R1, Canada

Armstrong, Billie Joe (Musician)
c/o Brian Bumbery *BB Gun Press*
9229 W Sunset Blvd Ste 305
Los Angeles, CA 90069-3403, USA

Armstrong, BJ (Athlete, Basketball Player)
SeS N Lake Shore Dr Apt 64e2
Chicago, IL 6e611-362S, USA

Armstrong, Brad (Adult Film Star)
c/o Staff Member *Vivid Entertainment*
1933 N Bronson Ave Apt 209
Los Angeles, CA 90068-5632, USA

Armstrong, Bruce (Athlete, Football Player)
12543 Brookwood Ct
Davie, FL 33330-1207, USA

Armstrong, Charlotte (Athlete, Baseball Player)
5838 N 81st St
Scottsdale, AZ 85250-6208, USA

Armstrong, Colby (Athlete, Hockey Player)

Armstrong, Curtis (Actor)
c/o Laura Ackerman *Advantage PR*
3900 W Alameda Ave Ste 1200
Burbank, CA 91505-4317, USA

Armstrong, Darrell (Athlete, Basketball Player)
337 Broadmoor Way
McDonough, GA 30253-4290, USA

Armstrong, Debbie (Athlete, Olympic Athlete, Skier)
681 Shekel Ln
Breckenridge, CO 80424-8931, USA

Armstrong, Derek (Athlete, Hockey Player)
602 N Juanita Ave # B
Redondo Beach, CA 90277-2934, USA

Armstrong, Dwight (Actor)
c/o Paul Greenstone *Paul Greenstone Entertainment*
1400 California Ave Apt 201
Santa Monica, CA 90403-4395, USA

Armstrong, George (Athlete, Hockey Player)
22 St Cuthberts Rd
East York, ON M4G 1V1, Canada

Armstrong, Gillian (Director)
Harry Linstead
500 Oxford St
Bondi Junction, NSW 02022, AUSTRALIA

Armstrong, Harvey (Athlete, Football Player)
2840 Olde Town Park Dr
Norcross, GA 30071-1837, USA

Armstrong, Hilton (Athlete, Basketball Player)
c/o Jeff Schwartz *Excel Sports Management*
1700 Broadway Fl 29
New York, NY 10019-6559, USA

Armstrong, Jack (Athlete, Baseball Player)
272 E River Park Dr
Jupiter, FL 33477-9381, USA

Armstrong, J D (Athlete, Football Player)
7906 W Meadow Pass Cir
Wichita, KS 67205-1611

Armstrong, Jonas (Actor)
c/o Andrew Kurland *ICM Partners*
10250 Constellation Blvd Fl 7
Los Angeles, CA 90067-6207, USA

Armstrong, Karen (Writer)
c/o Felicity Bryan *Felicity Bryan Literary Agency*
2a North Parade Ave
Oxford OX2 6LX, UNITED KINGDOM

Armstrong, Kelley (Writer)
RR 4 LCD MAIN
Aylmer, ON N5H 2R3, CANADA

Armstrong, Kerry (Actor)
Barbara Leane Mgmt
261 Miller St
North Sydney, NSW 02060, AUSTRALIA

Armstrong, Lance (Actor, Athlete, Cycler, Olympic Athlete)
LiveStrong
2201 E 6th St
Austin, TX 78702-3456, USA

Armstrong, Matthew John (Actor)
c/o David Ginsberg *Insight*
5358 Melrose Ave # 200W
Los Angeles, CA 90038-5117, USA

Armstrong, Mike (Athlete, Baseball Player)
525 Ashbrook Ct
Athens, GA 30605-3985, USA

Armstrong, Neil (Athlete, Hockey Player)
607-1295 Sandy Lane
Sarnia, ON N7V 4K5, Canada

Armstrong, Neill (Athlete, Football Player)
2804 Chatswood Dr
Trophy Club, TX 76262-3472, us

Armstrong, Otis (Athlete, Football Player)
7183 S Newport Way
Centennial, CO 80112-1613, USA

Armstrong, Quincy (Athlete, Football Player)
680 N Watters Rd Apt 119
Allen, TX 75013-5204, USA

Armstrong, Robb (Artist, Cartoonist)
c/o Wendi Niad *Niad Management*
15021 Ventura Blvd Ste 860
Sherman Oaks, CA 91403-2442, USA

Armstrong, Robert (Bob) (Athlete, Basketball Player)
6802 Packer Dr NE
Belmont, MI 49306-9240, USA

Armstrong, Roger (Cartoonist)
21701 Rushford Dr
Lake Forest, CA 92630-6510, USA

Armstrong, Samaire (Actor)
c/o Marianna Shafran *Shafran PR*
195 S Beverly Dr Ste 414
Beverly Hills, CA 90212-3044, USA

Armstrong, Tate (Athlete, Basketball Player)
14704 Westbury Rd
Rockville, MD 20853-1610, USA

Armstrong, Taylor (Reality Star)
1736 Family Crisis Center
2116 Arlington Ave Ste 200
Los Angeles, CA 90018-1353, USA

Armstrong, Thomas (Race Car Driver)
PacWest Racing Group
PO Box 1717
Bellevue, WA 98009-1717, USA

Armstrong, Trace (Athlete, Football Player)
10191 Winding Ridge Rd
Saint Louis, MO 63124-1157, USA

Armstrong, Trace (Athlete, Football Player)
8691 SW 28th Ln
Gainesville, FL 32608-9315, us

Armstrong, Ty (Athlete, Golfer)
11529 Kensington Dr
Eden Prairie, MN 55347-4943, USA

Armstrong, Valorie (Actor)
Contemporary Artists
610 Santa Monica Blvd Ste 202
Santa Monica, CA 90401-1645, USA

Armstrong, Vaughn (Actor)
1903 Apex Ave
Los Angeles, CA 90039-3115, USA

Armstrong, Wally (Athlete, Golfer)
Signature Sports Group
4150 Olson Memorial Hwy Ste 110
Minneapolis, MN 55422-4804, USA

Armstrong, William (Writer)
6 Roland St
Newton Highlands, MA 02461-1920, USA

Armtritraz, Ashok (Producer)
c/o Staff Member *Hyde Park Entertainment*
1857 N Victory Pl
Burbank, CA 91504-3424, USA

Arnason, Chuck (Athlete, Hockey Player)
39 Grimston Rd
Winnipeg, MB R3T 3T2, Canada

Arnason, Tyler (Athlete, Hockey Player)
881 N La Salle Dr
Chicago, IL 60610-3259, USA

Arnatt, John (Actor)
3 Warren Cottage Woodland Way
Surrey KT2 6NN, UK

Arnaud, Francois (Francis) (Actor)
c/o Allison Douglas *Wolf-Kasteler Public Relations*
6255 W Sunset Blvd Ste 1111
Los Angeles, CA 90028-7426, USA

Arnault, Bernard (Business Person)
Moet Hennessy Louis Vuitton
30 Ave Hoche
Paris 75008, FRANCE

Arnaz, Lucie (Actor)
3 Big Shop Ln Ste 4
Ridgefield, CT 06877-4565, USA

Arnaz Jr, Desi (Actor)
516 Avenue M
Boulder City, NV 89005-2831, USA

Arndt, Denis (Actor)
c/o Suzanne DeWalt *Dewalt & Musik Management*
623 N Parish Pl
Burbank, CA 91506-1701, USA

Arndt, Michael (Writer)
c/o Bill Weinstein *Verve Talent & Literary Agency*
6310 San Vicente Blvd Ste 100
Los Angeles, CA 90048-5498, USA

Arndt, Richard (Athlete, Football Player)
2130 Parkdale Dr
Kingwood, TX 77339-2351, USA

Arnelle, Jesse (Athlete, Basketball Player)
400 Urbano Dr
San Francisco, CA 94127-2827, USA

Arnesen, Lasse (Athlete, Skier)
Fagerborggata 34
Oslo N-0360, Norway

Arnesen, Liv (Skier)
119 N 4th St Ste 406
Minneapolis, MN 55401-1790, USA

Arneson, Jim (Athlete, Football Player)
12649 S 71st St
Tempe, AZ 85284-3105, USA

Arneson, Mark (Athlete, Football Player)
15902 Wetherburn Rd
Chesterfield, MO 63017-7341, USA

Arnett, Jon (Athlete, Football Player)
200 Greenridge Dr Apt 715
Lake Oswego, OR 97035-1475, us

Arnett, Jon D (Athlete, Football Player)
16869 SW 65th Ave Unit 330
Lake Oswego, OR 97035-7865, USA

Arnett, Peter (Journalist)
ForeignTV.com
162 5th Ave # 105A
New York, NY 10010-5902, USA

Arnett, Will (Actor, Comedian)
c/o Lewis Kay *Kovert Creative*
506 Santa Monica Blvd Ste 400
Santa Monica, CA 90401-2412, USA

Arnette, Jay (Athlete, Basketball Player, Olympic Athlete)
2 Hillside Ct
Austin, TX 78746-6436, USA

Arnette, Jeanetta (Actor)
466 N Harper Ave
Los Angeles, CA 90048-2221, USA

Arnezeder, Nora (Actor)
c/o Estelle Lasher *Lasher Group*
1133 Avenue of the Americas Fl 27
New York, NY 10036-6710, USA

Arnez J (Comedian)
c/o Staff Member *ICM Partners*
10250 Constellation Blvd Fl 7
Los Angeles, CA 90067-6207, USA

Arngrim, Alison (Actor)
PO Box 98
Tujunga, CA 91043-0098, USA

Arniel, Scott (Athlete, Hockey Player)
Columbus Blue Jackets
200 W Nationwide Blvd Unit 1
Columbus, OH 43215-2564, Canada

Arniel, Scott (Athlete, Hockey Player)
6 Edmond Muys Pl
Winnipeg, MB R3P 2Rl, Canada

Arning, Lisa (Actor)
c/o Julie Wolff *Morgan Agency, The*
1200 N Doheny Dr
Los Angeles, CA 90069-1723, USA

Arnold, Ben (Musician)
Golden Guru
227 Pine St
Philadelphia, PA 19106-4326, USA

Arnold, Ben (Race Car Driver)
309 Fair Oaks Dr
Fairfield, AL 35064-2418, USA

Arnold, Charles (Athlete, Baseball Player)
19537 Beaverland St
Detroit, MI 48219-5507, USA

Arnold, Charlotte (Actor)
c/o Norbert Abrams *Noble Caplan Abrams*
1260 Yonge St Fl 2
Toronto, ON M4T 1W5, CANADA

Arnold, Chris (Athlete, Baseball Player)
794 E 7th Ave
Denver, CO 80203-3820, USA

Arnold, David (Athlete, Football Player)
3079 Solar Dr NW
Warren, OH 44485-1611, us

Arnold, David (Athlete, Football Player)
1615 Stanley St
New Britain, CT 06053-2439, USA

Arnold, Debbie (Actor)
M Arnold Mgmt
12 Cambridge Park
Ease Twickenham
Middx TW1 2PF, UNITED KINGDOM (UK)

Arnold, Francis (Athlete, Football Player)
3312 W 80th St
Inglewood, CA 90305-1354, USA

Arnold, Jahine (Athlete, Football Player)
4534 W Beachway Dr
Tampa, FL 33609-4234, us

Arnold, Jahine (Athlete, Football Player)
10508 Greencrest Dr
Tampa, FL 33626-5201, USA

Arnold, James E (Athlete, Football Player)
4407 Waterford Cir
Nashville, TN 37221-2153, USA

Arnold, Jamie (Athlete, Baseball Player)
17132 W Tara Ln
Surprise, AZ 85388-1244, USA

Arnold, Jim (Athlete, Football Player)
4407 Waterford Cir
Nashville, TN 37221-2153, us

Arnold, Kristine (Musician)
Monty Hitchcock Mgmt
5101 Overton Rd
Nashville, TN 37220-1920, USA

Arnold, Lenna (Athlete, Baseball Player)
4312 Dodge Ave
Fort Wayne, IN 46815-6925, USA

Arnold, Lindsay (Dancer)
c/o Rebecca Lambrecht *Chicane Group*
6442 Santa Monica Blvd Ste 200B
Los Angeles, CA 90038-1530, USA

Arnold, Luke (Actor)
c/o Caryn Leeds *Wolf-Kasteler Public Relations*
6255 W Sunset Blvd Ste 1111
Los Angeles, CA 90028-7426, USA

Arnold, Mark (Actor)
c/o Jonathan Hall *Identity Agency Group (UK)*
95 Grays Inn Rd
London WC1X 8TX, UNITED KINGDOM

Arnold, Murray (Athlete, Basketball Player, Coach)
Western Kentucky University
Athletic Dept
Bowling Green, KY 42101, USA

Arnold, Richard R (Astronaut)
16302 Heather Bend Ct
Houston, TX 77059-5579, USA

Arnold, Scott (Athlete, Baseball Player)
3282 Gondola Dr
Lexington, KY 40513-1083, USA

Arnold, Tichina (Actor)
c/o Zenay Arnold *Tize & Company*
5886 Seminole Way
Fontana, CA 92336-5688, USA

Arnold, Tom (Actor, Comedian)
c/o Jean Sievers *Beachwood Entertainment Collective*
2271 Cheremoya Ave
Los Angeles, CA 90068-3006, USA

Arnold, Tony (Athlete, Baseball Player)
300 S Main St
Akron, OH 44308-1204, USA

Arnold, Walt (Athlete, Football Player)
8503 La Sala Grande NE
Albuquerque, NM 87111-4564, USA

Arnoldi, Charles A (Artist)
721 Hampton Dr
Venice, CA 90291-3018, USA

Arnott, Jason (Athlete, Hockey Player)
c/o Donald Meehan *Newport Sports Management*
201 City Centre Dr
Suite 400
Mississauga, ON L58 2T4, CANADA

Arnoul, Francoise (Actor)
53 Rue Censier
Paris 75005, FRANCE

Arnsberg, Brad (Athlete, Baseball Player)
706 Chaffee Ct
Arlington, TX 76006-2001, USA

Arnstein, Rolly (Music Group)
Bad Boy Entertainment
1540 Broadway Ste 3000
New York, NY 10036-4039, USA

Arntz, Jason (Athlete)
95A Finnegan Ln
Kendall Park, NJ 08824-1644, USA

Arnzen, Bob (Athlete, Basketball Player)
8 Grand Lake Dr
Fort Thomas, KY 41075-4100

Arnzen, Robert (Athlete, Basketball Player)
8 Grand Lake Dr
Fort Thomas, KY 41075-4100, USA

Arocha, Rene (Athlete, Baseball Player)
14652 SW 170th St
Miami, FL 33177-2040, USA

Aronofsky, Darren (Director)
c/o Staff Member *Protozoa Pictures Inc*
104 N 7th St
Brooklyn, NY 11249-3020, USA

Aronsohn, Lee (Writer)
14332 Roblar Pl
Sherman Oaks, CA 91423-4020, USA

Aronson, Doug (Athlete, Football Player)
36 Piermont Ter
Wayne, NJ 07470-3648, us

Aronson, Judie (Actor)
11543 Laurelcrest Dr
Studio City, CA 91604-3875, USA

Arpel, Adrien (Beauty Pageant Winner, Business Person)
Adrien Arpel Cosmetics
400 Hackensack Ave
Hackensack, NJ 07601-6310, USA

Arpey, Gerard (Business Person)
AMR Corp
433 Amon Carter Blvd
Forth Worth, TX 76155, USA

Arquette, David (Actor, Director, Producer)
c/o Staff Member *Coquette Productions*
9200 W Sunset Blvd Ph 22
West Hollywood, CA 90069-3601, USA

Arquette, Patricia (Actor)
c/o Molly Madden *3 Arts Entertainment*
9460 Wilshire Blvd Fl 7
Beverly Hills, CA 90212-2713, USA

Arquette, Rosanna (Actor)
PO Box 69646
W Hollywood, CA 90069-0646, USA

Arrants, Rod (Actor)
115 Maitland Dr
Alameda, CA 94502-6725, USA

Arras, Maria Celeste (Actor)
c/o Staff Member *Telemundo*
2470 W 8th Ave
Hialeah, FL 33010-2000, USA

Arredondo, Rosa (Actor)
c/o Suzanne (Sue) Wohl *TalentWorks*
3500 W Olive Ave Ste 1400
Burbank, CA 91505-5512, USA

Arriale, Lynne (Musician)
c/o Suzi Reynolds *Suzi Reynolds Associates*
2055 Center Ave PH A
Fort Lee, NJ 07024-4947, USA

Arrieta, Jake (Athlete, Baseball Player)
c/o Scott Boras *Boras Corporation*
18 Corporate Plaza Dr
Newport Beach, CA 92660-7901, USA

Arrigo, Gerry (Athlete, Baseball Player)
3740 Redthorne Dr
Amelia, OH 45102-1263, USA

Arrillaga, John (Business Person)
John Arrillaga Foundation
2450 Watson Ct
Palo Alto, CA 94303-3216, USA

Arrington, Buddy (Race Car Driver)
2820 Kings Mountain Rd
Martinsville, VA 24112-6751, USA

Arrington, Jill (Sportscaster)
CBS-TV
51 W 52nd St
New York, NY 10019-6119, USA

Arrington, J J (Athlete, Football Player)
1599 E Beretta Pl
Chandler, AZ 85286-1152, USA

Arrington, Kyle (Athlete, Football Player)

Arrington, LaVar (Athlete, Football Player)
1514 Cedar Lane Farm Rd
Annapolis, MD 21409-5625, USA

Arrington, Michael (Business Person, Internet Star)

Arrington, Richard (Athlete, Football Player)
2585 King Cir SE
Conyers, GA 30013-1981, USA

Arriola, Dante (Director)
c/o Staff Member *MJZ*
2201 S Carmelina Ave
Los Angeles, CA 90064-1001, USA

Arriota, Gus (Cartoonist)
PO Box 3275
Carmel, CA 93921-3275, USA

Arrobio, Charles (Chuck) (Athlete, Football Player)
35 Essex St Apt 5A
New York, NY 10002-4716, USA

Arrobio, Chuck (Athlete, Football Player)
481 Linda Vista Ave
Pasadena, CA 91105-1119, us

Arrojo, Luis (Athlete, Baseball Player)
5684 36th Ave N
Saint Petersburg, FL 33710-1914, USA

Arrolo, Rolando (Athlete, Baseball Player)
5684 36th Ave N
Saint Petersburg, FL 33710-1914, USA

Arroyo, Bronson (Athlete, Baseball Player)
9256 Scarlette Oak Ave
Fort Myers, FL 33967-5145, USA

Arroyo, Carlos (Athlete, Basketball Player)
1115 NW 126th Ct
Miami, FL 33182-2033, USA

Arroyo, Fernando (Athlete, Baseball Player)
5232 E Ingram St
Mesa, AZ 85205-3434, USA

Arroyo, Jose (Writer)
c/o Staff Member *Kaplan-Stahler Agency*
8383 Wilshire Blvd Ste 923
Beverly Hills, CA 90211-2443, USA

Arroyo, Rudolph (Athlete, Baseball Player)
828 Sierra Vista Ave
Mountain View, CA 94043-1706, USA

Arsenault, Pierre (Baseball Player)
17942 D'Amalfi St
Pierrefonds QC H9K 1M2 Canada, USA

Arsham, Daniel (Artist)
c/o Staff Member *Creative Artists Agency (CAA)*
2000 Avenue of the Stars Ste 100
Los Angeles, CA 90067-4705, USA

Arsmstrong, Colby (Athlete, Hockey Player)
8030 Sherwood Dr
Presto, PA 15142-1078, USA

Arteage, Rosalia (President)
Vice President's Office
Gobiemo Palacio
Garcia Morena, Quito, ECUADOR

Arterburn, Elmer (Athlete, Football Player)
3819 29th St
Lubbock, TX 79410-2508, USA

Arterburn, Stephen (Writer)
New Life Ministries
PO Box 1029
Lake Forest, CA 92609-1029, USA

Arterton, Gemma (Actor)
c/o Pippa Beng *Premier PR*
2-4 Bucknall St
London WC2H 8LA, UNITED KINGDOM

Arteta, Miguel (Director)
c/o Linda Lichter *Lichter Grossman Nichols Adler & Feldman Inc*
9200 W Sunset Blvd Ste 1200
Los Angeles, CA 90069-3607, USA

Arthur, Fred (Athlete, Hockey Player)
203-1408 Ernest Ave
London, ON N6E 3B2, Canada

Arthur, Fred Dr (Athlete, Hockey Player)
203-1408 Ernest Ave
London, ON N6E 3B2, Canada

Arthur, Joseph (Musician)
c/o Staff Member *Primary Talent International (UK)*
10-11 Jockeys Fields
The Primary Bldg
London WC1R 4BN, UNITED KINGDOM

Arthur, Maureen (Actor)
9171 Wilshire Blvd # 530
Beverly Hills, CA 90210-5530, USA

Arthur, Michelle (Actor)
c/o Steven Neibert *Imperium 7 Talent Agency*
5455 Wilshire Blvd Ste 1706
Los Angeles, CA 90036-4217, USA

Arthur, Mike (Athlete, Football Player)
10445 Sharondale Rd
Cincinnati, OH 45241-3077, USA

Arthur, Mike (Athlete, Football Player)
11271 Terwilligers Valley Ln
Cincinnati, OH 45249-2740, us

Arthur, Perry (Athlete, Golfer)
7513 Zurich Dr
Plano, TX 75025-3118, USA

Arthur, Rebeca (Actor)
Epstein-Wyckoff
280 S Beverly Dr Ste 400
Beverly Hills, CA 90212-3904, USA

Arthurs, John (Athlete, Basketball Player)
1429 Henry Clay Ave
New Orleans, LA 70118-6059, USA

Arthurs, Paul (Bonehead) (Musician)
Ignition Mgmt
54 Linhope St
London NW1 6HL, UNITED KINGDOM (UK)

Artist, Jacob (Actor, Musician)
c/o Michelle Schwartz *Rogers & Cowan*
909 3rd Ave Fl 9
New York, NY 10022-4752, USA

Artoe, Mike (Athlete, Football Player)
17 Canterbury Ct
Wilmette, IL 60091-2822, USA

Art of Noise, The (Music Group)
PO Box 199
London W11 4AN, UNITED KINGDOM (UK)

Artzt, Alice J (Musician)
51 Hawthorne Ave
Princeton, NJ 08540-3803, USA

Artzt, Edwin L (Business Person)
3849 Hedgewood Dr
Lawrenceburg, IN 47025-8047, USA

Arum, Bob (Athlete, Boxer, Coach)
36 Gulf Stream Ct
Las Vegas, NV 89113-1354, USA

Arute, Jack (Commentator, Race Car Driver)
342 Southwick Rd Apt 104
Westfield, MA 01085-4753, USA

Arvedson, Magnus (Athlete, Hockey Player)
Edsgatevagen 145
Karlstad 655 92, Sweden

Arvesen, Nina (Actor)
412 Culver Blvd Apt 9
Playa Del Rey, CA 90293-7765, USA

Arvie, Herman (Athlete, Football Player)
34565 Lakeview Dr
Solon, OH 44139-2019, USA

Arvizu, Reginald (Musician)
27511 Hidden Trail Rd
Laguna Hills, CA 92653-7841, USA

Arya (Actor)
c/o Staff Member *The Harbour Agency*
135 Forbes St
Woolloomooloo NSW 2011, Australia

Asad, Doug (Athlete, Football Player)
1701 Marquette Ct
Lake Forest, IL 60045-5115, us

Asadoorian, Rick (Athlete, Baseball Player)
c/o Terry Bross *Turn 2 Sports Management LLC*
PO Box 27345
Scottsdale, AZ 85255-0139, USA

Asay, Chuck (Cartoonist)
Colorada Springs Gazette
303 S Prospect St
Colorado Springs, CO 80903-3748, USA

Asbaek, Pilou (Actor)
c/o Ulrich Moeller-Joergensen *Art Management*
Kronprinsensgade 9A
Copenhagen K CPH 1114, DENMARK

Asbille, Kelsey (Actor)
c/o Jamie Harhay Skinner *Baker Winokur Ryder Public Relations*
9100 Wilshire Blvd
W Tower #500
Beverly Hills, CA 90212-3415, USA

Asbury, Kelly (Actor)
c/o Staff Member *Creative Artists Agency (CAA)*
2000 Avenue of the Stars Ste 100
Los Angeles, CA 90067-4705, USA

Asbury, Martin (Cartoonist)
Stoneworld
Pitch Green
Princes Risborough, Bucks HP27 9QG, UNITED KINGDOM (UK)

Ascencio, Nelson (Actor)
c/o Heidi Rotbart *Heidi Rotbart Management*
1810 Malcolm Ave Apt 207
Los Angeles, CA 90025-7610, USA

Asch, Peter (Athlete, Olympic Athlete, Water Polo Player)
1946 Green St
San Francisco, CA 94123-4811, USA

Aschbacher, Darrel (Athlete, Football Player)
1917 NE Squire Dr
Madras, OR 97741-9401, USA

Aschwege, David (Athlete, Baseball Player)
3027 S 27th St
Lincoln, NE 68502-5010, USA

Asghedom, Ermias (Nipsey Hussle) (Musician)
c/o John Pantle *Agency for the Performing Arts (APA)*
405 S Beverly Dr Ste 500
Beverly Hills, CA 90212-4425, USA

Ash, Brian (Producer, Writer)
c/o Simon Millar *Rumble Media*
1620 Broadway Ste C
Santa Monica, CA 90404-2777, USA

Ash, Lauren (Actor)
c/o Barb Godfrey *Parent Management*
84 Ontario St
Toronto, ON M5A 2V3, CANADA

Ash, Leslie (Actor)
c/o Michele Milburn *Milburn Browning Associates*
Holborn Hall - 4th Floor
London WC1V 7BD, UK

Ash, Ray (Athlete, Football Player)
3 Carriage Bay
Winnipeg, MB R2Y 0M4, Canada

Asham, Arron (Athlete, Hockey Player)
4121 Muirfield Cir
Presto, PA 15142-1070, CANADA

Ashanti (Musician)
c/o Rich Murphy *Emancipated Talent*
344 Grove St Ste 21
Jersey City, NJ 07302-5923, USA

Ashbrook, Dana (Actor)
Rigberg Roberts Rugolo
1180 S Beverly Dr Ste 601
Los Angeles, CA 90035-1158, USA

Ashbrook, Daphne (Actor)
Innovative Atrists
1505 10th St
Santa Monica, CA 90401-2805, USA

Ashbrook, Stephen (Musician)
Green Room
2280 NW Thurman St
Portland, OR 97210-2519, USA

Ashby, Alan (Athlete, Baseball Player)
17931 Spoke Hollow Ct
Cypress, TX 77433-4470, USA

Ashby, Andy (Athlete, Baseball Player)
2 Osborne Dr
Pittston, PA 18640-3751, USA

Ashby, Jeffrey S (Astronaut)
NASA
2101 NASA Road
Johnson Space Center
Webster, TX 77598-6202, USA

Ashby, Linden (Actor)
639 N Larchmont Blvd Ste 207
Los Angeles, CA 90004-1323, USA

Ashcroft, John (Politician)
5603 W Farm Road 54
Willard, MO 65781-8405, USA

Ashcroft, Richard (Musician, Songwriter)
c/o Marty Diamond *Paradigm*
140 Broadway Ste 2600
New York, NY 10005-1011, USA

Ashe, Christopher (Actor)
c/o John Pierce *The Group*
800 S Robertson Blvd Ste 5
Los Angeles, CA 90035-1634, USA

Asher, Jamie (Athlete, Football Player)
6840 S Arlington Ave
Indianapolis, IN 46237-9722, us

Asher, Jane (Actor)
10 Cheyne Walk
London SW3 5QZ, UNITED KINGDOM

Asher, Peter (Musician, Producer)
23446 Malibu Colony Rd
Malibu, CA 90265-4640, USA

Asher, Robert (Bob) (Athlete, Football Player)
4800 S Chicago Beach Dr Apt 612S
Chicago, IL 60615-3569, USA

Asher, Vanya (Actor)
c/o Tim Taylor *Luber Roklin Management*
5815 W Sunset Blvd Ste 208
Los Angeles, CA 90028-6481, USA

Asherson, Renee (Actor)
28 Elsworthy Road
London NW3, UNITED KINGDOM (UK)

Ashford, Mandy (Music Group)
Evolution Talent
1776 Broadway Ste 1500
New York, NY 10019-2032, USA

Ashford, Matthew (Actor)
c/o Staff Member *Tranquil Bay Entertainment*
330 Island Cove Rd
Norwood, NC 28128-6494, USA

Ashford, Michelle (Producer, Writer)
c/o Staff Member *WME/IMG*
9601 Wilshire Blvd
Beverly Hills, CA 90210-5213, USA

Ashford, Rob (Actor)
c/o Staff Member *Creative Artists Agency (CAA)*
2000 Avenue of the Stars Ste 100
Los Angeles, CA 90067-4705, USA

Ashford, Roslyn (Music Group)
Thomas Cassidy
11761 E Speedway Blvd
Tucson, AZ 85748-2017, USA

Ashford, Tucker (Athlete, Baseball Player)
122 E Church Ave
Covington, TN 38019-2504, USA

Ashford & Simpson (Music Group)
254 W 72nd St Apt 1A
New York, NY 10023-2851, USA

Ashida, Jun (Designer, Fashion Designer)
1-3-3 Aobadai
Meguroku
Tokyo 00153, JAPAN

Ashkenasi, Shmuel (Musician)
505 W 54th St Apt 326
New York, NY 10019-5011, USA

Ashkenazi, Rafi (Business Person)
Rational Group
Douglas Bay Complex, King Edward Rd
Onchan IM3 1DZ, Isle of Man

Ashley, Billy (Athlete, Baseball Player)
2787 Autumn Ridge Dr
Thousand Oaks, CA 91362-4934, USA

Ashley, Elizabeth (Actor)
1223 N Ogden Dr
West Hollywood, CA 90046-4706, USA

Ashley, Jennifer (Actor)
129 W Wilson St Ste 202
Costa Mesa, CA 92627-1586, USA

Ashley, Leon (Musician)
PO Box 567
Hendersonville, TN 37077-0567, USA

Ashley, Mike (Race Car Driver)
Gotham City Racing
201 Old Country Rd Ste 101
Melville, NY 11747-2731, USA

Ashley, Walker (Athlete, Football Player)
4 Dwight St
Jersey City, NJ 07305-4110, USA

Ashman, Duane (Athlete, Football Player)
2625 Antler Ct
Silver Spring, MD 20904-7157, USA

Ashmore, Aaron (Actor)
KG Talent
55 1/2 Sumach St
Toronto, ON M5A 3J6, Canada

Ashmore, Darryl (Athlete, Football Player)
8695 Thornbrook Terrace Pt
Boynton Beach, FL 33473-4882, USA

Ashmore, Frank (Actor)
c/o Staff Member *Howard Talent West*
PO Box 5403
Chatsworth, CA 91313-5403, USA

Ashmore, Shawn (Actor)
c/o Dominique Appel *Imprint PR*
6121 W Sunset Blvd
Neuehouse
Los Angeles, CA 90028-6442, USA

Ashrawl, Hanan (Politician)
Higher Education Ministry
PO Box 17360
Jerusalem, West Bank, ISRAEL

Ashton, Brent (Athlete, Hockey Player)
311 Brabant Cres
Saskatoon, SK S7J 4Y9, Canada

Ashton, Dean (Actor)

Ashton, John (Actor)
PO Box 272489
Fort Collins, CO 80527-2489, USA

Ashton, Susan (Music Group)
Bob Doyle Assoc
713 18th Ave S
Nashville, TN 37203-3214, USA

Ashton, Zawe (Actor)
c/o Lisa Kasteler *Wolf-Kasteler Public Relations*
6255 W Sunset Blvd Ste 1111
Los Angeles, CA 90028-7426, USA

Ashwell, Rachel (Business Person, Designer)
739 Superba Ave
Venice, CA 90291-3868, USA

Ashworth, Frank (Athlete, Hockey Player)
5110 Hot Springs Rd
Fairmont Hot Springs, BC V0B 1L1, Canada

Ashworth, Gerald (Gerry) (Athlete, Track Athlete)
PO Box 2
Ogunquit, ME 03907-0002, USA

Ashworth, Landon (Actor)
c/o Staff Member *Snyder Management*
PO Box 5728
Beverly Hills, CA 90209-5728, USA

Ashworth, Thomas (Athlete, Football Player)
10100 Commons St # B
Lone Tree, CO 80124-5645, USA

Asia (Music Group)
%Michael Rosen
7715 W Sunset Blvd Fl 3
Los Angeles, CA 90046-3912, USA

Asian Dub Foundation (Music Group)
c/o Staff Member *Paradigm (Monterey)*
404 W Franklin St
Monterey, CA 93940-2303, USA

Asiata, Matt (Athlete, Football Player)

As I Lay Dying (Music Group, Musician)
c/o Staff Member *Strong Management*
17625 Union Tpke # 405
Fresh Meadows, NY 11366-1515, USA

Askea, Mike (Athlete, Football Player)
Front Gate Cir
Ooltewah, TN 37363, us

Askea, Mike (Athlete, Football Player)
PO Box 2391
Ooltewah, TN 37363-2391, USA

Askew, B J (Athlete, Football Player)
4216 Lantana Dr
Lebanon, OH 45036-4022, USA

Askew, Desmond (Actor)
c/o Staff Member *Envision Entertainment*
8840 Wilshire Blvd Fl 3
Beverly Hills, CA 90211-2606, USA

Askew, Matthias (Athlete, Football Player)
220 Greenup St
Covington, KY 41011-1787, USA

Askew, Matthias (Athlete, Football Player)
3630 NW 6th St
Lauderhill, FL 33311-7526, us

Askey, Tom (Athlete, Hockey Player)
5732 S 6th St
Kalamazoo, MI 49009-9438, USA

Asking Alexandria (Music Group, Musician)
c/o Devin Timmons *The Artery Foundation*
PO Box 160451
Sacramento, CA 95816-0451, USA

Askson, Bert (Athlete, Football Player)
7713 Charlesmont St
Houston, TX 77016-3927, USA

Aslan, Reza (Religious Leader, Television Host)
c/o Staff Member *BoomGen Studios*
5 Devoe St Fl 2
Brooklyn, NY 11211-3504, USA

Asleep At The Wheel (Music Group)
PO Box 463
Austin, TX 78767-0463, USA

Aslyn (Musician)
c/o Staff Member *Paradigm (Monterey)*
404 W Franklin St
Monterey, CA 93940-2303, USA

Asmonga, Don (Athlete, Basketball Player)
124 Naylor Dr
Rostraver Township, PA 15012-4729, USA

Asmussen, Cash (Horse Racer)
111 Devonshire Ct
Laredo, TX 78041-2659, USA

Asner, Ed (Actor)
Quince Productions Inc
19574 Braewood Dr
Tarzana, CA 91356-5646, USA

Asner, Jules (Producer, Television Host)
5220 Los Bonitos Way
Los Angeles, CA 90027-1008, USA

Asomugha, Nnamdi (Athlete, Football Player)
1050 Armitage St
Alameda, CA 94502-7931, USA

Asomugha, Nnamdi (Athlete, Football Player)
22632 Felbar Ave
Torrance, CA 90505-2825, us

Aspen, Jennifer (Actor)
c/o Joel Stevens *Joel Stevens Entertainment*
5627 Allott Ave
Van Nuys, CA 91401-4502, USA

Aspromonte, Ken (Athlete, Baseball Player, Coach)
2 Derham Parc St
Houston, TX 77024-5200, USA

Assante, Armand (Actor)
c/o Michael Kaliski *Omniquest Entertainment (LA)*
1416 N La Brea Ave
Hollywood, CA 90028-7506, USA

Assaraf, John (Writer)

Asselstine, Brian (Athlete, Baseball Player)
1488 Country Ct
Santa Ynez, CA 93460-9754, USA

Asselstine, Ron (Athlete, Hockey Player)
338-224 Janefield Ave
Guelph, ON N1G 2L6, Canada

Assenmacher, Paul (Athlete, Baseball Player)
500 Covington Cv
Alpharetta, GA 30022-5574, USA

Assinger, Armin (Actor)
c/o Staff Member *ORF Enterprise*
Wurzburggasse 30
Wien A-1136, Austria

Assouline, Pierre (Writer)
78 Bd Flandrin
Paris 75116, France

Assuras, Thalia (Television Host)
c/o Staff Member *CBS News (NY)*
524 W 57th St Fl 8
New York, NY 10019-2930, USA

Astacio, Pedro (Athlete, Baseball Player)
123 Blue Heron Dr
Greenwood Village, CO 80121-2162, USA

Astaire, Robyn (Horse Racer)
1155 San Ysidro Dr
Beverly Hills, CA 90210-2102, USA

As Tall as Lions (Music Group)
c/o Staff Member *Paradigm (Monterey)*
404 W Franklin St
Monterey, CA 93940-2303, USA

Aster, Ari (Director, Producer)
c/o Dan Aloni *WME/IMG*
9601 Wilshire Blvd
Beverly Hills, CA 90210-5213, USA

Astin, John (Actor, Director)
3801 Canterbury Rd
Baltimore, MD 21218-2370, USA

Astin, Mackenzie (Actor)
9320 Wilshire Blvd Ste 300
Beverly Hills, CA 90212-3218, USA

Astin, Sean (Actor, Director, Producer)
c/o Teri Weigel *The Creative Group PR*
324 S Beverly Dr # 216
Beverly Hills, CA 90212-4801, USA

Astin, Skylar (Actor)
c/o Mike Smith *Principal Entertainment*
9255 W Sunset Blvd Ste 500
Los Angeles, CA 90069-3301, USA

Astley, Rick (Musician)
Unit 4 Plato St
72-74 Saint Dionis Road
London SW6 4UT, UNITED KINGDOM (UK)

Astrom, Hardy (Athlete, Hockey Player)
Bonasvagen 19B
Ornskoldsvik S-89072, Sweden

Astroth, Joe (Athlete, Baseball Player)
6035 Verde Trl S Apt J310
Boca Raton, FL 33433-4435, USA

Asuma, Linda (Actor)
c/o JR Dibbs *Malaky International*
205 S Beverly Dr Ste 211
Beverly Hills, CA 90212-3893, USA

Atack, Emily (Actor)
c/o Malcolm Browning *International Artistes*
Holborn Hall - 4th Floor
London WC1V 7BD, UK

Atari Teenage Riot (Music Group)
c/o Staff Member *Girlie Action*
243 W 30th St Fl 12
New York, NY 10001-2812, USA

Atchison, Scott (Race Car Driver)
Day Enterprises Racing
8528 Davis Blvd Ste 134
North Richland Hills, TX 76182-8302, USA

Atchley, Justin (Athlete, Baseball Player)
17958 Cove Ln
Mount Vernon, WA 98274-8126, USA

Aterciopelados (Musician)
c/o Staff Member *BMG*
1540 Broadway
New York, NY 10036-4039, USA

Atessis, Bill (Athlete, Football Player)
PO Box 616
Phoenix, AZ 85001-0616, USA

Atha, Dick (Athlete, Basketball Player)
PO Box 256
4E2 N JUSTUS
Oxford, IN 47971-0256, USA

Atha, Richard (Athlete, Basketball Player)
PO Box 256
402 N. Justus
Oxford, IN 47971-0256, USA

Athas, Pete (Athlete, Football Player)
1515 S 14th Ave Apt 16
Hollywood, FL 33020-6586, USA

Atherton, Keith (Athlete, Baseball Player)
1014 Cobbs Creek Ln
Cobbs Creek, VA 23035-2137, USA

Atherton, William (Actor)
c/o Staff Member *Artists & Representatives (Stone Manners Salners)*
6100 Wilshire Blvd Ste 1500
Los Angeles, CA 90048-5110, USA

Athie, Mamoudou (Actor)
c/o Staff Member *Gersh*
9465 Wilshire Blvd Ste 600
Beverly Hills, CA 90212-2605, USA

Athlete (Music Group)
c/o Staff Member *Paradigm (Monterey)*
404 W Franklin St
Monterey, CA 93940-2303, USA

A Thousand Horses (Music Group)
c/o Jake Basden *Big Machine Records*
1219 16th Ave S
Nashville, TN 37212-2901, USA

Atias, Moran (Actor)
c/o Carolyn Govers *Anonymous Content*
3532 Hayden Ave
Culver City, CA 90232-2413, USA

Atkin, Harvey (Actor)
527 S Curson Ave
Los Angeles, CA 90036-3252, USA

Atkins, Bob (Athlete, Football Player)
15871 Misty Loch Ln
Houston, TX 77084-6795, USA

Atkins, Christopher (Actor)
c/o Don Carroll *The Green Room*
7080 Hollywood Blvd Ste 1100
Los Angeles, CA 90028-6938, USA

Atkins, Chucky (Athlete, Basketball Player)
229 S Ortman Dr
Orlando, FL 32811-4219, USA

Atkins, Dave (Athlete, Football Player)
38140 Windy Hill Ln
Solon, OH 44139-3186, USA

Atkins, Dave (Athlete, Football Player)
737 W Wildwood Dr
Phoenix, AZ 85045-0632, us

Atkins, Eileen (Actor, Writer)
c/o Staff Member *ICM Partners*
10250 Constellation Blvd Fl 7
Los Angeles, CA 90067-6207, USA

Atkins, Essence (Actor)
11030 Sunnybrae Ave
Chatsworth, CA 91311-1651, USA

Atkins, Garrett (Athlete, Baseball Player)
92 Indigo Way
Castle Rock, CO 80108-9015, USA

Atkins, Gene (Athlete, Football Player)
3515 Sunnyside Dr
Tallahassee, FL 32305-6964, USA

Atkins, Gene (Athlete, Football Player)
3970 NW 84th Way
Pembroke Pines, FL 33024-5059, us

Atkins, Geno (Athlete, Football Player)
c/o Pat Dye Jr *SportsTrust Advisors*
3340 Peachtree Rd NE Fl 16
Atlanta, GA 30326-1000, USA

Atkins, George (Athlete, Football Player)
3445 Polo Downs
Hoover, AL 35226-3371, USA

Atkins, Kelvin (Athlete, Football Player)
4978 Timber Ridge Trl
Ocoee, FL 34761-8460, USA

Atkins, Larry (Athlete, Football Player)
1696 N Hughes Ave
Clovis, CA 93619-7547, USA

Atkins, Rhett (Musician)
c/o Kevin Neal *WME (Nashville)*
1201 Demonbreun St
Nashville, TN 37203-3140, USA

Atkins, Rodney (Musician)
751 Valhalla Ln
Brentwood, TN 37027-6414, USA

Atkins, Sharif (Actor)
c/o Scott Manners *Artists & Representatives (Stone Manners Salners)*
6100 Wilshire Blvd Ste 1500
Los Angeles, CA 90048-5110, USA

Atkins, Tom (Actor)
Paradigm Agency
10100 Santa Monica Blvd Ste 2500
Los Angeles, CA 90067-4116, USA

Atkinson, Al (Athlete, Football Player)
218 Wells Ln
Springfield, PA 19064-3038, USA

Atkinson, Bill (Athlete, Baseball Player)
15 Argyle Cres
Chatham, ON N7L 4T7, CANADA

Atkinson, Frank (Athlete, Football Player)
7 Franciscan Rdg
Portola Valley, CA 94028-8043, USA

Atkinson, George (Athlete, Football Player)
3570 Caldeira Dr
Livermore, CA 94550-6563, USA

Atkinson, Jayne (Actor)
Innovative Atrists
1505 10th St
Santa Monica, CA 90401-2805, USA

Atkinson, Jess (Athlete, Football Player)
2913 Southaven Dr
Annapolis, MD 21401-7125, USA

Atkinson, Matthew (Actor)
c/o Theo Swerissen *Theo Swerissen Management*
Prefers to be contacted via telephone or email
Los Angeles, CA, USA

Atkinson, Ray N (Business Person)
Guy F Atkinson Co
1001 Bayhill Dr
San Bruno, CA 94066-3062, USA

Atkinson, Rick (Journalist)
Kansas City Times
1729 Grand Blvd
Attn Editorial Dept
Kansas City, MO 64108-1413, USA

Atkinson, Ron (Soccer Player)
Nottingham Forest
Pavillion Road
Bridgeford
Nottingham N62 5JF, UNITED KINGDOM (UK)

Atkinson, Rowan (Actor)
Oliver
Drury Ln
Theatre Royal
Catherine St WC2B 5JF, UK

Atkinson, Steve (Athlete, Hockey Player)

Atkisson, Sharyl (Correspondent)
Cable News Network
News Dept 1051 Techwood Dr NW
Atlanta, GA 30318, USA

Atogwe, Oshiomogho (Athlete, Football Player)
496 Speyer Pl
Saint Charles, MO 63303-4208, USA

Atogwe, Oshiomogho (Athlete, Football Player)
18601 Turnbridge Dr
Dallas, TX 75252-5024, us

Atomic Kitten (Music Group)
c/o Staff Member *Concorde Intl Artists Ltd*
101 Shepherds Bush Rd
London W6 7LP, UNITED KINGDOM (UK)

Attal, Yvan (Actor, Director)
c/o Bertrand de Labbey *ArtMedia*
8 rue Danielle Casanova
Paris 75002, FRANCE

Attali, Jacques (Writer)
c/o Staff Member *Allen & Unwin*
PO Box 8500
St Leonards, NSW 08500, Australia

Attanasio, Paul (Producer, Writer)
236 Adelaide Dr
Santa Monica, CA 90402-1228, USA

Attaochu, Jeremiah (Athlete, Football Player)
c/o Pat Dye Jr *SportsTrust Advisors*
3340 Peachtree Rd NE Fl 16
Atlanta, GA 30326-1000, USA

Attardi, Michael (Athlete, Football Player)
11 Walada Ave
Port Monmouth, NJ 07758-1325, USA

Attell, Dave (Actor, Comedian, Producer)
c/o Josh Lieberman *Creative Artists Agency (CAA)*
2000 Avenue of the Stars Ste 100
Los Angeles, CA 90067-4705, USA

Attenborough, David F (Business Person, Writer)
5 Park Rd
Richmond, Surrey TW10 6NS, UK

Atterton, Edward (Actor)
PFD
Drury House
34-43 Russell St
London WC2B 5HA, UNITED KINGDOM (UK)

Attlee, Frank III (Business Person)
Monsanto Co
800 N Lindbergh Blvd
Saint Louis, MO 63167-0001, USA

Attles, Al (Athlete, Basketball Player, Coach)
195 Villanova Dr
Oakland, CA 94611-1108, USA

Attwell, Bob (Athlete, Hockey Player)
130 Rolling Hills Lane
Bolton, ON L7E 4E1, Canada

Attwell, Ron (Athlete, Hockey Player)
PO Box 292
Sundridge, ON P0A 1Z0, Canada

Atwater, Stephen D (Steve) (Athlete, Football Player)
2510 Sugarloaf Club Dr
Duluth, GA 30097-7407, USA

Atwater Rhodes, Amelia (Writer)
c/o Staff Member *Random House Publicity*
1745 Broadway Frnt 3
New York, NY 10019-4343, USA

Atwell, Hayley (Actor)
c/o Pippa Beng *Premier PR*
2-4 Bucknall St
London WC2H 8LA, UNITED KINGDOM

Atwood, Casey (Race Car Driver)
Day Enterprises Racing
107 Flat Ridge Rd
Goodlettsville, TN 37072-8509, USA

Atwood, Jensen (Actor)
c/o Jennifer Hebert *Brilliant Talent*
PO Box 58003
Sherman Oaks, CA 91413-3003, USA

Atwood, Margare (Writer)
c/o Ron Bernstein *ICM Partners*
10250 Constellation Blvd Fl 7
Los Angeles, CA 90067-6207, USA

Atwood, Roman (Comedian, Internet Star)
c/o Paul Cazers *Creative Artists Agency (CAA)*
2000 Avenue of the Stars Ste 100
Los Angeles, CA 90067-4705, USA

Atwood, Susie (Sue) (Swimmer)
5624 E 2nd St
Long Beach, CA 90803-3904, USA

Auber, Brigitte (Actor)
56 rue Guy-Moquet
Paris F-75017, FRANCE

Auberjonois, Rene (Actor)
3629 Wonder View Dr
Los Angeles, CA 90068-1539, USA

Aubert, KD (Actor)
c/o Scott Karp *The Syndicate*
10203 Santa Monica Blvd Fl 5
Los Angeles, CA 90067-6416, USA

Aubin, Normand (Athlete, Hockey Player)
1287 Rue des Berges
Sorel-Tracy, QC J3P 7X5, Canada

Aubin, Serge (Athlete, Hockey Player)
PO Box 105366
Atlanta, GA 30348-5366, USA

Aubrey, Emlyn (Athlete, Golfer)
2013 Surrey Ln
Bossier City, LA 71111-5534, USA

Aubrey, James (Actor)
Van Gelder
18-21 Jermyn St #300
London SW1Y 6HP, UNITED KINGDOM (UK)

Aubrey, Michael (Athlete, Baseball Player)
9622 Gardere Dr
Shreveport, LA 71115-4602, USA

Aubry, Cristina (Actor)
Carol Levi Co
Via Giuseppe Pisanelli
Rome 00196, ITALY

Aubry, Gabriel (Model)
c/o Staff Member *Beatrice International Models*
Via Vincenzo Monti 47
Milan 20123, ITALY

Aubry, Pierre (Athlete, Hockey Player)
110 Rue Buisson
Trois-Rivieres, QC G8V 1K4, Canada

Aubry, Serge (Hockey Player)

Aubuchon, Remi (Producer)
c/o Staff Member *United Talent Agency (UTA)*
9336 Civic Center Dr
Beverly Hills, CA 90210-3604, USA

Auburn, David (Writer)
97 W Elmwood Ave
Clawson, MI 48017-1228, USA

Aucoin, Adrian (Athlete, Hockey Player)
9820 E Thompson Peak Pkwy Unit 727
Scottsdale, AZ 85255-6657, USA

Aude, Rich (Athlete, Baseball Player)
4817 Natoma Ave
Woodland Hills, CA 91364-3416, USA

Audette, Donald (Athlete, Hockey Player)
15 Rue de Chinon
Blainville, QC J7B 1Y2, Canada

Audick, Daniel (Athlete, Football Player)
13253 Sparren Ave
San Diego, CA 92129-2324, USA

Auel, Jean M (Writer)
PO Box 8278
Portland, OR 97207-8278, USA

Auel, Jean Marie (Writer)
PO Box 8278
Portland, OR 97207-8278, USA

Auer, Barbara (Actor)
Agentur Carola Studlar
Neurieder Str 1C
Planegg 82152, GERMANY

Auer, Joe (Athlete, Football Player)
822 Clay St Ste 125
Winter Park, FL 32789-5463, USA

Auer, Scott (Athlete, Football Player)
2921 Burge Dr
Crown Point, IN 46307-8172, USA

Auerbach, Dan (Musician)
2013 19th Ave S
Nashville, TN 37212-4305, USA

Auerbach, Frank (Artist)
Marlborough Fine Art Gallery
6 Albermarle St
London W1X 4BY, UNITED KINGDOM (UK)

Auerbach, Rick (Athlete, Baseball Player)
2139 Stunt Rd
Calabasas, CA 91302-2358, USA

Auermann, Nadia (Model)
Elite Models
4 Rue de la Paiz
Paris 75002, FRANCE

Auermann, Nadja (Model)
c/o Staff Member *DNA Model Management*
555 W 25th St Fl 6
New York, NY 10001-5542, USA

AufDerMaur, Melissa (Music Group, Musician)
Artist Group International
9560 Wilshire Blvd Ste 400
Beverly Hills, CA 90212-2442, USA

Auferio, Tony (Athlete, Baseball Player)
493 Indian Rd
Wayne, NJ 07470-4922, USA

Augenstein, Bryan (Athlete, Baseball Player)
179 Cili)rona St
Sebastian, FL 32958-5607, USA

Auger, Brian (Music Group, Musician)
Earthtone
8306 Wilshire Blvd # 981
Beverly Hills, CA 90211-2304, USA

Auger, Claudine (Actor)
c/o Elisabeth Tanner *Time-Art*
8 rue Danielle Casanova
Paris 75002, FRANCE

Aughtman, Dowe (Athlete, Football Player)
2 Buckhead Ln
Opelika, AL 36804-7645, USA

Augmon, Stacey (Athlete, Basketball Player)
6936 Encino Ave
Van Nuys, CA 91406-4328, USA

August, Bille (Director)
2800 Lyngby
DENMARK

August, Don (Athlete, Baseball Player, Olympic Athlete)
N88W17812 Christman Rd
Menomonee Falls, WI 53051-2630, USA

August, John (Director, Musician, Producer)
644 S June St
Los Angeles, CA 90005-3821, USA

August, Pernilla (Actor)
Royal Dramatic Theater
Box 5037
Stockholm 102 41, SWEDEN

August, Steve (Athlete, Football Player)
6109 S 72nd East Ave
Tulsa, OK 74133-1124, USA

Augusta, Kim (Athlete, Golfer)
16 Rachella Ct
East Providence, RI 02914-3063, USA

Augusta, Patrik (Athlete, Hockey Player)
c/o Staff Member *Phoenix Coyotes*
6751 N White Out Way Ste 200
Glendale, AZ 85305-3213, USA

Augustain, Ira (Actor)
c/o Staff Member *Diamond Artists*
9200 W Sunset Blvd Ste 701
W Hollywood, CA 90069-3602, USA

Augustana (Music Group)
c/o Marty Diamond *Paradigm*
140 Broadway Ste 2600
New York, NY 10005-1011, USA

Augustine, Dave (Athlete, Baseball Player)
PO Box 1114
Saint Albans, WV 25177-1114, USA

Augustine, Jerry (Athlete, Baseball Player)
S74W13490 Courtland Ln
Muskego, WI 53150-3937, USA

Augustine, Norman R (Business Person)
Review of U.S. Human Space Flight Plans Committee
300 E St SW
Nasa Headquarters
Washington, DC 20024-3210, USA

Augustnyiak, Jerry (Music Group, Musician)
Agency for Performing Arts
9200 W Sunset Blvd Ste 900
Los Angeles, CA 90069-3604, USA

Augustus, Seimone (Athlete, Basketball Player)
Matheny Sears Linkert & Long, LLP
3638 American River Dr
Sacramento, CA 95864-5901, USA

Augustus, Sherman (Actor)
c/o Steve Rohr *Lexicon Public Relations*
1049 Havenhurst Dr # 365
West Hollywood, CA 90046-6002, USA

Augustyniak, Jerry (Musician)
c/o Staff Member *Agency for the Performing Arts (APA)*
405 S Beverly Dr Ste 500
Beverly Hills, CA 90212-4425, USA

Augustyniak, Mike (Athlete, Football Player)
10540 Castlebrook Dr
Jacksonville, FL 32257-6478, USA

Augustyniak, Mike (Athlete, Football Player)
244 Sweetbrier Branch Ln
Saint Johns, FL 32259-4407, us

Aukerman, Scott (Actor, Comedian, Television Host)
c/o Christie Smith *Rise Management*
6338 Wilshire Blvd
Los Angeles, CA 90048-5002, USA

Auktyon (Music Group, Musician)
c/o Staff Member *Skyline Music*
28 Union St
Whitefield, NH 03598-3503, USA

Auld, Alex (Athlete, Hockey Player)
2205 Swallow Cres
Thunder Bay, ON P7K 1G3, Canada

Ault, Chris (Coach, Football Coach)
University of Nevada
Athletic Dept
Reno, NV 89557-0001, USA

Ault, James M (Religious Leader)
1 Amoskegan Dr
Brunswick, ME 04011-9524, USA

Aumont, Michel (Actor)
c/o Staff Member *ArtMedia*
8 rue Danielle Casanova
Paris 75002, FRANCE

Aunon, Serena Dr (Astronaut)
2536 Goldeneye Ln
League City, TX 77573-6434, USA

Auriemma, Frank (Horse Racer)
21 Jacob Rd
Plainview, NY 11803-6462, USA

Auriemma, Geno (Athlete, Basketball Player, Coach)
180 Garth Rd
Manchester, CT 06040-5644, USA

Aurilia, Rich (Athlete, Baseball Player)
4525 E Cheery Lynn Rd
Phoenix, AZ 85018-6448, USA

Ausanio, Joe (Athlete, Baseball Player)
PO Box 213
Marlboro, NY 12542-0213, USA

Ausbie, Hubert (Athlete, Basketball Player)
902 Arthur Dr
Little Rock, AR 72204-1524, USA

Ausmus, Brad (Athlete, Baseball Player)
1644 Stratford Way
Del Mar, CA 92014-2444, USA

Ausoin, Derek (Athlete, Baseball Player)
233 W 77th St Apt 5E
New York, NY 10024-6809, USA

Aust, Dennis (Athlete, Baseball Player)
16252 Estuary Ct
Bokeelia, FL 33922-1535, USA

Auster, Paul (Director, Writer)
c/o Ron Bernstein *ICM Partners*
10250 Constellation Blvd Fl 7
Los Angeles, CA 90067-6207, USA

Austin, Alana (Actor)
c/o Lena Roklin *Luber Roklin Management*
5815 W Sunset Blvd Ste 208
Los Angeles, CA 90028-6481, USA

Austin, A Woody (Athlete, Golfer)
10906 W Havenhurst St
Maize, KS 67101-3712, USA

Austin, Billy (Athlete, Football Player)
12723 Timbermeadow Dr
Houston, TX 77070-4754, us

Austin, Charles (Athlete, Olympic Athlete, Track Athlete)
514 Duncan Dr
San Marcos, TX 78666-4900, USA

Austin, Cliff (Athlete, Football Player)
1652 Valencia Rd
Decatur, GA 30032-5263, USA

Austin, Cliff (Athlete, Football Player)
1278 Autumn Wood Trl
Sugar Hill, GA 30518-8627, us

Austin, Coco (Model, Reality Star)
c/o Soulgee McQueen *Trio Entertainment*
2014 Morris Ave Apt 3C
Bronx, NY 10453-4234, USA

Austin, Dallas (Musician, Producer, Songwriter)
5335 Northside Dr
Atlanta, GA 30327-4252, USA

Austin, Darlene (Musician, Songwriter)
PO Box 171143
Nashville, TN 37217-8143, USA

Austin, Darrell (Athlete, Football Player)
268 Austin Rd
Union, SC 29379-7658, USA

Austin, Darrell (Athlete, Football Player)
720A S Duncan Byp # A
Union, SC 29379-7830, us

Austin, Debbie (Athlete, Golfer)
6733 Bittersweet Ln
Orlando, FL 32819-4600, USA

Austin, Denise (Fitness Expert)
PrimeCare Systems, Inc
PO Box 796
Fairfax, VA 22038-0796, USA

Austin, Hise (Athlete, Football Player)
2538 Goldspring Ln
Spring, TX 77373-5849, USA

Austin, Ike (Athlete, Basketball Player)
1221 S 800 E
Salt Lake City, UT 84105-1207, USA

Austin, Jake (Actor)
c/o Steven Grossman *Untitled Entertainment*
350 S Beverly Dr Ste 200
Beverly Hills, CA 90212-4819, USA

Austin, Jeff (Musician)
c/o Staff Member *Paradigm (Monterey)*
404 W Franklin St
Monterey, CA 93940-2303, USA

Austin, Jeff (Athlete, Baseball Player)
6005 Mentmore Pl
Cary, NC 27519-1574, USA

Austin, Jim (Athlete, Baseball Player)
20974 Rootstown Ter
Ashburn, VA 20147-4839, USA

Austin, John (Athlete, Basketball Player)
1330 Riggs St NW
Washington, DC 20009-4325, USA

Austin, Johnny (Athlete, Basketball Player)
1330 Riggs St NW
Washington, DC 20009-4325, USA

Austin, Kent (Athlete, Football Player)
704 Legends Crest Dr
Franklin, TN 37069-4659, USA

Austin, Marvin (Athlete, Football Player)
c/o Peter Schaffer *Authentic Athletix*
400 S Steele St Unit 47
Denver, CO 80209-3535, USA

Austin, Miles (Athlete, Football Player)
c/o David Dunn *Athletes First*
23091 Mill Creek Dr
Laguna Hills, CA 92653-1258, USA

Austin, Ocie (Athlete, Football Player)
750 MacArthur Blvd Apt 301
Oakland, CA 94610-3702, USA

Austin, Pat (Race Car Driver)
14823 47th Ave E
Tacoma, WA 98446-4033, USA

Austin, Patti (Music Group)
3 Loudon Dr Unit 8
Fishkill, NY 12524-1870, USA

Austin, Reggie (Athlete, Football Player)
3339 Deerwood Ln
Rex, GA 30273-2475, USA

Austin, Rick (Athlete, Baseball Player)
6510 Claret
Kansas City, MO 64152-6086, USA

Austin, Scott (Race Car Driver)
Meads Creek Rd
Painted Post, NY 14870, USA

Austin, Sherrie (Musician)
Splash Publications
1520 16th Ave S Unit 2
Nashville, TN 37212-2938, USA

Austin, Steve (Stone Cold) (Athlete, Wrestler)
906 Howard St
Marina Del Rey, CA 90292-5519, USA

Austin, Teri (Actor)
4245 Laurelgrove Ave
Studio City, CA 91604-1624, USA

Austin, Thea (Musician)
c/o Stephen Ford *Diva Central Inc*
7510 W Sunset Blvd # 1445
Los Angeles, CA 90046-3408, USA

Austin, Thomas (Athlete, Football Player)
500 Almer Rd Apt 306
Burlingame, CA 94010-3966, USA

Austin, Tracy (Athlete, Tennis Player)
5 Williamsburg Ln
Rolling Hills, CA 90274-4056, USA

Austin, Walt (Race Car Driver)
Pro/Max Performance
5602 S Tacoma Way
Tacoma, WA 98409-4216, USA

Austin-Antelline, Charlotte (Actor)
3053 Valevista Trl
Los Angeles, CA 90068-1724, USA

Austin Jr, M P (Business Person)
BMC Software
2103 Citywest Blvd Ste 2100
Houston, TX 77042-2857, USA

Auston, Jim (Musician)
c/o Staff Member *Curb Records (Nashville)*
48 Music Sq E
Nashville, TN 37203-4639, USA

Austregesilo de Athayde, Belarmino M (Journalist)
Rua Cosme Velho 599
Rio de Janeiro RJ, BRAZIL

Austria, Steve (Congressman, Politician)
439 Cannon Hob
Washington, DC 20515-2801, USA

Auteuil, Daniel (Actor)
c/o Claire Blondel *ArtMedia*
8 rue Danielle Casanova
Paris 75002, FRANCE

Autrey, Billy (Athlete, Football Player)
9810 Knoboak Dr
Houston, TX 77080-6432, USA

Autry, Alan (Actor, Politician)
PO Box 989
Clovis, CA 93613-0989, USA

Autry, Albert (Al) (Athlete, Baseball Player)
3108 Lennox Dr
El Dorado Hills, CA 95762-5662, USA

Auyeung, Jin (Musician)
c/o Staff Member *Virgin Records (NY)*
150 5th Ave Fl 7
New York, NY 10011-4372, USA

Auzenne, Troy (Athlete, Football Player)
118 Oak Rd
Orinda, CA 94563-3348, us

Auzenne, Troy (Athlete, Football Player)
1501 Bluff Ct
Diamond Bar, CA 91765-4301, USA

Avala, Benny (Athlete, Baseball Player)
PO Box 222
Dorado, PR 00646-0222, USA

Avalon (Music Group)
PO Box 150867
Nashville, TN 37215-0867, USA

Avalon, Frankie (Actor, Musician)
4303 Spring Forest Ln
Westlake Village, CA 91362-5605, USA

Avant, Jason (Athlete, Football Player)
c/o Doug Hendrickson *Relativity Sports*
2029 Century Park E Ste 1550
Century City, CA 90067-3000, USA

Avant, Jason (Athlete, Football Player)
12136 S State St
Chicago, IL 60628-6629, USA

Avants, Nick (Athlete, Baseball Player)
3914 Mount Carmel Rd
Bryant, AR 72022-6209, USA

Avari, Erick (Actor)
c/o Michael Greene *Greene & Associates*
1901 Avenue of the Stars Ste 130
Los Angeles, CA 90067-6030, USA

Avary, Roger (Director)
c/o Brian Siberell *Creative Artists Agency (CAA)*
2000 Avenue of the Stars Ste 100
Los Angeles, CA 90067-4705, USA

Avdelsayed, Gabriel (Religious Leader)
Coptic Orthodox Curch
427 W Side Ave
Jersey City, NJ 07304-1403, USA

Avedon, Gregg (Model)
c/o Sid Craig *Craig Management*
2240 Miramonte Cir E Unit C
Palm Springs, CA 92264-5734, USA

Avellan, Elizabeth (Producer)
c/o Staff Member *ICM Partners*
10250 Constellation Blvd Fl 7
Los Angeles, CA 90067-6207, USA

Avellini, Bob (Athlete, Football Player)
1911 Maureen Dr
Hoffman Estates, IL 60192-4814, USA

Aven, Bruce (Athlete, Baseball Player)
4223 SW 141st Ave
Davie, FL 33330-5724, USA

Avenged Sevenfold (Music Group)
c/o Brian Bumbery *BB Gun Press*
9229 W Sunset Blvd Ste 305
Los Angeles, CA 90069-3403, USA

Avent, Anthony (Athlete, Basketball Player)
1166 Croton Rd
Flemington, NJ 08822-5607, USA

Averell, Tom (Athlete, Football Player)
100 Highland Pines Ct Apt 32
Pittsburgh, PA 15237-2038, USA

Averill Jr., Earl (Athlete, Baseball Player)
1806 19th Sr NE
Auburn, WA 98002-3465, USA

Averitt, William (Athlete, Basketball Player)
PO Box 802
Hopkinsville, KY 42241-0802, USA

Averre, Berton (Music Group, Musician)
17510 Posetano Rd
Pacific Palisades, CA 90272-4175, USA

Avery, Eric (Actor, Musician)
c/o Jeff Frasco *Creative Artists Agency (CAA)*
2000 Avenue of the Stars Ste 100
Los Angeles, CA 90067-4705, USA

Avery, John (Athlete, Football Player)
1301 Kensington Pl Apt B
Asheville, NC 28803-2393, us

Avery, John (Athlete, Football Player)
12 Ballantree Dr
Asheville, NC 28803-2018, USA

Avery, Ken (Athlete, Football Player)
625 Indian Ridge Dr
Nashville, TN 37221-4035, USA

Avery, Margaret (Actor)
2807 Pelham Pl
Los Angeles, CA 90068-2328, USA

Avery, Rick (Actor)
4 Blades Inc
11991 Wood Ranch Rd
Granada Hills, CA 91344-2144, USA

Avery, Sean (Athlete, Hockey Player)
c/o Donald Meehan *Newport Sports Management*
201 City Centre Dr
Suite 400
Mississauga, ON L58 2T4, CANADA

Avery, Shondrella (Actor)
c/o Jack Ketsoyan *EMC / Bowery*
8356 Fountain Ave Apt E1
W Hollywood, CA 90069-2968, USA

Avery, Steve (Athlete, Football Player)
2 Gleneagles Ct
Dearborn, MI 48120-1165, USA

Avery, Steve (Athlete, Baseball Player)
2 Gleneagles Ct
Dearborn, MI 48120-1165, USA

Avery, Val (Actor)
84 Grove St Apt 19
New York, NY 10014-3567, USA

Avery, William J (Business Person)
Crown Cork & Seal
770 Township Line Rd Ste 100
Yardley, PA 19067-4232, USA

Avgeropoulos, Marie (Actor)
c/o Darren Boghosian *United Talent Agency (UTA)*
9336 Civic Center Dr
Beverly Hills, CA 90210-3604, USA

Aviance, Kevin (Musician)
Kevin Aviance World
115 E 57th St Fl 11
New York, NY 10022-2120, USA

Avila, Alejandro (Actor)
c/o Staff Member *Televisa*
Blvd Adolfo Lopez Mateos 232
Colonia San Angel INN
DF CP 01060, MEXICO

Avila, Alex (Athlete, Baseball Player)
19164 SW 60th Ct
Southwest Ranches, FL 33332-3343, USA

Avila, Mariana (Actor)
c/o Staff Member *Televisa*
Blvd Adolfo Lopez Mateos 232
Colonia San Angel INN
DF CP 01060, MEXICO

Aviles, Mike (Athlete, Baseball Player)
13 Southgate Rd APT 27
Middletown, NY 10940-2035, USA

Aviles, Ramon (Athlete, Baseball Player)
C19 Calle Juan Morell Campos
Jard De Monaco 1
Manati, PR 00674-6618, USA

Avinger, Clarence (Athlete, Football Player)
2021 Chardonnay Way
Vestavia Hills, AL 35216-1650, USA

Avital, Mili (Actor)
c/o Craig Shapiro *ICM Partners*
10250 Constellation Blvd Fl 7
Los Angeles, CA 90067-6207, USA

Aviva (Actor)
4455 Los Feliz Blvd Apt 604
Los Angeles, CA 90027-2138, USA

Avnet, Jon (Director, Producer)
20911/20929 Colina Dr
Topanga, CA 90290, USA

Avni, Aki (Actor)
c/o Staff Member *Marshak/Zachary Company, The*
8840 Wilshire Blvd Fl 1
Beverly Hills, CA 90211-2606, USA

Avory, Mike (Musician)
Larry Page
29 Rushton Mews
London W11 1RB, UNITED KINGDOM (UK)

Avril, Cliff (Athlete, Football Player)

Awalt, Rob (Athlete, Football Player)
5424 U St
Sacramento, CA 95817-1650, USA

Awasom, Adrian (Athlete, Football Player)
12330 Grove Meadow Dr
Stafford, TX 77477-2204, USA

Awasom, Adrian (Athlete, Football Player)
5011 Highgrove Ct
Stafford, TX 77477, us

Awesome 3 (Music Group, Musician)
c/o Staff Member *Mission Control Artists Agency*
Unit 3 City Business Centre
St Olav's Court, Lower Road
London SE16 2XB, UNITED KINGDOM (UK)

Awkwafina (Actor, Comedian)
c/o Mackenzie Condon Roussos *United Talent Agency (UTA)*
888 7th Ave Fl 7
New York, NY 10106-0700, USA

Awrey, Donald W (Don) (Athlete, Hockey Player)
1015 Alaska Ave
Lehigh Acres, FL 33971-6447, USA

Awtrey, Dennis (Athlete, Basketball Player)
3823e James Rd
Nehalem, OR 97131-9602, USA

Ax, Emmanuel (Music Group, Musician)
c/o Staff Member *Askonas Holt Ltd*
Lincoln House
300 High Holborn
London WC1V 7JH, UK

Axelrod, Jack (Actor)
c/o Jennifer Lee Garland *Circle Talent Associates*
433 N Camden Dr Ste 400
Beverly Hills, CA 90210-4408, USA

Axelsson, P. J. (Athlete, Hockey Player)
50 Fleet St Ste 301
Boston, MA 02109-1129, USA

Axelsson, PJ (Athlete, Hockey Player)
121 Mount Vernon St
Boston, MA 02108-1104, USA

Axford, John (Athlete, Baseball Player)
961rma Crt
Ancaster, ON L9G 1K7, Canada

Axley, Eric (Athlete, Golfer)
1700 Cottage Wood Way
Knoxville, TN 37919-8881, USA

Axum, Donna (Beauty Pageant Winner)
6312 Indian Creek Dr
Ft Worth, TX 76116-1610, USA

Ayala, Alexis (Actor)
c/o Staff Member *Televisa*
Blvd Adolfo Lopez Mateos 232
Colonia San Angel INN
DF CP 01060, MEXICO

Ayala, Bobby (Athlete, Baseball Player)
11011 W Cottonwood Ln
Avondale, AZ 85392-4324, USA

Ayala, Paul (Boxer)
7524 Creek Meadow Dr
Fort Worth, TX 76123-1980, USA

Ayanbadejo, Brendon (Athlete, Football Player)
2800 NE 30th St Apt 2
Fort Lauderdale, FL 33306-1998, USA

Ayanbadejo, Obafemi (Athlete, Football Player)
707 President St APT 438
Baltimore, MD 21202-4477, us

Ayanbadejo, Obafemi (Athlete, Football Player)
707 President St APT 438
Baltimore, MD 21202-4477, USA

Ayanna, Charlotte (Actor)
Industry Entertainment
955 Carrillo Dr Ste 300
Los Angeles, CA 90048-5400, USA

Aybar, Erick (Athlete, Baseball Player)
1636 Orchard Dr Apt C
Placentia, CA 92870-5455, USA

Aybar, Manny (Athlete)
401 E Jefferson St
Phoenix, AZ 85004-2438

Aybar, Manuel (Athlete, Baseball Player)
3020 SW 189th Ter
Miramar, FL 33029-5861, USA

Ayckbourn, Alan (Director, Writer)
M Ramsay
14A Goodwins Ct
Saint Martin's Lane
London WC2N 4LL, UNITED KINGDOM (UK)

Aycock, Alice (Artist)
62 Greene St Apt 4
New York, NY 10012-4346, USA

Aycock, H David (Business Person)
Nucor Corp
2100 Rexford Rd
Charlotte, NC 28211-3589, USA

Aycox, Nicki (Actor)
c/o Jeb Brandon *Corner Booth Entertainment*
11872 La Grange Ave Fl 1
Los Angeles, CA 90025-5283, USA

Aydelette, William (Athlete, Football Player)
115 Woodward Rd
Trussville, AL 35173-1251, USA

Ayer, David (Producer)
Crave Films
3312 W Sunset Blvd
Los Angeles, CA 90026-2118, USA

Ayers, Akeem (Athlete, Football Player)
c/o Tom Condon *Creative Artists Agency (CAA)*
401 Commerce St PH
Nashville, TN 37219-2516, USA

Ayers, Chuck (Cartoonist)
c/o Staff Member *King Features Syndication*
300 W 57th St Fl 15
New York, NY 10019-5238, USA

Ayers, Dick (Cartoonist)
64 Beech St W
White Plains, NY 10604-2230, USA

Ayers, Randy (Athlete, Basketball Player, Coach)
Philadelphia 76ers
1st Union Center 3601 S Broad St
Philadelphia, PA 19148, USA

Ayers, Robert (Athlete, Football Player)
c/o Anthony J. Agnone *Eastern Athletic Services*
11350 McCormick Rd
Suite 800 - Executive Plaza
Hunt Valley, MD 21031-1002, USA

Ayers, Roy E Jr (Music Group, Musician)
Roy Ayers Ubiquity Inc
209 W 97th St Apt 4D
New York, NY 10025-5602, USA

Ayers, Sam (Actor)
c/o Staff Member *Bobby Ball Talent Agency*
4342 Lankershim Blvd
Universal City, CA 91602, USA

Aykroyd, Dan (Actor, Comedian)
PO Box 371
N Hollywood, CA 91603-0371, USA

Aylesworth, Reiko (Actor)
c/o Staff Member *Innovative Artists*
1505 10th St
Santa Monica, CA 90401-2805, USA

Aylward, John (Actor)
c/o Staff Member *Mitchell K Stubbs & Assoc*
8675 Washington Blvd Ste 203
Culver City, CA 90232-7486, USA

Aynsley, Brock (Athlete, Football Player)
3893 Casorso Rd
Kelowna, BC V1W 4R7, Canada

Ayodele, Akin (Athlete, Football Player)
7105 David Ln
Colleyville, TX 76034-6664, USA

Ayotte, Kelly (Senator)

Ayrault, Bob (Athlete, Baseball Player)
2395 S Arlington Ave
Reno, NV 89509-3605, USA

Ayrault, Joe (Athlete, Baseball Player)
PO Box 6756
Attn: Managers Office
Helena, MT 59604-6756, USA

Ayre, Calvin (Business Person)
Bodog
28th Floor, The Enterprise Center
6766 Ayala Avenue
Makati City, Philippines

Ayres, Robert Temple (Artist)
1578 Masters Dr
Banning, CA 92220-6630, USA

Ayres, Rosalind (Actor)
c/o Staff Member *Lou Coulson Agency*
37 Berwick St
1st Floor
London W1F 8RS, UNITED KINGDOM (UK)

Ayres, Travis (Race Car Driver)
Ayres Motorsports
RR 1 Box 188
Granville Summi, PA 16926, USA

Ayres Kalish, Leah (Actor)
15718 Milbank St
Encino, CA 91436-1637, USA

Aytes, Rochelle (Actor)
c/o Ryan Daly *Zero Gravity Management*
11110 Ohio Ave Ste 100
Los Angeles, CA 90025-3329, USA

Ayton, DeAndre (Athlete, Basketball Player)
c/o Nima Namakian *BDA Sports Management*
700 Ygnacio Valley Rd Ste 330
Walnut Creek, CA 94596-3838, USA

Azad, Afshan (Actor)
c/o Staff Member *Gordon and French*
12-13 Poland St
London W1F 8QB, UNITED KINGDOM (UK)

Azalea, Iggy (Musician)
c/o Sarah Stennett *Turn First Artists (UK)*
Grove Studios Adie Road
London W6 0PW, UNITED KINGDOM

Azar, Steve (Music Group)
1116 Harpeth Ridge Rd
Franklin, TN 37069-7054, USA

Azarenka, Victoria (Athlete, Tennis Player)
216 13th St
Manhattan Beach, CA 90266-4709, USA

Azaria, Hank (Actor)
8950 W Olympic Blvd Ste 402
Beverly Hills, CA 90211-3565, USA

Azcue, Jose (Joe) (Athlete, Baseball Player)
7609 W 115th St
Overland Park, KS 66210-2614, USA

Azelby, Joe (Athlete, Football Player)
14 Pierce Ave
Cresskill, NJ 07626-1126, USA

Azinger, Paul (Athlete, Golfer)
8910 21st Ave NW
Bradenton, FL 34209-9414, USA

Azizi, Anthony (Actor)
c/o Karen Embry *Sky Unlimited Arts*
7510 W Sunset Blvd # 554
Los Angeles, CA 90046-3408, USA

Azlynn, Valerie (Actor)
c/o Devon Jackson *Trademark Talent*
5900 Wilshire Blvd Ste 710
Los Angeles, CA 90036-5019, USA

Azoff, Irving (Business Person)
10224 Charing Cross Rd
Los Angeles, CA 90024-1815, USA

Azria, Max (Designer, Fashion Designer)
PO Box 3919
New York, NY 10163-3919, USA

Azul Azul (Music Group)
c/o Staff Member *Sony Music (Miami)*
404 Washington Ave Ste 700
Miami Beach, FL 33139-6615, USA

Azuma, Norio (Artist)
276 Riverside Dr
New York, NY 10025-5204, USA

Azumah, Jerry (Athlete, Football Player)
2337 W Montana St
Chicago, IL 60647-2007, USA

Azzara, Candice (Actor)

Azzaro, Chrissy (Designer, Fashion Designer)
c/o Staff Member *Perception Public Relations LLC*
3940 Laurel Canyon Blvd Ste 169
Studio City, CA 91604-3709, USA

Azzi, Jennifer (Athlete, Basketball Player, Olympic Athlete)
307 Lowell Ave
Mill Valley, CA 94941-3897, USA

B

B, Cardi (Musician)
c/o Kevin Lee *Quality Control Music*
1479 Metropolitan Pkwy SW
Atlanta, GA 30310-4453, USA

B, Jon (Musician, Songwriter, Writer)
Devour Mgmt
6399 Wilshire Blvd Ste 426
Los Angeles, CA 90048-5714, USA

B, Sandy (Musician)
c/o Stephen Ford *Diva Central Inc*
7510 W Sunset Blvd # 1445
Los Angeles, CA 90046-3408, USA

B2K (Music Group)
c/o Staff Member *Pyramid Entertainment Group*
377 Rector Pl Apt 21A
New York, NY 10280-1439, USA

B-52's, The (Music Group)

Baab, Mike (Athlete, Football Player)
1705 Windlea Dr
Euless, TX 76040-4016, USA

Baab, Mike (Athlete, Football Player)
PO Box 1808
Euless, TX 76039-1808, us

Baack, Steve (Athlete, Football Player)
14631 SW Buckhorn Pl
Terrebonne, OR 97760-9301, us

Baack, Steve (Athlete, Football Player)
12322 SW Autumn View St
Portland, OR 97224-2581, USA

Baas, David (Athlete, Football Player)
1701 Homestead Rd
Santa Clara, CA 95050-5257, USA

Baas, David (Athlete, Football Player)
7004 Lacantera Cir
Lakewood Ranch, FL 34202-5116, us

Babando, Pete (Athlete, Hockey Player)
95 Main St
South Porcupine, ON P0N 1H0, Canada

Babashoff, Jack (Athlete, Olympic Athlete, Swimmer)
16260 Mercury Dr
Westminster, CA 92683-7713, USA

Babashoff, Shirley (Athlete, Olympic Athlete, Swimmer)
16260 Mercury Dr
Westminster, CA 92683-7713, USA

Babatunde, Obba (Actor)
c/o Staff Member *Artists & Representatives (Stone Manners Salners)*
6100 Wilshire Blvd Ste 1500
Los Angeles, CA 90048-5110, USA

Babb, Charlie (Athlete, Football Player)
371 Heron Ave
Naples, FL 34108-2115, USA

Babb, Eugene (Gene) (Athlete, Football Player)
5110 W 9th Ave
Stillwater, OK 74074-1465, USA

Babbit, Jamie (Director, Producer, Writer)
c/o Staff Member *Innovative Artists*
1505 10th St
Santa Monica, CA 90401-2805, USA

Babbitt, Bruce E (Politician)
5169 Watson St NW
Washington, DC 20016-5330, USA

Babbs, Durrell (Tank) (Musician)
c/o Amy Malone *GIC Public Relations*
Prefers to be contacted via email or telephone
Los Angeles, CA 90069, USA

Babb-Sprague, Kristen (Swimmer)
4677 Pine Valley Cir
Stockton, CA 95219-1881, USA

Babcock, Barbara (Actor)
PO Box 222271
Carmel, CA 93922-2271, USA

Babcock, Bob (Athlete, Baseball Player)
7123 Fairway Dr
Butler, PA 16001-8597, USA

Babcock, Mike (Athlete, Coach, Hockey Player)
c/o Staff Member *Detroit Red Wings*
2645 Woodward Ave
Joe Luis Arena
Detroit, MI 48201-3028, USA

Babcock, Mike (Athlete, Hockey Player)
Detroit Red Wings
2645 Woodward Ave
Detroit, MI 48201-3028, USA

Babcock, Todd (Actor)
c/o Staff Member *The Gage Group*
5757 Wilshire Blvd Ste 659
Los Angeles, CA 90036-3682, USA

Babe, Warren (Athlete, Hockey Player)
15 Rocky Mtn Blvd W
Lethbridge, AB T1K 6V7, Canada

Baber, Billy (Athlete, Football Player)
6087 York Rd
Crozet, VA 22932-9448, USA

Babers, Roderick (Athlete, Football Player)
11838 Murr Way
Houston, TX 77048-2528, USA

Babic, Milos (Athlete, Basketball Player)
1500 Doris Dr
Cookeville, TN 38501-2026, USA

Babich, Bob (Athlete, Football Player)
4994 Mount Ashmun Dr
San Diego, CA 92111-3930, USA

Babilonia, Tai (Athlete, Figure Skater, Olympic Athlete)
13889 Valley Vista Blvd
Sherman Oaks, CA 91423-4662, USA

Babin, Jason (Athlete, Football Player)
2735 Peninsulas Dr
Missouri City, TX 77459-4317, USA

Babin, Mitch (Athlete, Hockey Player)
519 Pleasant St Apt 306
Leominster, MA 01453-6219, USA

Babineaux, Jonathan (Athlete, Football Player)
5659 Legends Club Cir
Braselton, GA 30517-6029, USA

Babineaux, Jordan (Athlete, Football Player)
720 N 10th St # 227
Renton, WA 98057-5525, USA

Babinecz, John (Athlete, Football Player)
810 Trout Run Dr
Malvern, PA 19355-3148, USA

Babitt, Shooty (Athlete, Baseball Player)
4912 Plaza Way
Richmond, CA 94804-4346, USA

Baby, John (Athlete, Hockey Player)
252 Brebeuf Ave
Sudbury, ON P3C 5H1, Canada

Baby, Peggy (Actor)
2219 Canyon Brook Ln
Newman, CA 95360-2407, USA

Babych, Dave (Athlete, Hockey Player)
1315 Wellington Cres
Winnipeg, MB R3N 0A9, Canada

Babych, Wayne (Athlete, Hockey Player)
1315 Wellington Cres
Winnipeg, MB R3N 0A9, Canada

Baca, Jason Aaron (Race Car Driver)
20770 Wildwood Way Apt 4
Saratoga, CA 95070-5898, USA

Baca, Jimmy Santiago (Writer)
c/o Staff Member *Blue Flower Arts*
PO Box 1361
Millbrook, NY 12545-1361, USA

Baca, Joe (Congressman, Politician)
2366 Rayburn Hob
Washington, DC 20515-3509, USA

Bacashihua, Jason (Athlete, Hockey Player)
23411 Annapolis St
Dearborn Heights, MI 48125-2200, USA

Baccaglio, Marty (Athlete, Football Player)
15030 Montebello Rd
Cupertino, CA 95014-5470, USA

Baccarin, Morena (Actor)
c/o Sarah Jackson *Seven Summits Pictures & Management*
8906 W Olympic Blvd
Beverly Hills, CA 90211-3550, USA

Bach, Barbara (Actor)
918 N Hillcrest Rd
Beverly Hills, CA 90210-2611, USA

Bach, Catherine (Actor)
c/o Steve Rohr *Lexicon Public Relations*
1049 Havenhurst Dr # 365
West Hollywood, CA 90046-6002, USA

Bach, David (Writer)
222 Broadway Fl 19
New York, NY 10038-2550, USA

Bach, Emmanuelle (Actor)
Artmedia
20 Ave Rapp
Paris 75007, FRANCE

Bach, Jillian (Actor)
c/o Staff Member *Metropolitan (MTA)*
4526 Wilshire Blvd
Los Angeles, CA 90010-3801, USA

Bach, John (Athlete, Basketball Player)
182 W Lake St Apt 21E6
Chicago, IL 60601-1049, USA

Bach, Richard (Writer)
Dell Publishing
1540 Broadway
New York, NY 10036-4039, USA

Bach, Sebastian (Actor, Music Group)
c/o David Gibson *New Ocean Media*
270 Doug Baker Blvd Ste 700
Birmingham, AL 35242-8300, USA

Bachar, Carmit (Musician)
c/o Cheryl McLean *Creative Public Relations*
3385 Oak Glen Dr
Los Angeles, CA 90068-1311, USA

Bacharach, Burt (Musician)
Tony Cee Associates
PO Box 410
Utica, NY 13503-0410, USA

Bachardy, Don (Writer)
145 Adelaide Dr
Santa Monica, CA 90402-1223, USA

Bachchan, Aisawarya Rai (Actor)
c/o Rick Genow *Stone, Meyer, Genow, Smelkinson and Binder*
9665 Wilshire Blvd Ste 500
Beverly Hills, CA 90212-2312, USA

Bachchan, Amitabh (Actor, Musician)
c/o Staff Member *AB Corp Ltd.*
16 New India Co-operative Housing Society Ltd.
13 North South Road
Juhu, Mumbai 400 049, India

Bachelart, Eric (Race Car Driver)
7326 W 88th St
Indianapolis, IN 46278-1106, USA

Bachelor, Andrew (Actor, Internet Star, Musician)
c/o Allan Haldeman *United Talent Agency (UTA)*
9336 Civic Center Dr
Beverly Hills, CA 90210-3604, USA

Bach Hasselhoff, Pamela (Actor)
c/o Nelson Parks *ESI Network*
5670 Wilshire Blvd Ste 1800
Los Angeles, CA 90036-5653, USA

Bachleda-Curus, Alicja (Actor)
c/o Laura Berwick *Berwick & Kovacik*
6230 Wilshire Blvd
Los Angeles, CA 90048-5126, USA

Bachman, Jay (Athlete, Football Player)
100 Carruthers Pond Dr
Cincinnati, OH 45246-3854, USA

Bachman, Michelle (Congressman, Politician)
103 Cannon Hob
Washington, DC 20515-2303, USA

Bachman, Randy (Music Group, Songwriter, Writer)
Entertainment Services
6400 Pleasant Park Dr
Chanhassen, MN 55317-8804, USA

Bachman, Tal (Music Group, Musician, Songwriter, Writer)
Q Prime
729 7th Ave Ste 1600
New York, NY 10019-6880, USA

Bachman, Ted (Athlete, Football Player)
2890 Huntington Blvd Apt 110
Fresno, CA 93721-2346, USA

Bachmann, Maria (Music Group, Musician)
c/o Staff Member *Above the Line*
Goethestr 17
Munich D-80336, GERMANY

Bachmann, Michele (Congressman, Politician)
412 Cannon Hob
Washington, DC 20515-2509, USA

Bachus, Spencer (Congressman, Politician)
2246 Rayburn Hob
Washington, DC 20515-3224, USA

Bacic, Steve (Actor, Producer)
c/o Staff Member *Pipeline Productions*
25715 Haskell St
Taylor, MI 48180-2076, USA

Backe, Brandon (Athlete, Baseball Player)
103 E Viejo Dr
Friendswood, TX 77546-5550, USA

Backer, Brian (Actor)
400 E 56th St Apt 17E
New York, NY 10022-4339, USA

Backes, David (Athlete, Hockey Player)
77 Monarch Way
Saint Paul, MN 55127-6163, USA

Backhaus, Robin (Athlete, Olympic Athlete, Swimmer)
PO Box 169
Captain Cook, HI 96704-0169, USA

Backis, Audrys Juozas Cardinal (Religious Leader)
Sventaragio 4
Vilnius, LITHUANIA

Backley, Stephen (Steve) (Athlete, Track Athlete)
Cambridge Harriers
56A-60 Glenhurst Ave
Bexley, Kent DA5 3QN, UNITED KINGDOM (UK)

Backlund, Bob (Athlete, Wrestler)
PO Box 973
Glastonbury, CT 06033-0973

Backman, Mike (Athlete, Hockey Player)
74 Dandy Dr
Cos Cob, CT 06807-2208, USA

Backman, Wally (Athlete, Baseball Player)
PO Box 598
Attn: Managers Office
Binghamton, NY 13902-0598, USA

Backman, Walter W (Wally) (Athlete, Baseball Player)
241 SE Mercury Ln
Prineville, OR 97754-2803, USA

Backstreet Boys (Music Group)
c/o John Marx *WME/IMG*
9601 Wilshire Blvd
Beverly Hills, CA 90210-5213, USA

Backstrom, Niklas (Athlete, Hockey Player)
2409 W 21st St
Minneapolis, MN 55405-2311, USA

Backstrom, Ralph (Athlete, Hockey Player)
220 Habitat Cir
Windsor, CO 80550-6196, USA

Backus, Billy (Boxer)
308 N Main St
Canastota, NY 13032-1070, USA

Backus, Gus (Musician)
Lustig Talent
PO Box 770850
Orlando, FL 32877-0850, USA

Backus, Jeff (Athlete, Football Player)
3627 Meadow View Dr
Dexter, MI 48130-9207, USA

Backus, Sharon (Coach)
University of California
Athletic Dept
Los Angeles, CA 90024, USA

Bacon, Henry (Athlete, Basketball Player)
10103 Grand Ave Apt 218
Louisville, KY 40299-3145, USA

Bacon, Kelvin (Actor)
PO Box 668
Sharon, CT 06069-0668, USA

Bacon, Kevin (Actor)
700 N San Vicente Blvd Ste G910
West Hollywood, CA 90069-5061, USA

Bacon, Michael (Actor)
12 Garnet Rd
Roxbury, CT 06783-2033, USA

Bacon, Sosie (Actor)
c/o Jill Littman *Impression Entertainment*
9229 W Sunset Blvd Ste 700
Los Angeles, CA 90069-3407, USA

Bacon, Waine (Athlete, Football Player)
2900 McFarland Blvd E
Apt 516
Tuscaloosa, AL 35405, USA

Bacon Brothers, The (Music Group)
c/o Staff Member *Paradigm (Monterey)*
404 W Franklin St
Monterey, CA 93940-2303, USA

Bacsik, Mike (Athlete, Baseball Player)
4014 Falcon Lake Dr
Arlington, TX 76016-4126, USA

Bacsik, Mike (Athlete, Baseball Player)
1126 N Clinton Ave
Dallas, TX 75208-3613, USA

Badalucco, Michael (Actor)
516 Highland Ave # 1A
Manhattan Beach, CA 90266-5747, USA

Badar, Rich (Athlete, Football Player)
5877 Riceland Dr
Newburgh, IN 47630-1892, USA

Bad Brains (Music Group)
c/o Jeremy Holgersen *UTA/The Agency Group*
888 7th Ave Fl 7
New York, NY 10106-0700, USA

Bad Company (Music Group)

Baddeley, Aaron (Athlete, Golfer)
c/o Jens Beck *Pro-Sport Management*
6157 E Indian School Rd
Scottsdale, AZ 85251-5441, USA

Baddiel, David (Actor, Writer)
c/o Staff Member *Lip Service Casting Ltd*
60-66 Wardour St
London W1F 0TA, UK

Badel, Sarah (Actor)
c/o Staff Member *The Rights House (UK)*
Drury House
34-43 Russell St
London WC2B 5HA, UNITED KINGDOM

Badelt, Klaus (Musician)
c/o John Tempereau *Soundtrack Music Assoc*
1460 4th St Ste 308
Santa Monica, CA 90401-3483, USA

Badenhop, Burke (Athlete, Baseball Player)
402 Berkshire Dr
Perrysburg, OH 43551-1281, USA

Bader, Beth (Athlete, Golfer)
713 S 7th St
Eldridge, IA 52748-1537, USA

Bader, Diedrich (Actor)
131 N June St
Los Angeles, CA 90004-1039, USA

Baderinwa, Sade (Correspondent)
WABC-TV
7 Lincoln Sq
New York, NY 10023-7219, USA

Badger, Brad (Athlete, Football Player)
2552 Milleford Ct
Pleasanton, CA 94588, USA

Badgley, Mark (Fashion Designer)
c/o Staff Member *Badgley Mischka*
133 W 52nd St # 5
New York, NY 10019-6003, USA

Badgley, Penn (Actor)
c/o Doug Wald *Anonymous Content*
3532 Hayden Ave
Culver City, CA 90232-2413, USA

Badham, John (Director)
Badham Company
344 Clerendon Road
Beverly Hills, CA 90210, USA

Badham, Mary (Actor)
3720 Whitehall Rd
Sandy Hook, VA 23153-2204, USA

Badie, Mina (Actor)
c/o Staff Member *Rugolo Entertainment*
195 S Beverly Dr Ste 400
Beverly Hills, CA 90212-3044, USA

Badler, Jane (Actor)
PO Box 43
S Yarra, VIC 03141, AUSTRALIA

Badly Drawn Boy (Music Group)
c/o Staff Member *Paradigm (Monterey)*
404 W Franklin St
Monterey, CA 93940-2303, USA

Badnarik, Michael (Politician)
Badnarik Campaign Headquarters
6633 E Highway 290
Austin, TX 78723-1172, USA

Badu, Erykah (Musician, Songwriter)
c/o Chris Chambers *The Chamber Group*
75 Broad St Rm 708
New York, NY 10004-3244, USA

Bae, Doona (Actor)
c/o David Wirtschafter *WME/IMG*
9601 Wilshire Blvd
Beverly Hills, CA 90210-5213, USA

Baechtold, James (Jim) (Athlete, Basketball Player)
225 W Irvine St
Richmond, KY 40475-2702, USA

Baeling, Becky (Musician)
c/o Staff Member *Diva Central Inc*
7510 W Sunset Blvd # 1445
Los Angeles, CA 90046-3408, USA

Baena, Marisa (Athlete, Golfer)
4036 Lantana Ln
Plano, TX 75093-7097, USA

Baer, Neal (Actor, Producer)
c/o Peter Benedek *United Talent Agency (UTA)*
9336 Civic Center Dr
Beverly Hills, CA 90210-3604, USA

Baerga, Carlos (Athlete, Baseball Player)
PO Box 1667
Bayamon, PR 00960-1667, USA

Baer Jr, Max (Actor, Director, Producer)
3456 Pueblo Way
Las Vegas, NV 89169-3337, USA

Baerwald, David (Musician)

Baetens, Veerle (Actor)
c/o Carter Cohn *ICM Partners*
10250 Constellation Blvd Fl 7
Los Angeles, CA 90067-6207, USA

Baez, Danys (Athlete, Baseball Player)
6190 SW 114th St
Miami, FL 33156-4953, USA

Baez, Eddie (DJ)
c/o Staff Member *Diva Central Inc*
7510 W Sunset Blvd # 1445
Los Angeles, CA 90046-3408, USA

Baez, Joan (Musician, Songwriter)
510 Whiskey Hill Rd
Woodside, CA 94062-1233, USA

Baez, Jose (Athlete, Baseball Player)
1028 E Jersey St Apt 2
Elizabeth, NJ 07201-2532, USA

Baez, Kevin (Athlete, Baseball Player)
72 Hollywood Dr
Oakdale, NY 11769-1941, USA

Baeza, Braulio (Horse Racer)
1588 Rosalind Ave
Elmont, NY 11003-1821, USA

Baeza, Paloma (Actor)
PFD
Drury House
34-43 Russell St
London WC2B 5HA, USA

Bafaro, Michael (Director, Writer)
c/o Staff Member *Lenhoff & Lenhoff*
324 S Beverly Dr
Beverly Hills, CA 90212-4801

Baffert, Bob (Horse Racer)
c/o Terry Ahern *Global PR*
5158 Clareton Dr Unit 2744
Agoura, CA 91376-7137, USA

Bagabandi, Ntsaagiyn (President)
President's Office
Great Hural
Ulan Bator, MONGOLIA

Bagach, Irene (Actor, Model)
Models One
12 Macklin St
Covent Garden
London WC2B 5SZ, UNITED KINGDOM

Bagans, Zak (Actor)
c/o Alec Shankman *Abrams Artists Agency*
750 N San Vicente Blvd
E Tower Fl 11
Los Angeles, CA 90069-5788, USA

Bagdasarian Jr, Ross (Actor, Producer)
c/o Staff Member *Bagdasarian Productions*
1192 E Mountain Dr
Montecito, CA 93108-1119

Bagge, Peter (Artist)
c/o Staff Member *Fantagraphics Books*
7563 Lake City Way NE
Seattle, WA 98115-4218, USA

Baggetta, Vincent (Actor)
3928 Madelia Ave
Sherman Oaks, CA 91403-4624, USA

Baggio, Roberto (Soccer Player)
Bologna FC
Via Casteldebole 10
Bologna 40132, ITALY

Bagian, James P (Astronaut)
21537 Holmbury Rd
Northville, MI 48167-1021, USA

Bagley, John (Athlete, Basketball Player)
1160 Stratford Ave Apt A2
Stratford, CT 06615-6317, USA

Bagley, Tom (Race Car Driver)
109 Walnut Dr
Shorewood, IL 60404-5302, USA

Bagley III, Marvin (Athlete, Basketball Player)
c/o Jeff Schwartz *Excel Sports Management*
1700 Broadway Fl 29
New York, NY 10019-6559, USA

Baglietto, Tara (Actor)
c/o Staff Member *Innovative Artists*
235 Park Ave S Fl 7
New York, NY 10003-1405, USA

Bagwell, Jeffrey R (Jeff) (Athlete, Baseball Player)
405 Timberwilde Ln
Houston, TX 77024-6927, USA

Baham, Curtis (Athlete, Football Player)
5936 Oxford Pl
New Orleans, LA 70131-3908, USA

Bahns, Maxine (Actor)
c/o Steven Jensen *Independent Group, The*
6363 Wilshire Blvd Ste 115
Los Angeles, CA 90048-5734, USA

Bahnsen, Ken (Athlete, Football Player)
671 N Masch Branch Rd
Denton, TX 76207-3633, USA

Bahnsen, Stan (Athlete, Baseball Player)
3500 Blue Lake Dr Apt 402
Pompano Beach, FL 33064-2026, USA

Bahr, Chris (Athlete, Football Player)
122 Kaywood Dr
Boalsburg, PA 16827-1686, USA

Bahr, Matthew D (Matt) (Athlete, Football Player)
53 Parkridge Ln
Pittsburgh, PA 15228-1105, USA

Bahrke, Shannon (Athlete, Olympic Athlete, Skier)
3556 S Crestwood Dr
Salt Lake City, UT 84109-3206, USA

Bai, Yang (Actor)
978 Huashan Road
Shanghai 200050, CHINA

Bailes, Margaret (Athlete, Olympic Athlete, Track Athlete)
11136 Vista Sorrento Pkwy Apt 203
San Diego, CA 92130-7606, USA

Bailes, Scott (Athlete, Baseball Player)
5895 S Teters Ct
Springfield, MO 65804-7720, USA

Bailey, Allen (Athlete, Football Player)
c/o Drew Rosenhaus *Rosenhaus Sports Representation*
3921 Alton Rd # 440
Miami Beach, FL 33140-3852, USA

Bailey, Amy (Actor)
c/o Matthew Lesher *Insight*
5358 Melrose Ave # 200W
Los Angeles, CA 90038-5117, USA

Bailey, Ben (Actor, Television Host)
c/o Amy Brownstein *PRStudio USA*
1875 Century Park E Ste 930
Los Angeles, CA 90067-2540, USA

Bailey, Buddy (Athlete, Baseball Player)

Bailey, Champ (Athlete, Football Player)
c/o Staff Member *Drew Eckl & Farnham*
303 Peachtree St NE Ste 3500
Atlanta, GA 30308-3263, USA

Bailey, Claron (Athlete, Football Player)
9624 E Navarro Ave
Mesa, AZ 85209-2491, USA

Bailey, Cory (Athlete, Baseball Player)
4422 Creek Nation Blacktop
Mulkeytown, IL 62865-3106, USA

Bailey, Cynthia (Model, Reality Star)
c/o Marcus Jackson *Caliber Models & Talent*
PO Box 79065
Atlanta, GA 30357-7065, USA

Bailey, Damon (Athlete, Basketball Player)
723 Diamond Rd
Heltonville, IN 47436-8559, USA

Bailey, Dan (Athlete, Football Player)
c/o Jordan Woy *Willis & Woy Management*
4890 Alpha Rd Ste 200
Dallas, TX 75244-4639, USA

Bailey, David (Athlete, Football Player)
1916 NE 29th St
Oklahoma City, OK 73111-3346, USA

Bailey, Don (Athlete, Football Player)
14831 NW 7th Ave
Miami, FL 33168-3105, USA

Bailey, Edwin (Athlete, Football Player)
3677 Cypress Point Dr
Augusta, GA 30907-9021, USA

Bailey, Eion (Actor)
c/o Brianna Smith *ID Public Relations*
7060 Hollywood Blvd Fl 8th
Los Angeles, CA 90028-6021, USA

Bailey, Elmer (Athlete, Football Player)
2459 Fillmore St
Hollywood, FL 33020-4305, USA

Bailey, Fenton (Producer)
c/o Staff Member *World of Wonder*
6650 Hollywood Blvd
Los Angeles, CA 90028-6219, USA

Bailey, F Lee (Attorney)
6231 Tidewater Island Cir
Fort Myers, FL 33908-4686, USA

Bailey, GW (Actor)
22415 La Rochelle Dr
Santa Clarita, CA 91350-1308, USA

Bailey, Harold (Athlete, Football Player)
22502 Prince George St
Katy, TX 77449-2723, USA

Bailey, HB (Race Car Driver)
PO Box 450288
Houston, TX 77245-0288, USA

Bailey, Homer (Athlete, Baseball Player)
4327 O Quinn Branch Rd # 0
La Grange, TX 78945-5695, USA

Bailey, Howard (Athlete, Baseball Player)
11674 156th Ave
West Olive, MI 49460-9388, USA

Bailey, Jeff (Athlete, Baseball Player)
709 N 18th Ave
Kelso, WA 98626-5036, USA

Bailey, Jerry (Athlete, Horse Racer)
105 Nurmi Dr
Ft Lauderdale, FL 33301-1404, USA

Bailey, Jim (Athlete, Baseball Player)
250 Cade Rd
Ten Mile, TN 37880-2149, USA

Bailey, Jim (Athlete, Football Player)
5219 Stone Creek Ct
Lawrence, KS 66049-4792, USA

Bailey, Karsten (Athlete, Football Player)
16 Salbide Ave
Newnan, GA 30263-2501, USA

Bailey, Mark (Athlete, Baseball Player)
32703 Waltham Xing
Fulshear, TX 77441-4203, USA

Bailey, Mark (Athlete, Baseball Player)
PO Box 694
Attn: Coaching Staff
Troy, NY 12181-0694, USA

Bailey, Mark (Athlete, Football Player)
3229 Corniche Ln
Roseville, CA 95661-3970, USA

Bailey, Otha (Athlete, Baseball Player)
937 6th Pl SW
Birmingham, AL 35211-1743, USA

Bailey, Palmer (Astronaut)
64710 Knob Hill Rd
Anchor Point, AK 99556-9160, USA

Bailey, Paul (Writer)
79 Davisville Road
London W12 9SH, UNITED KINGDOM (UK)

Bailey, Philip (Musician)
c/o Staff Member *Richard De La Font Agency*
3808 W South Park Blvd
Broken Arrow, OK 74011-1261, USA

Bailey, Preston (Actor)
c/o Staff Member *Elements Entertainment*
312 W 5th St Apt 815
Los Angeles, CA 90013-1750, USA

Bailey, Razzy (Musician, Songwriter, Writer)
Doc Sedelmeier
PO Box 146
Madison, SD 57042-0146, USA

Bailey, Robert M (Athlete, Football Player)
15325 SW 99th Ave
Miami, FL 33157-1708, USA

Bailey, Roger (Athlete, Baseball Player)
6186 Massive Peak Cir
Castle Rock, CO 80108-9484, USA

Bailey, Scott (Actor)
c/o Staff Member *Artists & Representatives (Stone Manners Salners)*
6100 Wilshire Blvd Ste 1500
Los Angeles, CA 90048-5110, USA

Bailey, Sean (Producer)
c/o Patrick Whitesell *WME/IMG*
9601 Wilshire Blvd
Beverly Hills, CA 90210-5213, USA

Bailey, Stacey (Athlete, Football Player)
3400 Lakewind Way
Alpharetta, GA 30005-6943, USA

Bailey, Steve (Athlete, Baseball Player)
4600 Queen Anne Ave
Lorain, OH 44052-5648, USA

Bailey, Steven W (Reality Star)
c/o Scott Fedro *Lone Star Entertainment*
139 S Beverly Dr Ste 314
Beverly Hills, CA 90212-3040, USA

Bailey, Teddy (Athlete, Football Player)
7825 Elbrook Ave
Cincinnati, OH 45237-2207, USA

Bailey, Thurl (Athlete, Basketball Player)
10265 N 6960 W
Highland, UT 84003-9337, USA

Bailey, Victor (Athlete, Football Player)
1405 Ogelthorpe Ave
Urbana, IL 61802-4749, USA

Bailey II, Irving W (Business Person)
Providian Corp
400 W Market St
Louisville, KY 40202-3346, USA

Bailey Rae, Corinne (Musician)
Running Media Group
14 Victoria Road
Douglas, Isle of Man IM2 4ER, BRITISH ISLES

Baillargeon, Joel (Athlete, Hockey Player)
165B Rue du Coutelier
Saint-Augustin-De-Desmaures, QC G3A 2J7, Canada

Bailon, Adrienne (Actor, Musician)
c/o Staff Member *FYI Public Relations*
174 5th Ave Ste 404
New York, NY 10010-5964, USA

Bailor, Bob (Athlete, Baseball Player)
1950 Swan Ln
Palm Harbor, FL 34683-6275, USA

Baily, Kirk (Actor)
c/o Staff Member *Independent Artists*
11500 W Olympic Blvd Ste 550
Los Angeles, CA 90064-1528, USA

Bain, Barbara (Actor)
Actors Studio
8341 De Longpre Ave
W Hollywood, CA 90069-2601, USA

Bain, William E (Bill) (Athlete, Football Player)
27661 Paseo Barona
San Juan Capistrano, CA 92675-2851, USA

Bainbridge, Merril (Musician, Songwriter, Writer)
001 Productions
PO Box 1760
Collingswood, VIC 03068, AUSTRALIA

Baines, Harold (Athlete, Baseball Player)
40 Grove St Ste 430
Wellesley, MA 02482-7774, USA

Baio, Scott (Actor)
20524 Chatsboro Dr
Woodland Hills, CA 91364-5652, USA

Baiocchi, Hugh (Athlete, Golfer)
3656 Half Moon Dr
Orlando, FL 32812-3816, USA

Bair, Doug (Athlete, Baseball Player)
11545 Kemper Woods Dr
Cincinnati, OH 45249-1753, USA

Baird, Allard (Commentator)
1425 Brickell Ave # 3D
Miami, FL 33131-3400, USA

Baird, Bill (Athlete, Football Player)
6050 E Heaton Ave
Fresno, CA 93727-5606, USA

Baird, Briny (Athlete, Golfer)
3340 SW Rivers End Way
Palm City, FL 34990-7603, USA

Baird, Butch (Athlete, Golfer)
PO Box 2663
Carefree, AZ 85377-2663, USA

Baird, Diora (Actor)
c/o Jessica Katz *Katz Public Relations*
14527 Dickens St
Sherman Oaks, CA 91403-3756, USA

Baird, James M (Religious Leader)
Presbyterian Church
PO Box 1428
Decatur, GA 30031-1428, USA

baird, jenni (Actor)
c/o Michael P Levine *Levine Management*
8549 Wilshire Blvd # 212
Beverly Hills, CA 90211-3104, USA

Baird, Ken (Athlete, Hockey Player)
Lot 4
Berry Bay
Snow Lake, MB R0B 1M0, Canada

Baird, Stuart (Director)
c/o Staff Member *Mirisch Agency*
8840 Wilshire Blvd Ste 100
Beverly Hills, CA 90211-2606, USA

Bairstow, Scott H (Actor)

Baisden, Michael (Producer, Radio Personality, Writer)
c/o Pamela Yvette Exum *PYE Enterprises Agency*
13901 Midway Rd Ste 102
Dallas, TX 75244-4388, USA

Baisley, Jeff (Athlete, Baseball Player)
16222 Pebblebrook Dr
Tampa, FL 33624-1072, USA

Baitz, Jon Robin (Producer)
c/o Simon Halls *Slate PR*
901 N Highland Ave
W Hollywood, CA 90038-2412, USA

Baiul, Oksana (Figure Skater)
Bob Young
PO Box 988
Niantic, CT 06357-0988, USA

Baiyewe, Tunde (Musician)
c/o Staff Member *Kitchenware Management*
The Stables
St. Thomas Street
Newcastle Upon Tyne NE1 4LE, UK

Bajardi, Lane (Television Host)
c/o Staff Member *Bloomberg Television*
731 Lexington Ave
New York, NY 10022-1331, USA

Bajema, Billy (Athlete, Football Player)
2605 SW 120th St
Oklahoma City, OK 73170-4735, USA

Bajenaru, Jeff (Athlete, Baseball Player)
2209 Ravinia Dr
Arlington, TX 76012-2934, USA

Bakalyan, Richard (Actor)
1070 S Bedford St
Los Angeles, CA 90035-2102, USA

Bakanic, Laddie (Athlete, Gymnast, Olympic Athlete)
7 David Ter
White Plains, NY 10603-3516, USA

Bakay, Nick (Actor)
c/o Lindsay Howard *Agency for the Performing Arts (APA)*
405 S Beverly Dr Ste 500
Beverly Hills, CA 90212-4425, USA

Baker, Al (Athlete, Football Player)
2784 Trinity Ct
Avon, OH 44011-1951, USA

Baker, Anita (Actor, Musician, Songwriter)
c/o Staff Member *Blue Note Label Group*
150 5th Ave
New York, NY 10011-4311, USA

Baker, Art (Athlete, Football Player)
24 Quail Hollow Rd # B
Mashpee, MA 02649-2824, us

Baker, Art (Athlete, Football Player)
247 Main St
Buzzards Bay, MA 02532-3232, USA

Baker, Bill (Athlete, Hockey Player, Olympic Athlete)
5638 Ojibwa Rd
Brainerd, MN 56401-7017, USA

Baker, Blanche (Actor)
2501 Palisade Ave Apt B2
Bronx, NY 10463-6104, USA

Baker, Brad (Race Car Driver)
565 Brick Church Park Dr
Nashville, TN 37207-3219, USA

Baker, Brenda (Actor)
Agency for Performing Arts
9200 W Sunset Blvd Ste 900
Los Angeles, CA 90069-3604, USA

Baker, Carroll (Actor)
Abrams Artists
9200 W Sunset Blvd Ste 1125
Los Angeles, CA 90069-3610, USA

Baker, Charles (Actor)
c/o Anna Kreynes *Advantage PR*
3900 W Alameda Ave Ste 1200
Burbank, CA 91505-4317, USA

Baker, Charles (Charlie) (Athlete, Football Player)
PO Box 112593
Carrollton, TX 75011-2593, USA

Baker, Chris (Athlete, Football Player)
c/o Neil Schwartz *Schwartz & Feinsod*
4 Hillandale Rd
Rye Brook, NY 10573-1705, USA

Baker, Chuck (Athlete, Baseball Player)
3035 Mescalero Dr
Lake Havasu City, AZ 86404-9605, USA

Baker, Colin (Actor)
Evans & Reiss
100 Fawe Park Road
London SW15 2EA, UNITED KINGDOM (UK)

Baker, Danny (Radio Personality)
c/o Staff Member *Noel Gay Artists*
2 Stephen St
London W1T 1AN, UNITED KINGDOM

Baker, Dave (Athlete, Baseball Player)
1207 N 6th St Apt 7
Indianola, IA 50125-4747, USA

Baker, Diane (Actor)
2733 Outpost Dr
Los Angeles, CA 90068-2061, USA

Baker, Doug (Athlete, Baseball Player)
116 Woodthrush Ln
Fallbrook, CA 92028-4149, USA

Baker, Dusty (Athlete, Baseball Player, Coach)
9090 Stockhorse Ln
Granite Bay, CA 95746-7165, USA

Baker, Dylan (Actor)
484 W 43rd St Apt 31H
New York, NY 10036-6333, USA

Baker, Edward (Athlete, Football Player)
74 Page Hill Rd
Far Hills, NJ 07931-2400, USA

Baker, Ellen Dr (Astronaut)
2207 Garden Stream Ct
Houston, TX 77062-3650, USA

Baker, Ellen Shulman (Astronaut)
2207 Garden Stream Ct
Houston, TX 77062-3650, USA

Baker, Ginger (Musician)
Twist Mgmt
4230 Del Rey Ave # 621
Marina Del Rey, CA 90292-5606, USA

Baker, Graham (Director)
10 Buckingham St
London WC2, UNITED KINGDOM (UK)

Baker, Jack (Athlete, Baseball Player)
5513 Hunters Hill Rd
Irondale, AL 35210-3011, USA

Baker, James A (Bubba) (Athlete, Football Player)
17408 Gulf Blvd Apt 953
Redington Shores, FL 33708-1314, USA

Baker, Jamie (Athlete, Hockey Player)
San Jose Sharks
525 W Santa Clara St
San Jose, CA 95113-1500

Baker, Jamie (Athlete, Hockey Player)
2300 Samaritan Pl APT 1
San Jose, CA 95124-3902, USA

Baker, Jason (Athlete, Football Player)
135 Union Chapel Dr
Mooresville, NC 28117-6700, USA

Baker, Jeff Baker (Athlete, Baseball Player)
4747 Timber Ridge Dr
Dumfries, VA 22025-1081, USA

Baker, Joe Don (Actor)
c/o Pippa Markham *Markham & Froggatt*
4 Windmill St
London W1T 1HZ, UNITED KINGDOM

Baker, John (Athlete, Baseball Player)
623 Alamatos Dr
Danville, CA 94526-2710, USA

Baker, Johnny (Athlete, Football Player)
466 Jan Kelly Ln
Houston, TX 77024-6511, us

Baker, John W (Athlete, Football Player)
72 Oak Village Blvd S
Homosassa, FL 34446-5945, USA

Baker, Kathy (Actor)
c/o Stephen Huvane *Slate PR*
901 N Highland Ave
W Hollywood, CA 90038-2412, USA

Baker, Keith (Athlete, Football Player)
3203 S Marsalis Ave
Dallas, TX 75216-5203, USA

Baker, Ken (Journalist)
1042 Augustana Dr
Naperville, IL 60565-3497, USA

Baker, Kitana (Actor)
PO Box 452
231 E Alessandro Blvd #A
Riverside, CA 92502-0452, USA

Baker, Laurie (Athlete, Hockey Player, Olympic Athlete)
85 Monsen Rd
Concord, MA 01742-1924, USA

Baker, Leslie David (Actor)
c/o David Rose *Innovative Artists*
1505 10th St
Santa Monica, CA 90401-2805, USA

Baker, Lewis (Musician)
Joe Terry Mgmt
PO Box 1017
Turnersville, NJ 08012-0837, USA

Baker, Loris (Athlete, Football Player)
1009 Brentwood Pl
Fircrest, WA 98466-5922, USA

Baker, Michael A Captain (Astronaut)
18138 Lakeside Ln
Houston, TX 77058-4331, USA

Baker, Michael A (Mike) (Astronaut)
NASA
2101 Nasa Pkwy Spc Johnsoncenter
Houston, TX 77058-3696, USA

Baker, Michael Andrew (Actor)
c/o David Chandler Secor *Daniel Hoff Agency*
5455 Wilshire Blvd Ste 1100
Los Angeles, CA 90036-4277, USA

Baker, Myron (Athlete, Football Player)
297 Peart Rd
Alexandria, LA 71302-9344, USA

Baker, Rae (Actor)
c/o Staff Member *Marmont Management*
Langham House
308 Regent St
London W1B 3AT, UNITED KINGDOM (UK)

Baker, Ralph (Athlete, Football Player)
36 Sunshine Cir
Lewistown, PA 17044-9264, USA

Baker, Randy (Race Car Driver)
Speed Tech
4333 Motorsports Dr SW
Concord, NC 28027-8977, USA

Baker, Ray (Actor)
11749 Chenault St
Los Angeles, CA 90049-4230, USA

Baker, Rick (Designer)
Cinovation Studios, Inc.
4260 Arcola Ave
Toluca Lake, CA 91602-2902, USA

Baker, Robby (Musician)
Management Trust
309B-219 Dufferin St
Toronto, ON M6K 3J1, CANADA

Baker, Robert (Actor)
c/o Amanda Glazer *The Kohner Agency*
9300 Wilshire Blvd Ste 555
Beverly Hills, CA 90212-3211, USA

Baker, Ron (Athlete, Football Player)
c/o Aaron Mintz *CAA Sports*
2000 Avenue of the Stars Ste 100
Los Angeles, CA 90067-4705, USA

Baker, Roy Ward (Director)
c/o Staff Member *Directors Guild Of Great Britain*
4 Windmill St
London W1T 2HZ, UK

Baker, Sam (Athlete, Football Player)
c/o Ben Dogra *Relativity Sports*
2029 Century Park E Ste 1550
Century City, CA 90067-3000, USA

Baker, Scott (Athlete, Baseball Player)
204 Highgate St
Henderson, NV 89074-2859, USA

Baker, Scott (Athlete, Baseball Player)
340 Johns Bluff Cir
Shreveport, LA 71106-4733, USA

Baker, Scott Thompson (Actor)
17651 Sidwell St
Granada Hills, CA 91344-1054, USA

Baker, Sean (Athlete, Football Player)

Baker, Shaun (Actor)
c/o Staff Member *Brady, Brannon & Rich Talent (BBR Talent)*
5670 Wilshire Blvd Ste 820
Los Angeles, CA 90036-5613, USA

Baker, Simon (Actor)
c/o Ina Treciokas *Slate PR*
901 N Highland Ave
W Hollywood, CA 90038-2412, USA

Baker, Stephen (Athlete, Football Player)
358 Rector St Apt 601
Perth Amboy, NJ 08861-4367, USA

Baker, Steve (Athlete, Baseball Player)
27527 Easy Acres Dr
Eugene, OR 97405-4500, USA

Baker, Steve (Athlete, Hockey Player)
10852 E Mirasol Cir
Scottsdale, AZ 85255-9061, USA

Baker, Terry (Athlete, Football Player, Heisman Trophy Winner)
3208 SW Fairmount Blvd
Portland, OR 97239-1443, USA

Baker, Tom (Actor, Writer)
c/o Edward Hill *Edward Hill Management*
Dolphin House
2-5 Manchester Street
London BN2 1TF, United Kingdom

Baker, Tony (Athlete, Football Player)
3847 Eagleston Ct
High Point, NC 27265-7928, us

Baker, Vin (Athlete, Basketball Player)
PO Box 179
Old Saybrook, CT 06475-0179, USA

Baker, Wayne (Athlete, Football Player)
209 Needmore Rd
Waco, KY 40385-9030, USA

Baker, W Thane (Athlete, Track Athlete)
6704 Saint John Ct
Granbury, TX 76049-4520, USA

Baker-Finch, Ian (Athlete, Golfer)
11309 Caladium Ln
Palm Beach Gardens, FL 33418-1506, USA

Baker III, James A (Politician)
Baker And Botts
1299 Pennsylvania Ave NW Ste 1200
NW Ste 1200
Washington, DC 20004-2408, USA

Bakhtair, Rudi (Correspondent)
Cable News Network
1050 Techwood Dr NW
News Dept
Atlanta, GA 30318-5695, USA

Bakhtiar, Jim (Athlete, Football Player)

Bakhtiari, David (Athlete, Football Player)

Bakke, Brenda (Actor)
c/o Staff Member *The House of Representatives*
3118 Wilshire Blvd Ste D
Santa Monica, CA 90403-2345, USA

Bakkedahl, Dan (Actor)
c/o Meg Mortimer *Authentic Talent and Literary Management (NY)*
20 Jay St Ste M17
Brooklyn, NY 11201-8300, USA

Bakken, James L (Jim) (Athlete, Football Player)
230 Glen Hollow Rd
Madison, WI 53705-1166, USA

Bakker, James O (Jim) (Religious Leader)
123 E End Rd
Branson, MO 65616-3701, USA

Bako, Brigitte (Actor)
8329 Anthony Cir
Los Angeles, CA 90046-1901, USA

Bako, Paul (Athlete, Baseball Player)
408 Worth Ave
Lafayette, LA 70508-6637, USA

Bakovic, Pete (Athlete, Hockey Player)
7991 S 47th St
Franklin, WI 53132-8468, USA

Bakshi, Ralph (Cartoonist)
PO Box 2858
Silver City, NM 88062-2858, USA

Bakula, Scott (Actor)
Bakula Pictures
16255 Ventura Blvd Ste 625
Encino, CA 91436-2307, USA

Bala, Chris (Athlete, Hockey Player)
271 Beacon Dr
Phoenixville, PA 19460-2046, USA

Balaban, Bob (Director, Producer)
310 Highland Terr
Bridgehampton, NY 11932, USA

Balaban, Liane (Actor)

Balaski, Belinda (Actor)
731 N Laurel Ave
Los Angeles, CA 90046-7007, USA

Balaz, John (Athlete, Baseball Player)
2916 Worden St
San Diego, CA 92110-5708, USA

Balazs, Andre (Business Person)
23 E 4th St
New York, NY 10003-7023, USA

Balboa, Marcelo (Soccer Player)
13139 Hedda Dr
Cerritos, CA 90703-6146, USA

Balboni, Steve (Athlete, Baseball Player)
117 Burlington Rd
New Providence, NJ 07974-2709, USA

Balcazar, Javier Hernández (Athlete, Soccer Player)
c/o Staff Member *Manchester United PLC*
Sir Matt Busby Way
Old Trafford
Manchester M160RA, UNITED KINGDOM

Balcer, Rene (Producer, Writer)
c/o Missy Malkin *Brillstein Entertainment Partners*
9150 Wilshire Blvd Ste 350
Beverly Hills, CA 90212-3453, USA

Baldacci, David (Writer)
c/o Aaron Priest *Aaron M. Priest Literary Agency*
708 3rd Ave Rm 2301
New York, NY 10017-4212, USA

Baldacci, John (Politician)
192 State St
Augusta, ME 04330-6406, USA

Baldacci, Lou (Athlete, Football Player)
983 Coral Dr
Pebble Beach, CA 93953-2538, USA

Baldachino, Gerald (Horse Racer)
208 Sweetmans Ln
Millstone Township, NJ 08535-8110, USA

Baldassin, Mike (Athlete, Football Player)
7914 Interlaaken Dr SW
Lakewood, WA 98498-5707, USA

Baldavin, Barbara (Actor)
228 17th St
Manhattan Beach, CA 90266-4634, USA

Baldelli, Rocco (Athlete, Baseball Player)
5301 Gulf Blvd Unit 610
St Pete Beach, FL 33706-2307, USA

Balderis, Helmut (Athlete, Hockey Player)
Latvian Ice Hockey Federation
Raunas lela 23
Riga LV-1039, Latvia

Balderson, Dick (Commentator)
1676 Raybrad Dr
Cordova, TN 38016-6038, USA

Balderstone, James S (Business Person)
115 Mont Albert Road
Canterbuy, VIC 03126, AUSTRALIA

Baldessari, John (Artist)
626 Vernon Ave
Venice, CA 90291-2737, USA

Balding, Rebecca (Actor)
2001 Winnetka Place
Woodland Hills, CA 91364, USA

Baldinger, Brian (Athlete, Football Player, Sportscaster)
21 Elmwood Rd S
Marlton, NJ 08053-2562, USA

Baldinger, Gary (Athlete, Football Player)
114 Adam Rd
Massapequa, NY 11758-8102, USA

Baldinger, Rich (Athlete, Football Player)
5401 Phelps Rd
Kansas City, MO 64136-1224, USA

Baldischwiler, Karl (Athlete, Football Player)
3033 N Willow Dr
Newcastle, OK 73065-6456, USA

Baldoni, Justin (Actor)
c/o Liz York *Principal Entertainment*
9255 W Sunset Blvd Ste 500
Los Angeles, CA 90069-3301, USA

Baldrige, Leticia (Writer)
Letitia Baldrige Enterprises Inc
2339 Massachusetts Ave NW
Washington, DC 20008-2803, USA

Baldry, Long John (Musician)
Macklam Feidman Mgmt
200-1505 2nd Ave W
Vancouver, BC V6H 3Y4, CANADA

Baldschun, Jack (Athlete, Baseball Player)
311 Erie Rd
Green Bay, WI 54311-7706, USA

Baldschun, Jack E (Athlete, Baseball Player)
311 Erie Rd
Green Bay, WI 54311-7706, USA

Baldwin, Adam (Actor)
c/o Abe Hoch *A Management Company*
16633 Ventura Blvd Ste 1450
Encino, CA 91436-1887, USA

Baldwin, Alec (Actor)
Alec Baldwin Foundation
509 Madison Ave Frnt 4
New York, NY 10022-5642, USA

Baldwin, Brooke (Journalist, Television Host)
c/o Staff Member *CNN (NY)*
10 Columbus Cir
Time Warner Center
New York, NY 10019-1158, USA

Baldwin, Daniel (Actor)
1999 Ave of Stars Ste 2850
Los Angeles, CA 90067-4627, USA

Baldwin, Dave (Athlete, Baseball Player)
PO Box 190
Yachats, OR 97498-0190, USA

Baldwin, Don (Athlete, Football Player)

Baldwin, Hailey (Actor)
c/o Joshua Otten *IMG Models (NY)*
304 Park Ave S PH N
New York, NY 10010-4303, USA

Baldwin, Hilaria (Television Host)
c/o Mark Mullett *Creative Artists Agency (CAA)*
2000 Avenue of the Stars Ste 100
Los Angeles, CA 90067-4705, USA

Baldwin, Howard (Producer)
c/o Staff Member *Baldwin Entertainment*
9200 W Sunset Blvd Ste 550
West Hollywood, CA 90069-3611, USA

Baldwin, Ireland (Actor, Model)
c/o Oren Segal *Management Production Entertainment (MPE)*
9229 W Sunset Blvd Ste 301
W Hollywood, CA 90069-3417, USA

Baldwin, Jack (Race Car Driver)
4748 Balmoral Way NE
Marietta, GA 30068-1604, USA

Baldwin, James (Athlete, Baseball Player)
18277 W Tecoma Rd
Goodyear, AZ 85338-3671, USA

Baldwin, Jeff (Athlete, Baseball Player)
269 Del Sol Ave
Davenport, FL 33837-6828, USA

Baldwin, Jerry (Business Person)
1400 Park Ave
Emeryville, CA 94608-3520, USA

Baldwin, Jonathan (Football Player)
c/o Ken Zuckerman *Priority Sports & Entertainment - (LA)*
15233 Ventura Blvd Ste 718
Sherman Oaks, CA 91403-2237, USA

Baldwin, Judy (Actor)
c/o Larry Metzger *Grant Savic Kopaloff & Associates*
4929 Wilshire Blvd Ste 259
Los Angeles, CA 90010-3816, USA

Baldwin, Kate (Actor)
c/o Sarah Yorke *Baker Winokur Ryder Public Relations*
200 5th Ave Fl 5
New York, NY 10010-3307, USA

Baldwin, Keith (Athlete, Football Player)
10788 Waterfall Rd
Strongsville, OH 44149-2150, USA

Baldwin, Margaret (Writer)
PO Box 1106
Williams Bay, WI 53191-1106, USA

Baldwin, Matisha (Actor)
c/o Marianne Golan *Golan & Blumberg*
2761 E Woodbury Dr
Arlington Heights, IL 60004-7247, USA

Baldwin, Randy (Athlete, Football Player)
862 S 9th St
Griffin, GA 30224-4823, USA

Baldwin, Reggie (Athlete, Baseball Player)
763 S Liebold St
Detroit, MI 48217-1219, USA

Baldwin, Rick (Athlete, Baseball Player)
2504 Hillbrook Way
Modesto, CA 95355-7824, USA

Baldwin, Stephen (Actor)
c/o Evan Mulvihill *Planet PR*
270 Lafayette St Ste 800
New York, NY 10012-3389, USA

Baldwin, Tammy (Congressman, Politician)
2446 Rayburn Hob
Washington, DC 20515-3703, USA

Baldwin, William (Billy) (Actor)
c/o Lee Wallman *Wallman Public Relations*
3859 Goldwyn Ter
Culver City, CA 90232-3103, USA

Bale, Christian (Actor)
9701 Wilshire Blvd Ste 1000
Beverly Hills, CA 90212-2010, USA

Bale, John (Athlete, Baseball Player)
9017 Roberts Rd
Odessa, FL 33556-1947, USA

Bales, Lee (Athlete, Baseball Player)
7422 Greatwood Lake Dr
Sugar Land, TX 77479-6302, USA

Bales, Michael (Athlete, Hockey Player)
470 Brunswick Ave
Toronto, ON M5R 2Z5, Canada

Bales, Mike (Athlete, Hockey Player)
470 Brunswick Ave
Toronto, ON M5R 2Z5, Canada

Balester, Collin (Athlete, Baseball Player)
7020 Pilliod Rd
Holland, OH 43528-8616, USA

Balfe, Caitriona (Actor)
c/o Cara Tripicchio *Shelter PR*
5670 Wilshire Blvd Ste 1200
Los Angeles, CA 90036-5621, USA

Balfour, Eric (Actor)
c/o Brian Medavoy *More/Medavoy Management*
10203 Santa Monica Blvd # 400
Los Angeles, CA 90067-6405, USA

Balfour, Grant (Athlete, Baseball Player)
c/o Seth Levinson *ACES*
188 Montague St Fl 6
Brooklyn, NY 11201-3609, USA

Baliani, Marco (Actor)
Carol Levi Co
Via Giuseppe Pisanelli
Rome 00196, ITALY

Baliles, Gerald L (Politician)
951 E Byrd St
Richmond, VA 23219-4040, USA

Balinska, Ella (Actor)
c/o Femi Oguns *Identity Agency Group (UK)*
95 Grays Inn Rd
London WC1X 8TX, UNITED KINGDOM

Balitran, Celine (Model)
c/o Staff Member *T G 6*
120 Ave Charles De Gaulle
Neuilly-Sur-Seine
Riverside, CA 92522-0001, FRANCE

Balk, Fairuza (Actor)
c/o Michael McConnell *Zero Gravity Management (II)*
5660 Silver Valley Ave
Agoura Hills, CA 91301-4000, USA

Balkenhol, Klaus (Athlete)
Narzissenweg 11A
Hilden 40723, GERMANY

Ball, Alan (Athlete, Football Player)
c/o Ryan Morgan *MAG Sports Agency*
8222 Melrose Ave Fl 2
Los Angeles, CA 90046-6825, USA

Ball, Alan (Producer)
7443 Woodrow Wilson Dr
Los Angeles, CA 90046-1322, USA

Ball, Ashleigh (Musician)
c/o Staff Member *Lauren Levitt & Associates Inc*
1525 W 8th Ave Fl 3
Vancouver BC V6J 1T5, CANADA

Ball, Blake (Athlete, Hockey Player)

Ball, Dave (Athlete, Football Player)
9234 Carrisbrook Ln
Brentwood, TN 37027-4883, us

Ball, Dave (Athlete, Football Player)
1020 Hillview Dr
Dixon, CA 95620-3729, USA

Ball, Edward (Writer)
Farrar Straus Giroux
19 Union Sq W
New York, NY 10003-3304, USA

Ball, Eric C (Athlete, Football Player)
10614 Margate Ter
Cincinnati, OH 45241-3000, USA

Ball, Ian (Musician)
c/o Staff Member *Paradigm (Monterey)*
404 W Franklin St
Monterey, CA 93940-2303, USA

Ball, Jason (Athlete, Football Player)
22 Coe Dr
Durham, NH 03824-2206, USA

Ball, Jeff (Athlete, Baseball Player)
1166 6th Ave Apt 9C
Vero Beach, FL 32960-5960, USA

Ball, Jerry L (Athlete, Football Player)

Ball, Larry (Athlete, Football Player)
8830 SW 57th St
Cooper City, FL 33328-5100, USA

Ball, Marcia (Musician)
PO Box 2629
Austin, TX 78768-2629, USA

Ball, Michael A (Actor, Musician)
PO Box 2073
Colchester, Essex CO4 3WS, UNITED KINGDOM (UK)

Ball, Montee (Athlete, Football Player)
c/o Neil Cornrich *NC Sports, LLC*
best to contact via email
Columbus, OH 43201, USA

Ball, Robert (Athlete, Football Player)
35 Summit Rd
Clifton, NJ 07012-2008, USA

Ball, Sam (Actor)
c/o Robert Stein *Robert Stein Management*
PO Box 3797
Beverly Hills, CA 90212-0797, USA

Ball, Sam (Athlete, Football Player)
1220 Glenshiel Dr
Henderson, KY 42420-2530, USA

Ball, Taylor (Actor)
c/o Shannon Barr *Rogers & Cowan*
1840 Century Park E Fl 18
Los Angeles, CA 90067-2101, USA

Ball, Terry (Athlete, Hockey Player)
4502 Torrington Ave
Parma, OH 44134-2163, USA

Balladur, Edouard (Politician)
5 Rue Jean Formige
Paris F-75015, FRANCE

Ballantine, Sara (Actor)
Talent Group
5670 Wilshire Blvd Ste 820
Los Angeles, CA 90036-5613, USA

Ballantyne (Designer, Fashion Designer)
c/o Staff Member *Ballantyne*
4-6 Savile Road
London, England W1S 3PD, United Kingdom

Ballard, Carroll (Director)
PO Box 556
Saint Helena, CA 94574-5056, USA

Ballard, Florence (Musician)
c/o Staff Member *Diva Central Inc*
7510 W Sunset Blvd # 1445
Los Angeles, CA 90046-3408, USA

Ballard, Frankie (Musician)
c/o Jensen Sussman *Sweet Talk PR*
700 12th Ave S Unit 201
Nashville, TN 37203-3329, USA

Ballard, Glen (Musician, Songwriter)
911 N Beverly Dr
Beverly Hills, CA 90210-2912, USA

Ballard, Greg (Athlete, Basketball Player)
100 Arborcrest Ct
Tyrone, GA 30290-1555, USA

Ballard, Howard (Athlete, Football Player)
PO Box 584
Ashland, AL 36251-0584, USA

Ballard, Jeff (Athlete, Baseball Player)
4828 Rimrock Rd
Billings, MT 59106-1317, USA

Ballard, J G (Writer)
36 Old Charlton Rd
Shepperton, Middlesex England, USA

Ballard, Jim (Athlete, Football Player)
3923 Darlington Ave NW
Canton, OH 44708-1721, us

Ballard, Kaye (Actor)
PO Box 922
Rancho Mirage, CA 92270-0922, USA

Ballard, Keith (Athlete, Hockey Player)
c/o Ben Hankinson *Octagon Hockey*
510 Marquette Ave Fl 13
Minneapolis, MN 55402-1102, USA

Ballard, Quinton (Athlete, Football Player)
4005 Saint Patrick Dr
Greensboro, NC 27406-6420, USA

Ballard, Vick (Athlete, Football Player)
c/o Bus Cook *Bus Cook Sports, Inc*
1 Willow Bend Dr
Hattiesburg, MS 39402-8552, USA

Ballas, Mark (Dancer, Reality Star)
c/o Rebecca Lambrecht *Chicane Group*
6442 Santa Monica Blvd Ste 200B
Los Angeles, CA 90038-1530, USA

Ballentine, Lonnie (Athlete, Football Player)
c/o Harold C Lewis *National Sports Agency*
12181 Prichard Farm Rd
Maryland Heights, MO 63043-4203, USA

Baller, Jay (Athlete, Baseball Player)
303 Spring Valley Rd
Reading, PA 19605-2747, USA

Ballerini, Edoardo (Actor)
3350 Atwater Ave
Los Angeles, CA 90039-2204, USA

Ballesteros, Roberto (Actor)
c/o Staff Member *Televisa*
Blvd Adolfo Lopez Mateos 232
Colonia San Angel INN
DF CP 01060, MEXICO

Ballestros, Anderson (Actor)
c/o J R Heermans *LatinActors*
920 Leavenworth St Apt 302
San Francisco, CA 94109-5192

Balley, Otha (Athlete, Baseball Player)
937 6th Pl SW
Birmingham, AL 35211-1743, USA

Ballina, Frank (Athlete, Baseball Player)
PO Box 54
Freeport, PA 16229-0054, USA

Ballinger, Colleen (Comedian, Internet Star)
c/o Tess Finkle *Metro Public Relations*
8671 Wilshire Blvd # 208
Beverly Hills, CA 90211-2926, USA

Ballmer, Steve (Business Person)
Microsoft Corp
1 Microsoft Way
Redmond, WA 98052-8300, USA

Ballon, Adrienne (Actor)
c/o Staff Member *ICM Partners*
10250 Constellation Blvd Fl 7
Los Angeles, CA 90067-6207, USA

Ballou, Mark (Actor)
c/o Staff Member *Imperium 7 Talent Agency*
5455 Wilshire Blvd Ste 1706
Los Angeles, CA 90036-4217, USA

Ballou, Tyson (Model)
c/o Staff Member *IMG*
304 Park Ave S Fl 12
New York, NY 10010-4314, USA

Balmaseda, Liz (Journalist)
Miami Herald
1 Herald Plz
Editorial Dept
Miami, FL 33132-1609, USA

Balmer, Earl (Race Car Driver)
7014 Jennifer Dr
Georgetown, IN 47122-8609, USA

Balmer, Jean-Francois (Actor, Director)
c/o Staff Member *ArtMedia*
8 rue Danielle Casanova
Paris 75002, FRANCE

Balmilero, Kimee (Actor)
c/o Staff Member *Rogers Orion Talent Agency*
3500 W Olive Ave Ste 300
Burbank, CA 91505-4647, USA

Balon, Dave (Athlete, Hockey Player)
D. 5-29-2007
USA

Balotelli, Mario (Athlete, Soccer Player)
c/o Staff Member *Manchester City FC*
City of Manchester Stadium
SportCity
Manchester M11 3FF, UK

Balsam, Talia (Actor)
c/o Gary Mantoosh *Baker Winokur Ryder Public Relations*
9100 Wilshire Blvd
W Tower #500
Beverly Hills, CA 90212-3415, USA

Balsamo, Tony (Athlete, Baseball Player)
21 Nikia Dr
Islip, NY 11751-2631, USA

Balsley, Darren (Athlete, Baseball Player, Coach)
1200 Harper Pl
Knoxville, TN 37922-5560, USA

Balsley, Phil (Musician)
1409 N Augusta St
Staunton, VA 24401-2402, USA

Baltes, Jameson (Actor)
Hervey/Grimes
PO Box 64249
Los Angeles, CA 90064-0249, USA

Baltica, Kremerata (Musician)
c/o Staff Member *ICM Partners*
10250 Constellation Blvd Fl 7
Los Angeles, CA 90067-6207, USA

Baltimore, Bryon (Athlete, Hockey Player)
McCaig Desrochers Ltd
2401-10088 102 Ave NW
Edmonton, AB T5J 2Z1, Canada

Baltron, Donna (Actor)
C N A Assoc
1925 Century Park E Ste 750
Los Angeles, CA 90067-2708, USA

Baluik, Stan (Athlete, Hockey Player)
809 8th Ter
Palm Beach Gardens, FL 33418-3607, USA

Bama, James (Artist)
PO Box 148
Wapiti, WY 82450-0148, USA

Bama, Jim (Artist)
PO Box 148
Wapiti, WY 82450-0148, USA

Bamber, Ellie (Actor)
c/o Pippa Beng *Premier PR*
2-4 Bucknall St
London WC2H 8LA, UNITED KINGDOM

Bamber, Jamie (Actor)
c/o Alan Siegel *Alan Siegel Entertainment*
9200 W Sunset Blvd Ste 804
West Hollywood, CA 90069-3603, USA

Bamford, Maria (Actor, Comedian)
c/o Bruce Smith *OmniPop Talent Group*
4605 Lankershim Blvd Ste 201
Toluca Lake, CA 91602-1874, USA

Bamman, Gerry (Actor)
c/o Julia Berman *Act One Management*
1501 Broadway Fl 12
New York, NY 10036-5505, USA

Bana, Eric (Actor, Comedian)
c/o Lauren Bergman *Lauren Bergman Management*
37 Browns Road, Main Ridge
Victoria 03928, Australia

Banach, Ed (Athlete, Olympic Athlete, Wrestler)
2128 Country Club Blvd
Ames, IA 50014-7061, USA

Banach, Lou (Athlete, Olympic Athlete, Wrestler)
1828 Tallgrass Cir
Waukesha, WI 53188-2661, USA

Banachowski, Andy (Athlete, Coach, Volleyball Player)
University of California
PO Box 24044
Athletic Dept - J.D. Morgan Center
Los Angeles, CA 90024-0044, USA

Banaszak, John A (Athlete, Football Player)
219 Maid Marion Ln
Canonsburg, PA 15317-2596, USA

Banaszak, Pete (Athlete, Football Player)
1021 Inverness Dr
Saint Augustine, FL 32092-2787, USA

Banaszynski, Jacqui (Journalist)
Saint Paul Pioneer Press
10 River Park Plz Ste 700
Editorial Dept
Saint Paul, MN 55107-1223, USA

Banbury, F H Frith (Director)
18 Park Saint James
Prince Albert Road
London NW8 7LE, UNITED KINGDOM (UK)

Bancroft, Cameron (Actor)
c/o Staff Member *Gersh*
9465 Wilshire Blvd Ste 600
Beverly Hills, CA 90212-2605, USA

Banda El Limon, Arrolladora (Music Group)
c/o Staff Member *Sony Music (Miami)*
404 Washington Ave Ste 700
Miami Beach, FL 33139-6615, USA

Banda Imperio (Music Group, Musician)
c/o Staff Member *Morena Music*
5021 Columbus Ave
Sherman Oaks, CA 91403-1251, USA

Banda Pachuco (Music Group)
c/o Staff Member *Sony Music (Miami)*
404 Washington Ave Ste 700
Miami Beach, FL 33139-6615, USA

Banderas, Antonio (Actor, Director, Musician, Producer)
c/o Staff Member *Green Moon Productions*
C/ Granada 33
Malaga 29015, SPAIN

B. Anderholf, Robert (Congressman, Politician)
2264 Rayburn Hob
Washington, DC 20515-3217, USA

Bandiera, Bob (Bobby) (Musician)
29C Court B
Brick, NJ 08724-2876, USA

Bando, Chris (Athlete, Baseball Player)
5811 S Mack Ave
Gilbert, AZ 85298-8709, USA

Bando, Sal (Athlete, Baseball Player)
c/o John Drana *The Drana Group*
789 N Water St Ste 480
Milwaukee, WI 53202-3562, USA

Band of Bees, A (Music Group)
c/o Staff Member *Paradigm (Monterey)*
404 W Franklin St
Monterey, CA 93940-2303, USA

Band of Horses (Music Group)
c/o Staff Member *Silva Artist Management (SAM)*
722 Seward St
Los Angeles, CA 90038-3504, USA

Bandura, Jeff (Athlete, Hockey Player)
27257 32B Ave
Aldergrove, BC V4W 3H8, Canada

Bandy, Don (Athlete, Football Player)
215 E Calvin St
Taft, CA 93268-2915, USA

Bandy, Moe (Musician, Songwriter)
2577 US 160
Reeds Spring, MO 65737, USA

Bane (Music Group)
c/o Staff Member *Equal Vision Records*
PO Box 38202
Albany, NY 12203-8202, USA

Bane, Eddie (Athlete, Baseball Player)
1132 Los Campaneros
San Marcos, CA 92078-5225, USA

Banes, Lisa (Actor)
c/o Tim Angle *Shelter Entertainment*
9255 W Sunset Blvd Ste 300
Los Angeles, CA 90069-3313, USA

Baney, Dick (Athlete, Baseball Player)
2231 Northup Dr
Tustin, CA 92782-1028, USA

Banfield, Ashleigh (Correspondent)
c/o Staff Member *NBC News (NY)*
30 Rockefeller Plz
New York, NY 10112-0015, USA

Banfield, Tony (Athlete, Football Player)
1102 Myrtlewood Dr
Friendswood, TX 77546-2015, us

Bang, Molly (Writer)
43 Drumlin Rd
Falmouth, MA 02540-2505, USA

Bangerter, Norman (Politician)
9947 S Congressional Way
South Jordan, UT 84095-3304, USA

Bangles, The (Music Group)
c/o Staff Member *UTA Music/The Agency Group (UK)*
361-373 City Rd
London EC1V 1PQ, UNITED KINGDOM

Bang Lime (Music Group)
c/o Staff Member *Paradigm (Monterey)*
404 W Franklin St
Monterey, CA 93940-2303, USA

Banham, Frank (Athlete, Hockey Player)
139 W Grayling Ln
Suffield, CT 06078-1960, USA

Banhart, Bobby (Reality Star)
c/o Elizabeth Much *East 2 West Collective*
11022 Santa Monica Blvd Ste 350
Los Angeles, CA 90025-7532, USA

Banhart, Devendra (Musician)
c/o Barry Dickins *International Talent Booking*
9 Kingsway
Fl 6
London WC2B 6XF, UNITED KINGDOM

Bani, John (President)
President's Office
Port Vila, VANUATU

Banister, Jeff (Athlete, Baseball Player)
1728 Biltmore Dr
Keller, TX 76262-9300, USA

Banke, Paul (Boxer)
1926 Bobolink Way
Pomona, CA 91767-2828, USA

Banker, Ted (Athlete, Football Player)
1862 Park Ave
East Meadow, NY 11554-4007, USA

Bankhead, Scott (Athlete, Baseball Player, Olympic Athlete)
1236 Idlewood Dr
Asheboro, NC 27205-4119, USA

Banks, Azealia (Actor, Musician)
c/o Staff Member *High Rise PR*
600 Luton Dr
Glendale, CA 91206-2626, USA

Banks, Brian (Athlete, Baseball Player)
3243 E Jacaranda Cir
Mesa, AZ 85213-3242, USA

Banks, Brianna (Adult Film Star)
c/o Staff Member *Atlas Multimedia Inc*
9005 Eton Ave Ste C
Canoga Park, CA 91304-6533, USA

Banks, Carl (Athlete, Football Player)
7 Glenview Dr
Warren, NJ 07059-5476, USA

Banks, Chip (Athlete, Football Player)
709 Albany Ave
Augusta, GA 30901-1807, USA

Banks, Chuck (Athlete, Football Player)
3705 Valley Hill Dr
Randallstown, MD 21133-4822, USA

Banks, Darren (Athlete, Hockey Player)
11 Millington Rd
Pleasant Ridge, MI 48069-1108, USA

Banks, David (Actor)
Shane Collins Assoc
2-5 Stedham Pl
Bloomsbury
London WC1A 1BU, ENGLAND

Banks, Elizabeth (Actor)
11635 Canton Pl
Studio City, CA 91604-4164, USA

Banks, Estes (Athlete, Football Player)
PO Box 6335
Buena Vista, CO 81211-6335, us

Banks, Fred (Athlete, Football Player)
PO Box 1571
Mableton, GA 30126-1009, USA

Banks, Gene (Athlete, Basketball Player)
Bluefield State College
219 Rock St
Athletic Dept
Bluefield, WV 24701-2198, USA

Banks, Gene (Athlete, Basketball Player)
1210 Sloan St
Greensboro, NC 27401-3442, USA

Banks, Gordon (Athlete, Football Player)
2644 E Trinity Mills Rd
Carrollton, TX 75006-2136, USA

Banks, Jonathan (Actor)
3922 Rambla Orienta
Malibu, CA 90265-5116, USA

Banks, Josh (Athlete, Baseball Player)
489 Old Orchard Cir
Millersville, MD 21108-2010, USA

Banks, Lloyd (Musician)
1 Fox Hunt Ct
Huntington, NY 11743-6542, USA

Banks, Lynne Reid (Writer)
c/o Staff Member *HarperCollins Publishers*
195 Broadway Fl 2
New York, NY 10007-3132, USA

Banks, Mike (Athlete, Football Player)
1615 1 Ave
Boone, IA 50036, us

Banks, Morwenna (Actor, Writer)
c/o Staff Member *ICM Partners*
10250 Constellation Blvd Fl 7
Los Angeles, CA 90067-6207, USA

Banks, Robert (Athlete, Football Player)
PO Box 1209
Hampton, VA 23661-0209, USA

Banks, Russell (Writer)
Princeton University
English Debt
Princeton, NJ 08544-0001, USA

Banks, Sandy (Journalist)
Los Angeles Times
2300 E Imperial Hwy
El Segundo, CA 90245-2813, USA

Banks, Skeeter (Athlete, Baseball Player)
3810 Castlewood Rd
Richmond, VA 23234-2612, USA

Banks, Steven (Actor, Comedian)
c/o Rob Kenneally *Creative Artists Agency (CAA)*
2000 Avenue of the Stars Ste 100
Los Angeles, CA 90067-4705, USA

Banks, Steven Gary (Producer, Writer)
c/o Staff Member *Evolution Entertainment*
10850 Wilshire Blvd Ste 600
Los Angeles, CA 90024-4319, USA

Banks, Ted (Coach)
Riverside Community College
Athletic Dept
Riverside, CA 92506, USA

Banks, Tom (Athlete, Football Player)
146 Revolutionary Way
Montevallo, AL 35115-5809, USA

Banks, Tony (Athlete, Football Player)
735 Laguna
Irving, TX 75039-3218, USA

Banks, Tyra (Actor, Model, Producer)
c/o Ivan Bart *IMG Models (NY)*
304 Park Ave S PH N
New York, NY 10010-4303, USA

Banks, Walker (Athlete, Basketball Player)
3207 Brentwood Dr
Champaign, IL 61821-3482, USA

Banks, Willie (Athlete, Baseball Player)
3443 Corte Sonrisa
Carlsbad, CA 92009-9341, USA

Bankston, Michael (Athlete, Football Player)
938 Kingwood Dr Apt 220
Humble, TX 77339-4446, USA

Bankston, Michael (Athlete, Football Player)
10851 W Montfair Blvd Apt 2122
Spring, TX 77382-2906, us

Bankston, Warren (Athlete, Football Player)
4201 Bordeaux Dr
Kenner, LA 70065-1739, USA

Bannan, Justin (Athlete, Football Player)
561 Mockingbird Dr Belgrade MT 59714-8139
Belgrade, MT 59714, us

Bannatyne, Duncan (Business Person, Writer)
Bannatyne Fitness Ltd
Powerhouse, Haughton Rd
Attn: Kim Crowther
Darlington DL1 1ST, UNITED KINGDOM

Banner, David (Actor, Musician, Producer)
c/o Tamra Goins *Innovative Artists*
1505 10th St
Santa Monica, CA 90401-2805, USA

Bannerman, Bill (Director, Producer)
Mirisch Agency
1875 Century Park E Ste 2025
C/O Lawrence Mirisch
Los Angeles, CA 90067-2337, USA

Bannerman, Isabella (Cartoonist)
41 South Dr
Hastings On Hudson, NY 10706-1813, USA

Bannerman, Murray (Athlete, Hockey Player)
826 Raintree Dr
Naperville, IL 60540-6381, USA

Bannister, Alan (Athlete, Baseball Player)
JDH Insurance Brokerage Services
20403 N Lake Pleasant Rd Ste 117
Peoria, AZ 85382-9707, USA

Bannister, Brian (Athlete, Baseball Player)
6701 E Caballo Dr
Paradise Valley, AZ 85253-2706, USA

Bannister, Floyd (Athlete, Baseball Player)
6701 E Caballo Dr
Paradise Valley, AZ 85253-2706, USA

Bannister, Ken (Athlete, Basketball Player)
2322 Broadgreen Dr
Missouri City, TX 77489-5002, USA

Bannister, Reggie (Actor, Musician)
Magic Inc
4450 California Pl # 315
Long Beach, CA 90807-2209, USA

Bannon, Bruce (Athlete, Football Player)

Bannon, Shaun (Musician)
Artist Group International
9560 Wilshire Blvd Ste 400
Beverly Hills, CA 90212-2442, USA

Banois, Vincent J (Athlete, Football Player)
24256J Tamarack Trl
Southfield, MI 48075, USA

Banta, Brad (Athlete, Football Player)
2069 Linwood Cir
Soddy Daisy, TN 37379-8139, USA

Banta, Brad (Athlete, Football Player)
1100 Smith Ave Birmingham MI48009-2031
Birmingham, MI 48009-2031, us

Banta-Cain, Tully (Athlete, Football Player)
111 Ruest Rd Attleboro MA2760-6610
North Attleboro, MA 02760-6610, us

Bantom, Mike (Athlete, Basketball Player, Olympic Athlete)
418 Egret Ln
Secaucus, NJ 07094-2219, USA

Banx, Brooke (Model)
8491 W Sunset Blvd # 285
W Hollywood, CA 90069-1911, USA

Baptist, Travis (Athlete, Baseball Player)
12269 Deersong Dr
Jacksonville, FL 32218-9038, USA

Baptista, Juan Alfonso (Actor)
c/o Gabriel Blanco *Gabriel Blanco Iglesias (Mexico)*
Rio Balsas 35-32
Colonia Cuauhtemoc
DF 06500, Mexico

Baptiste, Baron (Athlete)
c/o Staff Member *St Martins Press*
175 5th Ave
Publicity Dept
New York, NY 10010-7703, USA

Baquero, Ivana (Actor)
Eduardo González Valdivia
Isaac Peral 48
Suite 1B
Madrid 28040, SPAIN

Bar, Sendi (Actor)
c/o Peter Young *Sovereign Talent Group*
1642 Westwood Blvd Ste 202
Los Angeles, CA 90024-5609, USA

Barahona, Ralph (Athlete, Hockey Player)
4608 Bellflower Blvd
Lakewood, CA 90713-2502, USA

Barajas, Rod (Athlete, Baseball Player)
723 Avocado Pl
Del Mar, CA 92014-3943, USA

Barak, Ehud (Politician)
Israel Labor Party
16 Hayarkon St
Tel-Aviv 63571, ISRAEL

Baraka, Imiri (Writer)
State University Of New York
Dept of African Studies
Stony Brook, NY 11794-0001, USA

Baranova, Anastasia (Actor)
4HM
11340 Moorpark St
Studio City, CA 91602-2619, USA

Baranski, Christine (Actor)
316 Wood Creek Rd
Bethlehem, CT 06751-1012, USA

Barany, Istvan (Swimmer)
I Attila Utca 87
Budapest 01012, HUNGARY

Barash, Brandon (Actor)
c/o Martin (Marty) Berneman *Precision Entertainment*
6338 Wilshire Blvd
Los Angeles, CA 90048-5002, USA

Baratta, Adam (Actor)
c/o Gary Raskin *Raskin Peter Rubin & Simon*
1801 Century Park E Ste 2300
Los Angeles, CA 90067-2325, USA

Barbara, Kingsolver E (Writer)
c/o Staff Member *HarperCollins Publishers*
195 Broadway Fl 2
New York, NY 10007-3132, USA

Barbaro, Gary W (Athlete, Football Player)
1000 Giuffrias Ave
Metairie, LA 70001-3649, USA

Barbaro, Monica (Actor)
c/o Staff Member *Main Title Entertainment*
8383 Wilshire Blvd Ste 408
Beverly Hills, CA 90211-2435, USA

Barbat, Roxanne (Director, Producer, Writer)
c/o Staff Member *Fantastic Films*
3854 Clayton Ave
Los Angeles, CA 90027-4720, USA

Barbato, Randy (Producer)
c/o Staff Member *World of Wonder*
6650 Hollywood Blvd
Los Angeles, CA 90028-6219, USA

Barbeau, Adrienne (Actor, Musician)
PO Box 1839
Studio City, CA 91614-0839, USA

Barber, Aaron (Athlete, Basketball Player)
2830 Fillmore St NE
Minneapolis, MN 55418-2936, USA

Barber, Andrea (Actor)
1391 Beechwood Dr
Brea, CA 92821-2056, USA

Barber, Ava (Musician)
1508 N Courtney Oak Ln
Knoxville, TN 37938-4413, USA

Barber, Bill (Athlete, Hockey Player)
105 Harmon Dr
Blackwood, NJ 08012-5198, USA

Barber, Bob (Athlete, Football Player)
PO Box 552
Shreveport, LA 71162-0552, us

Barber, Brian (Athlete, Baseball Player)
347 Blue Stone Cir
Winter Garden, FL 34787-5231, USA

Barber, Celeste (Actor, Comedian)
PO Box 6607
Tweed Heads S NSW 2486, AUSTRALIA

Barber, Chris (Musician)
Cromwell Mgmt
45 High St
Huntington
Cambridgeshire PE29 3TE, UNITED KINGDOM (UK)

Barber, Christopher E (Athlete, Football Player)
2621 Monaco Cove Cir
Orlando, FL 32825-8442, USA

Barber, Don (Athlete, Hockey Player)
34165 6 Mile Rd
Livonia, MI 48152-3144, USA

Barber, Gary (Producer)
6114 Camino De La Costa
La Jolla, CA 92037-6520, USA

Barber, Glynis (Actor)
11-12 Dover St
Mayfair
London W1S 4LJ, UK

Barber, John (Athlete, Basketball Player)
1554 Mahan St
Orangeburg, SC 29118-3546, USA

Barber, Kurt (Athlete, Football Player)
400 E Main St
Frankfort, KY 40601-2334, USA

Barber, Kurt (Athlete, Football Player)
6850 Silver Eagle Ave Las Vegas NV89122-8387
Las Vegas, NV 89122-8387, us

Barber, Marion (Athlete, Football Player)
PO Box 46106
Minneapolis, MN 55446-0106, USA

Barber, Matt (Actor)
c/o Sarah Spear *Curtis Brown Ltd*
28-29 Hay Market
Hay Market House
London SW1Y 4SP, UNITED KINGDOM

Barber, Michael (Athlete, Football Player)
3020 Prosperity Church Rd Ste 1
Charlotte, NC 28269-7197, USA

Barber, Mike (Athlete, Football Player)
PO Box 2424
Desoto, TX 75123-2424, USA

Barber, Paul (Actor, Producer, Writer)
c/o Staff Member *Paradigm*
8942 Wilshire Blvd
Beverly Hills, CA 90211-1908, USA

Barber, Ronde (Athlete, Football Player)
17119 Journeys End Dr
Odessa, FL 33556-2442, USA

Barber, Rudy (Athlete, Football Player)
1411 NW 175th St
Miami, FL 33169-4660, USA

Barber, Shawn (Athlete, Football Player)
10511 W 159th Ter
Overland Park, KS 66221-8549, USA

Barber, Steve (Athlete, Baseball Player)
902 San Eduardo Ave
Henderson, NV 89002-8900, USA

Barber, Stewart C (Stew) (Athlete, Football Player)
2138 Country Manor Dr
Mount Pleasant, SC 29466-7448, USA

Barber, Tiki (Athlete, Football Player, Sportscaster)
c/o Mark Lepselter *Maxx Sports & Entertainment*
546 5th Ave Fl 6
New York, NY 10036-5000, USA

Barberie, Bret (Athlete, Baseball Player)
11607 Bos St
Cerritos, CA 90703-6744, USA

Barberie, Jillian (Actor, Television Host)
19413 Bilmoor Pl
Tarzana, CA 91356-4416, USA

Barberos, Alessandro (Business Person)
Fiat Spa
Corso G Marconi 10/20
New York, NY 10125-0001, ITALY

Barbieri, Jim (Athlete, Baseball Player)
13619 E 5th Ave
Spokane Valley, WA 99216-0600, USA

Barbon, Roberto (Athlete, Baseball Player)
Gabukun Dencho-2-Chome 6-Ban 460
Nishinomiya City
Hyogok, JAPAN

Barbosa, Derek Keith (Chino XL) (Musician)
c/o Staff Member *Universal Music Publishing Group (Latin)*
420 Lincoln Rd Ste 200
Miami Beach, FL 33139-3014, USA

Barbosa, Leandro (Athlete, Basketball Player)
c/o Dan Fegan *Relativity Sports*
2029 Century Park E Ste 1550
Century City, CA 90067-3000, USA

Barbour, Benny (Athlete, Football Player)
661 Barbour Rd
Smithfield, NC 27577-5579, USA

Barbour, Haley R (Politician)
648 Dogwood Dr
Yazoo City, MS 39194-8205, USA

Barbour, John (Actor, Comedian, Writer)
4254 Forman Ave
Toluca Lake, CA 91602-2908, USA

Barbre, Allen (Athlete, Football Player)

Barbree, Jay (Journalist)
9320 S Tropical Trl
Merritt Island, FL 32952-6821, USA

Barbusca, Brielle (Musician)
c/o April Mills *April Mills Entertainment*
PO Box 1983
Burbank, CA 91507-1983, USA

Barbusca, Thomas (Actor)
c/o April Mills *April Mills Entertainment*
PO Box 1983
Burbank, CA 91507-1983, USA

Barbutti, Pete (Musician)
Thomas Cassidy
11761 E Speedway Blvd
Tucson, AZ 85748-2017, USA

Barcelo, Lorenzo (Athlete, Baseball Player)
1520 N Blacklawn Ave
Tucson, AZ 85745-3356, USA

Barcelo, Rich (Athlete, Basketball Player)
5195 N Spring View Dr
Tucson, AZ 85749-7107, USA

Barcelona, Custo (Designer, Fashion Designer)
c/o Staff Member *Custo Barcelona*
2 Michael Road
1927 Bldg, North Entrance
London, England SW6 2AD, United Kingdom

Barclay, Dave (Actor)
c/o Staff Member *Coolwaters Productions*
10061 Riverside Dr # 531
Toluca Lake, CA 91602-2560, USA

Barclay, Don (Athlete, Football Player)
c/o Joe Linta *JL Sports*
1204 Main St Ste 179
Branford, CT 06405-3787, USA

Barclay, Paris (Director, Producer)
c/o Steve Lovett *Lovett Management*
1327 Brinkley Ave
Los Angeles, CA 90049-3619, USA

Bard, Josh (Athlete, Baseball Player)
2139 Beechnut Pl
Castle Rock, CO 80108-7827, USA

Bardem, Javier (Actor, Producer)
c/o Jose Marzilli *Jose Marzilli Represente de Actores*
Calle Rafael Calvo 42 5* Dcha
Madrid 28010, SPAIN

Barden, Brian (Athlete, Baseball Player)
3820 E Waltann Ln
Phoenix, AZ 85032-4042, USA

Barden, Jessica (Actor)
c/o Pandora Weldon *Public Eye Communications*
535 Kings Rd
#313 Plaza
London SW10 0SZ, UNITED KINGDOM

Bardot, Brigitte (Actor)
Fondation Brigitte Bardot
28, rue Vineuse
Paris F-75116, FRANCE

Bare, Bobby (Musician)
Bobby Bare Enterprises
112 the Lndg
Hendersonville, TN 37075-5213, USA

Barefoot, Ken (Athlete, Football Player)
1204 Lawrence Grey Dr
Virginia Beach, VA 23455-5605, USA

Bareikis, Arija (Actor)
c/o Rhonda Price *Gersh*
41 Madison Ave Ste 3301
New York, NY 10010-2210, USA

Bareikis, Arlia (Actor)
360 W 23rd St
New York, NY 10011-2258, USA

Bareilles, Sara (Musician)
235 Park Ave S Fl 9
New York, NY 10003-1405, USA

Barenaked Ladies (Music Group)
c/o Shaw Saltzberg *SL Feldman & Associates (Vancouver)*
200-1505 2nd Ave W
Vancouver, BC V6H 3Y4, CANADA

Barer, Libe (Actor)
c/o Jami Kandel *Vision PR*
2 Penn Plz Rm 2601
New York, NY 10121-0001, USA

Baretto, Ray (Musician)
Creative Music Consultants
181 Christle St #300
New York, NY 10002, USA

Barfield, Amanda (Actor)
Snyder Management
6409 Primrose Ave Ste 7
Los Angeles, CA 90068-2865, USA

Barfield, Jesse L (Athlete, Baseball Player)
5814 Spanish Moss Ct
Spring, TX 77379-6482, USA

Barfield, John (Athlete, Baseball Player)
2107 Hobson Ave
Hot Springs National Park, AR 71913-3037, USA

Barfield, Josh (Athlete, Baseball Player)
18082 N 93rd Pl
Scottsdale, AZ 85255-6055, USA

Barfield, Ron (Race Car Driver)
PO Box 6495
Florence, SC 29502-6495, USA

Bargar, Greg (Athlete, Baseball Player)
902 Felbar Ave
Torrance, CA 90503-5128, USA

Barger, Ralph (Sonny) (Actor)
c/o Staff Member *HarperCollins Publishers*
195 Broadway Fl 2
New York, NY 10007-3132, USA

Bargh, Renee (Television Host)
c/o Kyell Thomas *Octagon Entertainment*
1840 Century Park E Ste 200
Los Angeles, CA 90067-2114, USA

Bargnani, Andrea (Athlete, Basketball Player)
c/o Leon Rose *CAA Basketball*
405 Lexington Ave Fl 19
New York, NY 10174-1800, USA

Barhom, Ashraf (Actor)
c/o Alex Segal *InterTalent Rights Group*
46 Charlotte St
InterTalent House
London W1T 2GS, UNITED KINGDOM

Barhorst, Barney (Athlete, Basketball Player)
8004 River Bay Dr E
Indianapolis, IN 46240-2994, USA

Barinholtz, Ike (Actor, Comedian)
c/o Peter Principato *Artists First*
9465 Wilshire Blvd Ste 900
Beverly Hills, CA 90212-2608, USA

Barisich, Carl J (Athlete, Football Player)
10747 McGregor Dr
Columbia, MD 21044-4956, USA

Bark, Brian (Athlete, Baseball Player)
12308 Silver Cup Ct
Reisterstown, MD 21136-6481, USA

Barkauskas, Antanas S (President)
Akmenu 71
Vilnus, LITHUANIA

Barker, Bob (Game Show Host)
The DJ&T Foundation
PO Box 5109
West Hills, CA 91308-5109, USA

Barker, Bryan (Athlete, Football Player)
1225 Selva Marina Cir
Atlantic Beach, FL 32233-5525, USA

Barker, Clive (Producer, Writer)
c/o Staff Member *Seraphim Films*
1606 Argyle Ave
Hollywood, CA 90028-6408, USA

Barker, Ed (Athlete, Football Player)
12002 Clover Creek Dr SW
Lakewood, WA 98499-5210, USA

Barker, Glen (Athlete, Baseball Player)
363 2nd Ave
Albany, NY 12209-1924, USA

Barker, Jay (Athlete, Football Player, Talk Show Host)
4120 Montevallo Rd S
Mountain Brk, AL 35213-3114, USA

Barker, Jordan (Actor)
c/o Staff Member *Select Artists Ltd (CA-Westside Office)*
1138 12th St Apt 1
Santa Monica, CA 90403-5459, USA

Barker, Kevin (Athlete, Baseball Player)
PO Box 96
Mendota, VA 24270-0096, USA

Barker, Len (Athlete, Baseball Player)
10690 Locust Grove Dr
Chardon, OH 44024-8870, USA

Barker, Leo (Athlete, Football Player)
520 Grove Park Pl
Roswell, GA 30075-6873, USA

Barker, Lois (Athlete, Baseball Player)
195 W Main St Apt 6
Chester, NJ 07930-2451, USA

Barker, Pat (Writer)
Gillion Aitken
29 Fernshaw Road
London SW10 0TG, UNITED KINGDOM (UK)

Barker, Ray (Athlete, Baseball Player)
303 Greenbriar Rd
Martinsburg, WV 25401-2827, USA

Barker, Rich (Athlete, Baseball Player)
17 Landers Rd
Stoneham, MA 02180-1409, USA

Barker, Richard A (Religious Leader)
Orthodox Presbyterian Church
PO Box P
Willow Grove, PA 19090, USA

Barker, Roy (Athlete, Football Player)
23 Saint Marks Cir
Islandia, NY 11749-1728, USA

Barker, Sean (Athlete, Baseball Player)
1008 Tam O Shanter Dr
Bakersfield, CA 93309-2451, USA

Barker, Sue (Athlete, Tennis Player)
c/o Staff Member *BBC Artist Mail*
PO Box 1116
Belfast BT2 7AJ, United Kingdom

Barker, Tom (Actor)
London Mgmt
2-4 Noel St
London W1V 3RB, UNITED KINGDOM (UK)

Barker, Travis (Musician)
c/o Jenni Weinman *The Current Co. PR*
8671 Wilshire Blvd Ste 400
Beverly Hills, CA 90211-2912, USA

Barker-Lequia, Joan (Athlete, Baseball Player)
3236 34th St SW
Grandville, MI 49418-1905, USA

Barkett, Andy (Athlete, Baseball Player)
1016 Willa Lake Cir
Oviedo, FL 32765-6445, USA

Barkin, Ellen (Actor)
c/o Stephen Huvane *Slate PR*
901 N Highland Ave
W Hollywood, CA 90038-2412, USA

Barkley, Brian (Athlete, Baseball Player)
9208 Spring Ridge Cir
Woodway, TX 76712-8764, USA

Barkley, Charles (Athlete, Basketball Player, Olympic Athlete)
7615 E Vaquero Dr
Scottsdale, AZ 85258-2100, USA

Barkley, Dean M (Politician)
1300 W Medicine Lake Dr Apt 101
Minneapolis, MN 55441-4854, USA

Barkley, Doug (Athlete, Hockey Player)
583 63rd Ave.
Calgary, AB T3E 7N4, Canada

Barkley, Iran (Boxer)
2645 3rd Ave
Bronx, NY 10451-6329, USA

Barkley, Jeff (Athlete, Baseball Player)
264 3rd Ave NE
Hickory, NC 28601-5016, USA

Barkley, Matt (Athlete, Football Player)
c/o David Dunn *Athletes First*
23091 Mill Creek Dr
Laguna Hills, CA 92653-1258, USA

Barkley, Saquon (Athlete, Football Player)
c/o Kimblery Miale *Roc Nation*
1411 Broadway Fl 38
New York, NY 10018-3409, USA

Barkman, Tyler Jane (Janie) (Swimmer)
Princeton University
Athletic Dept
Princeton, NJ 08544-0001, USA

Barksdale, James (Jim) (Business Person)
Time Warner Inc.
1 Time Warner Ctr
New York, NY 10019-6038, USA

Barksdale, Lance (Athlete, Baseball Player)
136 Spring Oak Dr
Madison, MS 39110-9130, USA

Barksdale, LaQuanda (Athlete, Basketball Player)
San Antonio Silver Stars
1 at and T Center Pkwy
San Antonio, TX 78219-3604, USA

Barkum, Jerome P (Athlete, Football Player)
2720 Palmer Dr Apt J5
Gulfport, MS 39507-2854, USA

Barletta, Lou (Congressman, Politician)
510 Cannon Hob
Washington, DC 20515-1402, USA

Barlow, Bob (Athlete, Hockey Player)
4912 Wesley Rd
Victoria, BC V8Y 1Y5, Canada

Barlow, Corey (Athlete, Football Player)
1009 Narrows Point Dr
Birmingham, AL 35242-8675, USA

Barlow, Craig (Athlete, Golfer)
231 W Horizon Ridge Pkwy Apt 1515
Henderson, NV 89012-5427, USA

Barlow, Gary (Musician, Songwriter)
c/o Staff Member *WME/IMG (UK)*
103 New Oxford St WMA
Centrepoint
London WC1A 1DD, UNITED KINGDOM

Barlow, Kevan (Athlete, Football Player)
c/o Doug Hendrickson *Relativity Sports*
2029 Century Park E Ste 1550
Century City, CA 90067-3000, USA

Barlow, Mike (Athlete, Baseball Player)
4524 Francis Rd
Cazenovia, NY 13035-8470, USA

Barlow, Perry (Cartoonist)
New Yorker Magazine
4 Times Sq
Editorial Dept
New York, NY 10036-6518, USA

Barlow, Reggie (Athlete, Football Player)
8311 Timber Trace Ln
Pike Road, AL 36064-3444, USA

BarlowGirl (Music Group, Musician)
c/o Greg Oliver *Greg Oliver Agency Inc (GOA)*
278 Seaboard Ln Ste 10
Franklin, TN 37067-8315, USA

Barmes, Cllnt (Athlete, Baseball Player)
113 Mallard Ct
Mead, CO 80542-8802, USA

Barmore, Leon (Athlete, Basketball Player)
1100 Brookhaven Ave
Ruston, LA 71270-8505, USA

Barnaby, Matthew (Athlete, Hockey Player)
134 King Anthony Way
Getzville, NY 14068-1414, USA

Barnard, Aneurin (Actor)
c/o Romilly Bowlby *DDA Public Relations*
192-198 Vauxhall Bridge Rd
London SW1V 1DX, UNITED KINGDOM

Barndt, Tom (Athlete, Football Player)
11041 Romola St
Las Vegas, NV 89141-3410, USA

Barner, Kenjon (Athlete, Football Player)
c/o Frank Bauer *Sun West Sports*
7883 N Pershing Ave
Stockton, CA 95207-1749, USA

Barnes, Antwan (Athlete, Football Player)

Barnes, Ben (Actor)
c/o Lena Roklin *Luber Roklin Management*
5815 W Sunset Blvd Ste 208
Los Angeles, CA 90028-6481, USA

Barnes, Benny J (Athlete, Football Player)
5003 Fleming Ave
Richmond, CA 94804-4718, USA

Barnes, Billy Ray (Athlete, Football Player)
501 W Ryder Ave
Landis, NC 28088-1238, USA

Barnes, Brandon (Athlete, Football Player)
912 Westview Dr
Sikeston, MO 63801-4661, USA

Barnes, Brian (Athlete, Baseball Player)
860 River Cove Dr
Dacula, GA 30019-2090, USA

Barnes, Bruce (Athlete, Football Player)
7129 Alexandria Pl
Stockton, CA 95207-1503, USA

Barnes, Christopher Daniel (Actor)
1003 Blossom Ln
Redondo Beach, CA 90278-4951, USA

Barnes, Darian (Athlete, Football Player)
805 Lowell Ave
Toms River, NJ 08753-7722, USA

Barnes, Erich (Athlete, Football Player)
712 Warburton Ave
Yonkers, NY 10701-1501, USA

Barnes, Ernest E (Athlete, Football Player)
4435 Camellia Ave
North Hollywood, CA 91602-1905, USA

Barnes, Gary (Athlete, Football Player)
172 Falling Springs Rd
Central, SC 29630-9406, USA

Barnes, Jeff (Athlete, Football Player)
10738 Versailles Blvd
Clermont, FL 34711-7342, USA

Barnes, Jhane (Designer, Fashion Designer)
Jhane Barnes Inc
140 W 57th St Ste 5B
New York, NY 10019-3326, USA

Barnes, Jimmy (Musician)
Harbour Agency
135 Forbes St
Wooloomooloo, NSW 02011, AUSTRALIA

Barnes, Joanna (Actor)
PO Box 1103
Gualala, CA 95445-1103, USA

Barnes, Joe (Race Car Driver)
Barnes Racing
200 Neil Thompson Rd
Lackawaxen, PA 18435-9601, USA

Barnes, John (Athlete, Baseball Player)
1455 Godell St
Templeton, CA 93465-9424, USA

Barnes, Johnnie (Athlete, Football Player)
212 Charlemagne Dr
Suffolk, VA 23435-1453, USA

Barnes, Julian P (Writer)
P F D Drury House
34-43 Russell St
London WC2B 5HA, UNITED KINGDOM (UK)

Barnes, Khalif (Athlete, Football Player)
7967 Monterey Bay Dr
Jacksonville, FL 32256-2927, USA

Barnes, Kim (Writer)
c/o Staff Member *Knopf*
1745 Broadway Frnt 3
New York, NY 10019-4343, USA

Barnes, Larry (Athlete, Baseball Player)
11906 Crockett Ct
Bakersfield, CA 93312-5710, USA

Barnes, Larry (Athlete, Football Player)
2202 Belle Chase Cir
Tampa, FL 33634, USA

Barnes, Larry (Athlete, Football Player)
410 Navajo Ave
Simla, CO 80835, USA

Barnes, Linda (Writer)
56 Seaver St
Brookline, MA 02445-5749, USA

Barnes, Lute (Athlete, Baseball Player)
35911 Donny Cir
Palm Desert, CA 92211-2657, USA

Barnes, Marlon (Athlete, Football Player)
2693 Cherry St
Denver, CO 80207-3038, USA

Barnes, Matt (Athlete, Basketball Player)
c/o Toby Bailey *Paradigm Sports Management*
17461 Derian Ave Ste 108
Irvine, CA 92614-5807, USA

Barnes, Mike H (Athlete, Football Player)
205 Cindy St S
Keller, TX 76248-2341, USA

Barnes, Mike J (Athlete, Football Player)
27474 Plank Rd
Guys Mills, PA 16327-5434, USA

Barnes, Norm (Athlete, Hockey Player)
17 Meadow Xing
Simsbury, CT 06070-1006, USA

Barnes, Pat (Athlete, Football Player)
5 Willowglade
Trabuco Canyon, CA 92679-3813, USA

Barnes, Pricilla (Actor)

Barnes, Priscilla (Actor)
PO Box 684
La Canada, CA 91012-0684, USA

Barnes, Rashidi (Athlete, Football Player)
1036 Oak Grove Rd Apt 53
Concord, CA 94518-3238, USA

Barnes, Reggie (Athlete, Football Player)
505 W Springdale Ln
Grand Prairie, TX 75052-5122, USA

Barnes, Rich (Athlete, Baseball Player)
2845 Wilderness Rd
West Palm Beach, FL 33409-2030, USA

Barnes, Rick (Athlete, Basketball Player)
Texas University
Athletic Dept
Austin, TX 78713, USA

Barnes, Rod (Athlete, Basketball Player)
Mississippi State University
Athletic Dept
Mississippi State, MS 39762, USA

Barnes, Rodrigo (Athlete, Football Player)
4310 Gram Ln
Waco, TX 76705-2662, USA

Barnes, Roger (Actor)
3 Cardiff Crt
Whitby, ON L1N 5N8, Canada

Barnes, Ron (Athlete, Baseball Player)
5304 MacDonald Ave
El Cerrito, CA 94530-1636, USA

Barnes, Skeeter (Athlete, Baseball Player)
11544 Winding Wood Dr
Indianapolis, IN 46235-9731, USA

Barnes, Stu (Athlete, Hockey Player)
3955 Lively Ln
Dallas, TX 75220-1869, USA

Barnes, Stu (Athlete, Hockey Player)
Dallas Stars
2601 Avenue of the Stars Ste 100
Attn: Hockey Operations Dept
Frisco, TX 75034-9016, USA

Barnes, Tomur (Athlete, Football Player)
9550 Meyer Forest Dr APT 933
Houston, TX 77096-4350, USA

Barnes, Wallace (Business Person)
Barnes Group
123 Main St
Bristol, CT 06010-6376, USA

Barnes, William (Athlete, Baseball Player)
19792 Ardmore St
Detroit, MI 48235-1503, USA

Barnes Jr, Roosevelt (Athlete, Football Player)
3128 Covington Manor Rd
Fort Wayne, IN 46814-9126, USA

Barnes-McCoy, Joyce (Athlete, Baseball Player)
1313 E 19th Ave
Hutchinson, KS 67502-5061, USA

Barnett, Amy DuBois (Writer)
c/o Staff Member *Broadway Publicity*
1745 Broadway
New York, NY 10019-4640, USA

Barnett, Charlie (Actor)
c/o Randi Goldstein *Gersh*
41 Madison Ave Ste 3301
New York, NY 10010-2210, USA

Barnett, Dave (Commentator)
606 Witt Rd
Little Elm, TX 75068-5811, USA

Barnett, Dean (Athlete, Football Player)
8 Cozy Glen Cir
Henderson, NV 89074-1563, USA

Barnett, Dick (Athlete, Basketball Player)
1227 Pine Ridge
Bushkill, PA 18324, USA

Barnett, Douglas (Athlete, Football Player)
651 Park Ln
Billings, MT 59102-1930, USA

Barnett, Doyle (Writer)
c/o Staff Member *New World Library*
14 Pamaron Way Ste 1
Novato, CA 94949-6215, USA

Barnett, Errol (Correspondent, Journalist)
c/o Ali Spiesman *Creative Artists Agency (CAA)*
2000 Avenue of the Stars Ste 100
Los Angeles, CA 90067-4705, USA

Barnett, Fred (Athlete, Football Player)
428 N 13th St Apt 5F
Philadelphia, PA 19123-3629, USA

Barnett, Gary (Coach, Football Coach)
Colorado University
Athletic Dept
Boulder, CO 80309-0001, USA

Barnett, Jim (Athlete, Basketball Player)
7 Kittiwake Rd
Orinda, CA 94563-1716, USA

Barnett, Larry (Athlete, Baseball Player)
6298 Hughes Rd
Prospect, OH 43342-9602, USA

Barnett, Mandy (Musician)
320 Old Hickory Blvd Apt 1911
Nashville, TN 37221-1312, USA

Barnett, Mike (Athlete, Baseball Player)
465 Bramblewood Ln
Knoxville, TN 37922-4371, USA

Barnett, Nate (Athlete, Basketball Player)
71e N Jefferson St
Wilmington, DE 19801-1412, USA

Barnett, Nick (Athlete, Football Player)
3496 Country Winds Ct
Green Bay, WI 54311-6906, USA

Barnett, Oliver (Athlete, Football Player)
1133 Autumn Ridge Dr
Lexington, KY 40509-2055, USA

Barnett, Pam (Athlete, Golfer)
4908 E Rancho Tierra Dr
Cave Creek, AZ 85331-5912, USA

Barnett, Sloan (Correspondent, Writer)
c/o Staff Member *Simon & Schuster*
1230 Avenue of the Americas Fl CONC1
New York, NY 10020-1586, USA

Barnett, Steven (Steve) (Athlete, Football Player)
308 Romae Ct
Danville, CA 94526-1863, USA

Barnette, Curtis H (Business Person)
Bethlehem Steel
1170 8th Ave
Bethlehem, PA 18018-2255, USA

Barney, Darwin (Athlete, Baseball Player)
c/o Joe Urbon *Creative Artists Agency (CAA)*
405 Lexington Ave Fl 19
New York, NY 10174-1800, USA

Barney, Edith (Athlete, Baseball Player)
329 Blackburn Blvd
Venice, FL 34287-1507, USA

Barney, Tamra (Reality Star)
c/o Pamela Hicks *Hicks and Associates*
Prefers to be contacted via email or telephone
Los Angeles, CA 90069, USA

Barney Jr, Lemuel J (Lem) (Athlete, Football Player)
775 Kentbrook Dr
Commerce Township, MI 48382-5013, USA

Barnhardt, Tom (Athlete, Football Player)
503 Park St
China Grove, NC 28023-2154, USA

Barnhart, Vic (Athlete, Baseball Player)
13202 Unger Rd
Hagerstown, MD 21742-1429, USA

Barnhill, Herbert (Athlete, Baseball Player)
Jacksonville Red Caps
3712 Owen Ave
Jacksonville, FL 32208-2910, USA

Barnhill, John (Athlete, Basketball Player)
28511 Lomo Dr
Rancho Palos Verdes, CA 90275-3137, USA

Barnhill, Norton (Athlete, Basketball Player)
1718 Park Terrace Ln
Winston Salem, NC 27127-4794, USA

Barnhill, Scott (Model)
c/o Staff Member *IMG*
304 Park Ave S Fl 12
New York, NY 10010-4314, USA

Barnowski, Ed (Athlete, Baseball Player)
3812 Wax Myrtle Run
Naples, FL 34112-3374, USA

Barnwell, Chris (Athlete, Baseball Player)
1442 Fruit Cove Rd N
Saint Johns, FL 32259-2845, USA

Barnwell, Malcolm (Athlete, Football Player)
4045 Gullah Ave Apt 103
Charleston, SC 29405-6379, USA

Barnwell, Ysaye (Musician)
Sweet Honey Agency
PO Box 600099
Newtonville, MA 02460-0001, USA

Barocco, Rocco (Designer, Fashion Designer)
Via Occhio Marion
Capri/Napoli 80773, ITALY

Baron, Britt (Actor)
c/o Atil Singh *Principal Entertainment*
9255 W Sunset Blvd Ste 500
Los Angeles, CA 90069-3301, USA

Baron, Caroline (Producer)
c/o Paul Hook *ICM Partners*
10250 Constellation Blvd Fl 7
Los Angeles, CA 90067-6207, USA

Baron, Jimmy (Athlete, Baseball Player)
7402 Conner Ln
Edwardsville, IL 62025-4668, USA

Baron, Joanne (Actor)
940 N Tigertail Rd
Los Angeles, CA 90049-1419, USA

Baron, Murray (Athlete, Hockey Player)
23723 N. Scottsdale Rd.
#D-3
Scottsdale, AZ 85255, USA

Baron, Natalia (Actor)
c/o Michael Fuller *Fuller Law*
23501 Park Sorrento Ste 201
Calabasas, CA 91302-1374, USA

Barone, Anita (Actor)
c/o Dede Binder-Goldsmith *Defining Artists Agency*
8721 W Sunset Blvd Ste 209
W Hollywood, CA 90069-2272, USA

Barone, Daniel (Athlete, Baseball Player)
120 Joes Ln
Hollister, CA 95023-6353, USA

Barone, Dick (Athlete, Baseball Player)
1481 McDonald Cir
Hollister, CA 95023-6743, USA

Baron-Reid, Colette Baron-Reid (Writer)
c/o Staff Member *Hay House, Inc*
PO Box 5100
Carlsbad, CA 92018-5100, USA

Barr, Anthony (Athlete, Football Player)

Barr, Bob (Business Person, Politician)
Office of Bob Barr
4401 Northside Pkwy NW # 100
Atlanta, GA 30327-3065, USA

Barr, Cynthia (Athlete, Olympic Athlete, Swimmer)
3995 Aiken Rd
Pensacola, FL 32503-3301, USA

Barr, Dave (Athlete, Hockey Player)
c/o Staff Member *Guelph Storm Hockey Club*
55 Wyndham St N
Guelph, ON N1H 7T8, Canada

Barr, Dave (Golfer)
Duncan MacKenzie
10620 Southdale Rd
Richmond, BC V7A 2W7, CANADA

Barr, Doug (Actor)
PO Box 63
Rutherford, CA 94573-0063, USA

Barr, Jim (Athlete, Baseball Player)
6335 Oak Hill Dr
Granite Bay, CA 95746-8908, USA

Barr, Julia (Actor)
c/o Robert Attermann *Abrams Artists Agency*
275 7th Ave Fl 26
New York, NY 10001-6708, USA

Barr, Matt (Actor)
c/o Matt Luber *Luber Roklin Management*
5815 W Sunset Blvd Ste 208
Los Angeles, CA 90028-6481, USA

Barr, Mike (Athlete, Basketball Player)
350 38th St NW
Canton, OH 44709-1523, USA

Barr, Nevada (Writer)
G P Putnam's Sons
375 Hudson St
New York, NY 10014-3658, USA

Barr, Roseanne (Actor, Comedian, Producer)
c/o James Moore *Full Moon & High Tide Productions*
424 Main St
El Segundo, CA 90245-3002, USA

Barr, Steve (Athlete, Baseball Player)
470 Village Cir SW
Winter Haven, FL 33880-1668, USA

Barr, William (Politician)
1 Stamford Forum
Stamford, CT 06901-3516, USA

Barra, Mary (Business Person)
General Motors Company
P.O. Box 3170
Detroit, MI 48232, USA

Barragan, Cuno (Athlete, Baseball Player)
1824 Saint Ann Ct
Carmichael, CA 95608-5643, USA

Barranca, German (Athlete, Baseball Player)
199 Kreidler Ave
York, PA 17402-4976, USA

Barrasso, John (Senator)
307 Dirksen Senate Office Building
Washington, DC 20510-0001, USA

Barrasso, Tom (Athlete, Hockey Player)
1400 Edwards Mill Rd
Attn Coaching Staff
Raleigh, NC 27607-3624, USA

Barrasso, Tom (Athlete, Hockey Player)
12820 Rosalie St
Raleigh, NC 27614-7970, USA

Barratt, Michael R (Astronaut)
2102 Pleasant Palm Cir
League City, TX 77573-6670, USA

Barratt, Michael R Dr (Astronaut)
2102 Pleasant Palm Cir
League City, TX 77573-6670, USA

Barrault, Doug (Athlete, Hockey Player)
1305 Pine Dr
Golden, BC V0A 1H1, CANADA

Barrault, Marie-Christine (Actor)
Cineart
36 Rue de Ponthlieu
Paris 75008, FRANCE

Barraza, Adriana (Actor)
c/o Ivan De Paz *DePaz Management*
2011 N Vermont Ave
Los Angeles, CA 90027-1931, USA

Barraza, Maria (Actor)
c/o Staff Member *TV Caracol*
Calle 76 #11 - 35
Piso 10AA
Bogota DC 26484, COLOMBIA

Barrese, Sasha (Actor)
c/o Erik Kritzer *LINK Entertainment*
11872 La Grange Ave
Los Angeles, CA 90025-5282, USA

Barreto, Alexandra (Actor)
c/o Robert Marsala *Wishlab*
195 S Beverly Dr Ste 414
Beverly Hills, CA 90212-3044, USA

Barreto, Bruno (Director)
c/o Martin Spencer *Paradigm*
8942 Wilshire Blvd
Beverly Hills, CA 90211-1908, USA

Barreto, Rhianne (Actor)
c/o Paul Martin *Sainow Agency*
10-11 Lower John St.
Golden Square
London W1F 9EB, UNITED KINGDOM

Barrett, Alice (Actor)
Alliance Talent
9171 Wilshire Blvd Ste 441
Beverly Hills, CA 90210-5516, USA

Barrett, Bo (Actor)
c/o Staff Member *Badass Haircut Productions*
2718 Lakewood Ave
Los Angeles, CA 90039-2619, USA

Barrett, Brendan Ryan (Actor)
c/o Carol Elsner *AMT Artists*
14724 Ventura Blvd Ste 505
Sherman Oaks, CA 91403-3505, USA

Barrett, Brendon Ryan (Actor)
9255 W Sunset Blvd Ste 1010
West Hollywood, CA 90069-3307, USA

Barrett, Colleen (Business Person)
Southwest Airlines
PO Box 36611
2702 Love Field Dr
Dallas, TX 75235-1611, USA

Barrett, Craig R (Business Person)
Intel Corp
2200 Mission College Blvd
Santa Clara, CA 95054-1549, USA

Barrett, David (Athlete, Football Player)
1423 E Rose St
Blytheville, AR 72315-3714, USA

Barrett, Ernie (Athlete, Basketball Player)
2105 Grand Ridge Ct
Manhattan, KS 66503-8695, USA

Barrett, Fred (Athlete, Hockey Player)
3016 Leitrim Rd
Gloucester, ON K1T 3V9, Canada

Barrett, Jacinda (Actor)
c/o Joan Green *Joan Green Management*
1836 Courtney Ter
Los Angeles, CA 90046-2106, USA

Barrett, Jean (Athlete, Football Player)
7494 S Sleepy Hollow Dr
Tulsa, OK 74136-5919, USA

Barrett, John (Athlete, Hockey Player)
4570 Bank St
Gloucester, ON K1T 3W6, Canada

Barrett, Kelli (Actor)
c/o Emily Gerson Saines *Brookside Artists Management*
250 W 57th St Ste 1820
New York, NY 10107-1802, USA

Barrett, Malcolm (Actor)
c/o Beth Stein *Beth Stein and Associates*
925 N La Brea Ave # 4
West Hollywood, CA 90038-2321, USA

Barrett, Mario (Actor, Musician)
c/o Daniel Kim *Creative Artists Agency (CAA)*
2000 Avenue of the Stars Ste 100
Los Angeles, CA 90067-4705, USA

Barrett, Martin G (Marty) (Athlete, Baseball Player)
813 W Locust Dr
Chandler, AZ 85248-4355, USA

Barrett, Michael (Athlete, Baseball Player)
600 Galleria Pkwy SE Ste 1900
Atlanta, GA 30339-5990, USA

Barrett, Ted (Athlete, Baseball Player)
4380 E Sundance Ct
Gilbert, AZ 85297-9640, USA

Barrett, Tim (Athlete, Baseball Player)
5588 Jandel Dr
Aurora, IN 47001-3010, USA

Barrett, Tom (Athlete, Baseball Player)
381 S Silverbrush Dr
Chandler, AZ 85226-4427, USA

Barrett, Wade (Athlete, Wrestler)
c/o Staff Member *World Wrestling Entertainment (WWE)*
1241 E Main St
Stamford, CT 06902-3520, USA

Barrichello, Rubens (Race Car Driver)
c/o Staff Member *Jaguar Racing Ltd*
Bradbourne Drive
Tilbrook
Milton Keynes MK7 8BJ, United Kingdom

Barrie, Barbara (Actor)
c/o Staff Member *Innovative Artists*
1505 10th St
Santa Monica, CA 90401-2805, USA

Barrie, Chris (Actor, Comedian)
International Creative Mgmt
76 Oxford St
London W1N 0AX, UNITED KINGDOM (UK)

Barrie, Doug (Athlete, Hockey Player)
12130 46 St NW
Edmonton, AB T5W 2W4, Canada

Barrie, Len (Athlete, Hockey Player)
Bear Mountain Gold Club
208-2800 Bryn Maur Rd
Victoria, BC V9B 3T4, Canada

Barrie, Sebastian (Athlete, Football Player)
502 Heritage Meadows Rd
Pleasant Hill, CA 94523-3192, USA

Barrile, Anthony (Actor)
Alliance Talent
9171 Wilshire Blvd Ste 441
Beverly Hills, CA 90210-5516, USA

Barrino, Fantasia (Musician)
Jodiba Records
PO Box 306
High Point, NC 27261-0306, USA

Barrios, Jose (Athlete, Baseball Player)
6484 SW 25th St
Miami, FL 33155-2958, USA

Barris, Kenya (Director, Producer)
Khalabo Ink Society
500 S Buena Vista St
Burbank, CA 91521-0001, USA

Barriw, Barbara (Actor)
15 W 72nd St Apt 2A
New York, NY 10023-3419, USA

Barron, Alex (Athlete, Football Player)
630 Emerson Rd Apt 206
Saint Louis, MO 63141-6751, USA

Barron, Alex (Race Car Driver)
Dan Gurney's Racing
2334 S Broadway
Santa Ana, CA 92707-3250, USA

Barron, Chris (Music Group, Musician)
c/o Staff Member *Skyline Music*
28 Union St
Whitefield, NH 03598-3503, USA

Barron, Dana (Actor)
c/o Kevin Turner *Coast to Coast Talent Group*
3350 Barham Blvd
Los Angeles, CA 90068-1404, USA

Barron, Doug (Athlete, Golfer)
5080 Peg Ln
Memphis, TN 38117-2147, USA

Barron, Mark (Athlete, Football Player)
c/o Jimmy Sexton *CAA (Memphis)*
6060 Poplar Ave Ste 470
Memphis, TN 38119-0910, USA

Barron, Mark (Athlete, Baseball Player)
110 N Randolph Ave
Clarksville, IN 47129-2761, USA

Barron, Tony (Athlete, Baseball Player)
10301 Hipkins Rd SW
Lakewood, WA 98498-4439, USA

Barros, Dana (Athlete, Basketball Player)
10 Arborway
North Easton, MA 02356-1142, USA

Barrow, Barbara (Athlete, Golfer)
11427 Mayapple Way
San Diego, CA 92131-2928, USA

Barrow, Geoff (Musician)
Fruit
Saga Center
326 Kensal Road
London W10 5BZ, UNITED KINGDOM (UK)

Barrow, Michael (Athlete, Football Player)
1115 S Alhambra Cir Coral Gables, FL 33146, USA

Barrowman, John (Actor)
c/o Gavin Barker *Gavin Barker Assoc*
2D Wimpole St
London W1G 0EB, UNITED KINGDOM

Barrowman, Mike (Swimmer)
706 N Wamer St
Bay City, MI 48706, USA

Barrows, Scott (Athlete, Football Player)
3600 Kern Rd
Lake Orion, MI 48360-2351, USA

Barrows, Sydney Biddle (Business Person)
210 W 70th St Apt 209
New York, NY 10023-4363, USA

Barrueco, Manuel (Musician)
Columbia Artists Mgmt Inc
165 W 57th St
New York, NY 10019-2201, USA

Barry, A L (Religious Leader)
Lutheran Church Missouri Synod
1333 S Kirkwood Rd
Saint Louis, MO 63122-7295, USA

Barry, Allan (Athlete, Football Player)
700 S Myrtle Ave APT 230
Monrovia, CA 91016-8410, USA

Barry, Brent (Athlete, Basketball Player)
117 Coventry Ln
San Antonio, TX 78209-5445, USA

Barry, Daniel T (Dan) (Astronaut)
46 Ashton Ln
South Hadley, MA 01075-2143, USA

Barry, Daniel T Dr (Astronaut)
46 Ashton Ln
South Hadley, MA 01075-2143, USA

Barry, Dave (Journalist, Writer)
Miami Herald
1 Herald Plz
Editorial Dept
Miami, FL 33132-1609, USA

Barry, Jeff (Athlete, Baseball Player)
3816 Crystal Springs Dr
Medford, OR 97504-9113, USA

Barry, Jon (Athlete, Basketball Player)
3325 Piedmont Rd NE Unit 2307
Atlanta, GA 30305-1899, USA

Barry, Kevin (Athlete, Baseball Player)
160 Route 526
Allentown, NJ 08501-2015, USA

Barry, Len (Musician)
c/o Gary Cape *Cape Entertainment Inc*
8432 NW 31st Ct
Sunrise, FL 33351-8901, USA

Barry, Lynda (Cartoonist)
PO Box 447
Footville, WI 53537-0447, USA

Barry, Max (Writer)
c/o Staff Member *Scribe Publications Pty Ltd*
595 Drummond St
Carlton North Vic 03054, Australia

Barry, Odell (Athlete, Football Player)
2561 Ranch Reserve Rdg
Denver, CO 80234-2695, USA

Barry, Paul (Athlete, Football Player)
409 Kingswood Dr
El Paso, TX 79932-2217, USA

Barry, Randy (Reality Star)
c/o Michael Martin *MM Agency*
3937 Nobel Dr
San Diego, CA 92122-6156, USA

Barry, Raymond J (Actor)
c/o Bob McGowan *McGowan Management*
170 S Beverly Dr Ste 304
Beverly Hills, CA 90212-3000, USA

Barry, Rich (Athlete, Baseball Player)
12020 Hoffman St Apt K
Studio City, CA 91604-4760, USA

Barry, Rick (Athlete, Basketball Player)
5240 Broadmoor Bluffs Dr
Colorado Springs, CO 80906-7912, USA

Barry, Rod (Adult Film Star)
c/o Staff Member *Diva Central Inc*
7510 W Sunset Blvd # 1445
Los Angeles, CA 90046-3408, USA

Barry, Scott (Athlete, Baseball Player)
148 Lukesport Dr
Quincy, MI 49082-9595, USA

Barry, Seymour (Sy) (Artist, Cartoonist)
225 Fairfield Dr E
Holbrook, NY 11741-2866, USA

Barry, Todd (Comedian)
c/o John Griffin *Agency for the Performing Arts (APA)*
405 S Beverly Dr Ste 500
Beverly Hills, CA 90212-4425, USA

Barry III, Richard F D (Rick) (Athlete, Basketball Player)
KNBR Radio
55 Hawthorne St Ste 1100
San Francisco, CA 94105-3914, USA

Barrymore, Drew (Actor, Producer)
c/o Chris Miller *Flower Films Inc*
7119 W Sunset Blvd Ste 1123
West Hollywood, CA 90046-4411, USA

Bart, Peter (Writer)
c/o Daniel Strone *Trident Media Group LLC*
41 Madison Ave Fl 36
New York, NY 10010-2257, USA

Bart, Roger (Actor)
c/o Kimberlin Belloni *Artists First*
9465 Wilshire Blvd Ste 900
Beverly Hills, CA 90212-2608, USA

Bartecko, Lubos (Athlete, Hockey Player)
746 Whispering Forest Dr
Ballwin, MO 63021-4479, USA

Bartee, Kimera (Athlete, Baseball Player)
State College Spikes 112 Medlar Field at Lubrano Park 'Attn: Managers Office
University Park, PA 16802, USA

Bartee, William (Athlete, Football Player)
17 Talaquah Blvd
Ormond Beach, FL 32174-3705, USA

Bartek, Steve (Musician)
c/o Staff Member *Kraft-Engel Management*
15233 Ventura Blvd Ste 200
Sherman Oaks, CA 91403-2244, USA

Bartel, Robin (Athlete, Hockey Player)
210 Forsyth Crt
Saskatoon, SK S7N 4H2, Canada

Bartels, Jayden (Actor)
c/o Randy James *Randy James Management*
12711 Ventura Blvd Ste 345
Studio City, CA 91604-2416, USA

Barth, Robert (Religious Leader)
Churches of Christ in Christian Union
PO Box 30
Circleville, OH 43113-0030, USA

Bartha, Justin (Actor, Producer)
2220 N Berendo St
Los Angeles, CA 90027-1125, USA

Barthmaier, Jimmy (Athlete, Baseball Player)
445 Brook Cir
Roswell, GA 30075-7179, USA

Bartholomay, William C (Commentator)
180 E Pearson St Apt 3307
Chicago, IL 60611-6730, USA

Bartholomew, Brent (Athlete, Football Player)
809 N Lake Pleasant Rd
Apopka, FL 32712-3219, USA

Bartholomew, Jean (Athlete, Golfer)
411 Capistrano Dr
Palm Beach Gardens, FL 33410-4301, USA

Bartholomew, Logan (Actor)
c/o Joe Vance *Domain Talent*
1880 Century Park E Ste 1100
Los Angeles, CA 90067-1608, USA

Bartilson, Lynsey (Actor)
c/o Staff Member *Karen Renna & Associates*
PO Box 4227
Burbank, CA 91503-4227, USA

Bartirome, Tony (Athlete, Baseball Player)
1104 Palma Sola Blvd
Bradenton, FL 34209-3342, USA

Bartiromo, Maria (Correspondent)
c/o Staff Member *CNBC (DC)*
400 N Capitol St NW Ste 850
Washington, DC 20001-1555, USA

Bartkowski, Steven J (Steve) (Athlete, Football Player)
10745 Bell Rd
Duluth, GA 30097-1801, USA

Bartle, Cheryl (Actor)
8281 Melrose Ave Ste 200
Los Angeles, CA 90046-6890, USA

Bartles, Carl Bartles (Athlete, Football Player)
405 E 4th St
Kannapolis, NC 28083-3606, United States

Bartles, Edward (Athlete, Basketball Player)
105 Hemlock Dr
Killingworth, CT 06419-2225, USA

Bartlett, Bonnie (Actor, Musician)
12805 Hortense St
Studio City, CA 91604-1124, USA

Bartlett, Doug (Athlete, Football Player)
9133 26th St
Brookfield, IL 60513-1006, USA

Bartlett, Erinn (Actor)
c/o Randy James *Randy James Management*
12711 Ventura Blvd Ste 345
Studio City, CA 91604-2416, USA

Bartlett, Jason (Athlete, Baseball Player)
15476 Artesian Spring Rd
San Diego, CA 92127-5736, USA

Bartlett, Jennifer L (Artist)
Paula Cooper Gallery
526 W 26th St
New York, NY 10001-5517, USA

Bartlett, Jim (Athlete, Hockey Player)
8718 Chadwick Dr
Tampa, FL 33635-6212, USA

Bartlett, Murray (Actor)
c/o Rosanne Quezada *Paradigm*
8942 Wilshire Blvd
Beverly Hills, CA 90211-1908, USA

Bartlett, Robin (Actor)
2202 Pearl St
Santa Monica, CA 90405-2828, USA

Bartletti, Don (Journalist)
Los Angeles Times
2300 E Imperial Hwy
Editorial Dept
El Segundo, CA 90245-2813, USA

Bartlett O'Reilly, Alison (Actor)
c/o Carolyn Anthony *Anthony & Associates*
PO Box 910
New York, NY 10108-1201, USA

Bartley, Boyd (Athlete, Baseball Player)
7500 Noreast Dr
North Richland Hills, TX 76180-6736, USA

Bartley, Ephesians (Athlete, Football Player)
3552 Kittery Dr
Snellville, GA 30039-6033, USA

Bartmann, Bill (Business Person)
8556 E 101st St Ste C
Tulsa, OK 74133-7036, USA

Bartoe, John-David F (Astronaut)
7520 Ridgewood Ave Apt 802
Cape Canaveral, FL 32920-4803, 32920

Bartoletti, Louis (Athlete, Golfer)
1450 Longlea Ter
Wellington, FL 33414-9017, USA

Bartoli, Cecilia (Musician)
Decca Music Group Limited
8 St James's Square
London SW1Y 4JU, UNITED KINGDOM

Bartolome, Victor (Athlete, Basketball Player)
1025A Rinconada Rd # A
Santa Barbara, CA 93101-1424, USA

Barton, Austin (Artist)
100 N Lake St
Joseph, OR 97846-8500, USA

Barton, Bob (Athlete, Baseball Player)
29911 Cactus Pl
Temecula, CA 92592-2111, USA

Barton, Brian (Athlete, Baseball Player)
1217 W 76th St
Los Angeles, CA 90044-2411, USA

Barton, Daric (Athlete, Baseball Player)
950 Dogwood St
Costa Mesa, CA 92627-4161, USA

Barton, Dorie (Actor)
c/o Daniel Spilo *Industry Entertainment Partners*
955 Carrillo Dr Ste 300
Los Angeles, CA 90048-5400, USA

Barton, Eric (Athlete, Football Player)
23 Hayes Hill Dr
Northport, NY 11768-1331, USA

Barton, Glenys (Artist)
Angela Flowers Gallery
199-205 Richmond Road
London E8 3NJ, UNITED KINGDOM (UK)

Barton, Greg (Athlete, Football Player)
7799 SW Scholls Ferry Rd Apt 144
Beaverton, OR 97008-6542, USA

Barton, Greg (Athlete, Olympic Athlete)
Epic Kayaks Inc
2000 Jonesborough Rd
Erwin, TN 37650-4063, USA

Barton, Harris S (Athlete, Football Player)
334 Lincoln Ave
Palo Alto, CA 94301-2730, USA

Barton, Jim (Athlete, Football Player)
2126 Taylor Ln
Newark, OH 43055-6091, USA

Barton, Joe (Congressman, Politician)
2109 Rayburn Hob
Washington, DC 20515-4306, USA

Barton, Lou Ann (Musician)
c/o Cory L Moore *The Luther Wolf Agency*
PO Box 162078
Austin, TX 78716-2078, USA

Barton, Mischa (Actor)
c/o Adam Griffin *LINK Entertainment*
11872 La Grange Ave
Los Angeles, CA 90025-5282, USA

Barton, Peter (Actor)
10417 Eastborne Ave Apt 3
Los Angeles, CA 90024-6130, USA

Barton, Rachel (Musician)
I C M Artists
40 W 57th St
New York, NY 10019-4001, USA

Barton, Shawn (Athlete, Baseball Player)
1009 Helm Ln
Reading, PA 19605-3313, USA

Bartosh, Cliff (Athlete, Baseball Player)
939 Fairlawn Dr
Duncanville, TX 75116-3003, USA

Bartosik, Alison (Athlete, Olympic Athlete, Swimmer)
c/o Staff Member *Premier Management Group (PMG Sports)*
700 Evanvale Ct
Cary, NC 27518-2806, USA

Bartovic, Milan (Athlete, Hockey Player)
141 Bennington Hills Ct
West Henrietta, NY 14586-9768, USA

Bartrum, Mike (Athlete, Football Player)
43375 Carlton Pl
Pomeroy, OH 45769-9462, USA

Bartucelli, Jean-Louis (Actor)
9 rue Benard
Paris F-75014, France

Bartulis, Oskars (Athlete, Hockey Player)
45 Wimbledon Way
Marlton, NJ 08053-2087, USA

Bartz, Carol A (Business Person)
Autodesk Inc
111 McInnis Pkwy
San Rafael, CA 94903-2700, USA

Bartz, Randall (Athlete, Olympic Athlete, Speed Skater)
3820 Baker Rd
Hopkins, MN 55305-4908, USA

Baruchel, Jay (Actor)
c/o Hilary Hansen *Vision PR*
2 Penn Plz Rm 2601
New York, NY 10121-0001, USA

Barwin, Connor (Athlete, Football Player)
c/o Scott Smith *XAM Sports*
3509 Ice Age Dr
Madison, WI 53719-5409, USA

Baryshnikov, Mikhail (Actor, Dancer)
Baryshnikov Arts Center
455 W 35th St Apt 4
New York, NY 10001-1508, USA

Barzilauskas, Carl (Athlete, Football Player)
4444 Lower Schooner Rd
Nashville, IN 47448-9476, USA

Barzilla, Phil (Athlete, Baseball Player)
3310 Crystal Creek Dr
Sugar Land, TX 77478-4045, USA

Basa??ez, Sergio (Actor)
c/o Staff Member *TV Azteca*
Periferico Sur 4121
Colonia Fuentes del Pedregal
DF CP 14141, Mexico

Basana, Fred (Athlete, Baseball Player)
222 Diamond Oaks Rd
Roseville, CA 95678-1007, USA

Basaraba, Gary (Actor)
26 Rue Albus
Toulouse 31300, FRANCE

Basch, Harry (Actor)
8750 Burton Way
West Hollywood, CA 90048-3838, USA

Basche, David Allen (Actor)
c/o Staff Member *2 Wonder Full To Be*
21700 Oxnard St Ste 2050
Woodland Hills, CA 91367-7577, USA

Baschnagel, Brian D (Athlete, Football Player)
1824 Ridgewood Ln W
Glenview, IL 60025-2206, USA

Basco, Dante (Actor)
Don Buchwald
5900 Wilshire Blvd Ste 3100
Los Angeles, CA 90036-5030, USA

Basco, Derek (Actor)
c/o Staff Member *GVA Talent Agency Inc*
193 N Robertson Blvd
Beverly Hills, CA 90211-2103, USA

Basco, Dion (Actor)
Schiowitz/Clay/Rose
1680 Vine St # 1016
Los Angeles, CA 90028-8804, USA

Bash, Dana (Correspondent, Television Host)
5003 Belt Rd NW
Washington, DC 20016-4234, USA

Bashir, Idrees (Athlete, Football Player)
5579 Mountain View Pass
Stone Mountain, GA 30087-6020, USA

Bashir, Martin (Correspondent, Journalist, Television Host)
c/o Staff Member *John Miles Organisation*
Cadbury Camp Lane
Clapton in Gordano
Bristol BS20 7SB, United Kingdom

Bashkirov, Dmitri A (Musician)
25 Martirez Oblatos
Pozuelo
Madrid, SPAIN

Bashoff, Blake (Actor)
c/o Marni Rosenzweig *The Rosenzweig Group*
8840 Wilshire Blvd # 111
Beverly Hills, CA 90211-2606, USA

Basia (Music Group)
c/o Staff Member *Creative Artists Agency (CAA)*
2000 Avenue of the Stars Ste 100
Los Angeles, CA 90067-4705, USA

Basil, Toni (Musician)
830 S Ridgeley Dr
Los Angeles, CA 90036-4727, USA

Basinger, Kim (Actor)
c/o Annett Wolf *Wolf-Kasteler Public Relations*
6255 W Sunset Blvd Ste 1111
Los Angeles, CA 90028-7426, USA

Basinski, Ed (Athlete, Baseball Player)
8530 SW Curry Dr Unit B
Wilsonville, OR 97070-8448, USA

Basinski, Eddie (Athlete, Baseball Player)
220 E Hereford St
Gladstone, OR 97027-2165, USA

Basis, Austin (Actor)
c/o Sandy Erickson *Vic Ramos Management*
337 E 13th St Apt 6
New York, NY 10003-5852, USA

Baska, Richard (Rick) (Athlete, Football Player)
176 Josephine Ct
Central Point, OR 97502-3709, USA

Baskett, Hank (Athlete, Football Player, Reality Star)
4 Jillians Way
Voorhees, NJ 08043-9402, USA

Bass, Anthony (Athlete, Football Player)
120 Ridgewood Frst
Saint Albans, WV 25177-9502, USA

Bass, Ben (Actor)
c/o Ryan Stewart *Characters Talent Agency*
200-1505 2nd Ave W
Vancouver, BC V6H 3Y4, CANADA

Bass, Bob (Athlete, Basketball Player, Coach)
2266 Deerfield Dr
Fort Mill, SC 29715-6941, USA

Bass, Brian (Athlete, Baseball Player)
423 Seminole Dr
Montgomery, AL 36117-3905, USA

Bass, David (Athlete, Football Player)
c/o Harold C Lewis *National Sports Agency*
12181 Prichard Farm Rd
Maryland Heights, MO 63043-4203, USA

Bass, Doug (Actor)
c/o Jana Marimpietri *Mosaic Media Group*
407 N Maple Dr # 100
Beverly Hills, CA 90210-3818, USA

Bass, Glenn (Athlete, Football Player)
4185 Diplomacy Cir
Tallahassee, FL 32308-8720, USA

Bass, Jules (Director, Musician, Producer, Writer)
c/o Staff Member *Rankin/Bass Productions*
24 W 55th St
New York, NY 10019-5456, USA

Bass, Karen (Congressman, Politician)
405 Cannon Hob
Washington, DC 20515-4309, USA

Bass, Kevin (Athlete, Baseball Player)
3630 Maranatha Dr
Sugar Land, TX 77479-9665, USA

Bass, Lance (Musician)
c/o Bob Merrick *Lance Bass Productions*
130 N Brand Blvd Ste 400
Glendale, CA 91203-2631, USA

Bass, Michael T (Athlete, Football Player)
4703 NW 36th St
Gainesville, FL 32605-1017, USA

Bass, Mike (Athlete, Football Player)
4703 NW 36th St
Gainesville, FL 32605-1017, USA

Bass, Norm (Athlete, Football Player)
156 E 70th St
Los Angeles, CA 90003-2102, USA

Bass, Norm (Athlete, Baseball Player)
156 E 70th St
Los Angeles, CA 90003-2102, USA

Bass, Randy (Athlete, Baseball Player)
2709 SW Coombs Rd
Lawton, OK 73505-0809, USA

Bass, Ronald (Writer)
c/o Staff Member *Creative Artists Agency (CAA)*
2000 Avenue of the Stars Ste 100
Los Angeles, CA 90067-4705, USA

Bass, Ronald (Ron) (Actor, Producer, Writer)
c/o Staff Member *Writers Co-Op*
4000 Warner Blvd Bldg 1
Burbank, CA 91522-0001, USA

Bass, Sid (Business Person)
4824 Crestline Rd
Ft Worth, TX 76107-3708, USA

Bassen, Bob (Athlete, Coach, Hockey Player)
1742 Coldstone Dr
Frisco, TX 75034-2644, USA

Bassett, Angela (Actor)
c/o Staff Member *Bassett/Vance Productions*
1520 Ocean Park Blvd Apt C
Santa Monica, CA 90405-4853, USA

Bassett, Tim (Athlete, Basketball Player)
1143 Dorsey Pl
Plainfield, NJ 07062-2207, USA

Bassey, Dame Shirley (Musician)
24 Avenue Princess Grace
Monte Carlo 01200, Monaco

Bassey, Jennifer (Actor)
12 E 86th St Apt 1728
New York, NY 10028-0517, USA

Bassinger, Brec (Actor)
c/o Mitchell Gossett *Industry Entertainment Partners*
955 Carrillo Dr Ste 300
Los Angeles, CA 90048-5400, USA

Bassingthwaighte, Natalie (Actor)
c/o Staff Member *Mark Byrne Management*
1/2 Cooper St
Double Bay
Sydney, NSW 02028, Australia

Basslitz, Georg (Artist)
Schloss Demeberg
Holle 31188, GERMANY

Bassman, Herman (Red) (Athlete, Football Player)
910 Sunset Ave
Petersburg, VA 23805-2824, USA

Basso, Annalise (Actor)
c/o Daniel Spilo *Industry Entertainment Partners*
955 Carrillo Dr Ste 300
Los Angeles, CA 90048-5400, USA

Basso, Gabriel (Actor)
c/o David Eisenberg *Protege Entertainment*
710 E Angeleno Ave
Burbank, CA 91501-2213, USA

Bast, William (Producer)
6691 Whitley Ter
Los Angeles, CA 90068-3220, USA

Bastedo, Alexandra (Actor)
Charlesworth
68 Old Brompton Rd #280
London SW7 3LQ, UNITED KINGDOM (UK)

Bastel, Emily (Athlete, Golfer)
5377 County Highway 330
Upper Sandusky, OH 43351-9772, USA

Bastianich, Lidia (Chef)
c/o Max Stubblefield *United Talent Agency (UTA)*
9336 Civic Center Dr
Beverly Hills, CA 90210-3604, USA

Baston, Maceo (Athlete, Basketball Player)
c/o Mark Bartelstein *Priority Sports & Entertainment (Chicago)*
325 N La Salle Dr Ste 650
Chicago, IL 60654-8182, USA

Basu, Bipasha (Actor)
c/o Simone Sheffield *Canyon Entertainment*
PO Box 256
Palm Springs, CA 92263-0256, USA

Baswell, Jack (Athlete, Baseball Player)
9629 Bella Dr
Daphne, AL 36526-6271, USA

Batali, Dean (Writer)
c/o Bradford Bricken *The Cartel*
1108-1112 Tamarind Ave
Hollywood, CA 90038, USA

Batali, Mario (Chef, Television Host)
Otto Enoteca Pizzeria
1 5th Ave Frnt 2
New York, NY 10003-4312, USA

Batalla, Rick (Actor)
c/o Staff Member *Halpern Management*
PO Box 5042
Santa Monica, CA 90409-5042, USA

Batch, Baron (Athlete, Football Player)
c/o Jordan Woy *Willis & Woy Management*
4890 Alpha Rd Ste 200
Dallas, TX 75244-4639, USA

Batch, Charlie (Athlete, Football Player)
1844 Willow Oak Dr
Wexford, PA 15090-2506, USA

Batchelor, Rich (Athlete, Baseball Player)
860 S Whitehall Cir
Florence, SC 29501-8909, USA

Bateman, Brian (Athlete, Golfer)
2910 River Oaks Dr
Monroe, LA 71201-2028, USA

Bateman, Jason (Actor)
c/o Staff Member *Aggregate Films*
8409 Santa Monica Blvd
W Hollywood, CA 90069-4209, USA

Bateman, Justine (Actor)
7445 Woodrow Wilson Dr
Los Angeles, CA 90046-1322, USA

Bateman, Marv (Athlete, Football Player)
1022 W Smithsonian Way
Apple Valley, UT 84737-4830, USA

Bateman, Tom (Actor)
c/o Dallas Smith *United Agents*
12-26 Lexington St
London W1F OLE, UNITED KINGDOM

Bates, Alfred (Athlete, Track Athlete)
4215 Skymont Dr
Belmont, CA 94002-1245, USA

Bates, Bill (Athlete, Football Player)
1252 Neck Rd
Ponte Vedra Beach, FL 32082-4112, USA

Bates, Billy Ray (Athlete, Basketball Player)
340 Eastbrook Rd
Ridgewood, NJ 07450-2108, USA

Bates, Dick (Athlete, Baseball Player)
5859 W Cielo Grande
Glendale, AZ 85310-3631, USA

Bates, Dwayne (Athlete, Football Player)
555 W Madison St Apt 2901
Chicago, IL 60661-2848, USA

Bates, Emma (Actor)
c/o Marianne Golan *Golan & Blumberg*
2761 E Woodbury Dr
Arlington Heights, IL 60004-7247, USA

Bates, Jason (Athlete, Baseball Player)
4775 Silver Pine Dr
Castle Rock, CO 80108-7833, USA

Bates, Kathy (Actor)
243 S Muirfield Rd
Los Angeles, CA 90004-3730, USA

Bates, Mario (Athlete, Football Player)
PO Box 5832
Scottsdale, AZ 85261-5832, USA

Bates, Michael (Athlete, Football Player)
PO Box 69338
Tucson, AZ 85737-0014, USA

Bates, Pat (Athlete, Golfer)
215 Ward Cir Ste 200
Brentwood, TN 37027-2304, USA

Bates, Patrick J (Athlete, Football Player)
2745 N Collins St Apt 11123
Arlington, TX 76006-7108, USA

Bates, Shawn (Athlete, Hockey Player)
35 Bradshaw St
Medford, MA 02155-4819, USA

Bates, Ted (Athlete, Football Player)
4036 Paige St
Los Angeles, CA 90031-1437, USA

Bates, Tyler (Musician)
11733 Valleycrest Rd
Studio City, CA 91604-4227, USA

Bat for Lashes (Music Group)
c/o Staff Member *Red Light Management*
5800 Bristol Pkwy Ste 400
Culver City, CA 90230-6898, USA

Bathe, Bill (Athlete, Baseball Player)
1448 S Miller Creek Pl
Tucson, AZ 85748-7765, USA

Bathe, Frank (Athlete, Hockey Player)
2 Meadowood Dr
Scarborough, ME 04074-9421, USA

Bathe, Ryan Michelle (Actor)
c/o Atil Singh *Principal Entertainment*
9255 W Sunset Blvd Ste 500
Los Angeles, CA 90069-3301, USA

Batikis, Annastasia (Athlete, Baseball Player)
1023 Crab Tree Ln
Racine, WI 53406-4109, USA

Batinkoff, Randall (Actor)
1330 4th St
Santa Monica, CA 90401-1302, USA

Batista, Cardinal Giovanni (Religious Leader)
Palazzo Delle Congregazioni
Piazza Pio XII #10
Roma I-00193, ITALY

Batista, Eike (Business Person)
EBX
Praia Do Flamengo, 66, 10 Andar
Flamengo
Rio De Janerio, RJ 22210-903, Brazil

Batista, Tony (Athlete)
333 W Camden St
Baltimore, MD 21201-2496

Batiste, Kevin (Athlete, Baseball Player)
2501 Westridge St Apt 255
Houston, TX 77054-1519, USA

Batiste, Kim (Athlete, Baseball Player)
16163 Aikens Rd
Prairieville, LA 70769-4903, USA

Batiste, Michael (Athlete, Football Player)
2720 Edmonds St
Beaumont, TX 77705-1437, USA

Batiuk, Thomas M (Tom) (Cartoonist)
c/o Staff Member *King Features Syndication*
300 W 57th St Fl 15
New York, NY 10019-5238, USA

Batson, Susan (Actor)
Black Nexxus Inc.
311 W 43rd St Ste 201
New York, NY 10036-6034, USA

Batt, Bryan (Actor)
c/o Joanne Nici *Buchwald (NY)*
10 E 44th St
New York, NY 10017-3601, USA

Battaglia, Bates (Athlete, Hockey Player)
832 Graham St
Raleigh, NC 27605-1125, USA

Battaglia, Marco (Athlete, Football Player)
15832 79th St
Howard Beach, NY 11414-2907, USA

Battaglia, Matt (Actor)
c/o Stewart Strunk *Main Title Entertainment*
8383 Wilshire Blvd Ste 408
Beverly Hills, CA 90211-2435, USA

Battaglia, Rik (Actor)
Viale Montegrappa 10
Colle Verde Guidonia
Rome 00012, ITALY

Battelle, Ann (Athlete, Olympic Athlete, Skier)
Mogul Logic
4279 Monroe Dr Apt D
Boulder, CO 80303-8303, USA

Batten, Kim (Athlete, Olympic Athlete, Track Athlete)
24107 Plantation Dr NE
Atlanta, GA 30324-2942, USA

Batten, Pat (Athlete, Football Player)
9403 E 64th Ter
Raytown, MO 64133-4916, USA

Battie, Tony (Athlete, Basketball Player)
11264 Bridge House Rd
Windermere, FL 34786-5405

Battier, Shane (Athlete, Basketball Player)
4075 Bonita Ave
Miami, FL 33133-6336, USA

Battistelli, Francesca (Musician)
c/o Staff Member *Proper Management*
PO Box 68
Franklin, TN 37065-0068, USA

Battle, Allen (Athlete, Baseball Player)
106 Donette Loop
Daphne, AL 36526-7764, USA

Battle, Arnaz (Athlete, Football Player)
1091 Broadmoor Ln
Prosper, TX 75078-8940, USA

Battle, Greg (Athlete, Football Player)
1634 E Del Rio Dr
Tempe, AZ 85282-2766, USA

Battle, Howard (Athlete, Baseball Player)
238 Romana Ave SE
Albuquerque, NM 87102-5039, USA

Battle, Jackie (Athlete, Football Player)

Battle, James (Athlete, Football Player)
5 Oasis Crt
St. Albert, AB T8N 6X2, Canada

Battle, John (Athlete, Basketball Player)
234 Chadmore Ln
Tyrone, GA 30290-1573, USA

Battle, Julian (Athlete, Football Player)
196 Monterey Way
West Palm Beach, FL 33411-7817, USA

Battle, Kenny (Athlete, Basketball Player)
Northwest Sports and Entertainment Inc
835 W Warner Rd Ste 101-445
Gilbert, AZ 85233-7296, USA

Battle, Lois (Writer)
Viking Press
375 Hudson St
New York, NY 10014-3658, USA

Battle, Mike (Athlete, Football Player)
PO Box 1156
Amherst, VA 24521-1156, USA

Battle, Ralph (Athlete, Football Player)
184 Timber Oak Rd
Huntsville, AL 35806-4110, USA

Battle, Terry (Athlete, Football Player)
13108 Balfour Ave
Huntingtn Wds, MI 48070-1701, USA

Battle, Texas (Actor)
c/o Ryan Daly *Zero Gravity Management*
11110 Ohio Ave Ste 100
Los Angeles, CA 90025-3329, USA

Battles, Ainslev (Athlete, Football Player)
1237 Misty Valley Ct
Lawrenceville, GA 30045-2695, USA

Battles, Ainsley (Athlete, Football Player)
2859 Yellow Pine Dr
Jacksonville, FL 32277-3462, USA

Batton, Chris (Athlete, Baseball Player)
29806 Yorkton Rd
Murrieta, CA 92563-4748, USA

Batton, Dave (Athlete, Basketball Player)
8627 Hufsmith Rd APT 1221
Tomball, TX 77375-2874, USA

Batts, Lloyd (Athlete, Basketball Player)
500 S Denton Ave
Glenwood, IL 60425-2137, USA

Batts, Matt (Athlete, Baseball Player)
17927 Silver Creek Ct
Baton Rouge, LA 70810-8918, USA

Batts, Warren L (Business Person)
Premark International
3600 W Lake Ave
Glenview, IL 60026-1215, USA

Baty, Greg (Athlete, Football Player)
4 King St
Redwood City, CA 94062-1938, USA

Bauchau, Patrick (Actor)
1941 Lookout Dr
Agoura, CA 91301-2928, USA

Baucus, Max (Senator)
511 Hart Senate Office Bldg
Washington, DC 20510-0001, USA

Baudin, Belinda (Horse Racer, Olympic Athlete)
15939 NW 162nd Ter
Williston, FL 32696-4356, USA

Bauer, Alice (Athlete, Golfer)
LPGA Pioneer
77165 Avenida Arteaga
La Quinta, CA 92253-2552, USA

Bauer, Belinda (Actor)
c/o Staff Member *The Rights House (UK)*
Drury House
34-43 Russell St
London WC2B 5HA, UNITED KINGDOM

Bauer, Chris (Actor)
c/o Peg Donegan *Framework Entertainment*
9057 Nemo St # C
W Hollywood, CA 90069-5511, USA

Bauer, Donna (Business Person)
The Note Buyer
11006 Reading Rd Ste 201
Cincinnati, OH 45241-1980, USA

Bauer, Hank (Athlete, Football Player)
11150 Alejo Pl
San Diego, CA 92124-1521, USA

Bauer, Jaime Lyn (Actor)
4212 Camellia Ave
Studio City, CA 91604-2936, USA

Bauer, Linda Susan (Actor)
2476 Glendale Cir SE
Smyrna, GA 30080-1830, USA

Bauer, Rick (Athlete, Baseball Player)
6643 W Limelight Dr
Boise, ID 83714-6109, USA

Bauer, Steven (Actor)
c/o Liza Anderson *Anderson Group Public Relations*
8060 Melrose Ave Fl 4
Los Angeles, CA 90046-7038, USA

Bauer van Straten, Kristin (Actor)
c/o Ben Levine *LINK Entertainment*
11872 La Grange Ave
Los Angeles, CA 90025-5282, USA

Baugh, Gavin (Athlete, Baseball Player)
3605 Pasadena Dr
San Mateo, CA 94403-2947, USA

Baugh, Laura (Athlete, Golfer)
5225 Timberview Ter
Orlando, FL 32819-3924, USA

Baugh, Sammy (Athlete, Football Coach, Football Player)
General Delivery
Rotan, TX 79546-9999, USA

Baugh, Tom (Athlete, Football Player)
14716 S Bynum Rd
Lone Jack, MO 64070-9286, USA

Baughan, Maxie C (Athlete, Coach, Football Player)
42 Horizon Dr
Ithaca, NY 14850-9769, USA

Baughman, Justin (Athlete, Baseball Player)
4052 NE 21st Ave
Portland, OR 97212-1433, USA

Bauhaus (Music Group)
c/o Pete Riedling *Satellite Artist Management*
5653 1/2 Hollywood Blvd Ste 7
Los Angeles, CA 90028-7195, USA

Baum, Herbert M (Business Person)
Quarker State Corp
700 Milam St
Houston, TX 77002-2806, USA

Baum, John (Athlete, Basketball Player)
8550 Trumbauer Dr
Glenside, PA 19038-7451, USA

Bauman, Jon (Bowzer) (Musician)
3168 Oakshire Dr
Los Angeles, CA 90068-1743, USA

Bauman, Rashad (Athlete, Football Player)
14724 SE Loren Ln
Portland, OR 97267-1700, USA

Baumann, Charlie (Athlete, Football Player)
5434 Sago Palm Ct
Orlando, FL 32819-7174, USA

Baumann, Frank M (Athlete, Baseball Player)
7712 Sunray Ln
Saint Louis, MO 63123-1938, USA

Baumann, Kenny (Actor)
c/o Michael Valeo *Valeo Entertainment*
8581 Santa Monica Blvd Ste 570
West Hollywood, CA 90069-4120, USA

Baumbach, Noah (Actor)
c/o Jeremy Barber *United Talent Agency (UTA)*
9336 Civic Center Dr
Beverly Hills, CA 90210-3604, USA

Baumgardner, Larry (Athlete, Football Player)
1125 Loma Ave
Coronado, CA 92118-2835, USA

Baumgarten, Ross (Athlete, Baseball Player)
1020 Bluff Rd
Glencoe, IL 60022-1152, USA

Baumgartner, Brian (Actor)
c/o Tess Finkle *Metro Public Relations*
8671 Wilshire Blvd # 208
Beverly Hills, CA 90211-2926, USA

Baumgartner, Bruce (Athlete, Olympic Athlete, Wrestler)
12765 Forrest Dr
Edinboro, PA 16412-1281, USA

Baumgartner, John (Athlete, Baseball Player)
1215 Oxford Ct
Birmingham, AL 35242-4676, USA

Baumgartner, Ken (Athlete, Hockey Player)
261 Melrose St # 1
Auburndale, MA 02466-1917, USA

Baumgartner, Mary (Athlete, Baseball Player)
60 Lane
440 Jimmerson Lk
Fremont, IN 46737-9634, USA

Baumgartner, Mike (Athlete, Hockey Player)
31303 440th Ave
Roseau, MN 56751-8416, USA

Baumgartner, Steve (Athlete, Football Player)
144 Brookside Dr
Mandeville, LA 70471-3202, USA

Baumhower, Robert G (Bob) (Athlete, Football Player)
21201 Ayrshire Ln
Fairhope, AL 36532-4479, USA

Baumler, Hans-Jurgen (Actor)
18 chemin du Casteller
Le Rouret F-06650, France

Baun, Bob (Athlete, Hockey Player)
35 Pittmann Cres
Ajax, ON L1S 3G4, CANADA

Baun, Bobby (Athlete, Hockey Player)
576 Stonebridge Lane
Pickering, ON L1W 3B3, CANADA

Bause, Inka (Musician)
PF 08 03 04
Berlin 10003, Germany

Bauta, Ed (Athlete, Baseball Player)
3792 Long Grove Ln
Port Orange, FL 32129-8617, USA

Baute, Joseph A (Business Person)
Nashua Corp
11 Trafalgar Sq Ste 200
Nashua, NH 03063-1991, USA

Bautin, Sergei (Athlete, Hockey Player)
8580 E Lowry Blvd
Denver, CO 80230-6932, USA

Bautista, Danny (Athlete, Baseball Player)
901 E Van Buren St Apt 1063
Phoenix, AZ 85006-4014, USA

Bautista, Dave (Athlete, Wrestler)
c/o Jonathan Meisner *DMBV*
2020 Pennsylvania Ave NW # 179
Washington, DC 20006-1811, USA

Bautista, Franciso Javier Jr (Frankie J) (Musician)
c/o Staff Member *BMG*
1540 Broadway
New York, NY 10036-4039, USA

Bautista, Jose (Athlete, Baseball Player)
100 Shockoe Slip Fl 4
Richmond, VA 23219-4100, USA

Bavaro, David (Athlete, Football Player)
55 Ash St Unit 14
Danvers, MA 01923-2710, USA

Bavaro, Mark (Athlete, Football Player)
17 Long Hl
Boxford, MA 01921-2453, USA

Bavasi, Peter (Commentator)
1001 Genter St Unit 3G
La Jolla, CA 92037-5531, USA

Bawel, Edward (Athlete, Football Player)
1169 2nd Ave
Jasper, IN 47546-3411, USA

Bax, Kylie (Actor, Model)
c/o Reid Strathearn *Envision Entertainment*
8840 Wilshire Blvd Fl 3
Beverly Hills, CA 90211-2606, USA

Baxendale, Helen (Actor)
c/o Staff Member *Yakety Yak*
25 D'Arblay St
London W1F 8EJ, UNITED KINGDOM (UK)

Baxes, Mike (Athlete, Baseball Player)
4904 Clayton Rd Apt 104
Concord, CA 94521-4933, USA

Baxley, Rob (Athlete, Football Player)
39 Oak Creek Dr
Yorkville, IL 60560-9779, USA

Baxter, Fred (Athlete, Football Player)
PO Box 14
Brundidge, AL 36010-0014, USA

Baxter, Jeff (Skunk) (Music Group, Musician)
Monterey Peninsula Artists
509 Hartnell St
Monterey, CA 93940-2825, USA

Baxter, Lloyd (Athlete, Football Player)
2500 Homedale Dr
Austin, TX 78704-3837, USA

Baxter, Meredith (Actor)
c/o Alan Mills *Mills Kaplan Entertainment*
5225 Wilshire Blvd Ste 500
Los Angeles, CA 90036-5194, USA

Baxter, Paul (Athlete, Hockey Player)
106 Pembroke Ave
Nashville, TN 37205-3729, USA

Baxter, Stephen (Writer)
Tom Doherty Associates, LLC
175 5th Ave
New York, NY 10010-7703, USA

Baxter-Johnson, Patricia (Athlete, Golfer)
111 Bryn Mawr Dr
Lake Worth, FL 33460-6311, USA

Bay, James (Musician)
c/o Ryan Lofthouse *Closer Artists (UK)*
91 Peterborough Rd
Matrix Complex
London SW6 3BU, UNITED KINGDOM

Bay, Jason (Athlete, Baseball Player)
c/o Joe Urbon *Creative Artists Agency (CAA)*
405 Lexington Ave Fl 19
New York, NY 10174-1800, USA

Bay, Michael (Actor, Director, Producer)
c/o Staff Member *Bay Films*
631 Colorado Ave
Santa Monica, CA 90401-2507, USA

Bay, Susan (Actor)
801 Stone Canyon Rd
Los Angeles, CA 90077-2911, USA

Bay City Rollers (Music Group)
297 Kinderkamack Rd Ste 101
Oradell, NJ 07649-1535, USA

Baye, Nathalie (Actor)
Theatre De L'Atelier
1 Place Charles Dullin
Paris F-75 018, FRANCE

Bayer, Samuel (Director)
c/o Doreen Wilcox Little *Anonymous Content*
3532 Hayden Ave
Culver City, CA 90232-2413, USA

Bayle, Silvia (Actor)
c/o Staff Member *Telefe (Argentina)*
Pavon 2444
Buenos Aires C1248AAT, ARGENTINA

Bayless, Jerryd (Athlete, Basketball Player)
c/o Jeff Schwartz *Excel Sports Management*
1700 Broadway Fl 29
New York, NY 10019-6559, USA

Bayless, Martin (Athlete, Football Player)
757 Ernroe Dr
Dayton, OH 45417-3507, USA

Bayless, Rick (Athlete, Football Player)
885 Dawn Ave
Shoreview, MN 55126-6403, USA

Bayliss, Jonah (Athlete, Baseball Player)
41 Front St
Williamstown, MA 01267-2403, USA

Bayliss, Rachel (Musician)
Somerset Park Farm
Congelton Chelshire, UK

Baylon, Noah (Writer)
c/o James (Jamie) Feldman *Lichter Grossman Nichols Adler & Feldman Inc*
9200 W Sunset Blvd Ste 1200
Los Angeles, CA 90069-3607, USA

Baylor, Elgin (Athlete, Basketball Player)
2480 Briarcrest Rd
Beverly Hills, CA 90210-1820, USA

Baylor, John (Athlete, Football Player)
7436 Freeport Ln Apt A
Indianapolis, IN 46214-1037, USA

Baylor, Raymond (Athlete, Football Player)
5302 Heathercrest St
Houston, TX 77045-5230, USA

Baylor, Tim (Athlete, Football Player)
2305 River Pointe Cir
Minneapolis, MN 55411-4279, USA

Bayne, Howard (Athlete, Basketball Player)
11840 Yarnell Rd
Knoxville, TN 37932-2354, USA

Bayne, Trevor (Race Car Driver)
Trevor Bayne Inc
112 Argus Ln
Mooresville, NC 28117-6977, USA

Baynes, Michelle (Race Car Driver)
Bayshore Communications
2839 Ogletown Rd
Newark, DE 19713-1837, USA

Baynham, Craig (Athlete, Football Player)
370 River Wind Dr
North Augusta, SC 29841-6094, USA

Bayona, Alvaro (Actor)
c/o Gabriel Blanco *Gabriel Blanco Iglesias (Mexico)*
Rio Balsas 35-32
Colonia Cuauhtemoc
DF 06500, Mexico

Bayona, Juan Antonio (Director, Producer, Writer)
c/o Robert Newman *WME|IMG*
9601 Wilshire Blvd
Beverly Hills, CA 90210-5213, USA

Bays, Brandon (Writer)
The Journey Seminars LTD
P.O. Box 2
Cowbridge CF71 7WN, United Kingdom

Bays, Carter (Producer)
Bays Thomas Productions
1990 S Bundy Dr Ste 200
Los Angeles, CA 90025-5249, USA

Baze, Winiford (Athlete, Football Player)
5317 New Copeland Rd Apt 119
Tyler, TX 75703-3964, USA

Bazell, Josh (Writer)
c/o Staff Member *United Talent Agency (UTA)*
9336 Civic Center Dr
Beverly Hills, CA 90210-3604, USA

Bazell, Robert J (Correspondent)
NBC-TV News Dept
4001 Nebraska Ave NW
Washington, DC 20016-2795, USA

Bazemore, Whit (Race Car Driver)
50 Gasoline Aly Ste H
Indianapolis, IN 46222-5906, USA

BB Mak (Music Group)
c/o Staff Member *Hollywood Records*
500 S Buena Vista St
Burbank, CA 91521-0002, USA

BBMAK (Musician)
P.O. Box 22580
London W86YR, UK

Beach, Adam (Actor)
Bandwidth Digital Releasing
587 Ellice Ave
Winnipeg, MB R3B 1Z7, CANADA

Beach, Ed (Athlete, Football Player)
938 Sedgewick Ave
Scotch Plains, NJ 07076, USA

Beach, Michael (Actor)
7057 Sale Ave
West Hills, CA 91307-2370, USA

Beach, Pat (Athlete, Football Player)
2523 W Beach Rd
Oak Harbor, WA 98277-8865, USA

Beach, Roger C (Business Person)
Unocal Corp
2141 Rosecrans Ave
El Segundo, CA 90245-4747, USA

Beach, Sanjay (Athlete, Football Player)
2989 Riviera Ln
Westlake, OH 44145-6844, USA

Beacham, Stephanie (Actor)
c/o Staff Member *The Rights House (UK)*
Drury House
34-43 Russell St
London WC2B 5HA, UNITED KINGDOM

Beacher, Jeff (Producer, Television Host)
5777 W Century Blvd Ste 1600
Los Angeles, CA 90045-5671, USA

Beach House (Music Group)
c/o Staff Member *We Are Free*
61 Greenpoint Ave Ste 508
Brooklyn, NY 11222-1526, USA

Beachum, Kelvin (Athlete, Football Player)
c/o Eugene Parker *Independent Sports & Entertainment (ISE-IN)*
6435 W Jefferson Blvd # 197
Fort Wayne, IN 46804-6203, USA

Beadles, Zane (Athlete, Football Player)

Beady Eye (Music Group)
c/o David Levy *WME|IMG (UK)*
103 New Oxford St WMA
Centrepoint
London WC1A 1DD, UNITED KINGDOM

Beagle, Ronald G (Ron) (Athlete, Football Player)
3830 San Ysidro Way
Sacramento, CA 95864-5260, USA

Beahan, Kate (Actor)
c/o Suzan Bymel *Management 360*
9111 Wilshire Blvd
Beverly Hills, CA 90210-5508, USA

Beal, Andrew (Business Person)
Beal Bank
6000 Legacy Dr
Plano, TX 75024-3601, USA

Beal, Damien (Athlete, Baseball Player)
12836 Stanwyck Cir
Tampa, FL 33626-4465, USA

Beal, Jeremy (Athlete, Football Player)
3709 Furneaux Ln
Carrollton, TX 75007-2455, USA

Beal, Norm (Athlete, Football Player)
PO Box 688
Jefferson City, MO 65102-0688, USA

Beale, Betty (Writer)
2926 Garfield St NW
Washington, DC 20008-3536, USA

Beale, Simon Russell (Actor)
c/o Tony Lipp *Anonymous Content*
3532 Hayden Ave
Culver City, CA 90232-2413, USA

Beall, Bob (Athlete, Baseball Player)
513 NE Birchwood Rd
Hillsboro, OR 97124-3374, USA

Bealor, Bruce (Athlete, Football Player)
6010 Blue Ridge Dr Apt F
Highlands Ranch, CO 80130-3617, USA

Beals, Jennifer (Actor)
c/o Jill Fritzo *Jill Fritzo Public Relations*
208 E 51st St # 305
New York, NY 10022-6557, USA

Beals, Shawn (Athlete, Football Player)
250 Edward Ave
Pittsburg, CA 94565-4107, USA

Beals, Vaughn L Jr (Business Person)
Harley-Davidson Inc
3700 W Juneau Ave
Milwaukee, WI 53208-2818, USA

Beam, T J (Athlete, Baseball Player)
8505 E Pepper Tree Ln
Scottsdale, AZ 85250-4912, USA

Beaman, Lee Anne (Actor)
Cavaleri Assoc
178 S Victory Blvd Ste 205
Burbank, CA 91502-2881, USA

Beamer, Frank (Coach, Football Coach)
Virginia Polytechnic Institute
Athletic Dept
Blacksburg, VA 24061-0001, USA

Beamer, Lisa (Writer)
The Todd M Beamer Foundation
PO Box 32
Cranbury, NJ 08512-0032

Beamon, Autry (Athlete, Football Player)
2664 Lakeview Dr
Shakopee, MN 55379-9400, USA

Beamon, Trey (Athlete, Baseball Player)
2125 Highwood St
Mesquite, TX 75181-1727, USA

Beamon Jr, Charlie (Athlete, Baseball Player)
355 W Grant Line Rd Apt 212
Tracy, CA 95376-2579, USA

Beamon Sr, Charlie (Athlete, Baseball Player)
1717 Woodland Ave Apt 313
East Palo Alto, CA 94303-2313, USA

Bean, Andy (Athlete, Golfer)
2912 Grasslands Dr
Lakeland, FL 33803-5418, USA

Bean, Bill (Athlete, Baseball Player)
520 Brickell Key Dr
Miami, FL 33131-2660, USA

Bean, Bubba (Athlete, Football Player)
1117 Todd Trl
College Station, TX 77845-5145, USA

Bean, Colter (Athlete, Baseball Player)
2116 Shades Crest Rd
Vestavia Hills, AL 35216-1534, USA

Bean, Dawn Pawson (Swimmer)
11902 Redhill Ave
Santa Ana, CA 92705-3106, USA

Bean, Dexter (Race Car Driver)
Black Cat Racing
304 Performance Rd
Mooresville, NC 28115-9592, USA

Bean, Earnest (Athlete, Football Player)
1117 Todd Trl
College Station, TX 77845-5145, USA

Bean, Ed (Athlete, Baseball Player)
'827 3rd Ct SE
Winter Haven, FL 33880-4417, USA

Bean, Henry (Director)
c/o Staff Member *Fuller Films*
625 Santa Clara Ave
Venice, CA 90291-3445, USA

Bean, Noah (Actor)
c/o Elizabeth Morris *Rogers & Cowan*
1840 Century Park E Fl 18
Los Angeles, CA 90067-2101, USA

Bean, Orson (Actor, Comedian)
c/o Scott Manners *Artists & Representatives (Stone Manners Salners)*
6100 Wilshire Blvd Ste 1500
Los Angeles, CA 90048-5110, USA

Bean, Robert (Athlete, Football Player)
4197 Summit Crossing Dr
Decatur, GA 30034-3544, USA

Bean, Sean (Actor)
c/o Julie Nathanson *9.2.6pr*
3383 Tareco Dr
Los Angeles, CA 90068-1527, USA

Bean, Shoshana (Actor, Musician)
c/o Tim Marshal *Bauman Redanty & Shaul Agency*
5757 Wilshire Blvd
Suite 473
Beverly Hills, CA 90212, USA

Bean, Violette (Actor)
c/o Nilda Carrazana *Status PR*
PO Box 6191
Westlake Village, CA 91359-6191, USA

Beane, Billy (Commentator)
15 Saddleback Ct
Danville, CA 94506-3109, USA

Beard, Al (Athlete, Basketball Player)
1201 Orange St Apt 201
Fort Valley, GA 31030-3427, USA

Beard, Alana (Athlete, Basketball Player)
Washington Mystics
601 F St NW
Mcl Center
Washington, DC 20004-1605, USA

Beard, Amanda (Athlete, Olympic Athlete, Swimmer)
212 Fir Dr NW
Gig Harbor, WA 98335-5900, USA

Beard, Butch (Athlete, Basketball Player, Coach)
3834 Berleigh Hill Ct
Burtonsville, MD 20866-1392, USA

Beard, Dave (Athlete, Baseball Player)
4670 Hamptons Club Dr
Alpharetta, GA 30004-3974, USA

Beard, Ed (Athlete, Football Player)
4861 Strand Dr
Virginia Beach, VA 23462-6449, USA

Beard, Frank (Musician)
74066 De Anza Way
Palm Desert, CA 92260-3730, USA

Beard, Frank (Musician)
918 Pitts Rd
Richmond, TX 77406-1304, USA

Beard, Matthew (Actor)
c/o Sarah-Jayne Dines *Premier PR*
2-4 Bucknall St
London WC2H 8LA, UNITED KINGDOM

Beard, Mike (Athlete, Baseball Player)
90 Elcano Dr
Hot Springs Village, AR 71909-7833, USA

Beare, Gary (Athlete, Baseball Player)
17666 Tatia Ct
San Diego, CA 92128-2082, USA

Bearse, Amanda (Actor)
629 Elmwood Dr NE
Atlanta, GA 30306-3643, USA

Bearse, Kevin (Athlete, Baseball Player)
656 Saint Andrews Pl
Manalapan, NJ 07726-9551, USA

Beart, Emmanuelle (Actor)
c/o Laurent Gregoire *Agence Adequat*
21 Rue D'Uzes
Paris 75002, FRANCE

Beart, Guy (Musician, Songwriter, Writer)
Editions Temporel
2 Rue du Marquis de Mores
Garches 92380, FRANCE

Beartooth (Music Group)

Beasley, Aaron (Athlete, Football Player)
1635 Braid Hills Dr
Pasadena, MD 21122-3533, USA

Beasley, Allyce (Actor)
SBV
145 S Fairfax Ave Ste 310
Los Angeles, CA 90036-2176, USA

Beasley, Alyce (Actor)
c/o Staff Member *TalentWorks*
3500 W Olive Ave Ste 1400
Burbank, CA 91505-5512, USA

Beasley, Bruce M (Artist)
322 Lewis St
Oakland, CA 94607-1236, USA

Beasley, Charles (Athlete, Basketball Player)
6308 Winton St
Dallas, TX 75214-2645, USA

Beasley, Chris (Athlete, Baseball Player)
1013 W Cooley Dr
Gilbert, AZ 85233-2540, USA

Beasley, Cole (Athlete, Football Player)
c/o Staff Member *Carolinas Athletic Management Agency, LLC*
2 Shadow Moss Pl
North Myrtle Beach, SC 29582-2559, USA

Beasley, Derrick (Athlete, Football Player)
104 Bailey Rd
Andover, MA 01810-4235, USA

Beasley, Fred (Athlete, Football Player)
PO Box 242321
Montgomery, AL 36124-2321, USA

Beasley, John (Actor)

Beasley, John (Athlete, Basketball Player)
113 Oak Acres Dr W
Malakoff, TX 75148-3163, USA

Beasley, Lew (Athlete, Baseball Player)
24653 Newtown Rd
Bowling Green, VA 22427-2725, USA

Beasley, Michael (Athlete, Basketball Player)
c/o Jeff Schwartz *Excel Sports Management*
1700 Broadway Fl 29
New York, NY 10019-6559, USA

Beasley, Terry (Athlete, Football Player)
4052 Wellington Way
Moody, AL 35004-3507, USA

Beasley, Tom (Athlete, Football Player)
RR 1 Box 185
Hiltons, VA 24258, USA

Beasley, Tony (Athlete, Baseball Player)
4490 CCC Rd
Ruther Glen, VA 22546-2701, USA

Beasley, Vic (Athlete, Football Player)

Beastie Boys (Music Group)
c/o John Silva *SAM*
722 Seward St
Los Angeles, CA 90038-3504, USA

Beathard, Pete (Athlete, Football Player)
3350 McCue Rd Apt 1004
Houston, TX 77056-7123, USA

Beaton, Frank (Athlete, Hockey Player)
3327 Chapel Hills Pkwy
Fultondale, AL 35068-1596, USA

Beatrix, HM Queen (Royalty)
Kabinet Van De Koningin
Korte Vijverberg 3
The Hague 2513 AB, The Netherlands

Beatriz, Stephanie (Actor)
c/o Nicole Miller *NMA PR*
7916 Melrose Ave Ste 1
Los Angeles, CA 90046-7160, USA

Beattie, Jim (Athlete, Baseball Player)
PO Box 231
Quechee, VT 05059-0231, USA

Beattie, Joseph (Actor)
Ken McReddie Associates
36 - 40 Glasshouse St
London W1B 5DL, UNITED KINGDOM

Beattle, Ann (Writer)
Janklow & Nesbit
445 Park Ave Fl 13
New York, NY 10022-8628, USA

Beattle, Bob (Skier)
210 Aabc Ste N
Aspen, CO 81611-3537, USA

Beatty, Blaine (Athlete, Baseball Player)
867 Kolodzey Rd
Victoria, TX 77905-2445, USA

Beatty, Blaine (Athlete, Baseball Player)
Frederick Keys 21 Stadium Dr
Attn: Coaching Staff
Frederick, MD 21703-6553, USA

Beatty, Charles (Athlete, Football Player)
PO Box 2634
Waxahachie, TX 75168-8634, USA

Beatty, Jim (Athlete, Olympic Athlete, Track Athlete)
1516 Larochelle Ln
Charlotte, NC 28226-6868, USA

Beatty, Jordana (Actor)
c/o Steven Kavovit *Thruline Entertainment*
9250 Wilshire Blvd Fl Ground
Beverly Hills, CA 90212-3352, USA

Beatty, Ned (Actor)
c/o Deborah Miller *Shelter Entertainment*
9255 W Sunset Blvd Ste 300
Los Angeles, CA 90069-3313, USA

Beatty, Warren (Actor, Director, Producer)
c/o Richard Lovett *Creative Artists Agency (CAA)*
2000 Avenue of the Stars Ste 100
Los Angeles, CA 90067-4705, USA

Beatty, Will (Athlete, Football Player)
c/o Alan Herman *Sportstars Inc*
1370 Avenue of the Americas Fl 19
New York, NY 10019-4602, USA

Beaty, Zelmo (Athlete, Basketball Player)
2808 120th Ave NE
Bellevue, WA 98005-1515, USA

Beatz, Swizz (Musician, Producer)

Beau Brummels, The (Music Group, Musician)
PO Box 53664
C/O Jeff Hubbard
Indianapolis, IN 46253-0664, USA

Beauchamp, Al (Athlete, Football Player)
533 Pinegate Rd
Peachtree City, GA 30269-1120, USA

Beauchamp, Joe (Athlete, Football Player)
10525 Vista Sorrento Pkwy
Pkwy Ste 110
San Diego, CA 92121-2745, USA

Beauchemin, Francois (Athlete, Hockey Player)
Jandec Inc
803-3080 Le Carrefour Blvd
Attn Robert Sauve
Laval, QC H7T 2R5, Canada

Beaudin, Norm (Athlete, Hockey Player)
8625 Stone Harbour Loop
Bradenton, FL 34212-6322, USA

Beaudoin, Doug (Athlete, Football Player)
15143 Springview St
Tampa, FL 33624-2374, USA

Beaufait, Mark (Athlete, Hockey Player, Olympic Athlete)
5454 Longwood Ct SE
Ada, MI 49301-7755, USA

Beauford, Carter (Musician)
3000 Lonesome Mountain Rd
Charlottesville, VA 22911-6009, USA

Beaufoy, Simon (Director, Producer)
c/o Charlotte Knight *Knight Hall Agency*
7 Mallow St
Lower Ground Fl
London EC1Y 8RQ, UNITED KINGDOM

Beaule, Alain (Athlete, Hockey Player)
230 154e Rue
Saint-Georges, QC G5Y 7L8, Canada

Beaumon, Sterling (Actor)
c/o Lindsey Ludwig-Rahm *Viewpoint Inc*
89 5th Ave Ste 402
New York, NY 10003-3020, USA

Beaumont, Jimmy (Musician)
2109 Kansas Ave
White Oak, PA 15131-2307, USA

Beaumont, Thomas (Actor)
c/o Staff Member *Scott Stander & Associates*
4533 Van Nuys Blvd Ste 401
Sherman Oaks, CA 91403-2950, USA

Beaupre, Don (Athlete, Hockey Player)
2747 Thomas Ave S
Minneapolis, MN 55416-4346, USA

Beauregard, Robin (Athlete, Olympic Athlete, Water Polo Player)
467 Midvale Ave
Los Angeles, CA 90024-6707, USA

Beauregard, Stephane (Athlete, Hockey Player)
BMO Nesbitt Burns
991 Boul du Semina ire N
St-Jean-Sur-Richelieu, QC J3A IKI, Canada

Beauvais, Garcelle (Actor)
c/o Mona Loring *Status PR*
PO Box 6191
Westlake Village, CA 91359-6191, USA

Beaver, Jim (Actor)
c/o Teri Weigel *The Creative Group PR*
324 S Beverly Dr # 216
Beverly Hills, CA 90212-4801, USA

Beaver, Terry (Actor)
Paradigm Agency
10100 Santa Monica Blvd Ste 2500
Los Angeles, CA 90067-4116, USA

Beavers, Aubrey (Athlete, Football Player)
PO Box 321474
Houston, TX 77221-1474, USA

Beavers, Scott (Athlete, Football Player)
4030 Pittman Rd
College Park, GA 30349-1439, USA

Beban, Gary (Athlete, Football Player)
70 W Huron St APT 2308
Chicago, IL 60654-5351, USA

Bebout, Nick (Athlete, Football Player)
1719 E Park Ave
Riverton, WY 82501-4801, USA

Becerra, Xavier (Congressman, Politician)
1226 Longworth Hob
Washington, DC 20515-4208, USA

Bech, Brett (Athlete, Football Player)
206 Lairds Dr
Coppell, TX 75019-7922, USA

Bech, Debra (Actor)
Minnesota Public Radio
480 Cedar St
Saint Paul, MN 55101-2230, USA

Becht, Anthony (Athlete, Football Player)
1122 Oxbridge Dr
Lutz, FL 33549-9396, USA

Bechtel, Riley P (Business Person)
Bechtel Group
50 Beale St
San Francisco, CA 94105-1813, USA

Bechtel, Stefan (Writer)
c/o Ellen Levine *Trident Media Group LLC*
41 Madison Ave Fl 36
New York, NY 10010-2257, USA

Bechtel, Stephen D Jr (Business Person)
Bechtel Group
50 Beale St
San Francisco, CA 94105-1813, USA

Beck (Musician, Songwriter)
2528 Mandeville Canyon Rd
Los Angeles, CA 90049-1238, USA

Beck, Barry (Athlete, Hockey Player)
c/o Staff Member *Osoyoos Storm*
2 Killdeer Pl
Osoyoos, BC V0H 1V5, Canada

Beck, Braden (Athlete, Football Player)
691 Milverton Rd
Los Altos, CA 94022-3928, USA

Beck, Byron (Athlete, Basketball Player)
1909 S Williams St
Kennewick, WA 99338-1820, USA

Beck, Chip (Athlete, Golfer)
11 Pembroke Dr
Lake Forest, IL 60045-2147, USA

Beck, Corey (Athlete, Basketball Player)
9444 Austin Dr
Olive Branch, MS 38654-7647, USA

Beck, Ernie (Athlete, Basketball Player)
1132 Merrifield Dr
West Chester, PA 19380-6834, USA

Beck, Glenn (Radio Personality, Television Host)
8528 Davis Blvd Ste 134 PMB 357
North Richland Hills, TX 76182-8302, USA

Beck, Jeff (Musician)
c/o Phil Banfield *Coda Music Agency (UK)*
56 Compton St
Clerkenwell
London EC1V 0ET, UNITED KINGDOM

Beck, John (Athlete, Football Player)
5379 Paseo Gilberto
Yorba Linda, CA 92886-5706, USA

Beck, Jordan (Athlete, Football Player)
37301 County Road 27
Eaton, CO 80615-8427, USA

Beck, Kimberly (Actor)

Beck, Maria (Actor)
c/o Staff Member *Shamon Freitas Talent Agency*
3916 Oregon St
San Diego, CA 92104-2806, USA

Beck, Martha (Writer)
18011 N 14th Pl
Phoenix, AZ 85022-7201, USA

Beck, Martin (Actor)
c/o Dale Garrick *Dale Garrick International Agency*
1017 N La Cienega Blvd Ste 109
Los Angeles, CA 90069-4196, USA

Beck, Michael (Actor)
c/o Staff Member *Paradigm*
8942 Wilshire Blvd
Beverly Hills, CA 90211-1908, USA

Beck, Rich (Athlete, Baseball Player)
8218 N Sumter Ct
Spokane, WA 99208-5749, USA

Beck, Robin (Musician)
Cavaricci & White
156 W 56th St Ste 1803
New York, NY 10019-3899, USA

Beck, Tom (Athlete, Football Player)
806 Saddlewood Dr
Glen Ellyn, IL 60137-3202, USA

Beckel, Heather (Writer)
Milkshake Media
4203 Guadalupe St
Austin, TX 78751-4224, USA

Beckenbauer, Franz (Soccer Player)
Postfach 90 04 51
München 81504, Germany

Becker, Arthur (Athlete, Basketball Player)
1879 E Brentrup Dr
Tempe, AZ 85283-4275, USA

Becker, Boris (Athlete, Tennis Player)
c/o Staff Member *IMG (Cleveland)*
1360 E 9th St Ste 100
Cleveland, OH 44114-1730, USA

Becker, Donna (Athlete, Baseball Player)
5316 40th Ave
Kenosha, WI 53144-2707, USA

Becker, Doug (Athlete, Football Player)
3452 Fields Ertel Rd
Loveland, OH 45140-7394, USA

Becker, Gerry (Actor)
c/o Oliver Mossi *Paradigm*
8942 Wilshire Blvd
Beverly Hills, CA 90211-1908, USA

Becker, Gretchen (Actor)
Acme Talent
4727 Wilshire Blvd Ste 333
Los Angeles, CA 90010-3874, USA

Becker, Harold (Director, Producer)
c/o Jack Gilardi *ICM Partners*
10250 Constellation Blvd Fl 7
Los Angeles, CA 90067-6207, USA

Becker, Isaura (Actor)
c/o Staff Member *Televisa*
Blvd Adolfo Lopez Mateos 232
Colonia San Angel INN
DF CP 01060, MEXICO

Becker, Kuno (Actor)
c/o Ivan De Paz *DePaz Management*
2011 N Vermont Ave
Los Angeles, CA 90027-1931, USA

Becker, Kurt (Athlete, Football Player)
PO Box 1687
Aurora, IL 60507-1687, USA

Becker, Margaret (Musician)
Sparrow Communications
101 Winners Cir N
Brentwood, TN 37027-5352, USA

Becker, Rich (Athlete, Baseball Player)
210 Mary Senica Ct
La Salle, IL 61301-9676, USA

Becker, Rob (Actor, Comedian)
c/o Staff Member *WME|IMG*
9601 Wilshire Blvd
Beverly Hills, CA 90210-5213, USA

Becker, Thomas (Athlete)
Hagedomweg 6A
Solingen 42697, GERMANY

Becker, Tony (Actor)
Howard Talent West
10657 Riverside Dr
C/O Bonnie Howard
Toluca Lake, CA 91602-2341, USA

Becker, Walt (Director)
c/o Matt Luber *Luber Roklin Management*
5815 W Sunset Blvd Ste 208
Los Angeles, CA 90028-6481, USA

Beckerman, Kyle (Athlete, Soccer Player)
c/o Richard Motzkin *Wasserman Media Group*
10960 Wilshire Blvd Ste 1200
Los Angeles, CA 90024-3714, USA

Beckert, Glenn (Athlete, Baseball Player)
2391 Caraway Dr
Venice, FL 34292-4174, USA

Beckett, Bob (Athlete, Hockey Player)
38 Fonthill Blvd
Markham, ON L3R 1V7, Canada

Beckett, Josh (Athlete, Baseball Player)
4 Tudor Gln
San Antonio, TX 78257-1252, USA

Beckett, Robbie (Athlete, Baseball Player)
PO Box 731
Elgin, TX 78621-0731, USA

Beckett, Rogers (Athlete, Football Player)
635 Gaelic Ct
Apopka, FL 32712-4724, USA

Beckett, William (Musician)
c/o Bob McLynn *Crush Music Management*
60-62 E 11th St
Fl 7
New York, NY 10003, USA

Beckford, Roxanne (Actor)
9255 W Sunset Blvd Ste 401
Los Angeles, CA 90069-3302, USA

Beckford, Tyson (Actor, Model)
c/o Steven Hawthorne *The Cartel*
1108-1112 Tamarind Ave
Hollywood, CA 90038, USA

Beckham, Brice (Actor)
6561 E Espanita St
Long Beach, CA 90815-4635

Beckham, Cruz (Musician)
c/o Scooter Braun *SB Management*
755 N Bonhill Rd
Los Angeles, CA 90049-2303, USA

Beckham, David (Actor, Athlete, Soccer Player)
c/o Jeff Raymond *Rogers & Cowan*
1840 Century Park E Fl 18
Los Angeles, CA 90067-2101, USA

Beckham, Gordon (Athlete, Baseball Player)
8 Habersham Park NW
Atlanta, GA 30305-2856, USA

Beckham, Victoria (Actor, Musician)
c/o Simon Fuller *XIX Entertainment (UK)*
32/33 Ransomes Dock
London SW11 4NP, UNITED KINGDOM (UK)

Beckham Jr, Odell (Athlete, Football Player)
c/o Tammy Brook *FYI Public Relations*
174 5th Ave Ste 404
New York, NY 10010-5964, USA

Beckinsale, Kate (Actor)
c/o Jane Epstein *Independent Talent Group*
40 Whitfield St
London W1T 2RH, UNITED KINGDOM

Beckless, Ian (Athlete, Football Player)
4613 S Matanzas Ave
Tampa, FL 33611-2718, USA

Beckley, Gerry (Music Group, Musician)
Agency for Performing Arts
9200 W Sunset Blvd Ste 900
Los Angeles, CA 90069-3604, USA

Beckman, Cameron (Athlete, Golfer)
24008 Gran Palacio
San Antonio, TX 78261-2766, USA

Beckman, Ed (Athlete, Football Player)
4295 18th St NE
Naples, FL 34120-6409, USA

Beckman, Thomas (Athlete, Football Player)
3672 Cedar Shake Dr
Rochester Hills, MI 48309-1013, USA

Beckman, Tom (Athlete, Football Player)
3672 Cedar Shake Dr
Rochester Hills, MI 48309-1013, USA

Beckman, Witt (Athlete, Football Player)
568 Peachtree Pkwy
Cumming, GA 30041-7403, United States

Beckum, Travis (Athlete, Football Player)
c/o Roosevelt Barnes *Independent Sports & Entertainment (ISE-IN)*
6435 W Jefferson Blvd # 197
Fort Wayne, IN 46804-6203, USA

Beckwith, Alan (Actor)
3928 Carpenter Ave
Studio City, CA 91604-3764, USA

Beckwith, Darry (Athlete, Football Player)
c/o Jimmy Sexton *CAA (Memphis)*
6060 Poplar Ave Ste 470
Memphis, TN 38119-0910, USA

Beckwith, Joe (Athlete, Baseball Player)
2637 Danbury Dr
Auburn, AL 36830-6462, USA

Becquer, Julio (Athlete, Baseball Player)
1011 Feltl Ct Apt 233
Hopkins, MN 55343-3933, USA

Becton, C W (Religious Leader)
United Pentacostal Free Will Baptist Church
8855 Dunn Rd
Hazelwood, MO 63042-2212, USA

Bedard, Irene (Actor)
Don Buchwald
5900 Wilshire Blvd Ste 3100
Los Angeles, CA 90036-5030, USA

Bedard, James A (Athlete, Hockey Player)
c/o Staff Member *Detroit Red Wings*
2645 Woodward Ave
Joe Luis Arena
Detroit, MI 48201-3028, USA

Bedard, James L (Athlete, Hockey Player)
317 Crawford Ave E
Melfort, SK S0E 1A0, Canada

Bedard, Jim (Athlete, Hockey Player)
600 Civic Center Dr
Attn Coaching Staff
Detroit, MI 48226-4408, USA

Bedard, Jim (Athlete, Hockey Player)
139 Marine Dr
Windsor, ON N8N 3Z3, Canada

Bedard, Myriam (Athlete)
3329 Rue Pincourt
Quebec, QC G2B 2E4, CANADA

Bedard, Patrick (Race Car Driver)
1462 Indian Pass Rd
Port Saint Joe, FL 32456-7811, USA

Bedelia, Bonnie (Actor)
c/o Nevin Dolcefino *Innovative Artists*
1505 10th St
Santa Monica, CA 90401-2805, USA

Bedell, Bob (Athlete, Basketball Player)
3107 Kipling Way
Louisville, KY 40205-3005, USA

Bedell, Brad (Athlete, Football Player)
545 N Altura Rd
Arcadia, CA 91007-6059, USA

Bedell, Howie (Athlete, Baseball Player)
1187 Crestwood Dr
Pottstown, PA 19464-2931, USA

Bedford, Vance (Athlete, Football Player)
3200 Grandview St APT 9
Austin, TX 78705-2106, USA

Bedingfield, Daniel (Musician)
c/o David (Dave) Chumbley *Primary Talent International (UK)*
10-11 Jockeys Fields
The Primary Bldg
London WC1R 4BN, UNITED KINGDOM

Bedingfield, Natasha (Actor, Musician)
6149 Rockcliff Dr
Los Angeles, CA 90068-1649, USA

Bednarski, John (Athlete, Hockey Player)
1005 Windfaire Pl
Roswell, GA 30076-3310, USA

Bedore, Thomas (Athlete, Football Player)
211 73rd St
Niagara Falls, NY 14304-4028, USA

Bedore, Tom (Athlete, Football Player)
9 Catherine Ave
Latrobe, PA 15650-2602, USA

Bedrosian, Steve (Athlete, Baseball Player)
3915 Gordon Rd
Senoia, GA 30276-3041, USA

Bedsole, Hal (Athlete, Football Player)
5142 E Fernwood Ct
Cave Creek, AZ 85331-2305, USA

Bee, Samantha (Actor, Comedian, Producer, Television Host)
c/o Jenny Tversky *Shelter PR*
928 Broadway Ste 505
New York, NY 10010-8143, USA

Beebe, Don (Athlete, Football Player)
1246 Verona Ridge Dr
Aurora, IL 60506-6510, USA

Beech, Matt (Athlete, Baseball Player)
516 Sheffield Dr
Richardson, TX 75081-5610, USA

Beecham, Earl (Athlete, Football Player)
11 Terrace Cir Apt 1E
Great Neck, NY 11021-4143, USA

Beecham, Emily (Actor)
c/o Sarah Jackson *Seven Summits Pictures & Management*
8906 W Olympic Blvd
Beverly Hills, CA 90211-3550, USA

Beechen, Adam (Writer)
c/o Staff Member *Natural Talent Inc*
20265 Ventura Blvd Ste D
Woodland Hills, CA 91364-2550, USA

Beechler, Donnie (Race Car Driver)
212 N Harvey Rd
Greenwood, IN 46143-7383, USA

Beede, Frank (Athlete, Football Player)
1645 Somerset Pl
Antioch, CA 94509-2183, USA

Bee Gees, The (Music Group)
c/o Staff Member *United Talent Agency (UTA)*
9336 Civic Center Dr
Beverly Hills, CA 90210-3604, USA

Beekley, Bruce (Athlete, Football Player)
1351 Eaton Ave
San Carlos, CA 94070-4940, USA

Beem, Rich (Athlete, Golfer)
2510 Watkins Way
Austin, TX 78746-8027, USA

Beeman, Greg (Actor, Director, Producer, Writer)

Beene, Andy (Athlete, Baseball Player)
113 Forest Brook St
Red Oak, TX 75154-6028, USA

Beene, Fred (Athlete, Baseball Player)
PO Box 143
Oakhurst, TX 77359-0143, USA

Beer, Madison (Musician)
c/o Sarah Stennett *Turn First Artists (UK)*
Grove Studios Adie Road
London W6 0PW, UNITED KINGDOM

Beer, Tom (Athlete, Football Player)
186 New Wickham Dr
Penfield, NY 14526-2739, USA

Beers, Bob (Athlete, Hockey Player)
97 Blake Rd
Lexington, MA 02420-3212, USA

Beers, Bob (Athlete, Hockey Player)
Boston Bruins
100 Legends Way Ste 250
Attn: Broadcast Dept
Boston, MA 02114-1389, USA

Beers, Ed (Athlete, Hockey Player)
5-11442 Best St
Maple Ridge, BC V2X 7C7, Canada

Beers, Gary (Musician)
8 Hayes St
#1
Neutral Bay, NSW 20891, USA

Beesley, Max (Actor)
c/o Staff Member *Independent Talent Group*
40 Whitfield St
London W1T 2RH, UNITED KINGDOM

Beeson, Terry (Athlete, Football Player)
1302 Hibbard St
Coffeyville, KS 67337-1412, USA

Beetz, Zazie (Actor)
c/o Lindsay Porter *Gersh*
41 Madison Ave Ste 3301
New York, NY 10010-2210, USA

Bega, Leslie (Actor)
31 1/2 Buccaneer St
Marina Del Rey, CA 90292-5103, USA

Bega, Lou (Musician)
c/o Staff Member *Unicade Music*
Truderingerstrasse 259
Munchen 81821, Germany

Begala, Paul (Commentator, Television Host)
1581 Highland Glen Pl
McLean, VA 22101-4158, USA

Begay, Notah (Athlete, Golfer)
9228 Masini Ln NW
Albuquerque, NM 87114-6001, USA

Beghe, Jason (Actor)
3800 Decker Edison Rd
Malibu, CA 90265-2330, USA

Begler, Michael (Producer)
c/o Staff Member *WME|IMG*
9601 Wilshire Blvd
Beverly Hills, CA 90210-5213, USA

Begley, Hayden (Actor)
c/o Marina Anderson *Media Hound PR*
PO Box 261939
Encino, CA 91426-1939, USA

Begley Jr, Ed (Actor, Director)
c/o Marina Anderson *Media Hound PR*
PO Box 261939
Encino, CA 91426-1939, USA

Beglin, Elizabeth (Athlete, Hockey Player, Olympic Athlete)
2070 Silver Maple Trl
North Liberty, IA 52317-4765, USA

Begnaud, David (Journalist)
c/o Ali Spiesman *Creative Artists Agency (CAA)*
2000 Avenue of the Stars Ste 100
Los Angeles, CA 90067-4705, USA

Begovich, Mike (Actor)

Behagen, Ron (Athlete, Basketball Player)
1101 Juniper St NE Apt 401
Atlanta, GA 30309-7655, USA

Behar, Joy (Comedian, Talk Show Host, Television Host)
c/o Staff Member *The View*
57 W 66th St
New York, NY 10023-6201, USA

Beharie, Nicole (Actor, Musician)
c/o Jamie Harhay Skinner *Baker Winokur Ryder Public Relations*
9100 Wilshire Blvd
W Tower #500
Beverly Hills, CA 90212-3415, USA

Behe, Michael (Writer)
Lehigh University
Biochemistry Dept
Bethlehem, PA 18015, USA

Behle, Jochen (Skier)
Sonnenhof 1
Willingen 34508, GERMANY

Behm, Donald (Athlete, Olympic Athlete, Wrestler)
1398 Compton Ct
East Lansing, MI 48823-2386, USA

Behm, Forrest E (Athlete, Football Player)
10585 E San Salvador Dr
Scottsdale, AZ 85258-5745, USA

Behney, Mel (Athlete, Baseball Player)
2800 Woodshire Dr
Arlington, TX 76016-1553, USA

Behning, Mark (Athlete, Football Player)
1207 May St
Denton, TX 76209-4639, USA

Behnke, Elmer (Athlete, Basketball Player)
1717 Monteagle Dr
Hoover, AL 35244-6718, USA

Behnken, Robert L (Astronaut)
43708 Dejay St
Lancaster, CA 93536-5781, USA

Behr, Aaron (Actor)
c/o Garry Purdy *Momentum Talent and Literary Agency*
3500 W Olive Ave Ste 300
Burbank, CA 91505-4647, USA

Behr, Daniel (Politician)
C/O Deutscher Bundestag
Platz Der Republik, 1
Berlin D-11011, Germany

Behr, Ira Steven (Producer, Writer)
c/o Staff Member *Simon & Schuster*
1230 Avenue of the Americas Fl CONC1
New York, NY 10020-1586, USA

Behr, Jason (Actor)
c/o Robert Stein *Robert Stein Management*
PO Box 3797
Beverly Hills, CA 90212-0797, USA

Behrend, Marc (Athlete, Hockey Player, Olympic Athlete)
1808 Savannah Way
Waunakee, WI 53597-2307, USA

Behrendt, Greg (Actor, Writer)
c/o Staff Member *Simon & Schuster*
1230 Avenue of the Americas Fl CONC1
New York, NY 10020-1586, USA

Behrendt, Greg (Comedian, Radio Personality)
The Greg Behrendt Show
9336 Washington Blvd
Culver City, CA 90232-2628, USA

Behrens, Sam (Actor)
530 Bryant Dr
Canoga Park, CA 91304-1019, USA

Behrman, Dave (Athlete, Football Player)
10187 25 1/2 Mile Rd
Albion, MI 49224-9751, USA

Behrs, Beth (Actor)
c/o Chuck Binder *Binder & Associates*
1465 Lindacrest Dr
Beverly Hills, CA 90210-2519, USA

Beier, Thomas (Athlete, Football Player)
5055 Hammock Lake Dr
Coral Gables, FL 33156-2221, USA

Beimel, Joe (Athlete, Baseball Player)
4723 Boone Mountain Rd
Kersey, PA 15846-2109, USA

Beinfest, Larry (Commentator)
517 Via Con Dios
Camarillo, CA 93010-8456, USA

Beirne, Jim (Athlete, Football Player)
212 W Live Oak St
Fredericksbrg, TX 78624-4452, USA

Beirne, Kevin (Athlete, Baseball Player)
2 Cedar Chase Pl
Spring, TX 77381-3030, USA

Beisel, Elizabeth (Athlete, Olympic Athlete, Swimmer)
34 Pierce Rd
Saunderstown, RI 02874-3418, USA

Beisel, Monty (Athlete, Football Player)
16557 Goldenrod Pl
Encino, CA 91436-4141, USA

Beisler, Randy (Athlete, Football Player)
306 Ramona St
Palo Alto, CA 94301-1438, USA

Bejo, Berenice (Actor)
c/o Gregory Weill *Agence Adequat*
21 Rue D'Uzes
Paris 75002, FRANCE

Bekar, Derek (Athlete, Hockey Player)
29 Windjammer Rdg
Laconia, NH 03246-1841, USA

Bela, Dalila (Actor, Musician)
c/o Trudy Aronson *Premiere Talent Management*
Prefers to be contacted by email or phone.
Vancouver BC NA, CANADA

Belafonte, Harry (Actor, Musician)
Belafonte Enterprise
310 W 43rd St # 14
New York, NY 10036-3981, USA

Belafonte, Shari (Actor, Musician)
c/o Deborah Miller *Shelter Entertainment*
9255 W Sunset Blvd Ste 300
Los Angeles, CA 90069-3313, USA

Beland, Jessi Ann Gravel (Model)
c/o Staff Member *Models 1*
12 Macklin St
Covent Gardens
London WC2B 5SZ, UK

Belanger, Eric (Athlete, Hockey Player)
957 7th St
Hermosa Beach, CA 90254-4824, USA

Belanger, Ken (Athlete, Hockey Player)
KBX Hockey School
143-A Great Northern Rd
Suite 133
Sault Ste Marie, ON P6B 4Y9, Canada

Belbin, Tanith (Figure Skater)
c/o Staff Member *Champions on Ice*
3500 American Blvd W Ste 190
Minneapolis, MN 55431-4431, USA

Bel Biv Devoe (Music Group, Musician)
8942 Wilshire Blvd
Beverly Hills, CA 90211-1908, USA

Belcher, Kevin (Athlete, Baseball Player)
2400 State Highway 121 Apt 401
Euless, TX 76039-4064, USA

Belcher, Tim (Athlete, Baseball Player)
PO Box 153
Sparta, OH 43350-0153, USA

Belden, Bob (Athlete, Football Player)
6701 Militia Hill St NW
Canton, OH 44718-1391, USA

Belew, Adrian (Musician)
Umbrella Artists Mgmt
2612 Erie Ave
Cincinnati, OH 45208-2002, USA

Belew, Adrian (Musician)
2004 Hidden Ridge Ct
Mt Juliet, TN 37122-2366, USA

Belfi, Jordan (Actor)
c/o Lee Wallman *Wallman Public Relations*
3859 Goldwyn Ter
Culver City, CA 90232-3103, USA

Belford, Christine (Actor)
116 Inlet Ct
Hampstead, NC 28443-2558, USA

Belfort, Jordan (Business Person)
Global Motivation Inc
2711 N Sepulveda Blvd Ste 287
Manhattan Beach, CA 90266-2725, USA

Belfour, Ed (Athlete, Hockey Player)
544 Studebaker Rd
Whitewright, TX 75491-7288, USA

Belhumeur, Michel (Athlete, Hockey Player)
2230 Long Dr
Rockville, VA 23146-2017, USA

Belichick, Bill (Athlete, Football Coach, Football Player)
PO Box 715
Foxboro, MA 02035-0715, USA

Belichik, William S (Bill) (Coach, Football Coach)
New England Patriots
60 Washington St
Gillette Stadium RR1
Foxboro, MA 02035-1388, USA

Belinda, Stan (Athlete, Baseball Player)
4208 Reservoir Cir
Alexandria, PA 16611-2300, USA

Belisle, Danny (Athlete, Hockey Player)
3967 Glen Oaks Manor Dr
Sarasota, FL 34232-1045, USA

Belisle, Matt (Athlete, Baseball Player)
4009 Sierra Dr
Austin, TX 78731-3913, USA

Belitz, Todd (Athlete, Baseball Player)
17901 N Colton Ct
Colbert, WA 99005-9174, USA

Belk, Bill (Athlete, Football Player)
12 Ricemill Fry
Columbia, SC 29229-9034, USA

Belk, Tim (Athlete, Baseball Player)
14714 Carolcrest Dr
Houston, TX 77079-6408, USA

Belknap, Anna (Actor)
c/o Steve Stone *Cornerstone Talent Agency*
37 W 20th St Ste 1007
New York, NY 10011-3714, USA

Bell, Albert (Athlete, Football Player)
16222 Hunsaker Ave
Paramount, CA 90723-4762, USA

Bell, Andy (Musician)
c/o Stephen Ford *Diva Central Inc*
7510 W Sunset Blvd # 1445
Los Angeles, CA 90046-3408, USA

Bell, Anthony (Athlete, Football Player)
1564 Fitzgerald Dr
Pinole, CA 94564-2229, USA

Bell, Archie (Musician)
Billy Paul Management
7816 Rising Sun Ave
Philadelphia, PA 19111-2601, USA

Bell, Ashley (Actor)
c/o Michael Geiser *Jill Fritzo Public Relations*
208 E 51st St # 305
New York, NY 10022-6557, USA

Bell, Bill (Athlete, Baseball Player)
3401 Urbandale Ave
Des Moines, IA 50310-4006, USA

Bell, Billy Ray (Athlete, Football Player)
4006 Mossy Grove Ct
Humble, TX 77346-2498, USA

Bell, Bob (Athlete, Football Player)
700 Lower State Rd # 128G
North Wales, PA 19454-2167, USA

Bell, Brad (Athlete, Golfer)
6255 Oakridge Way
Sacramento, CA 95831-1829, USA

Bell, Brian (Musician)
3611 Sapphire Dr
Encino, CA 91436-4233, USA

Bell, Bruce (Athlete, Hockey Player)
101 Canyon Close W
Lethbridge, AB T1K 6W5, Canada

Bell, Buddy (Athlete, Baseball Player)
W 35th St Chicago White Sox 333
Attn Director of Player Development
Chicago, IL 60616-3696

Bell, Buddy (Athlete, Baseball Player, Coach)
420 E Ohio St Apt 40E
Chicago, IL 60611-4672, USA

Bell, Byron (Athlete, Football Player)
c/o Tom Condon *Creative Artists Agency (CAA)*
401 Commerce St PH
Nashville, TN 37219-2516, USA

Bell, Byron (Athlete, Basketball Player)
1141 Williams St
Lake Geneva, WI 53147-1260, USA

Bell, Carl (Musician)
10690 Fairfield Ave
Las Vegas, NV 89183-4636, USA

Bell, Carlos (Athlete, Football Player)
14411 Hartshill Dr
Houston, TX 77044-4925, USA

Bell, Catherine (Actor)
c/o Daniel (Danny) Sussman *Brillstein Entertainment Partners*
9150 Wilshire Blvd Ste 350
Beverly Hills, CA 90212-3453, USA

Bell, Charles (Business Person)
McDonald's Corp
1 McDonalds Dr
1 Kroc Dr
Oak Brook, IL 60523-1911, USA

Bell, Coby (Actor)
c/o Liza Anderson *Anderson Group Public Relations*
8060 Melrose Ave Fl 4
Los Angeles, CA 90046-7038, USA

Bell, Coleman (Athlete, Football Player)
3236 Gianna Way
Land O Lakes, FL 34638-7823, USA

Bell, David (Athlete, Baseball Player)
244 W Goldfinch Way
Chandler, AZ 85286-4547, USA

Bell, Dennis (Athlete, Basketball Player)
930 Misty Stream Dr
Cincinnati, OH 45231-7539, USA

Bell, Derek (Athlete, Baseball Player)
3404 Pine Top Dr
Valrico, FL 33594-7618, USA

Bell, Drake (Actor)
c/o Liza Anderson *Anderson Group Public Relations*
8060 Melrose Ave Fl 4
Los Angeles, CA 90046-7038, USA

Bell, Drew Tyler (Actor, Dancer)
c/o Mara Santino *Luber Roklin Management*
5815 W Sunset Blvd Ste 208
Los Angeles, CA 90028-6481, USA

Bell, Eddie (Athlete, Football Player)
4529 Tacoma Ter
Fort Worth, TX 76123-4005, USA

Bell, Eddie A (Actor)
4529 Tacoma Ter
Fort Worth, TX 76123-4005, USA

Bell, Emma (Actor)
c/o Justin Deanda *ICM Partners*
10250 Constellation Blvd Fl 7
Los Angeles, CA 90067-6207, USA

Bell, Eric (Athlete, Baseball Player)
1140 S 124th St
Chandler, AZ 85286-1121, USA

Bell, Gary (Athlete, Baseball Player)
2107 Oak Rnch
San Antonio, TX 78259-1819, USA

Bell, Gerard (Athlete, Football Player)
1347 Deerbourne Dr
Zephyrhills, FL 33543-6754, USA

Bell, Glen (Business Person)
Bell Charitable Foundation
PO Box 642
Rancho Santa Fe, CA 92067-0642, USA

Bell, Gordon (Athlete, Football Player)
205 Le Moyne Pkwy
Oak Park, IL 60302-1121, USA

Bell, Grantis (Athlete, Football Player)
1879 NW 96th Ave
Plantation, FL 33322-5626, USA

Bell, Greg (Athlete, Football Player)
5662 Calle Real
Goleta, CA 93117-2317, USA

Bell, Greg (Athlete, Track Athlete)
831 W Miami Ave
Logansport, IN 46947-2543, USA

Bell, Heath (Athlete, Baseball Player)
14224 Harrow Pl
Poway, CA 92064-2373, USA

Bell, Hilari (Writer)
PO Box 877
Chestertown, MD 21620-0877, USA

Bell, Jacob (Athlete, Football Player)
2175 W California St
San Diego, CA 92110, USA

Bell, Jaime (Actor)
c/o Staff Member *WME|IMG*
9601 Wilshire Blvd
Beverly Hills, CA 90210-5213, USA

Bell, Jamie (Actor)
c/o Brian Swardstrom *United Talent Agency (UTA)*
888 7th Ave Fl 7
New York, NY 10106-0700, USA

Bell, Jason (Athlete, Football Player)
3387 N Studebaker Rd
Long Beach, CA 90808-4258, USA

Bell, Jay (Athlete, Baseball Player)
3217 E Piro St
Phoenix, AZ 85044-3618, USA

Bell, Jerry (Athlete, Football Player)
1347 Deerbourne Dr
Zephyrhills, FL 33543-6754, USA

Bell, Jerry (Athlete, Baseball Player)
631 Audrey Rd
Mount Juliet, TN 37122-3844, USA

Bell, Jillian (Actor)
c/o Jillian Roscoe *ID Public Relations*
7060 Hollywood Blvd Fl 8th
Los Angeles, CA 90028-6021, USA

Bell, John (Musician)
Brown Cat Inc
400 Foundry St
Athens, GA 30601-2623, USA

Bell, John Anthony (Actor, Director)
Bell Shakespeare Co
88 George St
Level 1
Rocks, NSW 00200, AUSTRALIA

Bell, Joique (Athlete, Football Player)

Bell, Jorge A M (George) (Athlete, Baseball Player)
Lamiama #14
Bell 2nd Planto
San Pedro de Macoris, Dominican Republic

Bell, Joshua (Musician)
24 E 22nd St PH 7
New York, NY 10010-6146, USA

Bell, Ken (Athlete, Football Player)
8335 Fairmount Dr Unit 9-106
Denver, CO 80247-1137, us

Bell, Kendrell (Athlete, Football Player)
400 W Peachtree St NW Unit 1211
Atlanta, GA 30308-3547, USA

Bell, Kendrell (Athlete, Football Player)
1270 Caroline St NE Ste D120
Atlanta, GA 30307-2758, us

Bell, Kerwin (Athlete, Football Player)
525 3rd St N Apt 508
Jacksonville Beach, FL 32250-7039, USA

Bell, Kerwin (Athlete, Football Player)
1822 Waterbury Ln Fleming Island FL 32003-7749
Fleming Island, FL 32003, us

Bell, Kevin (Athlete, Baseball Player)
621 Sue St
Little Chute, WI 54140-2424, USA

Bell, Kevin (Athlete, Football Player)
5780 Phyllis Ln
Beaumont, TX 77713-9539, USA

Bell, Kristen (Actor)
c/o Marcel Pariseau *True Public Relations*
3575 Cahuenga Blvd W Ste 360
Los Angeles, CA 90068-1361, USA

Bell, Lake (Actor)
c/o Joannie Burstein *Burstein Company*
15304 W Sunset Blvd Ste 208
Pacific Palisades, CA 90272-3656, USA

Bell, Larry S (Artist)
PO Box 4101
Taos, NM 87571, USA

Bell, Lauralee (Actor)
23713 Malibu Colony Rd
Malibu, CA 90265-6629, USA

Bell, Le'Veon (Athlete, Football Player)
608 Herrogate Sq
Etna, OH 43147-8007, USA

Bell, Lynette (Swimmer)
149 Henry St
Merwether NSW 22, Australia

Bell, Madison Smartt (Writer)
Random House
1745 Broadway Frnt 3 # B1
New York, NY 10019-4343, USA

Bell, Marcus (Athlete, Football Player)
678 S School Bus Rd
Eagar, AZ 85925-9678, USA

Bell, Mark E (Athlete, Football Player)
2701 N Wild Rose St
Wichita, KS 67205-1607, USA

Bell, Marshall (Actor)
IFA Talent Agency
8730 W Sunset Blvd # 490
Los Angeles, CA 90069-2210, USA

Bell, Michael (Actor)
4906 Encino Ave
Encino, CA 91316-3816, USA

Bell, Michelle (Athlete, Golfer)
18895 Pond Cypress Ct
Jupiter, FL 33458-3735, USA

Bell, Mike (Athlete, Baseball Player)
8530 Woodland Brooke Trl
Cumming, GA 30028-5047, USA

Bell, Mike (Race Car Driver)
American Motorcycle Assn
13515 Yarmouth Dr
Pickerington, OH 43147-8273, USA

Bell, Mike J (Athlete, Football Player)
7405 W Lakewood Cir
Wichita, KS 67205-1608, USA

Bell, Mikw (Athlete)
244 W Goldfinch Way
Chandler, AZ 85286-4547, USA

Bell, Myron (Athlete, Football Player)
3027 Crawford Ave Gastonia NC28052-6076
Gastonia, NC 28052-6076, USA

Bell, Nick (Athlete, Football Player)
306 W South St
Anaheim, CA 92805-4516, USA

Bell, Raja (Athlete, Basketball Player)
22 E Cactus601 NE 36th St
Apt 1812 Wren Dr
Miami, FL 33137-3968, USA

Bell, Richard T (Athlete, Football Player)
12106 City View Ln SE
Chatfield, MN 55923-1719, USA

Bell, Ricky (Athlete, Football Player)
c/o Staff Member *Sosincere Entertainment*
2054 Nostrand Ave Apt 4F
Brooklyn, NY 11210-2526, USA

Bell, Rini (Actor)
c/o Sherry Marsh *Marsh Entertainment*
818 Warren Ave
Venice, CA 90291-2812, USA

Bell, Rob (Athlete, Baseball Player)
28 Blossom Hill Dr
Marlboro, NY 12542-6000, USA

Bell, Robert (Musician)
c/o Staff Member *J Bird Entertainment Agency*
4905 S Atlantic Ave
Ponce Inlet, FL 32127-7311, USA

Bell, Robert F (Athlete, Football Player)
7415 N 12th St
Melrose Park, PA 19027-3052, USA

Bell, Sean (Actor)
c/o Daniel Sladek *Daniel Sladek Entertainment Corporation*
8306 Wilshire Blvd # 510
Beverly Hills, CA 90211-2304, USA

Bell, Tatum (Athlete, Football Player)
18754 E Powers Dr
Aurora, CO 80015-3162, us

Bell, Terry (Athlete, Baseball Player)
8352 Normandy Creek Dr
Dayton, OH 45458-3284, USA

Bell, Tobin (Actor)
c/o Alan Saffron *Saffron Management*
9171 Wilshire Blvd Ste 441
Beverly Hills, CA 90210-5516, USA

Bell, Tom (Actor)
Shepherd & Ford
13 Randor Walk
London SW3 4BP, UNITED KINGDOM (uk)

Bell, Tone (Actor, Comedian)
c/o Steven Muller *Innovative Artists*
1505 10th St
Santa Monica, CA 90401-2805, USA

Bell, Townsend (Race Car Driver)
524 15th St
Santa Monica, CA 90402-2934, USA

Bell, Wally (Athlete, Baseball Player)
1675 W Western Reserve Rd Unit 3F
Youngstown, OH 44514-4507, USA

Bell, W Kamau (Comedian, Television Host)
c/o Staff Member *CNN (NY)*
10 Columbus Cir
Time Warner Center
New York, NY 10019-1158, USA

Bell, Yeremiah (Athlete, Football Player)
1886 Sirius Ln
Weston, FL 33327-2213, us

Bell, Zoe (Actor)
c/o Todd Diener *Untitled Entertainment*
350 S Beverly Dr Ste 200
Beverly Hills, CA 90212-4819, USA

Bella, John (Athlete, Baseball Player)
409 N Cypress Dr Apt 7
Jupiter, FL 33469-2656, USA

Bella, Nikki (Actor, Model, Wrestler)
June Entertainment
6350 Santa Monica Blvd
Los Angeles, CA 90038-1620, USA

Bella, Rachael (Actor)
c/o Brandy Gold *TalentWorks*
3500 W Olive Ave Ste 1400
Burbank, CA 91505-5512, USA

Bellamar, Ariane (Actor, Model)
c/o D'Anise Marie *Carolyns Model & Talent*
1965 Britannia Rd W Suite 210
Mississauga, ON L5M 4Y4, CANADA

Bellamy, Bill (Actor, Comedian)
c/o Alison Leslie *Marleah Leslie & Associates*
1645 Vine St Apt 712
Los Angeles, CA 90028-8812, USA

Bellamy, David J (Writer)
Mill House Bedbum
Bishop Auckland
County Durham DL13 3NN, UNITED KINGDOM (UK)

Bellamy, Ned (Actor)
c/o Laina Cohn *Cohn / Torgan Management*
Prefers to be contacted by telephone or email
Los Angeles, CA, USA

Belland, Neil (Athlete, Hockey Player)
868 Renaissance Dr
Oshawa, ON L1J 8K9, Canada

Bellani, Adrian (Actor)
8004 Woodrow Wilson Dr
Los Angeles, CA 90046-1117, USA

Bella Twins (Athlete, Wrestler)
c/o Staff Member *World Wrestling Entertainment (WWE)*
1241 E Main St
Stamford, CT 06902-3520, USA

Bell Calloway, Vanessa (Actor)
c/o Katie Mason Stern *Luber Roklin Management*
5815 W Sunset Blvd Ste 208
Los Angeles, CA 90028-6481, USA

Belle, Albert (Athlete, Baseball Player)
9299 E Marioosa Grande Dr
Scottsdale, AZ 85255-3789, USA

Belle, Camilla (Actor)
c/o Hilary Hansen *Vision PR*
2 Penn Plz Rm 2601
New York, NY 10121-0001, USA

Belle, David (Actor)
c/o Emanuel Nunez *Paradigm*
8942 Wilshire Blvd
Beverly Hills, CA 90211-1908, USA

Belle, Regina (Musician)
Green Light
24024 Saint Moritz Dr
Valencia, CA 91355-2033, USA

Bellefeuille, Blake (Athlete, Hockey Player)
716 Berlin Rd
Marlborough, MA 01752-4592, USA

Beller, Kathleen (Actor)
PO Box 806
Half Moon Bay, CA 94019-0806, USA

Bellflower, Nellie (Actor, Producer)
c/o Staff Member *Keylight Entertainment Group*
14159 Dickens St APT 201
Sherman Oaks, CA 91423-5806, USA

Bellhorn, Mark (Athlete, Baseball Player)
5624 E Hillery Dr
Scottsdale, AZ 85254-2448, USA

Bellhorn, Mark (Athlete, Basketball Player)
1447 Palomino Way
Oviedo, FL 32765-9304, USA

Belliard, Rafael (Athlete, Baseball Player)
10846 King Bay Dr
Boca Raton, FL 33498-4548, USA

Belliard, Ronnie (Athlete, Baseball Player)
2999 NW 96th St
Miami, FL 33147-2337, USA

Bellinger, Clay (Athlete, Baseball Player)
1390 E Horseshoe Dr
Chandler, AZ 85249-4761, USA

Bellinger, Rodney (Athlete, Football Player)
6721 SW 48th Ter
Miami, FL 33155-5745, USA

Bellingham, Lynda (Actor)
c/o Staff Member *Yakety Yak*
25 D'Arblay St
London W1F 8EJ, UNITED KINGDOM (UK)

Bellingham, Norman (Athlete, Olympic Athlete)
374 Irvington Ct
Colorado Springs, CO 80906-8276, USA

Bellino, Alexis (Reality Star)

Bellino, Dan (Athlete, Baseball Player)
8820 Belfield Rd
Crystal Lake, IL 60014-8503, USA

Bellino, Joe (Athlete, Football Player)
45 Hayden Ln
Bedford, MA 01730-1140, USA

Bellisario, Donald P (Actor, Director, Producer, Writer)
1565 Las Tunas Rd
Santa Barbara, CA 93108-1334, USA

Bellisario, Troian (Actor)
c/o Eric Kranzler *Management 360*
9111 Wilshire Blvd
Beverly Hills, CA 90210-5508, USA

Bell-Lundy, Sandra (Cartoonist)
255 Northwood Dr
Welland ON L3C 6V1, Canada

Bellman, Gina (Actor)
c/o Matthew Lesher *Insight*
5358 Melrose Ave # 200W
Los Angeles, CA 90038-5117, USA

Bellman-Balchunas, Lois (Athlete, Baseball Player)
1008 Southport Ave
Lisle, IL 60532-1346, USA

Bello, Maria (Actor)
c/o Heidi Schaeffer *PMK/BNC Public Relations*
1840 Century Park E Ste 1400
Los Angeles, CA 90067-2115, USA

Belloir, Rob (Athlete, Baseball Player)
PO Box 2933
Savannah, GA 31402-2933, USA

Bellore, Nick (Athlete, Football Player)
c/o Dave Butz *Sportstars Inc*
1370 Avenue of the Americas Fl 19
New York, NY 10019-4602, USA

Bellorin, Edwin (Athlete, Baseball Player)
c/o Alan Nero *Octagon (Chicago)*
875 N Michigan Ave Ste 2700
Chicago, IL 60611-1822, USA

Bellotti, Mike (Coach, Football Coach)
University of Oregon
Athletic Dept
Eugen, OR 97403, USA

Bellows, Brian (Athlete, Hockey Player)
6824 Valley View Rd
Edina, MN 55439-1646, USA

Bellows, Gil (Actor)
c/o Adam Stutt *Patterson Talent Management (PTM)*
1380 Queen St E
Toronto, ON M4L 1C9, CANADA

Bellucci, Monica (Actor, Model)
c/o Laurent Gregoire *Agence Adequat*
21 Rue D'Uzes
Paris 75002, FRANCE

Bellwood, Pamela (Actor)
2160 Veloz Dr
Santa Barbara, CA 93108-1538, USA

Bell X1 (Music Group)
c/o Staff Member *Paradigm (Monterey)*
404 W Franklin St
Monterey, CA 93940-2303, USA

Belm, Michaela (Model)
Agentur Talents
Ohmstr 5
Munich 80802, GERMANY

Belmares, Roland (DJ)
c/o Staff Member *Diva Central Inc*
7510 W Sunset Blvd # 1445
Los Angeles, CA 90046-3408, USA

Belmondo, Jean-Paul (Actor)
9 Rue des Saint Peres
Paris 75007, FRANCE

Belote, Melissa (Athlete, Olympic Athlete, Swimmer)
1504 E Coronado Dr
Tempe, AZ 85282-5763, USA

Belser, Ceaser (Athlete, Football Player)
1317 County Road 3673
Paradise, TX 76073-4512, USA

Belser, Jason (Athlete, Football Player)
20474 Middlebury St
Ashburn, VA 20147-3674, USA

Belton, Horace (Athlete, Football Player)
2047 General Lee Ave
Baton Rouge, LA 70810-6325

Beltran, Carlos (Athlete, Baseball Player)
300 E 79th St # Phcd
New York, NY 10075-0993, USA

Beltran, Rigo (Athlete, Baseball Player)
3950 Laurelwood Ln
Delray Beach, FL 33445-3503, USA

Beltran, Robert (Actor)
2210 Talmadge St
Los Angeles, CA 90027-2918, USA

Beltre, Adrian (Athlete, Baseball Player)
1204 Suncast Ln Ste 2
El Dorado Hills, CA 95762-9665, USA

Belushi, Jim (Actor)
c/o Marc Gurvitz *Brillstein Entertainment Partners*
9150 Wilshire Blvd Ste 350
Beverly Hills, CA 90212-3453, USA

Belushi-Pisano, Judith (Writer)
c/o Staff Member *CMG Worldwide*
429 N Pennsylvania St Ste 204
Indianapolis, IN 46204-1816, USA

Belvin, Art (Athlete, Football Player)
6506 Centre Place Cir
Spring, TX 77379-2937, USA

Belzer, Richard (Actor, Comedian)
c/o Rich Super *Gersh*
9465 Wilshire Blvd Ste 600
Beverly Hills, CA 90212-2605, USA

Beman, Deane R (Athlete, Golfer)
Golf HOF
5287 Commissioners Dr
Jacksonville, FL 32224-0886, USA

Bemiller, Al (Athlete, Football Player)
Buffalo Bills
5002 Armor Duells Rd
Orchard Park, NY 14127-4401, USA

Bemis, Cliff (Actor)
Beartooth Productions
11271 Ventura Blvd PMB 366
Studio City, CA 91604-3136, USA

Bemvenuti, Luciana (Athlete, Golfer)
3673 Wickford Ln
Peachtree Corners, GA 30096-2409, USA

Benami, Didi (Musician)
c/o Simon Fuller *XIX Entertainment (UK)*
32/33 Ransomes Dock
London SW11 4NP, UNITED KINGDOM (UK)

Benanti, Laura (Actor)
c/o Emily Gerson Saines *Brookside Artists Management*
250 W 57th St Ste 1820
New York, NY 10107-1802, USA

Benard, Marcus (Athlete, Football Player)
c/o Drew Rosenhaus *Rosenhaus Sports Representation*
3921 Alton Rd # 440
Miami Beach, FL 33140-3852, USA

Benard, Marvin (Athlete, Baseball Player)
11215 Rosemary Dr
Auburn, CA 95603-5910, USA

Benard, Maurice (Actor)
c/o Staff Member *Benard Management*
15300 Ventura Blvd Ste 315
Sherman Oaks, CA 91403-5870, USA

Benassi, Benny (Musician)
c/o Staff Member *Mission Control Artists Agency*
Unit 3 City Business Centre
St Olav's Court, Lower Road
London SE16 2XB, UNITED KINGDOM (UK)

Benatar, Pat (Musician, Songwriter)
c/o Tom Consolo *TC Management*
10960 Wilshire Blvd Ste 1415
Los Angeles, CA 90024-3729, USA

Benavides, Freddie (Athlete, Baseball Player)
3007 Wincrest Cir
Laredo, TX 78045-8149, USA

Benavides, Osvaldo (Actor)
c/o Staff Member *Televisa*
Blvd Adolfo Lopez Mateos 232
Colonia San Angel INN
DF CP 01060, MEXICO

Benben, Brian (Actor)
c/o Erwin More *More/Medavoy Management*
10203 Santa Monica Blvd # 400
Los Angeles, CA 90067-6405, USA

Bench, Johnny (Athlete, Baseball Player)
Johnny Bench Enterprises
3899 Ridgedale Dr
Cincinnati, OH 45247-6946, USA

Bendekovits, Joe (Athlete, Baseball Player)
9410 N Newport Ave
Tampa, FL 33612-7724, USA

Bender, Carey (Athlete, Football Player)
706 Antrim Meadow Ln
Cary, NC 27519-8857, USA

Bender, Gary N (Sportscaster)
TNT-TV
1050 Techwood Dr NW
Sports Dept
Atlanta, GA 30318-5604, USA

Bender, Jack (Director)
13055 Evanston St
Los Angeles, CA 90049-3642, USA

Bender, Jennie (Athlete, Olympic Athlete, Skier)
c/o Gigi Rock *Heraea Marketing*
10905 E Pear Tree Dr
Cornville, AZ 86325-5523, USA

Bender, Lawrence (Producer)
c/o Staff Member *Lawrence Bender Productions*
10100 Santa Monica Blvd
Los Angeles, CA 90067-4003, USA

Bender, Wes (Athlete, Football Player)
114 Skyline Dr
Burbank, CA 91501-1132, USA

Bendis, Brian Michael (Writer)
c/o David Engel *Circle of Confusion*
8931 Ellis Ave
Los Angeles, CA 90034-3336, USA

Bendix, Simone (Actor)
Joy Jameson
2/19 Plaza
535 Kings Road
London SW10 0SZ, UNITED KINGDOM (UK)

Bendlin, Kurt (Athlete, Track Athlete)
DLV
Asfelder Str 27
Leverkusen 64289, GERMANY

Bendross, Jesse (Athlete, Football Player)
5226 SW 22nd St
West Park, FL 33023-3118, USA

Bene, Bill (Athlete, Baseball Player)
1063 Bella Vista Ave
San Gabriel, CA 91775-2548, USA

Benedek, Joana (Actor)
c/o Staff Member *Televisa*
Blvd Adolfo Lopez Mateos 232
Colonia San Angel INN
DF CP 01060, MEXICO

Benedeti, Paulo (Actor)
1560 NW 13th Ave
Boca Raton, FL 33486-1217, USA

Benedict, Bruce (Athlete, Baseball Player)
125 Millpond Trce
Eatonton, GA 31024-5441, USA

Benedict, Dirk (Actor, Director)
c/o Ethan Dettenmaier *Arsenal Productions & Management*
11054 Ventura Blvd # 239
Studio City, CA 91604-3546, USA

Benedict, Robert Patrick (Actor)
c/o Charles Silver *SMS Talent*
8383 Wilshire Blvd Ste 230
Beverly Hills, CA 90211-2436, USA

Benedicto, Lourdes (Actor)
6223 Enfield Ave
Encino, CA 91316-7107, USA

Benedict XVI, Pope (Religious Leader)
Apostolic Palace
Vatican City 00120, ITALY

Benefield, Daved (Athlete, Football Player)
420 N Rodeo Dr Apt 15281
Beverly Hills, CA 90210-4502, USA

Benepe, Jim (Athlete, Golfer)
1955 1/2 Frackelton St
Sheridan, WY 82801-2526, USA

Benes, Alan (Athlete, Baseball Player)
754 Kraffel Ln
Chesterfield, MO 63017-8057, USA

Benes, Andy (Athlete, Baseball Player, Olympic Athlete)
1127 Highland Pointe Dr
Saint Louis, MO 63131-1420, USA

Benet, Eric (Actor, Musician)
c/o Anne Watkins *Primary Wave Talent*
116 E 16th St Fl 9
New York, NY 10003-2123, USA

Benetton, Giuliana (Business Person)
Benetton Group SpA
Via Minelli
Ponzano Treviso 31050, ITALY

Benetton, Lucianno (Business Person)
Benetton Group
Villa Minelli
Ponzano
Treviso 31050, Italy

Benetton, Luciano (Business Person)
Benetton Group SpA
Via Minelli
Ponzano Treviso 31050, ITALY

Benfatti, Lou (Athlete, Football Player)
29 Colonial Oaks Dr
Oak Ridge, NJ 07438-9196, USA

Benford, Gregory (Writer)
c/o Staff Member *Little, Brown Book Group*
100 Victoria Embankment
London EC4Y 0DY, UK

Bengis, Fred (Athlete, Baseball Player)
546 Quail Ct
Longs, SC 29568-8638, USA

Benglis, Lynda (Artist)
222 Bowery Apt 38
New York, NY 10012-4252, USA

Bengston, Billy Al (Artist)
805 Hampton Dr
Venice, CA 90291-3020, USA

Benigni, Roberto (Actor, Director)
Melampo Cinematografica
Via Ludovisi, 35
Rome IT-00187, Italy

Benignl, Roberto (Actor, Director)
Via Traversa 44
Vergaglio
Provinz di Prato, ITALY

Bening, Annette (Actor)
13671 Mulholland Dr
Beverly Hills, CA 90210-1135, USA

Benioff, David (Producer)
c/o Guymon Casady *Management 360*
9111 Wilshire Blvd
Beverly Hills, CA 90210-5508, USA

Beniquez, Juan (Athlete, Baseball Player)
87-12 Calle 99A
Carolina, PR 00985-4127, USA

Benirschke, Rolf J (Athlete, Football Player)
14770 Caminito Lorren
Del Mar, CA 92014-4109, USA

Benish, Dan (Athlete, Football Player)
1635 Brookmere Way
Cumming, GA 30040-1891, USA

Benishek, Dan (Congressman, Politician)
514 Cannon Hob
Washington, DC 20515-0103, USA

Benitez, Armando (Athlete, Baseball Player)
2205 Warwick Way Ste 200
Marriottsville, MD 21104-1632, USA

Benitez, Elsa (Model)
c/o Staff Member *M Fashion Model Management*
Via Monte Rosa, 80
Ashburn, VA 20149-0001, Italy

Benitez, Jellybean (Musician)
Jellybean Recordings
235 Park Ave S
New York, NY 10003-1405, USA

Benitez, Wilfred (Athlete, Boxer)
Wilfred Benitez Foundation, NFP
PO Box 2338
Temecula, CA 92593-2338, USA

Benitez, Yamil (Athlete, Baseball Player)
13 Calle Un
918 Caperra Terrace
San Juan, PR 00915-2401, USA

Benitz, Max (Actor)
c/o Michael Baum *Impression Entertainment*
9229 W Sunset Blvd Ste 700
Los Angeles, CA 90069-3407, USA

Benjamin, Andre 3000 (Artist, Musician)
c/o Keleigh Thomas Morgan *Sunshine Sachs*
720 Cole Ave
Los Angeles, CA 90038-3606, USA

Benjamin, Benoit (Athlete, Basketball Player)
28 Morning Grn
San Antonio, TX 78257-2602, USA

Benjamin, Guy (Athlete, Football Player)
91-443 Ewa Beach Rd Apt B
Ewa Beach, HI 96706-2974, USA

Benjamin, H Jon (Actor)
c/o Greg Cavic *United Talent Agency (UTA)*
9336 Civic Center Dr
Beverly Hills, CA 90210-3604, USA

Benjamin, Jill (Actor)
c/o Tom Chasin *Chasin Agency, The*
8281 Melrose Ave Ste 202
Los Angeles, CA 90046-6890, USA

Benjamin, Kelvin (Athlete, Football Player)
c/o Eugene Parker *Independent Sports & Entertainment (ISE-IN)*
6435 W Jefferson Blvd # 197
Fort Wayne, IN 46804-6203, USA

Benjamin, Mike (Athlete, Baseball Player)
25608 S 182nd Pl
Queen Creek, AZ 85142-8188, USA

Benjamin, Richard (Actor, Director)
c/o Staff Member *Gersh*
9465 Wilshire Blvd Ste 600
Beverly Hills, CA 90212-2605, USA

Benjamin, Ryan (Athlete, Football Player)
8332 Boyce Ct
New Port Richey, FL 34654-5602, USA

Benjamin, Travis (Athlete, Football Player)
c/o Mitchell Frankel *Impact Sports (FL)*
2799 NW 2nd Ave Ste 203
Boca Raton, FL 33431-6709, USA

Benn, Nigel (Boxer)
Matchroom Boxing
10 Western Road
Romford Essex RM1 3JT, UNITED KINGDOM

Benners, Fred (Athlete, Football Player)
5211 Shadywood Ln
Dallas, TX 75209-2207, USA

Bennet, Chloe (Actor)
c/o Patrick Baker *Fewlas Entertainment*
2831 Nichols Canyon Rd
Los Angeles, CA 90046-1308, USA

Bennet, Michael F. (Senator)
458 Russell Senate Office Building
Washington, DC 20510-0001, USA

Bennett, Adam (Athlete, Hockey Player)
3on3 Hockey
2193 Dunwin Dr
Mississauga, ON L5L 1X2, Canada

Bennett, A L (Athlete, Basketball Player)
5013 E 109th Pl
Tulsa, OK 74137-7269, USA

Bennett, Antoine (Athlete, Basketball Player)
5011 SW 173rd Ave
Miramar, FL 33029-5095, USA

Bennett, Barry (Athlete, Football Player)
22047 Ginseng Rd
Long Prairie, MN 56347-4754, USA

Bennett, Beck (Actor, Comedian)
c/o John Sacks *United Talent Agency (UTA)*
9336 Civic Center Dr
Beverly Hills, CA 90210-3604, USA

Bennett, Bennett (Actor)
c/o Andrew Rogers *ICM Partners*
10250 Constellation Blvd Fl 7
Los Angeles, CA 90067-6207, USA

Bennett, Bill (DJ)
c/o Staff Member *Diva Central Inc*
7510 W Sunset Blvd # 1445
Los Angeles, CA 90046-3408, USA

Bennett, Bill (Athlete, Hockey Player)
14 Glen Ave
Cranston, RI 02905-3702, USA

Bennett, Bob (Athlete, Olympic Athlete, Swimmer)
70 Rivo Alto Canal
Long Beach, CA 90803-4047, USA

Bennett, Bob (Musician, Songwriter, Writer)
c/o Vicki Jennette *The Benjamin Artist Agency*
PO Box 92348
Nashville, TN 37209-8348, USA

Bennett, Brad (Race Car Driver)
PO Box 16759
Stamford, CT 06905-8759, USA

Bennett, Brandon (Athlete, Football Player)
308 Daybrook Ct
Greenville, SC 29605-5963, us

Bennett, Brooke (Athlete, Olympic Athlete, Swimmer)
2585 Rowe Rd
Milford, MI 48380-2337, USA

Bennett, Carl (Athlete, Basketball Player)
2834 Little River Run
Fort Wayne, IN 46804-2573, USA

Bennett, Charles (Athlete, Football Player)
11935 Sunburst Marble Rd
Riverview, FL 33579-2138, USA

Bennett, Clay (Cartoonist)
Christian Science Monitor
Editorial Dept
1 Norway St
Boston, MA 02115, USA

Bennett, Cornelius (Athlete, Football Player)
818 S 7th Ave
Hollywood, FL 33019-1100, us

Bennett, Curt (Athlete, Hockey Player)
260 Awapuhi Pl
Wailuku, HI 96793-2117, USA

Bennett, Darren (Athlete, Football Player)
1437 E 38th St
Tulsa, OK 74105-3337, USA

Bennett, Dave (Athlete, Baseball Player)
101 S Fairchild St
Yreka, CA 96097-2263, USA

Bennett, Donnell (Athlete, Football Player)
129 NW 16th Ave
Pompano Beach, FL 33069-2803, USA

Bennett, Drew (Athlete, Football Player)
2335 Hyde St Apt 1
San Francisco, CA 94109-1352, us

Bennett, Edgar (Athlete, Football Player)
1880 Horseshoe Ln
De Pere, WI 54115-7947, USA

Bennett, Eliza (Actor)
c/o Brandi George *Advantage PR*
3900 W Alameda Ave Ste 1200
Burbank, CA 91505-4317, USA

Bennett, Elmer (Athlete, Basketball Player)
2820 Avenue of the Woods
Louisville, KY 40241-6232, USA

Bennett, Erik (Athlete, Baseball Player)
PO Box 4108
Salt Lake City, UT 84110-4108, USA

Bennett, Fran (Actor)
749 N La Fayette Park Pl
Los Angeles, CA 90026-2917, USA

Bennett, Gary (Athlete, Baseball Player)
14905 Creekside Path
Libertyville, IL 60048-1104, USA

Bennett, Haley (Actor)
c/o Kim Hodgert *Anonymous Content*
3532 Hayden Ave
Culver City, CA 90232-2413, USA

Bennett, Harvey (Athlete, Hockey Player)
1096 Warwick Neck Ave
Warwick, RI 02889-6815, USA

Bennett, Hywel (Actor)
Gavin Barker
45 S Molton St
London W1Y 3RD, UNITED KINGDOM (UK)

Bennett, Jeff (Athlete, Baseball Player)
544 Old Laguardo Rd W
Lebanon, TN 37087-8906, USA

Bennett, Jimmy (Actor)
c/o Pietra Ingenito *TalentWorks*
3500 W Olive Ave Ste 1400
Burbank, CA 91505-5512, USA

Bennett, Joel (Athlete, Baseball Player)
401 Riley Rd
Windsor, NY 13865-1043, USA

Bennett, Jonathan (Actor)
c/o Craig Schneider *Pinnacle Public Relations*
8721 Santa Monica Blvd # 133
W Hollywood, CA 90069-4507, USA

Bennett, Leeman (Athlete, Football Coach, Football Player)
6795 Kinnity Ct
Cumming, GA 30040-5793, USA

Bennett, Manu (Actor)
c/o Ruth Bornhauser *Sanders Armstrong Caserta*
4111 W Alameda Ave Ste 505
Burbank, CA 91505-4163, USA

Bennett, Martellus (Athlete, Football Player)
c/o Kennard McGuire *MS World LLC*
1270 Crabb River Rd Ste 600 PMB 104
Richmond, TX 77469-5635, USA

Bennett, Michael (Athlete, Football Player)
17110 Journeys End Dr
Odessa, FL 33556-2441, USA

Bennett, Monte (Athlete, Football Player)
2075 Avenue U
Sterling, KS 67579-8917, USA

Bennett, Nelson (Skier)
807 S 20th Ave
Yakima, WA 98902-4228, USA

Bennett, Nigel (Actor)
c/o Larry Goldhar *Characters Talent Agency (Toronto)*
8 Elm St Fl 2
Toronto, ON M5G 1G7, CANADA

Bennett, Paris (Musician)
c/o Stephen Ford *Diva Central Inc*
7510 W Sunset Blvd # 1445
Los Angeles, CA 90046-3408, USA

Bennett, Rick (Athlete, Hockey Player)
55 Evergreen Ave
Clifton Park, NY 12065-4032, USA

Bennett, Roy (Athlete, Football Player)
695 Wellington Way
Jonesboro, GA 30238-7607, USA

Bennett, Sean (Athlete, Football Player)
12163 E State Road 62
Saint Meinrad, IN 47577-9673, USA

Bennett, Tony (Athlete, Basketball Player)
3408 Cesford Grange
Keswick, VA 22947-9126, USA

Bennett, Tony (Musician)
Exploring the Arts
16 W 23rd St Fl 4
New York, NY 10010-5230, USA

Bennett, Tracie (Actor)
Annette Stone
9 Newburgh St
London W1V 1LA, UNITED KINGDOM (UK)

Bennett, Vinnie (Actor)
c/o Christiana Thomson *Johnson and Laird Management*
P.O. Box 78340
Grey Lynn Auckland 01245, NEW ZEALAND

Bennett, Wendell (Athlete, Hockey Player)
726 Maryland Dr
Vista, CA 92083-3333, USA

Bennett, William (Athlete, Hockey Player)
75 Tucker Ave
Cranston, RI 02905-3314, USA

Bennett, William J. (Politician)
1735 N Lynn St Ste 5007
Arlington, VA 22209-6432, USA

Bennett, Winston (Athlete, Basketball Player)
5108 Forest Grove Ct
Prospect, KY 40059-9672, USA

Bennett, Woody (Athlete, Football Player)
7175 Via Leonardo
Lake Worth, FL 33467-5236, us

Bennie, Dan (Musician)
22121 Cleveland St
Dearborn, MI 48124-3462, USA

Benning, Brian (Athlete, Hockey Player)
Interstate Batteries
11216 156 St NW
Edmonton, AB T5M 1Y3, Canada

Benning, Jim (Athlete, Hockey Player)
Boston Bruins
100 Legends Way Ste 250
Attn: Asst General Manager
Boston, MA 02114-1389, USA

Benning, Jim (Athlete, Hockey Player)
PO Box 1264
Sherwood, OR 97140-1264, USA

Benning, Norm (Race Car Driver)
3359 Babcock Blvd
Pittsburgh, PA 15237-2421, USA

Benny, Joan (Actor)
1131 Coldwater Canyon Dr
Beverly Hills, CA 90210-2402

Benoist, Melissa (Actor)
c/o Dara Gordon *Anonymous Content*
155 Spring St Frnt 3
New York, NY 10012-5208, USA

Benoit, David (Musician)
c/o Staff Member *Chapman & Co*
PO Box 55246
Sherman Oaks, CA 91413-0246, USA

Benoit, Morgan (Actor)
c/o Staff Member *Bluestone Entertainment*
9000 W Sunset Blvd Ste 700
Los Angeles, CA 90069-5807, USA

Benoni, Arne (Musician)
Arne Benoni Productions
Postbox 50
Sandefjord N-3209, Norway

Benrubi, Abraham (Actor)
c/o Erik Kritzer *LINK Entertainment*
11872 La Grange Ave
Los Angeles, CA 90025-5282, USA

Bensimon, Kelly Killoren (Model, Reality Star, Writer)
c/o Staff Member *Bravo TV (NY)*
30 Rockefeller Plz
New York, NY 10112-0015, USA

Benson, Amber (Actor)
c/o Ryan Revel *Good Fear Film + Management*
6255 W Sunset Blvd Ste 800
Los Angeles, CA 90028-7409, USA

Benson, Anna (Model, Reality Star)
3689 Guildhall Trl
Marietta, GA 30066-8523, USA

Benson, Ashley (Actor)
c/o Ruth Bernstein *Viewpoint Inc*
8820 Wilshire Blvd Ste 220
Beverly Hills, CA 90211-2622, USA

Benson, Brad (Athlete, Football Player)
840 Amwell Rd
Hillsborough, NJ 08844-3900, USA

Benson, Brendan (Musician)
235 Lauderdale Rd
Nashville, TN 37205-1821, USA

Benson, Cedric (Athlete, Football Player)
c/o Ashley Smith Becker *Relativity Sports*
2029 Century Park E Ste 1550
Century City, CA 90067-3000, USA

Benson, Charles (Athlete, Football Player)
2625 Empire Dr Apt 2114
Richardson, TX 75080-0061, USA

Benson, Cliff (Athlete, Football Player)
PO Box 821957
Vancouver, WA 98682-0045, USA

Benson, Darren (Athlete, Football Player)
PO Box 742614
Dallas, TX 75374-2614, USA

Benson, Doug (Comedian)
c/o Bruce Smith *OmniPop Talent Group*
4605 Lankershim Blvd Ste 201
Toluca Lake, CA 91602-1874, USA

Benson, George (Actor, Musician)
Spirit Media
PO Box 43591
Phoenix, AZ 85080-3591, USA

Benson, George (Race Car Driver)
16700 State Highway 96 Spc 16
Klamath River, CA 96050-9105, USA

Benson, Jodi (Actor)
c/o Staff Member *Innovative Artists*
1505 10th St
Santa Monica, CA 90401-2805, USA

Benson, Joyce (Athlete, Golfer)
5310 Papaya Cir
Harlingen, TX 78552-8956, USA

Benson, Kent (Athlete, Basketball Player)
3921 W Maybury Mall Apt 12
Bloomington, IN 47403-3738, USA

Benson, Kris (Athlete, Baseball Player, Business Person, Olympic Athlete)
c/o Staff Member *Superior Business Management Inc*
100 Galleria Pkwy SE Ste 1000
Atlanta, GA 30339-5954, USA

Benson, Robby (Actor)
c/o Staff Member *AKA Talent Agency*
325 N Larchmont Blvd
Los Angeles, CA 90004-3011, USA

Benson, Steve (Cartoonist)
Arizona Republic
200 E Van Buren St
Editorial Dept
Phoenix, AZ 85004-2238, USA

Benson, Thomas (Athlete, Football Player)
PO Box 701341
Dallas, TX 75370-1341, USA

Benson, Troy (Athlete, Football Player)
1038 Victoria Pl
Gibsonia, PA 15044-9200, USA

Benson-Landes, Wendy (Actor)
1236 N Doheny Dr
Los Angeles, CA 90069-1723, USA

Bent, Lyriq (Actor)
c/o Staff Member *Artists & Representatives (Stone Manners Salners)*
6100 Wilshire Blvd Ste 1500
Los Angeles, CA 90048-5110, USA

Bentham, Lee (Race Car Driver)
Forsythe Racing Inc
1111 Willis Ave
Wheeling, IL 60090-5816, USA

Bentley, Albert (Athlete, Football Player)
15970 Bayside Pointe W APT 303
Fort Myers, FL 33908-6935, USA

Bentley, Dierks (Musician)
c/o Coran Capshaw *Red Light Management*
455 2nd St NE
#500
Charlottesville, VA 22902-5791, USA

Bentley, Eric (Writer)
194 Riverside Dr Apt 4E
New York, NY 10025-7276, USA

Bentley, Kevin (Athlete, Football Player)
c/o Ken Zuckerman *Priority Sports & Entertainment - (LA)*
15233 Ventura Blvd Ste 718
Sherman Oaks, CA 91403-2237, USA

Bentley, Lecharles (Athlete, Football Player)
1177 Windsor Ave
Broadview Heights, OH 44147, USA

Bentley, Ray (Athlete, Football Player, Sportscaster)
4050 Redbush Dr SW
Grandville, MI 49418-3041, USA

Bentley, Scott (Athlete, Football Player)
7756 S Trenton Ct
Centennial, CO 80112-2636, us

Bentley, Wes (Actor)
c/o Susan Patricola *Patricola Public Relations*
369 S Doheny Dr # 1408
Beverly Hills, CA 90211-3508, USA

Benton, Barbi (Actor, Model)
840 N Starwood Dr
Aspen, CO 81611-9717, USA

Benton, Brad (Adult Film Star)
c/o Staff Member *Diva Central Inc*
7510 W Sunset Blvd # 1445
Los Angeles, CA 90046-3408, USA

Benton, Butch (Athlete, Baseball Player)
3 Cedar Cir
Ocala, FL 34472-2898, USA

Benton, Denee (Actor)
c/o Jodi Gottlieb *Independent Public Relations*
9601 Wilshire Blvd Ste 750
Beverly Hills, CA 90210-5228, USA

Benton, Fletcher (Artist)
250 Dore St
San Francisco, CA 94103-4308, USA

Benton, Robert (Director, Writer)
c/o Brian Siberell *Creative Artists Agency (CAA)*
2000 Avenue of the Stars Ste 100
Los Angeles, CA 90067-4705, USA

Bentrim, Jeff (Athlete, Football Player)
303 10A St NW Calgary
Canada, AB T2N, us

Bentz, Chad (Athlete, Baseball Player)
3027 Mountainwood Cir
Juneau, AK 99801-9624, USA

Benvenuti, Giovanni (Nino) (Boxer)
FPI Viaie Tiziano 70
Rome 00196, ITALY

Benvenuti, Leo (Director, Producer, Writer)
c/o John Elliott *Mosaic Media Group*
407 N Maple Dr # 100
Beverly Hills, CA 90210-3818, USA

Ben-Victor, Paul (Actor)
c/o Jack Kingsrud *Zero Gravity Management*
11110 Ohio Ave Ste 100
Los Angeles, CA 90025-3329, USA

Benward, Luke (Actor)
c/o Mitchell Gossett *Industry Entertainment Partners*
955 Carrillo Dr Ste 300
Los Angeles, CA 90048-5400, USA

Benwikere, Bene' (Athlete, Football Player)

Benymon, Chico (Actor)
c/o Staff Member *Gersh*
9465 Wilshire Blvd Ste 600
Beverly Hills, CA 90212-2605, USA

Benz, Amy (Athlete, Golfer)
85133 Shinnecock Hills Dr
Fernandina Beach, FL 32034-8177, USA

Benz, Julia (Actor)
Innovative Artists
1505 10th St
Santa Monica, CA 90401-2805, USA

Benz, Julie (Actor)
c/o Christy Hall *Paradigm*
8942 Wilshire Blvd
Beverly Hills, CA 90211-1908, USA

Benz, Larry (Athlete, Football Player)
1526 Brummel St
Evanston, IL 60202-3708, USA

Benz, Nikki (Actor, Adult Film Star, Model)
c/o Mike Esterman *Esterman.Com, LLC*
Prefers to be contacted via email
Baltimore, MD XXXXX, USA

Benz, Sepp (Athlete)
Kiefernweg 37
Zurich 08057, SWITZERLAND

Benza, AJ (Actor)
5670 Wilshire Blvd # 400W
Los Angeles, CA 90036-5679, USA

Benzali, Daniel (Actor)
c/o Staff Member *WME|IMG*
9601 Wilshire Blvd
Beverly Hills, CA 90210-5213, USA

Benzelock, Jim (Athlete, Hockey Player)
626 Greene Ave
Winnipeg, MB R2K 0M6, Canada

Benzinger, Todd (Athlete, Baseball Player)
8207 Coral Bell Ct
Liberty Township, OH 45044-8468, USA

Beotti, Valentina (Actor)
Carol Levi Co
Via Giuseppe Pisanelli
Rome 00196, ITALY

Berard, Bryan (Athlete, Hockey Player, Olympic Athlete)
160 Bleecker St Apt 5BW
New York, NY 10012-0128, USA

Berblinger, Jeff (Athlete, Baseball Player)
102 Swanee Dr
Goddard, KS 67052-9420, USA

Berce, Gene (Athlete, Basketball Player)
13900 W Burleigh Rd
Brookfield, WI 53005-3019, USA

Bercich, Bob (Athlete, Football Player)
19017 Edward Pkwy
Mokena, IL 60448-8565, USA

Bercich, Pete (Athlete, Football Player)
17448 Honeysuckle Ave
Lakeville, MN 55044-7824, USA

Bercu, Michaela (Actor, Model)
c/o Staff Member *Elite Model Management (NY)*
245 5th Ave Fl 24
New York, NY 10016-8728, USA

Berdal, Ingrid Bolso (Bols??) (Actor, Musician)
c/o Anne Lindberg *Lindberg Management*
Lavendelstaede 5-7
Baghuset, 4. Sal
Copenhagen K 1462, DENMARK

Berdy, Sean (Actor)
18685 Main St Ste 101 # 331
Huntington Beach, CA 92648-1719, USA

Berdych, Thomas (Athlete, Tennis Player)
c/o Staff Member *ATP Tour*
201 Atp Tour Blvd
Ponte Vedra Beach, FL 32082-3211, USA

Bere, Jason (Athlete, Baseball Player)
40 Berrington Pl
North Andover, MA 01845-2152, USA

Berehowsky, Drake (Athlete, Hockey Player)
20455 N 95th St
Scottsdale, AZ 85255-6629, USA

Berelc, Paris (Actor)
c/o Shannon Barr *Rogers & Cowan*
1840 Century Park E Fl 18
Los Angeles, CA 90067-2101, USA

Berendt, John (Writer)
c/o Suzanne Gluck *WME|IMG (NY)*
11 Madison Ave Fl 18
New York, NY 10010-3669, USA

Berenger, Tom (Actor)
c/o Matt Feil *Rowan & Maron*
3100 Donald Douglas Loop N
Santa Monica, CA 90405-3084, USA

Berenguer, Juan (Athlete, Baseball Player)
8616 Alisa Ct
Chanhassen, MN 55317-9373, USA

Berens, Ricky (Athlete, Swimmer)
1 Olympic Plz Bldg 2A
Colorado Springs, CO 80909-5746, USA

Berenson, Ken (Red) (Athlete, Coach, Hockey Player)
3555 Daleview Dr
Ann Arbor, MI 48105-9686, USA

Berenyi, bruce (Baseball Player)
10 Pine Grove Rd
Exeter, NH 03833-4718, USA

Berenyl, Bruce (Athlete, Baseball Player)
PO Box 133
Sherwood, OH 43556-0133, USA

Berenzweig, Andrew (Athlete, Hockey Player)
4603 Brookside Rd
Ottawa Hills, OH 43615-2207, USA

Beresford, Bruce (Director)
c/o Steve Kenis *Steve Kenis & Company*
Royalty House
72-74 Dean St
London W1D 3SG, UK

Berezan, Perry (Athlete, Hockey Player)
43 Mount Cascade Close SE
Calgary, AB T2Z 2K4, Canada

Berezhnaya, Yelena (Figure Skater)
Ice House Skating Rink
111 Midtown Bridge Approac
Hackensack, NJ 07601-7505, USA

Berezin, Sergei (Athlete, Hockey Player)
1645 SW 4th Ave
Boca Raton, FL 33432-7232, USA

Berfield, Justin (Actor, Director, Producer)
24944 Lorena Dr
Calabasas, CA 91302-3048, USA

Berg, Aaron (Actor)
c/o Cris Italia *CH Entertainment*
123 Bowery Apt 5F
New York, NY 10002-4919, USA

Berg, Aki (Athlete, Hockey Player)
7400 Metro Blvd Ste 280
Minneapolis, MN 55439-2363, USA

Berg, Aki-Petteri (Athlete, Hockey Player)
1751 Pinnacle Dr Ste 1500
McLean, VA 22102-3833, USA

Berg, Bill (Athlete, Hockey Player)
The NHL Network
9 Channel Nine Crt
Toronto, ON M1S 4B5, Canada

Berg, Dave (Athlete, Baseball Player)
PO Box 638
Jamestown, NY 14702-0638, USA

Berg, Dave (Baseball Player)
1917 Stonecastle Dr
Keller, TX 76262-4912, USA

Berg, justin (Baseball Player)
N3628 Heights Dr
Bryant, WI 54418-9563, USA

Berg, Kevin (Business Person)
c/o Staff Member *CBS Paramount Network Television*
4024 Radford Ave
Cbs Studios
Studio City, CA 91604-2190, USA

Berg, Laura (Athlete, Olympic Athlete, Softball Player)
2801 NE 50th St
Usa Softball
Oklahoma City, OK 73111-7203, USA

Berg, Matraca (Musician)
Joe's Garage
4405 Belmont Park Ter
Nashville, TN 37215-3609, USA

Berg, Peter (Actor)
c/o Staff Member *Film 44*
2045 S Barrington Ave # B
Los Angeles, CA 90025-1276, USA

Berg, Rick (Congressman, Politician)
323 Cannon Hob
Washington, DC 20515-0924, USA

Berg, Steve (Actor)
c/o Ilan Breil *Mosaic Media Group*
407 N Maple Dr # 100
Beverly Hills, CA 90210-3818, USA

Berg, Yehuda (Religious Leader)
Kabbalah Center International
1054 S Robertson Blvd
Los Angeles, CA 90035-1505, USA

Berganio, David Jr (Athlete, Golfer)
17811 Lahey St
Granada Hills, CA 91344-4030, USA

Berge, Francine (Actor)
Cineart
36 Rue de Ponthiew
Paris 75008, FRANCE

Bergen, Candice (Actor)
c/o Heidi Schaeffer *PMK/BNC Public Relations*
1840 Century Park E Ste 1400
Los Angeles, CA 90067-2115, USA

Bergen, Danny (Actor)
c/o Staff Member *Paul Lane Entertainment*
468 N Camden Dr
Beverly Hills, CA 90210-4507, USA

Bergen, Erich (Actor)
c/o Trevor Adley *Anonymous Content*
155 Spring St Frnt 3
New York, NY 10012-5208, USA

Bergen, Gary (Athlete, Basketball Player)
1386 Graham Cir
Erie, CO 80516-3617, USA

Berger, Brandon (Athlete, Baseball Player)
2276 Dixie Hwy
Ft Mitchell, KY 41017-2949, USA

Berger, Edward (Actor)
c/o Jodi Shields *Casarotto Ramsay & Associates Ltd (UK)*
Waverley House
7-12 Noel St
London W1F 8GQ, UNITED KINGDOM

Berger, Fred (Producer)
c/o Staff Member *Automatik Entertainment*
7122 Beverly Blvd Ste F
Los Angeles, CA 90036-2572, USA

Berger, Gerhard (Race Car Driver)
Berger Motorsport
Postfach 1121
Vaduz 09490, AUSTRIA

Berger, Helmut (Actor)

Berger, Isaac (Athlete, Olympic Athlete, Weightlifter)
206 E 31st St Apt 8A
New York, NY 10016-6357, USA

Berger, Lee (Actor)
57 Fellows Rd
Brentwood, NH 03833-6130, USA

Berger, Mike (Athlete, Hockey Player)
13171 Sweet Briar Pkwy
Fishers, IN 46038-5504, USA

Berger, Ronald (Athlete, Football Player)
22 Sierra Rosa Loop
Santa Fe, NM 87506-8212, USA

Berger, Senta (Actor)
Sentana Films
Gebsattelstr 30
Munich 81541, GERMANY

Bergerac, Jacques (Actor)
4 Rue Ferme
Neuilly-s-Seine 92200, France

Berger-Brown, Barbara (Athlete, Baseball Player)
1321 S Finley Rd Apt 109
Lombard, IL 60148-4355, USA

Berger-Knebl, Joan (Athlete, Baseball Player)
8 Lochmeath Way
Dover, DE 19904-6447, USA

Bergeron, J C (Athlete, Hockey Player)
c/o Staff Member *Reebok / CCM*
3400 Raymond-Lasnier St
Saint-Laurent, QC H4R 3L3, Canada

Bergeron, Marc-Andre (Athlete, Hockey Player)
Paraphe Sports Management
190 Rue Fusey
2nd Paul Corbeil
Trois-Rivieres, QC G8T 2V8, Canada

Bergeron, Michel (Athlete, Coach, Hockey Player)
T Q S
612 Rue Saint-Jacques
Montreal, QC H3C 1C8, CANADA

Bergeron, Patrice (Athlete, Hockey Player)
c/o Staff Member *Boston Bruins*
100 Legends Way Ste 250
Td Banknorth Garden
Boston, MA 02114-1389, USA

Bergeron, Peter (Athlete, Baseball Player)
3495 Manatee Dr SE
Saint Petersburg, FL 33705-4144, USA

Bergeron, Tom (Actor, Producer)
c/o Alejandra Cristina *Ace PR*
4122 Sunnyslope Ave
Sherman Oaks, CA 91423-4308, USA

Bergeron, Yves (Athlete, Hockey Player)
1035 Clearwater Ave
Bathurst, NB E2A 4H5, Canada

Berger-Taylor, Norma (Athlete, Baseball Player)
529 N Bierman Ave
Villa Park, IL 60181-1437, USA

Bergeson, Eric (Athlete, Football Player)
2397 E 1300 S
Salt Lake City, UT 84108-1940, USA

Bergeson, James (Athlete, Olympic Athlete, Water Polo Player)
7 Promontory
Trabuco Canyon, CA 92679-3811, USA

Bergeson, Pat (Musician)
3614 Central Ave
Nashville, TN 37205-2344, USA

Bergevin, Marc (Athlete, Hockey Player)
404 Canterbury Ct
Hinsdale, IL 60521-2826, USA

Bergevin, Marc (Athlete, Hockey Player)
Chicago Blackhawks
1901 W Madison St
Attn Assistant G M
Chicago, IL 60612-2459, USA

Bergey, Bruce (Athlete, Football Player)
7700 SW River Rd
Hillsboro, OR 97123-9108, USA

Bergey, William E (Bill) (Athlete, Football Player)
2 Hickory Ln
Chadds Ford, PA 19317-9715, USA

Berggren, Jenny (Musician)
Basic Music Mgmt
Norrtullsgatan 51
Stockholm 113 45, SWEDEN

Berggren, Jonas (Musician)
Basic Music Mgmt
Norrtullsgatan 51
Stockholm 11345, SWEDEN

Berggren, Malin (Musician)
Basic Music Mgmt
Norrtullsgatan 51
Stockholm 11345, SWEDEN

Berggren, Thommy (Actor)
Swedish Film Institute
PO Box 27126
Stockholm 102 52, SWEDEN

Bergh, Larry (Athlete, Basketball Player)
7020 Peoto Ln
Crossville, TN 38572-4501, USA

Berghman, Carl (Race Car Driver)
134 Bay State Rd
Rehobeth, 2769 MA, USA

Bergi, Emily (Actor)
Innovative Artists
1505 10th St
Santa Monica, CA 90401-2805, USA

Bergin, Michael (Actor, Model)
c/o Tom Chasin *Chasin Agency, The*
8281 Melrose Ave Ste 202
Los Angeles, CA 90046-6890, USA

Bergin, Patrick (Actor)
Hyler Mgmt
25 Sea Colony Dr
Santa Monica, CA 90405-5495, USA

Bergkamp, Dennis (Soccer Player)
Arsenal FC
Arsenal Stadium
Avenell Road
London N5 1BU, UNITED KINGDOM (UK)

Bergl, Emily (Actor)
c/o Bill Veloric *Innovative Artists*
235 Park Ave S Fl 7
New York, NY 10003-1405, USA

Bergland, Tim (Athlete, Hockey Player)
721 Labree Ave N
Thief River Falls, MN 56701-1632, USA

Berglind (Icey) (Television Host)
c/o Staff Member *E! Entertainment Television (LA)*
5750 Wilshire Blvd
Los Angeles, CA 90036-3697, USA

Bergloff, Bob (Athlete, Hockey Player)
10200 Harriet Ave S
Minneapolis, MN 55420-5233, USA

Berglund, Art (Athlete, Hockey Player)
3749 Blue Merion Ct
Colorado Springs, CO 80906-4444, USA

Berglund, Bo (Athlete, Hockey Player)
c/o Staff Member *Buffalo Sabres*
1 Seymour H Knox III Plz Ste 1
Buffalo, NY 14203-3096, USA

Bergman, Alan (Musician)
714 N Maple Dr
Beverly Hills, CA 90210-3411, USA

Bergman, Andrew C (Director, Writer)
c/o Robert (Bob) Bookman *Paradigm*
8942 Wilshire Blvd
Beverly Hills, CA 90211-1908, USA

Bergman, Dave (Athlete, Baseball Player)
PO Box 380135
Clinton Township, MI 48038-0060, USA

Bergman, Dusty (Athlete, Baseball Player)
1549 Koontz Ln
Carson City, NV 89701-6504, USA

Bergman, Jeff (Actor)
c/o Staff Member *Antland Productions*
686 E Passaic Ave
Bloomfield, NJ 07003-4420, USA

Bergman, Marilyn K (Musician)
714 N Maple Dr
Beverly Hills, CA 90210-3411, USA

Bergman, Peter (Actor)
120 Marine Ave
Newport Beach, CA 92662-1202, USA

Bergman, Sean (Athlete, Baseball Player)
14421 Scott Rd
Bryan, OH 43506-9624, USA

Bergman, Thommie (Athlete, Hockey Player)
c/o Staff Member *Toronto Maple Leafs*
Air Canada Centre
400-40 Bay St
Toronto, ON M5J 2X2, CANADA

Bergman Boreanaz, Jaime (Actor, Model)
c/o Staff Member *McCabe Group*
3211 Cahuenga Blvd W Ste 104
Los Angeles, CA 90068-1372, USA

Bergmann, Erma (Athlete, Baseball Player, Commentator)
6613 Morganford Rd
Saint Louis, MO 63116-2835, USA

Bergmann, Jay (Athlete, Baseball Player)
13 Abilene Ln
Manalapan, NJ 07726-4527, USA

Bergmann, S (Athlete, Baseball Player)

Bergoglio, Jose Mario Cardinal (Religious Leader)
Arzobispado
Rivadavia 415
Buenos Aires 01002, ARGENTINA

Bergomi, Giuseppe (Athlete, Football Player)
via Trento 1
Settala (MI) I-20090, Italy

Bergoust, Eric (Athlete, Olympic Athlete, Skier)
1430 Shadow Ln
Missoula, MT 59803-3405, USA

Bergstein, Eleanor (Director, Producer, Writer)
c/o Staff Member *Creative Artists Agency (CAA)*
2000 Avenue of the Stars Ste 100
Los Angeles, CA 90067-4705, USA

Berhe, Nat (Athlete, Football Player)
c/o Josh Arnold *Synergy Sports International LLC*
615 Esplanade Unit 105
Redondo Beach, CA 90277-4132, USA

Berhendt, Greg (Actor, Comedian)
c/o Staff Member *Avalon Management (UK)*
4A Exmoor St
London W10 6BD, UNITED KINGDOM

Berk, Michael (Producer)

Berkeley, Xander (Actor, Producer)
215 Drinkwater Point Rd
Yarmouth, ME 04096-5714, USA

Berkhoel, Adam (Athlete, Hockey Player)
1744 Manning AveS
Saint Paul, MN 55129-9251, USA

Berkley, Elizabeth (Actor, Producer)

Berkley, Shelley (Congressman, Politician)
405 Cannon Hob
Washington, DC 20515-4309, USA

Berkman, Lance (Athlete, Baseball Player)
5 Farnham Park Dr
Houston, TX 77024-7501, USA

Berkner, Laurie (Musician)
PO Box 250774
Columbia University Station
New York, NY 10025-1529, USA

Berkoff, David (Athlete, Swimmer)
Harvard University
Athletic Dept
Cambridge, MA 02138, USA

Berkoff, Steven (Actor)
c/o Luc Chaudhary *International Artists Management*
25-27 Heath St.
Hamstead NW3 6TR, UNITED KINGDOM

Berkowitz, Bob (Journalist, Television Host)
c/o Staff Member *CNBC (Main)*
900 Sylvan Ave
Englewood Cliffs, NJ 07632-3312, USA

Berkus, Nate (Designer, Television Host)
8195 Hollywood Blvd
Los Angeles, CA 90069-1643, USA

Berlanti, Greg (Producer)
PO Box 5623
Beverly Hills, CA 90209-5623, USA

Berlin, Eddie (Athlete, Football Player)
604 44th St
Des Moines, IA 50312-2302, USA

Berlin, Jeannie (Actor)
c/o Toni Howard *ICM Partners*
10250 Constellation Blvd Fl 7
Los Angeles, CA 90067-6207, USA

Berlin, Steve (Musician)
c/o Staff Member *Paradigm (Monterey)*
404 W Franklin St
Monterey, CA 93940-2303, USA

Berliner, Alain (Director)
United Talent Agency
9336 Civic Center Dr
Beverly Hills, CA 90210-3604, USA

Berlinger, Warren (Actor)
9761 Cactus Ave
Chatsworth, CA 91311-2630, USA

Berlinsky, Dmitri (Musician)
280 Rector Pl Apt 6O
New York, NY 10280-1140, USA

Berlioux, Daniel (Actor)
Cineart
36 Rue de Ponthieu
Paris 75008, FRANCE

Berman, Andy (Actor)
c/o Staff Member *Gersh*
9465 Wilshire Blvd Ste 600
Beverly Hills, CA 90212-2605, USA

Berman, Boris (Musician)
Columbia Artists Mgmt Inc
165 W 57th St
New York, NY 10019-2201, USA

Berman, Chris (Commentator, Sportscaster)
c/o Staff Member *ESPN (Main)*
935 Middle St
Espn Plaza
Bristol, CT 06010-1000, USA

Berman, David (Musician)
2406 Canyon Dr
Los Angeles, CA 90068-2414, USA

Berman, Josh (Producer)
c/o Staff Member *Creative Artists Agency (CAA)*
2000 Avenue of the Stars Ste 100
Los Angeles, CA 90067-4705, USA

Berman, Julie (Actor)
c/o Nicole Nassar *Nicole Nassar PR*
1111 10th St Unit 104
Santa Monica, CA 90403-5363, USA

Berman, Laura (Commentator, Doctor, Television Host)
2648 N Racine Ave
Chicago, IL 60614-1216, USA

Berman, Lazar N (Musician)
12 Nicola Ln
Nesconset, NY 11767-1550, USA

Berman, Shari Springer (Director)
c/o Staff Member *Creative Artists Agency (CAA)*
2000 Avenue of the Stars Ste 100
Los Angeles, CA 90067-4705, USA

Bermudez, Carolina (Musician)
c/o Staff Member *Buchwald*
5900 Wilshire Blvd Ste 3100
Los Angeles, CA 90036-5030, USA

Bermudez, Gustavo (Actor)
c/o Staff Member *Telefe (Argentina)*
Pavon 2444
Buenos Aires C1248AAT, ARGENTINA

Bermudez, Joe (DJ)
c/o Staff Member *Diva Central Inc*
7510 W Sunset Blvd # 1445
Los Angeles, CA 90046-3408, USA

Bernadeau, Mackenzy (Athlete, Football Player)

Bernal, Gael Garcia (Actor)
c/o Staff Member *Canana Films*
Zacatecas 142-A
Colonia Roma
Mexico City 06700, MEXICO

Bernard, Betsy (Business Person)
American Telephone & Telegraph Corp
32 Avenue of the Americas
New York, NY 10013-2473, USA

Bernard, Carlos (Actor)
8901 Wonderland Ave
Los Angeles, CA 90046-1853, USA

Bernard, Claire M A (Musician)
53 Rue Rabelais
Lyon 69003, FRANCE

Bernard, Crystal (Actor, Musician, Songwriter, Writer)
PO Box 202
Montrose, CA 91021-0202, USA

Bernard, Dwight (Athlete, Baseball Player)
5120 N Norwich Ln
Belle Rive, IL 62810-2703, USA

Bernard, Ed (Actor)
PO Box 7965
Northridge, CA 91327-7965, USA

Bernard, Giovani (Athlete, Football Player)
c/o JB Bernstein *Access Group*
3675 S Rainbow Blvd Ste 107
Las Vegas, NV 89103-1059, USA

Bernard, James (Race Car Driver)
PO Box 758
Mc Henry, MD 21541-0758, USA

Bernard, Molly (Actor)
c/o Michael Geiser *Jill Fritzo Public Relations*
208 E 51st St # 305
New York, NY 10022-6557, USA

Bernard, Robyn (Actor)
The Bernard Bookstore
PO Box 202
Montrose, CA 91021-0202, USA

Bernardi, Barry (Producer)
c/o Staff Member *Gersh*
9465 Wilshire Blvd Ste 600
Beverly Hills, CA 90212-2605, USA

Bernardi, Frank (Athlete, Football Player)
PO Box 1015
Broomfield, CO 80038-1015, USA

Bernazard, Tony (Athlete, Baseball Player)

Bernero, Adam (Athlete, Baseball Player)
11 Columbus Dr
Savannah, GA 31405-4101, USA

Bernero, Ed (Writer)
c/o Jeff Jacobs *Creative Artists Agency (CAA)*
2000 Avenue of the Stars Ste 100
Los Angeles, CA 90067-4705, USA

Bernet, Ed (Athlete, Football Player)
7967 Caruth Ct
Dallas, TX 75225-8135, USA

Bernet, Lee (Athlete, Football Player)
4689 Stoddart Ln
Saint Paul, MN 55127-2334, USA

Berney, Bob (President)
c/o Staff Member *Newmarket Films*
597 5th Ave Fl 7
New York, NY 10017-8264, USA

Bernhard, Sandra (Actor, Comedian, Musician)
c/o Jeremy Katz *Katz Company, The*
1674 Broadway Fl 7
New York, NY 10019-5838, USA

Bernhardt, Daniel (Actor)
6500 Wilshire Blvd Ste 2200
Los Angeles, CA 90048-4942

Bernhardt, Juan (Athlete, Baseball Player)
Eduardo Brito 13
San Pedro de Macoris, Dominican Republic

Bernhardt, Kevin (Writer)
c/o Luke Rivett *Anonymous Content*
3532 Hayden Ave
Culver City, CA 90232-2413, USA

Bernhardt, Roger (Athlete, Football Player)
PO Box 4631
Lawrence, KS 66046-1631, USA

Bernhardt, Tim (Athlete, Hockey Player)
RR 1
Schomberg, ON L0G 1T0, Canada

Bernheimer, Martin (Musician)
17350 W Sunset Blvd Apt 702C
Pacific Palisades, CA 90272-4109, USA

Bernice Johnson, Eddie (Congressman, Politician)
2468 Rayburn Hob
Washington, DC 20515-3306, USA

Bernich, Ken (Athlete, Football Player)
33 Okahatchee Cir SE
Fort Walton Beach, FL 32548-5754, USA

Bernier, Jean (Athlete, Hockey Player)
2350 Rue du Couvent-De-Lorette
St-Hyacinthe, QC J2T 4R3, Canada

Bernier, Serge (Athlete, Hockey Player)
534 Rue Elisabeth
Rimouski, QC G5L 3M9, Canada

Bernier, Sylvie (Race Car Driver)
Olympic Assn
Cite du Harve
Montreal QC H3C 3R4, CANADA

Berning, Susie (Athlete, Golfer)
80413 Portobello Dr
Indio, CA 92201-1877, USA

Berns, Rick (Athlete, Football Player)
127 Merry Trl San
Antonio, TX 78232, USA

Bernsen, Corbin (Actor)
11955 Addison St
Valley Village, CA 91607-3106, USA

Bernstein, Adam (Director, Producer, Writer)
c/o Sean Freidin *ICM Partners*
10250 Constellation Blvd Fl 7
Los Angeles, CA 90067-6207, USA

Bernstein, Al (Actor)

Bernstein, Assaf (Director)
c/o Lon Haber *Lon Haber & Co (IPPR)*
304 S Broadway
Los Angeles, CA 90013-1224, USA

Bernstein, Bonnie (Television Host)
c/o Staff Member *CBS Television*
51 W 52nd St
New York, NY 10019-6119, USA

Bernstein, Carl (Journalist, Writer)
9 Salt Meadow Ln
Sag Harbor, NY 11963-4324, USA

Bernstein, Josh (Television Host)
c/o Mark Schulman *3 Arts Entertainment*
9460 Wilshire Blvd Fl 7
Beverly Hills, CA 90212-2713, USA

Bernstein, Kenny (Race Car Driver)
King Racing
26231 Dimension Dr
Lake Forest, CA 92630-7805, USA

Bernstine, Rod (Athlete, Football Player)
6675 S Robertsdale Way
Aurora, CO 80016-7500, USA

Bernthal, Jon (Actor)
c/o Joannie Burstein *Burstein Company*
15304 W Sunset Blvd Ste 208
Pacific Palisades, CA 90272-3656, USA

Berra, Dale (Athlete, Baseball Player)
164 Eagle Rock Way
Montclair, NJ 07042-1623, USA

Berra, Steve (Skateboarder)
3716 Clayton Ave
Los Angeles, CA 90027-4614, USA

Berra, Tim (Athlete, Football Player)
23 Wilson Ter
West Caldwell, NJ 07006-7953, USA

Berra, Yogi (Athlete, Baseball Player, Coach)
The Yogi Berra Museum
8 Quarry Rd
Little Falls, NJ 07424-2161, USA

Berresford, Josh (Actor)
Auz & Associates PR
PO Box 601
Homewood, IL 60430-8601

Berri, Claude (Director, Producer)
Renn Espace d'Art Contemporain
7 Rue de Lille
Paris 75007, FRANCE

Berrian, Bernard (Athlete, Football Player)
7209 Tokay Cir
Winton, CA 95388-9358, USA

Berridge, Elizabeth (Actor)
Judy Schoen
606 N Larchmont Blvd Ste 309
Los Angeles, CA 90004-1309, USA

Berrier, Max (Race Car Driver)
6262 N.N.C. Hwy 109
High Point, NC 27265, USA

Berrington, Emily (Actor)
c/o Staff Member *Markham & Froggatt*
4 Windmill St
London W1T 1HZ, UNITED KINGDOM

Berroa, Geronimo (Athlete, Baseball Player)
3681 Broadwav Act 23
New York, NY 10031-1539, USA

Berry, Bert (Athlete, Football Player)
1402 E Coral Cove Dr
Gilbert, AZ 85234-2600, USA

Berry, Bill (Baseball Player)
Negro Baseball Leagues
2231 Dickinson St
Philadelphia, PA 19146-4204, USA

Berry, Bill (Musician)
1661 Old Farmington Rd
Watkinsville, GA 30677-3208, USA

Berry, Bob (Athlete, Football Player)
270 Hames Rd SPC 60
Watsonville, CA 95076-0220, USA

Berry, Brad (Athlete, Hockey Player)
Columbus Blue Jackets
200 W Nationwide Blvd Unit 1
Attn Coaching Staff
Columbus, OH 43215-2564, USA

Berry, Brad (Athlete, Hockey Player)
PO Box 5182
Grand Forks, ND 58206-5182, USA

Berry, David (Actor)
c/o Mark Morrissey *Morrissey Management*
16 Princess Ave
Rosebery
Sydney NSW 02018, AUSTRALIA

Berry, Ed (Athlete, Football Player)
4215 Skymont Dr
Belmont, CA 94002-1245, USA

Berry, Eric (Athlete, Football Player)
c/o Chad Speck *Allegiant Athletic Agency*
35 Market Sq Ste 201
Knoxville, TN 37902-1420, USA

Berry, Fred (Athlete, Hockey Player)
1330 Jaclyn Dr
Brookfield, WI 53045-4452, USA

Berry, Glen (Actor)
c/o Staff Member *The Rights House (UK)*
Drury House
34-43 Russell St
London WC2B 5HA, UNITED KINGDOM

Berry, Halle (Actor, Model)
c/o Meredith O'Sullivan Wasson *The Lede Company*
9701 Wilshire Blvd # 930
Beverly Hills, CA 90212-2020, USA

Berry, Jim (Artist, Cartoonist)
United Feature Syndicate
PO Box 5610
Cincinnati, OH 45201-5610, USA

Berry, Joy (Writer)
c/o Staff Member *Trident Media Group LLC*
41 Madison Ave Fl 36
New York, NY 10010-2257, USA

Berry, Ken (Athlete, Baseball Player)
1131 SW Camden Ln
Topeka, KS 66604-1980, USA

Berry, Ken (Athlete, Hockey Player)
14112 Marine Dr
White Rock, BC V4B 1A7, Canada

Berry, Kevin (Swimmer)
28 George St
Manly, NSW 02295, AUSTRALIA

Berry, Latin (Athlete, Football Player)
925 Prater Rd
Sulphur, LA 70663-4243, USA

Berry, Maleek (Producer)
StarBoy Entertainment
Prefers to be contacted by telephone or email

Berry, Mark (Athlete, Baseball Player)
5201 Keene Dr
Plant City, FL 33566-9798, USA

Berry, Matthew (Commentator)
c/o Jonathan Berry *3 Arts Entertainment*
9460 Wilshire Blvd Fl 7
Beverly Hills, CA 90212-2713, USA

Berry, Neil (Athlete, Baseball Player)
2405 University Ave
Kalamazoo, MI 49008-2430, USA

Berry, Ray (Athlete, Football Player)
12 Winged Foot Cir W
Abilene, TX 79606-5026, USA

Berry, Raymond E (Athlete, Football Coach, Football Player)
PO Box 332009
Murfreesboro, TN 37133, USA

Berry, Reggie (Athlete, Football Player)
1803 E Ocean Blvd Unit 402
Long Beach, CA 90802-6045, USA

Berry, Robert V (Bob) (Athlete, Coach, Hockey Player)
640 3rd St
Hermosa Beach, CA 90254-4710, USA

Berry, Royce (Athlete, Football Player)
PO Box 909
Comfort, TX 78013-0909, USA

Berry, Sean (Athlete, Baseball Player)
307 Susannah Ln
Paso Robles, CA 93446-7114, USA

Berry, Walter (Athlete, Basketball Player)
5206 Village Ct
Union City, GA 30291-5146, USA

Berry, Wendell E (Writer)
Lanes Landing Farm
PO Box 1
Port Royal, KY 40058-0001, USA

Berryhill, Damon (Athlete, Baseball Player)
11 Springbrook Rd
Laguna Niguel, CA 92677-5719, USA

Berryman, Michael (Actor)
PO Box 697
Clearlake, CA 95422-0697, USA

Bersia, John (Journalist)
Orlando Sentinel
633 N Orange Ave Lbby
Editorial Dept
Orlando, FL 32801-1349, USA

Bertelmann, Fred (Actor, Musician)
Am Hohenberg 9
Berg/Starnberger D-82335, Germany

Bertelsen, Jim (Athlete, Football Player)
2001 Days End Rd
Wimberley, TX 78676-9153, USA

Berteotti, Missy (Athlete, Golfer)
3065 Annandale Dr
Presto, PA 15142, USA

Berthiaume, Daniel (Athlete, Hockey Player)
PO Box 673
Hardy, VA 24101-0673, USA

Berthiaume-Wicken, Elizabeth (Baseball Player)
52 20th Ave E
Vancouver, BC V5V 1L6, CANADA

Berti, Joel (Actor)
c/o Melissa Hirschenson *Innovative Artists*
1505 10th St
Santa Monica, CA 90401-2805, USA

Bertie, Diego (Musician)
c/o Gabriel Blanco *Gabriel Blanco Iglesias (Mexico)*
Rio Balsas 35-32
Colonia Cuauhtemoc
DF 06500, Mexico

Bertinelli, Valerie (Actor)
c/o Marc Schwartz *Fusion Management*
2314 San Ysidro Dr
Beverly Hills, CA 90210-1556, USA

Bertone, Cardinal Tarcisio (Religious Leader)
Palazzo Del S Uffizio LI
Rome 00193, ITALY

Bertotti, Mike (Athlete, Baseball Player)
14 Jupiter Rd
Highland Mls, NY 10930-2916, USA

Bertram, Laura (Actor)
c/o Staff Member *Lucas Talent Inc*
1238 Homer St Suite 6
Vancouver, BC V6B 2Y5, CANADA

Bertsch, Jackie (Athlete, Golfer)
8215 E Bronco Trl
Scottsdale, AZ 85255-2171, USA

Bertuca, Tony (Athlete, Football Player)
2014 N Newcastle Ave
Chicago, IL 60707-3332, USA

Bertuzzi, Todd (Athlete, Hockey Player)
900 Deer Ridge Crt
Kitchener, ON N2P 2L3, Canada

Berube, Craig (Athlete, Hockey Player)
Philadelphia Flyers
3601 S Broad St Ste 2
Attn Coaching Staff
Philadelphia, PA 19148-5297, USA

Berube, Craig (Athlete, Hockey Player)
1341 Durham Rd
New Hope, PA 18938-9479, USA

Berumen, Andres (Athlete, Baseball Player)
PO Box 1436
Banning, CA 92220-0010, USA

Besana, Fred (Baseball Player)
Baltimore Orioles
3763 Westchester Dr
Roseville, CA 95747-6354, USA

Beschorner-Baskovich, Mary (Baseball Player)
211 Sandy Ln
Plano, IL 60545-2054, USA

Besedin, Vladimir (Figure Skater)
c/o Staff Member *Champions on Ice*
3500 American Blvd W Ste 190
Minneapolis, MN 55431-4431, USA

Beshore, Del (Athlete, Basketball Player)
1404 Cobblestone Ln
Pomona, CA 91767-3562, USA

Bess, Daniel (Actor)
c/o Raelle Koota *Anonymous Content*
3532 Hayden Ave
Culver City, CA 90232-2413, USA

Bess, Rufus (Athlete, Football Player)
6890 Betty Ln
Eden Prairie, MN 55344-7850, USA

Besser, Matt (Actor)
c/o Jonathan Weinstein *United Talent Agency (UTA)*
9336 Civic Center Dr
Beverly Hills, CA 90210-3604, USA

Bessillieu, Donald A (Don) (Athlete, Football Player)
4787 Gardiner Dr
Columbus, GA 31907-3441, USA

Besson, Luc (Director, Producer)
c/o Staff Member *Seaside Productions*
PO Box 69407
West Hollywood, CA 90069-0407, USA

Best, Art (Athlete, Football Player)
6276 Rider Rd
Reynoldsburg, OH 43068-2336, USA

Best, Greg (Athlete, Football Player)
2859 Darlington Rd
Beaver Falls, PA 15010-1054, USA

Best, Jahvid (Athlete, Football Player)
c/o Tony Fleming *Impact Sports (LA)*
12429 Ventura Ct
Studio City, CA 91604-2417, USA

Best, John O (Soccer Player)
1065 Lomita Blvd
Harbor City, CA 90710-1901, USA

Best, Karl (Athlete, Baseball Player)
PO Box 12698
Everett, WA 98206-2698, USA

Best, Kevin (Artist)
27 Dartford Rd
Thornleigh 02120, Australia

Best, Mat (Actor, Producer)
c/o Alan Rautbourt *Circle of Confusion*
8931 Ellis Ave
Los Angeles, CA 90034-3336, USA

Best, Pete (Musician)
8 Hymans Green
W Derby
Liverpool 00012, UNITED KINGDOM (UK)

Best, Travis (Athlete, Basketball Player)
703 Bradley Rd
Springfield, MA 01109-1424, USA

Bestar, Maria (Musician)
c/o Staff Member *Sony Music (Miami)*
404 Washington Ave Ste 700
Miami Beach, FL 33139-6615, USA

Bester, Allan (Athlete, Hockey Player)
12527 Crayford Ave
Orlando, FL 32837-8536, USA

Bestwick, Arnie (Race Car Driver)
10643 Court Rd
Morrison, IL 61270-9386, USA

Bestwicke, Martine (Actor)
Goldey Co
1156 S Carmelina Ave # B
Los Angeles, CA 90049-5812, USA

Beswick, Jim (Athlete, Baseball Player)
6512 3rd St
Lubbock, TX 79416-3718, USA

Beswicke, Martine (Actor)
Goldey Co
1156 S Carmelina Ave # 8
Los Angeles, CA 90049-5812, USA

Betancourt, Jeff (Director)
c/o Staff Member *Broder Webb Chervin Silbermann Agency, The (BWCS)*
10250 Constellation Blvd
Los Angeles, CA 90067-6200, USA

Betancourt, Yuniesky (Athlete, Baseball Player)
9500 SW 146th St
Miami, FL 33176-7871, USA

Betancurt, Natalia (Actor)
c/o Staff Member *TV Caracol*
Calle 76 #11 - 35
Piso 10AA
Bogota DC 26484, COLOMBIA

Bethea, Antoine (Athlete, Football Player)
6021 Gleneagles Cir
San Jose, CA 95138-2372, us

Bethea, Bill (Athlete, Baseball Player)
166 Penny ln
Georgetown, TX 78633-2016, USA

Bethea, Ellen (Actor)
Independent Artists
505 8th Ave Ste 2208
New York, NY 10018-6505, USA

Bethea, Elvin L (Athlete, Football Player)
16211 Leslie Ln
Missouri City, TX 77489-1012, USA

Bethel, Wilson (Actor)
c/o Ryan Daly *Zero Gravity Management*
11110 Ohio Ave Ste 100
Los Angeles, CA 90025-3329, USA

Bethell, Tabrett (Actor)
c/o El Erdmane *RGM Artists*
8-12 Ann St
Surry Hills, NSW 02010, AUSTRALIA

Beth Hart Band (Music Group, Musician)
c/o Staff Member *WME|IMG*
9601 Wilshire Blvd
Beverly Hills, CA 90210-5213, USA

Bethke, Jim (Athlete, Baseball Player)
4305 N Jarboe Ct
Kansas City, MO 64116-4655, USA

Bethune, Bobby (Athlete, Football Player)
PO Box 692
Leeds, AL 35094-0011, USA

Bethune, George (Athlete, Football Player)
2817 Gaslight Ln W
Mobile, AL 36695-3130, USA

Bethune, Patricia (Actor)
c/o Peter Himberger *Impact Artists Group LLC*
42 Hamilton Ter
New York, NY 10031-6403, USA

Bets, Maxim (Athlete, Hockey Player)
5566 Candlelight Dr
La Jolla, CA 92037-7711, USA

Bettany, Paul (Actor)
c/o Cara Tripicchio *Shelter PR*
5670 Wilshire Blvd Ste 1200
Los Angeles, CA 90036-5621, USA

Bettencourt, Nuno (Musician)
3001 Durand Dr
Los Angeles, CA 90068-1909, USA

Bettendorf, Jeff (Athlete, Baseball Player)
10349 SE Nicole Loop
Happy Valley, OR 97086-6881, USA

Betters, Doug L (Athlete, Football Player)
77 Better Way
Whitefish, MT 59937-3471, USA

Betterson, Doug (Athlete, Football Player)
2442 46th St
Pennsauken, NJ 08110-2018, USA

Betterson, James (Athlete, Football Player)
234 Allens Ln
Mullica Hill, NJ 08062-2005, USA

Bettiga, Mike (Athlete, Football Player)
PO Box 657
Hydesville, CA 95547-0657, USA

Bettis, Angela (Actor)
c/o Joe Weiner *Miloknay Weiner*
7162 Beverly Blvd Ste 345
Los Angeles, CA 90036-2547, USA

Bettis, Jerome (Athlete, Football Player)
1651 Randall Mill Pl NW
Atlanta, GA 30327-3136, USA

Bettis, Tom (Athlete, Football Coach, Football Player)
3523 N Peach Hollow Cir
Pearland, TX 77584-4007, USA

Bettman, Gary (Athlete, Hockey Player)
23 Baldwin Rd
Saddle River, NJ 07458-3203, USA

Bettridge, Ed (Athlete, Football Player)
505 Aqua Marine Blvd
Avon Lake, OH 44012-2588, USA

Betts, Daisy (Actor)
c/o Graciella Sanchez *Echo Lake Management*
421 S Beverly Dr Fl 8
Beverly Hills, CA 90212-4408, USA

Betts, Dickie (Musician)
FreeFalls
PO Box 604
Chagrin Falls, OH 44022-0604, USA

Betts, Erik (Actor)
9068 Hayvenhurst Ave
North Hills, CA 91343-3600, USA

Betts, Jack (Actor)
c/o Jon Simmons *Simmons & Scott Entertainment*
7942 Mulholland Dr
Los Angeles, CA 90046-1225, USA

Betts, Ladell (Athlete, Football Player)
42515 Regal Wood Dr
Brambleton, VA 20148-5629, USA

Betts, Richard (Dickey) (Musician)
325 Palmetto Ave
Osprey, FL 34229-9381, USA

Beuchel, Ted (Musician)
Variety Artists
1111 Riverside Ave Ste 501
Paso Robles, CA 93446-2683, USA

Beuerіein, Stephen T (Steve) (Athlete, Football Player)
15624 McCullers Ct
Charlotte, NC 28277-1478, USA

Beuerlein, Steve (Athlete, Football Player)
6 Roshelle Ln Ladera
Ranch, CA 92694, USA

Beukeboom, Jeff (Athlete, Hockey Player)
Sudbury Wolves
240 Elgin St
Attn Coaching Staff
Sudbury, ON P3E 3N6, Canada

Beukeboom, Jeff (Athlete, Hockey Player)
c/o Staff Member *Lindsay Muskies*
Lindsay Recreation Complex
Lindsay, ON K9V 4S3, Canada

Beutler, Tom (Athlete, Football Player)
7218 Longwater Dr
Maumee, OH 43537-8663, USA

Bevacqua, Kurt (Athlete, Baseball Player)
7679 Sitio Manana
Carlsbad, CA 92009-8960, USA

Bevan, Tim (Actor, Producer)
c/o Staff Member *Working Title Films*
100 Universal City Plz
Universal City, CA 91608-1002, USA

Beverley, Frankie (Musician)
115 Cherokee Rose Lane
Fairburn, GA 30213, USA

Beverley, Nick (Athlete, Coach, Hockey Player)
c/o Staff Member *Nashville Predators*
501 Broadway
Nashville, TN 37203-3980, USA

Beverley Sisters (Actor, Music Group)
Adam Nolan
80 Highcroft Ave Bispham
Blackpool, Lancashire FY20BW, UNITED KINGDOM

Beverlin, Jason (Athlete, Baseball Player)
1128 Old Shire Way
Statesboro, GA 30461-2994, USA

Beverly, David (Athlete, Football Player)
15 Wood Cove Dr
Spring, TX 77381-3312, USA

Beverly, Don (Race Car Driver)
1801 Coxendale Rd
Chester, VA 23836-2442, USA

Beverly, Ed (Athlete, Football Player)
13051 Golansville Rd
Ruther Glen, VA 22546-4029, USA

Beverly, Eric (Athlete, Football Player)
PO Box 24875
New Orleans, LA 70184-4875, USA

Beverly, Randy (Athlete, Football Player)
PO Box 425
Westbury, NY 11590-0130, USA

Bevil, Brian (Athlete, Baseball Player)
20103 Oakwood Ct
Humble, TX 77338-2500, USA

Bevill, Lisa (Musician)
Jeff Roberts
206 Bluebird Dr
Goodlettsville, TN 37072-2302, USA

Bevington, Terry (Athlete, Baseball Player, Coach)
2600 Halle Pkwy # Y
Collierville, TN 38017-8888, USA

Bevis, Muriel (Baseball Player)
538 Idlewood Dr
Mount Juliet, TN 37122-2118, USA

Bey, Andy (Musician)
Megaforce Entertainment
PO Box 779
New Hope, PA 18938-0779, USA

Bey, Turhan (Actor)
Paradisgasse Ave 47
Vienna, XIX 01190, AUSTRIA

Beyer, Andy (Sportscaster)
4237 Lenore Ln NW
Washington, DC 20008-3835, USA

Beyer, Brad (Actor)
c/o Mary Erickson *Mary Erickson Management*
3900 San Fernando Rd Unit 1507
Glendale, CA 91204-2866, USA

Beyer, Troy (Actor)
14333 Greenleaf St
Sherman Oaks, CA 91423-4013, USA

Beymer, Richard (Actor)
147 N Ridgewood Pl
Los Angeles, CA 90004-4002, USA

Beynon, Tom (Athlete, Football Player)
441 Winchester Dr
Waterloo, ON N2T 1H6, Canada

Bezic, Sandra (Figure Skater, Sportscaster)
c/o Staff Member *NBC Sports (NY)*
30 Rockefeller Plz
New York, NY 10112-0015, USA

Bezos, Jeff (Business Person)
Amazon Inc
PO Box 907
Bellevue, WA 98009-0907, USA

Bezos, MacKenzie (Business Person, Writer)
c/o Amanda Urban *ICM Partners (NY)*
730 5th Ave
New York, NY 10019-4105, USA

Bezucha, Thomas (Tom) (Director)
c/o Simon Halls *Slate PR*
901 N Highland Ave
W Hollywood, CA 90038-2412, USA

Bhakta, Raj (Business Person)
238 E 50th St
New York, NY 10022-7704, USA

Bhardwaj, Mohini (Athlete, Gymnast, Olympic Athlete)
53 Juergens Ave
Cincinnati, OH 45220-1227, USA

Bhaskar, Sanjeev (Actor)
c/o Staff Member *BBC Artist Mail*
PO Box 1116
Belfast BT2 7AJ, United Kingdom

Bhatt, Brinda (Actor)
c/o Staff Member *Innovative Artists*
1505 10th St
Santa Monica, CA 90401-2805, USA

Bhavsar, Raj (Athlete, Gymnast)
201 S Capitol Ave
Pan American Plaza, Suite 300
Indianapolis, IN 46225-1000

Bhise, Devika (Actor)
c/o Allison Levy *Innovative Artists*
235 Park Ave S Fl 7
New York, NY 10003-1405, USA

Biafra, Jello (Musician)
c/o Staff Member *Simon & Schuster*
1230 Avenue of the Americas Fl CONC1
New York, NY 10020-1586, USA

Biakabutuka, Tshimanga (Tim) (Athlete, Football Player)
6035 Hemby Rd
Matthews, NC 28104-8693, USA

Bialas, Dave (Baseball Player)
14080 N Bayshore Dr
Madeira Beach, FL 33708-2211, USA

Bialik, Mayim (Actor)
c/o Heather Weiss-Besignano *ICON PR*
8961 W Sunset Blvd Ste 1C
W Hollywood, CA 90069-1886, USA

Bialorucki, Larry (Athlete, Baseball Player)
5511 Armada Dr
Toledo, OH 43623-1709, USA

Bialosuknia, Wesley (Athlete, Basketball Player)
29 Bayberry Dr
Bristol, CT 06010-7604, USA

Bialowas, Dwight (Athlete, Hockey Player)
15616 Park Terrace Dr
Eden Prairie, MN 55346-2429, USA

Bialowas, Frank (Athlete, Hockey Player)
1640 New Brooklyn Rd
Williamstown, NJ 08094-3717, USA

Bianca, Viva (Actor)
c/o Matt Andrews *Marquee Management*
188 Oxford St Studio B
The Gatehouse
Paddington NSW 02021, AUSTRALIA

Biancalana, Buddy (Athlete, Baseball Player)
1204 Lakeview Dr
Fairfield, IA 52556-9670, USA

Bianchi, Al (Athlete, Baseball Player, Basketball Coach, Basketball Player, Coach)
4350 N 40th St
Phoenix, AZ 85018-4105, USA

Bianchi, Rosa Maria (Actor)
c/o Staff Member *Televisa*
Blvd Adolfo Lopez Mateos 232
Colonia San Angel INN
DF CP 01060, MEXICO

Bianchin, Wayne (Athlete, Hockey Player)
2091 Wellington Rd E
Nanaimo, BC V9S 5V2, Canada

Bianchl, Alfred (Al) (Athlete, Basketball Player, Coach)
Miami Heat
601 Biscayne Blvd
American Airlines Arena
Miami, FL 33132-1801, USA

Bianco, Esme (Actor)
c/o Norman Aladjem *Mainstay Entertainment*
9250 Beverly Blvd Fl 3
Beverly Hills, CA 90210-3710, USA

Bianco, Tom (Athlete, Baseball Player)
12 Knolltop Dr
Nesconset, NY 11767-2222, USA

Bianco, Tommy (Athlete, Baseball Player)
12 Knolltop Dr
Nesconset, NY 11767-2222, USA

Biao, Yuen (Actor)
c/o Staff Member *UTA/The Agency Group*
888 7th Ave Fl 7
New York, NY 10106-0700, USA

Biasucci, Dean (Athlete, Football Player)
3484 Sandy Beach Dr
Canandaigua, NY 14424-2348, USA

Bibb, John (Writer)
Nashville Tennessean
1100 Broadway
Editorial Dept
Nashville, TN 37203-3134, USA

Bibb, Laslie (Actor)
9615 Brighton Way Ste 300
Beverly Hills, CA 90210-5118, USA

Bibb, Leslie (Actor)
c/o John Carrabino *John Carrabino Management*
5900 Wilshire Blvd Ste 740
Los Angeles, CA 90036-5032, USA

Bibby, Henry (Athlete, Basketball Player)
Memphis Grizzlies
191 Beale St
Memphis, TN 38103-3715, USA

Bibby, Mike (Athlete, Basketball Player)
c/o David Falk *F.A.M.E*
Prefers to be contacted via telephone
Washington, DC, USA

Bice, Bo (Musician)
74 N Conrad Ave
Lecanto, FL 34461-8002, USA

Bichette, Dante (Athlete, Baseball Player)
1830 Gipson Green Ln
Winter Park, FL 32789-1480, USA

Bichir, Bruno (Actor)
c/o Sekka Scher *Ellipsis Entertainment Group*
175 Varick St Frnt 2
New York, NY 10014-4604, USA

Bichir, Demian (Actor)
c/o Amy Brownstein *PRStudio USA*
1875 Century Park E Ste 930
Los Angeles, CA 90067-2540, USA

Bickerstaff, Bernard T (Bernie) (Coach)
Charlotte Bobcats
129 W Trade St Ste 700
Charlotte, NC 28202-5301, USA

Bickett, Duane (Athlete, Football Player)
508 Van Dyke Ave
Del Mar, CA 92014-2545, USA

Bickford, Valerie (Actor)
c/o Staff Member *TLC*
1 Discovery Pl
Silver Spring, MD 20910-3354, USA

Bickle, Dick (Race Car Driver)
9l6-A Bambi Dr.
Destin, FL 32541, USA

Bickle, Mike (Religious Leader)
International House of Prayer
3535 E Red Bridge Rd
Kansas City, MO 64137-2135, USA

Bickle, Jr., Rich (Race Car Driver)
2119 W Glenmoor Ln
Janesville, WI 53545-9639, USA

Bicknell, Charlie (Athlete, Baseball Player)
304 E Summit St
Livingston, MT 59047-2126, USA

Bicks, Jenny (Producer)
c/o Jay Sures *United Talent Agency (UTA)*
9336 Civic Center Dr
Beverly Hills, CA 90210-3604, USA

Bicondova, Camren (Actor)
c/o Holly Williams *Williams Unlimited*
5010 Buffalo Ave
Sherman Oaks, CA 91423-1414

Bidart, Frank (Writer)
Wellesley College
106 Central St
English Dept
Wellesley, MA 02481-8203, USA

Biddle, Dennis (Bose) (Athlete, Baseball Player)
9418 N Green Bay Rd Apt 241
Milwaukee, WI 53209-1070, USA

Biddle, Rocky (Athlete, Baseball Player)
1313 5th Ave
Upland, CA 91786-3311, USA

Biden, Joe (Politician)
1212 Haines Ave
Wilmington, DE 19809-2713, USA

Biden, Joseph (Politician)
PO Box 3817
Wilmington, DE 19807-0817, USA

Biderman, Ann (Producer, Writer)
c/o Brian Siberell *Creative Artists Agency (CAA)*
2000 Avenue of the Stars Ste 100
Los Angeles, CA 90067-4705, USA

Bidner, Todd (Athlete, Hockey Player)
434 Oozloffsky St
Petrolia, ON N0N 1R0, Canada

Bidwell, Josh (Athlete, Football Player)
1380 W 40th Ave
Eugene, OR 97405-2001, USA

Bieber, Justin (Musician)
c/o Robert Mickelson *Creative Artists Agency (CAA)*
2000 Avenue of the Stars Ste 100
Los Angeles, CA 90067-4705, USA

Bieber, Nita (Actor)
PO Box 1889
Avalon, CA 90704-1889, USA

Biebl-Prelevic, Heidi (Skier)
Haus Olympia
Oberstaufen 87534, GERMANY

Biedenbach, Edward (Athlete, Basketball Player)
92 Kimberly Ave
Asheville, NC 28804-3607, USA

Biederman, Charles J (Artist)
5840 Collischan Rd
Red Wing, MN 55066-1113, USA

Biedermann, Jeanette (Actor)
Postfach 121004
Berlin 10599, Germany

Biedermann, Leo (Athlete, Football Player)
11640 Evergreen Creek Ln
Las Vegas, NV 89135-1650, USA

Biegler, David W (Business Person)
Texas Utilities Co
1601 Bryan St
Energy Plaza
Dallas, TX 75201-3431, USA

Biehn, Michael (Actor)
Blanc/Biehn Productions
10990 Wilshire Blvd Ste 800
Los Angeles, CA 90024-3931, USA

Biekert, Gregory (Athlete, Football Player)
2360 Fish Creek Pl
Danville, CA 94506-2063, USA

Biel, Jessica (Actor)
c/o Meredith O'Sullivan Wasson *The Lede Company*
9701 Wilshire Blvd # 930
Beverly Hills, CA 90212-2020, USA

Bielecki, Mike (Athlete, Baseball Player)
223 Heritage Preserve Run
Bradenton, FL 34212-3318, USA

Bielke, Don (Athlete, Basketball Player)
3768 Corte Cancion
Thousand Oaks, CA 91360-7017, USA

Biellmann, Denise (Figure Skater)
Im Brachli 25
Zurich 08053, SWITZERLAND

Bielski, Dick (Athlete, Football Player)
27 Malibu Ct
Towson, MD 21204-2047, USA

Bienen, Andy (Writer)
c/o Staff Member *United Talent Agency (UTA)*
9336 Civic Center Dr
Beverly Hills, CA 90210-3604, USA

Bieniemy, Eric (Athlete, Football Player)
3314 Fox Trl Dr NW
Prior Lake, MN 55372, USA

Bierbrodt, Nick (Athlete, Baseball Player)
1200 White Hawk Ranch Dr
Boulder, CO 80303-1668, USA

Biercevicz, Greg (Baseball Player)
21 Mead Farm Rd
Seymour, CT 06483-2453, USA

Bierko, Craig (Actor, Musician)
c/o Jill Littman *Impression Entertainment*
9229 W Sunset Blvd Ste 700
Los Angeles, CA 90069-3407, USA

Biermann, Kroy (Athlete, Football Player)
c/o Jack Ketsoyan *EMC / Bowery*
8356 Fountain Ave Apt E1
W Hollywood, CA 90069-2968, USA

Bies, Don (Athlete, Golfer)
1262 NW Blakely Ct
Seattle, WA 98177-4340, USA

Bieser, Steve (Athlete, Baseball Player)
1243 Timber Creek Dr
Cpe Girardeau, MO 63701-2621, USA

Bietila, Walter (Skier)
General Delivery
Iron Mountain, MI 49801, USA

Biffi, Giacomo Cardinal (Religious Leader)
Archdiocese of Bologna
Via Altabella 6
Bologna 40126, ITALY

Biffle, Greg (Race Car Driver)
319 Doolie Rd
Mooresville, NC 28117-5801, USA

Big & Rich (Music Group)
c/o Keith Miller *WME (Nashville)*
1201 Demonbreun St
Nashville, TN 37203-3140, USA

Big Bad Voodoo Daddy (Music Group)
c/o Chad Jensen *Jensen Artist Management*
1741 N Ventura Rd Apt 10
Oxnard, CA 93030-3315, USA

Bigbie, Larry (Athlete, Baseball Player)
140 Timber Point Ct
Valparaiso, IN 46385-9312, USA

Big Daddy Weave (Music Group)
c/o Jim Scherer *Whizbang Inc*
PO Box 100993
Nashville, TN 37224-0993, USA

Bigelow, Kathryn (Director, Producer)
c/o Kelly Bush Novak *ID Public Relations*
7060 Hollywood Blvd Fl 8th
Los Angeles, CA 90028-6021, USA

Bigelow, Tom (Race Car Driver)
Rt. 1
Box 158A
Winchester, IN 47394, USA

Biggers, E.J. (Athlete, Football Player)

Biggerstaff, Sean (Actor)
c/o Staff Member *Independent Talent Group*
40 Whitfield St
London W1T 2RH, UNITED KINGDOM

Biggert, Judy (Congressman, Politician)
2113 Rayburn Hob
Washington, DC 20515-0706, USA

Biggins, Al-Mela (Reality Star)

Biggio, Craig (Athlete, Baseball Player)
6520 Belmont St
Houston, TX 77005-3804, USA

Bigglo, Craig A (Baseball Player)
6520 Belmont St
Houston, TX 77005-3804, USA

Biggs, Don (Athlete, Hockey Player)
10050 Somerset Dr
Loveland, OH 45140-1863, USA

Biggs, Jason (Actor)
21700 Oxnard St Ste 2030
Woodland Hills, CA 91367-7545, USA

Biggs, John H (Business Person)
240 E 47th St # 47D
New York, NY 10017-2131, USA

Biggs-Dawson, Roxann (Actor)
Innovative Artists
1505 10th St
Santa Monica, CA 90401-2805, USA

Bignell, Larry (Athlete, Hockey Player)
51279 Range Road 223
Sherwood Park, AB T8C 1H2, Canada

Bignotti, George (Race Car Driver)
9413 Steeplehill Dr
Las Vegas, NV 89117-7271, USA

Big Preach (Musician)
c/o Staff Member *UGF Entertainment Inc*
3105 S Martin Luther King Jr Blvd # 313
Lansing, MI 48910-2939, USA

Big Sean (Musician)
c/o Chelsea Thomas *The Lede Company*
9701 Wilshire Blvd # 930
Beverly Hills, CA 90212-2020, USA

Big Tigger (Television Host)
c/o Staff Member *Britto Agency PR*
277 Broadway Ste 110
New York, NY 10007-2072, USA

Big Time Rush (Music Group)
c/o Erica Gerard *PMK/BNC Public Relations*
622 3rd Ave Fl 8
New York, NY 10017-6707, USA

Big Tymers (Music Group)
c/o Staff Member *ICM Partners*
10250 Constellation Blvd Fl 7
Los Angeles, CA 90067-6207, USA

Biittner, Larry (Athlete, Baseball Player)
915 3rd Ave NW
Pocahontas, IA 50574-1413, USA

Bila, Jedediah (Commentator, Television Host)
c/o Lia Aponte *United Talent Agency (UTA)*
888 7th Ave Fl 7
New York, NY 10106-0700, USA

Bila, Lucie (Actor, Musician)
Theate Ta Fantastika
Karlova Ul 8
Prague 1 110 00, CZECH REPUBLIC

Bilal (Musician)
c/o Jeff Epstein *M.A.G./Universal Attractions*
15 W 36th St Fl 8
New York, NY 10018-7927, USA

Bilardello, Dann (Athlete, Baseball Player)
2590 Everglades Blvd N
Naples, FL 34120-5560, USA

Bilderback, Nicole (Actor)
c/o Staff Member *Artists & Representatives (Stone Manners Salners)*
6100 Wilshire Blvd Ste 1500
Los Angeles, CA 90048-5110, USA

Biles, Simone (Athlete, Gymnast, Olympic Athlete)
c/o Ronald G Biles
6212 N Lazy Meadow Way
Spring, TX 77386-4152, USA

Bilheimer, Robert S (Religious Leader)
15256 Knightwood Rd
Cold Spring, MN 56320-9649, USA

Bill, Dunstan (Athlete, Football Player)
PO Box 514
Rancho Mirage, CA 92270-0514, USA

Bill, Tony (Actor, Director, Producer)
Barnstorm Films
73 Market St
Venice, CA 90291-3603, USA

Billard, Lani (Actor)
c/o Staff Member *Insight Production Company LTD*
489 King St W Suite 401
Toronto, ON M5V 1K4, Canada

Billick, Brian (Athlete, Football Coach, Football Player)
12500 Ivy Mill Rd
Reisterstown, MD 21136-5135, USA

Billie (Musician)
CIA
Concorde House
101 Shepherds Bush Road
London W6 7LP, UNITED KINGDOM (UK)

Billingham, Jack (Athlete, Baseball Player)
625 Faulkner St
New Smyrna Beach, FL 32168-6421, USA

Billings, Dick (Athlete, Baseball Player)
1917 Creek Wood Dr
Arlington, TX 76006-6611, USA

Billings, Earl (Actor)
c/o Staff Member *Artists & Representatives (Stone Manners Salners)*
6100 Wilshire Blvd Ste 1500
Los Angeles, CA 90048-5110, USA

Billingslea, Beau (Actor)
6025 Sepulveda Blvd Ste 201
Van Nuys, CA 91411-2513, USA

Billingslea, Shavonda (Reality Star)
c/o Michael Martin *MM Agency*
3937 Nobel Dr
San Diego, CA 92122-6156, USA

Billingsley, Brent (Athlete, Baseball Player)
16112 Medlar Ln
Chino Hills, CA 91709-3625, USA

Billingsley, Chad (Athlete, Baseball Player)
988 Leisure Dr
Lemoore, CA 93245-2575, USA

Billingsley, John (Actor)
c/o Devon Jackson *Trademark Talent*
5900 Wilshire Blvd Ste 710
Los Angeles, CA 90036-5019, USA

Billingsley, John (Athlete, Baseball Player)
3614 N 24th Pl
Milwaukee, WI 53206-1325, USA

Billingsley, Peter (Director)
Wild West Picture Show Productions
210 N La Brea Ave
W Hollywood, CA 90036, USA

Billingsley, Ray (Cartoonist)
c/o Staff Member *King Features Syndication*
300 W 57th St Fl 15
New York, NY 10019-5238, USA

Billingsley, Ron (Athlete, Football Player)
3819 Catlyn Woods Ave
Las Vegas, NV 89141-3308, USA

Billingsley, Sam (Baseball Player)
Memphis Red Sox
1426 W State St
Milwaukee, WI 53233-1249, USA

Billington, Craig (Athlete, Hockey Player)
3254 Elk View Dr
Evergreen, CO 80439-7972, USA

Billington, Craig (Athlete, Hockey Player)
c/o Staff Member *Colorado Avalanche*
1000 Chopper Cir
Pepsi Center
Denver, CO 80204-5805, USA

Billington, Kevin (Director)
33 Courtnell St
London W2 5BU, UNITED KINGDOM (UK)

Billmeyer, Mick (Baseball Player)
633 Tudor Dr
Hagerstown, MD 21742-9757, USA

Billups, Chauncey (Athlete, Basketball Player)
c/o Andy Miller *ASM Sports*
450 Fashion Ave Ste 1700
New York, NY 10123-1700, USA

Billups, Terry (Athlete, Football Player)
1801 E 12th St Apt 1721
Cleveland, OH 44114-3528, USA

Bill Wyman's Rhythm Kings (Music Group, Musician)
c/o Staff Member *Concerted Efforts*
PO Box 440326
Somerville, MA 02144-0004, USA

Billy Talent (Music Group)
Nettwerk Productions
1650 West 2nd Ave
Vancouver V6J 4R3, CANADA

Bilodeau, Gilles (Athlete, Hockey Player)
D. 8-12-2008
USA

Bilodeau, Jean-Luc (Actor)
c/o Allan Grifka *Alchemy Entertainment*
7024 Melrose Ave Ste 420
Los Angeles, CA 90038-3394, USA

Bilodeau, Yvon (Athlete, Hockey Player)
GD
Clyde, AB T0G 0P0, Canada

Bilson, Bruce (Director)
Downwind Enterprices
12505 Sarah St
Studio City, CA 91604-1113, USA

Bilson, Malcolm (Musician)
355 Savage Farm Dr
Ithaca, NY 14850-6504, USA

Bilson, Rachel (Actor)
c/o Troy Bailey *Bailey Brand Management*
1017 Ocean Ave Apt G
Santa Monica, CA 90403-3526, USA

Bilyk, Luke (Actor)
c/o Shari Quallenberg *AMI Artist Management*
464 King St E
Toronto, ON M5A 1L7, CANADA

Bilzerian, Dan (Athlete, Internet Star)
Rowdy Gentleman
PO Box 41478
Austin, TX 78704-0025, USA

bin Abdul-Aziz, Sheikh Sulaiman Al-Rajhi (Business Person)
Al Rajhi Bank
P.O. Box 22330
Riyadh 11495, Saudi Arabia

Binder, John (Religious Leader)
North American Baptist Conference
1S210 Summit Ave
Oakbrook Terrace, IL 60181-3994, USA

Binder, Mike (Actor, Director, Writer)
c/o Jason Hodes *WME|IMG (NY)*
11 Madison Ave Fl 18
New York, NY 10010-3669, USA

Binder, Steve (Director)
c/o Staff Member *Freeman, Heinecke and Sutton*
8961 W Sunset Blvd
Los Angeles, CA 90069-1807, USA

Bindler, Robb (Director, Writer)
c/o Susan Weaving *WME|IMG (NY)*
11 Madison Ave Fl 18
New York, NY 10010-3669, USA

Bing, Dave (Athlete, Basketball Player)
29555 Woodhaven Ln
Southfield, MI 48076-5281, USA

Bingaman, Jeff (Politician)
5028 Overlook Rd NW
Washington, DC 20016-1912, USA

Bingaman, Jeff (Senator)
703 Hart Senate Office Bldg
Washington, DC 20510-0001, USA

Bingbing, Fan (Actor)
c/o Daniel Manwaring *CAA (China)*
10/F Ste 1001, China View Tower 1
No.2 Jia, East Gongti Rd.
Beijing, Chaoyang Dist 100027, CHINA

Bingham, Craig (Athlete, Football Player)
PO Box 515
Carnegie, PA 15106-0515, USA

Bingham, Gregory R (Greg) (Athlete, Football Player)
3710 W Valley Dr
Missouri City, TX 77459-4320, USA

Bingham, Guy (Athlete, Football Player)
9214 Keegan Trl
Missoula, MT 59808-9382, USA

Bingham, Ryan (Musician)
c/o Jenna Adler *Creative Artists Agency (CAA)*
2000 Avenue of the Stars Ste 100
Los Angeles, CA 90067-4705, USA

Bingham, Traci (Actor, Model)
c/o Michael Blakey *Electra Star Management*
9229 W Sunset Blvd Ste 415
Los Angeles, CA 90069-3404, USA

Bingle, Lara (Model)
c/o Staff Member *TCN Nine Publicity*
TCN Nine Publicity
Willoughby, NSW 02068, Australia

Bingwa, Charmaine (Actor)
c/o Jessica Katz *Katz Public Relations*
14527 Dickens St
Sherman Oaks, CA 91403-3756, USA

Binkley, Gregg (Actor)
c/o Staff Member *Schachter Entertainment*
1157 S Beverly Dr Fl 2
Los Angeles, CA 90035-1119, USA

Binkley, Leslie J (Les) (Athlete, Hockey Player)
RR 3
Main Station
Hanover, ON N4N 3B9, Canada

Binn, Dave (Athlete, Football Player)
2005 Loring St
San Diego, CA 92109-1407, USA

Binnie, William B (Astronaut)
3039 Erica Ave
Rosamond, CA 93560-6776, USA

Binns, Malcolm (Musician)
233 Court Road
Orpington, Kent BR6 9BY, UNITED KINGDOM (UK)

Binoche, Juliette (Actor)
c/o Francois Samuelson *Intertalent*
16, Rue Henri Barbusse
Paris 75005, FRANCE

Binotto, John (Athlete, Football Player)
277 E McMurray Rd
Canonsburg, PA 15317-2929, USA

Binyon, Conrad (Actor)
17805 Margate St
Encino, CA 91316-2306, USA

Biodrowski, Denny (Athlete, Football Player)
821 Chase Cir
Hurst, TX 76053-4970, USA

Biondi, Frank J Jr (Business Person)
Seagram Co
1430 Peel St
Montreal, QC H3A 3T3, CANADA

Biondi, Matt (Athlete, Olympic Athlete, Swimmer)
Parker School
65-1224 Lindsey Rd
Mathematics Dept
Kamuela, HI 96743-8438, USA

Birch, Thora (Actor)
c/o Jack Birch *Keep the Peace Productions*
PO Box 691576
West Hollywood, CA 90069-9576, USA

Birchard, Bruce (Religious Leader)
Friends General Conference
1216 Arch St Ste 2B
Philadelphia, PA 19107-2835, USA

Birck, Michael J (Business Person)
Tellabs Inc
1415 W Diehl Rd
Naperville, IL 60563-9950, USA

Bird, Antonia (Director)
International Creative Mgmt
76 Oxford St
London W1N 0AX, UNITED KINGDOM (UK)

Bird, Brad (Director, Writer)
170 San Geronimo Valley Dr
Woodacre, CA 94973, USA

Bird, Cory (Athlete, Football Player)
443 Sycamore Ave
Egg Harbor Township, NJ 08234-9441, USA

Bird, Doug (Athlete, Baseball Player)
11821 Lady Anne Cir
Cape Coral, FL 33991-7548, USA

Bird, Jerry Lee (Athlete, Basketball Player)
1114 Scenic View Hts
Corbin, KY 40701-2156, USA

Bird, Larry (Athlete, Basketball Player, Olympic Athlete)
4715 Ellery Ln
Indianapolis, IN 46250-5677, USA

Bird, Rodger (Athlete, Football Player)
215 S Elm St
Henderson, KY 42420-3510, USA

Bird, Sue (Athlete, Basketball Player)
c/o Dan Levy *Wasserman Media Group (NC)*
4208 Six Forks Rd Ste 1020
Raleigh, NC 27609-5738, USA

Bird, Thora (Actor)
Old Loft 21 Leinster Mews
Lancaster Gate
London W2, UNITED KINGDOM (UK)

Bird-Phillips, Nalda (Baseball Player)
2033 Honeydew Ln NW
Kennesaw, GA 30152-5852, USA

Birdsell, Lilli (Actor)
c/o John Crosby *John Crosby Management*
1357 N Spaulding Ave
Los Angeles, CA 90046-4009, USA

Birdsong, Carl (Athlete, Football Player)
1807 Clubview Dr
Amarillo, TX 79124-1731, USA

Birdsong, Cindy (Musician)
c/o Staff Member *Diva Central Inc*
7510 W Sunset Blvd # 1445
Los Angeles, CA 90046-3408, USA

Birdsong, Mary (Actor, Writer)
c/o Stacy Abrams *Abrams Entertainment*
5225 Wilshire Blvd Ste 515
Los Angeles, CA 90036-4349, USA

Birdsong, Otis (Athlete, Basketball Player)
PO Box 316
Little Rock, AR 72203-0316, USA

Bires, Kally (Race Car Driver)
Black Cat Racing
304 Performance Rd
Mooresville, NC 28115-9592, USA

Bires, Kelly (Race Car Driver)
JTG Racing
304 Performance Rd
Mooresville, NC 28115-9592, USA

Birk, Matt (Athlete, Football Player)
620 Hidden Creek Trl
Saint Paul, MN 55118-3753, USA

Birk, Roger E (Business Person)
Federal National Mortgage Assn
3900 Wisconsin Ave NW
Washington, DC 20016-2806, USA

Birkbeck, Mike (Athlete, Baseball Player)
1705 W Hill Dr
Orrville, OH 44667-1331, USA

Birkell, Lauren (Actor)
c/o Joel King *Pakula/King & Associates*
9229 W Sunset Blvd Ste 315
Los Angeles, CA 90069-3403, USA

Birkett, Zoe (Musician)
Palace Theatre
Shaftesbury Ave
London W1V 8AY, UK

Birkin, David (Actor)
c/o Staff Member *Curtis Brown Ltd*
28-29 Hay Market
Hay Market House
London SW1Y 4SP, UNITED KINGDOM

Birkin, Jane (Actor)
Cineart
36 Rue de Ponthieu
Paris 75008, FRANCE

Birkins, Kurt (Athlete, Baseball Player)
24106 Vanowen St
West Hills, CA 91307-2932, USA

Birman, Len (Actor)
Michael Mann talent
617 S Olive St Ste 311
Los Angeles, CA 90014-1624, USA

Birmingham, Gil (Actor)
c/o Jean Sievers *Beachwood Entertainment Collective*
2271 Cheremoya Ave
Los Angeles, CA 90068-3006, USA

Birmingham, Stephen (Writer)
Brandt & Brandt
1501 Broadway Ste 2310
New York, NY 10036-5689, USA

Birnes, William J. (Writer)
c/o Staff Member *Simon & Schuster*
1230 Avenue of the Americas Fl CONC1
New York, NY 10020-1586, USA

Birney, David (Actor)
9942 Continental Dr
Huntingtn Bch, CA 92646-4256, USA

Birney, Earle (Writer)
1204-130 Carlton St
Toronto, ON M5A 4K3, CANADA

Birney, Frank (Actor)
c/o Staff Member *Bauman Redanty & Shaul Agency*
5757 Wilshire Blvd
Suite 473
Beverly Hills, CA 90212, USA

Biron, Martin (Athlete, Hockey Player)
Sport Prospects Inc
93 Whippoorwill Rd
Armonk, NY 10504-1143, USA

Biron, Mathieu (Athlete, Hockey Player)
5723 NW 199th Dr
Coral Springs, FL 33076, USA

Birrer, Babe (Athlete, Baseball Player)
9705 the Maples
Clarence, NY 14031-1594, USA

Birthistle, Eva (Actor)
c/o Staff Member *WME|IMG*
9601 Wilshire Blvd
Beverly Hills, CA 90210-5213, USA

Birtsas, Tim (Athlete, Baseball Player)
43 Robertson Ct
Clarkston, MI 48346-1547, USA

Biscaha, Joe (Athlete, Football Player)
700 N Delaware Ave
Apt 3
Beach Haven, NJ 08008, USA

Bischoff, Eric (Athlete, Wrestler)
29009 N Habitat Cir
Cave Creek, AZ 85331-8574, USA

Bisciotti, Steve (Business Person, Football Executive)
511 Point Field Dr
Millersville, MD 21108-2052, USA

Bisenius, Joe (Athlete, Baseball Player)
19254 Olive Plz
Gretna, NE 68028-6970, USA

Bishe, Kerry (Actor)
c/o Staff Member *Brookside Artists Management*
250 W 57th St Ste 1820
New York, NY 10107-1802, USA

Bishil, Summer (Actor)
c/o Mike Liotta *True Public Relations*
3575 Cahuenga Blvd W Ste 360
Los Angeles, CA 90068-1361, USA

Bishop, Ben (Athlete, Hockey Player)
4480 Market Commons Dr Unit 305
Fairfax, VA 22033-6058, USA

Bishop, Ben (Athlete, Hockey Player)
11 Huntleigh Trails Ln
Saint Louis, MO 63131-4801, USA

Bishop, Elvin (Musician)
DeLeon Artists
4031 Panama Ct
Piedmont, CA 94611-4930, USA

Bishop, Greg (Athlete, Football Player)
PO Box 2263
Lodi, CA 95241-2263, USA

Bishop, Harold (Athlete, Football Player)
4113 Woodland Hills Dr
Tuscaloosa, AL 35405-2777, USA

Bishop, Keith (Athlete, Football Player)
PO Box 133111
Spring, TX 77393-3111, USA

Bishop, Kelly (Actor)
c/o Robert Attermann *Abrams Artists Agency*
275 7th Ave Fl 26
New York, NY 10001-6708, USA

Bishop, Kevin (Actor)
c/o Staff Member *Gavin Barker Assoc*
2D Wimpole St
London W1G 0EB, UNITED KINGDOM

Bishop, Michael (Athlete, Football Player)
113 Philpot St
Willis, TX 77378, USA

Bishop, Rob (Congressman, Politician)
123 Cannon Hob
Washington, DC 20515-3805, USA

Bishop, Sonny (Athlete, Football Player)
22843 Hale Rd
Land O Lakes, FL 34639-4030, USA

Bishop, Stephen (Actor)
c/o Penny Vizcarra *PV Public Relations*
121 N Almont Dr Apt 203
Beverly Hills, CA 90211-1860, USA

Bisset, Jacqueline (Actor)
c/o Rona Menashe *Guttman Associates Public Relations*
118 S Beverly Dr Ste 201
Beverly Hills, CA 90212-3016, USA

Bissett, Josie (Actor)
8033 W Sunset Blvd # 4048
W Hollywood, CA 90046-2401, USA

Bissett, Tom (Athlete, Hockey Player)
3620 Arbor Chase Ct NE Apt 11
Grand Rapids, MI 49525-9453, United States

Bissinger, Buzz (Writer)
c/o Houghton Mifflin Company Trade Division
222 Berkeley St Ste 8
Boston, MA 02116-3753, USA

Bisson, Yannick (Actor)
c/o Jamie Levitt *Lauren Levitt & Associates Inc*
1525 W 8th Ave Fl 3
Vancouver BC V6J 1T5, CANADA

Bisutti, Kylie (Model)
c/o Anne Watkins *Primary Wave Talent*
116 E 16th St Fl 9
New York, NY 10003-2123, USA

Bitker, Joe (Athlete, Baseball Player)
39 Blackstone Ct
Chico, CA 95928-9428, USA

Bitonio, Joel (Athlete, Football Player)
c/o Bruce Tollner *REP 1 Sports Group*
80 Technology Dr
Irvine, CA 92618-2301, USA

Bitsui, Jeremiah (Actor)
c/o Siri Garber *Platform PR*
2666 N Beachwood Dr
Los Angeles, CA 90068-2308, USA

Bittan, Roy (Musician)
28929 Boniface Dr
Malibu, CA 90265-4207, USA

Bitterlich, Don (Athlete, Football Player)
101 Medinah Dr
Blue Bell, PA 19422-3213, USA

Bitterman, Shem (Writer)
c/o David Roberson *Roberson Public Relations*
7200 Franklin Ave Apt 501
Los Angeles, CA 90046-3085, USA

Bittiger, Jeff (Athlete, Baseball Player)
RR 5 Box 5348
Saylorsburg, PA 18353-9206, USA

Bittinger, Ned (Designer)
PO Box 4515
Santa Fe, NM 87502-4515, USA

Bittle, Ryan (Actor)
1345 Paseo Isabella
San Dimas, CA 91773-4076, USA

Bittner, Armin (Skier)
Rauchbergstr 30
Izell 83334, GERMANY

Bittner, Jayne (Baseball Player)
15536 Northville Forest Dr Apt U250
Plymouth, MI 48170-4901, USA

Bittner, Jaynne (Athlete, Baseball Player, Commentator)
1715 River Rd Apt 52
Saint Clair, MI 48079-3547, USA

Bittner, Lauren (Actor)
c/o Marnie Briskin *Circle of Confusion (NY)*
270 Lafayette St Ste 402
New York, NY 10012-3327, USA

Biya, Paul (President)
Palais Presidentiel
Rue de L'Exploration
Yaounde, CAMEROON REPUBLIC

Bizkit, Limp (Music Group)
c/o Chad Lehner *UTA Music*
1880 Century Park E Ste 711
Los Angeles, CA 90067-1618, USA

Bjarni V, Tryggvason (Astronaut)
Space Agency
Canadian Space Agency 6767 Rte de L'Aeroport Attn: Astronaut Office
Saint Hubert, QC J3Y 8Y9, CANADA

Bjedov-Gabrilo, Djurdjica (Swimmer)
Brace Santini 33
5800 Split
Serbia & Montenegro, SERBIA & MONTENEGRO

B. Jones, Walter (Congressman, Politician)
2333 Rayburn Hob
Washington, DC 20515-3223, USA

Bjorge, Jamie (Actor)
10061 Riverside Dr # 113
Toluca Lake, CA 91602-2560

Bjork (Musician)
160 Henry St PH
Brooklyn, NY 11201-2503, USA

Bjorkman, George (Athlete, Baseball Player)
3525 Teakwood Ln
Plano, TX 75075-1783, USA

Bjorkman, Jonas (Tennis Player)
Octagon
1751 Pinnacle Dr Ste 1500
McLean, VA 22102-3833, USA

Bjorkman, Reuben (Athlete, Hockey Player, Olympic Athlete)
504 Lake St NE
Warroad, MN 56763-2308, USA

Bjorlin, Nadia (Actor)
c/o Julia Buchwald *Buchwald*
5900 Wilshire Blvd Ste 3100
Los Angeles, CA 90036-5030, USA

Bjornson, Eric (Athlete, Football Player)
40 Orchard Rd
Orinda, CA 94563-3421, USA

Bjugstad, Scott (Athlete, Hockey Player, Olympic Athlete)
2874 Lisbon Ave N
Lake Elmo, MN 55042-8554, USA

Blab, Uwe (Athlete, Basketball Player)
5993 Mount Gainor
Wimberley, TX 78676-4278, USA

Blacc, Aloe (Musician)
3111 Paddington Rd
Glendale, CA 91206-1336, USA

Blachnik, Gabriele (Designer, Fashion Designer)
Blachnik Gabriele KG
Marstallstr 8
Munich 80539, GERMANY

Black, Alex (Actor)
c/o Julie Fulop *AKA Talent Agency*
325 N Larchmont Blvd
Los Angeles, CA 90004-3011, USA

Black, Avion (Athlete, Football Player)
7140 Park Glen Dr
Fairview, TN 37062-5129, USA

Black, Bibi (Musician)
Columbia Artists Mgmt Inc
165 W 57th St
New York, NY 10019-2201, USA

Black, BiBi (Musician)
c/o Staff Member *EMI Music Group (NY)*
150 5th Ave Fl 7
New York, NY 10011-4372, USA

Black, Bill (Baseball Player)
Detroit Tigers
264 Braeshire Dr
Ballwin, MO 63021-5659, USA

Black, Brantley (Actor)
c/o Taylor Jacobs *Cinema Talent Agency*
468 N Camden Dr # 200
Beverly Hills, CA 90210-4507, USA

Black, Bud (Athlete, Baseball Player)
PO Box 2133
Rancho Santa Fe, CA 92067-2133, USA

Black, Bud (Athlete, Baseball Player)
PO Box 122000
San Diego, CA 92112-2000, USA

Black, Cathie (Business Person, Writer)
c/o Staff Member *Hearst Magazines*
959 8th Ave Sutie 100
New York, NY 10019-3737, USA

Black, Claudia (Actor)
c/o Nicole Miller *NMA PR*
7916 Melrose Ave Ste 1
Los Angeles, CA 90046-7160, USA

Black, Clint (Actor, Musician)
141 Chickering Mdws
Nashville, TN 37215-5507, USA

Black, Debbie (Athlete, Basketball Player)
3709 Mary Anna Dr
Chattanooga, TN 37412-1519, USa

Black, Diane (Congressman, Politician)
1531 Longworth Hob
Washington, DC 20515-1310, USA

Black, Dustin Lance (Producer, Writer)
c/o Michael Donkis *PMK/BNC Public Relations*
1840 Century Park E Ste 1400
Los Angeles, CA 90067-2115, USA

Black, Holly (Writer)
10 Pleasant Ct
Amherst, MA 01002-1513, USA

Black, Jack (Actor, Comedian, Musician)
1735 Monte Cielo Ct
Beverly Hills, CA 90210-2422, USA

Black, James (Athlete, Hockey Player)
235 Callingwood Pl NW
Edmonton, AB T5T 2C6, Canada

Black, Jay (Musician)
c/o Staff Member *Charles Rapp Enterprises Inc*
88 Pine St Ste 1701
New York, NY 10005-1849, USA

Black, Kaitlyn (Actor)
c/o Spencer Robinson *Art/Work Entertainment*
5670 Wilshire Blvd Ste 900
Los Angeles, CA 90036-5699, USA

Black, Kodak (Musician)
c/o Ashley Kalmanowitz *Atlantic Records*
1290 Avenue of the Americas Fl 28
New York, NY 10104-0106, USA

Black, Leonard (Athlete, Football Player)
2705 Preston Woods Ln Apt 12
Fayetteville, NC 28304-3629, USA

Black, Lewis (Actor, Comedian)
c/o Glenn Schwartz *Glenn Schwartz Company*
4046 Declaration Ave
Calabasas, CA 91302-5741, USA

Black, Lisa Hartman (Actor)
c/o Staff Member *Innovative Artists*
1505 10th St
Santa Monica, CA 90401-2805, USA

Black, Lucas (Actor)
c/o Staff Member *Agency for the Performing Arts (APA)*
405 S Beverly Dr Ste 500
Beverly Hills, CA 90212-4425, USA

Black, Marina (Actor)
c/o Thomas Cushing *Innovative Artists*
1505 10th St
Santa Monica, CA 90401-2805, USA

Black, Mary (Musician)
International Music Network
278 Main St # 400
Gloucester, MA 01930-6022, USA

Black, Michael Ian (Actor, Comedian)
c/o Ted Schachter *Schachter Entertainment*
1157 S Beverly Dr Fl 2
Los Angeles, CA 90035-1119, USA

Black, Mike (Athlete, Football Player)
General Delivery
Acworth, GA 30101-9999, USA

Black, Mike D (Athlete, Football Player)
609 Grider Dr
Roseville, CA 95678-1244, USA

Black, Milt (Athlete, Hockey Player)
41 Willow Glen Dr
Kanata, ON K2M 1K9, Canada

Black, Pippa (Actor)
c/o Kimberlin Belloni *Artists First*
9465 Wilshire Blvd Ste 900
Beverly Hills, CA 90212-2608, USA

Black, Rebecca (Musician)

Black, Ronnie (Athlete, Golfer)
5118 N Ocean Ave
Tucson, AZ 85704-2545, USA

Black, Shane (Writer)
104 Fremont Pl
Los Angeles, CA 90005-3867, USA

Black, Stan (Athlete, Football Player)
470 Johnstone Dr
Madison, MS 39110-7586, USA

Black, Tim (Athlete, Football Player)
10520 Kilo Rd
Clarendon, TX 79226-5100, USA

Black, Todd (Producer)
c/o Staff Member *ICM Partners*
10250 Constellation Blvd Fl 7
Los Angeles, CA 90067-6207, USA

Black, Tori (Actor, Adult Film Star, Model)
c/o Staff Member *LA Direct Models*
3599 Cahuenga Blvd W Ste 4D
Los Angeles, CA 90068-1596, USA

Black 47 (Music Group, Musician)
c/o Staff Member *Skyline Music*
28 Union St
Whitefield, NH 03598-3503, USA

Blackabv, Ethan (Athlete, Baseball Player)
2002 W Sunnyside Dr APT 1314
Phoenix, AZ 85029-3553, USA

Blackaby, Ethan (Athlete, Baseball Player)
2002 W Sunnyside Dr Unit G12
Phoenix, AZ 85029-8501, USA

Blackberry Smoke (Music Group)

Black Box Recorder (Music Group)
c/o Staff Member *Paradigm (Monterey)*
404 W Franklin St
Monterey, CA 93940-2303, USA

Blackburn, Al (Astronaut)
1739 Kirby Rd
Mc Lean, VA 22101-4817, USA

Blackburn, Bob (Athlete, Hockey Player)
141 Robert St
PO Box 1761
New Liskeard, ON P0J 1P0, Canada

Blackburn, Chase (Athlete, Football Player)
562 Wagonwheel Ln
Marysville, OH 43040-1251, USA

Blackburn, Dan (Athlete, Hockey Player)
12 Carey Dr
Bedford, NY 10506-2025, USA

Blackburn, Don (Athlete, Hockey Player)
PO Box 8266
Longboat Key, FL 34228-8266, USA

Blackburn, Greta (Actor)
Dade/Schultz
6442 Coldwater Canyon Ave Ste 206
Valley Glen, CA 91606-1174, USA

Blackburn, Marsha (Congressman, Politician)
217 Cannon Hob
Washington, DC 20515-2507, USA

Blackburn, Tyler (Actor)
c/o Ruth Bernstein *Viewpoint Inc*
8820 Wilshire Blvd Ste 220
Beverly Hills, CA 90211-2622, USA

Blackburn, Woody (Athlete, Golfer)
PO Box 215
Orange Park, FL 32067-0215, USA

Black Crowes (Music Group)
c/o Staff Member *Mitch Schneider Organization (MSO)*
14724 Ventura Blvd Ste 410
Sherman Oaks, CA 91403-3537, USA

Black-D'Elia, Sofia (Actor)
c/o Ruth Bernstein *Viewpoint Inc*
8820 Wilshire Blvd Ste 220
Beverly Hills, CA 90211-2622, USA

Black Eyed Peas (Music Group)
c/o David Sonenberg *DAS Communications*
83 Riverside Dr
New York, NY 10024-5713, USA

Black Flag (Music Group)
c/o Heidi May *Rollins Management*
7510 W Sunset Blvd # 602
Los Angeles, CA 90046-3408, USA

Blackhurst, Rod (Director)
c/o Benjamin Rowe *Oasis Media Group*
9100 Wilshire Blvd Ste 210W
Beverly Hills, CA 90212-3555, USA

Blackiston, Caroline (Actor)
Caroline Dawson
125 Gloucester Road
London SW7 4IE, UNITED KINGDOM (UK)

Black Keys, The (Music Group)
c/o John Peets *Q Prime (TN)*
131 S 11th St
Nashville, TN 37206-2954, USA

Blackledge, Todd A (Athlete, Football Player, Sportscaster)
2711 Glenmont Rd NW
Canton, OH 44708-1345, USA

Blackley, Jamie (Actor)
c/o Pippa Beng *Premier PR*
2-4 Bucknall St
London WC2H 8LA, UNITED KINGDOM

Blackman, Don (Athlete, Football Player)
48 Shire Dr S
East Amherst, NY 14051-1814, USA

Blackman, Honor (Actor)
c/o Staff Member *Natasha Stevenson Mgmt*
Studio 7C Clapham North Arts Centre
Voltaire Rd
London SW4 6DH, UK

Blackman, Ken (Athlete, Football Player)
529 33rd Ave N
Clinton, IA 52732-1588, USA

Blackman, Robert (Athlete, Football Player)
70 Glenwood N
Van Vleck, TX 77482-6292, USA

Blackman, Rolando (Athlete, Basketball Player, Olympic Athlete)
2649 Peavy Rd
Dallas, TX 75228-4211, USA

Blackmar, Phil (Athlete, Golfer)
9 Imperial Dr
Trenton, NJ 08690-3100, USA

Blackmon, Don (Athlete, Football Player)
4340 Lansfaire Ter
Suwanee, GA 30024-6956, USA

Blackmon, Harold (Athlete, Football Player)
6937 S Crandon Ave Apt 4E
Chicago, IL 60649-2944, USA

Blackmon, Larry (Musician)
c/o Ben Petersonn *Primary Wave Talent*
116 E 16th St Fl 9
New York, NY 10003-2123, USA

Blackmon, Robert (Athlete, Football Player)
70 Glenwood N
Van Vleck, TX 77482-6292, USA

Blackmon, Roosevelt (Athlete, Football Player)
PO Box 1347
Belle Glade, FL 33430-6347, USA

Blackmon, Will (Athlete, Football Player)
c/o Eugene Parker *Independent Sports & Entertainment (ISE-IN)*
6435 W Jefferson Blvd # 197
Fort Wayne, IN 46804-6203, USA

Blackmon, Will (Athlete, Football Player)
37 Portalon Ct Ladera
Ranch, CA 92694, USA

Blackmore, Ritchie (Musician)
Blackmore Productions
PO Box 735
Nesconset, NY 11767-0735, USA

Blackmore, Stephanie (Actor)
1265 Leona Dr
Beverly Hills, CA 90210-2147, USA

Blacknall, Hubert (Athlete, Baseball Player)
46 Avenue A
Freehold, NJ 07728-1738, USA

Black Sabbath (Music Group)
c/o Rob Light *Creative Artists Agency (CAA)*
2000 Avenue of the Stars Ste 100
Los Angeles, CA 90067-4705, USA

Blackshear, Jeff (Athlete, Football Player)
9229 Christo Ct
Owings Mills, MD 21117-3596, USA

Blackthorne, Paul (Actor)
c/o Sarah Jackson *Seven Summits Pictures & Management*
8906 W Olympic Blvd
Beverly Hills, CA 90211-3550, USA

Black Veil Brides (Music Group)
c/o Staff Member *Eccentric Gent Organisation*
Castleham Business Centre
33 Stirling Road, St. Leonards-on-Sea
East Sussex TN38 9NP, UK

Blackwelder, Myra (Athlete, Golfer)
3789 Everetts Dl
Lexington, KY 40514-1190, USA

Blackwell, Alois (Athlete, Football Player)
2450 Louisiana St Ste 400
Houston, TX 77006-2318, USA

Blackwell, Chris (Business Person, Musician)
6 Hadley Gardens
C F Blackwell
London W4 4NX, UNITED KINGDOM

Blackwell, Nathaniel (Athlete, Basketball Player)
1926 S 22nd St
Philadelphia, PA 19145-2724, USA

Blackwell, Tim (Athlete, Baseball Player)
8854 Whiteport Ln
San Diego, CA 92119-2135, USA

Blackwell, Will (Athlete, Football Player)
6450 Dougherty Rd Apt 336
Dublin, CA 94568-7614, USA

Blackwell, Will (Athlete, Football Player)
6168 Seneca Cir
Discovery Bay, CA 94505-2632, USA

Blackwell, Willie (Athlete, Football Player)
152 Glenmore Ln
McDonough, GA 30253-8743, USA

Blackwood, Glenn (Athlete, Football Player)
3480 Ambassador Dr
Wellington, FL 33414-6815, USA

Blackwood, Lyle (Athlete, Football Player)
6315 Bandera Ave APT A
Dallas, TX 75225-3621, USA

Blackwood, Nina (DJ)
c/o Danny Sheridan *Entertainment Organization*
16161 Ventura Blvd Ste C714
Encino, CA 91436-2522, USA

Blackwood, Richard (Actor, Comedian)
c/o Lee Morgan *Lee Morgan Talent Management*
4 Bloomsbury Sq
London WC1A 2RP, UNITED KINGDOM

Blackwood, Sarah (Musician)
Primary Talent Int'l
2-12 Petonville Road
London N1 9PL, UNITED KINGDOM (UK)

Blackwood, Vas (Actor)
c/o David Ginsberg *Insight*
5358 Melrose Ave # 200W
Los Angeles, CA 90038-5117, USA

Blacque, Taurean (Actor)
5049 Rock Springs Rd
Lithonia, GA 30038-2239, USA

Bladd, Stephen Jo (Musician)
Nick Ben-Meir
2850 Ocean Park Blvd Ste 300
Santa Monica, CA 90405-6216, USA

Blade, Brian (Musician)
Ted Kurland
173 Brighton Ave
Boston, MA 02134-2003, USA

Blade, Willie (Athlete, Football Player)
331 Cobblestone Rd
Auburn, GA 30011-3022, USA

Blades, Bennie (Athlete, Football Player)
3409 NW 14th Ct Fort
Lauderdale, FL 33311, USA

Blades, Brian K (Athlete, Football Player)
1900 SW 70th Ter
Plantation, FL 33317-5010, USA

Blades, Jack (Musician)
2000 Warrington Rd
Santa Rosa, CA 95404-9775, USA

Blades, Ruben (Actor, Musician)
Instituto Panameñ De Turismo
Apartado 4421
Centro De Convenciones Atlapa
Vía Israel, San Francisco, Republic Of Panamá

Blados, Brian (Athlete, Football Player)
7087 Clawson Ridge Ct
Liberty Twp, OH 45011-9121, USA

Bladt, Rick (Athlete, Baseball Player)
8600 Wilco Hwy NE
Mount Angel, OR 97362-9747, USA

Blagden, George (Actor)
c/o Saskia Mulder *The Artists Partnership*
101 Finsbury Pavement
London EC2A 1RS, UNITED KINGDOM

Blagojevich, Rod (Politician)
2934 W Sunnyside Ave
Chicago, IL 60625-3845, USA

Blaha, John E (Astronaut)
346 Whitestone Dr
Spring Branch, TX 78070-6046, USA

Blahak, Joseph (Athlete, Football Player)
4040 N 21st St
Lincoln, NE 68521-1203, USA

Blahnik, Manolo (Designer, Fashion Designer)
49-51 Old Church St
London SW3 5BS, UNITED KINGDOM (UK)

Blahoski, Alana (Athlete, Hockey Player, Olympic Athlete)
60 E 9th St Apt 315
New York, NY 10003-6400, USA

Blain, Ser'Darius (Actor)
c/o Jessica Katz *Katz Public Relations*
14527 Dickens St
Sherman Oaks, CA 91403-3756, USA

Blaine, David (Magician)
354 Broadway Apt 1B
New York, NY 10013-3908, USA

Blaine, Ed (Athlete, Football Player)
3750 Miller Dr Apt 1114
Columbia, MO 65201-7699, USA

Blair, Bonnie (Athlete, Olympic Athlete, Speed Skater)
306 White Pine Rd
Delafield, WI 53018-1124, USA

Blair, Bre (Actor)
c/o Adri Palmieri *Baker Winokur Ryder Public Relations*
9100 Wilshire Blvd
W Tower #500
Beverly Hills, CA 90212-3415, USA

Blair, Charles (Athlete, Hockey Player)
869 Niagara Pky
Fort Erie, ON L2A 5M4, Canada

Blair, Dennis (Athlete, Baseball Player)
1706 Aurora Dr
Richardson, TX 75081-2115, USA

Blair, George (Athlete, Football Player)
1233 Karen Dr
Laurel, MS 39440-2186, USA

Blair, Isla (Actor)
Mayer & Eden
Grafton House
2/3 Golden House
London W1R 3AD, UNITED KINGDOM (UK)

Blair, Jayson (Actor)
c/o Todd Justice *Justice & Ponder*
PO Box 480033
Los Angeles, CA 90048-1033, USA

Blair, Ken (Athlete, Football Player)
1837 NE 51st St
Oklahoma City, OK 73111-7005, USA

Blair, Kimberly (Actor)
c/o John Elliott *Mosaic Media Group*
407 N Maple Dr # 100
Beverly Hills, CA 90210-3818, USA

Blair, Linda (Actor)
The Linda Blair WorldHeart Foundation
10061 Riverside Dr Ste 1003
Toluca Lake, CA 91602-2560, USA

Blair, Lionel (Dancer)
68 Old Brompton Road #200
London, England SW7 3LQ, United Kingdom

Blair, Matt (Athlete, Football Player)
5367 Barrington Way
Excelsior, MN 55331-7039, USA

Blair, Maybelle (Athlete, Baseball Player, Commentator)
PO Box 53
Sunset Beach, CA 90742-0053, USA

Blair, Natalie (Actor)
c/o Staff Member *RGM Artists*
8-12 Ann St
Surry Hills, NSW 02010, AUSTRALIA

Blair, Selma (Actor)
c/o Megan Moss *Narrative*
1601 Vine St Fl 6
Los Angeles, CA 90028-8802, USA

Blair, Stanley (Athlete, Football Player)
2255 Randle Rd
Pine Bluff, AR 71602, USA

Blair, Tony (Politician, Prime Minister)
PO Box 60519
London W2 7JU, UNITED KINGDOM

Blair, William (Athlete, Baseball Player)
1411 E Red Bird Ln
Dallas, TX 75241-2111, USA

Blair, William (Director)
c/o Staff Member *New Star Entertainment*
PO Box 84172
San Diego, CA 92138, USA

Blair, Willie (Athlete, Baseball Player)
Fort Wayne Tincaps 1301
Fort Wayne, IN 46802-3343, USA

Blais, Madeleine H (Journalist)
Miami Herald
1 Herald Plz
Editorial Dept
Miami, FL 33132-1609, USA

Blais, Richard (Chef, Reality Star)
c/o Meredith Sidman *Baltz and Company*
49 W 23rd St Ste 900
New York, NY 10010-4225, USA

Blaisdell, Mike (Athlete, Hockey Player)
458 Nicholl Ave
Regina Beach, SK S0G 4C0, Canada

Blaise, Kerlin (Athlete, Football Player)
37026 Aspen Dr
Farmington Hills, MI 48335-5482, USA

Blaise, Luna (Actor)
c/o Chelsea Thomas *The Lede Company*
9701 Wilshire Blvd # 930
Beverly Hills, CA 90212-2020, USA

Blake, Andre (Actor)
c/o Staff Member *Kerin-Goldberg Associates*
155 E 55th St Ste 5D
New York, NY 10022-4038, USA

Blake, Antwon (Athlete, Football Player)

Blake, Asha (Correspondent)
NBC-TV
30 Rockefeller Plz
News Dept
New York, NY 10112-0015, USA

Blake, Casey (Athlete, Baseball Player)
8224 150th Ave
Indianola, IA 50125-8683, USA

Blake, David (DJ Quik) (Musician)
c/o John Pantle *Agency for the Performing Arts (APA)*
405 S Beverly Dr Ste 500
Beverly Hills, CA 90212-4425, USA

Blake, Geoffrey (Writer)
9329 Kramerwood Pl
Los Angeles, CA 90034-2346, USA

Blake, Hamish (Radio Personality, Talk Show Host)
2DayFM Studios
Level 15
50 Goulburn St
Sydney, NSW 02000, AUSTRALIA

Blake, James (Athlete, Tennis Player)
645 Jocelyn Way
Encinitas, CA 92024-2487, USA

Blake, Jason (Athlete, Olympic Athlete)
11322 S Lake Eunice Rd
Detroit Lakes, MN 56501-7045, USA

Blake, Jay Don (Athlete, Golfer)
2859 Calle Del Sol
Saint George, UT 84790-7968, USA

Blake, Jeff (Athlete, Football Player)
1 Novacare Way
Philadelphia, PA 19145-5900, USA

Blake, Josh (Actor)
c/o Staff Member *Pakula/King & Associates*
9229 W Sunset Blvd Ste 315
Los Angeles, CA 90069-3403, USA

Blake, Julian W (Bud) (Cartoonist)
PO Box 146
Damariscotta, ME 04543-0146, USA

Blake, Kayla (Actor)
c/o Todd Diener *Untitled Entertainment*
350 S Beverly Dr Ste 200
Beverly Hills, CA 90212-4819, USA

Blake, Marcia (Writer)
c/o Staff Member *Creative Artists Agency (CAA)*
2000 Avenue of the Stars Ste 100
Los Angeles, CA 90067-4705, USA

Blake, Norman (Musician)
Scott O'Malley Assoc
433 E Cucharras St
Colorado Springs, CO 80903-3609, USA

Blake, Peter T (Artist)
Waddington Galleries
11 Cork St
London W1X 1PD, UNITED KINGDOM (UK)

Blake, Ricky (Athlete, Football Player)
13 Harper Dr
Fayetteville, TN 37334-6679, USA

Blake, Rob (Athlete, Hockey Player)
C A A Sports
2000 Avenue of the Stars Fl 3
Los Angeles, CA 90067-4704, USA

Blake, Robert (Actor)
c/o Thomas Mesereau
3055 Wilshire Blvd Ste 600
Los Angeles, CA 90010-1145, USA

Blake, Stephanie (Actor)
First Artists
1631 N Bristol St # 820
Santa Ana, CA 92706-3342, USA

Blake, Steve (Athlete, Basketball Player)
24915 SW Valley View Rd
West Linn, OR 97068-8638, USA

Blake, Susan (Correspondent)
News Center 4
1001 Van Ness Ave
San Francisco, CA 94109-6913, USA

Blake, Tchad (Musician)
Monterey International
72 W Adams St # 1000
Chicago, IL 60603-5107, USA

Blake, Teresa (Actor)
Stone Manners
6500 Wilshire Blvd # 550
Los Angeles, CA 90048-4920, USA

Blake, Theo (Adult Film Star)
c/o Staff Member *Diva Central Inc*
7510 W Sunset Blvd # 1445
Los Angeles, CA 90046-3408, USA

Blake, Tom (Athlete, Football Player)
2017 Tullis Dr
Middletown, OH 45042-2962, USA

Blake, Victoria (Actor)
23801 Calabasas Rd Ste 2023
Calabasas, CA 91302-1558, USA

Blakely, Rachel (Actor)
c/o Staff Member *Morrissey Management*
77 Glebe Point Road
Sydney NSW 2037, AUSTRALIA

Blakely, Sara (Business Person)
Spanx Inc.
3035 Peachtree Rd NE Ste A201
Atlanta, GA 30305-2761, USA

Blakely, Susan (Actor, Model)
c/o Stephen Jaffe *Jaffe & Company Strategic Media*
9663 Santa Monica Blvd # 663
Beverly Hills, CA 90210-4303, USA

Blakemore, Michael (Actor, Director, Writer)
18 Upper Park Rd
London NW3 2UP, UNITED KINGDOM (UK)

Blakemore, Sean (Actor)
c/o Steven Jang *SDB Partners Inc*
315 S Beverly Dr Ste 411
Beverly Hills, CA 90212-4301, USA

Blaker, Clay (Musician, Songwriter, Writer)
Texas Sounds Entertainment
2317 Pecan St
Dickinson, TX 77539-4949, USA

Blakley, Ronee (Actor, Musician)
8033 W Sunset Blvd # 693
West Hollywood, CA 90046-2401, USA

Blalock, Hank (Athlete, Baseball Player)
1541 Black Walnut Dr
San Marcos, CA 92078-7985, USA

Blalock, Jane (Athlete, Golfer)
75 Cambridge Pkwy # 809
Cambridge, MA 02142-1229, USA

Blalock, Jolene (Actor)
c/o Jason Trawick *WME/IMG*
9601 Wilshire Blvd
Beverly Hills, CA 90210-5213, USA

Blalock, Justin (Athlete, Football Player)
c/o Ben Dogra *Relativity Sports*
2029 Century Park E Ste 1550
Century City, CA 90067-3000, USA

Blamire, Larry (Actor, Director, Writer)
10878 Bloomfield St
Toluca Lake, CA 91602-2264, USA

Blanc, Georges (Chef)
Le Mere Blanc
Vonnas, Ain 01540, FRANCE

Blanc, Michel (Actor)
c/o Dominique Besnehard *ArtMedia*
8 rue Danielle Casanova
Paris 75002, FRANCE

Blanc, Raymond R A (Chef)
Le Manoir
Church Road
Great Milton, Oxford OX44 7PD, UNITED KINGDOM (UK)

Blancas, Homero (Athlete, Golfer)
6826 Queensclub Dr
Houston, TX 77069-1216, USA

Blanc-Biehn, Jennifer (Actor)
Blancbiehn Productions
10990 Wilshire Blvd Ste 800
Los Angeles, CA 90024-3931, USA

Blanchard, Ken (Business Person, Writer)
The Ken Blanchard Companies
125 State Pl
Escondido, CA 92029-1398, USA

Blanchard, Rachel (Actor)
c/o Christian Donatelli *MGMT Entertainment (The Schiff Company)*
9220 W Sunset Blvd Ste 106
W Hollywood, CA 90069-3500, USA

Blanchard, Rowan (Actor)
c/o Jillian Neal *Untitled Entertainment*
350 S Beverly Dr Ste 200
Beverly Hills, CA 90212-4819, USA

Blanchard, Tammy (Actor)
c/o Carol Bodie *art2perform*
9000 W Sunset Blvd Ste 1015
West Hollywood, CA 90069-5810, USA

Blanchard, Tim (Religious Leader)
Conservative Baptist Assn
20 Inverness Pl E
Englewood, CO 80112-5622, USA

Blanchard, Tom (Athlete, Football Player)
134 NE Bryce Ct
Grants Pass, OR 97526-3687, USA

Blanchard, Tully (Athlete, Wrestler)
922 Serenade Dr
San Antonio, TX 78213-1335, USA

Blanchett, Cate (Actor)
4 N Parade
Hunters Hill, NSW 02110, AUSTRALIA

Blanco, Gil (Athlete, Baseball Player)
18403 N 16th Pl
Phoenix, AZ 85022-1355, USA

Blanco, Henry (Athlete, Baseball Player)
5510 N 132nd Dr
Litchfield Park, AZ 85340-8328, USA

Blanco, Jorge (Musician)
c/o Siri Garber *Platform PR*
2666 N Beachwood Dr
Los Angeles, CA 90068-2308, USA

Blanco, Kathleen (Politician)
702 Myrtle Pl
Lafayette, LA 70506-3457, USA

Blanco-Cervantes, Raul (President)
Apdo 918
San Jose, COSTA RICA

Bland, Anthony (Tony) (Athlete, Football Player)
20429 Walnut Grove Ln
Tampa, FL 33647-3352, USA

Bland, Carl (Athlete, Football Player)
1985 Crossbridge Ct
Saint Charles, MO 63303-4810, USA

Bland, John (Athlete, Golfer)
PO Box 451436
Westlake, OH 44145-0638, USA

Bland, Nate (Athlete, Baseball Player)
1504 Oxmoor Rd
Birmingham, AL 35209-3908, USA

Bland, Tom (Athlete, Football Player)
66 S Winter Park Dr
Casselberry, FL 32707-4409, USA

Blandi, Oscar (Business Person)
Oscar Blandi Salon
746 Madison Ave
New York, NY 10065-7052, USA

Blandon, Roberto (Actor)
c/o Staff Member *TV Azteca*
Periferico Sur 4121
Colonia Fuentes del Pedregal
DF CP 14141, Mexico

Blaney, George (Athlete, Basketball Player)
1633 Main St
Glastonbury, CT 06033-3133, USA

Blank, Arthur (Business Person, Football Executive)
1080 W Paces Ferry Rd NW
Atlanta, GA 30327-2600, USA

Blank, Barbie (Actor, Wrestler)
c/o Staff Member *World Wrestling Entertainment (WWE)*
1241 E Main St
Stamford, CT 06902-3520, USA

Blank, Matt (Athlete, Baseball Player)
28332 Emerald Oaks
Magnolia, TX 77355-7546, USA

Blankenbuehler, Andy (Dancer, Writer)
c/o John Buzzetti *WME|IMG (NY)*
11 Madison Ave Fl 18
New York, NY 10010-3669, USA

Blankenship, Greg (Athlete, Football Player)
2067 La Con Ct Apt 1
Campbell, CA 95008-4315, USA

Blankenship, Kevin (Athlete, Baseball Player)
5014 Regency Dr
Rocklin, CA 95677-4420, USA

Blankenship, Lance (Athlete, Baseball Player)
340 Kimberwicke Ct
Alamo, CA 94507-2703, USA

Blankers-Koen, Fanny (Athlete, Track Athlete)
Olympic Committe
Surinamestraat 33
La Harve 02585, NETHERLANDS

Blanks, Billy (Actor, Athlete)
c/o Staff Member *WME|IMG*
9601 Wilshire Blvd
Beverly Hills, CA 90210-5213, USA

Blanks, Larvell (Athlete, Baseball Player)
PO Box 562
Del Rio, TX 78841-0562, USA

Blanks, Sid (Athlete, Football Player)
4402 Warm Springs Rd
Houston, TX 77035-6026, USA

Blanton, Dain (Athlete, Olympic Athlete, Volleyball Player)
1615 Stoner Ave Apt 3
Los Angeles, CA 90025-7340, USA

Blanton, Jerry (Athlete, Football Player)
1942 Calumet Ave
Toledo, OH 43607-1605, USA

Blanton, Joe (Athlete, Baseball Player)
636 Farragut Ave
Haddonfield, NJ 08033-3834, USA

Blanton, Robert (Athlete, Football Player)
c/o Scott Smith *XAM Sports*
3509 Ice Age Dr
Madison, WI 53719-5409, USA

Blaqk Audio (Music Group)
c/o Staff Member *Silva Artist Management (SAM)*
722 Seward St
Los Angeles, CA 90038-3504, USA

Blarikfield, Mark (Actor)
Artists Group
10 100 Santa Monica Blvd
#2490
Los Angeles, CA 90067, USA

B. Larson, John (Congressman, Politician)
1501 Longworth Hob
Washington, DC 20515-4708, USA

Blasberg, Erica (Athlete, Golfer)
2280 Treemont Pl Apt 206
Corona, CA 92879-7868, USA

Blasco, Chuck (Musician)
Media Promotion Enterprises
423 6th Ave Ste C
Huntington, WV 25701-1935, USA

Blaser, Cory (Athlete, Baseball Player)
10528 Ross Pl
Broomfield, CO 80021-3549, USA

Blasi, Rosa (Actor)
c/o Cheryl McLean *Creative Public Relations*
3385 Oak Glen Dr
Los Angeles, CA 90068-1311, USA

Blasingame, Wade (Athlete, Baseball Player)
5207 Riverhill Rd NE
Marietta, GA 30068-4865, USA

Blass, (Steve) (Athlete, Baseball Player)
PO Box 7000
Pittsburgh, PA 15212-0038, USA

Blasucci, Dick (Producer)
c/o Staff Member *Kaplan-Stahler Agency*
8383 Wilshire Blvd Ste 923
Beverly Hills, CA 90211-2443, USA

Blatche, Andray (Athlete, Basketball Player)
914 Jennings Mill Dr
Bowie, MD 20721-6223, USA

Blateric, Steve (Athlete, Baseball Player)
2855 S Monaco Pkwy Apt 2-304
Denver, CO 80222-7191, USA

Blatny, Zdenek (Athlete, Hockey Player)
c/o Staff Member *International Sports Advisors*
878 Ridge View Way
Franklin Lakes, NJ 07417-1524, USA

Blatt, Melanie (Musician)
c/o Staff Member *Concorde Intl Artists Ltd*
101 Shepherds Bush Rd
London W6 7LP, UNITED KINGDOM (UK)

Blatter, Joseph (Sepp) (Football Executive)
Federation Int'l Football Assn
PO Box 85
Gloucester City, NJ 08030-0085, SWITZERLAND

Blatz, Kelly (Actor, Musician)
c/o Lena Roklin *Luber Roklin Management*
5815 W Sunset Blvd Ste 208
Los Angeles, CA 90028-6481, USA

Blau, Daniel (Artist)
Belgradstr 26
Munich 80796, GERMANY

Blauser, Jeff (Athlete, Baseball Player)
6080 Carlisle Ln
Alpharetta, GA 30022-6279, USA

Blavatnik, Leonard (Business Person)
128 Porchuck Rd
Greenwich, CT 06831-2926, USA

Blaylock, Anthony (Athlete, Football Player)
604 Glen Iris Dr NE
Atlanta, GA 30308-2717, USA

Blaylock, Bob (Athlete, Baseball Player)
472933 E 1122 Rd
Muldrow, OK 74948-5589, USA

Blaylock, Caroline (Athlete, Golfer)
232 Hennon Dr NW # B
Rome, GA 30165-9725, USA

Blaylock, Daren """Mookie""" (Athlete, Basketball Player)
7601 Belmount Rd
Rowlett, TX 75089-7479, USA

Blaylock, Daron (Athlete, Basketball Player)
1017 Gresham Rd
Zebulon, GA 30295-3141, USA

Blaylock, Derrick (Athlete, Football Player)
1471 Edgewater Rd
Crown Point, IN 46307-8255, USA

Blaylock, Gary (Athlete, Baseball Player)
PO Box 241
Malden, MO 63863-0241, USA

Blazejowski, Carol (Athlete, Basketball Player, Olympic Athlete)
126 Walnut St
Nutley, NJ 07110-2851, USA

Blazelowski, Carol A (Athlete, Basketball Player)
New York Liberty
2 Penn Plz Fl 15
Madison Square Garden
New York, NY 10121-1700, USA

Blazer, Phil (Athlete, Football Player)
16 Tranquil Ave
Greenville, SC 29615-1516, USA

Blazier, Ron (Athlete, Baseball Player)
610 N 9th St
Bellwood, PA 16617-1524, USA

Blazitz, Micael (Athlete, Football Player)
27100 Bunert Rd
Warren, MI 48088-6013, USA

Bledel, Alexis (Actor, Model)
c/o Paul Brown *Industry Entertainment Partners*
955 Carrillo Dr Ste 300
Los Angeles, CA 90048-5400, USA

Bledsoe, Curtis (Athlete, Football Player)
1012 Red Oak Pl
Chula Vista, CA 91910-6750, USA

Bledsoe, Drew (Athlete, Football Player)
45 Hancock Dr
West Milford, NJ 07480-4506, USA

Bledsoe, Tempestt (Actor)
c/o Staff Member *GVA Talent Agency Inc*
193 N Robertson Blvd
Beverly Hills, CA 90211-2103, USA

Bleek (Cox), Memphis (Malik) (Artist, Musician)
Green Light Talent Agency
24024 Saint Moritz Dr
Valencia, CA 91355-2033, USA

Bleeth, Yasmine (Actor)
308 N Sycamore Ave Apt 202
Los Angeles, CA 90036-2661, USA

Bleick, Tom (Athlete, Football Player)
21 Ironaton Rd Apt 107
Talladega, AL 35160-5022, USA

Bleier, Robert P (Rocky) (Athlete, Football Player)
929 Osage Rd
Pittsburgh, PA 15243-1011, USA

Bleiler, Gretchen (Athlete, Olympic Athlete, Speed Skater)
USOC Headquarters
PO Box 5774
Snowmass Village, CO 81615-5774, USA

Blerk, Zac (Athlete, Hockey Player)
Team Shutout Goalie School
7044 Baskerville Run
Attn Manager of Plaver Development
Mississauga, ON L5W 1A2, Canada

Blessed, Brian (Actor)
Associated International Mgmt
5 Denmark St
London WC2H 8LP, UNITED KINGDOM (UK)

Blessen, Karen A (Journalist)
Karen Blessen Illustration
6327 Vickery Blvd
Dallas, TX 75214-3348, USA

Blessing, Jack (Actor)
c/o Marianne Golan *Golan & Blumberg*
2761 E Woodbury Dr
Arlington Heights, IL 60004-7247, USA

Blessitt, Ike (Athlete, Baseball Player)
19712 Anglin St
Detroit, MI 48234-1469, USA

Blethyn, Brenda (Actor)
61-63 Portobello Road
London W1N OAX, UNITED KINGDOM (UK)

Bleu, Corbin (Actor)
c/o Randy James *Randy James Management*
12711 Ventura Blvd Ste 345
Studio City, CA 91604-2416, USA

Blevins, Michael (Actor)
13 W 100th St Apt 2C
New York, NY 10025-4815, USA

Blewett III, John (Race Car Driver)
John Blewett Motorsports
246 Herbertsville Rd
Howell, NJ 07731-8787, USA

Blick, Richard (Dick) (Athlete, Swimmer)
1602 N Nye Ave
Fremont, NE 68025-3328, USA

Blier, Bertrand (Director)
11 Rue Margueritte
Paris 75017, FRANCE

Blige, Mary J (Musician)
c/o Dvora Vener Englefield *The Lede Company*
9701 Wilshire Blvd # 930
Beverly Hills, CA 90212-2020, USA

Bligen, Dennis (Athlete, Football Player)
PO Box 101
West Hempstead, NY 11552-0101, USA

Blind Boys of Alabama, The (Music Group, Musician)
192 Warren St SE
C/O Eric (Ricky) McKinnie
Atlanta, GA 30317-2243, USA

Blink-182 (Music Group)
c/o Karen Wiessen *Universal Music Group*
1755 Broadway Fl 6
New York, NY 10019-3768, USA

Blinka, Stan (Athlete, Football Player)
3304 Carriage Cir
Export, PA 15632-9213, USA

Blinks, Susan (Athlete, Horse Racer, Olympic Athlete)
3095 Florence St
West Palm Bch, FL 33414-4327, USA

Bliss, Boti Anne (Actor)
Chase/Goldberg Management
3400 San Marino St # A
Los Angeles, CA 90006-1106

Bliss, Caroline (Actor)
c/o Staff Member *The Rights House (UK)*
Drury House
34-43 Russell St
London WC2B 5HA, UNITED KINGDOM

Bliss, Mike (Race Car Driver)
185 Aztec Cir
Mooresville, NC 28117-6056, USA

Blitt, Ricky (Producer, Writer)
c/o Staff Member *Creative Artists Agency (CAA)*
2000 Avenue of the Stars Ste 100
Los Angeles, CA 90067-4705, USA

Blittner, Larry (Baseball Player)
Washington Senators
915 3rd Ave NW
Pocahontas, IA 50574-1413, USA

Blitz, Andy (Writer)
c/o Staff Member *3 Arts Entertainment*
9460 Wilshire Blvd Fl 7
Beverly Hills, CA 90212-2713, USA

Blitzer, Wolf (Correspondent, Television Host)
c/o Staff Member *CNN (DC)*
820 1st St NE Ste 1100
Washington, DC 20002-4247, USA

Bloch, Henry W (Business Person)
H & R Block Inc
4410 Main St
Kansas City, MO 64111-1812, USA

Bloch, Muriel (Writer)
Muriel Bloch
24 Blvd Saint-Denis
Paris 75010, France

Bloch, Phillip (Television Host)
c/o Chantal Cloutier *Cloutier Agency*
2632 La Cienega Ave
Los Angeles, CA 90034-2641, USA

Block, Francesca Lia (Writer)
c/o Angela Cheng Caplan *Cheng Caplan Co*
3863 Grand View Blvd # 2
Los Angeles, CA 90066-4414, USA

Block, Hunt (Actor)
PO Box 462
Greens Farms, CT 06838-0462, USA

Block, John (Athlete, Basketball Player)
Point Loma Nazarene College
1069 Santa Barbara St
San Diego, CA 92107-4160, USA

Block, Ken (Athlete, Hockey Player)
4901 Windrift Way
Carmel, IN 46033-9510, USA

Block, Lawrence (Writer)
299 W 12th St Apt 12D
New York, NY 10014-1829, USA

Block, Ron (Musician)
2065 Carters Creek Pike
Franklin, TN 37064-5914, USA

Blocker, Dirk (Actor)
5662 Calls Real
#251
Goleta, CA 93117, USA

Blocker, Terry (Athlete, Baseball Player)
745 Guide Post Ln
Stone Mountain, GA 30088-1943, USA

Bloc Party (Music Group)
c/o Staff Member *Toast Press*
Room 209, Bon Marche Building
241-251 Ferndale Rd
London SW9 8BJ, UK

Blodgett, Cindy (Athlete, Basketball Player)
25 Liberty St
Wakefield, RI 02879-2906, USA

Bloedorn, Greg (Athlete, Football Player)
816 N Catherine Ave
La Grange Park, IL 60526-1511, USA

Bloemberg, Jeff (Athlete, Hockey Player)
170 Diagonal Rd
Wingham, ON N0G 1W0, Canada

Blomberg, Ron (Athlete, Baseball Player)
11660 Mountain Laurel Dr
Roswell, GA 30075-1329, USA

Blomdahl, Ben (Athlete, Baseball Player)
22 Harveston
Mission Viejo, CA 92692-5116, USA

Blomgren, Michael (Actor)
c/o Staff Member *Select Artists Ltd (CA-Westside Office)*
1138 12th St Apt 1
Santa Monica, CA 90403-5459, USA

Blomquist, Rich (Actor)

Blomqvist, Timo (Athlete, Hockey Player)
HIFK Helsinki Ligaforeningen HIFK rd
Mantytie 23
Helsinki SF-00270, Finland

Blomsten, Arto (Athlete, Hockey Player)

Blondie (Music Group)
c/o Staff Member *10th Street Entertainment (NY)*
38 W 21st St Rm 300
New York, NY 10010-6979, USA

Blong, Jenni (Actor)
Austin Agency, The
6715 Hollywood Blvd Ste 204
Hollywood, CA 90028-4656

Blonsky, Nikki (Actor)
Alloy Entertainment
151 W 26th St # 1100
New York, NY 10001-6810, USA

Blood, Edward J (Skier)
2 Beech Hill Rd
Durham, NH 03824-1803, USA

Blood, Peter (Horse Racer)
290 SE 5th Ave
Pompano Beach, FL 33060-8024, USA

Bloodgood, Moon (Actor)
1238 S Holt Ave Apt 4
Los Angeles, CA 90035-5100, USA

Blood Red Shoes (Music Group)
c/o Angus Baskerville *13 Artists (UK)*
11-14 Kensington St
Brighton BN1 4AJ, UNITED KINGDOM

Bloodworth-Thomason, Linda (Producer, Writer)
c/o Staff Member *Mozark Productions*
4024 Radford Ave Bldg 5
Studio City, CA 91604-2101, USA

Bloom, Anne (Actor)
Abrams Artists
9200 W Sunset Blvd Ste 1125
Los Angeles, CA 90069-3610, USA

Bloom, Brian (Actor)
16760 Escalon Dr
Encino, CA 91436-3832, USA

Bloom, Claire (Actor)
c/o Staff Member *Conway van Gelder Grant*
8-12 Broadwick St
London W1F 8HW, UNITED KINGDOM

Bloom, Jeremy (Athlete, Olympic Athlete, Sportscaster)
c/o Staff Member *Maxx Sports & Entertainment*
546 5th Ave Fl 6
New York, NY 10036-5000, USA

Bloom, Lisa (Attorney, Commentator)
The Bloom Firm
22130 Clarendon St
Woodland Hills, CA 91367-6307, USA

Bloom, Luka (Music Group)
Mattie Fox Mgmt
Derryneel Ballinalee
Longford, IRELAND

Bloom, Mike (Athlete, Hockey Player)
3214 Marina Circle
Marina, CA 93933, USA

Bloom, Orlando (Actor)
c/o Jodi Gottlieb *Independent Public Relations*
9601 Wilshire Blvd Ste 750
Beverly Hills, CA 90210-5228, USA

Bloom, Rachel (Internet Star)
c/o Jeffrey Chassen *Imprint PR*
6121 W Sunset Blvd
Neuehouse
Los Angeles, CA 90028-6442, USA

Bloom, Samantha (Actor)
c/o Paul Lyon-Maris *Independent Talent Group*
40 Whitfield St
London W1T 2RH, UNITED KINGDOM

Bloom, Ursula (Writer)
Newton House Walls Dr Ravenglass
Cumbria, UNITED KINGDOM (UK)

Bloomauist, Willie (Athlete, Baseball Player)
7026 E Blue Sky Dr
Scottsdale, AZ 85266-7518, USA

Bloomberg, Michael (Business Person, Politician)
Bloomberg LP
499 Park Ave Ste 1500
New York, NY 10022-1240, USA

Bloomfield, Jack (Athlete, Baseball Player)
1310 W Iris Ave
McAllen, TX 78501-3995, USA

Bloomfield, Michael J (Mike) (Astronaut)
14302 Autumn Canyon Trce
Houston, TX 77062-2193, USA

Bloomfield, Willie (Athlete, Baseball Player)
3145 NE Magnolia St
Issaquah, WA 98029-3603, USA

Bloomquist, Scott (Race Car Driver)
219 Brooks Ln
Mooresburg, TN 37811-2113, USA

Blosser, Greg (Athlete, Baseball Player)
3059 Bay Oaks Dr
Sarasota, FL 34234-6420, USA

Blount, Alvin (Athlete, Football Player)
1943 Lakeshore Overlook Cir NW
Cir NW
Kennesaw, GA 30152-6711, USA

Blount, Corie (Athlete, Basketball Player)
5427 Kyles Ln
Liberty Township, OH 45044-9462, USA

Blount, Eric (Athlete, Football Player)
1388 Institute Rd
Kinston, NC 28504-7308, USA

Blount, Jeb (Athlete, Football Player)
1212 Daffodil Ln
Longview, TX 75604-2834, USA

Blount, John E (Athlete, Football Player)
1212 Daffodil Ln
Longview, TX 75604-2834, USA

Blount, Mark (Athlete, Basketball Player)
PO Box 33268
West Palm Bch, FL 33420, USA

Blount, Mel (Athlete, Football Player)
6 Mel Blount Dr
Claysville, PA 15323-1329, USA

Blount, Melvin C (Mel) (Athlete, Football Executive, Football Player)
6 Mel Blount Dr
Claysville, PA 15323-1329, USA

Blount, Winton M III (Business Person)
Blount Inc
4909 SE International Way
Portland, OR 97222-4679, USA

Blow, Kurtis (Music Group)
Entertainment Artists
2409 21st Ave S Ste 100
Nashville, TN 37212-5317, USA

Blowers, Mike (Athlete, Baseball Player)
PO Box 4100
Seattle, WA 98194-0100, USA

Blu, D K (Musician)
c/o Mike Rosen *Working Artists Agency*
13525 Ventura Blvd
Sherman Oaks, CA 91423-3801

Blucas, Marc (Actor)
c/o Sandra Chang *Anonymous Content*
3532 Hayden Ave
Culver City, CA 90232-2413, USA

Blue (Music Group)
c/o Billy Terry Wood *WME|IMG (UK)*
103 New Oxford St WMA
Centrepoint
London WC1A 1DD, UNITED KINGDOM

Blue (Musician)
c/o Staff Member *Concorde Intl Artists Ltd*
101 Shepherds Bush Rd
London W6 7LP, UNITED KINGDOM (UK)

Blue, Alfred (Athlete, Football Player)

Blue, Callum (Actor)
c/o Staff Member *Untitled Entertainment*
350 S Beverly Dr Ste 200
Beverly Hills, CA 90212-4819, USA

Blue, David (Actor)
c/o David Chien *Art/Work Entertainment*
5670 Wilshire Blvd Ste 900
Los Angeles, CA 90036-5699, USA

Blue, John (Athlete, Hockey Player)
2301 Half Moon Ln
Costa Mesa, CA 92627-6738, USA

Blue, Linda Bell (Producer)
c/o Staff Member *N.S. Bienstock*
888 7th Ave Fl 7
New York, NY 10106-0700, USA

Blue, Luther (Athlete, Football Player)
6952 Ravines Cir
West Bloomfield, MI 48322-2757, USA

Blue, Sam (Race Car Driver)
Blue Racing
1400 W 6th St
Red Wing, MN 55066-2174, USA

Blue, Sarayu (Actor)
c/o Staff Member *D2 Management*
10351 Santa Monica Blvd Ste 210
Los Angeles, CA 90025-6937, USA

Blue, Vida (Athlete, Baseball Player)
PO Box 1449
Pleasanton, CA 94566-0349, USA

Blues Traveler (Music Group)
c/o Keith Sarkisian *WME|IMG*
9601 Wilshire Blvd
Beverly Hills, CA 90210-5213, USA

Bluford, Guion (Astronaut)
PO Box 549
North Olmsted, OH 44070-0549, USA

Bluhm, Kay (Athlete)
Bahnorstr 104
Potsdam 14480, GERMANY

Blum, Geoff (Athlete, Baseball Player)
7 Calle Angelitos
San Clemente, CA 92673-6911, USA

Blum, Jason (Producer)
c/o Staff Member *Blumhouse International*
2401 Beverly Blvd
Los Angeles, CA 90057-1001, USA

Blum, John (Athlete, Coach, Hockey Player)
416 Marlborough St Apt 301
Boston, MA 02115-1559, USA

Blum, Stephanie (Comedian)
c/o Staff Member *Buchwald*
5900 Wilshire Blvd Ste 3100
Los Angeles, CA 90036-5030, USA

Blum, Steve (Actor)
c/o Staff Member *Arlene Thornton & Associates*
12711 Ventura Blvd Ste 490
Studio City, CA 91604-2477, USA

Blum, Walter (Horse Racer)
5710 NW 65th Way
Tamarac, FL 33321-5778, USA

Bluma, Jaime (Athlete, Baseball Player)
15219 Reeds St
Overland Park, KS 66223-3241, USA

Blumas, Trevor (Actor)
c/o Sandra Gillis *Premier Artists Management Ltd*
309 Cherry St
Toronto ON M5A 3L3, CANADA

Blume, Bernard (Athlete, Basketball Player)
626 SE 38th Dr
Gresham, OR 97080-8459, USA

Blume, Judy (Writer)
Tashmoo Productions
1075 Duval St Ste C21 # 236
Key West, FL 33040-3188, USA

Blumenauer, Earl (Congressman, Politician)
1502 Longworth Hob
Washington, DC 20515-1101, USA

Blumenthal, Richard (Senator)
702 Hart Senate Office Bldg
Washington, DC 20510-0001, USA

Blundell, Mark (Race Car Driver)
4001 Methanol Ln
Indianapolis, IN 46268-4855, USA

Blundin, Matt (Athlete, Football Player)
731 Milmont Ave
Swarthmore, PA 19081-2519, USA

Blunstone, Colin (Music Group)
Barry Collins
21A Cliftown Southend-on-Sea
Sussex SS1 1AB, UNITED KINGDOM (UK)

Blunt, Emily (Actor)
c/o BeBe Lerner *ID Public Relations*
7060 Hollywood Blvd Fl 8th
Los Angeles, CA 90028-6021, USA

Blunt, James (Musician)
c/o Todd Interland *Twenty-First Artists Ltd (UK)*
1 Blythe Rd
London W14 OHG, UK

Blunt, Roy (Senator)
260 Russell Senate Office Building
Washington, DC 20510-0001, USA

Blur (Music Group)
c/o Greg Janese *Paradigm (Nashville)*
222 2nd Ave S Ste 1600
Nashville, TN 37201-2375, USA

Blush (Music Group, Musician)
c/o Staff Member *Mitch Schneider Organization (MSO)*
14724 Ventura Blvd Ste 410
Sherman Oaks, CA 91403-3537, USA

Bluth, Don (Cartoonist)
10121 E Shangri La Rd
Scottsdale, AZ 85260-6302, USA

BLVD (Music Group, Musician)
c/o Staff Member *Skyline Music*
28 Union St
Whitefield, NH 03598-3503, USA

Bly, Dre' (Athlete, Football Player)
4312 Topsail Lndg
Chesapeake, VA 23321-6601, USA

Bly, Dre (Athlete, Football Player)
4312 Topsail Lndg
Chesapeake, VA 23321-6601, USA

Bly, Robert (Bob) (Athlete, Hockey Player)
7588 Av Henri-Julien
Montreal, QC H2R 2B5, Canada

Blyleven, Bert (Athlete, Baseball Player)
1 Twins Way
Minneapolis, MN 55403-1418, USA

Blynn, Sharon (Actor)
c/o Judy Katz *Judy Katz Public Relations*
1345 Avenue Of The Americas Fl 2
New York, NY 10105-0014, USA

Blyth, Ann (Actor)
PO Box 9754
Rancho Santa Fe, CA 92067-4754, USA

Blythe, Jamie (Reality Star)
c/o Mike Esterman *Esterman.Com, LLC*
Prefers to be contacted via email
Baltimore, MD XXXXX, USA

B. Maloney, Carolyn (Congressman, Politician)
2332 Rayburn Hob
Washington, DC 20515-3513, USA

B. McKinley, David (Congressman, Politician)
313 Cannon Hob
Washington, DC 20515-0925, USA

B. Nugent, Richard (Congressman, Politician)
1517 Longworth Hob
Washington, DC 20515-1004, USA

Board, Dwaine (Athlete, Football Player)
651 Arlington Rd
Redwood City, CA 94062-1842, USA

Boat, Billy (Race Car Driver)
23045 N 15th Ave
Phoenix, AZ 85027-1316, USA

Boath, Freddie (Actor)
c/o Staff Member *Sasha Leslie Management*
34 Pember Rd
London NW10 5LS, UNITED KINGDOM

Boatman, Michael (Actor)
678 Lookout Ln
Lake Havasu City, AZ 86403-3861, USA

Boatwright, Bon (Athlete, Football Player)
1801 E Main St
Henderson, TX 75652-3324, USA

Boatwright, Ron (Athlete, Football Player)
1801 E Main St
Henderson, TX 75652-3324, USA

Bob, Tim (Music Group, Musician)
c/o Staff Member *ArtistDirect*
9046 Lindblade St
Culver City, CA 90232-2513, USA

Bobadilla, Daniela (Actor)
c/o Bryan deCastro *East 2 West Collective*
11022 Santa Monica Blvd Ste 350
Los Angeles, CA 90025-7532, USA

Bobek, Nicole (Figure Skater)
19220 Seaview Rd # 100
Jupiter, FL 33469-2402, USA

Bober, Chris (Athlete, Football Player)
605 N 264th St
Waterloo, NE 68069-6238, USA

Bobko, Karol J (Astronaut)
32 Mansion Ct
Menlo Park, CA 94025-6658, USA

Bobo, DJ (Music Group)
Postfach
Wauwil 06242, SWITZERLAND

Bobo, Jonah (Actor)
c/o Ellen Gilbert *Abrams Artists Agency*
750 N San Vicente Blvd
E Tower Fl 11
Los Angeles, CA 90069-5788, USA

Bocachica, Hiram (Athlete, Baseball Player)
PO Box 364952
San Juan, PR 00936-4952, USA

Bocanegra, Carlos (Athlete, Soccer Player)
c/o Lyle York *Proactive Sports Management USA*
3233 M St NW
Washington, DC 20007-3556, USA

Boccabella, John (Athlete, Baseball Player)
1035 Lea Dr
San Rafael, CA 94903-3747, USA

Bocelli, Andrea (Musician)
c/o Staff Member *Almud*
Via Rosco Romagnola 742
Cascina, PI 55042, Italy

Bochefort, Dave (Athlete, Hockey Player)
7035 83 St NW
Edmonton, AB T6C 2Y1, Canada

Bochenski, Brandon (Athlete, Hockey Player)
10590 Kumquat St NW Apt 3
Minneapolis, MN 55448-1516, USA

Bochner, Hart (Actor)
c/o Nigel Mikoski *Connekt Creative*
136-1020 Mainland St
Vancouver, BC V6B 2T5, CANADA

Bochte, Bruce (Athlete, Baseball Player)
80 Century Ln
Petaluma, CA 94952-1218, USA

Bochtler, Doug (Athlete, Baseball Player)
PO Box 483
Yakima, WA 98907-0483, USA

Bochy, Bruce (Athlete, Baseball Player, Coach)
24 Willie Mays Plz
San Francisco, CA 94107-2134, USA

Bock, Charles (Writer)
c/o Staff Member *The Rights House (UK)*
Drury House
34-43 Russell St
London WC2B 5HA, UNITED KINGDOM

Bock, Edward J (Athlete, Business Person, Football Player)
2232 Clifton Forge Dr
Saint Louis, MO 63131-3107, USA

Bock, Joe (Athlete, Football Player)
35 Arrowhead Way N
Fairport, NY 14450-3303, USA

Bock, John (Athlete, Football Player)
232 NE 7th Ave
Delray Beach, FL 33483-5519, USA

Bock, Joseph (Athlete, Football Player)
35 Arrowhead Way N
Fairport, NY 14450-3303, USA

Bockhorn, Arlen (Athlete, Basketball Player)
3540 Big Tree Rd
Bellbrook, OH 45305-1971, USA

Bockus, Randy (Athlete, Baseball Player)
560 Helena Dr
Tallmadge, OH 44278-2667, USA

Bockwoldt, Colby (Athlete, Football Player)
1630 E 2450 S Unit 220
Saint George, UT 84790-6487, USA

Bocock, Brian (Baseball Player)
140 Cantermill Ln
Mount Crawford, VA 22841-2355, USA

Bodden, Alonzo (Actor, Comedian)
c/o Judi Brown *Levity Entertainment Group (LEG)*
6701 Center Dr W Ste 300
Los Angeles, CA 90045-2482, USA

Bodden, Leigh (Athlete, Football Player)
14409 Woodmore Oaks Ct
Bowie, MD 20721-3012, USA

Boddicker, Michael J (Mike) (Athlete, Basketball Player)
11324 W 121st Ter
Overland Park, KS 66213-1978, USA

Boddicker, Mike (Athlete, Baseball Player)
11324 W 121st Ter
Overland Park, KS 66213-1978, USA

Boddie, Tony (Athlete, Football Player)
330 Golden Pond St
Port Orchard, WA 98366-3300, USA

Boddy, Gregg (Athlete, Hockey Player)
2271 Sorrento Dr
Coquitlam, BC V3K 6P4, Canada

Boden, Lynn (Athlete, Football Player)
7103 N 146th St
Bennington, NE 68007-1527, USA

Bodenheimer, George W. (Business Person)
c/o Staff Member *ESPN (Main)*
935 Middle St
Espn Plaza
Bristol, CT 06010-1000, USA

Bodger, Doug (Athlete, Hockey Player)
Eddy's Hockey Shop
2827 James St
Duncan, BC V9L 2X9, Canada

Bodine, Geoff (Athlete, Race Car Driver)
Geoff Bodine Fan Club
812 Whimsical Ln
Malabar, FL 32950-3104, USA

Bodine, Geoffrey (Race Car Driver)
Gunselman Motorsports
208 Rolling Hill Rd
Mooresville, NC 28117-6845, USA

Bodine, Hunter (Actor)
c/o Paul Greenstone *Paul Greenstone Entertainment*
1400 California Ave Apt 201
Santa Monica, CA 90403-4395, USA

Bodine, Russell (Athlete, Football Player)

Bodine, Todd (Race Car Driver)
Team Onion Racing
PO Box 419
Mooresville, NC 28115-0419, USA

Bodine, Vance (Race Car Driver)
11881 Vance Davis Dr
Charlotte, NC 28269-7694, USA

Bodison, Wolfgang (Actor)
c/o Amy Macnow *Envoy Entertainment*
1640 S Sepulveda Blvd
Los Angeles, CA 90025-7510, USA

Bodrov, Sergei (Director)
c/o Steve Rabineau *WME|IMG*
9601 Wilshire Blvd
Beverly Hills, CA 90210-5213, USA

Boe, Alisha (Actor)
c/o Alyx Carr *42West*
600 3rd Ave Fl 23
New York, NY 10016-1914, USA

Boeheim, Jim (Athlete, Basketball Player, Coach)
702 Tiffany Cir
Fayetteville, NY 13066, USA

Boehm, Ron (Athlete, Hockey Player)
235 Simons Rd NW
Calgary, AB T2K 2X4, Canada

Boehmer, Len (Athlete, Baseball Player)
206 Townview Ct
Wentzville, MO 63385-2925, USA

Boehner, John (Congressman, Politician)
1011 Longworth Hob
Washington, DC 20515-3508, USA

Boehringer, Brian (Athlete, Baseball Player)
10 Sunset Dr
Fenton, MO 63026-4959, USA

Boehrs, Jessica (Actor)
Jondral Kunstlermanagement
Am Kliepesch 13a 50859
Cologne, Germany

Boeke, Jim (Athlete, Football Player)
34 Via Soria
San Clemente, CA 92673-7015, USA

Boen, Earl (Actor)
3015 Kalakaua Ave Apt 902
Honolulu, HI 96815-4750, USA

Boerigter, Marc (Athlete, Football Player)
220 W 2nd St Apt 2324
Kansas City, MO 64105-2174, USA

Boerner, Jacqueline (Speed Skater)
Bemhard-Bastlein-Str 55
Berlin 10367, USA

Boeschenstein, William W (Business Person)
1011 Sandusky St Ste L
Perrysburg, OH 43551-3171, USA

Boesel, Raul (Athlete, Race Car Driver)
150 SE 25th Rd Apt 4E
Miami, FL 33129-2403, USA

Boesen, Dannis L (Astronaut)
6613 Sandra Ave NE
Albuquerque, NM 87109-3639, USA

Boesen, Dennis (Astronaut)
6613 Sandra Ave NE
Albuquerque, NM 87109-3639, USA

Boever, Joe (Athlete, Baseball Player)
4701 Sawbuck St
St Augustine, FL 32092-3690, USA

Boffill, Angela (Music Group)
1385 York Ave Apt 6B
New York, NY 10021-3906, USA

Bogans, Keith (Athlete, Basketball Player)
9135 Country View Dr
Ypsilanti, MI 48197-6650, USA

Bogar, Tim (Athlete, Baseball Player)
4 Jersey St
Boston, MA 02215-4148, USA

Bogart, Andrea (Actor)
c/o Staff Member *Kazarian, Measures, Ruskin & Associates*
5200 Lankershim Blvd Ste 820
N Hollywood, CA 91601-3194, USA

Bogdan, Goran (Actor)
c/o Nicola Van Gelder *Conway van Gelder Grant*
8-12 Broadwick St
London W1F 8HW, UNITED KINGDOM

Bogdanovich, Peter (Director)
c/o Oren Segal *Management Production Entertainment (MPE)*
9229 W Sunset Blvd Ste 301
W Hollywood, CA 90069-3417, USA

Bogener, Terry (Athlete, Baseball Player)
311 Virginia Dr
Estes Park, CO 80517-9041, USA

Boggs, Bill (Journalist)
400 Central Park W Apt 18H
New York, NY 10025-5856, USA

Boggs, Brandon (Athlete, Baseball Player)
209 Riversgate Dr
Aot 41
Atlanta, GA 30339-2975, USA

Boggs, Mitchell Boggs (Athlete, Baseball Player)
901 W Walnut Ave
Dalton, GA 30720-3952, USA

Boggs, Taylor (Athlete, Football Player)
c/o Adam Heller *Vantage Management Group*
518 Reamer Dr
Carnegie, PA 15106-1845, USA

Boggs, Tommy (Athlete, Baseball Player)
1450 Long Mdw
Salado, TX 76571-5367, USA

Boggs, Wade (Athlete, Baseball Player)
6006 Windham Pl
Tampa, FL 33647-1149, USA

Bogguss, Suzy (Musician, Songwriter)
707 Sneed Rd W
Franklin, TN 37069-7045, USA

Bogle, Warren (Athlete, Baseball Player)
3400 Gulf Shore Blvd N Apt M8
N Aot M8
Naples, FL 34103-3609, USA

Bogle, Warren (Athlete, Baseball Player)
11605 SW 103rd Ave
Miami, FL 33176-4001, USA

Boglioli, Wendy (Athlete, Olympic Athlete, Swimmer)
General Delivery
Hood River, OR 97031-9999, USA

Bogner, Willy (Designer, Fashion Designer)
Bogner Film GmbH
Saint-Veit-Str 4
Munich 81673, GERMANY

Bogosian, Eric (Actor, Artist)
c/o Emily Gerson Saines *Brookside Artists Management*
250 W 57th St Ste 1820
New York, NY 10107-1802, USA

BOGRAKOS, Steve (Athlete, Football Player)
9051 E Chenango Ave
Greenwood Village, CO 80111-1320, USA

Bogues, Muggsy (Athlete, Basketball Player)
2318 Houston Branch Rd
Charlotte, NC 28270-0795, USA

Boguniecki, Eric (Athlete, Hockey Player)
58 Hine St
West Haven, CT 06516-4707, USA

Bogusevic, Brian (Athlete, Baseball Player)
1827 Fairoak Rd
Naperville, IL 60565-2821, USA

Bogush, Elizabeth (Actor)
c/o Craig Shapiro *ICM Partners*
10250 Constellation Blvd Fl 7
Los Angeles, CA 90067-6207, USA

Bohan, Marc (Designer, Fashion Designer)
35 Rue du Bourg a Mont
Chatillon Sur Seine 21400, FRANCE

Bohanon, Brian (Athlete, Baseball Player)
243 W Thorn Way
Houston, TX 77015-2069, USA

Bohanon, Tommy (Athlete, Football Player)
c/o Alan Herman *Sportstars Inc*
1370 Avenue of the Americas Fl 19
New York, NY 10019-4602, USA

Bohay, Heidi (Actor)
5004 Sanlo Pl
Woodland Hills, CA 91364-3528, USA

Bohbot, Daniel (Designer)
Hale Bob
2140 E 25th St
C/O Marc Springer
Vernon, CA 90058-1126, USA

Bohem, Les (Producer, Writer)
c/o Staff Member *United Talent Agency (UTA)*
9336 Civic Center Dr
Beverly Hills, CA 90210-3604, USA

Bohen, Ian (Actor)
c/o Angela Mach *Platform PR*
2666 N Beachwood Dr
Los Angeles, CA 90068-2308, USA

Bohling, Dewey (Athlete, Football Player)
5705 Cambria Rd NW
Albuquerque, NM 87120-2317, USA

Bohlke, Sanders (Musician)
c/o Staff Member *Paradigm (Monterey)*
404 W Franklin St
Monterey, CA 93940-2303, USA

Bohlmann, Ralph A (Religious Leader)
Lutheran Church Missouri Synod
1333 S Kirkwood Rd
Saint Louis, MO 63122-7295, USA

Bohn, Jason (Athlete, Golfer)
161 Graves Rd
Acworth, GA 30101-6117, USA

Bohn, T J (Athlete, Baseball Player)
PO Box 332
Millerstown, PA 17062-0332, USA

Bohnet, John (Athlete, Baseball Player)
224 Panorama Dr
Benicia, CA 94510-1523, USA

Bohringer, Romane (Actor)
c/o Laurent Gregoire *Agence Adequat*
21 Rue D'Uzes
Paris 75002, FRANCE

Boi, Big (Musician)
c/o Staff Member *HitCo Publishing Group*
500 Bishop St NW Ste A4
Atlanta, GA 30318-4380, USA

Boikov, Alexandre (Athlete, Hockey Player)
2138 Charleys Creek Rd
Culloden, WV 25510, USA

Boiman, Rocky (Athlete, Football Player)
9583 Dick Rd
Harrison, OH 45030-8417, USA

Boimistruck, Fred (Athlete, Hockey Player)
20 Cedar Ave
PO Box 92
Hornepayne, ON P0M 1Z0, Canada

Boiovic, Novo (Athlete, Football Player)
22097 Worcester Dr
Novi, MI 48374-3956, USA

Boireau, Michael (Athlete, Football Player)
1729 SW 101st Way
Miramar, FL 33025-6537, USA

Boisclair, Bruce (Athlete, Baseball Player)
3255 Briscoe Trl
San Antonio, TX 78253-5692, USA

Boisson, Christine (Actor)
Artmedia
21 Ave Rapp
Paris 75007, FRANCE

Boisvert, Gilles (Athlete, Hockey Player)
10213 Greenside Dr
Cockeysville, MD 21030-3332, USA

Boitano, Brian (Athlete, Figure Skater, Olympic Athlete)
Brian Boitano Enterprises
101 1st St # 370
Los Altos Hills, CA 94022-2750, USA

Boitano, Danny (Athlete, Baseball Player)
15400 Winchester Blvd Apt 43
Los Gatos, CA 95030-2346, USA

Boivin, Leo J (Athlete, Hockey Player)
PO Box 406
Prescott, ON K0E 1T0, Canada

Bok, Arthur (Athlete, Football Player)
3280 Early Rd
Dayton, OH 45415-2705, USA

Bokamper, Kim (Athlete, Football Player)
301 NW 127th Ave
Plantation, FL 33325-2318, USA

Bokelmann, Dick (Athlete, Baseball Player)
1538 Heather Ct Apt B2
Wheeling, IL 60090-5273, USA

Bola??os, Enrique (President)
President's Office
Casa de Gobierno #2398
Managua, Nicaragua

Bolden, Juran (Athlete, Football Player)
5003 Cumberland Dr
Tampa, FL 33617-8424, USA

Bolden, Omar (Athlete, Football Player)
c/o Joel Segal *Lagardere Unlimited (NY)*
456 Washington St Apt 9L
New York, NY 10013-1555, USA

Bolden, Rickey (Athlete, Football Player)
301 High Pointe Dr
Lagrange, GA 30240-9718, USA

Boldin, Anquan (Athlete, Football Player)
16225 Bridlewood Cir
Delray Beach, FL 33445-6675, USA

Boldirev, Ivan (Athlete, Hockey Player)
27408 Valois Dr
Bonita Springs, FL 34135-6024, USA

Boldman, Spencer (Actor)
c/o Meredith Fine *Coast to Coast Talent Group*
3350 Barham Blvd
Los Angeles, CA 90068-1404, USA

Boldon, Ato (Athlete, Track Athlete)
PO Box 3703
Santa Cruz, Trinidad, TRINIDAD & TOBAGO

Bolduc, Dan (Athlete, Hockey Player, Olympic Athlete)
27 Daisy Ln
Sidney, ME 04330-1809, USA

Bolduon, Kate (Commentator, Television Host)
c/o Staff Member *CNN (NY)*
10 Columbus Cir
Time Warner Center
New York, NY 10019-1158, USA

Bolek, Ken (Athlete, Baseball Player)
4816 1st Avenue Dr NW
Bradenton, FL 34209-2861, USA

Boles, Carl (Athlete, Baseball Player)
5618 Pine Bay Dr
Tampa, FL 33625-4025, USA

Boles, John E (Athlete, Baseball Player, Coach)
7901 Timberlake Dr
West Melbourne, FL 32904-2151, USA

Boley, Michael (Athlete, Football Player)
2324 N Gila Verde
Mesa, AZ 85207-9210, USA

Bolger, Bill (Athlete, Basketball Player)
525 Ahlstrand Rd
Glen Ellyn, IL 60137-6926, USA

Bolger, Emma (Actor)
c/o Abby Bluestone *Innovative Artists*
1505 10th St
Santa Monica, CA 90401-2805, USA

Bolger, Gary (Race Car Driver)
3632 Washington St
Lansing, IL 60438-2425, USA

Bolger, Jim (Athlete, Baseball Player)
5524 Sidney Rd
Cincinnati, OH 45238-3215, USA

Bolger, Sarah (Actor)
c/o Paul Nelson *Mosaic Media Group*
407 N Maple Dr # 100
Beverly Hills, CA 90210-3818, USA

Bolick, Frank (Athlete, Baseball Player)
381 Virginia Ln
Kulpmont, PA 17834-2024, USA

Bolin, Bobby D (Athlete, Baseball Player)
100 Medinah Dr
Easley, SC 29642-3126, USA

Boling, Clint (Athlete, Football Player)
c/o Pat Dye Jr *SportsTrust Advisors*
3340 Peachtree Rd NE Fl 16
Atlanta, GA 30326-1000, USA

Bolkiah, Hassanal (Royalty)
Office Of The Sultan
Istana Nurul Iman
Bandar Seri, Begawan BA1000, Brunei

Bolkovac, Nick (Athlete, Football Player)
1418 Humbolt Ave
Youngstown, OH 44502-2755, USA

Bollen, Roger (Cartoonist)
Tribune Media Services
435 N Michigan Ave Ste 1500
Chicago, IL 60611-4012, USA

Boller, Kyle (Athlete, Football Player)
14945 Via La Senda
Del Mar, CA 92014-4144, USA

Bollettieri, Nick (Coach, Tennis Player)
Nick Bollettieri Tennis Academy
5500 34th St W
Bradenton, FL 34210-3596, USA

Bolli, Justin (Athlete, Golfer)
3309 Buckhead Forest Mews NE
Atlanta, GA 30305-1706, USA

Bolling, Eric (Television Host)
c/o Staff Member *Fox News*
1211 Avenue of the Americas Lowr C1
New York, NY 10036-8705, USA

Bolling, Frank (Athlete, Baseball Player)
171 Fenwick Rd
Mobile, AL 36608-1743, USA

Bolling, Milt (Athlete, Baseball Player)
4009 Old Shell Rd Apt E11
Mobile, AL 36608-1385, USA

Bolling, Tiffany (Actor)
409 S Northwood Ave
Compton, CA 90220-2808, USA

Bollinger, Brian (Athlete, Football Player)
2835 N Highway A1a Apt 302
Indialantic, FL 32903-2106, USA

Bollinger, Brooks (Athlete, Football Player)
1465 Highview Ave
Saint Paul, MN 55121-1143, USA

Bollinger, Danielle (Musician)
c/o Len Evans *Project Publicity*
540 W 43rd St
New York, NY 10036, USA

Bollman, Ryan (Actor)
c/o Staff Member *Lichtman/Salners Company*
12216 Moorpark St
Studio City, CA 91604-5228, USA

Bollo, Greg (Athlete, Baseball Player)
4105 7th St
Wyandotte, MI 48192-7109, USA

Bolonchuk, Larry (Athlete, Hockey Player)
385 Woodlawn St
Winnipeg, MB R3J 2J2, Canada

Bolstorff, Douglas (Athlete, Basketball Player)
1553 Skyline Ct
Saint Paul, MN 55121-1148, USA

Bolt, Jackson (Actor)
c/o Jack Scagnetti *Jack Scagnetti Agency*
5118 Vineland Ave
North Hollywood, CA 91601-3814, USA

Bolt, Jeremy (Producer)
c/o Ken Kamins *Key Creatives*
1800 N Highland Ave Fl 5
Los Angeles, CA 90028-4523, USA

Bolt, Tommy (Athlete, Golfer)
8 Whispering Winds Tc
Cherokee Village, AR 72529, USA

Bolt, Usain (Athlete, Olympic Athlete, Track Athlete)
c/o Jason Hodes *WME/IMG (NY)*
11 Madison Ave Fl 18
New York, NY 10010-3669, USA

Bolton, Michael (Musician, Songwriter)
c/o Erin Culley *Creative Artists Agency (CAA)*
2000 Avenue of the Stars Ste 100
Los Angeles, CA 90067-4705, USA

Bolton, Rodney (Athlete, Baseball Player)
10682 Adlar Ct
Apison, TN 37302-5900, USA

Bolton, Ron (Athlete, Football Player)
408 Maiden Ln
Chesapeake, VA 23325-4607, USA

Bolton, Ruthie (Athlete, Basketball Player)
PO Box 188463
Sacramento, CA 95818-8463, USA

Bolton, Scott (Athlete, Football Player)
1635 Ashmoor Dr E
Mobile, AL 36695-4345, USA

Bolton, Tom (Athlete, Baseball Player)
2288 Rolling Hills Dr
Nolensville, TN 37135-9483, USA

Boltz, Ray (Musician)
Ray Boltz Music
5800 E Woodside Rd
Albany, IN 47320-9716, USA

Bolzan, Scott (Athlete, Football Player)
2074 E Linda Ln
Gilbert, AZ 85234-6210, USA

Bomback, Mark (Athlete, Baseball Player)
2482 Riverside Ave
Somerset, MA 02726-5149, USA

Bombard, Marc (Athlete, Baseball Player)
8612 Barkwood Pl
Tampa, FL 33615-1501, USA

Bombardir, Brad (Athlete, Hockey Player)
Minnesota Wild
317 Washington St
Player Development
Saint Paul, MN 55102-1667, USA

Bomer, Matt (Actor)
c/o Kami Putnam-Heist *Anonymous Content*
3532 Hayden Ave
Culver City, CA 90232-2413, USA

Bonaduce, Danny (Actor, Musician, Producer)
7124 Hollywood Blvd Apt 5
Los Angeles, CA 90046-3239, USA

Bonaly, Surya (Figure Skater)
c/o Staff Member *Champions on Ice*
3500 American Blvd W Ste 190
Minneapolis, MN 55431-4431, USA

Bonamassa, Joe (Musician)
c/o Staff Member *Premier Artists Services*
6278 NW 92nd Ave
Parkland, FL 33067-3746, USA

Bonamy, James (Musician)
Hallmark Direction
15 Music Sq W
Nashville, TN 37203-6200, USA

Bonanni, Angel (Actor)
c/o Hadas Mozes Lichtenstein *ADD Agency*
2 Raoul Wallenberg St
Ramat Hachayal
Tel Aviv 69719, Israel

Bonanno, Louis (Louie) (Actor)
PO Box 583
Laguna Beach, CA 92652-0583, USA

Bonar, Dan (Athlete, Hockey Player)
361 Mandeville St
Winnipeg, MB R3J 2G8, Canada

Bond, Edward (Writer)
Orchard Way
Great Wilbraham, Cambridge CB1 5KA, UNITED KINGDOM (UK)

Bond, Larry (Writer)
c/o Robert Gottlieb *Trident Media Group LLC*
41 Madison Ave Fl 36
New York, NY 10010-2257, USA

Bond, Phillip (Phil) (Athlete, Basketball Player)
208 Northwestern Pkwy
Louisville, KY 40212-2732, USA

Bond, Rhys Matthew (Actor)
c/o Bradford Bricken *The Cartel*
1108-1112 Tamarind Ave
Hollywood, CA 90038, USA

Bond, Samantha (Actor)
Conway Van Gelder Robinson
18-21 Jermyn St
London SW1Y 6NB, UNITED KINGDOM (UK)

Bond, Samatha (Actor)
c/o Staff Member *Innovative Artists*
1505 10th St
Santa Monica, CA 90401-2805, USA

Bond, Walter (Athlete, Basketball Player)
PO Box 87
Hamel, MN 55340-0087, USA

Bondar, Roberta L (Astronaut)
Space Agency
PO Box 7014 Stn Vanier
Ottawa, ON K1L 8E2, CANADA

Bondarchuk, Fyodor (Director)
Art Pictures Studio
Rochdelskaya 15
Bldg 23
Moscow 123022, RUSSIA

Bonderman, Jeremy (Athlete, Baseball Player)
=
10 Ridgeview Dr
Pasco, WA 99301-8808, USA

Bondra, Peter (Athlete, Hockey Player)
110 Highland Rd # 1
Somerville, MA 02144-2215, USA

Bonds, Barry (Athlete, Baseball Player)
3 Lagoon Dr Ste 300
Redwood City, CA 94065-1567, USA

Bonds, Gary US (Music Group)
c/o Marina Anderson *Media Hound PR*
PO Box 261939
Encino, CA 91426-1939, USA

Bondurant, Bob (Race Car Driver)
Firebird Racing School
20,000 S. Maricopa Rd
Box 5023
Chandler, AZ 85226, USA

Bondy, A.A. (Musician)
c/o Ken Weinstein *Big Hassle Media*
40 Exchange Pl Ste 1900
New York, NY 10005-2714, USA

Bone, Bizzy (Musician)
c/o Mary Bowlin *7th Sign Records*
145 Baker St
Marion, OH 43302-4111, USA

Boneham, Rupert (Reality Star)
c/o Staff Member *Abrams Artists Agency*
275 7th Ave Fl 26
New York, NY 10001-6708, USA

Bonehman, Rupert (Actor)
c/o Staff Member *Ruth Webb Enterprises*
10580 Des Moines Ave
Northridge, CA 91326-2926, USA

Bonelli, Ernest (Athlete, Football Player)
1290 Boyce Rd Apt C409
Pittsburgh, PA 15241-3991, USA

Bonerz, Peter (Actor, Comedian, Director)
3637 Lowry Rd
Los Angeles, CA 90027-1435, USA

Bones, Ricky (Athlete, Baseball Player)
908 NW lOOth Ave
Pembroke Pines, FL 33024-4371, USA

Bonet, Lisa (Actor)
1551 Will Geer Rd
Topanga, CA 90290-4291, USA

Boneta, Diego (Actor)
c/o Josh Glick *Grandview*
7122 Beverly Blvd Ste F
Los Angeles, CA 90036-2572, USA

Bong, Jung (Baseball Player)
Atlanta Braves
2917 Asteria Pointe
Duluth, GA 30097-5221, USA

Bongiovi, Tony (Musician, Producer)
Bongiovi Acoustics
649 SW Whitmore Dr
Port St Lucie, FL 34984-3567, USA

Bongo, Albert-Bernard Omar (President)
President's Office
Blvd de Independence
Libreville BP 546, GABON

Bonham, Bill (Athlete, Baseball Player)
2135 Holly Ln
Solvang, CA 93463-2207, USA

Bonham, Jason (Musician)
10324 El Caballo Ct
Delray Beach, FL 33446-2712, USA

Bonham, Ron (Athlete, Basketball Player)
12330 S County Road 400 E
Muncie, IN 47302-8435, USA

Bonham, Shane (Athlete, Football Player)
3431 Ardennes Dr
Maryville, TN 37801-9591, USA

Bonham, Tracy (Music Group, Songwriter)
c/o Staff Member *Paradigm (Monterey)*
404 W Franklin St
Monterey, CA 93940-2303, USA

Bonham Carter, Helena (Actor)
c/o Adam Isaacs *MGMT Entertainment (The Schiff Company)*
9220 W Sunset Blvd Ste 106
W Hollywood, CA 90069-3500, USA

Boniadi, Nazanin (Actor)
c/o Craig Bankey *Main Stage Public Relations*
Prefers to be contacted by phone or email.
Los Angeles, CA NA, USA

Bonifant, J Evan (Actor)
c/o Staff Member *Pacific Artists Management*
112 3rd Ave E Suite 210
Vancouver, BC V5T 1C8, CANADA

Bonikowski, Joe (Athlete, Baseball Player)
6701 Old Reid Rd
Charlotte, NC 28210-4622, USA

Bonilla, Hector (Actor)
c/o Staff Member *TV Azteca*
Periferico Sur 4121
Colonia Fuentes del Pedregal
DF CP 14141, Mexico

Bonilla, Juan (Athlete, Baseball Player)
2902 Orchidcrest Dr
Crestview, FL 32539-8528, USA

Bonilla, Roberto M A (Bobby) (Athlete, Baseball Player)
1774 Meadowood St
Sarasota, FL 34231-3014, USA

Bonin, Brian (Athlete, Hockey Player)
2279 8th St
Saint Paul, MN 55110-2869, USA

Bonin, Celeste Beryl (Athlete, Wrestler)
c/o Staff Member *World Wrestling Entertainment (WWE)*
1241 E Main St
Stamford, CT 06902-3520, USA

Bonin, Greg (Athlete, Baseball Player)
509 Boulder Creek Pkwy
Lafayette, LA 70508-1717, USA

Bonin, Marcel (Athlete, Hockey Player)
225-230 Rue du Juge-Guibault
Saint-Charles-Borromee, QC J6E 9B4, Canada

Bonine, Eddie (Athlete, Baseball Player)
15147 W Frontier Dr
Surprise, AZ 85387-6565, USA

Boniol, Chris (Athlete, Football Player)
3413 Monaghan St
Dublin, CA 94568-4569, USA

Bonjour, Daniel (Actor)
c/o Staff Member *Tinoco Management*
8033 W Sunset Blvd Ste 573
West Hollywood, CA 90046-2401, USA

Bon Jovi, Jon (Actor, Musician, Songwriter)
c/o Tiffany Shipp *Sunshine Sachs*
136 Madison Ave Fl 17
New York, NY 10016-6734, USA

Bonk, John (Athlete, Football Player)
54 Audubon St S
Stoney Creek, ON L8J 1J7, Canada

Bonk, Radek (Athlete, Hockey Player)
137 Allenhurst Cir
Franklin, TN 37067-7272, USA

Bonnaire, Sandrine (Actor)
36 rue de Ponthieu
Paris, FRANCE F-75008

Bonnell, Barry (Athlete, Baseball Player)
2102 179th Ct NE
Redmond, WA 98052-6064, USA

Bonner, Alan (Athlete, Football Player)
c/o Bus Cook *Bus Cook Sports, Inc*
1 Willow Bend Dr
Hattiesburg, MS 39402-8552, USA

Bonner, Anthony (Athlete, Basketball Player)
5854 Elmbank Ave
Saint Louis, MO 63120-1116, USA

Bonner, Bobby (Athlete, Baseball Player)
990 Manitou Rd
Hilton, NY 14468-9390, USA

Bonner, Jo (Congressman, Politician)
2236 Rayburn Hob
Washington, DC 20515-3312, USA

Bonner, Melvin (Athlete, Football Player)
2500 Fairway Dr Apt 102
Alvin, TX 77511-4628, USA

Bonness, Rik (Athlete, Football Player)
18914 Boyle Cir
Elkhorn, NE 68022-3953, USA

Bonneville, Hugh (Actor)
c/o Staff Member *Milk Publicity*
8-14 Vine Hill
The Entertainment Agency
London EC16 5DX, UNITED KINGDOM

Bonnke, Reinhard (Religious Leader)
Christ for All Nations
PO Box 590588
Orlando, FL 32859-0588, USA

Bono (Musician, Songwriter)
Regine Moylett
9 Ivebury Ct
325 Latimer Rd
London W10 6RA, UNITED KINGDOM

Bono, Chaz (Actor, Musician)
c/o Annie Jeeves *Cinematic Red*
PO Box 69392
West Hollywood, CA 90069-0392, USA

Bono, Steven C (Steve) (Athlete, Football Player)
1100 Hamilton Ave
Palo Alto, CA 94301-2216, USA

Bonoff, Karla (Musician, Songwriter)
2122 E Valley Rd
Santa Barbara, CA 93108-1513, USA

Bono Mack, Mary (Congressman, Politician)
104 Cannon Hob
Washington, DC 20515-0916, USA

Bonsall, Joe (Musician)
100 Surrey Hill Pt
Hendersonville, TN 37075-5212, USA

Bonsalle, George (Athlete, Basketball Player)
11804 Del Rey Ave NE
Albuquerque, NM 87122-2417, USA

Bonser, Boof (Athlete, Baseball Player)
9251 126th Ave
Largo, FL 33773-1247, USA

Bonsignore, Jason (Athlete, Hockey Player)
224 Ida Red Ln
Rochester, NY 14626-4448, USA

Bontemps, Ron (Athlete, Basketball Player, Olympic Athlete)
6358 N Allen Rd Unit 38
Peoria, IL 61614-3292, USA

Bonvicini, Joan (Athlete, Basketball Player, Coach)
University of Arizona
McKale Memorial Center
Atheletic Dept
Tucson, AZ 85721-0001, USA

Bonvie, Dennis (Athlete, Hockey Player)
45 Tamanini Dr
Wyoming, PA 18644-9371, USA

Boo, Jim (Athlete, Hockey Player)
416 4th St S
Stillwater, MN 55082-4912, USA

Boo, Katherine (Journalist, Writer)
c/o Staff Member *Random House Publicity*
1745 Broadway Frnt 3
New York, NY 10019-4343, USA

Booher, Paul (Race Car Driver)
653 Powers Dr
El Dorado Hills, CA 95762-4443, USA

Booka Shade (Music Group)
c/o Joel Zimmerman *WME/IMG (NY)*
11 Madison Ave Fl 18
New York, NY 10010-3669, USA

Booker, Buddy (Athlete, Baseball Player)
PO Box 59
Brookneal, VA 24528-0059, USA

Booker, Butch (Athlete, Basketball Player)
305 Barker Ave
Lansdowne, PA 19050-1215, USA

Booker, Chris (Athlete, Baseball Player)
2052 Perryville Rd
Monroeville, AL 36460-6852, USA

Booker, Greg (Athlete, Baseball Player)
1535 Charleigh Ct
Elon, NC 27244-9770, USA

Booker, Marty (Athlete, Football Player)
19920 NW 8th St
Pembroke Pines, FL 33029-3326, USA

Booker, Rod (Athlete, Baseball Player)
526 W Altadena Dr
Altadena, CA 91001-4204, USA

Booker, Vaughn (Athlete, Football Player)
56 E Mitchell Ave
Cincinnati, OH 45217-1520, USA

Booko, Daniel (Actor)
c/o Glenn Hughes III *Gem Entertainment Group*
10920 Wilshire Blvd Ste 150
Los Angeles, CA 90024-3990, USA

Bookwalter, JR (Director)
PO Box 6573
Akron, OH 44312-0573, USA

Boom, Benn (Actor)
c/o Staff Member *WME/IMG*
9601 Wilshire Blvd
Beverly Hills, CA 90210-5213, USA

Boomer, Linwood (Producer)
c/o Rick Rosen *WME/IMG*
9601 Wilshire Blvd
Beverly Hills, CA 90210-5213, USA

Boone, Aaron (Athlete, Baseball Player)
19860 N 97th St
Scottsdale, AZ 85255-6682, USA

Boone, Alex (Athlete, Football Player)
c/o Jonathan Feinsod *Schwartz & Feinsod*
4 Hillandale Rd
Rye Brook, NY 10573-1705, USA

Boone, Alfonso (Athlete, Football Player)
14290 W Lyle Ct
Libertyville, IL 60048-4835, USA

Boone, Bob (Athlete, Baseball Player)
1432 Misty Sea Way
San Marcos, CA 92078-1010, USA

Boone, Bret (Athlete, Baseball Player)
804 Midori Ct
Solana Beach, CA 92075-1291, USA

Boone, Danny (Athlete, Baseball Player)
320 Minnesota Ave
El Cajon, CA 92020-6118, USA

Boone, Debby (Actor, Musician)
6721 Andasol Ave
Van Nuys, CA 91406-5413, USA

Boone, Greg (Athlete, Football Player)
10426 Hunters Haven Blvd
Riverview, FL 33578-3362

Boone, James (Athlete, Football Player)
2529 Butler Bay Dr N
Windermere, FL 34786-6111, USA

Boone, Jim (Athlete, Football Player)
2529 Butler Bay Dr N
Windermere, FL 34786-6111, USA

Boone, Lesley (Actor)
12523 Landale St
Studio City, CA 91604-1306, USA

Boone, Megan (Actor)
c/o Sandra Chang *Anonymous Content*
3532 Hayden Ave
Culver City, CA 90232-2413, USA

Boone, Pat (Actor, Musician)
Pat Boone Enterprises, Inc.
9220 W Sunset Blvd Ste 310
Los Angeles, CA 90069-3503, USA

Boone, Ron (Athlete, Basketball Player)
2200 s 100 E
Salt Lake City, UT 84106-1836, USA

Boone, Steve (Music Group, Musician)
Pipeline Artists Mgmt
620 16th Ave S
Hopkins, MN 55343-7833, USA

Boone Junior, Mark (Actor)
c/o Michael Greenwald *Endorse Management Group*
9854 National Blvd # 454
Los Angeles, CA 90034-2713, USA

Booras, Steve (Athlete, Football Player)
1441 Parkhill Dr
Billings, MT 59102-3147, USA

Boorem, Mika (Actor)
c/o Naisha Arnold *Untitled Entertainment*
350 S Beverly Dr Ste 200
Beverly Hills, CA 90212-4819, USA

Boorman, Charley (Actor, Producer, Writer)
c/o Lindy King *United Agents*
12-26 Lexington St
London W1F OLE, UNITED KINGDOM

Boorman, John (Director)
Merlin Films
16 Upper Pembroke St
Dublin 2, IRELAND

Booros, James (Athlete, Golfer)
2615 W Pennsylvania St
Allentown, PA 18104-2921, USA

Boortz, Neal (Radio Personality)
1601 W Peachtree St NE
Atlanta, GA 30309-2641, USA

Boose, Dorian (Athlete, Football Player)
1630 NE Valley Rd Apt K102
Apt K102T Ct
Pullman, WA 99163-4464, USA

Boosler, Elayne (Actor, Comedian)
11061 Wrightwood Ln
Studio City, CA 91604-3959, USA

Booster, Joel Kim (Comedian)
c/o Zack Freedman *OmniPop Talent Group*
4605 Lankershim Blvd Ste 201
Toluca Lake, CA 91602-1874, USA

Bootcheck, Chris (Athlete, Baseball Player)
6105 Lakeaires Dr
Cumming, GA 30040-1109, USA

Booth, Brad (Athlete, Football Player)
2201 W 229th Pl
Torrance, CA 90501, USA

Booth, Calvin (Athlete, Basketball Player)
6001 E Horseshoe Rd
Paradise Valley, AZ 85253-8125, USA

Booth, Clarence (Athlete, Football Player)
33 Cor Dale Ct
Lafayette, IN 47904-1043, USA

Booth, Connie (Actor)
Kate Feast
Primrose Hill Studios
Fitzroy Rd
London NW1 8TR, UNITED KINGDOM (UK)

Booth, David (Athlete, Hockey Player)
Octagon Sports Management
132 Alea Ln
Lakeside, MT 59922-9553, USA

Booth, Douglas (Actor)
c/o Luke Windsor *Prosper PR (UK)*
535 Kings Rd
Suite 313 Plaza
London SW10 0SZ, UNITED KINGDOM

Booth, George (Cartoonist)
PO Box 1539
Stony Brook, NY 11790-0830, USA

Booth, Kellee (Athlete, Golfer)
9542 Crown Meadow Dr
Frisco, TX 75035-0320, USA

Booth, Kristin (Actor)
c/o Vicki McCarty *Covington International*
4237 Morro Dr
Woodland Hills, CA 91364-5521, USA

Booth, Lindy (Actor)
c/o Ronda Cooper *Characters Talent Agency*
200-1505 2nd Ave W
Vancouver, BC V6H 3Y4, CANADA

Booth, Tim (Musician)
1126 Bonilla Dr
Topanga, CA 90290-3600, USA

Boothe, Kevin (Athlete, Football Player)
c/o Peter Schaffer *Authentic Athletix*
400 S Steele St Unit 47
Denver, CO 80209-3535, USA

Boothie, Powers (Actor)
23629 Long Valley Rd
Hidden Hills, CA 91302-2406, USA

Booty, John (Athlete, Football Player)
1408 Flatwood Ct
Crofton, MD 21114-1440, USA

Booty, Josh (Athlete, Football Player)
6248 N Windermere Dr
Shreveport, LA 71129-3423, USA

Booty, Josh (Athlete, Baseball Player)
6248 N Windermere Dr
Shreveport, LA 71129-3423, USA

Boozer, Carlos (Athlete, Basketball Player)
c/o Rob Pelinka *Landmark Sports Agency*
10990 Wilshire Blvd Ste 1000
Los Angeles, CA 90024-3924, USA

Boozer, Emerson (Athlete, Football Player)
25 Windham Dr
Huntington Station, NY 11746-4541, USA

Borbon, Julio (Athlete, Baseball Player)
522 Vinings Oaks Run
Mableton, GA 30126-7239, USA

Borchard, Joe (Athlete, Baseball Player)
712 Camino Del Sol
Newbury Park, CA 91320-6701, USA

Borchardt, Jon (Athlete, Football Player)
18624 E Mainstreet Apt 5110
Parker, CO 80134-5055, USA

Borcky, Dennis (Athlete, Football Player)
18 Weathervane Rd
Aston, PA 19014-2616, USA

Bordano, Chris (Athlete, Football Player)
505 Cedar Trl
New Braunfels, TX 78130-6632, USA

Bordeleau, Christian (Athlete, Hockey Player)
1242 Rue Rabelais
Repentigny, QC JSV 3R7, Canada

Bordeleau, J P (Athlete, Hockey Player)
94 Lakemist Crt
Dartmouth, NS B3A 4Z1, Canada

Bordeleau, Paulin (Athlete, Hockey Player)
281A Rue Principale
La Sarre, QC J9Z 1Z1, Canada

Bordelon, Ben (Athlete, Football Player)
PO Box 250
Lockport, LA 70374-0250, USA

Bordelon, Kenneth (Athlete, Football Player)
1224 Octavia St
New Orleans, LA 70115-4223, USA

Borden, Amanda (Gymnast)
Cincinnati Gymnastics Academy
3536 Woodridge Blvd
Fairfield, OH 45014, USA

Borden, Lynn (Actor)
Associated Artists
6399 Wilshire Blvd Ste 211
Los Angeles, CA 90048-5705, USA

Borden, Robert (Producer)
c/o Staff Member *United Talent Agency (UTA)*
9336 Civic Center Dr
Beverly Hills, CA 90210-3604, USA

Borden, Scott (Actor)
c/o Staff Member *Progressive Artists Agency*
1041 N Formosa Ave
West Hollywood, CA 90046-6703, USA

Borden, Steve (Sting) (Athlete, Wrestler)
c/o Steve Martinez *Stonewood Entertainment*
Prefers to be contacted by telephone or email
Los Angeles, CA, USA

Borders, Nate (Athlete, Football Player)
950 Franklin St
Winchester, VA 22601-5810, USA

Borders, Pat (Athlete, Baseball Player, Olympic Athlete)
2650 Burns Ave
Lake Wales, FL 33898-7947, USA

Bordi, Rich (Athlete, Baseball Player)
948 Helene Ct
Rohnert Park, CA 94928-1457, USA

Bordick, Mike (Athlete, Baseball Player)
1302 Locust Ave
Towson, MD 21204-6619, USA

Bordley, Bill (Athlete, Baseball Player)
39 Moccasin Ln
Rolling Hills Estates, CA 90274-2506, USA

Boreanaz, David (Actor)
c/o Britney Ross *42West*
1840 Century Park E Ste 700
Los Angeles, CA 90067-2122, USA

Boren, Dan (Congressman, Politician)
2447 Rayburn Hob
Washington, DC 20515-4203, USA

Boren, Matt (Actor)
c/o Steven Jensen *Independent Group, The*
6363 Wilshire Blvd Ste 115
Los Angeles, CA 90048-5734, USA

Borg, Bjorn (Athlete, Tennis Player)
Tulegatan 11
Stockholm 113 53, SWEDEN

Borg, Flula (Musician)
c/o Staff Member *United Talent Agency (UTA)*
9336 Civic Center Dr
Beverly Hills, CA 90210-3604, USA

Borg-Aplin, Lorraine (Baseball Player)
5827 Laverne Cir Apt 2
Baxter, MN 56425-8231, USA

Borgen, Clint (Writer)

Borgeson, Don (Athlete, Hockey Player)
2211 Highway 49 W
Ashland City, TN 37015-5001, USA

Borgmann, Glenn (Athlete, Baseball Player)
16 Lundy Ter
Butler, NJ 07405-1926, USA

Borgognone, Dirk (Athlete, Football Player)
7148 Voyage Dr
Sparks, NV 89436-5427, USA

Boris, Paul (Athlete, Baseball Player)
28 Sunnyside Ln
Hillsborough, NJ 08844-4738, USA

Bork, Erik (Producer, Writer)
c/o Staff Member *Creative Artists Agency (CAA)*
2000 Avenue of the Stars Ste 100
Los Angeles, CA 90067-4705, USA

Bork, Frank (Athlete, Baseball Player)
8488 Dunsinane Dr
Dublin, OH 43017-9420, USA

Bork, George (Athlete, Football Player)
7316 Coventry Dr S
Spring Grove, IL 60081-9379, USA

Borkowski, Bob (Athlete, Baseball Player)
1362 Standish Ave
Dayton, OH 45432-3133, USA

Borkowski, David (Dave) (Athlete, Baseball Player)
2124 McIntosh Dr
Holland, OH 43528-7930, USA

Borland, Chris (Athlete, Football Player)
c/o Neil Cornrich *NC Sports, LLC*
best to contact via email
Columbus, OH 43201, USA

Borland, Toby (Athlete, Baseball Player)
8642 Quitman Hwy
Quitman, LA 71268-1282, USA

Borland, Tom (Athlete, Baseball Player)
624 W Cherokee Ave
Stillwater, OK 74075-1405, USA

Borle, Christian (Actor)
c/o Peter Kiernan *Free Association*
9111 Wilshire Blvd
Beverly Hills, CA 90210-5508, USA

Borlenghi, Matthew (Actor)
654 Portabello Ln
Marietta, GA 30068-4447, USA

Borman, Frank (Astronaut, Business Person)
PO Box 64
Bighorn, MT 59010-0064, USA

Born, Ruth (Athlete, Baseball Player, Commentator)
4205 Meridian Woods Dr
Valparaiso, IN 46385-7014, USA

Bornheimer, Kyle (Actor, Comedian)
3427 Ben Lomond Pl
Los Angeles, CA 90027-2908, USA

Bornstein, Jonathan (Athlete, Soccer Player)
c/o Lyle York *Proactive Sports Management USA*
3233 M St NW
Washington, DC 20007-3556, USA

Borntrager, Mary Christner (Writer)
c/o Staff Member *Herald Press*
616 Walnut Ave
Scottdale, PA 15683-1992, USA

Boron, Kathrin (Athlete)
Potsdamer RG
An Der Pirschheide
Potsdam 14471, GERMANY

Boros, Guy (Athlete, Golfer)
2900 NE 40th St
Ft Lauderdale, FL 33308-5743, USA

Borotsik, Jack (Athlete, Hockey Player)
Lakeview Road
Onanole, MB ROJ 1NO, Canada

Borowski, Joe (Athlete, Baseball Player)
13782 E Gail Rd
Scottsdale, AZ 85259-4642, USA

Borrego, Jesse (Actor)
c/o Kay Liberman *Liberman/Zerman Management*
252 N Larchmont Blvd Ste 200
Los Angeles, CA 90004-3754, USA

Borrero, Alejandra (Actor)
c/o Gabriel Blanco *Gabriel Blanco Iglesias (Mexico)*
Rio Balsas 35-32
Colonia Cuauhtemoc
DF 06500, Mexico

Borresen, Richard (Athlete, Football Player)
2291 Jefferson St
East Meadow, NY 11554-1907, USA

Borris, Angel (Actor)
c/o Lara Rosenstock *Lara Rosenstock Management*
8371 Blackburn Ave Apt 1
Los Angeles, CA 90048-4245, USA

Borsato, Luciano (Athlete, Hockey Player)
200-4 Tortoise Crt
Brampton, ON L6P 0A1, Canada

Borsavage, Ike (Athlete, Basketball Player)
5265 Roseberry Dr
Doylestown, PA 18902-1078, USA

Borschevsky, Nikolai (Athlete, Hockey Player)
3 Geranium Crt
Richmond Hill, ON L4C 7M7, Canada

Borschman, Laurie (Athlete, Hockey Player)
27 Delamere Dr
Stittsville, ON K2S 1G7, Canada

Borstein, Alex (Actor, Comedian)
c/o Maria Herrera *PMK/BNC Public Relations*
1840 Century Park E Ste 1400
Los Angeles, CA 90067-2115, USA

Borth, Michelle (Actor)
c/o Mark Rousso *Industry Entertainment Partners*
955 Carrillo Dr Ste 300
Los Angeles, CA 90048-5400, USA

Bortles, Blake (Athlete, Football Player)
c/o Ryan Tollner *REP 1 Sports Group*
80 Technology Dr
Irvine, CA 92618-2301, USA

Bortnick, Ethan (Actor, Musician)
c/o Michael Katcher *Creative Artists Agency (CAA)*
2000 Avenue of the Stars Ste 100
Los Angeles, CA 90067-4705, USA

Borton, Della (D B) (Writer)
Ohio Wesleyan University
Dept of English
Delaware, OH 43015, USA

Bortz, Mark (Athlete, Football Player)
PO Box 3504
Quincy, IL 62305-3504, USA

Boryla, Mike (Athlete, Football Player)
6092 Blue Terrace Cir
Castle Pines, CO 80108-8153, USA

Borzov, Valeri F (Athlete, Track Athlete)
Sport & Youth Ministry
Esplanadna St 42
Kiev 23 252023, UKRAINE

Bosa, John (Athlete, Football Player)
2101 NE 21st St
Ft Lauderdale, FL 33305-2522, USA

Bosarge, Wade (Athlete, Football Player)
8366 Via Rosa
Orlando, FL 32836-8788, USA

Bosch, Don (Athlete, Baseball Player)
14446 N State Highway 3
Fort Jones, CA 96032-9773, USA

Boschetti, Ryan (Athlete, Football Player)
c/o Brian Mackler *Sportstars Inc*
1370 Avenue of the Americas Fl 19
New York, NY 10019-4602, USA

Boschman, Laurie (Athlete, Hockey Player)
27 Delamere Dr
Stittsville, ON K2S 1G7, Canada

Bose, Eleanora (Model)
I M G Models
304 Park Ave S # 1200
New York, NY 10010-4301, USA

Bose, Miguel (Actor, Music Group, Songwriter, Writer)
RLM Producciones
Puerto Santa Maria 65
Madrid 28043, SPAIN

Bose, Priyanka (Actor)
c/o Siri Garber *Platform PR*
2666 N Beachwood Dr
Los Angeles, CA 90068-2308, USA

Bose, Rahul (Actor, Writer)
APM - Alpita Patel

Bose, Shonali (Director, Producer)
c/o Chaitanya Hegde *Tulsea*
93-B Mittal Ct
Mumbai MH 400021, INDIA

Boselll, Tony (Athlete, Football Player)
6 Glendenning Ln
Houston, TX 77024-6827, USA

Boselli, Pietro (Model)

Boselli, Tony (Athlete, Football Player)
356 San Juan Dr
Ponte Vedra Beach, FL 32082-2821, USA

Boseman, Chadwick (Actor)
c/o Nicki Fioravante *Viewpoint Inc*
8820 Wilshire Blvd Ste 220
Beverly Hills, CA 90211-2622, USA

Bosetti, Rick (Athlete, Baseball Player)
1471 Arroyo Manor Dr
Redding, CA 96003-9215, USA

Bosh, Chris (Athlete, Basketball Player)
c/o Danica Smith *Kovert Creative*
506 Santa Monica Blvd Ste 400
Santa Monica, CA 90401-2412, USA

Bosher, Matt (Athlete, Football Player)

Bosio, Chris (Athlete, Baseball Player)
Lawrence University
417 Hidden Ridges Way
Attn: Baseball Office
Combined Locks, WI 54113-1337, USA

Boskie, Shawn (Athlete, Baseball Player)
10220 N 55th St
Paradise Valley, AZ 85253-1168, USA

Boskovitch, Katie (Actor)
c/o Jon Orlando *Exposure Marketing Group*
348 Hauser Blvd Apt 414
Los Angeles, CA 90036-5590, USA

Bosley, Thad (Athlete, Baseball Player)
20660 Stevens Creek Blvd
Cupertino, CA 95014-2120, USA

Bosman, Dick (Athlete, Baseball Player)
3511 Landmark Trl
Palm Harbor, FL 34684-5015, USA

Boso, Casper (Athlete, Football Player)
8811 Calumet Dr
Indianapolis, IN 46236-9031, USA

Boss, Stephen (Twitch) (Actor, Dancer, DJ)
c/o Staff Member *Ellen DeGeneres Show*
3500 W Olive Ave Ste 1000
Burbank, CA 91505-5515, USA

Bosseler, Don J (Athlete, Football Player)
7782 SW 54th Ave
Miami, FL 33143-5851, USA

Bosson, Barbara (Actor)
742 Milwood Ave
Venice, CA 90291-3829, USA

Bossy, Michael (Mike) (Athlete, Hockey Player)
New York Islanders
200 Merrick Ave
East Meadow, NY 11554-1596, Canada

Bostelle, Tom (Artist)
Aeolian Palace Gallery
PO Box 8
Pocopson, PA 19366-0008, USA

Bostic, Jeff (Athlete, Football Player)
8250 Royal Saint Georges Ln
Duluth, GA 30097-1649, USA

Bostic, Jim (Athlete, Basketball Player)
111 Valentine Ln Apt 2D
Yonkers, NY 10705-3426, USA

Bostic, Joe (Athlete, Football Player)
3507 Bromley Wood Ln
Greensboro, NC 27410-2182, USA

Bostic, John (Athlete, Football Player)
611 Canaveral Ave
Titusville, FL 32796-7615, USA

Bostic, Jon (Athlete, Football Player)
c/o Tony Paige *Dream Point Sports*
1455 Pennsylvania Ave NW Ste 225
Washington, DC 20004-1026, USA

Bostic, Keith (Athlete, Football Player)
2419 Duchess Way
Stafford, TX 77477-6227, USA

Bostick, Brandon (Athlete, Football Player)
c/o Blake Baratz *The Institute for Athletes*
3600 Minnesota Dr Ste 550
Edina, MN 55435-7925, USA

Bostick, Devon (Actor)
c/o Norbert Abrams *Noble Caplan Abrams*
1260 Yonge St Fl 2
Toronto, ON M4T 1W5, CANADA

Boston (Music Group)
c/o Staff Member *Agency for the Performing Arts (APA)*
405 S Beverly Dr Ste 500
Beverly Hills, CA 90212-4425, USA

Boston, Daryl (Athlete, Baseball Player)
3136 Northchester Pl
Lithonia, GA 30038-2292, USA

Boston, David (Athlete, Football Player)
5580 SW 104th Ter
Cooper City, FL 33328-5635, USA

Boston, Lawrence (Athlete, Basketball Player)
93 Greencliff Dr
Bedford, OH 44146-3439, USA

Boston, McKinley (Athlete, Football Player)
PO Box 1303
Williamston, NC 27892-1303, USA

Boston, McKinley (Athlete, Football Player)
PO Box 1303
Williamston, NC 27892-1303, us

Boston, Rachel (Actor)
c/o Elizabeth Much *East 2 West Collective*
11022 Santa Monica Blvd Ste 350
Los Angeles, CA 90025-7532, USA

Boston, Ralph (Athlete, Olympic Athlete)
3301 Woodbine Ave
Knoxville, TN 37914-4448, USA

Boston, Tre (Athlete, Football Player)
c/o Bus Cook *Bus Cook Sports, Inc*
1 Willow Bend Dr
Hattiesburg, MS 39402-8552, USA

Bostridge, Ian (Musician)
c/o Staff Member *ICM Partners*
10250 Constellation Blvd Fl 7
Los Angeles, CA 90067-6207, USA

Bostrom, Zachary (Actor)
c/o Mike Baldridge *Momentum Talent and Literary Agency*
3500 W Olive Ave Ste 300
Burbank, CA 91505-4647, USA

Bostwick, Barry (Actor, Musician)
c/o Staff Member *Vanguard Management Group*
8060 Melrose Ave Fl 4
Los Angeles, CA 90046-7038, USA

Bostwick, Dunbar (Race Car Driver)
1623 Dewey Ave
Pompano Beach, FL 33060, USA

Boswell, Ken (Athlete, Baseball Player)
1103 Live Oak Dr
Marble Falls, TX 78654-7258, USA

Boswell, Thomas M (Writer)
Washington Post
1150 15th St NW
Washington, DC 20071-0002, USA

Boswell, Tom (Athlete, Basketball Player)
341 N Anton Dr
Montgomery, AL 36105-2112, USA

Bosworth, Brian (Actor, Athlete, Football Player)
8400 Hickory St Unit 952
Frisco, TX 75034-5595, USA

Bosworth, Kate (Actor)
c/o Jamie Arons *Rogers & Cowan*
1840 Century Park E Fl 18
Los Angeles, CA 90067-2101, USA

Bosworth, Lauren (Lo) (Reality Star)
c/o Bradley Singer *WME/IMG (NY)*
11 Madison Ave Fl 18
New York, NY 10010-3669, USA

Botchan, Ron (Athlete, Football Player)
55 Toscana Way E
Rancho Mirage, CA 92270-1977, USA

Botehho, Joao (Director)
Assicuacai de Realizadores
Rua de Palmeira 7 R/C
Lisbon 01200, PORTUGAL

Botelho, Derek (Athlete, Baseball Player)
1819 Orchard St
Burlington, IA 52601-6136, USA

Botero, Fernando (Artist)
2 Rue Honore Labarde
Principaute De Monaco 98 000, Monaco

Botha, Francois (Frans) (Boxer)
White Buffalo
PO Box 3982
Clearwater, FL 33767-8982, USA

Botha, Pieter W (President)
Die Anker
Wildemess, 6560 SOUTH AFRICA

Bothwell, Tim (Athlete, Coach, Hockey Player)
1769 7 Ave NW
Calgary, AB T2N 0Z5, CANADA

Botkin, Kirk (Athlete, Football Player)
7210 Shadow Brk
Texarkana, TX 75503-5450, USA

Botsford, Beth (Athlete, Olympic Athlete, Swimmer)
2210 River Bend Ct
White Hall, MD 21161-9214, USA

Botsford, Sara (Actor)
Kordek Agency
8490 W Sunset Blvd # 403
West Hollywood, CA 90069-1912, USA

Bottalico, Ricky (Athlete, Baseball Player)
37 Valley View Dr
Newington, CT 06111-5309, USA

Bottenfield, Kent (Athlete, Baseball Player)
12168 142nd Ct N
West Palm Beach, FL 33418-7901, USA

Botterill, Jason (Athlete, Hockey Player)
65 Middlesex Rd
Buffalo, NY 14216-3617, USA

Botti, Chris (Musician)
c/o Bobby Colomby *The Colomby Group*
4115 Glencoe Ave Apt 114
Marina Del Rey, CA 90292-3800, USA

Botting, Ralph (Athlete, Baseball Player)
7 Somerset
Trabuco Canyon, CA 92679-3701, USA

Botto, Juan Diego (Actor)
c/o David Koth *Untitled Entertainment*
350 S Beverly Dr Ste 200
Beverly Hills, CA 90212-4819, USA

Bottom, Joe (Swimmer)
PO Box 3840
Chico, CA 95927-3840, USA

Bottom, Joseph (Athlete, Olympic Athlete, Swimmer)
PO Box 3840
Chico, CA 95927-3840, USA

Bottoms, Joseph (Actor)
c/o Belle Zwerdling *Progressive Artists Agency*
9696 Culver Blvd Ste 110
Culver City, CA 90232-2737, USA

Bottoms, Timothy (Actor)
532 Hot Springs Rd
Montecito, CA 93108-2014, USA

Bottrell, David Dean (Actor, Writer)
c/o Alan Gasmer *Alan Gasmer Management Company*
10877 Wilshire Blvd Ste 603
Los Angeles, CA 90024-4348, USA

Botts, Jason (Athlete, Baseball Player)
405 Peachtree Ln
Paso Robles, CA 93446-2869, USA

Botts, Mike (Athlete, Football Player)
PO Box 247
105 S MARKET ST
Elizabethville, PA 17023-0247, USA

Botz, Bob (Athlete, Baseball Player)
14229 Desert Fire Ct
Horizon City, TX 79928-6422, USA

Boublil, Alain A (Songwriter, Writer)
Cameron Mackintosh Ltd
1 Bedford Square
London WCIB 3RA, UNITED KINGDOM (UK)

Boucha, Henry (Athlete, Hockey Player, Olympic Athlete)
7200 Biglerville Cir
Anchorage, AK 99507-2885, USA

Bouchard, Dan (Athlete, Hockey Player)
3111 Hillsdale Ct SE
Marietta, GA 30067-5431, USA

Bouchard, Daniel (Athlete, Hockey Player)
3111 Hillsdale Ct SE
Marietta, GA 30067-5431, USA

Bouchard, Eugenie (Athlete, Tennis Player)
c/o Fernando Soler *IMG (Spain)*
Via Augusta 200
Floor 4
Barcelona E-8021, SPAIN

Bouchard, Joel (Athlete, Hockey Player)
Club de Hockey Junior de Montreal
1410 Stanley St Suite 602
ATTN COACHING STAFF MONTREAL
Montreal, QC H3A 1P8, Canada

Bouchard, Ken (Race Car Driver)
520 Fairmount St
Fitchburg, MA 01420-5081, USA

Bouchard, Marc (Producer)
c/o Staff Member *Cirque du Soleil Inc*
8400 2e Av
Montreal, QC H1Z 4M6, CANADA

Bouchard, Pierre (Athlete, Hockey Player)
208 Marie-Victorian
Vercheres, QC J0L 2R0, Canada

Bouchard, Pierre-Marc (Athlete, Hockey Player)
9950 Wellington Ln
Woodbury, MN 55125-8459, USA

Bouchard, Ron (Race Car Driver)
300 Lunenburg St
Fitchburg, MA 01420-4504, USA

Bouchee, Ed (Athlete, Baseball Player)
1621 E Tremaine Ave
Gilbert, AZ 85234-8140, USA

Boucher, Brian (Athlete, Hockey Player)
3009 Allansford Ln
Raleigh, NC 27613-5468, USA

Boucher, Denis (Athlete, Baseball Player)
201-644 36e Av
Lachine, QC H8T 3M1, Canada

Boucher, Gaetan (Speed Skater)
Center Sportif
3850 Edger
Saint Hubert, QC J4T 368, CANADA

Boucher, Guy (Athlete, Hockey Player)
Tampa Bay Lightning
401 Channelside Dr
Attn Coaching Staff
Tampa, FL 33602-5400, USA

Boucher, Guy (Athlete, Hockey Player)
7211 Chatsworth Ct
University Park, FL 34201-2363, USA

Boucher, Philippe (Athlete, Hockey Player)
533 Rue Tessier
Rimouski, QC G5L 4L8, Canada

Boucher, Philippe (Athlete, Hockey Player)
Rimouski Oceanic Hockey Club
CP 816 Succ A
MANAGER
Rimouski, QC G5L 7C9, Canada

Boucher, Savannah (Actor)
H W A Talent
3500 W Olive Ave Ste 1400
Burbank, CA 91505-5512, USA

Bouchet, Barbara (Actor)

Bouchez, Elodie (Actor)
c/o Scott Zimmerman *Scott Zimmerman Management*
901 N Highland Ave
Los Angeles, CA 90038-2412, USA

Bouck, Brittany Paige (Actor)
c/o Henry Penner *Penner PR*
8225 Santa Monica Blvd
West Hollywood, CA 90046-5912

Boudia, David (Athlete, Olympic Athlete)
USA Diving Inc
201 S Capitol Ave
Pan American Plaza #430
Indianapolis, IN 46225-1000, USA

Boudreau, Bruce (Athlete, Hockey Player)
PO Box 59727
Potomac, MD 20859-9727, USA

Boudreau, Bruce (Athlete, Hockey Player)
627 N Glebe Rd Ste 850
Attn: Coaching Staff
Arlington, VA 22203-2129, United States

Boudrias, Andre (Athlete, Hockey Player)
1008-4300 Place des Cageux
Laval, QC H7W 4Z3, Canada

Bouette, Marc (Athlete, Football Player)
8787 Sienna Springs Blvd Apt 334
Missouri City, TX 77459-6070, USA

Bouffard, Danielle (Actor)

Bouffard, Danielle (Actor)
c/o Staff Member *King Talent*
36 Tiverton Ave
Toronto, ON M4M 2L9, Canada

Bouganim, Shirley (Model)
c/o Staff Member *Modelwerk Modelagentur GmbH*
Rothenbaum Chaussee 1
Hamburg 20148, Germany

Bouggess, Lee (Athlete, Football Player)
171 Villa Knoll Ct
Sicklerville, NJ 08081-2923, USA

Boughner, Barry (Athlete, Hockey Player)
52 Locke Ave
St Thomas, ON N5P 3X7, Canada

Boughner, Bob (Athlete, Hockey Player)
c/o Staff Member *Windsor Spitfires*
334 Wyandotte St E
Windsor, ON N9A 3H6, Canada

Boujenah, Michel (Actor)
c/o Staff Member *ArtMedia*
8 rue Danielle Casanova
Paris 75002, FRANCE

Boukadakis, Joey (Director, Producer, Writer)
c/o Michael Lasker *Mosaic Media Group*
407 N Maple Dr # 100
Beverly Hills, CA 90210-3818, USA

Boulanger, Pierre (Actor)
c/o Paul Nelson *Mosaic Media Group*
407 N Maple Dr # 100
Beverly Hills, CA 90210-3818, USA

Bouldin, Carl (Athlete, Baseball Player)
42 Fairway Dr
Southgate, KY 41071-3024, USA

Boulerice, Jesse (Athlete, Hockey Player)
900 Queensferry Rd
Cary, NC 27511-6423, USA

Boullion, Jean-Christophe (Race Car Driver)
Pescarolo
40 bis rue fabert
Paris F-75007, France

Boulos, Frenchy (Soccer Player)
20 Elvin St
Staten Island, NY 10314-4049, USA

Boulter, Roy (Actor, Producer)
c/o Peter MacFarlane *MacFarlane Chard (UK)*
113 Kingsway
London WC2B 6PP, UNITED KINGDOM

Boulton, Eric (Athlete, Hockey Player)
1867 Misty Woods Dr
Duluth, GA 30097-8108, USA

Boulud, Daniel (Chef)
Daniel Restaurant
60 E 65th St
New York, NY 10065-7056, USA

Boulware, Michael (Athlete, Football Player)
c/o Eugene Parker *Independent Sports & Entertainment (ISE-IN)*
6435 W Jefferson Blvd # 197
Fort Wayne, IN 46804-6203, USA

Boulware, Peter (Athlete, Football Player)
305 Leaning Tree Rd
Columbia, SC 29223-3010, USA

Bouman, Todd (Athlete, Football Player)
3070 Dartmouth Dr
Excelsior, MN 55331-7849, USA

Bouquet, Carole (Actor, Model)
Agents Associes Beaume
201 Faubourg Saint Honore
Paris 75008, FRANCE

Bourbeau, Allen (Athlete, Hockey Player, Olympic Athlete)
3539 Muirfield Dr
Titusville, FL 32780-3408, USA

Bourbonnais, Rick (Athlete, Hockey Player)
643 E Parkway Ct
Boise, ID 83706-6526, USA

Bourbonnals, Rick (Athlete, Hockey Player)
643 E Parkway Ct
Boise, ID 83706-6526, USA

Bource, Ludovic (Musician)
c/o Vasi Vangelos *First Artists Management*
4764 Park Granada Ste 110
Calabasas, CA 91302-3321, USA

Bourdeaux, Michael (Religious Leader)
Keston College
Heathfield Road Keston
Kent BR2 6BA, UNITED KINGDOM (UK)

Bourdian, Anthony (Chef)
Food Network
1180 Avenue of the Americas Ste 1220 # 1200
New York, NY 10036-8406, USA

Boures, Emil (Athlete, Football Player)
426 W Swissvale Ave
Pittsburgh, PA 15218-1637, USA

Bourgeois, Charles (Athlete, Hockey Player)
PO Box 1481 Stn Main
Stn Main
Moncton, NB E1C 8T6, Canada

Bourgeois, Charlie (Athlete, Hockey Player)
PO Box 1481 Stn Main
Moncton, NB E1C 8T6, Canada

Bourgeois, Jason (Athlete, Baseball Player)
16755 Ella Blvd
Ant 178
Houston, TX 77090-4224, USA

Bourgeois, Steve (Athlete, Baseball Player)
PO Box 143
Paulina, LA 70763-0143, USA

Bourgignon, Serge (Director)
18 Rue de General-Malterre
Paris 75016, FRANCE

Bourgoin, Louise (Actor)
c/o Jessica Kovacevic *WME|IMG*
9601 Wilshire Blvd
Beverly Hills, CA 90210-5213, USA

Bourjos, Chris (Athlete, Baseball Player)
10345 E Dreyfus Ave
Scottsdale, AZ 85260-9006, USA

Bourn, Michael (Athlete, Baseball Player)
14 Philbrook Way
The Woodlands, TX 77382-1378, USA

Bourne, Bob (Athlete, Hockey Player)
Bob Bourne Realty
1-1890 Cooper Rd
Kelowna, BC V1Y 8B7, Canada

Bourne, JR (Actor)
c/o Murray Gibson *Red Management*
415 Esplanade W Box 3
North Vancouver, BC V7M 1A6, CANADA

Bourne, Shae-Lynn (Figure Skater)
Connecticut Skating Center
300 Alumni Rd
Newington, CT 06111-1868, USA

Bournigal, Rafael (Athlete, Baseball Player)
230 Canterwood Ln
Mulberry, FL 33860-7637, USA

Bournissen, Chantal (Skier)
1983 Evolene
SWITZERLAND

Bourque, Pat (Athlete, Baseball Player)
PO Box 17593
Munds Park, AZ 86017-7593, USA

Bourque, Phil (Athlete, Hockey Player)
2000 Landmark Dr Unit 2105
Aliquippa, PA 15001-7318, USA

Bourque, Phil (Athlete, Hockey Player)
Pittsburgh Penguins
66 Mario Lemieux Pl Ste 2
Attn: Broadcast Dept
Pittsburgh, PA 15219-3504, USA

Bourque, Raymond J (Athlete, Hockey Player)
Tresca Restaurant
233 Hanover St
Boston, MA 02113-2310, USA

Bourque, Rene (Athlete, Hockey Player)
9110 93
Lac la Biche, AB TOA 2CO, Canada

Bourret, Caprice (Actor)
c/o Nadja Koglin *Richard Schwartz Management*
2934 1/2 N Beverly Glen Cir # 107
Los Angeles, CA 90077-1724, USA

Boushka, Dick (Athlete, Basketball Player, Olympic Athlete)
9844 Cypresswood Dr Apt 1803
Houston, TX 77070-3858, USA

Boutella, Sofia (Actor)
c/o Kate Buckley *42 Management (UK)*
8 Flitcroft St
London WC2H 8DL, UNITED KINGDOM

Boutette, Pat (Athlete, Hockey Player)
The Doctors House Restaurant
21 Nashville Road
Kleinburg, ON L0J 1C0, Canada

Boutiette, K C (Athlete, Olympic Athlete, Speed Skater)
1911 E 72nd St
Tacoma, WA 98404-5408, USA

Boutilier, Paul (Athlete, Hockey Player)
79 Lakemist Crt
Dartmouth, NS B3A 4Z1, Canada

Bouton, Jim (Athlete, Baseball Player)
PO Box 909
North Egremont, MA 01230-0909, USA

Boutte, Denise (Actor)
c/o Charles Newman *Newman-Thomas Management*
8306 Wilshire Blvd # 996
Beverly Hills, CA 90211-2304, USA

Boutte, Marc (Athlete, Football Player)
906 Derby Ln
Missouri City, TX 77489-3260, us

Boutwell, Thomas (Athlete, Football Player)
32353 Oaken Wood St
Denham Springs, LA 70726-1666, USA

Boutwell, Tommy (Athlete, Football Player)
32353 Oaken Wood St
Denham Springs, LA 70726-1666, us

Bouvet, Didier (Skier)
Bouvet-Sports
Abondance 74360, FRANCE

Bouwmeester, Jay (Athlete, Hockey Player)
McQuaig Desrochers LLP
28 Greenoch Cres NW
Attn Bryon Baltimore
Edmonton, AB T6L 1B4, Canada

Bouyer, Willie (Athlete, Football Player)
6560 Chesterbrook Dr
Elk Grove, CA 95758-6326, USA

Bouza, Matt (Athlete, Football Player)
1042 Via Nueva
Lafayette, CA 94549-2726, USA

Bouzeos, Phil (Athlete, Football Player)
10 Pembroke Ln
Oak Brook, IL 60523-1727, USA

Bova, Raoul (Actor)
c/o Alan Siegel *Alan Siegel Entertainment*
9200 W Sunset Blvd Ste 804
West Hollywood, CA 90069-3603, USA

Bovee, Mike (Athlete, Baseball Player)
11405 Affinity Ct Unit 236
San Diego, CA 92131-2718, USA

Boven, Don (Athlete, Basketball Player)
4434 Garth Rd
Charlottesville, VA 22901-5103, USA

Bowa, Lawrence R (Larry) (Athlete, Baseball Player, Coach)
302 Overlook Ln
Conshohocken, PA 19428-2634, USA

Bowab, John (Actor)
2598 Greenvalley Rd
Los Angeles, CA 90046-1438, USA

Bowdell III, Gordon (Athlete, Football Player)
14615 Harrison Ave
Allen Park, MI 48101-1802, USA

Bowden, Craig (Athlete, Golfer)
4651 S Amber Dr
Bloomington, IN 47401-8359, USA

Bowden, James (Commentator)
172 Capitol Island Rd
Southport, ME 04576-3241, USA

Bowden, Joe (Athlete, Football Player)
7026 Thistlewood Park Ct
Katy, TX 77494-4252, us

Bowden, Katrina (Actor)
c/o William Choi *Management 360*
9111 Wilshire Blvd
Beverly Hills, CA 90210-5508, USA

Bowden, Mark (Director, Writer)
c/o Ron Bernstein *ICM Partners*
10250 Constellation Blvd Fl 7
Los Angeles, CA 90067-6207, USA

Bowden, Michael (Athlete, Baseball Player)
2611 Cheshire Dr
Aurora, IL 60504-5237

Bowden, Robert (Bobby) (Athlete, Coach, Football Coach, Football Player)
2813 Shamrock St
Tallahassee, FL 32309, USA

Bowden, Terry (Coach, Football Coach, Sportscaster)
ABC-TV
77 W 66th St
New York, NY 10023-6201, USA

Bowden, Tommy (Coach, Football Coach)
Clemson University
Athletic Dept
Clemson, SC 29364, USA

Bowe, David (Actor)
c/o Staff Member *Commercial Talent*
12711 Ventura Blvd Ste 285
Studio City, CA 91604-2487, USA

Bowe, Dwayne (Athlete, Football Player)
2520 NE Bitter Creek Ct
Lees Summit, MO 64086-7100, us

Bowe, Riddick (Athlete, Boxer)
714 Amer Dr
Fort Washington, MD 20744-5943, USA

Bowe, Rosemarie (Actor)
321 St Pierre Rd
Los Angeles, CA 90077-3432, USA

Bowen, Andrea (Actor)
c/o Carri McClure *McClure and Associates Public Relations*
10153 1/2 Riverside Dr # 686
Toluca Lake, CA 91602-2561, USA

Bowen, Bruce (Athlete, Basketball Player)
1810 Settlers Ct
San Antonio, TX 78258-4764, USA

Bowen, Clare (Actor, Musician)
c/o Cielo Alano *Activist Artists Management (LA)*
8500 Melrose Ave # 200
W Hollywood, CA 90069-5145, USA

Bowen, Jason (Athlete, Hockey Player)
4900 W 14th Ave
Kennewick, WA 99338-1723, USA

Bowen, Jimmy (Music Group, Musician)
PO Box 454
Lebanon, TN 37088-0454, USA

Bowen, Julie (Actor)
c/o Kay Liberman *Liberman/Zerman Management*
252 N Larchmont Blvd Ste 200
Los Angeles, CA 90004-3754, USA

Bowen, Michael (Actor)
c/o Staff Member *SMS Talent*
8383 Wilshire Blvd Ste 230
Beverly Hills, CA 90211-2436, USA

Bowen, Nanci (Athlete, Golfer)
193 Tucker Rd
Macon, GA 31210-4423, USA

Bowen, Pamela (Actor)
c/o Staff Member *Henderson Hogan Agency (LA)*
8929 Wilshire Blvd Ste 312
Beverly Hills, CA 90211-1969, USA

Bowen, Rob (Athlete, Baseball Player)
389 Knight Dr
Ellijay, GA 30540-4381, USA

Bowen, Ryan (Athlete, Baseball Player)
3702 Frankford Rd Apt 18203
Dallas, TX 75287-7811, USA

Bowen, Sam (Athlete, Baseball Player)
8219 Victory Trl
Brentwood, TN 37027-7374, USA

Bowen, Stephen (Athlete, Football Player)
c/o Pat Dye Jr *SportsTrust Advisors*
3340 Peachtree Rd NE Fl 16
Atlanta, GA 30326-1000, USA

Bowen, Stephen G Cdr (Astronaut)
508 Oak Dr
Friendswood, TX 77546-5531, USA

Bowen, Wade (Musician)

Bowens, David (Athlete, Football Player)
12900 SW 33rd Dr
Davie, FL 33330-1246, USA

Bowens, Tim (Athlete, Football Player)
PO Box 93
Okolona, MS 38860-0093, USA

Bowens, Tom (Athlete, Basketball Player)
304 Martin Luther King St
Okolona, MS 38860-1330, USA

Bower, Antoinette (Actor)
1529 N Beverly Glen Blvd
Los Angeles, CA 90077-3129, USA

Bower, Michael (Actor)
c/o Karen Ammond *KBC Media Relations*
230 Kings Hwy E # 121
Haddonfield, NJ 08033-1907, USA

Bowers, Brent (Athlete, Baseball Player)
19257 Manchester Dr
Mokena, IL 60448-7747, USA

Bowers, Chris (Actor)
c/o Staff Member *Gersh*
9465 Wilshire Blvd Ste 600
Beverly Hills, CA 90212-2605, USA

Bowers, Dane (Actor, Musician)
Penshurst Place
90-92 SouthBridge Rd
Croydon, Surrey CRO 1AF, UNITED KINGDOM

Bowers, Da'Quan (Athlete, Football Player)
c/o Joe Flanagan *BTI Sports Advisors*
615 South Blvd Apt C
Oak Park, IL 60302-4606, USA

Bowers, John W (Religious Leader)
Foursquare Gospel Int'l Church
1100 Glendale Blvd
Los Angeles, CA 90026-3203, USA

Bowers, RJ (Athlete, Football Player)
109 Waterside Ln
Cross Junction, VA 22625-2469, USA

Bowers, Sam (Athlete, Football Player)
11211 John F Kennedy Dr Apt 311
Hagerstown, MD 21742-6768, USA

Bowers, Scotty (Writer)
c/o Staff Member *Grove / Atlantic, Inc*
841 Broadway Fl 4
New York, NY 10003-4704, USA

Bowers, Shane (Athlete, Baseball Player)
542 S Rancho Alegre Dr
Covina, CA 91724-3324, USA

Bowers, William (Athlete, Football Player)
43295 Lacovia Dr
Bermuda Dunes, CA 92203-8016, USA

Bowersox, Crystal (Musician)
c/o Susie Giang *Agency for the Performing Arts (APA-TN)*
150 4th Ave N Ste 2300
Nashville, TN 37219-2466, USA

Bowersox, Kenneth D (Astronaut)
16907 Soaring Forest Dr
Houston, TX 77059-4003, USA

Bowersox, Kenneth D Captain (Astronaut)
16907 Soaring Forest Dr
Houston, TX 77059-4003, USA

Bowes, Margie (Musician)
1502 Brentwood Pt
Brentwood, TN 37027-2801, USA

Bowick, Tony (Athlete, Football Player)
PO Box 234
Slocomb, AL 36375-0234

Bowick, Vantonio (Athlete, Football Player)
PO Box 234
Slocomb, AL 36375-0234, USA

Bowie, Heather (Athlete, Golfer)
3017 Elm River Dr
Ft Worth, TX 76116-0697, USA

Bowie, Jim (Athlete, Baseball Player)
1241 Swan Lake Dr
Fairfield, CA 94533-8137, USA

Bowie, John Ross (Actor, Comedian)
976 Sanborn Ave
Los Angeles, CA 90029-3061, USA

Bowie, Larry D (Athlete, Football Player)
739 Echo Shores Ct
Saint Paul, MN 55115-1473, USA

Bowie, Larry G (Athlete, Football Player)
260 Clarence St
Saint Paul, MN 55106-6572, USA

Bowie, Micah (Athlete, Baseball Player)
1710 Oak Rock
New Braunfels, TX 78132-3827, USA

Bowie, Michael (Athlete, Football Player)
c/o Peter Schaffer *Authentic Athletix*
400 S Steele St Unit 47
Denver, CO 80209-3535, USA

Bowie, Sam (Athlete, Basketball Player, Olympic Athlete)
PO Box 306
Lexington, KY 40588-0306, USA

Bowker, Gordon (Business Person, Writer)
c/o Staff Member *Little, Brown Book Group*
100 Victoria Embankment
London EC4Y 0DY, UK

Bowker, Judi (Actor)
66 Berkeley House 5 Hay Hill
London W1X 7LH, UNITED KINGDOM (UK)

Bowlby, April (Actor)
c/o Brian Wilkins *LINK Entertainment*
11872 La Grange Ave
Los Angeles, CA 90025-5282, USA

Bowler, Grant (Actor)
c/o Beth Holden-Garland *Untitled Entertainment*
350 S Beverly Dr Ste 200
Beverly Hills, CA 90212-4819, USA

Bowles, Brian (Athlete, Baseball Player)
1535 Steinhart Ave
Redondo Beach, CA 90278-2745, USA

Bowles, Charlie (Athlete, Golfer)
42009 Cherry Hill Rd
Novi, MI 48375-2518, USA

Bowles, Crandall C (Business Person)
Springs Industries
205 N White St
Fort Mill, SC 29715-1654, USA

Bowles, Erskine B (Politician)
6725 Old Providence Rd # A
Charlotte, NC 28226-7735, USA

Bowles, Lauren (Actor)
c/o Staff Member *Main Title Entertainment*
8383 Wilshire Blvd Ste 408
Beverly Hills, CA 90211-2435, USA

Bowles, Peter (Actor)
c/o Staff Member *Conway van Gelder Grant*
8-12 Broadwick St
London W1F 8HW, UNITED KINGDOM

Bowlin, Weldon (Hoss) (Athlete, Baseball Player)
PO Box 1026
Livingston, AL 35470-1026, USA

Bowling, Andy (Athlete, Football Player)
7421 Straightstone Rd
Long Island, VA 24569-2945, USA

Bowling, Orbie (Athlete, Basketball Player)
10179 Frank Rd
Collierville, TN 38017-3623, USA

Bowling, Steve (Athlete, Baseball Player)
524 E 117th St S
Jenks, OK 74037-3618, USA

Bowling for Soup (Music Group)
c/o Staff Member *UTA Music/The Agency Group (UK)*
361-373 City Rd
London EC1V 1PQ, UNITED KINGDOM

Bowman, Adarius (Athlete, Football Player)
c/o Brian E. Overstreet *E.O. Sports Management*
1314 Texas St Ste 1212
Houston, TX 77002-3525, USA

Bowman, Elizabeth (Athlete, Golfer)
82 Davidson St
Chula Vista, CA 91910-3002, USA

Bowman, Ernie (Athlete, Baseball Player)
123 Carter Dr Apt 8
Johnson City, TN 37601-2973, USA

Bowman, Jim (Athlete, Football Player)
12 Stony Field Rd
Norton, MA 02766-1143, USA

Bowman, Josh (Actor)
c/o Ruth Young *United Agents*
12-26 Lexington St
London W1F OLE, UNITED KINGDOM

Bowman, Ken (Athlete, Football Player)
13664 N Placita Montanas De Oro
Oro Valley, AZ 85755-8687, USA

Bowman, Kirk (Athlete, Hockey Player)
740 Point Pelee Dr
740 Point Pelee Dr RR 1
Leamington, ON N8H 3V4, Canada

Bowman, Navorro (Athlete, Football Player)
c/o Drew Rosenhaus *Rosenhaus Sports Representation*
3921 Alton Rd # 440
Miami Beach, FL 33140-3852, USA

Bowman, Scotty (Athlete, Coach, Hockey Player)
5760 Midnight Pass Rd Apt 104D
Sarasota, FL 34242-3023, CANADA

Bowman, Zack (Athlete, Football Player)
c/o W Vann McElroy *Select Sports Group*
2700 Post Oak Blvd Ste 1450
Houston, TX 77056-5785, USA

Bown, Chuck (Race Car Driver)
2503 Wedge Pl
Asheboro, NC 27205-0811, USA

Bown, Jim (Race Car Driver)
5045 Old NC 49
Asheboro, NC 27203, USA

Bownass, Rick (Athlete, Hockey Player)
Vancouver Canucks
800 Griffiths Way
Attn Coaching Staff
Vancouver, BC V6B 6G1, Canada

Bownes, Fabien (Athlete, Football Player)
8127 149th Pl NE Unit B112
Redmond, WA 98052-6582, USA

Bowness, Rick (Athlete, Hockey Player)
10 Shadowstone Ln
Lawrence Township, NJ 08648-1027, USA

Bowser, Charles (Athlete, Football Player)
1188 Dovetail Ct
Virginia Beach, VA 23464-8832, us

Bowsfield, Ted (Athlete, Baseball Player)
980 Briar Rose Ln
Nipomo, CA 93444-8989, USA

Bowyer, Clint (Race Car Driver)
828 Woodward Rd
Mocksville, NC 27028-5860, USA

Bowyer, William (Artist)
12 Cleveland Ave Chiswick
London W4 1SN, UNITED KINGDOM (UK)

Bowyer-Chapman, Jeffrey (Actor)
c/o Jaime Misher *Innovative Artists*
235 Park Ave S Fl 7
New York, NY 10003-1405, USA

Bowyer Jr, Walter (Athlete, Football Player)
203 Main St N
Bethlehem, CT 06751-1400, USA

Boxberger, Loa (Politician)
PO Box 708
Russell, KS 67665-0708, USA

Boxer, Barbara (Politician)
136 Yale Dr
Rancho Mirage, CA 92270-3677, USA

Boxerbaum, David (Actor)
c/o Staff Member *Agency for the Performing Arts (APA-TN)*
150 4th Ave N Ste 2300
Nashville, TN 37219-2466, USA

Boxleitner, Bruce (Actor, Writer)
c/o Cheryl Kagan *Cheryl Kagan Public Relations*
100 N Crescent Dr Ste 100
Beverly Hills, CA 90210-5447, USA

Box Tops, The (Music Group)
c/o Staff Member *Rick Levy Management*
Prefers to be contacted by telephone or email
Jacksonville, FL, USA

Boxx, Shannon (Athlete, Olympic Athlete, Soccer Player)
10111 NW Engleman St
Portland, OR 97229-7527, USA

Boy, Soulja (Musician)
Soulja Boy Music
113 Shadow Ln
Batesville, MS 38606-8789, USA

Boyar, Lombardo (Actor)
Greene & Associates
526 N Larchmont Blvd # 201
Los Angeles, CA 90004-1300

Boyarsky, Jerry (Athlete, Football Player)
RR 1 Box 357
Olyphant, PA 18447, USA

Boyce, Cameron (Actor)
c/o Emily Urbani *Osbrink Talent Agency*
4343 Lankershim Blvd # 100
North Hollywood, CA 91602-2705, USA

Boyce, Charles (Cartoonist)
1450 N King Edward Ct Apt 112
Palatine, IL 60067-2661, USA

Boyce, Kim (Music Group)
200 Nathan Dr
Hollister, MO 65672-6123, USA

Boyd, Billy (Actor)
c/o Helen Robinson *United Agents*
12-26 Lexington St
London W1F OLE, UNITED KINGDOM

Boyd, Bobby (Athlete, Football Player)
2105 Lansdowne Dr
Garland, TX 75040-3343, us

Boyd, Brandon (Musician)
515 Marguerita Ave
Santa Monica, CA 90402-1917, USA

Boyd, Brent (Athlete, Football Player)
948 N Coast Highway 101 Apt 185
Encinitas, CA 92024-2078, USA

Boyd, Cayden (Actor)
c/o Staff Member *WME/IMG*
9601 Wilshire Blvd
Beverly Hills, CA 90210-5213, USA

Boyd, Cletis L (Clete) (Baseball Player)
2034 20th Avenue Pkwy
Indian Rocks Beach, FL 33785-2967, USA

Boyd, Danny (Athlete, Football Player)
1709 32nd St W
Bradenton, FL 34205-3147, us

Boyd, Darren (Actor)
c/o Fiona McLoughlin *Independent Talent Group*
40 Whitfield St
London W1T 2RH, UNITED KINGDOM

Boyd, Davis (Oil Can) (Athlete, Baseball Player)
PO Box 8058
Meridian, MS 39303-8058, USA

Boyd, Dennis (Athlete, Baseball Player)
45 Swan St
East Providence, RI 02914-2406, USA

Boyd, Elmo (Athlete, Football Player)
219 S Short St
Troy, OH 45373-3360, USA

Boyd, Fred (Athlete, Basketball Player)
10915 Open Trail Rd
Bakersfield, CA 93311-2892, USA

Boyd, Gary (Athlete, Baseball Player)
15308 Haas Ave
Gardena, CA 90249-4239, USA

Boyd, Greg (Baseball Player)
9 Inez Way
Stafford, VA 22554-5515, USA

Boyd, Greg P (Athlete, Football Player)
5949 E Thomas Rd
Scottsdale, AZ 85251-7505, USA

Boyd, James (Athlete, Football Player)
3355 Sweetwater Rd Apt 10204
Lawrenceville, GA 30044-8544, USA

Boyd, Jason (Athlete, Baseball Player)
7962 State Route 140
Edwardsville, IL 62025-6110, USA

Boyd, Jenna (Actor)
c/o Staff Member *WME/IMG*
9601 Wilshire Blvd
Beverly Hills, CA 90210-5213, USA

Boyd, Johnny (Race Car Driver)
7635 N Gearhart Ave
Fresno, CA 93720-2548, USA

Boyd, Josh (Athlete, Football Player)

Boyd, Lavell (Athlete, Football Player)
4421 Charlotte Ann Dr
Louisville, KY 40216-3403, us

Boyd, Lynda (Actor)
c/o Michael Greene *Greene & Associates*
1901 Avenue of the Stars Ste 130
Los Angeles, CA 90067-6030, USA

Boyd, Malik (Athlete, Football Player)
5815 Fairway Manor Ln
Spring, TX 77373-4988, USA

Boyd, Randy (Athlete, Hockey Player)
1769 Blackwillow Dr
Marietta, GA 30066-1954, USA

Boyd, Robert (Athlete, Golfer)
828 Robert E Lee Dr
Wilmington, NC 28412-7138, USA

Boyd, Stephen (Athlete, Football Player)
6 Hollise Ct
Centerport, NY 11721-1108, USA

Boyd, Tommie (Athlete, Football Player)
46824 Amberwood Dr
Shelby Township, MI 48317-4100, us

Boye, Alex (Musician)
Go Marketing
925 S Fairview Ave
Salt Lake City, UT 84105-1703, USA

Boyega, John (Actor)
c/o Alan Nierob *Rogers & Cowan*
1840 Century Park E Fl 18
Los Angeles, CA 90067-2101, USA

Boyens, Philippa (Writer)
c/o Nick Reed *ICM Partners*
10250 Constellation Blvd Fl 7
Los Angeles, CA 90067-6207, USA

Boyer, Blaine (Athlete, Baseball Player)
4825 Bellingham Dr
Marietta, GA 30062-6412, USA

Boyer, Brant (Athlete, Football Player)
33 Sherwood Ave
Madison, NJ 07940-1758, USA

Boyer, Cloyd (Athlete, Baseball Player)
14528 County Road 210
Jasper, MO 64755-7226, USA

Boyer, Mark (Athlete, Football Player)
21942 Kaneohe Ln
Huntington Beach, CA 92646-7828, USA

Boyer, Verdi (Athlete, Football Player)
300 N Lake Ave Ste 930
Pasadena, CA 91101-4106, USA

Boyer, Wally (Athlete, Hockey Player)
400 Manly St
Midland, ON L4R 3E3, Canada

Boyes, Brad (Athlete, Hockey Player)
11711 Fawnridge Dr
Saint Louis, MO 63131-4235, USA

Boyett, Lon (Athlete, Football Player)
902 W Newgrove St
Lancaster, CA 93534-3012, USA

Boyette, Garland (Athlete, Football Player)
4003 E Valley Dr
Missouri City, TX 77459-4322, USA

Boykin, Brandon (Athlete, Football Player)
c/o Doug Hendrickson *Relativity Sports*
2029 Century Park E Ste 1550
Century City, CA 90067-3000, USA

Boykin, Deral (Athlete, Football Player)
3972 Lake Run Blvd
Stow, OH 44224-4351, USA

Boykin, Gerda (Athlete, Golfer)
3019 Colonnade Ct NW
Albuquerque, NM 87107-2961, USA

Boykin, Jarrett (Athlete, Football Player)
c/o Kevin Poston *Deal LLC*
28025 S Harwich Dr
Farmington Hills, MI 48334-4259, USA

Boyko, Darren (Athlete, Hockey Player)
1341 Wolseley Ave
Winnipeg, MB R3G 1H8, Canada

Boylan, Barbara (Dancer)
7945 S Eudora Cir
Centennial, CO 80122-3844, USA

Boylan, Dean (Athlete, Hockey Player)
14 Powers Rd
Andover, MA 01810-6070, USA

Boylan, Eileen (Actor)

Boylan, Jim (Athlete, Football Player)
1453 Highland Dr
Solana Beach, CA 92075-2101, USA

Boyland, Dorian (Athlete, Baseball Player)
548 Setting Sun Dr
Winter Garden, FL 34787-5933, USA

Boyle, Anthony (Actor)
c/o Donna Mills *Premier PR*
2-4 Bucknall St
London WC2H 8LA, UNITED KINGDOM

Boyle, Brian (Athlete, Hockey Player)
c/o Bobby Orr *The Orr Hockey Group (MA)*
PO Box 290836
Charlestown, MA 02129-0215, USA

Boyle, Clune Charlotte (Swimmer)
50 Browns Grv # 31
Scottsville, NY 14546-1302, USA

Boyle, Dan (Athlete, Hockey Player)
348 Sound Beach Ave
Old Greenwich, CT 06870-1930, USA

Boyle, Danny (Director)
c/o Robert Newman *WME/IMG*
9601 Wilshire Blvd
Beverly Hills, CA 90210-5213, USA

Boyle, Jim (Athlete, Football Player)
920 Beechmeadow Ln
Cincinnati, OH 45238-4350, USA

Boyle, Lara Flynn (Actor)
c/o Gina Rugolo *Rugolo Entertainment*
195 S Beverly Dr Ste 400
Beverly Hills, CA 90212-3044, USA

Boyle, Lisa (Actor, Model)
7336 Santa Monica Blvd # 776
West Hollywood, CA 90046-6670, USA

Boyle, Susan (Musician, Reality Star)
c/o Andy Stephens *Andy Stephens Management*
60A Highgate High St
London N6 5HX, UNITED KINGDOM (UK)

Boyle, T Coraghessan (Writer)
University of Southern California
English Dept
Los Angeles, CA 90089-0001, USA

Boyne, Walter (Writer)
10833 Margate Rd
Silver Spring, MD 20901-1615, USA

Boynes, Winford (Athlete, Basketball Player)
8979 Haflinger Way
Elk Grove, CA 95757-3262, USA

Boynton, George (Athlete, Football Player)
917 Sartain Dr
Andrews, TX 79714-3817, USA

Boynton, John (Athlete, Football Player)
PO Box 468
Pikeville, TN 37367-0468, USA

Boynton, Lucy (Actor)
c/o Olivia Homan *United Agents*
12-26 Lexington St
London W1F OLE, UNITED KINGDOM

Boynton, Nick (Athlete, Hockey Player)
3326 N Valencia Ln
Phoenix, AZ 85018-6611, USA

Boynton, Sandra (Artist, Writer)
c/o Staff Member *Simon & Schuster*
1230 Avenue of the Americas Fl CONC1
New York, NY 10020-1586, USA

Boysaw, Gregory (Athlete, Football Player)
PO Box 501762
Indianapolis, IN 46250-6762, USA

Boys Like Girls (Music Group)
c/o Staff Member *Primary Talent International (UK)*
10-11 Jockeys Fields
The Primary Bldg
London WC1R 4BN, UNITED KINGDOM

Boyz II Men (Music Group)
c/o Joe Mulvihill *LiveWire Entertainment (FL)*
7575 Dr Phillips Blvd Ste 255
Orlando, FL 32819-7220, USA

Boyzone (Music Group)
c/o Staff Member *Solo Agency Ltd (UK)*
53-55 Fulham High St
Fl 2
London SW6 3JJ, UNITED KINGDOM

Bozak, Tyler (Athlete, Hockey Player)
Newport Sports Management
400-201 City Centre Dr
Attn Wade Arnott
Mississauga, ON L5B 2T4, Canada

Bozarth, Marci (Athlete, Golfer)
30417 Briarcliff Dr
Georgetown, TX 78628, USA

Boze, Marshall (Athlete, Baseball Player)
432 Watson St
Davidson, NC 28036-9398, USA

Bozek, Steve (Athlete, Hockey Player)
8410 E Whispering Wind Dr
Scottsdale, AZ 85255-2863, USA

Bozilovic, Ivana (Actor)
c/o Jon Orlando *Exposure Marketing Group*
348 Hauser Blvd Apt 414
Los Angeles, CA 90036-5590, USA

Boznic, Josip Cardinal (Religious Leader)
Zagreb Archdiocese
Kaptol 31 PP 553
Zagreb Hrvatska 10001, CROATIA

Bozo, Laura (Actor)
c/o Staff Member *Telemundo*
2470 W 8th Ave
Hialeah, FL 33010-2000, USA

Bozza, Anthony (Writer)
c/o Staff Member *Random House Publicity (Toronto)*
1 Toronto St Suite 300
Toronto, ON M5C 2V6, Canada

BR5-49 (Music Group, Musician)
c/o Staff Member *Creative Artists Agency (CAA)*
401 Commerce St PH
Nashville, TN 37219-2516, USA

Braakensiek, Annalise (Actor, Model)

Braase, Ordell (Athlete, Football Player)
204 3rd St W Apt 201
Bradenton, FL 34205-8857, USA

Bracco, Lorraine (Actor)
c/o Heather Reynolds *One Entertainment (NY)*
347 5th Ave Rm 1404
New York, NY 10016-5034, USA

Bracelin, Greg (Athlete, Football Player)
5465 Calumet Ave
La Jolla, CA 92037-7604, USA

Bracey, Luke (Actor)
c/o Mark Morrissey *Morrissey Management*
16 Princess Ave
Rosebery
Sydney NSW 02018, AUSTRALIA

Bracht, Stephanie (Athlete, Golfer)
2004 Delancey Dr
Norman, OK 73071-3872, USA

Brack, Kenny (Race Car Driver)
Team Rahal
4601 Lyman Dr
Hilliard, OH 43026-1249, USA

Bracken, Don (Athlete, Football Player)
15950 W Diamond St
Goodyear, AZ 85338-2763, USA

Brackenbury, Curt (Athlete, Hockey Player)
W378N5861 Valley Rd
Oconomowoc, WI 53066-2246, USA

Brackens, Tony (Athlete, Football Player)
193 Private Road 407
Fairfield, TX 75840-6022, USA

Brackett, Gary (Athlete, Football Player)
7808 Parkdale Dr
Zionsville, IN 46077-8012, us

Brackett, Griffin (Model)
860 NE 73rd St
Miami, FL 33138-5228

Brackett, M L (Athlete, Football Player)
1216 Monte Vista Dr
Gadsden, AL 35904-3643, USA

Brackins, Charles (Athlete, Football Player)
7227 Haverton Dr
Apt 1907
Houston, TX 77016-2333, USA

Bradberry, Gary (Race Car Driver)
c/o Tri Star Motorsports
6006 Ball Park Rd
Thomasville, NC 27360-7942, USA

Bradbery, Danielle (Musician)
c/o Laurie Pozmantier *WME|IMG*
9601 Wilshire Blvd
Beverly Hills, CA 90210-5213, USA

Bradbury, Gary (Race Car Driver)
Hoover Motorsports
10705 Bringle Ferry Rd
Salisbury, NC 28146-9576, USA

Bradbury, Janette Lane (Actor)
2760 Arden Rd NW
Atlanta, GA 30327-1260, USA

Braddock, Paige (Cartoonist)
7596 Bodega Ave
Sebastopol, CA 95472-3654, USA

Braddy, Johanna (Actor)
c/o Frank Frattaroli *Circle of Confusion*
8931 Ellis Ave
Los Angeles, CA 90034-3336, USA

Braden, Gregg (Writer)
Wisdom Traditions
PO Box 14668
North Palm Beach, FL 33408-0668, USA

Bradey, Don (Athlete, Baseball Player)
330 Council Bluff Pkwy
Murfreesboro, TN 37127-8317, USA

Bradford, Barbara Taylor (Writer)
Bradford Enterprises
450 Park Ave # 2303
New York, NY 10022-2605, USA

Bradford, Buddy (Athlete, Baseball Player)
6440 Springpark Ave
Los Angeles, CA 90056-2222, USA

Bradford, Carl (Athlete, Football Player)
c/o David Dunn *Athletes First*
23091 Mill Creek Dr
Laguna Hills, CA 92653-1258, USA

Bradford, Chad (Athlete, Baseball Player)
218 Trace Cir
Raymond, MS 39154-9555, USA

Bradford, Corey (Athlete, Football Player)
13002 Highway 955 E
Ethel, LA 70730-3952, us

Bradford, Jesse (Actor)
22 Lowndes Ave
Norwalk, CT 06854-3722, USA

Bradford, Paul (Athlete, Football Player)
2239 Pulgas Ave
East Palo Alto, CA 94303-1755, USA

Bradford, Richard (Actor)
2511 Canyon Dr
Los Angeles, CA 90068-2415, USA

Bradford, Ronnie (Athlete, Football Player)
239 Bridlington St
Sugar Hill, GA 30518-6401, USA

Bradford, Sam (Athlete, Football Player)
c/o Tom Condon *Creative Artists Agency (CAA)*
401 Commerce St PH
Nashville, TN 37219-2516, USA

Bradfute, Byron (Athlete, Football Player)
939 Moonglow Ave
New Braunfels, TX 78130-6081, USA

Bradham, Nigel (Athlete, Football Player)
c/o Mitchell Frankel *Impact Sports (FL)*
2799 NW 2nd Ave Ste 203
Boca Raton, FL 33431-6709, USA

Bradley, Alonzo (Athlete, Basketball Player)
1713 Briaroaks Dr
Flower Mound, TX 75028-3482, USA

Bradley, Bert (Athlete, Baseball Player)
6039 Old State Rd
Mattoon, IL 61938-8815, USA

Bradley, Bill (Basketball Player, Olympic Athlete, Politician)
Betty Sue Flowers
200 Central Park S Apt 15B
New York, NY 10019-1443, USA

Bradley, Bob (Coach, Soccer Player)
Chicago Fire
980 N Michigan Ave Ste 1998
Chicago, IL 60611-7504, USA

Bradley, Brian (Athlete, Hockey Player)
27116 Winged Elm Dr
Wesley Chapel, FL 33544-7773, USA

Bradley, Brian (Astro) (Actor, Musician)
c/o Angela Mach *Platform PR*
2666 N Beachwood Dr
Los Angeles, CA 90068-2308, USA

Bradley, Carlos (Athlete, Football Player)
1316 E Cliveden St
Philadelphia, PA 19119-3948, USA

Bradley, Charles (Athlete, Basketball Player)
10810 Mountshire Cir
Highlands Ranch, CO 80126-7502, USA

Bradley, Christopher (Actor)
c/o Staff Member *Ford/Robert Black Agency*
9300 E Raintree Dr # 115
Scottsdale, AZ 85260-7304, USA

Bradley, Doug (Actor)
c/o Elaine Murphy *Elaine Murphy Associates*
50 High St
#1
London E11 2RJ, UNITED KINGDOM

Bradley, Dudley (Athlete, Basketball Player)
9830 Clanford Rd
Randallstown, MD 21133-2508, USA

Bradley, Ed (Athlete, Football Player)
206 Mossy Oak Dr
Winston Salem, NC 27127-9234, us

Bradley, Frank (Baseball Player)
Kansas City Monarchs
PO Box 516
Benton, LA 71006-0516, USA

Bradley, Gordon (Coach, Soccer Player)
14300 Bakerwood Pl
Haymarket, VA 20169-2638, USA

Bradley, Henry (Athlete, Football Player)
42927 Corte Siero
Temecula, CA 92592-3639, us

Bradley, John (Actor)
c/o Sandra Chalmers *Shepherd Management*
17-21 Garrick St
Floor 3, Joel House
London WC2E 9BL, UNITED KINGDOM (UK)

Bradley, Kathleen (Actor, Model)
c/o Staff Member *Kazarian, Measures, Ruskin & Associates*
5200 Lankershim Blvd Ste 820
N Hollywood, CA 91601-3194, USA

Bradley, Keegan (Athlete, Golfer)
c/o Ben Harrison *Lagardere Unlimited (AZ)*
13845 N Northsight Blvd Ste 200
Scottsdale, AZ 85260-3609, USA

Bradley, Luther (Athlete, Football Player)
45222 N Spring Dr
Canton, MI 48187-2544, USA

Bradley, Mark (Athlete, Baseball Player)
1605 S Nebraska St
Pine Bluff, AR 71601-6133, USA

Bradley, Michael (Athlete, Basketball Player)

Bradley, Michael (Athlete, Golfer)
3336 Anna George Dr
Valrico, FL 33596-6426, USA

Bradley, Milton (Athlete, Baseball Player)
5359 Oak Park Ave
Encino, CA 91316-2627, USA

Bradley, Myron (Athlete, Olympic Athlete, Water Polo Player)
262 Saint Joseph Ave
Long Beach, CA 90803-1720, USA

Bradley, Otha (Athlete, Football Player)
12612 S Wilmington Ave Unit 106
Compton, CA 90222-1648, USA

Bradley, Phil (Athlete, Baseball Player)
4604 Whispering Leaves Dr
Sarasota, FL 34243-3964, USA

Bradley, Rebecca (Athlete, Golfer)
14443 W Lee Shore Dr
Willis, TX 77318-7407, USA

Bradley, Ryan (Athlete, Baseball Player)
3454 Alder Pl
Chino Hills, CA 91709-2005, USA

Bradley, Scott (Athlete, Baseball Player)
PO Box 416
Pennington, NJ 08534-0416, USA

Bradley, Shawn (Athlete, Basketball Player)
6e6 Sunny Flowers Ln
Salt Lake City, UT 841e7-5411, USA

Bradley, Tom (Athlete, Baseball Player)
4104 Woodberry St
University Park, MD 20782-1169, USA

Bradley Baker, Dee (Actor)
13104 Bloomfield St
Sherman Oaks, CA 91423-3206, USA

Bradley Jr, Harold (Athlete, Football Player)
1302 Asbury Ave
Evanston, IL 60201-4108, USA

Bradley Jr, Timothy (Athlete, Boxer)
307 W Bon Air Dr
Palm Springs, CA 92262-1410, USA

Bradshaw (Wrestler)
139 Denny Ln
Athens, TX 75751

Bradshaw, Ahmad (Athlete, Football Player)
c/o Drew Rosenhaus *Rosenhaus Sports Representation*
3921 Alton Rd # 440
Miami Beach, FL 33140-3852, USA

Bradshaw, James A (Athlete, Football Player)
449 Tresham Rd
Gahanna, OH 43230-2224, USA

Bradshaw, Jim (Athlete, Football Player)
5653 Eagle Harbor Dr
Westerville, OH 43081-7085, us

Bradshaw, John (Actor, Director, Writer)
c/o Victoria Wisdom *Wisdom Literary*
287 S Robertson Blvd Ste 258
Beverly Hills, CA 90211-2810, USA

Bradshaw, Morris (Athlete, Football Player)
82 Steuben Bay
Alameda, CA 94502-6406, USA

Bradshaw, Sufe (Actor)
c/o Sarah Baker Grillo *Open Entertainment*
1051 Cole Ave
Los Angeles, CA 90038-2601, USA

Bradshaw, Terry (Athlete, Football Player, Sportscaster)
c/o Ira Stahlberger *IMG (Cleveland)*
1360 E 9th St Ste 100
Cleveland, OH 44114-1730, USA

Brady, Beau (Actor)
c/o Darren Gray *Darren Gray Management*
2 Marston Ln
Portsmouth
Hampshire PO3 5TW, UK

Brady, Brian (Athlete, Baseball Player)
920 W 23rd St
Odessa, TX 79763-2504, USA

Brady, Doug (Athlete, Baseball Player)
106 Tamarisk Dr
Springfield, IL 62704-3156, USA

Brady, Ed (Athlete, Football Player)
5755 White Path Ln
Liberty Twp, OH 45011-1273, USA

Brady, Jeff (Athlete, Football Player)
1506 NW 37th Pl
Cape Coral, FL 33993, USA

Brady, Jim (Athlete, Baseball Player)
9601 Southbrook Dr Apt N107
Jacksonville, FL 32256-0497, USA

Brady, Karren (Television Host)
c/o Gordon Poole *Gordon Poole Agency Limited*
The Limes
Brockley
Bristol BS48 3BB, United Kingdom

Brady, Kevin (Congressman, Politician)
301 Cannon Hob
Washington, DC 20515-1701, USA

Brady, Kyle (Athlete, Football Player)
2221 Alicia Ln
Atlantic Beach, FL 32233-5975, USA

Brady, Neil (Athlete, Hockey Player)
Anipet Animal Supplies
125-4300 26 St NE
Attn Warehouse Manager
Calgary, AB T1Y 7H7, Canada

Brady, Nicholas F (Politician)
Darby Overseas Investments
PO Box 1410W
Easton, MD 21601-8927, USA

Brady, Orla (Actor)
19534 Bowers Dr
Topanga, CA 90290-3100, USA

Brady, Pat (Cartoonist)
United Feature Syndicate
200 Madison Ave
New York, NY 10016-3903, USA

Brady, Patrick (Athlete, Football Player)
8990 Lombardi Rd
Reno, NV 89511-9537, USA

Brady, Ray (Correspondent)
CBS-TV
524 W 57th St
New York, NY 10019-2924, USA

Brady, Robert (Congressman, Politician)
102 Cannon Hob
Washington, DC 20515-0516, USA

Brady, Tom (Athlete, Football Player)
PO Box 961439
Boston, MA 02196-1439, USA

Brady, Wayne (Actor, Comedian, Musician, Producer)
c/o Norman Aladjem *Mainstay Entertainment*
9250 Beverly Blvd Fl 3
Beverly Hills, CA 90210-3710, USA

Braeden, Eric (Actor)
c/o Charles Sherman *Charles Sherman Public Relations*
8306 Wilshire Blvd Ste 2017
Beverly Hills, CA 90211-2304, USA

Braff, Zach (Actor, Writer)
c/o Danica Smith *Kovert Creative*
506 Santa Monica Blvd Ste 400
Santa Monica, CA 90401-2412, USA

Braga, Alice (Actor)
c/o Will Ward *Fourward*
10250 Constellation Blvd Ste 2710
Los Angeles, CA 90067-6227, USA

Braga, Brannon (Writer)
c/o Staff Member *WME|IMG*
9601 Wilshire Blvd
Beverly Hills, CA 90210-5213, USA

Braga, Sonia (Actor)
149 Avenue C Apt 2R
New York, NY 10009-5306, USA

Bragg, Billy (Musician)
Sincere Mgmt
6 Bravington Road
#6
London W9 3AH, UNITED KINGDOM (UK)

Bragg, Darren (Athlete, Baseball Player)
163 Patriot Rd
Southbury, CT 06488-1274, USA

Bragg, Don (Athlete, Olympic Athlete, Track Athlete)
965 Oak St
Clayton, CA 94517-1313, USA

Bragg, Melvyn (Writer)
12 Hampstead Hill Gardens
London NW3 2PL, UNITED KINGDOM (UK)

Bragg, Mike (Athlete, Football Player)
807 S 6th St
Saint Charles, MO 63301, USA

Bragg, Rick (Journalist)
229 W 43rd St
New York, NY 10036-3982, USA

Braggs, Byron (Athlete, Football Player)
19469 Mill Dam Pl
Leesburg, VA 20176-8428, USA

Braggs, Glenn (Athlete, Baseball Player)
28369 Falcon Crest Dr
Canyon Country, CA 91351-5016, USA

Braggs, Stephen (Athlete, Football Player)
4110 Pickfair St
Houston, TX 77026-3924, USA

Bragnalo, Rick (Athlete, Hockey Player)
515 Christina St E
Thunder Bay, ON P7E 4P3, Canada

Bragonier, Dennis (Athlete, Football Player)
PO Box 1206
Roseville, CA 95678-8206, USA

Braham, Rich (Athlete, Football Player)
19 Miramichi Trl
Morgantown, WV 26508-2928, USA

Brahaney, Thomas F (Tom) (Athlete, Football Player)
1602 W Cuthbert Ave
Midland, TX 79701-5724, USA

Brainard, Don (Horse Racer)
880 Banks Rd
Coconut Creek, FL 33063-4621, USA

Brainin, Nobert (Musician)
19 Prowse Ave
Busbey Heath
Herts WD2 1JS, UNITED KINGDOM (UK)

Brainville, Ives (Actor)
34 Cours de Vincennes
Paris F-75012, France

Brakes, The (Music Group)
c/o Staff Member *Paradigm (Monterey)*
404 W Franklin St
Monterey, CA 93940-2303, USA

Braman, Bryan (Athlete, Football Player)

Braman, Norman (Business Person, Football Executive)
1 Indian Creek Island Rd
Indian Creek Village, FL 33154-2903, USA

Bramhall, Mark (Actor)
c/o Alexandra Karrys *Divine Management*
3822 Latrobe St
Los Angeles, CA 90031-1446

Bramhill, Gina (Actor)
c/o Staff Member *ICM (London)*
76 Oxford St
London W1D 1BS, UNITED KINGDOM

Bramlet, Casey (Athlete, Football Player)
801 15th St
Wheatland, WY 82201-2709, US

Bramlett, John (Athlete, Football Player)
159 Cotton Ridge Cv S
Cordova, TN 38018-7409, USA

Brammell, Abby (Actor)
c/o Robert (Rob) Gomez *Precision Entertainment*
6338 Wilshire Blvd
Los Angeles, CA 90048-5002, USA

Brammer, Mark (Athlete, Football Player)
1680 Amherst St
Buffalo, NY 14214-2002, USA

Branagh, Kenneth (Actor, Director)
Kenneth Branagh Ltd
Sheppeton Studios
Studio Rd
Middlesex TW17 0QD, UNITED KINGDOM

Brancati, Paula (Actor)
AMI Artists Management
464 King St E
c/o Shari Quallenburg
Toronto, ON M5A 1L7, CANADA

Brancatisano, Richard (Actor)
c/o Jamie Harhay Skinner *Baker Winokur Ryder Public Relations*
9100 Wilshire Blvd
W Tower #500
Beverly Hills, CA 90212-3415, USA

Brancato, George (Athlete, Football Player)
25 Nancy Ave
Nepean, ON K2H 8L3, USA

Brancato, John D (JD) (Producer, Writer)
c/o Staff Member *Broder Webb Chervin Silbermann Agency, The (BWCS)*
10250 Constellation Blvd
Los Angeles, CA 90067-6200, USA

Brancato Jr, Lillo (Actor)
c/o Craig Shapiro *ICM Partners*
10250 Constellation Blvd Fl 7
Los Angeles, CA 90067-6207, USA

Branch, Adrian (Athlete, Basketball Player)
18008 Fence Post Ct
Gaithersburg, MD 20877-3794, USA

Branch, Alan (Athlete, Football Player)
c/o Blake Baratz *The Institute for Athletes*
3600 Minnesota Dr Ste 550
Edina, MN 55435-7925, USA

Branch, Andre (Athlete, Football Player)
c/o Hadley Engelhard *Enter-Sports Management*
6000 Lake Forrest Dr Ste 370
Atlanta, GA 30328-5902, USA

Branch, Clifford (Cliff) (Athlete, Coach, Football Coach, Football Player)
2071 Stonefield Ln
Santa Rosa, CA 95403-0952, USA

Branch, Colin (Athlete, Football Player)
8621 Creek Trail Ln Apt 906
Cornelius, NC 28031-6566, us

Branch, Deion (Athlete, Football Player)
13382 W Sherbern Dr
Carmel, IN 46032-1309, us

Branch, Harvey (Athlete, Baseball Player)
4995 Jolly Dr
Memphis, TN 38109-7123, USA

Branch, Michelle (Musician)
c/o Jeff Rabhan *Three Ring Projects (LA)*
9200 W Sunset Blvd Ste 810
Los Angeles, CA 90069-3603, USA

Branch, Reggie (Athlete, Football Player)
515 San Lanta Cir
Sanford, FL 32771-5903, USA

Branch, Roy (Athlete, Baseball Player)
5322 Terry Ave
Saint Louis, MO 63120-2021, USA

Branch, Tyvon (Athlete, Football Player)

Branch, Vanessa (Actor)
c/o Staff Member *3 Arts Entertainment*
9460 Wilshire Blvd Fl 7
Beverly Hills, CA 90212-2713, USA

Branch, William B (Writer)
53 Cortlandt Ave
New Rochelle, NY 10801-2032, USA

Brand, Colette (Skier)
Rigistr 24
Baar 06340, SWITZERLAND

Brand, Daniel (Dan) (Wrestler)
4321 Bridgeview Dr
Oakland, CA 94602-1910, USA

Brand, Elton (Athlete, Basketball Player)
942 S Mansfield Ave
Los Angeles, CA 90036-4940, USA

Brand, Glen (Athlete, Olympic Athlete, Wrestler)
PO Box 6069
Omaha, NE 68106-0069, USA

Brand, Jolene (Actor)
G.S. Prod
8321 Beverly Blvd
Los Angeles, CA 90048-2607, USA

Brand, Joshua (Producer)
c/o Staff Member *WME|IMG*
9601 Wilshire Blvd
Beverly Hills, CA 90210-5213, USA

Brand, Julie (Athlete, Golfer)
6 Emerald Way
Ocala, FL 34472-2333, USA

Brand, Neville (Actor)
c/o Staff Member *ICM Partners*
10250 Constellation Blvd Fl 7
Los Angeles, CA 90067-6207, USA

Brand, Robert (Designer)
508 W End Ave
New York, NY 10024-4328, USA

Brand, Ron (Athlete, Baseball Player)
1301 Hudson Ln
Prosper, TX 75078-5013, USA

Brand, Russell (Actor, Comedian)
c/o Angharad Wood *Tavistock Wood Management*
45 Conduit St
London W1S 2YN, UNITED KINGDOM

Brand, Simon (Director)
c/o Jon Huddle *Fourth Wall Management*
9336 Civic Center Dr
Beverly Hills, CA 90210-3604, USA

Brand, Steven (Actor)
c/o Brian Medavoy *More/Medavoy Management*
10203 Santa Monica Blvd # 400
Los Angeles, CA 90067-6405, USA

Brand, Vance D (Astronaut)
NASA Dryden Flight Center
21825 Hidden Canyon Dr
Tehachapi, CA 93561-9528, USA

Brandauer, Klaus Maria (Actor)
Novapool Gmbh
Paul Lincke Ufer 42-43
Berlin 10999, GERMANY

Brandenburg, Dan'''' (Athlete, Football Player)
PO Box 22533
Ft Lauderdale, FL 33335-2533, us

Brandenburg, Mark (Athlete, Baseball Player)
152 Cottonwood Dr
Coppell, TX 75019-2511, USA

Brandenstein, Daniel C (Astronaut)
12802 Tri City Beach Rd
Baytown, TX 77523-9216, USA

Brandenstein, Daniel C Captain (Astronaut)
15203 Greenleaf Ln
Houston, TX 77062-3672, USA

Brandes, John (Athlete, Football Player)
1414 Ravenwood Dr
Mansfield, TX 76063-6054, USA

Brandi (Model)
Next Model Mgmt
23 Watts St
New York, NY 10013, USA

Brandler, Shellylyn (Actor)
c/o Simon Millar *Rumble Media*
1620 Broadway Ste C
Santa Monica, CA 90404-2777, USA

Brandon, Barbara (Cartoonist)
Universal Press Syndicate
4520 Main St Ste 340
Kansas City, MO 64111-7705, USA

Brandon, Clark (Actor)
Jennings Assoc
28035 Dorothy Dr Ste 210A
Agoura, CA 91301-2685, USA

Brandon, Darrell (Athlete, Baseball Player)
590 White Cliff Dr
Plymouth, MA 02360-1483, USA

Brandon, David (Athlete, Football Player)
218 Crystal Downs Way
Suwanee, GA 30024-7630, us

Brandon, Jay (Writer)
PO Box 6764
San Antonio, TX 78209-0764, USA

Brandon, Jeb (Actor)
c/o Staff Member *WME|IMG*
9601 Wilshire Blvd
Beverly Hills, CA 90210-5213, USA

Brandon, John (Actor)
Coast to Coast Talent
3350 Barham Blvd
Los Angeles, CA 90068-1404, USA

Brandon, Michael (Actor)
c/o Peter Brooks *Creative Artists Management (CAM-UK)*
55-59 Shaftesbury Ave.
London W1D 6LD, UNITED KINGDOM

Brandon, Michael (Athlete, Football Player)
910 E Green St
Perry, FL 32347-3514, USA

Brandon, Sam (Athlete, Football Player)
7357 Country Fair Dr
Eastvale, CA 92880-0702, us

Brandon, Terrell (Athlete, Basketball Player)
3310 NE Shaver St
Portland, OR 97212-1860, USA

Brands, Terry (Athlete, Olympic Athlete, Wrestler)
3744 Lacina Dr SW
Iowa City, IA 52240-8620, USA

Brands, Tom (Wrestler)
4494 Taft Ave SE
Iowa City, IA 52240-8166, USA

Brands, X (Actor)
17171 Roscoe Blvd # 104
Northridge, CA 91325-4060, USA

Brandt, Betsy (Actor)
8033 W Sunset Blvd Ste 810
Los Angeles, CA 90046-2401, USA

Brandt, David'''' (Athlete, Football Player)
2214 Christine Ct SE
Grand Rapids, MI 49546-6468, us

Brandt, Hank (Actor)
Contemporary Artists
610 Santa Monica Blvd Ste 202
Santa Monica, CA 90401-1645, USA

Brandt, Jackie (Athlete, Baseball Player)
103 Sugar Maple Ave
Wildwood, FL 34785-9246, USA

Brandt, Jim (Athlete, Football Player)
714 Zumbro Dr NW
Rochester, MN 55901-2379, USA

Brandt, Jon (Musician)
Monterey Peninsula Artists
509 Hartnell St
Monterey, CA 93940-2825, USA

Brandt, Kyle (Actor, Reality Star)
c/o David Sweeney *Sweeney Entertainment*
1601 Vine St # 6
Los Angeles, CA 90028-8802, USA

Brandt, Lesley-Ann (Actor)
c/o Mia Hansen *Portrait PR*
5320 Sylmar Ave
Sherman Oaks, CA 91401-5612, USA

Brandt, Paul (Musician)
c/o Staff Member *WME|IMG*
9601 Wilshire Blvd
Beverly Hills, CA 90210-5213, USA

Brandt, Victor (Actor)
H David Moss
6063 Vineland Ave Apt B
North Hollywood, CA 91606-4986, USA

Branduardi, Angelo (Musician)
c/o Faustini Srl.
Via Veneto, 18
Pontoglio I-25 037, Italy

Brandy, J C (Actor)
Henderson/Hogan
8285 W Sunset Blvd Ste 1
West Hollywood, CA 90046-2420, USA

Brandywine, Marcia (Correspondent)
743 Huntley Dr
Los Angeles, CA 90069-5008, USA

B. Rangel, Charles (Congressman, Politician)
2354 Rayburn Hob
Washington, DC 20515-3215, USA

Brannagh, Brigid (Actor)
c/o Susan (Sue) Madore *Guttman Associates Public Relations*
118 S Beverly Dr Ste 201
Beverly Hills, CA 90212-3016, USA

Brannan, Solomon (Athlete, Football Player)
2500 Cascade Rd SW
Atlanta, GA 30311-3228, USA

Brannon, Ronald (Religious Leader)
Wesleyan Church
PO Box 50434
Indianapolis, IN 46250-0434, USA

Branshaw, David (Athlete, Golfer)
1617 Renaissance Way
Tampa, FL 33602-5981, USA

Branson, Brad (Athlete, Basketball Player)
7419 Cortes Dr
Houston, TX 77083-3617, USA

Branson, Jeff (Actor)
c/o Robert Attermann *Abrams Artists Agency*
275 7th Ave Fl 26
New York, NY 10001-6708, USA

Branson, Jeff (Athlete, Baseball Player)
10749 Spokane Ct
Union, KY 41091-7160, USA

Branson, Jeff (Athlete, Baseball Player)
501 W Maryland St
Attn Coaching Staff
Indianapolis, IN 46225-1041, USA

Branson, Jesse (Athlete, Basketball Player)
309 Forest Dr
Graham, NC 27253-4405, USA

Branson, Richard (Business Person)
c/o Staff Member *Virgin (UK)*
10-14 Bartley Wood Business Park
Hook RG27 9UP, UNITED KINGDOM

Branstad, Terry (Politician)
E Grand Ave
Des Moines, IA 50319, USA

Brant, Marshall (Athlete, Baseball Player)
604 Scotland Dr
Santa Rosa, CA 95409-4419, USA

Brant, Peter (Business Person)
385 Taconic Rd
Greenwich, CT 06831-2828, USA

Brant, Tim (Sportscaster)
ABC-TV
77 W 66th St
Sports Dept
New York, NY 10023-6201, USA

Brantley, Betsy (Actor)
c/o Staff Member *Mitchell K Stubbs & Assoc*
8675 Washington Blvd Ste 203
Culver City, CA 90232-7486, USA

Brantley, Chris (Athlete, Football Player)
257 Hamilton Rd
Teaneck, NJ 07666-6367, USA

Brantley, Cliff (Athlete, Baseball Player)
90 Grandview Ave
Staten Island, NY 10303-2000, USA

Brantley, Jeff (Athlete, Baseball Player)
104 Cherry Laurel Cv
Ridgeland, MS 39157-8643, USA

Brantley, Jeff (Athlete, Baseball Player)
100 Joe Nuxhall Way
Attn Broadcast Dept
Cincinnati, OH 45202-4109, USA

Brantley, John (Athlete, Football Player)
328 Jefferson Rd
Bishop, GA 30621-1517, USA

Brantley, Michael (Athlete, Baseball Player)
7640 NW 79th Ave
Apt L8
Tamarac, FL 33321-2868, USA

Brantley, Mickey (Athlete, Baseball Player)
3095 SW Boxwood Cir
Port Saint Lucie, FL 34953-6971, USA

Brantley, Ollie (Athlete, Baseball Player)
3647 Eden Dr
Dallas, TX 75287-6262, USA

Brantley, Rick (Musician)
c/o Staff Member *Paradigm (Monterey)*
404 W Franklin St
Monterey, CA 93940-2303, USA

Brantley, Scot (Athlete, Football Player)
11309 Galleria Dr
Tampa, FL 33618-8748, USA

Branton, Gene (Athlete, Football Player)
7008 Hazelhurst Ct
Tampa, FL 33615-2945, USA

Branyan, Russell (Athlete, Baseball Player)
3301 Running Springs Ct
Franklin, TN 37064-6257, USA

Brar, Karan (Actor)
c/o Bill Perlman *Foundation Media Partners*
23679 Calabasas Rd # 625
Calabasas, CA 91302-1502, USA

Brasar, Per-Olov (Athlete, Hockey Player)
Heden Lisshedsvagen 19
Leksand S-79329, Sweden

Brasco, Jim (Athlete, Basketball Player)
225 W Neck Rd
Huntington, NY 11743-2458, USA

Brashares, Ann (Writer)
c/o Jennifer Rudolph Walsh *WME|IMG (NY)*
11 Madison Ave Fl 18
New York, NY 10010-3669, USA

Braslow, Paul (Artist)
118 Saint Thomas Way
Belvedere Tiburon, CA 94920-1032, USA

Brassette, Amy (Actor)
c/o Marv Dauer *Marv Dauer Management*
11661 San Vicente Blvd Ste 104
Los Angeles, CA 90049-5150, USA

Brasseur, Claude (Actor)
Artmedia
20 Ave Rapp
Paris 75007, FRANCE

Brassfield, Darin (Race Car Driver)
541 Division St
Campbell, CA 95008-6905, USA

Bratkowski, Edmund R (Zeke) (Athlete, Coach, Football Player)
224 N Anchors Lake Dr
Santa Rosa Beach, FL 32459-4106, USA

Bratt, Benjamin (Actor)
c/o Staff Member *5 Stick Films*
7119 W Sunset Blvd Ste 915
Los Angeles, CA 90046-4411, USA

Bratton, Creed (Actor)
c/o Patrick Coleman *Persona Public Relations*
6255 W Sunset Blvd Ste 705
Hollywood, CA 90028-7408, USA

Bratton, Jason (Athlete, Football Player)
401 Phillips Dr
Gladewater, TX 75647-4831, USA

Bratz, Mike (Athlete, Basketball Player)
7503 Tillman Hill Rd
Colleyville, TX 76034-6929, USA

Bratzke, Chad (Athlete, Football Player)
10850 Ruby Ct
Carmel, IN 46032-9303, USA

Brauer, Arik (Artist)
Academy of Fine Arts
Schillerplatz 3
Vienna 01010, AUSTRIA

Braugher, Andre (Actor)
393 Charlton Ave
South Orange, NJ 07079-2405, USA

Braun, Carol Moseley (Politician)
PO Box 8155
Chicago, IL 60680-8155, USA

Braun, Colin (Race Car Driver)
c/o Staff Member *Roush Fenway Racing Team*
4202 Roush Pl NW
Concord, NC 28027-7112, USA

Braun, Nicholas (Actor)
c/o Ashley Partington *Abrams Artists Agency*
750 N San Vicente Blvd
E Tower Fl 11
Los Angeles, CA 90069-5788, USA

Braun, Pinkas (Actor, Director)
Unterdorf
8261
Hemishofen/SH, SWITZERLAND

Braun, Rick (Musician)
c/o Staff Member *APA Talent And Literary Agency (NY)*
45 W 45th St Ste 804
New York, NY 10036-4602, USA

Braun, Ryan (Athlete, Baseball Player)
3769 Puerco Canyon Rd
Malibu, CA 90265-4551, USA

Braun, Scooter (Business Person, Producer)
755 N Bonhill Rd
Los Angeles, CA 90049-2303, USA

Braun, Steve (Actor)
c/o Suzanne (Sue) Wohl *TalentWorks*
3500 W Olive Ave Ste 1400
Burbank, CA 91505-5512, USA

Braun, Steve (Athlete, Baseball Player)
108 Gainsboro Rd Apt 2
Lawrence Township, NJ 08648-3916, USA

Braun, Tamara (Actor)
c/o Steven Hawthorne *The Cartel*
1108-1112 Tamarind Ave
Hollywood, CA 90038, USA

Braun, Wendy (Actor)
c/o Staff Member *The House of Representatives*
3118 Wilshire Blvd Ste D
Santa Monica, CA 90403-2345, USA

Braunduardi, Angelo (Musician)
Faustini Srl.
Via Veneto, 18
Pontoglio I-25 037, Italy

Braunger, Matt (Actor, Comedian)
c/o David Martin *Avalon Management*
9171 Wilshire Blvd Ste 320
Beverly Hills, CA 90210-5516, USA

Braver, Rita (Correspondent)
CBS-TV
2020 M St NW
News Dept
Washington, DC 20036-3368, USA

Braverman, Bart (Actor)
c/o Staff Member *Henriksen Talent Management*
13024 Hesby St
Sherman Oaks, CA 91423-2134, USA

Braverman, Chuck (Director, Producer)
Braverman Productions Inc
3000 Olympic Blvd
Santa Monica, CA 90404-5073, USA

Bravo, Alex (Athlete, Football Player)
2316 Pine Ave
Manhattan Beach, CA 90266-2835, USA

Bravo, Ciara (Actor)
c/o Stella Alex *Savage Agency*
1041 N Formosa Ave
West Hollywood, CA 90046-6703, USA

Bravo, Duncan (Actor)
20929 Ventura Blvd
Woodland Hills, CA 91364-2334, USA

Braxton, David (Athlete, Football Player)
26898 Primrose Ln
Westlake, OH 44145-5487, USA

Braxton, Tamar (Actor, Musician)
c/o Nick Roses *Pantheon Talent*
1801 Century Park E Ste 1910
Los Angeles, CA 90067-2321, USA

Braxton, Toni (Musician, Songwriter)
LMA Productions
998C Old Country Rd # 409
Plainview, NY 11803-4917, USA

Braxton, Trlna (Musician, Reality Star)
c/o Staff Member *Primary Wave Talent*
116 E 16th St Fl 9
New York, NY 10003-2123, USA

Braxton, Tyrone S (Athlete, Football Player)
455 Keamey St
Denver, CO 80220, USA

Braxton III, Hezekiah (Athlete, Football Player)
12715 Norwood Ln
Fort Washington, MD 20744-6312, USA

Bray, Deanne (Actor)
c/o Sid Craig *Craig Management*
2240 Miramonte Cir E Unit C
Palm Springs, CA 92264-5734, USA

Bray, Kevin (Actor, Director, Producer)
c/o Simon Millar *Rumble Media*
1620 Broadway Ste C
Santa Monica, CA 90404-2777, USA

Bray, Tyler (Athlete, Football Player)
c/o Don Yee *Yee & Dubin Sports, LLC*
725 S Figueroa St Ste 3085
Los Angeles, CA 90017-5430, USA

Brayton, Tyler (Athlete, Football Player)
412 Hunter Ln
Charlotte, NC 28211-3043, USA

Brazadskas, Algirdas (President)
Tumiskiu 30
Vilnius 02016, LITHUANIA

Brazell, Craig (Athlete, Baseball Player)
8512 Rockbridge Cir
Montgomery, AL 36116-8807, USA

Brazelton, Dewon (Athlete, Baseball Player)
107 Scenic Dr
Tullahoma, TN 37388-5422, USA

Braziel, Larry (Athlete, Football Player)
831 Netherland Dr
Arlington, TX 76017-6019, USA

Brazier, Garry (Race Car Driver)
Stanton Racing
100 Memorial Dr
Nicholasville, KY 40356-1082, USA

Brazil, Jeff (Journalist)
Orlando Sentinel
633 N Orange Ave Lbby
Editorial Dept
Orlando, FL 32801-1349, USA

Brazile, Donna (Commentator, Politician)
c/o Matthew Latimer *Javelin*
203 S Union St Ste 200
Alexandria, VA 22314-3356, USA

Brazile, Trevor (Athlete)
715 County Road 3051
Decatur, TX 76234-4685, USA

Brazile Jr, Robert L (Athlete, Football Player)
813 Felder Ave
Mobile, AL 36612-1338, USA

Brazill, Mark (Producer)
c/o Dan Halsted *Manage-ment*
1103 1/2 Glendon Ave
Los Angeles, CA 90024-3501, USA

Brazzell, Chris (Athlete, Football Player)
1205 Las Palmas Cir
Alice, TX 78332-3169, USA

Brea, Leslie (Athlete, Baseball Player)
222 N 153rd Ave
Goodyear, AZ 85338-2966, USA

Bready, Richard L (Business Person)
166 President Ave
Providence, RI 02906-4616, USA

Breaker, Daniel (Actor)
c/o Brian Liebman *Liebman Entertainment*
29 W 46th St Fl 5
New York, NY 10036-4104, USA

Breaking Benjamin (Music Group)
c/o Staff Member *Hollywood Records*
500 S Buena Vista St
Burbank, CA 91521-0002, USA

B-Real (Artist, Musician)
17116 Labrador St
Northridge, CA 91325-1900, USA

Bream, Julian (Musician)
Hazard Chase
Richmond House
16-20 Regent St
Cambridge CB2 1DB, UNITED KINGDOM (UK)

Bream, Sid (Athlete, Baseball Player)
115 Sable Run
Zelienople, PA 16063-3141, USA

Breathed, Berkeley (Cartoonist)
Washington Post Writers Group
1150 15th St NW
Washington, DC 20071-0002, USA

Breathwaite, Edward (Writer)
University of West Indies
History Dept
Mona
Kingston 00007, JAMAICA

Breaux, Don (Athlete, Football Player)
19027 Southport Dr
Cornelius, NC 28031-6478, USA

Breaux, John (Politician)
25860 Royal Oak Road
Royal Oak, MD 21662, USA

Breaux, Tim (Athlete, Basketball Player)
845 Augusta Dr Apt E75
Apt E75
Houston, TX 77057-2029, USA

Breazeale, Jim (Athlete, Baseball Player)
2824 La Mesa St
Bay City, TX 77414-2798, USA

Breck, Jonathan (Actor)
c/o Eric Stevens *Rainbow High Entertainment*
10153 Riverside Dr # 583
Toluca Lake, CA 91602-2562, USA

Breckenridge, Alex (Actor)
c/o David (Dave) Fleming *Atlas Artists*
9220 W Sunset Blvd Ste 225
Los Angeles, CA 90069-3513, USA

Breckenridge, Laura (Actor)
c/o Glenn Rigberg *Inphenate*
9701 Wilshire Blvd Fl 10
Beverly Hills, CA 90212-2010, USA

Brecker, Randy (Musician)
Tropix International
163 3rd Ave # 206
New York, NY 10003-2523, USA

Bredahl, Charlotte (Athlete, Horse Racer, Olympic Athlete)
560 McMurray Rd
Buellton, CA 93427, USA

Brede, Brent (Athlete, Baseball Player)
1891 J Rock Rd
Trenton, IL 62293-2924, USA

Bredesen, Philip (Politician)
1724 Chickering Rd
Nashville, TN 37215-4908, USA

Breding, Ed (Athlete, Football Player)
126 Pritchard St NW
Harlowton, MT 59036-5069, USA

Bredsen, Espen (Skier)
Hellerud Gardsvei 18
Oslo 00671, NORWAY

Breech, Jim (Athlete, Football Player)
3189 Princeton Rd # 266
Fairfield Township, OH 45011-5338, USA

Breeden, Danny (Athlete, Baseball Player)
5111 B Ave
Loxley, AL 36551-4537, USA

Breeden, Hal (Athlete, Baseball Player)
665 Middle Rd S
Leesburg, GA 31763-3442, USA

Breeden, Joe (Athlete, Baseball Player)
1305 Bonaventure Dr
Melbourne, FL 32940-1904, USA

Breeden, Louis (Athlete, Football Player)
11264 Grooms Rd Ste E
Blue Ash, OH 45242-1418, USA

Breedlove, Craig (Race Car Driver)
200 N Front St
Rio Vista, CA 94571-1420, USA

Breedlove, Leory (Athlete, Baseball Player)
1910 N 16th St
Orange, TX 77630-3311, USA

Breedlove, Rod (Athlete, Football Player)
1664 Carlyle Dr Apt H
Crofton, MD 21114-1430, USA

Breeland, Bashaud (Athlete, Football Player)
c/o Joe Flanagan *BTI Sports Advisors*
615 South Blvd Apt C
Oak Park, IL 60302-4606, USA

Breen, Adrian (Athlete, Football Player)
261 Red Zone
Jackson, MO 63755-8741, USA

Breen, Gene (Athlete, Football Player)
1018 Henley Downs Pl
Lake Mary, FL 32746-1972, USA

Breen, George (Athlete, Olympic Athlete, Swimmer)
425 Pepper Mill Ct
Sewell, NJ 08080-2963, USA

Breen, John G (Business Person)
4951 Gulf Shore Blvd N Apt 553
Naples, FL 34103-2687, USA

Breen, Monica (Producer, Writer)
c/o Ilan Breil *Mosaic Media Group*
407 N Maple Dr # 100
Beverly Hills, CA 90210-3818, USA

Breen, Patrick (Actor)
c/o Abe Hoch *A Management Company*
16633 Ventura Blvd Ste 1450
Encino, CA 91436-1887, USA

Breen, Shelley (Musician)
8106 Patrice Dr
Brentwood, TN 37027-7126, USA

Breen, Stephen (Steve) (Cartoonist)
San Diego Union-Telegram
PO Box 120191
San Diego, CA 92112-0191, USA

Breer, Murle (Athlete, Golfer)
7008 Sand Rd
Savannah, GA 31410-2314, USA

Brees, Drew (Athlete, Football Player)
c/o Chris Stuart *Encore Sports and Entertainment*
4405 Manchester Ave Ste 205
Encinitas, CA 92024-7902, USA

Bregel, Jeff (Athlete, Football Player)
15431 Tulsa St Spc 33
Mission Hills, CA 91345-1349, USA

Bregman, Buddy (Actor)
c/o Staff Member *Paul Lane Entertainment*
468 N Camden Dr
Beverly Hills, CA 90210-4507, USA

Bregman, Tracey (Actor)
5630 Villa Mar Pl
Malibu, CA 90265, USA

Brehaut, Jeff (Athlete, Golfer)
1085 Leonello Ave
Los Altos, CA 94024-4914, USA

Breiman, Valerie (Director)
c/o Staff Member *Industry Entertainment Partners*
955 Carrillo Dr Ste 300
Los Angeles, CA 90048-5400, USA

Breining, Fred (Athlete, Baseball Player)
2120 Ticonderoga Dr
San Mateo, CA 94402-4045, USA

Breitenstein, Robert (Athlete, Football Player)
4215 WE 95th St
Tulsa, OK 74137-2311, USA

Breitenstien, Robert (Athlete, Football Player)
8524 S Winston Ave
Tulsa, OK 74137-1914, USA

Breitmayer, Peter (Actor)
PO Box 39499
Los Angeles, CA 90039-0499, USA

Breitner, Paul (Athlete, Soccer Player)
Eichendorfstrasse 10
Sauerlach, GERMANY 82054

Breitschwerdt, Werner (Business Person)
Daimler-Benz AG
Mercedesstr 136
Stuttgart 70322, GERMANY

Breland, Mark (Athlete, Boxer)
PO Box 980
Denmark, SC 29042-0980, USA

Bremer, Dick (Commentator)
15910 56th St NE
Saint Michael, MN 55376-3201, USA

Bremmer, Paul L (Politician, Writer)
c/o Staff Member *Simon & Schuster*
1230 Avenue of the Americas Fl CONC1
New York, NY 10020-1586, USA

Bremner, Ewen (Actor)
International Creative Mgmt
76 Oxford St
London W1N 0AX, UNITED KINGDOM (UK)

B. Renacci, James (Congressman, Politician)
130 Cannon Hob
Washington, DC 20515-3308, USA

Brenan, Gerald (Writer)
Alhaurin El Grande
Malaga, SPAIN

Brendel, Alfred (Musician)
Vanguard/Omega Classics
27 W 72nd St
New York, NY 10023-3498, USA

Brenden, Hallgeir (Skier)
2417 Torberget
NORWAY

Brendi, Pavel (Athlete, Hockey Player)
1400 Edwards Mill Rd
Raleigh, NC 27607-3624, USA

Brendon, Nicholas (Actor)
Platform
2666 N Beachwood Dr
Los Angeles, CA 90068-2308, USA

Brenly, Bob (Athlete, Baseball Player, Coach)
9726 E Laurel Ln
Scottsdale, AZ 85260-5959, USA

Brenly, Bob (Athlete, Basketball Player)
1060 W Addison St Ste 1
Attn: Broadcast Dept
Chicago, IL 60613-4383, USA

Brennaman, Marty (Commentator)
Cincinnati Reds
976 Wittshire Ln
Cincinnati, OH 45255-5702, USA

Brennaman, Thom (Commentator)
738 Park Ave
Terrace Park, OH 45174-1021, USA

Brennan, Brian (Athlete, Football Player)
2961 Edgewood Rd
Cleveland, OH 44124-5101, USA

Brennan, Christine (Writer)
Washington Post
Sports Dept
1150 15th Ave NW
Washington, DC 20071-0001, USA

Brennan, Dan (Athlete, Hockey Player)
1912 108 Ave
Dawson Creek, BC V1G 2T8, Canada

Brennan, Edward A (Business Person)
AMR Corp
433 Amon Carter Blvd
Fort Worth, TX 76155, USA

Brennan, Ian (Actor, Producer, Writer)
c/o Philip Raskind *WME|IMG*
9601 Wilshire Blvd
Beverly Hills, CA 90210-5213, USA

Brennan, Joseph E (Politician)
104 Frances St
Portland, ME 04102-2512, USA

Brennan, Kevin (Actor, Comedian)
United Talent Agency
9336 Civic Center Dr
Beverly Hills, CA 90210-3604, USA

Brennan, Maire (Musician, Songwriter, Writer)
Soho Agency
55 Fulham High St
London SW6 3JJ, UNITED KINGDOM (UK)

Brennan, Melissa (Actor)
6520 Platt Ave # 634
West Hills, CA 91307-3218, USA

Brennan, Mike (Athlete, Football Player)
33660 Fox Rd
Easton, MD 21601-6746, USA

Brennan, Neal (Actor, Comedian)
c/o Rachel Rusch *Creative Artists Agency (CAA)*
2000 Avenue of the Stars Ste 100
Los Angeles, CA 90067-4705, USA

Brennan, Rich (Athlete, Hockey Player)
96 Prospect St
Hingham, MA 02043-3442, USA

Brennan, Terrance P (Terry) (Athlete, Coach, Football Player)
1731 Wildberry Dr Unit C
Glenview, IL 60025-1742, USA

Brennan, Tom (Athlete, Baseball Player)
8204 Millbank Dr
Orland Park, IL 60462-1726, USA

Brennan, William (Athlete, Baseball Player)
1633 Wesleyan Dr # 220
Macon, GA 31210-0840, USA

Brenneman, Amy (Actor, Producer)
c/o Connie Tavel *Forward Entertainment*
1880 Century Park E Ste 1405
Los Angeles, CA 90067-1630, USA

Brenneman, John (Athlete, Hockey Player)
247 Radley Rd
Mississauga, ON L5G 2R6, Canada

Brenner, Dori (Actor)
210 W 101st St Apt 15C
New York, NY 10025-5040, USA

Brenner, Hoby (Athlete, Football Player)
40 Calle Ameno
San Clemente, CA 92672-2367, USA

Brenner, Lisa (Actor)
c/o Randy James *Randy James Management*
12711 Ventura Blvd Ste 345
Studio City, CA 91604-2416, USA

Brenner, Teddy (Boxer)
24 W 55th St Apt 9C
New York, NY 10019-5456, USA

Brescia, Justin (Bobby) (Musician, Reality Star)
Austin, TX, USA

Bresee, Bobbie (Actor)
8282 Hollywood Blvd
Los Angeles, CA 90069-1612, USA

Breslawsky, Marc C (Business Person)
Pitney Bowes Inc
1 Elmcroft Rd
Stamford, CT 06926-0700, USA

Breslin, Abigail (Actor)
c/o Maggie Bryant *Rogers & Cowan*
1840 Century Park E Fl 18
Los Angeles, CA 90067-2101, USA

Breslin, Spencer (Actor)
c/o Beth Cannon *Envision Entertainment*
8840 Wilshire Blvd Fl 3
Beverly Hills, CA 90211-2606, USA

Breslow, Craig (Athlete, Baseball Player)
26 Finchwood Dr
Trumbull, CT 06611-4040, USA

Bresnik, Randolph J Major (Astronaut)
14119 Lake Scene Trl
Houston, TX 77059-4406, USA

Bress, Eric (Director, Producer, Writer)
c/o Tobin Babst *Kaplan/Perrone Entertainment*
9171 Wilshire Blvd Ste 350
Beverly Hills, CA 90210-5523, USA

Bressoud, Eddie (Athlete, Baseball Player)
515 Marble Canyon Ln
San Ramon, CA 94582-4830, USA

Brest, Martin (Director, Producer)
c/o John Burnham *ICM Partners*
10250 Constellation Blvd Fl 7
Los Angeles, CA 90067-6207, USA

Bretherton, Billy (Reality Star)
Vexcon Inc.
1201 Linton Rd
Animal and Pest Control
Benton, LA 71006-8736, USA

Bretos, Max (Athlete, Soccer Player)
c/o Staff Member *Maxx Sports & Entertainment*
546 5th Ave Fl 6
New York, NY 10036-5000, USA

Brett, George (Athlete, Baseball Player)
PO Box 419969
Attn Vice President - Bb Operations
Kansas City, MO 64141-6969, USA

Brett, George (Athlete, Baseball Player)
6528 Seneca Rd
Mission Hills, KS 66208-1718, USA

Brett, Jonathan (Actor)
Agency for Performing Arts
9200 W Sunset Blvd Ste 900
Los Angeles, CA 90069-3604, USA

Brettschneider, Carl (Athlete, Football Player)
9325 Fresh Spring Dr
Las Vegas, NV 89134-8957, USA

Breuer, Grit (Athlete, Track Athlete)
Konrad-Adenauer-Str 16
Garbsen 30823, GERMANY

Breuer, Jim (Comedian)
c/o Staff Member *Rogers & Cowan*
1840 Century Park E Fl 18
Los Angeles, CA 90067-2101, USA

Breuer, Randy (Athlete, Basketball Player)
10481 Misty Morning Ln
Eden Prairie, MN 55347-5023, USA

Breunig, Robert P (Bob) (Athlete, Football Player)
9215 Westview Cir
Dallas, TX 75231-2502, USA

Brevak, Bob (Race Car Driver)
Brevak Racing
206 Performance Rd
Mooresville, NC 28115-9591, USA

Brew, Dorian (Athlete, Football Player)
1948 Lunenburg Dr
Saint Peters, MO 63376-8168, USA

Brewer, Aaron (Athlete, Football Player)
c/o Frank Bauer *Sun West Sports*
7883 N Pershing Ave
Stockton, CA 95207-1749, USA

Brewer, Billy (Athlete, Baseball Player)
7405 Woodway Dr
Woodway, TX 76712-6153, USA

Brewer, Craig (Director, Producer)
c/o Brad Gross *Brad Gross Agency, The*
161 S Arden Blvd
Los Angeles, CA 90004-3716, USA

Brewer, Dewell (Athlete, Football Player)
4804 Bloomfield Dr
Memphis, TN 38125-3356, USA

Brewer, Donald (Musician)
Lustig Talent
PO Box 770850
Orlando, FL 32877-0850, USA

Brewer, Eric (Athlete, Hockey Player)
7396 Stratford Ave
Saint Louis, MO 63130-4137, USA

Brewer, James (Athlete, Football Player)

Brewer, Jamie (Actor)
c/o Jenn Fernandez *Mosaic Public Relations*
856 N Hayworth Ave
Los Angeles, CA 90046-7107, USA

Brewer, Jamison (Athlete, Basketball Player)
1322 Wind Castle Trl
Indianapolis, IN 46280-2723, USA

Brewer, Jim (Athlete, Basketball Player, Olympic Athlete)
1814 S 23rd Ave
Maywood, IL 60153-2810, USA

Brewer, Madeline (Actor)
c/o Glenn Rigberg *Inphenate*
9701 Wilshire Blvd Fl 10
Beverly Hills, CA 90212-2010, USA

Brewer, Mike (Athlete, Baseball Player)
40 Amherst Ave
Menlo Park, CA 94025-3802, USA

Brewer, Rod (Athlete, Baseball Player)
2105 Carpathian Dr
Apopka, FL 32712-4711, USA

Brewer, Sean (Athlete, Football Player)
9232 Grangehill Dr
Riverside, CA 92508-9329, USA

Brewer, Tom (Athlete, Baseball Player)
205 Orange St
Darlington, SC 29532-3128, USA

Brewer, Tony (Athlete, Baseball Player)
659 Wildwood Ln
Palo Alto, CA 94303-3117, USA

Brewington, Jamie (Athlete, Baseball Player)
3370 S Roger Ct
Chandler, AZ 85286-2481, USA

Brewster, Darrel ""Pete"" (Athlete, Football Player)
PO Box 183
Peculiar, MO 64078-0183, USA

Brewster, Jordana (Actor)
c/o Heidi Lopata *Narrative*
1601 Vine St Fl 6
Los Angeles, CA 90028-8802, USA

Brewster, Paget (Actor)
c/o Joannie Burstein *Burstein Company*
15304 W Sunset Blvd Ste 208
Pacific Palisades, CA 90272-3656, USA

Brewster, Pete (Athlete, Football Player)
PO Box 183
Peculiar, MO 64078-0183, USA

Brewton, Maia (Actor)
525 W 49th St Apt 5A
New York, NY 10019-7148, USA

Brey, Mike (Coach)
Notre Dame University
Athletic Dept
Notre Dame, IN 46556, USA

Breyer, Stephen G (Attorney)
US Supreme Court
United States Supreme Court 11th St NE
Washington, DC 20543-0001, USA

Brezec, Primoz (Athlete, Basketball Player)
10030 Hazelview Dr
Charlotte, NC 28277-2948, USA

Brezina, Bobby (Athlete, Football Player)
1204 Pine Hollow Dr
Friendswood, TX 77546-4634, USA

Brezina, Greg (Athlete, Football Player)
155 Tillinghast Trce
Newnan, GA 30265-6000, USA

Brezina, Thomas (Writer)
ORF
Wurzburggasse 30
Wien 01136, Austria

Brian, Demarco (Athlete, Football Player)
4364 Tomahawk Ln
Vermilion, OH 44089-3323, USA

Brian duffy, colonel (Astronaut)
2625 Bay Area Blvd Spc V
Houston, TX 77058-1523, USA

Brice, Alan (Athlete, Baseball Player)
7612 Lake Vista Ct Unit 304
Lakewood Ranch, FL 34202-2117, USA

Brice, Alundis (Athlete, Football Player)
928 N Egypt Cir
Brookhaven, MS 39601-3556, USA

Brice, Lee (Musician)

Brice, Pierre (Actor)
c/o Staff Member *Thomas Claasen*
Bismarkstr 22
Itzehoe D-25524, Germany

Brice, Will (Athlete, Football Player)
1139 Craig Ave
Lancaster, SC 29720-8227, USA

Brice, William J (Artist)
427 Beloit Ave
Los Angeles, CA 90049-3405, USA

Bricekell, Beth (Director)
PO Box 119
Paron, AR 72122-0119, USA

Bricekell, Edie (Musician, Songwriter, Writer)
88 Central Park W
New York, NY 10023-5299, USA

Brickell, Beth (Actor)
3001 N Grant St
Little Rock, AR 72207-2819, USA

Brickell, Edie (Musician)
82 Brookwood Ln
New Canaan, CT 06840-3101, USA

Brickhouse, Smith N (Religious Leader)
Church of Christ
PO Box 472
Independence, MO 64051-0472, USA

Brickley, Andy (Athlete, Hockey Player)
Boston Bruins
100 Legends Way Ste 250
Attn: Broadcast Dept
Boston, MA 02114-1389, United States

Brickley, Andy (Athlete, Hockey Player)
5 Mill River Ln
Hingham, MA 02043-3455, USA

Brickman, Paul (Director)
4116 Holly Knoll Dr
Los Angeles, CA 90027-3222, USA

Brickowski, Frank (Athlete, Basketball Player)
589 7th St
Lake Oswego, OR 97034-2906, USA

Briclges, Roy D Maj Gen (Astronaut)
113 William Barksdale
Williamsburg, VA 23185-8211, USA

Bridgeforth, William (Athlete, Baseball Player)
4766 Drakes Branch Rd
Nashville, TN 37218-1436, USA

Bridgeman, Ulysses (Athlete, Basketball Player)
16e4 Cherokee Rd
Apt 5
Lousville, KY 40205-1349, USA

Bridgers, Sean (Actor)
c/o Darris Hatch *Daris Hatch Management*
10027 Rossbury Pl
Los Angeles, CA 90064-4825, USA

Bridges, Alan J S (Director)
28 High St
Shepperton
Middx TW7 9AW, UNITED KINGDOM (UK)

Bridges, Alicia (Musician)
c/o Richard Walters *Richard Walters Entertainment, Inc*
PO Box 2789
Toluca Lake, CA 91610-0789, USA

Bridges, Angelica (Actor, Model)
c/o Marv Dauer *Marv Dauer Management*
11661 San Vicente Blvd Ste 104
Los Angeles, CA 90049-5150, USA

Bridges, Beau (Actor)
3129 N Summit Pointe Dr
Topanga, CA 90290-4483, USA

Bridges, Bill (Athlete, Basketball Player)
2322 44rd St
Santa Monica, CA 90405-2102, USA

Bridges, Chloe (Actor)
c/o Kathy Bridges *Bridges Entertainment*
928 N San Fernando Blvd Ste J279
Burbank, CA 91504-4350, USA

Bridges, Jeff (Actor, Producer)
PO Box 20151
Santa Barbara, CA 93120-0151, USA

Bridges, Jeremy (Athlete, Football Player)
16213 S 31st Way
Phoenix, AZ 85048-7727, USA

Bridges, Jordan (Actor)
c/o Myrna Jacoby *MJ Management*
130 W 57th St Apt 11A
New York, NY 10019-3311, USA

Bridges, Krista (Actor)
c/o Murray Gibson *Red Management*
415 Esplanade W Box 3
North Vancouver, BC V7M 1A6, CANADA

Bridges, Leon (Musician)
c/o Michael McDonald *Mick Management*
35 Washington St
Brooklyn, NY 11201-1028, USA

Bridges, Rocky (Athlete, Baseball Player)
1128 W Shane Dr
Coeur D Alene, ID 83815-9788, USA

Bridges, Ruby (Activist)
Ruby Bridges Foundation
PO Box 430
Harvey, LA 70059-0430, USA

Bridges, Todd (Actor)
c/o Staff Member *DVFilmworks*
10850 Wilshire Blvd Ste 350
Los Angeles, CA 90024-4643, USA

Bridgewater, Brad (Athlete, Olympic Athlete, Swimmer)
4740 Paxton Ln
Frisco, TX 75034-2208, USA

Bridgewater, Dee Dee (Musician)
B H Hopper Mgmt
Elvirastr 25
Munich 80636, GERMANY

Bridgewater, Teddy (Athlete, Football Player)
c/o Kennard McGuire *MS World LLC*
1270 Crabb River Rd Ste 600 PMB 104
Richmond, TX 77469-5635, USA

Bridgman, Mel (Athlete, Hockey Player)
221 Concord St # 17
El Segundo, CA 90245-3799, USA

Bridgmohan, Shaun (Horse Racer)
4541 NW 5th St
Plantation, FL 33317-2132, USA

Brie, Alison (Actor)

Brief Smile, A (Music Group)
c/o Staff Member *Paradigm (Monterey)*
404 W Franklin St
Monterey, CA 93940-2303, USA

Briehl, Tom (Athlete, Football Player)
7752 N Via De La Montana
Scottsdale, AZ 85258-3320, USA

Briem, Anita (Actor)
c/o Steve Cohen *United Talent Agency (UTA)*
9336 Civic Center Dr
Beverly Hills, CA 90210-3604, USA

Brien, Doug (Athlete, Football Player)
55 Cambrian Ave
Piedmont, CA 94611-3606, USA

Brier, Kathy (Actor, Musician)
c/o Ricki Olshan *Buchwald (NY)*
10 E 44th St
New York, NY 10017-3601, USA

Briere, Daniel (Athlete, Hockey Player)
134 S Front St
Philadelphia, PA 19106-3115, USA

Brierley, Ronald A (Business Person)
Guinness Peat Group
21-26 Garlick Hill
London EC4 2AU, UNITED KINGDOM (UK)

Brigance, O J (Athlete, Football Player)
14 Woodfield Ct
Reisterstown, MD 21136-4639, USA

Brigati, Eddie (Musician, Songwriter, Writer)
Dassinger Creative
32 Ardsley Rd # 201
Montclair, NJ 07042-5002, USA

Briggs, Dan (Athlete, Baseball Player)
658 Little Rock Rd
Westerville, OH 43082-6423, USA

Briggs, Danny (Athlete, Golfer)
3730 Ravens Trace Ln
Franklin, TN 37064-4710, USA

Briggs, Greg (Athlete, Football Player)
11115 Harvest Dale Ave
Houston, TX 77065-3338, USA

Briggs, Johnny (Athlete, Baseball Player)
340 Tom Bell Rd Spc 133
Murphys, CA 95247-9735, USA

Briggs, Lance (Athlete, Football Player)
225 NE Mizner Blvd Ste 685
Boca Raton, FL 33432-4080, USA

Briggs, Raymond R (Cartoonist, Writer)
Weston
Underhill Lane
Westmeston near Hassocks
Sussex, UNITED KINGDOM (UK)

Briggs, Wilma (Athlete, Baseball Player, Commentator)
111 Summit Ave
Wakefield, RI 02879-2228, USA

Brigham, Jeremy (Athlete, Football Player)
1141 Catalina Dr
Livermore, CA 94550-5928, USA

Bright, Cameron (Actor)
c/o Vickie Petronio *Play Management*
220-807 Powell St
Vancouver, BC V6A 1H7, CANADA

Bright, Jason (Race Car Driver)
29103 Arnold Dr
Sonoma, CA 95476-9761, USA

Bright, Kevin (Director, Producer)
12903 Chalon Rd
Los Angeles, CA 90049-1253, USA

Bright, Leon (Athlete, Football Player)
1183 Dutton Ave
Deland, FL 32720-5011, USA

Brightbill, Susan (Actor, Writer)
c/o Michael Lasker *Mosaic Media Group*
407 N Maple Dr # 100
Beverly Hills, CA 90210-3818, USA

Brightman, Sarah (Musician)
c/o Whitney Tancred *42West*
1840 Century Park E Ste 700
Los Angeles, CA 90067-2122, USA

Brigman, D J (Athlete, Golfer)
8304 Calle Soquelle NE
Albuquerque, NM 87113-1771, USA

Briley, Greg (Athlete, Baseball Player)
2170 Sunnybrook Rd
Greenville, NC 27834-1164, USA

Briley, John (Writer)
c/o Jack Gilardi *ICM Partners*
10250 Constellation Blvd Fl 7
Los Angeles, CA 90067-6207, USA

Brill, Charlie (Actor)
3635 Wrightwood Dr
Studio City, CA 91604-3947, USA

Brill, Francesca (Actor)
Kate Feast Primrose Hill Studios
Fitzroy Road
London NW1 8TR, UNITED KINGDOM (UK)

Brilley, Greg (Athlete, Baseball Player)
2170 Sunnybrook Rd
Greenville, NC 27834-1164, usa

Brilz, Darrick (Athlete, Football Player)
794 Riverwatch Dr
Crescent Springs, KY 41017-5389, USA

Brim, James (Athlete, Football Player)
3772 Shadow Ridge Dr
High Point, NC 27265-8406, USA

Brimanis, Aris (Athlete, Hockey Player)
12909 Badger Ln
Anchorage, AK 99516-3034, USA

Brimley, Wilford (Actor)
2477 Riverfront Dr
Santa Clara, UT 84765-5437, USA

Brin, Sergey (Business Person)
c/o Staff Member *Google Inc*
1600 Amphitheatre Pkwy
Mountain View, CA 94043-1351, USA

Brind'amour, Rod (Athlete, Hockey Player)
Carolina Hurricanes
1400 Edwards Mill Rd Attn Coachingstaff
Raleigh, NC 27607-3624, USA

Brind'amour, Rod (Athlete, Hockey Player)
12304 Birchfalls Dr
Raleigh, NC 27614-7900, USA

Brindley, Doug (Athlete, Hockey Player)
Caledon Village Ontario Provincial Police
18473 Hurontario St
Caledon Village, ON L7K 0X8, Canada

Brinegar, Claude (Politician)
2444 Sharon Oaks Dr
Menlo Park, CA 94025-6829, USA

Bring Me the Horizon (Music Group)
c/o Craig Jennings *Raw Power Management*
Bridle House 36 Bridle Ln
London W1F 9BZ, UNITED KINGDOM

Brink, Brad (Athlete, Baseball Player)
2628 Surrey Ave
Modesto, CA 95355-4668, USA

Brink, Larry (Athlete, Football Player)
13310 Tierra Heights Rd13310 Tierra Heights Rd13310 Tierra Heights Rd
Redding, CA 96003-7489, USA

Brinker, Christopher (Producer)
c/o David Krintzman *Morris Yorn Barnes Levine Krintzman Rubenstein Kohner & Gellman*
2000 Avenue of the Stars Ste 300N
Tower N Fl 3
Los Angeles, CA 90067-4704, USA

Brinker, Nancy (Business Person)
The Susan G. Komen Breast Cancer Foundation, Inc
5005 Lyndon B Johnson Fwy Ste 526
Dallas, TX 75244-6169

Brinkley, Christie (Model)
c/o Brian Dubin *Artist Brand Alliance*
11 E 86th St Fl 9
New York, NY 10028-0501, USA

Brinkman, Chuck (Athlete, Baseball Player)
126 Country Club Rd
Bryan, OH 43506-9136, USA

Brinkman, Joe (Athlete, Baseball Player)
10351 NW 70th St
Chiefland, FL 32626-5042, USA

Brino, Lorenzo (Actor)
c/o Wendy Wilke *Media Partners*
636 Acanto St Apt 207
Los Angeles, CA 90049-2128, USA

Brino, Nikolas (Actor)
c/o Wendy Wilke *Media Partners*
636 Acanto St Apt 207
Los Angeles, CA 90049-2128, USA

Brino, Zachary (Actor)
c/o Wendy Wilke *Media Partners*
636 Acanto St Apt 207
Los Angeles, CA 90049-2128, USA

Brinson, Dana (Athlete, Football Player)
1100 Clark St
Valdosta, GA 31601-3744, USA

Brinson, Larry (Athlete, Football Player)
4614 Rainbow Run
Sugar Land, TX 77479-2039, USA

Brinson, Lewis (Athlete, Baseball Player)
c/o Kenny Felder *Excel Sports Management*
1700 Broadway Fl 29
New York, NY 10019-6559, USA

Brion, Francoise (Actor)
c/o Staff Member *Cineart*
28 Rue Mogador
Paris F-75009, FRANCE

Brisbin, David (Actor)
c/o Geneva Bray *GVA Talent Agency Inc*
193 N Robertson Blvd
Beverly Hills, CA 90211-2103, USA

Brisby, Vincent (Athlete, Football Player)
13102 Fallsview Ln Apt 5203
Houston, TX 77077-3643, USA

Brisco, Jack (Wrestler)
19018 Blake Rd
Odessa, FL 33556-4402, USA

Brisco, Marlin (Athlete, Football Player)
379 Newport Ave Apt 107
Long Beach, CA 90814-7011, USA

Brisco, Valerie (Athlete, Track Athlete)
USA Track & Field
4341 Starlight Dr
Indianapolis, IN 46239-1473, USA

Briscoe, Brent (Actor)
c/o Robert Enriquez *Red Baron Management*
1600 Rosecrans Ave
Manhattan Beach, CA 90266-3708, USA

Briscoe, John (Athlete, Baseball Player)
6815 Casa Loma Ave
Dallas, TX 75214-4003, USA

Briscoe, Ryan (Race Car Driver)
108 Hickory Hill Rd
Mooresville, NC 28117-8086, USA

Brisebois, Danielle (Musician, Producer)
1034 Garfield Ave
Venice, CA 90291-4935, USA

Brisebois, Patrice (Athlete, Hockey Player)
4723 Castle Cir
Broomfield, CO 80023-4079, USA

Brisson, Lance (Actor)
4570 Noeline Way
Encino, CA 91436-2108, USA

Brister, Walter A (Bubby) III (Athlete, Football Player)
4202 Ava Ln
Monroe, LA 71201-2099, USA

Bristol, Dave (Athlete, Baseball Player, Coach)
1748 Fairview Rd
Andrews, NC 28901-7426, USA

Bristor, John (Athlete, Football Player)
70 Rinehart Ln
Waynesburg, PA 15370-3412, USA

Bristow, Allan (Athlete, Basketball Player)
510 Sand Hill Ct
Marco Island, FL 34145-5859, USA

Bristow, Allan M (Athlete, Basketball Player, Coach)
PO Box 635
Gloucester Point, VA 23062-0635, USA

Brito, Jorge (Athlete, Baseball Player)
9348 Snake Rd
Athens, AL 35611-8031, USA

Brito, Michelle (Athlete, Tennis Player)
Tenis De Portugal
Rua Actor Chaby Pinheiro, 7 - A
Linda-A-Velha 2795 - 060, Portugal

Brito, Tilson (Athlete, Baseball Player)
6809 Fishers Farm Ln Unit F1
Charlotte, NC 28277-0334, USA

Britt, BJ (Actor)
c/o Jeff Morrone *Atlas Artists*
9220 W Sunset Blvd Ste 225
Los Angeles, CA 90069-3513, USA

Britt, Charley (Athlete, Football Player)
128 Savannah Pointe
North Augusta, SC 29841-3586, USA

Britt, Chris (Cartoonist)
State Journal-Register
1 Copley Plz
Editorial Dept
Springfield, IL 62701-1619, USA

Britt, James (Athlete, Football Player)
PO Box 371202
Decatur, GA 30037-1202, USA

Britt, Jessie (Athlete, Football Player)
4003 Coltrain Rd
Greensboro, NC 27455-2631, USA

Britt, Justin (Athlete, Football Player)
c/o Dave Butz *Sportstars Inc*
1370 Avenue of the Americas Fl 19
New York, NY 10019-4602, USA

Britt, Kenny (Athlete, Football Player)
c/o Bill Johnson *SportsTrust Advisors*
3340 Peachtree Rd NE Fl 16
Atlanta, GA 30326-1000, USA

Britt, May (Actor)
5059 Enfield Ave
Encino, CA 91316-3502, USA

Britt, Tyrone (Athlete, Basketball Player)
4631 Germantown Ave
Philadelphia, PA 19144-3010, USA

Britt, Wayman (Athlete, Basketball Player)
973 Paradise Lake Dr SE
Grand Rapids, MI 49546-3828, USA

Brittain, Michael (Mike) (Athlete, Basketball Player)
2101 Sunset Point Rd Apt 602
Clearwater, FL 33765-1277, USA

Brittany, Morgan (Actor, Model)
3434 Cornell Rd
Agoura Hills, CA 91301-2714, USA

Brittenum, John (Athlete, Football Player)
PO Box 3773
Fayetteville, AR 72702-3773, USA

Britton, Bill (Athlete, Golfer)
32 Western Reach
Red Bank, NJ 07701-5439, USA

Britton, Cameron (Actor)
c/o Nick Campbell *Velocity Entertainment Partners*
5455 Wilshire Blvd Ste 1502
Los Angeles, CA 90036-4204, USA

Britton, Chris (Athlete, Baseball Player)
7481 NW 11th Ct
Plantation, FL 33313-5913, USA

Britton, Christopher (Actor)
c/o Staff Member *Red Management*
415 Esplanade W Box 3
North Vancouver, BC V7M 1A6, CANADA

Britton, Connie (Actor, Musician)
c/o Sarah Yorke *Baker Winokur Ryder Public Relations*
200 5th Ave Fl 5
New York, NY 10010-3307, USA

Britton, Dave (Athlete, Basketball Player)
6321 Old Ox Rd
Dallas, TX 75241-2733, USA

Britton, Eben (Athlete, Football Player)
c/o Tom Condon *Creative Artists Agency (CAA)*
401 Commerce St PH
Nashville, TN 37219-2516, USA

Britton, Jim (Athlete, Baseball Player)
825 Forestwalk Dr
Suwanee, GA 30024-4243, USA

Britton, Tony (Actor)
c/o Staff Member *Independent Talent Group*
40 Whitfield St
London W1T 2RH, UNITED KINGDOM

Britton, Zach (Athlete, Baseball Player)
101 Heritage Ln
Weatherford, TX 76087-4422, USA

Britts, Sam (Athlete, Football Player)
10 Kingsbrook Ln
Saint Louis, MO 63132-3006, USA

Britz, Greg (Athlete, Hockey Player)
245 Ocean Ave
Marblehead, MA 01945-3700, USA

Britz, Jerilyn (Athlete, Golfer)
415 E Lincoln St Apt 7
Luverne, MN 56156-1643, USA

Brizendine, Louann (Writer)
UCSF School of Medicine
401 Parnassus Ave
Langporter
San Francisco, CA 94143-2211, USA

Brizzolara, Tony (Athlete, Baseball Player)
3424 Wise Way
The Villages, FL 32163-0172, USA

Broad, Eli (Business Person)
Eli & Edythe Broad Foundation
2121 Ave of Stars Ste 3000
Los Angeles, CA 90067-5058, USA

Broadbent, Jim (Actor)
c/o Sally Long-Innes *Independent Talent Group*
40 Whitfield St
London W1T 2RH, UNITED KINGDOM

Broadhead, James L (Business Person)
FPL Group
700 Universe Blvd
Juno Beach, FL 33408-2657, USA

Broadnax, Jerry (Athlete, Football Player)
429 Weaver St
Cedar Hill, TX 75104-9074, USA

Broadway, Lance (Athlete, Baseball Player)
4106 Greenwood Way
Mansfield, TX 76063-5562, USA

Broberg, Gus (Athlete, Basketball Player)
223 Peruvian Ave
Palm Beach, FL 33480-4635, USA

Broberg, Pete (Athlete, Baseball Player)
220 Monterey Rd
Palm Beach, FL 33480-3228, USA

Brocail, Doug (Athlete, Baseball Player)
8011 Meadow Vista Dr
Missouri City, TX 77459-5734, USA

Broccoli, Barbara (Producer)
709 N Hillcrest Rd
Beverly Hills, CA 90210-3516, USA

Brochtrup, Bill (Actor)
S D B Partners
1801 Ave of Stars
#902
Los Angeles, CA 90067, USA

Brochu, Stephane (Athlete, Hockey Player)
6029 Evergreen Ln
Grand Blanc, MI 48439-9643, USA

Brock, Chris (Athlete, Baseball Player)
7684 Markham Bend Pl
Sanford, FL 32771-8107, USA

Brock, Clyde (Athlete, Football Player)
5592 Yorkshire Pl
Lake Oswego, OR 97035-3382, USA

Brock, Dieter (Athlete, Football Player)
436 Cambrian Ridge Trl
Pelham, AL 35124-4832, USA

Brock, Greg (Athlete, Baseball Player)
3727 Valley Oak Dr
Loveland, CO 80538-8930, USA

Brock, Lou (Athlete, Baseball Player)
9716 Bonhomme Estates Dr
Saint Louis, MO 63132-4102, USA

Brock, Matt (Athlete, Football Player)
3105 SW 98th Ave
Portland, OR 97225-2924, USA

Brock, Pete (Athlete, Football Player)
111 Main St
Topsfield, MA 01983-1420, USA

Brock, Raheem (Athlete, Football Player)
25 Ave At Port Imperial Apt 1119
West New York, NJ 07093-8362, USA

Brock, Stanley J (Stan) (Athlete, Football Player)
2555 SW 81st Ave
Portland, OR 97225-3839, USA

Brock, Stevie (Actor, Musician)

Brock, Tarrik (Athlete, Baseball Player)
8111 Fairchild Ave
Winnetka, CA 91306-2012, USA

Brock, Tramaine (Athlete, Football Player)

Brock, Willie (Athlete, Football Player)
3732 NE 70th Ave
Portland, OR 97213-5141, USA

Brockel, Richie (Athlete, Football Player)

Brockermeyer, Blake (Athlete, Football Player)
PO Box 789
Wilson, WY 83014-0789, USA

Brock III, William E (Bill) (Politician)
16 Revell St
Annapolis, MD 21401-2611, USA

Brockington, John (Athlete, Football Player)
The Guardian 311 Camino Del Rio N Ste 1150
Suite1500
San Diego, CA 92108, USA

Brock Jr, Lou (Athlete, Football Player)
1015 Sandstone Dr
Saint Louis, MO 63146-5031, USA

Brocklander, Fred (Athlete, Baseball Player)
317 Eagles Lndg Ct Apt K
Odenton, MD 21113-5203, USA

Brockovich, Erin (Activist)
29365 Castlehill Dr
Agoura Hills, CA 91301-4432, USA

Broderick, Beth (Actor)
Innovative Artists
1505 10th St
Santa Monica, CA 90401-2805, USA

Broderick, Len (Athlete, Hockey Player)
216 Inverness Way
Easley, SC 29642-3116, USA

Broderick, Matthew (Actor)
PO Box 10459
Burbank, CA 91510-0459, USA

Broderson, Morris (Artist)
5707 Costello Ave
Valley Glen, CA 91401-4329, USA

Brodeur, Martin (Athlete, Hockey Player)
10 Sherwyn Ln
Saint Louis, MO 63141-7821, USA

Brodeur, Richard (Athlete, Hockey Player)
5007 Angus Dr
Vancouver, BC V6M 3M6, Canada

Brodie, John (Athlete, Football Player, Golfer)
49350 Avenida Fernando
La Quinta, CA 92253-2742, USA

Brodie, Kevin (Actor)
3925 Big Oak Dr Apt 5
Studio City, CA 91604-3800, USA

Brodowski, Dick (Athlete, Baseball Player)
82 Clark St
Lynn, MA 01902-1101, USA

Brodsky, Julian A (Business Person)
Comcast Corp
1500 Market St Fl 11E
Philadelphia, PA 19102-2107, USA

Brody, Adam (Actor)
1539 N Laurel Ave Apt 305
Los Angeles, CA 90046-2591, USA

Brody, Adrien (Actor)
c/o Alan Nierob *Rogers & Cowan*
1840 Century Park E Fl 18
Los Angeles, CA 90067-2101, USA

Brody, Jon Lee (Actor)
c/o Terry Cohen *Cohen Entertainment*
964 Hancock Ave Apt 305
West Hollywood, CA 90069-4091, USA

Brody, Lane (Music Group)
Black Stallion Country Productions
PO Box 368
Tujunga, CA 91043-0368, USA

Brogan, James (Athlete, Basketball Player)
6631 Hollycrest Ct
San Diego, CA 92121-4137, USA

Brogdon, Cindy (Athlete, Basketball Player, Olympic Athlete)
4160 Baxter Trl
Suwanee, GA 30024-8384, USA

Broglio, Ernie (Athlete, Baseball Player)
2838 Via Carmen
San Jose, CA 95124-1442, USA

Brogna, Rico (Athlete, Baseball Player)
2 Gate Post Ln
Woodbury, CT 06798-2136, USA

Brohamer, Jack (Athlete, Baseball Player)
39017 Narcissus Dr
Palm Desert, CA 92211-1882, USA

Brohawn, Troy (Athlete, Baseball Player)
1619 Taylors Island Rd
Woolford, MD 21677-1328, USA

Brohm, Jeff (Athlete, Football Player)
3820 Balmoral Dr
Champaign, IL 61822-8117, USA

Brokaw, Gary (Athlete, Basketball Player)
6614 Augustine Way
Charlotte, NC 28270-0891, USA

Brokaw, Tom (Journalist)
66 E 79th St Apt 11S
New York, NY 10075-0274, USA

Broken Lizard (Comedian)
c/o Staff Member *United Talent Agency (UTA)*
9336 Civic Center Dr
Beverly Hills, CA 90210-3604, USA

Brolin, James (Actor)
c/o Scott Hart *Scott Hart Entertainment*
14622 Ventura Blvd # 746
Sherman Oaks, CA 91403-3600, USA

Brolin, Josh (Actor)
c/o Staff Member *Brolin Productions*
1507 7th St Ste 566
Santa Monica, CA 90401-2605, USA

Brolly, Shane (Actor)
c/o Steven Siebert *Lighthouse Entertainment Group*
9229 W Sunset Blvd Ste 630
W Hollywood, CA 90069-3419, USA

Bromberg, David (Musician)
c/o Staff Member *UTA Music/The Agency Group*
9336 Civic Center Dr
Beverly Hills, CA 90210-3604, USA

Bromell, Loranzo (Athlete, Football Player)
18 Forest View Rd
Cumberland, VA 23040-2508, USA

Bromley, Gary (Athlete, Hockey Player)
1130 Munro St
Victoria, BC V9A 5P1, Canada

Bromley, Jay (Athlete, Football Player)

Bromstad, David (Designer)
c/o Ken Slotnick *AGI Entertainment*
150 E 58th St Fl 19
New York, NY 10155-1900, USA

Bron, Eleanor (Actor)
c/o Rebecca Blond *Rebecca Blond Associates*
69a Kings Rd
London SW3 4NX, UNITED KINGDOM

Bronfman, Charles (Commentator)
501 N Lake Way
Palm Beach, FL 33480-3520, USA

Bronfman, Hannah (Actor)
c/o Alexandra Crotin *The Lede Company*
9701 Wilshire Blvd # 930
Beverly Hills, CA 90212-2020, USA

Bronfman, Yefin (Musician)
I C M Artists
40 W 57th St
New York, NY 10019-4001, USA

Bronkey, Jeff (Athlete, Baseball Player)
622 Sunny Brook Dr
Edmond, OK 73034-4224, USA

Bronleewe, Matt (Musician)
Flood Burnstead McCready McCarthy
1700 Hayes St Ste 304
Nashville, TN 37203-3593, USA

Bronson, Ben (Athlete, Football Player)
13333 West Rd Apt 1717
Houston, TX 77041-6153, USA

Bronson, Po (Writer)
Random House
1745 Broadway Frnt 3 # B1
New York, NY 10019-4343, USA

Bronson, Zack (Athlete, Football Player)
5735 Jackie Ln
Beaumont, TX 77713-9261, USA

Bronstad, Jim (Athlete, Baseball Player)
63 One Main Pl
Benbrook, TX 76126-2206, USA

Bronstein, Elizabeth (Producer)
c/o Staff Member *Creative Artists Agency (CAA)*
2000 Avenue of the Stars Ste 100
Los Angeles, CA 90067-4705, USA

Brook, Apple (Actor)
c/o Staff Member *Grays Management & Associates*
Panther House
38 Mount Pleasant
London WC1X 0AP, UK

Brook, Holly (Musician)
c/o Staff Member *Paradigm (Monterey)*
404 W Franklin St
Monterey, CA 93940-2303, USA

Brook, Jayne (Actor)
c/o Leslie Siebert *Gersh*
9465 Wilshire Blvd Ste 600
Beverly Hills, CA 90212-2605, USA

Brook, Kelly (Actor)
c/o Evan Hainey *Untitled Entertainment*
350 S Beverly Dr Ste 200
Beverly Hills, CA 90212-4819, USA

Brook, Peter S P (Director)
CICT
13 Blvd de Rochechouart
Paris 75009, FRANCE

Brooke, Allison (Music Group, Songwriter, Writer)
2-K/EMI Records
6920 W Sunset Blvd
Los Angeles, CA 90028-7010, USA

Brooke, Ally (Musician)
c/o Carleen Donovan *Donovan Public Relations*
30 E 20th St Ste 2FE
New York, NY 10003-1310, USA

Brooke, Bob (Athlete, Hockey Player, Olympic Athlete)
15496 Stanburry Curv
Eden Prairie, MN 55347-2433, USA

Brooke, Jonatha (Musician, Songwriter, Writer)
Brooke
1255 5th Ave Apt 7J
New York, NY 10029-3848, USA

Brooke, Paul (Actor)
c/o Staff Member *Caroline Dawson Assoc.*
125 Gloucester Rd
2nd Floor
London SW7 4TE, UK

Brookens, Ike (Athlete, Baseball Player)
1053 Brookens Rd
Fayetteville, PA 17222-9314, USA

Brookens, Tom (Athlete, Baseball Player)
488 Black Gap Rd
Fayetteville, PA 17222-9717, USA

Brooker, Gary (Musician, Songwriter, Writer)
5 Cranley Gardens
London SW7, UNITED KINGDOM (UK)

Brooker, Tommy (Athlete, Football Player)
306 Woodridge Dr
Tuscaloosa, AL 35406-1923, USA

Brookes, Peter (Cartoonist)
London Times
Editorial Dept
1 Pennington St
London E98 1S5, UNITED KINGDOM (UK)

Brooke-Taylor, Tim (Actor, Comedian)
Jill Foster Ltd
3 Lonsdale Road
London SW13 9ED, UNITED KINGDOM (UK)

Brooking, Keith (Athlete, Football Player)
883 Lenox Ct NE
Atlanta, GA 30324-2982, USA

Brookins, Clarence (Athlete, Basketball Player)
8266 Fayette St
Philadelphia, PA 19150-2002, USA

Brookins, Gary (Cartoonist)
Richmond Newspapers
Editorial Dept
PO Box 85333
Richmond, VA 23293-0001, USA

Brookins, Jason (Athlete, Football Player)
523 N Wade St Apt C
Mexico, MO 65265-1880, USA

Brooks, Aaron (Athlete, Football Player)
1005 Middle Quarter Ct
Henrico, VA 23238-5920, USA

Brooks, Adam (Director)
c/o Jeff Gorin *WME|IMG*
9601 Wilshire Blvd
Beverly Hills, CA 90210-5213, USA

Brooks, Ahmad (Athlete, Football Player)

Brooks, Albert (Actor, Director, Writer)
3051 Antelo View Dr
Los Angeles, CA 90077-1607, USA

Brooks, Alex (Athlete, Hockey Player)
423 Glenmeadow Dr
Ballwin, MO 63011-3466, USA

Brooks, Amanda (Actor)
c/o Staff Member *Paradigm*
8942 Wilshire Blvd
Beverly Hills, CA 90211-1908, USA

Brooks, Angelle (Actor)
c/o Staff Member *Pakula/King & Associates*
9229 W Sunset Blvd Ste 315
Los Angeles, CA 90069-3403, USA

Brooks, Avery (Actor)
c/o Lilianna Laouri *Vanguard Management Group*
8060 Melrose Ave Fl 4
Los Angeles, CA 90046-7038, USA

Brooks, Barrett (Athlete, Football Player)
11 Berkshire Dr
Voorhees, NJ 08043-3448, USA

Brooks, Bill (Athlete, Football Player)
1088 Laurelwood
Carmel, IN 46032-8742, USA

Brooks, Bobby D (Athlete, Football Player)
7416 Red Osier Rd
Dallas, TX 75249-1349, USA

Brooks, Brandon (Athlete, Football Player)
c/o Joe Panos *Athletes First*
23091 Mill Creek Dr
Laguna Hills, CA 92653-1258, USA

Brooks, Bucky (Athlete, Football Player)
5124 Casland Dr
Raleigh, NC 27604-5449, USA

Brooks, Chet (Athlete, Football Player)
655 Shadyway Dr
Dallas, TX 75232-4821, USA

Brooks, Danielle (Actor)
c/o Jill McGrath *Door24*
115 W 29th St Rm 1102
New York, NY 10001-5106, USA

Brooks, Danny (Musician)
American Promotions
2011 Ferry Ave Apt U19
Camden, NJ 08104-1900, USA

Brooks, David Allen (David A) (Actor)
c/o Staff Member *Candy Entertainment Management*
8981 W Sunset Blvd Ste 310
West Hollywood, CA 90069-1848, USA

Brooks, Derrick (Athlete, Football Player)
Derrick Brooks Charities 10014 N Dale Mabry Hwy Ste 101
Tamna, FL 33618-4426, USA

Brooks, Donnie (Musician)
Al Lampkin Entertainment
1817 W Verdugo Ave
Burbank, CA 91506-2149, USA

Brooks, Ed (Athlete, Golfer)
6604 Augusta Rd
Fort Worth, TX 76132-4564, USA

Brooks, E R (Business Person)
Central & South West Corp
1616 Woodall Rodgers Fwy
Dallas, TX 75202-1234, USA

Brooks, Ethan (Athlete, Football Player)
8 Gatewood
Avon, CT 06001-3949, USA

Brooks, Garth (Musician, Songwriter)
c/o Bob Doyle *Bob Doyle & Associates*
1111 17th Ave S
Nashville, TN 37212-2203, USA

Brooks, Geraldine (Writer)
c/o Staff Member *Viking Press*
375 Hudson St
New York, NY 10014-3658, USA

Brooks, Golden (Actor)
c/o Ryan Revel *Good Fear Film + Management*
6255 W Sunset Blvd Ste 800
Los Angeles, CA 90028-7409, USA

Brooks, Greg (Athlete, Football Player)
3041 Alex Kornman Blvd
Harvey, LA 70058-2012, USA

Brooks, Hubert (Hubie) (Athlete, Baseball Player)
15001 Olive St
Hesperia, CA 92345-3306, USA

Brooks, Jamal (Athlete, Football Player)
8 Chestnut Bluffs Ct
Greensboro, NC 27407-6376, USA

Brooks, James (Athlete, Football Player)
2876 Sycamore Creek Dr
Independence, KY 41051-8410, USA

Brooks, James L (Actor, Director, Producer)
c/o Staff Member *Gracie Films*
10201 W Pico Blvd Bldg 41/42
Los Angeles, CA 90064-2606, USA

Brooks, Jason (Actor)
c/o Aaron Kogan *AK Management (LA)*
1680 Vine St
Taft Bldg #518
Los Angeles, CA 90028-8804, USA

Brooks, Jerry (Athlete, Baseball Player)
15152 Mountain View Ln
Frisco, TX 75035-6882, USA

Brooks, Jimmie (Athlete, Football Player)
10007 Shining Willow Dr Apt 207
Louisville, KY 40241-3148

Brooks, Jon (Athlete, Football Player)
104 Carver St
Saluda, SC 29138-1514, USA

Brooks, Karen (Musician)
5408 Clearview Ln
Waterford, WI 53185-2950, USA

Brooks, Kevin (Athlete, Football Player)
11620 Audelia Rd Apt 614
Dallas, TX 75243-5683, USA

Brooks, Kimberly A (Actor)
c/o Kevin Turner *Coast to Coast Talent Group*
3350 Barham Blvd
Los Angeles, CA 90068-1404, USA

Brooks, Kix (Musician, Songwriter)
Brooks & Dunn
PO Box 120669
Nashville, TN 37212-0669, USA

Brooks, Larry (Athlete, Football Player)
PO Box 9058 Attn: Football Coaching Staff
Petersburg, VA 23806-0001, USA

Brooks, Lee (Athlete, Football Player)
4206 Bamford Dr
Austin, TX 78731-1355, USA

Brooks, Macey (Athlete, Football Player)
693 Manhattan Cir
Oswego, IL 60543-9802, USA

Brooks, Mark (Athlete, Golfer)
4215 Pershing Ave
Fort Worth, TX 76107-4314, USA

Brooks, Mehcad (Actor)
c/o Monique Gonzalez *Persona Public Relations*
6255 W Sunset Blvd Ste 705
Hollywood, CA 90028-7408, USA

Brooks, Mel (Actor, Director)
c/o Staff Member *BrooksFilms Ltd / Culver Studios*
9336 Washington Blvd
Culver City, CA 90232-2600

Brooks, Meredith (Musician)
4197 NW Douglas Ave
Corvallis, OR 97330-1717, USA

Brooks, Michael (Athlete, Football Player)
30 Pine Tree Dr
Honey Brook, PA 19344-1254, USA

Brooks, Michael (Athlete, Football Player)
5002 Weatherstone Dr
Greensboro, NC 27406-8724, USA

Brooks, Mike (Athlete, Football Player)
716 2nd Ave
Ruston, LA 71270-6066, USA

Brooks, Nate (Athlete, Boxer, Olympic Athlete)
13717 Dressler Ave
Cleveland, OH 44125-5044, USA

Brooks, Nathan (Boxer)
13717 Dressler Ave
Cleveland, OH 44125-5044, USA

Brooks, Reggie (Athlete, Football Player)
1701 Portage Ave
South Bend, IN 46616-1919, USA

Brooks, Rich (Athlete, Coach, Football Coach, Football Player)
700 Delaney Woods
Nicholasville, KY 40356-8781, USA

Brooks, Richard (Actor)
333 Washington Blvd # 102
Marina Del Rey, CA 90292-5152, USA

Brooks, Robert (Athlete, Football Player)
8611 N 17th Pl # Pi
Phoenix, AZ 85020-3320, USA

Brooks, Ron (Athlete, Football Player)
c/o Pat Dye Jr *SportsTrust Advisors*
3340 Peachtree Rd NE Fl 16
Atlanta, GA 30326-1000, USA

Brooks, Ross (Athlete, Hockey Player)
196 Old River Rd Apt 215
Lincoln, RI 02865-1133, USA

Brooks, Scott (Athlete, Basketball Coach, Basketball Player, Coach)
c/o Warren LeGarie *Warren LeGarie Sports Management*
1108 Masonic Ave
San Francisco, CA 94117-2915, USA

Brooks, Steve (Athlete, Football Player)
3403 36th St
Lubbock, TX 79413-2233, USA

Brooks, Terry (Writer)
Del Rey Books
1540 Broadway
New York, NY 10036-4039, USA

Brooks, Tony (Athlete, Football Player)
19626 Northrop St
Cassopolis, MI 49031-9328, USA

Brooks & Dunn (Music Group, Musician)
PO Box 120669
PO Box 120669
Nashville, TN 37212-0669, USA

Brooks Jr, Cliff (Athlete, Football Player)
12023 Briar Forest Dr
Houston, TX 77077-3027, USA

Brooks Jr., Mo (Congressman, Politician)
1641 Longworth Hob
Washington, DC 20515-3005, USA

Brophy, Jay (Athlete, Football Player)
2117 Prestwick Dr
Uniontown, OH 44685-8847, USA

Brophy, Kevin (Actor)
15010 Hamlin St
Van Nuys, CA 91411-1408, USA

Brophy, Nancy (Athlete, Golfer)
141 Carpenter Ln
Rockingham, VA 22801-9777, USA

Brophy, Theodore F (Business Person)
60 Arch St
Greenwich, CT 06830-2507, USA

Broshears, Robert (Artist)
Robert Broshears Studio
8020 NW Holly Rd
Bremerton, WA 98312-9536, USA

Brosius, Scott D (Athlete, Baseball Player)
Linfield College
900 SE Baker St
Hhpa Complex, Mail Code A440
McMinnville, OR 97128-6894, USA

Brosnahan, Rachel (Actor)
c/o Samantha Hill *Wolf-Kasteler Public Relations*
6255 W Sunset Blvd Ste 1111
Los Angeles, CA 90028-7426, USA

Brosnan, Pierce (Actor, Producer)
c/o Jennifer Allen *Viewpoint Inc*
8820 Wilshire Blvd Ste 220
Beverly Hills, CA 90211-2622, USA

Brosnan, Sean (Actor)
c/o Sally Long-Innes *Independent Talent Group*
40 Whitfield St
London W1T 2RH, UNITED KINGDOM

Bross, Terry (Athlete, Baseball Player)
7952 E Camino Real
Scottsdale, AZ 85255-6136, USA

Brossart, Willie (Athlete, Hockey Player)
9318 Susquehanna Trl
Ashland, VA 23005-3382, USA

Brosseau, Frank (Athlete, Baseball Player)
41 Island Rd
Saint Paul, MN 55127-2635, USA

Brostek, Bern (Athlete, Football Player)
PO Box 44552
Kamuela, HI 96743-4552, USA

Broten, Aaron (Athlete, Hockey Player)
307 3rd Ave.
Roseau, SE 56751, USA

Broten, Neal (Athlete, Hockey Player, Olympic Athlete)
N8216 690th St
River Falls, WI 54022-4535, USA

Broten, Paul (Athlete, Hockey Player)
2971 Jordan Ct
Saint Paul, MN 55125-2821, USA

Brothers, Bellamy, The (Musician)
c/o Staff Member *Agency for the Performing Arts (APA)*
405 S Beverly Dr Ste 500
Beverly Hills, CA 90212-4425, USA

Brotherton, John (Actor)
c/o Elizabeth Much *East 2 West Collective*
11022 Santa Monica Blvd Ste 350
Los Angeles, CA 90025-7532, USA

Brotherton, Michael (Race Car Driver)
1317 Summertime Trl
Lewisville, TX 75067-5507, USA

Brough, Randi (Actor)
11684 Ventura Blvd # 476
Studio City, CA 91604-2699, USA

Broughton, Luther (Athlete, Football Player)
PO Box 371
Huger, SC 29450-0371, USA

Broughton, Willie (Athlete, Football Player)
1724 Lacy Ln
Mesquite, TX 75181-1560, USA

Brouhard, Mark (Athlete, Baseball Player)
6289 Jackie Ave
Woodland Hills, CA 91367-1424, USA

Broussard, Ben (Athlete, Baseball Player)
2067 Cedar Breaks Rd
Georgetown, TX 78633-8200, USA

Broussard, Fred (Athlete, Football Player)
2856 FM 1011 Rd
Liberty, TX 77575-7430, USA

Broussard, Israel (Actor)
c/o Jamie Harhay Skinner *Baker Winokur Ryder Public Relations*
9100 Wilshire Blvd
W Tower #500
Beverly Hills, CA 90212-3415, USA

Broussard, Marc (Musician)
c/o Staff Member *Paradigm (Monterey)*
404 W Franklin St
Monterey, CA 93940-2303, USA

Broussard, Rebecca (Actor)
413 Howland Canal
Venice, CA 90291-4619, USA

Broussard, Steve (Athlete, Football Player)
113 Waterland Way
Frederick, MD 21702-4094, USA

Brouwenstyn, Gerada (Actor)
Bachplein 3
Amsterdam NL-1077 GH, The Netherlands

Brow, Scott (Athlete, Baseball Player)
1194 W Remington Dr
Chandler, AZ 85286-6385, USA

Browder, Ben (Actor)
c/o Steven Siebert *Lighthouse Entertainment Group*
9229 W Sunset Blvd Ste 630
W Hollywood, CA 90069-3419, USA

Brower, Bob (Athlete, Baseball Player)
2703 N Van Buren St
Hutchinson, KS 67502-2017, USA

Brower, James (Jim) (Athlete, Baseball Player)
34W002 Cherry Ln
Geneva, IL 60134-4104, USA

Brower, Jordan (Actor)
9100 Wilshire Blvd Ste 503E
Beverly Hills, CA 90212-3419, USA

Brower, Jordan Lloyd (Actor)

Brower, Laurie (Athlete, Golfer)
6407 Peoria Ave
Lubbock, TX 79413-5127, USA

Brown, Aaron (Correspondent)
c/o Carole Cooper *N.S. Bienstock*
888 7th Ave Fl 7
New York, NY 10106-0700, USA

Brown, Aaron C (Athlete, Football Player)
3922 W Robson St
Tampa, FL 33614-2636, USA

Brown, A B (Athlete, Football Player)
224 Wesley St
Salem, NJ 08079-1714, USA

Brown, Adrian (Baseball Player)
Pittsburgh Pirates
604 Pike St
McComb, MS 39648-2250, USA

Brown, Alison (Musician, Songwriter, Writer)
SRO Artists
6629 University Ave Ste 206
Middleton, WI 53562-3037, USA

Brown, Allen (Athlete, Football Player)
454 Highway 569
Ferriday, LA 71334-4445, USA

Brown, Alton (Athlete, Baseball Player)
253 Consul Ave
Virginia Beach, VA 23462-3511, USA

Brown, Alton (Chef, Television Host)
441 Church St NE
Marietta, GA 30060-1319, USA

Brown, Amanda (Musician)
c/o Staff Member *ReverbNation (NY)*
15 E 36th St Apt 2D
New York, NY 10016-3308, USA

Brown, Andre (Athlete, Football Player)
11245 S Emerald Ave
Chicago, IL 60628-4706, USA

Brown, Andy (Athlete, Hockey Player)
6243 S 125 W
Trafalgar, IN 46181-8799, USA

Brown, Antonio (Athlete, Football Player)
c/o Tom Condon *Creative Artists Agency (CAA)*
401 Commerce St PH
Nashville, TN 37219-2516, USA

Brown, Antron (Race Car Driver)
45 Waln Rd
Trenton, NJ 08620, USA

Brown, Arnie (Athlete, Hockey Player)
GD
Woodview, ON K0L 3E0, Canada

Brown, Arnold (Athlete, Football Player)
8763 Stephens Church Rd
Wilmington, NC 28411-7985, USA

Brown, Arthur (Athlete, Football Player)
c/o Doug Hendrickson *Relativity Sports*
2029 Century Park E Ste 1550
Century City, CA 90067-3000, USA

Brown, Arthur (Musician)
c/o Staff Member *Artists2Events*
PO Box 64
Ammanford, Carmarthenshire
Wales SA18 9AB, UK

Brown, Ashley Nicole (Actor)
Hervey/Grimes
PO Box 64249
Los Angeles, CA 90064-0249, USA

Brown, Bill (Athlete, Football Player)
9365 Libby Ln
Eden Prairie, MN 55347-4282, USA

Brown, Bill (Commentator)
15910 Knolls Lodge Dr
Houston, TX 77095-1664, USA

Brown, Billy Aaron (Actor)
c/o John Goschin *Baker Winokur Ryder Public Relations*
9100 Wilshire Blvd Ste 850E
W Tower #500
Beverly Hills, CA 90212-3495, USA

Brown, Billy Ray (Athlete, Golfer)
4110 Woodlake Ln
Missouri City, TX 77459-4330, USA

Brown, Blair (Actor)
18 E 53rd St
#140
New York, NY 10022, USA

Brown, Bob (Athlete, Basketball Player)
7 Charleston St S
Sugar Land, TX 77478-3656, USA

Brown, Bob (Athlete, Football Player)
PO Box 211081
Saint Louis, MO 63121-9081, USA

Brown, Bobby (Athlete, Baseball Player)
700 Pleasant Ridge Ct
Chesapeake, VA 23322-2747, USA

Brown, Bobby (Athlete, Baseball Player)
1600 Texas St Apt 2304
Fort Worth, TX 76102-3494, USA

Brown, Bobby (Musician)
Bobby Brown Foods
21204 Vanowen St
Canoga Park, CA 91303-2823, USA

Brown, Booker (Athlete, Football Player)
3354 Arthur Ave
Mojave, CA 93501-1304, USA

Brown, Boyd (Athlete, Football Player)
PO Box 1852
Natchez, MS 39121-1852, USA

Brown, Brant (Athlete, Baseball Player)
7300 Rough Riders Trl
Frisco, TX 75034-9088, USA

Brown, Brene (Doctor, Writer)
c/o Jennifer Rudolph Walsh *WME|IMG (NY)*
11 Madison Ave Fl 18
New York, NY 10010-3669, USA

Brown, Brianna (Actor)
c/o Molly Schoneveld *S/W PR Shop*
584 N Larchmont Blvd # B
Los Angeles, CA 90004-1306, USA

Brown, Bryan (Actor)
c/o Staff Member *Steve Himber Entertainment*
211 S Beverly Dr # 601
Beverly Hills, CA 90212-3807, USA

Brown, Bryce (Athlete, Football Player)

Brown, Campbell (Correspondent, Journalist)
Partnership for Educational Justice
5252 11th St S
Arlington, VA 22204-3217, USA

Brown, Candace (Actor)
c/o Judy Orbach *Judy O Productions*
6136 Glen Holly St
Hollywood, CA 90068-2338, USA

Brown, Carlos (Athlete, Football Player)
1106 E Newhall Dr
Fresno, CA 93720-4084, USA

Brown, Cedric (Athlete, Football Player)
9005 Salsbury Ln Apt 11
Oklahoma City, OK 73132-2050, USA

Brown, Cedrick (Athlete, Football Player)
74 Arbor Meadow Dr
Sicklerville, NJ 08081-1754, USA

Brown, Chad (Athlete, Football Player)
10287 Dowling Way
Highlands Ranch, CO 80126-4769, USA

Brown, Charles (Athlete, Football Player)
2942 River Rd
Johns Island, SC 29455-8814, USA

Brown, Charles E (Athlete, Football Player)
7317 S Merrill Ave
Chicago, IL 60649-3208, USA

Brown, Charlie (Athlete, Football Player)
7317 S Merrill Ave # 5
Chicago, IL 60649-3208, USA

Brown, Charlie (Athlete, Football Player)
27 Buckeye Dr
Saint Louis, MO 63135-1514, USA

Brown, Charlie (Athlete, Football Player)
3113 Cherry Valley Cir
Fairfield, CA 94534-7510, USA

Brown, Charlie (Athlete, Hockey Player, Olympic Athlete)
4677 Parkridge Dr
Saint Paul, MN 55123-2130, USA

Brown, Charlie R (Athlete, Football Player)
5226 Washington Pl
Saint Louis, MO 63108-1117, USA

Brown, Chris (Musician)
c/o Nicole Perna *Imprint PR*
6121 W Sunset Blvd
Neuehouse
Los Angeles, CA 90028-6442, USA

Brown, Chris (Athlete, Football Player)
7161 Cypress Dr
Westerville, OH 43082-8111, USA

Brown, Chris (Athlete, Football Player)
2513 Broome St
Nolensville, TN 37135-5021, USA

Brown, Chuck (Race Car Driver)
5082 Old NC Highway 49
Asheboro, NC 27205-0118, USA

Brown, Chucky (Athlete, Basketball Player)
102 Balsamwood Ct
Cary, NC 27513-3456, USA

Brown, Chykie (Athlete, Football Player)
c/o Kevin Poston *Deal LLC*
28025 S Harwich Dr
Farmington Hills, MI 48334-4259, USA

Brown, Cindy (Athlete, Basketball Player)
2 Championship Dr
Auburn Hills, MI 48326-1753, USA

Brown, Clancy (Actor)
3141 Oakdell Ln
Studio City, CA 91604-4218, USA

Brown, Clay (Athlete, Football Player)
PO Box 904
Eagar, AZ 85925-0904, USA

Brown, Cleophus (Athlete, Baseball Player)
3912 Sharon Church Rd
Pinson, AL 35126-2660, USA

Brown, Clifford (Athlete, Baseball Player)
5104 N 37th St
Tampa, FL 33610-6421, USA

Brown, Cornell (Athlete, Football Player)
1600 Sangloe Pl
Lynchburg, VA 24502-1822, USA

Brown, Corrine (Congressman, Politician)
2336 Rayburn Hob
Washington, DC 20515-2305, USA

Brown, Corwin (Athlete, Football Player)
613 Primrose Ln
Matteson, IL 60443-1762, USA

Brown, Courtney (Athlete, Football Player)
1133 Schurlknight Rd
Saint Stephen, SC 29479-3617, USA

Brown, Curt (Athlete, Baseball Player)
8331 Sawpine Rd
Delray Beach, FL 33446-9796, USA

Brown, Curtis (Athlete, Baseball Player)
3200 Cloudview Dr
Sacramento, CA 95833-2700, USA

Brown, Curtis (Athlete, Football Player)
7370 San Diego Ave Apt 1
Saint Louis, MO 63121-2259, USA

Brown, Curtis (Athlete, Hockey Player)
467 Carroll St
Sunnyvale, CA 94086-6204, USA

Brown, Curtis L (Astronaut)
204 Starrwood
Hudson, WI 54016-7174, USA

Brown, Curtis L Jr (Astronaut)
204 Starrwood
Hudson, WI 54016-7174, USA

Brown, Dale (Writer)
c/o Robert Gottlieb *Trident Media Group LLC*
41 Madison Ave Fl 36
New York, NY 10010-2257, USA

Brown, Dale D (Coach, Sportscaster)
ESPN-TV
935 Middle St
Sports Dept Espn Plaza
Bristol, CT 06010-1000, USA

Brown, Dan (Writer)
c/o Michael Rudell *Franklin Weinrib Rudell & Vassallo*
488 Madison Ave Fl 22
New York, NY 10022-5704, USA

Brown, Dante (Athlete, Football Player)
c/o Liza Anderson *Anderson Group Public Relations*
8060 Melrose Ave Fl 4
Los Angeles, CA 90046-7038, USA

Brown, Daren (Athlete, Baseball Player)
2502 S Tyler St Attn Managersofc
Tacoma, WA 98405-1051, USA

Brown, Darrell (Athlete, Baseball Player)
Detroit Tigers
2808 Northampton Pl
Oklahoma City, OK 73120-3010, USA

Brown, Dave (Athlete, Hockey Player)
c/o Staff Member *Philadelphia Flyers*
3601 S Broad St Ste 2
First Union Spectrum
Philadelphia, PA 19148-5297, USA

Brown, Dee (Athlete, Baseball Player)
2018 Woodchase Cv
Cordova, TN 38016-5081, USA

Brown, Dee (Athlete, Basketball Player)
575 Birnamwood Dr
Suwanee, GA 30024-7577, USA

Brown, Dee (Athlete, Football Player)
3278 Margellina Dr
Charlotte, NC 28210-4086, USA

Brown, Derek (Athlete, Football Player)
13 Four Leaf Mnr
Rexford, NY 12148-1490, USA

Brown, Dermal (Baseball Player)
Kansas City Royals
2626 Balmoral Ct
Kissimmee, FL 34744-8442, USA

Brown, Don (Athlete, Football Player)
5167 SW 129th Ter
Miramar, FL 33027-5837, USA

Brown, Donald C (Athlete, Football Player)
2797 Union Ave
San Jose, CA 95124-1433, USA

Brown, Dorian (Actor)
c/o Staff Member *McKeon-Myones Management*
3500 W Olive Ave Ste 770
Burbank, CA 91505-5527, USA

Brown, Doug (Athlete, Hockey Player)
11 Chieftans Rd
Greenwich, CT 06831-3260, USA

Brown, Duane (Athlete, Football Player)
c/o Andy Ross *Select Sports Group*
2700 Post Oak Blvd Ste 1450
Houston, TX 77056-5785, USA

Brown, Dustin (Athlete, Hockey Player)
226 Bundy Rd
Ithaca, NY 14850-9249, USA

Brown, Eddie (Athlete, Football Player)
8400 SW 133rd Avenue Rd Apt 214
Miami, FL 33183-4543, USA

Brown, Emil (Athlete, Baseball Player)
17804 Paxton Ave
Lansing, IL 60438-1520, USA

Brown, Eric (Athlete, Football Player)
13011 Castlewind Ln
Pearland, TX 77584-6787, USA

Brown, Faith (Actor)
Million Dollar Music Co
12 Praed Mews
London W2 1QY, UNITED KINGDOM (UK)

Brown, Foxy (Musician)
c/o Marvet Britto *Britto Agency PR*
277 Broadway Ste 110
New York, NY 10007-2072, USA

Brown, Fred (Athlete, Basketball Player, Coach)
PO Box 1353
Mercer Island, WA 98040-1353, USA

Brown, Fred (Athlete, Football Player)
1050 Riverbend Club Dr SE
Atlanta, GA 30339-2805, USA

Brown, Fred R (Athlete, Football Player)
4128 Rigel Ave
Lompoc, CA 93436-1248, USA

Brown, Gary (Athlete, Football Player)
5 Crystal Ln
Brentwood, NY 11717-1114, USA

Brown, Gary (Athlete, Football Player)
35401 Saddle Crk
Avon, OH 44011-4917, USA

Brown, Gates (Athlete, Baseball Player)
17206 Santa Barbara Dr
Detroit, MI 48221-2525, USA

Brown, George (Athlete, Basketball Player)
24652 Santa Barbara St
Southfield, MI 48075-2526, USA

Brown, Georg Stanford (Actor)
2565 Greenvalley Rd
Los Angeles, CA 90046-1437, USA

Brown, Gilbert (Athlete, Football Player)
49374 Sherwood Ct
Belleville, MI 48111-8844, USA

Brown, Gordie (Comedian)
c/o Staff Member *WME|IMG*
9601 Wilshire Blvd
Beverly Hills, CA 90210-5213, USA

Brown, Greg (Athlete, Football Player)
1016 Hartley Ct
Sicklerville, NJ 08081-1109, USA

Brown, Greg (Athlete, Hockey Player)
43 Ladds Way
Scituate, MA 02066-1901, USA

Brown, Guy (Athlete, Football Player)
2233 Forest Hollow Park
Dallas, TX 75228-7826, USA

Brown, Hal (Athlete, Baseball Player)
2915 Crossfield Dr
Greensboro, NC 27408-6743, USA

Brown, Henry (Actor)
1101 E Pike St Ste 300
Seattle, WA 98122-3938, USA

Brown, Henry (Athlete, Baseball Player)
4075 N 61st St
Milwaukee, WI 53216-1210, USA

Brown, Heritage Doris (Athlete, Track Athlete)
Seattle Pacific College
Athletic Dept
Seattle, WA 98119, USA

Brown, Hubie (Basketball Coach, Coach)
120 Foxridge Rd
Atlanta, GA 30327-4310, USA

Brown, Ivory Lee (Athlete, Football Player)
9811 Dale Crest Dr Apt 1026
Dallas, TX 75220-3029, USA

Brown, Jackie (Athlete, Baseball Player)
65600 E 256 Rd
Grove, OK 74344-6135, USA

Brown, James (Sportscaster)
Fox-TV
205 E 67th St
Sports Dept
New York, NY 10065-6089, USA

Brown, James (Athlete, Football Player)
3723 SW 49th Pl
Fort Lauderdale, FL 33312-8231, USA

Brown, James (Musician)
c/o Charles Bobbit *James Brown Enterprises*
PO Box 1051
Augusta, GA 30903-1051, USA

Brown, Jamie (Athlete, Baseball Player)
4050 Bailey Acres Cir
Meridian, MS 39305-9263, USA

Brown, Jammal (Athlete, Football Player)
2223 NE 36th Street
Lawton, OK 73507, USA

Brown, Jarvis (Athlete, Baseball Player)
1537 Teal Dr
Lawrenceville, GA 30043-3296, USA

Brown, Jasmin Savoy (Actor)
c/o Nilda Carrazana *Status PR*
PO Box 6191
Westlake Village, CA 91359-6191, USA

Brown, Jason (Athlete, Football Player)
8810 Gilly Way
Randallstown, MD 21133-5300, USA

Brown, J B (Athlete, Football Player)
9103 Woodmore Center Dr
Lanham, MD 20706-1653, USA

Brown, J Cristopher (Cris) (Baseball Player)
5015 Brighton Ave
Los Angeles, CA 90062-2434, USA

Brown, Jeff (Athlete, Hockey Player)
800 Tara Oaks Dr
Chesterfield, MO 63005, USA

Brown, Jeremy (Athlete, Baseball Player)
704 Cobb St
Birmingham, AL 35209-6515, USA

Brown, J Glen (Horse Racer)
750 Michigan Ave
Columbus, OH 43215-1107, USA

Brown, Jim (Athlete, Football Player)
Amer-I-Can
269 S Beverly Dr # 1048
Beverly Hills, CA 90212-3851, USA

Brown, John (Athlete, Basketball Player)
1329 N Florissant Rd
Saint Louis, MO 63135-1153, USA

Brown, John (Athlete, Football Player)
101 Gadshill Pl
Pittsburgh, PA 15237-2341, USA

Brown, Johnny (Actor)
2732 Woodhaven Dr
Los Angeles, CA 90068-1934, USA

Brown, Jonathan (Athlete, Football Player)
c/o Chad Wiestling *Integrated Sports Management*
2120 Texas St Apt 2204
Houston, TX 77003-3054, USA

Brown, Jonathan Daniel (Actor)
c/o Staff Member *ICM Partners*
10250 Constellation Blvd Fl 7
Los Angeles, CA 90067-6207, USA

Brown, Jophrey (Athlete, Baseball Player)
3008 W 81st St
Inglewood, CA 90305-1425, USA

Brown, Julie (Downtown) (DJ, Television Host)
c/o Steven Jensen *Independent Group, The*
6363 Wilshire Blvd Ste 115
Los Angeles, CA 90048-5734, USA

Brown, Junior (Musician)
c/o Staff Member *Paradigm (Monterey)*
404 W Franklin St
Monterey, CA 93940-2303, USA

Brown, Justin (Athlete, Football Player)

Brown, Kaci (Musician)
c/o Staff Member *Interscope Records (LA) - Main*
2220 Colorado Ave
Santa Monica, CA 90404-3506, USA

Brown, Kale (Actor)
c/o Staff Member *The Gage Group*
5757 Wilshire Blvd Ste 659
Los Angeles, CA 90036-3682, USA

Brown, Katie (Designer, Television Host)

Brown, Keith (Athlete, Baseball Player)
139 Lakeshore Dr
Old Hickory, TN 37138-1110, USA

Brown, Keith (Athlete, Hockey Player)
4615 Sloan Rdg
Cumming, GA 30028-6932, USA

Brown, Ken (Athlete, Football Player)
1952 S Magnolia St Apt 3T
Denver, CO 80224-2208, USA

Brown, Ken (Athlete, Hockey Player)
2708 Checker Dr
Cedar Park, TX 78613-1640, USA

Brown, Ken J (Athlete, Football Player)
2004 Miramar Blvd
Oklahoma City, OK 73111-1808, USA

Brown, Kevin (Athlete, Baseball Player)
105 Browns Rdg
Macon, GA 31210-8614, USA

Brown, Kevin (Athlete, Baseball Player)
20 McKilt Ct
Sacramento, CA 95835-1334, USA

Brown, Kevin (Athlete, Baseball Player)
9201 Ryan Ct
Evansville, IN 47712-5410, USA

Brown, Kevin (Race Car Driver)
Jokers Wild Racing
99 S 1000 W
Clearfield, UT 84015-9234, USA

Brown, Kimberlin Ann (Actor)
c/o Staff Member *Pakula/King & Associates*
9229 W Sunset Blvd Ste 315
Los Angeles, CA 90069-3403, USA

Brown, Kimberly J (Actor)
Angry Puppy Productions
7119 W Sunset Blvd # 533
Los Angeles, CA 90046-4411, USA

Brown, Koffee (Musician)
Red Entertainment Group
481 8th Ave # 1750
New York, NY 10001-1809

Brown, Kris (Athlete, Football Player)
9715 Rockbrook Rd
Omaha, NE 68124-1928, USA

Brown, Kwame (Athlete, Basketball Player)
8713 Sagekirk Ct
Charlotte, NC 28278-9040, USA

Brown, Kwarne (Athlete, Basketball Player)
601 F St NW
Washington, DC 20004-1605, USA

Brown, Lacey (Musician)
c/o Staff Member *19 Entertainment*
35-37 Parkgate Rd #32/33
#32/33 Ransomes Dock
London SW11 4NP, UNITED KINGDOM

Brown, Larry (Athlete, Baseball Player)
13158 La Mirada Cir
Wellington, FL 33414-3997, USA

Brown, Larry (Athlete, Football Player)
1377 Glencoe Ave
Pittsburgh, PA 15205-4342, USA

Brown, Larry (Athlete, Football Player)
12004 Piney Glen Ln
Potomac, MD 20854-1417, USA

Brown, Larry (Athlete, Hockey Player)
21 Landing Dr
Dobbs Ferry, NY 10522-1181, USA

Brown, Larry (Athlete, Hockey Player)
5781 Eucalyptus Dr
Garden Valley, CA 95633-9622, USA

Brown, Larry (Basketball Coach, Basketball Player, Coach, Olympic Athlete)
1030 Green Valley Rd
Bryn Mawr, PA 19010-1912, USA

Brown, Leon (Athlete, Baseball Player)
7537 S La Rosa Dr
Tempe, AZ 85283-4627, USA

Brown, Leonard (Baseball Player)
Homestead Grays
4411 19th St NE
Washington, DC 20018-3305, USA

Brown, Les (Writer)

Brown, Levi (Athlete, Football Player)
c/o Joe Linta *JL Sports*
1204 Main St Ste 179
Branford, CT 06405-3787, USA

Brown, Lomas (Athlete, Football Player)
5049 Elizabeth Lake Rd
Waterford, MI 48327-2741, USA

Brown, Louis (Business Person)
Street Smart Systems
4426B Hugh Howell Rd Ste 200
Tucker, GA 30084-4905, USA

Brown, Mack (Coach)
University of Texas
Athletic Dept
Austin, TX 78712, USA

Brown, Malcom (Athlete, Football Player)
c/o David Mulugheta *Athletes First (TX)*
1139 Hidden Ridge Dr
Mesquite, TX 75181-4260, USA

Brown, Marc (Writer)
PO Box 873
West Tisbury, MA 02575-0873, USA

Brown, Mark (Athlete, Baseball Player)
108 NE 1st Street Ter
Blue Springs, MO 64014-2814, USA

Brown, Mark (Athlete, Football Player)
27615W 81st Way
Davie, FL 33328, USA

Brown, Mark N (Astronaut)
80 Earlsgate Rd
Beavercreek, OH 45440-3664, USA

Brown, Mark N Colonel (Astronaut)
4032 Linden Ave Attn Ofc
Dayton, OH 45432-3006, USA

Brown, Marlon (Athlete, Football Player)

Brown, Marty (Athlete, Baseball Player)
850 Las Vegas Blvd N Attn Managersofc
Las Vegas, NV 89101-2062, USA

Brown, Matt (Director)
c/o James Adams *Schreck Rose Dapello Adams Berlin & Dunham*
888 7th Ave Fl 19
New York, NY 10106-2599, USA

Brown, Matthew (Athlete, Baseball Player)
11259 N Cutlass St
Hayden, ID 83835-8654, USA

Brown, Max (Actor)
c/o Lena Roklin *Luber Roklin Management*
5815 W Sunset Blvd Ste 208
Los Angeles, CA 90028-6481, USA

Brown, Melanie (Mel B) (Dancer, Musician)
Spice Girls Ltd
66-68 Bell St
London NW1 6SP, UNITED KINGDOM

Brown, Mike (Athlete, Baseball Player)
941 SW Pine Tree Ln
Palm City, FL 34990-1942, USA

Brown, Mike (Athlete, Baseball Player)
2904 E Minton St
Mesa, AZ 85213-1697, USA

Brown, Mike (Basketball Coach)
304 Rays Mill Rd
Aberdeen, NC 28315-3323, USA

Brown, Miles (Actor)
c/o Emily Urbani *Osbrink Talent Agency*
4343 Lankershim Blvd # 100
North Hollywood, CA 91602-2705, USA

Brown, Milford (Athlete, Football Player)
21814 W Firemist Ct
Cypress, TX 77433-3514, USA

Brown, Millie Bobby (Actor)
c/o Cara Tripicchio *Shelter PR*
5670 Wilshire Blvd Ste 1200
Los Angeles, CA 90036-5621, USA

Brown, Myron (Athlete, Basketball Player)
722 Maple St
Bridgeville, PA 15017-2527, USA

Brown, Na (Athlete, Football Player)
PO Box 853
Fletcher, NC 28732-0853, USA

Brown, Norman (Musician)
c/o Staff Member *APA Talent And Literary Agency (NY)*
45 W 45th St Ste 804
New York, NY 10036-4602, USA

Brown, Norman W (Business Person)
Foote Cone Belding
101 E Erie St
Chicago, IL 60611-2802, USA

Brown, Norris (Athlete, Football Player)
320 Pinehaven St Ext
Laurens, SC 29360, USA

Brown, Olivia (Actor)

Brown, Ollie (Athlete, Baseball Player)
8462 Country Club Dr
Buena Park, CA 90621-1421, USA

Brown, Orlando (Actor)
c/o Sharyn Berg *Sharyn Talent Management*
PO Box 18033
Encino, CA 91416-8033, USA

Brown, Oscar (Athlete, Baseball Player)
19113 Gunlock Ave
Carson, CA 90746-2825, USA

Brown, Owsley II (Business Person)
Brown-Forman Corp
850 Dixie Hwy
Louisville, KY 40210-1038, USA

Brown, Patricia (Athlete, Baseball Player, Commentator)
821 Solar Ln
Glenview, IL 60025-4464, USA

Brown, Paul (Athlete, Baseball Player)
3617 Highway 75
Holdenville, OK 74848-9421, USA

Brown, Paul (Musician)
c/o Staff Member *Verve Music Group*
1755 Broadway Frnt 3
New York, NY 10019-3743, USA

Brown, Philip (Actor)
c/o Staff Member *Independent Artists*
11500 W Olympic Blvd Ste 550
Los Angeles, CA 90064-1528, USA

Brown, P J (Athlete, Basketball Player)
2142 Hampshire Dr
Slidell, LA 70461-5065, USA

Brown, Preston (Athlete, Football Player)
112 River Mill Rd
Huntsville, AL 35811-8074, USA

Brown, Ralph (Athlete, Football Player)
9395 Old Post Dr
Rancho Cucamonga, CA 91730-5765, USA

Brown, Randy (Baseball Player)
California Angels
PO Box 326
Plymouth, FL 32768-0326, USA

Brown, Ray (Athlete, Football Player)
1 Bills Dr
Orchard Park, NY 14127-2237, USA

Brown, Ray (Athlete, Football Player)
5530 Tupper Lake Dr
Houston, TX 77056-1627, USA

Brown, Ray (Athlete, Football Player)
2208 Woodside Xing
Savannah, GA 31405-8184, USA

Brown, Raymond (Athlete, Football Player)
2208 Woodside Xing
Savannah, GA 31405-8184, USA

Brown, Reb (Actor)
c/o Staff Member *Gyst Management*
9107 Wilshire Blvd Ste 450
Beverly Hills, CA 90210-5535, USA

Brown, Reggie (Athlete, Football Player)
950 Nix Rd
Alpharetta, GA 30004-2652, USA

Brown, Reggie (Athlete, Football Player)
2242 NW 93rd Ter
Miami, FL 33147-3068, USA

Brown, Reggie D (Athlete, Football Player)
17025 Tortoise St
Round Rock, TX 78664-8600, USA

Brown, Reggie V (Athlete, Football Player)
1325 Oxford Ln
Union, NJ 07083-5447, USA

Brown, Richard (Athlete, Football Player)
5652 Alfred Ave
Westminster, CA 92683-2810, USA

Brown, Rita Mae (Actor, Writer)
c/o Staff Member *Random House Publicity*
1745 Broadway Frnt 3
New York, NY 10019-4343, USA

Brown, Rob (Actor)
c/o Gabrielle (Gaby) Morgerman
WME|IMG
9601 Wilshire Blvd
Beverly Hills, CA 90210-5213, USA

Brown, Rob (Athlete, Hockey Player)
5204 84 St NW
Edmonton, AB T6E 5N8, Canada

Brown, Rob (Athlete, Hockey Player)
Edmonton Oilers
11230 110 St NW Dept Attn
Dept Broadcasting
Edmonton, AB T5G 3H7, Canada

Brown, Robert (Athlete, Football Player)
8624 Oak Chase Cir
Fairfax Station, VA 22039-3328, USA

Brown, Robert (Athlete, Football Player)
PO Box 3
Merigold, MS 38759-0003, USA

Brown, Robert Curtis (Actor)
2401 Pier Ave
Santa Monica, CA 90405-6053, USA

Brown, Robert D (Business Person)
Milacron Inc
2090 Florence Ave Ste 100
Cincinnati, OH 45206-2489, USA

Brown, Robert S (Bob) (Athlete, Football Player)
1200 Lakeshore Ave Apt 25G
Oakland, CA 94606-1689, USA

Brown, Roger (Athlete, Football Player)
9 N Point Dr
Portsmouth, VA 23703-3644, USA

Brown, Ron (Athlete, Football Player)
2212 Radcourt Dr
Hacienda Heights, CA 91745-5716, USA

Brown, Ronnie (Athlete, Football Player)
10751 Hawks Vista St
Plantation, FL 33324-8210, USA

Brown, Roosevelt (Athlete)
6551 Thea Ln Apt S17
Columbus, GA 31907-0822

Brown, Roosevelt (Athlete, Baseball Player)
308 Newitt Vick Dr
Vicksburg, MS 39183-8741, USA

Brown, Ruben (Athlete, Football Player)
339 Water Mill Towd Rd
Water Mill, NY 11976-2427, USA

Brown, Rush (Athlete, Football Player)
2425 Cartertown Rd
Clinton, NC 28328-7467, USA

Brown, Samantha (Actor)
c/o Erika Martineau *Brooks Group*
10 W 37th St Fl 5
New York, NY 10018-7396, USA

Brown, Samuel M (Athlete, Football Player)
25 Franklin Creek Rd N
Savannah, GA 31411-2826, USA

Brown, Sandra (Writer)
1306 W Abram St
Arlington, TX 76013-1703, USA

Brown, Sara (Actor)
Media Artists Group
6300 Wilshire Blvd Ste 1470
Los Angeles, CA 90048-5200, USA

Brown, Sarah (Actor)
c/o Staff Member *McKeon-Myones Management*
3500 W Olive Ave Ste 770
Burbank, CA 91505-5527, USA

Brown, Scott (Athlete, Baseball Player)
1238 Alton Pierce Rd
Dequincy, LA 70633-4501, USA

Brown, Scott P. (Senator)
359 Dirksen Senate Office Building
Washington, DC 20510-0001, USA

Brown, Selwyn (Athlete, Football Player)
3533 Inverrary Blvd W
Lauderhill, FL 33319-7114, USA

Brown, Shannon (Musician)
c/o Dale Morris *Morris Artists Management*
2001 Blair Blvd
Nashville, TN 37212-5007, USA

Brown, Shaun (Actor)
c/o Siri Garber *Platform PR*
2666 N Beachwood Dr
Los Angeles, CA 90068-2308, USA

Brown, Sheldon (Athlete, Football Player)
2616 Stonetrace Dr
Rock Hill, SC 29730-6664, USA

Brown, Sherrod (Senator)
713 Hart Senate Office Bldg
Washington, DC 20510-0001, USA

Brown, Simona (Actor)
c/o Emily Hargreaves *Multitude Media*
32 Bloomsbury St
London WC1B 3QJ, UNITED KINGDOM

Brown, Sky (Athlete, Skateboarder)
c/o Kristin Nava *Abrams Artists Agency*
750 N San Vicente Blvd
E Tower Fl 11
Los Angeles, CA 90069-5788, USA

Brown, Sonny (Athlete, Football Player)
825 Shadow Wood Dr
Edmond, OK 73034-7061, USA

Brown, Stan (Athlete, Basketball Player)
2201 Tremont St
Philadelphia, PA 19115-5041, USA

Brown, Stan (Athlete, Football Player)
PO Box 533
Benicia, CA 94510-0533, USA

Brown, Sterling K (Actor)
c/o Michael Geiser *Jill Fritzo Public Relations*
208 E 51st St # 305
New York, NY 10022-6557, USA

Brown, Steve (Athlete, Baseball Player)
9626 Cecilwood Dr
Santee, CA 92071-1428, USA

Brown, Steve (Athlete, Football Player)

Brown, Stevie (Athlete, Football Player)
c/o Blake Baratz *The Institute for Athletes*
3600 Minnesota Dr Ste 550
Edina, MN 55435-7925, USA

Brown, Susan (Actor)
11931 Addison St
N Hollywood, CA 91607-3106, USA

Brown, Tarell (Athlete, Football Player)
c/o Joel Segal *Lagardere Unlimited (NY)*
456 Washington St Apt 9L
New York, NY 10013-1555, USA

Brown, Tarrick (Baseball Player)
Chicago Cubs
18631 Collins St Apt 33
Tarzana, CA 91356-2178, USA

Brown, Ted (Athlete, Football Player)
2305 Abbey Pt
Shakopee, MN 55379-9475, USA

Brown, Terry (Athlete, Football Player)
605 W Apache St
Marlow, OK 73055-1831, USA

Brown, T Graham (Musician)
8437 Rolling Hills Dr
Nashville, TN 37221-5616, USA

Brown, Theotis (Athlete, Football Player)
9604 W 121st Ter
Overland Park, KS 66213-1691, USA

Brown, Thomas M (Athlete, Football Player)
6024 Approach Rd
Sarasota, FL 34238-5721, USA

Brown, Thomas W (Athlete, Football Player)
201 High Point Dr
Waco, TX 76705-1750, USA

Brown, Thomas Wilson (Actor)
c/o Staff Member *SDB Partners Inc*
315 S Beverly Dr Ste 411
Beverly Hills, CA 90212-4301, USA

Brown, Tim (Athlete, Football Player, Heisman Trophy Winner)
1307 Sunset Ridge Cir
Cedar Hill, TX 75104-4542, USA

Brown, Timmy (Athlete, Football Player)
505 S Farrell Dr Unit E28
Palm Springs, CA 92264-8071, USA

Brown, Tina (Talk Show Host, Writer)
c/o Staff Member *Ed Victor Ltd*
6 Bayley St
Bedford Square
London WC1B 3HB, UNITED KINGDOM

Brown, Tom (Athlete, Baseball Player)
2235 Rising Creek Ct
Dunedin, FL 34698-9405, USA

Brown, Tom (Athlete, Baseball Player)
600 Valencia Rd
Venice, FL 34285-2538, USA

Brown, Tom (Athlete, Football Player)
1008 Longmeadow Ln
Western Springs, IL 60558-2108, USA

Brown, Tommy (Athlete, Baseball Player)
8119 Shady Pl
Brentwood, TN 37027-7344, USA

Brown, Tom W (Athlete, Football Player)
201 High Point Dr
Waco, TX 76705-1750, USA

Brown, Tony (Athlete, Football Player)
11629 Garrick Ave
Sylmar, CA 91342-6533, USA

Brown, Travis (Athlete, Football Player)
30411 N 60th St
Cave Creek, AZ 85331-6087, USA

Brown, Troy (Athlete, Football Player)
124 Pine Hvn
Barnwell, SC 29812-2817, USA

Brown, Troy (Athlete, Football Player)
PO Box 452
Foxboro, MA 02035-0452, USA

Brown, Tyree (Actor)
c/o Nicole Jolley *Amsel, Eisenstadt & Frazier Talent Agency (AEF)*
5055 Wilshire Blvd Ste 860
Los Angeles, CA 90036-6108, USA

Brown, Vincent (Athlete, Football Player)
PO Box 71268
Henrico, VA 23255-1268, USA

Brown, Wayne (Athlete, Hockey Player)
50 Montgomery Blvd
Belleville, ON K8N 1H9, Canada

Brown, W Earl (Actor)
c/o Staff Member *WME/IMG*
9601 Wilshire Blvd
Beverly Hills, CA 90210-5213, USA

Brown, Wes (Actor)
c/o Stacy Abrams *Abrams Entertainment*
5225 Wilshire Blvd Ste 515
Los Angeles, CA 90036-4349, USA

Brown, William D (Bill) (Athlete, Coach, Football Player)
514 Northdale Blvd NW
Minneapolis, MN 55448-3357, USA

Brown, William F (Willie) (Athlete, Coach, Football Player)
27138 Lillegard Ct
Tracy, CA 95304-8866, USA

Brown, William S (Horse Racer)
750 Michigan Ave
Columbus, OH 43215-1107, USA

Brown, Willie (Baseball Player)
3430 John Hancock Dr
Tallahassee, FL 32312-1536, USA

Brown, Winston (Baseball Player)
12144 SW 50th St
Cooper City, FL 33330-4476, USA

Brown, Woody (Actor)
11844 Otsego St
Valley Village, CA 91607-3223, USA

Brown, Wren T (Actor)

Brown, Yvette Nicole (Actor)
c/o Jeremy Platt *Generate Management*
8750 Wilshire Blvd Ste 200
Beverly Hills, CA 90211-2707, USA

Brown, Zach (Athlete, Football Player)
c/o Carl Carey *Champion Pro Consulting Group*
3547 Ruth St
Houston, TX 77004-5515, USA

Brownback, Sam (Politician)
4826 SW Urish Rd
Topeka, KS 66610-9760, USA

Browne, Byron (Athlete, Baseball Player)
9708 W Riverside Ave
Tolleson, AZ 85353-8578, USA

Browne, Chris (Cartoonist)
c/o Staff Member *King Features Syndication*
300 W 57th St Fl 15
New York, NY 10019-5238, USA

Browne, E John P (Business Person)
BP Exploration Co
1 Finsbury Circus
London EC2M 7BA, UNITED KINGDOM (UK)

Browne, Gordie (Athlete, Football Player)
1001 Lakeridge Ct
Colleyville, TX 76034-2825, USA

Browne, Gordon (Athlete, Football Player)
1001 Lakeridge Ct
Colleyville, TX 76034-2825, USA

Browne, Jackson (Musician, Songwriter)
c/o Donald Miller *Donald Miller Management*
12746 Kling St
Studio City, CA 91604-1125, USA

Browne, Jerry (Athlete, Baseball Player)
Hagerstown Suns
274 Memorial Blvd E
Attn: Coaching Staff
Hagerstown, MD 21740-6200, USA

Browne, Kale (Actor)
c/o Staff Member *The Gage Group*
5757 Wilshire Blvd Ste 659
Los Angeles, CA 90036-3682, USA

Browne, Less (Athlete, Football Player)
19 Amblecote Pl
Hamilton, ON L8W 3E9, Canada

Browne, Olin (Athlete, Golfer)
9562 SE Sandpine Ln
Hobe Sound, FL 33455-6356, USA

Browne, Victor (Actor)
c/o Lara Rosenstock *Lara Rosenstock Management*
8371 Blackburn Ave Apt 1
Los Angeles, CA 90048-4245, USA

Browne, Zachary (Actor)
c/o Staff Member *Iris Burton Agency*
10100 Santa Monica Blvd Ste 1300
Los Angeles, CA 90067-4114, USA

Browner, Brandon (Athlete, Football Player)
c/o Peter Schaffer *Authentic Athletix*
400 S Steele St Unit 47
Denver, CO 80209-3535, USA

Browner, Jim (Athlete, Football Player)
6265 Crest Forest Ct E
Clarkston, MI 48348-4581, USA

Browner, Joey (Athlete, Football Player)
PO Box 22721
Saint Paul, MN 55122-0721, USA

Browner, Joey (Athlete, Football Player)
PO Box 571
Pierz, MN 56364-0571, USA

Browner, Keith (Athlete, Football Player)
5017 Chesley Ave
View Park, CA 90043-1836, USA

Browner, Ross (Athlete, Football Player)
7900 Indian Springs Dr
Nashville, TN 37221-1147, USA

Brown-Findlay, Jessica (Actor)
c/o Pippa Beng *Premier PR*
2-4 Bucknall St
London WC2H 8LA, UNITED KINGDOM

Browning, Bryant (Athlete, Football Player)
c/o Joe Flanagan *BTI Sports Advisors*
615 South Blvd Apt C
Oak Park, IL 60302-4606, USA

Browning, Cal (Athlete, Baseball Player)
111 N Eagle Dr
Ruidoso, NM 88345-6832, USA

Browning, Dave (Athlete, Football Player)
10117 S Lambs Ln
Mica, WA 99023-6031, USA

Browning, Emily (Actor)
c/o Michael D Aglion *Signpost Management*
100 N Brand Blvd Ste 200
Glendale, CA 91203-2642, USA

Browning, Kurt (Figure Skater)
c/o Nicole Cobuzio *Rob Bailey Communications*
310 State Rt 17
Upper Saddle River, NJ 07458-2308, USA

Browning, Logan (Actor)
c/o Ken Jacobson *Ken Jacobson Management*
Preferred to be contacted by phone or email
Los Angeles, CA 91367, USA

Browning, Ricou (Actor)
5221 SW 196th Ln
Southwest Ranches, FL 33332-1111, USA

Browning, Ryan (Actor)
United Talent Agency
9336 Civic Center Dr
Beverly Hills, CA 90210-3604, USA

Browning, Thomas L (Tom) (Athlete, Baseball Player)
3094 Friars Ln
Edgewood, KY 41017-8126, USA

Brown Jr, Larry (Athlete, Football Player)
5603 Sycamore Dr
Colleyville, TX 76034-5063, USA

Brown Jr, Neil (Actor)
c/o Nicole Miller *NMA PR*
7916 Melrose Ave Ste 1
Los Angeles, CA 90046-7160, USA

Brownlee, Claude (Athlete, Football Player)
2711 Hood St
Columbus, GA 31906-3251, USA

Brownlee, Sophia Grace (Musician)
c/o Jason Egenberg *Authentic Talent & Literary Management*
3615 Eastham Dr # 650
Culver City, CA 90232-2410, USA

Brownlow, Kevin (Producer)
Photoplay Productions
21 Princess Road
London NW1, UNITED KINGDOM (UK)

Brown-Miller, Lisa (Athlete, Hockey Player, Olympic Athlete)
1 Olympic Plz Bldg 4E
US Olympic Committee
Colorado Springs, CO 80909-5746, USA

Brownschidle, Jack (Athlete, Hockey Player)
35 Hidden Pines Ct
East Amherst, NY 14051-1688, USA

Brownson, Mark (Athlete, Baseball Player)
12161 Sunset Point Cir
Wellington, FL 33414-5595, USA

Brownstein, Carrie (Music Group, Musician)
Legends of 21st Century
7 Trinity Row
Florence, MA 01062-1931, USA

Broxton, Jonathan (Athlete, Baseball Player)
4751 Rocky Creek Church Rd
Waynesboro, GA 30830-4106, USA

Broyles, Ryan (Athlete, Football Player)

Brozer, Kim (Athlete, Golfer)
2700 N 16th St
Beaumont, TX 77703-4624, USA

Bruant, Joel (Chef)
Joel Restaurant 5-6-24 Minami Aoyama
Kyodo Building Minato-ku
Tokyo, Japan

Brubaker, Bruce (Athlete, Baseball Player)
Champion Ford
140 Southtown Blvd
Owensboro, KY 42303-7759, USA

Brubaker, Jeff (Athlete, Hockey Player)
1827 Oak Ridge Rd Unit A
Oak Ridge, NC 27310-9865, USA

Bruce, Aundray (Athlete, Football Player)
1730 Wentworth Dr
Montgomery, AL 36106-2639, USA

Bruce, Bob (Athlete, Baseball Player)
633 Mission Cir
Irving, TX 75063-6617, USA

Bruce, Bruce (Comedian)
c/o Staff Member *Agency for the Performing Arts (APA)*
405 S Beverly Dr Ste 500
Beverly Hills, CA 90212-4425, USA

Bruce, David (Athlete, Hockey Player)
3229 Northshore Rd
Bellingham, WA 98226-7828, USA

Bruce, Earle (Athlete, Football Player)
5988 Roundstone Pl
Dublin, OH 43016-9420, USA

Bruce, Ed (Musician)
PO Box 187
Monterey, TN 38574-0187, USA

Bruce, George (Writer)
c/o Staff Member *Counterpoint*
2117 4th St Ste D
Berkeley, CA 94710-2205, USA

Bruce, Isaac (Athlete, Football Player)
11301 NW 18th St
Plantation, FL 33323-2225, USA

Bruce, Thomas (Tom) (Swimmer)
122 Sea Terrace Way
Aptos, CA 95003-4521, USA

Bruce, Tom (Athlete, Swimmer)
13830 Hutchings Ct
Royal Oaks, CA 95076-5333, USA

Bruckheimer, Jerry (Director, Producer)
c/o Staff Member *Jerry Bruckheimer Films / Television*
1631 10th St
Santa Monica, CA 90404-3705, USA

Bruckner, Agnes (Actor)
c/o Oren Segal *Management Production Entertainment (MPE)*
9229 W Sunset Blvd Ste 301
W Hollywood, CA 90069-3417, USA

Bruckner, Amy (Actor)
c/o Susan Curtis *Curtis Talent Management*
9607 Arby Dr
Beverly Hills, CA 90210-1202, USA

Bruckner, Greg (Athlete, Golfer)
3906 E Potter Dr
Phoenix, AZ 85050-4837, USA

Bruckner, Les (Athlete, Football Player)
1325 Valley View Rd Apt 307
Glendale, CA 91202-4420, USA

Brud, Lulu (Actor)
c/o Greg Wapnick *Luber Roklin Management*
5815 W Sunset Blvd Ste 208
Los Angeles, CA 90028-6481, USA

Brudzinski, Robert L (Bob) (Athlete, Football Player)
1057 Lido Ct
Weston, FL 33326-2903, USA

Brue, Bob (Athlete, Golfer)
4316 N Sheffield Ave
Milwaukee, WI 53211-1432, USA

Brueckman, Charlie (Athlete, Football Player)
7439 Plott Rd
Charlotte, NC 28215-9440, USA

Bruel, Patrick (Music Group)
Artmedia
20 Ave Rapp
Paris 75007, FRANCE

Bruener, Mark (Athlete, Football Player)
26 Commanders Pl
Missouri City, TX 77459, USA

Bruening, Justin (Actor)
c/o Marnie Sparer *Power Entertainment Group*
195 S Beverly Dr Ste 414
Beverly Hills, CA 90212-3044, USA

Bruestle, Martin (Director)

Bruett, J T (Athlete, Baseball Player)
1437 Woods Creek Dr
Delano, MN 55328-9266, USA

Brugel, Amanda (Actor)
c/o Jennifer Rashwan *TouchwoodPR (ON)*
121 John St Fl 2
Toronto, ON M5V 2E2, CANADA

Bruguera, Sergi (Tennis Player)
C'Escipion 42
Barcelona 08023, SPAIN

Bruhert, Mike (Athlete, Baseball Player)
907 Center Dr
Franklin Square, NY 11010-2005, USA

Bruhin, John (Athlete, Football Player)
6960 Taylors View Ln
Knoxville, TN 37921-2843, USA

Bruhl, Daniel (Actor)
Amusement Park Films
Pappelallee 24
Berlin 10437, GERMANY

Brumbaugh, Cliff (Athlete, Baseball Player)
216 Moore Ave
New Castle, DE 19720-3559, USA

Brumbly, Charlie (Actor)
c/o Staff Member *DDO Artist Agency (LA)*
4605 Lankershim Blvd Ste 340
N Hollywood, CA 91602-1876, USA

Brumel, Valeryi (Actor)
Louknetzkaya Nab 8
Moscow, Russia

Brumfield, Jackson (Athlete, Football Player)
25644 Highway 25
Franklinton, LA 70438-5126, USA

Brumfield, Jacob D (Athlete, Baseball Player)
7970 Creekstone Way
Riverdale, GA 30274-3929, USA

Brumfield, Scott (Athlete, Football Player)
1150 E 900 S
Spanish Fork, UT 84660-2629, USA

Brumfield-White, Dolly (Athlete, Baseball Player, Commentator)
1604 Millcreek Dr
Arkadelphia, AR 71923-3024, USA

Brumfield-White, Dolores (Baseball Player)
1604 Millcreek Dr
Arkadelphia, AR 71923-3024, USA

Brumley, Duff (Athlete, Baseball Player)
8114 Fallen Maple Dr
Chattanooga, TN 37421-1245, USA

Brumley, Mike (Athlete, Baseball Player)
1020 Western Trl
Keller, TX 76248-4924, USA

Brumley, Robert L (Athlete, Football Player)
256 E Sunset Rd
San Antonio, TX 78209-2760, USA

Brumm, Donald D (Don) (Athlete, Football Player)
775 El Tampa Rd
Camdenton, MO 65020-4783, USA

Brummer, Glenn (Athlete, Baseball Player)
9 Blue Bird Dr
Kimberling City, MO 65686-9526, USA

Brummer, Renate (Astronaut)
NOAA/FSL
325 Broadway St
Boulder, CO 80305-3337, USA

Brummett, Greg (Athlete, Baseball Player)
1708 N Valleyview Ct
Wichita, KS 67212-1245, USA

Brumwell, Murray (Athlete, Hockey Player)
727 Tabriz Dr
Billings, MT 59105-2809, USA

Brunansky, Thomas A (Tom) (Athlete, Baseball Player)
13411 Summit Cir
Poway, CA 92064-2169, USA

Brundage, Dewey (Athlete, Football Player)
220 S 400 W
Orem, UT 84058-5329, USA

Brundage, Jennifer (Athlete, Olympic Athlete, Softball Player)
4487 Augusta Ct
Ann Arbor, MI 48108-9789, USA

Brundige, Bill (Athlete, Football Player)
2050 Roanoke St
Christiansburg, VA 24073-2510, USA

Brundtland, Gro Harlem (Politician)
Storting
Oslo, Norway

Brundy, Stan (Athlete, Basketball Player)
4644 Stephen Girard Ave
New Orleans, LA 70126-4756, USA

Brune, Jesse (Actor)
c/o Cat Josell *Synergy Management*
11271 Ventura Blvd Ste 495
Studio City, CA 91604-3136, USA

Brunell, Mark (Athlete, Football Player)
4550 Ortega Forest Dr
Jacksonville, FL 32210-5821, USA

Brunelli, Sam (Athlete, Football Player)
1080 Wisconsin Ave NW Apt 104
Washington, DC 20007-6052, USA

Bruner, Jack (Athlete, Football Player)
701 Lewiston St
Cottonwood, ID 83522-9750, USA

Bruner, Michael L (Mike) (Athlete, Olympic Athlete, Swimmer)
339 Garcia Ave
Half Moon Bay, CA 94019-1886, USA

Brunet, Andree Joly (Figure Skater)
2805 Boyne City Road
Boyne City, MI 49712, USA

Brunet, Bob (Athlete, Football Player)
25011 La Highway 1032
Denham Springs, LA 70726-5637, USA

Brunetta, Mario (Athlete, Hockey Player)
3874 de L'Hetriere St
Saint-Augustin-De-Desmaures, QC G3A 2X1, Canada

Brunette, Andrew (Athlete, Hockey Player)
2392 Morgan Ave N
Stillwater, MN 55082-1967, USA

Brunette, Justin (Athlete, Baseball Player)
11 Atherton
Irvine, CA 92620-2502, USA

Brunettes, The (Music Group)
c/o Staff Member *Paradigm (Monterey)*
404 W Franklin St
Monterey, CA 93940-2303, USA

Brunetti, Wayne H (Business Person)
New Century Energies
1225 17th St
Denver, CO 80202-5534, USA

Bruney, Brian (Athlete, Baseball Player)
PO Box 1053
Warrenton, OR 97146-1053, USA

Bruney, Fred (Athlete, Football Coach, Football Player)
1020 Piedmont Ave NE Unit 432
Atlanta, GA 30309-4153, USA

Bruni, Carla (Model, Musician)
Palais de l'Elysee
55 Rue Faubourg
Saint Honore
Paris 75008, FRANCE

Bruni, Frank (Writer)
c/o Staff Member *New York Times*
229 W 43rd St
New York, NY 10036-3982, USA

Brunkhorst, Brian (Athlete, Basketball Player)
PO Box 653
Elm Grove, WI 53122-0653, USA

Bruno, Billi (Actor)

Bruno, Chris (Actor)
3678 Alta Mesa Dr
Studio City, CA 91604-4003, USA

Bruno, Corbucci (Actor)
Via dei Colli della Farnesina
#144
Rome I-00194, Italy

Bruno, Dylan (Actor)
1481 W Paseo Del Mar
San Pedro, CA 90731-6055, USA

Bruno, Frank (Athlete, Boxer)
Little Billington
Leighton Buzzard
Bedfordshire LU7 9BS, UK

Bruno, Franklin R (Frank) (Boxer)
P O Box 2266 Brentwood
Essex CM15 0AQ, UNITED KINGDOM (UK)

Bruno, Tom (Athlete, Baseball Player)
316 Ft Sully Trl
Pierre, SD 57501-8309, USA

Bruns, George (Athlete, Basketball Player)
16 E Poplar St
Floral Park, NY 11001-3145, USA

Brunsberg, Ario (Athlete, Baseball Player)
883 104th Ln NW
Minneapolis, MN 55433-6542, USA

Brunson, Larry (Athlete, Football Player)
6104 E Peakview Pl
Centennial, CO 80111-4326, USA

Brunson, Will (Athlete, Baseball Player)
13119 Rudys Way
Streetman, TX 75859-7171, USA

Brunt, Maureen (Athlete, Olympic Athlete)
430 Silver Lake Dr
Portage, WI 53901-1340, USA

Bruntlett, Eric (Athlete, Baseball Player)
1106 Marconi St Apt A
Houston, TX 77019-4261, USA

Brupbacher, Ross (Athlete, Football Player)
200 Pembroke Ln
Lafayette, LA 70508-5616, USA

Bruschi, Tedy (Athlete, Football Player)
c/o Brad Blank *Brad Blank & Associates*
1800 Sunset Harbour Dr
#2402
Miami Beach, FL 33139, USA

Bruske, Jim (Athlete, Baseball Player)
5242 N Quail Run Pl
Paradise Valley, AZ 85253-7051, USA

Bruskin, Grisha (Artist)
236 W 26th St Rm 705
New York, NY 10001-6789, USA

Brusstar, Warren (Athlete, Baseball Player)
3320 Redwood Rd
Napa, CA 94558-9544, USA

Brutcher, Len (Baseball Player)
4510 Hallam Hill Ln
Lakeland, FL 33813-1808, USA

Bruton, David (Athlete, Football Player)
c/o David Dunn *Athletes First*
23091 Mill Creek Dr
Laguna Hills, CA 92653-1258, USA

Bruun, Kristian (Actor)
c/o Staff Member *TouchwoodPR (LA)*
7080 Hollywood Blvd Ste 1100
Los Angeles, CA 90028-6938, USA

Bry, Ellen (Actor)
Media Artists Group
6300 Wilshire Blvd Ste 1470
Los Angeles, CA 90048-5200, USA

Bryan, Ashley (Writer)
General Delivery
Islesford, ME 04646-9999, USA

Bryan, Billy (Athlete, Baseball Player)
16725 Brigadoon Trl
Gulf Shores, AL 36542-8252, USA

Bryan, Billy (Athlete, Football Player)
3408 Creekwood Dr
Tuscaloosa, AL 35453, USA

Bryan, Billy (Athlete, Football Player)
3408 Creekwood Dr
Vestavia, AL 35243-4435, USA

Bryan, Bob (Athlete, Tennis Player)
c/o John Tobias *TLA Worldwide (FL)*
1245 S Alhambra Cir
Coral Gables, FL 33146-3104, USA

Bryan, David (Musician)
45 Phalanx Rd
Colts Neck, NJ 07722-1510, USA

Bryan, Dora (Actor)
11 Marine Parade Brighton
Sussex, UNITED KINGDOM (UK)

Bryan, Jimmy (Race Car Driver)
PO Box 194
Novi, MI 48376-0194, USA

Bryan, Luke (Musician)
c/o Jessie Schmidt *Schmidt Relations*
3012 Business Park Cir Ste 500
Goodlettsville, TN 37072-3191, USA

Bryan, Mark (Musician)
816 Stone Pt
Awendaw, SC 29429-6131, USA

Bryan, Mary (Athlete, Golfer)
1735 Golf Garden Way
Apopka, FL 32712-2178, USA

Bryan, Mike (Athlete, Tennis Player)
c/o John Tobias *TLA Worldwide (FL)*
1245 S Alhambra Cir
Coral Gables, FL 33146-3104, USA

Bryan, Richard (Politician)
269 Russell
Washington, DC 20510-0001, USA

Bryan, Sabrina (Actor, Dancer)
c/o Staff Member *Puravida Enterprises*
2480 Corinth Ave Apt 3
Los Angeles, CA 90064-3266, USA

Bryan, Steve (Athlete, Football Player)
33659 E 147th St S
Coweta, OK 74429-7764, USA

Bryan, Walter (Athlete, Football Player)
757 Kenwood Dr
Abilene, TX 79601-5539, USA

Bryan, Zachery Ty (Actor)
c/o Staff Member *Lost Lane Entertainment*
6121 W Sunset Blvd
Los Angeles, CA 90028-6442, USA

Bryant, Aidy (Actor)
c/o Naomi Odenkirk *Odenkirk Provissiero Entertainment*
1936 N Bronson Ave
Raleigh Studios
Los Angeles, CA 90068-5602, USA

Bryant, Anita (Beauty Pageant Winner, Musician)
2377 NW 206th St
Edmond, OK 73012-9074, USA

Bryant, Anthony (Athlete, Football Player)
1136 County Road 16
Newbern, AL 36765-3712, USA

Bryant, Antonio (Athlete, Football Player)
c/o Staff Member *All Pro Sports and Entertainment*
50 S Steele St Ste 480
Denver, CO 80209-2836, USA

Bryant, Armonty (Athlete, Football Player)

Bryant, Bart (Athlete, Golfer)
1233 Lake Whitney Dr
Windermere, FL 34786-6069, USA

Bryant, Bill (Athlete, Football Player)
3516 Dewberry Dr
Shreveport, LA 71118-3606, USA

Bryant, Bobby (Athlete, Football Player)
192 Mariners Row
Columbia, SC 29212-8068, USA

Bryant, Bonnie (Athlete, Golfer)
2427 Wasabinang St
Hastings, MI 49058-8912, USA

Bryant, Brad (Athlete, Golfer)
3407 Bridgefield Dr
Lakeland, FL 33803-5914, USA

Bryant, Brad (Golfer)
3407 Bridgefield Dr
Lakeland, FL 33803-5914, USA

Bryant, Clark Rosalyn (Athlete, Track Athlete)
3901 Somerset Dr
Los Angeles, CA 90008-1704, USA

Bryant, Darrell (Race Car Driver)
171 Brenda Dr
Thomasville, NC 27360-8209, USA

Bryant, Derek (Athlete, Baseball Player)
1047 Redwood Dr
Lexington, KY 40511-1133, USA

Bryant, Desmond (Athlete, Football Player)
c/o Joby Branion *Vanguard Sports Group*
23091 Mill Creek Dr
Laguna Hills, CA 92653-1258, USA

Bryant, Dez (Athlete, Football Player)
c/o Ashley Smith Becker *Relativity Sports*
2029 Century Park E Ste 1550
Century City, CA 90067-3000, USA

Bryant, Domingo (Athlete, Football Player)
19703 Campfield Dr
Katy, TX 77449-6691, USA

Bryant, Don (Athlete, Baseball Player)
1844 Swiss Oaks St
Saint Johns, FL 32259-8954, USA

Bryant, Emmette (Athlete, Basketball Player)
PO Box 6229
Chicago, IL 60680-6229, USA

Bryant, Fernando (Athlete, Football Player)
1740 Hudson Bridge Rd
Stockbridge, GA 30281-6331, USA

Bryant, Gyude (President)
President's Office
Executive Mansion Capitol Hill
Monrovia, LIBERIA

Bryant, Hubie (Athlete, Football Player)
4804 Branch Rd
Roanoke, VA 24014-6702, USA

Bryant, Jeff (Athlete, Football Player)
2665 Tilson Rd
Decatur, GA 30032-5605, USA

Bryant, Joe (Athlete, Basketball Player)
1835 N 72nd St
Philadelphia, PA 19151-2311, USA

Bryant, Joshua (Actor)
216 Paseo Del Pueblo Norte Ste M
Taos, NM 87571-5912, USA

Bryant, Joy (Actor)
c/o David Schiff *MGMT Entertainment (The Schiff Company)*
9220 W Sunset Blvd Ste 106
W Hollywood, CA 90069-3500, USA

Bryant, Junior (Athlete, Football Player)

Bryant, Kevin (Athlete, Football Player)
701 E Church St
Tarboro, NC 27886-4505, USA

Bryant, Kobe (Athlete, Basketball Player)
Good Vibes Only Entertainment
10250 Constellation Blvd
Los Angeles, CA 90067-6200, USA

Bryant, Kris (Athlete, Basketball Player)
c/o Scott Boras *Boras Corporation*
18 Corporate Plaza Dr
Newport Beach, CA 92660-7901, USA

Bryant, Lucas (Actor)

Bryant, Mark (Athlete, Basketball Player)
2924 Firewheel Rd
Edmond, OK 73013-3825, USA

Bryant, Martavis (Athlete, Football Player)

Bryant, Matt (Athlete, Football Player)
c/o Jordan Woy *Willis & Woy Management*
4890 Alpha Rd Ste 200
Dallas, TX 75244-4639, USA

Bryant, Ralph (Athlete, Baseball Player)
35 Copper Leaf Ct
Villa Rica, GA 30180-4798, USA

Bryant, Red (Athlete, Football Player)
c/o Jimmy Sexton *CAA (Memphis)*
6060 Poplar Ave Ste 470
Memphis, TN 38119-0910, USA

Bryant, Ron (Baseball Player)
San Francisco Giants
90 Oak St # 1
Westerly, RI 02891-1737, USA

Bryant, Ronald Ray (Baby Bash) (Actor, Musician, Producer)
c/o Staff Member *Sony/BMG Music (NY)*
550 Madison Ave
New York, NY 10022-3211, USA

Bryant, Steve (Athlete, Football Player)
12618 Laleu Ln
Houston, TX 77071-3735, USA

Bryant, Taman (Athlete, Football Player)
2742 Bryant St
Vineland, NJ 08361-3021, USA

Bryant, Todd (Actor)

Bryant, Tony (Athlete, Football Player)
2351 Sombrero Blvd
Marathon, FL 33050-2468, USA

Bryant, Trent (Athlete, Football Player)
4801 S Tiemey Dr
Independence, MO 64055, USA

Bryant, Walter (Athlete, Football Player)
192 Mariners Row
Columbia, SC 29212-8068, USA

Bryant, Waymond (Athlete, Football Player)
2440 Covington Dr
Flower Mound, TX 75028-4666, USA

Bryant, Wendell (Athlete, Football Player)
PO Box 888
Phoenix, AZ 85001-0888, USA

Bryce, Ian (Producer)
Ian Bryce Productions
5555 Melrose Ave
Wallis Building, 105-106
Los Angeles, CA 90038-3989, USA

Bryden, T R (Athlete, Baseball Player)
1021 9th St
Clarkston, WA 99403-2505, USA

Brye, Steve (Athlete, Baseball Player)
621 S Spring St Apt 603
Los Angeles, CA 90014-3918, USA

Brylin, Sergei (Athlete, Hockey Player)
32 Robert Dr
Short Hills, NJ 07078-1507, USA

Bryson, Bill (Writer)
c/o Staff Member *Random House Publicity*
1745 Broadway Frnt 3
New York, NY 10019-4343, USA

Bryson, David (Musician)
PO Box 11289
Bainbridge Is, WA 98110-5289, USA

Bryson, Peabo (Music Group, Musician, Songwriter, Writer)
Agency for the Performing Arts
9200 W Sunset Blvd Ste 900
Los Angeles, CA 90069-3604, USA

Bryson, Peabo (Musician)
c/o Staff Member *Agency for the Performing Arts (APA)*
405 S Beverly Dr Ste 500
Beverly Hills, CA 90212-4425, USA

Bryson, Shawn (Athlete, Football Player)
41 Oakdale Dr
Franklin, NC 28734-9031, USA

Bryzgalov, Ilya (Athlete, Hockey Player)
4092 Santa Anita Ln
Yorba Linda, CA 92886-7014, USA

Brzeska, Magdalena (Athlete, Gymnast)
Vitesse Karcher GmbH
Porschestr 6
Fellbach 70736, GERMANY

Brzezinski, Mika (Talk Show Host)
c/o Henry Reisch *WME|IMG (NY)*
11 Madison Ave Fl 18
New York, NY 10010-3669, USA

B. Schiff, Adam (Congressman, Politician)
2411 Rayburn Hob
Washington, DC 20515-0511, USA

B-Side Players (Music Group, Musician)
c/o Staff Member *Skyline Music*
28 Union St
Whitefield, NH 03598-3503, USA

BTS (Music Group)
c/o Bang Si-hyuk *Big Hit Entertainment*
Seoul Gangnam-gu, 5 30-gil
Fl Yangjin Plz 5F
Hakdong-ro -, SOUTH KOREA

Buanne, Patrizio (Musician)
PO Box 293
Tadworth KT20 5SX, UNITED KINGDOM

Bubas, Vic (Athlete, Basketball Player, Coach)
133 Robert E Lee Ln
Bluffton, SC 29909-4424, USA

Bubela, Jaime (Athlete, Baseball Player)
14927 Royal Birkdale St
Houston, TX 77095-2812, USA

Bubka, Sergie N (Athlete, Track Athlete)
Andresi Kulikowski
Vasavagen 13
Solna 171 39, SWEDEN

Bubka, Surgei N (Athlete, Track Athlete)
Andresi Kulikowski
Vasavagen 13
Solna 171 39, SWEDEN

Bubla, Jiri (Athlete, Hockey Player)
405-1050 Bowron Crt
North Vancouver, BC V7H 2X7, Canada

Buble, Michael (Musician)
c/o Bruce Allen *Bruce Allen Talent*
425 Carrall St
Suite 400
Vancouver, BC V6B 6E3, CANADA

Bucannon, Deone (Athlete, Football Player)

Bucatinsky, Dan (Actor, Producer, Writer)
c/o Staff Member *Is or Isn't Entertainment*
8391 Beverly Blvd Ste 125
Los Angeles, CA 90048-2633, USA

Buccellato, Benedetta (Actor)
Carlo Levi Co
Via Giuseppe Pisanelli
Rome 00196, ITALY

Bucci, George (Athlete, Basketball Player)
15 Peter Ave
Newburgh, NY 12550-8812, USA

Buchanan, Bill (Athlete, Baseball Player)
94 Twill Valley Dr
Saint Peters, MO 63376-6566, USA

Buchanan, Bob (Athlete, Baseball Player)
2035 Bever Ave SE
Cedar Rapids, IA 52403-2716, USA

Buchanan, Brian (Athlete, Baseball Player)
8600 El Mirasol Ct
Estero, FL 33967-0521, USA

Buchanan, Charles (Athlete, Football Player)
1715 Windover Dr
Nashville, TN 37218-2410, USA

Buchanan, Edna (Writer)
156 5th Ave Ste 625
New York, NY 10010-7002, USA

Buchanan, Ian (Actor, Model)
Gold Marshak Liedtke
3500 W Olive Ave Ste 1400
Burbank, CA 91505-5512, USA

Buchanan, Jeff (Athlete, Hockey Player)
Wealth Management
1404 E Chocolate Ave
Hershey, PA 17033-1118, USA

Buchanan, Jensen (Actor)
Paradigm Agency
10100 Santa Monica Blvd Ste 2500
Los Angeles, CA 90067-4116, USA

Buchanan, Ken (Boxer)
45 Marmion Road Greenfaulds
Cumbemaul G67 4AN, SCOTLAND

Buchanan, Pat (Politician)
1017 Savile Ln
McLean, VA 22101-1830, USA

Buchanan, Phillip (Athlete, Football Player)
6185 Meadowview Cir
Fort Myers, FL 33916-4906, USA

Buchanan, Ray (Athlete, Football Player)
980 Winding Bridge Way
Duluth, GA 30097-8019, USA

Buchanan, Richard (Athlete, Football Player)
216 Brookwood Ln W
Bolingbrook, IL 60440-5511, USA

Buchanan, Robert S (Astronaut)
3 Lariat Ln
Rolling Hills Estates, CA 90274-4119, USA

Buchanan, Ron (Athlete, Hockey Player)
200 Telluride Trl
Ruidoso, NM 88345-7123, USA

Buchanan, Tanner (Actor)
c/o Debbie Palmer Beal *Beal Talent & Associates*
5850 Canoga Ave Fl 4
Woodland Hills, CA 91367-6554, USA

Buchanan, Tim (Athlete, Football Player)
888 Magnolia Ave Apt 1
Pasadena, CA 91106-3700, USA

Buchanan, Tom (Reality Star)
3130 Valley Rd
Saltville, VA 24370-4373

Buchanan, Vern (Congressman, Politician)
221 Cannon Hob
Washington, DC 20515-3515, USA

Buchanan, Willie J (Athlete, Football Player)
2742 Mesa Dr
Oceanside, CA 92054-3717, USA

Buchanon, Willie (Athlete, Football Player)
2742 Mesa Dr
Oceanside, CA 92054-3717, USA

Buchberger, Kelly (Athlete, Hockey Player)
c/o Staff Member *Springfield Falcons*
594 North St
Windsor Locks, CT 06096-1147, USA

Buchbinder, Rudolf (Music Group, Musician)
Columbia Artists Mgmt Inc
165 W 57th St
New York, NY 10019-2201, USA

Buchek, Jerry (Athlete, Baseball Player)
815 NW Flagler Ave Apt 303
Stuart, FL 34994-1158, USA

Buchel, Marco (Skier)
Ramschwagweg 55
Balzers 09496, SWITZERLAND

Buchholz, Christopher (Actor)
c/o Staff Member *TNA The New Agency*
Viale Parioli 41
Roma I-00197, Italy

Buchholz, Clay (Athlete, Baseball Player)
630 King Oaks St
Lumberton, TX 77657-7210, USA

Buchholz, Taylor (Athlete, Baseball Player)
321 Southcroft Rd
Springfield, PA 19064-1353, USA

Buchko, Steve (Athlete, Football Player)
460 Sinclair St
Winnipeg, MB R2X 1Y1, Canada

Buchli, James F Colonel (Astronaut)
14761A Innerarity Point Rd
Pensacola, FL 32507-8452, USA

Buchli, James F (Jim) (Astronaut)
1602 Fairoaks St
El Lago, TX 77586-5921, USA

Buck, Craig (Athlete, Olympic Athlete, Volleyball Player)
2110 Edgewater Way
Santa Barbara, CA 93109-1919, USA

Buck, Detlev (Director)
Agentur Sigrid Narjes
Goethestr 17
Munich 80336, GERMANY

Buck, Joe (Commentator, Television Host)
Joe Buck Inc
40 Overhills Dr
Saint Louis, MO 63124-1532, USA

Buck, John E (Artist)
11229 Cottonwood Rd
Bozeman, MT 59718-9576, USA

Buck, Mike E (Athlete, Football Player)
321 Fox Den Ct
Destin, FL 32541-4317, USA

Buck, Peter (Musician)
2033 2nd Ave Apt 2003
Seattle, WA 98121-2255, USA

Buck, Samantha (Actor)
c/o Elise Konialian *Untitled Entertainment (NY)*
215 Park Ave S Fl 8
New York, NY 10003-1622, USA

Buck, Scott (Producer)
c/o Ann Blanchard *Creative Artists Agency (CAA)*
2000 Avenue of the Stars Ste 100
Los Angeles, CA 90067-4705, USA

Buckcherry (Music Group)
c/o Andrew Goodfriend *The Kirby Organization (TKO-NY)*
9200 W Sunset Blvd Ste 600
Los Angeles, CA 90069-3196, USA

Buckels, Gary (Athlete, Baseball Player)
3510 E Longridge Dr
Orange, CA 92867-2021, USA

Buckens, Celine (Actor)
c/o Clair Dobbs *CLD Communications*
4 Broadway Ct
The Broadway
London SW191RG, UNITED KINGDOM

Buckey, Don (Athlete, Football Player)
8809 Audley Cir
Raleigh, NC 27615-3801, USA

Buckey, Jay C Dr (Astronaut)
1 Sargent St
Hanover, NH 03755-1912, USA

Buckey, Jay C Jr (Astronaut)
14 Valley Rd
Hanover, NH 03755-2228, USA

Buckhalter, Joe (Athlete, Basketball Player)
3900 Rose Hill Ave Apt 201A
Cincinnati, OH 45229-1467, USA

Buck III, Roland (Actor, Comedian)
c/o Matthew Lesher *Insight*
5358 Melrose Ave # 200W
Los Angeles, CA 90038-5117, USA

Buckingham, Gregory (Greg) (Swimmer)
338 Ridge Rd
San Carlos, CA 94070-4423, USA

Buckingham, Jane (Television Host)

Buckingham, Lindsay (Musician)
c/o Carl Stubner *Sanctuary Music Management*
15301 Arizona Ave
Bldg B #400
Santa Monica, CA 91403, USA

Buckingham, Lindsey (Musician)
c/o Tony Dimitriades *East End Management*
15260 Ventura Blvd Ste 2100
Sherman Oaks, CA 91403-5360, USA

Buckingham, Marcus (Business Person, Writer)
Simon & Schuster/Pocket/Summit
1230 Avenue of the Americas
New York, NY 10020-1513, USA

Buckinghams, The (Music Group)
Paradise Artists
PO Box 1821
Ojai, CA 93024-1821, USA

Buckland, Jonny (Musician)
21 Astor Pl Apt 6C
New York, NY 10003-6940, USA

Buckley, A J (Actor)
Innovative Artists
1505 10th St
Santa Monica, CA 90401-2805, USA

Buckley, Andy (Actor)
c/o Leanne Coronel *Coronel Group*
1100 Glendon Ave Fl 17
Los Angeles, CA 90024-3588, USA

Buckley, Betty (Actor, Director, Musician)
233 Russell Bend Rd
Weatherford, TX 76088-1217, USA

Buckley, Curtis (Athlete, Football Player)
2208 Cantura Dr
Mesquite, TX 75181-4653, USA

Buckley, D Terrell (Athlete, Football Player)
11111 Pine Lodge Trl
Davie, FL 33328-7317, USA

Buckley, James L (Politician)
8300 Burdette Rd Apt 555
Bethesda, MD 20817-2834, USA

Buckley, Jean (Athlete, Baseball Player, Commentator)
143 Monarch Dr
Fortuna, CA 95540-3451, USA

Buckley, Jessie (Actor, Musician)
c/o Ciara Parkes *Public Eye Communications*
535 Kings Rd
#313 Plaza
London SW10 0SZ, UNITED KINGDOM

Buckley, Kathy (Actor)

Buckley, Kevin (Athlete, Baseball Player)
34 Calvin St
Braintree, MA 02184-3814, USA

Buckley, Marcus W (Athlete, Football Player)
7100 Monterrey Dr
Fort Worth, TX 76112-4234, USA

Buckley, Mike (Race Car Driver)
Buckley Racing
424 Hollister Ct
Ann Arbor, MI 48103-9335, USA

Buckley, Robert (Actor)
c/o Gary Mantoosh *Baker Winokur Ryder Public Relations*
9100 Wilshire Blvd
W Tower #500
Beverly Hills, CA 90212-3415, USA

Buckley, Travis (Baseball Player)
10020 England Dr
Overland Park, KS 66212-4138, USA

Buckman, James E (Business Person)
Cendant Corp
9 W 57th St
New York, NY 10019-2701, USA

Buckman, Tara (Actor)
4525 Coldwater Canyon Ave Apt 2
Studio City, CA 91604-1088, USA

Buckman, Tom (Athlete, Football Player)
212 Foxford Dr
Keller, TX 76248-2532, USA

Buckner, Betty (Actor)
10643 Riverside Dr
Toluca Lake, CA 91602-2341, USA

Buckner, Bill (Athlete, Baseball Player)
1419 W Garfield St
Boise, ID 83706-4139, USA

Buckner, Brentson (Athlete, Football Player)
423 Leary Ct
Columbus, GA 31907-5403, USA

Buckner, Cleveland (Athlete, Basketball Player)
19227 S Grandee Ave
Carson, CA 90746-2805, USA

Buckner, Greg (Athlete, Baseball Player)
c/o Steve Kauffman *Kauffman Sports Management Group*
Prefers to be contacted by telephone
Malibu, CA, USA

Buckner, Quinn (Athlete, Basketball Player, Olympic Athlete)
857 Valencia Blvd
Irving, TX 75039-3057, USA

Buckner, Shelley (Actor)
c/o Pamela Kohl *3 Arts Entertainment*
9460 Wilshire Blvd Fl 7
Beverly Hills, CA 90212-2713, USA

Bucknor, C B (Athlete, Baseball Player)
46 Midwood St
Brooklyn, NY 11225-5004, USA

Bucknum, Jeff (Race Car Driver)
2428 Frederick Ln
Lake Havasu City, AZ 86404-9588, USA

Bucksey, Colin (Director)

Buckson, David P (Politician)
2710 Rismen Ct
Kissimmee, FL 34743-5370, USA

Bucshon, Larry (Congressman, Politician)
1123 Longworth Hob
Washington, DC 20515-4601, USA

Bucyk, John (Athlete, Hockey Player)
c/o Staff Member *Boston Bruins*
100 Legends Way Ste 250
Td Banknorth Garden
Boston, MA 02114-1389, USA

Bucyk, Randy (Athlete, Hockey Player)
23 Glenwood Cres
St. Albert, AB T8N 1X5, Canada

Buczkowski, Bob (Athlete, Football Player)
4515 Northern Pike
Monroeville, PA 15146-2915, USA

Budaj, Peter (Athlete, Hockey Player)
209 15th St
Manhattan Bch, CA 90266-4603, USA

Budaska, Mark (Athlete, Baseball Player)
15025 W Buttonwood Dr
Sun City West, AZ 85375-5750, USA

Budd, David (Athlete, Basketball Player)
40 N Woodland Ave
Woodbury, NJ 08096-2517, USA

Budd, Julie (Actor, Music Group)
Julie Budd Productions
163 Amsterdam Ave # 224
New York, NY 10023-5001, USA

Budd, Pieterse Zola (Athlete, Track Athlete)
General Delivery
Bloemfontein, SOUTH AFRICA

Budde, Brad E (Athlete, Football Player)
5121 W 159th Ter
Stilwell, KS 66085-8956, USA

Budde, Ed (Athlete, Football Player)
5121 W 159th Ter
Stilwell, KS 66085-8956, USA

Budde, Jordan (Producer, Writer)
c/o Ann Blanchard *Creative Artists Agency (CAA)*
2000 Avenue of the Stars Ste 100
Los Angeles, CA 90067-4705, USA

Budde, Ryan (Athlete, Baseball Player)
3109 N Peebly Dr
Oklahoma City, OK 73110-1509, USA

Budden, Joe (Actor)
c/o Staff Member *ICM Partners*
10250 Constellation Blvd Fl 7
Los Angeles, CA 90067-6207, USA

Buddie, Mike (Athlete, Baseball Player)
201 Siena Dr
Greenville, SC 29609-3070, USA

Budd-Pieterse, Zola (Athlete, Track Athlete)
c/o Staff Member *British Olympic Association*
1 Wandsworth Plain
London SW18 1EH, UK

Buddy, Brandon (Actor)
c/o Jon Simmons *Simmons & Scott Entertainment*
7942 Mulholland Dr
Los Angeles, CA 90046-1225, USA

Budenholzer, Mike (Basketball Coach)
c/o Michael Hawkins *Hawkins Law Firm*
1535 Mount Vernon Rd Ste 200
Atlanta, GA 30338-4149, USA

Budig, Gene (Commentator)
134 Fairbanks Oak Aly Unit 202
Daniel Island, SC 29492-6200, USA

Budig, Rebecca (Actor)
c/o Rob Kolker *Red Letter Entertainment*
550 W 45th St Apt 501
New York, NY 10036-3779, USA

Budka, Frank (Athlete, Football Player)
2637 SW Abel St
Port Saint Lucie, FL 34953-2834, USA

Budko, Walter (Athlete, Basketball Player)
2525 Pot Spring Rd Unit L703
Lutherville Timonium, MD 21093-2852, USA

Budness, Bill (Athlete, Football Player)
401 Huckle Hill Rd
Bernardston, MA 01337-9423, USA

Budrewicz, Tom (Athlete, Football Player)
13 Olde Farms Rd
Boxford, MA 01921-1915, USA

Budzinski, Mark (Athlete, Baseball Player)
4919 Packard Rd
Glen Allen, VA 23060-3536, USA

Buechele, Steve (Athlete, Baseball Player)
2600 Royal Glen Dr
Arlington, TX 76012-5553, USA

Buechler, John Carl (Director)
c/o Staff Member *Imageries Entertainment*
2815 Coldwater Canyon Dr
Beverly Hills, CA 90210-1305, USA

Buechler, Jud (Athlete, Basketball Player)
1515 West Ln
Del Mar, CA 92014-4137, USA

Buechrle, James (Baseball Player)
Chicago White Sox
Comiskey Park 333 W 35th St
Chicago, IL 60616, USA

Buehler, George (Athlete, Football Player)
63 Tara Rd
Orinda, CA 94563-3116, USA

Buehler, Jud (Athlete, Basketball Player)
4576 South Ln
Del Mar, CA 92014-4139, USA

Buehler, Walker (Athlete, Baseball Player)
c/o Kent Mercker *Excel Sports Management*
1700 Broadway Fl 29
New York, NY 10019-6559, USA

Buehrle, Mark (Athlete, Baseball Player)
5653 N Ridge Ave
Chicago, IL 60660-5549, USA

Buell, Bebe (Actor)
c/o Ivan Bart *IMG Models (NY)*
304 Park Ave S PH N
New York, NY 10010-4303, USA

Buer, Aaron (Actor)
c/o Staff Member *RPM Talent Agency*
11255 Yarmouth Ave
Granada Hills, CA 91344-4055, USA

Buerkle, Ann Marie (Congressman, Politician)
1630 Longworth Hob
Washington, DC 20515-2002, USA

Buerkle, Dick (Athlete, Olympic Athlete, Track Athlete)
3086 Dale Dr NE
Atlanta, GA 30305-2776, USA

Buetow, Brad (Athlete, Hockey Player)
1419 Alamo Ave
Colorado Springs, CO 80907-7301, USA

Buffett, Howard Graham (Business Person)
407 Southmoreland Pl
Decatur, IL 62521-3754, USA

Buffett, Jimmy (Musician)
Margaritaville
500 Duval St
Key West, FL 33040-6553, USA

Buffett, Peter (Musician)
c/o Staff Member *Paradigm (Monterey)*
404 W Franklin St
Monterey, CA 93940-2303, USA

Buffett, Warren (Business Person)
Berkshire Hathaway
1440 Kiewit Plaza
Omaha, NE 68131, USA

Buffone, Douglas J (Doug) (Athlete, Football Player)
1272 W Lexington St
Chicago, IL 60607-4110, USA

Bufman, Zev (Producer)
520 Brickell Key Dr # 612
Miami, FL 33131-2660, USA

Buford, Damon J (Athlete, Baseball Player)
3116 S Mill Ave Ste 512
Tempe, AZ 85282-3685, USA

Buford, Don (Athlete, Baseball Player)
15412 Valley Vista Blvd
Sherman Oaks, CA 91403-3812, USA

Buford, Maury (Athlete, Football Player)
241 Oak Hill Dr
Roanoke, TX 76262-5454, USA

Bugel, Joe (Athlete, Football Coach, Football Player)
7120 E Kierland Blvd Apt 318
Scottsdale, AZ 85254-3087, USA

Bugenhagen, Gary (Athlete, Football Player)
4337 Henneberry Rd
Manlius, NY 13104-8425, USA

Buggs, Dany (Athlete, Football Player)
3186 Evans Mill Rd
Lithonia, GA 30038-2420, USA

Buggs, Wamon (Athlete, Football Player)
5700 Sonoma Trce
Antioch, TN 37013-4273, USA

Buggy, Regina (Athlete, Hockey Player)
550 N Limekiln Pike
Chalfont, PA 18914-2739, USA

Bugner, Joe (Boxer)
22 Buckingham St
Surrey Hills, NSW 02010, AUSTRALIA

Buhl, Robbie (Race Car Driver)
28140 Center Ridge Rd
Westlake, OH 44145-3905, USA

Buhner, Jay (Athlete, Baseball Player)
David and Kay Buhner
2014 Sandy Coast Cir
League City, TX 77573-6618, USA

Buhrmaster, Robert C (Business Person)
Jostens Inc
7760 France Ave S Ste 400
Minneapolis, MN 55435-5844, USA

Buice, Dewayne (Athlete, Baseball Player)
PO Box 5185
Incline Village, NV 89450-5185, USA

Buie, Drew (Athlete, Football Player)
2815 Eland Dr
Winston Salem, NC 27127-7284, USA

Buitenhuis, Penelope (Director, Writer)
c/o Carl Lieberman *Characters Talent Agency*
200-1505 2nd Ave W
Vancouver, BC V6H 3Y4, CANADA

Bujnoch, Glenn (Athlete, Football Player)
7598 Fairwayglen Dr
Cincinnati, OH 45248-2800, USA

Bujold, Genevieve (Actor)
1327 Ocean Ave Ste J
Blake Agency
Santa Monica, CA 90401-1033, USA

Bukich, Rudy (Athlete, Football Player)
12764 Via Terceto
San Diego, CA 92130-2175, USA

Buktenica, Raymond (Actor)
Special Artists Agency
345 N Maple Dr # 302
Beverly Hills, CA 90210-3869, USA

Bukvich, Ryan (Athlete, Baseball Player)
605 Arbor Way
Brandon, MS 39047-7079, USA

Bulaga, Bryan (Athlete, Football Player)
c/o Ben Dogra *Relativity Sports*
2029 Century Park E Ste 1550
Century City, CA 90067-3000, USA

Bulaich, Norman B (Norm) (Athlete, Football Player)
421 Lynndale Ct
Hurst, TX 76054-2725, USA

Bulatovic, Momir (President)
Vlada Savezne Republike
Lenina 2
Belgrade 11070, SERBIA & MONTENEGRO

Bulger, Jason (Athlete, Baseball Player)
6720 Eastleigh Cir
Suwanee, GA 30024-5315, USA

Bulger, Marc (Athlete, Football Player)
c/o Tom Condon *Creative Artists Agency (CAA)*
401 Commerce St PH
Nashville, TN 37219-2516, USA

Bulifant, Joyce (Actor)
James/Levy/Jacobson
3500 W Olive Ave Ste 1470
Burbank, CA 91505-5514, USA

Bull, Ronald D (Ronnie) (Athlete, Football Player)
1417 Lahon St
Park Ridge, IL 60068-2521, USA

Bull, Scott (Athlete, Football Player)
2764 Quarry Ln
Fayetteville, AR 72704-6223, USA

Bullard, Courtland (Athlete, Football Player)
22200 SW 113th Ct
Miami, FL 33170-4762, us

Bullard, Kendricke (Athlete, Football Player)
PO Box 2330
North Little Rock, AR 72115-2330, US

Bullard, Matt (Athlete, Basketball Player)

Bullard, Mike (Athlete, Hockey Player)
1170 Shillington Ave
Ottawa, ON K1Z 7Z4, Canada

Bullet, Scott (Athlete, Baseball Player)
218 Vicky Bullett St
Martinsburg, WV 25404-4511, USA

Bullinger, Jim (Athlete, Baseball Player)
2504 Elise Ave
Metairie, LA 70003-1931, USA

Bullinger, Kirk (Athlete, Baseball Player)
509 Daniel St
Kenner, LA 70062-7507, USA

Bullington, Bryan (Athlete, Baseball Player)
20116 Oakwood Dr
Mokena, IL 60448-1395, USA

Bullins, Ed (Writer)
425 Lafayette St
New York, NY 10003-7021, USA

Bullmann, Maik (Wrestler)
AC Bavaria Goldbach
Postfach 1112
Goldbach 63769, GERMANY

Bulloch, Jeremy (Actor)
Fett Photos
10 Birchwood Rd
London SW17 9BQ, UNITED KINGDOM (UK)

Bullock, Bruce (Athlete, Hockey Player)
5226 W Redbird Rd
Phoenix, AZ 85083-6317, USA

Bullock, Eric (Athlete, Baseball Player)
2902 W Sweetwater Ave Apt 3214
Phoenix, AZ 85029-6301, USA

Bullock, Jim J (Actor)
c/o Staff Member *Bohemia Group*
1680 Vine St Ste 518
Los Angeles, CA 90028-8833, USA

Bullock, J R (Business Person)
Laidlaw Inc
3221 N Service Road
Burlington, ON L7R 3Y8, CANADA

Bullock, Randy (Athlete, Football Player)
c/o Eric Metz *Lock Metz Milanovic LLC*
6900 E Camelback Rd Ste 600
Scottsdale, AZ 85251-8044, USA

Bullock, Sandra (Actor, Producer)
c/o Staff Member *Fortis Films*
8581 Santa Monica Blvd Ste 1
West Hollywood, CA 90069-4120, USA

Bullock, Vicki (Athlete, Basketball Player)
Charlotte Sting
100 Hive Dr
Charlotte, NC 28217, USA

Bullocks, Amos (Athlete, Football Player)
17209 Dobson Ave
South Holland, IL 60473-3535, USA

Bullough, Hank (Athlete, Football Player)
4439 Copperhill Dr
Okemos, MI 48864-2067, USA

Bulluck, Keith (Athlete, Football Player)
874 Nialta Ln
Brentwood, TN 37027-8232, USA

Bulriss, Mark P (Business Person)
Great Lakes Chemical
9025 River Rd Ste 400
Indianapolis, IN 46240-6443, USA

Bum, Kim (Actor)
c/o Staff Member *Glory Entertainment*
1-25-5-3F Higashi Azabu
Minatoku
Tokyo 106-0044, Japan

Bumbeck, David (Artist)
Drew Lane RD 3
Middleburry, VT 05753, USA

Bumbry, Alonzo B (Al) (Athlete, Baseball Player)
28 Tremblant Ct
Lutherville Timonium, MD 21093-3748, USA

Bumgarner, Madison (Athlete, Baseball Player)
c/o Ashley Smith Becker *Relativity Sports*
2029 Century Park E Ste 1550
Century City, CA 90067-3000, USA

Bumgarner, Wayne (Actor)
PO Box 208
Claremont, NC 28610-0208, USA

Bump, Nate (Athlete, Baseball Player)
274 Caravelle Dr
Jupiter, FL 33458-8200, USA

Bumpas, Dick (Athlete, Football Player)
3612 Bellaire Dr N
Fort Worth, TX 76109-2115, USA

Bunbury, Kylie (Actor)
c/o Brett Ruttenberg *Imprint PR*
6121 W Sunset Blvd
Neuehouse
Los Angeles, CA 90028-6442, USA

Bunce, Gregory (Athlete, Basketball Player)
4447 Don Milagro Dr
Los Angeles, CA 90008-2831, USA

Bunce, Larry (Attorney, Basketball Player)
1000 Vintage Ln Apt 338
Mount Vernon, WA 98273-5532, USA

Bunch, Ashli (Athlete, Golfer)
1629 Country Club Dr
Morristown, TN 37814-3316, USA

Bunch, Jarrod (Athlete, Football Player)
1580 Hemlock Dr
Ashtabula, OH 44004-9360, USA

Bunch, Melvin (Athlete, Baseball Player)
782 Horseshoe Loop
Texarkana, TX 75501-1322, USA

Bunch, Sidney (Athlete, Baseball Player)
3285 Towne Village Rd
Antioch, TN 37013-1280, USA

Bund, Karlheinz (Business Person)
Huyssenallee 82-84
Essen Ruhr 45128, GERMANY

Bundchen, Gisele (Model)
c/o Anne Nelson *IMG Models (NY)*
304 Park Ave S PH N
New York, NY 10010-4303, USA

Bundini, Rudy (Model)
57 W 57th St
New York, NY 10019-2802, USA

Bundren, Jim (Athlete, Football Player)

Bundy, Brooke (Actor)
200 S Sycamore Ave Apt 7
Los Angeles, CA 90036-3047, USA

Bundy, Laura Bell (Actor, Musician)
c/o CeCe Yorke *True Public Relations*
3575 Cahuenga Blvd W Ste 360
Los Angeles, CA 90068-1361, USA

Bunker, Wallace E (Wally) (Athlete, Baseball Player)
325 Coosaw Way
Ridgeland, SC 29936-4931, USA

Bunkley, Broderick (Athlete, Football Player)
c/o Bill Johnson *SportsTrust Advisors*
3340 Peachtree Rd NE Fl 16
Atlanta, GA 30326-1000, USA

Bunkowsky-Scherbak, Barb (Athlete, Golfer)
8725 Marlamoor Ln
Palm Beach Gardens, FL 33412-1614, USA

Bunnell, John (Actor, Television Host)
c/o Greg Horangic *WME|IMG*
9601 Wilshire Blvd
Beverly Hills, CA 90210-5213, USA

Bunny, Lady (Comedian, DJ, Impersonator)
c/o Stephen Ford *Diva Central Inc*
7510 W Sunset Blvd # 1445
Los Angeles, CA 90046-3408, USA

Bunt, Dick (Actor)
11 Irving Pl
Greenlawn, NY 11740-3113, USA

Bunt, Richard (Athlete, Basketball Player)
90 Business Park Dr Unit 310
Armonk, NY 10504-1728, USA

Bunting, Eve (Writer)
Harper Collins Publishers
1512 Rose Villa St
Pasadena, CA 91106-3525, USA

Bunting, John (Athlete, Football Player)
395 Edgemere Way N
Naples, FL 34105-7148, USA

Bunting, William (Athlete, Basketball Player)
1084 Cornell Ct
Leland, NC 28451-4152, USA

Bunton, Emma (Music Group, Musician)
c/o Jeff Frasco *Creative Artists Agency (CAA)*
2000 Avenue of the Stars Ste 100
Los Angeles, CA 90067-4705, USA

Bunyan, John (Athlete, Football Player)
127 Belvidere Rd
Glen Rock, NJ 07452-3422, USA

Bunz, Dan (Athlete, Football Player)
4230 Rocklin Rd Apt 2
Rocklin, CA 95677-2869, USA

Buoniconti, Nicholas A (Nick) (Athlete, Business Person, Football Player)
PO Box 2037
Bridgehampton, NY 11932-2037, USA

Buono, Cara (Actor)
c/o Mitchell Gossett *Industry Entertainment Partners*
955 Carrillo Dr Ste 300
Los Angeles, CA 90048-5400, USA

Buono, Carla (Actor)
25 Sea Colony Dr
Santa Monica, CA 90405-5495, USA

Buraas, Hans-Peter (Skier)
Norges Skiforbund
Postboks 3853
Ulleval Hageby, Oslo 00805, NORWAY

Burakovsky, Robert (Athlete, Hockey Player)
John Lundvallsgatan 40
Bunkeflostrand S-21831, Sweden

Burba, Dave (Athlete, Baseball Player)
378 N Shore Ln
Gilbert, AZ 85233-4702, USA

Burbach, Bill (Athlete, Baseball Player)
147 Shenandoah Dr
Johnson City, TN 37601-5459, USA

Burbage, Cornell (Athlete, Football Player)
1309 Copper Run Blvd
Lexington, KY 40514-2217, us

Burbank, Daniel C Cdr (Astronaut)
364 Route 6A
Yarmouth Port, MA 02675-1820, USA

Burbank, Daniel C (Dan) (Astronaut)
3210 Water Elm Way
Houston, TX 77059, USA

Burbano, Mindy (Actor)
12 Fairway Pt
Newport Coast, CA 92657-1721, USA

Burch, Elliot (Race Car Driver)
402 Corey Ln
Middletown, RI 02842-5664, USA

Burch, Jerry (Athlete, Football Player)
1501 Plantation Dr
Simpsonville, SC 29681-4658, USA

Burch, Matt (Reality Star)
PO Box 802227
Santa Clarita, CA 91380-2227, USA

Burch, Rick (Musician)
c/o Staff Member *SAM*
722 Seward St
Los Angeles, CA 90038-3504, USA

Burch, Tory (Business Person, Designer)
Tory Burch
11 W 19th St Fl 7
New York, NY 10011-4277, USA

Burchard, Brendon (Business Person, Writer)
The Burchard Group
PO Box 5368
Portland, OR 97228-5368, USA

Burchart, Larry (Athlete, Baseball Player)
5310 E 94th St
Tulsa, OK 74137-4417, USA

Burchfield, Don (Athlete, Football Player)
26450 Summer Greens Dr
Bonita Springs, FL 34135-2328, USA

Burd, Steven A (Business Person)
Safeway Inc
5918 Stoneridge Mall Rd
Pleasanton, CA 94588-3229, USA

Burda, Bob (Athlete, Baseball Player)
5285 S Roanoke
Mesa, AZ 85206-2129, USA

Burden, Ross (Chef)
c/o Staff Member *Roseman Organisation, The*
51 Queen Anne St
London W1G 9HS, UK

Burden, Ticky (Athlete, Basketball Player)
4332 Grove Ave Apt C
Winston Salem, NC 27105-2837, USA

Burden, Willie (Athlete, Football Player)
112 Olde Towne Dr
Statesboro, GA 30458-1673, USA

Burdis, Ray (Actor)
c/o Roger Carey *Roger Carey Associates*
Suite 909, The Old House
Shepperton Film Studios, Studios Road
Shepperton, Mddx TW17 0QD, UNITED KINGDOM

Burditt, Joyce (Producer, Writer)
c/o Staff Member *WME|IMG*
9601 Wilshire Blvd
Beverly Hills, CA 90210-5213, USA

Burdon, Eric (Music Group, Songwriter, Writer)
Lustig Talent
PO Box 770850
Orlando, FL 32877-0850, USA

Bure, Pavel (Athlete, Hockey Player)
7632 Fisher Island Dr
Miami Beach, FL 33109-0780, USA

Bure, Valeri (Athlete, Hockey Player)
10371 Golden Eagle Ct
Plantation, FL 33324-2161, USA

Bureau, Marc (Athlete, Hockey Player)
3950 de Shawinigan-Sud Blvd
ECOLE DE POWER SKATING JULIE ROBITAILLE
Shawinigan, QC G9P 4T6, G9P 4T6

Burega, Bill (Athlete, Hockey Player)
122 Farmstead Crt
Kingston, ON K7P 3H9, Canada

Bureker-Stopper, Geraldine (Baseball Player)
2006 SE 41st Ave
Portland, OR 97214-5966, USA

Buress, Hannibal (Actor, Comedian)
c/o David (Dave) Becky *3 Arts Entertainment*
9460 Wilshire Blvd Fl 7
Beverly Hills, CA 90212-2713, USA

Burfeindt, Betty (Athlete, Golfer)
70 San Simeon Pl
Rancho Mirage, CA 92270-1951, USA

Burfict, Vontaze (Athlete, Football Player)

Burford, Christopher W (Chris) (Athlete, Football Player)
2187 Huntsdale Dr
Reno, NV 89521-8242, USA

Burg, Bob (Writer)
Burg Communications Inc
3607 Fairway Dr N
Jupiter, FL 33477-9525, USA

Burg, Mark (Producer)
14050 Aubrey Rd
Beverly Hills, CA 90210-1064, USA

Burger, Michael (Actor)
c/o Staff Member *Richard De La Font Agency*
3808 W South Park Blvd
Broken Arrow, OK 74011-1261, USA

Burger, Neil (Director)
c/o Staff Member *WME/IMG*
9601 Wilshire Blvd
Beverly Hills, CA 90210-5213, USA

Burgess, Annie (Athlete)
601 F St NW
Washington, DC 20004-1605

Burgess, Bobby (Actor)
11684 Ventura Blvd # 691
Studio City, CA 91604-2699, USA

Burgess, Dominic (Actor)
c/o Jonathan Hall *Identity Agency Group (UK)*
95 Grays Inn Rd
London WC1X 8TX, UNITED KINGDOM

Burgess, Mitchell (Writer)
c/o Staff Member *Broder Webb Chervin Silbermann Agency, The (BWCS)*
10250 Constellation Blvd
Los Angeles, CA 90067-6200, USA

Burgess, Ronnie (Athlete, Football Player)
303 Brandymill Blvd
Myrtle Beach, SC 29588-7227, USA

Burgess, Sharna (Dancer, Reality Star)
c/o Amy Malin *Trueheart Management*
20732 Wells Dr
Woodland Hills, CA 91364-3437, USA

Burgess, Tituss (Actor, Musician)
c/o Alla Plotkin *ID Public Relations (NY)*
40 Wall St Fl 51
New York, NY 10005-1385, USA

Burgess, Tom (Athlete, Football Player)
1399 Maryland Rd
Phelps, NY 14532-9508, USA

Burgess, Warren D (Religious Leader)
Reformed Church in America
475 Riverside Dr Ste 1606
New York, NY 10115-0093, USA

Burghoff, Gary (Actor)
c/o Jacqueline Stander *Scott Stander & Associates*
4533 Van Nuys Blvd Ste 401
Sherman Oaks, CA 91403-2950, USA

Burgi, Richard (Actor)
124 Sunset Ter
Laguna Beach, CA 92651-3967, USA

Burgio, Danielle (Actor)
c/o Carl Scott *Simmons & Scott Entertainment*
7942 Mulholland Dr
Los Angeles, CA 90046-1225, USA

Burgmeier, Ted (Athlete, Football Player)
861 Scenic Hts
East Dubuque, IL 61025-1041, USA

Burgmeler, Tom (Athlete, Baseball Player)
13118 Walmer St
Leawood, KS 66209-3618, USA

Burham, Daniel (Business Person)
Raytheon Co
870 Winter St
Waltham, MA 02451-1449, USA

Burish, Adam (Athlete, Hockey Player)
635 N Dearborn St Apt 2802
Chicago, IL 60654-6795, USA

Burk, Mack (Athlete, Baseball Player)
5710 Glen Pines Dr
Houston, TX 77069-1852, USA

Burk, Scott (Athlete, Football Player)
1330 Castlepoint Cir
Castle Pines, CO 80108-8295, USA

Burka, Vern (Athlete, Football Player)
580 Riviera Cir
Nipomo, CA 93444-8866, USA

Burkart, Phil (Race Car Driver)
114 Oriskany Blvd
Yorkville, NY 13495-1328, USA

Burke, Alexandra (Musician)
c/o Oliver Thomson *Cole Kitchenn Personal Management*
ROAR House
46 Charlotte St
London W1T 2GS, UNITED KINGDOM

Burke, Billy (Actor)
c/o Jennifer Allen *Viewpoint Inc*
8820 Wilshire Blvd Ste 220
Beverly Hills, CA 90211-2622, USA

Burke, Cheryl (Dancer, Reality Star)
Cheryl Burke Dance
5 Meadow Ln
Atherton, CA 94027-6468, USA

Burke, Chris (Actor)
c/o Staff Member *Abrams Artists Agency*
750 N San Vicente Blvd
E Tower Fl 11
Los Angeles, CA 90069-5788, USA

Burke, Chris (Athlete, Baseball Player)
15415 Crystal Springs Way
Louisville, KY 40245-5298, USA

Burke, Clement (Clem) (Musician)
Shore Fire Media
32 Court St Ste 1600
Brooklyn, NY 11201-4441, USA

Burke, Delta (Actor)
4270 Farmdale Ave
Studio City, CA 91604-2733, USA

Burke, Ed (Actor)
285 E Main St
Los Gatos, CA 95030-6106, USA

Burke, Edward (Athlete, Olympic Athlete)
16717 La Mirada Rd
Los Gatos, CA 95030-4118, USA

Burke, Ernest (Athlete, Baseball Player)
9451 Common Brook Rd Apt 302
Owings Mills, MD 21117-7582, USA

Burke, Hederman Lynn (Swimmer)
26 White Oak Tree Rd
Syosset, NY 11791-1210, USA

Burke, James (Correspondent)
Henley House
Terrace Bames
London SW13 0NP, UNITED KINGDOM (UK)

Burke, James D (Director)
Saint Louis Art Museum
Forest Park
Saint Louis, MO 63110, USA

Burke, James Lee (Writer)
c/o Joel Gotler *Intellectual Property Group (IPG)*
12400 Wilshire Blvd Ste 500
Los Angeles, CA 90025-1055, USA

Burke, Joe (Athlete, Football Player)
7 Maplewood St
Albany, NY 12208-2413, USA

Burke, John (Athlete, Baseball Player)
3490 Westbrook Ln
Highlands Ranch, CO 80129-1527, USA

Burke, John (Athlete, Football Player)
612 Oceanview Rd
Brielle, NJ 08730-1221, USA

Burke, Kathy (Actor)
Stephen Halton Mgmt
83 Shepperton Road
London N1 3DF, UNITED KINGDOM (UK)

Burke, Leo (Athlete, Baseball Player)
12916 Woodburn Dr
Hagerstown, MD 21742-2866, USA

Burke, Mark (Athlete, Football Player)
10 Maple Shade Dr
Marietta, OH 45750-1124, US

Burke, Michael Reilly (Actor)
c/o Staff Member *Paradigm*
8942 Wilshire Blvd
Beverly Hills, CA 90211-1908, USA

Burke, Mike (Athlete, Football Player)
720 Deodara Pl
Dixon, CA 95620-3639, USA

Burke, Patrick (Athlete, Golfer)
24 Saint Georges Ct
Trabuco Canyon, CA 92679-4926, USA

Burke, Philip (Artist)
L.B. Madison Fine Art
335 Buffalo Ave
Niagara Falls, NY 14303-1232, USA

Burke, Randall (Athlete, Football Player)
3420 Chestnut Hill Ln
Lexington, KY 40509-1916, USA

Burke, Randy (Athlete, Football Player)
3420 Chestnut Hill Ln
Lexington, KY 40509-1916, US

Burke, Robert John (Actor)
c/o Staff Member *Industry Entertainment Partners*
955 Carrillo Dr Ste 300
Los Angeles, CA 90048-5400, USA

Burke, Sarah (Reality Star)
c/o Mike Esterman *Esterman.Com, LLC*
Prefers to be contacted via email
Baltimore, MD XXXXX, USA

Burke, Sean (Athlete, Hockey Player)
16510 N 92nd St Unit 1015
Scottsdale, AZ 85260-2330, USA

Burke, Shawn (Athlete, Hockey Player)
6624 E Stallion Rd
Paradise Valley, AZ 85253-3158, USA

Burke, Soloman (Musician)
c/o Staff Member *Coalition Management*
Devonshire House
12 Barley Mow Passage
London W4 4PH, UK

Burke, Steve (Athlete, Baseball Player)
1812 Amber Leaf Way
Lodi, CA 95242-4468, USA

Burke, Steve (Athlete, Football Player)
RR 3 Box 553-F
Austin, TX 78754, USA

Burke, Tim (Athlete, Baseball Player)
12108 W Ida Ln
Littleton, CO 80127-3106, USA

Burke, Tom (Actor)
c/o Clair Dobbs *CLD Communications*
4 Broadway Ct
The Broadway
London SW191RG, UNITED KINGDOM

Burke-Charvet, Brooke (Actor, Model)
c/o Brit Reece *PMK/BNC Public Relations*
1840 Century Park E Ste 1400
Los Angeles, CA 90067-2115, USA

Burke Sr, Jack (Athlete, Golfer)
5602 Glen Pines Dr
Houston, TX 77069-1834, USA

Burkett, Chris (Athlete, Football Player)
296 Dover Ln
Madison, MS 39110-9726, USA

Burkett, Jackie (Athlete, Football Player)
895 Santa Rosa Blvd Apt 709
Fort Walton Beach, FL 32548-1913, USA

Burkett, John D (Athlete, Baseball Player)
2913 Alton Rd
Fort Worth, TX 76109-1204, USA

Burkhalter, Correll (Athlete, Football Player)
221 Robert Owens Rd
Mount Olive, MS 39119-4651, USA

Burkhardt, Lisa (Sportscaster)
Madison Square Garden Network
4 Pennsylvania Plaza
New York, NY 10001, USA

Burkhart, Morgan (Athlete, Baseball Player)
105 Turtle Rock Ct
Saint Charles, MO 63304-7679, USA

Burkhead, Rex (Athlete, Football Player)
c/o Neil Cornrich *NC Sports, LLC*
best to contact via email
Columbus, OH 43201, USA

Burkholder, Max (Actor)
c/o Brett Ruttenberg *Imprint PR*
6121 W Sunset Blvd
Neuehouse
Los Angeles, CA 90028-6442, USA

Burkholder, Owen E (Religious Leader)
421 S 2nd St Ste 600
Elkhart, IN 46516-3243, USA

Burkle, Ron (Business Person)
2607 Glendower Ave
Los Angeles, CA 90027-1114, USA

Burkman, Roger (Athlete, Basketball Player)
3242 Beals Branch Dr
Dallas, TX 75237-0861, USA

Burkovich, Shirley (Athlete, Baseball Player, Commentator)
67430 Ovante Rd
Cathedral City, CA 92234-8402, USA

Burks, Audra (Athlete, Golfer)
584 Brantley Terrace Way Unit 205
Altamonte Springs, FL 32714-0829, USA

Burks, Ellis R (Athlete, Baseball Player)
115 South Ln
Chagrin Falls, OH 44022-1145, USA

Burks, Randy (Athlete, Football Player)
300 Moyer Dr
Broken Bow, OK 74728-1519, USA

Burks, Shawn (Athlete, Football Player)
5752 Nottaway Dr
Baton Rouge, LA 70820-5415, USA

Burks, Steve (Athlete, Football Player)
2568 Mount Tabor Rd
Cabot, AR 72023-9596, USA

Burleson, Dyrol (Athlete, Olympic Athlete, Track Athlete)
12024 S Shadow Hills Ct SE
Turner, OR 97392-9353, USA

Burleson, Richard P (Rick) (Athlete, Baseball Player)
241 E Country Hills Dr
La Habra, CA 90631-7623, USA

Burleson, Tom (Athlete, Basketball Player, Olympic Athlete)
PO Box 861
Newland, NC 28657-0861, USA

Burley, Gary (Athlete, Football Player)
8228 Castlehill Rd
Birmingham, AL 35242-7233, USA

Burlinson, Tom (Actor)
c/o Staff Member *June Cann Management*
73 Jersey Rd
Woollahra 02025, AUSTRALIA

Burman, George (Athlete, Football Player)
1646 James St
Syracuse, NY 13203-2816, USA

Burn, Scott (Writer)
c/o Staff Member *Creative Artists Agency (CAA)*
2000 Avenue of the Stars Ste 100
Los Angeles, CA 90067-4705, USA

Burner, David L (Business Person)
B F Goodrich Co
2550 W Tyvola Rd
3 Coliseum Centre
Charlotte, NC 28217-4574, USA

Burnes, Karen (Correspondent)
CBS-TV
51 W 52nd St
News Dept
New York, NY 10019-6119, USA

Burnett, A J (Athlete, Baseball Player)
15208 Jarrettsville Pike
Monkton, MD 21111-2423, USA

Burnett, Anna (Actor)
c/o Suzy Kenway *Scott Marshall Partners Ltd*
49/50 Eagle Wharf Road
Holborn Studios
London N1 7ED, UNITED KINGDOM

Burnett, Bobby (Athlete, Football Player)
4521 N Diamond Leaf Dr
Castle Rock, CO 80109-8684, USA

Burnett, Carol (Actor, Comedian)
c/o Angie Horejsi *Mabel Cat*
9663 Santa Monica Blvd Ste 643
Beverly Hills, CA 90210-4303, USA

Burnett, Chester (Athlete, Football Player)
2610 Ivanhoe St
Denver, CO 80207-3409, USA

Burnett, Erin (Correspondent, Journalist, Television Host)
c/o Staff Member *CNN (NY)*
10 Columbus Cir
Time Warner Center
New York, NY 10019-1158, USA

Burnett, Kelly (Athlete, Hockey Player)
206-202 Walter Havill Dr
Halifax, NS B3N 3M4, Canada

Burnett, Mark (Producer)
c/o Staff Member *One Three Media*
3000 Olympic Blvd Bldg 2520
Santa Monica, CA 90404-5073, USA

Burnett, Molly (Actor)
c/o Shepard Smith *Luber Roklin Management*
5815 W Sunset Blvd Ste 208
Los Angeles, CA 90028-6481, USA

Burnett, Morgan (Athlete, Football Player)

Burnett, Nancy (Director)
Nancy Burnett Productions
32 Watson St
Unadilla, NY 13849-0735, USA

Burnett, Sean (Athlete, Baseball Player)
14016 Aster Ave
Wellington, FL 33414-2145, USA

Burnett, T-Bone (Musician, Producer, Songwriter)
c/o Staff Member *Paradigm (Monterey)*
404 W Franklin St
Monterey, CA 93940-2303, USA

Burnett, Webbie D (Athlete, Football Player)
5305 San Antonio Ave Apt 128
Orlando, FL 32839-2222, USA

Burnette, Dave (Athlete, Football Player)
4201 Senator St
Texarkana, AR 71854-1528, USA

Burnette, Olivia (Actor)
c/o Staff Member *RPM Talent Agency*
11255 Yarmouth Ave
Granada Hills, CA 91344-4055, USA

Burnette, Reggie (Athlete, Football Player)
7803 Chasewood Dr
Missouri City, TX 77489-1836, USA

Burnette, Rocky (Musician)
1900 Ave of Stars # 2530
Los Angeles, CA 90067-4301, USA

Burnham, Bo (Actor, Comedian)
c/o David (Dave) Becky *3 Arts Entertainment*
9460 Wilshire Blvd Fl 7
Beverly Hills, CA 90212-2713, USA

Burnine, Hank (Athlete, Football Player)
709 W Rieck Rd
Tyler, TX 75703-3559, USA

Burning, Spear (Musician)
13034 231st St
Laurelton, NY 11413-1832, USA

Burnitz, Jeromv (Athlete, Baseball Player)
PO Box 676032
Rancho Santa Fe, CA 92067-6032, USA

Burnitz, Jeromy (Athlete, Baseball Player)
18520 Old Coach Dr
Poway, CA 92064-6637, USA

Burnley, Benjamin (Musician)
c/o Staff Member *UTA Music/The Agency Group (UK)*
361-373 City Rd
London EC1V 1PQ, UNITED KINGDOM

Burnley, James H IV (Politician)
Shaw Pittman Potts Trowbridge
9401 Mount Vernon Cir
Alexandria, VA 22309-3221, USA

Burns, Annie (Musician, Songwriter, Writer)
Drake Assoc
177 Woodland Ave
Westwood, NJ 07675-3218, USA

Burns, Bob (Athlete, Golfer)
1687 N Mansfield Way
Eagle, ID 83616-6661, USA

Burns, Bob (Musician)
1687 N Mansfield Way
Eagle, ID 83616-6661, USA

Burns, Brent (Athlete, Hockey Player)
c/o Brent Burns *Icy Luck Inc*
720 Manhattan Ave
Manhattan Beach, CA 90266-5653, USA

Burns, Britt (Athlete, Baseball Player)
2315 Cactus Finch
Katy, TX 77494-2057, USA

Burns, Brooke (Actor, Model)
c/o John Griffin *Agency for the Performing Arts (APA)*
405 S Beverly Dr Ste 500
Beverly Hills, CA 90212-4425, USA

Burns, Charles (Artist)
c/o Staff Member *Fantagraphics Books*
7563 Lake City Way NE
Seattle, WA 98115-4218, USA

Burns, Charlie (Athlete, Hockey Player)
7 Fawn Dr
Wallingford, CT 06492-3307, USA

Burns, Christian (Musician)
Day Time
Crown House
225 Kensington High St
London W8 8SA, UNITED KINGDOM (UK)

Burns, David (Athlete, Basketball Player)
2623 Bainbridge Dr
Dallas, TX 75237-2801, USA

Burns, Edward (Actor, Director)
c/o Sean Cassidy *Dan Klores Communications (DKC)*
261 5th Ave Fl 2
New York, NY 10016-7601, USA

Burns, Eileen (Actor)
4000 W 43rd St.
New York, NY 10036, USA

Burns, Evers (Athlete, Basketball Player)
7216 Lost Spring Ct
Lanham, MD 20706-3834, USA

Burns, George (Athlete, Basketball Player)
16 E Poplar St
Floral Park, NY 11001-3145, USA

Burns, George (Athlete, Golfer)
10590 Limeberry Dr
Boynton Beach, FL 33436-5002, USA

Burns, Heather (Actor)
c/o Courtney Kivowitz *MGMT Entertainment (The Schiff Company)*
9220 W Sunset Blvd Ste 106
W Hollywood, CA 90069-3500, USA

Burns, James (Athlete, Basketball Player)
1500 Sheridan Rd Unit 3F
Wilmette, IL 60091-1845, USA

Burns, Jason (Athlete, Football Player)
8923 S Marshfield Ave
Chicago, IL 60620-4955, USA

Burns, Jeannie (Musician, Songwriter, Writer)
Drake Assoc
177 Woodland Ave
Westwood, NJ 07675-3218, USA

Burns, Jere (Actor)
c/o Mona Loring *Status PR*
PO Box 6191
Westlake Village, CA 91359-6191, USA

Burns, Jerry (Athlete, Football Coach, Football Player)
9520 Viking Dr
Eden Prairie, MN 55344-3825

Burns, Jim (Writer)
c/o Staff Member *Da Capo Press*
11 Cambridge Ctr
Cambridge, MA 02142-1400, USA

Burns, Keith (Athlete, Football Player)
7991 S Kittredge Way
Englewood, CO 80112-4631, USA

Burns, Kenneth L (Ken) (Director)
Florentine Films
Maple Grove Road
Walpole, NH 03608, USA

Burns, Lamont (Athlete, Football Player)
104 W Northwood St
Greensboro, NC 27401-1326, USA

Burns, M Anthony (Business Person)
Ryder System Inc
3600 NW 82nd Ave
Doral, FL 33166-6623, USA

Burns, Marie (Musician, Songwriter, Writer)
Drake Assoc
177 Woodland Ave
Westwood, NJ 07675-3218, USA

Burns, Megan (Actor)
c/o Kathryn Fleming *The Rights House (UK)*
Drury House
34-43 Russell St
London WC2B 5HA, UNITED KINGDOM

Burns, Michael (Business Person)
8365 Sunset View Dr
Los Angeles, CA 90069-1517, USA

Burns, Mike (Athlete, Football Player)
540 Stege Ave
Richmond, CA 94804-4133, USA

Burns, Pat (Coach)
New Jersey Devils
Continental Arena
50 RR 120 N
East Rutherford, NJ 07073, USA

Burns, Regan (Actor)
c/o Bruce Smith *OmniPop Talent Group*
4605 Lankershim Blvd Ste 201
Toluca Lake, CA 91602-1874, USA

Burns, Robin (Athlete, Hockey Player)
186 Sherwood Rd
Beaconsfield, QC H9W 2G8, Canada

Burns, Steven (Actor)
c/o Staff Member *Davis Spylios Management*
244 W 54th St Ste 707
New York, NY 10019-5515, USA

Burns, Todd (Athlete, Baseball Player)
PO Box 111
Princeton, AL 35766-0111, USA

Burnside, Pete (Athlete, Baseball Player)
1945 Chestnut Ave
Wilmette, IL 60091-1509, USA

Burnside, Sheldon (Athlete, Baseball Player)
7519 Wynford Cir
Montgomery, AL 36117-7483, USA

Burnstein, Nanette (Director, Producer)
c/o Scott Greenberg *Creative Artists Agency (CAA)*
2000 Avenue of the Stars Ste 100
Los Angeles, CA 90067-4705, USA

Burpo, George (Athlete, Baseball Player)
10101 Anaheim Ave NE
Albuquerque, NM 87122-3029, USA

Burr, Bill (Actor, Comedian)
c/o Michael O'Brien *Michael OBrien Entertainment*
Prefers to be contacted by telephone or email
New York, NY 10012, USA

Burr, Gary (Musician)
2316 Forest Lake Dr
Nashville, TN 37211-7026, USA

Burr, Richard (Senator)
217 Russell Senate Office Building
Washington, DC 20510-0001, USA

Burr, Shawn (Athlete, Hockey Player)
1615 River Rd
Saint Clair, MI 48079-3552, USA

Burrell, Anne (Chef, Television Host)
c/o Scott Feldman *Two Twelve Management*
PO Box 2305
New York, NY 10021-0056, USA

Burrell, George R (Athlete, Football Player)
129 W Upsal St
Philadelphia, PA 19119-4003, USA

Burrell, John (Athlete, Football Player)
376 Park Lake Dr
Mead, OK 73449-6352, USA

Burrell, Kenny (Musician)
c/o Staff Member *Concord Music Group, Inc*
900 N Rohlwing Rd
Itasca, IL 60143-1161, USA

Burrell, Leroy (Athlete, Track Athlete)
University of Houston
Athletic Dept
Houston, TX 77023, USA

Burrell, Orville (Shaggy) (Musician)
c/o Staff Member *Big Yard Music Group*
PO Box 1060
Valley Stream, NY 11582-1060, USA

Burrell, Pat (Athlete, Baseball Player)
40 Hidden Lake Dr
Burr Ridge, IL 60527-8371, USA

Burrell, Scott (Athlete, Basketball Player)
331 Evergreen Ave
Hamden, CT 06518-2745, USA

Burrell, Ty (Actor)
c/o Jillian Roscoe *ID Public Relations*
7060 Hollywood Blvd Fl 8th
Los Angeles, CA 90028-6021, USA

Burres, Brian (Athlete, Baseball Player)
533 SW Edgefield Meadows Ave
Troutdale, OR 97060-5451, USA

Burress, Hedy (Actor)
c/o David Lillard *Industry Entertainment Partners*
955 Carrillo Dr Ste 300
Los Angeles, CA 90048-5400, USA

Burress, Plaxico (Athlete, Football Player)
47 Huntington Ter
Totowa, NJ 07512-2181, USA

Burridge, Randy (Athlete, Hockey Player)
326 Desert Knolls St
Henderson, NV 89014-7809, USA

Burright, Larry (Athlete, Baseball Player)
1239 E Palm Dr
Glendora, CA 91741-2347, USA

Burris, Jeffrey L (Jeff) (Athlete, Football Player)
77 Reynolds St
Rock Hill, SC 29730-4368, USA

Burris, Miles (Athlete, Football Player)
c/o Ryan Tollner *REP 1 Sports Group*
80 Technology Dr
Irvine, CA 92618-2301, USA

Burris, Rav (Athlete, Baseball Player)
Erie Sea Wolves 110 E lOth St
Attn Coaching Staff Erie, PA 16501-1256, USA

Burris, Ray (Athlete, Baseball Player)
2708 Golden Creek Ln Apt 1208
Arlington, TX 76006-3557, USA

Burriss, Bo (Athlete, Football Player)
818 Pinemont Dr Apt 38
Houston, TX 77018-1529, USA

Burrough, Junior (Athlete, Basketball Player)
6950 Fernwood Dr Apt A
Charlotte, NC 28211-7210, USA

Burrough, Ken (Athlete, Football Player)
5823 Tallow Ln
Indianapolis, IN 46250, USA

Burroughs, Augusten (Writer)
197 Cedar Ln
Ossining, NY 10562-6211, USA

Burroughs, Jeffrey A (Jeff) (Athlete, Baseball Player)
6155 Laguna Ct
Long Beach, CA 90803-4812, USA

Burroughs, Jordan (Athlete, Olympic Athlete, Wrestler)
c/o Josh Weil *WME/IMG*
9601 Wilshire Blvd
Beverly Hills, CA 90210-5213, USA

Burroughs, Sean (Athlete, Baseball Player, Olympic Athlete)
6155 Laguna Ct
Long Beach, CA 90803-4812, USA

Burroughs, William S (Musician)
PO Box 147
Lawrence, KS 66044-0147, USA

Burrow, Bob (Athlete, Basketball Player)
2228 Oakbranch Cir
Franklin, TN 37064-7407, USA

Burrow, Curtis (Athlete, Football Player)
51 W Cadron Ridge Rd Apt A
Greenbrier, AR 72058-9102, USA

Burrow, Jim (Athlete, Football Player)
7961 Floyd Dr
The Plains, OH 45780-1403, USA

Burrow, Ken (Athlete, Football Player)
5371 Dunwoody Club Crk
Atlanta, GA 30360-1363, USA

Burrow, Robert (Athlete, Basketball Player)
2228 Oakbranch Cir
Franklin, TN 37064-7407, USA

Burrows, Darren E (Actor)
c/o Deborah Miller *Shelter Entertainment*
9255 W Sunset Blvd Ste 300
Los Angeles, CA 90069-3313, USA

Burrows, Dave (Athlete, Hockey Player)
RR 1 Stn Main Site 3x4
Parry Sound, ON P2A 2W7, CANADA

Burrows, James (Director)
10702 Levico Way
Los Angeles, CA 90077-1917, USA

Burrows, Saffron (Actor)
c/o Jillian Roscoe *ID Public Relations*
7060 Hollywood Blvd Fl 8th
Los Angeles, CA 90028-6021, USA

Burrows, Terrv (Athlete, Baseball Player)
7019 Burgandy Dr
Lake Charles, LA 70605-0252, USA

Burrows, Terry (Athlete, Baseball Player)
7019 Burgandy Dr
Lake Charles, LA 70605-0252, USA

Burruss, Kandi (Musician, Reality Star)
Kandi Koated Entertainment
PO Box 11349
Atlanta, GA 30310-0349, USA

Bursch, Daniel W (Astronaut)
1305 Buena Vista Ave
Pacific Grove, CA 93950-5505, USA

Burse, Isaiah (Athlete, Football Player)
c/o Jim Ivler *Sportstars Inc*
1370 Avenue of the Americas Fl 19
New York, NY 10019-4602, USA

Burson, Jim (Athlete, Football Player)
351 Heath Rd
Dawsonville, GA 30534-5603, USA

Burstyn, Ellen (Actor)
c/o Courtney Kivowitz *MGMT Entertainment (The Schiff Company)*
9220 W Sunset Blvd Ste 106
W Hollywood, CA 90069-3500, USA

Burt, Adam (Athlete, Hockey Player)
34 Smull Ave
Caldwell, NJ 07006-5012, USA

Burt, Jim (Athlete, Football Player)

Burtnett, Wellington (Athlete, Hockey Player)
1703 Pouliot Pl
Wilmington, MA 01887-4558, USA

Burton, Albert (Athlete, Football Player)
339 S Dr Martin Luther King Jr Blvd
Daytona Beach, FL 32114-4819, USA

Burton, Amanda (Actor)
c/o Staff Member *Independent Talent Group*
40 Whitfield St
London W1T 2RH, UNITED KINGDOM

Burton, Brandie (Athlete, Golfer)
2793 Forester Dr
La Verne, CA 91750-2360, USA

Burton, Brian (Danger Mouse) (Musician)
c/o Jeff Antebi *Waxploitation Music Corp.*
201 S Santa Fe Ave Ste 100
Los Angeles, CA 90012-4338, USA

Burton, Dan (Congressman, Politician)
2308 Raybunn Hob
Washington, DC 20515-0001, USA

Burton, Ed (Actor)
660 W Hile Rd
Norton Shores, MI 49441-5467, USA

Burton, Edward (Athlete, Basketball Player)
660 W Hile Rd
Norton Shores, MI 49441-5467, USA

Burton, Ellis (Athlete, Baseball Player)
15621 Beach Blvd Spc 7
Westminster, CA 92683-7120, USA

Burton, Gary (Musician)
Berklee College of Music
1140 Boylston St
Boston, MA 02215-3693, USA

Burton, Hilarie (Actor)
c/o Meg Mortimer *Authentic Talent and Literary Management (NY)*
20 Jay St Ste M17
Brooklyn, NY 11201-8300, USA

Burton, James (Athlete, Football Player)
458 W Altadena Dr
Altadena, CA 91001-4202, USA

Burton, James (Musician)
James Burton Foundation
714 Elvis Presley Ave
Shreveport, LA 71101-3406, USA

Burton, Jeff (Race Car Driver)
15555 Huntersville Concord Rd
Huntersville, NC 28078-6642, USA

Burton, Kate (Actor, Musician)
c/o Larry Taube *Principal Entertainment*
9255 W Sunset Blvd Ste 500
Los Angeles, CA 90069-3301, USA

Burton, Lance (Magician)
Monte Carlo Hotel
3770 Las Vegas Blvd S
Las Vegas, NV 89109-4323, USA

Burton, Lawrence (Athlete, Football Player)
41 San Gabriel
Rancho Santa Margarita, CA 92688-3127, USA

Burton, Leonard (Athlete, Football Player)
7728 Evening Shade Cv
Memphis, TN 38125-3103, USA

Burton, LeVar (Actor)
c/o Julie Nathanson *9.2.6pr*
3383 Tareco Dr
Los Angeles, CA 90068-1527, USA

Burton, Mike (Athlete, Olympic Athlete, Swimmer)
1119 N 31st St
Billings, MT 59101-0132, USA

Burton, Nelson (Athlete, Hockey Player)
609 Oakland Hills Ct Apt 201
Arnold, MD 21012-2472, USA

Burton, Shane (Athlete, Football Player)
PO Box 522
Hewitt Road
Catawba, NC 28609-0522, USA

Burton, Steve (Actor)
4814 Lemore Ave
Sherman Oaks, CA 91403, USA

Burton, Tim (Director, Producer)
1 5th Ave Apt 22D
New York, NY 10003-4340, USA

Burton, Trey (Athlete, Football Player)
c/o Hadley Engelhard *Enter-Sports Management*
6000 Lake Forrest Dr Ste 370
Atlanta, GA 30328-5902, USA

Burton, Ward (Race Car Driver)
The Ward Burton Wildlife Foundation
PO Box 519
Halifax, VA 24558-0519, USA

Burton, Willie (Athlete, Basketball Player)
18900 Fleming St
Detroit, MI 48234-1392, USA

Burton Carpenter, Jake (Athlete, Skier)
Burton Snowboards
80 Industrial Pkwy
Burlington, VT 05401-5434, USA

Burton Jr, John (Actor)
12711 Ventura Blvd Ste 490
Studio City, CA 91604-2477, USA

Burton-Woody, Patty (Baseball Player)
918 N Walnut St
Steele, MO 63877-1316, USA

Burtt, Dennis (Athlete, Baseball Player)
135 W Stadium Dr
Stockton, CA 95204-3117, USA

Burtt, Steve (Athlete, Basketball Player)
200 W 143rd St Apt 12D
New York, NY 10030-1527, USA

Burwell, Barbara (Actor)
1100 Millston Rd
Wayzata, MN 55391-9411, USA

Burwell, Dick (Athlete, Baseball Player)
6880 N 79th Pl
Scottsdale, AZ 85250-7940, USA

Bury, Pol (Artist)
12 Vallee da la Taupe-Perdreauville
Mantes-La-Jolie 78200, FRANCE

Busby, Cindy (Actor)
c/o Kalee Harris *Play Management*
220-807 Powell St
Vancouver, BC V6A 1H7, CANADA

Busby, Mike (Athlete, Baseball Player)
27399 N 84th Gln
Peoria, AZ 85383-4800, USA

Busby, Steve (Athlete, Baseball Player)
2701 Brittany Ln
Grapevine, TX 76051-4302, USA

Busby, Wayne (Athlete, Baseball Player)
287 S Tampa Ave
Orlando, FL 32805-2157, USA

Buscemi, Steve (Actor, Director)
c/o Lee Stollman *Gotham Group*
1041 N Formosa Ave # 200
West Hollywood, CA 90046-6703, USA

Busch, Adam (Actor)
c/o Ryan Revel *Good Fear Film + Management*
6255 W Sunset Blvd Ste 800
Los Angeles, CA 90028-7409, USA

Busch, August A III (Business Person)
Anheuser-Busch Cos
1 Busch Pl
Saint Louis, MO 63118-1852, USA

Busch, Charles (Actor)
c/o Brian Siberell *Creative Artists Agency (CAA)*
2000 Avenue of the Stars Ste 100
Los Angeles, CA 90067-4705, USA

Busch, Kurt (Race Car Driver)
Kurt Busch Inc
151 Lugnut Ln
Mooresville, NC 28117-9300, USA

Busch, Kyle (Race Car Driver)
351 Mazeppa Rd
Mooresville, NC 28115-7929, USA

Busch, Mike (Athlete, Baseball Player)
103 E 1st Ave
Donahue, IA 52746-9648, USA

Buscher, Brian (Athlete, Baseball Player)
876 Burnside Dr
Columbia, SC 29209-2505, USA

Buschhorn, Don (Athlete, Baseball Player)
560 Austin Pl
Reeds Spring, MO 65737-7325, USA

Buse, Don (Athlete, Basketball Player)
7300 W State Road 64
Huntingburg, IN 47542-9781, USA

Busemann, Frank (Athlete, Track Athlete)
Borkumstr 13A
Recklinghausen 45665, GERMANY

Buser, Martin (Race Car Driver)
PO Box 520997
Big Lake, AK 99652-0997, USA

Busey, Gary (Actor)
c/o Kieran Maguire *The Arlook Group*
11663 Gorham Ave Apt 5
Los Angeles, CA 90049-4749, USA

Busey, Jake (Actor)
c/o Amy Brownstein *PRStudio USA*
1875 Century Park E Ste 930
Los Angeles, CA 90067-2540, USA

Busfield, Timothy (Actor)
50265 Courtland Rd
Clarksburg, CA 95612-5026, USA

Bush (Music Group)
c/o Michael Moses *Baker Winokur Ryder Public Relations*
9100 Wilshire Blvd
W Tower #500
Beverly Hills, CA 90212-3415, USA

Bush, Barbara Pierce (Business Person)
Global Health Corps
5 Penn Plz
New York, NY 10001-1810, USA

Bush, Billy (Journalist, Television Host)
c/o Jill Fritzo *Jill Fritzo Public Relations*
208 E 51st St # 305
New York, NY 10022-6557, USA

Bush, Blair (Athlete, Football Player)
759 Heritage Arbor Dr
Wake Forest, NC 27587-3827, USA

Bush, Dave (Musician)
CMO Mgmt
Ransomes Dock
35-37 Parkgate Road
London SW11 4NP, UNITED KINGDOM (UK)

Bush, David (Athlete, Baseball Player)
518 Delancy Cir
Devon, PA 19333-1008, USA

Bush, Frank (Athlete, Football Player)
1126 W Armstrong Way
Chandler, AZ 85286-6306, USA

Bush, George (Politician)
Office Of George W. Bush
PO Box 259000
Dallas, TX 75225-9000, USA

Bush, Homer (Athlete, Baseball Player)
1703 Water Lily Dr
Southlake, TX 76092-5861, USA

Bush, Jarrett (Athlete, Football Player)
c/o Derrick Fox *Derrick Fox Management*
Prefers to be contacted by telephone
CA, USA

Bush, Jeb (Politician)
629 Altara Ave
Coral Gables, FL 33146-1303, USA

Bush, Josh (Athlete, Football Player)

Bush, Kate (Musician, Songwriter, Writer)
c/o Staff Member *Jukes Productions Ltd*
P.O. Box 13995
London W9 2FL, UK

Bush, Kristian (Musician)
917 Stratford Rd
Avondale Estates, GA 30002-1435, USA

Bush, Laura (Politician)
Office Of George W. Bush
PO Box 259000
Dallas, TX 75225-9000, USA

Bush, Randv (Athlete, Baseball Player)
1000 Chestnut Ct
Slidell, LA 70458-5486, USA

Bush, Randy (Athlete, Baseball Player)
368 S Mill View Way
Ponte Vedra Beach, FL 32082-4393, USA

Bush, Reggie (Athlete, Football Player)
Best
303 E Main St
#200
Louisville, KY 40202, USA

Bush, Sophia (Actor)
c/o Staff Member *Bekton Media Group*
37 Midbrook Ln
Old Greenwich, CT 06870-1427, USA

Bush, William Green (Actor)
Gold Marshak Liedtke
3500 W Olive Ave Ste 1400
Burbank, CA 91505-5512, USA

Bushbeck, Chuck (Athlete, Football Player)
2806 Angus Rd
Philadelphia, PA 19114-3414, USA

Bushell, Matt (Actor)
c/o Sandra Joseph *SLJ Management*
833 N Edinburgh Ave PH 11
Los Angeles, CA 90046-6999, USA

Bushing, Chris (Athlete, Baseball Player)
12830 NW 21st St
Pembroke Pines, FL 33028-2534, USA

Bushinsky, Joseph M (Jay) (Correspondent)
Rehov Hatsafon 5
Savyon 56540, ISRAEL

Bushnell, Bill (Director)
2751 Pelham Pl
Los Angeles, CA 90068-2326, USA

Bushnell, Candace (Producer, Writer)
PO Box 269
Roxbury, CT 06783-0269, USA

Bushrod, Jermon (Athlete, Football Player)
c/o Anthony J. Agnone *Eastern Athletic Services*
11350 McCormick Rd
Suite 800 - Executive Plaza
Hunt Valley, MD 21031-1002, USA

Bushy, Ronald (Ron) (Musician)
Entertainment Services Int'l
6400 Pleasant Park Dr
Chanhassen, MN 55317-8804, USA

Busick, Steve (Athlete, Football Player)
6246 W Long Dr
Littleton, CO 80123-5172, USA

Busino, Orlando (Cartoonist)
12 Shadblow Hill Rd
Ridgefield, CT 06877-5221, USA

Buskas, Rod (Athlete, Hockey Player)
182 Wentworth Dr
Henderson, NV 89074-1049, USA

Buskey, Mike (Athlete, Baseball Player)
11042 San Pedro St
Frisco, TX 75035-5318, USA

Buskey., Mike (Athlete, Baseball Player)
11042 San Pedro St
Frisco, TX 75035-5318, USA

Busniuk, Mike (Athlete, Hockey Player)
420 Sycamore Pl
Thunder Bay, ON P7C 1W9, Canada

Busniuk, Ron (Athlete, Hockey Player)
540 Laurentian Dr
Thunder Bay, ON P7C 5J8, Canada

Busse, Ray (Athlete, Baseball Player)
4265 Lemon St
Cocoa, FL 32926-2148, USA

Bussell, Gerry (Athlete, Football Player)
2922 Justin Ct
Orange Park, FL 32065-7338, USA

Bussey, Barney (Athlete, Football Player)
5059 Park Ridge Ct
West Chester, OH 45069-5552, USA

Bussey, Dexter (Athlete, Football Player)
2565 Bloomfield Xing
Bloomfield Hills, MI 48304-1707, US

Busted (Music Group)
c/o Staff Member *Helter Skelter (UK)*
535 Kings Rd
The Plaza
London SW10 0SZ, UNITED KINGDOM (UK)

Buster, Dolly (Adult Film Star)
Am Schornacker 66
Wesel D-46485, Germany

Bustion, Dave (Athlete, Basketball Player)
706 Tarrant Ct
Gadsden, AL 35901-3150, USA

Butala, Tony (Musician)
PO Box 151
Mc Kees Rocks, PA 15136-0151, USA

Butcher, Garth (Athlete, Hockey Player)
1524 Maple Ln
Bellingham, WA 98229-5242, USA

Butcher, Jade (Athlete, Football Player)
9730 N Moon Rd
Gosport, IN 47433-9517

Butcher, Jim (Writer)
c/o St. Martin's Press
175 5th Ave
Attn: Publicity Dept
New York, NY 10010-7703, USA

Butcher, John (Athlete, Baseball Player)
820 Woodridge Dr S
Chaska, MN 55318-1266, USA

Butcher, Mike (Athlete, Baseball Player)
324 33rd Ave
East Moline, IL 61244-3124, USA

Butcher, Paige (Model)
c/o Staff Member *Next Model Management (London)*
Ground Floor Blocks B and C
Morelands Building 5-23 Old Street
London EC1V9HL, UNITED KINGDOM

Butcher, Paul (Athlete, Football Player)
2239 Topanga Skyline Dr
Topanga, CA 90290-4051, US

Butcher, Rodney (Athlete, Golfer)
7333 Hideaway Trl
New Port Richey, FL 34655-4006, USA

Butcher-Marsh, Mary (Athlete, Baseball Player, Commentator)
PO Box 563
Lovelock, NV 89419-0563, USA

Butera, Sal (Athlete, Baseball Player)
324 Tersas Ct
Lake Mary, FL 32746-5143, USA

Buthelezi, Chief Mangosuthu G (Politician)
Home Affairs Ministry
Private Bag x741
Pretoria 00001, SOUTH AFRICA

Buthelezi, Minister Mangosuthu (Politician)
Parliament of the Republic of South Africa
Parliament St
Cape Town 08000, South Africa

Butkus, Dick (Actor, Athlete, Football Player)
The Butkus Foundation
18920 NE 227th Ave
Brush Prairie, WA 98606-8114, USA

Butler, Adam (Athlete, Baseball Player)
815 Providence Rd
Towson, MD 21286-2964, USA

Butler, Austin (Actor)
c/o Jeffrey Chassen *Imprint PR*
6121 W Sunset Blvd
Neuehouse
Los Angeles, CA 90028-6442, USA

Butler, Bernard (Musician)
Interceptor Enterprises
98 White Lion St
London N1 9PF, UNITED KINGDOM (UK)

Butler, Bill (Athlete, Baseball Player)
c/o Greg Genske *The Legacy Agency*
500 Newport Center Dr Ste 800
Newport Beach, CA 92660-7008, USA

Butler, Bob (Athlete, Football Player)
120 Holly Hills Dr
Mount Sterling, KY 40353-9738, USA

Butler, Bobby (Athlete, Hockey Player)
c/o John and Wendy Butler 56 Ethier Cir
Marlborough, MA 01752-7211, USA

Butler, Brent (Athlete, Baseball Player)
10441 Scotland Farm Rd
Laurinburg, NC 28352-7977, USA

Butler, Brett (Actor, Comedian)
c/o Staff Member *TalentWorks*
3500 W Olive Ave Ste 1400
Burbank, CA 91505-5512, USA

Butler, Brett M (Athlete, Baseball Player)
2989 N 44th St Unit 2012
Phoenix, AZ 85018-7308, USA

Butler, Brice (Athlete, Football Player)
c/o Tony Paige *Dream Point Sports*
1455 Pennsylvania Ave NW Ste 225
Washington, DC 20004-1026, USA

Butler, Brooke (Actor)
c/o Jack Kingsrud *Zero Gravity Management*
11110 Ohio Ave Ste 100
Los Angeles, CA 90025-3329, USA

Butler, Caron (Athlete, Basketball Player)
3808 Millard Way
Fairfax, VA 22033-2753, USA

Butler, Cecil (Athlete, Baseball Player)
263 Hickory Gap Trl
Dallas, GA 30157-5353, USA

Butler, Charles (Athlete, Basketball Player)
453 Arbor Cir
Youngstown, OH 44505-1915, USA

Butler, Charles W (Athlete, Football Player)
17932 Isabella Pl
Lathrop, CA 95330-8228, USA

Butler, Chuck (Athlete, Football Player)
5496N Celestial Dr
Atwater, CA 95301, US

Butler, Conrad (Actor)
Paradigm Agency
10100 Santa Monica Blvd Ste 2500
Los Angeles, CA 90067-4116, USA

Butler, Crezdon (Athlete, Football Player)
c/o Drew Rosenhaus *Rosenhaus Sports Representation*
3921 Alton Rd # 440
Miami Beach, FL 33140-3852, USA

Butler, Dan (Actor)
c/o Staff Member *ATA Management (NY)*
85 Broad St Fl 18
New York, NY 10004-2783, USA

Butler, Darius (Athlete, Football Player)
c/o Drew Rosenhaus *Rosenhaus Sports Representation*
3921 Alton Rd # 440
Miami Beach, FL 33140-3852, USA

Butler, David (Actor)
c/o Staff Member *The Rights House (UK)*
Drury House
34-43 Russell St
London WC2B 5HA, UNITED KINGDOM

Butler, Dean (Actor)
1310 Westholme Ave
Los Angeles, CA 90024-5016, USA

Butler, Donald (Athlete, Football Player)
c/o Ashley Smith Becker *Relativity Sports*
2029 Century Park E Ste 1550
Century City, CA 90067-3000, USA

Butler, Elbert (Athlete, Basketball Player)
153 Willow Ave
Rochester, NY 14609-1244, USA

Butler, Gary (Athlete, Football Player)
6660 S Piney Creek Cir
Centennial, CO 80016, USA

Butler, Gary C (Athlete, Football Player)
Automatic Data Processing
212 Oak Hollow St
Conroe, TX 77301-1747, USA

Butler, Gerard (Actor)
c/o Staff Member *G-BASE*
9200 W Sunset Blvd Ste 804
Los Angeles, CA 90069-3603, USA

Butler, Greg (Athlete, Basketball Player)
216 Beverly Rd
Scarsdale, NY 10583-1514, USA

Butler, James (Athlete, Football Player)
3181 Spring St
Atlanta, GA 30349-2345, USA

Butler, Jerry (Athlete, Hockey Player)
City of Winnipeg 83-30 Fort St Attn: Plan Examination Dept
Winnipeg, MB R3C 4X7, Canada

Butler, Jerry (Iceman) (Musician, Songwriter, Writer)
c/o Jeremy Plager *Creative Artists Agency (CAA)*
2000 Avenue of the Stars Ste 100
Los Angeles, CA 90067-4705, USA

Butler, Jerry O (Athlete, Football Player)
17117 Shaker Blvd
Cleveland, OH 44120-1635, USA

Butler, Jimmy (Athlete, Basketball Player)
c/o Ashley Smith Becker *Relativity Sports*
2029 Century Park E Ste 1550
Century City, CA 90067-3000, USA

Butler, Joe (Musician)
Pipeline Artists Mgmt
620 16th Ave S
Hopkins, MN 55343-7833, USA

Butler, John (Musician)
c/o Staff Member *Paradigm (Monterey)*
404 W Franklin St
Monterey, CA 93940-2303, USA

Butler, Jonathan (Musician)
294 Bell Canyon Rd
Bell Canyon, CA 91307-1112, USA

Butler, Keith (Athlete, Football Player)
805 Cavan Dr
Cranberry Twp, PA 16066-2333, USA

Butler, Kerry (Actor)
c/o Paul Reisman *Abrams Artists Agency*
275 7th Ave Fl 26
New York, NY 10001-6708, USA

Butler, Kevin (Athlete, Football Player)
3256 Bagley Psge
Duluth, GA 30097-3788, USA

Butler, LeRoy (Athlete, Football Player)
4119 Westloop Ln
Jacksonville, FL 32277-1729, USA

Butler, Lucy (Actor)
c/o Judy Orbach *Judy O Productions*
6136 Glen Holly St
Hollywood, CA 90068-2338, USA

Butler, Michael (Athlete, Football Player)
3107 Magdalene Forest Ct
Tampa, FL 33618-2509, USA

Butler, Mike (Athlete, Basketball Player)
3107 Magdalene Forest Ct
Tampa, FL 33618-2509, USA

Butler, Mitchell (Athlete, Basketball Player)
1468 Paseo De Oro
Pacific Palisades, CA 90272-1961, USA

Butler, Ray (Athlete, Football Player)
PO Box 1605
Fresno, TX 77545-1605, USA

Butler, Robert (Athlete, Football Player)
5567 Naylor Ct
Norcross, GA 30092-2072, USA

Butler, Robert (Director)
650 Club View Dr
Los Angeles, CA 90024-2624, USA

Butler, Robert Olen (Writer)
1009 Concord Rd Apt 230
Tallahassee, FL 32308-6294, USA

Butler, Robert olen (Writer)
3909 Reserve Dr Apt 1611
Tallahassee, FL 32311-1284, USA

Butler, Ross (Actor)
c/o Stephanie Jones *Jonesworks*
211 E 43rd St Rm 1502
New York, NY 10017-4746, USA

Butler, Skip (Athlete, Football Player)
1311 Spyglass Dr
Mansfield, TX 76063-4023, USA

Butler, Steve (Race Car Driver)
1820 S Buckeye St
Kokomo, IN 46902-2143, USA

Butler, Terence (Geezer) (Musician)
15165 Ventura Blvd Ste 230
Sherman Oaks, CA 91403-3373

Butler, William D (Athlete, Football Player)
200 E Liberty St
Berlin, WI 54923-1223, USA

Butler, William E (Athlete, Football Player)
3030 Cherry Hl
Manhattan, KS 66503-3011, USA

Butler, William E (Business Person)
Eaton Corp
1000 Eaton Blvd
Eaton Center
Beachwood, OH 44122-6058, USA

Butler, Yancy (Actor)
c/o Tom Monjack *Tom Monjack Celebrity Enterprises*
28650 Avenida Maravilla # A
Cathedral City, CA 92234-8115, USA

Butler Billv, Billv (Athlete, Baseball Player)
2007 Kansas Citv Rovals
7724 E Santa Catalina Dr, Scottsdale AZ, USA

Butler-Henderson, Vicki (Actor)
c/o Staff Member *Princess Productions*
Newcombe House
45 Notting Hill Gate
London W11 3LQ, UNITED KINGDOM

Butor, Michael (Writer)
A L'Ecart
Lucinges
Bonne 74380, FRANCE

Butsayev, Vyacheslav (Athlete, Hockey Player)
17555 Collins Ave Apt 1704
Sunny Isles Beach, FL 33160-2888, USA

Butsko, Harry (Athlete, Football Player)
4 Milo Cir
Duncannon, PA 17020-9647, USA

Butt, Brent (Actor, Comedian)
c/o Elizabeth Hodgson *Elizabeth Hodgson Management Group*
405-1688 Cypress St
Vancouver, BC V6J 5J1, CANADA

Butt, Charles (Business Person)
HEB Corp
646 S Main Ave
San Antonio, TX 78204-1210, USA

Buttafuoco, Joey (Actor)
10835 De Soto Ave
Chatsworth, CA 91311-1547, USA

Butterfield, Asa (Actor)
c/o Jane Brand *Independent Talent Group*
40 Whitfield St
London W1T 2RH, UNITED KINGDOM

Butterfield, Betty (Comedian)
c/o Staff Member *Diva Central Inc*
7510 W Sunset Blvd # 1445
Los Angeles, CA 90046-3408, USA

Butterfield, Deborah K (Artist)
11229 Cottonwood Rd
Bozeman, MT 59718-9576, USA

Butterfield, G. K. (Congressman, Politician)
2305 Rayburn Hob
Washington, DC 20515-2207, USA

Butterfly Boucher (Music Group)
c/o Staff Member *Paradigm (Monterey)*
404 W Franklin St
Monterey, CA 93940-2303, USA

Butters, Bill (Athlete, Hockey Player)
12579 Europa Ave N
Saint Paul, MN 55110-5957, USA

Butters, Tom (Athlete, Baseball Player)
4 Turnberry Ct
Durham, NC 27712-9465, USA

Butters, Torn (Athlete, Baseball Player)
4 Turnberry Ct
Durham, NC 27712-9465, USA

Butterworth, Dean (Musician)
3818 Carpenter Ave
Studio City, CA 91604-3729, USA

Butthole Surfers, The (Music Group, Musician)
c/o Staff Member *Mute Records*
1 Albion Pl
London W6 0QT, UK

Buttke, Nathan (Race Car Driver)
Mark III Motorsports
211 Greenwich Rd
Charlotte, NC 28211-2337, USA

Buttle, Gregory E (Greg) (Athlete, Football Player)
24 Buhl Ln
East Northport, NY 11731-5214, USA

Button, Dick (Athlete, Figure Skater, Olympic Athlete)
Candio Productions
765 Park Ave Apt 6B
New York, NY 10021-4271, USA

Button, Jenson (Race Car Driver)
Jenson Racing
67 Valkenburgerweg
Heerlen AP 06419, NETHERLANDS

Butts, Earl (Actor)
2741 N Salisbury St # 2116
West Lafayette, IN 47906-1431, USA

Butts, James (Athlete, Track Athlete)
16950 Belforest Dr
Carson, CA 90746-1113, USA

Butts, Marion (Athlete, Football Player)
4600 Lacosta Dr
Albany, GA 31721-9475, US

Butts, Robert (Athlete, Football Player)
108 Circle Dr
Flushing, OH 43977-9738, USA

Butz, David E (Dave) (Athlete, Football Player)
2324 Esther Ave
Saint Louis, MO 63139-2813, USA

Buxton, Sarah (Actor)
1416 Havenhurst Dr Apt 3C
West Hollywood, CA 90046-3885, USA

Buynak, Gordie (Athlete, Hockey Player)
11512 Douglas Lake Rd
Pellston, MI 49769-9100, USA

Buzin, Rich (Athlete, Football Player)
23004 Mastick Rd Apt 216
North Olmsted, OH 44070-3770, USA

Buzolic, Nathaniel (Actor)
c/o Jason Weinberg *Untitled Entertainment*
350 S Beverly Dr Ste 200
Beverly Hills, CA 90212-4819, USA

Buzolin, Mariah (Actor)
c/o Staff Member *Leslie Allan-Rice Management*
1007 Maybrook Dr
Beverly Hills, CA 90210-2715, USA

Buzzi, Ruth (Actor, Comedian)
31159 N State Highway 108
Mingus, TX 76463-6409, USA

B. West, Allen (Congressman, Politician)
1708 Longworth Hob
Washington, DC 20515-0403, USA

B*Witched (Music Group)
c/o Staff Member *Concorde Intl Artists Ltd*
101 Shepherds Bush Rd
London W6 7LP, UNITED KINGDOM (UK)

Byalikov, Henry (Dancer, Reality Star)
c/o Amy Malin *Trueheart Management*
20732 Wells Dr
Woodland Hills, CA 91364-3437, USA

Byars, Betsy C (Writer)
401 Rudder Rdg
Seneca, SC 29678-2035, USA

Byars, Keith (Athlete, Football Player)
5744 Rowena Dr
Dayton, OH 45415-2444, US

Byas, Rick (Athlete, Football Player)
19925 Greenwald Dr
Southfield, MI 48075-3956, US

Bybel, Carli (Internet Star)
c/o Seth Jacobs *Brillstein Entertainment Partners*
9150 Wilshire Blvd Ste 350
Beverly Hills, CA 90212-3453, USA

Byce, John (Athlete, Hockey Player)
9701 Hill Creek Dr
Verona, WI 53593-7984, USA

Bye, Karyn (Athlete, Hockey Player, Olympic Athlete)
322 Gandy Dancer Cir
Hudson, WI 54016-8186, USA

Byer, Nicole (Comedian)
c/o Rachel Wendler *Kovert Creative*
506 Santa Monica Blvd Ste 400
Santa Monica, CA 90401-2412, USA

Byers, Clinton (Athlete, Basketball Player)
4257 Leewood Rd
Stow, OH 44224-2555, USA

Byers, Ken (Athlete, Football Player)
5721 Kugler Mill Rd Apt A
Cincinnati, OH 45236-2156, USA

Byers, Lyndon (Athlete, Hockey Player)
654 Central St
20 Guest St, Suite 300
Holliston, MA 01746-2411, USA

Byers, Mike (Athlete, Hockey Player)
2743 Victoria Park Ave
Scarborough, ON M1T 1A8, Canada

Byers, Randy (Athlete, Baseball Player)
PO Box 1721
Bridgeton, NJ 08302-0470, USA

Byers, Scott (Athlete, Football Player)
6060 Buckingham Pkwy Apt 314
Culver City, CA 90230-6825, USA

Byers, Steve (Actor)
c/o Robyn Friedman *Artist Management Inc*
464 King St E
Toronto, ON M5A 1L7, CANADA

Byers, Trai (Actor)
c/o Alan Nierob *Rogers & Cowan*
1840 Century Park E Fl 18
Los Angeles, CA 90067-2101, USA

Byers, Walter (Athlete, Basketball Player)
521 W Bertrand Ave
Saint Marys, KS 66536-1618, USA

Byfuglien, Dustin (Athlete, Hockey Player)
33626 State Highway 11
Roseau, MN 56751-8107, USA

Bylsma, Dan (Athlete, Hockey Player)
207 S William St Unit 47
Ludington, MI 49431-2387, USA

Bylsma, Dan (Athlete, Hockey Player)
Pittsburgh Penguins 66 Mario Lemieux Pl Ste 2
Pittsburgh, PA 15219-3504, USA

Byman, Bob (Athlete, Golfer)
9325 Eagle Ridge Dr
Las Vegas, NV 89134-6345, USA

Byner, Earnest A (Athlete, Football Player)
1016 Sattui Ct
Franklin, TN 37064-7909, USA

Byner, John (Actor)
American Mgmt
19948 Mayall St
Chatsworth, CA 91311-3522, USA

Bynes, Amanda (Actor, Comedian)
4024 Benetton Way
Leander, TX 78641-3713, USA

Bynes, Josh (Athlete, Football Player)
c/o Chad Speck *Allegiant Athletic Agency*
35 Market Sq Ste 201
Knoxville, TN 37902-1420, USA

Bynum, Andrew (Athlete, Basketball Player)
c/o Philip Button *WME|IMG*
9601 Wilshire Blvd
Beverly Hills, CA 90210-5213, USA

Bynum, Freddie (Athlete, Baseball Player)
2987 Pope Farm Rd
Stantonsburg, NC 27883-8556, USA

Bynum, Juanita (Religious Leader, Television Host)
c/o Staff Member *Just Borne Mega Entertainment*
PO Box 668
Snellville, GA 30078-0668, USA

Bynum, Mike (Athlete, Baseball Player)
4576 Junction Dr
Middleburg, FL 32068-3254, USA

Bynum, Will (Athlete, Basketball Player)
c/o Brad Ames *Priority Sports & Entertainment - (LA)*
15233 Ventura Blvd Ste 718
Sherman Oaks, CA 91403-2237, USA

Byrd, Boris (Athlete, Football Player)
1376 Richpond Rockfield Rd
Bowling Green, KY 42101-7407, USA

Byrd, Dan (Actor)
c/o Daniel Spilo *Industry Entertainment Partners*
955 Carrillo Dr Ste 300
Los Angeles, CA 90048-5400, USA

Byrd, Darryl (Athlete, Football Player)
138 Mission Dr
East Palo Alto, CA 94303-2752, USA

Byrd, Dominique (Athlete, Football Player)
c/o Eugene Parker *Independent Sports & Entertainment (ISE-IN)*
6435 W Jefferson Blvd # 197
Fort Wayne, IN 46804-6203, USA

Byrd, Eugene (Actor)
c/o Staff Member *The Kohner Agency*
9300 Wilshire Blvd Ste 555
Beverly Hills, CA 90212-3211, USA

Byrd, George (Athlete, Football Player)
23 Wayside Rd
Westborough, MA 01581-3620, USA

Byrd, Gill (Athlete, Football Player)
5347 Notting Hill Rd
Gurnee, IL 60031-1008, US

Byrd, Isaac (Athlete, Football Player)
12521 Evening Shade Dr
Black Jack, MO 63033-8513, USA

Byrd, Israel (Athlete, Football Player)
5712 Astra Ave
Saint Louis, MO 63147-1012, USA

Byrd, Jairus (Athlete, Football Player)
c/o Ashley Smith Becker *Relativity Sports*
2029 Century Park E Ste 1550
Century City, CA 90067-3000, USA

Byrd, Jeff (Athlete, Baseball Player)
919 Sellwood Dr
Eagle Point, OR 97524-9069, USA

Byrd, Jim (Athlete, Baseball Player)
511 NW Woodridge Dr
Lawton, OK 73507-2265, USA

Byrd, Jonathan (Athlete, Golfer)
110 Meadow Bark
Saint Simons Island, GA 31522, USA

Byrd, Marlon (Athlete, Baseball Player)
3620 E Hamilton KY
West Palm Beach, FL 33411-6436, USA

Byrd, McArthur (Athlete, Football Player)
10291 Sheldon Rd
Elk Grove, CA 95624-9341, USA

Byrd, Paul (Athlete, Baseball Player)
29254 Grande Ct
Westlake, OH 44145-6707, USA

Byrd, Richard (Athlete, Football Player)
2230 Haley Rd
Terry, MS 39170-8820, USA

Byrd, Robin (Adult Film Star)
Robin Byrd Show
PO Box 305
Lenox Hill Station
New York, NY 10021-0009, USA

Byrd, Tom (Actor)
United Talent Agency
14011 Ventura Blvd Ste 213
Sherman Oaks, CA 91423-5222, USA

Byrd, Tracy (Musician)
4695 Monticello St
Beaumont, TX 77706-7710, USA

Byrdak, Tim (Athlete, Baseball Player)
15235 W Pantigo Ln
Homer Glen, IL 60491-6852, USA

Byrds, The (Music Group, Musician)
PO Box 1222
Pleasanton, CA 94566-0122, USA

Byrne, Chris (Actor)
c/o Staff Member *Kazarian, Measures, Ruskin & Associates*
5200 Lankershim Blvd Ste 820
N Hollywood, CA 91601-3194, USA

Byrne, David (Musician, Songwriter)
231 10th Ave # PH1
New York, NY 10011-4702, USA

Byrne, Gabriel (Actor)
211 Elizabeth St Apt 2N
New York, NY 10012-4290, USA

Byrne, Josh (Actor)
Hervey/Grimes
PO Box 64249
Los Angeles, CA 90064-0249, USA

Byrne, Michael (Actor)
Conway Van Gelder Robinson
18-21 Jermyn St
London SW1Y 6NB, UNITED KINGDOM (UK)

Byrne, Nicky (Musician)
c/o Staff Member *Solo Agency Ltd (UK)*
53-55 Fulham High St
Fl 2
London SW6 3JJ, UNITED KINGDOM

Byrne, Rhonda (Writer)
c/o Staff Member *Simon & Schuster*
1230 Avenue of the Americas Fl CONC1
New York, NY 10020-1586, USA

Byrne, Rose (Actor)
453 Warren St
Brooklyn, NY 11217-2505, USA

Byrne, Scarlett (Actor)
c/o Ashley Hanley *Agency for the Performing Arts (APA)*
405 S Beverly Dr Ste 500
Beverly Hills, CA 90212-4425, USA

Byrne, Steve (Musician)
c/o Kara Baker *Avalon Management*
9171 Wilshire Blvd Ste 320
Beverly Hills, CA 90210-5516, USA

Byrne, Thomas J (Tommy) (Athlete, Baseball Player)
1108 Fairway Villas Dr
Wake Forest, NC 27587-5179, USA

Byrnes, Edd (Actor)
PO Box 1623
Beverly Hills, CA 90213-1623, USA

Byrnes, Eric (Athlete, Baseball Player)
c/o Staff Member *WME|IMG*
9601 Wilshire Blvd
Beverly Hills, CA 90210-5213, USA

Byrnes, Eric (Athlete, Baseball Player)
24404 N 61st Dr
Glendale, AZ 85310-2704, USA

Byrnes, Jim (Actor)
c/o Staff Member *Characters Talent Agency*
200-1505 2nd Ave W
Vancouver, BC V6H 3Y4, CANADA

Byrnes, Marty (Athlete, Basketball Player)
8739 3rd Ave
Pleasant Prairie, WI 53158-4709, USA

Byrorn, Don (Musician)
Hans Wendl Productions
2220 California St
Berkeley, CA 94703-1608, USA

Byrorn, Monty (Musician, Songwriter, Writer)
Gurley Co
1204B Cedar Ln Apt B
Nashville, TN 37212-5910, USA

Byrum, Carl (Athlete, Football Player)
209 Castlewood Dr
Buffalo, NY 14227-2652, us

Byrum, Curt (Athlete, Golfer)
12441 N 86th St
Scottsdale, AZ 85260-5343, USA

Byrum, John W (Director)
7435 Woodrow Wilson Dr
Los Angeles, CA 90046-1322, USA

Byrum, Tom (Athlete, Golfer)
70 Sierra Oaks Dr
Sugar Land, TX 77479-5724, USA

Bystrom, Marty (Athlete, Baseball Player)
PO Box 89
Geigertown, PA 19523-0089, USA

Bzdelik, Jeff (Coach)
Denver Nuggets
1000 Chopper Cir
Pepsi Center
Denver, CO 80204-5805, USA

C

C, Melanie (Musician)
PO Box 25777
London SW20 8WE, UNITED KINGDOM

Caan, James (Actor, Director)
c/o Arnold Robinson *Rogers & Cowan*
1840 Century Park E Fl 18
Los Angeles, CA 90067-2101, USA

Caan, Scott (Actor)
c/o Stacy Boniello *Firm, The*
2049 Century Park E Ste 2550
Los Angeles, CA 90067-3110, USA

Caballero, Celestino (Athlete, Boxer)
c/o Jody Kohn *Talent Without Borders*
Prefers to be contacted by telephone
Las Vegas, NV 89145, USA

Caballero, Ralph (Putsy) (Athlete, Baseball Player)
6773 Milne Blvd
New Orleans, LA 70124-2242, USA

Cabana, Robert D (Astronaut)
18315 Cape Bahamas Ln
Houston, TX 77058-3406, USA

cabana, Robert d colonel (Astronaut)
1626 Manor Dr
Cocoa, FL 32922-6922, USA

Cabas (Musician)
c/o Staff Member *Creative Artists Agency (CAA)*
2000 Avenue of the Stars Ste 100
Los Angeles, CA 90067-4705, USA

Cabel, Barney (Athlete, Basketball Player)
1134 S Main St
Hampstead, MD 21074-2255, USA

Cabell, Enos M (Athlete, Baseball Player)
4103 Frost Lake Ct
Missouri City, TX 77459-2304, USA

Cabello, Camila (Musician)
All Parts Move
7601 SW 150th Ter
Palmetto Bay, FL 33158-2159, USA

Cable, Barney (Athlete, Basketball Player)
1134 S Main St
Hampstead, MD 21074-2255, USA

Cable, Candace (Athlete, Olympic Athlete)
1000 S Hope St Apt 313
Los Angeles, CA 90015-1489, USA

Cable, Tom (Athlete, Football Player)
c/o Don Yee *Yee & Dubin Sports, LLC*
725 S Figueroa St Ste 3085
Los Angeles, CA 90017-5430, USA

Cabot, Louis W (Business Person)
Brookings Institution
1775 Massachusetts Ave NW
Washington, DC 20036-2103, USA

Cabot, Meg (Writer)
PO Box 4904
Key West, FL 33041-4904, USA

Cabral, Angelique (Actor)
Lesly Kahn & Company
1720 N La Brea Ave
Los Angeles, CA 90046-3010, USA

Cabral, Brian (Athlete, Football Player)
5008 Ellsworth Pl
Boulder, CO 80303-1210, USA

Cabral, Richard (Actor)
c/o Jamie Harhay Skinner *Baker Winokur Ryder Public Relations*
9100 Wilshire Blvd
W Tower #500
Beverly Hills, CA 90212-3415, USA

Cabrera, John (Actor)
c/o Adam Griffin *LINK Entertainment*
11872 La Grange Ave
Los Angeles, CA 90025-5282, USA

Cabrera, Jolbert (Baseball Player)
c/o Staff Member *Los Angeles Dodgers*
1000 Elysian Park Ave
Los Angeles, CA 90012, USA

Cabrera, Melky (Athlete, Baseball Player)
c/o Peter Greenberg *TLA Worldwide (The Legacy Agency)*
1500 Broadway Ste 2501
New York, NY 10036-4082, USA

Cabrera, Miguel (Athlete, Baseball Player)
c/o Jason Spector *Independent Sports & Entertainment (LA)*
2029 Century Park E Ste 1550
Century City, CA 90067-3000, USA

Cabrera, Orlando (Athlete, Baseball Player)
9248 Scarlette Oak Ave
Fort Myers, FL 33967-5145, USA

Cabrera, Ryan (Musician)
c/o Staff Member *Central Entertainment Group*
250 W 40th St Fl 12
New York, NY 10018-4601, USA

Cabrera, Santiago (Actor)
100 Universal City Plz Bldg 5225
Universal City, CA 91608-1002, USA

Caccialanza, Lorenzo (Actor)
Ambrosio/Mortimer
PO Box 16758
Beverly Hills, CA 90209-2758, USA

Cacciavillan, Agnostino Cardinal (Religious Leader)
Patrimony of Holy See
Palazzo Apostolico
Vatican City 00120, VATICAN CITY

Cacek, Craig (Athlete, Baseball Player)
909 6th St Apt 3
Santa Monica, CA 90403-2700, USA

Caceres, Edgar (Athlete, Baseball Player)
2575 51st St
Sarasota, FL 34234-3215, USA

Caceres, Kurt (Actor)
c/o Robyn Holt *Genesis Entertainment Partners*
4145 Garden Ave
Los Angeles, CA 90039-1309, USA

Cackowski, Liz (Actor, Comedian)
c/o Staff Member *Creative Artists Agency (CAA)*
2000 Avenue of the Stars Ste 100
Los Angeles, CA 90067-4705, USA

Cadaret, Greg (Athlete, Baseball Player)
1447 E River Rd
Traverse City, MI 49696-8333, USA

Cadbury, Adrian (Business Person)
Bank of England
Threadneedle St
London EC2R 8AH, UNITED KINGDOM (UK)

Caddell, Patrick (Politician)
p
1048 Dominion Dr
Hanahan, SC 29410-2408, USA

Cade, Eddie (Athlete, Football Player)
501 W 4th St
Eloy, AZ 85131-2206, USA

Cade, Michael (Actor)

Cade, Mossy (Athlete, Football Player)
400 W Pasadena Ave Apt 19
Phoenix, AZ 85013-2367, USA

Cadell, Ava (Actor, Model)
c/o Rick Hersh *Celebrity Consultants LLC*
3340 Ocean Park Blvd Ste 1005
Santa Monica, CA 90405-3255, USA

Cadell, Dr. Ava (Adult Film Star)
Loveology University
9000 W Sunset Blvd Ste 1115
Los Angeles, CA 90069-5811, USA

Cadet, Travaris (Athlete, Football Player)

Cadigan, Dave (Athlete, Football Player)
14416 Katie Rd
Phoenix, MD 21131-1755, USA

Cadile, Jim (Athlete, Football Player)
1738 Spring St
Medford, OR 97504-6351, USA

Cadillac Three, The (Music Group)
c/o George Couri *Triple 8 Management*
1611 W 6th St
Austin, TX 78703-5059, USA

Cadogan, William J (Business Person)
ADC Communications
PO Box 1101
Minneapolis, MN 55440-1101, USA

Cadrez, Glenn (Athlete, Football Player)
1294 Mariposa Rd
Carlsbad, CA 92011-4208, USA

Caesar, Daniel (Musician)
c/o Caroline Yim *Creative Artists Agency (CAA)*
2000 Avenue of the Stars Ste 100
Los Angeles, CA 90067-4705, USA

Caesar, Shirley (Music Group)
Shirley Caesar Outreach Ministries
3310 Croasdaile Dr Ste 902
Durham, NC 27705-6806, USA

Caesars, The (Music Group)
c/o Staff Member *Paradigm (Monterey)*
404 W Franklin St
Monterey, CA 93940-2303, USA

Cafagna-Tesoro, Ashley (Actor)
c/o Staff Member *Tesoro Entertainment*
205D N Stephanie St # NO115
Henderson, NV 89074-8060, USA

Cafferty, Jack (Commentator)
41 Vincent Rd
Cedar Grove, NJ 07009-1337, USA

Caffery, Terry (Athlete, Hockey Player)
2743 Victoria Park Ave
Scarborough, ON M1T 1A8, Canada

Caffey, Charlotte (Musician)
4827 Glencairn Rd
Los Angeles, CA 90027-1135, USA

Caffey, Jason (Athlete, Basketball Player)
PO Box 131
Roswell, GA 30077-0131, USA

Caffrey, Bob (Athlete, Baseball Player, Olympic Athlete)
2305 Sunnyside Ave
Burlington, IA 52601-2537, USA

Cage, Byron (Musician)
c/o Staff Member *Verity Gospel Music Group*
25 Madison Ave Fl 19
New York, NY 10010-8601, USA

Cage, Michael (Athlete, Basketball Player)
21163 Newport Coast Dr
Dr
Newport Coast, CA 92657-1123, USA

Cage, Nicolas (Actor)
11661 San Vicente Blvd Ste 609
Los Angeles, CA 90049-5114, USA

Cage, Wavne (Athlete, Baseball Player)
1305 Davis Blvd
Ruston, LA 71270-6405, usa

Cage, Wayne (Athlete, Baseball Player)
1305 Davis Blvd
Ruston, LA 71270-6405, USA

Cagle, Buddy (Race Car Driver)
11713 E 118th St N
Collinsville, OK 74021-1011, USA

Cagle, Chris (Musician)
c/o Jeff Howard *Agency for the Performing Arts (APA-TN)*
150 4th Ave N Ste 2300
Nashville, TN 37219-2466, USA

Cagle, J Douglas (Business Person)
Cagle's Inc
1385 Collier Rd NW
Atlanta, GA 30318-7444, USA

Cagle, Jim (Athlete, Football Player)
745 Sharpshooters Rdg NW
Marietta, GA 30064-4731, USA

Cagle, Johnny (Athlete, Football Player)
1645 Citation Dr
Aiken, SC 29803-5223, USA

Cagle, Yvonne D (Astronaut)
c/o Staff Member *NASA-JSC*
2101 Nasa Pkwy # 1
Astronaut Office - Mail Code Cb
Houston, TX 77058-3607, USA

Caglini, Umperto (Actor)
via Don Crocetti #3
Fabriano (Ancona) I-60044, Italy

Cahill, Dave (Athlete, Football Player)
11 Kara E
Irvine, CA 92620-1855, us

Cahill, Eddie (Actor)
c/o David Seltzer *Management 360*
9111 Wilshire Blvd
Beverly Hills, CA 90210-5508, USA

Cahill, Erin (Actor)
c/o Staff Member *Ella Bee*
505 N Figueroa St Apt 400
Los Angeles, CA 90012-2190, USA

Cahill, Jason (Producer)
2316 Nottingham Ave
Los Angeles, CA 90027-1035, USA

Cahill, Laura (Writer)
c/o Staff Member *Broder Webb Chervin Silbermann Agency, The (BWCS)*
10250 Constellation Blvd
Los Angeles, CA 90067-6200, USA

Cahill, Leo (Athlete, Football Player)
161A Nelson St
Sarnia, ON N7T757, Canada

Cahill, Mike (Director)
c/o Craig Kestel *WME|IMG*
9601 Wilshire Blvd
Beverly Hills, CA 90210-5213, USA

Cahill, Thomas (Writer)
Doubleday Press
1540 Broadway
New York, NY 10036-4039, USA

Cahill, Trevor (Athlete, Baseball Player)
286 Juaneno Ave
Oceanside, CA 92057-4515, usa

Cahill, William (Bill) (Athlete, Football Player)
24328 Crystal Lake Way
Woodinville, WA 98077-9514, USA

Cahoon, Todd (Actor)
c/o Laura Pallas *Pallas Management*
4536 Greenbush Ave
Sherman Oaks, CA 91423-3112, US

Caifanes (Music Group)
c/o Staff Member *BMG*
1540 Broadway
New York, NY 10036-4039, USA

Caillat, Colbie (Musician)
c/o Chad Jensen *Jensen Artist Management*
1741 N Ventura Rd Apt 10
Oxnard, CA 93030-3315, USA

Cain, Betty Ann (Actor)
19379 Arkay Ct
Sonoma, CA 95476-6350, USA

Cain, Carl (Athlete, Basketball Player)
3045 Sun Valley Dr
Pickerington, OH 43147-9090, USA

Cain, Carl (Athlete, Basketball Player, Olympic Athlete)
3045 Sun Valley Dr
Pickerington, OH 43147-9090, USA

Cain, Christopher (Director)
Greenwomb Productions
11 Breeze Ave
Venice, CA 90291-3249, USA

Cain, Dean (Actor)
c/o Adam Griffin *LINK Entertainment*
11872 La Grange Ave
Los Angeles, CA 90025-5282, USA

Cain, Herman (Politician, Radio Personality)
c/o Staff Member *WSB Radio*
1601 W Peachtree St NE
Atlanta, GA 30309-2663, USA

Cain, Jeremy (Athlete, Football Player)
c/o Kristen Kuliga *Vanguard - K Sports Entertainment*
236 Huntington Ave Ste 209
Boston, MA 02115-4701, USA

Cain, Joe (Athlete, Football Player)
1219 W Piru St
Compton, CA 90222-1712, us

Cain, John Paul (Athlete, Golfer)
1404 Avondale St
Sweetwater, TX 79556-2614, USA

Cain, Jonathan (Musician)
311 Granny White Pike
Brentwood, TN 37027-5755, USA

Cain, Les (Athlete, Baseball Player)
31 Cutting Ct
Richmond, CA 94804-4217, USA

Cain, Lorenzo (Athlete, Baseball Player)
c/o Howard Kusnick *Diamond Sports Management*
300 NW 82nd Ave Ste 505
Plantation, FL 33324-7807, USA

Cain, Lynn (Athlete, Football Player)
PO Box 90881
Los Angeles, CA 90009-0881, USA

Cain, Matt (Athlete, Baseball Player)
c/o Jimmy Sexton *CAA (Memphis)*
6060 Poplar Ave Ste 470
Memphis, TN 38119-0910, USA

Cain, Mick (Actor)
7800 Beverly Blvd # 3371
Los Angeles, CA 90036-2112, USA

Cain, Scott (Race Car Driver)
6059 W Ashlan Ave
Fresno, CA 93723-9201, USA

Caine, Michael (Actor)
c/o Duncan Heath *Independent Talent Group*
40 Whitfield St
London W1T 2RH, UNITED KINGDOM

Caio, Francesco (Business Person)
Ing C Olivetti Co
Via G Jervos 77
Ivrea/Truin 10015, USA

Cairns, Eric (Athlete, Hockey Player)
1291 Treeland St
Burlington, ON L7R 3T5, Canada

Cairns, Leah (Actor)
Armada Partners
815 Moraga Dr
C/O David M Rudy
Los Angeles, CA 90049-1633, USA

Cairo, Miguel (Athlete, Baseball Player)
2262 Steven St
Clearwater, FL 33759-1419, USA

Cake (Music Group)
c/o Staff Member *The Umbrella Group*
151 W 28th St Rm 7E
New York, NY 10001-6112, USA

Calabrese, Gerry (Athlete, Basketball Player)
351 Esplanade Pl
Cliffside Park, NJ 07010-2708, USA

Calabro, Thomas (Actor)
4318 Ben Ave
Studio City, CA 91604-1703, USA

Calacurcio-Thomas, Aldine (Athlete, Baseball Player, Commentator)
5438 Nottingham Dr
Loves Park, IL 61111-3605, USA

Calafiore, Cody (Actor)
c/o Maury DiMauro *Innovative Artists*
1505 10th St
Santa Monica, CA 90401-2805, USA

Calaway, Mark (The Undertaker) (Athlete, Wrestler)
12904 Hacienda Rdg
Austin, TX 78738-7662, USA

Calcagni, Ron (Athlete, Football Player)
340 Savannah Park Cir
Conway, AR 72034-7277, USA

Calcavecchia, Mark (Athlete, Golfer)
1010 Loxahatchee Club Dr
Jupiter, FL 33458-7710, USA

Calder, David (Actor)
1 Winterwell Rd
London SW2 5TB, UK

Calder, Eric (Athlete, Hockey Player)
259 Stanley Dr
Waterloo, ON N2L 1H9, Canada

Calder, Kyle (Athlete, Hockey Player)
726 Monterey Blvd
Hermosa Beach, CA 90254-4549, USA

Calder, Nigel (Writer)
8 The Chase, Furnace Green
Crawley W. Sussex RH10 6HW, UK

Calderon, Leticia (Actor)
c/o Staff Member *Televisa*
Blvd Adolfo Lopez Mateos 232
Colonia San Angel INN
DF CP 01060, MEXICO

Calderon, Wilmer (Actor)
c/o Lena Roklin *Luber Roklin Management*
5815 W Sunset Blvd Ste 208
Los Angeles, CA 90028-6481, USA

Calderon Fournier, Rafael A (President)
Partido Unidad Social Cristiana
San Jose, COSTA RICA

Caldwell, Adrian (Athlete, Basketball Player)
10990 West Rd Apt 311
Houston, TX 77064-5496, USA

Caldwell, Alan (Athlete, Football Player)
1370 Kerner Rd
Kernersville, NC 27284-8943, USA

Caldwell, Andre (Athlete, Football Player)
c/o Tony Fleming *Impact Sports (LA)*
12429 Ventura Ct
Studio City, CA 91604-2417, USA

Caldwell, Bobby (Musician, Songwriter, Writer)
PO Box 6
Great Meadows, NJ 07838-0006, USA

Caldwell, Darryl (Athlete, Football Player)
4604 Malinta Ln
Chattanooga, TN 37416-3728, USA

Caldwell, Gail (Journalist)
c/o Staff Member *Zachary Shuster Harmsworth Talent Agency*
19 W 21st St Rm 501
New York, NY 10010-6874, USA

Caldwell, Jim (Athlete, Basketball Player)
705 Freedom Ln
Roswell, GA 30075-7911, USA

Caldwell, Joe (Athlete, Basketball Player, Olympic Athlete)
15 E Pebble Beach Dr
Tempe, AZ 85282-5127, USA

Caldwell, John (Cartoonist)
c/o Staff Member *King Features Syndication*
300 W 57th St Fl 15
New York, NY 10019-5238, USA

Caldwell, Kimberly (Musician, Reality Star)
c/o Anthony Cordova *Story Road Entertainment*
809 S Bundy Dr Apt 209
Los Angeles, CA 90049-5253, USA

Caldwell, Matt (Musician)
c/o Staff Member *Paradigm (Monterey)*
404 W Franklin St
Monterey, CA 93940-2303, USA

Caldwell, Mike (Athlete, Baseball Player)
1645 Brook Run Dr
Raleigh, NC 27614-9732, USA

Caldwell, Mike (Athlete, Football Player)
646 Robertsville Rd
Oak Ridge, TN 37830-4724, USA

Caldwell, Mike T (Athlete, Football Player)
41621 N Bent Creek Ct
Phoenix, AZ 85086-1903, USA

Caldwell, Ralph W (Athlete, Football Player)
4054 Charlene Dr
Los Angeles, CA 90043-1510, USA

Caldwell, Ralph W (Football Player)
4054 Charlene Dr
Los Angeles, CA 90043-1510, us

Caldwell, Ravin (Athlete, Football Player)
4415 Johnson St
Fort Smith, AR 72904-4531, USA

Caldwell, Scott (Athlete, Football Player)
1037 Tuskegee St
Grand Prairie, TX 75051-2637, USA

Caldwell, Tracy e dr (Astronaut)
827 Timber Cove Dr
Seabrook, TX 77586-4617, USA

Caldwell, Travis (Actor)
c/o Ellen Meyer *Ellen Meyer Management*
315 S Beverly Dr Ste 202
Beverly Hills, CA 90212-4310, USA

Caldwell, Zoe (Actor)
Whitehead-Stevens
1501 Broadway
New York, NY 10036-5601, USA

Cale, John (Music Group, Musician)
Firebrand Mgmt
12 Rickett St
West Brompton
London SW6 1RU, UNITED KINGDOM (UK)

Cale, Paula (Actor)
2518 Canyon Dr
Los Angeles, CA 90068-2416, USA

Cale, Puala (Actor)
Gersh Agency
232 N Canon Dr
Beverly Hills, CA 90210-5302, USA

Caleb, Jamie (Athlete, Football Player)
8889 Brandywine Rd
Northfield, OH 44067-2503, USA

Calero, Enriaue (Athlete, Baseball Player)
21465 65th Sts
1465 65th St, Emervville CA, 94608-1062

Calero, Kiko (Athlete, Baseball Player)
18 Danson Dr
Saint Peters, MO 63376-4028, USA

Calhoun, Bill (Athlete, Basketball Player)
3740 El Cerro View Cir
Reno, NV 89509-5610, USA

Calhoun, David (Athlete, Basketball Player)
17912 Lafayette Dr
Olney, MD 20832-2129, USA

Calhoun, Donald C (Don) (Athlete, Football Player)
PO Box 49104
Wichita, KS 67201-9104, USA

Calhoun, Jeff (Athlete, Baseball Player)
10002 Springwood Forest Dr
Houston, TX 77080-6419, USA

Calhoun, Jim (Athlete, Basketball Player, Coach)
PO Box 379
Pomfret Center, CT 06259-0379, USA

Calhoun, Kole (Athlete, Baseball Player)
c/o Page Odle *PSI Sports*
47 Dawson Dr
Suite 5S
Oxnard, CA 93036, USA

Calhoun, Monica (Actor)
Innovative Artists
1505 10th St
Santa Monica, CA 90401-2805, USA

Cali, Carmen (Athlete, Baseball Player)
5751 Copper Leaf Ln
Naples, FL 34116-6713, USA

Cali, Joseph (Actor)
25630 Edenwild Rd
Monte Nido, CA 91302-2265, USA

Calico, Tyrone (Athlete, Football Player)
3028 Brookview Forest Dr
Nashville, TN 37211-7049, USA

Caliendo, Frank (Actor)
298 Vinewood Oval
Avon Lake, OH 44012-1490, USA

Califano, Joseph A Jr (Politician)
Casa at Columbia
42 Morningside DrS
Westport, CT 06880-5413, USA

Caligiuri, Fred (Athlete, Baseball Player)
100 Baker St
Rimersburg, PA 16248-4324, USA

Calip, Demetrius (Athlete, Basketball Player)
7321 Lennox Ave Unit G5
Van Nuys, CA 91405-6262, USA

Calipari, John (Basketball Coach, Coach)
University of Kentucky
Athletic Dept
Lexington, KY 40506-0001, USA

Calis, Natasha (Actor)
c/o Jill Littman *Impression Entertainment*
9229 W Sunset Blvd Ste 700
Los Angeles, CA 90069-3407, USA

Calkins, Buzz (Race Car Driver)
1630 Chicago Ave Apt 904
Evanston, IL 60201-4589, USA

Call, Anthony (Actor)
Michael Thomas Agency
134 E 10th St
New York, NY 10021, USA

Call, Brandon (Actor)
c/o Staff Member *SDB Partners Inc*
315 S Beverly Dr Ste 411
Beverly Hills, CA 90212-4301, USA

Call, Jack (Athlete, Football Player)
PO Box 361
Churchville, MD 21028-0361, USA

Call, Kevin (Athlete, Football Player)
839 Carey Rd
Carmel, IN 46033-9324, USA

Callaghan-Maxwell, Margaret (Athlete, Baseball Player, Commentator)
5-250 15th Ave E
Vancouver, BC V5T 2P9, Canada

Callahan, Bill (Athlete, Coach, Football Coach, Football Player)
405 Christinas Ct
Cranberry Township, PA 16066-7805, USA

Callahan, John (Actor)
Levin Representatives
2402 4th St Apt 6
Santa Monica, CA 90405-3664, USA

Callan, Cecile (Actor)
SMZ
8730 W Sunset Blvd Ste 480
Los Angeles, CA 90069-2277, USA

Callan, K (Actor)
4957 Matilija Ave
Sherman Oaks, CA 91423-1921, USA

Callan, Michael (Actor)
1651 Camden Ave Apt 3
Los Angeles, CA 90025-3537, USA

Calland, Lee (Athlete, Football Player)
6624 Windwood Cir
Douglasville, GA 30135-1647, USA

Callander, Drew (Athlete, Hockey Player)
11 Edenwold Cres
Regina, SK S4R 8A6, Canada

Callander, Jock (Athlete, Hockey Player)
Lake Erie Monsters 1 Center Ice
Cleveland, OH 44115-4004, USA

Callaway, Mickey (Athlete, Baseball Player)
8061 Stonewyck Rd
Germantown, TN 38138-2351, USA

Callen, Bryan (Actor, Musician)
c/o Andrew Freedman *Andrew Freedman Public Relations*
35 E 84th St
New York, NY 10028-0871, USA

Callen, Jones Gloria (Swimmer)
1508 Chafton Rd
Charleston, WV 25314-1603, USA

Callender, Jock (Athlete, Hockey Player)
388 Lear Rd
Avon Lake, OH 44012-2079, USA

Callicutt, Ken (Athlete, Football Player)
919 Suchava Dr
White Lake, MI 48386-4558, USA

Callie, Dayton (Actor)
c/o Staff Member *Commercial Talent*
12711 Ventura Blvd Ste 285
Studio City, CA 91604-2487, USA

Callier, Frances (Comedian)
c/o Staff Member *Gekis Management*
4217 Verdugo View Dr
Los Angeles, CA 90065-4317, USA

Callies, Sarah Wayne (Actor)
c/o Erwin More *More/Medavoy Management*
10203 Santa Monica Blvd # 400
Los Angeles, CA 90067-6405, USA

Callighen, Brett (Athlete, Hockey Player)
PO Box 249
Bala, ON P0C 1A0, Canada

Calling, The (Music Group)
c/o Staff Member *WME|IMG*
9601 Wilshire Blvd
Beverly Hills, CA 90210-5213, USA

Callis, James (Actor, Director)
c/o Alan Siegel *Alan Siegel Entertainment*
9200 W Sunset Blvd Ste 804
West Hollywood, CA 90069-3603, USA

Callner, Marty (Director, Producer)
c/o David Steinberg *Morra Brezner Steinberg & Tenenbaum (MBST) Entertainment*
345 N Maple Dr Ste 200
Beverly Hills, CA 90210-5174, USA

Callow, Simon (Actor)
Marina Martin
12/13 Poland St
London WlV 3DE, UNITED KINGDOM (UK)

Calloway, AJ (Television Host)
c/o Mike Esterman *Esterman.Com, LLC*
Prefers to be contacted via email
Baltimore, MD XXXXX, USA

Calloway, Chris (Athlete, Football Player)
1277 Ponti Mews NW
Atlanta, GA 30318-4179, USA

Calloway, Ernie (Athlete, Football Player)
4027 Lenox Blvd
Orlando, FL 32811-4107, USA

Calloway, Jordan (Actor, Musician)
c/o Eunice Lee *Jordan Lee Talent*
8424 Santa Monica Blvd Ste 706 # A
Los Angeles, CA 90069-4267, USA

Calloway, Ron (Athlete, Baseball Player)
3868 Las Colinas Dr
Las Cruces, NM 88012-0693, USA

Callum, Keith Rennie (Actor)
c/o Staff Member *Elizabeth Hodgson Management Group*
405-1688 Cypress St
Vancouver, BC V6J 5J1, CANADA

Calmus, Dick (Athlete, Baseball Player)
2950 E 94th St Apt 403
Tulsa, OK 74137-8721, USA

Calmus, Rocky (Athlete, Football Player)
101 Gillespie Dr APT 11201
Franklin, TN 37067-7550, USA

Calombaris, George (Chef)
The Press Club
72 Flinders St
Melbourne, Vic 03000, Australia

Caltabiano, Tom (Comedian)
c/o Staff Member *United Talent Agency (UTA)*
9336 Civic Center Dr
Beverly Hills, CA 90210-3604, USA

Calvano, Sadie (Actor)
c/o Jack Kingsrud *Zero Gravity Management*
11110 Ohio Ave Ste 100
Los Angeles, CA 90025-3329, USA

Calvert, Ken (Congressman, Politician)
2269 Rayburn Hob
Washington, DC 20515-0005, USA

Calvert, Mark (Athlete, Baseball Player)
908 W Waco St
Broken Arrow, OK 74011-2819, USA

Calvert, Patricia (Writer)
c/o Staff Member *Simon & Schuster*
1230 Avenue of the Americas Fl CONC1
New York, NY 10020-1586, USA

Calvin, John (Actor)
2503 Ware Rd
Austin, TX 78741-5720, USA

Calvin, Mack (Athlete, Basketball Player)
333 N Main St # A
Hopkinsville, KY 42240-2417, USA

Calvin, Thomas (Athlete, Football Player)
2712 McTavish Ave SW
Decatur, AL 35603-1106, USA

Calvin, Tom (Athlete, Football Player)
2712 McTavish Ave SW
Decatur, AL 35603-1106, USA

Calzaghe, Joe (Boxer)
51 Caerbryn Pentwynmawar
Newbridge Gwent
South Wales, UNITED KINGDOM

Camacho, Ernie (Athlete, Baseball Player)
746 Saint Regis Way
Salinas, CA 93905-1642, USA

Camacho, Joe (Athlete, Baseball Player)
48 Massasoit Ave
Act 3-R
Fairhaven, MA 02719-3266, USA

Camarda, Charles (Astronaut)
2308 Beach Haven Dr Apt 303
Virginia Beach, VA 23451-1252, USA

Camareno, Joe (Actor)
c/o Staff Member *Conana Caroll & Associates*
6117 Rhodes Ave
N Hollywood, CA 91606-4601, Uninted States

Camarillo, Greg (Athlete, Football Player)
c/o JR Rickert *Authentic Athletix*
400 S Steele St Unit 47
Denver, CO 80209-3535, USA

Camarillo, Rich (Athlete, Football Player)
1941 E Clubhouse Dr
Phoenix, AZ 85048-4061, USA

Camastra, Danielle (Actor)
c/o Staff Member *Henderson Hogan Agency (LA)*
8929 Wilshire Blvd Ste 312
Beverly Hills, CA 90211-1969, USA

Cambal, Dennis (Athlete, Football Player)
24 Hedge Row
West Yarmouth, MA 02673-5813, USA

Cambria, Fred (Athlete, Baseball Player)
12 Iris Ct
Northport, NY 11768-3207, USA

Camby, Marcus (Athlete, Basketball Player)
6725 Fite Rd
Pearland, TX 77584-1089, USA

Camden, John (Business Person)
RMC Group
Coldgarbour Lane
Thorpe
Egham, Surrey TW20 8TD, UNITED KINGDOM (UK)

Cameo (Music Group)
1422 W Peachtree St NW # 816
Atlanta, GA 30309-2947, USA

Cameron, Al (Athlete, Hockey Player)
1225 Ormsby Lane NW
Edmonton, AB T5T 6R2, Canada

Cameron, Al (Athlete, Hockey Player)
1225 Ormsby Lane NW
Edmonton, AB T5T 6R2, Canada

Cameron, Bob (Athlete, Football Player)
349 Clare Ave
Winnipeg, MB R3L 1S2, Canada

Cameron, Dallas (Athlete, Football Player)
Hialeah-Miami Lakes High School
7977 W 12th Ave
Hialeah, FL 33014-3595, USA

Cameron, Dave (Athlete, Coach, Hockey Player)
c/o Staff Member *Mississauga St Michaels Majors*
5500 Rose Cherry Pl
Mississauga, ON L4Z 4B6, Canada

Cameron, David (Designer, Fashion Designer)
Schauspielschule Krauss
Weihburggasse 19
Vienna 01010, AUSTRIA

Cameron, Dean (Actor)
Landmark Artists Mgmt
4116 W Magnolia Blvd
Burbank, CA 91505-2782, USA

Cameron, Dove (Actor)
c/o Pamela Fisher *Abrams Artists Agency*
750 N San Vicente Blvd
E Tower Fl 11
Los Angeles, CA 90069-5788, USA

Cameron, Duncan (Music Group, Musician)
Sawyer Brown Inc
5200 Old Harding Rd
Franklin, TN 37064-9406, USA

Cameron, Dwayne (Actor)
c/o Scott Karp *The Syndicate*
10203 Santa Monica Blvd Fl 5
Los Angeles, CA 90067-6416, USA

Cameron, Glenn S (Athlete, Football Player)
8082 Steeplechase Dr
Palm Beach Gardens, FL 33418-7703, USA

Cameron, James (Director, Producer)
3211 Retreat Ct
Malibu, CA 90265-3448, USA

Cameron, Jordan (Athlete, Football Player)
c/o Tom Condon *Creative Artists Agency (CAA)*
401 Commerce St PH
Nashville, TN 37219-2516, USA

Cameron, Julia (Writer)
c/o Staff Member *HarperCollins Publishers*
195 Broadway Fl 2
New York, NY 10007-3132, USA

Cameron, Kenneth D (Astronaut)
Austvagen 13
Vastra Frotunda 42676, SWEDEN

Cameron, Kenneth d colonel (Astronaut)
11333 Gulf Beach Hwy
Pensacola, FL 32507-9100, USA

Cameron, Kevin (Athlete, Baseball Player)
26435 S Ivy Ln
Channahon, IL 60410-3341, USA

Cameron, Kirk (Actor)
c/o Staff Member *Pure Publicity*
188 Front St Ste 116 PMB 6
Franklin, TN 37064-5089, USA

Cameron, Laura (Actor)
8383 Wilshire Blvd # 954
Beverly Hills, CA 90211-2425, USA

Cameron, Mat (Music Group, Musician)
Susan Silver Mgmt
6523 California Ave SW # 348
Seattle, WA 98136-1833, USA

Cameron, Matt (Musician)
10910 Algonquin Rd
Woodway, WA 98020-6108, USA

Cameron, Mechelle (Swimmer)
Box 2 Site 1SS3
Calgary, AL T3C 3N9, CANADA

Cameron, Mike (Athlete, Baseball Player)
615 Champions Dr
McDonough, GA 30253-4284, USA

Cameron, Paul (Athlete, Football Player)
28072 Klamath Ct
Laguna Niguel, CA 92677-7018, USA

Cameron, Rhona (Actor)
c/o Staff Member *Jeremy Hicks Associates*
3 Stedham Place
London WC1A 1HU, UK

Cameron, Scotty (Golfer)
Acushnet Company
333 Bridge St
C/O Gordon Sanborn
Fairhaven, MA 02719-4900, USA

Cameron, Warren (Horse Racer)
1594 Bogie Dr
Big Pine Key, FL 33043-5016

Cameron, W Bruce (Writer)
c/o Scott Miller *Trident Media Group LLC*
41 Madison Ave Fl 36
New York, NY 10010-2257, USA

Cameron-Bure, Candace (Actor, Talk Show Host)
c/o Jeffery Brooks *Redrock Entertainment Development*
149 E Santa Anita Ave
Burbank, CA 91502-1926, USA

Camerota, Brett (Athlete, Olympic Athlete, Skier)
3118 Elk Run Dr
Park City, UT 84098-5300, USA

Camerota, Eric (Athlete, Olympic Athlete, Skier)
3118 Elk Run Dr
Park City, UT 84098-5300, USA

Camil, Jaime (Actor)
c/o Liza Anderson *Anderson Group Public Relations*
8060 Melrose Ave Fl 4
Los Angeles, CA 90046-7038, USA

Camiletti, Rob (Actor)
643 N La Cienega Blvd
Los Angeles, CA 90069-5201, USA

Camilleri, Louis C (Business Person)
Altria Group
120 Park Ave
New York, NY 10017-5577, USA

Camilleri, Terry (Actor)
c/o Staff Member *Barbara Gange Management (BGM)*
5/400 St Kilda Rd
Melbourne, VIC 03181, AUSTRALIA

Camilli, Doug (Athlete, Baseball Player)
4245 61st Ave
Vero Beach, FL 32967-8807, USA

Camilli, Lou (Athlete, Baseball Player)
1314 Sigma Chi Rd NE
Albuquerque, NM 87106-4544, USA

Camilo, Michael (Musician)
Joel Chriss
300 Mercer St Apt 3J
New York, NY 10003-6732, USA

Camilo, Michel (Music Group, Musician)
Redondo Music
590 W End Ave # 6
New York, NY 10024-1722, USA

Cammack, Eric (Athlete, Baseball Player)
605 Remington Dr
Bridge City, TX 77611-2234, USA

Cammalleri, Mike (Athlete, Hockey Player)
Pulver Sports
479 Bedford Park Ave
Attn tan Pulver
Toronto, ON M5M 1K2, Canada

Cammuso, Frank (Cartoonist)
PO Box 4915
Syracuse, NY 13221-4915, USA

Camp, Anna (Actor)
c/o Robert Glennon *Authentic Talent and Literary Management (NY)*
20 Jay St Ste M17
Brooklyn, NY 11201-8300, USA

Camp, Colleen (Actor)
473 N Tigertail Rd
Los Angeles, CA 90049-2807, USA

Camp, Dave (Congressman, Politician)
341 Cannon Hob
Washington, DC 20515-1806, USA

Camp, Jeremy (Musician)
c/o Steve Rohr *Lexicon Public Relations*
1049 Havenhurst Dr # 365
West Hollywood, CA 90046-6002, USA

Camp, John (Journalist)
Saint Paul Pioneer Press
10 River Park Plz Ste 700
Saint Paul, MN 55107-1223, USA

Camp, Rick (Athlete, Baseball Player)
F P C Montgomery ID # 11973-021
Maxwell Air Force Base
Montgomery, AL 36112, USA

Camp, Steve (Music Group)
Third Coast Artists
2021 21st Ave S Ste 220
Nashville, TN 37212-4348, USA

Campaneris, Bert (Athlete, Baseball Player)
9797 N 105th Pl
Scottsdale, AZ 85258-6071, USA

Campanis, Jim (Athlete, Baseball Player)
17082 Cascades Ave
Yorba Linda, CA 92886-4867, USA

Campbell, Alan (Actor)
Gersh Agency
41 Madison Ave Ste 3301
New York, NY 10010-2210, USA

Campbell, Ben Nighthorse (Politician)
PO Box 639
Ignacio, CO 81137-0639, USA

Campbell, Bill (Athlete, Baseball Player)
133 S Hale St
Palatine, IL 60067-6211, USA

Campbell, Billy (Actor)
c/o Sean Fay *LINK Entertainment*
11872 La Grange Ave
Los Angeles, CA 90025-5282, USA

Campbell, Brian (Athlete, Hockey Player)
4132 Grove Ave
Western Sprgs, IL 60558-1344, USA

Campbell, Bruce (Actor, Director, Producer)
735 Roca St
Ashland, OR 97520-3315, USA

Campbell, Bryan (Athlete, Hockey Player)
800 SE 20th Ave Apt 310
Deerfield Beach, FL 33441-5143, USA

Campbell, Calais (Athlete, Football Player)
c/o Tom Condon *Creative Artists Agency (CAA)*
401 Commerce St PH
Nashville, TN 37219-2516, USA

Campbell, Carter (Athlete, Football Player)
2085 Clementi Ln
Aurora, IL 60503-8579, USA

Campbell, Chad (Athlete, Golfer)
200 Glade Rd
Colleyville, TX 76034-3603, USA

Campbell, Cheryl (Actor)
Michael Whitehall
125 Gloucester Road
London SW7 4TE, UNITED KINGDOM (UK)

Campbell, Christa (Actor)
Campbell Grobman Films
9461 Charleville Blvd # 301
Beverly Hills, CA 90212-3017, USA

Campbell, Christian (Actor)
12533 Woodgreen St
Los Angeles, CA 90066-2723, USA

Campbell, Colin (Soupy) (Athlete, Coach, Hockey Player)
c/o Staff Member *National Hockey League (NHL)*
50 Bay St 11th Fl
Toronto, ON M5J 2X8, Canada

Campbell, Dan (Athlete, Football Player)
PO Box 977
Meridian, TX 76665-0977, USA

Campbell, Danielle (Actor)
c/o Mitchell Gossett *Industry Entertainment Partners*
955 Carrillo Dr Ste 300
Los Angeles, CA 90048-5400, USA

Campbell, Darren (Athlete, Track Athlete)
1 Wandsworth Plain
London SW18 1EH, UK

Campbell, Dave (Athlete, Baseball Player)
726 N Dundee Dr
Post Falls, ID 83854-8886, USA

Campbell, Dave (Athlete, Baseball Player)
3982 Lone Eagle Pl
Sanford, FL 32771-5810, USA

Campbell, Dick (Athlete, Football Player)
2557 Nicolet Dr
Green Bay, WI 54311-7225, USA

Campbell, Dick (Athlete, Football Player)
PO Box 198
Jensen Beach, FL 34958-0198, USA

Campbell, Earl (Athlete, Football Player)
The Tyler Rose
701 W 11th St
Austin, TX 78701-2067, USA

Campbell, Elden (Athlete, Basketball Player)
17252 Hawthome Blvd
#493
Torrance, CA 90504-1032, USA

Campbell, Gaetana (Actor)
1620 Richmond Cir Unit 105
Joliet, IL 60435-6751, USA

Campbell, Garry (Producer, Writer)
c/o Staff Member *Creative Artists Agency (CAA)*
2000 Avenue of the Stars Ste 100
Los Angeles, CA 90067-4705, USA

Campbell, Gary (Athlete, Football Player)
PO Box 775353
Steamboat Springs, CO 80477-5353, USA

Campbell, Gene (Athlete, Hockey Player)
1554 Wilshire Dr NE
Rochester, MN 55906-4363, USA

Campbell, Gregory (Athlete, Hockey Player)
RR 2
Tillsonburg, ON N4G 4G7, Canada

Campbell, Isobel (Music Group, Musician)
Legends of 21st Century
7 Trinity Row
Florence, MA 01062-1931, USA

Campbell, Jack (Politician)
PO Box 2208
Santa Fe, NM 87504-2208, USA

Campbell, Jason (Athlete, Football Player)
c/o Joel Segal *Lagardere Unlimited (NY)*
456 Washington St Apt 9L
New York, NY 10013-1555, USA

Campbell, Jeff (Athlete, Football Player)
2601 Berenson Ln
Austin, TX 78746-1963, USA

Campbell, Jeff (Baseball Player)
Homestead Grays
4194 San Miguel Ave
San Diego, CA 92113-1842, USA

Campbell, Jennifer Lynn (Actor)
11871 Dubarry Dr
Carmel, IN 46033-8259, USA

Campbell, Jesse (Athlete, Football Player)
875 Piney Neck Rd
Vanceboro, NC 28586-8677, USA

Campbell, Jessica (Actor)
Somers Teitelbaum David
8840 Wilshire Blvd # 200
Beverly Hills, CA 90211-2606, USA

Campbell, Jim (Athlete, Hockey Player)
32 Lemp Rd
Saint Louis, MO 63122-6947, USA

Campbell, Jim (Horse Racer)
31 Mill Pond Rd
Jackson, NJ 08527-4888, USA

Campbell, Joe (Athlete, Baseball Player)
330 Legends Ct
Bowling Green, KY 42103-2550, USA

Campbell, John (Congressman, Politician)
1507 Longworth Hob
Washington, DC 20515-4328, USA

Campbell, John (Horse Racer)
John D Campbell Stable
823 Allison Dr
River Vale, NJ 07675-6602, USA

Campbell, John W (Athlete, Football Player)
12908 Welcome Ln
Burnsville, MN 55337-3626, USA

Campbell, Joshua (Actor)
c/o Staff Member *Select Artists Ltd (CA-Westside Office)*
1138 12th St Apt 1
Santa Monica, CA 90403-5459, USA

Campbell, Julia (Actor)
c/o Staff Member *Innovative Artists*
1505 10th St
Santa Monica, CA 90401-2805, USA

Campbell, Kevin (Athlete, Baseball Player)
207 Ridout Dr
Des Arc, AR 72040-3335, USA

Campbell, Kim (Politician)
Canadian Consulate
550 S Hope St Ste 900
Los Angeles, CA 90071-2654, USA

Campbell, Lamar (Athlete, Football Player)
2511 W 7th St
Chester, PA 19013-2109, USA

Campbell, Larry Joe (Actor)
30306 Diamonte Ln
Rancho Palos Verdes, CA 90275-6395, USA

Campbell, Lewis B (Business Person)
Textron Inc
40 Westminster St Ste 500
Providence, RI 02903-2503, USA

Campbell, Luther (Musician)
16571 SW 18th St
Miramar, FL 33027-4468, USA

Campbell, Mark (Athlete, Football Player)
8303 SW 64th Pl # Pi
Gainesville, FL 32608-8545, USA

Campbell, Martin (Director)
International Creative Mgmt
8942 Wilshire Blvd # 219
Beverly Hills, CA 90211-1908, USA

Campbell, Matt (Athlete, Football Player)
9 Timberidge Dr
North Augusta, SC 29860-9725, USA

Campbell, Matthew (Matt) (Athlete, Football Player)
9 Timberidge Dr
North Augusta, SC 29860-9725, USA

Campbell, Michael (Athlete, Golfer)
c/o Adrian Mitchell *IMG (UK)*
McCormack House, Hogarth Business Park
Burlington Ln
Chiswick London W4 2TH, UNITED KINGDOM

Campbell, Mike (Athlete, Football Player)
383 Inverness Dr
Winston Salem, NC 27107-6030, USA

Campbell, Mike (Athlete, Baseball Player)
4500 36th Ave SW Apt 12
Seattle, WA 98126-2750, USA

Campbell, Mike (Athlete, Football Player)
383 Inverness Dr
Winston Salem, NC 27107-6030, USA

Campbell, Mike (Musician)
19950 Redwing St
Woodland Hills, CA 91364-2621, USA

Campbell, Naomi (Actor, Model)
c/o Cindi Berger *PMK/BNC Public Relations*
622 3rd Ave Fl 8
New York, NY 10017-6707, USA

Campbell, Nell (Actor)
246 W 14th St
New York, NY 10011-7201, USA

Campbell, Nell (Actor)
Andrew Taylor Management
P.O. Box 709
Broadway NSW 2007, Australia

Campbell, Neve (Actor)
c/o Paul Nelson *Mosaic Media Group*
407 N Maple Dr # 100
Beverly Hills, CA 90210-3818, USA

Campbell, Nicholas (Actor)
1206 N Orange Grove Ave
West Hollywood, CA 90046-5351, USA

Campbell, Paul (Actor)
c/o Staff Member *ROAR (LA)*
9701 Wilshire Blvd Fl 8
Beverly Hills, CA 90212-2008, USA

Campbell, Rich (Athlete, Football Player)
3176 Leeds Rd
Columbus, OH 43221-2625, USA

Campbell, Ron (Athlete, Baseball Player)
1104 Sweetbriar Ave NW
Cleveland, TN 37311-1657, USA

Campbell, Scott (Athlete, Football Player)
123 Oak Ln
Hershey, PA 17033-1748, USA

Campbell, Scott Michael (Actor)
MCK Productions
8306 Wilshire Blvd # 7055
Beverly Hills, CA 90211-2304, USA

Campbell, Sonny (Athlete, Football Player)
6250 N Desert Willow Dr
Tucson, AZ 85743-8701, USA

Campbell, Stacy Dean (Musician)
1105-C 16th Ave Sq
Nashville, TN 37212, USA

Campbell, Tevin (Musician)
c/o Staff Member *M.A.G./Universal Attractions*
15 W 36th St Fl 8
New York, NY 10018-7927, USA

Campbell, Tony (Athlete, Basketball Player)
1445 Teaneck Rd
Teaneck, NJ 07666-3627, USA

Campbell, Vivian (Musician)
3183 Olive Ave
Altadena, CA 91001-4261, USA

Campbell, Woodrow (Athlete, Football Player)
9122 Weymouth Dr
Houston, TX 77031-3034, USA

Campbell, Woody (Athlete, Football Player)
9122 Weymouth Dr
Houston, TX 77031-3034, USA

Campbell Bower, Jamie (Actor)
c/o Emma Jackson *Premier PR*
2-4 Bucknall St
London WC2H 8LA, UNITED KINGDOM

Campbell-Martin, Tisha (Actor)
c/o Michael Black *Michael Black Management*
9701 Wilshire Blvd Fl 10
Beverly Hills, CA 90212-2010, USA

Campeau, Rychard (Athlete, Hockey Player)
301 Rue Georges-Phaneuf
Saint-Jean-Sur-Richelieu, QC J3B 1J9, Canada

Campedelli, Dominic (Athlete, Hockey Player)
732 Jerusalem Rd
Cohasset, MA 02025-1032, USA

Campen, James (Athlete, Football Player)
2789 Ichabod Ln
Green Bay, WI 54313-3209, USA

Campfield, Billy (Athlete, Football Player)
930 Glenmore Way Apt K
Westerville, OH 43082-9429, USA

Campfield, William (Billy) (Athlete, Football Player)
532 Radcliff Dr
Westerville, OH 43082-6338, USA

Campion, Jane (Director)
c/o Kate Richter *HLA Management*
PO Box 1536
Strawberry Hills 02012, AUSTRALIA

Campisi, Sal (Athlete, Baseball Player)
644 77th Ave
St Pete Beach, FL 33706-1708, USA

Campo, Bobby (Actor)
c/o Tory Howard *Atlas Artists*
9220 W Sunset Blvd Ste 225
Los Angeles, CA 90069-3513, USA

Campo, Dave (Coach, Football Coach)
Celveland Browns
76 Lou Groza Blvd
Berea, OH 44017-1269, USA

Campos, Angel (Athlete, Baseball Player)
8410 W Calle Moheda
Tucson, AZ 85757-6815, USA

Campos, Antonio (Director)
c/o Staff Member *BorderLine Films*
545 8th Ave Fl 11
New York, NY 10018-4307, USA

Campos, Arsenio (Actor)
c/o Staff Member *Televisa*
Blvd Adolfo Lopez Mateos 232
Colonia San Angel INN
DF CP 01060, MEXICO

Campos, Bruno (Actor)
SDB Partners
1801 Ave of Stars
#902
Los Angeles, CA 90067, USA

Campos, Jorge (Soccer Player)
Federacion de Futbol Assn
Col Juarez
Mexico City 6, DF CP 06600, MEXICO

Cam'ron (Musician)
c/o Staff Member *ICM Partners*
10250 Constellation Blvd Fl 7
Los Angeles, CA 90067-6207, USA

Canada, Larry (Athlete, Football Player)
17691 Sarah Ln
Country Club Hills, IL 60478-4995, USA

Canada, Ron (Actor)
c/o Staff Member *Artists & Representatives (Stone Manners Salners)*
6100 Wilshire Blvd Ste 1500
Los Angeles, CA 90048-5110, USA

Canadas, Esther (Actor, Model)
Wilhelmina Models
300 Park Ave S # 200
New York, NY 10010-5313, USA

Canadian Brass (Music Group)
c/o Darcy Gregoire *UTA Music*
1880 Century Park E Ste 711
Los Angeles, CA 90067-1618, USA

Canadian Tenors, The (Music Group, Musician)
c/o Jeffrey Latimer *Jeffrey Latimer Entertainment*
280 Jarvis St Suite 301
Toronto, ON M5B 2C5, Canada

Canady, James (Jim) (Athlete, Football Player)
303 Sunset Dr
Burnet, TX 78611-9737, USA

Canagata, Bill (Baseball Player)
Indianapolis Clowns
25 W 132nd St Apt 10R
New York, NY 10037-3205, USA

Canale, George (Athlete, Baseball Player)
7333 Old Mill Rd
Roanoke, VA 24018-6712, USA

Canalis, Elisabetta (Actor, Model)
c/o Staff Member *Corsa Agency, The*
11849 W Olympic Blvd Ste 100
Los Angeles, CA 90064-1164, USA

Canals-Barrera, Maria (Actor)
c/o Megan Trevino *Status PR*
PO Box 6191
Westlake Village, CA 91359-6191, USA

Candaele, Casey (Athlete, Baseball Player)
2977 Flora St
San Luis Obispo, CA 93401-4627, USA

Candelaria, John (Athlete, Baseball Player)
3021 Merle St
Mobile, AL 36605-4161, USA

Candeloro, Philippe (Figure Skater)
Federation des Sports de Glace
35 Rue Felicien David
Paris 75016, FRANCE

Candeloro, Philippe (Figure Skater)
42 rue de Louvre
Paris F-75001, FRANCE

Candiotti, Thomas C (Tom) (Athlete, Baseball Player)
6061 E Jenan Dr
Scottsdale, AZ 85254-4972, USA

Candlebox (Music Group)
11410 NE 124th St # 627
Kirkland, WA 98034-4399, USA

Caneira, John (Athlete, Baseball Player)
18 Spruce Dr
Naugatuck, CT 06770-4231, USA

Canela, Jencarlos (Actor, Musician)
c/o Lauren Gold *Shelter PR*
5670 Wilshire Blvd Ste 1200
Los Angeles, CA 90036-5621, USA

Canerday, Natalie (Actor)
c/o Staff Member *The Agency Inc*
802 W 8th St
Little Rock, AR 72201-4016, USA

Canet, Guillaume (Actor, Director, Writer)
c/o Robert Newman *WME|IMG*
9601 Wilshire Blvd
Beverly Hills, CA 90210-5213, USA

Canete, Ariel (Athlete, Golfer)
Advantage International
1751 Pinnacle Dr Ste 1500
Mc Lean, VA 22102-3833, USA

Canfield, Jack (Business Person, Writer)
The Jack Canfield Companies
PO Box 30880
Santa Barbara, CA 93130-0880, USA

Cangelosi, John (Athlete, Baseball Player)
10914 Caribou Ln
Orland Park, IL 60467-7843, USA

Canidate, Trung (Athlete, Football Player)
1707 W Clarendon Ave
Phoenix, AZ 85015-5502, USA

Canipe, David (Athlete, Golfer)
505 Oakwood Ave
New Smyrna Beach, FL 32169-2715, USA

Canizales, Gaby (Boxer)
2205 Saint Maria Ave
Laredo, TX 78040, USA

Canizaro, Jay (Athlete, Baseball Player)
19523 Piney Lake Dr
Spring, TX 77388-3060, USA

Canley, Sheldon (Athlete, Football Player)
165 Village Circle Dr
Lompoc, CA 93436-5606, USA

Cannatella, Trishelle (Reality Star)
c/o Staff Member *Bunim/Murray Productions*
1015 Grandview Ave
Glendale, CA 91201-2205, USA

Cannava, Anthony (Tony) (Athlete, Football Player)
4 Arlington St Apt 31
Cambridge, MA 02140-2745, USA

Cannavale, Bobby (Actor)
c/o Marla Farrell *Shelter PR*
928 Broadway Ste 505
New York, NY 10010-8143, USA

Cannavino, Joe (Athlete, Football Player)
346 Claymore Blvd
Cleveland, OH 44143-1730, USA

Canned Heat (Music Group, Musician)
PO Box 3773
San Rafael, CA 94912-3773, USA

Cannida, James (Athlete, Football Player)
4504 Harmony Pl
Rohnert Park, CA 94928-1880, USA

Canning, Lisa (Actor, Correspondent)
880 Hilldale Ave Apt 12
West Hollywood, CA 90069-4920, USA

Canning, Sara (Actor)
c/o Laura Myones *McKeon-Myones Management*
3500 W Olive Ave Ste 770
Burbank, CA 91505-5527, USA

Cannizaro, Andy (Athlete, Baseball Player)
15250 Memorial Tower Dr
Baton Rouge, LA 70810-0301, USA

Cannizzaro, Chris (Athlete, Baseball Player)
PO Box 721011
San Diego, CA 92172-1011, USA

Cannon, Ace (Musician)
American Mgmt
19948 Mayall St
Chatsworth, CA 91311-3522, USA

Cannon, Carey (Actor)

Cannon, Danny (Producer)
c/o Staff Member *Creative Artists Agency (CAA)*
2000 Avenue of the Stars Ste 100
Los Angeles, CA 90067-4705, USA

Cannon, Dyan (Actor)
1100 Alta Loma Rd Apt 808
West Hollywood, CA 90069-2438, USA

Cannon, Freddy (Musician)
18641 Cassandra St
Tarzana, CA 91356-4509, USA

Cannon, Glenn (Actor)
University of Hawaii at Manoa
2500 Campus Rd
C/O Cinematic and Digital Arts
Honolulu, HI 96822-2217, USA

Cannon, Harold (Actor)
c/o Staff Member *Select Artists Ltd (CA-Valley Office)*
PO Box 4359
Burbank, CA 91503-4359, USA

Cannon, Joe (Soccer Player)
c/o Staff Member *Colorado Rapids Soccer Club*
1000 Chopper Cir
Pepsi Center
Denver, CO 80204-5805, USA

Cannon, Joe (J J) (Athlete, Baseball Player)
3017 Cedarwood Village Ln
Pensacola, FL 32514-6251, USA

Cannon, John (Athlete, Football Player)
2911 W Bay Vista Ave
Tampa, FL 33611-1609, USA

Cannon, Katherine (Actor)
1310 Westholme Ave
Los Angeles, CA 90024-5016, USA

Cannon, Larry (Athlete, Basketball Player)
12661 Kelly Sands Way Apt 113
Fort Myers, FL 33908-5917, USA

Cannon, Marcus (Athlete, Football Player)
c/o Tom Condon *Creative Artists Agency (CAA)*
401 Commerce St PH
Nashville, TN 37219-2516, USA

Cannon, Mark (Athlete, Football Player)
2604 Riveroaks Dr
Arlington, TX 76006-3638, USA

Cannon, Nick (Actor, Producer)
c/o Staff Member *N' Credible Entertainment*
3500 N San Fernando Blvd
Burbank, CA 91505-1000, USA

Cano, Christi (Athlete, Golfer)
834 Alametos
San Antonio, TX 78212-1331, USA

Cano, Roberto (Actor)
c/o Staff Member *TV Caracol*
Calle 76 #11 - 35
Piso 10AA
Bogota DC 26484, COLOMBIA

Cano, Robinson (Athlete, Baseball Player)
10234 45th Ave Apt 3
Corona, NY 11368-2833, USA

Canonero, Milena (Designer)
c/o Paul Hook *ICM Partners*
10250 Constellation Blvd Fl 7
Los Angeles, CA 90067-6207, USA

Canova, Diana (Actor)
Grand View Management
578 Washington Blvd Ste 688
Marina Del Rey, CA 90292-5442, USA

Canseco, Jose (Athlete, Baseball Player, Reality Star)
c/o Susan Haber *Haber Entertainment*
434 S Canon Dr Apt 204
Beverly Hills, CA 90212-4501, USA

Canseco, Ozzie (Athlete, Baseball Player)
10833 Wilshire Blvd Apt 525
Los Angeles, CA 90024-4157, USA

Cansino, Athena (Actor)
c/o Victor Kruglov *Kruglov & Associates*
6565 W Sunset Blvd Ste 280
Los Angeles, CA 90028-7219, USA

Cantafio, Jim (Actor)
c/o Laura Lichen *Laura Lichen Management*
PO Box 33051
Granada Hills, CA 91394-3051, USA

Cantano, Mark (Athlete, Football Player)
9036 Walton St
Indianapolis, IN 46231-1164, USA

Cantey, Charisie (Sportscaster)
ABC-TV
77 W 66th St
New York, NY 10023-6201, USA

Cantillo, Jose Pablo (Actor)
c/o Staff Member *New Wave Entertainment (LA)*
2660 W Olive Ave
Burbank, CA 91505-4525, USA

Canto, Adan (Actor)
c/o Kevin Volchok *United Talent Agency (UTA)*
9336 Civic Center Dr
Beverly Hills, CA 90210-3604, USA

Canton, Denio (Baseball Player)
New York Cubans
1330 NW 5th St Apt 5
Miami, FL 33125-4734, USA

Canton, Joanna (Actor)
c/o Lenore Zerman *Liberman/Zerman Management*
252 N Larchmont Blvd Ste 200
Los Angeles, CA 90004-3754, USA

Cantona, Eric (Actor)
French Federation de Football
60 Bis Ave D'Ilena
Paris 75783, France

Cantone, Mario (Actor)
c/o Jim Mannino *Jim Mannino PR*
27 W 76th St Apt 1C
New York, NY 10023-1554, USA

Cantor, Andres (Sportscaster)
c/o Staff Member *WME|IMG*
9601 Wilshire Blvd
Beverly Hills, CA 90210-5213, USA

Cantor, Eric (Congressman, Politician)
303 Cannon Hob
Washington, DC 20515-1501, USA

Cantoral, Itati (Actor)
c/o Gabriel Blanco *Gabriel Blanco Iglesias (Mexico)*
Rio Balsas 35-32
Colonia Cuauhtemoc
DF 06500, Mexico

Cantrell, Barry (Athlete, Football Player)
PO Box 541
Steinhatchee, FL 32359-0541, USA

Cantrell, Bill (Race Car Driver)
PO Box 194
Novi, MI 48376-0194, USA

Cantrell, Blu (Music Group)
c/o Staff Member *M.A.G./Universal Attractions*
15 W 36th St Fl 8
New York, NY 10018-7927, USA

Cantrell, Jerry (Musician)
11700 Valleycrest Rd
Studio City, CA 91604-4226, USA

Cantrell, Lana (Musician)
300 E 71st St Apt 19A
New York, NY 10021-5238, USA

Cantu, Jorge (Athlete, Baseball Player)
5009 S 24th St
McAllen, TX 78503-8936, USA

Cantwell, Maria (Politician)
904 7th AveS
Edmonds, WA 98020-4014, USA

Canty, Chris (Athlete, Football Player)
c/o Brad Blank *Brad Blank & Associates*
1800 Sunset Harbour Dr
#2402
Miami Beach, FL 33139, USA

Canyon, George (Musician)
c/o Staff Member *Paradigm (Monterey)*
404 W Franklin St
Monterey, CA 93940-2303, USA

Cap, Kelly (Athlete, Golfer)
3023 Alcazar Pl Apt 208
Palm Beach Gardens, FL 33410-2878, USA

Capalbo, Carmen C (Director, Producer)
500 2nd Ave Apt 20D
New York, NY 10016-8615, USA

Capaldi, Peter (Actor, Director)
c/o Lindy King *United Agents*
12-26 Lexington St
London W1F OLE, UNITED KINGDOM

Caparulo, John (Comedian)
c/o Staff Member *Brillstein Entertainment Partners*
9150 Wilshire Blvd Ste 350
Beverly Hills, CA 90212-3453, USA

Capece, Bill (Athlete, Football Player)
15 E Bradley St Lot 10
Miramar Beach, FL 32550-6870, USA

Capel, John (Athlete, Track Athlete)

Capel, Mike (Athlete, Baseball Player)
3901 Northshore Dr
Montgomery, TX 77356-5369, USA

Capellas, Michael (Business Person)
MCI
500 Clinton Center Dr Ste 2200
Clinton, MS 39056-5674, USA

Capellino, Ally (Designer, Fashion Designer)
N1R Metropolitan Wharf
Wapping Wall
London E1 9SS, UNITED KINGDOM (UK)

Capers, Dom (Athlete, Coach, Football Coach, Football Player)
669 Ponte Vedra Blvd Unit A
Ponte Vedra Beach, FL 32082-2984, USA

Capers, Wayne (Athlete, Football Player)
28 Greenlawn Dr
Pittsburgh, PA 15220-2503, USA

Capilla, Doug (Athlete, Baseball Player)
642 Nello Dr Apt 1
Campbell, CA 95008-4746, USA

Caplan, Lizzy (Actor)
c/o Julie Darmody *Rise Management*
6338 Wilshire Blvd
Los Angeles, CA 90048-5002, USA

Capleton (Musician)
c/o Staff Member *UTA/The Agency Group*
888 7th Ave Fl 7
New York, NY 10106-0700, USA

Capodice, John (Actor)

Capon, Edwin G (Religious Leader)
Swedenborgian Church
11 Highland Ave
Newtonville, MA 02460-1852, USA

Capone, Warren (Athlete, Football Player)
19050 Turnberry Ct
Baton Rouge, LA 70809-6606, USA

Caponera, John (Actor, Comedian)
Messina Baker Entertainment
955 Carrillo Dr Ste 100
Los Angeles, CA 90048-5400, USA

Caponi, Donna M (Athlete, Golfer)
2731 Silver River Trl
Orlando, FL 32828-7787, USA

Capp, Dick (Athlete, Football Player)
PO Box 2193
Cary, NC 27512-2193, USA

Cappadona, Robert (Bob) (Athlete, Football Player)
25 Summer St
Watertown, MA 02472-3457, USA

Cappelletti, Gino (Athlete, Football Player)
19 Louis Dr
Wellesley Hills, MA 02481-1164, USA

Cappelletti, John (Athlete, Football Player, Heisman Trophy Winner)
23791 Brant Ln
Laguna Niguel, CA 92677-1341, USA

Cappelman, Bill (Athlete, Football Player)
1506 Sydney Ln
Lynn Haven, FL 32444-2928, USA

Cappleman, William (Bill) (Athlete, Football Player)
1506 Sydney Ln
Lynn Haven, FL 32444-2928, USA

Capps, Lois (Congressman, Politician)
2231 Rayburn Hob
Washington, DC 20515-4321, USA

Capps, Matt (Athlete, Baseball Player)
6348 S Summers Cir
Douglasville, GA 30135-5450, USA

Capps, Ron (Race Car Driver)
Copenhagen Racing
1232 Distribution Way
Vista, CA 92081-8816, USA

Capps, Thomas E (Business Person)
Dominion Resources
120 Tredegar St
Richmond, VA 23219-4306, USA

Cappuzzello, George (Athlete, Baseball Player)
2024 Stillwood Pl
Windermere, FL 34786-8329, USA

Capra, Buzz (Athlete, Baseball Player)
15039 W Keswick Pl
Lockport, IL 60441-6251, USA

Capra, Francis (Actor)

Capra, Nick (Athlete, Baseball Player)
8024 E Mercer Ln
Scottsdale, AZ 85260-6562, USA

Capri, Ahna (Actor)
16547 Vanowen St Apt 209
Van Nuys, CA 91406-4710, USA

Capri, Mark (Actor)
The Blithe Spirit
225 W 44th St
the Shubert Theatre
New York, NY 10036-3964, USA

Capria, Carl (Athlete, Football Player)
6321 Colonial Dr
Whitestown, IN 46075-4001, USA

Capriati, Jennifer (Athlete, Olympic Athlete, Tennis Player)
5359 Kemkerry Rd
Zephyrhills, FL 33543-4426, USA

Caprice (Model, Music Group, Songwriter, Writer)
Mission Control
Business Center Lower Road
London SE16 2XB, UNITED KINGDOM (UK)

Caprice, Frank (Athlete, Hockey Player)
536 Lake Louise Cir Unit 202
Naples, FL 34110-7020, USA

Capshaw, Jessica (Actor)
PO Box 869
Pacific Palisades, CA 90272-0869, USA

Capshaw, Kate (Actor)
c/o Kevin Huvane *Creative Artists Agency (CAA)*
2000 Avenue of the Stars Ste 100
Los Angeles, CA 90067-4705, USA

Capuano, Chris (Athlete, Baseball Player)
19550 N Grayhawk Dr Unit 1112
Scottsdale, AZ 85255-3986, USA

Capuano, Dave (Athlete, Hockey Player)
145 Capuano Ave
Cranston, RI 02920-8200, USA

Capuano, Jack (Athlete, Coach, Hockey Player)
c/o Staff Member *Bridgeport Sound Tigers*
600 Main St Ste 1
Bridgeport, CT 06604-5106, USA

Capucill, Terese (Dancer)
Martha Graham dance Center
440 Lafayette St
New York, NY 10003-6919, USA

Caputo, Theresa (Astrologist/Medium/ Psychic, Reality Star)
33 Summer Ln
Hicksville, NY 11801-6326, USA

Capuzzi, Jim (Athlete, Football Player)
10538 Rancho Carmel Dr
San Diego, CA 92128-3627, USA

Cara, Alessia (Musician)
c/o Marty Diamond *Paradigm*
140 Broadway Ste 2600
New York, NY 10005-1011, USA

Cara, Irene (Actor, Musician)
Caramel Productions
7143 State Road 54 Ste 116
New Port Richey, FL 34653-6104, USA

Carafotes, Paul (Actor)
8033 W Sunset Blvd # 3554
West Hollywood, CA 90046-2401, USA

Caraluzzi, Joseph (Horse Racer)
40 Hudson St Apt A514
Freehold, NJ 07728-2241

Carano, Gina (Crush) (Athlete, Wrestler)
c/o Scott Karp *The Syndicate*
10203 Santa Monica Blvd Fl 5
Los Angeles, CA 90067-6416, USA

Carano, Glenn (Athlete, Football Player)
2551 E Lake Ridge Shrs
Reno, NV 89519-5787, USA

Carapella, Alfred (Al) (Athlete, Football Player)
10 Woodlot Rd
Eastchester, NY 10709-1204, USA

Carasco, DJ (Athlete, Baseball Player)
c/o Terry Bross *Turn 2 Sports Management LLC*
PO Box 27345
Scottsdale, AZ 85255-0139, USA

Carasco, Joe (King) (Music Group)
Texas Sounds
2317 Pecan St
Dickinson, TX 77539-4949, USA

Caravello, Joe (Athlete, Football Player)
633 W Palm Ave
El Segundo, CA 90245-2065, USA

Caray, Chip (Commentator)
355 Charlotte St
Saint Augustine, FL 32084-5034, USA

Carbajal, Michael (Athlete, Boxer, Olympic Athlete)
PO Box 510
Phoenix, AZ 85001-0510, USA

Carbo, Bernie (Athlete, Baseball Player)
6352 Woodside Dr S
Theodore, AL 36582-3992, USA

Carbonaro, Michael (Actor)

Carbone, Frank (Horse Racer)
6004 Dickens Ct
Norristown, PA 19403-1373, USA

Carbonell, Nestor (Actor)
128 S Larchmont Blvd
Los Angeles, CA 90004-3709, USA

Carbonneau, Guy (Athlete, Coach, Hockey Player)
c/o Staff Member *Montreal Canadiens*
1275 Rue Saint-Antoine O
Montreal, QC H3C 5L2, Canada

Carcaterra, Lorenzo (Producer, Writer)
c/o Staff Member *The Pitt Group*
275 Homewood Rd
Los Angeles, CA 90049-2709, USA

Carcieri, Donald (Politician)
PO Box 701
Saunderstown, RI 02874-0701, USA

Card, Andrew (Politician)
White House
10 Meetinghouse Rd
Jaffrey, NH 03452-5126, USA

Card, Michael (Music Group, Musician)
416 Brick Path Ln
Franklin, TN 37064-3174, USA

Card, Orson Scott (Writer)
401 Willoughby Blvd
Greensboro, NC 27408-3135, USA

Cardarople, Matty (Actor, Comedian)
c/o Marissa Mooney *Rogers & Cowan*
1840 Century Park E Fl 18
Los Angeles, CA 90067-2101, USA

Cardellini, Linda (Actor)
c/o Paul Nelson *Mosaic Media Group*
407 N Maple Dr # 100
Beverly Hills, CA 90210-3818, USA

Cardenal, Jose D (Athlete, Baseball Player)
118 Bridgewater Ct
Bradenton, FL 34212-9302, USA

Cardenas, Clayton (Actor)
c/o Marni Rosenzweig *The Rosenzweig Group*
8840 Wilshire Blvd # 111
Beverly Hills, CA 90211-2606, USA

Cardenas, Leo (Athlete, Baseball Player)
5412 Ravenna St
Cincinnati, OH 45227-1718, USA

Carder, Tank (Athlete, Football Player)
c/o Kelli Masters *Kelli Masters Management*
100 N Broadway Ave Ste 1700
Oklahoma City, OK 73102-8805, USA

Cardigans, The (Music Group)
c/o Larry Webman *Paradigm*
140 Broadway Ste 2600
New York, NY 10005-1011, USA

Cardille, Lori (Actor)
c/o Tracey Goldblum *Abrams Artists Agency*
275 7th Ave Fl 26
New York, NY 10001-6708, USA

Cardin, Benjamin L. (Senator)
509 Hart Senate Office Building
Washington, DC 20510-0001, USA

Cardin, Claude (Athlete, Hockey Player)
13 Rue Boucher
Sorel-Tracy, QC J3P 1E7, Canada

Cardin, Pierre (Designer, Fashion Designer)
59 Rue du Foubourg-St-Honore
Paris 75008, FRANCE

Cardinahl, Jessika (Actor)
Galerie Am Arkonaplatz
Wolliner Str. 11
Berlin D-10435, Germany

Cardinal, Brian (Athlete, Basketball Player)
1680 Lane 105
Lake James
Angola, IN 46703-8533, USA

Cardinal, Conrad (Athlete, Baseball Player)
162 E Hunter Ln
Central, UT 84722-3221, USA

Cardinal, Randy (Baseball Player)
Houston Colt 45's
3810 W Verde Way
North Las Vegas, NV 89031-4812, USA

Cardinale, Claudia (Actor)
Via Flaminia Km 77
Prima Porta
Rome 00188, ITALY

Cardinalem, Lindsey (Musician)

Cardle, Matt (Musician)
c/o Staff Member *Sony Music Entertainment (UK)*
9 Derry St
London W8 5HY, UK

Cardona, Manolo (Actor)
c/o Nina Shaw *Del Shaw Moonves Tanaka Finkelstein & Lezcano*
2029 Century Park E Ste 1750
Los Angeles, CA 90067-3036, USA

Cardone, Grant (Business Person, Writer)
c/o Sheri Hamilton *Grant Cardone Productions*
300 71st St Ste 620
Miami Beach, FL 33141-3089, USA

Cardone, Vivien (Actor)
c/o Staff Member *Persona Management*
40 E 9th St Apt 11J
Suite 11J
New York, NY 10003-6426, USA

Cardos, John Bud (Director)

Cardosa, Patricia (Director)
c/o Staff Member *ICM Partners*
10250 Constellation Blvd Fl 7
Los Angeles, CA 90067-6207, USA

Cardoso, Patricia (Director)
c/o Rosalie Swedlin *Anonymous Content*
3532 Hayden Ave
Culver City, CA 90232-2413, USA

Cardoza, Dennis (Congressman, Politician)
2437 Rayburn Hob
Washington, DC 20515-1010, USA

Care, Danny (Athlete, Rugby Player)
c/o Staff Member *Quins Rugby Union*
Twickenham Stoop Stadium
Langhorn Drive, Twickenham
Middlesex TW2 7SX, UNITED KINGDOM

Carell, Steve (Actor)
PO Box 339
Marshfield Hills, MA 02051-0339, USA

Carelli, Rick (Race Car Driver)
PO Box 1000
Arvada, CO 80001-1000, USA

Carenard, Brian (Saigon) (Musician)
Abandoned Nation Ent. Inc.
86-110 Orchard St Ste 2
Hackensack, NJ 07601-4833, USA

Caretto-Brown, Patty (Swimmer)
16079 Mesquite Cir
Santa Ana, CA 92708-1513, USA

Carew, Rod (Athlete, Baseball Player)
4271 Vale St
Irvine, CA 92604-2208, USA

Carey, Clare (Actor)
c/o Mark Measures *Kazarian, Measures, Ruskin & Associates*
5200 Lankershim Blvd Ste 820
N Hollywood, CA 91601-3194, USA

Carey, Danny (Musician)
2174 Canyon Dr
Los Angeles, CA 90068-3609, USA

Carey, Drew (Actor, Comedian)
c/o David DeCamillo *Gersh*
9465 Wilshire Blvd Ste 600
Beverly Hills, CA 90212-2605, USA

Carey, Duane G (Astronaut)
5938 Instone Cir
Colorado Springs, CO 80922-1716, USA

Carey, Duane G Lt Colonel (Astronaut)
5938 Instone Cir
Colorado Springs, CO 80922-1716, USA

Carey, Ezekiel (Music Group)
509 E Ridgecrest Blvd Apt A
Ridgecrest, CA 93555-3959, USA

Carey, George (Religious Leader)
University of Gloucestershire
Chancellors Office
Cheltenham GL50 2RH, UNITED KINGDOM

Carey, Jim (Athlete, Hockey Player)
5351 Hunt Club Way
Sarasota, FL 34238-4011, USA

Carey, Ka'Deem (Athlete, Football Player)
c/o Ken Zuckerman *Priority Sports & Entertainment - (LA)*
15233 Ventura Blvd Ste 718
Sherman Oaks, CA 91403-2237, USA

Carey, Marey (Adult Film Star)
c/o Pure Play Media
19800 Nordhoff Pl
Chatsworth, CA 91311-6607, USA

Carey, Mariah (Musician, Songwriter)
c/o Brett Ruttenberg *Imprint PR*
6121 W Sunset Blvd
Neuehouse
Los Angeles, CA 90028-6442, USA

Carey, Mary (Adult Film Star, Reality Star)

Carey, Michelle (Actor)
H David Moss
6063 Vineland Ave Apt B
North Hollywood, CA 91606-4986, USA

Carey, Paul (Athlete, Baseball Player)
5334 Olive Ave
Sarasota, FL 34231-2510, USA

Carey, Peter (Writer)
International Creative Mgmt
40 W 57th St Ste 1800
New York, NY 10019-4033, USA

Carey, Rick (Athlete, Swimmer)
119 Rockland Ave
Larchmont, NY 10538-1430, USA

Carey, Tony (Musician)
BMG Postfach 800149
Munich D-81601, Germany

Carey, Vernon (Athlete, Football Player)
16875 Stratford Ct
Southwest Ranches, FL 33331-1362, USA

Cargo, David F (Politician)
6422 Concordia Rd NE
Albuquerque, NM 87111-1228, USA

Carhart, Timothy (Actor)
29228 Circle Dr
Agoura Hills, CA 91301-2902, USA

Carides, Gia (Actor)
Robyn Gardiner Mgmt
397 Riley St
Surrey Hills, NSW 02010, AUSTRALIA

Carillo, Mary (Sportscaster)
390 Central Ave
Naples, FL 34102-5928, USA

Carimi, Gabe (Athlete, Football Player)

Cariou, Len (Actor)
c/o Clifford Stevens *Paradigm*
140 Broadway Ste 2600
New York, NY 10005-1011, USA

Carkner, Terry (Athlete, Hockey Player)
4 Remington Ln
Malvern, PA 19355-2896, USA

Carl, Harland (Athlete, Football Player)
1419 N Douglas St
Appleton, WI 54914-2517, USA

Carl, Jann (Television Host)
880 New Jersey Ave SE Unit 1228
Washington, DC 20003-3771, USA

Carle, Eric (Artist)
PO Box 485
Northampton, MA 01061-0485, USA

Carlei, Carlo (Director, Writer)
c/o Staff Member *Creative Artists Agency (CAA)*
2000 Avenue of the Stars Ste 100
Los Angeles, CA 90067-4705, USA

Carles Gordo, Ricardo M Cardinal (Religious Leader)
Carrer del Bisbe 5
Barcelona 08002, SPAIN

Carlesimo, PJ (Basketball Coach, Coach, Sportscaster)
1429 Willard Ave W
Seattle, WA 98119-3250, USA

Carleton, Wayne (Athlete, Hockey Player)
9846 Hwy 26 East
RR 2 LCD Collingwood
Collingwood, ON L9Y 3Z1, Canada

Carlile, Brandi (Musician)

Carlin, Brian (Athlete, Hockey Player)
103 Mt Norquay Pk SE
Calgary, AB T2Z 2R3, Canada

Carlin, John (Politician)
1208 Wyndham Heights Dr
Manhattan, KS 66503-8676, USA

Carlin, Vidal (Athlete, Football Player)
930 Palm Ave Apt 417
West Hollywood, CA 90069-4080, USA

Carlino, Lewis John (Director, Writer)
991 Oakmont St
Los Angeles, CA 90049-2228, USA

Carlisie, Rick (Basketball Player)
Boston Celtics
RR 4
Ogdensburg, NY 13669, USA

Carlisle, Belinda (Musician, Songwriter)
c/o JD Sobol *Almond Talent Management*
8217 Beverly Blvd Ste 8
W Hollywood, CA 90048-4534, USA

Carlisle, Cooper (Athlete, Football Player)
2032 Sorrelwood Ct
San Ramon, CA 94582-5004, USA

Carlisle, Jodi (Actor, Comedian)
c/o Staff Member *ICM Partners*
10250 Constellation Blvd Fl 7
Los Angeles, CA 90067-6207, USA

Carlisle, Rick (Athlete, Basketball Coach, Basketball Player, Coach)
2300 Wolf St Unit 21C
Dallas, TX 75201-7057, USA

Carlos, Bun (Musician)
6951 Belvidere Rd
Caledonia, IL 61011-9605, USA

Carlos, Emmons (Athlete, Football Player)
435 Verdi Ln
Atlanta, GA 30350-6619, USA

Carlos, Francisco (Cisco) (Athlete, Baseball Player)
6027 N 7th St
Phoenix, AZ 85014-1802, USA

Carlos, John (Athlete, Olympic Athlete, Track Athlete)
68640 Tortuga Rd
Cathedral City, CA 92234-3874, USA

Carlos, Jordan (Comedian)
c/o Scott Metzger *Paradigm*
140 Broadway Ste 2600
New York, NY 10005-1011, USA

Carlos, Roberto (Musician)
c/o Jorge Pinos *WME/IMG*
9601 Wilshire Blvd
Beverly Hills, CA 90210-5213, USA

Carlson, Amy (Actor)
c/o Estelle Lasher *Lasher Group*
1133 Avenue of the Americas Fl 27
New York, NY 10036-6710, USA

Carlson, Brendyn "'Tyce"' (Race Car Driver)
13436 Lorenzo Blvd
Carmel, IN 46074-8274, USA

Carlson, Cody (Athlete, Football Player)
3417 Foothill Ter
Austin, TX 78731-5826, USA

Carlson, Craig (Chef, Writer)
c/o Gail Parenteau *Parenteau Guidance*
132 E 35th St # J
New York, NY 10016-3892, USA

Carlson, Dale (Race Car Driver)
Mike Johnson Racing
7944 68th Loop SE
Olympia, WA 98513-5223, USA

Carlson, Dan (Athlete, Baseball Player)
Mobile Baybears 755 Boiling Brothers Blvd
Attn: Coaching Staff
Mobile, AL 36606-2505, USA

Carlson, Dan (Athlete, Baseball Player)
334 N Wickford Cir
Shreveport, LA 71115-2935, USA

Carlson, Gretchen (Television Host)
c/o Cindi Berger *PMK/BNC Public Relations*
622 3rd Ave Fl 8
New York, NY 10017-6707, USA

Carlson, Jack (Athlete, Hockey Player)
18259 Embers Ave
Farmington, MN 55024-9259, USA

Carlson, Jesse (Athlete, Baseball Player)
1461 Willard Ave Apt C
Newington, CT 06111-4545, USA

Carlson, Karen (Actor)
3700 Ventura Canyon Ave
Sherman Oaks, CA 91423-4709, USA

Carlson, Katrina (Actor)
c/o Staff Member *Sara Bennett Agency*
6404 Hollywood Blvd Ste 316
Los Angeles, CA 90028-6244, USA

Carlson, K C (Cartoonist)
DC Comics
2900 W Alameda Ave # 1
Burbank, CA 91505-4220, USA

Carlson, Kelly (Actor)
c/o Adam Griffin *LINK Entertainment*
11872 La Grange Ave
Los Angeles, CA 90025-5282, USA

Carlson, Kent (Athlete, Hockey Player)
58 Branch Tpke Unit 103
Concord, NH 03301-5779, USA

Carlson, Mark (Athlete, Baseball Player)
359 Tall Oak Trl
Tarpon Springs, FL 34688-7711, USA

Carlson, Paulette (Music Group)
Mark Sonder Music
250 W 57th St Ste 1830
New York, NY 10107-1802, USA

Carlson, Richard (Writer)
Pennsylvania State Univ
613 Moore Bldg
University Park, PA 16802-3106

Carlson, Steve (Athlete, Hockey Player)
PO Box 3476
Rancho Cordova, CA 95741-3476, USA

Carlson, Steve (Race Car Driver)
539 Brickl Rd
West Salem, WI 54669-1177, USA

Carlson, Stuart (Cartoonist)
Universal Press Syndicate
4520 Main St Ste 340
Kansas City, MO 64111-7705, USA

Carlson, Tucker (Correspondent, Journalist, Television Host)
PO Box 105366
Atlanta, GA 30348-5366, USA

Carlson, Vanessa (Musician)
c/o Kurt Steffek *Razor & Tie*
PO Box 585
New York, NY 10276-0585, USA

Carlson, Veronica (Actor)
7844 Kavanagh Ct
Sarasota, FL 34240-7906, USA

Carlton, Carl (Musician)
Randolph Enterprises
Oakland
Inkster, MI 48141, USA

Carlton, Larry (Musician)
c/o Staff Member *Paradigm (Monterey)*
404 W Franklin St
Monterey, CA 93940-2303, USA

Carlton, Steve (Athlete, Baseball Player)
Game Winner Sports
835 E 2nd Ave Ste 203
Durango, CO 81301-5488, USA

Carlton, Vanessa (Musician)
c/o Steve Kaul *UTA Music*
142 W 57th St Fl 6
New York, NY 10019-3300, USA

Carlton, Venessa (Music Group)
Peter Malkin Mgmt
410 Park Ave Ste 420
New York, NY 10022-9459, USA

Carlton, Wray (Athlete, Football Player)
29 Pine Ter
Orchard Park, NY 14127-3929, USA

Carlucci, Dave (Athlete, Baseball Player)
580 Pond St
Franklin, MA 02038-2710, USA

Carlyle, Buddy (Athlete, Baseball Player)
1532 Bardella Dr
Leander, TX 78641-3952, USA

Carlyle, Randy (Athlete, Coach, Hockey Player)
180 S Lakeview Ave
Anaheim, CA 92807-3606, USA

Carlyle, Randy (Athlete, Hockey Player)
2695 E Katella Ave
Attn Coaching Staff
Anaheim, CA 92806-5904, USA

Carlyle, Robert (Actor)
c/o Jon Rubinstein *Authentic Talent and Literary Management (NY)*
20 Jay St Ste M17
Brooklyn, NY 11201-8300, USA

Carmack, Chris (Actor)
c/o Lena Roklin *Luber Roklin Management*
5815 W Sunset Blvd Ste 208
Los Angeles, CA 90028-6481, USA

Carman, Don (Athlete, Baseball Player)
555 Murex Dr
Naples, FL 34102-5141, USA

Carman, Jon (Athlete, Football Player)
13 Nautilus Dr
Barnegat, NJ 08005-1302, USA

Carman, Patrick (Writer)
1887 Home Ave
Walla Walla, WA 99362-9059, USA

Carmazzi, Giovanni (Athlete, Football Player)
9401 Cook Riolo Rd
Roseville, CA 95747-9221, USA

Carmel, duke (Athlete, Baseball Player)
10 Pheasant Valley Dr
Coram, NY 11727-2320, USA

Carmen, Eric (Musician, Songwriter)
2155 Woodstock Rd
Gates Mills, OH 44040-9324, USA

Carmen, Julie (Actor)

Carmichael, Al (Athlete, Football Player)
72525 Desert Flower Dr
Palm Desert, CA 92260-6269, USA

Carmichael, Greg (Musician)
Monterey International
72 W Adams St # 1000
Chicago, IL 60603-5107, USA

Carmichael, Harold (Athlete, Football Player)
120 Liberty Way
Woodbury, NJ 08096-6803, USA

Carmichael, Jerrod (Comedian)
c/o Lindsay Krug *ID Public Relations*
7060 Hollywood Blvd Fl 8th
Los Angeles, CA 90028-6021, USA

Carmichael, Jesse (Musician)
8062 Woodrow Wilson Dr
Los Angeles, CA 90046-1117, USA

Carmichael, Laura (Actor)
c/o Charlotte Davies *United Agents*
12-26 Lexington St
London W1F OLE, UNITED KINGDOM

Carmichael, Paul (Athlete, Football Player)
550 Orange Ave Unit 335
Long Beach, CA 90802-7011, USA

Carmody, Steve (Athlete, Football Player)
PO Box 119
Jackson, MS 39205-0119, USA

Carmona, Cinthya (Actor)
c/o Tom Bixby *Bodhi Entertainment*
9903 Santa Monica Blvd Ste 625
Beverly Hills, CA 90212-1671, USA

Carn, Jean (Musician)
PO Box 27641
Philadelphia, PA 19118-0641, USA

Carnahan, Joe (Director)
7715 Southcliff Dr
Fair Oaks, CA 95628-7329, USA

Carnahan, Russ (Congressman, Politician)
1710 Longworth Hob
Washington, DC 20515-3206, USA

Carne, Jean (Music Group)
Walt Reeder Productions
PO Box 27641
Philadelphia, PA 19118-0641, USA

Carnegie, Dale (Business Person)
Dale Carnegie & Associates, Inc
58 S Service Rd Ste 301
Melville, NY 11747-2336, USA

Carnelly, Ray (Athlete, Football Player)
4650 Collier St Apt 135
Beaumont, TX 77706-6999, USA

Carner, Joanne (Athlete, Golfer)
3030 S Ocean Blvd Apt 325
Palm Beach, FL 33480-6610, USA

Carnes, Kim (Musician, Songwriter)
1829 Tyne Blvd
Nashville, TN 37215-4701, USA

Carnes, Ryan (Actor)
c/o Wendy Pineda *Supersonix Media*
560 W Main St Ste C PMB 337
Alhambra, CA 91801-3376, USA

Carnesecca, Lou (Basketball Coach, Coach)
18247 Midland Pkwy
Jamaica, NY 11432-1535, USA

Carnett, Eddie (Athlete, Baseball Player)
RR 1 Box 20C
Ringling, OK 73456-9701, USA

Carnevale, Mark (Athlete, Golfer)
24 Loggerhead Ln
Ponte Vedra Beach, FL 32082-2581, USA

Carney, John (Athlete, Football Player)
2950 Wishbone Way
Encinitas, CA 92024-7235, USA

Carney, Keith (Athlete, Hockey Player, Olympic Athlete)
8701 N 55th Pl # Pi
Paradise Valley, AZ 85253-2107, USA

Carney, Lester (Athlete, Olympic Athlete, Track Athlete)
986 Winton Ave
Akron, OH 44320-2846, USA

Carney, Patrick (Musician)
4330 Chickering Ln
Nashville, TN 37215-4916, USA

Carney, Reeve (Musician)
c/o Carleen Donovan *Donovan Public Relations*
30 E 20th St Ste 2FE
New York, NY 10003-1310, USA

Caro, Niki (Director, Writer)
c/o Sophy Holodnik *ICM Partners*
10250 Constellation Blvd Fl 7
Los Angeles, CA 90067-6207, USA

Caro, Robert A (Writer)
Robert A Caro Assoc
250 W 57th St Ste 2215
New York, NY 10107-2209, USA

Carolan, Brett (Athlete, Football Player)
3218 43rd Ave W
Seattle, WA 98199-2437, USA

Caroline, James C (J C) (Athlete, Football Player)
2501 Stanford Dr
Champaign, IL 61820-7634, USA

Carolla, Adam (Radio Personality, Talk Show Host)
c/o Staff Member *Jackhole Industries*
6834 Hollywood Blvd
Los Angeles, CA 90028-6116, USA

Carollo, Joe (Athlete, Football Player)
4634 Meyer Way
Carmichael, CA 95608-1144, USA

Caron, Alain (Athlete, Hockey Player)
6426 Moorings Point Cir Unit 201
Lakewood Ranch, FL 34202-1204, USA

Caron, Glenn Gordon (Director, Producer)
c/o Erwin Stoff *3 Arts Entertainment*
9460 Wilshire Blvd Fl 7
Beverly Hills, CA 90212-2713, USA

Caron, Jacques (Athlete, Hockey Player)
11105 Bullrush Ter
Lakewood Ranch, FL 34202-4149

Caron, Jason (Athlete, Golfer)
150 Silo Ridge Ln
Vilas, NC 28692-3002, USA

Caron, Leslie (Actor, Dancer)
c/o Staff Member *The Rights House (UK)*
Drury House
34-43 Russell St
London WC2B 5HA, UNITED KINGDOM

Caron, Roger (Athlete, Football Player)
10 Main St
Cheshire, CT 06410-2403, USA

Carothers, Veronica (Actor)
535 N Heatherstone Dr
Orange, CA 92869-2648, USA

Carpenetr, M scott cdr (Astronaut)
PO Box 3161
Vail, CO 81658-3161, USA

Carpenter, Andrew (Athlete, Baseball Player)
1894 SW Mistybrook Dr
Grants Pass, OR 97527-6441, USA

Carpenter, Bobby (Athlete, Football Player)
2410 Onandaga Dr
Columbus, OH 43221-3618, USA

Carpenter, Bobby (Athlete, Hockey Player)
17 Mill Pond
North Andover, MA 01845-2903, USA

Carpenter, Brian (Athlete, Football Player)
22018 Auction Barn Dr
Ashburn, VA 20148-4110, USA

Carpenter, Bubba (Athlete, Baseball Player)
4601 Saddlebrook Ave
Springdale, AR 72762-0503, USA

Carpenter, Carleton (Actor)
RR 2 Chardavoyne Road
Warwick, NY 10990, USA

Carpenter, Chad (Athlete, Football Player)
21311 S 187th Way
Queen Creek, AZ 85142-3668, USA

Carpenter, Charisma (Actor, Model)
c/o Gladys Gonzalez *John Carrabino Management*
5900 Wilshire Blvd Ste 740
Los Angeles, CA 90036-5032, USA

Carpenter, Chris (Athlete, Baseball Player)
809 S Warson Rd
Saint Louis, MO 63124-1258, USA

Carpenter, Cris (Athlete, Baseball Player)
1484 Heritage Pl
Gainesville, GA 30501-1249, USA

Carpenter, Dan (Athlete, Football Player)

Carpenter, Dave (Cartoonist)
PO Box 520
Emmetsburg, IA 50536-0520, USA

Carpenter, Ed (Race Car Driver)
Vision Racing
6803 Coffman Rd
Indianapolis, IN 46268-2561, USA

Carpenter, James (Football Player)
c/o Ken Zuckerman *Priority Sports & Entertainment - (LA)*
15233 Ventura Blvd Ste 718
Sherman Oaks, CA 91403-2237, USA

Carpenter, Jennifer (Actor)
c/o Stephanie Ritz *WME/IMG*
9601 Wilshire Blvd
Beverly Hills, CA 90210-5213, USA

Carpenter, John (Director)
PO Box 1334
Studio City, CA 91614-0334, USA

Carpenter, Katie (Actor)
c/o Ben Phelps *Emagine Content*
8033 W Sunset Blvd # 580
Los Angeles, CA 90046-2401, USA

Carpenter, Keion (Athlete, Football Player)
3820 Mabry Ridge Dr
Buford, GA 30518-1683, USA

Carpenter, Kip (Athlete, Olympic Athlete, Speed Skater)
2501 W Orange Grove Rd Unit 71
Tucson, AZ 85741-3417, USA

Carpenter, Marj C (Religious Leader)
Presbyterian Church USA
100 Witherspoon St
Louisville, KY 40202-6300, USA

Carpenter, Mary Chapin (Musician)
c/o Chris Tetzeli *Red Light Management*
455 2nd St NE
#500
Charlottesville, VA 22902-5791, USA

Carpenter, Patrick (Race Car Driver)
Team Players
500-2015 Rue Peel
Montreal, QC H3A 1T8, CANADA

Carpenter, Richard (Musician, Songwriter, Writer)
960 Country Valley Rd
Westlake Village, CA 91362-5631, USA

Carpenter, Rob (Athlete, Football Player)
1601 Wheeling Rd NE
Lancaster, OH 43130-8706, USA

Carpenter, Ron (Athlete, Football Player)
1500 Wade Haven Ct
McKinney, TX 75071-5985, USA

Carpenter, Ron (Athlete, Football Player)
1181 Chersonese Round
Mount Pleasant, SC 29464-9544, USA

Carpenter, Ron (Athlete, Football Player)
1500 Wade Haven Ct
McKinney, TX 75071-5985, USA

Carpenter, Sabrina (Actor, Musician)
c/o Bill Perlman *Foundation Media Partners*
23679 Calabasas Rd # 625
Calabasas, CA 91302-1502, USA

Carpenter, Teresa (Journalist)
Village Voice
36 Cooper Sq Frnt 1
Editorial Dept
New York, NY 10003-7118, USA

Carpenter, William S (Bill) Jr (Athlete, Football Player)
PO Box 4067
Whitefish, MT 59937-4067, USA

Carpenter, W M (Business Person)
Bausch & Lomb
1 Bausch and Lomb Pl
Rochester, NY 14604-2799, USA

Carpenter-Phinney, Connie (Athlete, Cycler, Olympic Athlete)
470 Juniper Ave
Boulder, CO 80304-1716, USA

Carper, Thomas R. (Politician)
600 W Matson Run Pkwy
Wilmington, DE 19802-1911, USA

Carpin, Frank (Athlete, Baseball Player)
4014 Park Ave
Richmond, VA 23221-1120, USA

Carpinello, James (Actor)
3721 Blue Canyon Dr
Studio City, CA 91604-3802, USA

Carr, Alan (Actor, Writer)
c/o Robin Morgan *Useful TV*
19-21 Crawford St
London W1H 2JG, UNITED KINGDOM

Carr, Antoine (Athlete, Basketball Player)
5724 Croyden Cir
Wichita, KS 67220-3119, USA

Carr, Austin (Athlete, Basketball Player)
4547 Saint Germain Blvd
Cleveland, OH 44128-6205, USA

Carr, Brandon (Athlete, Football Player)
c/o Tom Condon *Creative Artists Agency (CAA)*
401 Commerce St PH
Nashville, TN 37219-2516, USA

Carr, Catherine (Cathy) (Swimmer)
409 10th St
Davis, CA 95616-1941, USA

Carr, Chuck (Athlete, Baseball Player)
5419 E Greenway St
Mesa, AZ 85205-4360, USA

Carr, Darleen (Actor)
Abrams Artists
9200 W Sunset Blvd Ste 1125
Los Angeles, CA 90069-3610, USA

Carr, David (Athlete, Football Player)
c/o Timothy Younger *Younger & Associates*
10681 Foothill Blvd Ste 280
Rancho Cucamonga, CA 91730-7615, USA

Carr, Edwin (Athlete, Football Player)
1908 Scott Rd
Oreland, PA 19075-1519, USA

Carr, Fred (Athlete, Football Player)
6274 S 17th Pl
Phoenix, AZ 85042-4568, USA

Carr, Gene (Athlete, Hockey Player)
PO Box 57258
Sherman Oaks, CA 91413-2258, USA

Carr, Gerald (Astronaut)
49 Maple St Apt 123
Manchester Center, VT 05255-4485, USA

Carr, Gerald P Colonel (Astronaut)
49 Maple St Apt 123
Manchester Center, VT 05255-4485, USA

Carr, Gregg (Athlete, Football Player)
4314 Kennesaw Dr
Mountain Brk, AL 35213-3312, USA

Carr, Jane (Actor)
c/o Alex Irwin *Markham & Froggatt*
4 Windmill St
London W1T 1HZ, UNITED KINGDOM

Carr, Kenny (Athlete, Basketball Player, Olympic Athlete)
1210 W Adams Blvd Apt 106
Los Angeles, CA 90007-7700, USA

Carr, Levert (Athlete, Football Player)
21221 Prince Lake Ct
Crest Hill, IL 60403-1550, USA

Carr, Lloyd (Coach)
University of Michigan
Athletic Dept
Ann Arbor, MI 48109, USA

Carr, Lydell (Athlete, Football Player)
2217 Harrisburg Ln
Plano, TX 75025-5515, USA

Carr, Michael L (M L) (Athlete, Basketball Player, Coach)
134 Evergreen Dr
Marstons Mills, MA 02648-1256, USA

Carr, M L (Athlete, Basketball Player)
134 Evergreen Dr
Marstons Mills, MA 02648-1256, USA

Carr, M L (Basketball Player)
St Louis Spirits
134 Evergreen Dr
Marstons Mills, MA 02648-1256, USA

Carr, Nathaniel (Athlete, Olympic Athlete, Wrestler)
2815 Northridge Pkwy Unit 107
Ames, IA 50010-7172, USA

Carr, Roger D (Athlete, Football Player)
101 Green Forest Dr
Monroe, LA 71203-8860, USA

Carr, Steve (Director, Producer)
c/o Peter Principato *Artists First*
9465 Wilshire Blvd Ste 900
Beverly Hills, CA 90212-2608, USA

Carr, Vikki (Actor, Musician)
PO Box 780968
San Antonio, TX 78278-0968, USA

Carra, Alexis (Actor)
c/o JC Robbins *JC Robbins Management*
865 S Sherbourne Dr
Los Angeles, CA 90035-1809, USA

Carrabba, Chris (Musician)
323 NW 9th Terr
Boca Raton, FL 33486, USA

Carrack, Paul (Musician, Songwriter, Writer)
Firstars Mgmt
14724 Ventura Blvd PH
Sherman Oaks, CA 91403-3513, USA

Carradine, Cornellius ""Tank"" (Athlete, Football Player)

Carradine, Ever (Actor)
c/o Lainie Sorkin Becky *Management 360*
9111 Wilshire Blvd
Beverly Hills, CA 90210-5508, USA

Carradine, Keith (Actor, Musician, Songwriter)
c/o John Bauer *John Bauer Management*
Prefers to be contacted by email or phone.
Isaaquah, WA NA, USA

Carradine, Robert (Actor, Director, Producer)
Triple Tap Productions
5850 Canoga Ave Ste 200
Woodland Hills, CA 91367-6515, USA

Carragher, Jamie (Soccer Player)
The FA
25 Soho Square
London W1D 4FA, UNITED KINGDOM

Carrasco, Carlos (Actor)

Carrasco, D J (Athlete, Baseball Player)
1216 W 18th St
Safford, AZ 85546-3564, USA

Carre, Isabelle (Actor)
c/o Staff Member *Intertalent*
16, Rue Henri Barbusse
Paris 75005, FRANCE

Carreker, Alphonso (Athlete, Football Player)
5599 Asheforde Ln
Marietta, GA 30068-1851, USA

Carrell, Duane (Athlete, Football Player)
6525 Willow Springs Rd
Springfield, IL 62712-9501, USA

Carrell, John (Athlete, Football Player)
2303 Cliffs Edge Dr
Austin, TX 78733-6031, USA

Carreon, Mark (Athlete, Baseball Player)
413 Ashland Crk
Victoria, TX 77901-3687, USA

Carrera, Asia (Adult Film Star)
c/o Staff Member *Atlas Multimedia Inc*
9005 Eton Ave Ste C
Canoga Park, CA 91304-6533, USA

Carrera, Barbara (Actor)
9191 Burton Way
Beverly Hills, CA 90210-4932, USA

Carrera, Carlos (Director)
c/o Staff Member *Creative Artists Agency (CAA)*
2000 Avenue of the Stars Ste 100
Los Angeles, CA 90067-4705, USA

Carrera, Carmen (Actor, Model)
c/o Staff Member *Elite Model Management (Miami)*
119 Washington Ave Ste 501
Miami Beach, FL 33139-7228, USA

Carrere, Tia (Actor, Model, Producer)
c/o Kieran Maguire *The Arlook Group*
11663 Gorham Ave Apt 5
Los Angeles, CA 90049-4749, USA

Carretto, Joseph A Jr (Astronaut)
4534 E 85th St
Tulsa, OK 74137-1918, USA

Carrey, Jim (Actor, Comedian)
c/o Staff Member *JC 23 Entertainment*
11812 San Vicente Blvd
Los Angeles, CA 90049-5022, USA

Carrick, Michael (Soccer Player)
The FA
25 Soho Square
London W1D 4FA, UNITED KINGDOM

Carrie, T.J. (Athlete, Football Player)
c/o Dave Butz *Sportstars Inc*
1370 Avenue of the Americas Fl 19
New York, NY 10019-4602, USA

Carrier, Darel (Athlete, Basketball Player)
4224 Glasgow Rd
Oakland, KY 42159-6836, USA

Carrier, Derek (Athlete, Football Player)
c/o Ronald Slavin *BTI Sports Advisors*
615 South Blvd Apt C
Oak Park, IL 60302-4606, USA

Carrier, Mark A (Athlete, Football Player)
11231 Whimbrel Ct
Charlotte, NC 28278-0086, USA

Carriere, Jean P J (Writer)
Les Broussanes Domessargues
Ledignan 30350, FRANCE

Carriere, Larry (Athlete, Hockey Player)
94 Dawnbrook Ln
Buffalo, NY 14221-4932, USA

Carriere, Mathieu (Actor)
Agentur Schafer
Friesenstr 53
Cologne 50670, GERMANY

Carrigan, Anthony (Actor)
c/o Lee Wallman *Wallman Public Relations*
3859 Goldwyn Ter
Culver City, CA 90232-3103, USA

Carril, Pete (Athlete, Basketball Player, Coach)
372 Carter Rd
Princeton, NJ 08540-7422, USA

Carrillo, Cesar (Athlete, Baseball Player)
7801 Lamon Ave
Burbank, IL 60459-1522, USA

Carrillo, Elpidia (Actor)
Bresler Kelly Assoc
11500 W Olympic Blvd Ste 510
Los Angeles, CA 90064-1527, USA

Carrillo, Erick (Actor)
c/o Staff Member *Three Moons Entertainment Inc*
7040F W Sunset Blvd # 206
Los Angeles, CA 90028-7521, USA

Carrillo, Yadhira (Actor)
c/o Staff Member *Televisa*
Blvd Adolfo Lopez Mateos 232
Colonia San Angel INN
DF CP 01060, MEXICO

Carrington, Alex (Athlete, Football Player)
c/o Ashley Smith Becker *Relativity Sports*
2029 Century Park E Ste 1550
Century City, CA 90067-3000, USA

Carrington, Bob (Athlete, Basketball Player)
PO Box 131301
Carlsbad, CA 92013-1301, USA

Carrington, Chuck (Actor)
c/o Kate Edwards *Grand View Management*
578 Washington Blvd # 688
Marina Del Rey, CA 90292-5442, USA

Carrington, Darren (Athlete, Football Player)
14097 Montfort Ct
San Diego, CA 92128-4283, USA

Carrington, Debbie Lee (Actor)
Jonis
117 Wilton Dr
Los Angeles, CA 90004-4907, USA

Carrington, Rodney (Musician)
PMG Entertainment Group
1505 Atlantic St
Melbourne Beach, FL 32951-2326, USA

Carrithers, Don (Athlete, Baseball Player)
9367 Sunny Glade Ct
Elk Grove, CA 95758-4208, USA

Carroll, Ahmad (Athlete, Football Player)
1389 Pollard Dr SW
Atlanta, GA 30311-3451, USA

Carroll, Billy (Athlete, Hockey Player)
Carroll Home Improvements
239 Station St
Ajax, ON L1S 1S3, Canada

Carroll, Brian (Buckethead) (Musician)
915C W Foothill Blvd Ste 545
Claremont, CA 91711-3304, USA

Carroll, Bruce (Musician, Songwriter, Writer)
William Morris Agency
2100 W End Ave Ste 1000
Nashville, TN 37203-5240, USA

Carroll, Clay P (Athlete, Baseball Player)
12475 Burroughs Ln
Soddy Daisy, TN 37379-9119, USA

Carroll, Diahann (Actor, Musician)
9255 Doheny Rd Apt 1705
West Hollywood, CA 90069-3220, USA

Carroll, James (Athlete, Football Player)
13880 Stirling Rd
Southwest Ranches, FL 33330-3019, USA

Carroll, Jamey (Athlete, Baseball Player)
2789 Wyndham Way
Melbourne, FL 32940-5971, USA

Carroll, Jay (Athlete, Football Player)
117 Homedale Rd
Hopkins, MN 55343-8519, USA

Carroll, Jim (Athlete, Football Player)
13880 Stirling Rd
Southwest Ranches, FL 33330-3019, USA

Carroll, Joe (Athlete, Football Player)
4541 Fairfield St
Pittsburgh, PA 15201-2031, USA

Carroll, Joe Barry (Athlete, Basketball Player)
5220 Cascade Rd SW
Atlanta, GA 30331-7358, USA

Carroll, Julian (Politician)
413 Shelby St
Frankfort, KY 40601-2821, USA

Carroll, Leo (Athlete, Football Player)
78720 Iron Bark Dr
Palm Desert, CA 92211-2630, USA

Carroll, Lester (Les) (Cartoonist)
1715 Ivyhill Loop N
Columbus, OH 43229-5223, USA

Carroll, Madeline (Actor)
c/o Susan Curtis *Curtis Talent Management*
9607 Arby Dr
Beverly Hills, CA 90210-1202, USA

Carroll, Nolan (Athlete, Football Player)
c/o Chad Wiestling *Integrated Sports Management*
2120 Texas St Apt 2204
Houston, TX 77003-3054, USA

Carroll, Pat (Actor)
c/o Gabrielle Allabashi *Ellis Talent Group*
4705 Laurel Canyon Blvd Ste 300
Valley Village, CA 91607-5901, USA

Carroll, Pete (Athlete, Football Player)
c/o Staff Member *Seattle Seahawks*
12 Seahawks Way
Renton, WA 98056-1572, USA

Carroll, Rocky (Actor)
c/o Erik Kritzer *LINK Entertainment*
11872 La Grange Ave
Los Angeles, CA 90025-5282, USA

Carroll, Ron (Ronnie) (Athlete, Football Player)
3320 La Vista Ave
Bay City, TX 77414-2793, USA

Carroll, Sonny (Athlete, Baseball Player)
3311 Lawson St
Richmond, VA 23224-1853, USA

Carroll, Tom (Athlete, Baseball Player)
38572 Pheasant Hill Ln
Hamilton, VA 20158-3302, USA

Carroll, Tom (Tommy) (Athlete, Baseball Player)
304 Sonnet Ct
Peachtree City, GA 30269-3357, USA

Carroll, Wesley (Athlete, Football Player)
11740 SW 102nd St
Miami, FL 33186-2734, USA

Carroll, Willard (Director, Producer, Writer)
c/o Staff Member *Hyperion Pictures*
111 N Artsakh St Ste 300
Glendale, CA 91206-4097, USA

Carrozzi, Chris (Athlete, Hockey Player)
101 Marietta St NW Ste 1900
Atlanta, GA 30303-2771

Carruth, Paul (Athlete, Football Player)
388 Calumet Way
Trussville, AL 35173-3247, USA

Carruth, Rae (Athlete, Football Player)
12653 Tucker Crossing Ln
Charlotte, NC 28273-4746, USA

Carruthers, Dwight (Athlete, Hockey Player)
9513 W Nelson Dr
Nine Mile Falls, WA 99026-9620, USA

Carruthers, Garrey E (Politician)
1 Mansion Dr
Santa Fe, NM 87501-6904, USA

Carruthers, James H (Red) (Skier)
8 Malone Ave
Garnerville, NY 10923-1812, USA

Carruthers, Peter (Athlete, Figure Skater, Olympic Athlete)
5749 Valerie Ave
Woodland Hills, CA 91367-3968, USA

Carsey, Marcy (Producer)
c/o Staff Member *Carsey-Werner Company*
16027 Ventura Blvd Ste 600
Encino, CA 91436-2798, USA

Carson, Andre (Congressman, Politician)
425 Cannon Hob
Washington, DC 20515-2301, USA

Carson, Ben (Doctor)
Johns Hopkins University Medical Center
Pediatrics Surgery Dept
Baltimore, MD 21218, USA

Carson, Carlos A (Athlete, Football Player)
4747 W 150th Ter
Overland Park, KS 66224-3410, USA

Carson, Crystal (Actor)
6725 McLennan Ave
Van Nuys, CA 91406-5542, USA

Carson, David (Director)
c/o Chris Simonian *Creative Artists Agency (CAA)*
2000 Avenue of the Stars Ste 100
Los Angeles, CA 90067-4705, USA

Carson, Harold (Athlete, Football Player)
Harry Carson Inc
PO Box 882
Franklin Lakes, NJ 07417-0882, USA

Carson, Hunter (Actor)
c/o Staff Member *Elkins Entertainment*
8306 Wilshire Blvd # 438
Beverly Hills, CA 90211-2304, USA

Carson, James (Jimmy) (Athlete, Hockey Player)
1154 Ridgeway Dr
Rochester, MI 48307-1771, USA

Carson, Jeff (Musician)
1104 Hunting Creek Rd
Franklin, TN 37069-4754, USA

Carson, Leonardo (Athlete, Football Player)
9728 Windy Hollow Dr
Irving, TX 75063-5008

Carson, Lindsay (Athlete, Hockey Player)
5050 40th Street
NE, Calgary T3J 4P8, Canada

Carson, Lisa Nicole (Actor)
c/o Scott Zimmerman *Scott Zimmerman Management*
901 N Highland Ave
Los Angeles, CA 90038-2412, USA

Carson, Malcolm (Athlete, Football Player)
PO Box 11847
Birmingham, AL 35202-1847, USA

Carson, Matt (Athlete, Baseball Player)
33352 Madera De Playa
Temecula, CA 92592-9289, USA

Carson, Rachelle (Actor)
c/o Anthony Turk *Turk Entertainment Public Relations & Productions*
358 S Cochran Ave Apt 103
Los Angeles, CA 90036-3349, USA

Carson, Sofia (Actor)
c/o Meghan Prophet *PMK/BNC Public Relations*
1840 Century Park E Ste 1400
Los Angeles, CA 90067-2115, USA

Carstens, Jordan (Athlete, Football Player)
2487 140th St
Bagley, IA 50026-8558, USA

Carswell, Dwayne (Athlete, Football Player)
8202 Abbeyfield Dr
Jacksonville, FL 32277-0966, USA

Carswell, Robert (Athlete, Football Player)
6553 Wellington Chase Ct
Lithonia, GA 30058-6497, USA

Cartagena, Victoria (Actor)
c/o Larry Taube *Principal Entertainment*
9255 W Sunset Blvd Ste 500
Los Angeles, CA 90069-3301, USA

Carter, Aaron (Actor, Musician)
c/o Steve Honig *Honig Company, The*
4804 Laurel Canyon Blvd # 828
Studio City, CA 91607-3717, USA

Carter, Alex (Actor)
c/o Rich Caplan *Noble Caplan Abrams*
1260 Yonge St 2nd Fl
Toronto, ON M4T 1W5, CANADA

Carter, Allen (Athlete, Football Player)
13133 Le Parc Unit 609
Chino Hills, CA 91709-4025, USA

Carter, Andy (Athlete, Baseball Player)
106 Montgomery Ave
Glenside, PA 19038-8228, USA

Carter, Anson (Athlete, Hockey Player)
820 Haven Oaks Ct NE
Atlanta, GA 30342-4348, USA

Carter, Anthony (Athlete, Basketball Player)
4314 Danielson Dr
Lake Worth, FL 33467-3628, USA

Carter, Anthony (Athlete, Football Player)
4314 Danielson Dr
Lake Worth, FL 33467-3628, USA

Carter, Antonio (Athlete, Football Player)
7839 Maple Grove Dr
Lewis Center, OH 43035-9350, USA

Carter, Bernard (Athlete, Football Player)
261 Pinestraw Cir
Altamonte Springs, FL 32714-5416, USA

Carter, Betsy (Musician)
7561 Brush Lake Rd
North Lewisburg, OH 43060-9649

Carter, Billy (Athlete, Hockey Player)
28 Dale St RR 3
Ingleside, ON K0C 1M0, Canada

Carter, Bruce (Athlete, Football Player)
c/o Carl Carey *Champion Pro Consulting Group*
3547 Ruth St
Houston, TX 77004-5515, USA

Carter, Carl (Athlete, Football Player)
3256 Centennial Rd
Forest Hill, TX 76119-7103, USA

Carter, Carl (Athlete, Football Player)
7568 Kings Trl
Fort Worth, TX 76133-8346, USA

Carter, Cheryl (Actor)
CunninghamEscottDipene
10635 Santa Monica Blvd Ste 130
Los Angeles, CA 90025-8306, USA

Carter, Chris (Athlete, Football Player)
4219 Cornell Xing NW
Kennesaw, GA 30144-6128, USA

Carter, Chris (Producer)
566 Picacho Ln
Montecito, CA 93108-1223, USA

Carter, Clarence (Musician)
Rodgers Redding
1048 Tattnall St
Macon, GA 31201-1537, USA

Carter, Clarence (Athlete, Basketball Player)
300 Love St SW
Atlanta, GA 30315-1048, USA

Carter, Cris (Athlete, Football Player)
1970 Parkside Cir S
Boca Raton, FL 33486-8579, USA

Carter, Darren (Comedian)
c/o Staff Member *AKA Talent Agency*
325 N Larchmont Blvd
Los Angeles, CA 90004-3011, USA

Carter, David (Athlete, Football Player)
2401 Long Reach Dr
Sugar Land, TX 77478-4127, USA

Carter, Deana (Musician, Songwriter)
7708 Waring Ave
Los Angeles, CA 90046-7318, USA

Carter, Deanna (Actor, Musician)
c/o John Huie *Creative Artists Agency (CAA)*
401 Commerce St PH
Nashville, TN 37219-2516, USA

Carter, Dexter (Athlete, Football Player)
7130 Nesters Dr
Tallahassee, FL 32312-6740, USA

Carter, Dr Jay (Writer)
PO Box 6048
Wyomissing, PA 19610-0048, USA

Carter, Duane (Pancho) (Race Car Driver)
32 Forest
Brownsburg, IN 46112, USA

Carter, Dyshod (Athlete, Football Player)
16208 N 162nd Ln
Surprise, AZ 85374-5771, USA

Carter, Finn (Actor)
c/o Craig Dorfman *Frontline Management*
5670 Wilshire Blvd Ste 1370
Los Angeles, CA 90036-5649, USA

Carter, Fred (Athlete, Basketball Player)
2617 Dekalb Pike
Norristown, PA 19401-1845, USA

Carter, Frederick J (Fred) (Baseball Player, Coach)
5070 Parkside Ave # 3500
Philadelphia, PA 19131-4747, USA

Carter, Gerald (Athlete, Football Player)
3917 Cheshire Ct
Bryan, TX 77802-4905, USA

Carter, Graydon (Writer)
Vanity Fair Magazine
4 Times Sq
Basement C1B
New York, NY 10036-6518, USA

Carter, Hodding (Journalist)
1643 Brickell Ave Apt 3604
Miami, FL 33129-1297, USA

Carter, Howard (Athlete, Basketball Player)
8026 Jefferson Hwy Apt 112
Baton Rouge, LA 70809-1661, USA

Carter, Jake (Athlete, Basketball Player)
4632 Country Creek Dr Apt 1220
Dallas, TX 75236-1253, USA

Carter, Jay (Musician)
Brothers Mgmt
141 Dunbar Ave
Fords, NJ 08863-1551, USA

Carter, Jeff (Athlete, Baseball Player)
4625 River Overlook Dr
Valrico, FL 33596-7878, USA

Carter, Jim (Actor)
c/o Belinda Wright *CDA*
167-169 Kensington High St
London W8 6SH, UNITED KINGDOM

Carter, Jim (Athlete, Football Player)
1500 Morning Glory Ln
Wausau, WI 54401-7686, USA

Carter, Jim (Athlete, Golfer)
12575 N 130th Way
Scottsdale, AZ 85259-3542, USA

Carter, Jimmy (Politician)
The Carter Center
453 John Lewis Freedom Pkwy NE
Atlanta, GA 30307-1406, USA

Carter, Jodie (Athlete, Football Player)
5921 Timberview Rd
Little Rock, AR 72204-8559, USA

Carter, Joe (Athlete, Baseball Player)
3000 W 117th St
Leawood, KS 66211-2923, USA

Carter, Joelle (Actor)
c/o Bryan deCastro *East 2 West Collective*
11022 Santa Monica Blvd Ste 350
Los Angeles, CA 90025-7532, USA

Carter, John (Athlete, Hockey Player)
21 Chase Dr
Sharon, MA 02067-2961, USA

Carter, John (Musician)
Resort Attractions
2375 E Tropicana Ave # 304
Las Vegas, NV 89119-6564, USA

Carter, Kent (Athlete, Football Player)
18657 Klum Pl
Rowland Heights, CA 91748-4851, USA

Carter, Kevin (Athlete, Football Player)
1070 Vaughn Crest Dr
Franklin, TN 37069-7211, USA

Carter, Kevin (Athlete, Football Player)
17111 Journeys End Dr
Odessa, FL 33556-2442, USA

Carter, Ki-Jana (Athlete, Football Player)
1293 NW 121st Ave
Plantation, FL 33323-2441, USA

Carter, Lance (Athlete, Baseball Player)
13805 18th Pl E
Bradenton, FL 34212-9181, USA

Carter, Larry (Athlete, Baseball Player)
4305 Wilmette Dr
Denton, TX 76208-4823, USA

Carter, Louis (Athlete, Football Player)
8209 Swamp Rose Pl
Laurel, MD 20724-1963, USA

Carter, Lyle (Athlete, Hockey Player)
13 Hamilton Ave
Brookfield, NS B0N 1C0, Canada

Carter, Lynda (Actor)
c/o Staff Member *PSG/PR*
333 W 39th St Rm 604
New York, NY 10018-1460, USA

Carter, Marty (Athlete, Football Player)
1397 Waterford Green Dr
Marietta, GA 30068-2927, USA

Carter, Mel (Musician)
c/o Staff Member *Cape Entertainment Inc*
8432 NW 31st Ct
Sunrise, FL 33351-8901, USA

Carter, Michael (Actor)
London Mgmt
2-4 Noel St
London W1V 3RB, UNITED KINGDOM (UK)

Carter, Michael D (Athlete, Football Player)
901 Red Oak Creek Dr
Red Oak, TX 75154-3615, USA

Carter, Mike (Athlete, Football Player)
10705 Celeo Ln
San Jose, CA 95127-2706, USA

Carter, Mike (Baseball Player)
Atlanta Braves
12215 Magnolia Crescent Dr Apt D
Roswell, GA 30075-5568, USA

Carter, M L (Athlete, Football Player)
PO Box 1971
Seaside, CA 93955-1971, USA

Carter, M L (Athlete, Football Player)
1765 Napa St
Seaside, CA 93955-4018, USA

Carter, Nathan (Actor)
c/o Norbert Abrams *Noble Caplan Abrams*
1260 Yonge St Fl 2
Toronto, ON M4T 1W5, CANADA

Carter, Nick (Musician, Songwriter)
c/o Jack Ketsoyan *EMC / Bowery*
8356 Fountain Ave Apt E1
W Hollywood, CA 90069-2968, USA

Carter, Pat (Athlete, Football Player)
11321 Cambray Creek Loop
Riverview, FL 33579-3920, USA

Carter, Perry (Athlete, Football Player)
15719 Sweeney Park Ln
Houston, TX 77084-2281, USA

Carter, Quinton (Athlete, Football Player)
c/o Kelli Masters *Kelli Masters Management*
100 N Broadway Ave Ste 1700
Oklahoma City, OK 73102-8805, USA

Carter, Rodney (Athlete, Football Player)
4490 Jasmine Dr
Bethlehem, PA 18020-8840, USA

Carter, Rosalynn (Politician)
Carter Center
The Carter Center 453 Freedom Pkwy NE
Atlanta, GA 30307-1406, USA

Carter, Rubin (Athlete, Coach, Football Player)
PO Box 12773
Tallahassee, FL 32317-2773, USA

Carter, Rublin (Athlete, Football Player)
PO Box 12773
Tallahassee, FL 32317-2773, USA

Carter, Russell (Athlete, Football Player)
216 Lilac Ln
Douglassville, PA 19518-1121, USA

Carter, Sarah (Actor)
c/o Darren Goldberg *Global Creative*
1051 Cole Ave # B
Los Angeles, CA 90038-2601, USA

Carter, Steve (Athlete, Baseball Player)
13006 Innisbrook Dr
Beltsville, MD 20705-1196, USA

Carter, Terry (Actor)
244 Madison Ave # 332
New York, NY 10016-2817, USA

Carter, Thomas (Director)
140 N Tigertail Rd
Los Angeles, CA 90049-2706, USA

Carter, Tim (Athlete, Football Player)
4860 26th Ct S
Saint Petersburg, FL 33712-4322, USA

Carter, Tom (Athlete, Football Player)
4548 Bristol Ln
Cincinnati, OH 45229-1214, USA

Carter, Tom (Athlete, Golfer)
3787 County Line Rd
Quakertown, PA 18951-2085, USA

Carter, Tony (Athlete, Football Player)
c/o Sean Kiernan *Impact Sports (LA)*
12429 Ventura Ct
Studio City, CA 91604-2417, USA

Carter, Travis (Race Car Driver)
Carter Motorsports
2668 Peachtree Rd
Statesville, NC 28625-8252, USA

Carter, Troy (Business Person, Producer)
c/o Troy Carter *Atom Factory/Coalition Media Group*
PO Box 927
Culver City, CA 90232-0927, USA

Carter, Vince (Athlete, Basketball Player)
PO Box 9596
Daytona Beach, FL 32120-9596, USA

Carter, Virgil (Athlete, Football Player)
PO Box 9
Helendale, CA 92342-0009, USA

Carteris, Gabrielle (Actor)
c/o Staff Member *Screen Actors Guild (SAG)*
5757 Wilshire Blvd Ste 124
Los Angeles, CA 90036-3792, USA

Carter Jr, Wendell (Athlete, Basketball Player)
c/o Joby Branion *Vanguard Sports Group*
23091 Mill Creek Dr
Laguna Hills, CA 92653-1258, USA

Carter's Chord (Music Group)
c/o Staff Member *Paradigm (Monterey)*
404 W Franklin St
Monterey, CA 93940-2303, USA

Carthen, Jason (Athlete, Football Player)
10310 Townley Ct
Aurora, OH 44202-8147, USA

Carthy, Eliza (Musician)
c/o Staff Member *UTA/The Agency Group*
888 7th Ave Fl 7
New York, NY 10106-0700, USA

Cartier, Jean-Yves (Athlete, Hockey Player)
815 Bel-Air St
Montreal, QC H4C 2K4, Canada

Cartwright, Angela (Actor)
Rubber Boots
11333 Moorpark St # 433
N Hollywood, CA 91602-2618, USA

Cartwright, Bill (Athlete, Basketball Player)
PO Box 909
Lake Forest, IL 60045-0909, USA

Cartwright, Nancy (Actor)
The Nancy Show
9420 Reseda Blvd Bldg 572
Northridge, CA 91324-2932, USA

Cartwright, Rock (Athlete, Football Player)
231 Interstate 45 N Apt 21115
Conroe, TX 77304-2326, USA

Cartwright, Ryan (Actor)
c/o Jamie Hughes *Paradigm*
140 Broadway Ste 2600
New York, NY 10005-1011, USA

Cartwright, Veronica (Actor)
c/o Mitch Clem *Mitch Clem Management*
7080 Hollywood Blvd Ste 1100
Hollywood, CA 90028-6938, USA

Carty, Jay (Athlete, Basketball Player)
5425 Lower Honoapiilani Rd
Lahaina, HI 96761-8766, USA

Carty, Johndale (Athlete, Football Player)
PO Box 552076
Opa Locka, FL 33055-0076, USA

Carty, Rico (Athlete, Baseball Player)
5 Ens Enriquillo
San Pedro de Macoris, Dominician Republic

Caruana, Peter R (Politician)
Chief Minister's Office
10/3 Irish Town
GIBRALTAR

Caruso, David (Actor)
c/o Jason Weinberg *Untitled Entertainment*
350 S Beverly Dr Ste 200
Beverly Hills, CA 90212-4819, USA

Caruso, D.J. (Director)
c/o Geyer Kosinski *Media Talent Group*
9200 W Sunset Blvd Ste 550
Los Angeles, CA 90069-3611, USA

Caruso, Mike (Athlete, Baseball Player)
900 N Ocean Blvd Apt E
Pompano Beach, FL 33062-4045, USA

Caruso, Sophia Anne (Actor, Musician)
c/o Judy Katz *Judy Katz Public Relations*
1345 Avenue Of The Americas Fl 2
New York, NY 10105-0014, USA

Carver, Brent (Actor, Musician)
Live Entertainment
1500 Broadway Ste 902
New York, NY 10036-4055, USA

Carver, Charlie (Actor)
c/o Lindsey Ludwig-Rahm *Viewpoint Inc*
89 5th Ave Ste 402
New York, NY 10003-3020, USA

Carver, Dale (Athlete, Football Player)
939 Wc Stafford St
Titusville, FL 32780-7701, USA

Carver, Dana (Actor, Comedian)
775 E Blithedale Ave # 501
Mill Valley, CA 94941-1554, USA

Carver, Jeremy (Producer)
2004 La Brea Ter
Los Angeles, CA 90046-2314, USA

Carver, Johnny (Musician)
House of Talent
9 Lucy Ln
Sherwood, AR 72120-3612, USA

Carver, Max (Actor)
c/o Lindsey Ludwig-Rahm *Viewpoint Inc*
89 5th Ave Ste 402
New York, NY 10003-3020, USA

Carver, Melvin (Mel) (Athlete, Football Player)
10840 Breaking Rocks Dr
Lithia, FL 33547, USA

Carver, Randall (Actor)
Tyler Kjar
5144 Vineland Ave
North Hollywood, CA 91601-3849, USA

Carver, Shante (Athlete, Football Player)
2834 S Extension Rd Unit 2033
Mesa, AZ 85210-8290, USA

Carveth-Dunn, Betty (Athlete, Baseball Player, Commentator)
11531 77 Ave NW
Edmonton, AB T6G 0M2, CANADA

Carvey, Dana (Actor)
1 Roosevelt Ave
Mill Valley, CA 94941-1127, USA

Carvilie, C James Jr (Politician)
209 Pennsylvania Ave SE # 800
Washington, DC 20003-1107, USA

Carville, James (Journalist)
1711 Palmer Ave
New Orleans, LA 70118-6115, USA

Carville, James (Television Host)
424 S Washington St
Alexandria, VA 22314-4100, USA

Cary, Chuck (Athlete, Baseball Player)
1016 Stephen Dr
Niceville, FL 32578-2330, USA

Cary, Diane (Baby Peggy) Serra (Actor)
712 5th Ave
Gustine, CA 95322-1537, USA

Cary, Duane G (Astronaut)
5938 Instone Cir
Colorado Springs, CO 80922-1716, USA

Cary, W Sterling (Religious Leader)
2344 Vardon Ln
Flossmoor, IL 60422-1363, USA

Cary Brothers (Music Group)
c/o Staff Member *Paradigm (Monterey)*
404 W Franklin St
Monterey, CA 93940-2303, USA

Casablancas, Julian (Musician, Songwriter)

Casados, Eloy (Actor)
c/o Michelle Gordon *Michelle Gordon & Assoc*
401 Shirley Pl Apt 204
Beverly Hills, CA 90212-4135, USA

Casados, Rene (Actor)
c/o Staff Member *Televisa*
Blvd Adolfo Lopez Mateos 232
Colonia San Angel INN
DF CP 01060, MEXICO

Casady, Jack (Musician)
Ron Rainey Mgmt
315 S Beverly Dr Ste 407
Beverly Hills, CA 90212-4301, USA

Casale, Gerald (Musician)
7960 Fareholm Dr
Los Angeles, CA 90046-2113, USA

Casale, Jerry (Athlete, Baseball Player)
735 Stevens Ct
Paramus, NJ 07652-3706, USA

Casali, Kim (Cartoonist)
Times-Mirror Syndicate
Times-Mirror Square
Los Angeles, CA 90053, USA

Casals, Rosemary (Rosie) (Athlete, Tennis Player)
c/o Staff Member *Women's Tennis Association (WTA-US)*
1 Progress Plz Ste 1500
St Petersburg, FL 33701-4335, USA

Casanega, Ken (Athlete, Football Player)
37405 Westridge Ave
Palm Desert, CA 92211-1364, USA

Casanova, Paul (Athlete, Baseball Player)
5370 NW 183rd St
Miami Gardens, FL 33055-2304, USA

Casanova, Raul (Athlete, Baseball Player)
1670 Calle Marquesa
Ponce, PR 00716-0504, USA

Casanova, Thomas H (Tommy) (Athlete, Football Player)
345 Casanova Rd
Crowley, LA 70526-0504, USA

Casar, Amira (Actor)
c/o Barbara De Premilhat *Zzo*
8 Rue Royale
Paris 75008, FRANCE

Casares, Ricardo (Rick) (Athlete, Football Player)
4107 Starfish Ln
Tampa, FL 33615-5428, USA

Cascada (Musician)
Blue Art Event GmbH
c/o Frank Ehrlich
Varlar 41
D- 48720, Rosendahl, GERMANY

Cascadden, Chad (Athlete, Football Player)
2611 Winsor Dr
Eau Claire, WI 54703-1778, USA

Case, John (Writer)
Random House
1745 Broadway Frnt 3 # B1
New York, NY 10019-4343, USA

Case, J Scott (Athlete, Football Player)
4930 Price Dr
Suwanee, GA 30024-4186, USA

Case, Ronald (Ron) (Athlete, Football Player)
6960 Driskell Cir
Cumming, GA 30041-4714, USA

Case, Sharon (Actor)
265 S Linden Dr
Beverly Hills, CA 90212-3704, USA

Case, Steve (Business Person)
3303 Water St NW Unit 8F
Washington, DC 20007-3581, USA

Case, Stoney (Athlete, Football Player)
1813 E 49th St
Odessa, TX 79762-4524, USA

case, Walter (Horse Racer)
8795 Crow Dr
Macedonia, OH 44056-1647, USA

Case Jr, Walter (Race Car Driver)
142 Summer St
Lisbon Falls, ME 04252-9732, USA

Casel, Nitanju Bolade (Musician)
Sweet Honey Agency
PO Box 600099
Newtonville, MA 02460-0001, USA

Casella, Max (Actor)
c/o Sekka Scher *Ellipsis Entertainment Group*
175 Varick St Frnt 2
New York, NY 10014-4604, USA

Casely-Hayford, Joe (Designer, Fashion Designer)
c/o Staff Member *Joe Casely-Hayford*
128 Shoreditch High Street
London, England E1 6JE, United Kingdom

Casey, Dillon (Actor)
c/o Tim Taylor *Luber Roklin Management*
5815 W Sunset Blvd Ste 208
Los Angeles, CA 90028-6481, USA

Casey, Dwane (Basketball Coach)
c/o Warren LeGarie *Warren LeGarie Sports Management*
1108 Masonic Ave
San Francisco, CA 94117-2915, USA

Casey, Harry Wayne (Musician)
7530 Loch Ness Dr
Miami Lakes, FL 33014-6014, USA

Casey, James (Athlete, Football Player)
c/o W Vann McElroy *Select Sports Group*
2700 Post Oak Blvd Ste 1450
Houston, TX 77056-5785, USA

Casey, John D (Writer)
University of Virginia
English Dept
Charlottesville, VA 22903, USA

Casey, Jon (Athlete, Hockey Player)
32 E Lakeshore Dr
De Soto, MO 63020-3922, USA

Casey, Jurrell (Athlete, Football Player)
c/o Drew Rosenhaus *Rosenhaus Sports Representation*
3921 Alton Rd # 440
Miami Beach, FL 33140-3852, USA

Casey, Lawrence P. (Actor)
4139 Vanetta Pl
Studio City, CA 91604-2342, USA

Casey, Paddy (Musician)
c/o Staff Member *Helter Skelter (UK)*
535 Kings Rd
The Plaza
London SW10 0SZ, UNITED KINGDOM (UK)

Casey, Paul (Athlete, Golfer)
Paul Casey Foundation
72 Salcott Rd
London SW11 6DF, UNITED KINGDOM

Casey, Peter (Director)
Jim Preminger Agency
450 N Roxbury Dr Ste 1050
Beverly Hills, CA 90210-4235, USA

Casey, Sean (Athlete, Baseball Player)
40 Hartz Way Ste 10
Attn: on Air Personality
Secaucus, NJ 07094-2403, USA

Casey, Sean (Athlete, Baseball Player)
271 Trotwood Dr
Pittsburgh, PA 15241-2244, USA

Casey Jr, Robert P. (Senator)
393 Russell Senate Office Building
Washington, DC 20510-0001, USA

Cash, Antoine (Athlete, Football Player)
14441 Mirabelle Vista Cir
Tampa, FL 33626-3345, USA

Cash, Aya (Actor)
c/o Erica Gray *Viewpoint Inc*
8820 Wilshire Blvd Ste 220
Beverly Hills, CA 90211-2622, USA

Cash, Cornelius (Athlete, Basketball Player)
1661 Miami Chapel Rd
Dayton, OH 45417-4527, USA

Cash, Dave (Athlete, Baseball Player)
16308 Birkdale Dr
Odessa, FL 33556-2802, USA

Cash, Keith (Athlete, Football Player)
8505 NE 91st St
Kansas City, MO 64157-8685, USA

Cash, Kerry (Athlete, Football Player)
1414 Gator Creek Dr
Cedar Park, TX 78613-1442, USA

Cash, Kevin (Athlete, Baseball Player)
14607 Mirabelle Vista Cir
Tampa, FL 33626-3347, USA

Cash, Pat (Tennis Player)
281 Clarence St
Sydney NSW 2000, AUSTRALIA

Cash, Rick (Athlete, Football Player)
203 E Benton St
Savannah, MO 64485-1720, USA

Cash, Rosanne (Musician, Songwriter)
c/o Mike Leahy *Concerted Efforts*
PO Box 440326
Somerville, MA 02144-0004, USA

Cash, Roseanne (Musician)
1309 Boscobel St
Nashville, TN 37206-2917, USA

Cash, Sam (Athlete, Basketball Player)
25825 Karisa Cir
Moreno Valley, CA 92551-1968, USA

Cash, Swin (Athlete, Basketball Player)
Swin Cash Enterprises
1985 Lincoln Way Ste 23
White Oak, PA 15131-2415, USA

Cash, Tommy (Musician, Songwriter, Writer)
PO Box 1230
Hendersonville, TN 37077-1230, USA

Cashion, Red (Athlete, Football Player)
PO Box 3889
Bryan, TX 77805-3889, USA

Cashman, Brian (Commentator)
927 Weed St
New Canaan, CT 06840-4024, USA

Cashman, Terry (Musician)
15 Engle St
Englewood, NJ 07631-2936, USA

Cashman, Wayne (Athlete, Hockey Player)
5150 NW 80th Avenue Rd
Ocala, FL 34482-2028, USA

Cashner, Andrew (Athlete, Baseball Player)
14065 Amber Ln
Montgomery, TX 77316-2000, USA

Casian, Larry (Athlete, Baseball Player)
3845 Aberdeen St S
Salem, OR 97302-6804, USA

Casillas, Tony (Athlete, Football Player)
6201 Bay Valley Ct
Flower Mound, TX 75022-5573, USA

Casiraghi, Pierlulgi (Soccer Player)
Lazio Rorna
Via Novaro 32
Rome 00197, ITALY

Caskey, Craig (Athlete, Baseball Player)
17422 Palomino Dr
Bothell, WA 98012-6419, USA

Casnoff, Philip (Actor)
c/o Darris Hatch *Daris Hatch Management*
10027 Rossbury Pl
Los Angeles, CA 90064-4825, USA

Cason, Antoine (Athlete, Football Player)
c/o Drew Rosenhaus *Rosenhaus Sports Representation*
3921 Alton Rd # 440
Miami Beach, FL 33140-3852, USA

Cason, Aveion (Athlete, Football Player)
2916 Bahia
Grand Prairie, TX 75054-5517, USA

Caspary, Tina (Actor)
11350 Ventura Blvd Ste 206
Studio City, CA 91604-3140, USA

Casper, Colonel John H (Astronaut)
PO Box 923
Montreat, NC 28757-0923, USA

Casper, David J (Dave) (Athlete, Football Player)
11390 Kingsborough Trl
Cottage Grove, MN 55016-4664, USA

Casper, Robert (Actor)
CunninghamEscottDipene
10635 Santa Monica Blvd Ste 130
Los Angeles, CA 90025-8306, USA

Cass, Christopher (Actor)
Halpern Assoc
PO Box 5597
Santa Monica, CA 90409-5597, USA

Cassaday, Leann (Athlete, Golfer)
542 Orpheus Ave
Encinitas, CA 92024-2660, USA

Cassady, Howard (Hopalong) (Athlete, Football Player, Heisman Trophy Winner)
PO Box 7828
Talis Sports Management
Columbus, OH 43207-0828, USA

Cassar, Jon (Producer)
c/o Jeff Benson *Paradigm*
8942 Wilshire Blvd
Beverly Hills, CA 90211-1908, USA

Cassara, Frank (Athlete, Football Player)
9113 Brookshire Ave
Downey, CA 90240-2910, USA

Cassata, Rick (Athlete, Football Player)
62 Leydecker Rd Apt 3
Buffalo, NY 14224-4529, USA

Cassavetes, Nick (Actor, Director)
2067 Hercules Dr
Los Angeles, CA 90046-2014, USA

Cassel, Jack (Athlete, Baseball Player)
19427 Superior St
Northridge, CA 91324-1646, USA

Cassel, Matt (Athlete, Football Player)
150 Street of Dreams
Village Of Loch Lloyd, MO 64012-4179, USA

Cassel, Seymour (Actor)
c/o Harry Abrams *Abrams Artists Agency*
750 N San Vicente Blvd
E Tower Fl 11
Los Angeles, CA 90069-5788, USA

Cassel, Vincent (Actor)
c/o Staff Member *United Talent Agency (UTA)*
9336 Civic Center Dr
Beverly Hills, CA 90210-3604, USA

Cassell, Sam (Athlete, Basketball Player)
5205 N Charles St
Baltimore, MD 21210-2042, USA

Cassels, Andrew (Athlete, Hockey Player)
8614 Tartan Fields Dr
Dublin, OH 43017-8773, USA

Casserly, Charley (Commentator, Sportscaster)
c/o Staff Member *NFL Network*
10950 Washington Blvd Ste 100
Culver City, CA 90232-4032, USA

Cassese, Tom (Athlete, Football Player)
80 Van Buren St
Port Jefferson Station, NY 11776-3173, USA

Casseus, Gabriel (Actor)
c/o Dan Baron *Agency for the Performing Arts (APA)*
405 S Beverly Dr Ste 500
Beverly Hills, CA 90212-4425, USA

Cassevah, Bobby (Athlete, Baseball Player)
5581 Tucker Cir
Milton, FL 32571-1397, USA

Cassidy (Musician)
c/o Jeremy Katz *Katz Company, The*
1674 Broadway Fl 7
New York, NY 10019-5838, USA

Cassidy, Bill (Congressman, Politician)
1535 Longworth Hob
Washington, DC 20515-1410, USA

Cassidy, Bruce (Athlete, Coach, Hockey Player)
c/o Staff Member *Kingston Frontenacs*
PO Box 665 Stn Main
Stn Main
Kingston, ON K7L 4X1, Canada

Cassidy, Christopher (Astronaut)
1207 Spring Cress Ln
Seabrook, TX 77586-4721, USA

Cassidy, Elaine (Actor)
c/o Staff Member *ICM Partners*
10250 Constellation Blvd Fl 7
Los Angeles, CA 90067-6207, USA

Cassidy, Joanna (Actor)
c/o Bette Smith *Bette Smith Management*
499 N Canon Dr
Beverly Hills, CA 90210-4887, USA

Cassidy, Katie (Actor)
c/o Doreen Wilcox Little *Anonymous Content*
3532 Hayden Ave
Culver City, CA 90232-2413, USA

Cassidy, Michael (Actor)
c/o Vic Ramos *Vic Ramos Management*
337 E 13th St Apt 6
New York, NY 10003-5852, USA

Cassidy, Patrick (Actor)
c/o Alan Iezman *Shelter Entertainment*
9255 W Sunset Blvd Ste 300
Los Angeles, CA 90069-3313, USA

Cassidy, Ron (Athlete, Football Player)
2214 W 171st St
Torrance, CA 90504-2925

Cassidy, Ron (Athlete, Football Player)
2214 W 171st St
Torrance, CA 90504-2925, USA

Cassidy, Scott (Athlete, Baseball Player)
1006 4th St
Liverpool, NY 13088-4407, USA

Cassidy, Shaun (Actor, Musician)
Shaun Cassidy Productions
8530 Wilshire Blvd Ste 200
Beverly Hills, CA 90211-3130, USA

Cassie (Musician)
c/o James Cruz *Combs Enterprises*
1440 Broadway Frnt 3
New York, NY 10018-2301, USA

Cassivi, Frederic (Athlete, Hockey Player)
7521 Clover Lee Blvd
Harrisburg, PA 17112-8945, USA

Cassolato, Tony (Athlete, Hockey Player)
576 Camino El Dorado
Encinitas, CA 92024-3820, USA

Casson, Mel (Cartoonist)
c/o Staff Member *King Features Syndication*
300 W 57th St Fl 15
New York, NY 10019-5238, USA

Cast, Tricia (Actor)
1346 Pond Creek Rd
Ashland City, TN 37015-5517, USA

Casta, Laetitia (Actor)
Allarosa Productions
6 Bis Villa d'Alesia
Paris 75014, FRANCE

Castaneda, Pedro (Actor)
c/o Maggie Woods *Online Talent Group*
Prefers to be contacted via email or telephone
Los Angeles, CA 90069, USA

Castellaneta, Dan (Actor, Musician)
c/o Arlene Forster *Forster Entertainment*
12533 Woodgreen St
Los Angeles, CA 90066-2723, USA

Castellano, Pedro (Athlete, Baseball Player)
Parcela 63 #63-6
Cabudare Lara, Venezuela

Castellini, Clateo (Business Person)
Becton Dickinson Co
1 Becton Dr
Franklin Lakes, NJ 07417-1880, USA

Castellini, Robert (Commentator)
2180 Grandin Rd
Cincinnati, OH 45208-3306, USA

Castelluccio, Frederico (Actor)
c/o Robyn Ziegler *Robyn Ziegler Management*
30 Irving Pl Fl 6
New York, NY 10003-2303, USA

Caster, Rich (Athlete, Football Player)
8127 156th Ave
Howard Beach, NY 11414, USA

Castete, Jesse (Athlete, Football Player)
302 W Lee St
Sulphur, LA 70663-5440, USA

Castiglione, Joe (Commentator)
Boston Red Sox
100 King Phillips Pathe
Marshfield, MA 02050-5714, USA

Castilla, Vinny (Athlete, Baseball Player)
7680 Polo Ridge Dr
Littleton, CO 80128-2502, USA

Castille, Jeremiah (Athlete, Football Player)
2904 Kirkcaldy Ln
Birmingham, AL 35242-4117, USA

Castillio, Susie (Actor, Beauty Pageant Winner)
c/o Gordon Gilbertson *Gilbertson Management*
1334 3rd Street Promenade Ste 201
Santa Monica, CA 90401-1320, USA

Castillo, Alberto (Athlete, Baseball Player)
13600 Coco Palm Ct
Bakersfield, CA 93314-6662, USA

Castillo, Alberto (Athlete, Baseball Player)
400 SW Lakota Ave
Port Saint Lucie, FL 34953-3029, USA

Castillo, Carmen (Athlete, Baseball Player)
344 Prospect Ave Apt 6A
Hackensack, NJ 07601-2603, USA

Castillo, Joey (Musician)
1456 Angelus Ave
Los Angeles, CA 90026-2209, USA

Castillo, Luis (Athlete, Baseball Player)
10782 Hawks Vista St
Plantation, FL 33324-8212, USA

Castillo, Luis (Athlete, Football Player)
14165 Augusta Ct
Poway, CA 92064-6645

Castillo, Manny (Athlete, Baseball Player)
2300 El Jobean Rd
Port Charlotte, FL 33948-1109, USA

Castillo, Marty (Athlete, Baseball Player)
1700 Windover Pl
St Augustine, FL 32092-2426, USA

Castillo, Patricio (Actor)
c/o Staff Member *Televisa*
Blvd Adolfo Lopez Mateos 232
Colonia San Angel INN
DF CP 01060, MEXICO

Castillo, Rafael (De La Ghetto) (Musician)
c/o Staff Member *Baby Records Corp*
R104 Ave Galicia
Villa Venacia, Vistamar Marina
Carolina, PR 00983-1524, USA

Castillo, Raul (Actor)
c/o Michael Gasparro *Gasparro Management*
609 Degraw St
Brooklyn, NY 11217-3120, USA

Castillo, Rusney (Athlete, Baseball Player)
c/o Staff Member *Boston Red Sox*
4 Jersey St
Boston, MA 02215-4148, USA

Castillo, Tony (Athlete, Baseball Player)
6402 Silverwood Dr
Huntington Beach, CA 92647-3366, USA

Castillo Lara, Rosalio Jose Cardinal (Religious Leader)
Palazzo del Governatorato
00120, VATICAN CITY

Casting Crowns (Music Group, Musician)
c/o Stacey Jannette *Proper Management*
PO Box 68
Franklin, TN 37065-0068, USA

Castino, John (Athlete, Baseball Player)
6290 Bluestern Rd S
Hamel, MN 55340-4546, USA

Castle, Don (Athlete, Baseball Player)
560 Country Club Dr
Senatobia, MS 38668-6317, USA

Castle, Eric (Athlete, Football Player)
4833 SW Evans St
Portland, OR 97219-3303, USA

Castle, John (Actor)
c/o Simon Beresford *Dalzell & Beresford Ltd*
55 Charterhouse St
The Paddock Suite, The Courtyard
London EC1M 6HA, UNITED KINGDOM (UK)

Castle, Nick (Actor, Director, Writer)
PO Box 92136
Pasadena, CA 91109-2136, USA

Castle-Hughes, Keisha (Actor)
c/o Jennifer Rawlings *Omni Artists*
9465 Wilshire Blvd Ste 900
Beverly Hills, CA 90212-2608, USA

Castleman, Foster (Athlete, Baseball Player)
2208 Spruce Ln
Oxford, OH 45056-9106, USA

Castles, Neil (Race Car Driver)
1525 Stoneyridge Dr
Charlotte, NC 28214-8656, USA

Casto, Kory (Athlete, Baseball Player)
14820 SW Village Ln
Beaverton, OR 97007-3631, USA

Castonzo, Anthony (Athlete, Football Player)
c/o Tom Condon *Creative Artists Agency (CAA)*
401 Commerce St PH
Nashville, TN 37219-2516, USA

Castor, Chris (Athlete, Football Player)
206 Connors Cir
Cary, NC 27511-6100, USA

Castor, Kathy (Congressman, Politician)
137 Cannon Hob
Washington, DC 20515-2204, USA

Castro, Bill (Athlete, Baseball Player)
5217 W Harvard Dr
Franklin, WI 53132-8192, USA

Castro, Cristian (Musician)
c/o Staff Member *BMG*
1540 Broadway
New York, NY 10036-4039, USA

Castro, Daniela (Actor)
c/o Staff Member *Televisa*
Blvd Adolfo Lopez Mateos 232
Colonia San Angel INN
DF CP 01060, MEXICO

Castro, David (Actor)
c/o Staff Member *Persona Management*
40 E 9th St Apt 11J
Suite 11J
New York, NY 10003-6426, USA

Castro, Jason (Musician)
c/o Staff Member *Atlantic Recording Corporation*
1290 Avenue of the Americas
New York, NY 10104-0101, USA

Castro, Juan (Athlete, Baseball Player)
19402 N 62nd Ave
Glendale, AZ 85308-7666, USA

Castro, Ramon (Athlete, Baseball Player)
1230 Windway Cir
Kissimmee, FL 34744-2552, USA

Castro, Raquel (Actor)
c/o Staff Member *WME|IMG*
9601 Wilshire Blvd
Beverly Hills, CA 90210-5213, USA

Castroneves, Helio (Race Car Driver)
325 Seven Isles Dr
Ft Lauderdale, FL 33301-1532, USA

Castronuova, Cara (Actor, Reality Star)
c/o Seth Greenky *Green Key Mgmt (NY)*
251 W 89th St Ste 4-A
New York, NY 10024-1712, USA

Catalanotto, Frank (Athlete, Baseball Player)
PO Box 236
Frank Catalanotto Foundation
Saint James, NY 11780-0236, USA

Catan, Pete (Athlete, Football Player)
1261 Blakely St
Woodstock, IL 60098-3631, USA

Catanho, Alcides (Athlete, Football Player)
931 Pennington St Apt 1
Elizabeth, NJ 07202-1584, USA

Catanzaro, Tony (Dancer)
3496 NW 7th St
Miami, FL 33125-4014, USA

Catchings, Harvey (Athlete, Basketball Player)
17406 Edenwalk
Spring, TX 77379-8513, USA

Catchings, Tamika (Basketball Player)
Indiana Fever
125 S Pennsylvania St
Conseco Fieldhouse
Indianapolis, IN 46204-3610, USA

Catchings, Tamika (Athlete)
125 S Pennsylvania St
Indianapolis, IN 46204-3610

Catchings, Toney (Athlete, Football Player)
6213 Zoellners Pl
Fairfield Township, OH 45011-1001

Cate, Troy (Athlete, Baseball Player)
2770 Rainbow Valley Blvd
Fallbrook, CA 92028-8857, USA

Cater, Danny (Athlete, Baseball Player)
3268 Candlewood Trl
Plano, TX 75023-1320, USA

Cater, Greg (Athlete, Football Player)
19 Warwick Way SE
Rome, GA 30161-4058, USA

Cates, Challen (Actor)
179 S Hudson Ave
Los Angeles, CA 90004-1033, USA

Cates, Dariene (Actor)
13340 FM 740
Forney, TX 75126-6802, USA

Cates, Georgina (Actor)
c/o Louisa Spring *Louisa Spring Management*
404 Carroll Canal
Venice, CA 90291-4682, USA

Cates, Phoebe (Actor)
Blue Tree
1283 Madison Ave
New York, NY 10128-0575, USA

Cathcard, Patti (Musician)
Windham Hill Records
PO Box 5501
Beverly Hills, CA 90209-5501, USA

Cathcart, Sam (Athlete, Football Player)
PO Box 4816
Santa Barbara, CA 93140-4816, USA

Cather, Mike (Athlete, Baseball Player)
12215 Magnolia Crescent Dr
Roswell, GA 30075-5568, USA

Catherwood, Mike (Radio Personality, Reality Star)
c/o Staff Member *Core Entertainment*
14742 Ventura Blvd
Penthouse
Sherman Oaks, CA 91403, USA

Catledge, Terry (Athlete, Basketball Player)
170 Hall St
Houston, MS 38851-1605, USA

Catlett, Mary Jo (Actor)
4375 Farmdale Ave
Studio City, CA 91604-2737, USA

Cato, Keefe (Athlete, Baseball Player)
98 Maryton Rd
White Plains, NY 10603-2016, USA

Cato, Kelvin (Athlete, Basketball Player)
PO Box 1400
Missouri City, TX 77459-1400, USA

Caton Jones, Michael (Director)
c/o Staff Member *WME|IMG*
9601 Wilshire Blvd
Beverly Hills, CA 90210-5213, USA

Cattage, Bobby (Athlete, Basketball Player)
4838 US Highway 29 S
Auburn, AL 36830-8184, USA

Cattaneo, Peter (Director)
International Creative Mgmt
76 Oxford St
London W1N OAX, UNITED KINGDOM (UK)

Cattermole, Paul (Actor)
Eden Lifestyle
4 Flitcroft Street
London WC2H 8D, United Kingdom

Cattrall, Kim (Actor)
c/o Danica Smith *Kovert Creative*
506 Santa Monica Blvd Ste 400
Santa Monica, CA 90401-2412, USA

Caubere, Philippe (Actor)
La Comédie Nouvelle
23 Avenue Philippe-Auguste
Paris F-75011, France

Caudill, Bill (Athlete, Baseball Player)
11605 NE 41st St
Kirkland, WA 98033-8742, USA

Cauduro, Eugenia (Actor)
c/o Staff Member *Televisa*
Blvd Adolfo Lopez Mateos 232
Colonia San Angel INN
DF CP 01060, MEXICO

Cauffiel, Jessica (Actor)
c/o Michael Greene *Greene & Associates*
1901 Avenue of the Stars Ste 130
Los Angeles, CA 90067-6030, USA

Caufield, Jay (Athlete, Hockey Player)
106 Quail Hollow Ln
Wexford, PA 15090-7596, USA

Cauley-Stein, Willie (Athlete, Basketball Player)
c/o Rich Kleiman *Roc Nation*
1411 Broadway Fl 38
New York, NY 10018-3409, USA

Caulfield, Emma (Actor)
c/o Ellen Drantch-Billet *Media Artists Group*
8222 Melrose Ave Ste 304
Los Angeles, CA 90046-6839, USA

Caulfield, Lore (Designer, Fashion Designer)
2228 Cotner Ave
Los Angeles, CA 90064-1802, USA

Caulfield, Maxwell (Actor)
c/o Staff Member *Diamond Management*
31 Percy St
London W1T 2DD, UNITED KINGDOM

Caulkins, Tracy (Athlete, Olympic Athlete, Swimmer)
511 Oman St
Nashville, TN 37203-1234, USA

Causey, Wayne (Athlete, Baseball Player)
2905 Paynter Dr
Ruston, LA 71270-5242, USA

Causwell, Duane (Athlete, Baseball Player)
3 Pierce Dr
Stony Point, NY 10980-3701

Causwell, Duane (Athlete, Basketball Player)
3 Pierce Dr
Stony Point, NY 10980-3701, USA

Cauthen, Steve (Horse Racer)
15541 Porter Rd
Verona, KY 41092-9205, USA

Cavadini, Catherine (Cathy) (Actor)
c/o Staff Member *ICM Partners*
10250 Constellation Blvd Fl 7
Los Angeles, CA 90067-6207, USA

Cavalera, Max (Musician)
Variety Artists
1111 Riverside Ave Ste 501
Paso Robles, CA 93446-2683, USA

Cavaleri, Ray (Producer)
c/o Staff Member *Cavaleri & Associates*
3500 W Olive Ave Ste 300
Burbank, CA 91505-4647, USA

Cavallari, Kristin (Actor, Reality Star)
c/o Jack Ketsoyan *EMC / Bowery*
8356 Fountain Ave Apt E1
W Hollywood, CA 90069-2968, USA

Cavalli, Carmen (Athlete, Football Player)
6221 Madison Ct
Bensalem, PA 19020-1802, USA

Cavalli, Constanza (Actor)
c/o Gabriel Blanco *Gabriel Blanco Iglesias (Mexico)*
Rio Balsas 35-32
Colonia Cuauhtemoc
DF 06500, Mexico

Cavalli, Roberto (Designer, Fashion Designer)
Via del Cantone 29
Osmannoro Sesto Florentino
Firenze 50019, ITALY

Cavallini, Gino (Athlete, Hockey Player)
6614 Clayton Rd Unit 315
Saint Louis, MO 63117-1602, USA

Cavallini, Paul (Athlete, Hockey Player)
7201 Kingsbury Blvd
Saint Louis, MO 63130-4139, USA

Cavanagh, Megan (Actor)
c/o Staff Member *Framework Entertainment*
9057 Nemo St # C
W Hollywood, CA 90069-5511, USA

Cavanagh, Tom (Actor)
c/o Daniel Pancotto *Baker Street Media*
9601 Wilshire Blvd # 1141
Beverly Hills, CA 90210-5213, USA

Cavanaugh, Joe (Athlete, Hockey Player)
25 Nathaniel Green Dr
East Greenwich, RI 02818-2019, USA

Cavanaugh, Matt (Athlete, Football Player)
644 Robinwood Dr Apt C
Pittsburgh, PA 15216-1034, USA

Cavanaugh, Matthew A (Matt) (Athlete, Football Player)
8 Barstad Ct
Lutherville Timonium, MD 21093-3501, USA

Cavanaugh, Michael (Actor)
Ambrosio/Mortimer
165 W 46th St
New York, NY 10036-2501, USA

Cavanaugh, Page (Musician)
9420 Reseda Blvd
Northridge, CA 91324-2932, USA

Cavaretta, Philip J (Phil) (Athlete, Baseball Player, Coach)
4637 Kellogg Dr SW
Lilburn, GA 30047-4407, USA

Cavazos, Andy (Athlete, Baseball Player)
244 E Bernard St
Clute, TX 77531-4609, USA

Cavazos, Lauro (Politician)
173 Annursnac Hill Rd
Concord, MA 01742-5402, USA

Cavazos, Lumi (Actor)
Visionary Entertainment
8265 W Sunset Blvd Ste 203
West Hollywood, CA 90046-2470, USA

Cave, Jessie (Actor)
c/o Dallas Smith *United Agents*
12-26 Lexington St
London W1F OLE, UNITED KINGDOM

Cave, Nick (Musician, Songwriter, Writer)
Billions Corp
833 W Chicago Ave Ste 101
Chicago, IL 60642-8408, USA

Caven, Ingrid (Actor)
Green Ufos
Parque Pisa
C/Exposición, 8, 1º izq
Mairena del Aljarafe 41927, Spain

Cavenall, Ron (Athlete, Basketball Player)
PO Box 450983
Houston, TX 77245-0983, USA

Caver, James (Athlete, Football Player)
10722 Mersington Ave
Kansas City, MO 64137-1870, USA

Caver, Quinton (Athlete, Football Player)
PO Box 335
China, TX 77613-0335, USA

Caverly, Kristen (Athlete, Olympic Athlete, Swimmer)
9 Puerto Caravaca
San Clemente, CA 92672-6054, USA

Cavett, Dick (Actor)
c/o Joanne Nici *Buchwald (NY)*
10 E 44th St
New York, NY 10017-3601, USA

Cavic, Milorad (Mike) (Swimmer)
Cal Bears Athletics
Swimming
Haas Pavilion #4422
Berkeley, CA 94720-0001, USA

Caviezel, Jim (Actor)
c/o Karynne Tencer *Tencer and Associates*
411 N Oakhurst Dr
Beverly Hills, CA 90210-4037, USA

Cavil, Kwame (Athlete, Football Player)
2005 Dan Rowe St
Waco, TX 76704-1016, USA

Cavill, Henry (Actor)
c/o Dallas Smith *United Agents*
12-26 Lexington St
London W1F OLE, UNITED KINGDOM

Cavness, Grady (Athlete, Football Player)
7007 Roberson Rd
Missouri City, TX 77489-2508, USA

Cavuto, Neil (Television Host)
55 Prentice Ln
Mendham, NJ 07945-2723, USA

Cawley, Warren (Rex) (Athlete, Track Athlete)
1655 San Rafael Dr
Corona, CA 92882-6410, USA

Caylor, Lowell (Athlete, Football Player)
403 Woodway Dr
Greer, SC 29651-6869, USA

Cayne, Candis (Actor, Model, Reality Star)
c/o Ben Russo *EMC / Bowery*
8356 Fountain Ave Apt E1
W Hollywood, CA 90069-2968, USA

Cayo, Stephanie (Actor)

Cayo, Stephanie (Actor)
c/o Andres Budnik *Vision Entertainment*
119 Hurricane St
Marina Del Rey, CA 90292-5974, USA

Cazwell (Musician)
c/o Bill Coleman *Peace Bisquit*
963 Kent Ave Bldg E
Brooklyn, NY 11205-4461, USA

Cazzette (Music Group)
c/o Staff Member *D. Baron Media Relations*
1411 Cloverfield Blvd
Santa Monica, CA 90404-2917, USA

C. Burgess, Michael (Congressman, Politician)
2241 Rayburn Hob
Washington, DC 20515-3212, USA

C. Carney Jr., John (Congressman, Politician)
1429 Longworth Hob
Washington, DC 20515-2302, USA

Ceasar, Shirley (Actor, Musician)
c/o Staff Member *M.A.G./Universal Attractions*
15 W 36th St Fl 8
New York, NY 10018-7927, USA

Ceaser, Curtis (Athlete, Football Player)
4805 Corley St
Beaumont, TX 77707-4224, USA

Ceballos, Cedric (Athlete, Basketball Player)
3068 FM 1252 W
Kilgore, TX 75662-4830, USA

Ceberano, Kate (Musician)
Richard East Productions
Kildean Lane
Winchelsea, VIC 03241, AUSTRALIA

Cechmanek, Roman (Athlete, Hockey Player)
1111 S Figueroa St
Los Angeles, CA 90015-1300, USA

Cecil, Brett (Athlete, Baseball Player)
33 Ramsgate Dr
Saint Louis, MO 63132-4116, USA

Cedano, Roger (Athlete, Baseball Player)
9325 Byron Ave
Surfside, FL 33154-2437, USA

Cedar, Larry (Actor)
12949 Hartsook St
Sherman Oaks, CA 91423-1614, USA

Cedarstrom, Gary (Athlete, Baseball Player)
1610 18th St SE
Minot, ND 58701-6087, USA

Cedeno, Cesar (Athlete, Baseball Player)
9919 Sagedowne Ln
Houston, TX 77089-4309, USA

Cedeno, Matt (Actor)
c/o Cindy Collins *Collins & Associates PR*
358 S Cochran Ave Apt 103
Los Angeles, CA 90036-3349, USA

Cedeno, Roger (Athlete, Baseball Player)
2950 NE 188th St Apt 538
Miami, FL 33180-2737, USA

Cederstrom, Gary (Athlete, Baseball Player)
220 Lago Cir Apt 101
Melbourne, FL 32904-3359, USA

Cefalo, Jimmy (Athlete, Football Player)
6675 Roxbury Ln
Miami Beach, FL 33141-4532, USA

Ceika, Alex (Athlete, Golfer)
11589 Caldicot Dr
Las Vegas, NV 89138-1541, USA

Cejka, Alex (Athlete, Golfer)
11589 Caldicot Dr
Las Vegas, NV 89138-1541, USA

Cejudo, Henry (Athlete, Olympic Athlete, Wrestler)
Novuss Media
9943 E Bell Rd
Scottsdale, AZ 85260-2530, USA

Celeda (Musician)
c/o Staff Member *Diva Central Inc*
7510 W Sunset Blvd # 1445
Los Angeles, CA 90046-3408, USA

Celek, Brent (Athlete, Football Player)
3515 S Reserve Dr
Philadelphia, PA 19145-5752, us

Celek, Garrett (Athlete, Football Player)

Celestand, John (Athlete, Basketball Player, Sportscaster)
c/o Staff Member *Maxx Sports & Entertainment*
546 5th Ave Fl 6
New York, NY 10036-5000, USA

Celestin, Oliver (Athlete, Football Player)
PO Box 6963
New Orleans, LA 70174-6963, USA

Celi, AJ (Reality Star)
Playhouse Nightclub
6506 Hollywood Blvd
Los Angeles, CA 90028-6210, USA

Celi, Ari (Actor)
c/o Staff Member *SMS Talent*
8383 Wilshire Blvd Ste 230
Beverly Hills, CA 90211-2436, USA

Cellins, Art (Basketball Player)
Atlanta Hawks
5828 NW 19th Ave
Miami, FL 33142-7855, USA

Celmins, Vija (Artist)
49 Crosby St Apt 2
New York, NY 10012-4466, USA

Celotto, Mario (Athlete, Football Player)
47 Evirel Pl
Oakland, CA 94611-1323, USA

Celtic Woman (Music Group)
c/o Staff Member *Solo Agency Ltd (UK)*
53-55 Fulham High St
Fl 2
London SW6 3JJ, UNITED KINGDOM

Ce Marco, Cardinal (Religious Leader)
S Marco 318
Venice 30124, ITALY

Cena, John (Actor, Wrestler)
c/o Chris Gesue *World Wrestling Entertainment (WWE)*
1241 E Main St
Stamford, CT 06902-3520, USA

Cenci, John (Athlete, Football Player)
942 Rita Dr
Pittsburgh, PA 15221-3964, USA

Cenker, Robert J (Astronaut)
GORCA Inc
155 Hickory Corner Rd
East Windsor, NJ 08520-2417, USA

Centers, Larry (Athlete, Football Player)
5023 Stagecoach Way
Southlake, TX 76092-9519, USA

Centineo, Noah (Actor)
c/o Heidi Lopata *Narrative*
1601 Vine St Fl 6
Los Angeles, CA 90028-8802, USA

Cepeda, Angie (Actor)
c/o Katrina Bayonas *Kuranda Management*
Isla De Oza, 30
Madrid 28035, SPAIN

Cepeda, Orlando (Athlete, Baseball Player)
2305 Palmer Ct
Fairfield, CA 94534-7550, USA

Cepicky, Matt (Athlete, Baseball Player)
7 Upper Bluffs View Ct
Eureka, MO 63025-3724, USA

Cepicky, Scott (Athlete, Baseball Player, Olympic Athlete)
3937 Hopewell Rd
Culleoka, TN 38451-2045, USA

Cera, Michael (Actor)
c/o Amanda Rosenthal *Amanda Rosenthal Talent Agency*
315 Harbord St
Toronto, ON M6G 1G9, CANADA

Cerbone, Jason (Actor)

Cerbone, John (Race Car Driver)
2645 Old Yorktown Rd
Yorktown Heights, NY 10598-3136, USA

Cerda, Jaime (Athlete, Baseball Player)
2707 Northhill St
Selma, CA 93662-4313, USA

Ceresino, Gordy (Athlete, Football Player)
PO Box 675515
Rancho Santa Fe, CA 92067-5515, USA

Cerezo, Arevalo M Vincio (President)
Partido Democracia Cristiana
Avda Elena 20-66
Guatemala City, GUATEMALA

Cernadas, Segundo (Actor)
c/o Staff Member *Telefe (Argentina)*
Pavon 2444
Buenos Aires C1248AAT, ARGENTINA

Cerne, Joseph (Joe) (Athlete, Football Player)
536 Valley West Ct
West Des Moines, IA 50265-3900, USA

Cernik, Frantisek (Athlete, Hockey Player)
HC Vitkovice Steel CEZ
Arena Ruska 3077/135
Ostraka-Zabreh PSC 702 00, Czech Republic

Cerny, Amanda (Internet Star)
c/o Evan Silverberg *Management 360*
9111 Wilshire Blvd
Beverly Hills, CA 90210-5508, USA

Ceron, Laura (Actor)
c/o Lisa Blumenthal *Momentum Talent Management*
13935 Burbank Blvd Apt 102
Valley Glen, CA 91401-5078, USA

Cerone, Rick (Athlete, Baseball Player)
34 Winding Way
Woodland Park, NJ 07424-2669, USA

Cerqua, Marq (Athlete, Football Player)
18800 NE 29th Ave Apt 1122
Miami, FL 33180-2855, USA

Cerrone, Rick (Athlete)
100 Old Palisade Rd
Fort Lee, NJ 07024-7064

Cerruda, Ron (Golfer)
c/o Staff Member *Pro Golfers Association (PGA)*
112 TPC Blvd
Ponte Vedra Beach, FL 32082, USA

Cerruti, Nino (Designer, Fashion Designer)
3 Place de la Madeleine
Paris 75008, FRANCE

Certo, Tish (Athlete, Golfer)
151 Buffalo Ave Apt 211
Niagara Falls, NY 14303-1200, USA

Cervantes, Gary (Actor)
2240 Mardel Ave
Whittier, CA 90601-1532, USA

Cervelli, Francisco (Athlete, Baseball Player)
c/o Team Member *New York Yankees*
161st St & River Ave
Yankee Stadium
Bronx, NY 10451, USA

Cervenak, Mike (Athlete, Baseball Player)
27199 Carol Ln
New Boston, MI 48164-9636, USA

Cervenka, Exene (Musician)
Performers of the World
8901 Melrose Ave # 200
West Hollywood, CA 90069-5605, USA

Cerveris, Michael (Musician)
c/o Annick Muller *Wolf-Kasteler Public Relations*
40 Exchange Pl Ste 704
New York, NY 10005-2778, USA

Cervl, Alfred N (Al) (Basketball Player)
177 Dunrovin Ln
Rochester, NY 14618-4815, USA

Cervl, Valentina (Actor)
Artmedia
20 Ave Rapp
Paris 75007, FRANCE

Cesaire, Jacques (Athlete, Football Player)
13388 Greenstone Ct
San Diego, CA 92131-4242, USA

Cesare, Billy (Athlete, Football Player)
1655 Hendry Isles Blvd
Clewiston, FL 33440-5825, USA

Cespedes, Yoenis (Athlete, Baseball Player)
c/o Staff Member *New York Mets*
123-01 Roosevelt Avenue
Shea Stadium
Flushing, NY 11368-1699, USA

Cestaro, Alexander (Athlete, Football Player)
289 Devoe Ave
Yonkers, NY 10705-2709, USA

Cester, Chris (Musician)
2010 Holly Hill Ter
Los Angeles, CA 90068-3812, USA

Cetera, Peter (Musician, Songwriter)
6415 Jocelyn Hollow Rd
Nashville, TN 37205-3521, USA

Cetlinski, Matthew (Matt) (Swimmer)
13121 SE 93rd Terrace Rd
Summerfield, FL 34491-9347, USA

Cey, Ron (Athlete, Baseball Player)
22714 Creole Rd
Woodland Hills, CA 91364-3925, USA

Chabanol, Loan (Actor)
c/o Lena Roklin *Luber Roklin Management*
5815 W Sunset Blvd Ste 208
Los Angeles, CA 90028-6481, USA

Chabat, Alain (Actor, Producer)
Chez Wam
18, blvd Montmartre
Paris 75009, France

Chabert, Lacey (Actor)
9000 W Sunset Blvd Ste 525
W Hollywood, CA 90069-5805, USA

Chabon, Michael (Writer)
c/o Staff Member *United Talent Agency (UTA)*
9336 Civic Center Dr
Beverly Hills, CA 90210-3604, USA

Chabot, Frederic (Athlete, Hockey Player)
Edmonton Oilers
11230 110 St
Attn Coaching Staff Edmonton
NW, AB TSG 3H7, Canada

Chabot, John (Athlete, Coach, Hockey Player)
c/o Staff Member *New York Islanders*
1535 Old Country Rd
Plainview, NY 11803-5042, USA

Chabot, Steve (Congressman, Politician)
2351 Rayburn Hob
Washington, DC 20515-0525, USa

Chabria, Renee (Director)
c/o Staff Member *Management 360*
9111 Wilshire Blvd
Beverly Hills, CA 90210-5508, USA

Chacon, Alex Pineda (Soccer Player)
Los Angeles Galaxy
1010 Rose Bowl Dr
Pasadena, CA 91103, USA

Chacon, Shawn (Athlete, Baseball Player)
7610 19th Street Rd
Greeley, CO 80634-8628, USA

Chacurian, Chico (Soccer Player)
96 Stratford Rd
Stratford, CT 06615-7760, USA

Chadha, Gurinder (Director)
c/o Staff Member *ICM Partners*
10250 Constellation Blvd Fl 7
Los Angeles, CA 90067-6207, USA

Chadli, Bendjedid (President)
Palace Emir Abedelkader
Algiers, ALGERIA

Chadwick, Ed (Athlete, Hockey Player)
12 Bowen Rd
Fort Erie, ON L2A 2Y4, Canada

Chadwick, Jeff (Athlete, Football Player)
23062 Village Dr Apt A
Lake Forest, CA 92630-4955, USA

Chadwick, J Leslie (Les) (Musician)
Barry Collins
21A Cliftown Road
Southend-on-Sea
Essex SS1 1AB, UNITED KINGDOM (UK)

Chadwick, June (Actor)
Contemporary Artists
610 Santa Monica Blvd Ste 202
Santa Monica, CA 90401-1645, USA

Chadwick, Ray (Athlete, Baseball Player)
607 Gattis St
Durham, NC 27701-2831, USA

Chafee, Lincoln (Politician)
Brown University
International Studies Institute
Providence, RI 02912-0001, USA

Chafer, Derek (Actor)
Ugly Enterprises Ltd
Tigris House
256 Edgware Rd
London W2 1DS, UK

Chafetz, Sidney (Artist)
Ohio State University
Art Dept
Columbus, OH 43210, USA

Chaffee, Don (Director)
7020 La Presa Dr
Los Angeles, CA 90068-3105, USA

Chaffee, Susan (Suzy) (Athlete, Olympic Athlete, Skier)
55 Roadrunner Rd
Sedona, AZ 86336-5204, USA

Chaffetz, Jason (Congressman, Politician)
1032 Longworth Hob
Washington, DC 20515-3819, USA

Chaffey, Pat (Athlete, Football Player)
10415 SW Gardner Ct
Tualatin, OR 97062-7208, USA

Chafin, Bryan (Actor)
c/o Heather Collier *Collier Talent Agency*
2313 Lake Austin Blvd Ste 103
Austin, TX 78703-4545, USA

Chagall, Rachel (Actor)
251 S Van Ness Ave
Los Angeles, CA 90004-3920, USA

Chagnon, Marcel (Musician)
6535 Melinda Dr
Nashville, TN 37205-3934, USA

Chaiken, Ilene (Producer, Writer)
2614 Reppert Ct
Los Angeles, CA 90046-1605, USA

Chaikin, Carly (Actor)
c/o Lindsay Galin *Rogers & Cowan*
909 3rd Ave Fl 9
New York, NY 10022-4752, USA

Chainsmokers, The (Music Group)
c/o Adam Alpert *Disruptor Records*
25 Madison Ave Fl 19
New York, NY 10010-8601, USA

Chairmen of the Board (Musician)
c/o Staff Member *The Willis Blume Agency*
PO Box 509
Orangeburg, SC 29116-0509, USA

Chakiris, George (Actor, Dancer, Musician)
c/o Elisabeth Simpson *Agence Elisabeth Simpson*
62 Boulevard Du Montparnasse
Paris 75015, FRANCE

Chalamet, Timothee (Actor)
c/o Nicole Caruso *Relevant (NY)*
333 Hudson St Rm 502
New York, NY 10013-1033, USA

Chalayan, Hussein (Designer, Fashion Designer)
71 Endell Road
London WC2 9AJ, UNITED KINGDOM (UK)

Chalenski, Mike (Athlete, Football Player)
225 S Michigan Ave
Kenilworth, NJ 07033-1765, USA

Chalfant, Kathleen (Actor)
c/o Staff Member *Douglas Gorman Rothacker & Wilhelm Inc*
33 W 46th St Ste 801
New York, NY 10036-4103, USA

Chalk, Dave (Athlete, Baseball Player)
137 Cross Timbers Trl
Coppell, TX 75019-3731, USA

Chalke, Sarah (Actor)
c/o Staff Member *Carsey-Werner Company*
16027 Ventura Blvd Ste 600
Encino, CA 91436-2798, USA

Chalker, Will (Model)
c/o Staff Member *New York Model Management*
71 W 23rd St Ste 301
New York, NY 10010-3519, USA

Chalmers, Judith (Actor)
23 Eyot Gardens
London W10 5AT, UK

Chamberlain, Byron (Athlete, Football Player)
PO Box 326
Montclair, CA 91763-0326, USA

Chamberlain, Craig (Athlete, Baseball Player)
11292 Los Alamitos Blvd
Los Alamitos, CA 90720-3958, USA

Chamberlain, Dan (Athlete, Football Player)
6356 Puerto Dr
Rancho Murieta, CA 95683-9357, USA

Chamberlain, Emma (Internet Star)
c/o Staff Member *United Talent Agency (UTA)*
9336 Civic Center Dr
Beverly Hills, CA 90210-3604, USA

Chamberlain, Jimmy (Actor, Musician)
c/o Staff Member *WME/IMG*
9601 Wilshire Blvd
Beverly Hills, CA 90210-5213, USA

Chamberlain, Joba (Athlete, Baseball Player)
c/o Team Member *New York Yankees*
161st St & River Ave
Yankee Stadium
Bronx, NY 10451, USA

Chamberlain, Richard (Actor)
c/o Jean Diamond *Diamond Management*
31 Percy St
London W1T 2DD, UNITED KINGDOM

Chamberlain, Wes (Athlete, Baseball Player)
PO Box 1358
Homewood, IL 60430-0358, USA

Chambers, Al (Athlete, Baseball Player)
1303 N 14th St
Harrisburg, PA 17103-1206, USA

Chambers, Anne Cox (Business Person)
Cox Enterprises
1440 Lake Hearn Dr NE
Atlanta, GA 30319, USA

Chambers, Christina (Actor)
c/o Laura Gallagher *Klear PR*
827 N Hollywood Way Ste 506
Burbank, CA 91505-2814, USA

Chambers, Elizabeth (Actor)
c/o Stephanie Jones *Jonesworks*
211 E 43rd St Rm 1502
New York, NY 10017-4746, USA

Chambers, Erin (Actor)
c/o Ted Schachter *Schachter Entertainment*
1157 S Beverly Dr Fl 2
Los Angeles, CA 90035-1119, USA

Chambers, Faune (Actor)
c/o Mara Santino *Luber Roklin Management*
5815 W Sunset Blvd Ste 208
Los Angeles, CA 90028-6481, USA

Chambers, Jerry (Athlete, Basketball Player)
4135 Don Diablo Dr
Los Angeles, CA 90008-4305, USA

Chambers, Justin (Actor)
c/o Sandra Chang *Anonymous Content*
3532 Hayden Ave
Culver City, CA 90232-2413, USA

Chambers, Kasey (Musician)
c/o Bobby Cudd *Paradigm (Nashville)*
222 2nd Ave S Ste 1600
Nashville, TN 37201-2375, USA

Chambers, Kirk (Athlete, Football Player)
1294 Lakeview Dr
Provo, UT 84604-2933, USA

Chambers, Lester (Musician)
Lustig Talent
PO Box 770850
Orlando, FL 32877-0850, USA

Chambers, Munro (Actor)
c/o Laura Hubert *Hubert Talent Inc.*
6 Wellesley St W
Toronto, ON M4Y 1E7, Canada

Chambers, Shawn (Athlete, Hockey Player)
1267 Harbor Pl
Brainerd, MN 56401-6994, USA

Chambers, Tom (Athlete, Basketball Player)
7437 E Via Dona Rd
Scottsdale, AZ 85266-2154, USA

Chambers, Willie (Musician)
Noga Mgmt
PO Box 1428
Studio City, CA 91614-0428, USA

Chambers Watkins, Faune A (Actor)
c/o Loan Dang *Del Shaw Moonves Tanaka Finkelstein & Lezcano*
2029 Century Park E Ste 1750
Los Angeles, CA 90067-3036, USA

Chamblee, Al (Athlete, Football Player)
845 Garrow Rd
Newport News, VA 23608-3387, USA

Chamblee, Brandel (Athlete, Golfer)
728 Langston Ct
Orlando, FL 32804-6222, USA

Chamblee, Jim (Athlete, Baseball Player)
1408 Broadway St
Denton, TX 76201-2714, USA

Chambliss, Chris (Athlete, Baseball Player)
12755 Wyngate Trl
Alpharetta, GA 30005-7514, USA

Chambliss, Saxby (Politician)
27 Cherokee Rd
Moultrie, GA 31768-6541, USA

Chambliss, Saxby (Senator)
416 Russell Senate Office Building
Washington, DC 20510-0001, USA

Chamillionaire (Musician)
c/o Sara Ramaker *Paradigm*
8942 Wilshire Blvd
Beverly Hills, CA 90211-1908, USA

Chamitoff, Gregory E Dr (Astronaut)
4401 Ridgeside Ct
Austin, TX 78731-3726, USA

Champagne, Andre (Athlete, Hockey Player)
6936 E 75th St
Tulsa, OK 74133-3037, USA

Champion, Billy (Athlete, Baseball Player)
240 Triple H Farm Rd
Inman, SC 29349-8325, USA

Champion, Cari (Sportscaster)
c/o Sharon Chang *WME|IMG (NY)*
11 Madison Ave Fl 18
New York, NY 10010-3669, USA

Champion, Mike (Athlete, Baseball Player)
21884 Barbados
Mission Viejo, CA 92692-4609, USA

Champion, Sam (Commentator, Television Host)
c/o Staff Member *The Weather Channel*
300 Interstate North Pkwy SE Ste 300
Atlanta, GA 30339-2424, USA

Champion, Will (Musician)
Nettwerk Mgmt
1650 W 2nd Ave
Vancouver, BC V6J 4R3, CANADA

Champnella, Eric (Actor, Director, Writer)
c/o Paul Nelson *Mosaic Media Group*
407 N Maple Dr # 100
Beverly Hills, CA 90210-3818, USA

Champoux, Bob (Athlete, Hockey Player)
8861 Centaurus Way
San Diego, CA 92126-1916, USA

Chamuel, Michelle (Musician)
c/o Donnell Gavin *BMF Media*
50 W 23rd St Fl 7
New York, NY 10010-5205, USA

Chan, Ernie (Cartoonist)
4131 Vale Ave
Oakland, CA 94619-2223, USA

Chan, Gemma (Actor)
c/o Sally Long-Innes *Independent Talent Group*
40 Whitfield St
London W1T 2RH, UNITED KINGDOM

Chan, Jackie (Actor, Producer)
c/o Staff Member *Jackie & JJ Productions*
70 Pak To Ave
Clear Water Bay Rd
Kowloon NA, HONG KONG

Chan, Michael Paul (Actor)
4245 Colbath Ave
Sherman Oaks, CA 91423-4209, USA

Chance, Bob (Athlete, Baseball Player)
2258 Oakridge Dr
Charleston, WV 25311-1723, USA

Chance, Bobbie Shaw (Actor)
Expressions Unlimited
13317 Ventura Blvd
Studio G
Sherman Oaks, CA 91423-3966, USA

Chance, Greyson (Musician)
c/o Guy Oseary *Maverick Management*
9350 Civic Center Dr Ste 100
Beverly Hills, CA 90210-3629, USA

Chance, Larry (Musician)
Brothers Mgmt
141 Dunbar Ave
Fords, NJ 08863-1551, USA

Chancellor, Chris (Athlete, Football Player)
c/o Jordan Woy *Willis & Woy Management*
4890 Alpha Rd Ste 200
Dallas, TX 75244-4639, USA

Chancellor, Justin (Musician)
19805 Valley View Dr
Topanga, CA 90290-3260, USA

Chancellor, Kam (Athlete, Football Player)

Chancellor, Van (Coach)
Houston Comets
2 Greenway Plz Ste 400
Houston, TX 77046-0202, USA

Chance the Rapper (Musician)
c/o Cara Lewis *Cara Lewis Group*
7 W 18th St Fl 3
New York, NY 10011-4663, USA

Chancey, Robert (Athlete, Football Player)
PO Box 212
Coosada, AL 36020-0212, USA

Chanchez, Hosea (Actor)

Chandler, Al (Athlete, Football Player)
PO Box 21733
Oklahoma City, OK 73156-1733, USA

Chandler, Aubrey (Actor)
c/o John Pierce *The Group*
800 S Robertson Blvd Ste 5
Los Angeles, CA 90035-1634, USA

Chandler, Ben (Congressman, Politician)
1504 Longworth Hob
Washington, DC 20515-4101, USA

Chandler, Christopher M (Chris) (Athlete, Football Player)
1625 Lugano Ln
Del Mar, CA 92014-4126, USA

Chandler, Gene (Athlete, Football Player)
550 Southmoor Cir
Stockbridge, GA 30281-4974, USA

Chandler, Jeff (Boxer)
6242 Horner St
Philadelphia, PA 19144, USA

Chandler, Karl (Athlete, Football Player)
5 Plymouth Rd
Newtown Square, PA 19073-1409, USA

Chandler, Kyle (Actor)
222068 Topanga School Rd
Topanga, CA 90290, USA

Chandler, Scott (Athlete, Football Player)
c/o Ken Zuckerman *Priority Sports & Entertainment - (LA)*
15233 Ventura Blvd Ste 718
Sherman Oaks, CA 91403-2237, USA

Chandler, Thornton (Athlete, Football Player)
8646 Guinevere St
Houston, TX 77029-3357, USA

Chandler, Tom (Athlete, Football Player)
236 Mecca Dr
San Antonio, TX 78232-2209, USA

Chandler, Tyson (Athlete, Basketball Player)
21731 Ventura Blvd Ste 300
Woodland Hills, CA 91364-1851, USA

Chandler, Wesley S (Wes) (Athlete, Football Player)
207 Howard Ave
New Smyrna Beach, FL 32168-8195, USA

Chandler, Wilson (Athlete, Basketball Player)
c/o Chris Luchey *CGL Sports*
885 Woodstock Rd Ste 430 PMB 303
Roswell, GA 30075-2211, USA

Chando, Alexandra (Actor)
c/o Elise Koseff *MKSD Talent Management (NY)*
15 W 28th St Fl 9
New York, NY 10001-6430, USA

Chandor, JC (Director)
c/o Leslee Dart *42West*
600 3rd Ave Fl 23
New York, NY 10016-1914, USA

Chandrasekhar, Jay (Actor, Comedian, Director)
c/o Staff Member *Duck Attack Films*
1041 N Formosa Ave
Santa Monica Bldg W, Rm 218
West Hollywood, CA 90046-6703, USA

Chaneac, Delphine (Actor)
c/o Gavin Mills *Olivia Bell Management*
191 Wardour St.
London W1F 8ZE, UNITED KINGDOM

Chaney, Darrel (Athlete, Baseball Player)
906 Woodbrier
Sautee Nacoochee, GA 30571-5106, USA

Chaney, Don (Athlete, Basketball Player)
20711 Park Pine Dr
Katy, TX 77450-2811, USA

Chaney, John (Athlete, Basketball Player)
1639 Sharp Rd
Baton Rouge, LA 70815-4879, USA

Chaney, John (Coach)
Temple University
Athletic Dept
Philadelphia, PA 19122, USA

Chang, Christina (Actor)

Chang, David (Chef, Reality Star)
c/o Jonathan Rosen *WME|IMG (NY)*
11 Madison Ave Fl 18
New York, NY 10010-3669, USA

Chang, Emily (Actor)
c/o Scott Fish *Velocity Entertainment Partners*
5455 Wilshire Blvd Ste 1502
Los Angeles, CA 90036-4204, USA

Chang, Michael (Athlete, Tennis Player)
Chang Family Foundation
28562 Oso Pkwy # D343
Rancho Santa Margarita, CA 92688-5595, USA

Chang, Sarah (Musician)
I C M Artists
40 W 57th St
New York, NY 10019-4001, USA

Chang-Diaz, Franklin R (Astronaut)
NASA
2101 Nasa Pkwy Spc Johnsoncenter
Houston, TX 77058-3696, USA

Chang-Diaz, Franklin R (Astronaut)
1110 Pine Cir
Seabrook, TX 77586-4709, USA

Channing, Stockard (Actor)
c/o Christina Papadopoulos *Baker Winokur Ryder Public Relations*
200 5th Ave Fl 5
New York, NY 10010-3307, USA

Chant, Charlie (Athlete, Baseball Player)
930 Starlight Ct
Banning, CA 92220-1710, USA

Chantels, The (Music Group)
c/o Staff Member *Creative Entertainment Associates Inc*
6 Esterbrook Ln
Cherry Hill, NJ 08003-4002, USA

Chanticleer (Musician)
c/o Staff Member *ICM Partners*
10250 Constellation Blvd Fl 7
Los Angeles, CA 90067-6207, USA

Chantres, Carlos (Baseball Player)
67 Amherst St
Nashua, NH 03064-2561

Chao, Elaine (Politician)
2318 Dundee Rd
Louisville, KY 40205-2070, USA

Chao, Mark (Actor)
c/o Jaeson Ma *East West Artists*
5200 W Century Blvd # 701
Los Angeles, CA 90045-5928, USA

Chao, Rosalind (Actor)
305 15th St
Santa Monica, CA 90402-2211, USA

Chao, Vic (Actor)
c/o Staff Member *Osbrink Talent Agency*
4343 Lankershim Blvd # 100
North Hollywood, CA 91602-2705, USA

Chapa, Damian (Actor)
c/o Staff Member *New York Pictures*
2578 Broadway Ste 127
New York, NY 10025-5642, USA

Chapas, Shaun (Athlete, Football Player)
c/o Hadley Engelhard *Enter-Sports Management*
6000 Lake Forrest Dr Ste 370
Atlanta, GA 30328-5902, USA

Chapdelaine, Rene (Athlete, Hockey Player)
662 S Division Rd
Petoskey, MI 49770-8218, USA

Chapin, Darrin (Athlete, Baseball Player)
328 Portage Easterly Rd
Cortland, OH 44410-9510, USA

Chapin, Doug (Actor, Producer)
Doug Chapin Management
97 Seward St
San Francisco, CA 94114-2336, USA

Chapin, Lauren (Actor)
PO Box 322
Rancho Mirage, CA 92270-0322, USA

Chapin, Tom (Musician, Songwriter, Writer)
57 Piermont Pl
Piermont, NY 10968-1128, USA

Chaplin, Alexander (Actor)
c/o Tammy Rosen *Sanders Armstrong Caserta*
4111 W Alameda Ave Ste 505
Burbank, CA 91505-4163, USA

Chaplin, Ben (Actor)
c/o Louise Owen *Independent Talent Group*
40 Whitfield St
London W1T 2RH, UNITED KINGDOM

Chaplin, Geraldine (Actor, Writer)
c/o Staff Member *WME|IMG*
9601 Wilshire Blvd
Beverly Hills, CA 90210-5213, USA

Chaplin, Greg (Athlete, Baseball Player)
12426 Glenfield Ave
Tampa, FL 33626-2606, USA

Chaplin, Josephine (Actor)
Association Chaplin
58 Rue Jean Jacques Rousseau
Paris F-70001, FRANCE

Chaplin, Kiera (Actor, Producer)
c/o Staff Member *Creative Artists Agency (CAA)*
2000 Avenue of the Stars Ste 100
Los Angeles, CA 90067-4705, USA

Chaplin, Tom (Musician)
c/o Russell Warby *UTA Music/The Agency Group (UK)*
361-373 City Rd
London EC1V 1PQ, UNITED KINGDOM

Chapman, Beth Nielsen (Reality Star)
Sussman Assoc
1383 Queen Emma St
Honolulu, HI 96813-2301, USA

Chapman, Blair (Athlete, Hockey Player)
2068 Red Coach Rd
Allison Park, PA 15101-3231, USA

Chapman, Brian (Athlete, Hockey Player)
57 Penrose Dr
W Springfield, MA 01089-2456, USA

Chapman, Clarence (Athlete, Football Player)
14820 Parkside St
Detroit, MI 48238-2155, USA

Chapman, David S (Athlete, Football Player)
789 N Main St
New Martinsville, WV 26155-1414, USA

Chapman, Doug (Athlete, Football Player)
6215 Chesterfield Meadows Dr
Chesterfield, VA 23832-6597, USA

Chapman, Dr Philip K (Astronaut)
11460 E Helm Dr
Scottsdale, AZ 85255-1885, USA

Chapman, Duane Lee (Dog the Bounty Hunter) (Actor, Reality Star)
c/o Amy Weiss *Brillstein Entertainment Partners*
9150 Wilshire Blvd Ste 350
Beverly Hills, CA 90212-3453, USA

Chapman, Gary (Musician)
1115 Holly Hill Dr
Franklin, TN 37064-6709, USA

Chapman, Georgina (Designer)
Marchesa
601 W 26th St Rm 1425
New York, NY 10001-1160, USA

Chapman, Gil (Athlete, Football Player)
771 Cranford Ave
Westfield, NJ 07090-1308, USA

Chapman, Johnny (Race Car Driver)
Douglas & Sons Racing
1025 N Chipley Ford Rd
Statesville, NC 28625-1574, USA

Chapman, Josh (Athlete, Football Player)
c/o Pat Dye Jr *SportsTrust Advisors*
3340 Peachtree Rd NE Fl 16
Atlanta, GA 30326-1000, USA

Chapman, Judith (Actor)
c/o Staff Member *McCabe Group*
3211 Cahuenga Blvd W Ste 104
Los Angeles, CA 90068-1372, USA

Chapman, Kelvin (Athlete, Baseball Player)
9301 Laughlin Way
Redwood Valley, CA 95470-6425, USA

Chapman, Kevin (Actor)
c/o Suzanne (Sue) Wohl *TalentWorks*
3500 W Olive Ave Ste 1400
Burbank, CA 91505-5512, USA

Chapman, Lamar (Athlete, Football Player)
18513 N Whitedove Ln
Cleveland, OH 44130-8429, USA

Chapman, Lanei (Actor)
c/o Judy Page *Mitchell K Stubbs & Assoc*
8675 Washington Blvd Ste 203
Culver City, CA 90232-7486, USA

Chapman, Leland (Actor, Reality Star)

Chapman, Mark Lindsay (Actor)
c/o Michael Zanuck *Michael Zanuck Agency*
28035 Dorothy Dr Ste 120
Agoura Hills, CA 91301-4918, USA

Chapman, Mike (Athlete, Football Player)
9102 Highlands Cv
Boerne, TX 78006-4842, USA

Chapman, Nathan (Producer)
c/o Haverly Rauen *Adams and Reese LLP*
424 Church St Ste 2800
Nashville, TN 37219-2386, USA

Chapman, Nicki (Actor)
c/o Staff Member *Arlington Enterprises Ltd*
1-3 Charlotte St
London W1P 1HD, UNITED KINGDOM (UK)

Chapman, Paul (Actor)
The Spotlight
7 Leicester Pl
London WC2H 7RJ, UK

Chapman, Rex (Athlete, Basketball Player)
3812 Karen Ct
Lexington, KY 40510-9703, USA

Chapman, Steven Curtis (Musician, Songwriter)
Sparrow Records
PO Box 5010
Brentwood, TN 37024-5010, USA

Chapman, Thomas F (Business Person)
Equifax Inc
1550 Peachtree St NW
Atlanta, GA 30309-2468, USA

Chapman, Tracy (Musician, Songwriter)
c/o Lee Phillips *Manatt Phelps & Phillips LLP*
11355 W Olympic Blvd Fl 2
Los Angeles, CA 90064-1656, USA

Chapman, Travis (Athlete, Baseball Player)
5215 Hickson Rd
Jacksonville, FL 32207-5856, USA

Chapman, Wayne (Athlete, Basketball Player)
4030 Tates Creek Rd Apt 1139
Lexington, KY 40517-3078, USA

Chapoy, Pati (Actor)
c/o Staff Member *TV Azteca*
Periferico Sur 4121
Colonia Fuentes del Pedregal
DF CP 14141, Mexico

Chappas, Harry (Athlete, Baseball Player)
26 SE 1st Ave
Dania, FL 33004-3611, USA

Chappell, Crystal (Actor)
c/o Staff Member *Open Book Productions*
11271 Ventura Blvd # 489
Studio City, CA 91604-3136, USA

Chappell, Fred D (Writer)
305 Kensington Rd
Greensboro, NC 27403-1732, USA

Chappelle, Dave (Actor, Comedian, Producer)
3420 Grinnell Rd
Yellow Springs, OH 45387-9721, USA

Chapple, Dave (Athlete, Football Player)
5 Kara E
Irvine, CA 92620-1855, USA

Chapuisat, Stephane (Soccer Player)
Borussia Dortmund Soccer Club
Strobeialle
Dortmund 44139, GERMANY

Chapura, Richard (Dick) (Athlete, Football Player)
7853 Saddle Creek Trl
Sarasota, FL 34241-9550, USA

Chara, Zdeno (Athlete, Hockey Player)
211 Union Wharf
Boston, MA 02109-1204, USA

Charboneau, Joe (Athlete, Baseball Player)
33020 Leafy Mill Ln
North Ridgeville, OH 44039-2312, USA

Charbonneau, Patricia (Actor)
749 1/2 N La Fayette Park Pl
Los Angeles, CA 90026-6559, USA

Charbonneau, Stephane (Athlete, Hockey Player)
1 Wilderness Dr
Voorhees, NJ 08043-3415, USA

Charbonnier, CArole (Athlete, Golfer)
180 Walnut St Apt A57
Montclair, NJ 07042-2940, USA

Charen, Mona (Writer)
c/o Staff Member *HarperCollins Publishers*
195 Broadway Fl 2
New York, NY 10007-3132, USA

Charlap, Bill (Musician)
Abby Hoffer
223 1/2 E 48th St
New York, NY 10017, USA

Charlebois, Bob (Athlete, Hockey Player)
318 Duncairn Ave
Ottawa, ON K1Z 7G9, Canada

Charles, Bob (Athlete, Golfer)
5329 Sea Biscuit Rd
Palm Beach Gardens, FL 33418-7818, USA

Charles, Caroline (Designer, Fashion Designer)
56/57 Beauchamp Place
London SW3, UNITED KINGDOM (UK)

Charles, Craig (Actor)
PFD
Drury House
34-43 Russell St
London WC2B 5HA, UNITED KINGDOM (UK)

Charles, Daedra (Athlete, Basketball Player, Olympic Athlete)
Los Angeles Sparks
26730 Joy Rd Apt 3
Redford, MI 48239-1939, USA

Charles, Frank (Athlete, Baseball Player)
6029 Corinne Ln
Clarence Ctr, NY 14032-9517, USA

Charles, Gaius (Actor)
c/o Mike Smith *Principal Entertainment*
9255 W Sunset Blvd Ste 500
Los Angeles, CA 90069-3301, USA

Charles, Howard (Actor)
c/o Lindy King *United Agents*
12-26 Lexington St
London W1F OLE, UNITED KINGDOM

Charles, Jamaal (Athlete, Football Player)
c/o Staff Member *Kansas City Chiefs*
1 Arrowhead Dr
Kansas City, MO 64129-1651, USA

Charles, John (Athlete, Football Player)
5644 Westheimer Rd Apt 164
Houston, TX 77056-4002, USA

Charles, Josh (Actor)
c/o Bryna Rifkin *Narrative*
1601 Vine St Fl 6
Los Angeles, CA 90028-8802, USA

Charles, Ken (Athlete, Basketball Player)
621 Putnam Ave
Brooklyn, NY 11221-1601, USA

Charles, Max (Actor)
c/o Mona Loring *Status PR*
PO Box 6191
Westlake Village, CA 91359-6191, USA

Charles M Brig Gen, Duke (Astronaut)
PO Box 310345
New Braunfels, TX 78131-0345, USA

Charleson, Leslie (Actor)
4851 Cromwell Ave
Los Angeles, CA 90027-1141, USA

Charlesworth, Todd (Athlete, Hockey Player)
914 N Brookside Dr
Norton Shores, MI 49441-5365, USA

Charlie, Dupre (Athlete, Football Player)
407 Bay St N
Texas City, TX 77590-6427, USA

Charli XCX (Musician)
2917 Ledgewood Dr
Los Angeles, CA 90068-1957, USA

Charlton, Clifford (Athlete, Football Player)
3708 Carrington Pl
Tallahassee, FL 32303-2041, USA

Charlton, Norm (Athlete, Baseball Player)
312 Estes Dr
Rockport, TX 78382-9758, USA

Charlton, Robert (Bobby) (Soccer Player)
Garthollerton
Cleford Road
Ollerton near Knutsford, Cheshire, UNITED KINGDOM (UK)

Charm City Devils (Music Group, Musician)
c/o Frank Cimler *10th Street Entertainment*
700 N San Vicente Blvd # G410
W Hollywood, CA 90069-5060, USA

Charney, Jordan (Actor)
c/o Staff Member *Leading Artists*
145 W 45th St Rm 1000
New York, NY 10036-4032, USA

Charney, Kim (Actor)
4811 Seashore Dr
Newport Beach, CA 92663-2423, USA

Charo (Musician)
1801 Lexington Rd
Beverly Hills, CA 90210-3001, USA

Charron, Guy (Athlete, Hockey Player)
80 Country Village Cir NE
Calgary, AB T3K 6E2, Canada

Chartier, Dave (Athlete, Hockey Player)
SW 13-19-28 W
Binscarth, MB R0J 0G0, Canada

Chartoff, Melanie (Actor)
c/o Heylee Winters *Heylee Winters Associates*
8491 W Sunset Blvd # 268
W Hollywood, CA 90069-1911, USA

Charton, Pete (Athlete, Baseball Player)
27 Vincinda Ln
Harriman, TN 37748-3014, USA

Chartraw, Rick (Athlete, Hockey Player)
600 Chaparral Rd
Sierra Madre, CA 91024-1115, USA

Charvet, David (Actor)
c/o Nancy Iannios *Core Public PR*
1875 Century Park E Ste 930
Los Angeles, CA 90067-2540, USA

Charyk, Joseph V (Business Person)
7520 Old Dominion Dr
Mc Lean, VA 22102-2519, USA

Chase, Alison (Director)
Pilolobus Dance Theater
PO Box 388
Washington Depot, CT 06794-0388, USA

Chase, Alston (Writer)
c/o Deborah Clarke Grosvenor *The Bohrman Agency*
8899 Beverly Blvd Ste 811
Los Angeles, CA 90048-2452, USA

Chase, Bailey (Actor)
c/o Staff Member *McKeon-Myones Management*
3500 W Olive Ave Ste 770
Burbank, CA 91505-5527, USA

Chase, Barrie (Actor, Dancer)
446 Carroll Canal
Venice, CA 90291-4682, USA

Chase, Chevy (Actor, Comedian, Producer)
PO Box 257
Bedford, NY 10506-0257, USA

Chase, Daveigh (Actor)
c/o Debbie Palmer *Diverse Talent Group*
1875 Century Park E Ste 2250
Los Angeles, CA 90067-2563, USA

Chase, David (Producer)
c/o Leslee Dart *42West*
600 3rd Ave Fl 23
New York, NY 10016-1914, USA

Chase, Hayley (Actor)
c/o Staff Member *Bobby Ball Talent Agency*
4342 Lankershim Blvd
Universal City, CA 91602, USA

Chase, John (Athlete, Hockey Player)
170 Broadway Apt 609
New York, NY 10038-4154, USA

Chase, Jonathan (Actor)
c/o Tracy Steinsapir *Main Title Entertainment*
8383 Wilshire Blvd Ste 408
Beverly Hills, CA 90211-2435, USA

Chase, Kelly (Athlete, Hockey Player)
16984 Bottlebrush Ct
Chesterfield, MO 63005-4210, USA

Chase, Kristen (Writer)
c/o Staff Member *Adams Media Corporation*
57 Littlefield St Ste 3
Avon, MA 02322-1934, USA

Chase, Leah (Chef, Writer)
c/o Staff Member *Pelican Publishing Company*
1000 Burmaster St
Gretna, LA 70053-2246, USA

Chase, Lorraine (Actor)
c/o Staff Member *Peter Charlesworth & Assoc*
68 Old Brompton Rd
London SW7 3LQ, UK

Chase, Will (Actor)
c/o Randi Goldstein *Gersh*
41 Madison Ave Ste 3301
New York, NY 10010-2210, USA

Chasez, JC (Musician)
PO Box 962109
Orlando, FL 32869, USA

Chasin, Liza (Business Person)
c/o Staff Member *Working Title Films*
100 Universal City Plz
Universal City, CA 91608-1002, USA

Chass, Murray (Commentator)
22-20 Radburn Rd
Fair Lawn, NJ 07410-4524, USA

Chassey, Steve (Race Car Driver)
2409 Corsican Cir
Westfield, IN 46074-9383, USA

Chast, Roz (Comedian)
New Yorker Magazine
4 Times Sq
Editorial Dept
New York, NY 10036-6518, USA

Chastain, Brandi (Athlete, Olympic Athlete, Soccer Player)
1661 University Way
San Jose, CA 95126-1555, USA

Chastain, Jessica (Actor)
c/o Staff Member *Freckle Films*
205 W 57th St Apt 4B
New York, NY 10019-2112, USA

Chastel, Andre (Writer)
30 Rue de Lubeck
Paris 75116, FRANCE

Chatham, Matt (Athlete, Football Player)
565 Thurston St
Wrentham, MA 02093-1608, USA

Chatham, Russell (Artist)
General Delivery
Deep Creek
Livingston, MT 59047, USA

Chatham, Wes (Actor)
c/o Susan Patricola *Patricola Public Relations*
369 S Doheny Dr # 1408
Beverly Hills, CA 90211-3508, USA

Chatman, Jesse (Athlete, Football Player)
c/o Eugene Parker *Independent Sports & Entertainment (ISE-IN)*
6435 W Jefferson Blvd # 197
Fort Wayne, IN 46804-6203, USA

Chatwin, Justin (Actor)
c/o Theresa Peters *United Talent Agency (UTA)*
9336 Civic Center Dr
Beverly Hills, CA 90210-3604, USA

Chau, Francois (Actor)
c/o Geneva Bray *GVA Talent Agency Inc*
193 N Robertson Blvd
Beverly Hills, CA 90211-2103, USA

Chau, Hong (Actor)
c/o Lisa Kasteler *Wolf-Kasteler Public Relations*
6255 W Sunset Blvd Ste 1111
Los Angeles, CA 90028-7426, USA

Chavarria, Gabriel (Actor)
c/o Mike Baldridge *Momentum Talent and Literary Agency*
3500 W Olive Ave Ste 300
Burbank, CA 91505-4647, USA

Chavarria, Ossie (Athlete, Baseball Player)
3707 Cardiff St
Burnaby, BC V5G 2H1, Canada

Chaves, Richard J (Actor)
c/o Staff Member *Media Artists Group (NY)*
333 E 43rd St Apt 115
New York, NY 10017-4822, USA

Chavez, Anthony (Athlete, Baseball Player)
10569 S Varner Dr
Vail, AZ 85641-2582, USA

Chavez, Eric (Athlete, Baseball Player)
c/o Scott Leventhal *All Bases Covered Sports Management*
20669 N 101st St
Scottsdale, AZ 85255-3364, USA

Chavez, Jorge (Horse Racer)
1 Villa Ln
Smithtown, NY 11787-2330, USA

Chavez, Julio Cesar (Athlete, Boxer)
c/o Staff Member *Boxing Hall of Fame*
1 Hall of Fame Dr
Canastota, NY 13032-1180, USA

Chavez, Linda (Correspondent)
c/o Staff Member *Fox News*
1211 Avenue of the Americas Lowr C1
New York, NY 10036-8705, USA

Chavez, Marga (Actor)
c/o Staff Member *Select Artists Ltd (CA-Valley Office)*
PO Box 4359
Burbank, CA 91503-4359, USA

Chavira, Ricardo (Actor)
c/o Elizabeth Much *East 2 West Collective*
11022 Santa Monica Blvd Ste 350
Los Angeles, CA 90025-7532, USA

Chavous, Barney L (Athlete, Coach, Football Coach, Football Player)
601 Chavous Rd
Aiken, SC 29803-5031, USA

Chavous, Corey (Athlete, Football Player)
1218 S Main St
Saint Charles, MO 63301-3525, USA

Chayanne (Actor, Musician)
1717 N Bayshore Dr Apt 2146
Miami, FL 33132-1158, USA

Chazelle, Damien (Director)
c/o Gary Ungar *Exile Entertainment*
732 El Medio Ave
Pacific Palisades, CA 90272-3451, USA

Che, Michael (Actor)
c/o James Dixon *Dixon Talent*
375 Greenwich St Fl 5
New York, NY 10013-2376, USA

Cheadle, Don (Actor)
c/o Jennifer Allen *Viewpoint Inc*
8820 Wilshire Blvd Ste 220
Beverly Hills, CA 90211-2622, USA

Cheaney, Calbert (Athlete, Basketball Player)
4 Upper Dromara Ln
Saint Louis, MO 63124-1894, USA

CheapTrick (Music Group)
c/o Dave Frey *Red Light Management*
455 2nd St NE
#500
Charlottesville, VA 22902-5791, USA

Cheatham, Ernie (Athlete, Football Player)
400 Ashton Ave
Pittsburgh, PA 15207-1786, USA

Cheatham, Maree (Actor)
Yvette Schumer
8787 Shoreham Dr
West Hollywood, CA 90069-2231, USA

Cheban, Jonathan (Reality Star)
c/o Jonathan Cheban *Command PR*
265 W 14th St Ste 1102 # 90
New York, NY 10011-7166, USA

Checker, Chubby (Musician, Songwriter, Writer)
c/o Mary Parisi *Twisted Booking*
320 Fayette St Fl 2
Conshohocken, PA 19428-1960, USA

Checo, Robinson (Baseball Player)
Boston Red Sox
Romulo Bentan Cul #04
Santiago, DOMINICAN REPUBLIC

Cheechoo, Jonathan (Athlete, Hockey Player)
707 Iris Gardens Ct
San Jose, CA 95125-1642, USA

Cheek, Louis (Athlete, Football Player)
545 Woelke Rd
Seguin, TX 78155-9345, USA

Cheek, Molly (Actor)
c/o Staff Member *Pakula/King & Associates*
9229 W Sunset Blvd Ste 315
Los Angeles, CA 90069-3403, USA

Cheeks, Judy (Musician)
50 New Bond St.
London W1S 1RD, UK

Cheeks, Maurica E (Mo) (Athlete, Basketball Player, Coach)
7325 SW Childs Rd
Portland, OR 97224-7713, USA

Cheeks, Maurice (Athlete, Basketball Player)
5409 N Military Ave
Oklahoma City, OK 73118-4211, USA

Cheeseborough, Chandra (Athlete, Olympic Athlete, Track Athlete)
104 W Harbor
Hendersonville, TN 37075-3556, USA

Cheesman, Barry (Athlete, Golfer)
2901 Theresa Ln
Sarasota, FL 34239-7008, USA

Cheetwood, Derk (Actor)
1108 Arbor Run Pl
Brentwood, TN 37027-8474, USA

Cheever, Eddie (Race Car Driver)
6331 Sunset Ln
Indianapolis, IN 46260-4746, USA

Cheever, Michael (Athlete, Football Player)
2638 Weddington Pl NE
Marietta, GA 30068-3101, USA

Cheevers, Gary (Athlete, Hockey Player)
2 Jakobek Way
Merrimac, MA 01860-1017, USA

Cheevers, Gerry (Athlete, Hockey Player)
106 Appleton St
North Andover, MA 01845-3138, USA

Chekwa, Chimdi (Athlete, Football Player)
c/o Drew Rosenhaus *Rosenhaus Sports Representation*
3921 Alton Rd # 440
Miami Beach, FL 33140-3852, USA

Chelf, Donald(Don) (Athlete, Football Player)
7329 Bottle Brush Dr
Spring Hill, FL 34606-7023, USA

Cheli, Giovanni Cardinal (Religious Leader)
Pastoral Care of Migrants Council
Piazza Calisto 16
Rome 00153, ITALY

Cheli, Lt Colonel Maurizio (Astronaut)
Alenia Spazio Spa
Officio Piloti
Caselle Stud, Torino 1-10072, Italy

Cheli, Maurizio (Astronaut)
c/o Staff Member *NASA-JSC*
2101 Nasa Pkwy # 1
Astronaut Office - Mail Code Cb
Houston, TX 77058-3607, USA

Cheli-Merchez, Marianne (Astronaut)
132 Rue Van Aliard
Bruxelles 01180, BELGIUM

Chelios, Chris (Athlete, Hockey Player, Olympic Athlete)
790 Falmouth Dr
Bloomfield Hills, MI 48304-3308, USA

Chellgren, Paul W (Business Person)
Ashland Inc
PO Box 15391
Covington, KY 41015-0391, USA

Chelsom, Peter (Actor)
c/o Staff Member *Artists First*
9465 Wilshire Blvd Ste 900
Beverly Hills, CA 90212-2608, USA

Chemical Brothers (Music Group)
c/o Miles Leonard *Parlophone Records*
EMI House
43 Brook Green
London W6 7EF, United Kingdom

Chen, Bruce (Athlete, Baseball Player)
114 Dutchfork Creek Trl
Irmo, SC 29063-7834, USA

Chen, Camille (Actor)
c/o Scott Zimmerman *Scott Zimmerman Management*
901 N Highland Ave
Los Angeles, CA 90038-2412, USA

Chen, Da (Writer)
c/o Alex Glass *Trident Media Group LLC*
41 Madison Ave Fl 36
New York, NY 10010-2257, USA

Chen, Edith (Musician)
Columbia Artists Mgmt Inc
165 W 57th St
New York, NY 10019-2201, USA

Chen, Guang Biao (Business Person)
Jiangsu Huangpu Investment
Nanjing
Jiangsu Province, China

Chen, Joan (Actor, Director)
2601 Filbert St
San Francisco, CA 94123-3215, USA

Chen, John S (Business Person)
BlackBerry
2200 University Ave E
Waterloo, ON N2K 0A7, Canada

Chen, Joie (Correspondent)
Cable News Network
1050 Techwood Dr NW
News Dept
Atlanta, GA 30318-5695, USA

Chen, Julie (Reality Star, Television Host)
c/o Staff Member *CBS Paramount Network Television*
4024 Radford Ave
Cbs Studios
Studio City, CA 91604-2190, USA

Chen, Lu (Figure Skater)
Skating Assn
54 Baishiqiao Road
Haidian District
Beijing 10044, CHINA

Chen, Lynn (Actor)
c/o Staff Member *ICM Partners*
10250 Constellation Blvd Fl 7
Los Angeles, CA 90067-6207, USA

Chen, Robert (Musician)
Columbia Artists Mgmt Inc
165 W 57th St
New York, NY 10019-2201, USA

Chen, Shui-bian (President)
President's Office
Chieshshou Hall
Chung-King Road
Taipei 00100, TAIWAN

Chenault, Kenneth (Business Person)
1044 Brick Kiln Rd
Sag Harbor, NY 11963-2942, USA

Cheney, Dick (Politician)
American Enterprise Institute
1789 Massachusetts Ave NW
Washington, DC 20036-2103, USA

Cheney Holiday, Lauren (Athlete, Soccer Player)
c/o Dan Levy *Wasserman Media Group (NC)*
4208 Six Forks Rd Ste 1020
Raleigh, NC 27609-5738, USA

Cheng, Olivia (Actor)
c/o Elena Kirschner *Red Management*
415 Esplanade W Box 3
North Vancouver, BC V7M 1A6, CANADA

Cheng, Pei-pei (Actor)
c/o Andrew Ooi *Echelon Talent Management*
2915 Argo Pl
Burnaby, BC V3J 7G4, CANADA

Chenier, Phil (Athlete, Basketball Player)
907 Mount Holly St
Baltimore, MD 21229-1929, USA

Chenoweth, Kristin (Actor, Musician)
Micone Entertainment Group Inc.
1224 Great Oaks Dr
Wilmington, NC 28405-4203, USA

Cher (Actor, Director, Musician, Producer)
c/o Sean Patterson *SAM Worldwide*
92 Laight St Apt 9B
New York, NY 10013-2025, USA

Cherilus, Gosder (Athlete, Football Player)
c/o Adam Heller *Vantage Management Group*
518 Reamer Dr
Carnegie, PA 15106-1845, USA

Cherington, Ben (Commentator)
1 Forest Glen Rd
New Paltz, NY 12561-2607, USA

Chernin, Peter (Business Person)
2327 La Mesa Dr
Santa Monica, CA 90402-2330, USA

Chernoff, Mike (Athlete, Hockey Player)
864 Algoma Ave
Moose Jaw, SK S6H 3Z3, Canada

Chernomaz, Rich (Athlete, Hockey Player)
6041 Sierra Way
Nanaimo, BC V9V 1R8, Canada

Chernow, Ron (Writer)
63 Joralemon St
Brooklyn, NY 11201-4003, USA

Chernus, Michael (Actor)
c/o Jill Kaplan *Authentic Talent and Literary Management (NY)*
20 Jay St Ste M17
Brooklyn, NY 11201-8300, USA

Cherrelle (Musician)
c/o Staff Member *Associated Booking Corp*
PO Box 2055
New York, NY 10021-0051, USA

Cherry, Deron (Athlete, Football Player)
13800 S Pebblebrook Ln
Greenwood, MO 64034-8216, USA

Cherry, Dick (Athlete, Hockey Player)
PO Box 346
Bath, ON K0H 1G0, Canada

Cherry, Dick (Athlete, Hockey Player)
PO Box 346
RR 1
Bath, ON K0H 1G0, Canada

Cherry, Don S (Athlete, Coach, Hockey Player)
CBC TV
PO Box 500 Stn A
Attn: Hockey Night in Canada Attn Hockey Night in Canada
Toronto, ON M5W 1E6, Canada

Cherry, Jeirod (Athlete, Football Player)
993 Mimosa Dr
Macedonia, OH 44056-2391, USA

Cherry, Je'rod (Athlete, Football Player)
993 Mimosa Dr
Macedonia, OH 44056-2391, USA

Cherry, Jonathan (Actor)
c/o Jim Sheasgreen *Look Management*
1529 W 6th Ave #110
Vancouver V6J 1R, CANADA

Cherry, Marc (Producer, Writer)
4261 Hazeltine Ave
Sherman Oaks, CA 91423-4245, USA

Cherry, Matthew A (Athlete, Director, Football Player)
c/o Doug Johnson *ICM Partners*
10250 Constellation Blvd Fl 7
Los Angeles, CA 90067-6207, USA

Cherry, Mike (Athlete, Football Player)
4106 Central Pl
Texarkana, AR 71854-1617, USA

Cherry, Nena (Musician)
c/o Staff Member *Paradigm (Monterey)*
404 W Franklin St
Monterey, CA 93940-2303, USA

Cherry, Neneh (Musician)
PO Box 1622
London NW10 5TF, UNITED KINGDOM (UK)

Cherry, Rocky (Athlete, Baseball Player)
5624 Gleneagles Dr
Plano, TX 75093-5973, USA

Cherry Poppin' Daddies (Music Group, Musician)
c/o Jim Lenz *Paradise Artists*
108 E Matilija St
Ojai, CA 93023-2639, USA

Chertok, Jack (Producer)
515 Ocean Ave # 305
Santa Monica, CA 90402-2609, USA

Cherundolo, Charles (Chuck) (Athlete, Football Player)
4230 Simms Rd
Lakeland, FL 33810-0402, USA

Chervyakov, Denis (Athlete, Hockey Player)
21051 Roaming Shores Ter
Ashburn, VA 20147-3208, USA

Chesley, Al (Athlete, Football Player)
2604 32nd St SE
Washington, DC 20020-1448, USA

Chesney, Kenny (Musician)
PO Box 128529
Nashville, TN 37212-8529, USA

Chesnutt, Mark (Musician)
c/o Risha Rodgers *WME (Nashville)*
1201 Demonbreun St
Nashville, TN 37203-3140, USA

Chesson 3rd, Wes (Athlete, Football Player)
1028 Marlowe Rd
Raleigh, NC 27609-6962, USA

Chester, Chris (Athlete, Football Player)

Chester, Colby (Actor)
Talent Group
5670 Wilshire Blvd Ste 820
Los Angeles, CA 90036-5613, USA

Chester, Larry (Athlete, Football Player)
6359 Celtic Dr SW
Atlanta, GA 30331-9414, USA

Chester, Raymond (Athlete, Football Player)
4722 Grass Valley Rd
Oakland, CA 94605-5622, USA

Chester, Vanessa (Actor)
c/o Bill Perlman *Foundation Media Partners*
23679 Calabasas Rd # 625
Calabasas, CA 91302-1502, USA

Chestnut, Cyrus (Musician)
Avenue Management Group
250 W 57th St Ste 407
New York, NY 10107-0106, USA

Chestnut, Morris (Actor)
11551 Jerry St
Cerritos, CA 90703-7416, USA

Chetry, Kiran (Television Host)
c/o John Ferriter *The Alternative Company*
2980 N Beverly Glen Cir Ste 302
Los Angeles, CA 90077-1703, USA

Chetti, Joseph(Joe) (Athlete, Football Player)
7 Baur St
West Babylon, NY 11704-3320, USA

Chetwynd, Lionel (Producer, Writer)
c/o Bruce Vinokour *Creative Artists Agency (CAA)*
2000 Avenue of the Stars Ste 100
Los Angeles, CA 90067-4705, USA

Cheung, Maggie (Actor)
c/o Ted Schachter *Schachter Entertainment*
1157 S Beverly Dr Fl 2
Los Angeles, CA 90035-1119, USA

Chevalier, Tracy (Writer)
EP Dutton
375 Hudson St
New York, NY 10014-3658, USA

Chevelle (Music Group)
c/o Staff Member *Creative Artists Agency (CAA)*
2000 Avenue of the Stars Ste 100
Los Angeles, CA 90067-4705, USA

Chevrier, Alain (Athlete, Hockey Player)
6857 Rain Forest Dr
Boca Raton, FL 33434, USA

Chevrier, Alain (Athlete, Hockey Player)
5138 Greenwich Preserve Ct
Boynton Beach, FL 33436-5802, USA

Chew, Gloria Ann (Actor)
154 Sylvia Dr
Pleasant Hill, CA 94523-2910, USA

Cheylov, Milan (Director)
c/o Bill Douglass *Paradigm*
8942 Wilshire Blvd
Beverly Hills, CA 90211-1908, USA

Cheyunski, Jim (Athlete, Football Player)
821 W Locust St
Seaford, DE 19973-2122, USA

Chhetri, Sunil (Athlete)
c/o Bunty Sajdeh *Cornerstone Sport and Entertainment Pvt Ltd*
H1, Heliopolis, 157 A
Colaba Rd
Mumbai Maharashtra 400005, INDIA

Chia, Sandro (Artist)
Castello Romitorio
Montalcino, Siena, ITALY

Chiacchia, Darren (Athlete, Horse Racer, Olympic Athlete)
2775 NW 49th Ave UNIT 205
Ocala, FL 34482-6213, USA

Chiadel, Dana (Athlete)
5302 Flanders Ave
Kensington, MD 20895-1139, USA

Chiamparino, Scott (Athlete, Baseball Player)
179 Ortega Ave
Mountain View, CA 94040-1439, USA

Chianese, Dominic (Actor)
c/o Brian Liebman *Liebman Entertainment*
29 W 46th St Fl 5
New York, NY 10036-4104, USA

Chiarello, Michael (Chef)
Chiarello Family Vinyards
6525 Washington St
Yountville, CA 94599-1300, USA

Chiasson, Scott (Athlete, Baseball Player)
3660 N Lake Rd
Erieville, NY 13061-3106, USA

Chiaverini, Darrin (Athlete, Football Player)
11442 Springwood Ct
Riverside, CA 92505-5120, USA

Chicago (Music Group)
c/o Howard Rose *Howard Rose Agency Ltd, The*
9460 Wilshire Blvd Ste 310
Beverly Hills, CA 90212-2710, USA

Chick, Travis (Athlete, Baseball Player)
2201 Villa Dr
Tyler, TX 75703-1949, USA

Chickillo, Anthony (Tony) (Athlete, Football Player)
6920 Spanish Moss Cir
Tampa, FL 33625-6556, USA

Chieftans, The (Music Group)
c/o Staff Member *ICM Partners*
10250 Constellation Blvd Fl 7
Los Angeles, CA 90067-6207, USA

Chieng, Ronny (Actor)
c/o Joel Zadak *Artists First*
9465 Wilshire Blvd Ste 900
Beverly Hills, CA 90212-2608, USA

Chiesa, Fabrizio (Producer)
c/o Matt Leipzig *Original Artists*
2801 Hyperion Ave Ste 104
Los Angeles, CA 90027-2571, USA

Chievous, Derrick (Athlete, Basketball Player)
5607 Thornbrook Pkwy
Columbia, MO 65203-9799, USA

Chiffer, Floyd (Athlete, Baseball Player)
13055 San Jacinto St
La Mirada, CA 90638-3447, USA

Chiffons, The (Music Group, Musician)
c/o Staff Member *Lustig Talent Enterprises Inc*
PO Box 770850
Orlando, FL 32877-0850, USA

Chihuly, Dale P (Artist)
Chihuly Inc
1111 NW 50th St
Seattle, WA 98107-5120, USA

Chikezie (Musician)

Chikezie, Caroline (Actor)
c/o Jane Lehrer *Jane Lehrer Associates*
100A Chalk Farm Road
London NW1 8EH, UNITED KINGDOM

Chiklis, Michael (Actor, Director, Producer)
c/o Staff Member *Extravaganza Entertainment*
10990 Wilshire Blvd Fl 8
Los Angeles, CA 90024-3918, USA

Child, Desmond (Musician)
509 Tuckaway Ct
Nashville, TN 37205-3919, USA

Child, Jane (Musician)
2031 Holly Hill Ter
Los Angeles, CA 90068-3811, USA

Child, Lee (Writer)
c/o Staff Member *Delacorte Press*
1540 Broadway
New York, NY 10036-4039, USA

Child, Lincoln (Writer)
c/o Staff Member *Little, Brown Book Group*
100 Victoria Embankment
London EC4Y 0DY, UK

Childers, Ambyr (Actor)
c/o Jamie Harhay Skinner *Baker Winokur Ryder Public Relations*
9100 Wilshire Blvd
W Tower #500
Beverly Hills, CA 90212-3415, USA

Childers, Jason (Athlete, Baseball Player)
417 Aumond Rd
Augusta, GA 30909-3562, USA

Childers, Matt (Athlete, Baseball Player)
417 Aumond Rd
Augusta, GA 30909-3562, USA

Childress, Josh (Athlete, Basketball Player)
1433 Cherokee Trl
Lawrenceville, GA 30043-5807, USA

Childress, Kallie Flynn (Actor)
c/o TJ Stein *Stein Entertainment Group*
1351 N Crescent Heights Blvd Apt 312
West Hollywood, CA 90046-4549, USA

Childress, Randolph (Athlete, Basketball Player)
9900 Nicol Ct W
Bowie, MD 20721-2960

Childress, Raymond C (Ray) Jr (Athlete, Football Player)
639 Shady Hollow St
Houston, TX 77056-1635, USA

Childress, Richard (Race Car Driver)
Childress Racing
9543 Hampton Rd.
Lexington, NC 27295-9780, USA

Childress, Rocky (Athlete, Baseball Player)
5 Meadow Glen Ct
Santa Rosa, CA 95404-1845, USA

Childs, Billy (Musician)
Integrity Talent
PO Box 961
Burlington, MA 01803-5961, USA

Childs, Charissa (Athlete, Golfer)
25 Green Springs Cir
Columbia, SC 29223-6940, USA

Childs, Chris (Athlete, Basketball Player)
10830 Willow Meadow Cir
Cir
Alpharetta, GA 30022-6516, USA

Childs, Clarence (Athlete, Football Player)
1652 Lawrence Cir
Daytona Beach, FL 32117-3942, USA

Childs, Henry (Athlete, Football Player)
8304 Allman Rd
Lenexa, KS 66219-2705, USA

Chiles, Adrian (Actor)
The One Show
BBC Television Centre
Wood Ln
London W12 7RJ, UK

Chiles, Lois (Actor)
c/o Staff Member *Abrams Artists Agency*
750 N San Vicente Blvd
E Tower Fl 11
Los Angeles, CA 90069-5788, USA

Chiles, Rich (Athlete, Baseball Player)
18147 Mallard St
Woodland, CA 95695-6038, USA

Chilies, Lois (Actor)
c/o Staff Member *Abrams Artists Agency*
750 N San Vicente Blvd
E Tower Fl 11
Los Angeles, CA 90069-5788, USA

Chi-Lites, The (Music Group)
c/o Staff Member *M.A.G./Universal Attractions*
15 W 36th St Fl 8
New York, NY 10018-7927, USA

Chillar, Brandon (Athlete, Football Player)
1 Campanilla
San Clemente, CA 92673-2751, USA

Chillemi, Connie (Athlete, Golfer)
3150 NE 36th Ave Lot 422
Ocala, FL 34479-3167, USA

Chilton, Gene (Athlete, Football Player)
45828 US Highway 69 N
Jacksonville, TX 75766-8749, USA

Chilton, Kevin P (Astronaut)
16 Custer Dr
Offutt Afb, NE 68113-1018, USA

Chimera, Jason (Athlete, Hockey Player)
2468 Club Rd
Columbus, OH 43221-4007, USA

Chiminello, Bianca (Actor, Model)
c/o Staff Member *Matt Sherman Management*
8840 Wilshire Blvd # 109
Beverly Hills, CA 90211-2606, USA

Chin, Tessanne (Musician)
c/o Staff Member *ICM Partners*
10250 Constellation Blvd Fl 7
Los Angeles, CA 90067-6207, USA

Chin, Tsai (Actor)
c/o Donald Spradlin *Essential Talent Management*
7958 Beverly Blvd
Los Angeles, CA 90048-4511, USA

Chinlund, Nick (Actor)
c/o Gordon Gilbertson *Gilbertson Management*
1334 3rd Street Promenade Ste 201
Santa Monica, CA 90401-1320, USA

Chinnick, Rick (Athlete, Hockey Player)
55 Gregory Dr E
Chatham, ON N7L 2R5, Canada

Chiodo, Andy (Athlete, Hockey Player)
17 Fairhaven Dr
Etobicoke, ON M9P 2P8, Canada

Chiodos (Music Group)
c/o Staff Member *Equal Vision Records*
PO Box 38202
Albany, NY 12203-8202, USA

Chipchase, Jack (Athlete, Hockey Player)
143 Andrew St
Exeter, ON N0M 1S1, Canada

Chipperfield, Ron (Athlete, Hockey Player)
Optima World Sports
PO Box 248
Wilcox, SK S0G 5E0, Canada

Chishholm-Carrillo, Linda (Athlete, Volleyball Player)
17213 Vose St
Van Nuys, CA 91406-3633, USA

Chisholm, Art (Athlete, Hockey Player)
9 Jefferson Ct
Woburn, MA 01801-4326, USA

Chisholm, Ashleigh (Actor)
c/o Staff Member *Nickelodeon UK*
PO Box 6425
LONDON W1A 6UR, UNITED KINGDOM

Chism, Tom (Athlete, Baseball Player)
532 W Brookhaven Rd Apt F1
Brookhaven, PA 19015-1824, USA

Chissano, Joaquim A (President)
President's Office
Avda Julius Nyerere 2000
Maputo, MOZAMBIQUE

Chistov, Stanislav (Athlete, Hockey Player)
Puckagency LLC
555 Pleasantville Rd Ste 210N
Attn Jay Grossman
Briarcliff Manor, NY 10510-1900, USA

Chistov, Stanislaw (Athlete, Hockey Player)
c/o Jay Grossman *PuckAgency LLC*
555 Pleasantville Rd Ste 210N
North Building, Suite 210
Briarcliff Manor, NY 10510-1900, USA

Chitalada, Sot (Boxer)
Home Express Co
242/19 Moo 10
Sukhumvit Road
Washington, DC 20210-0001, THAILAND

Chitren, Steve (Athlete, Baseball Player)
808 Desert Oak Ct APT C
Las Vegas, NV 89145-2484, USA

Chittum, Nelson (Athlete, Baseball Player)
616 Bonita Pkwy
Hendersonville, TN 37075-4632, USA

Chitwood Jr, Joey (Race Car Driver)
Chicagoland Speedway
4410 W Alva St
Tampa, FL 33614-7639, USA

Chiu Wai, Tony Leung (Actor)
c/o Staff Member *WME/IMG*
9601 Wilshire Blvd
Beverly Hills, CA 90210-5213, USA

Chivers, Warren (Skier)
Vermont Academy
Saxtons River, WI 05154, USA

Chlebek, Ed (Athlete, Football Player)
6160 Waxmyrtle Way
Naples, FL 34109-5940, USA

Chlumsky, Anna (Actor)
c/o Cory Richman *Liebman Entertainment*
29 W 46th St Fl 5
New York, NY 10036-4104, USA

Chlupsa, Bob (Athlete, Baseball Player)
55 Willow St
Garden City, NY 11530-6316, USA

Chmerkovskiy, Maksim (Dancer, Reality Star)
c/o Amy Malin *Trueheart Management*
20732 Wells Dr
Woodland Hills, CA 91364-3437, USA

Chmerkovskiy, Val (Dancer, Reality Star)
c/o Brooks Butterfield *PMK/BNC Public Relations*
1840 Century Park E Ste 1400
Los Angeles, CA 90067-2115, USA

Chmura, Mark W (Athlete, Football Player)
S18W28948 Price Ct
Waukesha, WI 53188-9551, USA

Cho, Alina (Correspondent)
c/o John Ferriter *The Alternative Company*
2980 N Beverly Glen Cir Ste 302
Los Angeles, CA 90077-1703, USA

Cho, Catherine (Musician)
Columbia Artists Mgmt Inc
165 W 57th St
New York, NY 10019-2201, USA

Cho, Frank (Cartoonist)
Creators Syndicate
5777 W Century Blvd # 700
Los Angeles, CA 90045-5600, USA

Cho, Fujio (Business Person)
Toyota Motor Corp
1 Toyotacho
Toyota City, Aicji Prefecture 00471, JAPAN

Cho, Henry (Actor, Comedian, Writer)
c/o Alex Murray *Brillstein Entertainment Partners*
9150 Wilshire Blvd Ste 350
Beverly Hills, CA 90212-3453, USA

Cho, John (Actor)
2152 Panorama Ter
Los Angeles, CA 90039-3541, USA

Cho, Margaret (Actor, Comedian)
Cho & Taussig Productions
1815 Butler Ave Apt 120
Los Angeles, CA 90025-5462, USA

Cho, Smith (Actor)
c/o Amy Guenther *Gateway Management Company Inc*
860 Via De La Paz Ste F10
Pacific Palisades, CA 90272-3631, USA

Choate, Don (Athlete, Baseball Player)
9506 Maryann Dr
Fairview Heights, IL 62208-1625, USA

Choate, Jerry D (Business Person)
Allstate Insurance
2775 Sanders Rd
Allstate Plaza
Northbrook, IL 60062-6127, USA

Choate, Putt (Athlete, Football Player)
9800 Rockbrook Dr
Dallas, TX 75220-2041, USA

Choate, Randy (Athlete, Baseball Player)
316 Leon Pl
Devis, CA 95616-0236, USA

Choi, Hee Seop (Athlete, Baseball Player)
14310 SE 29th Cir
Vancouver, WA 98683-7691, USA

Choi, Kathy (Athlete, Golfer)
7912 Beachpoint Cir Apt 18
Huntington Beach, CA 92648-1478, USA

Choi, Kenneth (Actor)
c/o Tory Howard *Atlas Artists*
9220 W Sunset Blvd Ste 225
Los Angeles, CA 90069-3513, USA

Choi, KJ (Athlete, Golfer)
1360 E 9th St
Cleveland, OH 44114-1737, USA

Choi, Roy (Chef, Television Host)
c/o Lisa Shotland *CAA (London)*
3 Shortlands, Hammersmith
Fl 5
London W6 8DA, UNITED KINGDOM

Choi, Yun (Actor)
c/o Staff Member *Select Artists Ltd (CA-Westside Office)*
1138 12th St Apt 1
Santa Monica, CA 90403-5459, USA

Chokachi, David (Actor)
1036 S Ridgeley Dr
Los Angeles, CA 90019-2509, USA

Cholodenko, Lisa (Director, Producer, Writer)
c/o Bart Walker *ICM Partners*
10250 Constellation Blvd Fl 7
Los Angeles, CA 90067-6207, USA

Choma, John (Athlete, Football Player)
1544 Carol Ave
Burlingame, CA 94010-5231, USA

Chomet, Sylvain (Director, Writer)
c/o Robert Newman *WME/IMG*
9601 Wilshire Blvd
Beverly Hills, CA 90210-5213, USA

Chomsky, Marvin J (Director)
15200 W Sunset Blvd Ste 209
Pacific Palisades, CA 90272-3621

Chon, Justin (Actor)
c/o Jaeson Ma *East West Artists*
5200 W Century Blvd # 701
Los Angeles, CA 90045-5928, USA

Chonacas, Katie (Actor, Model)
c/o Staff Member *BMG Models & Talent*
5455 Wilshire Blvd Ste 900
Los Angeles, CA 90036-4250, USA

Chones, Jim (Athlete, Basketball Player)
26400 George Zeiger Dr
Dr Apt 305
Beachwood, OH 44122-7510, USA

Chong, Rae Dawn (Actor)
c/o David Fox *Myman Greenspan Fineman Fox Rosenberg & Light*
11601 Wilshire Blvd Ste 2200
Los Angeles, CA 90025-1758, USA

Chong, Tommy (Actor, Comedian)
1625 Casale Rd
Pacific Palisades, CA 90272-2717, USA

Chopra, Daniel (Athlete, Golfer)
9838 Laurel Valley Dr
Windermere, FL 34786-8911, USA

Chopra, Deepak (Doctor, Writer)
Chopra Well-Being Center
7620 Fay Ave
La Jolla, CA 92037, USA

Chopra, Priyanka (Actor)
c/o Troy Carter *Atom Factory/Coalition Media Group*
PO Box 927
Culver City, CA 90232-0927, USA

Chorske, Tom (Athlete, Hockey Player)
23 Cooper Cir
Minneapolis, MN 55436-1316, USA

Chorvat, Scarlett (Actor)
1727 N Crescent Heights Blvd
Los Angeles, CA 90069-1604, USA

Chou, Collin (Actor)
c/o Tim Kwok *Convergence Entertainment*
9150 Wilshire Blvd Ste 247
Beverly Hills, CA 90212-3429, USA

Chou, Jay (Musician)
c/o Staff Member *BMG*
1540 Broadway
New York, NY 10036-4039, USA

Choudhury, Sarita (Actor)
c/o Marisa Martins *The Lede Company*
401 Broadway Ste 206
New York, NY 10013-3033, USA

Chouinard, Bobby (Athlete, Baseball Player)
6298 S Netherland Cir
Centennial, CO 80016-1324, USA

Chouinard, Guy (Athlete, Hockey Player)
Quebec Remparts Laval University Peps
Rm 1564
Ste-Foy, QC G1K 7P4, Canada

Chouinard, Josee (Figure Skater)
c/o Staff Member *IMG (Canada)*
175 Bloor St E Twr 400
Toronto, ON M4W 3R8, CANADA

Choureau, Etchika (Actor)
9 rue du Docteur Blanche
Paris F-75016, France

Chow, Amy (Athlete, Gymnast, Olympic Athlete)
285 Tamarind Ln
Danville, CA 94526-4421, USA

Chow, China (Actor)
c/o David Unger *Artist International Group*
8439 W Sunset Blvd Ste 309
W Hollywood, CA 90069-1926, USA

Chow, Deborah (Actor)
c/o Gregory Shephard *Writ Large*
5815 W Sunset Blvd Ste 401
Los Angeles, CA 90028-6482, USA

Chow, Raymond (Producer)
c/o Staff Member *Golden Harvest Entertainment*
The Peninsula Office Tower
18 Middle Road 16/F Tsim Sha Tsui
Kowloon, Hong Kong

Chow, Stephen (Actor, Director, Writer)
Star Overseas
Rm 1201-1204 Sea Bird House
22-28 Wyndham Street
Hong Kong, China

Chow, Steven (Actor)
c/o Alan Grodin *Weissman Wolff Bergman Coleman Silverman Holmes*
9665 Wilshire Blvd Fl 9
Beverly Hills, CA 90212-2316, USA

Chrebet, Wayne (Athlete, Football Player)
147 Heulitt Rd
Colts Neck, NJ 07722-1427, USA

Chriqui, Emmanuelle (Actor)
c/o Chris Huvane *Management 360*
9111 Wilshire Blvd
Beverly Hills, CA 90210-5508, USA

Chris, Chris (Athlete, Hockey Player)
287 Brantwood Park Rd
Brantford, ON N3P 1H6, Canada

Chris, Mike (Athlete, Baseball Player)
31257 Corte Alhambra
Temecula, CA 92592-5420, USA

Chrisley, Neil (Athlete, Baseball Player)
280 Myrtle Greens Dr Apt B
Conway, SC 29526-9040, USA

Christ, Chad (Actor)
c/o Brian Liebman *Liebman Entertainment*
29 W 46th St Fl 5
New York, NY 10036-4104, USA

Christ, Dorothy (Athlete, Baseball Player, Commentator)
120 E Battell St Apt 108
Mishawaka, IN 46545-6660, USA

Christ, Fred (Athlete, Basketball Player)
514 Banyan Way
Melbourne Beach, FL 32951-2102, USA

Christensen, Bruce (Athlete, Baseball Player)
PO Box 178
Moroni, UT 84646-0178, USA

Christensen, Erika (Actor)
2505 Laurel Pass
Los Angeles, CA 90046-1403, USA

Christensen, Hayden (Actor)
PO Box 2459
San Rafael, CA 94912-2459, USA

Christensen, Helena (Model)
c/o Scott Lipps *One Management*
42 Bond St Fl 2
New York, NY 10012-2768, USA

Christensen, John (Athlete, Baseball Player)
2931 Yuma Dr
Lake Havasu City, AZ 86406-8568, USA

Christensen, Joss (Olympic Athlete, Skier)
US Ski And Snowboard Association
1 Victory Ln # 100
Park City, UT 84060-7463, USA

Christensen, McKay (Athlete, Baseball Player)
2720 W Shady Hollow Ln
Lehi, UT 84043-5713, USA

Christensen Jr, Erik (Athlete, Football Player)
308 Sentinel Ln
Newark, DE 19702-8504, USA

Christenson, Gary (Athlete, Baseball Player)
435 E Barbarita Ave
Gilbert, AZ 85234-4628, USA

Christenson, Larry (Athlete, Baseball Player)
1465 Le Boutillier Rd
Malvern, PA 19355-8741, USA

Christenson, Ryan (Athlete, Baseball Player)
100 Lismore Ct
Tyrone, GA 30290-2549, USA

Christenson, Ryan (Athlete, Baseball Player)
4021 Canario St Unit 136
Carlsbad, CA 92008-6102, USA

Christian, Andrew (Designer, Fashion Designer)
Andrew Christian Clothing
325 W Cerritos Ave
Glendale, CA 91204-2703, USA

Christian, Ash (Actor, Director, Writer)
c/o Simon Millar *Rumble Media*
1620 Broadway Ste C
Santa Monica, CA 90404-2777, USA

Christian, Bill (Athlete, Hockey Player, Olympic Athlete)
400 Fox Haven Dr Apt 4207
Naples, FL 34104-5134, USA

Christian, Bob (Athlete, Football Player)
16457 E 79th St N
Owasso, OK 74055-5743, USA

Christian, Christina (Actor, Musician)
c/o Irene Marie *Irene Marie Management Group*
728 Ocean Dr
Miami Beach, FL 33139-6220, USA

Christian, Claudia (Actor)
Zard Productions
8491 W Sunset Blvd # 140
West Hollywood, CA 90069-1911, USA

Christian, Cody (Actor)
c/o Holly Williams *Williams Unlimited*
5010 Buffalo Ave
Sherman Oaks, CA 91423-1414

Christian, Eddie (Baseball Player)
1126 NE Lija Loop
Portland, OR 97211-1318, USA

Christian, Gabrielle (Actor)
c/o Robert Haas *Innovative Artists*
1505 10th St
Santa Monica, CA 90401-2805, USA

Christian, Gordon (Athlete, Hockey Player)
604 Lake St NW
Warroad, MN 56763-2123, USA

Christian, Jeff (Athlete, Hockey Player)
2000 SE Manor Pl
Blue Springs, MO 64014-3823, USA

Christian, Richard (Actor)
c/o Staff Member *Select Artists Ltd (CA-Westside Office)*
1138 12th St Apt 1
Santa Monica, CA 90403-5459, USA

Christian, Shawn (Actor)
543 N Fuller Ave
Los Angeles, CA 90036-1940, USA

Christian-Jacque (Director, Writer)
42 Bis Rue de paris
Boulogne, Billancourt 92100, FRANCE

Christiansen, Clay (Athlete, Baseball Player)
7227 Eby Ave Apt 202
Overland Park, KS 66204-1643, USA

Christiansen, Jason (Athlete, Baseball Player)
1464 N Citrus Cove Cir
Mesa, AZ 85213-5604, USA

Christiansen, Robert S (Bob) (Athlete, Football Player)
5228 G St
Sacramento, CA 95819-3217, USA

Christianson, Bob (Musician)
c/o Mike Rosen *Working Artists Agency*
13525 Ventura Blvd
Sherman Oaks, CA 91423-3801

Christie, Chris (Politician)
Office of the Governor
PO Box 1
Trenton, NJ 08625-0001, USA

Christie, Doug (Athlete, Basketball Player)
PO Box 23609
Federal Way, WA 98093-0609, USA

Christie, Gwendoline (Actor)
c/o Claire Maroussas *Independent Talent Group*
40 Whitfield St
London W1T 2RH, UNITED KINGDOM

Christie, Julianna (Actor)
252 N Larchmont Blvd Ste 200
Los Angeles, CA 90004-3754, USA

Christie, Julianne (Actor)
252 N Larchmont Blvd Ste 200
Los Angeles, CA 90004-3754, USA

Christie, Julie (Actor, Model)
c/o Oriana Elia *Curtis Brown Ltd*
28-29 Hay Market
Hay Market House
London SW1Y 4SP, UNITED KINGDOM

Christie, Linford (Athlete, Track Athlete)
Nuff Respect
107 Sherland Road
Twickenham
Middx TW9 4HB, UNITED KINGDOM (UK)

Christie, Lou (Musician)
c/o Staff Member *Dick Fox Entertainment*
1650 Broadway
New York, NY 10019-6833, USA

Christie, Mike (Athlete, Hockey Player)
6093 S Krameria St
Centennial, CO 80111-4273, USA

Christie, Ryan (Athlete, Hockey Player)
4819 Union Rd
CHRISTIE'S DAIRY
Beamsville, ON L0R 1B4, Canada

Christie, Steve (Athlete, Football Player)
6150 Gulfport Blvd S Apt 102
Gulfport, FL 33707-3101, USA

Christie, Tony (Musician)
c/o Staff Member *Chris Davis Management Ltd.*
Tenbury House
36 Teme St, Tenbury Wells
Worcestershire WR15 8AA, UK

Christie, Warren (Actor)
c/o Vickie Petronio *Play Management*
220-807 Powell St
Vancouver, BC V6A 1H7, CANADA

Christie, William (Musician)
Les Arts Florissants
2 Rue de Saint-Petersbourg
Paris 75008, FRANCE

Christine, Andrew (Andy) (Cartoonist)
c/o Staff Member *King Features Syndication*
300 W 57th St Fl 15
New York, NY 10019-5238, USA

Christlieb, Peter (Pete) (Musician)
Thomas Cassidy
11761 E Speedway Blvd
Tucson, AZ 85748-2017, USA

Christman, Tim (Athlete, Baseball Player)
53 Joy Dr
Albany, NY 12211-1539, USA

Christmas, Steve (Athlete, Baseball Player)
600 Bentley St
Oviedo, FL 32765-8169, USA

Christoff, Steve (Athlete, Hockey Player, Olympic Athlete)
542 Fairview Ave S
Saint Paul, MN 55116-1466, USA

Christofferson, Debra (Actor)
5658 Lemp Ave
N Hollywood, CA 91601-1754, USA

Christo (Javacheff) (Artist)
48 Howard St Apt 2
New York, NY 10013-3074, USA

Christon, Shameka (Athlete, Basketball Player)
c/o Staff Member *New York Liberty*
2 Penn Plz Fl 15
New York, NY 10121-1700, USA

Christopher, Dennis (Actor)
BR&S
5757 Wilshire Blvd Ste 473
Los Angeles, CA 90036-3632, USA

Christopher, Gerald (Actor)
11900 Goshen Ave Apt 203
Los Angeles, CA 90049-6380, USA

Christopher, Gerard (Actor)

Christopher, Gretchen (Musician)
509 E Ridgecrest Blvd # 1A
Ridgecrest, CA 93555-3959, USA

Christopher, Herb (Athlete, Football Player)
PO Box 554
Redan, GA 30074-0554, USA

Christopher, Joe (Athlete, Baseball Player)
Chris Potter Sports 9722
Owings Mills, MD 71117-6341, USA

Christopher, Matt (Writer)
c/o Dale Christopher
PO Box 2511
Wilton, NY 12831-5511, USA

Christopher, Mike (Athlete, Baseball Player)
8707 Courthouse Rd
Church Road, VA 23833-2712, USA

Christopher, Patrick (Athlete, Basketball Player)
c/o Sam Goldfelder *Excel Sports Management (LA)*
9665 Wilshire Blvd Ste 500
Beverly Hills, CA 90212-2312, USA

Christopher, Ted (Race Car Driver)
Marsh Racing
81 Mile Creek Rd
Old Lyme, CT 06371-1763, USA

Christopher, Thom (Actor)
Ambrosio/Mortimer
PO Box 16758
Beverly Hills, CA 90209-2758, USA

Christopher, Tyler (Actor)
11523 Duque Dr
Studio City, CA 91604-4279, USA

Christopherson, James (Jim) (Athlete, Football Player)
526 Queens Ct
Moorhead, MN 56560-6777, USA

Christy, Barrett (Athlete, Olympic Athlete, Snowboarder)
131 Lois Ln
Sequim, WA 98382-3057, USA

Christy, Earl (Athlete, Football Player)
10825 S Prairie Ave
Chicago, IL 60628-3620, USA

Christy, Greg (Athlete, Football Player)
3 Concord St
Natrona Heights, PA 15065-9732, USA

Christy, Jeff (Athlete, Football Player)
138 Horseshoe Dr
Freeport, PA 16229-1712, USA

Chryplewicz, Pete (Athlete, Football Player)
11473 Claymont Cir
Windermere, FL 34786-5312, USA

Chrysostom, Bishop (Religious Leader)
Serbian Orthodox Church
PO Box 519
St Sava Monastery
Libertyville, IL 60048-0519, USA

Chrystal, Bob (Athlete, Hockey Player)
231 Rita St
Winnipeg, MB R3J 2Y3, Canada

Chu, Jon M (Director)
Electric Somewhere Co
7250 Beverly Blvd Ste 200
Los Angeles, CA 90036-2560, USA

Chu, Judy (Congressman, Politician)
1520 Longworth Hob
Washington, DC 20515-4605, USA

Chu, Julie (Athlete, Hockey Player, Olympic Athlete)
145 Primrose Ln
Fairfield, CT 06825-2309, USA

Chubb, Nick (Athlete, Football Player)
c/o Pat Dye Jr *SportsTrust Advisors*
3340 Peachtree Rd NE Fl 16
Atlanta, GA 30326-1000, USA

Chubin, Steve (Athlete, Basketball Player)
2324 S Gray Dr
Lakewood, CO 80227-3954, USA

Chuck, Chuck (Athlete, Football Player)
268 Babbitt Rd Apt M5
Bedford Hills, NY 10507-2123, USA

Chuck, Wendy (Designer)
c/o Heather Parker *Innovative Artists*
1505 10th St
Santa Monica, CA 90401-2805, USA

Chukwurah, Patrick (Athlete, Football Player)
12301 Olive Jones Rd
Tampa, FL 33625-3942

Chulack, Christopher (Director, Producer, Writer)
c/o Staff Member *Creative Artists Agency (CAA)*
2000 Avenue of the Stars Ste 100
Los Angeles, CA 90067-4705, USA

Chulk, Vinnie (Athlete, Baseball Player)
7580 SW 162nd St
Palmetto Bay, FL 33157-3822, USA

Chung, Alexa (Musician)
c/o Staff Member *Liz Matthews PR*
8 Smokehouse Yard
44-46 St. John St
London EC1M 4DF, United Kingdom

Chung, Connie (Correspondent, Journalist)
1 W 72nd St Apt 4
New York, NY 10023-3414, USA

Chung, Doo Ri (Designer)
c/o Meghan Wood *KCD Worldwide Inc*
475 10th Ave Fl 8
New York, NY 10018-9704, USA

Chung, Jamie (Actor, Reality Star)
c/o Sarah Shyn *3 Arts Entertainment*
9460 Wilshire Blvd Fl 7
Beverly Hills, CA 90212-2713, USA

Chung, Mark (Soccer Player)
Columbus Crew
2121 Velma Ave
Columbus, OH 43211-2085, USA

Chung, Myung-Whun (Musician)
Hans Ulrich Schmid
Postfach 1617
Hanover 30016, GERMANY

Church, Barry (Athlete, Football Player)
c/o Bruce Tollner *REP 1 Sports Group*
80 Technology Dr
Irvine, CA 92618-2301, USA

Church, Charlotte (Musician)
7 Dials Cambridge Bridge
Covent Garden
London WC2H 9HU, UNITED KINGDOM (UK)

Church, Eric (Musician)
c/o John Peets *Q Prime (TN)*
131 S 11th St
Nashville, TN 37206-2954, USA

Church, Ryan (Athlete, Baseball Player)
3500 Thurloe Dr
Rockledge, FL 32955-6066, USA

Churches, Brady J (Business Person)
Consolidated Stores
1105 N Market St
Wilmington, DE 19801-1216, USA

Churchill, Caryl (Writer)
Cassarotto
60/66 Wardour St
London W1V 4ND, UNITED KINGDOM (UK)

Churchman, Ricky (Athlete, Football Player)
445 Cherry Blossom Loop
Richland, WA 99352-7851, USA

Churla, Shane (Athlete, Hockey Player)
31826 Scotch Pine Ln
Bigfork, MT 59911-8275, USA

Churla, Steve (Athlete, Hockey Player)
19299 E. Shore Route
Bigfork, MT 55911, USA

Chvatal, Cynthia (Producer)
c/o Staff Member *United Talent Agency (UTA)*
9336 Civic Center Dr
Beverly Hills, CA 90210-3604, USA

Chwast, Seymour (Artist)
Push Pin Group
55 E 9th St Apt 1G
New York, NY 10003-6312, USA

Chychrun, Jeff (Athlete, Hockey Player)
6423 NW 32nd Way
Boca Raton, FL 33496-3396, USA

Chyna, Blac (Model, Reality Star)
c/o Walter Mosley Jr *Mosley & Associates*
1055 W 7th St PH 33
Los Angeles, CA 90017-2528, USA

Chynoweth, Dean (Athlete, Hockey Player)
131 Shawnee Rise SW
Calgary, AB T2Y 2S3, CANADA

Chyzowski, Dave (Athlete, Hockey Player)
c/o Staff Member *Kamloops Blazers*
300 Lorne St
Kamloops, BC V2C 1W3, Canada

Cialini, Julie (Artist, Model)
PO Box 55536
Valencia, CA 91385-0536, USA

Ciampi, Joe (Coach)
Auburn University
Athletic Dept
Auburn, AL 36831, USA

Ciampl, Joe (Coach)
Aubuin University
Athletic Dept
Auburn, AL 36831, USA

Cianfrocco, Archi (Athlete, Baseball Player)
12424 Addax Ct
San Diego, CA 92129-4141, USA

Ciara (Musician)
c/o Jenna Adler *Creative Artists Agency (CAA)*
2000 Avenue of the Stars Ste 100
Los Angeles, CA 90067-4705, USA

Ciaramello, Benny (Actor)
c/o Scott Zimmerman *Scott Zimmerman Management*
1644 Courtney Ave
Los Angeles, CA 90046-2708, USA

Ciardi, Mark (Athlete, Baseball Player)
21 Mitchell Ave
Piscataway, NJ 08854-5560, USA

Ciavaglia, Peter (Athlete, Hockey Player, Olympic Athlete)
1137 Carrie Ct
Rochester Hills, MI 48309-3766, USA

Cibak, Martin (Athlete, Hockey Player)
Nabrezie Dr Aurela Stodolu
1799/66
Liptovsky, Mikulas 03101, Slovakia

Cibrian, Eddie (Actor)
c/o Steve Sauer *Media Four*
10100 Santa Monica Blvd Ste 2300
Los Angeles, CA 90067-4135, USA

Cibulkova, Dominika (Athlete, Tennis Player)
WTA
1 Progress Plz Ste 1500
Saint Petersburg, FL 33701-4335, USA

Ciccarelli, Dino (Athlete, Hockey Player)
38371 Huron Pointe Dr
Harrison Twp, MI 48045-2838, USA

Ciccarelli, Dino (Athlete, Hockey Player)
1872 Clarence St.
Rome 1-00123, ITALY

Ciccolella, Jude (Actor)
705 N Screenland Dr
Burbank, CA 91505-3123, USA

Ciccolella, Mike (Athlete, Football Player)
8145 Station House Rd
Dayton, OH 45458-2931, USA

Ciccone, Christopher (Designer)
Bernhardt Design/Pacific Design Center
8687 Melrose Ave Ste B230
West Hollywood, CA 90069-5786

Ciccone, Enrico (Athlete, Hockey Player)
c/o Staff Member *Sports Prospects Inc*
77 Rue de Bleury
Rosemere, QC J7A 4L9, Canada

Cicerone, Aldo (Musician)
Gerhild Baron Mgmt
Dombacher Str 41/III/3
Vienna 01170, AUSTRIA

Cichocki, Chris (Athlete, Hockey Player)
3823 Spring Meadow Ln
Stockton, CA 95219-2547, USA

Cichowski, Gene (Chick) (Athlete, Football Player)
3903 Oak Ave
Northbrook, IL 60062-4922, USA

Cichowski, Tom (Athlete, Football Player)
443 N Hill Rd
Kalispell, MT 59901-8107, USA

Cichy, Joe J (Athlete, Football Player)
1220 N Mandan St
Bismarck, ND 58501-2608, USA

Cid, Celeste (Actor)
c/o Staff Member *Telefe (Argentina)*
Pavon 2444
Buenos Aires C1248AAT, ARGENTINA

Cidre, Cynthia (Producer, Writer)
c/o Ann Blanchard *Creative Artists Agency (CAA)*
2000 Avenue of the Stars Ste 100
Los Angeles, CA 90067-4705, USA

Cienfuegos, Mauricio (Soccer Player)
Los Angeles Galaxy
1010 Rose Bowl Dr
Pasadena, CA 91103, USA

Ciger, Zdeno (Athlete, Hockey Player)
Hotel 21 Nerudova 8
Bratislava 82104, Slovakia

Cigliuti, Natalia (Actor)
c/o Felicia Sager *Sager Management*
260 S Beverly Dr Ste 205
Beverly Hills, CA 90212-3812, USA

Cihocki, Al (Athlete, Baseball Player)
43 Cochise Cir
Medford, NJ 08055-9769, USA

Cilmi, Gabriella (Musician)
c/o David (Dave) Chumbley *Primary Talent International (UK)*
10-11 Jockeys Fields
The Primary Bldg
London WC1R 4BN, UNITED KINGDOM

Cimarro, Mario (Actor)
c/o Arlene Forster *Forster Entertainment*
12533 Woodgreen St
Los Angeles, CA 90066-2723, USA

Cimber, Matt (Director, Producer, Writer)
Cimero Enterprises
3620 Beverly Glen Blvd # 1A
Sherman Oaks, CA 91423-4403, USA

Cimellaro, Tony (Athlete, Coach, Hockey Player)
c/o Staff Member *Kingston Frontenacs*
PO Box 665 Stn Main
Stn Main
Kingston, ON K7L 4X1, Canada

Cimetta, Rob (Athlete, Hockey Player)
Cimetta Properties
207-834 Yonge St
Toronto, ON M4W 2H1, Canada

Cimino, Pete (Athlete, Baseball Player)
31 Douglas Rd
Dracut, MA 01826-4214, USA

Cimmo, Leonardo (Actor)
Michael Hartig Agency
156 5th Ave Ste 820
New York, NY 10010-7767, USA

Cimorelli, Frank (Athlete, Baseball Player)
8802 W Hadley St
Milwaukee, WI 53222-4632, USA

Cincotti, Peter (Musician)
c/o Staff Member *WME|IMG*
9601 Wilshire Blvd
Beverly Hills, CA 90210-5213, USA

Cinderella (Music Group)
Tom Keifer
6129 S Riverbend Dr
Nashville, TN 37221-3937, USA

Cindrich, Joe (Athlete, Football Player)
1310 Trinity Dr
Menlo Park, CA 94025-6680, USA

Cindrich, Ralph (Athlete, Football Player)
151 Fort Pitt Blvd Apt 1501
Pittsburgh, PA 15222-1572, USA

Cinematic Sunrise (Music Group)
c/o Staff Member *Equal Vision Records*
PO Box 38202
Albany, NY 12203-8202, USA

Cineson All-Stars (Music Group)
c/o Staff Member *Paradigm (Monterey)*
404 W Franklin St
Monterey, CA 93940-2303, USA

Cink, Stewart (Athlete, Golfer)
2195 Lockett Ct
Duluth, GA 30097-5012, USA

Cinninger, Jake (Musician)
19350 State Line Rd
South Bend, IN 46637-2080, USA

Cintron, Alex (Athlete, Baseball Player)
HC 2 Box 8575
Yabucoa, PR 00767-9599, USA

Cioffi, Charles (Actor)
c/o Staff Member *Paradigm*
8942 Wilshire Blvd
Beverly Hills, CA 90211-1908, USA

Cipa, Larry (Athlete, Football Player)
250 Torrent Ct
Rochester Hills, MI 48307-3871, USA

Cipriani, Frank (Athlete, Baseball Player)
14 Oakhill Dr
Buffalo, NY 14224-4214, USA

Cipriani Thorne, Juan Luis Cardinal (Religious Leader)
Arzobispado
Plaza de Armas S/N
Apartado 1512
Lima 00100, PERU

Circa Survive (Music Group)
c/o Brian Schechter *Riot Squad Management*
335 Cortlandt St Fl 2
Belleville, NJ 07109-3201, USA

Cirella, Joe (Athlete, Hockey Player)
600-1 Adelaide St E
TERANET
Toronto, ON M5C 2V9, Canada

Cirillo, Jeff (Athlete, Baseball Player)
PO Box 233
Medina, WA 98039-0233, USA

Cirrincione, Vincent (Producer)
Vincent Cirrincione Associates
1516 N Fairfax Ave
Los Angeles, CA 90046-2608, USA

Cisco, Galen (Athlete, Baseball Player)
604 Elmwood Ln
Celina, OH 45822-2966, USA

Cishek, Steven (Athlete, Baseball Player)
4 Clearwater Dr
East Falmouth, MA 02536-4768, USA

Cisneros, Henry (Politician)
2002 W Houston St
San Antonio, TX 78207-3419, USA

Cisowski, Steve (Athlete, Football Player)
1090 3rd St
Gilroy, CA 95020-5302, USA

Citarella, Ralph (Athlete, Baseball Player)
29 E Sherman Ave
Colonia, NJ 07067-1412, USA

Citro, Ralph (Boxer)
32 N Black Horse Pike
Blackwood, NJ 08012-3093, USA

Citti, Christine (Actor)
Artmedia
20 Ave Rapp
Paris 75007, FRANCE

Ciufo, Leonard (Athlete, Football Player)
1110 Trail View Pl
Nipomo, CA 93444-6689

Civiletti, Benjamin (Politician)
5900 Old Ocean Blvd Apt B3
Blvd Apt B3
Ocean Ridge, FL 33435-6228, USA

C. Johnson Jr., Henry (Congressman, Politician)
1427 Longworth Hob
Washington, DC 20515-1503, USA

CK, Louis (Actor, Comedian)
c/o John Sloss *Sloss Eckhouse LawCo*
555 W 25th St Fl 4
New York, NY 10001-5542, USA

Claar, Brian (Athlete, Golfer)
27 Bentgrass Pl
Spring, TX 77381-6122, USA

Clabo, Neal (Athlete, Football Player)
1100 Beaverton Rd Apt 1
Knoxville, TN 37919-7089, USA

Clabo, Neil (Athlete, Football Player)
1100 Beaverton Rd Apt 1
Knoxville, TN 37919-7089, USA

Clabo, Tyson (Athlete, Football Player)
c/o Chad Speck *Allegiant Athletic Agency*
35 Market Sq Ste 201
Knoxville, TN 37902-1420, USA

Clack, Darryl (Athlete, Football Player)
2050 E Runaway Bay Pl
Chandler, AZ 85249-4853, USA

Clackson, Kim (Athlete, Hockey Player)
342 Thomas Rd
Canonsburg, PA 15317-3534, USA

Clady, Ryan (Athlete, Football Player)

Claflin, Sam (Actor)
c/o Laura Colman *Premier PR*
2-4 Bucknall St
London WC2H 8LA, UNITED KINGDOM

Claggett, Anthony (Athlete, Baseball Player)
123 Arezzo Ct
Palm Desert, CA 92211-0715, USA

Claiborne, Morris (Athlete, Football Player)
c/o Bus Cook *Bus Cook Sports, Inc*
1 Willow Bend Dr
Hattiesburg, MS 39402-8552, USA

Claiborne, Preston (Athlete, Baseball Player)
c/o Terry Bross *Turn 2 Sports Management LLC*
PO Box 27345
Scottsdale, AZ 85255-0139, USA

Claire, Fred (Commentator)
1458 Rutherford Dr
Pasadena, CA 91103-2773, USA

Clairmont, Patsy (Writer)
Milk n Honey Inc
PO Box 36
Brighton, MI 48116-0036, USA

Claitt, Rickey (Athlete, Football Player)
5830 Grand Canyon Dr
Orlando, FL 32810-3232, USA

Clampett, Bobby (Athlete, Golfer)
5722 Belmont Valley Ct
Raleigh, NC 27612-6464, USA

Clampi, Joe (Coach)
Auburn University
Athletic Dept
Auburn, AL 36831, USA

Clancy, Jack (Athlete, Football Player)
Landmark Graphics AS PO Box 200
Stavanger, N-Norway 04065

Clancy, Jim (Athlete, Baseball Player)
2598 Gary Cir Apt 502
Dunedin, FL 34698-1789, USA

Clancy, Sam (Athlete, Football Player)
1308 Crest Ln
Oakdale, PA 15071-1748, USA

Clancy, Sean (Athlete, Football Player)
211 Bal Cross Dr
Bal Harbour, FL 33154-1318, USA

Clancy, Terry (Athlete, Hockey Player)
65 Golfdale Rd
Toronto, ON M4N 2B5, Canada

Clanton, Jimmy (Musician)
Jimmy Clanton Enterprises
409 Pencroft Dr S
Holtwood, PA 17532-9711, USA

Clapinski, Chris (Athlete, Baseball Player)
83328 Wagon Rd
Indio, CA 92203-2837, USA

Clapp, Gordon (Actor)
c/o Cynthia Snyder *Cynthia Snyder Public Relations*
5739 Colfax Ave
N Hollywood, CA 91601-1636, USA

Clapp, Nicholas R (Producer)
PO Box 1019
Borrego Springs, CA 92004-1019, USA

Clapp, Stubby (Athlete, Baseball Player)
140 P Haynes Ln
Savannah, TN 38372-3517, USA

Clapp, Thomas (Athlete, Football Player)
804 Live Oak St
Metairie, LA 70005-1216, USA

Clapton, Eric (Musician)
c/o Kristen Foster *PMK/BNC Public Relations*
1840 Century Park E Ste 1400
Los Angeles, CA 90067-2115, USA

Clap Your Hands Say Yeah (Music Group)
c/o Staff Member *Big Hassle Media*
40 Exchange Pl Ste 1900
New York, NY 10005-2714, USA

Clarence, Ellis (Athlete, Football Player)
5849 Leisure South Dr SE
Grand Rapids, MI 49548-6855, USA

Clarey, Doug (Athlete, Baseball Player)
2116 Hillhurst Ave
Los Angeles, CA 90027-2004, USA

Claridge, Dennis (Athlete, Football Player)
2621 Calvert St
Lincoln, NE 68502-4935, USA

Clarizio, Louis (Athlete, Baseball Player)
133 Lela Ln
Schaumburg, IL 60193-1339, USA

Clark, Al (Athlete, Baseball Player)
1185 SW 5th Ave
Boca Raton, FL 33432-7140, USA

Clark, Alan (Musician)
Damage Mgmt
16 Lambton Place
London W11 2SH, UNITED KINGDOM (UK)

Clark, Annie (Actor)
c/o Norbert Abrams *Noble Caplan Abrams*
1260 Yonge St Fl 2
Toronto, ON M4T 1W5, CANADA

Clark, Annie (St Vincent) (Musician)
c/o Staff Member *Lever and Beam*
15 W 26th St Fl 12
New York, NY 10010-1023, USA

Clark, Anthony (Actor, Comedian)
c/o Mark Rousso *Industry Entertainment Partners*
955 Carrillo Dr Ste 300
Los Angeles, CA 90048-5400, USA

Clark, Archie (Athlete, Basketball Player)
4268 10th St
Ecorse, MI 48229-1219, USA

Clark, Bernard (Athlete, Football Player)
7231 Peregrina Loop
Wesley Chapel, FL 33545-5071, USA

Clark, Blake (Actor)
c/o Brett Cates *Luber Roklin Management*
5815 W Sunset Blvd Ste 208
Los Angeles, CA 90028-6481, USA

Clark, Bobby (Athlete, Baseball Player)
575 S Lyon Ave Spc 60
Hemet, CA 92543-5753, USA

Clark, Brady (Athlete, Baseball Player)
19275 Green Lakes Loop
Bend, OR 97702-1171, USA

Clark, Brandy (Musician)

Clark, Bret (Athlete, Football Player)
815 Manes Ct
Lincoln, NE 68505-2021, USA

Clark, Brett (Athlete, Hockey Player)
8745 Aberdeen Cir
Highlands Ranch, CO 80130-3952, USA

Clark, Brian (Athlete, Football Player)
752 Hunt Club Run
Charleston, SC 29414-9100, USA

Clark, Bruce (Athlete, Football Player)
3150 Shellers Bnd
State College, PA 16801-2772, USA

Clark, Bryan (Athlete, Football Player)
44290 Delco Blvd
Sterling Heights, MI 48313-1018, USA

Clark, Bryan (Baseball Player)
Seattle Mariners
508 E Clark St
Madera, CA 93638-1662, USA

Clark, Candy (Actor)
13935 Hatteras St
Van Nuys, CA 91401-4342, USA

Clark, Carol Hiqgins (Writer)
300 E 56th St
New York, NY 10022-4136, USA

Clark, Charles D (Actor)
Woodbridge, VA 22193, USA

Clark, Chris (Athlete, Football Player)

Clark, Chris (Athlete, Hockey Player)
160 Pine Tree Ln
South Windsor, CT 06074-3219, USA

Clark, Dallas (Athlete, Football Player)
PO Box 44
Livermore, IA 50558-0044, USA

Clark, Daniel (Actor)
c/o Staff Member *Schachter Entertainment*
1157 S Beverly Dr Fl 2
Los Angeles, CA 90035-1119, USA

Clark, Danny (Athlete, Football Player)
213 Seneca Trl
Bloomingdale, IL 60108-2432, USA

Clark, Dave (Athlete, Baseball Player)
4842 Mayfield Rd W
Collierville, TN 38017-3309, USA

Clark, Desmond (Athlete, Football Player)
2190 Shadow Creek Ct
Vernon Hills, IL 60061-4567

Clark, Doug (Athlete, Baseball Player)
106 Piedmont St
Springfield, MA 01104-2042, USA

Clark, Earl (Swimmer)
1145 NE 126th St Apt 4
North Miami, FL 33161-5027, USA

Clark, Gail (Athlete, Football Player)
337 Colton Ave
Bellefontaine, OH 43311-1872, USA

Clark, Gene (Musician)
Artists International Mgmt
9850 Sandaltoot Road
#458
Boca Raton, FL 33428, USA

Clark, Glen (Athlete, Baseball Player)
5605 Marblehead Dr
Dallas, TX 75232-2356, USA

Clark, Gordie (Athlete, Hockey Player)
28 Rockingham St
Portsmouth, NH 03801-3940, USA

Clark, Harry (Athlete, Football Player)
1121 Patton Dr
Morgantown, WV 26505-3756, USA

Clark, Howie (Athlete, Baseball Player)
14204 439th Ave SE
North Bend, WA 98045-9209, USA

Clark, Jack (The Ripper) (Athlete, Baseball Player)
7601 Orvale Rd Apt 8416
Plano, TX 75024-5997, USA

Clark, Jerald (Athlete, Baseball Player)
12325 Crisscross Ln
San Diego, CA 92129-3766, USA

Clark, Jermaine (Athlete, Baseball Player)
2 Ute Ct
San Ramon, CA 94583-2455, USA

Clark, Jessie (Athlete, Football Player)
7611 S 9th Way
Phoenix, AZ 85042-6621, USA

Clark, Jim (Athlete, Baseball Player)
659 S Indian Hill Blvd Apt C
Claremont, CA 91711-5486, USA

Clark, Kelly (Athlete, Skier)
178 Route 100
West Dover, VT 05356-0725, USA

Clark, Kelvin (Athlete, Football Player)
3812 Evesham Dr
Plano, TX 75025-3818, USA

Clark, Keon (Basketball Player)
Utah Jazz Delta Center
301 W South Temple
Salt Lake City, UT 84101-1219, USA

Clark, Kevin Alexander (Actor)

Clark, Leroy (Athlete, Football Player)
5458 Osprey Dr
Houston, TX 77048-1109, USA

Clark, L Hill (Business Person)
Crane Co
100 Stamford Pl Ste 300
Stamford, CT 06902-6740, USA

Clark, Louis S (Athlete, Football Player)
6149 Kissengen Springs Ct
Jacksonville, FL 32258-5136, USA

Clark, Marcia (Attorney, Television Host)
c/o Jason Richman *United Talent Agency (UTA)*
9336 Civic Center Dr
Beverly Hills, CA 90210-3604, USA

Clark, Mario (Athlete, Football Player)
48100 Sandia Creek Dr
Temecula, CA 92590-4130, USA

Clark, Mark (Athlete, Baseball Player)
18262 E CR 520N
Kilbourne, IL 62655-6628, USA

Clark, Marlene (Actor)
c/o Staff Member *Sutton Barth & Vennari Inc*
5900 Wilshire Blvd Ste 700
Los Angeles, CA 90036-5009, USA

Clark, Mary Ellen (Athlete, Swimmer)

Clark, Mary Higgins (Writer)
MHC-Clark
15 Werimus Brook Rd
Saddle River, NJ 07458-3118, USA

Clark, Mary Higgins (Writer)
210 Central Park S Apt 16B
New York, NY 10019-1425, USA

Clark, Matt (Actor)
1199 Park Ave Apt 15D
New York, NY 10128-1791, USA

Clark, Mystro (Actor, Comedian)
c/o Staff Member *ICM Partners*
10250 Constellation Blvd Fl 7
Los Angeles, CA 90067-6207, USA

Clark, Nate (Comedian)
c/o Lon Haber *Lon Haber & Co (IPPR)*
304 S Broadway
Los Angeles, CA 90013-1224, USA

Clark, Perry (Coach)
Miami University
Athletic Dept
Coral Gables, FL 33124, USA

Clark, Petula (Musician)
5415 Collins Ave # Phf
Miami Beach, FL 33140-2575, USA

Clark, Phil (Athlete, Baseball Player)
112 Hicks Rd
Dawson, GA 39842-4002, USA

Clark, Phil (Athlete, Football Player)
PO Box 3021
Barrington, IL 60011-3021, USA

Clark, Ramsey (Politician)
37 W 12th St Apt 2B
New York, NY 10011-8503, USA

Clark, Rickey (Athlete, Baseball Player)
8953 Emerald Waters Ct
Las Vegas, NV 89147-6501, USA

Clark, Robert C (Artist)
34 Monterey Ct
Manhattan Beach, CA 90266-7237, USA

Clark, Ron (Athlete, Baseball Player)
700 Starkey Rd Unit 511
Largo, FL 33771-2344, USA

Clark, Ryan (Athlete, Football Player)
1236 Camarta Dr
Pittsburgh, PA 15227-3956, USA

Clark, Sedric (Athlete, Football Player)
7819 Chasewood Dr
Missouri City, TX 77489-1836, USA

Clark, Spencer Treat (Actor)
c/o Britney Ross *42West*
1840 Century Park E Ste 700
Los Angeles, CA 90067-2122, USA

Clark, Stephen E (Steve) (Swimmer)
29 Martling Rd
San Anselmo, CA 94960-1172, USA

Clark, Susan (Actor)
7943 Woodrow Wilson Dr
Los Angeles, CA 90046-1215, USA

Clark, Terry (Athlete, Baseball Player)
1607 E Tam O Shanter St
Ontario, CA 91761-6356, USA

Clark, Tim (Athlete, Golfer)
22400 N 97th St
Scottsdale, AZ 85255-4431, USA

Clark, Tony (Athlete, Baseball Player)
35 Rickland Rd
Old Tappan, NJ 07675-6856, USA

Clark, Vinnie (Athlete, Football Player)
1120 Virescent Ct
Cincinnati, OH 45224-2789, USA

Clark, Wayne (Athlete, Football Player)
14241 Lambeth Way
Tustin, CA 92780-2230, USA

Clark, Wendel (Athlete, Hockey Player)
c/o Staff Member *Toronto Maple Leafs*
Air Canada Centre
400-40 Bay St
Toronto, ON M5J 2X2, CANADA

Clark, Wendel (Athlete, Hockey Player)
14922 Bathurst St
King City, ON L7B 1K5, Canada

Clark, Will (Adult Film Star)
c/o Staff Member *Diva Central Inc*
7510 W Sunset Blvd # 1445
Los Angeles, CA 90046-3408, USA

Clark, Will (Athlete, Baseball Player, Olympic Athlete)
18555 Saint Andrews Ct E
Prairieville, LA 70769-3248, USA

Clark-Cole, Dorinda (Musician)
c/o Keith Douglas *RKD Music Management*
PO Box 11611
Beverly Hills, CA 90213-4611, USA

Clark-Diggs, Joetta (Athlete, Olympic Athlete, Track Athlete)
1856 Clarence Dr
Hellertown, PA 18055-2701, USA

Clarke, Allan (Music Group, Musician)
Hill Farm Hackleton
Northantshire NN7 2DH, UNITED KINGDOM (UK)

Clarke, Angela (Actor)
3930 Weeping Willow Dr
Moorpark, CA 93021-2842, USA

Clarke, Bob (Cartoonist)
10326 Windtree Ln
Charlotte, NC 28215-9018, USA

Clarke, Bobby (Athlete, Hockey Player)
Philadelphia Flyers
3601 S Broad St Ste 2
Philadelphia, PA 19148-5297, USA

Clarke, Brian Patrick (Actor)
c/o Staff Member *Orange Grove Group, The*
12178 Ventura Blvd Ste 205
Studio City, CA 91604-2540, USA

Clarke, Darren (Athlete, Golfer)
c/o Andrew ""Chubby"" Chandler *International Sports Management Ltd (ISM UK)*
Cherry Tree Farm
Cherry Tree Lane
Rostherne, Cheshire WA14 3RZ, UNITED KINGDOM

Clarke, Elis E I (President)
16 Frederick St
Port of Spain, TRINADAD & TOBAGO

Clarke, Emilia (Actor)
c/o Michael Emptage *Emptage Hallett*
34-35 Eastcastle St
Fl 3
London W1W 8DW, UNITED KINGDOM (UK)

Clarke, Emily (Actor)
c/o Darren Goldberg *Global Creative*
1051 Cole Ave # B
Los Angeles, CA 90038-2601, USA

Clarke, Emmy (Actor)
c/o Darren Goldberg *Global Creative*
1051 Cole Ave # B
Los Angeles, CA 90038-2601, USA

Clarke, Gary (Actor, Writer)
6701 Rialto Blvd Apt 5402
Austin, TX 78735-8640, USA

Clarke, Gilby (Music Group, Musician)
Sammy Boyd Entertainment
212 Allen Ave
Allenhurst, NJ 07711-1006, USA

Clarke, Hagood (Athlete, Football Player)
2500 NE 37th Dr
Fort Lauderdale, FL 33308-6323, USA

Clarke, Hansen (Congressman, Politician)
1319 Longworth Hob
Washington, DC 20515-1305, USA

Clarke, Horace (Athlete, Baseball Player)
9611 Dixon St
Laurel, MD 20723-1926, USA

Clarke, Jason (Actor)
c/o Erin O'Connor *RGM Artists*
8-12 Ann St
Surry Hills, NSW 02010, AUSTRALIA

Clarke, John (Actor)
Days of Our Lives Show
3000 W Alameda Ave
Burbank, CA 91523-0001, USA

Clarke, Kate (Actor)
1470 Angelus Ave
Los Angeles, CA 90026-2209, USA

Clarke, Ken (Athlete, Football Player)
7610 Willoughby Ct
Alpharetta, GA 30005-3028, USA

Clarke, Lenny (Actor)
c/o Staff Member *Paradigm*
8942 Wilshire Blvd
Beverly Hills, CA 90211-1908, USA

Clarke, Melinda (Actor)
c/o Michael (Mike) Jelline *United Talent Agency (UTA)*
9336 Civic Center Dr
Beverly Hills, CA 90210-3604, USA

Clarke, Noah (Athlete, Hockey Player)
4683 Oberle Ct
La Verne, CA 91750-2126, USA

Clarke, Noel (Actor, Director, Writer)
c/o Staff Member *Liz Matthews PR*
8 Smokehouse Yard
44-46 St. John St
London EC1M 4DF, United Kingdom

Clarke, Sarah (Actor)
c/o Staff Member *Levine Management*
8549 Wilshire Blvd # 212
Beverly Hills, CA 90211-3104, USA

Clarke, Stan (Athlete, Baseball Player)
5333 Sanders Dr
Toledo, OH 43615-6860, USA

Clarke, Stanley (Musician)
880 Greenleaf Canyon Rd
Topanga, CA 90290-4111, USA

Clarke, Susanna (Writer)
Tom Doherty Associates, LLC
175 5th Ave
New York, NY 10010-7703, USA

Clarke, Thomas E (Business Person)
Nice Inc
1 SW Bowerman Dr
Beaverton, OR 97005-0979, USA

Clark II, Michael (Athlete, Golfer)
511 Williamsburg Dr
Dalton, GA 30720-8145, USA

Clark-Sheard, Karen (Musician)
c/o Staff Member *M.A.G./Universal Attractions*
15 W 36th St Fl 8
New York, NY 10018-7927, USA

Clarkson, Jeremy (Television Host)
c/o Staff Member *XS Promotions*
57 Fonthill Rd
Aberdeen AB11 6UQ, UNITED KINGDOM (UK)

Clarkson, Kelly (Musician, Songwriter)
c/o Narvel Blackstock *Starstruck Entertainment*
40 Music Sq W
Nashville, TN 37203-3206, USA

Clarkson, Patricia (Actor)
c/o Tony Lipp *Anonymous Content*
3532 Hayden Ave
Culver City, CA 90232-2413, USA

Clary, Jeromey (Athlete, Football Player)
c/o David Dunn *Athletes First*
23091 Mill Creek Dr
Laguna Hills, CA 92653-1258, USA

Clary, Julian (Actor)
PO Box 976
Swindon
SN5 7HN, UNITED KINGDOM

Clary, Marty (Athlete, Baseball Player)
205 Yorktown Ct
Easley, SC 29642-9042, USA

Clary, Robert (Actor)
10001 Sundial Ln
Beverly Hills, CA 90210-2719, USA

Clasby, Bob (Athlete, Football Player)
5959 N 78th St Unit 2131
Scottsdale, AZ 85250-6195, USA

Clatney, Paul (Athlete, Football Player)
302-190 Manitoba St
Toronto, ON M8Y 3Y8, Canada

Claudel, Philippe (Director)
c/o Staff Member *ArtMedia*
8 rue Danielle Casanova
Paris 75002, FRANCE

Claudio, Sabrina (Musician)
c/o Brian Edelman *WME/IMG*
9601 Wilshire Blvd
Beverly Hills, CA 90210-5213, USA

Clausen, Jimmy (Athlete, Football Player)
c/o David Dunn *Athletes First*
23091 Mill Creek Dr
Laguna Hills, CA 92653-1258, USA

Clauss, Jared (Athlete, Football Player)
105 Fox Lndg
Waukee, IA 50263-9539, USA

Claussen, Brandon (Athlete, Baseball Player)
2626 29th St
Lubbock, TX 79410-3320, USA

Clavier, Christian (Actor)
Agents Associes Beaume
201 Faubourg Saint Honore
Paris 75008, FRANCE

Clawson, John (Athlete, Basketball Player, Olympic Athlete)
30 Eagle Lake Pl Unit 31
San Ramon, CA 94582-4858, USA

Claxton, Craig (Speedy) (Athlete, Basketball Player)
Golden State Warriors
57 Hitchcock Ln
Old Westbury, NY 11568-1403, USA

Claxton, Paul (Athlete, Golfer)
PO Box 485
Claxton, GA 30417-0485, USA

Clay, Andrew Dice (Comedian)
c/o Liza Anderson *Anderson Group Public Relations*
8060 Melrose Ave Fl 4
Los Angeles, CA 90046-7038, USA

Clay, Bryan (Athlete, Olympic Athlete)
c/o Staff Member *USA Track & Field*
130 E Washington St Ste 800
Indianapolis, IN 46204-4619, USA

Clay, Charles (Athlete, Football Player)

Clay, Danny (Athlete, Baseball Player)
151 Illinois Ave
Westerville, OH 43081-2325, USA

Clay, Hayward (Athlete, Football Player)
PO Box 234
Snyder, TX 79550-0234, USA

Clay, John (Athlete, Football Player)
1441 S 10th St
Saint Louis, MO 63104-3724, USA

Clay, Walter (Athlete, Football Player)
2827 Arlington Ave
Pueblo, CO 81003-1315, USA

Clay, Willie (Athlete, Football Player)
1460 Hawthorne St
Pittsburgh, PA 15201-2025, USA

Clayborn, Raymond D (Ray) (Athlete, Football Player)
20610 Aspen Canyon Dr
Katy, TX 77450-7091, USA

Claybrooks, Devon (Athlete, Football Player)
725 Auburn Pl
Martinsville, VA 24112-4502, USA

Clayderman, Richard (Musician)
Denis Vaughan Management
P O Box 28286
London N21 3WT, UNITED KINGDOM (UK)

Claydon, Phil (Director)
c/o Jason Burns *United Talent Agency (UTA)*
9336 Civic Center Dr
Beverly Hills, CA 90210-3604, USA

Claypool, Les (Musician)
c/o Brad Sands *Red Light Management*
455 2nd St NE
#500
Charlottesville, VA 22902-5791, USA

Clayson, Jane (Correspondent)
c/o Staff Member *CBS Television*
51 W 52nd St
New York, NY 10019-6119, USA

Clayton, Adam (Music Group, Musician)
Principle Mgmt
30-32 Sir John Rogersons Quay
Dublin @, IRELAND

Clayton, Amber (Actor)
c/o Steve Glick *Glick Agency*
1321 7th St Ste 203
Santa Monica, CA 90401-1631, USA

Clayton, Garrett (Actor)
7916 Melrose Ave Ste 1
Los Angeles, CA 90046-7160, USA

Clayton, Harvey (Athlete, Football Player)
15303 SW 143rd St
Miami, FL 33196-2879, USA

Clayton, John (Correspondent, Writer)
c/o Staff Member *ESPN (Main)*
935 Middle St
Espn Plaza
Bristol, CT 06010-1000, USA

Clayton, Keenan (Athlete, Football Player)
c/o Ashley Smith Becker *Relativity Sports*
2029 Century Park E Ste 1550
Century City, CA 90067-3000, USA

Clayton, Mark (Athlete, Football Player)
16426 Canyon Chase Dr
Houston, TX 77095-6532, USA

Clayton, Michael (Athlete, Football Player)
8501 Kentucky Derby Dr
Odessa, FL 33556-2446, USA

Clayton, Ralph (Athlete, Football Player)
6356 Selkirk St
Detroit, MI 48211-1836, USA

Clayton, Royce (Athlete, Baseball Player)
5924 Paseo Canyon Dr
Malibu, CA 90265-3130, USA

Clayton, Thomas David (Music Group, Musician)
Music Avenue Inc
43 Washington St
Groveland, MA 01834-1142, USA

Cleamons, Jim (Athlete, Basketball Player)
29 Sausalito Cir W
Manhattan Beach, CA 90266-7234, USA

Clear, Mark (Athlete, Baseball Player)
15654 S Rene St
Olathe, KS 66062-4676, USA

Clearwater, Keith (Athlete, Golfer)
42712 Azure St
Temecula, CA 92592-4705, USA

Clearwater, Ray (Athlete, Hockey Player)
98 George St
East Haven, CT 06512-4726, USA

Cleary, Beverly (Writer)
c/o Staff Member *HarperCollins Publishers*
195 Broadway Fl 2
New York, NY 10007-3132, USA

Cleary, Jon Stephen (Writer)
HarperCollins
23 Ryde Road
Pymble, NSW 02073, AUSTRALIA

Cleary, William J (Bill) Jr (Athlete, Hockey Player, Olympic Athlete)
27 Kingswood Rd
Auburndale, MA 02466-1013, USA

Cleave, Dr Mary L (Astronaut)
7101 Bay Front Dr Apt 118
Annapolis, MD 21403-3628, USA

Cleave, Mary L (Astronaut)
NASA
Earth Science Office
Code AS Room 7R86
Washington, DC 20546-0001, USA

Cleaver, Alan (Designer, Fashion Designer)
Via Vallone 11
Monte Conero
Sirolo, ITALY

Cleaver, Emanuel (Congressman, Politician)
1433 Longworth Hob
Washington, DC 20515-0104, USA

Cleeland, Cam (Athlete, Football Player)
23160 Lanyard Ln
Mount Vernon, WA 98274-8379, USA

Cleese, John (Actor, Comedian, Writer)
c/o Tony Lipp *Anonymous Content*
3532 Hayden Ave
Culver City, CA 90232-2413, USA

Clef (Music Group, Musician)
DAS Communications
83 Riverside Dr
New York, NY 10024-5713, USA

Clegg, Johnny (Music Group, Musician)
c/o Staff Member *Monterey International (Chicago)*
72 W Adams St # 1000
Chicago, IL 60603-5107, USA

Cleghorne, Ellen (Actor, Comedian)
c/o Frederick Levy *Management 101*
11271 Ventura Blvd # 102
Studio City, CA 91604-3136, USA

Cleland, Max (Politician)
2460 Peachtree Rd NW Apt 1406
Atlanta, GA 30305-4223, USA

Clemens, Barry (Athlete, Basketball Player)
3111 Clinton Ave
Cleveland, OH 44113-2973, USA

Clemens, Donella (Religious Leader)
Mononnite Church
722 N Main St
Newton, KS 67114-1819, USA

Clemens, Doug (Athlete, Baseball Player)
4799 Lower Mountain Rd
New Hope, PA 18938-9454, USA

Clemens, Kellen (Athlete, Football Player)
c/o David Dunn *Athletes First*
23091 Mill Creek Dr
Laguna Hills, CA 92653-1258, USA

Clemens, Robert (Bob) (Athlete, Football Player)
2007 Poole Dr NW Ste D
Huntsville, AL 35810-4900, USA

Clemens, Roger (Athlete, Baseball Player)
11535 Quail Hollow Ln
Houston, TX 77024-6508, USA

Clemenson, Christian (Actor)
2666 La Cuesta Dr
Los Angeles, CA 90046-1337, USA

Clement, Anthony (Athlete, Football Player)
141 Navajo Ln
Opelousas, LA 70570-0324, USA

Clement, Aurore (Actor)
c/o Elisabeth Tanner *Time-Art*
8 rue Danielle Casanova
Paris 75002, FRANCE

Clement, Bill (Athlete, Hockey Player)
8 Elfreths Ct
Newtown, PA 18940-1150, USA

Clement, Jeff (Athlete, Baseball Player)
33730 585th Ave
Cambridge, IA 50046-8595, USA

Clement, Jemaine (Actor, Writer)
c/o Jason Heyman *United Talent Agency (UTA)*
9336 Civic Center Dr
Beverly Hills, CA 90210-3604, USA

Clement, Matt (Athlete, Baseball Player)
143 Milt Miller Rd
Renfrew, PA 16053-9613, USA

Clement, Skip (Athlete, Football Player)
620 Tennis Club Dr Apt 106
Fort Lauderdale, FL 33311-4030, USA

Clemente, Fransesco (Artist)
684 Broadway Apt 2E
New York, NY 10012-1122, USA

Clementi, Kassandra (Actor)
c/o Siri Garber *Platform PR*
2666 N Beachwood Dr
Los Angeles, CA 90068-2308, USA

Clements, Dick (Director, Producer, Writer)
c/o Bruce Kaufman *ICM Partners*
10250 Constellation Blvd Fl 7
Los Angeles, CA 90067-6207, USA

Clements, Kim (Writer)
c/o Staff Member *Creative Artists Agency (CAA)*
2000 Avenue of the Stars Ste 100
Los Angeles, CA 90067-4705, USA

Clements, Lennie (Athlete, Golfer)

Clements, Nate (Athlete, Football Player)
1 Bills Dr
Orchard Park, NY 14127-2237, USA

Clements, Pat (Athlete, Baseball Player)
14 Barker Ct
Chico, CA 95928-3842, USA

Clements, Ronald (Director, Producer, Writer)
c/o Staff Member *Creative Artists Agency (CAA)*
2000 Avenue of the Stars Ste 100
Los Angeles, CA 90067-4705, USA

Clements, Suzanne (Designer, Fashion Designer)
Clements Ribeiro Ltd
48 S Molton St
London W1X 1HE, UNITED KINGDOM (UK)

Clements, Tom (Athlete, Football Player)
999 N Doheny Dr Apt 1008
West Hollywood, CA 90069-3152, USA

Clements, Vincent (Vin) (Athlete, Football Player)
8217 Rusty Sandstone Ct
Las Vegas, NV 89131-1439, USA

Clemmensen, Scott (Athlete, Hockey Player)
Edge Sports Management
26 Autumn Ridge Rd
Pound Ridge, NY 10576-1400, USA

Clemmer, Ronnie (Producer)
c/o Staff Member *Longbow Productions*
PO Box 240
Van Nuys, CA 91408-0240, USA

Clemons, Charlie (Athlete, Football Player)
1973 Bertha Ct
Hampton, GA 30228-4006, USA

Clemons, Chris (Athlete, Football Player)
c/o Drew Rosenhaus *Rosenhaus Sports Representation*
3921 Alton Rd # 440
Miami Beach, FL 33140-3852, USA

Clemons, Chris (Athlete, Baseball Player)
521 Karen Dr
Robinson, TX 76706-5122, USA

Clemons, Craig (Athlete, Football Player)
2764 Audubon Trl
Columbus, OH 43231-5842, USA

Clemons, Duane (Athlete, Football Player)
259 Bishops Glen Dr
Frederick, MD 21702-1157, USA

Clemons, Kiersey (Actor)
c/o Starr Andreeff *Maple Jam Music Group (MJMG)*
4108 W Riverside Dr Ste 3
Burbank, CA 91505-4192, USA

Clemons, Toney (Athlete, Football Player)

Clendenin, Robert (Bob) (Actor)
2343 N Reese Pl
Burbank, CA 91504-2214, USA

Clennon, David (Actor)
2309 27th St
Santa Monica, CA 90405-1921, USA

Clervoy, Jean-Francois (Astronaut)
NASA
EAC Postfach 90 26 96
Koln, Germany D-51127, USA

Cleveland, Davis (Actor)
c/o Mara Santino *Luber Roklin Management*
5815 W Sunset Blvd Ste 208
Los Angeles, CA 90028-6481, USA

Cleveland, Reggie (Athlete, Baseball Player)
11708 Beach St
Frisco, TX 75036-6435, USA

Clevlen, Brent (Athlete, Baseball Player)
14100 Avery Ranch Blvd Unit 1703
Austin, TX 78717-4012, USA

Cliburn, Stan (Athlete, Baseball Player)
Sioux City Explorers 3400
C;ioull Ciru, LA 51106, USA

Cliburn, Stew (Athlete, Baseball Player)
425 William Dr
Pleasant View, TN 37146-7910, USA

Cliche, Karen (Actor)
c/o Sandy Martinez *Martinez Creative Management*
7012 St Laurent Blvd Suite 200
Montreal, QC H2S 3E2, Canada

Click, Shannan (Model)
1672 Mountcrest Ave
Los Angeles, CA 90069-1426, USA

Cliff, Jimmy (Music Group, Songwriter, Writer)
51 Lady Musgrave Rd
Kingston, JAMAICA

Clifford, Chris (Athlete, Hockey Player)
600 Compass Crt
Kingston, ON K7M 8V9, Canada

Clifford, Linda (Music Group)
c/o Staff Member *Diva Central Inc*
7510 W Sunset Blvd # 1445
Los Angeles, CA 90046-3408, USA

Clifford, Michael R (Astronaut)
601 Hillside Dr N Apt 2344
North Myrtle Beach, SC 29582-8918, USA

Clifford, M Richard (Rich) (Astronaut)
3700 Bay Area Blvd
Houston, TX 77058-1160, USA

Clifford, Steve (Basketball Coach)
c/o Steve Kauffman *Kauffman Sports Management Group*
Prefers to be contacted by telephone
Malibu, CA, USA

Clifford, Tokala (Black Elk) (Actor)
c/o Darryl Mork *Darryl Mork Talent Management*
12012-133A Ave
Edmonton T5E 1GB, CANADA

Clifton, Chad (Athlete, Football Player)
346 Heidelberg Ct
Green Bay, WI 54302-4949, USA

Clifton, Greg (Athlete, Football Player)
5701 Statesville Rd
Charlotte, NC 28269-2836, USA

Clifton, Kyle (Athlete, Football Player)
777 S Point Ct
Aledo, TX 76008-4134, USA

Clifton, Scott (Actor)
3527 Coldwater Canyon Ave
Studio City, CA 91604-4060, USA

Clijsters, Kim (Athlete, Tennis Player)
213 9th Ave
Belmar, NJ 07719-2303, USA

Cliks, The (Music Group)
c/o Staff Member *Paradigm (Monterey)*
404 W Franklin St
Monterey, CA 93940-2303, USA

Climie, Ron (Athlete, Hockey Player)
5 Ackland St
Stoney Creek, ON L8J 1H5, Canada

Cline, Bruce (Athlete, Hockey Player)
8-890 Rue St Pierre
Drummondville, QC J2C 3X3, Canada

Cline, Ernest (Writer)
c/o Dan Farah *Farah Films & Management*
11640 Mayfield Ave Apt 208
Los Angeles, CA 90049-5728, USa

Cline, Jackie (Athlete, Football Player)
5935 High Forest Dr
Mc Calla, AL 35111-4205, USA

Cline, Richard (Cartoonist)
New Yorker Magazine
4 Times Sq
Editorial Dept
New York, NY 10036-6518, USA

Cline, Ty (Athlete, Baseball Player)
37 Wappoo Creek Pl
Charleston, SC 29412-2121, USA

Clines, Gene (Athlete, Baseball Player)
5303 9th Avenue Dr W
Bradenton, FL 34209-4205, USA

Cline Sr, Tony (Athlete, Football Player)
59 Chestnut Pl
Danville, CA 94506-4542, USA

Clinkscale, F Dextor (Athlete, Football Player)
206 Michaux Dr
Greenville, SC 29605-3156, USA

Clinkscales, Joey (Athlete, Football Player)
10207 Shrewsbury Run W
Collierville, TN 38017-8304, USA

Clinkscales, Sherard (Baseball Player)
7314 N Layman Ave
Indianapolis, IN 46250-2634, USA

Clinton, Bill (Politician)
3067 Whitehaven St NW
Washington, DC 20008-3620, USA

Clinton, Chelsea (Politician)
21 E 26th St Apt 2
New York, NY 10010-1406, USA

Clinton, George (Musician, Songwriter)
1300 Hendrix Rd
Tallahassee, FL 32301-4904, USA

Clinton, Hillary Rodham (Politician)
Hillary for America
PO Box 5256
New York, NY 10185-5256, USA

Clinton, Kate (Comedian)
230 W End Ave Apt 10C
New York, NY 10023-3664, USA

Clinton-Dix, Ha Ha (Athlete, Football Player)

Clippard, Tyler (Athlete, Baseball Player)
2160 Chianti Pl Unit 118
Palm Harbor, FL 34683-7736, USA

Clippingdale, Steve (Athlete, Hockey Player)
5560 Swordfern Pl
North Vancouver, BC V7R 4T1, Canada

Clique Girlz (Music Group, Musician)
c/o Staff Member *Clique Entertainment Productions*
11 Forest View Ct
Egg Harbor Township, NJ 08234-7132, USA

Clisters, Kim (Tennis Player)
Assn of Tennis Professionals
200 Tournament Road
Ponte Vedra Beach, FL 32082, USA

Clohessy, Robert (Actor)
Don Buchwald
5900 Wilshire Blvd Ste 3100
Los Angeles, CA 90036-5030, USA

Cloke, Kristen (Actor)
c/o Staff Member *Mitchell K Stubbs & Assoc*
8675 Washington Blvd Ste 203
Culver City, CA 90232-7486, USA

Cloninger, Tony (Athlete, Baseball Player)
PO Box 1500
Denver, NC 28037-1500, USA

Clontz, Brad (Athlete, Baseball Player)
735 Eider Down Ct
Alpharetta, GA 30022-6198, USA

Clooney, Amal (Attorney)
c/o Steven Lashever *Creative Artists Agency (CAA)*
2000 Avenue of the Stars Ste 100
Los Angeles, CA 90067-4705, USA

Clooney, George (Actor, Producer)
c/o Staff Member *Smoke House Productions*
10066 Valley Spring Ln
Toluca Lake, CA 91602-2928, USA

Clooney, Nick (Writer)
American University
4400 Massachusetts Ave NW
School of Communication, Room 330A
Washington, DC 20016-8200, USA

Close, Bill (Basketball Player)
555 Byron St Apt 409
Palo Alto, CA 94301-2038, USA

Close, Chuck (Artist)
20 Bond St
New York, NY 10012-2689, USA

Close, Eric (Actor)
c/o Beth Holden-Garland *Untitled Entertainment*
350 S Beverly Dr Ste 200
Beverly Hills, CA 90212-4819, USA

Close, Glenn (Actor)
c/o Staff Member *Trillium Productions*
PO Box 1560
New Canaan, CT 06840-1560, USA

Close, Joshua (Actor)
c/o Barb Godfrey *Parent Management*
84 Ontario St
Toronto, ON M5A 2V3, CANADA

Closser, J D (Athlete, Baseball Player)
2202_U._32nd Ave
Alexandria, IN .JI0602-46, USA

Closter, Al (Athlete, Baseball Player)
1101 Haxall Point Unit 1015
Richmond, VA 23219-3953, USA

Closure In Moscow (Music Group, Musician)
c/o Andrew Cook *Run Artist Management*
5753 Cobblestone Dr
Rocklin, CA 95765-4103, USA

Clotworthy, Bob (Athlete, Olympic Athlete, Swimmer)
7170 S Brookhill Dr
Salt Lake City, UT 84121-3604, USA

Cloud, Mike (Athlete, Football Player)
5126 Miller Ave
Dallas, TX 75206-6419, USA

Cloude, Ken (Athlete, Baseball Player)
1414 Martin Meadows Dr
Fallston, MD 21047-2221, USA

Cloutier, Dan (Athlete, Hockey Player)
Vaughan Vipers
9201 Islington Ave
Goaltending Coach
Woodbridge, ON L4L 1A6, CANADA

Cloutier, Jacques (Athlete, Hockey Player)
12172 Triple Crown Dr
Parker, CO 80134-7747, USA

Cloutier, Real (Athlete, Hockey Player)
1798 Rue de la Petite-Oasis
Quebec, QC G3E 1K7, Canada

Clowe, Ryane (Athlete, Hockey Player)
c/o Kent Hughes *MFIVE Sports*
6 Windmill Ln
Westwood, MA 02090-2951, USA

Clowes, Dan (Artist)
c/o Staff Member *Fantagraphics Books*
7563 Lake City Way NE
Seattle, WA 98115-4218, USA

Clowes, Daniel (Writer)
Fantagraphics
7563 Lake City Way NE
Seattle, WA 98115-4218, USA

Clowney, Jadeveon (Actor, Football Player)
c/o Bus Cook *Bus Cook Sports, Inc*
1 Willow Bend Dr
Hattiesburg, MS 39402-8552, USA

Clune, Don (Athlete, Football Player)
327 Meetinghouse Ln Apt 8
Media, PA 19063-1657, USA

Clunes, Martin (Actor)
c/o Samira Higham *Independent Talent Group*
40 Whitfield St
London W1T 2RH, UNITED KINGDOM

Clunie, Michelle Renee (Actor)
c/o Dominic Friesen *Bridge and Tunnel Communications*
8149 Santa Monica Blvd # 407
West Hollywood, CA 90046-4912, USA

Clutch (Music Group, Musician)
c/o Paul Ryan *UTA Music/The Agency Group (UK)*
361-373 City Rd
London EC1V 1PQ, UNITED KINGDOM

Clutterbuck, Bryan (Athlete, Baseball Player)
7998 Grand St Apt 1
Dexter, MI 48130-1357, USA

Clwson, John (Basketball Player)
Oakland Oaks
33 San Ysidro Ct
Danville, CA 94526-1545, USA

Clyde, Ben (Basketball Player)
Bosten Celtics
8356 A Street Apt
#1
Saint Petersburg, FL 33701, USA

Clyde, David (Athlete, Baseball Player)
7806 Pinehurst Shadows Dr
Humble, TX 77346-1511, USA

Clyde, KC (Actor)
c/o Ted Schachter *Schachter Entertainment*
1157 S Beverly Dr Fl 2
Los Angeles, CA 90035-1119, USA

Clymer, Ben (Athlete, Hockey Player)
3700 Landings Dr
Excelsior, MN 55331-9711, USA

Clyne, Nikki (Actor)
c/o David Miner *3 Arts Entertainment*
9460 Wilshire Blvd Fl 7
Beverly Hills, CA 90212-2713, USA

CM Punk (Athlete, Wrestler)
1456 N Milwaukee Ave
Chicago, IL 60622-9225, USA

Coachman, Bobby (Baseball Player)
California Angels
PO Box 44
Cottonwood, AL 36320-0044, USA

Coachman, Pete (Athlete, Baseball Player)
8795 S County 55 Rd
Cottonwood, AL 36320-3323, USA

Coady, Richard (Rich) (Athlete, Football Player)
17106 Spanky Pl
Dallas, TX 75248-1533, USA

Coakley, Dexter (Athlete, Football Player)
1304 Sunset Ridge Cir
Cedar Hill, TX 75104-4541, USA

Coal Chamber (Music Group)
c/o Tim Borror *Sound Talent Group*
1870 Joe Crosson Dr
Hangar 111
El Cajon, CA 92020-1271, USA

Coalter, Gary (Athlete, Hockey Player)
Lot 23 Concession 6 RR 1
South River, ON P0A 1X0, Canada

Coan, Bert (Athlete, Football Player)
14517 N US Highway 59
Nacogdoches, TX 75965-9004, USA

Coan, Gil (Athlete, Baseball Player)
PO Box 668
Brevard, NC 28712-0668, USA

Coates, Ben (Athlete, Football Player)
1740 Deer Creek Dr Ste 1
Xenia, OH 45385-8069, USA

Coates, Brian (Athlete, Hockey Player)
PO Box 213
Roland, MB R0G 1T0, Canada

Coates, Jim (Athlete, Baseball Player)
1098 Oak Hill Rd
Lancaster, VA 22503-4009, USA

Coates, Kim (Actor)
c/o Gayle Abrams *Oscars Abrams Zimel & Associates*
438 Queen St E
Toronto, ON M5A 1T4, CANADA

Coates, Phyllis (Actor)
PO Box 1969
Boyes Hot Springs, CA 95416-1969, USA

Coates, Ray (Athlete, Football Player)
6219 Louis XIV St
New Orleans, LA 70124-3024, USA

Coates, Sherrod (Athlete, Football Player)
12233 Silveroak Ln
Charlotte, NC 28277-1582, USA

Coates, Steve (Athlete, Hockey Player)
Philadelphia Flyers
3601 S Broad St Ste 2
Philadelphia, PA 19148-5297

Coates, Steve (Athlete, Hockey Player)
102 Stoney Creek Dr
Egg Harbor Township, NJ 08234-7559, USA

Coates, Ta-Nehisi (Writer)
c/o Staff Member *United Talent Agency (UTA)*
9336 Civic Center Dr
Beverly Hills, CA 90210-3604, USA

Coats, Daniel (Athlete, Football Player)
419 S 380 W
Tooele, UT 84074-2958, USA

Coats, Daniel (Senator)
United States Senate SR-493
Washington, DC 20510-0001, USA

Coats, Kristi (Athlete, Golfer)
185 Wildwood Trl
Petal, MS 39465-2681, USA

Coats, Michael L (Astronaut)
3203 Acorn Wood Way
Houston, TX 77059-3175, USA

Coats, Michael L Captain (Astronaut)
3203 Acorn Wood Way
Houston, TX 77059-3175, USA

Cobb, Charles (Athlete, Football Player)
6075 N Forkner Ave
Fresno, CA 93711-1827, USA

Cobb, Dave (Musician)
c/o Sandy Robertson *World's End Inc*
183 N Martel Ave Ste 270
Los Angeles, CA 90036-2755, USA

Cobb, David (Politician)
c/o Staff Member *The Green Party of the United States*
PO Box 57065
Washington, DC 20037, USA

Cobb, Garry (Athlete, Football Player)
112 Society Hill Blvd
Cherry Hill, NJ 08003-2402, USA

Cobb, Julie (Actor)
S D B Partners
1801 Ave of the Stars #902
Los Angeles, CA 90067, USA

Cobb, Keith Hamilton (Actor)
c/o Philip Adelman *BRS / Gage Talent Agency (NY)*
1650 Broadway Ste 1410
New York, NY 10019-6957, USA

Cobb, Marvin (Athlete, Football Player)
655 S Flower St Unit 290
Los Angeles, CA 90017-2805, USA

Cobb, Randall (Athlete, Football Player)
c/o Jimmy Sexton *CAA (Memphis)*
6060 Poplar Ave Ste 470
Memphis, TN 38119-0910, USA

Cobb, Randall (Tex) (Athlete, Baseball Player)
1928 18th Ave S
Nashville, TN 37212-3804, USA

Cobb, Reggie (Athlete, Football Player)
13315 Orchard Harvest Dr
Richmond, TX 77407-3219, USA

Cobb, Trevor (Athlete, Football Player)
2001 Bering Dr Apt 2H
Houston, TX 77057-3762, USA

Cobbin, James (Athlete, Baseball Player)
389 Redondo Rd
Youngstown, OH 44504-1451, USA

Cobbs, Bill (Actor, Producer)
c/o Staff Member *Forster Entertainment*
12533 Woodgreen St
Los Angeles, CA 90066-2723, USA

Cobbs, Cedric (Athlete, Football Player)
4710 Fairlee Dr
Little Rock, AR 72209-5218, USA

Cobbs, Tasha (Musician)
4209 Northeast Expy
Atlanta, GA 30340-3802, USA

Coble, Drew (Athlete, Baseball Player)
3098 Marsh Island Dr
Myrtle Beach, SC 29579-5320, USA

Coble, Howard (Congressman, Politician)
2188 Rayburn Hob
Washington, DC 20515-1303, USA

Coblenz, Walter (Director, Producer)
4310 Cahuenga Blvd Unit 401
Toluca Lake, CA 91602-2713, USA

Cobra Starship (Music Group)
c/o Jonathan Daniel *Crush Music Management*
60-62 E 11th St
Fl 7
New York, NY 10003, USA

Coburn, Braydon (Athlete, Hockey Player)
c/o Gerry Johansson *The Sports Corporation*
2735 Toronto Dominion Tower
10088-102 Ave
Edmonton ABc T5J 2Z1, CANADA

Coburn, Tom (Senator)
172 Russell Senate Office Bldg
Washington, DC 20510-0001, USA

Cocanower, James S (Jaime) (Athlete, Baseball Player)
10777 Gram B Cir
Lowell, AR 72745-8446, USA

Coccioletti, Philip (Actor)
c/o Carmen Lavia *Fifi Oscard Agency*
110 W 40th St Rm 1601
New York, NY 10018-8512, USA

Cochereau, Pierre (Musician)
15 Bis des Ursins
Paris 75004, FRANCE

Cochran, Antonio (Athlete, Football Player)
8433 Manchester Hwy
Woodland, GA 31836-2038, USA

Cochran, Barbara (Athlete, Olympic Athlete, Skier)
213 Brown Hl W
Starksboro, VT 05487-7283, USA

Cochran, John (Athlete, Football Player)
1249 Driftwood Dr
De Pere, WI 54115-1813, USA

Cochran, John (Correspondent)
ABC-TV
5010 Creston St
Hyattsville, MD 20781-1216, USA

Cochran, Robert (Producer, Writer)
c/o Staff Member *Agency for the Performing Arts (APA)*
405 S Beverly Dr Ste 500
Beverly Hills, CA 90212-4425, USA

Cochran, Russ (Athlete, Golfer)
23 Bayview Rd
Jupiter, FL 33469-2012, USA

Cochran, Shannon (Actor)
Stubbs
1450 S Robertson Blvd
Los Angeles, CA 90035-3402, USA

Cochran, Thad (Politician)
386A Highway 7 S
Oxford, MS 38655-8247, USA

Cochran, Thad (Senator)
113 Dirksen Senate Office Building
Washington, DC 20510-0001, USA

Cochrane, Annalisa (Actor)
c/o Garry Purdy *Momentum Talent and Literary Agency*
3500 W Olive Ave Ste 300
Burbank, CA 91505-4647, USA

Cochrane, Dave (Athlete, Baseball Player)
11 Muirfield
Trabuco Canyon, CA 92679-3427, USA

Cochrane, Glen (Athlete, Hockey Player)
405 Collett Rd
Kelowna, BC V1W 1K6, Canada

Cochrane, Rory (Actor)
c/o Beth Holden-Garland *Untitled Entertainment*
350 S Beverly Dr Ste 200
Beverly Hills, CA 90212-4819, USA

Cockburn, Bruce (Musician)
c/o Staff Member *UTA/The Agency Group*
888 7th Ave Fl 7
New York, NY 10106-0700, USA

Cocker, Jarvis (Musician, Songwriter)
c/o Staff Member *Paradigm (Monterey)*
404 W Franklin St
Monterey, CA 93940-2303, USA

Cockerill, Kay (Athlete, Golfer)
131 Beulah St
San Francisco, CA 94117-2717, USA

Cockrell, Gene (Athlete, Football Player)
8652 County Road 21
Pampa, TX 79065-1313, USA

Cockrell, Kenneth D (Astronaut)
2300 Richmond Ave Apt 350
Houston, TX 77098-3265, USA

Cockrell, Ross (Athlete, Football Player)
c/o Joby Branion *Vanguard Sports Group*
23091 Mill Creek Dr
Laguna Hills, CA 92653-1258, USA

Cock Robin (Music Group, Musician)
Loft Recording Studio
48 Dellwood Pl
Cheektowaga, NY 14225-2617, USA

Cockroft, Don (Athlete, Football Player)
2418 Dunkeith Dr NW
Canton, OH 44708-1326, USA

Cocks, Burling (Race Car Driver)
PO Box 512
Unionville, PA 19375-0512, USA

Code, Merl (Athlete, Football Player)
100 Rearden Dr
Greenville, SC 29605-3261, USA

Coder, Ron (Athlete, Football Player)
25 N Bryant Ave
Pittsburgh, PA 15202-3346, USA

Codey, Lawrence R (Business Person)
Public Service Enterprise
PO Box 1171
80 PARK PLAZA
Newark, NJ 07101-1171, USA

Codiroli, Chris (Athlete, Baseball Player)
2700 Hillcrest Dr
Cameron Park, CA 95682-9279, USA

Codrescu, Andrei (Writer)
Louisiana State University
English Dept
Baton Rouge, LA 70803-0001, USA

Coduri, Camille (Actor)
c/o Staff Member *Independent Talent Group*
40 Whitfield St
London W1T 2RH, UNITED KINGDOM

Cody, Bill (Athlete, Football Player)
209 Orleans Dr
Fairhope, AL 36532-4218, USA

Cody, Commander (Musician)
Skyline Music
Old Cherry Mountain Road
Jefferson, NH 03583, USA

Cody, Dan (Athlete, Football Player)
205 Park Dr
Ada, OK 74820-8355, USA

Cody, Diablo (Writer)
8024 Mulholland Dr
Los Angeles, CA 90046-1129, USA

Cody, Terrence (Athlete, Football Player)
c/o Peter Schaffer *Authentic Athletix*
400 S Steele St Unit 47
Denver, CO 80209-3535, USA

Coe, David Allan (Musician)
129 Caldwell Dr
Hendersonville, TN 37075-2045, USA

Coe, Sabastian N (Athlete, Track Athlete)
Starswood High Barn Road
Effingham
Surrey KT24 5PW, UNITED KINGDOM (UK)

Coe, Sebastian (Athlete, Politician)
London 2012
One Churchill Place
Canary Wharf
London E14 5LN, UK

Coe, Sue (Artist)
527 W 26th St
New York, NY 10001, USA

Coelen, Chris (Director, Producer, Writer)

Coelho, Paulo (Writer)
Instituto Paulo Coelho
Henrique Pechman
Av Copacabana 1133 salas 601 / 602
Rio de Janeiro 22070-010, BRAZIL

Coelho, Susie (Actor)
1347 Rossmoyne Ave
Glendale, CA 91207-1852, USA

Coen, Ethan (Director, Writer)
c/o Jim Berkus *United Talent Agency (UTA)*
9336 Civic Center Dr
Beverly Hills, CA 90210-3604, USA

Coen, Joel (Director, Writer)
23 Rafael Ave
Bolinas, CA 94924, USA

Coetzee, Gerrie (Boxer)
22 Sydney Road
Ravenswood, Boksburg 01460, SOUTH AFRICA

Coetzer, Amanda (Tennis Player)
Octagon
1751 Pinnacle Dr Ste 1500
McLean, VA 22102-3833, USA

Cofer, J Michael (Mike) (Athlete, Football Player)
2688 Hollowvale Ln
Henderson, NV 89052-2846, USA

Cofer, Mike (Athlete, Football Player)
2688 Hollowvale Ln
Henderson, NV 89052-2846, USA

Cofer, Mike (Athlete, Football Player)
270 Ridgewood Dr
Fayetteville, GA 30215-8165, USA

Cofer, Mike (Race Car Driver)
Racing West
1772 Los Arboles
#J-186
Thousand Oaks, CA 91362, USA

Coffee, Claire (Actor)
c/o Liza Anderson *Anderson Group Public Relations*
8060 Melrose Ave Fl 4
Los Angeles, CA 90046-7038, USA

Coffey, Don (Athlete, Football Player)
231 Redfield Dr
Jackson, TN 38305-8534, USA

Coffey, Junior L (Athlete, Football Player)
17228 32nd Ave S Apt E-12
Seatac, WA 98188-4402, USA

Coffey, Kellie (Musician)
c/o Staff Member *WME (Nashville)*
1201 Demonbreun St
Nashville, TN 37203-3140, USA

Coffey, Ken (Athlete, Football Player)
3322 Medinah Ct
Sugar Land, TX 77479-2459, USA

Coffey, Paul D (Athlete, Hockey Player)
Paul Coffey's Bolton Toyota
13050 Albion-Vaughan Rd.
Bolton, ON L7E 1S7, Canada

Coffey, Richard (Athlete, Basketball Player)
7021 McCauley Trl S
Edina, MN 55439-1027, USA

Coffey, Tabatha (Business Person, Reality Star)
c/o Tanya Taylor *Triple 7 PR (Nashville)*
11693 San Vicente Blvd # 333
Los Angeles, CA 90049-5105, USA

Coffey, Todd (Athlete, Baseball Player)
320 Widd Lawing Ln
Union Mills, NC 28167-8588, USA

Coffield, Kelly (Actor)
c/o Staff Member *Innovative Artists*
235 Park Ave S Fl 7
New York, NY 10003-1405, USA

Coffield, Randy (Athlete, Football Player)
7110 Lake Basin Rd
Tallahassee, FL 32312-6708, USA

Coffin, Edmund (Tad) (Horse Racer)
General Delivery
Strafford, VT 05072, USA

Coffin, Jeff (Musician)
5201 Elkins Ave
Nashville, TN 37209-3328, USA

Coffman, Chase (Athlete, Football Player)
c/o Tom Condon *Creative Artists Agency (CAA)*
401 Commerce St PH
Nashville, TN 37219-2516, USA

Coffman, Kevin (Athlete, Baseball Player)
12503 Mooremeadow Ln
Houston, TX 77024-1104, USA

Coffman, Mike (Congressman, Politician)
1222 Longworth Hob
Washington, DC 20515-1307, USA

Coffman, Paul (Athlete, Football Player)
14103 E 195th St
Peculiar, MO 64078-9199, USA

Coffman, Vance D (Business Person)
Lockheed Martin Corp
6801 Rockledge Dr
Bethesda, MD 20817-1877, USA

Cofield, Fred (Athlete, Basketball Player)
833 Frederick St
Ypsilanti, MI 48197-5270, USA

Cofield, Tim (Athlete, Football Player)
312 NE Warrington Ct
Lees Summit, MO 64064-1603, USA

Coflin, Hugh (Athlete, Hockey Player)
244 Murphy Dr W
Delta, BC V4M 3P2, Canada

Cogdill, Gail (Athlete, Football Player)
12922 E 36th Ave
Spokane Valley, WA 99206-8405, USA

Coggin, David (Athlete, Baseball Player)
861 Emerson St
Upland, CA 91784-1227, USA

Coggins, Rich (Athlete, Baseball Player)
4095 Fruit St Spc 219
La Verne, CA 91750-2930, USA

Coghill, George (Athlete, Football Player)
307 Chancellor Pl
Fredericksburg, VA 22401-2104, USA

Coghlan, Eamon (Athlete, Track Athlete)
Int'l Mgmt Group
1 Erieview Plz
1360 E 9th St #1300
Cleveland, OH 44114-1738, USA

Cogliano, Andrew (Athlete, Hockey Player)
c/o Staff Member *Edmonton Oilers*
11230 110 St NW
Edmonton, AB T5G 3H7, Canada

Cohan, Lauren (Actor)
c/o Sean Grumman *WME|IMG*
9601 Wilshire Blvd
Beverly Hills, CA 90210-5213, USA

Coheed and Cambria (Music Group)
c/o Nick Storch *ICM Partners (NY)*
730 5th Ave
New York, NY 10019-4105, USA

Cohen, Adam (Writer)
c/o Staff Member *Penguin Press HC*
375 Hudson St Bsmt 3
New York, NY 10014-7465, USA

Cohen, Andy (Producer, Reality Star, Television Host)
Watch What Happens Live!
325 Hudson St Fl 6
New York, NY 10013-1045, USA

Cohen, Avishai (Music Group, Musician)
Ron Moss Mgmt
2635 Griffith Park Blvd
Los Angeles, CA 90039-2519, USA

Cohen, Ben (Business Person)
Ben & Jerry's
30 Community Dr Ste 1
South Burlington, VT 05403-6828, USA

Cohen, Bruce (Actor, Producer)
Bruce Cohen Productions
274 W 11th St Apt 5R
New York, NY 10014-2467, USA

Cohen, Emory (Actor)
c/o Donnalyn Carfi *Harvest Talent Management*
127 W 83rd St Unit 887
New York, NY 10024-0814, USA

Cohen, Etan (Director, Producer)
c/o Amanda Lundberg *42West*
600 3rd Ave Fl 23
New York, NY 10016-1914, USA

Cohen, Gary (Commentator)
136 Haviland Rd
Ridgefield, CT 06877-2822, USA

Cohen, Hy (Athlete, Baseball Player)
35734 Donny Cir
Palm Desert, CA 92211-2695, USA

Cohen, John (Musician, Photographer)
Deborah Bell Photographs
511 W 25th St Ste 703
New York, NY 10001-5584, USA

Cohen, Landon (Athlete, Football Player)
c/o Drew Rosenhaus *Rosenhaus Sports Representation*
3921 Alton Rd # 440
Miami Beach, FL 33140-3852, USA

Cohen, Linda (Musician)
c/o Staff Member *Greenspan Artist Management*
8760 W Sunset Blvd
West Hollywood, CA 90069-2206, USA

Cohen, Lynn (Actor)
c/o Josh Pultz *Amplified Entertainment*
33 W 46th St Ste 801
New York, NY 10036-4103, USA

Cohen, Matt (Actor)
c/o Sharon Lane *Lane Management Group*
4370 Tujunga Ave Ste 130
Studio City, CA 91604-2769, USA

Cohen, Michael (Race Car Driver)
Cohen Motorsports
1210 S 56th Ave
Hollywood, FL 33023-1924, USA

Cohen, Rob (Director)
Nowita Pictures
2900 Olympic Blvd # 345
Santa Monica, CA 90404-4127, USA

Cohen, Sacha Baron (Actor, Producer)
c/o Staff Member *Four by Two Films*
9100 Wilshire Blvd Ste 1000W
Beverly Hills, CA 90212-3463, USA

Cohen, Sarah (Journalist)
Washington Post
1150 15th St NW
Washington, DC 20071-0002, USA

Cohen, Sasha (Athlete, Figure Skater)
c/o Staff Member *Champions on Ice*
3500 American Blvd W Ste 190
Minneapolis, MN 55431-4431, USA

Cohen, Scott (Actor)
c/o Heather Reynolds *One Entertainment (NY)*
347 5th Ave Rm 1404
New York, NY 10016-5034, USA

Cohen, Steve (Actor)
c/o Staff Member *WME|IMG*
9601 Wilshire Blvd
Beverly Hills, CA 90210-5213, USA

Cohen, Steve (Business Person)
SAC Capital Advisors
72 Cummings Ave
Stamford, CT 06902, USA

Cohen, Steve (Congressman, Politician)
1005 Longworth Hob
Washington, DC 20515-0701, USA

Cohen, Steven A (Business Person)
S.A.C. Capital Advisors
72 Cummings Point Rd
Stamford, CT 06902-7912, USA

Cohen, William (Politician)
The Cohen Group
500 8th St NW # 200
Washington, DC 20004-2131, USA

Cohn, Ethan (Actor)
c/o Darren Goldberg *Global Creative*
1051 Cole Ave # B
Los Angeles, CA 90038-2601, USA

Cohn, Gary (Journalist)
Balitmore Sun
501 N Calvert St
Baltimore, MD 21278-1000, USA

Cohn, Marc (Musician)
c/o Ryan Owens *Monterey International*
72 W Adams St # 1000
Chicago, IL 60603-5107, USA

Cohn, Mindy (Actor)
c/o Patrick Welborn *Allegory Creative Management*
13261 Moorpark St Ste 103
Sherman Oaks, CA 91423-5156, USA

Cohoon Friedman, Patti (Actor)
11630 Dona Teresa Dr
Studio City, CA 91604, USA

Coil, Austin (Race Car Driver)
John Force Racing
22722 Old Canal Rd
Yorba Linda, CA 92887-4602, USA

Coiro, Rhys (Actor)
2233 Baxter St
Los Angeles, CA 90039-3601, USA

Coke, Phil (Athlete, Baseball Player)
c/o Team Member *New York Yankees*
161st St & River Ave
Yankee Stadium
Bronx, NY 10451, USA

Coker, Larry (Coach, Football Coach)
Miami University
Athletic Dept
Coral Gables, FL 33124, USA

Cokes, Curtis (Boxer)
618 Calcutta Dr
Dallas, TX 75241-1001, USA

Cola, Angelo (Athlete, Football Player)
11 McDermott Pl
Brigantine, NJ 08203-2934, USA

Colangelo, Jerry (Commentator)
70 E Country Club Dr
Phoenix, AZ 85014-5435, USA

Colangelo, Mike (Athlete, Baseball Player)
5751 Fincastle Dr
Manassas, VA 20112-5439, USA

Colangelo, Sarah (Director)
c/o Courtney Kivowitz *MGMT Entertainment (The Schiff Company)*
9220 W Sunset Blvd Ste 106
W Hollywood, CA 90069-3500, USA

Colantoni, Enrico (Actor)
c/o Lee Wallman *Wallman Public Relations*
3859 Goldwyn Ter
Culver City, CA 90232-3103, USA

Colasanti, Robert (Horse Racer)
4 Duke Pass
Colts Neck, NJ 07722-1761, USA

Colavito, Rocky (Athlete, Baseball Player)
656 Scenic Dr
Bernville, PA 19506-8257, USA

Colavito, Steve (Athlete, Football Player)
57 Fairview Ct Apt 1
Nanuet, NY 10954-3230, USA

Colbert, Craig (Athlete, Baseball Player)
6635 SE 42nd Ave
Portland, OR 97206-7703, USA

Colbert, Darrell (Athlete, Football Player)
6514 River Bluff Dr
Houston, TX 77085-1306, USA

Colbert, Jim (Athlete, Golfer)
118 Wanish Pl
Palm Desert, CA 92260-7316, USA

Colbert, Keary (Athlete, Football Player)

Colbert, Nate (Athlete, Baseball Player)
2756 N Green Valley Pkwy
Henderson, NV 89014-2120, USA

Colbert, Rondy (Athlete, Football Player)
5622 Cedarburg Dr
Houston, TX 77048-1821, USA

Colbert, Stephen (Producer, Television Host)
Ed Sullivan Theater
1697 Broadway Ste 906
New York, NY 10019-5900, USA

Colbert, Steve (Actor, Talk Show Host, Writer)
The Colbert Report
513 W 54th St
New York, NY 10019-5014, USA

Colbert, Vince (Athlete, Baseball Player)
18071 Blandford Rd
Cleveland, OH 44121-1040, USA

Colborn, James W (Jim) (Athlete, Baseball Player)
2932 Solimar Beach Dr
Ventura, CA 93001-9754, USA

Colborn, Richard (Musician)
Legends of 21st Century
7 Trinity Row
Florence, MA 01062-1931, USA

Colbrunn, Greg (Athlete, Baseball Player)
3196 Pignatelli Cres
Mount Pleasant, SC 29466-8060, USA

Colby, Angel (Actor)
Hobsons International
62 Chiswick High Rd
London W4 1SY, UK

Colby, Danielle (Reality Star)
4 Miles 2 Memphis
303 S 2nd St
Le Claire, IA 52753-9551, USA

Colchico, Dan (Athlete, Football Player)
5160 Paul Scarlet Dr
Concord, CA 94521-3134, USA

Coldplay (Music Group)
c/o Ambrosia Healy *The Fun Star*
8439 W Sunset Blvd Ste 2
Los Angeles, CA 90069-1925, USA

Cold War Kids (Music Group)
c/o Staff Member *Paradigm (Monterey)*
404 W Franklin St
Monterey, CA 93940-2303, USA

Cole, Alex (Athlete, Baseball Player)
6545 N Stevens Hollow Dr
Chesterfield, VA 23832-8548, USA

Cole, Artemas (Cartoonist)
15 Regency Mnr Apt 15-8
Rutland, VT 05701-5310, USA

Cole, Ashley (Athlete, Soccer Player)
c/o Staff Member *Chelsea Football Club*
Stamford Bridge
Fulham Road
London SW6 1HS, UNITED KINGDOM

Cole, Audie (Athlete, Football Player)

Cole, Bob (Sportscaster)
Molstar Communications
805-250 Bloor St E
Toronto, ON M4W 1E6, CANADA

Cole, Bobby (Athlete, Golfer)
204 W 2nd Ave
Windermere, FL 34786-8507, USA

Cole, Bradley (Actor)
c/o Staff Member *The Rights House (UK)*
Drury House
34-43 Russell St
London WC2B 5HA, UNITED KINGDOM

Cole, Cecil (Baseball Player)
Newark Eagles
201 N 12th St
Connellsville, PA 15425-2422, USA

Cole, Cheryl (Musician)
c/o Solomon Parker *WME|IMG (UK)*
103 New Oxford St WMA
Centrepoint
London WC1A 1DD, UNITED KINGDOM

Cole, Chris (Athlete, Football Player)
6642 Hudnall Rd
Orange, TX 77632-3589, USA

Cole, Christina (Actor)
c/o Lorrie Bartlett *ICM Partners*
10250 Constellation Blvd Fl 7
Los Angeles, CA 90067-6207, USA

Cole, Colin (Athlete, Football Player)

Cole, Danton (Athlete, Hockey Player)
9263 Lookout Cir
Grand Ledge, MI 48837-8246, USA

Cole, Deon (Actor)
c/o Dan Baron *Agency for the Performing Arts (APA)*
405 S Beverly Dr Ste 500
Beverly Hills, CA 90212-4425, USA

Cole, Dick (Athlete, Baseball Player)
5 First American Way
Santa Ana, CA 92707-5913, USA

Cole, Emerson (Athlete, Football Player)
1661 Indiana Ave
Toledo, OH 43607-3966, USA

Cole, Erik (Athlete, Hockey Player, Olympic Athlete)
Sports Consulting Group
65 Monroe Ave Ste D
Pittsford, NY 14534-1318, USA

Cole, Finn (Actor)
c/o Kat Gosling *Troika*
10A Christina St.
London EC2A 4PA, UNITED KINGDOM

Cole, Ford (Athlete, Football Player)
PO Box 3218
Olympic Valley, CA 96146-3218, USA

Cole, Fred (Athlete, Football Player)
10 Tuscan Rd
Livingston, NJ 07039-2919, USA

Cole, Gary (Actor)
c/o Barbara Gale *Envoy Entertainment*
1640 S Sepulveda Blvd
Los Angeles, CA 90025-7510, USA

Cole, Gerrit (Athlete, Basketball Player)
c/o Scott Boras *Boras Corporation*
18 Corporate Plaza Dr
Newport Beach, CA 92660-7901, USA

Cole, Holly (Musician)
Alert Music
41 Britain St
#305
Toronto, ON M5A 1R7, CANADA

Cole, J (Musician)
c/o Julius Garcia *ByStorm Entertainment*
198 W 21st St # 721
New York, NY 10011-3202, USA

Cole, Joanna (Writer)
c/o Staff Member *Scholastic Entertainment*
557 Broadway
New York, NY 10012-3962, USA

Cole, Joe (Actor)
c/o Alexa Pearson *Beaumont Communications*
189-190 Shoreditch High St
Unit 2
London E1 6HU, UNITED KINGDOM

Cole, John (Cartoonist)
Durham Herald-Sun
2828 Pickett Rd
Durham, NC 27705-5613, USA

Cole, Julie Dawn (Actor)
Barry Burnett
31 Coventry St
London W1V 8AS, UNITED KINGDOM (UK)

Cole, Kenneth (Designer)
Kenneth Cole Productions Inc
601 W 50th St
New York, NY 10019, USA

Cole, Keyshia (Musician)
c/o Ernest Dukes *The Nottingham Group*
1800 Century Park E Ste 210
Los Angeles, CA 90067-1505, USA

Cole, Kimberly (Musician)
c/o Amanda Cee *Amanda Cee*
3355 Wilshire Blvd Apt 1202
Los Angeles, CA 90010-1808, USA

Cole, Kyla (Adult Film Star)
Adrian Daskalov
Nabrezi SPB 446
Ostrava 70800, CZECH REPUBLIC

Cole, Larry R (Athlete, Football Player)
5432 Chinkapin Ln
Fort Worth, TX 76244-6783, USA

Cole, Lily (Actor, Model)
c/o Staff Member *Storm Model Management*
5 Jubilee Pl
1st Floor
London SW3 3TD, UK

Cole, Linzy (Athlete, Football Player)
7700 Creekbend Dr Apt 18
Houston, TX 77071-1728, USA

Cole, Lloyd (Musician)
Supervision Mgmt
109B Regents Park Road
London NW1 8UR, UNITED KINGDOM (UK)

Cole, Michael (Actor)
5121 Varna Ave
Sherman Oaks, CA 91423-1526, USA

Cole, Nigel (Director, Writer)
c/o Rosalie Swedlin *Anonymous Content*
3532 Hayden Ave
Culver City, CA 90232-2413, USA

Cole, Paula (Musician)
c/o Bobby Colomby *The Colomby Group*
4115 Glencoe Ave Apt 114
Marina Del Rey, CA 90292-3800, USA

Cole, Robin (Athlete, Football Player)
9 Brook Ln
Eighty Four, PA 15330-2603, USA

Cole, Stu (Athlete, Baseball Player)
6527 Willow Gate Ln
Charlotte, NC 28215-4014, USA

Cole, Taylor (Actor)
c/o Joannie Burstein *Burstein Company*
15304 W Sunset Blvd Ste 208
Pacific Palisades, CA 90272-3656, USA

Cole, Tina (Actor)
778 University Ave
Junior League of Sacramento
Sacramento, CA 95825-6703, USA

Cole, Tom (Congressman, Politician)
2458 Rayburn Hob
Washington, DC 20515-4323, USA

Cole, Trent (Athlete, Football Player)
c/o Anthony J. Agnone *Eastern Athletic Services*
11350 McCormick Rd
Suite 800 - Executive Plaza
Hunt Valley, MD 21031-1002, USA

Cole, Victor (Athlete, Baseball Player)
138 Estonallie Rd
Mercer, TN 38392-7102, USA

Coleman, Andre (Athlete, Football Player)
2955 Megan Cir
Youngstown, OH 44505-4384, USA

Coleman, Ben (Athlete, Basketball Player)
206 Mallard Dr
Shakopee, MN 55379-9375, USA

Coleman, Casey (Athlete, Football Player)
11901 Northumberland Dr
Tampa, FL 33626-1327

Coleman, Catherine (Cady) (Astronaut)
30 Frank Williams Rd
Shelburne Falls, MA 01370-9724, USA

Coleman, Chad L (Actor)
c/o Liza Anderson *Anderson Group Public Relations*
8060 Melrose Ave Fl 4
Los Angeles, CA 90046-7038, USA

Coleman, Chris (Athlete, Football Player)
2425 Evans St SW
Lenoir, NC 28645-6358, USA

Coleman, Cleopatra (Actor)
c/o Samantha Hill *Wolf-Kasteler Public Relations*
6255 W Sunset Blvd Ste 1111
Los Angeles, CA 90028-7426, USA

Coleman, Cosey (Athlete, Football Player)
9021 Westbay Blvd
Tampa, FL 33615-2749, USA

Coleman, Dabney (Actor)
13659 Victory Blvd Ste 339
Van Nuys, CA 91401-1735, USA

Coleman, Derrick (Athlete, Basketball Player)
Derrick Coleman Elite
29488 Woodward Ave
Royal Oak, MI 48073-0903, USA

Coleman, Don E (Athlete, Football Player)
424 McPherson Ave
Lansing, MI 48915-1158, USA

Coleman, Eric (Athlete, Football Player)
2933 Elm St
Denver, CO 80207-2658, USA

Coleman, George E (Musician)
63 E 9th St Apt 4G
New York, NY 10003-6331, USA

Coleman, Greg (Athlete, Football Player)
2313 River Pointe Cir
Minneapolis, MN 55411-4279, USA

Coleman, Harry (Athlete, Football Player)
c/o Tony Paige *Dream Point Sports*
1455 Pennsylvania Ave NW Ste 225
Washington, DC 20004-1026, USA

Coleman, Jack (Actor)
3816 Goodland Ave
Studio City, CA 91604-2314, USA

Coleman, Jenna (Actor)
c/o Conor McCaughan *Troika*
10A Christina St.
London EC2A 4PA, UNITED KINGDOM

Coleman, Karon (Athlete, Football Player)
19503 E 58th Ave
Aurora, CO 80019-2014, USA

Coleman, Kelly (Athlete, Basketball Player)
PO Box 55
Wayland, KY 41666-0055, USA

Coleman, Kenyon (Athlete, Football Player)
c/o Jordan Woy *Willis & Woy Management*
4890 Alpha Rd Ste 200
Dallas, TX 75244-4639, USA

Coleman, Leonard (Athlete, Football Player)
125 NE 13th Ave
Boynton Beach, FL 33435-3124, USA

Coleman, Lincoln (Athlete, Football Player)
PO Box 496
Seguin, TX 78156-0496, USA

Coleman, Marcus (Athlete, Football Player)
1736 Mapleleaf Dr
Wylie, TX 75098-8166, USA

Coleman, Michael (Mike) (Athlete, Baseball Player)
1053 Mallow Dr
Madison, TN 37115-4219, USA

Coleman, Mike (Actor, Producer, Writer)
c/o Melanie Turner *Pacific Artists Management*
112 3rd Ave E Suite 210
Vancouver, BC V5T 1C8, CANADA

Coleman, Monique (Actor)
c/o Salvador Yanez *Fridam*
1600 Vine St Apt 456
Los Angeles, CA 90028-8824, USA

Coleman, Monte (Athlete, Football Player)
4700 S Beech St
Pine Bluff, AR 71603-7327, USA

Coleman, Norm (Politician)
909 Osceola Ave
Saint Paul, MN 55105-3209, USA

Coleman, Oliver (Actor)
c/o Troy Zien *3 Arts Entertainment*
9460 Wilshire Blvd Fl 7
Beverly Hills, CA 90212-2713, USA

Coleman, Paul (Athlete, Baseball Player)
2704 Brentwood Dr
Tyler, TX 75701-5902, USA

Coleman, Roderick (Rod) (Athlete, Football Player)
6735 Great Water Dr
Flowery Branch, GA 30542-6639, USA

Coleman, Sidney (Athlete, Football Player)
8034 King Rd
Meridian, MS 39305-9261, USA

Coleman, Signy (Actor)
c/o Staff Member *Abrams Artists Agency*
750 N San Vicente Blvd
E Tower Fl 11
Los Angeles, CA 90069-5788, USA

Coleman, Steve (Athlete, Football Player)
81 W Johnson St
Philadelphia, PA 19144-1937, USA

Coleman, Walter (Baseball Player)
New York Yankees
HC 1 Box 236
New Russia, NY 12964-9705, USA

Coles, Bimbo (Athlete, Basketball Player)
1102 Washington St E
Lewisburg, WV 24901-2523, USA

Coles, Darnell (Athlete, Baseball Player)
10021 Brompton Dr
Tampa, FL 33626-5408, USA

Coles, Janet (Athlete, Golfer)
6083 Alumni Gym
Hanover, NH 03755-3501, USA

Coles, Kim (Actor, Comedian)
9000 Cynthia St Apt 403
West Hollywood, CA 90069-4871, USA

Coles, Laveranues (Athlete, Football Player)
87 Coles Ct
Saint Johns, FL 32259-8898, USA

Coletta, Chris (Athlete, Baseball Player)
206 SW 45th St
Cape Coral, FL 33914-5906, USA

Coley, Daryl (Musician)
Daryl Coley Ministries
417 E Regent St
Inglewood, CA 90301-1315, USA

Coley, James (Athlete, Football Player)
111 Pebble Park Rd
Starr, SC 29684-9259, USA

Coley, John Ford (Musician, Songwriter, Writer)
Earthtone
8306 Wilshire Blvd # 981
Beverly Hills, CA 90211-2304, USA

Colfer, Chris (Actor, Musician)
2654 Charl Pl
Los Angeles, CA 90046-1023, USA

Colfer, Eoin (Writer)
c/o Staff Member *HarperCollins Publishers*
195 Broadway Fl 2
New York, NY 10007-3132, USA

Colicchio, Tom (Chef, Reality Star, Television Host)
Craft Restaurant
43 E 19th St Frnt 1
New York, NY 10003-1304, USA

Colier, Jason (Basketball Player)
Houston Rockets
19318 Kristen Pine Dr
Humble, TX 77346-2084, USA

Colin, Charlie (Musician)
Jon Landau
80 Main St
Greenwich, CT 06830, USA

Colin, Margaret (Actor)
c/o Christina Papadopoulos *Baker Winokur Ryder Public Relations*
200 5th Ave Fl 5
New York, NY 10010-3307, USA

Colinet, Stalin (Athlete, Football Player)
5227 Riverstone Crossing Dr
Sugar Land, TX 77479-4821, USA

C'Oliveira, Damon (Actor)
c/o Staff Member *LeFeaver Talent Management Ltd*
202-2 College St
Toronto, ON M5G 1K3, CANADA

Coll, Stephen W (Journalist)
Washington Post
Editorial Dept
1150 15th St NW
Washington, DC 20071-0001, USA

Collard, Jean-Philippe (Musician)
c/o Staff Member *Véronique Jourdain Artists Management*
29 rue Violet
Paris F-75015, FRANCE

Collective Soul (Music Group)
c/o Tim Beeding *Creative Artists Agency (CAA)*
401 Commerce St PH
Nashville, TN 37219-2516, USA

Colledge, Daryn (Athlete, Football Player)
c/o Jeff Sperbeck *The Novo Agency*
1537 Via Romero Ste 100
Alamo, CA 94507-1527, USA

Collee, John (Writer)
c/o Alex Lerner *Kaplan/Perrone Entertainment*
9171 Wilshire Blvd Ste 350
Beverly Hills, CA 90210-5523, USA

Collen, Phil (Musician)
26971 Highwood Cir
Laguna Hills, CA 92653-7828, USA

Collet, Christopher (Actor)
232 President St
Brooklyn, NY 11231-4339, USA

Collett, Elmer (Athlete, Football Player)
PO Box 522
10 AVENIDA
Stinson Beach, CA 94970-0522, USA

Collette, Toni (Actor)
848 N Las Palmas Ave
Los Angeles, CA 90038-3516, USA

Colletti, Roseanne (Correspondent)
WNBC-TV
30 Rockefeller Plz Fl 7
New York, NY 10112-0015, USA

Colletti, Stephen (Reality Star)
c/o Chris Rossi *Status PR*
PO Box 6191
Westlake Village, CA 91359-6191, USA

Collett-Serra, Jaume (Director)
c/o Staff Member *Ombra Films*
12444 Ventura Blvd Ste 103
Studio City, CA 91604-2409, USA

Colley, Dana (Musician)
Creative Performance Group
48 Laight St
New York, NY 10013-2156, USA

Colley, Ed (Artist, Cartoonist)
11 Blaisdell Ter
Ipswich, MA 01938-1706, USA

Colley, Kenneth (Actor)
Kenneth McReddie
91 Regent St
London W1R 7TB, UNITED KINGDOM (UK)

Colley, Tom (Athlete, Hockey Player)
71 Dillon Dr
Collingwood, ON L9Y 4S4, Canada

Colley-Lee, Myrna (Designer)
Mississippi State University Libraries
PO Box 5408
395 Hardy Road
Mississippi State, MS 39762-5408

Collie, Bruce (Athlete, Football Player)
9595 Ranch Road 12 Ste 13
Wimberley, TX 78676-5248, USA

Collie, Mark (Actor, Musician, Songwriter)
c/o Jim Mazza *Dreamcatcher Entertainment*
2910 Poston Ave
Nashville, TN 37203-1312, USA

Collier, James (Athlete, Football Player)
922 Bromley Dr
Baton Rouge, LA 70808-5814, USA

Collier, Jim (Athlete, Football Player)
1670 Terral Island Rd
Farmerville, LA 71241-4013, USA

Collier, Lou (Athlete, Baseball Player)
5140 S Hyde Park Blvd Apt 17B
Chicago, IL 60615-4266, USA

Collier, Mark (Actor)
c/o John Crosby *John Crosby Management*
1357 N Spaulding Ave
Los Angeles, CA 90046-4009, USA

Collier, Steve (Athlete, Football Player)
3473 S King Dr
Chicago, IL 60616-4108, USA

Collier, Timothy (Tim) (Athlete, Football Player)
3116 50th St
Dallas, TX 75216-7343, USA

Collingwood, Chris (Musician, Songwriter, Writer)
MOB Agency
6404 Wilshire Blvd Ste 505
Los Angeles, CA 90048-5507, USA

Collins, Alfred (Sonny) (Athlete, Football Player)
2455 Cedar Canyon Ct SE
Marietta, GA 30067-6617, USA

Collins, Anthony (Athlete, Football Player)
c/o Todd France *Creative Artists Agency (CAA) Sports*
3500 Lenox Rd NE
Atlanta, GA 30326-4228, USA

Collins, Art (Athlete, Basketball Player)
5828 NW 19th Ave
Miami, FL 33142-7855, USA

Collins, Arthur D Jr (Business Person)
7000 Central Ave NE
Medtronic Inc
Minneapolis, MN 55432-3568, USA

Collins, Bill (Athlete, Hockey Player)
5000 Town Ctr Ste 505
Southfield, MI 48075-1112, USA

Collins, Billy (Writer)
PO Box 2487
Winter Park, FL 32790-2487, USA

Collins, Bootsy (Musician)
c/o Bruce Solar *Agency for the Performing Arts (APA)*
405 S Beverly Dr Ste 500
Beverly Hills, CA 90212-4425, USA

Collins, Brett W (Athlete, Football Player)
6550 E 35th Rd
Yuma, AZ 85365-8202, USA

Collins, Clifton (Actor)
12933 Bloomfield St
Studio City, CA 91604-1402, USA

Collins, David S (Dave) (Athlete, Baseball Player)
92 Lauretta Mae Dr Unit A
Lebanon, OH 45036-2652, USA

Collins, Donald E (Don) (Athlete, Baseball Player)
127 Deerwood Trl
Sharpsburg, GA 30277-2002, USA

Collins, Douglas (Doug) (Athlete, Basketball Player, Coach, Sportscaster)
10040 E Happy Valley Rd Unit 617
Scottsdale, AZ 85255-2355, USA

Collins, Duane E (Business Person)
Parker Hannifin Corp
6035 Parkland Blvd
Cleveland, OH 44124-4186, USA

Collins, Dwight (Athlete, Football Player)
821 12th St
Beaver Falls, PA 15010-4416, USA

Collins, Gary (Athlete, Hockey Player)
1908-1320 Islington Ave
Etobicoke, ON M9A 5C6, Canada

Collins, Gary J (Athlete, Football Player)
840 S Franklin St
Palmyra, PA 17078-3327, USA

Collins, Gemma (Reality Star)
c/o Mark Thomas *TM Media*
45 Circus Rd
London NW8 9JH, UNITED KINGDOM

Collins, George (Athlete, Football Player)
2043 Northside Rd
Perry, GA 31069-2224, USA

Collins, Glen L (Athlete, Football Player)
17 Autumn Park
Jackson, MS 39206-6241, USA

Collins, Jack (Actor)
Contemporary Artists
610 Santa Monica Blvd Ste 202
Santa Monica, CA 90401-1645, USA

Collins, Jamie (Athlete, Football Player)
c/o Bus Cook *Bus Cook Sports, Inc*
1 Willow Bend Dr
Hattiesburg, MS 39402-8552, USA

Collins, Jarron (Athlete, Basketball Player)
11173 Cashmere St
Los Angeles, CA 90049-3233, USA

Collins, Jason (Athlete, Basketball Player)
12639 Promontory Rd
Los Angeles, CA 90049-1186, USA

Collins, Jed (Athlete, Football Player)
c/o Derrick Fox *Derrick Fox Management*
Prefers to be contacted by telephone
CA, USA

Collins, Jerome (Athlete, Football Player)
25540 Soya Ln
Warrenville, IL 60555, USA

Collins, Jessica (Actor)
c/o Marnie Sparer *Power Entertainment Group*
195 S Beverly Dr Ste 414
Beverly Hills, CA 90212-3044, USA

Collins, Jim (Athlete, Football Player)
2140 E Oceanfront
Newport Beach, CA 92661-1525, USA

Collins, Joan (Actor)
c/o Ashley Vallance *InterTalent Rights Group*
46 Charlotte St
InterTalent House
London W1T 2GS, UNITED KINGDOM

Collins, Joely (Actor)
c/o Staff Member *TalentWorks*
3500 W Olive Ave Ste 1400
Burbank, CA 91505-5512, USA

Collins, Judy (Musician, Songwriter, Writer)
Rocky Mountains Production
PO Box 1296
New York, NY 10025-1296, USA

Collins, Kate (Actor)
1410 York Ave Apt 4D
New York, NY 10021-3401, USA

Collins, Kerry (Athlete, Football Player)
1090 Stockett Dr
Nashville, TN 37221-4431, USA

Collins, Kevin (Athlete, Baseball Player)
9121 Point Charity Dr
Pigeon, MI 48755-9624, USA

Collins, Lauren (Actor)
c/o Steven Kavovit *Thruline Entertainment*
9250 Wilshire Blvd Fl Ground
Beverly Hills, CA 90212-3352, USA

Collins, Lily (Actor)
c/o Rick Yorn *LBI Entertainment*
2000 Avenue of the Stars
N Tower Fl 3
Los Angeles, CA 90067-4700, USA

Collins, Lynn (Actor)
c/o Christine Tripicchio *Shelter PR*
5670 Wilshire Blvd Ste 1200
Los Angeles, CA 90036-5621, USA

Collins, Mark (Athlete, Football Player)
PO Box 23056
2X CHAMP SPORTS
Overland Park, KS 66283-0056, USA

Collins, Michael (Astronaut)
c/o Staff Member *Farrar, Straus and Giroux*
175 Varick St Fl 9
New York, NY 10014-7407, USA

Collins, Michael Brig Gen (Astronaut)
272 Polynesia Ct
Marco Island, FL 34145-3826, USA

Collins, Michelle (Actor)
c/o Tanya Kleckner *Henderson Represents*
11846 Ventura Blvd Ste 302
Studio City, CA 91604-2620, USA

Collins, Misha (Actor)
c/o Carolyn Govers *Anonymous Content*
3532 Hayden Ave
Culver City, CA 90232-2413, USA

Collins, Mo (Actor, Comedian)
c/o Harold Augenstein *Kazarian, Measures, Ruskin & Associates*
5200 Lankershim Blvd Ste 820
N Hollywood, CA 91601-3194, USA

Collins, Patrick (Actor)

Collins, Paul (Athlete, Football Player)
3704 Masters Ct
League City, TX 77573-4401, USA

Collins, Paul (Athlete, Football Player)
24463 Bashian Dr
Novi, MI 48375-2932, USA

Collins, Pauline (Actor)
c/o Sarah Camlett *Independent Talent Group*
40 Whitfield St
London W1T 2RH, UNITED KINGDOM

Collins, Phil (Musician, Songwriter)
Phil Collins Ltd
25 Ives Street
London SW3 2ND, UK

Collins, Roosevelt (Athlete, Football Player)
3600 Holly St
Denison, TX 75020-3714, USA

Collins, Shane (Athlete, Football Player)
PO Box 11090
Bozeman, MT 59719-1090, USA

Collins, Shanna (Actor)
c/o Stephanie Simon *Untitled Entertainment*
350 S Beverly Dr Ste 200
Beverly Hills, CA 90212-4819, USA

Collins, Shawn (Athlete, Football Player)
2744 Preece St
San Diego, CA 92111-5416, USA

Collins, Shawn (Athlete, Football Player)
PO Box 711933
San Diego, CA 92171-1933, USA

Collins, Stephen (Actor)
c/o Beth Cannon *Envision Entertainment*
8840 Wilshire Blvd Fl 3
Beverly Hills, CA 90211-2606, USA

Collins, Steve (Athlete, Boxer)
c/o Staff Member *Thomas Murphy PR*
Prefers to be contacted by email or phone.
London NA, UNITED KINGDOM

Collins, Susan (Senator)
413 Dirksen Senate Office Building
Washington, DC 20510-0001, USA

Collins, Suzanne (Actor)
c/o Tracey Bell *Red Door Actors Management*
21/22 Great Castle St
London W1 G0HZ, UK

Collins, Suzanne (Writer)
c/o Rosemary B. Stimola *Stimola Literary Studio*
306 Chase Ct
Edgewater, NJ 07020-1601, USA

Collins, Terry (Athlete, Baseball Player, Coach)
Roosevelt Ave Attn
NEWYORKMETS12301MANAGERSO
Flushing, NY 11368-9993, USA

Collins, Todd F (Athlete, Football Player)
1279 Collins Rd
New Market, TN 37820-3837, USA

Collins, Todd S (Athlete, Football Player)
26 Cambridge Cir
Victor, NY 14564-1503, USA

Collins, Tony (Athlete, Football Player)
10709 N Preserve Way Apt 203
Miramar, FL 33025-6553, USA

Collinsworth, Cris (Athlete, Football Player, Sportscaster)
31 Crow Hill Rd
Fort Thomas, KY 41075-1801, USA

Collis, Shannon (Actor)

Collison, Darren (Athlete, Basketball Player)
c/o Bill Duffy *BDA Sports Management*
700 Ygnacio Valley Rd Ste 330
Walnut Creek, CA 94596-3838, USA

Collison, Nick (Athlete, Basketball Player)
c/o Mike Higgins *Excel Sports Management (LA)*
9665 Wilshire Blvd Ste 500
Beverly Hills, CA 90212-2312, USA

Collyard, Bob (Athlete, Hockey Player)
5300 Knox Ave N
Minneapolis, MN 55430-3058, USA

Colman, Booth (Actor)
2160 Century Park E Apt 603
Los Angeles, CA 90067-2214, USA

Colman, Olivia (Actor)
c/o Ciara Parkes *Public Eye Communications*
535 Kings Rd
#313 Plaza
London SW10 0SZ, UNITED KINGDOM

Colman, Wayne (Athlete, Football Player)
604 N Somerset Ave
Ventnor City, NJ 08406-1551, USA

Colmenares, Grecia (Actor)
c/o Staff Member *Telefe (Argentina)*
Pavon 2444
Buenos Aires C1248AAT, ARGENTINA

Colo, Don (Athlete, Football Player)
26625 N 61st St
Scottsdale, AZ 85266-8770, USA

Coloma, Marcus (Actor)
c/o Paul Rosicker *Gersh*
9465 Wilshire Blvd Ste 600
Beverly Hills, CA 90212-2605, USA

Colombini, Aldo (Director, Producer)
PO Box 829
Newbury Park, CA 91319-0829, USA

Colombo, Marc (Athlete, Football Player)
1250 Biltmore Dr
Southlake, TX 76092-3462, USA

Colomby, Bobby (Musician)
1423 Holmby Ave
Los Angeles, CA 90024-5104, USA

Colomby, Scott (Actor)
Borinstein Oreck Bogart
3172 Dona Susana Dr
Studio City, CA 91604-4356, USA

Colon, Bartolo (Athlete, Baseball Player)
14 Federal St # 1
Passaic, NJ 07055-3209, USA

Colon, Harry (Athlete, Football Player)
10337 Alvarado Way
Charlotte, NC 28277-3459, USA

Colon, Willie (Athlete, Football Player)
c/o Joe Linta *JL Sports*
1204 Main St Ste 179
Branford, CT 06405-3787, USA

Colonna, Sarah (Actor)
c/o Staff Member *Brillstein Entertainment Partners*
9150 Wilshire Blvd Ste 350
Beverly Hills, CA 90212-3453, USA

Colorito, Tony (Athlete, Football Player)
17805 SW Cicero Ct
Beaverton, OR 97007-9036, USA

Colpaert, Dick (Athlete, Baseball Player)
47412 Eldon Dr
Shelby Township, MI 48317-2912, USA

Colquitt, Britton (Athlete, Football Player)

Colquitt, Craig (Athlete, Football Player)
4305 Franklin Rd
Lebanon, TN 37090-8067, USA

Colquitt, Dustin (Athlete, Football Player)
1905 Pitts Field Ln
Knoxville, TN 37922-6197, USA

Colquitt, Jimmy (Athlete, Football Player)
11722 Hardin Valley Rd
Knoxville, TN 37932-2319, USA

Colson, Loyd A (Athlete, Baseball Player)
309 E Sycamore St
Hollis, OK 73550-1233, USA

Colston, Marques (Athlete, Football Player)
c/o Joel Segal *Lagardere Unlimited (NY)*
456 Washington St Apt 9L
New York, NY 10013-1555, USA

Colston, Tim (Athlete, Football Player)
6804 N 47th St
Tampa, FL 33610-1808, USA

Colt, Marshall (Actor)
1150 Anchorage Ln Unit 612
San Diego, CA 92106-3124, USA

Colter, Jessie (Musician)
Shout Factory
2042-A Armacost Ave
Los Angeles, CA 90025, USA

Colter, Mike (Actor)
c/o Kelli M Jones *Status PR (NY)*
PO Box 6191
Westlake Village, CA 91359-6191, USA

Colter, Steve (Athlete, Basketball Player)
802 E Mountain Sage Dr
Phoenix, AZ 85048-4428, USA

Colton, Graham (Musician)
c/o Staff Member *Red Light Management*
5800 Bristol Pkwy Ste 400
Culver City, CA 90230-6898, USA

Colton, Lawrence R (Larry) (Athlete, Baseball Player)
3027 NE 68th Ave
Portland, OR 97213-5215, USA

Colton, Michael (Writer)
c/o Tony Etz *Creative Artists Agency (CAA)*
2000 Avenue of the Stars Ste 100
Los Angeles, CA 90067-4705, USA

Coltraine, Robbie (Actor)
19 Sydney Mews
London SW3 6HL, United Kingdom

Coltrane, Ellar (Actor)
c/o Staff Member *Cinetic Media*
555 W 25th St Fl 4
New York, NY 10001-5542, USA

Coltrane, Robbie (Actor)
Caroline Dawson & Associates
125 Gloucester Road
2nd Fl
London SW7 4TE, UNITED KINGDOM

Coluccio, Bob (Athlete, Baseball Player)
369 Flower St
Costa Mesa, CA 92627-2352, USA

Columbus, Chris (Director, Producer)
c/o Staff Member *1492 Pictures*
1606 Stockton St
San Francisco, CA 94133-3300, USA

Colunga, Fernando (Actor)
c/o Staff Member *Crossover Agency*
801 SW 3rd Ave Ste 302
Miami, FL 33130-3576, USA

Colussy, Dan A (Business Person)
20 Saint Thomas Dr
West Palm Beach, FL 33418-4598, USA

Colvin, James (Jim) (Athlete, Football Player)
4583 S Deer Poppy Cir
Saint George, UT 84790-4722, USA

Colvin, Roosevelt (Athlete, Football Player)
12170 Annette Ln
Fishers, IN 46037-8197, USA

Colvin, Shawn (Musician, Songwriter)
615 Pressler St
Austin, TX 78703-5125, USA

Colvin, Tyler (Athlete, Baseball Player)
777 Bradburn Dr
Mount Pleasant, SC 29464-5114, USA

Colwill, Les (Athlete, Hockey Player)
714 20 St N
Lethbridge, AB T1H 3N6, Canada

Colyar, Michael (Actor, Comedian)
c/o Vanzil Burke *Burke Management*
231 S Gale Dr
Beverly Hills, CA 90211-3405, USA

Colyer, Steve (Athlete, Baseball Player)
205 S Saint Jacques St
Florissant, MO 63031-6950, USA

Colzie, Jim (Athlete, Baseball Player)
3140 Day Ave
Miami, FL 33133-5111, USA

Comaneci, Nadia (Athlete, Gymnast)
Marion Hatter
3214 Bart Conner Dr
Norman, OK 73072-2406, USA

Combe, Geoff (Athlete, Baseball Player)
743 Tudor Cir
Thousand Oaks, CA 91360-5246, USA

Combes, Willard W (Cartoonist)
1266 Oakridge Dr
Cleveland, OH 44121-1623, USA

Combichrist (Music Group, Musician)
c/o Staff Member *Metropolis Records*
PO Box 974
Media, PA 19063-0974, USA

Combs, Chris (Athlete, Football Player)
2018 Guernsdel St
Durham, NC 27705-2418, USA

Combs, Glenn (Athlete, Basketball Player)
3627 Dogwood Ln SW
Roanoke, VA 24015-4503, USA

Combs, Holly Marie (Actor, Producer, Writer)
223 Saddlebow Rd
Bell Canyon, CA 91307-1035, USA

Combs, Jeffrey (Actor)
6478 Pinion St
Oak Park, CA 91377-1211, USA

Combs, Jessi (Reality Star)
PO Box 21859
Long Beach, CA 90801-4859, USA

Combs, Leroy (Athlete, Basketball Player)
1631 Glenn Bo Dr
Norman, OK 73071-2813, USA

Combs, Patrick D (Pat) (Athlete, Baseball Player)
203 Timber Lake Way
Southlake, TX 76092-7217, USA

Combs, Rodney (Race Car Driver)
201 Old Country Rd Ste 101
Melville, NY 11747-2731, USA

Combs, Sean (Musician, Producer)
c/o James Cruz *Combs Enterprises*
1440 Broadway Frnt 3
New York, NY 10018-2301, USA

Comden, Danny (Director)
c/o Ruthanne Secunda *ICM Partners*
10250 Constellation Blvd Fl 7
Los Angeles, CA 90067-6207, USA

Comeau, Andy (Actor)
c/o Staff Member *Rugolo Entertainment*
195 S Beverly Dr Ste 400
Beverly Hills, CA 90212-3044, USA

Comeau, Rey (Athlete, Hockey Player)
4 Rue de Cernay
Lorraine, QC J6Z 2Z1, Canada

Comeaux, Darren (Athlete, Football Player)
2450 N 142nd Dr
Goodyear, AZ 85395-1660, USA

Comeaux, John (Athlete, Basketball Player)
PO Box 327
Carencro, LA 70520-0327, USA

Comegys, Dallas (Athlete, Basketball Player)
4330 Wayne Ave
Philadelphia, PA 19140-1745, USA

Comella, Greg (Athlete, Football Player)
90 Fairbanks Ave
Wellesley Hills, MA 02481-5256, USA

Comer, Anjanette (Actor)
Dade/Schultz
6442 Coldwater Canyon Ave Ste 206
Valley Glen, CA 91606-1174, USA

Comer, Steve (Athlete, Baseball Player)
425 Chan Vw Apt 314
Chanhassen, MN 55317-8403, USA

Comer, Wayne (Athlete, Baseball Player)
145 Marcus St
Shenandoah, VA 22849-3917, USA

Comess, Aaron (Musician)
DAS Communications
83 Riverside Dr
New York, NY 10024-5713, USA

Comey, James (Attorney)
c/o Keith Urbahn *Javelin*
203 S Union St Ste 200
Alexandria, VA 22314-3356, USA

Comi, Paul (Actor)
2395 Ridgeway Rd
San Marino, CA 91108-2116, USA

Comiskey, Chuck (Athlete, Football Player)
2502 Convent Ave
Pascagoula, MS 39567-4517, USA

Commerford, Tim (Musician)
5908 Zumirez Dr
Malibu, CA 90265-4004, USA

Commings, Sanders (Athlete, Football Player)

Commodore, Mike (Athlete, Hockey Player)
Newport Sports Management
400-201 City Centre Dr
Attn Wade Arnott
Mississauga, ON L5B 2T4, Canada

Commodores, The (Music Group, Musician)
1920 Benson Ave
Saint Paul, MN 55116-3214, USA

Common (Musician)
c/o Alexandra Crotin *The Lede Company*
9701 Wilshire Blvd # 930
Beverly Hills, CA 90212-2020, USA

Compaore, Blaise (President)
President's Office
Boile Postale 7031
Ouagadougou, BURKINA FASO

Complete Stone Roses, The (Music Group)
c/o Ross Morrison *Primary Talent International (UK)*
10-11 Jockeys Fields
The Primary Bldg
London WC1R 4BN, UNITED KINGDOM

Compte, Maurice (Actor)
c/o Brit Reece *PMK/BNC Public Relations*
1840 Century Park E Ste 1400
Los Angeles, CA 90067-2115, USA

Compton, Clint (Athlete, Baseball Player)
77 Glen St # AJT1
Augusta, ME 04330-3916, USA

Compton, Dick (Athlete, Football Player)
3408 Briarcliff Ct S
Irving, TX 75062-3206, USA

Compton, Mike (Athlete, Baseball Player)
8624 Leighton Dr
Tampa, FL 33614-1723, USA

Compton, Ogden (Athlete, Football Player)
13918 Preston Valley Pl # Pb
Dallas, TX 75240-4769, USA

Compton, Stacy (Race Car Driver)
2050 Easome Rd
Hurt, VA 24563-3650, USA

Compton, Tom (Athlete, Football Player)
c/o Joel Segal *Lagardere Unlimited (NY)*
456 Washington St Apt 9L
New York, NY 10013-1555, USA

Comrie, Mike (Athlete, Hockey Player)
10800 Wilshire Blvd Apt 1703
Los Angeles, CA 90024-4217, USA

Comrie, Paul (Athlete, Business Person, Hockey Player)
The Brick Group Income Fund
16930 114 Ave NW Ofc of
Attn the President
Edmonton, AB T5M 3S2, Canada

Comstock, Keith (Athlete, Baseball Player)
9615 E Desert Trl
Scottsdale, AZ 85260-4624, USA

Conacher, Brian (Athlete, Hockey Player)
202-500 Avenue Rd
Toronto, ON M4V 2J6, Canada

Conacher, Jim (Athlete, Hockey Player)
422-980 Lynn Valley Rd
North Vancouver, BC V7J 3V7, Canada

Conacher, Pat (Athlete, Hockey Player)
PO Box 104 Stn Main
Regina, SK S4P 2Z5, Canada

Conacher, Pete (Athlete, Hockey Player)
3 Conifer Dr
Etobicoke, ON M9C 1X3, Canada

Conant, Sean (Actor)
c/o Staff Member *Rising Picture*
PO Box 2
North Hampton, NH 03862-0002, USA

Conatser, Clint (Athlete, Baseball Player)
26701 Quail Crk Apt 191
Laguna Hills, CA 92656-3010, USA

Conatsor, Clint (Athlete, Baseball Player)
26701 Quail Crk Apt 191
Laguna Hills, CA 92656-3010, USA

Conaty, William (Bill) (Athlete, Football Player)
203 Country Club Dr
Moorestown, NJ 08057-3977, USA

Conaway, Cristi (Actor)
443 14th St
Santa Monica, CA 90402-2131, USA

Conaway, K. Michael (Congressman, Politician)
2430 Rayburn Hob
Washington, DC 20515-3705, USA

Concepcion, David I (Davey) (Athlete, Baseball Player)
Urbanizacion el Castano
Botalon 5-D
Maracay, Venezuela, Venezuela

Concepcion, Onix (Athlete, Baseball Player)
1486 Steeplechase Ln
Deltona, FL 32725-4752, USA

Concha, Billy (Actor)
PO Box 1129
Hermosa Beach, CA 90254-1129, USA

Concrete Blonde (Music Group)
Concrete Blonde Touring Company Inc
15821 Ventura Blvd Ste 270
Encino, CA 91436-4775, USA

Concretes, The (Music Group)
c/o Staff Member *Paradigm (Monterey)*
404 W Franklin St
Monterey, CA 93940-2303, USA

Conde, Ninel (Actor)
c/o Gabriel Blanco *Gabriel Blanco Iglesias (Mexico)*
Rio Balsas 35-32
Colonia Cuauhtemoc
DF 06500, Mexico

Conde, Ramon (Athlete, Baseball Player)
PO Box 57
Juana Diaz, PR 00795-0057, USA

Condit, Philip M (Business Person)
Boeing Co
PO Box 3707
Seattle, WA 98124-2207, USA

Condo, Jon (Athlete, Football Player)
c/o Chad Wiestling *Integrated Sports Management*
2120 Texas St Apt 2204
Houston, TX 77003-3054, USA

Condon, Bill (Director, Writer)
c/o Amanda Lundberg *42West*
600 3rd Ave Fl 23
New York, NY 10016-1914, USA

Condon, Tom (Athlete, Football Player)
c/o Staff Member *CAA Sports*
2000 Avenue of the Stars Ste 100
Los Angeles, CA 90067-4705, USA

Condor, Lana (Actor)
c/o Jordyn Palos *Persona Public Relations*
6255 W Sunset Blvd Ste 705
Hollywood, CA 90028-7408, USA

Condra, Julie (Actor)
c/o Rick Ax *Gold Coast Management*
935 Victoria Ave Frnt
Venice, CA 90291-3933, USA

Condredge, Holloway (Athlete, Football Player)
8137 Faircrest Ln
Knoxville, TN 37919-2038, USA

Condren, Glen (Athlete, Football Player)
8557 N 175th East Ave
Owasso, OK 74055-5638, USA

Condren, Steve (Horse Racer)
36-130 Robert St
Milton, ON L9T 6E3, Canada

Condrey, Clay (Athlete, Baseball Player)
412 N 8th St
Navasota, TX 77868-2927, USA

Cone, David B (Athlete, Baseball Player)
303 E 83rd St Apt 6A
New York, NY 10028-4316, USA

Cone, Fred (Athlete, Football Player)
PO Box 1819
Blairsville, GA 30514-1819, USA

Confederate Railroad (Music Group)
The Bobby Roberts Company Inc
PO Box 1547
Goodlettsville, TN 37070-1547, USA

Conforti, Gino (Actor)
Orange Gove Group
12178 Ventura Blvd Ste 205
Studio City, CA 91604-2540, USA

Conforto, Michael (Athlete, Baseball Player)
c/o Scott Boras *Boras Corporation*
18 Corporate Plaza Dr
Newport Beach, CA 92660-7901, USA

Congdon, Jeff (Athlete, Basketball Player)
13712 S 500 E
Draper, UT 84020-8926, USA

Congemi, John (Athlete, Football Player)
1015 Trailmore Ln
Weston, FL 33326-2820

Coniar, Larry (Athlete, Football Player)
PO Box 5133
Evanston, IL 60204-5133, USA

Conigliaro, Billy (Athlete, Baseball Player)
501 Cabot St Unit 2
Beverly, MA 01915-2580, USA

Conine, Jeff (Athlete, Baseball Player)
3166 Inverness
Weston, FL 33332-1816, USA

Conjar, Larry (Athlete, Football Player)
542 Sheridan Rd Apt 2
Evanston, IL 60202-3124, USA

Conklin, Cary (Athlete, Football Player)
13425 W Waldemar St
Boise, ID 83713, USA

Conklin, Ty (Athlete, Hockey Player)
K 0 Sports
501 S Cherry St Ste 580
Attn Kurt Overhardt
Denver, CO 80246-1327, USA

Conlan, Shane P (Athlete, Football Player)
521 East Dr
Sewickley, PA 15143-1114, USA

Conlee, John (Musician)
John Conlee Enterprises
713 18th Ave S
Nashville, TN 37203-3214, USA

Conley, Bob (Athlete, Baseball Player)
16A Canton Dr
Whiting, NJ 08759-1977, USA

Conley, Darby (Cartoonist)
c/o Staff Member *United Press Media*
200 Madison Ave
New York, NY 10016-3903, USA

Conley, Earl Thomas (Musician, Songwriter)
657 Baker Rd
Smyrna, TN 37167-4777, USA

Conley, Jack (Actor)
c/o Julia Buchwald *Buchwald*
5900 Wilshire Blvd Ste 3100
Los Angeles, CA 90036-5030, USA

Conley, Joe (Actor)
8300 Burdette Rd Apt 432
Bethesda, MD 20817-2830, USA

Conley, Larry (Athlete, Basketball Player)
5422 Forest Springs Dr
Atlanta, GA 30338-3606, USA

Conley, Michael (Mike) (Athlete, Track Athlete)
University of Arkansas
Athletic Dept
Fayetteville, AR 72701, USA

Conley, Mike (Athlete, Basketball Player)
334 Dubray Manor Dr
Collierville, TN 38017-3950, USA

Conley, Steve (Athlete, Football Player)
1745 N Independence Pl
Fayetteville, AR 72704-5789, USA

Conlin, Chris (Athlete, Football Player)
4864 Tropicana Ave
Cooper City, FL 33330-4428, USA

Conlin, Edward (Athlete, Basketball Player)
153 N Mountain Ave
Montclair, NJ 07042-2347, USA

Conlin, Michaela (Actor)
c/o Jillian Roscoe *ID Public Relations*
7060 Hollywood Blvd Fl 8th
Los Angeles, CA 90028-6021, USA

Conlon, Marty (Athlete, Basketball Player)
180 Woodbine Dr
East Hampton, NY 11937-1747, USA

Conn, Didi (Actor, Musician)
c/o Staff Member *The House of Representatives*
3118 Wilshire Blvd Ste D
Santa Monica, CA 90403-2345, USA

Conn, Richard (Dick) (Athlete, Football Player)
144 Sugarmill Ln
Moore, SC 29369-9497, USA

Conn, Terri (Actor)
c/o Staff Member *Innovative Artists*
1505 10th St
Santa Monica, CA 90401-2805, USA

Connally, Fritzie (Athlete, Baseball Player)
615 Portofino Dr
Arlington, TX 76012-2700, USA

Conneff, Kevin (Musician)
Macklam Feldman Mgmt
200-1505 2nd Ave W
Vancouver, BC V6H 3Y4, CANADA

Connell, Albert (Athlete, Football Player)
3328 Clevemont Way
Ellenwood, GA 30294-1323, USA

Connell, Chad (Actor)
c/o Marc Hamou *Thruline Entertainment*
9250 Wilshire Blvd Fl Ground
Beverly Hills, CA 90212-3352, USA

Connelly, Jennifer (Actor)
c/o Meredith O'Sullivan Wasson *The Lede Company*
9701 Wilshire Blvd # 930
Beverly Hills, CA 90212-2020, USA

Connelly, Lynn (Athlete, Golfer)
19 E Elm St
Greenwich, CT 06830-6519, USA

Connelly, Michael (Writer)
847 S Newport Ave
Tampa, FL 33606-2934, USA

Connelly, Mike (Athlete, Football Player)
9513 Alta Mira Dr
Dallas, TX 75218-3506, USA

Connelly, Steve (Athlete, Baseball Player)
1863 Litchfield Ave
Long Beach, CA 90815-3037, USA

Connelly, Wayne (Athlete, Hockey Player)
Site 2 Box 61
RR 2
Swastika, ON P0K 1T0, Canada

Conner, Bart (Athlete, Gymnast, Olympic Athlete)
4421 Hidden Hill Rd
Norman, OK 73072-2899, USA

Conner, Chris (Actor)
c/o Gregg A Klein *AKA Talent Agency*
325 N Larchmont Blvd
Los Angeles, CA 90004-3011, USA

Conner, Darion (Athlete, Football Player)
9444 Prairie Point Rd
Macon, MS 39341-8084, USA

Conner, Frank (Golfer)
c/o Staff Member *Pro Golfers Association (PGA)*
112 TPC Blvd
Ponte Vedra Beach, FL 32082, USA

Conner, Jimmy Dan (Athlete, Basketball Player)
Kentucky Colonels
5009 Old Federal Rd
Louisville, KY 40207-1200, USA

Conner, Jimmy Dan (Athlete, Basketball Player)
5009 Old Federal Rd
Louisville, KY 40207-1200, USA

Conner, Lester (Athlete, Basketball Player)
12517 Daniels Gate Dr
Castle Pines, CO 80108-9420, USA

Conners, Dan (Athlete, Football Player)
1895 Partridge Dr
San Luis Obispo, CA 93405-6321, USA

Connery, Jason (Actor)
c/o Staff Member *Unconditional Entertainment*
3607 W Magnolia Blvd Ste 3
Burbank, CA 91505-2962, USA

Connery, Sean (Actor)
Lyford Cay
P.O. Box N-7776
Nassau, BAHAMAS

Conney, Terry (Athlete, Baseball Player)
3205 Filbert Ave
Clovis, CA 93611-6050, USA

Connick Jr, Harry (Actor, Musician, Reality Star, Talk Show Host)
Harry TV
530 W 57th St
Cbs Broadcast Center
New York, NY 10019-2902, USA

Conniff, Cal (Skier)
157 Pleasantview Ave
Longmeadow, MA 01106-1021, USA

Connolly, Billy (Actor, Musician, Producer)
c/o Victoria Belfrage *Julian Belfrage & Associates*
9 Argyll St Fl 3
London W1F 7TG, UNITED KINGDOM

Connolly, Kevin (Actor)
c/o Troy Zien *3 Arts Entertainment*
9460 Wilshire Blvd Fl 7
Beverly Hills, CA 90212-2713, USA

Connolly, Kristen (Actor)
525 Rialto Ave
Venice, CA 90291-4247, USA

Connolly, Olga Fikotova (Athlete, Track Athlete)
514 Huntington St
Huntington Beach, CA 92648-4929, USA

Connolly, Tim (Athlete, Hockey Player)
772 Forest Ave
Buffalo, NY 14209-1042, USA

Connor, Cam (Athlete, Hockey Player)
2716 118 St NW
Edmonton, AB T6J 3P9, Canada

Connor, Chris (Musician)
Maxine Harvard Unlimited
7942 W Bell Rd Ste C5
Glendale, AZ 85308-8710, USA

Connor, Christopher M (Business Person)
Sherwin-Williams Co
101 W Prospect Ave Ste 1020
Cleveland, OH 44115-1027, USA

Connor, Jodie (Musician)
c/o Staff Member *Primary Talent International (UK)*
10-11 Jockeys Fields
The Primary Bldg
London WC1R 4BN, UNITED KINGDOM

Connor, Mark (Athlete, Baseball Player)
7400 Nubbin Ridge Dr
Knoxville, TN 37919-8155, USA

Connor, Patrick (Athlete, Football Player)
3 Spring Bank
New Mills, Stockport SK12 4AS, UNITED KINGDOM

Connor, Sarah (Musician)
Postfach 3053
Hannover 30030, GERMANY

Connor, Shannon (Model)
4 Rockage Rd
Warren, NJ 07059-5506

Connors, Carol (Musician, Songwriter)
1709 Ferrari Dr
Beverly Hills, CA 90210-1603, USA

Connors, Jimmy (Athlete, Tennis Player)
c/o Michael Blakey *Electra Star Management*
9229 W Sunset Blvd Ste 415
Los Angeles, CA 90069-3404, USA

Connors, Patrick (Athlete, Baseball Player)
1038 S Oakwood Rd
Oshkosh, WI 54904-8167, USA

Connot, Scott (Athlete, Football Player)
47069 220th St
Brookings, SD 57006-7153, USA

Conover, Scott (Athlete, Football Player, Sportscaster)
17 Mimosa Ct
Jackson, NJ 08527-1239, USA

Conoway, Cristi (Actor)
Cristi Conaway Design
2433 Main St # C
Santa Monica, CA 90405-3539, USA

Conrad, Bobby Joe (Athlete, Football Player)
140 County Road 3270
Clifton, TX 76634-4678, USA

Conrad, Brooks (Athlete, Baseball Player)
3964 E Wateka Ct
Gilbert, AZ 85297-9497, USA

Conrad, Chris (Athlete, Football Player)
984 Orangewood Dr
Brea, CA 92821-2514, USA

Conrad, David (Actor)
c/o Marion Campbell Kammer *TalentWorks*
3500 W Olive Ave Ste 1400
Burbank, CA 91505-5512, USA

Conrad, Kent (Politician, Senator)
530 Hart Senate Office Building
Washington, DC 20003-1340, USA

Conrad, Kimberly (Actor)
10236 Charing Cross Rd
Los Angeles, CA 90024-1815

Conrad, Lauren (Reality Star)
c/o Nicole Perez-Krueger *PMK/BNC Public Relations*
1840 Century Park E Ste 1400
Los Angeles, CA 90067-2115, USA

Conrad, Robert (Actor)
Wildwest 2L
10487 Sunland Blvd
Sunland, CA 91040-1905, USA

Conradt, Jody (Athlete, Basketball Player, Coach)
8546 Adirondack Trl Apt 8
Austin, TX 78759-7906, USA

Conran, Jasper A T (Designer, Fashion Designer)
Jasper Conran Ltd
2 Munden St
London W14 0RH, UNITED KINGDOM (UK)

Conran, Terence O (Designer)
22 SHad Thames
London SE1 2YU, UNITED KINGDOM (UK)

Conroy, Christopher (Athlete, Baseball Player)
3910 Cephas Child Rd UNIT 12
Doylestown, PA 18902-9089, USA

Conroy, Craig (Athlete, Hockey Player, Olympic Athlete)
PO Box 549
Henderson Harbor, NY 13651-0549, USA

Conroy, Frances (Actor)
c/o Paul Martino *Martino Management*
149 W 72nd St Apt 1D
New York, NY 10023-3228, USA

Conroy, Jeff (Producer)
Original Productions
308 W Verdugo Ave
Burbank, CA 91502-2340, USA

Conroy, Kevin (Actor)
c/o Staff Member *Imperium 7 Talent Agency*
5455 Wilshire Blvd Ste 1706
Los Angeles, CA 90036-4217, USA

Conroy, Tim (Athlete, Baseball Player)
109 Moonlight Dr
Monroeville, PA 15146-2028, USA

Conroy, Zack (Actor)
c/o Danielle Quinoa *Stewart Talent Agency (NY)*
318 W 53rd St Rm 201
New York, NY 10019-5742, USA

Considine, John (Actor)
5200 Cape George Rd
Port Townsend, WA 98368-9035, USA

Considine, Paddy (Actor, Writer)
c/o Staff Member *Creative Artists Agency (CAA)*
2000 Avenue of the Stars Ste 100
Los Angeles, CA 90067-4705, USA

Considine, Tim (Actor)
3708 Mountain View Ave
Los Angeles, CA 90066-3112, USA

Conspirator (Music Group)
c/o Staff Member *Paradigm (Monterey)*
404 W Franklin St
Monterey, CA 93940-2303, USA

Constantin, Charles (Athlete, Hockey Player)
1277 Av de Merici
Quebec, QC G1S 3H8, Canada

Constantine, Kevin (Coach)
5928 Jenny Lind Ct
San Jose, CA 95120-1789, USA

Constantine, Michael (Actor)
1604 Bern St
Reading, PA 19604-1630, USA

Consuelos, Mark (Actor)
c/o Staff Member *Milojo Productions*
157 Columbus Ave Fl 5
New York, NY 10023-6083, USA

Conte, Chris (Athlete, Football Player)
c/o Ryan Tollner *REP 1 Sports Group*
80 Technology Dr
Irvine, CA 92618-2301, USA

Conte, Lansana (President)
President's Office
Conakry, GUINEA

Conti, Bill (Musician)
117 Fremont Pl
Los Angeles, CA 90005-3868, USA

Conti, Guy (Athlete, Baseball Player)
448 53rd Sq
Vero Beach, FL 32968-1021, USA

Conti, Jason (Athlete, Baseball Player)
740 N April Dr
Chandler, AZ 85226-1632, USA

Conti, Tom (Actor)
Chatto & Linnit
Prince of Wales Coventry St
London W1V 7FE, UNITED KINGDOM(UK)

Contini, Joe (Athlete, Hockey Player)
302 Domville St
Arthur, ON N0G 1A0, Canada

Contostavlos, Tulisa (Model)
c/o Alex Segal *InterTalent Rights Group*
ROAR House
46 Charlotte St
London W1T 2GS, UNITED KINGDOM

Contoulis, John (Athlete, Football Player)
404 Champion Cir
Throop, PA 18512-1451, USA

Contours, The (Music Group)
c/o Jeff Epstein *M.A.G./Universal Attractions*
15 W 36th St Fl 8
New York, NY 10018-7927, USA

Contreras, Jose (Athlete, Baseball Player)
8501 Lithia Pinecrest Rd
Lithia, FL 33547-2807, USA

Contreras, Nardi (Athlete, Baseball Player)
5052 Lurgan Rd Land 0
Lakes, FL 34638-7653, USA

Contz, Bill (Athlete, Football Player)
106 Grace Dr
Cranberry Twp, PA 16066-2308, USA

Converse, Frank (Actor)
c/o Phil Sutfin *ICM Partners*
10250 Constellation Blvd Fl 7
Los Angeles, CA 90067-6207, USA

Converse, Jim (Athlete, Baseball Player)
11865 Cobble Brook Dr
Rancho Cordova, CA 95742-8008, USA

Converse-Roberts, William (Actor)
Innovative Artists
1505 10th St
Santa Monica, CA 90401-2805, USA

Convery, Brandon (Athlete, Hockey Player)
PO Box 2556
Manhattan Beach, CA 90267-2556, USA

Conway, Billy (Music Group, Musician)
Creative Performance Group
48 Laight St
New York, NY 10013-2156, USA

Conway, Brett (Athlete, Football Player)
568 Park Dr NE
Atlanta, GA 30306-3671, USA

Conway, Curtis (Athlete, Football Player)

Conway, Gary (Actor)
2035 Mandeville Canyon Rd
Los Angeles, CA 90049-2226, USA

Conway, James (Race Car Driver)
420 Fair Hill Dr # 1
Elkton, MD 21921-2573, USA

Conway, James L (Director, Producer)
c/o Andrea Simon *Andrea Simon Entertainment*
6345 Balboa Blvd Ste 138
Encino, CA 91316-1510, USA

Conway, John W (Business Person)
Crown Cork & Seal
770 Township Line Rd Ste 100
Yardley, PA 19067-4232, USA

Conway, Kellyanne (Business Person)
c/o Staff Member *White House, The*
1600 Pennsylvania Ave NW
Washington, DC 20500-0004, USA

Conway, Kevin (Actor)
c/o Mary Erickson *Mary Erickson Management*
3900 San Fernando Rd Unit 1507
Glendale, CA 91204-2866, USA

Conway, Tim (Actor, Comedian)
c/o Howard Bragman *LaBrea Media*
8306 Wilshire Blvd # 4002
Beverly Hills, CA 90211-2304, USA

Conwell, Angell (Actor)
c/o Staff Member *Evolution Entertainment*
10850 Wilshire Blvd Ste 600
Los Angeles, CA 90024-4319, USA

Conwell, Ernie (Athlete, Football Player)
5301 McGavock Rd
Brentwood, TN 37027-5185, USA

Conwell, Joseph (Joe) (Athlete, Football Player)
1301 Stoney River Dr
Ambler, PA 19002-1159, USA

Conwell, Tommy (Music Group, Musician)
Brothers Mgmt
141 Dunbar Ave
Fords, NJ 08863-1551, USA

Conyers Jr., John (Congressman, Politician)
2426 Rayburn Hob
Washington, DC 20515-2214, USA

Cooder, Ry (Musician)
326 Entrada Dr
Santa Monica, CA 90402-1202, USA

Coody, Charles (Athlete, Golfer)
1555 Oldham Ln
Abilene, TX 79602-4143, USA

Coogan, Keith (Actor)
c/o Drew Elliot *Artist International*
333 E 43rd St Apt 115
New York, NY 10017-4822, USA

Coogan, Steve (Actor, Producer)
Baby Cow Productions
5-6 Portland Mews
London W1F 8JG, UNITED KINGDOM

Coogler, Ryan (Director)
c/o Craig Kestel *WME|IMG*
9601 Wilshire Blvd
Beverly Hills, CA 90210-5213, USA

Cook, Aaron (Athlete, Baseball Player)
1004 Tara Dr
Burleson, TX 76028-8243, USA

Cook, AJ (Actor)
c/o Siri Garber *Platform PR*
2666 N Beachwood Dr
Los Angeles, CA 90068-2308, USA

Cook, Andy (Athlete, Baseball Player)
3312 Central Ave
Memphis, TN 38111-4402, USA

Cook, Ann Turner (Model, Writer)
12401 N 22nd St Apt E501
Tampa, FL 33612-4625, USA

Cook, Anthony (Athlete, Football Player)
111 Elm St
Salisbury, NC 28144-6115, USA

Cook, Bert (Athlete, Basketball Player)
2571 W 5725 S
Roy, UT 84067-1326, USA

Cook, Bob (Athlete, Football Player)
100 Sioux Ct
Hendersonville, TN 37075-4634, USA

Cook, Carole (Actor, Comedian)
8829 Ashcroft Ave
West Hollywood, CA 90048-2401, USA

Cook, Chris (Athlete, Football Player)
c/o Hadley Engelhard *Enter-Sports Management*
6000 Lake Forrest Dr Ste 370
Atlanta, GA 30328-5902, USA

Cook, Cliff (Athlete, Baseball Player)
605 E Williamsburg Mnr
Arlington, TX 76014-1145, USA

Cook, Daequan (Basketball Player)
c/o Staff Member *Miami Heat*
601 Biscayne Blvd
American Airlines Arena
Miami, FL 33132-1801, USA

Cook, Dalvin (Athlete, Football Player)
c/o Zac Hiller *ZHS*
6 Zeck Ct
Suffern, NY 10901-3426, USA

Cook, Dane (Actor)
c/o Staff Member *Superfinger Entertainment*
2660 W Olive Ave
Burbank, CA 91505-4525, USA

Cook, Darwin (Athlete, Basketball Player)
PO Box 4078
Lancaster, CA 93539-4078, USA

Cook, David (Musician)
c/o Staff Member *CinemaNow*
4553 Glencoe Ave Ste 200
Marina Del Rey, CA 90292-7909, USA

Cook, Dennis (Athlete, Baseball Player)
3413 Serene Hills Ct
Austin, TX 78738-1230, USA

Cook, Doris (Athlete, Baseball Player, Commentator)
4435 Cedar Ln
Norton Shores, MI 49441-5649, USA

Cook, Edward J (Athlete, Football Player)
902 Briarwood Ct
Sewell, NJ 08080-3508, USA

Cook, Fred (Athlete, Football Player)
4402 Market St
Pascagoula, MS 39567-2224, USA

Cook, Gayle (Business Person)
Cook Group Inc
PO Box 489
Bloomington, IN 47402-0489, USA

Cook, Glen (Athlete, Baseball Player)
424 Scarlet Sage Dr
League City, TX 77573-6426, USA

Cook, Jameel (Athlete, Football Player)
PO Box 131647
Houston, TX 77219-1647, USA

Cook, Jared (Athlete, Football Player)

Cook, Jason (Actor)
c/o Katie Mason Stern *Luber Roklin Management*
5815 W Sunset Blvd Ste 208
Los Angeles, CA 90028-6481, USA

Cook, Jeff (Athlete, Basketball Player)
4908 E Doubletree Ranch Rd
Paradise Valley, AZ 85253-1556, USA

Cook, Jeff (Music Group, Musician)
P O Box 35967
Fort Payne, AL 35967, USA

Cook, Jerry (Race Car Driver)
117 Palmetto Dr
Mooresville, NC 28117-9406, USA

Cook, John (Athlete, Golfer)
8815 Conroy Windermere Rd # 40
Orlando, FL 32835-3129, USA

Cook, Katie (Television Host)
c/o Evan Warner *WME|IMG*
9601 Wilshire Blvd
Beverly Hills, CA 90210-5213, USA

Cook, Kristy Lee (Musician)
c/o Marty Rendleman *Rendleman Management Group, Inc.*
PO Box 670366
Dallas, TX 75367-0366, USA

Cook, Kyle (Musician)
626 Calverton Ln
Brentwood, TN 37027-8989, USA

Cook, Marv (Athlete, Football Player)
425 Butternut Ln
Iowa City, IA 52246-2782, USA

Cook, Mike (Athlete, Baseball Player)
216 Harlech Way
Charleston, SC 29414-6876, USA

Cook, Paul (Music Group, Musician)
Solo Agency
55 Fulham High St
London SW6 3JJ, UNITED KINGDOM(UK)

Cook, Paul M (Business Person)
SRI International
333 Ravenswood Ave
Menlo Park, CA 94025-3493, USA

Cook, Rachael Leigh (Actor)
Moongate Management
4570 Van Nuys Blvd Ste 171
Sherman Oaks, CA 91403-2913, USA

Cook, Rashard (Athlete, Football Player)
517 Ocean Breeze Way
Chula Vista, CA 91914-2022, USA

Cook, Robert (Athlete, Baseball Player)
179 Royal Farm E
Blacklick, OH 43004-9209, USA

Cook, Robin (Writer)
16 Louisburg Sq
Boston, MA 02108-1203, USA

Cook, Robin (Writer)
4601 Gulf Shore Blvd N # P4
Naples, FL 34103-2221, USA

Cook, Ron (Athlete, Baseball Player)
1918 Franklin Dr
Longview, TX 75601-4111, USA

Cook, Terry (Race Car Driver)
177 Knob Hill Rd
Mooresville, NC 28117-6847, USA

Cook, Thomas A (Writer)
Bantam Books
1540 Broadway
New York, NY 10036-4039, USA

Cook, Tim (Business Person)
Apple Computer
1 Infinite Loop
Cupertino, CA 95014-2084, USA

Cook, Toi (Athlete, Football Player)
5064 Llano Dr
Woodland Hills, CA 91364-3029, USA

Cooke, Amelia (Actor)
c/o Darren Goldberg *Global Creative*
1051 Cole Ave # B
Los Angeles, CA 90038-2601, USA

Cooke, Christian (Actor)
c/o Chris Huvane *Management 360*
9111 Wilshire Blvd
Beverly Hills, CA 90210-5508, USA

Cooke, David (Athlete, Basketball Player)
PO Box 270591
San Diego, CA 92198-2591, USA

Cooke, Ed (Athlete, Football Player)
2093 Wake Forest St
Virginia Beach, VA 23451-1421, USA

Cooke, Janis (Journalist)
Washington Post
1150 15th St NW
Washington, DC 20071-0002, USA

Cooke, Joe (Athlete, Football Player)
2550 E River Rd Unit 3101
Tucson, AZ 85718-9504, USA

Cooke, Josh (Actor)
c/o Elise Konialian *Untitled Entertainment (NY)*
215 Park Ave S Fl 8
New York, NY 10003-1622, USA

Cooke, Olivia (Actor)
c/o Josh Glick *Grandview*
7122 Beverly Blvd Ste F
Los Angeles, CA 90036-2572, USA

Cooke, Steve (Athlete, Baseball Player)
9791 Jefferson Pkwy Apt A3
Englewood, CO 80112-5962, USA

Cooke, William (Bill) (Athlete, Football Player)
1851 Hillside Rd
Fairfield, CT 06824-2017, USA

Cooks, Brandin (Athlete, Football Player)

Cooks, Johnie (Athlete, Football Player)
2170 Sun Creek Rd
Starkville, MS 39759-8436, USA

Cooks, Kerry (Athlete, Football Player)
5358 Lismore Ln
Fitchburg, WI 53711-7680, USA

Cooks, Rayford (Athlete, Football Player)
1839 Nomas St
Dallas, TX 75212-3806, USA

Cooksey, Dave (Religious Leader)
Brethren Church
27 High St
Ashland, OH 44805-8705, USA

Cooksey, Patricia (Patti) (Athlete, Horse Racer)
Kentucky Horse Racing Commission
4063 Iron Works Pkwy Bldg B
Lexington, KY 40511-8511, USA

Cookson, Brent (Athlete, Baseball Player)
1232 Manzanita Dr
Santa Paula, CA 93060-1239, USA

Cookson, Sophie (Actor)
c/o Romilly Bowlby *DDA Public Relations*
192-198 Vauxhall Bridge Rd
London SW1V 1DX, UNITED KINGDOM

Coolbaugh, Scott (Athlete, Baseball Player)
6708 Carriage Ln
Colleyville, TX 76034-5771, USA

Cooley, Chris (Athlete, Football Player)
PO Box 144
Hamilton, VA 20159-0144, USA

Cooley, Ryan (Actor)
c/o Norbert Abrams *Noble Caplan Abrams*
1260 Yonge St Fl 2
Toronto, ON M4T 1W5, CANADA

Cooley, Tonya (Reality Star)
c/o Staff Member *Bunim/Murray Productions*
1015 Grandview Ave
Glendale, CA 91201-2205, USA

Cooleyb, Chelsea (Beauty Pageant Winner)
c/o Staff Member *Miss Universe Organization, The*
1370 Avenue of the Americas Fl 16
New York, NY 10019-4602, USA

Coolidge, Jennifer (Actor)
c/o Ali Benmohamed *United Talent Agency (UTA)*
9336 Civic Center Dr
Beverly Hills, CA 90210-3604, USA

Coolidge, Martha (Director)
760 N La Cienega Blvd
Los Angeles, CA 90069-5204, USA

Coolidge, Rita (Musician)
7520 Proctor Rd
Tallahassee, FL 32309-7600, USA

Coolio (Actor, Musician)
c/o Susan Haber *Haber Entertainment*
434 S Canon Dr Apt 204
Beverly Hills, CA 90212-4501, USA

Coombs, Danny (Athlete, Baseball Player)
14130 Cleobrook Dr
Houston, TX 77070-3744, USA

Coombs, Torrance (Actor)
c/o Danielle Allman-Del *D2 Management*
10351 Santa Monica Blvd Ste 210
Los Angeles, CA 90025-6937, USA

Coombs-Mueller, Carol (Actor)
5200 Irvine Blvd Spc 364
Irvine, CA 92620-2060, USA

Coomer, Ron (Athlete, Baseball Player)
13184 Spencer Sweet Pea Ln
Eden Prairie, MN 55347-2187, USA

Coon, Carrie (Actor)
c/o Jason Kendziera *Sanders Armstrong Caserta*
4111 W Alameda Ave Ste 505
Burbank, CA 91505-4163, USA

Coon, Christopher (Senator)
127A Russell Senate Office Building
Washington, DC 20510-0001, USA

Coonce, Ricky (Music Group, Musician)
Thomas Cassidy
11761 E Speedway Blvd
Tucson, AZ 85748-2017, USA

Cooney, Gerry (Boxer)
370 North Ave
Fanwood, NJ 07023-1320, USA

Cooney, Mark (Athlete, Football Player)
8035 Flower Ct
Arvada, CO 80005-2445, USA

Coonts, Stephen (Writer)
116 W 14th St Apt 8S
New York, NY 10011-7315, USA

Coonts, Stephen (Writer)
40 Upland Rd
Colorado Springs, CO 80906-4246

Coooinger, Rocky (Athlete, Baseball Player)
7208 Alto Rey Ave
El Paso, TX 79912-2100

Cooper, Adrian (Athlete, Football Player)
3120 N Saint Paul St
Denver, CO 80205-4840, USA

Cooper, Alice (Musician)
8033 W Sunset Blvd # 745
W Hollywood, CA 90046-2401, USA

Cooper, Amari (Athlete, Football Player)
c/o Joel Segal *Lagardere Unlimited (NY)*
456 Washington St Apt 9L
New York, NY 10013-1555, USA

Cooper, Anderson (Correspondent, Journalist, Television Host)
c/o Staff Member *CNN (NY)*
10 Columbus Cir
Time Warner Center
New York, NY 10019-1158, USA

Cooper, Artis (Athlete, Basketball Player)
5013 Millstone Way
Granite Bay, CA 95746-6126, USA

Cooper, Bert (Athlete, Football Player)
3152 Aldon Ave
Las Vegas, NV 89121-5610, USA

Cooper, Bill (Athlete, Football Player)
16056 Greenwood Rd
Monte Sereno, CA 95030-3018, USA

Cooper, Blake (Actor)
c/o Andrew Freedman *Andrew Freedman Public Relations*
35 E 84th St
New York, NY 10028-0871, USA

Cooper, Bonnie (Athlete, Baseball Player, Commentator)
PO Box 26
119 SAMPSON STREET
Tremont, IL 61568-0026, USA

Cooper, Bradley (Actor)
733 Brooktree Rd
Pacific Palisades, CA 90272-3902, USA

Cooper, Brian (Athlete, Baseball Player)
San Jose Giants
PO Box 21727
San Jose, CA 95151-1727, USA

Cooper, Brian (Athlete, Baseball Player)
346 W Ada Ave
Glendora, CA 91741-4248, USA

Cooper, Camille (Basketball Player)
New York Liberty
2 Penn Plz Fl 15
Madison Square Garden
New York, NY 10121-1700, USA

Cooper, Carl (Athlete, Golfer)
4823 Scenic Woods Trl
Kingwood, TX 77345-2323, USA

Cooper, Cecil (Athlete, Baseball Player)
7208 Alto Rey Ave
El Paso, TX 79912-2100, USA

Cooper, Charles (Actor)
c/o Joel Kleinman *Baier/Kleinman International*
3575 Cahuenga Blvd W Ste 500
Los Angeles, CA 90068-1344, USA

Cooper, Chris (Actor)
c/o Lisa Kasteler *Wolf-Kasteler Public Relations*
6255 W Sunset Blvd Ste 1111
Los Angeles, CA 90028-7426, USA

Cooper, Christin (Athlete, Olympic Athlete, Skier)
1001 E Hyman Ave
Aspen, CO 81611-2612, USA

Cooper, Darin (Actor)
c/o Marianne Golan *Golan & Blumberg*
2761 E Woodbury Dr
Arlington Heights, IL 60004-7247, USA

Cooper, Dave (Artist)
c/o Staff Member *Fantagraphics Books*
7563 Lake City Way NE
Seattle, WA 98115-4218, USA

Cooper, Dominic (Actor)
c/o Joel Lubin *Creative Artists Agency (CAA)*
2000 Avenue of the Stars Ste 100
Los Angeles, CA 90067-4705, USA

Cooper, Don (Athlete, Baseball Player)
2109 Willowmet Dr
Brentwood, TN 37027-1812, USA

Cooper, Don (Athlete, Baseball Player)
2320 Arborfield Ln
Sarasota, FL 34235-1807, USA

Cooper, Duane (Athlete, Basketball Player)
13813 Ocana Ave
Bellflower, CA 90706-2528, USA

Cooper, Earl (Athlete, Football Player)
2224 E Highway 21
Lincoln, TX 78948-6496, USA

Cooper, Eric (Athlete, Baseball Player)
5404 Longview Ct Unit 4
Johnston, IA 50131-2706, USA

Cooper, Gary (Athlete, Baseball Player)
1136 Birch Cir
Alpine, UT 84004-1212, USA

Cooper, Gary (Baseball Player)
Atlanta Braves
402 E Victory Dr
Savannah, GA 31405-2254, USA

Cooper, Hal (Director)
2651 Hutton Dr
Beverly Hills, CA 90210-1213, USA

Cooper, Imogen (Music Group, Musician)
Van Walsum Mgmt
4 Addison Bridge Place
London W14 8XP, UNITED KINGDOM(UK)

Cooper, Jilly (Writer)
c/o Staff Member *Transworld Publishers*
20 Vauxhall Bridge Road
London SW1V 2SA, UK

Cooper, Jim (Athlete, Football Player)
12910 Low Meadow Ct
Charlotte, NC 28277-4030, USA

Cooper, Jim (Congressman, Politician)
1536 Longworth Hob
Washington, DC 20515-4205, USA

Cooper, Jonathan (Athlete, Football Player)
c/o Todd France *Creative Artists Agency (CAA) Sports*
3500 Lenox Rd NE
Atlanta, GA 30326-4228, USA

Cooper, Lester I (Producer)
45 Morningside Dr S
Westport, CT 06880-5414, USA

Cooper, Louis (Athlete, Football Player)
200 Gregg Ave
Marion, SC 29571-3824, USA

Cooper, Marcus Ramone (Pleasure P) (Musician)
c/o Staff Member *Atlantic Records*
1290 Avenue of the Americas Fl 28
New York, NY 10104-0106, USA

Cooper, Mark S (Athlete, Football Player)
18295 Cottonwood Dr Apt 104
Parker, CO 80138-8983, USA

Cooper, Oliver (Actor)
c/o Greg Longstreet *Polaris PR*
8135 W 4th St Fl 2
Los Angeles, CA 90048-4415, USA

Cooper, Riley (Athlete, Football Player)
c/o Joel Segal *Lagardere Unlimited (NY)*
456 Washington St Apt 9L
New York, NY 10013-1555, USA

Cooper, Ryan (Actor)
c/o Cristina DiCocco *Persona PR*
401 Park Ave S # 861
New York, NY 10016-8808, USA

Cooper, Scott (Actor, Director)
c/o Annalee Paulo *42West*
1840 Century Park E Ste 700
Los Angeles, CA 90067-2122, USA

Cooper, Scott (Athlete, Baseball Player)
7 Fairways Cir Apt F
Saint Charles, MO 63303-3353, USA

Cooper, Stephen (Business Person)
Enron Corp
1400 Smith St Ste 11195
Houston, TX 77002-3800, USA

Cooper, Wayne (Athlete, Basketball Player)
5013 Millstone Way
Granite Bay, CA 95746-6126, USA

Cooper, Wayne (Artist)
PO Box 106
Depew, OK 74028-0106, USA

Cooper, Wima Lee (Musician)
c/o Staff Member *Charles Rapp Enterprises Inc*
88 Pine St Ste 1701
New York, NY 10005-1849, USA

Cooperwheat, Lee (Designer, Fashion Designer)
Cooperwheat Blundell
14 Cheshire St
London E2 6EH, UNITED KINGDOM (UK)

Coover, Robert (Writer)
Brown University
Linden Press
49 George St
Providence, RI 02912-0001, USA

Copa, Tom (Athlete, Basketball Player)
10068 Circleview Dr
Austin, TX 78733-6302, USA

Cope, Amber (Race Car Driver)
PO Box 44337
Tacoma, WA 98448-0337, USA

Cope, Derrike (Race Car Driver)
CLR Racing
1037 Briarhill Rd
Mooresville, NC 28115-2333, USA

Cope, Jonathan (Dancer)
Royal Ballet
Covent Garden
Bow St
London WC2E 9DD, UNITED KINGDOM (UK)

Cope, Julian (Musician, Songwriter, Writer)
International Talent Group
729 7th Ave Ste 1600
New York, NY 10019-6880, USA

Cope, Mike (Race Car Driver)
60th St. North
Clearwater, FL 34620, USA

Copeland, Adam (Edge) (Wrestler)
c/o Kerry Rodgerson *World Wrestling Entertainment (WWE)*
1241 E Main St
Stamford, CT 06902-3520, USA

Copeland, Damian (Athlete, Football Player)

Copeland, Danny (Athlete, Football Player)
186 Old Newton Rd
Pelham, GA 31779-4043, USA

Copeland, Gloria (Religious Leader)
Kenneth Copeland Ministries
14355 Morris Dido Rd
Newark, TX 76071-9501, USA

Copeland, Hollis (Athlete, Basketball Player)
257 Upland Ave
Ewing, NJ 08638-2331, USA

Copeland, Horace (Athlete, Football Player)
4195 Blakemore Pl
Spring Hill, FL 34609-0694, USA

Copeland, Joan (Actor)
88 Central Park W Apt 11W
New York, NY 10023-6045, USA

Copeland, John (Athlete, Football Player)
4226 Maxwell Dr
Mason, OH 45040-6504, USA

Copeland, Kenneth (Religious Leader)
Kenneth Copeland Ministries
14355 Morris Dido Rd
Newark, TX 76071-9501, USA

Copeland, Kristina (Actor)
Collingwood Management
1572 4th Ave W 2nd Fl
Vancouver, BC V6J 1L7, CANADA

Copeland, Lanard (Athlete, Basketball Player)
4115 Pierce Rd
Atlanta, GA 30349-3648, USA

Copeland, Miles (Musician)
1830 N Sierra Bonita Ave
Los Angeles, CA 90046-2233, USA

Copeland, Misty (Dancer)
American Ballet Theatre
890 Broadway Fl 3
New York, NY 10003-1278, USA

Copeland, Stewart (Musician)
2420 Arbutus Dr
Los Angeles, CA 90049-1209, USA

Copeland Jr., Zane (Lil Zane) (Musician)
c/o Gail Del Corral *Del Corral and Associates*
1010 Common St Ste 2550
New Orleans, LA 70112-2461, USA

Coples, Quinton (Athlete, Football Player)
c/o Chad Speck *Allegiant Athletic Agency*
35 Market Sq Ste 201
Knoxville, TN 37902-1420, USA

Copley, Sharlto (Actor)
c/o Brandon Liebman *WME/IMG*
9601 Wilshire Blvd
Beverly Hills, CA 90210-5213, USA

Copley, Teri (Actor, Model)
13351 Riverside Dr # D513
Sherman Oaks, CA 91423-2542, USA

Copon, Michael (Actor)
c/o Lena Roklin *Luber Roklin Management*
5815 W Sunset Blvd Ste 208
Los Angeles, CA 90028-6481, USA

Coppenbarger, Ron (Athlete, Football Player)
7890 James Island Trl
Jacksonville, FL 32256-7355, USA

Coppens, Gus (Athlete, Football Player)
2413 Deerpark Dr
Fullerton, CA 92835-3001, USA

Copperfield, David (Magician)
Magic of David Copperfield
3650 W Russell Rd
Las Vegas, NV 89118-2423, USA

Coppinger, Rocky (Athlete, Baseball Player)
7208 Alto Rey Ave
El Paso, TX 79912-2100, USA

Coppo, Paul (Athlete, Hockey Player)
3458 Solitude Rd
De Pere, WI 54115-8617, USA

Coppock, Laurel (Actor)
The Groundlings Theatre
7307 Melrose Ave
Los Angeles, CA 90046-7512, USA

Coppola, Alicia (Actor)
c/o Leslie Allan-Rice *Leslie Allan-Rice Management*
1007 Maybrook Dr
Beverly Hills, CA 90210-2715, USA

Coppola, Chris (Actor)
c/o Laura Pallas *Pallas Management*
4536 Greenbush Ave
Sherman Oaks, CA 91423-3112, US

Coppola, Francis Ford (Director)
c/o Staff Member *American Zoetrope*
1641 Ivar Ave
Los Angeles, CA 90028-6304, USA

Coppola, Roman (Director)
6740 Milner Rd
Los Angeles, CA 90068-3215, USA

Coppola, Sofia (Actor, Director, Writer)
46 Morton St
New York, NY 10014-4549, USA

Coppolla, Alicia (Actor)
c/o Jeff Witjas *Agency for the Performing Arts (APA)*
405 S Beverly Dr Ste 500
Beverly Hills, CA 90212-4425, USA

CopQO, Paul (Athlete, Hockey Player)
3458 Solitude Rd
De Pere, WI 54115-8617, USA

Coquillette, Trace (Athlete, Baseball Player)
5200 Mississippi Bar Dr
Orangevale, CA 95662-5717, USA

Cora, Alex (Athlete, Baseball Player)
F12 Calle 14
Caguas, PR 00727-6935, USA

Cora, Cat (Chef)
c/o BeBe Lerner *ID Public Relations*
7060 Hollywood Blvd Fl 8th
Los Angeles, CA 90028-6021, USA

Cora, Joey (Athlete, Baseball Player)
423 Labrador Ln
Clairton, PA 15025-5240, USA

Cora, Joey (Athlete, Baseball Player)
Florida Marlins
2267 NW 199th St
Miami Gardens, FL 33056-2664, USA

Cora, Jose M (Joey) (Athlete, Baseball Player)
F12 Calle 14
Villa Nueva
Caguas, PR 00727-6935, USA

Corabi, John (Musician)
c/o Staff Member *Union Entertainment Group*
4952 Warner Ave
Huntington Beach, CA 92649-4479, USA

Coraci, Frank (Director)
9738 Arby Dr
Beverly Hills, CA 90210-1203, USA

Coral, The (Music Group)
c/o Staff Member *Paradigm (Monterey)*
404 W Franklin St
Monterey, CA 93940-2303, USA

Corazzini, Carl (Athlete, Hockey Player)
583 Winter St
Framingham, MA 01702-5634, USA

Corbero, Ursula (Actor)
c/o Pedro Garay *Garay Talent*
Calle de las Navas de Tolosa 3
Madrid 28013, SPAIN

Corbet, Brady (Actor)
c/o Brian Young *Three Six Zero (LA)*
7175 Willoughby Ave Fl 2
Los Angeles, CA 90046-6711, USA

Corbet, Rene (Athlete, Hockey Player)
68 Aspen Stone Way SW
Calgary, AB T3H 0H5, Canada

Corbett, Doug (Athlete, Baseball Player)
75083 Edwards Rd
Yulee, FL 32097-2660, USA

Corbett, Gretchen (Actor)
6932 N Vincent Ave
Portland, OR 97217-5133, USA

Corbett, James (Athlete, Football Player)
2723 Marlo Way
Lakeside Park, KY 41017-2121, USA

Corbett, John (Actor, Musician)
c/o Steve Lovett *Lovett Management*
1327 Brinkley Ave
Los Angeles, CA 90049-3619, USA

Corbett, Luke R (Business Person)
Kerr-McGee Corp
Kerr-McGee Center
Oklahoma City, OK 73125, USA

Corbett, Michael (Actor)
c/o Milton B Suchin *Suchin Company, The*
15315 Magnolia Blvd Ste 101
Sherman Oaks, CA 91403-1100, USA

Corbett, Mike (Athlete, Football Player)
PO Box 2809
Oakhurst, CA 93644-2809, USA

Corbett, Sherman (Athlete, Baseball Player)
7031 Washita Way
San Antonio, TX 78256-2310, USA

Corbett, Steve (Athlete, Football Player)
3 Wake Robin Rd
Sudbury, MA 01776-1726, USA

Corbin, Archie (Athlete, Baseball Player)
7525 Tram Rd
Beaumont, TX 77713-8723, USA

Corbin, Barry (Actor)
c/o Staff Member *Dick Delson & Associates*
4520 Bakman Ave
Studio City, CA 91602-2013, USA

Corbin, Easton (Musician)
c/o Staff Member *WME (Nashville)*
1201 Demonbreun St
Nashville, TN 37203-3140, USA

Corbin, Ray (Athlete, Baseball Player)
922 Liberty St SW
Live Oak, FL 32064-3619, USA

Corbin, Tyrone (Athlete, Basketball Coach, Basketball Player, Coach)
c/o Steve Kauffman *Kauffman Sports Management Group*
Prefers to be contacted by telephone
Malibu, CA, USA

Corbus, William (Athlete, Football Player)
1100 Union St Apt 1100
San Francisco, CA 94109-2019, USA

Corchiani, Chris (Athlete, Basketball Player)
1106 Harvey St
Raleigh, NC 27608-2205, USA

Corcoran, Barbara (Business Person, Reality Star)
1192 Park Ave
New York, NY 10128-1314, USA

Corcoran, Donna (Actor)
22408 Kanaina Ct
Chatsworth, CA 91311-1275, USA

Corcoran, Roy (Athlete, Baseball Player)
PO Box 173
Slaughter, LA 70777-0173, USA

Corcoran, Tim (Athlete, Baseball Player)
PO Box 173
Slaughter, LA 70777-0173, USA

Corcoran, Tim (Athlete, Baseball Player)
4349 Friar Cir
La Verne, CA 91750-2718, USA

Cord, Alex (Actor)
c/o Staff Member *Coast to Coast Talent Group*
3350 Barham Blvd
Los Angeles, CA 90068-1404, USA

Corday, Barbara (Business Person)
1949 Coldwater Canyon Dr
Beverly Hills, CA 90210-1730, USA

Corday, Mara (Actor)
25932 Mendoza Dr
Valencia, CA 91355-2159, USA

Corddry, Nate (Actor)
c/o Jill McGrath *Door24*
115 W 29th St Rm 1102
New York, NY 10001-5106, USA

Corddry, Rob (Actor)
c/o Peter Principato *Artists First*
9465 Wilshire Blvd Ste 900
Beverly Hills, CA 90212-2608, USA

Corden, James (Actor, Comedian, Talk Show Host)
Fulwell 73
7a Bayham St
Camden
London NW1 0EY, UNITED KINGDOM

Cordero, Angel (Horse Racer)
4 Osborne Ln
Greenvale, NY 11548-1141, USA

Cordero, Chad (Athlete, Baseball Player)
2825 Live Oak Ave
Fullerton, CA 92835-2237, USA

Cordero, Francisco (Athlete, Baseball Player)
3103 N Chassy Ave
Fayetteville, AR 72703-3679, USA

Cordero, Joaquin (Actor)
c/o Staff Member *Televisa*
Blvd Adolfo Lopez Mateos 232
Colonia San Angel INN
DF CP 01060, MEXICO

Cordero, Wilfredo N (Wil) (Baseball Player)
Montreal Expos
25844 Kensington Dr
Westlake, OH 44145-1472, USA

Cordes-Elliott, Gloria (Athlete, Baseball Player, Commentator)
86 Malone Ave
Staten Island, NY 10306-4110, USA

Cordes-Elliott, Gloria (Baseball Player)
86 Malone Ave
Staten Island, NY 10306-4110, USA

Cordileone, Lou (Athlete, Football Player)
5312 Mark Ct
Agoura Hills, CA 91301-5200, USA

Cordova, Francisco (Athlete, Baseball Player)
c/o Staff Member *San Diego Padres*
100 Park Blvd
San Diego, CA 92101-7405, USA

Cordova, Ismael Cruz (Actor)
c/o Liz Mahoney *Narrative*
7080 Hollywood Blvd Ste 1100
Los Angeles, CA 90028-6938, USA

Cordova, Jorge (Athlete, Football Player)
10800 Scripps Ranch Blvd Apt 108
San Diego, CA 92131-6012, USA

Cordova, Marty (Athlete, Baseball Player)
47 Club Vista Dr
Henderson, NV 89052-6603, USA

Cordova-Buckley, Natalia (Actor)
c/o Maria Herrera *PMK/BNC Public Relations*
1840 Century Park E Ste 1400
Los Angeles, CA 90067-2115, USA

Corduner, Allan (Actor)
c/o Staff Member *Conway van Gelder Grant*
8-12 Broadwick St
London W1F 8HW, UNITED KINGDOM

Corea, Chick (Musician)
Chick Corea Productions
10400 Samoa Ave
Tujunga, CA 91042-1921, USA

Corev, Brvan (Athlete, Baseball Player)
7829 E Riverdale Cir
Mesa, AZ 85207-0804, USA

Corey, Bryan (Athlete, Baseball Player)
7829 E Riverdale Cir
Mesa, AZ 85207-0804, USA

Corey, Jill (Musician)
64 Division Ave
Levittown, NY 11756-2999, USA

Corey, Mark (Athlete, Baseball Player)
9321 Cornell Cir
Highlands Ranch, CO 80130-4143, USA

Corey, Mark (Athlete, Baseball Player)
PO Box 113
Austin, PA 16720-0113, USA

Corey, Walt (Athlete, Football Player)

Corgan, Billy (Musician, Songwriter)
1249 Sheridan Rd
Highland Park, IL 60035-4107, USA

Cori, Carl T (Business Person)
Sigma-Aldrich Corp
3050 Spruce St
Saint Louis, MO 63103-2530, USA

Cori, Yarckin (Musician)
GreeneHouse Management, Inc
PO Box 151234
Altamonte Springs, FL 32715-1234, USA

Corinealdi, Emayatzy (Actor)
c/o Jeff Morrone *Atlas Artists*
9220 W Sunset Blvd Ste 225
Los Angeles, CA 90069-3513, USA

Corker, Bob (Senator)
Dirksen Senate Office Building SD-185
Washington, DC 20510-0001, USA

Corker, John (Athlete, Football Player)
825 Martin Luther King Jr Blvd
Baltimore, MD 21201-2306, USA

Corkins, Mike (Athlete, Baseball Player)
3760 Chemehuevi Blvd
Lake Havasu City, AZ 86406-6449, USA

Corkum, Bob (Athlete, Hockey Player)
165 Scotland Rd
Newbury, MA 01951-1004, USA

Corley, Al (Actor)
Code Entertainment
280 S Beverly Dr Ste 513
Beverly Hills, CA 90212-3908, USA

Corley, Annie (Actor)
c/o Renee Jennett *Renee Jennett Management*
5757 Wilshire Blvd Ste 473
Los Angeles, CA 90036-3632, USA

Corley, Anthony (Athlete, Football Player)
7465 Rodin Ct
Sun Valley, NV 89433-6691, USA

Corley, Ray (Athlete, Basketball Player)
590 Elwood Rd
East Northport, NY 11731-5629, USA

Cormack, Danielle (Actor)
c/o Staff Member *Platform PR*
2666 N Beachwood Dr
Los Angeles, CA 90068-2308, USA

Corman, Avery (Writer)
International Creative Mgmt
40 W 57th St Ste 1800
New York, NY 10019-4033, USA

Corman, Roger (Actor, Director, Producer)
2501 La Mesa Dr
Santa Monica, CA 90402-2334, USA

Cormier, Joe (Athlete, Football Player)
9110 La Salle Ave
Los Angeles, CA 90047-3608, USA

Cormier, Lance (Athlete, Baseball Player)
17949 Romulus Rd
Ralph, AL 35480-9111, USA

Cormier, Rheal (Athlete, Baseball Player)
6750 Cody Trl
Park City, UT 84098-6394, USA

Corn, Laura (Writer)
c/o Staff Member *Literary Group International*
330 W 38th St Rm 408
New York, NY 10018-8473, USA

Corneille (Artist)
Society of Independent Artists
Cours la Reine
Paris 75008, FRANCE

Corneisen, Rufus (Religious Leader)
415 S Chester Rd
Swarthmore, PA 19081-2303, USA

Cornejo, Mardie (Athlete, Baseball Player)
321 E 3rd St
Wellington, KS 67152-2706, USA

Cornejo, Nate (Athlete, Baseball Player)
1600 N B St
Wellington, KS 67152-4405, USA

Cornelison, Jerry (Athlete, Football Player)
12713 Cedar St
Leawood, KS 66209-1873, USA

Cornelius, Charles (Athlete, Football Player)
8865 Okeechobee Blvd Apt 306
West Palm Beach, FL 33411-5125, USA

Cornelius, James (Business Person)
Guidant Corp
111 Monument Cir
Indianapolis, IN 46204-5100, USA

Cornelius, Jemalle (Athlete, Football Player)
c/o Chad Speck *Allegiant Athletic Agency*
35 Market Sq Ste 201
Knoxville, TN 37902-1420, USA

Cornelius, Kathy (Athlete, Golfer)
5744 W Del Rio St
Chandler, AZ 85226-6825, USA

Cornelius, Reid (Athlete, Baseball Player)
10117 Hunt Club Ln
Palm Beach Gardens, FL 33418-4568, USA

Corneliussen, Stephanie (Actor, Model)
c/o Patrick Corcoran *PCM International*
450 N Rossmore Ave
Studio 303
Los Angeles, CA 90004-2406, USA

Cornell, Harry M Jr (Business Person)
leggett & Platt Inc
1 Leggett Rd
Carthage, MO 64836-9649, USA

Cornell, Jeff (Athlete, Baseball Player)
1644 SW Jeffrey Cir
Lees Summit, MO 64081-4115, USA

Cornell, Lydia (Actor)
269 S Beverly Dr
Beverly Hills, CA 90212-3851, USA

Cornell, Robert (Bo) (Athlete, Football Player)
2605 239th Ave SE
Sammamish, WA 98075-9442, USA

Cornett, Betty Jane (Athlete, Baseball Player)
99 Corbett Ct Apt 410
Pittsburgh, PA 15237-3030, USA

Cornett, Brad (Athlete, Baseball Player)
1704 N Avenue I
Lamesa, TX 79331-3140, USA

Cornett, Leanza (Actor)
c/o Staff Member *WME|IMG*
9601 Wilshire Blvd
Beverly Hills, CA 90210-5213, USA

Cornfeld, Stuart (Producer)
59 W 12th St Apt 6H
New York, NY 10011-8535, USA

Cornforth, Mark (Athlete, Hockey Player)
11 Indian Spring Rd
Milton, MA 02186-3716, USA

Cornick, Paul (Athlete, Football Player)

Cornish, Abbie (Actor)
c/o Cara Tripicchio *Shelter PR*
5670 Wilshire Blvd Ste 1200
Los Angeles, CA 90036-5621, USA

Cornish, Frank (Athlete, Football Player)
406 20th St Apt 29
Gretna, LA 70053-5736, USA

Cornish, Nick (Actor)
c/o Robert Stein *Robert Stein Management*
PO Box 3797
Beverly Hills, CA 90212-0797, USA

Cornutt, Terry (Athlete, Baseball Player)
179 W Hazel St
Roseburg, OR 97471-2211, USA

Cornwell, Fred (Athlete, Football Player)
2107 Windward Ln
Newport Beach, CA 92660-3820, USA

Cornwell, Johnny (Musician)
Overland Productions
156 W 56th St # 500
New York, NY 10019-3800, USA

Cornwell, Justin (Actor)
c/o Doug Wald *Anonymous Content*
3532 Hayden Ave
Culver City, CA 90232-2413, USA

Cornwell, Patricia (Actor, Producer, Writer)
c/o Sheryl Main *Main1 Communications*
703 Pier Ave Ste B229
Hermosa Beach, CA 90254-3949, USA

Cornyn, John (Politician)
1348 S Carolina Ave SE
Washington, DC 20003-2371, USA

Cornyn, John (Senator)
517 Hart Senate Office Bldg
Washington, DC 20510-0001, USA

Coronado, Bob (Athlete, Football Player)
1539 Sereno Dr
Vallejo, CA 94589-2726, USA

Corone, Antoni (Actor)
c/o Bonni Allen *Allen + Oleary*
74223 Santa Rosa Cir
Palm Desert, CA 92260-3034, USA

Coronel, Al (Actor)
c/o Wendy Pineda *Supersonix Media*
560 W Main St Ste C PMB 337
Alhambra, CA 91801-3376, USA

Coronel, Felipe (Immortal Technique) (Musician)
c/o Staff Member *Viper Records*
230 Mott St Frnt A
New York, NY 10012-4147, USA

Corr, Andrea (Musician)
c/o Staff Member *Luber Roklin Management*
5815 W Sunset Blvd Ste 208
Los Angeles, CA 90028-6481, USA

Corr, Caroline (Music Group)
John Hughes
6 Martello Terr Sandycove
Dunlaoughaire
Dublin, IRELAND

Corr, Jim (Music Group)
John Hughes
6 Martello Terr Sandycove
Dunlaoughaire
Dublin, IRELAND

Corr, Ryan (Actor)
c/o Catherine Poulton *Catherine Poulton Management*
105 Rupert St
Collingwood
Melbourne, Victoria 03066, AUSTRALIA

Corr, Sharon (Musician)
c/o Staff Member *Solo Agency Ltd (UK)*
53-55 Fulham High St
Fl 2
London SW6 3JJ, UNITED KINGDOM

Corrado, Fred (Business Person)
Great A & P Tea Co
19 Spear Rd Ste 310
Ramsey, NJ 07446-1223, USA

Corrado, Gabriel (Actor)
c/o Staff Member *Telefe (Argentina)*
Pavon 2444
Buenos Aires C1248AAT, ARGENTINA

Corral, Frank (Athlete, Football Player)
Riverside Municipal Building
3900 Main St
Attn Graffiti Control Coordinator
Riverside, CA 92522-0001, USA

Corrales, Pat (Athlete, Baseball Player, Coach)
2 W Wesley Rd NW Apt 18
Atlanta, GA 30305-3500, USA

Correa, Carlos (Athlete, Baseball Player)
c/o Greg Genske *The Legacy Agency*
500 Newport Center Dr Ste 800
Newport Beach, CA 92660-7008, USA

Correa, Ed (Athlete, Baseball Player)
A2 Calle Milagros Cabezas
Urb Carolina Alta
Carolina, PR 00987-7101, USA

Correal, Charles (Athlete, Football Player)
110 Springbrooke Dr
Venetia, PA 15367-1054, USA

Correale, Pete (Musician)
c/o Staff Member *Monterey International (Chicago)*
72 W Adams St # 1000
Chicago, IL 60603-5107, USA

Correia, Kevin (Athlete, Baseball Player)
San Francisco Giants
1200 Crestview Dr
Cardiff By The Sea, CA 92007-1400, USA

Correia, Rod (Athlete, Baseball Player)
82 Perrwille Rd
Rehoboth, MA 02769-1808, USA

Correll, Vic (Athlete, Baseball Player)
119 Kentucky Downs
Perry, GA 31069-8514, USA

Corrente, Michael (Actor, Director, Producer)
c/o David Greenblatt *Greenlit*
1800 N Highland Ave Ste 500
Los Angeles, CA 90028-4527, USA

Correnti, John D (Business Person)
Nucor Corp
2100 Rexford Rd
Charlotte, NC 28211-3589, USA

Corretja, Alex (Tennis Player)
Assn of Tennis Professionals
200 Tournament Road
Ponte Vedra Beach, FL 32082, USA

Corri, Andrienne (Actor)
c/o Staff Member *Rolf Kruger Management*
205 Chudleigh R
London SE4 1EG, UNITED KINGDOM (UK)

Corridon-Mortell, Marie (Swimmer)
13 Heritage Vlg # A
Southbury, CT 06488-1601, USA

Corrie, Emily (Actor)
c/o Kathryn Fleming *The Rights House (UK)*
Drury House
34-43 Russell St
London WC2B 5HA, UNITED KINGDOM

Corrigal, Jim (Athlete, Football Player)
560 Deerwood Dr
Tallmadge, OH 44278-2008, USA

Corrigan, Kevin (Actor)
c/o Lisa Lieberman *Innovative Artists*
235 Park Ave S Fl 7
New York, NY 10003-1405, USA

Corrigan, Mike (Athlete, Hockey Player)
21 Birchwood Rd
Enfield, CT 06082-2701, USA

Corrigan, Wilfred J (Business Person)
LSI Logic
1621 Barber Ln
Milpitas, CA 95035-7455, USA

Corrington, Kip (Athlete, Football Player)
6407 Olympic Ct
Greensboro, NC 27410-8412, USA

Corripio Ahumada, Ernesto Cardinal (Religious Leader)
Apotinar Nieto 40 Col Tetlameyer
Mexico City 04730, MEXICO

Corriveau, Yvon (Athlete, Hockey Player)
130 Hazelmere Rd
New Britain, CT 06053-2116, USA

Corrock-Luby, Susan (Athlete, Olympic Athlete, Skier)
3809 S Geiger Blvd Apt 603
Spokane, WA 99224-5427, USA

Corry, Megan (Actor)
c/o Staff Member *Mary Anne Claro Talent Agency*
1513 W Passyunk Ave
Philadelphia, PA 19145-3029, USA

Corsaro, Frank A (Director)
33 Riverside Dr
New York, NY 10023-8012, USA

Corsi, Jim (Athlete, Baseball Player)
48 Eastview Rd
Hopkinton, MA 01748-1853, USA

Corsi, Jim (Athlete, Hockey Player)
785 Rue Maugue
L'Ile-Bizard, QC H9C 2T7, Canada

Corsi, Richard (Race Car Driver)
Cormac Motorsports
7954 S Castle Bay St
Tucson, AZ 85747-9232, USA

Corson, Shayne (Athlete, Hockey Player)
Tappo Restaurant and Wine Bar
55 Mill St
Bldg 3
Toronto, ON N5A 3C4, Canada

Cort, Barry (Athlete, Baseball Player)
1812 E Okaloosa Ave
Tampa, FL 33604-2032, USA

Cort, Bud (Actor)
5707 W Sandstone Ct
Homosassa, FL 34446-2761, USA

Cortazar, Esteban (Designer, Fashion Designer)
Esteban Cortazar Inc
1 NE 1st St Ste 9
Miami, FL 33132-2460, USA

Cortes, Ron (Journalist)
Philadelphia Inquirer
400 N Broad St
Philadelphia, PA 19130-4015, USA

Cortese, Dan (Actor)
c/o Amy Abell *BRS / Gage Talent Agency (LA)*
6300 Wilshire Blvd Ste 1430
Los Angeles, CA 90048-5216, USA

Cortese, Genevieve (Actor)
c/o Joannie Burstein *Burstein Company*
15304 W Sunset Blvd Ste 208
Pacific Palisades, CA 90272-3656, USA

Cortese, Joe (Actor)
100 S Hayworth Ave Apt 201
Los Angeles, CA 90048-3658, USA

Cortese, Valentina (Actor)
Pretta S Erasmo 6
Milan 20121, ITALY

Cortez, Alfonso (Actor)
CunninghamEscottDipene
10635 Santa Monica Blvd Ste 130
Los Angeles, CA 90025-8306, USA

Corver, Clayton (Athlete, Football Player)
1401 8th St SE
Orange City, IA 51041-7463

Corvino, Anthony (Athlete, Football Player)
PO Box 57
North Haven, CT 06473-0057, USA

Corvo (Musician)
c/o Staff Member *Sony Music (Miami)*
404 Washington Ave Ste 700
Miami Beach, FL 33139-6615, USA

Corvo, Joe (Athlete, Hockey Player)
943 Wenonah Ave
Oak Park, IL 60304-1810, USA

Corwin, Jeff (Actor)
c/o Staff Member *WME|IMG*
9601 Wilshire Blvd
Beverly Hills, CA 90210-5213, USA

Corwin, Lola (Reality Star)
c/o Cindy Osbrink *Osbrink Talent Agency*
4343 Lankershim Blvd # 100
North Hollywood, CA 91602-2705, USA

Coryatt, Quentin (Athlete, Football Player)
611 Cannon Ln
Sugar Land, TX 77479-5846, USA

Corzine, Dave (Athlete, Basketball Player)
1161 W Hunting Dr
Palatine, IL 60067-6673, USA

Corzine, Jon (Politician)
PO Box 1276
Hoboken, NJ 07030-1276, USA

Corzine, Lester (Athlete, Football Player)
38423 Nasturtium Way
Palm Desert, CA 92211-5075, USA

Cosbie, Doug (Athlete, Football Player)
2284 Paddock Ln
Newcastle, CA 95658-9389, USA

Cosby, Bill (Actor, Comedian)
c/o David Brokaw *Brokaw Company*
PO Box 462
Culver City, CA 90232-0462, USA

Cosby, Rita (Correspondent, Journalist, Television Host)

Coscarelli, Don (Director, Producer, Writer)
c/o Staff Member *Starway International*
12021 Wilshire Blvd # 661
Los Angeles, CA 90025-1206, USA

Coscina, Dennis (Athlete, Golfer)
211 Main St
East Windsor, CT 06088-9518, USA

Cosentino, Frank (Athlete, Football Player)
PO Box 316
Eganville, ON K0J 1T0, Canada

Cosey, Ray (Athlete, Baseball Player)
139 Byxbee St
San Francisco, CA 94132-2602, USA

Cosgrove, Daniel (Actor)
c/o Staff Member *Randy James Management*
12711 Ventura Blvd Ste 345
Studio City, CA 91604-2416, USA

Cosgrove, Mike (Athlete, Baseball Player)
8813 W Corrine Dr
Peoria, AZ 85381-8166, USA

Cosgrove, Miranda (Actor)
c/o Michael Sugar *Anonymous Content*
3532 Hayden Ave
Culver City, CA 90232-2413, USA

Cosiga, Fransesco (President)
Palazzo Giustiniani
Via Della Dogana Vecchia 29
Rome 00186, ITALY

Coslet, Bruce N (Athlete, Coach, Football Coach, Football Player)
1778 Ivy Pointe Ct
Naples, FL 34109-3375, USA

Cosman, Jim (Athlete, Baseball Player)
299 Northgate Trce
Roswell, GA 30075-2329, USA

Cosmovici, Cristiano B (Astronaut)
Istituto Fisica Spazio Interplanetario
CP 27
Frascati 00044, ITALY

Cosner, Don (Athlete, Football Player)
141 NW Carter Farms Ct
Bremerton, WA 98310-2090, USA

Cosnett, Rick (Actor)
c/o Mona Loring *Status PR*
PO Box 6191
Westlake Village, CA 91359-6191, USA

Cosper, Kina (Music Group)
Green Light Talent Agency
24024 Saint Moritz Dr
Valencia, CA 91355-2033, USA

Costa, David J (Dave) (Athlete, Football Player)
40 Halili Ln Apt 4M
Kihei, HI 96753-6070, USA

Costa, Gal (Music Group)
Bridge Agency
35 Clark St Apt A5
Brooklyn Heights, NY 11201-2374, USA

Costa, Jim (Congressman, Politician)
1314 Longworth Hob
Washington, DC 20515-4908, USA

Costa, Nikka (Musician)
23821 Crosson Dr
Woodland Hls, CA 91367-4072, USA

Costa, Paul (Athlete, Football Player)
1475 Bent Creek Dr
Southlake, TX 76092-9407, USA

Costa, Shane (Athlete, Baseball Player)
127 E Arlen Ave
Visalia, CA 93277-7691, USA

Costabile, David (Actor)
c/o Sean Liebowitz *ICM Partners (NY)*
730 5th Ave
New York, NY 10019-4105, USA

Costa-Gavras (Director, Producer, Writer)
c/o Bertrand de Labbey *ArtMedia*
8 rue Danielle Casanova
Paris 75002, FRANCE

Costanza, John (Race Car Driver)
Demand Flow Racing
6625 S. Galena St.
Englewood, CO 80112, USA

Costanzo, Paulo (Actor)
c/o Madeline Ryan *Ryan Management*
461 S Ogden Dr
Los Angeles, CA 90036-3119, USA

Costanzo, Robert (Actor)
832 Masselin Ave
Los Angeles, CA 90036-4722, USA

Costas, Bob (Commentator)
22 Coral Cay
Newport Coast, CA 92657-1908, USA

Coste, Chris (Athlete, Baseball Player)
33595 Charlie Trapp Rd
Dent, MN 56528-9012, USA

Costello, Brad (Athlete, Football Player)
9 Stout Rd
Princeton, NJ 08540-7440, USA

Costello, Elvis (Musician, Songwriter)
c/o Sam Feldman *Feldman Agency (Toronto)*
200-1505 2nd Ave W
Vancouver, BC V6H 3Y4, CANADA

Costello, John (Athlete, Baseball Player)
16614 Willow Glen Dr
Grover, MO 63040-1750, USA

Costello, Mariclare (Actor)
Borinstein Oreck Bogart
3172 Dona Susana Dr
Studio City, CA 91604-4356, USA

Costello, Mark (Writer)
Fordham Univesity
Law School
New York, NY 10458, USA

Costello, Murray (Athlete, Hockey Player)
105 Kenilworth St
Ottawa, ON K1Y 3Y8, Canada

Costello, Rich (Athlete, Hockey Player)
242 Monarch Bay Dr
Dana Point, CA 92629-3435, USA

Costello, Sean (Actor, Producer)
c/o Staff Member *Concerted Efforts*
PO Box 440326
Somerville, MA 02144-0004, USA

Costello, Sue (Actor)
United Talent Agency
9336 Civic Center Dr
Beverly Hills, CA 90210-3604, USA

Costello, Thomas (Tom) (Athlete, Football Player)
PO Box 299
Rocky Point, NY 11778-0299, USA

Costello, Vince (Athlete, Football Player)
12300 Perry St
Overland Park, KS 66213-1811, USA

Costelloe, Paul (Designer, Fashion Designer)
Moygashel Mills
Dungannon BT71 7PB, NORTHERN IRELAND

Coster, Nicolas (Actor)
c/o Staff Member *Momentum Talent and Literary Agency*
3500 W Olive Ave Ste 300
Burbank, CA 91505-4647, USA

Coster, Ritchie (Actor)
c/o Glenn Daniels *Glenn Daniels Arts Management*
56 Warren St Apt 5E
New York, NY 10007-1097, USA

Coster Waldau, Nikolaj (Actor)
c/o Anne Lindberg *Lindberg Management*
Lavendelstaede 5-7
Baghuset, 4. Sal
Copenhagen K 1462, DENMARK

Costner, Kevin (Actor, Director)
c/o Staff Member *Kevin Costner & Modern West*
122 Ocean Park Blvd Unit 508
Santa Monica, CA 90405-3564, USA

Costo, Tim (Athlete, Baseball Player)
3107 Pintail Ln
Signal Mountain, TN 37377-1439, USA

Cota, Chad (Athlete, Football Player)
216 Island Pointe Dr
Medford, OR 97504-9453, USA

Cota, Humberto (Baseball Player)
c/o Staff Member *Pittsburgh Pirates*
115 Federal St Ste 115B
Pnc Park
Pittsburgh, PA 15212-5740, USA

Cotchery, Jerricho (Athlete, Football Player)
c/o Brian Levy *Goal Line Football Management*
1025 Kane Concourse Ste 207
Bay Harbor Islands, FL 33154-2118, USA

Cote, Alain (Athlete, Hockey Player)
1352 Rue Gabrielle-Roy
Quebec, QC G1Y 3K3, Canada

Cote, David (Business Person)
TRW Inc
1900 Richmond Road
Cleveland, OH 44124, USA

Cote, Del (Horse Racer)
PO Box 124
Cream Ridge, NJ 08514-0124, USA

Cote, Ray (Athlete, Hockey Player)
5802 E Leland St
Mesa, AZ 85215-2716, CANADA

Cote, Riley (Athlete, Hockey Player)
1485 Kearsley Rd
Sicklerville, NJ 08081-5215, USA

Cote, Sylvain (Athlete, Hockey Player)
836 Boxwood Trl
Crownsville, MD 21032-1837, USA

Cotham, Frank (Cartoonist)
7763 Sunny Trail Dr
Memphis, TN 38135-0418, USA

Cothran, Jeff (Athlete, Football Player)
5671 Oakview Ter
Liberty Twp, OH 45011-2494, USA

Cothren, Paige (Athlete, Football Player)
1332 Highway 15 S
Woodland, MS 39776-9741, USA

Cotillard, Marion (Actor)
c/o Laurent Gregoire *Agence Adequat*
21 Rue D'Uzes
Paris 75002, FRANCE

Cotler, Kami (Actor)
7425 Arizona Ave
Los Angeles, CA 90045-1324, USA

Cotney, Mark (Athlete, Football Player)
4809 Cheval Blvd
Lutz, FL 33558-5338, USA

Cotrona, DJ (Actor)
c/o Christian Donatelli *MGMT Entertainment (The Schiff Company)*
9220 W Sunset Blvd Ste 106
W Hollywood, CA 90069-3500, USA

Cotroneo, Vince (Commentator)
4455 E Palmdale Ln
Gilbert, AZ 85298-4024, USA

Cotten, Joanna (Musician)
c/o Staff Member *WME (Nashville)*
1201 Demonbreun St
Nashville, TN 37203-3140, USA

Cottet, Mia (Actor)
c/o Sheila Wenzel *Wenzel Entertainment*
9350 Wilshire Blvd Ste 203
Beverly Hills, CA 90212-3204, USA

Cotti, Flavio (President)
Christian Democratic Party
Klaraweg 6
Bem 03001, SWITZERLAND

Cottier, Chuck (Athlete, Baseball Player, Coach)
7129 Lake Ballinger Way
Edmonds, WA 98026-8545, USA

Cottier, George Cardinal (Religious Leader)
Convento Santa Sabina
Piazza Pierro d'Illiria
Rome 00193, ITALY

Cottingham, Robert (Artist)
PO Box 604
Newtown, CT 06470-0604, USA

Cotto, Delilah (Actor)
c/o Ivan De Paz *DePaz Management*
2011 N Vermont Ave
Los Angeles, CA 90027-1931, USA

Cotto, Henry (Athlete, Baseball Player)
1141 W Thomas Rd
Phoenix, AZ 85013-4206, USA

Cotto, Miguel (Athlete, Boxer)
c/o Staff Member *Top Rank Inc.*
3908 Howard Hughes Pkwy
#580
Las Vegas, NV 89109, USA

Cotton, Barney (Athlete, Football Player)
2402 Sundown Dr
Ames, IA 50014-8220, USA

Cotton, Blaine (Actor)
Jack Scagnetti Talent
5118 Vineland Ave # 102
North Hollywood, CA 91601-3814, USA

Cotton, Craig (Athlete, Football Player)
5020 Trabuco Canyon Dr
Bakersfield, CA 93307-6932, USA

Cotton, Fearne (Actor)
c/o Staff Member *Rabbit Vocal Management*
27 Poland St
Fl 3
London W1F 8QW, UNITED KINGDOM

Cotton, John (Athlete, Basketball Player)
11426 Country Road 4 South
Alamosa, CO 81101-9630, USA

Cotton, Josie (Music Group)
2794 Hume Rd
Malibu, CA 90265-3435, USA

Cotton, Marcus (Athlete, Football Player)
484 Lake Park Ave Apt 280
Oakland, CA 94610-2730, USA

Cotton, Mason Vale (Actor)
c/o Matt Fletcher *TalentWorks*
3500 W Olive Ave Ste 1400
Burbank, CA 91505-5512, USA

Cotton, Maxwell Perry (Actor)
c/o Matt Fletcher *TalentWorks*
3500 W Olive Ave Ste 1400
Burbank, CA 91505-5512, USA

Cottrell, Dana (Athlete, Football Player)
1 Driftwood Ln
North Billerica, MA 01862-1222, USA

Cottrell, Erin (Actor)
c/o Abbey Sibucao-MacDonald *New Wave Entertainment (LA)*
2660 W Olive Ave
Burbank, CA 91505-4525, USA

Cottrell, Ted (Athlete, Football Player)
135 Spring Meadow Dr Apt 5
Buffalo, NY 14221-8436, USA

Cottrell, William (Bill) (Athlete, Football Player)
39675 Patterson Ln
Solon, OH 44139-6705, USA

Cottringer, Tom (Athlete, Hockey Player)
6 Fernwood Terr
Welland, ON L3C 2R8, Canada

Cotts, Neal (Athlete, Baseball Player)
14383 W Wycombe Ct
Aot 1
Libertyville, IL 60048-4839, USA

Couch, Chris (Athlete, Golfer)
307 Johns Creek Pkwy
Saint Augustine, FL 32092-5064, USA

Couch, Tim (Athlete, Football Player)
2110 N Ocean Blvd Apt 28D
Fort Lauderdale, FL 33305-1946, USA

Couchee, Mike (Athlete, Baseball Player)
3060 N Ridgecrest Unit 155
Mesa, AZ 85207-1080, USA

Coughlan, Marisa (Actor)
11725 Laurelcrest Dr
Studio City, CA 91604-3816, USA

Coughlan, Mary (Musician)
c/o Staff Member *MPI (Management Promotion International)*
The Gasworks
10 Upper Grand Canal St
Dublin 00002, Ireland

Coughlin, Mike (Race Car Driver)
Jeg's High Performance Racing
751 E 11th Ave
Columbus, OH 43211-2695, USA

Coughlin, Natalie (Athlete, Olympic Athlete, Swimmer)
4139 Coralee Ln
Lafayette, CA 94549-3356, USA

Coughlin, Tom (Coach, Football Coach)
New York Giants
Giants Stadium
East Rutherford, NJ 07073, USA

Coughlin, Troy (Race Car Driver)
Jeg's High Performance Racing
751 E 11th Ave
Columbus, OH 43211-2695, USA

Coughlin, Jr., Jeg (Race Car Driver)
Jeg's High Performance Racing
751 E 11th Ave
Columbus, OH 43211-2695, USA

Coughran, John (Athlete, Basketball Player)
5476 Morningside Dr
San Jose, CA 95138-2244, USA

Coughtry, Marlan (Athlete, Baseball Player)
5504 NE 55th St
Vancouver, WA 98661-2168, USA

Coulier, Dave (Actor)
38014 Lakeshore Dr
Harrison Township, MI 48045-2855, USA

Coulson, Christian (Actor)
c/o Staff Member *Artists Rights Group (ARG)*
4A Exmoor St
London W10 6BD, UNITED KINGDOM

Coulter, Allen (Director)
c/o Paul Alan Smith *Equitable Stewardship for Artists (ESA)*
6363 Wilshire Blvd Ste 650
Los Angeles, CA 90048-5725, USA

Coulter, Ann (Writer)
c/o Suzanne Gluck *WME/IMG (NY)*
11 Madison Ave Fl 18
New York, NY 10010-3669, USA

Coulter, Brian (Music Group, Musician)
Ashley Talent
2002 Hogback Rd Ste 20
Ann Arbor, MI 48105-9736, USA

Coulter, Catherine (Writer)
PO Box 17
Mill Valley, CA 94942-0017, USA

Coulter, Chip (Athlete, Baseball Player)
718 Trenton St
Toronto, OH 43964-1269, USA

Coulter, Phil (Music Group)
87th Street Ltd
24 Upper Mount St
Dublin, IRELAND

Coulthard, David (Race Car Driver)
Red Bull
Am Brunnen 1
Puschi, am See 05330, AUSTRIA

Coulthard, Philippa (Actor)
c/o Jamie Harhay Skinner *Baker Winokur Ryder Public Relations*
9100 Wilshire Blvd
W Tower #500
Beverly Hills, CA 90212-3415, USA

Council, Keith (Athlete, Football Player)
4418 Lenox Blvd
Orlando, FL 32811-4541, USA

Counsell, Craig (Athlete, Baseball Player)
992 E Circle Dr
Milwaukee, WI 53217-5361, USA

Counting Crows (Music Group)
c/o Kristen Foster *PMK/BNC Public Relations*
1840 Century Park E Ste 1400
Los Angeles, CA 90067-2115, USA

Counts, Mel (Athlete, Basketball Player, Olympic Athlete)
717 Castle Pines Dr N
Keizer, OR 97303-7480, USA

Coupe, Eliza (Actor)
c/o Rhett Usry *ID Public Relations (NY)*
40 Wall St Fl 51
New York, NY 10005-1385, USA

Coupland, Douglas (Writer)
c/o Staff Member *The Wylie Agency*
250 W 57th St Ste 2114
New York, NY 10107-2114, USA

Couples, Fred (Athlete, Golfer)
127 S Carmelina Ave
Los Angeles, CA 90049-3901, USA

Couric, Katie (Journalist, Television Host)
c/o Matthew Hiltzik *Hiltzik Strategies*
381 Park Ave S Rm 1201
New York, NY 10016-8820, USA

Courier, Jim (Athlete, Olympic Athlete, Tennis Player)
Saddlebrook Resort
5700 Saddlebrook Way
Wesley Chapel, FL 33543-4499, USA

Cournoyer, Yvan (Athlete, Hockey Player)
c/o Staff Member *Montreal Canadiens*
1275 Rue Saint-Antoine O
Montreal, QC H3C 5L2, Canada

Court, Alyson (Actor)
c/o Staff Member *Newton-Landry Management*
19 Isabella St
Toronto, ON M4Y 1M7, Canada

Courtemanche, Michael (Actor)
c/o Staff Member *Encore Management*
406-6300 Av du Parc
Montreal, QC H2V 4H8, CANADA

Courtenay, Ed (Athlete, Hockey Player)
1422 Whispering Oaks Trl
Mount Pleasant, SC 29466-8584, USA

Courtenay, Tom (Actor)
Jonathan Altaras
13 Shorts Gardens
London WC2H 9AT, UNITED KINGDOM(UK)

Courtin, Steve (Athlete, Basketball Player)
1109 Grinnell Rd
Wilmington, DE 19803-5125, USA

Courtnall, Geoff (Athlete, Hockey Player)
1270 Dallas Rd
Victoria, BC V8V 1C4, Canada

Courtnall, Russ (Athlete, Hockey Player)
c/o Staff Member *Victoria Atom B Hockey*
3651 Shelbourne St
Victoria, BC V8P 4H1, Canada

Courtney, Jai (Actor)
c/o Sam Maydew *Silver Lining Entertainment*
421 S Beverly Dr Fl 7
Beverly Hills, CA 90212-4408, USA

Courtney, Joe (Congressman, Politician)
215 Cannon Hob
Washington, DC 20515-0702, USA

Courtney, Joel (Actor)
c/o Nicki Fioravante *Viewpoint Inc*
8820 Wilshire Blvd Ste 220
Beverly Hills, CA 90211-2622, USA

Courtney, Patricia (Baseball Player)
8 Eagle Loop Ln
Freedom, NH 03836-5311, USA

Courtney, Stephanie (Actor)
c/o Naomi Odenkirk *Odenkirk Provissiero Entertainment*
1936 N Bronson Ave
Raleigh Studios
Los Angeles, CA 90068-5602, USA

Courtney, Thomas W (Tom) (Athlete, Olympic Athlete, Track Athlete)
336 Edgemere Way E
Naples, FL 34105-7151, USA

Courtright, John (Athlete, Baseball Player)
316 S Roosevelt Ave
Columbus, OH 43209-1829, USA

Court Yard Hounds (Music Group, Musician)
c/o Staff Member *Columbia Records UK*
Bedford House
69-79 Fulham High St
London SW6 3JW, United Kingdom

Courville, Larry (Athlete, Hockey Player)
559 Royal Rd
Palmyra, PA 17078-9017, USA

Courville, Vince (Athlete, Football Player)
5123 Avenue R
Galveston, TX 77551-5282, USA

Coury, Dick (Athlete, Football Player)
4553 Campus Ave Apt 6
San Diego, CA 92116-1162, USA

Coury, Steve (Athlete, Football Player)
6003 Newcastle Dr
Lake Oswego, OR 97035-8757, USA

Cousin, Terry (Athlete, Football Player)
4061 Blossom Hill Dr
Matthews, NC 28104-7742, USA

Cousineau, Tom (Athlete, Football Player)
910 Eaton Ave
Akron, OH 44303-1312, USA

Cousino, Brad (Athlete, Football Player)
5061 Lord Alfred Ct
Cincinnati, OH 45241-2181, USA

Cousins, Christopher (Actor)
c/o Deborah Miller *Shelter Entertainment*
9255 W Sunset Blvd Ste 300
Los Angeles, CA 90069-3313, USA

Cousins, Derryl (Athlete, Baseball Player)
78136 Desert Mountain Cir
Bermuda Dunes, CA 92203-8151, USA

Cousins, Jomo (Athlete, Football Player)
12425 Bramfield Dr
Riverview, FL 33579-7771, USA

Cousins, Kirk (Athlete, Football Player)
c/o Michael McCartney *Priority Sports & Entertainment (Chicago)*
325 N La Salle Dr Ste 650
Chicago, IL 60654-8182, USA

Cousins, Oniel (Athlete, Football Player)

Cousins, Robin (Athlete, Figure Skater)
Billy Marsh
174-8 N Gower St
London NW1 2NB, UNITED KINGDOM(UK)

Coustas, Mary (Actor)
c/o Nanette Fox *Nanette Fox Artist Representation & Development*
P.O. Box 138
Fitzroy, Victoria 03065, Australia

Cousteau, Fabien (Activist, Producer)
c/o Justin Green *Hays Entertainment LLC*
161 E 35th St Frnt 2F
New York, NY 10016-4119, USA

Cousteau, Jean-Michel (Producer)
Ocean Futures Society
325 Chapala St
Santa Barbara, CA 93101-3407, USA

Cousy, Robert J (Bob) (Athlete, Basketball Player)
427 Salisbury St
Worcester, MA 01609-1266, USA

Coutlangus, Jon (Athlete, Baseball Player)
428 Starbridge Ct
Pleasant Hill, CA 94523-4723, USA

Coutu, Rich (Athlete, Hockey Player)
22 Rue Florian-Paiement
Salaberry-De-Valleyfield, QC J6S 5Z9, Canada

Couture, Randy (Athlete, Wrestler)
c/o Samantha Hill *Wolf-Kasteler Public Relations*
6255 W Sunset Blvd Ste 1111
Los Angeles, CA 90028-7426, USA

Covelli, Coco Crisp (Athlete, Baseball Player)
508 Judy Dr
Redondo Beach, CA 90277-3830, USA

Coverdale, David (Musician)
757 Champagne Rd
Incline Village, NV 89451-8001, USA

Covert, Allen (Actor, Comedian)
c/o Cindy Guagenti *Baker Winokur Ryder Public Relations*
9100 Wilshire Blvd
W Tower #500
Beverly Hills, CA 90212-3415, USA

Covert, James (Jimbo) (Athlete, Football Player)
2647 Nelson Ct
Weston, FL 33332-1835, USA

Covey, Richard O Colonel (Astronaut)
1155 High Lake Vw
Colorado Springs, CO 80906-8717, USA

Covington, John (Athlete, Football Player)
1598 Legrand Cir
Lawrenceville, GA 30043-8191, USA

Covington, Scott (Athlete, Football Player)
7444 W 81st St
Los Angeles, CA 90045-2304, USA

Covington, Tony (Athlete, Football Player)
11160 S Lakes Dr # C1
Reston, VA 20191-4327, USA

Covington, Warren (Music Group)
1627 Open Field Loop
Brandon, FL 33510-2096, USA

Cowan, Billy (Athlete, Baseball Player)
1539 Via Coronel
Palos Verdes Estates, CA 90274-1941, USA

Cowan, Caylee (Actor)
c/o Megan Moss *Narrative*
1601 Vine St Fl 6
Los Angeles, CA 90028-8802, USA

Cowan, Dr. Connell (Writer)
c/o Staff Member *Reece Halsey North*
98 Main St # 704
Tiburon, CA 94920-2517, USA

Cowan, Elliot (Actor)
c/o Laura Berwick *Berwick & Kovacik*
6230 Wilshire Blvd
Los Angeles, CA 90048-5126, USA

Cowan, Lawrence (Larry) (Athlete, Football Player)
1456 McCluer Rd
Jackson, MS 39212-6224, USA

Cowan, Ralph Wolfe (Artist)
243 29th St
West Palm Beach, FL 33407-5207, USA

Coward, Herbert (Actor)
1399 Worley Cove Rd
Canton, NC 28716-7069, USA

Cowart, Sam (Athlete, Football Player)
11110 Fallgate Point Ct
Jacksonville, FL 32256-4833, USA

Cowboy Mouth (Music Group, Musician)
c/o Konrad Leh *Creative Talent Group*
1900 Avenue of the Stars Ste 2475
Los Angeles, CA 90067-4512, USA

Cowell, Simon (Producer, Reality Star)
717 N Palm Dr
Beverly Hills, CA 90210-3416, USA

Cowens, Dave (Athlete, Basketball Player)
132 Deep Cv
Raymond, ME 04071-6523, USA

Cowher, Bill (Athlete, Football Coach, Football Player)
188 E 64th St Apt 3604
New York, NY 10065-0279, USA

Cowick, Bruce (Athlete, Hockey Player)
2953 Cressida Cres
Victoria, BC V9B 5W7, Canada

Cowie, Colin (Designer)
Colin Cowie Trademarks, LLC
256 W 36th St Fl 4
New York, NY 10018-7712, USA

Cowley, Joe (Athlete, Baseball Player)
243 W Vista St
Lexington, KY 40503-1326, USA

Cowley, Wayne (Athlete, Hockey Player)
700-22 Front St W
BOTTOM LINE RESTAURANT
Toronto, ON M5J 2W5, Canada

Cowlings, Al (Athlete, Football Player)
PO Box 1064
Pacific Palisades, CA 90272-1064, USA

Cowper, Nicola (Actor)
Brunskill Mgmt
169 Queens Gate #A8
London SW7 5EH, UNITED KINGDOM(UK)

Cowper, Steve (Politician)
PO Box A
Juneau, AK 99811, USA

Cowsill, Susan (Musician)
c/o Valerie Turner Polishook *V Public Relations LLC*
PO Box 341810
Bethesda, MD 20827-1810, USA

Cox, Alex (Actor, Director)
United Talent Agency
9336 Civic Center Dr
Beverly Hills, CA 90210-3604, USA

Cox, Billy (Athlete, Football Player)
5192 Marsh Field Ln
Sarasota, FL 34235-7029, USA

Cox, Bobby (Commentator)
261 Indian Hills Ct
Marietta, GA 30068-3972, USA

Cox, Brian (Actor)
c/o Matthew Lesher *Insight*
5358 Melrose Ave # 200W
Los Angeles, CA 90038-5117, USA

Cox, Bryan (Athlete, Football Player)
3040 Peachtree Rd NW Unit 1206
Atlanta, GA 30305-2290, USA

Cox, Casey (Athlete, Baseball Player)
2840 La Concha Dr
Clearwater, FL 33762-2203, USA

Cox, Charlie (Actor)
c/o Nick Frenkel *3 Arts Entertainment*
9460 Wilshire Blvd Fl 7
Beverly Hills, CA 90212-2713, USA

Cox, Chris (Musician)
c/o Staff Member *Diva Central Inc*
7510 W Sunset Blvd # 1445
Los Angeles, CA 90046-3408, USA

Cox, Christina (Actor)
Rysher Entertainment
3400 W Riverside Dr # 600
Burbank, CA 91505-4669, USA

Cox, C Jay (Director, Producer)
c/o Scott Zimmerman *Scott Zimmerman Management*
901 N Highland Ave
Los Angeles, CA 90038-2412, USA

Cox, Courteney (Actor, Producer)
9255 Doheny Rd Apt 2505
West Hollywood, CA 90069-3207, USA

Cox, Danny (Athlete, Baseball Player)
306 Feagin Mill Rd
Warner Robins, GA 31088-6208, USA

Cox, Darron (Athlete, Baseball Player)
3331 E 140th Pl
Thornton, CO 80602-8887, USA

Cox, Deborah (Musician, Songwriter)
8348 NW 62nd Pl
Parkland, FL 33067-5019, USA

Cox, Fletcher (Athlete, Football Player)
c/o Todd France *Creative Artists Agency (CAA) Sports*
3500 Lenox Rd NE Ste 1500
Atlanta, GA 30326-4231, USA

Cox, Frederick W (Fred) (Athlete, Football Player)
401 E River St
Monticello, MN 55362-9397, USA

Cox, Jeff (Athlete, Baseball Player)
2155 E Garvey Ave N Ste B6
West Covina, CA 91791-1509, USA

Cox, Jennifer Elise (Actor)
c/o Lisa DiSante-Frank *DiSante Frank & Company*
10061 Riverside Dr Ste 377
Toluca Lake, CA 91602-2560, USA

Cox, Jim (Athlete, Baseball Player)
25854 S New Town Dr
Sun Lakes, AZ 85248-6731, USA

Cox, John (Athlete, Football Player)
5201 Desoto Rd APT 112
Sarasota, FL 34235-3616, USA

Cox, Johnny (Athlete, Basketball Player, Coach)
849 N Main St
Hazard, KY 41701-1345, USA

Cox, Joshua (Actor)
7185 Pacific View Dr
Los Angeles, CA 90068-2039, USA

Cox, Kris (Athlete, Golfer)
5350 Richard Ave
Dallas, TX 75206-6712, USA

Cox, Larry (Athlete, Football Player)
10326 Catlett Ln
La Porte, TX 77571-4218, USA

Cox, Laverne (Actor)
c/o Jessica Pierson *Vision PR*
2 Penn Plz Rm 2601
New York, NY 10121-0001, USA

Cox, Lynne (Swimmer)
Advanced Sport Research
4141 Ball Road #142
Cypress, CA 90630, USA

Cox, Mark (Tennis Player)
Oaks Astead Woods
Astead
Surrey KT21 2ER, UNITED KINGDOM(UK)

Cox, Morgan (Athlete, Football Player)
c/o Jimmy Sexton *CAA (Memphis)*
6060 Poplar Ave Ste 470
Memphis, TN 38119-0910, USA

Cox, Nathalie (Actor)
c/o Chuck James *ICM Partners*
10250 Constellation Blvd Fl 7
Los Angeles, CA 90067-6207, USA

Cox, Nikki (Actor)
c/o Martin Lesak *United Talent Agency (UTA)*
9336 Civic Center Dr
Beverly Hills, CA 90210-3604, USA

Cox, Perrish (Athlete, Football Player)
c/o Jordan Woy *Willis & Woy Management*
4890 Alpha Rd Ste 200
Dallas, TX 75244-4639, USA

Cox, Prof Brian (Doctor)
Apollo's Children
101 Clapham High St.
Suite 45
London SW4 7TB, UNITED KINGDOM

Cox, Ralph (Athlete, Hockey Player)
1 Harborside Dr Ste 200S
East Boston, MA 02128-2905, USA

Cox, Ronny (Actor)
13948 Magnolia Blvd
Sherman Oaks, CA 91423-1230, USA

Cox, Stephen J (Artist)
154 Barnsbury Road
Islington
London N1 0ER, UNITED KINGDOM (UK)

Cox, Steve (Athlete, Baseball Player)
22678 Avenue 188
Strathmore, CA 93267-9680, USA

Cox, Steve (Athlete, Football Player)
Rainwater & Cox LLC
915 Enterprise Dr
Jonesboro, AR 72401-9201, USA

Cox, Ted (Athlete, Baseball Player)
3990 E Seward Rd
Guthrie, OK 73044-9854, USA

Cox, Terry (Athlete, Baseball Player)
707 N Broadway St
Aot 302
Pittsburg, KS 66762-3905, USA

Cox, Thomas (Race Car Driver)
2321 Race Track Rd
Sophia, NC 27350-8901, USA

Cox, Tom (Athlete, Football Player)
2121 S Mill Ave Apt 231
Tempe, AZ 85282-2138, USA

Cox, Tony (Actor)
c/o Staff Member *New Wave Entertainment (LA)*
2660 W Olive Ave
Burbank, CA 91505-4525, USA

Cox, Torrie (Athlete, Football Player)
42 NW 92nd St
Miami Shores, FL 33150-2227, USA

Cox, Veanne (Actor)
c/o Nyle Brenner *Brenner Management*
Prefers to be contacted via telephone or email
CA, USA

Coxe, Craig (Athlete, Hockey Player)
W3059 Oak St
Saint Ignace, MI 49781-9849, USA

Coy, Chris (Actor)
c/o Jamie Harhay Skinner *Baker Winokur Ryder Public Relations*
9100 Wilshire Blvd
W Tower #500
Beverly Hills, CA 90212-3415, USA

Coyle, Brendan (Actor)
c/o Kenny Goodman *Goodmanagement*
137 N Larchmont Blvd
Los Angeles, CA 90004-3704, USA

Coyle, Eric (Athlete, Football Player)
397 County Road 26
Longmont, CO 80504-9515, USA

Coyle, Nadine (Actor, Musician)
c/o Julie Colbert *WME|IMG*
9601 Wilshire Blvd
Beverly Hills, CA 90210-5213, USA

Coyle, Ross (Athlete, Football Player)
PO Box 68
Blanchard, OK 73010-0068, USA

Coyne, Colleen (Athlete, Hockey Player, Olympic Athlete)
79 Cedar St
Amesbury, MA 01913-1821, USA

Coyne, Dale (Race Car Driver)
13400 S Budler Rd
Plainfield, IL 60544-9493, USA

Coyne, Jonny (Actor)
c/o Oliver Azis *Independent Talent Group*
40 Whitfield St
London W1T 2RH, UNITED KINGDOM

Coyne, Wayne (Musician)
1715 NW 13th St
Oklahoma City, OK 73106-2005, USA

Coyote, Peter (Actor)
774 Marin Dr
Mill Valley, CA 94941-3919, USA

Cozart, Keith (Chief Keef) (Musician)
c/o Staff Member *Interscope Records (LA) - Main*
2220 Colorado Ave
Santa Monica, CA 90404-3506, USA

Cozler, Jimmy (Musician, Songwriter, Writer)
J Racords
745 5th Ave Ste 600
New York, NY 10151-0004, USA

C. Peters, Gary (Congressman, Politician)
1609 Longworth Hob
Washington, DC 20515-0538, USA

C. Peterson, Collin (Congressman, Politician)
2211 Rayburn Hob
Washington, DC 20515-1317, USA

Crabapple, Molly (Artist, Writer)
Molly Crabapple Inc
347 5th Ave Ste 1402-605
New York, NY 10016-5010, USA

Crabb, Claude (Athlete, Football Player)
49851 Wayne St
Indio, CA 92201, USA

Crabb, Joey (Athlete, Hockey Player)
9100 Granite Pl
Anchorage, AK 99507-3947, USA

Crabbe, Cullen (Actor)
4175 E Laurel Ave
Gilbert, AZ 85234-7911, USA

Crable, Bob (Athlete, Football Player)
995 Paxton Guinea Rd
Loveland, OH 45140-8587, USA

Crabtree, Eric (Athlete, Football Player)
3342 Arapahoe St
Denver, CO 80205-2741, USA

Crabtree, Michael (Athlete, Football Player)
c/o Ashley Smith Becker *Relativity Sports*
2029 Century Park E Ste 1550
Century City, CA 90067-3000, USA

Crabtree, Tim (Athlete, Baseball Player)
1503 Kingswood Ln
Colleyville, TX 76034-5580, USA

Cracknell, James (Athlete, Olympic Athlete)
Headway
190 Bagnall Rd
Old Basford
Nottingham, Nottinghamshire NG6 8SF, UNITED KINGDOM

Craddock, Billy (Crash) (Musician, Songwriter, Writer)
3007 Old Martinsville Road
Greensboro, NC 27455, USA

Cradle, Rickey (Athlete, Baseball Player)
1311 Dry Gap Pike
Knoxville, TN 37918-9785, USA

Cradle Of Filth (Music Group, Musician)
c/o Staff Member *In Phase Management*
P O Box 756A
Surbiton KT6 6YZ, UK

Craft, Jason (Athlete, Football Player)
11688 Amistad Ct
Jacksonville, FL 32256-2925, USA

Craft, Sammi (Actor)
c/o Staff Member *Paradigm*
8942 Wilshire Blvd
Beverly Hills, CA 90211-1908, USA

Craft, Terry (Athlete, Baseball Player)
16 Sheldon Ave
Castle Rock, CO 80104-8820, USA

Crafter, Jane (Athlete, Golfer)
1007 S Butte Crest Cir
Payson, AZ 85541-5603, USA

Crafts, Hannah (Writer)
c/o Staff Member *Creative Artists Agency (CAA)*
2000 Avenue of the Stars Ste 100
Los Angeles, CA 90067-4705, USA

Cragg, Anthony D (Tony) (Artist)
Adolt-Vorwerk-Str 24
Wuppertal 42287, GERMANY

Craggs, George (Soccer Player)
6223 6th Ave NW
Seattle, WA 98107-2131, USA

Craig, Adam Jamal (Actor)
c/o Staff Member *SMS Talent*
8383 Wilshire Blvd Ste 230
Beverly Hills, CA 90211-2436, USA

Craig, Daniel (Actor)
c/o Laura Symons *Premier PR*
2-4 Bucknall St
London WC2H 8LA, UNITED KINGDOM

Craig, Demeyune (Athlete, Football Player)
5102 31st Ave
Valley, AL 36854-5214, USA

Craig, Elijah (Actor)
Agency for Performing Arts
9200 W Sunset Blvd Ste 900
Los Angeles, CA 90069-3604, USA

Craig, Jenny (Business Person, Doctor)
5770 Fleet St
Carlsbad, CA 92008-4700, USA

Craig, Jim (Athlete, Hockey Player, Olympic Athlete)
29907 County Road 3
Merrifield, MN 56465-4402, USA

Craig, Larry (Politician)
8935 W Cornwall Dr
Boise, ID 83704-4310, USA

Craig, Michael (Actor)
Chatto & Linnit
Prince of Wales
Coventry St
London W1V 7FE, UNITED KINGDOM (UK)

Craig, Mike (Athlete, Hockey Player)
29907 County Road 3
Merrifield, MN 56465-4402, USA

Craig, Neal (Athlete, Football Player)
11267 Lodgeview Ct
Cincinnati, OH 45240-2207, USA

Craig, Paco (Athlete, Football Player)
23668 Marguerite Cir
Moreno Valley, CA 92557-2853, USA

Craig, Pete (Athlete, Baseball Player)
5915 Carmel Ln
Raleigh, NC 27609-3953, USA

Craig, Rod (Athlete, Baseball Player)
1200 E Kay St Apt C
Compton, CA 90221-1573, USA

Craig, Roger (Athlete, Baseball Player, Coach)
15526 Indian Head Ct
Ramona, CA 92065-4512, USA

Craig, Roger (Athlete, Football Player)
271 Vista Verde Way
Portola Valley, CA 94028-8149, USA

Craig, William (Bill) (Swimmer)
PO Box 629
Newport Beach, CA 92661-0629, USA

Craighead, John (Athlete, Hockey Player)
JC's Extreme Hockey
2595 Barnet Hwy
Coquitlam, BC V3E 1K9, Canada

Crain, Jesse (Athlete, Baseball Player)
20702 Hartford Way
Lakeville, MN 55044-4438, USA

Crain, William (Director)

Crais, Robert (Writer)
1647 Blue Jay Way
Los Angeles, CA 90069-1216, USA

Cram, Jerry (Athlete, Baseball Player)
20638 Furr Rd
Round Hill, VA 20141-1802, USA

Cram, Stephen (Steve) (Athlete, Track Athlete)
General Delivery
Jarrow, UNITED KINGDOM (UK)

Cramer, Grant (Actor)
Richard Sindell
1910 Holmby Ave Apt 1
Los Angeles, CA 90025-5936, USA

Cramer, James (Television Host)
c/o Staff Member *CNBC (Main)*
900 Sylvan Ave
Englewood Cliffs, NJ 07632-3312, USA

Cramer, Jim (Business Person, Television Host)
c/o Staff Member *CNBC (Main)*
900 Sylvan Ave
Englewood Cliffs, NJ 07632-3312, USA

Cramer, Peggy (Athlete, Baseball Player, Commentator)
1160 E Old Andrew Johnson Hwy
Talbott, TN 37877-3103, USA

Cramps, The (Music Group)
c/o Stormy Shepherd *Leave Home Booking*
1400 S Foothill Dr Ste 34
Salt Lake City, UT 84108-2392, USA

Crampton, Barbara (Actor)
c/o Nancy Scanlon *Au Courant*
5000 S Centinela Ave Apt 313
Los Angeles, CA 90066-6965, USA

Crampton, Bruce (Athlete, Golfer)
112 Belfalls Dr
Georgetown, TX 78633-4941, USA

Cranberries, The (Music Group)
Curtain Call
12-13 O'Connell St
Limerick, IRELAND

Crandall, Del (Athlete, Baseball Player, Coach)
1355 Clear Lake Pl
Brea, CA 92821-2807, USA

Crane, Brian (Cartoonist)
PO Box 51771
Sparks, NV 89435-1771, USA

Crane, Caprice (Actor, Writer)
c/o Brad Petrigala *Brillstein Entertainment Partners*
9150 Wilshire Blvd Ste 350
Beverly Hills, CA 90212-3453, USA

Crane, David (Director, Producer, Writer)
c/o Staff Member *Bright Kauffman Crane Productions*
4000 Warner Blvd Bldg 750
Burbank, CA 91522-0001

Crane, Gary (Athlete, Football Player)
6 Greystone
Bentonville, AR 72712-4098, USA

Crane, John (Writer)
c/o Staff Member *Agency for the Performing Arts (APA)*
405 S Beverly Dr Ste 500
Beverly Hills, CA 90212-4425, USA

Crane, Kenneth G (Director)
6627 Lindenhurst Ave
Los Angeles, CA 90048-4611, USA

Crane, Paul (Athlete, Football Player)
12 N Monterey St
Mobile, AL 36604-1317, USA

Crane, Tony (Actor)
Abrams Artists
9200 W Sunset Blvd Ste 1125
Los Angeles, CA 90069-3610, USA

Cranston, Bryan (Actor)
Moonshot Entertainment
15821 Ventura Blvd Ste 500
Encino, CA 91436-2945, USA

Crapo, Michael (Politician)
3212nd St SE
Washington, DC 20003-1902, USA

Crapo, Mike (Senator)
239 Dirksen Senate Building
Washington, DC 20510-0001, USA

Crashley, Bart (Athlete, Hockey Player)
90 Goacher Rd RR 1
Campbellford, ON K0L 1L0, Canada

Crash Test Dummies (Music Group, Musician)
c/o Staff Member *UTA/The Agency Group*
888 7th Ave Fl 7
New York, NY 10106-0700, USA

Cravaack, Chip (Congressman, Politician)
508 Cannon Hob
Washington, DC 20515-2210, USA

Cravalho, Auli'i (Actor, Musician)
c/o Pedro Tapia *Cunningham Escott Slevin & Doherty (CESD)*
10635 Santa Monica Blvd Ste 130
Los Angeles, CA 90025-8306, USA

Craven, Bill (Athlete, Football Player)
4363 N Buckhead Dr NE
Atlanta, GA 30342-3451, USA

Craven, Gemma (Actor)
c/o Jonathan Arun *Jonathan Arun Talent*
37 Pearman St
Waterloo
London SE1 7RB, UNITED KINGDOM

Craven, Matt (Actor)
c/o Craig Dorfman *Frontline Management*
5670 Wilshire Blvd Ste 1370
Los Angeles, CA 90036-5649, USA

Craven, Murray (Athlete, Hockey Player)
2802 Rest Haven Dr
Whitefish, MT 59937-8015, USA

Craven, Ricky (Race Car Driver)
PO Box 472
Concord, NC 28026-0472, USA

Cravens, Greg (Cartoonist)
312 N McLean Blvd
Memphis, TN 38112-5341, USA

Craver, Aaron (Athlete, Football Player)
821 W Maple St
Compton, CA 90220-1829, USA

Crawford, Bill Dr (Athlete, Football Player)
701 Redwood Dr
Qualicum Beach, BC V9K 2J2, Canada

Crawford, Bob (Athlete, Hockey Player)
6 Progress Dr
Cromwell, CT 06416-1055, USA

Crawford, Brad (Athlete, Football Player)
RR2
Winamac, IL 46996, USA

Crawford, Carl (Athlete, Baseball Player)
15618 Bristol Lake Dr
Houston, TX 77070-3865, USA

Crawford, Carlos (Athlete, Baseball Player)
1605 Martin Luther King Ave E
Bradenton, FL 34208-2801, USA

Crawford, Chace (Actor)
c/o Eric Podwall *Podwall Entertainment*
710 N Orlando Ave Apt 203
Loft 203
Los Angeles, CA 90069-5549, USA

Crawford, Christina (Writer)
7 Springs Farm Sanders Road
Tensed, ID 83870-9615, USA

Crawford, Cindy (Actor, Model)
c/o Annett Wolf *Wolf-Kasteler Public Relations*
6255 W Sunset Blvd Ste 1111
Los Angeles, CA 90028-7426, USA

Crawford, Clayne (Actor)
c/o Tom Lawless *Vox*
5670 Wilshire Blvd Ste 820
Los Angeles, CA 90036-5613, USA

Crawford, Ed (Athlete, Football Player)
204 Country Club Rd
Oxford, MS 38655-2606, USA

Crawford, Eric (Congressman, Politician)
1408 Longworth Hob
Washington, DC 20515-3102, USA

Crawford, Fred (Athlete, Basketball Player)
24 W Lawn Dr
Teaneck, NJ 07666-5612, USA

Crawford, Hilton (Athlete, Football Player)
262 Hagen St
Buffalo, NY 14215-3959, USA

Crawford, Jack (Athlete, Football Player)
c/o Anthony J. Agnone *Eastern Athletic Services*
11350 McCormick Rd
Suite 800 - Executive Plaza
Hunt Valley, MD 21031-1002, USA

Crawford, Jamal (Basketball Player)
Chicago Bulls United Center
1901 W Madison St
Chicago, IL 60612-2459, USA

Crawford, Jerry (Athlete, Baseball Player)
111 9th St E
Saint Petersburg, FL 33715-2204, USA

Crawford, Jim (Athlete, Baseball Player)
7711 S Barlow Dr
Gilbert, AZ 85298-0062, USA

Crawford, Joan (Athlete, Basketball Player)
4728 S Harvard Ave Apt 22
Tulsa, OK 74135-3045, USA

Crawford, Joe (Athlete, Baseball Player)
5428 US Highway 50
Hillsboro, OH 45133-7533, USA

Crawford, Johnny (Actor, Musician)
Crawford Music Services
PO Box 7073
Burbank, CA 91510-7073, USA

Crawford, Keith (Athlete, Football Player)
RR 5 Box 5008
Palestine, TX 75801, USA

Crawford, Kirsty (Musician)
c/o Zoe Sobol *Rocket Music Management*
1 Blythe Rd
London W14 0HG, UNITED KINGDOM

Crawford, Lou (Athlete, Hockey Player)
50 New Gower St
St. John's, NL A1C 1J3, Canada

Crawford, Marc (Athlete, Coach, Hockey Player)
c/o Staff Member *Los Angeles Kings*
1111 S Figueroa St Ste 3100
Los Angeles, CA 90015-1333, USA

Crawford, Michael (Actor, Musician)
c/o Steve Levine *ICM Partners*
10250 Constellation Blvd Fl 7
Los Angeles, CA 90067-6207, USA

Crawford, Paxton (Athlete, Baseball Player)
PO Box 345
Plumerville, AR 72127-0345, USA

Crawford, Rachael (Actor)
c/o Staff Member *Coast to Coast Talent Group*
3350 Barham Blvd
Los Angeles, CA 90068-1404, USA

Crawford, Randy (Musician)
911 Park St SW
Grand Rapids, MI 49504-6241, USA

Crawford, Steve (Athlete, Baseball Player)
912 N Dorothy Ave
Claremore, OK 74017-6505, USA

Crawford, Vernon (Athlete, Football Player)
2001 Gemini St Apt 1305
Houston, TX 77058-2062, USA

Crawley, Pauline (Baseball Player)
68670 Raposa Rd
Cathedral City, CA 92234-8148, USA

Crawley, Sylvia (Athlete, Basketball Player)
125 S Pennsylvania St
Indianapolis, IN 46204-3610, USA

Cray, Robert (Musician)
c/o Chad Jensen *Jensen Artist Management*
1741 N Ventura Rd Apt 10
Oxnard, CA 93030-3315, USA

Craybas, Jill (Athlete, Tennis Player)
23412 Pacific Park Dr Unit 28L
Aliso Viejo, CA 92656-3347, USA

Craymer, Judy (Producer)
Winter Garden Theater
1634 Broadway Ofc
New York, NY 10019-6894, USA

Crayton, Patrick (Athlete, Football Player)
2301 Silver Table Dr
Lewisville, TX 75056-5679, USA

Creamer, Paula (Athlete, Golfer)
4812 Alexandra Garden Ct
Windermere, FL 34786-8838, USA

Creamer, Roger W (Writer)
180 E Hartsdale Ave Apt 2E
Hartsdale, NY 10530-3540, USA

Creamer, Timothy J (Astronaut)
5103 Carefree Dr
League City, TX 77573-3195, USA

Creamer, Timothy J Lt Colonel (Astronaut)
5103 Carefree Dr
League City, TX 77573-3195, USA

Crear, Mark (Athlete, Olympic Athlete, Track Athlete)
Octagon
9420 Reseda Blvd Ste 600
Northridge, CA 91324-2932, USA

Crecion, Gabe (Athlete, Football Player)
4800 Coyote Wells Cir
Westlake Village, CA 91362-4712, USA

Crede, Joe (Athlete, Baseball Player)
42 Dry Creek Trl
Linn, MO 65051-2617, USA

Creech, Bob (Athlete, Football Player)
1905 Windsor Dr
Mesquite, TX 75181-2358, USA

Creech, Sharon (Writer)
10 E 53rd St Frnt
New York, NY 10022-5244, USA

Creed (Music Group)
c/o Ken Fermaglich *UTA Music*
142 W 57th St Fl 6
New York, NY 10019-3300, USA

Creed, Clifford Ann (Athlete, Golfer)
240 N Rosemont Dr
Sulphur, LA 70665-7994, USA

Creed-Miles, Esme (Actor)
c/o Nicola Van Gelder *Conway van Gelder Grant*
8-12 Broadwick St
London W1F 8HW, UNITED KINGDOM

Creek, Doug (Athlete, Baseball Player)
12440 Oakview Ct
Newburg, MD 20664-2209, USA

Creel, Gavin (Actor)
c/o Amy Brownstein *PRStudio USA*
1875 Century Park E Ste 930
Los Angeles, CA 90067-2540, USA

Creel, Keith (Athlete, Baseball Player)
527 Trail Ridge Dr
Duncanville, TX 75116-2433, USA

Creel, Monica (Actor)
c/o Mike Eistenstadt *Amsel, Eisenstadt & Frazier Talent Agency (AEF)*
5055 Wilshire Blvd Ste 860
Los Angeles, CA 90036-6108, USA

Cregar, Bill (Athlete, Football Player)
22 Locust Ct
Spring Lake, NJ 07762-2109, USA

Creighton, Adam (Athlete, Hockey Player)
Boston Bruins
100 Legends Way Ste 250
Scouting Dept
Boston, MA 02114-1389, USA

Creighton, Jim (Athlete, Basketball Player)
5297 S Geneva St
Englewood, CO 80111-6210, USA

Creighton, John O (Astronaut)
2111 SW 174th St
Burien, WA 98166-3259, USA

Creighton, John O Captain (Astronaut)
2111 SW 174th St
Burien, WA 98166-3259, USA

Creighton Sr, Dave (Athlete, Hockey Player)
5202 Spectacular Bid Dr
Wesley Chapel, FL 33544-1576, USA

Creme, Lol (Musician)
Heronden Hall
Tenferden
Kent, UNITED KINGDOM (UK)

Cremins, Bobby (Coach)
150 Bobby John Road
Atlanta, GA 30332-0001, USA

Crennel, Carl (Athlete, Football Player)
204 Hawthorne Sq
Oakdale, PA 15071-1060, USA

Crennel, Romeo (Athlete, Football Coach, Football Player)
80 Cayman Pl
Palm Beach Gardens, FL 33418-8096, USA

Crenshaw, Ander (Congressman, Politician)
440 Cannon Hob
Washington, DC 20515-1504, USA

Crenshaw, Ben (Athlete, Golfer)
PO Box 50568
Austin, TX 78763-0568, USA

Crenshaw, Marshall (Musician)
c/o Staff Member *MCT Management*
520 8th Ave Rm 2205
New York, NY 10018-4160, USA

Crenshaw, Willis (Athlete, Football Player)
22 Carly Rd
Woodstock, NY 12498-2524, USA

Creole, Kid (Musician)
Ron Rainey Mgmt
315 S Beverly Dr Ste 407
Beverly Hills, CA 90212-4301, USA

Creskoff, Rebecca (Actor)
c/o Steven Levy *Framework Entertainment*
9057 Nemo St # C
W Hollywood, CA 90069-5511, USA

Crespino, Robert (Athlete, Football Player)
191 Avery St
Decatur, GA 30030-3802, USA

Crespo, Elvis (Musician)
A-P R Media
8334 Lefferts Blvd Apt 3C
Kew Gardens, NY 11415-2507, USA

Crespo, Felipe (Athlete, Baseball Player)
C2 Calle 6
Caguas, PR 00725-2019, USA

Cresse, Mark (Athlete, Baseball Player)
3222 Clay St
Newport Beach, CA 92663-4207, USA

Cressend, Jack (Athlete, Baseball Player)
2409 W Ranch Dr
Friendswood, TX 77546-5579, USA

Cressman, Dave (Athlete, Hockey Player)
University of Waterloo
200 University Ave W
Attn: Hockey Program
Waterloo, ON N2L 3G1, Canada

Cressman, Glen (Athlete, Hockey Player)
8778 Cuyamaca St
Santee, CA 92071-4255

Cressy, Jr., Dale (Race Car Driver)
1336 Paralllount Parkway
Batavia, IL 60510, USA

Creswell, Smiley (Athlete, Football Player)
132 Academy Way
Monroe, WA 98272-2047, USA

Cretler, Jean-Luc (Skier)
153 Ave du Marechal Lereic
BP 20
Bourq Saint Maurice 73700, FRANCE

Cretton, Destin Daniel (Director, Producer)
c/o Leslee Dart *42West*
600 3rd Ave Fl 23
New York, NY 10016-1914, USA

Crevalle, Laura (Actor)
PO Box 557
Old Orchard Beach, ME 04064-0557, USA

Crew, Amanda (Actor)
c/o Vickie Petronio *Play Management*
220-807 Powell St
Vancouver, BC V6A 1H7, CANADA

Crewdson, John M (Journalist)
435 N Michigan Ave Ste 200
Chicago, IL 60611-4067, USA

Crews, Albert (Astronaut)
444 Sllja terway Dr
Satellite Beach, FL 32937-3834, USA

Crews, Gina (Reality Star)
10211 W State Road 235
Alachua, FL 32615-4947, USA

Crews, Terry (Actor)
c/o Liza Anderson *Anderson Group Public Relations*
8060 Melrose Ave Fl 4
Los Angeles, CA 90046-7038, USA

Crewson, Wendy (Actor)
438 Queen St E
Toronto, ON M5A 1T4, CANADA

Crha, Jiri (Athlete, Hockey Player)
23026 Clear Echo Dr Unit 6
Boca Raton, FL 33433-6452, USA

Crha, Jiri (Athlete, Hockey Player)
8023 Laurel Ridge Ct
Delray Beach, FL 33446-9537, USA

Crialese, Emanuele (Director)
c/o Staff Member *WME|IMG*
9601 Wilshire Blvd
Beverly Hills, CA 90210-5213, USA

Cribbins, Barnard (Actor)
Hamm Court
Weybridge, Surrey, UNITED KINGDOM (UK)

Cribbs, Joe S (Athlete, Football Player)
203 Weatherly Way
Pelham, AL 35124-2803, USA

Cribbs, Joshua (Athlete, Football Player)
9333 W Hampton Dr
North Royalton, OH 44133-2884, USA

Crichlow, Lenora (Actor)
c/o Brantley Brown *Authentic Talent & Literary Management*
3615 Eastham Dr # 650
Culver City, CA 90232-2410, USA

Crichton, Scott (Athlete, Football Player)
c/o Doug Hendrickson *Relativity Sports*
2029 Century Park E Ste 1550
Century City, CA 90067-3000, USA

Crick, Jared (Athlete, Football Player)
c/o David Dunn *Athletes First*
23091 Mill Creek Dr
Laguna Hills, CA 92653-1258, USA

Crickhowell of Pont Esgob, Nicholas E (Politician)
4 Henning St
London SW11 3DR, UNITED KINGDOM (UK)

Crider, Melissa (Missy) (Actor)
Paradigm Agency
10100 Santa Monica Blvd Ste 2500
Los Angeles, CA 90067-4116, USA

Crier, Catherine (Correspondent, Television Host)
Catherine Crier Live
600 3rd Ave
Courtroom Television Network
New York, NY 10016-1901, USA

Crier, Catherine (Journalist)
190 Marietta St NW Ste 280
Atlanta, GA 30303-2766, USA

Crile, Susan (Artist)
168 W 86th St
New York, NY 10024-4022, USA

Crim, Chuck (Athlete, Baseball Player)
50039 Golden Horse Dr
Oakhurst, CA 93644-9497, USA

Crim, Chuck (Athlete, Baseball Player)
Chattanooga Lookouts
PO Box 11002
Attn: Coaching Staff
Chattanooga, TN 37401-2002, USA

Crimian, Jack (Athlete, Baseball Player)
3012 Green St
Claymont, DE 19703-2026, USA

Cripe, Dave (Athlete, Baseball Player)
1835 Montara Way
San Jacinto, CA 92583-5832, USA

Crippen, Robert L (Astronaut)
781 Harbour Isle Pl
West Palm Beach, FL 33410-4408, USA

Crippen, Robert L Captain (Astronaut)
781 Harbour Isle Pl
West Palm Beach, FL 33410-4408, USA

Criqui, Don (Sportscaster)
CBS-TV
51 W 52nd St
Sports Dept
New York, NY 10019-6119, USA

Criscione, Dave (Athlete, Baseball Player)
87 Hamlet St
Fredonia, NY 14063-2143, USA

Crisman, Joel (Athlete, Football Player)
10200 Park Meadows Dr Unit 1416
Lone Tree, CO 80124-5465, USA

Crisostomo, Manny (Journalist, Photographer)
Pacific Daily News
PO Box Dn
Hagatna, GU 96932-7643, USA

Crisp, Coco (Athlete, Baseball Player)
508 Judy Dr
Redondo Beach, CA 90277-3830, USA

crisp, terry (Athlete, Hockey Player)
Nashville Predators
501 Broadway
Nashville, TN 37203-3980

Crisp, Terry A (Athlete, Coach, Hockey Player)
805 Cherry Laurel Ct
Nashville, TN 37215-6173, USA

Crispin, Anne C (Writer)
175 5th Ave
Tom Doherty Associates, Llc
New York, NY 10010-7703, USA

Criss, Charles (Athlete, Basketball Player)
4310 Melanie Ln
Atlanta, GA 30349-2849, USA

Criss, Darren (Actor, Musician)
c/o Ricky Rollins *Hyphenate Creative Management*
8149 Santa Monica Blvd # 111
West Hollywood, CA 90046-4912, USA

Criss, Peter (Musician)
GHR Entertainment
16601 Ventura Blvd Ste 506
Encino, CA 91436-1921, USA

Crist, Charlie (Attorney)
Charlie Crist for Governor
PO Box 311
Tallahassee, FL 32302-0311, USA

Crist, Chuck (Athlete, Football Player)
3 N Forest Beach Dr Apt 203
Hilton Head Island, SC 29928-6480, USA

Crist, John (Comedian)
c/o Joe Eshenbaugh *Innovative Artists*
1505 10th St
Santa Monica, CA 90401-2805, USA

Cristal, Linda (Actor)
9129 Hazen Dr
Beverly Hills, CA 90210-1825, USA

Cristofer, Michael (Director, Writer)
c/o Geyer Kosinski *Media Talent Group*
9200 W Sunset Blvd Ste 550
Los Angeles, CA 90069-3611, USA

Cristofer, Michael (Writer)
9830 Wilshire Blvd
Beverly Hills, CA 90212-1804, USA

Criswell, Jeff (Athlete, Football Player)
1101 Walnut St
Kansas City, MO 64106-2110, USA

Critchfield, Russell (Athlete, Basketball Player)
7 Patches Dr
Chico, CA 95928-4353, USA

Crite, Winston (Athlete, Basketball Player)
8812 Heely Ct
Bakersfield, CA 93311-1923, USA

Critelli, Michael (Business Person)
Pitney Bowes Inc
1 Elmcroft Rd
Stamford, CT 06926-0700, USA

Criter, Ken (Athlete, Football Player)
PO Box 441343
Aurora, CO 80044-1343, USA

Crittenden, Ray (Athlete, Football Player)
6206 Secret Hollow Ln
Centreville, VA 20120-1156, USA

Crivello, Anthony (Actor)
c/o Neil Bagg *Buchwald*
5900 Wilshire Blvd Ste 3100
Los Angeles, CA 90036-5030, USA

Croce, Pat (Basketball Player, Business Person, Sportscaster)
c/o Staff Member *WME/IMG*
9601 Wilshire Blvd
Beverly Hills, CA 90210-5213, USA

Crocicchia, James (Athlete, Football Player)
11 Lanesboro Rd
Ladera Ranch, CA 92694-0712, USA

Crocicchia, Jim (Athlete, Football Player)
2867 Calle Heraldo
San Clemente, CA 92673-3536, USA

Crocicchia, Olivia (Actor)
c/o Laura Ackerman *Advantage PR*
3900 W Alameda Ave Ste 1200
Burbank, CA 91505-4317, USA

Crocker, Chris (Actor, Reality Star)
44 Blue Productions
3900 W Alameda Ave Lbby
Burbank, CA 91505-4370, USA

Crocker, Dillard (Athlete, Basketball Player)
5601 Holiday Park Blvd
North Port, FL 34287-2615, USA

Crocker, Ian (Athlete, Olympic Athlete, Swimmer)
8901 Ovalla Dr
Austin, TX 78749-5100

Crocker, Mary Lou (Athlete, Golfer)
1403 Sutton Dr
Carrollton, TX 75006-2943, USA

Crockett, Bobby (Athlete, Football Player)
PO Box 26
Harriet, AR 72639-0026, USA

Crockett, Gibson (Cartoonist)
4713 Great Oak Rd
Rockville, MD 20853-1607, USA

Crockett, Ivory (Athlete, Track Athlete)
PO Box 31403
Saint Louis, MO 63131-0403, USA

Crockett, Monte (Athlete, Football Player)
2696 Halleck Dr
Columbus, OH 43209-3220, USA

Crockett, Ray (Athlete, Football Player)
361 S White Chapel Blvd
Southlake, TX 76092-7312, USA

Crockett, Willis (Athlete, Football Player)
493 Bojo Ella Dr
Douglas, GA 31533-0607, USA

Crockett, Zack (Athlete, Football Player)
6136 NW 120th Ter
Coral Springs, FL 33076-1913, USA

Croel, Mike (Athlete, Football Player)
8305 Lookout Mountain Ave
Los Angeles, CA 90046-1548, USA

Croft, Don (Athlete, Football Player)
511 Larry Dr
Irving, TX 75060-2847, USA

Croft, Parker (Actor)
c/o Staff Member *ROAR (LA)*
9701 Wilshire Blvd Fl 8
Beverly Hills, CA 90212-2008, USA

Croftcheck, Don (Athlete, Football Player)
120 Mine Street
Allison, PA 15413, USA

Crofts, Dash (Musician, Songwriter, Writer)
Nationwide Entertainment
2756 N Green Valley Pkwy
Henderson, NV 89014-2120, USA

Croghan, Emma-Kate (Director)
Hilary Linstead
500 Oxford St
Bondi Junction, NSW 02022, AUSTRALIA

Cromartie, Antonio (Athlete, Football Player)
c/o Ben Dogra *Relativity Sports*
2029 Century Park E Ste 1550
Century City, CA 90067-3000, USA

Cromartie, Warren (Athlete, Baseball Player)
20450 NW 2nd Ave Waxy 790
Attn: Talkin' Hardball
Miami, FL 33169-2505, USA

Crombeen, Mike (Athlete, Hockey Player)
817 Foxcroft Blvd
Newmarket, ON L3X 1M8, Canada

Crombie, Ed (Race Car Driver)
10 Davoren Rd
Clearwater, BC V0E 1N2, Canada

Crombie, Robert B (Astronaut)
20632 Queens Park Ln
Huntington Beach, CA 92646-6018, USA

Cromer, D T (Athlete, Baseball Player)
134 Ridge Top Rd
Lexington, SC 29072-7130, USA

Cromer, Tripp (Athlete, Baseball Player)
32 W Tombee Ln
Columbia, SC 29209-0844, USA

Cromwell, James (Actor)
c/o Staff Member *Koshari Films*
13251 Ventura Blvd Ste 1
Studio City, CA 91604-1838, USA

Cromwell, Nolan (Athlete, Coach, Football Coach, Football Player)
30312 Point Marina Dr
Canyon Lake, CA 92587-7412, USA

Cron, Chris (Athlete, Baseball Player)
Erie Sea Wolves 110 E lOth St
Attn: Managers Office
Erie, PA 16501-1256, USA

Cron, Chris (Athlete, Baseball Player)
14879 S 43rd Pl
Phoenix, AZ 85044-6788, USA

Cronan, Pete (Athlete, Football Player)
13 Saddle Hill Rd
Hopkinton, MA 01748-1151, USA

Crone, Ray (Athlete, Baseball Player)
508 Panorama
Waxahachie, TX 75165-5919, USA

Cronenberg, David (Actor)
c/o Robert Newman *WME/IMG*
9601 Wilshire Blvd
Beverly Hills, CA 90210-5213, USA

Cronin, Eugene (Athlete, Football Player)
2445 37th Ave
Sacramento, CA 95822-3613, USA

Cronin, Kevin (Musician)
1547 Pathfinder Ave
Westlake Village, CA 91362-5299, USA

Cronin, Mark (Producer)
1435 Crest Dr
Altadena, CA 91001-1836, USA

Cronin, Rachel (Actor)
c/o Lisa King *King Talent*
36 Tiverton Ave
Toronto, ON M4M 2L9, Canada

Cronin, Shawn (Athlete, Hockey Player)
4163 SE Oakland St
Stuart, FL 34997-5415, USA

Cronkite, Kathy (Actor)
PO Box 5261
Austin, TX 78763-5261, USA

Cronnenberg, David (Director)
Toronto Antenna
244 DuPont St #200
Toronto, ON M5R 1V7, CANADA

Cronyn, Christopher (Producer)
c/o Staff Member *Lichter Grossman Nichols Adler & Feldman Inc*
9200 W Sunset Blvd Ste 1200
Los Angeles, CA 90069-3607, USA

Cronyn, Susan Cooper (Producer, Writer)
c/o Ron Bernstein *ICM Partners*
10250 Constellation Blvd Fl 7
Los Angeles, CA 90067-6207, USA

Crook, Edward Jr (Boxer)
PO Box 12021
Columbus, GA 31917-2021, USA

Crook, Lorianne (Musician)
1111 Wilson Pike
Brentwood, TN 37027-6736, USA

Crooke, Edward A (Business Person)
Constellation Energy Group
39 W Lexington St Apt 1503
Baltimore, MD 21201-3955, USA

Crooks, Shree (Actor)
c/o Doreen Wilcox Little *Anonymous Content*
3532 Hayden Ave
Culver City, CA 90232-2413, USA

Croom, Corey (Athlete, Football Player)
414 Lawrence St
Sandusky, OH 44870-2318, USA

Croom, Sylvester (Athlete, Coach, Football Player)
1410 18th Ave E # 301
Tuscaloosa, AL 35404-3950, USA

Crooms, Chris (Athlete, Football Player)
810 Laindon Springs Ln
Spring, TX 77373-8461, USA

Crooms, Chris (Athlete, Football Player)
1522 Beaumont Rd
Baytown, TX 77520-3104, USA

Cropper, Marshall (Athlete, Football Player)
2932 Fort Baker Dr SE
Washington, DC 20020-7222, USA

Cropper, Steve (Musician)
819 Tyne Blvd
Nashville, TN 37220-1504, USA

Crosbie, Annette (Actor)
c/o Staff Member *Independent Talent Group*
40 Whitfield St
London W1T 2RH, UNITED KINGDOM

Crosbie, John C (Politician)
235 Water St
Saint John's Nf, NL A1C 5L3, CANADA

Crosby, Bobby (Athlete, Baseball Player)
11463 Anticost Way
Cypress, CA 90630-5429, USA

Crosby, Bubba (Athlete, Baseball Player)
4309 Jane St
Bellaire, TX 77401-4605, USA

Crosby, Caitlin (Musician)
c/o Gerry Cagle *Crysis Management*
8424 Santa Monica Blvd
West Hollywood, CA 90069-6233, USA

Crosby, Cathy Lee (Actor)
1223 Wilshire Blvd # 404
Santa Monica, CA 90403-5406, USA

Crosby, Cleveland (Athlete, Football Player)
2703 Sandal Walk
Pearland, TX 77584-3365, USA

Crosby, David (Musician)
c/o Staff Member *Blue Castle Records*
37 Burlington Ave
Wilmington, MA 01887-3902, USA

Crosby, Denise (Actor, Model)
935 Embury St
Pacific Palisades, CA 90272-3811, USA

Crosby, Ed (Athlete, Baseball Player)
6952 Brightwood Ln Apt 9
Garden Grove, CA 92845-2976, USA

Crosby, Elaine (Athlete, Golfer)
2580 Meadowbrook Ln
Jackson, MI 49201-7702, USA

Crosby, Ken (Athlete, Baseball Player)
PO Box 680306
Park City, UT 84068-0306, USA

Crosby, Lucinda (Actor)
4942 Vineland Ave Ste 200
North Hollywood, CA 91601-5649, USA

Crosby, Mason (Athlete, Football Player)
2050 S Point Rd
Green Bay, WI 54313-5445, USA

Crosby, Norm (Actor, Comedian)
c/o Staff Member *WME/IMG*
9601 Wilshire Blvd Ste 1
Beverly Hills, CA 90210-5213, USA

Crosby, Paul (Musician)
Helter Skelter
Plaza
535 Kings Road
London SW10 0S, UNITED KINGDOM (UK)

Crosby, Phil (Athlete, Football Player)
13439 Hyperion Hills Ln
Charlotte, NC 28278-8137, USA

Crosby, Sidney (Athlete, Hockey Player)
c/o Staff Member *Pittsburgh Penguins*
1001 5th Ave
Pittsburgh, PA 15219-6201, USA

Crosby, Steve (Athlete, Coach, Football Coach, Football Player)
Vanderbitt University
2201 W End Ave
Attn: Football Coaching Staff
Nashville, TN 37235-0001, USA

Crosby, Steve (Athlete, Football Player)
PO Box 609609
San Diego, CA 92160-9609, USA

Crosby Stills & Nash (Music Group)
c/o Carole Kinzel *Creative Artists Agency (CAA)*
2000 Avenue of the Stars Ste 100
Los Angeles, CA 90067-4705, USA

Croshere, Austin (Athlete, Basketball Player)
21766 Azurelee Dr
Malibu, CA 90265-3401, USA

Cross, Ben (Actor)
c/o Jeff Goldberg *Jeff Goldberg Management*
817 Monte Leon Dr
Beverly Hills, CA 90210-2629, USA

Cross, Billy (Athlete, Football Player)
PO Box 103
Canadian, TX 79014-0103, USA

Cross, Burton (Politician)
8 Lonsdale Rd
Farmingdale, ME 04344, USA

Cross, Christopher (Musician, Songwriter)
c/o Steve Levine *ICM Partners*
10250 Constellation Blvd Fl 7
Los Angeles, CA 90067-6207, USA

Cross, Cory (Athlete, Hockey Player)
2963 W Bayshore Ct
Tampa, FL 33611, USA

Cross, David (Actor, Comedian)
c/o Chris Kanarick *ID Public Relations (NY)*
40 Wall St Fl 51
New York, NY 10005-1385, USA

Cross, Howard (Athlete, Football Player)
60 Mulberry Ct
Paramus, NJ 07652-1361, USA

Cross, Irv (Athlete, Football Player, Sportscaster)
2196 Marion Rd
Saint Paul, MN 55113-3824, USA

Cross, Jeff (Athlete, Basketball Player)
5 Patterson Cir
Exeter, NH 03833-6542, USA

Cross, Jeff (Athlete, Football Player)
8045 SW 100th St
Miami, FL 33156-2523, USA

Cross, Jeff (Athlete, Football Player)
2715 Walkers Way
Weston, FL 33331-3021, USA

Cross, Joseph (Actor)
c/o Matt Luber *Luber Roklin Management*
5815 W Sunset Blvd Ste 208
Los Angeles, CA 90028-6481, USA

Cross, Justin (Athlete, Football Player)
10 Longwood Dr
Hampton, NH 03842-1122, USA

Cross, Kendall (Athlete, Olympic Athlete, Wrestler)
2209 Kings Pass
Rockwall, TX 75032-5921

Cross, Marcia (Actor)
c/o Heidi Lopata *Narrative*
1601 Vine St Fl 6
Los Angeles, CA 90028-8802, USA

Cross, Randall L (Randy) (Athlete, Football Player, Sportscaster)
155 Travertine Trl
Alpharetta, GA 30022-5196, USA

Cross, Roger (Actor)
c/o Staff Member *SMS Talent*
8383 Wilshire Blvd Ste 230
Beverly Hills, CA 90211-2436, USA

Cross, Russell (Basketball Player)
Elmhurst College
190 S Prospect Ave
Athletic Dept
Elmhurst, IL 60126-3296, USA

Crossan, Dave (Athlete, Football Player)
3590 Round Bottom Rd
Cincinnati, OH 45244-3026, USA

Crosse, Liris (Actor, Model)
c/o Staff Member *Cinematic Management*
249 1/2 E 13th St
New York, NY 10003-5602, USA

Crossley, Charlotte (Actor, Musician)
Stone Manners Agency
6500 Wilshire Blvd # 550
Los Angeles, CA 90048-4920, USA

Crossley-Holland, Kevin (Writer)
c/o Staff Member *Random House Publicity (Toronto)*
1 Toronto St Suite 300
Toronto, ON M5C 2V6, Canada

Crossman, Doug (Athlete, Hockey Player)
PO Box 634
Somers Point, NJ 08244-0634, USA

Crossman, Kimberley (Actor)
c/o Penny Vizcarra *PV Public Relations*
121 N Almont Dr Apt 203
Beverly Hills, CA 90211-1860, USA

Crosswhite, Leon (Athlete, Football Player)
1955 E 120th St Rear
Cleveland, OH 44106-2138, USA

Croston, Dave (Athlete, Football Player)
6280 Tiger Dr
Sioux City, IA 51106-7136, USA

Croteau, Gary (Athlete, Hockey Player)
6638 Green River Dr Unit B
Highlands Ranch, CO 80130-6752, USA

Crotty, Jim (Athlete, Football Player)
215 S 195th St # 5
Des Moines, WA 98148-2137, USA

Crotty, John (Athlete, Basketball Player)
685 Destacada Ave
Miami, FL 33156-8001, USA

Crouch, Eric (Athlete, Football Player, Heisman Trophy Winner)
1505 N 138th St
Omaha, NE 68154-3888, USA

Crouch, Jan (Religious Leader)
1973 Port Chelsea Pl
Newport Beach, CA 92660-5349, USA

Crouch, Lindsay (Actor)
15115 1/2 W Sunset Blvd Ste A
Pacific Palisades, CA 90272-3751, USA

Crouch, Matthew (Producer)
3556 Multiview Dr
Los Angeles, CA 90068-1222, USA

Crouch, Robbie (Race Car Driver)
106 Pierremount Ave
New Britain, CT 06053-2345, USA

Crouch, Roger K (Astronaut)
120 6th St NE Apt B
Washington, DC 20002-8307, USA

Crouch, Sandra (Musician, Songwriter, Writer)
Sparrow Communications Group
101 Winners Cir N
Brentwood, TN 37027-5352, USA

Crouch, William T (Bill) (Journalist, Photographer)
5660 Valley Oaks Ct
Placerville, CA 95667-9363, USA

Crouch, Zach (Athlete, Baseball Player)
9418 San Paulo Cir
Elk Grove, CA 95624-2126, USA

Crouse, Lindsay (Actor)
263 Monte Grigio Dr
Pacific Palisades, CA 90272-3109, USA

Croushore, Rich (Athlete, Baseball Player)
3110 Bastogne Way
Benton, AR 72019-2943, USA

Croushore, Rick (Athlete, Baseball Player)
4001 Tanglewilde St Apt 101
Houston, TX 77063-5164, USA

Crouthamel, Jake (Athlete, Football Player)
385 Elliott Rd
Centerville, MA 02632-3666, USA

Crouther, Lance (Actor, Producer, Writer)

Crow, Al (Athlete, Football Player)
6191 Occoquan Forest Dr
Manassas, VA 20112-3034, USA

Crow, Bill (Athlete, Basketball Player)
21300 River Rd # 15
Perris, CA 92570-8390, USA

Crow, Dean (Athlete, Baseball Player)
11507 Wickchester Ln
Houston, TX 77043-4521, USA

Crow, Don (Athlete, Baseball Player)
1023 E Lincoln Ave
Nampa, ID 83686-5321, USA

Crow, Lindon (Athlete, Football Player)
2869 Riachuelo
San Clemente, CA 92673-4050, USA

Crow, Mark (Athlete, Basketball Player)
501 W Bay St
Jacksonville, FL 32202-4428, USA

Crow, Rachel (Actor, Musician)
c/o Christian Carino *Creative Artists Agency (CAA)*
2000 Avenue of the Stars Ste 100
Los Angeles, CA 90067-4705, USA

Crow, Sheryl (Musician, Songwriter)
PO Box 4084
Santa Monica, CA 90411-4084, USA

Crow, Wayne (Athlete, Football Player)
16561 Fawn St
Truckee, CA 96161-3534, USA

Crowder, Bruce (Athlete, Hockey Player)
7 Kyle Dr
Nashua, NH 03062-4539, USA

Crowder, Channing (Athlete, Football Player)
8921 Southern Orchard Rd N
Davie, FL 33328-6986, USA

Crowder, Corey (Athlete, Basketball Player)
725 Ballard Bridge Rd
Carrollton, GA 30117-9104, USA

Crowder, Keith (Athlete, Hockey Player)
PO Box 95 Stn Main
Stn Main
Essex, ON N8M 2Y1, Canada

Crowder, Randy (Athlete, Football Player)
613 S 8th St
Philadelphia, PA 19147-2001, USA

Crowder, Troy (Athlete, Hockey Player)
Adventure North Hockey
103 Panache North Shore Rd
Whitefish, ON P0M 3E0, Canada

Crowe, Cameron (Director)
1016 Amalfi Dr
Pacific Palisades, CA 90272-4028, USA

Crowe, James (J.D.) (Musician)
JD Crowe Festival
201 S Lexington Ave
Wilmore, KY 40390-1200, USA

Crowe, John (Writer)
c/o Staff Member *Troubador Publishing Ltd*
5 Weir Rd
Kibworth Beauchamp
Leicester LE8 0LQ, UK

Crowe, Mia (Actor, Model)
Mia Crowe Official Fan Club
7336 Santa Monica Blvd # 633
West Hollywood, CA 90046-6670, USA

Crowe, Pat (Horse Racer)
202-100 Millside Dr
Milton, ON L9T 5E2, USA

Crowe, Phil (Athlete, Hockey Player)
1409 Pintail Ct
Windsor, CO 80550-6144, USA

Crowe, Russell (Actor)
c/o Robin Baum *Slate PR*
901 N Highland Ave
W Hollywood, CA 90038-2412, USA

Crowe, Tonya (Actor)
159 N Clark Dr APT 1
Beverly Hills, CA 90211-4705, USA

Crowell, Angelo (Athlete, Football Player)
5309 Dockery Dr
Charlotte, NC 28209-3668, USA

Crowell, Germane (Athlete, Football Player)
2575 Viola Ct
Winston Salem, NC 27127-5992, USA

Crowell, Jim (Athlete, Baseball Player)
4003 Sleighbell Ln
Valparaiso, IN 46383-1943, USA

Crowell, Rodney (Musician)
1238 Saddle Springs Dr
Thompsons Station, TN 37179-5419, USA

Crowley, Ben (Actor)
c/o Staff Member *Kass Management*
1011 Euclid St Unit B
Santa Monica, CA 90403-4296, USA

Crowley, Candy (Correspondent)
5709 Ridgefield Rd
Bethesda, MD 20816-1250, USA

Crowley, Joseph (Congressman, Politician)
2404 Rayburn Hob
Washington, DC 20515-3605, USA

Crowley, Kevin (Actor)
c/o Lorraine Berglund *Lorraine Berglund Management*
11537 Hesby St
North Hollywood, CA 91601-3618, USA

Crowley, Monica (Television Host)
c/o Staff Member *Fox News*
1211 Avenue of the Americas Lowr C1
New York, NY 10036-8705, USA

Crowley, Pat (Actor)
551 Perugia Way
Los Angeles, CA 90077-3708, USA

Crowley, Paul (Athlete, Hockey Player)
Canadian Hockey Enterprises
727 Lansdowne St W
Peterborough, ON K9J 1Z2, Canada

Crowley, Ted (Athlete, Hockey Player)
248 Seaward Bnd Apt 53-2
Teaticket, MA 02536-5843, USA

Crowley, Terry (Athlete, Baseball Player)
333 W Camden St
Attn: Coaching Staff
Baltimore, MD 21201-2496, USA

Crowley, Terry (Athlete, Baseball Player)
18405 Ensor Farm Ct
Parkton, MD 21120-9685, USA

Crown, Lester (Business Person)
Henry Crown & Co
222 N La Salle St Ste 2000
Chicago, IL 60601-1120

Crowton, Gary (Coach, Football Coach)
Brigham Young University
Athletic Dept
Provo, UT 84602, USA

Croyle, Brodie (Athlete, Football Player)
105 Apple Blossom Dr
Brandon, MS 39047-7443, USA

Croyle, Philip (Athlete, Football Player)
5883 Treetop Ct
San Jose, CA 95123-4346, USA

Crozier, Eric (Athlete, Baseball Player)
3142 Clermont Rd
Columbus, OH 43227-1833, USA

Crozier, Joseph R (Joe) (Athlete, Coach, Hockey Player)
299 Randwood Dr
Buffalo, NY 14221-1444, USA

Crudale, Mike (Athlete, Baseball Player)
2319 Tree Creek Pl
Danville, CA 94506-2065, USA

Crudup, Billy (Actor)
c/o Simon Halls *Slate PR*
901 N Highland Ave
W Hollywood, CA 90038-2412, USA

Cruikshank, Dave (Athlete, Olympic Athlete, Speed Skater)
1223 Aspen Ct
Delafield, WI 53018-1300, USA

Cruikshank, Lucas (Actor)
c/o Evan Weiss *Collective Digital Studio*
8383 Wilshire Blvd Ste 1050
Beverly Hills, CA 90211-2415, USA

Cruikshank, Thomas H (Business Person)
5949 Sherry Ln Ste 1035
Dallas, TX 75225-6521, USA

Cruise, Asia (Musician)
c/o Staff Member *Zomba Records (NY)*
137-139 W 25th St
New York, NY 10001, USA

Cruise, Earl (Horse Racer)
151 Liberty St Apt 16
Little Ferry, NJ 07643-1790, USA

Cruise, Jimmy (Horse Racer)
34431 Windley Cir
Eustis, FL 32736-7265, USA

Cruise, Tom (Actor, Director, Producer)
c/o Amanda Lundberg *42West*
600 3rd Ave Fl 23
New York, NY 10016-1914, USA

Cruisie, Jennifer (Writer)
c/o Argh Ink LLC
285 5th Ave # 470
Brooklyn, NY 11215-2578, USA

Crum, E Denzel (Denny) (Athlete, Basketball Player, Coach)
6901 Routt Rd
Louisville, KY 40299-5243, USA

Crumb, Robert (Artist, Cartoonist)
c/o Staff Member *Fantagraphics Books*
7563 Lake City Way NE
Seattle, WA 98115-4218, USA

Crumb, Robert (R) (Cartoonist)
20 Rue du Pont Vieux
Sauve 30610, FRANCE

Crumley Jr, James R (Religious Leader)
108 Castle Church Rd
Chapin, SC 29036-7853, USA

Crump, Diane (Horse Racer)
PO Box 297
Linden, VA 22642-0297, USA

Crump, Dwayne (Athlete, Football Player)
35708 Marciel Ave
Madera, CA 93636-8414, USA

Crump, Harry (Athlete, Football Player)
9601 Collins Ave PH 201
Bal Harbour, FL 33154-2220, USA

Crumpler, Alge (Athlete, Football Player)
787 Blackfoot Trl
Suwanee, GA 30024-1753, USA

Crumpler, Carlester (Athlete, Football Player)
4355 River Gate Ln Unit B
Little River, SC 29566-6833, USA

Crusan, Doug (Athlete, Football Player)
6263 Hanover Ct
Fishers, IN 46038-1799, USA

Crutchfield, Dwayne (Athlete, Football Player)
6936 Rebecca Dr
Niagara Falls, NY 14304-3053, USA

Cruz, Alexis (Actor)
c/o Staff Member *Abrams Artists Agency*
750 N San Vicente Blvd
E Tower Fl 11
Los Angeles, CA 90069-5788, USA

Cruz, Cirilio (Baseball Player)
St Louis Cardinals
E8 Calle H
Arroyo, PR 00714-2236, USA

Cruz, Deivi (Baseball Player)
Detroit Tigers
611 Woodward Ave
Detroit, MI 48226-3408, USA

Cruz, Hector (Athlete, Baseball Player)
1646 N Monticello Ave
Chicago, IL 60647-4719, USA

Cruz, Henry (Athlete, Baseball Player)
Los Angeles Dodgers
PO Box 70012
Fajardo, PR 00738-7012, USA

Cruz, Ivan (Athlete, Baseball Player)
3874 Bright Leaf Ct
Jacksonville, FL 32246-7660, USA

Cruz, Jacob (Athlete, Baseball Player)
600 California St FL 18
San Francisco, CA 94108-2711, USA

Cruz, Juan (Athlete, Baseball Player)
c/o Staff Member *Chicago Cubs*
1060 W Addison St
Wrigley Field
Chicago, IL 60613-4397, USA

Cruz, Julio (Athlete, Baseball Player)
6599 170th Pl SE
Bellevue, WA 98006-6012, USA

Cruz, Mike (DJ)
c/o Staff Member *Diva Central Inc*
7510 W Sunset Blvd # 1445
Los Angeles, CA 90046-3408, USA

Cruz, Monica (Actor)
c/o Antonio Rubial *A6 Cinema*
Conde De Xiquena 13
#3D
Madrid 28004, SPAIN

Cruz, Nelson (Athlete, Baseball Player)
2021 Stone Canyon Ct
Arlington, TX 76012-5762, USA

Cruz, Nicky (Religious Leader)
Nicky Cruz Outreach
PO Box 62010
Colorado Springs, CO 80962-2010, USA

Cruz, Penelope (Actor, Model)
c/o Katrina Bayonas *Kuranda Management*
Isla De Oza, 30
Madrid 28035, SPAIN

Cruz, Raymond (Actor)
c/o Raphael Berko *Media Artists Group*
8222 Melrose Ave Ste 304
Los Angeles, CA 90046-6839, USA

Cruz, Smith Martin (Writer)
Random House
1745 Broadway Frnt 3 # B1
New York, NY 10019-4343, USA

Cruz, Taio (Musician)
c/o Michael Moses *Baker Winokur Ryder Public Relations*
9100 Wilshire Blvd
W Tower #500
Beverly Hills, CA 90212-3415, USA

Cruz, Ted (Politician, Senator)
c/o Staff Member *Javelin*
203 S Union St Ste 200
Alexandria, VA 22314-3356, USA

Cruz, Tommy (Athlete, Baseball Player)
E8 Calle H
Arroyo, PR 00714-2236, USA

Cruz, Tommy (Athlete, Baseball Player)
12000 Stadium Rd
Attn Coaching Staff
Adelanto, CA 92301-3400, USA

Cruz, Valerie (Actor)
c/o Staff Member *Innovative Artists*
1505 10th St
Santa Monica, CA 90401-2805, USA

Cruz, Victor (Athlete, Football Player)
c/o Tom Condon *Creative Artists Agency (CAA)*
401 Commerce St PH
Nashville, TN 37219-2516, USA

Cruz, Wilson (Actor)
c/o Tammy Rosen *Sanders Armstrong Caserta*
4111 W Alameda Ave Ste 505
Burbank, CA 91505-4163, USA

Cruz Jr, Jose (Athlete, Baseball Player)
7421 SW 56th Ct
Miami, FL 33143-5606, USA

Cruz Sr, Jose D (Athlete, Baseball Player)
2309 Delta Bridge Dr
Pearland, TX 77584-1566, USA

Crvenkovski, Branko (President)
President's Office
Skopje, MACEDONIA

Cryder, Robert (Athlete, Football Player)
9054 Crescent Bar Rd NW Unit 16
Quincy, WA 98848-8966, USA

Crye, John B (Actor, Producer, Writer)
c/o Staff Member *Fewdio*
13348 Reedley St
Panorama City, CA 91402-4061, USA

Cryer, Gretchen (Actor, Songwriter, Writer)
885 W End Ave Apt 1A
New York, NY 10025-3512, USA

Cryer, Jon (Actor)
c/o Karen Samfilippo *IMPR*
1158 26th St # 548
Santa Monica, CA 90403-4698, USA

Cryer, Morgan (Actor)
c/o Sylvia Hutson *Hutson Talent Agency*
35 Burtis St
Portsmouth, VA 23702-2703, USA

Cryer, Suzanne (Actor)
c/o Elizabeth Much *East 2 West Collective*
11022 Santa Monica Blvd Ste 350
Los Angeles, CA 90025-7532, USA

Crystal, Billy (Actor, Comedian)
c/o Staff Member *Face Productions*
1250 6th St Ste 405
Santa Monica, CA 90401-1638, USA

Crystals (Music Group)
27-L Ambiance Ct
Bardonia, NY 10954-1421, USA

C. Scott, Robert (Congressman, Politician)
1201 Longworth Hob
Washington, DC 20515-0520, USA

Csokas, Marton (Actor)
c/o George Freeman *WME|IMG*
9601 Wilshire Blvd
Beverly Hills, CA 90210-5213, USA

Csonka, Larry (Athlete, Football Player)
37256 Hunter Camp Rd
Lisbon, OH 44432-9464, USA

Csupo, Gabor (Animator, Director, Producer)
c/o Staff Member *Grand Allure Entertainment*
12835 Mulholland Dr
Beverly Hills, CA 90210-1247, USA

Ctvrtlik, Bob (Athlete, Olympic Athlete, Volleyball Player)
5525 E Seaside Walk Apt B
Long Beach, CA 90803-4427, USA

Cua, Rick (Musician)
1086 Rip Steele Rd
Columbia, TN 38401-7745, USA

Cuaron, Alfonso (Director)
c/o Staff Member *Esperanto Filmoj*
37 W 20th St
New York, NY 10011-3706, USA

Cuban, Mark (Business Person, Reality Star)
c/o Staff Member *Dallas Mavericks*
1333 N Stemmons Fwy Ste 105
Dallas, TX 75207-3722, USA

Cubbage, Mike (Athlete, Baseball Player, Coach)
3349 Carroll Creek Rd
Keswick, VA 22947-9156, USA

Cube, Ice (Actor, Director, Musician)
c/o Staff Member *CubeVision*
9000 W Sunset Blvd Ste 650A
W Hollywood, CA 90069-5806, USA

Cubillan, Darwin (Athlete, Baseball Player)
11505 Clumbet Ln
Lehigh Acres, FL 33971-3748, USA

Cubitt, David (Actor)
c/o Shelley Browning *Magnolia Entertainment*
9595 Wilshire Blvd Ste 601
Beverly Hills, CA 90212-2506, USA

Cuccurullo, Waren (Musician)
DD Productions
93A Westbourne Park Villas
London W2 5ED, UNITED KINGDOM (UK)

Cuche, Didier (Skier)
Les Bugnenets
Le Paquier 02058, SWITZERLAND

Cucinotta, Maria Grazia (Actor)
c/o Staff Member *Seven Dreams Production*
Piazza A. Capponi, 13
Rome 00193, ITALY

Cuddie, Steve (Athlete, Hockey Player)
18 Hill Country Dr
Gormley, ON L4A 3T2, Canada

Cuddle, Steve (Athlete, Hockey Player)
24 Dodie St
Aurora, ON L4G 2L2, Canada

Cuddy, Jim (Musician)
c/o Staff Member *UTA/The Agency Group*
888 7th Ave Fl 7
New York, NY 10106-0700, USA

Cuddyer, Michael (Athlete, Baseball Player)
10240 Washingtonia Palm Way Apt 2024
Fort Myers, FL 33966-6915, USA

Cudi, Scott (Kid) (Musician)
c/o Stephen (Steve) Levinson *Leverage Management*
3030 Pennsylvania Ave
Santa Monica, CA 90404-4112, USA

Cudlitz, Michael (Actor)
c/o Ame VanIden *VanIden Public Relations*
4070 Wilson Pike
Franklin, TN 37067-8126, USA

Cudmore, Daniel (Actor)
c/o Murray Gibson *Red Management*
415 Esplanade W Box 3
North Vancouver, BC V7M 1A6, CANADA

Cuellar, Bobby (Athlete, Baseball Player)
1 Morrie Silver Way
Attn Coaching Staff
Rochester, NY 14608-1754, USA

Cuellar, Bobby (Athlete, Baseball Player)
705 E 6th St
Alice, TX 78332-4651, USA

Cueller, Henry (Congressman, Politician)
2463 Rayburn Hob
Washington, DC 20515-4315, USA

Cueto, Al (Athlete, Basketball Player)
5714 Riviera Dr
Coral Gables, FL 33146-2751, USA

Cueto, Johnny (Athlete, Basketball Player)
c/o Team Member *San Francisco Giants*
24 Willie Mays Plz
Sbc Park
San Francisco, CA 94107-2199, USA

Culbertson Jr, Frank L (Astronaut)
15700 Columbus Mountain Dr
Broomfield, CO 80023-9446, USA

Culbreath, Jim (Athlete, Football Player)
212 Elder Ave
Lansdowne, PA 19050-3028, USA

Culbreath, Joshua (Josh) (Athlete, Track Athlete)
Central State University
Athletic Dept
Wilberforce, OH 45384, USA

Culbreth, Feildin (Athlete, Baseball Player)
224 Claiborne Ct
Spartanburg, SC 29301-5345, USA

Culhane, Jim (Athlete, Hockey Player)
Western Michigan University
PO Box 19765
Kalamazoo, MI 49019-0765, USA

Culkin, Kieran (Actor)
c/o Emily Gerson Saines *Brookside Artists Management*
250 W 57th St Ste 1820
New York, NY 10107-1802, USA

Culkin, Macaulay (Actor)
704 Broadway Fl 8
New York, NY 10003-9504, USA

Culkin, Rory (Actor)
c/o Emily Gerson Saines *Brookside Artists Management*
250 W 57th St Ste 1820
New York, NY 10107-1802, USA

Cullars, Willie (Athlete, Football Player)
1034 Garfield Ave
Kansas City, KS 66104, USA

Cullen, Barry (Athlete, Hockey Player)
Cullen Motors
905 Woodlawn Rd W
Guelph, ON N1K 1B7, Canada

Cullen, Betsy (Athlete, Golfer)
4144 Greystone Way Apt 707
Sugar Land, TX 77479-3014, USA

Cullen, Brett (Actor)
2229 Glyndon Ave
Venice, CA 90291-4042, USA

Cullen, Brian (Athlete, Hockey Player)
Brian Cullen Motors
386 Ontario St
St Catharines, ON L2R 5L8, Canada

Cullen, Jack (Athlete, Baseball Player)
164 Alexander Ave
Nutley, NJ 07110-1002, USA

Cullen, John (Athlete, Hockey Player)
1002 Legacy Hills Dr
McDonough, GA 30253-8824, USA

Cullen, Kimberly (Actor)
8916 Ashcroft Ave
West Hollywood, CA 90048-2404, USA

Cullen, Matt (Athlete, Hockey Player)
530 Tessa Dr
Moorhead, MN 56560-5631, USA

Cullen, Peter (Actor)
c/o Kevin Motley *Tisherman Gilbert Motley Drozdoski Talent Agency (TGMD)*
6767 Forest Lawn Dr # 101
Los Angeles, CA 90068-1027, USA

Cullen, Ray (Athlete, Hockey Player)
20 Sydenham Dr RR 2
Ilderton, ON N0M 2A0, Canada

Cullen, Tim (Athlete, Baseball Player)
159 W G St
Benicia, CA 94510-3114, USA

Cullens, E Van (Business Person)
Harris Corp
1025 W Nasa Blvd
Melbourne, FL 32919-0001, USA

Culligan, Joe (Writer)
Research Investigative Services
650 NE 126th St
North Miami, FL 33161-4821, USA

Cullimore, Jassen (Athlete, Hockey Player)
5509 S Washington St
Hinsdale, IL 60521-4965, USA

Cullity, Dave (Athlete, Football Player)
3155 Oak Creek Dr E
Colorado Spgs, CO 80906-4549, USA

Culliver, Chris (Athlete, Football Player)
c/o Chafie Fields *Lagardere Unlimited (Miami)*
845 United Nations Plz
New York, NY 10017-3540, USA

Cullocks, Josh (Athlete, Football Player)
5511 Eastover Dr S
New Orleans, LA 70128-3658, USA

Cullum, Jamie (Musician)
c/o Martin Kirkup *Direct Management Group*
8332 Melrose Ave
Los Angeles, CA 90069-5420, USA

Cullum, John (Actor)
c/o Jeff Berger *Jeff Berger Management*
301 W 53rd St Apt 10J
New York, NY 10019-5794, USA

Cullum, Kaitlin (Actor)
c/o Norma Robbins *Abrams Artists Agency*
750 N San Vicente Blvd
E Tower Fl 11
Los Angeles, CA 90069-5788, USA

Cullum, Kimberly (Actor)
8916 Ashcroft Ave
West Hollywood, CA 90048-2404

Culos, Chris (Musician)
845 Windstone Blvd
Brentwood, TN 37027-6215, USA

Culp, Curley (Athlete, Football Player)
16811 Gravesend Rd
Pflugerville, TX 78660-1830, USA

Culp, Ray (Athlete, Baseball Player)
7400 Waterline Rd
Austin, TX 78731-2055, USA

Culp, Steven (Actor)
1680 Las Lunas St
Pasadena, CA 91106-1303, USA

Culpepper, Brad (Athlete, Football Player)
136 W Davis Blvd
Tampa, FL 33606-3540, USA

Culpepper, Daunte (Athlete, Football Player)
16730 Berkshire Ct
Southwest Ranches, FL 33331-1331, USA

Culpepper, Ed (Athlete, Football Player)
9293 Poplar Ave Apt 338
Germantown, TN 38138-7925, USA

Culpepper, Robert E (Athlete, Football Player)
1535 45th Ave E
Ellenton, FL 34222-2643, USA

Culpo, Olivia (Actor)
c/o Jill Fritzo *Jill Fritzo Public Relations*
208 E 51st St # 305
New York, NY 10022-6557, USA

Culver, George (Athlete, Baseball Player)
5409 Rustic Canyon St
Bakersfield, CA 93306-7315, USA

Culver, Michael (Actor)
77 Beak St.
London, ENGLAND W1F 9ST

Culver, Molly (Actor)
4537 Finley Ave
Los Angeles, CA 90027-2601, USA

Cumberbatch, Benedict (Actor)
c/o Staff Member *Sunnymarch*
Maxwell Building
Elstree Film Studios
Borehamwood Hertfordshire WD6 1JG, UNITED KINGDOM

Cumberland, John (Athlete, Baseball Player)
1771 Muddy Creek Rd
Dandridge, TN 37725-6674, USA

Cumby, George E (Athlete, Football Player)
12090 Cross Fence Trl
Tyler, TX 75706-4239, USA

Cumming, Alan (Actor, Musician)
c/o Nikola Barisic *Untitled Entertainment (NY)*
215 Park Ave S Fl 8
New York, NY 10003-1622, USA

Cummings, Ashleigh (Actor)
c/o Lisa Mann *Lisa Mann Creative Management*
19-25 Cope St
Redfern NSW 02016, AUSTRALIA

Cummings, Burton (Musician, Songwriter)
3758 Woodcliff Rd
Sherman Oaks, CA 91403-5050, USA

Cummings, Ed (Athlete, Football Player)
237 Schearbrook Ln
Stevensville, MT 59870-6405, USA

Cummings, Erin (Actor)
Mittens for Detroit
PO Box 448
Clawson, MI 48017-0448, USA

Cummings, Jim (Actor)
c/o Heather Vergo *Atlas Talent Agency (NY)*
15 E 32nd St Fl 6
New York, NY 10016-5570, USA

Cummings, Joe (Athlete, Football Player)
2552 Snaffle Bit Way
Missoula, MT 59808-5214, USA

Cummings, John (Athlete, Baseball Player)
21 Park Paseo
Laguna Niguel, CA 92677-5317, USA

Cummings, Midre (Athlete, Baseball Player)
7226 Hummingbird Ln
New Prt Rchy, FL 34655-4011, USA

Cummings, Quinn (Actor)
3870 Glenfeliz Blvd
Los Angeles, CA 90039-1742, USA

Cummings, Steve (Athlete, Baseball Player)
1805 Branch Hill Dr
Pearland, TX 77581-6198, USA

Cummings, Terry (Athlete, Basketball Player)
2400 Parkland Dr NE Unit 108
Atlanta, GA 30324-3592, USA

Cummings, Terry (Athlete, Basketball Player)
12820 W Golden Ln
San Antonio, TX 78249-2231, USA

Cummings, Whitney (Actor)
c/o Chelsea Thomas *The Lede Company*
9701 Wilshire Blvd # 930
Beverly Hills, CA 90212-2020, USA

Cummins, Barry (Athlete, Hockey Player)
155 Marsden St
Kimberley, BC V1A 1G8, Canada

Cummins, Dan (Comedian)
c/o Maggie Houlehan *Parallel Entertainment (LA)*
15025 Altata Dr
Pacific Palisades, CA 90272-4450, USA

Cummins, Gregory Scott (Actor)
Schiowitz/Clay/Rose
1680 Vine St # 1016
Los Angeles, CA 90028-8804, USA

Cummins, Jim (Athlete, Hockey Player)
25640 Kinyon St
Taylor, MI 48180-3281, USA

Cumpsty, Michael (Actor)
c/o Staff Member *Innovative Artists*
1505 10th St
Santa Monica, CA 90401-2805, USA

Cundieff, Rusty (Actor)
c/o Rich Freeman *Code Entertainment*
280 S Beverly Dr Ste 513
Beverly Hills, CA 90212-3908, USA

Cundiff, Billy (Athlete, Football Player)
2989 N 44th St Unit 2046
Phoenix, AZ 85018-7309, USA

Cunnane, Will (Athlete, Baseball Player)
123 Sleepy Hollow Ln
Congers, NY 10920-1515, USA

Cunneyworth, Randy (Athlete, Coach, Hockey Player)
c/o Staff Member *Rochester Americans*
1 War Memorial Sq Ste 228
Rochester, NY 14614-2192, USA

cunneyworth, randy (Athlete, Hockey Player)
Montreal Canadiens
0-1275 Rue Saint-Antoine O
Montreal, QC H3C 5L2, Canada

Cunniff, Jill (Musician)
Metropolitan Entertainment
2 Penn Plz # 2600
New York, NY 10121-0101, USA

Cunniff, John (Athlete, Hockey Player)

Cunning, Kat (Actor, Musician)
c/o Matt Galle *Paradigm*
140 Broadway Ste 2600
New York, NY 10005-1011, USA

Cunningham, Bennie L (Athlete, Football Player)
PO Box 1086
Seneca, SC 29679-1086, USA

Cunningham, Bill (Musician)
Horizon Mgmt
PO Box 8770
Endwell, NY 13762-8770, USA

Cunningham, Bill (Radio Personality)
8044 Montgomery Rd Ste 650
Cincinnati, OH 45236-2959, USA

Cunningham, Brian (Race Car Driver)
PTG Racing
441 Victory Rd
Winchester, VA 22602-4567, USA

Cunningham, Carl (Athlete, Football Player)
4471 Saddleworth Cir
Orlando, FL 32826-4123, USA

Cunningham, Colin (Actor)
c/o Staff Member *Characters Talent Agency (Toronto)*
8 Elm St Fl 2
Toronto, ON M5G 1G7, CANADA

Cunningham, Dick (Athlete, Basketball Player)
13102 Cypress Hill Dr
Hudson, FL 34669-2829, USA

Cunningham, Dick (Athlete, Football Player)
205 Edgewater Way
Peachtree City, GA 30269-1736, USA

Cunningham, Doug (Athlete, Football Player)
5060 Harling Pl
Jackson, MS 39211, USA

Cunningham, Ed (Athlete, Football Player)
4154 Vinton Ave
Culver City, CA 90232-3420, USA

Cunningham, Gunther (Athlete, Coach, Football Coach, Football Player)
4558 Forest Edge Ln
West Bloomfield, MI 48323-2182, USA

Cunningham, Jay (Athlete, Football Player)
3617 Farland Rd
Cleveland, OH 44118-3016, USA

Cunningham, Jermaine (Athlete, Football Player)

Cunningham, Joe (Athlete, Baseball Player)
RR 1 Box 80A
Koshkonong, MO 65692-9526, USA

Cunningham, Katherine (Actor)
c/o Jean-Pierre (JP) Henraux *Henraux Management*
Prefers to be contacted by telephone
CA, USA

Cunningham, Kristan (Actor, Television Host)
c/o Cat Josell *Synergy Management*
11271 Ventura Blvd Ste 495
Studio City, CA 91604-3136, USA

Cunningham, Leon (Athlete, Football Player)
5484 Brookwood Dr SW
Mableton, GA 30126-2028, USA

Cunningham, Liam (Actor)
c/o Sarah Camlett *Independent Talent Group*
40 Whitfield St
London W1T 2RH, UNITED KINGDOM

Cunningham, Michael (Writer)
Farrar Straus Giroux
19 Union Sq W
New York, NY 10003-3304, USA

Cunningham, Randall (Athlete, Football Player)
9367 Jeremy Blaine Ct
Las Vegas, NV 89139-8358, USA

Cunningham, Richard (Athlete, Football Player)
205 Edgewater Way
Peachtree City, GA 30269-1736, USA

Cunningham, Richie (Athlete, Football Player)
610 Cheyenne Dr
Houma, LA 70360-6060, USA

Cunningham, Sam (Athlete, Football Player)
9316 S 4th Ave # 5
Inglewood, CA 90305-3002, USA

Cunningham, Sean (Director, Producer)
4420 Hayvenhurst Ave
Encino, CA 91436-3248, USA

Cunningham, T J (Athlete, Football Player)
11640 E Walsh Pl
Aurora, CO 80012-3264, USA

Cunningham, Walter (Astronaut)
AVD
PO Box 604
Glenn Dale, MD 20769-0604, USA

Cunningham, Walter Colonel (Astronaut)
1707 Post Oak Blvd Ste 263
Houston, 77056-3801 TX, USA

Cunningham, William J (Billy) (Athlete, Basketball Player, Coach)
Cunningham's Court Restaurant
31 Front St # 33
Conshohocken, PA 19428-2867, USA

Cuoco-Sweeting, Kaley (Actor)
c/o Melissa Kates *Viewpoint Inc*
8820 Wilshire Blvd Ste 220
Beverly Hills, CA 90211-2622, USA

Cuomo, Andrew (Politician)
Office of the Governor
NYS State Capitol Building
Albany, NY 12224, USA

Cuomo, Chris (Correspondent, Journalist, Television Host)
c/o Staff Member *CNN (NY)*
10 Columbus Cir
Time Warner Center
New York, NY 10019-1158, USA

Cuomo, Rivers (Musician)
515 Marguerita Ave
Santa Monica, CA 90402-1917, USA

Cuozzo, Gary S (Athlete, Football Player)
911 Middletown Lincroft Rd
Middletown, NJ 07748-3109, USA

Cura, Francesco (Actor)

Curatola, Vincent (Actor)
26 Possum Trl
Upper Saddle River, NJ 07458-1825, USA

Curb, Mike (Musician, Producer)
c/o Staff Member *Curb Records (Nashville)*
48 Music Sq E
Nashville, TN 37203-4639, USA

Curbeam, Robert L Cdr (Astronaut)
13727 Briaridge Ct
Highland, MD 20777-9539, USA

Curbeam, Robert L Jr (Astronaut)
15806 Virginia Fern Way
Houston, TX 77059-3002, USA

Curci, Francis (Athlete, Football Player)
14707 Croydon Pl
Tampa, FL 33618-2160, USA

Curcic, Danica (Actor)
c/o Anne Lindberg *Lindberg Management*
Lavendelstaede 5-7
Baghuset, 4. Sal
Copenhagen K 1462, DENMARK

Curcillo, Anthony (Athlete, Football Player)
23887 Corte Emerado
Murrieta, CA 92562-3539, USA

Curcio, Michael (Athlete, Football Player)
165 Lincoln Ave
Hightstown, NJ 08520-4117, USA

Curd, Francis (Athlete, Football Player)
14707 Croydon Pl
Tampa, FL 33618-2160, USA

Cure, Robert (Athlete, Football Player)
145 Main St
Los Altos, CA 94022-2912, USA

Cure, The (Music Group)
c/o Rick Roskin *Creative Artists Agency (CAA)*
2000 Avenue of the Stars Ste 100
Los Angeles, CA 90067-4705, USA

Cureton, Earl (Athlete, Basketball Player)
7306 Balsam Ct
West Bloomfield, MI 48322-2821, USA

Cureton, Will (Athlete, Football Player)
1700 Cedar Springs Rd Apt 1805
Dallas, TX 75202-1219, USA

Curfman, Shannon (Musician)
Monterey International
72 W Adams St # 1000
Chicago, IL 60603-5107, USA

Curl, Carolyn (Skier)
Robert U Curt
405 N Westridge Dr
Idaho Falls, ID 83402-5447, USA

Curlander, Paul J (Business Person)
Lexmark International
740 W New Circle Rd
Lexington, KY 40511-1876, USA

Curley, Bill (Athlete, Basketball Player)
377 Autumn Ave
Duxbury, MA 02332-4614, USA

Curley, Marianne (Writer)
43 Nariah Cres
Toormina NSW 2452, AUSTRALIA

Curnen, Monique (Actor)
c/o Sheree Cohen *Buchwald*
5900 Wilshire Blvd Ste 3100
Los Angeles, CA 90036-5030, USA

Curran, Brian (Athlete, Coach, Hockey Player)
c/o Staff Member *Quad City Mallards*
1509 3rd Avenue A
Moline, IL 61265-1363, USA

Curran, Brian (Athlete, Hockey Player)
3600 Vanrick Dr
Attn: Director of Hockey Operations
Kalamazoo, MI 49001-0805, USA

Curran, Mike (Athlete, Hockey Player, Olympic Athlete)
7615 Lanewood Ln N
Osseo, MN 55311-2608, USA

Curran, Pat (Athlete, Football Player)
1525 Glenwood Dr
San Diego, CA 92103-4732, USA

Curran, Tony (Actor)
c/o Tammy Rosen *Sanders Armstrong Caserta*
4111 W Alameda Ave Ste 505
Burbank, CA 91505-4163, USA

Currence, Lafayette (Athlete, Baseball Player)
113 Rock Springs Way
Rock Hill, SC 29730-6149, USA

Currie, Bill (Athlete, Baseball Player)
242 Lakeside Dr SW
Arlington, GA 39813-2345, USA

Currie, Brian (Writer)
c/o David Krintzman *Morris Yorn Barnes Levine Krintzman Rubenstein Kohner & Gellman*
2000 Avenue of the Stars Ste 300N
Tower N Fl 3
Los Angeles, CA 90067-4704, USA

Currie, Cherie (Musician)
Cherie Currie's Chainsaw Art Gallery
8511 Hanna Ave
West Hills, CA 91304-2322, USA

Currie, Daniel (Dan) (Athlete, Football Player)
6650 W Flamingo Rd Apt 152
Las Vegas, NV 89103-2144, USA

Currie, Gordon (Actor)
c/o Jennifer Goldhar *Characters Talent Agency (Toronto)*
8 Elm St Fl 2
Toronto, ON M5G 1G7, CANADA

Currie, Louise (Actor)
1317 Delresto Dr
Beverly Hills, CA 90210-2100, USA

Currie, Malcolm R (Business Person)
Hughes Aircraft Co
PO Box 956
El Segundo, CA 90245-0956, USA

Currie, Nancy J (Astronaut)
NASA Johnson Space Center
2101 Nasa Pkwy
Houston, TX 77058-3696, USA

Currie, Sondra (Actor)
3951 Longridge Ave
Sherman Oaks, CA 91423-4923, USA

Currie, Tony (Athlete, Hockey Player)
2600-2 Bloor St W
Toronto, ON M4W 3E2, Canada

Currier, William(Bill) (Athlete, Football Player)
8661 Monticello Rd
Columbia, SC 29203-9706, USA

Currie-Wood, Wallis (Actor)
c/o Dara Gordon *Anonymous Content*
155 Spring St Frnt 3
New York, NY 10012-5208, USA

Currin, James A (Athlete, Football Player)
11770 Thayer Ln
Cincinnati, OH 45249-1566, USA

Currington, Billy (Musician)
c/o John Dennis *Dennis Entertainment*
209 10th Ave S Ste 506
Nashville, TN 37203-0790, USA

Curry, Adrianne (Model, Reality Star)
c/o Phil Viardo *The Viardo Agency*
8484 Wilshire Blvd Ste 220
Beverly Hills, CA 90211-3223, USA

Curry, Alana (Actor)
c/o JD Sobol *Almond Talent Management*
8217 Beverly Blvd Ste 8
W Hollywood, CA 90048-4534, USA

Curry, Ann (Television Host)
181 Ferris Hill Rd
New Canaan, CT 06840-3826, USA

Curry, Ayesha (Chef)
c/o Robert Flutie *Flutie Entertainment*
5161 Lankershim Blvd Ste 400
North Hollywood, CA 91601-4964, USA

Curry, Bill (Athlete, Coach, Football Coach, Football Player)
Wellborn, Wallace & Woodard LLC
1175 Peachtree St NE Ste 300
100 Colony Sq. #300 (Attn: Susan Wellborn)
Atlanta, GA 30361-3538, USA

Curry, Buddy (Athlete, Football Player)
4407 Trestle Way
Buford, GA 30518-6055, USA

Curry, Craig (Athlete, Football Player)
5419 Pine Wood Meadows Ln
Spring, TX 77386-3979, USA

Curry, Dell (Athlete, Basketball Player)
1615 Rutledge Ave
Charlotte, NC 28211-2752, USA

Curry, Demarcus (Athlete, Football Player)
765 Forest Crossing Dr SW
Atlanta, GA 30331-7387, USA

Curry, Denise (Athlete, Basketball Player, Coach)
21 Maple Dr
Aliso Viejo, CA 92656-4273, USA

Curry, Denzel (Musician)
c/o Mike Malak *Coda Music Agency (UK)*
56 Compton St
Clerkenwell
London EC1V 0ET, UNITED KINGDOM

Curry, Don (Athlete, Boxer, Olympic Athlete)
2509 McKenzie St
Fort Worth, TX 76105-3940, USA

Curry, Don (DC) (Actor, Comedian)
c/o Tony Spires *Full Circle Entertainment*
6320 Canoga Ave Ste 1550
Woodland Hills, CA 91367-2563, USA

Curry, Eddy (Athlete, Basketball Player)
17 Magnolia Dr
Purchase, NY 10577-1137, USA

Curry, Eric F (Athlete, Football Player)
PO Box 17321
Jacksonville, FL 32245-7321, USA

Curry, Mark (Actor)
12200 W Olympic Blvd Ste 499
Los Angeles, CA 90064-1041, USA

Curry, Mike (Athlete, Basketball Player)
2880 Wells Dr
Augusta, GA 30906-5373, USA

Curry, Ronald (Athlete, Football Player)
1881 Brawley School Rd
Mooresville, NC 28117-7084, USA

Curry, Roy (Athlete, Football Player)
9045 S Paxton Ave
Chicago, IL 60617-3814, USA

Curry, Stephen (Athlete, Basketball Player)
c/o Jeff Austin *Octagon Home Office*
7950 Jones Branch Dr # 700N
Mc Lean, VA 22107-0002, USA

Curry, Steve (Athlete, Baseball Player)
10725 Obee Rd
Whitehouse, OH 43571-9250, USA

Curry, Tim (Actor, Musician)
c/o Gilly Sanquinetti *The Artists Partnership*
101 Finsbury Pavement
London EC2A 1RS, UNITED KINGDOM

Curry, Valorie (Actor)
c/o Ron West *Thruline Entertainment*
9250 Wilshire Blvd Fl Ground
Beverly Hills, CA 90212-3352, USA

Curry, Vinny (Athlete, Football Player)
c/o Jimmy Sexton *CAA (Memphis)*
6060 Poplar Ave Ste 470
Memphis, TN 38119-0910, USA

Curtale, Tony (Athlete, Hockey Player)
6450 Double Eagle Dr APT 605
Woodridge, IL 60517-1599, USA

Curtin, Catherine (Actor)
c/o Lucy Middleweek *Middleweek Newton Talent Management*
47 Bedford St
London WC2E 9HA, UNITED KINGDOM

Curtin, Jane (Actor)
c/o Toni Howard *ICM Partners*
10250 Constellation Blvd Fl 7
Los Angeles, CA 90067-6207, USA

Curtin, Valerie (Actor)
15622 Meadowgate Rd
Encino, CA 91436-3431, USA

Curtis, Ben (Actor)
c/o Staff Member *Abrams Artists Agency*
275 7th Ave Fl 26
New York, NY 10001-6708, USA

Curtis, Ben (Athlete, Golfer)
8959 Bevington Ln
Orlando, FL 32827-7058, USA

Curtis, Bonnie (Producer)
c/o Staff Member *Mockingbird Pictures, LLC*
2312 Lorenzo Dr
Los Angeles, CA 90068-2726, USA

Curtis, Chad (Athlete, Baseball Player)
621 Eagle Point Rd
Lake Odessa, MI 48849-9445, USA

Curtis, Cliff (Actor)
c/o Joseph (Joe) Rice *JR Talent Group*
Prefers to be contacted by email or phone.
Los Angeles, CA NA, USA

Curtis, Don (Wrestler)
920 Middleton Rd
Jacksonville, FL 32211-6273, USA

Curtis, Isaac F (Athlete, Football Player)
711 Clinton Springs Ave
Cincinnati, OH 45229-1300, USA

Curtis, Jack (Athlete, Baseball Player)
4949 Ike Starnes Rd
Granite Falls, NC 28630-8631, USA

Curtis, Jamie Lee (Actor)
c/o Heidi Schaeffer *PMK/BNC Public Relations*
1840 Century Park E Ste 1400
Los Angeles, CA 90067-2115, USA

Curtis, John (Athlete, Baseball Player)
1800 Roundhill Rd Apt 1207
Charleston, WV 25314-1559, USA

Curtis, John (Athlete, Baseball Player)
3125 Leeman Ferry Rd SW
Attn Coaching Staff
Huntsville, AL 35801-5331, USA

Curtis, Kelly (Actor)
651 N Kilkea Dr
Los Angeles, CA 90048-2213, USA

Curtis, Kenneth (Politician)
15 Piper Rd Apt J103
Scarborough, ME 04074-7561, USA

Curtis, King (Baseball Player)
St Louis Cardinals
2538 Beechwood Dr
Vineland, NJ 08361-2932, USA

Curtis, Liane (Actor)
11749 Palms Blvd
Los Angeles, CA 90066-2030, USA

Curtis, Mike (Athlete, Football Player)
940 Water Lily Ct NE
Saint Petersburg, FL 33703-3136, USA

Curtis, Nicole (Designer, Reality Star, Television Host)
Keller Williams Realty
1350 Lagoon Ave Ste 900
Minneapolis, MN 55408-2692, USA

Curtis, Paul (Athlete, Hockey Player)
PO Box 6325
Abilene, TX 79608-6325, USA

Curtis, Richard (Writer)
c/o Anthony Jones *United Agents*
12-26 Lexington St
London W1F OLE, UNITED KINGDOM

Curtis, Robin (Actor)
1147 Beverly Hill Dr
Cincinnati, OH 45208-4323, USA

Curtis, Scott (Athlete, Football Player)
31661 Prairie Dunes Ct
Evergreen, CO 80439-5902, USA

Curtis, Todd (Actor)
2046 14th St Apt 10
Santa Monica, CA 90405-1641, USA

Curtis, Tom (Athlete, Football Player)
5433 NW 94th Doral Pl
Doral, FL 33178, USA

Curtis, Travis (Athlete, Football Player)
9905 Sorrel Ave
Potomac, MD 20854-4703, USA

Curtola, Bobby (Musician)
ESP Productions
720 Spadina Ave PH 2
Toronto, ON M5S 2T9, CANADA

Cusack, Ann (Actor)
Innovative Artists
1505 10th St
Santa Monica, CA 90401-2805, USA

Cusack, Joan (Actor, Comedian)
60 E Cedar St
Chicago, IL 60611-1179, USA

Cusack, John (Actor)
941 S Vermont Ave Ste 101
Los Angeles, CA 90006-1686, USA

Cusack, Sinead (Actor)
Markham & Froggatt Julian House
4 Windmill St.
London W1P 1HF, UNITED KINGDOM (UK)

Cuschieri, Paul (Writer)
c/o Naren Desai *Brillstein Entertainment Partners*
9150 Wilshire Blvd Ste 350
Beverly Hills, CA 90212-3453, USA

Cuse, Carlton (Producer)
c/o Staff Member *WME|IMG*
9601 Wilshire Blvd
Beverly Hills, CA 90210-5213, USA

Cushenan, Ian (Athlete, Hockey Player)
4014 Dryden Dr
North Olmsted, OH 44070-1928, USA

Cushing, Brian (Athlete, Football Player)
c/o Drew Rosenhaus *Rosenhaus Sports Representation*
3921 Alton Rd # 440
Miami Beach, FL 33140-3852, USA

Cushing, Matt (Athlete, Football Player)
5752 Lyman Ave
Downers Grove, IL 60516-1401, USA

Cushman, Karen (Writer)
17804 Thorsen Rd SW
Vashon, WA 98070-4502, USA

Cusick, Henry Ian (Actor)
c/o Abi Harris *The Artists Partnership*
101 Finsbury Pavement
London EC2A 1RS, UNITED KINGDOM

Cusick, Pete (Athlete, Football Player)
807 Esplanade
Redondo Beach, CA 90277-4734, USA

Cussler, Clive (Writer)
c/o Bert Fields *Greenberg Glusker*
1900 Avenue of the Stars Ste 2100
Los Angeles, CA 90067-4502, USA

Cust, Jack (Athlete, Baseball Player)
9 Club House Dr
Whitehouse Station, NJ 08889-3366, USA

Custer, Brian (Commentator, Sportscaster)
c/o Staff Member *Showtime Networks*
1633 Broadway
New York, NY 10019-6708, USA

Cutcliffe, David (Coach, Football Coach)
University of Mississippi
Athletic Dept
University, MS 38677, USA

Cut Copy (Music Group)
c/o Allie Larson *Girlie Action*
243 W 30th St Fl 12
New York, NY 10001-2812, USA

Cute Is What We Aim For (Music Group)
Fueled By Ramen
PO Box 1803
Tampa, FL 33601-1803, USA

Cuthbert, Elisha (Actor)
c/o Dominique Appel *Imprint PR*
6121 W Sunset Blvd
Neuehouse
Los Angeles, CA 90028-6442, USA

Cuthbert, Randy (Athlete, Football Player)
6169 Valley Forge Dr
Coopersburg, PA 18036, USA

Cutkosky, Ethan (Actor)
c/o Marni Rosenzweig *The Rosenzweig Group*
8840 Wilshire Blvd # 111
Beverly Hills, CA 90211-2606, USA

Cutler, Alexander M (Business Person)
Eaton Corp
1000 Eaton Blvd
Eaton Center
Beachwood, OH 44122-6058, USA

Cutler, Dave (Athlete, Football Player)
4980 Cordova Bay Rd
Victoria, BC V8Y 2K2, Canada

Cutler, Jay (Athlete, Football Player)
c/o Bus Cook *Bus Cook Sports, Inc*
1 Willow Bend Dr
Hattiesburg, MS 39402-8552, USA

Cutler, Jay (Athlete)
c/o Brad Marks *Blue Five Media*
9150 Wilshire Blvd Ste 103
Beverly Hills, CA 90212-3428, USA

Cutler, RJ (Director, Producer)
c/o Amanda Lundberg *42West*
600 3rd Ave Fl 23
New York, NY 10016-1914, USA

Cutliffe, Molly (Actor)
Herney/Grimes
PO Box 64249
Los Angeles, CA 90064-0249, USA

Cutrone, Kelly (Business Person, Reality Star)
People's Revolution Inc
62 Grand St Apt 3
New York, NY 10013-2245, USA

Cutrufello, Mary (Musician, Songwriter, Writer)
Joe's Garage
4405 Belmont Park Ter
Nashville, TN 37215-3609, USA

Cutsinger, Gary (Athlete, Football Player)
600 Mountain Dew
Horseshoe Bay, TX 78657-6341, USA

Cutter, Kiki (Skier)
PO Box 1317
Carbondale, CO 81623-1317, USA

Cutter, Lise (Actor)
36 Poplar St
Sag Harbor, NY 11963-1718, USA

Cutter, Slade D (Athlete, Football Player)
9214 River Crescent Dr
Annapolis, MD 21401-7770, USA

Cutts, Don (Athlete, Hockey Player)
222 15th St NW
Main Floor
Calgary, AB T2N 2A7, CANADA

Cuwinski, Kevin (Race Car Driver)
Brevak Racing
206 Performance Rd
Mooresville, NC 28115-9591, USA

Cuyler, Milt (Athlete, Baseball Player)
962 Lamar Rd
Macon, GA 31210-7109, USA

Cuzzi, Phil (Athlete, Baseball Player)
32 Mapes Ave
Nutley, NJ 07110-1410, USA

Cwiklinski, Stanley (Athlete, Olympic Athlete)
2840 Maple St
San Diego, CA 92104-4940, USA

C. Woolsey, Lynn (Congressman, Politician)
2263 Rayburn Hob
Washington, DC 20515-0506, USA

Cyler, RJ (Actor)
c/o Nic de Armendi *JLA Talent Agency*
9151 W Sunset Blvd
West Hollywood, CA 90069-3106, USA

C. Young, Todd (Congressman, Politician)
1721 Longworth Hob
Washington, DC 20515-4326, USA

Cypher, Jon (Actor)
498 Manzanita Ave
Ventura, CA 93001-2227, USA

Cyphers, Charles (Actor)
c/o Chris Roe *Chris Roe Management*
PO Box 761
Burbank, CA 91503-0761, USA

Cypress Hill (Music Group)
c/o David Benveniste *Velvet Hammer*
9014 Melrose Ave
Los Angeles, CA 90069-5610, USA

Cyprien, Jonathan (Athlete, Football Player)
c/o Drew Rosenhaus *Rosenhaus Sports Representation*
3921 Alton Rd # 440
Miami Beach, FL 33140-3852, USA

Cyr, Denis (Athlete, Hockey Player)
9816 N Townsend Dr
Peoria, IL 61615-1388, USA

Cyrus, Billy Ray (Musician, Songwriter)
c/o Bob Kinkead *The Kinkead Entertainment Agency*
253 Jackson Meadows Dr
Hermitage, TN 37076-1426, USA

Cyrus, Brandi (Actor)
c/o Staff Member *United Talent Agency (UTA)*
9336 Civic Center Dr
Beverly Hills, CA 90210-3604, USA

Cyrus, Miley (Actor, Musician)
c/o Evelyn O'Neill *Management 360*
9111 Wilshire Blvd
Beverly Hills, CA 90210-5508, USA

Cywinski, Kevin (Race Car Driver)
709 Performance Rd
Mooresville, NC 28115-9596, USA

Czajkowski, Jim (Athlete, Baseball Player)
1648 Rivergate Dr
Sevierville, TN 37862-9321, USA

Czemy, Henry (Actor)
438 Queen St E
Toronto, ON M5A 1T4, CANADA

Czerny, Henry (Actor)

Czuchery, Matt (Actor)
c/o Ashley Franklin *Thruline Entertainment*
9250 Wilshire Blvd Fl Ground
Beverly Hills, CA 90212-3352, USA

Czuchry, Matt (Actor)
c/o Jeff Golenberg *Silver Lining Entertainment*
421 S Beverly Dr Fl 7
Beverly Hills, CA 90212-4408, USA

Czyz, Bobby (Athlete, Boxer)

D

D, Chuck (Musician)
c/o Walter F. Leaphart Jr *Creamworks*
8391 Beverly Blvd Ste 352
Los Angeles, CA 90048-2633, USA

D, Deezer (Actor)
c/o Staff Member *Commercial Talent*
12711 Ventura Blvd Ste 285
Studio City, CA 91604-2487, USA

D, Mike (Musician)
7126 Fernhill Dr
Malibu, CA 90265-4243, USA

D-12 (Musician)
Evolution Talent Agency
1776 Broadway Fl 15
New York, NY 10019-2002

D12 (Music Group)
c/o Staff Member *WME|IMG (NY)*
11 Madison Ave Fl 18
New York, NY 10010-3669, USA

Daal, Omar (Athlete, Baseball Player)
2130 E Aris Dr
Gilbert, AZ 85298-1203, USA

Daanen, Jerome (Athlete, Football Player)
1011 S Erie St
De Pere, WI 54115-3109, USA

D'Abaldo, Chris (Musician)
Helter Skelter Plaza
535 Kings Road
London SW10 0S, UNITED KINGDOM (UK)

Da Band (Music Group)
c/o Staff Member *Combs Enterprises*
1440 Broadway Frnt 3
New York, NY 10018-2301, USA

Dabich, Mike (Athlete, Basketball Player)
PO Box 236
Hudson, WY 82515-0236, USA

Dabney, Carlton (Athlete, Football Player)
2522 Northumberland Ave
Richmond, VA 23220-1504, USA

D'Abo, Maryam (Actor)
Artist Independent
32 Tavistock St
London WC2E 7PB, UNITED KINGDOM (UK)

D'Abo, Olivia (Actor)
8500 Melrose Ave Ste 208
W Hollywood, CA 90069-5169, USA

Da Brat (Musician)
c/o Staff Member *WME|IMG*
9601 Wilshire Blvd
Beverly Hills, CA 90210-5213, USA

Dacascos, Mark (Actor)
2811 Stonecutter St
Thousand Oaks, CA 91362-5786, USA

Dackell, Andreas (Athlete, Hockey Player)
Tegnervagan 1
Gavle 822 67, Sweden

Da Costa, Rebecca (Actor)
c/o Liza Anderson *Anderson Group Public Relations*
8060 Melrose Ave Fl 4
Los Angeles, CA 90046-7038, USA

Dacquisto, John (Athlete, Baseball Player)
32010 N 20th Ln
Phoenix, AZ 85085-7081, USA

D'Acquisto, John F (Athlete, Baseball Player)
1441 Santa Lucia Rd Unit 615
Chula Vista, CA 91913-3600, USA

Dacruz Policarpo, Jose Cardinal (Religious Leader)
Curia Patriarcal
Camo dos Martires da Patria 45
Lisbon 01150, PORTUGAL

Dacus, Don (Actor)
8455 Fountain Ave Unit 512
Los Angeles, CA 90069-2543, USA

Daddario, Alexandra (Actor)
c/o Lindsay Galin *Rogers & Cowan*
909 3rd Ave Fl 9
New York, NY 10022-4752, USA

Daddario, Matthew (Actor, Musician)
c/o Donnalyn Carfi *Harvest Talent Management*
127 W 83rd St Unit 887
New York, NY 10024-0814, USA

Dade, Paul (Athlete, Baseball Player)
5212 66th Street Ct W
University Place, WA 98467-3337, USA

da Don, Polow (Musician)
c/o Laura Wright *Avid Exposure*
1179 W A St Ste 233
Hayward, CA 94541-7006, USA

Dadswell, Doug (Athlete, Hockey Player)
54-10030 Oakmoor Way SW
Calgary, AB T2V 4S8, Canada

Daehlie, Bjorn (Skier)
Cathinka Guldbergs Veg 64
Holler 02034, NORWAY

Daetweiler, Louella (Baseball Player)
415 S Poplar Ave
Brea, CA 92821-6650, USA

Dafoe, Byron (Athlete, Hockey Player)
6620 Lakeshore Rd
Kelowna, BC V1W 4J5, Canada

Dafoe, Willem (Actor)
c/o Frank Frattaroli *Circle of Confusion*
8931 Ellis Ave
Los Angeles, CA 90034-3336, USA

Daft, Douglas (Business Person)
Coca Cola Co
1 Coca Cola Plz NW
310 North Ave NW
Atlanta, GA 30313-2499, USA

Daft, Kevin (Athlete, Football Player)
6033 Old Quarry Loop
Oakland, CA 94605-3375, USA

Daft Punk (Music Group)
c/o Peter Elliot *Primary Talent International (UK)*
10-11 Jockeys Fields
The Primary Bldg
London WC1R 4BN, UNITED KINGDOM

Daggett, Jensen (Actor)
682 Palisades Dr
Pacific Palisades, CA 90272-2853, USA

Daggett, Timothy (Tim) (Gymnast)
3730 N Ocean Dr Unit 12B
Riviera Beach, FL 33404-3287, USA

Daghe, Noelle (Athlete, Golfer)
1300 Tamarac St
Denver, CO 80220-3325, USA

Dagleish, John (Actor)
c/o Romilly Bowlby *DDA Public Relations*
192-198 Vauxhall Bridge Rd
London SW1V 1DX, UNITED KINGDOM

D'Agosto, Nicholas (Actor)
c/o Faras Rabadi *Emerald Talent Group*
3500 W Olive Ave Ste 300
Burbank, CA 91505-4647, USA

Dagres, Angie (Athlete, Baseball Player)
35 Railroad Ave
Rowley, MA 01969-1202, USA

Dagworthy Prew, Wendy A (Designer, Fashion Designer)
18 Melrose Terrace
London W6, UNITED KINGDOM (UK)

Dahan, Olivier (Director)
c/o David Vatinet *Agents Associes (AA)*
201 Rue Du Faubourg Saint
Honore Ile-de-france 75008, FRANCE

Dahl, Ariene (Actor)
Dahlmark Productions
PO Box 116
Sparkill, NY 10976-0116, USA

Dahl, Arlene (Actor)
PO Box 116
Sparkill, NY 10976-0116, USA

Dahl, Bob (Athlete, Football Player)
363 Elliots Hill Ln
Lexington, VA 24450-7202, USA

Dahl, Craig (Athlete, Football Player)
62503 Shorewood Ln
Madison Lake, MN 56063-4434, USA

Dahl, Dave (Correspondent)
KSTP
3415 University Ave SE
Minneapolis, MN 55414-3365, USA

Dahl, John (Director, Writer)
c/o Jason Spitz *WME|IMG*
9601 Wilshire Blvd
Beverly Hills, CA 90210-5213, USA

Dahl, Kevin (Athlete, Hockey Player)
4000 Astoria Way
Avon, OH 44011-3426, USA

Dahl, Sophie (Actor, Model)
c/o Lindy King *United Agents*
12-26 Lexington St
London W1F OLE, UNITED KINGDOM

Dahlen, Ulf (Athlete, Hockey Player)
2500 Victory Ave
Dallas, TX 75219-7601, USA

Dahler, Ed (Athlete, Basketball Player)
511 E Tremont St
Hillsboro, IL 62049-1801, USA

Dahlin, Kjell (Athlete, Hockey Player)
Sidvallsgatan 5
Karlstad 654 65, Sweden

Dahllof, Eva (Athlete, Golfer)
419 Glen Crest Dr
Moore, SC 29369-9287, USA

Dahlquist, Chris (Athlete, Hockey Player)
10859 Purdey Rd
Eden Prairie, MN 55347-5236, USA

Dahm, Jaclyn (Actor)
c/o Amy Godsick *Candy Entertainment Management*
8981 W Sunset Blvd Ste 310
West Hollywood, CA 90069-1848, USA

Dai, Sijie (Writer)
c/o Staff Member *Knopf*
1745 Broadway Frnt 3
New York, NY 10019-4343, USA

Daiches, David (Writer)
22 Belgrave Crescent
Edinburgh EH4 3AL, SCOTLAND

Daigle, Alain (Athlete, Hockey Player)
3510 Rue de Bordeaux
Trois-Rivieres, QC G8Y 3P7, Canada

Daigle, Alexander (Athlete, Hockey Player)
3510 Rue de Bordeaux
Trois-Rivieres, QC G8Y 3P7, Canada

Daigle, Casey (Athlete, Baseball Player)
2607 Wpa Rd
Sulphur, LA 70663-9408, USA

Daigneau, Maurice (Athlete, Football Player)
32 Redmond Ave
Buffalo, NY 14216-1511, USA

Daigneault, J J (Athlete, Coach, Hockey Player)
c/o Staff Member *Hartford Wolf Pack*
196 Trumbull St Fl 3
Hartford, CT 06103-2207, USA

Daigneault, Rejean (Horse Racer)
95 Hildreth Pl
Yonkers, NY 10704-2220, USA

Dailey, Bill (Athlete, Baseball Player)
5019 Meadow Way
Dublin, VA 24084-5721, USA

Dailey, Dianne (Athlete, Golfer)
4220 Stonehenge Ln
Lakeland, FL 33813, USA

Daily, Elizabeth (EG) (Actor, Musician)
6 Star Ventures
100 S Doheny Dr
Los Angeles, CA 90048-2955, USA

Daily, Parker (Religious Leader)
Baptist Bible Fellowship International
PO Box 191
Springfield, MO 65801-0191, USA

Daingerfield, Michael (Actor)
c/o Staff Member *Kirk Talent Agencies Inc*
196 3rd Ave W Suite 102
Vancouver, BC V5Y 1E9, CANADA

Daisey, Gene (Horse Racer)
5335 Havasu Ct
Lake Worth, FL 33467-5533, USA

Dajani, Nadia (Actor)
22 Perry St # 3C/D
New York, NY 10014-2775, USA

Dalberto, Michel (Musician)
13 Blvd Henri Plumof
Vevey 01800, SWITZERLAND

Daldry, Stephen (Director)
c/o Leslee Dart *42West*
600 3rd Ave Fl 23
New York, NY 10016-1914, USA

Dale, Alan (Actor)
c/o Dan Baron *Agency for the Performing Arts (APA)*
405 S Beverly Dr Ste 500
Beverly Hills, CA 90212-4425, USA

Dale, Carl (Athlete, Baseball Player)
4916 Cedar Creek Cir
Cookeville, TN 38501-9621, USA

Dale, Carroll (Athlete, Football Player)
9533 Coeburn Mountain Rd
Wise, VA 24293-7331, USA

Dale, Dick (Actor)
PO Box 1713
Twentynine Palms, CA 92277-1000, USA

Dale, James Badge (Actor)
255 E 7th St Apt 3F
New York, NY 10009-6077, USA

Dale, Jerry (Athlete, Baseball Player)
2112 Middlewood Dr
Maryville, TN 37803-6374, USA

Dale, Jim (Actor)
Mark Sendroff
230 W 56th St Apt 63B
New York, NY 10019-0077, USA

Dale & Grace (Music Group)
Sea Cruise Productions
PO Box 1875
Gretna, LA 70054-1875, USA

Dalembert, Samuel (Athlete, Basketball Player)
899 NE Orchid Bay Dr
Boca Raton, FL 33487-1751, USA

Dalena, Pete (Athlete, Baseball Player)
4951 N Thorne Ave
Fresno, CA 93704-2935, USA

D'Aleo, Angelo (Musician)
Paramount Entertainment
PO Box 12
Far Hills, NJ 07931-0012, USA

Dalesandro, Mark (Athlete, Baseball Player)
1908 Arbor Fields Dr
Plainfield, IL 60586-5729, USA

Dale Scott, Cynthia (Actor)
c/o Derek Maki *Coolwaters Productions*
10061 Riverside Dr # 531
Toluca Lake, CA 91602-2560, USA

Dales-Schuman, Stacey (Basketball Player)
Washington Mystics
601 F St NW
Mcl Center
Washington, DC 20004-1605, USA

D'Alessio, Diana (Athlete, Golfer)
6955 Nunn Rd
Lakeland, FL 33813-3821, USA

D'Alessio, Diana (Golfer)
6955 Nunn Rd
Lakeland, FL 33813-3821, USA

Daley, Bill (Athlete, Baseball Player)
SBC Communications
4370 Brookside Ct Apt 302
Minneapolis, MN 55436-1441, USA

Daley, Bud (Athlete, Baseball Player)
922 Moose Dr
Riverton, WY 82501-2537, USA

Daley, Joe (Athlete, Hockey Player)
Joe Daley's Cards
666 St James St
Winnipeg, MB R3G 3J6, Canada

Daley, John (Golfer)
c/o Staff Member *Pro Golfers Assoc of America (PGA)*
112 TPC Blvd
Ponte Vedra Beach, FL 32082-3077, USA

Daley, John (Golfer)
10015 E Mountain View Rd Apt 2126
Scottsdale, AZ 85258-5221, USA

Daley, John Francis (Actor)
c/o Maria Herrera *PMK/BNC Public Relations*
1840 Century Park E Ste 1400
Los Angeles, CA 90067-2115, USA

Daley, Matt (Athlete, Baseball Player)
173 Kildare Rd
Garden City, NY 11530-1120, USA

Daley, Patrick (Athlete, Hockey Player)
118 Mount Olive Dr
Toronto, ON M9V 2E2, Canada

Daley, Pete (Athlete, Baseball Player)
4019 Calle Mira Monte
Newbury Park, CA 91320-1932, USA

Daley, Richard M (Politician)
Mayor's Office
121 N La Salle St
City Hall
Chicago, IL 60602-1202, USA

Daley, Tom (Athlete, Olympic Athlete, Swimmer)
c/o Staff Member *James Grant Group Ltd*
94 Strand On the Green
Chiswick
London W4 3NN, UNITED KINGDOM

Dalgarno, Brad (Athlete, Hockey Player)
1146 Fairfield Pl
Oakville, ON L6M 2L9, Canada

Dalgilsh, Kenneth M (Kenny) (Coach, Soccer Player)
c/o Staff Member *Liverpool FC Football Club*
69/71 Anfield Road
Liverpool L4 OTQ, UNITED KINGDOM

Dalheimer, Patrick (Musician)
Freedman & Smith
350 W End Ave Apt 1
New York, NY 10024-6818, USA

Dali, Tracy (Actor, Model)
JAS Entertainment Squad
7119 W Sunset Blvd # 261
P.O. Box 261
Los Angeles, CA 90046-4411, USA

Dalian, Susan (Actor)
c/o Staff Member *GVA Talent Agency Inc*
193 N Robertson Blvd
Beverly Hills, CA 90211-2103, USA

Dalie, Beatrice (Actor)
Artmedia
20 Ave Rapp
Paris 75007, FRANCE

Dalkas, Nicole (Athlete, Golfer)
288 Green Mountain Dr
Palm Desert, CA 92211-3246, USA

Dalkowski, Steve (Baseball Player)
Walnut Hill Care Center 55 Grand St
New Britain, CT 06052-2021, USA

Dall, Bobby (Musician)
160 Ocean Oaks Dr
Indialantic, FL 32903-2732, USA

Dallafior, Ken (Athlete, Football Player)
188 Four Seasons Dr
Lake Orion, MI 48360-2645, USA

Dallas, Cameron (Internet Star)
c/o Cynthia Pett-Dante *Brillstein Entertainment Partners*
9150 Wilshire Blvd Ste 350
Beverly Hills, CA 90212-3453, USA

Dallas, Joshua (Actor)
c/o John Carrabino *John Carrabino Management*
5900 Wilshire Blvd Ste 740
Los Angeles, CA 90036-5032, USA

Dallas, Matt (Actor)
c/o Staff Member *Astoria Entertainment*
1145 N Hudson Ave
Los Angeles, CA 90038-1405, USA

Dallas Cowboys Cheerleaders (Athlete, Dancer, Music Group)
Dallas Cowboys Football
1 Cowboys Way Ste 100
Frisco, TX 75034-1977, USA

Dallenbach Jr., Wally (Race Car Driver)
2561 Frying Pan Rd
Basalt, CO 81621-9715, USA

Dallesandro, Joe (Actor)
c/o Stann Findelle *Stann Findelle Management*
2029 Century Park E Ste 900
Los Angeles, CA 90067-2910, USA

Dalley, Amy (Musician)
c/o Staff Member *Curb Records (Nashville)*
48 Music Sq E
Nashville, TN 37203-4639, USA

Dallimore, Brian (Athlete, Baseball Player)
10531 Haywood Dr
Las Vegas, NV 89135-2850, USA

Dallman, Marty (Athlete, Hockey Player)
3843 Main St
Niagara Falls, ON L2G 6B4, Canada

Dalmacci, Ricardo (Actor)
c/o Gabriel Blanco *Gabriel Blanco Iglesias (Mexico)*
Rio Balsas 35-32
Colonia Cuauhtemoc
DF 06500, Mexico

Dalmas, Yannick (Race Car Driver)
Rue Raimus
83330 Le Beaunet
FRANCE

Dalrymple, Clay (Athlete, Baseball Player)
28248 Mateer Rd
Gold Beach, OR 97444-9618, USA

Dalton, Andy (Athlete, Football Player)
c/o W Vann McElroy *Select Sports Group*
2700 Post Oak Blvd Ste 1450
Houston, TX 77056-5785, USA

Dalton, Audrey (Actor)
22461 Labrusca
Mission Viejo, CA 92692-1325, USA

Dalton, Brett (Actor)
c/o Emily Gerson Saines *Brookside Artists Management*
250 W 57th St Ste 1820
New York, NY 10107-1802, USA

Dalton, Jake (Athlete, Gymnast, Olympic Athlete)
c/o Staff Member *Radegen Sports Management, LLC*
30 W 36th St Rm 301
New York, NY 10018-8013, USA

Dalton, Kristen (Actor)
c/o Sharon Vitro *Zero Gravity Management*
11110 Ohio Ave Ste 100
Los Angeles, CA 90025-3329, USA

Dalton, Lacy J (Musician)
820 Cartwright Rd
Reno, NV 89521-7134, USA

Dalton, Lional (Athlete, Football Player)
9858 Clint Moore Rd Ste 128
Boca Raton, FL 33496-1033, USA

Dalton, Mike (Athlete, Baseball Player)
42410 Palm Ave
Fremont, CA 94539-4729, USA

Dalton, Nic (Musician)
c/o Staff Member *UTA/The Agency Group*
888 7th Ave Fl 7
New York, NY 10106-0700, USA

Dalton, Nicole (Actor)
c/o Staff Member *Commonwealth Talent Group*
PO Box 36514
Los Angeles, CA 90036-0514, USA

Dalton, Oakley (Athlete, Football Player)
3647 Highway 131
Washburn, TN 37888-4015, USA

Dalton, Piercey (Actor)
c/o Ben Phelps *Emagine Content*
8033 W Sunset Blvd # 580
Los Angeles, CA 90046-2401, USA

Dalton, Timothy (Actor)
8322 Marmont Ln
Los Angeles, CA 90069-1637, USA

Daltrey, Roger (Actor, Musician)
c/o Harry Gold *TalentWorks*
3500 W Olive Ave Ste 1400
Burbank, CA 91505-5512, USA

Daluiso, Brad (Athlete, Football Player)
13258 Glencliff Way
San Diego, CA 92130-1309, USA

Daly, Andy (Actor, Comedian)
c/o Lewis Kay *Kovert Creative*
506 Santa Monica Blvd Ste 400
Santa Monica, CA 90401-2412, USA

Daly, Carson (Television Host)
133 Elderfields Rd
Manhasset, NY 11030-1648, USA

Daly, Derek (Race Car Driver)
18300 Deshane Ave
Noblesville, IN 46060-9627, USA

Daly, John (Athlete, Golfer)
10093 Par St
Dardanelle, AR 72834-8793, USA

Daly, Rad (Actor)

Daly, Robert (Baseball Player)
Los Angeles Dodgers
10779 Bellagio Rd
Los Angeles, CA 90077-3731, USA

Daly, Tess (Model, Television Host)
c/o Staff Member *John Noel Management*
10A Belmont St
Floor 2
London NW1 8HH, UNITED KINGDOM (UK)

Daly, Tim (Actor, Producer)
c/o Amy Guenther *Gateway Management Company Inc*
860 Via De La Paz Ste F10
Pacific Palisades, CA 90272-3631, USA

Daly, Tyne (Actor)
1617 N Sierra Bonita Ave
Los Angeles, CA 90046-2815, USA

Daly-Donofrio, Heather (Athlete, Golfer)
1285 Sunningdale Ln
Ormond Beach, FL 32174-1406, USA

Damageplan (Music Group)
2706 Monterrey St
Arlington, TX 76015-1323, USA

Damas, Bertila (Actor)
PO Box 17193
Beverly Hills, CA 90209-3193, USA

Damaska, Jack (Athlete, Baseball Player)
252 Blackhawk Rd
Beaver Falls, PA 15010-1404, USA

D'Amato, Lisa (Musician)
c/o Staff Member *Brendan Vaughn*
Prefers to be contact via telephone or email
Los Angeles, CA 90069, USA

D'Amato, Mike (Athlete, Football Player)
17961 Bonita National Blvd Unit 531
Bonita Springs, FL 34135-8715, USA

DaMatta, Cristiano (Race Car Driver)
Newman-Haas Racing
500 Tower Pkwy
Lincolnshire, IL 60069-3642, USA

Dames, Romi (Actor)
c/o Nicole Walter *Metro Public Relations*
8671 Wilshire Blvd # 208
Beverly Hills, CA 90211-2926, USA

Dameshek, David (Actor, Writer)
c/o Staff Member *Creative Artists Agency (CAA)*
2000 Avenue of the Stars Ste 100
Los Angeles, CA 90067-4705, USA

Damian, Alexa (Actor)
c/o Staff Member *Televisa*
Blvd Adolfo Lopez Mateos 232
Colonia San Angel INN
DF CP 01060, MEXICO

Damian, Michael (Actor, Musician)
SCS
4412 Whitsett Ave
C/O Estelle Harrison
Studio City, CA 91604-1361, USA

Damiani, Damiano (Director)
Via Delle Terme Deciane 2
Rome 00153, ITALY

D'Amico, Jeff (Athlete, Baseball Player)
30 Evelyn Ct
Oldsmar, FL 34677-2322, USA

Damico, Jeff (Athlete, Baseball Player)
2223 Muirfield Way
Oldsmar, FL 34677-1942, USA

Damico, Jeff (Athlete, Baseball Player)
9567 NE North Town Loop
Bainbridge Island, WA 98110-3532, USA

D'Amico, William D (Athlete)
30 Greenwood St
Lake Placid, NY 12946-1214, USA

Damkroger, Maury (Athlete, Football Player)
1722 S 166th Cir
Omaha, NE 68130-1502, USA

Dammerman, Dennis D (Business Person)
General Electric Co
3135 Easton Tumpike
Fairfield, CT 06828, USA

Damon, Grey (Actor)
c/o Toni Benson *Thirdhill Entertainment*
195 S Beverly Dr Ste 400
Beverly Hills, CA 90212-3044, USA

Damon, Johnny (Athlete, Baseball Player)
PO Box 8540
Stockton, CA 95208-0540, USA

Damon, Mark (Actor)
2781 Benedict Canyon Dr
Beverly Hills, CA 90210-1024, USA

Damon, Matt (Actor)
Pearl Street Films
1660 Euclid St
Santa Monica, CA 90404-3724, USA

Damon, Stuart (Actor)
16321 Pacific Coast Hwy Spc 152
Pacific Palisades, CA 90272-4771, USA

Damon, Una (Actor)
c/o Suzanne DeWalt *Dewalt & Musik Management*
623 N Parish Pl
Burbank, CA 91506-1701, USA

Damore, John (Athlete, Football Player)
627 Citadel Dr
Westmont, IL 60559-1297, USA

D'Amour, Marc (Athlete, Hockey Player)
70 Jacobs Creek Dr
Hershey, PA 17033-8918, USA

Damphousse, Vincent (Athlete, Hockey Player)
c/o Staff Member *NHL Players Association*
1700-20 Bay St
Toronto, ON M5J 2N8, Canada

Dampier, Erick (Athlete, Basketball Player)
18724 Wainsborough Ln
Dallas, TX 75287-5525, USA

Dampier, Louie (Athlete, Basketball Player)
2808 New Moody Ln
La Grange, KY 40031-9453, USA

Dampler, Louie (Basketball Player)
Dampler Ditributing
2808 New Moody Ln
La Grange, KY 40031-9453, USA

Damron, Robert (Athlete, Golfer)
5632 Bay Side Dr
Orlando, FL 32819-4045, USA

Damus, Mike (Actor)
c/o Staff Member *United Talent Agency (UTA)*
9336 Civic Center Dr
Beverly Hills, CA 90210-3604, USA

Dan, Dercher (Athlete, Football Player)
3448 W 131st St
Leawood, KS 66209-4112, USA

Dan, Reeder (Athlete, Football Player)
703 Southwood Rd
Hockessin, DE 19707-1040, USA

Dan, Rice (Athlete, Football Player)
247 Bramblebush Rd
Stoughton, MA 02072-3096, USA

Dana, Justin (Actor)
13111 Ventura Blvd Ste 102
Studio City, CA 91604-2218, USA

Danare, Malcolm (Actor)
c/o Monique Moss *Integrated PR*
9025 Wilshire Blvd Ste 400
Beverly Hills, CA 90211-1828, USA

Danby, John (Athlete, Hockey Player)
20 Jb Dr
Marstons Mills, MA 02648-1521, USA

Dance, Charies (Actor)
7812 Forsythe St
Sunland, CA 91040-2502, USA

Dance, Charles (Actor)

Dancer, Donald (Horse Racer)
30 Amherst Rd
Marlboro, NJ 07746-1557, USA

Dancer, James (Horse Racer)
1273 Edgewater Cir
Bradenton, FL 34209-7386, USA

Dancer, Rachel (Horse Racer)
4051 NE 31st Ave
Lighthouse Point, FL 33064-8436, USA

Dancer, Ronald (Horse Racer)
PO Box 235
New Egypt, NJ 08533-0235, USA

Dancer, Stanley F (Race Car Driver)
1300 S Ocean Blvd Apt 101
Pompano Beach, FL 33062-6916, USA

Dancy, Bill (Athlete, Baseball Player)
2225 Hemerick Pl
Clearwater, FL 33765-2228, USA

Dancy, Hugh (Actor)
19 Downing St
New York, NY 10014-4748, USA

Dancy, John (Correspondent)
Harvard University
Kennedy Government School
Cambridge, MA 02138, USA

Dandenault, Mathieu (Athlete, Hockey Player)
2615 Dorchester Rd
Birmingham, MI 48009-5990, USA

Dando, Evan (Musician)
c/o Staff Member *Good Cop Public Relations*
425 W 13th St # 502
New York, NY 10014-1123, USA

Dandridge, Bob (Athlete, Basketball Player)
1708 Saint Denis Ave
Norfolk, VA 23509-1004, USA

Dandy Warholds, The (Music Group)
c/o Staff Member *Tsunami Entertainment*
1600 E Desert Inn Rd Ste 270
Las Vegas, NV 89169-2576, USA

Dandy Warhols (Music Group)
c/o Staff Member *Tsunami Entertainment*
1600 E Desert Inn Rd Ste 270
Las Vegas, NV 89169-2576, USA

Dane, Alexandra (Actor)
Rolf Kruger Mgmt
205 Chudliegh Road
London SE4 1EG, UNITED KINGDOM (UK)

Dane, Eric (Actor)
c/o Susan Patricola *Patricola Public Relations*
369 S Doheny Dr # 1408
Beverly Hills, CA 90211-3508, USA

Dane, Lloyd (Race Car Driver)
4165 Amarillo Dr SW
Concord, NC 28027-0404, USA

Danehe, Dick (Athlete, Football Player)
23871 Willows Dr Apt 378
Laguna Hills, CA 92653-1951, USA

Daneker, Pat (Athlete, Baseball Player)
107 Van Buren Rd Apt 5
Voorhees, NJ 08043-2409, USA

Danelli, Dino (Musician)
Rascals Cassidy
11761 E Speedway Blvd
Tucson, AZ 85748-2017, USA

Danelo, Joe (Athlete, Football Player)
3601 Roxbury St
San Pedro, CA 90731-6440, USA

Danenhauer, Bill (Athlete, Football Player)
10 Kirkby Cir
Bella Vista, AR 72715-2349, USA

Danenhauer, Eldon (Athlete, Football Player)
1222 SW 29th Ter Apt 105
Topeka, KS 66611-1886, USA

Danes, Claire (Actor)
19 Downing St
New York, NY 10014-4748, USA

Daney_ko, Ken (Athlete, Hockey Player)
10 Mahogany Way
Randolph, NJ 07869-3734

Daneyko, Ken (Athlete, Hockey Player)
11 Combs Hollow Rd
Mendham, NJ 07945-2204, USA

Danforth, Douglas D (Athlete, Baseball Player, Business Person)
5039 Indianola Way
La Canada Flintridge, CA 91011-2657, USA

Danforth, Fred (Artist)
PO Box 828
Middlebury, VT 05753-0828, USA

Danforth, John (Politician)
HC 1 Box 91
Newburg, MO 65550, USA

D'Angelo (Musician, Songwriter)
c/o Kevin Liles *KWL Management*
112 Madison Ave Fl 4
New York, NY 10016-7416, USA

D'Angelo, Beverly (Actor)
8033 W Sunset Blvd Ste 247
West Hollywood, CA 90046-2401, USA

Daniel, Brittany (Actor)
c/o Glenn Rigberg *Inphenate*
9701 Wilshire Blvd Fl 10
Beverly Hills, CA 90212-2010, USA

Daniel, Chase (Athlete, Football Player)
10Star Apparel
912 113th St
Arlington, TX 76011-5407, USA

Daniel, Elizabeth A (Beth) (Athlete, Golfer)
219 Palm Trl
Delray Beach, FL 33483-5526, USA

Daniel, Eugene (Athlete, Football Player)
PO Box 80345
Baton Rouge, LA 70898-0345, USA

Daniel, Kenny (Athlete, Football Player)
2911 Center Ave
Richmond, CA 94804-3022, USA

Daniel, Robert (Athlete, Football Player)
9860 Scyene Rd Apt 518
Dallas, TX 75227-1951, USA

Daniel, Willie (Athlete, Football Player)
8323 Oktoc Rd
Starkville, MS 39759-6461, USA

Danielle, Juliette (Actor)
PO Box 18557
Encino, CA 91416-8557, USA

Daniels, Anthony (Actor)
c/o Fifi Oscard *Fifi Oscard Agency*
110 W 40th St Rm 1601
New York, NY 10018-8512, USA

Daniels, Antonio (Basketball Player)
Seatle SuperSonics
351 Elliott Ave W Ste 500
Seattle, WA 98119-4153, USA

Daniels, Ben (Actor)
c/o Christian Hodell *Hamilton Hodell Ltd*
20 Golden Sq
Fl 5
London W1F 9JL, UNITED KINGDOM

Daniels, Bennie (Athlete, Baseball Player)
938 W 156th St
Compton, CA 90220-3504, USA

Daniels, Charlie (Musician, Songwriter)
c/o Staff Member *CDB Inc*
17060 Central Pike
Lebanon, TN 37090-8019, USA

Daniels, Clem (Athlete, Football Player)
8683 Mountain Blvd
Oakland, CA 94605-4545, USA

Daniels, Dexter (Athlete, Football Player)
518 E Magnolia St
Valdosta, GA 31601-5860, USA

Daniels, Erin (Actor)
c/o Mary Ellen Mulcahy *Framework Entertainment*
9057 Nemo St # C
W Hollywood, CA 90069-5511, USA

Daniels, Fred (Athlete, Baseball Player)
PO Box 6208
Statesville, NC 28687-6208, USA

Daniels, Greg (Actor)
c/o Howard Klein *3 Arts Entertainment*
9460 Wilshire Blvd Fl 7
Beverly Hills, CA 90212-2713, USA

Daniels, Jack (Athlete, Baseball Player)
811 S Lombard Ave
Evansville, IN 47714-0428, USA

Daniels, Jeff (Actor)
c/o Alan Nierob *Rogers & Cowan*
1840 Century Park E Fl 18
Los Angeles, CA 90067-2101, USA

Daniels, Jeff (Athlete, Hockey Player)
108 Delaplane Ct
Morrisville, NC 27560-6987, USA

Daniels, Jenna (Athlete, Golfer)
85140 Amagansett Dr
Fernandina Beach, FL 32034-8711, USA

Daniels, Jerome (Athlete, Football Player)
311 Park Ave
Bloomfield, CT 06002-3103, USA

Daniels, Jon (Athlete, Baseball Player)
602 Aberdeen Way
Southlake, TX 76092-9553, USA

Daniels, Jon (Commentator)
602 Aberdeen Way
Southlake, TX 76092-9553, USA

Daniels, Kal (Athlete, Baseball Player)
PO Box 9632
Warner Robins, GA 31095-9632, USA

Daniels, Kevin (Actor)
c/o Staff Member *Insight*
5358 Melrose Ave # 200W
Los Angeles, CA 90038-5117, USA

Daniels, Lee (Director, Producer)
c/o Brooke Blumberg *Sunshine Sachs*
720 Cole Ave
Los Angeles, CA 90038-3606, USA

Daniels, Leshun (Athlete, Football Player)
593 Magnolia St
Dekalb, IL 60115-5954, USA

Daniels, Marquis (Athlete, Basketball Player)
c/o Staff Member *Dallas Mavericks*
1333 N Stemmons Fwy Ste 105
Dallas, TX 75207-3722, USA

Daniels, Marquis (Athlete, Basketball Player)
2501 Sutton Place Dr S
Carmel, IN 46032-8694, USA

Daniels, Mike (Athlete, Football Player)
c/o Denise White *EAG Sports Management*
909 N Pacific Coast Hwy Ste 360
El Segundo, CA 90245-3864, USA

Daniels, Owen (Athlete, Football Player)
740 Pifer Rd
Houston, TX 77024-5422, USA

Daniels, Phillip (Athlete, Football Player)
112 Cherry Farm Ln
West Chester, PA 19382-8345, USA

Daniels, Scott (Athlete, Hockey Player)
36 Deer Run
Southwick, MA 01077-9523, USA

Daniels, Shane (Actor)
c/o Cheryl Lynch *Lynch Archer PR*
5115 Wilshire Blvd Apt 400
Los Angeles, CA 90036-4372, USA

Daniels, Spencer (Actor)
c/o Staff Member *Artists & Representatives (Stone Manners Salners)*
6100 Wilshire Blvd Ste 1500
Los Angeles, CA 90048-5110, USA

Daniels, Stormy (Adult Film Star, Model)
Digital Playground Inc
16134 Hart St
Van Nuys, CA 91406-3903, USA

Daniels, Susan (Athlete, Golfer)
251 N Lake Blvd
Tahoe City, CA 96145, USA

Daniels, Travis (Athlete, Football Player)
4665 SW 75th Way Unit 104
Davie, FL 33314-4113, USA

Daniels, William (Actor)
12805 Hortense St
Studio City, CA 91604-1124, USA

Danielsen, Egil (Athlete, Track Athlete)
Roreks Gate 9
Hamar 02300, NORWAY

Danielson, Gary D (Athlete, Football Player)
10112 Magnolia Bnd
Estero, FL 34135-8109, USA

Daniloff, Nicholas (Journalist)
PO Box 892
Chester, VT 05143-0892, USA

Danity Kane (Music Group)
c/o Tammy Brook *FYI Public Relations*
174 5th Ave Ste 404
New York, NY 10010-5964, USA

Danks, John (Athlete, Baseball Player)
702 Oaklands Dr
Round Rock, TX 78681-4029, USA

Danley, Kerwin (Athlete, Baseball Player)
2455 E Desert Broom Pl
Chandler, AZ 85286-2336, USA

Danmeier, Rick (Athlete, Football Player)
4917 Ridge Rd
Minneapolis, MN 55436-1012, USA

Danna, Mychael (Musician)
c/o Robert Messinger *Fortress Talent Management*
23901 Calabasas Rd Ste 2016
Calabasas, CA 91302-1593, USA

Danner, Blythe (Actor)
c/o Tony Lipp *Anonymous Content*
3532 Hayden Ave
Culver City, CA 90232-2413, USA

Danning, Sybil (Actor, Model)
Adventuress Productions International
8491 W Sunset Blvd # 361
W Hollywood, CA 90069-1911, USA

Danny & The Juniors (Music Group)
PO Box 279
Williamstown, NJ 08094-0279

Dano, Paul (Actor)
c/o Sandra Chang *Anonymous Content*
3532 Hayden Ave
Culver City, CA 90232-2413, USA

Dansby, Karlos (Athlete, Football Player)
16850 Stratford Ct
Southwest Ranches, FL 33331-1359, USA

Danson, Ted (Actor)
2850 Ocean Park Blvd Ste 300
Santa Monica, CA 90405-6216, USA

Dante, Joe (Director)
Metaluna Productions
1438 N Gower St Ste 15
Los Angeles, CA 90028-8306, USA

Dante, Michael (Actor)
71372 Biskra Rd
Rancho Mirage, CA 92270-4200, USA

Dante, Peter (Actor)
5815 Ramirez Canyon Rd
Malibu, CA 90265-4420, USA

Dante Bichette, Alphonse (Baseball Player)
2298 Robin Rd
Orlando, FL 32814-6548, USA

Dantine, Nikki (Actor)
707 N Palm Dr
Beverly Hills, CA 90210-3416, USA

Dantley, Adrian (Athlete, Basketball Player, Olympic Athlete)
9 Barn Ridge Ct
Silver Spring, MD 20906-1105, USA

Danton, Mike (Athlete, Hockey Player)
PO Box 1000
Fort Dix F C I
Fort Dix, NJ 08640-0902, USA

D'Antoni, Mike (Basketball Coach)
9 Hunter Ln
Rye, NY 10580-1614, USA

Dantoni, Mike (Athlete, Basketball Player)
9 Hunter Ln
Rye, NY 10580-1614, USA

Danz, Shirley (Athlete, Baseball Player, Commentator)
330 Greystone Dr
Hendersonville, NC 28792-9173, USA

Danza, Tony (Actor)
16030 Ventura Blvd Ste 300
Encino, CA 91436-2754, USA

Danzig (Music Group)
PO Box 884563
San Francisco, CA 94188-4563, USA

Danziger, Cory (Actor)
c/o Staff Member *Iris Burton Agency*
10100 Santa Monica Blvd Ste 1300
Los Angeles, CA 90067-4114, USA

Dao, Chloe (Fashion Designer)
Lot 8 Boutique
6127 Kirby Dr
Houston, TX 77005-3148, USA

Daoust, Dan (Athlete, Hockey Player)
55 John Stiver Cres
Markham, ON L3R 9B6, Canada

Dapkus-Wolf, Eleanor (Baseball Player)
9150 Mallard Cv
Saint John, IN 46373-9019, USA

Dara, Olu (Actor)
c/o Staff Member *Monterey International (Chicago)*
72 W Adams St # 1000
Chicago, IL 60603-5107, USA

D'Arabian, Melissa (Chef)
c/o Josh Bider *WME/IMG (NY)*
11 Madison Ave Fl 18
New York, NY 10010-3669, USA

Darabont, Frank (Director)
8225 Manjares
Monterey, CA 93940-7322, USA

D'Arbanville, Patti (Actor)
c/o Rob Kolker *Red Letter Entertainment*
550 W 45th St Apt 501
New York, NY 10036-3779, USA

Darbo, Patrika (Musician)
Boyles Agency
PO Box 13334
Durham, NC 27709-3334, USA

Darboven, Hanne (Artist)
Am Burgberg 26
Hamburg 21079, GERMANY

Darby, Chartric (Athlete, Football Player)
14335 Simonds Rd NE Apt A302
Kirkland, WA 98034-9277, USA

Darby, Craig (Athlete, Hockey Player)
40 Vista Dr
Saratoga Springs, NY 12866-8772

Darby, Kim (Actor)
8149 Quinault Rd
Blaine, WA 98230-9548, USA

Darby, Matt (Athlete, Football Player)
501 Sagecreek Ct
Winter Springs, FL 32708-2731, USA

Darby, Rhys (Actor)
c/o Hugo Young *Independent Talent Group*
40 Whitfield St
London W1T 2RH, UNITED KINGDOM

Darc, Mireille (Actor)
Agents Associes Beaume
201 Faubourg Saint Honore
Paris 75008, FRANCE

Darcey, Pete (Athlete, Basketball Player)
17600 N Anderson Rd
Arcadia, OK 73007-7113, USA

Darche, Jean-Philippe (Athlete, Football Player)
9507 W 160th Ter
Stilwell, KS 66085-8127, USA

Darcum, Max (Skier)
PO Box 189
Dillon, CO 80435-0189, USA

D'Arcy (Musician)
Cohen Brothers Mgmt
500 Molino St Ste 104
Los Angeles, CA 90013-2264, USA

Darcy, Dame (Artist)
c/o Staff Member *Fantagraphics Books*
7563 Lake City Way NE
Seattle, WA 98115-4218, USA

D'Arcy, James (Actor)
c/o Pippa Markham *Markham & Froggatt*
4 Windmill St
London W1T 1HZ, UNITED KINGDOM

D'Arcy, Margaretta (Writer)
Cassarotto
60/66 Wardour St
London W1V 4ND, UNITED KINGDOM (UK)

Darcy, Pat (Athlete, Baseball Player)
515 S Columbus Blvd
Tucson, AZ 85711-4753, USA

D'Arcy James, Brian (Actor)
c/o Amy Brownstein *PRStudio USA*
1875 Century Park E Ste 930
Los Angeles, CA 90067-2540, USA

Dar Dar, Kirby (Athlete, Football Player)
PO Box 2872
Syracuse, NY 13220-2872, USA

Darden, Christopher (Attorney)
19150 Allandale Dr
Tarzana, CA 91356-5821, USA

Darden, Dexter (Actor)
c/o Siri Garber *Platform PR*
2666 N Beachwood Dr
Los Angeles, CA 90068-2308, USA

Darden, Thom (Athlete, Football Player)
637 20th Ave SW
Cedar Rapids, IA 52404-5520, USA

Darego, Agbani (Model)
c/o Staff Member *Miss World Ltd*
21 Golden Sq
London W1R 3PA, UNITED KINGDOM (UK)

Darensbourg, Vic (Athlete, Baseball Player)
4151 Abernethy Forest Pl
Las Vegas, NV 89141-4336, USA

Dareus, Marcell (Football Player)
c/o Todd France *Creative Artists Agency (CAA) Sports*
3500 Lenox Rd NE
Atlanta, GA 30326-4228, USA

Darin, Ricardo (Actor)
c/o Jesus Garcia Ciordia *Reacting Talent*
Avenida De Dos Castillas 33
Atico 4 B A
Madrid 28224, SPAIN

Darish, Frank (Horse Racer)
11 March Ln
Westbury, NY 11590-6301, USA

Darius, Donovin (Athlete, Football Player)
1357 Lawrence Rd
Danville, CA 94506-4735, USA

Dark, Al (Athlete, Baseball Player, Coach)
103 Cranberry Way
Easley, SC 29642-3200, USA

Dark, Mike (Athlete, Hockey Player)
741 Wellington St
Sarnia, ON N7T 1J3, Canada

Darke, Erin (Actor)
c/o Scott Boute *Serge PR*
339 W 12th St
New York, NY 10014-1721, USA

Darkins, Chris (Athlete, Football Player)
10903 Shawnbrook Dr
Houston, TX 77071-1515, USA

Dark Star Orchestra (Music Group)
PO Box 1282
Evanston, IL 60204-1282, USA

Darling, Chuck (Athlete, Basketball Player, Olympic Athlete)
3237 Summer Wind Ln APT 1413
Hghlnds Ranch, CO 80129-2482, USA

Darling, Devard (Athlete, Football Player)
10544 Sentinel Dr
Gig Harbor, WA 98332-5109, USA

Darling, Gary (Athlete, Baseball Player)
16422 S 36th Pl
Phoenix, AZ 85048-7977, USA

Darling, Jennifer (Actor)
13351 Riverside Dr # 427
Sherman Oaks, CA 91423-2542, USA

Darling, Joan (Actor)
PO Box 6700
Tesuque, NM 87574-6700, USA

Darling, Ron (Athlete, Baseball Player)
c/o Staff Member *SportsNet New York*
75 Rockefeller Plz
New York, NY 10019-6908, USA

Darmaatmadja, Julius Riyadi Cardinal (Religious Leader)
Keuskupan Agung
Jl Katedral 7
Jakarta 10710, INDONESIA

d'Arnaud, Travis (Athlete, Baseball Player)
c/o Joel Wolfe *Wasserman Media Group*
10960 Wilshire Blvd Ste 1200
Los Angeles, CA 90024-3714, USA

Darnell, Erik (Race Car Driver)
Darmer Motorsports Ltd
3627 Washington St
Park City, IL 60085-4767, USA

Darnell, Mike (Producer)
24962 Lorenzo Ct
Calabasas, CA 91302-3088, USA

Darnold, Sam (Athlete, Football Player)
c/o Team Member *New York Jets*
1 Jets Dr
Florham Park, NJ 07932-1215, USA

Darragh, Dan (Athlete, Football Player)
201 Sewickley Ridge Ct
Sewickley, PA 15143-8973, USA

Darren, James (Actor, Musician)
Spafax Inflight Entertainment
575 Anton Blvd Ste 1020
Costa Mesa, CA 92626-7029, USA

Darrian, Raquel (Adult Film Star)
49 Eaton Ct
Manhasset, NY 11030-4052

Darrow, Barry (Athlete, Football Player)
2406 Chief Victor Camp Rd
Victor, MT 59875-9410, USA

Darrow, Nathan (Actor)
c/o James Suskin *Suskin Management*
2 Charlton St Apt 5K
New York, NY 10014-4970, USA

Dart, Iris Rainer (Writer)
938 Coral Dr
Pebble Beach, CA 93953-2503, USA

Darvill, Arthur (Actor)
c/o Jeff Golenberg *Silver Lining Entertainment*
421 S Beverly Dr Fl 7
Beverly Hills, CA 90212-4408, USA

Darvish, Yu (Athlete, Baseball Player)
c/o Joel Wolfe *Wasserman Media Group*
10960 Wilshire Blvd Ste 1200
Los Angeles, CA 90024-3714, USA

Darwin, Bobby (Athlete, Baseball Player)
6516 Pleasant Hill Cir
Eastvale, CA 92880-3015, USA

Darwin, Danny (Athlete, Baseball Player)
11131 Lakecrest Dr
Sanger, TX 76266-3446, USA

Darwin, Jeff (Athlete, Baseball Player)
PO Box 323
Dodd City, TX 75438-0323, USA

Darwin, Matt (Athlete, Football Player)
414 Love Bird Ln
Murphy, TX 75094-3263, USA

Darwitz, Natalie (Athlete, Hockey Player, Olympic Athlete)
c/o Staff Member *US Olympic Committee*
1750 E Boulder St
Alumni Relations
Colorado Springs, CO 80909-5793, USA

Das, Alisha (Actor)
19583 Bowers Dr
Topanga, CA 90290-3102, USA

Das, Nandita (Actor)
c/o Aude Powell *Brunskill Management*
169 Queen's Gate
#8A
London NW1 4JR, UNITED KINGDOM

Das, Vir (Actor, Comedian)
Weird Ass Comedy
Chez Nous
12 St Sebastian Rd
Bandra, Mumbai Maharashtra 400050, INDIA

Dascascos, Marc (Actor)
PO Box 1549
Studio City, CA 91614-0549, USA

Dascenzo, Doug (Athlete, Baseball Player)
111 Eastgate Rd
Uniontown, PA 15401-5615, USA

Daschle, Thomas (Politician)
1020 N Jay St Apt 212
Aberdeen, SD 57401-2478, USA

D'Ascoli, Bernard (Musician)
Clarion/Seven Muses
47 Whitehall Park
London N19 3TW, UNITED KINGDOM (UK)

Dash, Damon (Actor, Director, Producer)
c/o Staff Member *Fortitude*
8619 Washington Blvd
Culver City, CA 90232-7441, USA

Dash, Julie (Actor, Director, Producer, Writer)
c/o Kimber Wheeler *TalentWorks*
3500 W Olive Ave Ste 1400
Burbank, CA 91505-5512, USA

Dash, Leon O Jr (Journalist)
Washington Post
Editorial Dept
1150 15th Ave NW
Washington, DC 20071-0001, USA

Dash, Stacey (Actor)
c/o Siri Garber *Platform PR*
2666 N Beachwood Dr
Los Angeles, CA 90068-2308, USA

Dashboard Confessional (Music Group)

da Silva, Luiz Inacio Lula (Politician)
Partido Dos Trabalhadores
Setor Comercial Sul - Quadra 2
Bloco C - Nº 256
Edifício Toufic, Brasília DF, CEP: 70302-, Brazil

Daskalakis, Cleon (Athlete, Hockey Player)
752 Main St
Boxford, MA 01921-1127, USA

Dassier, Uwe (Swimmer)
Stolze-Schrey-Str 6
Wilday 15745, GREECE

Datsyuk, Pavel (Athlete, Hockey Player)
3166 Rosedale St
Ann Arbor, MI 48108-1884, USA

Dattilo, Bryan (Actor)
7039 Shoshone Ave
Van Nuys, CA 91406-3529, USA

Dattilo, Kristin (Actor)

Datz, Jeff (Athlete, Baseball Player)
4775 Elen Ct
Shingle Springs, CA 95682-9519, USA

Daubach, Brian (Athlete, Baseball Player)
2709 Timberline Dr
Belleville, IL 62226-4933, USA

Dauer, Rich (Athlete, Baseball Player)
4435 Manor Creek Dr
Cumming, GA 30040-6817, USA

Daugherty, Brad (Athlete, Basketball Player)
10 Inspiration Way
Swannanoa, NC 28778-8106, USA

Daugherty, Brant (Actor)
c/o David Sweeney *Sweeney Entertainment*
1601 Vine St # 6
Los Angeles, CA 90028-8802, USA

Daugherty, Doc (Athlete, Baseball Player)
314 Summers Dr
Lancaster, PA 17601-5884, USA

Daugherty, Jack (Athlete, Baseball Player)
20360 N 95th Pl
Scottsdale, AZ 85255-6646, USA

Daughtry, Chris (Musician)
c/o Simon Fuller *XIX Entertainment (UK)*
32/33 Ransomes Dock
London SW11 4NP, UNITED KINGDOM (UK)

Dauline, Marie (Musician)
Todo Mundo
PO Box 652
Cooper Station
New York, NY 10276-0652, USA

Daurey, Dana (Actor)

Davalillo, Vic (Athlete, Baseball Player)
Calle Trujillo 7
Mariperez Q V
Caracas, Venezuela

Davalos, Alexa (Actor)
c/o Staff Member *Anonymous Content*
3532 Hayden Ave
Culver City, CA 90232-2413, USA

Davalos, Richard (Actor)
23388 Mulholland Dr # 28
Woodland Hills, CA 91364-2733, USA

Davanon, Jeff (Athlete, Baseball Player)
2811 Piedmont Ave
Los Alamitos, CA 90720-4244, USA

Davanon, Jerry (Athlete, Baseball Player)
350 Greypine W
Montgomery, TX 77356-8192, USA

Dave, Al (Athlete, Football Player)
5173 Waring Rd Apt 441
San Diego, CA 92120-2705, USA

Dave Matthews Band (Music Group)
c/o Coran Capshaw *Red Light Management*
455 2nd St NE
#500
Charlottesville, VA 22902-5791, USA

Davenport, Adell (Baseball Player)
Topps
PO Box 462490
Garland, TX 75046-2490, USA

Davenport, Charles (Athlete, Football Player)
206 Wapiti Dr
Spring Lake, NC 28390-1530, USA

Davenport, Jack (Actor)
c/o Lorraine Hamilton *Hamilton Hodell Ltd*
20 Golden Sq
Fl 5
London W1F 9JL, UNITED KINGDOM

Davenport, Jim (Athlete, Baseball Player, Coach)
1016 Hewitt Dr
San Carlos, CA 94070-3601, USA

Davenport, Joe (Athlete, Baseball Player)
10102 Wycliffe St
Santee, CA 92071-1176, USA

Davenport, Ken (Producer)
Davenport Theatrical Enterprises
250 W 49th St Ste 301
New York, NY 10019-7437, USA

Davenport, Lindsay (Athlete, Olympic Athlete, Tennis Player)
PO Box 10179
Newport Beach, CA 92658-0179, USA

Davenport, Lindsey (Tennis Player)
PO Box 10179
Newport Beach, CA 92658-0179, USA

Davenport, Madison (Actor)
c/o Erik Kritzer *LINK Entertainment*
11872 La Grange Ave
Los Angeles, CA 90025-5282, USA

Davenport, Najeh (Athlete, Football Player)
c/o Brian Lammi *Lammi Sports Management*
310 E Buffalo St
Milwaukee, WI 53202-5808, USA

Davenport Cabinet (Music Group)
c/o Staff Member *Equal Vision Records*
PO Box 38202
Albany, NY 12203-8202, USA

Davenport Jr, Guy M (Writer)
621 Sayre Ave
Lexington, KY 40508-2317, USA

Davey, Don (Athlete, Football Player)
1525 Beach Ave
Atlantic Beach, FL 32233-5735, USA

Davey, Mike (Athlete, Baseball Player)
902 W Melinda Ln
Spokane, WA 99203-1363, USA

Davey, Rohan (Athlete, Football Player)
24696 Plank Rd
Slaughter, LA 70777-9703, USA

Davey, Tom (Athlete, Baseball Player)
13125 Andover Dr
Plymouth, MI 48170-8208, USA

Davi, Robert (Actor)
10044 Calvin Ave
Northridge, CA 91324-1111, USA

Daviault, Ray (Athlete, Baseball Player)
2864 Ch des Pins RR 1
Notre-Dame-De-La-Merci, QC J0T 2A0, Canada

Davich, Jacob (Actor, Musician)
c/o Brad Schenck *ICM Partners*
10250 Constellation Blvd Fl 7
Los Angeles, CA 90067-6207, USA

David, Andre (Athlete, Baseball Player)
18483 W Paradise Ln
Surprise, AZ 85388-1809, USA

David, Charlie (Actor)
CTM International
205-309 W Cordova St
Vancouver BC V6B 1E5, Canada

David, Craig (Musician)
c/o Peter Nash *WME|IMG*
9601 Wilshire Blvd
Beverly Hills, CA 90210-5213, USA

David, Duke (Politician)
240 Garden Ave
Mandeville, LA 70471-2910, USA

David, George A L (Business Person)
United Technologies Corp
United Technologies Building
Hartford, CT 06101, USA

David, Keith (Actor)
c/o Janell Barrett-Jones *Harlot Unlimited*
468 N Camden Dr Ste 300
Beverly Hills, CA 90210-4507, USA

David, Larry (Actor, Producer, Writer)
1078 Napoli Dr
Pacific Palisades, CA 90272-4038, USA

David, Lavonte (Athlete, Football Player)
c/o Mitchell Frankel *Impact Sports (FL)*
2799 NW 2nd Ave Ste 203
Boca Raton, FL 33431-6709, USA

David, Peter (Writer)
PO Box 239
Bayport, NY 11705-0239, USA

David, Richie (Athlete, Football Player)
3712 NE 110th St
Vancouver, WA 98686-3991, USA

David, Stacey (Reality Star)
c/o Staff Member *Elite Talent Agency*
1200 Clinton St Ste 212
Nashville, TN 37203-2894, USA

David, Stan (Athlete, Football Player)
502 Baja Cir
Denver City, TX 79323-3747, USA

David, Yuval (Actor, Musician)
c/o Gary Krasny *The Krasny Office*
1501 Broadway Ste 1507
New York, NY 10036-5505, USA

David Bossert, David Bossert (Director, Producer)
c/o Staff Member *Disney Animation (LA)*
500 S Buena Vista St
Burbank, CA 91521-9500, USA

David Crowder Band (Musician)
c/o Shelley Giglio *Six Steps Records*
515 Garson Dr NE
Atlanta, GA 30324-3344, USA

Davidoff, Dov (Actor)
c/o Stephanie Davis *Wet Dog Entertainment*
2458 Crest View Dr
Los Angeles, CA 90046-1407, USA

Davidovich, Bella (Musician)
c/o Staff Member *Columbia Artists Mgmt Inc*
1790 Broadway Fl 6
New York, NY 10019-1537, USA

Davidovich, Lolita (Actor)
c/o Ben Press *Primary Wave Entertainment*
10850 Wilshire Blvd Fl 6
Los Angeles, CA 90024-4319, USA

Davids, Hollace (Producer)
c/o Staff Member *Universal Pictures*
100 Universal City Plz
Universal City, CA 91608-1085, USA

Davidson, Adam (Actor)
c/o Andrea Simon *Andrea Simon Entertainment*
6345 Balboa Blvd Ste 138
Encino, CA 91316-1510, USA

Davidson, Amy (Actor)
c/o Caitlin Wellner *Framework Entertainment*
9057 Nemo St # C
W Hollywood, CA 90069-5511, USA

Davidson, Beau (Actor, Musician)
1307 Enclave Cir
1307 Enclave Cir
Nashville, TN 37211-7457, USA

Davidson, Bob (Athlete, Baseball Player)
91 Deerwood Dr
Littleton, CO 80127-2626, USA

Davidson, Bob (Athlete, Baseball Player)
1420 Bruton Parish Way
Fairfield, OH 45014-4536, USA

Davidson, Cleatus (Athlete, Baseball Player)
112 Lincoln Ave
Dundee, FL 33838-4394, USA

Davidson, Cotton (Athlete, Football Player)
435 Old Osage Rd
Gatesville, TX 76528-3362, USA

Davidson, Dallas (Musician)
4320 Wallace Ln
Nashville, TN 37215-3234, USA

Davidson, Diane Mott (Writer)
c/o Author Mail *Bantam-Dell Publishing (NY)*
1745 Broadway
New York, NY 10019-4640, USA

Davidson, Doug (Actor)
295 Toro Canyon Rd
Carpinteria, CA 93013-3040, USA

Davidson, Eileen (Actor, Reality Star)
c/o Fran Blain *Blaine & Associates*
8840 Wilshire Blvd
Beverly Hills, CA 90211-2606, USA

Davidson, Gary L (Athlete, Hockey Player)
245 Fischer Ave Ste D1
Costa Mesa, CA 92626-4539, USA

Davidson, George A Jr (Business Person)
Consolidated Natural Gas
625 Liberty Ave
Pittsburgh, PA 15222-3110, USA

Davidson, Jeff (Athlete, Football Player)
10036 Gristmill Rdg
Eden Prairie, MN 55347-4759, USA

Davidson, Jeremy (Actor)
c/o Matthew Lesher *Insight*
5358 Melrose Ave # 200W
Los Angeles, CA 90038-5117, USA

Davidson, Jim (Actor)
c/o Staff Member *International Artistes*
Holborn Hall - 4th Floor
London WC1V 7BD, UK

Davidson, John (Athlete, Hockey Player)
c/o Josh Pultz *Amplified Entertainment*
33 W 46th St Ste 801
New York, NY 10036-4103, USA

Davidson, John (Actor, Musician)
8605 Santa Monica Blvd
W Hollywood, CA 90069-4109, USA

Davidson, John (Athlete, Hockey Player)
6 Briarbrook Trl
Saint Louis, MO 63131-3947, USA

Davidson, Ken (Athlete, Football Player)
1922 Thompson Crossing Dr
Richmond, TX 77406-6707, USA

Davidson, Mark (Athlete, Baseball Player)
806 Marina Pointe Ct
Seneca, SC 29672-4728, USA

Davidson, Matthew (Athlete, Golfer)
3 Westminster Pl
Cranbury, NJ 08512-3217, USA

Davidson, Owen (Athlete, Tennis Player)
39 N Lakemist Harbour Pl
Spring, TX 77381-3344, USA

Davidson, Pete (Actor, Comedian)
c/o Ayala Cohen *ICM Partners*
10250 Constellation Blvd Fl 7
Los Angeles, CA 90067-6207, USA

Davidson, Satch (Athlete, Baseball Player)
2400 Westheimer Rd Apt 209W
Houston, TX 77098-1305, USA

Davidson, Tommy (Actor, Comedian)
c/o Monique Moss *Integrated PR*
9025 Wilshire Blvd Ste 400
Beverly Hills, CA 90211-1828, USA

Davidtz, Embeth (Actor)
c/o Sarah Clossey *United Talent Agency (UTA)*
9336 Civic Center Dr
Beverly Hills, CA 90210-3604, USA

Davie, Donald A (Writer)
4 High St
Silverton
Exeter EX5 4JB, UNITED KINGDOM (UK)

Davie, Jerry (Athlete, Baseball Player)
2800 US Highwav 17 92 W Ofc
Haines Citv, FL 33844-7375, USA

Davies, Dave (Musician)
Larry Page
29 Ruston Mews
London W11 1RB, UNITED KINGDOM (UK)

Davies, Dennis Russell (Musician)
Am Wichelshof 24
Bonn 53111, GERMANY

Davies, Gail (Musician)
246 Cherokee Rd
Nashville, TN 37205-1818, USA

Davies, Geralnt Wyn (Actor)
Oscars Abrams Zimel
438 Queen St E
Toronto, ON M5A 1T4, CANADA

Davies, Jeremy (Actor)
c/o Jack Kingsrud *Zero Gravity Management*
11110 Ohio Ave Ste 100
Los Angeles, CA 90025-3329, USA

Davies, Kyle (Athlete, Baseball Player)
5436 Glenridge Vw
Atlanta, GA 30342-1737, USA

Davies, Lane (Actor)
PO Box 20531
Thousand Oaks, CA 91358, USA

Davies, Laura (Athlete, Golfer)
I M G
1360 E 9th St Ste 100
Cleveland, OH 44114-1730, USA

Davies, Linda (Writer)
Calle Once 286
La Molona
Lima, PERU

Davies, Russel T (Writer)
c/o Lisa Harrison *WME|IMG*
9601 Wilshire Blvd
Beverly Hills, CA 90210-5213, USA

Davies, Tamara (Actor)
c/o Staff Member *Bauman Redanty & Shaul Agency*
5757 Wilshire Blvd
Suite 473
Beverly Hills, CA 90212, USA

Davies, Terence (Director)
c/o Tony Peake *Peake Associates*
14 Grafton Crescent
London NW1 8SL, UK

Davies, Warrick (Actor)
International Creative Mgmt
76 Oxford St
London W1N 0AX, UNITED KINGDOM (UK)

Davies, Wyn (Actor)
c/o Staff Member *Screen Actors Guild (SAG)*
5757 Wilshire Blvd Ste 124
Los Angeles, CA 90036-3792, USA

Davis, A Dano (Business Person)
Winn-Dixie Stores
5050 Edgewood Ct
Jacksonville, FL 32254-3699, USA

Davis, A.J. (Athlete, Football Player)
c/o Pat Dye Jr *SportsTrust Advisors*
3340 Peachtree Rd NE Fl 16
Atlanta, GA 30326-1000, USA

Davis, Alecia (Actor)
c/o Jonathan Clements *Nashville Agency*
501 Metroplex Dr Ste 116
Nashville, TN 37211-3131, USA

Davis, Alvin (Athlete, Baseball Player)
7983 Arma101osa Dr
Riverside, CA 92S08-8713, USA

Davis, Andra (Athlete, Football Player)
21230 Greenfield Pl
Strongsville, OH 44149-9218, USA

Davis, Andra (Athlete, Football Player)
5839 Pinehurst Ct
Lake View, NY 14085-9719, USA

Davis, Andre (Athlete, Football Player)
11407 Jutland Rd
Houston, TX 77048-2631, USA

Davis, Andrew (Director)
c/o Laurence Becsey *Intellectual Property Group (IPG)*
12400 Wilshire Blvd Ste 500
Los Angeles, CA 90025-1055, USA

Davis, Andy (Athlete, Football Player)
14500 Fiske Dr
Silver Spring, MD 20906-1737, USA

Davis, Angela (Activist, Politician)
SpeakOut
PO Box 22748
Oakland, CA 94609-5348, USA

Davis, Anthony (Athlete, Basketball Player)
c/o Thad Foucher *Wasserman Media Group*
10960 Wilshire Blvd Ste 1200
Los Angeles, CA 90024-3714, USA

Davis, Anthony (Athlete, Football Player)
c/o Drew Rosenhaus *Rosenhaus Sports Representation*
3921 Alton Rd # 440
Miami Beach, FL 33140-3852, USA

Davis, Anthony (Athlete, Football Player)
A D 28 Development Inc 29 Firwood
Irvine, CA 92604-4632, USA

Davis, Anthony (Athlete, Football Player)
8500 W 131st Ter Apt 1834
Overland Park, KS 66213-5157, USA

Davis, Antone (Athlete, Football Player)
2252 Red Bud Rd
Sevierville, TN 37876, USA

Davis, Antonio (Athlete, Basketball Player)
1883 Cedar Glenn Way
Atlanta, GA 30339-8563, USA

Davis, Ardie A (Writer)
c/o Staff Member *Harvard Common Press, The*
535 Albany St Ste 47
Boston, MA 02118-2559, USA

Davis, Aree (Actor)
c/o Myrna Lieberman *Myrna Lieberman Management*
3001 Hollyridge Dr
Hollywood, CA 90068-1951, USA

Davis, Arthur (Athlete, Football Player)
8260 SW Woodbridge Ct
Wilsonville, OR 97070-7458, USA

Davis, Bard (Basketball Player)
Los Angeles Lakers
2703 Ridge Top Ln
Arlington, TX 76006-2729, USA

Davis, Baron (Athlete, Basketball Player)
c/o Staff Member *BDA Sports Management*
700 Ygnacio Valley Rd Ste 330
Walnut Creek, CA 94596-3838, USA

Davis, Barry (Athlete, Olympic Athlete, Wrestler)
PO Box 2
Mauston, WI 53948-0002, USA

Davis, Ben (Athlete, Baseball Player)
2 Pine Ln
Chadds Ford, PA 19317-9730, USA

Davis, Ben (Athlete, Football Player)
1144 Brandon Rd
Cleveland, OH 44112-3632, USA

Davis, Bill (Athlete, Baseball Player)
6638 Knox AveS
Minneapolis, MN 55423-2161, USA

Davis, Bill (Race Car Driver)
11 N Robbins St
Thomasville, NC 27360-8970, USA

Davis, Billy (Athlete, Football Player)
5813 Tautoga Dr
El Paso, TX 79924-5620, USA

Davis, Bob (Athlete, Baseball Player)
PO Box 1123
Salina, OK 74365-1123, USA

Davis, Brad (Athlete, Basketball Player)
2703 Ridge Top Ln
Arlington, TX 76006-2729, USA

Davis, Brian (Athlete, Football Player)
9874 Red Sumac Pl
Parker, CO 80138-7868, USA

Davis, Brian (Athlete, Golfer)
10545 Down Lakeview Cir
Windermere, FL 34786-7911, USA

Davis, Brianne (Actor)
c/o Liza Anderson *Anderson Group Public Relations*
8060 Melrose Ave Fl 4
Los Angeles, CA 90046-7038, USA

Davis, Brock (Athlete, Baseball Player)
23759 Heliotrope Way
Moreno Valley, CA 92557-2858, USA

Davis, Buddy (Athlete, Basketball Player, Olympic Athlete)

Davis, Butch (Athlete, Baseball Player)
1108 Brucemont Dr
Garner, NC 27529-4505, USA

Davis, Carole (Actor)
c/o Judy Orbach *Judy O Productions*
6136 Glen Holly St
Hollywood, CA 90068-2338, USA

Davis, Charles (Athlete, Basketball Player)
615 Main St
Nashville, TN 37206-3603, USA

Davis, Charles (Chili) (Athlete, Baseball Player)
c/o Team Member *San Francisco Giants*
24 Willie Mays Plz
Sbc Park
San Francisco, CA 94107-2199, USA

Davis, Charles ""Chili (Athlete, Baseball Player)
4625 Lake Washington Blvd SE
Bellevue, WA 98006-2625, USA

Davis, Charles D (Athlete, Football Player)
8935 Aspen Meadow Dr
Houston, TX 77071-3256, USA

Davis, Charles M (Athlete, Football Player)
2391 Crescent Park Dr
Houston, TX 77077-6756, USA

Davis, Charles Michael (Actor)
c/o Mary Erickson *Mary Erickson Management*
3900 San Fernando Rd Unit 1507
Glendale, CA 91204-2866, USA

Davis, Charlie (Athlete, Basketball Player)
302 Heather Ridge Ct
Greensboro, NC 27455-8360, USA

Davis, Chip (Musician)
c/o Staff Member *Brokaw Company*
PO Box 462
Culver City, CA 90232-0462, USA

Davis, Chris (Athlete, Baseball Player)
c/o Scott Boras *Boras Corporation*
18 Corporate Plaza Dr
Newport Beach, CA 92660-7901, USA

Davis, Christine (Writer)
Lighthearted Press Inc
PO Box 90125
Portland, OR 97290-0125, USA

Davis, Christopher (Chris) W (Athlete, Football Player)
PO Box 5000
Ogdensburg, NY 13669-5000, USA

Davis, Clarence (Athlete, Football Player)
171 Longleaf St
Pickerington, OH 43147-7940, USA

Davis, Clifton (Actor)
c/o Staff Member *Agency for the Performing Arts (APA)*
405 S Beverly Dr Ste 500
Beverly Hills, CA 90212-4425, USA

Davis, Clive (Business Person, Producer)
c/o Allen Grubman *Grubman Shire & Meiselas*
152 W 57th St Fl 31
New York, NY 10019-3310, USA

Davis, Dana (Actor)
c/o Darryl Marshak *Marshak/Zachary Company, The*
8840 Wilshire Blvd Fl 1
Beverly Hills, CA 90211-2606, USA

Davis, Daniel (Actor)
c/o Gary Gersh *Innovative Artists*
235 Park Ave S Fl 7
New York, NY 10003-1405, USA

Davis, Demario (Athlete, Football Player)
c/o Alan Herman *Sportstars Inc*
1370 Avenue of the Americas Fl 19
New York, NY 10019-4602, USA

Davis, DeRay (Actor)
c/o April Lim *Global Artists Agency*
6253 Hollywood Blvd Apt 508
Los Angeles, CA 90028-8251, USA

Davis, Dexter (Athlete, Football Player)
5078 Old Mountain Trl
Powder Spgs, GA 30127-4317, USA

Davis, Dick (Athlete, Football Player)
1626 N 137th St
Omaha, NE 68154-3826, USA

Davis, Dick (Athlete, Baseball Player)
11091 Sultan St
Moreno Valley, CA 92557-4917, USA

Davis, Dick (Athlete, Football Player)
1626 N 137th St
Omaha, NE 68154-3826, USA

Davis, Domanick (Athlete, Football Player)
1023 Johnson Rd
Breaux Bridge, LA 70517-7018, USA

Davis, Dominique (Athlete, Football Player)
c/o Adisa P Bakari *Kelley Drye & Warren LLP*
3050 K St NW Ste 400
Washington, DC 20007-5100, USA

Davis, Donald (Athlete, Football Player)
739 E 48th St
Los Angeles, CA 90011-4008, USA

Davis, Don H Jr (Business Person)
Rockwell International
777 E Wisconsin Ave Ste 1400
Milwaukee, WI 53202-5317, USA

Davis, Dorsett (Athlete, Football Player)
605 Rosemary Rd
Cleveland, MS 38732-2048, USA

Davis, Doug (Athlete, Baseball Player)
279 Whites Church Rd
Bloomsburg, PA 17815-7156, USA

Davis, Doug (Athlete, Baseball Player)
26125 N 116th St Unit 7
Scottsdale, AZ 85255-8721, USA

Davis, Drew (Athlete, Football Player)
c/o Derrick Fox *Derrick Fox Management*
Prefers to be contacted by telephone
CA, USA

Davis, Dwight (Athlete, Basketball Player)
PO Box 324
Newfields, NH 03856-0324, USA

Davis, Ed (Athlete, Basketball Player)
36750 US Highway 19 N # 26-3437
Palm Harbor, FL 34684-1239, USA

Davis, Elizabeth (Musician)
Rave Booking
PO Box 310780
Jamaica, NY 11431-0780, USA

Davis, Eric K (Athlete, Baseball Player)
1370 E San Carlos Way
Chandler, AZ 85249-4718, USA

Davis, Eric W (Athlete, Football Player)
3737 Coyote Cyn
Soquel, CA 95073-3034, USA

Davis, Frenchie (Musician)
c/o Stephen Ford *Diva Central Inc*
7510 W Sunset Blvd # 1445
Los Angeles, CA 90046-3408, USA

Davis, Gary (Athlete, Football Player)
10750 San Marcos Rd
Atascadero, CA 93422-2126, USA

Davis, Geena (Actor)
8033 W Sunset Blvd Ste 367
W Hollywood, CA 90046-2401, USA

Davis, Geoff (Congressman, Politician)
1119 Longworth Hob
Washington, DC 20515-0531, USA

Davis, George (Athlete, Baseball Player)
3092 Kimball Ave
Memphis, TN 38114-4070, USA

Davis, Gerry (Athlete, Baseball Player)
2440 Stroebe Island Dr
Appleton, WI 54914-8758, USA

Davis, Gray (Politician)
10430 Wilshire Blvd Apt 605
Los Angeles, CA 90024-4653, USA

Davis, Greg (Athlete, Football Player)
793 Vernon Rd NE
Rome, GA 30165-6445, USA

Davis, Harper (Athlete, Football Player)
1224 Springdale Dr
Jackson, MS 39211-3130, USA

Davis, Harrison (Athlete, Football Player)
6409 Lesser Dr
Greeley, CO 80634-9595, USA

Davis, Harry (Athlete, Basketball Player)
1966 E 75th St
Cleveland, OH 44103-4125, USA

Davis, Hope (Actor)
152 Jermain Ave
Sag Harbor, NY 11963-3413, USA

Davis, Hubert (Athlete, Basketball Player)
204 Lancaster Dr
Chapel Hill, NC 27517-3429, USA

Davis, Jack (Athlete, Football Player)
203 Creek St
Heavener, OK 74937-2210, USA

Davis, Jacke (Athlete, Baseball Player)
6806 Castle Pines Ct
Tyler, TX 75703-5890, USA

Davis, James (Athlete, Football Player)
5701 S St Andrews Pl
Los Angeles, CA 90062-2649, USA

Davis, James (Basketball Player)
Rochesster Royals
44 Van Ter
Sparkill, NY 10976-1406, USA

Davis, James (Cartoonist)
5440 E Country Rd 450 N
Albany, IN 47320-9728, USA

Davis, Jamie (Actor)
c/o Sarah Spear *Curtis Brown Ltd*
28-29 Hay Market
Hay Market House
London SW1Y 4SP, UNITED KINGDOM

Davis, Jason (Athlete, Baseball Player)
2245 NO Pone Rd NW
Georgetown, TN 37336-4710, USA

Davis, Jay (Athlete, Golfer)
2152 S State St
Springfield, IL 62704-4526, USA

Davis, Jeff (Actor)
c/o Staff Member *United Talent Agency (UTA)*
9336 Civic Center Dr
Beverly Hills, CA 90210-3604, USA

Davis, Jeff (Athlete, Football Player)
162 Heritage Place Dr
Pendleton, SC 29670-1250, USA

Davis, Jeremy (Musician)
c/o Randy Dease *Fly South Music Group*
37 N Orange Ave Ste 790
Orlando, FL 32801-2450, USA

Davis, Jerome (Athlete, Football Player)
515 N 4th St
Palatka, FL 32177-3523, USA

Davis, Jerry (Baseball Player)
San Diego Padres
72 Theresa St
Ewing, NJ 08618-1531, USA

Davis, Jesse (Musician)
Concord Records
100 N Crescent Dr Ste 275
Beverly Hills, CA 90210-5412, USA

Davis, Jill A (Writer)
Random House
1745 Broadway Frnt 3 # B1
New York, NY 10019-4343, USA

Davis, Jimmy (Athlete, Football Player)
616 Briar Patch Ter
Waxhaw, NC 28173-6822, USA

Davis, JJ (Athlete, Baseball Player)
2112 Heath Lake Dr
Mint Hill, NC 28227-4608, USA

Davis, Jody (Athlete, Baseball Player)
5631 N 79th St Unit 4
Scottsdale, AZ 85250-6546, USA

Davis, Joe (Sportscaster)

Davis, Joel (Athlete, Baseball Player)
609 Matterhorn Rd
Jacksonville, FL 32216-9166, USA

Davis, John (Actor, Director, Producer)
c/o Staff Member *DJ Classicz*
150 S Barrington Pl
Los Angeles, CA 90049-3306, USA

Davis, John (Athlete, Baseball Player)
76871 Castle Ct
Palm Desert, CA 92211-7100, USA

Davis, John (Athlete, Football Player)
901 Forest Pond Dr
Marietta, GA 30068-4420, USA

Davis, Johnny (Athlete, Basketball Player, Coach)
28 S Kaufman Stone Way
Biltmore Lake, NC 28715-7722, USA

Davis, Johnny (Athlete, Football Player)
PO Box 550
Edgewater, NJ 07020-0550, USA

Davis, Josie (Actor)
c/o Rebecca Lyle *Authentic Talent & Literary Management*
3615 Eastham Dr # 650
Culver City, CA 90232-2410, USA

Davis, Judy (Actor)
c/o Ann Churchill-Brown *Shanahan Management*
Level 3 Berman House
Surry Hills 02010, AUSTRALIA

Davis, Kane (Athlete, Baseball Player)
1558 Noble Rdg
Reedy, WV 25270-9540, USA

Davis, Kara (Adult Film Star)
PO Box 9465
Newport Beach, CA 92658-9465, USA

Davis, Keith B (Athlete, Football Player)
1343 Marvin Gdns
Lancaster, TX 75134-1684, USA

Davis, Kenneth E (Athlete, Football Player)
1224 Brooklawn Dr
Arlington, TX 76018-2952, USA

Davis, Kim (Athlete, Hockey Player)
14 Shorecrest Dr
Winnipeg, MB R3P 1N2, Canada

Davis, Knile (Athlete, Football Player)

Davis, Kristin (Actor)
c/o Ame Vanlden *Vanlden Public Relations*
4070 Wilson Pike
Franklin, TN 37067-8126, USA

Davis, Kyle (Athlete, Football Player)
104 Futurity Ln
Weatherford, TX 76087-4606, USA

Davis, Lance (Athlete, Baseball Player)
5845 Old Berkley Rd
Auburndale, FL 33823-8361, USA

Davis, L Edward (Religious Leader)
Evangelical Presbyterian Church
26049 5 Mile Rd
Detroit, MI 48239-3235, USA

Davis, Lee (Director)
Gersh Agency
232 N Canon Dr
Beverly Hills, CA 90210-5302, USA

Davis, Lee (Athlete, Basketball Player)
5024 Fieldgreen Xing Apt B2
Stone Mountain, GA 30088-3103, USA

Davis, Leonard (Athlete, Football Player)
5105 Monterey Dr
Frisco, TX 75034-4081, USA

Davis, Linda (Musician)
PO Box 767
Hermitage, TN 37076-0767, USA

Davis, Lorenzo (Athlete, Football Player)
149 Vista Luna Dr
Davie, FL 33325-6929, USA

Davis, Lucy (Actor, Director)
c/o Rebecca Taylor *PMK/BNC Public Relations*
1840 Century Park E Ste 1400
Los Angeles, CA 90067-2115, USA

Davis, Mac (Actor, Musician, Songwriter)
346 N Tigertail Rd
Los Angeles, CA 90049-2806, USA

Davis, Mackenzie (Actor)
c/o Alexandra Kahn *Relevant (NY)*
333 Hudson St Rm 502
New York, NY 10013-1033, USA

Davis, Mark (Athlete, Baseball Player)
8867 E Sierra Pinta Dr
Scottsdale, AZ 85255-9174, USA

Davis, Mark A (Athlete, Basketball Player)
108 Government Cir # A
Thibodaux, LA 70301-6615, USA

Davis, Mark G (Basketball Player)
Milwaukee Bucks
3120 Aaron Dr
Chesapeake, VA 23323-2600, USA

Davis, Mark W (Athlete, Baseball Player)
8867 E Sierra Pinta Dr
Scottsdale, AZ 85255-9174, USA

Davis, Martha (Musician)
c/o Trip Brown *Paradise Artists*
108 E Matilija St
Ojai, CA 93023-2639, USA

Davis, Marv (Butch) (Athlete, Football Player)
700 Ponce De Leon Ave
Clewiston, FL 33440-2413, USA

Davis, Mary (Athlete, Football Player)
700 Ponce De Leon Ave
Clewiston, FL 33440-2413, USA

Davis, Matthew (Actor)
1958 Glencoe Way
Los Angeles, CA 90068-3113, USA

Davis, Melvyn (Athlete, Basketball Player)
PO Box 29
Suffern, NY 10901-0029, USA

Davis, Meryl (Athlete, Figure Skater, Olympic Athlete)
c/o Hailey Ohnuki *IMG World*
200 5th Ave Fl 7
New York, NY 10010-3307, USA

Davis, Michael (Athlete, Basketball Player)
110 W Clay St
Richmond, VA 23220-3913, USA

Davis, Michael A (Athlete, Football Player)
4913 W 11th Street Rd Unit 7
Greeley, CO 80634-1908, USA

Davis, Michael L (Athlete, Football Player)
PO Box 614
Beaver Falls, PA 15010-0614, USA

Davis, Mike (Athlete, Baseball Player)
c/o Staff Member *Oakland Athletics*
7000 Coliseum Way Ste 3
Oakland, CA 94621-1992, USA

Davis, Mike (Athlete, Basketball Player)
100 W 92nd St Apt 29E
New York, NY 10025-7546, USA

Davis, Mike (Athlete, Football Player)
37039 N 109th St
Scottsdale, AZ 85262-3582, USA

Davis, Monti (Athlete, Basketball Player)
328 Tod Ln
Youngstown, OH 44504-1403, USA

Davis, N Jan (Astronaut)
4105 Cumberland Pass Apt 814
Fort Worth, TX 76116-0753, USA

Davis, Odie (Athlete, Baseball Player)
7314 Hidden His N
San Antonio, TX 78244-1504, USA

Davis, Oliver (Athlete, Football Player)
1527 Evanston Ct
Marietta, GA 30062-2148, USA

Davis, Paige (Television Host)
c/o Staff Member *WME|IMG*
9601 Wilshire Blvd
Beverly Hills, CA 90210-5213, USA

Davis, Paschall (Athlete, Football Player)
937 Plumeria Dr
Arlington, TX 76002-2402, USA

Davis, Patti (Writer)
c/o Staff Member *Hay House, Inc*
PO Box 5100
Carlsbad, CA 92018-5100, USA

Davis, Paul (Athlete, Football Player)
227 Oval Park Pl # Pi
Chapel Hill, NC 27517-8116, USA

Davis, Phyllis (Actor)
29330 SE Hillyard Dr # D14
Boring, OR 97009-8502, USA

Davis, Preston (Athlete, Football Player)
1282 W 100th Pl # Pi
Northglenn, CO 80260-6208, USA

Davis, Raiai (Athlete, Baseball Player)
9 Pear Grv
East Lyme, CT 06333-1177, USA

Davis, Ralph (Athlete, Basketball Player)
2624 S Kathwood Cir
Cincinnati, OH 45236-1026, USA

Davis, Rennie (Politician)
Birth of a New Nation
905 S Gilpin St
Denver, CO 80209-4520, USA

Davis, Reuben (Athlete, Football Player)
7105 Kepley Rd
Chapel Hill, NC 27517-8792, USA

Davis, Richard (Musician)
SRO Artists
6629 University Ave Ste 206
Middleton, WI 53562-3037, USA

Davis, Ricky (Athlete, Basketball Player)
c/o Jeff Schwartz *Excel Sports Management*
1700 Broadway Fl 29
New York, NY 10019-6559, USA

Davis, Ricky (Athlete, Football Player)
5715 Whirlaway Rd
Palm Beach Gardens, FL 33418-7739, USA

Davis, Robbie (Horse Racer)
756 Stone Church Rd
Middle Grove, NY 12850-1131, USA

Davis, Roger (Actor)
Janette Anderson Talent Agency
9682 Via Torino
Burbank, CA 91504-1410, USA

Davis, Roger (Athlete, Football Player)
27950 Belcourt Rd
Cleveland, OH 44124-5614, USA

Davis, Ron (Athlete, Basketball Player)
11748 N 90th Pl # Pi
Scottsdale, AZ 85260-6841, USA

Davis, Ronald (Ron) (Artist)
PO Box 293
Arroyo Hondo, NM 87513-0293, USA

Davis, Ronald (Ron) (Athlete, Football Player)
4717 Pompton Ln
Chester, VA 23831-4335, USA

Davis, Ross (Athlete, Baseball Player)
8042 Highway 71
Garwood, TX 77442-4158, USA

Davis, Russ (Athlete, Baseball Player)
3351 Crescent Dr
Bessemer, AL 35023-2919, USA

Davis, Russell (Athlete, Football Player)
605 Jones Ferry Rd
Carrboro, NC 27510-2106, USA

Davis, Russell (Athlete, Football Player)
1208 Tanbark Ln E
Jackson, MI 49203-1275, USA

Davis, Russell A (Athlete, Football Player)
4236 Crosswood Dr
Burtonsville, MD 20866-1350, USA

Davis, Russell S (Russ) (Baseball Player)
3351 Crescent Dr
Hueytown, AL 35023-2919, USA

Davis, Ruth (Athlete, Baseball Player, Commentator)
1917 Park Ave
Cheyenne, WY 82007-3395, USA

Davis, Sam (Athlete, Football Player)
423 Edgemont St
Mt Washington, PA 15211-2405, USA

Davis, Sammy (Athlete, Football Player)
4020 Murphy Canyon Rd
San Diego, CA 92123-4407, USA

Davis, Stephen (Athlete, Football Player)
16 Dunleith Ct
Irmo, SC 29063-8042, USA

Davis, Steve (Athlete, Baseball Player)
601186th St
Lubbock, TX 79424-6708, USA

Davis, Steve (Athlete, Baseball Player)
6011 86th St
Lubbock, TX 79424-6708, USA

Davis, Steve (Athlete, Football Player)
906 E 26th St
Buena Vista, VA 24416-1804, USA

Davis, Storm (Athlete, Baseball Player)
8469 Mizner Cir E
Jacksonville, FL 32217-4326, USA

Davis, Storm George (Baseball Player)
7931 Dawsons Creek Dr
Jacksonville, FL 32222-4905, USA

Davis, Susan (Congressman, Politician)
1526 Longworth Hob
Washington, DC 20515-3305, USA

Davis, Tamra (Director)
7126 Fernhill Dr
Malibu, CA 90265-4243, USA

Davis, Ted (Athlete, Football Player)
4220 Lower Roswell Rd # 232
Marietta, GA 30068-4128, USA

Davis, Terrell (Athlete, Football Player)
30949 Central Park Dr
Murrieta, CA 92563-8820, USA

Davis, Terry (Athlete, Basketball Player)
2933 Kenmore Rd
Richmond, VA 23225-1429, USA

Davis, Thomas (Athlete, Football Player)
c/o Todd France *Creative Artists Agency (CAA) Sports*
3500 Lenox Rd NE
Atlanta, GA 30326-4228, USA

Davis, Tim (Athlete, Baseball Player)
16161 NW Lakeside Ln
Bristol, FL 32321-3932, USA

Davis, Todd (Actor)
245 S Keystone St
Burbank, CA 91506-2727, USA

Davis, Tommy (Athlete, Baseball Player)
JD Legends Promotions
Chris Potter Sports 9722
Owin11s Mills, MD 21117- 634, USA

Davis, Travis (Athlete, Football Player)
PO Box 35196
Detroit, MI 48235-0196, USA

Davis, Trench (Athlete, Baseball Player)
306 40th Street Cir W
Palmetto, FL 34221-9516, USA

Davis, Troy (Athlete, Football Player)
11861 SW 190th St
Miami, FL 33177-3940, USA

Davis, Vernon (Athlete, Football Player)
c/o John Goschin *Baker Winokur Ryder Public Relations*
9100 Wilshire Blvd
W Tower #500
Beverly Hills, CA 90212-3415, USA

Davis, Vicki (Actor)
c/o Staff Member *Innovative Artists*
1505 10th St
Santa Monica, CA 90401-2805, USA

Davis, Viola (Actor)
c/o Staff Member *JuVee Productions*
3500 W Olive Ave Ste 1470
Burbank, CA 91505-5514, USA

Davis, Vontae (Athlete, Football Player)
c/o Todd France *Creative Artists Agency (CAA) Sports*
3500 Lenox Rd NE
Atlanta, GA 30326-4228, USA

Davis, Wade (Writer)
c/o Staff Member *Simon & Schuster*
1230 Avenue of the Americas Fl CONC1
New York, NY 10020-1586, USA

Davis, Wade (Athlete, Baseball Player)
39 Reservoir Rd
Marlboro, NY 12542-5011, USA

Davis, Walter (Athlete, Basketball Player, Olympic Athlete)
5200 E Donald Ave Apt A
Denver, CO 80222-5539, USA

Davis, Warren (Athlete, Basketball Player)
44429 Oriole Dr Unit 1E1
Fort Mill, SC 29707-5947, USA

Davis, Warwick (Actor)
c/o Paul Lyon-Maris *Independent Talent Group*
40 Whitfield St
London W1T 2RH, UNITED KINGDOM

Davis, Wendell (Athlete, Football Player)
180 Rinconada Ave
Palo Alto, CA 94301-3725, USA

Davis, Wendell (Athlete, Football Player)
10850 Green Mountain Cir Unit 117
Columbia, MD 21044-2300, USA

Davis, Will (Athlete, Football Player)
c/o Doug Hendrickson *Relativity Sports*
2029 Century Park E Ste 1550
Century City, CA 90067-3000, USA

Davis, William (Actor)
c/o Staff Member *Lucas Talent Inc*
1238 Homer St Suite 6
Vancouver, BC V6B 2Y5, CANADA

Davis, William E (Business Person)
Niagara Mohawk Holdings
300 Erie Blvd W
Syracuse, NY 13202-4250, USA

Davis, William L (Business Person)
R R Donnelley & Sons
77 W Wacker Dr
Chicago, IL 60601-1604, USA

Davis, Willie (Athlete, Football Player)
7352 Vista Del Mar Ln
Playa Del Rey, CA 90293-7650, USA

Davis Jr, Greg (Actor, Comedian, Internet Star)
c/o Colleen Schlegel *Schlegel Entertainment*
1119 Colorado Ave Ste 12
Santa Monica, CA 90401-3009, USA

Davison, Beverly C (Religious Leader)
American Baptist Churches
PO Box 851
Valley Forge, PA 19482-0851, USA

Davison, Bruce (Actor)
c/o Beverly Magid *Guttman Associates Public Relations*
118 S Beverly Dr Ste 201
Beverly Hills, CA 90212-3016, USA

Davison, Mike (Athlete, Baseball Player)
578 Prospect St NE
Hutchinson, MN 55350-1715, USA

Davison, Peter (Actor)
'Legally Blonde', Savoy Theatre
The Strand
London WC2R 0ET, UK

Davison, Sam (Religious Leader)
International Baptist Bible Fellowship
720 E Kearney St
Springfield, MO 65803-3428, USA

Davison, Scott (Athlete, Baseball Player)
4507 Sharynne Ln
Torrance, CA 90505-3454, USA

Davis-Wrightsil, Clarissa (Basketball Player)
Phoenix Mercury
201 E Jefferson St
American West Arena
Phoenix, AZ 85004-2412, USA

Davitian, Ken (Actor)
c/o Tess Finkle *Metro Public Relations*
8671 Wilshire Blvd # 208
Beverly Hills, CA 90211-2926, USA

Davkin, Tony (Athlete, Football Player)
5204 Cross Ridge Cir
Woodstock, GA 30188-4381, USA

Davoli, Andrew (Actor)
c/o Greg Clark *Untitled Entertainment*
350 S Beverly Dr Ste 200
Beverly Hills, CA 90212-4819, USA

Daw, Jeff (Athlete, Hockey Player)
150 Union St Apt 208
Providence, RI 02903-1792, USA

Dawber, Pam (Actor)
c/o Staff Member *TalentWorks*
3500 W Olive Ave Ste 1400
Burbank, CA 91505-5512, USA

Dawe, Jason (Athlete, Hockey Player)
9077 Drayton Ln
Fort Mill, SC 29707-6484, USA

Dawes, Dominique (Athlete, Gymnast, Olympic Athlete)
c/o Evan Morgenstein *Premier Management Group (PMG Sports)*
700 Evanvale Ct
Cary, NC 27518-2806, USA

Dawes, Joseph (Cartoonist)
20 Church Ct
Closter, NJ 07624-2803, USA

Dawkins, Brian (Athlete, Football Player)
10010 Tavistock Rd
Orlando, FL 32827-7053, USA

Dawkins, Dale (Athlete, Football Player)
1113 37th Ave SW
Vero Beach, FL 32968-4918, USA

Dawkins, Joe (Athlete, Football Player)
9200 S Harvard Blvd
Los Angeles, CA 90047-3801, USA

Dawkins, Joe (Athlete, Football Player)
4235 Ensenada Dr
Woodland Hills, CA 91364-5403, USA

Dawkins, Johnny (Athlete, Basketball Player)
Central Florida University
4000 Central Florida Blvd
Athletic Dept
Orlando, FL 32816-8005, USA

Dawkins, Paul (Athlete, Basketball Player)
2728 N Hampton Dr
Grand Prairie, TX 75052-4201, USA

Dawkins, Pete (Business Person, Football Player, Heisman Trophy Winner, Politician)
PO Box 218
Rumson, NJ 07760-0218, USA

Dawkins, Sean (Athlete, Football Player)
826 Weichert Dr
Morgan Hill, CA 95037-3785, USA

Dawkins, Travis (Athlete, Baseball Player, Olympic Athlete)
1290 Calhoun Rd
Greenwood, SC 29649-1244, USA

Dawley, Bill (Athlete, Baseball Player)
111 N Silver Manor Cir
Montgomery, TX 77316-1455, USA

Dawley, Joey (Athlete, Baseball Player)
27951 Cactus Ave Unit A
Moreno Valley, CA 92555-3609, USA

Dawley, Joseph W (Joe) (Artist)
13 Wholly St
Cranford, NJ 07016, USA

Dawn, Karena (Fitness Expert)
Tone It Up LLC
703 Pier Ave Ste B # 806
Hermosa Beach, CA 90254-3943, USA

Dawsey, Lawrence (Athlete, Football Player)
4341 Cheval Blvd
Lutz, FL 33558-5328, USA

Dawson, Andre (Athlete, Baseball Player)
Andre Dawson Foundation
PO Box 431339
Miami, FL 33243-1339, USA

Dawson, Ashley Taylor (Actor)
c/o Staff Member *Blackburn Sachs Associates*
88-90 Crawford St
London W1H 2BS, UNITED KINGDOM (UK)

Dawson, Buck (Swimmer)
Swimming Hall of Fame
1 Hall of Fame Dr
Fort Lauderdale, FL 33316-1694, USA

Dawson, Dale (Athlete, Football Player)
1710 E Oak Knoll Cir
Davie, FL 33324-6424, USA

Dawson, Dermontti (Athlete, Football Player)
PO Box 712481
San Diego, CA 92171-2481, USA

Dawson, Devin (Musician)
c/o Jason Owen *Sandbox Entertainment*
3810 Bedford Ave Ste 200
Nashville, TN 37215-2555, USA

Dawson, Douglas A (Doug) (Athlete, Football Player)
Dawson Financial Services
1 Riverway Ste 900
Houston, TX 77056-1906, USA

Dawson, Jajuan (Athlete, Football Player)
2302 Sun Shadow Ln
Spring, TX 77386-1871, USA

Dawson, Jim (Athlete, Basketball Player)
61 Glendale Ave
Rye, NY 10580-1547, USA

Dawson, Keyunta (Athlete, Football Player)
8417 Codesa Way
Indianapolis, IN 46278-5067, USA

Dawson, Lake (Athlete, Football Player)
33228 37th Pl SW
Federal Way, WA 98023-2959, USA

Dawson, Lake (Athlete, Football Player)
33228 37th Pl SW
Federal Way, WA 98023-2959, USA

Dawson, Len (Athlete, Football Player)
1025 W 59th Ter
Kansas City, MO 64113-1335, USA

Dawson, Lenny (Athlete, Football Player, Sportscaster)
1030 W 59th Ter
Kansas City, MO 64113-1336, USA

Dawson, Marco (Athlete, Golfer)
4360 Stillwater Dr
Merritt Island, FL 32952-6320, USA

Dawson, Phil (Athlete, Football Player)
13321 Coleto Creek Trl
Austin, TX 78732-2070, USA

Dawson, Phil (Athlete, Football Player)
1770 Arlington Row
Westlake, OH 44145-3561, USA

Dawson, Rhett (Athlete, Football Player)
1252 Bearkat Canyon Dr
Dripping Spgs, TX 78620-4279, USA

Dawson, Rosario (Actor)
c/o Chelsea Thomas *The Lede Company*
9701 Wilshire Blvd # 930
Beverly Hills, CA 90212-2020, USA

Dawson, Roxann (Actor)
227 Bell Canyon Rd
Bell Canyon, CA 91307-1111, USA

Dawson, Shane (Actor)
c/o Matthew Labov *Forefront Media*
1669 Virginia Rd
Los Angeles, CA 90019-5935, USA

Dawson, Trent (Actor)
c/o Michael Mann *Michael Mann Management*
1728 S Robertson Blvd Apt 4
Los Angeles, CA 90035-4346, USA

Day, Andra (Musician)
c/o Staff Member *Creative Artists Agency (CAA)*
2000 Avenue of the Stars Ste 100
Los Angeles, CA 90067-4705, USA

Day, Bill (Cartoonist)
Memphis Commercial-Appeal
495 Union Ave
Editorial Dept
Memphis, TN 38103-3221, USA

Day, Boots (Athlete, Baseball Player)
1154 Vespasian Way
Chesterfield, MO 63017-3016, USA

Day, Charlie (Actor)
c/o Michelle Benson Margolis *The Lede Company*
9701 Wilshire Blvd # 930
Beverly Hills, CA 90212-2020, USA

Day, Chon (Cartoonist)
127 Main St
Ashaway, RI 02804-2239, USA

Day, Dewon (Athlete, Baseball Player)
1935 Marshall Pl
Jackson, MS 39213-4450, USA

Day, Doris (Actor)
Doris Day Animal Foundation
8033 W Sunset Blvd Ste 845
Los Angeles, CA 90046-2401, USA

Day, Felicia (Actor)
c/o Ari Greenburg *WME|IMG*
9601 Wilshire Blvd
Beverly Hills, CA 90210-5213, USA

Day, Glen (Athlete, Golfer)
25 Valley Estates Ct
Little Rock, AR 72212, USA

Day, Howie (Musician)
c/o Staff Member *Supreme Entertainment Artists*
PO Box 15601
Boston, MA 02215-0011, USA

Day, Inaya (Musician)
c/o Staff Member *Diva Central Inc*
7510 W Sunset Blvd # 1445
Los Angeles, CA 90046-3408, USA

Day, Jason (Actor)
c/o Julio Caro *Caro Entertainment*
3221 Hutchison Ave Ste H
Los Angeles, CA 90034-3298, USA

Day, Jason (Athlete, Golfer)
c/o Bud Martin *Wasserman Media Group / SFX Golf*
11921 Freedom Dr Ste 1180
Reston, VA 20190-5634, USA

Day, Joe (Athlete, Hockey Player)
805 Shoreline Rd
Lake Barrington, IL 60010-3878, USA

Day, Matt (Actor)
Robyn Gardiner Mgmt
397 Riley St
Surrey Hills, NSW 02010, AUSTRALIA

Day, Mikey (Actor)
c/o Michael Goldman *Michael Goldman Management*
7471 Melrose Ave Ste &11
Los Angeles, CA 90046-7551, USA

Day, Morris (Musician)
805 Hampton Bluff Dr
Alpharetta, GA 30004-3074, USA

Day, Pat (Horse Racer)
14703 Isleworth Ct
Louisville, KY 40245-5256, USA

Day, Terry (Athlete, Football Player)
PO Box 85
Pickens, MS 39146-0085, USA

Day, Wallis (Actor)

Day, Zach (Athlete, Baseball Player)
11220 Brookbridge Dr
Cincinnati, OH 45249-2201, USA

Dayal, Manish (Actor)
c/o Laura Hersh *Industry Entertainment Partners*
955 Carrillo Dr Ste 300
Los Angeles, CA 90048-5400, USA

Dayan, Isaac (Actor)
c/o Staff Member *TV Caracol*
Calle 76 #11 - 35
Piso 10AA
Bogota DC 26484, COLOMBIA

Daye, Darren (Athlete, Basketball Player)
17 Elderberry
Irvine, CA 92603-3703, USA

Dayett, Brian (Athlete, Baseball Player)
276 Phillips Dr
Winchester, TN 37398-4268, USA

Daykin, Anthony (Athlete, Football Player)
5204 Cross Ridge Cir
Woodstock, GA 30188-4381, USA

Day-Lewis, Daniel (Actor)
c/o Victoria Belfrage *Julian Belfrage & Associates*
9 Argyll St Fl 3
London W1F 7TG, UNITED KINGDOM

Dayley, Ken (Athlete, Baseball Player)
1300 Windgate Way Ct
Chesterfield, MO 63005-4497, USA

Dayne, Bella (Actor)
c/o Jonathan Hall *Identity Agency Group (UK)*
95 Grays Inn Rd
London WC1X 8TX, UNITED KINGDOM

Dayne, Ron (Athlete, Football Player, Heisman Trophy Winner)
2135 Regent St
Madison, WI 53726-3941, USA

Dayne, Taylor (Actor, Musician)
c/o Konrad Leh *Creative Talent Group*
1900 Avenue of the Stars Ste 2475
Los Angeles, CA 90067-4512, USA

Dayton, Jonathan (Director)
505 Radcliffe Ave
Pacific Palisades, CA 90272-4330, USA

Dayton, June (Actor)
Abrams Artists
9200 W Sunset Blvd Ste 1125
Los Angeles, CA 90069-3610, USA

Dayton, Mark (Politician)
330 Maryland Ave NE
Washington, DC 20002-5712, USA

Daze, Eric (Athlete, Hockey Player)
445 E 4th St
Hinsdale, IL 60521-4659, USA

D. Bishop Jr., Sanford (Congressman, Politician)

D. Clarke, Yvette (Congressman, Politician)
1029 Longworth Hob
Washington, DC 20515-2304, USA

dc Talk (Music Group, Musician)
c/o Staff Member *True Artist Management*
227 3rd Ave N
Franklin, TN 37064-2504, USa

D (DelVecchio), Pauly (DJ, Reality Star)
c/o Michael Schweiger *Central Entertainment Group*
250 W 40th St Fl 12
New York, NY 10018-4601, USA

D. Dicks, Norman (Congressman, Politician)
2467 Rayburn Hob
Washington, DC 20515-4706, USA

Dea, Bill (Athlete, Hockey Player)
2636 W Bartlett Way
Queen Creek, AZ 85142-6611, USA

Deacon, John (Musician)
The Mill Mill Lane
367 Windsor Hwy
New Windsor, NY 12553-7900, USA

Deacon, Richard (Artist)
Lisson Gallery
67 Lisson St
London NW1 5DA, UNITED KINGDOM (UK)

Dead Can Dance (Music Group)
c/o Staff Member *WME|IMG*
9601 Wilshire Blvd
Beverly Hills, CA 90210-5213, USA

Deaderick, Brandon (Athlete, Football Player)
c/o Tony Paige *Dream Point Sports*
1455 Pennsylvania Ave NW Ste 225
Washington, DC 20004-1026, USA

Dead marsh, Adam (Athlete, Hockey Player)
Colorado Avalanche
1000 Chopper Cir
Denver, CO 80204-5805

Deadmarsh, Adam (Athlete, Hockey Player, Olympic Athlete)
519 Backcountry Ln
Highlands Ranch, CO 80126-5633, USA

Deadmarsh, Butch (Athlete, Hockey Player)
282 Diamond Dr SE
Calgary, AB T2J 7E2, Canada

deadmau5 (Music Group)
c/o Joel Zimmerman *WME|IMG (NY)*
11 Madison Ave Fl 18
New York, NY 10010-3669, USA

Deadsy (Music Group)

Dead, The (Music Group)
c/o Staff Member *Paradigm (Monterey)*
404 W Franklin St
Monterey, CA 93940-2303, USA

Deakin, Paul (Musician)
AristoMedia
1620 16th Ave S
Nashville, TN 37212-2908, USA

Deal, Cot (Athlete, Baseball Player)
9009 N May Ave Apt 164
Oklahoma City, OK 73120-4464, USA

Deal, Ellis (Athlete, Baseball Player)
9009 N May Ave Apt 164
Oklahoma City, OK 73120-4464, USA

Deal, Kelley (Musician)
Wire & Twine
4089 Langland St
Cincinnati, OH 45223-2298, USA

Deal, Kim (Musician)
c/o Richard Jones *Key Music Group (UK)*
Edenhurst 87 Station Road
Marple
Cheshire SK6 6NY, UK

Deal, Lance (Athlete, Olympic Athlete)
4715 Fox Hollow Rd
Eugene, OR 97405-5302, USA

Deal, Nathan (Politician)
The Office of the Governor
203 State Capitol SW
State of Georgia
Atlanta, GA 30334-1600, USA

de Almeida, Joaquim (Actor)
c/o Alsira Garcia Maroto *Alsira Garcia-Maroto Talent Agency*
Calle De Los Invencibles 8
Bajo
Madrid 28019, SPAIN

Dean, Barry (Athlete, Hockey Player)
315 Marsh
Maple Creek, SK S0N 1N0, Canada

Dean, Billy (Musician)
PO Box 354
Smithville, TN 37166-0354, USA

Dean, Christopher (Dancer)
124 Ladies Mile Road
Brighton
East Sussex BN1 8TE, UNITED KINGDOM (UK)

Dean, Eddie (Actor, Musician)
32161 Sailview Ln
Westlake Village, CA 91361-3620, USA

Dean, Ester (Actor, Musician)
Hummingbird Talent
2220 Colorado Ave
Santa Monica, CA 90404-3506, USA

Dean, Fred (Athlete, Football Player)
3911 Whitchurch Dr
Houston, TX 77066-4535, USA

Dean, Fred (Athlete, Football Player)
2411 Highway 3061
Ruston, LA 71270-9626, USA

Dean, Howard (Politician)
325 S Cove Rd
Burlington, VT 05401-5447, USA

Dean, Ira (Musician)
Graham Agency
6999 E Business 20
Odessa, TX 79762-5483, USA

Dean, John (Politician)
9496 Rembert Ln
Beverly Hills, CA 90210-1720, USA

Dean, Kevin (Athlete, Hockey Player)
c/o Staff Member *Lowell Devils*
300 Martin Luther King Jr Way
Lowell, MA 01852-1050, USA

Dean, Kiley (Musician)
c/o Staff Member *Interscope Records (LA) - Main*
2220 Colorado Ave
Santa Monica, CA 90404-3506, USA

Dean, Loren (Actor)
c/o Amy Guenther *Gateway Management Company Inc*
860 Via De La Paz Ste F10
Pacific Palisades, CA 90272-3631, USA

Dean, Randy (Athlete, Football Player)
11850 N Sandhill Cir
Mequon, WI 53092-2995, USA

Dean, Ted (Athlete, Football Player)
16474 W Lava Dr
Surprise, AZ 85374-6250, USA

Dean, Tommy (Athlete, Baseball Player)
PO Box 1014
Iuka, MS 38852-6014, USA

Dean, Vernon (Athlete, Football Player)
2223 Fall Meadow Dr
Missouri City, TX 77459-3337, USA

DeAnda, Paula (Musician)
c/o Staff Member *RCA Label Group UK*
9 Derry St
London W8 5HY, UK

DeAngelis, Barbara (Writer)
c/o Staff Member *St Martins Press*
175 5th Ave
Publicity Dept
New York, NY 10010-7703, USA

Deangelis, Billy (Athlete, Basketball Player)
14 Pickering Dr
Trenton, NJ 08691-2332, USA

DeAngelis, Meg (Actor)
c/o Ben Davis *WME/IMG (NY)*
11 Madison Ave Fl 18
New York, NY 10010-3669, USA

De Aragon, Maria (Actor)
c/o Staff Member *Coolwaters Productions*
10061 Riverside Dr # 531
Toluca Lake, CA 91602-2560, USA

Dearden, James (Director)
International Creative Mgmt
8942 Wilshire Blvd # 219
Beverly Hills, CA 90211-1908, USA

Deardorff, Jeff (Athlete, Baseball Player)
16823 Rockwell Heights Ln
Clermont, FL 34711-7907, USA

Deardurff-Schmidt, Deena (Swimmer)
742 Murray Dr
El Cajon, CA 92020-5640, USA

De Armas, Ana (Actor)
c/o Jill Littman *Impression Entertainment*
9229 W Sunset Blvd Ste 700
Los Angeles, CA 90069-3407, USA

de Armas, Roly (Baseball Player)
2650 Countryside Blvd Apt B102
Clearwater, FL 33761-3604, USA

DeArmond, Frank (Astronaut)
5620 E Colby St
Mesa, AZ 85205-7418, USA

Deas, Justin (Actor)
41 Bradford Ave
Montclair, NJ 07043-1024, USA

Death Cab for Cutie (Music Group)
c/o Jordan Kurland *Zeitgeist Artist Management*
600 York St Ste 216
San Francisco, CA 94110-2119, USA

Deavenport, Earnest Jr (Business Person)
Eastman Chemical Co
100 N Eastman Rd
Kingsport, TN 37660-5299, USA

Deaver, Jeffrey (Writer)
Pocket Star Books
1230 Avenue of the Americas
New York, NY 10020-1513, USA

Deb, Debbie (Musician)
c/o Staff Member *Green Light Talent Agency*
24024 Saint Moritz Dr
Valencia, CA 91355-2033, USA

DeBarge, Eldra (El) (Musician)
c/o Carlos Keyes *Red Entertainment Agency*
3537 36th St Ste 2
Astoria, NY 11106-1347, USA

DeBarge, Kristinia (Musician)
c/o Staff Member *Edmonds Entertainment Group*
3352 Clerendon Rd
Beverly Hills, CA 90210-1059, USA

Debarr, Denny (Athlete, Baseball Player)
33843 Juliet Cir
Fremont, CA 94555-3452, USA

de Beaufort, India (Actor)
c/o Cassandra Vargas *PMK/BNC Public Relations*
1840 Century Park E Ste 1400
Los Angeles, CA 90067-2115, USA

De Becker, Gain (Commentator)
5064 Lemona Ave
Sherman Oaks, CA 91403-1341, USA

DeBell, Kristine (Actor)
c/o Ted Elston *Karma Talent Management*
453 S Rexford Dr
Beverly Hills, CA 90212-4711, USA

De Bello, James (Actor, Musician)
c/o Craig Shapiro *ICM Partners*
10250 Constellation Blvd Fl 7
Los Angeles, CA 90067-6207, USA

DeBello, James (Actor)
c/o Craig Shapiro *ICM Partners*
10250 Constellation Blvd Fl 7
Los Angeles, CA 90067-6207, USA

Debenedet, Nelson (Athlete, Hockey Player)
38142 N Vista Dr
Livonia, MI 48152-1066, USA

De Benning, Burr (Actor)
4235 Kingfisher Rd
Calabasas, CA 91302-1842, USA

DeBenning, Burr (Actor)
4235 Kingfisher Rd
Calabasas, CA 91302-1842, USA

DeBerg, Steve (Athlete, Coach, Football Player)
17920 Simms Rd
Odessa, FL 33556-4751, USA

Debicki, Elizabeth (Actor)
c/o Lisa Kasteler *Wolf-Kasteler Public Relations*
6255 W Sunset Blvd Ste 1111
Los Angeles, CA 90028-7426, USA

Deblois, Lucien (Athlete, Hockey Player)
c/o Staff Member *Vancouver Canucks*
800 Griffiths Way
Vancouver, BC V6B 6G1, Canada

Debnam-Carey, Alycia (Actor)
c/o Lisa Mann *Lisa Mann Creative Management*
19-25 Cope St
Redfern NSW 02016, AUSTRALIA

Debney, John (Musician)
2906 Olney Pl
Burbank, CA 91504-1840, USA

DeBoer, Harm E (Business Person)
Russell Corp
755 Lee St
Alexander City, AL 35010-2638, USA

DeBoer, Nicole (Actor)
c/o Jeff Witjas *Agency for the Performing Arts (APA)*
405 S Beverly Dr Ste 500
Beverly Hills, CA 90212-4425, USA

Deboer, Peter (Athlete, Hockey Player)
New Jersey Devils
165 Mulberry St
Newark, NJ 07102-3607

DeBoer, Rick (Actor)
Pacific Artists
1404-510 Hastings St W
Vancouver, BC V6B 1L8, CANADA

Debol, Dave (Athlete, Hockey Player)
288 Clark St Apt 7
Saline, MI 48176-1247, USA

De Bont, Jan (Director, Producer)
c/o Martin Bauer *Bauer Company, The*
9720 Wilshire Blvd Ste 710
Beverly Hills, CA 90212-2016, USA

DeBorda, Dorothy (Actor)
PO Box 2723
Livermore, CA 94551-2723, USA

DeBose, Ariana (Actor)
c/o Alyx Carr *42West*
600 3rd Ave Fl 23
New York, NY 10016-1914, USA

De Bruijn, Inge (Athlete, Olympic Athlete, Swimmer)
Top voor Talent
Van Ostadestraat 368-2
Amsterdam 1074 XA, NETHERLANDS

DeBrunhoff, Laurent (Writer)
527 W 26th St
New York, NY 10001-5503, USA

Debrusk, Louie (Athlete, Hockey Player)
Edmonton Oilers
11230 110 St NW Dept
Edmonton, AB T5G 3H7, Canada

DeBurgh, Chris (Musician, Songwriter, Writer)
Kenny Thomson Mgmt
754 Fulham Road
London, SW6 5SW, UNITED KINGDOM (UK)

Debus, Jon (Baseball Player, Basketball Coach)
3702 N Highway A1a Apt 703
Hutchinson Island, FL 34949-8550, USA

De Cadenet, Amanda (Actor)
c/o Alyssa Schimel *Kovert Creative*
506 Santa Monica Blvd Ste 400
Santa Monica, CA 90401-2412, USA

De Caestecker, Iain (Actor)
c/o Clair Dobbs *CLD Communications*
4 Broadway Ct
The Broadway
London SW191RG, UNITED KINGDOM

Decambra-Kelley, Lillian (Athlete, Baseball Player, Commentator)
250 South St
Somerset, MA 02726-5616, USA

DeCarlo, Mark (Actor, Television Host)
3292 Carse Dr
Los Angeles, CA 90068-1707, USA

DeCasabianca, Carnille (Actor)
Artmedia
20 Ave Rapp
Paris 75007, FRANCE

DeCastelia, F Robert (Athlete, Track Athlete)
Australian Institute of Sport
PO Box 176
Belconnen, ACT 02616, AUSTRALIA

DeCastro, David (Athlete, Football Player)
c/o Tom Condon *Creative Artists Agency (CAA)*
401 Commerce St PH
Nashville, TN 37219-2516, USA

DeCesare, Carmella (Actor, Model)
c/o Staff Member *Alpha Talent Group*
1201 24th St
Santa Monica, CA 90404-1321, USA

DeCicco, Dom (Athlete, Football Player)

Decinces, Doug (Athlete, Baseball Player)
115 Garnet Ave
Newport Beach, CA 92662-1008, USA

Deck, Inspectah (Musician)
A&E Entertainment
13280 NE Freeway #F328
Houston, TX 77040, USA

Decker, Brooklyn (Actor)
c/o Chris Kiely *Authentic Talent and Literary Management (NY)*
20 Jay St Ste M17
Brooklyn, NY 11201-8300, USA

Decker, Eric (Athlete, Football Player)
c/o Todd France *Creative Artists Agency (CAA) Sports*
3500 Lenox Rd NE
Atlanta, GA 30326-4228, USA

Decker, Jessie James (Musician)
c/o Meghan Prophet *PMK/BNC Public Relations*
1840 Century Park E Ste 1400
Los Angeles, CA 90067-2115, USA

Decker, Marty (Athlete, Baseball Player)
1630 Youngs Ln
Yuba City, CA 95991-1925, USA

Decker, Max (Actor)
c/o Staff Member *TalentWorks*
3500 W Olive Ave Ste 1400
Burbank, CA 91505-5512, USA

Decker, Steve (Athlete, Baseball Player)
1024 Laurelridge St NE
Keizer, OR 97303-7208, USA

Decker, Susan (Business Person)
33 Old Coach Rd
Napa, CA 94558-3858, USA

Deckers, Daphne (Actor)
Nagtzaan
Hoge Naardenweg 44
Hilversum, AG 01217, NETHERLANDS

Deckert, Scott (Actor)
c/o Whitney Tancred *42West*
1840 Century Park E Ste 700
Los Angeles, CA 90067-2122, USA

DeConcini, Dennis (Politician)
6014 Chesterbrook Rd
McLean, VA 22101-3210, USA

de Cordova, Fred (Actor, Director, Producer)
1875 Carla Rdg
Beverly Hills, CA 90210-1936

DeCosta, Roger (Race Car Driver)
MC Sports
1919 Torrance Blvd
Torrance, CA 90501-2722, USA

DeCosta, Sara (Athlete, Hockey Player, Olympic Athlete)
200 Cowesett Green Dr
Warwick, RI 02886-8570, USA

DeCoster, Roger (Race Car Driver)
MC Sports
1919 Torrance Blvd
Torrance, CA 90501-2722, USA

Decter, Midge (Writer)
120 E 81st St
New York, NY 10028-1428, USA

De De, Dorsey (Athlete, Football Player)
6522 Southern Trace Dr
Leeds, AL 35094-6605, USA

de Dios, Silvia (Actor)
c/o Staff Member *TV Caracol*
Calle 76 #11 - 35
Piso 10AA
Bogota DC 26484, COLOMBIA

Dedmon, Jeff (Athlete, Baseball Player)
21102 Broadwell Ave
Torrance, CA 90502-1636, USA

Dedrick, Jim (Athlete, Baseball Player)
2929 NW Kennedy Ct
Portland, OR 97229-8099, USA

Dee, Aisha (Actor)
c/o Brett Ruttenberg *Imprint PR*
6121 W Sunset Blvd
Neuehouse
Los Angeles, CA 90028-6442, USA

Dee, Donald (Athlete, Basketball Player, Olympic Athlete)
7924 N Pennsylvania Ave
Kansas City, MO 64118-1416, USA

Dee, Donnie (Athlete, Football Player)
633 Rolling Hills Rd
Vista, CA 92081-7513, USA

Dee, Francine (Adult Film Star)
Extreme Models
PO Box 472170
Reseda, CA 91337, USA

Dee, Joey (Musician)
Horizon Mgmt
PO Box 8770
Endwell, NY 13762-8770, USA

Dee, Sally (Athlete, Golfer)
3508 W Barcelona St
Tampa, FL 33629-7010, USA

Dee, Toni (Fitness Expert)
Toni Dee Fitness
PO Box 834
Corte Madera, CA 94976-0834, USA

Deegan, Bill (Athlete, Baseball Player)
8883 Christie Dr
Largo, FL 33771-6408, USA

Deeley, Cat (Actor)
c/o Danica Smith *Kovert Creative*
506 Santa Monica Blvd Ste 400
Santa Monica, CA 90401-2412, USA

Dee-Lite (Musician)
428 Cedar Street NW
Washington, DC 20012, USA

Deemer, Audrey (Athlete, Baseball Player, Commentator)
241 Neff St
Powhatan Point, OH 43942-1328, USA

Deen, James (Actor, Adult Film Star)
c/o Bill McCoy *Nocturnal Entertainment*
11735 Dorothy St Apt 302
Los Angeles, CA 90049-5567, USA

Deen, Paula (Chef, Television Host)
818 Wilmington Island Rd
Savannah, GA 31410-4503, USA

Deepa, Mehta (Director)
Deepa Mehta Films
460 College St Suite 301
Toronto, ON M6G 1A1, CANADA

Deep Purple (Music Group)
c/o Staff Member *UTA Music/The Agency Group (UK)*
361-373 City Rd
London EC1V 1PQ, UNITED KINGDOM

Deer, Rob (Athlete, Baseball Player)
PO Box 27516
Scottsdale, AZ 85255-0141, USA

Deering, John (Cartoonist)
6701 Westover Dr
Little Rock, AR 72207-3447, USA

Dees, Archie (Athlete, Basketball Player)
4405 N Hillview Dr
Bloomington, IN 47408-9770, USA

Dees, Charlie (Athlete, Baseball Player)
1286 Glynview Cir
Lawrenceville, GA 30043-5633, USA

Dees, Rick (DJ, Radio Personality)
Dees Entertainment
3601 W Olive Ave Ste 675
Burbank, CA 91505-4622, USA

Deese, Derrick (Athlete, Football Player)
PO Box 3356
Cerritos, CA 90703-3356, USA

De Eugenia, Coco (Actor)
c/o Nancy Harding *Powerhouse Talent*
PO Box 261939
Encino, CA 91426-1939, USA

Deezen, Eddie (Actor)
c/o Staff Member *Coolwaters Productions*
10061 Riverside Dr # 531
Toluca Lake, CA 91602-2560, USA

Default (Music Group)
c/o Staff Member *UTA/The Agency Group*
888 7th Ave Fl 7
New York, NY 10106-0700, USA

Defauw, Brad (Athlete, Hockey Player)
Jane And Russell Defauw
13030 Florida Ct
Saint Paul, MN 55124-7943, USA

Defazio, Dean (Athlete, Hockey Player)
2475 Logan Ave
Oakville, ON L6H 6P3, Canada

DeFazio, Peter (Congressman, Politician)
2134 Rayburn Hob
Washington, DC 20515-3704, USA

Defebo, Brian (Race Car Driver)
Magic Motorsports
122 E Front St
Berwick, PA 18603-4818, USA

Defee, Lois (Dancer, Model)
223 Wink Rd
Oak Grove, LA 71263-6973, USA

DeFelitta, Raymond (Director, Writer)
c/o Gary Ungar *Exile Entertainment*
732 El Medio Ave
Pacific Palisades, CA 90272-3451, USA

DeFer, Kaylee (Actor)
c/o Staff Member *Abrams Artists Agency*
750 N San Vicente Blvd
E Tower Fl 11
Los Angeles, CA 90069-5788, USA

de Ferran, Gil (Race Car Driver)
Penske Racing
13400 W Outer Dr
Detroit, MI 48239-1309, USA

DeFina, Barbara (Producer)
Columbia University
School of Arts
513 Dodge Hall, Mail Code 1808, 2960 Broadway
New York, NY 10027, USA

Def Leppard (Music Group)
Mercury Records
136-144 New Kings Rd
London SW6 4LZ, UNITED KINGDOM

DeForest, Roy (Artist)
2785 Kurtz St Ste 10
San Diego, CA 92110-3111, USA

DeForrest, Jeff (Sportscaster)
825 S Ocean Blvd
Pompano Beach, FL 33062-6315, USA

DeFrancesco, Tony (Basketball Coach)
7159 E Quince St
Mesa, AZ 85207-1841, USA

DeFranco, Philip (Actor, Writer)
c/o Staff Member *Creative Artists Agency (CAA)*
2000 Avenue of the Stars Ste 100
Los Angeles, CA 90067-4705, USA

DeFrank, Joe (Horse Racer)
PO Box 655
Lake Pleasant, NY 12108-0655, USA

Deftones (Music Group)
c/o David Benveniste *Velvet Hammer*
9014 Melrose Ave
Los Angeles, CA 90069-5610, USA

DeGarmo, Diana (Musician)
c/o Drew Elliot *Artist International*
333 E 43rd St Apt 115
New York, NY 10017-4822, USA

Degen, Bruce (Writer)
62 Castle Meadow Rd
Newtown, CT 06470-2502, USA

DeGeneres, Ellen (Actor, Comedian, Talk Show Host)
c/o Staff Member *Ellen DeGeneres Show*
3500 W Olive Ave Ste 1000
Burbank, CA 91505-5515, USA

Degerick, Mike (Athlete, Baseball Player)
612 Hummingbird Ln
Delray Beach, FL 33445-1845, USA

DeGette, Diana (Congressman, Politician)
2335 Rayburn Hob
Washington, DC 20515-4329, USA

Degg, Jakki (Actor, Model)
Neon Management
34 Clare Ln
London N13DB, UNITED KINGDOM

DeGiorgi, Salvatore Cardinal (Religious Leader)
Curia Archivescovile
Corso Vittorio Emanuele 461
Los Angeles, CA 90134-0001, ITALY

Degnan, John J (Business Person)
Chubb Corp
202 Halls Mill Rd
Whitehouse Station, NJ 08889-3435, USA

De Gouw, Jessica (Actor)
c/o Theresa Huska *Independent Management Company*
87-103 Epsom Rd
#15
Rosebery NSW 2018, AUSTRALIA

Degraffenreid, Allen (Athlete, Football Player)
3823 E Thunderheart Trl
Gilbert, AZ 85297-7874, USA

DeGrate, Tony (Athlete, Football Player)
203 Newport Landing Pl
Round Rock, TX 78665-2856, USA

DeGrate Jr, Donald Earle (DeVante Swing) (Musician)
c/o Staff Member *De Swing Mob Inc / EMI April Music Inc*
810 7th Ave
C/O Emi Music Publishing
New York, NY 10019-5818, USA

DeGraw, Gavin (Musician)
c/o Jeff Frasco *Creative Artists Agency (CAA)*
2000 Avenue of the Stars Ste 100
Los Angeles, CA 90067-4705, USA

Degray, Dale (Athlete, Hockey Player)
c/o Staff Member *Owen Sound Attack*
PO Box 1420 Stn Main
Stn Main
Owen Sound, ON N4K 6T5, Canada

deGrom, Jacob (Athlete, Baseball Player)
c/o Staff Member *New York Mets*
123-01 Roosevelt Avenue
Shea Stadium
Flushing, NY 11368-1699, USA

Deguise, Michel (Athlete, Hockey Player)
380 Rue Moge
Sorel-Tracy, QC J3P 7A6, Canada

Dehaan, Dane (Actor)
c/o Christian Donatelli *MGMT Entertainment (The Schiff Company)*
9220 W Sunset Blvd Ste 106
W Hollywood, CA 90069-3500, USA

Dehaan, Kory (Athlete, Baseball Player)
19040 E Superstition Dr
Queen Creek, AZ 85142-6884, USA

DeHaan, Richard W (Religious Leader)
3000 Kraft Ave SE
Grand Rapids, MI 49512-2024, USA

Dehart, Rick (Athlete, Baseball Player)
811 NE Wabash Ave
Topeka, KS 66616-1443, USA

DeHaven, Penny (Musician)
PO Box 83
Brentwood, TN 37024-0083, USA

de Havilland, Olivia (Actor)
3 Rue Benouville
Paris 75016, FRANCE

De Heer, Rolf (Director, Producer, Writer)
c/o Staff Member *Vertigo Productions Pty Ltd*
3 Butler Dr
Hendon SA 05014, AUSTRALIA

Dehere, Terry (Athlete, Basketball Player)
120 Wayne St
Jersey City, NJ 07302-3406, USA

Deidel, Jim (Athlete, Baseball Player)
14312 Wright Way
Broomfield, CO 80023-4045, USA

Deidrick, Casey (Actor)
c/o Jon Simmons *Simmons & Scott Entertainment*
7942 Mulholland Dr
Los Angeles, CA 90046-1225, USA

Deidrick, Casey Jon (Actor)
c/o Chantal Artur *Sunshine Sachs*
720 Cole Ave
Los Angeles, CA 90038-3606, USA

Deitch, Donna (Director)
International Creative Mgmt
8942 Wilshire Blvd # 219
Beverly Hills, CA 90211-1908, USA

Deja (Musician)
c/o Anthony Embry *AE Entertainment Public Relations*
124 Evening Shade Dr
Charleston, SC 29414-9144, USA

Deja, Andreas (Animator)
3494 Berry Dr
Studio City, CA 91604-4152, USA

Dejdel, Jim (Baseball Player)
New York Yankees
14312 Wright Way
Broomfield, CO 80023-4045, USA

DeJean, Mike (Athlete, Baseball Player)
144 Delouche Rd
West Monroe, LA 71291-8717, USA

Dejesus, David (Athlete, Baseball Player)
2009 Burnham Pl
Wheaton, IL 60189-8155, USA

Dejesus, Ivan (Athlete, Baseball Player)
14608 Velleux Dr
Orlando, FL 32837-5467, USA

Dejesus, Jose (Athlete, Baseball Player)
Kansas City Royals
479 Sect Justo Rodriguez
Cidra, PR 00739-2168, USA

De Jesus, Wanda (Actor)
c/o Bob McGowan *McGowan Management*
170 S Beverly Dr Ste 304
Beverly Hills, CA 90212-3000, USA

Dejohn, Mark (Athlete, Baseball Player)
84 Osgood Ave
New Britain, CT 06053-2834, USA

DeJong, Jordan (Athlete, Baseball Player)
5305 Via Cartagena
Yorba Linda, CA 92886-4561, USA

DeJordy, Denis E (Athlete, Hockey Player)
472 Ch des Patriotes
St-Charles-Sur-Richelieu, QC J0H 2G0, Canada

DeJoria, John Paul (Business Person)
Paul Mitchell Systems
26455 Golden Valley Rd
Santa Clarita, CA 91350-2973, USA

Dejurnett, Charles (Athlete, Football Player)
1355 Heritage Ct
Escondido, CA 92027-3972, USA

DeKay, Tim (Actor)
4649 Willowcrest Ave
Toluca Lake, CA 91602-1464, USA

Dekker, Fred (Director)
4151 Tujunga Ave
Studio City, CA 91604-3065, USA

Dekker, Thomas (Actor, Director)
c/o Mimi DiTrani *MGMT Entertainment (The Schiff Company)*
9220 W Sunset Blvd Ste 106
W Hollywood, CA 90069-3500, USA

Deklin, Mark (Actor)
c/o Jamie Harhay Skinner *Baker Winokur Ryder Public Relations*
9100 Wilshire Blvd
W Tower #500
Beverly Hills, CA 90212-3415, USA

de La Baume, Josephine (Actor)
c/o Pandora Weldon *Public Eye Communications*
535 Kings Rd
#313 Plaza
London SW10 0SZ, UNITED KINGDOM

de la Cruz, Melissa (Writer)
c/o Richard Abate *3 Arts Entertainment*
9460 Wilshire Blvd Fl 7
Beverly Hills, CA 90212-2713, USA

DeLaCruz, Rosie (Model)
Willhelmina Models
300 Park Ave S # 200
New York, NY 10010-5313, USA

De La Cruz, Veronica (Commentator, Television Host)
c/o Staff Member *CNN (Atlanta)*
1 Cnn Ctr NW
PO Box 105366
Atlanta, GA 30303-2762, USA

De La Fuente, Cristian (Actor)
c/o Luis Balaguer *Latin World Entertainment (LA)*
9777 Wilshire Blvd Ste 915
Beverly Hills, CA 90212-1902, USA

DeLaFuente, Joel (Actor)
LMRK
130 W 42nd St Ste 1906
New York, NY 10036-7902, USA

de la Fuente, Marian (Actor)
c/o Staff Member *Telemundo*
2470 W 8th Ave
Hialeah, FL 33010-2000, USA

De La Garza, Alana (Actor)
c/o Jai Khanna *Brillstein Entertainment Partners*
9150 Wilshire Blvd Ste 350
Beverly Hills, CA 90212-3453, USA

de la Garza, Gabriela (Actor)
c/o Patricia Mora *Metro Public Relations*
8671 Wilshire Blvd # 208
Beverly Hills, CA 90211-2926, USA

Delahoussaye, Eddie (Horse Racer)
1024 S 4th Ave
Arcadia, CA 91006-4218, USA

Delahoussaye, Ryan (Musician)
Ashley Talent
2002 Hogback Rd Ste 20
Ann Arbor, MI 48105-9736, USA

De La Hoya, Oscar (Athlete, Boxer)
c/o Richard Schaefer *Golden Boy Promotions*
626 Wilshire Blvd Ste 350
Los Angeles, CA 90017-3581, USA

De La Hoz, Mike (Athlete, Baseball Player)
PO Box 441233
Miami, FL 33144-1233, USA

de la Huerta, Paz (Actor)
c/o Tracy Christian *TCA Mgmt*
8447 Wilshire Blvd Ste 100
Beverly Hills, CA 90211-3228, USA

Delain, Moneca (Actor)
c/o Staff Member *Pacific Artists Management*
112 3rd Ave E Suite 210
Vancouver, BC V5T 1C8, CANADA

De La Maza, Roland (Athlete, Baseball Player)
28533 Silverking Trl
Santa Clarita, CA 91390-5248, USA

DeLamielleure, Joseph M (Joe) (Athlete, Football Player)
210 Village Stone Cir
Summerville, SC 29486-8195, USA

Del Amitri (Musician, Songwriter)
c/o Staff Member *Progressive Global Agency*
PO Box 50294
Nashville, TN 37205-0294, USA

DeLancie, John (Actor)
1313 Brunswick Ave
South Pasadena, CA 91030-3509, USA

Delaney, Don (Basketball Coach, Coach)
25 High Point Ln
Willoughby, OH 44094-6968, USA

Delaney, Jeff (Athlete, Football Player)
369 Valley View Rd
Eighty Four, PA 15330-2461, USA

Delaney, Kim (Actor, Model)
c/o Lisa Wright *LINK Entertainment*
11872 La Grange Ave
Los Angeles, CA 90025-5282, USA

Delano, Diane (Actor)
Gold Marshak Liedtke
3500 W Olive Ave Ste 1400
Burbank, CA 91505-5512, USA

Delano, Michael (Actor)
c/o Cody Garden *McCarty Agency*
2600 W Olive Ave Fl 5
Burbank, CA 91505-4572, USA

Delany, Dana (Actor)
2522 Beverley Ave
Santa Monica, CA 90405-3719, USA

DeLap, Tony (Artist)
225 Jasmine Ave
Corona Del Mar, CA 92625-3035, USA

De La Paz, Danny (Actor)

De La Puente, Brian (Athlete, Football Player)
c/o Bruce Tollner *REP 1 Sports Group*
80 Technology Dr
Irvine, CA 92618-2301, USA

Del Arco, Jonathan (Actor)
c/o Kyle Fritz *Kyle Fritz Management*
6325 Heather Dr
Los Angeles, CA 90068-1633, USA

DelArco, Jonathan (Actor)
Michael Slessinger
8730 W Sunset Blvd Ste 220W
Los Angeles, CA 90069-2275, USA

de la Reguera, Ana (Actor)
c/o Liza Anderson *Anderson Group Public Relations*
8060 Melrose Ave Fl 4
Los Angeles, CA 90046-7038, USA

DeLaria, Lea (Actor)

DeLaRocha, Zack (Musician)
GAS Entertainment
8935 Lindblade St
Culver City, CA 90232-2438, USA

De La Rosa, Jo (Actor)

DeLaRosa, Yvonne (Actor)
c/o Theo Caesar *90210 Talent Agency*
16430 Ventura Blvd Ste 200
Encino, CA 91436-2135, USA

Delasin, Dorothy (Athlete, Golfer)
20 Longview Dr
Daly City, CA 94015-4714, USA

De La Soul (Music Group)
2697 Heath Ave
Bronx, NY 10463-7546, USA

DeLatour, David (Actor)

De La Tour, Frances (Actor)
c/o Carl Scott *Simmons & Scott Entertainment*
7942 Mulholland Dr
Los Angeles, CA 90046-1225, USA

De Laurentiis, Giada (Chef)
c/o Alex Schack *Slate PR*
901 N Highland Ave
W Hollywood, CA 90038-2412, USA

De Laurentiis, Raffaella (Actor, Producer)
Rafaella Productions
100 Universal City Plz
Bungalow 5162
Universal City, CA 91608-1002, USA

Delavan, Burt (Athlete, Football Player)
1161 Jacob Ln
Carmichael, CA 95608-6202, USA

DeLay, Tom (Politician)
242 Cannon Hob
Washington, DC 20515-4322, USA

Delays Delirium (Music Group)
c/o Staff Member *Paradigm (Monterey)*
404 W Franklin St
Monterey, CA 93940-2303, USA

Del Bello, Jack (Athlete, Football Player)
391 Belfast Ter
Sebastian, FL 32958-5509, USA

del Boca, Andrea (Actor)
c/o Staff Member *Telefe (Argentina)*
Pavon 2444
Buenos Aires C1248AAT, ARGENTINA

Delcarmen, Manny (Athlete, Baseball Player)
68 Surrey Ln
East Bridgewater, MA 02333-3110, USA

del Castillo, Eric (Actor)
c/o Staff Member *Televisa*
Blvd Adolfo Lopez Mateos 232
Colonia San Angel INN
DF CP 01060, MEXICO

Del Castillo, Kate (Actor)
c/o Jennifer Rawlings *Omni Artists*
6121 W Sunset Blvd
Los Angeles, CA 90028-6442, USA

Del Castillo-Kinney, Ysora (Athlete, Baseball Player, Commentator)
1555 W 44th Pl Apt 216C
Hialeah, FL 33012-7837, USA

deLeeuw, Rob (Actor)
5075 Trail Canyon Dr
Jurupa Valley, CA 91752-1685, USA

DeLeo, Dean (Musician)
Q Prime
729 7th Ave Ste 1600
New York, NY 10019-6880, USA

DeLeo, Robert (Musician)
2225 Via Cerritos
Palos Verdes Estates, CA 90274-2141, USA

Deleon, Jose (Athlete, Baseball Player)
Pittsburgh Pirates
348 Herbert St Apt 1
Perth Amboy, NJ 08861-3708, USA

de Leon, Miguel (Actor)
c/o Staff Member *Televisa*
Blvd Adolfo Lopez Mateos 232
Colonia San Angel INN
DF CP 01060, MEXICO

de Leon, Patricia (Actor)
c/o Jerry Shandrew *Shandrew Public Relations*
1050 S Stanley Ave
Los Angeles, CA 90019-6634, USA

Deleone, Tom (Athlete, Football Player)
PO Box 681472
Park City, UT 84068-1472, USA

de Lesseps, LuAnn (Countess) (Musician, Reality Star)
c/o Pete Sanders *O&M Co.*
213 W 35th St Rm 403
New York, NY 10001-0215, USA

Delevingne, Cara (Model)
c/o Katie Greenthal *The Lede Company*
9701 Wilshire Blvd # 930
Beverly Hills, CA 90212-2020, USA

Delevingne, Poppy (Actor)
c/o Kimberley Donovan *The Artists Partnership*
101 Finsbury Pavement
London EC2A 1RS, UNITED KINGDOM

Delfino, Carlos Francisco (Basketball Player)
Detroit Pistons
2 Championship Dr
Palace
Auburn Hills, MI 48326-1753, USA

Delfino, Majandra (Actor)
c/o Bradley Frank *Platform PR*
2666 N Beachwood Dr
Los Angeles, CA 90068-2308, USA

Delfino, Marieh (Actor)
c/o Amanda Glazer *The Kohner Agency*
9300 Wilshire Blvd Ste 555
Beverly Hills, CA 90212-3211, USA

Delgado, Carlos (Athlete, Baseball Player)
9 Repto Ramos
Aguadilla, PR 00603-5944, USA

Delgado, Chiquinquira (Actor)
c/o Gabriel Blanco *Gabriel Blanco Iglesias (Mexico)*
Rio Balsas 35-32
Colonia Cuauhtemoc
DF 06500, Mexico

Delgado, Felix Avila (Cuban Link) (Musician)
c/o Staff Member *Mob Records*
Unit 2A Queens Studios
21 Salusbury Rd
London NW6 6RG, USA

Delgado, Frankie (Actor)
c/o Eric Podwall *Podwall Entertainment*
710 N Orlando Ave Apt 203
Loft 203
Los Angeles, CA 90069-5549, USA

Delgado, Issac (Musician)
Ralph Mercado Mgmt
568 Broadway Rm 806
New York, NY 10012-3253, USA

Delgado, Jose Maria Gil Roble (Politician)
97-113 Rue Belliard
Brussels 01047, Belgium

Del Gaizo, Jim (Athlete, Football Player)
9581 NW 13th St
Plantation, FL 33322-4809, USA

Del Greco, Al (Athlete, Football Player)
1012 Little Turtle Cir
Birmingham, AL 35242-3282, USA

Del Greco, Bobby (Athlete, Baseball Player)
625 Southview Dr
Pittsburgh, PA 15226-2540, USA

Delguidice, Matt (Athlete, Hockey Player)
25 Church St
North Branford, CT 06471-1418, USA

Delhomme, Jake (Athlete, Football Player)
2896 Rocky Ridge Dr
Westlake, OH 44145-6848, USA

Delhoyo, George (Actor)
c/o Staff Member *TalentWorks*
3500 W Olive Ave Ste 1400
Burbank, CA 91505-5512, USA

D'Elia, Chris (Actor, Comedian)
c/o Lewis Kay *Kovert Creative*
506 Santa Monica Blvd Ste 400
Santa Monica, CA 90401-2412, USA

D'Elia, Federico (Actor)
c/o Staff Member *Telefe (Argentina)*
Pavon 2444
Buenos Aires C1248AAT, ARGENTINA

Delia, Joseph (Athlete, Football Player)
PO Box 19654
Irvine, CA 92623-9654, USA

Delilah (Radio Personality)
Radio Delilah Media Group
15260 Ventura Blvd Ste 400
Sherman Oaks, CA 91403-5300, USA

DeLillo, Don (Writer)
57 Rossmore Ave
Bronxville, NY 10708-5615, USA

DeLine, Donald (Producer)
120 N Hudson Ave
Los Angeles, CA 90004-1032, USA

Delinsky, Barbara (Writer)
c/o Staff Member *Simon & Schuster*
1230 Avenue of the Americas Fl CONC1
New York, NY 10020-1586, USA

de Lint, Derek (Actor)
c/o Vanessa Henneman *Features Creative Managment*
76a Entrepotdok
Amsterdam 1018 AD, NETHERLANDS

DeLisle, Grey (Actor)
c/o Lisa Perkins *Baker Winokur Ryder Public Relations*
9100 Wilshire Blvd
W Tower #500
Beverly Hills, CA 90212-3415, USA

Delisle, Jim (Athlete, Football Player)
26301 W Cedar Niles Cir
Olathe, KS 66061-7478, USA

Delizia, Cara (Actor)
c/o Mark Measures *Kazarian, Measures, Ruskin & Associates*
5200 Lankershim Blvd Ste 820
N Hollywood, CA 91601-3194, USA

Delk, Joan (Athlete, Golfer)
830 Forest Path Ln
Alpharetta, GA 30022-6468, USA

Delk, Tony (Athlete, Basketball Player)
1843 Glenhill Dr
Lexington, KY 40502-2817, USA

Dell, Donald (Athlete, Tennis Player)
Lagardere Unlimited
5335 Wisconsin Ave NW Ste 360
Washington, DC 20015-2054, USA

Dell, Michael (Business Person)
Dell Inc
1 Dell Way
Round Rock, TX 78682-7000, USA

Dell'Abate, Gary (Producer)
c/o Tony D. Burton *Buchwald (NY)*
10 E 44th St
New York, NY 10017-3601, USA

Dellaero, Jason (Athlete, Baseball Player)
3240 Chapel Creek Cir
Wesley Chapel, FL 33544-7700, USA

Dellanos, Myrka (Actor)
c/o Staff Member *Univision*
605 3rd Ave Fl 12
New York, NY 10158-0034, USA

Dellenbach, Jeff (Athlete, Football Player)
1002 Pine Branch Dr
Weston, FL 33326-2840, USA

Dellinger, Bill (Athlete, Olympic Athlete, Track Athlete)
1993 Fircrest Dr
Eugene, OR 97403-3112, USA

Dellinger, Dustin (Dusty) (Athlete, Baseball Player)
5203 Grindstone Ln
Granite Falls, NC 28602-5533, USA

Dellucci, David (Athlete, Baseball Player)
5512 Summer Lake Dr
Baton Rouge, LA 70817-4313, USA

Delmas, Louis (Athlete, Football Player)
c/o Drew Rosenhaus *Rosenhaus Sports Representation*
3921 Alton Rd # 440
Miami Beach, FL 33140-3852, USA

Del Negro, Matthew (Actor)
c/o Becca Kovacik *Berwick & Kovacik*
6230 Wilshire Blvd
Los Angeles, CA 90048-5126, USA

Del Negro, Vinny (Athlete, Basketball Player)
7320 N 71st St
Paradise Valley, AZ 85253-3616, USA

Delo, Ken (Actor)
161 Avondale Dr # 93-8
Branson, MO 65616-3646, USA

DeLoach, Nikki (Actor)
c/o Carrie Wick *Carrie Wick Public Relations*
1455 4th St Apt 415
Santa Monica, CA 90401-2324, USA

Delock, Ike (Athlete, Baseball Player)
433 Cypress Way E
Naples, FL 34110-1107, USA

Delon, Alain (Actor)
Alain Delon International
7 Rue Des Battoirs
Geneva 01205, SWITZERLAND

Delon, Anthony (Actor)
Intertalent
5 Rue Clement-Marot
Paris 75008, FRANCE

Delong, Greg (Athlete, Football Player)
8265 Riverway Rd
Lewisville, NC 27023-9844, USA

DeLong, Keith A (Athlete, Football Player)
1850 Greywell Rd
Knoxville, TN 37922-9454, USA

Delong, Nate (Athlete, Basketball Player)
PO Box 485
Hayward, WI 54843-0485, USA

DeLonge, Tom (Actor, Musician)
18433 Via Candela Rancho
Santa Fe, CA 92091, USA

DeLongis, Anthony (Actor)
PO Box 2445
Canyon Country, CA 91386-2445, USA

Deloplaine, Jack (Athlete, Football Player)
215 Montana St
Pittsburgh, PA 15214-1630, USA

Delora, Jennifer (Actor)
Gilla Roos
9744 Wilshire Blvd Ste 203
Beverly Hills, CA 90212-1812, USA

Delorenzi, Ray (Athlete, Hockey Player)
735 N Highway A1a Apt 201
Indialantic, FL 32903-3048, USA

DeLorenzo, Michael (Actor)
c/o Staff Member *Shelter Entertainment*
9255 W Sunset Blvd Ste 300
Los Angeles, CA 90069-3313, USA

Delorme, Gilbert (Athlete, Hockey Player)
Le Rocket de Montreal
195 Boul Sir-Wilfrid-Laurier
Saint-Basile-Le-Grand, QC J3N 1R1, Canada

Delorme, Ron (Athlete, Hockey Player)
94 Ravine Dr
Port Moody, BC V3H 4T8, Canada

De Los Santos, Valerio (Athlete, Baseball Player)
9838 N 119th Pl # Pi
Scottsdale, AZ 85259-5069, USA

Delparte, Guy (Athlete, Hockey Player)
74 Harrison Ave
Saco, ME 04072-3250, USA

Del Piero, Alessandro (Soccer Player)
Juventus FC
Piazza Crimea 7
New York, NY 10131-0001, ITALY

Delpino, Robert L (Athlete, Football Player)
621 Sun Valley Ln Apt 103
Corona, CA 92879-6587, USA

Delpy, Julie (Actor)
c/o Ruth Bernstein *Viewpoint Inc*
8820 Wilshire Blvd Ste 220
Beverly Hills, CA 90211-2622, USA

Del Rey, Lana (Musician)
c/o Ed Millett *TAP Management*
Unit G4, Union Wharf 23
Wenlock Road
London N1 7SB, UNITED KINGDOM

del Rincon, Fernando (Actor)
c/o Staff Member *Univision*
605 3rd Ave Fl 12
New York, NY 10158-0034, USA

Del Rio, Bianca (Impersonator, Reality Star)
c/o Len Evans *Project Publicity*
540 W 43rd St
New York, NY 10036, USA

Del Rio, Jack (Athlete, Football Coach, Football Player)
285 Twisted Pine Trl
Santa Rsa Bch, FL 32459-3223, USA

Del Rio, Rebekah (Musician)
2280 Grass Valley Hwy # 138
Auburn, CA 95603-2536, USA

Delsing, Jay (Athlete, Golfer)
1833 Aston Way
Chesterfield, MO 63005-4579, USA

del Solar, Fernando (Actor)
c/o Staff Member *TV Azteca*
Periferico Sur 4121
Colonia Fuentes del Pedregal
DF CP 14141, Mexico

Delson, Brad (Musician)
12097 Summit Cir
Beverly Hills, CA 90210-1376, USA

Delta Spirit (Music Group)
c/o Staff Member *Paradigm (Monterey)*
404 W Franklin St
Monterey, CA 93940-2303, USA

Del Toro, Benicio (Actor)
c/o Robin Baum *Slate PR*
901 N Highland Ave
W Hollywood, CA 90038-2412, USA

Del Toro, Guillermo (Director, Producer)
c/o Staff Member *del Toro Productions*
1000 Flower St
Glendale, CA 91201-3007, USA

Deluca, Annette (Athlete, Golfer)
7 Turtle Creek Dr Apt D
Jupiter, FL 33469-1530, USA

De Luca, Mike (Producer)
Michael De Luca Productions
10202 Washington Blvd
Astaire Bldg Ste 3028
Culver City, CA 90232-3119, USA

DeLucas, Lawrence J (Astronaut)
909 19th St S
Birmingham, AL 35205, USA

Delucas, Lawrence J Dr (Astronaut)
90819th St S
Birmingham, AL 35205-3704, USA

Deluca-Verley, Ava (Actor)
c/o Pearl Servat *PMK/BNC Public Relations*
1840 Century Park E Ste 1400
Los Angeles, CA 90067-2115, USA

Delucca, Jerry (Athlete, Football Player)
27 Pulaski St
Peabody, MA 01960-1831, USA

Delucia, Rich (Athlete, Baseball Player)
4 Rick Rd
Reading, PA 19607-9704, USA

DeLuise, David (Actor)
1225 N Olive Dr
Los Angeles, CA 90069-2706, USA

Deluise, Michael (Actor)
11661 San Vicente Blvd Ste 600
Los Angeles, CA 90049-5114, USA

Deluise, Peter (Actor, Director, Producer)
c/o Lee Dinstman *Agency for the Performing Arts (APA)*
405 S Beverly Dr Ste 500
Beverly Hills, CA 90212-4425, USA

DeLuna, Kat (Musician)
c/o Damon DeGraff *dGi Management*
401 Broadway Ste 1705
New York, NY 10013-3019, USA

Delvecchio, Alexander P (Alex) (Athlete, Hockey Player)
Pen Pro
2602 Stoodleigh Dr
Rochester Hills, MI 48309-2836, USA

Del-Vikings, The (Music Group)
PO Box 770850
Orlando, FL 32877-0850, USA

Del Zotto, Michael (Athlete, Hockey Player)
37 Elia Dr
Stouffville, ON L4A 3V8, Canada

Demaestri, Joe (Athlete, Baseball Player)
22 Corte Del Norte
Greenbrae, CA 94904-1843, USA

Demao, Al (Athlete, Football Player)
16206 Atlantis Dr
Bowie, MD 20716-3839, USA

Demar, Enoch (Athlete, Football Player)
1579 Olympian Cir SW
Atlanta, GA 30310-2440, USA

Demarco, Bob (Athlete, Football Player)
13055 Midfield Ter
Saint Louis, MO 63146-6053, USA

DeMarco, Guido (President)
President's Office
Palace
Valletta, MALTA

DeMarco, Jean (Artist)
Cervaro
Prov-Frosinore 03044, ITALY

Demarco, Robert (Bob) (Athlete, Football Player)
13055 Midfield Ter
Saint Louis, MO 63146-6053, USA

DeMarco, Tony (Boxer)
PO Box 53664
Indianapolis, IN 46253-0664, USA

DeMarcus, Jay (Musician)
24 Inveraray
Nashville, TN 37215-4129, USA

Demarie, John (Athlete, Football Player)
2019 Choupique Rd
Sulphur, LA 70663-8430, USA

Demars, Billy (Athlete, Baseball Player)
770 Island Way Apt 305
Clearwater, FL 33767-1824, USA

de Matteo, Drea (Actor)
c/o Evan Hainey *Untitled Entertainment*
350 S Beverly Dr Ste 200
Beverly Hills, CA 90212-4819, USA

Dembo, Fennis (Athlete, Basketball Player)
430 N Pine St
San Antonio, TX 78202-2850, USA

de Medeiros, Maria (Actor, Director)
c/o Alsira Garcia Maroto *Alsira Garcia-Maroto Talent Agency*
Calle De Los Invencibles 8
Bajo
Madrid 28019, SPAIN

Demel, Sam (Athlete, Baseball Player)
18650 N 120th Pl
Scottsdale, AZ 85259, USA

DeMenezes, Fradique (President)
President's Office
Pargo do Povo
Sao Tome, SAO TOME & PRINCIPE

Demens, Kenny (Athlete, Football Player)
c/o Blake Baratz *The Institute for Athletes*
3600 Minnesota Dr Ste 550
Edina, MN 55435-7925, USA

DeMent, Iris (Songwriter, Writer)
c/o Staff Member *Paradigm (Monterey)*
404 W Franklin St
Monterey, CA 93940-2303, USA

Dement, Kenneth (Athlete, Football Player)
8 Bel Air Dr
Sikeston, MO 63801-1916, USA

Dementieva, Elena (Tennis Player)
c/o Staff Member *Octagon (VA)*
7100 Forest Ave Ste 201
Richmond, VA 23226-3742, USA

DeMeo, Adriana (Actor)
c/o Michael Gasparro *Gasparro Management*
609 Degraw St
Brooklyn, NY 11217-3120, USA

DeMerchant, Paul (Religious Leader)
Missionary Church
PO Box 9127
Fort Wayne, IN 46899-9127, USA

Demerit, John (Athlete, Baseball Player)
550 W Walters St
Port Washington, WI 53074-1430, USA

DeMerritt, Marty (Athlete, Baseball Player)
7511 Creekridge Ln
Citrus Heights, CA 95610-3273, USA

Demery, Larry (Athlete, Baseball Player)
10627 Kurt St
Sylmar, CA 91342-6838, USA

Demeter, Don (Athlete, Baseball Player)
108 Church Way
Oklahoma City, OK 73139-8626, USA

Demeter, Steve (Athlete, Baseball Player)
6032 Ravine Blvd
Cleveland, OH 44134-3047, USA

Demetral, Chris (Actor)
c/o Jamie Gold *JMG Management*
18000 Coastline Dr Apt 8
Malibu, CA 90265-5727, USA

Demetriadis, Phoklon (Cartoonist)
3rd September St 174
Athens, GREECE

Demetrios (Religious Leader)
Greek Orthodox Church
89 E 79th St
#19
New York, NY 10021, USA

Demeulemeester, Ann (Designer, Fashion Designer)
c/o Staff Member *Ann Demeulemeester*
6 Rue Milne Edwards
Paris 75017, France

Demic, Larry (Athlete, Basketball Player)
680 S Lassen Ct
Anaheim, CA 92804-3123, USA

Demie, Alexa (Actor)
c/o Meredith Rothman *Anonymous Content*
3532 Hayden Ave
Culver City, CA 90232-2413, USA

DeMille, Nelson (Writer)
61 Hilton Ave Ste 23
Garden City, NY 11530-2813, USA

Demmings, Pancho (Actor)
c/o Judy Orbach *Judy O Productions*
6136 Glen Holly St
Hollywood, CA 90068-2338, USA

de Mol, John (Producer)
Talpa
PO Box 154
Laren, Noord Holland 1250 AD, The Netherlands

Demola, Don (Athlete, Baseball Player)
352 Village Dr
Hauppauge, NY 11788-3225, USA

de Molina, Raul (Actor)
c/o Staff Member *Univision*
605 3rd Ave Fl 12
New York, NY 10158-0034, USA

Demong, Bill (Athlete, Olympic Athlete, Skier)
1546 Mallard Cir
Park City, UT 84098-5410, USA

Demon Hunter (Music Group)
c/o Staff Member *UTA/The Agency Group*
888 7th Ave Fl 7
New York, NY 10106-0700, USA

DeMont, Rick (Athlete, Swimmer)
PO Box 1453
Waianae, HI 96792-6453, USA

Demorest, Jude (Actor)
c/o Gordon Gilbertson *Gilbertson Management*
1334 3rd Street Promenade Ste 201
Santa Monica, CA 90401-1320, USA

DeMornay, Rebecca (Actor)
2179 Castilian Dr
Los Angeles, CA 90068-2610, USA

Demory, Joe (Athlete, Football Player)

Demos, Adam (Actor)
c/o Sophie Jermyn *Sophie Jermyn Management*
PO Box 7333
Bondi Beach NSW 02026, AUSTRALIA

Demoss, Bob (Athlete, Football Player)
15750 Bethpage Trl
Carmel, IN 46033-5513, USA

Demoss, Darcy (Actor)
7550 Mulholland Dr
Los Angeles, CA 90046-1239, USA

Demps, Quintin (Athlete, Football Player)
c/o Dave Butz *Sportstars Inc*
1370 Avenue of the Americas Fl 19
New York, NY 10019-4602, USA

Demps, Will (Athlete)
c/o Staff Member *EAG Sports Management*
909 N Pacific Coast Hwy Ste 360
El Segundo, CA 90245-3864, USA

Dempsey, Clint (Athlete, Soccer Player)
c/o Lyle Yorks *James Grant Sports Ltd (USA)*
3233 M St NW
Washington, DC 20007-3556, USA

Dempsey, George (Athlete, Basketball Player)
6945 Cedar Ave
Pennsauken, NJ 08109-2713, USA

Dempsey, Mark (Athlete, Baseball Player)
673 W Martindale Rd
Englewood, OH 45322-3043, USA

Dempsey, Michael (Actor)
c/o Lorraine Berglund *Lorraine Berglund Management*
11537 Hesby St
North Hollywood, CA 91601-3618, USA

Dempsey, Nathan (Athlete, Hockey Player)
c/o Art Breeze *Pro-Rep Entertainment Consulting*
113-276 Midpark Gdns SE
Calgary, AB T2X 1T3, Canada

Dempsey, Pat (Baseball Player)
10116 Oro Vista Ave
Sunland, CA 91040-3238, USA

Dempsey, Patrick (Actor)
c/o Staff Member *Shifting Gears Productions*
15304 W Sunset Blvd Ste 208
Pacific Palisades, CA 90272-3656, USA

Dempsey, Rick (Athlete, Baseball Player)
1673 Crown Ridge Ct
Westlake Village, CA 91362-4731, USA

Dempsey, Tanya (Actor)
c/o Dino May *Dino May Management*
13223 Bloomfield St
Sherman Oaks, CA 91423-3207, USA

Dempsey, Thomas (Tom) (Athlete, Football Player)
541 Julius Ave
New Orleans, LA 70121-1613, USA

Dempster, Ryan (Athlete, Baseball Player)
3537 N Greenview Ave
Chicago, IL 60657-1317, USA

Demsey, Todd (Athlete, Golfer)
8140 E Arroyo Seco Rd
Scottsdale, AZ 85266-1056, USA

DeMunn, Jeffrey (Actor)
PO Box 373
Round Top, NY 12473-0373, USA

Demus, Jorg (Musician)
LYRA
Doblinger Hauptstr 77-A/10
Vienna 01190, AUSTRIA

Demus, Lashinda (Athlete, Track Athlete)
c/o Staff Member *Pure Perception PR*
10535 Rose Ave Apt 2
Los Angeles, CA 90034-4648, USA

Demuth, Dana (Athlete, Baseball Player)
1156 W Wagner Dr
Gilbert, AZ 85233-7980, USA

Denard, Michael (Dancer)
Paris Opera Ballet
Place de l'Opera
Paris 75009, FRANCE

Denberg, Lori Beth (Actor)
c/o Staff Member *Acme Talent & Literary*
4727 Wilshire Blvd Ste 333
Los Angeles, CA 90010-3874, USA

Denbo, Gary (Athlete, Baseball Player)
13374 Alton Rd
Palm Beach Gardens, FL 33418-6023, USA

Dench, Judi (Actor)
Wasp Green Millers Ln
Outwood
Redhill, West Sussex RH15PY, UNITED KINGDOM

Dencik, David (Actor)
c/o Alissa Goodman (Feldman) *Authentic Talent & Literary Management*
3615 Eastham Dr # 650
Culver City, CA 90232-2410, USA

Denehy, Bill (Athlete, Baseball Player)

Denes, Agnes C (Artist)
595 Broadway Fl 5
New York, NY 10012-3222, USA

Deneuve, Catherine (Actor)
c/o Melody Korenbrot *Block-Korenbrot Public Relations*
6100 Wilshire Blvd Ste 170
Los Angeles, CA 90048-5109, USA

Deng, Luol (Athlete, Basketball Player)
5925 N Bayshore Dr
Miami, FL 33137-2305, USA

Denham, Jeff (Congressman, Politician)
1605 Longworth Hob
Washington, DC 20515-1406, USA

Den Herder, Vern W (Athlete, Football Player)
2342 Riviera Rd
Sioux Center, IA 51250-2943, USA

Denicourt, Marianne (Actor)
Artmedia
20 Ave Rapp
Paris 75007, FRANCE

Denino, Paul (Ice Poseidon) (Internet Star)
c/o Brent Kaskel *NRG Esports*
Prefers to be contacted by email.
NA NA, USA

De Niro, Robert (Actor)
c/o Staff Member *Tribeca Productions*
375 Greenwich St Fl 7
New York, NY 10013-2379, USA

Denis, Louis (Athlete, Hockey Player)
412-1450 First St E
Cornwall, ON K6H 6H2, Canada

Denis, Marc (Athlete, Hockey Player)
Montreal Canadiens
1275 Rue Saint-Antoine 0
Montreal, QC H3C SL2, Canada

Denisof, Alexis (Actor)
c/o Chris Kanarick *ID Public Relations (NY)*
40 Wall St Fl 51
New York, NY 10005-1385, USA

Denison, Anthony (Actor)
10100 Santa Monica Blvd Ste 1060
Los Angeles, CA 90067-4151, USA

Deniz, Burak (Actor, Model)
c/o Nathan Kucuk *GDE Team Talent Agency*
Evliya Celebi Mah. Mesrutiyet Cad.
Ersoy Han No:102 Sishane_Beyoglu
Istanbul D:04, TURKEY

Denker, Travis (Athlete, Baseball Player)
701 W Valley View Dr
Fullerton, CA 92835-4077, USA

Denkinger, Don (Athlete, Baseball Player)
3505 Kingswood Pl
Waterloo, IA 50701-4524, USA

Denman, Brian (Athlete, Baseball Player)
16 Cindy Dr
Buffalo, NY 14221-3002, USA

Denman, David (Actor)
c/o Becca Kovacik *Berwick & Kovacik*
9465 Wilshire Blvd Ste 420
Beverly Hills, CA 90212-2603, USA

Denman, Tony (Actor)
c/o Nathan Higgins *Commercial Talent*
12711 Ventura Blvd Ste 285
Studio City, CA 91604-2487, USA

Dennard, Alfonzo (Athlete, Football Player)
c/o David Dunn *Athletes First*
23091 Mill Creek Dr
Laguna Hills, CA 92653-1258, USA

Dennard, Darqueze (Athlete, Football Player)
c/o Chafie Fields *Lagardere Unlimited (Miami)*
845 United Nations Plz
New York, NY 10017-3540, USA

Dennard, Kenny (Athlete, Basketball Player)
6641 Westchester Ave
Houston, TX 77005-3755, USA

Dennard, Mark (Athlete, Football Player)
4990 Afton Oaks Dr
College Station, TX 77845-7666, USA

Dennard, Preston (Athlete, Football Player)
4545 Greene Ave NW
Albuquerque, NM 87114-4296, USA

Dennehy, Brian (Actor)
141 Joy Rd
Woodstock, CT 06281-2206, USA

Dennehy, Kathleen (Actor)
Susan Nathe
8281 Melrose Ave Ste 200
Los Angeles, CA 90046-6823, USA

Dennen, Barry (Actor, Musician)
5044 Willowcrest Ave
North Hollywood, CA 91601-4049, USA

Dennen, Brett (Musician)
c/o Michael McDonald *Mick Management*
35 Washington St
Brooklyn, NY 11201-1028, USA

Dennerlein, Barbara (Musician)
Tsingtauer Str 66
Munich 81827, GERMANY

Dennert-Hill, Pauline (Athlete, Baseball Player, Commentator)
415 Clinton St
Owosso, MI 48867-2718, USA

Denney, John (Athlete, Football Player)

Denney, Kyle (Athlete, Baseball Player)
PO Box 300
Prague, OK 74864-0300, USA

Denney, Mike (Athlete, Football Player)
6419 Oakley St
Philadelphia, PA 19111-5218, USA

Denney, Ryan (Athlete, Football Player)
646 N Country Manor Ln
Alpine, UT 84004-1940, USA

Denning, Blaine (Athlete, Basketball Player)
1283 NW Bentley Cir Apt A
Port Saint Lucie, FL 34986-1834, USA

Denning, Hazel M (Writer)
Llewellyn Worldwide
PO Box 64383
St Paul, MN 55164-0383

Denning, Jon (Race Car Driver)
Dobbs Motorsports
23 Springfield Ave
Springfield, NJ 07081-1312, USA

Dennings, Kat (Actor)
c/o Nicole King *Management 360*
9111 Wilshire Blvd
Beverly Hills, CA 90210-5508, USA

Dennis, Cathy (Musician)
19 Music
Ransomes Gate #32
35-37 Parkgate
London SW11 4NP, UNITED KINGDOM (UK)

Dennis, Clark (Athlete, Golfer)
4117 Sarita Dr
Fort Worth, TX 76109-4743, USA

Dennis, Donna F (Artist)
131 Duane St
New York, NY 10013-3850, USA

Dennis, Gabrielle (Actor)
c/o Staff Member *Much and House Public Relations*
8075 W 3rd St Ste 500
Los Angeles, CA 90048-4325, USA

Dennis, Guy (Athlete, Football Player)
PO Box 2500
Hawthorne, FL 32640-2500, USA

Dennis, Hugh (Actor)
c/o Staff Member *United Agents*
12-26 Lexington St
London W1F OLE, UNITED KINGDOM

Dennis, Jim (Race Car Driver)
1810 Little Mastens Corner Rd
Harrington, DE 19952-3219, USA

Dennis, Marc (Athlete, Hockey Player)
16336 Bumiston Drive
Tampa, FL 33647-2763, USA

Dennis, Mark (Athlete, Football Player)
7 Londonderry Ln
Lincolnshire, IL 60069-3901, USA

Dennis, Mike (Athlete, Football Player)
332 Long Cove Dr
Madison, MS 39110-9183, USA

Dennis, Mike (Musician)
American Promotions
2011 Ferry Ave Apt U19
Camden, NJ 08104-1900, USA

Dennis, Mike (Athlete, Football Player)
332 Long Cove Dr
Madison, MS 39110-9183, USA

Dennis, Norm (Athlete, Hockey Player)
1531 3B Hwy
Fruitvale, BC V0G 1L1, Canada

Dennis, Pamela (Designer, Fashion Designer)
c/o Jerry Shandrew *Shandrew Public Relations*
1050 S Stanley Ave
Los Angeles, CA 90019-6634, USA

Dennis, Pat (Athlete, Football Player)
600 S MacArthur Blvd Apt 2821
Coppell, TX 75019-6733, USA

Dennison, Bonnie (Actor)

Dennison, Doug (Athlete, Football Player)
2309 Daybreak Trl
Plano, TX 75093-3808, USA

Dennison, Glenn (Athlete, Football Player)
1104 Tucker Ln
Ashton, MD 20861-9766, USA

Dennison, Julian (Actor)
c/o Jude Lane *Red Rocket Actors*
25/27 Majoribanks St
Mt Victoria Wellington 06011, NEW ZEALAND

Dennison, Rick (Athlete, Football Player)
12322 Overcup Dr
Houston, TX 77024-4913, USA

Denny, Christopher (Musician)
c/o Staff Member *Paradigm (Monterey)*
404 W Franklin St
Monterey, CA 93940-2303, USA

Denny, Dorothy (Actor)
15707 La Verida Dr
Victorville, CA 92395-3413, USA

Denny, John (Athlete, Baseball Player)
9403 Tower Pine Dr
Winter Garden, FL 34787-9613, USA

Denny, Robyn (Artist)
20/30 Wilds Rents
#4B
London SE14QG, UNITED KINGDOM (UK)

Denny, Simone (Musician)
c/o Stephen Ford *Diva Central Inc*
7510 W Sunset Blvd # 1445
Los Angeles, CA 90046-3408, USA

Denorfia, Chris (Athlete, Baseball Player)
8 Hawks Nest Dr
Southington, CT 06489-1372, USA

DenOuden, Wilerninintie (Willy) (Swimmer)
Goudsewagenstraat 23B
Rotterdam, HOLLAND

Densham, Gary (Race Car Driver)
Densham Racing
16661 Grand Ave
Bellflower, CA 90706-5037, USA

Densham, Pen (Director)
International Creative Mgmt
8942 Wilshire Blvd # 219
Beverly Hills, CA 90211-1908, USA

Densmore, Elizabeth (Actor)
c/o Sharon Lane *Lane Management Group*
4370 Tujunga Ave Ste 130
Studio City, CA 91604-2769, USA

Densmore, John (Musician)
49 Haldeman Rd
Santa Monica, CA 90402-1003, USA

Denson, Al (Athlete, Football Player)
6019 Bart Rd
Jacksonville, FL 32209-1809, USA

Denson, Autry (Athlete, Football Player)
1025 S Beach St Apt 30
Daytona Beach, FL 32114-6223, USA

Denson, Keith (Athlete, Football Player)
28024 Eagle Peak Ave
Canyon Country, CA 91387-3105, USA

Denson, Moses (Athlete, Football Player)
14005 Drake Dr
Rockville, MD 20853-2641, USA

Dent, Akeem (Athlete, Football Player)
c/o Hadley Engelhard *Enter-Sports Management*
6000 Lake Forrest Dr Ste 370
Atlanta, GA 30328-5902, USA

Dent, Bucky (Athlete, Baseball Player, Coach)
6693 Via Alfieri
Lake Worth, FL 33467-7087, USA

Dent, Burnell (Athlete, Football Player)
2904 Essex Ave
La Place, LA 70068-2241, USA

Dent, Catherine (Actor)
c/o Susan (Sue) Madore *Guttman Associates Public Relations*
118 S Beverly Dr Ste 201
Beverly Hills, CA 90212-3016, USA

Dent, Frederick (Politician)
221 Montgornery St
Spartanburg, SC 29302-3443, USA

Dent, Jim (Athlete, Golfer)
PO Box 290656
Tampa, FL 33687-0656, USA

Dent, Richard L (Athlete, Coach, Football Coach, Football Player)
4453 RFD
Long Grove, IL 60047-6900, USA

Dent, Robert (Bob) (Athlete, Football Player)
6669 Embarcadero Dr Apt 7
Stockton, CA 95219-3378, USA

Dent, Russell E (Bucky) (Athlete, Baseball Player)
Bucky Dent Baseball School
490 Dotterel Rd
Delray Beach, FL 33444-3201, USA

Dent, Taylor (Athlete, Tennis Player)
7143 Hawks Harbor Cir
Bradenton, FL 34207-5863, USA

Denters, Esmee (Musician)
c/o Staff Member *WME/IMG (UK)*
103 New Oxford St WMA
Centrepoint
London WC1A 1DD, UNITED KINGDOM

Denton, James (Actor)
1620 Lamego Dr
Glendale, CA 91207-1208, USA

Denton, Jeremiah (Politician)
4509 Wishart Rd
Virginia Bch, VA 23455-5526, USA

Denton, Judy (Writer)
400 Main St S
Atwater, MN 56209, USA

Denton, Kelly (Race Car Driver)
Henderson Motosports
532 E Main St
Abingdon, VA 24210-3410, USA

Denton, Mona (Baseball Player)
1880 S Newton St
Denver, CO 80219-4503, USA

Denton, Randy (Athlete, Basketball Player)
509 Sunnybrook Rd
Raleigh, NC 27610-2850, USA

Denton, Sandi (Pepa) (Musician)
Famous Artists Agency
250 W 57th St
New York, NY 10107-0001, USA

Denton, Sandra (Pepa) (Musician)
570/580 Johnson Ave
Aspen, CO 81611, USA

Denvir, John (Athlete, Football Player)
23250 Walker Basin Rd
Caliente, CA 93518-2103, USA

DeOre, Bill (Cartoonist)
Dallas News
Editorial Dept
Communications Center
Dallas, TX 75265, USA

Deossie, Steve (Athlete, Football Player)
835 Chestnut St
North Andover, MA 01845-6020, USA

DeOssie, Zak (Athlete, Football Player)

de Pablo, Cote (Actor)
c/o Jennifer Abel *PMK/BNC Public Relations*
1840 Century Park E Ste 1400
Los Angeles, CA 90067-2115, USA

De Palma, Brian (Director)
82 Pantigo Rd
East Hampton, NY 11937-2642, USA

Depalo, Jim (Baseball Player)
TCMA
4727 7th Ave SW
Naples, FL 34119-4039, USA

DePalva, James (Actor)
PO Box 11152
Greenwich, CT 06831-1152, USA

DePaola, Tomie (Actor, Writer)
c/o Staff Member *Penguin Putnam Books for Young Readers*
345 Hudson St Fl 14
New York, NY 10014-4592

Depaolo, Terri (Producer)
43 Rossmore Ave
Bronxville, NY 10708-5615, USA

Depardieu, Gerard (Actor)
3 Ashley Ln
Hendon
London NW4 1HF, UNITED KINGDOM

Departure, Themm (Music Group)
c/o Staff Member *Paradigm (Monterey)*
404 W Franklin St
Monterey, CA 93940-2303, USA

Depaso, Tom (Athlete, Football Player)
2108 Polo Pointe Dr
Vienna, VA 22181-2804, USA

de Passe, Suzanne (Producer)
9701 Oak Pass Rd
Beverly Hills, CA 90210-1222, USA

Depastino, Joe (Athlete, Baseball Player)
12853 Sheringham Way
Sarasota, FL 34240-8762, USA

Depaula, Sean (Athlete, Baseball Player)
2 Thomas St
Derry, NH 03038-2988, USA

Depeche Mode (Music Group)
Venusnote
PO Box 5239
Christchurch, Dorset BH23 2ZJ, UNITED KINGDOM

DePew, Charlie (Actor)
c/o Jill Fritzo *Jill Fritzo Public Relations*
208 E 51st St # 305
New York, NY 10022-6557, USA

Deply, Julie (Actor)
c/o Glenn Rigberg *Inphenate*
9701 Wilshire Blvd Fl 10
Beverly Hills, CA 90212-2010, USA

Depodesta, Paul (Commentator)
2775 Costebelle Dr
La Jolla, CA 92037-3518, USA

DePoyster, Jerry D (Athlete, Football Player)
PO Box 3029
Rock Springs, WY 82902-3029, USA

Depp, Johnny (Actor, Director)
c/o Staff Member *Spanky Taylor*
3010 Adornos Way
Burbank, CA 91504-1609, USA

Depre, Joe (Athlete, Basketball Player)
207 National Dr Apt 78
Murfreesboro, TN 37128-6810, USA

DePree, Hopwood (Actor)
c/o Staff Member *ROAR (LA)*
9701 Wilshire Blvd Fl 8
Beverly Hills, CA 90212-2008, USA

DePrume, Cathryn (Actor)
c/o Staff Member *Flick Commercials*
9057 Nemo St # A
W Hollywood, CA 90069-5511, USA

Dequenne, Emilie (Actor)
c/o Danielle Gain *Cineart*
28 Rue Mogador
Paris F-75009, FRANCE

Dequenne, Emilie (Cartoonist)
Houston Post
4888 Loop Central Dr # 390
Editorial Dept
Houston, TX 77081-2227, USA

de Ravin, Emilie (Actor)
c/o Allison Band *Gersh*
9465 Wilshire Blvd Ste 600
Beverly Hills, CA 90212-2605, USA

Derbez, Eugenio (Comedian, Producer)
Jaime Nuno 109
Col. Guadalupe Inn
Mexico, DF 01090, MEXICO

Derbez, Silvia (Actor)
c/o Staff Member *Televisa*
Blvd Adolfo Lopez Mateos 232
Colonia San Angel INN
DF CP 01060, MEXICO

Derby, Dean (Athlete, Football Player)
1682 Corkrum Rd
Walla Walla, WA 99362-8628, USA

Derek, Bo (Actor, Model)
c/o Rona Menashe *Guttman Associates Public Relations*
118 S Beverly Dr Ste 201
Beverly Hills, CA 90212-3016, USA

Dereuck, Colleen (Athlete)
4172 Saint Croix St
Boulder, CO 80301, USA

Dergan, Lisa (Actor, Model, Television Host)
PO Box 482325
Los Angeles, CA 90049, USA

Derhak, Rob (Musician)
45 Hadlock Rd
Falmouth, ME 04105-2559, USA

Derlago, Bill (Athlete, Hockey Player)
Seven View Chrysler
2685 Highway 7
Concord, ON L4K 1V8, Canada

Derline, Rodney (Athlete, Basketball Player)
12612 SE 215th St
Kent, WA 98031-2287, USA

Dern, Bruce (Actor)
PO Box 1581
Santa Monica, CA 90406-1581, USA

Dern, Laura (Actor)
c/o Annett Wolf *Wolf-Kasteler Public Relations*
6255 W Sunset Blvd Ste 1111
Los Angeles, CA 90028-7426, USA

Dernier, Bob (Athlete, Baseball Player)
1242 SW Arbormill Ter
Lees Summit, MO 64082-4165, USA

Deroo, Brian (Athlete, Football Player)
49224 Escalante St
Indio, CA 92201-8850, USA

Derosa, Mark (Athlete, Baseball Player)
4814 Kettle River Pt
Suwanee, GA 30024-8804, USA

Derosier, Michael (Musician)
Borman Entertainment
1250 6th St Ste 401
Santa Monica, CA 90401-1638, USA

De Rosnay, Tatiana (Writer)
Éitions Héloïse d'Ormesson
3 rue Rollin
Paris 75005, FRANCE

de Rossi, Portia (Actor)
c/o Scott Henderson *WME|IMG*
9601 Wilshire Blvd
Beverly Hills, CA 90210-5213, USA

de Rothschild, David (Producer)
Adventure Ecology
Zetland House
5/25 Scrutton St
London EC2A 4HJ, UK

Derr, Kenneth T (Business Person)
Chevron Corp
6001 Bollinger Canyon Rd
San Ramon, CA 94583-5737, USA

Derrick, Edward (Athlete, Baseball Player)
PO Box 158473
Nashville, TN 37215-8473, USA

Derricks, Cleavant (Actor)
480 Burano Court
Agoura Hills, CA 91377, USA

Derrickson, Scott (Director, Producer)
c/o Philip Raskind *WME|IMG*
9601 Wilshire Blvd
Beverly Hills, CA 90210-5213, USA

D'Errico, Donna (Actor, Model)
c/o Wendy Peldon *Caviar Entertainment*
2934 N Beverly Glen Cir # 115
Los Angeles, CA 90077-1724, USA

Derringer, Rick (Musician)
c/o Steve Peck *Fantasma Productions Inc*
854 Conniston Rd
West Palm Beach, FL 33405-2131, USA

Derrington, Bob (Race Car Driver)
1704 Aspen Ln
Seabrook, TX 77586-2912, USA

Derrington, Jim (Athlete, Baseball Player)
711 Sandlewood Ave
La Habra, CA 90631-7248, USA

Derryberry, Debi (Actor)
PO Box 2726
Toluca Lake, CA 91610-0726, USA

Dersch, Hans (Swimmer)
7217 E 55th Pl
Tulsa, OK 74145-7704, USA

Dershowitz, Alan (Attorney)
Harvard University Law School
1575 Massachusetts Ave
Hauser Hall 520
Cambridge, MA 02138-2801, USA

Derulo, Jason (Musician)
5000 Vanalden Ave
Tarzana, CA 91356-3906, USA

Derwin, Mark (Actor)
708 N Hillcrest Rd
Beverly Hills, CA 90210-3517, USA

Desai, Anita (Writer)
Deborah Rogers Ltd
20 Powis Mews
London W11 1JN, UNITED KINGDOM (UK)

Desai, Anoop (Musician)
c/o Mona Loring *Status PR*
PO Box 6191
Westlake Village, CA 91359-6191, USA

Desai-Barochia, Anand (Actor)
c/o Ashley Moore *Rogers & Cowan*
1840 Century Park E Fl 18
Los Angeles, CA 90067-2101, USA

Desailly, Marcel (Soccer Player)
FC Chelsea Stamford Bridge
Fulham Road
London SW6 1HS, UNITED KINGDOM (UK)

Desalvo, Matt (Athlete, Baseball Player)
10 Village Gate Blvd
Delaware, OH 43015-8844, USA

DeSantis, Jaclyn (Actor)
c/o Sarah Fargo *Paradigm*
140 Broadway Ste 2600
New York, NY 10005-1011, USA

DeSantis, John (Actor)
c/o Kathy Carpenter *KC Talent*
109-119 Pender St W
Vancouver, BC V6B 1S5, CANADA

Desanto, Tom (Producer)
c/o Jodi Lederman *Wolf-Kasteler Public Relations*
6255 W Sunset Blvd Ste 1111
Los Angeles, CA 90028-7426, USA

Des Barres, Michael (Actor)
c/o Pam Ellis *Ellis Talent Group*
4705 Laurel Canyon Blvd Ste 300
Valley Village, CA 91607-5901, USA

Descalso, Daniel (Athlete, Baseball Player)
1937 Eaton Ave
San Carlos, CA 94070-4740, USA

Deschaine, Dick (Athlete, Football Player)
424 Cleveland St Apt 202
Winneconne, WI 54986-9678, USA

Deschanel, Emily (Actor)
c/o Rhonda Price *Gersh*
41 Madison Ave Ste 3301
New York, NY 10010-2210, USA

Deschanel, Mary Jo (Actor)
844 Chautauqua Blvd
Pacific Palisades, CA 90272-3801, USA

Deschanel, Zooey (Actor)
c/o Lauren Auslander *LUNA*
116 Nassau St # 615
New York, NY 10038-2402, USA

Descher, Sandra (Actor)
4544 Arcola Ave
Toluca Lake, CA 91602-1517, USA

Descombes-Dinehart, Nancy (Baseball Player)
59607 County Road 11
Elkhart, IN 46517-9178, USA

DesCombes Lesko, Jeneane (Baseball Player)
17410 87th Ave SE TRLR 1
Snohomish, WA 98296-8005, USA

Descombes-Lesko, Jeneane (Athlete, Baseball Player, Commentator)
11227 NE 109th Ln Apt L108
Kirkland, WA 98033-5029, USA

Desert, Alex (Actor)
1292 S Highland Ave
Los Angeles, CA 90019-1732, USA

deSeve, Peter (Artist)
25 Park Pl
Brooklyn, NY 11217-3207, USA

Deshaies, Jim (Baseball Player)
151 N TID'ior Point Dr
Spring, TX 77382-1240, USA

Deshales, Jim (Athlete, Baseball Player)
151 N Taylor Point Dr
Spring, TX 77382-1240, USA

DeShannon, Jackie (Musician)
606 N Arden Dr
Beverly Hills, CA 90210-3510, USA

DeShields, Delino L (Athlete, Baseball Player)
3399 Kiveton Ct
Norcross, GA 30092-3374, USA

Deshler, Jimmy (Actor)
c/o Shelly DeMarre *JST Management*
7606 N Courage Way
Van Nuys, CA 91405-5649, USA

Desiderio, Robert (Actor)
1475 Sierra Vista Dr
Aspen, CO 81611-1044, USA

Desiigner (Musician)
c/o Tammy Brook *FYI Public Relations*
174 5th Ave Ste 404
New York, NY 10010-5964, USA

Desilva, John (Athlete, Baseball Player)
32750 Airport Rd
Fort Bragg, CA 95437-9514, USA

de Silva, Jorge (Actor)
c/o Staff Member *Televisa*
Blvd Adolfo Lopez Mateos 232
Colonia San Angel INN
DF CP 01060, MEXICO

DeSimone, Livio D (Desi) (Business Person)
Minnesota Mining & Manufacturing
3M Center
Saint Paul, MN 55144-0002, USA

Desjardins, Eric (Athlete, Hockey Player)
9 Woodglen Ln
Voorhees, NJ 08043-9559, USA

Desjardins, Gerry (Athlete, Hockey Player)
252 Suffolk Pl
London, ON N6G 3S4, Canada

DesJarlais, Scott (Congressman, Politician)
413 Cannon Hob
Washington, DC 20515-3301, USA

Deskins, Donald (Athlete, Football Player)
3240 Pittsview Dr
Ann Arbor, MI 48108-1946, USA

Desman, Shawn (Musician)
c/o Staff Member *BMG*
1540 Broadway
New York, NY 10036-4039, USA

Desmond, Ian (Athlete, Baseball Player)
c/o Staff Member *Colorado Rockies*
2001 Blake St
Coors Field
Denver, CO 80205-2000, USA

Desormeaux, Kent (Horse Racer)
Desmormeaux Racing Stable
385 W Huntington Dr
Arcadia, CA 91007, USA

De Sousa, Melissa (Actor)
c/o Mark Rousso *Industry Entertainment Partners*
955 Carrillo Dr Ste 300
Los Angeles, CA 90048-5400, USA

De Souza, Steven (Producer, Writer)
c/o Alan Gasmer *Alan Gasmer Management Company*
10877 Wilshire Blvd Ste 603
Los Angeles, CA 90024-4348, USA

Des'ree (Musician)
Solo Agency
55 Fulham High St
London SW6 3JJ, UNITED KINGDOM (UK)

Dess, Darrell (Athlete, Football Player)
224 Sumner Ave
New Castle, PA 16105-2579, USA

Dessens, Elmer (Athlete, Baseball Player)
5542 E Estrid Ave
Scottsdale, AZ 85254-2973, USA

DeStefano, Pete (Producer)
c/o Babette Perry *Innovative Artists*
1505 10th St
Santa Monica, CA 90401-2805, USA

Destiny, Ryan (Actor)
c/o Dawn Irons *717 Management*
Prefers not to be contacted by email.
New York, NY NA, USA

Destrade, Orestes (Athlete, Baseball Player)
20425 Walnut Grove Ln
Tampa, FL 33647-3352, USA

Desutter, Wayne (Athlete, Football Player)
4450 Antietam Creek Trl
Leesburg, FL 34748-1203, USA

Deters, Harold (Athlete, Football Player)
1602 Woods Creek Dr
Garner, NC 27529-4761, USA

Detherage, Bob (Athlete, Baseball Player)
322 Turf Ln
Carl Junction, MO 64834-9575, USA

Detmer, Amanda (Actor)
c/o John Carrabino *John Carrabino Management*
5900 Wilshire Blvd Ste 740
Los Angeles, CA 90036-5032, USA

Detmer, Koy (Athlete, Football Player)
6419 N Vandiver Rd Apt 1212
San Antonio, TX 78209-4481, USA

Detmer, Ty (Athlete, Football Player, Heisman Trophy Winner)
102 S Aspen Dr
Mapleton, UT 84664-4724, USA

Detmers, Maruschka (Actor)
c/o Staff Member *Agence Alvares Correa*
34, Rue Jouffroy D'Abbans
Paris 75017, France

Detorie, Rick (Cartoonist)
Creators Syndicate
5777 W Century Blvd # 700
Los Angeles, CA 90045-5600, USA

Detroit, Marcella (Musician, Songwriter, Writer)
MCM Mgmt
40 Langham St
#300
London W1N 5RG, UNITED KINGDOM (UK)

Dettlaff, Bill (Athlete, Golfer)
133 Clearlake Dr
Ponte Vedra Beach, FL 32082-2178, USA

Dettmer, John (Athlete, Baseball Player)
1868 E Chimney Stone Ct
Draper, UT 84020-2510, USA

Dettore, Tom (Athlete, Baseball Player)
1120 McEwen Ave
Canonsburg, PA 15317-1928, USA

Detweiler, Ducky (Athlete, Baseball Player)
22027 Gannon Dr
Preston, MD 21655-1236, USA

Detwiler, Chuck (Athlete, Football Player)
79898 Viento Dr
La Quinta, CA 92253-8811, USA

Detwiler, Ross (Baseball Player)
359 Brown Swiss Cir
Duncansville, PA 16635-8061, USA

Deutch, Howard (Director)
International Creative Mgmt
8942 Wilshire Blvd # 219
Beverly Hills, CA 90211-1908, USA

Deutch, Howie (Actor, Director, Producer, Writer)
c/o Daniel J Talbot *ICM Partners*
10250 Constellation Blvd Fl 7
Los Angeles, CA 90067-6207, USA

Deutch, John (Politician)
51 Clifton St
Belmont, MA 02478-3353, USA

Deutch, Madelyn (Actor)
c/o Mona Loring *Status PR*
PO Box 6191
Westlake Village, CA 91359-6191, USA

Deutch, Zoey (Actor)
c/o Gordon Gilbertson *Gilbertson Management*
1334 3rd Street Promenade Ste 201
Santa Monica, CA 90401-1320, USA

Deutsch, Dave (Athlete, Basketball Player)
24 Dell Ln
Bernville, PA 19506-9590, USA

Deutsch, Donny (Television Host)
Deutsch
330 W 34th St Fl 13
New York, NY 10001-2406, USA

DeValeria, Dennis (Sportscaster)
213 Hillendale Rd
Pittsburgh, PA 15237-1803, USA

Devane, William (Actor)
c/o Deborah Miller *Shelter Entertainment*
9255 W Sunset Blvd Ste 300
Los Angeles, CA 90069-3313, USA

Devar, Sharmila (Actor)
c/o Mike Eistenstadt *Amsel, Eisenstadt & Frazier Talent Agency (AEF)*
5055 Wilshire Blvd Ste 860
Los Angeles, CA 90036-6108, USA

Devarez, Cesar (Athlete, Baseball Player)
35 Arden St Apt B
New York, NY 10040-1318, USA

DeVarona, Donna (Athlete, Olympic Athlete, Swimmer)
TWI
3 Avon Ln
Greenwich, CT 06830-3926, USA

de Vasconcelos, Tasha (Actor)
c/o Samira Higham *Independent Talent Group*
40 Whitfield St
London W1T 2RH, UNITED KINGDOM

DeVasquez, Devin (Model)
9903 Santa Monica Blvd Ste 169
Beverly Hills, CA 90212-1671, USA

Devaughn, Dennis (Athlete, Football Player)
2416 Clear Field Dr
Plano, TX 75025-5184, USA

DeVaughn, Raheem (Actor, Musician)
c/o Eva Arthur *M.A.G./Universal Attractions*
15 W 36th St Fl 8
New York, NY 10018-7927, USA

Devault, Calvin (Actor)
c/o John Frazier *Amsel, Eisenstadt & Frazier Talent Agency (AEF)*
5055 Wilshire Blvd Ste 860
Los Angeles, CA 90036-6108, USA

Develin, James (Athlete, Football Player)

Devellano, Jim (Athlete, Hockey Player)
300 Riverfront Dr Unit 23G
Detroit, MI 48226-4584

Devenzio, Dick (Athlete, Basketball Player)
1116 Home Pl
Matthews, NC 28105-6891, USA

Dever, Kaitlyn (Actor)
c/o Emily Urbani *Osbrink Talent Agency*
4343 Lankershim Blvd # 100
North Hollywood, CA 91602-2705, USA

Dever, Seamus (Actor)
c/o Craig Schneider *Pinnacle Public Relations*
8721 Santa Monica Blvd # 133
W Hollywood, CA 90069-4507, USA

Deveraux, Jude (Writer)
Pocket Books
1230 Avenue of the Americas Fl CONC1
New York, NY 10020-1586, USA

Devereaux, Boyd (Athlete, Hockey Player)
10766 E Palm Ridge Dr
Scottsdale, AZ 85255-1719, USA

Devereaux, Mike (Athlete, Baseball Player)
2236 W Doublegrove St
West Covina, CA 91790-5607, USA

Devers, Gail (Athlete, Olympic Athlete, Track Athlete)
3245 Morgan Rd
Buford, GA 30519-5398, USA

Devicq, Paula (Actor, Model)
c/o Joanne Horowitz *Joanne Horowitz Management*
928 N Beverly Dr
Beverly Hills, CA 90210-2913, USA

Deville, CC (Musician)
c/o Mike Esterman *Esterman.Com, LLC*
Prefers to be contacted via email
Baltimore, MD XXXXX, USA

Deville, Michael (Director)
36 Rue Reinhardt
Boulogne 92100, FRANCE

Devin, Michael (Actor, Musician)
c/o Noelle Kim *National Talent LA*
5670 Wilshire Blvd # 1867
Los Angeles, CA 90036-5679, USA

Devine, Adam (Actor)
c/o Isaac Horne *Avalon Management*
9171 Wilshire Blvd Ste 320
Beverly Hills, CA 90210-5516, USA

Devine, Adrian (Athlete, Baseball Player)
900 Lilac Arbor Rd
Dacula, GA 30019-2477, USA

Devine, Harold (Boxer)
595 Wyckoff Ave
Wyckoff, NJ 07481-1337, USA

Devine, Joey (Athlete, Baseball Player)
805 Morning Oaks Dr
Holly Springs, NC 27540-6170, USA

Devine, Loretta (Actor)
c/o Alex Spieller *Baker Winokur Ryder Public Relations*
200 5th Ave Fl 5
New York, NY 10010-3307, USA

DeVink, Lodewijk J R (Business Person)
Warner-Lambert Co
201 Tabor Rd
Morris Plains, NJ 07950-2614, USA

DeVito, Danny (Actor, Comedian, Director)
c/o Staff Member *Jersey Films*
PO Box 491246
Los Angeles, CA 90049-9246, USA

Devito, Louie (DJ, Musician)
c/o Len Evans *Project Publicity*
540 W 43rd St
New York, NY 10036, USA

Devito, Mike (Athlete, Football Player)

Devitt, John (Swimmer)
46 Beacon Ave
Beacon Hill, NSW 02100, AUSTRALIA

DeVitto, Torrey (Actor)
c/o Matthew Lesher *Insight*
5358 Melrose Ave # 200W
Los Angeles, CA 90038-5117, USA

Devliegher, Charles (Chuck) (Athlete, Football Player)
27307 N 89th Ave
Peoria, AZ 85383-4854, USA

Devlin, Barry (Director, Writer)

Devlin, Bruce (Athlete, Golfer)
176 Brook Hollow Ln
Weatherford, TX 76088-7630, USA

Devlin, Chris (Athlete, Football Player)
100 Meadow Lark Ln
Boalsburg, PA 16827-1800, USA

Devlin, Dean (Actor, Director, Producer)
Electric Entertainment
1438 N Gower St Ste 24
Los Angeles, CA 90028-8306, USA

Devlin, Joseph (Athlete, Football Player)
3715 Schintzius Rd
Eden, NY 14057-9790, USA

Devlin, Mike (Athlete, Football Player)
5719 Waterwalk Ct
Richmond, TX 77469-7352, USA

Devlin, Robert M (Business Person)
American General Corp
2929 Allen Pkwy Ste 3800
Houston, TX 77019-2155, USA

Devlins, The (Music Group)
c/o Staff Member *Paradigm (Monterey)*
404 W Franklin St
Monterey, CA 93940-2303, USA

Devo (Music Group, Musician)
c/o Ian Fintak *ICM Partners*
10250 Constellation Blvd Fl 7
Los Angeles, CA 90067-6207, USA

DeVoe, Ronnie (Musician)
c/o Staff Member *Pyramid Entertainment Group*
377 Rector Pl Apt 21A
New York, NY 10280-1439, USA

Devon, Dayna (Actor, Television Host)
545 S Plymouth Blvd
Los Angeles, CA 90020-4709, USA

Devore, Doug (Athlete, Baseball Player)
5247 Willow Grove Pl S
Dublin, OH 43017-2116, USA

Devorski, Paul (Athlete, Hockey Player)
6292 Farmers Ln
Harrisburg, PA 17111-7066

DeVos, Betsy (Politician)
1025 S Shore Dr
Holland, MI 49423-4500, USA

Devries, Greg (Athlete, Hockey Player)
25 Colonel Winstead Dr
Brentwood, TN 37027-8937, USA

Devries, Jared (Athlete, Football Player)
15342 Lambert Dr
Clear Lake, IA 50428-8637, USA

Devries, Jed (Athlete, Football Player)
2433 W 1425 S
Syracuse, UT 84075-6996, USA

deVry, William (Actor)
3268 Bennett Dr
Los Angeles, CA 90068-1702, USA

Dewan, Jenna (Actor)
c/o Lena Roklin *Luber Roklin Management*
5815 W Sunset Blvd Ste 208
Los Angeles, CA 90028-6481, USA

Dewan Tatum, Jenna (Actor, Dancer)
c/o Gabriel Cohen *Management 360*
9111 Wilshire Blvd
Beverly Hills, CA 90210-5508, USA

Dewar, Susan (Cartoonist)
Universal Press Syndicate
4520 Main St Ste 340
Kansas City, MO 64111-7705, USA

Deward, Scott (Race Car Driver)
479 Bay Rd
South Easton, MA 02375-1424, USA

Dewberry, Michelle (Reality Star)
Taylor Herring
11 Westway Centre
69 St Marks Road
London W10 6JG, UNITED KINGDOM

Dewese, Mohandas (Kool mo Dee) (Actor)
c/o Staff Member *Identity Talent Agency (ID)*
9107 Wilshire Blvd Ste 500
Beverly Hills, CA 90210-5526, USA

DeWet, Shaun (Model)
c/o Staff Member *Elite Model Management (NY)*
245 5th Ave Fl 24
New York, NY 10016-8728, USA

Dewey, Mark (Athlete, Baseball Player)
28150 Rivermont Dr
Meadowview, VA 24361-2822, USA

Dewey, Tommy (Actor)
c/o Paul Brown *Industry Entertainment Partners*
955 Carrillo Dr Ste 300
Los Angeles, CA 90048-5400, USA

DeWilde, Edy (Director)
Stedelijk Museum
Amsterdam, NETHERLANDS

Dewillis, Jeff (Athlete, Baseball Player)
4804 Sherman Blvd
Galveston, TX 77551-5953, USA

Dewine, Mike (Politician)
336 Phillips St
Yellow Springs, OH 45387-1724, USA

De Winne, Frank Major (Astronaut)
European Astronaut Centre Linder Hohe
Potsfach 90 60 96 Koln
D-51142, Germany

Dewitt, Blake (Athlete, Baseball Player)
212 Holmes Dr
Sikeston, MO 63801-4907, USA

DeWitt, Doug (Boxer)
2035 Central Ave
Yonkers, NY 10710, USA

DeWitt, Joyce (Actor)
c/o Staff Member *JG Business Management Inc*
PO Box 7309
Santa Monica, CA 90406-7309, USA

Dewitt, Matt (Athlete, Baseball Player)
10188 Calabro Ct
Las Vegas, NV 89178-8043, USA

DeWitt, Rosemarie (Actor)
c/o Meredith O'Sullivan Wasson *The Lede Company*
9701 Wilshire Blvd # 930
Beverly Hills, CA 90212-2020, USA

Dewitt, William 0 (Commentator)
5825 Drewry Farm Ln
Cincinnati, OH 45243-3441, USA

Dewitt, William O (Baseball Player)
St Louis Cardinals
5825 Drewry Farm Ln
Cincinnati, OH 45243-3441, USA

DeWitt, Willie (Boxer)
605 N Water St
Burnet, TX 78611-1728, USA

Dews, Bobby (Athlete, Baseball Player)
2509 Ridgewood Ln
Albany, GA 31707-3047, USA

DeWulf, Noureen (Actor)
c/o Scott Newman *Slate PR*
901 N Highland Ave
W Hollywood, CA 90038-2412, USA

DeWyze, Lee (Musician)
c/o Simon Fuller *XIX Entertainment (UK)*
32/33 Ransomes Dock
London SW11 4NP, UNITED KINGDOM (UK)

Dexter, Mary (Director)
Hank Tani
14542 Delaware Dr
Moorpark, CA 93021-3560, USA

Dexter, Pete (Writer)
c/o Author Mail *Doubleday*
1745 Broadway Frnt 3
New York, NY 10019-4641, USA

Dexter, Peter W (Writer)
Sacramento Bee
Editorial Dept
21st & Q Sts
Sacramento, CA 95852, USA

Dexter-Jones, Annabelle (Actor)
c/o Bianca Bianconi *42West*
600 3rd Ave Fl 23
New York, NY 10016-1914, USA

Dey, Susan (Actor)
c/o Toni Howard *ICM Partners*
10250 Constellation Blvd Fl 7
Los Angeles, CA 90067-6207, USA

Deyn, Agyness (Actor)
c/o Danie Streisand *United Talent Agency (UTA)*
888 7th Ave Fl 7
New York, NY 10106-0700, USA

DeYoung, Cliff (Actor)
481 Savona Way
Oak Park, CA 91377-4842, USA

DeYoung, Dennis (Musician)
12/13 Ambriance Dr
Burr Ridge, IL 60527, USA

Dezelan, Frank (Athlete, Baseball Player)
7423 Lighthouse Pt
Pittsburgh, PA 15221-2553, USA

Dhananjay, Siddharth (Actor, Musician)
c/o Siri Garber *Platform PR*
2666 N Beachwood Dr
Los Angeles, CA 90068-2308, USA

Dhavernas, Caroline (Actor)
c/o Marla Farrell *Shelter PR*
928 Broadway Ste 505
New York, NY 10010-8143, USA

Dial, Quinton (Athlete, Football Player)

Diallo, Mmadou (Soccer Player)
New England Revolution
1 Patriot Pl
Cmgi Field
Foxboro, MA 02035-1388, USA

Diamandis, Maria (Musician)
c/o Marty Diamond *Paradigm*
140 Broadway Ste 2600
New York, NY 10005-1011, USA

Diamandis, Peter (Business Person)
XPRIZE Foundation
800 Corporate Pointe Ste 350
Culver City, CA 90230-7692, USA

Diamantopoulos, Chris (Actor)
c/o Ruth Bernstein *Viewpoint Inc*
8820 Wilshire Blvd Ste 220
Beverly Hills, CA 90211-2622, USA

Diamond, Charles (Athlete, Football Player)
7300 SW 69th Ct
Miami, FL 33143-4420, USA

Diamond, Chris (Race Car Driver)
J&L Racing
5171 Icard Ridge Rd
Hickory, NC 28601-8968, USA

Diamond, Diane (Television Host)
c/o Staff Member *Court TV*
600 3rd Ave Fl 2
New York, NY 10016-1919, USA

Diamond, Dustin (Actor)
c/o Staff Member *Jack Koshick Presents*
PO Box 511385
Milwaukee, WI 53203-0231, USA

Diamond, Joel (Producer)
Joel Diamond Entertainment
3940 Laurel Canyon Blvd Ste 441
Studio City, CA 91604-3709, USA

Diamond, Michael (Mike D) (Musician)
GAS Entertainment
8935 Lindblade St
Culver City, CA 90232-2438, USA

Diamond, Michael T (DJ)
c/o Staff Member *Diva Central Inc*
7510 W Sunset Blvd # 1445
Los Angeles, CA 90046-3408, USA

Diamond, Neil (Musician)
PO Box 3357
Los Angeles, CA 90078-3357, USA

Diamond, Reed (Actor)
c/o David Weise *David Weise and Associates*
16000 Ventura Blvd Ste 600
Encino, CA 91436-2753, USA

Diamond, Thomas (Athlete, Baseball Player)
310 Edgewood Ln
La Place, LA 70068-8964, USA

Diamond Rio (Music Group)
c/o Renee Behrman-Greiman *Modern Management*
1625 Broadway Ste 600
Nashville, TN 37203-3141, USA

Diamonds, The (Music Group)
561 Keystone Ave # 224
Reno, NV 89503-4304, USA

Diamont, Don (Actor)
c/o Staff Member *Craig Management*
2240 Miramonte Cir E Unit C
Palm Springs, CA 92264-5734, USA

Diana, Rich (Athlete, Football Player)
2 Munson Dr Unit 7
Wallingford, CT 06492-5366, USA

Diaw, Boris (Athlete, Basketball Player)
8632 N Via La Serena
Paradise Valley, AZ 85253-2130, USA

Diaz, Aaron (Actor)

Diaz, Alyssa (Actor)
c/o Cindy Guagenti *Baker Winokur Ryder Public Relations*
9100 Wilshire Blvd
W Tower #500
Beverly Hills, CA 90212-3415, USA

Diaz, Cameron (Actor)
14320 Ventura Blvd # 636
Sherman Oaks, CA 91423-2717, USA

Diaz, Carlos (Athlete, Baseball Player)
45-236 Ka Hanahou Cir
Kaneohe, HI 96744-3009, USA

Diaz, Carlos (Athlete, Baseball Player)
3037 Homestead Oaks Dr
Clearwater, FL 33759-1626, USA

Diaz, David (Athlete, Boxer)
c/o Staff Member *Top Rank Inc.*
3908 Howard Hughes Pkwy
#580
Las Vegas, NV 89109, USA

Diaz, Einar (Athlete, Baseball Player)
4315 70th Ave E
Ellenton, FL 34222-7329, USA

Diaz, Guillermo (Actor)
c/o Meghan Schumacher *Meghan Schumacher Management*
13351D Riverside Dr Ste 387
Sherman Oaks, CA 91423-2508, USA

Diaz, Helga (Actor)
c/o Gabriel Blanco *Gabriel Blanco Iglesias (Mexico)*
Rio Balsas 35-32
Colonia Cuauhtemoc
DF 06500, Mexico

Diaz, Izzy (Actor)
c/o Scott Zimmerman *Scott Zimmerman Management*
901 N Highland Ave
Los Angeles, CA 90038-2412, USA

Diaz, Joey (Actor)
c/o Justin Edbrooke *Creative Artists Agency (CAA)*
2000 Avenue of the Stars Ste 100
Los Angeles, CA 90067-4705, USA

Diaz, Jorge (Athlete, Football Player)
9282 123rd Ave
Largo, FL 33773-2523, USA

Diaz, Laura (Golfer)
c/o Staff Member *Ladies Pro Golf Association (LPGA)*
100 International Golf Dr
Daytona Beach, FL 32124-1092, USA

Diaz, Lazaro (Athlete, Baseball Player)
13557 Meadow Bay Loop
Orlando, FL 32824-5082, USA

Diaz, Manny (Politician)
Mayor's Office
3500 Pan American Dr
Miami, FL 33133-5504, USA

Diaz, Mario (Athlete, Baseball Player)
90 Calle Menta
Gurabo, PR 00778-9655, USA

Diaz, Matt (Athlete, Baseball Player)
1124 Afton St
Lakeland, FL 33803-3202, USA

Diaz, Melonie (Actor)
c/o Ashley Franklin *Thruline Entertainment*
9250 Wilshire Blvd Fl Ground
Beverly Hills, CA 90212-3352, USA

Diaz, Mike (Athlete, Baseball Player)
225 Hillside Dr
Pacifica, CA 94044-3032, USA

Diaz, Robison (Actor)
c/o Staff Member *TV Caracol*
Calle 76 #11 - 35
Piso 10AA
Bogota DC 26484, COLOMBIA

Diaz, Rocsi (Actor)
c/o Daniel Ryan Kinney *Artist and Brand Management - NY*
250 Hudson St Fl 2
New York, NY 10013-1413, USA

Diaz Balart, Jose (Actor)
c/o Staff Member *Telemundo*
2470 W 8th Ave
Hialeah, FL 33010-2000, USA

Diaz-Balart, Jose (Correspondent)
CBS-TV
51 W 52nd St
News Dept
New York, NY 10019-6119, USA

Diaz-Balart, Mario (Congressman, Politician)
436 Cannon Hob
Washington, DC 20515-3203, USA

Diaz-Infante, David (Athlete, Football Player)
24723 E Park Crescent Dr
Aurora, CO 80016-3190, USA

Diaz-Rahi, Yamila (Model)
Next Model Mgmt
23 Watts St
New York, NY 10013, USA

Dibaba, Tirunesh (Athlete, Olympic Athlete, Track Athlete)
c/o Staff Member *Global Athletics & Marketing, Inc.*
437 Boylston St Ste 400
Boston, MA 02116-3374, USA

Di Bauda, Faustino (Actor)
c/o Chris Lewis *Aries Entertainment*
PO Box 771
Harlan, KY 40831-0771, USA

Dibble, Dorne (Athlete, Football Player)
18601 Jamestown Cir
Northville, MI 48168-1834, USA

Dibble, Rob (Athlete, Baseball Player)
30020 Trail Creek Dr
Agoura Hills, CA 91301-4041, USA

Dibel, John C (Business Person)
Meade Instruments Corp
6001 Oak Cyn
Irvine, CA 92618-5200, USA

Dibernardo, Rick (Athlete, Football Player)
229 Encantado Cyn
Rcho Sta Marg, CA 92688-2997, USA

DiBiase, Ted (Athlete, Wrestler)
Heart of David Ministry
PO Box 1291
Clinton, MS 39060-1291, USA

DiBlasio, Raul (Musician)
Esterfan Enterprises
420 Jefferson Ave
Miami Beach, FL 33139-6503, USA

Diblassio, Raul (Musician)
c/o Staff Member *BMG*
1540 Broadway
New York, NY 10036-4039, USA

di Bonaventura, Lorenzo (Producer)
c/o Staff Member *Di Bonaventura Pictures*
5555 Melrose Ave
Demille Bldg Fl 2
Los Angeles, CA 90038-3989, USA

Dibos, Alicia (Athlete, Golfer)
112 River Run
Greenwich, CT 06831-4149, USA

DiCamillo, Brandon (Actor)
c/o Staff Member *Stoic Management*
947 Trinity Ln
King Of Prussia, PA 19406-3603, USA

Dicamillo, Gary T (Business Person)
1001 Saint Georges Rd
Baltimore, MD 21210-1412, USA

DiCaprio, Leonardo (Actor, Producer)
c/o Staff Member *Appian Way*
9255 W Sunset Blvd Ste 615
West Hollywood, CA 90069-3303, USA

Di Cione, Sevy (Actor)
c/o Cindy Sheffield *The Sheffield Agency*
14020 NW Passage Apt 104
Marina Del Rey, CA 90292-7407, USA

Dick, Andy (Actor, Comedian)
c/o Scott Carlsen *Scott Carlsen Entertainment*
5328 Alhama Dr
Woodland Hills, CA 91364-2013, USA

Dick, Degen (Athlete, Football Player)
15871 Springdale St
Huntington Beach, CA 92649-1727

Dick, Douglas (Actor)
16530 Ventura Blvd Ste 404
Encino, CA 91436-5057, USA

Dick, Ed (Baseball Player)
TCMA
501 Washington Ave
Ocean Springs, MS 39564-4631, USA

Dickau, Dan (Athlete, Basketball Player)
c/o Mark Bartelstein *Priority Sports & Entertainment (Chicago)*
325 N La Salle Dr Ste 650
Chicago, IL 60654-8182, USA

Dickel, Dan (Athlete, Football Player)
832 Normandy Dr
Iowa City, IA 52246-2931, USA

Dicken, Paul (Athlete, Baseball Player)
2775 NW 49th Ave Unit 205
Ocala, FL 34482-6213, USA

Dickens, Kim (Actor)
c/o Stephen Hirsh *Gersh*
9465 Wilshire Blvd Ste 600
Beverly Hills, CA 90212-2605, USA

Dickenson, Herb (Athlete, Hockey Player)
55-6 McCarthy Cres
3
Angus, ON L0M 1B3, Canada

Dicker, Cintia (Model)
c/o Staff Member *Nova Models Munich*
Siegesstrasse 3
Munich 80802, Germany

Dickerson, Dan (Baseball Player)
7950 Brookwood Dr
Clarkston, MI 48348-4471, USA

Dickerson, Eric (Athlete, Football Player, Sportscaster)
26815 Mulholland Hwy
Calabasas, CA 91302-1947, USA

Dickerson, Ernest (Director)
c/o David Gersh *Gersh*
9465 Wilshire Blvd Ste 600
Beverly Hills, CA 90212-2605, USA

Dickerson, Henry (Athlete, Basketball Player)
3204 Skybrook Ln
Durham, NC 27703-5983, USA

Dickerson, John (Athlete, Baseball Player)
1702 26th St N
Columbus, MS 39701-2606, USA

Dickerson, Kenneth (Athlete, Football Player)
2406 Alabama Ave
Tuskegee Institute, AL 36088-2410, USA

Dickerson, Marty (Athlete, Golfer)
4225 Luzon Way
Sarasota, FL 34241-5728, USA

Dickerson, Sam (Athlete, Football Player)
551 Waddell Way
Modesto, CA 95357-1477, USA

Dickerson, Sandra (Actor)
Howes & Prior
Berkeley House
Hay Hill
London W1X 7LH, UNITED KINGDOM (UK)

Dickey, Boh A (Business Person)
SAFECO Corp
Safeco Plaza
Seattle, WA 98185-0001, USA

Dickey, Charlie (Athlete, Football Player)
1992 E Farm Cir
Sandy, UT 84093-6296, USA

Dickey, Curtis (Athlete, Football Player)
702 Glenview Dr
Mansfield, TX 76063-6743, USA

Dickey, Lynn (Athlete, Football Player)
9220 Pawnee Ln
Leawood, KS 66206-1758, USA

Dickey, RA (Athlete, Baseball Player)
c/o Bo McKinnis *McKinnis Sports Management*
209 10th Ave S Ste 405
Nashville, TN 37203-0764, USA

Dickey, Richard (Athlete, Basketball Player)
1109 Red Maple Dr
Plymouth, IN 46563-3697, USA

Dickey, Wallace (Athlete, Football Player)
220 E Montana Dr
Shiner, TX 77984-6240, USA

Dickinson, Angie (Actor)
c/o Tom Monjack *Tom Monjack Celebrity Enterprises*
28650 Avenida Maravilla # A
Cathedral City, CA 92234-8115, USA

Dickinson, Bruce (Musician)
c/o Staff Member *UTA Music/The Agency Group (UK)*
361-373 City Rd
London EC1V 1PQ, UNITED KINGDOM

Dickinson, David (Actor)
Bargain Hunt
PO Box 229
Bristol BS99 7JN, ENGLAND

Dickinson, Harris (Actor)
c/o Kristin Tarry *TCG Artist Management*
14a Goodwin's Ct
Covent Garden
London WC2N 4LL, UNITED KINGDOM

Dickinson, Janice (Model, Reality Star)
c/o Staff Member *WME|IMG*
9601 Wilshire Blvd
Beverly Hills, CA 90210-5213, USA

Dickinson, Judy (Athlete, Golfer)
18277 SE Heritage Dr
Jupiter, FL 33469-1439, USA

Dickinson, Parnell (Athlete, Football Player)
1646 Wallace Rd
Lutz, FL 33549-3933, USA

Dickinson, Richard (Athlete, Football Player)
PO Box 166
New Augusta, MS 39462-0166, USA

Dickinson, Steve (Cartoonist)
c/o Staff Member *King Features Syndication*
300 W 57th St Fl 15
New York, NY 10019-5238, USA

Dickman, James B (Journalist)
1471 Peach Creek Dr
Splendora, TX 77372, USA

Dickson, Bob (Athlete, Golfer)
140 Woodlands Creek Dr
Ponte Vedra Beach, FL 32082-3217, USA

Dickson, Bruce (Bad) (Race Car Driver)
1370 Bridge Rd
West Chester, PA 19382-2033, USA

Dickson, Ed (Athlete, Football Player)

Dickson, Jason (Athlete, Baseball Player)
15 Edison St
St Margarets, NB E1N 5B4, Canada

Dickson, Jennifer (Artist, Photographer)
20 Osborne St
Ottawa, ON K1S 4Z9, CANADA

Dickson, Jim (Athlete, Baseball Player)
685 Franklin Ave
Astoria, OR 97103-4615, USA

Dickson, John (Athlete, Basketball Player)
4646 Wynmeade Park NE
Marietta, GA 30067-4098, USA

Dickson, Lance (Athlete, Baseball Player)
4615 N Placita Roca Blanca
Tucson, AZ 85718-7476, USA

Dickson, Neil (Actor)
c/o Lorraine Berglund *Lorraine Berglund Management*
11537 Hesby St
North Hollywood, CA 91601-3618, USA

Dickson, Ngila (Designer)
c/o Staff Member *Sandra Marsh Management*
9150 Wilshire Blvd Ste 220
Beverly Hills, CA 90212-3429, USA

Dicus, Charles (Chuck) (Athlete, Football Player)
7 Valley Club Cir
Little Rock, AR 72212-3436, USA

Didier, Bob (Athlete, Baseball Player)
1819 N Lynch
Mesa, AZ 85207-3179, USA

Didier, Clint (Athlete, Football Player)
5015 S Regal St Apt L3089
Spokane, WA 99223-7975, USA

Didion, Joan (Writer)
c/o Lynn Nesbit *Janklow & Nesbit Associates*
285 Madison Ave Fl 21
New York, NY 10017-6427, USA

Dido (Musician, Songwriter)
c/o Staff Member *Paradigm*
140 Broadway Ste 2600
New York, NY 10005-1011, USA

Diduck, Gerald (Athlete, Hockey Player)
3303 Drexel Dr
Dallas, TX 75205-2914

Die Antwoord (Music Group)
c/o Joel Zimmerman *WME|IMG (NY)*
11 Madison Ave Fl 18
New York, NY 10010-3669, USA

Diebel, Nelson (Athlete, Olympic Athlete, Swimmer)
401 Webb Rd
Newark, DE 19711-2652, USA

Diebold, John (Business Person)
Diebold Group
PO Box 515
Bedford Hills, NY 10507-0515, USA

Diehl, August (Actor)
c/o Marie-Louise Schmidt *Die Agenten*
Motzstraße 60
Berlin 10777, GERMANY

Diehl, David (Athlete, Football Player)
116 Liberty Ridge Trl
Totowa, NJ 07512-1600, USA

Diehl, John (Actor)
c/o Sandi Dudek *Paradigm*
8942 Wilshire Blvd
Beverly Hills, CA 90211-1908, USA

Diehl, John A (Athlete, Football Player)
900 S Henry St
Williamsburg, VA 23185-3989, USA

Dieken, Doug H (Athlete, Football Player)
29876 Lake Rd
Bay Village, OH 44140-1276, USA

Diem, Ryan (Athlete, Football Player)
11522 Willow Ridge Dr
Zionsville, IN 46077-7823, USA

Diener, Robert (Business Person)
9 Indian Creek Island Rd
Indian Creek Village, FL 33154-2903, USA

Diener, Travis (Athlete, Basketball Player)
1007 Springs Rd
Fond Du Lac, WI 54935-7613, USA

Dienhart, Mark (Athlete, Football Player)
1944 Bayard Ave
Saint Paul, MN 55116-1216, USA

Diercks, Justin (Race Car Driver)
c/o Steve Diercks
1030 E. 4th St.
Davenport, IA 52807, USA

Dierdof, Dan (Athlete, Football Player, Sportscaster)
1316 Litzsinger Woods Ln
Saint Louis, MO 63124-1495, USA

Diering, Chuck (Athlete, Baseball Player)
1 Nob Hill Dr
Saint Louis, MO 63138-1400, USA

Dierker, Larry (Athlete, Baseball Player, Coach)
8318 N Tahoe Dr
Jersey Village, TX 77040-1258, USA

Dierking, Scott (Athlete, Football Player)
1862 Wingate Ln
Wheaton, IL 60189-7881, USA

Dierkop, Charles (Actor)
c/o Staff Member *The Actors Studio*
432 W 44th St
New York, NY 10036-5205, USA

Dierks, Dieter (Musician)
Dierk's Recording Mobile
Hauptstrasse 33
Pulheim-Stommeln 50259, Germany

Diesel (Music Group)
c/o Staff Member *The Harbour Agency*
135 Forbes St
Woolloomooloo NSW 2011, Australia

Diesel, Vin (Actor, Director, Producer)
c/o Jeff Raymond *Rogers & Cowan*
1840 Century Park E Fl 18
Los Angeles, CA 90067-2101, USA

Dieselboy (DJ, Musician)
c/o Joel Zimmerman *WME|IMG (NY)*
11 Madison Ave Fl 18
New York, NY 10010-3669, USA

Dieterich, Chris (Athlete, Football Player)
804 Edisto River Rd
Myrtle Beach, SC 29588-7439, USA

Dietrich, Dena (Actor)
23388 Mulholland Dr Ste 224
Woodland Hills, CA 91364-2733, USA

Dietrich, Don (Athlete, Hockey Player)
310 Finlay Ave E
Deloraine, MB R0M 0M0, Canada

Dietrich, William A (Bill) (Journalist)
Seattle Times Fairview Avenue NAnd John Street
Attn: Editorial Dept
Seattle, WA 98111, USA

Dietrick, Coby (Athlete, Basketball Player)
644 Patterson Ave
San Antonio, TX 78209-5655, USA

Dietzel, Roy (Athlete, Baseball Player)
8421 Coulwood Oak Ln
Charlotte, NC 28214-1165, USA

Dietzen, Brian (Actor)
c/o Staff Member *Sweeney Entertainment*
1601 Vine St # 6
Los Angeles, CA 90028-8802, USA

DiEugenio, James (Writer)
310 Amherst Dr Apt F
Burbank, CA 91504-4209, USA

Difelice, Mark (Athlete, Baseball Player)
1215 Belfield Ave
Drexel Hill, PA 19026-4110, USA

Difelice, Mike (Athlete, Baseball Player)
14369 N Dale Mabry Hwy
Tampa, FL 33618-2017, USA

Diffie, Joe (Musician)
Third Rock Entertainment
1114 17th Ave S Ste 105
Nashville, TN 37212-2215, USA

Diffrient, Niels (Designer)
General Delivery
Ridgefield, CT 06877, USA

DiFranco, Ani (Musician, Songwriter)
c/o Scot Fisher
PO Box 95
Ellicott Station
Buffalo, NY 14205-0095, USA

Digby, Marie (Musician)
c/o Staff Member *Nettwerk Management (LA)*
1545 Wilcox Ace
Suite 200
Los Angeles, CA 90028, USA

Diggins, Ben (Athlete, Baseball Player)
4804 E Merrell St
Phoenix, AZ 85018-7876, USA

Diggins, Skylar (Athlete, Basketball Player)
108 Guadalupe Dr
Irving, TX 75039-3333, USA

Diggs, Daveed (Actor, Musician)
c/o Alexandra Crotin *The Lede Company*
9701 Wilshire Blvd # 930
Beverly Hills, CA 90212-2020, USA

Diggs, Nail (Athlete, Football Player)
2006 Connonade Dr
Waxhaw, NC 28173-0109, USA

Diggs, Shelton (Athlete, Football Player)
261 Washington Ave Apt 3R
New Rochelle, NY 10801-5967, USA

Diggs, Stefon (Athlete, Football Player)
c/o Adisa P Bakari *Kelley Drye & Warren LLP*
3050 K St NW Ste 400
Washington, DC 20007-5100, USA

Diggs, Taye (Actor)
c/o Staff Member *OTaye Productions*
12001 Ventura Pl Ste 340
Studio City, CA 91604-2629, USA

Digiacomo, Curt (Athlete, Football Player)
830 Ida Ave
Solana Beach, CA 92075-2439, USA

Digible Planets (Music Group)
345 N Maple Dr Ste 123
Beverly Hills, CA 90210-5185, USA

Digitalism (Music Group)
c/o Staff Member *Girlie Action*
243 W 30th St Fl 12
New York, NY 10001-2812, USA

DiGregorio, Ernie (Athlete, Basketball Player)
60 Chestnut Ave
Narragansett, RI 02882-6113, USA

Dilauro, Jack (Athlete, Baseball Player)
102 Sea Oats Dr
Panama City Beach, FL 32413-2763, USA

Dilba (Musician)
United Stage Production
PO Box 11029
Stockholm 10061, SWEDEN

Dildarian, Steve (Actor)
2481 N Edgemont St
Los Angeles, CA 90027-1054, USA

Dilfer, Trent (Athlete, Football Player, Sportscaster)
7024 Cielo Azul Pass
Austin, TX 78732-1643, USA

Dilger, Ken (Athlete, Football Player)
10403 Windemere
Carmel, IN 46032-8594, USA

Dill, Craig (Athlete, Basketball Player)
4277 N Autumn Ridge Ct
Saginaw, MI 48603-8605, USA

Dill, Laddie John (Artist)
1625 Electric Ave
Venice, CA 90291-4803, USA

Dill, Terry (Athlete, Golfer)
7003 Western Oaks Blvd
Austin, TX 78749-2229, USA

Dillahunt, Garret (Actor)
1077 E Santa Anita Ave
Burbank, CA 91501-1509, USA

Dillam, Bradford (Actor)
770 Hot Springs Rd
Santa Barbara, CA 93108-1107, USA

Dillane, Stephen (Actor)
Michelle Braidman
10/11 Lower John St
#300
London W1R 3PE, UNITED KINGDOM (UK)

Dillard, Alex (Business Person)
Dillard's Inc
1600 Cantrell Rd
Little Rock, AR 72201-1145, USA

Dillard, Annie (Writer)
Russell Volkering
50 W 29th St
New York, NY 10001-4227, USA

Dillard, Don (Athlete, Baseball Player)
45 Bream Ln
Waterloo, SC 29384-4868, USA

Dillard, Gordon (Athlete, Baseball Player)
840 Via Manzana
Aromas, CA 95004-9026, USA

Dillard, Harrison (Athlete, Olympic Athlete, Track Athlete)
306 Knollwood Trl
Cleveland, OH 44143-1482, USA

Dillard, Harrison H. (Athlete, Olympic Athlete, Track Athlete)
3842 E 147th St
Cleveland, OH 44128-1027, USA

Dillard, Mickey (Athlete, Basketball Player)
224 SW 11th Ave
Dania, FL 33004-3515, USA

Dillard, Phillip (Athlete, Football Player)
c/o Roosevelt Barnes *Independent Sports & Entertainment (ISE-IN)*
6435 W Jefferson Blvd # 197
Fort Wayne, IN 46804-6203, USA

Dillard, Stacey (Athlete, Football Player)
3188 County Road 4220
Annona, TX 75550-4037, USA

Dillard, Steve (Athlete, Baseball Player)
154 Drive 841
Saltillo, MS 38866-9362, USA

Dillard, Tim (Athlete, Baseball Player)
2682 Avery Park Dr
Nashville, TN 37211-7182, USA

Dillard, Victoria (Actor)
c/o Craig Dorfman *Frontline Management*
5670 Wilshire Blvd Ste 1370
Los Angeles, CA 90036-5649, USA

Dillard, William T Jr (Business Person)
Dillard's Inc
1600 Cantrell Rd
Little Rock, AR 72201-1145, USA

Dille, Bob (Athlete, Basketball Player)
200 Albi Rd Apt 3
Naples, FL 34112-6108, USA

Diller, Barry (Business Person)
IAC/InterActive Corp
555 W 18th St
New York, NY 10011-2822, USA

Dillion, Wayne (Athlete, Hockey Player)
Hockey Development Centre of Ontario
301-1185 Eglinton Ave E
North York, ON M3C 3C6, Canada

Dillman, Bill (Athlete, Baseball Player)
PO Box 5167
Winter Park, FL 32793-5167, USA

Dillman, Brooke (Actor)
1632 S Point View St
Los Angeles, CA 90035-4508, USA

Dillon, Austin (Race Car Driver)
Childress Racing
236 Industrial Dr
Welcom, NC 27374, USA

Dillon, Bobby (Athlete, Football Player)
1289 Morgan Dr
Temple, TX 76502-4245, USA

Dillon, Corey (Athlete, Football Player)
31574 Foxfield Dr
Westlake Village, CA 91361-4764, USA

Dillon, David B (Business Person)
Kroger Co
1014 Vine St Ste 2200
Cincinnati, OH 45202-1116, USA

Dillon, Denny (Actor, Comedian)
International Creative Mgmt
8942 Wilshire Blvd # 219
Beverly Hills, CA 90211-1908, USA

Dillon, Joe (Athlete, Baseball Player)
1220 Islemere Dr
Rockwall, TX 75087-2412, USA

Dillon, Kevin (Actor)
1259 S Stanley Ave
Los Angeles, CA 90019-6616, USA

Dillon, Matt (Actor, Director)
c/o Staff Member *Banyan Tree*
1 Worth St Fl 2
New York, NY 10013-2930, USA

Dillon, Melinda (Actor)
4065 Michael Ave
Los Angeles, CA 90066-5115, USA

Dillon, Mike (Race Car Driver)
PO Box 30414
Winston Salem, NC 27130-0414, USA

Dillon, Steve (Athlete, Baseball Player)
511 Wateredge Ave
Baldwin, NY 11510-3728, USA

Dillon, Wayne (Athlete, Hockey Player)
312-3 Concorde Gate
Toronto, ON M3C 3N7, Canada

Dilmancheff, Babe (Athlete, Football Player)
3917 Edgehill Dr
Los Angeles, CA 90008-2617, USA

Dilone, Miguel (Athlete, Baseball Player)
Calle El Sol #190
Santiago, Dominican Republic

Dils, Steve (Athlete, Football Player)
10285 Midway Ave
Alpharetta, GA 30022-6028, USA

Dilts, Bucky (Athlete, Football Player)
240 McCaslin Blvd # 101
Louisville, CO 80027-2911, USA

Dilts, Douglas (Athlete, Football Player)
1180 Drewsbury Ct SE
Smyrna, GA 30080-3949, USA

Dilweg, Anthony (Athlete, Football Player)
5310 S Alston Ave Ste 210
Durham, NC 27713-4381, USA

Dilworth, John (Animator, Director)
Stretch Films
561 Hudson St # 21
New York, NY 10014-2463, USA

DiMaggio, John (Actor)
c/o Paul Rosicker *Gersh*
9465 Wilshire Blvd Ste 600
Beverly Hills, CA 90212-2605, USA

Dimaio, Rob (Athlete, Hockey Player)
c/o Staff Member *Dallas Stars*
2601 Avenue of the Stars Ste 100
Frisco, TX 75034-9016, USA

DiManche, Jayson (Athlete, Football Player)
c/o Joe Linta *JL Sports*
1204 Main St Ste 179
Branford, CT 06405-3787, USA

DiMarco, Chris (Athlete, Golfer)
508 N Washington St
Denver, CO 80203-3812, USA

DiMarco, Nyle (Dancer, Model)
c/o Chris Rossi *Status PR*
PO Box 6191
Westlake Village, CA 91359-6191, USA

DiMarco, Patrick (Athlete, Football Player)

Dimas, Trent (Gymnast)
Gold Cup Gymnastics School
6009 Carmel Ave NE
Albuquerque, NM 87113-1741, USA

Dimbort, Danny (Producer)
Capstone Group
2049 Century Park E Ste 810
Los Angeles, CA 90067-9502, USA

DiMeo, Paul (Actor, Reality Star)

Di Meola, Al (Musician)
c/o Staff Member *Entourage Talent Associates*
150 W 28th St Ste 1503
New York, NY 10001-6180, USA

Dimichele, Frank (Athlete, Baseball Player)
119 Clemens Cir
Norristown, PA 19403-3087, USA

Dimitrakos, Niko (Athlete, Hockey Player)
149 Timber Ct
Wood Dale, IL 60191-1356

Dimitriades, Alex (Actor)
c/o Staff Member *Shanahan Management*
Level 3 Berman House
Surry Hills 02010, AUSTRALIA

Dimmel, Mike (Athlete, Baseball Player)
526 Country Ln
Coppell, TX 75019-5129, USA

Dimmick, Thomas (Athlete, Football Player)
204 Broadmoor Blvd
Lafayette, LA 70503-5114, USA

Dimon, James (Jamie) (Business Person)
J P Morgan Chase
270 Park Ave Fl 12
New York, NY 10017-2089, USA

Di Montezemolo, Luca (Business Person, Race Car Driver)
c/o Staff Member *Jaguar Racing Ltd*
Bradbourne Drive
Tilbrook
Milton Keynes MK7 8BJ, United Kingdom

Dimry, Charles (Athlete, Football Player)
3530 Calle Palmito
Carlsbad, CA 92009-8958, USA

DiMucci, Dion (Actor, Musician)
3099 NW 63rd St
Boca Raton, FL 33496-3309, USA

Dimuro, Mike (Athlete, Baseball Player)
525 Oak Point Ct
Liberty Hill, TX 78642-2013, USA

Dimuro, Ray (Athlete, Baseball Player)
9625 N 33rd St
Phoenix, AZ 85028-4919, USA

Dinapoli, Gennaro (Athlete, Football Player)
10 White Oak Farm Rd
Newtown, CT 06470-2501, USA

diNapoli, Marc (Actor)
8 rue de Georges-de-Porto-Riche
Paris F-75014, France

DiNardo, Gerry (Coach, Football Coach)
Indiana University
Athletic Dept
Bloomington, IN 47405, USA

Dinardo, Lenny (Athlete, Baseball Player)
23015 NW 227th Dr
High Springs, FL 32643-9031, USA

Dindal, Mark (Director)
c/o Peter Nichols *Lichter Grossman Nichols Adler & Feldman Inc*
9200 W Sunset Blvd Ste 1200
Los Angeles, CA 90069-3607, USA

Dine, James (Artist)
Pace Gallery
32 E 57th St Fl 4
New York, NY 10022-2530, USA

Dineen, gord (Athlete, Hockey Player)
Toronto Marlies
100 Princes Blvd
Toronto, ON M6K 3C3, Canada

Dineen, Gord (Athlete, Hockey Player)
51 Fitzgerald Rd
Queensbury, NY 12804-1344

Dineen, Kenny (Athlete, Baseball Player)
112 S Ranch St
Santa Maria, CA 93454-5319, USA

Dineen, Kevin (Athlete, Hockey Player)
360 N Oak St
Hinsdale, IL 60521-3848

Dineen, Kevin (Athlete, Hockey Player)
Florida Panthers
1 Panther Pkwy
Sunrise, FL 33323-5315

Dineen, Peter (Athlete, Hockey Player)
65 Birch Rd
Lake George, NY 12845-4323

Dinerstein, James (Artist)
Salander-O'Reilly Gallery
20 E 79th St
New York, NY 10075-0106, USA

Dingle, Adrian (Athlete, Football Player)
650 Ocean Ave Unit 430
Revere, MA 02151-1374, USA

Dingle, Mike (Athlete, Football Player)
512 Menlo Dr
Columbia, SC 29210-6537, USA

Dingman, Chris (Athlete, Hockey Player)
9220 Pine Island Ct
Tampa, FL 33647-2301

Dingman, Craig (Athlete, Baseball Player)
3573 W Del Sienno St
Wichita, KS 67203-4349, USA

Dini, Paul (Actor, Producer, Writer)
c/o Staff Member *United Talent Agency (UTA)*
9336 Civic Center Dr
Beverly Hills, CA 90210-3604, USA

Dinkel, Tom (Athlete, Football Player)
4883 Dartmouth Dr
Burlington, KY 41005-9186, USA

Dinkelman, Brian (Athlete, Baseball Player)
20 Edgewood Ln N
Centralia, IL 62801-3708, USA

Dinkins, Byron (Athlete, Basketball Player)
10326 Tallent Ln
Huntersville, NC 28078-5903, USA

Dinkins, Darnell (Athlete, Football Player)
301 Cottingham Dr
Allison Park, PA 15101-2054, USA

Dinkins, Howard (Athlete, Football Player)
5980 Covered Creek Ln
Jacksonville, FL 32277-1447, USA

Dinklage, Peter (Actor)
c/o David Ginsberg *Insight*
5358 Melrose Ave # 200W
Los Angeles, CA 90038-5117, USA

Dinnel, Harry (Athlete, Basketball Player)
1427 El Nido Dr
Fallbrook, CA 92028-8697, USA

Dinner, Michael (Director)
c/o Staff Member *Creative Artists Agency (CAA)*
2000 Avenue of the Stars Ste 100
Los Angeles, CA 90067-4705, USA

Dinnigan, Collette (Designer, Fashion Designer)
22-24 Hutchinson St
Surry Hills
Sydney, NSW 02010, AUSTRALIA

Dinwiddle, Ryan (Athlete, Football Player)
2931 S Zach Pl
Boise, ID 83706-6807

DioGuardi, Kara (Musician, Reality Star, Songwriter)
c/o Jonathan Swaden *Creative Artists Agency (CAA)*
2000 Avenue of the Stars Ste 100
Los Angeles, CA 90067-4705, USA

Dion (Musician)
3099 NW 63rd St
Boca Raton, FL 33496-3309, USA

Dion, Celine (Actor, Musician)
Caesars Palace - The Colosseum
3570 Las Vegas Blvd S
Las Vegas, NV 89109-8933, USA

Dion, Colleen (Actor)
Abrams Artists
9200 W Sunset Blvd Ste 1125
Los Angeles, CA 90069-3610, USA

Dion, Michel (Athlete, Hockey Player)
33 Mulrain Way
Bluffton, SC 29910-6530, USA

Dion, Terry (Athlete, Football Player)
106 E Libby Rd
Shelton, WA 98584-8132, USA

Dionisi, Stefano (Actor)
Carol Levi Co
Via Giuseppe Pisanelli
Rome 00196, ITALY

Dionne, Gilbert (Athlete, Hockey Player)
196 Bender Ave
Tavistock, ON N0B 2R0, Canada

Dionne, Marcel E (Athlete, Hockey Player)
Marcel Dionne Inc
PO Box 2596
Niagara Falls, NY 14302-2596

Diop, Anna (Actor)
c/o Marianna Shafran *Shafran PR*
195 S Beverly Dr Ste 414
Beverly Hills, CA 90212-3044, USA

Diop, DeSagana (Athlete, Basketball Player)
4300 Haddonfield Rd Ste 309
Pennsauken, NJ 08109-3376, USA

Diop, Majhemout (President)
210 HCM Guediawaye
Dakar, SENEGAL

Diorio, Nick (Soccer Player)
273 Clark St
Lemoyne, PA 17043-2010, USA

Diorio, Ron (Athlete, Baseball Player)
2 White Oak Ln
Waterbury, CT 06705-1835, USA

DiPersia, Alexander (Actor)
c/o Staff Member *Grandview*
7122 Beverly Blvd Ste F
Los Angeles, CA 90036-2572, USA

Dipierro, Ramon (Athlete, Football Player)
1750 Brownstone Blvd Apt H
Toledo, OH 43614-1362, USA

Dipietro, Rick (Athlete, Hockey Player, Olympic Athlete)
Pulver Sports
479 Bedford Park Ave
Attn I an Pulver
Toronto, ON M5M 1K2, Canada

Dipietro, Rocky (Athlete, Football Player)
1 Logan St
St Catharines, ON L2N 2B6, Canada

Dipino, Frank (Athlete, Baseball Player)
141 Northwood Way
Camillus, NY 13031-1255, USA

Diplo (DJ, Musician)
Big Dada HQ
PO Box 4296
London SE11 4WW, UNITED KINGDOM

Dipoto, Jerry (Commentator)
15130 E Camelview Dr
Fountain Hills, AZ 85268-6405, USA

Dippold, Katie (Actor, Comedian, Writer)
c/o Greg Walter *3 Arts Entertainment*
9460 Wilshire Blvd Fl 7
Beverly Hills, CA 90212-2713, USA

DiPreta, Tony (Cartoonist)
North American Syndicate
235 E 45th St
New York, NY 10017-3305, USA

DiPrete, Edward D (Politician)
125 Midway Rd
Cranston, RI 02920-5757, USA

Dirda, Michael (Journalist)
Washington Post
Editorial Dept
1150 15th St NW
Washington, DC 20071-0001, USA

Dirden, Brandon J (Actor)
c/o David Williams *David Williams Management*
269 S Beverly Dr # 1408
Beverly Hills, CA 90212-3851, USA

Dirden, Johnnie (Athlete, Football Player)
1403 S Ulster St
Denver, CO 80231-2744, USA

Director, Kim (Actor)
c/o Jessica Cohen *JCPR*
9903 Santa Monica Blvd # 983
Beverly Hills, CA 90212-1671, USA

Direnzo, Daniel (Dan) (Athlete, Football Player)
PO Box 958
Albrightsville, PA 18210-0958, USA

Direnzo, Fred (Athlete, Football Player)
5 Togno St
Netcong, NJ 07857-1608, USA

Diresta, John (Actor, Comedian)
c/o Ruthanne Secunda *ICM Partners*
10250 Constellation Blvd Fl 7
Los Angeles, CA 90067-6207, USA

Dirk, Robert (Athlete, Hockey Player)
Okanagan Hockey School
201-853 Eckhardt Ave W
Penticton, BC V2A 9C4, Canada

Dirnt, Mike (Musician)
Adeline Records
5900 Wilshire Blvd # 1720
Los Angeles, CA 90036-5013, USA

Dirty Pretty Things (Music Group)
c/o Staff Member *Paradigm (Monterey)*
404 W Franklin St
Monterey, CA 93940-2303, USA

Disarcina, Gary (Athlete, Baseball Player)
PO Box 1532
Plymouth, MA 02362-1532, USA

Dischinger, Terry (Athlete, Basketball Player, Olympic Athlete)
PO Box 87
Lake Oswego, OR 97034-0012, USA

Disco Biscuits, The (Music Group)
c/o Staff Member *Red Light Management*
5800 Bristol Pkwy Ste 400
Culver City, CA 90230-6898, USA

Disel, Vin (Actor, Director)
c/o Stacy Boniello *Firm, The*
2049 Century Park E Ste 2550
Los Angeles, CA 90067-3110, USA

Dishman, Chris E (Athlete, Football Player)
1561 Raymond Rd
Garland, NE 68360-9347, USA

Dishman, Cris (Athlete, Football Player)
5019 Mariposa Cir
Fresno, TX 77545-9219, USA

Dishman, Glenn (Athlete, Baseball Player)
4318 N Verrado Way
Buckeye, AZ 85396-7533, USA

Dishy, Bob (Actor)
20 E 9th St
New York, NY 10003-5944, USA

Disi, Ursula (Skier)
Krumme Gasse 10A
Ruhpolding 83324, GERMANY

Disick, Scott (Reality Star)
PO Box 9332
Calabasas, CA 91372-9331, USA

Disney, Abigail (Producer)
c/o Staff Member *Fork Films*
25 E 21st St Fl 7
New York, NY 10010-6235, USA

Disney, Bill (Athlete, Olympic Athlete, Speed Skater)
1610 Kirk Dr Lake
Havasu City, AZ 86404-2449

Disney, William (Speed Skater)
1610 Kirk Dr
Lake Havasu City, AZ 86404-2449, USA

DiSpirito, Rocco (Chef, Reality Star)
c/o Amanda Molina *Much and House Public Relations*
8075 W 3rd St Ste 500
Los Angeles, CA 90048-4325, USA

Di Stefano, Andrea (Actor, Director)
c/o Mike Simpson *WME|IMG*
9601 Wilshire Blvd
Beverly Hills, CA 90210-5213, USA

Distefano, Benny (Athlete, Baseball Player)
9911 Murray Lndg
Missouri City, TX 77459-6417, USA

Distler, Natalie (Actor)
c/o Siri Garber *Platform PR*
2666 N Beachwood Dr
Los Angeles, CA 90068-2308, USA

Disturbed (Music Group)
c/o Mitch Schneider *Mitch Schneider Organization (MSO)*
14724 Ventura Blvd Ste 410
Sherman Oaks, CA 91403-3537, USA

DiSuvero, Mark (Artist)
PO Box 2218
Astoria, NY 11102, USA

Ditka, Mike (Athlete, Coach, Football Coach, Football Player)
161 E Chicago Ave Unit 39F
Chicago, IL 60611-2623, USA

Ditmar, Arthur J (Art) (Athlete, Baseball Player)
6687 Wisteria Dr
Myrtle Beach, SC 29588-6481, USA

Di Tomasso, Daniel (Actor)
c/o Vikram Dhawer *Authentic Talent and Literary Management (NY)*
20 Jay St Ste M17
Brooklyn, NY 11201-8300, USA

DiTomasso, Daniel (Actor)
c/o Vikram Dhawer *Authentic Talent and Literary Management (NY)*
20 Jay St Ste M17
Brooklyn, NY 11201-8300, USA

Ditto, Beth (Musician)
c/o Heidi Lopata *Narrative*
1601 Vine St Fl 6
Los Angeles, CA 90028-8802, USA

Dityatin, Aleksandr N (Gymnast)
Nevski Prosp 18
#25
Saint Petersburg, RUSSIA

Ditz, Nancy (Athlete, Track Athlete)
524 Moore Rd
Woodside, CA 94062-1109, USA

Divac, Vlade (Athlete, Basketball Player)
c/o Marc Fleisher *Entersport-World HQ*
128 Heather Dr
New Canaan, CT 06840-5224, USA

DiVello, Adam (Producer)
1235 N Kenter Ave
Los Angeles, CA 90049-1317, USA

Divine Comedy, The (Music Group)
c/o Staff Member *Paradigm (Monterey)*
404 W Franklin St
Monterey, CA 93940-2303, USA

Divins, Charles (Actor)

Divis, Reinhard (Athlete, Hockey Player)
Unterer Hubertusweg 5
Thuringen 06712, Austriil

Divoff, Andrew (Actor)
c/o Staff Member *Marshak/Zachary Company, The*
8840 Wilshire Blvd Fl 1
Beverly Hills, CA 90211-2606, USA

Dixie Chicks (Music Group)
c/o Cindi Berger *PMK/BNC Public Relations*
622 3rd Ave Fl 8
New York, NY 10017-6707, USA

Dixie Cups, The (Music Group)
2535 Noble St
North Las Vegas, NV 89030-3819, USA

Dixon, Al (Athlete, Football Player)
386 Somerset St Apt 1
North Plainfield, NJ 07060-4758, USA

Dixon, Alan J (Politician)
7606 Foley Dr
Belleville, IL 62223-2322, USA

Dixon, Alesha (Musician)
c/o Staff Member *Independent Talent Group*
40 Whitfield St
London W1T 2RH, UNITED KINGDOM

Dixon, Becky (Sportscaster)
ABC-TV
77 W 66th St
Sports Dept
New York, NY 10023-6201, USA

Dixon, Brandon (Athlete, Football Player)
c/o Peter Schaffer *Authentic Athletix*
400 S Steele St Unit 47
Denver, CO 80209-3535, USA

Dixon, Brandon Victor (Actor, Musician)
c/o David Seltzer *Management 360*
9111 Wilshire Blvd
Beverly Hills, CA 90210-5508, USA

Dixon, Brian (Athlete, Football Player)
c/o Peter Schaffer *Authentic Athletix*
400 S Steele St Unit 47
Denver, CO 80209-3535, USA

Dixon, Cal (Athlete, Football Player)
125 E Crisafulli Rd
Merritt Island, FL 32953-7304, USA

Dixon, Craig (Athlete, Olympic Athlete, Track Athlete)
10630 Wellworth Ave
Los Angeles, CA 90024-5012, USA

Dixon, David (Athlete, Football Player)
4795 W 131 1/2 St
Savage, MN 55378-2505, USA

Dixon, Dennis (Athlete, Football Player)
c/o Jeff Sperbeck *The Novo Agency*
1537 Via Romero Ste 100
Alamo, CA 94507-1527, USA

Dixon, Donna (Actor)
7708 Woodrow Wilson Dr
Los Angeles, CA 90046-1212, USA

Dixon, Dwayne (Athlete, Football Player)
78 Westfield Pl
Athens, OH 45701-3857, USA

Dixon, Floyd (Musician)
Folklore Prod
PO Box 7003
Santa Monica, CA 90406-7003, USA

Dixon, Gerald (Athlete, Football Player)
1315 Big Rock Ct
Fort Mill, SC 29708-6950, USA

Dixon, Juan (Basketball Player)
Washington Wizards
601 F St NW
Washington, DC 20004-1605, USA

Dixon, Ken (Athlete, Baseball Player)
4317 Highview Ave
Baltimore, MD 21229-5303, USA

Dixon, Larry (Race Car Driver)
Don Prudhomme Racing
1232 Distribution Way
Vista, CA 92081-8816, USA

Dixon, Leslie (Director, Producer, Writer)
c/o Todd Feldman *Creative Artists Agency (CAA)*
2000 Avenue of the Stars Ste 100
Los Angeles, CA 90067-4705, USA

Dixon, Mark (Athlete, Football Player)
4016 Ivy Ln
Kitty Hawk, NC 27949-4347, USA

Dixon, Randolph C (Randy) (Athlete, Football Player)
9910 Summerlakes Dr
Carmel, IN 46032-9307, USA

Dixon, Rodney (Rod) (Athlete, Track Athlete)
22 Entrican Ave
Remuera
Auckland 00005, NEW ZEALAND

Dixon, Ronnie (Athlete, Football Player)
1440 W Kemper Rd Apt 510
Cincinnati, OH 45240-1652, USA

Dixon, Scott (Race Car Driver)
Target Chip Ganassi Racing
7161 Zionville Rd.
Indianapolis, IN 46250, USA

Dixon, Steve (Athlete, Baseball Player)
6510 Hollow Tree Rd
Louisville, KY 40228-1336, USA

Dixon, Tamecka (Basketball Player)
Los Angeles Sparks
1111 S Figueroa St
Staples Center
Los Angeles, CA 90015-1300, USA

Dixon, Tom (Athlete, Baseball Player)
1815 Monastery Rd
Orange City, FL 32763-6320, USA

Dixon, Tony (Athlete, Football Player)
1521 Riverchase Trl
Hoover, AL 35244-2043, USA

Dixon, Zachary (Athlete, Football Player)
19365 Hottinger Cir
Germantown, MD 20874-1504, USA

Dizzia, Maria (Actor)
c/o Erica Tuchman *Perennial Entertainment*
157 Columbus Ave Fl 4
New York, NY 10023-6083, USA

Djalili, Omid (Actor)
c/o Brian Stern *AGI Entertainment*
150 E 58th St Fl 19
New York, NY 10155-1900, USA

DJ Ashba (Musician)
c/o Jill Siegel *10th Street Entertainment*
700 N San Vicente Blvd # G410
W Hollywood, CA 90069-5060, USA

DJ Cassidy (DJ, Musician)
c/o Linda Carbone *Press Here Publicity*
138 W 25th St Ste 900
New York, NY 10001-7470, USA

DJ Jazzy Jeff (Actor, Musician)
c/o Jeff Epstein *M.A.G./Universal Attractions*
15 W 36th St Fl 8
New York, NY 10018-7927, USA

DJ Mendez (Musician)
c/o Leopoldo Mendez *Macabro Records*
Bolidenvagen 10
Johanneshov 121 63, SWEDEN

DJ Mustard (DJ, Musician)
c/o Ayanna Wilks *Roc Nation*
1411 Broadway Fl 38
New York, NY 10018-3409, USA

Djodjov Pejoski, Marjan (Designer, Fashion Designer)
c/o Staff Member *Marjan Djodjov Pejoski*
75 Garden Flat
Warwick Avenue
London, England W1Y 1DH, United Kingdom

Djokovic, Novak (Athlete, Tennis Player)
c/o Fernando Soler *IMG (Spain)*
Via Augusta 200
Floor 4
Barcelona E-8021, SPAIN

DJ Snake (DJ, Musician)
c/o Edward Shapiro *Reed Smith*
599 Lexington Ave Fl 26
New York, NY 10022-7684, USA

Djukanovic, Milo (President)
Executive Council
Bul Lenjina 2
Novi Belgrad 11075, SERBIA & MONTENEGRO

Dlouhy, Lukas (Athlete, Tennis Player)
c/o Staff Member *ATP Tour*
201 Atp Tour Blvd
Ponte Vedra Beach, FL 32082-3211, USA

D. Lucas, Frank (Congressman, Politician)
2311 Rayburn Hob
Washington, DC 20515-2404, USA

D'Lyn, Shae (Actor)
c/o Michael Kaleda *Bold Management & Production*
8228 W Sunset Blvd # 106
West Hollywood, CA 90046-2414, USA

Dmitriev, Artur (Figure Skater)
Russian Skating Federation
Luchneksaia Nab 8
Moscow 119871, RUSSIA

DNCE (Music Group)
c/o Brian Manning *Creative Artists Agency (CAA)*
2000 Avenue of the Stars Ste 100
Los Angeles, CA 90067-4705, USA

Doan, Shane (Athlete, Hockey Player)
9820 E Thompson Peak Pkwy Unit 728
Scottsdale, AZ 85255-6657, CANADA

Dobbek, Dan (Athlete, Baseball Player)
4042 SE Yamhill St
Portland, OR 97214-4445, USA

Dobbin, Brian (Athlete, Hockey Player)
5075 Shiloh Line
Petrolia, ON N0N 1R0, Canada

Dobbins, Herb (Athlete, Football Player)
10 Keating Pt
St. Albert, AB T8N 5W8, Canada

Dobbins, Oliver (Athlete, Football Player)
11126 Piscataway Rd
Clinton, MD 20735-9519, USA

Dobbins, Tim (Athlete, Football Player)
c/o Harold C Lewis *National Sports Agency*
12181 Prichard Farm Rd
Maryland Heights, MO 63043-4203, USA

Dobbs, Demarcus (Athlete, Football Player)

Dobbs, Greg (Athlete, Baseball Player)
2255 Richey Dr
La Canada Flintridge, CA 91011-1350, USA

Dobbs, Lou (Television Host)
7112 Eagle Ter
West Palm Beach, FL 33412-3101, USA

Dobek, Bob (Athlete, Hockey Player, Olympic Athlete)
3813 Observation Pl
Escondido, CA 92025-7933, USA

Dobek, Michelle (Athlete, Golfer)
292 Chicopee St
Chicopee, MA 01013-1744, USA

Dobkin, Alix (Musician)
PO Box 761
Woodstock, NY 12498-0761, USA

Dobkin, David (Director)
HSI Productions
9465 Wilshire Blvd Ste 300
Beverly Hills, CA 90212-2624, USA

Dobkins, Carl Jr (Musician)
7640 Cheviot Rd Apt 212
Cincinnati, OH 45247-4011, USA

Dobler, Conrad F (Athlete, Football Player)
12600 Fairway Rd
Leawood, KS 66209-2453, USA

Dobler, David (Religious Leader)
Presbyterian Church USA
100 Witherspoon St
Louisville, KY 40202-6300, USA

Dobo, Kata (Actor)
c/o Sara Ramaker *Paradigm*
8942 Wilshire Blvd
Beverly Hills, CA 90211-1908, USA

Dobre Brothers (Internet Star, Music Group)
c/o Brian Sokolik *Fullscreen Media (LA)*
12180 Millennium Ste 100
Los Angeles, CA 90094-2951, USA

Dobrev, Nina (Actor)
c/o Kami Putnam-Heist *Anonymous Content*
3532 Hayden Ave
Culver City, CA 90232-2413, USA

Dobslow, Bill (Musician)
945 Handlebar Rd
Mishawaka, IN 46544-6647, USA

Dobson, Aaron (Athlete, Football Player)
c/o Chad Speck *Allegiant Athletic Agency*
35 Market Sq Ste 201
Knoxville, TN 37902-1420, USA

Dobson, Chuck (Athlete, Baseball Player)
4208 Locust St
Kansas City, MO 64110-1017, USA

Dobson, Dominic (Race Car Driver)
2719 63rd Ave SE
Mercer Island, WA 98040-2433, USA

Dobson, Fefe (Musician)
c/o Staff Member *Island Records*
825 8th Ave Rm C2
New York, NY 10019-7472, USA

Dobson, Helen (Athlete, Golfer)
7638 Eagle Creek Dr
Sarasota, FL 34243-4613, USA

Dobson, James C (Religious Leader)
Focus on the Family
8605 Explorer Dr
Colorado Springs, CO 80920-1051, USA

Dobson, Kevin (Actor)
c/o Roger Neal *Neal Public Relations & Management*
3042 N Keystone St
Burbank, CA 91504-1621, USA

Dobson, Peter (Actor)
1351 N Crescent Heights Blvd Apt 318
West Hollywood, CA 90046-4579, USA

Dockery, Derrick (Athlete, Football Player)
7102 Jack Franzen Dr
Garland, TX 75043-6600, USA

Dockery, John (Athlete, Football Player)
17 Garden Pl
Brooklyn, NY 11201-4501, USA

Dockery, Michelle (Actor)
c/o Sandra Chang *Anonymous Content*
3532 Hayden Ave
Culver City, CA 90232-2413, USA

Dockett, Darnell (Athlete, Football Player)
6815 Sand Cherry Way
Clinton, MD 20735-4246, USA

Docter, Mary (Athlete, Olympic Athlete, Speed Skater)
3400 S Russel Rd
New Berlin, WI 53151-4637, USA

Docter, Pete (Actor, Director)
c/o Staff Member *Pixar Animation Studios*
1200 Park Ave
Emeryville, CA 94608-3677, USA

Doctorow, Cory (Internet Star)
Box 306 456-458
Strand, London WC2R0DZ, UNITED KINGDOM

Dodani, Nik (Actor)
c/o Whitney Tancred *42West*
1840 Century Park E Ste 700
Los Angeles, CA 90067-2122, USA

Dodd, Alice (Model)
574 N Irving Blvd
Los Angeles, CA 90004-1407, USA

Dodd, Carolyn (Actor)
c/o Marsha McManus *Principal Entertainment*
9255 W Sunset Blvd Ste 500
Los Angeles, CA 90069-3301, USA

Dodd, Christopher (Politician)
87th St NE
Washington, DC 20002-6022, USA

Dodd, Deryl (Musician, Songwriter, Writer)
823 Mgmt
PO Box 186
Waring, TX 78074-0186, USA

Dodd, Jamie (Actor)
c/o Staff Member *Nikki Bond Management*
Aspect Court
47 Park Square East
Leeds LS1 2NL, United Kingdom

Dodd, Maurice (Cartoonist)
Daily Mirror
Editorial Dept
1 Canada Square
London E14 5AP, UNITED KINGDOM (UK)

Dodd, Michael T (Mike) (Athlete, Volleyball Player)
AVP Pro Beach Volleyball Tour
960 Knox St Bldg A
Torrance, CA 90502-1086, USA

Dodd, Patty D (Athlete, Volleyball Player)
Fonz
1017 Manhattan Ave
Manhattan Beach, CA 90266-5452, USA

Dodd, Robert (Athlete, Baseball Player)
3467 Overhill Dr
Frisco, TX 75033-1112, USA

Dodd, Tom (Athlete, Baseball Player)
2206 NE 155th Ave
Portland, OR 97230-5298, USA

Dodds, Megan (Actor)
c/o Jason Shapiro *Silver Lining Entertainment*
421 S Beverly Dr Fl 7
Beverly Hills, CA 90212-4408, USA

Dodds, Trevor (Athlete, Golfer)
9730 Plummer St
Houston, TX 77029-4230, USA

Dodge, Brooks (Skier)
PO Box C
Jackson, NH 03846-0802, USA

Dodge, Dedrick (Athlete, Football Player)
1109 Bowlin Dr
Locust Grove, GA 30248-7079, USA

Dodge, Kirk (Athlete, Football Player)
9412 Tudor Ln
Garden Grove, CA 92841-3429, USA

Dodrill, Dale (Athlete, Football Player)
2579 S Independence St
Lakewood, CO 80227-2847, USA

Dodson, Pat (Athlete, Baseball Player)
1034 Hillside Rd
Grove, OK 74344-3514, USA

Dodson, Quintin (Reality Star)
4571 Haskell Ave Apt 15
Encino, CA 91436-3156, USA

Dodson, Richard (Athlete, Football Player)
PO Box 81302
Phoenix, AZ 85069-1302, USA

Doe, Cathy Jeneen (Actor)

Doelling, Fred (Athlete, Football Player)
60 South St
Valparaiso, IN 46383-6445, USA

Doerger, Jerome (Athlete, Football Player)
8309 Ridgevalley Ct
Cincinnati, OH 45247-3597, USA

Doering, Chris (Athlete, Football Player)
3843 SW 92nd Ter
Gainesville, FL 32608, USA

Doering, Jason (Athlete, Football Player)
24 Milford St Apt 1
Boston, MA 02118-3612, USA

Doerre-Heinig, Katrin (Athlete, Track Athlete)
Westring 53
Erbach 06471, GERMANY

Dogg, Snoop (Actor, Musician)
Doggy Style Records
1142 S Diamond Bar Blvd # 504
Diamond Bar, CA 91765-2203, USA

Doggett, Lloyd (Congressman, Politician)
201 Cannon Hob
Washington, DC 20515-4310, USA

Dogins, Kevin (Athlete, Football Player)
8861 Cameron Crest Dr
Tampa, FL 33626-4732, USA

Dog Star (Music Group)
1900 Avenue of the Stars # 1040
Los Angeles, CA 90067-4301, USA

Dohan, Meital (Actor, Musician)
c/o Cory Richman *Liebman Entertainment*
29 W 46th St Fl 5
New York, NY 10036-4104, USA

Doherty, James (Horse Racer)
9 Jane St
East Rutherford, NJ 07073-1420, USA

Doherty, John (Athlete, Baseball Player)
109 Wakefield St
Reading, MA 01867-1854, USA

Doherty, Peter (Musician)
c/o Staff Member *Bucks Music Group*
Onward House
11 Uxbridge Street
London W8 7TQ, United Kingdom

Doherty, Robert (Producer)
c/o Staff Member *United Talent Agency (UTA)*
9336 Civic Center Dr
Beverly Hills, CA 90210-3604, USA

Doherty, Shannen (Actor)
c/o Steven Grossman *Untitled Entertainment*
350 S Beverly Dr Ste 200
Beverly Hills, CA 90212-4819, USA

Doherty, Thomas (Actor)
c/o Harriet Long *Olivia Bell Management*
191 Wardour St.
London W1F 8ZE, UNITED KINGDOM

Dohm, Gaby (Actor)
Omnis Agentur
Wiedenmayerstr 11
Munich 80538, GERMANY

Dohmann, Scott (Athlete, Baseball Player)
3222 W Paxton Ave
Tampa, FL 33611-3920, USA

Dohner, Mark (Actor, Internet Star)
c/o Maxwell Mitcheson *Abrams Artists Agency*
750 N San Vicente Blvd
E Tower Fl 11
Los Angeles, CA 90069-5788, USA

Dohring, Jason (Actor)
c/o Joel Stevens *Joel Stevens Entertainment*
5627 Allott Ave
Van Nuys, CA 91401-4502, USA

Dohrmann, Angela (Actor)
Innovative Artists
1505 10th St
Santa Monica, CA 90401-2805, USA

Dohrmann, George (Journalist)
Saint Paul Pioneer Press
10 River Park Plz Ste 700
Editorial Dept
Saint Paul, MN 55107-1223, USA

Doi, Takao (Astronaut)
NASDA
Tsukuba Space Ctr
2-1-2 Sengern
Tukubashi, Ibaraki, JAPAN

Doi, Takao Dr (Astronaut)
NASDA, Tsukuba Space Center 2-1-1, Sengen
Tukuba-shi Ibaraka 00305, Japan

Doig, Jason (Athlete, Hockey Player)
2153 Broderick Ave
Duarte, CA 91010-3508, USA

Doig, Lex (Actor)
Andromeda Productions
8651 Eastlake Dr
Burnaby, BC V5A 4T7

Doig, Lexa (Actor)

Doig, Steve (Athlete, Football Player)
PO Box 3082
Gloucester, MA 01931-3082, USA

Dokey, Merritt (Horse Racer)
439 Yerkes St
Northville, MI 48167-1683, USA

Dokish, Wanita (Athlete, Baseball Player, Commentator)
403 Todd Farm Rd
Rostraver Township, PA 15012-3869, USA

Dokken, Don (Music Group)
c/o John Domagall *ARM Entertainment*
1257 Arcade St
Saint Paul, MN 55106-2022, USA

Doktor, Martin (Athlete)
Canoe Prosport Sezemice
Slinecni 627
Sezemice 533 04, CZECH REPUBLIC

Dolan, Chuck (Business Person)
330 Cove Neck Rd
Oyster Bay, NY 11771, USA

Dolan, Don (Actor)
14228 Emelita St
Van Nuys, CA 91401-4208, USA

Dolan, Ellen (Actor)
Don Buchwald
10 E 44th St Frnt 1
New York, NY 10017-3654, USA

Dolan, Grayson (Comedian, Internet Star)
c/o Ben Davis *WME/IMG (NY)*
11 Madison Ave Fl 18
New York, NY 10010-3669, USA

Dolan, Lawrence J (Commentator)
16 Windward Way
Chagrin Falls, OH 44023-6705, USA

Dolan, Tom (Athlete, Olympic Athlete, Swimmer)
12 S Manchester St
Arlington, VA 22204-1075

Dolan, Xavier (Actor, Director)
c/o Gregory Weill *Agence Adequat*
21 Rue D'Uzes
Paris 75002, FRANCE

Dolbin, Jack (Athlete, Football Player)
1775 Howard Ave
Pottsville, PA 17901-3215, USA

Dolby, Thomas (Musician, Songwriter, Writer)
Inteinational Talent Group
729 7th Ave Ste 1600
New York, NY 10019-6880, USA

Dolce (Musician)
c/o Staff Member *Diva Central Inc*
7510 W Sunset Blvd # 1445
Los Angeles, CA 90046-3408, USA

Dolce, Domenico (Designer, Fashion Designer)

Dold, R Bruce (Journalist)
501 N Park Rd # Hse
La Grange Park, IL 60526-5516, USA

Dole, Bob (Politician)
The Atlantic Building
950 F St NW Fl 10
Washington, DC 20004-1439, USA

Dole, Elizabeth H (Politician)
c/o Staff Member *WME|IMG*
9601 Wilshire Blvd
Beverly Hills, CA 90210-5213, USA

Doleac, Michael (Athlete, Basketball Player)
1155 Old Rail Ln
Park City, UT 84098-6640, USA

Doleman, Chris (Athlete, Football Player)
7020 Sentara Pl
Alpharetta, GA 30005-3017, USA

Dolenz, Ami (Actor)
1860 Bel Air Rd
Los Angeles, CA 90077-2729, USA

Dolenz, Micky (Actor, Musician)
22 Baymare Rd
Bell Canyon, CA 91307-1101, USA

D'Oliveira, Luisa (Actor)
c/o Morgan Moss *M Public Relations*
6121 W Sunset Blvd
Los Angeles, CA 90028-6442, USA

Dolla $ign, Ty (Musician)
c/o Kevin Liles *KWL Management*
112 Madison Ave Fl 4
New York, NY 10016-7416, USA

Dollar, Aubrey (Actor)
c/o Rhonda Price *Gersh*
41 Madison Ave Ste 3301
New York, NY 10010-2210, USA

Dollar, Creflo (Religious Leader)
Creflo Dollar Ministries
PO Box 490124
College Park, GA 30349-0124, USA

Dollar, Linda (Coach)
Southwest Missouri State University
Athletic Dept
Springfield, MO 65804, USA

Dollar, Taffi (Religious Leader)
Creflo Dollar Ministries
PO Box 490124
College Park, GA 30349-0124, USA

Dollard, Christopher Edward (Actor)
Gold Marshak Liedtke
3500 W Olive Ave Ste 1400
Burbank, CA 91505-5512, USA

Dollas, Bobby (Athlete, Hockey Player)
c/o Staff Member *Contact Image*
185 Rue du Seminaire
Montreal, QC H3C 2A3, Canada

Dollaz, Rich (Producer)
Dollaz Unlimited
171 Hasbrouck Ave
Hasbrouck Heights, NJ 07604-2703, USA

Dollens, Ronald (Business Person)
Guidant Corp
111 Monument Cir
Indianapolis, IN 46204-5100, USA

Dolley, Jason (Actor)
c/o Nils Larsen *Management 360*
9465 Wilshire Blvd Ste 900
Beverly Hills, CA 90212-2608, USA

Dolmayan, John (Musician)
Velvet Hammer
9911 W Pico Blvd # 350
Los Angeles, CA 90035-2703, USA

Doman, Brandon (Athlete, Football Player)
4616 N Pheasant Ridge Trl
Lehi, UT 84043-5288, USA

Doman, John (Actor)
c/o Staff Member *Peter Strain & Associates Inc (LA)*
10901 Whipple St Apt 322
N Hollywood, CA 91602-3245, USA

Dombasle, Arielle (Actor)
Agence Intertalent
5 Rue Clemet Marot
Paris 75008, FRANCE

Dombroski, Paul (Athlete, Football Player)
19122 Beckett Dr
Odessa, FL 33556-2274, USA

Dombrowski, Dave (Commentator)
Detroit Tigers
232 Woodland Rd
Chestnut Hill, MA 02467-2205, USA

Dombrowski, James M (Jim) (Athlete, Football Player)
220 Evangeline Dr
Mandeville, LA 70471-1874, USA

Domenichelli, Hnat (Athlete, Hockey Player)
1500 Mansell Rd
Alpharetta, GA 30009-4709, USA

Domi, Tie (Athlete, Hockey Player)
1-7357 Woodbine Ave
Suite 415
Markham, ON L3R 6L3, Canada

Domi, Tim (Athlete, Hockey Player)
46 Florence St
Ottawa, ON K2P 0W7, Canada

Dominczyk, Dagmara (Actor)
c/o Bill Butler *Industry Entertainment Partners*
1133 Broadway Ste 630
New York, NY 10010-8072, USA

Dominczyk, Marika (Actor)
c/o Sally Ware *Gersh*
41 Madison Ave Ste 3301
New York, NY 10010-2210, USA

Dominguez, Fernandez Adolfo (Designer, Fashion Designer)
Polingono Industrial Calle 4
San Ciprian de Vinas, Ourense 32901, SPAIN

Dominguez, Mario (Race Car Driver)
Herdez Racing
57 Gasoline Aly Ste A
Indianapolis, IN 46222-5932, USA

Dominguez, Matt (Athlete, Football Player)
4804 Counts Cv
Austin, TX 78749-3755, USA

Dominic, Rhodes (Athlete, Football Player)
6411 Canyon Lake Dr
Dallas, TX 75249-3021, USA

Dominik, Andrew (Director)
c/o Alex Mebed *Creative Artists Agency (CAA)*
2000 Avenue of the Stars Ste 100
Los Angeles, CA 90067-4705, USA

Dominique, Andy (Athlete, Baseball Player)
2016 Lamego Way
El Dorado Hills, CA 95762-7557, USA

Domres, Martin F (Marty) (Athlete, Football Player)
Deutsche Bank
1 South St Ste 2400
Baltimore, MD 21202-3348, USA

Don, Stefflon (Musician)
c/o Erin Larsen *Paradigm*
140 Broadway Ste 2600
New York, NY 10005-1011, USA

Donahew, Casey (Musician)
c/o Vanessa Parker-Davis *Splash Publicity*
1520 16th Ave S Unit 2
Nashville, TN 37212-2938, USA

Donahue, Elinor (Actor)
78533 Sunrise Mountain Vw
Palm Desert, CA 92211-2403, USA

Donahue, Heather (Actor)
Rigberg Roberts Rugolo
118D S Bevedy Dr
#601
Los Aneles, CA 90035, USA

Donahue, Mitch (Athlete, Football Player)
2220 Beloit Dr
Billings, MT 59102-5706, USA

Donahue, Phil (Talk Show Host)
244 Madison Ave Ste 707
New York, NY 10016-2817, USA

Donahue, Terry (Athlete, Baseball Player, Commentator)
215 N 3rd Ave
Saint Charles, IL 60174-2005, USA

Donald, Luke (Athlete, Golfer)
178 Bears Club Dr
Jupiter, FL 33477-4203, USA

Donald, Mike (Athlete, Golfer)
2400 N 65th Way
Hollywood, FL 33024-4046, USA

Donaldson, Colby (Actor, Reality Star)
c/o Brian Samuels *Evolution Management + Marketing*
901 N Highland Ave
Los Angeles, CA 90038-2412, USA

Donaldson, James (Athlete, Basketball Player)
2843 34th Ave W
Seattle, WA 98199-2602, USA

Donaldson, Jeff (Athlete, Football Player)
4529 Stover St
Fort Collins, CO 80525-3261, USA

Donaldson, John (Athlete, Baseball Player)
3913 Yates Ct
Charlotte, NC 28215-3955, USA

Donaldson, John (Athlete, Football Player)
3913 Yates Ct
Charlotte, NC 28215-3955, USA

Donaldson, Ray (Athlete, Football Player)
3128 Crestwell Dr
Indianapolis, IN 46268-8655, USA

Donaldson, Roger (Director, Producer)
c/o Jane Cameron *Cameron Creswell Agency*
61 Marlborough St
Fl 7
Surry Hills, NSW 02010, AUSTRALIA

Donaldson, Sam (Journalist)
1211 Crest Ln
Mc Lean, VA 22101-1837, USA

Donaldson, Samuel (Sam) (Correspondent)
1125 Crest Ln
McLean, VA 22101-1805, USA

Donan, Holland R (Athlete, Football Player)
212 Valley Vw
Pompton Plains, NJ 07444-2166, USA

Do Nascimento, Alexandre Cardinal (Religious Leader)
Arcebispado
CP 87
Luanda 1230 C, ANGOLA

Donatelli, Clark (Athlete, Hockey Player)
351 Reynolds St
Kingston, PA 18704-5207

Donatelli, Don (Athlete, Football Player)
54846 Seneca Lake Rd
Quaker City, OH 43773-9659, USA

Donato, Ted (Athlete, Hockey Player, Olympic Athlete)
34 Whitcomb Rd
Scituate, MA 02066-1123

Donchez, Tom (Athlete, Football Player)
3369 Green Meadow Dr
Bethlehem, PA 18017-1942, USA

Doncic, Luka (Athlete, Basketball Player)
c/o Bill Duffy *BDA Sports Management*
700 Ygnacio Valley Rd Ste 330
Walnut Creek, CA 94596-3838, USA

Donckers, William (Athlete, Football Player)
13708 SE 141st St
Renton, WA 98059-5416, USA

Doneen, Derek (Director, Producer)
c/o Matthew Baskharoon *WME|IMG*
9601 Wilshire Blvd
Beverly Hills, CA 90210-5213, USA

Donegan, Dan (Musician)
c/o Staff Member *Mitch Schneider Organization (MSO)*
14724 Ventura Blvd Ste 410
Sherman Oaks, CA 91403-3537, USA

Donella, Chad E (Actor)
c/o Staff Member *TalentWorks*
3500 W Olive Ave Ste 1400
Burbank, CA 91505-5512, USA

Donelly, Tanya (Music Group, Songwriter, Writer)
Helter Skelter
Plaza 535 Kings Road
London SW10 0S, UNITED KINGDOM (UK)

Donlan, Yolande (Actor)
11 Mellina Place
London NW8, UNITED KINGDOM (UK)

Donlavey, Junie (Race Car Driver)
5011 Old Midlothian Tpke
Richmond, VA 23224-1119, USA

Donley, Doug (Athlete, Football Player)
8005 Pullam Cir
Plano, TX 75024-6849, USA

Donnahoo, Roger (Athlete, Football Player)
20 Rock Brook Cv
Rossville, GA 30741-5355, USA

Donnalley, Kevin (Athlete, Football Player)
8910 Dove Stand Ln
Charlotte, NC 28226-2671, USA

Donnalley, Rick (Athlete, Football Player)
1796 Danforth Dr
Marietta, GA 30062-5544, USA

Donnellan, Declan (Director)
Cheek by Jowl Theatre Co
Aveline St
London SW11 5DQ, UNITED KINGDOM (UK)

Donnelley, James R (Business Person)
R R Donnelley & Sons
77 W Wacker Dr
Chicago, IL 60601-1604, USA

Donnelly, Andrew (Actor)
c/o Ruthanne Secunda *ICM Partners*
10250 Constellation Blvd Fl 7
Los Angeles, CA 90067-6207, USA

Donnelly, Brendan (Athlete, Baseball Player)
2815 E Arrowhead Trl
Gilbert, AZ 85297-5270, USA

Donnelly, Declan (Actor, Television Host)
c/o Staff Member *Rabbit Vocal Management*
27 Poland St
Fl 3
London W1F 8QW, UNITED KINGDOM

Donnelly, George (Athlete, Football Player)
2S530 Beechwood Rd
Glen Ellyn, IL 60137-6955, USA

Donnelly, Gord (Athlete, Coach, Hockey Player)
c/o Staff Member *Hockey Montreal International*
4612 Royal Ave
Montreal, QC H4A 2M8, Canada

Donnelly, Jennifer (Writer)
c/o Staff Member *Simon & Schuster*
1230 Avenue of the Americas Fl CONC1
New York, NY 10020-1586, USA

Donnelly, Laura (Actor)
c/o Lainie Sorkin Becky *Management 360*
9111 Wilshire Blvd
Beverly Hills, CA 90210-5508, USA

Donnelly, Meg (Actor)
c/o Jordyn Palos *Persona Public Relations*
6255 W Sunset Blvd Ste 705
Hollywood, CA 90028-7408, USA

Donnelly, Mike (Athlete, Hockey Player)
18429 Stoneridge Ct
Northville, MI 48168-8571, USA

Donnelly, Rich (Athlete, Baseball Player)
101 Bryden Rd
Steubenville, OH 43953-3429, USA

Donnelly, Rick (Athlete, Football Player)
PO Box 20441
Cheyenne, WY 82003-7011, USA

Donnels, Chris (Athlete, Baseball Player)
5 Stone Pne
Aliso Viejo, CA 92656-2131, USA

Donner, Jom J (Director)
Pohjoisranta 12
Helsinki 17 00170, FINLAND

Donner, Lauren Shuler (Producer)

Donner, Richard (Director)
1444 Forest Knoll Dr
Los Angeles, CA 90069-1332, USA

Donnie, Elder (Athlete, Football Player)
16613 Norwood Dr
Tampa, FL 33624-1168, USA

Donoahoe, John (Business Person)
10 Palmer Ln
Portola Valley, CA 94028-7918, USA

D'Onofrio, Mark (Athlete, Football Player)
295 Harmon Ave
Fort Lee, NJ 07024-4446, USA

D'Onofrio, Vincent (Actor, Producer)
c/o Sam Maydew *Silver Lining Entertainment*
421 S Beverly Dr Fl 7
Beverly Hills, CA 90212-4408, USA

Donohoe, Amanda (Actor)
Markham & Froggatt
Julian House
4 Windmill Street
London W1P 1HF, UNITED KINGDOM (UK)

Donohoe, Michael (Athlete, Football Player)
505 Juneberry Rd
Riverwoods, IL 60015-3715, USA

Donohoe, Peter (Music Group, Musician)
82 Hampton Lane Solihull
West Midlands B91 2RS, UNITED KINGDOM (UK)

Donohue, Jim (Athlete, Baseball Player)
16 Huntleigh Downs
Saint Louis, MO 63131-3416, USA

Donohue, Leon (Athlete, Football Player)
1904 Bechelli Ln
Redding, CA 96002-0132, USA

Donohue, Timothy (Business Person)
Nextel Communications
2001 Edmund Halley Dr
Reston, VA 20191-1132, USA

Donohue, Tom (Athlete, Baseball Player)
249 Liberty Ave
Westbury, NY 11590-2135, USA

Donoso, Jose (Writer)
Calceite
Province of Teruel, SPAIN

Donovan (Music Group, Songwriter, Writer)
P O Box 1119
London SW9 9JW, UNITED KINGDOM (UK)

Donovan, Billy (Athlete, Basketball Player)
2009 Huntington Ave
Nichols Hills, OK 73116-5112, USA

Donovan, Brian (Journalist)
Newsday
1735 York Ave APT 12C
New York, NY 10128-6857, USA

Donovan, Elisa (Actor)
c/o Patrick Millsaps *Londonderry Entertainment*
8383 Wilshire Blvd Ste 445
Beverly Hills, CA 90211-2449, USA

Donovan, Harry (Athlete, Basketball Player)
8303 Bayonet Point Ct Apt C
Fredericksburg, VA 22407-2125, USA

Donovan, Jason S (Actor, Music Group)
Richard East Productions
PO Box 342
South Yarra, VIC 03141, AUSTRALIA

Donovan, Jeffrey (Actor)
21042 Entrada Rd
Topanga, CA 90290-3531, USA

Donovan, Landon (Athlete, Soccer Player)
c/o Staff Member *Los Angeles Galaxy*
18400 Avalon Blvd Ste 200
Carson, CA 90746-2181, USA

Donovan, Martin (Actor)
c/o Pam Winter *Gary Goddard Agency (GGA)*
304-250 The Esplanade
Toronto, ON M5A 1J2, CANADA

Donovan, Pat (Athlete, Football Player)
113 S Prairiesmoke Cir
Whitefish, MT 59937-8182, USA

Donovan, Raymond J (Politician)
1600 Paterson Park Rd
Secaucus, NJ 07094-4019, USA

Donovan, Shean (Athlete, Hockey Player)
11 Mountain Rd
Lexington, MA 02420-1308, USA

Donovan, Tate (Actor)
9514 San Lucas
Austin, TX 78737-1232, USA

Donovan, Trevor (Actor)
c/o Michael Yanni *Michael Yanni*
1642 N Fairfax Ave
Los Angeles, CA 90046-2610, YSA

Donowho, Ryan (Actor)
c/o Staff Member *Brookside Artists Management*
250 W 57th St Ste 1820
New York, NY 10107-1802, USA

Doobie Brothers (Music Group)
PO Box 878
Sonoma, CA 95476-0878, USA

Doocy, Steve (Television Host)
c/o Staff Member *Fox News*
1211 Avenue of the Americas Lowr C1
New York, NY 10036-8705, USA

Doody, Alison (Actor)
Julian Belfarge
46 Albermarle St
London W1X 4PP, UNITED KINGDOM (UK)

Doolan, Wendy (Athlete, Golfer)
3412 Turnberry Ln
Lakeland, FL 33803-5465, USA

Dooley, Paul (Actor)
c/o Andrew Freedman *Andrew Freedman Public Relations*
35 E 84th St
New York, NY 10028-0871, USA

Dooley, Taylor (Actor)
c/o Heather Reynolds *One Entertainment (NY)*
347 5th Ave Rm 1404
New York, NY 10016-5034, USA

Dooley, Thomas (Athlete, Soccer Player)
South Coast Bayern Futbol Club
18141 Beach Blvd Ste 110
Huntington Beach, CA 92648-1354, USA

Dooley, Vincent J (Vince) (Athlete, Coach, Football Coach, Football Player)
University of Georgia
PO Box 1472
Athletic Dept
Athens, GA 30603-1472, USA

Dooling, Brendan (Actor)
c/o Elise Koseff *MKSD Talent Management (NY)*
15 W 28th St Fl 9
New York, NY 10001-6430, USA

Dooling, Keyon (Athlete, Basketball Player)
Los Angeles Clippers
6001 N Ocean Dr Apt 302
Hollywood, FL 33019-4616, USA

Doolittle, Eliza (Musician)
c/o James Whitting *Coda Music Agency (UK)*
56 Compton St
Clerkenwell
London EC1V 0ET, UNITED KINGDOM

Doolittle, Melinda (Musician, Reality Star)
1524 Braden Cir
Franklin, TN 37067-8595, USA

Doom, Ryan (Actor)
c/o Katie Rhodes *Untitled Entertainment*
350 S Beverly Dr Ste 200
Beverly Hills, CA 90212-4819, USA

Doornink, Dan (Athlete, Football Player)
402 S 12th Ave
Yakima, WA 98902-3115, USA

Dopazo, Cecilia (Actor)
c/o Staff Member *Telefe (Argentina)*
Pavon 2444
Buenos Aires C1248AAT, ARGENTINA

Dope, Edsel (Musician)
c/o Bob Ringe *Survival Management*
30765 Pacific Coast Hwy Ste 325
Malibu, CA 90265-3643, USA

Dopson, John (Athlete, Baseball Player)
3337 Old Gamber Rd
Finksburg, MD 21048-2223, USA

Dora Brown, Kathryne (Actor)
1617 N Sierra Bonita Ave
Los Angeles, CA 90046-2815, USA

Doran, Bill (Athlete, Baseball Player)
1230 Shawnee Run Dr
Maineville, OH 45039-7231, USA

Dore, Andre (Athlete, Hockey Player)
73 Betsys Ln
New Canaan, CT 06840-5202, USA

Dore, Daniel (Athlete, Hockey Player)
c/o Staff Member *Boston Bruins*
100 Legends Way Ste 250
Td Banknorth Garden
Boston, MA 02114-1389, USA

Dore, Jimmy (Comedian)
c/o Alex Murray *Brillstein Entertainment Partners*
9150 Wilshire Blvd Ste 350
Beverly Hills, CA 90212-3453, USA

Dore, Jon (Actor)
c/o Lorne Perlmutar *Diamondfield Entertainment*
124 Portland St
Toronto, ON M5V 2N5, Canada

Dore, Patricia (Actor)
Cineart
36 Rue de Ponthieu
Paris 75008, FRANCE

Doremus, David (Actor)
28965 Rock Canyon Dr
Santa Clarita, CA 91390-5282, USA

Dorenbos, Jon (Athlete, Football Player)
c/o Ken Harris *Optimum Sports Management*
3225 S Macdill Ave Ste 330
Tampa, FL 33629-8171, USA

Dorensky, Sergey L (Music Group, Musician)
Bryusov Per 8/10 #75
Moscow 103009, RUSSIA

Dorey, Jim (Athlete, Hockey Player)
105 Aaron Pl
Amherstview, ON K7N 2A1, Canada

Dorff, Stephen (Actor)
c/o Oren Segal *Management Production Entertainment (MPE)*
9229 W Sunset Blvd Ste 301
W Hollywood, CA 90069-3417, USA

Dorfman, Andi (Reality Star)
c/o Liz Decesare *Authentic Talent and Literary Management (NY)*
20 Jay St Ste M17
Brooklyn, NY 11201-8300, USA

Dorfman, Ariel (Writer)
Duke University
2122 Campus Dr
International Studies Center
Durham, NC 27708-9963, USA

Dorfman, Cliff (Writer)
c/o Rich Green *ICM Partners*
10250 Constellation Blvd Fl 7
Los Angeles, CA 90067-6207, USA

Dorfman, David (Actor)
c/o Wendi Green *Paradigm*
8942 Wilshire Blvd
Beverly Hills, CA 90211-1908, USA

Dorfman, Tommy (Actor)
c/o Brett Ruttenberg *Imprint PR*
6121 W Sunset Blvd
Neuehouse
Los Angeles, CA 90028-6442, USA

Dorfmeister, Michaela (Skier)
Quellensteig
Neusiedl 02763, AUSTRIA

Dorgan, Byron (Politician)
1702 Esquire Ln
Mc Lean, VA 22101-4754, USA

Dorin, Francoise (Actor, Writer)
Artmedia
20 Ave Rapp
Paris 75007, FRANCE

Dorio, Gabriella (Athlete, Track Athlete)
Federation of Light Athletics
Viale Tialano 70
Rome 00196, ITALY

Dorion, Dan (Athlete, Hockey Player)
10910 Queens Blvd Apt 12H
Forest Hills, NY 11375-5319, USA

Dormann, Dana (Athlete, Golfer)
4887 Arlene Pl
Pleasanton, CA 94566-7824, USA

Dormeker, Jerry (Race Car Driver)
Bad Moon Rising
2243 Ravenna St
Hudson, OH 44236-3453, USA

Dormer, Natalie (Actor)
c/o Jason Weinberg *Untitled Entertainment*
350 S Beverly Dr Ste 200
Beverly Hills, CA 90212-4819, USA

Dorn, Michael (Actor)
c/o Marilyn Atlas *Marilyn Atlas Management*
132 S Lasky Dr Ste 200
Beverly Hills, CA 90212-1706, USA

Dornan, Jamie (Actor)
708 S Barrington Ave Apt 205
Los Angeles, CA 90049-4582, USA

Dornan, Robert (Politician)
8623 Beaver Pond Ln
Fairfax Station, VA 22039-2725, USA

Dornbrook, Thom (Athlete, Football Player)
5918 Emerald Lakes Dr
Medina, OH 44256-7464, USA

Dorney, Keith R (Athlete, Football Player)
2450 Blucher Valley Rd
Sebastopol, CA 95472-5355, USA

Dornhoefer, Gary (Athlete, Hockey Player)
12 Lordship Ln
Dover, DE 19901-6130

Dornseif, Dave (Athlete, Hockey Player)
3989 E Phillips Cir
Centennial, CO 80122-3647, USA

Doronina, Tatyana (Actor)
Gorky Arts Theater
22 Tverskoi Blvd
Moscow 119146, RUSSIA

Dorough, Howie (Musician)
PO Box 110697
Palm Bay, FL 32911-0697, USA

Dorrell, Karl (Coach, Football Coach)
University of California
Athletic Dept
Los Angeles, CA 90024, USA

Dorris, Andrew (Athlete, Football Player)
RR 22 Box 549
Conroe, TX 77303, USA

Dorris, Derek (Athlete, Football Player)
437 Corriente Trl
Azle, TX 76020-3642, USA

D'Orsay, Brooke (Actor)

Dorsch, Hank (Athlete, Football Player)
801 Shannon Rd
Regina, SK S4S 5K1, Canada

Dorsch, Travis (Athlete, Football Player)
PO Box 2086
West Lafayette, IN 47996-2086, USA

Dorsett, Brian (Athlete, Baseball Player)
700 Dobbs Glen St
Terre Haute, IN 47803-2480, USA

Dorsett, Phillip (Athlete, Football Player)
c/o Tony Fleming *Impact Sports (LA)*
12429 Ventura Ct
Studio City, CA 91604-2417, USA

Dorsett, Tony (Athlete, Football Player, Heisman Trophy Winner)
Tony Dorsett Foundation
6505 W Park Blvd Ste 306 # 283
Plano, TX 75093-6212, USA

Dorsett Jr, Anthony (Athlete, Football Player)
3817 Bowser Ave Apt C
Dallas, TX 75219-4385, USA

Dorsey, Christopher (BG) (Musician)
c/o Staff Member *Sosincere Entertainment*
2054 Nostrand Ave Apt 4F
Brooklyn, NY 11210-2526, USA

Dorsey, Eric (Athlete, Football Player)
5 London Ct
Teaneck, NJ 07666-6461, USA

Dorsey, Jack (Business Person)
1355 Market St Ste 900
San Francisco, CA 94103-1337, USA

Dorsey, Jacky (Athlete, Basketball Player)
1231 S Teal Estates Cir
Fresno, TX 77545-8652, USA

Dorsey, Jim (Athlete, Baseball Player)
335 Elm St
Seekonk, MA 02771-1724, USA

Dorsey, John (Athlete, Football Player)
425 Arrowhead Dr
Green Bay, WI 54301-2635, USA

Dorsey, Ken (Athlete, Football Player)
7108 Presidio Gln
Lakewood Ranch, FL 34202-5038, USA

Dorsey, Kerris (Actor)
c/o Brett Ruttenberg *Imprint PR*
6121 W Sunset Blvd
Neuehouse
Los Angeles, CA 90028-6442, USA

Dorsey, Nate (Athlete, Football Player)
5023 S 87th St
Tampa, FL 33619-7209, USA

Dorsey, Omar (Actor)
c/o Janice Lee *Rogers & Cowan*
1840 Century Park E Fl 18
Los Angeles, CA 90067-2101, USA

Dorsey, Ron (Athlete, Basketball Player)
3925 Mallard Way
Cumming, GA 30028-4862, USA

Dorsey, Ryan (Actor)
c/o Danielle Allman-Del *D2 Management*
10351 Santa Monica Blvd Ste 210
Los Angeles, CA 90025-6937, USA

Dorsey Brothers Orchestra (Music Group, Musician)
PO Box 643176
Vero Beach, FL 32964-3176, USA

Dorta, Melvin (Athlete, Baseball Player)
21 Williamsburg Building
Hershey, PA 17033-2241, USA

Doss, Barrett (Actor)
c/o Marisa Martins *The Lede Company*
401 Broadway Ste 206
New York, NY 10013-3033, USA

Doss, Tandon (Athlete, Football Player)

Dos Santos, Alexandre J M Cardinal (Religious Leader)
Paco Arquiepiscopal
Avenida Eduardo Mondlane
CP Maputo 01448, MOZAMBIQUE

Doster, David (Athlete, Baseball Player)
4123 Sugarhill Run
New Haven, IN 46774-2736, USA

Dotel, Octavio (Athlete, Baseball Player)
382 Oakland Rd
Lawrenceville, GA 30044-3726, USA

Dotson, Al (Athlete, Football Player)
Coyues 24 Las Playas
Acapulco 39390, Mexico

Dotson, Dewayne (Athlete, Football Player)
PO Box 425
White House, TN 37188-0425, USA

Dotson, Earl (Athlete, Football Player)
1112 Azalea Dr
Longview, TX 75601-3214, USA

Dotson, Richard E (Rich) (Athlete, Baseball Player)
7 Colonel Watson Dr
New Richmond, OH 45157-9002, USA

Dotson, Santana (Athlete, Football Player)
PO Box 79134
Houston, TX 77279-9134, USA

Dotter, Bobby (Race Car Driver)
MPH Racing
118 Stutt Road
Mooresville, NC 28117, USA

Dotter, Gary (Athlete, Baseball Player)
7413 Ravenswood Rd
Granbury, TX 76049-4742, USA

Dotter, Robert (Race Car Driver)
3632 N Pacific Ave
Chicago, IL 60634-2012, USA

Dottley, John (Athlete, Football Player)
1438 Wisteria Dr
Vicksburg, MS 39180-4757, USA

Douaihy, Saliba (Artist)
Vining Road
Windham, NY 12496, USA

Doubleday, Kaitlin (Actor)
c/o Mary Putnam Greene *MPG Management*
7162 Beverly Blvd Ste 332
Los Angeles, CA 90036-2547, USA

Doucett, Linda (Actor, Model)
c/o Michael Slessinger *Michael Slessinger & Associates*
8730 W Sunset Blvd Ste 1125
W Hollywood, CA 90069-2210, USA

Doucette, Paul (Musician)
8071 Woodrow Wilson Dr
Los Angeles, CA 90046-1116, USA

Doug, Doug E (Musician)
4024 Radford Ave # 3
Studio City, CA 91604-2101, USA

Doughboys (Musician)
PO Box 5559 Stn H
Montreal, QC H3G 2L6, Canada

Dougherty, Ed (Athlete, Golfer)
448 SW Fairway Vis
Port Saint Lucie, FL 34986-2131, USA

Dougherty, Jim (Athlete, Baseball Player)
102 Pinnacle Ct
Kitty Hawk, NC 27949-5911, USA

Dougherty, Joseph (Joe) (Director, Producer, Writer)
c/o Ken Freimann *Circle of Confusion*
8931 Ellis Ave
Los Angeles, CA 90034-3336, USA

Dougherty, Richard (Athlete, Hockey Player, Olympic Athlete)
1501 W Paulson Rd
Green Bay, WI 54313-6025, USA

Doughty, Glenn (Athlete, Football Player)
1825 Seven Pines Dr
Saint Louis, MO 63146-3715, USA

Doughty, Kenny (Actor)
c/o Alan Siegel *Alan Siegel Entertainment*
9200 W Sunset Blvd Ste 804
West Hollywood, CA 90069-3603, USA

Douglas, Aaron (Actor)
c/o Russ Mortensen *Pacific Artists Management*
112 3rd Ave E Suite 210
Vancouver, BC V5T 1C8, CANADA

Douglas, Barry (Musician)
c/o Staff Member *Opus 3 Artists (NY)*
470 Park Ave S # 900N
New York, NY 10016-6819, USA

Douglas, Bobby (Coach, Wrestler)
Iowa State University
Athletic Dept
Ames, IA 50011-0001, USA

Douglas, Carl (Attorney)
6611 Shenandoah Ave
Los Angeles, CA 90056-2115, USA

Douglas, Carol (Music Group)
Famous Artists Agency
250 W 57th St
New York, NY 10107-0001, USA

Douglas, Charles (Whammy) (Athlete, Baseball Player)
1711 Catherine Lake Rd
Jacksonville, NC 28540-8755, USA

Douglas, David (Athlete, Football Player)
505 Willard St
Maryville, TN 37803-3135, USA

Douglas, Gabby (Athlete, Gymnast, Olympic Athlete)
Buckeye Gymnastics
7159 Northgate Way
Westerville, OH 43082-9478, USA

Douglas, Harry (Athlete, Football Player)
c/o Todd France *Creative Artists Agency (CAA) Sports*
3500 Lenox Rd NE
Atlanta, GA 30326-4228, USA

Douglas, Hugh (Athlete, Football Player)
5 Pennbrook Ln
Glen Mills, PA 19342-1663, USA

Douglas, Ileana (Actor)
c/o Staff Member *Baumgarten Management*
11925 Wilshire Blvd Ste 310
Los Angeles, CA 90025-6649, USA

Douglas, Illeana (Actor, Director, Producer)
Illeanarama
11812 San Vicente Blvd Ste 200
Los Angeles, CA 90049-6622, USA

Douglas, James (Buster) (Athlete, Boxer)
PO Box 342
Johnstown, OH 43031-0342, USA

Douglas, Jay (Athlete, Football Player)
2909 Laurel Cherry Way
The Woodlands, TX 77380-4004, USA

Douglas, Jerry (Actor)
739 Rodney Dr
Nashville, TN 37205-3015, USA

Douglas, Jordy (Athlete, Hockey Player)
Courts Financial Group
200-1215 Henderson Hwy
Winnipeg, MB R2G 1L8, Canada

Douglas, Katie (Basketball Player)
Connecticut Sun
Mohegan Sun Arena
Uncasville, CT 06382, USA

Douglas, Kirk (Actor, Producer)
805 N Rexford Dr
Beverly Hills, CA 90210-2908, USA

Douglas, Leon (Athlete, Basketball Player)
PO Box 58
Leighton, AL 35646-0058, USA

Douglas, Merrill (Athlete, Football Player)
2185 E 3970 S
Salt Lake City, UT 84124-1754, USA

Douglas, Michael (Actor, Director, Producer)
151 Central Park W Apt 9C
New York, NY 10023-1577, USA

Douglas, Nik (Writer)
c/o Staff Member *Simon & Schuster*
1230 Avenue of the Americas Fl CONC1
New York, NY 10020-1586, USA

Douglas, Santiago (Actor)
c/o Charlton Blackburne *Charlton Blackburne Management*
4022 Los Feliz Blvd
Los Angeles, CA 90027-2305, USA

Douglas, Sarah (Actor)
c/o Staff Member *Vic Murray Talent*
185 A Latchmere Rd
London SW11 2JZ, UK

Douglas, Sherman (Athlete, Basketball Player)
1330 West Ave Apt 1107
Miami Beach, FL 33139-0905, USA

Douglass, Bobby (Athlete, Football Player)
151 E Laurel Ave Apt 203
Lake Forest, IL 60045-1296, USA

Douglass, Dale (Athlete, Golfer)
6601 E San Miguel Ave
Paradise Valley, AZ 85253-5983, USA

Douglass, Maurice (Athlete, Football Player)
1021 Sunset Dr
Englewood, OH 45322-2252, USA

Douglass, Mike (Athlete, Football Player)
1725 Porterfield Pl
El Cajon, CA 92019-4122, USA

Douglass, Robyn (Actor)
407 S Dearborn St Unit 1675
Chicago, IL 60605-1113, USA

Douglass, Sean (Athlete, Baseball Player)
43956 Johns Ct
Lancaster, CA 93536-8213, USA

Doumit, Ryan (Athlete, Baseball Player)
17716 E Apollo Rd
Spokane Valley, WA 99016-5068, USA

Doumit, Sam (Actor)
c/o Staff Member *Baker Winokur Ryder Public Relations*
9100 Wilshire Blvd
W Tower #500
Beverly Hills, CA 90212-3415, USA

Dourdan, Gary (Actor)
c/o Becky Poliakoff *aTa Management (LA)*
2508 N Vermont Ave # 702
Los Angeles, CA 90027-1243, USA

Dourif, Brad (Actor)
137 S Robertson Blvd # 126
Beverly Hills, CA 90211-2801, USA

Dourif, Fiona (Actor)
PO Box 1444
Issaquah, WA 98027-0059, USA

Douris, Peter (Athlete, Hockey Player)
PO Box 488
York Beach, ME 03910-0488, USA

Douse, Joseph (Athlete, Baseball Player)
16722 Fenmore St
Detroit, MI 48235-3423, USA

Douthitt, Earl (Athlete, Football Player)
8100 Central Ave Apt 211
Cleveland, OH 44104-2173, USA

Douzable, Leger (Athlete, Football Player)

Dove, Dennis (Athlete, Baseball Player)
306 W 3rd St
Ocilla, GA 31774-1732, USA

Dove, Eddie (Athlete, Football Player)
1750 Poppy Ave
Menlo Park, CA 94025-5738, USA

Dove, Grace (Actor)
c/o Jack Kingsrud *Zero Gravity Management*
11110 Ohio Ave Ste 100
Los Angeles, CA 90025-3329, USA

Dove, Rita F (Writer)
1757 Lambs Rd
Charlottesville, VA 22901-8911, USA

Dove, Ronnie (Music Group)
c/o Staff Member *Time Machine*
2109 S Wilbur Ave
Walla Walla, WA 99362-9048, USA

Doves (Music Group)
c/o Staff Member *Paradigm (Monterey)*
404 W Franklin St
Monterey, CA 93940-2303, USA

Dovolani, Tony (Choreographer, Dancer, Reality Star)
c/o Cynthia Snyder *Cynthia Snyder Public Relations*
5739 Colfax Ave
N Hollywood, CA 91601-1636, USA

Dow, Peggy (Actor)
2121 S Yorktown Ave
Tulsa, OK 74114-1426, USA

Dow, Tony (Actor)
c/o David Moss *David Moss Company*
6063 Vineland Ave Apt B
N Hollywood, CA 91606-4986, USA

Dowd, Ann (Actor)
c/o Adam Kersh *Brigade Marketing*
116 W 23rd St Fl 5
New York, NY 10011-2599, USA

Dowd, Jim (Athlete, Hockey Player)
708 New Jersey Ave
Point Pleasant Beach, NJ 08742-2970, USA

Dowd, Maureen (Writer)
c/o Staff Member *21st Century Speakers*
1352 Lake Ave
Gouldsboro, PA 18424, USA

Dowdell, Marcus (Athlete, Football Player)
16 Charleston Park Dr
Houston, TX 77025-5647, USA

Dowdy, Adam (Athlete, Baseball Player)
909 E Chestnut St
Pontiac, IL 61764-1407, USA

Dowell, Ken (Athlete, Baseball Player)
5221 Helen Way
Sacramento, CA 95822-2868, USA

Dower, John W (Writer)
Massachusetts Institute of Technology
History Dept
Cambridge, MA 02139, USA

Dowhower, Rod (Athlete, Football Coach, Football Player)
3412 Lindenridge Cir
Buford, GA 30519-7235, USA

Dowie, Bruce (Athlete, Hockey Player)
3277 Star Lane
Burlington, ON L7M 5A4, Canada

Dowle, David (Music Group, Musician)
Int'l Talent Booking
27A Floral St #300
London WC2E 9DQ, UNITED KINGDOM (UK)

Dowler, Boyd H (Athlete, Football Player)
3013 Grove View Ct
Dacula, GA 30019-6896, USA

Dowling, Brian (Athlete, Football Player)
114 Arboretum Way
Burlington, MA 01803-3827, USA

Dowling, Dave (Athlete, Baseball Player)
173 Whelan Way
Manteca, CA 95336-5945, USA

Dowling, Jonathan (Athlete, Football Player)

Dowling, Peter (Director)
703 3rd St S
Stillwater, MN 55082-6259, USA

Dowling, Timothy (Actor)
c/o Staff Member *WME/IMG*
9601 Wilshire Blvd
Beverly Hills, CA 90210-5213, USA

Dowling, Vincent (Director, Writer)
322 E River Rd
Huntington, MA 01050-9645, USA

Down, Lesley-Anne (Actor)
6525 Paseo Canyon Dr
Malibu, CA 91604, USA

Down, Leslie-Anne (Actor)
6252 Paseo Canyon Dr
Malibu, CA 90265-3135, USA

Down, Rick (Athlete, Baseball Player)
10908 Salford Dr
Las Vegas, NV 89144-4498, USA

Down, Sarah (Cartoonist)
Playboy Magazine
680 N Lake Shore Dr
Chicago, IL 60611-4546, USA

Downes, Robin Atkin (Actor)
c/o Staff Member *Gordon Agency*
260 S Beverly Dr Ste 308
Beverly Hills, CA 90212-3814, USA

Downey, Bill (Athlete, Basketball Player)
1035 S Moorings Dr
Arlington Heights, IL 60005-3217, USA

Downey, James (Writer)
c/o Staff Member *3 Arts Entertainment*
9460 Wilshire Blvd Fl 7
Beverly Hills, CA 90212-2713, USA

Downey, Jim (Writer)
c/o Staff Member *3 Arts Entertainment*
9460 Wilshire Blvd Fl 7
Beverly Hills, CA 90212-2713, USA

Downey, Roma (Actor)
c/o Staff Member *One Three Media*
3000 Olympic Blvd Bldg 2520
Santa Monica, CA 90404-5073, USA

Downey, Susan (Producer)
Team Downey
1311 Abbot Kinney Blvd
Venice, CA 90291-3739, USA

Downey Jr, Robert (Actor)
Team Downey
1311 Abbot Kinney Blvd
Venice, CA 90291-3739, USA

Downie, Steve (Athlete, Hockey Player)
c/o Darren Ferris *Definitive Hockey Group*
200-65 International Blvd
Etobicoke, ON M9W 6L9, Canada

Downing, Al (Athlete, Baseball Player)
25343 Silver Aspen Way Apt 325
Wav Ant 735
Valencia, CA 91381-0689, USA

Downing, Alphonso E (Al) (Athlete, Baseball Player)
25343 Silver Aspen Way Apt 735
Valencia, CA 91381-0698, USA

Downing, Brian J (Athlete, Baseball Player)
8095 County Road 135
Celina, TX 75009-2539, USA

Downing, Jim (Race Car Driver)
5096 Peachtree Rd
Atlanta, GA 30341-3134, USA

Downing, Sara (Actor)
c/o Mike Eistenstadt *Amsel, Eisenstadt & Frazier Talent Agency (AEF)*
5055 Wilshire Blvd Ste 860
Los Angeles, CA 90036-6108, USA

Downing, Steve (Athlete, Basketball Player)
6433 Lakeside Woods Cir
Indianapolis, IN 46278-1663, USA

Downing, Walt (Athlete, Football Player)
1141 Durham Cir NW
Massillon, OH 44646-2121, USA

Downs, Dave (Athlete, Baseball Player)
925 E 1050 N
Bountiful, UT 84010-2620, USA

Downs, Gary (Athlete, Football Player)
5026 Apple Grove Rd
Buford, GA 30519-3405, USA

Downs, Hugh (Correspondent, Journalist)
c/o Rick Hersh *Celebrity Consultants LLC*
3340 Ocean Park Blvd Ste 1005
Santa Monica, CA 90405-3255, USA

Downs, Jonathan (Writer)
Centre for Fortean Zoology
Myrtle Cottage
Woolfardisworthy
Bideford, North Devon EX39 5QR, UK

Downs, Kelly (Athlete, Baseball Player)
6459 Willow Creek Rd
Morgan, UT 84050-6746, USA

Downs, Lila (Musician)
c/o Bill Traut *Open Door Management*
Prefers to be contacted by email or phone.
Pacific Palisades, CA 90272, USA

Downs, Matt (Athlete, Baseball Player)
448 Cruise Ave
Centreville, AL 35042-6653, USA

Downs, Michael (Athlete, Football Player)
1405 Knob Hill Dr
Desoto, TX 75115-5335, USA

Downs, Nicholas (Actor)
c/o Andrew Stawiarski *ADS Management*
269 S Beverly Dr Ste 441
Beverly Hills, CA 90212-3851, USA

Downs, Robert (Athlete, Football Player)
28024 High Vista Dr
Escondido, CA 92026-7215, USA

Downs, Scott (Athlete, Baseball Player)
6814 Barbrook Rd
Louisville, KY 40258-2668, USA

Doyle, Allen (Athlete, Golfer)
512 Riverside Dr
Lagrange, GA 30240-9633, USA

Doyle, Brian (Athlete, Baseball Player)
PO Box 9156
Winter Haven, FL 33883-9156, USA

Doyle, Dennis (Race Car Driver)
DRG Motorsports
37 Meghan Blvd
Plymouth, CT 06782-2019, USA

Doyle, Denny (Athlete, Baseball Player)
PO Box 9156
Winter Haven, FL 33883-9156, USA

Doyle, Jack (Athlete, Football Player)

Doyle, James (Politician)
2001 Hawks Ridge Dr
Verona, WI 53593-9195, USA

Doyle, Jeff (Athlete, Baseball Player)
830 SE Bayshore Cir
Corvallis, OR 97333-3206, USA

Doyle, Kevin (Actor)
c/o Charlotte Davies *United Agents*
12-26 Lexington St
London W1F OLE, UNITED KINGDOM

Doyle, Paul (Athlete, Baseball Player)
19361 Brookhurst St Spc 15
Snc 15
Huntington Beach, CA 92646-2949, USA

Doyle, Roddy (Writer)
Secker & Warburg
38A West Road Bromsgrove
Worc B60 2NQ, UNITED KINGDOM (UK)

Doyle, Shawn (Actor)
3744 San Rafael Ave
Los Angeles, CA 90065-3217, USA

Doyle & Debbie Show, The (Music Group)
c/o Staff Member *Paradigm (Monterey)*
404 W Franklin St
Monterey, CA 93940-2303, USA

Doyle-Childress, Cartha (Athlete, Baseball Player, Commentator)
1516 Carowinds Cir
Maryville, TN 37803-7704, USA

Doyle Kennedy, Maria (Actor)
c/o Ruth Young *United Agents*
12-26 Lexington St
London W1F OLE, UNITED KINGDOM

Doyle-Murray, Brian (Actor, Comedian)
c/o Lisa Marber-Rich *Atlas Talent Agency (NY)*
15 E 32nd St Fl 6
New York, NY 10016-5570, USA

Doyne, Cory (Athlete, Baseball Player)
20228 County Line Rd
Lutz, FL 33558-5074, USA

Doyon, Mario (Athlete, Hockey Player)
12530 Windsor Dr
Carmel, IN 46033-3148

Dozier, Dakota (Athlete, Football Player)
c/o Anthony J. Agnone *Eastern Athletic Services*
11350 McCormick Rd
Suite 800 - Executive Plaza
Hunt Valley, MD 21031-1002, USA

Dozier, D J (Athlete, Baseball Player)
5821 N Cherokee Cluster
Virginia Beach, VA 23462-3214, USA

Dozier, Jan Davis Dr (Astronaut)
4105 Cumberland Pass Apt 814
Fort Worth, TX 76116-0753, USA

Dozier, Terry (Athlete, Basketball Player)
521 Sparkleberry Ln
Columbia, SC 29229-8609, USA

Dozier, Tom (Athlete, Baseball Player)
1231 Willow Ave Apt D7
Hercules, CA 94547-1200, USA

Drabble, Margaret (Writer)
P F D
Drury House 34-43 Russell St
London WC2B 5HA, UNITED KINGDOM (UK)

Drabek, Doug (Athlete, Baseball Player)
15 Ivy Pond Pl
Spring, TX 77381-6326, USA

Drabek, Kyle (Athlete, Baseball Player)
18 Cokeberry St
Spring, TX 77380-1885, USA

Drabinsky, Garth H (Producer)
Livent Inc
600-165 Avenue Rd
Toronto, ON M5R 3S4, CANADA

Draffen, Willis (Music Group)
16103 Vista Del Mar Dr
Houston, TX 77083-2309, USA

Draft, Chris (Athlete, Football Player)
970 E Oak St
Anaheim, CA 92805-4138, USA

Dragila, Stacy (Athlete, Olympic Athlete, Track Athlete)
PO Box 30931
Phoenix, AZ 85046-0931, USA

Draglia, Stacy (Athlete, Track Athlete)
1112 E Monte Cristo Ave
Phoenix, AZ 85022-3150, USA

Drago, Billy (Actor)
c/o Deborah Miller *Shelter Entertainment*
9255 W Sunset Blvd Ste 300
Los Angeles, CA 90069-3313, USA

Drago, Richard A (Dick) (Athlete, Baseball Player)
4703 Belle Chase Cir
Tampa, FL 33634-4256, USA

Drahman, Brian (Athlete, Baseball Player)
9984 Nob Hill Ln
Sunrise, FL 33351-4671, USA

Drahos, Nick (Athlete, Football Player)
3228 Beckie Dr SW
Wyoming, MI 49418-9014, USA

Drai, Victor (Producer)
10527 Bellagio Road
Beverly Hills, CA 90210, USA

Draiman, Dave (Musician)
c/o Staff Member *UTA/The Agency Group*
888 7th Ave Fl 7
New York, NY 10106-0700, USA

Drake (Actor, Musician)
Young Money Entertainment
2800 Veterans Memorial Blvd
Metairie, LA 70002-6130, USA

Drake, Bebe (Actor)
c/o Staff Member *Baron Entertainment*
13848 Ventura Blvd Ste A
Sherman Oaks, CA 91423-3654

Drake, Dallas (Athlete, Hockey Player)
11472 S Cedar Bay Trl
Traverse City, MI 49684-6841

Drake, Jerry (Athlete, Football Player)
2857 Regal Cir Apt E
Vestavia Hills, AL 35216-4632, USA

Drake, Jerry (Athlete, Football Player)
1893 Colonnade Rd
Cleveland, OH 44112-1567, USA

Drake, Jessica (Actor, Adult Film Star, Model)
Wicked Pictures
9040 Eton Ave
Canoga Park, CA 91304-1616, USA

Drake, Judith (Actor)
20th Century Artists
4605 Lankershim Blvd Ste 305
North Hollywood, CA 91602-1875, USA

Drake, Robert (Athlete, Baseball Player)
5409 Barrett Cir
Buena Park, CA 90621-1352, USA

Drake, Solly (Athlete, Baseball Player)
1732 S Corning St
Los Angeles, CA 90035-4302, USA

Drake, Stephanie (Actor)
c/o Samantha Chalk *Gersh*
41 Madison Ave Ste 3301
New York, NY 10010-2210, USA

Drakeford, Tyronne (Athlete, Football Player)
7786 Cedar Branch Dr
Gainesville, VA 20155-1994, USA

Drane, Dwight (Athlete, Football Player)
200 NW 107th Ave
Plantation, FL 33324-1700, USA

Dransfeldt, Kelly (Athlete, Baseball Player)
2011 Prairie Rose Dr
Morris, IL 60450-6851, USA

Draper, Courtnee (Actor)
PO Box 25985
Prescott Valley, AZ 86312-5985, USA

Draper, Denny (Athlete, Football Player)
11105 Baker Creek Rd
McMinnville, OR 97128-8000, USA

Draper, E Lynn Jr (Business Person)
American Electric Power
1 Riverside Plz Fl 1
Columbus, OH 43215-2373, USA

Draper, Kris (Athlete, Hockey Player)
3418 Westchester Rd
Bloomfield Hills, MI 48304-2573

Draper, Mike (Athlete, Baseball Player)
7608 NW 18th St
Act 105
Margate, FL 33063-3100, USA

Draper, Polly (Actor)
3856 Berry Dr
Studio City, CA 91604-3859, USA

Draper, Tim (Athlete, Hockey Player)
76 Blackstone Ave
Binghamton, NY 13903-1328, USA

Dratch, Rachel (Actor, Comedian)
c/o Scott Metzger *Paradigm*
140 Broadway Ste 2600
New York, NY 10005-1011, USA

Dravecky, Dave (Athlete, Baseball Player)
475 W 12th Ave Unit 8F
Denver, CO 80204-3687, USA

Draven, Jamie (Actor)
c/o Staff Member *Independent Talent Group*
40 Whitfield St
London W1T 2RH, UNITED KINGDOM

Draves, Victoria (Vickie) (Athlete, Swimmer)
23842 Shady Tree Cir
Laguna Niguel, CA 92677-1704, USA

Dray, Jim (Athlete, Football Player)

Drayton, Charlie (Music Group, Musician)
Direct Mangement Group
947 N La Cienega Blvd Ste G
Los Angeles, CA 90069-4700, USA

Drayton, Poppy (Actor)
c/o Peter Brooks *Creative Artists Management (CAM-UK)*
55-59 Shaftesbury Ave.
London W1D 6LD, UNITED KINGDOM

Drayton, Troy (Athlete, Football Player)
700 SW 78th Ave APT 813
Plantation, FL 33324-3377, USA

Dr DisRespect (Internet Star)
c/o Peter Letz *Creative Artists Agency (CAA)*
2000 Avenue of the Stars Ste 100
Los Angeles, CA 90067-4705, USA

Dr Dog (Musician)
c/o Staff Member *Paradigm (Monterey)*
404 W Franklin St
Monterey, CA 93940-2303, USA

Dr Dre (Actor, Musician)
c/o Staff Member *Aftermath Entertainment/Crucial Films*
2220 Colorado Ave Fl 5
Santa Monica, CA 90404-3506, USA

Dreamstreet (Music Group)
c/o Staff Member *Adonis Productions*
175 Skillman St
Brooklyn, NY 11205-3537, USA

Drechsler, Dave (Athlete, Football Player)
1135 Arabian Farms Rd
Clover, SC 29710-8562, USA

Drechsler, Heike (Athlete, Track Athlete)
LAC Chemnitz
Reichenhainer Str 154
Chmnitz 09135, GERMANY

Dreckman, Bruce (Athlete, Baseball Player)
110 N Maple St
Marcus, IA 51035-7175, USA

Drees, Tom (Athlete, Baseball Player)
18638 Bearpath Trl
Eden Prairie, MN 55347-3459, USA

Dreesen, Tom (Actor, Comedian)
14538 Benefit St Unit 301
Sherman Oaks, CA 91403-5507, USA

Dreifort, Darren (Athlete, Baseball Player, Olympic Athlete)
463 Wynola St
Pacific Palisades, CA 90272-4243, USA

Dreifuss, Ruth (President)
Federal Chancellery
Bundeshaus-W
Bundesgasse
Beme 03033, SWITZERLAND

Dreiling, Greg (Athlete, Basketball Player)
5952 Willowross Way
Plano, TX 75093-4776, USA

Dreilling, Greg (Athlete, Basketball Player)
5952 Willowross Way
Plano, TX 75093-4776, USA

Drescher, Aviva (Reality Star)
c/o Michael Schweiger *Central Entertainment Group*
250 W 40th St Fl 12
New York, NY 10018-4601, USA

Drescher, Fran (Actor)
c/o Bonnie Liedtke *Authentic Talent & Literary Management*
3615 Eastham Dr # 650
Culver City, CA 90232-2410, USA

Drescher, Justin (Athlete, Football Player)
c/o Derrick Fox *Derrick Fox Management*
Prefers to be contacted by telephone
CA, USA

Drese, Ryan (Athlete, Baseball Player)
2201 Bear Lake Dr
Euless, TX 76039-6058, USA

Dressel, Chris (Athlete, Football Player)
410 Whiskey Hill Rd
Woodside, CA 94062-2571, USA

Dressendorfer, Kirk (Athlete, Baseball Player)
1105 Oaklands Dr
Round Rock, TX 78681-2704, USA

Dressler, Doug (Athlete, Football Player)
118 Frostwood Dr
Westwood, CA 96137-9647, USA

Dressler, Rob (Athlete, Baseball Player)
2037 17th Ave
Forest Grove, OR 97116-2709, USA

Drew, Cameron (Athlete, Baseball Player)
31 Highbridge Rd
Trenton, NJ 08620-9632, USA

Drew, David Jonathan (J D) (Athlete, Baseball Player)
5006 Old US 41 N
Hahira, GA 31632-4405, USA

Drew, Heather (Athlete, Golfer)
78160 Desert Mountain Cir
Bermuda Dunes, CA 92203-8151, USA

Drew, JD (Athlete, Baseball Player)
c/o Scott Boras *Boras Corporation*
18 Corporate Plaza Dr
Newport Beach, CA 92660-7901, USA

Drew, John (Athlete, Basketball Player)
2303 W Tidwell Rd Apt 3404
Houston, TX 77091-4766, USA

Drew, Larry (Athlete, Basketball Player)
c/o J.R. Hensley *ASM Sports*
450 Fashion Ave Ste 1700
New York, NY 10123-1700, USA

Drew, Malaya (Actor)
c/o Ray Moheet *Mainstay Entertainment*
9250 Beverly Blvd Fl 3
Beverly Hills, CA 90210-3710, USA

Drew, Sarah (Actor)
c/o Adam Griffin *LINK Entertainment*
11872 La Grange Ave
Los Angeles, CA 90025-5282, USA

Drew, Stephen (Athlete, Baseball Player)
2801 Country Club Dr
Valdosta, GA 31602-1665, USA

Drew, Tim (Athlete, Baseball Player)
5006 Old US 41 N
Hahira, GA 31632-4405, USA

Drewiske, Davis (Athlete, Hockey Player)
3327 Humboldt AveS# B
Minneapolis, MN 55408-3331

Drewrey, Willie (Athlete, Football Player)
2714 Cheryl Ct
Missouri City, TX 77459-2930, USA

Drexler, Clyde (Basketball Player, Coach)
Dade/Schultz
6442 Coldwater Canyon Ave Ste 206
North Hollywood, CA 91606-1174, USA

Drexler, Clyde (Athlete, Basketball Player, Olympic Athlete)
4045 Piping Rock Ln
Houston, TX 77027-3916, USA

Drexler, Millard (Business Person)
J. Crew
1 Ivy Cres
Lynchburg, VA 24513-1002, USA

Dreyer, Pamela (Athlete, Hockey Player, Olympic Athlete)
111 E 88th St Apt 4A
New York, NY 10128-1158, USA

Dreyer, Steve (Athlete, Baseball Player)
6018 Greywood Cir
Johnston, IA 50131-1687, USA

Dreyfuss, Richard (Actor, Producer)
PO Box 10459
Burbank, CA 91510-0459, USA

Drier, David (Congressman, Politician)
233 Cannon Hob
Washington, DC 20515-1308, USA

Drier, Moosey (Actor)
3501 Camino De La Cumbre
Sherman Oaks, CA 91423-4516, USA

Drier, Moosie (Actor, Director)
3501 Camino De La Cumbre
Sherman Oaks, CA 91423-4516, USA

Driessen, Dan (Athlete, Baseball Player)
208 Mitchellville Rd
Hilton Head Island, SC 29926-2820, USA

Drills, David (Athlete, Cycler, Olympic Athlete)
3736 Brookside Rd
Ottawa Hills, OH 43606-2614

Drinkwater, Carol (Writer)
c/o Ken McReddie *Ken McReddie Ltd*
101 Finsbury Pavement
London EC2A 1RS, UK

Drinkwater-Simmons, Maxine (Athlete, Baseball Player, Commentator)
18 Belmont Ave
Camden, ME 04843-2028, USA

Driscoll, Edward ""Terry"" (Athlete, Basketball Player)
101 Tayloe Cir
Williamsburg, VA 23185-8248, USA

Driscoll, Edward (Terry) (Athlete, Basketball Player)
William & Mary University
PO Box 399
Athletics Department
Williamsburg, VA 23187-0399, USA

Driscoll, Jean (Athlete, Olympic Athlete)
Pat Fettig
8142 Traverse Ct
Montgomery, OH 45242-7224, USA

Driscoll, Jim (Athlete, Baseball Player)
8050 E Indian School Rd
Scottsdale, AZ 85251-2612, USA

Driscoll, John (Actor)

Driscoll, Peter (Athlete, Hockey Player)
422 N Cypress Dr Apt B
Jupiter, FL 33469-3712, USA

Driscoll, Peter (Athlete, Hockey Player)
14839 Senator Way
Carmel, IN 46032-5128, USA

Driskill, Travis (Athlete, Baseball Player)
2308 Bunker Hill Cir
Plano, TX 75075-2924, USA

Driver, Adam (Actor)
c/o Randi Goldstein *Gersh*
41 Madison Ave Ste 3301
New York, NY 10010-2210, USA

Driver, Bruce (Athlete, Hockey Player)
21A Crest Ter
Montville, NJ 07045-9370

Driver, Donald (Athlete, Football Player)
1501 Noble Way
Flower Mound, TX 75022-8117, USA

Driver, Minnie (Actor)
c/o Lisa Kasteler *Wolf-Kasteler Public Relations*
6255 W Sunset Blvd Ste 1111
Los Angeles, CA 90028-7426, USA

Dr John (Musician)
53 Millstone Brook Rd
Southampton, NY 11968-2220, USA

Drobny, Jaroslav (Actor)
23 Kenilworth Court
Lower Richmond Road
London SW15 1EW, United Kingdom

Drogba, Didier (Athlete, Soccer Player)
c/o Staff Member *IMG Artists Worldwide (UK)*
The Light Box
111 Power Road
London W4 5PY, United Kingdom

Drolet, Claude (Horse Racer)
156 Greeley Lake Rd
Greeley, PA 18425-9765, USA

Drolet, Jean (Horse Racer)
101 10th St
Matamoras, PA 18336-1822, USA

Drollinger, Ralph (Athlete, Basketball Player)
22831 Market St
Newhall, CA 91321-3605, USA

Droppa, Ivan (Athlete, Hockey Player)
Palucanska 632/89
Liptovsky Mikulas 031 01, Slovakia

Drosdick, John G (Business Person)
Sunoco Inc
10 Penn Center 1801 Market St
Philadelphia, PA 19103, USA

Drougas, Tom (Athlete, Football Player)
821 Silver Star Dr
Hailey, ID 83333-5059, USA

Droughns, Reuben (Athlete, Football Player)
5955 S Elkhart Ct
Centennial, CO 80016-4710, USA

Drouin, Jude (Athlete, Hockey Player)
44479 Maltese Falcon Sq
Ashburn, VA 20147-3886

Drowning Pool (Music Group)
c/o Frank Cimler *10th Street Entertainment*
700 N San Vicente Blvd # G410
W Hollywood, CA 90069-5060, USA

Drozdov, Darren (Athlete, Football Player)

Druce, John (Athlete, Hockey Player)
Freedom 55 Financial 405-360 George St N
Peterborough, ON K9H 7E7, Canada

Druckenmiller, Jim (Athlete, Football Player)
8273 Still Oaks Cv
Cordova, TN 38018-9140, USA

Drucker, Eugene (Music Group, Musician)
I M G Artists
3 Burlington Lane
Chiswick
London W4 2TH, UNITED KINGDOM (UK)

Drudge, Matt (Internet Star, Journalist)
22661 SW 157th Ave
Miami, FL 33170-5906, USA

Drugg, Herb (Race Car Driver)
PO Box 916
Troy, NH 03465-0916, USA

Dru Hill (Music Group)
c/o Staff Member *WME/IMG*
9601 Wilshire Blvd
Beverly Hills, CA 90210-5213, USA

Druid, Devin (Actor)
c/o Gina Hoffman *Vision PR*
2 Penn Plz Rm 2601
New York, NY 10121-0001, USA

Druken, Harold (Athlete, Hockey Player)
16 Shaw Dr
Wayland, MA 01778-3214, USA

Drulia, Stan (Athlete, Hockey Player)
3939 Essex Pl
Fort Gratiot, MI 48059-3762, USA

Drummond, Alice (Actor)
351 E 50th St Apt 1
New York, NY 10022-7975, USA

Drummond, Ann Marie (Ree) (Chef, Writer)
c/o Ennis Kamcili *United Talent Agency (UTA)*
9336 Civic Center Dr
Beverly Hills, CA 90210-3604, USA

Drummond, Jonathan (Jon) (Athlete, Track Athlete)
c/o Staff Member *HS International Sports Management, Inc.*
9871 Irvine Center Dr
Irvine, CA 92618-4361, USA

Drummond, Roscoe (Writer)
6637 MacLean Dr Olde Dominion Square
McLean, VA 22101, USA

Drummond, Ryan (Actor)
c/o Staff Member *Bobby Ball Talent Agency*
4342 Lankershim Blvd
Universal City, CA 91602, USA

Drummond, Tim (Athlete, Baseball Player)
102 Haldane Ct
La Plata, MD 20646-4308, USA

Drungo, Elbert (Athlete, Football Player)
216 Lake Chateau Dr
Hermitage, TN 37076-3072, USA

Drury, Chris (Athlete, Hockey Player, Olympic Athlete)
25 Central Park W Apt 27J
New York, NY 10023-7200, USA

Drury, James (Actor)
12126 Osage Park Dr
Houston, TX 77065-3812, USA

Drury, Ted (Athlete, Hockey Player)
28 Cottage Pl
Trumbull, CT 06611-5227, USA

Drury, Ted (Athlete, Hockey Player)
2507 Greenwood Ave
Wilmette, IL 60091-1303, USA

Druschel, Rick (Athlete, Football Player)
724 Cochran Dr
Greensburg, PA 15601-4610, USA

Drut, Guy J (Athlete, Track Athlete)
Maine
Coulommiers 77120, FRANCE

Dry, Tim (Actor)
c/o Staff Member *Coolwaters Productions*
10061 Riverside Dr # 531
Toluca Lake, CA 91602-2560, USA

Dryden, Dave (Athlete, Hockey Player)
2257 All Saints Cres
Oakville, ON L6J 5N1, Canada

Dryden, Kenneth (Ken) (Athlete, Hockey Player)
House of Commons
58 Poplar Plains Rd
Toronto, ON M4V 2M8, Canada

Dryer, Fred (Actor, Athlete, Football Player)
1700 W Burbank Blvd # 100
Burbank, CA 91506-1355, USA

Drynan, Jeanie (Actor)
c/o Monica Keightley *Mollison Keightley Management*
139 Cathedral St
Woolloomooloo
Sydney NSW 02011, AUSTRALIA

Drysdale, Cliff (Sportscaster, Tennis Player)
Landfall
1801 Eastwood Road #F
Wilmington, NC 28403, USA

Drzewiecki, Ron (Athlete, Football Player)
10412 W White Manor Ct
Franksville, WI 53126-9572, USA

D. Schakowsky, Janice (Congressman, Politician)
2367 Rayburn Hob
Washington, DC 20515-1304, USA

DSquared2 (Fashion Designer)
DSquared2
220 W 19th St Fl 11
New York, NY 10011-4035, USA

DuArt, Louise (Religious Leader, Television Host)

Dubble, Curtis (Religious Leader)
Church of Brethren
1451 Dundee Ave
Elgin, IL 60120-1694, USA

Dube, Joseph (Joe) (Athlete, Wrestler)
8821 Eaton Ave
Jacksonville, FL 32211-0306, USA

Dube, Norm (Athlete, Hockey Player)
1590 Rue John-Griffith
Sherbrooke, QC J1J 4L4, Canada

Dubee, Rich (Athlete, Baseball Player)
8517 Eagle Preserve Way
Sarasota, FL 34241-8505, USA

Dubenion, Elbert (Athlete, Football Player)
867 High St Ste B
Worthington, OH 43085-4154, USA

Duberman, Justin (Athlete, Hockey Player)
5635 S Oak St
Hinsdale, IL 60521-5062

Dubielewicz, Wade (Athlete, Hockey Player)
132 Wintergreen Ave
Hamden, CT 06514-3346

Dubinsky, Brandon (Athlete, Hockey Player)
10110 Salix Cir
Anchorage, AK 99507-4138, USA

Dubinsky, Steve (Athlete, Hockey Player)
1367 Cavell Ave
Highland Park, IL 60035-2805, USA

Dublinski, James L (Athlete, Football Player)
939 S Donner Way Apt 304
Salt Lake City, UT 84108-2148, USA

Dublinski, Tom (Athlete, Football Player)
509 Aurora Ave Unit 613
Naperville, IL 60540-6262, USA

Dubner, Stephen J (Writer)
c/o Suzanne Gluck *WME/IMG (NY)*
11 Madison Ave Fl 18
New York, NY 10010-3669, USA

Dubois, Allison (Astrologist/Medium/Psychic)
Smarter Than They Think, LLC
11111 N Scottsdale Rd Ste 205
Scottsdale, AZ 85254-6732, USA

Dubois, Brian (Athlete, Baseball Player)
3 Soartan Pl
Sorinefield, IL 62703-4715, USA

Dubois, Janet (Actor)
c/o Staff Member *Cunningham Escott Slevin & Doherty (CESD)*
10635 Santa Monica Blvd Ste 130
Los Angeles, CA 90025-8306, USA

Dubois, Jason (Athlete, Baseball Player)
2204 Lord Seaton Cir
Virginia Beach, VA 23454-2923, USA

DuBois, Marta (Actor)
Three Moons Entertainment
5441 E Beverly Blvd Ste G
Los Angeles, CA 90022-2243, USA

Dubois, Phil (Athlete, Football Player)
405 Speedway Ave
Missoula, MT 59802-5475, USA

Dubose, Brian (Baseball Player)
Ted Williams
15336 Oakfield St
Detroit, MI 48227-1532, USA

Dubose, Eric (Athlete, Baseball Player)
326 County Road 8
Gilbertown, AL 36908-2211, USA

DuBose, James (Director, Producer)
Visceral Media Group
8484 Wilshire Blvd # 850A
Beverly Hills, CA 90211-3227, USA

Dubose, Jimmy (Athlete, Football Player)
11420 Walker Rd
Thonotosassa, FL 33592-3616, USA

Dubovsky, Dana (Producer)
American World Pictures
21700 Oxnard St Ste 1770
Woodland Hills, CA 91367-7594, USA

Dubrow, Heather (Actor, Reality Star)
c/o Lance Klein *WME/IMG*
9601 Wilshire Blvd
Beverly Hills, CA 90210-5213, USA

Dubzinski, Walt (Athlete, Football Player)
158 Lovewell St
Gardner, MA 01440-3552, USA

Ducasse, Alain (Chef)
Groupe Alain Ducasse
Hotel de Paris Louis XV Restaurant
Monte Carlo, Monaco, USA

Ducasse, Vladimir (Athlete, Football Player)
c/o Joe Linta *JL Sports*
1204 Main St Ste 179
Branford, CT 06405-3787, USA

Ducey, Rob (Athlete, Baseball Player)
699 Richmond Close
Tarpon Springs, FL 34688-8423, USA

Duchesnay, Isamelle (Dancer)
Im Steinach 30
Oberstdorf 87561, GERMANY

Duchesnay, Paul (Figure Skater)
Bundesleistungszentrum
Rossbichstr 2-6
Oberstdorf 87561, GERMANY

Duchesne, Steve (Athlete, Hockey Player)
2108 Collins Path
Colleyville, TX 76034-7323, USA

Duchovny, David (Actor, Producer)
320 Central Park W # 19A
New York, NY 10025-7659, USA

Duchscherer, Justin (Athlete, Baseball Player)
3405 E Birchwood Pl
Chandler, AZ 85249-4564, USA

Duck Dynasty (Reality Star)
Duck Commander
117 Kings Ln
West Monroe, LA 71292-9430, USA

Duckett, Forey (Athlete, Football Player)
7518 Winona Ave N
Seattle, WA 98103-4838, USA

Duckett, Mahlon (Athlete, Baseball Player)
5325 Old York Rd Apt 611
Philadelphia, PA 19141-2952, USA

Duckett, Richard (Athlete, Basketball Player)
10 Wyckham Rd
Spring Lake, NJ 07762-2255, USA

Duckett, TJ (Athlete, Football Player)
c/o Joel Segal *Lagardere Unlimited (NY)*
456 Washington St Apt 9L
New York, NY 10013-1555, USA

Ducksworth, Sheila (Producer)
c/o Staff Member *Creative Artists Agency (CAA)*
2000 Avenue of the Stars Ste 100
Los Angeles, CA 90067-4705, USA

Duckworth, Brandon (Athlete, Baseball Player)
4460 W 6095 S
Salt Lake City, UT 84118-5289, USA

Duckworth, Jim (Athlete, Baseball Player)
1881 Brittlebush Ln
Johns Island, SC 29455-6716, USA

Duckworth, Tyler (Reality Star)
c/o Len Evans *Project Publicity*
540 W 43rd St
New York, NY 10036, USA

Duda, Lucas (Athlete, Baseball Player)
c/o Dan Horwitz *Beverly Hills Sports Council*
1666 20th St Ste 200A
Santa Monica, CA 90404-3828, USA

Duda, Mark (Athlete, Football Player)
1707 Cherry St
Scranton, PA 18505-3972, USA

Dudek, Anne (Actor)
c/o Michael Geiser *Jill Fritzo Public Relations*
208 E 51st St # 305
New York, NY 10022-6557, USA

Dudek, Joseph A (Joe) (Athlete, Football Player)
6 Veterans Rd Apt 12
Amherst, NH 03031-2738, USA

Dudek, Mitch (Athlete, Football Player)
1241 Forest Ave
Wilmette, IL 60091-1656, USA

Duden, H Richard (Dick) Jr (Athlete, Football Player)
11 Old Station Rd
Severna Park, MD 21146-4601, USA

Dudikoff, Michael (Actor)
PO Box 7000-602
Redondo Beach, CA 90277, USA

Dudley, Brian (Athlete, Football Player)
6319 London Ave
Rancho Cucamonga, CA 91737-3646, USA

Dudley, Charles (Athlete, Basketball Player)
4032 42nd Ave S
Seattle, WA 98118-1121, USA

Dudley, Chris (Athlete, Basketball Player)
1150 Fairway Rd
Lake Oswego, OR 97034-2818, USA

Dudley, James (Baseball Player)
Baltimore Elite Giants
607 Delafield Pl NW
Washington, DC 20011-4054, USA

Dudley, Olivia Taylor (Actor)
c/o Brett Ruttenberg *Imprint PR*
6121 W Sunset Blvd
Neuehouse
Los Angeles, CA 90028-6442, USA

Dudley, Rick (Athlete, Coach, Hockey Player)
5150 Oakhill Dr
Lewiston, NY 14092-1857, USA

Dudley, Rickey (Athlete, Football Player)
4110 Arron Ct
Lewisville, TX 75077-7916, USA

Duell, Chad (Actor)
c/o Joseph Le *Joseph Le Talent Agency*
3500 W Olive Ave Ste 300
Burbank, CA 91505-4647, USA

Duenkel, Ginny (Athlete, Olympic Athlete, Swimmer)
2132 NE 17th Ter Fl 5
Wilton Manors, FL 33305-2414, USA

Duenkel Fuldner, Virginia (Swimmer)
2132 NE 17th Ter # 500
Wilton Manors, FL 33305-2414, USA

Duensing, Brian Duensing (Athlete, Baseball Player)
7710 N 207th Cir
Elkhorn, NE 68022-1154, USA

Duerod, Terry (Athlete, Basketball Player)
6S42 Chirrewa St
Westland, MI 48185-2807, USA

Dues, Hal (Athlete, Baseball Player)
3932 Amanda Dr
Dickinson, TX 77539-6405, USA

Dueto Voces del Rancho (Musician)
c/o Staff Member *Sony Music (Miami)*
404 Washington Ave Ste 700
Miami Beach, FL 33139-6615, USA

Dufek, Don (Athlete, Football Player)
570 S Maple Rd
Ann Arbor, MI 48103-3837, USA

Dufek, Joe (Athlete, Football Player)
17015 N 7th St Ste 1
Phoenix, AZ 85022-2404, USA

Duff, Haylie (Actor, Musician)
c/o Lauren Auslander *LUNA*
116 Nassau St # 615
New York, NY 10038-2402, USA

Duff, Hilary (Actor, Musician)
c/o Kristen Foster *PMK/BNC Public Relations*
1840 Century Park E Ste 1400
Los Angeles, CA 90067-2115, USA

Duff, Jamal (Athlete, Football Player)
PO Box 20058
Long Beach, CA 90801-3058, USA

Duff, John (Athlete, Football Player)
PO Box 20058
Long Beach, CA 90801-3058, USA

Duff, Matt (Athlete, Baseball Player)
Major League Bowhunter
500 N Highway 18
Chandler, OK 74834-1218, USA

Duff, T Richard (Dick) (Athlete, Hockey Player)
4-7 Elmwood Ave S
Mississauga, ON L5G 3J6, Canada

Duffalo, Jim (Athlete, Baseball Player)
1505 Savannah St
Mesquite, TX 75149-8715, USA

Duffer, Matt (Director, Producer)
c/o Joe Cohen *Creative Artists Agency (CAA)*
2000 Avenue of the Stars Ste 100
Los Angeles, CA 90067-4705, USA

Duffer, Ross (Director, Producer)
c/o Joe Cohen *Creative Artists Agency (CAA)*
2000 Avenue of the Stars Ste 100
Los Angeles, CA 90067-4705, USA

Duffie, John (Athlete, Baseball Player)
177 Lakeside Cir
Douglas, GA 31535-6627, USA

Duffield, David (Business Person)
PeopleSoft Inc
4460 Hacienda Dr
Pleasanton, CA 94588-2761, USA

Duffner, Mark (Coach, Football Coach)
University of Maryland
Athletic Dept
College Park, MD 20740, USA

Duffus, Parris (Athlete, Hockey Player)
8609 Timbermill Pl
Fort Wayne, IN 46804-3411, USA

Duffy, Aimee Anne (DUFFY) (Musician)
c/o Staff Member *Island Records*
825 8th Ave Rm C2
New York, NY 10019-7472, USA

Duffy, Brian (Astronaut)
14805 Pristine Dr
Colorado Springs, CO 80921-3549, USA

Duffy, Chris (Athlete, Baseball Player)
14332 N 174th Ln
Surprise, AZ 85388-7845, USA

Duffy, Dorothy (Actor)
PFD
Drury House
34-43 Russell St
London WC2B 5HA, UNITED KINGDOM (UK)

Duffy, Frank (Athlete, Baseball Player)
3750 N Country Club Rd APT 27
Tucson, AZ 85716-1262, USA

Duffy, Julia (Actor)
540 Live Oak Circle Dr
Calabasas, CA 91302-2139, USA

Duffy, Karen (Actor, Model)
c/o Staff Member *Rebel Entertainment Partners*
5700 Wilshire Blvd Ste 470
Los Angeles, CA 90036-4379, USA

Duffy, Keith (Music Group)
Carol Assoc-War Mgmt
Bushy Park Road 57 Meadowgate
Dublin, IRELAND

Duffy, Matt (Athlete, Baseball Player)
c/o Paul Cohen *TWC Sports Management (LA)*
445 W Erie St Ste 205
Chicago, IL 60654-5733, USA

Duffy, Patrick (Actor, Director, Producer)
c/o Annick Muller *Wolf-Kasteler Public Relations*
40 Exchange Pl Ste 704
New York, NY 10005-2778, USA

Duffy, Roger (Athlete, Football Player)
6509 Lutz Ave NW
Massillon, OH 44646-9512, USA

Duffy, Ryan (Correspondent)
c/o Staff Member *United Talent Agency (UTA)*
9336 Civic Center Dr
Beverly Hills, CA 90210-3604, USA

Duffy, Troy (Actor, Director, Writer)
c/o David Krintzman *Morris Yorn Barnes Levine Krintzman Rubenstein Kohner & Gellman*
2000 Avenue of the Stars Ste 300N
Tower N Fl 3
Los Angeles, CA 90067-4704, USA

Dufner, Jason (Athlete, Golfer)
c/o Clarke Jones *IMG (Cleveland)*
1360 E 9th St Ste 100
Cleveland, OH 44114-1730, USA

Dufour, Luc (Athlete, Hockey Player)
334 Rue des Champs-Elysees
Chicoutimi, QC G7H 2V8, Canada

Dufresne, Donald (Athlete, Coach, Hockey Player)
c/o Staff Member *Rimouski Oceanic Hockey Club*
CP 816 Succ A
Rimouski, QC G5L 7C9, Canada

Dugan, Dennis (Actor, Director)
4505 Woodley Ave
Encino, CA 91436-2721, USA

Dugan, Fred (Athlete, Football Player)
1827 Tamiami Trl N
Nokomis, FL 34275, USA

Dugan, Jeff (Athlete, Football Player)
13701 Ashcroft Rd
Savage, MN 55378-2374, USA

Dugans, Ron (Athlete, Football Player)
1549 Coleman St
Tallahassee, FL 32310-6016, USA

Duggan, Catherine (Athlete, Golfer)
5923 Marilyn Dr
Knoxville, TN 37914-5149, USA

Duggan, Jim (Athlete, Wrestler)
1328 Hornsby Cir Apt A
Lugoff, SC 29078-9722, USA

Duggan, Jim (Athlete, Football Player)
1328 Hornsby Cir Apt A
Lugoff, SC 29078-9722, USA

Duggar, Michelle (Reality Star)
548 Arbor Acres Ave
Springdale, AR 72762-6256, USA

Dugger, John S (Artist)
410 Evelyn Ave Apt 201
Albany, CA 94706-1358, USA

Duguary, Ron (Actor, Athlete, Hockey Player)
982 Ponte Vedra Blvd
Ponte Vedra Beach, FL 32082-4068, USA

Duguay, Ron (Athlete, Hockey Player)
20 Sea Winds Ln N
Ponte Vedra, FL 32082-2731, USA

Duhamel, Josh (Actor)
c/o Ruth Bernstein *Viewpoint Inc*
8820 Wilshire Blvd Ste 220
Beverly Hills, CA 90211-2622, USA

Duhe, Adam J (A J) Jr (Athlete, Football Player)
379 Coconut Cir
Weston, FL 33326-3320, USA

Duhon, Chris (Athlete, Basketball Player)
c/o Bill Duffy *BDA Sports Management*
700 Ygnacio Valley Rd Ste 330
Walnut Creek, CA 94596-3838, USA

Duhon, Josh (Actor)
c/o Abby Bluestone *Innovative Artists*
1505 10th St
Santa Monica, CA 90401-2805, USA

Duhon, Robert (Bobby) (Athlete, Football Player)
4384 Whitewater Creek Rd NW
Atlanta, GA 30327-3958, USA

Duich, Steve (Athlete, Football Player)
PO Box 2
Descanso, CA 91916-0002, USA

Dujardin, Jean (Actor)
JD Prod
28 Avenue De Messine
Paris 75018, FRANCE

Dukakis, Olympia (Actor)
684 Broadway Apt 6E
New York, NY 10012-1123, USA

Duke, Bill (Actor, Director, Producer)
Duke Media
7510 W Sunset Blvd Ste 523
Los Angeles, CA 90046-3408, USA

Duke, Clark (Actor)
c/o Dan Weiner *Paradigm (Monterey)*
404 W Franklin St
Monterey, CA 93940-2303, USA

Duke, Ken (Athlete, Golfer)
25 Island Rd
Stuart, FL 34996-7006, USA

Duke, Randolph (Fashion Designer)
c/o Diana Bianchini *Di Moda Public Relations*
2525 Main St Ste 203
Santa Monica, CA 90405-3538, USA

Duke, Robin (Actor)
c/o Staff Member *Oscars Abrams Zimel & Associates*
438 Queen St E
Toronto, ON M5A 1T4, CANADA

Duke, Winston (Actor)
c/o Marianna Shafran *Shafran PR*
195 S Beverly Dr Ste 414
Beverly Hills, CA 90212-3044, USA

Duke, Zach (Athlete, Baseball Player)
221 Harper Ct
Keller, TX 76248-3022, USA

Dukes, Elijah (Athlete, Baseball Player)
2430 Cedar Trace Cir # B
Tampa, FL 33613-5628, USA

Dukes, Jamie (Athlete, Football Player)
2452 Stone Manor Dr
Buford, GA 30519-7686, USA

Dukes, Jan (Athlete, Baseball Player)
959 Helena Dr
Sunnyvale, CA 94087-4126, USA

Dukes, Michael (Athlete, Football Player)
115 N 23rd St
Nederland, TX 77627-5909, USA

Dukes, The (Music Group)
11 Chartfield Square
London, England SW15, United Kingdom

Dukes, Tom (Athlete, Baseball Player)
325 Monte Vista Rd
Arcadia, CA 91007-6147, USA

Duke Spirit, The (Music Group)
c/o Staff Member *Paradigm (Monterey)*
404 W Franklin St
Monterey, CA 93940-2303, USA

Dukochitz, Jonathan (Actor, Musician)
c/o Staff Member *Innovative Artists*
1505 10th St
Santa Monica, CA 90401-2805, USA

Dulany, Caitlin (Actor)
Gersh Agency
232 N Canon Dr
Beverly Hills, CA 90210-5302, USA

Duley, Ed (Athlete, Football Player)
5219 N Casa Blanca Dr
Paradise Valley, AZ 85253-6201, USA

Dulgan, John (Director)
54A Tite St
London SW3 4JA, UNITED KINGDOM (UK)

Dulhalde, Eduardo (President)
Casa de Gobiemo
Balcarce 50
Buenos Aires 01064, ARGENTINA

Duliba, Bob (Athlete, Baseball Player)
327 Philadelphia Ave
West Pittston, PA 18643-2146, USA

Dullea, Keir (Actor)
c/o Staff Member *Bret Adams Agency*
448 W 44th St
New York, NY 10036-5220, USA

Dulli, Greg (Musician)
3211 Hamilton Way
Los Angeles, CA 90026-2147, USA

Dumars III, Joe (Athlete, Basketball Player)
1400 Scenic Ct
Bloomfield Hills, MI 48302-2351, USA

Dumas, Marlene (Artist)
Tolstraat 94 HS
Amsterdam 1073 BE, The Netherlands

Dumas, Michel (Athlete, Hockey Player)
c/o Staff Member *Chicago Blackhawks*
1901 W Madison St
Chicago, IL 60612-2459, USA

Dumas, Mike (Athlete, Football Player)
2686 Mohican Ave SE
Grand Rapids, MI 49546-6988, USA

Dumas, Tony (Athlete, Basketball Player)
7806 Spinnaker Cv
Rowlett, TX 75089-2622, USA

Dumatrait, Phil (Athlete, Baseball Player)
1412 Stub Oak Ave
Bakersfield, CA 93307-6917, USA

Dumbauld, Jonathan (Athlete, Football Player)
1530 E Sagebrush Ct
Gilbert, AZ 85296-2522, USA

Dumelie, Larry (Athlete, Football Player)
3619 4th Line Rd
Osgoode, ON KOA 2WO, Canada

Dumervil, Elvis (Athlete, Football Player)
1717 N Bayshore Dr Apt A-2641
Miami, FL 33132-1180, USA

Dumler, Doug (Athlete, Football Player)
1526 Peterson St
Fort Collins, CO 80524-4130, USA

Dummit, Dennis (Athlete, Football Player)
111 Via Di Roma Walk
Long Beach, CA 90803-4156, USA

Dumont, Emma (Actor)
c/o Jennifer Merlino *Untitled Entertainment*
350 S Beverly Dr Ste 200
Beverly Hills, CA 90212-4819, USA

Dumont, J P (Athlete, Hockey Player)
1512 Kimberleigh Ct
Franklin, TN 37069-7226, USA

Dumont, Sky (Actor)
ZBF Agentur
Leopoldstr 19
Munich 80802, GERMANY

Dumont, Tom (Musician)
326 Glendora Ave
Long Beach, CA 90803-1924, USA

Dumoulin, Dan (Athlete, Baseball Player)
3 Green Hills Ct
Greentown, IN 46936-1039, USA

Dunagan, Donnie (Actor)
422 S Bishop St
San Angelo, TX 76901-4126, USA

Dunagin, Ralph (Cartoonist)
North American Syndicate
235 E 45th St
New York, NY 10017-3305, USA

Dunaway, Craig (Athlete, Football Player)
1000 Westchester Way
Birmingham, MI 48009-2954, USA

Dunaway, Faye (Actor)
c/o Tony Cloer *Blue Ridge Entertainment*
3 Columbus Cir Fl 15
New York, NY 10019-8716, USA

Dunaway, James E (Athlete, Football Player)
170 Mount Carmel Church Rd
Sandy Hook, MS 39478-9793, USA

Dunbar, Bonnie J (Astronaut)
2200 Todville Rd
Seabrook, TX 77586-3005, USA

Dunbar, Dale (Athlete, Hockey Player)
41 Nahant Ave
Winthrop, MA 02152-1514, USA

Dunbar, Dr. bonnie j (Astronaut)
2200 Todville Rd
Seabrook, TX 77586-3005, USA

Dunbar, Huey (Musician)
c/o Staff Member *Sony Music (Miami)*
404 Washington Ave Ste 700
Miami Beach, FL 33139-6615, USA

Dunbar, Lance (Athlete, Football Player)
c/o Brian E. Overstreet *E.O. Sports Management*
1314 Texas St Ste 1212
Houston, TX 77002-3525, USA

Dunbar, Matt (Athlete, Baseball Player)
6328 County Donegal Ct
Charlotte, NC 28277-9652, USA

Dunbar, Rockmond (Actor)
Flypaper Films
20700 Ventura Blvd Ste 328
Woodland Hills, CA 91364-6282, USA

Dunbar, Vaughn (Athlete, Football Player)
1085 Greatwood Mnr
Alpharetta, GA 30005-7459, USA

Duncan, Allison (Race Car Driver)
McNally Racing
8636 Antelope North Rd
Antelope, CA 95843-3930, USA

Duncan, Andy (Basketball Player)
Rochester Royals
608 Berry Pl
Marion, VA 24354-4168, USA

Duncan, Angus (Actor)
Thomas Jennings
28035 Dorothy Dr Ste 210A
Agoura, CA 91301-2685, USA

Duncan, Brian (Athlete, Football Player)
739 Elm St
Graham, TX 76450-3018, USA

Duncan, Chris (Athlete, Baseball Player)
1220 N La Cienega Blvd APT E1
W Hollywood, CA 90069-2413, USA

Duncan, Courtney (Athlete, Baseball Player)
121 Adalene Ln
Madison, AL 35757-8423, USA

Duncan, Curtis (Athlete, Football Player)
4915 Glen Hollow St
Sugar Land, TX 77479-3804, USA

Duncan, Dan (Business Person)
Enterprise Products Partners L.P
1100 Louisiana St
Houston, TX 77002-5227, USA

Duncan, Dave (Athlete, Baseball Player)
205 Hunters Glenn Ln
Ln
Kimberling City, MO 65686-9862, USA

Duncan, Dennis (Athlete, Baseball Player)
7650 N Zack Rd
Columbia, MO 65202-9240, USA

Duncan, Donna (Race Car Driver)
Mike Murphy Racing
PO Box 3936
Portsmouth, VA 23701-0936, USA

Duncan, Iain (Athlete, Hockey Player)
1956 W Alexis Rd Apt 406
Toledo, OH 43613-5406, USA

Duncan, Jamie (Athlete, Football Player)
217 Remi Dr
New Castle, DE 19720-5624, USA

Duncan, Jeff (Congressman, Politician)
116 Cannon Hob
Washington, DC 20515-0913, USA

Duncan, Jeff (Athlete, Baseball Player)
825 Lincoln Ln
Frankfort, IL 60423-1087, USA

Duncan, Jeff (Congressman, Politician)
116 Cannon Hob
Washington, DC 20515-0913, USA

Duncan, Ken (Athlete, Football Player)
4 Christina Ave
Camarillo, CA 93012-8102, USA

Duncan, lain (Athlete, Hockey Player)
453 Cedarwood Rd
Avon Lake, OH 44012-3141, USA

Duncan, Leslie (Speedy) (Athlete, Football Player)
1607 Porter Way
Stockton, CA 95207-4126, USA

Duncan, Lindsay (Actor)
c/o Simon Beresford *Dalzell & Beresford Ltd*
55 Charterhouse St
The Paddock Suite, The Courtyard
London EC1M 6HA, UNITED KINGDOM (UK)

Duncan, Mariano (Athlete, Baseball Player)
11142 NW 71st Ter
Doral, FL 33178-3789, USA

Duncan, Melvin (Athlete, Baseball Player)
PO Box 980407
470 Bedford Dr
Ypsilanti, MI 48198-0407, USA

Duncan, Meredith (Athlete, Golfer)
244 Arthur Ave
Shreveport, LA 71105-3626, USA

Duncan, Mike (Race Car Driver)
PO Box 21235
Bakersfield, CA 93390-1235, USA

Duncan, Patrick S (Director, Producer, Writer)
c/o David Kanter *Anonymous Content*
3532 Hayden Ave
Culver City, CA 90232-2413, USA

Duncan, Sandy (Actor)
c/o Andrew Lawler *Douglas Gorman Rothacker & Wilhelm Inc*
33 W 46th St Ste 801
New York, NY 10036-4103, USA

duncan, Shelley (Athlete, Baseball Player)
6547 N Turnberry Dr
Tucson, AZ 85718-2600, USA

Duncan, Speedy (Athlete, Football Player)
1607 Porter Way
Stockton, CA 95207-4126, USA

Duncan, Tim (Athlete, Basketball Player)
21321 Babcock Rd Lot 3
San Antonio, TX 78255-2231, USA

Duncanson, Craig (Athlete, Hockey Player)
Laurentian University
935 Ramsey Lake Dr
Attn: Hockey Program
Sudbury, ON P3E 2C6, Canada

Dundas, Jason (Reality Star)
c/o Michelle Elliot
PO Box 128
Surry Hills NSW 2010, AUSTRALIA

Dundas, Rocky (Athlete, Hockey Player)
14 Nantucket Dr
Richmond Hill, ON L4E 3V1, Canada

Dunegan, Jim (Athlete, Baseball Player)
20246 180th St
New London, IA 52645-8555, USA

Dungey, Merrin (Actor)
2906 Nichols Canyon Rd
Los Angeles, CA 90046-1241, USA

Dungy, Tony (Athlete, Coach, Football Coach, Football Player)
16604 Villalenda De Avila
Tampa, FL 33613-5200, USA

Dunham, Archie W (Business Person)
ConocoPhilips Inc
600 N Dairy Ashford Rd
Houston, TX 77079-1100, USA

Dunham, Chip (Cartoonist)
Universal Press Syndicate
4520 Main St Ste 340
Kansas City, MO 64111-7705, USA

Dunham, Duane R (Business Person)
Bethlehem Steel Corp
1170 8th Ave
Bethlehem, PA 18018-2255, USA

Dunham, Jeff (Comedian)
c/o Judi Brown *Levity Entertainment Group (LEG)*
6701 Center Dr W Ste 300
Los Angeles, CA 90045-2482, USA

Dunham, John L (Business Person)
May Department Stores
611 Olive St
Saint Louis, MO 63101-1702, USA

Dunham, Lena (Actor, Writer)
Lenny
8383 Wilshire Blvd Ste 1050
Beverly Hills, CA 90211-2415, USA

Dunham, Michael (Mike) (Athlete, Hockey Player, Olympic Athlete)
511 Elm St
Concord, MA 01742-2212, USA

Dunigan, Matt (Athlete, Football Player)
CanWest Global Communications
3100 CanWest Global
Place Attn: Road Grill Show
Winnipeg, MB R3B 3L7, Canada

Dunkie, Nancy (Basketball Player)
University of California
Campus Police
Berkeley, CA 94720-0001, USA

Dunkle, Nancy (Athlete, Basketball Player, Olympic Athlete)

Dunlap, Alexander W (Astronaut)
721 Parkside Dr
Woodstock, GA 30188-6057, USA

Dunlap, Carlos (Athlete, Football Player)
c/o Drew Rosenhaus *Rosenhaus Sports Representation*
3921 Alton Rd # 440
Miami Beach, FL 33140-3852, USA

Dunlap, Grant (Athlete, Baseball Player)
1440 Paseo De Las Flores
Encinitas, CA 92024-2363, USA

Dunlap, King (Athlete, Football Player)

Dunlap, Page (Athlete, Golfer)
8728 Misty Creek Dr
Sarasota, FL 34241-9561, USA

Dunlap, Scott (Athlete, Golfer)
104 Summerour Vale
Duluth, GA 30097-2464, USA

Dunleavy, Michael J (Mike) (Athlete, Basketball Player, Coach)
127 S Carmelina Ave
Los Angeles, CA 90049-3901, USA

Dunleavy, Mike (Athlete, Basketball Player)
Golden State Warriors
127 S Carmelina Ave
Los Angeles, CA 90049-3901, USA

Dunleavy Jr, Mike (Athlete, Basketball Player)
127 S Carmelina Ave
Los Angeles, CA 90049-3901, USA

Dunleavy Sr, Mike (Athlete, Basketball Player, Coach)
c/o Warren LeGarie *Warren LeGarie Sports Management*
1108 Masonic Ave
San Francisco, CA 94117-2915, USA

Dunlop, Andy (Music Group, Musician)
Wildlife Entertainment
21 Heathmans Road
London SW6 4TJ, UNITED KINGDOM (UK)

Dunlop, Blake (Athlete, Hockey Player)
8112 Maryland Ave
Saint Louis, MO 63105-3729, USA

Dunn, Adam (Athlete, Baseball Player)
11109 Beinhorn Rd
Houston, TX 77024-4507, USA

Dunn, Alan (Athlete, Baseball Player)
8536 Glenfield Dr
Baton Rouge, LA 70809-5214, USA

Dunn, Colton (Actor)
c/o Joel Zadak *Artists First*
9465 Wilshire Blvd Ste 900
Beverly Hills, CA 90212-2608, USA

Dunn, Dave (Athlete, Hockey Player)
1433 Hamilton St
Regina, SK S4R 7V4, Canada

Dunn, Douglas (Writer)
c/o Staff Member *The Rights House (UK)*
Drury House
34-43 Russell St
London WC2B 5HA, UNITED KINGDOM

Dunn, Gary (Athlete, Football Player)
243 Navajo St
Tavernier, FL 33070-2119, USA

Dunn, Gertie (Baseball Player)
PO Box 88
Chadds Ford, PA 19317-0088, USA

Dunn, Jim (Race Car Driver)
840 Kallin Ave
Long Beach, CA 90815-5004, USA

Dunn, Jourdan (Actor, Model)
c/o Kate Rosen *The Lede Company*
401 Broadway Ste 206
New York, NY 10013-3033, USA

Dunn, Justin (Athlete, Baseball Player)
c/o Staff Member *New York Mets*
123-01 Roosevelt Avenue
Shea Stadium
Flushing, NY 11368-1699, USA

Dunn, Keldrick (K.D.) (Athlete, Football Player)
1640 Township Ter
McDonough, GA 30252-6813, USA

Dunn, Kevin (Actor)
c/o Steven Siebert *Lighthouse Entertainment Group*
9229 W Sunset Blvd Ste 630
W Hollywood, CA 90069-3419, USA

Dunn, Mike (Race Car Driver)
Team Mopar
PO Box 128
Wrightsville, PA 17368-0128, USA

Dunn, Moira (Athlete, Golfer)
15803 Bridgewater Ln
Tampa, FL 33624-1044, USA

Dunn, Nora (Actor, Comedian)
c/o Steven Siebert *Lighthouse Entertainment Group*
9229 W Sunset Blvd Ste 630
W Hollywood, CA 90069-3419, USA

Dunn, Patricia (Tricia) (Athlete, Hockey Player, Olympic Athlete)
4 Huson Ave
Derry, NH 03038-4217, USA

Dunn, Perry Lee (Athlete, Football Player)
64 Glenway Pl
Brandon, MS 39042-2545, USA

Dunn, Ron (Athlete, Baseball Player)
1161 Husted Ave
San Jose, CA 95125-3633, USA

Dunn, Ronnie (Musician, Songwriter)
c/o Jake Basden *Big Machine Records*
1219 16th Ave S
Nashville, TN 37212-2901, USA

Dunn, Sarah Jayne (Actor)
RDF Management
c/o Michael Ford
3-6 Kenrick Place
London W1U 6HD, UNITED KINGDOM

Dunn, Scott (Athlete, Baseball Player)
1331 Arizona Ash St
San Antonio, TX 78232-3409, USA

Dunn, Steve (Athlete, Baseball Player)
484 Broadmoor Dr
Maryville, TN 37803-6575, USA

Dunn, Todd (Athlete, Baseball Player)
12030 London Lake Dr W
Jacksonville, FL 32258-3317, USA

Dunn, T R (Athlete, Basketball Player)
1014 19th St SW
Birmingham, AL 35211-3623, USA

Dunn, Warrick (Athlete, Football Player)
6016 Beacon Shores St
Tampa, FL 33616-1317, USA

Dunne, Griffin (Actor, Director)
26 E 10th St # 1011F
New York, NY 10003-5977, USA

Dunne, Mike (Athlete, Baseball Player, Olympic Athlete)
5115 W Ancient Oak Dr
Peoria, IL 61615-2247, USA

Dunne, Robin (Actor)
c/o Jennifer Goldhar *Characters Talent Agency (Toronto)*
8 Elm St Fl 2
Toronto, ON M5G 1G7, CANADA

Dunne, Roisin (Music Group, Musician)
Rave Booking
PO Box 310780
Jamaica, NY 11431-0780, USA

Dunnigan, T Kevin (Business Person)
Thomas & Betts Corp
8155 Thomas & Betts Blvd
Memphis, TN 38125, USA

Dunning, Debbe (Actor, Model)
290 Rancho Santa Fe Rd
Encinitas, CA 92024-6424, USA

Dunning, Steve (Athlete, Baseball Player)

Dunphry, Jessica (Actor)
c/o Staff Member *Station3 (LA)*
1051 Cole Ave Ste B
Los Angeles, CA 90038-2601, USA

Dunphy, Marv (Athlete, Coach, Volleyball Player)
33370 Decker School Rd
Malibu, CA 90265-2344, USA

Dunphy, T J Dermot (Business Person)
Sealed Air Corp
Park 80 Plaza E
Saddle Park, NJ 07663, USA

Dunsmore, Barrie (Correspondent)
ABC-TV
5010 Creston St
News Dept
Hyattsville, MD 20781-1216, USA

Dunst, Kirsten (Actor)
c/o Stephen Huvane *Slate PR*
901 N Highland Ave
W Hollywood, CA 90038-2412, USA

Dunstan, William (Athlete, Football Player)
PO Box 514
Rancho Mirage, CA 92270-0514, USA

Dunston, Shawon D (Athlete, Baseball Player)
957 Corte Del Sol
Fremont, CA 94539-4925, USA

Dunwoody, Todd (Athlete, Baseball Player)
4212 S Monolith Ct
West Lafayette, IN 47906-5670, USA

Dunye, Cheryl (Actor, Director, Producer, Writer)
c/o Staff Member *Broder Webb Chervin Silbermann Agency, The (BWCS)*
10250 Constellation Blvd
Los Angeles, CA 90067-6200, USA

Duos, Deena (Adult Film Star)
3661 S Maryland Pkwy # 31
PMB 285
Las Vegas, NV 89169-3003, USA

Dupard, Reggie (Athlete, Football Player)
1316 Green Hills Ct
Duncanville, TX 75137-2842, USA

Duper, Mark (Athlete, Football Player)
1905 Banks Rd
Margate, FL 33063-7713, USA

Dupere, Denis (Athlete, Hockey Player)
Tournament Embroidery
26 Lorraine Ave
Kitchener, ON N2B 2M8, Canada

Duplass, Jay (Director, Producer)
c/o Naomi Odenkirk *Odenkirk Provissiero Entertainment*
1936 N Bronson Ave
Raleigh Studios
Los Angeles, CA 90068-5602, USA

Duplass, Mark (Director, Producer)
c/o Adam Kersh *Brigade Marketing*
116 W 23rd St Fl 5
New York, NY 10011-2599, USA

Dupont, Andre (Athlete, Hockey Player)
905 Rue Guilbert
Trois-Rivieres, QC G8T 5V5, Canada

Dupont, Jacques (Politician)
Minister of State's Office
Boite Postale 522
Monaco-Cedex 98015, MONACO

Dupont, Jerry (Athlete, Hockey Player)
216 Rosemar Gdns
Richmond Hill, ON L4C 3Z9, Canada

Dupont, Norman (Athlete, Hockey Player)
3289 Rue Alfred-De Musset
Laval, QC H7P 0A7, Canada

Dupont, Tiffany (Actor)
c/o Todd Diener *Untitled Entertainment*
350 S Beverly Dr Ste 200
Beverly Hills, CA 90212-4819, USA

Dupre, Ashley (Model, Musician)
c/o David Kokakis *Foundry Media Group*
598 Broadway Fl 3
New York, NY 10012-3351, USA

Dupree, Alvin (Bud) (Athlete, Football Player)

Dupree, Billy Joe (Athlete, Football Player)
3621 Llano River Trl
McKinney, TX 75070-6137, USA

Dupree, Donald (Don) (Athlete)
3 Center St
Saranac Lake, NY 12983, USA

Dupree, Marcus (Athlete, Football Player)
3661 John F Kennedy Blvd
Jackson, MS 39213-2918, USA

Dupree, Mike (Athlete, Baseball Player)
2358 E Richmond Ave
Fresno, CA 93720-0438, USA

Dupree, Myron (Athlete, Football Player)
1553 Tadlock Ave
Rocky Mount, NC 27801-3035, USA

Dupri, Jermaine (Musician)
c/o Jeff Rabhan *Three Ring Projects (LA)*
111 Westwood Pl Ste 101
Brentwood, TN 37027-5057, USA

Dupuis, Bob (Athlete, Hockey Player)
867 Main St N
Callander, ON P0H 1H0, CANADA

Dupuis, Roy (Actor)
c/o Robert Stein *Robert Stein Management*
PO Box 3797
Beverly Hills, CA 90212-0797, USA

Duque, Bernardo (Musician)
c/o Gabriel Blanco *Gabriel Blanco Iglesias (Mexico)*
Rio Balsas 35-32
Colonia Cuauhtemoc
DF 06500, Mexico

Duque, Pedro (Astronaut)
ESTEC Postbus 299
Noordwijk, NL 02200, Netherlands

Duque, Ximena (Actor, Reality Star)
c/o Staff Member *Univision*
605 3rd Ave Fl 12
New York, NY 10158-0034, USA

Duquette, Dan (Commentator)
112 W Acton Rd
Stow, MA 01775-2141, USA

Duran, Clarence (Athlete, Football Player)
201 W 54th St
Los Angeles, CA 90037-3803, USA

Duran, Dan (Athlete, Baseball Player)
493 Maxine Ct
Sunnyvale, CA 94086-6338, USA

Duran, Micki (Actor)
c/o Staff Member *DDO Artist Agency (LA)*
4605 Lankershim Blvd Ste 340
N Hollywood, CA 91602-1876, USA

Duran, Roberto (Boxer)
Nuevo Reperto El Carmen
PANAMA

Durance, Erica (Actor)
c/o Staff Member *Gersh*
9465 Wilshire Blvd Ste 600
Beverly Hills, CA 90212-2605, USA

Durand, Kevin (Actor)
5205 Newcastle Ln
Calabasas, CA 91302-3118, USA

Duran Duran (Music Group)
c/o Staff Member *DD Productions*
122 Av. Des Champs-Élysées
Paris 75008, FRANCE

Durant, Joe (Athlete, Golfer)
PO Box 910
Gulf Breeze, FL 32562-0910, USA

Durant, Justin (Athlete, Football Player)
7818 Mount Ranier Dr
Jacksonville, FL 32256-2998, USA

Durant, Kevin (Athlete, Basketball Player)
c/o Jay-Z *Roc Nation*
9348 Civic Center Dr
Beverly Hills, CA 90210-3624, USA

Durant, Mike (Athlete, Baseball Player)
9437 Cape Wrath Dr
Dublin, OH 43017-7624, USA

Durazo, Erubiel (Athlete, Baseball Player)
3800 S Cantabria Cir Unit 1079
Chandler, AZ 85248-4250, USA

Durbin, Chad (Athlete, Baseball Player)
18652 Montclair Ct
Baton Rouge, LA 70809-6709, USA

Durbin, James (Musician)
c/o Simon Fuller *XIX Entertainment (UK)*
32/33 Ransomes Dock
London SW11 4NP, UNITED KINGDOM (UK)

Durbin, J D (Athlete, Baseball Player)
1913 E Pinto Dr
Gilbert, AZ 85296-3214, USA

Durbin, Richard (Politician, Senator)
1525 S Bates Ave
Springfield, IL 62704-3347, USA

Durcal, Rocio (Musician)
c/o Staff Member *BMG*
1540 Broadway
New York, NY 10036-4039, USA

Duren, Clarence (Athlete, Football Player)
201 W 54th St
Los Angeles, CA 90037-3803, USA

Duren, John (Athlete, Basketball Player)
151 Q St NE Apt 3204
Washington, DC 20002-2174, USA

Duren, Steven (Musician)
35316 Mulholland Hwy
Malibu, CA 90265-2363, USA

Durfee, Peter (Athlete, Baseball Player)
54 Lobelia Ct
Chico, CA 95973-8241, USA

Durham, Don (Athlete, Baseball Player)
2627 Pennington Bend Rd
Nashville, TN 37214-1107, USA

Durham, Hugh (Basketball Player, Coach)
Jacksonville University
Athletic Dept
Jacksonville, FL 32211, USA

Durham, Jarrett (Athlete, Basketball Player)
18 McKelvey Ave
Pittsburgh, PA 15218-1454, USA

Durham, Joe (Athlete, Baseball Player)
9715 Mendoza Rd
Randallstown, MD 21133-2530, USA

Durham, Judith (Musician)
c/o Greg Thomas *Musicoast Pty Ltd*
P.O. Box 555
South Yarra, Vic 03141, Australia

Durham, Kris (Athlete, Football Player)

Durham, Leon (Athlete, Baseball Player)
1553 Williamson Dr
Cincinnati, OH 45240-1549, USA

Durham, Ray (Sugar Ray) (Athlete, Baseball Player)
PO Box 679
Colfax, CA 95713-0679, USA

Duris, Romain (Actor)
c/o Abi Harris *The Artists Partnership*
101 Finsbury Pavement
London EC2A 1RS, UNITED KINGDOM

Duris, Slava (Athlete, Hockey Player)
1-92 Walmer Rd
Toronto, ON M5R 2X7, Canada

Duritz, Adam (Musician, Songwriter)
52 Cooper Sq
#5B
New York, NY 10003, USA

Durkee, Charlie (Athlete, Football Player)
1210 Danbury Dr
Mansfield, TX 76063-3809, USA

Durko, Sandy (Athlete, Football Player)
2020 Paseo Del Mar
Palos Verdes Estates, CA 90274-2659, USA

Durkota, Jeff (Athlete, Football Player)
1020 Lititz Ave
Lancaster, PA 17602-1921, USA

Durnbaugh, Bobby (Athlete, Baseball Player)
1638 N Central Dr
Beavercreek, OH 45432-2118, USA

Durocher, Jayson (Athlete, Baseball Player)
3997 E Robin Ln
Phoenix, AZ 85050-5416, USA

Durr, Jason (Actor)
536 N Gower St
Los Angeles, CA 90004-1302, USA

Durrant, Devin (Athlete, Basketball Player)
1846 N 1350 W
Provo, UT 84604-1151, USA

Durr Browning, Francoise (Tennis Player)
195 Rue de Lourmel
Paris, 75015, FRANCE

Durrington, Trent (Athlete, Baseball Player)
499 N Canon Dr Apt 400
Beverly Hills, CA 90210-4887, USA

Durst, Fred (Musician)
c/o Joanne Roberts Wiles *ICM Partners*
10250 Constellation Blvd Fl 7
Los Angeles, CA 90067-6207, USA

Durst, Will (Actor, Comedian)
Durstco
PO Box 225126
San Francisco, CA 94122-5126, USA

Durupt, Lisa (Actor)
c/o Dylan Collingwood *Collingwood Management*
1572 4th Ave W 2nd Fl
Vancouver, BC V6J 1L7, CANADA

Dusan, Gene (Athlete, Baseball Player)
2241 SE Pilatus Ln
Bend, OR 97702-2498, USA

Dusay, Debra (Actor)
Susan Nathe
8281 Melrose Ave Ste 200
Los Angeles, CA 90046-6823, USA

Dusay, Mari (Actor)
320 W 66th St
New York, NY 10023-6304, USA

Dusay, Marj (Actor)
Susan Nathe
8281 Melrose Ave Ste 200
Los Angeles, CA 90046-6823, USA

Dusbabek, Mark (Athlete, Football Player)
11452 Dona Dorotea Dr
Studio City, CA 91604-4246, USA

Dusek, Brad (Athlete, Football Player)
The 4th Quarter Ranch 8311 Fm 2086
Temple, TX 76501, USA

Dusenberry, Ann (Actor)
1615 San Leandro Lane
Montecito, CA 93108, USA

Duser, Carl (Athlete, Baseball Player)
133 W Union Blvd Apt 411
Bethlehem, PA 18018-3862, USA

Dushku, Eliza (Actor, Producer)
2548 Laurel Pass
Los Angeles, CA 90046-1404, USA

Dushku, Nate (Actor)
c/o Staff Member *Peter Strain & Associates Inc (LA)*
10901 Whipple St Apt 322
N Hollywood, CA 91602-3245, USA

Dusick, Ryan (Musician)
c/o Brian Manning *Creative Artists Agency (CAA)*
2000 Avenue of the Stars Ste 100
Los Angeles, CA 90067-4705, USA

Dusk, Matt (Musician)
c/o Garry Kief *Stiletto Entertainment*
9696 Culver Blvd Ste 105
Culver City, CA 90232-2737, USA

Dussault, Nancy (Actor)
c/o Robert Malcolm *The Artists Group*
1650 Broadway # 711
New York, NY 10019-6833, USA

Dussault, Rebecca (Athlete, Olympic Athlete, Skier)
313 N Taylor St
Gunnison, CO 81230-2135

Dustal, Bob (Athlete, Baseball Player)
625 Marian Ln
Lakeland, FL 33813-1412, USA

Dustrude-Roberson, Beverly (Baseball Player)
2422 Lobelia Dr
Oxnard, CA 93036-6260, USA

Dutch, Deborah (Actor)
850 N Kings Rd # 100
West Hollywood, CA 90069-5442, USA

du Tertre, Celine (Actor)
c/o Donnalyn Carfi *Harvest Talent Management*
127 W 83rd St Unit 887
New York, NY 10024-0814, USA

Du Toit, Elize (Actor)

Dutt, Hank (Music Group, Musician)
Kronos Quartet
1235 9th Ave
San Francisco, CA 94122-2306, USA

Dutton, Charles S (Actor)
c/o Steven Siebert *Lighthouse Entertainment Group*
9229 W Sunset Blvd Ste 630
W Hollywood, CA 90069-3419, USA

Dutton, James P Major (Astronaut)
1604 Mossy Stone Dr
Friendswood, TX 77546-5576, USA

Dutton, John O (Athlete, Football Player)
5706 Moss Creek Trl
Dallas, TX 75252-2380, USA

Dutton, Lawrence (Music Group, Musician)
I M G Artists
3 Burlington Lane Chiswick
London W4 2TH, UNITED KINGDOM (UK)

Dutton, Simon (Actor)
Marmont Management
Langham House 302/8 Regent St
London W1R 5AL, UNITED KINGDOM (UK)

Duty, Kenton (Actor)
c/o Randy James *Randy James Management*
12711 Ventura Blvd Ste 345
Studio City, CA 91604-2416, USA

Duval, David (Athlete, Golfer)
1250 Selva Marina Cir
Atlantic Bch, FL 32233-5526, USA

Duval, Dennis (Athlete, Basketball Player)
8105 Verbeck Dr
Manlius, NY 13104-9306, USA

Duval, James (Actor)
c/o Ryan Revel *Good Fear Film + Management*
6255 W Sunset Blvd Ste 800
Los Angeles, CA 90028-7409, USA

Duval, Juliette (Actor)
Cineart
36 Rue de Ponthieu
Paris 75008, FRANCE

Duval, Michel (Actor, Musician)
c/o Ruby Castillo *TOR Entertainment (MX)*
Heriberto Frias 846
Col Del Valle
Mexico City DF 03100, MEXICO

Duval, Mike (Athlete, Baseball Player)
14329 Mindello Dr
Fort Myers, FL 33905-5680, USA

Duvall, Brad (Baseball Player)
Bowman
438 Sycamore Trl
Woodstock, GA 30189-7423, USA

Duvall, Carol (Television Host)
c/o Staff Member *HGTV*
9721 Sherrill Blvd
Knoxville, TN 37932-3330, USA

DuVall, Clea (Actor)
4504 Lennox Ave
Sherman Oaks, CA 91423-2613, USA

Duvall, Jed (Correspondent)
ABC-TV
5010 Creston St
Hyattsville, MD 20781-1216, USA

Duvall, Robert (Actor)
PO Box 520
The Plains, VA 20198-0520, USA

Duvall, Sammy (Skier)
PO Box 871
Windermere, FL 34786-0871, USA

Duvall, Shelley (Actor)
c/o Staff Member *Gersh*
9465 Wilshire Blvd Ste 600
Beverly Hills, CA 90212-2605, USA

Duvall, Wayne (Actor)
c/o Mitchell Stubbs *Mitchell K Stubbs & Assoc*
8675 Washington Blvd Ste 203
Culver City, CA 90232-7486, USA

Duvall-Hero, Camille (Skier)
PO Box 871
Windermere, FL 34786-0871, USA

DuVernay, Ava (Director)
c/o Staff Member *DuVernay Agency, The*
180 Glendale Blvd
Los Angeles, CA 90026-5826, USA

Duvernay-Tardif, Laurent (Athlete, Football Player)
c/o Chad Speck *Allegiant Athletic Agency*
35 Market Sq Ste 201
Knoxville, TN 37902-1420, USA

Duvignaud, Jean (Writer)
28 Rue Saint-Leonard
La Rochelle 01700, FRANCE

Duvillard, Henri (Skier)
Le Monte d'Arbois
Megere 74120, FRANCE

Duwelius, Richard L (Rich) (Athlete, Olympic Athlete, Volleyball Player)
266 Stoddards Wharf Rd
Gales Ferry, CT 06335-1130, USA

Dvorak, Radek (Athlete, Hockey Player)
10342 Lexington Estates Blvd
Boca Raton, FL 33428-4290, USA

Dvorak, Richard (Rick) (Athlete, Football Player)
13587 SE 230 Rd
Spearville, KS 67876-7506, USA

Dwight, Edward Captain (Astronaut)
3824 Dahlia St Studio Gallery
Denver, CO 80207-1020, USA

Dwight, Edward Jr (Astronaut)
4022 Montview Blvd
Denver, CO 80207-3713, USA

Dwight, Tim (Athlete, Football Player)
26164 Indigo Dr
Park Rapids, MN 56470-5189, USA

Dworaczyk, Hope (Model)
c/o Liza Anderson *Anderson Group Public Relations*
8060 Melrose Ave Fl 4
Los Angeles, CA 90046-7038, USA

Dwyer, Bil (Comedian, Game Show Host, Television Host)
c/o Bruce Smith *OmniPop Talent Group*
4605 Lankershim Blvd Ste 201
Toluca Lake, CA 91602-1874, USA

Dwyer, Clark (Race Car Driver)
3935 Elisa Ct
Colorado Springs, CO 80904-1056, USA

Dwyer, Conor (Athlete, Olympic Athlete, Swimmer)
1170 Lindenwood Dr
Winnetka, IL 60093-3722, USA

Dwyer, Jim (Athlete, Baseball Player)
825 Hancock Bridge Pkwy
Cape Coral, FL 33990-1236, USA

Dwyer, Jonathan (Athlete, Football Player)
c/o Adisa P Bakari *Kelley Drye & Warren LLP*
3050 K St NW Ste 400
Washington, DC 20007-5100, USA

Dwyer, Karyn (Actor)
Oscars Abrams Zimel
438 Queen St E
Toronto, ON M5A 1T4, CANADA

Dwyer, Mary (Athlete, Golfer)
460 Sunningdale Dr
Rancho Mirage, CA 92270-1443, USA

Dyal, Mike (Athlete, Football Player)
2844 Rock Barn Dr
Kerrville, TX 78028-8054, USA

Dybdahl, Thomas (Musician)
c/o Staff Member *Paradigm (Monterey)*
404 W Franklin St
Monterey, CA 93940-2303, USA

Dybzinski, Jerry (Athlete, Baseball Player)
1626 Haywood Pl
Fort Collins, CO 80526-2289, USA

Dye, Cameron (Actor)
13035 Woodbridge St
Studio City, CA 91604-1431, USA

Dye, Dale (Actor)
16129 Tupper St
North Hills, CA 91343-3047, USA

Dye, Jermaine (Athlete, Baseball Player)
6655 N 66th Pl
Paradise Valley, AZ 85253-4340, USA

Dyer, Clint (Actor)
c/o Femi Oguns *Identity Agency Group (UK)*
95 Grays Inn Rd
London WC1X 8TX, UNITED KINGDOM

Dyer, Danny (Actor)
c/o Staff Member *ICM Partners*
10250 Constellation Blvd Fl 7
Los Angeles, CA 90067-6207, USA

Dyer, Duffy (Athlete, Baseball Player)
742 W Las Palmaritas Dr
Phoenix, AZ 85021-5545, USA

Dyer, Hector (Athlete, Track Athlete)
1620 E Chapman Ave # 214
Fullerton, CA 92831-4016, USA

Dyer, Henry (Athlete, Football Player)
23464 Reames Rd
Zachary, LA 70791-6603, USA

Dyer, Joseph W Jr (Athlete, Football Player)
46 Windy Way
Alexander City, AL 35010-9407, USA

Dyer, Mike (Athlete, Baseball Player)
22392 Manacor
Mission Viejo, CA 92692-1188, USA

Dyer, Natalia (Actor)
c/o Anthony Aiello *One Entertainment (NY)*
347 5th Ave Rm 1404
New York, NY 10016-5034, USA

Dyer, Natalie (Actor)
c/o Anthony Aiello *One Entertainment (NY)*
347 5th Ave Rm 1404
New York, NY 10016-5034, USA

Dykema, Craig (Athlete, Basketball Player)
10525 Destino St
Bellflower, CA 90706-7125, USA

Dykes, Hart Lee (Athlete, Football Player)
30 Dorothea Ln
Sugar Land, TX 77479-2446, USA

Dykes, Keilen (Athlete, Football Player)
2329 W Melody Dr
Phoenix, AZ 85041-7634, USA

Dykes, Sean (Athlete, Football Player)
7186 Copperfield Cir
Lake Worth, FL 33467-7129, USA

Dykes Bower, John (Music Group, Musician)
4Z Artillery Mansions Westminster
London SW1, UNITED KINGDOM (UK)

Dykhoff, Radhames (Baseball Player)
Baltimore Orioles
105 Angelfish Ln
Jupiter, FL 33477-7227, USA

Dykinga, Jack (Journalist, Photographer)
1519 E Tascal Loop
Tucson, AZ 85737-8570, USA

Dykstra, Chloe (Actor, Comedian)
c/o Jenine Leigh-Pollard *Agency for the Performing Arts (APA)*
405 S Beverly Dr Ste 500
Beverly Hills, CA 90212-4425, USA

Dykstra, John (Animator, Artist)
15060 Encanto Dr
Sherman Oaks, CA 91403-4408, USA

Dykstra, Lenny (Athlete, Baseball Player)
1072 Newbern Ct
Thousand Oaks, CA 91361-5346, USA

Dylan, Bob (Musician, Songwriter)
c/o Elliott Mintz *Elliot Mintz Public Relations*
2934 1/2 N Beverly Glen Cir
Los Angeles, CA 90077-1724, USA

Dylan, Jakob (Musician)
c/o Marty Diamond *Paradigm*
140 Broadway Ste 2600
New York, NY 10005-1011, USA

Dylan, Jesse (Director)
2741 Woodstock Rd
Los Angeles, CA 90046-1118, USA

Dynamo (Magician)
c/o Darin Friedman *Management 360*
9111 Wilshire Blvd
Beverly Hills, CA 90210-5508, USA

Dynevor, Phoebe (Actor)
c/o Lena Roklin *Luber Roklin Management*
5815 W Sunset Blvd Ste 208
Los Angeles, CA 90028-6481, USA

Dyrdek, Rob (Actor, Athlete, Skateboarder)
c/o Benjamin Simone *WME|IMG (NY)*
11 Madison Ave Fl 18
New York, NY 10010-3669, USA

Dyroen-Lancer, Rebekah (Athlete, Olympic Athlete, Swimmer)

Dyson, Andre (Athlete, Football Player)
3367 N Shoreline Cir
Layton, UT 84040-7128, USA

Dyson, James (Business Person)
James Dyson Foundation
600 W Chicago Ave Ste 275
Chicago, IL 60654-2813, USA

Dyson, Kevin (Athlete, Football Player)
905 Calib Ct
Franklin, TN 37067-1372, USA

Dyson, Michael Eric (Writer)
DePaul University
English Dept
Chicago, IL 60604, USA

Dziedzic, Joe (Athlete, Hockey Player)
2195 Marion Rd Apt 102
Saint Paul, MN 55113-3805, USA

Dziedzic, Stanley (Athlete, Olympic Athlete, Wrestler)
835 Hedgegate Ct
Roswell, GA 30075-2281, USA

Dziena, Alexis (Actor)
c/o Adam Schweitzer *ICM Partners (NY)*
730 5th Ave
New York, NY 10019-4105, USA

Dzienny, Gracie (Actor)
c/o Cameron Curtis *Curtis Talent Management*
9607 Arby Dr
Beverly Hills, CA 90210-1202, USA

Dziubinska, Anulka (Kitamura) (Actor, Model)
Playboy Promotions
9346 Civic Center Dr Ste 200
Beverly Hills, CA 90210-3604, USA

Dziura, Jennifer (Comedian)
334 15th St # 1
Brooklyn, NY 11215-5006, USA

Dzundza, George (Actor)
PO Box 133
Netarts, OR 97143-0133, USA

E 40 (Music Group)
BME Recordings
2144 Hills Ave NW Ste D
Atlanta, GA 30318-2805, USA

E-40 (Music Group)
c/o Fred Zahedinia *Paradigm*
8942 Wilshire Blvd
Beverly Hills, CA 90211-1908, USA

Eaben, Bill (Athlete, Basketball Player)
12254 Colliers Reserve Dr
Naples, FL 34110-0910, USA

Eackles, Ledell (Athlete, Basketball Player)
9134 Elmgrove Garden Dr
Baton Rouge, LA 70807-4307, USA

Eadie, Betty J. (Writer)
c/o Staff Member *Random House Publicity*
1745 Broadway Frnt 3
New York, NY 10019-4343, USA

Eads, George (Actor)
c/o Jim Osborne *Agency for the Performing Arts (APA)*
405 S Beverly Dr Ste 500
Beverly Hills, CA 90212-4425, USA

Eads, Ora W (Religious Leader)
Christian Congregation
804 E Hemlock St
La Follette, TN 37766-3758, USA

Eagan, James (Writer)
c/o Greg Cavic *United Talent Agency (UTA)*
9336 Civic Center Dr
Beverly Hills, CA 90210-3604, USA

Eagle, Ian (Sportscaster)
CBS-TV
51 W 52nd St
Sports Dept
New York, NY 10019-6119, USA

Eagles, Mike (Athlete, Hockey Player)
Saint Thomas University 51 Dineen Drive
Attn: Hockey Coaching Staff
Fredericton, NB E3B 5G3, Canada

Eagleson, Alan (Athlete, Hockey Player)
53 Georgian Manor Dr
Collingwood, ON L9Y 3Z1, Canada

Eagles, The (Music Group)
c/o Irving Azoff *Azoff Music Management*
1100 Glendon Ave Ste 2000
Los Angeles, CA 90024-3524, USA

Eakes, Bobbie (Actor)
c/o Staff Member *WME|IMG*
9601 Wilshire Blvd
Beverly Hills, CA 90210-5213, USA

Eakin, Thomas C (Business Person)
245 Sandover Dr
Aurora, OH 44202-8774, USA

Eakins, Dallas (Athlete, Hockey Player)
21579 N 81st St
Scottsdale, AZ 85255-6477, USA

Eakins, Dallas (Athlete, Hockey Player)
Toronto Marlies 100 Princes Blvd
Attn Coaching Staff
Toronto, ON M6K 3C3, Canada

Eakins, Gretchen (Actor)
Mattie Management
1438 N Gower St Ste 34
C/O Mattie Semradek
Los Angeles, CA 90028-8362, USA

Eakins, Jim (Athlete, Basketball Player)
2575 E Little Cottonwood Rd
Sandy, UT 84092-3469, USA

Eaks, RW (Athlete, Golfer)
9359 E Windrose Dr
Scottsdale, AZ 85260-4595, USA

Ealey, Chuck (Athlete, Football Player)
37 Links Lane
Brampton, ON L6Y 5H2, Canada

Ealy, Kony (Athlete, Football Player)
c/o Andy Ross *Select Sports Group*
2700 Post Oak Blvd Ste 1450
Houston, TX 77056-5785, USA

Ealy, Michael (Actor)
c/o Jessica Cohen *JCPR*
9903 Santa Monica Blvd # 983
Beverly Hills, CA 90212-1671, USA

Earl, Acie (Athlete, Basketball Player)
301 S Iowa St
Solon, IA 52333-9428, USA

Earl, Anthony (Politician)
2810 Arbor Dr Unit B
Madison, WI 53711-1809, USA

Earl, Denny (Athlete, Football Player)
3600 Ozark Acres Dr
Bentonville, AR 72713-7111, USA

Earl, Glenn (Athlete, Football Player)
838 N Doheny Dr Apt 1207
West Hollywood, CA 90069-4851, USA

Earl, Robin D (Athlete, Football Player)
1457 E Evergreen Dr Apt 303
Palatine, IL 60074-8739, USA

Earl, Roger (Musician)
Lustig Talent
PO Box 770850
Orlando, FL 32877-0850, USA

Earl, Scott (Athlete, Baseball Player)
8102 Salt Fork Way
Indianapolis, IN 46256-1679, USA

Earle, Ed (Athlete, Basketball Player)
1940 Burton Ln
Park Ridge, IL 60068-1572, USA

Earle, Steve (Actor, Musician)
c/o Danny Goldberg *Gold Village Entertainment*
260 W 35th St Ste 700
New York, NY 10001-2522, USA

Earle, Sylvia (Writer)
12812 Skyline Blvd
Oakland, CA 94619-3125, USA

Earley, Anthony F Jr (Business Person)
Detroit Edison
2000 2nd Ave
Detroit, MI 48226-1203, USA

Earley, Bill (Athlete, Baseball Player)
19408 Cub Cir
Bloomsburg, PA 17815-8558, USA

Earley, Liz (Athlete, Golfer)
24 Morton Dr
Buffalo, NY 14226-3338, USA

Earley, Michael M (Business Person)
Triton Group
550 W C St
San Diego, CA 92101-3540, USA

Earley, Quinn (Athlete, Football Player)
PO Box 675752
Rancho Santa Fe, CA 92067-5752, USA

Early, David (Actor)
PO Box 154
Homestead, PA 15120-0154, USA

Early, Gerald L (Writer)
Washington University
English Dept
Saint Louis, MO 63130, USA

Early, Quinn (Athlete, Football Player)
5770 Aster Meadows Pl
San Diego, CA 92130-6907, USA

Earnhardt, Jeffrey (Race Car Driver)
c/o Staff Member *Rick Ware Racing*
111 Sunrise Center Dr
Thomasville, NC 27360-4928, USA

Earnhardt, Kelley (Race Car Driver)
Dale Earnhardt Inc
1675 Coddle Creek Hwy
Mooresville, NC 28115-8245, USA

Earnhardt, Kerry (Race Car Driver)
Kerry Earnhardt Fan Club
1675 Coddle Creek Hwy
Mooresville, NC 28115-8245, USA

Earnhardt Jr, Dale (Race Car Driver)
c/o Staff Member *Hendrick Motorsports*
4400 Papa Joe Hendrick Blvd
Charlotte, NC 28262-5703, USA

Earnie, Rhone (Athlete, Football Player)
3603 Potomac Ave
Texarkana, TX 75503-3519, USA

Earon, Blaine (Athlete, Football Player)
1141 Bald Eagle Trce
Hoschton, GA 30548-1991, USA

Earp, Mildred (Athlete, Baseball Player, Commentator)
217 Dolly Dr
West Fork, AR 72774-9109, USA

Earth Wind & Fire (Music Group)
c/o Damien Smith *Azoff Music Management*
1100 Glendon Ave Ste 2000
Los Angeles, CA 90024-3524, USA

Easler, Mike (Athlete, Baseball Player)
3709 White Lion Ln
N Las Vegas, NV 89084-2334, USA

Easley, Bill (Musician)
Hot Jazz Mgmt
328 W 43rd St
#4FW
New York, NY 10036, USA

Easley, Damion (Athlete, Baseball Player)
24415 N 93rd Dr
Peoria, AZ 85383-4049, USA

Easley, Dominique (Athlete, Football Player)

Easley, Kenny (Athlete, Football Player)
3906 Kegagie Dr
Norfolk, VA 23518-1500, USA

Easley, Logan (Athlete, Baseball Player)
753 W Cagney St
Meridian, ID 83646-5299, USA

Easley, Marcus (Athlete, Football Player)
c/o Ed Wasielewski *EMG Sports - PA*
PO Box 2
Richboro, PA 18954-0002, USA

Easley, Michael (Politician)
216 River Dr
Southport, NC 28461-4108, USA

Easmon, Ricky (Athlete, Football Player)
6605 N Riviera Manor Dr Apt A4
Tampa, FL 33604-6444, USA

Eason, Eric (Actor, Director, Writer)
c/o Simon Millar *Rumble Media*
1620 Broadway Ste C
Santa Monica, CA 90404-2777, USA

Eason, Tony (Athlete, Football Player)
PO Box 340
Walnut Grove, CA 95690-0340, USA

East, Anderson (Musician)
c/o Jonathan Levine *Paradigm (Nashville)*
222 2nd Ave S Ste 1600
Nashville, TN 37201-2375, USA

East, Dave (Musician)
c/o Peter DeSantis *United Talent Agency (UTA)*
9336 Civic Center Dr
Beverly Hills, CA 90210-3604, USA

East, Jeff (Actor)
c/o Vaughn Hart *Vaughn Hart & Associates*
12304 Santa Monica Blvd Ste 111
Los Angeles, CA 90025-2586, USA

East, Ron (Athlete, Football Player)
2024 I Ave
Anacortes, WA 98221-3715, USA

Easterbrook, Leslie (Actor)
c/o Peter Young *Sovereign Talent Group*
1642 Westwood Blvd Ste 202
Los Angeles, CA 90024-5609, USA

Easterly, David E (Business Person)
Cox Enterprises
1400 Lake Heam Dr NE
Atlanta, GA 30319, USA

Easterly, Dick (Athlete, Football Player)
206 S Gardenia Ave
Tampa, FL 33609-2506, USA

Easterly, Jamie (Athlete, Baseball Player)
1306 Plantation Dr
Crockett, TX 75835-2314, USA

Easterly, Richard (Athlete, Football Player)
206 S Gardenia Ave
Tampa, FL 33609-2506, USA

Eastern Conference Champions (Music Group)
c/o Staff Member *Paradigm (Monterey)*
404 W Franklin St
Monterey, CA 93940-2303, USA

Eastin, Steve (Actor)
c/o Staff Member *Agency for the Performing Arts (APA)*
405 S Beverly Dr Ste 500
Beverly Hills, CA 90212-4425, USA

Eastman, Kevin (Cartoonist)
1932 Coldwater Canyon Dr
Beverly Hills, CA 90210-1731, USA

Eastman, Madeline (Musician)
Prince/SF Productions
1316 Oakmont Dr Apt 4
Walnut Creek, CA 94595-2434, USA

Eastman, Marilyn (Actor)
Hardman-Eastman Studios
138 Hawthome St
Pittsburgh, PA 15218, USA

Eastman, Rodney (Actor)
c/o Justin Evans *The Independent Group*
6363 Wilshire Blvd Ste 115
Los Angeles, CA 90048-5734, USA

Easton, Michael (Actor)
c/o Danielle Allman-Del *D2 Management*
10351 Santa Monica Blvd Ste 210
Los Angeles, CA 90025-6937, USA

Easton, Millard E (Bill) (Coach)
1704 NW Weatherstone Dr
Blue Springs, MO 64015-6317, USA

Easton, Sheena (Musician)
Emmis Mgmt
18136 Califa St
Tarzana, CA 91356-1718, USA

Eastwick, Rawly (Athlete, Baseball Player)
301 Preserve Trl
Waverly, GA 31565-2692, USA

Eastwood, Alison (Actor, Model)
c/o Bob McGowan *McGowan Management*
170 S Beverly Dr Ste 304
Beverly Hills, CA 90212-3000, USA

Eastwood, Bob (Athlete, Golfer)
3826 Falmouth Ct
Stockton, CA 95219-3203, USA

Eastwood, Clint (Actor, Producer)
c/o Staff Member *Malpaso Productions*
4000 Warner Blvd
Burbank, CA 91522-0001, USA

Eastwood, Dina (Correspondent, Reality Star)
California Museum
1020 O St
Sacramento, CA 95814-5704, USA

Eastwood, Francesca (Actor)
c/o Staff Member *Brillstein Entertainment Partners*
9150 Wilshire Blvd Ste 350
Beverly Hills, CA 90212-3453, USA

Eastwood, Mike (Athlete, Hockey Player)
Sports Radio 1200 - The Team
87 George St
Attn: Hockey Broadcast Dept
Ottawa, ON K1N 9H7, Canada

Eastwood, Scott (Actor)
c/o Jennifer Allen *Viewpoint Inc*
8820 Wilshire Blvd Ste 220
Beverly Hills, CA 90211-2622, USA

Easy, Omar (Athlete, Football Player)
102 Fernwood Ct
State College, PA 16803-1661, USA

Eathorne, A J (Athlete, Golfer)
23023 N 25th Pl
Phoenix, AZ 85024-7567, USA

Eaton, Adam (Athlete, Baseball Player)
17404 NE 126th Pl # Pi
Redmond, WA 98052-2296, USA

Eaton, Andrew (Producer)
c/o Staff Member *Revolution Films*
9A Dallington St
London EC1V 0BQ, UNITED KINGDOM (UK)

Eaton, Brando (Actor)
c/o Jade Moser *NLE PR*
24965 Lorena Dr
Calabasas, CA 91302-3049, USA

Eaton, Chad (Athlete, Football Player)
1285 SE Sunnymead Way
Pullman, WA 99163-5475, USA

Eaton, Courtney (Actor)
c/o Christine Fox *Viviens Model Management*
90 King St
Level 1
Perth, WA 06000, AUSTRALIA

Eaton, Craig (Athlete, Baseball Player)
119 Lunata Ct
Jupiter, FL 33478-5472, USA

Eaton, Mark (Athlete, Basketball Player)
PO Box 982108
Park City, UT 84098-2108, USA

Eaton, Mark (Athlete, Hockey Player)
28 Hathaway Ln
Manhasset, NY 11030-4120, USA

Eaton, Mark (Basketball Player)
Utah Jazz
2104 Dayton Ave NE
Renton, WA 98056-2719, USA

Eaton, Meredith (Actor)
c/o Staff Member *Bresler Kelly & Associates*
11500 W Olympic Blvd Ste 510
Los Angeles, CA 90064-1527, USA

Eaton, Scott (Athlete, Football Player)
3950 W Lake Sammamish Pkwy SE
Bellevue, WA 98008-5836, USA

Eaton, Shirley (Actor)
Guild House
Upper Saint Martin's Lane
London WC2H PEG, UNITED KINGDOM

Eaton, Tracey (Athlete, Football Player)
788 110th Ave NE Apt N3101
Bellevue, WA 98004-8429, USA

Eaton, Vic (Athlete, Football Player)
100 Promenade Ave APT 515
Wayzata, MN 55391-4556, USA

Eatough, Jeff (Athlete, Hockey Player)
2050 Insley Rd
Mississauga, ON L4Y 1P9, Canada

Eave, Gary (Athlete, Baseball Player)
1601 King Ave
Bastrop, LA 71220-4957, USA

Eaves, Jerry (Athlete, Basketball Player)
3714 Mizell Rd APT F
Greensboro, NC 27405-4719, USA

Eaves, Mike (Athlete, Hockey Player)
3615 Culver Trl
Faribault, MN 55021-7366, USA

Eaves, Murray (Athlete, Hockey Player)
Shattuck-St Mary's School
3610 Archer Ln N
Minneapolis, MN 55446-2685, USA

Eaves, Patrick (Athlete, Hockey Player)
3615 Culver Trl
Faribault, MN 55021-7366, USA

Ebanks, Devin (Athlete, Basketball Player)
c/o David Bauman *F.A.M.E*
Prefers to be contacted via telephone
Washington, DC, USA

Ebanks, Selita (Actor, Model)
c/o Staff Member *Full Picture Management (NY)*
915 Broadway Fl 20
New York, NY 10010-7131, USA

Ebben, Bill (Basketball Player)
Detroit Pistons
12254 Colliers Reserve Dr
Naples, FL 34110-0910, USA

Ebebole, Christine (Actor)
c/o Barry McPherson *Agency for the Performing Arts*
135 W 50th St Fl 17
New York, NY 10020-1201, USA

Ebel, Dino (Athlete, Baseball Player)
c/o Staff Member *Los Angeles Dodgers*
1000 Elysian Park Ave
Los Angeles, CA 90012, USA

Eber, Richard (Athlete, Football Player)
13 Stoney Pt
Laguna Niguel, CA 92677-1000, USA

Eber, Rick (Athlete, Football Player)
13 Stoney Pt
Laguna Niguel, CA 92677-1000, USA

Eberhard, Al (Athlete, Basketball Player)
2300 Bennett Springs Dr Apt 114
Columbia, MO 65201-7255, USA

Eberharter, Stefan (Athlete, Skier)
Dorfstr 21
6272 Stumm
AUSTRIA

Eberle, Jordan (Athlete, Hockey Player)
c/o Craig Oster *Newport Sports Management*
201 City Centre Dr
Suite 400
Mississauga, ON L58 2T4, CANADA

Eberle, Markus (Skier)
Unterwestweg 27
Rieztem 87567, GERMANY

Eberle, William D (Business Person)
PO Box 1568
Concord, MA 01742-6568, USA

Ebersole, Christine (Actor)
c/o Barry McPherson *Agency for the Performing Arts*
135 W 50th St Fl 17
New York, NY 10020-1201, USA

Ebersole, Dick (Business Person)
174 West St # 54
Litchfield, CT 06759-3434, USA

Ebersole, Drew (Actor)
c/o Staff Member *The House of Representatives*
3118 Wilshire Blvd Ste D
Santa Monica, CA 90403-2345, USA

Ebersole, John (Athlete, Football Player)
1470 Village Sq
Mount Pleasant, SC 29464-4626, USA

Ebert, Derrin (Athlete, Baseball Player)
13785 W Acapulco Ln
Surprise, AZ 85379-8303, USA

Ebert, Jeremy (Athlete, Football Player)
c/o Michael McCartney *Priority Sports & Entertainment (Chicago)*
325 N La Salle Dr Ste 650
Chicago, IL 60654-8182, USA

Ebert, Peter (Musician)
Col di Mura
06010 Lippiano, ITALY

Ebertharter, Stefan (Skier)
Dorfstr 21
6272 Stumm
Austria

Ebi, Ndudi (Basketball Player)
Minnesota Timberwolves
600 1st Ave N
Target Center
Minneapolis, MN 55403-1400, USA

Ebner, Nate (Athlete, Football Player)
c/o Neil Cornrich *NC Sports, LLC*
best to contact via email
Columbus, OH 43201, USA

Ebrahim, Vincent (Actor)
c/o Staff Member *BBC Artist Mail*
PO Box 1116
Belfast BT2 7AJ, United Kingdom

Ebron, Eric (Athlete, Football Player)
c/o Bus Cook *Bus Cook Sports, Inc*
1 Willow Bend Dr
Hattiesburg, MS 39402-8552, USA

Ebron, Roy (Athlete, Basketball Player)
7100 Virgilian St
New Orleans, LA 70126-2633, USA

Ebsen, Bonnie (Actor)
PO Box 356
Agoura, CA 91376-0356, USA

E. Capuano, Michael (Congressman, Politician)
1414 Longworth Hob
Washington, DC 20515-3103, USA

Eccleston, Christopher (Actor)
c/o Claire Maroussas *Independent Talent Group*
40 Whitfield St
London W1T 2RH, UNITED KINGDOM

Ecclestone, Bernie (Race Car Driver)
26 Chelsea Square
London, England SW3 6LQ, UK

Ecclestone, Timothy J (Tim) (Athlete, Hockey Player)
10095 Fairway Village Dr
Roswell, GA 30076-3718, USA

Ecclestone Stunt, Petra (Model)
c/o Howard Bragman *LaBrea Media*
8306 Wilshire Blvd # 4002
Beverly Hills, CA 90211-2304, USA

Echevarria, Angel (Athlete, Baseball Player)
23830 231st Pl SE
Maple Valley, WA 98038-5257, USA

Echeverria, Sandra (Actor)
c/o Amy Brownstein *PRStudio USA*
1875 Century Park E Ste 930
Los Angeles, CA 90067-2540, USA

Echikunwoke, Megalyn (Actor)
c/o Ira Belgrade *Ira Belgrade Management*
5850 W 3rd St Ste E
Los Angeles, CA 90036-2836, USA

Echols, Terry (Athlete, Football Player)
6123 Sissonville Dr
Charleston, WV 25312, USA

Echosmith (Music Group)
c/o Jill Fritzo *Jill Fritzo Public Relations*
208 E 51st St # 305
New York, NY 10022-6557, USA

Eck, Keith (Athlete, Football Player)
7426 Solano St
Carlsbad, CA 92009-7527, USA

Eckenstahler, Eric (Athlete, Baseball Player)
24250 W Alpine Ct
Lake Villa, IL 60046-8637, USA

Ecker, Guy (Actor)
Bossa Sales Inc.
PO Box 490001
Los Angeles, CA 90049-0001, USA

Eckersley, Dennis (Athlete, Baseball Player)
6 Macy Ln
Ipswich, MA 01938-1185, USA

Eckert, Robert (Business Person)
Mattel Inc
333 Continental Blvd
El Segundo, CA 90245-5032, USA

Eckert, Shari (Actor)
PO Box 5761
Sherman Oaks, CA 91413-5761, USA

Eckhart, Aaron (Actor, Producer)
c/o Staci Wolfe *Polaris PR*
8135 W 4th St Fl 2
Los Angeles, CA 90048-4415, USA

Eckholdt, Steven (Actor)
137 N Larchmont Blvd # 138
Los Angeles, CA 90004-3704, USA

Eckhouse, James (Actor, Director)
c/o Tracy Steinsapir *Main Title Entertainment*
8383 Wilshire Blvd Ste 408
Beverly Hills, CA 90211-2435, USA

Ecko, Marc (Fashion Designer, Producer)
c/o Kisha Maldonado *5W Public Relations*
230 Park Ave Fl 32
New York, NY 10169-3204, USA

Eckstein, David (Athlete, Baseball Player)
1917 Lake Markham Preserve Trl
Sanford, FL 32771-8103, USA

Eckwood, Jerry (Athlete, Football Player)
496 Pickett Rd
Memphis, TN 38109-7365, USA

E. Clyburn, James (Congressman, Politician)
2135 Rayburn Hob
Washington, DC 20515-0005, USA

E. Connolly, Gerald (Congressman, Politician)
424 Cannon Hob
Washington, DC 20515-0306, USA

Econoline Crush (Musician)
c/o Staff Member *JMA Talent*
115 George St Suite 716
Oakville, ON L6J 0A2, Canada

E. Cummings, Elijah (Congressman, Politician)
2235 Rayburn Hob # B
Washington, DC 20515-0923, USA

Ed, Reynolds (Athlete, Football Player)
173 Moyer Rd
Stoneville, NC 27048-8462, USA

Edberg, Rolf (Athlete, Hockey Player)
Helmerdalsve 4
Farst S-12352, Sweden

Edberg, Stefan (Athlete, Tennis Player)
International Tennis Hall Of Fame
194 Bellevue Ave
Newport, RI 02840-3586, USA

Eddie, Patrick (Basketball Player)
New York Knicks
4424 N 76th St Apt 3
Milwaukee, WI 53218-5336, USA

Eddie X (DJ)
c/o Staff Member *Diva Central Inc*
7510 W Sunset Blvd # 1445
Los Angeles, CA 90046-3408, USA

Eddings, Doug (Athlete, Baseball Player)
1405 5th St
Las Cruces, NM 88005-1942, USA

Eddings, Floyd (Athlete, Football Player)
988 S Brampton Ave # 5
Rialto, CA 92376-7833, USA

Edds, A.J. (Athlete, Football Player)

Eddy, Chris (Athlete, Baseball Player)
47 Winterbury Cir
Wilmington, DE 19808-1429, USA

Eddy, Don (Athlete, Baseball Player)
421 1st St N
Rockwell, IA 50469-1002, USA

Eddy, Duane (Musician)
1083 Cedarview Ln
Franklin, TN 37067-4074, USA

Eddy, Nicholas M (Nick) (Athlete, Football Player)
2225 London Cir
Modesto, CA 95356-0731, USA

Eddy, Sonya (Actor)
c/o Staff Member *Marshak/Zachary Company, The*
8840 Wilshire Blvd Fl 1
Beverly Hills, CA 90211-2606, USA

Eddy, Steve (Athlete, Baseball Player)
1113 W Kaibab Dr
Chandler, AZ 85248-9105, USA

Edelen, Joe (Athlete, Baseball Player)
PO Box 22
Gracemont, OK 73042-0022, USA

Edelin, Kent (Athlete, Basketball Player)
10950 Clara Barton Dr
Fairfax Station, VA 22039-1431, USA

Edelman, Brad M (Athlete, Football Player)
537 Bienville St
New Orleans, LA 70130-2206, USA

Edelman, John (Athlete, Baseball Player)
922 Monte Vista Dr
West Chester, PA 19380-6030, USA

Edelman, Julian (Athlete, Football Player)
c/o Carter Chow *Yee & Dubin Sports, LLC*
725 S Figueroa St Ste 3085
Los Angeles, CA 90017-5430, USA

Edelstein, Eric (Actor)
c/o Olivia Gerke *3 Arts Entertainment*
9460 Wilshire Blvd Fl 7
Beverly Hills, CA 90212-2713, USA

Edelstein, Lisa (Actor)
c/o Wendy Murphey *LBI Entertainment*
2000 Avenue of the Stars
N Tower Fl 3
Los Angeles, CA 90067-4700, USA

Edelstein, Michael (Producer)
c/o Staff Member *Industry Entertainment Partners*
955 Carrillo Dr Ste 300
Los Angeles, CA 90048-5400, USA

Edelstein, Victor (Designer, Fashion Designer)
3 Stanhope Mews West
London SW7 5RB, UNITED KINGDOM (UK)

Eden, Barbara (Actor)
c/o Gene Schwam *Hanson & Schwam Public Relations*
9350 Wilshire Blvd Ste 315
Beverly Hills, CA 90212-3206, USA

Eden, Harry (Actor)
c/o Peter McGrath *Echo Lake Management*
421 S Beverly Dr Fl 8
Beverly Hills, CA 90212-4408, USA

Eden, Mike (Athlete, Baseball Player)
11531 Forest Hills Dr
Tampa, FL 33612-5121, USA

Eden, Richard (Actor)
The Agency
1800 Avenue of the Stars Ste 400
Los Angeles, CA 90067-4206, USA

Eden, Sondi (Echo) (Race Car Driver)
Eden Racing
1962 W Crescent Dr
Crawfordsville, IN 47933-8938, USA

Edenfield, Ken (Athlete, Baseball Player)
4627 Aylesbury Dr
Knoxville, TN 37918-7049, USA

Edens, Tom (Athlete, Baseball Player)
2033 Quailridge Ct
Clarkston, WA 99403-1787, USA

Eder, Linda (Actor)
c/o Staff Member *UTA Music/The Agency Group*
9336 Civic Center Dr
Beverly Hills, CA 90210-3604, USA

Edestrand, Darryl (Athlete, Hockey Player)
391 Beachwood Ave
London, ON N6J 3J9, Canada

E. Deutch, Theodore (Congressman, Politician)
1024 Longworth Hob
Washington, DC 20515-1409, USA

Edgar, David (Dave) (Swimmer)
2633 Middle River Dr Apt 3
Fort Lauderdale, FL 33306-1437, USA

Edgar, James (Politician)
1007 W Nevada St Attn
Instituteofgovernment
Urbana, IL 61801-3812, USA

Edgar, Robert W (Religious Leader)
National Council of Churches
475 Riverside Dr # 1880
New York, NY 10115-0002, USA

Edge (Musician)
Regine Moylet
145A Ladbroke Grove
London W10 6HJ, UNITED KINGDOM (UK)

Edge, Butch (Athlete, Baseball Player)
63553 Gold Spur Way
Bend, OR 97703-9182, USA

Edge, Claude (Butch) Edge (Athlete, Baseball Player)
63553 Gold Spur Way
Bend, OR 97703-9182, USA

Edge, Mitzi (Athlete, Golfer)
118 Kings Chapel Rd
Augusta, GA 30907-4002, USA

Edge, Shayne (Athlete, Football Player)
350 SW Legacy Gin
Lake City, FL 32025, USA

Edge, Steve (Actor)
c/o Staff Member *Independent Talent Group*
40 Whitfield St
London W1T 2RH, UNITED KINGDOM

Edgerson, Booker (Athlete, Football Player)
68 Union Cmn
Buffalo, NY 14221-7744, USA

Edgerton, Bill (Athlete, Baseball Player)
501 Cotton Creek Dr Unit 755
Gulf Shores, AL 36542-9081, USA

Edgerton, Joel (Director)
c/o Staff Member *Blue-Tongue Films*
PO Box 873
Darlinghurst
Sydney NSW 01300, AUSTRALIA

Edgley, Gigi (Actor)
Forster - Delaney Management
12533 Woodgreen St
Los Angeles, CA 90066-2723, USA

Ed Hardy, Don (Artist, Business Person, Designer)
Ed Hardy's Tattoo City
700 Lombard St
San Francisco, CA 94133-2317, USA

Edinger, Paul (Athlete, Football Player)
2313 York Pl
Lakeland, FL 33810-4883, USA

Edler, Dave (Athlete, Baseball Player)
1504 S 34th Ave
Yakima, WA 98902-4808, USA

Edmonds, James P (Jim) (Athlete, Baseball Player)
25 Boulder Vw
Irvine, CA 92603-0409, USA

Edmonds, Kenneth (Babyface) (Musician, Producer)
c/o Susan Markheim *Azoff Music Management*
1100 Glendon Ave Ste 2000
Los Angeles, CA 90024-3524, USA

Edmonds, Noel (Television Host)
c/o Staff Member *Talking Heads*
2-4 Noel St
London W1F 8GB, UNITED KINGDOM

Edmonds, Tracey E (Producer)
c/o Staff Member *Edmonds Entertainment Group*
3352 Clerendon Rd
Beverly Hills, CA 90210-1059, USA

Edmondson, Brian (Athlete, Baseball Player)
304 Ridgeview Trce
Canton, GA 30114-7000, USA

Edmunds, Dave (Musician, Songwriter, Writer)
Entertainment Services
227 Laurel Rd Ste 106
Voorhees, NJ 08043-8303, USA

Edmunds, Ferrell (Athlete, Football Player)
PO Box 414
Blairs, VA 24527-0414, USA

Edmunds, Randall (Athlete, Football Player)
2307 Amity Woodlawn Rd
Lincolnton, GA 30817-1910, USA

Edmunds, Randy (Athlete, Football Player)
2307 Amity Woodlawn Rd
Lincolnton, GA 30817-1910, USA

Edna, Dame (Actor, Comedian)

Edner, Ashley (Actor)
c/o Nicole Cataldo *Diverse Talent Group*
1875 Century Park E Ste 2250
Los Angeles, CA 90067-2563, USA

Edner, Bobby (Actor)
c/o Kendall Park *JLA Talent Agency*
9151 W Sunset Blvd
West Hollywood, CA 90069-3106, USA

Edney, Tyus (Athlete, Basketball Player)
1800 S Floyd Ct
La Habra, CA 90631-2058, USA

Edson, Hilary (Actor)
400 S Beverly Dr Ste 216
Beverly Hills, CA 90212-4404, USA

Edson, James (Actor)
c/o Staff Member *Synergy Talent*
13251 Ventura Blvd Ste 2
Studio City, CA 91604-1838, USA

Eduardo dos Santos, Jose (President)
President's Office
Palacio do Povo
Luanda, ANGOLA

Edur, Tom (Athlete, Hockey Player)
Puhanga 77
Tallinn 10316, Estonia

Edward, John (Astrologist/Medium/Psychic)
c/o Gina Rugolo *Rugolo Entertainment*
195 S Beverly Dr Ste 400
Beverly Hills, CA 90212-3044, USA

Edwards, Al (Athlete, Football Player)
3225 Arkansas Ave
Kenner, LA 70065-3612, USA

Edwards, Anthony (Actor, Producer)
141 E 88th St PH S
New York, NY 10128-2398, USA

Edwards, Antonio (Athlete, Football Player)
716 2nd St NW
Moultrie, GA 31768-3330, USA

Edwards, Antuan (Athlete, Football Player)
8108 Connestee Dr
McKinney, TX 75070-4820, USA

Edwards, Barbara (Actor, Model)
Hansen
7767 Hollywood Blvd Apt 202
Los Angeles, CA 90046-2643, USA

Edwards, Bill (Athlete, Basketball Player)
6670 Linzie Ct
Franklin, OH 45005-5373, USA

Edwards, Brad (Athlete, Football Player)
202 Southwood Dr
Columbia, SC 29205-3222, USA

Edwards, Braylon (Athlete, Football Player)
2266 Attard
Birmingham, MI 48009-6814, USA

Edwards, Carl (Race Car Driver)
c/o Staff Member *Joe Gibbs Racing*
13415 Reese Blvd W
Huntersville, NC 28078-7933, USA

Edwards, Cid (Athlete, Football Player)
5343 Adobe Falls Rd
San Diego, CA 92120-4403, USA

Edwards, Danny (Athlete, Golfer)
8361 E Evans Rd Ste 106
Scottsdale, AZ 85260-3617, USA

Edwards, Dave (Athlete, Baseball Player)
7356 Walling Cir
Dallas, TX 75231-7332, USA

Edwards, David (Athlete, Golfer)
5 Champion Pl
Stillwater, OK 74074-1065, USA

Edwards, Doc (Athlete, Baseball Player, Coach)
3706 Driftwood Dr
San Angelo, TX 76904-5972, USA

Edwards, Don (Athlete, Hockey Player)
c/o Staff Member *Saginaw Spirit*
PO Box 6157
Saginaw, MI 48608-6157, USA

Edwards, Don (Musician, Songwriter)
Scott O'Malley Assoc
433 S Cuchamas St
Colorado Springs, CO 80903, USA

Edwards, Doug (Athlete, Basketball Player)
3001 Brookville Dr
Manhattan, KS 66502-8434, USA

Edwards, Dwan (Athlete, Football Player)
c/o Frank Bauer *Sun West Sports*
7883 N Pershing Ave
Stockton, CA 95207-1749, USA

Edwards, Earl (Athlete, Football Player)
1534 W Saint Thomas Dr
Gilbert, AZ 85233-6534, USA

Edwards, Eddie (Athlete, Football Player)
2701 NW 1st St APT 2
Pompano Beach, FL 33069-2550, USA

Edwards, Edwin (Politician)
2225 Edinburgh Ave
Baton Rouge, LA 70808-3920, USA

Edwards, Gareth (Soccer Player)
211 West Rd
Nottage
Porthcawl, Mid-Clamorgan CF363RT, WALES

Edwards, Gary (Athlete, Hockey Player)
6818 Pecan Ave
Moorpark, CA 93021-1661, USA

Edwards, Glen (Athlete, Football Player)
4115 31st St S
St Petersburg, FL 33712-4049, USA

Edwards, Herm (Athlete, Football Coach, Football Player)
140 E Rio Salado Pkwy Unit 710
Tempe, AZ 85281-5495, USA

Edwards, James (Athlete, Basketball Player)
227S0 Civic Center Dr Apt B4
Southfield, MI 48033-7149, USA

Edwards, Jay (Athlete, Basketball Player)
121 N Washington St Apt 506
Marion, IN 46952-2865, USA

Edwards, Jennifer (Actor)
4123 Saint Clair Ave
Studio City, CA 91604-1608, USA

Edwards, Joe F Cdr (Astronaut)
24051 Hunters Trail Ln
Aldie, VA 20105-2760, USA

Edwards, Joe F Jr (Astronaut)
Enron Broadband Services
PO Box 1188
Houston, TX 77251-1188, USA

Edwards, Joel (Athlete, Golfer)
280 Benson Ln
Coppell, TX 75019-4548, USA

Edwards, John (Musician)
Buddy Allen Mgmt
3750 Hudson Manor Ter Apt 3AE
Bronx, NY 10463-1167, USA

Edwards, John (Politician)
1201 Old Greensboro Rd
Chapel Hill, NC 27516-5224, USA

Edwards, Johnny (Athlete, Baseball Player)
2511 E Blue Lake Dr
Magnolia, TX 77354-4827, USA

Edwards, Jonathan (Athlete, Track Athlete)
MTC
10 Kendall Place
London, England W1H3AH, United Kingdom

Edwards, Jonathan (Music Group, Songwriter, Writer)
Northern Lights
437 Live Oak Loop NE
Albuquerque, NM 87122-1406, USA

Edwards, Kadeem (Athlete, Football Player)

Edwards, Kalimba (Athlete)
c/o Staff Member *Detroit Lions*
222 Republic Dr
Allen Park, MI 48101-3650, USA

Edwards, Kalimba (Athlete, Football Player)
6140 Sibling Pine Dr
Durham, NC 27705-7802, USA

Edwards, Kelvin (Athlete, Football Player)
1716 Brookarbor Ct
Arlington, TX 76018-2420, USA

Edwards, Kevin (Athlete, Basketball Player)
84 Warrington Dr
Lake Bluff, IL 60044-1321, USA

Edwards, Lavar (Athlete, Football Player)
c/o Brian E. Overstreet *E.O. Sports Management*
1314 Texas St Ste 1212
Houston, TX 77002-3525, USA

Edwards, Luke (Actor)
Ensemble Entertainment
10474 Santa Monica Blvd # 380
Los Angeles, CA 90025-6929, USA

Edwards, Marc (Athlete, Football Player)
6426 Autumn Crest Ct
Westerville, OH 43082-8963, USA

Edwards, Mario (Athlete, Football Player)
PO Box 216
Prosper, TX 75078-0216, USA

Edwards, Marshall (Baseball Player)
5059 Quail Run Rd Apt 75
Riverside, CA 92507-6485, USA

Edwards, Marv (Athlete, Hockey Player)
3277 1st Ave Lot 40
Mims, FL 32754-3136, USA

Edwards, Michelle (Athlete, Basketball Player)
992 Village Dr E # B
North Brunswick, NJ 08902-2821, USA

Edwards, Mike (Athlete, Baseball Player)
11370 Moreno Beach Dr
Moreno Valley, CA 92555-5240, USA

Edwards, Mike (Athlete, Baseball Player)
502 Sharon Ave
Mechanicsburg, PA 17055-6630, USA

Edwards, Paul A. (Producer)
c/o Geoffrey Brandt *Course Management*
142 Porto Vecchio Way
Palm Beach Gardens, FL 33418-6223, USA

Edwards, Randy (Athlete, Football Player)
1369 Mountain Park Dr NW
Kennesaw, GA 30152-4780, USA

Edwards, Reign (Actor)
c/o Brett Ruttenberg *Imprint PR*
6121 W Sunset Blvd
Neuehouse
Los Angeles, CA 90028-6442, USA

Edwards, Robert (Athlete, Football Player)
931 Knight Rd
Tennille, GA 31089-4210, USA

Edwards, Stacy (Actor)
Paradigm Agency
10 100 Santa Monica Blvd
#2500
Los Angeles, CA 90067, USA

Edwards, Stephanie (Actor)
c/o Staff Member *Tisherman Gilbert Motley Drozdoski Talent Agency (TGMD)*
6767 Forest Lawn Dr # 101
Los Angeles, CA 90068-1027, USA

Edwards, Steve (Musician)
c/o Staff Member *Gorfaine/Schwartz Agency Inc*
4111 W Alameda Ave Ste 509
Burbank, CA 91505-4171, USA

Edwards, Teresa (Athlete, Basketball Player, Olympic Athlete)
1303 Emerson Ave SE
Cairo, GA 39828-3539, USA

Edwards, Theodore (Blue) (Athlete, Basketball Player)
10914 Lee Manor Ln
Charlotte, NC 28277-2751, USA

Edwards, Tommy Lee (Cartoonist)
DC Comics
2900 W Alameda Ave # 1
Burbank, CA 91505-4220, USA

Edwards, Tonya (Basketball Player)
Phoenix Mercury
201 E Jefferson St
American West Arena
Phoenix, AZ 85004-2412, USA

Edwards, Troy (Athlete, Football Player)
401 Bentley Dr
Midlothian, TX 76065-1667, USA

Edwards, Wayne (Athlete, Baseball Player)
26441 Circle Knoll Ct
Newhall, CA 91321-1320, USA

Edwards, Williams (Monk) (Athlete, Football Player)
3518 Teakwood Dr
Pearland, TX 77584-2530, USA

Edwards III, Dixon (Athlete, Football Player)
8959 Zodiac Dr
Cincinnati, OH 45231-4168, USA

Eenhoorn, Robert (Athlete, Baseball Player)
Zermilieplaats 15 3068J
Rotterdam, Netherlands, USA

Efron, Zac (Actor)
c/o Staff Member *Ninjas Runnin' Wild Productions*
7024 Melrose Ave Ste 420
Los Angeles, CA 90038-3394, USA

Egan, Christopher (Actor)
c/o Sandra Chang *Anonymous Content*
3532 Hayden Ave
Culver City, CA 90232-2413, USA

Egan, Dick (Athlete, Baseball Player)
709 Carnoustie Ct
Garland, TX 75044-5054, USA

Egan, Jennifer (Writer)
Doubleday Press
1540 Broadway
New York, NY 10036-4039, USA

Egan, John (Johnny) (Athlete, Basketball Player)
2124 Nantucket Dr Apt B
Houston, TX 77057-2906, USA

Egan, John L (Business Person)
130 Wilton Road
London, England SW1V 1LQ, UNITED KINGDOM

Egan, Kian (Musician)
c/o Staff Member *Solo Agency Ltd (UK)*
53-55 Fulham High St
Fl 2
London SW6 3JJ, UNITED KINGDOM

Egan, Peter (Actor)
James Sharkey
21 Golden Square
London, England W1R 3PA, UNITED KINGDOM

Egan, Richard J (Business Person)
ECM Corp
35 Parkwood Dr
Hopkinton, MA 01748-1699, USA

Egan, Susan (Actor)
1680 Vine St Ste 614
Los Angeles, CA 90028-8833, USA

Egan, Tom (Athlete, Baseball Player)
184 E Myrna Ln
Tempe, AZ 85284-3118, USA

Egbert, Dave (Television Host)
PO Box 537
Lakehead, CA 96051-0537, USA

Ege, Julie (Actor)
Guild House
Upper Saint Martins
London, England WC2H 9EG, UNITED KINGDOM

Egender, Joe (Actor)
c/o Derek Kroeger *Myman Greenspan Fineman Fox Rosenberg & Light*
11601 Wilshire Blvd Ste 2200
Los Angeles, CA 90025-1758, USA

Eger, David (Athlete, Golfer)
3508 Winslow Green Dr
Charlotte, NC 28210-3488, USA

Egers, Jack (Athlete, Hockey Player)
1-24 Zinkann Cres RR 1
Wellesley, ON N0B 2T0, Canada

Egerszegi, Krisztina (Swimmer)
Budapest Spartacus
Koer Utca 1/A
1103 Budapest, HUNGARY

Egerton, Tamsin (Actor)
c/o Sandra Chang *Anonymous Content*
3532 Hayden Ave
Culver City, CA 90232-2413, USA

Egerton, Taron (Actor)
c/o Clair Dobbs *CLD Communications*
4 Broadway Ct
The Broadway
London SW191RG, UNITED KINGDOM

Eggar, Robin (Writer)
c/o Staff Member *Simon & Schuster*
1230 Avenue of the Americas Fl CONC1
New York, NY 10020-1586, USA

Eggar, Samantha (Actor)
5005 Varna Ave
Sherman Oaks, CA 91423-1524, USA

Eggeling, Dale (Athlete, Golfer)
8918 Magnolia Chase Cir
Tampa, FL 33647-2219, USA

Eggers, Dave (Writer)
Simon & Schuster
1230 Avenue of the Americas Fl CONC1
New York, NY 10020-1586, USA

Eggers, Doug (Athlete, Football Player)
12803 Cedarbrook Ln
Laurel, MD 20708-2449, USA

Eggert, Nicole (Actor)
c/o JD Sobol *Almond Talent Management*
8217 Beverly Blvd Ste 8
W Hollywood, CA 90048-4534, USA

Egglesfield, Colin (Actor)
c/o Colton Gramm *Brillstein Entertainment Partners*
9150 Wilshire Blvd Ste 350
Beverly Hills, CA 90212-3453, USA

Eggleston, Rachel (Actor)
c/o Meredith Fine *Coast to Coast Talent Group*
3350 Barham Blvd
Los Angeles, CA 90068-1404, USA

Eggold, Ryan (Actor)
c/o Siri Garber *Platform PR*
2666 N Beachwood Dr
Los Angeles, CA 90068-2308, USA

Egloff, Bruce (Athlete, Baseball Player)
3136 S Emporia Ct
Denver, CO 80231-4739, USA

Egloff, Ron (Athlete, Football Player)
975 N Lincoln St Apt 5G
Denver, CO 80203-2757, USA

Egnew, Danielle (Musician)
Danielle Egnew Spiritual Advisory
15030 Ventura Blvd Ste 843
Sherman Oaks, CA 91403-5470, USA

Egoyan, Atom (Actor)
Ego Film Artiosts
80 Niagara St
Toronto ON M5V 1C5, CANADA

Ehle, Jennifer (Actor)
c/o Sally Long-Innes *Independent Talent Group*
40 Whitfield St
London W1T 2RH, UNITED KINGDOM

Ehlers, Beth (Actor)
c/o Staff Member *Artists & Representatives (Stone Manners Salners)*
6100 Wilshire Blvd Ste 1500
Los Angeles, CA 90048-5110, USA

Ehlers, Edwin (Athlete, Basketball Player)
PO Box 303
Notre Dame, IN 46556-0303, USA

Ehlers, Tom (Athlete, Football Player)
13898 Layton Rd
Mishawaka, IN 46544-9498, USA

Ehlo, Craig (Athlete, Basketball Player)
3323 E 77th Ave
Spokane, WA 99223-1943, USA

Ehrenreich, Alden (Actor)
c/o Jessica Kolstad *Relevant*
400 S Beverly Dr Ste 220
Beverly Hills, CA 90212-4404, USA

Ehret, Gloria (Athlete, Golfer)
3335 Royal Ln
Dallas, TX 75229-5062, USA

Ehrhoff, Christian (Athlete, Hockey Player)
4517 Carlyle Ct
Santa Clara, CA 95054-3917, USA

Ehrlich, Robert (Politician)
110 State Cir
Annapolis, MD 21401-1924, USA

Ehrmann, Joe (Athlete, Football Player)
15 Battersea Bridge Ct
Lutherville Timonium, MD 21093-3947, USA

Eichelberger, Dave (Athlete, Golfer)
4348 Waialae Ave # 649
Honolulu, HI 96816-5767, USA

Eichelberger, Juan (Athlete, Baseball Player)
14674 Silverset St
Poway, CA 92064-6408, USA

Eichhorn, Lisa (Actor)
c/o Staff Member *Conway van Gelder Grant*
8-12 Broadwick St
London W1F 8HW, UNITED KINGDOM

Eichhorn, Mark (Athlete, Baseball Player)
147 Norma Ct
Aptos, CA 95003-9789, USA

Eichhorst, Richard (Athlete, Basketball Player)
2701 Sheridan Rd
Saint Louis, MO 63125-4168, USA

Eichner, Billy (Comedian)
c/o Molly Kawachi *ID Public Relations (NY)*
40 Wall St Fl 51
New York, NY 10005-1385, USA

Eick, Dick (Producer, Writer)
Dick Eick Productions
100 Universal City Plz Bldg E
Universal City, CA 91608-1002, USA

Eidem, Erik (Actor, Producer)
c/o Scott Zimmerman *Scott Zimmerman Management*
901 N Highland Ave
Los Angeles, CA 90038-2412, USA

Eidson, Jim (Athlete, Football Player)
3116 Purdue Ave
Dallas, TX 75225-7721, USA

Eifert, Tyler (Athlete, Football Player)
c/o Ben Dogra *Relativity Sports*
2029 Century Park E Ste 1550
Century City, CA 90067-3000, USA

Eifrid, Jim (Athlete, Football Player)
2710 Tyler Ave
Fort Wayne, IN 46808-1944, USA

Eigeman, Chris (Actor)
c/o Thomas Cushing *Innovative Artists*
1505 10th St
Santa Monica, CA 90401-2805, USA

Eigenberg, David (Actor)
c/o Sheree Cohen *Buchwald*
5900 Wilshire Blvd Ste 3100
Los Angeles, CA 90036-5030, USA

Eigsti, Roger H (Business Person)
SAFECO Corp
Safeco Plaza
Seattle, WA 98185-0001, USA

Eikenberry, Jill (Actor)
c/o Wes Stevens *Vox*
5670 Wilshire Blvd Ste 820
Los Angeles, CA 90036-5613, USA

Eiland, Dave (Athlete, Baseball Player)
2824 Blue Springs Pl
Wesley Chapel, FL 33544-8746, USA

Eilbacher, Lisa (Actor)
4600 Petit Ave
Encino, CA 91436-3216, USA

Eilber, Janet (Actor, Dancer)
Martha Graham Dance Center Of Contemporary Dance
344 E 59th St
New York, NY 10022-1593, USA

Eilers, Dave (Athlete, Baseball Player)
602 Perkins Ln
Brenham, TX 77833-4394, USA

Eilers, Pat (Athlete, Football Player)
58 Indian Hill Rd
Winnetka, IL 60093-3938, USA

Eilish, Billie (Actor)
c/o Stephanie Miles *Paradigm*
8942 Wilshire Blvd
Beverly Hills, CA 90211-1908, USA

Einaudi, Ludovico (Musician)
c/o Staff Member *Ponderosa Music & Art*
Piazza Santa Maria Delle Grazie, 1
Milano 20123, Italy

Einertson, Darrell (Athlete, Baseball Player)
221 Hawthorne Dr
Norwalk, IA 50211-9665, USA

Einziger, Mike (Musician)
c/o Staff Member *ArtistDirect*
9046 Lindblade St
Culver City, CA 90232-2513, USA

Eischeid, Mike (Athlete, Football Player)
306 Auburn St
West Union, IA 52175-1067, USA

Eischen, Joey (Athlete, Baseball Player)
Asheville Tourists
30 Buchanan Pl
Asheville, NC 28801-4243, USA

Eischen, Joey (Athlete, Baseball Player)
10408 Bryant Rd
Lithia, FL 33547-2510, USA

Eisen, Erez (Musician)

Eisen, Hal (Actor)
c/o Staff Member *Caldwell Jeffery*
943 Queen St E Fl 2
Toronto, ON M4M 1J6, CANADA

Eisen, Tripp (Music Group)
Andy Gould Mgmt
9100 Wilshire Blvd Ste 400W
Beverly Hills, CA 90212-3464, USA

Eisenberg, Jesse (Actor)
c/o Jennifer Allen *Viewpoint Inc*
8820 Wilshire Blvd Ste 220
Beverly Hills, CA 90211-2622, USA

Eisenberg, Warren (Business Person)
Bed Bath & Beyond
650 Liberty Ave
Union, NJ 07083-8107, USA

Eisenhauer, Lawrence (Larry) (Athlete, Football Player)
Pro Action
2 Winter St Ste 402B
Waltham, MA 02451-0961, USA

Eisenhauer, Stephen S (Steve) (Athlete, Football Player)
105 Abbey Rd
Winchester, VA 22602-7402, USA

Eisenhooth, John (Athlete, Football Player)
8870 Avery Rd
Baldwinsville, NY 13027-9632, USA

Eisenhower, David (Politician)
255 Foxall Ln
Berwyn, PA 19312-1843, USA

Eisenreich, Jim (Athlete, Baseball Player)
11 Emerald Shore Dr
Blue Springs, MO 64015-9658, USA

Eisenstein, Michael (Music Group)
Little Big Man
155 Avenue of the Americas Rm 700
New York, NY 10013-1507, USA

Eisler, Lloyd (Athlete, Figure Skater, Olympic Athlete)
211-800 Montarville
Boucherville PQ JYB 125, Canada

Eisley, Howard (Athlete, Basketball Player)
20250 Rodeo Ct
Southfield, MI 48075-1285, USA

Eisley, India (Actor)
c/o Todd Justice *Justice & Ponder*
PO Box 480033
Los Angeles, CA 90048-1033, USA

Eisman, Hy (Cartoonist)
99 Boulevard
Glen Rock, NJ 07452-2003, USA

Eisner, Breck (Director)
c/o Gregory McKnight *United Talent Agency (UTA)*
9336 Civic Center Dr
Beverly Hills, CA 90210-3604, USA

Eisner, Michael (Business Person)
Vuguru
315 S Beverly Dr Ste 315
Beverly Hills, CA 90212-4309, USA

E. Issa, Darrell (Congressman, Politician)
2347 Rayburn Hob
Washington, DC 20515-0915, USA

Eitzel, Mark (Music Group, Songwriter, Writer)
Legends of 21st Century
7 Trinity Row
Florence, MA 01062-1931, USA

Ejiofor, Chiwetel (Actor)
c/o Emma Jackson *Premier PR*
2-4 Bucknall St
London WC2H 8LA, UNITED KINGDOM

Ejogo, Carmen (Actor)
c/o Eric Kranzler *Management 360*
9111 Wilshire Blvd
Beverly Hills, CA 90210-5508, USA

Ek, Daniel (Business Person)
c/o Staff Member *Spotify*
150 Greenwich St Fl 62
4 World Trade Center
New York, NY 10007-2366, USA

Ekberg, Ulf (Musician)
Basic Music Mgmt
Norrtullsgatan 52
Stockholm 113 45, SWEDEN

Eker, T Harv (Business Person)
True Power International Limited
300 N Commercial
Be, WA 98227-5008

E. Kildee, Dale (Congressman, Politician)
2107 Rayburn Hob
Washington, DC 20515-2205, USA

Ekland, Britt (Actor)
c/o Gareth Owen *Bondstars*
Pinewood Studios
Iver Heath
Bucks SL0 0NH, UNITED KINGDOM

Eklund, Brian (Athlete, Hockey Player)
66 Blossom Rd
Braintree, MA 02184-3806, USA

Eklund, Fredrik (Business Person, Reality Star)
Douglas Elliman
936 Broadway
New York, NY 10010-6013, USA

Eklund, Greg (Music Group)
Pinnacle Entertainment
30 Glenn St
White Plains, NY 10603-3254, USA

Eklund, Pelle (Athlete, Hockey Player)
c/o Staff Member *San Jose Sharks*
525 W Santa Clara St
San Jose, CA 95113-1500, USA

Ekstran, Garner (Athlete, Football Player)
10867 Samish Beach Ln
Bow, WA 98232-9405

Ekstrom, Mike (Athlete, Baseball Player)
1616 SE 282nd Ave
Gresham, OR 97080-9014, USA

Ekuban, Ebenezer (Athlete, Football Player)
5391 Moonlight Way
Parker, CO 80134-4535, USA

El, Antwaan Randle (Athlete, Football Player)
The El Foundation
1218 Grandview Ave
Pittsburgh, PA 15211-1239, USA

Elam, Jason (Athlete, Football Player)
1503 Shadow Forest Dr
Matthews, NC 28105-7227, USA

Elam, Matt (Athlete, Football Player)

Elarton, Scott (Athlete, Baseball Player)
13501 County Road 33
Karval, CO 80823-9305, USA

E. Latta, Robert (Congressman, Politician)
1323 Longworth Hob
Washington, DC 20515-4704, USA

Elba, Idris (Actor)
c/o Katie Greenthal *The Lede Company*
9701 Wilshire Blvd # 930
Beverly Hills, CA 90212-2020, USA

El Bambino, Tito (Musician)
c/o Staff Member *EMI Music Publishing (Latin America)*
1688 Meridian Ave Ste 900
Miami Beach, FL 33139-2712, USA

Eldard, Ron (Actor)
c/o William Choi *Management 360*
9111 Wilshire Blvd
Beverly Hills, CA 90210-5508, USA

Eldebrink, Anders (Athlete, Hockey Player)
Batsmansgrand 4
Mariefred 64730, Sweden

Elder, Christian (Race Car Driver)
Atkins Motorsports
222 Raceway Dr
Mooresville, NC 28117-6510, USA

Elder, Dave (Athlete, Baseball Player)
2642 High St SW
Conyers, GA 30094-6843, USA

Elder, George (Athlete, Baseball Player)
423 Amethyst Dr
Fruita, CO 81521-8813, USA

Elder, Larry (Actor)
c/o Ari Emanuel *WME/IMG*
9601 Wilshire Blvd
Beverly Hills, CA 90210-5213, USA

Elder, Lee (Athlete, Golfer)
PO Box 667200
Pompano Beach, FL 33066-7200, USA

Elder, Ray (Race Car Driver)
15252 S Cherry Ave
Caruthers, CA 93609-9754, USA

Eldred, Brad (Athlete, Baseball Player)
12402 175th Rd N
Jupiter, FL 33478-4624, USA

Eldred, Cal (Athlete, Baseball Player)
1893 Horn Rd
Mount Vernon, IA 52314-9517, USA

Eldredge, Allison (Music Group)
C M Artists
40 W 25th St
New York, NY 10010-2707, USA

Eldredge, Brett (Musician)
c/o Staff Member *WME/IMG*
9601 Wilshire Blvd
Beverly Hills, CA 90210-5213, USA

Eldredge, Todd (Athlete, Olympic Athlete, Speed Skater)
20030 Buttermere Ct
Estero, FL 33928-7724, USA

Electra, Carmen (Actor, Model)
c/o Jack Ketsoyan *EMC / Bowery*
8356 Fountain Ave Apt E1
W Hollywood, CA 90069-2968, USA

Electrik Red (Music Group, Musician)
c/o Staff Member *Island Def Jam Group*
825 8th Ave Fl 28
New York, NY 10019-7416, USA

Elegant, Robert S (Writer)
Manor House
Middle Green near Langley
Bucks SL3 6BS, UNITED KINGDOM (UK)

Eleniak, Erika (Actor, Model)
c/o Danielle Bilodeau *Cue Agency*
560 Beatty St Suite L100
Vancouver, BC V6B 2L3, CANADA

El Fadil, Siddig (Actor)
Paramount
5555 Melrose Ave
Los Angeles, CA 90038-3197, USA

Elfman, Bodhi (Actor)
c/o Staff Member *Artists & Representatives (Stone Manners Salners)*
6100 Wilshire Blvd Ste 1500
Los Angeles, CA 90048-5110, USA

Elfman, Danny (Musician)
Musica de la Muerte
1901 Avenue of the Stars Ste 1450
Los Angeles, CA 90067-6087, USA

Elfman, Jenna (Actor, Model, Producer)
c/o David McIlvain *Brillstein Entertainment Partners*
9150 Wilshire Blvd Ste 350
Beverly Hills, CA 90212-3453, USA

Elfont, Harry (Director, Writer)
c/o Staff Member *WME|IMG*
9601 Wilshire Blvd
Beverly Hills, CA 90210-5213, USA

Elgaard, Ray (Athlete, Football Player)
8821 Smokey Dr
Las Vegas, NV 89134-8422, United States

Elgort, Ansel (Actor)
c/o Lindsay Galin *Rogers & Cowan*
909 3rd Ave Fl 9
New York, NY 10022-4752, USA

Elia, Lee (Athlete, Baseball Player)
11613 Innfields Dr
Odessa, FL 33556-5407, USA

Elias, Eliane (Musician)
c/o Anders-Chan Tidemann *Word of Mouth Music*
235 E 22nd St Apt 9F
New York, NY 10010-4636, USA

Elias, Keith (Athlete, Football Player)
24 Dover St
Toms River, NJ 08753-7454, USA

Elias, Patrik (Athlete, Hockey Player)
1005 Smith Manor Blvd
West Orange, NJ 07052-4227, USA

Elice, Rick (Actor, Writer)
c/o Joe Machota *Creative Artists Agency (CAA)*
405 Lexington Ave Fl 19
New York, NY 10174-1800, USA

Elich, Matt (Athlete, Hockey Player)
276 McKinley Ave
Grosse Pointe Farms, MI 48236-3460, USA

Elie, Mario (Athlete, Basketball Player)
1 Mott Ln
Houston, TX 77024-7315, USA

Eliff, Tom (Religious Leader)
Southern Baptist Convention
901 Commerce St Ste 750
Nashville, TN 37203-3600, USA

Eliopulos, Jim (Athlete, Football Player)
2500 Macero St
Roseville, CA 95747-5000, USA

Eliot, Darren (Athlete, Hockey Player)
1001 Cadieux Rd
Grosse Pointe Park, MI 48230-1511, USA

Elise, Christine (Actor, Writer)
c/o Tim Angle *Shelter Entertainment*
9255 W Sunset Blvd Ste 300
Los Angeles, CA 90069-3313, USA

Elise, Kimberly (Actor)
c/o Evan Hainey *Untitled Entertainment*
350 S Beverly Dr Ste 200
Beverly Hills, CA 90212-4819, USA

Elisha, Walter Y (Business Person)
Springs Industries
205 N White St
Fort Mill, SC 29715-1654, USA

Eli Young Band (Music Group)
c/o George Couri *Triple 8 Management*
1611 W 6th St
Austin, TX 78703-5059, USA

Elizabeth, Shannon (Actor, Producer)
c/o Staff Member *Ganesh Productions*
7336 Santa Monica Blvd Ste 690
West Hollywood, CA 90046-6670, USA

Elizondo, Hector (Actor)
c/o Mark Teitelbaum *Teitelbaum Artists Group*
8840 Wilshire Blvd Fl 3
Beverly Hills, CA 90211-2606, USA

Elk, Jim (Actor)
Dade/Schultz
6442 Coldwater Canyon Ave Ste 206
Valley Glen, CA 91606-1174, USA

Elkington, Steve (Athlete, Golfer)
7010 Kelsey Rae Ct
Houston, TX 77069-1102, USA

Elkins, Corey (Athlete, Hockey Player)
2668 Silverside Rd
Waterford, MI 48328-1762, USA

Elkins, Larry (Athlete, Football Player)
4407 McArthur Cir
Brownwood, TX 76801-7334, USA

Elkins, Lawrence C (Larry) (Athlete, Football Player)
1 Keats Avenue Norden
Rochdale, Lancestershire OL12 7PZ, UK

Elkins, Mike (Athlete, Football Player)
743 Drifting Wind Run
Dripping Springs, TX 78620-4487, USA

Ell, Lindsay (Musician)
c/o Todd Jordan *Paquin Entertainment Agency (Winnipeg)*
468 Stradbrook Ave
Winnipeg MB M6K 3J1, CANADA

Ellacott, Ken (Athlete, Hockey Player)
131 Crawford Cres
Cambridge, ON N1T 1X6, Canada

Ellard, Henry A (Athlete, Football Player)
29 Knob Hill Dr
Summit, NJ 07901-3024, USA

Ellenbogen, Bill (Athlete, Football Player)
777 Pelham Rd Apt 2G
New Rochelle, NY 10805-1137, USA

Ellenstein, Robert (Actor)
5212 Sepulveda Blvd # 23F
Culver City, CA 90230-5214, USA

Eller, Carl (Athlete, Football Player)
1035 Washburn Ave N
Minneapolis, MN 55411-3557, USA

Ellerbe, Dannell (Athlete, Football Player)
c/o Hadley Engelhard *Enter-Sports Management*
6000 Lake Forrest Dr Ste 370
Atlanta, GA 30328-5902, USA

Ellerbee, Linda (Journalist)
LRB Services Inc
3930 Secor Ave Apt 1
C/O Lori Seidner
Bronx, NY 10466-2416, USA

Ellerson, Gary (Athlete, Football Player)
S86W18643 Sue Marie Ln
Muskego, WI 53150-8718, USA

Ellett, Dave (Athlete, Hockey Player)
20660 N 40th St Unit 2018
Phoenix, AZ 85050-7312, USA

Ellin, Doug (Actor, Director, Producer, Writer)
c/o Staff Member *Westward Productions*
11693 San Vicente Blvd # 324
Los Angeles, CA 90049-5105, USA

Elling, Kurt (Music Group, Musician)
c/o Ted Kurland *Ted Kurland Associates*
173 Brighton Ave
Boston, MA 02134-2003, USA

Ellingsen, Bruce (Athlete, Baseball Player)
5873 Daneland St
Lakewood, CA 90713-1830, USA

Ellingson, Evan (Actor)
c/o Staff Member *Reel Talent Management*
PO Box 491035
Los Angeles, CA 90049-9035, USA

Ellington, andre (Athlete, Football Player)

Ellington, Bruce (Athlete, Football Player)
c/o Eugene Parker *Independent Sports & Entertainment (ISE-IN)*
6435 W Jefferson Blvd # 197
Fort Wayne, IN 46804-6203, USA

Elliot, Ernie (Race Car Driver)
PO Box 476
Dawsonville, GA 30534-0009, USA

Elliot, Graham (Chef, Television Host)

Elliot, Larry (Athlete, Baseball Player)
13010 Caminito Bracho
San Diego, CA 92128-1808, USA

Elliot, Lin (Athlete, Football Player)
540 Lost Hunters Cyn
China Spring, TX 76633-3455, USA

Elliot, Tony (Athlete, Football Player)
45907 Riverwoods Dr
Macomb, MI 48044-5788, USA

Elliott, Abby (Actor, Comedian)
c/o Dianne McGunigle *MGMT Entertainment (The Schiff Company)*
9220 W Sunset Blvd Ste 106
W Hollywood, CA 90069-3500, USA

Elliott, Alecia (Actor, Music Group)
PO Box 3075
Muscle Shoals, AL 35662-3075, USA

Elliott, Alison (Actor)
2 Ironsides #18
Marina Del Rey, CA 90292, USA

Elliott, Beverley (Actor)
c/o Richard Lucas *Lucas Talent Inc*
1238 Homer St Suite 6
Vancouver, BC V6B 2Y5, CANADA

Elliott, Bill (Race Car Driver)
Bill Elliott Racing
109 Ruby Ln
Dawsonville, GA 30534-6978, USA

Elliott, Brennan (Actor)
c/o Staff Member *Artists & Representatives (Stone Manners Salners)*
6100 Wilshire Blvd Ste 1500
Los Angeles, CA 90048-5110, USA

Elliott, Brooke (Actor)
Powerline Entertainment
1158 Linda Flora Dr
Los Angeles, CA 90049-1730, USA

Elliott, Chalmers (Bump) (Coach, Football Coach, Football Player)
University of Iowa
Athletic Dept
Iowa City, IA 52242, USA

Elliott, Chris (Actor, Comedian)
c/o Ben Feigin *Anonymous Content*
3532 Hayden Ave
Culver City, CA 90232-2413, USA

Elliott, David James (Actor)
c/o Erik Kritzer *LINK Entertainment*
11872 La Grange Ave
Los Angeles, CA 90025-5282, USA

Elliott, Dennis (Music Group)
Hard to Handle Mgmt
16501 Ventura Blvd Ste 602
Encino, CA 91436-2072, USA

Elliott, Donnie (Athlete, Baseball Player)
1206 Bayou Vista Dr
Deer Park, TX 77536-6902, USA

Elliott, Ezekiel (Athlete, Football Player)
c/o Rocky Arceneaux *Alliance Management Group*
11469 Olive Blvd Ste 276
Saint Louis, MO 63141-7108, USA

Elliott, Gordon (Chef, Producer)
c/o Staff Member *Follow Productions*
589 8th Ave Fl 12
New York, NY 10018-3086, USA

Elliott, Harry (Athlete, Baseball Player)
9608 Los Coches Rd
Lakeside, CA 92040-4240, USA

Elliott, Herbert (Herb) (Athlete, Track Athlete)
Athletics Australia
431 St Kilda Rd
#22
Melbourne, VIC 03004, AUSTRALIA

Elliott, Joe (Musician)
c/o Rod MacSween *International Talent Booking*
9 Kingsway
Fl 6
London WC2B 6XF, UNITED KINGDOM

Elliott, John (Athlete, Golfer)
235 Lexington Rd
Glastonbury, CT 06033-1289, USA

Elliott, John (Jumbo) (Athlete, Football Player)
17 Fieldstone Ln
Oyster Bay, NY 11771-3122, USA

Elliott, Matt (Athlete, Football Player)
540 Lost Hunters Cyn
China Spring, TX 76633-3455, USA

Elliott, Missy (Actor, Musician, Producer)
Monami Entertainment
649 W 27th St
New York, NY 10001-1105, USA

Elliott, Randy (Athlete, Baseball Player)
PO Box 834
Somis, CA 93066-0834, USA

Elliott, Robert (Athlete, Basketball Player)
6760 E Fieldstone Ln
Tucson, AZ 85750-2075, USA

Elliott, Sam (Actor)
c/o Lisa Kasteler *Wolf-Kasteler Public Relations*
6255 W Sunset Blvd Ste 1111
Los Angeles, CA 90028-7426, USA

Elliott, Sean (Athlete, Basketball Player)
250 Lismore
San Antonio, TX 78260-4313, USA

Elliott, Stephen (Writer)
The Rumpus
490 2nd St Ste 200
San Francisco, CA 94107-1419, USA

Elliott, Steve (Horse Racer)
1070 Club House Blvd
New Smyrna, FL 32168-7964, USA

Elliott, Ted (Writer)
c/o Brian Siberell *Creative Artists Agency (CAA)*
2000 Avenue of the Stars Ste 100
Los Angeles, CA 90067-4705, USA

Ellis, A J (Athlete, Baseball Player)
301 Keene Manor Cir
Nicholasville, KY 40356-7009, USA

Ellis, Alex (Athlete, Basketball Player)
914 S Front St
Hamilton, OH 45011-3016, USA

Ellis, Allan (Athlete, Football Player)
7359 S Dante Ave # 2
Chicago, IL 60619-2116, USA

Ellis, Aunjanue (Actor)
c/o Howard Axel *TMT Entertainment Group*
648 Broadway # 1002
New York, NY 10012-2348, USA

Ellis, Bo (Athlete, Basketball Player)
516 North 14th Street
Milwaukee, WI 53233, USA

Ellis, Bret Easton (Writer)
c/o Staff Member *Vintage Books*
1745 Broadway Frnt 3 # 12-1
New York, NY 10019-4343, USA

Ellis, Caroline (Actor)
14600 Overhill Rd
Whitewater, CA 92282-2813, USA

Ellis, Chris (Athlete, Football Player)
c/o Adam Heller *Vantage Management Group*
518 Reamer Dr
Carnegie, PA 15106-1845, USA

Ellis, Cliff (Basketball Player, Coach)
Auburn University
Athletic Dept
Auburn, AL 36831, USA

Ellis, Dale (Athlete, Basketball Player)
3564 W Hampton Dr NW
Marietta, GA 30064-1775, USA

Ellis, Dan (Athlete, Hockey Player)
1505 N 188th St
Elkhorn, NE 68022-4522, USA

Ellis, Danny (Athlete, Golfer)
1543 Cherry Lake Way
Lake Mary, FL 32746-1906, USA

Ellis, Gerry (Athlete, Football Player)
250 Cavil Way
De Pere, WI 54115-3772, USA

Ellis, Gregory (Athlete, Football Player)
PO Box 96075
Southlake, TX 76092-0111, USA

Ellis, Harold (Athlete, Basketball Player)
9420 Parkwood Ave
Douglasville, GA 30135-7504, USA

Ellis, Hunter (Actor, Reality Star)
c/o Lauren Feeney *Ideal Management*
172 81st St
Brooklyn, NY 11209-3502, United States

Ellis, Janet (Actor)
Arlington Entertainments
1/3 Charlotte St
London W1P 1HD, UNITED KINGDOM (UK)

Ellis, Jay (Actor)
c/o Rachel Karten *ID Public Relations*
7060 Hollywood Blvd Fl 8th
Los Angeles, CA 90028-6021, USA

Ellis, Jim (Athlete, Baseball Player)
13608 Avenue 224
Tulare, CA 93274-9304, USA

Ellis, Joe (Athlete, Basketball Player)
Perfect Shot Skills
PO Box 8055
Foster City, CA 94404-8055, USA

Ellis, John (Athlete, Baseball Player)
Connecticut Sports Foundation
15 N Main St
Old Saybrook, CT 06475-4204, USA

Ellis, Joseph J (Writer)
Mount Holyoke College
History Dept
South Hadley, MA 01075, USA

Ellis, Kathleen (Kathy) (Swimmer)
3024 Woodshore Ct
Carmel, IN 46033-3643, USA

Ellis, Kenneth (Athlete, Football Player)
13826 Brantley Dr
Baker, LA 70714-4634, USA

Ellis, Kenrick (Athlete, Football Player)
c/o Brian Levy *Goal Line Football Management*
1025 Kane Concourse Ste 207
Bay Harbor Islands, FL 33154-2118, USA

Ellis, LaPhonso (Athlete, Basketball Player)
51215 Shannon Brook Ct
Granger, IN 46530-7905, USA

Ellis, Luther (Athlete, Football Player)
527 Riverside Ave
Mancos, CO 81328, USA

Ellis, Mark (Athlete, Baseball Player)
19301 N 100th Way
Scottsdale, AZ 85255-2606, USA

Ellis, Mary Elizabeth (Actor)
2175 W Live Oak Dr
Los Angeles, CA 90068-3640, USA

Ellis, Maurice (Bo) (Athlete, Basketball Player)
1229 E 158th St
South Holland, IL 60473-1804, USA

Ellis, Michelle (Athlete, Golfer)
30842 Temple Stand Ave
Wesley Chapel, FL 33543-7105, USA

Ellis, Ray (Athlete, Football Player)
10555 E Corbin Ave
Mesa, AZ 85212-9486, USA

Ellis, Rob (Athlete, Baseball Player)
2020 Krislin Dr NE
Grand Rapids, MI 49505-7160, USA

Ellis, Robert (Athlete, Baseball Player)
2066 75th Ave
Baton Rouge, LA 70807-5836, USA

Ellis, Romallis (Athlete, Boxer, Olympic Athlete)
2062 San Marco Dr
Ellenwood, GA 30294-1009, USA

Ellis, Ronald J E (Ron) (Athlete, Hockey Player)
c/o Staff Member *Hockey Hall of Fame*
Brookfield Place
30 Yonge St
Toronto, ON M5E 1X8, CANADA

Ellis, Samuel J (Sam) (Baseball Player)
12511 Forest Highlands Dr
Dade City, FL 33525-8273, USA

Ellis, Scott (Director)
420 Central Park W Apt 5B
New York, NY 10025-4315, USA

Ellis, Sean (Actor)
c/o Jessica Sykes *Independent Talent Group*
40 Whitfield St
London W1T 2RH, UNITED KINGDOM

Ellis, Sedrick (Athlete, Football Player)
c/o Eugene Parker *Independent Sports & Entertainment (ISE-IN)*
6435 W Jefferson Blvd # 197
Fort Wayne, IN 46804-6203, USA

Ellis, Shuan (Athlete, Football Player)
1000 Fulton Ave
Hempstead, NY 11550-1030, USA

Ellis, Terry (Music Group)
East West Records
75 Rockefeller Plz Ste 1200
New York, NY 10019-7849, USA

Ellis, Tom (Actor)
c/o Lauren Gold *Shelter PR*
5670 Wilshire Blvd Ste 1200
Los Angeles, CA 90036-5621, USA

Ellis-Bextor, Sophie (Actor, Musician)
c/o Staff Member *Universal Music Ltd (UK)*
22 St Peters Square
London W6 9NW, UNITED KINGDOM

Ellis Brothers (Music Group, Musician)
PO Box 50221
Nashville, TN 37205-0221, USA

Ellis Jr, Clarence J (Athlete, Football Player)
120 Hights Holw
Fayetteville, GA 30215-5139, USA

Ellison, Chase (Actor)
c/o Staff Member *Artistry Management*
340 N Camden Dr Ste 302
Beverly Hills, CA 90210-5116, USA

Ellison, David (Actor)

Ellison, Jason (Athlete, Baseball Player)
3745 248th Ave SE
Sammamish, WA 98029-7717, USA

Ellison, Jennifer (Actor)
c/o Colette Fenlon *Colette Fenlon Management*
2A Eaton Rd
West Derby
Liverpool L2 7JJ, UNITED KINGDOM

Ellison, Keith (Congressman, Politician)
1027 Longworth Hob
Washington, DC 20515-2101, USA

Ellison, Larry (Business Person)
Oracle Systems
500 Oracle Pkwy
Redwood City, CA 94065-1677, USA

Ellison, Lawrence J (Business Person)
Oracle Systems
500 Oracle Pkwy
Redwood City, CA 94065-1677, USA

Ellison, Megan (Producer)
1 Electra Ct
Los Angeles, CA 90046-2061, USA

Ellison, Pervis (Athlete, Basketball Player)
4602 Kettering Dr NE
Roswell, GA 30075-3190, USA

Ellison, Rhett (Athlete, Football Player)
c/o Tony Paige *Dream Point Sports*
1455 Pennsylvania Ave NW Ste 225
Washington, DC 20004-1026, USA

Ellison, Riki (Athlete, Football Player)
11 Wharf St
Alexandria, VA 22314-3881, USA

Ellison, William H (Willie) (Athlete, Football Player)
3902 Belgrade Dr
Houston, TX 77045-3404, USA

Elliss, Luther (Athlete, Football Player)
1324 Franklin Rd
Moscow, ID 83843-8208, USA

Ellroy, James (Writer)
Sobel Weber Assoc
146 E 19th St
New York, NY 10003-2404, USA

Ellsberg, Daniel (Politician)
90 Norwood Ave
Kensington, CA 94707-1150, USA

Ellsburv, Jacoby (Athlete, Baseball Player)
2007 Boston Red Sox
3636 SE Midvale Dr, Corvallis OR, 97333-3229

Ellsbury, Jacoby (Athlete, Baseball Player)
c/o Scott Boras *Boras Corporation*
18 Corporate Plaza Dr
Newport Beach, CA 92660-7901, USA

Ellsworth, Dick (Athlete, Baseball Player)
1099 W Morris Ave
USA

Ellsworth, Kiko (Actor)
c/o Staff Member *Psycho Rock Productions*
PO Box 55305
Sherman Oaks, CA 91413-0305, USA

Ellsworth, Percy (Athlete, Football Player)
11261 Fortsville Rd
Drewryville, VA 23844, USA

Ellsworth, Steve (Athlete, Baseball Player)
546 W Enterprise Ave
Clovis, CA 93619-8356, USA

Ellzey, Charley (Athlete, Football Player)
116 Roosevelt St
Quitman, MS 39355-2018, USA

Elman, Jamie (Actor)
c/o Staff Member *The Kohner Agency*
9300 Wilshire Blvd Ste 555
Beverly Hills, CA 90212-3211, USA

Elmendorf, Dave (Athlete, Football Player)
17990 FM 1452 W
Normangee, TX 77871-4174, USA

Elmore, Henry (Athlete, Baseball Player)
4311 43rd Pl N
Birmingham, AL 35217-3925, USA

Elmore, Len (Athlete, Basketball Player)
PO Box 22
Highland, MD 20777-0022, USA

El Moussa, Christina (Reality Star)
c/o Antranig Balian *Mortar Media*
9465 Wilshire Blvd Ste 300
Beverly Hills, CA 90212-2624, USA

Eloani, Sandra (Actor)
c/o Stefan Jacobs *Heretic Entertainment*
1205 Electric Ave
Venice, CA 90291-3324, USA

Elordi, Jacob (Actor)
c/o Nicky Gluyas *Nicky Gluyas Management*
PO Box 564
Avalon Beach NSW 02107, AUSTRALIA

Elrod, Jack (Cartoonist)
770 Old Loganville Rd
Loganville, GA 30052-2578, USA

Elrod, Scott (Actor)
c/o Steven Muller *Innovative Artists*
1505 10th St
Santa Monica, CA 90401-2805, USA

Els, Ernie (Athlete, Golfer)
c/o Andrew ""Chubby"" Chandler
International Sports Management Ltd (ISM UK)
Cherry Tree Farm
Cherry Tree Lane
Rostherne, Cheshire WA14 3RZ, UNITED KINGDOM

Elshire, Neil (Athlete, Football Player)
2441 NW Torsway St
Bend, OR 97703-8647, USA

Elsna, Hebe (Writer)
Curtis Brown
162/168 Regent St
London W1R 5TB, UNITED KINGDOM (UK)

Elsner, Hannelore (Actor)
ZBF Leopoldstr. 19
Munich, GERMANY D-80802

Elson, Francisco (Athlete, Basketball Player)
92 Foxton Drive
San Antonio, TX 78260-7749, USA

Elson, Karen (Model)
Ford Models Agence
9 Rue Scribe
Paris 75009, FRANCE

Elster, Kevin (Athlete, Baseball Player)
5801 Marshall Dr
Huntington Beach, CA 92649-2727, USA

Elston, Darrell (Athlete, Basketball Player)
113 Edward St
Tipton, IN 46072-8945, USA

Elston, Gene (Commentator)
10810 Ashcroft Dr
Houston, TX 77096-6021, USA

Elsworth, Michael (Actor)
Sharon Power
PO Box 1243
Wellington, NEW ZEALAND

Elswrit, Richard (Rik) (Music Group)
Artists Int'l Mgmt
9850 Sandalwood Blvd #458
Boca Raton, FL 33428, USA

Elton, Ben (Actor, Comedian)
Phil McIntyre Management
35 Soho Sq
London W1D 3QX, UNITED KINGDOM

E. Lungren, Daniel (Congressman, Politician)
2313 Rayburn Hob
Washington, DC 20515-1401, USA

Elvira (Actor, Television Host)
Queen B Productions
PO Box 3022
Newport Beach, CA 92659-0556, USA

Elvira, Narciso (Athlete, Baseball Player)
Dom Conocida El
Concuite Mun Tlalix, Mexico, USA

Elway, John A (Athlete, Football Player)
Elway's
4763 S Elizabeth Ct
Englewood, CO 80113-7105, USA

Elwes, Cary (Actor)
c/o Britney Ross *42West*
1840 Century Park E Ste 700
Los Angeles, CA 90067-2122, USA

Ely, Alexandre (Soccer Player)
5526 N 2nd St
Philadelphia, PA 19120-2904, USA

Ely, Joe (Musician, Songwriter)
8949 Appaloosa Run
Austin, TX 78737-4016, USA

Ely, Larry (Athlete, Football Player)
12190 Waters Edge Ct
Loveland, OH 45140-4828, USA

Ely, Melvin (Basketball Player)
Los Angeles Clippers
Staples Center 1111 S Figueroa St
Los Angeles, CA 90015, USA

Elynuik, Pat (Athlete, Hockey Player)
143 Aspen Green
Calgary, AB T3Z 3B9, Canada

Emanuel, Alphonsia (Actor)
Marina Martin
12/13 Poland St
London W1V 2DE, UNITED KINGDOM (UK)

Emanuel, Ari (Business Person)
1647 Mandeville Canyon Rd
Los Angeles, CA 90049-2523, USA

Emanuel, Bert (Athlete, Football Player)
15 Bees Creek Ct
Missouri City, TX 77459-6734, USA

Emanuel, Elizabeth F (Designer, Fashion Designer)
42A Warrington Crescent
Maida Vale
London W9 1EP, UNITED KINGDOM (UK)

Emanuel, Frank (Athlete, Football Player)
10211 Deercliff Dr
Tampa, FL 33647-2941, USA

Emanuel, Rahm (Politician)
Mayor's Office
121 N Salle St
Suite 507
Chicago, IL 60602, USA

Embach, Carsten (Athlete)
BSR Rennsteig e V
Grafenrodaer Str 2
Oberhof 98559, GERMANY

Emberg, Kelly (Actor, Model)
PO Box 675401
Rancho Santa Fe, CA 92067-5401, USA

Emblem3 (Music Group)
18685 Main St Ste 101
Huntington Beach, CA 92648-1719, USA

Embrace (Music Group)
c/o Staff Member *Paradigm (Monterey)*
404 W Franklin St
Monterey, CA 93940-2303, USA

Embree, Alan (Athlete, Baseball Player)
238 NW Outlook Vista Dr
Bend, OR 97703-5473, USA

Embree, Jon (Athlete, Football Player)
2300 S Rock Creek Pkwy Apt 14201
Superior, CO 80027-4409, USA

Embry, Ethan (Actor)
c/o Brad Schenck *ICM Partners*
10250 Constellation Blvd Fl 7
Los Angeles, CA 90067-6207, USA

Emerick, Kate (Actor)

Emerson, Chris (Actor)
c/o Lorraine Berglund *Lorraine Berglund Management*
11537 Hesby St
North Hollywood, CA 91601-3618, USA

Emerson, Douglas (Actor)
1450 Belfast Dr
Los Angeles, CA 90069-1327, USA

Emerson, Jo Ann (Congressman, Politician)
2230 Rayburn Hob
Washington, DC 20515-1404, USA

Emerson, Max (Actor, Model)
c/o Mark Pfeffer *Luber Roklin Management*
5815 W Sunset Blvd Ste 208
Los Angeles, CA 90028-6481, USA

Emerson, Michael (Actor)
c/o Staff Member *Vanguard Management Group*
8060 Melrose Ave Fl 4
Los Angeles, CA 90046-7038, USA

Emerson, Nelson (Athlete, Hockey Player)
717 33rd St
Manhattan Beach, CA 90266-3425, USA

Emerson, Roy (Athlete, Tennis Player)
2221 Alta Vista Dr
Newport Beach, CA 92660-4128, USA

Emerson Drive (Music Group)
c/o Staff Member *Creative Artists Agency (CAA)*
401 Commerce St PH
Nashville, TN 37219-2516, USA

Emery, Brent (Athlete, Cycler, Olympic Athlete)
N62W15 Teepee Court
Menomonee Falls, WI 53051

Emery, Gareth (DJ, Musician)
c/o David Lewis *Buchwald (NY)*
10 E 44th St
New York, NY 10017-3601, USA

Emery, John (Athlete)
2001 Union St
San Francisco, CA 94123-4114, USA

Emery, Julie Ann (Actor)
c/o Mona Loring *Status PR*
PO Box 6191
Westlake Village, CA 91359-6191, USA

Emery, Oren D (Religious Leader)
Wesleyan International
6060 Castleway West Dr
Indianapolis, IN 46250-1906, USA

Emery, Ralph (DJ)
RFD-TV / Rural Media Group
1 Valmont Plz Ste 400
Omaha, NE 68154-5301, USA

Emery, Victor (Athlete)
61 Walton St
London SW 3J, UNITED KINGDOM (UK)

Emick, Jarrod (Actor)
Gersh Agency
232 N Canon Dr
Beverly Hills, CA 90210-5302, USA

Emilio (Music Group)
Refugee Mgmt
209 10th Ave S #347 Cummins Station
Nashville, TN 37203, USA

Emin, Tracey (Director)
European Graduate School
Alter Kehr 20
Leuk-Stadt CH-3953, Switzerland

Eminem (Musician)
c/o Paul Rosenberg *Goliath Artists*
151 Lafayette St Rm 6
New York, NY 10013-3617, USA

Eminger, Steve (Athlete, Hockey Player)
145 Triton Ave
Woodbridge, ON L4L 6R8, Canada

Emma, David (Athlete, Hockey Player, Olympic Athlete)
6702 Stonegate Dr
Naples, FL 34109-7224, USA

Emmanuel (Musician)
Sendyk Leonard
532 Colorado Ave
Santa Monica, CA 90401-2408, USA

Emmanuel, Nathalie (Actor)
c/o Meredith O'Sullivan Wasson *The Lede Company*
9701 Wilshire Blvd # 930
Beverly Hills, CA 90212-2020, USA

Emmanuel, Tommy (Musician)
c/o Staff Member *Paradigm (Monterey)*
404 W Franklin St
Monterey, CA 93940-2303, USA

Emmanuel, Tommy (Musician)
CPR Entertainment (Gina Mendello)
PO Box 121983
Nashville, TN 37212-1983, USA

Emme (Model)
c/o Daniel Strone *Trident Media Group LLC*
41 Madison Ave Fl 36
New York, NY 10010-2257, USA

Emmel, Paul (Athlete, Baseball Player)
8462 Idlewood Ct
Lakewood Ranch, FL 34202-2216, USA

Emmerich, Noah (Actor, Producer)
c/o Jason Gutman *Gersh*
41 Madison Ave Ste 3301
New York, NY 10010-2210, USA

Emmerich, Roland (Director, Producer)
c/o Staff Member *Centropolis Entertainment*
818 N La Brea Ave # 1
Los Angeles, CA 90038-3341, USA

Emmerton, Bill (Athlete, Track Athlete)
615 Ocean Ave
Santa Monica, CA 90402-2611, USA

Emmons, John (Athlete, Hockey Player)
67589 Rachael Ln
Washington, MI 48095-1844, USA

Emory, Sonny (Musician)
Great Scott Productions
137 N Wetherly Dr Apt 403
Los Angeles, CA 90048-2866, USA

Emotions (Music Group)
c/o Staff Member *Diva Central Inc*
7510 W Sunset Blvd # 1445
Los Angeles, CA 90046-3408, USA

Emrick, Mike (Doc) (Athlete, Hockey Player)
PO Box 246
Marysville, MI 48040-0246, USA

Emtman, Steven C (Steve) (Athlete, Football Player)
19601 S Cheney Spangle Rd
Cheney, WA 99004-9040, USA

Ena, Justin (Athlete, Football Player)
1252 W 2050 S
Syracuse, UT 84075-9566, USA

Enan, Susan (Musician)
c/o Staff Member *Paradigm (Monterey)*
404 W Franklin St
Monterey, CA 93940-2303, USA

Enau, Ron (Race Car Driver)
Bunch Racing
9009 Topsail Cove Dr Apt B
Huntersville, NC 28078-4904, USA

Enberg, Alexander (Actor)
c/o Staff Member *TalentWorks*
3500 W Olive Ave Ste 1400
Burbank, CA 91505-5512, USA

En Blanco Y Negro (Music Group)
c/o Staff Member *Sony Music (Miami)*
404 Washington Ave Ste 700
Miami Beach, FL 33139-6615, USA

Enbom, John (Writer)
c/o Staff Member *Creative Artists Agency (CAA)*
2000 Avenue of the Stars Ste 100
Los Angeles, CA 90067-4705, USA

Encarnacion, Luis (Athlete, Baseball Player)
6 las Cabos De Herrer
Manz 9 Santo Domingo, Dominican Republic, USA

Endean, Craig (Athlete, Hockey Player)
650 Garnet Rd
Kamloops, BC V2B 6K1, Canada

Endelman, Stephen (Musician)
c/o Staff Member *Robert Urband & Associates*
1200 Esplanade Apt 222
Redondo Beach, CA 90277-4951, USA

Ender, Grummt Kornelia (Swimmer)
DSV
Postfach 420140
Kassel 34070, GERMANY

Enders, Erica (Race Car Driver)
Enders Racing
18000 Groeschke Rd
Hanger A2
Houston, TX 77084-5675, USA

Enders, Trevor (Athlete, Baseball Player)
25906 Silver Timbers Ln
Katy, TX 77494-0726, USA

Endicott, Lori (Athlete, Olympic Athlete, Volleyball Player)
351 Dogwood Rdg
Rogersville, MO 65742-8183, USA

Endicott, Shane (Athlete, Hockey Player)
1025 2nd St E
Saskatoon, SK S7H 1R2, Canada

End of Fashion (Music Group)
c/o Staff Member *Paradigm (Monterey)*
404 W Franklin St
Monterey, CA 93940-2303, USA

Endress, Albert (al) (Athlete, Football Player)
201 Oregon Ave
Louisville, OH 44641-2332, USA

Endress, Belinda (Race Car Driver)
God Speed on Wheels
PO Box 501
Newbury Park, CA 91319-0501, USA

Endress, Ned (Athlete, Basketball Player)
1632 Highbridge Rd
Cuyahoga Falls, OH 44223-2363, USA

E. Neal, Richard (Congressman, Politician)
2208 Rayburn Hob
Washington, DC 20515-0522, USA

Enemkpali, IK (Athlete, Football Player)

Engblom, Brian (Athlete, Hockey Player)
410 Barcelona Dr
Saint Petersburg, FL 33716-1206, USA

Engel, Bob (Athlete, Baseball Player)
350 Calloway Dr Unit A329
Bakersfield, CA 93312-2981, USA

Engel, Georgia (Actor)
c/o Staff Member *Peter Strain & Associates Inc (LA)*
10901 Whipple St Apt 322
N Hollywood, CA 91602-3245, USA

Engel, Steve (Athlete, Baseball Player)
6212 Old Stone Ct
Fairfield Township, OH 45011-0003, USA

Engelberger, John (Athlete, Football Player)
8176 Cliffview Ave
Springfield, VA 22153-2623, USA

Engelhard, David H (Religious Leader)
Cristian Reformed Church
2850 Kalamazoo Ave SE
Grand Rapids, MI 49560-1500, USA

Engen, D Travis (Business Person)
ITT Industries
4 W Red Oak Ln Ste 200
White Plains, NY 10604-3603, USA

Enger, John (Athlete, Golfer)
c/o Jim Lehrman *Medalist Management Inc*
36855 W Main St Ste 200
Purcellville, VA 20132-3561, USA

Engibous, Thomas J (Business Person)
Texas Instruments
PO Box 660199
Dallas, TX 75266-0199, USA

England, Anthony W Dr (Astronaut)
3520 Blue Heron Ct
Ypsilanti, MI 48198-9609, USA

England, Tyler (Music Group)
Buddy Lee
665 Whyte Ave
Roseville, CA 95661-5240, USA

Engle, Dave (Athlete, Baseball Player)
5343 Castle Hills Dr
San Diego, CA 92109-1926, USA

Engle, Doug (Baseball Player)
Montreal Expos
17282 Heiser Rd
Berlin Center, OH 44401-9784, USA

Engle, Eleanor (Commentator)
Archives
319 W Main St
Camp Hill, PA 17011-6333, USA

Engle, Joe (Astronaut)
PO Box 58386
Houston, TX 77258-8386, USA

Engle, Jon (Race Car Driver)
Engle Motorsports
960 Saint Andrews Ln
Louisville, CO 80027-9589, USA

Engle, Rick (Athlete, Baseball Player)
6413 Seneca Trl
Mentor, OH 44060-3416, USA

Engleberg, Mort (Producer)
Mort Engelberg Productions, Inc.
1504 Rising Glen Rd
Los Angeles, CA 90069-1226, USA

Englehorn, Shirley (Athlete, Golfer)
849 Shrine Vw
Colorado Springs, CO 80906-8500, USA

Engler, James (Politician)
PO Box 3037
Mount Pleasant, ML 48804, USA

Engler, Michael (Director, Producer)
c/o Staff Member *United Talent Agency (UTA)*
9336 Civic Center Dr
Beverly Hills, CA 90210-3604, USA

Englert, Alice (Actor)
c/o Heidi Lopata *Narrative*
1601 Vine St Fl 6
Los Angeles, CA 90028-8802, USA

Engles, Rick (Athlete, Football Player)
11307 S Vine St
Jenks, OK 74037-2466, USA

English, A J (Athlete, Basketball Player)
305 Green Ct
Middletown, DE 19709-6803, USA

English, Alex (Athlete, Basketball Player)
596 Rimer Pond Rd
Blythewood, SC 29016-9448, USA

English, Claude (Athlete, Basketball Player)
14041 Switzer Rd
Overland Park, KS 66221-9735, USA

English, Corri (Actor)
c/o Staff Member *SMS Talent*
8383 Wilshire Blvd Ste 230
Beverly Hills, CA 90211-2436, USA

English, Diane (Writer)
c/o Staff Member *Shukovsky/English Entertainment*
4605 Lankershim Blvd Ste 510
North Hollywood, CA 91602-1877

English, Edmond J (Business Person)
TJX Companies
770 Cochituate Rd
Framingham, MA 01701-4698, USA

English, Floyd L (Business Person)
Andrew Corp
10500 W 153rd St
Orland Park, IL 60462-3071, USA

English, JoJo (Athlete, Basketball Player)
133 Ramblewood Dr
Columbia, SC 29209-4439, USA

English, Kim (Musician)
c/o Staff Member *Diva Central Inc*
7510 W Sunset Blvd # 1445
Los Angeles, CA 90046-3408, USA

English, Larry (Athlete, Football Player)
c/o Todd France *Creative Artists Agency (CAA) Sports*
3500 Lenox Rd NE
Atlanta, GA 30326-4228, USA

English, L Douglas (Doug) (Athlete, Football Player)
4306 Bennedict Ln
Austin, TX 78746-1940, USA

English, Madeline (Athlete, Baseball Player)
55 Clinton St
Everett, MA 02149-4640, USA

English, Michael (Music Group)
Trifecta Entertainment
1404 51st Ave N
Nashville, TN 37209-1520, USA

English, Paul (Actor)
Wurzel Talent Mgmt
19528 Ventura Blvd # 501
Tarzana, CA 91356-2917, USA

English, Ralna (Musician)
9321 N 115th St
Scottsdale, AZ 85259-5849, USA

English, Scott (Athlete, Basketball Player)
9303 E Spur Crossing Pl
Tucson, AZ 85749-9240, USA

English, Todd (Chef)
c/o Staff Member *Grand Productions*
2811 Champion Rd
Naperville, IL 60564-4958, USA

Englund, Robert (Actor)
1278 Glenneyre St PMB 73
Laguna Beach, CA 92651-3103, USA

Engram, Simon (Bobby) (Athlete, Football Player)
1104 Black River Rd
Camden, SC 29020-9720, USA

Engstrom, Molly (Athlete, Hockey Player, Olympic Athlete)
7560 Southshore Dr
Siren, WI 54872

Engvall, Bill (Actor, Comedian, Producer)
c/o J P Williams *Parallel Entertainment (LA)*
15025 Altata Dr
Pacific Palisades, CA 90272-4450, USA

Enigma (Music Group)
c/o Staff Member *Virgin Records (NY)*
150 5th Ave Fl 7
New York, NY 10011-4372, USA

Enis, Curtis (Athlete, Football Player)
10972 Comanche Dr
Sidney, OH 45365-9586, USA

Enis, Hunter (Athlete, Football Player)
2521 Marley Rd
Jacksboro, TX 76458-3808, USA

Enke, Fred (Athlete, Football Player)
206 E McMurray Blvd
Casa Grande, AZ 85122-3415, USA

Enke-Kania, Karin (Athlete, Skier)
Tolstoistr 3
Dresden 01326, GERMANY

Enlow, Johnny (Religious Leader, Writer)
DAYSTAR
3434 Pleasantdale Rd
Atlanta, GA 30340-4204, USA

Enn, Hans (Skier)
Hinterglemm 400
Saalbach 05754, AUSTRIA

Ennis, Jessica (Athlete, Olympic Athlete)
JCCM Ltd
Matrix Studios
91 Peterborough Rd
London SW6 3BU, UK

Ennis, John (Athlete, Baseball Player)
2231 Agate Ct
Simi Valley, CA 93065-1841, USA

Ennis, Ralph (Musician)
2 Kirklake Bank
Formby
Liverpool L37 2Y5, UNITED KINGDOM (UK)

Ennis, Ray (Musician)
2 Kirklake Bank
Formby
Liverpool L37 2Y5, UNITED KINGDOM (UK)

Ennis Sisters, The (Music Group)
c/o Staff Member *Paradigm (Monterey)*
404 W Franklin St
Monterey, CA 93940-2303, USA

Eno, Brian (Musician)
c/o Bryan Loucks *Creative Artists Agency (CAA)*
2000 Avenue of the Stars Ste 100
Los Angeles, CA 90067-4705, USA

Enoch, Alfred (Actor)
c/o Estelle Lasher *Lasher Group*
1133 Avenue of the Americas Fl 27
New York, NY 10036-6710, USA

Enos, John (Actor)
c/o Susan Ferris *Bohemia Group*
1680 Vine St Ste 518
Los Angeles, CA 90028-8833, USA

Enos, Lisa (Actor, Producer)
c/o Staff Member *ICM Partners*
10250 Constellation Blvd Fl 7
Los Angeles, CA 90067-6207, USA

Enos, Mireille (Actor)
c/o Heidi Lopata *Narrative*
1601 Vine St Fl 6
Los Angeles, CA 90028-8802, USA

Enos, Randal (Cartoonist)
402 N Park Ave
Easton, CT 06612-1248, USA

Enright, Barry (Athlete, Baseball Player)
11627 E Regal Ct
Chandler, AZ 85249-4545, USA

Enright, George (Athlete, Baseball Player)
3075 Strawflower Way
Lake Worth, FL 33467-1465, USA

Ensberg, Morgan (Athlete, Baseball Player)
5535 Memorial Dr Ste F PMB 114
Houston, TX 77007-8023, USA

Ensign, Michael (Actor)
Abrams Artists
9200 W Sunset Blvd Ste 1125
Los Angeles, CA 90069-3610, USA

Ensler, Eve (Actor, Producer, Writer)
c/o Staff Member *Little, Brown Book Group*
100 Victoria Embankment
London EC4Y 0DY, UK

Entner, Warren (Music Group)
Thomas Cassidy
11761 E Speedway Blvd
Tucson, AZ 85748-2017, USA

Entremont, Philippe (Musician)
10 Rue de Castuglione
Paris 75001, FRANCE

En Vogue (Music Group)
c/o Joe Mulvihill *LiveWire Entertainment (FL)*
7575 Dr Phillips Blvd Ste 255
Orlando, FL 32819-7220, USA

Enya (Musician)
Manderley Castle
Victoria Road
Dalkey Co, Dublin, Ireland

Enzensberger, Hans M (Writer)
Lindenstr 29
Frankfurt am Maim 60325, GERMANY

Enzi, Michael (Politician)
431 Circle Dr
Gillette, WY 82716-4903, USA

E. Petri, Thomas (Congressman, Politician)
2462 Rayburn Hob
Washington, DC 20515-4906, USA

Ephraim, Alonzo (Athlete, Football Player)
1713 Five Acre Rd
Dolomite, AL 35061-1038, USA

Ephraim, Molly (Actor)
c/o Josh Katz *United Talent Agency (UTA)*
9336 Civic Center Dr
Beverly Hills, CA 90210-3604, USA

Epic (Artist, Musician)
Wyze Mgmt
34 Maple St
London W1 5GD, UNITED KINGDOM (UK)

Epik High (Music Group)
c/o Staff Member *WME|IMG*
9601 Wilshire Blvd
Beverly Hills, CA 90210-5213, USA

Epler, Jim (Race Car Driver)
1600 W Struck Ave # 11
Orange, CA 92867-3427, USA

Eppard, Jim (Athlete, Baseball Player)
23115 153rd Ave
Rapid City, SD 57703-9041, USA

Epperson-Doumani, Brenda (Actor)
kazarian/Spencer
11365 Ventura Blvd Ste 100
Studio City, CA 91604-3148, USA

Epple, Maria (Skier)
Gunzesried 3
Blaicach 87544, GERMANY

Epple-Beck, Irene (Skier)
Autmberg 235
Seeg 87637, GERMANY

Epps, Bobby (Athlete, Football Player)
934 Illinois Ave
Pittsburgh, PA 15221-4718, USA

Epps, Jeanette J (Astronaut)
4727 Five Knolls Dr
Friendswood, TX 77546-3160, USA

Epps, Mike (Actor, Comedian)
c/o Danica Smith *Kovert Creative*
506 Santa Monica Blvd Ste 400
Santa Monica, CA 90401-2412, USA

Epps, Omar (Actor, Producer)
c/o Staff Member *BrooklynWorks Films*
3532 Hayden Ave
Culver City, CA 90232-2413, USA

Epps, Raymond (Athlete, Basketball Player)
4030 Old Warwick Rd
Richmond, VA 23234-1975, USA

E. Price, David (Congressman, Politician)
2162 Rayburn Hob
Washington, DC 20515-3304, USA

Epstein, Daniel M (Writer)
843 W University Pkwy
Baltimore, MD 21210-2911, USA

Epstein, Mike (Athlete, Baseball Player)
1265 Nightfire Cir
Castle Rock, CO 80104-7707, USA

Epstein, Theo (Commentator)
c/o Staff Member *Chicago Cubs*
1060 W Addison St
Wrigley Field
Chicago, IL 60613-4397, USA

Erardi, Greg (Athlete, Baseball Player)
42 Westgate Rd
Massapequa Park, NY 11762-1953, USA

Erasure (Music Group)
c/o Kirk Sommer *WME|IMG*
9601 Wilshire Blvd
Beverly Hills, CA 90210-5213, USA

Erat, Martin (Athlete, Hockey Player)
4 Crooked Stick Ln
Brentwood, TN 37027-8938, USA

Erautt, Eddie (Athlete, Baseball Player)
7252 Waite Dr
La Mesa, CA 91941-7631, USA

Erb, Christy (Athlete, Golfer)
4043 Country Trl
Bonita, CA 91902-3025, USA

Erbe, Kathryn (Actor)
c/o Gary Gersh *Innovative Artists*
235 Park Ave S Fl 7
New York, NY 10003-1405, USA

Erdman, Dennis (Actor, Director, Producer)
c/o Staff Member *ICM Partners*
10250 Constellation Blvd Fl 7
Los Angeles, CA 90067-6207, USA

Erdman, Paul E (Writer)
1817 Lytton Springs Rd
Healdsburg, CA 95448-9145, USA

Erdman, Richard (Actor)
PO Box 715
Van Nuys, CA 91408-0715, USA

Erdmann, Susi-Lisa (Athlete)
Karwendelstr 8A
Munich 81369, GERMANY

Erdo, Peter Cardinal (Religious Leader)
Mindszenty Hercegprimas Ter 2
Esztergom Magyarirszay 02501, HUNGARY

Erdos, Todd (Athlete, Baseball Player)
406 Honey Locust Dr
Cranberry Township, PA 16066-3764, USA

Erenberg, Richard (Athlete, Football Player)
318 Snowberry Cir
Venetia, PA 15367-1043, USA

Ergenc, Halit (Actor)
c/o Ayse Barim *Id Iletisim*
Safran Sok. No.5
Levent
Istanbul NA, TURKEY

Erhuero, Oris (Actor)
c/o Staff Member *Midwest Talent Management Inc*
4821 Lankershim Blvd Ste F149
N Hollywood, CA 91601-4538, USA

Eric, B (Music Group, Musician)
Rush Artists
1600 Varick St
New York, NY 10013, USA

Eric Kaplan, Bruce (Producer)
c/o Staff Member *WME|IMG*
9601 Wilshire Blvd
Beverly Hills, CA 90210-5213, USA

Ericks, John (Athlete, Baseball Player)
17000 Oketo Ave
Tinley Park, IL 60477-2630, USA

Erickson, Bryan (Athlete, Hockey Player)
5012 Prosperity Way S
Fargo, ND 58104-7567, USA

Erickson, Bud (Athlete, Football Player)
14523 165th Pl NE
Woodinville, WA 98072-9037, USA

Erickson, Chad (Athlete, Hockey Player)
56213 349th St
Warroad, MN 56763-9127, USA

Erickson, Craig (Athlete, Football Player)
420 N Country Club Dr
Lake Worth, FL 33462-1004, USA

Erickson, Dennis (Athlete, Coach, Football Coach, Football Player)
4949 Marie P Debartolo Way
Santa Clara, CA 95054-1156, USA

Erickson, Ethan (Actor)
c/o Staff Member *Diverse Talent Group*
1875 Century Park E Ste 2250
Los Angeles, CA 90067-2563, USA

Erickson, Grant (Athlete, Hockey Player)
222 Parks St
Whitewood, SK S0G 5C0, Canada

Erickson, Keith (Athlete, Basketball Player, Volleyball Player)
333 23rd St
Santa Monica, CA 90402-2513, USA

Erickson, Matt (Athlete, Baseball Player)
1408 S Fidelis St
Appleton, WI 54915-4069, USA

Erickson, Millard J. (Writer)
c/o Staff Member *Crossway Books*
1300 Crescent St
Wheaton, IL 60187-5815, USA

Erickson, Roger (Athlete, Baseball Player)
PO Box 235
Sautee Nacoochee, GA 30571-0235, USA

Erickson, Scott (Actor)
c/o Staff Member *ICM Partners*
10250 Constellation Blvd Fl 7
Los Angeles, CA 90067-6207, USA

Erickson, Scott G (Athlete, Baseball Player)
1183 Corral Ave
Sunnyvale, CA 94086-7010, USA

Erickson, Steve (Writer)
Poseidon Press
1230 Avenue of the Americas
New York, NY 10020-1513, USA

Erickson-Sauer, Louise (Athlete, Baseball Player, Commentator)
917 Pleasant Ave
Arcadia, WI 54612-1859, USA

Ericson, John (Actor)
7 Avenida Vista Grande # 310
Santa Fe, NM 87508-9198, USA

Ericsson, Jonathan (Athlete, Hockey Player)
c/o Staff Member *Newport Sports Management*
201 City Centre Dr
Suite 400
Mississauga, ON L58 2T4, CANADA

E. Rigell, Scott (Congressman, Politician)
327 Cannon Hob
Washington, DC 20515-4320, USA

Erik, Erik (Athlete, Olympic Athlete, Skier)
731 Martingale Ln
Park City, UT 84098-7559, USA

Eriksson, Roland (Athlete, Hockey Player)
Falkvagen 6
Vasteras S-72223, Sweden

Erin Gray, Erin Gray (Actor)

Erivo, Cynthia (Actor)
c/o Meg Mortimer *Authentic Talent and Literary Management (NY)*
20 Jay St Ste M17
Brooklyn, NY 11201-8300, USA

Erixon, Jan (Athlete, Hockey Player)
Stenbackav 58
Skelleftea S-93142, Sweden

Erkiletian, Lynda (Reality Star)
c/o Staff Member *Bravo TV (NY)*
30 Rockefeller Plz
New York, NY 10112-0015, USA

Erlandson, Eric (Songwriter, Writer)
Artist Group International
9560 Wilshire Blvd Ste 400
Beverly Hills, CA 90212-2442, USA

Erlandson, Tom Sr (Athlete, Football Player)
5950 S Ogden Ct
Centennial, CO 80121-2484, USA

Erman, John (Director)
c/o Staff Member *Paradigm*
8942 Wilshire Blvd
Beverly Hills, CA 90211-1908, USA

Erna, Sully (Actor, Music Group)
c/o Staff Member *WME|IMG*
9601 Wilshire Blvd Ste 500
Beverly Hills, CA 90210-5207, USA

Ernaga, Frank (Athlete, Baseball Player)
50 N Roop St
Susanville, CA 96130-3926, USA

Ernest, Dixon (Athlete, Football Player)
324 Viceroy Curv
Stockbridge, GA 30281-9140, USA

Erni, Hans (Artist)
6045 Meggen
Lucerne, SWITZERLAND

Ernie, Nimmons (Athlete, Baseball Player)
500 Pine Hollow Blvd Apt 103D
Lorain, OH 44055-3003, USA

Ernman, Malena (Musician)
c/o Staff Member *Eliasson Artists Stockholm*
Skeppargatan 86
Stockholm 114 59, Sweden

Ernst, Bret (Actor, Comedian)
c/o Joan Green *Joan Green Management*
1836 Courtney Ter
Los Angeles, CA 90046-2106, USA

Ernster, Paul (Athlete, Football Player)
6954 S Fultondale Cir
Aurora, CO 80016-4142, USA

Eroy, Iran (Actor)
c/o Staff Member *Televisa*
Blvd Adolfo Lopez Mateos 232
Colonia San Angel INN
DF CP 01060, MEXICO

Errazuriz Ossa, Francisco J Cardinal (Religious Leader)
Casilla 30D
Erasmo Escala 1894
Santiago, CHILE

Errey, Bob (Athlete, Hockey Player)
156 Hickory Heights Dr
Bridgeville, PA 15017-1076, USA

Errico, Melissa (Actor)
c/o Staff Member *Stewart Talent Agency (NY)*
318 W 53rd St Rm 201
New York, NY 10019-5742, USA

Erskine, Carl D (Athlete, Baseball Player)
1111 Primrose Ct
Anderson, IN 46011-9537, USA

Erskine, Peter (Musician)
1727 Hill St
Santa Monica, CA 90405-4843, USA

Erstad, Darin C (Athlete, Baseball Player)
12 Secret Cv
Newport Coast, CA 92657-2107, USA

Ertel, Mark (Athlete, Basketball Player)
1721 Cloister Dr
Indianapolis, IN 46260-1066, USA

Ertl, Martina (Skier)
Erthofe 17
Lenggries 83661, GERMANY

Ertl, Sue (Athlete, Golfer)
4707 Sabal Key Dr
Bradenton, FL 34203-3126, USA

Ertz, Zach (Athlete, Football Player)

Eruzione, Mike (Athlete, Hockey Player, Olympic Athlete)
1 Silber Way Fl 7
Boston, MA 02215-1703, USA

Ervin, Anthony (Athlete, Olympic Athlete, Swimmer)
USOC Alumni Relations
1750 W Boulder St
Colorado Springs, CO 80904, USA

Erving, Cameron (Athlete, Football Player)
c/o Isaac Conner *Allegiant Athletic Agency*
35 Market Sq Ste 201
Knoxville, TN 37902-1420, USA

Erving, Julius (Athlete, Basketball Player)
PO Box 914100
Longwood, FL 32791, USA

Ervins, Ricky (Athlete, Football Player)
20984 Nightshade Pl
Ashburn, VA 20147-4703, USA

Ervolino, Frank (Politician)
Laundry & Dry Cleaning Union
107 Delaware Ave
Buffalo, NY 14202-2810, USA

Erwin, Andrew (Director, Producer)
c/o Staff Member *Erwin Brothers Entertainment*
270 Doug Baker Blvd
Birmingham, AL 35242-2693, USA

Erwin, Jon (Cinematographer, Director)
c/o Staff Member *Erwin Brothers Entertainment*
270 Doug Baker Blvd
Birmingham, AL 35242-2693, USA

Erwin, Mike (Actor)
c/o Mia Hansen *Portrait PR*
5320 Sylmar Ave
Sherman Oaks, CA 91401-5612, USA

Erwin, Terry (Athlete, Football Player)
5596 S Lansing Way
Englewood, CO 80111-4104, USA

Erxleban, Russell (Athlete, Football Player)
306 Saddlehorn Dr
Dripping Springs, TX 78620-2740, USA

Erxleben, Russell A (Athlete, Football Player)
306 Saddlehorn Dr
Dripping Springs, TX 78620-2740, USA

Esasky, Nick (Athlete, Baseball Player)
1779 Starlight Dr
Marietta, GA 30062-1942, USA

Esau, Len (Athlete, Hockey Player)
809 1st St W
Meadow Lake, SK S9X 1E2, Canada

Esbjornson, David (Director)
Mason Gross Performing Arts Center
85 George St
New Brunswick, NJ 08901-1452, USA

Escalera, Nino (Athlete, Baseball Player)
DK20 Calle 201
Carolina, PR 00983-3715, USA

Escamilla, Franco (Comedian)
c/o Staff Member *United Talent Agency (UTA)*
9336 Civic Center Dr
Beverly Hills, CA 90210-3604, USA

Escarpeta, Arlen (Actor)
c/o Laura Ackerman *Advantage PR*
3900 W Alameda Ave Ste 1200
Burbank, CA 91505-4317, USA

Esch, Eric (Butterbean) (Boxer)
Rt 13 Box 254
Jasper, MI 35501, USA

Esche, Robert (Athlete, Hockey Player, Olympic Athlete)
6750 W Carter Rd
Rome, NY 13440-1326, USA

Eschelman, Vaughn (Athlete, Baseball Player)
30106 Falher Dr
Spring, TX 77386-1683, USA

Eschen, larrv (Athlete, Baseball Player)
3649 Garden Blvd
Gainesville, GA 30506-1552, USA

Eschen, Larry (Athlete, Baseball Player)
3649 Garden Blvd
Gainesville, GA 30506-1552, USA

Eschenbach, Christoph (Musician)
Maspalomas
Monte Leon 760625
Gran Canaria, SPAIN

Eschert, Jurgen (Athlete)
Tornowstr 8
Potsdam 01447, GERMANY

Esco, Lina (Actor)
c/o Lena Roklin *Luber Roklin Management*
5815 W Sunset Blvd Ste 208
Los Angeles, CA 90028-6481, USA

Escobar, Gavin (Athlete, Football Player)
c/o Alan Herman *Sportstars Inc*
1370 Avenue of the Americas Fl 19
New York, NY 10019-4602, USA

Escobar, Kelvim (Athlete, Baseball Player)
1292 Biscaya Dr
Surfside, FL 33154-3316, USA

Escobar, Yunel (Athlete, Baseball Player)
15763 SW 43rd St
Miami, FL 33185-3815, USA

Escolar, Irene (Actor)
c/o Carlos Bobadilla *Valor Entertainment*
811 W 7th St Ste 1200
Los Angeles, CA 90017-3423, USA

Escovedo, Pete (Musician)
PO Box 1741
C/O Victor Pamiroyan
Alameda, CA 94501-0199, USA

E. Serrano, Jose (Congressman, Politician)
2227 Rayburn Hob
Washington, DC 20515-3216, USA

Esiason, Norman J (Boomer) (Athlete, Football Player)
25 Heights Rd
Manhasset, NY 11030-1412, USA

Eskridge, Jack (Athlete, Basketball Player)
15297 K4 Hwy
Valley Falls, KS 66088-1293, USA

Esmail, Sam (Director, Producer)
c/o Chad Hamilton *Anonymous Content*
1804 Lincoln Blvd
Venice, CA 90291-3969, USA

Espada, Joey (Athlete, Baseball Player)
220 New Haven Blvd
Jupiter, FL 33458-2831, USA

Esparaza, Michael (Actor)
c/o Carl Scott *Simmons & Scott Entertainment*
7942 Mulholland Dr
Los Angeles, CA 90046-1225, USA

Esparza, Marlen (Athlete, Boxer)
c/o Staff Member *United Talent Agency (UTA)*
9336 Civic Center Dr
Beverly Hills, CA 90210-3604, USA

Esparza, Moctesuma (Producer)
c/o Staff Member *ICM Partners*
10250 Constellation Blvd Fl 7
Los Angeles, CA 90067-6207, USA

Esparza, Raul (Actor)
c/o Elin McManus-Flack *Elin Flack Management*
435 W 57th St Apt 3M
New York, NY 10019-1724, USA

Espenson, Jane (Producer)
c/o Melanie Marquez *M4 Publicity*
11684 Ventura Blvd # 213
Studio City, CA 91604-2699, USA

Esper, Michael (Actor, Dancer)
c/o Sarah Yorke *Baker Winokur Ryder Public Relations*
200 5th Ave Fl 5
New York, NY 10010-3307, USA

Esperon, Natalia (Actor)
c/o Staff Member *Televisa*
Blvd Adolfo Lopez Mateos 232
Colonia San Angel INN
DF CP 01060, MEXICO

Espineli, Geno (Athlete, Baseball Player)
1222 Park Ln
Katy, TX 77450-4613

Espino, Gaby (Actor)
c/o Gabriel Blanco *Gabriel Blanco Iglesias (Mexico)*
Rio Balsas 35-32
Colonia Cuauhtemoc
DF 06500, Mexico

Espinosa, Danny (Athlete, Baseball Player)
2326 N Towner St
Santa Ana, CA 92706-1942, USA

Espinoza, Alvaro (Athlete, Baseball Player)
1601 SE Airoso Blvd
Port Saint Lucie, FL 34984-3736, USA

Espinoza, Mark (Actor)
c/o Staff Member *Howard Entertainment*
16530 Ventura Blvd Ste 305
Encino, CA 91436-4594, USA

Esposito, Brian (Athlete, Baseball Player)
364 Twinbark Ave
Holbrook, NY 11741-5722, USA

Esposito, Cameron (Comedian)
c/o Lexi Klein *Rogers & Cowan*
1840 Century Park E Fl 18
Los Angeles, CA 90067-2101, USA

Esposito, Giancarlo (Actor)
c/o Jeffrey Chassen *Imprint PR*
6121 W Sunset Blvd
Neuehouse
Los Angeles, CA 90028-6442, USA

Esposito, Jennifer (Actor)
Jennifer's Way Bakery
263 E 10th St Apt 18
New York, NY 10009-4815, USA

Esposito, Laura (Actor)
Gersh Agency
232 N Canon Dr
Beverly Hills, CA 90210-5302, USA

Esposito, Mike (Athlete, Football Player)
241 Drakeside Rd Unit 1300
Hampton, NH 03842-1825, USA

Esposito, Philip A (Phil) (Athlete, Hockey Player)
4003 W Tacon St
Tampa, FL 33629-8544, USA

Esposito, Sammy (Athlete, Baseball Player)
8303 Amber Leaf Ct
Raleigh, NC 27612-7388, USA

Esposito, Tony (Athlete, Hockey Player)
418 55th Ave
St Pete Beach, FL 33706-2311, USA

Espy, Cecil (Athlete, Baseball Player)
5480 Encina Dr
San Diego, CA 92114-6307, USA

Espy, Mike (Politician)
819 7th St NW Ste 205
Washington, DC 20001-3762, USA

Esquivel, Laura (Actor, Producer, Writer)
c/o Staff Member *Doubleday/ RandomHouse*
1745 Broadway
New York, NY 10019-4640, USA

Essany, Michael (Actor, Talk Show Host)
Michael Essany Show
139 Concord Cir
C/O Mike Randazzo
Valparaiso, IN 46385-8070, USA

Essegian, Chuck (Athlete, Baseball Player)
15639 Bronco Dr
Canyon Country, CA 91387-4717, USA

Essensa, Bob (Athlete, Hockey Player)
1130 Iroquois Trl
Oxford, MI 48371-6621, USA

Esser, Mark (Athlete, Baseball Player)
208 Ridge Rd
Jupiter, FL 33477-9652, USA

Essex, David (Musician)
PO Box 390
Billinghurst, West Sussex RH14 4BE, UNITED KINGDOM

Essex, Trai (Athlete, Football Player)
c/o Eugene Parker *Independent Sports & Entertainment (ISE-IN)*
6435 W Jefferson Blvd # 197
Fort Wayne, IN 46804-6203, USA

Essian, James (Jim) (Athlete, Baseball Player, Coach)
134 Eckford Dr
Troy, MI 48085-4745, USA

Essink, Ron (Athlete, Football Player)
PO Box 265
Hamilton, MI 49419-0265, USA

Esslinger, Hartmut (Designer)
FrogDesign
1327 Chesapeake Ter
Sunnyvale, CA 94089-1104, USA

Essman, Susie (Comedian)
c/o Scott Metzger *Paradigm*
140 Broadway Ste 2600
New York, NY 10005-1011, USA

Estabrook, Mike (Athlete, Baseball Player)
502 Titus Rd
Lambertville, NJ 08530-2235, USA

Estabrook, Wayne (Athlete, Football Player)
6219 S Los Lagos Cv
Fort Mohave, AZ 86426-7046, USA

Estacea, Elizabeth (Musician)
PO Box 691481
Charlotte, NC 28227-7025

Estalella, Bobby (Athlete, Baseball Player)
674 Milan Dr
Kissimmee, FL 34758-4303, USA

Esteban, Samantha (Actor)
c/o Nick Terzian *NTA Talent Agency*
1445 N Stanley Ave Fl 2
Los Angeles, CA 90046-4015, USA

Estefan, Emilio (Business Person, Musician)
Estefan Enterprises
420 Jefferson Ave
Miami Beach, FL 33139-6503, USA

Estefan, Gloria (Musician)
39 Star Island Dr
Miami Beach, FL 33139-5146, USA

Estefan, Lili (Actor)
c/o Staff Member *Univision*
605 3rd Ave Fl 12
New York, NY 10158-0034, USA

Estelle (DJ, Musician)
c/o Kevin Liles *KWL Management*
112 Madison Ave Fl 4
New York, NY 10016-7416, USA

Estelle, Dick (Athlete, Baseball Player)
2221 Taylor St
Point Pleasant Boro, NJ 08742-3839, USA

Esten, Charles (Chip) (Actor)
519 Arden Wood Pl
Brentwood, TN 37027-5659, USA

Estern, Neil (Artist)
432 Cream Hill Rd
West Cornwall, CT 06796-1210, USA

Estes, A Shawn (Athlete, Baseball Player)
6659 E Meadowlark Ln
Paradise Valley, AZ 85253-3620, USA

Estes, Bob (Athlete, Golfer)
4408 Long Champ Dr Apt 21
Austin, TX 78746-1186, USA

Estes, Clarissa Pinkola (Writer)
c/o Staff Member *Random House Publicity*
1745 Broadway Frnt 3
New York, NY 10019-4343, USA

Estes, James (Cartoonist)
1103 Callahan St
Amarillo, TX 79106-4201, USA

Estes, Larry (Athlete, Football Player)
135 Iever St
Hammond, LA 70401-2136, USA

Estes, Rob (Actor)
1020 91st Ave NE
Bellevue, WA 98004-3901, USA

Estes, Will (Actor)
c/o Jason Barrett *Alchemy Entertainment*
7024 Melrose Ave Ste 420
Los Angeles, CA 90038-3394, USA

Estevez, Emilio (Actor, Director)
c/o Staff Member *Estevez Sheen Productions*
99 S Raymond Ave Ste 601
Pasadena, CA 91105-2046, USA

Estevez, Ramon (Actor)
837 Ocean Ave
#101
Santa Monica, CA 90402, USA

Estevez, Renee (Actor)
Michael Mann Talent
617 S Olive St Ste 311
Los Angeles, CA 90014-1624, USA

Esthero (Musician)
c/o Staff Member *ArtistDirect*
9046 Lindblade St
Culver City, CA 90232-2513, USA

Estill, Michelle (Athlete, Golfer)
642 Yacavona St
Kent, OH 44240-3318, USA

Estleman, Loren Daniel (Writer)
5552 Walsh Rd
Whitmore Lake, MI 48189-9673, USA

Estrada, Charle L (Chuck) (Athlete, Baseball Player)
1289 Manzanita Way
San Luis Obispo, CA 93401-7838, USA

Estrada, Erik (Actor, Producer)
c/o Konrad Leh *Creative Talent Group*
1900 Avenue of the Stars Ste 2475
Los Angeles, CA 90067-4512, USA

estrada, Johnny (Athlete, Baseball Player)
20 Winged Foot Rdg
Newnan, GA 30265-2083, USA

Estrada, Marco (Athlete, Baseball Player)
c/o Paul Cohen *TWC Sports Management (LA)*
445 W Erie St Ste 205
Chicago, IL 60654-5733, USA

Estrella, Alberto (Actor)
c/o Staff Member *Televisa*
Blvd Adolfo Lopez Mateos 232
Colonia San Angel INN
DF CP 01060, MEXICO

Estrella, Leo (Athlete, Baseball Player)
5462 NW Boydga Ave
Port Saint Lucie, FL 34986-4038, USA

Estrin, Dan (Musician)
24616 Stagg St
Canoga Park, CA 91304-6143, USA

Estrin, Zack (Writer)
c/o Staff Member *WME|IMG*
9601 Wilshire Blvd
Beverly Hills, CA 90210-5213, USA

Eszterhas, Joe (Writer)
c/o Craig Baumgarten *Zero Gravity Management*
11110 Ohio Ave Ste 100
Los Angeles, CA 90025-3329, USA

Etchebarren, Andy (Athlete, Baseball Player)
1488 Vermeer Dr
Nokomis, FL 34275-4470, USA

Etchegaray, Roger Cardinal (Religious Leader)
Piazza San Calisto
Vatican City 00120

Etcheverry, Marco (Soccer Player)
DC United
14120 Newbrook Dr
Chantilly, VA 20151-2273, USA

Etcheverry, Michel (Actor)
47 Rue du Borrego
Paris 75020, FRANCE

Etebari, Eric (Actor)
c/o Staff Member *D2 Management*
10351 Santa Monica Blvd Ste 210
Los Angeles, CA 90025-6937, USA

Etel, Alex (Actor)
c/o Staff Member *ICM Partners*
10250 Constellation Blvd Fl 7
Los Angeles, CA 90067-6207, USA

Etharton, Seth (Baseball Player)
Anaheim Angels
16 Saint John
Dana Point, CA 92629-4127, USA

Ethelle, Chuck (Race Car Driver)
124-126 Pomfret St.
Putnam, CT 06260, USA

Etheredge, Carlos (Athlete, Football Player)
1231 Tuscumbia Rd
Collierville, TN 38017-3418, USA

Etheridge, Bobby (Athlete, Baseball Player)
118 Portland Rd
Eudora, AR 71640-2174, USA

Etheridge, Joe (Athlete, Football Player)
900 E Bryan St
Kermit, TX 79745-3623, USA

Etheridge, Melissa (Musician, Songwriter)
c/o Emily Clay *True Public Relations*
3575 Cahuenga Blvd W Ste 360
Los Angeles, CA 90068-1361, USA

Etherton, Seth (Athlete, Baseball Player)
16 Saint John
Dana Point, CA 92629-4127, USA

Ethier, Andre (Athlete, Baseball Player)
c/o Nez Balelo *CAA Sports*
2000 Avenue of the Stars Ste 100
Los Angeles, CA 90067-4705, USA

Etienne, Treva (Actor)
c/o Staff Member *London Flair PR*
7119 W Sunset Blvd # 170
Los Angeles, CA 90046-4411, USA

Etienne-Martin (Artist)
7 Rue du Pot de Fer
Paris 75005, FRANCE

Eto'o, Samuel (Athlete, Soccer Player)
c/o Staff Member *Chelsea Football Club*
Stamford Bridge
Fulham Road
London SW6 1HS, UNITED KINGDOM

Etrog, Sorel (Artist)
23 Yonge Blvd
PO Box 67034
Toronto, ON M5M 3G6, CANADA

Etsou-Nzabi-Bamungwabi, Frederic (Religious Leader)
Archdiocese of Kinshasa
BP 8431
Kinshasa 1, CONGO DEMOCRATIC REPUBLIC

Etter, Bob (Athlete, Football Player)
8609 La Riviera Dr Apt F
Sacramento, CA 95826-1775, USA

Ettles, Mark (Athlete, Baseball Player)
3-10 Rose Avenue
South Perth, AU 06151, Australia

Eubank, Chris (Boxer)
9 Upper Dr
Hove, East Sussex BN3 6GR, UNITED KINGDOM

Eubank, Shari (Actor)
2965 N 625 East Rd
Farmer City, IL 61842-7000, USA

Eubanks, Bob (Game Show Host, Television Host)
c/o Cheryl Kagan *Cheryl Kagan Public Relations*
100 N Crescent Dr Ste 100
Beverly Hills, CA 90210-5447, USA

Eubanks, Dwight (Reality Star)
Purple Door Salon
321 Edgewood Ave SE
Atlanta, GA 30312-4003, USA

Eubanks, Kevin (Musician)
c/o Staff Member *NBC News (NY)*
30 Rockefeller Plz
New York, NY 10112-0015, USA

Eufemia, Frank (Athlete, Baseball Player)
433 6th Ave
Seaside Heights, NJ 08751-1304, USA

Euhus, Tim (Athlete, Football Player)
1625 SW Brooklane Dr
Corvallis, OR 97333-1632, USA

Eunice, Cecil (Race Car Driver)
Rt. 3
Box 77
Blackshear, GA 31515, USA

Eure, Wesley (Actor)
Irv Schechter
9300 Wilshire Blvd Ste 410
Beverly Hills, CA 90212-3228, USA

Europe (Music Group, Musician)
Box 22036
Stockholm S-10422, Sweden

Europe, Tom (Athlete, Football Player)
Groundwork Athletics
10-736 Granville St
Vancouver, BC V6Z 1G3, Canada

Eusebio, Tony (Athlete, Baseball Player)
2078 Shannon Lakes Blvd
Kissimmee, FL 34743-3648, USA

Evancho, Jackie (Musician)
Integrity Music
1000 Cody Rd S
Mobile, AL 36695-3425, USA

Evanescence (Music Group)
c/o Dennis Rider *Dennis Rider Management*
927 Hilldale Ave
W Hollywood, CA 90069-4404, USA

Evangelista, Christine (Actor)
c/o Myrna Jacoby *MJ Management*
130 W 57th St Apt 11A
New York, NY 10019-3311, USA

Evangelista, Daniella (Actor)
c/o Steve Chasman *Current Entertainment*
9378 Wilshire Blvd Ste 210
Beverly Hills, CA 90212-3167, USA

Evangelista, Linda (Actor, Model)
c/o Didier Fernandez *DNA Model Management*
555 W 25th St Fl 6
New York, NY 10001-5542, USA

Evanovich, Janet (Writer)
c/o Robert Gottlieb *Trident Media Group LLC*
41 Madison Ave Fl 36
New York, NY 10010-2257, USA

Evans, Aja (Actor)
c/o Staff Member *Precision Entertainment*
6338 Wilshire Blvd
Los Angeles, CA 90048-5002, USA

Evans, Alice (Actor)
c/o Mary Ellen Mulcahy *Framework Entertainment*
9057 Nemo St # C
W Hollywood, CA 90069-5511, USA

Evans, Barry (Athlete, Baseball Player)
8303 Seven Oaks Dr
Jonesboro, GA 30236-4025, USA

Evans, Bart (Athlete, Baseball Player)
8323 Rolling Hills Dr
Nixa, MO 65714-7392, USA

Evans, Bentley Kyle (Director, Producer)
c/o Richard Lovett *Creative Artists Agency (CAA)*
2000 Avenue of the Stars Ste 100
Los Angeles, CA 90067-4705, USA

Evans, Bill (Athlete, Basketball Player, Olympic Athlete)
24360 Sandpiper Isle Way Unit 105
Bonita Springs, FL 34134-4933, USA

Evans, Byron (Athlete, Football Player)
1763 E Carter Rd
Phoenix, AZ 85042-5754, USA

Evans, Caryl (Athlete, Hockey Player)
22403 Marjorie Ave
Torrance, CA 90505-2241, USA

Evans, Charlie (Athlete, Football Player)
406 Ozzie St NW
Orting, WA 98360-7405, USA

Evans, Chris (Actor)
c/o Megan Moss *Narrative*
1601 Vine St Fl 6
Los Angeles, CA 90028-8802, USA

Evans, Dale (Athlete, Football Player)
8878 N State Highway 5 Unit 3
Camdenton, MO 65020-4599, USA

Evans, Dan (Commentator)
113 Mineola Ct
Boulder, CO 80303-4417, USA

Evans, Daniel J (Politician)
4000-D NE 41st St
Seattle, WA 98105, USA

Evans, Darrell (Athlete, Baseball Player)
4109 S Hulen St Apt 322
Fort Worth, TX 76109-4956, USA

Evans, Daryl (Athlete, Hockey Player)
22403 Marjorie Ave
Torrance, CA 90505-2241, USA

Evans, David (Edge) (Musician)
c/o Allen Grubman *Grubman Shire & Meiselas*
152 W 57th St Fl 31
New York, NY 10019-3310, USA

Evans, David Mickey (Director)
c/o Staff Member *Bill Thompson Management*
5956 Kanan Dume Rd
Malibu, CA 90265-4027, USA

Evans, Demetric (Athlete, Football Player)
3820 Appleton Ln
Flower Mound, TX 75022-2932, USA

Evans, Dick (Writer)
121 Morning Dove Ct
Daytona Beach, FL 32119-8739, USA

Evans, Donald (Athlete, Football Player)
1008 Brighton Rd
Raleigh, NC 27610-1643, USA

Evans, Donna (Actor)
c/o Staff Member *United Stuntwomen's Association*
3518 Cahuenga Blvd W # 206B
Hollywood, CA 90068-1304, USA

Evans, Doug (Athlete, Hockey Player)
869 Clonsilla Ave
Peterborough, ON K9J OB7, Canada

Evans, Dwayne (Athlete)
PO Box 91219
Phoenix, AZ 85066-1219, USA

Evans, Dwight (Athlete, Baseball Player)
c/o Staff Member *Boston Red Sox*
4 Jersey St
Boston, MA 02215-4148, USA

Evans, Evans (Actor)
10112 Empyrean Way Apt 104
Los Angeles, CA 90067-3809, USA

Evans, Faith (Musician)
7518 Agnew Ave
Los Angeles, CA 90045-1006, USA

Evans, Frank (Athlete, Baseball Player)
c/o Jeanette Kimble 6617 S Monroe St
Tacoma, WA 98409-2437, USA

Evans, George (Cartoonist)
c/o Staff Member *King Features Syndication*
300 W 57th St Fl 15
New York, NY 10019-5238, USA

Evans, Greg (Cartoonist)
216 Country Garden Ln
San Marcos, CA 92069-9759, USA

Evans, Heath (Athlete, Football Player)
242 Surfview Dr
Pacific Palisades, CA 90272-2911, USA

Evans, Indiana (Actor)
c/o Claudine Kermond *Kermond Management*
293 A Riley Street
Surry Hills NSW 02010, AUSTRALIA

Evans, Jahri (Athlete, Football Player)

Evans, James B (Jim) (Baseball Player)
1801 Rogge Ln
Austin, TX 78723-3416, USA

Evans, Janet (Athlete, Olympic Athlete, Swimmer)
c/o Staff Member *Premier Management Group (PMG Sports)*
700 Evanvale Ct
Cary, NC 27518-2806, USA

Evans, Jay (Athlete, Football Player)
8878 N State Highway 5
Camdenton, MO 65020-4278, USA

Evans, Jerry (Athlete, Football Player)
4139 Ivanhoe Dr
Lorain, OH 44053-1560, USA

Evans, Joan (Actor)
2289 Merrimack Ave
Henderson, NV 89044, USA

Evans, John (Business Person)
Alcan Aluminium
100-1188 Sherbrooke Rue O
Montreal, QC H3A 3G2, CANADA

Evans, John A (Athlete, Football Player)
North Carolina State University
P O Box 8501
Attn: Alumni Association
Raleigh, NC 27695-0001, USA

Evans, John E (Business Person)
Allied Group
701 5th Ave
Des Moines, IA 50391-9997, USA

Evans, Josh (Athlete, Football Player)
PO Box 273309
Boca Raton, FL 33427-3309, USA

Evans, Karena (Actor, Director)
c/o Daniel Birnbaum *Talent House (Toronto)*
204-A St George St
Toronto, ON M5R 2N6, CANADA

Evans, Kellylee (Musician)
c/o Staff Member *SL Feldman & Associates (Toronto)*
8 Elm St
Toronto, ON M5G 1G7, Canada

Evans, Larry (Athlete, Football Player)
5316 S Broadway Cir Apt 8-208
Englewood, CO 80113-6735, USA

Evans, Lee (Actor, Comedian, Writer)
c/o Staff Member *Off The Kerb Productions*
Hammer House, 3rd Fl
113-117 Wardour St
London W1F 0UN, UK

Evans, Linda (Actor)
PO Box 29
Rainier, WA 98576-0029, USA

Evans, Luke (Actor)
c/o Lena Roklin *Luber Roklin Management*
5815 W Sunset Blvd Ste 208
Los Angeles, CA 90028-6481, USA

Evans, Lynn (Musician)
Richard Paul Assoc
16207 Mott Dr
Macomb, MI 48044-5650, USA

Evans, Marc (Director)
c/o Jane Villiers *Tessa Sayle Agency*
11 Jubilee Pl
London SW3 3TE, UNITED KINGDOM (UK)

Evans, Mary Beth (Actor, Director)
c/o Michael Bruno *The Michael Bruno Group*
13576 Cheltenham Dr
Sherman Oaks, CA 91423-4818, USA

Evans, Mike (Athlete, Football Player)
c/o Deryk Gilmore *Priority Sports & Entertainment (Chicago)*
325 N La Salle Dr Ste 650
Chicago, IL 60654-8182, USA

Evans, Mike (Athlete, Basketball Player)
9931 Cottoncreek Dr
Highlands Ranch, CO 80130-3825, USA

Evans, Mike (Athlete, Football Player)
4 Autumn Leaf Ln
Westford, MA 01886-4316, USA

Evans, Murray (Journalist)
46 Courtside Cir
San Antonio, TX 78216-7843, USA

Evans, Nicholas (Nick) (Writer)
Delacorte Press
1540 Broadway
New York, NY 10036-4039, USA

Evans, Norm (Athlete, Football Player)
100 Timber Ridge Way NW Unit 1404
Issaquah, WA 98027-2958, USA

Evans, Norm E (Athlete, Football Player)
4143 Via Marina
Marina Del Rey, CA 90292-5303, USA

Evans, Paul (Athlete, Hockey Player)
1033 Silverdale Rd
Peterborough, ON K9J 7W5, Canada

Evans, Reggie (Athlete, Football Player)
2813 Juniper St
Merrifield, VA 22116, USA

Evans, Richard (Sportscaster)
Madison Square Garden
4 Pennsylvania Plaza
New York, NY 10001, USA

Evans, Richard Paul (Writer)
Richard Paul Evans Inc.
PO Box 712137
Salt Lake City, UT 84171-2137, USA

Evans, Rob (Coach)
Arizona State University
Athletic Dept
Tempe, AZ 85287-0001, USA

Evans, Robert (Producer)
Robert Evans Productions
5555 Melrose Ave
Paramount Pictures
Los Angeles, CA 90038-3989, USA

Evans, Robert S (Business Person)
Crane Co
100 Stamford Pl Ste 300
Stamford, CT 06902-6740, USA

Evans, Sara (Musician)
c/o Brenner Van Meter *Modern Management*
1625 Broadway Ste 600
Nashville, TN 37203-3141, USA

Evans, Shaun (Actor)
c/o Christopher Farrar *Hamilton Hodell Ltd*
20 Golden Sq
Fl 5
London W1F 9JL, UNITED KINGDOM

Evans, Thom (Athlete, Model)
c/o Tim Beaumont *Beaumont Communications*
189-190 Shoreditch High St
Unit 2
London E1 6HU, UNITED KINGDOM

Evans, Tom (Athlete, Baseball Player)
32533 SE 68th St
Issaquah, WA 98027-8729, USA

Evans, Tracy (Athlete, Olympic Athlete, Skier)
1317 Ptarmigan Loop
Park City, UT 84098-5989, USA

Evans, Tristan (Musician)
c/o Ryan Craven *Paradigm (Chicago)*
2209 W North Ave
Chicago, IL 60647-6084, USA

Evans, Troy (Actor)
4757 N Figueroa St
Los Angeles, CA 90042-4406, USA

Evans, Vince (Athlete, Football Player)
14084 Bronte Dr
Whittier, CA 90602-2608, USA

Evans, Walker (Race Car Driver)
Walker Evans Racing
PO Box 2469
Riverside, CA 92516-2469, USA

Evans, William (Basketball Player, Olympic Athlete)
3110 Springstead Cir
Louisville, KY 40241-4416, USA

Evanshen, Terry (Athlete, Football Player)
19 Dorset St RR 1
Hampton, ON L0B 1J0, Canada

Evashevski, Forest (Coach, Football Coach)
5820 Clubhouse Dr
Vero Beach, FL 32967-7552, USA

Evason, Dean (Athlete, Hockey Player)
c/o Staff Member *Washington Capitals*
627 N Glebe Rd Ste 850
Arlington, VA 22203-2129, USA

Evastina, Liisa (Actor)
c/o Celia Campbell *Murphy Kidman Edwards*
45 Manchester St
London W1U 7LS, UK

Eve (Actor, Musician)
c/o Elizabeth Morris *Rogers & Cowan*
1840 Century Park E Fl 18
Los Angeles, CA 90067-2101, USA

Eve (Actor, Producer)
c/o Steven Grossman *Untitled Entertainment*
350 S Beverly Dr Ste 200
Beverly Hills, CA 90212-4819, USA

Eve, Alice (Actor)
c/o Jason Weinberg *Untitled Entertainment*
350 S Beverly Dr Ste 200
Beverly Hills, CA 90212-4819, USA

Eve, Diva (Athlete, Wrestler)
c/o Staff Member *World Wrestling Entertainment (WWE)*
1241 E Main St
Stamford, CT 06902-3520, USA

Eve, Trevor J (Actor)
c/o Matthew Lesher *Insight*
5358 Melrose Ave # 200W
Los Angeles, CA 90038-5117, USA

Eveland, Dana (Athlete, Baseball Player)
37138 Liana Ln
Palmdale, CA 93551-6237, USA

Evelyn, Lionel (Athlete, Baseball Player)
2508 Edgemere Ave
Far Rockaway, NY 11691-2716, USA

Everclear (Music Group)
c/o Jeff Epstein *M.A.G./Universal Attractions*
15 W 36th St Fl 8
New York, NY 10018-7927, USA

Everett, Adam (Athlete, Baseball Player, Olympic Athlete)
1311 Marietta Country Club Dr NW
Kennesaw, GA 30152-4729, USA

Everett, Bridget (Actor, Comedian)
c/o Seth Seigle *WME|IMG (NY)*
11 Madison Ave Fl 18
New York, NY 10010-3669, USA

Everett, Bruce (Producer)
Prefers to be contacted via telephone or email

Everett, Carl E (Athlete, Baseball Player)
19108 Harborbridge Ln
Lutz, FL 33558-9717, USA

Everett, Chad (Actor)
6 Meridian Ln
San Rafael, CA 94901-1384, USA

Everett, Danny (Athlete)
Santa Monica Track Club
1801 Ocean Park Blvd Apt 112
Santa Monica, CA 90405-4925, USA

Everett, Jim (Athlete, Football Player)
555 N El Camino Real Ste A445
San Clemente, CA 92672-6740, USA

Everett, Major (Athlete, Football Player)
PO Box 1441
Pine Lake, GA 30072-1441, USA

Everett, Mark Oliver (Musician)
4046 Cromwell Ave
Los Angeles, CA 90027-1352, USA

Everett, Rupert (Actor)
c/o Francoise Salimov *ArtMedia*
8 rue Danielle Casanova
Paris 75002, FRANCE

Everett, Thomas G (Athlete, Football Player)
PO Box 795337
Dallas, TX 75379-5337, USA

Everham, Ray (Race Car Driver)
18917 Peninsula Point Dr
Cornelius, NC 28031-7599, USA

Everhard, Nancy (Actor)
Kazarian /Spencer
11365 Ventura Blvd Ste 100
Studio City, CA 91604-3148, USA

Everhart, Angie (Actor, Producer)
11725 San Vicente Blvd
#368
Los Angeles, CA 90049, USA

Everitt, Leon (Athlete, Baseball Player)
367 Henry Everitt Rd
Marshall, TX 75672-3919, USA

Everitt, Mike (Athlete, Baseball Player)
4215 162nd St
Urbandale, IA 50323-2509, USA

Everitt, Mike (Baseball Player)
12381 Walnut Ridge Ct
Clive, IA 50325-8127, USA

Everitt, Steve (Athlete, Football Player)
17252 Snapper Ln
Summerland Key, FL 33042-3669, USA

Everlast (Actor, Musician)
3455 Rubio Crest Dr
Altadena, CA 91001-1529, USA

Everly Brothers (Music Group, Musician)
c/o Neil Warnock *UTA Music/The Agency Group (UK)*
361-373 City Rd
London EC1V 1PQ, UNITED KINGDOM

Evermore (Music Group)
c/o Staff Member *Paradigm (Monterey)*
404 W Franklin St
Monterey, CA 93940-2303, USA

Evernham, Ray (Race Car Driver)
18917 Peninsula Point Dr
Cornelius, NC 28031-7599, USA

Evers, Bill (Athlete, Baseball Player)
PO Box 507
Durham, NC 27702-0507, USA

Evers, Charles (Politician)
1072 J R Lynch St
Jackson, MS 39203-3344, USA

Evers, Jackson (Actor)
232 N Crescent Dr Apt 101
Beverly Hills, CA 90210-4827, USA

Evers, John (Comedian)
PO Box 169
Mount Airy, NC 27030-0169, USA

Eversgerd, Bryan (Baseball Player, Coach)
Swing of the Quad Cities
PO Box 3496
Attn: Coaching Staff
Davenport, IA 52808-3496, USA

Eversley, Frederick J (Artist)
1110 W Albert Kinney Blvd
Venice, CA 90219, USA

Eversman, Nick (Actor)
c/o Brian Medavoy *More/Medavoy Management*
10203 Santa Monica Blvd # 400
Los Angeles, CA 90067-6405, USA

Everson, Cory (Actor, Athlete)
39 Hackamore Ln
Bell Canyon, CA 91307-1019, USA

Evert, Chris (Athlete, Olympic Athlete, Tennis Player)
8563 Horseshoe Ln
Boca Raton, FL 33496-1231, USA

Every Move A Picture (Music Group)
c/o Staff Member *Paradigm (Monterey)*
404 W Franklin St
Monterey, CA 93940-2303, USA

Everything But The Girl (Music Group, Musician)
c/o Staff Member *High Road Touring*
751 Bridgeway Fl 2
Sausalito, CA 94965-2174, USA

Everything Everything (Music Group)
c/o Duncan Ellis *Scruffy Bird Management*
26 Shacklewell Ln
3rd Floor
London E8 2EZ, UK

Evigan, Briana (Actor)
c/o Matt Luber *Luber Roklin Management*
5815 W Sunset Blvd Ste 208
Los Angeles, CA 90028-6481, USA

Evigan, Greg (Actor)
5070 Arundel Dr
Woodland Hills, CA 91364-3602, USA

Evo, Bill (Athlete, Hockey Player)
2723 Roundtree Dr
Troy, MI 48083-2327, USA

Evora, Cesar (Actor)
c/o Staff Member *Televisa*
Blvd Adolfo Lopez Mateos 232
Colonia San Angel INN
DF CP 01060, MEXICO

Evraire, Ken (Athlete, Football Player)
73 Fairlawn Ave
Toronto, ON M5M 1S6, Canada

Evre, Willie (Athlete, Baseball Player)
364 S 100 E Apt 211
Cedar City, UT 84720-3810, USA

Ewald, Esther (Athlete, Baseball Player, Commentator)
808 E Crescent Dr
Arlington Heights, IL 60005-3263, USA

Ewell, Dwight (Actor)

Ewell, Kayla (Actor)
c/o Ryan Daly *Zero Gravity Management*
11110 Ohio Ave Ste 100
Los Angeles, CA 90025-3329, USA

Ewen, Todd (Athlete, Hockey Player)
420 Arlington Terrace Dr
Wildwood, MO 63040-1701, USA

Ewing, Barbara (Actor)
Flat 4
1 Candover St
York House, London W1W 7DG, UNITED KINGDOM (UK)

Ewing, Bradie (Athlete, Football Player)
c/o Scott Smith *XAM Sports*
3509 Ice Age Dr
Madison, WI 53719-5409, USA

Ewing, Patrick (Athlete, Basketball Player, Coach, Olympic Athlete)
2127 Brickell Ave Apt 3802
Miami, FL 33129-2109, USA

Ewing, Reid (Actor)
c/o Donovan Daughtry *Untitled Entertainment*
350 S Beverly Dr Ste 200
Beverly Hills, CA 90212-4819, USA

Ewing, Sam (Athlete, Baseball Player)
1048 Cedarview Ln
Franklin, TN 37067-4068, USA

Example (Music Group)
c/o Doug Smith *Coda Music Agency (UK)*
56 Compton St
Clerkenwell
London EC1V 0ET, UNITED KINGDOM

Exarchopoulos, Adele (Actor)

Exelby, Garnet (Athlete, Hockey Player)
1182 Saint Louis Pl NE
Atlanta, GA 30306-4834, USA

Exelby, Randy (Athlete, Hockey Player)
10040 E Happy Valley Rd Unit 210
Scottsdale, AZ 85255-2368, USA

Exerins, Leo (Athlete, Football Player)
595 Valour Rd
Winnipeg, MB R3G 3A7, Canada

Exies, The (Music Group)
c/o Frank Cimler *10th Street Entertainment*
700 N San Vicente Blvd # G410
W Hollywood, CA 90069-5060, USA

Expose (Music Group)
c/o Stephen Ford *Diva Central Inc*
7510 W Sunset Blvd # 1445
Los Angeles, CA 90046-3408, USA

Extreme (Music Group)
c/o Rod MacSween *International Talent Booking*
9 Kingsway
Fl 6
London WC2B 6XF, UNITED KINGDOM

Exum, Antone (Athlete, Football Player)

Eyharts, Leopold Colonel (Astronaut)
2371 Calypso Ln
League City, TX 77573-0758, USA

Eyre, Richard (Director)
c/o Staff Member *Creative Artists Agency (CAA)*
2000 Avenue of the Stars Ste 100
Los Angeles, CA 90067-4705, USA

Eyre, Scott (Athlete, Baseball Player)
6804 205th St E
Bradenton, FL 34211-7302, USA

Eyre, Willie (Athlete, Baseball Player)
17569 Cherry Ridge Ln
Fort Myers, FL 33967-5138, USA

Ezarik, Justine (iJustine) (Internet Star)
c/o Denisse Montfort *Sunshine Sachs*
720 Cole Ave
Los Angeles, CA 90038-3606, USA

Ezell, Glenn (Athlete, Baseball Player)
PO Box 5004
Tucson, AZ 85703-0004, USA

Ezersky, John (Athlete, Basketball Player)
2564 Walnut Blvd Apt 103
Walnut Creek, CA 94596-4251, USA

Ezor, Blake (Athlete, Football Player)
10622 Salmon Leap St
Las Vegas, NV 89183-4917, USA

Ezra, George (Musician)
c/o Ryan Lofthouse *Closer Artists (UK)*
91 Peterborough Rd
Matrix Complex
London SW6 3BU, UNITED KINGDOM

Ezrin, Bob (Producer)
Nimbus School of Recording Arts Ltd.
238 2nd Ave E Suite 300
Vancouver, BC V5T 1B7, Canada

F

Fa, Sione (Reality Star)
43258 W Chisholm Dr
Maricopa, AZ 85138-1500, USA

Fabac-Bretting, Elizabeth (Baseball Player)
1455 Mesa St
Redding, CA 96001-2310, USA

Fabares, Shelley (Actor)
c/o Staff Member *Innovative Artists*
1505 10th St
Santa Monica, CA 90401-2805, USA

Fabel, Brad (Athlete, Golfer)
247 Windsor Terrace Dr
Nashville, TN 37221-2279, USA

Faber, David (Actor, Writer)
c/o Staff Member *CNBC (Main)*
900 Sylvan Ave
Englewood Cliffs, NJ 07632-3312, USA

Fabian, John M (Astronaut)
100 Shine Rd
Port Ludlow, WA 98365-9274, USA

Fabian, John M Dr (Astronaut)
100 Shine Rd
Port Ludlow, WA 98365-9274, USA

Fabian, Lara (Musician, Songwriter, Writer)
9 productions SPRL
58 avenue du Manoir
Waterloo 01410, BELGIUM

Fabian, Patrick (Actor)
c/o Jamie Harhay Skinner *Baker Winokur Ryder Public Relations*
9100 Wilshire Blvd
W Tower #500
Beverly Hills, CA 90212-3415, USA

Fabini, Jason (Athlete, Football Player)
17 Tappanwood Dr
Locust Valley, NY 11560-1321, USA

Fabio (Actor, Model)
19620 Wells Dr
Tarzana, CA 91356-3829, USA

Fabregas, Francesc (Soccer Player)
Arsenal Football Club
Highbury House
75 Drayton Park
London N5 1BU, UNITED KINGDOM

Fabregas, Jorge (Athlete, Baseball Player)
4936 SW 6th St
Coral Gables, FL 33134-1346, USA

Fabro, Sam (Athlete, Football Player)
724 South Dr
Winnipeg, MB R3T 0C3, Canada

Fabulous, Moolah (Wrestler)
101 Moolah Dr
Columbia, SC 29223-3931, USA

Face, Elroy L (Roy) (Athlete, Baseball Player)
425 Elizabeth St
North Versailles, PA 15137-1239, USA

Facinelli, Peter (Actor)
c/o Staff Member *A7SLE Films*
10061 Riverside Dr Ste 418
Toluca Lake, CA 91602-2560, USA

Faedo, Len (Lenny) (Athlete, Baseball Player)
2920 W Collins St
Tampa, FL 33607-6702, USA

Faerch, Daeg (Actor)
c/o Kieran Maguire *The Arlook Group*
11663 Gorham Ave Apt 5
Los Angeles, CA 90049-4749, USA

Fagan, Julian (Athlete, Football Player)
PO Box 920
Madison, MS 39130-0920, USA

Fagan, Kevin (Athlete, Football Player)
11441 Camp Dr
Dunnellon, FL 34432-8321, USA

Fagan, kevin (Cartoonist)
26771 Ashford
Mission Viejo, CA 92692-4106, USA

Fagen, Clifford B (Basketball Player)
1021 Royal Saint George Dr
Naperville, IL 60563-2322, USA

Fagen, Donald (Musician, Songwriter, Writer)
c/o Barry Dickins *International Talent Booking*
9 Kingsway
Fl 6
London WC2B 6XF, UNITED KINGDOM

Fagerbakke, Bill (Actor)
c/o Justin Baxter *Abrams Artists Agency*
750 N San Vicente Blvd
E Tower Fl 11
Los Angeles, CA 90069-5788, USA

Faggins, Demarcus (Athlete, Football Player)
3002 Southworth Ln
Manvel, TX 77578-4323, USA

Faggs, Starr H Mae (Athlete, Track Athlete)
10152 Shady Ln
Cincinnati, OH 45215-1322, USA

Fahey, Bill (Athlete, Baseball Player)
5740 Mona Ln
Dallas, TX 75236-1722, USA

Fahey, Brandon (Athlete, Baseball Player)
5740 Mona Ln
Dallas, TX 75236-1722, USA

Fahey, Damien (Television Host)
c/o Mike Esterman *Esterman.Com, LLC*
Prefers to be contacted via email
Baltimore, MD XXXXX, USA

Fahey, Jeff (Actor)
c/o Dede Binder-Goldsmith *Defining Artists Agency*
8721 W Sunset Blvd Ste 209
W Hollywood, CA 90069-2272, USA

Fahey, Jim (Athlete, Hockey Player)
117 Plymouth Ave
Milton, MA 02186-5440, USA

Fahey, Siobhan (Musician)
1208 Poinsettia Dr
West Hollywood, CA 90046-5714, USA

Fahey, Trevor (Athlete, Hockey Player)
7629 Bayhill Ct
New Port Richey, FL 34654-6100, USA

Fahnhorst, Jim (Athlete, Football Player)

Fahnhorst, Keith (Athlete, Football Player)
12216 Chadwick Ln
Eden Prairie, MN 55344-3292, USA

Fahr, Alicia (Actor)
c/o Staff Member *Televisa*
Blvd Adolfo Lopez Mateos 232
Colonia San Angel INN
DF CP 01060, MEXICO

Fahy, Bill (Horse Racer)
465 Hewitt Ave
Washington, PA 15301-1538, USA

Faia, Renee (Actor)
c/o Marni Anhalt *Imperium 7 Talent Agency*
5455 Wilshire Blvd Ste 1706
Los Angeles, CA 90036-4217, USA

Faiers, Sam (Model)
Minnie's Boutique
8 Ropers Yard
Brentwood, Essex CM14 4AX, UK

Fain, Richard (Athlete, Football Player)
2705 62nd St W
Lehigh Acres, FL 33971-5849, USA

Faine, Jeff K (Athlete, Football Player)
Forty VII
108 Estates Cir Unit A
Lake Mary, FL 32746-3023, USA

Fair, Lorrie (Athlete, Olympic Athlete, Soccer Player)
300 3rd St Apt 1515
San Francisco, CA 94107-1259

Fair, Terry (Athlete, Football Player)
9948 Winding Hill Ln
Knoxville, TN 37931-4659, USA

Fairbairn, Bill (Athlete, Hockey Player)
10-20W Magnacca Cres
Brandon, MB R7B 2N9, Canada

Fairbairn, Robert (Bruce) (Actor)
4573 Branciforte Dr
Santa Cruz, CA 95065-9620, USA

Fairchild, Chad (Athlete, Baseball Player)
7208 Presidio Gln
Lakewood Ranch, FL 34202-5040, USA

Fairchild, Greg (Athlete, Football Player)
6604 Heege Rd
Saint Louis, MO 63123-2608, USA

Fairchild, John (Athlete, Basketball Player)
9801 Chantilly Rd NW
Albuquerque, NM 87114-4402, USA

Fairchild, Karen (Musician)
56 Annandale
Nashville, TN 37215-5819, USA

Fairchild, Kelly (Athlete, Hockey Player)
4505 Juneau Ln N
Plymouth, MN 55446-2115, USA

Fairchild, Morgan (Actor)
PO Box 57593
Sherman Oaks, CA 91413-2593, USA

Fairchild, Paul (Athlete, Football Player)
22249 W 183rd St
Olathe, KS 66062-9284, USA

Faircloth, Arthur (Athlete, Football Player)
10010 Sandwedge Ct
Fredericksburg, VA 22408-9546, USA

Faircloth, D McLauchlin (Lauch) (Politician)
803 Beaman St
Clinton, NC 28328-2607, USA

Fairey, Jim (Athlete, Baseball Player)
218 Strawberry Ln
Clemson, SC 29631-1363, USA

Fairey, Shepard (Artist)
c/o Bradley Frank *Platform PR*
2666 N Beachwood Dr
Los Angeles, CA 90068-2308, USA

Fairholm, Jeff (Athlete, Football Player)
110 Rue Pierre-Panet
L'Ile-Bizard, QC H9C 2X3, Canada

Fairley, Nick (Athlete, Football Player)
c/o Jamie Fritz *Fritz Martin Management*
8550 W Charleston Blvd Ste 102 PMB 335
Las Vegas, NV 89117-9086, USA

Fairly, Ronald R (Ron) (Athlete, Baseball Player)
75369 Spyglass Dr
Indian Wells, CA 92210-7650, USA

Fairs, Eric (Athlete, Football Player)
32707 Wales Cir
Fulshear, TX 77441-4250, USA

Faison, Adam (Actor)
c/o Stephen Belden *More/Medavoy Management*
10203 Santa Monica Blvd # 400
Los Angeles, CA 90067-6405, USA

Faison, Donald (Actor)
c/o Glenn Rigberg *Inphenate*
9701 Wilshire Blvd Fl 10
Beverly Hills, CA 90212-2010, USA

Faison, Matthew (Actor)
13701 E Kagel Canyon Road
Sylmar, CA 91342, USA

Faison, Tiffani (Chef, Reality Star)
Sweet Cheeks Q
1381 Boylston St
Boston, MA 02215-3936, USA

Faison, William (Earl) (Athlete, Football Player)
2279 Sequoia Dr
Prescott, AZ 86301-4326, USA

Faith, Paloma (Musician)
c/o Olivia Woodward *Curtis Brown Ltd*
28-29 Hay Market
Hay Market House
London SW1Y 4SP, UNITED KINGDOM

Faithfull, Marianne (Actor, Songwriter)
Susan Dewsap
235 Gootscray Rd
New Eltham
London SE9 2EL, UNITED KINGDOM (UK)

Faithless (Music Group)
c/o Staff Member *Paradigm (Monterey)*
404 W Franklin St
Monterey, CA 93940-2303, USA

Faith No More (Music Group)
Ipecac Records
PO Box 1778
Orinda, CA 94563-0678, USA

Fakhri, Nargis (Actor)
c/o Kristin Konig *MGMT Entertainment (The Schiff Company)*
9220 W Sunset Blvd Ste 106
W Hollywood, CA 90069-3500, USA

Fakih, Rima (Beauty Pageant Winner)
The Miss Universe Organization
1370 Avenue of the Americas Fl 16
New York, NY 10019-4602, USA

Fakir, Abdul (Duke) (Music Group)
c/o Staff Member *ICM Partners (NY)*
730 5th Ave
New York, NY 10019-4105, USA

Falahee, Jack (Actor)
c/o Geoffrey Soffer *Soffer/Namoff Entertainment*
450 W 42nd St Apt 30E
New York, NY 10036-6877, USA

Falana, Lola (Dancer, Musician)
c/o Bill Carpenter *Capital Entertainment*
217 Seaton Pl NE
Washington, DC 20002-1528, USA

Falcam, Leo A (President)
President's Office
Palikjr
Kolonia
Pohnpei, FM 96941, MICRONESIA

Falcao, Jose Freire Cardinal (Religious Leader)
QL 12-CJ12
Lote 1
Lago Sul, Brasilia DF 71630-325, BRAZIL

Falcao, Jose Friere Cardinal (Religious Leader)
QL 12-CJ 12 Lote 1 Lago Sul
Brasilia DF 71630-325, BRAZIL

Falchuk, Brad (Producer)
8383 Wilshire Blvd Ste 400
Beverly Hills, CA 90211-2400, USA

Falco, Edie (Actor)
c/o David Seltzer *Management 360*
9111 Wilshire Blvd
Beverly Hills, CA 90210-5508, USA

Falcon, Veronica (Actor)
c/o Estelle Lasher *Lasher Group*
1133 Avenue of the Americas Fl 27
New York, NY 10036-6710, USA

Falcone, Ben (Actor, Comedian)
c/o Courtney Kivowitz *MGMT Entertainment (The Schiff Company)*
9220 W Sunset Blvd Ste 106
W Hollywood, CA 90069-3500, USA

Falcone, Lisa Maria (Producer)
c/o Staff Member *Everest Entertainment*
450 Park Ave Fl 31
New York, NY 10022-2637, USA

Falcone, Pete (Athlete, Baseball Player)
2232 Thornton Ct
Alexandria, LA 71301-5147, USA

Falconi, Irina (Athlete, Tennis Player)
c/o Dan Nagler *South Beach Sports Agency*
770 Claughton Island Dr Apt 1510
Miami, FL 33131-2630, USA

Faldo, Nick (Athlete, Golfer)
19 Russell St
Berkshire, Windsor SL4 1HQ, UNITED KINGDOM

Falk, Paul (Figure Skater)
Sybelstr 21
Dusseldorf 40239, GERMANY

Falk, Randall M (Religious Leader)
Temple
5015 Harding Pike
Nashville, TN 37205-2890, USA

Falkenberg, Bob (Athlete, Hockey Player)
7251 190A St NW
Edmonton, AB T5T 5S9, Canada

Falkenborg, Brian (Athlete, Baseball Player)
30233 N 125th Dr
Peoria, AZ 85383-3429, USA

Falkenstein, Claire (Artist)
719 Ocean Front Walk
Venice, CA 90291-3212, USA

Falkman, Craig (Athlete, Hockey Player)
2057 Ruffino Dr
Colorado Springs, CO 80921-7698, USA

Falkner, Keith (Musician)
Low Cottages Ilketshall Saint Margaraet
Bungay
Suffolk, UNITED KINGDOM (UK)

Fall, Jim (Actor)
c/o Staff Member *United Talent Agency (UTA)*
9336 Civic Center Dr
Beverly Hills, CA 90210-3604, USA

Fall, Timothy (Actor)
Gersh Agency
232 N Canon Dr
Beverly Hills, CA 90210-5302, USA

Fallon, Bob (Athlete, Baseball Player)
1830 N Lauderdale Ave Apt 4416
North Lauderdale, FL 33068-4253, USA

Fallon, Jimmy (Actor, Comedian, Talk Show Host)
Tonight Show with Jimmy Fallon
30 Rockefeller Plz
New York, NY 10112-0015, USA

Fallon, Tiffany (Model, Reality Star)
c/o Cheryl McLean *Creative Public Relations*
3385 Oak Glen Dr
Los Angeles, CA 90068-1311, USA

Falloon, Pat (Athlete, Hockey Player)
112-155 10th St
Birtle, MB R0M 0C0, Canada

Fall Out Boy (Music Group)
c/o Bob McLynn *Crush Music Management*
60-62 E 11th St
Fl 7
New York, NY 10003, USA

Falls, Mike (Athlete, Football Player)
5831 Secrest Dr
Austin, TX 78759-2416, USA

Falteisek, Steve (Athlete, Baseball Player)
12 Verbena Ave
Floral Park, NY 11001-2712, USA

Faltskog, Agnetha (Musician)
Agnetha Faltskog Productions
Sodra Brobanken 41A
Stockholm 111 49, Sweden

Faludi, Susan C (Journalist)
1032 Irving St # 204
San Francisco, CA 94122-2216, USA

Falvey, Justin (Producer)
c/o Staff Member *Dreamworks Television*
100 Universal Plaza Bldg 5125
Universal City, CA 91608, USA

Fambrough, Charles (Musician)
Zane Mgmt
Bellvue
Broad & Walnut Sts
Philadelphia, PA 19102, USA

Fambrough, Henry (Music Group)
Buddy Allen Management
3750 Hudson Manor Ter # 3AG
Bronx, NY 10463-1126, USA

Famiglietti, Mark (Actor)
c/o Robert Stein *Robert Stein Management*
PO Box 3797
Beverly Hills, CA 90212-0797, USA

Familia, Jeurys (Athlete, Baseball Player)
c/o Sam Levinson *ACES*
188 Montague St Fl 6
Brooklyn, NY 11201-3609, USA

Famuyiwa, Rick (Director)
c/o Benjamin Rowe *Oasis Media Group*
9100 Wilshire Blvd Ste 210W
Beverly Hills, CA 90212-3555, USA

Fancher, Hampton (Director)
262 Old Topanga Canyon Rd
Topanga, CA 90290-3810, USA

Fancy, Richard (Actor)
c/o Paul Kohner *The Kohner Agency*
9300 Wilshire Blvd Ste 555
Beverly Hills, CA 90212-3211, USA

Faneca, Alan (Athlete, Football Player)
214 Friedrichs Ave
Metairie, LA 70005-4517, USA

Faneyte, Rikkert (Baseball Player)
San Francisco Giants
7408 E Osborn Rd
Scottsdale, AZ 85251-6424, USA

Fangio II, Juan Manuel (Race Car Driver)
All-American Racers
2334 S Broadway
Santa Ana, CA 92707-3250, USA

Fankhouser, Scott (Athlete, Hockey Player)
826 Alpine Dr
Jasper, GA 30143-3427, USA

Fann, Al (Actor)
PO Box 1288
Agoura Hills, CA 91376-1288, USA

Fanning, Brent (Race Car Driver)
Udder Nonsense Racing
Rt. 4
Box 80
Stephenville, TX 76401, USA

Fanning, Dakota (Actor)
c/o Brittany Kahan *Echo Lake Management*
421 S Beverly Dr Fl 8
Beverly Hills, CA 90212-4408, USA

Fanning, Elle (Actor)
c/o Brittany Kahan *Echo Lake Management*
421 S Beverly Dr Fl 8
Beverly Hills, CA 90212-4408, USA

Fanning, Michael L (Mike) (Athlete, Football Player)
7107 S Yale Ave # 330
Tulsa, OK 74136-6308, USA

Fanning, Neil (Actor)
c/o Staff Member *International Casting Service & Associates*
2/218 Crown St (via Kings Lane)
Darlinghurst NSW 2010, Australia

Fanning, Shawn (Business Person)
c/o Staff Member *Roxio Inc*
455 El Camino Real
Santa Clara, CA 95050-4377, USA

Fannypack (Music Group)
Famous Celebrity Sound
29 John St Ste 230
New York, NY 10038-4005, USA

Fanok, Harry (Athlete, Baseball Player)
12373 Old State Rd
Chardon, OH 44024-9560, USA

Fansler, Stan (Athlete, Baseball Player)
32 Bunting Ln
Beckley, WV 25801-3656, USA

Fanta 4 (Music Group)
c/o Staff Member *Sony Music Entertainment Germany*
Neumarkter Str. 28
Muenchen 81673, Germany

Fante, Ricky (Musician)
c/o Staff Member *Virgin Records (NY)*
150 5th Ave Fl 7
New York, NY 10011-4372, USA

Fantetti, Ken (Athlete, Football Player)
1211 SE 175th Pl
Portland, OR 97233-4631, USA

Fanucchi, Ledio (Athlete, Football Player)
5650 W Dakota Ave
Fresno, CA 93722-9749, USA

Fanucci, Mike (Athlete, Football Player)
1357 N Tercera Ave
Chandler, AZ 85226-1339, USA

Fanzone, Carmen (Athlete, Baseball Player)
5114 Ranchito Ave
Sherman Oaks, CA 91423-1235, USA

Faracy, Stephanie (Actor)
8765 Lookout Mountain Ave
Los Angeles, CA 90046-1861, USA

Farah, Mo (Athlete, Track Athlete)
c/o Staff Member *Pace Sports Management*
6 The Causeway
Teddington
Middlesex TW11 OHE, UNITED KINGDOM

Farahan, Reza (Reality Star)
c/o Steven Grossman *Untitled Entertainment*
350 S Beverly Dr Ste 200
Beverly Hills, CA 90212-4819, USA

Faraldo, Joe (Horse Racer)
12510 Queens Blvd Apt 1206
Kew Gardens, NY 11415-1528, USA

Faralla, Lillian (Athlete, Baseball Player, Commentator)
102 Antigua Ct
Coronado, CA 92118-3315, USA

Farasopoulos, Chris (Athlete, Football Player)
195 Migues Mountain Ln
Aptos, CA 95003-9628, USA

Farber, Barry (Journalist)
2211 Broadway Apt 3A
New York, NY 10024-6264, USA

Farber, Hap (Athlete, Football Player)
200 Dominican Dr
Madison, MS 39110-8630, USA

Farber, Stacey (Actor)
c/o Yanick Landry *Newton-Landry Management*
19 Isabella St
Toronto, ON M4Y 1M7, Canada

Farda, Richard (Athlete, Hockey Player)
Sonnenrain 10
Hor-gen, 8810, SWITZERLAND

Far East Movement (Music Group)
c/o Staff Member *Stampede Management*
12530 Beatrice St
Los Angeles, CA 90066-7002, USA

Farenthold, Blake (Congressman, Politician)
2110 Rayburn Hob
Washington, DC 20515-1306, USA

Fargas, Antonio (Actor)
H David Moss
6063 Vineland Ave Apt B
North Hollywood, CA 91606-4986, USA

Fargas, Justin (Athlete, Football Player)
9839 Kessler Ave
Chatsworth, CA 91311-5506, USA

Fargis, Joe (Athlete, Horse Racer, Olympic Athlete)
11744 Marblestone Ct
Wellington, FL 33414-6041, USA

Fargo, Donna (Musician)
PO Box 210877
Nashville, TN 37221-0877, USA

Farhadi, Asghar (Director)
c/o Keya Khayatian *United Talent Agency (UTA)*
9336 Civic Center Dr
Beverly Hills, CA 90210-3604, USA

Faries, Paul (Athlete, Baseball Player)
3299 Beechwood Dr
Lafayette, CA 94549-4661, USA

Farina, Battista (Pinin) (Designer)
Pinitarina SpA
Via Lesna 78
Turin
Grugliasco 10095, ITALY

Farina, David (Religious Leader)
Chrishtian Church of North America
41 Sherbrooke Rd
Ewing, NJ 08638-2416, USA

Farina, Johnny (Music Group)
Bellrose Music
308 E 6th St Apt 13
New York, NY 10003-8760, USA

Faris, Anna (Actor)
c/o Doug Wald *Anonymous Content*
3532 Hayden Ave
Culver City, CA 90232-2413, USA

Faris, Paula (Correspondent, Journalist)
c/o Staff Member *ABC News*
77 W 66th St Fl 3
New York, NY 10023-6201, USA

Faris, Sean (Actor)
c/o Dino May *Dino May Management*
13223 Bloomfield St
Sherman Oaks, CA 91423-3207, USA

Faris, Valerie (Director, Producer)
Bob Industries
1313 5th St
Santa Monica, CA 90401-1414, USA

Fariss, Monty (Athlete, Baseball Player)
PO Box 1854
Weatherford, OK 73096-1854, USA

Farkas, Jeff (Athlete, Hockey Player)
284 Patrice Ter
Buffalo, NY 14221-3922, USA

Farley, Bob (Athlete, Baseball Player)
1325 Sycamore Rd
Montoursville, PA 17754-9511, USA

Farley, Dale (Athlete, Football Player)
1048 Mount Carmel Church Rd
Sparta, TN 38583-5203, USA

Farley, Dick (Athlete, Football Player)
117 Candlewood Dr
Williamstown, MA 01267-2973, USA

Farley, Jenni (JWoww) (Reality Star)
c/o Robyn Santiago *Illumination PR*
6 Rye Ridge Plz
Rye Brook, NY 10573-2820, USA

Farley, Kevin (Actor, Comedian)
c/o Jonathan Mason *Buchwald (NY)*
10 E 44th St
New York, NY 10017-3601, USA

Farm, Ali (Athlete)
PO Box 160
Berrien Springs, MI 49103-0160

Farman, Melissa (Actor)
c/o Staff Member *Prodigy Talent Group*
Prefers to be contacted by telephone or email
Beverly Hills, CA, USA

Farmar, Jordan (Athlete, Basketball Player)
172 Middlesex Ave
Englewood Cliffs, NJ 07632-1532, USA

Farmer, Billy (Baseball Player)
18987 E Wilshire Blvd
Jones, OK 73049-5917, USA

Farmer, Charles (Red) (Race Car Driver)
143 Foust Ave
Hueytown, AL 35023-2068, USA

Farmer, Danny (Athlete, Football Player)
332 Lorraine Blvd
Los Angeles, CA 90020-4728, USA

Farmer, Darci Lynne (Artist, Impersonator, Reality Star)
c/o Staff Member *Magna Talent Agency*
PO Box 1637
Norman, OK 73070-1637, USA

Farmer, Dave (Athlete, Football Player)
141 Via Medici
Aptos, CA 95003-5838, USA

Farmer, Ed (Athlete)
333 W 35th St
Chicago, IL 60616-3621

Farmer, Ed (Athlete, Baseball Player)
4581 Camino Del Sol
Calabasas, CA 91302-3836, USA

Farmer, Evan (Actor, Television Host)
c/o Robert Attermann *Abrams Artists Agency*
275 7th Ave Fl 26
New York, NY 10001-6708, USA

Farmer, Gary (Actor)
c/o Staff Member *Gonzo Dr. Records*
PO Box 31096
Santa Fe, NM 87594-1096, USA

Farmer, George (Athlete, Football Player)
332 Lorraine Blvd
Los Angeles, CA 90020-4728, USA

Farmer, George III (Athlete, Football Player)
PO Box 2752
Gardena, CA 90247, USA

Farmer, Howard (Athlete, Baseball Player)
1675 W 10th Pl
Gary, IN 46404-1501, USA

Farmer, James (Athlete, Basketball Player)
214 Ashborough Cir
Dothan, AL 36301-1267, USA

Farmer, Mike (Athlete, Basketball Player, Coach)
2520 Lakeview Dr
Santa Rosa, CA 95405-8657, USA

Farmer, Mimsy (Actor)
Cineart
36 Rue de Ponthieu
Paris 75008, FRANCE

Farmer, Robert (Athlete, Football Player)
481 Bergen Ave
Jersey City, NJ 07304-2416, USA

Farmiga, Taissa (Actor)
c/o Dara Gordon *Anonymous Content*
155 Spring St Frnt 3
New York, NY 10012-5208, USA

Farmiga, Vera (Actor)
c/o Jon Rubinstein *Authentic Talent and Literary Management (NY)*
20 Jay St Ste M17
Brooklyn, NY 11201-8300, USA

Farm, The (Music Group, Musician)
900 Division St
Nashville, TN 37203-4111, USA

Farner, Mark (Music Group, Musician)
Bobby Roberts
PO Box 1547
Goodlettsville, TN 37070-1547, USA

Farnham, John (Musician)
Box 6500 St. Kilda Rd.
Central Melbourne, AUSTRALIA 03004

Farnham, John P (Music Group)
TalentWorks
663 Victoria St
Abbottsford, VIC 03067, AUSTRALIA

Farnsworth, Jeff (Athlete, Baseball Player)
704 50th Ave W
Bradenton, FL 34207-2683, USA

Farnsworth, Kyle (Athlete, Baseball Player)
1400 Stickley Ave
Kissimmee, FL 34747-4024, USA

Farr, Diane (Actor)
c/o Jeff Golenberg *Silver Lining Entertainment*
421 S Beverly Dr Fl 7
Beverly Hills, CA 90212-4408, USA

Farr, Dmarco (Athlete, Football Player)
2175 Del Monte Dr
San Pablo, CA 94806-1016, USA

Farr, Jaime (Actor)
2316 Delaware Ave Ste 266
Buffalo, NY 14216-2638, USA

Farr, Jamie (Actor)
53 Ranchero Rd
Bell Canyon, CA 91307-1032, USA

Farr, Jim (Athlete, Baseball Player)
3 Tyndal Ct
Williamsburg, VA 23188-1552, USA

Farr, Kimberly (Actor)
Tisherman Agency
6767 Forest Lawn Dr # 101
Los Angeles, CA 90068-1027, USA

Farr, Michael (Athlete, Football Player)
3950 Paran Rdg NW
Atlanta, GA 30327-3030, USA

Farr, Miller (Athlete, Football Player)
11815 Rowood Dr
Houston, TX 77070-5349, USA

Farr, Norman (Rocky) (Athlete, Hockey Player)
3850 Overton Park Dr W
Fort Worth, TX 76109-3405, USA

Farr, Sam (Congressman, Politician)
1124 Longworth Hob
Washington, DC 20515-4001, USA

Farrakhan, Louis (Religious Leader)
Nation of Islam
734 W 79th St
Chicago, IL 60620-2424, USA

Farrar, Frank L (Politician)
203 9th Ave
Britton, SD 57430, USA

Farrel, Franklin (Athlete, Hockey Player)
89 Notch Hill Road
Apt 223
North Branford, CT 06471, USA

Farrell, Colin (Actor)
c/o Danica Smith *Kovert Creative*
506 Santa Monica Blvd Ste 400
Santa Monica, CA 90401-2412, USA

Farrell, Dave (Musician)
7 Sawgrass
Trabuco Canyon, CA 92679-4906, USA

Farrell, John (Athlete, Baseball Player)
2400 Beacon St Unit 107
Chestnut Hill, MA 02467-1468, USA

Farrell, Margaux (Athlete, Olympic Athlete, Swimmer)
Bob Farrell
55 Wepawaug Rd
Woodbridge, CT 06525-2424, USA

Farrell, Mike (Actor)
c/o Alan Iezman *Shelter Entertainment*
9255 W Sunset Blvd Ste 300
Los Angeles, CA 90069-3313, USA

Farrell, Paul (Athlete, Football Player)
PO Box 804
Dennis Port, MA 02639-0804, USA

Farrell, Perry (Musician)
c/o Rod MacSween *International Talent Booking*
9 Kingsway
Fl 6
London WC2B 6XF, UNITED KINGDOM

Farrell, Sean (Athlete, Football Player)
17754 Esprit Dr
Tampa, FL 33647-2508, USA

Farrell, Sharon (Actor)
c/o Staff Member *Sherri Lynn Talent Management*
6680 Medford Ct
Chino, CA 91710-3887, USA

Farrell, Shea (Actor)
Artists Agency
1180 S Beverly Dr Ste 301
Los Angeles, CA 90035-1154, USA

Farrell, Terry (Actor)
c/o Becca Kovacik *Berwick & Kovacik*
6230 Wilshire Blvd
Los Angeles, CA 90048-5126, USA

Farrelly, Bobby (Director, Producer, Writer)
c/o Amanda Lundberg *42West*
600 3rd Ave Fl 23
New York, NY 10016-1914, USA

Farrelly, Peter (Director, Producer, Writer)
c/o Amanda Lundberg *42West*
600 3rd Ave Fl 23
New York, NY 10016-1914, USA

Farrelly, Stephen (Athlete, Wrestler)
c/o Staff Member *World Wrestling Entertainment (WWE)*
1241 E Main St
Stamford, CT 06902-3520, USA

Farren, Paul (Athlete, Football Player)
21 Gammons Rd
Cohasset, MA 02025-1405, USA

Farrer, Kathy (Athlete, Golfer)
4500 Sojourn Dr Apt 2503
Addison, TX 75001-5069, USA

Farrier, David (Director, Television Host)
c/o Karen Kay *Karen Kay Management*
2/25 Sale St
Freemans Bay, Auckland 01010, New Zealand

Farrimond, Richard A (Athlete, Baseball Player)
Metra Marconi Center
Gunnels Wood Rd Stevenage
Herts, Kittv Hawk 27949-3522, UNITED KINGDOM (UK)

Farrimond, Richard Major (Astronaut)
Paradigm Secure Communications
Gunnels Wood Road Stevenage
Hertfordshire SGI 2AS, England

Farrington, Richard (Horse Racer)
32 Spring St
Wallington, NJ 07057-2045, USA

Farrington, Robert (Horse Racer)
105 Country Pl
Sanford, FL 32771-6502, USA

Farrington, Robert G (Bob) (Race Car Driver)
201 Lake Hinsdale Dr Apt 211
Willowbrook, IL 60527-2688, USA

Farrior, James (Athlete, Football Player)
1004 Summerset Dr
Pittsburgh, PA 15217-2535, USA

Farris, Dionne (Music Group)
c/o Staff Member *Creative Artists Agency (CAA)*
2000 Avenue of the Stars Ste 100
Los Angeles, CA 90067-4705, USA

Farris, Joseph (Cartoonist)
16 Long Meadow Ln
Bethel, CT 06801-2612, USA

Farris, Kris (Athlete, Football Player)
24 Allbrook Ct
Ladera Ranch, CA 92694-0246, USA

Farris, Lindsay (Actor)
c/o Lital Spitzer *3 Arts Entertainment*
9460 Wilshire Blvd Fl 7
Beverly Hills, CA 90212-2713, USA

Farris, Rachel (Musician)
c/o Staff Member *Logic House Media*
109 Indigo Heights Ct
Azle, TX 76020-1635, USA

Farrish, Dave (Athlete, Hockey Player)
2695 E Katella Ave
Attn Coaching Staff
Anaheim, CA 92806-5904, USA

Farriss, Andrew (Music Group)
8 Hayes St #1
Neutral Bay, NSW 20891, AUSTRALIA

Farriss, Jon (Music Group, Musician)
8 Hayes St #1
Neutral Bay, NSW 20891, AUSTRALIA

Farriss, Tim (Music Group, Musician)
8 Hayes St #1
Neutral Bay, NSW 20891, AUSTRALIA

Farro, Zac (Musician)
c/o Randy Dease *Fly South Music Group*
37 N Orange Ave Ste 790
Orlando, FL 32801-2450, USA

Farrow, Mallory (Actor)
Hervey/Grimes
PO Box 64249
Los Angeles, CA 90064-0249, USA

Farrow, Mia (Actor)
124 Henry Sanford Rd Apt A
Bridgewater, CT 06752-1213, USA

Farrow, Ronan (Journalist)
The New Yorker
1 World Trade Ctr Fl 38
New York, NY 10007-0090, USA

Farrow, Yvonne (Actor)
Geddes Agency
8430 Santa Monica Blvd Ste 200
West Hollywood, CA 90069-4221, USA

Farrow-Rapp, Elizabeth (Baseball Player)
401 Quail Run
Metamora, IL 61548-8360, USA

Farwell, Heath (Athlete, Football Player)
c/o Bruce Tollner *REP 1 Sports Group*
80 Technology Dr
Irvine, CA 92618-2301, USA

Farwig, Stephanie (Athlete, Golfer)
2308 E Taro Ln
Phoenix, AZ 85024-2416, USA

Faryniarz, Brett (Athlete, Football Player)
415 S Laureltree Dr
Anaheim, CA 92808-1648, USA

Fasano, Anthony (Athlete, Football Player)
1016 S Rio Vista Blvd
Ft Lauderdale, FL 33316-1371, USA

Fasano, Sal (Athlete, Baseball Player)
905 Catherine Gln
Minooka, IL 60447-4528, USA

Fassbender, Michael (Actor)
c/o Staff Member *DMC Film*
25 Atlantic Avenue
Ballycastle
Antrim BT54 6AL, NORTHERN IRELAND

Fassel, Jim (Athlete, Coach, Football Coach, Football Player)
345 N Quentin Rd Ste 100
Palatine, IL 60067-4896, USA

Fassero, Jeff (Athlete, Baseball Player)
7313 E Citrus Way
Scottsdale, AZ 85250-5525, USA

Fast, Darcy (Athlete, Baseball Player)
2981 Harrison Ave
Centralia, WA 98531-9356, USA

Fast, Darrell (Religious Leader)
Mennonite Church General Conference
PO Box 347
Newton, KS 67114-0347, USA

Faszholz, Jack (Athlete, Baseball Player)
18338 Maries Road 308
Belle, MO 65013-2125, USA

Faszhotz, Jack (Athlete, Baseball Player)
18338 Maries Road 308
Belle, MO 65013-2125, USA

Fatafehi, Mario (Athlete, Football Player)
7625 Nancy Ann Dr
Painesville, OH 44077-9240

Fatboy Slim (Musician)
c/o David Levy *WME/IMG (UK)*
103 New Oxford St WMA
Centrepoint
London WC1A 1DD, UNITED KINGDOM

Fatefehi, Mario (Athlete, Football Player)
279 W 1360 N
American Fork, UT 84003-2739, USA

Fatel, Mitch (Musician)
c/o Staff Member *Paradigm (Monterey)*
404 W Franklin St
Monterey, CA 93940-2303, USA

Fath, Farah (Actor)
c/o Kurt Patino *Patino Management Company*
10201 Riverside Dr Ste 207
Toluca Lake, CA 91602-2538, USA

Fat Joe (Actor, Musician)
c/o Staff Member *Jim Havey Public Relations*
2817 W End Ave Ste 126 PMB 203
Nashville, TN 37203-1453, USA

Fatone, Joey (Dancer, Musician)
c/o Joe Mulvihill *LiveWire Entertainment (FL)*
7575 Dr Phillips Blvd Ste 255
Orlando, FL 32819-7220, USA

Fator, Terry (Actor, Comedian)
c/o Sean Perry *WME/IMG*
9601 Wilshire Blvd
Beverly Hills, CA 90210-5213, USA

Fattah, Chaka (Congressman, Politician)
2301 Rayburn Hob
Washington, DC 20515-3802, USA

Faubert, Mario (Athlete, Hockey Player)
4 Ch du Canal RR 1
Saint-Stanislas-De-Kostka, QC J0S 1W0, Canada

Faucette, Chuck (Athlete, Football Player)
9714 Broadmoor Ln
Rowlett, TX 75089-8373, USA

Faucette, Mark (Athlete, Hockey Player)
1100 Haley Ln
Dunedin, FL 34698-6120, USA

Faucher, William (Horse Racer)
42 Old Stage Rd
Hinsdale, NH 03451-2308, USA

Faulconer, Martha (Athlete, Golfer)
374 Stratford Dr
Lexington, KY 40503-1813, USA

Faulk, Amy (Race Car Driver)
Hypertech Inc
1215 Appling Rd.
Bartlett, TN 38135, USA

Faulk, Kevin (Athlete, Football Player)
190 Summer St
South Walpole, MA 02071-1014, USA

Faulk, Marshall (Athlete, Football Player)
c/o Jon Orlando *Exposure Marketing Group*
348 Hauser Blvd Apt 414
Los Angeles, CA 90036-5590, USA

Faulk, Trev (Athlete, Football Player)
307 Martin Oaks Dr
Lafayette, LA 70501-2507, USA

Faulkner, Alex (Athlete, Hockey Player)
17 Adams Ave
Bishops Falls, NL A0H 1C0, Canada

Faulkner, Chris (Athlete, Football Player)
1596 E 400 S
Tipton, IN 46072-8440, USA

Faulkner, Eric (Musician)
27 Preston Grange
Preston Pans E
Lothian, SCOTLAND

Faulkner, Harris (Television Host)
c/o Staff Member *Fox News*
1211 Avenue of the Americas Lowr C1
New York, NY 10036-8705, USA

Faulkner, Jeff (Athlete, Football Player)
14150 Carlton Dr
Davie, FL 33330-4659, USA

Faumui, Taase (Athlete, Football Player)
1574 Linapuni St
Honolulu, HI 96819-3507, USA

Fauntleroy, James (Musician)

Fauria, Christian (Athlete, Football Player)
1908 SE Abbey St
Blue Springs, MO 64014-4015, USA

Fauria, Joseph (Athlete, Football Player)
c/o David Dunn *Athletes First*
23091 Mill Creek Dr
Laguna Hills, CA 92653-1258, USA

Fauser, Mark (Actor)
c/o Staff Member *United Talent Agency (UTA)*
9336 Civic Center Dr
Beverly Hills, CA 90210-3604, USA

Fauss, Ted (Athlete, Hockey Player)
6861 Lowell Rd
Rome, NY 13440-1228, USA

Faust, Andre (Athlete, Hockey Player)
250 Heritage Rd
Cherry Hill, NJ 08034-3150, USA

Faust, August (Athlete, Hockey Player)
250 Heritage Rd
Cherry Hill, NJ 08034-3150, USA

Faust, Chad (Actor)
c/o Evan Hainey *Untitled Entertainment*
350 S Beverly Dr Ste 200
Beverly Hills, CA 90212-4819, USA

Faust, Paul (Athlete, Football Player)
5522 Highwood Dr W
Minneapolis, MN 55436-1227, USA

Faustino, David (Actor)
c/o Elizabeth Much *East 2 West Collective*
11022 Santa Monica Blvd Ste 350
Los Angeles, CA 90025-7532, USA

Faut-Eastman, Jean (Athlete, Baseball Player, Commentator)
406 Warrington Pl
Rock Hill, SC 29732-7408, USA

Fauts, Dan (Athlete, Football Player)
4020 Murphy Canyon Rd
San Diego, CA 92123-4407, USA

Favela, Marlene (Actor)
Broadcast Music Inc
320 W 57th St
New York, NY 10019-3705, USA

Favell, Doug (Athlete, Hockey Player)
8 Captain Tenbrock Terr
St Catharines, ON L2W 1B2, CANADA

Favier, Jean-Jacques Dr (Astronaut)
20 rue Jeanne Marvig
Toulouse 31400, France

Favino, Pierfrancesco (Actor)
c/o Graziella Bonacchi *TNA*
Viale Parioli, 41
Rome 00197, ITALY

Favor, Mike (Athlete, Football Player)
8409 Shadow Creek Dr
Osseo, MN 55311-1570, USA

Favor-Hamilton, Suzy (Athlete, Olympic Athlete, Track Athlete)
1014 Beloit Ct
Madison, WI 53705-2233

Favors, Gregory (Athlete, Football Player)
230 Merritt Dr
Roswell, GA 30076-3936, USA

Favre, Brett (Athlete, Football Player)
1 Willow Bend Dr
Hattiesburg, MS 39402-8552, USA

Favreau, Jon (Actor)
c/o Ina Treciokas *Slate PR*
901 N Highland Ave
W Hollywood, CA 90038-2412, USA

Fawcett, John (Director)
c/o Scott Yoselow *Gersh*
41 Madison Ave Ste 3301
New York, NY 10010-2210, USA

Fawcett, Joy (Athlete, Olympic Athlete, Soccer Player)
11 Calle Marta Rancho
Santa Margarita, CA 92688-3500, USA

Faxon, Nat (Actor)
c/o Jillian Roscoe *ID Public Relations*
7060 Hollywood Blvd Fl 8th
Los Angeles, CA 90028-6021, USA

Faxon Jr, Brad (Athlete, Golfer)
c/o Staff Member *Pro Golfers Association (PGA)*
112 TPC Blvd
Ponte Vedra Beach, FL 32082, USA

Fay, David B (Golfer)
US Golf Assn
Golf House
Liberty Corner Road
Far Hills, NJ 07931, USA

Fay, Meagan (Actor)
c/o Staff Member *Paradigm*
8942 Wilshire Blvd
Beverly Hills, CA 90211-1908, USA

Fay, Meagen (Actor)
c/o Staff Member *Main Title Entertainment*
8383 Wilshire Blvd Ste 408
Beverly Hills, CA 90211-2435, USA

Faydoedeelay (Music Group, Musician)
Q Prime
729 7th Ave Ste 1600
New York, NY 10019-6880, USA

Fazal, Ali (Actor)
c/o Victoria Belfrage *Julian Belfrage & Associates*
9 Argyll St Fl 3
London W1F 7TG, UNITED KINGDOM

Fazande, Jermaine (Athlete, Football Player)
460 Wilson St
Marrero, LA 70072-1124, USA

Fazio, Ernie (Athlete, Baseball Player)
2310 Royal Oaks Dr
Alamo, CA 94507-2223, USA

F. Bass, Charles (Congressman, Politician)
2350 Rayburn Hob
Washington, DC 20515-0550, USA

F. Costello, Jerry (Congressman, Politician)
2408 Rayburn Hob
Washington, DC 20515-0922, USA

F. Doyle, Michael (Congressman, Politician)
401 Cannon Hob
Washington, DC 20515-3814, USA

Feacher, Ricky (Athlete, Football Player)
1522 Ferman Ave
Cleveland, OH 44109-3642, USA

Feagles, Jeff (Athlete, Football Player)
221 Avondale Rd
Ridgewood, NJ 07450-1303, USA

Feamster, Dave (Athlete, Hockey Player)
1058 S May Valley Dr
Pueblo, CO 81007-5033, USA

Feamster, Tom (Athlete, Football Player)
1805 Virginia Ct
Tavares, FL 32778-2135, USA

Fear Before (Music Group, Musician)
c/o Staff Member *Equal Vision Records*
PO Box 38202
Albany, NY 12203-8202, USA

Fearnley-Whittingstall, Hugh (Chef)
c/o Staff Member *BBC Artist Mail*
PO Box 1116
Belfast BT2 7AJ, United Kingdom

Fears, Willie (Athlete, Football Player)
1414 S Summit St
Little Rock, AR 72202-5821, USA

Feaster, Allison (Athlete, Basketball Player)
6022 Kentworth Dr
Holly Springs, NC 27540-7670, USA

Featherson, Ashley Blaine (Actor, Comedian)
c/o Mike Smith *Principal Entertainment*
9255 W Sunset Blvd Ste 500
Los Angeles, CA 90069-3301, USA

Featherston, Katie (Actor)
c/o Jillian Roscoe *ID Public Relations*
7060 Hollywood Blvd Fl 8th
Los Angeles, CA 90028-6021, USA

Featherstone, Glen (Athlete, Hockey Player)
8 Larrabee Ave
Danvers, MA 01923-1828, USA

Featherstone, Tony (Athlete, Hockey Player)
Allstate Insurance Agency
3003 Danforth Ave Danforth Shoppers World #9
Toronto, ON M4C 1M9, CANADA

Febles, Carlos (Athlete, Baseball Player, Coach)
Lancaster Jethawks
45116 Valley Central Way
Attn: Coaching Staff
Lancaster, CA 93536-1508, USA

Fedderly, Bernie (Race Car Driver)
John Force Racing
22722 Old Canal Rd
Yorba Linda, CA 92887-4602, USA

Fede, Terrence (Athlete, Football Player)
c/o Joe Linta *JL Sports*
1204 Main St Ste 179
Branford, CT 06405-3787, USA

Federer, Mike (Race Car Driver)
Mike Federer Racing
23210 54th St E
Buckley, WA 98321-9759, USA

Federer, Roger (Athlete, Tennis Player)
Lynette Federer
Postfach
Bottmingen CH-4103, Switzerland

Federico, Anthony (Athlete, Football Player)
12306 Van Nuys Blvd
Sylmar, CA 91342-6049, USA

Federico, Creig (Athlete, Football Player)
303 Ridgewood Dr
Bloomingdale, IL 60108-2533, USA

Federko, Bernie (Athlete, Hockey Player)
2219 Devonsbrook Dr
Chesterfield, MO 63005-4519, USA

Federko, Bernie (Athlete, Hockey Player)
St Louis Blues 1401 Clark Ave
Attn Broadcast Dept
Saint Louis, MO 63103-2700, USA

Federline, Kevin (Actor, Dancer, Musician)
24812 Paseo Del Rancho
Calabasas, CA 91302-3092, USA

Federov, Sergei (Athlete, Hockey Player)
1865 Huntingwood Ln
Bloomfield Hills, MI 48304-2313, USA

Federspiel, Joe (Athlete, Football Player)
2016 Lakeside Dr
Lexington, KY 40502-3017, USA

Fedewa, Tim (Race Car Driver)
1737 Onondaga Rd
Holt, MI 48842-8600, USA

Fedor, Dave (Athlete, Basketball Player)
4510 Audubon Ave
De Leon Springs, FL 32130-3033

Fedorov, Sergei (Athlete, Hockey Player)
1975 Tiverton Rd
Bloomfield Hills, MI 48304-2348, USA

Fedorov, Sergey (Athlete, Hockey Player)
c/o Staff Member *CAA Sports*
2000 Avenue of the Stars Ste 100
Los Angeles, CA 90067-4705, USA

Fedoruk, Paul (Athlete, Hockey Player)
4578 Liam Dr
Frisco, TX 75034-2139, USA

Fedoruk, Todd (Athlete, Hockey Player)
25 Mallard Dr
Mount Laurel, NJ 08054-3084, USA

Fedotenko, Ruslan (Athlete, Hockey Player)
230 W 56th St Apt 54E
New York, NY 10019-0077, USA

Fedotov, Maxim V (Musician)
Tolbukhin Str 8 #6
Moscow 121596, RUSSIA

Fedotowsky, Ali (Actor, Reality Star)

F. Edwards, Donna (Congressman, Politician)
318 Cannon Hob
Washington, DC 20515-3101, USA

Fedyk, Brent (Athlete, Hockey Player)
1741 Holland St
Birmingham, MI 48009-7804, USA

Fee, Melinda (Actor)
145 S Fairfax Ave Ste 310
Los Angeles, CA 90036-2176, USA

Feeder (Music Group)
Feeder Central
PO Box 2539
London W1A 3HZ, UNITED KINGDOM

Feehery, Gerry (Athlete, Football Player)
5 Sharpless Ln
Media, PA 19063-3931, USA

Feehily, Mark (Musician)
c/o Staff Member *Solo Agency Ltd (UK)*
53-55 Fulham High St
Fl 2
London SW6 3JJ, UNITED KINGDOM

Feeley, A J (Athlete, Football Player)
477 Zuni Or
Del Mar, CA 92014-2445, USA

Feely, Jay (Athlete, Football Player)
7808 River Ridge Dr
Temple Terrace, FL 33637-4933, USA

Fegan, Roshon (Actor, Musician)
c/o Jennifer Merlino *Untitled Entertainment*
350 S Beverly Dr Ste 200
Beverly Hills, CA 90212-4819, USA

Fegley, Jr., Don (Race Car Driver)
RD 1
Box 148-J
New Ringgold, PA 17960, USA

Feher, Raymond (Athlete, Basketball Player)
62 Cool Springs Rd
Signal Mountain, TN 37377-2075, USA

Feherty, David (Athlete, Golfer)
6422 Prestonshire Ln
Dallas, TX 75225-2309, USA

Fehr, Brendan (Actor)
c/o Christopher Burbidge *Fourward*
10250 Constellation Blvd Ste 2710
Los Angeles, CA 90067-6227, USA

Fehr, Donald (Commentator)
34 Rockinghorse Trl
Rye Brook, NY 10573-1038, USA

Fehr, Oded (Actor)
c/o Karen Samfilippo *IMPR*
1158 26th St # 548
Santa Monica, CA 90403-4698, USA

Fehr, Rick (Athlete, Golfer)
2869 W Haley Dr
Anthem, AZ 85086-1749, USA

Feick, Jamie (Athlete, Basketball Player)
7561 Darlington Rd S
Fredericktown, OH 43019-9247, USA

Feierabend, Ryan (Athlete, Baseball Player)
366 Windsor Dr
Elyria, OH 44035-1732, USA

Feiffer, Jules (Cartoonist, Writer)
PO Box 1777
Shelter Island, NY 11964-1777, USA

Feig, Paul (Actor, Director)
c/o Staff Member *Powderkeg Media*
3500 W Olive Ave # 350
Burbank, CA 91505-4628, USA

Feige, Kevin (Business Person, Producer)
c/o Staff Member *Marvel Studios Inc*
500 S Buena Vista St
Burbank, CA 91521-0001, USA

Feinberg, Alan (Musician)
Cramer/Marder Artists
3436 Springhill Rd
Lafayette, CA 94549-2535, USA

Feingold, Russell (Politician)
3736 Pheasant Branch Rd
Middleton, WI 53562-1133, USA

Feinstein, Dianne (Politician)
c/o Staff Member *United States Senate (Hart Office)*
316 Hart Senate Office Building
Washington, DC 20510-0001, USA

Feinstein, Michael (Music Group, Musician)
4647 Kingswell Ave # 110
Los Angeles, CA 90027-4301, USA

Feist, Leslie (Musician)

Feitle, Dave (Athlete, Basketball Player)
120 Cathedral Vw
Sedona, AZ 86351-9508, USA

Fekkai, Frederic (Business Person)
Frederic Fekkai Salon
444 N Rodeo Dr
Beverly Hills, CA 90210-4502, USA

Felber, Dean (Music Group, Musician)
FishCo Mgmt
P O Box 5456
Columbia, SC 29250, USA

Felder, Benny (Athlete, Baseball Player)
5012 N 39th St
Tampa, FL 33610-6628, USA

Felder, Bobby (Athlete, Football Player)
c/o Ashanti Webb *EMG Sports - OH*
8055 Reynoldswood Dr
Reynoldsburg, OH 43068-9348, USA

Felder, Don (Musician)
PO Box 6051
Malibu, CA 90264-6051, USA

Felder, Kenny (Athlete, Baseball Player)
2902 W Amberwood Dr
Phoenix, AZ 85045-2289, USA

Felder, Mike (Athlete, Baseball Player)
322 S 17th St
Richmond, CA 94804-2606, USA

Felder, Raoul Lionel (Attorney)
437 Madison Ave Ste 3000
New York, NY 10022-7030, USA

Feldhausen, Paul (Athlete, Football Player)
W137S6949 Clarendon Pl
Muskego, WI 53150-3207, USA

Feldman, Bella (Artist)
12 Summit Ln
Berkeley, CA 94708-2213, USA

Feldman, Ben (Actor)
c/o Danica Smith *Kovert Creative*
506 Santa Monica Blvd Ste 400
Santa Monica, CA 90401-2412, USA

Feldman, Corey (Actor)
c/o Samantha Waranch *JAG Entertainment*
4605 Lankershim Blvd Ste 807
North Hollywood, CA 91602-1879, 91505

Feldman, Donna (Actor, Model)
c/o Allee Newhoff *DAS Model Management*
2228 Park Ave # 2
Miami Beach, FL 33139-1722, USA

Feldman, Marty (Athlete, Football Player)
100 Louise Ct
Los Gatos, CA 95032-1608, USA

Feldman, Scott (Athlete, Baseball Player)
2848 Woodside St Apt 302
Dallas, TX 75204-2587, USA

Feldman, Tamara (Actor)
c/o John Pierce *The Group*
800 S Robertson Blvd Ste 5
Los Angeles, CA 90035-1634, USA

Feldon, Barbara (Actor, Model)
14 E 74th St Apt 1
New York, NY 10021-2628, USA

Feldott, Jennifer (Athlete, Golfer)
1730 Lakeshore Dr
Fennville, MI 49408-9721, USA

Feldshuh, Tovah (Actor)
c/o Christina Papadopoulos *Baker Winokur Ryder Public Relations*
200 5th Ave Fl 5
New York, NY 10010-3307, USA

Feldstein, Beanie (Actor)
c/o Stacy O'Neil *Brillstein Entertainment Partners*
9150 Wilshire Blvd Ste 350
Beverly Hills, CA 90212-3453, USA

Felici, Angelo Cardinal (Religious Leader)
Piazza della Citta Leonina 9
Rome 00193, ITALY

Feliciano, Jose (Musician)
c/o Guy Richard *UTA Music/The Agency Group*
9336 Civic Center Dr
Beverly Hills, CA 90210-3604, USA

Felix, Allyson (Athlete, Olympic Athlete, Track Athlete)
5656 W 63rd St
Los Angeles, CA 90056-2013, USA

Felix, Junior (Athlete, Baseball Player)
7545 Treadway Rd
Gresham, SC 29546-4210, USA

Feliz, Rhenzy (Actor)
c/o Lisa Wright *LINK Entertainment*
11872 La Grange Ave
Los Angeles, CA 90025-5282, USA

Felke, Petra (Athlete, Track Athlete)
SC Motor Jena
Wollnitzevstr 42
Jena 07749, GERMANY

Felker, Gene (Athlete, Football Player)
945 N Pasadena Unit 160
Mesa, AZ 85201-4319, USA

Fell, Sam (Animator, Director)
c/o Staff Member *United Talent Agency (UTA)*
9336 Civic Center Dr
Beverly Hills, CA 90210-3604, USA

Feller, Happy (Athlete, Football Player)
4225 Camacho St
Austin, TX 78723-5389, USA

Feller, Jack (Athlete, Baseball Player)
145 Oakwood Dr
Coldwater, MI 49036-8606, USA

Fellner, Eric (Producer)
c/o Simon Halls *Slate PR*
901 N Highland Ave
W Hollywood, CA 90038-2412, USA

Fellowes, Julian (Actor)
c/o Jeff Sanderson *Chasen & Company*
8560 W Sunset Blvd Ste 210
Los Angeles, CA 90069-2345, USA

Fellows, Mark (Athlete, Football Player)
PO Box 517
Choteau, MT 59422-0517, USA

Fellows, Ron (Athlete, Football Player)
202 Creekview Dr
Wylie, TX 75098-7481, USA

Fells, Daniel (Athlete, Football Player)

Fells, Darren (Athlete, Football Player)

Felske, John (Athlete, Baseball Player, Coach)
300 Faith Rd
Blue Eye, MO 65611-7264, USA

Felsner, Brian (Athlete, Hockey Player)
26563 Autumn Lake Dr
Chesterfield, MI 48051-1988, USA

Felsner, Denny (Athlete, Hockey Player)
16094 Haverhill Dr
Macomb, MI 48044-1946, USA

Felt, Richard (Athlete, Football Player)
3993 N 750 E
Provo, UT 84604-4773, USA

Felton, Dennis (Basketball Player)
University of Georgia
Athletic Dept
Athens, GA 30602-0001, USA

Felton, Eric (Athlete, Football Player)
PO Box 1355
Coppell, TX 75019-1310, USA

Felton, Jerome (Athlete, Football Player)
c/o Sean Howard *Octagon Football*
600 Battery St Fl 2
San Francisco, CA 94111-1820, USA

Felton, John (Musician)
GMS
PO Box 1031
Montrose, CA 91021-1031, USA

Felton, Raymond (Athlete, Basketball Player)
15109 Redwood Valley Ln
Charlotte, NC 28277-3282, USA

Felton, Terry (Athlete, Baseball Player)
1253 Cordoba Dr
Zachary, LA 70791-6212, USA

Felton, Tom (Actor)
c/o Michael Duff *Troika*
10A Christina St.
London EC2A 4PA, UNITED KINGDOM

Feltrin, Tony (Athlete, Hockey Player)
PO Box 560
Lake Cowichan, BC V0R 2G0, Canada

Felts, Narvel (Musician, Songwriter, Writer)
2005 Narvel Felts Dr
Malden, MO 63863-1243, USA

Feltsman, Vladimir (Musician)
Columbia Artists Mgmt Inc
165 W 57th St
New York, NY 10019-2201, USA

Feltus, Alan E (Artist)
Porziano 68
Assisi PG 06081, ITALY

Feltz, Vanessa (Actor)
c/o Staff Member *XS Promotions*
57 Fonthill Rd
Aberdeen AB11 6UQ, UNITED KINGDOM (UK)

Fencik, J Gary (Athlete, Football Player)
1134 W Schubert Ave
Chicago, IL 60614-1309, USA

Fendrich, Rainhard (Musician)
c/o Staff Member *Agentur Rehling*
Kirchenstrasse 17c
Germering D-82110, Germany

Fenech, Edwige (Actor)
Carol Levi Co
Via Giuseppe Pisanelli
Rome 00196, ITALY

Fenech, Jeff (Boxer)
PO Box 21
Hardys Bay, NSW 02257, AUSTRALIA

Fenenbock, Charles (Athlete, Football Player)
6000 S Land Park Dr Apt 105
Sacramento, CA 95822-3362, USA

Fenerty, Gill (Athlete, Football Player)
2452 Brookhaven Ct NE
Atlanta, GA 30319-5243, USA

Fenn, Sherilyn (Actor)
Water Street Anthem Entertainment
5225 Wilshire Blvd Ste 615
Los Angeles, CA 90036-4350, USA

Fennema, Carl (Athlete, Football Player)
2470 Dexter Ave N Apt 402
Seattle, WA 98109-2248, USA

Fenner, Derrick (Athlete, Football Player)
7533 33rd Ave NW
Seattle, WA 98117-4712, USA

Fenner, Lane (Athlete, Football Player)
412 Labarre Ct
Saint Johns, FL 32259-4024, USA

Fenney, Rick (Athlete, Football Player)
41594 Margarita Rd
Temecula, CA 92591-2922, USA

Fenoli, Randy (Designer, Reality Star)
c/o Staff Member *Creative Artists Agency (CAA)*
2000 Avenue of the Stars Ste 100
Los Angeles, CA 90067-4705, USA

Fenson, Pete (Athlete, Olympic Athlete)
3769 Crest Ct NE
Bemidji, MN 56601-6083, USA

Fenton, James (Writer)
P F D Drury House
34-43 Russell St
London WC2B 5HA, UNITED KINGDOM (UK)

Fenton, Paul (Athlete, Hockey Player)
501 Broadway
Attn: Asst General Manager
Nashville, TN 37203-3980, USA

Fenton, Paul (Athlete, Hockey Player)
16 Bridle Path Rd
Brewster, MA 02631-1611, USA

Fenton, Peggy (Athlete, Baseball Player, Commentator)
11131 Cottonwood Dr Unit A
Palos Hills, IL 60465-2528, USA

Fenwick, Bobby (Athlete, Baseball Player)
51201 Hutchinson Rd
Three Rivers, MI 49093-9029, USA

Fenyves, Dave (Athlete, Hockey Player)
940 Parish Pl
Hummelstown, PA 17036-8986, USA

Feore, Colm (Actor)
c/o Leanne Coronel *Coronel Group*
1100 Glendon Ave Fl 17
Los Angeles, CA 90024-3588, USA

Feraud, Gianfranco (Designer, Fashion Designer)
25 Rue Saint Honore
Paris 75001, FRANCE

Ferdinand, Franz (Musician)
c/o Staff Member *Paradigm (Monterey)*
404 W Franklin St
Monterey, CA 93940-2303, USA

Ferdinand, Marie (Athlete, Basketball Player)
San Antonio Silver Stars
1 at and T Center Pkwy
San Antonio, TX 78219-3604, USA

Ferdinand, Rio (Soccer Player)
c/o Staff Member *Manchester United PLC*
Sir Matt Busby Way
Old Trafford
Manchester M160RA, UNITED KINGDOM

Ferdinand, Ron (Cartoonist)
PO Box 1997
Monterey, CA 93942-1997

Ference, Andrew (Athlete, Hockey Player)
220 Commercial St Unit 2F
Boston, MA 02109-6304, USA

Ference, Brad (Athlete, Hockey Player)
2424 Gold Canyon Dr
San Antonio, TX 78259-3568, USA

Ferentz, Kirk (Coach, Football Coach)
University of Iowa
Athletic Dept
Iowa City
IA 52242, USA

Fergie (Actor, Musician)
c/o William Derella *DAS Communications*
83 Riverside Dr
New York, NY 10024-5713, USA

Fergon, Vicki (Athlete, Golfer)
44 Partridge Ln
Aliso Viejo, CA 92656-1701, USA

Fergus, Keith (Athlete, Golfer)
11903 Royal Rose Dr
Houston, TX 77082-6863, USA

Fergus, Tom (Athlete, Hockey Player)
Blue Leaf Ltd
1240 Springwood Cres
Oakville, ON L6M 1V8, Canada

Ferguson, Alex (Business Person)
c/o Staff Member *Manchester United PLC*
Sir Matt Busby Way
Old Trafford
Manchester M160RA, UNITED KINGDOM

Ferguson, Charley (Athlete, Football Player)
81 Stonecroft Ln
Buffalo, NY 14226-4129, USA

Ferguson, Christopher (Astronaut)
425 Pierce Ave UNIT 310
Cpe Canaveral, FL 32920-3179, USA

Ferguson, Colin (Actor)
c/o Staff Member *GEP Productions Inc*
3500 Cornett Rd Bldg B
Vancouver, BC V5M 2H5, Canada

Ferguson, Craig (Actor, Comedian, Television Host)
c/o Staff Member *Green Mountain West*
2700 Colorado Ave Ste 200
Santa Monica, CA 90404-5502, USA

Ferguson, Cullum Cathy (Athlete, Olympic Athlete, Swimmer)
3107 San Gabriel Ave
Clovis, CA 93619-9272, USA

Ferguson, D'Brickashaw (Athlete, Football Player)
c/o Brad Blank *Brad Blank & Associates*
1800 Sunset Harbour Dr
#2402
Miami Beach, FL 33139, USA

Ferguson, George (Athlete, Hockey Player)
306 Old Lesnett Rd
Pittsburgh, PA 15241-3517, USA

Ferguson, Jason (Athlete, Football Player)
15139 SW 34th St
Davie, FL 33331-2714, USA

Ferguson, Jay R (Actor)
c/o Jennifer Sims *Imprint PR*
375 Hudson St
New York, NY 10014-3658, USA

Ferguson, Jesse Tyler (Actor)
c/o Jillian Roscoe *ID Public Relations*
7060 Hollywood Blvd Fl 8th
Los Angeles, CA 90028-6021, USA

Ferguson, Joe (Athlete, Baseball Player)
11322 River Run Ln
Berlin, MD 21811-3288, USA

Ferguson, Joe (Athlete, Football Player)
12 Mason Ln
Bella Vista, AR 72715-5548, USA

Ferguson, Keith (Athlete, Football Player)
PO Box 19006
Sugar Land, TX 77496-9006, USA

Ferguson, Lynda (Actor)
606 N Larchmont Blvd Ste 309
Los Angeles, CA 90004-1309, USA

Ferguson, Nick (Athlete, Football Player)
1114 Arlington Ave SW
Atlanta, GA 30310-3832, USA

Ferguson, Norm (Athlete, Hockey Player)
71 Causeway Dr
Sydney, NS B1L 1C5, Canada

Ferguson, Rebecca (Actor)
c/o Romilly Bowlby *DDA Public Relations*
192-198 Vauxhall Bridge Rd
London SW1V 1DX, UNITED KINGDOM

Ferguson, Robert (Athlete, Football Player)
15102 Oldtown Bridge Ct
Sugar Land, TX 77498-1298, USA

Ferguson, Sarah (Royalty)
c/o Karen Sellars *ICM Partners*
10250 Constellation Blvd Fl 7
Los Angeles, CA 90067-6207, USA

Ferguson, Thomas A Jr (Business Person)
Newell Rubbermaid Inc
29 E Stephenson St
Newell Center
Freeport, IL 61032-0943, USA

Ferguson, Vasquero D (Vagas) (Athlete, Football Player)
Richmond High School
380 Hub Etchison Pkwy
Richmond, IN 47374-5398, USA

Ferguson, William (Athlete, Football Player)
9433 N Newport Hwy
Spokane, WA 99218, USA

Ferguson-Winn, Mabel (Athlete, Track Athlete)
2575 Steele Rd Apt 206
San Bernardino, CA 92408-3979, USA

Fergus-Thompson, Gordo (Musician)
150 Audley Road
Hendon
London NW4 3EG, UNITED KINGDOM (UK)

Ferigno, Lou (Actor)
Lou Ferrigno Enterprises Inc
PO Box 1671
Santa Monica, CA 90406-1671, USA

Ferland, E James (Business Person)
Public Service Enterprise
80 Park Plz
PO Box 1171
Newark, NJ 07102-4194, USA

Ferland, Jodelle (Actor)
c/o Vickie Petronio *Play Management*
220-807 Powell St
Vancouver, BC V6A 1H7, CANADA

Ferlinghetti, Lawrence (Writer)
City Lights Booksellers
261 Columbus Ave
San Francisco, CA 94133-4586, USA

Ferlito, Vanessa (Actor)
c/o Jason Barrett *Alchemy Entertainment*
7024 Melrose Ave Ste 420
Los Angeles, CA 90038-3394, USA

Fermin, Felix (Athlete, Baseball Player)
Akron Aeros
300 S Main St
Attn: Coaching Staff
Akron, OH 44308-1204, USA

Fern, Cody (Actor)
c/o Heidi Lopata *Narrative*
1601 Vine St Fl 6
Los Angeles, CA 90028-8802, USA

Fernandes, Ron (Athlete, Football Player)
900 Fairwood St
Inkster, MI 48141-4003, USA

Fernandez, Adrian (Race Car Driver)
Fernandez Racing
PO Box 68828
Indianapolis, IN 46268-0828, USA

Fernandez, Alejandro (Musician)
Hauser Entertainment
11003 Rooks Rd
Whittier, CA 90601-1624, USA

Fernandez, Alex (Athlete, Baseball Player)
12323 SW 55th St Ste 107
Cooper City, FL 33330-3312, USA

Fernandez, Bernardo (Athlete, Baseball Player)
6701 Dorita Ave Unit 202
Las Vegas, NV 89108-0355, USA

Fernandez, Chico (Athlete, Baseball Player)
1310 SW 97th Ave
Miami, FL 33174-1384, USA

Fernandez, Chico (Athlete, Baseball Player)
27920 Shiawassee Rd
Farmington Hills, MI 48336-6064, USA

Fernandez, Craig (Director, Writer)
c/o Staff Member *Gotham Group*
1041 N Formosa Ave # 200
West Hollywood, CA 90046-6703, USA

Fernandez, C Sidney (Sid) (Athlete, Baseball Player)
25 Aulike St Apt 218
Kailua, HI 96734-2747, USA

Fernandez, Frank (Athlete, Baseball Player)
118 Windermere Rd
Staten Island, NY 10305-2724, USA

Fernandez, Gigi (Athlete, Tennis Player)
Gigi Tennis Camp
4202 E Fowler Ave # 214
Tampa, FL 33620-9951, USA

Fernandez, Giselle (Television Host)
NHD International Service
PO Box 498
Quakertown, PA 18951-0498, USA

Fernandez, Jacqueline (Actor)
c/o Staff Member *Spice PR (India)*
D 43, Self Help
St Francis Road, Ville Parle (West)
Mumbai Maharashtra NA, INDIA

Fernandez, Jared (Athlete, Baseball Player)
4298 S 4625 W
Salt Lake City, UT 84120-4964, USA

Fernandez, Juan (Actor)
Don Buchwald
5900 Wilshire Blvd Ste 3100
Los Angeles, CA 90036-5030, USA

Fernandez, Lisa (Athlete, Olympic Athlete, Softball Player)
1460 Homewood Rd Apt 95B
Seal Beach, CA 90740-4627, USA

Fernandez, Manny (Athlete, Hockey Player)
Sport Prospects Inc
77 Rue de Bleury
Attn: Gilles Lupien
Rosemere, QC J7A 4L9, Canada

Fernandez, Manny (Athlete, Football Player)
1709 Poplar Ridge Rd
Ellaville, GA 31806-5935, USA

Fernandez, Mary Joe (Athlete, Olympic Athlete, Tennis Player)
3215 Roundwood Rd
Chagrin Falls, OH 44022-6635, USA

Fernandez, Mervyn (Athlete, Football Player)
2567 Branden Pl
Manteca, CA 95337-2020, USA

Fernandez, O Antonio (Tony) (Athlete, Baseball Player)
19232 N Gardenia Ave
Weston, FL 33332-4409, USA

Fernández, Pedro (Musician)
c/o Staff Member *Machete Music*
2220 Colorado Ave
Santa Monica, CA 90404-3506, USA

Fernandez, Pedro (Musician, Songwriter)
Exclusive Artists Productions
PO Box 65948
Los Angeles, CA 90065-0948, USA

Fernandez, Shiloh (Actor)
c/o Justin Grey Stone *Management 360*
9111 Wilshire Blvd
Beverly Hills, CA 90210-5508, USA

Fernandez, Vicente (Musician)
c/o Staff Member *Hauser Entertainment*
3703 San Gabriel River Pkwy
Pico Rivera, CA 90660-1404, USA

Fernandez-Versini, Cheryl (Musician)

Fernsten, Eric (Athlete, Basketball Player)
5634 Linden St
Dublin, CA 94568-7704

Ferragamo, Vince (Athlete, Football Player)
Touchdown Real Estate
6200 E Canyon Rim Rd Ste 204
Anaheim, CA 92807-4315, USA

Ferragni, Chiara (Designer)
TBS Crew Srl
Piazza Cavour 3
Milano 20121, ITALY

Ferrante, Orlando (Athlete, Football Player)
1223 Adair St
San Marino, CA 91108-1806, USA

Ferrara, Abel (Director)
International Creative Mgmt
8942 Wilshire Blvd # 219
Beverly Hills, CA 90211-1908, USA

Ferrara, Adam (Actor)
c/o Rory Rosegarten *Conversation Company*
1044 Northern Blvd Ste 304
Roslyn, NY 11576-1589, USA

Ferrara, Al (Athlete, Baseball Player)
4901 Whitsett Ave Apt 207
Valley Village, CA 91607-3550, USA

Ferrara, Al (Athlete, Baseball Player)
4901 Whitsett Ave Apt 207
Valley Village, CA 91607-3550, USA

Ferrara, Jerry (Actor)
c/o Stephen (Steve) Levinson *Leverage Management*
3030 Pennsylvania Ave
Santa Monica, CA 90404-4112, USA

Ferrare, Cristina (Actor, Model, Television Host)
c/o Lori Jonas *Jonas Public Relations*
1327 Ocean Ave Ste F
Santa Monica, CA 90401-1024, USA

Ferrarese, Don (Athlete, Baseball Player)
15290 Myalon Rd
Apple Valley, CA 92307-4938, USA

Ferrari, Al (Athlete, Basketball Player)
162 Ameren Way Apt 827
Ballwin, MO 63021-3316, USA

Ferrari, Anthony (Athlete, Baseball Player)
17 Bretano Way
Greenbrae, CA 94904-1180, USA

Ferrari, Tina (Dancer, Wrestler)
2901 Las Vegas Blvd S
Las Vegas, NV 89109-1933, USA

Ferrario, Bill (Athlete, Football Player)
116 Hensy Ct
Scranton, PA 18504, USA

Ferraris, Jan (Athlete, Golfer)
7108 N 13th Pl
Phoenix, AZ 85020-5408, USA

Ferraro, Chris (Athlete, Hockey Player)
PO Box 155
Sound Beach, NY 11789-0155, USA

Ferraro, Christina (Actor)
c/o Steve Rodriguez *McGowan Management*
170 S Beverly Dr Ste 304
Beverly Hills, CA 90212-3000, USA

Ferraro, Mike (Athlete, Baseball Player, Coach)
5201 Rim View Ln
Las Vegas, NV 89130-3658, USA

Ferraro, Peter (Athlete, Hockey Player)
PO Box 155
Sound Beach, NY 11789-0155, USA

Ferraro, Ray (Athlete, Hockey Player)
c/o Staff Member *Rogers Sportsnet*
181 Keefer Pl Suite 221
Vancouver, BC V6B 6C1, Canada

Ferras (Musician)
c/o Staff Member *Monterey International (Chicago)*
72 W Adams St # 1000
Chicago, IL 60603-5107, USA

Ferratti, Rebecca (Actor, Model)
10061 Riverside Dr # 721
Toluca Lake, CA 91602-2560, USA

Ferrazzi, Ferruccio (Artist)
Piazza delle Muse
Via G G Porro 27
Rome 00197, ITALY

Ferrazzi, Pierpaolo (Athlete)
EuroGrafica
Via del Progresso
Marano Vicenza 36035, ITALY

Ferre, Gianfranco (Designer, Fashion Designer)
Villa Della Spiga 19/A
Milan 20121, ITALY

Ferree, Jim (Athlete, Golfer)
12 Kings Tree Rd
Hilton Head Island, SC 29928-6101, USA

Ferreira, Sky (Musician)
c/o Robin Baum *Slate PR*
901 N Highland Ave
W Hollywood, CA 90038-2412, USA

Ferreira, Tony (Athlete, Baseball Player)
611 Fair Oaks Dr
Tarpon Spgs, FL 34689-3917, USA

Ferreira, Wayne (Tennis Player)
Int'l Mgmt Group
1 Erieview Plz
1360 E 9th St #1300
Cleveland, OH 44114-1738, USA

Ferrell, Bob (Athlete, Football Player)
PO Box 343
Beaumont, CA 92223-0343, USA

Ferrell, Conchata (Actor)
1335 Seward St
Los Angeles, CA 90028-7816, USA

Ferrell, Earl (Athlete, Football Player)
107 E Forest Trl
South Boston, VA 24592-4366, USA

Ferrell, Rachel (Musician)
Vida Music Group
19800 Cornerstone Sq Apt 415
Ashburn, VA 20147-4250, USA

Ferrell, Rachelle (Musician)
Vida Music Group
19800 Cornerstone Sq Apt 415
Ashburn, VA 20147-4250, USA

Ferrell, Tyra (Actor)
c/o Staff Member *Gersh*
9465 Wilshire Blvd Ste 600
Beverly Hills, CA 90212-2605, USA

Ferrell, Will (Actor, Comedian, Producer)
c/o Jimmy Miller *Mosaic Media Group*
407 N Maple Dr # 100
Beverly Hills, CA 90210-3818, USA

Ferrell Edmonson, Barbara A (Athlete, Olympic Athlete, Track Athlete)
University of Newada
239 N Hillcrest Blvd
Inglewood, CA 90301-1310, USA

Ferrer, Alex (Judge, Reality Star)
c/o Babette Perry *Innovative Artists*
1505 10th St
Santa Monica, CA 90401-2805, USA

Ferrer, Danay (Musician)
Evolution Talent
1776 Broadway Ste 1500
New York, NY 10019-2032, USA

Ferrer, David (Athlete, Tennis Player)
Amador Martinez Rocha (Poeta) 1
Valencia 46025, Spain

Ferrer, Sergio (Athlete, Baseball Player)
37 Coughlan Ave
Staten Island, NY 10310-3149, USA

Ferrer, Tessa (Actor)
c/o Estelle Lasher *Lasher Group*
1133 Avenue of the Americas Fl 27
New York, NY 10036-6710, USA

Ferrera, America (Actor)
c/o Molly Kawachi *ID Public Relations (NY)*
40 Wall St Fl 51
New York, NY 10005-1385, USA

Ferrero, Louis P (Business Person)
PO Box 675744
Rancho Santa Fe, CA 92067-5744, USA

Ferrigno, Lou (Actor)
Lou Ferrigno Enterprises Inc
PO Box 1671
Santa Monica, CA 90406-1671, USA

Ferrigno Jr, Lou (Actor)
c/o Matt Gogal *Abrams Artists Agency*
750 N San Vicente Blvd
E Tower Fl 11
Los Angeles, CA 90069-5788, USA

Ferrin, Arnie (Athlete, Basketball Player)
91e Donner Way
Apt 301
Salt Lake City, UT 84158-4119, USA

Ferrin, Jennifer (Actor)

Ferris, Bob (Athlete, Baseball Player)
18259 Glen Oak Way
Leesburg, VA 20176-3992, USA

Ferris, John (Swimmer)
1961 Klamath River Dr
Rancho Cordova, CA 95670-2910, USA

Ferris, Michael (Mike) (Producer, Writer)
c/o Staff Member *Broder Webb Chervin Silbermann Agency, The (BWCS)*
10250 Constellation Blvd
Los Angeles, CA 90067-6200, USA

Ferris, Pamela (Actor)
16601 Marquez Ave Unit 405
Pacific Palisades, CA 90272-3263

Ferriss, Dave (Athlete, Baseball Player)
510 Robinson Dr
Cleveland, MS 38732-2214, USA

Ferriss, David M (Boo) (Athlete, Baseball Player)
510 Robinson Dr
Cleveland, MS 38732-2214, USA

Ferriss, Tim (Business Person, Internet Star, Talk Show Host, Writer)
c/o Staff Member *Random House Publicity*
1745 Broadway Frnt 3
New York, NY 10019-4343, USA

Ferro, Cindy (Athlete, Golfer)
1901 Brookside Dr
Scotch Plains, NJ 07076-2601, USA

Ferron (Musician, Songwriter)
JR Productions
4930 Paradise Dr
Belvedere Tiburon, CA 94920-1060, USA

Ferry, Bryan (Musician, Songwriter)
c/o Linda Carbone *Press Here Publicity*
138 W 25th St Ste 900
New York, NY 10001-7470, USA

Ferry, Daniel J W (Danny) (Athlete, Basketball Player)
19300 S Park Blvd
Shaker Heights, OH 44122-1859, USA

Ferry, David R (Writer)
Wellesley College
English Dept
Wellesley, MA 02181, USA

Ferry, Robert (Bob) (Athlete, Basketball Player)
2129 Beach Haven Rd
Annapolis, MD 21409-5744, USA

Fersen, Paul (Athlete, Football Player)
205 Old Post Rd
Centerville, MA 02632-2922, USA

Fest, Howard (Athlete, Football Player)
133 Forest Cir
Bandera, TX 78003-4015, USA

Festinger, Robert (Writer)
c/o Bryan Besser *Verve Talent & Literary Agency*
6310 San Vicente Blvd Ste 100
Los Angeles, CA 90048-5498, USA

Fetisov, Viachesiav (Slava) (Athlete, Hockey Player)
65 Avon Dr
Essex Fells, NJ 07021-1717, USA

Fetisov, Viacheslav (Athlete, Hockey Player)
65 Avon Dr
Essex Fells, NJ 07021-1717, USA

Fetter, Laurie (Actor, Model)
c/o Jon Orlando *Exposure Marketing Group*
348 Hauser Blvd Apt 414
Los Angeles, CA 90036-5590, USA

Fetter, Trevor (Business Person)
13737 Noel Rd Ste 100
Dallas, TX 75240-2017, USA

Fetterhoff, Robert (Religious Leader)
Fellowship of Grace Brethem
PO Box 386
Winona Lake, IN 46590-0386, USA

Fetters, Mike (Athlete, Baseball Player)
2411 E Cedar Pl
Chandler, AZ 85249-3761, USA

Fettig, Jeff M (Business Person)
Whirlpool Corp
2000 N State St
RR 63
Benton Harbor, MI 49022, USA

Fetting, Katie (Actor)
c/o Ramses Ishak *United Talent Agency (UTA)*
9336 Civic Center Dr
Beverly Hills, CA 90210-3604, USA

Fetting, Ralner (Artist)
Hasenhelde 61
Berlin 00061, GERMANY

Fettman, Martin (Astronaut)
1572 N Saguaro Cliffs Ct
Tucson, AZ 85745-8839, USA

Fettman, Martin J (Astronaut)
1572 N Saguaro Cliffs Ct
Tucson, AZ 85745-8839, USA

Feuer, Debra (Actor)
c/o Staff Member *United Talent Agency (UTA)*
9336 Civic Center Dr
Beverly Hills, CA 90210-3604, USA

Feuerstein, Mark (Actor)
1714 N Orange Grove Ave
Los Angeles, CA 90046-2132, USA

Feustel, Andrew J (Astronaut)
4003 Elm Crest Trl
Houston, TX 77059-3281, USA

Fey (Musician)
RAC Paseo Palmas 1005
#1
Chapultapec Lomas
Mexico City 11000, MEXICO

Fey, Michael (Cartoonist)
United Feature Syndicate
200 Madison Ave
New York, NY 10016-3903, USA

Fey, Tina (Actor, Comedian)
c/o Cara Tripicchio *Shelter PR*
5670 Wilshire Blvd Ste 1200
Los Angeles, CA 90036-5621, USA

Fezler, Forrest (Athlete, Golfer)
6270 Old Water Oak Rd
Tallahassee, FL 32312-3861, USA

F. H. Faleomavaega Jr., Eni (Congressman, Politician)
2422 Rayburn Hob
Washington, DC 20515-5201, USA

Fiala, John (Athlete, Football Player)
12113 268th Dr NE
Duvall, WA 98019-9610, USA

Fiala, Neil (Athlete, Baseball Player)
4709 Woody Terrace Ct
Saint Louis, MO 63129-1683, USA

Fialkowska, Janina (Musician)
Ingpen & Williams
7 St George's Ct
131 Putney Bridge Rd
London SW15 2PA, UNITED KINGDOM (UK)

Fiasco, Lupe (Musician)
1st & 15th Records
437 Brookwood Dr
Olympia Fields, IL 60461-1503, USA

Fibiger, Jesse (Athlete, Hockey Player)
3336 Ocean Blvd
Victoria, BC V9C 1W6, Canada

Ficca, Dan (Athlete, Football Player)
151 Kansas Ln
Kulpmont, PA 17834-2005, USA

Fichaud, Eric (Athlete, Hockey Player)
191 Rue Charron
Lemoyne, QC J4R 2K6, Canada

Fichtel, Anja (Athlete, Olympic Athlete)
Stauferring 104
Tauberbischofsheim D-97941, Germany

Fichter, Mike (Athlete, Baseball Player)
8821 Jackson Ct
Munster, IN 46321-2410, USA

Fichtner, Ross (Athlete, Football Player)
46833 Danbridge St
Plymouth, MI 48170-3079, USA

Fichtner, William (Actor)
c/o Christopher Hart *United Talent Agency (UTA)*
9336 Civic Center Dr
Beverly Hills, CA 90210-3604, USA

Fick, Robert (Athlete, Baseball Player)
164 Brodia Way
Walnut Creek, CA 94598-4920, USA

Fiddler, Vern (Athlete, Hockey Player)
3659 Hickory Grove Ln
Frisco, TX 75033-2875, USA

Fidler, Mike (Athlete, Hockey Player)
7723 Gleason Rd
Minneapolis, MN 55439-2563, USA

Fiedler, Jay (Athlete, Football Player)
25 Russell Rd
Garden City, NY 11530-1947, USA

Fiedler, Jens (Athlete, Cycler, Olympic Athlete)
Bruno-Granz-Str. 48
Chemnitz D-09122, Germany

Field, Arabella (Actor)
c/o Staff Member *SMS Talent*
8383 Wilshire Blvd Ste 230
Beverly Hills, CA 90211-2436, USA

Field, Ayda (Actor)
c/o Staff Member *Brillstein Entertainment Partners*
9150 Wilshire Blvd Ste 350
Beverly Hills, CA 90212-3453, USA

Field, Chelsea (Actor)
c/o Jay Schwartz *Jay D Schwartz & Associates*
6767 Forest Lawn Dr Ste 211
Los Angeles, CA 90068-1051, USA

Field, Nate (Athlete, Baseball Player)
332 W Jamison Pl Unit 58
Littleton, CO 80120-5248, USA

Field, Patricia (Business Person)
c/o Ivana Savic *Grant Savic Kopaloff & Associates*
4929 Wilshire Blvd Ste 259
Los Angeles, CA 90010-3816, USA

Field, Sally (Actor)
c/o Heidi Schaeffer *PMK/BNC Public Relations*
1840 Century Park E Ste 1400
Los Angeles, CA 90067-2115, USA

Field, Shirley Arin (Actor)
c/o Paul Pearson *London Theatrical*
18 Leamore St
London W6 0JZ, UNITED KINGDOM

Field, Todd (Actor, Director)
c/o Ari Emanuel *WME/IMG*
9601 Wilshire Blvd
Beverly Hills, CA 90210-5213, USA

Fielder, Cecil (Athlete, Baseball Player)
Charlotte County Redfish
6907 Smokey Brook Ln
Katy, TX 77494-1607, USA

Fielder, Guyle (Athlete, Hockey Player)
2253 Leisure World
Mesa, AZ 85206-5384, USA

Fielder, Prince (Athlete, Baseball Player)
c/o Scott Boras *Boras Corporation*
18 Corporate Plaza Dr
Newport Beach, CA 92660-7901, USA

Fieldgate, Norm (Athlete, Football Player)
2510 Colwood Dr
North Vancouver, BC V7R 2R1, Canada

Fielding, Helen (Writer)
c/o Beth Swofford *Creative Artists Agency (CAA)*
2000 Avenue of the Stars Ste 100
Los Angeles, CA 90067-4705, USA

Fielding, Joy (Writer)
Atria Books
1230 Avenue of the Americas
New York, NY 10020-1513, USA

Fielding, Susannah (Actor)
c/o Kim Callahan *Industry Entertainment Partners*
955 Carrillo Dr Ste 300
Los Angeles, CA 90048-5400, USA

Fielding, Yvette (Actor)
Antix Productions
128 Grove Ln
Cheadle Hulme
Cheshire SK8 7ND, UNITED KINGDOM

Fields, Brandon (Athlete, Football Player)
4509 Holt Rd
Sylvania, OH 43560-9795, USA

Fields, Bruce (Athlete, Baseball Player)
2401 Ontario St
Cleveland, OH 44115-4003, USA

Fields, Debbi (Business Person)
Mrs. Fields
1717 S 4800 W
Salt Lake City, UT 84104-5324, USA

Fields, Debbi (Business Person)
Mrs. Fields Training R&D Ctr
1290 W 2320 S Ste A
Salt Lake City, UT 84119-1483, USA

Fields, Edgar (Athlete, Football Player)
435 Musket Entry
Roswell, GA 30076-3411, USA

Fields, Holly (Actor)
Don Buchwald
5900 Wilshire Blvd Ste 3100
Los Angeles, CA 90036-5030, USA

Fields, Jitter (Athlete, Football Player)
5776 Kensington Ave
Detroit, MI 48224-2071, USA

Fields, Joseph C (Joe) Jr (Athlete, Football Player)
1 University Pl
Chester, PA 19013-5700, USA

Fields, Josh (Athlete, Baseball Player)
4819 61st Avenue Dr W
Bradenton, FL 34210-4033, USA

Fields, Kenny (Athlete, Basketball Player)
lese E Ramon Rd Unit 81
Palm Springs, CA 92264-7775, USA

Fields, Kim (Actor)
c/o Art Rutter *Critical Mass Management*
1158 26th St Ste 414
Santa Monica, CA 90403-4698, USA

Fields, Landry (Athlete, Basketball Player)
c/o Chris Emens *Octagon (AZ)*
16055 N Dial Blvd Ste 8
Scottsdale, AZ 85260-1642, USA

Fields, Mark (Athlete, Football Player)
887 W Palo Brea Dr
Litchfield Park, AZ 85340-6009, USA

Fields, Scott (Athlete, Football Player)
7513 Santa Lucia St
Fontana, CA 92336-3603, USA

Fields, Stephen (Athlete, Baseball Player)
8306 Wickham Rd
Springfield, VA 22152-1708, USA

Fields, Stephen (Baseball Player)
8306 Wickham Rd
Springfield, VA 22152-1708, USA

Fien, Casey (Athlete, Baseball Player)
7200 Santa Clara St
Buena Park, CA 90620-3116, USA

Fiennes, Joseph (Actor)
c/o Sandra Chang *Anonymous Content*
3532 Hayden Ave
Culver City, CA 90232-2413, USA

Fiennes, Ralph (Actor)
c/o Simon Beresford *Dalzell & Beresford Ltd*
55 Charterhouse St
The Paddock Suite, The Courtyard
London EC1M 6HA, UNITED KINGDOM (UK)

Fieri, Guy (Chef, Television Host)
c/o Rebecca Brooks *Brooks Group*
10 W 37th St Fl 5
New York, NY 10018-7396, USA

Fiers, Mike (Athlete, Baseball Player)
c/o Robert Garber *RMG Baseball*
445 W Erie St Ste 205
Chicago, IL 60654-5733, USA

Fierstein, Harvey (Actor, Musician, Writer)
c/o Ron Fierstein *RF Entertainment Inc.*
29 Haines Rd Ste 200
Bedford Hills, NY 10507-1237, USA

Fife, Dan (Danny) (Athlete, Baseball Player)
5854 Misty Hill Dr
Clarkston, MI 48346-3033, USA

Fifth Harmony (Music Group)
c/o Larry Rudolph *Maverick*
9350 Civic Center Dr
Beverly Hills, CA 90210-3629, USA

Figaro, Cedric (Athlete, Football Player)
205 Staten St
Lafayette, LA 70501-1745, USA

Figga, Mike (Athlete, Baseball Player)
16434 Turnbury Oak Dr
Odessa, FL 33556-2896, USA

Figg-Currier, Cindy (Athlete, Golfer)
109 Blue Jay Dr
Lakeway, TX 78734-5101, USA

Figgins, Chone (Athlete, Baseball Player)
16 San Sovino
Newport Coast, CA 92657-1313, USA

Figgins, Desmond '''Chone''' (Athlete, Baseball Player)
6SO Bellevue Wav NE
Bellevue, WA 98004-5045, USA

Figgis, Michael (Mike) (Director)
c/o Robert Newman *WME|IMG*
9601 Wilshire Blvd
Beverly Hills, CA 90210-5213, USA

Figini, Michela (Skier)
Ariolo
Prato Lavenina 06799, SWITZERLAND

Figliuzzi, Frank (Politician)
ETS Risk Management
7315 Wisconsin Ave Ste 400W
Bethesda, MD 20814-3224, USA

Figlo-Gill, Josephine (Athlete, Baseball Player, Commentator)
437 N Fork Dr
Lakeland, FL 33809-1426, USA

Figner, George (Athlete, Football Player)
2329 N Recker Rd Unit 116
Mesa, AZ 85215-2766, USA

Figo, Luis (Soccer Player)
Real Madrid FC
Avda Cincha Espina 1
Madrid 28036, SPAIN

Figueras, Nacho (Athlete)
c/o Tony Godsick *Team 8 Global*
30650 Pinetree Rd Ste 1
Pepper Pike, OH 44124-5920, USA

Figueras-Dotti, Marta (Athlete, Golfer)
6174 Palomino Cir
Bradenton, FL 34201-2384, USA

Figueroa, Bien (Athlete, Baseball Player)
3272 Addison Ln
Tallahassee, FL 32317-9045, USA

Figueroa, Ed (Athlete, Baseball Player)
A-N15 Calle 41
Santa Juanita, PR 00619, USA

Figueroa, Efrain (Actor)
c/o Staff Member *Mitchell K Stubbs & Assoc*
8675 Washington Blvd Ste 203
Culver City, CA 90232-7486, USA

Figueroa, Nelson (Athlete, Baseball Player)
19 Hamilton Ave
Weehawken, NJ 07086-6905, USA

Figura, Maria Louisa (Actor)
The Figura Studio
5716 Cahuenga Blvd
North Hollywood, CA 91601-2105, USA

Figures, Deon (Athlete, Football Player)
1520 S Visalia Ave
Compton, CA 90220-3947, USA

Fikac, Jeremy (Athlete, Baseball Player)
PO Box 2187
Wimberley, TX 78676-7087, USA

Fike, Dan (Athlete, Football Player)
23479 Wingedfoot Dr
Westlake, OH 44145-4371, USA

Fila, Ivan (Writer)
c/o David Krintzman *Morris Yorn Barnes Levine Krintzman Rubenstein Kohner & Gellman*
2000 Avenue of the Stars Ste 300N
Tower N Fl 3
Los Angeles, CA 90067-4704, USA

Filan, Shane (Musician)
c/o Staff Member *RCA Label Group UK*
9 Derry St
London W8 5HY, UK

Filardi, Peter (Director, Producer, Writer)
c/o Robert Marsala *Wishlab*
195 S Beverly Dr Ste 414
Beverly Hills, CA 90212-3044, USA

Filarski-Steffes, Helen (Athlete, Baseball Player, Commentator)
19623 Damman St
Harper Woods, MI 48225-1753, USA

File, Bob (Athlete, Baseball Player)
203 Nathan Dr
Cinnaminson, NJ 08077-1582, USA

Filer, Tom (Athlete, Baseball Player)
501 W Maryland St Attn Coachingstaff
Indianapolis, IN 46225-1041, USA

Files, Jim (Athlete, Football Player)
8808 Ridgeview Cv
Sherwood, AR 72120-4264, USA

Files, Jimmy (Athlete, Football Player)
8808 Ridgeview Cv
Sherwood, AR 72120-4264, USA

Filicia, Thom (Designer, Television Host)
c/o Staff Member *WME|IMG*
9601 Wilshire Blvd
Beverly Hills, CA 90210-5213, USA

Filiol, Jalme (Tennis Player)
Advantage International
1025 Thomas Jefferson St NW # 430
Washington, DC 20007-5201, USA

Filion, Renald (Horse Racer)
3-95 Rue des Erables
Lachute, QC J8H 1A6, J8H lAG Canada

Filion, Rheo (Horse Racer)
187 S Franklin St # 251
Wilkes Barre, PA 18766-0998, USA

Filipek, Ron (Athlete, Basketball Player)
PO Box 3647
Cookeville, TN 38502-3647, USA

Filipelli, John (Horse Racer)
1949 NE 1st St
Deerfield Beach, FL 33441-4504, USA

Filippo (Fillipo/Filippo), Fabrizio (Fab) (Actor)
c/o David Lillard *Industry Entertainment Partners*
955 Carrillo Dr Ste 300
Los Angeles, CA 90048-5400, USA

Fill, Shannon (Actor)
260 S Beverly Dr Ste 200
Beverly Hills, CA 90212-3812, USA

Fillion, Nathan (Actor)
c/o Tracy Brennan *Creative Artists Agency (CAA)*
2000 Avenue of the Stars Ste 100
Los Angeles, CA 90067-4705, USA

Fillip, Chet (Race Car Driver)
PO Box 220
Ozona, TX 76943-0220, USA

Fillmore, Greg (Athlete, Basketball Player)
12449 Blueberry Woods Cir E Apt E
Jacksonville, FL 32258-4174

Filner, Bob (Congressman, Politician)
2428 Rayburn Hob
Washington, DC 20515-0551, USA

Filppula, Valttieri (Athlete, Hockey Player)
20883 Richmond Dr
Northville, MI 48167-9501, USA

Filson, Pete (Athlete, Baseball Player)
1725 Packer Ave
Philadelphia, PA 19145-4119, USA

Filter (Music Group)
c/o Staff Member *Warner Bros Records (NY)*
75 Rockefeller Plz
New York, NY 10019-6908, USA

Fimmel, Travis (Actor, Model)
c/o Natasha Dubin-Collatos *Independent Public Relations*
9601 Wilshire Blvd Ste 750
Beverly Hills, CA 90210-5228, USA

Fimple, Jack (Athlete, Baseball Player)
684 Road N
Redwood Valley, CA 95470-9776, USA

Fina, John (Athlete, Football Player)
5180 E Fort Lowell Rd
Tucson, AZ 85712-1309, USA

Finch, James (Race Car Driver)
Phoenix Racing
1718 Tennessee Ave
Lynn Haven, FL 32444, USA

Finch, Jennie (Athlete, Olympic Athlete, Softball Player)
Finch Windmill
PO Box 97
Finch Windmill
La Mirada, CA 90637-0097, USA

Finch, Joel (Athlete, Baseball Player)
68571 Oak Springs Rd
Edwardsburg, MI 49112-9502, USA

Finch, Jon (Actor)
London Mgmt
2-4 Noel St
London W1V 3RB, UNITED KINGDOM (UK)

Finch, Karl (Athlete, Football Player)
4408 Copper Crest Ln
Modesto, CA 95355-8970, USA

Finch, Tyrone (Comedian)
c/o Staff Member *United Talent Agency (UTA)*
9336 Civic Center Dr
Beverly Hills, CA 90210-3604, USA

Finchem, Timothy W (Athlete, Golfer)
c/o Staff Member *Pro Golfers Association (PGA)*
112 TPC Blvd
Ponte Vedra Beach, FL 32082, USA

Fincher, Alfred (Athlete, Football Player)
1267 Avenue Du Chateau
Covington, LA 70433-6424, USA

Fincher, David (Director)
7 Harrison St Apt 2N
New York, NY 10013-2832, USA

Fincke, Edward M (Astronaut)
15107 Bronze Bay Ct
Houston, TX 77059-6453, USA

Fincke, E Michael (Mike) (Astronaut)
15107 Bronze Bay Ct
Houston, TX 77059-6453, USA

Finckel, David (Musician)
I M G Artists
3 Burlington Lane
London W4 2TH, UNITED KINGDOM (UK)

Findlay, Katie (Actor)
c/o Chris Henze *Thruline Entertainment*
9250 Wilshire Blvd Fl Ground
Beverly Hills, CA 90212-3352, USA

Fine, David (Director, Writer)
c/o Melissa Myers *WME|IMG*
9601 Wilshire Blvd
Beverly Hills, CA 90210-5213, USA

Fine, Travis (Actor)
Vaughn D Hart
200 N Robertson Blvd # 219
Beverly Hills, CA 90211-1769, USA

Finfera, Joe (Actor)
c/o Staff Member *Select Artists Ltd (CA-Westside Office)*
1138 12th St Apt 1
Santa Monica, CA 90403-5459, USA

Fingaz, Sticky (Artist, Musician)
c/o David Guc *Vanguard Management Group*
8060 Melrose Ave Fl 4
Los Angeles, CA 90046-7038, USA

Finger Eleven (Music Group)
c/o Robert Lanni *Coalition Entertainment Management*
10271 Yonge St Suite 302
Richmond Hill, ON L4C 3B5, Canada

Fingers, Rollie (Athlete, Baseball Player)
PO Box 230729
Las Vegas, NV 89105-0729, USA

Fink, Ashley (Actor)
c/o Marni Rosenzweig *The Rosenzweig Group*
8840 Wilshire Blvd # 111
Beverly Hills, CA 90211-2606, USA

Fink, Jason (Athlete, Football Player)
2619 Regatta Ln
Davis, CA 95618-6409, USA

Fink, Lucie (Internet Star)
c/o Henry Huang *Heroes and Villains Entertainment*
1041 N Formosa Ave
Formosa Bldg, Suite 202
West Hollywood, CA 90046-6703, USA

Fink, Natascha (Athlete, Golfer)
Golfclub Murhof Adriach 54
Frohnleiten A-8130, Austria

Finkel, Henry (Hank) (Athlete, Basketball Player)
2 Pocahontas Way
Lynnfield, MA 01940-1042, USA

Finkelstein, Norman G (Writer)
2245 Ocean Pkwy Apt 3A
Brooklyn, NY 11223-4859, USA

Finkes, Matt (Athlete, Football Player)
5442 Cedar Spgs
Columbus, OH 43228-7200, USA

Finley, Brian (Athlete, Hockey Player)
84 Greenview Lane
Sault Ste. Marie, ON P6A 6K9, Canada

Finley, Charles E (Chuck) (Athlete, Baseball Player)
500 McCormick Rd
West Monroe, LA 71291-1921, USA

Finley, Greg (Actor)
c/o Jamie Harhay Skinner *Baker Winokur Ryder Public Relations*
9100 Wilshire Blvd
W Tower #500
Beverly Hills, CA 90212-3415, USA

Finley, Jeff (Race Car Driver)
Team Rensi Motorsports
4011 Hands Mill Hwy
York, SC 29745-9647, USA

Finley, Jermichael (Athlete, Football Player)

Finley, John L (Astronaut)
700 Colonial Rd Ste 120
Memphis, TN 38117-5191, USA

Finley, Karen (Artist)
Creative Time
59 E 4th St Ste 6E
New York, NY 10003-8991, USA

Finley, Margot (Actor)
c/o Staff Member *Pacific Artists Management*
112 3rd Ave E Suite 210
Vancouver, BC V5T 1C8, CANADA

Finley, Michael (Athlete, Basketball Player)
11 Highgate Dr
San Antonio, TX 78257-1714, USA

Finley, Steven (Steve) (Athlete, Baseball Player)
c/o Lew Weitzman *Preferred Artists*
16633 Ventura Blvd Ste 1421
Encino, CA 91436-1885, USA

Finn, Craig (Musician)
c/o Jay Belin *WME|IMG*
9601 Wilshire Blvd
Beverly Hills, CA 90210-5213, USA

Finn, Jim (Athlete, Football Player)
12-14 Western Dr
Fair Lawn, NJ 07410-2213, USA

Finn, John (Actor)
c/o Gabrielle Krengel *Domain Talent*
1880 Century Park E Ste 1100
Los Angeles, CA 90067-1608, USA

Finn, Neil (Musician, Songwriter, Writer)
c/o Staff Member *WME|IMG*
9601 Wilshire Blvd
Beverly Hills, CA 90210-5213, USA

Finn, Patrick (Actor)
c/o Staff Member *Brillstein Entertainment Partners*
9150 Wilshire Blvd Ste 350
Beverly Hills, CA 90212-3453, USA

Finn, Steve (Athlete, Hockey Player)
5 de Cheverny St
Blainville, QC J7B 1M7, Canada

Finn, Steven (Athlete, Hockey Player)
8 Rue D'Angers
Blainville, QC J7B 1Y8, Canada

Finn, Tim (Musician)
Grant Thomas Mgmt
98 Surrey St
Darlinghurst, NSW 02010, AUSTRALIA

Finn, Veronica (Musician)
Evolution Talent
1776 Broadway Ste 1500
New York, NY 10019-2032, USA

Finnegan, Christian (Comedian)
c/o Kara Welker *Generate Management*
8750 Wilshire Blvd Ste 200
Beverly Hills, CA 90211-2707, USA

Finnegan, Cortland (Athlete, Football Player)
9254 Wardley Park Ln
Brentwood, TN 37027-4465, USA

Finneran, Brian (Athlete, Football Player)
1905 Sugarloaf Club Dr
Duluth, GA 30097-7448, USA

Finneran, Garry (Athlete, Football Player)
17021 Paulette Pl
Granada Hills, CA 91344-1651, USA

Finneran, Gary (Athlete, Football Player)
17021 Paulette Pl
Granada Hills, CA 91344-1651, USA

Finneran, Katie (Actor)
c/o Jonathan Howard *Innovative Artists*
1505 10th St
Santa Monica, CA 90401-2805, USA

Finneran, Rittenhouse Sharon (Swimmer)
212 Harbor Dr
Santa Cruz, CA 95062-3442, USA

Finnerty, Dan (Actor, Musician)

Finnessey, Shandi (Beauty Pageant Winner)
c/o Staff Member *Miss Universe Organization, The*
1370 Avenue of the Americas Fl 16
New York, NY 10019-4602, USA

Finney, Allison (Athlete, Golfer)
78160 Desert Mountain Cir
Bermuda Dunes, CA 92203-8151, USA

Finney, Tom (Soccer Player)
Preston North End FC
Deepdale
Sir Finney Way
Preston PR1 6RU, UNITED KINGDOM (UK)

Finnie, Linda A (Musician)
16 Golf Course Girvan
Ayrshire KA26 9HW, UNITED KINGDOM (UK)

Finnie, Roger (Athlete, Football Player)
937 NW 58th St
Miami, FL 33127-1321, USA

Finnigan, Jennifer (Actor)
c/o John Carrabino *John Carrabino Management*
5900 Wilshire Blvd Ste 740
Los Angeles, CA 90036-5032, USA

Finnvold, Gar (Athlete, Baseball Player)
1204 NE 4th Ave
Boca Raton, FL 33432-2808, USA

Finsterwald, Dow (Athlete, Golfer)
6330 Masters Blvd
Orlando, FL 32819-4869, USA

Finzer, Dave (Athlete, Football Player)
1435 Kaywood Ln
Glenview, IL 60025-2341, USA

Fiona, Melanie (Musician)
c/o Dennis Ashley *ICM Partners*
10250 Constellation Blvd Fl 7
Los Angeles, CA 90067-6207, USA

Fiore, Dave (Athlete, Football Player)
868 Southampton Dr
Palo Alto, CA 94303-3439, USA

Fiore, Kathryn (Actor)
c/o Michael P Levine *Levine Management*
8549 Wilshire Blvd # 212
Beverly Hills, CA 90211-3104, USA

Fiore, Mike (Athlete, Baseball Player)
17 Silver St
Malverne, NY 11565-1116, USA

Fiore, Tony (Athlete, Baseball Player)
19021 Fishermans Bend Dr
Lutz, FL 33558-9754, USA

Fiorentini, Jeff (Athlete, Baseball Player)
4200 Chardonnay Dr
Rockledge, FL 32955-5133, USA

Fiorentino, Linda (Actor)
c/o Staff Member *Paradigm*
8942 Wilshire Blvd
Beverly Hills, CA 90211-1908, USA

Fiorentino, Peter (Athlete, Hockey Player)
5570 Belmont Ave
Niagara Falls, ON L2H 1J7, Canada

Fiori, Ed (Athlete, Golfer)
4411 Winding River Dr
Richmond, TX 77406-9218, USA

Fiori, Fernando (Actor)
c/o Staff Member *Latin World Entertainment (FL)*
3470 NW 82nd Ave Ste 670
Doral, FL 33122-1026, USA

Fiorina, Carly (Politician)
11201 Gunston Rd
Lorton, VA 22079-4006, USA

Fiorito, Jaelle (Actor, Television Host)
c/o Staff Member *Rebel Entertainment Partners*
5700 Wilshire Blvd Ste 470
Los Angeles, CA 90036-4379, USA

Fireovid, Steve (Athlete, Baseball Player)
1408 Woodstream Dr
Bryan, OH 43506-9049, USA

Fires, Earlie S (Horse Racer)
16337 Rivervale Lane
Rivervale, AR 60640-7034, USA

Firestone, Andrew (Actor, Reality Star)
c/o Staff Member *Paradigm*
8942 Wilshire Blvd
Beverly Hills, CA 90211-1908, USA

Firestone, Dennis (Race Car Driver)
5380 Via Morena
Yorba Linda, CA 92886-5008, USA

Firestone, Roy (Sportscaster)
Seizen/Wallach Productions
257 S Rodeo Dr
Beverly Hills, CA 90212-3803, USA

Firova, Dan (Athlete, Baseball Player)
208 Saint John St
Refugio, TX 78377-3436, USA

Firth, Colin (Actor)
c/o Jessica Kolstad *Relevant*
400 S Beverly Dr Ste 220
Beverly Hills, CA 90212-4404, USA

Firth, Peter (Actor)
Markham & Froggatt
Julian House
4 Windmill St
London W1P 1HF, UNITED KINGDOM (UK)

Fiscella, Nicole (Model)
c/o Staff Member *New York Model Management*
71 W 23rd St Ste 301
New York, NY 10010-3519, USA

Fischbach, Mark (Markiplier) (Internet Star)
c/o Lewis Kay *Kovert Creative*
506 Santa Monica Blvd Ste 400
Santa Monica, CA 90401-2412, USA

Fischbacher, Andrea (Athlete, Skier)
Hauptstr. 255
Eben/PG A-5531, Austria

Fischer, Bill (Athlete, Baseball Player)
139 Upland Dr
Council Bluffs, IA 51503-4823, USA

Fischer, Bill (Athlete, Football Player)
23191 Shady Oak Ln
Estero, FL 33928-4383, USA

Fischer, Brad (Athlete, Baseball Player)
6110 Forest Ridge Ct
Mc Farland, WI 53558-9020, USA

Fischer, Erich (Athlete, Olympic Athlete, Water Polo Player)
542 Cress St
Laguna Beach, CA 92651-3128, USA

Fischer, Hank (Athlete, Baseball Player)
7212 Reef Rd
Navarre, FL 32566-8787, USA

Fischer, Heinz (President)
Prasidentschaftskanzlei
Hofburg
Alderstiege
Vienna 01010, AUSTRIA

Fischer, Jeff (Athlete, Baseball Player)
215 Worth Ct N
West Palm Beach, FL 33405-2751, USA

Fischer, Jenna (Actor)
c/o Naomi Odenkirk *Odenkirk Provissiero Entertainment*
1936 N Bronson Ave
Raleigh Studios
Los Angeles, CA 90068-5602, USA

Fischer, Jiri (Athlete, Hockey Player)
20101 Westview Dr
Northville, MI 48167-9206, USA

Fischer, Lisa (Musician)
Alive Enterprices
3264 S Kihei Rd
Kihei, HI 96753-9605, USA

Fischer, Pat (Athlete, Football Player)
45800 Jona Dr APT 314
Sterling, VA 20165-5690, USA

Fischer, Schmidt Birgit (Athlete)
Kuckuckswald 11
Kleinmachnow 14532, GERMANY

Fischer, Sven (Athlete)
Schillerhoehe 7
Schmalkalden 98574, GERMANY

Fischer, Todd (Athlete, Baseball Player)
12734 Newtown Rd
Unionville, TN 37180-5004, USA

Fischer, Todd (Athlete, Golfer)
11800 Kaymak Ln
Seminole, FL 33772-2607, USA

Fischer, Van (Director)
Gersh Agency
232 N Canon Dr
Beverly Hills, CA 90210-5302, USA

Fischerspooner (Music Group)
c/o Staff Member *Paradigm (Monterey)*
404 W Franklin St
Monterey, CA 93940-2303, USA

Fischetti, Brad (Musician)
Evolution Talent Agency
1776 roadway
15th Floor
New York, NY 10019

Fischler, Patrick (Actor)
c/o Stewart Strunk *Main Title Entertainment*
8383 Wilshire Blvd Ste 408
Beverly Hills, CA 90211-2435, USA

Fischlin, Mike (Athlete, Baseball Player)
1010 Curtright Pl
Greensboro, GA 30642-7432, USA

Fiset, Stephane (Athlete, Hockey Player)
c/o Staff Member *Newport Sports Management*
1042 Rue Charcot Suite 304
Boucherville, QC J4B 8R4, Canada

Fish, Ginger (Musician)
c/o Staff Member *Interscope Records (LA) - Main*
2220 Colorado Ave
Santa Monica, CA 90404-3506, USA

Fish, Mardy (Athlete, Tennis Player)
c/o John Tobias *TLA Worldwide (FL)*
1245 S Alhambra Cir
Coral Gables, FL 33146-3104, USA

Fish, Matt (Athlete, Basketball Player)
4138 E Waterman Ct
Gilbert, AZ 85297-3574, USA

Fishbacher, Siegfried (Magician)
Mirage Hotel & Casino
3400 Las Vegas Blvd S
Las Vegas, NV 89109-8907, USA

Fishback, Dominique (Actor)
c/o Shani Rosenzweig *United Talent Agency (UTA)*
9336 Civic Center Dr
Beverly Hills, CA 90210-3604, USA

Fishback, Joe (Athlete, Football Player)
148 Fairoaks Cir
Stockbridge, GA 30281-1189, USA

Fishburne, Laurence (Actor)
c/o Helen Sugland *Landmark Artists*
4116 W Magnolia Blvd Ste 101
Burbank, CA 91505-2700, USA

Fishel, Danielle (Actor)
c/o Christopher Nathaniel *Industry Entertainment Partners*
955 Carrillo Dr Ste 300
Los Angeles, CA 90048-5400, USA

Fishel, John (Athlete, Baseball Player)
329 Marjoram Dr
Columbus, OH 43230-7027, USA

Fisher, Anna L (Astronaut)
1912 Elmen St
Houston, TX 77019-6144, USA

Fisher, Brian (Athlete, Baseball Player)
3660 S Uravan St
Aurora, CO 80013-3458, USA

Fisher, Bryan (Actor)
c/o Jamie Freed *Paris Hilton Entertainment*
2934 1/2 N Beverly Glen Cir # 383
Los Angeles, CA 90077-1724, USA

Fisher, Charles (Athlete, Football Player)
PO Box 133
Aliquippa, PA 15001-0133, USA

Fisher, Derek (Athlete, Basketball Player)
c/o Staff Member *New York Knicks*
2 Pennsylvania Plz
New York, NY 10121, USA

Fisher, Doug (Athlete, Football Player)
4040 Hancock St Apt 204
San Diego, CA 92110-5154, USA

Fisher, Ed (Athlete, Football Player)
4734 E Redfield Rd
Phoenix, AZ 85032-5520, USA

Fisher, Eddie G (Athlete, Baseball Player)
408 Cardinal Cir S
Altus, OK 73521-1714, USA

Fisher, Eric (Athlete, Football Player)
c/o Joel Segal *Lagardere Unlimited (NY)*
456 Washington St Apt 9L
New York, NY 10013-1555, USA

Fisher, Evan (Musician)
GEMS
PO Box 1031
Montrose, CA 91021-1031, USA

Fisher, Frances (Actor)
c/o Elizabeth Much *East 2 West Collective*
11022 Santa Monica Blvd Ste 350
Los Angeles, CA 90025-7532, USA

Fisher, Fritz (Athlete, Baseball Player)
3703 Barcelona Dr
Toledo, OH 43615-1203, USA

Fisher, Isla (Actor)
c/o Julie Darmody *Rise Management*
6338 Wilshire Blvd
Los Angeles, CA 90048-5002, USA

Fisher, Jack (Athlete, Baseball Player)
4407 Nicholas St
Easton, PA 18045-4930, USA

Fisher, Jeff (Athlete, Football Coach, Football Player)
385 Lake Valley Dr
Franklin, TN 37069-4652, USA

Fisher, Jeff (Coach, Football Coach)
460 Great Circle Rd
Nashville, TN 37228-1404, USA

Fisher, Joel (Artist)
PO Box 65
Palisades, NY 10964-0065, USA

Fisher, Joely (Actor)
c/o Brit Reece *PMK/BNC Public Relations*
1840 Century Park E Ste 1400
Los Angeles, CA 90067-2115, USA

Fisher, Jordan (Actor)
c/o Laura Ackerman *Advantage PR*
3900 W Alameda Ave Ste 1200
Burbank, CA 91505-4317, USA

Fisher, Kimberly (Model)
c/o Staff Member *ISA Talent Management*
PO Box 5467
North Hollywood, CA 91616-5467, USA

Fisher, Maurice (Maury) (Athlete, Baseball Player)
15920 Lucerne Rd
Fredericktown, OH 43019-9531, USA

Fisher, Miles (Actor)
c/o Steven Fisher *Underground Management*
1180 S Beverly Dr Ste 509
Los Angeles, CA 90035-1157, USA

Fisher, Noel (Actor)
c/o Paul Brown *Industry Entertainment Partners*
955 Carrillo Dr Ste 300
Los Angeles, CA 90048-5400, USA

Fisher, Ray (Actor)
c/o Holly Jeter *WME|IMG*
9601 Wilshire Blvd
Beverly Hills, CA 90210-5213, USA

Fisher, Red (Writer)
Montreal Gazette
250 Saint Antoine W
Montreal, QC H2Y 3R7, CANADA

Fisher, Robert (Business Person)
Gap Inc
2 Folsom St
San Francisco, CA 94105-1205, USA

Fisher, Roger (Musician)
Borman Entertainment
1250 6th St Ste 401
Santa Monica, CA 90401-1638, USA

Fisher, Sarah (Actor)
Armstrong Acting Studios
9 Davies Ave
Toronto, ON M4M 2A6, CANADA

Fisher, Sarah (Race Car Driver)
c/o Staff Member *NASCAR*
1801 W Speedway Blvd
Daytona Beach, FL 32114-1243, USA

Fisher, Steve (Coach)
San Diego State University
Athletic Dept
San Diego, CA 92182-0001, USA

Fisher, Tom (Athlete, Baseball Player)
7127 E County Road 200 N
Avon, IN 46123-8550, USA

Fisher, Tony (Athlete, Football Player)

Fisher, William F (Astronaut)
1119 Woodland Dr
El Lago, TX 77586-6044, USA

Fisher-Stevens, Lorraine (Baseball Player)
120 Birdsell St
Jackson, MI 49203-4670, USA

Fishman, Jerald G (Business Person)
Analog Devices Inc
1 Technology Way
Norwood, MA 02062-2666, USA

Fishman, Jon (Musician)
Dionysian Productions
431 Pine St
Burlington, VT 05401-4726, USA

Fishman, Michael (Actor)
c/o Staff Member *Carsey-Werner Company*
16027 Ventura Blvd Ste 600
Encino, CA 91436-2798, USA

Fisichella, Giancarlo (Race Car Driver)
Benetton Formula Ltd
Whiteways Tech Centre
Enstone
Chipping Norton, Oxfordshire OX8 6XZ, UNITED KINGDOM

Fisk, Carlton (Athlete, Baseball Player)
18705 63rd Ave E
Bradenton, FL 34211-7025, USA

Fisk, Schuyler (Actor)
c/o Weiman Seid *Fat Dot*
87 Bedford St Apt 1
New York, NY 10014-3769, USA

Fisser, Christoph (Producer)
c/o Staff Member *Babelsberg Film*
August-Bebelstr. 26-53
Potsdam 14482, Germany

Fister, Doug (Athlete, Baseball Player)
3279 Leaf Dr
Merced, CA 95340-8304, USA

Fit, Chrissie (Actor)
c/o Mona Loring *Status PR*
PO Box 6191
Westlake Village, CA 91359-6191, USA

Fitch, Bill (Basketball Coach, Coach)
3714 Walden Estates Dr
Montgomery, TX 77356-8043, USA

Fitch, Leigh (Horse Racer)
RR 114
Sebag, ME 04029, USA

Fitchner, Bob (Athlete, Hockey Player)
138 Ross Pl
Carman, MB R0G 0J0, Canada

Fites, Donald V (Business Person)
Caterpillar Inc
100 NE Adams St
Peoria, IL 61629-0002, USA

Fittipaldi, Christian (Race Car Driver)
282 Alphaville Barueri
Sao Paulo 64500, BRAZIL

Fittipaldi, Emerson (Race Car Driver)
735 Crandon Blvd Apt 503
Miami, FL 33149-2526, USA

Fittipaldi, Lisa (Artist)
Mind's Eye Foundation
215 Beauregard San Antonio,
TX 78204-1304, USA

Fitzgerald, Brian (Athlete, Baseball Player)
94 Wood Landing Rd
Fredericksbrg, VA 22405-3531, USA

Fitzgerald, Caitlin (Actor)
c/o Adam Schweitzer *ICM Partners (NY)*
730 5th Ave
New York, NY 10019-4105, USA

Fitzgerald, Ed (Athlete, Baseball Player)
431 Christopher St
Folsom, CA 95630-1706, USA

Fitzgerald, Fern (Actor)
41685 Anza Rd
Temecula, CA 92592-9517, USA

FitzGerald, Frances (Writer)
Simon & Schuster
1230 Avenue of the Americas Fl CONC1
New York, NY 10020-1586, USA

Fitzgerald, Glenn (Actor)
c/o Steve Tisherman *Tisherman Gilbert Motley Drozdoski Talent Agency (TGMD)*
6767 Forest Lawn Dr # 101
Los Angeles, CA 90068-1027, USA

FitzGerald, Helen (Actor)
Paul Lohner
9300 Wilshire Blvd Ste 555
Beverly Hills, CA 90212-3211, USA

Fitzgerald, Jack (Actor)
William Kerwin Agency
1605 N Cahuenga Blvd # 202
Los Angeles, CA 90028-6201, USA

Fitzgerald, John (Athlete, Baseball Player)
1913 Greve Ave Apt 1
Spring Lake, NJ 07762-2354, USA

Fitzgerald, John (Athlete, Football Player)
408 Arborcrest Dr
Richardson, TX 75080-2606, USA

Fitzgerald, Larry (Athlete, Football Player)
6920 E Hummingbird Ln
Paradise Valley, AZ 85253-3643, USA

Fitzgerald, Marcus (Athlete, Football Player)
c/o Roosevelt Barnes *Independent Sports & Entertainment (ISE-IN)*
6435 W Jefferson Blvd # 197
Fort Wayne, IN 46804-6203, USA

Fitzgerald, Melissa (Actor)

Fitzgerald, Mickey (Athlete, Football Player)
4579 Somerset Rd SW
Smyrna, GA 30082-4538, USA

Fitzgerald, Mike (Athlete, Baseball Player)
33 Verna Dr
Springfield, IL 62702-4608, USA

Fitzgerald, Mike (Athlete, Baseball Player)
502 Flint Ave
Long Beach, CA 90814-2039, USA

Fitzgerald, Mosley Benita (Athlete)
Women in Cable/Telecommunications
14555 Avion Pkwy Ste 250
Chantilly, VA 20151-1117, USA

FitzGerald, Niali W A (Business Person)
Unilever NV
Weena 455
Rotterdam, DK 03000, NETHERLANDS

Fitzgerald, Pat (Athlete, Football Player)
2271 Bracken Ln
Northfield, IL 60093-2902

Fitzgerald, Rusty (Athlete, Hockey Player)
4213 Chambersburg Ave
Duluth, MN 55811-5614, USA

Fitzgerald, Tac (Actor)
c/o Staff Member *Iris Burton Agency*
10100 Santa Monica Blvd Ste 1300
Los Angeles, CA 90067-4114, USA

Fitzgerald, Tara (Actor)
c/o Lindy King *United Agents*
12-26 Lexington St
London W1F OLE, UNITED KINGDOM

Fitzgerald, Thom (Director)
c/o Gloria Bonelli *Gloria Bonelli & Associates*
11 Victoria Ter
Goshen, NY 10924-2205, USA

Fitzgerald, Tom (Athlete, Hockey Player)
Pittsburgh Penguins 66 Mario Lemieux Pl Ste 2
Attn: Asst To General Manager
Pittsburgh, PA 15219-3504, USA

Fitzgerald, Tom (Athlete, Hockey Player)
3 Samuel Phelps Way
North Reading, MA 01864-2990, USA

Fitzgerald-Leclair, Meryle (Baseball Player)
909 E Hanson Ave
Mitchell, SD 57301-3635, USA

Fitz-Henley, Parisa (Actor)
c/o Dominique Appel *Imprint PR*
6121 W Sunset Blvd
Neuehouse
Los Angeles, CA 90028-6442, USA

Fitzhugh, Steve (Athlete, Football Player)
1030 Feltl Ct Apt 330
Hopkins, MN 55343-3904, USA

Fitzkee, Scott (Athlete, Football Player)
1611 Grafton Shop Rd
Forest Hill, MD 21050-2535, USA

Fitzmaurice, Shaun (Athlete, Baseball Player)
1911 Normandstone Dr
Midlothian, VA 23113-9669, USA

Fitzmorris, Al (Athlete, Baseball Player)
17512 W 159th Ter
Olathe, KS 66062-4017, USA

Fitzpatrick, Hugh (Producer)
c/o Staff Member *Teakwood Lane Productions*
11845 W Olympic Blvd Ste 1125
Los Angeles, CA 90064-5096, USA

Fitzpatrick, Mark (Athlete, Hockey Player)
10571 SW Kelsey Way
Port Saint Lucie, FL 34987-1989, USA

Fitzpatrick, Michael (Baseball Player)
262 Lodge Ln
Kalamazoo, MI 49009-9161, USA

Fitzpatrick, Mike (Athlete, Baseball Player)
262 Lodge Ln
Kalamazoo, MI 49009-9161, USA

Fitzpatrick, Rory (Athlete, Hockey Player)
580 Colebrook Dr
Rochester, NY 14617-2009, USA

Fitzpatrick, Ross (Athlete, Hockey Player)
PO Box 459
Hershey, PA 17033-0459, USA

Fitzpatrick, Ryan (Athlete, Football Player)
c/o Jimmy Sexton *CAA (Memphis)*
6060 Poplar Ave Ste 470
Memphis, TN 38119-0910, USA

Fitzpatrick, Sandy (Athlete, Hockey Player)
11250 Lakerim Rd
San Diego, CA 92131-2311, USA

Fitzsimmons, Greg (Comedian)
c/o Kara Welker *Generate Management*
8750 Wilshire Blvd Ste 200
Beverly Hills, CA 90211-2707, USA

Five (5ive) (Music Group)
c/o Paul Franklin *CAA (London)*
3 Shortlands, Hammersmith
Fl 5
London W6 8DA, UNITED KINGDOM

Five Finger Death Punch (Music Group, Musician)
c/o Ron Opaleski *WME/IMG*
9601 Wilshire Blvd
Beverly Hills, CA 90210-5213, USA

Five for Fighting (Music Group)
c/o Staff Member *Paradigm*
140 Broadway Ste 2600
New York, NY 10005-1011, USA

Fix, Oliver (Athlete)
Ringstr 6
Stadtbergen, GERMANY

Fizer, Marcus (Basketball Player)
Charlotte Bobcats
129 W Trade St Ste 700
Charlotte, NC 28202-5301, USA

Flacco, Joe (Athlete, Football Player)
c/o Joe Linta *JL Sports*
1204 Main St Ste 179
Branford, CT 06405-3787, USA

Flack, Enya (Actor)
c/o Marv Dauer *Marv Dauer Management*
11661 San Vicente Blvd Ste 104
Los Angeles, CA 90049-5150, USA

Flack, Roberta (Musician)
556 State Route 385 # 2
Athens, NY 12015-5611, USA

Flagg, Fannie (Actor, Comedian)
c/o Sally Willcox *Creative Artists Agency (CAA)*
2000 Avenue of the Stars Ste 100
Los Angeles, CA 90067-4705, USA

Flagg, Josh (Business Person, Reality Star)
1133 Cory Ave
West Hollywood, CA 90069-1701, USA

Flagler, Randy (Actor)
c/o Jenine Leigh-Pollard *Agency for the Performing Arts (APA)*
405 S Beverly Dr Ste 500
Beverly Hills, CA 90212-4425, USA

Flaherty, Harry (Athlete, Football Player)
10 Rossiter Pl
Oceanport, NJ 07757-1368, USA

Flaherty, John (Athlete, Baseball Player)
29 Cherrywood Ct
Westwood, NJ 07675-6487, USA

Flaherty, Wade (Athlete, Hockey Player)
c/o Art Breeze *Pro-Rep Entertainment Consulting*
113-276 Midpark Gdns SE
Calgary, AB T2X 1T3, Canada

Flair, Ric (Athlete, Wrestler)
c/o Darren Prince *Prince Marketing Group*
18 Seneca Trl
Sparta, NJ 07871-1514, USA

Flake, Jeff (Congressman, Politician)
240 Cannon Hob
Washington, DC 20515-1802, USa

Flame, Penny (Adult Film Star)
19422 Archwood St
Reseda, CA 91335-4903, USA

Flame, Waka Flocka (Musician)
103 Bayberry Hls
McDonough, GA 30253-4293, USA

Flaming Lips, The (Music Group, Musician)
c/o Robby Fraser *WME/IMG*
9601 Wilshire Blvd
Beverly Hills, CA 90210-5213, USA

Flanagan, Barry (Artist)
5E Fawe St
London E14 6PD, UNITED KINGDOM (UK)

Flanagan, Crista (Actor)
c/o Kay Liberman *Liberman/Zerman Management*
252 N Larchmont Blvd Ste 200
Los Angeles, CA 90004-3754, USA

Flanagan, Ed (Athlete, Football Player)

Flanagan, Fionnula (Actor)
c/o Dick Guttman *Guttman Associates Public Relations*
118 S Beverly Dr Ste 201
Beverly Hills, CA 90212-3016, USA

Flanagan, Flonnula (Actor)
Guttman
118 S Beverly Dr Ste 201
Beverly Hills, CA 90212-3016, USA

Flanagan, Mike (Athlete, Football Player)
4631 Waring St
Houston, TX 77027-6217, USA

Flanagan, Shalane (Athlete, Track Athlete)
410 NW 18th Ave
Portland, OR 97209-2237, USA

Flanagan, Tommy (Actor)
c/o Beth Holden-Garland *Untitled Entertainment*
350 S Beverly Dr Ste 200
Beverly Hills, CA 90212-4819, USA

Flanery, Sean Patrick (Actor)
c/o Jeff Golenberg *Silver Lining Entertainment*
421 S Beverly Dr Fl 7
Beverly Hills, CA 90212-4408, USA

Flanigan, Jim (Athlete, Football Player)
3820 Sand Bay Point Rd
Sturgeon Bay, WI 54235-8418, USA

Flanigan, Jim (Athlete, Football Player)
4511 Wyandot Trl
Green Bay, WI 54313-6789, USA

Flanigan, Joe (Actor)
c/o Michael Lazo *Untitled Entertainment*
350 S Beverly Dr Ste 200
Beverly Hills, CA 90212-4819, USA

Flanigan, Tom (Athlete, Baseball Player)
114 E 40th St Apt 1
Covington, KY 41015-1802, USA

Flannery, John (Athlete, Baseball Player)
109 Sarahs Ln
Liberty Hill, TX 78642-4035, USA

Flannery, John (Athlete, Football Player)
7514 Dawn Mist Ct
Sugar Land, TX 77479-6323, USA

Flannery, Kate (Actor)
c/o Kristopher Koller *Seven Summits Pictures & Management*
8906 W Olympic Blvd
Beverly Hills, CA 90211-3550, USA

Flannery, Susan (Actor)
Flannery-Daedy-Leona
6977 Shepard Mesa Rd
Carpinteria, CA 93013-3134, USA

Flannery, Tim (Athlete, Baseball Player)
715 Hymettus Ave
Encinitas, CA 92024-2148, USA

Flannigan, Maureen (Actor)
Gold Marshak Liedtke
3500 W Olive Ave Ste 1400
Burbank, CA 91505-5512, USA

Flash, Grandmaster (DJ, Musician)
Grandmaster Flash Enterprises
600 Johnson Ave Ste E7
Bohemia, NY 11716-2664, USA

Flaska, Carrie (Actor)
3440 29th St
Astoria, NY 11106-3572, USA

Flatley, Michael (Actor, Dancer)
c/o Staff Member *Creative Artists Agency (CAA)*
2000 Avenue of the Stars Ste 100
Los Angeles, CA 90067-4705, USA

Flatley, Patrick (Pat) (Athlete, Hockey Player)
c/o Staff Member *National Hockey League (NHL)*
50 Bay St 11th Fl
Toronto, ON M5J 2X8, Canada

Flatley, Paul R (Athlete, Football Player)
795 Woods Rd
Richmond, IN 47374-9409, USA

Flav, Flavor (Actor, Comedian, Reality Star)
c/o Ruby Martin *Media Artists Group*
8222 Melrose Ave Ste 304
Los Angeles, CA 90046-6839, USA

Flavin, Jennifer (Model)
30 Beverly Park
Beverly Hills, CA 90210-1546, USA

Flavin, John (Athlete, Baseball Player)
23060 16th St
Newhall, CA 91321-1054, USA

Flavio, Alfaro (Athlete, Baseball Player, Olympic Athlete)
3240 N Bass Island Rd
West Sacramento, CA 95691-5848, USA

Flay, Bobby (Chef, Television Host)
Bold Food
PO Box 1102
New York, NY 10159-1102, USA

Flchter, Michael (Baseball Player)
8821 Jackson Ct
Munster, IN 46321-2410, USA

Flea (Actor, Musician)
c/o Peter Mensch *Q Prime (NY)*
729 7th Ave Fl 16
New York, NY 10019-6831, USA

Flebotte, Dave (Producer)
c/o Ann Blanchard *Creative Artists Agency (CAA)*
2000 Avenue of the Stars Ste 100
Los Angeles, CA 90067-4705, USA

Fleck, Bela (Musician)
c/o Ted Kurland *Ted Kurland Associates*
173 Brighton Ave
Boston, MA 02134-2003, USA

Fleckman, Marty (Athlete, Golfer)
17802 Mound Rd Apt 29105
Cypress, TX 77433-0092, USA

Fleder, Gary (Director)
c/o Staff Member *Mojo Films*
4024 Radford Ave
Studio City, CA 91604-2101, USA

Fleener, Coby (Athlete, Football Player)
c/o Frank Bauer *Sun West Sports*
7883 N Pershing Ave
Stockton, CA 95207-1749, USA

Fleeshman, Richard (Actor)
c/o Paul Lyon-Maris *Independent Talent Group*
40 Whitfield St
London W1T 2RH, UNITED KINGDOM

Fleetwood, Ken (Designer, Fashion Designer)
14 Savile Row
London SW1, UNITED KINGDOM (UK)

Fleetwood, Mick (Musician)
c/o Carl Stubner *Sanctuary Music Management*
15301 Arizona Ave
Bldg B #400
Santa Monica, CA 91403, USA

Fleigel, Bernie (Athlete, Basketball Player)
21 Granville Rd # 3
Cambridge, MA 02138-6806, USA

Fleischer, Daniel (Religious Leader)
201 Princess Dr
Corpus Christi, TX 78410-1615, USA

Fleischman, Paul (Writer)
PO Box 646
Aromas, CA 95004-0646, USA

Fleischmann, Peter (Director, Producer)
Filmzentrum Babelsberg
August-Bebel-Str 26-53
Potsdam 14482, GERMANY

Fleisher, Brett (Actor)
c/o Alan Somers *Pure Arts Entertainment/ Rose Group*
9925 Jefferson Blvd
Culver City, CA 90232-3505, USA

Fleisher, Bruce (Athlete, Golfer)
11722 Cardena Ct
Palm Beach Gardens, FL 33418-1564, USA

Fleisher, Leon (Musician)
20 Merrymount Rd
Baltimore, MD 21210-1909, USA

Fleiss, Heidi (Business Person)
PO Box 93607
Pasadena, CA 91109-3607, USA

Fleiss, Mike (Director, Producer)
c/o Staff Member *Next Entertainment*
3601 W Olive Ave Ste 700
Burbank, CA 91505-4655, USA

Fleiss, Noah (Actor)
c/o Ellen Gilbert *Paradigm*
140 Broadway Ste 2600
New York, NY 10005-1011, USA

Fleming, Cameron (Athlete, Football Player)

Fleming, Cory (Athlete, Football Player)
2500 Whitney Pl Apt 8108
Metairie, LA 70002-6257, USA

Fleming, David (Dave) (Athlete, Baseball Player)
15 Scuppo Rd UNIT 102
Danbury, CT 06811-5304, USA

Fleming, Eric (Director)
c/o David Krintzman *Morris Yorn Barnes Levine Krintzman Rubenstein Kohner & Gellman*
2000 Avenue of the Stars Ste 300N
Tower N Fl 3
Los Angeles, CA 90067-4704, USA

Fleming, George (Athlete, Football Player)
1100 Lake Washington Blvd S
Seattle, WA 98144-3316, USA

Fleming, Gerry (Athlete, Hockey Player)
c/o Staff Member *Florida Everblades*
11000 Everblades Pkwy
Estero, FL 33928-9412, USA

Fleming, Jamell (Athlete, Football Player)
c/o Ken Landphere *Octagon Football*
600 Battery St Fl 2
San Francisco, CA 94111-1820, USA

Fleming, John (Congressman, Politician)
416 Cannon Hob
Washington, DC 20515-3220, USA

Fleming, Marv (Athlete, Football Player)
909 Howard St
Marina Del Rey, CA 90292-5518, USA

Fleming, Peggy (Athlete, Figure Skater, Olympic Athlete)
c/o Staff Member *IMG World*
304 Park Ave S Fl 11
New York, NY 10010-4305, USA

Fleming, Renee (Musician)
c/o Staff Member *IMG Artists Worldwide (UK)*
The Light Box
111 Power Road
London W4 5PY, United Kingdom

Fleming, Rhonda (Actor)
10281 Century Woods Dr
Los Angeles, CA 90067-6312, USA

Fleming, Troy (Athlete, Football Player)
115 Reveille Ct
Franklin, TN 37064-2332, USA

Fleming, Troy (Athlete, Football Player)
PO Box 789
Knoxville, TN 37901-0789, USA

Fleming, Vern (Athlete, Basketball Player, Olympic Athlete)
10713 Brixton Ln
Fishers, IN 46037-8707, USA

Fleming, Willie (Athlete, Football Player)
10295 Maggira Pl
Las Vegas, NV 89135-3249, USA

Flemming, John (Artist)
1409 Cambronne St
New Orleans, LA 70118-1301, USA

Flemming, William N (Bill) (Sportscaster)
ABC-TV Sports Dept
77 W 66th St
New York, NY 10023-6201, USA

Flemyng, Gordon (Director)
1 Albert Road
Wilmslow
Cheshire SK9 5HT, UNITED KINGDOM (UK)

Flemyng, Jason (Actor)
Conway Van Gelder Robinson
18-21 Jermyn St
London SW1Y 6NB, UNITED KINGDOM (UK)

Flemyng, Robert (Actor)
4 Netherbourne Road
London SW4, UNITED KINGDOM (UK)

Flener, Huck (Athlete, Baseball Player)
2186 North Ave
Chico, CA 95926-1430, USA

Flerstein, Harvey F (Actor, Musician, Writer)
1479 Carla Ridge Dr
Beverly Hills, CA 90210, USA

Flesch, John (Athlete, Hockey Player)
74101 8th Ave
South Haven, MI 49090-9750, USA

Flesch, Steve (Athlete, Golfer)
10710 Meadow Stable Ln
Union, KY 41091-7986, USA

Flessel, Craig (Cartoonist)
40 Camino Alto Apt 2306
Mill Valley, CA 94941-2964, USA

Fletcher, Andrew (Baseball Player)
3282 Kinderhill Ln
Germantown, TN 38138-8210, USA

Fletcher, Andy (Athlete, Baseball Player)
7304 Lauren Ln
Olive Branch, MS 38654-1333, USA

Fletcher, Andy (Musician)
Reach Media
295 Greenwich St # 109
New York, NY 10007-1049, USA

Fletcher, Billy (Athlete, Football Player)
3216 Winners Cir
Germantown, TN 38138-8220, USA

Fletcher, Bradley (Athlete, Football Player)

Fletcher, Brendan (Actor)
Seven Summits Mgmt
8447 Wilshire Blvd Ste 200
Beverly Hills, CA 90211-3207, USA

Fletcher, Chris (Athlete, Football Player)
4818 La Cruz Dr
La Mesa, CA 91941-4489, USA

Fletcher, Cliff (Athlete, Hockey Player)
3030 Grand Bay Blvd Unit 314
Longboat Key, FL 34228-4407, USA

Fletcher, Dane (Athlete, Football Player)

Fletcher, Darrin (Athlete, Baseball Player)
9146 E 2100 North Rd
Oakwood, IL 61858-6285, USA

Fletcher, Derrick (Athlete, Football Player)
79 Terra Bella Dr
Manvel, TX 77578-3339, USA

Fletcher, Dexter (Actor)
c/o Sally Long-Innes *Independent Talent Group*
40 Whitfield St
London W1T 2RH, UNITED KINGDOM

Fletcher, Diane (Actor)
Ken McReddie
91 regent St
London W1R 7TB, UNITED KINGDOM (UK)

Fletcher, Ernest L (Politician)
811 Landing Pt
Stockbridge, GA 30281-9064, USA

Fletcher, Guy (Musician)
Damage Mgmt
16 Lambton Place
London W11 2SH, UNITED KINGDOM (UK)

Fletcher, Jamar (Athlete, Football Player)
11063 Worchester Dr
Saint Louis, MO 63136-5828, USA

Fletcher, London (Athlete, Football Player)
18898 Shropshire Ct
Leesburg, VA 20176-8493, USA

Fletcher, Louis (Athlete, Football Player)
18278 Buccaneer Ter
Leesburg, VA 20176-8479, USA

Fletcher, Louise (Actor)
1520 Camden Ave Apt 105
Los Angeles, CA 90025-3443, USA

Fletcher, Maria (Beauty Pageant Winner)
117 Regency Dr
Conway, SC 29526-9018, USA

Fletcher, Martin (Correspondent)
NBC-TV
4001 Nebraska Ave NW
News Dept
Washington, DC 20016-2795, USA

Fletcher, Paul (Athlete, Baseball Player)
431 Harpold Ave
Ravenswood, WV 26164-1333, USA

Fletcher, Scott B (Athlete, Baseball Player)
375 Sage Ln
Fayetteville, GA 30214-4295, USA

Fletcher, Simon (Athlete, Football Player)
2225 S Ensenada St
Aurora, CO 80013-6230, USA

Fletcher, Terrell (Athlete, Football Player)
22457 N Summit Ridge Cir
Chatsworth, CA 91311-2691, USA

Fletcher, Tom (Athlete, Baseball Player)
9287 E 2085 North Rd
Oakwood, IL 61858-6252, USA

Fleury, Marc-Andre (Athlete, Hockey Player)
Octagon Sports Management
1751 Pinnacle Dr Ste 1500
McLean, VA 22102-3833, USA

Fleury, Theoren (Theo) (Athlete, Hockey Player)
Fleury's Concrete Coatings
542 Patterson Grove SW
Calgary, AB T3H 3N6, Canada

Flichel, Todd (Athlete, Hockey Player)
Bowling Green State University Athletic
9564 Taberna Ln
Olmsted Twp, OH 44138-4257, USA

Flick, Bob (Musician)
Bob Flick Productions
300 Vine St Ste 14
Seattle, WA 98121-1465, USA

Flick, Tom (Athlete, Football Player)
9718 208th Ave NE
Redmond, WA 98053-5216, USA

Flinn, John (Athlete, Baseball Player)
6221 Lake Providence Ln
Charlotte, NC 28277-0565, USA

Flinn, Ryan (Athlete, Hockey Player)
21611 N 37th St
Phoenix, AZ 85050-4945, USA

Flint, George (Athlete, Football Player)
PO Box 2486
Prescott, AZ 86302-2486, USA

Flint, Judson (Athlete, Football Player)
807 Lee Ave
Farrell, PA 16121-1928, USA

Flippin, Lucy Lee (Actor)
50785 Grand Traverse Ave
La Quinta, CA 92253-5845, USA

Flitcroft, Garry (Soccer Player)
c/o Staff Member *Blackburn Rovers Football Club*
Ewood Park
Blackburn
Lancashire BB2 4JF, UNITED KINGDOM

Flitter, Josh (Actor)
c/o Ellen Gilbert *Paradigm*
140 Broadway Ste 2600
New York, NY 10005-1011, USA

Float, Jeffrey (Athlete, Olympic Athlete, Swimmer)
1906 University Park Dr
Sacramento, CA 95825-8210, USA

Flobots (Music Group)
c/o Corrie Christopher Martin *Paradigm*
8942 Wilshire Blvd
Beverly Hills, CA 90211-1908, USA

Flockhart, Calista (Actor)
c/o Melissa Kates *Viewpoint Inc*
8820 Wilshire Blvd Ste 220
Beverly Hills, CA 90211-2622, USA

Flockhart, Ron (Athlete, Hockey Player)
PO Box 234
Sicamous, BC V0E 2V0, Canada

Flock of Seagulls (Music Group)
c/o Carlos Keyes *Red Entertainment Agency*
3537 36th St Ste 2
Astoria, NY 11106-1347, USA

Floethe, Chris (Baseball Player)
5634 Mount Hood Ct
Martinez, CA 94553-5837, USA

Floetry (Music Group)
c/o Cara Lewis *Cara Lewis Group*
7 W 18th St Fl 3
New York, NY 10011-4663, USA

Flogging Molly (Music Group)
c/o Gary Schwindt *Villam Artist Management*
820 Hyperion Ave
Los Angeles, CA 90029-3106, USA

Flood, Ann (Actor)
15 E 91st St
New York, NY 10128-0648, USA

Flood, Staci (Model, Musician)
Clear Talent Group
10950 Ventura Blvd
Studio City, CA 91604-3340, USA

Flora, Kevin (Athlete, Baseball Player)
25035 Portsmouth
Mission Viejo, CA 92692-2812, USA

Flora, Lars (Athlete, Olympic Athlete, Track Athlete)
6500 Michigan Blvd
Anchorage, AK 99516-1818, USA

Florance, Sheila (Actor)
Melbourne Artists
643 Saint Kikla Road
Melbourne, VIC 03004, AUSTRALIA

Florek, Dann (Actor)
c/o Staff Member *Access Talent Management*
630 9th Ave Ste 415
New York, NY 10036-4750, USA

Florence, Don (Athlete, Baseball Player)
144 Bedford Rd
New Boston, NH 03070-4301, USA

Florence, Tyler (Chef, Television Host)
c/o Lisa Shotland *CAA (London)*
3 Shortlands, Hammersmith
Fl 5
London W6 8DA, UNITED KINGDOM

Florence + The Machine (Music Group)
c/o Mairead Nash *LuvLuvLuv Management*
106 Leonard St Fl 1
London EC2A 4RH, UNITED KINGDOM (UK)

Flores, Alba (Actor)
c/o Katrina Bayonas *Kuranda Management*
Isla De Oza, 30
Madrid 28035, SPAIN

Flores, Bill (Congressman, Politician)
1505 Longworth Hob
Washington, DC 20515-3313, USA

Flores, Francisco (President)
President's Office
Casa Presidencial
San Salvador, El SALVADOR

Flores, Jose (Athlete, Baseball Player)
PO Box 81533
Corpus Christi, TX 78468-1533, USA

Flores, Nikki (Musician)
c/o Staff Member *Sony/BMG Music (NY)*
550 Madison Ave
New York, NY 10022-3211, USA

Flores, Patrick F (Religious Leader)
Archbishop's Residence
2600 W Woodlawn Ave
San Antonio, TX 78228-5122, USA

Flores, Randy (Athlete, Baseball Player)
7 Enfield Rd
Saint Louis, MO 63132-4317, USA

Flores, Ron (Athlete, Baseball Player)
7309 Ramey Rd
Whittier, CA 90606-2566, USA

Flores, Thomas R (Tom) (Athlete, Coach, Football Coach, Football Executive, Football Player)
77741 Cove Pointe Cir
Indian Wells, CA 92210-6101, USA

Flores, Wilmer (Athlete, Baseball Player)
c/o Jim McNamara *McNamara Baseball Group*
Prefers to be contacted by phone.
Phoenix, AZ NA, USA

Florida Georgia Line (Music Group)
c/o Kevin 'Chief' Zaruk *Big Loud Mountain*
1111 16th Ave S Ste 201
Nashville, TN 37212-2336, USA

Florie, Bryce (Athlete, Baseball Player)
1118 Lands End Dr
Hanahan, SC 29410-4752, USA

Florin, Susan (Athlete, Golfer)
1883 Lexington Pl
Tarpon Springs, FL 34688-4965, USA

Florio, James (Politician)
416 Edgemoor Dr
Moorestown, NJ 08057-3404, USA

Florio, Thomas A (Actor)
New Yorker Magazine
4 Times Sq
Publisher's Office
New York, NY 10036-6518, USA

Flory, Med (Actor)
6044 Ensign Ave
North Hollywood, CA 91606-4905, USA

Flournoy, Craig (Journalist)
Dallas News
Editorial Dept
Communications Center
Dallas, TX 75265, USA

Flower, Joseph R (Religious Leader)
Assemblies of God
1445 N Boonville Ave
Springfield, MO 65802-1894, USA

flower, tyler (Athlete, Baseball Player)
109 Newcastle Walk
Woodstock, GA 30188-6088, USA

Flowers, Bernard (Athlete, Football Player)
3819 Old Farm Rd
Lafayette, IN 47909-3521, USA

Flowers, Brandon (Athlete, Football Player)
c/o Katrina Leonce *EAG Sports Management*
909 N Pacific Coast Hwy Ste 360
El Segundo, CA 90245-3864, USA

Flowers, Brandon (Musician)
c/o Linda Carbone *Press Here Publicity*
138 W 25th St Ste 900
New York, NY 10001-7470, USA

Flowers, Bruce (Athlete, Basketball Player)
276 W Grantley Ave
Elmhurst, IL 60126-2238, USA

Flowers, Charles (Charlie) (Athlete, Football Player)
6170 Mount Brook Way NW
Atlanta, GA 30328, USA

Flowers, Ereck (Athlete, Football Player)

Flowers ', Erik (Athlete, Football Player)
712 Mandalay Pkwy
McDonough, GA 30253-6109, USA

Flowers, Frank E (Director, Writer)
c/o David McIlvain *Brillstein Entertainment Partners*
9150 Wilshire Blvd Ste 350
Beverly Hills, CA 90212-3453, USA

Flowers, Gennifer (Actor, Model)
4859 Cedar Springs Rd Apt 241
Dallas, TX 75219-1215

Flowers, Richmond (Athlete, Football Player)
3434 Indian Lake Dr
Pelham, AL 35124-2713, USA

Floyd, Bobby (Athlete, Baseball Player)
9040 Laurel Ridge Dr
Mount Dora, FL 32757-9115, USA

Floyd, Bobby Jack (Athlete, Football Player)
4133 Tahoe Vista Dr
Rocklin, CA 95765-5089, USA

Floyd, C Clifford (Cliff) (Athlete, Baseball Player)
11640 SW 1st Ct
Plantation, FL 33325-2923, USA

Floyd, Dixon (Athlete, Football Player)
4285 Pierre Dr
Beaumont, TX 77705-1018, USA

Floyd, Eddie (Musician, Songwriter, Writer)
Jason West
Gables House
Saddlebow Kings Lynn PE34 3AR, UNITED KINGDOM (UK)

Floyd, Eric (Athlete, Football Player)
18047 Sailfish Dr
Lutz, FL 33558-7771, USA

Floyd, Eric (Sleepy) (Athlete, Basketball Player)
3101 Ivy Creek Rd
Gastonia, NC 28056-0301, USA

Floyd, Gavin (Athlete, Baseball Player)
9809 Milano Dr
Trinity, FL 34655-4668, USA

Floyd, George (Athlete, Football Player)
7056 Burlington Pike
Attn: Faculty Staff
Florence, KY 41042-1681, USA

Floyd, Larry (Athlete, Hockey Player)
3780 Hancock St
San Diego, CA 92110-4340, USA

Floyd, Leslie (Baseball Player)
Detroit Tigers
PO Box 7619
Texarkana, TX 75505-7619, USA

Floyd, Malcolm (Athlete, Football Player)

Floyd, Marlene (Athlete, Golfer)
5370 Clubhouse Ln
Hope Mills, NC 28348-9794, USA

Floyd, Michael (Athlete, Football Player)
c/o David Dunn *Athletes First*
23091 Mill Creek Dr
Laguna Hills, CA 92653-1258, USA

Floyd, Raymond (Athlete, Golfer)
505 S Flagler Dr Ste 910
West Palm Beach, FL 33401-5948, USA

Floyd, Sharrif (Athlete, Football Player)

Floyd, Tim (Coach)
New Orleans Hornets
1501 Girod St
New Orleans Arena
New Orleans, LA 70113-3124, USA

Floyd, William (Athlete, Football Player)
7827 Glen Echo Rd N
Jacksonville, FL 32211-6028, USA

Flueger, Patrick (Actor)
c/o Nancy Kremer *Nancy Kremer Management*
4545 Morse Ave
Studio City, CA 91604-1008, USA

Fluevog, John (Fashion Designer)
John Fluevog Shoes
837 Granville St
Vancouver, BC V6Z 1K7, Canada

Fluker, D.J. (Athlete, Football Player)

Fluno, Jere D (Business Person)
W W Grainger Inc
5500 Howard St
Skokie, IL 60077-2620, USA

Flutie, Darren (Athlete, Football Player)
29 Pine St
Natick, MA 01760-1203, USA

Flutie, Doug (Athlete, Football Player, Heisman Trophy Winner)
Doug Flutie Foundation
PO Box 2157
Framingham, MA 01703-2157, USA

Fly, DC Young (Actor, Comedian, Internet Star)
c/o Anwar Patterson *Archive Entertainment*
264 19th St NW Unit 2404
Atlanta, GA 30363-1151, USA

Flyleaf (Music Group)
c/o Rod MacSween *International Talent Booking*
9 Kingsway
Fl 6
London WC2B 6XF, UNITED KINGDOM

F. Lynch, Stephen (Congressman, Politician)
2348 Rayburn Hob
Washington, DC 20515-4611, USA

Flynn, Barbara (Actor)
Markham & Froggatt
Julian House
4 Windmill St
London W1P 1HF, UNITED KINGDOM (UK)

Flynn, Beau (Director)
c/o Adam Kaller *Hansen, Jacobson, Teller, Hoberman, Newman, Warren & Richman*
450 N Roxbury Dr Fl 8
Beverly Hills, CA 90210-4222, USA

Flynn, Brandon (Actor)
c/o Kim Hodgert *Anonymous Content*
3532 Hayden Ave
Culver City, CA 90232-2413, USA

Flynn, Colleen (Actor)
LGM
10390 Santa Monica Blvd Ste 300
Los Angeles, CA 90025-5091, USA

Flynn, Doug (Athlete, Baseball Player)
2465 Vale Dr
Lexington, KY 40514-1421, USA

Flynn, Gillian (Writer)
c/o Stephanie Kip Rostan *Levine Greenberg Literary Agency*
307 7th Ave Rm 2407
New York, NY 10001-6062, USA

Flynn, Jackie (Comedian)
c/o Staff Member *Buchwald*
5900 Wilshire Blvd Ste 3100
Los Angeles, CA 90036-5030, USA

Flynn, Luke (Actor, Producer, Writer)

Flynn, Matt (Athlete, Football Player)
c/o Pat Dye Jr *SportsTrust Advisors*
3340 Peachtree Rd NE Fl 16
Atlanta, GA 30326-1000, USA

Flynn, Mell (Actor)
PO Box 7695
Van Nuys, CA 91409-7695, USA

Flynn, Mike (Athlete, Basketball Player)
2138 Woodbourne Ave
Louisville, KY 40205-1912, USA

Flynn, Mike (Athlete, Football Player)
c/o Staff Member *Cindrich & Company*
552 Washington Ave
Carnegie, PA 15106-2848, USA

Flynn, Neil (Actor)
c/o Dan Baron *Agency for the Performing Arts (APA)*
405 S Beverly Dr Ste 500
Beverly Hills, CA 90212-4425, USA

Flynn, Sean (Actor)
c/o Danielle Lenniger *Luber Roklin Management*
5815 W Sunset Blvd Ste 208
Los Angeles, CA 90028-6481, USA

Flynn, Tom (Athlete, Football Player)
4008 Holiday Park Dr
Murrysville, PA 15668-8529, USA

Flynn, Willam (Billy) (Actor)
c/o Patrick Corcoran *PCM International*
450 N Rossmore Ave
Studio 303
Los Angeles, CA 90004-2406, USA

Flynville Train (Music Group)
c/o Staff Member *Paradigm (Monterey)*
404 W Franklin St
Monterey, CA 93940-2303, USA

Flythe, Mark (Athlete, Football Player)
505 Pheasant Run
Monmouth Junction, NJ 08852-1929, USA

F. Napolitano, Grace (Congressman, Politician)
1610 Longworth Hob
Washington, DC 20515-2213, USA

Foa, Barrett (Actor)
c/o Ethan Salter *Greene & Associates*
1901 Avenue of the Stars Ste 130
Los Angeles, CA 90067-6030, USA

Foale, C Michael (Mike) (Astronaut)
2101 Todville Rd # 11
Seabrook, TX 77586-3723, USA

Foden, Ben (Athlete, Rugby Player)
c/o Leigh Hinton *Big Red Management*
Woodcock House
Gibbard Mews, High Street, Wimbledon Village
London SW19 5BY, UNITED KINGDOM

Foeger, Luggi (Skier)
Christopher Foeger
230 S Balsamina Way
Portola Valley, CA 94028-7503, USA

Fogdoe, Tomas (Athlete, Skier)
Skogsvagen 18
Gallvare 970 02, SWEDEN

Fogel, Susanna (Director, Producer)
c/o Joy Fehily *PMK/BNC Public Relations*
1840 Century Park E Ste 1400
Los Angeles, CA 90067-2115, USA

Fogelman, Dan (Producer)
Rhode Island Ave Productions
11766 Wilshire Blvd
Los Angeles, CA 90025-6538, USA

Fogelnest, Jake (Actor)
c/o Kara Welker *Generate Management*
8750 Wilshire Blvd Ste 200
Beverly Hills, CA 90211-2707, USA

Fogerty, John (Musician, Songwriter)
2700 White Stallion Rd
Thousand Oaks, CA 91361-5012, USA

Fogg, Josh (Athlete, Baseball Player)
4910 S Quincy St
Tampa, FL 33611-3820, USA

Fogg, Kirk (Actor)

Foggie, Fred (Athlete, Football Player)
360 Jackson Rd
Inman, SC 29349-9533, USA

Foggs, Edward L (Religious Leader)
Church of God
PO Box 2420
Anderson, IN 46018-2420, USA

Fogle, Larry (Athlete, Basketball Player)
72 Beechwood Street
Rochester, NY 14609, USA

Fogler, Dan (Actor, Producer)
c/o Staff Member *Studio 13*
28 College Pl
Brooklyn, NY 11201-2404, USA

Fogler, Eddie (Basketball Player)
University of South Carolina
Athletic Dept
Columbia, SC 53233, USA

Fogolin Jr, Lee (Athlete, Hockey Player)
352 Lessard Dr NW
Edmonton, AB T6M 1A5, Canada

Foiles, Hank (Athlete, Baseball Player)
4333 Silverleaf Ct
Virginia Beach, VA 23462-5738, USA

Foiles, Lisa (Actor)
Boutique Talent Agency
C/O Nancy Schmidt Sanford
10 Universal City Plaza #2000
Universal City, CA 91608, USA

Folau, Spencer (Athlete, Football Player)
14003 Woodens Ln
Reisterstown, MD 21136-4536, USA

Folco, Peter (Athlete, Hockey Player)
6463 Rue Bannantyne
Verdun, QC H4H 1J8, Canada

Folds, Ben (Musician, Songwriter)
c/o Staff Member *ICM Partners*
10250 Constellation Blvd Fl 7
Los Angeles, CA 90067-6207, USA

Foles, Nick (Athlete, Football Player)
c/o David Dunn *Athletes First*
23091 Mill Creek Dr
Laguna Hills, CA 92653-1258, USA

Foley, Christopher (Actor)
c/o Staff Member *Innovative Artists*
1505 10th St
Santa Monica, CA 90401-2805, USA

Foley, Dave (Comedian)
c/o Bradie Steinlauf *Agency for the Performing Arts (APA)*
405 S Beverly Dr Ste 500
Beverly Hills, CA 90212-4425, USA

Foley, Dave (Athlete, Football Player)
2656 Galway Dr
Springfield, OH 45503-1177, USA

Foley, Gerry (Athlete, Hockey Player)
352 Skead Rd
Garson, ON P3L 1N4, Canada

Foley, Glenn (Athlete, Football Player)
3204 Buxmont Rd
Marlton, NJ 08053-8506, USA

Foley, Jeremy (Actor)
Academy Kids Mgmt
4942 Vineland Ave Ste 103
North Hollywood, CA 91601-5649, USA

Foley, John (Athlete, Basketball Player)
PO Box 143
Barre, MA 01005-0143, USA

Foley, Marv (Athlete, Baseball Player)
10166 Glenmore Ave
Bradenton, FL 34202-4049, USA

Foley, Mick (Actor, Wrestler)
c/o Elaine Gillespie *Gillespie Agency, The*
3007 Millwood Ave
Columbia, SC 29205-1855, USA

Foley, Scott (Actor)
c/o Staff Member *Primary Wave Entertainment*
10850 Wilshire Blvd Fl 6
Los Angeles, CA 90024-4319, USA

Foley, Steve (Athlete, Football Player)
6321 S Newport Ct
Centennial, CO 80111-4630, USA

Foley, Tim (Athlete, Football Player)
9816 Fairway Cir
Leesburg, FL 34788-3623, USA

Foley, Tim J (Athlete, Football Player)
2851 Old Clifton Rd
Springfield, OH 45502-9455, USA

Foley, Tom (Athlete, Baseball Player)
5237 Karlsburg Pl
Palm Harbor, FL 34685-3696, USA

Folger, Franklin (Cartoonist)
c/o Staff Member *King Features Syndication*
300 W 57th St Fl 15
New York, NY 10019-5238, USA

Foli, Tim (Athlete, Baseball Player)
74 Apian Way
Ormond Beach, FL 32174-1872, USA

Foligno, Mike (Athlete, Hockey Player)
c/o Staff Member *Sudbury Wolves*
240 Elgin St
Sudbury, ON P3E 3N6, Canada

Folk, Nick (Athlete, Football Player)
c/o Gary Uberstine *PSE Management*
1500 Rosecrans Ave Ste 500
Manhattan Beach, CA 90266-3771, USA

Folkenberg, Robert S (Religious Leader)
Seventh-Day Adventists
12501 Old Columbia Pike
Silver Spring, MD 20904-6600, USA

Folkers, Rich (Athlete, Baseball Player)
7100 3rd Ave N
Saint Petersburg, FL 33710-7502, USA

Folkins, Lee (Athlete, Football Player)
8749 the Esplanade Apt 13
Orlando, FL 32836-7734, USA

Folkl, Kristin (Athlete, Olympic Athlete, Volleyball Player)
4847 Langtree Dr
Saint Louis, MO 63128-2728, USA

Foll, Tim (Baseball Player)
New York Mets
1003 Hilltop Ln
Kodak, TN 37764-1838, USA

Follese, Ryan (Musician)
135 Holly Frst
Nashville, TN 37221-2226, USA

Follet, George (Athlete, Football Player)
6254 Parima St
Long Beach, CA 90803-2108, USA

Follett, Ken (Writer)
Box 4
Knebworth SG3 6UT, UNITED KINGDOM (UK)

Followill, Caleb (Musician)
c/o Andy Mendelsohn *Vector Management*
276 5th Ave Rm 604
New York, NY 10001-4527, USA

Followill, Matthew (Musician)
c/o Andy Mendelsohn *Vector Management*
276 5th Ave Rm 604
New York, NY 10001-4527, USA

Follows, Megan (Actor)

Folman, Ari (Director)
c/o Maha Dakhil *Creative Artists Agency (CAA)*
2000 Avenue of the Stars Ste 100
Los Angeles, CA 90067-4705, USA

Folon, Jean-Michel (Artist)
Burcy
Beaumont-du-Gatinais 77890, FRANCE

Folse, John (Chef)
Chef John Folse and Company
2517 S Philippe Ave
Gonzales, LA 70737-3750, USA

Folsom, James (Politician)
1482 Orchard Dr NE
Cullman, AL 35055-2145, USA

Folsom, Steve (Athlete, Football Player)
6 Woodhollow Trl
Round Rock, TX 78665-9739, USA

Folston, James (Athlete, Football Player)
1450 Victoria Blvd
Rockledge, FL 32955-4312, USA

Fonda, Bridget (Actor)
c/o Nancy Seltzer *Nancy Seltzer & Associates*
6220 Del Valle Dr
Los Angeles, CA 90048-5306, USA

Fonda, Jane (Actor)
Fonda Foundation
PO Box 5840
Atlanta, GA 31107-0840, USA

Fonda, Peter (Actor)
c/o Beth Holden-Garland *Untitled Entertainment*
350 S Beverly Dr Ste 200
Beverly Hills, CA 90212-4819, USA

Fonoti, Toniu (Athlete, Football Player)
370 Ulupaina St Apt D
Kailua, HI 96734-2412, USA

Fonseca (Musician)
c/o Staff Member *WME/IMG (Miami)*
119 Washington Ave Ste 400
Miami Beach, FL 33139-7202, USA

Fonseca, Adriana (Actor)
c/o Staff Member *Televisa*
Blvd Adolfo Lopez Mateos 232
Colonia San Angel INN
DF CP 01060, MEXICO

Fonseca, Chris (Actor)
Strauss-McGarr Entertainment
1199 Boise Way
Costa Mesa, CA 92626-2704, USA

Fonseca, David (Musician)
c/o Staff Member *Universal Music Publishing Group (Latin)*
420 Lincoln Rd Ste 200
Miami Beach, FL 33139-3014, USA

Fonseca, Lyndsy (Actor)
c/o Felicia Sager *Sager Management*
260 S Beverly Dr Ste 205
Beverly Hills, CA 90212-3812, USA

Fonsi, Luis (Musician)
Tony Mojena Entertainment Inc
463 Sergio Cuevas Bustamante
San Juan, PR 00918, USA

Fontaine, Levi (Athlete, Basketball Player)
805 Rollins Rd Apt 2
Burlingame, CA 94010-2664, USA

Fontana, Isabeli (Model)
UNO BCN
Av. Marques de l'Argentera 5
Principal 3
Barcelona 08003, Spain

Fontana, Santino (Actor)
c/o Emily Gerson Saines *Brookside Artists Management*
250 W 57th St Ste 1820
New York, NY 10107-1802, USA

Fontana, Tom (Producer, Writer)
c/o Peter Benedek *United Talent Agency (UTA)*
9336 Civic Center Dr
Beverly Hills, CA 90210-3604, USA

Fontana, Wayne (Musician)
Brian Gannon Mgmt
PO Box 106
Rochdale OL16 4HW, UNITED KINGDOM (UK)

Fontas, Jon (Athlete, Hockey Player)
9 Boggs Cir
Nashua, NH 03060-4861, USA

Fontenot, Albert (Athlete, Football Player)
4919 Gammage St
Houston, TX 77021-3205, USA

Fontenot, Jerry (Athlete, Football Player)
938 Bristol Dr
Deerfield, IL 60015-4843, USA

Fontenot, Joe (Athlete, Baseball Player)
2231 Doc Hughes Rd
Buford, GA 30519-4240, USA

Fontenot, Ray (Athlete, Baseball Player)
1674 S Crestview Dr
Lake Charles, LA 70605-5280, USA

Fontes, Wayne H (Athlete, Coach, Football Coach, Football Player)
10700 Ruffino Ct
Trinity, FL 34655-7062, USA

Fonteyne, Val (Athlete, Hockey Player)
5403 52 Ave
Wetaskiwin, AB T9A 0X8, Canada

Fonville, Chad (Athlete, Baseball Player)
2338 Piney Green Rd
Midway Park, NC 28544-1112, USA

Fonville, Charles (Athlete, Track Athlete)
1845 Wintergreen Ct
Ann Arbor, MI 48103-9727, USA

Fonzi, Dolores (Actor)
c/o Staff Member *Kuranda Management*
Isla De Oza, 30
Madrid 28035, SPAIN

Foo, Jon (Actor)
c/o Mark Schumacher *Schumacher Management*
Prefers to be contacted by email or phone.
Los Angeles, CA 90064, USA

Foo Fighters (Music Group)
c/o Michele Hug *Nasty Little Man*
285 W Broadway Rm 310
New York, NY 10013-2257, USA

Foor, Jim (Athlete, Baseball Player)
2018 Bolsover St
Houston, TX 77005-1616, USA

Foose, Chip (Actor)
Foose Design Inc
17811 Sampson Ln Ste A
Huntington Beach, CA 92647-7199, USA

Foote, Adam (Athlete, Hockey Player)
1573 S Pennsylvania St
Denver, CO 80210-2636, USA

Foote, Barry (Athlete, Baseball Player)
92 Lassiter Pond Rd
Smithfield, NC 27577-7956, USA

Foote, Chris (Athlete, Football Player)
1140 Harbin Ridge Ln
Knoxville, TN 37909-2382, USA

Foote, Larry (Athlete, Football Player)
c/o Brian Levy *Goal Line Football Management*
1025 Kane Concourse Ste 207
Bay Harbor Islands, FL 33154-2118, USA

Footman, Dan (Athlete, Football Player)
7189 Nottinghamshire Dr
Jacksonville, FL 32219-4338, USA

Foppert, Jesse (Athlete, Baseball Player)
PO Box 150682
San Rafael, CA 94915-0682, USA

Forbert, Steve (Musician, Songwriter, Writer)
Mongrel Music
743 Center Blvd
Fairfax, CA 94930-1764, USA

Forbes, Colin (Writer)
Elaine Green Ltd 37 Gold Hawk Road
London, W12 8QQ, England

Forbes, Dave (Athlete, Hockey Player)
4020 Reserve Pt
Colorado Springs, CO 80904-1043, USA

Forbes, Michelle (Actor)
c/o Laura Berwick *Berwick & Kovacik*
6230 Wilshire Blvd
Los Angeles, CA 90048-5126, USA

Forbes, Mike (Athlete, Hockey Player)
547 Waverly Ave
Grand Haven, MI 49417-2127, USA

Forbes, P J (Athlete, Baseball Player)
10236 W Westlakes Ct
Wichita, KS 67205-5219, USA

Forbes, West (Musician)
Paramount Entertainment
PO Box 12
Far Hills, NJ 07931-0012, USA

Force, John (Race Car Driver)
John Force Racing
22722 Old Canal Rd
Yorba Linda, CA 92887-4602, USA

Ford, Alan (Actor)
c/o Malcolm Browning *International Artistes*
Holborn Hall - 4th Floor
London WC1V 7BD, UK

Ford, Alan (Athlete, Football Player)
1251 McNiven Ave
Regina, SK S4S 3X7, Canada

Ford, Ben (Athlete, Baseball Player)
1717 Applewood Pl NE
Cedar Rapids, IA 52402-3321, USA

Ford, Brian (Athlete, Hockey Player)
311 Queen St
Fredericton, NB E3B 1B1, CANADA

Ford, Charlie (Athlete, Football Player)
2995 South St
Beaumont, TX 77702-2108, USA

Ford, Cheryl (Basketball Player)
Detroit Shock Palace
2 Championship Dr
Auburn Hills, MI 48326-1753, USA

Ford, Chris (Athlete, Basketball Player, Coach)
424 N Vendome Ave
Margate City, NJ 08402-1265, USA

Ford, Clementine (Actor)
c/o Staff Member *AKA Talent Agency*
325 N Larchmont Blvd
Los Angeles, CA 90004-3011, USA

Ford, Colton (Musician)
c/o Bill Coleman *Peace Bisquit*
963 Kent Ave Bldg E
Brooklyn, NY 11205-4461, USA

Ford, Curt (Athlete, Baseball Player)
5825 Armide St
North Las Vegas, NV 89081-3400, USA

Ford, Dale (Athlete, Baseball Player)
106 Rhudy Ln
Jonesborough, TN 37659-4962, USA

Ford, Dan (Athlete, Baseball Player)
1271 Linton Rd
Benton, LA 71006-8736, USA

Ford, Darren (Baseball Player)
7640 NW 79th Ave Apt L8
Tamarac, FL 33321-2868, USA

Ford, Dave (Athlete, Baseball Player)
19523 N Sagamore Rd
Cleveland, OH 44126-1662, USA

Ford, David (Musician)
c/o Staff Member *Paradigm (Monterey)*
404 W Franklin St
Monterey, CA 93940-2303, USA

Ford, Dee (Athlete, Football Player)
c/o Adisa P Bakari *Kelley Drye & Warren LLP*
3050 K St NW Ste 400
Washington, DC 20007-5100, USA

Ford, Don (Athlete, Basketball Player)
519 W Quinto St Apt B
Santa Barbara, CA 93105-4800

Ford, Don (Athlete, Basketball Player)
519 W Quinto St Apt B
Santa Barbara, CA 93105-4800, USA

Ford, Doug (Athlete, Golfer)
3737 Gulfstream Rd
Delray Beach, FL 33483-7411, USA

Ford, Eileen (Business Person)
c/o Staff Member *Ford Models (NY)*
238 E 4th St
New York, NY 10009-7425, USA

Ford, Ervin (Baseball Player)
Indianapolis Clowns
429 Banks St
Greensboro, NC 27401-3105, USA

Ford, Faith (Actor)
c/o Becca Kovacik *Berwick & Kovacik*
6230 Wilshire Blvd
Los Angeles, CA 90048-5126, USA

Ford, Frederick (Adult Film Star)
c/o Staff Member *Diva Central Inc*
7510 W Sunset Blvd # 1445
Los Angeles, CA 90046-3408, USA

Ford, Garrett (Athlete, Football Player)
682 Westview Ave
Morgantown, WV 26505-2418, USA

Ford, Gib (Athlete, Basketball Player, Olympic Athlete)
152 Amblewood Ln
Naples, FL 34105-7146, USA

Ford, Harrison (Actor)
c/o Ina Treciokas *Slate PR*
901 N Highland Ave
W Hollywood, CA 90038-2412, USA

Ford, Henry (Athlete, Football Player)
7222 Shannon Rd
Verona, PA 15147-2036, USA

Ford, Henry (Athlete, Football Player)
809 Glendevon Dr
McKinney, TX 75071-6543, USA

Ford, Jack (Correspondent)
CBS-TV
51 W 52nd St
News Dept
New York, NY 10019-6119, USA

Ford, James L (Athlete, Football Player)
2168 College Cir N
Jacksonville, FL 32209-5980, USA

Ford, Kevin A (Astronaut)
1002 Oak Park Ln
Friendswood, TX 77546-3584, USA

Ford, Lew (Athlete, Baseball Player)
2201 Lady Cornwall Dr
Lewisville, TX 75056-5615, USA

Ford, Lita (Actor, Musician)
c/o Andrew Goodfriend *The Kirby Organization (TKO-NY)*
141 Halstead Ave PH
Mamaroneck, NY 10543-2607, USA

Ford, Matt (Athlete, Baseball Player)
10837 Cypress Glen Dr
Coral Springs, FL 33071-8164, USA

Ford, Melissa (Model)
c/o Mike Esterman *Esterman.Com, LLC*
Prefers to be contacted via email
Baltimore, MD XXXXX, USA

Ford, Melyssa (Model)
c/o Theo Caesar *90210 Talent Agency*
16430 Ventura Blvd Ste 200
Encino, CA 91436-2135, USA

Ford, Mick (Actor)
c/o Staff Member *CDA*
167-169 Kensington High St
London W8 6SH, UNITED KINGDOM

Ford, Mike (Athlete, Football Player)
9798 FM 1565
Terrell, TX 75160-8516, USA

Ford, Mike (Athlete, Hockey Player)
65 Kingscrest Dr
la Salle, MB ROG OAl, Canada

Ford, Patricia (Model)

Ford, Phil (Athlete, Basketball Player, Olympic Athlete)
PO Box 90623
Raleigh, NC 27675-0623, USA

Ford, Richard (Writer)
c/o Staff Member *HarperCollins Publishers*
195 Broadway Fl 2
New York, NY 10007-3132, USA

Ford, Robert (Athlete, Basketball Player)
202 Pathway Ln
West Lafayette, IN 47906-2162, USA

Ford, Ruth (Actor)
Dakota Hotel
1 W 72nd St Apt 68
New York, NY 10023-3423, USA

Ford, Scott (Business Person)
Alltel Corp
PO Box 96019
Charlotte, NC 28296-0019, USA

Ford, Sherell (Athlete, Basketball Player)
1509 S 6th Ave
Maywood, IL 60153-2014, USA

Ford, Ted (Athlete, Baseball Player)
3713 N 25th Ln
McAllen, TX 78501-6285, USA

Ford, T J (Basketball Player)
Milwaukee Bucks
1543 N 2nd St Fl 6
Bradley Center
Milwaukee, WI 53212-4036, USA

Ford, Tom (Designer, Fashion Designer)
c/o Simon Halls *Slate PR*
901 N Highland Ave
W Hollywood, CA 90038-2412, USA

Ford, Trent (Actor)
c/o Staff Member *Paradigm*
8942 Wilshire Blvd
Beverly Hills, CA 90211-1908, USA

Ford, Whitey (Athlete, Baseball Player)
WhiteyFord.com
3750 Galt Ocean Dr Apt 1411
Fort Lauderdale, FL 33308-7623, USA

Ford, Willa (Musician)
c/o Brad Marks *Blue Five Media*
9150 Wilshire Blvd Ste 103
Beverly Hills, CA 90212-3428, USA

Ford, William C Jr (Business Person)
Ford Motor Co
American Road
Dearborn, MI 48121, USA

Ford Bales, Susan (Writer)
2712 Piersall Dr
McKinney, TX 75072-3406, USA

Forde, Brian (Athlete, Football Player)
20225 Bothell Everett Hwy Apt 1131
Bothell, WA 98012-8186, USA

Fordham, Julia (Musician, Songwriter, Writer)
Vanguard Records
2700 Pennsylvania Ave Ste 1100
Santa Monica, CA 90404-4059, USA

Fordham, Tom (Athlete, Baseball Player)
14559 Miguel Ln
El Cajon, CA 92021-2843, USA

Fordham, Willie (Baseball Player)
Negro Baseball Leagues
3608 Tudor Dr
Harrisburg, PA 17109-1235, USA

Fordyce, Brook (Athlete, Baseball Player)
5 River Crest Ct
Stuart, FL 34996-6515, USA

Foreigner (Music Group, Musician)
c/o Dan Weiner *Paradigm (Monterey)*
404 W Franklin St
Monterey, CA 93940-2303, USA

Foreman, Amanda (Actor)

Foreman, Chuck (Athlete, Football Player)
9716 Mill Creek Dr
Eden Prairie, MN 55347-4307, USA

Foreman, Deborah (Actor)
PO Box 2305
Big Bear City, CA 92314-2305, USA

Foreman, D'Onta (Athlete, Football Player)
c/o Graylan Crain *Select Sports Group*
2700 Post Oak Blvd Ste 1450
Houston, TX 77056-5785, USA

Foreman, George (Athlete, Boxer, Olympic Athlete)
George Foreman Enterprises
PO Box 1405
Huffman, TX 77336-1405, USA

Foreman, Walter E (Chuck) (Athlete, Football Player)
574 Prairie Center Dr Ste 165
Eden Prairie, MN 55344-7945, USA

Forest, Michael (Actor)
1327 N Vista St Apt 203
Los Angeles, CA 90046-4832, USA

Forester, Herschel (Athlete, Football Player)
15250 Prestonwood Blvd Apt 230
Dallas, TX 75248-4796, USA

Forester, Nicole (Actor)
c/o Doug Kesten *Paradigm*
140 Broadway Ste 2600
New York, NY 10005-1011, USA

Foret, Sarah (Actor)

Forey, Conley (Athlete, Hockey Player)
412-2929 4th Ave W
Vancouver, BC V6K 4T3, Canada

Forget, Guy (Tennis Player)
Rue des Pacs 2
Neuchatel 02000, SWITZERLAND

Forlani, Claire (Actor)
c/o Paul Nelson *Mosaic Media Group*
407 N Maple Dr # 100
Beverly Hills, CA 90210-3818, USA

Form, Andrew (Producer)
c/o Staff Member *Platinum Dunes*
631 Colorado Ave
Santa Monica, CA 90401-2507, USA

Forman, Don (Athlete, Basketball Player)
1532 Gormican Ln
Naples, FL 34110-0920, USA

Forman, Stanley (Journalist, Photographer)
17 Cherry Rd
Beverly, MA 01915-1511, USA

Forman, Tom (Cartoonist)
10544 James Rd
Celina, TX 75009-3744, USA

Formia, Osvaldo (Horse Racer)
6501 Winfield Blvd # A10
Margate, FL 33063-7168, USA

Forney, Carl (Athlete, Baseball Player)
169 Ridley St
Marion, NC 28752-4629, USA

Forney, Kynan (Athlete, Football Player)
2046 Skybrooke Ln
Hoschton, GA 30548-6295, USA

Foronjy, Richard (Actor)
c/o Staff Member *The House of Representatives*
3118 Wilshire Blvd Ste D
Santa Monica, CA 90403-2345, USA

Forrest, Bayard (Athlete, Basketball Player)
300A Squaw Valley Pl # A
Pagosa Springs, CO 81147-9773, USA

Forrest, Frederic (Actor)
11300 W Olympic Blvd Ste 610
Los Angeles, CA 90064-1643, USA

Forrest, Katherine Virginia (Writer)
PO Box 31613
San Francisco, CA 94131-0613

Forrest, Lili (Designer)
600 Moulton Ave Apt 205
Los Angeles, CA 90031-3485, USA

Forrester, Patrick G (Astronaut)
3923 Park Circle Way
Houston, TX 77059-3019, USA

Forrester Sisters (Music Group)
c/o Staff Member *Warner Music*
4000 Warner Blvd
Burbank, CA 91522-0002, USA

Forsberg, Fred (Athlete, Football Player)
1727 223rd Ave SE
Sammamish, WA 98075-9570, USA

Forsberg, Peter (Athlete, Hockey Player)
Forspro AB
Viktoriaesplanaden 1,
Ornskoldsvik 89123, Sweden

Forsch, Ken (Athlete, Baseball Player)
881 S Country Glen Way
Anaheim, CA 92808-2635, USA

Forsey, Brock (Athlete, Football Player)
8346 W Sundisk St
Boise, ID 83714-2509, USA

Forslund, Constance (Actor)
4528 1/2 Laurel Canyon Blvd
Studio City, CA 91607-4183, USA

Forsman, Dan (Athlete, Golfer)
88 W 4500 N
Provo, UT 84604-5517, USA

Forst, Bill (Cartoonist)
2320 Byer Rd
Santa Cruz, CA 95062-1949, USA

Forstchen, William (Writer)
c/o Staff Member *Spectrum Literary Agency*
320 Central Park W Ste 1-D
New York, NY 10025-7659, USA

Forster, Brian (Actor)
c/o Merrilee Neely *Parmeter Group, The*
Prefers to be contacted by telephone or email
Santa Monica, CA 90405, USA

Forster, Marc (Director, Producer)
Apparatus Productions
11634 Huston St
N Hollywood, CA 91601-4314, USA

Forster, Robert (Actor)
c/o Eli Selden *Anonymous Content*
3532 Hayden Ave
Culver City, CA 90232-2413, USA

Forster, Scott (Athlete, Baseball Player)
901 Sturgis Ln
Ambler, PA 19002-2022, USA

Forster, Terry (Baseball Player)
Chicago White Sox
PO Box 711658
Santee, CA 92072-1658, USA

Forsyth, Bill (Director)
P F D
Drury House
34-43 Russell St
London WC2B 5HA, UNITED KINGDOM (UK)

Forsyth, Chris (Actor)
c/o Bob McGowan *McGowan Management*
170 S Beverly Dr Ste 304
Beverly Hills, CA 90212-3000, USA

Forsyth, Frederick (Writer)
Trans World Publishers
61-63 Oxbridge Rd
Ealing
London W5 5SA, UNITED KINGDOM (UK)

Forsythe, Rosemary (Actor)
1591 Benedict Canyon Dr
Beverly Hills, CA 90210-2023, USA

Forsythe, William (Actor)
Frankfurt Ballet
Untermainanlage 11
Frankfurt 60311, GERMANY

Forte, Deborah (Producer)
c/o Staff Member *Scholastic Entertainment*
557 Broadway
New York, NY 10012-3962, USA

Forte, Fabian (Actor)
PO Box 951
Connellsville, PA 15425-0951, USA

Forte, Ike (Athlete, Football Player)
5811 Winchester Dr
Texarkana, TX 75503-4602, USA

Forte, Joseph (Basketball Player)
355 Elmcroft Blvd # 621
Rockville, MD 20850-5662, USA

Forte, Matt (Athlete, Football Player)
c/o Adisa P Bakari *Kelley Drye & Warren LLP*
3050 K St NW Ste 400
Washington, DC 20007-5100, USA

Forte, Will (Actor, Writer)
c/o Julie Darmody *Rise Management*
6338 Wilshire Blvd
Los Angeles, CA 90048-5002, USA

Fortenberry, Jeff (Congressman, Politician)
1514 Longworth Hob
Washington, DC 20515-0537, USA

Fortier, Dave (Athlete, Hockey Player)
150 Kingsmount Blvd
Sudbury, ON P3E 1K9, Canada

Fortier, Laurie (Actor)
c/o Danielle Allman-Del *D2 Management*
10351 Santa Monica Blvd Ste 210
Los Angeles, CA 90025-6937, USA

Fortin, Ray (Athlete, Hockey Player)
899 109e Av
Drummondville, QC J2B 4M1, Canada

Fortin, Roman (Athlete, Football Player)
4342 Club Dr NE
Atlanta, GA 30319-1120, USA

Fortner, Nell (Coach)
Auburn University
Athletic Dept
Auburn, AL 36849-0001, USA

Fortson, Danny (Athlete, Basketball Player)
360 Cleveland Ave
Glendale, OH 45246-4624, USA

Fortt, Khairi (Athlete, Football Player)

Fortugno, Tim (Athlete, Baseball Player)
3604 Babson Dr
Elk Grove, CA 95758-4576, USA

Fortunato, Don (Athlete, Football Player)
222 Regent Wood Rd
Northfield, IL 60093-2767, USA

Fortunato, Joseph F (Joe) (Athlete, Football Player)
PO Box 934
Natchez, MS 39121-0934, USA

Fortune, Jimmy (Musician)
American Major Talent
8747 W Commerce St
Hernando, MS 38632-8445, USA

Foruria, John (Athlete, Football Player)
5603 W Edson St
Boise, ID 83705-1852, USA

Forward, Susan (Writer)
c/o Staff Member *HarperCollins Publishers*
195 Broadway Fl 2
New York, NY 10007-3132, USA

Forzano, Rick (Athlete, Football Coach, Football Player)
3216 Interlaken St
West Bloomfield, MI 48323-1824, USA

Fosbury, Dick (Athlete, Olympic Athlete, Track Athlete)
PO Box 1791
Ketchum, ID 83340-1781

Fosnow, Jerry (Athlete, Baseball Player)
7028 W Waters Ave
Tampa, FL 33634-2292, USA

Foss, Anita (Athlete, Baseball Player, Commentator)
9630 Sombra Valley Dr
Sunland, CA 91040-1524, USA

Foss, Larry (Athlete, Baseball Player)
4303 E English St
Wichita, KS 67218-1320, USA

Fossas, Tony (Athlete, Baseball Player)
11302 NW 9th St
Plantation, FL 33325-1501, USA

Fosse, Ray (Athlete, Baseball Player)
PO Box 567
Diablo, CA 94528-0567, USA

Fossey, Brigitte (Actor)
18 Rue Troyon
Paris 75017, FRANCE

Fossum, Casey (Athlete, Baseball Player)
18032 Glenville Cv
Austin, TX 78738-7651, USA

Fossum, Michael E (Astronaut)
822 Rolling Run Ct
Houston, TX 77062-2100, USA

Foster, Alan (Athlete, Baseball Player)
10330 Grandview Dr
La Mesa, CA 91941-6844, USA

Foster, Alex (Athlete, Hockey Player)
721 S Livernois Rd
Rochester Hills, MI 48307-2770, USA

Foster, Arian (Athlete, Football Player)
c/o Michael McCartney *Priority Sports & Entertainment (Chicago)*
325 N La Salle Dr Ste 650
Chicago, IL 60654-8182, USA

Foster, Barry (Athlete, Football Player)
1905 Ashton Ct
Colleyville, TX 76034-4401, USA

Foster, Ben (Actor)
c/o Annie Schmidt *Untitled Entertainment (NY)*
215 Park Ave S Fl 8
New York, NY 10003-1622, USA

Foster, Brendan (Athlete, Track Athlete)
Whitegates
31 Meadowfield Road
Stocksfield, Northumberland, UNITED KINGDOM (UK)

Foster, Corey (Athlete, Hockey Player)
71 Pine Ridge Dr
Arnprior, ON K7S 3G8, Canada

Foster, David (Musician, Songwriter)
David Foster Productions
5555 Melrose Ave
Bungalow 9
Los Angeles, CA 90038-3989, ISA

Foster, Deshaun (Athlete, Football Player)
2391 Apple Tree Dr
Tustin, CA 92780-7134, USA

Foster, Dwight (Athlete, Hockey Player)
721 S Livernois Rd
Rochester Hills, MI 48307-2770, USA

Foster, George (Athlete, Baseball Player)
c/o Brian Lammi *Lammi Sports Management*
310 E Buffalo St
Milwaukee, WI 53202-5808, USA

Foster, George (Athlete, Football Player)
4057 Meadowbrook Dr
Macon, GA 31204-4752, USA

Foster, Jeff (Athlete, Basketball Player)
333 Pickwick Ct
Noblesville, IN 46062-9071, USA

Foster, Jerome (Athlete, Football Player)
18900 Goldwin St
Southfield, MI 48075-7218, USA

Foster, Jodie (Actor, Director)
c/o Jennifer Allen *Viewpoint Inc*
8820 Wilshire Blvd Ste 220
Beverly Hills, CA 90211-2622, USA

Foster, John (Actor)

Foster, John (Athlete, Baseball Player)
519 Airway Ave
Lewiston, ID 83501-4503, USA

Foster, Jon (Actor)
c/o Ken Jacobson *Ken Jacobson Management*
Preferred to be contacted by phone or email
Los Angeles, CA 91367, USA

Foster, Kris (Athlete, Baseball Player)
131 Morgan Rd
Hendersonville, NC 28739-9753, USA

Foster, Larry (Athlete, Baseball Player)
205 W Obell St
Whitehall, MI 49461-1742, USA

Foster, Leo (Athlete, Baseball Player)
699 Glensprings Dr
Cincinnati, OH 45246-2129, USA

Foster, Mark (Musician)
3549 N Knoll Dr
Los Angeles, CA 90068-1523, USA

Foster, Marty (Athlete, Baseball Player)
1718 Arrowhead Dr
Beloit, WI 53511-3808, USA

Foster, Marty (Baseball Player)
319 W 5th Ave
Denver, CO 80204-5118, USA

Foster, Meg (Actor)
c/o Chris Roe *Chris Roe Management*
PO Box 761
Burbank, CA 91503-0761, USA

Foster, Norm (Athlete, Hockey Player)
632 Rewold Dr
Rochester, MI 48307-2233, USA

Foster, Radney (Musician, Songwriter, Writer)
c/o Staff Member *WME|IMG*
9601 Wilshire Blvd
Beverly Hills, CA 90210-5213, USA

Foster, Ramon (Athlete, Football Player)
c/o Joel Segal *Lagardere Unlimited (NY)*
456 Washington St Apt 9L
New York, NY 10013-1555, USA

Foster, Rod (Athlete, Basketball Player)
1246 Armacost Ave Apt 105
Los Angeles, CA 90025-6432, USA

Foster, Ron (Athlete, Football Player)
18360 Cantara St Unit 2
Reseda, CA 91335-7519, USA

Foster, Roy A (Athlete, Football Player)
5824 Shenandoah Ave
Los Angeles, CA 90056-1424, USA

Foster, Sara (Actor)
c/o Brad Marks *Blue Five Media*
9150 Wilshire Blvd Ste 103
Beverly Hills, CA 90212-3428, USA

Foster, Scott M (Actor)
c/o John Tae Lee *Shapiro/West & Associates*
141 El Camino Dr Ste 205
Beverly Hills, CA 90212-2786, USA

Foster, Scott Michael (Actor)
c/o John Tae Lee *Shapiro/West & Associates*
141 El Camino Dr Ste 205
Beverly Hills, CA 90212-2786, USA

Foster, Steve (Athlete, Baseball Player)
5707 Pine Park St
Schofield, WI 54476-3566, USA

Foster, Sutton (Actor)
c/o Joe Machota *Creative Artists Agency (CAA)*
405 Lexington Ave Fl 19
New York, NY 10174-1800, USA

Foster, Todd (Boxer)
249 21st Ave NW
Great Falls, MT 59404-1425, USA

Foster, Yolanda (Reality Star)
c/o Brian Dow *Agency for the Performing Arts (APA)*
405 S Beverly Dr Ste 500
Beverly Hills, CA 90212-4425, USA

Foster the People (Music Group)
c/o Ian Montone *Monotone Inc.*
820 Seward St
Los Angeles, CA 90038-3602, USA

Foti, Tony (Race Car Driver)
LAPD Racing Team
10250 Etiwanda Ave
Northridge, CA 91325-1015, USA

Fotiu, Nick (Athlete, Hockey Player)
16 Backus River Rd
East Falmouth, MA 02536-5205, USA

Fou, Ts'ong (Musician)
62 Aberdeen Park
London N5 2BL, UNITED KINGDOM (UK)

Foucault, Steve (Athlete, Baseball Player)
23813 Coral Ridge Ln
Land O Lakes, FL 34639-4879, USA

Fouch, Allison (Athlete, Golfer)
2949 Oakwood Dr SE
Grand Rapids, MI 49506-4235, USA

Foudy, Judy (Julie) (Model, Soccer Player)
US Soccer Federation
1801 S Prairie Ave
Chicago, IL 60616-1356, USA

Fought, John (Athlete, Golfer)
5747 E Via Los Ranchos
Paradise Valley, AZ 85253, USA

Foules, Elbert (Athlete, Football Player)
PO Box 1061
Greenville, MS 38702-1061, USA

Foulke, Keith (Athlete, Baseball Player)
4844 W Electra Ln
Glendale, AZ 85310-3833, USA

Foulkes, Llyn (Artist)
6010 Eucalyptus Ln
Los Angeles, CA 90042-1244, USA

Fountaine, Jamal (Athlete, Football Player)
245 SW Lincoln St Apt 122
Portland, OR 97201-5083, USA

Fountains of Wayne (Music Group)
c/o Ken Weinstein *Big Hassle Media*
40 Exchange Pl Ste 1900
New York, NY 10005-2714, USA

Fouraker, Chase (Musician)
c/o Austin Mullins *WME (Nashville)*
1201 Demonbreun St
Nashville, TN 37203-3140, USA

Fourcade, John (Athlete, Football Player)
2749 Long Branch Dr
Marrero, LA 70072-5856, USA

Four Freshmen, The (Music Group)
c/o Staff Member *International Ventures*
25115 Avenue Stanford Ste 102
Valencia, CA 91355-4777, USA

Fournette, Leonard (Athlete, Football Player)
c/o Ari Nissim *Roc Nation*
1411 Broadway Fl 38
New York, NY 10018-3409, USA

Foust, Nina (Athlete, Golfer)
901 East Dr
Morehead City, NC 28557-3009, USA

Fouts, Dan (Athlete, Football Player)
16820 Varco Rd
Bend, OR 97703-9135, USA

Fowler, Blair (Actor)
c/o Brian Dow *Agency for the Performing Arts (APA)*
405 S Beverly Dr Ste 500
Beverly Hills, CA 90212-4425, USA

Fowler, Bobby (Athlete, Football Player)
5259 Denmans Loop
Belton, TX 76513-4940, USA

Fowler, Chris (Sportscaster)
c/o Staff Member *ESPN (Main)*
935 Middle St
Espn Plaza
Bristol, CT 06010-1000, USA

Fowler, Dan (Athlete, Football Player)
2660 Links End
Roswell, GA 30076-3582, USA

Fowler, David (Athlete, Football Player)
511 Cove Rd
Shelbyville, KY 40065-7941, USA

Fowler, Elle (Internet Star)
c/o Brian Dow *Agency for the Performing Arts (APA)*
405 S Beverly Dr Ste 500
Beverly Hills, CA 90212-4425, USA

Fowler, Jim (Actor)
Wild Kingdom
Mutual of Omaha
Mutual of Omaha Plaza
Omaha, NE 68175-0001, USA

Fowler, Kevin (Musician)
c/o George Couri *Triple 8 Management*
1611 W 6th St
Austin, TX 78703-5059, USA

Fowler, Melvin (Athlete, Football Player)
2850 Amsdell Rd Apt 27
Hamburg, NY 14075-7800, USA

Fowler, Peggy Y (Business Person)
Portland General Electric
121 SW Salmon St
Portland, OR 97204-2977, USA

Fowler, Ryan (Athlete, Football Player)
1713 Montclair Blvd
Brentwood, TN 37027-8073, USA

Fowler, Todd (Athlete, Football Player)
10024 FM 3053 N
Kilgore, TX 75662-4721, USA

Fowler, Willmer (Athlete, Football Player)
471 Linwood Ave
Buffalo, NY 14209-1630, USA

Fowler Jr, Dante (Athlete, Football Player)
c/o Ben Dogra *Relativity Sports*
2029 Century Park E Ste 1550
Century City, CA 90067-3000, USA

Fowlkes, Alan (Athlete, Baseball Player)
405 Emerald Lake Dr
Lumberton, NC 28358-8022, USA

Fox, Allen (Coach, Tennis Player)
Pepperdine University
Athletic Dept
Malibu, CA 90265, USA

Fox, Andy (Athlete, Baseball Player)
9087 Tarmac Ct
Fair Oaks, CA 95628-8142, USA

Fox, Bernard (Actor)
6601 Burnet Ave
Van Nuys, CA 91405-4515, USA

Fox, Billy (Producer)
c/o Gil Harari *Agency for the Performing Arts (APA)*
405 S Beverly Dr Ste 500
Beverly Hills, CA 90212-4425, USA

Fox, Chad (Athlete, Baseball Player)
7930 Wooded Way Dr
Spring, TX 77389-4161, USA

Fox, Dan (Athlete, Football Player)

Fox, Edward (Actor)
25 Maida Ave
London W2, UNITED KINGDOM (UK)

Fox, Emilia (Actor)
125 Glouster Rd
London SW7 4TE, UNITED KINGDOM

Fox, Eric (Athlete, Baseball Player)
5061 N Spangle Ave
Meridian, ID 83646-5689, USA

Fox, Greg (Athlete, Hockey Player)
635 Glendalough Ct
Alpharetta, GA 30004-3056, USA

Fox, Harold (Athlete, Basketball Player)
6511 Wilburn Dr
Capitol Heights, MD 20743-3351, USA

Fox, Jake (Athlete, Baseball Player)
7028 Bellona Ave
Baltimore, MD 21212-1111, USA

Fox, James (Actor)
International Creative Mgmt
76 Oxford St
London W1N 0AX, UNITED KINGDOM (UK)

Fox, Jason (Athlete, Football Player)
c/o Drew Rosenhaus *Rosenhaus Sports Representation*
3921 Alton Rd # 440
Miami Beach, FL 33140-3852, USA

Fox, Jessica (Actor)
Associated International Management
Nederlander House 7 Great Russell Street
London
WC1B 3NH UK

Fox, Jim (Athlete, Basketball Player)
4136 N 52nd St
Phoenix, AZ 85018-4402, USA

Fox, Jim (Athlete, Hockey Player)
224 S Juanita Ave # A
Redondo Beach, CA 90277-3438, USA

Fox, John (Athlete, Coach, Football Coach, Football Player)
11137 McClure Manor Dr
Charlotte, NC 28277-3027, USA

Fox, Jorja (Actor)
c/o Peg Donegan *Framework Entertainment*
9057 Nemo St # C
W Hollywood, CA 90069-5511, USA

Fox, Matthew (Actor)
c/o Danica Smith *Kovert Creative*
506 Santa Monica Blvd Ste 400
Santa Monica, CA 90401-2412, USA

Fox, Matthew (Athlete, Baseball Player)
8609 Lovett Ave
Orlando, FL 32832-4983, USA

Fox, Megan (Actor)
c/o Lorrie Bartlett *ICM Partners*
10250 Constellation Blvd Fl 7
Los Angeles, CA 90067-6207, USA

Fox, Michael J (Actor)
The Michael J. Fox Foundation For Parkinson's Research
PO Box 4777
Grand Central Station
New York, NY 10163-4777, USA

Fox, Neil (Actor)
c/o Staff Member *MPC Entertainment*
MPC House
15-16 Maple Mews
London NW6 5UZ, UNITED KINGDOM

Fox, Rick (Actor, Athlete, Basketball Player)
c/o Jill Smoller *WME/IMG*
9601 Wilshire Blvd
Beverly Hills, CA 90210-5213, USA

Fox, Samantha (Model, Musician)
c/o JD Sobol *Almond Talent Management*
8217 Beverly Blvd Ste 8
W Hollywood, CA 90048-4534, USA

Fox, Spencer (Actor)
c/o Maggie Schuster *MKSD Talent Management (NY)*
15 W 28th St Fl 9
New York, NY 10001-6430, USA

Fox, Terry (Athlete, Baseball Player)
2312 Sugar Mill Rd
New Iberia, LA 70563-8648, USA

Fox, Tim (Athlete, Football Player)
11 Glover Ave
Hull, MA 02045-1464, USA

Fox, Tim (Athlete, Football Player)
10 Longmeadow Dr
Westwood, MA 02090-1079, USA

Fox, Vernon (Athlete, Football Player)
6704 Willow River Ct
Las Vegas, NV 89108-5033, USA

Fox, Vicente (Politician, President)
Patacio Nacional
Patio de Honor
2 Piso
Mexico City DF 06067, MEXICO

Fox, Vivica A (Actor)
Foxy Brown Productions
PO Box 6305
Woodland Hills, CA 91365-6305, USA

Foxworth, Domonique (Athlete, Football Player)
3533 S Sherwood Rd SE # 5
Smyrna, GA 30082-2833, USA

Foxworth, Robert (Actor)
c/o Chris Schmidt *Paradigm*
8942 Wilshire Blvd
Beverly Hills, CA 90211-1908, USA

Foxworthy, Jeff (Actor, Comedian)
Foxworthy Outdoors
PO Box 505
Hamilton, GA 31811-0505, USA

Foxx, Corinne (Actor, Model)
c/o James Barnett *LBI Entertainment*
2000 Avenue of the Stars
N Tower Fl 3
Los Angeles, CA 90067-4700, USA

Foxx, Dion (Athlete, Football Player)
6457 Springcrest Ln
Henrico, VA 23231-5325, USA

Foxx, Jamie (Actor, Comedian)
c/o Alan Nierob *Rogers & Cowan*
1840 Century Park E Fl 18
Los Angeles, CA 90067-2101, USA

Foxx, Shyla (Adult Film Star)
c/o Staff Member *Atlas Multimedia Inc*
9005 Eton Ave Ste C
Canoga Park, CA 91304-6533, USA

Foxx, Tanya (Adult Film Star)
901 W Victoria St Ste G
Compton, CA 90220-5819, USA

Foxx, Virginia (Congressman, Politician)
1230 Longworth Hob
Washington, DC 20515-0547, USA

Foy, Claire (Actor)
c/o Pippa Beng *Premier PR*
2-4 Bucknall St
London WC2H 8LA, UNITED KINGDOM

Foy, Eddie III (Actor)
3003 W Olive Ave
Burbank, CA 91505-4538, USA

Foy, Mackenzie (Actor)
c/o Scott Wexler *Lighthouse Management and Media*
9000 W Sunset Blvd Ste 1520
Los Angeles, CA 90069-5815, USA

Foyle, Adonal (Athlete, Basketball Player)
174 Crestview Dr
Orinda, CA 94563-3922, USA

Foyt, Larry (Race Car Driver)
AJ Foyt Racing
128 Commercial Dr
Mooresville, TN 28116, USA

Foytack, Paul (Athlete, Baseball Player)
1910 Portview Dr
Spring Hill, TN 37174-8249, USA

Foyt IV, A.J. (Race Car Driver)
Vision Racing
19480 Stokes Rd
Waller, TX 77484-8785, USA

Foyt, Jr., A.J. (Race Car Driver)
19480 Stokes Rd
Waller, TX 77484-8785, USA

Frabotta, Don (Actor)
PO Box 962
Douglas, MA 01516-0962, USA

Fradon, Dana (Cartoonist)
2 Brushy Hill Road
Newtown, CT 06470, USA

Fradon, Ramona (Cartoonist)
Tribune Media Services
435 N Michigan Ave Ste 1500
Chicago, IL 60611-4012, USA

Frailing, Ken (Athlete, Baseball Player)
2150 Shadow Oaks Rd
Sarasota, FL 34240-9324, USA

Frain, James (Actor)
c/o Melanie Greene *Affirmative Entertainment*
6525 W Sunset Blvd # 7
Los Angeles, CA 90028-7212, USA

Fraiture, Nikolai (Musician)
3 Sheridan Sq Apt 9C # 9C
New York, NY 10014-6832, USA

Frakes, Jonathan (Actor, Director)
5315 Oakdale Ave
Woodland Hills, CA 91364-3635, USA

Fralic, William (Bill) (Athlete, Football Player)
280 Galsworthy Ct
Roswell, GA 30075-6354, USA

Frampton, Mia Rose (Actor)
c/o Mona Loring *Status PR*
PO Box 6191
Westlake Village, CA 91359-6191, USA

Frampton, Peter (Musician, Songwriter)
c/o Nicki Loranger *Vector Management*
1100 Glendon Ave Ste 2000
Los Angeles, CA 90024-3524, USA

France, Brian (Race Car Driver)
1151 N Halifax Ave
Daytona Beach, FL 32118-3654, USA

France, Doug (Athlete, Football Player)
6056 Great Falls Ave
Las Vegas, NV 89110-2709, USA

France, Jim (Business Person)
Nascar
PO Box 2875
Daytona Beach, FL 32120, USA

Francella, Meaghan (Athlete, Golfer)
36000 Portofino Cir APT 110
Palm Bch Gdns, FL 33418-1284, USA

Franceschetti, Lou (Athlete, Hockey Player)
72 Orchardcroft Cres
Toronto, ON M3J 1S8, Canada

Franchitti, Dario (Race Car Driver)
Team Green
7615 Zionsville Rd
Indianapolis, IN 46268-2174, USA

Franci, Jason (Athlete, Football Player)
336 Vintage Glen Ct
Santa Rosa, CA 95403-7567, USA

Franciosi, Aisling (Actor)
c/o Emma Jackson *Premier PR*
2-4 Bucknall St
London WC2H 8LA, UNITED KINGDOM

Francis, Betty (Baseball Player)
2602 River Bend Ln
Plainfield, IL 60586-6691, USA

Francis, Black (Musician)
3970 N Shasta Loop
Eugene, OR 97405-4436, USA

Francis, Bob (Athlete, Coach, Hockey Player)
23725 N 75th Pl
Scottsdale, AZ 85258-6128, USA

Francis, Connie (Actor, Musician)
6413 NW 102nd Ter
Parkland, FL 33076-2357, USA

Francis, Dillon (Musician)
c/o Staff Member *Paradigm (Chicago)*
2209 W North Ave
Chicago, IL 60647-6084, USA

Francis, Emile (Athlete, Hockey Player)
7220 Crystal Lake Dr
West Palm Beach, FL 33411-5713, USA

Francis, Emile P (Coach)
7220 Crystal Lake Dr
West Palm Beach, FL 33411-5713, USA

Francis, Fred (Correspondent)
NBC-TV
4001 Nebraska Ave NW
News Dept
Washington, DC 20016-2795, USA

Francis, Genie (Actor)
5315 Oakdale Ave
Woodland Hills, CA 91364-3635, USA

Francis, Harrison (Athlete, Football Player)
207 S Susan Ave
Wagoner, OK 74467-4843, USA

Francis, James (Athlete, Football Player)
1201 E Old Settlers Blvd Apt 1201
Round Rock, TX 78664-2413, USA

Francis, Jeff (Athlete, Baseball Player)
600 California St FL 18
San Francisco, CA 94108-2711, USA

Francis, Joe (Athlete, Football Player)
45-570 Kaaluna Pl
Kaneohe, HI 96744-3410, USA

Francis, Joe (Producer)
c/o Staff Member *Mantra Films*
PO Box 150
Hollywood, CA 90078-0150, USA

Francis, Paul (Actor)
c/o Staff Member *Gilbertson Management*
1334 3rd Street Promenade Ste 201
Santa Monica, CA 90401-1320, USA

Francis, Pope (Religious Leader)
Palazzo Apostolico Vaticano
Vatican City 00120, ITALY

Francis, Ron (Athlete, Football Player)
3315 Ashton Park Dr
Houston, TX 77082-5307, USA

Francis, Ron (Athlete, Hockey Player)
12312 Birchfalls Dr
Raleigh, NC 27614-7900, USA

Francis, Russ (Athlete, Football Player)
800 Putney Rd
Brattleboro, VT 05301-9058, USA

Francis, Steve (Athlete, Basketball Player)
632 Pifer Rd
Houston, TX 77024-5434, USA

Francis, Wallace (Athlete, Football Player)
2452 Wilshire Way
Douglasville, GA 30135-8129, USA

Francis, Wally (Athlete, Football Player)
1307 Walton Ln SE
Smyrna, GA 30082-3875, USA

Francis, William (Bill) (Musician)
Artists International
9850 Sandalwood Blvd
#458
Boca Raton, FL 33428, USA

Francisco, Aaron (Athlete, Football Player)
2849 E Citadel Ct
Gilbert, AZ 85298-5726, USA

Francisco, Ben (Athlete, Baseball Player)
689 S Scout Trl
Anaheim, CA 92807-4757, us

Francisco, Don (Television Host)
c/o Staff Member *Univision*
605 3rd Ave Fl 12
New York, NY 10158-0034, USA

Francisco, Pablo (Comedian)
c/o Debbie Keller *Personal Publicity*
12831 S 71st St
Tempe, AZ 85284-3103, USA

Franckowiak, Mike (Athlete, Football Player)
73 Fitch Way
Princeton, NJ 08540-7609, USA

Francks, Rainbow Sun (Actor)
c/o Staff Member *Sci-FI Channel, The*
100 Universal Plaza
Bldg 1280/12
Universal City, CA 91608, USA

Franco, Brian (Athlete, Football Player)
155 Oceanwalk Dr S
Atlantic Beach, FL 32233-4679

Franco, Carlos (Athlete, Golfer)
10561 NW 51st St
Doral, FL 33178-3209, USA

Franco, Dave (Actor)
c/o Evelyn Karamanos *Relevant*
400 S Beverly Dr Ste 220
Beverly Hills, CA 90212-4404, USA

Franco, James (Actor, Director, Writer)
c/o Staff Member *Elysium Bandini Studios*
3278 Wilshire Blvd
Los Angeles, CA 90010-1402, USA

Franco, John (Athlete, Baseball Player)
111 Cliffwood Ave
Staten Island, NY 10304, USA

Franco, Julio (Athlete, Baseball Player)
651 NE 23rd Ct
Pompano Beach, FL 33064-5504, USA

Franco, Liliana (Actor)
c/o Staff Member *Eileen O'farrell Personal Management*
11653 Blix St Apt 5
Studio City, CA 91602-1051, United States

Franco, Matt (Athlete, Baseball Player)
4271 Flintlock Ln
Westlake Village, CA 91361-4604, USA

Franco, Samuel (Writer)
c/o Parker Davis *Verve Talent & Literary Agency*
6310 San Vicente Blvd Ste 100
Los Angeles, CA 90048-5498, USA

Francoeur, Jeff (Athlete, Baseball Player)
3111 Willowstone Dr
Duluth, GA 30096-4023, USA

Francona, Terry (Athlete, Baseball Player, Coach)
750 Newton St
Chestnut Hill, MA 02467-2606, USA

Frandsen, Kevin (Athlete, Baseball Player)
1044 Camino Ricardo
San Jose, CA 95125-4305, USA

Frangoulis, Mario (Musician)
c/o Staff Member *Sony/BMG Music (NY)*
550 Madison Ave
New York, NY 10022-3211, USA

Frank, Barney (Politician)
Congressman Barney Frank
2252 Rayburn Hob
Washington, DC 20515-2104, USA

Frank, Charles (Actor)
S D B Partners
1801 Ave of Stars
#902
Los Angeles, CA 90067, USA

Frank, Darryl (Producer)
c/o Staff Member *Dreamworks Television*
100 Universal Plaza Bldg 5125
Universal City, CA 91608, USA

Frank, Diana (Actor)
The Agency
1800 Avenue of the Stars Ste 400
Los Angeles, CA 90067-4206, USA

Frank, Donald (Athlete, Football Player)
2039 Weston Green Loop
Cary, NC 27513-2268, USA

Frank, Gary (Actor)
1401 S Bentley Ave Apt 202
Los Angeles, CA 90025-8031, USA

Frank, Howard (Business Person)
Carnival Corp
3655 NW 87th Ave
Doral, FL 33178-2428, USA

Frank, Jason David (Actor, Comedian)
Richard Stone
2 Henrietta St
London WC2E 8PS, UNITED KINGDOM (UK)

Frank, Joanna (Actor)
1274 Capri Dr
Pacific Palisades, CA 90272-4001, USA

Frank, John (Athlete, Football Player)
Medical Hair Restoration
200 W End Ave Apt 17E
New York, NY 10023-4856, USA

Frank, Larry (Race Car Driver)
Larry Frank Auto Body Works
832 Fork Shoals Rd
Greenville, SC 29605-5832, USA

Frank, Mike (Athlete, Baseball Player)
1740 Seven Oakes Rd # 108
Escondido, CA 92026-3308, USA

Frank, Phil (Cartoonist)
500 Turney St
Sausalito, CA 94965-1840, USA

Frank, Scott (Actor, Director, Writer)
c/o Staff Member *Arroyo Films*
302 W 12th St Apt 15G
New York, NY 10014-6034, USA

Frank, Tellis (Athlete, Basketball Player)
4936 Van Noord Ave
Sherman Oaks, CA 91423-2214, USA

Frank-Dummerth, Edna (Baseball Player)
5044 Tealby Ln
Saint Louis, MO 63128-2952, USA

Franke, Robert (Writer)
c/o Allen Fischer *Artists First*
9465 Wilshire Blvd Ste 900
Beverly Hills, CA 90212-2608, USA

Frankel, Bethenny (Business Person, Chef, Reality Star, Talk Show Host)
c/o Jill Fritzo *Jill Fritzo Public Relations*
208 E 51st St # 305
New York, NY 10022-6557, USA

Frankel, David (Director)
c/o Rosalie Swedlin *Anonymous Content*
3532 Hayden Ave
Culver City, CA 90232-2413, USA

Frankel, Felice (Artist, Photographer)
Massachusetts Institute of Technology
Edgerton Center
Cambridge, MA 02139, USA

Frankel, Max (Journalist)
229 W 43rd St Attn Dept
New York, NY 10036-3982, USA

Franken, Al (Actor, Comedian, Senator)
US Senate
Hart Office Bldg
Washington, DC 20510-0001, USA

Frankl, Peter (Musician)
5 Gresham Gardens
London NW11 8NX, UNITED KINGDOM (UK)

Frankl, Viktor (Writer)
Mariannengasse 1
Vienna A-1090, Austria

Franklin, Anthony R (Tony) (Athlete, Football Player)
117 Shady Trail St
San Antonio, TX 78232-1313, USA

Franklin, Arnold (Athlete, Football Player)
131 Ruskin Dr
Cincinnati, OH 45246-2418, USA

Franklin, Aubrayo (Athlete, Football Player)
1 Castleton Ct
Johnson City, TN 37615-4949, USA

Franklin, Bobby (Athlete, Football Player)
114 Claire Cv
Senatobia, MS 38668-4084, USA

Franklin, Byron (Athlete, Football Player)
2613 Singapore Dr
Birmingham, AL 35211-6924, USA

Franklin, Carl (Actor, Director, Writer)
c/o Alex Goldstone *Anonymous Content*
3532 Hayden Ave
Culver City, CA 90232-2413, USA

Franklin, Cleveland (Athlete, Football Player)
60 Hillary Cir
New Castle, DE 19720-8620, USA

Franklin, Dennis (Athlete, Football Player)
15474 Edmore Dr
Detroit, MI 48205-1351, USA

Franklin, DeVon (Producer)
c/o Cassandra Vargas *PMK/BNC Public Relations*
1840 Century Park E Ste 1400
Los Angeles, CA 90067-2115, USA

Franklin, Diane (Actor)
Third Hill Entertainment
195 S Beverly Dr Ste 400
Beverly Hills, CA 90212-3044, USA

Franklin, Don (Actor)
Paradigm Agency
10100 Santa Monica Blvd Ste 2500
Los Angeles, CA 90067-4116, USA

Franklin, Farrah (Musician)
8391 Beverly Blvd
Los Angeles, CA 90048-2633, USA

Franklin, George (Athlete, Football Player)
6727 Feather Creek Dr
Houston, TX 77086-2005, USA

Franklin, Howard (Director, Writer)
c/o Staff Member *Agency for the Performing Arts (APA)*
405 S Beverly Dr Ste 500
Beverly Hills, CA 90212-4425, USA

Franklin, Jay (Baseball Player)
San Diego Padres
2450 Massanutten Ter
Winchester, VA 22601-2774, USA

Franklin, Jerrell (Athlete, Football Player)
2512 Nettleton St
Houston, TX 77004-2042, USA

Franklin, Jethro (Athlete, Football Player)
4806 Keneshaw St
Sugar Land, TX 77479-3984, USA

Franklin, John (Actor)
Gilla Roos
9744 Wilshire Blvd Ste 203
Beverly Hills, CA 90212-1812, USA

Franklin, Jon D (Journalist)
9650 Strickland Rd
Raleigh, NC 27615-1902, USA

Franklin, Kirk (Musician)
PO Box 8169
Inglewood, CA 90308, USA

Franklin, Larry (Athlete, Football Player)
9390 Afton Grove Rd
Cordova, TN 38018-7519, USA

Franklin, Micah (Athlete, Baseball Player)
3948 E Lafayette Ave
Gilbert, AZ 85298-9139, USA

Franklin, Missy (Athlete, Olympic Athlete, Swimmer)
Colorado Stars Swim Club
6400 S Lewiston Way
Aurora, CO 80016-3000, USA

Franklin, Orlando (Athlete, Football Player)
c/o Drew Rosenhaus *Rosenhaus Sports Representation*
3921 Alton Rd # 440
Miami Beach, FL 33140-3852, USA

Franklin, P J (Athlete, Football Player)
903 S Laurel St
Amite, LA 70422-3525, USA

Franklin, Robert (Business Person)
Placer Dome Inc
1600-1055 Dunsmuir St
Vancouver, BC V7X 1P1, CANADA

Franklin, Roshawn (Actor)
c/o Staff Member *Freeze Frame Entertainment*
5225 Wilshire Blvd Ste 303
Los Angeles, CA 90036-4347, USA

Franklin, Ryan (Athlete, Baseball Player, Olympic Athlete)
1009 Muirfield Dr
Shawnee, OK 74801-0515, USA

Franklin, Shirley (Politician)
Mayor's Office
55 Trinity Ave SW Ste 1600
City Hall
Atlanta, GA 30303-3534, USA

Franklin, Wayne (Athlete, Baseball Player)
15 S Mauldin Ave
North East, MD 21901-4023, USA

Franklin, Willie (Athlete, Football Player)
PO Box 62
Lake Dallas, TX 75065-0062, USA

Franklyn, Sabina (Actor)
CCA Mgmt
4 Court Lodge
48 Sloane Square
London SW1W 8AT, UNITED KINGDOM (UK)

Franks, Daniel (Bubba) (Athlete, Football Player)
1 Cavil Way
De Pere, WI 54115, USA

Franks, Dennis (Athlete, Football Player)
18601 Peninsula Club Dr
Cornelius, NC 28031-5113, USA

Franks, Dominique (Athlete, Football Player)

Franks, Elvis (Athlete, Football Player)
2147 Rusk St
Beaumont, TX 77701-2525, USA

Franks, Hermine (Baseball Player)
422 Pecor St
Oconto, WI 54153-1800, USA

Franks, Michael (Musician, Songwriter, Writer)
c/o Staff Member *Agency for the Performing Arts (APA)*
405 S Beverly Dr Ste 500
Beverly Hills, CA 90212-4425, USA

Franks, Ray (Race Car Driver)
PO Box 151
New Carlisle, OH 45344-0151, USA

Franks, Trent (Congressman, Politician)
2435 Rayburn Hob
Washington, DC 20515-4318, USA

Frankston, Robert M (Bob) (Designer)
State Corp
15035 N 73rd St
Scottsdale, AZ 85260-2468, USA

Fransioli, Thomas A (Artist)
55 Dodges Row
Wenham, MA 01984-1627, USA

Franta, Connor (Internet Star)
c/o Chelsea Brandon *Core Public PR*
1875 Century Park E Ste 930
Los Angeles, CA 90067-2540, USA

Franti, Michael (Actor, Musician)
c/o Bernie Cahill *Activist Artists Management (LA)*
8500 Melrose Ave # 200
W Hollywood, CA 90069-5145, USA

Frantz, Adrienne (Actor)
c/o Marnie Sparer *Power Entertainment Group*
1505 10th St
Santa Monica, CA 90401-2805, USA

Frantz, Chris (Musician)
Premier Talent
3 E 54th St # 1100
New York, NY 10022-3108, USA

Franz, Arthur (Art) (Athlete, Baseball Player)
PO Box 974
El Prado, NM 87529-0974, USA

Franz, Dennis (Actor)
PO Box 5370
Santa Barbara, CA 93150-5370, USA

Franz, Frederick W (Religious Leader)
Jehovah's Witnesses
900 Red Mills Rd
Wallkill, NY 12589-5200, USA

Franz, Nolan (Athlete, Football Player)
327 31st St
Gulfport, MS 39507-2341, USA

Franz, Rodney T (Rod) (Athlete, Football Player)
1448 Engberg Ct
Carmichael, CA 95608-5812, USA

Franz, Ron (Athlete, Basketball Player)
2 Garniers Post Rd
Fort Walton Beach, FL 32547-1828, USA

Franz, Todd (Athlete, Football Player)
5629 N Classen Blvd
Oklahoma City, OK 73118-4015, USA

Franzen, Johan (Athlete, Hockey Player)
22726 Summer Ln
Novi, MI 48374-3648, USA

Franzen, Jonathan (Writer)
c/o Susan Galomb *Writers House*
21 W 26th St
New York, NY 10010-1083, USA

Frappi, Luigi (Artist)
Via Del Cirone, 6
Bevagna I-06031, Italy

Frascatore, John (Athlete, Baseball Player)
3121 Saturn Rd
Brooksville, FL 34604-7032, USA

Frase, Paul (Athlete, Football Player)
124 Crossroad Lakes Dr
Ponte Vedra Beach, FL 32082-4031, USA

Fraser, Antonia (Writer)
Curtis Brown
Haymarket House
28/29 Haymarket
London SW1Y 4SP, UNITED KINGDOM (UK)

Fraser, Brad (Writer)
Great North Artists Mgmt
350 Dupont St
Toronto, ON M5R 1V9, CANADA

Fraser, Brendan (Actor)
c/o JoAnne Colonna *Brillstein Entertainment Partners*
9150 Wilshire Blvd Ste 350
Beverly Hills, CA 90212-3453, USA

Fraser, Brooke (Musician)
c/o Jonathan Adelman *Paradigm*
140 Broadway Ste 2600
New York, NY 10005-1011, USA

Fraser, Curt (Athlete, Hockey Player)
Grand Rapids Griffins 130 Fulton St W Ste 111
Grand Rapids, ML 49503-2601, USA

Fraser, Dawn (Athlete, Swimmer)
87 Birchgrove Road
Balmain NSW, Australia

Fraser, George MacDonald (Writer)
Curtis Brown
28/29 Haymarket
London SW1Y 4SP, UNITED KINGDOM (UK)

Fraser, Hugh (Actor)
Jonathan Altaras
13 Shorts Gardens
London WC2H 9AT, UNITED KINGDOM (UK)

Fraser, Laura (Actor)
c/o Tammy Rosen *Sanders Armstrong Caserta*
4111 W Alameda Ave Ste 505
Burbank, CA 91505-4163, USA

Fraser, Mat (Actor)
c/o Michele Milburn *Milburn Browning Associates*
91, Brick Lane
The Old Truman Brewery
London E1 6QL, UNITED KINGDOM

Fraser, Neale (Tennis Player)
21 Bolton Ave
Hampton, VIC 03188, AUSTRALIA

Fraser, Ware Dawn (Swimmer)
403 Darling St
Balmain, NSW 02041, AUSTRALIA

Fraser, Willie (Athlete, Baseball Player)
3 Turano
Laguna Niguel, CA 92677-8927, USA

Frashilla, Fran (Coach)
New Mexico University
Athletic Dept
Albuquerque, NM 87131-0001, USA

Frasor, Jason (Athlete, Baseball Player)
12611 SE Old Cypress Dr
Hobe Sound, FL 33455-7923, USA

Fratello, Michael R (Mike) (Athlete, Basketball Player, Coach, Sportscaster)
7642 Fisher Island Dr
Miami Beach, FL 33109-0783, USA

Fratianne, Linda S (Athlete, Figure Skater, Olympic Athlete)
14411 Starr Rd SE
Olalla, WA 98359-8597, USA

Frattare, Lanny (Commentator)
Pittsburgh Pirates
3006 Shoreline Ln
Mc Donald, PA 15057-3062, USA

Frauenfelder, Mark (Internet Star)
Boing Boing
13547 Ventura Blvd # 91
Sherman Oaks, CA 91423-3825, USA

Frayn, Michael (Writer)
Greene & Heaton
37A Goldhawk Road
London W12 8QQ, UNITED KINGDOM (UK)

Frazar, Harrison (Athlete, Golfer)
3208 Villanova St
Dallas, TX 75225-4839, USA

Frazer, Liz (Actor)
Peter Charlesworth
68 Old Brompton Road
#200
London SW7 3LQ, UNITED KINGDOM (UK)

Frazier, Al (Athlete, Football Player)
17240 133rd Ave Apt 12A
Jamaica, NY 11434-3965, USA

Frazier, Albert (Baseball Player)
Jacksonville Red Caps
5749 Copper Hill Ln E
Jacksonville, FL 32218-7311, USA

Frazier, Andre (Athlete, Football Player)
9650 Fallshill Cir
Cincinnati, OH 45231-2886, USA

Frazier, Charles (Writer)
c/o Staff Member *Curtis Brown Ltd*
28-29 Hay Market
Hay Market House
London SW1Y 4SP, UNITED KINGDOM

Frazier, Charley (Athlete, Football Player)
4018 Brookston St
Houston, TX 77045-3412, USA

Frazier, Dallas (Musician, Songwriter, Writer)
RR 5 Box 133
Longhollow Pike
Gallatin, TN 37066, USA

Frazier, George (Athlete, Baseball Player)
6886 S Evanston Ave
Tulsa, OK 74136-4554, USA

Frazier, Guy (Athlete, Football Player)
3944 Dickson Ave
Cincinnati, OH 45229-1306, USA

Frazier, Herman (Athlete, Olympic Athlete, Track Athlete)
1777 Ala Moana Blvd
Honolulu, HI 96815-1603, USA

Frazier, Ian (Writer)
Farrar Straus Giroux
19 Union Sq W
New York, NY 10003-3304, USA

Frazier, Kevin (Actor, Television Host)
c/o Nick Khan *Creative Artists Agency (CAA)*
2000 Avenue of the Stars Ste 100
Los Angeles, CA 90067-4705, USA

Frazier, Leslie (Athlete, Football Player)
867 Normandy Trace Rd
Tampa, FL 33602-5763, USA

Frazier, Lisa (Musician)
c/o Staff Member *Diva Central Inc*
7510 W Sunset Blvd # 1445
Los Angeles, CA 90046-3408, USA

Frazier, Lou (Athlete, Baseball Player)
1371 N Concord Ave
Chandler, AZ 85225-8624, USA

Frazier, Mavis (Boxer)
2917 N Broad St
Philadelphia, PA 19132-2402, USA

Frazier, Owsley B (Business Person)
Brown-Forman Corp
850 Dixie Hwy
Louisville, KY 40210-1038, USA

Frazier, Sheila (Actor)
c/o Daniel Hoff *Daniel Hoff Agency*
5455 Wilshire Blvd Ste 1100
Los Angeles, CA 90036-4277, USA

Frazier, Todd (Athlete, Baseball Player)
c/o Staff Member *New York Mets*
123-01 Roosevelt Avenue
Shea Stadium
Flushing, NY 11368-1699, USA

Frazier, Walt (Athlete, Basketball Player)
381 Malcolm X Blvd Ph C
New York, NY 10027-2174, USA

Frazier, Will (Athlete, Basketball Player)
PO Box 380772
Duncanville, TX 75138-0772, USA

Frazier, Willie (Athlete, Football Player)
6203 Bankside Dr
Houston, TX 77096-5608, USA

Frears, Stephen A (Actor, Director, Producer)
93 Talbot Road
London W2, UNITED KINGDOM (UK)

Frechette, Peter (Actor)
c/o Staff Member *Buchwald*
5900 Wilshire Blvd Ste 3100
Los Angeles, CA 90036-5030, USA

Frecheville, James (Actor)
c/o Kenny Goodman *Goodmanagement*
9220 W Sunset Blvd Ste 106
W Hollywood, CA 90069-3500, USA

Freddie, Douglas (Athlete, Football Player)
24 Pheasant Run Dr
Cabot, AR 72023-3608, USA

Frederic, Dreux (Lil Fizz) (Musician)
c/o Douglas Mark *Mark Music and Media Law*
Prefers to be contacted via telephone
Los Angeles, CA 90069, USA

Frederick, Andrew B (Athlete, Football Player)
7247 Alexander Dr
Dallas, TX 75214-3216, USA

Frederick, Kevin (Athlete, Baseball Player)
20512 N Clarice Ave
Lincolnshire, IL 60069-9618, USA

Frederick, Mike (Athlete, Football Player)
425 Fairmont Dr
Chester Springs, PA 19425-3657, USA

Fredericks, Frank (Frankie) (Athlete, Track Athlete)
4497 Wimbledon Dr
Provo, UT 84604-5394, USA

Fredericks, Fred (Cartoonist)
PO Box 475
Eastham, MA 02642-0475, USA

Frederickson, Ivan C (Tucker) (Athlete, Football Player)
17277 SE Galway Ct
Jupiter, FL 33469-1703, USA

Frederickson, Rob (Athlete, Football Player)
5942 E Caballo Ln
Paradise Valley, AZ 85253-2216, USA

Frederickson, Scott (Athlete, Baseball Player)
20703 Turning Leaf Lake Ct
Cypress, TX 77433-4612, USA

Fredette, Jimmer (Athlete, Basketball Player)
26 Ogden St
Glens Falls, NY 12801-2215, USA

Fredrickson, Rob (Athlete, Football Player)
8312 N 50th St
Paradise Valley, AZ 85253-2005, USA

Fredrickson, Scott (Athlete, Baseball Player)
20703 Turning Leaf Lake Ct
Cypress, TX 77433-4612, USA

Fredriksson, Gert (Athlete)
Bruunsgat 13
Nykoping 61122, SWEDEN

Fredriksson, Marie (Musician, Songwriter, Writer)
D &D Mgmt
Lilla Nygatan 19
Stockholm 11128, SWEDEN

Free (Actor, Musician)
c/o Damu Bobb *Identity Talent Agency (ID)*
9107 Wilshire Blvd Ste 500
Beverly Hills, CA 90210-5526, USA

Free, Doug (Athlete, Football Player)
c/o Jimmy Sexton *CAA (Memphis)*
6060 Poplar Ave Ste 470
Memphis, TN 38119-0910, USA

Free, World B (Athlete, Basketball Player, Coach)
PO Box 741
Sicklerville, NJ 08081-0741, USA

Freed, Andy (Commentator)
13140 Peregrin Cir
Bradenton, FL 34212-2928, USA

Freedman, Alix M (Journalist)
Wall Street Journal
200 Liberty St
Editorial Dept
New York, NY 10281-1003, USA

Freeh, Louis (Misc)
Freeh Group International Solutions, LLC
3711 Kennett Pike Ste 130
Wilmington, DE 19807-2156, USA

Freehan, Bill (Athlete, Baseball Player)
6999 Indian Garden Rd
Petoskey, MI 49770-8708, USA

Freelon, Nnenna (Musician)
Ted Kurland
173 Brighton Ave
Boston, MA 02134-2003, USA

Freelon, Solomon (Athlete, Football Player)
2021 Burg Jones Ln
Monroe, LA 71202-4406, USA

Freeman, Antonio (Athlete, Football Player)
11201 NW 18th St
Plantation, FL 33323-2226, USA

Freeman, Arturo (Athlete, Football Player)
14420 Stirling Rd
Southwest Ranches, FL 33330-2908, USA

Freeman, Bernard (Bun B) (Musician)
c/o Marty Diamond *Paradigm*
140 Broadway Ste 2600
New York, NY 10005-1011, USA

Freeman, Cassidy (Actor)
c/o James Weir *Anderson Group Public Relations*
8060 Melrose Ave Fl 4
Los Angeles, CA 90046-7038, USA

Freeman, Cathy (Athlete, Track Athlete)
PO Box 700
South Melbourne, VIC 03205, AUSTRALIA

Freeman, Crispin (Actor, Writer)
c/o Staff Member *Arlene Thornton & Associates*
12711 Ventura Blvd Ste 490
Studio City, CA 91604-2477, USA

Freeman, Dalton (Athlete, Football Player)
c/o Anthony J. Agnone *Eastern Athletic Services*
11350 McCormick Rd
Suite 800 - Executive Plaza
Hunt Valley, MD 21031-1002, USA

Freeman, Devonta (Athlete, Football Player)
c/o Tony Fleming *Impact Sports (LA)*
12429 Ventura Ct
Studio City, CA 91604-2417, USA

Freeman, Freddie (Athlete, Baseball Player)
c/o Casey Close *Excel Sports Management*
1700 Broadway Fl 29
New York, NY 10019-6559, USA

Freeman, Gary (Athlete, Basketball Player)
PO Box 1399
Albany, OR 97321-0548, USA

Freeman, Gregory A (Writer)
4880 Lower Roswell Rd Ste 165210
Marietta, GA 30068-4375, USA

Freeman, Isaac (Musician)
Keith Case Assoc
1025 17th Ave S Fl 2
Nashville, TN 37212-2211, USA

Freeman, Issac (Fatman Scoop) (Musician)
c/o Staff Member *PhreQuency Entertainment*
1830 South Rd Ste 24 # 178
Wappingers Falls, NY 12590-1372, USA

Freeman, J E (Actor)
Gersh Agency
232 N Canon Dr
Beverly Hills, CA 90210-5302, USA

Freeman, Jennifer (Actor)
c/o Nils Larsen *Management 360*
9111 Wilshire Blvd
Beverly Hills, CA 90210-5508, USA

Freeman, Jimmy (Athlete, Baseball Player)
4716 E 106th St
Tulsa, OK 74137-6805, USA

Freeman, K Todd (Actor)
c/o Staff Member *D2 Management*
10351 Santa Monica Blvd Ste 210
Los Angeles, CA 90025-6937, USA

Freeman, La Vel (Athlete, Baseball Player)
8941 Laguna Place Way
Elk Grove, CA 95758-5351, USA

Freeman, Martin (Actor)
c/o Laura Colman *Premier PR*
2-4 Bucknall St
London WC2H 8LA, UNITED KINGDOM

Freeman, Marvin (Athlete, Baseball Player)
2494 Sinclair Trce
Powder Springs, GA 30127-5098, USA

Freeman, Michael William (Actor)
c/o Scott Zimmerman *Scott Zimmerman Management*
901 N Highland Ave
Los Angeles, CA 90038-2412, USA

Freeman, Mike (Athlete, Football Player)
6020 Danny Kaye Dr Apt 1502
San Antonio, TX 78240-1946, USA

Freeman, Morgan (Actor)
c/o Staff Member *Revelations Entertainment*
1990 S Bundy Dr Ste 850
Los Angeles, CA 90025-5253, USA

Freeman, Phil (Athlete, Football Player)
1222 S Stanley Ave
Los Angeles, CA 90019-6617, USA

Freeman, Reggie (Athlete, Football Player)
285 Berenger Walk
Royal Palm Beach, FL 33414-4347, USA

Freeman, Robin (Athlete, Golfer)
115 Chelsea Cir
Palm Desert, CA 92260-4688, USA

Freeman, Rod (Athlete, Basketball Player)
6308 Murray Ln
Brentwood, TN 37027-6210, USA

Freeman, Royce (Athlete, Football Player)
c/o Joel Segal *Lagardere Unlimited (NY)*
456 Washington St Apt 9L
New York, NY 10013-1555, USA

Freeman, Russ (Athlete, Football Player)
4090 Summit Crossing Dr
Decatur, GA 30034-3542, USA

Freeman, Russell (Football Coach, Football Player)
4090 Summit Crossing Dr
Decatur, GA 30034-3542, USA

Freeman, Sandi (Correspondent)
Cable News Network
820 1st St NE Ste 1000
News Dept
Washington, DC 20002-4363, USA

Freeman, Steve (Athlete, Football Player)
Mississippi State University
PO Box 5308
Attn: Alumni Association
Mississippi State, MS 39762-5308, USA

Freeman, Yvette (Actor, Musician)
Stone Manners
6500 Wilshire Blvd # 550
Los Angeles, CA 90048-4920, USA

Freeney, Dwight (Athlete, Football Player)
11021 Hintocks Cir
Carmel, IN 46032, USA

Freeny, Jonathan (Athlete, Football Player)

Freer, Mark (Athlete, Hockey Player)
218 Maple Ave
Hershey, PA 17033-1548, USA

Freese, David (Athlete, Baseball Player)
16559 Thunderhead Canyon Ct
Wildwood, MO 63011-1853, USA

Freese, Gene (Athlete, Baseball Player)
6504 Glendale St
Metairie, LA 70003-3011, USA

Freese, Louis (Musician)
c/o Jack Iannaci *Brass Artists & Associates*
4749 Bandini Ave
Riverside, CA 92506-1004, USA

Fregoso, Ramon (Actor)
c/o Staff Member *TV Azteca*
Periferico Sur 4121
Colonia Fuentes del Pedregal
DF CP 14141, Mexico

Frehley, Ace (Musician)
1347/1357/1363 Spring Valley Rd
Ossining, NY 10562, USA

Freidheim, Cyrus (Business Person)
Chiquita Brands International
250 E 5th St
Cincinnati, OH 45202-4119, USA

Freilicher, Jane (Artist)
Fishbach Gallery
20 Island Ave Apt 1104
Miami Beach, FL 33139-1311, USA

Freire, Nelson (Musician)
Columbia Artists Mgmt Inc
165 W 57th St
New York, NY 10019-2201, USA

Frei Ruiz-Tagle, Eduardo (President)
President's Office
Palacio de la Monedo
Santiago, CHILE

Freisleben, Dave (Athlete, Baseball Player)
53 Monterrey Rd W
Montgomery, TX 77356-8182, USA

Freitas, Jesse (Athlete, Football Player)
8405 Florissant Ct
San Diego, CA 92129-4408, USA

Freitas, Rocky (Athlete, Football Player)
2667 E Manoa Rd
Honolulu, HI 96822-1817, USA

French, Dawn (Actor, Comedian)
P F D Drury House
34-43 Russell St
London WC2B 5HA, UNITED KINGDOM (UK)

French, Ernest (Athlete, Football Player)
1004 Moran St
Bay Minette, AL 36507-2443, USA

French, Heather (Beauty Pageant Winner)
1361 Tyler Park Dr
Louisville, KY 40204-1539, USA

French, Jane (Musician)
c/o Staff Member *Pixie Publishing*
9611 Ross Ave
Montgomery, OH 45242-7123

French, Jim (Athlete, Baseball Player)
PO Box 39
49594 KE RD
Mesa, CO 81643-0039, USA

French, John (Athlete, Hockey Player)
142 Woodbury Cres
Newmarket, ON L3X 2S5, Canada

French, Kate (Actor)
c/o Brooklyn Weaver *Energy Entertainment*
6121 W Sunset Blvd Lbby
Los Angeles, CA 90028-6450, USA

French, Leigh (Actor)
1850 N Vista St
Los Angeles, CA 90046-2237, USA

French, Luke (Athlete, Baseball Player)
14070 Sierra Ridge Cir
Parker, CO 80134-9508, USA

French, Marilyn (Writer)
Charlotte Sheedy Agency
65 Bleecker St # 1200
New York, NY 10012-2420, USA

French, Niki (Musician)
Mega Artists Mgmt
PO Box 89
Edam, ZJ 01135, NETHERLANDS

French, Paige (Actor)
Gersh Agency
232 N Canon Dr
Beverly Hills, CA 90210-5302, USA

French, Rufus (Athlete, Football Player)
PO Box 10628
Green Bay, WI 54307-0628, USA

French, Sarah (Model, Television Host)
221 Trumbull St
Hartford, CT 06103-1500, USA

Frentzen, Heinz-Harald (Race Car Driver)
Formula One Ltd
Silverstone Circuit
Northamptonshire NN12 8TN, UNITED KINGDOM (UK)

Freon, Franck (Race Car Driver)
434 E .Ma i n St.
Brownsburg, IN 46112, USA

Freotte, Gus (Athlete, Football Player)
10040 Litzsinger Rd
Saint Louis, MO 63124-1132, USA

Freotte, Mitch (Athlete, Football Player)
445 Reynolds Ave
Kittanning, PA 16201-2713, USA

Frerotte, Gus (Athlete, Football Player)
10040 Litzsinger Rd
Saint Louis, MO 63124-1132, USA

Fresco, Paolo (Business Person)
Fiat SpA
Corso Marconi 10/20
New York, NY 10125-0001, ITALY

Fresh, Doug E (Musician)
c/o Drew Elliot *Artist International*
333 E 43rd St Apt 115
New York, NY 10017-4822, USA

Fresh, Mannie (Musician, Producer)
c/o Staff Member *Universal Music Group*
100 Universal City Plz
Universal City, CA 91608-1002, USA

Freston, Kathy (Writer)
c/o Staff Member *St Martins Press*
175 5th Ave
Publicity Dept
New York, NY 10010-7703, USA

Freud, Bella (Designer, Fashion Designer)
48 Rawstorne St
London EC1V 7ND, UNITED KINGDOM (UK)

Freudenthal, David (Politician)
10020 Yellowstone Rd
Cheyenne, WY 82009-8943, USA

Freudenthal, Thor (Director)
c/o Peter McHugh *Gotham Group*
1041 N Formosa Ave # 200
West Hollywood, CA 90046-6703, USA

Freundlich, Bart (Director, Producer, Writer)
c/o Bart Walker *ICM Partners*
10250 Constellation Blvd Fl 7
Los Angeles, CA 90067-6207, USA

Frewer, Matt (Actor)
c/o Gordon Gilbertson *Gilbertson Management*
1334 3rd Street Promenade Ste 201
Santa Monica, CA 90401-1320, USA

Frey, Bob (Race Car Driver)
605 Harvest Ln
Waterford Works, NJ 08089-2117, USA

Frey, CeCe (Musician)
c/o Mike Esterman *Esterman.Com, LLC*
Prefers to be contacted via email
Baltimore, MD XXXXX, USA

Frey, Isaiah (Athlete, Football Player)
c/o Brian E. Overstreet *E.O. Sports Management*
1314 Texas St Ste 1212
Houston, TX 77002-3525, USA

Frey, James (Writer)
c/o Alicia Gordon *WME/IMG*
9601 Wilshire Blvd
Beverly Hills, CA 90210-5213, USA

Frey, Jim (Commentator)
247 Marsh Hollow Rd
Ponte Vedra, FL 32081-4343, USA

Frey, Richard (Athlete, Football Player)
PO Box 1967
Tomball, TX 77377-1967, USA

Frey, Sami (Actor)
21 Place des Vosges
Paris F-75003, FRANCE

Frey, Steve (Athlete, Baseball Player)
1414 2nd Street Pike
Southampton, PA 18966-3931, USA

Freyndlikh, Alisa B (Actor)
Rubinstein Str 11
#7
Saint Petersburg 191002, RUSSIA

Frezza, Alberto (Actor)
c/o Abby Bluestone *Innovative Artists*
1505 10th St
Santa Monica, CA 90401-2805, USA

Friberg, Arnold (Artist)
Friberg Fine Arts
5206 S Pinemont Dr
Salt Lake City, UT 84123-4607, USA

Frick, Stephen (Astronaut)
27998 Mercurio Rd
Carmel, CA 93923-8429, USA

Fricke, Janie (Musician)
Janie Fricke Concerts
PO Box 798
Lancaster, TX 75146-0798, USA

Fricker, Brenda (Actor)
c/o Cassie Mayer *Cassie Mayer*
5 Old Garden House
The Lanterns, Bridge Lane
London SW11 3AD, UNITED KINGDOM

Frickman, Andy (Director)
c/o Staff Member *WME/IMG*
9601 Wilshire Blvd
Beverly Hills, CA 90210-5213, USA

Friday, Bill (Athlete, Hockey Player)
34 South brook Dr Unit 43
Binbrook, ON LOR lCO, Canada

Friday, Tim (Athlete, Hockey Player)
81 Fisher Rd
Southborough, MA 01772-1004, USA

Fridgen, Dan (Athlete, Hockey Player)
1524 Bouton Rd
Troy, NY 12180-3630, USA

Fridman, Mikhail (Business Person)
Alfa Group
1 Arbat St
Moscow 119019, Russia

Fridriksson, Fridrik T (Director)
Bjarkgata 8
Reykjavik 00101, ICELAND

Friede, Mike (Athlete, Football Player)
6943 County Road 56
Johnstown, CO 80534-8237, USA

Friedericy, Bonita (Actor)
c/o Devon Jackson *Trademark Talent*
5900 Wilshire Blvd Ste 710
Los Angeles, CA 90036-5019, USA

Friedgen, Ralph (Coach, Football Coach)
University of Maryland
Athletic Dept
College Park, MD 20742-0001, USA

Friedkin, William (Director)
c/o Peter Trinh *ICM Partners*
10250 Constellation Blvd Fl 7
Los Angeles, CA 90067-6207, USA

Friedlander, Judah (Comedian, Writer)
c/o Andrew Russell *WME/IMG (NY)*
11 Madison Ave Fl 18
New York, NY 10010-3669, USA

Friedlander, Lee (Artist, Photographer)
44 S Mountain Rd
New City, NY 10956-2315, USA

Friedle, Gerry (DJ Otzi) (Musician)
C/O Karin Neuwirth
Pollau 31
Jagerberg A-8091, Austria

Friedle, Will (Actor)
c/o Staff Member *Cunningham Escott Slevin & Doherty (CESD)*
10635 Santa Monica Blvd Ste 130
Los Angeles, CA 90025-8306, USA

Friedman, Andrew (Commentator)
1265 Snell Isle Blvd NE
Saint Petersburg, FL 33704-3035, USA

Friedman, Doug (Athlete, Hockey Player)
226 Falmouth Rd
Falmouth, ME 04105-2053, USA

Friedman, Kinky (Writer)
1101 Crown Ridge Path
Austin, TX 78753-4511, USA

Friedman, Lennie (Athlete, Football Player)
1300 Adams Mountain Rd
Raleigh, NC 27614-8191, USA

Friedman, Peter (Actor, Musician)
J Michael Bloom
233 Park Ave S # 1000
New York, NY 10003-1606, USA

Friedman, Philip (Writer)
Ivy Books/Random House Inc
1745 Broadway Frnt 3
New York, NY 10019-4343, USA

Friedman, Thomas (Commentator, Journalist)
c/o Esther Newberg *ICM Partners (NY)*
730 5th Ave
New York, NY 10019-4105, USA

Friedmann, Phil (Musician)
Overland Productions
156 W 56th St # 500
New York, NY 10019-3800, USA

Friel, Anna (Actor)
c/o Abi Harris *The Artists Partnership*
101 Finsbury Pavement
London EC2A 1RS, UNITED KINGDOM

Friels, Colin (Actor)
129 Brooke St
Woollomooloo
Sydney, NSW 02011, AUSTRALIA

Friend, Rupert (Actor)
c/o Boomer Malkin *WME/IMG*
9601 Wilshire Blvd Ste 500
Beverly Hills, CA 90210-5207, USA

Frier, Mike (Athlete, Football Player)
2378 Capella Cir SW
Atlanta, GA 30331-3869, USA

Friese, Ajay (Actor)
c/o Ben Levine *LINK Entertainment*
11872 La Grange Ave
Los Angeles, CA 90025-5282, USA

Friesen, David (Musician)
Thomas Cassidy
11761 E Speedway Blvd
Tucson, AZ 85748-2017, USA

Friesen, Don (Musician)
c/o Staff Member *Paradigm (Monterey)*
404 W Franklin St
Monterey, CA 93940-2303, USA

Friesen, Jeff (Athlete, Hockey Player)
47 Christopher St
Ladera Ranch, CA 92694-1527, USA

Friesinger, Anni (Speed Skater)
WIGE Media AG
Geilbelweg 24
Fellbach 70736, GERMANY

Friest, Ron (Athlete, Hockey Player)
456 St John St
Windsor, ON N8S 3T7, Canada

Friesz, John (Athlete, Football Player)
1454 E Pebblestone Ct
Hayden, ID 83835-7999, USA

Frig, Len (Athlete, Hockey Player)
7556 S Wynford St
Salt Lake City, UT 84121-5449, USA

Friis, Janus (Business Person)
50 New Bond St
London W1S 1BJ, UK

Frimout, Dirk D (Astronaut)
c/o Staff Member *NASA-JSC*
2101 Nasa Pkwy # 1
Astronaut Office - Mail Code Cb
Houston, TX 77058-3607, USA

Frimout, Dirk D Dr (Astronaut)
Laurierlaan 1
Sint-Pieters-Woluwe B-1150, Belgium

Frisbee, Rob (Athlete)
c/o Jerry Shandrew *Shandrew Public Relations*
1050 S Stanley Ave
Los Angeles, CA 90019-6634, USA

Frisch, Byron (Athlete, Football Coach, Football Player)
3304 Corte Cadiz
Carlsbad, CA 92009-8956, USA

Frisch, David (Athlete, Football Player)
3 Pebble Acres Ct
High Ridge, MO 63049-1665, USA

Frischmann, Justine (Musician)
CMO Mgmt
Ransomes Dock
357-37 Parkgate Road
London SW11 4NP, UNITED KINGDOM (UK)

Frisell, William R (Bill) (Musician)
Nonesuch Records
75 Rockefeller Plz
New York, NY 10019-6908, USA

Frist, William (Politician)
703 Bowling Ave
Nashville, TN 37215-1048, USA

Frist Jr, Thomas (Business Person)
HCA
1 Park Plz
Nashville, TN 37203-6527, USA

Fritsche, Dan (Athlete, Hockey Player)
116 Olentangy Pt
Columbus, OH 43202-1905, USA

Fritsche, Jim (Athlete, Basketball Player)
470 Emerson Ave W
Saint Paul, MN 55118-2034, USA

Fritsch Jr, Ted (Athlete, Football Player)
5014 Odins Way
Marietta, GA 30068-1660, USA

Fritz, Frank (Reality Star)
Antique Archaeology
1300 Clinton St Ste 130
Nashville, TN 37203-7014, USA

Fritz, Nikki (Actor)
PO Box 57764
Sherman Oaks, CA 91413-2764, USA

Frizzell, David (Musician)
4694 E Robertson Rd
Cross Plains, TN 37049-4827, USA

Frizzelle, William J (Athlete, Football Player)
8001 Tylerton Dr
Raleigh, NC 27613-1557, USA

Frnka, Alex (Actor)
c/o Pedro Tapia *Cunningham Escott Slevin & Doherty (CESD)*
10635 Santa Monica Blvd Ste 130
Los Angeles, CA 90025-8306, USA

Frobel, Doug (Athlete, Baseball Player)
169 Springwater Dr
Kanata, ON K2M 1Z8, Canada

Froboess, Cornelia (Musician)
Rinklhof
Kleinholzhausen
Raubling, GERMANY D-83064

Froemming, Bruce (Athlete, Baseball Player)
702 W Haddonstone Pl
Thiensville, WI 53092-5966, USA

Froese, Bob (Athlete, Hockey Player)
11701 Clarence Center Rd
Akron, NY 14001-9747, USA

Froggatt, Joanne (Actor)
c/o Mike Smith *Principal Entertainment*
9255 W Sunset Blvd Ste 500
Los Angeles, CA 90069-3301, USA

Frogren, Jonas (Athlete, Hockey Player)
Newport Sports Management
400-201 City Centre Dr
Attn Don Meehan
Mississauga, ON L5B 2T4, Canada

Frohwirth, Todd (Athlete, Baseball Player)
S66W24360 Skyline Ave
Waukesha, WI 53189-9254, USA

Frolov, Alexander (Athlete, Hockey Player)
24 Grenada Ct
Manhattan Beach, CA 90266-7216, USA

Frolov, Diane (Actor)
c/o Richard Weitz *WME|IMG*
9601 Wilshire Blvd
Beverly Hills, CA 90210-5213, USA

Fron, Kenneth (Designer)
Kenneth Fron Designs
333 W North Ave # 133
Chicago, IL 60610-1293, USA

Frongillo, John (Athlete, Football Player)
10230 Elmhurst Dr NW
Albuquerque, NM 87114-4617, USA

Froning-O'Meara, Mary (Athlete, Baseball Player, Commentator)
417 Bay Hill Dr
Madison, WI 53717-2650, USA

Fronius, Hans (Artist)
Guggenberggasse 18
Perchtoldadorf bel Vienna 02380, AUSTRIA

Frost, Dave (Athlete, Baseball Player)
2206 Ocana Ave
Long Beach, CA 90815-2125, USA

Frost, David (Producer)
c/o Nick Ranceford-Hadley *Noel Gay Artists*
2 Stephen St
London W1T 1AN, UNITED KINGDOM

Frost, Jo (Actor, Reality Star)
c/o Juliette Harris *It Girl Public Relations*
3763 Eddingham Ave
Calabasas, CA 91302-5835, USA

Frost, Ken (Athlete, Football Player)
22842 Stinnett Hollow Rd
Athens, AL 35614-3516, USA

Frost, Lindsay (Actor)
c/o Staff Member *Allman/Rea Management*
141 Barrington Walk
#E
Los Angeles, CA 90049, USA

Frost, Mark (Writer)
c/o Staff Member *Creative Artists Management (CAM-UK)*
55-59 Shaftesbury Ave.
London W1D 6LD, UNITED KINGDOM

Frost, Nick (Actor)
c/o Tom Drumm *Think Tank Management*
8748 Holloway Dr
Los Angeles, CA 90069-2327, USA

Frost, Sadie (Actor)
Julian Belfarge
46 Albermarle St
London W1X 4PP, UNITED KINGDOM (UK)

Frost, Scott (Athlete, Football Player)
99 Thomas Lk
Ashland, NE 68003, USA

Froud, Brian (Artist)
c/o Robert Gould *IMAGINOSIS*
4195 Crisp Canyon Rd
Sherman Oaks, CA 91403-4602, USA

Froud, Wendy (Artist)
c/o Robert Gould *IMAGINOSIS*
4195 Crisp Canyon Rd
Sherman Oaks, CA 91403-4602, USA

Fruh, Eugen (Artist)
Romergasse 9
Zurich 08001, SWITZERLAND

Fruhwirth, Amy (Athlete, Golfer)
26431 N 44th Way
Phoenix, AZ 85050-8579, USA

Frusciante, John (Musician)
Boeing
8942 Wilshire Blvd
Everett, WA 98208, USA

Fry, Bob (Athlete, Football Player)
1604 Bexley Dr
Wilmington, NC 28412-2049, USA

Fry, Hayden (Athlete, Football Player)
2580 W Camp Wisdom Rd Ste 100
Grand Prairie, TX 75052-3089, USA

Fry, Jay (Athlete, Football Player)
PO Box 53
College Corner, OH 45003-0053, USA

Fry, Jerry (Athlete, Baseball Player)
3300 Stanton St
Springfield, IL 62703-4830, USA

Fry, Jordan (Actor)
c/o Carlyne Grager *Dramatic Artists Agency*
103 W Alameda Ave Ste 139
Burbank, CA 91502-2253, USA

Fry, Michael (Cartoonist)
United Feature Syndicate
200 Madison Ave
New York, NY 10016-3903, USA

Fry, Robert (Athlete, Football Player)
1604 Bexley Dr
Wilmington, NC 28412-2049, USA

Fry, Stephen J (Actor, Comedian)
Sprout Pictures
33 Foley St
#100
London W1W 7TL, UNITED KINGDOM

Fryar, Irving D (Athlete, Football Player, Sportscaster)
3207 Millenium Dr
Willingboro, NJ 08046-1049, USA

Fryberger, Dates (Athlete, Hockey Player, Olympic Athlete)
PO Box 564
114 GIN RIDGE RD
Sun Valley, ID 83353-0564, USA

Fryce, Trevor (Athlete, Football Player)
20293 E Lake Cir
Centennial, CO 80016-1282, USA

Frye, Channing (Athlete, Basketball Player)
c/o Rob Pelinka *Landmark Sports Agency*
10990 Wilshire Blvd Ste 1000
Los Angeles, CA 90024-3924, USA

Frye, Jeff (Athlete, Baseball Player)
4236 Calmont Ave
Fort Worth, TX 76107-4311, USA

Frye, Kelly (Actor)
c/o Katie Mason Stern *Luber Roklin Management*
5815 W Sunset Blvd Ste 208
Los Angeles, CA 90028-6481, USA

Frye, Soleil Moon (Actor)
The Little Seed
219 N Larchmont Blvd
Los Angeles, CA 90004-3706, USA

Fryer, Bernie (Athlete, Basketball Player)
91 Fircrest Dr
Sequim, WA 98382-8235, USA

Fryling, Victor J (Business Person)
CMS Energy Fairlane Plaza South
330 Town Center Dr
Dearborn, MI 48126-2738, USA

Fryman, Travis (Athlete, Baseball Player)
2600 Highway 196
Molino, FL 32577-9502, USA

F. Sensenbrenner Jr., James (Congressman, Politician)
2449 Rayburn Hob
Washington, DC 20515-4905, USA

Ftorek, Robert B (Robbie) (Athlete, Hockey Player, Olympic Athlete)
79 Sunset Point Rd
Wolfeboro, NH 03894-4907, USA

Fu, Mingxia (Swimmer)
General Physical Culture Bureau
9 Tiyuguan Road
Bejing, CHINA

Fucarino, Frank (Athlete, Basketball Player)
21 Heathcote Ct
Shirley, NY 11967-4423, USA

Fuchs, Jason (Actor, Producer)
c/o Heidi Lopata *Narrative*
1601 Vine St Fl 6
Los Angeles, CA 90028-8802, USA

Fuchs, Michael J (Television Host)
Home Box Office
1100 Ave of Americans
New York, NY 10036, USA

Fuchsberger, Joachim (Actor)
Hubertusstr 62
Grunwald 82031, GERMANY

Fuente, David I (Business Person)
Office Depot Inc
2200 Germantown Rd
Delray Beach, FL 33445-8223, USA

Fuente, Luis (Dancer)
98 Rue Lepic
Paris 75018, FRANCE

Fuentes, Brian (Athlete, Baseball Player)
1342 El Portal Dr
Merced, CA 95340-0774, USA

Fuentes, Daisy (DJ, Model, Television Host)
c/o Ray McKigney *Shelter Entertainment*
9255 W Sunset Blvd Ste 300
Los Angeles, CA 90069-3313, USA

Fuentes, Mike (Athlete, Baseball Player)
9626 Sycamore Ct
Davie, FL 33328-6768, USA

Fuentes, Rigoberto (Tito) (Athlete, Baseball Player)
61 S Maddux Dr
Reno, NV 89512-1832, USA

Fuentes, Tito (Athlete, Baseball Player)
61 S Maddux Dr
Reno, NV 89512-1832, USA

Fugard, Athol H (Writer)
PO Box 5090
Walmer
Port Elizabeth 06065, SOUTH AFRICA

Fugate, Katherine (Writer)
c/o Alex Hertzberg *Hertzberg Media*
645 W 9th St Ste 110 PMB 386
Los Angeles, CA 90015-1662, USA

Fugelsang, John (Actor, Comedian)
c/o Monique Moss *Integrated PR*
9025 Wilshire Blvd Ste 400
Beverly Hills, CA 90211-1828, USA

Fugere, Joe (Athlete, Baseball Player)
1150 Hillsboro Mile Apt 404
Hillsboro Beach, FL 33062-1737, USA

Fugere, Joe (Baseball Player)
1150 Hillsboro Mile Apt 404
Hillsboro Beach, FL 33062-1737, USA

Fugett, Jean (Athlete, Football Player)
4801 Westparkway
Baltimore, MD 21229-1336, USA

Fugit, Patrick (Actor)
c/o Brett Norensberg *Gersh*
9465 Wilshire Blvd Ste 600
Beverly Hills, CA 90212-2605, USA

Fuglesang, Christer (Astronaut)

Fuhrman, Isabelle (Actor)
c/o Suzan Bymel *Management 360*
9111 Wilshire Blvd
Beverly Hills, CA 90210-5508, USA

Fuhrman, Mark (Attorney)
PO Box 333
Sagle, ID 83860-0333, USA

Fujita, Scott (Athlete, Football Player)
27350 Upper Forty Dr
Carmel Valley, CA 93924-9250, USA

Fukuhara, Karen (Actor)
c/o Jamie Harhay Skinner *Baker Winokur Ryder Public Relations*
9100 Wilshire Blvd
W Tower #500
Beverly Hills, CA 90212-3415, USA

Fukunaga, Cary (Director, Producer)
c/o Michael Sugar *Anonymous Content*
3532 Hayden Ave
Culver City, CA 90232-2413, USA

Fukuto, Maru (Director)
Jim Preminger Agency
450 N Roxbury Dr Ste 1050
Beverly Hills, CA 90210-4235, USA

Fulcher, Bill (Athlete, Football Player)
18 Eagle Pointe Dr
Augusta, GA 30909-6056, USA

Fulcher, David (Athlete, Football Player)
4140 Fieldsedge Dr
Mason, OH 45040-8538, USA

Fulcher, Modriel (Athlete, Football Player)
6010 S Westmoreland Rd Apt 1012
Dallas, TX 75237-2061, USA

Fulchino, Jeff (Athlete, Baseball Player)
48 Arrowhead Dr
Monroe, CT 06468-1067, USA

Fuld, Sam (Athlete, Baseball Player)
318 W Highland Ave
Philadelphia, PA 19118-3731, USA

Fulgham, John (Athlete, Baseball Player)
769 Cricklewood Ter
Lake Mary, FL 32746-5310, USA

Fulghum, Robert (Writer)
c/o Staff Member *HarperCollins Publishers*
195 Broadway Fl 2
New York, NY 10007-3132, USA

Fulghum, Robert (Writer)
Random House
1015 Violeta Dr
Alhambra, CA 91801-5332, USA

Fulhage, Scott (Athlete, Football Player)
2340 N Rd
Beloit, KS 67420, USA

Fulks, Robbie (Musician, Songwriter, Writer)
Mongrel Music
743 Center Blvd
Fairfax, CA 94930-1764, USA

Fuller, Amanda (Actor)
c/o Siri Garber *Platform PR*
2666 N Beachwood Dr
Los Angeles, CA 90068-2308, USA

Fuller, Bob B (Writer)
37 Langton Way
London 05000, UNITED KINGDOM (UK)

Fuller, Bryan (Writer)
c/o Ari Greenburg *WME/IMG*
9601 Wilshire Blvd
Beverly Hills, CA 90210-5213, USA

Fuller, Carl (Athlete, Basketball Player)
8302 Kirkville Dr
Houston, TX 77089-2194, USA

Fuller, Corey (Athlete, Football Player)
4161 Ballard Rd
Tallahassee, FL 32305-6308, USA

Fuller, Curtis D (Athlete, Football Player)
Denon Records
4045 Flowering Peach Rd
Marvin, NC 28173-6219, USA

Fuller, Deiores (Actor, Songwriter, Writer)
3628 Ottawa Cir
Las Vegas, NV 89169-3301, USA

Fuller, Drew (Actor)
c/o Stephanie Simon *Untitled Entertainment*
350 S Beverly Dr Ste 200
Beverly Hills, CA 90212-4819, USA

Fuller, Eddie (Athlete, Football Player)
36422 the Bluffs Ave
Prairieville, LA 70769-3197, USA

Fuller, Jeff (Race Car Driver)
Jeff Fuller Motorsports
PO Box 3336
Mooresville, NC 28117-3336, USA

Fuller, Jim (Athlete, Baseball Player)
5107 Bur Oak Dr
Pasadena, TX 77505-3028, USA

Fuller, Joe (Athlete, Football Player)
8906 Farnsworth Ave N
Minneapolis, MN 55443-1752, USA

Fuller, John (Athlete, Baseball Player)
31912 Paseo Terraza
San Juan Capistrano, CA 92675-3060, USA

Fuller, Johnny (Athlete, Football Player)
1925 Highland Dr
Salado, TX 76571-5792, USA

Fuller, Kurt (Actor)
c/o Rick Ax *Gold Coast Management*
935 Victoria Ave Frnt
Venice, CA 90291-3933, USA

Fuller, Kyle (Athlete, Football Player)
c/o Greg Barnett *Lagarde Unlimited (GA)*
1525 Senoia Rd Ste E
Tyrone, GA 30290-3602, USA

Fuller, Mark (Artist)
Wet Design
90 Universal City Plz
Universal City, CA 91608-1002, USA

Fuller, Mike (Athlete, Football Player)
4241 Abingdon Trl
Mountain Brk, AL 35243-1737, USA

Fuller, Penny (Actor)
12428 Hesby St
North Hollywood, CA 91607-3020, USA

Fuller, Randy (Athlete, Football Player)
1126 Ashley Station Blvd Apt 103
Columbus, GA 31904-8626, USA

Fuller, Robert (Actor)
PO Box 272
Era, TX 76238-0272, USA

Fuller, Rod (Race Car Driver)
David Powers Motorsports
10205 Westheimer Rd Ste 100
Houston, TX 77042-3164, USA

Fuller, Simon (Producer)
c/o Staff Member *XIX Entertainment (UK)*
32/33 Ransomes Dock
London SW11 4NP, UNITED KINGDOM (UK)

Fuller, Steve (Athlete, Football Player)
81 Oak Tree Rd
Bluffton, SC 29910-4960, USA

Fuller, Tony (Athlete, Basketball Player)
4222 Lost Springs Dr
Agoura Hills, CA 91301-5326, USA

Fuller, Vem (Athlete, Baseball Player)
9004 Hampton Cir
Aurora, OH 44202-9254, USA

Fuller, Vern (Athlete, Baseball Player)
9004 Hampton Cir
Aurora, OH 44202-9254, USA

Fuller, Vincent (Athlete, Football Player)
180 Water St APT 1812
New York, NY 10038-5316, USA

Fuller, William H Jr (Athlete, Football Player)
1004 Poquoson Xing
Chesapeake, VA 23320-0667, USA

Fullerton, Ed (Athlete, Football Player)
5846 Elizabeth Ann Way
Fort Myers, FL 33912-2236, USA

Fullerton, Fiona (Actor)
London Mgmt
2-4 Noel St
London W1V 3RB, UNITED KINGDOM (UK)

Fullington, Darrell (Athlete, Football Player)
1023 W Patrick Cir
Daytona Beach, FL 32117-4565, USA

Fullmer, Brad (Athlete, Baseball Player)
18115 Kingsport Dr
Malibu, CA 90265-5633, USA

Fullone, Sam (Race Car Driver)
Fullone Motorsports
10743 Mileback Rd
North Collins, NY 14111, USA

Fullwood, Brent (Athlete, Football Player)
4002 Maybreeze Rd
Marietta, GA 30066-2734, USA

Fullwood, Troy (Athlete, Baseball Player)
317 Manning Ln
Hampton, VA 23666-5023, USA

Fulmer, Phillip (Coach, Football Coach)
University of Tennessee
Athletic Dept
Knoxville, TN 37996-0001, USA

Fulton, Bill (Athlete, Baseball Player)
3001 Lexington Ct
Export, PA 15632-9061, USA

Fulton, Eileen (Actor, Musician)
""As the World Turns Show"" CBS-TV
524 W 57th St
New York, NY 10019-2924, USA

Fulton, Grace (Actor)
c/o Norman Aladjem *Mainstay Entertainment*
9250 Beverly Blvd Fl 3
Beverly Hills, CA 90210-3710, USA

Fulton, Robert (Politician)
PO Box 2634
Waterloo, IA 50704-2634, USA

Fulton, Soren (Actor)
c/o Staff Member *Savage Agency*
1041 N Formosa Ave
West Hollywood, CA 90046-6703, USA

Fulton, Zach (Athlete, Football Player)

Fultz, Aaron (Athlete, Baseball Player)
PO Box 41
Munford, TN 38058-0041, USA

Fultz, Frank (Athlete, Baseball Player)
310 Willow Glade Pt
Alpharetta, GA 30022-1025, USA

Fultz, Jeff (Race Car Driver)
JCR3 Racing
PO Box 561001
Charlotte, NC 28256-1001, USA

Fultz, Mike (Athlete, Football Player)
1900 W Foothills Rd
Lincoln, NE 68523-9389, USA

Fu Manchu (Music Group, Musician)
c/o Staff Member *Agency for the Performing Arts (APA)*
405 S Beverly Dr Ste 500
Beverly Hills, CA 90212-4425, USA

Fumero, David (Actor)
c/o Jerome Martin *Jerome Martin Management*
1655 N Cherokee Ave
2nd Floor
Hollywood, CA 90028, USA

Fumero, Melissa (Actor)
200 W 60th St
New York, NY 10023-8502, USA

Fumusa, Dominic (Actor)
c/o Robert Stein *Robert Stein Management*
PO Box 3797
Beverly Hills, CA 90212-0797, USA

Fun. (Music Group, Musician)
c/o Dalton Sim *Nettwerk - Boston*
33 Richdale Ave Ste 121
Cambridge, MA 02140-2627, USA

Funaki, Kazuyoshi (Skier)
Japanese Olympic Committee
1-1-1 Jinan Shilbuya-Ku
Tokyo 00150, JAPAN

Funches, Ron (Actor, Comedian)
c/o Melanie Truhett *Truhett / Garcia Management*
12031 Ventura Blvd Ste 4
Studio City, CA 91604-2636, USA

Funchess, Tom (Athlete, Football Player)
1015 Funchess St
Crystal Springs, MS 39059-3017, USA

Fund, John (Writer)
c/o Staff Member *The American Spectator*
1611 N Kent St Ste 901
Arlington, VA 22209-2111, USA

Funderburk, Mark (Athlete, Baseball Player)
6924 Old Providence Rd
Charlotte, NC 28226-7740, USA

Funderburke, Lawrence (Athlete, Basketball Player)
1688 Meadoway Ct
Blacklick, OH 43004-9759, USA

Funk, Caribbean (Music Group)
c/o Staff Member *Sony Music (Miami)*
404 Washington Ave Ste 700
Miami Beach, FL 33139-6615, USA

Funk, Frank (Athlete, Baseball Player)
4022 S Alamandas Way
Gold Canyon, AZ 85118-1899, USA

Funk, Fred (Athlete, Golfer)
24729 Harbour View Dr
Ponte Vedra Beach, FL 32082-1509, USA

Funk, Nolan Gerard (Actor)
c/o Kim Callahan *Industry Entertainment Partners*
955 Carrillo Dr Ste 300
Los Angeles, CA 90048-5400, USA

Funk, Terry (Athlete, Wrestler)
418 N Shore Dr
Amarillo, TX 79118-8004, USA

Funk, Tom (Athlete, Baseball Player)
6952 N Olive St
Kansas City, MO 64118-2876, USA

Funkmaster Flex (DJ, Musician)
c/o Michael Schweiger *Central Entertainment Group*
250 W 40th St Fl 12
New York, NY 10018-4601, USA

Fuqua, Antoine (Director)
c/o Chase Lehner *Slate PR*
901 N Highland Ave
W Hollywood, CA 90038-2412, USA

Fuqua, John (Athlete, Football Player)
13983 Glastonbury Ave
Detroit, MI 48223-2921, USA

Furay, Richie (Musician)
c/o Staff Member *UTA/The Agency Group*
888 7th Ave Fl 7
New York, NY 10106-0700, USA

Furcal, Rafael (Athlete, Baseball Player)
397 Sweet Bay Ave
Plantation, FL 33324-8227, USA

Furey, John (Actor)
c/o Staff Member *Hartig Hilepo Agency Ltd*
2728 Thomson Ave Unit 602
Long Island City, NY 11101-2932, USA

Furgler, Kurt (President)
Dufourstr 34
Saint-Gail 09000, SWITZERLAND

Furian, Mira (Actor)
6410 Blarney Stone Ct
Springfield, VA 22152-2129, USA

Furie, Sidney (Director, Producer, Writer)
c/o Jack Gilardi *ICM Partners*
10250 Constellation Blvd Fl 7
Los Angeles, CA 90067-6207, USA

Furjanic, Anthony (Athlete, Football Player)
1501 W Water St Ste 27
New Buffalo, MI 49117-1081, USA

Furlan, Mira (Actor)
c/o Georg Georgi *Das Imperium*
Torstrasse 129
Berlin 10119, GERMANY

Furlong, Edward (Actor)

Furlong, Shirley (Athlete, Golfer)
16412 S 18th Dr
Phoenix, AZ 85045-1628, USA

Furman, Andrew (Race Car Driver)
Latonio Racing
PO Box 75007
Cincinnati, OH 45275-0007, USA

Furmaniak, J J (Athlete, Baseball Player)
12502 Larkspur Ln
Plainfield, IL 60585-5545, USA

Furmann, Benno (Actor)
c/o Staff Member *Artists Independent Management (UK)*
32 Tavistock St
London WC2E 7PB, UNITED KINGDOM (UK)

Furness, Deborra-Lee (Actor, Director, Producer)
c/o David (Dave) Fleming *Atlas Artists*
9220 W Sunset Blvd Ste 225
Los Angeles, CA 90069-3513, USA

Furniss, Bruce (Athlete, Olympic Athlete, Swimmer)
18452 Old Lamplighter Cir
Villa Park, CA 92861-4528, USA

Furniss, Steve (Athlete, Olympic Athlete, Swimmer)
6478 Frampton Cir
Huntington Beach, CA 92648-6620, USA

Furno, Carlo Cardinal (Religious Leader)
Piazza Della Citta Leonina
Rome 92807, ITALY

Furr, Brad (Race Car Driver)
8242 Creekside Dr
Dublin, CA 94568-3512, USA

Furrer, Will (Athlete, Football Player)
420 Logan Ranch Rd
Georgetown, TX 78628-1211, USA

Furrey, Mike (Athlete, Football Player)
8579 Newbury Ct N
Canton, MI 48187-4444, USA

Furst, Alan (Writer)
c/o Sally Marvin *Random House Publicity*
1745 Broadway Frnt 3
New York, NY 10019-4343, USA

Furst, Anthony (Athlete, Football Player)
3001 Big Hill Rd
Dayton, OH 45419-1303, USA

Furst, Nathan (Musician)
c/o Mike Rosen *Working Artists Agency*
13525 Ventura Blvd
Sherman Oaks, CA 91423-3801

Furstenfeld, Jeremy (Musician)
Ashley Talent
2002 Hogback Rd Ste 20
Ann Arbor, MI 48105-9736, USA

Furstenfeld, Justin (Musician)
827 W Hopkins St
San Marcos, TX 78666-4200, USA

Furtado, Nelly (Musician, Songwriter)
c/o Staff Member *SL Feldman & Associates (Vancouver)*
200-1505 2nd Ave W
Vancouver, BC V6H 3Y4, CANADA

Furtick, Steven (Writer)
Elevation Church
11416 E Independence Blvd Ste N
Matthews, NC 28105-4947, USA

Furuhashi, Hironshin (Swimmer)
3-9-11 Nozawa
Setagayaku
Tokyo, JAPAN

Furukawa, Masaru (Swimmer)
5-5-12 Shinohara Honmachi
Nadaku
Kobe, JAPAN

Furukawa, Satoshi (Astronaut)
NASDA
Tsukuba Space Center
2-1-1 Sengen
Tukuhashi, Ibaraka 00305, JAPAN

Furukawa, Satoshi Dr (Astronaut)
NASDA, Tsukuba Space Center 2-1-1 Sengen
Tukuba-shi Ibaraka 00305, Japan

Furuseth, Ole Christian (Skier)
John Colletts Alle 74
Oslo 00854, NORWAY

Fury, Ed (Actor)
6729 Babcock Ave
N Hollywood, CA 91606-1310

Furyk, Jim (Athlete, Golfer)
240 Deer Haven Dr
Ponte Vedra Beach, FL 32082-2107, USA

Fusco, Cosimo (Actor)
Studio Segre
Piazzale Di Ponte Milvio 28
Rome 00191, Italy

Fusco, John (Writer)
c/o Michael Sugar *Anonymous Content*
3532 Hayden Ave
Culver City, CA 90232-2413, USA

Fusco, Mark (Athlete, Hockey Player, Olympic Athlete)
155 Grove St
Westwood, MA 02090-1027, USA

Fusco, Scott (Athlete, Hockey Player, Olympic Athlete)
41 Wedgemere Ave
Winchester, MA 01890-2439, USA

Fusina, Chuck A (Athlete, Football Player)
1548 King James Dr
Pittsburgh, PA 15237-1588, USA

Fussell, Chris (Athlete, Baseball Player)
424 Foxridge Ln
Oregon, OH 43616-2474, USA

Futterman, Dan (Actor)
Gersh Agency
232 N Canon Dr
Beverly Hills, CA 90210-5302, USA

Future (Musician)
Freebandz/Epic Records
9830 Wilshire Blvd
Beverly Hills, CA 90212-1804, USA

Futureheads, The (Music Group)
c/o Staff Member *Paradigm (Monterey)*
404 W Franklin St
Monterey, CA 93940-2303, USA

Fyhrie, Mike (Athlete, Baseball Player)
4 Wellesley Ct
Trabuco Canyon, CA 92679-4725, USA

G

G, Becky (Musician)
c/o Erin Culley *Creative Artists Agency (CAA)*
2000 Avenue of the Stars Ste 100
Los Angeles, CA 90067-4705, USA

G, Franky (Actor)
c/o Jimmy Darmody *Creative Artists Agency (CAA)*
2000 Avenue of the Stars Ste 100
Los Angeles, CA 90067-4705, USA

G, Kenny (Musician)
c/o Mark Young *Fame Factory*
8581 Santa Monica Blvd Ste 495
West Hollywood, CA 90069-4120, USA

Gabai, Sasson (Actor)
c/o Estelle Lasher *Lasher Group*
1133 Avenue of the Americas Fl 27
New York, NY 10036-6710, USA

Gabaldon, Diana (Writer)
10810 N Tatum Blvd Ste 102 PMB 321
Phoenix, AZ 85028-6056, USA

Gabalier, Andreas (Musician)
c/o Staff Member *Armin Rahn Agency and Management*
Dreimuehlenstr. 7
Muenchen 80469, Germany

Gabarra, Carin (Athlete, Olympic Athlete, Soccer Player)
305 Rosslare Dr
Arnold, MD 21012-3007, USA

Gabbana, Stefano (Designer, Fashion Designer)

Gabbard, Kason (Athlete, Baseball Player)
855 D011town Dr
Savannah, TN 38372-3713, USA

Gabbard, Steve (Athlete, Football Player)
7038 Bradfordville Rd
Tallahassee, FL 32309-1806, USA

Gabbert, Blaine (Athlete, Football Player)
c/o Team Member *Tennessee Titans*
460 Great Circle Rd
Nashville, TN 37228-1404, USA

Gabel, Elyes (Actor)
c/o Gary O'Sullivan *Troika*
10A Christina St.
London EC2A 4PA, UNITED KINGDOM

Gabel, Seth (Actor)
c/o Alex Schack *Slate PR*
901 N Highland Ave
W Hollywood, CA 90038-2412, USA

Gaberino, Geoffrey (Athlete, Olympic Athlete, Swimmer)
4 Minnich Ct
Fairhope, AL 36532-2320, USA

Gable, Brian (Cartoonist)
444 Front St W
THE GLOBE AND MAIL
Toronto, ON M5V 2S9, CANADA

Gable, Brian (Cartoonist)
67 Riverside Dr Apt 1D
New York, NY 10024-6155, USA

Gable, Daniel M (Danny) (Athlete, Olympic Athlete, Wrestler)
4343 Treefarm Ln NE
Iowa City, IA 52240-7829, USA

Gable, John Clark (Actor)
c/o David Rubini *David Rubini Artist Management*
3100 Main St # 3
Dallas, TX 75226-1535, USA

Gabler, Bill (Baseball Player)
Chicago Cubs
4443 Mattis Rd
Saint Louis, MO 63128-3136, USA

Gabler, Wally (Athlete, Football Player)
RR 1
Heathcote, ON N0H 1N0, Canada

Gabor, William (Athlete, Basketball Player)
110 Mangrove Bay Way Apt 1403
Jupiter, FL 33477-6406, USA

Gaborik, Marian (Athlete, Hockey Player)
Icy Luck Inc
720 Manhattan Ave
Manhattan Beach, CA 90266-5653, USA

Gabriel, Betty (Actor)
c/o Annick Oppenheim *Wolf-Kasteler Public Relations*
6255 W Sunset Blvd Ste 1111
Los Angeles, CA 90028-7426, USA

Gabriel, Michael (Artist)
Dlouha 32
Prague 1 110 00, CZECH REPUBLIC

Gabriel, Peter (Musician, Songwriter)
c/o Staff Member *Real World Records*
Box Mill
Box Corsham
Wiltshire SN1 38PN, United Kingdom

Gabriel, Roman (Athlete, Football Player)
16817 McKee Rd
Charlotte, NC 28278-8406, USA

Gabriel, Seychelle (Actor)
c/o TJ Stein *Stein Entertainment Group*
1351 N Crescent Heights Blvd Apt 312
West Hollywood, CA 90046-4549, USA

Gabriel Jr, Roman I (Athlete, Football Player)
PO Box 4173
Calabash, NC 28467-0373, USA

Gabrielle, Josefina (Actor)
c/o Staff Member *Artists & Representatives (Stone Manners Salners)*
6100 Wilshire Blvd Ste 1500
Los Angeles, CA 90048-5110, USA

Gabrielle, Monique (Actor, Model)
Purrfect Productions
1231 NE 28th Ave
Pompano Beach, FL 33062-3822, USA

Gabrielson, Len (Athlete, Baseball Player)
24230 Hillview Rd
Los Altos, CA 94024-5221, USA

Gachkar, Andrew (Athlete, Football Player)

Gacki, Sebastian (Actor)
c/o Staff Member *Lizbell Agency*
216-309 Cordova St W
Vancouver, BC V6B 1E5, USA

Gad, Josh (Actor)
c/o Melissa Raubvogel *Imprint PR*
375 Hudson St
New York, NY 10014-3658, USA

Gaddis, Robert (Athlete, Football Player)
1022 Gaddis Rd
Edwards, MS 39066-8007, USA

Gade, Ariel (Actor)
c/o Jennifer Millar *Paradigm*
8942 Wilshire Blvd
Beverly Hills, CA 90211-1908, USA

Gadinsky, Brian (Producer)
c/o Staff Member *WME|IMG*
9601 Wilshire Blvd
Beverly Hills, CA 90210-5213, USA

Gadiot, Peter (Actor)
c/o Annick Oppenheim *Wolf-Kasteler Public Relations*
6255 W Sunset Blvd Ste 1111
Los Angeles, CA 90028-7426, USA

Gadon, Sarah (Actor)
c/o Dani De Lio *Creative Drive Artists*
20 Minowan Miikan Lane
Toronto, ON M6J 0E5, CANADA

Gadot, Gal (Actor)
c/o Melissa Raubvogel *Imprint PR*
375 Hudson St
New York, NY 10014-3658, USA

Gadsby, Hannah (Actor, Musician)
c/o Janette Linden *PBJ Management*
22 Rathbone St
London W1T 1LA, UNITED KINGDOM

Gadsden, Oronde (Athlete, Football Player)
1427 SW 110th Way
Davie, FL 33324-7185, USA

Gadzuric, Dan (Athlete, Basketball Player)
1051 Olsen St Ste 311
Henderson, NV 89011-3039, USA

Gaechter, Mike (Athlete, Football Player)
13 Horizon Pt
Frisco, TX 75034-6840, USA

Gaerte, Joe (Race Car Driver)
Gaerte Engines
615 Monroe St
Rochester, IN 46975-1426, USA

Gaetti, Gary (Athlete, Baseball Player)
2704 Barbara Ln
Houston, TX 77005-3420, USA

Gaff, Brent (Athlete, Baseball Player)
5925 S State Road 9
Albion, IN 46701-9623, USA

Gaffigan, Jim (Actor, Comedian)
c/o Alex Murray *Brillstein Entertainment Partners*
9150 Wilshire Blvd Ste 350
Beverly Hills, CA 90212-3453, USA

Gaffney, Derrick T (Athlete, Football Player)
11750 Cherry Bark Dr E
Jacksonville, FL 32218-7674, USA

Gaffney, Drew Dr (Astronaut)
6613 Chatsworth Pl
Nashville, TN 37205-3955, USA

Gaffney, Jabar (Athlete, Football Player)
10142 Hatton Cir
Orlando, FL 32832-6174, USA

Gaffney, Janice (Athlete, Skier)
8118 Vantage Ave
North Hollywood, CA 91605-1437, USA

Gaffney, Mo (Actor)
c/o Staff Member *Artists & Representatives (Stone Manners Salners)*
6100 Wilshire Blvd Ste 1500
Los Angeles, CA 90048-5110, USA

Gaffney, Tyler (Athlete, Football Player)
c/o Ryan Tollner *REP 1 Sports Group*
80 Technology Dr
Irvine, CA 92618-2301, USA

Gafford, Thomas (Athlete, Football Player)

Gaga, Lady (Dancer, Musician)
c/o Amanda Silverman *The Lede Company*
401 Broadway Ste 206
New York, NY 10013-3033, USA

Gage, Jody (Athlete, Hockey Player)
91 W Forest Dr
Rochester, NY 14624-3755, USA

Gage, Nicholas (Journalist, Writer)
37 Nelson St
North Grafton, MA 01536-1424, USA

Gagliano, Phil (Athlete, Baseball Player)
1095 Crescent Dr
Hollister, MO 65672-4884, USA

Gagliano, Ralph (Athlete, Baseball Player)
1756 Overton Park Ave
Memphis, TN 38112-5344, USA

Gagliano, Robert F (Bob) (Athlete, Football Player)
822 Fitzgerald Ave
Ventura, CA 93003-0228, USA

Gagne, Eric S (Athlete, Baseball Player)
c/o Scott Boras *Boras Corporation*
18 Corporate Plaza Dr
Newport Beach, CA 92660-7901, USA

Gagne, Greg (Athlete, Baseball Player)
746 Whetstone Hill Rd
Somerset, MA 02726-3702, USA

Gagne, Paul (Athlete, Hockey Player)
Lot 13 Aurora
Iroquois Falls, ON P0K 6K1, Canada

Gagne, Simone (Athlete, Hockey Player)
116710th St
Manhattan Beach, CA 90266-6019, USA

Gagner, Dave (Athlete, Coach, Hockey Player)
c/o Staff Member *London Knights*
99 Dundas St
London, ON N6A 6K1, Canada

Gagner, Larry (Athlete, Football Player)
205 W Curtis St
Tampa, FL 33603-3649, USA

Gagner, Sam (Athlete, Hockey Player)
Pulver Sports
479 Bedford Park Ave
Attn Ian Pulver
Toronto, ON M5M 1K2, Canada

Gagnier, Holly (Actor)
Stone Manners
6500 Wilshire Blvd # 550
Los Angeles, CA 90048-4920, USA

Gagnon, Dave (Athlete, Hockey Player)
34684 Richard O Dr
Sterling Heights, MI 48310-6128, USA

Gago, Jenny (Actor)
c/o Bill Rogin *Bill Rogin Management*
427 N Canon Dr Ste 215
Beverly Hills, CA 90210-4840, USA

Gagosian, Larry (Business Person)
Gagosian Gallery
980 Madison Ave PH
New York, NY 10075-1859, USA

Gahan, Dave (Musician)
27 S Davis Ave
Montauk, NJ 11954, USA

Gaikowski, Steve (Athlete, Baseball Player)
416 Turner St NE
Olympia, WA 98506-4663, USA

Gail, Max (Actor)
Full Circle Productions
PO Box 4160
Malibu, CA 90264-4160, USA

Gailey, T Chandler (Chan) (Athlete, Coach, Football Coach, Football Player)
401 North St
Clarkesville, GA 30523-6035, USA

Gaillard, Bob (Coach)
50 Bonnie Brae Dr
Novato, CA 94949-5851, USA

Gaillard, Eddie (Athlete, Baseball Player)
134 Sweet Bay Cir
Jupiter, FL 33458-2816, USA

Gaiman, Neil (Writer)
Cat Mihos
4470 W Sunset Blvd # 339
Los Angeles, CA 90027-6302, USA

Gainer, Derrick (Athlete, Football Player)
733 E McDonald Rd
Plant City, FL 33567-3529, USA

Gainer, Jay (Athlete, Baseball Player)
1035 E 8th St
Panama City, FL 32401-3594, USA

Gaines, Bill (Athlete, Basketball Player)
921 Beverly Cir
Cedar Hill, TX 75104-1236, USA

Gaines, Boyd (Actor, Musician)
c/o Elin McManus-Flack *Elin Flack Management*
435 W 57th St Apt 3M
New York, NY 10019-1724, USA

Gaines, Chip (Designer, Reality Star, Television Host)
Magnolia Market
601 Webster Ave
Waco, TX 76706-1164, USA

Gaines, Clark (Athlete, Football Player)
21364 Scara Pl
Broadlands, VA 20148-3602, USA

Gaines, Corey (Athlete, Basketball Player)
3968 Windansea St
Las Vegas, NV 89147-6544, USA

Gaines, Ernest J (Writer)
PO Box 81
Oscar, LA 70762-0081, USA

Gaines, Joanna (Designer, Reality Star, Television Host)
Magnolia Market
601 Webster Ave
Waco, TX 76706-1164, USA

Gaines, Joe (Athlete, Baseball Player)
77 Anair Way
Oakland, CA 94605-4874, USA

Gaines, Lawrence (Athlete, Football Player)
4963 Cherry Blossom Cir
West Bloomfield, MI 48324-1297, USA

Gaines, Reese (Baseball Player)
Houston Rockets
2 Greenway Plz
Toyota Center
Houston, TX 77046-0297, USA

Gaines, Roger (Athlete, Football Player)

Gaines, Rowdy (Athlete, Olympic Athlete, Swimmer)
c/o Evan Morgenstein *Premier Management Group (PMG Sports)*
700 Evanvale Ct
Cary, NC 27518-2806, USA

Gaines, Wentford (Athlete, Football Player)
97 Bayview Ave
Jersey City, NJ 07305-3306, USA

Gaines, William C (Journalist)
Chicago Tribune
1326 Marks Ave
Jackson, MS 39213-7113, USA

Gainey, Mike (M.C.) (Actor)
c/o Staff Member *Miriam Milgrom Management*
3614 Lankershim Blvd
Los Angeles, CA 90068-1218, USA

Gainey, Robert M (Bob) (Athlete, Coach, Hockey Player)
c/o Staff Member *Montreal Canadiens*
1275 Rue Saint-Antoine O
Montreal, QC H3C 5L2, Canada

Gainey, Steve (Athlete, Hockey Player)
900 McGill Road Box 3010
Attn: Hockey Coaching Staff
Kamloops, BC V2C SN3, USA

Gainey, Telmanch '''Ty''' (Athlete, Baseball Player)
123 Presidential Dr Aot D
19807-3213, DE Wilmine:to, USA

Gains, Courtney (Actor)
c/o Chris Roe *Chris Roe Management*
PO Box 761
Burbank, CA 91503-0761, USA

Gainsbourg, Charlotte (Actor)
c/o Kate Buckley *42 Management (UK)*
8 Flitcroft St
London WC2H 8DL, UNITED KINGDOM

Gaiser, George (Athlete, Football Player)
28752 Kalkallo Dr
Boerne, TX 78015-4614, USA

Gaison, Blane (Athlete, Football Player)
45-444 Koa Kahiko St
Kaneohe, HI 96744-2008, USA

Gaitan, Paulina (Actor)
c/o Ruby Castillo *TOR Entertainment (MX)*
Heriberto Frias 846
Col Del Valle
Mexico City DF 03100, MEXICO

Gaiter, Tony (Athlete, Football Player)
9235 NW 35th Ct
Miami, FL 33147-2829, USA

Gaiters, Bob (Athlete, Football Player)
6909 Knowlton Pl Apt 206
Los Angeles, CA 90045-2036, USA

Gaither, Bill (Musician, Songwriter)
Gaither Music Co
PO Box 737
Alexandria, VA 22314, USA

Gajan, Hokie (Athlete, Football Player)
213 Cottonwood Ln
Mandeville, LA 70471-2552, USA

Gajdusek, Karl (Writer)
c/o Jill McElroy *Management 360*
9111 Wilshire Blvd
Beverly Hills, CA 90210-5508, USA

Gajkowski, Steve (Athlete, Baseball Player)
416 Turner St NE
Olympia, WA 98506-4663, USA

Gakeler, Dan (Athlete, Baseball Player)
378 Lakeshore Dr
Lexington, NC 27292-7960, USA

Gal, Sandra (Athlete, Golfer)
Callaway Golf Company
2180 Rutherford Rd
Carlsbad, CA 92008-7328, USA

Galanos, Mike (Television Host)
Prime News Tonight
1 Time Warner Ctr
CNN
New York, NY 10019-6038, USA

Galante, Matt (Baseball Player, Coach)
Houston Astros
85 Hei11hts Ter
Middletown, NJ 07748-3405, USA

Galarraga, Andres (Athlete, Baseball Player)
1639 Enclave Cir
West Palm Beach, FL 33411-1862, USA

Galasso, Bob (Athlete, Baseball Player)
267 Adelaide Rd
Connellsville, PA 15425-6215, USA

Galati, Frank J (Director)
580 Bellora Way
Sarasota, FL 34234-4574, USA

Galavis, Juan Pablo (Athlete, Reality Star, Soccer Player)
c/o Staff Member *DMT Event*
21 Alessio Ter
Hamilton, NJ 08620-9772, USA

Galbraith, Clint (Horse Racer)
PO Box 902
Scottsville, NY 14546-0902, USA

Galbraith, Scott (Athlete, Football Player)
3700 Plymouth Dr
North Highlands, CA 95660-3312, USA

Galbreath, Scott (Athlete, Football Player)
3649 Plymouth Dr
North Highlands, CA 95660-3309, USA

Galbreath, Tony (Athlete, Football Player)
411 W 9th St
Fulton, MO 65251-1178, USA

Gale, Ed (Actor)
c/o Cindy Osbrink *Osbrink Talent Agency*
4343 Lankershim Blvd # 100
North Hollywood, CA 91602-2705, USA

Gale, Elan (Producer)
c/o Jordyn Palos *Persona Public Relations*
6255 W Sunset Blvd Ste 705
Hollywood, CA 90028-7408, USA

Gale, Megan (Actor)
c/o Ann Churchill-Brown *Shanahan Management*
Level 3 Berman House
Surry Hills 02010, AUSTRALIA

Gale, Mike (Athlete, Basketball Player)
18003 4th Ave S
Burien, WA 98148-1803, USA

Gale, Rich (Athlete, Baseball Player)
869 Center Park St
Daniel Island, SC 29492-7569, USA

Gale, Tommy (Race Car Driver)
PO Box 375
Elizabeth, PA 15037-0375, USA

Galecki, Johnny (Actor)
c/o Tom Monjack *Tom Monjack Celebrity Enterprises*
28650 Avenida Maravilla # A
Cathedral City, CA 92234-8115, USA

Galeotti, Bethany Joy (Actor)
c/o Jill Fritzo *Jill Fritzo Public Relations*
208 E 51st St # 305
New York, NY 10022-6557, USA

Galette, Junior (Athlete, Football Player)

Galiena, Anna (Actor)
c/o Dominique Besnehard *ArtMedia*
8 rue Danielle Casanova
Paris 75002, FRANCE

Galifianakis, Zach (Actor, Producer, Writer)
c/o Marc Gurvitz *Brillstein Entertainment Partners*
9150 Wilshire Blvd Ste 350
Beverly Hills, CA 90212-3453, USA

Galigher, Ed (Athlete, Football Player)
1025 Prospect St Ste 150
La Jolla, CA 92037-4163, USA

Galik, Denise (Actor)
Badgley Connor Talent
9229 W Sunset Blvd Ste 311
Los Angeles, CA 90069-3403, USA

Galina, Stacy (Actor)
c/o Mark Scroggs *David Shapira & Associates*
193 N Robertson Blvd
Beverly Hills, CA 90211-2103, USA

Galindo, Rudy (Figure Skater)
c/o Staff Member *Champions on Ice*
3500 American Blvd W Ste 190
Minneapolis, MN 55431-4431, USA

Galitzine, Nicholas (Actor)
c/o Meredith Rothman *Anonymous Content*
3532 Hayden Ave
Culver City, CA 90232-2413, USA

Gall, Ellie (Actor)
c/o Peter McGrath *Echo Lake Management*
421 S Beverly Dr Fl 8
Beverly Hills, CA 90212-4408, USA

Gall, John (Athlete, Baseball Player)
20 Corte Del Sol
Millbrae, CA 94030-2111, USA

Gallacher, Kevin (Soccer Player)
Blackbum Rovers
Ewood Park
Blackbum
Lancashire BB2 4JF, UNITED KINGDOM (UK)

Gallagher, Al (Athlete, Baseball Player)
1810 N Parkwood Dr
Harlingen, TX 78550-8027, USA

Gallagher, Bob (Athlete, Baseball Player)
315 Fair Ave
Santa Cruz, CA 95060-6343, USA

Gallagher, Bronagh (Actor)
Marmont Mgmt
Langham House
302/8 Regent St
London W1R 5AL, UNITED KINGDOM (UK)

Gallagher, Chad (Athlete, Basketball Player)
482 Wynstone Way
Rockton, IL 61072-3434, USA

Gallagher, Dave (Athlete, Baseball Player)
29 Carrs Tavern Rd
Millstone Township, NJ 08510-1505, USA

Gallagher, Dave (Athlete, Football Player)
2740 California Ct
Columbus, IN 47201-2924, USA

Gallagher, David (Actor)
c/o Staff Member *DC Talent Management*
25523 Via Ventana
Valencia, CA 91381-0641, USA

Gallagher, Doug (Athlete, Baseball Player)
11 Cherokee Dr
Hamilton, OH 45013-4909, USA

Gallagher, Frank (Athlete, Football Player)
6572 Enclave Dr
Clarkston, MI 48348-4859, USA

Gallagher, Helen (Actor, Musician)
260 W End Ave Apt 4A
New York, NY 10023-3658, USA

Gallagher, Leo (Comedian)
c/o Craig Marquardo *Fathom Artist Management*
Prefers to be contacted by phone or email.
Portland, OR NA, USA

Gallagher, Liam (Musician)
160 Central Park S # 1709
New York, NY 10019-1502, USA

Gallagher, Mary (Actor)
c/o Michael Greenwald *Endorse Management Group*
9854 National Blvd # 454
Los Angeles, CA 90034-2713, USA

Gallagher, Megan (Actor)
c/o Tim Angle *Shelter Entertainment*
9255 W Sunset Blvd Ste 300
Los Angeles, CA 90069-3313, USA

Gallagher, Mike (Radio Personality)
Gallagher Networks
350 5th Ave Ste 1818
New York, NY 10118-1818, USA

Gallagher, Noel (Musician, Songwriter, Writer)
c/o Staff Member *Ignition Management*
54 Linhope St
London NW1 6HL, UNITED KINGDOM

Gallagher, Patrick (Actor)
c/o Harold Augenstein *Kazarian, Measures, Ruskin & Associates*
5200 Lankershim Blvd Ste 820
N Hollywood, CA 91601-3194, USA

Gallagher, Peter (Actor)
c/o John Carrabino *John Carrabino Management*
5900 Wilshire Blvd Ste 740
Los Angeles, CA 90036-5032, USA

Gallagher, Sean (Athlete, Baseball Player)
4434 NW 99th Ter
Sunrise, FL 33351-4747, USA

Gallagher Jr, Jim (Athlete, Golfer)
PO Box 507
Greenwood, MS 38935-0507, USA

Gallagher Jr, John (Actor)
c/o Byron Wetzel *Byron Wetzel Management*
200 Park Ave S Fl 8
New York, NY 10003-1526, USA

Gallagher-Smith, Jackie (Athlete, Golfer)
193 Paradise Cir
Jupiter, FL 33458-2853, USA

Gallant, Gerard (Athlete, Coach, Hockey Player)
c/o Staff Member *New York Islanders*
1535 Old Country Rd
Plainview, NY 11803-5042, USA

Gallant, Matt (Actor, Television Host)
608 Idaho Ave Unit 8
Santa Monica, CA 90403-2712, USA

Gallardo, Camillio (Actor)
Innovative Artists
1505 10th St
Santa Monica, CA 90401-2805, USA

Gallardo, Carlos (Actor)
c/o Michael Henderson *Heresun Management*
4119 W Burbank Blvd
Burbank, CA 91505-2122, USA

Gallardo, Yovani (Athlete, Baseball Player)
8556 Waterfront Ct
Fort Worth, TX 76179-2504, USA

Gallegly, Elton (Congressman, Politician)
2309 Rayburn Hob
Washington, DC 20515-3211, USA

Gallego, Gina (Actor)
The Agency
1800 Avenue of the Stars Ste 400
Los Angeles, CA 90067-4206, USA

Gallego, Mike (Athlete, Baseball Player)
11 Sunnin11dale
Trabuco Canvon, CA 92679-5103, USA

Gallery, Robert (Athlete, Football Player)
3163 20th St
Masonville, IA 50654, USA

Galles, Jamie (Race Car Driver)
109 Gasoline Aly Ste C
Indianapolis, IN 46222-5934, USA

Galletti, Carl (Business Person)
PO Box 3934
Sedona, AZ 86340-3934, USA

Galley, Garry (Athlete, Hockey Player)
PO Box 500 Stn A
Toronto, ON M5W 1E6, Canada

Galliano, John (Designer, Fashion Designer)
House of Dior
60 Rue D'Avron
Paris 75020, FRANCE

Galligan, Zach (Actor, Comedian)
c/o Aine Leicht *Horror & Hilarity*
Prefers to be contacted by email or phone.
Los Angeles, CA 90067, USA

Gallimore, Jamie (Athlete, Hockey Player)
10931 62 Ave NW
Edmonton, AB T6H 1N3, Canada

Gallison, Joe (Actor)
PO Box 10187
Wilmington, NC 28404-0187, USA

Gallman, Kuki (Writer)
The Gallmann Memorial Foundation
P. O. Box 63704
Nairobi 00619, KENYA

Gallner, Kyle (Actor)
c/o Sarah Shyn *3 Arts Entertainment*
9460 Wilshire Blvd Fl 7
Beverly Hills, CA 90212-2713, USA

Gallo, Carla (Actor)
c/o Stacy Abrams *Abrams Entertainment*
5225 Wilshire Blvd Ste 515
Los Angeles, CA 90036-4349, USA

Gallo, Frank (Artist)
University of Illinios
Art Dept
Urbana, IL 61801, USA

Gallo, George (Director)
c/o Todd Hoffman *ICM Partners*
10250 Constellation Blvd Fl 7
Los Angeles, CA 90067-6207, USA

Gallo, Mike (Athlete, Baseball Player)
1415 Christine St
Houston, TX 77017-4003, USA

Gallo, Vincent (Actor, Director)
c/o Staff Member *Gray Daisy Films Agency*
8033 W Sunset Blvd Ste 833
Los Angeles, CA 90046-2401, USA

Gallop, Tom (Actor)
c/o Dan Baron *Agency for the Performing Arts (APA)*
405 S Beverly Dr Ste 500
Beverly Hills, CA 90212-4425, USA

Galloway, David (Athlete, Football Player)
5441 NW 184th St
Miami Gardens, FL 33055-5344, USA

Galloway, Jean (Religious Leader)
Volunteers of America
1660 Duke St Ste 100
Alexandria, VA 22314-3427, USA

Galloway, Joey (Athlete, Football Player)
4340 Hanna Hills Dr
Dublin, OH 43016-9518, USA

Gallup, Michael (Athlete, Football Player)
c/o Michael Gallup *Capital Sports Advisors*
1919 14th St # 410
Boulder, CO 80302-5310, USA

Galvez, Balvino (Athlete, Baseball Player)
3986 SW 190th Ave
Miramar, FL 33029-2726, USA

Galvin, Emma (Actor)
c/o Steve Maihack *44 West Entertainment*
151 Petaluma Blvd S Apt 311
Petaluma, CA 94952-5185, USA

Galvin, James (Writer)
University of Iowa
Writer's Workshop
Iowa City, IA 52242, USA

Galvin, John R (Athlete, Football Player)
136 Parkview Ave
Lowell, MA 01852-3811, USA

Galvin, Noah (Actor)
c/o Smith (Stevie) Stephanie *Station3 (LA)*
1051 Cole Ave Ste B
Los Angeles, CA 90038-2601, USA

Galway, James (Musician)
Benzeholzstr 11
Meggen 06045, SWITZERLAND

Galyon, Gregory (Athlete, Football Player)
2352 Monticello Dr
Maryville, TN 37803-7528, USA

Galyon, Scott (Athlete, Football Player)
4631 Horseshoe Trl
Morristown, TN 37814-8035, USA

Gambee, Dave (Athlete, Basketball Player)
5615 SW Knightsbridge Dr
Portland, OR 97219-4993, USA

Gamble, Chris (Athlete, Football Player)
13335 Pierre Reverdy Dr
Davidson, NC 28036-7008, USA

Gamble, David (Athlete, Football Player)
16804 Royal Poinciana Dr
Weston, FL 33326-1582, USA

Gamble, Ed (Cartoonist)
Florida Times-Union
1 Riverside Ave
Editorial Dept
Jacksonville, FL 32202-4904, USA

Gamble, Fred (Race Car Driver)
PO Box 5274
Snowmass Village, CO 81615-5274, USA

Gamble, John (Athlete, Baseball Player)
369 Caliente St
Reno, NV 89509-2729, USA

Gamble, Kenny (Ken) (Athlete, Football Player)
4 Algonquin Dr
Wilbraham, MA 01095-2373, USA

Gamble, Kevin (Athlete, Basketball Player)
41 W Huckleberry Rd
Lynnfield, MA 01940-2615, USA

Gamble, Mason (Actor)
United Talent Agency
9336 Civic Center Dr
Beverly Hills, CA 90210-3604, USA

Gamble, Nathan (Actor)
c/o Jessica Katz *Katz Public Relations*
14527 Dickens St
Sherman Oaks, CA 91403-3756, USA

Gamble, Oscar (Athlete, Baseball Player)
9705 Bent Brook Dr
Montgomery, AL 36117-7445, USA

Gamble, Troy (Athlete, Hockey Player)
12038 Terraza Cove Ln
Houston, TX 77041-6230, USA

Gamboa, Juan Pablo (Actor)
c/o Staff Member *Televisa*
Blvd Adolfo Lopez Mateos 232
Colonia San Angel INN
DF CP 01060, MEXICO

Gamboa, Tom (Athlete, Baseball Player)
318 Loch Lomond Rd
Rancho Mirage, CA 92270-5606, USA

Gambol, Chris (Athlete, Football Player)
PO Box 2154
Glen Ellyn, IL 60138-2154, USA

Gambon, Michael (Actor)
c/o Paul Lyon-Maris *Independent Talent Group*
40 Whitfield St
London W1T 2RH, UNITED KINGDOM

Gambon, Michael J (Actor)
International Creative Mgmt
40 W 57th St Ste 1800
New York, NY 10019-4033, USA

Gambon, Sir Michael (Actor)
c/o Staff Member *ICM Partners*
10250 Constellation Blvd Fl 7
Los Angeles, CA 90067-6207, USA

Gambrell, Bill (Athlete, Football Player)
341 Osceola Ave
Bogart, GA 30622-1511, USA

Gambrell, David (Politician)
3747 Peachtree Rd NE Apt 1715
Atlanta, GA 30319-1377, USA

Gambril, Don (Coach)
4409 Spring Row
Northport, AL 35473-5231, USA

Gambucci, Gary (Athlete, Hockey Player)
9241 Yukon Ave S
Minneapolis, MN 55438-1446, USA

Gamester, Russ (Race Car Driver)
150 W Warren St
Peru, IN 46970-2754, USA

Gamez, Robert (Athlete, Golfer)
1128 Wilde Dr
Kissimmee, FL 34747-4046, USA

Gammino, Thomas (Race Car Driver)
875 Phenix Ave
Cranston, RI 02921-1107, USA

Gammon, John (Actor)
c/o Liza Anderson *Anderson Group Public Relations*
8060 Melrose Ave Fl 4
Los Angeles, CA 90046-7038, USA

Gammon, Kendall (Athlete, Football Player)
16225 Wedd St
Stilwell, KS 66085-7857, USA

Gammons, Peter (Commentator)
Boston Globe
PO Box 755
Cataumet, MA 02534-0755, USA

Ganassi, Floyd (Chip) (Race Car Driver)
7777 Woodland Dr
Indianapolis, IN 46278-1794, USA

Ganatra, Nisha (Director)
c/o Kevin Crotty *ICM Partners*
10250 Constellation Blvd Fl 7
Los Angeles, CA 90067-6207, USA

Ganchar, Perry (Athlete, Hockey Player)
4176 Bangle Ct
Dublin, OH 43016-7333, USA

Gand, Gale (Chef, Television Host)
c/o Staff Member *The Food Network.com*
1180 Avenue of the Americas Fl 14
New York, NY 10036-8401, USA

Gandarillas, Gus (Athlete, Baseball Player)
6320 NW 114th St
Hialeah, FL 33012-2334, USA

Gandee, Sherman (Sonny) (Athlete, Football Player)
148 Viking Way
Naples, FL 34110-1136, USA

Gandler, Markus (Skier)
Sinwell 22
Kitzbuhel 06370, AUSTRIA

Gandolfo, Joseph (Horse Racer)
4 Cameron Rd
Saddle River, NJ 07458-2934, USA

Gandy, David (Model)
c/o Angharad Wood *Tavistock Wood Management*
45 Conduit St
London W1S 2YN, UNITED KINGDOM

Gandy, Dylan (Athlete, Football Player)
41302 Scarborough Ln
Novi, MI 48375-2893, USA

Gandy, Mike (Athlete, Football Player)
5331 E Valle Vista Rd
Phoenix, AZ 85018-1933, USA

Gandy, Wayne L (Athlete, Football Player)
406 Pinecrest Rd NE
Atlanta, GA 30342-3827, USA

Gangel, Jamie (Correspondent)
NBC-TV News Dept
30 Rockefeller Plz
New York, NY 10112-0015, USA

Gangloff, Mark (Athlete, Olympic Athlete, Swimmer)
5318 Camden Dr
Stow, OH 44224-5526, USA

Gang of Four (Music Group)
c/o Staff Member *Paradigm (Monterey)*
404 W Franklin St
Monterey, CA 93940-2303, USA

Gann, Mike (Athlete, Football Player)
1479 Ashford Pl NE
Brookhaven, GA 30319-1888, USA

Gannascoli, Joseph (Joe) (Actor)
c/o Jeffrey Leavitt *Leavitt Talent Group*
11500 W Olympic Blvd Ste 400
Los Angeles, CA 90064-1525, USA

Gannon, Rich (Athlete, Football Player, Sportscaster)
6472 Smithtown Rd
Excelsior, MN 55331-8211, USA

Gano, Graham (Athlete, Football Player)
c/o Dave Butz *Sportstars Inc*
1370 Avenue of the Americas Fl 19
New York, NY 10019-4602, USA

Gans, Christoph (Director)
c/o Craig Gering *Creative Artists Agency (CAA)*
2000 Avenue of the Stars Ste 100
Los Angeles, CA 90067-4705, USA

Gansa, Alex (Producer)
c/o BeBe Lerner *ID Public Relations*
7060 Hollywood Blvd Fl 8th
Los Angeles, CA 90028-6021, USA

Gansler, Bob (Coach, Soccer Player)
Kansas City Wizards
2 Arrowhead Dr
Kansas City, MO 64129, USA

Ganson, Arthur (Artist)
Massachusetts Institute of Technology
Compton Gallery
Cambridge, MA 02139, USA

Gant, Harry (Race Car Driver)
7531 Millersville Rd
Taylorsville, NC 28681-8946, USA

Gant, Kenneth (Athlete, Football Player)
1820 W 10th St
Lakeland, FL 33805-3308, USA

Gant, Kenneth (Kenny) (Athlete, Football Player)
3906 Carrollwood Place Cir Apt 243
Tampa, FL 33624-3064, USA

Gant, Mtume (Actor)
c/o Maggie Woods *Online Talent Group*
Prefers to be contacted via email or telephone
Los Angeles, CA 90069, USA

Gant, Reuben (Athlete, Football Player)
PO Box 3051
Tulsa, OK 74101-3051, USA

Gant, Robert (Actor)
c/o Brit Reece *PMK/BNC Public Relations*
1840 Century Park E Ste 1400
Los Angeles, CA 90067-2115, USA

Gant, Ron (Athlete, Baseball Player)
40 Hartz Way Ste 10
Secaucus, NJ 07094-2403, USA

Gantin, Bernardin Cardinal (Religious Leader)
Congregation for Bishops
Plazza Pio XII 10
Rome 00193, ITALY

Gantner, Jim (Athlete, Baseball Player)
PO Box 156
Eden, WI 53019-0156, USA

Gantos, Jack (Writer)
Farrar Straus Giroux
19 Union Sq W
New York, NY 10003-3304, USA

Gantt, Jerome (Athlete, Football Player)
2035 Long Point Trl
Sanford, NC 27332-7449, USA

Gantt, Jerry (Athlete, Football Player)
1511 Atwick Dr
Fayetteville, NC 28304-3901, USA

Gantt, Mark (Actor)
c/o Paul Greenstone *Paul Greenstone Entertainment*
1400 California Ave Apt 201
Santa Monica, CA 90403-4395, USA

Ganz, Bruno (Actor)
Mgmt Ema Baumbauer
Keplerstrasse 2
München 81679, GERMANY

Ganzel, Teresa (Actor)
Irv Schechter
9300 Wilshire Blvd Ste 410
Beverly Hills, CA 90212-3228, USA

Gao, Xiang (Musician)
Columbia Artists Mgmt Inc
165 W 57th St
New York, NY 10019-2201, USA

Gaona, Jessica (Actor)
c/o Staff Member *Abrams Artists Agency*
750 N San Vicente Blvd
E Tower Fl 11
Los Angeles, CA 90069-5788, USA

Garagozzo, Keith (Athlete, Baseball Player)
787 Cornwallis Dr
Mount Laurel, NJ 08054-3209, USA

Garai, Romola (Actor)
c/o Billy Lazarus *United Talent Agency (UTA)*
9336 Civic Center Dr
Beverly Hills, CA 90210-3604, USA

Garalczyk, Mark (Athlete, Football Player)
8096 N 85th Way Ste 101
Scottsdale, AZ 85258-4322, USA

Garamendi, John (Congressman, Politician)
228 Cannon Hob
Washington, DC 20515-3307, USA

Garant, Robert Ben (Actor, Director, Producer, Writer)
c/o Matthew Labov *Forefront Media*
1669 Virginia Rd
Los Angeles, CA 90019-5935, USA

Garas, Kaz (Actor)
10145 N Buchanan Ave
Portland, OR 97203, USA

Garavani, Valentino (Designer, Fashion Designer)
Palazzo Mignanelli
Piazza Mignanelli 22
Rome 00187, Italy

Garbacz, Lori (Athlete, Golfer)
777 Albany Post Rd
Briarcliff Manor, NY 10510-2400, USA

Garbage (Music Group)
c/o Jenna Adler *Creative Artists Agency (CAA)*
2000 Avenue of the Stars Ste 100
Los Angeles, CA 90067-4705, USA

Garbarek, Jan (Musician)
Niels Juels Gate 42
Oslo 00257, NORWAY

Garber, Gene (Athlete, Baseball Player)
771 Stonemill Dr
Elizabethtown, PA 17022-9717, USA

Garber, Terri (Actor)
38 E 1st St # 2B
New York, NY 10003-9345, USA

Garber, Victor (Actor)
c/o Bill Butler *Industry Entertainment Partners*
1133 Broadway Ste 630
New York, NY 10010-8072, USA

Garbey, Barbaro (Athlete, Baseball Player)
14094 Woodside St
Livonia, MI 48154-5206, USA

Garces, Paula (Actor)
c/o Jason Newman *Untitled Entertainment*
350 S Beverly Dr Ste 200
Beverly Hills, CA 90212-4819, USA

Garces, Rich (Athlete, Baseball Player)
605 Swigert St
Kerrville, TX 78028-3140, USA

Garci, Jose Luis (Director)
Direccion General del Libro
Paseo de la Castellana 109
Madrid 00016, SPAIN

Garcia, Adam (Actor)
c/o Peter Safran *The Safran Company*
8748 Holloway Dr
Los Angeles, CA 90069-2327, USA

Garcia, Aimee (Actor)
c/o William (Willie) Mercer *Thruline Entertainment*
9250 Wilshire Blvd Fl Ground
Beverly Hills, CA 90212-3352, USA

Garcia, Andrew (Musician)
c/o Simon Fuller *XIX Entertainment (UK)*
32/33 Ransomes Dock
London SW11 4NP, UNITED KINGDOM (UK)

Garcia, Andy (Actor, Musician)
4323 Forman Ave
Toluca Lake, CA 91602-2909, USA

Garcia, Carlos (Athlete, Baseball Player)
5208 William St
Lancaster, NY 14086-9448, USA

Garcia, Danay (Actor)
c/o Steve Honig *Honig Company, The*
4804 Laurel Canyon Blvd # 828
Studio City, CA 91607-3717, USA

Garcia, Danna (Actor)
c/o Staff Member *Telemundo*
2470 W 8th Ave
Hialeah, FL 33010-2000, USA

Garcia, Danny (Athlete, Baseball Player)
22 Silo Ln
Levittown, NY 11756-3807, USA

Garcia, Eddie (Athlete, Football Player)
4912 Oreilly Rd
Omro, WI 54963-9643, USA

Garcia, Freddy A (Athlete, Baseball Player)
Quisquella Qta
Etapa M22 #52
La Romana, DOMINICAN REPUBLIC

Garcia, Guillermo (Athlete, Baseball Player)
3806 Shoma Dr
Royal Palm Beach, FL 33414-4374, USA

Garcia, Hiram (Producer)
c/o Stephanie Jones *Jonesworks*
211 E 43rd St Rm 1502
New York, NY 10017-4746, USA

Garcia, James (Athlete, Football Player)
999 E Basse Rd Ste 180
San Antonio, TX 78209-1807, USA

Garcia, Jeff (Athlete, Football Player)
PO Box 8977
Rancho Santa Fe, CA 92067-8977, USA

Garcia, Jim (Athlete, Football Player)
999 E Basse Rd Ste 180
San Antonio, TX 78209-1807, USA

Garcia, Joanna (Actor)
c/o Pamela Kohl *3 Arts Entertainment*
9460 Wilshire Blvd Fl 7
Beverly Hills, CA 90212-2713, USA

Garcia, Jorge (Actor)
c/o Erik Kritzer *LINK Entertainment*
11872 La Grange Ave
Los Angeles, CA 90025-5282, USA

Garcia, Jsu (Actor)
c/o Phyllis Carlyle *Carlyle Productions & Management*
2050 Laurel Canyon Blvd
Los Angeles, CA 90046-2065, USA

Garcia, Juan Carlos (Actor)
c/o Gabriel Blanco *Gabriel Blanco Iglesias (Mexico)*
Rio Balsas 35-32
Colonia Cuauhtemoc
DF 06500, Mexico

Garcia, Karim (Athlete, Baseball Player)
38 Agnew Farm Rd
Armonk, NY 10504-1371, USA

Garcia, Kiko (Athlete, Baseball Player)
526 Trailview Cir
Martinez, CA 94553-3563, USA

Garcia, Leo (Athlete, Baseball Player)
11264 W Buchanan St
Avondale, AZ 85323-6824, USA

Garcia, Leonardo (Actor)
c/o Staff Member *TV Azteca*
Periferico Sur 4121
Colonia Fuentes del Pedregal
DF CP 14141, Mexico

Garcia, Martina (Actor)
c/o Florent Lamy *Elevate Artists Management (FR)*
5, Rue Au Maire
Paris 75003, FRANCE

Garcia, Mike (Athlete, Baseball Player)
25931 Calle Agua
Moreno Valley, CA 92551-1620, USA

Garcia, Nina (Business Person, Reality Star)
Elle Magazine
1633 Broadway Fl 44
New York, NY 10019-6708, USA

Garcia, Odalys (Actor)
c/o Staff Member *Univision*
605 3rd Ave Fl 12
New York, NY 10158-0034, USA

Garcia, Pedro (Athlete, Baseball Player)
L4 Parq Del Condado
Caguas, PR 00727-1224, USA

Garcia, Ralph (Athlete, Baseball Player)
7441 Brian Ln
La Palma, CA 90623-1312, USA

Garcia, Rich (Athlete, Baseball Player)
P.O. Box 3276
Clearwater Beach, FL 33767, USA

Garcia, Rich (Baseball Player)
PO Box 3276
Clearwater Beach, FL 33767-8276, USA

Garcia, Rodrigo (Director)
c/o Adriana Alberghetti *WME/IMG*
9601 Wilshire Blvd
Beverly Hills, CA 90210-5213, USA

Garcia, Teddy (Athlete, Football Player)
2203 Cook Rd
Oak Grove, LA 71263-3705, USA

Garcia-Lorido, Dominik (Actor)
c/o Jamie Harhay Skinner *Baker Winokur Ryder Public Relations*
9100 Wilshire Blvd
W Tower #500
Beverly Hills, CA 90212-3415, USA

Garciaparra, Nomar (Athlete, Baseball Player, Olympic Athlete)
613 15th St
Manhattan Beach, CA 90266-4804, USA

Garcia-Rulfo, Manuel (Actor)
c/o Wendy Murphey *LBI Entertainment*
2000 Avenue of the Stars
N Tower Fl 3
Los Angeles, CA 90067-4700, USA

Garcon, Pierre (Athlete, Football Player)
c/o Bradley Cicala *Terra Firma Sports Management*
330 W Spring St Ste 355
Columbus, OH 43215-7305, USA

Gardeazabal, Marcela (Actor)

Gardell, Billy (Actor)
c/o Nick Nuciforo *United Talent Agency (UTA)*
9336 Civic Center Dr
Beverly Hills, CA 90210-3604, USA

Gardener, Daryl (Athlete, Football Player)
8925 Legacy Ct Apt 106
Kissimmee, FL 34747-3018, USA

Gardenhire, Ron (Athlete, Baseball Player, Coach)
c/o John Boggs *John Boggs & Associates*
6265 Greenwich Dr Ste 240
San Diego, CA 92122-5921, USA

Gardin, Ron (Athlete, Football Player)
PO Box 66051
Tucson, AZ 85728-6051, USA

Gardiner, Bruce (Athlete, Hockey Player)
29 Sperling Dr
BARRIE POLICE HEADQUARTERS
Barrie, ON L4M 6K9, Canada

Gardiner, Mike (Athlete, Baseball Player)
26 Read Dr
Hanover, MA 02339-2632, USA

Gardner, Andrew (Actor, Athlete, Football Player)

Gardner, Art (Athlete, Baseball Player)
1953 Highway 35 S
Walnut Grove, MS 39189-5025, USA

Gardner, Ashley (Actor)
c/o Staff Member *Forster Entertainment*
12533 Woodgreen St
Los Angeles, CA 90066-2723, USA

Gardner, Barry (Athlete, Football Player)
15415 Ashland Ave
Harvey, IL 60426-3620, USA

Gardner, Bill (Athlete, Hockey Player)
c/o Staff Member *Chicago Wolves*
2301 Ravine Way
Glenview, IL 60025-7627, USA

Gardner, Billy (Athlete, Baseball Player, Coach)
35 Dayton Rd
Waterford, CT 06385-4205, USA

Gardner, Brett (Athlete, Baseball Player)
331 Foxglove Ave
Summerville, SC 29483-5567, USA

Gardner, Carwell (Athlete, Football Player)
9603 Galene Dr
Louisville, KY 40299-3231, USA

Gardner, Chris (Athlete, Baseball Player)
5318 County Road 125
Wildwood, FL 34785-7942, USA

Gardner, Christopher (Business Person, Writer)
Rubenstein Communications
1345 Avenue of the Americas Fl 30
C/O Rachel Nagler
New York, NY 10105-0109, USA

Gardner, Cory (Congressman, Politician)
213 Cannon Hob
Washington, DC 20515-0919, USA

Gardner, Dave (Athlete, Hockey Player)
Brick Brewing
181 King St S
Waterloo, ON N2J 1P7, Canada

Gardner, Dede (Producer)
c/o Staff Member *Plan B Entertainment*
9150 Wilshire Blvd Ste 350
Beverly Hills, CA 90212-3453, USA

Gardner, Guy (Astronaut)
c/o Staff Member *NASA-JSC*
2101 Nasa Pkwy # 1
Astronaut Office - Mail Code Cb
Houston, TX 77058-3607, USA

Gardner, James H (Basketball Player, Coach)
5465 Bromely Dr
Oak Park, CA 91377-4750, USA

Gardner, Jeff (Athlete, Baseball Player)
28451 Sheridan Dr
Laguna Niguel, CA 92677-1457, USA

Gardner, John (Dancer)
American Ballet Theatre
890 Broadway Fl 3
New York, NY 10003-1278, USA

Gardner, Ken (Athlete, Basketball Player)
3795 S Hawkeye St
Salt Lake City, UT 84120-3390, USA

Gardner, Lee (Athlete, Baseball Player)
1354 Blue Heron Dr
Highland, MI 48357-3910, USA

Gardner, Mark (Athlete, Baseball Player)
15216 Mesa View Ave
Friant, CA 93626-9780, USA

Gardner, Martin (Writer)
c/o St. Martin's Press
175 5th Ave
Attn: Publicity Dept
New York, NY 10010-7703, USA

Gardner, Moe (Athlete, Football Player)
4101 Glen Vista Ct
Duluth, GA 30097-7651, USA

Gardner, Paul (Athlete, Hockey Player)
3687 May Pointe Cv
Southaven, MS 38672-6513, USA

Gardner, Racine (Race Car Driver)
PO Box 934
Buellton, CA 93427-0934, USA

Gardner, Randy (Athlete, Figure Skater, Olympic Athlete)
4640 Glencoe Ave Unit 6
Marina Del Rey, CA 90292-6388, USA

Gardner, Rob (Athlete, Baseball Player)
2001 Gasrilla Rd Lot D21
Placida, FL 33946-2635, USA

Gardner, Rod (Athlete, Football Player)
3351 Tybee Island Cv
Lawrenceville, GA 30044-3484, USA

Gardner, Rulon (Athlete, Olympic Athlete, Wrestler)
Elite Training Center
981 S Main St Ste 130
Logan, UT 84321-6054, USA

Gardner, Slick (Race Car Driver)
PO Box 277
Buellton, CA 93427-0277, USA

Gardner, Wee Willie (Athlete, Basketball Player)
Harlem Globetrotters
5445 Triangle Pkwy Ste 300
Peachtree Corners, GA 30092-2568, USA

Gardner, Wes (Athlete, Baseball Player)
305 Ruth
Benton, AR 72019-2226, USA

Gardocki, Christopher A (Chris) (Athlete, Football Player)
63 Yorkshire Dr
Hilton Head Island, SC 29928-3368, USA

Gardos, Eva (Director)
c/o Staff Member *ICM Partners*
10250 Constellation Blvd Fl 7
Los Angeles, CA 90067-6207, USA

Gare, Danny (Athlete, Hockey Player)
Buffalo Sabres 1 Seymour H Knox III Plz Ste 1
Attn: Broadcast Dept
Buffalo, NY 14203-3096, USA

Gare, Danny (Athlete, Hockey Player)
6 Regent St
Nelson, BC V1L 2P1, Canada

Garelick, Jeremy (Producer)
c/o Staff Member *Artists First*
9465 Wilshire Blvd Ste 900
Beverly Hills, CA 90212-2608, USA

Garfat, Jance (Musician)
Artists Int'l Mgmt
9850 Sandalwood Blvd
#458
Boca Raton, FL 33428, USA

Garfield, Allen (Actor)
c/o Brian McCabe *Venture IAB*
3211 Cahuenga Blvd W Ste 104
Los Angeles, CA 90068-1372, USA

Garfield, Andrew (Actor)
c/o Mara Buxbaum *ID Public Relations*
7060 Hollywood Blvd Fl 8th
Los Angeles, CA 90028-6021, USA

Garfinkel, Jack (Athlete, Basketball Player)
300 Ocean Pkwy Apt 2E
Brooklyn, NY 11218-4078, USA

Garfinkle, David (Producer)
c/o Staff Member *Renegade 83 Entertainment*
12925 Riverside Dr Bldg 413
Sherman Oaks, CA 91423-5263, USA

Garfunkel, Art (Musician)
c/o Ken DiCamillo *WME/IMG (NY)*
11 Madison Ave Fl 18
New York, NY 10010-3669, USA

Garibaldi, Bob (Athlete, Baseball Player)
2143 Oregon Ave
Stockton, CA 95204-4617, USA

Garity, Troy (Actor)
c/o Jason Weinberg *Untitled Entertainment*
350 S Beverly Dr Ste 200
Beverly Hills, CA 90212-4819, USA

Garko, Ryan (Athlete, Baseball Player)
9267 E Trailside Vw
Scottsdale, AZ 85255-6214, USA

Garland, Beverly (Actor)
4222 Vineland Ave
N Hollywood, CA 91602-3318, USA

Garland, Jon (Athlete, Baseball Player)
16833 Armstead St
Granada Hills, CA 91344-2704, USA

Garland, Travis (Musician)
c/o Simon Fuller *XIX Entertainment (UK)*
32/33 Ransomes Dock
London SW11 4NP, UNITED KINGDOM (UK)

Garland, Wayne (Athlete, Baseball Player)
7556 Mossback St
Las Vegas, NV 89123-1581, USA

Garland, Winston (Athlete, Basketball Player)
234 Highland Villa Cir
Nashville, TN 37211-7320, USA

Garlick, Scott (Athlete, Soccer Player)
Cushman & Wakefield
201 N Franklin St Ste 3300
Tampa, FL 33602-5818, USA

Garlin, Jeff (Actor, Comedian)
c/o BeBe Lerner *ID Public Relations*
7060 Hollywood Blvd Fl 8th
Los Angeles, CA 90028-6021, USA

Garlits, Don (Big Daddy) (Race Car Driver)
Garlits Racing Museum
13700 SW 16th Ave
Ocala, FL 34473-3918, USA

Garmaker, Dick (Athlete, Basketball Player)
11517 S 66th East Ave
Bixby, OK 74008-8222, USA

Garman, Mike (Athlete, Baseball Player)
15144 Kings Row Rd
Caldwell, ID 83607-8371, USA

Garman-Hosted, Ann (Athlete, Baseball Player, Commentator)
6582 N 100 E
Wawaka, IN 46794-9724, USA

Garmendia, German (Comedian, Internet Star, Musician)
c/o Staff Member *WME|IMG*
9601 Wilshire Blvd
Beverly Hills, CA 90210-5213, USA

Garmon, Kelvin (Athlete, Football Player)
1424 Creekview Dr
Lewisville, TX 75067-4994, USA

Garn, Jake Brig Gen (Astronaut)
1267 E Chandler Cir
Salt Lake City, UT 84103-4237, USA

Garneau, Jean-Claude (Athlete, Hockey Player)
497 Av Glazier
Quebec, QC G1M 3R6, Canada

Garneau, Marc (Astronaut)
Space Agency
6767 Rte de L'Aeroport
Saint-Hubert, QC J3Y 8Y9, CANADA

Garneau, Marc Capt (Astronaut)
5282 Rue Drolet
Montreal, QC H2T 2H4, CANADA

Garner, Charlie (Athlete, Football Player)
12944 Royal George Ave
Odessa, FL 33556-5709, USA

Garner, Hal (Athlete, Football Player)
5524 Skyline Pkwy
Ogden, UT 84403-4837, USA

Garner, Jennifer (Actor)
c/o Chelsea Thomas *The Lede Company*
9701 Wilshire Blvd # 930
Beverly Hills, CA 90212-2020, USA

Garner, Julia (Actor)
c/o Dara Gordon *Anonymous Content*
155 Spring St Frnt 3
New York, NY 10012-5208, USA

Garner, Kelli (Actor)
c/o Elizabeth Morris *Rogers & Cowan*
1840 Century Park E Fl 18
Los Angeles, CA 90067-2101, USA

Garner, Nate (Athlete, Football Player)

Garner, Phil (Athlete, Baseball Player, Coach)
2 Sapling Pl
Spring, TX 77382-2636, USA

Garner, Tyrone (Athlete, Hockey Player)
Halton Regional Police Department 3800 Southampton Blvd
Burlington, ON L7M 3Y2, Canada

Garner, William S (Cartoonist)
Memphis Commercial Appeal
495 Union Ave
Editorial Dept
Memphis, TN 38103-3221, USA

Garnes, Sam (Athlete, Football Player)
101 Hearthstone Dr
West Milford, NJ 07480-3751, USA

Garnett, Dave (Athlete, Football Player)
4527 Tyrone Ave
Sherman Oaks, CA 91423-2628, USA

Garnett, Kevin (Athlete, Basketball Player)
c/o Andy Miller *ASM Sports*
450 Fashion Ave Ste 1700
New York, NY 10123-1700, USA

Garnett, Scott (Athlete, Football Player)
1637 28th St SE
Puyallup, WA 98372-5188, USA

Garnett, Winfield (Athlete, Football Player)
2029 S 16th Ave
Broadview, IL 60155-3015, USA

Garofalo, Janeane (Actor)
c/o Kara Welker *Generate Management*
8750 Wilshire Blvd Ste 200
Beverly Hills, CA 90211-2707, USA

Garoppolo, Jimmy (Athlete, Football Player)
4949 Marie P Debartolo Way
Santa Clara, CA 95054-1156, USA

Garouste, Gerard (Artist)
La Mesangere
Marcilly-sur-Eure 27810, FRANCE

Garpeniov, Johan (Athlete, Hockey Player)
Vikvagen 1
Tyreso S-13562, Sweden

Garpenlov, Johan (Athlete, Hockey Player)
Breviksvagen 133
Tyresso A-13569, Sweden

Garr, Ralph (Athlete, Baseball Player)
22314 Auburn Canyon Ln
Richmond, TX 77469-5639, USA

Garr, Teri (Actor)
c/o Marc Gurvitz *Brillstein Entertainment Partners*
9150 Wilshire Blvd Ste 350
Beverly Hills, CA 90212-3453, USA

Garrard, David (Athlete, Football Player)
12450 Royal Troon Ln
Jacksonville, FL 32224-5675, USA

Garrard, Rose (Artist)
105 Carpenters Road
#21
London E18, UNITED KINGDOM (UK)

Garrells, Josh (Musician)
Small Voice Records
PO Box 11500
Portland, OR 97211-0500, USA

Garrelts, Scott (Athlete, Baseball Player)
11070 Ashland Way
Shreveport, LA 71106-9348, USA

Garret, Peter (Musician)
PO Box 249
Foxboro, MA 02035-0249, Australia

Garrett, Adrian (Athlete, Baseball Player)
401 E Main St
Louisville, KY 40202-1110, USA

Garrett, Alvin (Athlete, Football Player)
2016 Richelieu Ct
Vestavia Hills, AL 35216-6804, USA

Garrett, Beau (Actor)
c/o Sean Fay *LINK Entertainment*
11872 La Grange Ave
Los Angeles, CA 90025-5282, USA

Garrett, Brad (Actor, Comedian)
c/o Eryn Brown *Management 360*
9111 Wilshire Blvd
Beverly Hills, CA 90210-5508, USA

Garrett, Carl (Athlete, Football Player)
25 Pleasant Vly
Sanger, TX 76266-5784, USA

Garrett, Clifton (Athlete, Baseball Player)
7504 Kenicott Ln
Plainfield, IL 60586-4173, USA

Garrett, Dick (Athlete, Basketball Player)
7100 N Park Manor Dr
Milwaukee, WI 53224-4642, USA

Garrett, Drake (Athlete, Football Player)
32600 Concord Dr Apt 724
Madison Heights, MI 48071-1114, USA

Garrett, Jason (Athlete, Football Player)
c/o David Dunn *Athletes First*
23091 Mill Creek Dr
Laguna Hills, CA 92653-1258, USA

Garrett, Jeremy (Actor)
c/o Staff Member *Paradigm*
8942 Wilshire Blvd
Beverly Hills, CA 90211-1908, USA

Garrett, John (Athlete, Hockey Player)
c/o Staff Member *Rogers Sportsnet*
181 Keefer Pl Suite 221
Vancouver, BC V6B 6C1, Canada

Garrett, John (Athlete, Football Player)
1402 Meadow Ln
Southlake, TX 76092-8339, USA

Garrett, Judd (Athlete, Football Player)
3015 Southwestern Blvd
Dallas, TX 75225-7841, USA

Garrett, Kathleen (Actor)
The Agency
1800 Avenue of the Stars Ste 400
Los Angeles, CA 90067-4206, USA

Garrett, Kenny (Musician)
Von Productions
1915 Cullen Ave
Austin, TX 78757-2435, USA

Garrett, LaMonica (Actor)
c/o Tom Spriggs *Coronel Group*
1100 Glendon Ave Fl 17
Los Angeles, CA 90024-3588, USA

Garrett, Leif (Actor, Musician)
c/o Barbara Papageorge *Barbara Papageorge PR*
790 Amsterdam Ave Apt 4E
New York, NY 10025-5710, USA

Garrett, Len (Athlete, Football Player)
9413 W Tampa Dr
Baton Rouge, LA 70815-8951, USA

Garrett, Lila (Director)
1245 Laurel Way
Beverly Hills, CA 90210, USA

Garrett, Mike (Athlete, Football Player, Heisman Trophy Winner)

Garrett, Myles (Athlete, Football Player)
c/o Bus Cook *Bus Cook Sports, Inc*
1 Willow Bend Dr
Hattiesburg, MS 39402-8552, USA

Garrett, Pat (Musician, Songwriter, Writer)
Patrick Sickafus
PO Box 84
Strausstown, PA 19559-0084, USA

Garrett, Peter (Musician, Politician)
P.O. Box 186
Glebe NSW 2037, Australia

Garrett, Reggie (Athlete, Football Player)
3 Martino Way
Somerset, NJ 08873-4952, USA

Garrett, Rowland (Athlete, Basketball Player)
219 Western Hills Dr
Jackson, MS 39212-3216, USA

Garrett, Scott (Congressman, Politician)
2244 Rayburn Hob
Washington, DC 20515-0921, USA

Garrett, Spencer (Actor)
c/o Erik Kritzer *LINK Entertainment*
11872 La Grange Ave
Los Angeles, CA 90025-5282, USA

Garrett, Wayne (Athlete, Baseball Player)
4331 Linwood St
Sarasota, FL 34232-3905, USA

Garrick, Tom (Athlete, Basketball Player)
235 Providence St
West Warwick, RI 02893-2552, USA

Garrido, Gil (Athlete, Baseball Player)
11311 SW 200th St Apt 110D
Miami, FL 33157-8281, USA

Garrido, Norberto (Athlete, Football Player)
15633 Briarbank St
La Puente, CA 91744-1106, USA

Garriott, Owen K (Astronaut)
111 Lost Tree Dr SW
Huntsville, AL 35824-1313, USA

Garris, John (Athlete, Basketball Player)
308 Carroll St
New Bedford, MA 02740-1415, USA

Garris, Kiwane (Athlete, Basketball Player)
23 E Rocket Cir
Park Forest, IL 60466-1613, USA

Garrison, David (Actor)
630 Estrada Redona
Santa Fe, NM 87501, USA

Garrison, Gary (Athlete, Football Player)
7757 Caminito Encanto Unit 102
Carlsbad, CA 92009-8666, USA

Garrison, John (Athlete, Hockey Player)
Old Concord Rd
Lincoln, MA 01773, USA

Garrison, Lane (Actor)
c/o Dannielle Thomas *Untitled Entertainment*
350 S Beverly Dr Ste 200
Beverly Hills, CA 90212-4819, USA

Garrison, Walt (Athlete, Football Player)
3475 E Hickory Hill Rd
Argyle, TX 76226-3133, USA

Garrison, Webster (Athlete, Baseball Player)
2038 Rue Racine
Marrero, LA 70072-4729, USA

Garrison, Zina (Athlete, Olympic Athlete, Tennis Player)
All Court Tennis Foundation
12335 Kingsride Ln # 106
Houston, TX 77024-4116, USA

Garrity, Gregg (Athlete, Football Player)
86 Seldom Seen Rd
Bradfordwoods, PA 15015-1320, USA

Garrity, Pat (Athlete, Basketball Player)
85 Harrison Ave
New Canaan, CT 06840-5802, USA

Garrix, Martin (DJ)
c/o Scooter Braun *SB Management*
755 N Bonhill Rd
Los Angeles, CA 90049-2303, USA

Garron, Larry (Athlete, Football Player)
987 Pleasant St
Framingham, MA 01701-8853, USA

Garror, Leon (Athlete, Football Player)
259 Stocking St
Mobile, AL 36604-1948, USA

Garrum, Larry (Athlete, Hockey Player)
987 Pleasant St
Framingham, MA 01701-8853, USA

Garson, Willie (Actor)
c/o Gladys Gonzalez *John Carrabino Management*
5900 Wilshire Blvd Ste 740
Los Angeles, CA 90036-5032, USA

Garten, Ina (Chef, Television Host)
Barefoot Contessa
46 Newtown Ln Ste 3
East Hampton, NY 11937-2484, USA

Garth, Jennie (Actor)
PO Box 1944
Studio City, CA 91614-0944, USA

Gartner, Claus-Theo (Actor)
Postfach 230313
Essen, GERMANY 45071

Gartner, Mike (Athlete, Hockey Player)
c/o Staff Member *Hockey Hall of Fame*
Brookfield Place
30 Yonge St
Toronto, ON M5E 1X8, CANADA

Garver, Cathy (Actor)
550 Mountain Home Rd
Woodside, CA 94062-2515, USA

Garver, Kathy (Actor)
170 Woodridge Rd
Hillsborough, CA 94010-7263, USA

Garvey, Mike (Race Car Driver)
Competitive Edge
1033 Louisiana Ave.
#1101
Winter Park, FL 32789, USA

Garvey, Steve (Athlete, Baseball Player)
74720 Old Prospector Trl
Palm Desert, CA 92260-5635, USA

Garvin, Jerry (Athlete, Baseball Player)
1797 E 700 S
Springville, UT 84663-3241, USA

Garvin, Terence (Athlete, Football Player)

Garwasiuk, Ron (Athlete, Hockey Player)
34 Fieldstone Dr
Spruce Grove, AB T7X 3C2, Canada

Gary, Cleveland (Athlete, Football Player)
720 SE Martin Luther King Jr Blvd
Stuart, FL 34994-2368, USA

Gary, Cleveland E (Athlete, Football Player)
1446 SW 169th Ave
Indiantown, FL 37956, USA

Gary, Dunn (Athlete, Football Player)
243 Navajo St
Tavernier, FL 33070-2119, USA

Gary, Keith (Athlete, Football Player)
1401 N Taft St APT 821
Arlington, VA 22201-2650, USA

Gary, Leonard (Athlete, Basketball Player)
3318 N Decatur Blvd Unit 2086
Las Vegas, NV 89130-3253, USA

Gary, Lorraine (Actor)
1158 Tower Rd
Beverly Hills, CA 90210-2131, USA

Garza, David (Musician)
Partisan Arts
PO Box 5085
Larkspur, CA 94977-5085, USA

Garza, Joselle (Race Car Driver)
865 Comstock Ave Apt 11A
Los Angeles, CA 90024-2585, USA

Garza, Matt (Athlete, Baseball Player)
c/o Nez Balelo *CAA Sports*
2000 Avenue of the Stars Ste 100
Los Angeles, CA 90067-4705, USA

Garza, Nicole (Actor)
c/o David Rudy *Armada Partners*
815 Moraga Dr
Los Angeles, CA 90049-1633, USA

Garza, Roberto (Athlete, Football Player)

Gascoigne, Paul J (Soccer Player)
Arran Gardner
Holborn Hall
10 Grays Inn Road
London WC1X 8BY, UNITED KINGDOM (UK)

Gascoine, Jill (Actor)
Marina Martin
12/13 Poland St
London W1V 3DE, UNITED KINGDOM (UK)

Gascon, Eileen (Athlete, Baseball Player, Commentator)
249 Trowbridge Rd
Elk Grove Village, IL 60007-3820, USA

Gascon, Elleen (Baseball Player)
249 Trowbridge Rd
Elk Grove Village, IL 60007-3820, USA

Gash, Samuel L (Sam) (Athlete, Football Player)
46544 Galway Dr
Novi, MI 48374-3871, USA

Gash, Thane (Athlete, Football Player)
201 Whispering Hills Dr
Hendersonville, NC 28792-1213, USA

Gaskill, Brian (Actor)
c/o Marie Mathews *Marie Mathews Management*
1158 26th St Ste 800
Santa Monica, CA 90403-4698, USA

Gasol, Pau (Athlete, Basketball Player, Olympic Athlete)
415 S Front St # 20
Memphis, TN 38103-6404, USA

Gaspar, Rod (Athlete, Baseball Player)
28771 Peach Blossom
Mission Viejo, CA 92692-1072, USA

Gassert, Ron (Athlete, Football Player)
11 Sheffield Pl
Southampton, NJ 08088-1306, USA

Gassman, Alessandro (Actor)
Christian Cucchini Mgmt
Lungotevere del Mellini 10
Rome 00193, ITALY

Gassner, Dave (Athlete, Baseball Player)
N1376 Woodland Dr
Greenville, WI 54942-8035, USA

Gassoff, Brad (Athlete, Hockey Player)
PO Box 85
Wells, BC V0K 2R0, Canada

Gast, Paul (Race Car Driver)
120 Industrial Dr
Grand Island, NY 14072-1219, USA

Gasteyer, Ana (Actor, Comedian)
c/o Frank Frattaroli *Circle of Confusion*
8931 Ellis Ave
Los Angeles, CA 90034-3336, USA

Gastineau, Brittny (Actor, Reality Star)
c/o Dana-Lee Schuman *ICM Partners*
10250 Constellation Blvd Fl 7
Los Angeles, CA 90067-6207, USA

Gastineau, Lisa (Actor, Reality Star)

Gastineau, Marcus D (Mark) (Athlete, Football Player)
22202 N 48th St
Phoenix, AZ 85054-6171, USA

Gastineau, Mark (Athlete, Football Player)
PO Box 816
Eagar, AZ 85925-0816, USA

Gastini, Marta (Actor)
c/o Tiziana Di Matteo *TT Agency*
Via Della Giuliana 35
Rome 00195, ITALY

Gaston, Cito (Athlete, Baseball Player, Coach)
1454 Woodstream Dr
Oldsmar, FL 34677-4832, USA

Gaston, Hiram (Baseball Player)
Birmingham Black Barons
18 Burntwood Cres
Winnipeg, MB R2J 3A1, CANADA

Gaston, Michael (Actor)
c/o Lisa Lieberman *Innovative Artists*
235 Park Ave S Fl 7
New York, NY 10003-1405, USA

Gates, Antonio (Athlete, Football Player)
c/o Staff Member *EAG Sports Management*
909 N Pacific Coast Hwy Ste 360
El Segundo, CA 90245-3864, USA

Gates, Bill (Business Person)
1835 73rd Ave NE
Medina, WA 98039-2328, USA

Gates, Brent (Athlete, Baseball Player)
2125 Shawnee Dr SE
Grand Rapids, MI 49506-5332, USA

Gates, Daryl (Actor)
24876 Sunstar Ln
Dana Point, CA 92629-1930, USA

Gates, David (Musician, Songwriter, Writer)
Paradise Artists
108 E Matilija St
Ojai, CA 93023-2639, USA

Gates, Gareth (Musician)
c/o Staff Member *19 Entertainment*
35-37 Parkgate Rd #32/33
#32/33 Ransomes Dock
London SW11 4NP, UNITED KINGDOM

Gates, Josh (Actor)
c/o Staff Member *Brady, Brannon & Rich Talent (BBR Talent)*
5670 Wilshire Blvd Ste 820
Los Angeles, CA 90036-5613, USA

Gates, Kevin (Musician)
c/o Chelsey Northern *Atlantic Records*
3400 W Olive Ave Fl 2
Burbank, CA 91505-5538, USA

Gates, Melinda (Business Person)
Bill & Melinda Gates Foundation
1835 73rd Ave NE
Medina, WA 98039-2328, USA

Gates, Mike (Athlete, Baseball Player)
131 Edgewater Rd
Kooskia, ID 83539-5024, USA

Gatewood, Aubrey (Athlete, Baseball Player)
5 Pine Tree Loop
North Little Rock, AR 72116-8313, USA

Gatewood, Kimmy (Actor)
c/o Jennie Cooper-Church *Haven Entertainment*
8111 Beverly Blvd Ste 201
Los Angeles, CA 90048-4531, USA

Gatewood, Les (Athlete, Football Player)
508 W Drew St
Kirbyville, TX 75956-1716, USA

Gatewood, Tom (Athlete, Football Player)
53489 Hansel Ln
South Bend, IN 46637-5248, USA

Gatewood, Yusuf (Actor)
c/o Patrick Havern *The Green Room*
7080 Hollywood Blvd Ste 1100
Los Angeles, CA 90028-6938, USA

Gathegi, Edi (Actor)
c/o Whitney Tancred *42West*
1840 Century Park E Ste 700
Los Angeles, CA 90067-2122, USA

Gatherum, Dave (Athlete, Hockey Player)
1457 Mountain Rd
Thunder Bay, ON P7J 1C5, Canada

Gathright, Joey (Athlete, Baseball Player)
20100 Park Row Dr Apt 1307
Katy, TX 77449-4985, USA

Gatlin, Justin (Athlete, Track Athlete)
c/o Staff Member *USA Track & Field*
130 E Washington St Ste 800
Indianapolis, IN 46204-4619, USA

Gatlin, Larry (Musician)
5100 Harris Ave
Kansas City, MO 64133-2331, USA

Gatlin, Steve (Musician)
5103 Fountainhead Dr
Brentwood, TN 37027-5809, USA

Gatling, Chris (Athlete, Basketball Player)
175 Canon Dr
Orinda, CA 94563-2218, USA

Gatt, Joseph (Actor)
c/o Mike Liotta *True Public Relations*
3575 Cahuenga Blvd W Ste 360
Los Angeles, CA 90068-1361, USA

Gatti, Bill (Athlete, Football Player)
1400 Regal Springs Ct
Louisville, KY 40205-3334

Gatti, Jennifer (Actor)
S D B Partners
1801 Ave of Stars
#902
Los Angeles, CA 90067, USA

Gattison, Kenny (Athlete, Basketball Player)
1115 I St NE
Washington, DC 20002-7117, USA

Gatto, Joe (Actor, Producer)
c/o Dexter Scott *Vector Management*
276 5th Ave Rm 604
New York, NY 10001-4527, USA

Gattorno, Francisco (Actor)
c/o Gabriel Blanco *Gabriel Blanco Iglesias (Mexico)*
Rio Balsas 35-32
Colonia Cuauhtemoc
DF 06500, Mexico

Gattuso, Tyler (Model)
c/o Staff Member *Wilhelmina Models (Miami)*
1100 West Ave
Miami Beach, FL 33139-4749, USA

Gatzos, Steve (Athlete, Hockey Player)
McThirsty's Pint
172 Lansdowne St E
PORCH AND PINT
Peterborough, ON K9J 7N9, Canada

Gaubatz, Dennis (Athlete, Football Player)
1250 County Road 943
West Columbia, TX 77486-9454, USA

Gaudet, Jim (Athlete, Baseball Player)
3336 Vineville Ave
Macon, GA 31204-2328, USA

Gaudin, Chad (Athlete, Baseball Player)
108 Citrus Rd
New Orleans, LA 70123-2504, USA

Gaudreau, Rob (Athlete, Hockey Player)
22 Briarbrooke Ln
Cranston, RI 02921-2111, USA

Gaughan, Brendan (Race Car Driver)
Rusty Wallace Racing
1459 Knob Hill Rd.
Mooresville, NC 28117, USA

Gaul, Frank (Athlete, Football Player)
3420 Balsam Dr
Westlake, OH 44145-4407, USA

Gaul, Gilbert M (Journalist)
Philadelphia Inquirer
400 N Broad St
Editorial Dept
Philadelphia, PA 19130-4015, USA

Gaul, Michael (Athlete, Hockey Player)
Webster Hockey Academy
22 Av D'Hampton Gardens
Staff
Pointe-Claire, QC H9S 5B8, Canada

Gaulin, Jean-Marc (Athlete, Hockey Player)
273 Rue Principale
St-Basile-Le-Grand, QC J3N 1J7, Canada

Gault, Bill (Athlete, Football Player)
PO Box 105
Bangs, TX 76823-0105, USA

Gault, William Campbell (Writer)
481 Mountain Dr
Santa Barbara, CA 93103-1700, USA

Gault, Willie (Athlete, Football Player)
15460 La Maida St
Sherman Oaks, CA 91403-1043, USA

Gaultier, Jean Paul (Designer, Fashion Designer)
30, rue du Faubourg St Antoine
Paris 75012, FRANCE

Gaume, Dallas (Athlete, Hockey Player)
4350 Gallaghers Fairway S
Kelowna, BC V1W 4X4, Canada

Gaustad, Paul (Athlete, Hockey Player)
508 Huckleberry Rd
Nashville, TN 37205-2635, USA

Gauthier, Dan (Actor)

Gauthier, Daniel (Athlete, Hockey Player)
136B Rue St Alexis
Charlemagne, QC J5Z 1E8, CANADA

Gauthier, Jean (Athlete, Hockey Player)
415 Av Vinet
Dorval, QC H9S 2M7, Canada

Gauthier, Luc (Athlete, Hockey Player)
c/o Staff Member *Colorado Avalanche*
1000 Chopper Cir
Pepsi Center
Denver, CO 80204-5805, USA

Gauthier, Jr., Denis (Athlete, Hockey Player)
1658 9th St
Manhattan Beach, CA 90266-6129, USA

Gauthreaux, Joe (DJ, Musician)
c/o Staff Member *Diva Central Inc*
7510 W Sunset Blvd # 1445
Los Angeles, CA 90046-3408, USA

Gautlier, Jean-Paul (Designer, Fashion Designer)
Jean-Paul Gaultier SA
325 Rue Du Faubaurg St Martin
Paris 75003, FRANCE

Gauvreau, Jocelyn (Athlete, Hockey Player)
19 Rue Le Vasseur
Gatineau, QC J8V 2M8, Canada

Gava, Cassandra (Actor)
1745 Camino Palmero St Apt 210
Los Angeles, CA 90046-2918, USA

Gavankar, Janina (Actor)
c/o Julie Nathanson *9.2.6pr*
3383 Tareco Dr
Los Angeles, CA 90068-1527, USA

Gavaris, Jordan (Actor)
c/o Pam Winter *Gary Goddard Agency (GGA)*
304-250 The Esplanade
Toronto, ON M5A 1J2, CANADA

Gavin, Charles E (Chuck) (Athlete, Football Player)
2800 Grape St
Denver, CO 80207-2730, USA

Gavin, Diarmuid (Actor, Designer)
Diarmuid Gavin Designs
Block B, Imperial Works
Perren Street
London NW5 3ED, UNITED KINGDOM

Gavin, Erica (Actor)

Gaviria, Trujillo Cesar (President)
Organization of American States
17th & Constitution NW
Washington, DC 20006, USA

Gavrilov, Andrei V (Musician)
c/o Mark Stephan *Mark Stephan Buhl Artists Management*
Geylinggasse 1
Wien 01130, AUSTRIA

Gavron, Rafi (Actor)
c/o Melanie Greene *Affirmative Entertainment*
6525 W Sunset Blvd # 7
Los Angeles, CA 90028-7212, USA

Gay, Billy (Athlete, Football Player)
824 Lisdowney Dr
Lockport, IL 60441-2794, USA

Gay, Brian (Athlete, Golfer)
6809 Valhalla Way
Windermere, FL 34786-5627, USA

Gay, Everett (Athlete, Football Player)
700 E Johnson St
Waco, TX 76705-3816, USA

Gay, Randall (Athlete, Football Player)
116 Cocasset St Apt 14
Foxboro, MA 02035-2067, USA

Gay, Rudy (Athlete, Basketball Player)
16875 Berkshire Ct
Southwest Ranches, FL 33331-1356, USA

Gay, William (Athlete, Football Player)
8200 E Jefferson Ave Apt 804
Detroit, MI 48214-2681, USA

Gaydos, Joey (Actor)
c/o Staff Member *Cunningham Escott Slevin & Doherty (CESD)*
10635 Santa Monica Blvd Ste 130
Los Angeles, CA 90025-8306, USA

Gaydos, Kent (Athlete, Football Player)
1500 Lakeside Dr
Bluff Dale, TX 76433-4385, USA

Gaydos Jr, Joey (Actor)
20436 Martinsville Rd
Belleville, MI 48111-8706, USA

Gaye, Nona (Actor)
c/o Steven Muller *Innovative Artists*
1505 10th St
Santa Monica, CA 90401-2805, USA

Gayheart, Rebecca (Actor, Model)
c/o Gary Mantoosh *Baker Winokur Ryder Public Relations*
9100 Wilshire Blvd
W Tower #500
Beverly Hills, CA 90212-3415, USA

Gayle, Crystal (Actor, Musician)
c/o Staff Member *Agency for the Performing Arts (APA)*
405 S Beverly Dr Ste 500
Beverly Hills, CA 90212-4425, USA

Gayle, Sami (Actor)
c/o Annick Oppenheim *Wolf-Kasteler Public Relations*
6255 W Sunset Blvd Ste 1111
Los Angeles, CA 90028-7426, USA

Gayle, Shaun (Athlete, Football Player)
1530 N Elk Grove Ave Apt I
Chicago, IL 60622-2059, USA

Gaylor, Trevor (Athlete, Football Player)
5855 Hammond Dr
Norcross, GA 30071-3412, USA

Gaylord, Frank (Artist)
25 Delmont Ave
Barre, VT 05641-3630, USA

Gaylord, Mitch (Athlete, Gymnast, Olympic Athlete)
9601 Bowman Dr
Fort Worth, TX 76244-9180, USA

Gaylord, Scott (Race Car Driver)
Scott Gaylord Racing
1451 Depew St
Lakewood, CO 80214-2236, USA

Gaynor, Gloria (Music Group, Musician)
c/o Staff Member *Richard De La Font Agency*
3808 W South Park Blvd
Broken Arrow, OK 74011-1261, USA

Gaynor, Mitzi (Actor, Dancer, Musician)
c/o Rene Reyes *Polly O. Entertainment*
12659 Moorpark St Apt 15
Studio City, CA 91604-1318, USA

Gayton, Joe (Writer)
c/o David Saunders *Agency for the Performing Arts (APA)*
405 S Beverly Dr Ste 500
Beverly Hills, CA 90212-4425, USA

Gayton, Tony (Writer)
c/o Matt Ochacher *Agency for the Performing Arts (APA)*
405 S Beverly Dr Ste 500
Beverly Hills, CA 90212-4425, USA

Gaze, Andrew (Athlete, Basketball Player)
Australian Basketball Resources
P.O. Box 2222
Ivanhoe, East 03029, Australia

Gbagbo, Laurent (President)
President's Office
Boulevard Clozel
Abidijan, IVORY COAST

Gbaja-Biamila, Akbar (Athlete, Football Player)
1050 Armitage St
Alameda, CA 94502-7931, USA

Gbajabiamila, Akbar (Actor, Athlete, Football Player, Television Host)
c/o Liza Anderson *Anderson Group Public Relations*
8060 Melrose Ave Fl 4
Los Angeles, CA 90046-7038, USA

Gbaja-Biamila, Kabeer (Athlete, Football Player)
1071 Hill Dr
Oneida, WI 54155-9114, USA

Geale, Rob (Athlete, Hockey Player)
4167 NW 178th Pl
Portland, OR 97229-7703, USA

Gealey, Grace (Actor)
c/o Angela Mach *Platform PR*
2666 N Beachwood Dr
Los Angeles, CA 90068-2308, USA

Gearing, Ashley (Musician)
Violator Mainstar
2805 Azalea Pl
Nashville, TN 37204-3117, USA

Geary, Anthony (Actor)
4312 Woodman Ave Ste 200
Sherman Oaks, CA 91423-5548, USA

Geary, Cynthia (Actor)
Baumgarten/Prophet
1041 N Formosa Ave # 200
West Hollywood, CA 90046-6703, USA

Geary, Geoff (Athlete, Baseball Player)
2735 Callaway Ln
Kissimmee, FL 34744-8533, USA

Geater, Ron (Athlete, Football Player)
3012 Oceanside Ct
Plainfield, IL 60586-5123, USA

Geathers, Clifton (Athlete, Football Player)
c/o Bill Johnson *SportsTrust Advisors*
3340 Peachtree Rd NE Fl 16
Atlanta, GA 30326-1000, USA

Geathers, James (Athlete, Football Player)
200 Tony Dr
Georgetown, SC 29440-2059, USA

Geathers, Robert (Athlete, Football Player)
1 Dab Dr
Georgetown, SC 29440-6059, USA

G-Eazy (Musician)
c/o Gee Roberson *Blueprint Group*
9348 Civic Center Dr
Beverly Hills, CA 90210-3624, USA

Gebhard, Bob (Commentator)
5242 E Otero Pl
Centennial, CO 80122-3889, USA

Gebrselassie, Haile (Athlete, Track Athlete)
Ethiopian Athletic Federation
P O Box 3241
Addis Ababa, ETHIOPIA

Geddes, Bob (Athlete, Football Player)
79251 Tom Fazio Ln S
La Quinta, CA 92253-8031, USA

Geddes, Jane (Athlete, Golfer)
4918 W San Rafael St
Tampa, FL 33629-5404, USA

Geddes, Jim (Athlete, Baseball Player)
4897 Blossom Way
Grove City, OH 43123-8260, USA

Geddes, Ken (Athlete, Football Player)
7702 147th Ave NE
Redmond, WA 98052-4168, USA

Gedman, Rich (Athlete, Baseball Player)
10 Parmenter Rd
Framingham, MA 01701-3019, USA

Gedmintas, Ruta (Actor)
c/o Olivia Homan *United Agents*
12-26 Lexington St
London W1F OLE, UNITED KINGDOM

Gedney, Chris (Athlete, Football Player)
26111 Upton Crk
San Antonio, TX 78260-2407, USA

Gedrick, Jason (Actor)
c/o Michael Garnett *Leverage Management*
3030 Pennsylvania Ave
Santa Monica, CA 90404-4112, USA

Gee, Dillon (Athlete, Baseball Player)
413 S Hill Dr
Cleburne, TX 76033-4539, USA

Gee, James D (Religious Leader)
Penecostal Church of God
4901 Pennsylvania
Joplin, MO 64804, USA

Gee, Prunella (Actor)
Michael Ladkin Mgmt
1Duchess St #1
London W1N 3DE, UNITED KINGDOM (UK)

Geer, Ellen (Actor)
21418 Entrada Rd
Topanga, CA 90290-3539, USA

Geer, Josh (Athlete, Baseball Player)
10836 Peach Cir
Forney, TX 75126-6666, USA

Geeson, Judy (Actor)
c/o Chris Roe *Chris Roe Management*
PO Box 761
Burbank, CA 91503-0761, USA

Geeson, Sally (Actor)
c/o Staff Member *Michael Summerton Management*
Martin Taylor-Brown
Mimosa House, Mimosa St
London SW6 4DS, UK

Gee-Soo, Kim (Actor)
Sidus HQ
88 Sam-sung dong
Sambo Building 1st Fl.
Kang-nam gu, Seoul 135 090, Korea

Geffen, David (Business Person, Producer)
Geffen Playhouse
10886 Le Conte Ave
Los Angeles, CA 90024-3021, USA

Geffner, Glenn (Commentator)
4058 Palm Pl
Weston, FL 33331-5035, USA

Geha, Maggie (Actor)
c/o Tigran Babadjanian *Principal Entertainment*
9255 W Sunset Blvd Ste 500
Los Angeles, CA 90069-3301, USA

Gehlfuss, Nick (Actor)
c/o Annick Oppenheim *Wolf-Kasteler Public Relations*
6255 W Sunset Blvd Ste 1111
Los Angeles, CA 90028-7426, USA

Gehlhausen, Spike (Race Car Driver)
5456 Meadowood Dr
Speedway, IN 46224-3338, USA

Gehringer, Rick (Musician)
c/o Staff Member *Brothers Management Associates Inc*
141 Dunbar Ave
Fords, NJ 08863-1551

Gehrke, Jack (Athlete, Football Player)
9200 E Cherry Creek South Dr Apt 40
Denver, CO 80231-4019, USA

Gehry, Frank (Designer)
Gehry Partners
12541 Beatrice St
Los Angeles, CA 90066-7001, USA

Geiberger, Al (Athlete, Golfer)
73091 Country Club Dr Ste A4
Palm Desert, CA 92260-2338, USA

Geiberger, Brent (Athlete, Golfer)
113 Chelsea Cir
Palm Desert, CA 92260-4688, USA

Geiger, Ken (Journalist, Photographer)
Dallas Mornig News
Communications Center
Dallas, TX 75265, USA

Geiger, Matt (Athlete, Basketball Player)
12506 Twin Branch Acres Rd
Tampa, FL 33626-4423, USA

Geiger, Teddy (Musician)
c/o Ollie Hammett *Spark Management*
360 Hamilton Ave Ste 100
White Plains, NY 10601-1847, USA

Geisel, Dave (Athlete, Baseball Player)
4 Blacksmith Ln
Media, PA 19063-4411, USA

Geishert, Vern (Athlete, Baseball Player)
1440 W Seminary St
Richland Ctr, WI 53581-2036, USA

Geisinger, Justin (Athlete, Football Player)
441 Summit Oaks Dr
Nashville, TN 37221-1317, USA

Geist, William (Bill) (Commentator, Writer)
c/o Staff Member *CBS News (NY)*
524 W 57th St Fl 8
New York, NY 10019-2930, USA

Geist, Willie (Commentator, Journalist, Television Host)
c/o Staff Member *NBC News (NY)*
30 Rockefeller Plz
New York, NY 10112-0015, USA

Gelbaugh, Stan (Athlete, Football Player)
10819 Hob Nail Ct
Potomac, MD 20854-2560, USA

Geldart, Gary (Athlete, Hockey Player)
565 Demarett Dr
Lago Vista, TX 78645-8515, USA

Geldof, Bob (Actor, Musician)
c/o Rick Shoor *Red Entertainment Agency*
3537 36th St Ste 2
Astoria, NY 11106-1347, USA

Gelfant, Alan (Actor)
Peter Strain
5724 W 3rd St Ste 302
Los Angeles, CA 90036-3085, USA

Gelinas, Gratien (Actor, Writer)
207-316 Girouard St
Oka, QC J0N 1E0, CANADA

Gelinas, Martin (Athlete, Hockey Player)
c/o Staff Member *National Sports Development Ltd*
7475 Flint Rd SE
Calgary, AB T2H 1G3, Canada

Gellar, Sarah Michelle (Actor)
2435 Mandeville Canyon Rd
Los Angeles, CA 90049-1235, USA

Gellard, Sam (Athlete, Hockey Player)
35 Dancers Dr
Markham, ON L6C 2C4, Canada

Geller, Glenn (Business Person)
c/o Staff Member *CBS Paramount Network Television*
4024 Radford Ave
Cbs Studios
Studio City, CA 91604-2190, USA

Geller, Uri (Actor)
c/o Staff Member *Celeb Agents*
77 Oxford St
London ON W1D 2ES, UNITED KINGDOM (UK)

Gelman, Larry (Actor)
5121 Greenbush Ave
Sherman Oaks, CA 91423-1507, USA

Gelman, Michael (Producer)
7 Lincoln Sq
New York, NY 10023-7219

Gelnar, John (Athlete, Baseball Player)
1811 Suzanne Dr Apt 2
Weatherford, OK 73096-2383, USA

Gemar, Charles D (Astronaut)
7660 N 159th Street Ct E
Benton, KS 67017-8926, USA

Gemar, Charles D Lt Colonel (Astronaut)
7660 N 159th Street Ct E
Benton, KS 67017-8926, USA

GEM Sisters (Comedian, Internet Star)
c/o Tim Weissman *Buchwald*
5900 Wilshire Blvd Ste 3100
Los Angeles, CA 90036-5030, USA

Gendron, Jean-Guy (Athlete, Hockey Player)
122 Rue Jacques-Bigot
Levis, QC G7A 2R8, Canada

Gene, Marc (Race Car Driver)
Minardi Team
Via Spallanzani 21
Faenza 48018, ITALY

Genesis (Music Group)
c/o Staff Member *Hit and Run Music Ltd*
25 Ives Street
South Kensington
London SW3 2ND, United Kingdom

Genilas, Eric (Athlete, Hockey Player)
165 Mulberry St
Newark, NJ 07102-3607, USA

Genitallica (Music Group)
c/o Staff Member *Sony Music (Miami)*
404 Washington Ave Ste 700
Miami Beach, FL 33139-6615, USA

Genovese, George (Athlete, Baseball Player)
11615 Killion St
North Hollywood, CA 91601-2639, USA

Gentile, Jim (Athlete, Baseball Player)
1016 S Neptune Rd
Edmond, OK 73003-6071, USA

Gentile, Troy (Actor)
c/o Matt Goldman *Silver Lining Entertainment*
421 S Beverly Dr Fl 7
Beverly Hills, CA 90212-4408, USA

Gentilozzi, Paul (Race Car Driver)
3400 West Rd
East Lansing, MI 48823-7309, USA

Gentry, Craig (Athlete, Baseball Player)
1209 Cartwright St
Van Buren, AR 72956-2809, USA

Gentry, Curtis (Athlete, Football Player)
387 Meadow Green Ln
Round Lake Beach, IL 60073-1326, USA

Gentry, Dennis (Athlete, Football Player)
916 Queen Elizabeth Dr
Mc Gregor, TX 76657-4000, USA

Gentry, Harvey (Athlete, Baseball Player)
109 Eaton Ln
Bristol, TN 37620-2820, USA

Gentry, Montgomery (Music Group)
c/o John Dorris Sr *Hallmark Direction Company*
713 18th Ave S
Nashville, TN 37203-3214, USA

Gentry, Teddy W (Music Group, Musician)
P O Box 529
Fort Payne, AL 35968, USA

Genzel, Carrie (Actor)
Pakula/King
9229 W Sunset Blvd Ste 315
Los Angeles, CA 90069-3403, USA

Genzman, Andy (Race Car Driver)
Genzman Racing
2145 Napoleon Rd
Fremont, OH 43420-1502, USA

Geoffrion, Dan (Athlete, Hockey Player)
413 Overall Dr
Brentwood, TN 37027-7649, USA

Geoffrion, Daniel (Athlete, Hockey Player)
413 Overall Dr
Brentwood, TN 37027-7649, USA

Geoffrion, Scott (Race Car Driver)
Team Mopar
27608 La Paz
#506
Laguna Rills, CA 92656, USA

George, Alex (Athlete, Baseball Player)
8024 Granada Rd
Prairie Village, KS 66208-5061, USA

George, Boy (Musician)
c/o Dawn Miller *Miller PR*
750 N San Vicente Blvd # 800
W Hollywood, CA 90069-5788, USA

George, Chris (Athlete, Baseball Player, Olympic Athlete)
428 Kathy Lynn Dr
Pittsburgh, PA 15239-1708, USA

George, Christopher S (Chris) (Baseball Player)
121 E Maranta Rd
Mooresville, NC 28117-6335, USA

George, Devean (Athlete, Basketball Player)
1285 French Creek Dr
Wayzata, MN 55391-9105, USA

George, Ed (Athlete, Football Player)
1220 S Orange Ave
Sarasota, FL 34239-2028, USA

George, Eddie (Athlete, Football Player, Heisman Trophy Winner, Television Host)
9538 Sanctuary Pl
Brentwood, TN 37027-8498, USA

George, Elizabeth (Writer)
c/o Robert Gottlieb *Trident Media Group LLC*
41 Madison Ave Fl 36
New York, NY 10010-2257, USA

George, Eric (Actor)
Lasher McManus Robinson
1964 Westwood Blvd Ste 400
Los Angeles, CA 90025-4695, USA

George, Gotz (Actor)
c/o Ute Nicolai *Agentur Ute Nicolai*
Gosslerstrasse 2
Berlin 12161, Germany

George, Helen (Actor)
c/o Pandora Weldon *Public Eye Communications*
535 Kings Rd
#313 Plaza
London SW10 0SZ, UNITED KINGDOM

George, Jason Winston (Actor)
c/o Barry McPherson *Agency for the Performing Arts*
135 W 50th St Fl 17
New York, NY 10020-1201, USA

George, Jeffrey S (Jeff) (Athlete, Football Player)
1908 Schwier Ct
Indianapolis, IN 46229-2154, USA

George, Matt (Athlete, Football Player)
24403 Newhall Ave Apt 3
Newhall, CA 91321-2771, USA

George, Max (Musician)
c/o Scooter Braun *SB Management*
755 N Bonhill Rd
Los Angeles, CA 90049-2303, USA

George, Melissa (Actor)
c/o Pamela Kohl *3 Arts Entertainment*
9460 Wilshire Blvd Fl 7
Beverly Hills, CA 90212-2713, USA

George, Paul (Athlete, Basketball Player)
13715 W 109th St Ste 110
Lenexa, KS 66215-4332, USA

George, Peter (Athlete, Olympic Athlete, Weightlifter)
1649 Kalakaua Ave Ste 204
Honolulu, HI 96826-2494, USA

George, Phyllis (Beauty Pageant Winner, Television Host)
c/o Staff Member *The Miss America Organization*
PO Box 1919
Atlantic City, NJ 08404-1919, USA

George, Ron (Athlete, Football Player)
10136 Middlebrooks Ter
Nokesville, VA 20181-3669, USA

George, Steve (Athlete, Football Player)
5922 W Airport Blvd
Houston, TX 77035-5302, USA

George, Susan (Actor)
McKorkindale & Holton
1-2 Langham Place
London W1A 3DD, UNITED KINGDOM (UK)

George, Tate (Athlete, Basketball Player)
55 Georgetown Rd
Bristol, CT 06010-5510, USA

George, Terry (Writer)
c/o Ari Emanuel *WME/IMG*
9601 Wilshire Blvd
Beverly Hills, CA 90210-5213, USA

George, Tim (Athlete, Football Player)
77 Saddle Ln
Easton, PA 18045-3115, USA

George, Tony (Race Car Driver)
Vison Racing
6803 Coffman Rd
Indianapolis, IN 46268-2561, USA

George, Wes (Athlete, Hockey Player)
442 O'Regan Crt
Saskatoon, SK S7L 6N8, Canada

George, William W (Business Person)
Medtronic Inc
7000 Central Ave NE
Minneapolis, MN 55432-3576, USA

George-McFaul, Jean (Baseball Player)
2432 Kilkeer Ste 9
N Battleford, SK S9I 3Y5, CANADA

Georges, Anne (Baseball Player)
407 Oak St
Des Plaines, IL 60016-4429, USA

Georgian, Theodore J (Religious Leader)
Orthodox Presbyterian Church
P O Box P
Willow Grove, PA 19090, USA

Georgije, Bishop (Religious Leader)
Serbian Orthodox Church
PO Box 519
Libertyville, IL 60048-0519, USA

Georgoulis, Alexis (Actor)
c/o Ali Sages *Sages Entertainment Group*
9107 Wilshire Blvd Ste 450
Beverly Hills, CA 90210-5535, USA

Gephardt, Richard (Politician)
DLA Piper
PO Box 9945
Mc Lean, VA 22102-0945, USA

Geraci, Sonny (Music Group)
Mars Talent
27 L Ambiance Ct
Bardonia, NY 10954-1421, USA

Geraghty, Brian (Actor)
c/o Lena Roklin *Luber Roklin Management*
5815 W Sunset Blvd Ste 208
Los Angeles, CA 90028-6481, USA

Gerard, Caitlin (Actor)
c/o Mara Buxbaum *ID Public Relations*
7060 Hollywood Blvd Fl 8th
Los Angeles, CA 90028-6021, USA

Gerard, Gil (Actor)
c/o Michael Einfeld *Michael Einfeld Management*
10630 Moorpark St Unit 101
Toluca Lake, CA 91602-2797, USA

Gerard, Gus (Athlete, Basketball Player)
614 Cypresswood Dr
Spring, TX 77388-5913, USA

Gerber, Craig (Athlete, Baseball Player)
366 I St
Chula Vista, CA 91910-5627, USA

Gerber, H Joseph (Business Person)
Gerber Scientific Inc
24 Industrial Park Rd W
Tolland, CT 06084-2806, USA

Gerber, Kaia (Actor, Model)
c/o Jillian Neal *Untitled Entertainment*
350 S Beverly Dr Ste 200
Beverly Hills, CA 90212-4819, USA

Gerber, Michael (Business Person, Writer)
E-Myth Worldwide
2235 Mercury Way Ste 200
Santa Rosa, CA 95407-5472, USA

Gerber, Rande (Business Person)
Crawdaddy Productions
3340 Ocean Park Blvd # 300
Santa Monica, CA 90405-3204, USA

Gerberman, George (Athlete, Baseball Player)
1501 Michael St
El Campo, TX 77437-9345, USA

Gercke, Lena (Model)
c/o Staff Member *REDSEVEN Artists & Events GmbH*
Medienallee 7
Unterfoehring D-85774, Germany

Gere, Richard (Actor)
Richard Gere Foundation
10100 Santa Monica Blvd Ste 1700
Los Angeles, CA 90067-4156, USA

Geredine, Tom (Athlete, Football Player)
1155 Woodlands Dr
Kyle, TX 78640-5530, USA

Gerela, Roy (Athlete, Football Player)
3933 Ramrod Frg
Las Cruces, NM 88012-6008, USA

Geren, Bob (Athlete, Baseball Player, Coach)
32 Bottlebrush Ct
Danville, CA 94506-4743, USA

Gerena, Samuel (Gringo) (Musician)
c/o Staff Member *Universal Music Publishing Group (Latin)*
420 Lincoln Rd Ste 200
Miami Beach, FL 33139-3014, USA

Gerg, Hilde (Skier)
Brauneck Tolzer Hutte
Lenggries 83661, GERMANY

Gergen, David R (Politician)
31 Ash St
Cambridge, MA 02138-4840, USA

Gerg-Leitner, Michaela (Skier)
Jachenauer Str 26
Lenggries 83661, GERMANY

Gerhardt, Alben (Musician)
Columbia Artists Mgmt Inc
165 W 57th St
New York, NY 10019-2201, USA

Gerhardt, Don (Athlete, Football Player)
1465 Waterford Dr
Golden Valley, MN 55422-4274, USA

Gerhardt, Jason (Actor)
Hollywood Entertainment
9255 W Sunset Blvd Ste 803
C/O Ron Scott
Los Angeles, CA 90069-3305, USA

Gerhardt, Rusty (Athlete, Baseball Player)
PO Box 426
New London, TX 75682-0426, USA

Gerhart, Bobby (Race Car Driver)
305 Lights St.
Lebanon, PA 17042, USA

Gerhart, Garth (Athlete, Football Player)
c/o David Dunn *Athletes First*
23091 Mill Creek Dr
Laguna Hills, CA 92653-1258, USA

Gerhart, Ken (Athlete, Baseball Player)
1603 Ashford Ct
Murfreesboro, TN 37129-5888, USA

Gerhart, Toby (Athlete, Football Player)
c/o Joby Branion *Vanguard Sports Group*
23091 Mill Creek Dr
Laguna Hills, CA 92653-1258, USA

Gering, Galen (Actor)
c/o Mark Schumacher *Schumacher Management*
Prefers to be contacted by email or phone.
Los Angeles, CA 90064, USA

Gering, Jenna (Actor)
c/o Jonathan Bluman *WME|IMG*
9601 Wilshire Blvd
Beverly Hills, CA 90210-5213, USA

Gerlach, Jim (Congressman, Politician)
2442 Rayburn Hob
Washington, DC 20515-3011, USA

Germain, Dorothy (Athlete, Golfer)
3443 Waterwheel Cir
Winston Salem, NC 27103-6478, USA

Germain, Eric (Athlete, Hockey Player)
46 Dawes Ave
Hamden, CT 06517-2331, USA

Germain, Stephanie (Producer)
c/o Staff Member *Creative Artists Agency (CAA)*
2000 Avenue of the Stars Ste 100
Los Angeles, CA 90067-4705, USA

German, Jammi (Athlete, Football Player)
3702 Highland Ave
Fort Myers, FL 33916-6529, USA

German, Lauren (Actor)
c/o Doug Wald *Anonymous Content*
3532 Hayden Ave
Culver City, CA 90232-2413, USA

Germani, Fernando (Music Group, Musician)
Via Delle Terme Decians 11
Rome, ITALY

Germann, Greg (Actor, Director)
c/o Liza Anderson *Anderson Group Public Relations*
8060 Melrose Ave Fl 4
Los Angeles, CA 90046-7038, USA

Germano, Justin (Athlete, Baseball Player)
1006 NE 15th St
Cape Coral, FL 33909-1455, USA

Germano, Lisa (Music Group, Musician)
Artists & Audience Entertainment
PO Box 35
Pawling, NY 12564-0035, USA

Germany, Reggie (Athlete, Football Player)
145 Prince Rd SW
Etna, OH 43062-8358, USA

Germany, Willie (Athlete, Football Player)
4401 Pratt St
Omaha, NE 68111-2533, USA

Germar, Manfred (Athlete, Track Athlete)
DLV
Alsfelder Str 27
Darmstadt 642889, GERMANY

Germeshausen, Bernhard (Athlete)
Hinter Dem Salon 39
Schwansee 99195, GERMANY

Gernander, Ken (Athlete, Hockey Player)
355 Eddy Glover Blvd
New Britain, CT 06053-2411, USA

Gernert, Dick (Athlete, Baseball Player)
1801 Cambridge Ave Apt C12
Reading, PA 19610-2669, USA

Gernhardt, Michael L (Astronaut)
2022 Lakeside Lndg
Seabrook, TX 77586-8301, USA

Gernon, Bruce (Writer)
c/o Staff Member *Llewellyn Worldwide, LTD*
2143 Wooddale Dr
Saint Paul, MN 55125-2989, USA

Geronimo, Cesar F (Baseball Player)
Tefeda Flo #46
Santo Domingo, DOMINICAN REPUBLIC

Gerrard, Steven (Athlete, Soccer Player)
c/o Dan Levy *Wasserman Media Group (NC)*
4208 Six Forks Rd Ste 1020
Raleigh, NC 27609-5738, USA

Gerring, Cathy (Athlete, Golfer)
3328 Tarrant Springs Trl
Fort Wayne, IN 46804-6161, USA

Gersbach, Carl (Athlete, Football Player)
PO Box 433
Devon, PA 19333-0433, USA

Gershman, Benj (Musician)
275 Greenwich St # 9JS
New York, NY 10007-2150, USA

Gershon, Gina (Actor)
c/o Annie Schmidt *Untitled Entertainment (NY)*
215 Park Ave S Fl 8
New York, NY 10003-1622, USA

Gerstell, A Frederick (Business Person)
CalMat Co
3200 N San Fernando Rd
Los Angeles, CA 90065-1415, USA

Gerstner, Lou (Business Person)
IBM Corp
1 N Castle Dr Ste 2
Armonk, NY 10504-1784, USA

Gertz, Jami (Actor)
c/o Jason Barrett *Alchemy Entertainment*
7024 Melrose Ave Ste 420
Los Angeles, CA 90038-3394, USA

Gerut, Jody (Athlete, Baseball Player)
623 Rochdale Cir
Lombard, IL 60148-4730, USA

Gerut, Joseph ""Jody"" (Athlete, Baseball Player)
746 N Cuyler Ave
Oak Park, IL 60302-1775, USA

Gervais, Ricky (Actor, Director, Producer)
c/o Duncan Hayes *United Agents*
12-26 Lexington St
London W1F OLE, UNITED KINGDOM

Gervin, Derrick (Athlete, Basketball Player)
8147 Babe Ruth St
San Antonio, TX 78240-2902, USA

Gervin, George (Athlete, Basketball Player, Coach)
44 Gervin Pass
Spring Branch, TX 78070-6370, USA

Gerwig, Greta (Actor, Director)
c/o Evelyn O'Neill *Management 360*
9111 Wilshire Blvd
Beverly Hills, CA 90210-5508, USA

Geschke, Charles (Business Person)
Adobe Systems
345 Park Ave
San Jose, CA 95110-2704, USA

Gesek, John (Athlete, Football Player)
105 Sand Point Ct
Coppell, TX 75019-5359, USA

G. Eshoo, Anna (Congressman, Politician)
205 Cannon Hob
Washington, DC 20515-0514, USA

Gessford, Jim (Athlete, Football Player)
8537 Chaparral Cir
Lincoln, NE 68520-1180

Gessle, Per (Musician)
c/o Staff Member *D&D Management*
Drottning Gatan 55
Stockholm 11121, SWEDEN

Gethard, Chris (Actor, Comedian)
c/o Brian Stern *AGI Entertainment*
150 E 58th St Fl 19
New York, NY 10155-1900, USA

Getherall, Joey (Athlete, Football Player)
3105 Las Marias Ave
Hacienda Heights, CA 91745-6219, USA

Gethers, Peter (Writer)
c/o Catherine Brackey *ICM Partners*
10250 Constellation Blvd Fl 7
Los Angeles, CA 90067-6207, USA

Gets, Malcolm (Actor)
c/o Lisa Loosemore *Viking Entertainment*
445 W 23rd St Ste 1A
New York, NY 10011-1445, USA

Gettinger, Ruby (Reality Star)
c/o Glenn Rigberg *Inphenate*
9701 Wilshire Blvd Fl 10
Beverly Hills, CA 90212-2010, USA

Gettis, Byron (Athlete, Baseball Player)
6313 Whalen Ave
East Saint Louis, IL 62207-1051, USA

Getty, Balthazar (Actor)
c/o Cheryl Lynch *Lynch Archer PR*
5115 Wilshire Blvd Apt 400
Los Angeles, CA 90036-4372, USA

Getty, Charlie (Athlete, Football Player)
1446 Hudson Lndg
Saint Charles, MO 63303-6174, USA

Get Up Kids (Music Group)
c/o Staff Member *Creative Artists Agency (CAA)*
2000 Avenue of the Stars Ste 100
Los Angeles, CA 90067-4705, USA

Getz, John (Actor)
4124 Wade St
Los Angeles, CA 90066-5732, USA

Getzlaf, Ryan (Athlete, Hockey Player)
The Sports Corporation
2735-10088 102 Ave NW
Attn Rich Winter
Edmonton, AB T5J 2Z1, Canada

Getzlaff, James (Actor)
c/o Staff Member *Douglas Gorman Rothacker & Wilhelm Inc*
33 W 46th St Ste 801
New York, NY 10036-4103, USA

Gevinson, Tavi (Actor)
c/o Jordan Berkus *United Talent Agency (UTA)*
9336 Civic Center Dr
Beverly Hills, CA 90210-3604, USA

Geyer, Dean (Actor)
c/o Mike Gillespie *Primary Wave Entertainment*
10850 Wilshire Blvd Fl 6
Los Angeles, CA 90024-4319, USA

Geyer, Georgie Anne (Journalist)
The Plaza Suite 800 25th St NW
Washington, DC 20037-2208, USA

Geyer, Hugh (Music Group)
2218 Ridge Rd
McKeesport, PA 15135-3037, USA

G. Fitzpatrick, Michael (Congressman, Politician)
1224 Longworth Hob
Washington, DC 20515-0553, USA

G. Grimm, Michael (Congressman, Politician)
512 Cannon Hob
Washington, DC 20515-1012, USA

Ghadie, Samia (Actor)
c/o Granada TV
Quay Street
Manchester M60 9EA

Ghaffari, Matt (Athlete, Olympic Athlete, Wrestler)
32834 Fox Chappel Ln
Avon Lake, OH 44012-2331, USA

Ghanime, Mark (Actor, Producer)
c/o Nicole Miller *NMA PR*
7916 Melrose Ave Ste 1
Los Angeles, CA 90046-7160, USA

Ghattas, Stephenos II Cardinal (Religious Leader)
Patriarcat Copte Catholique
BP 69 Rue Ibn Sandar
Cairo 11712, EGYPT

Ghauri, Yasmeen (Model)
c/o Staff Member *Next Model Management (NY)*
15 Watts St Fl 6
New York, NY 10013-1677, USA

Ghelfi, Tony (Athlete, Baseball Player)
3414 Geneva Ln
La Crosse, WI 54601-8302, USA

Gheorghiu, Ion A (Artist)
27-29 Emil Pangratti St
Bucharest, ROMANIA

Ghesquiere, Nicolas (Fashion Designer)
11 Avenue dlena
Balenciaga, Paris 75016, UNITED KINGDOM

Ghiglia, Oscar A (Music Group, Musician)
Helfembergstr 14
Basel 04059, SWITZERLAND

Ghigliotti, Marilyn (Actor)
Redrock Entertainment Development
149 E Santa Anita Ave
Burbank, CA 91502-1926, USA

Gholston, William (Athlete, Football Player)
c/o Blake Baratz *The Institute for Athletes*
3600 Minnesota Dr Ste 550
Edina, MN 55435-7925, USA

Ghost, Amanda (Musician)
c/o Staff Member *Basina Recording Company*
PO Box 8121
Pittsburgh, PA 15217-0121, USA

Ghostface, Killa (Music Group, Musician)
Famous Artists Agency
250 W 57th St
New York, NY 10107-0001, USA

Ghostland Observatory (Music Group)
c/o Ken Weinstein *Big Hassle Media*
40 Exchange Pl Ste 1900
New York, NY 10005-2714, USA

Ghuman Jr, JB (Actor)
c/o Harry Gold *TalentWorks*
3500 W Olive Ave Ste 1400
Burbank, CA 91505-5512, USA

Giacchino, Michael (Musician)
c/o Brad Shenfeld *Shenfeld Law*
16255 Ventura Blvd Ste 201
Encino, CA 91436-2300, USA

Giacomarro, Ralph (Athlete, Football Player)
512 Sackman Falls Ct
Canton, GA 30114-8147, USA

Giacomin, Edward (Eddie) (Athlete, Hockey Player)
6575 Red Maple Ln
Bloomfield Hills, MI 48301-3225, USA

Giacomini, Breno (Athlete, Football Player)

Giaffone, Felipe (Race Car Driver)
Conquest Racing
5062 W 79th St
Indianapolis, IN 46268-1645, USA

Giallombardo, Bob (Athlete, Baseball Player)
7903 Antique Cir
Waxhaw, NC 28173-7858, USA

Giallonardo, Mario (Athlete, Hockey Player)
94 Queen Mary Ave
Burlington, ON L7T 2G7, Canada

Giamatti, Paul (Actor)
c/o Perri Kipperman *Kipperman Management*
345 7th Ave Rm 503
New York, NY 10001-5054, USA

Giambalvo, Louis (Actor)
c/o Staff Member *Judy Schoen & Associates*
606 N Larchmont Blvd Ste 309
Los Angeles, CA 90004-1309, USA

Giambi, Jason (Athlete, Baseball Player)
3 Crystal Tree Pass
Henderson, NV 89052-6701, USA

Giambi, Jeremy (Athlete, Baseball Player)
18512 Carlson Ln
Elgin, TX 78621-3839, USA

Giambra, Joey (Boxer)
7950 W Flamingo Rd Unit 1188
Las Vegas, NV 89147-4234, USA

Giambrone, Art (Horse Racer)
398 Brickyard Rd
Freehold, NJ 07728-8414, USA

Giammona, Louie (Athlete, Football Player)
525 Parrish St
Philadelphia, PA 19123-2111, USA

Gian, Joseph (Joey) (Actor, Musician)
Joey Gian Entertainment
13351D Riverside Dr # 294
Sherman Oaks, CA 91423-2508, USA

Giancanelli, Hal (Athlete, Football Player)
2227 Portola Ln
Westlake Village, CA 91361-1748, USA

Giancola, Sammi (Reality Star)
c/o Sal Bonaventura *Central Entertainment Group*
250 W 40th St Fl 12
New York, NY 10018-4601, USA

Gianelli, John (Athlete, Basketball Player)
PO Box 1097
Pinecrest, CA 95364-0097, USA

Giannelli, Ray (Athlete, Baseball Player)
56 E Saltaire Rd
Lindenhurst, NY 11757-6829, USA

Giannini, Andriano (Actor)
c/o Lindy King *United Agents*
12-26 Lexington St
London W1F OLE, UNITED KINGDOM

Giannini, Giancario (Actor)
Via Salaria 292
Rome 00199, ITALY

Giannoulas, Ted (Commentator)
6549 Mission Gorge Rd Ste 247
San Diego, CA 92120-2306, USA

Gianopoulos, David (Actor)
c/o Staff Member *GVA Talent Agency Inc*
193 N Robertson Blvd
Beverly Hills, CA 90211-2103, USA

Giaquinto, Nick (Athlete, Football Player)
1613 Stone Moss Reach Apt D
Chesapeake, VA 23320-7468, USA

Giarraputo, Jack (Producer)
c/o Staff Member *Happy Madison Productions*
10202 Washington Blvd
Judy Garland Bldg
Culver City, CA 90232-3119, USA

Giarratano, Tony (Athlete, Baseball Player)
145 Leedom Way
Newtown, PA 18940-2307, USA

Gibb, Barry (Musician, Songwriter)
PO Box 8179
Miami, FL 33139, USA

Gibb, Cynthia (Actor)
c/o Scott Hart *Scott Hart Entertainment*
14622 Ventura Blvd # 746
Sherman Oaks, CA 91403-3600, USA

Gibb, Donald (Actor)
Ashby/Rojo Entertainment
1485 S Beverly Dr
Los Angeles, CA 90035-3021, USA

Gibbard, Ben (Musician)
c/o Staff Member *Zeitgeist Artist Management*
600 York St Ste 216
San Francisco, CA 94110-2119, USA

Gibbon, Joe (Athlete, Baseball Player)
26 County Road 24142
Newton, MS 39345-8946, USA

Gibbons, Beth (Music Group, Songwriter, Writer)
Fruit
Saga Center 326 Kensal Road
London W10 5BZ, UNITED KINGDOM (UK)

Gibbons, Billy (Musician)
c/o Rick Canny *Favor the Artist Management*
Prefers to be contacted by email or phone.
Los Angeles, CA NA, USA

Gibbons, Brian (Athlete, Baseball Player)
51788 Whitestable Ln
South Bend, IN 46637-1370, USA

Gibbons, Brian (Athlete, Hockey Player)
4 Twillingate Pl
St. John's, NL AlE 3R4, Canada

Gibbons, Gail (Writer)
c/o Staff Member *Simon & Schuster*
1230 Avenue of the Americas Fl CONC1
New York, NY 10020-1586, USA

Gibbons, Jay (Athlete, Baseball Player)
29408 Malibu View Ct
Agoura Hills, CA 91301-6237, USA

Gibbons, Jim (Athlete, Football Player)
891 Valley Rd
Carbondale, CO 81623-9712, USA

Gibbons, John (Athlete, Baseball Player, Coach)
PO Box 782294
San Antonio, TX 78278-2294, USA

Gibbons, Kaye (Writer)
c/o Lynn Pleshette *Lynn Pleshette Literary Agency*
2700 N Beachwood Dr
Los Angeles, CA 90068-1922, USA

Gibbons, Leeza (Producer, Television Host)
9025 Ashcroft Ave
West Hollywood, CA 90048-1704, USA

Gibbons, Tim (Producer)
c/o Staff Member *ICM Partners*
10250 Constellation Blvd Fl 7
Los Angeles, CA 90067-6207, USA

Gibbons, Walter (Athlete, Baseball Player)
8515 N Temple Ave
Tampa, FL 33617-6934, USA

Gibbs, Barry (Athlete, Hockey Player)
6176 Stinson Way NW
Edmonton, AB T6R 0K3, Canada

Gibbs, Bob (Congressman, Politician)
329 Cannon Hob
Washington, DC 20515-4607, USA

Gibbs, Connor (Actor)
c/o Geoff Cheddy *Brillstein Entertainment Partners*
9150 Wilshire Blvd Ste 350
Beverly Hills, CA 90212-3453, USA

Gibbs, Coy (Race Car Driver)
c/o Staff Member *NASCAR*
1801 W Speedway Blvd
Daytona Beach, FL 32114-1243, USA

Gibbs, H Jarrell (Business Person)
Texas Utilities Co
Energy Plaza 1601 Bryan St
Dallas, TX 75201, USA

Gibbs, Jake (Athlete, Baseball Player)
223 Saint Andrews Cir
Oxford, MS 38655-2518, USA

Gibbs, Joe (Athlete, Football Coach, Football Player, Race Car Driver)
Joe Gibbs Racing
19122 Peninsula Point Dr.
Cornelius, NC 2803-7603, USA

Gibbs, Marla (Actor, Music Group)
3500 W Manchester Blvd Unit 267
Inglewood, CA 90305-4267, USA

Gibbs, Mickey (Race Car Driver)
3 Grandview Cir
Gadsden, AL 35905-8837, USA

Gibbs, Pat (Athlete, Football Player)
4835 Corley St
Beaumont, TX 77707-4224, USA

Gibbs, Sonny (Athlete, Football Player)
2708 Halbert St
Fort Worth, TX 76112-5531, USA

Gibbs, Terri (Musician, Songwriter)
1439 Clary Cut Rd
Appling, GA 30802, USA

Gibbs, Terry (Music Group, Musician)
Thomas Cassidy
11761 E Speedway Blvd
Tucson, AZ 85748-2017, USA

Gibbs, Timothy (Actor)
c/o Julia Buchwald *Buchwald*
5900 Wilshire Blvd Ste 3100
Los Angeles, CA 90036-5030, USA

Gibgot, Adam (Writer)
c/o Adriana Alberghetti *WME/IMG*
9601 Wilshire Blvd
Beverly Hills, CA 90210-5213, USA

Giblin, Robert (Athlete, Football Player)
2818 Reynolds Ln
Port Neches, TX 77651-5410, USA

Gibney, Alex (Producer)
c/o Staff Member *Jigsaw Productions*
419 Park Ave S Rm 600
New York, NY 10016-8410, USA

Gibney, Rebecca (Actor)
128 Rupert St.
Collingwood, Vic. 03066, AUSTRALIA

Gibney, Susan (Actor)
c/o Matthew Lesher *Insight*
5358 Melrose Ave # 200W
Los Angeles, CA 90038-5117, USA

Gibralter, Steve (Athlete, Baseball Player)
2512 Crooked Crk
Mesquite, TX 75181-4214, USA

Gibraltor, Steve (Athlete, Baseball Player)
3651 Asbury St
Dallas, TX 75205-1848, USA

Gibson, Aaron (Athlete, Football Player)
1777 Timber Creek Rd Apt 2122
Flower Mound, TX 75028-7342, USA

Gibson, Andy (Musician)
c/o Staff Member *Curb Records (Nashville)*
48 Music Sq E
Nashville, TN 37203-4639, USA

Gibson, Antonio (Athlete, Football Player)
2320 Jaguar Dr Apt 502
Bryan, TX 77807-2346, USA

Gibson, Bob (Athlete, Baseball Player)
215 Bellevue Blvd S
Bellevue, NE 68005-2442, USA

Gibson, Bob (Athlete, Basketball Player)
1524 Cuming St Apt 519
Omaha, NE 68102-4436, USA

Gibson, Brandon (Athlete, Football Player)

Gibson, Charles (Charlie) (Journalist, Television Host)
25 E End Ave PH
New York, NY 10028-7052, USA

Gibson, Claude (Athlete, Football Player)
47 Gladstone Rd
Asheville, NC 28805-2454, USA

Gibson, Damon (Athlete, Football Player)
4332 Dell Rd Apt J
Lansing, MI 48911-8126, USA

Gibson, Deborah (Debbie) (Actor, Musician)
PO Box 1154
Katy, TX 77492-1154, USA

Gibson, Dennis (Athlete, Football Player)
912 SW Elm St
Ankeny, IA 50023-2850, USA

Gibson, Derrick (Athlete, Baseball Player)
138 Buckeye Loop Rd
Winter Haven, FL 33881-2703, USA

Gibson, Derrick (Athlete, Football Player)
303 Avenue 0 NW
Winter Haven, FL 33881-4906, USA

Gibson, Doug (Athlete, Hockey Player)
1220 Cartier Blvd
Peterborough, ON K9H 6S1, Canada

Gibson, Edward (Astronaut)
1594 E Copper Holw
San Tan Valley, AZ 85140-5347, USA

Gibson, Ellie (Athlete, Golfer)
35705 N 29th Ln
Phoenix, AZ 85086-4219, USA

Gibson, Ernest (Athlete, Football Player)
1749 Kinsmon Cv
Marietta, GA 30062-8173, USA

Gibson, Fred (Athlete, Golfer)
432 Shorewood Ln
New Smyrna Beach, FL 32168-8384, USA

Gibson, Greg (Athlete, Baseball Player)
20305 Country Club Dr
Catlettsburg, KY 41129-8602, USA

Gibson, Greg (Baseball Player)
3628 Briarwood Dr
Catlettsburg, KY 41129-9298, USA

Gibson, Janice (Athlete, Golfer)
9747 S Granite Ave
Tulsa, OK 74137-4931, USA

Gibson, Kelly (Athlete, Golfer)
700 S Peters St Apt 419
New Orleans, LA 70130-1606, USA

Gibson, Kirk (Athlete, Baseball Player)
33 Sunset Ln
Grosse Pointe Farms, MI 48236-3730, USA

Gibson, Laurieann (Dancer)
c/o Jeff Raymond *Rogers & Cowan*
1840 Century Park E Fl 18
Los Angeles, CA 90067-2101, USA

Gibson, Leah (Actor)
c/o Kim Matuka *Schuller Talent (LA)*
332 S Beverly Dr Ste 100
Beverly Hills, CA 90212-4812, USA

Gibson, Mark (Race Car Driver)
Mark Gibson Racing
308 Wages Rd
Auburn, GA 30011-2856, USA

Gibson, Mel (Actor, Director, Producer)
c/o Staff Member *Icon Productions*
808 Wilshire Blvd Fl 4
Santa Monica, CA 90401-1889, USA

Gibson, Milo (Actor)
c/o Amy Brownstein *PRStudio USA*
9255 W Sunset Blvd # 10
W Hollywood, CA 90069-3309, USA

Gibson, Oliver (Athlete, Football Player)
1448 E 52nd St # 406
Chicago, IL 60615-4122, USA

Gibson, Paul (Athlete, Baseball Player)
23421 Water Cir
Boca Raton, FL 33486-8547, USA

Gibson, Robert L Captain (Astronaut)
1709 Shagbark Trl
Murfreesboro, TN 37130-1136, USA

Gibson, Robert L (Hoot) (Astronaut)
1709 Shagbark Trl
Murfreesboro, TN 37130-1136, USA

Gibson, Russ (Athlete)
495 Gardners Neck Rd
Swansea, MA 02777-3131, USA

Gibson, Thomas (Actor, Director)
c/o Liza Anderson *Anderson Group Public Relations*
8060 Melrose Ave Fl 4
Los Angeles, CA 90046-7038, USA

Gibson, Tyrese (Actor, Musician, Producer)
c/o Staff Member *HQ Pictures*
15260 Ventura Blvd Ste 2100
Sherman Oaks, CA 91403-5360, USA

Gibson, William (Writer)
G P Putnam's Sons
375 Hudson St
New York, NY 10014-3658, USA

Gick, George (Athlete, Baseball Player)
875 Elston Rd
Lafayette, IN 47909-6322, USA

Gidada, Negasso (President)
President's Office
P O Box 5707
Addis Ababa, ETHIOPIA

Giddish, Kelli (Actor)
c/o Jean-Louis Diamonika *One Entertainment (NY)*
347 5th Ave Rm 1404
New York, NY 10016-5034, USA

Gideon, Brett (Athlete, Baseball Player)
PO Box 822
Georgetown, TX 78627-0822, USA

Gideon, Jim (Athlete, Baseball Player)
2509 McCallum Dr
Austin, TX 78703-2520, USA

Gideon, Raynold (Actor, Writer)
3524 Multiview Dr
Los Angeles, CA 90068-1222, USA

Giella, Joseph (Cartoonist)
191 Morris Dr
East Meadow, NY 11554-1317, USA

Gien, Pamela (Actor, Writer)
c/o Heather Schroder *ICM Partners (NY)*
730 5th Ave
New York, NY 10019-4105, USA

Gierer, Vincent A Jr (Business Person)
UST Inc
100 W Putnam Ave
Greenwich, CT 06830-5361, USA

Gierowski, Stefen (Artist)
Ul Gagarina 15 m 97
Warsaw 00-753, POLAND

Gierszal, Jakub (Actor)
c/o Rose Parkinson *Lisa Richards Agency (UK)*
33 Old Compton St
London W1D 5JU, UNITED KINGDOM

Giesler, Jon (Athlete, Football Player)
129 Umbrella Pl
Jupiter, FL 33458-1622, USA

Giessinger, Andrew (Athlete, Football Player)
1667 Union Ave
Barberton, OH 44203-7644, USA

Gietzen, Pam (Athlete, Golfer)
603 Woodland West Dr
Woodway, TX 76712-3514, USA

Giffin, Lee (Athlete, Hockey Player)
RR 4
Blenheim, ON N0P 1A0, Canada

Gifford, Cassidy (Actor)
c/o Jenny Tversky *Shelter PR*
928 Broadway Ste 505
New York, NY 10010-8143, USA

Gifford, Gloria (Actor)
Schiowitz/Clay/Rose
1680 Vine St # 1016
Los Angeles, CA 90028-8804, USA

Gifford, Kathie Lee (Television Host)
c/o Staff Member *The Today Show*
30 Rockefeller Plz
New York, NY 10112-0015, USA

Giffords, Gabby (Congressman, Politician)
Americans For Responsible Solutions PAC
PO Box 92560
Washington, DC 20090-2560, USA

Gift, Roland (Actor, Music Group)
Primary Talent Int'l
1-12 Petonville Road
London N1 9PL, UNITED KINGDOM (UK)

Gigandet, Cam (Actor)
c/o Ina Treciokas *Slate PR*
901 N Highland Ave
W Hollywood, CA 90038-2412, USA

Giggie, Bob (Athlete, Baseball Player)
8 Royal Lake Dr Apt 3
Braintree, MA 02184-5457, USA

Gigli, Romeo (Designer, Fashion Designer)
37 W 57th St Ste 900
New York, NY 10019-3411, USA

Gigliotti, Lou (Race Car Driver)
LG Motorsports
4314 Action St
Garland, TX 75042-6805, USA

Gigon, Norm (Athlete, Baseball Player)
2503 Rio Vista Dr
Mahwah, NJ 07430-4506, USA

Gigot, Paul (Journalist)
Wall Street Journal
200 Liberty St
New York, NY 10281-1003, USA

Giguere, Jean-Sebastien (Athlete, Hockey Player)
2066 Port Bristol Cir
Newport Beach, CA 92660-5413, USA

Giguere, Russ (Music Group, Musician)
Variety Artists
1111 Riverside Ave Ste 501
Paso Robles, CA 93446-2683, USA

Giheno, John (President)
Prime Minister's Office
Marera Hau
Port Moresby, PAPUA NEW GUINEA

Gil, Ariadna (Actor)
Cineart
36 Rue de Ponthieu
Paris 75008, FRANCE

Gil, Benii (Athlete, Baseball Player)
12712 Steadman Farms Dr
Keller, TX 76244-1786, USA

Gil, Geronimo (Athlete, Baseball Player)
c/o Staff Member *Baltimore Orioles*
333 W Camden St Ste 1
Baltimore, MD 21201-2476, USA

Gil, Gilberto (Music Group, Songwriter, Writer)
BPR
36 Como St Ramford
Essex RM 7 7DR, UNITED KINGDOM (UK)

Gil, Gus (Athlete, Baseball Player)
2240 SW 42nd Ter
Fort Lauderdale, FL 33317-6618, USA

Gil, R Benjamin (Benji) (Athlete, Baseball Player)
504 Unbridled Ln
Keller, TX 76248-8724, USA

Gilberry, Wallace (Athlete, Football Player)
c/o Jimmy Sexton *CAA (Memphis)*
6060 Poplar Ave Ste 470
Memphis, TN 38119-0910, USA

Gilbert, Brad (Athlete, Tennis Player)
ProServe
1101 Woodrow Wilson Blvd #1800
Arlington, VA 22209, USA

Gilbert, Brantley (Musician)
c/o Jake Basden *Big Machine Records*
1219 16th Ave S
Nashville, TN 37212-2901, USA

Gilbert, Buddy (Athlete, Baseball Player)
1913 Belcaro Dr
Knoxville, TN 37918-3709, USA

Gilbert, Chris (Athlete, Football Player)
6619 Blue Hills Rd
Houston, TX 77069-2412, USA

Gilbert, Daren (Athlete, Football Player)
885 Mallorca Ct
Riverside, CA 92501, USA

Gilbert, David (Cartoonist)
c/o Staff Member *King Features Syndication*
300 W 57th St Fl 15
New York, NY 10019-5238, USA

Gilbert, Ed (Athlete, Hockey Player)
657 Jacksonville Rd
Warminster, PA 18974-1508, USA

Gilbert, Elizabeth (Writer)
c/o Sarah Chalfant *The Wylie Agency*
250 W 57th St Ste 2114
New York, NY 10107-2114, USA

Gilbert, Freddie (Athlete, Football Player)
110 Camden Rd
Griffin, GA 30223-1677, USA

Gilbert, Gary (Producer)
c/o Staff Member *Gilbert Films*
1835 Deloz Ave
Los Angeles, CA 90027-4617, USA

Gilbert, Gibby (Athlete, Golfer)
7070 Sunset Mountain Dr
Chattanooga, TN 37421, USA

Gilbert, Gilles (Athlete, Hockey Player)
9964 Rue de la Fariniere
Quebec, QC G2K 1L7, Canada

Gilbert, Greg (Athlete, Coach, Hockey Player)
c/o Staff Member *Toronto Marlies*
100 Princes Blvd
Toronto, ON M6K 3C3, Canada

Gilbert, Joe (Athlete, Baseball Player)
512 W Martin Luther King Blvd
Jasper, TX 75951-2527, USA

Gilbert, Justin (Athlete, Football Player)
c/o Jimmy Sexton *CAA (Memphis)*
6060 Poplar Ave Ste 470
Memphis, TN 38119-0910, USA

Gilbert, Kenneth A (Music Group, Musician)
23 Cloitre Notre-Dame
Chartres 28000, FRANCE

Gilbert, Lewis (Athlete, Football Player)
6331 SW 1st St
Plantation, FL 33317-3407, USA

Gilbert, Marcus (Athlete, Football Player)
c/o Drew Rosenhaus *Rosenhaus Sports Representation*
3921 Alton Rd # 440
Miami Beach, FL 33140-3852, USA

Gilbert, Mark (Athlete, Baseball Player)
2340 NW 45th St
Boca Raton, FL 33431-8437, USA

Gilbert, Melissa (Actor)
c/o Ame VanIden *VanIden Public Relations*
4070 Wilson Pike
Franklin, TN 37067-8126, USA

Gilbert, O'Neill (Athlete, Coach, Football Coach, Football Player)
460 Great Circle Rd
Nashville, TN 37228-1404, USA

Gilbert, Peter (Director)
Innovative Artists
1505 10th St
Santa Monica, CA 90401-2805, USA

Gilbert, Rodrique G (Rod) (Athlete, Hockey Player)
52 E End Ave Apt 33A
New York, NY 10028-8116, USA

Gilbert, Sara (Actor, Talk Show Host)
c/o Staff Member *CBS Paramount Network Television*
4024 Radford Ave
Cbs Studios
Studio City, CA 91604-2190, USA

Gilbert, Sean (Athlete, Football Player)
7219 Grassy Knob Ct
Charlotte, NC 28273-3171, USA

Gilbert, Shawn (Athlete, Baseball Player)
6392 Rosemary Dr
Cypress, CA 90630-4052, USA

Gilbert, Simon (Musician)
Interceptor Enterprises
98 White Lion St
London N1 9PF, UNITED KINGDOM (UK)

Gilbert, S J Sr (Religious Leader)
Baptist Convention of America
6717 Centennial Blvd
Nashville, TN 37209-1017, USA

Gilberto, Astrud (Music Group)
Absolute Artists
530 Howard St Ste 200
San Francisco, CA 94105-3018, USA

Gilberto, Bebel (Music Group)
Miracle Prestige
1 Water Lane Camden Town
London NW1 8NZ, UNITED KINGDOM (UK)

Gilbertson, Bob (Race Car Driver)
2250 Toomey Ave
Charlotte, NC 28203-4635, USA

Gilbertson, Harrison (Actor)
c/o Ame VanIden *VanIden Public Relations*
4070 Wilson Pike
Franklin, TN 37067-8126, USA

Gilbertson, Keith (Coach, Football Coach)
University of Washington
Athletic Dept
Seattle, WA 98195-0001, USA

Gilbertson, Stan (Athlete, Hockey Player)
2924 Mosswood Dr
Lodi, CA 95242-2051, USA

Gilbreath, Rod (Athlete, Baseball Player)
1438 Ridgeland Way SW
Lilburn, GA 30047-4352, USA

Gilbreth, Bill (Athlete, Baseball Player)
709 Gary Ln
Abilene, TX 79601-5537, USA

Gilbride, Kevin (Athlete, Coach, Football Player)
3400 S Water St
Pittsburgh, PA 15203-2349, USA

Gilburg, Tom (Athlete, Football Player)
437 Patriots Way
Lititz, PA 17543-7318, USA

Gilchrist, Brent (Athlete, Hockey Player)
Bank of Montreal
200-3200 30 Ave
Vernon, BC V1T 2C5, Canada

Gilchrist, Guy (Cartoonist)
20 Bristol Dr
Canton, CT 06019-2214, USA

Gilchrist, Jeanne (Baseball Player)
218-67 Miner St
New Westminster, BC V3L 5N5, CANADA

Gilchrist, Keir (Actor)
c/o Samantha Hill *Wolf-Kasteler Public Relations*
6255 W Sunset Blvd Ste 1111
Los Angeles, CA 90028-7426, USA

Gilchrist, Marcus (Athlete, Football Player)
c/o Hadley Engelhard *Enter-Sports Management*
6000 Lake Forrest Dr Ste 370
Atlanta, GA 30328-5902, USA

Gilchrist, Pual R (Religious Leader)
Presbyterian Church in America
1862 Century Place
Atlanta, GA 30345, USA

Gilder, Bob (Athlete, Golfer)
2600 NW Century Dr Apt 243
Corvallis, OR 97330-4733, USA

Gildon, Jason (Athlete, Football Player)
1562 Barrington Dr
Wexford, PA 15090-9377, USA

Gile, Don (Athlete, Baseball Player)
624 W Cherokee Ave
Stillwater, OK 74075-1405, USA

Giles, Bill (Commentator)
Philadelphia Phillies
1400 Waverly Rd APT B-317
Gladwyne, PA 19035-1269, USA

Giles, Brian (Athlete, Baseball Player)
c/o Brett Bick *Pro Star Management*
312 Walnut St Ste 1600
1600 Scripps Center
Cincinnati, OH 45202-4038, USA

Giles, Curt (Athlete, Hockey Player)
5225 Grandview Sq Apt 402
Minneapolis, MN 55436-1691, USA

Giles, Jimmie (Athlete, Football Player)
3959 Van Dyke Rd # 298
Lutz, FL 33558-8025, USA

Giles, Marcus (Athlete, Baseball Player)
26132 Old Highway 80
Descanso, CA 91916-9797, USA

Giles, Nancy (Actor)
12047 178th St
Jamaica, NY 11434-2719, USA

Giles, Selina (Actor)
Edward Hill Management
Dolphin House
2-5 Manchester St
BN2 1TF, United Kingdom

Giletti, Alain (Figure Skater)
103 Place de L'Eglise
Chamonix 74400, FRANCE

Gilfillan, Jason (Athlete, Baseball Player)
153 Gilfillan Rd
Blacksburg, SC 29702-8521, USA

Gilford, David (Athlete, Golfer)
Andrew Murray
19 Higher Lane
Lymm Cheshire WA13 0AR, United Kingdom

Gilford, Zach (Actor)
c/o Charles Mastropietro *Circle of Confusion*
8931 Ellis Ave
Los Angeles, CA 90034-3336, USA

Gilgorov, Kiro (President)
President's Office
Skopje, MACEDONIA

Gilhen, Randy (Athlete, Hockey Player)
c/o Staff Member *Manitoba Moose*
260 Hargrave St
Winnipeg, MB R3C 5S5, Canada

Gilinksy, Jack (Actor, Musician)
c/o Carleen Donovan *Donovan Public Relations*
30 E 20th St Ste 2FE
New York, NY 10003-1310, USA

Gilk, Shelley (Athlete, Golfer)
10537 Toledo Dr N
Minneapolis, MN 55443-5424, USA

Gilkey, Bernard (Athlete, Baseball Player)
2200 Dunhill Way Ct
Chesterfield, MO 63005-4511, USA

Gilkey, Garrett (Athlete, Football Player)

Gill, Hal (Athlete, Hockey Player)
115 Westhampton Pl
Nashville, TN 37205-3438, USA

Gill, Janis (Music Group)
Monty Hitchcock Mgmt
5101 Overton Rd
Nashville, TN 37220-1920, USA

Gill, Johnny (Actor)
9229 W Sunset Blvd Ste 311
West Hollywood, CA 90069-3403, USA

Gill, Katie (Actor)
c/o Kelly-Marie Smith *Status PR*
PO Box 6191
Westlake Village, CA 91359-6191, USA

Gill, Kendall (Athlete, Basketball Player)
c/o Staff Member *Milwaukee Bucks*
1543 N 2nd St Fl 6
Milwaukee, WI 53212-4036, USA

Gill, Michael (Actor)
c/o David Williams *David Williams Management*
269 S Beverly Dr # 1408
Beverly Hills, CA 90212-3851, USA

Gill, Thea (Actor)
c/o Barry Krost *Barry Krost Management*
9220 W Sunset Blvd Ste 106
Los Angeles, CA 90069-3500, USA

Gill, Todd (Athlete, Hockey Player)
c/o Staff Member *Brockville Braves*
1030 Montrose St
Brockville, ON K6V 7G1, Canada

Gill, Tonya (Athlete, Golfer)
3655 Habersham Rd NE Apt B2229
Atlanta, GA 30305-1142, USA

Gill, Vince (Musician, Songwriter)
515 Park Center Ave
Nashville, TN 37205-3429, USA

Gillan, Ian (Musician)
Miracle Prestige
1 Water Lane
Camden Town
London NW1 8N2, UNITED KINGDOM (UK)

Gillan, Karen (Actor)
c/o Sarah Stephenson *Troika*
10A Christina St.
London EC2A 4PA, UNITED KINGDOM

Gillanders, David (Athlete, Olympic Athlete, Swimmer)
1617 Briarwood Dr
Jonesboro, AR 72401-4632, USA

Gillaspie, Conor (Athlete, Baseball Player)
5601 Pacific St
Omaha, NE 68106-1640, USA

Gillbreath, Rod (Baseball Player)
Atlanta Braves
1438 Ridgeland Way SW
Lilburn, GA 30047-4352, USA

Gillen, Aidan (Actor)
c/o Leanne Coronel *Coronel Group*
1100 Glendon Ave Fl 17
Los Angeles, CA 90024-3588, USA

Gillen, Don (Athlete, Hockey Player)
21 Capilano Dr
Saskatoon, SK S7K 4A4, Canada

Gilles, Daniel (Writer)
161 Ave Churchill
Brussels 01180, BELGIUM

Gilles, Tom (Athlete, Baseball Player)
14615 W Southern St
Princeville, IL 61559-9375, USA

Gillespie, Ann (Actor)
Greene Assoc
7080 Hollywood Blvd Ste 1017
Los Angeles, CA 90028-6937, USA

Gillespie, Cole (Athlete, Baseball Player)
6810 NE Alameda St
Portland, OR 97213-5902, USA

Gillespie, Craig (Director)
c/o Simon Millar *Rumble Media*
1620 Broadway Ste C
Santa Monica, CA 90404-2777, USA

Gillespie, Damon (Actor)
c/o Dawn Gray *Gray Talent Group (IL)*
727 S Dearborn St Apt 312
Chicago, IL 60605-3822, USA

Gillespie, Darlene (Actor)
2117 Bermuda Dunes Pl
Oxnard, CA 93036-2787, USA

Gillespie, Jack (Athlete, Basketball Player)
600 6th Ave N
Great Falls, MT 59401-2342, USA

Gillespie, Rhondda (Music Group, Musician)
2 Princess Road
Saint Leonards-on-Sea
East Sussex TN37 6EL, UNITED KINGDOM (UK)

Gillespie, Willie (Athlete, Football Player)
102 Aztec Dr
Starkville, MS 39759-2006, USA

Gillette (Musician)
c/o Staff Member *Diva Central Inc*
7510 W Sunset Blvd # 1445
Los Angeles, CA 90046-3408, USA

Gillette, Anita (Actor)
501 S Beverly Dr Fl 3
Beverly Hills, CA 90212-4520, USA

Gillette, Walker (Athlete, Football Player)
401 N College Dr
Franklin, VA 23851-2401, USA

Gilley, Mickey (Musician)
Gilley's Interests
PO Box 1242
Pasadena, TX 77501-1242, USA

Gilliam, Dondre (Athlete, Football Player)
6858 Sturbridge Dr Apt D
Baltimore, MD 21234-7426, USA

Gilliam, Elijah (Baseball Player)
Birmingham Black Barons
1617 5th Ave N
Birmingham, AL 35203-1953, USA

Gilliam, John (Athlete, Football Player)
4045 Moheb St SW
Atlanta, GA 30331-6418, USA

Gilliam, Jon (Athlete, Football Player)
440 S Walnut Grove Rd
Midlothian, TX 76065-6206, USA

Gilliam, Seth (Actor)
c/o Jason Gutman *Gersh*
41 Madison Ave Ste 3301
New York, NY 10010-2210, USA

Gilliam, Terry (Actor, Animator, Writer)
Old Hall South Grove
Highgate
London N6 6BP, UNITED KINGDOM

Gilliand, David (Race Car Driver)
7777 Woodland Dr
Indianapolis, IN 46278-1794, USA

Gilliand, Herman (Baseball Player)
Chicago Cubs
1833 Kern Mountain Way
Antioch, CA 94531-7497, USA

Gilliard, Cory (Athlete, Football Player)
3951 Zinsle Ave
Cincinnati, OH 45213-2348, USA

Gillick, Pat (Commentator)
3011 W Garfield St
Seattle, WA 98199-4243, USA

Gillie, Nick (Producer)
c/o Staff Member *Metropolitan (MTA)*
4526 Wilshire Blvd
Los Angeles, CA 90010-3801, USA

Gillies, Ben (Music Group, Musician)
John Watson Mgmt
P O Box 281
Sunny Hills, NSW 02010, AUSTRALIA

Gillies, Clark (Athlete, Hockey Player)
17 Pinta Ct
Greenlawn, NY 11740-2314, USA

Gillies, Daniel (Actor, Director)
PO Box 15
Merewether, HSW 02291, AUSTRALIA

Gillies, Elizabeth (Actor)
c/o Lindsay Krug *ID Public Relations*
7060 Hollywood Blvd Fl 8th
Los Angeles, CA 90028-6021, USA

Gillies, Isabel (Actor, Writer)
315 W 106th St Apt 8A
New York, NY 10025-3475, USA

Gilliford, Paul (Athlete, Baseball Player)
7 Woodland Dr
Malvern, PA 19355-3308, USA

Gillig, Tony (Race Car Driver)
Gillig Motorsports
PO Box 823
Lake Zurich, IL 60047-0823, USA

Gilligan, Vince (Producer, Writer)
c/o Staff Member *High Bridge Productions*
2120 Colorado Ave Ste 200
Santa Monica, CA 90404-3561, USA

Gillilan, William J III (Business Person)
Centex Corp
9111 Cypress Waters Blvd Ste 200
Coppell, TX 75019-4858, USA

Gilliland, Butch (Race Car Driver)
Gilliland Racing
912 N Anaheim Blvd
Anaheim, CA 92805-1903, USA

Gilliland, David (Race Car Driver)
The Racers Group
292 Rolling Hill Rd
Mooresville, NC 28117-6845, USA

Gilliland, Richard (Actor)
c/o Anthony DeMichele *Beacon Talent Agency*
170 Apple Ridge Rd
Woodcliff Lk, NJ 07677-8149, USA

Gillingwater, Leah (Reality Star)

Gillis, Don (Athlete, Football Player)
4658 Oso Pkwy
Corpus Christi, TX 78413-5269, USA

Gillis, Louis (Baseball Player)
Birmingham Black Barons
2920 33rd Way N
Birmingham, AL 35207-3720, USA

Gillis, Mike (Athlete, Hockey Player)
Gillis and Association
Vancouver Canucks 800 Griffiths Way
Attn: General Manager Vancouver Canucksmanager
Vancouver, BC V6B 6G1, Canada

Gillis, Tom (Athlete, Golfer)
527 Tanview Dr
Oxford, MI 48371-4769, USA

Gillom, Jennifer (Basketball Player)
c/o Staff Member *LA Sparks*
555 N Nash St
El Segundo, CA 90245-2818, USA

Gillow, Russ (Athlete, Hockey Player)
1517 W Songbird Dr
St George, UT 84790-7261, USA

Gilman, Billy (Music Group)
c/o Rodney Essig *Creative Artists Agency (CAA)*
401 Commerce St PH
Nashville, TN 37219-2516, USA

Gilman, Kenneth B (Business Person)
Limited Inc
3 Limited Pkwy
P O Box 1600
Columbus, OH 43230-1467, USA

Gilmartin, Paul (Comedian)
c/o Staff Member *Agency for the Performing Arts (APA)*
405 S Beverly Dr Ste 500
Beverly Hills, CA 90212-4425, USA

Gilmartin, Raymond V (Business Person)
Merck Co
PO Box 100
Whitehouse Station, NJ 08889-0100, USA

Gilmer, Harry V (Athlete, Football Player)
7467 Highway N
O Fallon, MO 63368-7003, USA

Gilmore, Artis (Athlete, Basketball Player)
11043 Turnbridge Dr
Jacksonville, FL 32256-2329, USA

Gilmore, Bryan (Athlete, Football Player)
123 Houston St
Lufkin, TX 75904, USA

Gilmore, Jared (Actor)
c/o David Dean Portelli *David Dean Management*
Prefers to be contacted via telephone or email
Los Angeles, CA, USA

Gilmore, Jim (Politician)
Jim Gilmore for America
PO Box 29322
Henrico, VA 23242-0322, USA

Gilmore, Jimmie Dale (Musician, Songwriter)
c/o David Whitehead *Maine Road Management*
PO Box 1412
Woodstock, NY 12498-8412, USA

Gilmore, Stephon (Athlete, Football Player)
c/o Alan Herman *Sportstars Inc*
1370 Avenue of the Americas Fl 19
New York, NY 10019-4602, USA

Gilmore, Tom (Athlete, Hockey Player)
Partition Systems
1647 70 Ave NW
Edmonton, AB T6P 1N5, Canada

Gilmore, Walt (Athlete, Basketball Player)
257 Benjamin Blvd
Bear, DE 19701-1693, USA

Gilmour, Buddy (Horse Racer)
50 Merrick Ave Unit 410
East Meadow, NY 11554-1593, USA

Gilmour, David (Musician)
PO Box 62
Heathfield
E Sussex TN21 8ZE, UNITED KINGDOM

Gilmour, Doug (Athlete, Hockey Player)
c/o Staff Member *Toronto Maple Leafs*
Air Canada Centre
400-40 Bay St
Toronto, ON M5J 2X2, CANADA

Gilmour, Doug (Athlete, Hockey Player)
PO Box 665 Stn Main
Attn: General Manager
Kingston, ON K7L 4X1, Canada

Gilmour, George (Horse Racer)
1445 NW 69th Ave
Margate, FL 33063-2552, USA

Gilmur, Chuck (Athlete, Basketball Player)
PO Box 64290
Tacoma, WA 98464-0290, USA

Gilpin, Betty (Actor)
c/o Jenny Tversky *Shelter PR*
928 Broadway Ste 505
New York, NY 10010-8143, USA

Gilpin, Peri (Actor)
c/o Joannie Burstein *Burstein Company*
15304 W Sunset Blvd Ste 208
Pacific Palisades, CA 90272-3656, USA

Gilroy, Tom (Actor, Director, Producer, Writer)
c/o Staff Member *WME|IMG*
9601 Wilshire Blvd
Beverly Hills, CA 90210-5213, USA

Gilroy, Tony (Director, Writer)
c/o Cynthia Swartz *Strategy PR*
630 9th Ave Ste 709
New York, NY 10036-3747, USA

Gilsig, Jessalyn (Actor)
c/o Steven Levy *Framework Entertainment*
9057 Nemo St # C
W Hollywood, CA 90069-5511, USA

Gilson, Hal (Athlete, Baseball Player)
15247 E Sage Dr
Fountain Hills, AZ 85268-4373, USA

Gimenez, Chris (Athlete, Baseball Player)
781 Eschenburg Dr
Gilroy, CA 95020-5610, USA

Gimenez, Jennifer (Actor, Model)
c/o Marki Costello *Creative Management Entertainment Group (CMEG)*
2050 S Bundy Dr Ste 280
Los Angeles, CA 90025-6128, USA

Gimeno, Andres (Tennis Player)
Paseo de la Bnanova 38
Barcelona 6, SPAIN

Gina G (Music Group)
What Mgmt
PO Box 1463
Culver City, CA 90232-1463, USA

Gin Blossoms (Music Group)
PO Box 429094
San Francisco, CA 94142, USA

Ging, Jack (Actor)
48701 San Pedro St
La Quinta, CA 92253-6229, USA

Gingras, Gaston (Athlete, Hockey Player)
50 Rue du Docteur
Pierrefonds, QC H8Z 1L2, Canada

Gingrey, Phil (Congressman, Politician)
442 Cannon Hob
Washington, DC 20515-0106, USA

Gingrich, Callista (Cally) (Business Person, Writer)
Gingrich Productions
4501 Fairfax Dr Ste 900
Arlington, VA 22203-1660, USA

Gingrich, Newt (Politician)
Gingrich Productions
4501 Fairfax Dr Ste 900
Arlington, VA 22203-1660, USA

Ginn, Chad (Athlete, Golfer)
c/o Staff Member *Signature Sports Group*
4150 Olson Memorial Hey
Suite 110
Minneapolis, MN 55422, USA

Ginn, Hubert (Athlete, Football Player)
14 E State St
Savannah, GA 31401-3713, USA

Ginn Jr, Ted (Athlete, Football Player)
c/o Randy Mims *LRMR Marketing*
3800 Embassy Pkwy Ste 360
Akron, OH 44333-8389, USA

Ginobili, Manu (Athlete, Basketball Player)
10 Grand Ter
San Antonio, TX 78257-0002, USA

Ginsberg, Joe (Athlete, Baseball Player)
12635 SW Kingsway Cir # D1
Lake Suzy, FL 34269-4585, USA

Ginter, Keith (Athlete, Baseball Player)
2907 Maple Ave
Fullerton, CA 92835-2126, USA

Ginter, Matt (Athlete, Baseball Player)
3320 Boonesboro Rd
Winchester, KY 40391-9292, USA

Ginter-Brooker, Susan (Athlete, Golfer)
314 Yorkshire Dr
Greenville, SC 29615-1133, USA

Ginuwine (Musician)
Silverman Sclar Shin & Byrne
381 Park Ave S Rm 1600
New York, NY 10016-8812, USA

Ginzburg, Esti (Actor)
c/o Michael Williams *Frankfurt Kurnit Klein & Selz*
488 Madison Ave Fl 10
New York, NY 10022-5754, USA

Gioia (Musician)
c/o Staff Member *Diva Central Inc*
7510 W Sunset Blvd # 1445
Los Angeles, CA 90046-3408, USA

Gionta, Brian (Athlete, Hockey Player, Olympic Athlete)
Sports Consulting Group
65 Monroe Ave Ste D
Pittsford, NY 14534-1318, USA

Giordano, Tommy (Athlete, Baseball Player)
3348 Sterling Ln
Orlando, FL 32817-1663, USA

Giosia, Nadia (Nadia G) (Chef)
c/o Jason Pinyan *Innovative Artists*
1505 10th St
Santa Monica, CA 90401-2805, USA

Giovanni, Nikki E (Writer)
Virginia Polytechnic Institute
English Dept
Blacksburg, VA 24061-0001, USA

Giovanola, Ed (Athlete, Baseball Player)
1741 Nomark Ct
San Jose, CA 95125-3948, USA

Giovinazzo, Carmine (Actor)
c/o Jai Khanna *Brillstein Entertainment Partners*
9150 Wilshire Blvd Ste 350
Beverly Hills, CA 90212-3453, USA

Gipson, Charles (Athlete, Baseball Player)
632 S Earlham St
Orange, CA 92869-5406, USA

Gipsy Kings (Music Group)
Pascal Imbert Enterprises
350 Lincoln Rd # 415
Miami Beach, FL 33139-3154, USA

Giradelll, Marc (Skier)
9413 Oberegg-Sulzbach
SWITZERLAND

Giraldo, Neil (Musician, Producer)
0 Hana Hwy
Hana, HI 96713, USA

Girard, Ken (Athlete, Hockey Player)
6-519 Riverside Dr
London, ON N6H 5J3, Canada

Girardi, Dan (Athlete, Hockey Player)
Newport Sports Management
400-201 City Centre Dr
Attn Don Meehan
Mississauga, ON L5B 2T4, Canada

Girardi, Joseph E (Joe) (Athlete, Baseball Player)
6 Fairway Dr
Purchase, NY 10577-1139, USA

Giraud, Joyce (Beauty Pageant Winner, Model, Reality Star)
c/o Robert S Monaghan *Wunder Agency*
332 S Beverly Dr
Beverly Hills, CA 90212-4812, USA

Giraudeau, Bernard (Actor)
Cineart
36 Rue de Ponthieu
Paris 75008, FRANCE

Girone, Remo (Actor)
Cineart
36 Rue de Ponthieu
Paris 75008, FRANCE

Giroux, Bonny (Actor)
c/o Staff Member *Deborah Harry Talent*
408-1917 4th Ave W
Vancouver, BC V6J 1M7, CANADA

Giroux, Claude (Athlete, Hockey Player)
c/o Larry Kelly *Octagon Hockey - Ottawa*
66 Slater St
Ottawa, ON K1P 5H1, Canada

Giroux, Larry (Athlete, Hockey Player)
10 Colleen Dr
Edwardsville, IL 62025-4242, USA

Giroux, Rejean (Athlete, Hockey Player)
1060 Av de Salaberry
Quebec, QC G1R 2V5, Canada

Giscard, d'Estaing Valery (Politician, President)
11 Rue Benouville
Paris F-75116, FRANCE

Gish, Annabeth (Actor)
c/o Joan Hyler *Hyler Management*
20 Ocean Park Blvd Unit 25
Santa Monica, CA 90405-3590, USA

Gisler, Mike (Athlete, Football Player)
407 Tampa Dr
Victoria, TX 77904-1649, USA

Gismonti, Egberto (Music Group, Musician)
International Music Network
278 Main St # 400
Gloucester, MA 01930-6022, USA

Gissell, Chris (Athlete, Baseball Player)
4310 NW 121st Cir
Vancouver, WA 98685-2052, USA

Gissinger, Andy (Athlete, Football Player)
1667 Union Ave
Barberton, OH 44203-7644, USA

Gitomer, Jeffrey (Business Person)
BuyGitomer Inc
310 Arlington Ave Unit 329
Charlotte, NC 28203-4296, USA

Giudice, Teresa (Reality Star)
c/o James J Leonard Jr *Leonard Law Group LLC*
1200 Atlantic Ave
Atlantic City, NJ 08401-7327, USA

Giuffre, James P (Jimmy) (Music Group, Musician)
Legacy Records
550 Madison Ave Frnt 1
New York, NY 10022-3211, USA

Giuliani, Rudy (Politician)
Giuliani Partners
445 Park Ave Ste 1801
New York, NY 10022-8622, USA

Giuliano, Jeff (Athlete, Hockey Player)
46 Lutheran Dr
Nashua, NH 03063-2914, USA

Giuliano, Louis J (Business Person)
ITT Industries
4 W Red Oak Ln Ste 200
White Plains, NY 10604-3603, USA

Giuliano, Tom (Music Group)
6929 N Hayden Rd
Scottsdale, AZ 85250-7978, USA

Giuntoli, David (Actor)
c/o Warren Zavala *WME|IMG*
9601 Wilshire Blvd
Beverly Hills, CA 90210-5213, USA

Giuranna, Bruno (Music Group, Musician)
Via Bembo 96
Asolo TV 31011, ITALY

Giusti, David J (Dave) (Athlete, Baseball Player)
524 Clair Dr
Pittsburgh, PA 15241-2013, USA

Givaty, Sarai (Actor)
c/o Staff Member *Yitzug1*
Ben Yahuda 99
Tel Aviv NA, ISRAEL

Givens, Adele (Actor, Comedian)
c/o Ricky Anderson *Anderson & Smith P.C.*
7322 Southwest Fwy Ste 2010
1 Arena Pl
Houston, TX 77074-2077, USA

Givens, Brian (Athlete, Baseball Player)

Givens, Robin (Actor)
c/o James Grant *JGPR*
NA
New York, NY NA, USA

Givins, Brian (Athlete, Baseball Player)
9055 Sanderling Way
Littleton, CO 80126-5295, USA

Givins, Ernest (Athlete, Football Player)
924 58th St S
Gulfport, FL 33707-2548, USA

Gjertsen, Douglas (Athlete, Olympic Athlete, Swimmer)
7130 Havenridge Way
McDonough, GA 30253-8511, USA

Gladden, Danny (Dan) (Athlete, Baseball Player)
6543 Pinnacle Dr
Eden Prairie, MN 55346-1906, USA

Gladding, Fred (Athlete, Baseball Player)
436 Marsh Pointe Dr
Columbia, SC 29229-7025, USA

Gladieux, Robert (Athlete, Football Player)
802 Arch Ave
South Bend, IN 46601-3204, USA

Gladis, Michael (Actor)
c/o Lisa Gallant *Gallant Management*
1112 Montana Ave # 454
Santa Monica, CA 90403-1652, USA

Gladstone, Lily (Actor)
c/o Jordyn Palos *Persona Public Relations*
6255 W Sunset Blvd Ste 705
Hollywood, CA 90028-7408, USA

Gladwell, Malcolm (Writer)
c/o Staff Member *Black Bay / Little Brown*
3 Center Plz
Boston, MA 02108-2003, USA

Glance, Harvey (Athlete, Track Athlete)
4804 Cambridge Dr
Northport, AL 35473-1061, USA

Glanville, Brandi (Model, Reality Star)
c/o Staff Member *Persona Public Relations*
6255 W Sunset Blvd Ste 705
Hollywood, CA 90028-7408, USA

Glanville, Doug (Athlete, Baseball Player)
209 Hillcrest Rd
Raleigh, NC 27605-1719, USA

Glanville, Jerry (Athlete, Coach, Football Coach, Football Player, Sportscaster)
Jerry Glanville Motorsports
550 Twinflower Ct
Roswell, GA 30075-5531, USA

Glasbergen, Randy (Cartoonist)
c/o Staff Member *King Features Syndication*
300 W 57th St Fl 15
New York, NY 10019-5238, USA

Glaser, Jim (Music Group)
Joe Taylor Artist Agency
2802 Columbine Pl
Nashville, TN 37204-3104, USA

Glaser, Jon (Actor, Writer)
c/o Staff Member *3 Arts Entertainment*
9460 Wilshire Blvd Fl 7
Beverly Hills, CA 90212-2713, USA

Glaser, Nikki (Comedian)
c/o Brittany Gilpin *Kovert Creative*
506 Santa Monica Blvd Ste 400
Santa Monica, CA 90401-2412, USA

Glaser, Paul Michael (Actor, Director)
c/o Mark Teitelbaum *Teitelbaum Artists Group*
8840 Wilshire Blvd Fl 3
Beverly Hills, CA 90211-2606, USA

Glaser, Rose Mary (Athlete, Baseball Player, Commentator)
8929 Long Ln
Cincinnati, OH 45231-5024, USA

Glasgow, Brian (Athlete, Football Player)
5 Sage Ct
Bolingbrook, IL 60490-3220, USA

Glasgow, Nesby (Athlete, Football Player)
7311 Beverly Blvd
Everett, WA 98203-5724, USA

Glass, Chip (Athlete, Football Player)
7704 NE 140th St
Bothell, WA 98011, USA

Glass, David (Commentator)
Kansas City Royals
17 Glenbrook
Bentonville, AR 72712-3840, USA

Glass, Gerald (Athlete, Basketball Player)
1123 Tillman Rd
Port Gibson, MS 39150-2890, USA

Glass, Glenn (Athlete, Football Player)
7116 W Arbor Trace Dr Apt 902
Knoxville, TN 37909-3060, USA

Glass, Ira (Writer)
c/o Steven Barclay *Steven Barclay Agency*
12 Western Ave
Petaluma, CA 94952-2907, USA

Glass, Leland (Athlete, Football Player)
9 Bayou Ct
Sacramento, CA 95831-2403, USA

Glass, Nancy (Journalist)
Glass DiFede Productions
345 Montgomery Ave
Bala Cynwyd, PA 19004-2801

Glass, Philip (Musician)
48 E 3rd St # 2
New York, NY 10003-9271, USA

Glass, Todd (Actor)
c/o Alex Murray *Brillstein Entertainment Partners*
9150 Wilshire Blvd Ste 350
Beverly Hills, CA 90212-3453, USA

Glass, William S (Bill) (Athlete, Football Player)
Bill Glass Ministries
PO Box 761101
Dallas, TX 75376-1101, USA

Glasser, Erika (Actor)
c/o Gabriel Blanco *Gabriel Blanco Iglesias (Mexico)*
Rio Balsas 35-32
Colonia Cuauhtemoc
DF 06500, Mexico

Glassford, Bill (Athlete, Football Player)
3212 N Miller Rd Apt 216
Scottsdale, AZ 85251-6985, USA

Glassic, Tom (Athlete, Football Player)
1030 S Pine Dr
Bailey, CO 80421-2333, USA

Glassman, Adam (Commentator)
O: The Oprah Magazine
300 W 57th St Fl 36
New York, NY 10019-5915, USA

Glasson, Bill (Athlete, Golfer)
4801 W Crestview Ave
Stillwater, OK 74074-1313, USA

Glasvegas (Music Group, Musician)
c/o Ben Winchester *Primary Talent International (UK)*
10-11 Jockeys Fields
The Primary Bldg
London WC1R 4BN, UNITED KINGDOM

Glatter, Lesli L (Director)
United Talent Agency
9336 Civic Center Dr
Beverly Hills, CA 90210-3604, USA

Glatz, Fred (Athlete, Football Player)
224 Perkins Row
Topsfield, MA 01983-1532, USA

Glau, Summer (Actor)
c/o Nancy Gates *United Talent Agency (UTA)*
888 7th Ave Fl 7
New York, NY 10106-0700, USA

Glauber, Keith (Athlete, Baseball Player)
50 Beth Page Dr
Monroe Township, NJ 08831-8835, USA

Glaudini, Lola (Actor, Producer)
c/o James Suskin *Suskin Management*
2 Charlton St Apt 5K
New York, NY 10014-4970, USA

Glaus, Troy (Athlete, Baseball Player)
4300 Bibleway Ct
Holly Springs, NC 27540-3305, USA

Glave, Matthew (Actor)
17628 McCormick St
Encino, CA 91316-2551, USA

Glavine, Mike (Athlete, Baseball Player)
89 Treble Cove Rd
North Billerica, MA 01862-2215, USA

Glavine, Tom (Athlete, Baseball Player)
920 Hurleston Ln
Alpharetta, GA 30022-6251, USA

Glazer, Ilana (Actor, Comedian)
c/o Rhett Usry *ID Public Relations (NY)*
40 Wall St Fl 51
New York, NY 10005-1385, USA

Glazer, Jay (Sportscaster)
CBS-TV
51 W 52nd St
New York, NY 10019-6119, USA

Glazer, Jonathan (Director)
c/o Chris Donnelly *LBI Entertainment*
2000 Avenue of the Stars
N Tower Fl 3
Los Angeles, CA 90067-4700, USA

Glazer, Mitch (Producer)
c/o Staff Member *Creative Artists Agency (CAA)*
2000 Avenue of the Stars Ste 100
Los Angeles, CA 90067-4705, USA

Glazier, Nancy (Artist)
Somerset House Publishing
10688 Haddington Dr
Houston, TX 77043-3229, USA

Glazunov, Ilya S (Artist)
Razhviz Academy
Kamergersky Per 2
Moscow 103009, RUSSIA

Gleason, Joanna (Actor)
c/o Vera Mihailovich *Forward Entertainment*
1880 Century Park E Ste 1405
Los Angeles, CA 90067-1630, USA

Gleason, Mary Pat (Actor, Writer)
c/o Scott Manners *Artists & Representatives (Stone Manners Salners)*
6100 Wilshire Blvd Ste 1500
Los Angeles, CA 90048-5110, USA

Gleason, Roy (Athlete, Baseball Player)
35218 Fir Ave SPC 93
Yucaipa, CA 92399-3078, USA

Gleason, Tim (Athlete, Hockey Player)
4316 Brinleys Cove Ct
Raleigh, NC 27614-0001, USA

Gleaton, Jerry Don (Athlete, Baseball Player)
3008 Avenue K
Brownwood, TX 76801-6016, USA

Gleeson, Brendan (Actor)
c/o Danica Smith *Kovert Creative*
506 Santa Monica Blvd Ste 400
Santa Monica, CA 90401-2412, USA

Gleeson, David (Director)
c/o Staff Member *Wide Eye Films*
70, Sir John Rogerson's Quay
Dublin 00002, IRELAND

Gleeson, Domhnall (Actor)
c/o Karl Hayden *The Agency (Ireland)*
25 Leeson Street Lower
Dublin 2 D02 XD77, IRELAND

Gleeson, Jack (Actor)
c/o Staff Member *ITW Agency*
8 Terminus Mills
Clonskeagh Road
Ranelagh, Dublin 00006, Ireland

Glemp, Jozef Cardinal (Religious Leader)
Sekretariat Prymasa Kolski
Ul Miodowa 17
Warsaw 00 246, POLAND

Glen, John (Director)
Spyros Skouras
1015 Gayley Ave Ste 300
Los Angeles, CA 90024-3440, USA

Glenn, Aaron (Athlete, Football Player)
507 Montego Ct
Avon Lake, OH 44012-2952, USA

Glenn, Cordy (Athlete, Football Player)
c/o Pat Dye Jr *SportsTrust Advisors*
3340 Peachtree Rd NE Fl 16
Atlanta, GA 30326-1000, USA

Glenn, Dorsey (Athlete, Football Player)
4242 NE Edmonson Ct
Lees Summit, MO 64064-1681, USA

Glenn, Jason (Athlete, Football Player)
15530 Ella Blvd Apt 501
Houston, TX 77090-5309, USA

Glenn, Kimiko (Actor)
c/o Jennifer Sims *Imprint PR*
375 Hudson St
New York, NY 10014-3658, USA

Glenn, Mike (Athlete, Basketball Player)
3571 Kilpatrick Ln
Snellville, GA 30039-8643, USA

Glenn, Scott (Actor)
491 10th St E # A12
Ketchum, ID 83340-9403, USA

Glenn, Stanley (Athlete, Baseball Player)
9 Baily Rd
Lansdowne, PA 19050-2817, USA

Glenn, Tarik (Athlete, Football Player)
10481 Titan Run
Carmel, IN 46032-8232, USA

Glenn, Vencie (Athlete, Football Player)
718 Casita Ln
San Marcos, CA 92069-7397, USA

Glennie, Brian (Athlete, Hockey Player)
4 Curling Rd
Bracebridge, ON P1L 1M6, Canada

Glennie, Evelyn E A (Music Group, Musician)
P O Box 6 Sawtry Huntingdon
Cambs PE17 5WE, UNITED KINGDOM (UK)

Glennon, Matt (Athlete, Hockey Player)
6 Gardner Street
Hingham, MA 02043, USA

Gless, Sharon (Actor)
Rosenzweig Productions
PO Box 48005
Los Angeles, CA 90048-0005, USA

Glick, Alexis (Correspondent)
c/o Staff Member *Fox News*
1211 Avenue of the Americas Lowr C1
New York, NY 10036-8705, USA

Glick, Frederick (Freddie) (Athlete, Football Player)
4226 Antlers Ct
Fort Collins, CO 80526-6411, USA

Glick, Gary (Athlete, Football Player)
2267 Hiawatha Ct
Fort Collins, CO 80525-1840, USA

Glidden, Bob (Race Car Driver)
PO Box 236
Rt. 1
Whiteland, IN 46184-0236, USA

Glinatsis, George (Athlete, Baseball Player)
13742 W 59th Ave
Arvada, CO 80004-3740, USA

Glitter, Gary (Music Group, Songwriter, Writer)
Jef Hanlon Mgmt
1 York St
London W1H 1PZ, UNITED KINGDOM (UK)

Glizzy, Shy (Musician)
c/o Mari Davies *ICM Partners*
10250 Constellation Blvd Fl 7
Los Angeles, CA 90067-6207, USA

Gload, Ross (Athlete, Baseball Player)
23 Harrison Ave
East Hampton, NY 11937-2051, USA

Gloag, Ann (Business Person)
Kinfauns Castle
Perth, Scotland

Globensky, Alan (Athlete, Hockey Player)
20 Myrtle St Apt 2
Augusta, ME 04330-4736

Globke, Rob (Athlete, Hockey Player)
5514 Cambridge Club Cir APT 105
Ann Arbor, MI 48103-9252, USA

Gloden, Fred (Athlete, Football Player)
2203 Emerson St
Philadelphia, PA 19152-2507, USA

Gloeckner, Lorry (Athlete, Hockey Player)
11671 King Rd
Richmond, BC V7A 3B5, Canada

Gloor, Danny (Athlete, Hockey Player)
172 Henry St
Mitchell, ON N0K 1N0, Canada

Gloriana (Music Group)
c/o Haley Melikian *Matchbook Company*
220 E 23rd St Ste 1005
New York, NY 10010-4692, USA

Glory, New Found (Music Group)
c/o Staff Member *Ellis Industries Inc*
234 Shoreward Dr
Great Neck, NY 11021-2734, USA

Glosson, Clyde (Athlete, Football Player)
5803 Lake Falls Dr
San Antonio, TX 78222-2405, USA

Glotzbach, Charlie (Race Car Driver)
2513 Coopers Ln
Sellersburg, IN 47172-9564, USA

Glotzbatch, Charles (Race Car Driver)
2513 Coopers Ln
Sellersburg, IN 47172-9564, USA

Glouberman, Michael (Producer)
c/o Staff Member *United Talent Agency (UTA)*
9336 Civic Center Dr
Beverly Hills, CA 90210-3604, USA

G Love & Special Sauce (Music Group)
c/o Staff Member *Paradigm (Monterey)*
404 W Franklin St
Monterey, CA 93940-2303, USA

Glover, Andrew (Athlete, Football Player)
12414 Colt Ct
Magnolia, TX 77354-4911, USA

Glover, Brian (Actor)
DeWolfe
Manfield House
376/378 Strand
London WC2R OLR, UNITED KINGDOM

Glover, Bruce (Actor)
11449 Woodbine St
Los Angeles, CA 90066-1229, USA

Glover, Chris (Musician)
c/o Staff Member *Paradigm (Monterey)*
404 W Franklin St
Monterey, CA 93940-2303, USA

Glover, Clarence (Athlete, Basketball Player)
811 Lake Forest Pkwy
Louisville, KY 40245-5138, USA

Glover, Crispin (Actor, Director, Producer)
3573 Carnation Ave
Los Angeles, CA 90026-1103, USA

Glover, Danny (Actor)
c/o Staff Member *Louverture Films*
101 W 23rd St # 283
New York, NY 10011-2490, USA

Glover, Dion (Athlete, Basketball Player)
3691 Seton Hall Way
Decatur, GA 30034-5509, USA

Glover, Donald (Actor, Writer)
c/o Dianne McGunigle *MGMT Entertainment (The Schiff Company)*
9220 W Sunset Blvd Ste 106
W Hollywood, CA 90069-3500, USA

Glover, Gary (Athlete, Baseball Player)
19704 Kell Estates Ln
Lutz, FL 33549-4092, USA

Glover, Howie (Athlete, Hockey Player)
15 Wendy Cres
Kitchener, ON N2A 3T4, Canada

Glover, John (Actor)
c/o Nevin Dolcefino *Innovative Artists*
1505 10th St
Santa Monica, CA 90401-2805, USA

Glover, Julian (Actor)
200 Fulham Road
London SW10 9PN, United Kingdom

Glover, Kevin B (Athlete, Football Player)
14502 Highbury Ln
Laurel, MD 20707-3120, USA

Glover, La'Roi (Athlete, Football Player)
PO Box 2521
Rancho Santa Fe, CA 92067-2521, USA

Glover, Lucas (Athlete, Golfer)
105 Annas Pl
Simpsonville, SC 29681-4813, USA

Glover, Richard E (Rich) (Athlete, Football Player)
215 Claremont Ave
Jersey City, NJ 07305-3623, USA

Glover, Stephen (Musician, Producer)
c/o Ryan Feldman *WME|IMG*
9601 Wilshire Blvd
Beverly Hills, CA 90210-5213, USA

Gloy, Tom (Race Car Driver)
Rahal/Gloy Racing
804A Performance Rd
Mooresville, NC 28115-9597, USA

Gluck, Griffin (Actor)
c/o Leslie Allan-Rice *Leslie Allan-Rice Management*
1007 Maybrook Dr
Beverly Hills, CA 90210-2715, USA

Gluck, Louise E (Writer)
14 Ellsworth Park
Cambridge, MA 02139-1011, USA

Glueck, Larry (Athlete, Football Player)
PO Box 141
Ocean View, DE 19970-0141, USA

Glusman, Karl (Actor)
c/o Annick Oppenheim *Wolf-Kasteler Public Relations*
6255 W Sunset Blvd Ste 1111
Los Angeles, CA 90028-7426, USA

Glymph, Junior (Athlete, Football Player)
7300 Fontana Dr
Columbia, SC 29209-3248, USA

Glynn, Bill (Athlete, Baseball Player)
6916 51st St
San Diego, CA 92120-1212, USA

Glynn, Brian (Athlete, Hockey Player)
City of Prince Albert
City of Prince Albert 1084 Central Ave
Attn: Police Dept
Prince Albert, SK S6V 7P3, Canada

Glynn, Carlin (Actor)
1165 5th Ave
New York, NY 10029-6931, USA

Glynn, Ed (Athlete, Baseball Player)
5212 Stratford Chase Dr
Virginia Beach, VA 23464-5621, USA

Glynn, Gene (Athlete, Baseball Player)
15329 Snake Trl
Waseca, MN 56093-4733, USA

Glynn, Robert D Jr (Business Person)
PG&E Corp
1 Market St
San Francisco, CA 94105-1420, USA

Glynn, Ryan (Athlete, Baseball Player)
14010 W Hyde Park Dr Apt 201
Fort Myers, FL 33912-0207, USA

G. McCotter, Thaddeus (Congressman, Politician)
1632 Longworth Hob
Washington, DC 20515-2007, USA

G. Miller, Gary (Congressman, Politician)
2349 Rayburn Hob
Washington, DC 20515-2209, USA

Gminski, Mike (Athlete, Basketball Player, Sportscaster)
1309 Canterbury Hill Cir
Charlotte, NC 28211-1454, USA

Gnarls Barkley (Music Group)
Downtown Records
73 Spring St Rm 504
New York, NY 10012-5802, USA

Goad, Tim (Athlete, Football Player)
138 Birchwood Dr
Pittsboro, NC 27312-8737, USA

Goalby, Bob (Athlete, Golfer)
904 Briar Hill Rd
Belleville, IL 62223-1133, USA

Goaz, Harry (Actor)
c/o David J Stieve *AKA Talent Agency*
325 N Larchmont Blvd
Los Angeles, CA 90004-3011, USA

Gob, Art (Athlete, Football Player)
123 Hiscott Dr
Pittsburgh, PA 15241-1105, USA

Gobble, Jimmy (Athlete, Baseball Player)
150 Lake View Estates Dr
Bristol, TN 37620-1307, USA

Goble, Les (Athlete, Football Player)
21 Dodge Ave
Waverly, NY 14892-9651, USA

Goc, Marcel (Athlete, Hockey Player)
8342 Delcrest Dr UNIT 419
Saint Louis, MO 63124-2249, USA

Gocong, Chris (Athlete, Football Player)
PO Box 93
Berea, OH 44017-0093, USA

Godard, Eric (Athlete, Hockey Player)
2330 Larkins Way
Pittsburgh, PA 15203-2218, USA

Godard, Jean-Luc (Director)
15 Rue du Nord
Roulle 01180, SWITZERLAND

Godboldo, Dale (Actor)
c/o Joannie Burstein *Burstein Company*
15304 W Sunset Blvd Ste 208
Pacific Palisades, CA 90272-3656, USA

Godby, Danny (Athlete, Baseball Player)
551 Airport Rd
Chapmanville, WV 25508-5708, USA

Godchaux, Stephen (Producer)
c/o Staff Member *WME|IMG*
9601 Wilshire Blvd
Beverly Hills, CA 90210-5213, USA

Goddard, Daniel (Actor)
c/o Staff Member *Luber Roklin Management*
5815 W Sunset Blvd Ste 208
Los Angeles, CA 90028-6481, USA

Goddard, Joe (Athlete, Baseball Player)
304 Ridgepark Dr
Beckley, WV 25801-9593, USA

Goddard, Mark (Actor)
PO Box 778
Middleboro, MA 02346-0778, USA

Godden, Ernie (Athlete, Hockey Player)
31 Rinaldo Rd
Keswick, ON L4P 3X9, Canada

Godecki, Marzena (Actor)
Jonethan M. Shiff Productions
373 Bay Street
Port Melbourne
Victoria, Australia 03207

Godfread, Dan (Athlete, Basketball Player)
315 Jonathan St Apt J
Eagle River, WI 54521-9536, USA

Godfrey (Actor, Comedian)
c/o Matt Luber *Luber Roklin Management*
5815 W Sunset Blvd Ste 208
Los Angeles, CA 90028-6481, USA

Godfrey, Charles (Athlete, Football Player)
c/o Doug Hendrickson *Relativity Sports*
2029 Century Park E Ste 1550
Century City, CA 90067-3000, USA

Godfrey, Chris (Athlete, Football Player)
52383 Swanson Dr
South Bend, IN 46635-1067, USA

Godfrey, Randall (Athlete, Football Player)
4102 Mount Zion Church Rd
Valdosta, GA 31605-6506, USA

Godin, Seth (Business Person, Writer)
Do You Zoom Inc
PO Box 305
Irvington, NY 10533-0305, USA

Godley, Georgina (Designer, Fashion Designer)
42 Bassett Road
London W10 6UL, UNITED KINGDOM (UK)

Godley, Kevin (Music Group, Musician)
Heronden Hall Tenterden
Kent, UNITED KINGDOM (UK)

Godmanis, Ivars (Politician)
Palasta St 1
Riga 01954, LATVIA

Godreche, Judith (Actor)
c/o Laura Meerson *Agence Adequat*
21 Rue D'Uzes
Paris 75002, FRANCE

Godsmack (Music Group)
c/o John Branigan *WME|IMG*
9601 Wilshire Blvd
Beverly Hills, CA 90210-5213, USA

Godwin, Gail K (Writer)
PO Box 946
Woodstock, NY 12498-0946, USA

Godwin, John (Reality Star)
c/o Theresa Brown *WME|IMG*
9601 Wilshire Blvd
Beverly Hills, CA 90210-5213, USA

Godynyuk, Alexander (Athlete, Hockey Player)
217 Follen Rd
Lexington, MA 02421-5802, USA

Goeas, Leo (Athlete, Football Player)
113 Shady Ln
Longwood, FL 32750-2867, USA

Goebel, Brad (Athlete, Football Player)
PO Box 4006
Horseshoe Bay, TX 78657-4006, USA

Goebel, Timothy (Athlete, Figure Skater, Olympic Athlete)
c/o Staff Member *Champions on Ice*
3500 American Blvd W Ste 190
Minneapolis, MN 55431-4431, USA

Goeddeke, George (Athlete, Football Player)
45575 N Stonewood Rd
Canton, MI 48187-6645, USA

Goellner, Marc-Kevin (Athlete, Tennis Player)
Blau-Weiss Neuss
Tennishall Jahnstrasse
Neuss 41464, GERMANY

Goen, Bob (Game Show Host, Television Host)
c/o Staff Member *Rebel Entertainment Partners*
5700 Wilshire Blvd Ste 470
Los Angeles, CA 90036-4379, USA

Goepper, Nick (Olympic Athlete, Skier)
US Ski And Snowboard Association
1 Victory Ln # 100
Park City, UT 84060-7463, USA

Goestenkors, Gail (Basketball Player, Coach)
Duke University
Athletic Dept
Durham, NC 27708-0001, USA

Goestschi, Renate (Skier)
Schwarzenbach 3
Obdach 08742, AUSTRIA

Goetz, Dick (Athlete, Golfer)
4301 Fillbrook Ln
Tyler, TX 75707-5465, USA

Goetz, Peter Michael (Actor)
c/o Staff Member *SMS Talent*
8383 Wilshire Blvd Ste 230
Beverly Hills, CA 90211-2436, USA

Goetz, Russ (Athlete, Baseball Player)
12909 Riffle Ford Ct
Gaithersburg, MD 20878-2158, USA

Goetz, Russ (Baseball Player)
12909 Riffle Ford Ct
Gaithersburg, MD 20878-2158, USA

Goetze-Ackerman, Vicki (Athlete, Golfer)
3621 Sally Parrish Trl
Valrico, FL 33596-8433, USA

Goetzman, Gary (Producer)
c/o Staff Member *Creative Artists Agency (CAA)*
2000 Avenue of the Stars Ste 100
Los Angeles, CA 90067-4705, USA

Goff, Jerry (Athlete, Baseball Player)
3 Oak Valley Dr
Novato, CA 94947-1964, USA

Goff, Mike (Athlete, Baseball Player)
153 Norton Pl APT D
Mobile, AL 36607-2235, USA

Goff, Mike (Athlete, Football Player)
2225 5th St
Peru, IL 61354-2506, USA

Goff, Willard (Athlete, Football Player)
441 E 10th Ave
Springfield, CO 81073, USA

Goffin, David (Producer)
c/o Staff Member *Creative Artists Agency (CAA)*
2000 Avenue of the Stars Ste 100
Los Angeles, CA 90067-4705, USA

Goffin, Louise (Musician)
c/o Staff Member *Evolution Music Partners*
1680 Vine St Ste 500
Hollywood, CA 90028-8800, USA

Goforth, Bart (Athlete, Football Player)
7000 Greenbriar Dr Apt 20
Houston, TX 77030-3244, USA

Gofourth, Derrel (Athlete, Football Player)
1119 S Woodcrest Dr
Stillwater, OK 74074-1433, USA

Gogan, Kevin (Athlete, Football Player)
385 SW Mount Baker Dr
Issaquah, WA 98027-3663, USA

Goganious, Keith (Athlete, Football Player)
4173 Cheswick Ln
Virginia Beach, VA 23455-6560, USA

Gogel, Matt (Athlete, Golfer)
3509 W 68th St # 0
Mission Hills, KS 66208-2142, USA

Goggin, Chuck (Athlete, Baseball Player)
305 Windemere Woods Dr
Nashville, TN 37215-2458, USA

Goggins, Walton (Actor, Producer)
c/o Darris Hatch *Daris Hatch Management*
10027 Rossbury Pl
Los Angeles, CA 90064-4825, USA

Gogolak, Charlie (Athlete, Football Player)
PO Box 361
Northeast Harbor, ME 04662-0361, USA

Gogolak, Peter (Pete) (Athlete, Football Player)
24 Arrowhead Way
Darien, CT 06820-5505, USA

Gogolewski, Bill (Athlete, Baseball Player)
1522 Graham Ave
Oshkosh, WI 54902-2623, USA

Go-Go's, The (Music Group)
c/o Brett Steinberg *Creative Artists Agency (CAA)*
2000 Avenue of the Stars Ste 100
Los Angeles, CA 90067-4705, USA

Go-Go's, The (Music Group)
c/o Martin Kirkup *Direct Management Group*
8332 Melrose Ave
Los Angeles, CA 90069-5420, USA

Goh, Michelle (Actor)
c/o Andrew Ooi *Echelon Talent Management*
2915 Argo Pl
Burnaby, BC V3J 7G4, CANADA

Goh, Rex (Music Group, Musician)
Agency for Performing Arts
9200 W Sunset Blvd Ste 900
Los Angeles, CA 90069-3604, USA

Gohmert, Louie (Congressman, Politician)
2440 Rayburn Hob
Washington, DC 20515-2508, USA

Gohr, Greg (Athlete, Baseball Player)
77 Scotland Rd
Reading, MA 01867-3323, USA

Goich, Dan (Athlete, Football Player)
PO Box 19068
Las Vegas, NV 89132-0068, USA

Going, Joanna (Actor)
c/o Liza Anderson *Anderson Group Public Relations*
8060 Melrose Ave Fl 4
Los Angeles, CA 90046-7038, USA

Goings, E V (Business Person)
Tupperware Corp
PO Box 2353
Orlando, FL 32802-2353, USA

Goings, Nick (Athlete)
c/o Staff Member *Carolina Panthers*
800 S Mint St
Ericsson Stadium
Charlotte, NC 28202-1640, USA

Goings, Nick (Athlete, Football Player)
9603 Sunset Grove Dr
Huntersville, NC 28078-0640, USA

Gokey, Danny (Musician)
2698 McLemore Rd
Franklin, TN 37064-1128, USA

Golay, Jeanne (Athlete, Cycler, Olympic Athlete)
PO Box 1697
Glenwood Springs, CO 81602-1697, USA

Gold, Ari (Musician)

Gold, Brandy (Actor)
Gold Marshak Liedtke
3500 W Olive Ave Ste 1400
Burbank, CA 91505-5512, USA

Gold, Elon (Actor, Comedian)
c/o Ruthanne Secunda *ICM Partners*
10250 Constellation Blvd Fl 7
Los Angeles, CA 90067-6207, USA

Gold, Herbert (Writer)
1051 Broadway # A
San Francisco, CA 94133-4205, USA

Gold, Ian (Athlete, Football Player)
10275 Tradition Pl
Lone Tree, CO 80124-8505, USA

Gold, Jack (Director)
24 Wood Vale
London N1O 3DP, UNITED KINGDOM (UK)

Gold, Judy (Comedian)
c/o Jodi Schoenbrun Carter *1022m*
407 W 43rd St Fl 3
New York, NY 10036-5330, USA

Gold, Murray (Musician)
Manners McDade Artist Management
c/o Catherine Manners
18 Broadwick St 4th Fl
London W1F 8HS, UNITED KINGDOM

Gold, Seth (Reality Star)
c/o Linda Shafran *Linda Shafran*
424 Wisconsin Ave Apt 1N
Oak Park, IL 60302-3678, USA

Gold, Tracey (Actor)
c/o Harry Gold *TalentWorks*
3500 W Olive Ave Ste 1400
Burbank, CA 91505-5512, USA

Goldberg, Adam (Actor, Comedian)
1990 S Bundy Dr Ste 200
Los Angeles, CA 90025-5249, USA

Goldberg, Bernard (Writer)
c/o Staff Member *HarperCollins Publishers*
195 Broadway Fl 2
New York, NY 10007-3132, USA

Goldberg, Bill (Actor, Athlete, Football Player, Wrestler)
Extreme Power Gym
3753 Mission Ave Ste 105
Oceanside, CA 92058-1472, USA

Goldberg, Eric (Animator)
c/o Ellen Goldsmith-Vein *Gotham Group*
1041 N Formosa Ave # 200
West Hollywood, CA 90046-6703, USA

Goldberg, Hank (Sportscaster)
1480 Paseo Verde Pkwy APT 3208
Henderson, NV 89012-6510, USA

Goldberg, Leonard (Producer)
Spectradyne Inc
1198 Commerce Dr
Richardson, TX 75081-2307, USA

Goldberg, Marshall (Biggie) (Artist)
222 Bowery Apt 6
New York, NY 10012-4251, USA

Goldberg, Whoopi (Actor, Comedian, Talk Show Host)
c/o Staff Member *Whoop Inc*
1650 Broadway Ste 1400
New York, NY 10019-6985, USA

Goldberger, Andreas (Skier)
Bleckenwegen 4
Waldzell 04924, AUSTRIA

Goldblum, Jeff (Actor)
c/o Marla Farrell *Shelter PR*
928 Broadway Ste 505
New York, NY 10010-8143, USA

Golden, Arthur (Writer)
c/o Lynn Pleshette *Lynn Pleshette Literary Agency*
2700 N Beachwood Dr
Los Angeles, CA 90068-1922, USA

Golden, Brittan (Athlete, Football Player)

Golden, Clyde (Athlete, Baseball Player)
PO Box 6188
Jacksonville, FL 32236, USA

Golden, Jim (Athlete, Baseball Player)
8630 SW 10th Ave
Topeka, KS 66615-9688, USA

Golden, Josh (Musician)
c/o Rich Green *ICM Partners*
10250 Constellation Blvd Fl 7
Los Angeles, CA 90067-6207, USA

Golden, Kate (Athlete, Golfer)
969 Hunterwood Dr
Jasper, TX 75951-2821, USA

Golden, Kit (Producer)
c/o Staff Member *Manhattan Project*
1775 Broadway Ste 410
New York, NY 10019-1903, USA

Golden, Robert (Athlete, Football Player)
c/o Jim Ivler *Sportstars Inc*
1370 Avenue of the Americas Fl 19
New York, NY 10019-4602, USA

Golden, Tim (Athlete, Football Player)
PO Box 278052
Miramar, FL 33027-8052, USA

Golden, William Lee (Musician, Songwriter)
1764 Saundersville Rd
Hendersonville, TN 37075-8534, USA

Goldenthal, Elliot (Musician)
c/o Sam Schwartz *Gorfaine/Schwartz Agency Inc*
4111 W Alameda Ave Ste 509
Burbank, CA 91505-4171, USA

Goldfaden, Ben (Athlete, Basketball Player)
5819 Bounty Cir
Tavares, FL 32778-9293, USA

Goldfrapp, Alison (Musician)
c/o Staff Member *Mute Records*
1 Albion Pl
London W6 0QT, UK

Goldin, Ricky Paull (Actor)
c/o Staff Member *Artists & Representatives (Stone Manners Salners)*
6100 Wilshire Blvd Ste 1500
Los Angeles, CA 90048-5110, USA

Golding, Henry (Actor)
c/o Nick LoPiccolo *Paradigm*
8942 Wilshire Blvd
Beverly Hills, CA 90211-1908, USA

Golding, Meta (Actor)
c/o Charlton Blackburne *Charlton Blackburne Management*
4022 Los Feliz Blvd
Los Angeles, CA 90027-2305, USA

Goldman, Bo (Producer, Writer)
c/o David O'Connor *Creative Artists Agency (CAA)*
2000 Avenue of the Stars Ste 100
Los Angeles, CA 90067-4705, USA

Goldman, Duff (Chef)
Charm City Cakes
2936 Remington Ave
Baltimore, MD 21211-2830, USA

Goldman, Julie (Actor, Comedian)
c/o Staff Member *Ellis Talent Group*
4705 Laurel Canyon Blvd Ste 300
Valley Village, CA 91607-5901, USA

Goldman, Les (Athlete, Football Player)
800 E Cypress Creek Rd Ste 203
Fort Lauderdale, FL 33334-3522, USA

Gold-Onwude, Rosalyn (Commentator, Sportscaster)
c/o Lou Oppenheim *ICM Partners (NY)*
730 5th Ave
New York, NY 10019-4105, USA

Goldsberry, Renee Elise (Actor)
c/o Nina Shreiber *Sweet 180*
141 W 28th St Rm 300
New York, NY 10001-6187, USA

Goldsboro, Bobby (Musician, Songwriter)
La Rana Productions
PO Box 5250
Ocala, FL 34478-5250, USA

Goldschmidt, Neil (Politician)
1150 SW King Ave
Portland, OR 97205-1116, USA

Goldsman, Akiva (Director, Producer)
c/o Staff Member *Weed Road Pictures*
4000 Warner Blvd Bldg 115
Burbank, CA 91522-0001, USA

Goldsmith, Bethany (Baseball Player)
1000 E Michigan St Apt A
Orlando, FL 32806-4736, USA

Goldsmith, Jonathan (Actor)
c/o Stephanie Gabriel *Randy James Management*
12711 Ventura Blvd Ste 345
Studio City, CA 91604-2416, USA

Goldsmith, Paul (Race Car Driver)
1705 E Main St
Griffith, IN 46319-2941, USA

Goldsmith, Stephen (Politician)
Governor's Office
State House
Indianapolis, IN 46204, USA

Goldson, Dashon (Athlete, Football Player)
c/o Tom Condon *Creative Artists Agency (CAA)*
401 Commerce St PH
Nashville, TN 37219-2516, USA

Goldspink, Calvin (Actor)
c/o Staff Member *Reel Talent Management*
PO Box 491035
Los Angeles, CA 90049-9035, USA

Goldstein, Jonathan (Producer)
c/o Maria Herrera *PMK/BNC Public Relations*
1840 Century Park E Ste 1400
Los Angeles, CA 90067-2115, USA

Goldstein, Lonnie (Athlete, Baseball Player)
3401 Premier Dr Apt 213
Plano, TX 75023-7093, USA

Goldthwait, Bob (Bobcat) (Actor, Comedian)
c/o Staff Member *Personal Publicity*
12831 S 71st St
Tempe, AZ 85284-3103, USA

Goldup, Glenn (Athlete, Hockey Player)
31 Elizabeth St
Etobicoke, ON M8V 2R9, Canada

Goldwyn, Tony (Actor, Director)
c/o Karen Samfilippo *IMPR*
1158 26th St # 548
Santa Monica, CA 90403-4698, USA

Golembrosky, Frank (Athlete, Hockey Player)
4 Francis Cir
Newark, DE 19711-2625

Golenbock, Peter (Sportscaster)
849 Jennings Ave N
Saint Petersburg, FL 33704-1142, USA

Golic, Bob (Athlete, Football Player, Sportscaster)
6130 Loch Lomond Ct
Solon, OH 44139-5945, USA

Golic, Mike (Athlete, Football Player)
c/o Staff Member *ESPN (Main)*
935 Middle St
Espn Plaza
Bristol, CT 06010-1000, USA

Golino, Valeria (Actor, Producer)
c/o Frederique Moidon *ArtMedia*
8 rue Danielle Casanova
Paris 75002, FRANCE

Golisano, B Thomas (Business Person)
Paychex Inc
911 Panorama Trl S
Rochester, NY 14625-2396, USA

Golisano, Tom (Business Person)
911 Panorama Trl S
Rochester, NY 14625-2311, USA

Gollat, Mike (Baseball Player)
Philadelphia Phillies
2650 Greenlawn Dr
Seven Hills, OH 44131-3623, USA

Golodryga, Bianna (Television Host)

Golonka, Arlene (Actor)
c/o David Moss *David Moss Company*
6063 Vineland Ave Apt B
N Hollywood, CA 91606-4986, USA

Golovin, Tatiana (Athlete, Tennis Player)
c/o Staff Member *Women's Tennis Association (WTA (UK))*
Palliser House
Palliser Rd
London W149EB, UK

Golson, Greg (Athlete, Baseball Player)
2670 Ravenwood Dr
Round Rock, TX 78665-7926, USA

Golsteyn, Jerry (Athlete, Football Player)
243 Tadcaster Ct
Raeford, NC 28376-6623, USA

Golston, Kedric (Athlete, Football Player)

Goltz, Dave (Athlete, Baseball Player)
1009 Stony Brook Mnr
Fergus Falls, MN 56537-4413, USA

Gomes, Jessica (Actor, Model)
c/o Christopher Burbidge *Fourward*
10250 Constellation Blvd Ste 2710
Los Angeles, CA 90067-6227, USA

Gomes, Jonny (Athlete, Baseball Player)
17692 N 77th Pl
Scottsdale, AZ 85255-0409, USA

Gomes, Wayne (Athlete, Baseball Player)
5104 W Creek Ct
Suffolk, VA 23435-3523, USA

Gomez (Music Group)
c/o Jason Colton *Red Light Management*
455 2nd St NE
#500
Charlottesville, VA 22902-5791, USA

Gomez, Andres (Tennis Player)
ProServe
1101 Woodrow Wilson Blvd #1800
Arlington, VA 22209, USA

Gomez, Carlos (Actor)
c/o Billy Miller *Billy Miller Management*
8322 Ridpath Dr
Los Angeles, CA 90046-7710, USA

Gomez, Carlos (Athlete, Baseball Player)
15520 Flyboat Ln
Saint Paul, MN 55124-6021, USA

Gomez, Chris (Athlete, Baseball Player)
2618 San Miguel Dr # 183
Newport Beach, CA 92660-5437, USA

Gomez, Edgar (Eddie) (Music Group, Musician)
Integrity Talent
PO Box 961
Burlington, MA 01803-5961, USA

Gomez, Hector (Actor)
c/o Staff Member *Televisa*
Blvd Adolfo Lopez Mateos 232
Colonia San Angel INN
DF CP 01060, MEXICO

Gomez, Ian (Actor)
c/o Jamie Harhay Skinner *Baker Winokur Ryder Public Relations*
9100 Wilshire Blvd
W Tower #500
Beverly Hills, CA 90212-3415, USA

Gomez, Javier (Actor)
c/o Gabriel Blanco *Gabriel Blanco Iglesias (Mexico)*
Rio Balsas 35-32
Colonia Cuauhtemoc
DF 06500, Mexico

Gomez, Jeff (Cartoonist)
5 Union Sq W Attn of
New York, NY 10003-3306, USA

Gomez, Juan "'A Orlando"' (Athlete, Baseball Player)
Frederick Keys
21 Stadium Dr
Attn: Manager's Office
Frederick, MD 21703-6553, USA

Gomez, Leo (Athlete, Baseball Player)
273 Portofino Dr
North Venice, FL 34275-6654, USA

Gomez, Luis (Athlete, Baseball Player)
676 Chesterfield Dr
Lawrenceville, GA 30044-5624, USA

Gomez, Marga (Comedian)
PO Box 460368
San Francisco, CA 94146-0368, USA

Gomez, Natalie (Actor)
c/o Staff Member *Advance LA*
7904 Santa Monica Blvd Ste 200
West Hollywood, CA 90046-5170

Gomez, Nick (Director)
c/o Staff Member *Evolution Entertainment*
10850 Wilshire Blvd Ste 600
Los Angeles, CA 90024-4319, USA

Gomez, Panchito (Actor)
240 N Hollywood Way
Burbank, CA 91505-3431, USA

Gomez, Pat (Athlete, Baseball Player)
3102 Poseidon Ln
Roseville, CA 95661-3974, USA

Gomez, Randy (Athlete, Baseball Player)
707 Grandview Dr
Hudson, WI 54016-1839, USA

Gomez, Rick (Actor)
c/o Sam Maydew *Silver Lining Entertainment*
421 S Beverly Dr Fl 7
Beverly Hills, CA 90212-4408, USA

Gomez, Scott (Athlete, Hockey Player, Olympic Athlete)
Pulver Sports
479 Bedford Park Ave
Attn Ian Pulver
Toronto, ON M5M 1K2, Canada

Gomez, Selena (Actor)
c/o Aleen Keshishian *Lighthouse Management and Media*
9000 W Sunset Blvd Ste 1520
Los Angeles, CA 90069-5815, USA

Gomez, Wilfredo (Athlete, Boxer)
Boxing Hall of Fame
1 Hall of Fame Dr
Canastota, NY 13032-1180, USA

Gomez-Preston, Reagan (Actor)
c/o Shannon Barr *Rogers & Cowan*
1840 Century Park E Fl 18
Los Angeles, CA 90067-2101, USA

Gomez-Preston, Reagen (Actor)
c/o Staff Member *Jeff Morrone Entertainment*
9350 Wilshire Blvd Ste 224
Beverly Hills, CA 90212-3204, USA

Gomez-Rejon, Alfonso (Director, Producer)
c/o Roger Green *WME|IMG*
9601 Wilshire Blvd
Beverly Hills, CA 90210-5213, USA

Gompers, Bill (Athlete, Football Player)
551 Casa Bella Dr Unit 505
Cape Canaveral, FL 32920-4350, USA

Gonchar, Sergei (Athlete, Hockey Player)
3401 Cornell Ave
Dallas, TX 75205-2901, USA

Gondrezick, Grant (Athlete, Basketball Player)
5906 Etiwanda Ave Unit 19
Tarzana, CA 91356-1649, USA

Gondry, Michel (Director, Writer)
c/o Dan Aloni *WME|IMG*
9601 Wilshire Blvd
Beverly Hills, CA 90210-5213, USA

Gonick, Larry (Cartoonist)
247 Missouri St
San Francisco, CA 94107-2404, USA

Gonshaw, Francesca (Actor)
Greg Mellard
12 D'Arblay St #200
London W1V 3FP, UNITED KINGDOM (UK)

Gonsoulin, Austin (Goose) (Athlete, Football Player)
5966 Reeves Dr
Silsbee, TX 77656-8987, USA

Gonzaga, Ginger (Actor)
c/o Eric Kranzler *Management 360*
9111 Wilshire Blvd
Beverly Hills, CA 90210-5508, USA

Gonzales, Dan (Athlete, Baseball Player)
429 W Silvertip Rd
Tucson, AZ 85737-3704, USA

Gonzales, Jaslene (Model)
c/o Lizzie Grubman *Lizzie Grubman Public Relations*
1201 Broadway Ste 810
New York, NY 10001-5656, USA

Gonzales, Larry (Athlete, Baseball Player)
3800 Bradford St Spc 248
La Verne, CA 91750-3151, USA

Gonzales, Raul (Soccer Player)
Sergio Cerro Luengas
Alcala 694 1
Madrid 28019, SPAIN

Gonzales, Rene (Athlete, Baseball Player)
755 E Orangewood Dr
Covina, CA 91723-3620, USA

Gonzalez, Alex (Athlete, Baseball Player)
7743 SW 119th Ct
Miami, FL 33183-3854, USA

Gonzalez, Anthony (Athlete, Football Player)
13271 Dumbarton St
Carmel, IN 46032-7321, USA

Gonzalez, Araceli (Actor)
c/o Staff Member *Telefe (Argentina)*
Pavon 2444
Buenos Aires C1248AAT, ARGENTINA

Gonzalez, Charles (Congressman, Politician)
1434 Longworth Hob
Washington, DC 20515-0004, USA

Gonzalez, Edgar (Athlete, Baseball Player)
1818 Camino Mojave
Chula Vista, CA 91914-4614, USA

Gonzalez, Edith (Actor)
c/o Staff Member *Televisa*
Blvd Adolfo Lopez Mateos 232
Colonia San Angel INN
DF CP 01060, MEXICO

Gonzalez, Eiza (Actor, Musician)
c/o Ina Treciokas *Slate PR*
901 N Highland Ave
W Hollywood, CA 90038-2412, USA

Gonzalez, Fredi (Athlete, Baseball Player, Coach)
8 Great Woods Ln
Malvern, PA 19355-9698, USA

Gonzalez, Gabe (Athlete, Baseball Player)
920 Cerritos Ave
Long Beach, CA 90813-4812, USA

Gonzalez, Hector (Religious Leader)
Baptist Churches USA
PO Box 851
Valley Forge, PA 19482-0851, USA

Gonzalez, Jeremi (Athlete, Baseball Player)
1120 N La Salle Dr Apt 14N
Chicago, IL 60610-7609, USA

Gonzalez, Juan (Athlete, Baseball Player)
c/o Staff Member *Texas Rangers*
1000 Ballpark Way Ste 400
Arlington, TX 76011-5170, USA

Gonzalez, Juan A (Baseball Player)
Ext Catoni A9
Vega Baja, PR 00693, USA

Gonzalez, Lazaro Naranjo (Cholly) (Athlete, Baseball Player)
8306 NW 7th St Apt 32
Miami, FL 33126-3924, USA

Gonzalez, Leon (Athlete, Football Player)
4025 Leonnie Rd
Jacksonville, FL 32208-2947, USA

Gonzalez, Luis (Athlete, Baseball Player)
8902 Ilona Ln Apt 8
Houston, TX 77025-3636, USA

Gonzalez, Mike (Athlete, Baseball Player)
2414 Pine Brook Ct
Deer Park, TX 77536-1518, USA

Gonzalez, Nicholas (Actor)
c/o Siri Garber *Platform PR*
2666 N Beachwood Dr
Los Angeles, CA 90068-2308, USA

Gonzalez, Orlando (Athlete, Baseball Player)
4309 SW 164th Ct
Miami, FL 33185-5294, USA

Gonzalez, Pedro (Athlete, Baseball Player)
104 Gen Cabral
San Pedro de Macoris, Dominican Republic

Gonzalez, Phoenix (Actor)
c/o Staff Member *Select Artists Ltd (CA-Westside Office)*
1138 12th St Apt 1
Santa Monica, CA 90403-5459, USA

Gonzalez, Raul (Soccer Player)
Real Madrid FC
Avda Concha Espina 1
Madrid 28036, SPAIN

Gonzalez, Rick (Actor)
c/o Staff Member *Ziffren Brittenham*
1801 Century Park W Fl 7
Los Angeles, CA 90067-6406, USA

Gonzalez, Susana (Actor)
c/o Staff Member *Televisa*
Blvd Adolfo Lopez Mateos 232
Colonia San Angel INN
DF CP 01060, MEXICO

Gonzalez, Tony (Athlete, Football Player, Television Host)
8011 SW 196th Ter
Cutler Bay, FL 33189-2103, USA

Gonzalez, Victor (Actor)
c/o Gabriel Blanco *Gabriel Blanco Iglesias (Mexico)*
Rio Balsas 35-32
Colonia Cuauhtemoc
DF 06500, Mexico

Gonzalez Zumarraga, Antonio J Cardinal (Religious Leader)
Arzobispado
Apartado 17-01-00106
Called Chile
Quito 01140, ECUADOR

Gonzalo, Julie (Actor)
c/o Ben Levine *LINK Entertainment*
11872 La Grange Ave
Los Angeles, CA 90025-5282, USA

Gooch, Brad (Model, Writer)
c/o Joy Harris *Joy Harris Literary Agency*
1501 Broadway Ste 2310
New York, NY 10036-5600, USA

Gooch, Jeff (Athlete, Football Player)
9225 Fox Sparrow Rd
Tampa, FL 33626-2657, USA

Good, Andrew (Athlete, Baseball Player)
1433 S Belcher Rd Apt G4
Clearwater, FL 33764-2863, USA

Good, David (Reality Star, Writer)
c/o Inna Shamis *AvantGarde Communications Group*
Prefers to be contacted via telephone or email
USA

Good, Hugh W (Religious Leader)
Primitive Advent Christian Church
273 Frame Road
Elkview, WV 25071, USA

Good, Meagan (Actor)
c/o Marcel Pariseau *True Public Relations*
3575 Cahuenga Blvd W Ste 360
Los Angeles, CA 90068-1361, USA

Good, Melanie (Actor)
c/o Staff Member *Bobby Ball Talent Agency*
4342 Lankershim Blvd
Universal City, CA 91602, USA

Good, Michael T (Astronaut)
2617 Broussard Ct
Seabrook, TX 77586-3361, USA

Goodacre, Connick Jill (Model)
Harry Connick
323 Broadway
Cambridge, MA 02139-1801, USA

Goodall, Caroline (Actor)
P F D Drury House
34-43 Russell St
London WC2B 5HA, UNITED KINGDOM (UK)

Goodall, Jane (Writer)
The Jane Goodall Institute
1595 Spring Hill Rd Ste 550
Vienna, VA 22182-4100, USA

Goodburn, Kelly (Athlete, Football Player)
3710 W 52nd Pl
Roeland Park, KS 66205-2766, USA

Good Charlotte (Music Group)
81 Pondfield Rd # 358
Bronxville, NY 10708-3818, USA

Goode, Chris (Athlete, Football Player)
1428 Egret Ln
Birmingham, AL 35214-3410, USA

Goode, David R (Business Person)
Norfolk Southern Corp
3 Commercial Pl Ste 1A
Norfolk, VA 23510-2108, USA

Goode, Irvin (Irv) (Athlete, Football Player)
1030 Woods Mill Plz
Chesterfield, MO 63017-0606, USA

Goode, Kerry (Athlete, Football Player)
639 Herron Ct
Fairburn, GA 30213-2398, USA

Goode, Matthew (Actor)
c/o Craig Bankey *Main Stage Public Relations*
Prefers to be contacted by phone or email.
Los Angeles, CA NA, USA

Goode, Najee (Athlete, Football Player)
c/o Tony Paige *Dream Point Sports*
1455 Pennsylvania Ave NW Ste 225
Washington, DC 20004-1026, USA

Goode, Rob (Athlete, Football Player)
1902 Oakridge Trl
Bridgeport, TX 76426-2620, USA

Goode, Tom (Athlete, Football Player)
9190 Tom Goode Rd
West Point, MS 39773, USA

Goodell, Brian S (Athlete, Olympic Athlete, Swimmer)
27040 S Ridge Dr
Mission Viejo, CA 92692-5015, USA

Goodell, Roger (Business Person, Football Executive)
National Football League
280 Park Ave Fl 12W
Commissioner's Office
New York, NY 10017-1298, USA

Gooden, Drew (Basketball Player)
Orlando Magic
8701 Maitland Summit Blvd
Waterhouse Center
Orlando, FL 32810-5915, USA

Gooden, Dwight (Athlete, Baseball Player)
55 North Dr
Westbury, NY 11590-1011, USA

Gooden, Harry (Athlete, Football Player)
524 10th Ct W
Birmingham, AL 35204-2924, USA

Gooden, Zaviar (Athlete, Football Player)
c/o Andy Ross *Select Sports Group*
2700 Post Oak Blvd Ste 1450
Houston, TX 77056-5785, USA

Goodenough, Larry (Athlete, Hockey Player)
3677 Spruce Hill Rd
Ottsville, PA 18942-9508, USA

Goodeve, Charles P (Athlete, Football Player)
30177 Tattersail Way
Menifee, CA 92584-7366, USA

Goodeve, Grant (Actor)
21416 NE 68th Ct
Redmond, WA 98053-2393, USA

Goodfriend, Lynda (Actor)
338 S Beachwood Dr
Burbank, CA 91506-2713, USA

Goodfriend, Lynda (Actor)
c/o Lynda Goodfriend *Lynda Goodfriend Management*
338 S Beachwood Dr
Burbank, CA 91506-2713, USA

Gooding, Omar (Actor)
c/o David Lederman *Innovative Artists*
1505 10th St
Santa Monica, CA 90401-2805, USA

Gooding Jr, Cuba (Actor)
19356 Vista Grande Way
Porter Ranch, CA 91326-1234, USA

Goodlatte, Bob (Congressman, Politician)
2240 Rayburn Hob
Washington, DC 20515-4606, USA

Goodman, Allegra (Writer)
Dial Press
375 Hudson St
New York, NY 10014-3658, USA

Goodman, Amy (Journalist)
Democracy Now!
207 W 25th St Fl 11
New York, NY 10001-7161, USA

Goodman, Andre (Athlete, Football Player)
101 Walden Place Cir
Elgin, SC 29045-8225, USA

Goodman, Brian (Actor)
c/o Paul Santana *Agency for the Performing Arts (APA)*
405 S Beverly Dr Ste 500
Beverly Hills, CA 90212-4425, USA

Goodman, Brian (Athlete, Football Player)
15009 S 14th Pl
Phoenix, AZ 85048-6242, USA

Goodman, David A. (Director)
c/o Jon Huddle *Fourth Wall Management*
9336 Civic Center Dr
Beverly Hills, CA 90210-3604, USA

Goodman, Drew (Commentator)
5721 Green Oaks Dr
Greenwood Village, CO 80121-1336, USA

Goodman, Harvey (Athlete, Football Player)
2689 County Road 318
Westcliffe, CO 81252-8704, USA

Goodman, John (Actor, Musician, Producer)
c/o Staff Member *Carsey-Werner Company*
16027 Ventura Blvd Ste 600
Encino, CA 91436-2798, USA

Goodman, John (Athlete, Football Player)
800 E 9th St
Edmond, OK 73034-5407, USA

Goodman, Malliciah (Athlete, Football Player)
c/o Chad Speck *Allegiant Athletic Agency*
35 Market Sq Ste 201
Knoxville, TN 37902-1420, USA

Goodman, Richard (Producer)
c/o Staff Member *WME|IMG*
9601 Wilshire Blvd
Beverly Hills, CA 90210-5213, USA

Goodnight, James (Jim) (Business Person)
SAS Institute Inc
100 Sas Campus Dr
Cary, NC 27513-8617, USA

Goodrem, Delta (Actor, Musician)
c/o Jimmy Cundiff *Cundiff & Co.*
1710 Buckingham Rd
Los Angeles, CA 90019-5905, USA

Goodrich, Dwayne (Athlete, Football Player)
533 Oakcrest Dr
Coppell, TX 75019-4082, USA

Goodrich, Gail (Actor, Athlete, Basketball Player, Sportscaster)
PO Box 6999
Ketchum, ID 83340-6999, USA

Goodrich, Jon (Baseball Player)
123 W Agua Caliente Rd
Sonoma, CA 95476-3340, USA

Goodrich Jr, Gail C (Athlete, Basketball Player)
270 Oceano Dr
Los Angeles, CA 90049-4124, USA

Goodrum, Charles (Athlete, Football Player)
117 Pico Rd
East Palatka, FL 32131, USA

Goodson, Ed (Athlete, Baseball Player)
PO Box 327
Fries, VA 24330-0327, USA

Goodwill, Oliver (Actor)
Asylum Entertainment
7920 W Sunset Blvd Fl 2
C/O Marcello Robinson
Los Angeles, CA 90046-3300, USA

Goodwin, Curtis (Athlete, Baseball Player)
4203 Loch Ln
San Leandro, CA 94578-4552, USA

Goodwin, Danny (Athlete, Baseball Player)
1555 Linksview Close
Stone Mountain, GA 30088-3768, USA

Goodwin, Doug (Athlete, Football Player)
915 Eagle View Dr
Charleston, SC 29414-5768, USA

Goodwin, Ginnifer (Actor)
c/o John Carrabino *John Carrabino Management*
5900 Wilshire Blvd Ste 740
Los Angeles, CA 90036-5032, USA

Goodwin, Hunter (Athlete, Football Player)
1011 Lyceum Ct
College Station, TX 77840-2342, USA

Goodwin, Jonathan (Athlete, Football Player)
c/o Ben Dogra *Relativity Sports*
2029 Century Park E Ste 1550
Century City, CA 90067-3000, USA

Goodwin, Marquise (Athlete, Football Player)
c/o Joby Branion *Vanguard Sports Group*
23091 Mill Creek Dr
Laguna Hills, CA 92653-1258, USA

Goodwin, Michael (Actor)
8271 Melrose Ave Ste 110
Los Angeles, CA 90046-6800, USA

Goodwin, Randy (Race Car Driver)
Randy Goodwin Racing
2009 Somerset Lane
Fullerton, CA 92633, USA

Goodwin, Tom (Athlete, Baseball Player, Olympic Athlete)
8 Maple St
Massapequa, NY 11758-5717, USA

Goodwin, Trudie (Actor)
Bosun House
1 Deer Park Rd
Merton
London SW19 3TL, ENGLAND

Goodyear, Scott (Race Car Driver)
Scott Goodyear Racing
PO Box 589
Carmel, IN 46082-0589, USA

Goo Goo Dolls (Music Group)
c/o David Levine *WME|IMG*
9601 Wilshire Blvd
Beverly Hills, CA 90210-5213, USA

Goolagong-Cawley, Evonne (Athlete, Tennis Player)
c/o Staff Member *Ovations*
P.O. Box 1337
Rozelle, NSW 02039, Australia

Goolagong Cawley, Evonne F (Tennis Player)
Private Bag 6060
Richmond, SV 03121, AUSTRALIA

Goorjian, Michael (Actor)
Evolution Entertainment
10850 Wilshire Blvd Ste 600
Los Angeles, CA 90024-4319, USA

Goosen, Retief (Athlete, Golfer)
14 N Park
Sunninghill
Ascot SL59B, United Kingdom

Gorani, Hala (Correspondent)
c/o Staff Member *CNN (Atlanta)*
1 Cnn Ctr NW
PO Box 105366
Atlanta, GA 30303-2762, USA

Goranson, Alicia (Actor)
c/o Staff Member *Carsey-Werner Company*
16027 Ventura Blvd Ste 600
Encino, CA 91436-2798, USA

Goransson, Ludwig (Composer, Musician)
c/o Ray Costa *Costa Communications*
8265 W Sunset Blvd Ste 101
West Hollywood, CA 90046-2433, USA

Gorbachev, Mikhail S (Politician)
Leningradsky Prospekt 49
Moscow 125468, RUSSIA

Gorbachev, Yuri (Artist)
Adrienne Editions
377 Geary St
San Francisco, CA 94102-1801, USA

Gordeeva, Ekaterina (Athlete, Figure Skater)
c/o Staff Member *IMG (LA)*
2049 Century Park E Ste 2460
Los Angeles, CA 90067-3126, USA

Gorder, Genevieve (Designer, Television Host)
c/o Ken Slotnick *AGI Entertainment*
150 E 58th St Fl 19
New York, NY 10155-1900, USA

Gordin, Charles (Actor)
187 Chestnut Hill Rd
Wilton, CT 06897-4108, USA

Gordon, Aaron (Athlete, Basketball Player)
c/o Bill Duffy *BDA Sports Management*
700 Ygnacio Valley Rd Ste 330
Walnut Creek, CA 94596-3838, USA

Gordon, Barry (Actor, Music Group)
1912 Kaweah Dr
Pasadena, CA 91105-3604, USA

Gordon, Ben (Athlete, Basketball Player)
c/o Raymond Brothers *International Athlete Management, Inc*
433 N Camden Dr Ste 600
Beverly Hills, CA 90210-4416, USA

Gordon, Bert I (Director)
9640 Arby Dr
Beverly Hills, CA 90210-1202, USA

Gordon, Bobby (Race Car Driver)
6300 Valley View St
Buena Park, CA 90620-1032, USA

Gordon, Bridgette (Athlete, Basketball Player, Olympic Athlete)
3400 Sweetwater Rd Apt 1309
Lawrenceville, GA 30044-2495, USA

Gordon, Cornell (Athlete, Football Player)
4029 Spring Meadow Cres
Chesapeake, VA 23321-3117, USA

Gordon, Danso (Actor)
c/o Paul Nicholls *Industry Entertainment Partners*
955 Carrillo Dr Ste 300
Los Angeles, CA 90048-5400, USA

Gordon, Darrien (Athlete, Football Player)
1500 Pecos Dr
Southlake, TX 76092-5933, USA

Gordon, Dick (Athlete, Football Player)
5017 Anderson Pl
Cincinnati, OH 45227-1601, USA

Gordon, Don (Actor)
Acme Talent
4727 Wilshire Blvd Ste 333
Los Angeles, CA 90010-3874, USA

Gordon, Don (Athlete, Baseball Player)
711 Sunset Mountain Dr
Chattanooga, TN 37421-2076, USA

Gordon, Don (Athlete, Baseball Player)
711 Sunset Mountain Dr
Dr
Chattanooga, TN 37421-2076, USA

Gordon, Ed (Correspondent)
NBC-TV
30 Rockefeller Plz
New York, NY 10112-0015, USA

Gordon, Eve (Actor)
10100 Santa Monica Blvd Ste 2500
Los Angeles, CA 90067-4116

Gordon, Hannah Taylor (Actor)
Hutton Mgmt
4 Old Manor Close Askett
Buckinghamshire HP27 9NA, UNITED KINGDOM (UK)

Gordon, Harold P (Business Person)
Hasbro Inc
1027 Newport Ave
Pawtucket, RI 02861-2500, USA

Gordon, Howard (Producer, Writer)
c/o Rick Rosen *WME|IMG*
9601 Wilshire Blvd
Beverly Hills, CA 90210-5213, USA

Gordon, Ira (Athlete, Football Player)
PO Box 24526
Federal Way, WA 98093-1526, USA

Gordon, Jack (Athlete, Hockey Player)
17-1725 Southmere Cres
Surrey, BC V4A 7A7, Canada

Gordon, Jeff (Race Car Driver)
Jeff Gordon Children's Foundation
210 Barton Springs Rd Ste 500
Austin, TX 78704-1223, USA

Gordon, John (Commentator)
13011 Milford Pl
Fort Myers, FL 33913-8454, USA

Gordon, Josh (Athlete, Football Player)
c/o Drew Rosenhaus *Rosenhaus Sports Representation*
3921 Alton Rd # 440
Miami Beach, FL 33140-3852, USA

Gordon, Keith (Actor, Director, Writer)
c/o Dan Aloni *WME|IMG*
9601 Wilshire Blvd
Beverly Hills, CA 90210-5213, USA

Gordon, Keith (Athlete, Baseball Player)
4601 Thornhurst Dr
Olney, MD 20832-1826, USA

Gordon, Kiowa (Actor)
c/o Jade Moser *NLE PR*
24965 Lorena Dr
Calabasas, CA 91302-3049, USA

Gordon, Lamar (Athlete, Football Player)
4331 N 16th St
Milwaukee, WI 53209-6924, USA

Gordon, Lancaster (Athlete, Basketball Player)
550 Robinhood Rd
Jackson, MS 39206-5403, USA

Gordon, Lawrence (Business Person)
Largo Entertainment
10201 W Pico Blvd
Los Angeles, CA 90064-2606, USA

Gordon, Mark (Producer)
Mark Gordon Productions
1447 Cloverfield Blvd Ste 200
Santa Monica, CA 90404-2979, USA

Gordon, Melvin (Athlete, Football Player)
c/o Fletcher Smith *Revolution Sports*
270 17th St NW Unit 3001
Atlanta, GA 30363-1261, USA

Gordon, Mikalah (Musician)
c/o Stephen Ford *Diva Central Inc*
7510 W Sunset Blvd # 1445
Los Angeles, CA 90046-3408, USA

Gordon, Mike (Musician)
c/o Jason Colton *Red Light Management*
455 2nd St NE
#500
Charlottesville, VA 22902-5791, USA

Gordon, Molly (Actor)
c/o Dominique Appel *Imprint PR*
6121 W Sunset Blvd
Neuehouse
Los Angeles, CA 90028-6442, USA

Gordon, Nina (Musician)
c/o Staff Member *Paradigm (Monterey)*
404 W Franklin St
Monterey, CA 93940-2303, USA

Gordon, Robby (Race Car Driver)
Robby Gordon Motorsports
10615 Twin Lakes Pkwy
Charlotte, NC 28269-7659, USA

Gordon, Scott (Athlete, Coach, Hockey Player)
c/o Staff Member *Providence Bruins*
1 La Salle Sq
Providence, RI 02903-1888, USA

Gordon, Sean (Model)
c/o Staff Member *IMG*
304 Park Ave S Fl 12
New York, NY 10010-4314, USA

Gordon, Seth (Director)
c/o David McIlvain *Brillstein Entertainment Partners*
9150 Wilshire Blvd Ste 350
Beverly Hills, CA 90212-3453, USA

Gordon, Shep (Producer)
c/o Staff Member *Alive Enterprises*
3264 S Kihei Rd
Kihei, HI 96753-9605, USA

Gordon, Stuart (Director, Producer)
c/o Staff Member *Red Hen Productions*
3607 W Magnolia Blvd Ste L
Burbank, CA 91505-2988, USA

Gordon, Tom (Athlete, Baseball Player)
2006 Lake Lotela Dr
Avon Park, FL 33825-8030, USA

Gordon, Tracy (Race Car Driver)
Beal's General Store
Main St.
Strong, ME 02983, USA

Gordon, Zachary (Actor)
c/o Daniel Spilo *Industry Entertainment Partners*
955 Carrillo Dr Ste 300
Los Angeles, CA 90048-5400, USA

Gordon-Levitt, Joseph (Actor)
3847 Franklin Ave
Los Angeles, CA 90027-4621, USA

Gordy, Berry (Musician, Producer)
801 Sarbonne Rd
Los Angeles, CA 90077-3303, USA

Gordy, Josh (Athlete, Football Player)

Gordy, Kenneth (Rockwell) (Music Group)
c/o Francesco Caccamo *WME|IMG*
9601 Wilshire Blvd
Beverly Hills, CA 90210-5213, USA

Gore, Al (Politician)
The Office of Al & Tipper Gore
3810 Bedford Ave Ste 250
Nashville, TN 37215-2563, USA

Gore, Frank (Athlete, Football Player)
16820 NE 8th Pl
North Miami Beach, FL 33162-2511, USA

Gore, Kristin (Writer)
c/o Rich Green *ICM Partners*
10250 Constellation Blvd Fl 7
Los Angeles, CA 90067-6207, USA

Gore, Martin (Musician)
c/o Staff Member *Mute Records*
1 Albion Pl
London W6 0QT, UK

Gore, Tipper (Politician)
The Office of Al & Tipper Gore
3810 Bedford Ave Ste 250
Nashville, TN 37215-2563, USA

Gorecki, Reid (Athlete, Baseball Player)
1017 Crestdale
Crossing Dr
Avon Park, FL 33825-8030, USA

Gorecki, Rick (Athlete, Baseball Player)
8703 Powers Ct
Orland Park, IL 60462-5695, USA

Gorence, Tom (Athlete, Hockey Player)
120 Hanapepe Loop
Honolulu, HI 96825-2110, USA

Gores, Tom (Business Person)
78 Beverly Park Ln
Beverly Hills, CA 90210-1573, USA

Goreski, Brad (Designer, Reality Star, Television Host)
c/o Nicole Perez-Krueger *PMK/BNC Public Relations*
1840 Century Park E Ste 1400
Los Angeles, CA 90067-2115, USA

Goretta, Claude (Director)
10 Tour de Boel
Geneva 01204, SWITZERLAND

Gorga, Melissa (Musician, Reality Star)
c/o Jaime Cassavechia *EJ Media Group*
349 5th Ave Fl 3
New York, NY 10016-5021, USA

Gorgal, Ken (Athlete, Football Player)
4 the Court of Harborside
Northbrook, IL 60062-3207, USA

Gorgl, Elisabeth (Athlete, Skier)
Kapfenberger Sportvereinigung
Franz Fekete Stadion
J.-Brandl-Gasse 25
Kapfenberg A-8605, Austria

Gorham, Christopher (Actor)
c/o Glenn Rigberg *Inphenate*
9701 Wilshire Blvd Fl 10
Beverly Hills, CA 90212-2010, USA

Gorie, Dominic L Pudwill (Astronaut)
13656 Hidden Valley Ln
Salida, CO 81201-9760, USA

Gorillaz (Music Group)
c/o Chris Morrison *CMO Management Int Ltd*
Fourth Floor, Phoenix Brewery
13 Bramley Rd
London W10 6SP, UK

Gorin, Brandon (Athlete, Football Player)
11470 Burkwood Dr
Carmel, IN 46033-3990, USA

Goring, Robert T (Butch) (Athlete, Hockey Player)
1255 Hempstead Tpke
Attn: Broadcast Dept
Uniondale, NY 11553-1260, USA

Gorinski, Bob (Athlete, Baseball Player)
758 Claypike Rd
Acme, PA 15610-2177, USA

Gorman, Brian (Athlete, Baseball Player)
1381 Via Latina Dr
Camarillo, CA 93012-9294, USA

Gorman, Brian (Baseball Player)
PO Box 1208
Somis, CA 93066-1208, USA

Gorman, Burn (Actor)
c/o Chris Huvane *Management 360*
9111 Wilshire Blvd
Beverly Hills, CA 90210-5508, USA

Gorman, Dave (Actor, Producer, Writer)
c/o Staff Member *Avalon Management (UK)*
4A Exmoor St
London W10 6BD, UNITED KINGDOM

Gorman, Dave (Athlete, Hockey Player)
6821 Domenic Cres
Niagara Falls, ON L2J 4L5, Canada

Gorman, E J (Writer)
PO Box 669
Cedar Rapids, IA 52406-0669, USA

Gorman, Joseph T (Business Person)
TRW Inc
1900 Richmond Road
Cleveland, OH 44124, USA

Gorman, R C (Artist)
PO Box 1258
El Prado, NM 87529-1258, USA

Gorman, Steve (Musician)
c/o Staff Member *Mitch Schneider Organization (MSO)*
14724 Ventura Blvd Ste 410
Sherman Oaks, CA 91403-3537, USA

Gorman, Tom (Athlete, Baseball Player)
1615 SW 5th Ave
Portland, OR 97201-5403, USA

Gorman, Tom (Tennis Player)
ProServe
1101 Woodrow Wilson Blvd
#1800
Arlington, VA 22209, USA

Gormley, Antony (Artist)
13 South Villas
London NW1 9BS, UNITED KINGDOM (UK)

Gorneault, Nick (Athlete, Baseball Player)
94 Seymour Ave
Springfield, MA 01109-1330, USA

Gorney, Karen Lynn (Actor)
Karen Company
Po Box 23-1060
New York, NY 10023, USA

Gorrell, Bob (Cartoonist)
Creators Syndicate
5777 W Century Blvd # 700
Los Angeles, CA 90045-5600, USA

Gorrer, Danny (Athlete, Football Player)
c/o David Dunn *Athletes First*
23091 Mill Creek Dr
Laguna Hills, CA 92653-1258, USA

Gorris, Marleen (Director, Writer)

Gorski, Mark (Athlete, Cycler, Olympic Athlete)
17 Colonial Hills Pkwy
Saint Louis, MO 63141-7765, USA

Gorski, Tamara (Actor)
Steve Young & Associates
18 Gloucester Lane #200
Toronto M4Y 1L5, CANADA

Gortman, Shaunzinski (Basketball Player)
Charlotte Sting
100 Hive Dr
Charlotte, NC 28217, USA

Gortner, Marjoe (Actor)
PO Box 356
Sun Valley, ID 83353-0356, USA

Gorvl, John (Athlete, Baseball Player)
1888 Cranberrv Isles
Way
Apopka, FL 32712-2138, USA

Goryl, John (Athlete, Baseball Player, Coach)
528 Dry Run Rd
Monongahela, PA 15063-1223, USA

Gorzelanny, Tom (Athlete, Baseball Player)
10522 Louetta Ln
Orland Park, IL 60467-1350, USA

Gosar, Paul (Congressman, Politician)
504 Cannon Hob
Washington, DC 20515-4204, USA

Gosger, Jim (Athlete, Baseball Player)
1823 7th St
Port Huron, MI 48060-6301, USA

Gosling, Mike (Athlete, Baseball Player)
2016 Crest Dr
Encinitas, CA 92024-5218, USA

Gosling, Ryan (Actor)
c/o Megan Senior *Slate PR*
901 N Highland Ave
W Hollywood, CA 90038-2412, USA

Gosnell, Raja (Director)
c/o Staff Member *Creative Artists Agency (CAA)*
2000 Avenue of the Stars Ste 100
Los Angeles, CA 90067-4705, USA

Goss, Luke (Actor)
Insomnia Media Group
100 Universal Dr Bungalow 7151
Universal City, CA 91608, USA

Goss, Matt (Actor)
c/o Staff Member *Andrew Freedman Public Relations*
35 E 84th St
New York, NY 10028-0871, USA

Gossage, Goose (Athlete, Baseball Player)
Wish You Were Here Productions
303 E 83rd St Apt 6A
New York, NY 10028-4316, USA

Gossage, Rich (Athlete, Baseball Player)
35 Marland Rd
Colorado Springs, CO 80906-4328, USA

Gosselaar, Mark-Paul (Actor)
c/o Genevieve Penn *Luber Roklin Management*
5815 W Sunset Blvd Ste 208
Los Angeles, CA 90028-6481, USA

Gosselin, Guy (Athlete, Hockey Player, Olympic Athlete)
Mlkern sports
131 Bissen St
Caledonia, MN 55921-1811, USA

Gosselin, Jonathan (Reality Star)
c/o Mike Heller *Talent Resources*
124 E 36th St Ste A
New York, NY 10016-3402, USA

Gosselin, Kate (Reality Star)
c/o Julie May *Media Motion International (MMI)*
15332 Antioch St # 726
Pacific Palisades, CA 90272-3628, USA

Gosselin, Mario (Athlete, Hockey Player)
c/o Staff Member *Ecole de Hockey Energie*
70 Rue des Fauvettes
Saint-Basile-Le-Grand, QC J3N 1P4, Canada

Gosselin, Mario (Race Car Driver)
Wing's Racing
270 Parkside Ln
Rocky Mount, VA 24151-2671, USA

Gossett, David (Athlete, Golfer)
4501 Spanish Oaks Club Blvd Unit 9
Austin, TX 78738-6618, USA

Gossett, D Bruce (Athlete, Football Player)
6109 Puerto Dr
Rancho Murieta, CA 95683-9320, USA

Gossett, Jeff (Athlete, Football Player)
6 Lake Forest Ct
Roanoke, TX 76262-5504, USA

Gossett, Robert (Actor)
c/o Staff Member *Leavitt Talent Group*
11500 W Olympic Blvd Ste 400
Los Angeles, CA 90064-1525, USA

Gossett Jr, Louis (Actor)
c/o Staff Member *Logo Entertainment*
22337 Pacific Coast Hwy # 202
Malibu, CA 90265-5030, USA

Gossick Crockatt, Sue (Swimmer)
13768 Christian Barrett Dr
Moorpark, CA 93021-2802, USA

Gossin, Tom (Musician)
3322 Dovecote Ave
Wilmington, NC 28409-1500, USA

Gossip (Music Group)
c/o Sara Newkirk Simon *WME/IMG*
9601 Wilshire Blvd
Beverly Hills, CA 90210-5213, USA

Gossom, Thom (Athlete, Football Player)
25 Bay Dr SE
Fort Walton Beach, FL 32548-5701, USA

Gostkowski, Stephen (Athlete, Football Player)
c/o Jimmy Sexton *CAA (Memphis)*
6060 Poplar Ave Ste 470
Memphis, TN 38119-0910, USA

Goth, Mia (Actor)
c/o Sarah Spear *Curtis Brown Ltd*
28-29 Hay Market
Hay Market House
London SW1Y 4SP, UNITED KINGDOM

Gothard, Preston (Athlete, Football Player)
448 Merry Way
Pike Road, AL 36064-2282, USA

Gotshalk, Len (Athlete, Football Player)
1200 Butler Creek Rd
Ashland, OR 97520-9370, USA

Gotshalk, Leonard (Athlete, Football Player)
1200 Butler Creek Rd
Ashland, OR 97520-9370, USA

Gott, Jim (Athlete, Baseball Player)
2275 Huntil'lgton
Dr Unit 177
San Marino, CA 91108-2640, USA

Gott, Karel (Musician)
Nad Bertramkou 18
Prague 160 00, CZECH REPUBLIC

Gottfried, Brian (Tennis Player)
9255 Sunrise Breeze Cir
Jacksonville, FL 32256-9614, USA

Gottfried, Gilbert (Actor, Comedian)
c/o Glenn Schwartz *Glenn Schwartz Company*
4046 Declaration Ave
Calabasas, CA 91302-5741, USA

Gotti, Carmine (Reality Star)

Gotti, John, Jr (Reality Star)

Gotti, Victoria (Actor, Producer, Reality Star)
6 Birch Hill Ct
Old Westbury, NY 11568-1218, USA

Gottlieb, Bill (Writer)
c/o Staff Member *Simon & Schuster*
1230 Avenue of the Americas Fl CONC1
New York, NY 10020-1586, USA

Gottlieb, Bill J (Producer)
c/o Staff Member *Gorilla Pictures*
2000 W Olive Ave
Burbank, CA 91506-2642, USA

Gottman, John (Writer)
The Gottman Institute, Inc
PO Box 15644
Seattle, WA 98115-0644, USA

Gottwald, Lukasz (Dr. Luke) (Producer)
Kemosabe Entertainment, LLC
9111 W Sunset Blvd
Los Angeles, CA 90069-3106, USA

Gotye (Music Group, Musician)
c/o Alix Wenmouth *Wasted Youth PR*
53 Corsica St
London N5 1JT, UK

Goude, Ingrid (Model)
511 Las Fuentes Dr
Santa Barbara, CA 93108-2250, USA

Gough, Alfred (Producer, Writer)
c/o Staff Member *Millar/Gough Ink*
3800 Barham Blvd Ste 503
Los Angeles, CA 90068-1042, USA

Gough, Tommy (Musician)
Brothers Mgmt
141 Dunbar Ave
Fords, NJ 08863-1551, USA

Goulart, Izabel (Actor, Model)
c/o Staff Member *Women Model Management*
199 Lafayette St Fl 7
New York, NY 10012-4281, USA

Gould, Alexander (Actor)
c/o Matt Gogal *Abrams Artists Agency*
750 N San Vicente Blvd
E Tower Fl 11
Los Angeles, CA 90069-5788, USA

Gould, Bob (Athlete, Hockey Player)
3651 Oil Springs Line
Oil Springs, ON N0N 1P0, Canada

Gould, Dana (Actor, Producer, Writer)

Gould, Elliott (Actor)
c/o Jeff Witjas *Agency for the Performing Arts (APA)*
405 S Beverly Dr Ste 500
Beverly Hills, CA 90212-4425, USA

Gould, Hal (Athlete, Baseball Player)
126 Rogers Ave
Millville, NJ 08332-9723, USA

Gould, John (Athlete, Hockey Player)
99 Main St W
Beeton, ON L0G 1A0, Canada

Gould, Kelly (Actor)
c/o TJ Stein *Stein Entertainment Group*
1351 N Crescent Heights Blvd Apt 312
West Hollywood, CA 90046-4549, USA

Gould, Matt Kennedy (Reality Star)
c/o Staff Member *WME/IMG*
9601 Wilshire Blvd
Beverly Hills, CA 90210-5213, USA

Gould, Nolan (Actor)
c/o Nicole Nassar *Nicole Nassar PR*
1111 10th St Unit 104
Santa Monica, CA 90403-5363, USA

Gould, Terry (Producer)
c/o Staff Member *Lenhoff & Lenhoff*
324 S Beverly Dr
Beverly Hills, CA 90212-4801

Goulding, Ellie (Musician)
c/o Ed Millett *TAP Management*
Unit G4, Union Wharf 23
Wenlock Road
London N1 7SB, UNITED KINGDOM

Gould Innes, Shane (Swimmer)
207 Kent St
Level 18
Sydney, NSW 02000, AUSTRALIA

Goulet, Michael (Athlete, Hockey Player)
17 Viking Dr
Englewood, CO 80113-7054, USA

Goulet, Michel (Athlete, Hockey Player)
17 Viking Dr
Englewood, CO 80113-7054, USA

Gourdine, Jerome (Musician)
10270 Camelback Ln
Boca Raton, FL 33498-4727, USA

Gourrier, Dana (Actor)
c/o Lori Jonas *Jonas Public Relations*
1327 Ocean Ave Ste F
Santa Monica, CA 90401-1024, USA

Gouveia, Kurt (Athlete, Football Player)
138 Seagrove Ln
Mooresville, NC 28117-8976, USA

Govan, Gerald (Athlete, Basketball Player)
30 Newport Pkwy Apt 2112
Jersey City, NJ 07310-1512, USA

Gove, David (Athlete, Hockey Player)
397 Prince Hinckley Rd
Centerville, MA 02632-2198

Gove, Jeff (Athlete, Golfer)
21323 31st Ave SE
Bothell, WA 98021-7871, USA

Govedaris, Chris (Athlete, Hockey Player)
325 Brewster Rd
Bristol, CT 06010-5277, USA

Govedaris, David (Athlete, Hockey Player)
3838B Lower Union Rd
Orlando, FL 32814-6508, USA

Goverde, David (Athlete, Hockey Player)
3838B Lower Union Rd
Orlando, FL 32814-6508

Govich, Milena (Actor)
c/o Rhonda Price *Gersh*
41 Madison Ave Ste 3301
New York, NY 10010-2210, USA

Gov't Mule (Music Group)
c/o Staff Member *Paradigm (Monterey)*
404 W Franklin St
Monterey, CA 93940-2303, USA

Gowan, Caroline (Athlete, Golfer)
209 Crescent Ave
Greenville, SC 29605-2814, USA

Gowdy, Cornell (Athlete, Football Player)
4611 John St
Suitland, MD 20746-3772, USA

Gowdy, Trey (Congressman, Politician)
1237 Longworth Hob
Washington, DC 20515-0302, USA

Gowell, Larry (Athlete, Baseball Player)
45 Seventh St Apt 2
Auburn, ME 04210-5692, USA

Gower, Jessica (Actor)

Gowin, Toby (Athlete, Football Player)
1605 Oak Creek Cir
Tyler, TX 75703-0433, USA

Goycoechea, Sergio (Soccer Player)
Argentine Football Assn
Via Monte 1366-76
Buenos Aires 01053, ARGENTINA

Goydos, Paul (Athlete, Golfer)
1864 Stearnlee Ave
Long Beach, CA 90815-3040, USA

Goyer, David (Director, Producer, Writer)
c/o Dan Aloni *WME/IMG*
9601 Wilshire Blvd
Beverly Hills, CA 90210-5213, USA

Goyer, Gerry (Athlete, Hockey Player)
205-1963 Durnin Rd
Kelowna, BC V1X 7Y4, Canada

Goyette, Danielle (Athlete, Hockey Player, Olympic Athlete)
131 Silver Springs Dr NW
Calgary, AB T3B 3G6, Canada

Goyette, J G Philippe (Phil) (Athlete, Hockey Player)
815 38e Ave
Lachine, QC H8T 2C4, Canada

Goyo, Dakota (Actor)
c/o Steven Kavovit *Thruline Entertainment*
9250 Wilshire Blvd Fl Ground
Beverly Hills, CA 90212-3352, USA

Goyri, Sergio (Actor)
c/o Staff Member *Televisa*
Blvd Adolfo Lopez Mateos 232
Colonia San Angel INN
DF CP 01060, MEXICO

Gozzo, Mauro (Athlete, Baseball Player)
156 Newton St
Berlin, CT 06037-1254, USA

Grabarkewitz, Billy (Athlete, Baseball Player)
3912 Ivy Glenn Ct
Colleyville, TX 76034-1145, USA

Grabe, Ronald J (Astronaut)
2652 E Scorpio Pl
Chandler, AZ 85249-5253, USA

Grabe, Ronald J Colonel (Astronaut)
145 Ball Park Rd
Auburntown, TN 37016-6055, USA

Grabeel, Lucas (Actor)
c/o Samir Karar *LINK Entertainment*
11872 La Grange Ave
Los Angeles, CA 90025-5282, USA

Graber, Bill (Athlete, Track Athlete)
PO Box 5019
Upland, CA 91785-5019, USA

Graber, Rod (Athlete, Baseball Player)
4674 Mount Armet Dr
San Diego, CA 92117-4719, USA

Grabow, John (Athlete, Baseball Player)
19415 E Via Del Palo
Queen Creek, AZ 85142-8276, USA

Grabowski, James S (Jim) (Athlete, Football Player)
1523 Withorn Ln
Inverness, IL 60067-4367, USA

Grabowski, Jason (Athlete, Baseball Player)
131 Beach Park Rd
Clinton, CT 06413-2335, USA

Grace, Alexis (Musician)

Grace, April (Actor)
c/o Lenore Zerman *Liberman/Zerman Management*
252 N Larchmont Blvd Ste 200
Los Angeles, CA 90004-3754, USA

Grace, Bud (Cartoonist)
PO Box 92
Newcomb, MD 21653-0092, USA

Grace, Maggie (Actor)
c/o Brett Ruttenberg *Imprint PR*
6121 W Sunset Blvd
Neuehouse
Los Angeles, CA 90028-6442, USA

Grace, Mark (Athlete, Baseball Player)
5624 E Via Buena Vis
Paradise Valley, AZ 85253-8129, USA

Grace, McKenna (Actor)
c/o Brett Ruttenberg *Imprint PR*
6121 W Sunset Blvd
Neuehouse
Los Angeles, CA 90028-6442, USA

Grace, Mike (Athlete, Baseball Player)
12791 Big Lake Rd
Davisburg, MI 48350-3419, USA

Grace, Nancy (Attorney, Television Host)
3384 Peachtree Rd NE Ste 450
Atlanta, GA 30326-1183, USA

Grace, Robert Bud (Cartoonist)
3037 Fox Den Ln
Oakton, VA 22124-1307, USA

Grace, Topher (Actor)
c/o Aleen Keshishian *Lighthouse Management and Media*
9000 W Sunset Blvd Ste 1520
Los Angeles, CA 90069-5815, USA

Graceffa, Joey (Actor)
PO Box 5344
Culver City, CA 90231-5344, USA

Gracey, Michael (Director)
c/o Le-Wei Chu *Partizan*
19-23 Kingsland Rd
London E2 8AA, UNITED KINGDOM

Grach, Eduard D (Musician)
1st Smolensky Per 9
#98
Moscow 113324, RUSSIA

Grachvogel, Maria (Designer, Fashion Designer)
c/o Staff Member *Maria Grachvogel*
5 South Molton Street
London, England W11 1LT, United Kingdom

Gracie, Charlie (Musician)
Jeff Hubbard Productions
PO Box 53664
Indianapolis, IN 46253-0664, USA

Gracie, Royce (Athlete, Wrestler)
KhonKhor Enterprises Inc
9806 Zackery Ave
Charlotte, NC 28277-2124, USA

Gracin, Joshua (Musician)
c/o Ken Madson *Average Joes Management*
3738 Keystone Ave
Nashville, TN 37211-3321, USA

Graddy, Sam (Athlete, Football Player)
4792 Brasac Dr
Stone Mountain, GA 30083-5100, USA

Gradin, Thomas (Athlete, Hockey Player)
c/o Staff Member *Vancouver Canucks*
800 Griffiths Way
Vancouver, BC V6B 6G1, Canada

Gradishar, Randy C (Athlete, Football Player)
3060 S Birch St
Denver, CO 80222-6713, USA

Gradison, Ronnie (Athlete, Basketball Player)
6151 Chappellfield Dr
West Chester, OH 45069-6648, USA

Gradkowski, Bruce (Athlete, Football Player)
c/o Michael McCartney *Priority Sports & Entertainment (Chicago)*
325 N La Salle Dr Ste 650
Chicago, IL 60654-8182, USA

Gradkowski, Gino (Athlete, Football Player)
c/o Joe Linta *JL Sports*
1204 Main St Ste 179
Branford, CT 06405-3787, USA

Grady, James T (Politician)
International Teamsters Brotherhood
25 Louisiana Ave NW
Washington, DC 20001-2198, USA

Grady, Wayne (Athlete, Golfer)
PO Box 78
Coolum Beach QLD 4573, Australia

Graeber, Clark (Tennis Player)
411 Harbor Road
Fairfield, CT 06431, USA

Graef, Jed (Athlete, Olympic Athlete, Swimmer)
PO Box 880
Shelburne, VT 05482-0880, USA

Graf, Dave (Athlete, Football Player)
1825 Bel Air Ave
Pompano Beach, FL 33062-7672, USA

Graf, Richard (Athlete, Football Player)
11108 Bluestem Ln
Eden Prairie, MN 55347-4731, USA

Graf, Rick (Athlete, Football Player)
6609 Biscayne Blvd
Minneapolis, MN 55436-1703, USA

Graf, Stefanie (Steffi) (Athlete, Tennis Player)
8921 Andre Dr
Las Vegas, NV 89148-1405, USA

Graff, Ilena (Actor)
11455 Sunshine Ter
Studio City, CA 91604-3129, USA

Graff, Neil (Athlete, Football Player)
Graff Capital Management
200 E 10th St Ste 500
Sioux Falls, SD 57104-6375, USA

Graff, Randy (Actor)
Peter Strawn Assoc
1501 Broadway Ste 2900
New York, NY 10036-5600, USA

Graff, Todd (Actor)
547 Hudson St
New York, NY 10014-3290, USA

Graffanino, Tony (Athlete, Baseball Player)
6875 W Cottontail Ln
Peoria, AZ 85383-7090, USA

Graffman, Gary (Musician)
Curtis Institute of Music
1726 Locust St
Philadelphia, PA 19103-6187, USA

Gragg, Chris (Athlete, Football Player)
c/o Joel Segal *Lagardere Unlimited (NY)*
456 Washington St Apt 9L
New York, NY 10013-1555, USA

Gragg, Scott (Athlete, Football Player)
4113 Stevensville River Rd
Stevensville, MT 59870-6421, USA

Graham, Art (Athlete, Football Player)
80 Nickerson Rd
Orleans, MA 02653-3316, USA

Graham, Ashley (Model)
c/o Christanna Ciabattoni *Skai Blue Media*
732 S Broad St
Philadelphia, PA 19146-2203, USA

Graham, Bill (Athlete, Football Player)
11013 Sierra Verde Trl
Austin, TX 78759-5129, USA

Graham, Bob (Politician)
14814 Breckness Pl
Miami Lakes, FL 33016-1458, USA

Graham, Brandon (Athlete, Football Player)
c/o Joel Segal *Lagardere Unlimited (NY)*
456 Washington St Apt 9L
New York, NY 10013-1555, USA

Graham, Brendan (Musician, Writer)
c/o Staff Member *PeerMusic USA*
3260 Blume Dr Ste 405
Richmond, CA 94806-5277, USA

Graham, Brian (Athlete, Baseball Player)
11995 El Camino Real
San Diego, CA 92130-2539, USA

Graham, Chris (Director)
c/o Simon Millar *Rumble Media*
1620 Broadway Ste C
Santa Monica, CA 90404-2777, USA

Graham, Corey (Athlete, Football Player)

Graham, Currie (Actor)
c/o Matt Luber *Luber Roklin Management*
5815 W Sunset Blvd Ste 208
Los Angeles, CA 90028-6481, USA

Graham, Dan (Athlete, Baseball Player)
6444 Little Pine Way
Las Vegas, NV 89108-3420, USA

Graham, David (Athlete, Golfer)
4201 Lomo Alto Dr Apt 305
Dallas, TX 75219-1515, USA

Graham, Derrick (Athlete, Football Player)
203 Pine Hill Rd
West End, NC 27376-8848, USA

Graham, Dick (Athlete, Hockey Player)
13580 Technology Dr Apt 3314
Eden Prairie, MN 55344-2317, USA

Graham, Dirk (Athlete, Coach, Hockey Player)
17001 S Blackfoot Dr
Lockport, IL 60441-4367

Graham, Ed (Musician)
c/o Sue Whitehouse *Whitehouse Management*
PO Box 43829
London NW6 3PJ, UNITED KINGDOM

Graham, Franklin (Religious Leader)
Samantan's Purse
PO Box 3000
Boone, NC 28607-3000, USA

Graham, Gail (Golfer)
Landmark Sport Group 277 Richmond St NW
Toronto, ON M5V 1X1, CANADA

Graham, Garrett (Athlete, Football Player)
c/o David Dunn *Athletes First*
23091 Mill Creek Dr
Laguna Hills, CA 92653-1258, USA

Graham, Gerrit (Actor)
S M S Talent
8730 W Sunset Blvd Ste 440
Los Angeles, CA 90069-2277, USA

Graham, Glen (Musician)
Shapiro Co
10990 Wilshire Blvd Fl 8
Los Angeles, CA 90024-3918, USA

Graham, Greg (Athlete, Basketball Player)
100 Elena St Apt 122
Cranston, RI 02920-4381, USA

Graham, Hason (Athlete, Football Player)
140 Shoreline Dr
Fayetteville, GA 30215-4663, USA

Graham, Heather (Actor, Producer)
Slush Pile Productions
1104 Malaga Ave
Coral Gables, FL 33134-6321, USA

Graham, Jeff (Athlete, Football Player)
1840 Infirmary Rd
Dayton, OH 45417-5730, USA

Graham, Jimmy (Athlete, Football Player)
800 Occidental Ave S
Seattle, WA 98134-1200, USA

Graham, John R (Writer)
University of California
Astronomy # 607
Berkeley, CA 94720-0001, USA

Graham, Jorie (Writer)
General Delivery
12 Quincy St
Cambridge, MA 02138-3804, USA

Graham, Kat (Actor, Musician)
c/o JoAnne Colonna *Brillstein Entertainment Partners*
9150 Wilshire Blvd Ste 350
Beverly Hills, CA 90212-3453, USA

Graham, Kenny (Athlete, Football Player)
PO Box 7402
Santa Monica, CA 90406-7402, USA

Graham, Kent (Athlete, Football Player)
1001 N Washington St
Wheaton, IL 60187-3857, USA

Graham, Larry (Musician)
c/o Staff Member *Groove Entertainment Inc*
1005 N Alfred St Apt 2
Los Angeles, CA 90069-4757, USA

Graham, Lauren (Actor)
c/o Cheryl Maisel *PMK/BNC Public Relations*
1840 Century Park E Ste 1400
Los Angeles, CA 90067-2115, USA

Graham, Lee (Athlete, Baseball Player)
481 Richmond Rd
Cleveland, OH 44143-2745, USA

Graham, Lindsey (Politician)
PO Box 486
Seneca, SC 29679-0486, USA

Graham, Lou (Athlete, Golfer)
85 Concord Park W
Nashville, TN 37205-4707, USA

Graham, Lukas (Musician)
c/o Jeffrey Azoff *Full Stop Management*
Prefers to be contacted by email.
NA NA, USA

Graham, Mal (Athlete, Basketball Player)
122 Christina St
Newton Highlands, MA 02461-1916, USA

Graham, Mikey (Musician)
JC Music
84A Strand on the Green
London W43 PU, UNITED KINGDOM (UK)

Graham, Milt (Athlete, Football Player)
17 Granite Dr
Wilton, CT 06897-1318, USA

Graham, Parker (Musician)
Performers of the World
8901 Melrose Ave # 200
West Hollywood, CA 90069-5605, USA

Graham, Pat (Athlete, Hockey Player)
Dundas University Health Clinic
200-438 University Ave
Toronto, ON M5G 2K8, Canada

Graham, Paul (Athlete, Basketball Player)
5255 N Marshall St
Philadelphia, PA 19120-3134, USA

Graham, Roger (Athlete, Football Player)
1996 Jacksonville Jaguars
Monroe, NY 10950-4946, USA

Graham, Samaria (Actor)
8730 W Sunset Blvd Ste 600
Los Angeles, CA 90069-2279, USA

Graham, Shayne (Athlete, Football Player)
c/o David Dunn *Athletes First*
23091 Mill Creek Dr
Laguna Hills, CA 92653-1258, USA

Graham, Stedman (Business Person)
737 N Michigan Ave Ste 1050
Chicago, IL 60611-7019, USA

Graham, Stephen (Actor)
c/o Ben Levine *LINK Entertainment*
11872 La Grange Ave
Los Angeles, CA 90025-5282, USA

Graham, TJ (Athlete, Football Player)
c/o Alan Herman *Sportstars Inc*
1370 Avenue of the Americas Fl 19
New York, NY 10019-4602, USA

Graham, Tommy (Athlete, Football Player)
4084 S Wisteria Way
Denver, CO 80237-1714, USA

Graham, Wayne (Athlete, Baseball Player)
40 Logansport Ct
Montgomery, TX 77356-8464, USA

Graham, William B (Business Person)
40 Devonshire Ln
Kenilworth, IL 60043-1205, USA

Graham-Douglas, Mary Lou (Baseball Player)
9990 N Hillview Dr
Tucson, AZ 85737-7940, USA

Grahame, John (Athlete, Hockey Player, Olympic Athlete)
9000 E Jewell Cir
Denver, CO 80231-3450

Grahame, Ron (Athlete, Hockey Player)
9000 E Jewell Cir
Denver, CO 80231-3450

Grahame-Smith, Seth (Writer)
c/o Melissa Kates *Viewpoint Inc*
8820 Wilshire Blvd Ste 220
Beverly Hills, CA 90211-2622, USA

Grahe, Joe (Athlete, Baseball Player)
2317 N Wallen Dr
West Palm Beach, FL 33410-2558, USA

Grahn, Nancy Lee (Actor)
4910 Agnes Ave
North Hollywood, CA 91607-3705, USA

Grainger, David W (Business Person)
WW Grainger Inc
100 Grainger Pkwy
Lake Forest, IL 60045-5202, USA

Grainger, Holliday (Actor)
c/o Pippa Beng *Premier PR*
2-4 Bucknall St
London WC2H 8LA, UNITED KINGDOM

Gralish, Tom (Journalist, Photographer)
203 E Cottage Ave
Haddonfield, NJ 08033-1824, USA

Graman, Alex (Athlete, Baseball Player)
450 E Sunset Dr
Huntingburg, IN 47542-9316, USA

Gramanis, Paul (Athlete, Football Player)
989 Parkview Dr
Tallahassee, FL 32311-1245, USA

Gramatica, Guillermo (Bill) (Athlete, Football Player)
3912 Northampton Way
Tampa, FL 33618-8443, USA

Gramatica, Martin (Athlete, Football Player)
8905 Promise Dr
Tampa, FL 33626-5122, USA

Gramly, Tommy (Athlete, Baseball Player)
16485 Red Wood Cir W
McKinney, TX 75071-6198, USA

Gramm, Lou (Musician)
c/o Staff Member *Creative Artists Agency (CAA)*
2000 Avenue of the Stars Ste 100
Los Angeles, CA 90067-4705, USA

Gramm, W Philip (Phil) (Politician)
UBS Warburg
PO Box 1559
Helotes, TX 78023-1559, USA

Grammas, Alex (Athlete, Baseball Player, Coach)
4030 Vestview Dr
Vestavia, AL 35242-2554, USA

Grammer, Andy (Musician)
c/o Ben Singer *Silverberg Management Group (SMG)*
3030 Nebraska Ave Ste 201
Santa Monica, CA 90404-4140, USA

Grammer, Camille (Actor, Reality Star)
c/o Howard Bragman *LaBrea Media*
8306 Wilshire Blvd # 4002
Beverly Hills, CA 90211-2304, USA

Grammer, Greer (Actor)
c/o Sara Lambley *PV Public Relations*
121 N Almont Dr Apt 203
Beverly Hills, CA 90211-1860, USA

Grammer, Kathy (Actor)
Artists Agency
1180 S Beverly Dr Ste 301
Los Angeles, CA 90035-1154, USA

Grammer, Kelsey (Actor)
c/o Staff Member *Grammnet Productions*
2461 Santa Monica Blvd Ste 521
Santa Monica, CA 90404-2138, USA

Grammer, Spencer (Actor)
c/o Evan Hainey *Untitled Entertainment*
350 S Beverly Dr Ste 200
Beverly Hills, CA 90212-4819, USA

Granaderos, Timothy (Actor)
c/o Jade Wiselogle *Persona Public Relations*
6255 W Sunset Blvd Ste 705
Hollywood, CA 90028-7408, USA

Granat, Cary (Producer)
c/o Staff Member *Bedrock Studios*
2115 Colorado Ave
Santa Monica, CA 90404-3503, USA

Granato, Catherine (Cammi) (Athlete, Hockey Player, Olympic Athlete)
Hockey Hall of Fame Brookfield Place 30 Yonge St
Toronto, ON MSE 1X8, Canada

Granato, Tony (Athlete, Hockey Player)
Pittsburgh Penguins
66 Mario Lemieux Pl Ste 2
Pittsburgh, PA 15219-3504

Granato, Tony (Athlete, Hockey Player, Olympic Athlete)
44537 Spring Hill Rd
Northville, MI 48168-4365

Granby, John (Athlete, Football Player)
61 Butternut Ln
Basking Ridge, NJ 07920-3303, USA

Grand, Steve (Musician)
PO Box 129
Lemont, IL 60439-0129, USA

Grandberry, Ken (Athlete, Football Player)
1223 Garston
San Antonio, TX 78253-5830, USA

Grandberry, Omarion (Actor)
c/o Raphael Berko *Media Artists Group*
8222 Melrose Ave Ste 304
Los Angeles, CA 90046-6839, USA

Grande, Ariana (Actor)
c/o Jules Ferree *Scooter Braun Projects*
1755 Broadway
New York, NY 10019-3743, USA

Grande, George (Commentator)
70 Four Rod Rd
Hamden, CT 06514-1615, USA

Grandelius, Everett (Sonny) (Athlete, Football Player)
31531 Robinhood Dr
Beverly Hills, MI 48025-3532, USA

Granderson, Curtis (Athlete, Baseball Player)
1450 S Emerald St
Chicago, IL 60607-4440, USA

Granderson, Rufus (Athlete, Football Player)
1717 Paris Ave SE
Grand Rapids, MI 49507-2633, USA

Grand Funk Railroad (Musician)
c/o Staff Member *Paradigm (Monterey)*
404 W Franklin St
Monterey, CA 93940-2303, USA

Grandholm, Jim (Athlete, Basketball Player)
211 Spring Park Ave
Sawyer, MI 49125-8353, USA

Grandison, Ronnie (Athlete, Basketball Player)
6151 Chappellfield Dr
West Chester, OH 45069-6648, USA

Grand-Pierre, Jean-Luc (Athlete, Hockey Player)
8432 Galdino Dr
New Albany, OH 43054-7149

Grandpre, Mary (Designer)
Scholastic Press
555 Broadway
New York, NY 10012-3919, USA

Grandy, Fred (Politician)
9417 Spruce Tree Cir
Bethesda, MD 20814-1654, USA

Granger, Charley (Athlete, Football Player)
621 Burbridge St
Port Allen, LA 70767-2128, USA

Granger, Danny (Athlete, Basketball Player)
3801 Pete Dye Blvd
Carmel, IN 46033-8170, USA

Granger, David (Athlete)
Ingalls & Snyder
61 Broadway Fl 31
New York, NY 10006-2803, USA

Granger, Hoyle (Athlete, Football Player)
10611 Cranbrook Rd
Houston, TX 77042-1436, USA

Granger, Jeff (Athlete, Baseball Player)
2905 Glasgow Dr
Arlington, TX 76015-2226, USA

Granger, Kay (Congressman, Politician)
320 CAJ1LLLON Hob
Washington, DC 20515-0001, USA

Granger, Stewart (Athlete, Basketball Player)
552 E 53rd St
Brooklyn, NY 11203-5323, USA

Granger, Wayne (Athlete, Baseball Player)
133 Redtail Pl
Winter Springs, FL 32708-5626, USA

Granholm, Jennifer (Politician)
2066 Asilomar Dr
Oakland, CA 94611-2646, USA

Granik, Debra (Director)
c/o Frank Wuliger *Gersh*
9465 Wilshire Blvd Ste 600
Beverly Hills, CA 90212-2605, USA

Grant, Alan (Athlete, Football Player)
2474 40th Ave
San Francisco, CA 94116-2115, USA

Grant, Alexander (Alex da Kid) (Musician)
9126 Cordell Dr
Los Angeles, CA 90069-1718, USA

Grant, Allie (Actor)
c/o David Doan *Cunningham Escott Slevin & Doherty (CESD)*
10635 Santa Monica Blvd Ste 130
Los Angeles, CA 90025-8306, USA

Grant, Amy (Musician, Songwriter)
c/o Staff Member *The M Collective*
PO Box 273
Franklin, TN 37065-0273, USA

Grant, Beth (Actor)
c/o Staff Member *Big Leap Productions*
12439 Magnolia Blvd Ste 282
Valley Village, CA 91607-2450, USA

Grant, Bob (Athlete, Football Player)
10153 Riverside Dr
Toluca Lake, CA 91602-2562, USA

Grant, Boyd (Coach)
Colorado State University
Athletic Dept
Fort Collins, CO 80523-0001, USA

Grant, Brea (Actor)
c/o Nicole Perna *Imprint PR*
6121 W Sunset Blvd
Neuehouse
Los Angeles, CA 90028-6442, USA

Grant, Brian (Athlete, Basketball Player)
24152 SW Petes Mountain Rd
West Linn, OR 97068-4500, USA

Grant, Bud (Athlete, Football Coach, Football Player)
8134 Oakmere Rd
Minneapolis, MN 55438-1333, USA

Grant, Charles (Actor)
Spotlight
7 Leicester Pl
London WC2H 7RJ, UNITED KINGDOM

Grant, Charles (Athlete, Football Player)
c/o Bill Johnson *SportsTrust Advisors*
3340 Peachtree Rd NE Fl 16
Atlanta, GA 30326-1000, USA

Grant, Clare (Actor, Musician)
c/o Ryan Thomson *Velocity Entertainment Partners*
5455 Wilshire Blvd Ste 1502
Los Angeles, CA 90036-4204, USA

Grant, Danny (Athlete, Hockey Player)
1163 Route 101
Nasonworth, NB E3C 2C3, Canada

Grant, Darryl (Athlete, Football Player)
6931 Compton Ln
Centreville, VA 20121-5009, USA

Grant, David (Athlete, Football Player)
c/o Michael Katcher *Creative Artists Agency (CAA)*
2000 Avenue of the Stars Ste 100
Los Angeles, CA 90067-4705, USA

Grant, Deborah (Actor)
Larry Datzall
17 Broad Ct #12
London WC2B 5QN, UNITED KINGDOM

Grant, Deon (Athlete, Football Player)
2001 Carolina Panthers
Evans, GA 30809-4526, USA

Grant, Edmond (Eddy) (Musician, Songwriter, Writer)
Consolidated Ale
PO Box 87
Tarporley CW6 9FN, UNITED KINGDOM (UK)

Grant, Faye (Actor)
13000 Brentwood Ter
Los Angeles, CA 90049-4807, USA

Grant, Frank (Athlete, Football Player)
2126 Glencourse Ln
Reston, VA 20191-1315, USA

Grant, Gil (Producer)
c/o Staff Member *Principal Entertainment*
9255 W Sunset Blvd Ste 500
Los Angeles, CA 90069-3301, USA

Grant, Harry (Race Car Driver)
7531 Millersville Rd
Taylorsville, NC 28681-8946, USA

Grant, Harvey (Athlete, Basketball Player)
11802 Woodbrook Ct
Bowie, MD 20721-4102, USA

Grant, Horace (Athlete, Basketball Player)
195 Michael Ln
Arroyo Grande, CA 93420-5323, USA

Grant, Hugh (Actor)
Underarm Services
1A Hammond St
London NW1 8DN, UNITED KINGDOM

Grant, Hugh (Horse Racer)
35 E 84th St Apt 8B
New York, NY 10028-0871, USA

Grant, James T (Mudcat) (Athlete, Baseball Player)
1020 S Dunsmuir Ave
Los Angeles, CA 90019-6754, USA

Grant, Jenessa (Actor)
c/o Maggie Dunlop *Oldfield Management*
320-20 Soho St
Toronto, ON M5T 1Z7, Canada

Grant, Jennifer (Actor)
c/o Mark Teitelbaum *Teitelbaum Artists Group*
8840 Wilshire Blvd Fl 3
Beverly Hills, CA 90211-2606, USA

Grant, Jim '''Mudcat''' (Athlete, Baseball Player)
1020 S Dunsmuir Ave
Los Angeles, CA 90019-6754, USA

Grant, John (Athlete, Football Player)
623 Clayton St
Denver, CO 80206-3812, USA

Grant, Josh (Athlete, Basketball Player)
3191 S Davis Blvd
Bountiful, UT 84010-5764, USA

Grant, Kate Jennings (Actor)
c/o Alex Spieller *Baker Winokur Ryder Public Relations*
200 5th Ave Fl 5
New York, NY 10010-3307, USA

Grant, Lee (Actor, Director)
Feury/Grant Entertainment
610 W End Ave Apt 7B
New York, NY 10024-1644, USA

Grant, Leonard (Uncle Murda) (Musician)

Grant, Mark (Commentator)
2837 Via Dieguenos
Alpine, CA 91901-3638, USA

Grant, Martin (Athlete, Hockey Player)
17 Mount View Crt
Collingwood, ON L9Y 5A9, Canada

Grant, Mickie (Actor)
250 W 94th St # 6G
New York, NY 10025-6954, USA

Grant, Orantes (Athlete, Football Player)
5103 Ashford Gables Dr
Atlanta, GA 30338-6780, USA

Grant, Orantes (Athlete, Football Player)
385 Creekview Blvd
Covington, GA 30016-3080, USA

Grant, Paul (Basketball Player)
Milwaukee Bucks
1543 N 2nd St Fl 6
Bradley Center
Milwaukee, WI 53212-4036, USA

Grant, Rachel (Actor)
Bloomfields Management
34 South Molton Street
London W1K 5BP, UNITED KINGDOM

Grant, Reginald (Athlete, Football Player)
PO Box 15602
Los Angeles, CA 90015-0602, USA

Grant, Richard E (Actor)
c/o Staff Member *Artists Rights Group (ARG)*
4A Exmoor St
London W10 6BD, UNITED KINGDOM

Grant, Rodney A. (Actor)

Grant, Ryan (Athlete, Football Player)
c/o Alan Herman *Sportstars Inc*
1370 Avenue of the Americas Fl 19
New York, NY 10019-4602, USA

Grant, Shalita (Actor)
c/o Danielle Allman-Del *D2 Management*
10351 Santa Monica Blvd Ste 210
Los Angeles, CA 90025-6937, USA

Grant, Steve (Athlete, Football Player)
20134 SW 123rd Dr
Miami, FL 33177-5201, USA

Grant, Susannah (Director, Writer)
c/o Risa Gertner *Creative Artists Agency (CAA)*
2000 Avenue of the Stars Ste 100
Los Angeles, CA 90067-4705, USA

Grant, Tom (Athlete, Baseball Player)
230 Holmes Rd
North Attleboro, MA 02760-6213, USA

Grant, Travis (Athlete, Basketball Player)
3314 Pointe Bleue Ct
Decatur, GA 30034-5118, USA

Grant, Wes (Athlete, Football Player)
3014 North St # B
Atlanta, GA 30344-4355, USA

Grant, Wesley (Athlete, Football Player)
3870 Crenshaw Blvd Apt 926
Los Angeles, CA 90008-1837, USA

Granville, Billy (Athlete, Football Player)
PO Box 3426
Sugar Land, TX 77487-3307, USA

Grapenthin, Dick (Athlete, Baseball Player)
5040 170th Ave
Linn Grove, IA 51033-8023, USA

Grapenthin, Rick (Athlete, Baseball Player)
500 Argylls Crst
Alpharetta, GA 30022-6118, USA

Grasmanis, Paul (Athlete, Football Player)
1073 Watkins Creek Dr
Franklin, TN 37067-7830, USA

Grasmick, Lou (Athlete, Baseball Player)
6715 Quad Ave
Rosedale, MD 21237-2406, USA

Grass, Darren (Athlete, Baseball Player, Olympic Athlete)
1086 174th St
Hammond, WI 54015-4831, USA

Grassie, Karen (Actor)
PO Box 913
Pacific Palisades, CA 90272-0913, USA

Grassle, Karen (Actor)
2646 Francisco Way
El Cerrito, CA 94530-1531, USA

Grassley, charles (Politician)
2342 S Rolfe St
Arlington, VA 22202-1545, USA

Grata, Enrique (Actor)
c/o Staff Member *Univision*
605 3rd Ave Fl 12
New York, NY 10158-0034, USA

Grate, Carl (Athlete, Football Player)
205 Wind Ship Ln
Woodstock, GA 30189-5286, USA

Grate, Don (Athlete, Baseball Player)
4721 SW 25th Ter
Fort Lauderdale, FL 33312-5908, USA

Grate, Don (Athlete, Basketball Player)
4721 SW 25th Ter
Fort Lauderdale, FL 33312-5908, USA

Grater, Mark (Athlete, Baseball Player)
1136 Indiana Ave
Monaca, PA 15061-2025, USA

Graterol, Belker (Athlete, Baseball Player)
2301 Lakeland Hills Blvd
Lakeland, FL 33805-2909, USA

Gratham, Larry (Athlete, Football Player)
1971 Tissington Dr
Horn Lake, MS 38637-3752, USA

Gratton, Chris (Athlete, Hockey Player)
8801 Fazio Ct
Tampa, FL 33647-2292

Gratton, Gilles (Athlete, Hockey Player)
4980 des Chenes St
Sainte-Catherine, QC J5C 1L1, CANADA

Gratton, Jean-Guy (Athlete, Hockey Player)
1320 Rue des Patriotes
Laval, QC H7L 2N6, Canada

Gratz, Dwayne (Athlete, Football Player)

Grau, Shirley Ann (Writer)
12 Nassau Dr
Metairie, LA 70005-4434, USA

Grauer, Ona (Actor)
c/o Michelle Gauvin *Performers Management*
5-636 Clyde Ave
West Vancouver, BC V7T 1E1, CANADA

Grausman, Philip (Artist)
21 Barnes Rd
Washington, CT 06793-1402, USA

Gravano, Karen (Reality Star)
c/o Ernest Dukes *The Nottingham Group*
1800 Century Park E Ste 210
Los Angeles, CA 90067-1505, USA

Gravel, Gerry (Ge Ge) (Race Car Driver)
52 Mount Auburn St
Somersworth, NH 03878-2417, USA

Gravel, Maurice R (Mike) (Politician)
3133 Frontera Way Apt 341
Burlingame, CA 94010-5767, USA

Gravelle, Gordon (Athlete, Football Player)
2208 Cordoba Ct
Antioch, CA 94509-5861, USA

Graves, Adam (Athlete, Hockey Player)
c/o Staff Member *New York Rangers*
2 Pennsylvania Plaza
Rm 2200
New York, NY 10121, USA

Graves, Alex (Producer)
c/o Staff Member *ICM Partners*
10250 Constellation Blvd Fl 7
Los Angeles, CA 90067-6207, USA

Graves, Danny (Athlete, Baseball Player)
5041 Rishley Run Way
Mount Dora, FL 32757-8010, USA

Graves, Earl (Athlete, Basketball Player)
123 Random Farms Dr
Chappaqua, NY 10514-1018, USA

Graves, Earl G (Writer)
130 5th Ave
New York, NY 10011-4306, USA

Graves, Hilliard (Athlete, Hockey Player)
AMCA Sales Ltd
100 Simmonds Dr
Dartmouth, NS B3B 1N9, Canada

Graves, Marsharne (Athlete, Football Player)
7544 E Hannibal Cir
Mesa, AZ 85207-4824, USA

Graves, Ray (Athlete, Coach, Football Coach, Football Player)
4230 Hartwood Ln
Tampa, FL 33618-7536, USA

Graves, Rory (Athlete, Football Player)
7585 Shadow Wood Dr
Jonesboro, GA 30236-7302, USA

Graves, Rupert (Actor)
c/o Barry McPherson *Agency for the Performing Arts*
135 W 50th St Fl 17
New York, NY 10020-1201, USA

Graves, Sam (Congressman, Politician)
1415 Longworth Hob
Washington, DC 20515-2306, USA

Graves, Tom (Athlete, Football Player)
1902 Montclair Ave
Norfolk, VA 23523-2322, USA

Graves, Tom (Congressman, Politician)
1113 Longworth Hob
Washington, DC 20515-0401, USA

Graves, White (Athlete, Football Player)
2610 Birchwood Dr
Monroe, LA 71201-2337, USA

Gravitte, Beau (Actor)
Paradigm Agency
10100 Santa Monica Blvd Ste 2500
Los Angeles, CA 90067-4116, USA

Gray, Alasdair J (Writer)
McAlpine
2 Marchmont Terrace
Glasgow G12 9LT, SCOTLAND

Gray, Alec (Actor)
c/o Delaney Andrews *Strategic Talent Group*
4804 Laurel Canyon Blvd # 149
Valley Village, CA 91607-3717, USA

Gray, Billy (Actor)
19612 Grand View Dr
Topanga, CA 90290-3353, USA

Gray, Bryshere (Yazz) (Musician)
c/o Jeff Kolodny *Paradigm*
8942 Wilshire Blvd
Beverly Hills, CA 90211-1908, USA

Gray, Carlton (Athlete, Football Player)
638 Brunner Dr
Cincinnati, OH 45240-3822, USA

Gray, Cyrus (Athlete, Football Player)
c/o David Dunn *Athletes First*
23091 Mill Creek Dr
Laguna Hills, CA 92653-1258, USA

Gray, Dave (Athlete, Baseball Player)
416 E 1050 N
Ogden, UT 84404-3643, USA

Gray, David (Musician, Songwriter)
c/o Rob Holden *Mondo Management*
26-32 Voltaire Rd #2D
London SW6 6DH, UNITED KINGDOM (UK)

Gray, Dick (Athlete, Baseball Player)
503 S Hampton St
Anaheim, CA 92804-2233, USA

Gray, Doug (Musician)
Ron Rainey Mgmt
315 S Beverly Dr Ste 407
Beverly Hills, CA 90212-4301, USA

Gray, Duicie (Actor)
Barry Burnett
31 Coventry St
London W1V 8AS, UNITED KINGDOM (UK)

Gray, Earnest (Athlete, Football Player)
6746 Kirby Oaks Ln
Memphis, TN 38119-8328, USA

Gray, Ed (Basketball Player)
Houston Rockets
2 Greenway Plz
Toyota Center
Houston, TX 77046-0297, USA

Gray, Erin (Actor)
c/o Geneva Bray *GVA Talent Agency Inc*
193 N Robertson Blvd
Beverly Hills, CA 90211-2103, USA

Gray, Erin (Actor, Model)
10921 Alta View Dr
Studio City, CA 91604-3904, USA

Gray, F Gary (Director)
c/o Staff Member *HSI Productions*
601 W 26th St Rm 1420
New York, NY 10001-1136, USA

Gray, Gary (Athlete, Basketball Player)
541 Janice Ln
La Place, LA 70068-5680, USA

Gray, Gary G. (Athlete, Baseball Player)
PO Box 98
La Place, LA 70069-0098, USA

Gray, Hector (Athlete, Football Player)
Miami Springs High School
751 Dove Ave
Miami Springs, FL 33166-3299, USA

Gray, James (Director, Writer)
c/o Todd Feldman *Creative Artists Agency (CAA)*
2000 Avenue of the Stars Ste 100
Los Angeles, CA 90067-4705, USA

Gray, Jeff (Athlete, Baseball Player)
10302 Marsh Harbor Way APT 2
Riverview, FL 33578-3553, USA

Gray, Jerry (Athlete, Football Player)
PO Box 280869
Nashville, TN 37228-0869, USA

Gray, Jim (Actor)
3325 Blair Dr
Los Angeles, CA 90068-1409, USA

Gray, John (Athlete, Hockey Player)
23 Bear Path
Hampton, NH 03842-1300

Gray, John (Director, Writer)
c/o Robert Wolken *Rain Management Group*
11162 La Grange Ave
Los Angeles, CA 90025-5632, USA

Gray, John (Writer)
John Gray's Mars Venus
20 Sunnyside Ave # A130
Mill Valley, CA 94941-1933, USA

Gray, Johnnie (Athlete, Football Player)
220 Short St
Wrightstown, WI 54180-1154, USA

Gray, Ken (Athlete, Football Player)
1202 Lacey Oak Loop
Round Rock, TX 78681-2183, USA

Gray, Linda (Actor)
PO Box 5064
Sherman Oaks, CA 91413-5064, USA

Gray, Lorenzo (Athlete, Baseball Player)
2680 E 19th St Apt 1
Signal Hill, CA 90755-1106, USA

Gray, Macy (Musician, Songwriter)
c/o Ron Alvarez *Stampede Management*
12530 Beatrice St
Los Angeles, CA 90066-7002, USA

Gray, MarQueis (Athlete, Football Player)
c/o Eugene Parker *Independent Sports & Entertainment (ISE-IN)*
6435 W Jefferson Blvd # 197
Fort Wayne, IN 46804-6203, USA

Gray, Mel (Athlete, Football Player)
4507 Skyline Dr
Rockford, IL 61107-3718, USA

Gray, Mel (Athlete, Football Player)
137 Winterset Pass
Williamsburg, VA 23188-1758, USA

Gray, Mike (Actor)
c/o Michele Large *Epic Talent Management*
1263 N Flores St Apt G1
W Hollywood, CA 90069-2973, USA

Gray, Moses (Athlete, Football Player)
1331 Aggie Ln
Indianapolis, IN 46260-4096, USA

Gray, Nel (Athlete, Football Player)
6549 Samantha Ln
Rockford, IL 61107-6307, USA

Gray, Scott (Cartoonist)
c/o Staff Member *Marvel Entertainment, Inc.*
417 5th Ave
New York, NY 10016-2204, USA

Gray, Sonny (Athlete, Baseball Player)
c/o Bo McKinnis *McKinnis Sports Management*
209 10th Ave S Ste 405
Nashville, TN 37203-0764, USA

Gray, Spaiding (Artist, Writer)
22 Wooster St
New York, NY 10013-2300, USA

Gray, Stuart (Athlete, Basketball Player)
601 Spadeleaf Park
Lexington, KY 40509-8310, USA

Gray, Sylvester (Athlete, Basketball Player)
4929 Bilrae Cir S
Millington, TN 38053-1612, USA

Gray, Tamrya (Actor)
c/o Staff Member *19 Entertainment*
35-37 Parkgate Rd #32/33
#32/33 Ransomes Dock
London SW11 4NP, UNITED KINGDOM

Gray, Tamyra (Musician)
c/o Jeff Frasco *Creative Artists Agency (CAA)*
2000 Avenue of the Stars Ste 100
Los Angeles, CA 90067-4705, USA

Gray, Terry (Athlete, Hockey Player)
PO Box 371
Richmond, ON K0A 2Z0, Canada

Gray, Tim (Athlete, Football Player)
6109 Crane St
Houston, TX 77026-4234, USA

Gray, Torrian (Athlete, Football Player)
417 SW 129th Ter
Newberry, FL 32669-2761, USA

Gray Cabey, Noah (Actor)
c/o Blake Bandy *LINK Entertainment*
11872 La Grange Ave
Los Angeles, CA 90025-5282, USA

Grayden, Sprague (Actor)
c/o Katie Rhodes *Untitled Entertainment*
350 S Beverly Dr Ste 200
Beverly Hills, CA 90212-4819, USA

Graye, Devon (Actor)
c/o Adam Griffin *LINK Entertainment*
11872 La Grange Ave
Los Angeles, CA 90025-5282, USA

Grayer, Jeff (Athlete, Basketball Player)
1617 Barbara Dr
Flint, MI 48504-1637, USA

Grayhm, Steven (Actor, Director, Writer)
c/o Adam Griffin *LINK Entertainment*
11872 La Grange Ave
Los Angeles, CA 90025-5282, USA

Graynor, Ari (Actor)
c/o Jill Kaplan *Authentic Talent and Literary Management (NY)*
20 Jay St Ste M17
Brooklyn, NY 11201-8300, USA

Grayson, David Lee (Athlete, Football Player)
5962 Rancho Mission Rd Unit 218
San Diego, CA 92108-2552, USA

Grayson Sr, Dave (Athlete, Football Player)
7116 Los Soneto Ct
San Diego, CA 92114-5918, USA

Gray-Stanford, Jason (Actor)
c/o Scott Zimmerman *Scott Zimmerman Management*
1644 Courtney Ave
Los Angeles, CA 90046-2708, USA

Grazer, Brian (Producer)
1605 San Vicente Blvd
Santa Monica, CA 90402-2207, USA

Graziadei, Michael (Actor)
c/o Amy Abell *BRS / Gage Talent Agency (LA)*
6300 Wilshire Blvd Ste 1430
Los Angeles, CA 90048-5216, USA

Graziani, Ariel (Soccer Player)
San Jose Earthquakes
3550 Stevens Creek Blvd Ste 200
San Jose, CA 95117-1031, USA

Graziano, Renee (Reality Star)
c/o Ernest Dukes *The Nottingham Group*
1800 Century Park E Ste 210
Los Angeles, CA 90067-1505, USA

Grazioso, Claudia (Producer, Writer)
c/o Nicole Clemens *ICM Partners*
10250 Constellation Blvd Fl 7
Los Angeles, CA 90067-6207, USA

Grba, Eli (Athlete, Baseball Player)
106 Fox Run
Florence, AL 35633-1465, USA

Grbac, Elvis (Athlete, Football Player)
17361 Coldwater Trl
Chagrin Falls, OH 44023-1413, USA

Greacen, Bob (Athlete, Basketball Player)
15 Commanders Dr
Washington Crossing, PA 18977-1145, USA

Greason, Bill (Athlete, Baseball Player)
4536 Hillman Dr SW
Birmingham, AL 35221-1816, USA

Greason, William (Baseball Player)
Birmingham Black Barons
4536 Hillman Dr SW
Birmingham, AL 35221-1816, USA

Great Big Sea (Musician)
Fleming & Associates
733-735 North Main
Ann Arbor, MI 48104-1030

Greaves, Gary (Athlete, Football Player)
4340 Windover Way
Melbourne, FL 32934-8517, USA

Grebeck, Craig (Athlete, Baseball Player)
24202 Juanita Dr
Laguna Niguel, CA 92677-4064, USA

Grebenshchikov, Boris (Musician)
2 Marata St
#3
Saint Petersburg, RUSSIA

Greco, Emilio (Artist)
Viale Cortina d'Ampezzo 132
Rome 00135, ITALY

Greco, John (Athlete, Football Player)
c/o Adam Heller *Vantage Management Group*
518 Reamer Dr
Carnegie, PA 15106-1845, USA

Greco, Juliette (Actor, Musician)
Maurice Maraouani
37 Rue Marbeuf
Paris 75008, FRANCE

Greco, Marco (Race Car Driver)
11717 W. Rockville Rd.
Indianapolis, IN 46232, USA

Greco, Michael (Actor)
c/o Pedro Pinto *Gregg Millard Management*
38 Barton House
Sable St
London N1 2AF, UK

Greczyn, Alice (Actor)
c/o Adam Griffin *LINK Entertainment*
11872 La Grange Ave
Los Angeles, CA 90025-5282, USA

Greeley, Andrew M (Andy) (Writer)
6030 S Ellis Ave
Chicago, IL 60637-2608, USA

Green, A C (Athlete, Basketball Player)
904 Silver Spur Rd Ste 270
Rolling Hills Estates, CA 90274-4266, USA

Green, AC (Athlete, Basketball Player)
904 Silver Spur Rd # 416
Rolling Hills Estates, CA 90274-3800, USA

Green, Adolph (Musician)
211 Central Park W # 19E
New York, NY 10024-6020, USA

Green, Ahman (Athlete, Football Player)
1750 Limestone Trl
De Pere, WI 54115-7973, USA

Green, AJ (Athlete, Football Player)
c/o Ben Dogra *Relativity Sports*
2029 Century Park E Ste 1550
Century City, CA 90067-3000, USA

Green, Al (Musician)
Al Green Music
PO Box 456
Millington, TN 38083-0456, USA

Green, Al (Congressman, Politician)
220.1 Rayburn Hob
Washington, DC 20515-0001, USA

Green, Al (Musician, Religious Leader, Songwriter)
PO Box 456
Millington, TN 38083-0456, USA

Green, Andy (Athlete, Baseball Player)
1025 Lakefront Dr
Lexington, KY 40517-2658, USA

Green, Anthony (Athlete, Football Player)
9611 Wesland Cir
Randallstown, MD 21133-2043, USA

Green, Barrett (Athlete, Football Player)
1004 Green Pine Blvd Apt D1
West Palm Beach, FL 33409-7013, USA

Green, Benny (Musician)
Jazz Tree
211 Thompson St Apt 1D
New York, NY 10012-1335, USA

Green, B Eric (Athlete, Football Player)
13131 Luntz Point Ln
Windermere, FL 34786-5802, USA

Green, Boyce (Athlete, Football Player)
4156 1st Street Pl NW
Hickory, NC 28601-8075, USA

Green, Brian Austin (Actor, Director, Producer)
1605 San Vicente Blvd
Santa Monica, CA 90402-2207, USA

Green, Cee Lo (Musician)
JL Entertainment
18653 Ventura Blvd # 340
Tarzana, CA 91356-4103, USA

Green, Charlie (Athlete, Football Player)
255 S Kyrene Rd Unit 214
Chandler, AZ 85226-4460, USA

Green, Charlie (Athlete, Football Player)
c/o Staff Member *Bryan Bantry*
119 W 57th St Ste 1211
New York, NY 10019-2400, USA

Green, Chris (Athlete, Baseball Player)
4054 Uppergate Ln
Charlotte, NC 28215-3831, USA

Green, Chris (Athlete, Football Player)
331 Patio Village Ter
Weston, FL 33326-1622, USA

Green, Cleveland (Athlete, Football Player)
5537 Robinson Road Ext
Jackson, MS 39204-4142, USA

Green, Cornell (Athlete, Football Player)
2106 Trinidad Dr
Dallas, TX 75232-2750, USA

Green, Darrell (Athlete, Football Player)
20998 Rostormel Ct
Ashburn, VA 20147-4780, USA

Green, Dave (Athlete, Football Player)
8311 Pat Blvd
Tampa, FL 33615-1810, USA

Green, David (Director)
International Creative Mgmt
76 Oxford St
London W1N 0AX, UNITED KINGDOM (UK)

Green, David (Athlete, Baseball Player)
Colinia Managua Grupo H47
Managua, Nicaragua

Green, David (Race Car Driver)
118 Reel Brook Lane
Mooreslli11e, NC 28117-8801, USA

Green, David E (Athlete, Football Player)
8311 Pat Blvd
Tampa, FL 33615-1810, USA

Green, David Gordon (Director, Producer, Writer)
c/o Staff Member *Gotham Group*
1041 N Formosa Ave # 200
West Hollywood, CA 90046-6703, USA

Green, Debbie (Athlete, Olympic Athlete, Volleyball Player)
239 5th St
Seal Beach, CA 90740-6116, USA

Green, Dick (Athlete, Baseball Player)
3924 Ridgemoor Dr
Rapid City, SD 57702-5328, USA

Green, Donnie (Athlete, Football Player)
11 S Walnut St Apt 316
Hagerstown, MD 21740-5499, USA

Green, Draymond (Athlete, Basketball Player, Olympic Athlete)
c/o BJ Armstrong *Wasserman Media Group*
10960 Wilshire Blvd Ste 1200
Los Angeles, CA 90024-3714, USA

Green, E G (Athlete, Football Player)
3505 45th Ter W Unit 105
Bradenton, FL 34210-3177, USA

Green, E.G. (Athlete, Football Player)
26620 Castleview Way
Wesley Chapel, FL 33544-4739, USA

Green, EG (Athlete, Football Player)
242 Echo Cir
Fort Walton Beach, FL 32548-6315, USA

Green, Eric (Athlete, Football Player)
PO Box 204
Clewiston, FL 33440-0204, USA

Green, Ernie (Athlete, Football Player)
424 Rue Marseille
Dayton, OH 45429-1878, USA

Green, Eva (Actor)
c/o Angharad Wood *Tavistock Wood Management*
45 Conduit St
London W1S 2YN, UNITED KINGDOM

Green, Gary (Athlete, Baseball Player)
939 Kennebec St
Pittsburgh, PA 15217-2604, USA

Green, Gary F (Athlete, Football Player)
PO Box 701133
San Antonio, TX 78270-1133, USA

Green, Gaston (Athlete, Football Player)
13524 Stanford Ave
Los Angeles, CA 90059-3538, USA

Green, Gene (Congressman, Politician)
2470 Rayburn Hob
Washington, DC 20515-4327, USA

Green, George (Athlete, Baseball Player)
1718 S Oxford Ave Apt 1
Los Angeles, CA 90006-5130, USA

Green, Gerald (Writer)
88 Arrowhead Trl
New Canaan, CT 06840-3441, USA

Green, Harold (Athlete, Football Player)
145 Folk Rd
Blythewood, SC 29016-9031, USA

Green, Hugh (Athlete, Football Player)
4758 Highway 61
Fayette, MS 39069-5422, USA

Green, Jacob (Athlete, Football Player)
4921 Whistling Straits Loop
College Station, TX 77845-3866, USA

Green, Jacquez (Athlete, Football Player)
5102 Madison Lakes Cir W
Davie, FL 33328-4519, USA

Green, Janine (Actor)
c/o David Sweeney *Sweeney Entertainment*
1601 Vine St # 6
Los Angeles, CA 90028-8802, USA

Green, Jarvis (Athlete, Football Player)
10438 Dunsford Dr
Lone Tree, CO 80124-9796, USA

Green, Jeff (Athlete, Basketball Player)
c/o Staff Member *Oklahoma City Thunder*
211 N Robinson Ave Ste N300
Two Leadership Square
Oklahoma City, OK 73102-7191, USA

Green, Jeff (Race Car Driver)
Haas CNC Racing
6001 Haas Way
Kannapolis Gateway Business Park
Kannapolis, NC 28081-7730, USA

Green, Jenna Leigh (Actor)
c/o Aaron Kogan *AK Management (LA)*
1680 Vine St Ste 200
Taft Bldg #518
Los Angeles, CA 90028-8829, USA

Green, Jessica (Actor)
c/o Jonathan Perry *Agency for the Performing Arts (APA)*
405 S Beverly Dr Ste 500
Beverly Hills, CA 90212-4425, USA

Green, Jessie (Athlete, Football Player)
638 County Road 2470
Mount Pleasant, TX 75455-9255, USA

Green, Jimmy (Athlete, Golfer)
PO Box 1607
Auburn, AL 36831, USA

Green, John (Writer)
PO Box 8147
Missoula, MT 59807-8147, USA

Green, John M (Johnny) (Athlete, Basketball Player)
9 Susan Ln
Dix Hills, NY 11746-5140, USA

Green, Jordan-Claire (Actor)
c/o Staff Member *Cunningham Escott Slevin & Doherty (CESD)*
10635 Santa Monica Blvd Ste 130
Los Angeles, CA 90025-8306, USA

Green, Kate (Writer)
Bantam/Delacorte/Dell/Doubleday Press
1540 Broadway
New York, NY 10036-4039, USA

Green, Ken (Athlete, Golfer)
4520 Feivel Rd Apt 56
West Palm Beach, FL 33417-8078, USA

Green, Kerri (Actor)
c/o Lisa Loosemore *Viking Entertainment*
445 W 23rd St Ste 1A
New York, NY 10011-1445, USA

Green, Ladarius (Athlete, Football Player)
c/o Adisa P Bakari *Kelley Drye & Warren LLP*
3050 K St NW Ste 400
Washington, DC 20007-5100, USA

Green, Lamar (Athlete, Basketball Player)
PO Box 490208
Chicago, IL 60649-0019, USA

Green, Lenny (Athlete, Baseball Player)
18693 Sunset St
Detroit, MI 48234-2043, USA

Green, Leonard I (Business Person)
Rite Aid Corp
30 Hunter Ln
Camp Hill, PA 17011-2400, USA

Green, Litterial (Athlete, Basketball Player)
160 McIntosh Place Dr
Fayetteville, GA 30214-7318, USA

Green, Marilyn (Race Car Driver)
601 Norwalk St
Greensboro, NC 27407-1409, USA

Green, Mark (Race Car Driver)
Hensley Racing
1542 Js Holland Rd
Ridgeway, VA 24148-3726, USA

Green, Mark (Race Car Driver)
Trackside Marketing Group
345 Marblerock Way
Lexington, KY 40503-6321, USA

Green, Mark A (Athlete, Football Player)
1087 Creek Bend Dr
Vernon Hills, IL 60061-3307, USA

Green, Mike (Athlete, Football Player)
15271 Peach St
Chino Hills, CA 91709-2565, USA

Green, Nick (Athlete, Baseball Player)
1380 Lake Washington Cir
Cir
Lawrenceville, GA 30043-6664, USA

Green, Pat (Musician)
HB Public Relations & Mgmt
4611 Dakota Ave
Nashville, TN 37209-3525, USA

Green, Patricia (Producer, Writer)
c/o David Greenblatt *Greenlit*
1800 N Highland Ave Ste 500
Los Angeles, CA 90028-4527, USA

Green, Paul (Athlete, Football Player)
1635 N Formosa Ave Apt 208
Los Angeles, CA 90046-3993, USA

Green, Pumpsie (Athlete, Baseball Player)
2105 Harper St
El Cerrito, CA 94530-1724, USA

Green, Ray (Athlete, Football Player)
2738 S University Dr Apt 15A
Davie, FL 33328-1428, USA

Green, Reinaldo Marcus (Producer)
c/o Craig Kestel *WME/IMG*
9601 Wilshire Blvd
Beverly Hills, CA 90210-5213, USA

Green, Rick (Athlete, Hockey Player)
1260 W. de la Gauchettiere St.
Montreal, QC H3B 5E8, Canada

Green, Rick (Producer)
c/o Glenn Cockburn *Meridian Artists*
2 College St Suite 207
Toronto, ON M5G 1K3, Canada

Green, Rickey (Athlete, Basketball Player)
9 Hampton Ct
Flossmoor, IL 60422-2293, USA

Green, Robin (Writer)
c/o Staff Member *Broder Webb Chervin Silbermann Agency, The (BWCS)*
10250 Constellation Blvd
Los Angeles, CA 90067-6200, USA

Green, Robson (Actor)
c/o Staff Member *Coastal Productions*
25B Broadchare
The Quayside
Newcastle-Upon-Tyne NE1 3DQ, UNITED KINGDOM (UK)

Green, Sarah (Producer)
c/o Staff Member *ICM Partners*
10250 Constellation Blvd Fl 7
Los Angeles, CA 90067-6207, USA

Green, Scarborough (Athlete, Baseball Player)
2020 Crimson Meadows Dr
O Fallon, MO 63366-4186, USA

Green, Seth (Actor, Comedian, Producer)
c/o Steven Nossokoff *Untitled Entertainment*
350 S Beverly Dr Ste 200
Beverly Hills, CA 90212-4819, USA

Green, Shawn (Athlete, Baseball Player)

Green, Sidney (Basketball Player, Coach)
Florida Atlantic University
Athletic Dept
Boca Raton, FL 33431, USA

Green, Skylar (Athlete, Football Player)
3121 Thomas Ave Apt D
Dallas, TX 75204-2605, USA

Green, Steve (Athlete, Basketball Player)
13483 Chrisfield Ln
McCordsville, IN 46055-9646, USA

Green, Suzy (Athlete, Golfer)
26006 Carol Ave
Franklin, MI 48025-1107, USA

Green, Tammie (Athlete, Golfer)
4990 Township Road 147 NE
Somerset, OH 43783-9753, USA

Green, Taylor (Athlete, Baseball Player)
7640 NW 79th Ave
Apt L8
Tamarac, FL 33321-2868, USA

Green, Tim (Athlete, Football Player, Sportscaster)
1194 Greenfield Ln
Skaneateles, NY 13152-9666, USA

Green, Tom (Actor, Comedian)
c/o Ann Gurrola *Marleah Leslie & Associates*
1645 Vine St Apt 712
Los Angeles, CA 90028-8812, USA

Green, Travis (Athlete, Hockey Player)
2 Riverside
Irvine, CA 92602-0903, USA

Green, Trent (Athlete, Football Player)
12109 Alhambra St
Leawood, KS 66209-2254, USA

Green, Tyler (Athlete, Baseball Player)
15065 S 39th St
Phoenix, AZ 85044-6676, USA

Green, Van (Athlete, Football Player)
311 Leta St
Auburndale, FL 33823-4313, USA

Green, Victor (Athlete, Football Player)
802 Jamont Cir
Alpharetta, GA 30022-7681, USA

Green, Virgil (Athlete, Football Player)
c/o Scott Smith *XAM Sports*
3509 Ice Age Dr
Madison, WI 53719-5409, USA

Green, Vivian (Actor)
c/o Staff Member *WME/IMG*
9601 Wilshire Blvd
Beverly Hills, CA 90210-5213, USA

Green, Willie (Athlete, Football Player)
152 Farmington Rd
Shelby, NC 28150-8698, USA

Green, Woody (Athlete, Football Player)
702 SE Palmblad Pl
Portland, OR 97080-1496, USA

Green, Yatil (Athlete, Football Player)
2000 Island Blvd Apt 3002
Aventura, FL 33160-4966, USA

Greenaway, Peter (Director)
Allarts Ltd
387B King St
London W6 9NH, UNITED KINGDOM (UK)

Greenberg, Adam (Athlete, Baseball Player)
256A Woodard Rd
Arnold, MD 21012-2252, USA

Greenberg, Bryan (Actor)
c/o Jodi Gottlieb *Independent Public Relations*
9601 Wilshire Blvd Ste 750
Beverly Hills, CA 90210-5228, USA

Greenberg, Carl (Journalist)
6001 Canterbury Dr
Culver City, CA 90230-6876, USA

Greenberg, Evan (Business Person)
ACE Limited
Barengasse 32
Zurich 08001, Switzerland

Greenberg, Maurice R (Business Person)
American International Group
70 Pine St Apt 920
New York, NY 10005-0018, USA

Greenberg, Mike (Sportscaster, Television Host)
c/o Staff Member *ESPN (Main)*
935 Middle St
Espn Plaza
Bristol, CT 06010-1000, USA

Greenberg, Peter (Television Host)

Greenberg, Ross (Producer, Writer)
c/o Staff Member *Shed Media US*
3800 Barham Blvd Ste 410
Los Angeles, CA 90068-1042, USA

Greenblatt, Stephen J (Writer)
Harvard University
English Dept
Cambridge, MA 02138, USA

Greenburg, Dan (Writer)
323 E 50th St
New York, NY 10022-7901, USA

Greenburg, Michael (Producer)
c/o Staff Member *Big Pix*
2401 Main St
C/O Murphy & Kress
Santa Monica, CA 90405-3515, USA

Greenburg, Paul (Journalist)
5900 Scenic Dr
Little Rock, AR 72207-2833, USA

Greenbush, Rachel Lindsay (Actor)
Gold Marshak Liedtke
3500 W Olive Ave Ste 1400
Burbank, CA 91505-5512, USA

Greenbush, Sidney Robin (Actor)
Gold Marshak Liedtke
3500 W Olive Ave Ste 1400
Burbank, CA 91505-5512, USA

Green Day (Music Group)
c/o Brian Bumbery *BB Gun Press*
9229 W Sunset Blvd Ste 305
Los Angeles, CA 90069-3403, USA

Greene, A J (Athlete, Football Player)
3900 Braxton Dr
Charlotte, NC 28226-7003, USA

Greene, Ashley (Actor)
c/o Ryan Daly *Zero Gravity Management*
11110 Ohio Ave Ste 100
Los Angeles, CA 90025-3329, USA

Greene, Billoah (Actor)
c/o Staff Member *The House of Representatives*
3118 Wilshire Blvd Ste D
Santa Monica, CA 90403-2345, USA

Greene, Bob (Fitness Expert)
c/o Bill Stankey *Westport Entertainment Associates*
1120 W State Route 89A Ste B1
Sedona, AZ 86336-5763, USA

Greene, Charles E (Charlie) (Athlete, Olympic Athlete, Track Athlete)
PO Box 6938
Lincoln, NE 68506-0938, USA

Greene, Charlie (Athlete, Baseball Player)
1449 Oldfield Dr
Tallahassee, FL 32308-0534, USA

Greene, David (Football Coach, Football Player)
c/o Lenore Zerman *Liberman/Zerman Management*
252 N Larchmont Blvd Ste 200
Los Angeles, CA 90004-3754, USA

Greene, Ellen (Musician)
Innovative Artists
1505 10th St
Santa Monica, CA 90401-2805, USA

Greene, Graham (Actor)
c/o Gerry Jordan *Jordan & Associates*
125-720 King St W
Toronto, ON M5V 3S5, CANADA

Greene, Joe (Athlete, Football Player)
PO Box 270953
Flower Mound, TX 75027-0953, USA

Greene, Kai (Fitness Expert)
101 Bedford Ave Apt D510
Brooklyn, NY 11211-3780, USA

Greene, Ken (Athlete, Football Player)
PO Box 195
Bayview, ID 83803-0195, USA

Greene, Kevin (Athlete, Football Player)
c/o David Dunn *Athletes First*
23091 Mill Creek Dr
Laguna Hills, CA 92653-1258, USA

Greene, Khalil (Athlete, Baseball Player)
24731 Ellesmere
San Antonio, TX 78257-1368, USA

Greene, Khaseem (Athlete, Football Player)

Greene, Maurice (Athlete, Track Athlete)
c/o Jon Orlando *Exposure Marketing Group*
348 Hauser Blvd Apt 414
Los Angeles, CA 90036-5590, USA

Greene, Michele (Actor, Musician)
PO Box 29117
Los Angeles, CA 90029-0117, USA

Greene, Pat (Writer)
c/o Staff Member *Playscripts, Inc.*
450 7th Ave Ste 1502
New York, NY 10123-0083, USA

Greene, Paul (Actor)
c/o Jessica Cohen *JCPR*
9903 Santa Monica Blvd # 983
Beverly Hills, CA 90212-1671, USA

Greene, Shecky (Actor, Comedian)
312 Quiet Harbor Dr
Henderson, NV 89052-2344, USA

Greene, Shonn (Athlete, Football Player)
c/o Sean Howard *Octagon Football*
600 Battery St Fl 2
San Francisco, CA 94111-1820, USA

Greene, Todd (Athlete, Baseball Player)
725 Pine Leaf Ct
Alpharetta, GA 30022-1026, USA

Greene, Tommy (Athlete, Baseball Player)
6001 Dalecross Way
Glen Allen, VA 23059-6962, USA

Greene, Tony (Athlete, Football Player)
1890 Briarcliff Cir NE Apt D
Atlanta, GA 30329-2574, USA

Greene, Tony (Athlete, Football Player)
9001 Brookville Rd
Silver Spring, MD 20910-1819, USA

Greene, Willie (Athlete, Baseball Player)
1044 GA Highway 22 E
Haddock, GA 31033-2360, USA

Greenfield, James L (Journalist)
12 Ives Rd
Washington Depot, CT 06794-1116, USA

Greenfield, Jeff (Correspondent)
Cable News Network
820 1st St NE Ste 1000
News Dept
Washington, DC 20002-4363, USA

Greenfield, Lauren (Director, Photographer, Producer)
Lauren Greenfield Photography
2417 McKinley Ave
Venice, CA 90291-4625, USA

Greenfield, Luke (Director)
c/o Staff Member *WideAwake*
17530 Ventura Blvd Ste 201
Encino, CA 91316-3889, USA

Greenfield, Max (Actor, Producer)
c/o Jillian Roscoe *ID Public Relations*
7060 Hollywood Blvd Fl 8th
Los Angeles, CA 90028-6021, USA

Greenfield-Sanders, Timothy (Artist, Photographer)
821 Broadway Fl 4
New York, NY 10003-4702, USA

Greengrass, Jim (Athlete, Baseball Player)
119 Remington Dr SW
Cartersville, GA 30120-5784, USA

Greengrass, Paul (Director)
c/o Beth Swofford *Creative Artists Agency (CAA)*
2000 Avenue of the Stars Ste 100
Los Angeles, CA 90067-4705, USA

Greenlaw, Jeff (Athlete, Hockey Player)
9213 Colberg Dr
Austin, TX 78749-4151, USA

Greenlaw, Linda (Writer)

Greenlay, Mike (Athlete, Hockey Player)
c/o Staff Member *Minnesota Wild*
317 Washington St
Saint Paul, MN 55102-1667, USA

Greenlay, Mike (Athlete, Hockey Player)
3338 Richmond Bay
Saint Paul, MN 55129-4925

Greenlee, David (Actor)
1811 Whitley Ave Apt 800
Los Angeles, CA 90028-4960, USA

Greenspan, Alan (Politician)
Greenspan Associates LLC
2710 Chain Bridge Rd NW
Washington, DC 20016-3404, USA

Greenspan, Jerry (Athlete, Basketball Player)
605 Sterling Dr
Florham Park, NJ 07932-3030, USA

Greenspan, Melissa (Actor)
c/o Jeff Danis *Danis, Panaro, Nist Talent (DPN)*
9201 W Olympic Blvd
Beverly Hills, CA 90212-4605, USA

Greenstein, Jeff (Producer)
c/o Staff Member *ICM Partners*
10250 Constellation Blvd Fl 7
Los Angeles, CA 90067-6207, USA

Greenville, Georgina (Model)
Next Model Mgmt
188 Rue de Rivoli
Paris 75001, FRANCE

Greenway, Chad (Athlete, Football Player)
39448 250th St
Mount Vernon, SD 57363-5005, USA

Greenwell, Emma (Actor)
c/o Alexa Pearson *Beaumont Communications*
189-190 Shoreditch High St
Unit 2
London E1 6HU, UNITED KINGDOM

Greenwell, Mike (Athlete, Baseball Player)
18500 State Road 31
Alva, FL 33920-3016, USA

Greenwood, Bruce (Actor)
c/o Jean Sievers *Beachwood Entertainment Collective*
2271 Cheremoya Ave
Los Angeles, CA 90068-3006, USA

Greenwood, Clarence (Citizen Cope) (Musician, Producer)
c/o Neil Warnock *UTA Music/The Agency Group (UK)*
361-373 City Rd
London EC1V 1PQ, UNITED KINGDOM

Greenwood, Colin (Musician)
Nasty Little Man
72 Spring St # 1100
New York, NY 10012-4019, USA

Greenwood, David (Athlete, Basketball Player)
18857 Whitney Pl
Rowland Heights, CA 91748-4873, USA

Greenwood, Jonny (Musician)
Nasty Little Man
72 Spring St # 1100
New York, NY 10012-4019, USA

Greenwood, L C (Athlete, Football Player)
PO Box 3528
Parkersburg, WV 26103-3528, USA

Greenwood, Lee (Musician, Songwriter)
c/o Roger Neal *Neal Public Relations & Management*
3042 N Keystone St
Burbank, CA 91504-1621, USA

Greenwood, Morlon (Athlete, Football Player)
2 Waters Lake Blvd
Missouri City, TX 77459-6553, USA

Greer, Brian (Athlete, Baseball Player)
307 Bagnall Ave
Placentia, CA 92870-1904, USA

Greer, Brodie (Actor)
11911 Mayfair Ave
#3
Los Angeles, CA 90049, USA

Greer, Donovan (Athlete, Football Player)
3423 Shadowside Ct
Houston, TX 77082-8303, USA

Greer, Germaine (Writer)
Atkin & Stone
Atkin and Stone29 Fernshaw Road
London SW10 0TG, UNITED KINGDOM

Greer, Judy (Actor)
c/o David Gardner *Artists First*
9465 Wilshire Blvd Ste 900
Beverly Hills, CA 90212-2608, USA

Greer, Kenny (Athlete, Baseball Player)
17 Hill St
Cohasset, MA 02025-2218, USA

Greer, Raeden (Actor)
c/o Mona Loring *Status PR*
PO Box 6191
Westlake Village, CA 91359-6191, USA

Greer, Rusty (Athlete, Baseball Player)
4703 Patterson Ln
Colleyville, TX 76034-4507, USA

Greezyn, Alice (Actor)

Gregerson, Luke (Athlete, Baseball Player)
109 N Aldine Ave
Park Ridge, IL 60068-3007, USA

Gregg, Clark (Actor)
c/o Tom Lassally *3 Arts Entertainment*
9460 Wilshire Blvd Fl 7
Beverly Hills, CA 90212-2713, USA

Gregg, Forrest (Athlete, Coach, Football Coach, Football Executive, Football Player)
2985 Plaza Azul
Santa Fe, NM 87507-5337, USA

Gregg, Judd A (Politician)
1234 Ocean Blvd
Rye, NH 03870-2209, USA

Gregg, Kelly (Athlete, Football Player)
13800 Hollow Glen Rd
Edmond, OK 73013-7278, USA

Gregg, Kevin (Athlete, Baseball Player)
1907 SW Brooklane Dr
Corvallis, OR 97333-1627, USA

Gregg, Randy (Athlete, Hockey Player)
13021 104 Ave NW
Edmonton, AB T5N 0V9, Canada

Gregg, Stephen (Writer)
c/o Staff Member *Creative Artists Agency (CAA)*
2000 Avenue of the Stars Ste 100
Los Angeles, CA 90067-4705, USA

Gregg, Tommy (Athlete, Baseball Player)
12356 Ballpark Way
Attn: Coaching Staff
Papillion, NE 68046-4817, USA

Gregg, Tommy (Athlete, Baseball Player)
10 Cambridge Ln
Sharpsburg, GA 30277-2462, USA

Gregoire, Gabriel (Athlete, Football Player)
575 Rang Saint-Joseph RR 2
Sainte-Martine, QC J0S 1V0, Canada

Gregoire, Stephan (Race Car Driver)
Dick Simon Racing
25801 Victoria Blvd
Dana Point, CA 92624-1124, USA

Gregor, Bob (Athlete, Football Player)
14128 180th Ave NE
Redmond, WA 98052-1220, USA

Gregor, Gary (Athlete, Basketball Player)
139 Club Ridge Rd
Elgin, SC 29045-8326, USA

Gregorio, Rose (Actor)
29 W 10th St Apt 3
New York, NY 10011-8739, USA

Gregorio, Tom (Athlete, Baseball Player)
2929 W Windsong Dr
Phoenix, AZ 85045-1204, USA

Gregory, Adam (Actor)
c/o Peter Gallagher *Gallagher Management*
955 Carrillo Dr Ste 100
Los Angeles, CA 90048-5400, USA

Gregory, Bettina L (Correspondent)
ABC-TV
5010 Creston St
News Dept
Hyattsville, MD 20781-1216, USA

Gregory, Bill (Athlete, Football Player)
4317 Cityview Dr
Plano, TX 75093-3236, USA

Gregory, Claude (Athlete, Basketball Player)
14621 Blackburn Rd
Burtonsville, MD 20866-1303, USA

Gregory, Damian (Athlete, Football Player)
717 Albert Pl
Ridgewood, NJ 07450-5310, USA

Gregory, David A (Actor)
c/o Staff Member *Leading Artists*
145 W 45th St Rm 1000
New York, NY 10036-4032, USA

Gregory, Dorian (Actor, Television Host)
c/o Staff Member *Creative Management Entertainment Group (CMEG)*
2050 S Bundy Dr Ste 280
Los Angeles, CA 90025-6128, USA

Gregory, Frederick D (Astronaut)
506 Tulip Rd
Annapolis, MD 21403-1326, USA

Gregory, Glynn (Athlete, Football Player)
7007 Joyce Way
Dallas, TX 75225-1728, USA

Gregory, Jim (Athlete, Hockey Player)
c/o Staff Member *National Hockey League (NHL)*
50 Bay St 11th Fl
Toronto, ON M5J 2X8, Canada

Gregory, Kathy (Cartoonist)
Playboy Magazine
680 N Lake Shore Dr
Reader Services
Chicago, IL 60611-4546, USA

Gregory, Kimberly Hebert (Actor)
c/o Michael Geiser *Jill Fritzo Public Relations*
208 E 51st St # 305
New York, NY 10022-6557, USA

Gregory, Lee (Athlete, Baseball Player)
6456 N Teilman Ave
Fresno, CA 93711-1315, USA

Gregory, Nick (Actor)
c/o Staff Member *Kerin-Goldberg Associates*
155 E 55th St Ste 5D
New York, NY 10022-4038, USA

Gregory, Paul (Actor)
PO Box 415
Desert Hot Springs, CA 92240-0415, USA

Gregory, Philippa (Writer)
c/o Staff Member *Independent Talent Group*
40 Whitfield St
London W1T 2RH, UNITED KINGDOM

Gregory, Roberta (Artist)
c/o Staff Member *Fantagraphics Books*
7563 Lake City Way NE
Seattle, WA 98115-4218, USA

Gregory, Stephen (Actor)
Carey
64 Thomton Ave
London W4 1QQ, UNITED KINGDOM (UK)

Gregory, William G (Astronaut)
2027 E Freeport Ln
Gilbert, AZ 85234-2829, USA

Gregory, William G Lt Colonel (Astronaut)
2027 E Freeport Ln
Gilbert, AZ 85234-2829, USA

Gregory, William Jr (Athlete, Football Player)
4317 Cityview Dr
Plano, TX 75093-3236, USA

Gregory, Wilton D (Religious Leader)
Illinois Diocese
222 S 3rd St
Chancery Office
Belleville, IL 62220-1916, USA

Gregson, Glenn (Athlete, Baseball Player)
719 Touchstone Dr
Helena, MT 59601-5488, USA

Gregson-Williams, Harry (Musician)
Overseer Enterprises
9541 W Frank Ave
Peoria, AZ 85382-5394, USA

Greif, Bill (Athlete, Baseball Player)
807 E 31st St
Austin, TX 78705-3205, USA

Greig, John (Athlete, Basketball Player)
2031 218th Pl NE
Sammamish, WA 98074-4049, USA

Greig, Mark (Athlete, Hockey Player)
c/o Art Breeze *Pro-Rep Entertainment Consulting*
113-276 Midpark Gdns SE
Calgary, AB T2X 1T3, Canada

Greiner, Lori (Business Person, Reality Star, Television Host)
400 N Saint Paul St Ste 1040
Dallas, TX 75201-6845, USA

Greiner-Petter-Memm, Simone (Athlete)
Am Sportplatz 14
Waldau 98667, GERMANY

Greinke, Zack (Athlete, Baseball Player)
c/o Casey Close *Excel Sports Management*
1700 Broadway Fl 29
New York, NY 10019-6559, USA

Greise, Bob (Athlete)
3195 Ponce De Leon Blvd Ste 412
Coral Gables, FL 33134-6801

Greisen, Chris (Athlete, Football Player)
1710 Arabian Dr
Green Bay, WI 54313-4388, USA

Greisen, Nick (Athlete, Football Player)
c/o Brad Leshnock *BTI Sports Advisors*
615 South Blvd Apt C
Oak Park, IL 60302-4606, USA

Greisinger, Seth (Athlete, Baseball Player, Olympic Athlete)
6460 Overbrook St
Falls Church, VA 22043-1914, USA

Greist, Kim (Actor)
Innovative Artists
1505 10th St
Santa Monica, CA 90401-2805, USA

Grelf, Michael (Director)
La Jolla Playhouse
PO Box 12039
La Jolla, CA 92039-2039, USA

Grenier, Adrian (Actor)
c/o Staff Member *Reckless Productions*
425 Riverside Dr Apt 13D
New York, NY 10025-7732, USA

Grenier, Richard (Athlete, Hockey Player)
234 Rue Lanoue
Repentigny, QC J6A 1W1, Canada

Grenier, Zach (Actor)
c/o Staff Member *Hartig Hilepo Agency Ltd*
2728 Thomson Ave Unit 602
Long Island City, NY 11101-2932, USA

Grentz, Theresa Shank (Coach)
University of Illinois
Athletic Dept
Champaign, IL 61820, USA

Greschner, Ron (Athlete, Hockey Player)
8389 Ironhorse Ct
West Palm Beach, FL 33412-2422, USA

Gresham, Bob (Athlete, Football Player)
314 Meadowview Dr Apt 709
Boone, NC 28607-5229, USA

Gresham, Jermaine (Athlete, Football Player)
c/o Ben Dogra *Relativity Sports*
2029 Century Park E Ste 1550
Century City, CA 90067-3000, USA

Gretch, Joel (Actor)
c/o Molly Madden *3 Arts Entertainment*
9460 Wilshire Blvd Fl 7
Beverly Hills, CA 90212-2713, USA

G. Retcnert, David (Congressman, Politician)
1730 Longworth Hob
Washington, DC 20515-3510, USA

Gretsch, Joel (Actor)
c/o David (Dave) Fleming *Atlas Artists*
9220 W Sunset Blvd Ste 225
Los Angeles, CA 90069-3513, USA

Gretzky, Paulina (Actor)
c/o Staff Member *3 Arts Entertainment*
9460 Wilshire Blvd Fl 7
Beverly Hills, CA 90212-2713, USA

Gretzky, Wayne (Athlete, Hockey Player)
c/o Ira Stahlberger *IMG (Cleveland)*
1360 E 9th St Ste 100
Cleveland, OH 44114-1730, USA

Grevers, Matt (Athlete, Olympic Athlete, Swimmer)
821 N Waukegan Rd
Lake Forest, IL 60045-1628, USA

Grevey, Kevin (Athlete, Basketball Player)
528 River Bend Rd
Great Falls, VA 22066-2716, USA

Grevioux, Kevin (Actor)
c/o Scott Agostini *WME|IMG*
9601 Wilshire Blvd
Beverly Hills, CA 90210-5213, USA

Grewal, Alexi (Athlete, Cycler, Olympic Athlete)
88 Forsythe Rd
Nederland, CO 80466-9693, USA

Grey, Alex (Artist)
CoSM
46 Deer Hill Rd
Wappingers Falls, NY 12590-3911, USA

Grey, Dick (Athlete, Baseball Player)
503 S Hampton St
Anaheim, CA 92804-2233, USA

Grey, Jennifer (Actor)
c/o Greg Clark *Untitled Entertainment*
350 S Beverly Dr Ste 200
Beverly Hills, CA 90212-4819, USA

Grey, Joel (Actor)
c/o Nevin Dolcefino *Innovative Artists*
1505 10th St
Santa Monica, CA 90401-2805, USA

Grey, Laura (Actor)
c/o Fred Hashagen *United Talent Agency (UTA)*
888 7th Ave Fl 7
New York, NY 10106-0700, USA

Grey, Sasha (Actor, Adult Film Star)
PO Box 1480
Studio City, CA 91614-0480, USA

Grey, Skylar (Musician)
c/o Jessica Erskine *Rogers & Cowan*
1840 Century Park E Fl 18
Los Angeles, CA 90067-2101, USA

Grey, Zena (Actor)
c/o Abby Bluestone *Innovative Artists*
1505 10th St
Santa Monica, CA 90401-2805, USA

Gribbon, Melissa (Actor)
c/o Dianne Hooper *Starcraft Talent Agency*
265 E Orange Grove Ave Ste D
Burbank, CA 91502-1229, USA

Grich, Bobby (Athlete, Baseball Player)
7668 El Camino Real
Ste 104-435
Carlsbad, CA 92009-7932, USA

Grieco, Richard (Actor)
c/o Zack Teperman *ZTPR*
9000 W Sunset Blvd Ste 709
West Hollywood, CA 90069-5828, USA

Grieder, William (Journalist)
Simon & Schuster
1230 Avenue of the Americas Fl CONC1
New York, NY 10020-1586, USA

Griem, Helmut (Actor)
Mgmt Erna Baumbauer
Keplerstr 2
Munich 81679, GERMANY

Grier, David Alan (Actor, Comedian)
c/o Cielo Alano *Activist Artists Management (LA)*
8500 Melrose Ave # 200
W Hollywood, CA 90069-5145, USA

Grier, Marrio (Athlete, Football Player)
826 Almora Dr
Charlotte, NC 28216-3069, USA

Grier, Mike (Athlete, Hockey Player)
72 Stonecrest Dr
Needham, MA 02492-2783

Grier, Nash (Actor, Internet Star)
c/o Melinda Morris Zanoni *Legacy Talent & Entertainment*
1300 Baxter St Ste 100A
Charlotte, NC 28204-3806, USA

Grier, Pam (Actor)
c/o Harry Gold *TalentWorks*
3500 W Olive Ave Ste 1400
Burbank, CA 91505-5512, USA

Grier, Rosey (Athlete, Football Player)
1250 4th St Fl 6
Santa Monica, CA 90401-1418, USA

Grierson, Don (Athlete, Hockey Player)
2066 Mountain Grove Ave
Burlington, ON L7P 2H9, Canada

Gries, Jonathan (Jon) (Actor, Director, Producer)
c/o Steve Lovett *Lovett Management*
1327 Brinkley Ave
Los Angeles, CA 90049-3619, USA

Griese, Brian (Athlete, Football Player)
17 Polo Club Dr
Denver, CO 80209-3309, USA

Griese, Robert A (Bob) (Athlete, Football Player, Sportscaster)
12044 SE Birkdale Run
Jupiter, FL 33469-1740, USA

Grieve, Ben (Athlete, Baseball Player)
6906 Fairway Rd
La Jolla, CA 92037-5619, USA

Grieve, Brent (Athlete, Hockey Player)
Cardinal Group of Companies Ltd
1595 16th Ave Suite 602
Richmond Hill, ON L4B 3N9, Canada

Grieve, Pierson M (Business Person)
Ecolab Inc
370 Wabasha St N Ste 1700
Ecolab Center
Saint Paul, MN 55102-1334, USA

Grieve, Tom (Athlete, Baseball Player)
PO Box 90111
Attn Broadcast Dept
Arlington, TX 76004-3111, USA

Grieve, Tom (Commentator)
4107 Carnation Dr
Arlington, TX 76016-3922, USA

Griffen, Everson (Athlete, Football Player)
c/o David Dunn *Athletes First*
23091 Mill Creek Dr
Laguna Hills, CA 92653-1258, USA

Griffey Jr, Ken (Athlete, Baseball Player)
c/o Adam Limle *Creative Sports Entertainment*
312 Walnut St Ste 1151
Cincinnati, OH 45202-4026, USA

Griffey Sr, Ken (Athlete, Baseball Player)
c/o Brian Marc Goldberg *Creative Sports Entertainment*
312 Walnut St Ste 1151
Cincinnati, OH 45202-4026, USA

Griffin, Alfredo (Athlete, Baseball Player)
9731 NW 41st St
Doral, FL 33178-2944, USA

Griffin, Alfredo (Athlete, Baseball Player)
2000 E Gene Autry Way
Attn: Coaching Staff
Anaheim, CA 92806-6143, USA

Griffin, Archie (Athlete, Football Player, Heisman Trophy Winner)
6845 Temperance Point Pl
Westerville, OH 43082-8704, USA

Griffin, Blake (Athlete, Basketball Player)
c/o Staff Member *Detroit Pistons*
2 Championship Dr
Auburn Hills, MI 48326-1753, USA

Griffin, Cedric (Athlete, Football Player)
10567 Parker Dr
Eden Prairie, MN 55347-5249, USA

Griffin, Cornelius (Athlete, Football Player)
224 Countryside Dr
Troy, AL 36079-9191, USA

Griffin, Courtney (Athlete, Football Player)
PO Box 1386
Fresno, CA 93716-1386, USA

Griffin, Damon (Athlete, Football Player)
1608 Radford Pl
Monrovia, CA 91016-4431, USA

Griffin, David (Athlete, Football Player)
PO Box 1443
Roswell, GA 30077-1443, USA

Griffin, Doug (Athlete, Baseball Player)
15811 El Soneto Dr
Whittier, CA 90603-1446, USA

Griffin, Eddie (Actor, Comedian, Producer)
c/o Dana Sims *ICM Partners*
10250 Constellation Blvd Fl 7
Los Angeles, CA 90067-6207, USA

Griffin, Emily (Writer)
c/o Rich Green *ICM Partners*
10250 Constellation Blvd Fl 7
Los Angeles, CA 90067-6207, USA

Griffin, Eric (Boxer)
PO Box 964
Jasper, TN 37347-0964, USA

Griffin, Forrest (Athlete, Wrestler)
c/o Jervis L Cole
5 E River Park Pl W Ste 203
Fresno, CA 93720-1557, USA

Griffin, Greg (Athlete, Basketball Player)
12051 Bayport St Apt 1-208
Garden Grove, CA 92840-4404, USA

Griffin, Jim (Athlete, Football Player)
217 Packing House Rd
Lake Charles, LA 70615-5207, USA

Griffin, John-Ford (Athlete, Baseball Player)
PO Box 1359
Sarasota, FL 34230-1359, USA

Griffin, John W (Athlete, Football Player)
10315 Herons Ridge Dr
Lakeland, TN 38002-8292, USA

Griffin, Kathy (Actor, Comedian, Reality Star)
c/o Cindy Guagenti *Baker Winokur Ryder Public Relations*
9100 Wilshire Blvd
W Tower #500
Beverly Hills, CA 90212-3415, USA

Griffin, Keith (Athlete, Football Player)
4330 Canada Hills Ct
Waldorf, MD 20602-3106, USA

Griffin, Larry (Athlete, Football Player)
5617 Silchester Ln
Charlotte, NC 28215-5327, USA

Griffin, Leonard (Athlete, Football Player)
PO Box 480
Calhoun, LA 71225-0480, USA

Griffin, Mike (Athlete, Baseball Player)
1620 Grove Ave
Woodland, CA 95695-5149, USA

Griffin, Mike (Athlete, Baseball Player)
150 Park Ave
Attn Coaching Staff
Norfolk, VA 23510-2712, USA

Griffin, Nikki (Actor)
c/o Staff Member *Agency for the Performing Arts (APA)*
405 S Beverly Dr Ste 500
Beverly Hills, CA 90212-4425, USA

Griffin, Patty (Musician, Songwriter)
c/o Paul Fenn *Asgard Promotions*
125 Parkway
London NW1 7PS, UNITED KINGDOM

Griffin, Paul (Athlete, Basketball Player)
19220 Reata Trl
San Antonio, TX 78258-4025, USA

Griffin, Ray (Athlete, Football Player)
5395 Anacala Ct
Westerville, OH 43082-8352, USA

Griffin, Ryan (Athlete, Football Player)

Griffin, Taylor (Athlete, Basketball Player)
c/o Jeff Schwartz *Excel Sports Management*
1700 Broadway Fl 29
New York, NY 10019-6559, USA

Griffin, Timothy (Congressman, Politician)
1232 Longworth Hob
Washington, DC 20515-2108, USA

Griffin, Tom (Athlete, Baseball Player)
13147 Avenida La Valencia
Poway, CA 92064-1905, USA

Griffin, Tony (Actor, Director, Writer)
c/o Staff Member *Commercial Talent*
12711 Ventura Blvd Ste 285
Studio City, CA 91604-2487, USA

Griffin, Ty (Athlete, Baseball Player, Olympic Athlete)
7803 N River Shore Dr
Tampa, FL 33604-3903, USA

Griffin, Wade (Athlete, Football Player)
2937 Highway 72
Holly Springs, MS 38635-9512, USA

Griffin, Warren (Warren G) (Actor, Musician)
c/o Portia Scott *Coast to Coast Talent Group*
3350 Barham Blvd
Los Angeles, CA 90068-1404, USA

Griffing, Glynn (Athlete, Football Player)
2318 Irving Pl
Jackson, MS 39211-6133, USA

Griffin III, Robert (Athlete, Football Player)
110 April Breeze St
Montgomery, TX 77356-5882, USA

Griffith, Bill (Cartoonist)
Pinhead Productions
PO Box 88
Hadlyme, CT 06439-0088, USA

Griffith, Calvin (Baseball Player)
Minnesota Twins
501 Chicago Ave
Minneapolis, MN 55415-1517, USA

Griffith, Clint (Athlete, Football Player)
878 13th Ave S
Jacksonville Beach, FL 32250-4122, USA

Griffith, Darrell (Athlete, Basketball Player)
PO Box 24841
Louisville, KY 40224-0841, USA

Griffith, Derrell (Athlete, Baseball Player)
201 E Central Blvd
Anadarko, OK 73005-3431, USA

Griffith, H. Morgan (Congressman, Politician)
1108 Longworth Hob
Washington, DC 20515-3809, USA

Griffith, Howard (Athlete, Football Player)
9152 S Clyde Ave
Chicago, IL 60617-3740, USA

Griffith, James (Business Person)
Timken Co
1835 Dueber Ave SW
Canton, OH 44706-2798, USA

Griffith, Melanie (Actor, Producer)
c/o Robin Baum *Slate PR*
901 N Highland Ave
W Hollywood, CA 90038-2412, USA

Griffith, Rhiana (Actor)
c/o Staff Member *Darlene Kaplan Entertainment*
4450 Balboa Ave
Encino, CA 91316-4101, USA

Griffith, Robert (Athlete, Football Player)
3525 Del Mar Heights Rd Unit 331
San Diego, CA 92130-2199, USA

Griffith, Thomas Ian (Actor)
c/o Lou Pitt *The Pitt Group*
275 Homewood Rd
Los Angeles, CA 90049-2709, USA

Griffith, Thomas Ian (Actor)
Endeavor Talent Agency
9701 Wilshire Blvd Ste 1000
Beverly Hills, CA 90212-2010, USA

Griffith, Wendy (Religious Leader, Television Host)

Griffith, Yolanda (Basketball Player)
Sacramento Monarchs
1 Sports Pkwy
Arco Arena
Sacramento, CA 95834-2300, USA

Griffiths, Brian (Baseball Player)
16022 SE Goosehollow Dr
Clackamas, OR 97015-7859, USA

Griffiths, Jeremy (Athlete, Baseball Player)
120 Beachdale Dr
Avon Lake, OH 44012-1611, USA

Griffiths, Lucy (Actor)
c/o Larry Taube *Principal Entertainment*
9255 W Sunset Blvd Ste 500
Los Angeles, CA 90069-3301, USA

Griffiths, Rachel (Actor)
c/o Michael D Aglion *Signpost Management*
100 N Brand Blvd Ste 200
Glendale, CA 91203-2642, USA

Griggs, Acle (Baseball Player)
Birmingham Black Barons
820 Newwau Ave SW
Birmingham, AL 35221-3854, USA

Griggs, Perry (Athlete, Football Player)
1275 Carlysle Park Dr
Lawrenceville, GA 30044-2242, USA

Griggs, William E (Athlete, Football Player)
18 Summerhill Ln
Medford, NJ 08055-2365, USA

Grigorian, Irina (Figure Skater)
c/o Staff Member *Champions on Ice*
3500 American Blvd W Ste 190
Minneapolis, MN 55431-4431, USA

Grigsby, Benji (Baseball Player)
118 Teakwood Dr SW
Huntsville, AL 35801-3453, USA

Grijalva, Lucy (Writer)
PO Box 1634
Benicia, CA 94510-4634

Grijalva, Victor E (Business Person)
Schlumberger Ltd
277 Park Ave
New York, NY 10172-0003, USA

Grilli, Guido (Athlete, Baseball Player)
250 Sloan Ln
Locust Grove, AR 72550-9000, USA

Grilli, Jason (Athlete, Baseball Player)
9037 Point Cypress Dr
Orlando, FL 32836-5475, USA

Grilli, Steve (Athlete, Baseball Player)
8824 River Rd
Baldwinsville, NY 13027-9227, USA

Grillo, Frank (Actor)
c/o Bianca Bianconi *42West*
600 3rd Ave Fl 23
New York, NY 10016-1914, USA

Grim, Robert (Bob) (Athlete, Football Player)
18 NW Saginaw Ave
Bend, OR 97703-1221, USA

Grimaldi, Dan (Actor)

Grimaud, Helene (Musician)
I C M Artists
40 W 57th St
New York, NY 10019-4001, USA

Grimes (Musician)
c/o Dvora Vener Englefield *The Lede Company*
9701 Wilshire Blvd # 930
Beverly Hills, CA 90212-2020, USA

Grimes, Brent (Athlete, Football Player)
c/o Ben Dogra *Relativity Sports*
2029 Century Park E Ste 1550
Century City, CA 90067-3000, USA

Grimes, Karolyn (Actor)
PO Box 432
Manchester, WA 98353-0432, USA

Grimes, Luke (Actor)
c/o Kim Hodgert *Anonymous Content*
3532 Hayden Ave
Culver City, CA 90232-2413, USA

Grimes, Martha (Writer)
115 D St SE Apt G6
Washington, DC 20003-1822, USA

Grimes, Randy (Athlete, Football Player)
13214 Halifax St
Houston, TX 77015-2829, USA

Grimes, Scott (Actor)
c/o Staff Member *Agency for the Performing Arts (APA)*
405 S Beverly Dr Ste 500
Beverly Hills, CA 90212-4425, USA

Grimes, Shenae (Actor)
c/o Amanda Rosenthal *Amanda Rosenthal Talent Agency*
315 Harbord St
Toronto, ON M6G 1G9, CANADA

Grimes, Tinsley (Actor)
c/o Staff Member *Innovative Artists*
1505 10th St
Santa Monica, CA 90401-2805, USA

Griminelli, Andrea (Musician)
Columbia Artists Mgmt Inc
165 W 57th St
New York, NY 10019-2201, USA

Grimm, Dan (Athlete, Football Player)
6209 Gold Springs Way
Denver, NC 28037-6249, USA

Grimm, Russ (Athlete, Coach, Football Coach, Football Player)
2654 E Mead Pl
Chandler, AZ 85249, USA

Grimm, Tim (Actor)
Abrams Artists
9200 W Sunset Blvd Ste 1125
Los Angeles, CA 90069-3610, USA

Grimsley, Jason (Athlete, Baseball Player)
51 Birch Canoe Dr
Tomball, TX 77375-1453, USA

Grimsley, Ross (Athlete, Baseball Player)
Richmond Flying Squirrels
3001 N Boulevard
Richmond, VA 23230-4331, USA

Grimsley, Ross (Athlete, Baseball Player)
92 Conewago Ct
Owings Mills, MD 21117-5049, USA

Grimson, Stu (Athlete, Hockey Player)
c/o Staff Member *NHL Players Association*
1700-20 Bay St
Toronto, ON M5J 2N8, Canada

Grimsson, Olafur Ragnar (President)
President's Office
Sto'marradshusini v/Lackjartog
Reykjavik, ICELAND

Grinberg, Anouk (Actor)
Artmedia
20 Ave Rapp
Paris 75007, FRANCE

Grindenko, Tatyana T (Musician)
Moscow State Philharmonic
Tverskaya Str 31
Moscow 103050, RUSSIA

Grinder, Scott (Athlete, Baseball Player)
1323 14th Ave N
Birmingham, AL 35173-5218, USA

Grinder, Scott (Baseball Player)
1323 14th Ave N
Birmingham, AL 35204-2712, USA

Griner, Brittney (Athlete, Basketball Player)
c/o Staff Member *Phoenix Mercury*
201 E Jefferson St
Phoenix, AZ 85004-2412, USA

Griner, Paul (Writer)
Random House
1745 Broadway Frnt 3 # B1
New York, NY 10019-4343, USA

Grinham, Rawley Judy (Swimmer)
103 Green Lane Northwood
Middx HA6 1AP, UNITED KINGDOM (UK)

Grinnell, Todd (Actor)
c/o Nick Collins *Gersh*
9465 Wilshire Blvd Ste 600
Beverly Hills, CA 90212-2605, USA

Grinstead, Irish (Musician)
c/o Staff Member *Creative Artists Agency (CAA)*
2000 Avenue of the Stars Ste 100
Los Angeles, CA 90067-4705, USA

Grinstead, LeMisha (Musician)
c/o Staff Member *Creative Artists Agency (CAA)*
2000 Avenue of the Stars Ste 100
Los Angeles, CA 90067-4705, USA

Grinstein, Gerald (Business Person)
Delta Airlines
Hartsfield International Airport
Atlanta, GA 30320, USA

Grint, Rupert (Actor)
c/o Clair Dobbs *CLD Communications*
4 Broadway Ct
The Broadway
London SW191RG, UNITED KINGDOM

Grinville, Patrick (Writer)
Academie Goncourt
38 Rue du Faubourg Saint Jacques
Paris 75014, FRANCE

Grisdale, John (Athlete, Hockey Player)
A-455 Bromley St
Coquitlam, BC V3K 6N7, Canada

Grisham, John (Writer)
c/o David Gernert *Gernert Company*
136 E 57th St Fl 18
New York, NY 10022-2923, USA

Grishin, Evgenil (Speed Skater)
Committee of Physical Culture
Skatertny Pl 4
Moscow, RUSSIA

Grissom, Marquis (Athlete, Baseball Player)
6545 Old Riverside Dr
Atlanta, GA 30328-2744, USA

Grissom, Scott (Race Car Driver)
Grissom Motorsports
395 Sawdust Rd # 2019
The Woodlands, TX 77380-2242, USA

Grissom, Steve (Race Car Driver)
Source International
5901 Orr Rd
Charlotte, NC 28213-6321, USA

Grizzard, George (Baseball Player, Basketball Player)
Champion Lakes
PO Box 288
Bolivar, PA 15923-0288, USA

Groat, Dick (Athlete, Basketball Player)
320 Beech St
Pittsburgh, PA 15218-1406, USA

Groat, Dick (Athlete, Baseball Player)
320 Beech St
Pittsburgh, PA 15218-1406, USA

Grob, Mike (Athlete, Golfer)
3611 Quimet Cir
Billings, MT 59106-1009, USA

Groban, Josh (Musician)
c/o Peter Mensch *Q Prime (NY)*
729 7th Ave Fl 16
New York, NY 10019-6831, USA

Groce, Clifton (Clif) (Athlete, Football Player)
1632 Park Pl # A
College Station, TX 77840-3123, USA

Groce, Dejuan (Athlete, Football Player)
1443 Oxbow Dr
Cedar Hill, TX 75104-4007, USA

Groce, Ron (Athlete, Football Player)
3624 5th Ave S
Minneapolis, MN 55409-1329, USA

Grocholewski, Zenon Cardinal (Religious Leader)
Palazzo della Congregazioni
Piazzo Pio XII #3
Rome 00193, ITALY

Grode, Jarrett (Actor)
c/o Ruthanne Secunda *ICM Partners*
10250 Constellation Blvd Fl 7
Los Angeles, CA 90067-6207, USA

Groener, Harry (Actor)

Groening, Matt (Cartoonist)
Matt Groening Productions
1650 21st St
Santa Monica, CA 90404-3915, USA

Groetzinger Jr, Jon (Business Person)
American Greetings Corp
1 American Rd
Cleveland, OH 44144-2354, USA

Groff, Jonathan (Actor)
c/o Cara Tripicchio *Shelter PR*
5670 Wilshire Blvd Ste 1200
Los Angeles, CA 90036-5621, USA

Groff, Mike (Race Car Driver)
270 Wigmore Dr
Pasadena, CA 91105-3337, USA

Grogan, John (Writer)
c/o Laurie Abkemeier *DeFiore and Company*
47 E 19th St Fl 3
New York, NY 10003-1323, USA

Grogan, Steven J (Steve) (Athlete, Football Player)
6 Country Club Ln
Foxboro, MA 02035-2756, USA

Groh, Al (Coach, Football Coach)
University of Virginia
Athletic Dept
Charlottesburg, VA 22903, USA

Groh, Gary (Athlete, Golfer)
331 Signe Ct
Lake Bluff, IL 60044-1219, USA

Grohl, Dave (Musician)
c/o Steve Martin *Nasty Little Man*
285 W Broadway Rm 310
New York, NY 10013-2257, USA

Grollman, Rabbi Earl (Religious Leader, Writer)
c/o Staff Member *Beacon Press*
25 Beacon St
Boston, MA 02108-2800, USA

Groman, Bill (Athlete, Football Player)
7906 Scherzo Ln
Houston, TX 77040-2529, USA

Groman, William (Athlete, Football Player)
7906 Scherzo Ln
Houston, TX 77040-2529, USA

Gronberg, Mathias (Athlete, Golfer)
247 Plymouth Rd
West Palm Beach, FL 33405-3324, USA

Gronemeyer, Herbert (Musician)
c/o Antje Winter *Agentur Winter*
Meienbergstr. 24
Erfurt 99084, Germany

Gronk (Artist)
Saxon-Lee Gallery
7525 Beverly Blvd
Los Angeles, CA 90036-2722, USA

Gronkiewicz, Lee (Athlete, Baseball Player)
227 S Marion St Apt D
Columbia, SC 29205-3271, USA

Gronkowski, Rob (Athlete, Football Player)
c/o Jerry Shandrew *Shandrew Public Relations*
1050 S Stanley Ave
Los Angeles, CA 90019-6634, USA

Gronman, Tuomas (Athlete, Hockey Player)
66 Mario Lemieux Pl
Pittsburgh, PA 15219-3504, USA

Gronstrand, Jari (Athlete, Hockey Player)
c/o Staff Member *Toronto Maple Leafs*
Air Canada Centre
400-40 Bay St
Toronto, ON M5J 2X2, CANADA

Groom, Buddy (Athlete, Baseball Player)
1991 Saint Andrews Dr
Red Oak, TX 75154-5837, USA

Groom, Sam (Actor)
8730 W Sunset Blvd Ste 440
Los Angeles, CA 90069-2277, USA

Groom, Winston (Writer)
18096 Woodland Dr
Point Clear, AL 36564, USA

Grootegoed, Matt (Athlete, Football Player)
17302 Destry Cir
Huntington Beach, CA 92647-6135, USA

Gros, Earl (Athlete, Football Player)
17424 Airline Hwy Ste 12
Prairieville, LA 70769-3352, USA

Grosek, Michal (Athlete, Hockey Player)
5 Samba Cir
Sandwich, MA 02563-2597

Gross, Al (Athlete, Football Player)

Gross, Alfred E (Athlete, Football Player)
8227 Grandstaff Dr
Sacramento, CA 95823-5970, USA

Gross, Arye (Actor)
c/o Leanne Coronel *Coronel Group*
1100 Glendon Ave Fl 17
Los Angeles, CA 90024-3588, USA

Gross, David (Comedian)
c/o Staff Member *United Talent Agency (UTA)*
9336 Civic Center Dr
Beverly Hills, CA 90210-3604, USA

Gross, Don (Athlete, Baseball Player)
1299 E Farrand Rd
Clio, MI 48420-9137, USA

Gross, Gabe (Athlete, Baseball Player)
1756 Ravmer Pl
Auburn, AL 36830-2185, USA

Gross, Greg (Athlete, Baseball Player)
802 Hallowell Dr
West Chester, PA 19382-5243, USA

Gross, Henry (Musician)
c/o Pat Horgan *Pat Horgan Talent*
2789 W Main St Ste 5
Wappingers Falls, NY 12590-1524, USA

Gross, Jordan (Athlete, Football Player)
12725 Ninebark Trl
Charlotte, NC 28278-6838, USA

Gross, Kevin (Athlete, Baseball Player)
2058 N Mills Ave
PO Box 144
Claremont, CA 91711-2812, USA

Gross, Kip (Athlete, Baseball Player)
2015 Ridgeview Ct
Redlands, CA 92373-6979, USA

Gross, Lance (Actor)
c/o Kenny Goodman *Goodmanagement*
137 N Larchmont Blvd
Los Angeles, CA 90004-3704, USA

Gross, Lee (Athlete, Football Player)
871 Holland Rd
Newton, AL 36352-8035, USA

Gross, Mary (Actor, Comedian)
c/o Staff Member *Pakula/King & Associates*
9229 W Sunset Blvd Ste 315
Los Angeles, CA 90069-3403, USA

Gross, Michael (Actor)
4431 Woodleigh Ln
La Canada Flintridge, CA 91011-3542, USA

Gross, Michael (Swimmer)
Paul-Ehrlich-Str 6
Frankfurt/Main 60596, GERMANY

Gross, Paul (Actor)
c/o John S Kelly *Bresler Kelly & Associates*
11500 W Olympic Blvd Ste 510
Los Angeles, CA 90064-1527, USA

Gross, Ricco (Athlete)
Waldbahnstr 34A
Ruhpolding 83324, GERMANY

Gross, Robert (Bob) (Athlete, Basketball Player)
13466 SE Red Rose Ln
Happy Valley, OR 97086-9752, USA

Gross, Terry R (Correspondent)
WHYY-Radio
News Dept
Independence Mall W
Philadelphia, PA 19104, USA

Gross, Wayne (Athlete, Baseball Player)
45 Leonard Ct
Danville, CA 94526-1911, USA

Grosscup, Lee (Athlete, Football Player)
703 Atlantic Ave Apt 110
Alameda, CA 94501-2177, USA

Grossman, Burt (Athlete, Football Player)
4429 Loma Paseo
Bonita, CA 91902-2347, USA

Grossman, Judith (Athlete, Football Player)
1000 Football Dr
Lake Forest, IL 60045, USA

Grossman, Judith (Writer)
Warren Wilson College
English Dept
Swannanoa, NC 28778, USA

Grossman, Leslie (Actor)
c/o Staff Member *Metropolitan (MTA)*
4526 Wilshire Blvd
Los Angeles, CA 90010-3801, USA

Grossman, Naomi (Actor)
c/o Wendi Niad *Niad Management*
15021 Ventura Blvd Ste 860
Sherman Oaks, CA 91403-2442, USA

Grossman, Randy (Athlete, Football Player)
1460 Jefferson Heights Rd
Pittsburgh, PA 15235-5220, USA

Grossman, Rex (Athlete, Football Player)
2552 S Smith Rd
Bloomington, IN 47401-8923, USA

Grossman, Rex (Athlete, Football Player)
715 SE 8th St
Delray Beach, FL 33483-5122, USA

Grote, Jerry (Athlete, Baseball Player)
2608 N Main St Ste B
#21
Belton, TX 76513-1547, USA

Grote, Jerry C. (Athlete, Basketball Player)
3 Balboa Way
Hot Springs Village, AR 71909-6913, USA

Grotewold, Jeff (Athlete, Baseball Player)
PO Box 3439
Crestline, CA 92325-3439, USA

Groth, Jeff (Athlete, Football Player)
13824 Driftwood Dr
Carmel, IN 46033-8510, USA

Groth, Johnny (Athlete, Baseball Player)
170 N Ocean Blvd Apt 307
Palm Beach, FL 33480-3931, USA

Grott, Matt (Athlete, Baseball Player)
6209 E McKellips Rd Lot 256
Mesa, AZ 85215-2848, USA

Grottkau, Bob (Athlete, Football Player)
255 Atlantic Dr
Rio Vista, CA 94571-2168, USA

Grottkau, Robert (Athlete, Football Player)
5105 S Muirfield Ln
Spokane, WA 99223-6362, USA

Grouch, Roger K (Astronaut)
Life/Microgravity Sciences Office
Nasa Headquarters
Washington, DC 20546-0001, USA

Groulx, Pierre (Coach, Hockey Player)
156 NW 118th Dr
Coral Springs, FL 33071-8072, USA

Groulx, Wayne (Athlete, Hockey Player)
552 Montee de L'Eglise
St-Colomban, QC J5K 2J2, Canada

Grove, David-Paul (Actor)
c/o Kim Edwards *Kirk Talent Agencies Inc*
196 3rd Ave W Suite 102
Vancouver, BC V5Y 1E9, CANADA

Groves, Napiera Danielle (Actor)
c/o Christine Thomas *Sweet Mud Group*
648 Broadway # 1002
New York, NY 10012-2348, USA

Grow, Carol (Actor, Model)
c/o Jon Orlando *Exposure Marketing Group*
348 Hauser Blvd Apt 414
Los Angeles, CA 90036-5590, USA

Grroms, Charles R (Red) (Artist)
85 Walker St
New York, NY 10013-3523, USA

Grubar, Richard (Athlete, Basketball Player)
1804 Milan Rd
Greensboro, NC 27410-3028, USA

Grubb, John (Athlete, Baseball Player)
60 Carnoustie Rd APT 905
Hilton Head, SC 29928, USA

Grubb, Kevin (Race Car Driver)
c/o Grubb Motorsports
5120 Jefferson Davis Hwy
North Chesterfield, VA 23234-2252, USA

Grubb, Robert (Actor)
c/o Staff Member *Shanahan Management*
Level 3 Berman House
Surry Hills 02010, AUSTRALIA

Grubb, Wayne (Race Car Driver)
Grubb Motorsports
5120 Jefferson Davis Hwy
North Chesterfield, VA 23234-2252, USA

Grubbs, Ben (Athlete, Football Player)
c/o Pat Dye Jr *SportsTrust Advisors*
3340 Peachtree Rd NE Fl 16
Atlanta, GA 30326-1000, USA

Grubbs, Gary (Actor)
Parasigm Agency
10100 Santa Monica Blvd Ste 2500
Los Angeles, CA 90067-4116, USA

Grubbs, Teilor (Actor)
c/o Emily Urbani *Osbrink Talent Agency*
4343 Lankershim Blvd # 100
North Hollywood, CA 91602-2705, USA

Gruber, Bob (Athlete, Football Player)
1704 W Call St Apt 107
Tallahassee, FL 32304-4959, USA

Gruber, Jonathan (Director)
c/o Josh Adler *New Wave Entertainment (LA)*
2660 W Olive Ave
Burbank, CA 91505-4525, USA

Gruber, Kelly (Athlete, Baseball Player)
16703 Black Kettle Dr
Leander, TX 78641-3052, USA

Gruber, Paul (Athlete, Football Player)
PO Box 4239
Edwards, CO 81632-4239, USA

Grubnic, Dave (Race Car Driver)
John Mitchell Racing
392 Highway 287
Ennis, MT 29729, USA

Gruden, John (Athlete, Hockey Player)
1287 Essex Dr
Rochester Hills, MI 48307-3139

Gruden, Jon (Athlete, Coach, Football Coach, Football Player)
216 Red Pine Ct
Danville, CA 94506-4505, USA

Grudzielanek, Mark (Athlete, Baseball Player)
PO Box 1581
Rancho Santa Fe, CA 92067-1581, USA

Gruen, Danny (Athlete, Hockey Player)
RR 1
South Gillies, ON P0T 2V0, Canada

Gruen, Sara (Writer)
c/o Staff Member *HarperCollins Publishers*
195 Broadway Fl 2
New York, NY 10007-3132, USA

Gruenberg, Erich (Musician)
80 Northway
Hampstead Garden Suburb
London NW11 6PA, UNITED KINGDOM (UK)

Gruenwald, Jim (Athlete, Olympic Athlete, Wrestler)
0N727 Peter Rd
Wheaton, IL 60187-2979, USA

Gruffudd, Ioan (Actor)
c/o Peg Donegan *Framework Entertainment*
9057 Nemo St # C
W Hollywood, CA 90069-5511, USA

Gruhl, Scott (Athlete, Hockey Player)
8732 Laumic Dr
North Chesterfield, VA 23235-4655

Grum, Anselm (Religious Leader)
Sekretariat P Anselm Grun
Schweinfurter Strabe 40
Munsterschwarzach, Abtei 97359, GERMANY

Grum, Clifford J (Business Person)
Temple-Inland Inc
303 S Temple Dr
Diboll, TX 75941-2419, USA

Grumman, Cornelia (Journalist)
Chicago Tribune
160 N Stetson Ave
Editorial Dept
Chicago, IL 60601-6707, USA

Grunberg, Adrian (Director)
c/o Staff Member *Redrum*
Callejon Del Aguacate 32
Barrio De Santa Catarina
Coyoacan DF 04010, MEXICO

Grunberg, Greg (Actor)
c/o Susan Calogerakis *SC Management*
9465 Wilshire Blvd Fl 7
Beverly Hills, CA 90212-2606, USA

Grundman, Bernie (Musician)
Bernie Grundman Mastering
1640 N Gower St
Hollywood, CA 90028-6518, USA

Grundt, Ken (Athlete, Baseball Player)
5244 N Melvina Ave
Chicago, IL 60630-1037, USA

Grundy, Hugh (Musician)
Lustig Talent
PO Box 770850
Orlando, FL 32877-0850, USA

Gruneisen, Sam (Athlete, Football Player)
569 Finsbay Ct
Ocoee, FL 34761-5658, USA

Grunfeld, Ernie (Athlete, Basketball Player, Olympic Athlete)
10121 Counselman Rd
Potomac, MD 20854-5021, USA

Grunhard, Tim (Athlete, Football Player)
2005 Arno Rd
Mission Hills, KS 66208-2246, USA

Grunseth, Jon (Politician)
Lennonville Orchards 259 Lennon Road
North Bruny TAS 7150, Australia

Grunsfeld, John M (Astronaut)
PO Box 279
Highland, MD 20777-0279, USA

Grunwald, Ernie (Actor)
c/o Suzanne (Sue) Wohl *TalentWorks*
3500 W Olive Ave Ste 1400
Burbank, CA 91505-5512, USA

Grupo Mania (Music Group)
c/o Staff Member *Sony Music (Miami)*
404 Washington Ave Ste 700
Miami Beach, FL 33139-6615, USA

Grupp, Robert (Athlete, Football Player)
305 Hill Ave
Langhorne, PA 19047-2819, USA

Gruttadauria, Mike (Athlete, Football Player)
4250 Swift Rd
Sarasota, FL 34231-6547, USA

Gryboski, Kevin (Athlete, Baseball Player)
127 Castlebrooke Dr
Venetia, PA 15367-1391, USA

Grygiel, George (Athlete, Baseball Player)
451 W Bazille Way
Green Valley, AZ 85614-5270, USA

Grylls, Bear (Television Host)
Second Assn
Gilwell Park
Chingford
London E4 7QW, UNITED KINGDOM

Grymes, Darrell (Athlete, Football Player)
1737 Minnesota Ave SE Apt 1
Washington, DC 20020-4755, USA

Gryp, Bob (Athlete, Hockey Player)
11 Duren Ave
Woburn, MA 01801-5304

Grzanich, Mike (Athlete, Baseball Player)
176 Holliday Trce
Raymond, MS 39154-9569, USA

Grzebien, Anna (Athlete, Golfer)
c/o Staff Member *Ladies Pro Golf Association (LPGA)*
100 International Golf Dr
Daytona Beach, FL 32124-1092, USA

Grzenda, Joe (Athlete, Baseball Player)
40 Hillcrest Dr
Covington Township, PA 18424-7852, USA

G. Thompson, Bennie (Congressman, Politician)
2466 Rayburn Hob
Washington, DC 20515-3807, USA

Guadagnino, Kathy Baker (Athlete, Golfer)
1535 SW 4th Cir
Boca Raton, FL 33486-4414, USA

Guadagnino, Luca (Director)
First Sun
Vicolo del Cefalo 12
Roma 00186, ITALY

Guadagnino, Vinny (Reality Star)
431 Bradley Ave
Staten Island, NY 10314-6945, USA

Guangbiao, Chen (Business Person)
Jiangsu Huangpu Investment
Nanjing, Jiangsu Province, China

Guardado, Eddie (Athlete, Baseball Player)
11268 Overlook Pt
Tustin, CA 92782-4314, USA

Guardino, Harry (Actor)
2949 E Via Vaquero Rd
Palm Springs, CA 92262-7941, USA

Guardiola, Herizen (Actor, Musician)
c/o Cara Tripicchio *Shelter PR*
5670 Wilshire Blvd Ste 1200
Los Angeles, CA 90036-5621, USA

Guare, John (Writer)
1 Dag Hammarskjold Plz
New York, NY 10017-2201, USA

Guarilia, Gene (Athlete, Basketball Player)
86 Main St
Duryea, PA 18642-1023, USA

Guarini, Justin (Musician)
c/o Jeff Ballard *Jeff Ballard PR*
4814 Lemona Ave
Sherman Oaks, CA 91403-2010, USA

Guarnaschelli, Alex (Chef)
Butter Restaurant
70 W 45th St
New York, NY 10036-4202, USA

Guaty, Camille (Actor)
c/o Michael Baum *Impression Entertainment*
9229 W Sunset Blvd Ste 700
Los Angeles, CA 90069-3407, USA

Guay, Paul (Athlete, Hockey Player, Olympic Athlete)
34 Kirkbrae Dr
Lincoln, RI 02865-1019

Gubanich, Creighton (Athlete, Baseball Player)
205 Red Rock Cir
Limerick, PA 19468-1193, USA

Gubelmann, Fiona (Actor)
c/o Brady McKay *Haven Entertainment*
8111 Beverly Blvd Ste 201
Los Angeles, CA 90048-4531, USA

Guber, Peter (Producer)
Mandaly Entertainment
10202 Washington Blvd # 1070
Culver City, CA 90232-3119, USA

Gubicza, Mark (Athlete, Baseball Player)
11808 Macoda Ln
Chatsworth, CA 91311-1271, USA

Gubler, Matthew Gray (Actor, Director, Writer)
c/o Colton Gramm *Brillstein Entertainment Partners*
9150 Wilshire Blvd Ste 350
Beverly Hills, CA 90212-3453, USA

Gubner, Gary (Athlete, Olympic Athlete, Weightlifter)
7134 Great Falls Cir
Boynton Beach, FL 33437-0900, USA

Gucci (Designer, Fashion Designer)
Gucci
Rembrandt Tower, 1
Amstelplein 1096 HA
Amsterdam, The Netherlands

Gucciardo, Pat (Athlete, Football Player)
2406 Kenmoore Rd
Maumee, OH 43537-1121, USA

Guccione, Chris (Athlete, Baseball Player)
88 Paloma Ave
Brighton, CO 80601-8791, USA

Guccione, Christopher (Baseball Player)
88 Paloma Ave
Brighton, CO 80601-8791, USA

Guckert, Elmer (Athlete, Baseball Player)
1212 Balmoral Dr
Pittsburgh, PA 15237-6222, USA

Guckert, Elmer (Baseball Player)
1212 Balmoral Dr
Pittsburgh, PA 15237-6222, USA

Gudmundson, Scott (Athlete, Football Player)
11 Guindola Way Apt 268
Hot Springs Village, AR 71909-7128, USA

Gudmundsson, Petur (Athlete, Basketball Player)
2423 Vibrant Oak
San Antonio, TX 78232-2616, USA

Guelleh, Ismail Omar (President)
President's Office
8-10 Ahmed Nessim St
Djibouti, DJIBOUTI

Guennel, Joe (Soccer Player)
835 Front Range Rd
Littleton, CO 80120-4005, USA

Gueno, James (Athlete, Football Player)
8173 Drexel Ct
Eden Prairie, MN 55347-2189, USA

Guerard, Michael E (Chef)
Les Pres d'Eugenie
Eugenie les Bains 40320, FRANCE

Guerard, Stephane (Athlete, Hockey Player)
123 Rue Principale
Saint-Flavien, QC G0S 2M0, Canada

Guerin, Bill (Athlete, Hockey Player)
Pittsburgh Penguins
66 Mario Lemieux Pl Ste 2
Pittsburgh, PA 15219-3504

Guerin, Bill (Athlete, Hockey Player, Olympic Athlete)
12 North Rd
Oyster Bay, NY 11771-1904

Guerin, Richie (Athlete, Basketball Player)
1355 Bear Island Dr
West Palm Beach, FL 33409-2042, USA

Guerra, Blanca (Actor)
c/o Staff Member *Televisa*
Blvd Adolfo Lopez Mateos 232
Colonia San Angel INN
DF CP 01060, MEXICO

Guerra, Jackie (Comedian)
c/o Staff Member *Brillstein Entertainment Partners*
9150 Wilshire Blvd Ste 350
Beverly Hills, CA 90212-3453, USA

Guerra, Juan Luis (Musician)
c/o Staff Member *EMI Music Group (NY)*
150 5th Ave Fl 7
New York, NY 10011-4372, USA

Guerra, Saverio (Actor)
c/o Susan Ferris *Bohemia Group*
1680 Vine St Ste 518
Los Angeles, CA 90028-8833, USA

Guerra, Vida (Actor, Model)
c/o Staff Member *Britto Agency PR*
277 Broadway Ste 110
New York, NY 10007-2072, USA

Guerrero, Diane (Actor)
c/o Josh Taylor *Vamnation Entertainment*
2 Main St Ste 8
Roslyn, NY 11576-6106, USA

Guerrero, Julen (Soccer Player)
AC Bilbao
Alameda Mazarredo 23
Bilbao 48009, SPAIN

Guerrero, Mario (Athlete, Baseball Player)
Calle Duarte#450
Santa Domingo, Dominican Republic, USA

Guerrero, Pedro (Athlete, Baseball Player)
903 Country Club Dr SE Apt A
Rio Rancho, NM 87124-5816, USA

Guerrero, Roberto (Race Car Driver)
PO Box 381
Clay, KY 42404-0381, USA

Guerrero, Vladimir (Athlete, Baseball Player)
5160 E Copa De Oro Dr
Anaheim, CA 92807-3639, USA

Guerrero Coles, Lisa (Actor, Journalist, Sportscaster)
c/o Mike Liotta *True Public Relations*
3575 Cahuenga Blvd W Ste 360
Los Angeles, CA 90068-1361, USA

Guerrier, Manouschka (Chef)
c/o Jason Pinyan *Innovative Artists*
1505 10th St
Santa Monica, CA 90401-2805, USA

Guerrier, Matt (Athlete, Baseball Player)
200 Highland View Dr
Birmingham, AL 35242-6874, USA

Guest, Christopher (Actor, Director)
c/o Staff Member *Go Film*
11725 Brookdale Ln
Studio City, CA 91604-4203, USA

Guest, Cornelia (Model)
1419 Donhill Dr
Beverly Hills, CA 90210-2216, USA

Guetary, Francois (Actor)
Cineart
36 Rue de Ponthieu
Paris 75008, FRANCE

Guetta, David (DJ, Musician)
Astralwerks Records
101 Avenue of the Americas # 400
New York, NY 10013-1941, USA

Guetterman, Lee (Athlete, Baseball Player)
108 1/2 E Broadway St
Lenoir City, TN 37771-2908, USA

Guevara, Carlos (Athlete, Baseball Player)
501 S Crisp St
Uvalde, TX 78801-5905, USA

Guevara, Zabryna (Actor)
c/o Michael Geiser *Jill Fritzo Public Relations*
208 E 51st St # 305
New York, NY 10022-6557, USA

Guevremont, Jocelyn (Athlete, Hockey Player)
627 Siesta Key Cir Apt 3117
Deerfield Beach, FL 33441-8128, USA

Guffey, Cary (Actor)
236 Eagle Park Ln
Birmingham, AL 35242, USA

Guffey Jr, John W (Business Person)
Coltec Industries
2550 W Tyvola Rd
Charlotte, NC 28217-4574, USA

Gugelmin, Mauricio (Race Car Driver)
PacWest Reacing Group
4476 60 602
Cuiriba, PR 80250-210, BRAZIL

Guggemos, Neal (Athlete, Football Player)
8173 Drexel Ct
Eden Prairie, MN 55347-2189, USA

Guggenheim, Marc (Actor)

Gugino, Carla (Actor)
c/o Meredith O'Sullivan Wasson *The Lede Company*
9701 Wilshire Blvd # 930
Beverly Hills, CA 90212-2020, USA

Guglielmi, Ralph (Athlete, Football Player)
159 Red Berry Dr
Wallace, NC 28466-2376, USA

Gugliotta, Tom (Athlete, Basketball Player)
992 Wadsworth Dr NW
Atlanta, GA 30318-1654, USA

Guice, Jackson (Cartoonist)
DC Comics
2900 W Alameda Ave # 1
Burbank, CA 91505-4220, USA

Guidinger, Jay (Athlete, Basketball Player)
N39W22702 Grandview Dr
Pewaukee, WI 53072-2735, USA

Guidoni, Umberto (Astronaut)
Via Leonardo Libera 34
Rome 00173, Italy

Guidry, Kevin (Athlete, Football Player)
4045 W Briarfield St
Lake Charles, LA 70607-3658, USA

Guidry, Paul (Athlete, Football Player)
3420 Colebrook Dr
Thompsons Station, TN 37179-9611, USA

Guidry, Ron (Athlete, Baseball Player)
PO Box 666
Scott, LA 70583-0666, USA

Guiel, Aaron (Athlete, Baseball Player)
18944 69 Ave
Surrey, BC V4N 5K1, Canada

Guilbaut, Jeremy (Actor)
c/o Russ Mortensen *Pacific Artists Management*
112 3rd Ave E Suite 210
Vancouver, BC V5T 1C8, CANADA

Guilbe, Felix (Baseball Player)
Baltimore Elite Giants
Los Cabos Calle Carambala
Ponce, PR 00716, USA

Guilford, Eric (Athlete, Football Player)
8111 W Wacker Rd Unit 51
Peoria, AZ 85381-4943, USA

Guilfoyle, Kimberly (Television Host)
c/o Staff Member *Fox News*
1211 Avenue of the Americas Lowr C1
New York, NY 10036-8705, USA

Guilfoyle, Paul (Actor)
15226 Dickens St
Sherman Oaks, CA 91403-3335, USA

Guill, Juliana (Actor)
c/o Tim Taylor *Luber Roklin Management*
5815 W Sunset Blvd Ste 208
Los Angeles, CA 90028-6481, USA

Guillemots (Music Group, Musician)
c/o Staff Member *MCT Management*
520 8th Ave Rm 2205
New York, NY 10018-4160, USA

Guillen, Francesca (Actor)
c/o Staff Member *Televisa*
Blvd Adolfo Lopez Mateos 232
Colonia San Angel INN
DF CP 01060, MEXICO

Guillen, Ozzie (Athlete, Baseball Player)
Florida Marlins
2267 NW 199th St
Miami Gardens, FL 33056-2664, USA

Guillen, Ozzie (Athlete, Baseball Player)
19462 38th Ct
Golden Beach, FL 33160-2298, USA

Guillerman, John (Director)
309 S Rockingham Ave
Los Angeles, CA 90049-3637, USA

Guillo, Dominque (Actor)
Cineart
36 Rue de Ponthieu
Paris 75008, FRANCE

Guillory, Sienna (Actor)
c/o Staff Member *42West*
1840 Century Park E Ste 700
Los Angeles, CA 90067-2122, USA

Guillory, Tony (Athlete, Football Player)
2605 Blanchette St
Beaumont, TX 77701-6615, USA

Guindon, Bob (Athlete, Baseball Player)
2109 Tsse Jourdain
Sainte-Sophie, QC J5J 1K1, Canada

Guindon, Bob (Athlete, Hockey Player)
2109 Tsse Jourdain
Sainte-Sophie, QC J5J 1K1, Canada

Guindon, Richard G (Cartoonist)
321 W Lafayette Blvd Lbby
Detroit, MI 48226-2703, USA

Guinee, Tim (Actor)
c/o Larry Taube *Principal Entertainment*
9255 W Sunset Blvd Ste 500
Los Angeles, CA 90069-3301, USA

Guiney, Bob (Game Show Host, Reality Star)
c/o Anthony Embry *AE Entertainment Public Relations*
124 Evening Shade Dr
Charleston, SC 29414-9144, USA

Guinn, Skip (Athlete, Baseball Player)
PO Box 911
Stilwell, OK 74960-0911, USA

Guinney, Bob (Reality Star)
c/o Kim Jakwerth *KMJ PR*
1645 Vine St Apt 712
Los Angeles, CA 90028-8812, USA

Guinta, Frank (Congressman, Politician)
1223 Longworth Hob
Washington, DC 20515-3810, USA

Guion, Letroy (Athlete, Football Player)
c/o Joe Linta *JL Sports*
1204 Main St Ste 179
Branford, CT 06405-3787, USA

Guirgis, Stephen Adly (Comedian)
c/o Sandra Chang *Anonymous Content*
3532 Hayden Ave
Culver City, CA 90232-2413, USA

Guiry, Thomas (Actor)
c/o Rhonda Price *Gersh*
41 Madison Ave Ste 3301
New York, NY 10010-2210, USA

Guisewite, Cathy L (Cartoonist)
4039 Camellia Ave
Studio City, CA 91604-3007, USA

Guite, Ben (Athlete, Hockey Player)
c/o Allain Roy *RSG Hockey, LLC*
9675 Ladue Rd
Saint Louis, MO 63124-1344, USA

Guite, Pierre (Athlete, Hockey Player)
96085 Marsh Lakes Dr
Fernandina Beach, FL 32034-0825

Gulager, Clu (Actor)
Clu Gulager Acting
320 Wilshire Blvd
Santa Monica, CA 90401-1315, USA

Gulan, Mike (Athlete, Baseball Player)
4409 Fairway Dr
Steubenville, OH 43953-3305, USA

Gulbinowicx, Henryk Roman Cardinal (Religious Leader)
Metropolita Wroclawski
UL Katedraina 11
Wroclaw 50-328, POLAND

Gulbis, Natalie (Athlete, Golfer)
30 Strada Principale
Henderson, NV 89011-3603, USA

Guldelli, Giovanni (Actor)
Carol Levi Co
Via Giuseppe Pisanelli
Rome 00196, ITALY

Gulden, Brad (Athlete, Baseball Player)
15820 Lundstead Rd
Carver, MN 55315-9702, USA

Guliford, Eric (Athlete, Football Player)
8111 W Wacker Rd Unit 51
Peoria, AZ 85381-4943, USA

Gulka, Budd (Athlete, Hockey Player)
20945 42 Ave
Langley, BC V3A 4Z9, Canada

Gulledge, David (Athlete, Football Player)
1064 Inverness Cove Way
Birmingham, AL 35242-4217, USA

Gullett, Don (Athlete, Baseball Player)
237 Dotson Ln
South Shore, KY 41175-7879, USA

Gulli, Franco (Musician)
Columbia Artists Mgmt Inc
165 W 57th St
New York, NY 10019-2201, USA

Gullickson, William L (Bill) (Athlete, Baseball Player)
217 Blanca Isles Ln
Jupiter, FL 33478-5477, USA

Gullikson, Tom (Athlete, Coach, Tennis Player)
Tim & Tom Gullikson Foundation
8000 Sears Tower
Chicago, IL 60606

Gullit, Ruud (Soccer Player)
FC Chelsea
Stamford Bridge
Fulham Road
London SW6 1HS, UNITED KINGDOM (UK)

Gulliver, Glenn (Athlete, Baseball Player)
8123 Cortland Ave
Allen Park, MI 48101-2215, USA

Gulman, Gary (Musician)
c/o Staff Member *Paradigm (Monterey)*
404 W Franklin St
Monterey, CA 93940-2303, USA

Gulseth, Don (Athlete, Football Player)
100 2nd St SE Apt 202
Minneapolis, MN 55414-2128, USA

Gulutzan, Glen (Athlete, Hockey Player)
Dallas Stars
2601 Avenue of the Stars Ste 100
Frisco, TX 75034-9016

Guman, Michael D (Mike) (Athlete, Football Player)
3913 Pleasant Ave
Allentown, PA 18103-9773, USA

Gumbel, Bryant C (Sportscaster)
NFL Network
30 Rockefeller Plz Ste 1508
New York, NY 10112-0015, USA

Gumbel, Greg (Sportscaster, Television Host)
c/o Staff Member *CBS Television*
51 W 52nd St
New York, NY 10019-6119, USA

Gumenick, Amy (Actor)
c/o Kristopher Koller *Seven Summits Pictures & Management*
8906 W Olympic Blvd
Beverly Hills, CA 90211-3550, USA

Gummer, Grace (Actor)
c/o Kim Hodgert *Anonymous Content*
3532 Hayden Ave
Culver City, CA 90232-2413, USA

Gummer, Henry (Musician)
c/o Matthew Berkson *Undermountain Records*
1918 Weepah Way
Los Angeles, CA 90046-7723, USA

Gummer, Mamie (Actor)
c/o Tony Lipp *Anonymous Content*
3532 Hayden Ave
Culver City, CA 90232-2413, USA

Gummersall, Devon (Actor)
c/o Peg Donegan *Framework Entertainment*
9057 Nemo St # C
W Hollywood, CA 90069-5511, USA

Gummoe, John (Musician)
6812 Apperson St
Tujunga, CA 91042-2018, USA

Gump, Scott (Athlete, Golfer)
11225 Willow Gardens Dr
Windermere, FL 34786-6020, USA

Gumpert, Dave (Athlete, Baseball Player)
68371 Fleetwood Dr
South Haven, MI 49090-8357, USA

Gun, Jang Dong (Actor)
152-4-4 bukit gembira condo
off jalan kuchai lama
kuala lumpur, wilayah
persekutuan 58200, Mylasia

Gunderman, Robert (Athlete, Football Player)
11 Post Brook Rd S
West Milford, NJ 07480-4518, USA

Gunderson, Eric (Athlete, Baseball Player)
19809 SE 10th St
Camas, WA 98607-7273, USA

Gundi (Actor)
RR 1
Roseneath, ON K0K 2X0, CANADA

G Unit (Music Group)
c/o Staff Member *Interscope Records*
1755 Broadway Fl 6
New York, NY 10019-3768, USA

Gunmuddsson, Petur (Athlete, Basketball Player)
2423 Vibrant Oak
San Antonio, TX 78232-2616, USA

Gunn, Anna (Actor)
c/o Christian Donatelli *MGMT Entertainment (The Schiff Company)*
9220 W Sunset Blvd Ste 106
W Hollywood, CA 90069-3500, USA

Gunn, Billy (Athlete, Wrestler)
Northeast Wrestling Inc
PO Box 454
Cornwall On Hudson, NY 12520-0454, USA

Gunn, Chanda (Athlete, Hockey Player, Olympic Athlete)
74 Rockcroft Rd
Weymouth, MA 02188, USA

Gunn, James (Actor, Director)
c/o Maria Herrera *PMK/BNC Public Relations*
1840 Century Park E Ste 1400
Los Angeles, CA 90067-2115, USA

Gunn, Lance (Athlete, Football Player)
1301 Fernglade
Cedar Park, TX 78613-4562, USA

Gunn, Richard (Actor)
c/o Chris Henze *Thruline Entertainment*
9250 Wilshire Blvd Fl Ground
Beverly Hills, CA 90212-3352, USA

Gunn, Sean (Actor)
c/o Mitch Clem *Mitch Clem Management*
7080 Hollywood Blvd Ste 1100
Hollywood, CA 90028-6938, USA

Gunn, Tim (Designer, Reality Star, Television Host)
c/o CeCe Yorke *True Public Relations*
3575 Cahuenga Blvd W Ste 360
Los Angeles, CA 90068-1361, USA

Gunnell, Sally (Athlete, Track Athlete)
18 Shepherd's Croft
Brighton
East Sussex, UNITED KINGDOM (UK)

Gunnels, Riley (Athlete, Football Player)
1731 Route 9 Unit 124
Ocean View, NJ 08230-1385, USA

Gunner, Harry (Athlete, Football Player)
248 Emory Ln
Port Arthur, TX 77642-4769, USA

Gunsberg, Andrew (Actor)

Guns N' Roses (Music Group)
c/o Ken Fermaglich *UTA Music*
142 W 57th St Fl 6
New York, NY 10019-3300, USA

Gunter, Dan (Actor)
Century Artists
PO Box 59747
Santa Barbara, CA 93150, USA

Gunther, David (Athlete, Basketball Player)
4510 Cherry St
Grand Forks, ND 58201-7742, USA

Gunton, Bob (Actor)
34300 Lantern Bay Dr Unit 60
Dana Point, CA 92629-3804, USA

Gunvalson, Vicki (Reality Star)
30021 Tomas Ste 200
Rancho Santa Margarita, CA 92688-2160, USA

Guokas Jr, Matt (Athlete, Basketball Player, Coach)
2410 S 19th St
Philadelphia, PA 19145-4226, USA

Guolla, Steve (Athlete, Hockey Player)
729 Rutgers Rd
Rochester Hills, MI 48309-2546

Gupta, Arjun (Actor)
c/o Lisa Perkins *Baker Winokur Ryder Public Relations*
9100 Wilshire Blvd
W Tower #500
Beverly Hills, CA 90212-3415, USA

Gupta, Raj (Business Person)
Rohm & Haas Co
100 S Independence Mall W # 1A
Philadelphia, PA 19106-2320, USA

Gupta, Sanjay (Correspondent, Doctor)
Emory Clinic
550 Peachtree St NE Frnt
Atlanta, GA 30308-2245, USA

Gura, Larry C (Athlete, Baseball Player)
PO Box 94
Litchfield Park, AZ 85340-0094, USA

Guren, Peter (Cartoonist)
Creators Syndicate
5777 W Century Blvd # 700
Los Angeles, CA 90045-5600, USA

Gurewitz, Brett (Musician)
c/o Staff Member *WME/IMG*
9601 Wilshire Blvd
Beverly Hills, CA 90210-5213, USA

Gurganus, Alan (Writer)
Vintage/Anchor Publicity
1745 Broadway Fl 20
New York, NY 10019-4651, USA

Gurian, Michael (Writer)
417 W 32nd Ave
Spokane, WA 99203-1777, USA

Gurira, Danai (Actor)
c/o Sarah Yorke *Baker Winokur Ryder Public Relations*
200 5th Ave Fl 5
New York, NY 10010-3307, USA

Gurley, Buck (Athlete, Football Player)
103 Neetle Close Dr
Woodstock, GA 30188-7077, USA

Gurley, Todd (Athlete, Football Player)
c/o Ari Nissim *Roc Nation*
1411 Broadway Fl 38
New York, NY 10018-3409, USA

Gurley, Tori (Athlete, Football Player)

Gurney, Alex (Race Car Driver)
Dan Gurney Racing
2334 S Broadway
Santa Ana, CA 92707-3250, USA

Gurney, Hilda (Horse Racer)
8430 Waters Rd
Moorpark, CA 93021-8715, USA

Gurney, James (Writer)
PO Box 693
Rhinebeck, NY 12572-0693, USA

Gurney, Scott (Actor)
c/o Staff Member *Guttman Associates Public Relations*
118 S Beverly Dr Ste 201
Beverly Hills, CA 90212-3016, USA

Gurode, Andre (Athlete, Football Player)
15827 Maple Shores Dr
Houston, TX 77044-4485, USA

Gurry, Kick (Actor)
c/o Robert Stein *Robert Stein Management*
PO Box 3797
Beverly Hills, CA 90212-0797, USA

Gursky, Al (Athlete, Football Player)
54 Securda Rd
Reading, PA 19607-2521, USA

Gurwitch, Annabelle (Actor)
Don Buchwald
5900 Wilshire Blvd Ste 3100
Los Angeles, CA 90036-5030, USA

Gusarov, Alexei (Athlete, Hockey Player)
9695 E Kansas Cir Apt 41
Denver, CO 80247-2319

Gusev, Sergei (Athlete, Hockey Player)
16001 Ridley Pl Apt 2-A
Tampa, FL 33647-2050, USA

Gus Gus (Music Group)

Gushiken, Koji (Gymnast)
Nippon Physical Education College
Judo School
Tokyo, JAPAN

Gusmao, Jose Alexandre (Xanana) (President)
President's Office
Dili, EAST TIMOR

Gustafson, Derek (Athlete, Hockey Player)
2002 NE 180th Pl
Vancouver, WA 98684-0773

Gustafson, Ed (Athlete, Football Player)
6209 Mineral Point Rd Apt 1007
Madison, WI 53705-4555, USA

Gustafson, Sophie (Athlete, Golfer)
6043 Jamestown Park
Orlando, FL 32819-4435, USA

Gustafson, Steven (Musician)
Agency for Performing Arts
9200 W Sunset Blvd Ste 900
Los Angeles, CA 90069-3604, USA

Gustafsson, Bjorn (Actor)
c/o Marisa Martins *The Lede Company*
401 Broadway Ste 206
New York, NY 10013-3033, USA

Gustafsson, Per (Athlete, Hockey Player)
5605 NE 3rd Ave
Fort Lauderdale, FL 33334-1705, USA

Gustav, H.M. King Carl XVI (Royalty)
Kungl. Slottet
Stockholm SE-111 30, Sweden

Guster (Music Group)
c/o Dalton Sim *Nettwerk - Boston*
33 Richdale Ave Ste 121
Cambridge, MA 02140-2627, USA

Gustin, Grant (Actor)
c/o Robert Stein *Robert Stein Management*
PO Box 3797
Beverly Hills, CA 90212-0797, USA

Gutensohn-Knopf, Katrin (Skier)
Oberfeldweg 12
Oberaudorf 83080, GERMANY

Guterman, Lawrence M (Director)
c/o Staff Member *WME|IMG*
9601 Wilshire Blvd
Beverly Hills, CA 90210-5213, USA

Gutfeld, Greg (Television Host)
c/o Staff Member *Fox News*
1211 Avenue of the Americas Lowr C1
New York, NY 10036-8705, USA

Guth, Bucky (Athlete, Baseball Player)
202 Morris Dr
Salisbury, MD 21804-7229, USA

Gutherie, Arlo (Actor, Musician)
c/o Dora Whitaker *Whitaker Agency, The*
Prefers to be contacted by email or phone.
N Hollywood, CA 91601, USA

Gutherie, Jeremy (Athlete, Baseball Player)
1004 Clay St
Ashland, OR 97520-3613, USA

Guthrie, Arlo (Musician, Songwriter)
c/o Annie Guthrie *Rising Son Records*
218 Beach Rd
Clamzo's Court
Washington, MA 01223-9680, USA

Guthrie, Brett (Congressman, Politician)
308 Cannon Hob
Washington, DC 20515-4701, USA

Guthrie, Janet (Race Car Driver)
Janet Guthrie Racing
PO Box 505
Aspen, CO 81612-0505, USA

Guthrie, Jennifer (Actor)
Don Buchwald
5900 Wilshire Blvd Ste 3100
Los Angeles, CA 90036-5030, USA

Guthrie, Jeremy (Athlete, Baseball Player)
3810 Springhill Ln
Sugar Land, TX 77479-2255, USA

Guthrie, Mark (Athlete, Baseball Player)
3129 Donald Ross Rd E
Sarasota, FL 34240-7628, USA

Guthrie, Savannah (Correspondent)
c/o Staff Member *The Today Show*
30 Rockefeller Plz
New York, NY 10112-0015, USA

Gutierrez, Brock (Athlete, Football Player)
1040 Pueblo Pass
Weidman, MI 48893-9322, USA

Gutierrez, Carlos M (Business Person)
Kellogg Co
1 Kellogg Sq
PO Box 3599
Battle Creek, MI 49017-3517, USA

Gutierrez, Diego (Actor)
c/o Chris Harbert *Creative Artists Agency (CAA)*
2000 Avenue of the Stars Ste 100
Los Angeles, CA 90067-4705, USA

Gutierrez, Franklin (Athlete, Baseball Player)
5130 Preferred Pl
Hilliard, OH 43026-7046, USA

Gutierrez, Horacio (Music Group, Musician)
I C M Artists
40 W 57th St
New York, NY 10019-4001, USA

Gutierrez, Jackie (Athlete, Baseball Player)
10631 SW 126th Ave
Miami, FL 33186-3744, USA

Gutierrez, Luclo (President)
Palacio de Gobiemo
Garcia Moreno
Quito 01043, ECUADOR

Gutierrez, Ricky (Athlete, Baseball Player)
13803 NW lOth Ct
Pembroke Pines, FL 33028-2350, USA

Gutierrez, Sebastian (Director, Writer)
c/o Craig Brody *Creative Artists Agency (CAA)*
2000 Avenue of the Stars Ste 100
Los Angeles, CA 90067-4705, USA

Gutierrez, Sidney M (Astronaut)
324 Sarah Ln NW
Albuquerque, NM 87114-1026, USA

Gutierrez, Sidney M Colonel (Astronaut)
324 Sarah Ln NW
Albuquerque, NM 87114-1026, USA

Gutman, Natalia G (Music Group, Musician)
Askonas Holt Ltd
27 Chancery Lane
London WC2A 1PF, UNITED KINGDOM (UK)

Gutman, Roy W (Journalist)
1349 Windy Hill Rd
McLean, VA 22102-2803, USA

Gutoskie, Kristen (Actor)
c/o Sandra Gillis *Premier Artists Management Ltd*
309 Cherry St
Toronto ON M5A 3L3, CANADA

Gutowski, Eva (Actor, Internet Star)
c/o Brittany Gilpin *Kovert Creative*
506 Santa Monica Blvd Ste 400
Santa Monica, CA 90401-2412, USA

Gutsche, TorstenHans- (Athlete)
Hans-Marchwitza-Ring 51
Potsdam 14473, GERMANY

Gutschewski, Scott (Basketball Player, Golfer)
20110 Douglas St
Elkhorn, NE 68022-1600, USA

Guttenberg, Steve (Actor)
c/o Staff Member *Binder & Associates*
1465 Lindacrest Dr
Beverly Hills, CA 90210-2519, USA

Guttierez, Froy (Actor)
c/o Sean Reilly *The Brand Partners*
6404 Wilshire Blvd Ste 500
Los Angeles, CA 90048-5507, USA

Guttman, Ronald (Actor)
c/o Sebastien Perrolat *Time-Art*
59 Rue De Richelieu
Paris 75002, FRANCE

Gutz, Julie (Athlete, Baseball Player, Commentator)
9940 Gappa Rd
Kabetogama, MN 56669-8048, USA

Guy, Buddy (Music Group, Musician)
Buddy Guy Legends
734 S Wabash Ave
Chicago, IL 60603, USA

Guy, Francois-Frederic (Music Group, Musician)
Van Walsum Mgmt
4 Addison Bridge Place
London W14 8XP, UNITED KINGDOM (UK)

Guy, Jasmine (Actor)
c/o Staff Member *Artists & Representatives (Stone Manners Salners)*
6100 Wilshire Blvd Ste 1500
Los Angeles, CA 90048-5110, USA

Guy, Kevan (Athlete, Hockey Player)
10127 S Dunsinane Dr
South Jordan, UT 84009-9066

Guy, Lou (Athlete, Football Player)
2127 Sheffield Dr
Jackson, MS 39211-5851, USA

Guy, Melwood (Athlete, Football Player)
345 Castle St
Lowell, IN 46356-1810, USA

Guy, Ray (Athlete, Football Player)
936 Central Rd SW
Thomson, GA 30824-8278, USA

Guy, Sebastien (Actor)
c/o Staff Member *Acme Talent & Literary*
4727 Wilshire Blvd Ste 333
Los Angeles, CA 90010-3874, USA

Guyer, Cindy (Actor)
c/o Marta Michaud *Cinematic Management*
249 1/2 E 13th St
New York, NY 10003-5602, USA

Guyot, Paul (Actor, Producer, Writer)
c/o Kathy White *Creative Artists Agency (CAA)*
2000 Avenue of the Stars Ste 100
Los Angeles, CA 90067-4705, USA

Guyton, Myron (Athlete, Football Player)
302 Shadow Gln
McDonough, GA 30253-4294, USA

Guzikowski, Aaron (Writer)
c/o Adam Kolbrenner *Madhouse Entertainment*
10390 Santa Monica Blvd Ste 110
Los Angeles, CA 90025-5093, USA

Guzman, Alejandra (Musician)
c/o Staff Member *BMG*
1540 Broadway
New York, NY 10036-4039, USA

Guzman, Andrea (Actor)
c/o Staff Member *TV Caracol*
Calle 76 #11 - 35
Piso 10AA
Bogota DC 26484, COLOMBIA

Guzman, Cristian (Athlete, Baseball Player)
10727 Cory Lake Dr
Tampa, FL 33647-2725, USA

Guzman, Jose (Athlete, Baseball Player)
903 Suffolk Ct
Southlake, TX 76092-4223, USA

Guzman, Juan (Athlete, Baseball Player)
176 Dockside Cir
Weston, FL 33327-1100, USA

Guzman, Luis (Actor)
Gersh Agency
232 N Canon Dr
Beverly Hills, CA 90210-5302, USA

Guzman, Paloma (Actor)
c/o Jonathan Perry *Agency for the Performing Arts (APA)*
405 S Beverly Dr Ste 500
Beverly Hills, CA 90212-4425, USA

Guzman, Ryan (Actor)
c/o Mona Loring *Status PR*
PO Box 6191
Westlake Village, CA 91359-6191, USA

Guzman, Santiago (Baseball Player)
St Louis Cardinals
1712 N Douty St
Hanford, CA 93230-2155, USA

Guzy, Carol (Journalist, Photographer)
2412 Fort Scott Dr
Arlington, VA 22202-2266, USA

Gwinn, Mary Ann (Journalist)
Seattle Times
Seattle Times Fairview Avenue NAnd John Street Attn: Editorial Dept
Seattle, WA 98111, USA

Gwinn, Ross (Athlete, Football Player)
1736 Washington St
Natchitoches, LA 71457-4926, USA

Gwosdz, Doug (Athlete, Baseball Player)
505 Sugar Trail Dr
League City, TX 77573-7415, USA

Gwyn, Marcus (Athlete, Baseball Player)
23923 E Roxbury Pl
Aurora, CO 80016-7545, USA

Gwynn, Chris (Athlete, Baseball Player, Olympic Athlete)
10975 Hillside Rd
Rancho Cucamonga, CA 91737-2458, USA

Gwynn, Darrell (Race Car Driver)
3225 Aviation Ave Ste 500
Miami, FL 33133-4741, USA

Gyll, J Soren (Business Person)
Volvo AB
Goteborg 405 08, SWEDEN

Gyllenhaal, Jake (Actor)
c/o Mara Buxbaum *ID Public Relations*
7060 Hollywood Blvd Fl 8th
Los Angeles, CA 90028-6021, USA

Gyllenhaal, Maggie (Actor)
c/o Amanda Silverman *The Lede Company*
401 Broadway Ste 206
New York, NY 10013-3033, USA

Gyllenhaal, Stephen G (Director, Producer, Writer)
c/o Staff Member *WME/IMG*
9601 Wilshire Blvd
Beverly Hills, CA 90210-5213, USA

Gyllenhammer, Pehr G (Business Person)
CHU PLC Saint Helen's 1 Undershaft
London EC3P 3DQ, UNITED KINGDOM (UK)

Gym Class Heroes (Music Group)
c/o Bob McLynn *Crush Music Management*
60-62 E 11th St
Fl 7
New York, NY 10003, USA

Gyokuban, Sal (Chef)
Kanmeiho Restaurant
7-6-47 Akasaka Akasaka New Plaza 105
USA

GZA (Musician)
c/o Staff Member *UTA/The Agency Group*
888 7th Ave Fl 7
New York, NY 10106-0700, USA

H

Haas, Dave (Athlete, Baseball Player)
1826 S Red Oaks St
Wichita, KS 67207-5772, USA

Haas, Eddie (Athlete, Baseball Player, Coach)
8314 Alpena Way
Louisville, KY 40242-2502, USA

Haas, Hunter (Athlete, Golfer)
4078 Lively Ln
Dallas, TX 75220-1825, USA

Haas, Jay (Athlete, Golfer)
4 Tuscany Ct
Greer, SC 29650-4021, USA

Haas, Jerry (Race Car Driver)
Jerry Haas Motorsports
350 Haas Ln
Fenton, MO 63026-4673, USA

Haas, Lukas (Actor)
c/o Whitney Tancred *42West*
1840 Century Park E Ste 700
Los Angeles, CA 90067-2122, USA

Haas, Moose (Athlete, Baseball Player)
4351 E Lariat Ln
Phoenix, AZ 85050-8905, USA

Haas, Richard J (Artist)
29 Overcliff St
Yonkers, NY 10705-1418, USA

Haas, Tommy (Athlete, Tennis Player)
c/o Staff Member *Lagardere Unlimited (DC)*
5335 Wisconsin Ave NW Ste 850
Washington, DC 20015-2052, USA

Haas, Waltraut (Actor)
Kuniglberggasse 45
Wien A-1130, Austria

Haase, Andy (Athlete, Football Player)

Haayer, Adam (Athlete, Football Player)
2114 Tree Top Ct
Granbury, TX 76049-8067, USA

Habel, Sarah (Actor)
c/o Ashley Franklin *Thruline Entertainment*
9250 Wilshire Blvd Fl Ground
Beverly Hills, CA 90212-3352, USA

Habermann, Eva (Actor)
c/o Sascha Wunsch *Agentur Sascha Wuensch*
Stubenrauchstr. 57
Berlin 12161, Germany

Habib, Brian (Athlete, Football Player)
17235 Sangallo Ln
San Diego, CA 92127-2807, USA

Habibie, Baharuddin Jusuf (President)
President's Office
15 Jalan Merdeka Utara
Jakarta, INDONESIA

Habscheid, Marc (Athlete, Hockey Player)
6 Sussex Rd
Winchester, MA 01890-3848, USA

Habyan, John (Athlete, Baseball Player)
4 Dorfer Ln
Nesconset, NY 11767-1067, USA

Hachten, Bill (Athlete, Football Player)
6175 Mineral Point Rd
Madison, WI 53705-4457, USA

Hachten, William (Athlete, Football Player)
6175 Mineral Point Rd
Madison, WI 53705-4457, USA

Hack, Olivia (Actor)
c/o Bonnie Ventis *Clear Talent Group (LA)*
10950 Ventura Blvd
Studio City, CA 91604-3340, USA

Hack, Shelley (Actor, Model)
c/o Staff Member *Smash Media*
1208 Georgina Ave
Santa Monica, CA 90402-2120, USA

Hackbart, Dale (Athlete, Football Player)
2541 Cowley Dr
Lafayette, CO 80026-9175, USA

Hacker, Eric (Athlete, Baseball Player)
526 Shelly Ct
Duncanville, TX 75137-4128, USA

Hacker, Rich (Athlete, Baseball Player)
115 State Route 13
Marissa, IL 62257-1715, USA

Hackett, Dino (Athlete, Football Player)
1152 Kearns Hackett Rd
Pleasant Garden, NC 27313-8218, USA

Hackett, D.J. (Athlete, Football Player)
6510 S Delmar Pl
Gilbert, AZ 85298-4061, USA

Hackett, Grant (Athlete, Olympic Athlete, Swimmer)
International Quarterback Pty LTD
Suite 9
36 Agnes St
Fortitude Valley, QLD 04006, Australia

Hackett, Jeff (Athlete, Hockey Player)
c/o Staff Member *Colorado Avalanche*
1000 Chopper Cir
Pepsi Center
Denver, CO 80204-5805, USA

Hackett, Joey (Athlete, Football Player)
1147 Kearns Hackett Rd
Pleasant Garden, NC 27313-8218, USA

Hackett, Martha (Actor)
Vaughn D Hart
8899 Beverly Blvd Ste 815
Los Angeles, CA 90048-2452, USA

Hackett, Paul (Politician)
Hackett for US Senate
PO Box 43281
Cincinnati, OH 45243-0281, USA

Hackett, Rudy (Athlete, Baseball Player)
10330 Downey Ave Unit 30
Downey, CA 90241-5914, USA

Hackett, Ryan (Race Car Driver)
J&R Supply Corp.
4380 Hackett Pl
White Plains, MD 20695-3059, USA

Hackford, Taylor (Director, Producer, Writer)
c/o Stan Rosenfield *Stan Rosenfield & Associates*
2029 Century Park E Ste 1190
Los Angeles, CA 90067-2931, USA

Hackl, Georg (Athlete)
Caftehaus Soamatl Ramsauerstr 100
Berchtesgaden-Engedey 83471, GERMANY

Hackman, Gene (Actor)
c/o Susan (Sue) Madore *Guttman Associates Public Relations*
118 S Beverly Dr Ste 201
Beverly Hills, CA 90212-3016, USA

Hackman, Luther (Athlete, Baseball Player)
50 Powers Pl
Columbus, MS 39702-8680, USA

Hackney, David (Artist)
19-B Buckingham Avenue
Slough Berks, England SLl 4QB, USA

Hackney, Lisa (Basketball Player, Golfer)
c/o Staff Member *Signature Sports Group*
4150 Olson Memorial Hey
Suite 110
Minneapolis, MN 55422, USA

Hackwith, Scott (Musician, Songwriter)

Haddad, Drew (Athlete, Football Player)
2597 Wakefield Ln
Westlake, OH 44145-3838, USA

Haddad, Janie (Actor)
3018 Gracia St
Los Angeles, CA 90039-2306, USA

Haddish, Tiffany (Actor, Comedian)
c/o Lewis Kay *Kovert Creative*
506 Santa Monica Blvd Ste 400
Santa Monica, CA 90401-2412, USA

Haddix, Margaret (Writer)
c/o Joshua Adams *Adams Literary*
7845 Colony Rd
C4 #215
Charlotte, NC 28226-7681, USA

Haddix, Michael (Athlete, Football Player)
614 Fox Run Rd
Sewell, NJ 08080-4254, USA

Haddix, Wayne (Athlete, Football Player)
8117 S Pole CvDr
Memphis, TN 38125-4610, USA

Haddock, Karen (Race Car Driver)
Haddock Racing
PO Box 2455
2811 Ocean Hwy.
Shallotte, NC 28459-2455, USA

Haddock, Laura (Actor)
c/o Sarah-Jayne Dines *Premier PR*
2-4 Bucknall St
London WC2H 8LA, UNITED KINGDOM

Haddon, Dayle (Actor, Model)
Hyperion Books
114 5th Ave Fl 13
New York, NY 10011-5690, USA

Haddon, Lawrence (Actor)
14950 Sutton St
Sherman Oaks, CA 91403-4018, USA

Haddon, Lloyd (Athlete, Hockey Player)
16806 94 Ave NW
Edmonton, AB T5R 5L5, Canada

Haddon, Tallulah (Actor)
c/o Pandora Weldon *Public Eye Communications*
535 Kings Rd
#313 Plaza
London SW10 0SZ, UNITED KINGDOM

Haden, Joe (Athlete, Football Player)
c/o Drew Rosenhaus *Rosenhaus Sports Representation*
3921 Alton Rd # 440
Miami Beach, FL 33140-3852, USA

Haden, Nate (Actor)
c/o Staff Member *Diverse Talent Group*
1875 Century Park E Ste 2250
Los Angeles, CA 90067-2563, USA

Haden, Nick (Athlete, Football Player)
114 Julianna Dr
Coraopolis, PA 15108-3763, USA

Haden, Patrick C (Pat) (Athlete, Football Player, Sportscaster)
1525 Wilson Ave
San Marino, CA 91108-2364, USA

Haden Church, Thomas (Actor)
2366 Station C Rd
Vanderpool, TX 78885-8523, USA

Hader, Bill (Actor)
c/o Matthew Labov *Forefront Media*
1669 Virginia Rd
Los Angeles, CA 90019-5935, USA

Hader, Josh (Athlete, Baseball Player)
c/o Staff Member *Milwaukee Brewers*
1 Brewers Way Stop 4
Miller Park
Milwaukee, WI 53214-3691, USA

Hadfield, Chris (Astronaut)
PO Box 1645
Corunna, ON N0N 1G0, CANADA

Hadfield, Vic (Athlete, Hockey Player)
438-1011 Upper Middle Rd E
Oakville, ON L6H 5Z9, Canada

Hadid, Bella (Model)
c/o Luiz Mattos *IMG World*
200 5th Ave Fl 7
New York, NY 10010-3307, USA

Hadid, Gigi (Model)
c/o Charlie Dougiello *The Door*
37 W 17th St Fl 5
New York, NY 10011-5521, USA

Hadid, Momahed (Business Person)
Hadid Development
11301 W Olympic Blvd Ste 537
Los Angeles, CA 90064-1653, USA

Hadl, John W (Athlete, Football Player)
University of Kansas 1651 Drive Naismith
105 Parrott Athletic Center
Lawrence, KS 66045-0001, USA

Hadley, Brett (Actor)
5070 Woodley Ave
Encino, CA 91436-1411, USA

Hadley, Ron (Athlete, Football Player)
2220 Salt Wind Way
Mt Pleasant, SC 29466-8690, USA

Hadley, Tony (Music Group, Musician)
c/o Staff Member *Shout! Promotions*
P.O. Box 42
Manchester M46 0WX, UK

Hadnot, James (Athlete, Football Player)
5521 48th St Apt 84
Lubbock, TX 79414-1413, USA

Hadnot, Rex (Athlete, Football Player)
2677 Center Court Dr
Dr
Weston, FL 33332-1833, USA

Haebler, Ingrid (Music Group, Musician)
Ibbs & Tillett
420-452 Edgware Road
London W2 1EG, UNITED KINGDOM (UK)

Haefner, Ruby (Athlete, Baseball Player)
1436 Union Rd Apt 329
Gastonia, NC 28054-2310, USA

Haegg, Gunder (Athlete, Track Athlete)
Swedish Olympic Committee
Idrottens Hus
Farsta 12387, SWEDEN

Haendel, Ida (Music Group, Musician)
Harlod Holt
31 Sinclair Road
London W14 0NS, UNITED KINGDOM (UK)

Hafen, Barney (Athlete, Football Player)
1125 Goldenrod Cir
Saint George, UT 84790-7512, USA

Hafer, Fred D (Business Person)
GPU Inc
300 Madison Ave
Morristown, NJ 07960-6169, USA

Haffner, Scott (Athlete, Basketball Player)
5e62 Sweetwater Dr
Noblesville, IN 46e62-7164, USA

Hafner, Travis (Athlete, Baseball Player)
4526 W Rosemere Rd
Tampa, FL 33609-4210, USA

Hafstrom, Mikael (Director)
c/o Robert Newman *WME/IMG*
9601 Wilshire Blvd
Beverly Hills, CA 90210-5213, USA

Hag, Sid (Actor)
Kathleen Schultz Associates Talent Agency
6442 Coldwater Canyon Ave Ste 206
Valley Glen, CA 91606-1174, USA

Hagan, Cliff (Athlete, Basketball Player)
8839 Lakeside Cir
Vero Beach, FL 32963-4082, USA

Hagan, Derek (Football Player)
830 Madison St Apt 523
Hoboken, NJ 07030-6857, USA

Hagan, Glenn (Athlete, Basketball Player)
34 Roth St
Rochester, NY 14621-5320, USA

Hagan, Mallory (Beauty Pageant Winner)
c/o Lee White *WME/IMG*
9601 Wilshire Blvd
Beverly Hills, CA 90210-5213, USA

Hagan, Marianne (Actor)
c/o Scott Zimmerman *Scott Zimmerman Management*
901 N Highland Ave
Los Angeles, CA 90038-2412, USA

Hagan, Molly (Actor)
c/o Staff Member *The Kohner Agency*
9300 Wilshire Blvd Ste 555
Beverly Hills, CA 90212-3211, USA

Hagan, Sarah (Actor)
c/o Staff Member *Mark Robert Management*
2208 Patricia Ave
Los Angeles, CA 90064-2318, USA

Hagar, Sammy (Musician, Songwriter)
c/o Hannah Kampf *HK Integrated PR*
260 S Beverly Dr Ste 205
Beverly Hills, CA 90212-3812, USA

Hagee, Pastor John (Religious Leader)
John Hagee Ministries
PO Box 1400
San Antonio, TX 78295-1400, USA

Hagel, Chuck (Politician, Senator)
920 Towlston Rd
Mc Lean, VA 22102-1036, USA

Hageman, Dan (Writer)
c/o Trevor Engelson *Underground Management*
1180 S Beverly Dr Ste 509
Los Angeles, CA 90035-1157, USA

Hageman, Fred (Athlete, Football Player)
4608 Merion Ct
Lawrence, KS 66047-1811, USA

Hageman, Kevin (Writer)
c/o Trevor Engelson *Underground Management*
1180 S Beverly Dr Ste 509
Los Angeles, CA 90035-1157, USA

Hageman, Ra'Shede (Athlete, Football Player)

Hagen, Cosma Shiva (Actor)
c/o Nicole Walter *Metro Public Relations*
8671 Wilshire Blvd # 208
Beverly Hills, CA 90211-2926, USA

Hagen, Halvor (Athlete, Football Player)
32 Algonquin Rd
Canton, MA 02021-1202, USA

Hagen, Kevin (Athlete, Baseball Player)
24826 164th Ave SE
Covington, WA 98042-5232, USA

Hager, Britt (Athlete, Football Player)
6200 Indian Canyon Dr
Austin, TX 78746-6352, USA

Hager, Jenna Bush (Correspondent)
c/o Staff Member *HarperCollins Publishers*
195 Broadway Fl 2
New York, NY 10007-3132, USA

Hager, Kristen (Actor)
c/o Shelley Browning *Magnolia Entertainment*
9595 Wilshire Blvd Ste 601
Beverly Hills, CA 90212-2506, USA

Hager, Robert (Correspondent)
NBC-TV
4001 Nebraska Ave NW
Washington, DC 20016-2795, USA

Hagerty, Julie (Actor)
c/o Steven Levy *Framework Entertainment*
9057 Nemo St # C
W Hollywood, CA 90069-5511, USA

Hagerty, Mike (Actor)
c/o Staff Member *Mark Holder Management*
5225 Wilshire Blvd Ste 600
Los Angeles, CA 90036-4351, USA

Haggans, Clark (Athlete, Football Player)
3165 S Alma School Rd Ste 29
Chandler, AZ 85248-3764, USA

Haggard, Ted (Religious Leader)
PO Box 62474
Colorado Springs, CO 80962-2474, USA

Hagge, Marlene (Athlete, Golfer)
PO Box 2212
Palm Desert, CA 92261-2212, USA

Haggerty, Jonathan (Athlete, Football Player)
c/o Staff Member *Synergy Sports, Inc.*
14001 Dallas Pkwy Ste 1200
Dallas, TX 75240-7369, USA

Haggerty, Sean (Athlete, Hockey Player)
200 Highland Rd
Rye, NY 10580-1883

Haggerty, Steve (Athlete, Football Player)
3313 E Costilla Ave
Centennial, CO 80122-1849, USA

Haggerty, Tim (Cartoonist)
United Feature Syndicate
200 Madison Ave
New York, NY 10016-3903, USA

Haggins, Odell (Athlete, Football Player)
8125 Blenheim Ln
Tallahassee, FL 32312-6803, USA

Haggins, Raymond (Athlete, Baseball Player)
2825 E Lynchburg Ct
Montgomery, AL 36116-3335, USA

Haggis, Paul (Director, Producer, Writer)
423 15th St
Santa Monica, CA 90402-2231, USA

Hagin, Wayne (Commentator)
2236 Thistle Ridge Cir
Highlands Ranch, CO 80126-2638, USA

Hagin Jr, Kenneth (Religious Leader)
Kenneth Hagin Ministries
PO Box 50126
Tulsa, OK 74150-0126, USA

Hagins, Isaac (Ike) (Athlete, Football Player)
9008 Tudor Dr Apt 105
Tampa, FL 33615-3749, USA

Hagler, Marvin (Boxer)
c/o Valerie Swett *Deutsch Williams*
160 Federal St Fl 15
Boston, MA 02110-1700

Hagman, Matti (Athlete, Hockey Player)
Finnish Hockey Hall of Fame
PO Box 487
Tampere F-33101, Finland

Hagman, Niklas (Athlete, Hockey Player)
Thompson, Dorfman, Sweatman
PO Box 639 Stn Main
Attn: Donald Baizley
Winnipeg, MB R3C 2K6, Canada

Hagn, Johanna (Athlete)
ASG Elsdorf
Behrgasse 6
Elsdorf 50198, GERMANY

Hagner, Meredith (Actor)
c/o Ruth Bernstein *Viewpoint Inc*
8820 Wilshire Blvd Ste 220
Beverly Hills, CA 90211-2622, USA

Hagon, Garrick (Actor)
c/o Staff Member *Coolwaters Productions*
10061 Riverside Dr # 531
Toluca Lake, CA 91602-2560, USA

Hahn, Don (Athlete, Baseball Player)
1046 Boise Dr
Campbell, CA 95008-0306, USA

Hahn, Hilary (Music Group, Musician)
Hans Ulrich Schmid
Postfach 1617
Hanover 30016, GERMANY

Hahn, James (Politician)
Mayor's Office
200 N Spring St
Los Angeles, CA 90012-4801, USA

Hahn, Joseph (Music Group)
Artist Group International
9560 Wilshire Blvd Ste 400
Beverly Hills, CA 90212-2442, USA

Hahn, Kathryn (Actor)
c/o Lindsay Krug *ID Public Relations*
7060 Hollywood Blvd Fl 8th
Los Angeles, CA 90028-6021, USA

Hahn, Mary Downing (Writer)
c/o Staff Member *Clarion Books*
3 Park Ave Rm 3618
New York, NY 10016-5902, USA

Hai, Do Thi (Actor)
c/o Barry McPherson *Agency for the Performing Arts*
135 W 50th St Fl 17
New York, NY 10020-1201, USA

Haid, Charles (Athlete, Baseball Player)
4376 Forman Ave
Toluca Lake, CA 91602-2944, USA

Haig, Georgina (Actor)
c/o Sue Barnett *Sue Barnett and Associates*
1/96 Albion Street
Surrey Hills, NSW 02010, AUSTRALIA

Haig, Sid (Actor)

Haigh, Denise (Athlete, Golfer)
198 Barbados Dr
Jupiter, FL 33458-2920, USA

Haight, Mike (Athlete, Football Player)
210 Tartan Dr
North Liberty, IA 52317-8001, USA

Haik, Mac (Athlete, Football Player)
11738 Wood Ln
Houston, TX 77024-5129, USA

Hailer, Bill (Athlete, Baseball Player)
1211 N 6th St APT 1
Vandalia, IL 62471-1259, USA

Hailey, Ken (Athlete, Football Player)
241 Festival Dr
Oceanside, CA 92057-5135, USA

Hailey, Leisha (Actor, Musician, Songwriter)
c/o Geordie Frey *GEF Entertainment*
533 N Las Palmas Ave
Los Angeles, CA 90004-1017, USA

Haill, Gary H (Athlete, Football Player)
6207 Surflanding Ln
Huntington Beach, CA 92648-7507, USA

HAIM (Music Group)
c/o Brandon Creed *The Creed Company*
10960 Wilshire Blvd Fl 5
Los Angeles, CA 90024-3708, USA

Haimovitz, Matt (Music Group, Musician)
Columbia Artists Mgmt Inc
165 W 57th St
New York, NY 10019-2201, USA

Haine-Daniels, Audrey (Athlete, Baseball Player, Commentator)
618 Revere Dr
Bay Village, OH 44140-1971, USA

Haines, Byron (Athlete, Football Player)
16625 1st Ave S Apt 202
Burien, WA 98148-1472, USA

Haines, Emily (Musician)
c/o Staff Member *Paradigm (Monterey)*
404 W Franklin St
Monterey, CA 93940-2303, USA

Haines, John (Athlete, Football Player)
4000 Chamisa Dr
Austin, TX 78730-3310, USA

Haines, Kris (Athlete, Football Player)
2828 N Talman Ave Unit K
Chicago, IL 60618-7829, USA

Haines, Lee M (Religious Leader)
Wesleyan Church
PO Box 50434
Indianapolis, IN 46250-0434, USA

Haines, Martha (Athlete, Baseball Player, Commentator)
3375 Moxahala Park Rd
Zanesville, OH 43701-8359, USA

Haines, Randa (Director)
1429 Avon Park Ter
Los Angeles, CA 90026-2007, USA

Haines, Sara (Correspondent, Television Host)
c/o Staff Member *Good Morning America (GMA)*
44th St & Broadway
New York, NY 10112, USA

Hainsev, Ron (Athlete, Hockey Player)
2154 Wynnton Pt
Duluth, GA 30097-5007

Hainsey, Ron (Athlete, Hockey Player)
Olympic Sports Management
9 Alden Rd
Wellesley, MA 02481-6702, USA

Hair, Harlod (Athlete, Baseball Player)
1645 W 20th St
Jacksonville, FL 32209-4817, USA

Hair, Harold (Athlete, Baseball Player)
1645 W 20th St
Jacksonville, FL 32209-4817, USA

Haire, John E (Business Person)
Highland Capital Partners
92 Hayden Ave
Lexington, MA 02421-7951, USA

Hairston, Alan (Athlete, Basketball Player)
6120 S 125th St
Seattle, WA 98178-3546, USA

Hairston, Carl (Athlete, Football Player)
3514 Spyglass Hill Dr
Green Bay, WI 54311-6122, USA

Hairston, Chris (Athlete, Football Player)
c/o Joe Linta *JL Sports*
1204 Main St Ste 179
Branford, CT 06405-3787, USA

Hairston, Harold (Baseball Player)
Homestead Grays
542 E 107th St
Cleveland, OH 44108-1432, USA

Hairston, John (Johnny) (Athlete, Baseball Player)
4226 NE 22nd Ave
Portland, OR 97211-5757, USA

Hairston, PJ (Athlete, Basketball Player)
c/o Jonathan Stahler *Upside Media Group (UMG) Global*
201 S Biscayne Blvd Fl 28
Miami, FL 33131-4309, USA

Hairston, Scott (Athlete, Baseball Player)
17920 E Bronco Dr
Queen Creek, AZ 85142-5665, USA

Hairston, Stacey (Athlete, Football Player)
668 Piedmont St
Wilmington, OH 45177-2523, USA

Hairston Jr, Jerry (Athlete, Baseball Player)
2205 Warwick Way Ste 200
Marriottsville, MD 21104-1632, USA

Hairston Sr, Jerry (Athlete, Baseball Player)
7831 W Peace Pipe Rd
Tucson, AZ 85743-5207, USA

Haise, Fred (Astronaut)
PO Box 5765
Pasadena, TX 77508-5765, USA

Haise, Jim (Baseball Player)
Washington Senators
2425 Albion Ave
Orlando, FL 32833-3981, USA

Haislip, Marcus (Basketball Player)
Milwaukee Bucks
Bradley Center 1001 N 4th St
Milwaukee, WI 53203, USA

Hajdu, Richard (Athlete, Hockey Player)
1236 Janet Pl
Duncan, BC V9L5R6, Canada

Hajek, Andreas (Athlete)
Weissbundenweg 18
Halle/Saale 06128, GERMANY

Hajek, Dave (Athlete, Baseball Player)
4107 Park Haven Vw
Colorado Springs, CO 80917-2604, USA

Ha Jin (Writer)
Emory University
English Dept
Atlanta, GA 30332-0001, USA

Haji-Sheikh, Ali (Athlete, Football Player)
550 S Spinningwheel Ln
Bloomfield Township, MI 48304-1318, USA

Hajt, Bill (Athlete, Hockey Player)
215 Old Lyme Dr # 0
Buffalo, NY 14221-2208

Hajt, Chris (Athlete, Hockey Player)
12 Eugene Dr
Guelph, ON N1L 1P6, Canada

Hakim, Az-Zahir (Athlete, Football Player)
210 Canaan Glen Way SW
Atlanta, GA 30331-8055, USA

Hakkinen, Mikka (Race Car Driver)
McLaren International
Albert Dr
Woking
Surrey GU21 5JY, UNITED KINGDOM (UK)

Hal, Andre (Athlete, Football Player)
c/o Tony Paige *Dream Point Sports*
1455 Pennsylvania Ave NW Ste 225
Washington, DC 20004-1026, USA

Halama, John (Athlete, Baseball Player)
7615 Fort Hamilton Pkwy
Brooklyn, NY 11228-2325, USA

Halbert, Charles (Athlete, Basketball Player)
100 E Whidbey Ave Apt 35
Oak Harbor, WA 98277-2579, USA

Halbert, David (Business Person)
Advance PCS
750 W John Carpenter Fwy Ste 1200
Irving, TX 75039-2507

Haldeman, Tim (Actor)
4257 Lincoln Ave
Culver City, CA 90232-3217, USA

Haldiman, Phillip (Actor)
Haldi Enterprises
749 E Montebello Ave UNIT 129
Phoenix, AZ 85014-2539, USA

Haldorson, Burdette (Athlete, Basketball Player, Olympic Athlete)
2868 Stonewall Hts
Colorado Springs, CO 80909-1735, USA

Hale, Bob (Athlete, Baseball Player)
616 Overhill Ave
Park Ridge, IL 60068-3455, USA

Hale, Chanin (Actor)
c/o Staff Member *RRB Consultants*
17300 Ballinger St
Northridge, CA 91325-2005, USA

Hale, Chip (Athlete, Baseball Player)
190 Driftwood Ct
Aptos, CA 95003-5769, USA

Hale, Chris (Athlete, Football Player)
327 E El Sur St
Monrovia, CA 91016-4802, USA

Hale, Dave (Athlete, Football Player)
1015 S Mulberry St
Ottawa, KS 66067-3326, USA

Hale, David (Athlete, Hockey Player)

Hale, Demarlo (Athlete, Baseball Player)
318 SW 34th Ter
Deerfield Beach, FL 33442-2370, USA

Hale, Georgina (Actor)
74A St John's Wood High St
London NW8, UNITED KINGDOM (UK)

Hale, John (Athlete, Baseball Player)
2200 Pine St
Bakersfield, CA 93301-3429, USA

Hale, Larry (Athlete, Hockey Player)
795 Chase Ave
Penticton, BC V2A 2H8, Canada

Hale, Lucy (Actor)
c/o Elissa Leeds-Fickman *Reel Talent Management*
PO Box 491035
Los Angeles, CA 90049-9035, USA

Hale, Tony (Actor)
c/o Steven Levy *Framework Entertainment*
9057 Nemo St # C
W Hollywood, CA 90069-5511, USA

Hale, Walter (Chip) (Athlete, Baseball Player)
7555 E Sabino Vista Dr
Tucson, AZ 85750-2710, USA

Halestorm (Music Group)
c/o Staff Member *In De Goot Entertainment*
119 W 23rd St Ste 609
New York, NY 10011-2594, USA

Haley, Charles J (Athlete, Football Player)
3787 Royal Cove Dr
Dallas, TX 75229-5237, USA

Haley, Dick (Athlete, Football Player)
5248 Shoreline Cir
Sanford, FL 32771-7168, USA

Haley, Jack (Athlete, Basketball Player)
5e9 Ocean Ave
Seal Beach, CA 9e74e-6le6, USA

Haley, Jackie Earle (Actor)
c/o Leslie Allan-Rice *Leslie Allan-Rice Management*
1007 Maybrook Dr
Beverly Hills, CA 90210-2715, USA

Haley, Jermaine (Athlete, Football Player)
16806 Heather Knolls Pl
Hamilton, VA 20158-9403, USA

Haley, Katie (Athlete, Golfer)
24312 138th Ave SE
Kent, WA 98042-5168, USA

Haley, Len (Athlete, Hockey Player)
724 Balmer Cres
Creston, BC V0B 1G0, Canada

Halford, Rob (Music Group)
International Creative Mgmt
40 W 57th St Ste 1800
New York, NY 10019-4033, USA

Halfpenny, Jill (Actor)
c/o Staff Member *Talking Heads*
2-4 Noel St
London W1F 8GB, UNITED KINGDOM

Hali, Tamba (Athlete, Football Player)
13227 Outlook St
Leawood, KS 66209-4022, USA

Haliburton, Ronnie (Athlete, Football Player)
3460 Lake Arthur Dr
Port Arthur, TX 77642-7604, USA

Halicki, Ed (Athlete, Baseball Player)
19605 Paddlewheel Ln
Reno, NV 89521-7850, USA

Halimon, Shaler (Athlete, Basketball Player)
9535 SW Millen Dr
Portland, OR 97224-6510, USA

Halkidis, Bob (Athlete, Hockey Player)
Hal kid is Hockey Training
3419 Lake Park Rd
Indian Trail, NC 28079-6561

Halko, Steve (Athlete, Hockey Player)
124 Crystlewood Ct
Morrisville, NC 27560-7569

Hall, Adam (Athlete, Hockey Player)
1230 Fletcher Ave
Kalamazoo, MI 49006-2432

Hall, Ahmard (Athlete, Football Player)
4541 Winfield Dr
Nashville, TN 37211-8553, USA

Hall, Alaina Reed (Actor)
10636 Rathburn Ave
Northridge, CA 91326-3127, USA

Hall, Albert (Athlete, Baseball Player)
1628 Spaulding Ishkooda Rd
Birmingham, AL 35211-5520, USA

Hall, Alex (Athlete, Football Player)

Hall, Andy (Athlete, Football Player)
4601 Bayview Dr
Fort Lauderdale, FL 33308-5333, USA

Hall, Anthony Michael (Actor)
c/o Amy Brownstein *PRStudio USA*
1875 Century Park E Ste 930
Los Angeles, CA 90067-2540, USA

Hall, Arsenio (Actor, Musician, Television Host)
c/o Thomas Repicci *Octagon Entertainment*
1840 Century Park E Ste 200
Los Angeles, CA 90067-2114, USA

Hall, Art (Athlete, Football Player)
Cardinal Gibbons High School
4601 Bayview Dr
Fort Lauderdale, FL 33308-5332, USA

Hall, Barbara (Producer, Writer)
c/o Claire Best *Claire Best & Associates*
736 Seward St
Los Angeles, CA 90038-3504, USA

Hall, Bill (Athlete, Baseball Player)
PO Box 4104
Scottsdale, AZ 85261-4104, USA

Hall, Brandon Micheal (Actor)
c/o Nicki Fioravante *Viewpoint Inc*
8820 Wilshire Blvd Ste 220
Beverly Hills, CA 90211-2622, USA

Hall, Brett A. (Athlete, Hockey Player)
3520 Eben Way
Stillwater, MN 55082-8102, USA

Hall, Bridget (Model)
c/o Scott Lipps *One Management*
42 Bond St Fl 2
New York, NY 10012-2768, USA

Hall, Brittany S (Actor)
c/o Brad Stokes *LINK Entertainment*
11872 La Grange Ave
Los Angeles, CA 90025-5282, USA

Hall, Bruce Michael (Actor)
c/o Jerry Shandrew *Shandrew Public Relations*
1050 S Stanley Ave
Los Angeles, CA 90019-6634, USA

Hall, Bug (Actor)
c/o Laina Cohn *Cohn / Torgan Management*
Prefers to be contacted by telephone or email
Los Angeles, CA, USA

Hall, Carla (Chef, Television Host)
c/o Sarah Fuller *True Public Relations*
3575 Cahuenga Blvd W Ste 360
Los Angeles, CA 90068-1361, USA

Hall, Chad (Athlete, Football Player)
c/o Chad Speck *Allegiant Athletic Agency*
35 Market Sq Ste 201
Knoxville, TN 37902-1420, USA

Hall, Charlie (Football Player)
602 Lavaca St
Yoakum, TX 77995-4136, USA

Hall, Cory (Athlete, Football Player)
1202 E Swift Ave
Fresno, CA 93704-3836, USA

Hall, Courtney (Athlete, Football Player)
19912 Enslow Dr
Carson, CA 90746-3028, USA

Hall, Dana (Athlete, Football Player)
9730 Diamond St
Yucaipa, CA 92399-2946, USA

Hall, Dante (Athlete)
c/o Staff Member *Kansas City Chiefs*
1 Arrowhead Dr
Kansas City, MO 64129-1651, USA

Hall, Dante (Athlete, Football Player)
13314 Barbstone Dr
Houston, TX 77044-4957, USA

Hall, Darren (Athlete, Baseball Player)
4009 Oak Park Dr
Flower Mound, TX 75028-1374, USA

Hall, Darryl (Athlete, Football Player)
21013 E Crestline Cir
Centennial, CO 80015-3619, USA

Hall, Daryl (Musician, Songwriter)
PO Box 450
Mansfield, MA 02048-0450, USA

Hall, Deangelo (Athlete, Football Player)
20998 Rostormel Ct
Ashburn, VA 20147-4780, USA

Hall, Dean Scott (Race Car Driver)
PO Box 2589
Olympic Valley, CA 96146-2589, USA

Hall, Debi (Actor)
DH Productions
4838 Sunnyslope Ave Apt C
Sherman Oaks, CA 91423-2436, USA

Hall, Deidre (Actor)
1223 Wilshire Blvd # 825
Santa Monica, CA 90403-5406, USA

Hall, Del (Athlete, Hockey Player)
1057 E 6160 S
Salt Lake City, UT 84121-6712

Hall, Delores (Actor, Music Group)
Agency for Performing Arts
485 Madison Ave
New York, NY 10022-5803, USA

Hall, Delton (Athlete, Football Player)
9 Mystic Ct
Greensboro, NC 27406-5724, USA

Hall, Dick (Athlete, Baseball Player)
403 Plumbridge Ct Unit 403
Lutherville Timonium, MD 21093-8131, USA

Hall, Dino (Football Player)
355 Chestnut Neck Rd
Port Republic, NJ 08241-9703, USA

Hall, Donald J (Business Person)
Hallmark Cards
2501 McGee St
Kansas City, MO 64108-2600, USA

Hall, Donald R (Athlete, Football Player)
355 Chestnut Neck Rd
Port Republic, NJ 08241-9703, USA

Hall, Drew (Athlete, Baseball Player)
4107 Spreading Oaks Ct
Waxhaw, NC 28173-7814, USA

Hall, Ervin (Erv) (Athlete, Track Athlete)
Citicorp Mortgage
670 Mason Ridge Center Dr
Saint Louis, MO 63141-8650, USA

Hall, Galen (Coach, Football Coach, Football Player)
Pennsylvania State University
200 Presidents Dr
State College, PA 16803-1802, USA

Hall, Glenn H (Athlete, Hockey Player)
PO Box 2483 Stn Main
Stony Plain, AB T7Z 1X9, Canada

Hall, Greff Kaye (Swimmer)
906 3rd St
Mukilteo, WA 98275-1634, USA

Hall, Hanna R (Actor)
c/o Joel Dean *TalentWorks*
3500 W Olive Ave Ste 1400
Burbank, CA 91505-5512, USA

Hall, Irma P. (Actor)
3202 O Bannon Dr
Dallas, TX 75224-3239, USA

Hall, James E (Jim) (Race Car Driver)
RR 7 Box 640
Midland, TX 79706, USA

Hall, Jeff (Athlete, Football Player)
2201 Lake Ave Apt 205
Knoxville, TN 37916-2814, USA

Hall, Jerry (Actor, Model)
c/o Staff Member *Ford Models (LA)*
9200 W Sunset Blvd Ste 805
W Hollywood, CA 90069-3603, USA

Hall, Jimmie (Athlete, Baseball Player)
8622 Carter Grove Dr
Elm City, NC 27822-7926, USA

Hall, Joe (Athlete, Baseball Player)
961 Peachers Mill Rd
Clarksville, TN 37042-7629, USA

Hall, Joe B (Basketball Player, Coach)
Central Bank & Trust Co
300 W Vine St Ste 3
Lexington, KY 40507-1666, USA

Hall, Josh (Athlete, Baseball Player)
3512 Hawkins Mill Rd
Lynchburg, VA 24503-4923, USA

Hall, Ken (Athlete, Football Player)
PO Box 567
Fredericksburg, TX 78624-0567, USA

Hall, Kristen (Musician)
c/o Staff Member *BMI (TN)*
10 Music Sq E
Nashville, TN 37203-4321, USA

Hall, Lani (Music Group)
31930 Pacific Coast Hwy
Malibu, CA 90265-2524, USA

Hall, Lemanski (Athlete, Football Player)
185 Carronbridge Way
Franklin, TN 37067-6223, USA

Hall, Lena (Actor, Musician)
c/o Sean Liebowitz *ICM Partners (NY)*
730 5th Ave
New York, NY 10019-4105, USA

Hall, Leon (Athlete, Football Player)
2343 Clydes Xing
Cincinnati, OH 45244-2800, USA

Hall, Lloyd M Jr (Religious Leader)
Congregation Christian Church Assn
PO Box 1620
Oak Creek, MI 53154, USA

Hall, L Parker (Athlete, Football Player)
4712 Cole Rd
Memphis, TN 38117-4013, USA

Hall, Michael C (Actor, Producer)
c/o Jon Rubinstein *Authentic Talent and Literary Management (NY)*
20 Jay St Ste M17
Brooklyn, NY 11201-8300, USA

Hall, Murray (Athlete, Hockey Player)
21-1357 Ontario St
Burlington, ON L7S 1E9, Canada

Hall, Natasha (Actor)
c/o Gary Ousdahl *Advanced Management*
8033 W Sunset Blvd # 935
Los Angeles, CA 90046-2401, USA

Hall, Nigel J (Artist)
11 Kensington Park Gardens
London W11 3HD, UNITED KINGDOM (UK)

Hall, Philip Baker (Actor)

Hall, Pooch (Actor)
c/o Marni Rosenzweig *The Rosenzweig Group*
8840 Wilshire Blvd # 111
Beverly Hills, CA 90211-2606, USA

Hall, Randy (Athlete, Football Player)
PO Box 447
Genesee, ID 83832-0447, USA

Hall, Reamy (Actor)
c/o Gloria Hinojosa *Amsel, Eisenstadt & Frazier Talent Agency (AEF)*
5055 Wilshire Blvd Ste 860
Los Angeles, CA 90036-6108, USA

Hall, Rebecca (Actor)
c/o Victoria Belfrage *Julian Belfrage & Associates*
9 Argyll St Fl 3
London W1F 7TG, UNITED KINGDOM

Hall, Regina (Actor)
c/o Amanda Nesbitt *The Lede Company*
9701 Wilshire Blvd # 930
Beverly Hills, CA 90212-2020, USA

Hall, Rhett (Athlete, Football Player)
1059 Bent Dr
Campbell, CA 95008-3603, USA

Hall, Robert David (Actor)
c/o Cynthia Snyder *Cynthia Snyder Public Relations*
5739 Colfax Ave
N Hollywood, CA 91601-1636, USA

Hall, Samuel (Sam) (Athlete, Swimmer)
5759 Wilcke Way
Dayton, OH 45459-1637, USA

Hall, Shane (Race Car Driver)
Stegall Motorsports
515 Putman Rd
Fountain Inn, SC 29644-1305, USA

Hall, Tamron (Correspondent, Television Host)
c/o Henry Reisch *WME/IMG (NY)*
11 Madison Ave Fl 18
New York, NY 10010-3669, USA

Hall, Toby (Athlete, Baseball Player)
5206 Avenue La Crosse
Lutz, FL 33558-2827, USA

Hall, Todrick (Internet Star, Reality Star)
c/o Jules Ferree *Scooter Braun Projects*
1755 Broadway
New York, NY 10019-3743, USA

Hall, Tom (Athlete, Baseball Player)
3592 Lillian St
Riverside, CA 92504-3609, USA

Hall, Tom (Athlete, Football Player)
75 the Laurels
Enfield, CT 06082-2356, USA

Hall, Tom T (Musician, Songwriter)
Tom T Hall Enterprises
PO Box 1246
Franklin, TN 37065-1246, USA

Hall, Walter (Athlete, Golfer)
271 Orchard Park Dr
Advance, NC 27006-7481, USA

Hall, Willie (Athlete, Football Player)
717 S Hacienda St
Anaheim, CA 92804-2658, USA

Hall, Windlan (Athlete, Football Player)
13609 Pleasant Ln
Burnsville, MN 55337-4547, USA

Hall, Zuri (Actor)
c/o Jordyn Palos *Persona Public Relations*
6255 W Sunset Blvd Ste 705
Hollywood, CA 90028-7408, USA

Halla, Brian L (Business Person)
National Semiconductor
2900 Semiconductor Dr
Santa Clara, CA 95051-0695, USA

Hall & Oates (Music Group)
c/o Jonathan Wolfson *Wolfson Entertainment*
2659 Townsgate Rd Ste 119
Westlake Village, CA 91361-2767, USA

Hallberg, Gary (Athlete, Golfer)
c/o Staff Member *Pro Golfers Association (PGA)*
112 TPC Blvd
Ponte Vedra Beach, FL 32082, USA

Halldorson, Dan (Athlete, Golfer)
209 South Rd
Cambridge, IL 61238-1429, USA

Hallen, Bob (Athlete, Football Player)
7052 Rushmore Way
Painesville, OH 44077-2301, USA

Haller, Alan (Athlete, Football Player)
1265 Lobelia Ln
Dewitt, MI 48820-7409, USA

Haller, Bill (Baseball Player)
1211 N 6th St Apt 1
Vandalia, IL 62471-1259, USA

Haller, Gordon (Athlete)
20514 E Caley Dr
Centennial, CO 80016-3800, USA

Haller, Kevin (Athlete, Hockey Player)
c/o Staff Member *Hockey Ministries International*
1100 de la Gauchetiere St W Unit 265
7
Montreal, QC H3B 2S2, Canada

Hallervorden, Dieter (Actor)
Nurnberger Str. 33
Berlin, GERMANY D-10777

Hallet, Jim (Athlete, Golfer)
18 Oliver St
South Yarmouth, MA 02664-2902, USA

Hall-Garmes, Ruth (Actor)
432 Alandele Ave
Los Angeles, CA 90036-3153, USA

Halliburton, Jeff (Athlete, Basketball Player)
322 Myna Dr
Lake Saint Louis, MO 63367-1817, USA

Hallick, Tom (Actor)
13900 Tahiti Way Apt 108
Marina Del Rey, CA 90292-6568, USA

Halliday, Nathan (Actor)
c/o Sharon Lane *Lane Management Group*
4370 Tujunga Ave Ste 130
Studio City, CA 91604-2769, USA

Hallier, Lori (Actor)
c/o Richard Lucas *Lucas Talent Inc*
1238 Homer St Suite 6
Vancouver, BC V6B 2Y5, CANADA

Hallin, Mats (Athlete, Hockey Player)
c/o Staff Member *Chicago Blackhawks*
1901 W Madison St
Chicago, IL 60612-2459, USA

Hallinan, Joseph T (Journalist)
Random House
1745 Broadway Frnt 3 # B1
New York, NY 10019-4343, USA

Hallion, Tom (Athlete, Baseball Player)
4040 Ormond Rd
Louisville, KY 40207-2036, USA

Hallion, Tom (Baseball Player)
4040 Ormond Rd
Louisville, KY 40207-2036, USA

Hallisay, Brian (Actor)
c/o Gary Mantoosh *Baker Winokur Ryder Public Relations*
9100 Wilshire Blvd
W Tower #500
Beverly Hills, CA 90212-3415, USA

Hallisey, Caroline (Athlete, Olympic Athlete, Speed Skater)
44 New Zealand Rd Apt 26
Seabrook, NH 03874-4181, USA

Halliwell, Geri (Musician)
All Girl Productions
5800 W Sunset Blvd
Los Angeles, CA 90028-6607, USA

Hall Jr, Gary (Athlete, Olympic Athlete, Swimmer)
2409 E Luke Ave
Phoenix, AZ 85016-2808, USA

Hallman, Tom Jr (Journalist)
Portland Oregonian
1320 SW Broadway
Editorial Dept
Portland, OR 97201-3427, USA

Hallman, Victoria (Actor)
2006 Lombardy Ave
Nashville, TN 37215-1306, USA

Hallock, Ty (Athlete, Football Player)
3676 Hunters Way Dr SE
Ada, MI 49301-8351, USA

Hall Sr, Gary (Athlete, Olympic Athlete, Swimmer)
The Race Club
151 Kahiki Dr
Tavernier, FL 33070-2409, USA

Hallstrom, Lasse (Director)
c/o Staff Member *Laha Films*
137 W 57th St
7th Floor
New York, NY 10019, USA

Hallstrom, Ron (Athlete, Football Player)
PO Box 379
Woodruff, WI 54568-0379, USA

Hallwachs, Hans-Peter (Actor)
Lindenstr. 9a
Grunwald, GERMANY 83021

Halonen Tarja, Kaarina (President)
Presidential Palace
Pohjoisesplandi 1
Helsinki 17 00170, FINLAND

Halpern, Daniel (Writer)
9 Mercer St
Princeton, NJ 08540-6807, USA

Halpern, Jeff (Athlete, Hockey Player)
9212 Sprinklewood Ln
Potomac, MD 20854-2255, USA

Halpin, Brandan Dean (Actor)

Halpin, Luke (Actor)
227 Caddy Rd
Rotonda West, FL 33947-2223, USA

Halsell, James D Colonel (Astronaut)
2101 Nasa Pkwy Spc Centerattn
Houston, TX 77058-3607, USA

Halsell Jr, James D (Astronaut)
257 River Cove Rd
Huntsville, AL 35811-8010, USA

Halsey (Musician)
c/o Jennie Boddy *Capital Music Group*
NA
Na, NY NA, USA

Halstead, Greg (Model, Reality Star)
c/o Anthony Embry *AE Entertainment Public Relations*
124 Evening Shade Dr
Charleston, SC 29414-9144, USA

Halter, Shane (Athlete, Baseball Player)
2701 W 140th St
Overland Park, KS 66224-3940, USA

Halterman, Aaron (Athlete, Football Player)
5067 Worthington Dr
Bargersville, IN 46106-9047, USA

Haluska, Jim (Athlete, Football Player)
4325 W Cleveland Ave
Milwaukee, WI 53219-3209, USA

Halverson, Dean (Athlete, Football Player)
3819 Fairmont Ln NW
Olympia, WA 98502-3744, USA

Halward, Doug (Athlete, Hockey Player)
16 Creekstone Pl
Port Moody, BC V3H 4L6, Canada

Ham, Darvin (Athlete, Basketball Player)
13e8 Yucatan Dr SE
Rio Rancho, NM 87124-8922, USA

Ham, Jack (Athlete, Football Player)
Jack Ham Enterprises Inc
540 Lindbergh Dr
Coraopolis, PA 15108-2750, USA

Ham, Kenneth T (Astronaut)
19 Plum Hollow Dr
Henderson, NV 89052-6420, USA

Ham, Kenneth T Cdr (Astronaut)
19 Plum Hollow Dr
Henderson, NV 89052-6420, USA

Ham, Tracy (Athlete, Football Player)
164 Cotton Creek Dr
McDonough, GA 30252-9012, USA

Hamasaki, Ayumi (Actor, Musician)
c/o Staff Member *Avex Entertainment*
3-1-30-7F Minami Aoyama
Minato
Tokyo 107-0062, Japan

Hambling, Maggi (Artist)
Morley College
Westminster Bridge Road
London SE1 7HT, UNITED KINGDOM (UK)

Hambrick, Darren (Athlete, Football Player)
38632 Patti Lane
Lacoochee, FL 33537, USA

Hambrick, Troy (Athlete, Football Player)
1103 Pinelane Rd
Columbia, SC 29223-1974, USA

Hambright, Roger (Athlete, Baseball Player)
8709 NE 37th Ave
Vancouver, WA 98665-1065, USA

Hamburger, Michael P L (Writer)
John Johnson
45/47 Clerkenwell Green
London EC1R 0HT, UNITED KINGDOM (UK)

Hamed, Nihad (Religious Leader)
Islamic Assn in US/Canada
25351 Five Mile Road
Redford Township, MI 48239, USA

Hamed, Prince Naseem (Athlete, Boxer)
Mowbray House
Mowbray Street
Stockport, Cheshire SK1 3EJ, UNITED KINGDOM

Hamel, Dean (Athlete, Football Player)
110 Live Oak Ln
Hendersonville, NC 28791-2956, USA

Hamel, Gilles (Athlete, Hockey Player)
1484 Rue du Macon
Sherbrooke, QC J1N 1V4, Canada

Hamel, Jean (Athlete, Hockey Player)
5 Rue Lebeau
Asbestos, QC J1T 4L4, Canada

Hamel, Pierre (Athlete, Hockey Player)
1613 Beechwood Rd
Yadkinville, NC 27055-6604, USA

Hamel, Veronica (Actor, Model)
c/o Staff Member *Freedman, Broder & Company*
11100 Santa Monica Blvd Ste 400
Los Angeles, CA 90025-0520, USA

Hamel, William (Religious Leader)
Evangelical Free Church
901 E 78th St
Minneapolis, MN 55420-1300, USA

Hamelin, Bob (Athlete, Baseball Player)
51 Patton Ct SE
Concord, NC 28025-3742, USA

Hamels, Cole (Athlete, Baseball Player)
c/o Jon Orlando *Exposure Marketing Group*
348 Hauser Blvd Apt 414
Los Angeles, CA 90036-5590, USA

Hamhuis, Dan (Athlete, Hockey Player)
9553 Hampton Reserve Dr
Brentwood, TN 37027-8485, USA

Hamill, Dorothy (Athlete, Figure Skater, Olympic Athlete)
10045 Red Run Blvd Ste 250
Owings Mills, MD 21117-5907, USA

Hamill, Mark (Actor)
c/o Natanya Rose *Danis, Panaro, Nist Talent (DPN)*
9201 W Olympic Blvd
Beverly Hills, CA 90212-4605, USA

Hamilton, Al (Athlete, Hockey Player)
2452 115 St NW
Edmonton, AB T6J 3S1, Canada

Hamilton, Allan G (Al) (Athlete, Hockey Player)
2452 115 St NW
Edmonton, AB T6J 3S1, Canada

Hamilton, Anthony (Musician)
c/o Mark Cheatham *Creative Artists Agency (CAA)*
405 Lexington Ave Fl 19
New York, NY 10174-1800, USA

Hamilton, Arthur Lee (Athlete, Baseball Player)
2243 College Cir N
Jacksonville, FL 32209-5916, USA

Hamilton, Ashley (Actor)
c/o Staff Member *TalentWorks*
3500 W Olive Ave Ste 1400
Burbank, CA 91505-5512, USA

Hamilton, Ben (Athlete, Football Player)
5240 Golden Ridge Ct
Parker, CO 80134-4546, USA

Hamilton, Bethany (Athlete)
PO Box 863
Hanalei, HI 96714-0863, USA

Hamilton, Bobby Jr (Race Car Driver)
Motorsports Decisions
PO Box 190
Greenbrier, TN 37073-0190, USA

Hamilton, Charles (Musician)
c/o Staff Member *Interscope Records*
1755 Broadway Fl 6
New York, NY 10019-3768, USA

Hamilton, Conrad (Athlete, Football Player)
19619 N 35th Pl
Phoenix, AZ 85050, USA

Hamilton, Darrell (Athlete, Football Player)
22 Sunrise Ct
Randallstown, MD 21133-3629, USA

Hamilton, Darryl (Athlete, Baseball Player)
4721 Southwind Dr
Baton Rouge, LA 70816-4738, USA

Hamilton, Dave (Athlete, Baseball Player)
9464 Cherry Hills Ln
San Ramon, CA 94583-3935, USA

Hamilton, Davey (Race Car Driver)
6415 Toledo St
Houston, TX 77008-6236, USA

Hamilton, Derek (Actor)
c/o PJ Shapiro *Ziffren Brittenham*
1801 Century Park W Fl 7
Los Angeles, CA 90067-6406, USA

Hamilton, Derrick (Athlete, Football Player)

Hamilton, George (Actor)
c/o Tim Angle *Shelter Entertainment*
9255 W Sunset Blvd Ste 300
Los Angeles, CA 90069-3313, USA

Hamilton, Hamish (Director, Producer)
Done and Dusted
151 Wardour St.
London W1F 8WE, UNITED KINGDOM

Hamilton, Harry (Athlete, Football Player)
PO Box 986
Lemont, PA 16851-0986, USA

Hamilton, Jakar (Athlete, Football Player)

Hamilton, James (Athlete, Football Player)
242 McGirt Rd
Hamlet, NC 28345-9124, USA

Hamilton, Jeff (Athlete, Baseball Player)
702 Aldrich St
Linden, MI 48451-9050, USA

Hamilton, Joe (Athlete, Basketball Player)
9e2 Loveall Ln
Louisville, KY 40223-3470, USA

Hamilton, Joey (Athlete, Baseball Player)
215 Lake Heights Ct
Alpharetta, GA 30022-5642, USA

Hamilton, Josh (Athlete, Baseball Player)
PO Box 10370
Liberty, TX 77575-7870, USA

Hamilton, Keith (Athlete, Football Player)
6 Bonnieview Ln
Towaco, NJ 07082-1289, USA

Hamilton, Laird (Athlete, Producer)
c/o Jane Kachmer *Jane Kachmer Management*
PO Box 2246
Malibu, CA 90265-7246, USA

Hamilton, Laurell K (Writer)
Ma Petite Enterprises, L.L.C.
PO Box 270375
Saint Louis, MO 63127-0375, USA

Hamilton, Lee H (Politician)
Wilson Int'l Schorlars Center
1300 Pennsylvania Ave NW
Washington, DC 20004-3002, USA

Hamilton, Leonard (Basketball Player, Coach)
Florida State University
Athletic Dept
Tallahassee, FL 32306-0001, USA

Hamilton, Lewis (Race Car Driver)
Hamilton Motorsport Ltd.
Corporatec Ltd.
32 St. James°S St
London SW1A 1HD, UNITED KINGDOM

Hamilton, Linda (Actor)
c/o Bobbie Edrick *Bobbie Edrick*
8955 Norma Pl
Los Angeles, CA 90069-4818, USA

Hamilton, LisaGay (Actor)
c/o Michael Greene *Greene & Associates*
1901 Avenue of the Stars Ste 130
Los Angeles, CA 90067-6030, USA

Hamilton, Lynn (Actor)
7453 Pierce Pl
Merrillville, IN 46410-4679

Hamilton, Marcus (Actor)
Hank Ketchum Enterprises
PO Box 1997
Monterey, CA 93942-1997, USA

Hamilton, Marcus (Cartoonist)
12225 Ranburne Rd
Mint Hill, NC 28227-5623, USA

Hamilton, Michael (Artist)
2012 N 19th St
Boise, ID 83702-0821, USA

Hamilton, Michael (Athlete, Football Player)
6755 Mira Mesa Blvd Ste 123 PMB 227
San Diego, CA 92121-4311, USA

Hamilton, Mike (Athlete, Baseball Player)
1070 Thorndale Cir
Prosper, TX 75078-9391, USA

Hamilton, Natasha (Musician)
c/o Staff Member *Concorde Intl Artists Ltd*
101 Shepherds Bush Rd
London W6 7LP, UNITED KINGDOM (UK)

Hamilton, Paula (Actor)
PFD Drury House
34-43 Russell St
London WC2B 5HA, UNITED KINGDOM (UK)

Hamilton, Ray (Athlete, Football Player)
PO Box 3233
Windermere, FL 34786-3233, USA

Hamilton, Richard (Athlete, Basketball Player)
23el W Big Beaver Rd Ste 535
Troy, MI 48084-3320, USA

Hamilton, Roy Lee (Athlete, Basketball Player)
10535 Wilshire Blvd Apt 555
Los Angeles, CA 90024-4514, USA

Hamilton, Ruffin (Athlete, Football Player)
236 Sumac Trl
Woodstock, GA 30188-5154, USA

Hamilton, Scott (Athlete, Figure Skater, Olympic Athlete)
c/o Larry Thompson *Larry A Thompson Organization*
9663 Santa Monica Blvd Ste 801
Beverly Hills, CA 90210-4303, USA

Hamilton, Suzanna (Actor)
Julian Belfarge
46 Albermarie St
London W1X 4PP, UNITED KINGDOM (UK)

Hamilton, Tanya (Director)
c/o Adam Robinson *Southfield Village*
8228 W Sunset Blvd # 190
West Hollywood, CA 90046-2414, USA

Hamilton, Todd (Athlete, Golfer)
2004 Rock Dove Ct
Westlake, TX 76262-9076, USA

Hamilton, Tom (Commentator)
31704 Sailors Cv
Avon Lake, OH 44012-2931, USA

Hamilton, Tom (Musician)
PO Box 67039
Chestnut Hill, MA 02467-0001, USA

Hamilton, Tyler (Artist, Cycler, Olympic Athlete)
40 Cloutmans Ln
Marblehead, MA 01945-1545, USA

Hamilton, Victoria (Actor)
c/o Michael Lazo *Untitled Entertainment*
350 S Beverly Dr Ste 200
Beverly Hills, CA 90212-4819, USA

Hamiter, Uhuru (Athlete, Football Player)
5737 Hazel Ave
Philadelphia, PA 19143-1910, USA

Hamlin, Brooke (Actor)
c/o Staff Member *Coast to Coast Talent Group*
3350 Barham Blvd
Los Angeles, CA 90068-1404, USA

Hamlin, Delilah Belle (Actor, Model)
c/o Jill Fritzo *Jill Fritzo Public Relations*
208 E 51st St # 305
New York, NY 10022-6557, USA

Hamlin, Denny (Race Car Driver)
Denny Hamlin Racing, Inc
13415 Reese Blvd W
Huntersville, NC 28078-7933, USA

Hamlin, Eugene (Athlete, Football Player)
3571 Silver Farms Ln
Traverse City, MI 49684-8827, USA

Hamlin, Harry (Actor)
3007 Lake Glen Dr
Beverly Hills, CA 90210-1313, USA

Hamlin, Ken (Athlete, Baseball Player)
5242 County Road 413
Mc Millan, MI 49853-9266, USa

Hamlin, Shelley (Athlete, Golfer)
4311 W Ardmore Rd
Laveen, AZ 85339-2112, USA

Hamm, Harold (Business Person)
Continental Resources, Inc
20 N Broadway
Oklahoma City, OK 73102-9213, USA

Hamm, Jon (Actor)
c/o Annett Wolf *Wolf-Kasteler Public Relations*
6255 W Sunset Blvd Ste 1111
Los Angeles, CA 90028-7426, USA

Hamm, Mia (Athlete, Olympic Athlete, Soccer Player)
Mia Hamm Foundation
5315 Highgate Dr Ste 204
Durham, NC 27713-6623, USA

Hamm, Morgan (Athlete, Gymnast, Olympic Athlete)
W229S3827 Milky Way Rd
Waukesha, WI 53189-7909, USA

Hamm, Nick (Director)
International Creative Mgmt
8942 Wilshire Blvd # 219
Beverly Hills, CA 90211-1908, USA

Hamm, Paul (Athlete, Gymnast, Olympic Athlete)
c/o Sandy Hamm
W230S3827 Milky Way Rd
Waukesha, WI 53189-7909, USA

Hamm, Pete (Athlete, Baseball Player)
525 Lockhart Gulch Rd
Scotts Valley, CA 95066-3034, USA

Hamm, Richard L (Religious Leader)
Christian Church Disciples of Christ
PO Box 1986
Indianapolis, IN 46206-1986, USA

Hammaker, Atlee (Athlete, Baseball Player)
12740 Manning Ln
Knoxville, TN 37932-1001, USA

Hammarlund, Kaisa (Actor)
c/o Philip Belfield *Belfield & Ward*
26 - 28 Neal St
London WC2H 9QQ, UNITED KINGDOM

Hammarstrom, Inge (Athlete, Hockey Player)
c/o Staff Member *Philadelphia Flyers*
3601 S Broad St Ste 2
First Union Spectrum
Philadelphia, PA 19148-5297, USA

Hammel, Penny (Athlete, Golfer)
4786 Orchard Ln
Delray Beach, FL 33445-5306, USA

Hammer, AJ (Television Host)
c/o Staff Member *CNN (NY)*
10 Columbus Cir
Time Warner Center
New York, NY 10019-1158, USA

Hammer, Armie (Actor)
c/o Evelyn Karamanos *Relevant*
400 S Beverly Dr Ste 220
Beverly Hills, CA 90212-4404, USA

Hammer, MC (Actor, Musician, Songwriter)
PO Box 884988
San Francisco, CA 94188-4988, USA

Hammergren, John H (Business Person)
McKesson HBOC Inc
1 Post St Ste 107
San Francisco, CA 94104-5203, USA

Hammer Jr, Jan (Musician)
Elliott Sears Management
7 Dunham Dr
New Fairfield, CT 06812-4022, USA

Hammett, Kirk (Music Group, Musician)
2505 Divisadero St
San Francisco, CA 94115-1119, USA

Hammink, Geert (Athlete, Basketball Player)
2619 Clementon Park Ct
Orlando, FL 32835-6160, USA

Hammock, Robby (Athlete, Baseball Player)
2215 W Buckhorn Trl
Phoenix, AZ 85085-5774, USA

Hammon, Becky (Athlete, Basketball Player)
c/o Mike Cound *Sportalents*
Ctra de l'Escladella, 11
El Meu Poblet - Bloc 3E
La Massana, Andorra

Hammon, Ira (Athlete, Football Player)
17715 NE 38th Way
Vancouver, WA 98682-3683, USA

Hammond, Beres (Musician)
c/o Jeff Epstein *M.A.G./Universal Attractions*
15 W 36th St Fl 8
New York, NY 10018-7927, USA

Hammond, Bobby (Athlete, Football Player)
2535 Butler St
East Elmhurst, NY 11369-1628, USA

Hammond, Chris (Athlete, Baseball Player)
908 Old Highway 431
Wedowee, AL 36278-4612, USA

Hammond, Darrell (Actor, Comedian)
c/o Geoff Cheddy *Brillstein Entertainment Partners*
9150 Wilshire Blvd Ste 350
Beverly Hills, CA 90212-3453, USA

Hammond, Donnie (Athlete, Golfer)
516 Pickfair Ter
Lake Mary, FL 32746-5807, USA

Hammond, Fred (Music Group)
Face to Face
21421 Hilltop St Ste 20
Southfield, MI 48033-4002, USA

Hammond, Gary (Athlete, Football Player)
5321 Seascape Ln
Plano, TX 75093-4121, USA

Hammond, James T (Religious Leader)
Pentecostal Free Will Baptist Church
PO Box 1568
Dunn, NC 28335-1568, USA

Hammond, John (Music Group, Musician)
c/o Staff Member *Shore Fire Media*
32 Court St Fl 16
Brooklyn, NY 11201-4441, USA

Hammond, Josh (Actor)
c/o Staff Member *Hines and Hunt Entertainment*
1213 W Magnolia Blvd
Burbank, CA 91506-1829, USA

Hammond, Julie (Athlete, Basketball Player)
2943 S Ulster St
Denver, CO 80231-4170, USA

Hammond, Ken (Athlete, Hockey Player)
37 Ibis Dr
Akron, OH 44319-5808, USA

Hammond, Kim (Athlete, Football Player)
9 Creek Bluff Run
Flagler Beach, FL 32136-5106, USA

Hammond, L Blaine Colonel (Astronaut)
17595 Harvard Ave
Irvine, CA 92614-8516, USA

Hammond, Richard (Actor, Correspondent)
c/o Staff Member *BBC Television Centre*
Incoming Mail
Wood Lane
London W12 7RJ, UNITED KINGDOM

Hammond, Steve (Athlete, Baseball Player)
11104 Lake Butler Blvd
Windermere, FL 34786-7808, USA

Hammond, Tom (Sportscaster)
NBC-TV
30 Rockefeller Plz
New York, NY 10112-0015, USA

Hammonds, Jeffrey (Jeff) (Athlete, Baseball Player, Olympic Athlete)
113 Grand Cove Pl # Pi
Madison, AL 35758-3034, USA

Hammonds, Tom (Athlete, Basketball Player)
122 Windsor Dr
Crestview, FL 32539-8601, USA

Hammons, David (Artist)
Studio Museum in Harlem
144 W 125th St Fl 2
New York, NY 10027-4498, USA

Hammons, Roger (Religious Leader)
Primitive Advent Christian Church
273 Frame Road
Elkview, WV 25071, USA

Hamnett, Katharine (Designer, Fashion Designer)
Katharine Hamnett Ltd
202 New North Road
London N1, UNITED KINGDOM (UK)

Hampel, Olaf (Athlete)
Pommenweg 2
Bielefeld 33689, GERMANY

Hampshire, Emily (Actor)
c/o Dani De Lio *Creative Drive Artists*
20 Minowan Miikan Lane
Toronto, ON M6J 0E5, CANADA

Hampshire, Susan (Actor)
123A Kings Rd
London SW3 4PL, UNITED KINGDOM (UK)

Hampson, Blake (Actor)
c/o Staff Member *Nickelodeon UK*
PO Box 6425
LONDON W1A 6UR, UNITED KINGDOM

Hampson, Justin (Athlete, Baseball Player)
1202 W Main St
Alhambra, IL 62001-2132, USA

Hampson, Ted (Athlete, Hockey Player)
4436 Claremore Dr
Minneapolis, MN 55435-4136, USA

Hampton, Brenda (Producer)
c/o Clifford Gilbert-Lurie *Ziffren Brittenham*
1801 Century Park W Fl 7
Los Angeles, CA 90067-6406, USA

Hampton, Casey (Athlete, Football Player)
105 Conover Rd
Pittsburgh, PA 15208-2601, USA

Hampton, Christopher J (Writer)
2 Kensington Park Gardens
London W11, UNITED KINGDOM (UK)

Hampton, Daniel O (Dan) (Athlete, Football Player)
9191 Falling Waters Dr E
Burr Ridge, IL 60527-0716, USA

Hampton, Ike (Baseball Player)
New York Mets
4415 E Ridge Gate Rd
Anaheim, CA 92807-3507, USA

Hampton, James (Actor)
102 Forest Hill Dr
Roanoke, TX 76262-5522, USA

Hampton, Locksley (Slide) (Music Group, Musician)
Charismic Productions
2604 Mozart Pl NW
Washington, DC 20009-3601, USA

Hampton, Lorenzo (Athlete, Football Player)
1251 Nottoway Trl
Marietta, GA 30066-7811, USA

Hampton, Mike (Athlete, Baseball Player)
c/o Mark Rodgers *Frontline Athlete Management*
PO Box 2612
Palm City, FL 34991-2612, USA

Hampton, Millard (Athlete, Track Athlete)
201 W Mission St
San Jose, CA 95110-1701, USA

Hampton, Ralph C Jr (Religious Leader)
Free Will Baptist Bible College
PO Box 479
Gallatin, TN 37066-0479, USA

Hampton, Rick (Athlete, Hockey Player)
King City Community Center
King City Community_ Center 25 Doctors Lane
King City, ON L7B 1G2, Canada

Hampton, Rodney (Athlete, Football Player)
5603 Grand Floral Blvd
Houston, TX 77041-5563, USA

Hampton, Shanola (Actor)
c/o Elissa Leeds-Fickman *Reel Talent Management*
PO Box 491035
Los Angeles, CA 90049-9035, USA

Hamri, Sanaa (Director)
c/o Larry Kennar *Code Entertainment*
280 S Beverly Dr Ste 513
Beverly Hills, CA 90212-3908, USA

Hamrlik, Roman (Athlete, Hockey Player)
56 Alhambra Dr
Oceanside, NY 11572-5425, USA

Hamulack, Tim (Athlete, Baseball Player)
530 Campbell Rd
York, PA 17402-3335, USA

Hamway, Mark (Athlete, Hockey Player)
2865 Rubbins Rd
Howell, MI 48843-7924, USA

Hamway, Marl (Athlete, Hockey Player)
3758 Loch Bend Dr
Commerce Township, MI 48382-4336, USA

Han, Chin (Actor)
c/o Andrew Ooi *Echelon Talent Management*
2915 Argo Pl
Burnaby, BC V3J 7G4, CANADA

Han, Heejun (Musician)
c/o Staff Member *19 Entertainment*
401 Wilshire Blvd Ste 1070
Santa Monica, CA 90401-1428, USA

Hanauer, Terri (Actor, Director)
8271 Melrose Ave Ste 110
Los Angeles, CA 90046-6800, USA

Hanburger, Christian (Chris) Jr (Athlete, Football Player)
708 Winter Hill Dr
Apex, NC 27502-1376, USA

Hancock, Anthony (Athlete, Football Player)
8233 Corteland Dr
Knoxville, TN 37909-2116, USA

Hancock, Eddie(murphy) (Athlete, Baseball Player)
2104 W 15th St
Pueblo, CO 81003-1126, USA

Hancock, Garry (Athlete, Baseball Player)
11311 Mossy Branch Ct
Riverview, FL 33578-4677, USA

Hancock, Herbie (Musician)
c/o Bruce Eskowitz *Red Light Management*
5800 Bristol Pkwy Ste 400
Culver City, CA 90230-6898, USA

Hancock, John D (Director)
7355 Fail Rd
La Porte, IN 46350-7108, USA

Hancock, John Lee (Director, Producer, Writer)
790 Pinehurst Dr
Pasadena, CA 91106-4535, USA

Hancock, Lee (Athlete, Baseball Player)
8338 Brentwood Blvd
Brentwood, CA 94513-1113, USA

Hancock, Leroy (Athlete, Baseball Player)
2010 Haywood Ave
Forrest City, AR 72335-4518, USA

Hancock, Mike (Athlete, Football Player)
5513 Coloma Cir
Simi Valley, CA 93063-5029, USA

Hancock, Phillip (Athlete, Golfer)
3215 W Swann Ave Apt 30
Tampa, FL 33609-4663, USA

Hancock, Ryan (Athlete, Baseball Player)
542 W Aiden Ridge Dr
Draper, UT 84020-7305, USA

Hancock, Terri (Athlete, Golfer)
115 Devereux Dr
Athens, GA 30606-1634, USA

Hand, Jon T (Athlete, Football Player)
13013 Broad St
Carmel, IN 46032-7226, USA

Hand, Larry (Athlete, Football Player)
3410 Meridian Way
Winston Salem, NC 27104-1835, USA

Hand, Rich (Athlete, Baseball Player)
3824 Bay Ct
Fort Worth, TX 76179-3831, USA

Handelsman, J B (Cartoonist)
New Yorker Magazine
4 Times Sq
New York, NY 10036-6518, USA

Handford, Martin (Cartoonist)
Walker Books
87 Vauxhall Walk
London SE11 5HU, UNITED KINGDOM (UK)

Handler, Chelsea (Comedian, Television Host)
c/o Amanda Silverman *The Lede Company*
401 Broadway Ste 206
New York, NY 10013-3033, USA

Handler, Evan (Actor)
c/o Tammy Rosen *Sanders Armstrong Caserta*
4111 W Alameda Ave Ste 505
Burbank, CA 91505-4163, USA

Handley, Ray (Athlete, Football Coach, Football Player)
PO Box 355
Glenbrook, NV 89413-0355, USA

Handley, Taylor (Actor)
c/o Booh Schut *Booh Schut Company*
11365 Sunshine Ter
Studio City, CA 91604-3141, USA

Handrahan, Vern (Athlete, Baseball Player)
36 Newland Cres
Charlottetown, PE C1A 4H5, Canada

Hands, Terence (Director)
Clwyd Theater Cymru
Mold
Flintshire, NORTH WALES

Hands, William A (Bill) (Athlete, Baseball Player)
PO Box 334
Orient, NY 11957-0334, USA

Handy, John (Music Group, Musician)
Integrity Talent
PO Box 961
Burlington, MA 01803-5961, USA

Handzus, Michal (Athlete, Hockey Player)
123 29th St
Hermosa Beach, CA 90254-2358, USA

Hanescu, Victor (Athlete, Tennis Player)
c/o Staff Member *SFX Sports Management*
5335 Wisconsin Ave NW Ste 850
Washington, DC 20015-2052, USA

Haney, Chris (Athlete, Baseball Player)
PO Box 135
Barboursville, VA 22923-0135, USA

Haney, Hank (Golfer)
Hank Haney Golf Ranch
2791 S Stemmons Fwy
Lewisville, TX 75067-4138, USA

Haney, Larry (Athlete, Baseball Player)
PO Box 157
Barboursville, VA 22923-0157, USA

Haney, Lee (Writer)
Lee Haney Enterprises
105 Trail Point Circle
Fairburn, GA 30213, USA

Haney, Merv (Athlete, Hockey Player)
249 Lindsay St
Kimberley, BC V1A 1L4, Canada

Haney, Todd (Athlete, Baseball Player)
3615 Fieldstone Cir
Waco, TX 76708-2363, USA

Hanford, Dixon (Athlete, Football Player)
1512 Hunters Chase Dr Apt 2C
Westlake, OH 44145-6126, USA

Hangartner, Geoff (Athlete, Football Player)
805 Park Slope Dr
Charlotte, NC 28209-2049, USA

Hangsleben, Alan (Athlete, Hockey Player)
5760 Little Rd
Lothian, MD 20711-9543

Hanie, Caleb (Athlete, Football Player)
10933 Helms Trl
Forney, TX 75126-7070, USA

Hanifan, Jim (Athlete, Football Coach, Football Player)
1217 Grey Fox Run
Weldon Spring, MO 63304-0307, USA

Hanin, Roger (Actor)
9 rue du Boccador
Paris 75008, FRANCE

Hanke, Christopher (Actor)
c/o Dannielle Thomas *Untitled Entertainment*
350 S Beverly Dr Ste 200
Beverly Hills, CA 90212-4819, USA

Hankerson, Leonard (Athlete, Football Player)
c/o Drew Rosenhaus *Rosenhaus Sports Representation*
3921 Alton Rd # 440
Miami Beach, FL 33140-3852, USA

Hankins, Jay (Athlete, Baseball Player)
26509 E Outer Belt Rd
Greenwood, MO 64034-9387, USA

Hankins, Jonathan (Athlete, Football Player)
c/o Kevin Poston *Deal LLC*
28025 S Harwich Dr
Farmington Hills, MI 48334-4259, USA

Hankinson, Ben (Athlete, Hockey Player)
125 Hawthorne Rd
Hopkins, MN 55343-8509, USA

Hankinson, Casey (Athlete, Hockey Player)
5221 Kellogg Ave
Minneapolis, MN 55424-1304, USA

Hankinson, Tim (Coach, Soccer Player)
Columbus Crew
2121 Velma Ave
Columbus, OH 43211-2085, USA

Hanks, Colin (Actor)
PO Box 5623
Beverly Hills, CA 90209-5623, USA

Hanks, Merton (Athlete, Football Player)
1409 S Lamar St Apt 903
Dallas, TX 75215-6851, USA

Hanks, Sam (Race Car Driver)
17766 Tramonto Dr
Pacific Palisades, CA 90272-3131, USA

Hanks, Tom (Actor, Producer)
c/o Morgan Pesante *42West*
1840 Century Park E Ste 700
Los Angeles, CA 90067-2122, USA

Hanks, Zach (Actor)
c/o Michael Henderson *Heresun Management*
4119 W Burbank Blvd
Burbank, CA 91505-2122, USA

Hankton, Cortez (Athlete, Football Player)
11180 Castlemain Cir W
Jacksonville, FL 32256-4828, USA

Hankton, Karl (Athlete, Football Player)
12532 Hennigan Place Ln
Charlotte, NC 28214-1464, USA

Hanley, Bridget (Actor)
c/o David Moss *David Moss Company*
6063 Vineland Ave Apt B
N Hollywood, CA 91606-4986, USA

Hanley, Dick (Athlete, Olympic Athlete, Swimmer)
266 Lake Dr
Hurley, WI 54534, USA

Hanley, Jenny (Actor)
MGA
Southbank House
Black Prince Road
London SE1 7SJ, UNITED KINGDOM (UK)

Hanley, Kay (Music Group)
c/o Staff Member *Paradigm (Monterey)*
404 W Franklin St
Monterey, CA 93940-2303, USA

Hanley, Richard (Swimmer)
E266 Lake Rd
Ironwood, MI 49938-9736, USA

Hanlon, Glen (Athlete, Hockey Player)
c/o Staff Member *Washington Capitals*
627 N Glebe Rd Ste 850
Arlington, VA 22203-2129, USA

Hanlon, Glen (Athlete, Hockey Player)
100 Renfrew St N
Attn Coaching Staff Vancouver Giants
Vancouver, BC V5K 3N7, Canada

Hann, Judith (Actor)
56 Wood Lane
London, ENGLAND W12 7RJ

Hanna, Gabbie (Internet Star)
c/o Andrew Graham *Creative Artists Agency (CAA)*
2000 Avenue of the Stars Ste 100
Los Angeles, CA 90067-4705, USA

Hanna, Jack (Activist)
PO Box 400
Powell, OH 43065-0400, USA

Hanna, James (Athlete, Football Player)

Hanna, Jen (Athlete, Golfer)
9 Zelma Dr
Greenville, SC 29617-7213, USA

Hanna, Jerome (Music Group)
Paramount Entertainment
PO Box 12
Far Hills, NJ 07931-0012, USA

Hanna, Preston (Athlete, Baseball Player)
5555 Mayfair Dr
Pensacola, FL 32506-5390, USA

Hannah, Bob (Baseball Player, Coach)
University of Delaware
Athletic Dept
Newark, DE 19716, USA

Hannah, Charles A (Charley) (Athlete, Football Player)
PO Box 2671
Lutz, FL 33548-2671, USA

Hannah, Daryl (Actor)
c/o Mark Rousso *Industry Entertainment Partners*
955 Carrillo Dr Ste 300
Los Angeles, CA 90048-5400, USA

Hannah, John (Actor)
c/o Sue Latimer *Artists Rights Group (ARG)*
4A Exmoor St
London W10 6BD, UNITED KINGDOM

Hannah, John (Athlete, Football Player)
2407 Hideaway Pl SE
Decatur, AL 35603-5602, USA

Hannah, Travis (Athlete, Football Player)
10807 Lemoli Ave
Inglewood, CA 90303-2023, USA

Hannah, Wayne (Religious Leader)
Fellowship of Grace Brethren Churches
PO Box 386
Winona Lake, IN 46590-0386, USA

Hannahan, Jack (Athlete, Baseball Player)
1995 Bayard Ave
Saint Paul, MN 55116-1214, USA

Hannahs, Gerald (Gerry) (Athlete, Baseball Player)
1411 Andover Rdg
Little Rock, AR 72227-3971, USA

Hannam, Ryan (Athlete, Football Player)
213 S School St
Saint Ansgar, IA 50472-1495, USA

Hannan, Dave (Athlete, Hockey Player)
408 Timberlake Dr
Venetia, PA 15367-1394, USA

Hannan, Jim (Athlete, Baseball Player)
3907 Cherry Hill Way
Annandale, VA 22003-2220, USA

Hannan, Scott (Athlete, Hockey Player)
c/o Mark Guy *Newport Sports Management*
201 City Centre Dr
Suite 400
Mississauga, ON L58 2T4, CANADA

Hannawald, Sven (Skier)
WH Sport Int'l GmbH
Im Sabel 4
Trier 54294, GERMANY

Hannelius, Geneveive (Actor)
c/o Karl Hofheinz *Synergy Talent*
13251 Ventura Blvd Ste 2
Studio City, CA 91604-1838, USA

Hannelius, Genevieve (Actor)
c/o Brett Ruttenberg *Imprint PR*
6121 W Sunset Blvd
Neuehouse
Los Angeles, CA 90028-6442, USA

Hanneman, Craig (Athlete, Football Player)
4350 Gibson Rd NW
Salem, OR 97304-9547, USA

Hanneman, Steve (Actor)
c/o Staff Member *Abrams Artists Agency*
750 N San Vicente Blvd
E Tower Fl 11
Los Angeles, CA 90069-5788, USA

Hannigan, Alyson (Actor)
c/o Cari Ross *Balance Public Relations*
Prefers to be contacted by email or phone.
New York, NY 10013, USA

Hannigan, Mackenzie (Actor)
c/o Staff Member *Martin Weiss Management*
PO Box 5656
Santa Monica, CA 90409-5656, USA

Hannigan, Ray (Athlete, Hockey Player)
1717 S Woodland Dr Spc 36
Kalispell, MT 59901-9103, USA

Hannity, Sean (Correspondent)
c/o Staff Member *Fox News*
1211 Avenue of the Americas Lowr C1
New York, NY 10036-8705, USA

Hannon, Tom (Athlete, Football Player)
17398 Roxbury Ave
Southfield, MI 48075-7609, USA

Hannuia, Dick (Coach, Swimmer)
1021 S Westley Dr
Tacoma, WA 98465-1426, USA

Hanrahan, Don (Athlete, Basketball Player)
416 Valley Rd
Cos Cob, CT 06807-1622, USA

Hanrahan, Joel (Athlete, Baseball Player)
c/o Larry Reynolds *Reynolds Sports Management*
3850 Vine St Ste 230
Riverside, CA 92507-4225, USA

Hanratty, Sammi (Actor)
c/o Ryan Daly *Zero Gravity Management*
11110 Ohio Ave Ste 100
Los Angeles, CA 90025-3329, USA

Hanratty, Terrance R (Terry) (Athlete, Football Player)
31 Gower Rd
New Canaan, CT 06840-6630, USA

Hans, Rollen (Athlete, Basketball Player)
12607 100th Ln NE Unit L156
Kirkland, WA 98034-8830, USA

Hansbrough, Tyler (Athlete, Basketball Player)
c/o Jeff Schwartz *Excel Sports Management*
1700 Broadway Fl 29
New York, NY 10019-6559, USA

Hansell, Greg (Athlete, Baseball Player)
1791 W Prescott Dr
Chandler, AZ 85248-4845, USA

Hansen, Bob (Athlete, Baseball Player)
19 N Kelsey Ave
Evansville, IN 47711-6051, USA

Hansen, Bob (Athlete, Basketball Player)
1838 P Ave
Marengo, IA 52301-8554, USA

Hansen, Brendan (Athlete, Olympic Athlete, Swimmer)
311 Blue Ridge Trl
Austin, TX 78746-5408, USA

Hansen, Brian (Athlete, Football Player)
101 W Hazeltine Ln
Sioux Falls, SD 57108-6422, USA

Hansen, Bruce (Athlete, Football Player)
480 N 1100 E
American Fork, UT 84003-1992, USA

Hansen, Chai (Actor)
c/o Staff Member *Independent Management Company*
87-103 Epsom Rd
#15
Rosebery NSW 2018, AUSTRALIA

Hansen, Chris (Correspondent, Television Host)

Hansen, Courtney (Actor)
c/o Liza Anderson *Anderson Group Public Relations*
8060 Melrose Ave Fl 4
Los Angeles, CA 90046-7038, USA

Hansen, Craig (Athlete, Baseball Player)
1180 Washington St Apt 508
Boston, MA 02118-2154, USA

Hansen, David (Dave) (Athlete, Baseball Player)
9852 Orchard Ln
Villa Park, CA 92861-3105, USA

Hansen, Don (Athlete, Football Player)
3290 Spain Rd
Snellville, GA 30039-8503, USA

Hansen, Frederick M (Fred) (Athlete, Track Athlete)
201 Vanderpool Ln Apt 12
Houston, TX 77024-6151, USA

Hansen, Gale (Actor)
c/o Staff Member *Relativity Media*
9242 Beverly Blvd Ste 300
Beverly Hills, CA 90210-3728, USA

Hansen, Gunnar (Actor)
PO Box 368
Northeast Harbor, ME 04662-0368, USA

Hansen, Gus (Actor)
c/o Staff Member *Poker Royalty, LLC*
10789 W Twain Ave Ste 200
Las Vegas, NV 89135-3030, USA

Hansen, Guy (Athlete, Baseball Player)
3876 Red Rock St
Las Vegas, NV 89103-2333, USA

Hansen, Jacqueline (Athlete, Track Athlete)
1133 9th St
Santa Monica, CA 90403-5247, USA

Hansen, Jed (Athlete, Baseball Player)
1534 12th Ln
Fox Island, WA 98333-9664, USA

Hansen, Josh (Athlete, Motorcycle Racer)
c/o Cheryl Lynch *Lynch Archer PR*
5115 Wilshire Blvd Apt 400
Los Angeles, CA 90036-4372, USA

Hansen, Kourtney (Actor)

Hansen, Lars (Athlete, Basketball Player)
1230 Horn Ave Apt 504
West Hollywood, CA 90069-2175, USA

Hansen, Mark Victor (Business Person, Writer)
Mark Victor Hansen and Associates
711 W 17th St Ste D2
Costa Mesa, CA 92627-4344, USA

Hansen, Neil (Race Car Driver)
4018 E 5th Ave
Spokane, WA 99202-5043, USA

Hansen, Patti (Model)
Redlands W Wittering
Chichester
Sussex, UNITED KINGDOM (UK)

Hansen, Phil (Athlete, Football Player)
24921 N Melissa Dr
Detroit Lakes, MN 56501-7266, USA

Hansen, Rich (Athlete, Hockey Player)
78 Eatons Neck Rd
Northport, NY 11768-1105, USA

Hansen, Rick (Athlete)
Rick Hansen Man In Motion Foundation
520 West 6th Ave 5th Fl
Vancouver, BC V5Z 1A1, CANADA

Hansen, Roger (Athlete, Baseball Player)
14618 Kayak Point Rd
Stanwood, WA 98292-5301, USA

Hansen, Ron (Athlete, Baseball Player)
13602 Alliston Dr
Baldwin, MD 21013-9748, USA

Hansen, Roscoe (Athlete, Football Player)
638 Sooy Ln
Absecon, NJ 08201-1325, USA

Hansen, Ryan (Actor)
4123 Van Noord Ave
Studio City, CA 91604-2202, USA

Hansen, Sig (Reality Star)
c/o Rich Super *Gersh*
9465 Wilshire Blvd Ste 600
Beverly Hills, CA 90212-2605, USA

Hansen, Tavis (Athlete, Hockey Player)
3821 51st Ave SW
Seattle, WA 98116-3614, USA

Hansen-Love (L??ve), Mia (Director)
c/o Francois Samuelson *Intertalent*
16, Rue Henri Barbusse
Paris 75005, FRANCE

Hansis, Ron (Athlete, Hockey Player)
112 Stegal Cir
Longs, SC 29568-8841

Hansis, Van (Actor)

Hanson (Music Group)
PO Box 884563
San Francisco, CA 94188-4563, USA

Hanson, Dave (Athlete, Hockey Player)
304 Timberlake Dr
Venetia, PA 15367-1376

Hanson, Erik (Athlete, Baseball Player)
20333 N 83rd Pl
Scottsdale, AZ 85255-3931, USA

Hanson, Isaac (Musician)
c/o Jeffrey Hasson *Paradigm (Nashville)*
222 2nd Ave S Ste 1600
Nashville, TN 37201-2375, USA

Hanson, Jason D (Athlete, Football Player)
27272 Ovid Ct
Franklin, MI 48025-1036, USA

Hanson, Jennifer (Musician)
c/o Staff Member *Creative Artists Agency (CAA)*
401 Commerce St PH
Nashville, TN 37219-2516, USA

Hanson, Joselio (Athlete, Football Player)
2531 Hudspeth St
Inglewood, CA 90303-2432, USA

Hanson, Taylor (Musician, Songwriter)
c/o Neil Warnock *UTA Music/The Agency Group (UK)*
361-373 City Rd
London EC1V 1PQ, UNITED KINGDOM

Hanson, Tracy (Athlete, Golfer)
451 Pine Wood Ct
Holland, MI 49424-6625, USA

Hanson, William R (Artist)
78 W Notre Dame St
Glens Falls, NY 12801-2721, USA

Hanson, Zac (Musician)
c/o Jeffrey Hasson *Paradigm (Nashville)*
222 2nd Ave S Ste 1600
Nashville, TN 37201-2375, USA

Hanson-Sfingi, Beverly (Athlete, Golfer)
79915 Horseshoe Rd
La Quinta, CA 92253-4309, USA

Hanspard, Byron (Athlete, Football Player)
PO Box 792
Desoto, TX 75123-0792, USA

Hantak, Bob (Athlete, Baseball Player)
526 Summerplace Ct
Saint Louis, MO 63125-5545, USA

Hantla, Bob (Athlete, Football Player)
7815 E Monte Vista Rd
Scottsdale, AZ 85257-2209, USA

Hantla, Robert (Athlete, Football Player)
7815 E Monte Vista Rd
Scottsdale, AZ 85257-2209, USA

Hantuchova, Daniela (Tennis Player)
c/o Staff Member *Women's Tennis Association (WTA-US)*
1 Progress Plz Ste 1500
St Petersburg, FL 33701-4335, USA

Ha-nui (Hanee), Lee (Actor)
c/o Sonya Kim *Saram Entertainment*
157, Seongmisan-Ro, Mapo-Gu
SARAM Entertainment, 2^4F
Seoul 03980, REPUBLIC OF KOREA

Hanulak, Chet (Athlete, Football Player)
225 Canal Park Dr Apt 6
Salisbury, MD 21804-7266, USA

Hanzal, Martin (Athlete, Hockey Player)
19550 N Grayhawk Dr Unit 1091
Scottsdale, AZ 85255-3993, USA

Hanzlik, Bill (Athlete, Basketball Player, Olympic Athlete)
5701 Green Oaks Dr
Greenwood Village, CO 80121-1336, USA

Hape, Patrick (Athlete, Football Player)
105 Sutton Cir
Birmingham, AL 35242-7075, USA

Hapka, Mark (Actor)
c/o Stephen Rice *Pantheon Talent*
1801 Century Park E Ste 1910
Los Angeles, CA 90067-2321, USA

Happ, J A (Athlete, Baseball Player)
3832 N Ashland Ave Apt 3S
Chicago, IL 60613-5235, USA

Hara, Mikie (Adult Film Star)
c/o Staff Member *Oscar Promotion*
3-6-7-5F Kita Aoyama
Minato
Tokyo 107-0061, Japan

Harada, Masahiko (Fighting) (Boxer)
2-21-5 Azabu-Juban
Minatoku
Tokyo 00106, JAPAN

Haralson, Parys (Athlete, Football Player)
c/o Sean Kiernan *Impact Sports (LA)*
12429 Ventura Ct
Studio City, CA 91604-2417, USA

Harang, Aaron (Athlete, Baseball Player)
6411 Glenroy St
San Diego, CA 92120-2713, USA

Harang, Aaron (Athlete, Baseball Player)
6392 Camino Corto
San Diego, CA 92120-3108, USA

Harb, Fred (Race Car Driver)
815 E Fairfield Rd
High Point, NC 27263-2353, USA

Harbaugh, David (Cartoonist)
1649 Stone Mansion Dr
Sewickley, PA 15143-8600, USA

Harbaugh, Gregory J (Astronaut)
N5684 County Road F
Sullivan, WI 53178-9736, USA

Harbaugh, James (jim) (Athlete, Football Player)
c/o David Dunn *Athletes First*
23091 Mill Creek Dr
Laguna Hills, CA 92653-1258, USA

Harbaugh, John (Athlete, Coach, Football Coach)
c/o Bryan Harlan *Harlan Sports Management*
400 N Michigan Ave Ste 710
Chicago, IL 60611-4105, USA

Harbor, Clay (Athlete, Football Player)

Harbour, David (Actor)
c/o Meg Mortimer *Authentic Talent and Literary Management (NY)*
20 Jay St Ste M17
Brooklyn, NY 11201-8300, USA

Harcourt, Ed (Musician)
c/o Staff Member *Paradigm (Monterey)*
404 W Franklin St
Monterey, CA 93940-2303, USA

Hard, Darlene R (Tennis Player)
22924 Erwin St
Woodland Hills, CA 91367-3215, USA

Hardaway, Anfemee (Penny) (Athlete, Basketball Player, Olympic Athlete)
3217 Point Hill Cv
Memphis, TN 38125-8890, USA

Hardaway, Anfernee (Penny) (Athlete, Basketball Player, Olympic Athlete)
410 Goodwyn St
Memphis, TN 38111-3312, USA

Hardaway, Tim (Athlete, Basketball Player, Olympic Athlete)
c/o Mark Bartelstein *Priority Sports & Entertainment (Chicago)*
325 N La Salle Dr Ste 650
Chicago, IL 60654-8182, USA

Hardeman, Buddy (Athlete, Football Player)
5711 Heming Ave
Springfield, VA 22151-2714, USA

Hardeman, Don (Athlete, Football Player)
901 S Valley Mills Dr Apt 207-B
Waco, TX 76711-1160, USA

Harden, Bobby (Athlete, Football Player)
1750 NW 36th Ter
Lauderhill, FL 33311-4128, USA

Harden, James (Athlete, Basketball Player)
c/o Rob Pelinka *Landmark Sports Agency*
10990 Wilshire Blvd Ste 1000
Los Angeles, CA 90024-3924, USA

Harden, Marcia Gay (Actor)
c/o Jamie Harhay Skinner *Baker Winokur Ryder Public Relations*
9100 Wilshire Blvd
W Tower #500
Beverly Hills, CA 90212-3415, USA

Harden, Michael (Athlete, Football Player)
7150 Leetsdale Dr Apt 315
Denver, CO 80224-1999, USA

Harden, Mike (Athlete, Football Player)
21512 E Portland Pl
Aurora, CO 80016-2343, USA

Hardenberger, Hahan (Music Group, Musician)
Columbia Artists Mgmt Inc
165 W 57th St
New York, NY 10019-2201, USA

Hardesty, Brandon (Actor)
c/o Brandt Joel *WME|IMG*
9601 Wilshire Blvd
Beverly Hills, CA 90210-5213, USA

Hardie, Kate (Actor)
Jonathan Altaras
13 Shorts Gardens
London WC2H 9AT, UNITED KINGDOM (UK)

Hardin, Melora (Actor)
c/o Mary Ellen Mulcahy *Framework Entertainment*
9057 Nemo St # C
W Hollywood, CA 90069-5511, USA

Harding, Daniel (Musician)
c/o Staff Member *ICM Partners*
10250 Constellation Blvd Fl 7
Los Angeles, CA 90067-6207, USA

Harding, Ian (Actor)
c/o Vikram Dhawer *Authentic Talent and Literary Management (NY)*
20 Jay St Ste M17
Brooklyn, NY 11201-8300, USA

Harding, Sarah (Musician)
c/o Sarah Camlett *Independent Talent Group*
40 Whitfield St
London W1T 2RH, UNITED KINGDOM

Harding, Tonya (Athlete, Figure Skater)
300 S Stagecoach Trl Apt 2305
San Marcos, TX 78666-5120, USA

Hardingham, Abigail (Actor)
c/o Barnaby Welch *Bloomfields Welch Management*
The Leaather Market Lafone House
Weston St
London SE1 3ER, UNITED KINGDOM

Hardison, Dee (Athlete, Football Player)
756 Belvin Maynard Rd
Harrells, NC 28444-9308, USA

Hardison, Kadeem (Actor)
19743 Valley View Dr
Topanga, CA 90290-3257, USA

Hardman, Cedrick (Athlete, Football Player)
250 Moss St
Laguna Beach, CA 92651-3624, USA

Hardnett, Charles (Charlie) (Athlete, Basketball Player, Coach)
1906 Swainsboro Dr
Louisville, KY 40218-2417, USA

Hardrict, Cory (Actor)
c/o Matt Luber *Luber Roklin Management*
5815 W Sunset Blvd Ste 208
Los Angeles, CA 90028-6481, USA

Hardtke, Jason (Athlete, Baseball Player)
6486 Pfeiffer Ranch Rd
San Jose, CA 95120-1622, USA

Hardwick, Chris (Actor, Game Show Host, Television Host)
c/o Staff Member *PUNY*
PO Box 1760
Santa Monica, CA 90406-1760, USA

Hardwick, Gary C (Director, Producer, Writer)
c/o Bruce Kaufman *ICM Partners*
10250 Constellation Blvd Fl 7
Los Angeles, CA 90067-6207, USA

Hardwick, Nick (Athlete, Football Player)
c/o David Dunn *Athletes First*
23091 Mill Creek Dr
Laguna Hills, CA 92653-1258, USA

Hardwick, Omari (Actor)
c/o Annick Muller *Wolf-Kasteler Public Relations*
40 Exchange Pl Ste 704
New York, NY 10005-2778, USA

Hardwicke, Catherine (Director)
c/o BeBe Lerner *ID Public Relations*
7060 Hollywood Blvd Fl 8th
Los Angeles, CA 90028-6021, USA

Hardy, Adrian (Athlete, Football Player)
7530 Kingsport Blvd
New Orleans, LA 70128-2114, USA

Hardy, Alan (Athlete, Basketball Player)
13841 Gratiot Ave
Detroit, MI 48205-2805, USA

Hardy, Bruce A (Athlete, Football Player)
7901 E State Route 69 Lot 38
Prescott Valley, AZ 86314-8468, USA

Hardy, Carroll (Athlete, Baseball Player, Football Player)
3377 Mill Vista Rd Unit 3505
Highlands Ranch, CO 80129-2408, USA

Hardy, Darrell (Athlete, Basketball Player)
3126 Knoll St
Houston, TX 77080-3011, USA

Hardy, David (Athlete, Football Player)
PO Box 1270
New Waverly, TX 77358-1270, USA

Hardy, Greg (Athlete, Football Player)
c/o Drew Rosenhaus *Rosenhaus Sports Representation*
3921 Alton Rd # 440
Miami Beach, FL 33140-3852, USA

Hardy, James (Athlete, Football Player)
c/o Eugene Parker *Independent Sports & Entertainment (ISE-IN)*
6435 W Jefferson Blvd # 197
Fort Wayne, IN 46804-6203, USA

Hardy, James (Athlete, Basketball Player)
1243 E Brickyard Rd Apt 340
Salt Lake City, UT 84106-5621, USA

Hardy, Jeff (Athlete, Wrestler)
TNA Wrestling
209 10th Ave S Ste 302
Nashville, TN 37203-0730, USA

Hardy, Jessica (Athlete, Olympic Athlete, Swimmer)
5622 Campo Walk
Long Beach, CA 90803-3947, USA

Hardy, Jim (Athlete, Football Player)
48490 San Vicente St
La Quinta, CA 92253-6253, USA

Hardy, J J (Athlete, Baseball Player)
5070 S Roosevelt St
Tempe, AZ 85282-6599, USA

Hardy, Joe (Athlete, Hockey Player)
1256 Rte de Fossambault RR 2
Saint-Augustin-De-Desmaures, QC G3A 1W8, Canada

Hardy, John (Jack) (Athlete, Baseball Player)
1260 NW 192nd Ln
Pembroke Pines, FL 33029-4520, USA

Hardy, Kevin (Athlete, Football Player)
1228 Windsor Harbor Dr
Jacksonville, FL 32225-2651, USA

Hardy, Kevin (Athlete, Football Player)
298 Paraiso Dr
Danville, CA 94526-4950, USA

HardY, Larry (Athlete, Baseball Player)
17 Jennifer Ct
Roanoke, TX 76262-5402, USA

Hardy, Larry (Athlete, Baseball Player)
7 Jennifer Ct
Roanoke, TX 76262-5402, USA

Hardy, Larry (Athlete, Football Player)
1711 Fairwood Dr
Jackson, MS 39213-7918, USA

Hardy, Mark (Athlete, Hockey Player)
220 21st St # B
Manhattan Beach, CA 90266-4547, USA

Hardy, Matt (Wrestler)
c/o Kerry Rodgerson *World Wrestling Entertainment (WWE)*
1241 E Main St
Stamford, CT 06902-3520, USA

Hardy, Rob (Actor)
c/o Adam Robinson *Southfield Village*
8228 W Sunset Blvd # 190
West Hollywood, CA 90046-2414, USA

Hardy, Terry (Athlete, Football Player)
3109 S Rick Dr
Montgomery, AL 36108-3821, USA

Hardy, Tom (Actor)
c/o Staff Member *Hardy, Son & Baker*
26 Aybrook St
London W1U 4AN, UNITED KINGDOM

Hare, David (Writer)
95 Linden Gardens
London WC2, UNITED KINGDOM (UK)

Hare, Eddie (Athlete, Football Player)
802 Walker School Rd
Sugar Land, TX 77479-5807, USA

Hare, Shawn (Athlete, Baseball Player)
5030 Rockport Ave
Franklin, TN 37064-1488, USA

Harelik, Mark (Actor)

Haren, Dan (Athlete, Baseball Player)
c/o Staff Member *Los Angeles Dodgers*
1000 Elysian Park Ave
Los Angeles, CA 90012, USA

Harewood, David (Actor)
c/o Vikram Dhawer *Authentic Talent and Literary Management (NY)*
20 Jay St Ste M17
Brooklyn, NY 11201-8300, USA

Harewood, Dorian (Actor)
c/o Tracy Quinn *Quinn Management*
17328 Ventura Blvd Ste 416
Encino, CA 91316-3904, USA

Hargain, Tony (Athlete, Football Player)
PO Box 116
Fair Oaks, CA 95628-0116, USA

Hargan, Steve (Athlete, Baseball Player)
2502 E Morongo Trl
Palm Springs, CA 92264-4839, USA

Harge, Ira (Athlete, Basketball Player)
328 Yucca Dr NW
Albuquerque, NM 87105-1935, USA

Hargesheimer, Al (Athlete, Baseball Player)
196 Old Wick Ln
Inverness, IL 60067-8018, USA

Hargesheimer, Alan (Athlete, Baseball Player)
196 Old Wick Ln
Inverness, IL 60067-8018, USA

Hargett, Edd (Athlete, Football Player)
5203 Kinloch Dr
College Station, TX 77845-2501, USA

Hargis, Gary (Athlete, Baseball Player)
157 Gemini St
Lompoc, CA 93436-1244, USA

Hargitay, Mariska (Actor)
c/o Keleigh Thomas Morgan *Sunshine Sachs*
720 Cole Ave
Los Angeles, CA 90038-3606, USA

Hargreaves, Amy (Actor)
c/o Kelli M Jones *Status PR (NY)*
59 Chelsea Piers
Level 3
New York, NY 10011-1008, USA

Hargrove, D Michael (Mike) (Athlete, Baseball Player, Coach)
3925 Ramblewood Dr
Richfield, OH 44286-9642, USA

Hargrove, Jim (Athlete, Football Player)
805 S Key Ave
Lampasas, TX 76550-3153, USA

Hargrove, Linda (Coach)
Washington Mystics
601 E St NW
Mcl Center
Washington, DC 20049-0001, USA

Hargrove, Marion (Writer)
401 Montana Ave # 6
Santa Monica, CA 90403-1303, USA

Hari, Vani (Activist)
c/o Amanda Kogan *WME/IMG*
9601 Wilshire Blvd
Beverly Hills, CA 90210-5213, USA

Harikkala, Tim (Athlete, Baseball Player)
W6132 Everglade Rd
Greenville, WI 54942-8590, USA

Harington, Kit (Actor)
c/o Marianna Shafran *Shafran PR*
195 S Beverly Dr Ste 414
Beverly Hills, CA 90212-3044, USA

Haris, Niki (Musician)
c/o Staff Member *Diva Central Inc*
7510 W Sunset Blvd # 1445
Los Angeles, CA 90046-3408, USA

Harkavy, Juliana (Actor)
c/o Lee Wallman *Wallman Public Relations*
3859 Goldwyn Ter
Culver City, CA 90232-3103, USA

Harker, Al (Athlete, Soccer Player)
409 2nd St
Lafayette Hill, PA 19444-1403, USA

Harket, Morten (Music Group)
Bandana Mgmt
11 Elvaston Place #300
London SW7 5QC, UNITED KINGDOM (UK)

Harkey, Mike (Athlete, Baseball Player)
23930 Strange Creek Dr
Diamond Bar, CA 91765-1144, USA

Harkey, Steve (Athlete, Football Player)
6582 Cherry Tree Ln
Atlanta, GA 30328-3319, USA

Harkin, Kenan (Sportscaster)
c/o Staff Member *WME/IMG*
9601 Wilshire Blvd
Beverly Hills, CA 90210-5213, USA

Harkins, Brett (Athlete, Hockey Player)
14756 Spinnaker Way
Naples, FL 34114-8790, USA

Harkleroad, Ashley (Tennis Player)
c/o Jill Smoller *WME/IMG*
9601 Wilshire Blvd
Beverly Hills, CA 90210-5213, USA

Harkless, Burkley (Athlete, Football Player)
2308 E Windsor Dr
Denton, TX 76209-1447, USA

Harkness, Deborah (Writer)
c/o Rich Green *ICM Partners*
10250 Constellation Blvd Fl 7
Los Angeles, CA 90067-6207, USA

Harkness, Jerry (Athlete, Basketball Player)
8340 Misty Dr
Indianapolis, IN 46236-9190, USA

Harkness, Tim (Athlete, Baseball Player)
70 Homefield Sq
Courtice, ON L1E 1L3, Canada

Harkrider, Kip (Athlete, Baseball Player, Olympic Athlete)
172 County Road 491
Carthage, TX 75633-3309, USA

Harlan, Bob (Business Person, Football Executive)
2621 Forestville Dr
Green Bay, WI 54304-1359, USA

Harlan, Kevin (Commentator, Sportscaster)
c/o Lou Oppenheim *ICM Partners (NY)*
730 5th Ave
New York, NY 10019-4105, USA

Harley, Steve (Music Group)
Work Hard
19D Pinfold Road
London SW16 2SL, UNITED KINGDOM (UK)

Harlicka, Skip (Athlete, Basketball Player)
2645 1/2 Saint Marys St
Raleigh, NC 27609-7644, USA

Harlin, Renny (Director, Producer)
c/o Staff Member *Midnight Sun Features*
2029 Century Park E Ste 1500
Los Angeles, CA 90067-2935, USA

Harlock, David (Athlete, Hockey Player)
1805 W Huron River Dr
Ann Arbor, MI 48103-2236, USA

Harlow, Eve (Actor)
c/o Gayle Abrams *Oscars Abrams Zimel & Associates*
438 Queen St E
Toronto, ON M5A 1T4, CANADA

Harlow, Larrv (Athlete, Baseball Player)
26348 W Burnett Rd
Buckeye, AZ 85396-9239, USA

Harlow, Larry (Athlete, Baseball Player)
26348 W Burnett Rd
Buckeye, AZ 85396-9239, USA

Harlow, Pat (Athlete, Football Player)
230 W Avenida San Antonio
San Clemente, CA 92672-4356, USA

Harlow, Scott (Athlete, Hockey Player)
6 Butter Cup Ln
Raynham, MA 02767-1872, USA

Harlow, Shalom (Model)
c/o Drew MacKenzie *Great North Artists Management*
350 Dupont St
Toronto, ON M5R 1V9, CANADA

Harman, Jane (Congressman, Politician)
2400 Rayburn Hob
Washington, DC 20515-0536, USA

Harmon, Andrew P (Athlete, Football Player)
1258 Waters Edge Dr
Dayton, OH 45458-3937, USA

Harmon, Andy (Football Player)
1258 Waters Edge Dr
Dayton, OH 45458-3937, USA

Harmon, Angie (Actor)
c/o John Carrabino *John Carrabino Management*
5900 Wilshire Blvd Ste 740
Los Angeles, CA 90036-5032, USA

Harmon, Chuck (Athlete, Baseball Player)
PO Box 12243
Cincinnati, OH 45212, USA

Harmon, Clarence (Athlete, Football Player)
PO Box 571
Verona, MS 38879-0571, USA

Harmon, Dan (Comedian)
c/o Blair Kohan *United Talent Agency (UTA)*
9336 Civic Center Dr
Beverly Hills, CA 90210-3604, USA

Harmon, Duron (Athlete, Football Player)
c/o Brian Levy *Goal Line Football Management*
1025 Kane Concourse Ste 207
Bay Harbor Islands, FL 33154-2118, USA

Harmon, Ed (Football Player)
136 Juniper Hill Rd NE
Albuquerque, NM 87122-1913, USA

Harmon, Joy (Actor)
9901 Poole Ave
Sunland, CA 91040-1335, USA

Harmon, Kelly (Actor, Model)
13224 Old Oak Ln
Los Angeles, CA 90049-2502, USA

Harmon, Mark (Actor)
c/o Karen Samfilippo *IMPR*
1158 26th St # 548
Santa Monica, CA 90403-4698, USA

Harmon, Merle (Sportscaster)
424 E Lamar Blvd Ste 210
Arlington, TX 76011-3606, USA

Harmon, Michael (Athlete, Football Player)
336 Hayat Loop
Oxford, MS 38655-9017, USA

Harmon, Mike (Race Car Driver)
Donlavey Racing
5011 Old Midlothian Tpke
Richmond, VA 23224-1119, USA

Harmon, Nigel (Astronaut)
Church Crookham
Aldershot, UNITED KINGDOM (UK)

Harmon, Richard (Actor)
c/o Naisha Arnold *Untitled Entertainment*
350 S Beverly Dr Ste 200
Beverly Hills, CA 90212-4819, USA

Harmon, Robert (Director)
c/o Andrew Ruf *Paradigm*
8942 Wilshire Blvd
Beverly Hills, CA 90211-1908, USA

Harmon, Ronnie K (Athlete, Football Player)
13022 218th St
Laurelton, NY 11413-1231, USA

Harmon, Terry (Athlete, Baseball Player)
62 Oakwood Dr
Medford, NJ 08055-8824, USA

Harmon, Tom (Athlete, Baseball Player)
6101 Bon Terra Dr
Austin, TX 78731-3849, USA

Harms, Kristin (Producer)
c/o Staff Member *Creative Artists Agency (CAA)*
2000 Avenue of the Stars Ste 100
Los Angeles, CA 90067-4705, USA

Harnden, Arthur (Art) (Athlete, Olympic Athlete, Track Athlete)
7218 Pepper Ridge Rd
Corpus Christi, TX 78413-5005, USA

Harnell, Tony (Musician)
c/o Tiziana Hurd *SolMusic Management Inc.*
Prefers to be contacted by telephone or email
Canada

Harnes, Robert (Baseball Player)
Chicago Giants
833 E Drexel Sq # 1
Chicago, IL 60615-3705, USA

Harney, Michael (Actor)
c/o Christopher Wright *Wright Entertainment*
14724 Ventura Blvd Ste 1201
Sherman Oaks, CA 91403-3512, USA

Harnick, Sheldon (Writer)
122 E 42nd St Fl 31
New York, NY 10168-3100, USA

Harnisch, Peter T (Pete) (Athlete, Baseball Player)
35 Bretwood Dr S
Colts Neck, NJ 07722-2402, USA

Harnois, Elisabeth (Actor)
c/o Ted Schachter *Schachter Entertainment*
1157 S Beverly Dr Fl 2
Los Angeles, CA 90035-1119, USA

Harnos, Christine (Actor)
Gersh Agency
232 N Canon Dr
Beverly Hills, CA 90210-5302, USA

Harnoy, Ofra (Musician)
437 Spadina Rd
PO Box 23046
Toronto, ON M5P 2W3, CANADA

Harold, Gale (Actor)
c/o Larry Taube *Principal Entertainment*
9255 W Sunset Blvd Ste 500
Los Angeles, CA 90069-3301, USA

Harout, Magda (Actor)
20950 Oxnard St APT 3
Woodland Hls, CA 91367-5227, USA

Harper, Alvin C (Athlete, Football Player)
8517 Paragon Ct
Upper Marlboro, MD 20772-6403, USA

Harper, Ben (Musician, Songwriter)
2314 La Mesa Dr
Santa Monica, CA 90402-2331, USA

Harper, Bob (Fitness Expert)
c/o Jennifer Wentzo (Wilson) *CodedPR*
54 W 39th St Fl 10
New York, NY 10018-2066, USA

Harper, Brandon (Athlete, Baseball Player)
1612 Iris St
Broomfield, CO 80020-3433, USA

Harper, Brian (Athlete, Baseball Player)
8319 E Shetland Trl
Scottsdale, AZ 85258-1343, USA

Harper, Bruce (Athlete, Football Player)
311 Lindbergh Ave
Closter, NJ 07624-2732, USA

Harper, Bryce (Athlete, Baseball Player)
c/o Scott Boras *Boras Corporation*
18 Corporate Plaza Dr
Newport Beach, CA 92660-7901, USA

Harper, Charlie (Athlete, Football Player)
2115 Augusta
McKinney, TX 75072-4301, USA

Harper, Dave (Athlete, Football Player)
4494 Cedar St
Eureka, CA 95503-8901, USA

Harper, David (Athlete, Football Player)
4494 Cedar St
Eureka, CA 95503-8901, USA

Harper, Derek (Athlete, Basketball Player)
5665 Arapaho Rd Apt 1223
Dallas, TX 75248-3492, USA

Harper, Deveron (Athlete, Football Player)
2749 Huntsville St
Kenner, LA 70062-5124, USA

Harper, Dwayne (Athlete, Football Player)
104 Cue St
Orangeburg, SC 29115-7593, USA

Harper, Gregg (Congressman, Politician)
307 Cq,Nnqn Hob
Washington, DC 20515-0001, USA

Harper, Herschel (Baseball Player)
Negro Baseball Leagues
3302 Hazelwood Dr SW
Atlanta, GA 30311-3038, USA

Harper, Hill (Actor)
c/o Lena Roklin *Luber Roklin Management*
5815 W Sunset Blvd Ste 208
Los Angeles, CA 90028-6481, USA

Harper, Jessica (Actor, Musician)
c/o Ellen Lubin Sanitsky *Wright Entertainment*
14724 Ventura Blvd Ste 1201
Sherman Oaks, CA 91403-3512, USA

Harper, Mark (Athlete, Football Player)
2162 Albany Ave
Memphis, TN 38108-3011, USA

Harper, Michael (Athlete, Basketball Player)
2387 College Hill Pl
West Linn, OR 97068-1222, USA

Harper, Nick (Athlete, Football Player)
9549 Sanctuary Pl
Brentwood, TN 37027-8499, USA

Harper, Robert (Actor)
c/o Jim Weissenbach *Weissenbach Management*
5951 Airdrome St
Los Angeles, CA 90035-4635, USA

Harper, Roger (Athlete, Football Player)
1921 Holburn Ave
Columbus, OH 43207-1683, USA

Harper, Roland (Athlete, Football Player)
5702 Wildspring Dr
Lk In The Hls, IL 60156-6416, USA

Harper, Roman (Athlete, Football Player)
c/o Pat Dye Jr *SportsTrust Advisors*
3340 Peachtree Rd NE Fl 16
Atlanta, GA 30326-1000, USA

Harper, Ron (Actor)
c/o Staff Member *Tisherman Gilbert Motley Drozdoski Talent Agency (TGMD)*
6767 Forest Lawn Dr # 101
Los Angeles, CA 90068-1027, USA

Harper, Ron (Athlete, Basketball Player)
24 Post Ln
Montvale, NJ 07645-1013, USA

Harper, Shane (Actor)
c/o Nicole David *WME|IMG*
9601 Wilshire Blvd
Beverly Hills, CA 90210-5213, USA

Harper, Terry (Athlete, Baseball Player)
2831 Aunt Pitty Pat Ln
Douglasville, GA 30135-2109, USA

Harper, Terry (Athlete, Hockey Player)
PO Box 5227
El Dorado Hills, CA 95762-0005, USA

Harper, Tess (Actor)
c/o David Guc *Vanguard Management Group*
8060 Melrose Ave Fl 4
Los Angeles, CA 90046-7038, USA

Harper, Tommy (Athlete, Baseball Player)
5 Cow Hill Rd
Sharon, MA 02067-2987, USA

Harper, Travis (Athlete, Baseball Player)
10 Brook Ridge Ln
Morgantown, WV 26508-2542, USA

Harper, Valerie (Actor)
PO Box 7187
Beverly Hills, CA 90212-7187, USA

Harper, Willie M (Athlete, Football Player)
2525 Berryessa Ct
Tracy, CA 95304-5825, USA

Harper-Nelson, Dawn (Athlete, Olympic Athlete, Track Athlete)
c/o Staff Member *Wasserman Media Group*
10960 Wilshire Blvd Ste 1200
Los Angeles, CA 90024-3714, USA

Harpring, Matt (Athlete, Basketball Player)
c/o Staff Member *Utah Jazz*
301 W South Temple
Salt Lake City, UT 84101-1219, USA

Harrah, Colbert D (Toby) (Athlete, Baseball Player, Coach)
316 Leewood Cir
Azle, TX 76020-4913, USA

Harrah, Dennis W (Athlete, Football Player)
925 Rockin One Way
Paso Robles, CA 93446-8433, USA

Harraway, Charley (Athlete, Football Player)
7961 Megan Hammock Way
Sarasota, FL 34240-8244, USA

Harraway, Charlie (Athlete, Football Player)
7961 Megan Hammock Way
Sarasota, FL 34240-8244, USA

Harrell, Anthony (Actor)

Harrell, Graham (Athlete, Football Player)
c/o Chad Speck *Allegiant Athletic Agency*
35 Market Sq Ste 201
Knoxville, TN 37902-1420, USA

Harrell, James (Athlete, Football Player)
14615 Middlefield Ln
Odessa, FL 33556-3634, USA

Harrell, John (Athlete, Baseball Player)
3218 Denton Ct
Pleasanton, CA 94566-4681, USA

Harrell, Justin (Athlete, Football Player)
c/o Eugene Parker *Independent Sports & Entertainment (ISE-IN)*
6435 W Jefferson Blvd # 197
Fort Wayne, IN 46804-6203, USA

Harrell, Lucas (Athlete, Baseball Player)
2453 E Raynell St
Springfield, MO 65804-4510, USA

Harrell, Lynn M (Musician)
I M G Artists
420 W 45th St
New York, NY 10036-3501, USA

Harrell, Sam (Athlete, Football Player)
5758 Hirondel St
Houston, TX 77033-2302, USA

Harrell, Tom (Music Group, Musician)
Joel Chriss
300 Mercer St Apt 3J
New York, NY 10003-6732, USA

Harrell, Willard (Athlete, Football Player)
8 Scarlet Oak Ct
Lake Saint Louis, MO 63367-2143, USA

Harrelson, Bill (Athlete, Baseball Player)
6900 Kimberly Ave
Bakersfield, CA 93308-3923, USA

Harrelson, Brett (Actor)
Agency for Performing Arts
9200 W Sunset Blvd Ste 900
Los Angeles, CA 90069-3604, USA

Harrelson, Derrell M (Bud) (Athlete, Baseball Player, Coach)
357 Ridgefield Rd
Hauppauge, NY 11788-2314, USA

Harrelson, Ken (Commentator)
9006 Shawn Park Pl
Orlando, FL 32819-4830, USA

Harrelson, Woody (Actor)
PO Box 327
Kula, HI 96790-0327, USA

Harrer, Tim (Athlete, Hockey Player)
7030 W 113th St
Minneapolis, MN 55438-2446, USA

Harrick, Jim (Basketball Player, Coach)
Denver Nuggets
1000 Chopper Cir
Pepsi Center
Denver, CO 80204-5805, USA

Harrier, Laura (Actor)
c/o Geoffrey Soffer *Soffer/Namoff Entertainment*
450 W 42nd St Apt 30E
New York, NY 10036-6877, USA

Harriet, Judy (Actor)
12400 Ventura Blvd
Studio City, CA 91604-2406, USA

Harrigan, Lori (Athlete, Olympic Athlete, Softball Player)
828 Rainbow Rock St
Las Vegas, NV 89123-3121, USA

Harriger, Denny (Athlete, Baseball Player)
902 N Water St
Kittanning, PA 16201-1121, USA

Harring, Laura Elena (Actor, Beauty Pageant Winner)
c/o Jason Zenowich *Abrams Artists Agency*
750 N San Vicente Blvd
E Tower Fl 11
Los Angeles, CA 90069-5788, USA

Harrington, Al (Athlete, Basketball Player)
16124 Chancellors Ridge Way
Westfield, IN 46062-7137, USA

Harrington, Bill (Athlete, Baseball Player)
7219 Cleveland School Rd
Garner, NC 27529-8928, USA

Harrington, David (Music Group, Musician)
Kronos Quartet
1235 9th Ave
San Francisco, CA 94122-2306, USA

Harrington, Dennis (Athlete, Golfer)
5668 S Rex Rd Ste 101
Stanford Roberts
Memphis, TN 38119-3829, USA

Harrington, Desmond (Actor)
c/o Stephanie Simon *Untitled Entertainment*
350 S Beverly Dr Ste 200
Beverly Hills, CA 90212-4819, USA

Harrington, Jay (Actor)
c/o Abe Hoch *A Management Company*
16633 Ventura Blvd Ste 1450
Encino, CA 91436-1887, USA

Harrington, Joey (Athlete, Football Player)
2000 NE 42nd Ave PMB 336
Portland, OR 97213-1399, USA

Harrington, John (Athlete, Hockey Player, Olympic Athlete)
635 Orchid Ln N
Minneapolis, MN 55447-3739, USA

Harrington, Kevin (Business Person, Reality Star)
Top Performance Group
7796 N Country Rd. 100
E. Bainbridge, IN 60586, USA

Harrington, Mickev (Athlete, Baseball Player)
135 Scenic Dr
Hattiesburg, MS 39401-8403, USA

Harrington, Mike (Mickey) (Athlete, Baseball Player)
135 Scenic Dr
Hattiesburg, MS 39401-8403, USA

Harrington, Othella (Athlete, Basketball Player)
1602 Rika Pt
Houston, TX 77077-3432, USA

Harrington, Padraig (Golfer)
c/o Staff Member *Pro Golfers Association (PGA)*
112 TPC Blvd
Ponte Vedra Beach, FL 32082, USA

Harrington, Perry (Athlete, Football Player)
1302 Roxbury Ct
Jackson, MS 39211-6367, USA

Harrington, Robert (Race Car Driver)
2609 Woodshade Ave
Kannapolis, NC 28127, USA

Harrington, Scott (Race Car Driver)
920 Ardmore Dr
Louisville, KY 40217-2312, USA

Harris, Al (Athlete, Football Player)
4200 NW 96th Ave
Coral Springs, FL 33065-1518, USA

Harris, Al (Athlete, Football Player)
2041 Ivy Ridge Dr
Hoffman Estates, IL 60192-4153, USA

Harris, Alonzo (Candy) (Athlete, Baseball Player)
7378 Tyler Ln
Fontana, CA 92336-5408, USA

Harris, Andy (Congressman, Politician)
506 Callinon Hob
Washington, DC 20515-0001, USA

Harris, Antwan (Athlete, Football Player)
7413 Ray Rd
Raleigh, NC 27613-8801, USA

Harris, Archie (Athlete, Football Player)
17 Hawthorne Ct NE
Washington, DC 20017-1014, USA

Harris, Arlen (Athlete, Football Player)
144 Woodspur Dr
Wentzville, MO 63385-4674, USA

Harris, Barry (DJ, Music Group, Musician)
Brad Simon Organization
122 E 57th St # 300
New York, NY 10022-2623, USA

Harris, Bernard A Jr (Astronaut)
3411 Erin Knoll Ct
Houston, TX 77059-3716, USA

Harris, Billy (Athlete, Baseball Player)
205 Fellowship Dr
Hamlet, NC 28345-3507, USA

Harris, Billy (Athlete, Hockey Player)
PO Box 233
Rosseau, ON P0C 1J0, Canada

Harris, Bo (Athlete, Football Player)
PO Box 52539
Shreveport, LA 71135-2539, USA

Harris, Boyd (Gail) (Athlete, Baseball Player)
9008 Weir St
Manassas, VA 20110-4913, USA

Harris, Brandon (Athlete, Football Player)

Harris, Brendan (Athlete, Baseball Player)
1703 Sun Gazer Dr
Rockledge, FL 32955-6323, USA

Harris, Buddy (Athlete, Baseball Player)
2305 Carol Ln
Norristown, PA 19401-2046, USA

Harris, Callard (Actor)
c/o Amy Slomovits *Haven Entertainment*
8111 Beverly Blvd Ste 201
Los Angeles, CA 90048-4531, USA

Harris, Calvin (DJ, Musician)
c/o Dvora Vener Englefield *The Lede Company*
9701 Wilshire Blvd # 930
Beverly Hills, CA 90212-2020, USA

Harris, Charlaine (Writer)
c/o Steven Fisher *Underground Management*
1180 S Beverly Dr Ste 509
Los Angeles, CA 90035-1157, USA

Harris, Charles (Bubba) (Athlete, Baseball Player)
PO Box 159
Nobleton, FL 34661-0159, USA

Harris, Chris (Athlete, Basketball Player)
1ee Oakmont Ln Apt 8e8
Belleair, FL 33756-1975, USA

Harris, Clark (Athlete, Football Player)
c/o Brad Leshnock *BTI Sports Advisors*
615 South Blvd Apt C
Oak Park, IL 60302-4606, USA

Harris, Cliff (Athlete, Football Player)
722 Kentwood Dr
Rockwall, TX 75032-7506, USA

Harris, Corey (Athlete, Football Player)
933 N Tremont St
Indianapolis, IN 46222-3738, USA

Harris, Cristi Ellen (Actor)
c/o Staff Member *The House of Representatives*
3118 Wilshire Blvd Ste D
Santa Monica, CA 90403-2345, USA

Harris, Damian (Director)
International Creative Mgmt
8942 Wilshire Blvd # 219
Beverly Hills, CA 90211-1908, USA

Harris, Dan (Television Host)
c/o Staff Member *ABC News*
77 W 66th St Fl 3
New York, NY 10023-6201, USA

Harris, Danielle (Actor)
c/o Nathan Habben *Zero Gravity Management*
11110 Ohio Ave Ste 100
Los Angeles, CA 90025-3329, USA

Harris, Danneel (Actor)
c/o Lewis Kay *Kovert Creative*
506 Santa Monica Blvd Ste 400
Santa Monica, CA 90401-2412, USA

Harris, Del (Basketball Coach, Coach)
1134 Osage Cir
St George, UT 84790-6810, USA

Harris, Demetrius (Athlete, Football Player)

Harris, Devin (Athlete, Basketball Player)
8 Green Park Dr
Dallas, TX 75248-2798, USA

Harris, Dickie (Athlete, Football Player)
801 Fuller Ave
Kelowna, BC V1Y 6X2, Canada

Harris, Donald (Athlete, Baseball Player)
909 Hubert St
Waco, TX 76704-1935, USA

Harris, Duriel (Athlete, Football Player)
8822 Dandy Ave
Jacksonville, FL 32211-8016, USA

Harris, Dwayne (Athlete, Football Player)
c/o Chad Speck *Allegiant Athletic Agency*
35 Market Sq Ste 201
Knoxville, TN 37902-1420, USA

Harris, Ed (Actor)
c/o Jill Fritzo *Jill Fritzo Public Relations*
208 E 51st St # 305
New York, NY 10022-6557, USA

Harris, Emmylou (Musician, Songwriter)
PO Box 158568
Nashville, TN 37215-8568, USA

Harris, Ernest (Athlete, Baseball Player)
1007 46th Street Ensley
Birmingham, AL 35208-1434, USA

Harris, Estelle (Actor)

Harris, Franco (Athlete, Football Player)
200 Chaucer Ct S
Sewickley, PA 15143-8726, USA

Harris, Gail (Baseball Player)
New York Giants
9008 Weir St
Manassas, VA 20110-4913, USA

Harris, Gail Robyn (Actor)
Don Gerler
3349 Cahuenga Blvd W Ste 1
Los Angeles, CA 90068-1379, USA

Harris, George (Athlete, Hockey Player)
1467 Miller Dr
Sarnia, ON N7S 3M5, Canada

Harris, Greg (Athlete, Baseball Player)
12613 Richmond Run Dr
Raleigh, NC 27614-6419, USA

Harris, Greg (Athlete, Baseball Player)
PO Box 2665
Orleans, MA 02653-6665, USA

Harris, Hernando (Pep) (Athlete, Baseball Player)
995 Ten Oaks Dr
Lancaster, SC 29720-9039, USA

Harris, Hugh (Athlete, Hockey Player)
9784 Herons Cv
Indianapolis, IN 46280-2787, USA

Harris, Ike (Athlete, Football Player)
Bellsouth Corporation
26 N Waterview Dr
Palm Coast, FL 32137-1619, USA

Harris, Jackie (Athlete, Football Player)
716 W Barraque St
Pine Bluff, AR 71601-4064, USA

Harris, James L (Athlete, Football Player)
9838 Old Baymeadows Rd
Jacksonville, FL 32256-8101, USA

Harris, Jared (Actor)
c/o Amy Guenther *Gateway Management Company Inc*
860 Via De La Paz Ste F10
Pacific Palisades, CA 90272-3631, USA

Harris, Jay (Cartoonist)
c/o Staff Member *King Features Syndication*
300 W 57th St Fl 15
New York, NY 10019-5238, USA

Harris, Jeff (Athlete, Baseball Player)
Lake County Captains 35300 Vine St Attn: Coaching Staff, OH 44095-3142, USA

Harris, Jeremy (Athlete, Football Player)
c/o Don Yee *Yee & Dubin Sports, LLC*
725 S Figueroa St Ste 3085
Los Angeles, CA 90017-5430, USA

Harris, Jeremy O (Actor)
c/o Sarah R Kelly *ICM Partners (NY)*
730 5th Ave
New York, NY 10019-4105, USA

Harris, Jillian (Television Host)
c/o Bill Stankey *Westport Entertainment Associates*
1120 W State Route 89A Ste B1
Sedona, AZ 86336-5763, USA

Harris, Joe (Athlete, Football Player)
4747 River Rd
Ellenwood, GA 30294-1507, USA

Harris, John (Athlete, Baseball Player)
7109 Rochelle Ln
Amarillo, TX 79109-6856, USA

Harris, John (Athlete, Football Player)
270 NW 120th St
Miami, FL 33168-3525, USA

Harris, John (Athlete, Golfer)
7505 W Shore Dr
Minneapolis, MN 55435-4023, USA

Harris, John (Athlete, Hockey Player)
Somerset Downs
11-4311 20 St
Vernon, BC V1T 4E4, Canada

Harris, Jon (Athlete, Football Player)
110 Cedar Ct
Swedesboro, NJ 08085-5054, USA

Harris, Joshua (Actor)
1800 Vine St # 305
Los Angeles, CA 90028-5250, USA

Harris, Keraun (King Keraun) (Comedian, Internet Star)
c/o Shawn Naim *Abrams Artists Agency*
750 N San Vicente Blvd
E Tower Fl 11
Los Angeles, CA 90069-5788, USA

Harris, Kwame (Athlete, Football Player)
4949 Marie P Debartolo Way
Santa Clara, CA 95054-1156, USA

Harris, Lara (Actor)
c/o Peter Kaiser *Talent House (NY)*
325 W 38th St Rm 605
New York, NY 10018-9642, USA

Harris, Larry (Athlete, Football Player)
41 Alta Ave
Yonkers, NY 10705-1402, USA

Harris, Laura (Actor)
c/o Kami Putnam-Heist *Anonymous Content*
3532 Hayden Ave
Culver City, CA 90232-2413, USA

Harris, Lenny (Athlete, Baseball Player)
JD Legends Promotions
10808 Foothill Blvd Ste 160 PMB 454
Attn: Jack Delance
Rancho Cucamonga, CA 91730-0601, USA

Harris, Leon (Correspondent)
Cable News Network
1050 Techwood Dr NW
News Dept
Atlanta, GA 30318-5695, USA

Harris, Leonard (Athlete, Football Player)
1817 Trilogy Park Dr
Hoschton, GA 30548-6237, USA

Harris, Leotis (Athlete, Football Player)
2815 Stephanie Dr
Little Rock, AR 72206-5421, USA

Harris, Leroy (Athlete, Football Player)
1919 Live Oak St
Savannah, GA 31404-3336, USA

Harris, Lou (Athlete, Football Player)
5606 Windsor Ct
Suitland, MD 20746-4410, USA

Harris, Lucious (Athlete, Basketball Player)
1149 W 62nd St
Los Angeles, CA 90044-3733, USA

Harris, Major (Athlete, Football Player)
c/o Staff Member *College Football Hall Of Fame*
111 Saint Joseph St S
South Bend, IN 46601-1939, USA

Harris, Mel (Actor)
c/o Joannie Burstein *Burstein Company*
15304 W Sunset Blvd Ste 208
Pacific Palisades, CA 90272-3656, USA

Harris, Mike (Athlete, Football Player)
c/o Joe Linta *JL Sports*
1204 Main St Ste 179
Branford, CT 06405-3787, USA

Harris, M L (Athlete, Football Player)
M L Harris Outreach
15589 Apple Valley Rd
Apple Valley, CA 92307-4575, USA

Harris, Moira (Actor)
c/o Staff Member *Creative Artists Agency (CAA)*
2000 Avenue of the Stars Ste 100
Los Angeles, CA 90067-4705, USA

Harris, Naomie (Actor)
c/o Angharad Wood *Tavistock Wood Management*
45 Conduit St
London W1S 2YN, UNITED KINGDOM

Harris, Napoleon (Athlete, Football Player)
c/o Staff Member *EAG Sports Management*
909 N Pacific Coast Hwy Ste 360
El Segundo, CA 90245-3864, USA

Harris, Neil Patrick (Actor)
c/o Simon Halls *Slate PR*
901 N Highland Ave
W Hollywood, CA 90038-2412, USA

Harris, Nick (Athlete, Football Player)
2035 Kingsway Dr
Troy, MI 48098-4173, USA

Harris, Niki (Musician)
c/o Stephen Ford *Diva Central Inc*
7510 W Sunset Blvd # 1445
Los Angeles, CA 90046-3408, USA

Harris, Odie L Jr (Athlete, Football Player)
821 S Polk St Apt 127
Desoto, TX 75115-7591, USA

Harris, Quentin (Athlete, Football Player)
3013 W Glass Ln
Phoenix, AZ 85041-6366, USA

Harris, Rachael (Actor, Comedian)
c/o Peter Principato *Artists First*
9465 Wilshire Blvd Ste 900
Beverly Hills, CA 90212-2608, USA

Harris, Raymont (Athlete, Football Player)
795 N 6th St
Columbus, OH 43215-1800, USA

Harris, Reggie (Athlete, Baseball Player)
35 Ashleigh Dr
Waynesboro, VA 22980-6547, USA

Harris, Rickie (Athlete, Football Player)
4225 Mozart Brigade Ln Apt 1
Fairfax, VA 22033-3960, USA

Harris, Robert (Athlete, Football Player)
8837 Elliotts Ct
Orlando, FL 32836-5028, USA

Harris, Rolf (Musician, Television Host)
c/o Suzanne Westrip *Billy Marsh Associates*
76A Grove End Rd
St John's Wood
London NW8 9ND, UNITED KINGDOM

Harris, Ron (Athlete, Hockey Player)
7 Bachman Terr
Kanata, ON K2L 1W2, Canada

Harris, Ronald W (Ronnie) (Boxer)
1365 Glennview St NE
Canton, OH 44721-1916, USA

Harris, Ronnie (Athlete, Football Player)
16911 123rd Pl NE
Bothell, WA 98011-7135, USA

Harris, Rosemary (Actor)
International Creative Mgmt
76 Oxford St
London W1N 0AX, UNITED KINGDOM (UK)

Harris, Ryan (Athlete, Football Player)
c/o Ashley Smith Becker *Relativity Sports*
2029 Century Park E Ste 1550
Century City, CA 90067-3000, USA

Harris, Sam (Writer)
c/o Anne Edelstein *AE Literary Agency*
20 W 22nd St Ste 1603
New York, NY 10010-5848, USA

Harris, Samantha (Correspondent, Television Host)
c/o Siri Garber *Platform PR*
2666 N Beachwood Dr
Los Angeles, CA 90068-2308, USA

Harris, Sean (Athlete, Football Player)
2255 W Germann Rd Apt 1162
Chandler, AZ 85286-7270, USA

Harris, Sidney (Cartoonist)
302 W 86th St Apt 9A
New York, NY 10024-3154, USA

Harris, Steve (Actor)
c/o Colton Gramm *Brillstein Entertainment Partners*
9150 Wilshire Blvd Ste 350
Beverly Hills, CA 90212-3453, USA

Harris, Steve (Athlete, Basketball Player)
3005 W Fort Worth St
Broken Arrow, OK 74012-3276, USA

Harris, Steve (Musician)
Sanctuary Music Mgmt
82 Bishop's Bridge Road
London W2 6BB, UNITED KINGDOM (UK)

Harris, Susan (Producer)
LaGrange Management
7120 Hayvenhurst Ave Ste 104
Van Nuys, CA 91406-3813, USA

Harris, Tameka (Tiny) (Musician)
c/o Ernest Dukes *The Nottingham Group*
1800 Century Park E Ste 210
Los Angeles, CA 90067-1505, USA

Harris, Ted (Athlete, Hockey Player)
1015 Sibley Memorial Hwy Apt 229
Saint Paul, MN 55118-5605, USA

Harris, Thomas (Director, Writer)
c/o Robert (Bob) Bookman *Paradigm*
8942 Wilshire Blvd
Beverly Hills, CA 90211-1908, USA

Harris, Tim (Athlete, Football Player)
843 N N St
Livermore, CA 94551-2057, USA

Harris, Tobias (Athlete, Basketball Player)
c/o Henry Thomas *CAA Sports*
2000 Avenue of the Stars Ste 100
Los Angeles, CA 90067-4705, USA

Harris, Tomas (Writer)
c/o Robert (Bob) Bookman *Paradigm*
8942 Wilshire Blvd
Beverly Hills, CA 90211-1908, USA

Harris, Tommie (Athlete, Football Player)
1000 Football Dr
Lake Forest, IL 60045, USA

Harris, Tony (Athlete, Football Player)
530 Venice Way Apt 6
Inglewood, CA 90302-2841, USA

Harris, Tyrone (Gene) (Athlete, Baseball Player)
1267 NE 16th Ave
Okeechobee, FL 34972-3066, USA

Harris, Vic (Athlete, Baseball Player)
5420 S Garth Ave
Los Angeles, CA 90056-1116, USA

Harris, Walt (Athlete, Football Player)
4103 Shinault Ln
Olive Branch, MS 38654-8039, USA

Harris, Wendell (Athlete, Football Player)
10338 Westwood Ave
Baton Rouge, LA 70809-3268, USA

Harris, William M (Athlete, Football Player)
2118 Laurel Forest Way
Houston, TX 77014-2452, USA

Harris, Willie (Athlete, Baseball Player)
1176 Willie C Harris Dr
Cairo, GA 39828-3367, USA

Harris, Wilmer (Baseball Player)
Philadelphia Stars
441 Tomlinson Rd Apt F3
Philadelphia, PA 19116-3227, USA

Harris, Wood (Actor)
Gersh Agency
232 N Canon Dr
Beverly Hills, CA 90210-5302, USA

Harris III, James S. (Jimmy Jam) (Musician)
c/o Staff Member *Flyte Tyme Productions*
PO Box 398045
Edina, MN 55439-8045, USA

Harrison, Alvin (Athlete, Track Athlete)
Octagon
1751 Pinnacle Dr Ste 1500
McLean, VA 22102-3833, USA

Harrison, Bob (Athlete, Baseball Player)
16777 Loch Cir
Noblesville, IN 46060-4482, USA

Harrison, Bob (Athlete, Football Player)
3 Westwind Cir
Stamford, TX 79553-6117, USA

Harrison, Brett (Actor)
1539 N Laurel Ave Apt 305
Los Angeles, CA 90046-2591, USA

Harrison, Chris (Reality Star)
15301 Ventura Blvd Bldg E
Sherman Oaks, CA 91403-5885, USA

Harrison, Chuck (Athlete, Baseball Player)
222 Buckskin Rd
Abilene, TX 79602-4508, USA

Harrison, Corey (Reality Star)
Gold & Silver Pawn Shop
713 Las Vegas Blvd S
Las Vegas, NV 89101-6755, USA

Harrison, Damon (Athlete, Football Player)
c/o Jimmy Sexton *CAA (Memphis)*
6060 Poplar Ave Ste 470
Memphis, TN 38119-0910, USA

Harrison, David (Athlete, Basketball Player)
11593 Larkspur Ln
Carmel, IN 46032-8614, USA

Harrison, Dennis (Athlete, Football Player)
900 Todd Preis Dr
Nashville, TN 37221-2407, USA

Harrison, Dhani (Musician)
c/o Robert Messinger *Fortress Talent Management*
23901 Calabasas Rd Ste 2016
Calabasas, CA 91302-1593, USA

Harrison, Dwight (Athlete, Football Player)
2265 Buchanan St
Beaumont, TX 77703-2255, USA

Harrison, Glynn (Athlete, Football Player)
485 Huntington Rd Ste 203
Athens, GA 30606-1845, USA

Harrison, Greg (Actor)
6708 Green Hollow Ct
Wake Forest, NC 27587-6292, USA

Harrison, Gregory (Actor)
c/o Steve Himber *Steve Himber Entertainment*
211 S Beverly Dr # 601
Beverly Hills, CA 90212-3807, USA

Harrison, James (Athlete, Football Player)
2525 Matterhorn Dr
Wexford, PA 15090-7963, USA

Harrison, Jenilee (Actor)
JLeeCorp
19528 Ventura Blvd # 365
Tarzana, CA 91356-2917, USA

Harrison, Jerome (Athlete, Football Player)
7500 Paradise Rd Lot 75
San Antonio, TX 78244-2293, USA

Harrison, Jerry (Musician)
Sire/Warner Bros Records
3300 Warner Blvd
Burbank, CA 91505-4694, USA

Harrison, Jim (Athlete, Football Player)
6038 Royal Crk
San Antonio, TX 78239-1614, USA

Harrison, Jim (Athlete, Hockey Player)
102-645 Barrera Rd
Kelowna, BC V1W 3C9, Canada

Harrison, Kathryn (Writer)
Random House
1745 Broadway Frnt 3 # B1
New York, NY 10019-4343, USA

Harrison, Linda (Actor)
9846 Portola Dr
Beverly Hills, CA 90210-1421, USA

Harrison, Lisi (Writer)
c/o Staff Member *Little, Brown Book Group*
100 Victoria Embankment
London EC4Y 0DY, UK

Harrison, Martin (Athlete, Football Player)
6160 S Featherstone Cir
Reno, NV 89511-4349, USA

Harrison, Marvin (Athlete, Football Player)
c/o Tom Condon *Creative Artists Agency (CAA)*
401 Commerce St PH
Nashville, TN 37219-2516, USA

Harrison, Matt (Athlete, Baseball Player)
160llrvil'lg Pl
Creedmoo, NC 27522-7028, USA

Harrison, Matthew (Director)
Rigberg Roberts Rugolo
1180 S Beverly Dr Ste 601
Los Angeles, CA 90035-1158, USA

Harrison, (Mya) Marie (Actor)
c/o Melissa Berger *Melissa Berger Public Relations*
437 S Cochran Ave Apt 6
Los Angeles, CA 90036-3308, USA

Harrison, Nolan (Athlete, Football Player)
2121 N Westmoreland St Apt 543
Arlington, VA 22213-1069, USA

Harrison, Olivia (Actor, Producer)
Friar Park
Badgemore
Henley-on-Thames RG9 4NR, UK

Harrison, Paul (Athlete, Hockey Player)
486 Elm St S
Timmins, ON P4N 1X9, Canada

Harrison, Randy (Actor, Producer)
c/o Staff Member *Paradigm*
8942 Wilshire Blvd
Beverly Hills, CA 90211-1908, USA

Harrison, Reggie (Athlete, Football Player)
1912 Halifax Rd
Woodbridge, VA 22191-2407, USA

Harrison, Rick (Reality Star)
Gold & Silver Pawn Shop
713 Las Vegas Blvd S
Las Vegas, NV 89101-6755, USA

Harrison, Robert (Athlete, Basketball Player)
2413 Central Park Dr
Melbourne, FL 32935-2122, USA

Harrison, Rodney (Athlete, Football Player)
2825 Darlington Pointe
Duluth, GA 30097-4318, USA

Harrison, Roric (Athlete, Baseball Player)
18662 MacArthur Blvd Ste 200
Irvine, CA 92612-1285, USA

Harrison, Rorie (Athlete, Baseball Player)
680 Glenneyre St
Laguna Beach, CA 92651-2420, USA

Harrison, Tom (Athlete, Baseball Player)
2932 Channing Way
Los Alamitos, CA 90720-4049, USA

Harrison, Tony (Writer)
Gordon Dickinson
2 Crescent Grove
London SW4 7AH, UNITED KINGDOM (UK)

Harrison, Tyreo (Athlete, Football Player)
27011 Sage Crk
Boerne, TX 78006-4803, USA

Harrison Breetzke, Joan (Swimmer)
16 Clevedon Road
East London 05201, SOUTH AFRICA

Harris-Stewart, Luisa (Basketball Player, Olympic Athlete)
1002 Cherry St
Greenwood, MS 38930-6506, USA

Harris-Stewart, Lusia M (Lucy) (Athlete, Basketball Player, Olympic Athlete)
1002 Cherry St
Greenwood, MS 38930-6506, USA

Harrold, Peter (Athlete, Hockey Player)
9385 Baldwin Rd
Mentor, OH 44060-8055, USA

Harron, Mary (Director, Producer, Writer)
c/o Charles Mastropietro *Circle of Confusion*
8931 Ellis Ave
Los Angeles, CA 90034-3336, USA

Harry, Debbie (Actor, Musician, Songwriter)
c/o Linda Carbone *Press Here Publicity*
138 W 25th St Ste 900
New York, NY 10001-7470, USA

Harry, Emile (Athlete, Football Player)
34 Villa Vista Dr
Brownsville, TX 78520-4649, USA

Harry, Jackee (Actor, Director)
c/o Staff Member *Pure Publicity*
188 Front St Ste 116 PMB 6
Franklin, TN 37064-5089, USA

Harsch, Eddie (Musician)
c/o Staff Member *Mitch Schneider Organization (MSO)*
14724 Ventura Blvd Ste 410
Sherman Oaks, CA 91403-3537, USA

Harshman, Jack (Athlete, Baseball Player)
320 Yukon Ter
Georgetown, TX 78633-5098, USA

Harshman, Margo (Actor)
c/o Paul Brown *Industry Entertainment Partners*
955 Carrillo Dr Ste 300
Los Angeles, CA 90048-5400, USA

Harshman, Marv (Athlete, Basketball Player, Coach)
1653 S Geiger St
Tacoma, WA 98465-1509, USA

Hart, Bo (Athlete, Baseball Player)
PO Box 1761
Freedom, CA 95019-1761, USA

Hart, Bret (Athlete, Wrestler)
435 Patina Pl SW
Calgary, AB T3H 2P5, CANADA

Hart, Carey (Athlete)
1470 Count Fleet St
Santa Ynez, CA 93460-9531, USA

Hart, Clinton (Athlete, Football Player)
2894 CR 730
Webster, FL 33597-4084, USA

Hart, Corey (Athlete, Baseball Player)
1445 Lambert Close #300
Montreal, CANADA 42101-5220, USA

Hart, Dick (Athlete, Football Player)
273 Oarlock Cir
East Syracuse, NY 13057-3123, USA

Hart, Dolores Hart (Actor)
Regina Laudis Abbey
275 Flanders Road
Bethlehem, CT 06751, USA

Hart, Doug (Athlete, Football Player)
2192 Medina Rd
Long Lake, MN 55356-9501, USA

Hart, Dudley (Athlete, Golfer)
5130 Rockledge Dr
Clarence, NY 14031-2442, USA

Hart, Gary (Politician, Senator)
730 17th St Ste 300
Denver, CO 80202-3513, USA

Hart, Gerry (Athlete, Hockey Player)
10 Parkridge Ct
Huntington, NY 11743-3671, USA

Hart, Harold J (Athlete, Football Player)
1016 Brook View Ave
Atlanta, GA 30340-3842, USA

Hart, Ian (Actor)
c/o Robert Marsala *Wishlab*
195 S Beverly Dr Ste 414
Beverly Hills, CA 90212-3044, USA

Hart, James V (Director, Producer, Writer)
c/o Stuart Rosenthal *Bloom Hergott Diemer Rosenthal Laviolette Feldman Schenkman & Goodman*
150 S Rodeo Dr Fl 3
Beverly Hills, CA 90212-2410, USA

Hart, Jason (Athlete, Baseball Player)
19317 Nestor Ave
Carson, CA 90746-2607, USA

Hart, Jeff (Athlete, Football Player)
1307 SE 14th Ave
Canby, OR 97013-6341, USA

Hart, Jeff (Athlete, Golfer)
105 Guanajuato Ct
Solana Beach, CA 92075-2510, USA

Hart, Jim (Athlete, Football Player)
3141 Dominica Way
Naples, FL 34119-1606, USA

Hart, Jo (Actor)
c/o Luc Chaudhary *International Artists Management*
25-27 Heath St.
Hamstead NW3 6TR, UNITED KINGDOM

Hart, John (Athlete, Baseball Player)
5205 Latrobe Dr
Windermere, FL 34786-8959, USA

Hart, John (Commentator)
5205 Latrobe Dr
Windermere, FL 34786-8959, USA

Hart, Kevin (Actor, Comedian)
Hartbeat Productions
15910 Ventura Blvd # 15
Encino, CA 91436-2802, USA

Hart, Kevin (Athlete, Baseball Player)
5605 Plantation Cir
Plano, TX 75093-4205, USA

Hart, Larry (Athlete, Football Player)
c/o Jordan Woy *Willis & Woy Management*
4890 Alpha Rd Ste 200
Dallas, TX 75244-4639, USA

Hart, Leo (Athlete, Football Player)
1014 Arbor Trce NE
Brookhaven, GA 30319-5378

Hart, Linda (Actor)
c/o Staff Member *The Gage Group*
5757 Wilshire Blvd Ste 659
Los Angeles, CA 90036-3682, USA

Hart, Marcy (Athlete, Golfer)
1607 Kinloch Dr
Winston Salem, NC 27107-8031, USA

Hart, Mary (Television Host)
9440 Santa Monica Blvd Ste 407
Beverly Hills, CA 90210-4607, USA

Hart, Melissa Joan (Actor)
c/o Gordon Gilbertson *Gilbertson Management*
1334 3rd Street Promenade Ste 201
Santa Monica, CA 90401-1320, USA

Hart, Mickey (Music Group, Musician)
c/o Staff Member *UTA/The Agency Group*
888 7th Ave Fl 7
New York, NY 10106-0700, USA

Hart, Mike (Athlete, Baseball Player)
409 Larkspur Ave
Portage, MI 49002-6243, USA

Hart, Mike (Athlete, Baseball Player)
16552 W Crescent Dr
New Berlin, WI 53151-6514, USA

Hart, Miranda (Actor)
c/o Duncan Hayes *United Agents*
12-26 Lexington St
London W1F OLE, UNITED KINGDOM

Hart, Richard (Athlete, Football Player)
273 Oarlock Cir
East Syracuse, NY 13057-3123, USA

Hart, Terry J (Astronaut)
PO Box V
Hellertown, PA 18055-0218, USA

Hart, Terry J Dr (Astronaut)
PO Box V
Hellertown, PA 18055-0218, USA

Hart, Tommy (Athlete, Football Player)
3503 Highland Ave
Redwood City, CA 94062-3109, USA

Hartenstein, Chuck (Athlete, Baseball Player)
10735 Cassia Dr
Austin, TX 78759-6452, USA

Hartenstine, Michael A (Mike) (Athlete, Football Player)
322 Winchester Ct
Lake Bluff, IL 60044-1930, USA

Hartgraves, Dean (Athlete, Baseball Player)
1741 S Sierra Vista Dr
Tempe, AZ 85281-6633, USA

Hartigan, Grace (Artist)
1701 1/2 Eastern Ave
Baltimore, MD 21231-2439, USA

Hartigan, Mark (Athlete, Hockey Player)
17925 48th Ct N
Minneapolis, MN 55446-1948, USA

Hartings, Jeff (Athlete, Football Player)
500 W Orange Rd
Delaware, OH 43015-7070, USA

Hartler, Vicky (Congressman, Politician)
1023 Longworth Hob
Washington, DC 20515-3701, USA

Hartley, Bob (Athlete, Coach, Hockey Player)
13 South Ave SE
Atlanta, GA 30315, USA

Hartley, Bob (Athlete, Hockey Player)
2713 Bonar Hall Path
Duluth, GA 30097-7463, USA

Hartley, Frank (Athlete, Football Player)
4022 Fishermans Cove Ct
Lutz, FL 33558-9749, USA

Hartley, Hal (Director)
c/o Staff Member *Possible Films*
779 Riverside Dr Apt B25
New York, NY 10032-7309, USA

Hartley, Justin (Actor)
c/o Jordyn Palos *Persona Public Relations*
6255 W Sunset Blvd Ste 705
Hollywood, CA 90028-7408, USA

Hartley, Ken (Athlete, Football Player)
4615 S Bridge Ave
Weslaco, TX 78596-1393, USA

Hartley, Mariette (Actor)
c/o Chris Roe *Chris Roe Management*
PO Box 761
Burbank, CA 91503-0761, USA

Hartley, Mike (Athlete, Baseball Player)
9485 Quail Canyon Rd
El Cajon, CA 92021-6709, USA

Hartley, Nina (Actor, Adult Film Star, Director, Model, Producer)
7095 Hollywood Blvd Ste 648
Los Angeles, CA 90028-8912, USA

HartleyJ, Bob (Athlete, Hockey Player)
110-1000 Palladium Dr
Attn: Broadcast Dept Ottawa Senators
Ottawa, ON K2V 1A5, Canada

Hartline, Brian (Athlete, Football Player)
c/o Drew Rosenhaus *Rosenhaus Sports Representation*
3921 Alton Rd # 440
Miami Beach, FL 33140-3852, USA

Hartline, Mary (Actor)
c/o Staff Member *Pierce & Shelly*
13775A Mono Way # 220
Sonora, CA 95370-8813, USA

Hartman, J C (Athlete, Baseball Player)
3425 Rosedale St
Houston, TX 77004-6312, USA

Hartman, Kevin (Soccer Player)
Los Angeles Galaxy
1010 Rose Bowl Dr
Pasadena, CA 91103, USA

Hartman, Mike (Athlete, Hockey Player)
2 12th St Ph 7
Hoboken, NJ 07030-6787, USA

Hartman, Rhonda (Race Car Driver)
5611 Hwy.
81 North
Williamston, SC 29697, USA

Hartman, Richard (Race Car Driver)
1340 Keone Cir
Williamston, SC 29697-9245, USA

Hartmann, Thom (Radio Personality, Writer)
c/o Staff Member *Red Wheel / Weiser /Conari*
65 Parker St Ste 7
Newburyport, MA 01950-4600, USA

Hartnell, Scott (Athlete, Hockey Player)
111 Church St
Philadelphia, PA 19106-2209, USA

Hartnett, Josh (Actor)
c/o Susan Patricola *Patricola Public Relations*
369 S Doheny Dr # 1408
Beverly Hills, CA 90211-3508, USA

Hartog, Jan de (Writer)
Andrew Numberg Assoc
45/47 Clerkenwell Green
London EC1R 0HT, UNITED KINGDOM (UK)

Harts, Greg (Athlete, Baseball Player)
829 Humphries St SW
Atlanta, GA 30310-2165, USA

Harts, Shaunard (Athlete, Football Player)
5304 Tamarindo Ln
Elk Grove, CA 95758-6821, USA

Hartsburg, Craig (Athlete, Hockey Player)
c/o Staff Member *Soo Greyhounds Hockey Club*
201-212 Queen St E
Sault Ste. Marie, ON P6A 5X8, Canada

Hartsfield, Roy (Athlete, Baseball Player)
159 Preserve Pkwy
Ball Ground, GA 30107-3233, USA

Hartshorn, Lawrence (Athlete, Football Player)
PO Box 1542
Cedar Ridge, CA 95924-1542, USA

Hartsock, Ben (Athlete, Football Player)
1274 Wheatley Forest Dr
Brentwood, TN 37027-8342, USA

Hartsock, Desiree (Reality Star)
c/o Staff Member *Next Entertainment*
3601 W Olive Ave Ste 700
Burbank, CA 91505-4655, USA

Hartsock, Jeffrey (Jeff) (Athlete, Baseball Player)
1720 Swannanoa Dr
Greensboro, NC 27410-3932, USA

Hartung, James (Athlete, Gymnast, Olympic Athlete)
6425 Tanglewood Ln
Lincoln, NE 68516-2355, USA

Hartwell, Edgerton (Athlete, Football Player)
2427 Country Valley Ct
N Las Vegas, NV 89030-4702, USA

Hartwell, Erin (Athlete, Cycler, Olympic Athlete)
PO Box 917
Trexlertown, PA 18087-0917, USA

Hartwell, Lisa Wu (Reality Star)
c/o Staff Member *Bravo TV (NY)*
30 Rockefeller Plz
New York, NY 10112-0015, USA

Hartwig, Carter (Athlete, Football Player)
5539 FM 762 Rd
Richmond, TX 77469-8320, USA

Hartwig, Justin (Athlete, Football Player)
4009 Overland Dr
Lawrence, KS 66049-4122, USA

Hartzell, Paul (Athlete, Baseball Player)
PO Box 2860
Hailey, ID 83333-2860, USA

Harvard, Russell (Actor)
c/o Bill Veloric *Innovative Artists*
235 Park Ave S Fl 7
New York, NY 10003-1405, USA

Harvey, Antonio (Athlete, Basketball Player)
59e6 Yaupon Ave
Moss Point, MS 39563-6046, USA

Harvey, Bryan (Athlete, Baseball Player)
1224 Astoria Pkwy
Catawba, NC 28609-8885, USA

Harvey, Claude (Athlete, Football Player)
2918 Dragonwick Dr
Houston, TX 77045-4708, USA

Harvey, David R (Business Person)
Sigme-Aldrich Corp
3050 Spruce St
Saint Louis, MO 63103-2530, USA

Harvey, Donnell (Basketball Player)
Orlando Magic
8701 Maitland Summit Blvd
Waterhouse Center
Orlando, FL 32810-5915, USA

Harvey, Guy (Artist)
Guy Harvey Enterprises
4350 Oakes Rd Ste 518
Davie, FL 33314-2224, USA

Harvey, James B (Athlete, Football Player)
3685 Clairice Cv
Memphis, TN 38133-0979, USA

Harvey, Jim (Athlete, Football Player)
3685 Clairice Cv
Memphis, TN 38133-0979, USA

Harvey, Ken (Athlete, Baseball Player)
5012 Grand Ave Apt C
Kansas City, MO 64112-2761, USA

Harvey, Ken (Athlete, Football Player)
11600 Great Falls Way
Great Falls, VA 22066-1150, USA

Harvey, Marvin (Athlete, Football Player)
901 Riggins Rd Apt 522
Tallahassee, FL 32308-2202, USA

Harvey, Matt (Athlete, Basketball Player)
c/o Scott Boras *Boras Corporation*
18 Corporate Plaza Dr
Newport Beach, CA 92660-7901, USA

Harvey, Maurice (Athlete, Football Player)
440 Baldwin Ave APT 58
Rochester, MI 48307-2126, USA

Harvey, Nancy (Athlete, Golfer)
7006 E Jensen St Unit 62
Mesa, AZ 85207-2833, USA

Harvey, PJ (Musician)
c/o Marsha Vlasic *Artist Group International (NY)*
150 E 58th St Fl 19
New York, NY 10155-1900, USA

Harvey, Richard (Athlete, Football Player)
3414 Baltimore Ave
Pascagoula, MS 39581-4236, USA

Harvey, Steve (Actor, Comedian, Television Host)
The Steve Harvey Show
100 Universal City Plz
Universal City, CA 91608-1002, USA

Harvey, Terry (Baseball Player)
US Olympic Team
215 Annandale Dr
Cary, NC 27511-6503, USA

Harvey, Todd (Athlete, Hockey Player)
353 McCarthy Rd
PO BOX 818 HOCKEY TRAINING ABOVE
Stratford, ON N5A 7S7, Canada

Harvick, Kevin (Race Car Driver)
Kevin Harvick Foundation
PO Box 222098
Charlotte, NC 28222-2098, USA

Harville, Chad (Athlete, Baseball Player)
450 Cedar Cove Ln
Savannah, TN 38372-5620, USA

Harvin, Percy (Athlete, Football Player)
1929 Summit Ridge Rd
Fleming Island, FL 32003-4967, USA

Harwell, Steve (Actor, Music Group)
c/o Staff Member *Creative Artists Agency (CAA)*
2000 Avenue of the Stars Ste 100
Los Angeles, CA 90067-4705, USA

Hary, Armin (Athlete, Track Athlete)
Schloss
Diessen/Ammersee 86911, GERMANY

Hasegawa, Shigetoshi (Athlete, Baseball Player)
105 Interval
Irvine, CA 92618-0864, USA

Hasek, Dominik (Athlete, Hockey Player)
c/o Dominator Areal Dutreva, Delnicka
54/1020 Praha 7
Holesovice 170 00, Czech Republic

Haselman, Bill (Athlete, Baseball Player)
14501 SE 85th St
Newcastle, WA 98059-9218, USA

Haselrig, Carlton (Athlete, Football Player)
386 William Penn Ave
Johnstown, PA 15901-1253, USA

Haseltine, Dan (Music Group)
Flood Bumstead McCarthy
1700 Hayes St Ste 304
Nashville, TN 37203-3593, USA

Hasen, Irvin H (Cartoonist)
68 E 79th St Apt E
New York, NY 10075-0224, USA

Hasenmayer, Don (Athlete, Baseball Player)
721 Golf Dr
Warrington, PA 18976-2053, USA

Hasham, Josephine (Athlete, Baseball Player, Commentator)
575 SW 11th St
Miami, FL 33129-1034, USA

Hashimoto, Ryutaro (Politician)
Prime Ministers Office 6-1 Nagata-cho 1 chome Chiyoda-Ku
Tokyo, Japan 35214-4826, USA

Hashu, Nick (Athlete, Basketball Player)
2514 W Orangethorpe Ave Spc 27
Fullerton, CA 92833-4238, USA

Haskell, Colleen Marie (Actor)
c/o Andy Cohen *Gersh*
9465 Wilshire Blvd Ste 600
Beverly Hills, CA 90212-2605, USA

Haskell, James (Athlete, Rugby Player)

Haskin, Scott (Athlete, Basketball Player)
3078 Roxbury Dr
West Linn, OR 97068-8295, USA

Haskins, Clem (Athlete, Basketball Player, Coach)
2632 Roberts Rd
Campbellsville, KY 42718, USA

Haskins, Dennis (Actor)
c/o Jay Schachter *Abrams Artists Agency*
750 N San Vicente Blvd
E Tower Fl 11
Los Angeles, CA 90069-5788, USA

Haskins, Jon (Athlete, Football Player)
4055 Higel Ave
Sarasota, FL 34242-1138, USA

Haslam, Annie (Musician)
c/o Benjamin Shprits *Entourage Talent Associates*
150 W 28th St Ste 1503
New York, NY 10001-6180, USA

Haslem, Udonis (Athlete, Basketball Player)
1331 Brickell Bay Dr Apt 3311
Miami, FL 33131-3685, USA

Haslett, James D (Jim) (Athlete, Coach, Football Coach, Football Player)
118 Crandon Dr
Saint Louis, MO 63105-3606, USA

Hass, Robert (Writer)
University of California
English Dept
Berkeley, CA 94720-0001, USA

Hassan, Ahmed (Television Host)
5417 Prewett Ranch Dr
Antioch, CA 94531-8522, USA

Hassan, Fred (Business Person)
Schering-Plough Corp
1 Giralda Farms
Madison, NJ 07940-1021, USA

Hassel, Trenton (Athlete, Baseball Player)
4776 Mickle Ln
Clarksville, TN 37043-8263, U S A

Hasselbach, Harald (Athlete, Football Player)
17919 E Dorado Dr
Centennial, CO 80015-5916, USA

Hasselbeck, Donald W (Don) (Athlete, Football Player)
38 Noon Hill Ave
Norfolk, MA 02056-1145, USA

Hasselbeck, Elisabeth (Reality Star, Television Host)
1110 Nichol Ln
Nashville, TN 37205-4418, USA

Hasselbeck, Matt (Athlete, Football Player)
9027 NE 1st St
Bellevue, WA 98004-4814, USA

Hasselbeck, Tim (Athlete, Football Player)
38 Noon Hill Ave
Norfolk, MA 02056-1145, USA

Hasselhoff, David (Actor, Musician)
c/o Larry Thompson *Larry A Thompson Organization*
9663 Santa Monica Blvd Ste 801
Beverly Hills, CA 90210-4303, USA

Hasselhoff, Hayley (Actor, Model)
c/o Liza Anderson *Anderson Group Public Relations*
8060 Melrose Ave Fl 4
Los Angeles, CA 90046-7038, USA

Hassenfeld, Alan G (Business Person)
Hasbro Inc
1027 Newport Ave
Pawtucket, RI 02861-2500, USA

Hassett, Joe (Athlete, Basketball Player)
28 Marigold Cir
North Providence, RI 02904-3891, USA

Hassett, Marilyn (Actor)
8905 Rosewood Ave
West Hollywood, CA 90048-2409, USA

Hassey, Ron (Athlete, Baseball Player)
4751 Main St Attn Ofc
Jupiter, FL 33458-5203, USA

Hassler, Andy (Athlete, Baseball Player)
1855 W Wickenburg Way Lot 114
Wickenburg, AZ 85390-3239, USA

Hasson, Maddie (Actor)
c/o Richard Beddingfield *Beddingfield Company, The*
13600 Ventura Blvd Ste B
Sherman Oaks, CA 91423-5050, USA

Hasson, Maurice (Musician)
18 West Heath Court
North End Road
London NW11, UNITED KINGDOM (UK)

Hastert, J Dennis (Politician)
PO Box 153
Plano, IL 60545-0153, USA

Hastings, Andre (Athlete, Football Player)
700 N Dobson Rd Unit 37
Chandler, AZ 85224-6940, USA

Hastings, Doc (Congressman, Politician)
1203 Longworth Hob
Washington, DC 20515-3505, USA

Hastings, Don (Actor)
524 W 57th St # 5330
New York, NY 10019-2930, USA

Hastings, Scott (Athlete, Basketball Player)
5414 E Nichols Pl
Centennial, CO 80122-3800, USA

Haston, Kirk (Athlete, Basketball Player)
2600 S Main St
Lobelville, TN 37097, USA

Hasty, James (Athlete, Football Player)
8212 127th Ave SE
Newcastle, WA 98056-9146, USA

Hatalsky, Morris (Athlete, Golfer)
201 S Ocean Grande Dr PH 5
Ponte Vedra Beach, FL 32082-6514, USA

Hatch, Annia (Athlete, Gymnast, Olympic Athlete)
1800 Sans Souci Blvd Apt 239
North Miami, FL 33181-3069, USA

Hatch, Richard (Actor, Reality Star)
c/o Charles Lago *DTLA Entertainment Group*
301 N Palm Canyon Dr Ste A
Palm Springs, CA 92262-5672, USA

Hatchell, Sylvia (Basketball Player)
University of North Carolina
Athletic Dept
Chapell Hill, NC 27515, USA

Hatcher, Billy (Athlete, Baseball Player)
100 Joe Nuxhall Way
Cincinnati, OH 45202-4109, USA

Hatcher, Chris (Athlete, Baseball Player)
4514 Navajo St
Council Bluffs, IA 51501-8707, USA

Hatcher, Derian (Athlete, Hockey Player)
3601 S Broad St Ste 2
Attn Coaching Staff
Philadelphia, PA 19148-5250, USA

Hatcher, Derian (Athlete, Hockey Player, Olympic Athlete)
1159 S Water St
Marine City, MI 48039-1699, USA

Hatcher, Jason (Athlete, Football Player)
c/o Jordan Woy *Willis & Woy Management*
4890 Alpha Rd Ste 200
Dallas, TX 75244-4639, USA

Hatcher, Kevin (Athlete, Hockey Player, Olympic Athlete)
14668 Westwind Ct
Washington, MI 48094-3236, USA

Hatcher, Mickey (Athlete, Baseball Player)
2000 E Gene Autry Way
Attn Coaching Staff
Anaheim, CA 92806-6143, USA

Hatcher, R Dale (Athlete, Football Player)
906 White Plains Rd
Gaffney, SC 29340-5473, USA

Hatcher, Teri (Actor)
c/o Staff Member *ISBE Productions*
1925 Century Park E Ste 2200
Los Angeles, CA 90067-2723, USA

Hatchett, Derrick (Athlete, Football Player)
7811 Westshire Dr
San Antonio, TX 78227-2760, USA

Hatchett, Glenda (Judge, Reality Star)
c/o Elizabeth Much *East 2 West Collective*
11022 Santa Monica Blvd Ste 350
Los Angeles, CA 90025-7532, USA

Hatchette, Matthew (Athlete, Football Player)
3222 Winding Pine Trl
Longwood, FL 32779-3170, USA

Hatfield, Juliana (Musician, Songwriter)
c/o Staff Member *Concerted Efforts*
PO Box 440326
Somerville, MA 02144-0004, USA

Hathaway, Anne (Actor)
c/o Jennifer Plante *Slate PR (NY)*
307 7th Ave Rm 2401
New York, NY 10001-6019, USA

Hathaway, Hilly (Athlete, Baseball Player)
13341 Low Tide Way
Jacksonville, FL 32258-5207, USA

Hathaway, Noah (Actor)
5150 Choppers & Hot Rods
228 Grand Ave
Perryville, MO 63775-1806, USA

Hathaway, Paige (Fitness Expert, Internet Star)
c/o Lion Shirdan *UPRISE Management*
2317 Mount Olympus Dr
Los Angeles, CA 90046-1639, USA

Hathaway, Ray (Athlete, Baseball Player)
25 Leisure Mountain Rd
Asheville, NC 28804-1147, USA

Hathcock, Dave (Athlete, Football Player)
1717 Stoney Hill Ln
Spring Hill, TN 37174-6187, USA

Hatori, Miho (Music Group)
Billions Corp
833 W Chicago Ave Ste 101
Chicago, IL 60642-8408, USA

Hatosy, Shawn (Actor)
H2F Entertainment
644 N Cherokee Ave
Los Angeles, CA 90004-1009, USA

Hatoum, Ed (Athlete, Hockey Player)
Hatoum Auto Sales 5711 No 3 Rd
Richmond, BC VGX 2C9, Canada

Hatteberg, Scott (Athlete, Baseball Player)
802 Berg Ct NW
Gig Harbor, WA 98335-7709, USA

Hatten, Tom (Actor)
1759 Sunset Plaza Dr
Los Angeles, CA 90069-1311, USA

Hattestad, Stine Lise (Skier)
Sundlia 1B
Nesoya 01315, NORWAY

Hatton, Ricky (Athlete, Boxer)
Banner Promotions
1231 Bainbridge St
Philadelphia, PA 19147-1805, USA

Hatton, Vernon (Vern) (Athlete, Basketball Player)
1492 Copper Run Blvd
Lexington, KY 40514-2221, USA

Hattori, Shige (Race Car Driver)
4377 Triple Crown Dr.
Concord, NC 28027, USA

Hattori, Shigeaki (Race Car Driver)
Bettenhausen Motorsports
57 Gasoline Aly Ste A
Indianapolis, IN 46222-5932, USA

Hauck, Frederick H (Rick) (Astronaut)
2 Redwood Ln
Falmouth, ME 04105-1368, USA

Hauck, Frederick H "'Rick"' Captain (Astronaut)
2 Redwood Ln
Falmouth, ME 04105-1368, USA

Hauck, Tim (Athlete, Football Player)
460 Great Circle Rd
Nashville, TN 37228-1404, USA

Haudenschild, Jack (Race Car Driver)
Wildchild Designs
628 Maple St.
Vermillion, OH 44089, USA

Hauer, Brett (Athlete, Hockey Player)
2921 Branch St
Duluth, MN 55812-2340, USA

Hauer, Rutger (Actor)
c/o Joan Hyler *Hyler Management*
20 Ocean Park Blvd Unit 25
Santa Monica, CA 90405-3590, USA

Hauerwas, Stanley (Religious Leader)
Duke University
Divinity School
Durham, NC 27706, USA

Haughey, Chris (Athlete, Baseball Player)
4117 Stevenson Blvd Apt 283
Fremont, CA 94538-5001, USA

Haught, Gary (Athlete, Baseball Player)
16445 Lynn St
Choctaw, OK 73020-7926, USA

Haun, Darla (Actor)
300 S Raymond Ave Ste 11
Pasadena, CA 91105-2639, USA

Haun, Lindsey (Actor)
c/o Claudine Vacca *The House of Representatives*
3118 Wilshire Blvd Ste D
Santa Monica, CA 90403-2345, USA

Hauschka, Steven (Athlete, Football Player)
c/o Neil Cornrich *NC Sports, LLC*
best to contact via email
Columbus, OH 43201, USA

Hauser, Art (Athlete, Football Player)
2816 Walsh Rd
Cincinnati, OH 45208-3426, USA

Hauser, Cole (Actor)
c/o Jason Weinberg *Untitled Entertainment*
350 S Beverly Dr Ste 200
Beverly Hills, CA 90212-4819, USA

Hauser, Erich (Artist)
Saline 36
Rottweil 78628, GERMANY

Hauser, Wings (Actor)
9450 Chivers Ave
Sun Valley, CA 91352-2654, USA

Hausman, Tom (Athlete, Baseball Player)
3165 Westfield Cir
Las Vegas, NV 89121-3332, USA

Hauss, Lenard M (Len) (Athlete, Football Player)
110 Portmere Dr
Jesup, GA 31546-4738, USA

Havelid, Niclas (Athlete, Hockey Player)
Prestige Hocey Group
PO Box 129
Point Roberts, WA 98281-0129, USA

Haven, Annette (Actor)
PO Box 1244
Sausalito, CA 94966-1244, USA

Haven, James (Actor)
c/o Staff Member *Saffron Management*
9171 Wilshire Blvd Ste 441
Beverly Hills, CA 90210-5516, USA

Havens, Brad (Athlete, Baseball Player)
3227 Eden Trl
Brighton, MI 48114-9185, USA

Havens, Frank B (Athlete)
PO Box 221
Belle Haven, VA 23306-0221, USA

Haverdink, Kevin (Athlete, Football Player)
15844 Prairie Ronde Rd
Schoolcraft, MI 49087-9124, USA

Havers, Nigel (Actor)
c/o John Crosby *John Crosby Management*
1357 N Spaulding Ave
Los Angeles, CA 90046-4009, USA

Havig, Dennis (Athlete, Football Player)
5964 Old Stilesboro Rd NW
Acworth, GA 30101-4304, USA

Havili, Stanley (Athlete, Football Player)

Havins, Alexa (Actor)
c/o Rhonda Price *Gersh*
41 Madison Ave Ste 3301
New York, NY 10010-2210, USA

Havlicek, John (Athlete, Basketball Player)
Naismith Basketball Hall of Fame
1150 W Columbus Ave
Springfield, MA 01105-2502, USA

Havlish, Jean (Athlete, Baseball Player, Commentator)
PO Box 122
Rockville, MN 56369-0122, USA

Havok, Davey (Musician)
5842 Mendocino Ave
Oakland, CA 94618-1809, USA

Havrilak, Sam (Athlete, Football Player)
1 Trojan Horse Dr
Phoenix, MD 21131-1345, USA

Hawass, Zahi (Writer)
Supreme Council of Antiquities
3 Al-Adel Bakr St
Zamalek, Cairo, EGYPT

Hawblitzel, Ryan (Athlete, Baseball Player)
4 Bigleaf Ct
Homosassa, FL 34446-4956, USA

Hawerchuck, Dale (Athlete, Hockey Player)
Grande Farms
RR 5
LCD Main
Orangeville, ON L9W 2Z2, Canada

Hawerchuk, Dale (Athlete, Hockey Player)
Grande Farms RR 5 LCD Main
Orangeville, ON L9W 2Z2, CANADA

Hawes, Roy (Athlete, Baseball Player)
79 Crestwood Dr
Ringgold, GA 30736-3260, USA

Hawes, Steve (Athlete, Basketball Player)
400 W Highland Dr
Seattle, WA 98119-3532, USA

Hawgood, Greg (Athlete, Hockey Player)
1230 Saint Andrews Way
Kamloops, BC V1S 1S6, Canada

Hawk, Abigail (Actor)
c/o Rosella Olson *Rosella Olson Management*
319 W 105th St Apt 1F
New York, NY 10025-9112, USA

Hawk, AJ (Athlete, Football Player)
4349 Windemer Ln
Oneida, WI 54155-8648, USA

Hawk, Ronni (Actor)
c/o Emily Urbani *Osbrink Talent Agency*
4343 Lankershim Blvd # 100
North Hollywood, CA 91602-2705, USA

Hawk, Tony (Actor, Athlete, Skateboarder)
Tony Hawk Inc
1611A S Melrose Dr # 362
Vista, CA 92081-5471, USA

Hawke, Ethan (Actor)
c/o Mara Buxbaum *ID Public Relations*
7060 Hollywood Blvd Fl 8th
Los Angeles, CA 90028-6021, USA

Hawke, Jason (Adult Film Star)
c/o Staff Member *Diva Central Inc*
7510 W Sunset Blvd # 1445
Los Angeles, CA 90046-3408, USA

Hawke, Maya (Actor)
c/o Annett Wolf *Wolf-Kasteler Public Relations*
6255 W Sunset Blvd Ste 1111
Los Angeles, CA 90028-7426, USA

Hawker, Kari (Actor)
c/o Staff Member *Talent Management Group, Inc.*
339 E 3900 S Ste 210
Salt Lake City, UT 84107-1691, USA

Hawkes, John (Actor)
c/o Karen Samfilippo *IMPR*
1158 26th St # 548
Santa Monica, CA 90403-4698, USA

Hawking, Lucy (Writer)
c/o Staff Member *Simon & Schuster*
1230 Avenue of the Americas Fl CONC1
New York, NY 10020-1586, USA

Hawkins, Alex (Athlete, Football Player)
215 Bonanza Rd
Denmark, SC 29042-9311, USA

Hawkins, Andy (Athlete, Baseball Player)
PO Box 90111
Arlington, TX 76004-3111, USA

Hawkins, Artrell (Athlete, Football Player)
12166 Peak Dr
Cincinnati, OH 45246-1400, USA

Hawkins, Barbara (Music Group)
Superstars Unlimited
PO Box 371371
Las Vegas, NV 89137-1371, USA

Hawkins, Benjamin C (Ben) (Athlete, Football Player)
703 15th Ave
Belmar, NJ 07719-2711, USA

Hawkins, Bill (Athlete, Football Player)
19183 SE Jupiter River Dr
Jupiter, FL 33458-1023, USA

Hawkins, Brad (Actor)
5815 W Sunset Blvd Ste 206
Los Angeles, CA 90028-6481, USA

Hawkins, Corey (Actor)
c/o Christine Tripicchio *Shelter PR*
5670 Wilshire Blvd Ste 1200
Los Angeles, CA 90036-5621, USA

Hawkins, Corey (Athlete, Basketball Player)
c/o Chris Emens *Octagon (AZ)*
16055 N Dial Blvd Ste 8
Scottsdale, AZ 85260-1642, USA

Hawkins, Courtney (Athlete, Football Player)
8305 Gale Rd
Goodrich, MI 48438-9436, USA

Hawkins, Dan (Musician)
c/o Sue Whitehouse *Whitehouse Management*
PO Box 43829
London NW6 3PJ, UNITED KINGDOM

Hawkins, Frank (Athlete, Football Player)
2300 Alta Dr
Las Vegas, NV 89107-4616, USA

Hawkins, Hersey (Athlete, Basketball Player, Olympic Athlete)
18168 W Narramore Rd
Goodyear, AZ 85338-5055, USA

Hawkins, Jennifer (Actor, Beauty Pageant Winner)
c/o Staff Member *Ovations*
P.O. Box 1337
Rozelle, NSW 02039, Australia

Hawkins, Justin (Musician)
Must Destroy Music
PO Box 40008
London N6 5XT, UNITED KINGDOM

Hawkins, Laroyce (Actor)
c/o Staff Member *Stewart Talent Agency (Chicago)*
58 W Huron St
Chicago, IL 60654-3806, USA

Hawkins, Latroy (Athlete, Baseball Player)
3521 Amberwood Ln
Prosper, TX 75078-9126, USA

Hawkins, Mike (Athlete, Football Player)
2320 Bordeaux Dr
Bay City, TX 77414-8512, USA

Hawkins, Paula (Writer)
c/o Lizzy Kremer *David Higham Associates*
5-8 Lower John St
Golden Square
London W1F 9HA, UNITED KINGDOM

Hawkins, Rip (Athlete, Football Player)
100 Tower Carlile Rd
Devils Tower, WY 82714, USA

Hawkins, Ronnie (Music Group)
Agency Group Ltd
59 Berkeley St
Toronto, ON M5A 2W5, CANADA

Hawkins, Rosa (Music Group)
Superstars Unlimited
PO Box 371371
Las Vegas, NV 89137-1371, USA

Hawkins, Sally (Actor)
c/o John Grant *Conway van Gelder Grant*
8-12 Broadwick St
London W1F 8HW, UNITED KINGDOM

Hawkins, Sophie B (Music Group, Musician, Songwriter, Writer)
Trumpet Swan Productions
520 Washington Blvd #337
Marina Del Rey, CA 90292, USA

Hawkins, Todd (Athlete, Hockey Player)
300 Lamoreaux Dr
Elk Rapids, MI 49629-9737, USA

Hawkins, Wayne (Athlete, Football Player)
72750 Country Club Dr Apt 238
Rancho Mirage, CA 92270-4096, USA

Hawkins, Wynn (Athlete, Baseball Player)
5326 Cottage Dr
Cortland, OH 44410-9521, USA

Hawkinson, Tanner (Athlete, Football Player)

Hawkinson, Tim (Artist)
Ace Gallery
3435 Wilshire Blvd Ste 990
Los Angeles, CA 90010-1998, USA

Hawksworth, Blake (Athlete, Baseball Player)
24641 Julie Ave
Laguna Hills, CA 92653-4330, USA

Hawley, Frank (Race Car Driver)
Frank Hawley Drag Racing School
County Road 225
Gainesville, FL 32609, USA

Hawley, Joe (Athlete, Football Player)
c/o Harold C Lewis *National Sports Agency*
12181 Prichard Farm Rd
Maryland Heights, MO 63043-4203, USA

Hawley, Richard (Musician)
c/o Staff Member *Alias Production*
22, Rue Douai
Paris F-75009, France

Hawley, Steven (Astronaut)
University of Kansas
3303 Calvin Dr
Lawrence, KS 66049-9003, USA

Hawn, Goldie (Actor, Director, Producer)
c/o Jason Weinberg *Untitled Entertainment*
350 S Beverly Dr Ste 200
Beverly Hills, CA 90212-4819, USA

Haworth, Alan (Athlete, Hockey Player)
2614 Rue de la Commune
Drummondville, QC J2B 0B5, Canada

Haworth, Gord (Athlete, Hockey Player)
2780 Rue Lalancette
Drummondville, QC J2B 3X9, CANADA

Hawpe, Brad (Athlete, Baseball Player)
2001 Blake St
Denver, CO 80205-2060, USA

Hawryliw, Neil (Athlete, Hockey Player)
1366 Seminole Rd
Norton Shores, MI 49441-4349, Canada

Hawthorne, David (Athlete, Football Player)

Hawthorne, Duane (Athlete, Football Player)
11481 Pineview Crossing Dr
Maryland Heights, MO 63043-5103, USA

Hawthorne, Greg (Athlete, Football Player)
1428 E Jefferson Ave
Fort Worth, TX 76104-5714, USA

Hax, Carolyn (Writer)
Washington Post
Editorial Dept
1150 15th St NW
Washington, DC 20071-0001, USA

Hay, Bill (Athlete, Hockey Player)
4020 Crestview Rd SW
Calgary, AB T2T 2L4, Canada

Hay, Colin (Music Group)
TPA
PO Box 125
Round Corner, NSW 02158, AUSTRALIA

Hay, Don (Athlete, Hockey Player)
100 Renfrew St N
Attn Coaching Staff Vancouver Giants
Vancouver, BC V5K 3N7, Canada

Hayashida, Erica (Athlete, Golfer)
1470 NW 107th Ave Ste R
Sweetwater, FL 33172-2735, USA

Haydel, Hal (Athlete, Baseball Player)
304 Lynwood Dr
Houma, LA 70360-6228, USA

Hayden, Aaron (Athlete, Football Player)
504 Stone Oaks Cv
Collierville, TN 38017-9124, USA

Hayden, D.J. (Athlete, Football Player)

Hayden, Gene (Athlete, Baseball Player)
424 W Locust St
Lodi, CA 95240-2018, USA

Hayden, John (Race Car Driver)
Hayden Enterprises
107 Flat Ridge Rd
Goodlettsville, TN 37072-8509, USA

Hayden, Leo (Athlete, Football Player)
33 Preston Rd
Columbus, OH 43209-1652, USA

Hayden, Linda (Actor)
Michael Ladkin Mgmt
1 Duchess St #1
London W1N 3DE, UNITED KINGDOM (UK)

Hayden, Mary Elise (Actor)

Hayden, Michael (Actor)
H W A Talent
3500 W Olive Ave Ste 1400
Burbank, CA 91505-5512, USA

Hayden, Michael (Politician)
5809 Sagamore Ct
Lawrence, KS 66047-2071, USA

Hayden, Nick (Athlete, Football Player)
c/o Brad Leshnock *BTI Sports Advisors*
615 South Blvd Apt C
Oak Park, IL 60302-4606, USA

Hayden, Tom (Politician)
152 Wadsworth Ave
Santa Monica, CA 90405-3510, USA

Haydon, Jones Ann (Tennis Player)
85 Westerfield Road
Edgloaston
Birmingham 15, UNITED KINGDOM (UK)

Haye, David (Athlete, Boxer)
Hayemaker Boxing
57 Jackson Rd
Bromley
Kent BR2 8NT, UK

Hayek, Peter (Athlete, Hockey Player)
4367 Colorado Ave N
Minneapolis, MN 55422-1018, USA

Hayek, Salma (Actor, Model, Producer)
c/o Evelyn O'Neill *Management 360*
9111 Wilshire Blvd
Beverly Hills, CA 90210-5508, USA

Hayers, Sidney A (Director)
John Redway
5 Denmark St
London WC2H 8LP, UNITED KINGDOM (UK)

Hayes, Amy (Model, Sportscaster)
641 N Hardin Hts
Harrodsburg, KY 40330-9234, USA

Hayes, Ben (Athlete, Baseball Player)
3501 10th St NE
Saint Petersburg, FL 33704-1605, USA

Hayes, Bill (Athlete, Baseball Player)
24 Willie Mays Plz
San Francisco, CA 94107-2134, USA

Hayes, Bill (Actor)
4528 Beck Ave
North Hollywood, CA 91602-1904, USA

Hayes, Billie (Athlete, Football Player)
2876 Avalon St
Riverside, CA 92509-2013, USA

Hayes, Charlie (Athlete, Baseball Player)
22503 Holly Creek Trl
Tomball, TX 77377-3656, USA

Hayes, Chris (Race Car Driver)
R&H Motorsports
10134 6th St Ste G
Rancho Cucamonga, CA 91730-5856, USA

Hayes, Darren (Music Group, Musician)
PO Box 193
Sabattus, ME 04280-0193, AUSTRALIA

Hayes, Elvin (Athlete, Basketball Player)
14 Canaveral Creek Ln
Sugar Land, TX 77479-2724, USA

Hayes, Erinn (Actor)
c/o David Sweeney *Sweeney Entertainment*
1601 Vine St # 6
Los Angeles, CA 90028-8802, USA

Hayes, Gemma (Musician)
c/o Staff Member *Paradigm (Monterey)*
404 W Franklin St
Monterey, CA 93940-2303, USA

Hayes, Gerald (Athlete, Football Player)
PO Box 94917
Phoenix, AZ 85070-4917, USA

Hayes, Hana (Actor)
c/o Alexandra Heller *Advantage PR*
3900 W Alameda Ave Ste 1200
Burbank, CA 91505-4317, USA

Hayes, Hunter (Musician)
c/o Rodney Essig *Creative Artists Agency (CAA)*
401 Commerce St PH
Nashville, TN 37219-2516, USA

Hayes, Jarvis (Basketball Player)
Washington Wizards
MCI Center 601 F St NW
Washington, DC 30326-1240, USA

Hayes, Jim (Athlete, Basketball Player)
31 Curley St
Long Beach, NY 11561-2705, USA

Hayes, Jonathan (Athlete, Football Player)
1231 Obannon Creek Ln
Loveland, OH 45140-6027, USA

Hayes, J P (Athlete, Golfer)
740 Camino Real Ave
El Paso, TX 79922-2010, USA

Hayes, Larry (Athlete, Football Player)
4215 Harding Pike Apt 759
Nashville, TN 37205-2028, USA

Hayes, Louis S (Music Group, Musician)
PO Box 482
Desoto, TX 75123-0482, USA

Hayes, Mark (Athlete, Golfer)
1014 Saint Andrews Dr
Edmond, OK 73025-2645, USA

Hayes, Mercury (Athlete, Football Player)
138 W Whitney St
Houston, TX 77018-4515, USA

Hayes, Patty (Athlete, Golfer)
3436 Sipsey St
The Villages, FL 32162-6666, USA

Hayes, Ray (Athlete, Football Player)
5000 Laur Rd
North Branch, MI 48461-9782, USA

Hayes, Reggie (Actor)
c/o Staff Member *TalentWorks*
3500 W Olive Ave Ste 1400
Burbank, CA 91505-5512, USA

Hayes, Rudy (Athlete, Football Player)
354 Red Hill Rd
Pickens, SC 29671-9188, USA

Hayes, Sean (Actor)
c/o Bria Schreiber *Viewpoint Inc*
8820 Wilshire Blvd Ste 220
Beverly Hills, CA 90211-2622, USA

Hayes, Steve (Athlete, Basketball Player)
1630 Mercoal Dr
Spring, TX 77386-1626, USA

Hayes, Von (Athlete, Baseball Player)
435 E Illinois Rd
Lake Forest, IL 60045-2354, USA

Hayes, Wade (Musician)
c/o Dale Morris *Morris Artists Management*
2001 Blair Blvd
Nashville, TN 37212-5007, USA

Hayes, Wendell (Athlete, Football Player)
1935 E 30th St Apt 23
Oakland, CA 94606-3485, USA

Hayes, William (Athlete, Football Player)

Haygood, Herb (Athlete, Football Player)
1735 Central Ave
Sarasota, FL 34234-8410, USA

Hayhoe, Bill (Athlete, Football Player)
5146 Santa Anita Dr
Sparks, NV 89436-0801, USA

Hayhurst, Dirk (Athlete, Baseball Player)
1534 Woodlake Blvd
Stow, OH 44224-2456, USA

Haylett, Alice (Athlete, Baseball Player)
243 Pearl Ave
Lakeland, FL 33815-3737, USA

Hayman, Conway (Athlete, Football Player)
9613 Rustic Gate Rd
La Porte, TX 77571-3986, USA

Hayman, David (Actor, Director)
c/o Staff Member *Independent Talent Group*
40 Whitfield St
London W1T 2RH, UNITED KINGDOM

Hayman, James (Director)
c/o Staff Member *Creative Artists Agency (CAA)*
2000 Avenue of the Stars Ste 100
Los Angeles, CA 90067-4705, USA

Haymond, Alvin (Athlete, Football Player)
2857 Mantis Dr
San Jose, CA 95148-2136, USA

Haynes, Abner (Athlete, Football Player)
1950 FM 489
Oakwood, TX 75855-8409, USA

Haynes, Betsy (Writer)
5973 Sandhill Cir
The Colony, TX 75056-3678, USA

Haynes, Colton (Actor)
c/o Eric Podwall *Podwall Entertainment*
710 N Orlando Ave Apt 203
Loft 203
Los Angeles, CA 90069-5549, USA

Haynes, Heath (Athlete, Baseball Player)
1525 S Carmelina Ave
Los Angeles, CA 90025-3621, USA

Haynes, Jimmy (Athlete, Baseball Player)
516 Riverside Dr
Lagrange, GA 30240-9633, USA

Haynes, Mark (Athlete, Football Player)
220 S Oneida St
Denver, CO 80230-6951, USA

Haynes, Michael (Athlete, Football Player)
2375 Saddlesprings Dr
Alpharetta, GA 30004-3254, USA

Haynes, Michael (Athlete, Football Player)
1580 Arbour Glenn Dr
Lawrenceville, GA 30043-7154, USA

Haynes, Mike (Athlete, Football Player)
8141 Santaluz Village Gm n S
San Diego, CA 92127-2518, USA

Haynes, Mike (Athlete, Football Player)
8 Morningside Ln
Westport, CT 06880-3815, USA

Haynes, Nathan (Athlete, Baseball Player)
609 N Ventura St Apt 4
Anaheim, CA 92801-3740, USA

Haynes, Reggie (Athlete, Football Player)
2324 Antiqua Ct
Reston, VA 20191-1706, USA

Haynes, Roy O (Musician)
Ted Kurland
173 Brighton Ave
Boston, MA 02134-2003, USA

Haynes, Todd (Director)
c/o Staff Member *Creative Artists Agency (CAA)*
2000 Avenue of the Stars Ste 100
Los Angeles, CA 90067-4705, USA

Haynes, Verron (Athlete, Football Player)
2500 Northwinds Pkwy Ste 275
Alpharetta, GA 30009-2265, USA

Haynes, Warren (Musician)
c/o Staff Member *Paradigm (Monterey)*
404 W Franklin St
Monterey, CA 93940-2303, USA

Haynes Jr, Cornell (Nelly) (Musician)
c/o Dana Sims *ICM Partners*
10250 Constellation Blvd Fl 7
Los Angeles, CA 90067-6207, USA

Haynesworth, Albert (Athlete, Football Player)
c/o Chad Speck *Allegiant Athletic Agency*
35 Market Sq Ste 201
Knoxville, TN 37902-1420, USA

Haynie, Jim (Actor)
c/o Geneva Bray *GVA Talent Agency Inc*
193 N Robertson Blvd
Beverly Hills, CA 90211-2103, USA

Haynie, Sandra (Athlete, Golfer)
6 Brookfield Ct
Roanoke, TX 76262-5468, USA

Hays, Harold (Athlete, Football Player)
5612 Wedgefield Rd
Granbury, TX 76049-4413, USA

Hays, Kathryn (Actor)

Hays, Robert (Actor)
919 Victoria Ave
Venice, CA 90291-3933, USA

Haysbert, Dennis (Actor)
c/o Marianna Shafran *Shafran PR*
195 S Beverly Dr Ste 414
Beverly Hills, CA 90212-3044, USA

Hayter, David (Writer)
c/o Staff Member *Kaplan/Perrone Entertainment*
9171 Wilshire Blvd Ste 350
Beverly Hills, CA 90210-5523, USA

Hayward, Adam (Athlete, Football Player)
c/o Derrick Fox *Derrick Fox Management*
Prefers to be contacted by telephone
CA, USA

Hayward, Brian (Athlete, Hockey Player)
2695 E Katella Ave
Attn Broadcast Dept
Anaheim, CA 92806-5904, USA

Hayward, Brian (Athlete, Hockey Player)
7648 E Hollow Oak Rd
Anaheim, CA 92808-1425, USA

Hayward, Casey (Athlete, Football Player)
c/o Scott Smith *XAM Sports*
3509 Ice Age Dr
Madison, WI 53719-5409, USA

Hayward, Gordon (Athlete, Baseball Player)
76 Brandywine Ct
Brownsburg, IN 46112-1076, U S A

Hayward, Hurley (Race Car Driver)
1445 Ponte Vedra Blvd
Ponte Vedra Beach, FL 32082-4505, USA

Hayward, Justin (Musician)
The Threshold Record Co Ltd
53 High St
Cobham, Surrey KT11 3DP, UNITED KINGDOM (UK)

Hayward, Kara (Actor)
c/o Christine Tripicchio *Shelter PR*
5670 Wilshire Blvd Ste 1200
Los Angeles, CA 90036-5621, USA

Hayward, Lazar (Athlete, Basketball Player)
c/o Sam Goldfelder *Excel Sports Management (LA)*
9665 Wilshire Blvd Ste 500
Beverly Hills, CA 90212-2312, USA

Hayward, Ray (Athlete, Baseball Player)
5113 Deerhurst Dr
Norman, OK 73072-3882, USA

Hayward, Reggie (Athlete, Football Player)

Haywood, Alfred (Athlete, Football Player)
69 Waters Edge Way
Fayetteville, GA 30215-8509, USA

Haywood, Bill (Athlete, Baseball Player)
867 Villa Dr
North Myrtle Beach, SC 29582-2575, USA

Haywood, Spencer (Athlete, Basketball Player, Olympic Athlete)
Spencer Haywood Foundation
4300 Val Dechiana Ave
Las Vegas, NV 89141-4258, USA

Hayworth, Nan (Congressman, Politician)
1440 Longworth Hob
Washington, DC 20515-0307, USA

Hayworth, Tracy (Athlete, Football Player)
155 Knights Church Rd
Decherd, TN 37324-3279, USA

Hazanavicius, Michael (Director)
c/o Maha Dakhil *Creative Artists Agency (CAA)*
2000 Avenue of the Stars Ste 100
Los Angeles, CA 90067-4705, USA

Haze, Jonathan (Actor)
3636 Woodhill Canyon Rd
Studio City, CA 91604-3658, USA

Haze, Scott (Actor)
c/o Jamie Harhay Skinner *Baker Winokur Ryder Public Relations*
9100 Wilshire Blvd
W Tower #500
Beverly Hills, CA 90212-3415, USA

Hazell, Keeley (Actor)
98 De Beauvoir Rd
London N1 4EN, United Kingdom

Hazelton, Major (Athlete, Football Player)
6803 S Crandon Ave # 3
Chicago, IL 60649-1210, USA

Hazen, Maya (Actor)
c/o Adam Griffin *LINK Entertainment*
11872 La Grange Ave
Los Angeles, CA 90025-5282, USA

Hazewood, Drungo (Athlete, Baseball Player)
1716 X St
Sacramento, CA 95818-2335, USA

Haziza, Shlomi (Artist)
H Studio
8640 Tamarack Ave
Sun Valley, CA 91352-2504, USA

Hazzard, Johnny (Adult Film Star)
c/o Staff Member *Diva Central Inc*
7510 W Sunset Blvd # 1445
Los Angeles, CA 90046-3408, USA

Hazzard, Shirley (Writer)
200 E 66th St
New York, NY 10065-9175, USA

H. Bishop, Timothy (Congressman, Politician)
306 Cannon Hob
Washington, DC 20515-0303, USA

Head, Anthony (Actor)
Gordon & French
12-13 Poland St
London W1F 8QB, ENGLAND

Head, Anthony Stewart (Actor)

Head, Don (Athlete, Hockey Player)
15240 NE Knott St
Portland, OR 97230-5280, USA

Head, Emily (Actor)
c/o Kate Bryden *Gordon and French*
12-13 Poland St
London W1F 8QB, UNITED KINGDOM (UK)

Head, John (Baseball Player)
Kansas City Monarchs
12677 Tremblewood Dr
Florissant, MO 63033-4729, USA

Head, Murray (Actor, Musician)
c/o Staff Member *Zelig Films*
57 rue Reaumur
Paris 75002, France

Head, Roy (Musician)
Texas Sounds Entertainment
2317 Pecan St
Dickinson, TX 77539-4949, USA

Headden, Susan M (Journalist)
Indianapolis Star
130 S Meridian St
Editorial Dept
Indianapolis, IN 46225-1046, USA

Head East (Music Group)
c/o John Domagall *ARM Entertainment*
1257 Arcade St
Saint Paul, MN 55106-2022, USA

Headen, Andy (Athlete, Football Player)
PO Box 821
Liberty, NC 27298-0821, USA

Headey, Lena (Actor)
2 Hillbury Rd
Unit 2
London SW17 8JT, UNITED KINGDOM

Headley, Chase (Athlete, Baseball Player)
1128 Re2alitv Wav
Knoxville, TN 37923-6799, USA

Headley, Heather (Actor, Musician)
40 W 56th St Apt 5F
New York, NY 10019-3813, USA

Headley, Shari (Actor)
11226 178th St
Jamaica, NY 11433-4118, USA

Headon, Topper (Musician)
c/o Staff Member *Premier Talent*
3 E 54th St # 1100
New York, NY 10022-3108, USA

Heafner, Vance (Athlete, Golfer)
6212 Godfrey Dr
Raleigh, NC 27612-6717, USA

Heald, Anthony (Actor)
Endeavor Talent Agency
9701 Wilshire Blvd Ste 1000
Beverly Hills, CA 90212-2010, USA

Healey, Mary (Actor)
c/o Staff Member *Rabbit Vocal Management*
27 Poland St
Fl 3
London W1F 8QW, UNITED KINGDOM

Healey, Rich (Athlete, Hockey Player)
1085 Carter Crest Rd NW
Edmonton, AB T6R 2N2, Canada

Healy, Chip (Football Player)
1903 Lathan Ct
Nashville, TN 37207-4812, USA

Healy, Don (Athlete, Football Player)
3427 Boca Ciega Dr
Naples, FL 34112-6809, USA

Healy, Fran (Athlete, Baseball Player)
1 Primrose Ln
Holyoke, MA 01040-1523, USA

Healy, Fran (Magician)
2267 El Contento Dr
Los Angeles, CA 90068-2813, USA

Healy, Glenn (Athlete, Hockey Player)
PO Box 500 Stn A
Attn: Hockey Night in Canada CBC TV
Toronto, ON M5W 1E6, Canada

Healy, Jane E (Journalist)
Orlando Sentinel
633 N Orange Ave Lbby
Editrial Dept
Orlando, FL 32801-1349, USA

Healy, Matthew L. (Matt) (Writer)
c/o Simon Millar *Rumble Media*
1620 Broadway Ste C
Santa Monica, CA 90404-2777, USA

Healy, Pat (Actor)
c/o Adam Kersh *Brigade Marketing*
116 W 23rd St Fl 5
New York, NY 10011-2599, USA

Heames, Darin (Actor)
c/o Andrew Stawiarski *ADS Management*
269 S Beverly Dr Ste 441
Beverly Hills, CA 90212-3851, USA

Heaney, Brian (Athlete, Basketball Player)
153 Spinnaker Dr
Halifax, NS B3N 3C3, Canada

Heap, Imogen (Musician)
The Round House
Broxhill Rd
Havering-atte-Bower
Romford Essex RM4 1QH, UNITED KINGDOM

Heap, Todd (Athlete, Football Player)
4320 N Essex Cir
Mesa, AZ 85207-7167, USA

Heaphy, Shawn (Athlete, Hockey Player)
73 Lakeview Dr
Charlton, MA 01507-5429, USA

Heard, Amber (Actor)
c/o Jodi Gottlieb *Independent Public Relations*
9601 Wilshire Blvd Ste 750
Beverly Hills, CA 90210-5228, USA

Heard, Garfield (Athlete, Basketball Player)
1735 Peachtree St NE Unit 133
Atlanta, GA 30309-7004, USA

Heard, Jerry (Athlete, Golfer)
293 Talowah Rd
Purvis, MS 39475-5047, USA

Heard Jr, Herman (Athlete, Football Player)

Hearn, Ed (Athlete, Baseball Player)
5737 Theden St
Shawnee, KS 66218-9199, USA

Hearn, George (Actor, Music Group)
211 S Beverly Dr # 211
Beverly Hills, CA 90212-3807, USA

Hearn, J Woodrow (Religious Leader)
United Methodist Church
PO Box 320
Nashville, TN 37202-0320, USA

Hearn, Kevin (Musician)
c/o Staff Member *Six Shooter Management*
98038-970 Queen St E
Toronto, ON M4M 1J8, Canada

Hearn, Tom (Golfer)
Links Mmg
5068 W Plano Pkwy Ste 256
Plano, TX 75093-4441, USA

Hearne, Bill (Music Group, Musician)
Class Act Entertainment
PO Box 160236
Nashville, TN 37216-0236, USA

Hearns, Shane (Athlete, Baseball Player, Olympic Athlete)
8165 Brians Ct
Lambertville, MI 48144-9583, USA

Hearns, Tommy (Boxer)
c/o Staff Member *National Organization of Professional Athletes*
1806 Watermere Ln
Windermere, FL 34786-6121, USA

Hearron, Jeff (Athlete, Baseball Player)
5820 Hill Rd
Powder Springs, GA 30127-4041, USA

Hearst, Amanda Randolph (Model)
c/o Keya Morgan *Keya Morgan Productions*
PO Box 18447
Beverly Hills, CA 90209-4447, USA

Hearst, Garrison (Athlete, Football Player)
3753 Augusta Hwy
Lincolnton, GA 30817-4402, USA

Hearst, Lydia (Model)
c/o Oren Segal *Management Production Entertainment (MPE)*
9229 W Sunset Blvd Ste 301
W Hollywood, CA 90069-3417, USA

Hearst, Patricia (Writer)
110 5th St
San Francisco, CA 94103-2918

Hearst, Patricia (Patty) (Actor)
110 5th St
San Francisco, CA 94103-2918, USA

Hearst, Rick (Actor)
Stone Manners
6500 Wilshire Blvd # 550
Los Angeles, CA 90048-4920, USA

Heart (Musician)
c/o Jeff Frasco *Creative Artists Agency (CAA)*
2000 Avenue of the Stars Ste 100
Los Angeles, CA 90067-4705, USA

Heaslip, Mark (Athlete, Hockey Player)
11 Leland Ct
Chevy Chase, MD 20815-4906, USA

Heater, Don (Athlete, Football Player)
8704 Manchester Ave
Kansas City, MO 64138-4167, USA

Heater, Larry (Athlete, Football Player)
3711 Royal Fern Cir
Las Vegas, NV 89115-1257, USA

Heath, Albert (Tootie) (Music Group, Musician)
Ted Kurland
173 Brighton Ave
Boston, MA 02134-2003, USA

Heath, Bill (Athlete, Baseball Player)
1626 Lake Charlotte Ln
Richmond, TX 77406-7016, USA

Heath, Brandon (Musician)
c/o Staff Member *Creative Trust, Inc.*
5141 Virginia Way Ste 320
Brentwood, TN 37027-2317, USA

Heath, Carey (Race Car Driver)
Carey Heath Motorsports
12 Worster Rd.
Eliot, ME 03903, USA

Heath, Jeff (Athlete, Football Player)
c/o Derrick Fox *Derrick Fox Management*
Prefers to be contacted by telephone
CA, USA

Heath, Kelly (Athlete, Baseball Player)
2936 Mulberry Ln Unit C
Greenville, NC 27858-5741, USA

Heath, Mike (Athlete, Baseball Player)
2107 Timothy Ter
Valrico, FL 33594-3145, USA

Heath, Rodney (Athlete, Football Player)
6673 Red Pine Dr
Liberty Township, OH 45044-8765, USA

Heath, Tommy (Musician)
c/o JD Sobol *Almond Talent Management*
8217 Beverly Blvd Ste 8
W Hollywood, CA 90048-4534, USA

Heathcock, Jeff (Athlete, Baseball Player)
24962 Calle Vecindad
Lake Forest, CA 92630-2105, USA

Heathcote, Bella (Actor)
c/o Ame VanIden *VanIden Public Relations*
4070 Wilson Pike
Franklin, TN 37067-8126, USA

Heathcott, Mike (Athlete, Baseball Player)
12445 E Saddlehorn Trl
Scottsdale, AZ 85259-6125, USA

Heatherly, Eric (Actor)
c/o Staff Member *The Bazel Group Inc*
4636 Lebanon Pike # 308
Hermitage, TN 37076-1316, USA

Heatherton, Erin (Actor)
c/o Maja Chiesi *IMG Models (NY)*
304 Park Ave S PH N
New York, NY 10010-4303, USA

Heatherton, Joey (Actor)

Heath-Stubbs, John F A (Writer)
22 Artesian Road
London W2 5AR, UNITED KINGDOM (UK)

Heaton, Charlie (Actor)
c/o Ruth Bernstein *Viewpoint Inc*
8820 Wilshire Blvd Ste 220
Beverly Hills, CA 90211-2622, USA

Heaton, Neal (Athlete, Baseball Player)
3 Nursery Ct
East Patchogue, NY 11772-6152, USA

Heaton, Patricia (Actor)
c/o Staff Member *FourBoys Films*
4000 Warner Blvd
Warner Bros. Studios
Burbank, CA 91522-0001, USA

Heaver, Paul (Athlete, Hockey Player)
20 Raiford St
Aurora, ON L4G 6J2, Canada

Heaverlo, Dave (Athlete, Baseball Player)
3720 W Lakeshore Dr
Moses Lake, WA 98837-3003, USA

Hebenton, Clay (Athlete, Hockey Player)
11040 E Singletree Trl
Dewey, AZ 86327-5414, USA

Hebert, Ashley (Reality Star)
University Of Pennsylvania
240 S 40th St Ste 1
School of Dental Medicine
Philadelphia, PA 19104-6030, USA

Hebert, Austin (Actor)
c/o Marni Rosenzweig *The Rosenzweig Group*
8840 Wilshire Blvd # 111
Beverly Hills, CA 90211-2606, USA

Hebert, Bobby (Athlete, Football Player)
530 Avala Ct
Alpharetta, GA 30022-5576, USA

Hebert, Bud (Athlete, Football Player)
PO Box 250342
Plano, TX 75025-0342, USA

Hebert, Guy (Athlete, Hockey Player, Olympic Athlete)
8 Gleneagles Dr
Newport Beach, CA 92660-4296, USA

Hebert, Johnny (Race Car Driver)
Team Lotus
Kettering Hamm Hall
Wymondham
Norfolk NR18 7HW, UNITED KINGDOM (UK)

Hebert, Ken (Athlete, Football Player)
7001 Mount Sharp Rd
Wimberley, TX 78676-4245, USA

Hebner, Rich (Richie) (Athlete, Baseball Player)
6 Tetreault Dr
Walpole, MA 02081-2224, USA

Hebron, Vaughn (Athlete, Football Player)
154 Madison Ct
Southampton, PA 18966-2728, USA

Hebson, Bryan (Athlete, Baseball Player)
1151 Fairmont Ln
Auburn, AL 36830-2105, USA

Heche, Anne (Actor)
c/o Jason Weinberg *Untitled Entertainment*
350 S Beverly Dr Ste 200
Beverly Hills, CA 90212-4819, USA

Hecht, Albie (Producer, Writer)
c/o Staff Member *Spike TV*
1515 Broadway
New York, NY 10036-8901, USA

Hecht, Jessica (Actor)
c/o Staff Member *Innovative Artists*
1505 10th St
Santa Monica, CA 90401-2805, USA

Hecht, Jochen (Athlete, Hockey Player)
95 Levin Ln
East Amherst, NY 14051-2243, USA

Hechter, Daniel (Designer, Fashion Designer)
4 Ave Ter Hoche
Paris 75008, FRANCE

Hecht-Herskowitz, Gina (Actor)
5930 Foothill Dr
Los Angeles, CA 90068-3524, USA

Heck, Andy (Athlete, Football Player)
221 Deer Haven Dr
Ponte Vedra Beach, FL 32082-2108, USA

Heck, Bob (Athlete, Football Player)
1939 Tarpon Rd
Naples, FL 34102-1565, USA

Heck, Ralph (Athlete, Football Player)
1906 Wicks Ridge Ln
Marietta, GA 30062-6777, USA

Heck, Robert (Athlete, Football Player)
1939 Tarpon Rd
Naples, FL 34102-1565, USA

Heckard, Steve (Athlete, Football Player)
398 Quinby Way
Rock Hill, SC 29732-8288, USA

Heckard, Tae (Actor)
c/o Staff Member *Pakula/King & Associates*
9229 W Sunset Blvd Ste 315
Los Angeles, CA 90069-3403, USA

Heckerling, Amy (Director, Producer)
1330 Schuyler Rd
Beverly Hills, CA 90210-2539, USA

Heckscher, August (Writer)
333 E 68th St Apt 8A
New York, NY 10065-5604, USA

Hecox, Ian (Comedian, Internet Star, Producer)
c/o Brent Weinstein *United Talent Agency (UTA)*
9336 Civic Center Dr
Beverly Hills, CA 90210-3604, USA

Hector, Johnny (Athlete, Football Player)
101 Grandville Dr
Lafayette, LA 70508-6448, USA

Hector, Willie (Athlete, Football Player)
138 Lower Ter
San Francisco, CA 94114-1443, USA

Hedaya, Dan (Actor)
Gersh Agency
232 N Canon Dr
Beverly Hills, CA 90210-5302, USA

Hedberg, Anders (Athlete, Hockey Player)
7305 Campeau Dr
Kanata, ON K2K 3M2, Canada

Hedberg, Johan (Athlete, Hockey Player)
c/o Jay Grossman *PuckAgency LLC*
555 Pleasantville Rd Ste 210N
North Building, Suite 210
Briarcliff Manor, NY 10510-1900, USA

Hedberg, Randy (Athlete, Football Player)
6802 23rd St S
Fargo, ND 58104-7807, USA

Hedderick, Herman (Athlete, Basketball Player)
2913 Homestead Dr
Erie, PA 16506-2131, USA

Heder, Jon (Actor, Producer)
c/o Julie Darmody *Rise Management*
6338 Wilshire Blvd
Los Angeles, CA 90048-5002, USA

Hedford, Eric (Music Group, Musician)
Monqui Mgmt
PO Box 5908
Portland, OR 97228-5908, USA

Hedgepeth, Whitney (Athlete, Olympic Athlete, Swimmer)
9801 Westward Dr
Austin, TX 78733-3145, USA

Hedges, Lucas (Actor)
c/o Mara Buxbaum *ID Public Relations*
7060 Hollywood Blvd Fl 8th
Los Angeles, CA 90028-6021, USA

Hedges, Peter (Director, Writer)
c/o Richard Lovett *Creative Artists Agency (CAA)*
2000 Avenue of the Stars Ste 100
Los Angeles, CA 90067-4705, USA

Hedican, Bret (Athlete, Hockey Player, Olympic Athlete)
290 Las Quebradas
Alamo, CA 94507-1732, USA

Hedin, Pierre (Athlete, Hockey Player)
Lakasund 158
Bonassund 891 78, Sweden

Hedington, Tim (Producer)
c/o Staff Member *GK Films*
1411 5th St Ste 200
Santa Monica, CA 90401-2480, USA

Hedison, Alexandra (Actor)
Hedison Photography
PO Box 691636
Los Angeles, CA 90069-9636, USA

Hedison, Bret (Athlete, Hockey Player)
1848 Torrington St
Raleigh, NC 27615-2575, USA

Hedison, David (Actor)
779 Carissa Dr
Royal Palm Beach, FL 33411-3412, USA

Hedley (Music Group, Musician)
c/o Adrienne Butcher *Watchdog Management*
200-1505 2nd Ave W
Vancouver, BC V6H 3Y4, Canada

Hedlund, Garrett (Actor)
c/o Cynthia Pett-Dante *Brillstein Entertainment Partners*
9150 Wilshire Blvd Ste 350
Beverly Hills, CA 90212-3453, USA

Hedlund, Mike (Athlete, Baseball Player)
2412 Klinger Rd
Arlington, TX 76016-1143, USA

Hedren, Tippi (Actor)
PO Box 189
Acton, CA 93510-0189, USA

Hedrick, Chad (Athlete, Olympic Athlete, Speed Skater)
18203 Stockton Springs Dr
Spring, TX 77379-6926, USA

Hedrick, Joan (Writer)
300 Summit St
Hartford, CT 06106-3100, USA

Hedrick, Larry (Race Car Driver)
Larry Hedrick Motorsports
PO Box 511
114 Victory Lane
Statesville, NC 28687-0511, USA

Heelan, Briga (Actor)
c/o Lindsey Ludwig-Rahm *Viewpoint Inc*
89 5th Ave Ste 402
New York, NY 10003-3020, USA

Heenan, Pat (Athlete, Football Player)
28344 Seaford Rd
Laurel, DE 19956-3712, USA

Heep, Danny (Athlete, Baseball Player)
18610 Crosstimber
San Antonio, TX 78258-4587, USA

Heeter, Gene (Athlete, Football Player)
11 Symphony Dr
Lake Grove, NY 11755-1313, USA

Heffern, Meghan (Actor)
c/o Barb Godfrey *Parent Management*
84 Ontario St
Toronto, ON M5A 2V3, CANADA

Heffernan, Bert (Athlete, Baseball Player)
130 Eagle Ct
Locust Grove, VA 22508-5432, USA

Heffernan, Dave (Athlete, Football Player)
8101 SW 79th Ter
Miami, FL 33143, USA

Heffernan, Kevin (Actor, Comedian, Producer)
Broken Lizard Industries
PO Box 642809
Los Angeles, CA 90064-8279, USA

Heffner, Bob (Athlete, Baseball Player)
910 N 12th St
Allentown, PA 18102-1102, USA

Heffner, Kyle (Actor)
c/o Melanie Sharp *Sharp Talent*
117 N Orlando Ave
Los Angeles, CA 90048-3403, USA

Heffron, John (Actor, Comedian)
c/o Peter Rosegarten *Conversation Company*
1044 Northern Blvd Ste 304
Roslyn, NY 11576-1589, USA

Heffron, Richard T (Director)
c/o Staff Member *Shapiro-Lichtman Talent Agency*
1333 Beverly Green Dr
Los Angeles, CA 90035-1018, USA

Heflin, Bronson (Athlete, Baseball Player)
1043 Parsons Way
Hendersonville, TN 37075-6313, USA

Heflin, Vince (Athlete, Football Player)
4811 Lake Ontario Way
Bowie, MD 20720-3694, USA

Hefner, Larry (Athlete, Football Player)
1208 Arboretum Dr
Lewisville, NC 27023-8658, USA

Hefner, Lene (Adult Film Star)
15127 Califa St
Van Nuys, CA 91411-3021, USA

Heft, Robert (Bob) (Designer)
PO Box 20404
Saginaw, MI 48602, USA

Hegamin, George (Athlete, Football Player)
1409 S Lamar St Apt 616
Dallas, TX 75215-6834, USA

Heger, Rene (Actor)
c/o Jerry Shandrew *Shandrew Public Relations*
1050 S Stanley Ave
Los Angeles, CA 90019-6634, USA

Hegerland, Anita (Musician)
C/O Medienburo Elke Kruger
Bornicker Str. 35
Berlin 13595, Germany

Hegg, Steve (Athlete, Cycler, Olympic Athlete)

Heggtveit, Ann Hamilton (Skier)
General Delivery
Grand Isle, VT 05458, USA

Hegland, Jean (Writer)
5450 Mill Creek Rd
Healdsburg, CA 95448-9760, USA

Hegman, Bob (Athlete, Baseball Player)
3529 NW Winding Woods Dr
Lees Summit, MO 64064-1879, USA

Hegman, Mike (Athlete, Football Player)
2958 Suesand Dr
Memphis, TN 38128-5941, USA

Hehn, Sascha (Actor)
C/O Tanja Junginger
Stifterweg 75
Ulm D-89075, Germany

Heidei, James (Athlete, Football Player)
1425 Wisteria Dr
Vicksburg, MS 39180-4756, USA

Heidemann, Jack (Athlete, Baseball Player)
1816 S Salida Del Sol Cir
Mesa, AZ 85202-5529, USA

Heiden, Beth (Athlete, Olympic Athlete, Speed Skater)

Heiden, Eric (Athlete, Olympic Athlete, Speed Skater)
1219 Cottonwood Ln
Park City, UT 84098-7602, USA

Heiden, Steve (Athlete, Football Player)
18186 Lake Forest Cir
Lakeville, MN 55044-5284, USA

Heiden, Steve (Athlete, Football Player)
2600 Rushford Village
Rushford, MN 55971, USA

Heidmann, Manfred (Actor)
Borbecker Str. 237
Essen D-45355, Germany

Heidt, Mike (Athlete, Hockey Player)
8 Creekside Way
Spruce Grove, AB T7X 3Y7, Canada

Heidt Jr, Horace (Musician)
4155 Witzel Dr
Sherman Oaks, CA 91423-4613, USA

Heigl, Katherine (Actor, Model)
c/o Jill Fritzo *Jill Fritzo Public Relations*
208 E 51st St # 305
New York, NY 10022-6557, USA

Heilbron, Lorna (Actor)
Brunskill
169 Queen's Gate
London SW7 5HE, UNITED KINGDOM (UK)

Heilman, Aaron (Athlete, Baseball Player)
39W272 Sheldon Ln
Geneva, IL 60134-6045, USA

Heim, Val (Athlete, Baseball Player)
1050 Louden St
Superior, NE 68978-2303, USA

Heimbold, Charles A Jr (Business Person)
Bristol-Myers Squibb
345 Park Ave Bsmt LC3
New York, NY 10154-0019, USA

Heimburger, Craig (Athlete, Football Player)
311 Flagstone Dr
Belleville, IL 62221-5821, USA

Heimkreiter, Steve (Athlete, Football Player)
45 Devils Den Apt 208
Fort Thomas, KY 41075-4045, USA

Heim-McDaniel, Kay (Athlete, Baseball Player, Commentator)
3390 143rd St W
Rosemount, MN 55068-4057, USA

Heimrath, Jr., Ludwig (Race Car Driver)
26117 34th Ave E
Spanaway, WA 98387-9439, USA

Heimueller, Gorman (Athlete, Baseball Player)
2148 W Glen Ave
Riverton, UT 84065-7079, USA

Heimuli, Lakei (Athlete, Football Player)
1963 W 1870 S
Woods Cross, UT 84087-2181, USA

Heine, Cariba (Actor)
c/o Natasha Harrison *United Management*
Marlborough House
Ste 45, Level 4, 61 Marlborough St
Surry HillsNSW 02010, AUSTRALIA

Heine, Jutta (Athlete, Track Athlete)
Blaue Muhle
Burglahr 57614, GERMANY

Heineman, Ken (Athlete, Football Player)
15982 Serenity Point Ln
Rogers, AR 72756-8615, USA

Heinen, Mike (Athlete, Golfer)
4518 E Meadow Ln
Lake Charles, LA 70605-5318, USA

Heinkel, Don (Athlete, Baseball Player)
508 Covington Ave
Birmingham, AL 35206-3057, USA

Heinle, Amelia (Actor)
c/o John Carrabino *John Carrabino Management*
5900 Wilshire Blvd Ste 740
Los Angeles, CA 90036-5032, USA

Heinrich, Keith (Athlete, Football Player)
21011 Pricewood Manor Ct
Cypress, TX 77433-2075, USA

Heinrich, Martin (Congressman, Politician)
336 Cannon Hob
Washington, DC 20515-3506, USA

Heins, Thorsten (Business Person)
BlackBerry
295 Phillip St
Research in Motion
Waterloo, ON N2L 3W8, CANADA

Heinsohn, Tom (Athlete, Basketball Player, Coach)
PO Box 422
Newton Upper Falls, MA 02464-0002, USA

Heintz, Bob (Athlete, Golfer)
2213 Highland Woods Dr
Dunedin, FL 34698-9407, USA

Heintz, Chris (Athlete, Baseball Player)
7128 Wareham Dr
Tampa, FL 33647-1132, USA

Heintzelman, Tom (Athlete, Baseball Player)
435 W Gleneagles Dr
Phoenix, AZ 85023-5256, USA

Heinz, Bob (Athlete, Football Player)
516 Mansion Ct Unit 502
Santa Clara, CA 95054-4336, USA

Heinz, Rick (Athlete, Hockey Player)
264 Van Allen Gate
Milton, ON L9T 5Y8, Canada

Heinz, W C (Sportscaster, Writer)
1150 Nichols Hill Rd
Dorset, VT 05251-9536, USA

Heinze, Steve (Athlete, Hockey Player, Olympic Athlete)
4659 La Espada Dr
Santa Barbara, CA 93111-1301, USA

Heinzer, Franz (Skier)
Lauenen
Rickenbach/Schwyz 06432, SWITZERLAND

Heise, Bob (Athlete, Baseball Player)
537 Live Oak Dr
Angels Camp, CA 95222-9898, USA

Heiser, Roy (Athlete, Baseball Player)
1038 Grovehill Rd
Halethorpe, MD 21227-3802, USA

Heiserman, Rick (Athlete, Baseball Player)
17252 Adams St
Omaha, NE 68135-3078, USA

Heiskala, Earl (Athlete, Hockey Player)
982 Ocean Ln
Imperial Beach, CA 91932-2420, USA

Heiss Jenkins, Carol (Athlete, Figure Skater, Olympic Athlete)
3183 Regency Pl
Westlake, OH 44145-6735, USA

Heisten, Barrett (Athlete, Hockey Player)
13360 Seacloud Cir
Anchorage, AK 99516-3469, USA

Heitmann, Eric (Athlete, Football Player)
21511 Grand Hollow Ln
Katy, TX 77450-8809, USA

Heizer, Miles (Actor)
c/o Jenny Tversky *Shelter PR*
928 Broadway Ste 505
New York, NY 10010-8143, USA

Hejda, Jan (Athlete, Hockey Player)
8236 S Old Hammer Ln
Aurora, CO 80016-2074, USA

Hejduk, Milan (Athlete, Hockey Player)
7895 Forest Keep Cir
Parker, CO 80134-6412, USA

Helander, Peter (Athlete, Hockey Player)
Vastergatan 3A
Goteborg 411 23, Sweden

Helberg, Simon (Actor)
2549 N Catalina St
Los Angeles, CA 90027-1132, USA

Helbig, Grace (Internet Star)
c/o Ken Treusch *Bleecker Street Entertainment*
853 Broadway Ste 1214
New York, NY 10003-4717, USA

Held, Franklin (Bud) (Athlete, Olympic Athlete, Track Athlete)
13367 Caminito Mar Villa
Del Mar, CA 92014-3613, USA

Held, Mel (Athlete, Baseball Player)
103 Hogan Ln
Bryan, OH 43506-9161, USA

Held, Paul (Athlete, Football Player)
29055 Blue Moon Dr
Menifee, CA 92584-7302, USA

Heldt, Mike (Athlete, Football Player)
12711 Corral Rd
Tampa, FL 33626-4405, USA

Helfand, Eric (Athlete, Baseball Player)
7314 Jackson Dr
San Diego, CA 92119-2317, USA

Helfer, Tricia (Actor)
c/o Gordon Gilbertson *Gilbertson Management*
1334 3rd Street Promenade Ste 201
Santa Monica, CA 90401-1320, USA

Helford, Bruce (Producer, Writer)
c/o Staff Member *United Talent Agency (UTA)*
9336 Civic Center Dr
Beverly Hills, CA 90210-3604, USA

Helgeland, Brian (Director)
c/o Robert Newman *WME/IMG*
9601 Wilshire Blvd
Beverly Hills, CA 90210-5213, USA

Helgenberger, Marg (Actor)
c/o Nancy Sanders *Sanders Armstrong Caserta*
4111 W Alameda Ave Ste 505
Burbank, CA 91505-4163, USA

Hellemond, Andy Van (Athlete, Hockey Player)
4 St Catharine St
Guelph, ON N1E 4L5, Canada

Heller, Jane (Writer)
1325 Snell Isle Blvd NE Unit 606
Saint Petersburg, FL 33704-2419, USA

Heller, Jeffrey M (Business Person)
Electronic Data Systems
5400 Legacy Dr
Plano, TX 75024-3199, USA

Heller, Ron (Athlete, Football Player)
538 Stillwater River Rd
Absarokee, MT 59001-6218, USA

Hellestrae, Dale (Athlete, Football Player)
11705 E Charter Oak Dr
Scottsdale, AZ 85259-2743, USA

Hellickson, Russell (Russ) (Athlete, Olympic Athlete, Wrestler)
6893 Lauren Pl
Columbus, OH 43235-2188, USA

Helling, Rick A (Ricky) (Athlete, Baseball Player, Olympic Athlete)
3672 Landings Dr
Excelsior, MN 55331-9709, USA

Hellman, Monte (Director)
73434 Irontree Dr
Palm Desert, CA 92260-6904, USA

Hellmann, Martina (Athlete, Track Athlete)
Neue Leipziger Str 14
Leipzig 04205, GERMANY

Helluin, Francis (Athlete, Football Player)
3930 Southdown Mandalay Rd
Houma, LA 70360-3001, USA

Helluin, Jerry (Athlete, Football Player)
3930 Southdown Mandalay Rd
Houma, LA 70360-3001, USA

Hellwig, Jim (Athlete, Wrestler)
Ultimate Creations, Inc.
815 E Palace Ave Apt 29
Santa Fe, NM 87501-6432, USA

Hellyeah (Music Group)
c/o Dan Devita *The Kirby Organization (TKO-UK)*
6 Walter Ln
Camden
London NW1 8NZ, UNITED KINGDOM

Helm, Darren (Athlete, Hockey Player)
c/o Staff Member *Detroit Red Wings*
2645 Woodward Ave
Joe Luis Arena
Detroit, MI 48201-3028, USA

Helm, Val (Athlete, Baseball Player)
Chicago White Sox
PO Box 423
Superior, NE 68978-0423, USA

Helman, Josh (Actor)
c/o Brad Stokes *LINK Entertainment*
11872 La Grange Ave
Los Angeles, CA 90025-5282, USA

Helmerich, Hans C (Business Person)
Helmerich & Payne Inc
Utica & 21st St
Tulsa, OK 74114, USA

Helmerich, Walter H III (Business Person)
Helmerich & Payne Inc
Utica & 21st St
Tulsa, OK 74114, USA

Helmerson, Frans (Music Group, Musician)
Columbia Artists Mgmt Inc
165 W 57th St
New York, NY 10019-2201, USA

Helms, Ed (Actor, Comedian)
c/o Peter Principato *Artists First*
9465 Wilshire Blvd Ste 900
Beverly Hills, CA 90212-2608, USA

Helms, Jimmy (Race Car Driver)
6230 Rock Island Rd
Charlotte, NC 28278-6508, USA

Helms, Susan J (Astronaut)
NASA
2101 Nasa Pkwy Spc Johnsoncenter
Houston, TX 77058-3696, USA

Helms, Tommy (Athlete, Baseball Player, Coach)
5427 Bluesky Dr
Cincinnati, OH 45247-7865, USA

Helms, Wes (Athlete, Baseball Player)
9314 Bear Creek Rd
Sterrett, AL 35147-9166, USA

Helnwein, Gottfried (Artist)
Aul der Burg 2
Burgbrol 56659, GERMANY

Heloise, (Cruse Evans) (Journalist)
PO Box 795000
San Antonio, TX 78279-5000, USA

Helprin, Mark (Writer)
c/o Staff Member *The Wendy Weil Agency, Inc.*
232 Madison Ave Rm 1300
New York, NY 10016-2922, USA

Heltau, Michael (Actor, Music Group)
Sulzweg 11
Vienna 01190, AUSTRIA

Helton, Barry (Athlete, Football Player)
3325 Clubview Ter
Colorado Springs, CO 80906-4479, USA

Helton, Mike (Race Car Driver)
PO Box 2875
Daytona Beach, FL 32120, USA

Helton, RJ (Musician)
PO Box 246
1400 Market Place Blvd
Cumming, GA 30028-0246, USA

Helton, Todd (Athlete, Baseball Player)
12128 Warrior Trl
Knoxville, TN 37922-5459, USA

Helu, Roy (Athlete, Football Player)
c/o Ken Zuckerman *Priority Sports & Entertainment - (LA)*
15233 Ventura Blvd Ste 718
Sherman Oaks, CA 91403-2237, USA

Helvin, Marie (Model)
IMG Models
23 Eyot Gardens
London W6 9TN, UNITED KINGDOM (UK)

Hely, Steve (Actor)
c/o Cori Wellins *WME/IMG*
9601 Wilshire Blvd
Beverly Hills, CA 90210-5213, USA

Heman, Russ (Athlete, Baseball Player)
5555 Canyon Crest Dr Apt 3D
Riverside, CA 92507-6453, USA

Hemandez, Angel (Baseball Player)
500 Cypress Xing
Wellington, FL 33414-6368, USA

Hemecker, Ralph (Director)
c/o Staff Member *Mythic Films*
225 E Broadway Ste 115B
Glendale, CA 91205-1008, USA

Hemingway, Dree (Actor)
c/o Sarah R Kelly *ICM Partners (NY)*
730 5th Ave
New York, NY 10019-4105, USA

Hemingway, Gerardine (Designer, Fashion Designer)
Red or Dead Ltd
Courtney Road Bldg 201
Wembley
Middx HA9 7PP, UNITED KINGDOM (UK)

Hemingway, Junior (Athlete, Football Player)

Hemingway, Mariel (Actor, Model)
c/o Staff Member *Progressive Artists Agency*
9696 Culver Blvd
Culver City, CA 90232-2700, USA

Hemingway, Rose (Actor)
c/o Charles Mastropietro *Circle of Confusion*
8931 Ellis Ave
Los Angeles, CA 90034-3336, USA

Hemingway, Toby (Actor)
c/o Sarah Shyn *3 Arts Entertainment*
9460 Wilshire Blvd Fl 7
Beverly Hills, CA 90212-2713, USA

Hemingway, Wayne (Designer, Fashion Designer)
Red or Dead Ltd
Courtney Road Bldg 201
Wembley
Middx HA9 7PP, UNITED KINGDOM (UK)

Hemme, Christy (Actor)
c/o Liza Anderson *Anderson Group Public Relations*
8060 Melrose Ave Fl 4
Los Angeles, CA 90046-7038, USA

Hemmens, Heather (Actor)
c/o Mike Gillespie *Primary Wave Entertainment*
10850 Wilshire Blvd Fl 6
Los Angeles, CA 90024-4319, USA

Hemmer, Bill (Correspondent, Television Host)
c/o Staff Member *Fox News*
1211 Avenue of the Americas Lowr C1
New York, NY 10036-8705, USA

Hemmi, Heini (Skier)
Chalet Bel-Lia
Valbella 07077, SWITZERLAND

Hemmis, Paige (Actor, Reality Star)

Hemond, Roland (Commentator)
1332 W Edgemont Ave
Phoenix, AZ 85007-1117, USA

Hemond, Scott (Athlete, Baseball Player)
263 Florida Ave
Dunedin, FL 34698-7530, USA

Hemphill., Bret (Athlete, Baseball Player)
2721 Ashland Dr
Roseville, CA 95661-7960, United States

Hemphill, Darryl (Athlete, Football Player)
10218 Aurora Fld
San Antonio, TX 78245-2622, USA

Hemphill, Joel (Music Group)
Harper Agency
PO Box 144
Goodlettsville, TN 37070-0144, USA

Hemphill, Labreeska (Music Group)
Harper Agency
PO Box 144
Goodlettsville, TN 37070-0144, USA

Hemphill, Richard (Baseball Player)
Kansas City Monarchs
422 Barnes St
Rock Hill, SC 29730-5044, USA

Hempstead, Hessley (Athlete, Football Player)
14823 Dunbeth Dr
Huntersville, NC 28078-3308, USA

Hempstead Wright, Isaac (Actor)
c/o Claire Comisky *Artists Rights Group (ARG)*
4A Exmoor St
London W10 6BD, UNITED KINGDOM

Hemric, Dick (Athlete, Basketball Player)
1220 7th St NE
North Canton, OH 44720-2116, USA

Hemsky, Ales (Athlete, Hockey Player)
Jiri Crha Sports Representation
16390 Braeburn Ridge Trl
Delray Beach, FL 33446-9508, USA

Hemsley, Nate (Athlete, Football Player)
26 Roberts Pl
Willingboro, NJ 08046-2514, USA

Hemsley, Stephen J (Business Person)
United HealthCare Corp
9900 Bren Rd E Ste 300W
Opus Center
Minnetonka, MN 55343-4402, USA

Hemsworth, Chris (Actor)
c/o Mark Morrissey *Morrissey Management*
16 Princess Ave
Rosebery
Sydney NSW 02018, AUSTRALIA

Hemsworth, Liam (Actor)
c/o Christopher Burbidge *Fourward*
10250 Constellation Blvd Ste 2710
Los Angeles, CA 90067-6227, USA

Hemsworth, Luke (Actor)
c/o Fleur Griffin *Morrissey Management*
16 Princess Ave
Rosebery
Sydney NSW 02018, AUSTRALIA

Hemus, Solly (Athlete, Baseball Player, Coach)
5100 San Felipe St Unit 194E
Houston, TX 77056-3688, USA

Henao, Zulay (Actor)
c/o Jean-Louis Diamonika *One Entertainment (NY)*
347 5th Ave Rm 1404
New York, NY 10016-5034, USA

Henckel von Donnersmarck, Florian (Director)
c/o Craig Gering *Creative Artists Agency (CAA)*
2000 Avenue of the Stars Ste 100
Los Angeles, CA 90067-4705, USA

Hencken, John F (Athlete, Olympic Athlete, Swimmer)
PO Box 2540
Weaverville, NC 28787-2540, USA

Hendershot, Larry (Athlete, Football Player)
2820 N Mohawk Trl
Chino Valley, AZ 86323-8679, USA

Hendershot, Ray (Artist)
1007 Lakeview Ter
Pennsburg, PA 18073-1611, USA

Henderson, Alan (Basketball Player)
Atlanta Hawks
190 Marietta St NW Ste 405
Atlanta, GA 30303-2717, USA

Henderson, Anthony (Krayzie Bone) (Musician)
c/o Staff Member *RBC Records*
150 E Olive Ave Ste 114
Burbank, CA 91502-1849, USA

Henderson, Cedric (Athlete, Basketball Player)
PO Box 148
Smyrna, GA 30081-0148, USA

Henderson, Chris (Soccer Player)
Columbus Crew
2121 Velma Ave
Columbus, OH 43211-2085, USA

Henderson, David (Athlete, Basketball Player)
805 Sweet Hollow Ct
Middletown, DE 19709-8645, USA

Henderson, Devery (Athlete, Football Player)
835 E Bellevue St
Opelousas, LA 70570, USA

Henderson, Felicia (Writer)
c/o Scott Schwartz *Vision Art Management*
750 N San Vicente Blvd Ste RE800
West Hollywood, CA 90069-5778, USA

Henderson, Gerald (Athlete, Basketball Player)
185 Birkdale Dr
Blue Bell, PA 19422-3276, USA

Henderson, James A (Business Person)
Cummins Engine Co
PO Box 3005
500 Jackson St
Columbus, IN 47202-3005, USA

Henderson, Jerome (Athlete, Basketball Player)
3208 Potterstone Way
Avon, OH 44011-4202, USA

Henderson, Jerome (Athlete, Football Player)
11051 Berkely Club Dr Apt 201
Raleigh, NC 27617-8543, USA

Henderson, Joe (Athlete, Baseball Player)
14468 Bryce Dr
Horizon City, TX 79928-6971, USA

Henderson, John (Athlete, Football Player)
11667 Blackstone River Dr
Jacksonville, FL 32256-2919, USA

Henderson, John (Athlete, Football Player)
18130 19th Ave N
Plymouth, MN 55447-2634, USA

Henderson, Josh (Actor)
c/o Jacob Fenton *United Talent Agency (UTA)*
9336 Civic Center Dr
Beverly Hills, CA 90210-3604, USA

Henderson, Julie (Model)
596 Broadway # 701
New York, NY 10012-3396, USA

Henderson, Keith (Athlete, Football Player)
PO Box 2754
Cartersville, GA 30120-1696, USA

Henderson, Ken (Athlete, Baseball Player)
200 Winchester Cir Apt D104
Los Gatos, CA 95032-1872, USA

Henderson, Kevin (Athlete, Basketball Player)
2960 Champion Way Apt 2203
Tustin, CA 92782-1238, USA

Henderson, Logan (Musician)
c/o Remington Franklin *Resolution (LA)*
10250 Constellation Blvd Fl 7
Los Angeles, CA 90067-6207, USA

Henderson, Martin (Actor)
c/o Danica Smith *Kovert Creative*
506 Santa Monica Blvd Ste 400
Santa Monica, CA 90401-2412, USA

Henderson, Neale (Athlete, Baseball Player)
341 Los Soneto Dr
San Diego, CA 92114-5922, USA

Henderson, Othello (Athlete, Football Player)
323 Silent Spring Dr
Cedar Park, TX 78613-4217, USA

Henderson, Paul (Athlete, Hockey Player)
1292 Whitewater Lane
Mississauga, ON L5V 1L8, CANADA

Henderson, Paul III (Journalist)
Seattle Times
1120 John St
Editorial Dept
Seattle, WA 98109-5321, USA

Henderson, Reuben (Athlete, Football Player)
3918 Hunters Ridge Dr Apt 4
Lansing, MI 48911-1106, USA

Henderson, Richard (Actor, Musician)

Henderson, Rickey (Athlete, Baseball Player)
10561 Englewood Dr
Oakland, CA 94605-5013, USA

Henderson, Rod (Athlete, Baseball Player)
4484 Logans Fort Ln
Lexington, KY 40509-8552, USA

Henderson, Seantrel (Athlete, Football Player)
c/o Joel Segal *Lagardere Unlimited (NY)*
456 Washington St Apt 9L
New York, NY 10013-1555, USA

Henderson, Shirley (Actor)
c/o Lorraine Hamilton *Hamilton Hodell Ltd*
20 Golden Sq
Fl 5
London W1F 9JL, UNITED KINGDOM

Henderson, Steve (Athlete, Baseball Player)
10509 Gretna Green Dr
Tampa, FL 33626-1830, USA

Henderson, Thomas (Athlete, Basketball Player, Olympic Athlete)
6822 Baron Gate Ct
Spring, TX 77379-5094, USA

Henderson, Thomas (Athlete, Football Player)
3106 E 13th St
Austin, TX 78702-2506, USA

Henderson, Wymon (Athlete, Football Player)
634 Braidwood Dr NW
Acworth, GA 30101-3529, USA

Henderson, Zachary (Athlete, Football Player)
16005 Sheffield Blvd
Edmond, OK 73013-2043, USA

Henderson III, Joe (Race Car Driver)
1435 W Morehead St # 170
Charlotte, NC 28208-5208, USA

Hendley, Bob (Athlete, Baseball Player)
645 Wimbish Rd
Macon, GA 31210-4328, USA

Hendley, Dick (Athlete, Football Player)
6 Sun Flare Ct
Greer, SC 29650-4419, USA

Hendra, Tony (Writer)
c/o Staff Member *Simon & Schuster*
1230 Avenue of the Americas Fl CONC1
New York, NY 10020-1586, USA

Hendren, Jerry (Athlete, Football Player)
14826 N Chesapeake Ln
Mead, WA 99021-9270, USA

Hendrick, George (Athlete, Baseball Player)
1 Tropicana Dr
Saint Petersburg, FL 33705-1703, USA

Hendricks, Christina (Actor)
c/o Britney Ross *42West*
1840 Century Park E Ste 700
Los Angeles, CA 90067-2122, USA

Hendricks, L H (Baseball Player)
Negro Baseball Leagues
12 Sunset Blvd
Beaufort, SC 29907-1421, USA

Hendricks, Matt (Athlete, Hockey Player)
19865 Lakeview Ave
Excelsior, MN 55331-9353, USA

Hendricks, Theodore P (Ted) (Athlete, Football Player)
1232 W Weston Dr
Arlington Heights, IL 60004-7946, USA

Hendrickson, Darby (Athlete, Hockey Player, Olympic Athlete)
317 Washington St
Saint Paul, MN 55102-1609, USA

Hendrickson, Elizabeth (Actor)
c/o Suzanne (Sue) Wohl *TalentWorks*
3500 W Olive Ave Ste 1400
Burbank, CA 91505-5512, USA

Hendrickson, Jack (Athlete, Hockey Player)
4161 Jeddo Rd
Burtchville, MI 48059-1121, USA

Hendrickson, Mark (Athlete, Baseball Player)
1585 Wyndham Dr
York, PA 17403-5925, USA

Hendrickson, Steve (Athlete, Football Player)
210 W 15th Ave
Escondido, CA 92025-5714, USA

Hendrix, Elaine (Actor)
c/o Staff Member *EHx Productions*
8721 Santa Monica Blvd Ste 255
West Hollywood, CA 90069-4507, USA

Hendrix, Harville (Writer)
c/o Staff Member *Henry Holt & Company*
175 5th Ave Ste 400
New York, NY 10010-7726, USA

Hendrix, Terri (Musician)
Wilory Records
PO Box 2340
San Marcos, TX 78667-2340, USA

Hendrix, Tim (Athlete, Football Player)
7251 Hamilton Dr
Midlothian, TX 76065-6974, USA

Hendry, Gloria (Actor)
256 S Robertson Blvd
Beverly Hills, CA 90211-2811, USA

Hendry, Jim (Commentator)
507 Doucet Rd
Lafayette, LA 70503-3557, USA

Hendry, Joel (Athlete, Golfer)
c/o Jim Lehrman *Medalist Management Inc*
36855 W Main St Ste 200
Purcellville, VA 20132-3561, USA

Hendry, Ted (Athlete, Baseball Player)
14740 N 90th Pl
Scottsdale, AZ 85260-2700, USA

Hendry, Ted (Baseball Player)
14740 N 90th Pl
Scottsdale, AZ 85260-2700, USA

Hendryx, Nona (Musician)
Black Rock
6201 Sunset Blvd #329
Hollywood, CA 90028, USA

Hendy, John (Athlete, Football Player)
590 N Bayview Ave
Sunnyvale, CA 94085-3633, USA

Henenlotter, Frank (Director)
81 Bedford St Apt 6E
New York, NY 10014-5749, USA

Henery, Alex (Athlete, Football Player)
c/o Neil Cornrich *NC Sports, LLC*
best to contact via email
Columbus, OH 43201, USA

Hengel, Dave (Athlete, Baseball Player)
2642 Kingfisher Ln
Lincoln, CA 95648-8753, USA

Henggeler, Courtney (Actor)
c/o Marissa Mooney *Rogers & Cowan*
1840 Century Park E Fl 18
Los Angeles, CA 90067-2101, USA

Henin-Hardenne, Justine (Tennis Player)
Octagon
1751 Pinnacle Dr Ste 1500
McLean, VA 22102-3833, USA

Henke, Brad (Athlete, Football Player)
650 S Hill St Ste C9
Los Angeles, CA 90014-1783, USA

Henke, Brad William (Actor)
c/o Dan Baron *Agency for the Performing Arts (APA)*
405 S Beverly Dr Ste 500
Beverly Hills, CA 90212-4425, USA

Henke, Ed (Athlete, Football Player)
906 Turaco Ct
Lincoln, CA 95648-7825, USA

Henke, Karl (Athlete, Football Player)
1180 Bogota Ct
Oxnard, CA 93035-2608, USA

Henke, Nolan (Athlete, Golfer)
1323 Florida Ave
Fort Myers, FL 33901-7707, USA

Henke, Tom (Athlete, Baseball Player)
6200 Saint Francis Dr
Jefferson City, MO 65101-9292, USA

Henkel, Herbert L (Business Person)
Ingersoll-Rand Co
PO Box 6820
Piscataway, NJ 08855-6820, USA

Henley, Bob (Athlete, Baseball Player)
11050 Moreland Dr E
Grand Bay, AL 36541-6626, USA

Henley, Carey (Athlete, Football Player)
1611 S Clayton Ave
Chattanooga, TN 37412-1107, USA

Henley, Darryl (Athlete, Football Player)
10178 Woodridge Dr
Rancho Cucamonga, CA 91737-6834, USA

Henley, Don (Musician, Songwriter)
c/o Larry Solters *Scoop Marketing*
12754 Ventura Blvd Ste C
Studio City, CA 91604-2441, USA

Henley, Drewe (Actor)
Granary Cottage Bed & Breakfast
1 Granary Cottages
Combpyne, Axminster
Devon EX13 8SX, UK

Henley, Gail (Athlete, Baseball Player)
4315 Saint Mark Ave
La Verne, CA 91750-2848, USA

Henley, Garney (Athlete, Football Player)
857 Nebraska Ave SW
SW
Huron, SD 57350-2347, USA

Henley, Georgie (Actor)
c/o Christian Hodell *Hamilton Hodell Ltd*
20 Golden Sq
Fl 5
London W1F 9JL, UNITED KINGDOM

Henman, Graham (Director)
Agency for Performing Arts
9200 W Sunset Blvd Ste 900
Los Angeles, CA 90069-3604, USA

Henman, Tim (Tennis Player)
14497 N Dale Mabry Hwy Ste 205
Tampa, FL 33618-2047, USA

Henn, Mark (Animator)
c/o Staff Member *Disney Animation (FL)*
PO Box 10200
Orlando, FL 32830-0200, USA

Henn, Sean (Athlete, Baseball Player)
3658 Snow Creek Dr
Aledo, TX 76008-3677, USA

Hennagan, Monique (Athlete, Olympic Athlete, Track Athlete)
505 Winter View Way
Stockbridge, GA 30281-7799, USA

Henne, Chad (Athlete, Football Player)
c/o David Dunn *Athletes First*
23091 Mill Creek Dr
Laguna Hills, CA 92653-1258, USA

Henneman, Brian (Music Group)
Hard Head Productions
180 Varick St Rm 810
New York, NY 10014-5416, USA

Henneman, Mike (Athlete, Baseball Player)
c/o Staff Member *Athlete Connection LLC*
PO Box 380135
Clinton Township, MI 48038-0060, USA

Hennen, Thomas J (Astronaut)
Atlantis Foundation
PO Box 402
Seabrook, TX 77586-0402, USA

Henner, Marilu (Actor)
c/o Rory Rosegarten *Conversation Company*
1044 Northern Blvd Ste 304
Roslyn, NY 11576-1589, USA

Hennessey, Brad (Athlete, Baseball Player)
9402 Northcreek Woods
Lambertville, MI 48144-8707, USA

Hennessey, Wally (Horse Racer)
4141 NW 9th Ct
Coconut Creek, FL 33066-1644, USA

Hennessy, Jill (Actor)
c/o Cara Tripicchio *Shelter PR*
5670 Wilshire Blvd Ste 1200
Los Angeles, CA 90036-5621, USA

Henney, Daniel (Actor)
c/o Brian Medavoy *More/Medavoy Management*
10203 Santa Monica Blvd # 400
Los Angeles, CA 90067-6405, USA

Hennig, Shelley (Actor)
c/o Allan Grifka *Alchemy Entertainment*
7024 Melrose Ave Ste 420
Los Angeles, CA 90038-3394, USA

Hennigan, Charley (Athlete, Football Player)
PO Box 180
Huffman, TX 77336, USA

Hennigan, John (Athlete, Wrestler)
c/o Staff Member *World Wrestling Entertainment (WWE)*
1241 E Main St
Stamford, CT 06902-3520, USA

Hennigan, Mike (Athlete, Football Player)
542 N Washington Ave
Cookeville, TN 38501-2657, USA

Hennigan, Phil (Athlete, Baseball Player)
PO Box 1212
Center, TX 75935-1212, USA

Henning, Dan (Athlete, Football Coach, Football Player)
116 Meeting Way
Ponte Vedra Beach, FL 32082-3947, USA

Henning, Linda (Actor)
10765 Wrightwood Ln
Studio City, CA 91604-3951, USA

Henning, Lorne (Athlete, Coach, Hockey Player)
800 Griffiths Way
VANCOUVER CANUCKS
Vancouver, BC V6B 6G1, Canada

Henning, Paul (Athlete, Hockey Player)
4250 Navajo Ave
Toluca Lake, CA 91602-2914, USA

Henninger, Brian (Athlete, Golfer)
25481 SW Newland Rd
Wilsonville, OR 97070, USA

Henninger, Rick (Athlete, Baseball Player)
2505 Clover Glen Dr
Edmond, OK 73013-2869, USA

Hennings, Chad W (Athlete, Football Player)
6101 Bay Valley Ct
Flower Mound, TX 75022-5575, USA

Henning-Walker, Anne (Athlete, Olympic Athlete, Speed Skater)
12359 E Lasalle Pl
Aurora, CO 80014-1921, USA

Hennis, Randy (Athlete, Baseball Player)
1747 Sienna Dr
Melbourne, FL 32934-9030, USA

Henrich, Bobby (Athlete, Baseball Player)
1531 Via Los Coyotes
La Habra, CA 90631-7655, USA

Henrichs, Jeff (Athlete, Baseball Player)
6192 Riverside Blvd Apt C46
Sacramento, CA 95831-1222, USA

Henrichsen, Brett (DJ, Musician)
c/o Len Evans *Project Publicity*
540 W 43rd St
New York, NY 10036, USA

Henricks, Jon N (Swimmer)
254 Laurel Ave
Des Plaines, IL 60016, USA

Henricks, Terence Colonel (Astronaut)
3811 Cole Ave
Dallas, TX 75204-1514, USA

Henricks, Terence T (Tom) (Astronaut)
Timken Aerospace
7 Optical Ave
Keene, NH 03431-4320, USA

Henrie, David (Actor)
c/o Jason Weinberg *Untitled Entertainment*
350 S Beverly Dr Ste 200
Beverly Hills, CA 90212-4819, USA

Henriksen, Jan (Horse Racer)
PO Box 176
Crosswicks, NJ 08515-0176, USA

Henriksen, Lance (Actor)
c/o Jeff Witjas *Agency for the Performing Arts (APA)*
405 S Beverly Dr Ste 500
Beverly Hills, CA 90212-4425, USA

Henrique, Adam (Athlete, Hockey Player)
285 E Quarter Townline Rd
Burford, ON N0E 1A0, Canada

Henriquez, Ron (Actor)
PO Box 38027
Los Angeles, CA 90038, USA

Henry, Albert (Athlete, Basketball Player)
2410 N 52nd St
Philadelphia, PA 19131-1409, USA

Henry, Anthony (Athlete, Football Player)
1619 N La Brea Ave APT 511
Los Angeles, CA 90028-6476, USA

Henry, Brad (Politician)
Governor's Office
State Capitol Bldg #212
Oklahoma City, OK 73105, USA

Henry, Brad (Politician)
PO Box 156
Shawnee, OK 74802-0156, USA

Henry, Brian Tyree (Actor)
c/o Michael Geiser *Jill Fritzo Public Relations*
208 E 51st St # 305
New York, NY 10022-6557, USA

Henry, Buck (Actor, Writer)
117 E 57th St Apt 40B
New York, NY 10022-2095, USA

Henry, Buck (Writer)
117 W 57th St
New York, NY 10019-2209, USA

Henry, Butch (Athlete, Baseball Player)
12072 Paseo De Amor Ln
El Paso, TX 79936-4499, USA

Henry, Chris (Athlete, Football Player)
545 Summit Oaks Ct
Nashville, TN 37221-1429, USA

Henry, Chuck (Correspondent)
KNBC
3000 W Alameda Ave
Burbank, CA 91523-0002, USA

Henry, Clarence (Forgman) (Music Group, Songwriter, Writer)
3309 Lawrence St
New Orleans, LA 70114-3230, USA

Henry, Conner (Athlete, Basketball Player)
1122 N College Ave
Claremont, CA 91711-3927, USA

Henry, Dale (Attorney, Hockey Player)
8611 Datapoint Dr Apt 43
San Antonio, TX 78229-5922, USA

Henry, David (Actor)
c/o Dallas Smith *United Agents*
12-26 Lexington St
London W1F OLE, UNITED KINGDOM

Henry, Doug (Athlete, Baseball Player)
2804 Burries Rd
Hartland, WI 53029-8823, USA

Henry, Dwayne (Athlete, Baseball Player)
2675 Chandler Grove Dr
Buford, GA 30519-7085, USA

Henry, Gloria (Actor)
849 N Harper Ave
Los Angeles, CA 90046-6803, USA

Henry, Gregg (Actor)
8956 Appian Way
Los Angeles, CA 90046-7737, USA

Henry, J J (Athlete, Golfer)
6901 Sanctuary Ln
Fort Worth, TX 76132-7101, USA

Henry, Joe (Music Group, Songwriter, Writer)
Monterey Peninsula Artists
509 Hartnell St
Monterey, CA 93940-2825, USA

Henry, Joe (Athlete, Baseball Player)
220 N 7th St
Lovejoy, IL 62059-1001, USA

Henry, John (Baseball Player)
Florida Marlins
4698 Sanctuary Ln
Boca Raton, FL 33431-5206, USA

Henry, John (Commentator)
40 Cottage St
Brookline, MA 02445-5938, USA

Henry, Joshua (Actor, Musician)
c/o Christina Papadopoulos *Baker Winokur Ryder Public Relations*
200 5th Ave Fl 5
New York, NY 10010-3307, USA

Henry, Justin (Actor)
c/o Staff Member *Phoenix Organization, The*
540 San Vicente Blvd Apt 21
Santa Monica, CA 90402-1865, USA

Henry, Kevin (Athlete, Football Player)
1428 Mill Pointe Ct
Lawrenceville, GA 30043-9111, USA

Henry, Lenny (Actor)
c/o Staff Member *WME|IMG*
9601 Wilshire Blvd
Beverly Hills, CA 90210-5213, USA

Henry, Mark (Athlete, Wrestler)
c/o Staff Member *World Wrestling Entertainment (WWE)*
1241 E Main St
Stamford, CT 06902-3520, USA

Henry, Mike (Actor)
Pittsburgh Steelers
10803 Blix St Unit 3
North Hollywood, CA 91602-3822, USA

Henry, Ron (Athlete, Baseball Player)
1708 Mystic Dr
Durham, NC 27712-2099, USA

Henry, Steve (Athlete, Football Player)
1907 Darlene Way
Emporia, KS 66801-6024, USA

Henry, Thierry (Athlete, Soccer Player)
c/o Nicola Richardson *QVoice*
161 Drury Ln, Covent Garden
3rd Floor
London WC2B 5PN, UK

Henry, Travis (Athlete, Football Player)
c/o Hadley Engelhard *Enter-Sports Management*
6000 Lake Forrest Dr Ste 370
Atlanta, GA 30328-5902, USA

Henry, Tyler (Astrologist/Medium/Psychic)
44 Blue Productions
3900 W Alameda Ave Ste 700
Burbank, CA 91505-4308, USA

Henry, Wally (Athlete, Football Player)
3444 Bernadette Ct Apt A
West Covina, CA 91792-4702, USA

Henry, Xavier (Athlete, Basketball Player)
c/o Arn Tellem *Wasserman Media Group*
10960 Wilshire Blvd Ste 1200
Los Angeles, CA 90024-3714, USA

Hensarling, Jeb (Congressman, Politician)
129 Cannon Hob
Washington, DC 20515-3501, USA

Hensby, Mark (Athlete, Golfer)
6814 E Monterey Way
Scottsdale, AZ 85251-6834, USA

Hensel, Robert M (Athlete)
wheelierecord@yahoo.com
138 E 3rd St # A
Oswego, NY 13126-2607, USA

Henshall, Daniel (Actor)
c/o Erin O'Connor *RGM Artists*
8-12 Ann St
Surry Hills, NSW 02010, AUSTRALIA

Hensley, Chuck (Athlete, Baseball Player)
511 S Clearview Ave
Mesa, AZ 85208-1920, USA

Hensley, Clay (Athlete, Baseball Player)
3601 Dogwood Blossom Ct
Pearland, TX 77581-5038, USA

Hensley, Dick (Athlete, Football Player)
6319 Roberto Dr
Huntington, WV 25705-2529, USA

Hensley, Jimmy (Race Car Driver)
2570 Horsepasture Price Rd
Ridgeway, VA 24148-3707, USA

Hensley, John (Actor)
c/o Markus Rudolph Goerg *Heroes and Villains Entertainment*
1041 N Formosa Ave
Formosa Bldg, Suite 202
West Hollywood, CA 90046-6703, USA

Hensley, Jon (Actor)

Hensley, Kirby J (Religious Leader)
Universal Life Church
601 3rd St
Modesto, CA 95351-3395, USA

Henson, Brian (Actor, Director, Producer)

Henson, Champ (Athlete, Football Player)
PO Box 3
Ashville, OH 43103-0003, USA

Henson, Darrin Dewitt (Actor)
c/o Adam Griffin *LINK Entertainment*
11872 La Grange Ave
Los Angeles, CA 90025-5282, USA

Henson, Drew (Athlete, Football Player)
4629 Lorraine Ave
Dallas, TX 75209-6013, USA

Henson, Drew (Athlete, Baseball Player)
4629 Lorraine Ave
Dallas, TX 75209-6013, USA

Henson, Elden (Actor)
c/o Jelani Johnson *Creative Artists Agency (CAA)*
2000 Avenue of the Stars Ste 100
Los Angeles, CA 90067-4705, USA

Henson, Gary (Athlete, Football Player)

Henson, Harold (Athlete, Football Player)
15367 Lockbourne Eastern Rd
Ashville, OH 43103-9476, USA

Henson, John (Actor, Comedian)
c/o Rory Rosegarten *Conversation Company*
1044 Northern Blvd Ste 304
Roslyn, NY 11576-1589, USA

Henson, John (Athlete, Basketball Player)
c/o Staff Member *Milwaukee Bucks*
1543 N 2nd St Fl 6
Milwaukee, WI 53212-4036, USA

Henson, Lisa (Producer)
c/o Staff Member *Jim Henson Company*
1416 N La Brea Ave
Hollywood, CA 90028-7506, USA

Henson, Lou (Basketball Player, Coach)
New Mexico State University
Athletic Dept
Las Cruces, NM 88033, USA

Henson, Luther (Athlete, Football Player)
5395 Maple Grove Ave
Blanchester, OH 45107-1533, USA

Henson, Sammie (Athlete, Olympic Athlete, Wrestler)
US Military Academy
Athletic Dept
West Point, NY 10996, USA

Henson, Taraji P (Actor)
c/o Amanda Nesbitt *The Lede Company*
9701 Wilshire Blvd # 930
Beverly Hills, CA 90212-2020, USA

Henstridge, Elizabeth (Actor)
c/o Amy Slomovits *Haven Entertainment*
8111 Beverly Blvd Ste 201
Los Angeles, CA 90048-4531, USA

Henstridge, Natasha (Actor, Model)
c/o Marcel Pariseau *True Public Relations*
3575 Cahuenga Blvd W Ste 360
Los Angeles, CA 90068-1361, USA

Hentgen, Pat (Athlete, Baseball Player)
1 Blue Jays Way Suite 3200
TORONTO BLUE JAYS ATTN SPECIAL ASSISTANT
Toronto, ON M5V 1J1, USA

Henton, Anthony (Athlete, Football Player)
1026 Avenue G
Bessemer, AL 35020-7200, USA

Henton, John (Actor)
c/o Staff Member *Gersh*
9465 Wilshire Blvd Ste 600
Beverly Hills, CA 90212-2605, USA

Hentrich, Craig (Athlete, Football Player)
604 Canters Ct
Franklin, TN 37067-5047, USA

Hentschel, Falk (Actor)
c/o Elisa Christophe *Public Eye Communications*
535 Kings Rd
#313 Plaza
London SW10 0SZ, UNITED KINGDOM

Henwick, Jessica (Actor)
c/o Sophie Patterson *Tavistock Wood Management*
45 Conduit St
London W1S 2YN, UNITED KINGDOM

Hepburn, Cassandra (Actor)
c/o Mara Santino *Luber Roklin Management*
5815 W Sunset Blvd Ste 208
Los Angeles, CA 90028-6481, USA

Hepburn, Lonnie (Athlete, Football Player)
1875 NW 59th St
Miami, FL 33142-2429, USA

Hephner, Jeff (Actor)
c/o Jillian Roscoe *ID Public Relations*
7060 Hollywood Blvd Fl 8th
Los Angeles, CA 90028-6021, USA

Hepler, Bill (Athlete, Baseball Player)
12518 Fort King Rd
Dade City, FL 33525-5609, USA

Hepple, Alan (Athlete, Hockey Player)
1000 Chopper Cir
Denver, CO 80204-5805, USA

Heppner, Peter (Musician)
c/o Staff Member *Warner Music (Germany)*
Alter Wandrahm 14
Hamburg D-20457, GERMANY

Herb, Marvin (Business Person)
Coca-Cola Bottling Company of Chicago
7400 N Oak Park Ave
Niles, IL 60714-3818

Herbers, Ian (Athlete, Hockey Player)
1135 Ridgeway Rd
Brookfield, WI 53045-2423, USA

Herbers, Katja (Actor)
c/o Janey van Ireland *nummer19*
Ottersingel 1
Culemborg VW 04105, THE NETHERLANDS

Herbert, Doug (Race Car Driver)
1443 E Gaston St
Lincolnton, NC 28092-4401, USA

Herbert, Holly (Journalist)
Celebrity Justice c/o Warner Bros
4000 Warner Blvd
Burbank, CA 91522-0002, USA

Herbert, Johnny (Race Car Driver)
PP Sayber AG
Wildbachstr 9
Hinwil 08340, SWITZERLAND

Herbert, Raymond E (Ray) (Athlete, Baseball Player)
15281 Newburgh Rd
Livonia, MI 48154-5038, USA

Herbert, Vincent (Musician, Producer)
c/o Kenneth (Kenny) Meiselas *Grubman Shire & Meiselas*
152 W 57th St Fl 31
New York, NY 10019-3310, USA

Herbstreit, Kirk (Sportscaster)
c/o Staff Member *ESPN (Main)*
935 Middle St
Espn Plaza
Bristol, CT 06010-1000, USA

Herd, Richard (Actor)
PO Box 57155
Sherman Oaks, CA 91413-2155, USA

Heredia, Felix (Athlete, Baseball Player)
PO Box 4842
Hialeah, FL 33014-0842, USA

Heredia, Gil (Athlete, Baseball Player)
Missoula Osprey 412 WAlder St Attn Coaching Staff
Missoula, MT 59802-4122, USA

Heredia, Wilson (Actor)
c/o Sarah Fargo *Paradigm*
140 Broadway Ste 2600
New York, NY 10005-1011, USA

Heredia, Wilson Jermaine (Actor, Musician)
c/o Mitch Clem *Mitch Clem Management*
7080 Hollywood Blvd Ste 1100
Hollywood, CA 90028-6938, USA

Herek, Stephen R (Director)
Endeavor Talent Agency
9701 Wilshire Blvd Ste 1000
Beverly Hills, CA 90212-2010, USA

Herera, Sue (Correspondent, Television Host)
c/o Staff Member *CNBC (Main)*
900 Sylvan Ave
Englewood Cliffs, NJ 07632-3312, USA

Herger, Wally (Congressman, Politician)
242 Cannon Hob
Washington, DC 20515-4322, USA

Hergert, Joe (Athlete, Football Player)
875 Tater Rd
New Smyrna Beach, FL 32168-9140, USA

Herges, Matt (Athlete, Baseball Player)
21019 N 79th Pl
Scottsdale, AZ 85255-6421, USA

Herjavec, Robert (Business Person, Reality Star)
c/o Penny Vizcarra *PV Public Relations*
121 N Almont Dr Apt 203
Beverly Hills, CA 90211-1860, USA

Herkenhoff, Matt (Athlete, Football Player)
16000 Baywood Ln
Eden Prairie, MN 55346-2409, USA

Herles, Kathleen (Actor)
c/o Shirley Grant *Shirley Grant Management*
PO Box 866
Teaneck, NJ 07666-0866, USA

Herlihy, Tim (Actor, Comedian)
c/o Staff Member *WME|IMG*
9601 Wilshire Blvd
Beverly Hills, CA 90210-5213, USA

Herline, Alan (Athlete, Football Player)
610 Post Oak Cir
Brentwood, TN 37027-5189, USA

Herman, Alexis (Politician)
892 Linganore Dr
Mc Lean, VA 22102-2141, USA

Herman, Bill (Athlete, Basketball Player)
200 Laurel Lake Dr Apt 305
Hudson, OH 44236-2175, USA

Herman, Bill (Horse Racer)
478 Sycamore Springs St
Debary, FL 32713-4828, USA

Herman, Dave (Athlete, Football Player)
19 Stephens Ln
Valhalla, NY 10595-1601, USA

Herman, David J (Business Person)
Adam Opel AG
Bahnhofplatz 1
Russelsheim 65429, GERMANY

Herman, Jerry (Musician)
455 N Palm Dr Apt 3
Beverly Hills, CA 90210-4894, USA

Herman, Micah (Director)
c/o Joannie Burstein *Burstein Company*
15304 W Sunset Blvd Ste 208
Pacific Palisades, CA 90272-3656, USA

Herman, Pee-Wee (Actor, Comedian)
PO Box 29373
Los Angeles, CA 90029-0373

Hermann, Mark (Athlete, Football Player)
8525 Tidewater Dr
Indianapolis, IN 46236-8917, USA

Hermann, Peter (Actor)
c/o Randi Goldstein *Gersh*
41 Madison Ave Ste 3301
New York, NY 10010-2210, USA

Hermannson, Dustin M (Baseball Player)
9002 E Rimrock Dr
Scottsdale, AZ 85255-9133, USA

Hermansen, Chad (Athlete, Baseball Player)
2104 Rhonda Ter
Henderson, NV 89074-0651, USA

Hermanson, Dustin (Athlete, Baseball Player)
9002 E Rimrock Dr
Scottsdale, AZ 85255-9133, USA

Hermeling, Terry (Athlete, Football Player)
717 NW 16th Ave
Portland, OR 97209-2301, USA

Hermida, Jeremy (Athlete, Baseball Player)
1821 Berkshire Pass
Atlanta, GA 30338-5029, USA

Hermits s/ Peter Noone, Herman's (Music Group, Musician)
Herman's Hermits Inc
1482 E Valley Rd Ste 515
Montecito, CA 93108-1200, USA

Hermlin, Stephan (Writer)
Hermann-Hesse-Str 39
Berlin 13156, GERMANY

Herms, George (Artist)
Jack Rutberg Fine Arts
PO Box 48739
Los Angeles, CA 90048-0739, USA

Hern, Tom (Actor)
c/o Simon Millar *Rumble Media*
1620 Broadway Ste C
Santa Monica, CA 90404-2777, USA

Hernandez, Adrian (Athlete, Baseball Player)
1723 Alden Rd Apt 1
Janesville, WI 53545-0886, USA

Hernandez, Angel (Athlete, Baseball Player)
501 Cypress Xing
Wellington, FL 33414-6369, USA

Hernandez, Carlos (Athlete, Baseball Player)
San Diego Padres
PO Box 122000
Attn: Player Development Dept
San Diego, CA 92112-2000, USA

Hernandez, Chuck (Athlete, Baseball Player)
9704 Hidden Cove Ct
Tampa, FL 33618-4542, USA

Hernandez, David (Musician)
c/o Stephen Ford *Diva Central Inc*
7510 W Sunset Blvd # 1445
Los Angeles, CA 90046-3408, USA

Hernandez, David (Athlete, Baseball Player)
9618 McKenn(l D(
Elk Grove, CA 95757-4024, USA

Hernandez, Evelio (Athlete, Baseball Player)
3004 SW 113th Ave
Miami, FL 33165-2228, USA

Hernandez, Felix (Athlete, Baseball Player)
c/o Alan Nero *Octagon (Chicago)*
875 N Michigan Ave Ste 2700
Chicago, IL 60611-1822, USA

Hernandez, Jackie (Athlete, Baseball Player)
13390 NE 7th Ave Apt 103
North Miami, FL 33161-7509, USA

Hernandez, Jay (Actor)
c/o Jason Barrett *Alchemy Entertainment*
7024 Melrose Ave Ste 420
Los Angeles, CA 90038-3394, USA

Hernandez, Jeremy (Athlete, Baseball Player)
861 Hemlock Ridge Ct
Simi Valley, CA 93065-5540, USA

Hernandez, Jose (Astronaut)
4015 N Water Iris Ct
Houston, TX 77059-3013, USA

Hernandez, Jose (Athlete, Baseball Player)
22 Calle S
Vega Alta, PR 00692-7073, USA

Hernandez, Joseline (Musician, Reality Star)
c/o Everett Johnson *WME|IMG*
9601 Wilshire Blvd
Beverly Hills, CA 90210-5213, USA

Hernandez, Keith (Athlete, Baseball Player)
c/o Staff Member *SportsNet New York*
75 Rockefeller Plz
New York, NY 10019-6908, USA

Hernandez, Laurie (Athlete, Gymnast, Olympic Athlete)
c/o Sheryl Shade *Shade Global*
171 W 57th St Apt 8A
New York, NY 10019-2222, USA

Hernandez, Leo (Athlete, Baseball Player)
1352 SW 75th Ave
Miami, FL 33144-4422, USA

Hernandez, Livan (Athlete, Baseball Player)
560 Gate Ln
Miami, FL 33137-3361, USA

Hernandez, Los Bros (Artist)
c/o Staff Member *Fantagraphics Books*
7563 Lake City Way NE
Seattle, WA 98115-4218, USA

Hernandez, Matt (Athlete, Football Player)
PO Box 682
Eastpointe, MI 48021-0682, USA

Hernandez, Michel (Athlete, Baseball Player)
18857 Maisons Dr
Lutz, FL 33558-2879, USA

Hernandez, Orlando (Athlete, Baseball Player)
1001 Brickell Bay Dr Ste 1710
Miami, FL 33131-4939, USA

Hernandez, Ramon (Athlete, Baseball Player)
19498 S Coquina Way
Weston, FL 33332-2423, USA

Hernandez, Roberto (Athlete, Baseball Player)
5965 Bayview Cir S
Gulfport, FL 33707-3929, USA

Hernandez, Rudy (Athlete, Baseball Player)
8 Calle Rodriguez Serra
San Juan, PR 00907-1456, USA

Hernandez, Rudy (Athlete, Baseball Player)
Beloit Snappers
PO Box 855
Attn: Coaching Staff
Beloit, WI 53512-0855, USA

Hernandez, Runelvys (Athlete, Baseball Player)
18717 E 24th Street Ct S
Independence, MO 64057-2474, USA

Hernandez, Willie (Athlete, Baseball Player)
PO Box 125
Calle C Buzon
Aguada, PR 00602-0125, USA

Hernandez, Xavier (Athlete, Baseball Player)
21302 Falls Frost Dr
Richmond, TX 77407-1026, USA

Herndon, David (Athlete, Baseball Player)
337 Dusty Ln
Panama City, FL 32409-2203, USA

Herndon, Junior (Athlete, Baseball Player)
139 W 8th St
Craig, CO 81625-2403, USA

Herndon, Kelly (Athlete, Football Player)
1968 Cambridge St
Twinsburg, OH 44087-2008, USA

Herndon, Larry (Athlete, Baseball Player)
2125 N Lake Ave
Attn: Coaching Staff
Lakeland, FL 33805-5012

Herndon, Larry (Athlete, Baseball Player)
6149 Brunswick Rd
Arlington, TN 38002-6936, USA

Herndon, Mark J (Music Group, Musician)
RR 1 Box 239A
Mentone, AL 35984, USA

Herndon, Ty (Music Group)
PO Box 121858
Nashville, TN 37212-1858, USA

Heroux, Yves (Athlete, Hockey Player)
8 Village Ln
Middletown, NJ 07748-1854, CANADA

Herr, Matt (Athlete, Hockey Player)
1951 Holly Creek Pl
Concord, CA 94521-1550, USA

Herr, Tom (Athlete, Baseball Player)
1077 Olde Forge Xing
Lancaster, PA 17601-1738, USA

Herranz Casado, Julian Cardinal (Religious Leader)
Legislative Texts Curia
Piazza Pio XII #10
Rome 00193, ITALY

Herremans, Todd (Athlete, Football Player)

Herren, James (Athlete, Football Player)
224 Monongahela Ave
Glassport, PA 15045-1319, USA

Herrera, Alfonso (Actor, Musician)
c/o Fabiola Pena *TOR Entertainment (LA)*
Heriberto Frias 846
Col Del Valle
Mexico City DF 03100, MEXICO

Herrera, Anthony (Athlete, Football Player)
c/o Chad Speck *Allegiant Athletic Agency*
35 Market Sq Ste 201
Knoxville, TN 37902-1420, USA

Herrera, Augustine (Race Car Driver)
Marty Kane Motorsports
PO Box 908
Brea, CA 92822-0908, USA

Herrera, Carolina (Designer, Fashion Designer)
Carolina Herrera Ltd
501 Fashion Ave Fl 17
New York, NY 10018-5911, USA

Herrera, Caroline (Designer, Fashion Designer)
501 Seventh Ave Fl 17
New York, NY 10018, USA

Herrera, Efren (Athlete, Football Player)
861 Atlanta Ct
Claremont, CA 91711-2515, USA

Herrera, Jaime (Congressman, Politician)
1130 Longworth Hob
Washington, DC 20515-0606, USA

Herrera, Johnny (Race Car Driver)
Johnny Herrera Racing Inc
2333 E Southern Ave Unit 1013
Tempe, AZ 85282-7639, USA

Herrera, Kristin (Actor)
c/o Abby Bluestone *Innovative Artists*
1505 10th St
Santa Monica, CA 90401-2805, USA

Herriman, Damon (Actor)
c/o Lisa Mann *Lisa Mann Creative Management*
19-25 Cope St
Redfern NSW 02016, AUSTRALIA

Herriman, Don (Athlete, Hockey Player)
640 Homewood Ave
Peterborough, ON K9J 4V6, Canada

Herring, Harold (Athlete, Football Player)
8673 Laurel Dr N
Pinellas Park, FL 33782-4304, USA

Herring, Joanne (Actor)
c/o Brad Littlefield *Open Range Pictures*
11124 Washington Blvd
Culver City, CA 90232-3902, USA

Herring, Lynn (Actor)
37900 Road 800
Raymond, CA 93653-9714, USA

Herring-James, Katie (Athlete, Baseball Player, Commentator)
143 Grouse Ridge Rd
Tamaqua, PA 18252-5442, USA

Herrington, John B (Astronaut)
4367 Bays Water Dr
Colorado Springs, CO 80920-7636, USA

Herrman, Ed (Athlete, Baseball Player)
13153 Tobiasson Rd
Poway, CA 92064-4308, USA

Herrmann, Don (Athlete, Football Player)
PO Box 318
Brookside, NJ 07926-0318, USA

Herrmann, Mark (Athlete, Football Player)
8525 Tidewater Dr
Indianapolis, IN 46236-8917, USA

Herrnstein, John (Athlete, Baseball Player)
603 Seminole Rd
Chillicothe, OH 45601-1547, USA

Herrod, Jeff (Athlete, Football Player)
20129 Tamiami Ave
Tampa, FL 33647-3370, USA

Herron, Bruce (Athlete, Football Player)
8504 S Calumet Ave
Chicago, IL 60619-6026, USA

Herron, Cindy (Music Group)
East West Records
75 Rockefeller Plz Ste 1200
New York, NY 10019-7849, USA

Herron, Denis (Athlete, Hockey Player)
12841 Marsh Pointe Way
West Palm Beach, FL 33418-6973, USA

Herron, Keith (Athlete, Basketball Player)
5374 Chew Ave Apt G2
Philadelphia, PA 19138-2815, USA

Herron, Tim (Athlete, Golfer)
20440 Linden Rd
Excelsior, MN 55331-9371, USA

Herrscher, Rick (Athlete, Baseball Player)
4436 Belclaire Ave
Dallas, TX 75205-3037, USA

Hersch, Fred (Music Group, Musician)
SRO Artists
PO Box 9532
Madison, WI 53715, USA

Herschler, E David (Artist)
1206 Coast Village Cir Ste I
Santa Barbara, CA 93108-2710, USA

Hersh, Earl (Athlete, Baseball Player)
682 Morning Glory Dr
Hanover, PA 17331-7828, USA

Hersh, Kristin (Musician)
c/o Staff Member *Concerted Efforts*
PO Box 440326
Somerville, MA 02144-0004, USA

Hersh, Seymour (Journalist, Writer)
1211 Connecticut Ave NW Ste 320
Washington, DC 20036-2709, USA

Hershey, Barbara (Actor)
c/o Jill Littman *Impression Entertainment*
9229 W Sunset Blvd Ste 700
Los Angeles, CA 90069-3407, USA

Hershey, Erin (Actor)
PO Box 16212
Irvine, CA 92623-6212, USA

Hershey-Reeser, Esther Anne (Athlete, Baseball Player, Commentator)
3450 Compass Rd
Gap, PA 17527-9006, USA

Hershiser, Orel (Athlete, Baseball Player)
2167 Orchard Mist St
Las Vegas, NV 89135-1563, USA

Herskovitz, Marshall (Producer)
c/o Staff Member *Bedford Falls Company, The*
409 Santa Monica Blvd PH
Santa Monica, CA 90401-2232, USA

Herta, Bryan (Race Car Driver)
Bryan Herta Racing, Inc
25083 Blue Ridge Way
Stevenson Rnh, CA 91381-1821, USA

Hertel, Rob (Athlete, Football Player)
1707 Camden Pkwy
S Pasadena, CA 91030-4913, USA

Herter, Jason (Athlete, Hockey Player)
5325 Roosevelt Dr
Hermantown, MN 55811-3679, USA

Hertford, Chelsea (Actor)
345 E Tujunga Ave Apt G
Burbank, CA 91502-1339, USA

Hertweck, Neal (Athlete, Baseball Player)
3020 Thistle Trl
Suwanee, GA 30024-1044, USA

Hertz, Steve (Athlete, Baseball Player)
10211 SW 96th Ter
Miami, FL 33176-2704, USA

Hertzberg, Daniel (Journalist)
Wall Street Journal
200 Liberty St
Editorial Dept
New York, NY 10281-1003, USA

Hervey, Jason (Actor)
c/o Staff Member *Bischoff/Hervey Entertainment*
1033 N Hollywood Way Ste F
Burbank, CA 91505-2550, USA

Hervey, Jillian (Actor, Musician)
c/o Brian Edwards *Enter Talking Client Relations*
645 W 9th St Ste 110
Los Angeles, CA 90015-1662, USA

Hervey, Matt (Athlete, Hockey Player)
38635 Maracaibo Cir W
Palm Springs, CA 92264-0208, USA

Herzfeld, John (Director)
c/o Staff Member *WME|IMG*
9601 Wilshire Blvd
Beverly Hills, CA 90210-5213, USA

Herzfeld, John M (Director)
Industry Entertainment
955 Carrillo Dr Ste 300
Los Angeles, CA 90048-5400, USA

Herzigova, Eva (Model)
c/o Scott Lipps *One Management*
42 Bond St Fl 2
New York, NY 10012-2768, USA

Herzlich, Mark (Athlete, Football Player)
c/o Tom Condon *Creative Artists Agency (CAA)*
401 Commerce St PH
Nashville, TN 37219-2516, USA

Herzlinger, Brian (Director)
c/o Naren Desai *Brillstein Entertainment Partners*
9150 Wilshire Blvd Ste 350
Beverly Hills, CA 90212-3453, USA

Herzog, Arthur III (Writer)
4 E 81st St
New York, NY 10028-0235, USA

Herzog, Werner (Director)
Werner Herzog Filmproduktion
Spiegelgasse 9
Vienna 01010, Austria

Herzog, Whitey (Athlete, Baseball Player, Coach)
9426 Sappington Estates Dr
Saint Louis, MO 63127-1664, USA

Hesketh, Joe (Athlete, Baseball Player)
202 Glenridge Rd
East Aurora, NY 14052-2625, USA

Heskin, Kam (Actor)
c/o Susan Calogerakis *SC Management*
9465 Wilshire Blvd Fl 7
Beverly Hills, CA 90212-2606, USA

Heslov, Grant (Actor, Director)
c/o Rick Ax *Gold Coast Management*
935 Victoria Ave Frnt
Venice, CA 90291-3933, USA

Hess, Bob (Athlete, Hockey Player)
PO Box 598
Chesterfield, MO 63006-0598, USA

Hess, Erika (Skier)
Aeschi
Gratenort 06388, SWITZERLAND

Hess, Jared (Director, Writer)
Moxie Pictures
2644 30th St Ste 100
Santa Monica, CA 90405-3051, USA

Hess, John B (Business Person)
Amerada Hess Corp
1185 Avenue of the Americas Fl 39
New York, NY 10036-2665, USA

Hess, Sandra (Actor)
7410 Rosewood Ave
Los Angeles, CA 90036-5750, USA

Hesseman, Howard (Actor)
Innovative Artists
1505 10th St
Santa Monica, CA 90401-2805, USA

Hession, Therese (Athlete, Golfer)
3871 Stonesthrow Ln
Hilliard, OH 43026-5712, USA

Hessler, Gordon (Director)
8910 Holly Pl
Los Angeles, CA 90046-1836, USA

Hessman, Mike (Athlete, Baseball Player)
566 Flowering Branch Ave
Little River, SC 29566-6787, USA

Hest, Ari (Musician)
c/o Staff Member *Paradigm (Monterey)*
404 W Franklin St
Monterey, CA 93940-2303, USA

Hester, Dan (Athlete, Basketball Player)
13846 N Sunset Dr
Fountain Hills, AZ 85268-3173, USA

Hester, Devin (Athlete, Football Player)
c/o Ashley Smith Becker *Relativity Sports*
2029 Century Park E Ste 1550
Century City, CA 90067-3000, USA

Hester, Jessie L (Athlete, Football Player)
12813 Pineacre Ct
Wellington, FL 33414-4140, USA

Hester, John (Athlete, Baseball Player)
125 Okoni Ln
Eatonton, GA 31024-1098, USA

Heston, Fraser (Actor)
7990 Briar Summit Dr
Los Angeles, CA 90046-1125, USA

Hetfield, James (Musician)
c/o Staff Member *Q Prime (NY)*
729 7th Ave Fl 16
New York, NY 10019-6831, USA

Hetki, Johnny (Athlete, Baseball Player)
4004 Stary Dr
Cleveland, OH 44134-5823, USA

Hetrick, Jennifer (Actor)
c/o Staff Member *AKA Talent Agency*
325 N Larchmont Blvd
Los Angeles, CA 90004-3011, USA

Hettema, Dave (Athlete, Football Player)
31 Desert Sky Rd SE
Albuquerque, NM 87123-3983, USA

Hetzel, Eric (Athlete, Baseball Player)
2271 Hetzel Rd
Crowley, LA 70526-8318, USA

Hetzel, Fred (Athlete, Basketball Player)
218 Cornwall St NW
Leesburg, VA 20176-2701, USA

Heughan, Sam (Actor)
c/o Theresa Peters *United Talent Agency (UTA)*
9336 Civic Center Dr
Beverly Hills, CA 90210-3604, USA

Heuring, Lori (Actor)
c/o Sheree Cohen *Buchwald*
5900 Wilshire Blvd Ste 3100
Los Angeles, CA 90036-5030, USA

Heusinger, Patrick (Actor)
c/o Jeffrey Chassen *Imprint PR*
6121 W Sunset Blvd
Neuehouse
Los Angeles, CA 90028-6442, USA

Heverly-Williams, Ruth (Baseball Player)
520 Tennis Ave
Ambler, PA 19002-6015, USA

Heveron, Doug (Race Car Driver)
PO Box 250
Denver, NC 28037-0250, USA

Heward, Jamie (Athlete, Hockey Player)
159 Bentley Dr
Regina, SK S4N 4S7, Canada

Hewett, Howard (Music Group)
GHR Entertainment
6014 N Pointe Pl
Woodland Hills, CA 91367-5500, USA

Hewgley, Claude (Athlete, Football Player)
55 Silvermont Dr
Spring, TX 77382-2007, USA

Hewitt, Angela (Musician)
Cramer/Marder Artists
3436 Springhill Rd
Lafayette, CA 94549-2535, USA

Hewitt, Bill (Athlete, Baseball Player)
923 Vance Jackson Apt 1107
San Antonio, TX 78201-2739, USA

Hewitt, Bob (Tennis Player)
822 Boylston St Ste 203
Chestnut Hill, MA 02467-2504, USA

Hewitt, Christopher (Actor)
154 E 66th St
New York, NY 10065-6643, USA

Hewitt, Jennifer Love (Actor)
c/o Ruth Bernstein *Viewpoint Inc*
8820 Wilshire Blvd Ste 220
Beverly Hills, CA 90211-2622, USA

Hewitt, John (Race Car Driver)
Hewitt Racing
37 Hewitt Dr
Troy, NY 12180-8121, USA

Hewitt, Martin (Actor)
1346 Madonna Rd
San Luis Obispo, CA 93405-6504, USA

Hewitt, Paul (Basketball Player, Coach)
Georgia Institute of Technology
Athletic Dept
Atlanta, GA 30332-0001, USA

Hewitt, Peter (Director, Producer, Writer)
c/o Jenne Casarotto *Casarotto Ramsay & Associates Ltd (UK)*
Waverley House
7-12 Noel St
London W1F 8GQ, UNITED KINGDOM

Hewko, Robert (Athlete, Football Player)
100 Lincoln Rd Apt 634
Miami Beach, FL 33139-2013, USA

Hewlett, David (Actor)
c/o Shelley Browning *Magnolia Entertainment*
9595 Wilshire Blvd Ste 601
Beverly Hills, CA 90212-2506, USA

Hewlett, Howard (Music Group)
Green Light Talent Agency
24024 Saint Moritz Dr
Valencia, CA 91355-2033, USA

Hewson, Eve (Actor)
c/o Cynthia Pett-Dante *Brillstein Entertainment Partners*
9150 Wilshire Blvd Ste 350
Beverly Hills, CA 90212-3453, USA

Hewson, Jack (Athlete, Basketball Player)
114 Tahlequah Ln
Loudon, TN 37774-3143, USA

Hewson, Liv (Actor)
c/o Aran Michael *Aran Michael Management*
PO Box 8696
Armadale VC 03143, AUSTRALIA

Hextall, Dennis H (Athlete, Hockey Player)
2728 Long Winter Ln
Oakland, MI 48363-2154, USA

Hextall, Ronald (Ron) (Athlete, Hockey Player)
1111 S Figueroa St Ste 3100
Los Angeles, CA 90015-1333, USA

Hextall Jr, Brian (Athlete, Hockey Player)
908-6880 Wallace Dr
Brentwood Bay, BC V8M 1N8, Canada

Hey, Virginia (Actor)

Heydeman, Greg (Athlete, Baseball Player)
702 Ramona Ave
Monterey, CA 93940-5430, USA

Heyer, Kirk (Athlete, Football Player)
4264 Center Street
Omaha, NE 68105, USA

Heyer, Shane (Athlete, Hockey Player)
345 Toyon Ter
San Marcos, CA 92069-8120, USA

Heyerdahl, Christopher (Actor)
c/o Michael Greene *Greene & Associates*
1901 Avenue of the Stars Ste 130
Los Angeles, CA 90067-6030, USA

Heyman, Paul (Athlete, Wrestler)
4 Cherrywood Rd
Scarsdale, NY 10583-4606, USA

Hey! Ocean (Music Group)
c/o Staff Member *Nettwerk Management (Canada)*
1850 W Second Ave
Vancouver BC V6J 4R3, CANADA

Heyward, Cameron (Athlete, Football Player)
c/o Michael Perrett *Element Sports Group*
3180 N Point Pkwy Ste 106
Alpharetta, GA 30005-4349, USA

Heyward, Jason (Athlete, Baseball Player)
1685 Mount Paran Rd NW
Atlanta, GA 30327-3805, USA

Heyward, Nick (Musician)
c/o Staff Member *Little Giant Entertainment*
2 Hermitage House
Gerrard Road
London N1 8AT, UK

Heyward-Bey, Darrius (Athlete, Football Player)
c/o Tom Condon *Creative Artists Agency (CAA)*
401 Commerce St PH
Nashville, TN 37219-2516, USA

Heywood, Anne (Actor)
9966 Liebe Dr
Beverly Hills, CA 90210-1037, USA

H. Hoyer, Steney (Congressman, Politician)
1705 Longworth Hob
Washington, DC 20515-2005, USA

Hiatt, Jack (Athlete, Baseball Player)
715 E 1st St
Coquille, OR 97423-1904, USA

Hiatt, John (Music Group, Musician, Songwriter, Writer)
c/o Staff Member *United Talent Agency (UTA)*
9336 Civic Center Dr
Beverly Hills, CA 90210-3604, USA

Hiatt, Phil (Athlete, Baseball Player)
30 Littleton St
Cantonment, FL 32533-6558, USA

Hiatt, Shana (Actor, Model)
c/o Jerry Shandrew *Shandrew Public Relations*
1050 S Stanley Ave
Los Angeles, CA 90019-6634, USA

Hibbard, Greg (Athlete, Baseball Player)
Mahoning Valley Scrappers 111 Eastwood Mall Blvd
Attn Coaching Staff
Niles, OH 44446-4841, USA

Hibbard, Greg (Athlete, Baseball Player)
5575 Lamb Rd
Arlington, TN 38002-9316, USA

Hibbert, Edward (Actor)
Gage Group
14724 Ventura Blvd Ste 505
Sherman Oaks, CA 91403-3505, USA

Hibbs, Jim (Athlete, Baseball Player)
4659 Foothill Rd
Ventura, CA 93003-1903, USA

Hick, John H (Religious Leader)
144 Oak Tree Lane
Selly Oak
Birmingham B29 6HU, UNITED KINGDOM (UK)

Hick', Ray (Athlete, Football Player)
801 Evergreen Dr
Friendswood, TX 77546-4757, USA

Hickam, Homer (Writer)
9532 Hemlock Dr SE
Huntsville, AL 35803-1165, USA

Hickam, Homer H Jr (Writer)
9532 Hemlock Dr SE
Huntsville, AL 35803-1165, USA

Hicke, Ernie (Athlete, Hockey Player)
5287 S Sugarberry Ct
Gilbert, AZ 85298-4657, USA

Hickenbottom, Michael (Wrestler)
c/o Kerry Rodgerson *World Wrestling Entertainment (WWE)*
1241 E Main St
Stamford, CT 06902-3520, USA

Hickerson, Bryan (Athlete, Baseball Player)
275 S Hunters Rdg
Warsaw, IN 46582-5645, USA

Hickerson, Gene (Athlete)
4471 Nagel Rd
Avon, OH 44011-2735, USA

Hickey, Bo (Athlete, Football Player)
94 Field Crest Rd
New Canaan, CT 06840-6330, USA

Hickey, Jim (Athlete, Baseball Player)
216 Maryland Ave
Saint Cloud, FL 34769-2424, USA

Hickey, John Benjamin (Actor)
c/o Sarah Fargo *Paradigm*
140 Broadway Ste 2600
New York, NY 10005-1011, USA

Hickey, Pat (Athlete, Hockey Player)
2 Alexis St
Red Deer, AB T4R 3E6, Canada

Hickey, William V (Business Person)
Sealed Air Corp
Park 80 E
Saddle Brook, NJ 07663, USA

Hickland, Catherine (Actor)
255 W 84th St Apt 2A
New York, NY 10024-4322, USA

Hickman, Dallas (Athlete, Football Player)
6521 E Dreyfus Ave
Scottsdale, AZ 85254-3915, USA

Hickman, Darryl (Actor)
171 Hermosillo Rd
Santa Barbara, CA 93108-2414, USA

Hickman, Dwayne (Actor)
PO Box 17226
Encino, CA 91416-7226, USA

Hickman, Fred (Sportscaster)
Cable News Network
1050 Techwood Dr NW
Sports Dept
Atlanta, GA 30318-5695, USA

Hickman, Jesse (Athlete, Baseball Player)
2004 Simmons St # A
Alexandria, LA 71301-3739, USA

Hickman, Jim (Race Car Driver)
PO Box 455
Henning, TN 38041-0455, USA

Hickman, Larry (Athlete, Football Player)
11245 Shoreline Dr Apt 210
Tyler, TX 75703-7466, USA

Hickman, Tracy (Writer)
c/o Staff Member *HarperCollins Publishers*
195 Broadway Fl 2
New York, NY 10007-3132, USA

Hickox, Edwin (Athlete, Baseball Player)
239 Coral Reef Way
Daytona Beach, FL 32124-1107, USA

Hickox, Edwin (Attorney, Baseball Player)
239 Coral Reef Way
Daytona Beach, FL 32124-1107, USA

Hicks, Adam (Actor)
c/o Mona Loring *Status PR*
PO Box 6191
Westlake Village, CA 91359-6191, USA

Hicks, Alex (Athlete, Hockey Player)
7500 E Deer Valley Rd Unit 158
Scottsdale, AZ 85255-4869, USA

Hicks, Artis (Athlete, Football Player)
1804 Woods Edge Dr NE
Leesburg, VA 20176-6618, USA

Hicks, Betty (Athlete, Golfer)
10357 Mary Ave
Cupertino, CA 95014-1340, USA

Hicks, Brandon (Athlete, Baseball Player)
4907 Pocahontas Dr
Pasadena, TX 77505-2915, USA

Hicks, Buddy (Athlete, Baseball Player)
1526 N Dixie Downs Rd Unit 26
Saint George, UT 84770-4105, USA

Hicks, Catherine (Actor)
c/o Margrit Polak *Margrit Polak Management*
1920 Hillhurst Ave Ste 405
Los Angeles, CA 90027-2712, USA

Hicks, Doug (Athlete, Hockey Player)
117 Selkirk Blvd
Red Deer, AB T4N 0G8, Canada

Hicks, Dwight (Athlete, Football Player)
PO Box 342
Sierra Madre, CA 91025-0342, USA

Hicks, Eric (Athlete, Football Player)
10410 W 168th Ter
Overland Park, KS 66221-4597, USA

Hicks, Esther (Writer)
PO Box 690070
San Antonio, TX 78269-0070, USA

Hicks, Glenn (Athlete, Hockey Player)
2 Alexis St
Red Deer, AB T4R 3E6, Canada

Hicks, Jim (Athlete, Baseball Player)
2927 Highland Lakes Dr
Missouri City, TX 77459-4218, USA

Hicks, Jimmy (Musician)
4110 N Shore Dr
West Palm Beach, FL 33407-3202, USA

Hicks, Joe (Athlete, Baseball Player)
2707 Brookmere Rd
Charlottesville, VA 22901-1106, USA

Hicks, Michele (Actor)
c/o Eric Black *Crestview Entertainment*
521 Montana Ave
Santa Monica, CA 90403-1313, USA

Hicks, Michelle (Actor)
c/o Staff Member *Innovative Artists*
1505 10th St
Santa Monica, CA 90401-2805, USA

Hicks, Robert (Athlete, Football Player)
2544 Hightower Ct NW
Atlanta, GA 30318-7412, USA

Hicks, Scott (Director)
PO Box 824
Kent Town 05071, SOUTH AFRICA

Hicks, "Sonny" Osceola (Athlete, Football Player)
1626 Wood Grove Rd
Memphis, TN 38117-2350, USA

Hicks, Sylvester (Athlete, Football Player)
144 Sweetbay Dr
Jackson, TN 38301-3569, USA

Hicks, Taylor (Musician)
c/o Cole Johnstone *Johnstone Management*
Prefers to be contacted by email or phone.
Nashville, TN 37201, USA

Hicks, Thomas O (Commentator)
Texas Rangers
2200 Ross Ave # 50
Dallas, TX 75201-2708, USA

Hicks, Tom (Athlete, Football Player)
207 Rivershire Ln Apt 106
Lincolnshire, IL 60069-3808, USA

Hicks, Wayne (Athlete, Hockey Player)
7500 E Deer Valley Rd Unit 158
Scottsdale, AZ 85255-4869, USA

Hicks, W K (Athlete, Football Player)
10149 Kemp Forest Dr
Houston, TX 77080-2509, USA

Hiddleston, Tom (Actor)
c/o Michael Symons *Hamilton Hodell Ltd*
20 Golden Sq
Fl 5
London W1F 9JL, UNITED KINGDOM

Hide, Herbie (Boxer)
Matchroom
10 Western Road
Romford
Essex RM1 3JT, UNITED KINGDOM (UK)

Hidi, Andre (Athlete, Hockey Player)
38 Avoca Ave
Toronto, ON M4T 2B9, Canada

Hieb, Richard J (Astronaut)
Allied Signal Tech Services
7010 Olde Stage Rd
Boulder, CO 80302-3402, USA

Hiemstra, Ed (Athlete, Football Player)
100 Hamilton Ct Unit D
Manhattan, MT 59741-8162, USA

Hieronymus, Clara W (Journalist)
50 Spring St
Savannah, TN 38372-1454, USA

Hietala, Brad (Race Car Driver)
85 North St
Enfield, CT 06082-3933, USA

Hietpas, Joe (Athlete, Baseball Player)
611 E Timberline Dr
Appleton, WI 54913-7104, USA

Hi-Five (Music Group)
PO Box 313030
Jamaica, NY 11431-3030, USA

Higashi, Satoshi (Athlete, Golfer)
Bridgestone Sports
45 Higashi-Matsushita-Cho Kanda
Chiyoda-ku
Tokyo 00101, Japan

Higdon, Bruce (Cartoonist)
210 Canvasback Ct
Murfreesboro, TN 37130-8855, USA

Higgins, Al (Producer)
c/o Staff Member *Creative Artists Agency (CAA)*
2000 Avenue of the Stars Ste 100
Los Angeles, CA 90067-4705, USA

Higgins, Anthony (Actor)
c/o Staff Member *Independent Talent Group*
40 Whitfield St
London W1T 2RH, UNITED KINGDOM

Higgins, Brian (Congressman, Politician)
2459 Rayburn Hob
Washington, DC 20515-4311, USA

Higgins, Chris (Athlete, Hockey Player)
34 Colgate Dr
Smithtown, NY 11787-2017, USA

Higgins, David (Actor)
c/o Ben Feigin *Anonymous Content*
3532 Hayden Ave
Culver City, CA 90232-2413, USA

Higgins, Dennis (Athlete, Baseball Player)
1123 Boonville Rd
Jefferson City, MO 65109-0621, USA

Higgins, Earle (Athlete, Basketball Player)
29128 Chateau Ct
Farmington Hills, MI 48334-4112, USA

Higgins, Jack (Cartoonist)
7 Timber Vw
Lemont, IL 60439-8740, USA

Higgins, Jack (Writer)
September Tide
Mont de la Rocque Jersey
Channel Island, UNITED KINGDOM (UK)

Higgins, John (Coach, Swimmer)
40 Williams Dr
Annapolis, MD 21401-2265, USA

Higgins, John Michael (Actor)
c/o Jo Yao *United Talent Agency (UTA)*
9336 Civic Center Dr
Beverly Hills, CA 90210-3604, USA

Higgins, Kevin (Athlete, Baseball Player)
10551 Haywood Dr
Las Vegas, NV 89135-2851, USA

Higgins, Mark (Athlete, Baseball Player)
2999 Abbotts Oak Way
Duluth, GA 30097-2193, USA

Higgins, Mike (Athlete, Basketball Player)
137 48th Ave
Greeley, CO 80634-4307, USA

Higgins, Missy (Musician)
c/o Staff Member *EMI Music (Australia)*
PO Box 311
98-100 Glover St
Westwood, MA 02090-0311, Australia

Higgins, Pam (Athlete, Golfer)
5 Pea Pine Ln
Newport Beach, CA 92660, USA

Higgins, Paul (Athlete, Hockey Player)
c/o Staff Member *Toronto Young Nationals Hockey Club*
233-1080 Tapscott Rd
Scarborough, ON M1X 1E7, Canada

Higgins, Robert (Business Person)
Fleet Boston Corp
1 Federal St
Boston, MA 02110-2012, USA

Higgins, Rod (Athlete, Basketball Player)
743 Mendenhall Ct
Fort Mill, SC 29715-7852, USA

Higgins, Scott (Athlete, Baseball Player)
3591 Indian Clover St
Plumas Lake, CA 95961-8740, USA

Higgins, Tim (Athlete, Hockey Player)
c/o Staff Member *Chicago Blackhawks*
1901 W Madison St
Chicago, IL 60612-2459, USA

Higgins, Tom (Athlete, Football Player)
506-251 Queens Quay W
Toronto, ON M5J 2N6, Canada

Higginson, Bobby (Athlete, Baseball Player)
2039 Indian Sky Cir
Lakeland, FL 33813-4859, USA

Higginson, Torri (Actor)
c/o Peter Young *Sovereign Talent Group*
1642 Westwood Blvd Ste 202
Los Angeles, CA 90024-5609, USA

Higgs, Kenny (Athlete, Basketball Player)
746 Sargent Dr
Owensboro, KY 42301-8332, USA

Higgs, Mark (Athlete, Football Player)
45 NW 156th Ln
Pembroke Pines, FL 33028-1500, USA

Higham, Scott (Journalist)
Washington Post
Editorial Dept
1150 15th St NW
Washington, DC 20071-0001, USA

Highley, Ray (Race Car Driver)
Red Line Racing
1650 Linda Vista Dr
San Marcos, CA 92078-3810, USA

Highmore, Freddie (Actor)
c/o Sue Latimer *Artists Rights Group (ARG)*
4A Exmoor St
London W10 6BD, UNITED KINGDOM

Highsmith, Alonzo (Athlete, Football Player)
3703 E Valley Dr
Missouri City, TX 77459-4305, USA

Highsmith, Don (Athlete, Football Player)
221 S 9th Ave
Highland Park, NJ 08904-3145, USA

High Speed Scene, The (Music Group)
c/o Staff Member *Paradigm (Monterey)*
404 W Franklin St
Monterey, CA 93940-2303, USA

Hightower, Chelsie (Actor)
c/o Cynthia Snyder *Cynthia Snyder Public Relations*
5739 Colfax Ave
N Hollywood, CA 91601-1636, USA

Hightower, Dont'a (Athlete, Football Player)
c/o Michael Perrett *Element Sports Group*
3340 Peachtree Rd NE Fl 16
Atlanta, GA 30326-1000, USA

Higuera, Teddy (Athlete, Baseball Player)
1567 S Sycamore Pl
Chandler, AZ 85286-6818, USA

Hii, Remy (Actor)
c/o Trent Baker *RGM Artists*
8-12 Ann St
Surry Hills, NSW 02010, AUSTRALIA

Hiii-Westerman, Joyce (Athlete, Baseball Player, Commentator)
1565 47th Ave
Kenosha, WI 53144-1289, USA

Hijeulos, Oscar (Writer)
132 E 43rd St
New York, NY 10017-4019, USA

Hikaru, Utada (Musician)
c/o Staff Member *Island Records*
825 8th Ave Rm C2
New York, NY 10019-7472, USA

Hilario, Maybyner (Nene) (Basketball Player)
Denver Nuggets
1000 Chopper Cir
Pepsi Center
Denver, CO 80204-5805, USA

Hilario, Nene (Athlete, Basketball Player)
c/o Dan Fegan *Relativity Sports*
2029 Century Park E Ste 1550
Century City, CA 90067-3000, USA

Hilbert, Andy (Athlete, Hockey Player)
419 N Michigan Ave
Howell, MI 48843-1505, USA

Hilbert, Jon (Athlete, Football Player)
10505 Colonel Hancock Dr
Louisville, KY 40291-4081, USA

Hildebrand, Brianna (Actor)
c/o Dominique Appel *Imprint PR*
6121 W Sunset Blvd
Neuehouse
Los Angeles, CA 90028-6442, USA

Hildebrand, Jeffrey (Business Person)
3780 Willowick Rd
Houston, TX 77019-1116, USA

Hildebrand, Madison (Business Person, Reality Star)
Coldwell Banker
29178 Heathercliff Rd Ste 3
Malibu, CA 90265-4168, USA

Hildebrandt, Greg (Cartoonist)
Dark Horse
10956 SE Main St
Milwaukie, OR 97222-7644, USA

Hilderbrand, Elin (Writer)
c/o Katharine Mayers *Little, Brown & Co.*
1290 Avenue of the Americas
New York, NY 10104-0101, USA

Hilderth, Mark (Actor)
c/o Staff Member *SMS Talent*
8383 Wilshire Blvd Ste 230
Beverly Hills, CA 90211-2436, USA

Hilfiger, Tommy (Designer, Fashion Designer)
Tommy Hilfiger USA
601 W 26th St Rm 500
New York, NY 10001-1142, USA

Hilgenberg, Jay W (Athlete, Football Player)
1296 Kimmer Ct
Lake Forest, IL 60045-3669, USA

Hilgenberg, Joel (Athlete, Football Player)
2027 Ridgeway Dr
Iowa City, IA 52245-3239, USA

Hilgenbrinck, Tad (Actor)
c/o Jonathan Howard *Innovative Artists*
1505 10th St
Santa Monica, CA 90401-2805, USA

Hilgendorf, Tom (Athlete, Baseball Player)
PO Box 124
Camanche, IA 52730-0124, USA

Hilger, Rusty (Athlete, Football Player)
2625 SW 67th St
Oklahoma City, OK 73159-2735, USA

Hiljus, Erik (Athlete, Baseball Player)
2253 Demaray Dr
Grants Pass, OR 97527-9147, USA

Hilker, Nadia (Actor)
c/o Annick Oppenheim *Wolf-Kasteler Public Relations*
6255 W Sunset Blvd Ste 1111
Los Angeles, CA 90028-7426, USA

Hill, Aaron (Actor)
c/o Siri Garber *Platform PR*
2666 N Beachwood Dr
Los Angeles, CA 90068-2308, USA

Hill, Aaron (Athlete, Baseball Player)
1147 Skye Ln
Palm Harbor, FL 34683-1460, USA

Hill, A Derek (Artist)
National Art Collections Fund
20 John Islip St
London SW1, UNITED KINGDOM (UK)

Hill, Al (Athlete, Hockey Player)
4807 Margaret Ln
Harrisburg, PA 17110-3365, United States

Hill, Al (Athlete, Hockey Player)
4807 Margaret Ln
Harrisburg, PA 17110-3365, USA

Hill, Armand (Athlete, Basketball Player)
1626 Laurens Way SW
Atlanta, GA 30311-3718, USA

Hill, Bernard (Actor)
c/o Staff Member *Seven Summits Pictures & Management*
8906 W Olympic Blvd
Beverly Hills, CA 90211-3550, USA

Hill, Bob (Basketball Coach, Coach)
2215 Cedar Springs Rd Apt 1607
Dallas, TX 75201-1863, USA

Hill, Bobby (Athlete, Baseball Player)
1874 Dry Creek Rd
San Jose, CA 95124-1005, USA

Hill, Brendan (Musician)
c/o Staff Member *ArtistDirect*
9046 Lindblade St
Culver City, CA 90232-2513, USA

Hill, Bruce (Athlete, Football Player)
1919 E Citation Ln
Tempe, AZ 85284-4704, USA

Hill, Calvin (Athlete, Football Player)
10300 Walker Lake Dr
Great Falls, VA 22066-3557, USA

Hill, Carolyn (Athlete, Golfer)
5906 Skimmer Point Blvd S
Gulfport, FL 33707-3938, USA

Hill, Cindy (Athlete, Golfer)
2852 NW 8th St
Fort Lauderdale, FL 33311-6637, USA

Hill, Damon G D (Race Car Driver)
PO Box 100
Nelson
Lanscashire BB9 8AQ, UNITED KINGDOM (UK)

Hill, Dan (Musician, Songwriter)
Paquin Entertainment
1067 Sherwin Rd
Winnipeg, MB R3H 0T8, CANADA

Hill, Daniel W (Dan) (Athlete, Football Player)
171 Montrose Dr
Durham, NC 27707-3929, USA

Hill, Dave (Athlete, Baseball Player)
4950 Colonnades Cir W
Lakeland, FL 33811-1572, USA

Hill, David H (Athlete, Football Player)
921 Clements Cir
Moody, AL 35004-2512, USA

Hill, Derek (Athlete, Football Player)
8939 Gallatin Rd
Pico Rivera, CA 90660-1693, USA

Hill, Donnie (Athlete, Baseball Player)
6 Knob Hl
Laguna Niguel, CA 92677-5903, USA

Hill, Dule (Actor)
c/o Marisa Martins *The Lede Company*
401 Broadway Ste 206
New York, NY 10013-3033, USA

Hill, Dusty (Music Group, Musician)
Lone Wolf Mgmt
PO Box 163690
Austin, TX 78716-3690, USA

Hill, Eddie (Race Car Driver)
National Hot Rod Association
2035 E Financial Way
Glendora, CA 91741-4602, USA

Hill, Eric (Athlete, Football Player)
5500 Palm Cir
Galveston, TX 77551-5566, USA

Hill, Erica (Television Host)
Prime News Tonight
1 Time Warner Ctr
CNN
New York, NY 10019-6038, USA

Hill, Faith (Musician)
c/o Kristen Foster *PMK/BNC Public Relations*
1840 Century Park E Ste 1400
Los Angeles, CA 90067-2115, USA

Hill, Fred (Athlete, Football Player)
31441 Paseo Riobo
San Juan Capistrano, CA 92675-5524, USA

Hill, Garry (Athlete, Baseball Player)
9602 Willowglen Trl
Charlotte, NC 28215-9767, USA

Hill, Gary (Athlete, Basketball Player, Football Player)
9957 Hickory Hollow Rd
Shawnee, OK 74804-9059, USA

Hill, George (Athlete, Basketball Player)
c/o Staff Member *Indiana Pacers*
125 S Pennsylvania St
Indianapolis, IN 46204-3610, USA

Hill, Glenallen (Athlete, Baseball Player)
108 Calvin Pl
Santa Cruz, CA 95060-3124, USA

Hill, Grant (Athlete, Basketball Player, Olympic Athlete, Sportscaster)
c/o Jim Tanner *Tandem Sports & Entertainment*
2900 Crystal Dr Ste 420
Arlington, VA 22202-3556, USA

Hill, Greg (Athlete, Football Player)
Audio Video Unplugged
14580 E Beltwood Pkwy
Farmers Branch, TX 75244-3200, USA

Hill, Greg (Athlete, Football Player)
P.O. Box 43210
Port Hueneme, CA 93044, USA

Hill, Greg L (Athlete, Football Player)
P.O. Box 43210
Port Hueneme, CA 93044, USA

Hill, Gregory (Director)
c/o Staff Member *Paul Lane Entertainment*
468 N Camden Dr
Beverly Hills, CA 90210-4507, USA

Hill, Ike (Athlete, Football Player)
412 Randolph St
Oak Park, IL 60302-3260, USA

Hill, Jack (Director, Producer)
c/o Alan Shafer *Careyes Entertainment*
8447 Wilshire Blvd Ste 401
Beverly Hills, CA 90211-3209, USA

Hill, J D (Athlete, Football Player)
2543 N 53rd Dr
Phoenix, AZ 85035-1910, USA

Hill, J.D. (Athlete, Football Player)
1550 S Yucca St
Chandler, AZ 85286-6859, USA

Hill, Jeremy (Athlete, Football Player)
10050 Gooding Dr
Dallas, TX 75229-6209, USA

Hill, Jim (Sportscaster)
ABC-TV
77 W 66th St
Sprots Dept
New York, NY 10023-6201, USA

Hill, Jim (Athlete, Football Player)
4120 Parva Ave
Los Angeles, CA 90027-1365, USA

Hill, Jody (Director, Producer)
c/o Staff Member *Rough House Pictures*
1726 Whitley Ave
Hollywood, CA 90028-4809, USA

Hill, John S (Athlete, Football Player)
2005 Boyce Bridge Rd
Creedmoor, NC 27522-8023, USA

Hill, Jonah (Actor, Comedian)
c/o Rick Yorn *LBI Entertainment*
2000 Avenue of the Stars Fl 11
N Tower Fl 3
Los Angeles, CA 90067-4732, USA

Hill, Jordan (Athlete, Basketball Player)
c/o Bill Duffy *BDA Sports Management*
700 Ygnacio Valley Rd Ste 330
Walnut Creek, CA 94596-3838, USA

Hill, Ken (Athlete, Baseball Player)
1360 Shady Oaks Dr
Southlake, TX 76092-4208, USA

Hill, Kenneth (Athlete, Football Player)
121 Hawkins Pl
Boonton, NJ 07005-1127, USA

Hill, Kent (Athlete, Football Player)
630 Hawthorne Pl
Fayetteville, GA 30214-1218, USA

Hill, Kent A (Athlete, Football Player)
630 Hawthorne Pl
Fayetteville, GA 30214-1218, USA

Hill, Kim (Music Group)
Ambassador Artist Agency
PO Box 50358
Nashville, TN 37205-0358, USA

Hill, King (Athlete, Football Player)
7611 Sands Terrace Ln
Spring, TX 77389-2131, USA

Hill, Koyie (Athlete, Baseball Player)
2405 NW 151st St
Edmond, OK 73013-9227, USA

Hill, Koyle (Athlete, Baseball Player)
5216 N Valentine Rd
Park City, KS 67219-2718, USA

Hill, Lauryn (Actor, Musician)
441 Twin Oak Rd
South Orange, NJ 07079-1219, USA

Hill, Madre (Athlete, Football Player)
18 Charleston Ct
Elgin, SC 29045-8521, USA

Hill, Marc (Athlete, Baseball Player)
203 Maple St
Elsberry, MO 63343-1604, USA

Hill, Michael (Commentator)
11231 NW 18th St
Plantation, FL 33323-2226, USA

Hill, Mike (Athlete, Golfer)
4008 Nevel Cv
Clarklake, MI 49234-9733, USA

Hill, Milt (Athlete, Baseball Player)
8401 Avalon Ct
Cumming, GA 30041-5724, USA

Hill, Norm (Athlete, Football Player)
340 Dromore Ave
Winnipeg, MB R3M 0J5, Canada

Hill, Pat (Football Player)
California State University
Athletic Dept
Fresno, CA 93740-0001, USA

Hill, Perry (Athlete, Baseball Player)
8916 Wyatt Cir
Argyle, TX 76226-6513, USA

Hill, Randal (Athlete, Football Player)
5360 SW 130th Ter
Miramar, FL 33027-5411, USA

Hill, Rich (Athlete, Baseball Player)
17 Spafford Rd
Milton, MA 02186-4408, USA

Hill, Ron (Athlete, Track Athlete)
PO Box 11
Hyde
Cheshire SK14 1RD, UNITED KINGDOM (UK)

Hill, Roy (Race Car Driver)
Roy Hill Drag Racing School
4926 Walker Mill Rd
Sophia, NC 27350-9246, USA

Hill, Samme (Athlete, Football Player)
c/o Brian Levy *Goal Line Football Management*
1025 Kane Concourse Ste 207
Bay Harbor Islands, FL 33154-2118, USA

Hill, Sean (Athlete, Hockey Player, Olympic Athlete)
2735 E Carob Dr
Chandler, AZ 85286-3118, USA

Hill, Shaun (Athlete, Football Player)

Hill, Simmie (Athlete, Basketball Player)
1470 Elizabeth Blvd
Pittsburgh, PA 15221-1223, USA

Hill, Susan E (Writer)
Longmoor Farmhouse Ebrington
Chipping Campden
Glos GL55 6NW, UNITED KINGDOM (UK)

Hill, Tamia (Musician)
c/o Staff Member *HUFF Events and PR*
325 W 38th St Rm 805
New York, NY 10018-9622, USA

Hill, Taylor Marie (Model)
c/o Aleen Keshishian *Lighthouse Management and Media*
9000 W Sunset Blvd Ste 1520
Los Angeles, CA 90069-5815, USA

Hill, Terence (Actor)
3 Los Pinos Rd
Santa Fe, NM 87507-4300, USA

Hill, Thomas (Tom) (Athlete, Track Athlete)
428 Elmcrest Dr
Norman, OK 73071-7053, USA

Hill, Tony (Athlete, Football Player)
729 Forest Bend Dr
Plano, TX 75025-3205, USA

Hill, Tye (Athlete, Football Player)
c/o Doug Hendrickson *Relativity Sports*
2029 Century Park E Ste 1550
Century City, CA 90067-3000, USA

Hill, Tyrone (Baseball Player)
Pinnacle
5594 Electric Ave
San Bernardino, CA 92407-2713, USA

Hill, Virgil (Athlete, Boxer)
1618 Santa Gertrudis Loop
Bismarck, ND 58503-0866, USA

Hill, Walter (Director)
c/o John Burnham *ICM Partners*
10250 Constellation Blvd Fl 7
Los Angeles, CA 90067-6207, USA

Hill, Will (Athlete, Football Player)
c/o Adisa P Bakari *Kelley Drye & Warren LLP*
3050 K St NW Ste 400
Washington, DC 20007-5100, USA

Hillaby, John (Writer)
Constable Co
Lanchesters
102 Fulham Palace Road
London W6 9ER, UNITED KINGDOM (UK)

Hillan, Patrick (Actor)
11005 Morrison St Apt 206
N Hollywood, CA 91601-3899

Hillebrand, Gerald (Athlete, Football Player)
23 Madison Cir
Davenport, IA 52806-2812, USA

Hillegas, Shawn (Athlete, Baseball Player)
1409 116th Dr SE
Lake Stevens, WA 98258-7935, USA

Hillen, Bobby (Race Car Driver)
Donlavey Racing
5011 Midlothian Turnpike
Richmond, VA 23225, USA

Hillenbrand, Daniel A (Business Person)
Hillenbrand Industries
700 State RR 46 E
Batesville, IN 47006, USA

Hillenbrand, Laura (Writer)
c/o Tina Bennett *WME|IMG (NY)*
11 Madison Ave Fl 18
New York, NY 10010-3669, USA

Hillenbrand, Shea (Athlete, Baseball Player)
2614 E Via De Palmas
Gilbert, AZ 85298-2068, USA

Hiller, Arthur (Director)
1230 N Doheny Dr
Los Angeles, CA 90069-1723, USA

Hiller, Jim (Athlete, Coach, Hockey Player)
c/o Staff Member *Chilliwack Bruins*
45323 Hodgins Ave
Chilliwack, BC V2P 8G1, Canada

Hiller, John (Athlete, Baseball Player)
W8085 Becker Dr
Iron Mountain, MI 49801-9385, USA

Hiller, Lee (Journalist)
c/o Staff Member *Artistic Agency*
PO Box 68538
Portland, OR 97268-0538, USA

Hillery, Patrick J (President)
Grasmere Greenfield Road
Sutton
Dublin 13, IRELAND

Hill Hearth, Amy (Writer)
c/o Staff Member *Trident Media Group LLC*
41 Madison Ave Fl 36
New York, NY 10010-2257, USA

Hilliard, Corey (Athlete, Football Player)
c/o Mitchell Frankel *Impact Sports (FL)*
2799 NW 2nd Ave Ste 203
Boca Raton, FL 33431-6709, USA

Hilliard, Dalton (Athlete, Football Player)
23 Hermitage Dr
Destrehan, LA 70047-3701, USA

Hilliard, Ike (Athlete, Football Player)
c/o Neil Schwartz *Schwartz & Feinsod*
4 Hillandale Rd
Rye Brook, NY 10573-1705, USA

Hilliard, Issac (Athlete, Football Player)
8240 SW 164th Ter
Palmetto Bay, FL 33157-3653, USA

Hillier, Randy (Athlete, Hockey Player)
308 Brookhaven Ln
Pittsburgh, PA 15241-2582, USA

Hillier, Steve (Music Group, Musician)
Primary Talent Int'l
2-12 Petonville Road
London N1 9PL, UNITED KINGDOM (UK)

Hillin Jr, Bobby (Race Car Driver)
c/o Staff Member *NASCAR*
1801 W Speedway Blvd
Daytona Beach, FL 32114-1243, USA

Hillis, Ali (Actor, Producer)
c/o Craig Schneider *Pinnacle Public Relations*
8721 Santa Monica Blvd # 133
W Hollywood, CA 90069-4507, USA

Hillis, Peyton (Athlete, Football Player)
c/o Drew Rosenhaus *Rosenhaus Sports Representation*
3921 Alton Rd # 440
Miami Beach, FL 33140-3852, USA

Hillis, Robert (Rib) (Actor)
c/o Charles Riley *Charles Riley*
7122 Beverly Blvd Ste F
Los Angeles, CA 90036-2572, USA

Hillman, Avriel (Actor)
203 W Comstock St Apt 11
Seattle, WA 98119-3557, USA

Hillman, Chris (Music Group, Musician, Songwriter, Writer)
McMullen Co
433 N Camden Dr Ste 400
Beverly Hills, CA 90210-4408, USA

Hillman, Darnell (Athlete, Basketball Player)
6011 Medora Dr
Indianapolis, IN 46228-1397, USA

Hillman, Dave (Athlete, Baseball Player)
849 Mimosa Dr
Kingsport, TN 37660-2563, USA

Hillman, Eric (Athlete, Baseball Player)
157 Bellaire St
Denver, CO 80220-5632, USA

Hillman, Larry (Athlete, Hockey Player)
57 Westland St
St Catharines, ON L2S 3W8, Canada

Hillman, Ronnie (Athlete, Football Player)
c/o Ashley Smith Becker *Relativity Sports*
2029 Century Park E Ste 1550
Century City, CA 90067-3000, USA

Hillman, Trey (Athlete, Baseball Player, Coach)
301 Appaloosa Run
Liberty Hill, TX 78642-3862, USA

Hills, Carla (Politician)
5610 Wisconsin Ave Ph 20C
Chevy Chase, MD 20815-4443, USA

Hills, Nate (Danja) (Musician, Producer)
8045 Mulholland Dr
Los Angeles, CA 90046-1128, USA

Hillsong (Music Group)
Hillsong Church
1-5 Solent Circuit
Baulkham Hills, NSW 02153, AUSTRALIA

Hillton, Dave (Athlete, Baseball Player)
4910 E Sunnyside Dr
Scottsdale, AZ 85254-4671, USA

Hill-Westerman, Joyce (Baseball Player)
1565 47th Ave
Kenosha, WI 53144-1289, USA

Hilmar, Hera (Actor)
c/o Donna Mills *Premier PR*
2-4 Bucknall St
London WC2H 8LA, UNITED KINGDOM

Hilmers, David C (Astronaut)
2846 Bellefontaine St
Houston, TX 77025-1610, USA

Hilmers, David C Colonel (Astronaut)
2846 Bellefontaine St
Houston, TX 77025-1610, USA

Hilson, Keri (Musician)
c/o Sherlen Archibald *The Chamber Group*
75 Broad St Rm 708
New York, NY 10004-3244, USA

Hil St Soul (Music Group)
c/o Staff Member *Paradigm (Monterey)*
404 W Franklin St
Monterey, CA 93940-2303, USA

Hilton, Barron (Business Person)
Hilton Hotels Corp
7930 Jones Branch Dr Ste 1100
McLean, VA 22102-3313, USA

Hilton, Dave (Athlete, Baseball Player)
4910 E Sunnyside Dr
Scottsdale, AZ 85254-4671, USA

Hilton, Fred (Athlete, Basketball Player)
6169 Mourning Dove Dr
Baton Rouge, LA 70817-1107, USA

Hilton, Janet (Music Group, Musician)
Holly House E Downs Road
Bowdon Altrincham
Cheshire WA14 2LH, UNITED KINGDOM (UK)

Hilton, John J (Athlete, Football Player)
2927 Stockbridge Way
Dacula, GA 30019-6865, USA

Hilton, Kathy (Reality Star)

Hilton, Nicky (Designer)
c/o Dawn Miller *Miller PR*
750 N San Vicente Blvd # 800
W Hollywood, CA 90069-5788, USA

Hilton, Paris (Designer, DJ, Model, Reality Star)
c/o Jamie Freed *Paris Hilton Entertainment*
2934 1/2 N Beverly Glen Cir # 383
Los Angeles, CA 90077-1724, USA

Hilton, Perez (Internet Star, Writer)
c/o Ben Russo *EMC / Bowery*
8356 Fountain Ave Apt E1
W Hollywood, CA 90069-2968, USA

Hilton, Rick (Business Person)
Hilton & Hyland
257 N Canon Dr
Beverly Hills, CA 90210-5301, USA

Hilton, Roy (Athlete, Football Player)
8332 Merrymount Dr
Baltimore, MD 21244-2242, USA

Hilton, TY (Athlete, Football Player)
c/o Michael Katz *Katz Brothers Sports*
600 Galleria Pkwy SE Ste 900
Atlanta, GA 30339-8121, USA

Hilton, Tyler (Actor, Musician)
c/o Becca Kovacik *Berwick & Kovacik*
6230 Wilshire Blvd
Los Angeles, CA 90048-5126, USA

Hilty, Megan (Actor)
c/o Jill Fritzo *Jill Fritzo Public Relations*
208 E 51st St # 305
New York, NY 10022-6557, USA

Hiltz, Nichole (Actor)
c/o Staff Member *Metropolitan (MTA)*
4526 Wilshire Blvd
Los Angeles, CA 90010-3801, USA

Hiltzik, Michael A (Journalist)
Los Angeles Times
2300 E Imperial Hwy
Editorial Dept
El Segundo, CA 90245-2813, USA

Hilworth, John (Athlete, Hockey Player)
11084 State Road 37 E
New Haven, IN 46774-9770, USA

HIM (Music Group, Musician)
c/o Tim Edwards *Flowerbooking*
2616 N Richmond St
Chicago, IL 60647-1710, USA

Himelstein, Aaron (Actor)
c/o Paul Brown *Industry Entertainment Partners*
955 Carrillo Dr Ste 300
Los Angeles, CA 90048-5400, USA

Himes, Dick (Athlete, Football Player)
431 Prairie Ln
Luxemburg, WI 54217-1054, USA

Himes, James (Congressman, Politician)
119 Cannon Hob
Washington, DC 20515-0501, USA

Himes, Larry (Commentator)
6516 W Montego Ln
Glendale, AZ 85306-3144, USA

Himmelman, Peter (Musician)
230 22nd. Street
Brentwood, CA 94513, USA

Hinault, Bernard (Athlete)
Les Poteries
Quessoy
Yffiniac F-22120, France

Hincapie, George (Athlete, Cycler, Olympic Athlete)
11 Bella Citta Ct
Greenville, SC 29609-2724, USA

Hinch, AJ (Athlete, Baseball Player)
59 W Double Green Cir
Spring, TX 77382-1098, USA

Hinchliffe, Brett (Athlete, Baseball Player)
5117 Melbourne St Unit 4204
Punta Gorda, FL 33980-3034, USA

Hinckley, Mike (Athlete, Baseball Player)
525 Allison Ln
Moore, OK 73160-0006, USA

Hinder (Music Group)
c/o Kevin 'Chief' Zaruk *Big Loud Mountain*
1111 16th Ave S Ste 201
Nashville, TN 37212-2336, USA

Hindi, Dion (Race Car Driver)
Hindi Motorsports
1421 Wagon Train Dr SE
Albuquerque, NM 87123-4296, USA

Hindle, Art (Actor)
Buzz Halliday & Assoc
8899 Beverly Blvd # 715
Los Angeles, CA 90048-2412, USA

Hindman, Stan (Athlete, Football Player)
824 Creed Rd
Oakland, CA 94610-1827, USA

Hindmarch, Dave (Athlete, Hockey Player)
3341 Beach Ave
Roberts Creek, BC V0N 2W2, Canada

Hinds, Aisha (Actor)
c/o Michael Greene *Greene & Associates*
1901 Avenue of the Stars Ste 130
Los Angeles, CA 90067-6030, USA

Hinds, Ciaran (Actor)
c/o Larry Dalzell *Dalzell & Beresford Ltd*
55 Charterhouse St
The Paddock Suite, The Courtyard
London EC1M 6HA, UNITED KINGDOM (UK)

Hinds, Cirian (Actor)
c/o Staff Member *WME/IMG*
9601 Wilshire Blvd
Beverly Hills, CA 90210-5213, USA

Hinds, Sam (Athlete, Baseball Player)
2151 Sunnyside Ave Apt 132
Clovis, CA 93611-4045, USA

Hinds, William (Cartoonist)
1301 Spring Oaks Cir
Houston, TX 77055-4703, USA

Hiner, Glen H (Business Person)
Owens-Coming
1 Owens Coming Parkway
Toledo, OH 43659-0001, USA

Hines, Andre (Athlete, Football Player)
6515 W 103rd St
Overland Park, KS 66212-1728, USA

Hines, Ben (Athlete, Baseball Player)
2709 2nd St
La Verne, CA 91750-5006, USA

Hines, Brendan (Actor)
c/o Heather Weiss-Besignano *ICON PR*
8961 W Sunset Blvd Ste 1C
W Hollywood, CA 90069-1886, USA

Hines, Bruce (Athlete, Baseball Player)
4155 E Fairfield St
Mesa, AZ 85205-5008, USA

Hines, Byron (Race Car Driver)
14010 Marquardt Ave
Santa Fe Springs, CA 90670-5019, USA

Hines, Cheryl (Actor)
c/o Ann Gurrola *Marleah Leslie & Associates*
1645 Vine St Apt 712
Los Angeles, CA 90028-8812, USA

Hines, Clint (Race Car Driver)
Hines Racing
8324 140th St W
Taylor Ridge, IL 61284-9769, USA

Hines, Deni (Music Group)
Peter Rix Mgmt
49 Hume St #200
Crows Nest, NSW 02065, AUSTRALIA

Hines, Glen Ray (Athlete, Football Player)
1429 Windsor Ave
Springdale, AR 72764-9301, USA

Hines, Grainger (Actor, Producer)
c/o Marianne Golan *Golan & Blumberg*
2761 E Woodbury Dr
Arlington Heights, IL 60004-7247, USA

Hines, Mimi (Actor)
2540 S Maryland Pkwy
Las Vegas, NV 89109-1627

Hines, Nyheim (Athlete, Football Player)
c/o Ed Wasielewski *EMG Sports - PA*
PO Box 2
Richboro, PA 18954-0002, USA

Hingis, Martina (Athlete, Tennis Player)
Inselweg 28
Hurden CH-8640, Switzerland

Hingsen, Jurgen (Athlete, Track Athlete)
655 Circle Dr
Santa Barbara, CA 93108-1001, USA

Hinkle, Lon (Athlete, Golfer)
PO Box 1347
Bigfork, MT 59911-1347, USA

Hinkle, Marin (Actor)
c/o Staff Member *Innovative Artists*
1505 10th St
Santa Monica, CA 90401-2805, USA

Hinkle, Robert (Actor)
389 Old Wagon Rd
Royse City, TX 75189-6761, USA

Hinkley, Brent (Actor)
c/o Staff Member *The Gage Group*
5757 Wilshire Blvd Ste 659
Los Angeles, CA 90036-3682, USA

Hinn, Benny (Religious Leader)
PO Box 162000
Irving, TX 75016-2000, USA

Hinnant, Michael (Athlete, Football Player)
43 Ashford Way
Schwenksville, PA 19473-1693, USA

Hinojosa, Ruben (Congressman, Politician)
2262 Rayburn Hob
Washington, DC 20515-0703, USA

Hinojosa, Tish (Music Group, Songwriter, Writer)
PO Box 3304
Austin, TX 78764-3304, USA

Hinote, Dan (Athlete, Hockey Player)
200 W Nationwide Blvd Unit 1
Columbus, OH 43215-2561, USA

Hinrich, Kirk (Basketball Player)
c/o Staff Member *Chicago Bulls*
1901 W Madison St
Chicago, IL 60612-2459, USA

Hinrichs, Paul (Athlete, Baseball Player)
1982 Brett Dr
Madisonville, KY 42431-9115, USA

Hinse, Andre (Athlete, Hockey Player)
PO Box 237
Fort Cobb, OK 73038-0237, USA

Hinshaw, Alex (Athlete, Baseball Player)
3367 Yankton Ave
Claremont, CA 91711-2004, USA

Hinshaw, George (Athlete, Baseball Player)
15125 S Raymond Ave Apt 14
Gardena, CA 90247-3433, USA

Hinske, Eric (Athlete, Baseball Player)
9460 E Sierra Pinta Dr
Scottsdale, AZ 85255-9196, USA

Hinsley, Jerry (Athlete, Baseball Player)
4255 Holliday Ln
Las Cruces, NM 88007-5760, USA

Hinson, Jordan (Actor)
c/o Sandra Siegal *Siegal Company, The*
9025 Wilshire Blvd Ste 400
Beverly Hills, CA 90211-1828, USA

Hinson, Larry (Athlete, Golfer)
3179 GA Highway 32 E
Douglas, GA 31533-1723, USA

Hinson, Roy (Athlete, Basketball Player)
4272 State Highway 27
Monmouth Junction, NJ 08852, USA

Hinson, Roy (Athlete, Basketball Player)
8804 Lakes Blvd
West Palm Beach, FL 33412-1549, USA

Hinterseer, Ernst (Skier)
Hahnenkammstr
Kitzbuhel 06370, AUSTRIA

Hinterseer, Hans (Hansi) (Athlete, Musician, Skier)
Charlet-Sonnenhofweg 16
Kitzbuhel A-6370, Austria

Hinton, Charles R (Athlete, Football Player)
124 Tanglewood Rd
Natchez, MS 39120-4526, USA

Hinton, Chris (Athlete, Football Player)
650 Galway Dr
Roswell, GA 30076-5132, USA

Hinton, Christopher J (Chris) (Athlete, Football Player)
5136 Falcon Chase Ln
Atlanta, GA 30342, USA

Hinton, Chuck (Athlete, Football Player)
124 Tanglewood Rd
Natchez, MS 39120-4526, USA

Hinton, Chuck (Athlete, Baseball Player)
6330 16th St NW
Washington, DC 20011-8010, USA

Hinton, Darby (Actor)
1267 Bel Air Road
Los Angeles, CA 90077, USA

Hinton, Eddie (Athlete, Football Player)
34 Auburn Rdg
Spring Branch, TX 78070-6014, USA

Hinton, James David (Actor)
c/o Staff Member *Cunningham Escott Slevin & Doherty (CESD)*
10635 Santa Monica Blvd Ste 130
Los Angeles, CA 90025-8306, USA

Hinton, Jerrika (Actor)
c/o Alyx Carr *42West*
600 3rd Ave Fl 23
New York, NY 10016-1914, USA

Hinton, Jill (Athlete, Golfer)
8976 SW 44th Ln
Gainesville, FL 32608-4140, USA

Hinton, Marcus (Athlete, Football Player)
63 Farrell Breland Rd
Wiggins, MS 39577-9119, USA

Hinton, Rich (Athlete, Baseball Player)
7447 Hawkins Rd
Sarasota, FL 34241-9376, USA

Hinton, Sam (Musician, Songwriter)
1719 Addison St
Berkeley, CA 94703-1501, USA

Hinton, S E (Writer)
8955 Beverly Blvd
West Hollywood, CA 90048-2423, USA

Hintz, Donald C (Business Person)
Entergy Corp
10055 Grogans Mill Rd Ste 150
The Woodlands, TX 77380-1048, USA

Hinzo, Tommy (Athlete, Baseball Player)
635 Imperial Beach Blvd
Imperial Beach, CA 91932-2720, USA

Hipp, I M (Athlete, Football Player)
1216 Hickman Arch
Virginia Beach, VA 23454-5878, USA

Hipp, Paul (Actor)
c/o Staff Member *Artists & Representatives (Stone Manners Salners)*
6100 Wilshire Blvd Ste 1500
Los Angeles, CA 90048-5110, USA

Hipple, Eric (Athlete, Football Player)
7155 Driftwood Dr
Fenton, MI 48430-4304, USA

Hipps, Claude (Athlete, Football Player)
3930 Hidden Oaks Ln
Melbourne, FL 32934-7738, USA

Hirase, Mayumi (Athlete, Golfer)
I M G
1360 E 9th St Ste 100
Cleveland, OH 44114-1730, USA

Hirata-Chalfin, Gail (Athlete, Golfer)
15539 Quiet Oak Dr
Chino Hills, CA 91709-4254, USA

Hire, Kathryn P Cdr (Astronaut)
PO Box 580146
Houston, TX 77258-0146, USA

Hire, Kathryn P (Kay) (Astronaut)
PO Box 580146
Houston, TX 77258-0146, USA

Hires, Justin (Actor, Comedian)
c/o CeCe Yorke *True Public Relations*
3575 Cahuenga Blvd W Ste 360
Los Angeles, CA 90068-1361, USA

Hirosue, Ryoyo (Actor)
c/o Omiotek Maciej *OmniotComp*
Sowinskiego 27A
Grodzisk
Mazowiecki, POLAND

Hirsch, Corey (Athlete, Hockey Player)
c/o Staff Member *Hockey Canada*
2424 University Dr NW
Calgary, AB T2N 3Y9, Canada

Hirsch, David (Actor)
6255 W Sunset Blvd # 627
Los Angeles, CA 90028-7403, USA

Hirsch, Emile (Actor)
c/o Sam Maydew *Silver Lining Entertainment*
421 S Beverly Dr Fl 7
Beverly Hills, CA 90212-4408, USA

Hirsch, Hallee (Actor, Musician)
c/o Amy Abell *BRS / Gage Talent Agency (LA)*
6300 Wilshire Blvd Ste 1430
Los Angeles, CA 90048-5216, USA

Hirsch, Judd (Actor)
c/o Harry Gold *TalentWorks*
3500 W Olive Ave Ste 1400
Burbank, CA 91505-5512, USA

Hirsch, Laurence E (Business Person)
Centex Corp
2728 N Harwood St Ste 200
Dallas, TX 75201-1579, USA

Hirsch, Lee (Director)
c/o Mark Ross *Paradigm*
8942 Wilshire Blvd
Beverly Hills, CA 90211-1908, USA

Hirsch, Robert P (Actor)
1 Pl du Palais Bourbon
Paris 75007, FRANCE

Hirsch, Tom (Athlete, Hockey Player)
8469 Zanzibar Ln N
Osseo, MN 55311-1814, USA

Hirschbeck, John (Athlete, Baseball Player)
495 Via Avelino St
North Lima, OH 44452-9604, USA

Hirschbeck, Mark (Athlete, Baseball Player)
15 Blackberry Ln
Shelton, CT 06484-3774, USA

Hirschbeck, Mark (Baseball Player)
15 Blackberry Ln
Shelton, CT 06484-3774, USA

Hirschbiegel, Oliver (Director)
c/o Tobin Babst *Kaplan/Perrone Entertainment*
9171 Wilshire Blvd Ste 350
Beverly Hills, CA 90210-5523, USA

Hirscher, Marcel (Athlete, Skier)
Atomic GMBH
Lackengasse 301
Altenmarkt A-5541, Austria

Hirsh, Hallee (Actor)
c/o Staff Member *Dorit Simone Management & Productions*
1012 S Robertson Blvd Ste E
Los Angeles, CA 90035-1551, USA

Hirson, Alice (Actor)
Halpem Assoc
PO Box 5597
Santa Monica, CA 90409-5597, USA

Hirst, Damien (Artist)
White Cube Gallery
44 Duke St
St James's
London SW1Y 6DD, UNITED KINGDOM (UK)

Hisaishi, Joe (Musician)
c/o Staff Member *Greenspan Artist Management*
8760 W Sunset Blvd
West Hollywood, CA 90069-2206, USA

Hiser, Gene (Athlete, Baseball Player)
1450 Caldwell Ln
Hoffman Estates, IL 60169-1202, USA

Hiskey, Babe (Athlete, Golfer)
1706 12th St
Galena Park, TX 77547-2302, USA

Hisle, Larry (Athlete, Baseball Player)
10603 N Hidden Reserve Cir
Mequon, WI 53092-5579, USA

Hislop, Ian (Actor)
c/o Jenne Casarotto *Casarotto Ramsay & Associates Ltd (UK)*
Waverley House
7-12 Noel St
London W1F 8GQ, UNITED KINGDOM

Hislop, Jamie (Athlete, Hockey Player)
10852 Mapleshire Cres SE
Calgary, AB T2J 1Y9, Canada

Hisner, Harley (Athlete, Baseball Player)
9925 Grotrian Rd
Monroeville, IN 46773-9580, USA

Hitchcock, Jimmy (Athlete, Football Player)
616 Briar Patch Ter
Waxhaw, NC 28173-6822, USA

Hitchcock, Ken (Athlete, Hockey Player)
St Louis Blues 1401 Clark
Ave Attn Coaching Staff
Saint Louis, MO 63103-2700, USA

Hitchcock, Michael (Actor)
c/o Josh Hornstock *United Talent Agency (UTA)*
9336 Civic Center Dr
Beverly Hills, CA 90210-3604, USA

Hitchcock, Patricia (Actor)
2648 Stafford Rd
Thousand Oaks, CA 91361-5039, USA

Hitchcock, Ray (Athlete, Football Player)
2190 Arcade St
Saint Paul, MN 55109-2572, USA

Hitchcock, Robyn (Musician, Songwriter)
c/o Ken Weinstein *Big Hassle Media*
40 Exchange Pl Ste 1900
New York, NY 10005-2714, USA

Hitchcock, Russell (Musician)
Agency for Performing Arts
9200 W Sunset Blvd Ste 900
Los Angeles, CA 90069-3604, USA

Hitchcock, Sterling (Athlete, Baseball Player)
255 Yucca Rd
Naples, FL 34102-5318, USA

Hitchens, Anthony (Athlete, Football Player)

Hite, Shere (Writer)
75 Haywood St Apt 312
Asheville, NC 28801-0075, USA

Hite-James, Kathy (Athlete, Golfer)
38651 Nyasa Dr
Palm Desert, CA 92211-7009, USA

Hitt, Joel (Athlete, Football Player)
800 Founders Pointe Blvd
Franklin, TN 37064-0752, USA

Hitt, Lee (Athlete, Football Player)
4318 N Hall St
Dallas, TX 75219-2731, USA

Hix, William (Athlete, Football Player)
5070 White Dr
Batesville, AR 72501-9138, USA

Hjejle, Iben (Actor, Writer)
c/o Staff Member *Kasper Notlev*
Gl. Kongevej 86A 3.Th
Frederiksberg C1850, Denmark

Hjertstedt, Gabriel (Athlete, Golfer)
100 Sawgrass Corners Dr
Ponte Vedra Beach, FL 32082-3567, USA

Hjorth, Maria (Athlete, Golfer)
608 Henley Cir
Davenport, FL 33896-3072, USA

Hlavac, Jan (Athlete, Hockey Player)
1033 Royal Pass Rd
Tampa, FL 33602-5724, USA

Hlushko, Todd (Athlete, Hockey Player)
16 Elderberry Crt
Guelph, ON N1L 1K3, Canada

H. Michaud, Michael (Congressman, Politician)
1724 Longworth Hob
Washington, DC 20515-0509, USA

Hnath, Lucas (Writer)
c/o George Freeman *WME/IMG*
9601 Wilshire Blvd
Beverly Hills, CA 90210-5213, USA

Hnatiuk, Glen (Athlete, Golfer)
8746 Mississippi Run
Weeki Wachee, FL 34613-4046, USA

Hnidy, Shane (Athlete, Hockey Player)
3 Iris
Irvine, CA 92620-2212, USA

Hnilicka, Milan (Athlete, Hockey Player)
1111 S Figueroa St
Los Angeles, CA 90015-1300, USA

Hoag, Judith W (Actor)
c/o Lori Jonas *Jonas Public Relations*
1327 Ocean Ave Ste F
Santa Monica, CA 90401-1024, USA

Hoag, Tami (Writer)
c/o Andrea Cirillo *Jane Rotrosen Agency*
318 E 51st St
New York, NY 10022-7803, USA

Hoage, Terrell L (Terry) (Athlete, Football Player)
870 Arbor Rd
Paso Robles, CA 93446-8609, USA

Hoagland, Ashley (Athlete, Golfer)
803 26th Ave W
Palmetto, FL 34221-3576, USA

Hoagland, Edward (Writer)
283 Village Ln
Bennington, VT 05201-9824, USA

Hoagland, Jahiem (Musician)
c/o Staff Member *Atlantic Records*
1290 Avenue of the Americas Fl 28
New York, NY 10104-0106, USA

Hoagland, Jimmie L (Jim) (Journalist)
Washington Post
Editorial Dept
1150 15th St NW
Washington, DC 20071-0001, USA

Hoaglin, Fred (Athlete, Coach, Football Coach, Football Player)
7 Governors Rd
Hilton Head, SC 29928-3018, USA

Hoak, Dick (Athlete, Football Player)
1103 Scepter Ln E
Greensburg, PA 15601-9401, USA

Hoard, Leroy (Athlete, Football Player)
3143 SW 141st Ter
Davie, FL 33330-4679, USA

Hoban, Mike (Athlete, Football Player)
1917 Holly Ave
Darien, IL 60561-3518, USA

Hobart, Ken (Athlete, Football Player)
531 18th Ave
Lewiston, ID 83501-3823

Hobart, Nick (Cartoonist)
4410 Glenview Ln
Winter Park, FL 32792-9058, USA

Hobaugh, Charles 0 Lt Colonel (Astronaut)
2009 Charter Pointe Ct
League City, TX 77573-9021, USA

Hobaugh, Charles O (Astronaut)
NASA
2101 Nasa Pkwy Spc Johnsoncenter
Houston, TX 77058-3696, USA

Hobaugh, Ed (Athlete, Baseball Player)
1420 3rd Ave
Ford City, PA 16226-1303, USA

Hobbie, Glen (Athlete, Baseball Player)
2115 N 835 St
Ramsey, IL 62080-4437, USA

Hobbs, Becky (Musician)
Entertainment Artists
2409 21st Ave S Ste 100
Nashville, TN 37212-5317, USA

Hobbs, Chelsea (Actor)

Hobbs, Ellis (Athlete, Football Player)
8885 Old Southwick Pass
Alpharetta, GA 30022-7137, USA

Hobbs, Jack (Athlete, Baseball Player)
3 Wade Dr
Cherry Hill, NJ 08034-1741, USA

Hobbs, Rebecca (Actor)
c/o Kathryn Rawlings *Kathryn Rawlings Actors Agency*
4/28 Williamson Ave.
Grey Lynn
Auckland, New Zealand

Hobby, Marion (Athlete, Football Player)
708 Nytol Cir
Irondale, AL 35210-2919, USA

Hobel, Mara (Actor)
17 Cunningham Dr
Lagrangeville, NY 12540-6841, USA

Hobgood, CJ (Athlete)
c/o Steven Astephen *Wasserman Media Group - Carlsbad*
2251 Faraday Ave # 200
Carlsbad, CA 92008-7209, USA

Hoblit, Gregory (Director, Producer)
c/o Harley Copen *ICM Partners*
10250 Constellation Blvd Fl 7
Los Angeles, CA 90067-6207, USA

Hobson, Clell L (Butch) (Athlete, Baseball Player)
5904 Saltaire Village Ct
Wilmington, NC 28412-2761, USA

Hobson, Mellody (Producer)
c/o Staff Member *DreamWorks SKG*
1000 Flower St
Glendale, CA 91201-3007, USA

Hoch, Carin (Athlete, Golfer)
I M G
1360 E 9th St Ste 100
Cleveland, OH 44114-1730, USA

Hoch, Danny (Artist)
c/o Sekka Scher *Ellipsis Entertainment Group*
175 Varick St Frnt 2
New York, NY 10014-4604, USA

Hoch, Greg (Horse Racer)
18 Summer Wind Loop
Murrells Inlet, SC 29576-5690, USA

Hoch, Scott (Athlete, Golfer)
8800 Lake Sheen Ct
Orlando, FL 32836-5482, USA

Hochevar, Luke (Athlete, Baseball Player)
2452 Glen Meadow Rd
Knoxville, TN 37909-1092, USA

Hochhuth, Rolf (Writer)
PO Box 661
Alfred, ME 04002-0661, SWITZERLAND

Hochstein, Lisa (Reality Star)
c/o Zachary Solov *Z Group LA*
Prefers to be contacted by email or phone.
Beverly Hills, CA 90048, USA

Hochstein, Russ (Athlete, Football Player)
43 Massand Rd
N Attleboro, MA 02760-6724, USA

Hochwald, Bari (Actor)
Tuscan Film Commission
Via San Gallo, 25
Florence 50129, Italy

Hocke, Stefan (Skier)
Sportgymnasium
Am Harzwald 3
Oberhof 98558, GERMANY

Hockenberry, Chuck (Athlete, Baseball Player)
1546 Birka Ln
Onalaska, WI 54650-2087, USA

Hockenberry, John (Actor, Correspondent, Writer)
c/o Sally Willcox *Creative Artists Agency (CAA)*
2000 Avenue of the Stars Ste 100
Los Angeles, CA 90067-4705, USA

Hockenbery, Chuck (Athlete, Baseball Player)
1546 Birka Ln
Onalaska, WI 54650-2087, USA

Hocking, Dennis (Athlete, Baseball Player)
2592 N Falconer Way
Orange, CA 92867-6493, USA

Hocking, Denny (Athlete, Baseball Player)
7384 E Villanueva Dr
Orange, CA 92867-6440, USA

Hocking, Justin (Athlete, Hockey Player)
3726 E 52nd Ct
Spokane, WA 99223-8604, USA

Hockney, David (Artist)
7508 Santa Monica Blvd
West Hollywood, CA 90046-6407, USA

Hocott, Brenda (Athlete, Golfer)
261 Cave Ln
San Antonio, TX 78209-2242, USA

Hodder, Kane (Actor)
3701 Senda Calma
Calabasas, CA 91302-3066, USA

Hoddick, Steve (Race Car Driver)
782 Aero Dr
Cheektowaga, NY 14225-1408, USA

Hoddle, Glenn (Soccer Player)
Football Assn
16 Lancaster Gate
London W2 3LW, UNITED KINGDOM (UK)

Hodel, Donald (Politician)
10922 Zephyr St
Broomfield, CO 80021-2630, USA

Hodel, Nathan (Athlete, Football Player)
19197 W Fairview Dr
Mundelein, IL 60060-3497, USA

Hodge, Aldis (Actor)
c/o Alyx Carr *42West*
600 3rd Ave Fl 23
New York, NY 10016-1914, USA

Hodge, Daniel A (Dan) (Wrestler)
General Delivery
Perry, OK 73077-9999, USA

Hodge, Douglas (Actor)
c/o Lindy King *United Agents*
12-26 Lexington St
London W1F OLE, UNITED KINGDOM

Hodge, Ed (Athlete, Baseball Player)
127 Jewell St
Johnson City, TN 37601-5209, USA

Hodge, Edwin (Actor)
c/o Matt Luber *Luber Roklin Management*
5815 W Sunset Blvd Ste 208
Los Angeles, CA 90028-6481, USA

Hodge, Patricia (Actor)
International Creative Mgmt
76 Oxford St
London W1N 0AX, UNITED KINGDOM (UK)

Hodge, Sedrick (Athlete, Football Player)
4140 Will Lee Rd
Atlanta, GA 30349-1952, USA

Hodge, Stephanie (Actor)
Gersh Agency
232 N Canon Dr
Beverly Hills, CA 90210-5302, USA

Hodge, Sue (Actor)
82 Constance Rd. Twickenham
Middlesex A TW2 7J, UK

Hodge Jr, Kenneth R (Ken) (Athlete, Hockey Player)
1115 Main St
Lynnfield, MA 01940-1030, USA

Hodges, Bill (Basketball Player, Coach)
Georgia College
Athletic Dept
Milledgeville, GA 31061, USA

Hodges, Bob (Athlete, Hockey Player)
43 Karch St
Cambridge, ON N3C 1Y4, Canada

Hodges, Craig (Athlete, Basketball Player)
67 Elm St
Park Forest, IL 60466-1702, USA

Hodges, Gerald (Athlete, Football Player)
c/o Michael McCartney *Priority Sports & Entertainment (Chicago)*
325 N La Salle Dr Ste 650
Chicago, IL 60654-8182, USA

Hodges, Kevin (Athlete, Baseball Player)
19506 Kuykendahl Rd
Spring, TX 77379-3408, USA

Hodges, Louise (Actor)
31A St. George's Rd Leyton
London ElO 5RH, UK

Hodges, Mike (Director)
Wesley Farm Durweston
Blanford Forum
Dorset DT11 0QG, UNITED KINGDOM (UK)

Hodges, Morris (Athlete, Baseball Player)
1520 River Haven Ln
Hoover, AL 35244-1259, USA

Hodges, Morris (Athlete, Baseball Player)
404 Park Lake Ter
Helena, AL 35080-3287, USA

Hodges, Pat (Actor, Musician)
c/o Staff Member *Diva Central Inc*
7510 W Sunset Blvd # 1445
Los Angeles, CA 90046-3408, USA

Hodges, Ron (Athlete, Baseball Player)
55 Hajo Ln
Rocky Mount, VA 24151-6819, USA

Hodges, Trey (Athlete, Baseball Player)
19506 Kuykendahl Rd
Spring, TX 77379-3408, USA

Hodge Sr, Ken (Athlete, Hockey Player)
13 Longfellow Dr
Newburyport, MA 01950-3325, USA

Hodgman, John (Actor)
c/o Jay Gassner *United Talent Agency (UTA)*
9336 Civic Center Dr
Beverly Hills, CA 90210-3604, USA

Hodgson, James D (Politician)
28802 Grayfox St
Malibu, CA 90265-4253, USA

Hodgson, Pat (Athlete, Football Player)
816 Commons Park
Statham, GA 30666-2539, USA

Hodgson, Roger (Musician)
c/o Staff Member *UTA/The Agency Group*
888 7th Ave Fl 7
New York, NY 10106-0700, USA

Hodgson, Ted (Athlete, Hockey Player)
PO Box 162
Hobbema, AB T0C 1N0, Canada

Hodo, David (Music Group)
8255 W Sunset Blvd
West Hollywood, CA 90046-2417, USA

Hodson, Kevin (Athlete, Hockey Player)
390 McNabb St
Unit 2
Sault Sainte Marie, ON P6B 1, Canada

Hodson, Tom (Athlete, Football Player)
1653 Obrien Dr
Baton Rouge, LA 70810-2927, USA

Hoebel, Bret (Reality Star)
c/o Staff Member *Abrams Artists Agency*
750 N San Vicente Blvd
E Tower Fl 11
Los Angeles, CA 90069-5788, USA

Hoechlin, Tyler (Actor)
c/o Evelyn Karamanos *Relevant*
400 S Beverly Dr Ste 220
Beverly Hills, CA 90212-4404, USA

Hoegh, Leo (Politician)
1472 W Desert Hills Dr
Green Valley, AZ 85622-8287, USA

Hoeks, Sylvia (Actor)
c/o Robin Baum *Slate PR*
901 N Highland Ave
W Hollywood, CA 90038-2412, USA

Hoelscher, David (Athlete, Football Player)
8931 N Star Fort Loramie Rd
Yorkshire, OH 45388-9750, USA

Hoelscher, Joel (Athlete, Football Player)
8931 N Star Fort Loramie Rd
Yorkshire, OH 45388-9750, USA

Hoelzer, Margaret (Athlete, Olympic Athlete, Swimmer)
500 Renton Ave S
Renton, WA 98057-6012, USA

Hoene, Ohil (Athlete, Hockey Player)
1110 Mississippi Ave
Duluth, MN 55811-4920, USA

Hoene, Phil (Athlete, Hockey Player)
5831 N Brooklet Pl
Boise, ID 83713-1353, USA

Hoenig, Michael (Musician)
c/o Staff Member *Gorfaine/Schwartz Agency Inc*
4111 W Alameda Ave Ste 509
Burbank, CA 91505-4171, USA

Hoernig, Otto W Lt Colonel (Astronaut)
12930 Worldgate Dr Ste 700
Herndon, VA 20170-6036, USA

Hoerr, Irv (Race Car Driver)
541 Division St
Campbell, CA 95008-6905, USA

Hoest, Bunny (Cartoonist)
William Hoest Enterprises
27 Watch Way
Lloyd Neck
Lloyd Harbor, NY 11743-9707, USA

Hoeven, john (Politician)
PO Box 2572
Bismarck, ND 58502-2572, USA

Hoey, George (Athlete, Football Player)
13635 Clermont Ct
Thornton, CO 80602-6965, USA

Hoey, Jim (Athlete, Baseball Player)
2360 Highwav 33
Ste 207
Trenton, NJ 08691-1417, USA

Hofer, Paul (Athlete, Football Player)
7093 Cedardale Rd
Olive Branch, MS 38654-1307, USA

Hoff, Katie (Athlete, Olympic Athlete, Swimmer)
c/o Staff Member *USA Swimming Association*
1 Olympic Plz Bldg 2A
Colorado Springs, CO 80909-5770, USA

Hoff, Philip (Politician)
Hoff Wilson Powell Lang
PO Box 123
Essex Junction, VT 05453-0123, USA

Hoffman, Al (Race Car Driver)
Al Hoffman Racing
17818 County Road 450A
Umatilla, FL 32784-9205, USA

Hoffman, Alice (Writer)
PO Box 381485
Cambridge, MA 02238-1485, USA

Hoffman, Barbara (Athlete, Baseball Player, Commentator)
318 E Mill St
Millstadt, IL 62260-1218, USA

Hoffman, Basil (Actor)
64 Glenflow Ct
Glendale, CA 91206-1730, USA

Hoffman, Dustin (Actor, Director, Producer)
PO Box 492359
Los Angeles, CA 90049-8359, USA

Hoffman, Elizabeth (Actor)
Bauman Assoc
5750 Wilshire Blvd # 473
Los Angeles, CA 90036-3697, USA

Hoffman, Glenn E (Athlete, Baseball Player)
201 S Old Bridge Rd
Anaheim, CA 92808-1326, USA

Hoffman, Guy (Athlete, Baseball Player)
1705 Longden Ave
Bloomington, IL 61701-8306, USA

Hoffman, Ingrid (Chef, Television Host)
c/o Staff Member *The Food Network.com*
1180 Avenue of the Americas Fl 14
New York, NY 10036-8401, USA

Hoffman, Jackie (Actor)
c/o Michael Geiser *Jill Fritzo Public Relations*
208 E 51st St # 305
New York, NY 10022-6557, USA

Hoffman, Jamie (Athlete, Baseball Player)
909 N Jefferson St
New Ulm, MN 56073-1433, USA

Hoffman, Jeffrey A (Astronaut)
US Embassy
2 Ave Gabriel
PSC 116/NASA
Paris Cedex 75382, FRANCE

Hoffman, Jeffrey A Dr (Astronaut)
100 Lovejoy Wharf Unit 12J
Boston, MA 02114-2164, USA

Hoffman, John (Athlete, Football Player)
18092 E Lake Ave
Aurora, CO 80016-3105, USA

Hoffman, John Robert (Writer)
c/o Rosalie Swedlin *Anonymous Content*
3532 Hayden Ave
Culver City, CA 90232-2413, USA

Hoffman, Jorg (Swimmer)
Saarmunder Str 74
Potsdam 14478, GERMANY

Hoffman, Kara (Actor)
c/o Rod Baron *Baron Entertainment*
13848 Ventura Blvd Ste A
Sherman Oaks, CA 91423-3654

Hoffman, Matt (Actor)
c/o Staff Member *Liberation Management*
1412 12th Ave
Los Angeles, CA 90019-4316, USA

Hoffman, Michael (Director)
c/o Doug MacLaren *ICM Partners*
10250 Constellation Blvd Fl 7
Los Angeles, CA 90067-6207, USA

Hoffman, Reid (Business Person)
LinkedIn
1000 W Maude Ave
Sunnyvale, CA 94085-2810, USA

Hoffman, Rick (Actor)
c/o Steven Levy *Framework Entertainment*
9057 Nemo St # C
W Hollywood, CA 90069-5511, USA

Hoffman, Robert (Actor, Dancer)
c/o Jeffrey Chassen *Imprint PR*
6121 W Sunset Blvd
Neuehouse
Los Angeles, CA 90028-6442, USA

Hoffman, Toby (Music Group, Musician)
Columbia Artists Mgmt Inc
165 W 57th St
New York, NY 10019-2201, USA

Hoffman, Trevor (Athlete, Baseball Player)
2220 Ocean Front
Del Mar, CA 92014-2134, USA

Hoffmann, Christian (Skier)
Frunwald 7
Aigen 04160, AUSTRIA

Hoffmann, Frank N (Nordy) (Athlete, Football Player)
400 N Capitol St NW Apt 327
Washington, DC 20001-1511, USA

Hoffmann, Gaby (Actor)
c/o John Sacks *United Talent Agency (UTA)*
9336 Civic Center Dr
Beverly Hills, CA 90210-3604, USA

Hoffmann, Isabella (Actor)
c/o Kevin Turner *Daniel Hoff Agency*
5455 Wilshire Blvd Ste 1100
Los Angeles, CA 90036-4277, USA

Hoffmeyer, Bob (Athlete, Hockey Player)
c/o Staff Member *New Jersey Devils*
165 Mulberry St
Continental Arena
Newark, NJ 07102-3607, USA

Hofford, Jim (Athlete, Hockey Player)
63 Filkins St
Fairport, NY 14450-2452, USA

Hoffort, Bruce (Athlete, Hockey Player)
N1778 Hyacinth Ln
Greenville, WI 54942-9005, USA

Hoffpauir, Jarrett (Athlete, Baseball Player)
2043 Viking St
Vidalia, LA 71373-3011, USA

Hoffpauir, Micah (Athlete, Baseball Player)
2105 Stanford St
Jacksonville, TX 75766-5246, USA

Hoffs, Susanna (Musician)
Bangles Mall
1341 W Fullerton Ave # 180
Chicago, IL 60614-2362, USA

Hofheimer, Charlie (Actor)
c/o Abby Bluestone *Innovative Artists*
1505 10th St
Santa Monica, CA 90401-2805, USA

Hofmann, Al (Race Car Driver)
PO Box 346
Umatilla, FL 32784-0346, USA

Hofmann, Detief (Athlete)
Saarlandstr 164
Karlsruhe 76187, GERMANY

Hofmann, Douglas (Artist)
8602 Saxon Cir
Baltimore, MD 21236-2559, USA

Hofmann, Isabella (Actor)
Don Buchwald
5900 Wilshire Blvd Ste 3100
Los Angeles, CA 90036-5030, USA

Hofmann, Kenneth (Commentator)
Oakland A's
1380 Galaxy Way
Concord, CA 94520-4912, USA

Hofschneider, Marco (Actor)
Progressive Artists Agency
400 S Beverly Dr Ste 216
Beverly Hills, CA 90212-4404, USA

Hofstetter, Steve (Writer)
c/o David Krintzman *Morris Yorn Barnes Levine Krintzman Rubenstein Kohner & Gellman*
2000 Avenue of the Stars Ste 300N
Tower N Fl 3
Los Angeles, CA 90067-4704, USA

Hogaboam, Bill (Athlete, Hockey Player)
1317 Mountainview St
Kelowna, BC V1Y 4M9, Canada

Hogan, Brooke (Musician, Reality Star)
c/o Staff Member *SoBe Entertainment*
820 Lincoln Rd
Miami Beach, FL 33139, USA

Hogan, Chris (Actor)
c/o Tim Curtis *WME|IMG*
9601 Wilshire Blvd
Beverly Hills, CA 90210-5213, USA

Hogan, Chuck (Writer)
c/o Ron Bernstein *ICM Partners*
10250 Constellation Blvd Fl 7
Los Angeles, CA 90067-6207, USA

Hogan, Darrell (Athlete, Football Player)
14988 Scenic Loop Rd
Helotes, TX 78023-3701, USA

Hogan, Hulk (Athlete, Wrestler)
HH World Media
5025 W Lemon St
Tampa, FL 33609-1101, USA

Hogan, John (Horse Racer)
4947 State Route 40
Argyle, NY 12809-3468, USA

Hogan, Linda (Actor)
c/o Peter Young *Sovereign Talent Group*
1642 Westwood Blvd Ste 202
Los Angeles, CA 90024-5609, USA

Hogan, Linda (Writer)
University of Colorado
English Dept
Boulder, CO 80309-0001, USA

Hogan, Marc (Athlete, Football Player)
3761 Colby St
Pittsburgh, PA 15214-2134, USA

Hogan, Michael (Actor)
c/o Jamie Levitt *Lauren Levitt & Associates Inc*
1525 W 8th Ave Fl 3
Vancouver BC V6J 1T5, CANADA

Hogan, Mike (Athlete, Football Player)
11 Walton Creek Dr SW
Rome, GA 30165-7228, USA

Hogan, Nick (Actor, Reality Star)
c/o Darren Prince *Prince Marketing Group*
18 Seneca Trl
Sparta, NJ 07871-1514, USA

Hogan, Paul (Actor)
7022 Grasswood Ave
Malibu, CA 90265-4247, USA

Hogan, Paul (PJ) (Director, Producer, Writer)
c/o Richard Lovett *Creative Artists Agency (CAA)*
2000 Avenue of the Stars Ste 100
Los Angeles, CA 90067-4705, USA

Hogan, Robert (Actor)
344 W 89th St Apt 1B
New York, NY 10024-2176, USA

Hogan, Susan (Actor)
c/o Lisa King *Northern Exposure Talent Management*
1111 Alberni St Suite 2808
Vancouver, BC V6E 4V2, CANADA

Hoganson, Paul (Athlete, Hockey Player)
1070 W Eagle Landing Pl
Tucson, AZ 85737-9230, USA

Hoge, Merril (Athlete, Football Player)
105 Stanbery Rdg
Fort Thomas, KY 41075-1068, USA

Hogeboom, Gary (Athlete, Football Player)
15062 Copper Pl
Grand Haven, MI 49417-9770, USA

Hogestyn, Drake (Actor)
28913 W Beach Ln
Malibu, CA 90265-4078, USA

Hogg, Christopher A (Business Person)
Courtaulds
18 Hanover Square
London W1A 2BB, UNITED KINGDOM (UK)

Hoggard, Jay (Music Group, Musician)
Creative Music Consultants
181 Chrystie St # 300
New York, NY 10002-1275, USA

Hoggarth, Ron (Athlete, Hockey Player)
1109 Woodland Dr
Oro-Medonte, ON L3V 0R8, CANADA

Hogh Andersen, Alex (Actor)
c/o Lene Seested *Panorama Agency (Denmark)*
Ryesgade 103B
CopenHagen DK-2100, DENMARK

Hogland, Doug (Athlete, Football Player)
1514 4th St
Tillamook, OR 97141-3426, USA

Hoglund, Jonas (Athlete, Hockey Player)
Ringvagen 28
Skoghall 66333, Sweden

Hogosta, Goran (Athlete, Hockey Player)
Hosjostrand 109
Falun S-79147, Sweden

Hogue, Beniot (Athlete, Hockey Player)
488 Village Oaks Ln
Babylon, NY 11702-3124, USA

Hogue, Benoit (Athlete, Hockey Player)
488 Village Oaks Ln
Babylon, NY 11702-3124, USA

Hohensee, Mike (Athlete, Football Player)
859 Pheasant Trl
Saint Charles, IL 60174-8802, USA

Hohlmayer, Alice (Athlete, Baseball Player, Commentator)
5155 Cedarwood Rd Apt 47
Bonita, CA 91902-1946, USA

Hohn, Bill (Athlete, Baseball Player)
1406 Royal Oak Dr
Blue Bell, PA 19422-2166, USA

Hohn, Robert (Athlete, Football Player)
2624 N 78th St
Lincoln, NE 68507-2965, USA

Hoiberg, Fred (Basketball Coach)
2129 Quail Ridge Rd
Ames, IA 50010-9476, USA

Hoiles, Chris (Athlete, Baseball Player)
8688 Jerry City Rd
Wayne, OH 43466-9837, USA

Hoisington, Allan (Athlete, Football Player)
71371 Biskra Rd
Rancho Mirage, CA 92270-4251, USA

Hoke, Chris (Athlete, Football Player)
121 Cardinal Cir
Pittsburgh, PA 15237-1067, USA

Hoke, Jon (Athlete, Football Player)
404 Fetterbush Rd
Elgin, SC 29045-9195, USA

Hoku (Musician)
c/o Staff Member *United Talent Agency (UTA)*
9336 Civic Center Dr
Beverly Hills, CA 90210-3604, USA

Holberg, Fred (Athlete, Basketball Player)
2851 Timberview Trl
Chaska, MN 55318-1113, USA

Holbert, Aaron (Athlete, Baseball Player)
32015 Teague Way
Wesley Chapel, FL 33545-1612, USA

Holbert, Ray (Athlete, Baseball Player)
18436 W Palo Verde Ave
Waddell, AZ 85355-4330, USA

Holbrook, Bill (Cartoonist)
c/o Staff Member *King Features Syndication*
300 W 57th St Fl 15
New York, NY 10019-5238, USA

Holbrook, Bill (Cartoonist)
465 Chelsea Cir NE
Atlanta, GA 30307-1268, USA

Holbrook, Boyd (Actor)
c/o Elan Ruspoli *Creative Artists Agency (CAA)*
2000 Avenue of the Stars Ste 100
Los Angeles, CA 90067-4705, USA

Holbrook, Hal (Actor)
c/o Staff Member *Century Public Relations*
1901 Avenue of the Stars Fl 2
Los Angeles, CA 90067-6001, USA

Holbrook, Sam (Athlete, Baseball Player)
12812 Guildford Ter
Fort Myers, FL 33913-8479, USA

Holbrook, Terry (Athlete, Hockey Player)
251 Meriden Rd
Painesville, OH 44077-3733, USA

Holcomb, Corey (Comedian)
c/o April King *ICM Partners*
10250 Constellation Blvd Fl 7
Los Angeles, CA 90067-6207, USA

Holcroft, Edward (Actor)
c/o Romilly Bowlby *DDA Public Relations*
192-198 Vauxhall Bridge Rd
London SW1V 1DX, UNITED KINGDOM

Holden, Alexandra (Actor)
c/o Mary Putnam Greene *MPG Management*
7162 Beverly Blvd Ste 332
Los Angeles, CA 90036-2547, USA

Holden, Amanda (Actor, Television Host)
c/o John Ferriter *The Alternative Company*
2980 N Beverly Glen Cir Ste 302
Los Angeles, CA 90077-1703, USA

Holden, Carl (Athlete, Baseball Player)
12755 Henderson Ln
Madison, AL 35756-3327, USA

Holden, Gina (Actor)
c/o Staff Member *Collective Digital Studio*
8383 Wilshire Blvd Ste 1050
Beverly Hills, CA 90211-2415, USA

Holden, Joyce (Actor)
444 N El Camino Real Spc 89
Encinitas, CA 92024-1313

Holden, Laurie (Actor)
c/o Jeff Raymond *Rogers & Cowan*
1840 Century Park E Fl 18
Los Angeles, CA 90067-2101, USA

Holden, Mari (Athlete, Cycler, Olympic Athlete)
2109 Caminito Del Barco
Del Mar, CA 92014-3603, USA

Holden, Mariean (Actor)
L A Talent
8335 W Sunset Blvd Ste 200
Los Angeles, CA 90069-1534, USA

Holden, Mark (Athlete, Hockey Player)
4837 Spruce Pine Way
North Ridgeville, OH 44039-2341, USA

Holden, Robert (Politician)
1937 Windriver Dr
Jefferson City, MO 65101-4375, USA

Holden, Steve (Athlete, Football Player)
1202 N Nevada Way
Mesa, AZ 85203-4323, USA

Holden, Tim (Congressman, Politician)
2417 Rayburn Hob
Washington, DC 20515-3817, USA

Holden-Reid, Kristen (Actor)
c/o Staff Member *Paradigm*
8942 Wilshire Blvd
Beverly Hills, CA 90211-1908, USA

Holden-Ried, Kris (Actor)
c/o Alyssa Beinhaker *MLC PR*
5757 Wilshire Blvd Ste 370
Los Angeles, CA 90036-3628, USA

Holder, Christopher (Actor)
H David Moss
6063 Vineland Ave Apt B
North Hollywood, CA 91606-4986, USA

Holder, Livingston L (Astronaut)
18422 SE 58th St
Issaquah, WA 98027-8618, USA

Holder, Meagan (Actor)
c/o Sarah Jackson *Seven Summits Pictures & Management*
8906 W Olympic Blvd
Beverly Hills, CA 90211-3550, USA

Holderness, Joan (Athlete, Baseball Player, Commentator)
1037 Summerwind Dr
Crossville, TN 38571-3691, USA

Holderness, Sue (Actor)
10 Rectory Close Windsor
Berks., ENGLAND SL4 5ER

Holdman, Warrick (Athlete, Football Player)

Holdorf, Willi (Athlete, Track Athlete)
Adidas KG
Herzogenaurach 91074, GERMANY

Holdridge, David (Athlete, Baseball Player)
39364 N Parisi Cir
San Tan Valley, AZ 85140-5721, USA

Holdsclaw, Chamique (Basketball Player)
Washington Mystics
601 F St NW
Mcl Center
Washington, DC 20004-1605, USA

Holdsworth, Fred (Athlete, Baseball Player)
578 Upland Hills Dr
Chelsea, MI 48118-9650, USA

Holecek, John (Athlete, Football Player)
1876 N Wilmot Ave
Chicago, IL 60647-4417, USA

Holiday, Corey (Athlete, Football Player)
315 Columbia Pl E
Chapel Hill, NC 27516-2161, USA

Holiday, Debby (Musician)
c/o Staff Member *Diva Central Inc*
7510 W Sunset Blvd # 1445
Los Angeles, CA 90046-3408, USA

Holiday, Kene (Actor)
c/o Staff Member *Abrams Artists Agency*
275 7th Ave Fl 26
New York, NY 10001-6708, USA

Holiday, Ron (Athlete, Football Player)
229 Balance Meeting Rd
Peach Bottom, PA 17563-9772, USA

Holiday, Ryan (Writer)
2405 Saint Charles Ave Apt 2
New Orleans, LA 70130-5839, USA

Holik, Bobby (Athlete, Hockey Player)
PO Box 9236
Jackson, WY 83002-9236, USA

Holker, Allison (Dancer)
c/o Lee Wallman *Wallman Public Relations*
3859 Goldwyn Ter
Culver City, CA 90232-3103, USA

Holladay, Robert (Athlete, Football Player)
2369 Timberland Dr NE
Conyers, GA 30207, USA

Holland, Agnieszka (Director, Writer)
Agence Nicole Cann
1 Rue Alfred de Vigny
Paris 75008, FRANCE

Holland, Al (Athlete, Baseball Player)
4443 Lewiston St NW
Roanoke, VA 24017-1009, USA

Holland, Al (Athlete, Baseball Player)
4443 Lewiston St NW
Roanoke, VA 24017-1009, USA

Holland, Andre (Actor, Director, Producer)
c/o Alexandra Crotin *The Lede Company*
9701 Wilshire Blvd # 930
Beverly Hills, CA 90212-2020, USA

Holland, Bill (Race Car Driver)
4790 W 16th St
Indianapolis, IN 46222-2550, USA

Holland, Brad (Athlete, Basketball Player)
1374 Sparrow Rd
Carlsbad, CA 92011-3961, USA

Holland, Darius (Athlete, Football Player)
13972 Meadowbrook Dr
Broomfield, CO 80020-6148, USA

Holland, Derek (Athlete, Baseball Player)
13316 W Ocotillo Ln
Surprise, AZ 85374-5255, USA

Holland, Dexter (Musician)
Rebel Waltz
PO Box 9215
Laguna Beach, CA 92652-7212, USA

Holland, Jamie L (Athlete, Football Player)
Ohio State University
410 Woody Hayes Dr
Attn: Alumni Association
Columbus, OH 43210-1104, USA

Holland, Jennifer (Actor)
c/o Jon Simmons *Simmons & Scott Entertainment*
7942 Mulholland Dr
Los Angeles, CA 90046-1225, USA

Holland, Jennifer (Writer)
c/o Lisa Blum *723 Productions*
Prefers to be contacted by telephone or email
Los Angeles, CA, USA

Holland, Jerry (Athlete, Hockey Player)
115 Douglasbank Pl SE
Calgary, AB T2Z 2J4, Canada

Holland, John (Athlete, Football Player)
3117 Flagstone Dr
Garland, TX 75044-5882, USA

Holland, Johnny (Athlete, Football Player)
4208 Stonebridge Dr
Missouri City, TX 77459-3264, USA

Holland, John R (Religious Leader)
Foursquare Gospel Int'l Church
1910 W Sunset Blvd Ste 200
Los Angeles, CA 90026-3279, USA

Holland, Jools (Music Group)
c/o Staff Member *Miracle Artists*
1 York Street
London
England W1U 6PA, United Kingdom

Holland, Josh (Actor)
4533 Willis Ave
Sherman Oaks, CA 91403-2710, USA

Holland, Juliam M (Jools) (Musician)
One Fifteen
Gallery 28 Wood Wharf
Horseferry
London SE10 9BT, UNITED KINGDOM (UK)

Holland, Ken (Athlete, Hockey Player)
600 Civic Center Dr
Attn: General Manager
Detroit, MI 48226-4408, USA

Holland, Ken (Athlete, Hockey Player)
967 McDonald Dr
Northville, MI 48167-1072, USA

Holland, Paul (Musician)
Variety Artists
1111 Riverside Ave Ste 501
Paso Robles, CA 93446-2683, USA

Holland, Richard (Actor)
453 Frederick St
San Francisco, CA 94117-2719, USA

Holland, Todd (Director)
c/o David Lonner *Oasis Media Group*
9100 Wilshire Blvd Ste 210W
Beverly Hills, CA 90212-3555, USA

Holland, Tom (Actor)
c/o Olivia Woodward *Curtis Brown Ltd*
28-29 Hay Market
Hay Market House
London SW1Y 4SP, UNITED KINGDOM

Holland, Wilbur (Athlete, Basketball Player)
538 Georgia Dr
Columbus, GA 31907-5091, USA

Holland, Willa (Actor)
c/o Ruth Bernstein *Viewpoint Inc*
8820 Wilshire Blvd Ste 220
Beverly Hills, CA 90211-2622, USA

Hollander, Dan (Figure Skater)
c/o Staff Member *Champions on Ice*
3500 American Blvd W Ste 190
Minneapolis, MN 55431-4431, USA

Hollander, Lorin (Musician)
I C M Artists
40 W 57th St
New York, NY 10019-4001, USA

Hollander, Zander (Writer)
3805 Yuma St NW
Washington, DC 20016-2213, USA

Hollandsworth, Todd M (Athlete, Baseball Player)
8735 Watercrest Cir E
Parkland, FL 33076-2853, USA

Hollas, Donald (Athlete, Football Player)
22015 Gold Leaf Trl
Cypress, TX 77433-4643, USA

Holle, Eric (Athlete, Football Player)
6646 Whitemarsh Valley Walk
Austin, TX 78746-6363, USA

Holle, Gary (Athlete, Baseball Player)
820 5th Ave
Watervliet, NY 12189-3612, USA

Holler, Ed (Athlete, Football Player)
4500 Ivy Hall Dr
Columbia, SC 29206-1229, USA

Holleran, Leslie (Producer)
c/o Staff Member *Laha Films*
137 W 57th St
7th Floor
New York, NY 10019, USA

Hollerer, Walter F (Writer)
Heerstr 99
Berlin 14055, GERMANY

Holliday, Charles O (Business Person)
E I DuPont de Nemours
1007 N Market St
Wilmington, DE 19801-1227, USA

Holliday, Cheryl (Writer)
c/o Staff Member *United Talent Agency (UTA)*
9336 Civic Center Dr
Beverly Hills, CA 90210-3604, USA

Holliday, Fred (Actor)
4610 Forman Ave
Toluca Lake, CA 91602-1617, USA

Holliday, Jennifer (Actor, Music Group)
c/o Jeff Epstein *M.A.G./Universal Attractions*
15 W 36th St Fl 8
New York, NY 10018-7927, USA

Holliday, Johnny (Commentator)
1500 S Capitol St SE
Attn: Broadcast Dept
Washington, DC 20003-3599, USA

Holliday, Polly D (Actor, Music Group)
c/o Staff Member *The Blake Agency*
23441 Malibu Colony Rd
Malibu, CA 90265-4640, USA

Holliday, Trindon (Athlete, Football Player)
c/o Drew Rosenhaus *Rosenhaus Sports Representation*
3921 Alton Rd # 440
Miami Beach, FL 33140-3852, USA

Hollie, Doug (Athlete, Football Player)
3917 Midvale Ave
Oakland, CA 94602-3940, USA

Hollier, Dwight (Athlete, Football Player)
5012 Woodview Ln
Matthews, NC 28104-8057, USA

Holliman, Earl (Actor)
4249 Bellingham Ave
Studio City, CA 91604-1604, USA

Hollimon, Mike (Athlete, Baseball Player)
753 Avalon Dr
Rockwall, TX 75032-2062, USA

Hollimon, Ulysses (Athlete, Baseball Player)
3818 Loyola Ct
Decatur, GA 30034-5533, USA

Hollings, Ernest (Politician)
1415 N Utah St
Arlington, VA 22201-4823, USA

Hollings, Michael R (Religious Leader)
Saint Mary of Angels
Moorhouse Road Bayswater
London W2 5DJ, UNITED KINGDOM (UK)

Hollingsworth, Ben (Actor)
c/o Shelley Browning *Magnolia Entertainment*
9595 Wilshire Blvd Ste 601
Beverly Hills, CA 90212-2506, USA

Hollingsworth, Shawn (Athlete, Football Player)
6 Broyhill Ct
Stafford, VA 22554-7757, USA

Hollinquest, Lamont (Athlete, Football Player)
13709 S San Pedro St
Los Angeles, CA 90061-2619, USA

Hollins, Damon (Athlete, Baseball Player)
1135 Camellia Ln
Suisun City, CA 94585-3804, USA

Hollins, Dave (Athlete, Baseball Player)
3221 Southwestern Blvd
Orchard Park, NY 14127-1230, USA

hollins, Essie (Athlete, Basketball Player)
9102 NW 48th St
Sunrise, FL 33351-5214, USA

Hollins, Lionel (Athlete, Basketball Player, Coach)
7594 Tagg Dr
Germantown, TN 38138-5827, USA

Hollis, Essie (Athlete, Basketball Player)
9102 NW 48th St
Sunrise, FL 33351-5214, USA

Hollis, James (Writer)
2501 Wisconsin Ave NW APT 301
Washington, DC 20007-4543, USA

Hollis, Michael (Athlete, Football Player)
24 Falling Waters
Oakland, NJ 07436-2341, USA

Hollis, Rachel (Business Person, Writer)
c/o Antranig Balian *Mortar Media*
9465 Wilshire Blvd Ste 300
Beverly Hills, CA 90212-2624, USA

Hollister, Dave (Actor, Music Group)
c/o Staff Member *Richard De La Font Agency*
3808 W South Park Blvd
Broken Arrow, OK 74011-1261, USA

Hollister, Ken (Athlete, Football Player)
8772 Linksway Dr
Powell, OH 43065-8299, USA

Hollit, Raye (Zapp) (Actor)
2554 Lincoln Blvd. #638
Marina Del Rey, CA 90292

Holloman, DeVonte (Athlete, Football Player)

Holloman, Laurel (Actor)
c/o Tammy Rosen *Sanders Armstrong Caserta*
4111 W Alameda Ave Ste 505
Burbank, CA 91505-4163, USA

Hollomon, Gus (Athlete, Football Player)
2489 County Road 139
Cameron, TX 76520-3614, USA

Holloway, Brenda (Musician)
Universal Attractions
145 W 57th St # 1500
New York, NY 10019-2220, USA

Holloway, Brian (Athlete, Football Player)
742 New York Route 43
Stephentown, NY 12168, USA

Holloway, Johnny (Athlete, Football Player)
1500 W 9th St Apt 5
Lawrence, KS 66044-2462, USA

Holloway, Josh (Actor)
c/o Jai Khanna *Brillstein Entertainment Partners*
9150 Wilshire Blvd Ste 350
Beverly Hills, CA 90212-3453, USA

Holloway, Ken (Music Group)
World Class/Berry Mgmt
1848 Tyne Blvd
Nashville, TN 37215-4702, USA

Holloway, Matt (Writer)
c/o Matt Rosen *Grandview*
7122 Beverly Blvd Ste F
Los Angeles, CA 90036-2572, USA

Hollowell, Matt (Athlete, Baseball Player)
8 Oldwick Rd
Whitehouse Station, NJ 08889-3719, USA

Hollowell, Matt (Baseball Player)
8 Oldwick Rd
Whitehouse Station, NJ 08889-3719, USA

Hollweg, Ryan (Athlete, Hockey Player)
340 Treeline Park Apt 1226
San Antonio, TX 78209-1843, USA

Holly, Jeff (Athlete, Baseball Player)
611 S Blaine St APT 111
Newberg, OR 97132-3382, USA

Holly, Lauren (Actor)
c/o James Weir *Anderson Group Public Relations*
8060 Melrose Ave Fl 4
Los Angeles, CA 90046-7038, USA

Holly, Molly (Wrestler)
c/o Staff Member *World Wrestling Entertainment (WWE)*
1241 E Main St
Stamford, CT 06902-3520, USA

Hollyday, Christopher (Musician)
Ted Kurland
173 Brighton Ave
Boston, MA 02134-2003, USA

Hollywood Undead (Music Group, Musician)
c/o Starr Andreeff *Maple Jam Music Group (MJMG)*
4108 W Riverside Dr Ste 3
Burbank, CA 91505-4192, USA

Holm, Anders (Actor)
c/o Isaac Horne *Avalon Management*
9171 Wilshire Blvd Ste 320
Beverly Hills, CA 90210-5516, USA

Holm, Holly (Athlete, Boxer)
9513 Peralta Rd NE
Albuquerque, NM 87109-6359, USA

Holm, Ian (Actor)
Markham & Froggatt
Julian House
4 Windmill St
London W1P 1HF, UNITED KINGDOM (UK)

Holm, Steve (Athlete, Baseball Player)
3620 N Sycamore Dr
Boise, ID 83703-4140, USA

Holman, Brad (Athlete, Baseball Player)
4720 N Ridge Rd
Wichita, KS 67205-8837, USA

Holman, Brian (Athlete, Baseball Player)
15821 Parkhill St
Overland Park, KS 66221-2549, USA

Holman, C Ray (Business Person)
Mallinckrodt Inc
675 McDonell Blvd
Saint Louis, MO 63134, USA

Holman, Gary (Athlete, Baseball Player)
8073 Camino Montego
Carlsbad, CA 92009-9545, USA

Holman, Rodney (Athlete, Football Player)
41460 Herwig Bluff Rd
Slidell, LA 70461-5040, USA

Holman, Scott (Athlete, Baseball Player)
25 Delbert Ln
Santa Rosa Beach, FL 32459-3678, USA

Holman, Scott (Athlete, Football Player)
4 Comiso
Irvine, CA 92614-0224, USA

Holman, Shawn (Athlete, Baseball Player)
105 Edgewood Rd
Sewickley, PA 15143-9681, USA

Holmberg, Dennis (Athlete, Baseball Player)
458 Grant St
Dunedin, FL 34698-4950, USA

Holmberg, Mark (Musician)
MOB Agency
6404 Wilshire Blvd Ste 505
Los Angeles, CA 90048-5507, USA

Holmberg, Rob (Athlete, Football Player)
316 Coppersmith Ln
Strasburg, PA 17579-1021, USA

Holmes, A M (Writer)
Columbia University
English Dept
New York, NY 10027, USA

Holmes, Andre (Athlete, Football Player)
c/o Ashanti Webb *EMG Sports - OH*
8055 Reynoldswood Dr
Reynoldsburg, OH 43068-9348, USA

Holmes, Ashton (Actor)
c/o Jeff Morrone *Atlas Artists*
9220 W Sunset Blvd Ste 225
Los Angeles, CA 90069-3513, USA

Holmes, Charlie (Athlete, Hockey Player)
3205 Fifield Rd
Pleasant Grove, CA 95668-9702, USA

Holmes, Clayton (Athlete, Football Player)
1142 Hollings Ave
Florence, SC 29506-6725, USA

Holmes, Clint (Music Group)
Conversation Co
697 Middle Neck Rd
Great Neck, NY 11023-1216, USA

Holmes, Dame Kelly (Athlete)
International Association of Athletics Federations
17 rue Princesse Florestine
BP 359
MC98007, MONACO

Holmes, Darren (Athlete, Baseball Player)
1 Emerald Ct
Arden, NC 28704-9594, USA

Holmes, Earl (Athlete, Football Player)
2978 Stonybrook Ct
Tallahassee, FL 32309-2167, USA

Holmes, Eric (Race Car Driver)
Beebe Racing
801 10th St Fl 5-1
Modesto, CA 95354-2311, USA

Holmes, Howdy (Race Car Driver)
301 Barton Shore Dr
Ann Arbor, MI 48105-1025, USA

Holmes, JB (Athlete, Golfer)
5175 Latrobe Dr
Windermere, FL 34786-8959, USA

Holmes, Jennifer (Actor)
PO Box 6303
Carmel, CA 93921-6303, USA

Holmes, Jerry (Athlete, Football Player)
107 Chatham Ter
Hampton, VA 23666-4105, USA

Holmes, Katie (Actor)
c/o John Carrabino *John Carrabino Management*
5900 Wilshire Blvd Ste 740
Los Angeles, CA 90036-5032, USA

Holmes, Kenneth (Athlete, Football Player)
PO Box 273309
Boca Raton, FL 33427-3309, USA

Holmes, Khaled (Athlete, Football Player)
c/o Joe Panos *Athletes First*
23091 Mill Creek Dr
Laguna Hills, CA 92653-1258, USA

Holmes, Lamar (Athlete, Football Player)
c/o Bus Cook *Bus Cook Sports, Inc*
1 Willow Bend Dr
Hattiesburg, MS 39402-8552, USA

Holmes, Larry (Boxer)
91 Larry Holmes Dr Ste 200
Easton, PA 18042-7745, USA

Holmes, Lester (Athlete, Football Player)
3760 Motor Ave
Los Angeles, CA 90034-6404, USA

Holmes, Pat (Athlete, Football Player)
221 Mack Hollimon Dr
Kerrville, TX 78028-6628, USA

Holmes, Priest (Athlete, Football Player)
c/o Todd France *Creative Artists Agency (CAA) Sports*
3500 Lenox Rd NE
Atlanta, GA 30326-4228, USA

Holmes, Rudell (Athlete, Football Player)
1713 Lisa Ave
Vista, CA 92084-3057, USA

Holmes, Rudy (Athlete, Football Player)
2151 Ronda Granada Unit A
Laguna Woods, CA 92637-0718, USA

Holmes, Santonio (Athlete, Football Player)
PO Box 1023
Pickerington, OH 43147-5023, USA

Holmes, Susan (Actor, Model)
c/o Jerry Shandrew *Shandrew Public Relations*
1050 S Stanley Ave
Los Angeles, CA 90019-6634, USA

Holmes, Tina (Actor)
c/o Mike Smith *Principal Entertainment*
9255 W Sunset Blvd Ste 500
Los Angeles, CA 90069-3301, USA

Holmes Norton, Eleanor (Congressman, Politician)
2136 Rayburn Hob
Washington, DC 20515-5100, USA

Holmgren, Mike (Athlete, Coach, Football Coach, Football Player)
905 Lake St S Apt 191
Kirkland, WA 98033-6428, USA

Holmgren, Paul (Athlete, Coach, Hockey Player)
724 Southwick Cir
Somerdale, NJ 08083-2312, USA

Holmoe, Tom (Athlete, Football Player)
1674 N 1670 W
Provo, UT 84604-7210, USA

Holmquest, Donald L (Astronaut)
205 Princeton Rd
Menlo Park, CA 94025-5217, USA

Holmquest, Donald L Dr (Astronaut)
205 Princeton Rd
Menlo Park, CA 94025-5217, USA

Holmstrom, Carl (Skier)
1703 E 3rd St Apt 101
Duluth, MN 55812-1743, USA

Holmstrom, Peter (Musician)
Monqui Mgmt
PO Box 5908
Portland, OR 97228-5908, USA

Holmstrom, Tomas (Athlete, Hockey Player)
43479 McLean Ct
Novi, MI 48375-4017, USA

Holohan, Pete (Athlete, Football Player)
2945 Curie St
San Diego, CA 92122-4105, USA

Holroyd, Michael (Writer)
85 Saint Marks Road
London W10 6JS, UNITED KINGDOM (UK)

Holroyd, Scott (Actor)
c/o Scott Manners *Artists & Representatives (Stone Manners Salners)*
6100 Wilshire Blvd Ste 1500
Los Angeles, CA 90048-5110, USA

Holst, Per (Producer)
Per Holst Film A/S
Rentemestervej 69A
Copenhagen, NV 02400, DENMARK

Holt, Chris (Athlete, Baseball Player)
413 Waterview Dr
Coppell, TX 75019-6671, USA

Holt, Claire (Actor)
c/o Melanie Greene *Affirmative Entertainment*
6525 W Sunset Blvd # 7
Los Angeles, CA 90028-7212, USA

Holt, David Lee (Musician)
AristoMedia
1620 16th Ave S
Nashville, TN 37212-2908, USA

Holt, Gary (Athlete, Hockey Player)
5820 S Sorrel Ct
Spokane, WA 99224-8298, USA

Holt, Glenn L (Athlete, Football Player)
North Miami High School
800 NE 137th St
North Miami, FL 33161-3299, USA

Holt, Glynn Dr (Astronaut)
110 Cummington Mall
Boston, MA 02215-2407, USA

Holt, Harry (Athlete, Football Player)
5608 S Vine Ave
Tucson, AZ 85706-2116, USA

Holt, Issac (Athlete, Football Player)
4028 Fairmont Pl
Birmingham, AL 35207-2732, USA

Holt, Issiac (Athlete, Football Player)
4028 Fairmont Pl
Birmingham, AL 35207-2732, USA

Holt, Jim (Athlete, Baseball Player)
150 Judge Sharpe Rd
Graham, NC 27253-8202, USA

Holt, Lester (Correspondent)
NBC-TV
30 Rockefeller Plz
News Dept
New York, NY 10112-0015, USA

Holt, Milton (Athlete, Football Player)
1461 N School St
Honolulu, HI 96817-1915, USA

Holt, Olivia (Actor, Musician)
c/o Alexandra Heller *Advantage PR*
3900 W Alameda Ave Ste 1200
Burbank, CA 91505-4317, USA

Holt, Pierce (Athlete, Football Player)
3840 County Road 339
Christoval, TX 76935-3000, USA

Holt, Robert J (Athlete, Football Player)
6337 Elder Grove Dr
Dallas, TX 75232-2919, USA

Holt, Roger (Athlete, Baseball Player)
804 Hilltop St
Fruitland Park, FL 34731-2061, USA

Holt, Sandrine (Actor)
c/o Christina Papadopoulos *Baker Winokur Ryder Public Relations*
200 5th Ave Fl 5
New York, NY 10010-3307, USA

Holt, Torry (Athlete, Football Player)
c/o Mark Lepselter *Maxx Sports & Entertainment*
546 5th Ave Fl 6
New York, NY 10036-5000, USA

Holtgrave, Vern (Athlete, Baseball Player)
389 N 8th St
Breese, IL 62230-1107, USA

Holt Jr., Rush (Congressman, Politician)
1214 Longworth Hob
Washington, DC 20515-1408, USA

Holton, Brian (Athlete, Baseball Player)
3214 Estate Dr
Oakdale, PA 15071-1445, USA

Holton, Linwood (Politician)
3883 Black Stump Rd
Weems, VA 22576-2017, USA

Holton, Mark (Actor)
c/o Staff Member *The Gage Group*
5757 Wilshire Blvd Ste 659
Los Angeles, CA 90036-3682, USA

Holton, Michael (Athlete, Basketball Player, Coach)
7225 SW Sharon Ln
Portland, OR 97225-2056, USA

Holtz, Louis L (Lou) (Athlete, Coach, Football Coach, Football Player)
9209 Cromwell Park Pl
Orlando, FL 32827-7005, USA

Holtz, Mike (Athlete, Baseball Player)
515 Double Dam Rd
Northern Cambria, PA 15714-7404, USA

Holtzman, Jerome (Baseball Player, Writer)
1225 Forest Ave
Evanston, IL 60202-1409, USA

Holtzman, Kenneth D (Ken) (Athlete, Baseball Player)
256 Waterside Dr
Grover, MO 63040-1632, USA

Holub, Dick (Athlete, Basketball Player)
16159 W Wildflower Dr
Surprise, AZ 85374-5048, USA

Holub, E J (Athlete, Football Player)
2311 S County Road 1120
Midland, TX 79706-4942, USA

Holum, Dianne (Athlete, Olympic Athlete, Speed Skater)
5801 N Banana River Blvd APT 942
Cpe Canaveral, FL 32920-3984, USA

Holum, Kirstin (Athlete, Olympic Athlete, Speed Skater)
961 E 1st Ave Apt 605
Broomfield, CO 80020-3724, USA

Holy, Steve (Musician)
c/o Staff Member *Paradigm (Nashville)*
222 2nd Ave S Ste 1600
Nashville, TN 37201-2375, USA

Holyfield, Evander (Athlete, Boxer)
c/o Chris Smith *ICM Partners*
10250 Constellation Blvd Fl 7
Los Angeles, CA 90067-6207, USA

Holz, Gordon (Athlete, Football Player)
3601 Wooddale Ave S Apt 523
Minneapolis, MN 55416-2459, USA

Holzemer, Mark (Athlete, Baseball Player)
10044 Macalister Trl
Highlands Ranch, CO 80129-6248, USA

Holzer, Jenny (Artist)
80 Hewitts Rd
Hoosick Falls, NY 12090-4000, USA

Holzer, Kristine (Athlete, Olympic Athlete, Speed Skater)
10410 W Whispering Cliffs Dr
Boise, ID 83704-1911, USA

Holzier, James (Actor)
c/o Bob Willems *Champion Entertainment*
2620 Fountain View Dr Ste 220
Houston, TX 77057-7627, USA

Holzinger, Brian (Athlete, Hockey Player)
1005 Ledgemont Dr
Broadview Heights, OH 44147-4021, USA

Homan, Dennis (Athlete, Football Player)
1950 Charlotte Ct
Florence, AL 35630-6768, USA

Homfeld, Conrad (Athlete, Horse Racer, Olympic Athlete)
Sandron
11744 Marblestone Ct
Wellington, FL 33414-6041, USA

Honda, Yuka (Music Group)
Billions Corp
833 W Chicago Ave Ste 101
Chicago, IL 60642-8408, USA

Honegger, Fritz (President)
Schloss-Str 29
Ruschlidon 08803, SWITZERLAND

Honeycutt, Rick (Athlete, Baseball Player)
207 Forrest Rd
Fort Oglethorpe, GA 30742-3706, USA

Honeycyt (Music Group)
c/o Staff Member *Paradigm (Monterey)*
404 W Franklin St
Monterey, CA 93940-2303, USA

Honeyghan, Lloyd (Boxer)
50 Barnfield Wood Road
Park Langley
Beckenham
Kent, UNITED KINGDOM (UK)

Honeymoon Suite (Music Group)
c/o Staff Member *ARM Entertainment*
1257 Arcade St
Saint Paul, MN 55106-2022, USA

Hong, James (Actor)
8235 Sunset Blvd #202
West Hollywood, CA 90046, USA

Honig, Donald (Commentator)
2322 Cromwell Hills Dr
Cromwell, CT 06416-1803, USA

Honore, Jean Cardinal (Religious Leader)
Archeveche
BP 1117
27 Rue Jules-Simon
Tours Cedex 37011, FRANCE

Hoobastank (Music Group)

Hood, Ace (Musician)
c/o Jon Moskowitz *M.A.G./Universal Attractions*
15 W 36th St Fl 8
New York, NY 10018-7927, USA

Hood, Calum (Musician)
c/o Matt Emsell *Wonder Management*
10-16 Scrutton St
Level 4
London EC2A 4RU, UNITED KINGDOM

Hood, Don (Athlete, Baseball Player)
20753 Charing Cross Cir
Estero, FL 33928-2542, USA

Hood, Estus (Athlete, Football Player)
2105 W Grace St
Kankakee, IL 60901-4590, USA

Hood, Gavin (Director)
c/o Michael Sugar *Anonymous Content*
3532 Hayden Ave
Culver City, CA 90232-2413, USA

Hood, Kenneth (Religious Leader)
5799 Bloomfield Ave
Verona, NJ 07044, USA

Hook, Chris (Athlete, Baseball Player)
30 Northfield Dr
Florence, KY 41042-8924, USA

Hook, Jay (Athlete, Baseball Player)
PO Box 90
Maple City, MI 49664-0090, USA

Hooker, Charles R (Artist)
28 Whippingham Road
Brighton
Sussex BN2 3PG, UNITED KINGDOM (UK)

Hooker, Fair (Athlete, Football Player)
3728 Rutherford Ct
Inglewood, CA 90305-2244, USA

Hooks, Kevin (Director)
International Creative Mgmt
8942 Wilshire Blvd # 219
Beverly Hills, CA 90211-1908, USA

Hooks, Robert (Actor)
145 N Valley St
Burbank, CA 91505-4036, USA

Hooks, Roland (Athlete, Football Player)
3724 Calgary Dr
Reno, NV 89511-6096, USA

Hoomanawanui, Michael (Athlete, Football Player)
c/o Mark Bartelstein *Priority Sports & Entertainment (Chicago)*
325 N La Salle Dr Ste 650
Chicago, IL 60654-8182, USA

Hoop, Jesca (Musician)
c/o Staff Member *Paradigm (Monterey)*
404 W Franklin St
Monterey, CA 93940-2303, USA

Hooper, Bobby Joe (Athlete, Basketball Player)
825 Ivywood St Apt 4
Dayton, OH 45420-1751, USA

Hooper, C Darrow (Athlete, Olympic Athlete, Track Athlete)
6608 Lakeshore Dr
Dallas, TX 75214-3741, USA

Hooper, Kevin (Athlete, Baseball Player)
2701 Century Dr
Lawrence, KS 66049-2523, USA

Hooper, Lance (Race Car Driver)
195 Poplar Grove Rd
Mooresville, NC 28117-6813, USA

Hooper, Tom (Director)
c/o Doug MacLaren *ICM Partners*
10250 Constellation Blvd Fl 7
Los Angeles, CA 90067-6207, USA

Hoopes, Mitch (Athlete, Football Player)
5000 S Murray Blvd Apt F1
Salt Lake City, UT 84123-2674, USA

Hooser, Carroll (Athlete, Basketball Player)
6317 Kings Rd
Double Oak, TX 75077-7314, USA

Hooten, Leon (Athlete, Baseball Player)
524 S 7th St
Coos Bay, OR 97420-1302, USA

Hootie & The Blowfish (Music Group)
917 Huger St
Columbia, SC 29201-3621, USA

Hooton, Burt C (Athlete, Baseball Player)
3619 Granby Ct
San Antonio, TX 78217-4653, USA

Hoover, Brad (Athlete, Football Player)
415 Turtleback Rdg
Matthews, NC 28104-0022, USA

Hoover, Houston (Athlete, Football Player)
1216 Mareed Ave
Yazoo City, MS 39194-2831, USA

Hoover, Mikaela (Actor)
c/o James Cole *Primary Wave Entertainment*
10850 Wilshire Blvd Fl 6
Los Angeles, CA 90024-4319, USA

Hoover, Paul (Athlete, Baseball Player)
307 Baronsway Dr
Cuyahoga Fls, OH 44223-2892, USA

Hoover, Tom (Athlete, Basketball Player)
9 Apple Manor Ln
East Brunswick, NJ 08816-2872, USA

Hoover, Tom (Race Car Driver)
918 Boundary Blvd
Rotonda West, FL 33947-2873, USA

Hoovler, Skip (Athlete, Football Player)
8249 Broad St SW
Pataskala, OH 43062-7831, USA

Hope, Alec D (Writer)
PO Box 7949
Alice Springs, NT 00871, AUSTRALIA

Hope, Jim (Producer)
c/o Staff Member *WME|IMG*
9601 Wilshire Blvd
Beverly Hills, CA 90210-5213, USA

Hope, John (Athlete, Baseball Player)
1141 NW 70th Ter
Plantation, FL 33313-6031, USA

Hope, Leslie (Actor)
c/o Lee Wallman *Wallman Public Relations*
3859 Goldwyn Ter
Culver City, CA 90232-3103, USA

Hope, Maurice (Boxer)
582 Kingsland Road
London E8, UNITED KINGDOM (UK)

Hope, Tamara (Actor, Musician)
c/o Matt Schwartz *Wright Entertainment*
3207 Winnie Dr
Los Angeles, CA 90068-1439, USA

Hopkins, Andy (Athlete, Football Player)
2335 Walnut Ridge Dr
Missouri City, TX 77489-5005, USA

Hopkins, Anna (Actor)
Armstrong Acting Studios
9 Davies Avenue
Toronto, ON M4M 2A6, CANADA

Hopkins, Anthony (Actor)
c/o Arnold Robinson *Rogers & Cowan*
1840 Century Park E Fl 18
Los Angeles, CA 90067-2101, USA

Hopkins, Bernard (Athlete, Boxer)
c/o Staff Member *Golden Boy Promotions*
626 Wilshire Blvd Ste 350
Los Angeles, CA 90017-3581, USA

Hopkins, Bo (Actor)
6628 Ethel Ave
North Hollywood, CA 91606-1018, USA

Hopkins, Bob (Athlete, Basketball Player)
8421 SE 71st St
Mercer Island, WA 98040-5409, USA

Hopkins, DeAndre (Athlete, Football Player)
4904 S Shepherd Dr
Houston, TX 77098-5320, USA

Hopkins, Demetrius (Boxer)
c/o Staff Member *Top Rank Inc.*
3908 Howard Hughes Pkwy
#580
Las Vegas, NV 89109, USA

Hopkins, Don (Athlete, Baseball Player)
PO Box 8817
Benton Harbor, MI 49023-8817, USA

Hopkins, Dustin (Athlete, Football Player)

Hopkins, Gail (Athlete, Baseball Player)
120 Canterbury Dr
Parkersburg, WV 26104-8048, USA

Hopkins, Gareth (Business Person)
c/o Staff Member *EMI Recorded Music (UK)*
27 Wrights Lane
London W8 5SW, UK

Hopkins, Jan (Correspondent)
Cable News Network
1050 Techwood Dr NW
News Dept
Atlanta, GA 30318-5695, USA

Hopkins, Jerry (Athlete, Football Player)
6688 E State Highway 6
Waco, TX 76705-5385, USA

Hopkins, Josh (Actor)
Gersh Agency
232 N Canon Dr
Beverly Hills, CA 90210-5302, USA

Hopkins, Kaitlin (Actor)
19528 Ventura Blvd # 559
Tarzana, CA 91356-2917, USA

Hopkins, Larry (Athlete, Hockey Player)
4008 S Yellowood Ave
Broken Arrow, OK 74011-1372, USA

Hopkins, Michael S Ltcolonel (Astronaut)
910 White Pine Dr
Friendswood, TX 77546-3570, USA

Hopkins, Stephen (Director)
c/o Frank Frattaroli *Circle of Confusion*
8931 Ellis Ave
Los Angeles, CA 90034-3336, USA

Hopkins, Sy (Music Group)
Paramount Entertainment
PO Box 12
Far Hills, NJ 07931-0012, USA

Hopkins, Tamburo (Athlete, Football Player)
2740 Maitland Crossing Way Apt 2208
Orlando, FL 32810-7130, USA

Hopkins, Telma (Actor, Musician)
4122 Don Luis Dr
Los Angeles, CA 90008-4215, USA

Hopkins, Tom (Business Person, Writer)
Tom Hopkins International
7531 E 2nd St
Scottsdale, AZ 85251-4503, USA

Hopkins, Wesley (Athlete, Football Player)
7412 White Oak Rd
Fairfield, AL 35064-2454, USA

Hoppe, Fred (Artist)
7401 NW 105th St
Malcolm, NE 68402-9700, USA

Hoppe, Wolfgang (Athlete)
Dieterstedter Str 11
Apolda 99510, GERMANY

Hoppen, Dave (Athlete, Basketball Player)
16341 Webster St
Omaha, NE 68118-2513, USA

Hopper, C Darrow (Athlete, Football Player)
6 Braemore Pl
Dallas, TX 75230-1958, USA

Hopper, Norris (Athlete, Baseball Player)
902 Hampton St
Shelby, NC 28152-6412, USA

Hopper, Tom (Actor)
c/o Nicki Fioravante *Viewpoint Inc*
8820 Wilshire Blvd Ste 220
Beverly Hills, CA 90211-2622, USA

Hopperdeitz, Anna (Actor)
c/o Staff Member *Agentur Fuhrmann*
Lindenstr 8A
Isen-Pemmering 84424, Germany

Hoppock, Doug (Athlete, Football Player)
13212 W 115th St
Shawnee Mission, KS 66210-3540, USA

Hoppus, Mark (Actor, Musician, Producer)
c/o Geyer Kosinski *Media Talent Group*
9200 W Sunset Blvd Ste 550
Los Angeles, CA 90069-3611, USA

Hopsin, Marcus (Musician, Producer)
Funk Volume
8447 Wilshire Blvd Ste 450
Beverly Hills, CA 90211-3236, USA

Hopson, Dennis (Athlete, Basketball Player)
4064 Hillandale Rd Apt 2
Ottawa Hills, OH 43606-2562, USA

Horacek, Tony (Athlete, Hockey Player)
71 Clover Pl
Lebanon, PA 17042-9400, USA

Horan, James (Actor)
c/o Raphael Berko *Media Artists Group*
8222 Melrose Ave Ste 304
Los Angeles, CA 90046-6839, USA

Horan, Machael W (Mike) (Athlete, Football Player)
1232 Edgeview Dr
Santa Ana, CA 92705-2339, USA

Horan, Niall (Musician)
c/o Harry Magee *Modest! Management*
91A Peterborough Rd
London SW6 3BU, UNITED KINGDOM

Horbiger, Christiane (Actor)
Frankengasse 28
Zurich CH-8001, SWITZERLAND

Horbul, Doug (Athlete, Hockey Player)
2562 Statts
Fruitvale, BC VOG 1LO, Canada

Hordges, Cedrick (Athlete, Basketball Player)
237 W 127th St Apt 28
New York, NY 10027-2901, USA

Hordichuk, Darcy (Athlete, Hockey Player)
8237 NW 107th Ter
Parkland, FL 33076-4766, USA

Horford, Al (Athlete, Basketball Player)
c/o Arn Tellem *Wasserman Media Group*
10960 Wilshire Blvd Ste 1200
Los Angeles, CA 90024-3714, USA

Horgan, Joe (Athlete, Baseball Player)
16108 Rim Rd
Edmond, OK 73013-3215, USA

Horgan, Patrick (Actor)
201 E 89th St
New York, NY 10128-3421, USA

Horlen, Joel (Athlete, Baseball Player)
7702 Parkwood Way
San Antonio, TX 78249-4724, USA

Horn, Don (Athlete, Football Player)
8611 Mallard Pl
Highlands Ranch, CO 80126-2961, USA

Horn, Joe (Athlete, Football Player)
2408 Shenley Park Ct
Duluth, GA 30097-4961, USA

Horn, Roy (Magician)
Mirage Hotel & Casino
3400 Las Vegas Blvd S
Las Vegas, NV 89109-8907, USA

Horn, Sam (Athlete, Baseball Player)
1305 Narragansett Blvd
Cranston, RI 02905-3825, USA

Horn, Shriley (Music Group)
1007 Towne Ln
Charlottesville, VA 22901-3173, USA

Horn, Thomas (Actor)
c/o Jennifer Allen *Viewpoint Inc*
8820 Wilshire Blvd Ste 220
Beverly Hills, CA 90211-2622, USA

Hornacek, Jeff (Athlete, Basketball Player)
1360 E 9th St
Cleveland, OH 44114-1737, USA

Hornaday, Ron (Race Car Driver)
Miss Estelle's Place
101 S Broad St
Mooresville, NC 28115-3102, USA

Hornbuckle, Alexis (Athlete, Basketball Player)
125 Juniper St
Lake Jackson, TX 77566-5025, USA

Hornby, Nick (Writer)
c/o Jenne Casarotto *Casarotto Ramsay & Associates Ltd (UK)*
Waverley House
7-12 Noel St
London W1F 8GQ, UNITED KINGDOM

Horne, Donald R (Writer)
53 Grosvenor St
Woollahra
Sydney, NSW 02025, AUSTRALIA

Horne, John R (Business Person)
Navistar International
PO Box 1488
Warrenville, IL 60555-7488, USA

Horneff, Wil (Actor)
c/o Staff Member *Creative Artists Agency (CAA)*
2000 Avenue of the Stars Ste 100
Los Angeles, CA 90067-4705, USA

Horner, Bob (Athlete, Baseball Player)
209 Steeplechase Dr
Irving, TX 75062-3823, USA

Horner, Craig (Actor)
c/o Matt Andrews *Marquee Management*
188 Oxford St Studio B
The Gatehouse
Paddington NSW 02021, AUSTRALIA

Horner, Sam (Athlete, Football Player)
681 Duck Thurmond Rd
Dawsonville, GA 30534-2811, USA

Hornish Jr, Sam (Race Car Driver)
Penske Racing
200 Penske Way
Mooresville, NC 28115-8022, USA

Hornsby, Bruce (Musician)
PO Box 3545
Williamsburg, VA 23187-3545, USA

Hornsby, Ron (Athlete, Football Player)
2028 Washington St
Franklinton, LA 70438-2533, USA

Hornsby, Russell (Actor)
c/o Steve Small *aTa Management (LA)*
2508 N Vermont Ave # 702
Los Angeles, CA 90027-1243, USA

Hornung, Paul (Athlete, Football Player, Heisman Trophy Winner)
325 W Main St Ste 1116
Waterfront Plaza
Louisville, KY 40202-4255, USA

Horovitz, Adam (King Ad-Rock) (Artist, Music Group, Musician)
c/o Staff Member *WME/IMG*
9601 Wilshire Blvd
Beverly Hills, CA 90210-5213, USA

Horovitz, Israel A (Writer)
146 W 11th St
New York, NY 10011-8306, USA

Horowitz, Jordan (Producer)
c/o Risa Gertner *Creative Artists Agency (CAA)*
2000 Avenue of the Stars Ste 100
Los Angeles, CA 90067-4705, USA

Horowitz, Sari (Journalist)
Washington Post
Editorial Dept
1150 15th St NW
Washington, DC 20071-0001, USA

Horowitz, Scott J (Astronaut)
5491 Freestyle Way
Park City, UT 84098-7621, USA

Horowitz, Scott J Colonel (Astronaut)
5491 Freestyle Way
Park City, UT 84098-7621, USA

Horry, Robert (Athlete, Basketball Player)
2618 Sara Ridge Ln
Katy, TX 77450-5374, USA

Horschel, Billy (Athlete, Golfer)
4300 S Beach Pkwy Apt 3213
Jacksonville Beach, FL 32250-8181, USA

Horsford, Anna Maria (Actor)
PO Box 48082
Los Angeles, CA 90048-0082, USA

Horsley, Jack (Athlete, Olympic Athlete, Swimmer)
608 N Sampson St
Ellensburg, WA 98926-3162, USA

Horsley, Lee A (Actor)
c/o Laura Walsh *Central Artists*
1023 N Hollywood Way Ste 102
Burbank, CA 91505-2554, USA

Horsman, Vince (Athlete, Baseball Player)
1941 Pinehurst Dr
Clearwater, FL 33763-2228, USA

Horstman, Catherine (Athlete, Baseball Player, Commentator)
708 Oakwood Dr
Minster, OH 45865-1335, USA

Horton, Ethan S (Football Player, Sportscaster)
4602 Fairvista Dr
Charlotte, NC 28269-1098, USA

Horton, Greg (Athlete, Football Player)
1053 Lytle St
Redlands, CA 92374-6240, USA

Horton, Jonathan (Athlete, Gymnast, Olympic Athlete)
c/o Staff Member *USA Gymnastics*
130 E Washington St Ste 700
Indianapolis, IN 46204-4621, USA

Horton, Larry (Athlete, Football Player)
215 Emerald St
Harrisburg, PA 17110-1013, USA

Horton, Lawrence (Athlete, Football Player)
1442 S 13th St
Harrisburg, PA 17104-3107, USA

Horton, Mark (Race Car Driver)
Summit Racing
PO Box 535
Richfield, OH 44286-0535, USA

Horton, Nathan (Athlete, Hockey Player)
The Orr Hockey Group
PO Box 290836
Charlestown, MA 02129-0215, USA

Horton, Peter (Actor)
409 Santa Monica Blvd PH
Santa Monica, CA 90401-2232, USA

Horton, Ray (Athlete, Football Player)
3400 S Water St
Pittsburgh, PA 15203-2349, USA

Horton, Ricky (Athlete, Baseball Player)
16026 Aston Ct
Chesterfield, MO 63005-4575, USA

Horton, Tony (Athlete, Baseball Player)
17001 Livorno Dr
Pacific Palisades, CA 90272-3232, USA

Horton, Tony (Athlete, Fitness Expert, Television Host)
BeachBody
3301 Exposition Blvd Fl 3
Santa Monica, CA 90404-5082, USA

Horton, Wes (Athlete, Football Player)
c/o Bruce Tollner *REP 1 Sports Group*
80 Technology Dr
Irvine, CA 92618-2301, USA

Horton, Willie (Athlete, Baseball Player)
The Athlete Connection
PO Box 380135
Clinton Township, MI 48038-0060, USA

Horvath, Bronco J (Athlete, Hockey Player)
27 Oliver St
South Yarmouth, MA 02664-2901, USA

Horvitz, Louis J (Director, Producer)
c/o Bob Gersh *Gersh*
9465 Wilshire Blvd Ste 600
Beverly Hills, CA 90212-2605, USA

Horwitz, Brian (Athlete, Baseball Player)
19313 N 69th Ave
Glendale, AZ 85308-5769, USA

Horwitz, Tony (Journalist)
Wall Street Journal
200 Liberty St
Editorial Dept
New York, NY 10281-1003, USA

Hosbein, Marion (Athlete, Baseball Player, Commentator)
1347 Cliff Barnes Dr
Kalamazoo, MI 49009-8329, USA

Hosea, Bobby (Actor)
c/o Sara Schedeen *Metropolitan (MTA)*
4526 Wilshire Blvd
Los Angeles, CA 90010-3801, USA

Hosey, Dwayne (Athlete, Baseball Player)
164 N Plum Ave
Ontario, CA 91764-4137, USA

Hosey, Steve (Athlete, Baseball Player)
2351 W Lorna Linda Ave
Fresno, CA 93711-0417, USA

Hoshide, Akihiko (Astronaut)
NASDA, Tsukuba Space Center 2-1-1, Sengen
Tukuba-shi, Ibaraka 00305, japan

Hosket, Bill (Athlete, Basketball Player, Olympic Athlete)
7461 Worthington Galena Rd
Worthington, OH 43085-1529, USA

Hoskins, Derrick (Athlete, Football Player)
10491 Road 842
Philadelphia, MS 39350-8204, USA

Hosley, Jayron (Athlete, Football Player)
c/o Mitchell Frankel *Impact Sports (FL)*
2799 NW 2nd Ave Ste 203
Boca Raton, FL 33431-6709, USA

Hospodar, Ed (Athlete, Hockey Player)
217 Orchard Way
Wayne, PA 19087-4805, USA

Hoss, Clark (Athlete, Football Player)
2709 Ridge Ln
West Linn, OR 97068-2986, USA

Hossa, Marian (Athlete, Hockey Player)
The Sports Corporation
2735-10088 102 Ave NW
Attn Rich Winter
Edmonton, AB T5J 2Z1, Canada

Hossein, Robert (Actor, Director)
Ghislaine de Wing
10 Rue du Docteur Roux
Paris 75015, FRANCE

Hostak, Al (Boxer)
11501 161st Ave SE
Renton, WA 98059-6145, USA

Hostak, Martin (Athlete, Hockey Player)
Ceska Televize odd. kontaktu s divakem
Kavci hory
Praha 4 140 70, Czech Republic

Hostetler, Dave (Athlete, Baseball Player)
3404 Steeplechase Trl
Arlington, TX 76016-2325, USA

Hostetler, David L (Artist)
PO Box 989
Athens, OH 45701-0989, USA

Hostetler, Jeff (Athlete, Football Player)
2032 Magnolia Dr
Morgantown, WV 26508-4467, USA

Hostetter, G Richard (Religious Leader)
Presbyterian Church in America
1852 Century Pl NE Ste 201
Atlanta, GA 30345-4305, USA

Hostin, Sunny (Commentator)
c/o Staff Member *The View*
57 W 66th St
New York, NY 10023-6201, USA

Hoston, Ricky (Baseball Player)
St Louis Cardinals
16026 Aston Ct
Chesterfield, MO 63005-4575, USA

Hoston, Tony (Baseball Player)
Boston Red Sox
17001 Livorno Dr
Pacific Palisades, CA 90272-3232, USA

Hot Chelle Rae (Music Group)
c/o Staff Member *Jive Records*
550 Madison Ave Frnt 1
New York, NY 10022-3211, USA

Hotchkiss, Rob (Musician)
Jon Landau
80 Mason St
Greenwich, CT 06830-5515, USA

Hotchner, Aaron Edward (Producer, Writer)
c/o Staff Member *HarperCollins Publishers*
195 Broadway Fl 2
New York, NY 10007-3132, USA

Hotham, Greg (Athlete, Hockey Player)
40 Ridgeway Ave
Barrie, ON L4N 5L2, Canada

Hottman, Ken (Athlete, Baseball Player)
9537 2nd Ave
Elk Grove, CA 95624-1936, USA

Houbregs, Bob (Athlete, Basketball Player)
1949 Arena Ct SE
Tumwater, WA 98501-6874, USA

Houda, Doug (Athlete, Hockey Player)
536 Graten St
Birmingham, MI 48009-6516, USA

Hough, Charlie (Athlete, Baseball Player)
2266 Shadetree Cir
Brea, CA 92821-4423, USA

Hough, Derek (Dancer, Reality Star)
c/o Staff Member *Silver Lining Entertainment*
421 S Beverly Dr Fl 7
Beverly Hills, CA 90212-4408, USA

Hough, Jim (Athlete, Football Player)
2440 Christian Dr
Chaska, MN 55318-1993, USA

Hough, John (Director)
Associated International Mgmt
5 Denmark St
London WC2H 8LP, UNITED KINGDOM (UK)

Hough, Julianne (Actor, Dancer, Musician)
PO Box 682425
Park City, UT 84068-2425, USA

Hough, Mike (Athlete, Hockey Player)
25 Marsh Harbr
Aurora, ON L4G 5Y7, Canada

Hough, Stephen A G (Musician)
Harrison/Parrott
12 Penzance Place
London W11 4PA, UNITED KINGDOM (UK)

Houghton, Katherine (Actor)
Ambrosio/Mortimer
165 W 46th St
New York, NY 10036-2501, USA

Hougland, Bill (Athlete, Basketball Player, Olympic Athlete)
504 Canyon Dr
Lawrence, KS 66049-2400, USA

Houider, Bill (Athlete, Hockey Player)
220 Maple Cove
RR 2 North Bay, ON P1B 8G3, Canada

Houle, Rejean (Athlete, Hockey Player)
7941 Boul Lasalle
Lasalle, QC H8P 3R1, Canada

Houlemard, Michael (Athlete, Baseball Player)
111 S Orange Grove Blvd Apt 104
Pasadena, CA 91105-1756, USA

Hoult, Nicholas (Actor)
c/o Kate Buckley *42 Management (UK)*
8 Flitcroft St
London WC2H 8DL, UNITED KINGDOM

Houlton, D J (Athlete, Baseball Player)
2357 N Campus Ave
Upland, CA 91784-1303, USA

Hounsou, Djimon (Actor, Model, Producer)
c/o Peter Safran *The Safran Company*
8748 Holloway Dr
Los Angeles, CA 90069-2327, USA

Hourde, Daniel (Artist)
37, rue Galande
Paris 75005, France

House, Craig (Athlete, Baseball Player)
8614 Brock Cir
Austin, TX 78745-6368, USA

House, David (Dave) (Business Person)
Nortel Networks Corp
8200 Dixie Rd
Brampton, ON L6T 4B8, CANADA

House, Davon (Athlete, Football Player)
c/o Ken Zuckerman *Priority Sports & Entertainment - (LA)*
15233 Ventura Blvd Ste 718
Sherman Oaks, CA 91403-2237, USA

House, J R (Athlete, Baseball Player)
34 River Ridge Trl
Ormond Beach, FL 32174-4340, USA

House, Karen Eliot (Journalist)
1 World Financial Ctr Attn of
New York, NY 10281-1003, USA

House, Karen Ellot (Journalist)
58 Cleveland Ln
Princeton, NJ 08540-3077, USA

House, Kevin (Athlete, Football Player)
615 Canyon Oaks Dr APT A
Oakland, CA 94605-5923, USA

House, Pat (Athlete, Baseball Player)
2053 S White Pine Ln
Boise, ID 83706-4048, USA

House, Pat (Athlete, Baseball Player)
2554 W Penick Pointe Ct
Meridian, ID 83646-5182, USA

House, Rick (Athlete, Football Player)
1538 McCreary Rd
Winnipeg, MB R3P 0M7, Canada

House, Tom (Athlete, Baseball Player)
12794 Via Felino
Del Mar, CA 92014-3806, USA

House, Yoanna (Model, Television Host)

Householder, Paul (Athlete, Baseball Player)
521 N Swinton Ave
Delray Beach, FL 33444-3969, USA

HouseJ, Eddie (Athlete, Basketball Player)
35 Kings Way
Waltham, MA 02451-9041, USA

House of Pain (Music Group)
c/o Staff Member *WME/IMG*
9601 Wilshire Blvd
Beverly Hills, CA 90210-5213, USA

Houser, Jerry (Actor)
8325 Skyline Dr
Los Angeles, CA 90046-1038, USA

Houser, John (Athlete, Football Player)
2197 Creekside Dr
Solvang, CA 93463-2238, USA

Houser, Kevin (Athlete, Football Player)
941 Montclair Cir
Westlake, OH 44145-1445, USA

Houser, Randy (Musician)
c/o Staff Member *Fitzgerald Hartley Co (Nashville)*
1908 Wedgewood Ave
Nashville, TN 37212-3733, USA

Houshmandzadeh, T J (Athlete, Football Player)
16703 Greenbrook Cir
Cerritos, CA 90703-1188, USA

Housie, Wayne (Athlete, Baseball Player)
25315 Picasso Ct
Moreno Valley, CA 92553-7101, USA

Housler, Rob (Athlete, Football Player)

Housley, Phil (Athlete, Hockey Player, Olympic Athlete)
2877 Itasca Ave S
Lakeland, MN 55043-9742, USA

Houston (Adult Film Star)
c/o Staff Member *Atlas Multimedia Inc*
9005 Eton Ave Ste C
Canoga Park, CA 91304-6533, USA

Houston, Allan (Athlete, Basketball Player, Olympic Athlete)
Allan Houston Foundation
350 5th Ave Fl 59
New York, NY 10118-5999, USA

Houston, Andy (Race Car Driver)
835F Williamson Rd # 36
C/O Global Performance Co
Mooresville, NC 28117-8597, USA

Houston, Bobby (Athlete, Football Player)
4640 Vendue Range Dr
Raleigh, NC 27604-5078, USA

Houston, Byron (Athlete, Basketball Player)
16116 Cantera Creek Dr
Edmond, OK 73013-1473, USA

Houston, Cissy (Musician)
The New Hope Baptist Church Youth Choir
106 Sussex Ave
Newark, NJ 07103-3698, USA

Houston, Edwin A (Business Person)
Ryder System Inc
3600 NW 82nd Ave
Doral, FL 33166-6623, USA

Houston, Jim (Athlete, Football Player)
925 Trimble Pl
Northfield, OH 44067-2239, USA

Houston, Justin (Athlete, Football Player)
c/o Chafie Fields *Lagardere Unlimited (Miami)*
927 Lincoln Rd Ste 200
Miami Beach, FL 33139-2618, USA

Houston, Kenneth R (Ken) (Athlete, Football Player)
3603 Forest Village Dr
Kingwood, TX 77339-1819, USA

Houston, Lamarr (Athlete, Football Player)
c/o Mitchell Frankel *Impact Sports (FL)*
2799 NW 2nd Ave Ste 203
Boca Raton, FL 33431-6709, USA

Houston, Marques (Actor, Musician)
DePasse Entertainment
9200 W Sunset Blvd Ste 510
West Hollywood, CA 90069-3507, USA

Houston, Marquis (Actor, Musician)

Houston, Mike (Actor)
c/o Kelli M Jones *Status PR (NY)*
PO Box 6191
Westlake Village, CA 91359-6191, USA

Houston, Penelope (Music Group)
Absolute Artists
8490 W Sunset Blvd # 403
West Hollywood, CA 90069-1912, USA

Houston, Russell (Artist)
General Delivery
Eagar, AZ 85925-9999, USA

Houston, Thelma (Musician)
c/o Stephen Ford *Diva Central Inc*
7510 W Sunset Blvd # 1445
Los Angeles, CA 90046-3408, USA

Houston, Tyler (Athlete, Baseball Player)
325 Pleasant Summit Dr
Henderson, NV 89012-3486, USA

Houston, Wade (Basketball Player, Coach)
University of Tennessee
Athletic Dept
Knoxville, TN 37901, USA

Houston Calls (Music Group)
c/o Staff Member *Drive Thru Records*
3019 Olympic Blvd
Santa Monica, CA 90404-5001, USA

Hovan, Chris (Athlete, Football Player)
17301 Ladera Estates Blvd
Lutz, FL 33548-4817, USA

Hover, Don (Athlete, Football Player)
19 Wolf Creek Rd
Winthrop, WA 98862-9767, USA

Hovind, David J (Business Person)
PACCAR Inc
777 106th Ave NE
Bellevue, WA 98004-5027, USA

Hovis, Guy (Musician)
207 Morningside N
Ridgeland, MS 39157-9755, USA

Hovland, Tim (Athlete, Volleyball Player)
431 Main St
El Segundo, CA 90245-3003, USA

Hovley, Steve (Athlete, Baseball Player)
PO Box 655
Oak View, CA 93022-0655, USA

Hovsepian, Vatche (Religious Leader)
Armenian Church of America West
1201 Vine St
Los Angeles, CA 90038-1695, USA

Howard, Adina (Musician)
International Creative Mgmt
40 W 57th St Ste 1800
New York, NY 10019-4033, USA

Howard, Andrew (Actor)
c/o Michelle Czernin von Chudenitz
Popular Press Media Group (PPMG)
468 N Camden Dr Ste 105A
Beverly Hills, CA 90210-4507, USA

Howard, Arliss (Actor, Director, Writer)
c/o Staff Member *WME/IMG*
9601 Wilshire Blvd
Beverly Hills, CA 90210-5213, USA

Howard, Austin (Athlete, Football Player)

Howard, Ben (Athlete, Baseball Player)
45 Cross Brook Cv
Jackson, TN 38305-3548, USA

Howard, Bob (Athlete, Football Player)
2444 56th St
San Diego, CA 92105-5012, USA

Howard, Bobby (Athlete, Football Player)
4725 Bald Eagle Way
Douglasville, GA 30135-7475, USA

Howard, Brian (Athlete, Basketball Player)
619 Vermont Ave
Fort Walton Beach, FL 32547-3033, USA

Howard, Bruce (Athlete, Baseball Player)
8705 Misty Creek Dr
Sarasota, FL 34241-9562, USA

Howard, Bryce Dallas (Actor)
c/o Stephen Huvane *Slate PR*
901 N Highland Ave
W Hollywood, CA 90038-2412, USA

Howard, Chris (Athlete, Baseball Player)
8655 Jones Rd Apt 301
Jersey Village, TX 77065-5104, USA

Howard, Chris (Athlete, Baseball Player)
17 Sea View Ave
Nahant, MA 01908-1548, USA

Howard, Clark (Commentator, Radio Personality, Television Host, Writer)
Newstalk 750 WSB
1601 W Peachtree St NE
Atlanta, GA 30309-2641, USA

Howard, Clint (Actor)
c/o Harry Gold *TalentWorks*
3500 W Olive Ave Ste 1400
Burbank, CA 91505-5512, USA

Howard, Dana (Athlete, Football Player)
347 Forest Oaks Dr
Caseyville, IL 62232-2821, USA

Howard, David (Athlete, Baseball Player)
22846 Chesterview Loop
Loopapt 111
Land O Lakes, FL 34639-5341, USA

Howard, David (Athlete, Football Player)
5516 E Rosedale St
Fort Worth, TX 76112-6859, USA

Howard, Desmond (Athlete, Football Player, Heisman Trophy Winner)
12206 Mount Overlook Ave
Cleveland, OH 44120-1034, USA

Howard, Doug (Athlete, Baseball Player)
8038 S Deer Creek Rd
Salt Lake City, UT 84121-5762, USA

Howard, Dwight (Athlete, Basketball Player)
c/o Alan Nierob *Rogers & Cowan*
1840 Century Park E Fl 18
Los Angeles, CA 90067-2101, USA

Howard, Eddie (Athlete, Football Player)
1130 E Workman Ave
West Covina, CA 91790-2357, USA

Howard, Emma (Actor)
c/o Angela Mach *Platform PR*
2666 N Beachwood Dr
Los Angeles, CA 90068-2308, USA

Howard, Erik (Athlete, Football Player)
23255 FM 150 W
Driftwood, TX 78619-9155, USA

Howard, Frank (Athlete, Baseball Player, Coach)
24178 Lenah Woods Pl
Aldie, VA 20105-2369, USA

Howard, Frank O (Athlete, Baseball Player)
24178 Lenah Woods Pl
Aldie, VA 20105-2369, USA

Howard, Fred (Athlete, Baseball Player)
250 Lake Lulu Dr
Winter Haven, FL 33880-4461, USA

Howard, Gene (Athlete, Football Player)
11051 Lavender Ave
Fountain Valley, CA 92708-2457, USA

Howard, George (Musician)
David Rubinson
PO Box 411197
San Francisco, CA 94141-1197, USA

Howard, Greg (Athlete, Basketball Player)
4517 W 16th Pl Apt 2
Los Angeles, CA 90019-5164, USA

Howard, Greg (Cartoonist)
3403 W 28th St
Minneapolis, MN 55416-4302, USA

Howard, James Newton (Musician)
815 Myrtle Ave
Glendora, CA 91741-3657, USA

Howard, Jan (Music Group)
c/o Staff Member *Tessier-Marsh Talent*
505 Canton Pass
Madison, TN 37115-5449, USA

Howard, Jaye (Athlete, Football Player)
c/o Drew Rosenhaus *Rosenhaus Sports Representation*
3921 Alton Rd # 440
Miami Beach, FL 33140-3852, USA

Howard, Jim (Athlete, Hockey Player)
518 Hamilton St
Ogdensburg, NY 13669-2714, USA

Howard, Joe (Athlete, Football Player)
2501 Joseph Dr
Clinton, MD 20735-4540, USA

Howard, John (Politician)
GPO Box 59
Sydney, AUSTRALIA NSW 2001, AUSTRALIA

Howard, Josh (Athlete, Basketball Player)
PO Box 802851
Dallas, TX 75380-2851, USA

Howard, Juwan (Athlete, Basketball Player)
11714 Bistro Ln
Houston, TX 77082-2726, USA

Howard, Kyle (Actor)
c/o Steve Himber *Steve Himber Entertainment*
211 S Beverly Dr # 601
Beverly Hills, CA 90212-3807, USA

Howard, Larry (Athlete, Baseball Player)
207 Innwood Dr
Georgetown, TX 78628-8311, USA

Howard, Lee (Athlete, Baseball Player)
4650 Dulin Rd Spc 203
Fallbrook, CA 92028-8766, USA

Howard, Leo (Actor)
c/o Randy James *Randy James Management*
12711 Ventura Blvd Ste 345
Studio City, CA 91604-2416, USA

Howard, Lisa (Actor)
c/o Lisa Sharon Goldberg *Lisa Sharon Goldberg*
88 Leonard St Apt 607
New York, NY 10013-3495, USA

Howard, Matt (Athlete, Baseball Player)
31896 Jaybee Ln
Temecula, CA 92592-4174, USA

Howard, Mike (Athlete, Baseball Player)
101 Kenbridge Ln
Madison, MS 39110-9773, USA

Howard, Miki (Musician)
c/o Mike Gardner *Gardener Entertainment*
5683 Hazelcrest Cir
Westlake Village, CA 91362-5426, USA

Howard, OJ (Athlete, Football Player)
c/o Todd France *Creative Artists Agency (CAA) Sports*
3500 Lenox Rd NE
Atlanta, GA 30326-4228, USA

Howard, Otis (Athlete, Basketball Player)
231 Manhattan Ave
Oak Ridge, TN 37830-7544, USA

Howard, Paige (Actor)
c/o Meredith Wechter *WME|IMG*
9601 Wilshire Blvd
Beverly Hills, CA 90210-5213, USA

Howard, Paul (Athlete, Football Player)
8502 S Jebel Way
Aurora, CO 80013, USA

Howard, Percy (Athlete, Football Player)
3525 Neely Rd
Memphis, TN 38109-3811, USA

Howard, Rebecca Lynn (Musician)
c/o Staff Member *Paradigm (Monterey)*
404 W Franklin St
Monterey, CA 93940-2303, USA

Howard, Reggie (Athlete, Baseball Player)
4332 Crimson Leaf Cv
Memphis, TN 38125-2905, USA

Howard, Reggie (Athlete, Football Player)
775 Tucker St
Dyersburg, TN 38024-3791, USA

Howard, Richard (Writer)
23 Waverly Pl Apt 5X
New York, NY 10003-6717, USA

Howard, Robert (Hardcore Holly) (Wrestler)
c/o Kerry Rodgerson *World Wrestling Entertainment (WWE)*
1241 E Main St
Stamford, CT 06902-3520, USA

Howard, Ron (Actor, Director, Producer, Writer)
c/o Richard Lovett *Creative Artists Agency (CAA)*
2000 Avenue of the Stars Ste 100
Los Angeles, CA 90067-4705, USA

Howard, Ron (Athlete, Football Player)
14701 NE 61st Ct
Redmond, WA 98052-4751, USA

Howard, Ryan (Athlete, Baseball Player)
16543 Clayton Rd
Wildwood, MO 63011-1720, USA

Howard, Sherman (Athlete, Football Player)
5125 Thomas Dr
Richton Park, IL 60471-1639, USA

Howard, Sherri (Actor)
c/o Michael Henderson *Heresun Management*
4119 W Burbank Blvd
Burbank, CA 91505-2122, USA

Howard, Sherri (Athlete, Track Athlete)
14059 Bridle Ridge Rd
Sylmar, CA 91342-1060, USA

Howard, Stephen (Athlete, Basketball Player)
3941 Legacy Dr Ste 204 # A193
Plano, TX 75023-8331, USA

Howard, Steven (Athlete, Baseball Player)
4712 Shetland Ave
Oakland, CA 94605-5629, USA

Howard, Susan (Actor)
PO Box 1456
Boerne, TX 78006-1456, USA

Howard, Terrence (Actor)
c/o Howard Bragman *LaBrea Media*
8306 Wilshire Blvd # 4002
Beverly Hills, CA 90211-2304, USA

Howard, Thomas (Athlete, Baseball Player)
340 Clark St
Middletown, OH 45042-2041, USA

Howard, Tim (Athlete, Soccer Player)
c/o Richard Motzkin *Wasserman Media Group*
10960 Wilshire Blvd Ste 1200
Los Angeles, CA 90024-3714, USA

Howard, Todd (Athlete, Football Player)
17325 Palo Duro Cyn
College Station, TX 77845-4584, USA

Howard, Traylor (Actor)
c/o John Carrabino *John Carrabino Management*
5900 Wilshire Blvd Ste 740
Los Angeles, CA 90036-5032, USA

Howard, Wilbur (Athlete, Baseball Player)
643 Walston Ln
Houston, TX 77060-5846, USA

Howarth, Jim (Athlete, Baseball Player)
275 Santini St
Biloxi, MS 39530-2958, USA

Howarth, Roger (Actor)
K&H
1212 Avenue of the Americas # 3
New York, NY 10036-1602, USA

Howatch, Susan (Writer)
Atiken & Stone
29 Fernshaw Road
London SW10 0TG, UNITED KINGDOM (UK)

Howatt, Garry (Athlete, Hockey Player)
20314 E Bronco Dr
Queen Creek, AZ 85142-6007, USA

Howe, Arthur (Journalist)
Philadelphia Inquirer
400 N Broad St
Editorial Dept
Philadelphia, PA 19130-4015, USA

Howe, Brian (Musician)
c/o Samantha Crisp *The Kohner Agency*
9300 Wilshire Blvd Ste 555
Beverly Hills, CA 90212-3211, USA

Howe, Delles (Athlete, Football Player)
1907 Crescent Dr
Monroe, LA 71202-3023, USA

Howe, Garry (Athlete, Football Player)
5226 NE Hillcrest Dr
Ankeny, IA 50021-6827, USA

Howe, Marie (Writer)
822 Palmer Rd Apt 2A
Bronxville, NY 10708-3317, USA

Howe, Mark (Athlete, Hockey Player, Olympic Athlete)
9 Inverness Ln
Jackson, NJ 08527-4046, USA

Howe, Marty (Athlete, Hockey Player)
40 Plank Ln
Glastonbury, CT 06033-2523, USA

Howe, Oscar (Artist)
5900 S Prairie View Ct
Sioux Falls, SD 57108-2003, USA

Howe, Sean (Writer)
c/o Staff Member *HarperCollins Publishers*
195 Broadway Fl 2
New York, NY 10007-3132, USA

Howe, Tina (Writer)
750 Columbus Ave APT 11J
New York, NY 10025-6481, USA

Howe Jr, Arthur H (Art) (Athlete, Baseball Player, Coach)
17214 Calico Peak Way
Cypress, TX 77433-2113, USA

Howell, Alex (Cartoonist)
c/o Staff Member *King Features Syndication*
300 W 57th St Fl 15
New York, NY 10019-5238, USA

Howell, Bailey (Athlete, Basketball Player)
1567 Montgomery Rd
Starkville, MS 39759-5431, USA

Howell, C Thomas (Actor, Director, Producer, Writer)
Global 3 Media
224 Tulip Trail Bnd
Cedar Park, TX 78613-3775, USA

Howell, David (Golfer)
c/o Staff Member *International Sports Management Ltd (ISM UK)*
Cherry Tree Farm
Cherry Tree Lane
Rostherne, Cheshire WA14 3RZ, UNITED KINGDOM

Howell, Delano (Athlete, Football Player)

Howell, Delles (Athlete, Football Player)
1907 Crescent Dr
Monroe, LA 71202-3023, USA

Howell, Jack (Athlete, Baseball Player)
822 S Lehigh Dr
Tucson, AZ 85710-4741, USA

Howell, Jay (Athlete, Baseball Player)
4560 Colony Pt
Suwanee, GA 30024-3010, USA

Howell, J P (Athlete, Baseball Player)
1706 11th St Apt 11
Sacramento, CA 95811-6547, USA

Howell, Kanin (Actor)

Howell, Ken (Athlete, Baseball Player)
22090 Buckingham Dr
Farmington Hills, MI 48335-5423, USA

Howell, Margaret (Designer, Fashion Designer)
5 Garden House
8 Battersea Park Road
London SW8, UNITED KINGDOM (UK)

Howell, Mike (Athlete, Football Player)
200 Charlotte St
Monroe, LA 71202-3906, USA

Howell, Pat (Athlete, Football Player)
7692 N Kincaid Ave
Fresno, CA 93711-0363, USA

Howell, Patrick (Pat) (Athlete, Baseball Player)
3081 Lacoste Rd
Mobile, AL 36618-4617, USA

Howell, Roy (Athlete, Baseball Player)
276 El Portal Dr
Pismo Beach, CA 93449-1504, USA

Howell-Baptiste, Kirby (Actor)
c/o Jodi Gottlieb *Independent Public Relations*
9601 Wilshire Blvd Ste 750
Beverly Hills, CA 90210-5228, USA

Howell III, Charles (Athlete, Golfer)
c/o Thomas Parker *GPR Sports Management*
11715 Spinnaker Way
Hollywood, FL 33026-1233, USA

Hower, Elisabeth (Actor)
c/o Ken Treusch *Bleecker Street Entertainment*
853 Broadway Ste 1214
New York, NY 10003-4717, USA

Howerdel, Billy (Musician)
4373 Beck Ave
Studio City, CA 91604-2702, USA

Howerton, Glenn (Actor)
c/o Sean Elliott *Authentic Talent & Literary Management*
3615 Eastham Dr # 650
Culver City, CA 90232-2410, USA

Howery, Lil Rel (Actor, Comedian)
c/o Michelle Watts *Aziza Work Group*
6701 Eton Ave Apt 123
Woodland Hills, CA 91303-4032, USA

Howes, Lewis (Athlete, Business Person, Football Player, Internet Star)
418 Media LLC
838 N Doheny Dr Apt 1106
W Hollywood, CA 90069-4851, USA

Howes, Sally Ann (Actor, Music Group, Musician)
Saraband
265 Liverpool Road
London N1 1LX, UNITED KINGDOM (UK)

Howey, Steve (Actor)
c/o Brian Swardstrom *United Talent Agency (UTA)*
888 7th Ave Fl 7
New York, NY 10106-0700, USA

Howfield, Bobby (Athlete, Football Player)
5529 S Lowell Blvd
Littleton, CO 80123-2840, USA

Howfield, Ian (Athlete, Football Player)
4520 Palisades Canyon Cir
Las Vegas, NV 89129-5364, USA

Howison, Ryan (Athlete, Golfer)
160 Barbados Dr
Jupiter, FL 33458-2920, USA

Howitt, Dann (Athlete, Baseball Player)
2035 Woodlark Dr
Holland, MI 49424-7643, USA

Howitt, Peter (Actor, Director)
c/o Stephen Marks *Evolution Entertainment*
10850 Wilshire Blvd Ste 600
Los Angeles, CA 90024-4319, USA

Howland, Ben (Basketball Player, Coach)
University of California
Athletic Dept
Los Angeles, CA 90024, USA

Howle, Paul (Cartoonist)
United Feature Syndicate
200 Madison Ave
New York, NY 10016-3903, USA

Howley, Chuck (Athlete, Football Player)
5234 Ravine Dr
Dallas, TX 75220-2260, USA

Howry, Bobby (Athlete, Baseball Player)
26225 N 100th Ln
Peoria, AZ 85383-8944, USA

Howry, Keenan (Athlete, Football Player)
1961 Cassia Rd APT 301
Carlsbad, CA 92011-4182, USA

Howson, Scott (Athlete, Hockey Player)
c/o Staff Member *Edmonton Oilers*
11230 110 St NW
Edmonton, AB T5G 3H7, Canada

Howze, Leonard Earl (Actor)
c/o Ben Levine *LINK Entertainment*
11872 La Grange Ave
Los Angeles, CA 90025-5282, USA

Hoy, Peter (Athlete, Baseball Player)
26 Woods Dr
Canton, NY 13617-1061, USA

Hoyda, Dave (Athlete, Hockey Player)
3305 Bahama Dr
Sand Springs, OK 74063-2912, USA

Hoye, James (Athlete, Baseball Player)
1830 Oak Hammock Ct
Lutz, FL 33558-7304, USA

Hoyem, Steve (Athlete, Football Player)
28 Twilight Blf
Newport Coast, CA 92657-2126, USA

Hoyer, Brian (Athlete, Football Player)
c/o Joe Linta *JL Sports*
1204 Main St Ste 179
Branford, CT 06405-3787, USA

Hoyer, Jed (Commentator)
118 Huntington Ave
Boston, MA 02116-5743, USA

Hoying, Bobby (Athlete, Football Player)
9071 Tartan Fields Dr
Dublin, OH 43017-8873, USA

Hoyos, Luis Fernando (Actor)
c/o Gabriel Blanco *Gabriel Blanco Iglesias (Mexico)*
Rio Balsas 35-32
Colonia Cuauhtemoc
DF 06500, Mexico

Hoyt, D LaMarr (Athlete, Baseball Player)
500 Harbison Blvd APT 1002
Columbia, SC 29212-1719, USA

Hozier (Musician)
c/o Kimberly Harris *Sony Music Entertainment*
25 Madison Ave Fl 19
New York, NY 10010-8601, USA

Hrabosky, Alan T (Al) (Athlete, Baseball Player, Sportscaster)
9 Frontenac Estates Dr
Saint Louis, MO 63131-2613, USA

Hrbek, Kent A (Athlete, Baseball Player)
2611 W 112th St
Bloomington, MN 55431-3965, USA

Hrdina, Jiri (Athlete, Hockey Player)
c/o Staff Member *Dallas Stars*
2601 Avenue of the Stars Ste 100
Frisco, TX 75034-9016, USA

Hriniak, Walt (Athlete, Baseball Player)
18 Stacy Dr
North Andover, MA 01845-1832, USA

Hrivnak, Gary (Athlete, Football Player)
651 Rocky Brook Dr
Cordova, TN 38018-6548, USA

Hrivnak, Jim (Athlete, Hockey Player)
835 Rue Pierre-Marc-Masson
L'Ile-Bizard, QC H9E 0A3, Canada

Hrkac, Tony (Athlete, Hockey Player)
592 N Midvale Blvd
Madison, WI 53705-3238, USA

Hrudey, Kelly (Athlete, Hockey Player)
P.O Box 500
Box 500
Toronto, ON M5W 1E6, CANADA

Hrycuik, Jim (Athlete, Hockey Player)
1011 Konihowski Rd
Saskatoon, SK S7S 1K5, Canada

Hrynewich, Tim (Athlete, Hockey Player)
3597 Henry St Ste 103
Norton Shores, MI 49441-6723, USA

H. Smith, Christopher (Congressman, Politician)
2373 Rayburn Hob
Washington, DC 20515-3004, USA

Hu, Jintao (President)
Communist Party Central Committee
1 Zhong Nan Hai
Beijing, CHINA

Hu, Kelly (Actor)
c/o Cheryl McLean *Creative Public Relations*
3385 Oak Glen Dr
Los Angeles, CA 90068-1311, USA

Huang, Helen (Musician)
I C M Artists
40 W 57th St
New York, NY 10019-4001, USA

Huang, James (Actor)
c/o Staff Member *Cunningham Escott Slevin & Doherty (CESD)*
10635 Santa Monica Blvd Ste 130
Los Angeles, CA 90025-8306, USA

Huang, Ying (Musician)
c/o Staff Member *Sony BMG/Jive Records*
2100 Colorado Ave
Santa Monica, CA 90404-3504, USA

Huard, Bill (Athlete, Hockey Player)
41 Massier Ln
Foothill Ranch, CA 92610-2305, USA

Huard, Brock (Athlete, Football Player)
11688 179th Pl NE
Redmond, WA 98052, USA

Huard, Damon (Athlete, Football Player)
9508 NE 18th St
Clyde Hill, WA 98004-2539, USA

Huard, John (Athlete, Football Player)
148 Breakwater Dr Unit 11
South Portland, ME 04106-1638, USA

Huarte, John (Athlete, Football Player, Heisman Trophy Winner)
Arizona Tile
8829 S Priest Dr
Tempe, AZ 85284-1905, USA

Hub (Musician)
William Morris Agency
1325 Avenue of the Americas
New York, NY 10019-6026, USA

Hubbard, Erica (Actor)
c/o Jenny Delaney *Jenny Delaney Management*
10636 Wilshire Blvd Apt 207
Los Angeles, CA 90024-7326, USA

Hubbard, Glenn (Athlete, Baseball Player)
1515 Kings Xing
Stone Mountain, GA 30087-1914, USA

Hubbard, Gregg (Hobbie) (Music Group, Musician)
Sawyer Brown Inc
5200 Old Harding Rd
Franklin, TN 37064-9406, USA

Hubbard, John (Artist)
Chilcombe House
Chilcombe near Bridport
Dorset, UNITED KINGDOM (UK)

Hubbard, Mike (Athlete, Baseball Player)
2619 Lancraft Rd
North Chesterfield, VA 23235-3007, USA

Hubbard, Phil (Athlete, Basketball Player, Olympic Athlete)
5130 Pleasant Forest Dr
Centreville, VA 20120-1248, USA

Hubbard, Ray Wylie (Musician)
c/o Staff Member *Davis McLarty Agency*
708 S Lamar Blvd Ste D
Austin, TX 78704-1541, USA

Hubbard, Robert (Athlete, Basketball Player)
353 Piper Rd
West Springfield, MA 01089-1757, USA

Hubbard, Trenidad (Athlete, Baseball Player)
4206 Clearwater Ct
Missouri City, TX 77459-1668, USA

Hubbard, Trent (Baseball Player)
Colorado Rockies
2654 E 77th St
Chicago, IL 60649-4725, USA

Hubbauer, Matt (Athlete, Hockey Player)
c/o Staff Member *Toronto Maple Leafs*
Air Canada Centre
400-40 Bay St
Toronto, ON M5J 2X2, CANADA

Hubbert, Brad (Athlete, Football Player)
3100 Landington Dr
Austell, GA 30106-3538, USA

Huber, Anke (Tennis Player)
Dieselstr 10
Karlsdorf-Neuthard 76689, GERMANY

Huber, Jon (Athlete, Baseball Player)
4409 S Angeline St
Seattle, WA 98118-1857, USA

Huber, Kevin (Athlete, Football Player)
c/o Joe Flanagan *BTI Sports Advisors*
615 South Blvd Apt C
Oak Park, IL 60302-4606, USA

Huber, Max (Athlete, Football Player)
1047 Riverside Ln
Orem, UT 84097-6601, USA

Huber, Mike (Athlete, Baseball Player)
509 N Hena St
Greenville, IL 62246-1313, USA

Hubert, Janet (Actor)
10061 Riverside Dr Apt 204
Toluca Lake, CA 91602-2560, USA

Hubick, Greg (Athlete, Hockey Player)
225 Angus St
Regina, SK S4R 3K5, Canada

Hubka, Gene (Athlete, Football Player)
217 Laurel Ct
West Creek, NJ 08092-2819, USA

Hubley, Season (Actor)
31 Mansfield Ave
Essex Junction, VT 05452-3732, USA

Huck, Fran (Athlete, Hockey Player)
Fran Huck and Associates
550 El Camino Rd
Kelowna, BC V1X 2R9, Canada

Huckabee, Cooper (Actor)
1800 El Cerrito Pl Apt 34
Los Angeles, CA 90068-3743, USA

Huckabee, Mike (Politician)
Blue Diamond Media
PO Box 242058
Little Rock, AR 72223-0019, USA

Huckaby, Ken (Athlete, Baseball Player)
4490 S Rio Dr
Chandler, AZ 85249-3382, USA

Huckaby, Rick (Musician)
c/o Dale Morris *Morris Artists Management*
2001 Blair Blvd
Nashville, TN 37212-5007, USA

Huckleby, Harlan (Athlete, Football Player)
7473 Franklin Ridge Way
West Bloomfield, MI 48322-4128, USA

Hucknall, Mick (Musician)
c/o Staff Member *Silentway Managment Ltd*
34 Percy St
London W1T 2DG, UK

Huclack, Dan (Athlete, Football Player)
B-11 Apple Lane
Winnipeg, MB R2Y 2G9, Canada

Hucles, Angela (Athlete, Olympic Athlete, Soccer Player)
1641 Tether Keep
Virginia Beach, VA 23454-1332, USA

Hucul, Fred (Athlete, Hockey Player)
4550 N Flowing Wells Rd Unit 226
Tucson, AZ 85705-2387, USA

Huddy, Charlie (Athlete, Hockey Player)
c/o Staff Member *Edmonton Oilers*
11230 110 St NW
Edmonton, AB T5G 3H7, Canada

Hudecek, Vaclav (Musician)
Londynska 25
Prague 2 120 00, CZECH REPUBLIC

Hudek, John (Athlete, Baseball Player)
John Hudek's All Star Baseball Academy
7603 Shady Way Dr
Sugar Land, TX 77479-6284, USA

Hudepohl, Joe (Athlete, Olympic Athlete, Swimmer)
2784 Mornington Dr NW
Atlanta, GA 30327-1216, USA

Hudgens, Dave (Athlete, Baseball Player)
5802 E Windsor Ave
Scottsdale, AZ 85257-1039, USA

Hudgens, Vanessa (Actor)
c/o Katie Greenthal *The Lede Company*
9701 Wilshire Blvd # 930
Beverly Hills, CA 90212-2020, USA

Hudis, Mark (Writer)
c/o Staff Member *United Talent Agency (UTA)*
9336 Civic Center Dr
Beverly Hills, CA 90210-3604, USA

Hudler, Jiri (Athlete, Hockey Player)
111 Willits St Apt 502
Birmingham, MI 48009-3332, USA

Hudler, Rex (Athlete, Baseball Player)
11745 Riehl Ave
Tustin, CA 92782-3372, USA

Hudlin, Reginald (Director, Producer)
c/o Staff Member *Hudlin Entertainment*
369 S Doheny Dr Ste 172
Beverly Hills, CA 90211-3508, USA

Hudson, Bill (Actor)
2808 Westbrook Ave
Los Angeles, CA 90046-1249, USA

Hudson, Bob (Athlete, Football Player)
6122 Magnolia Ln
Rowlett, TX 75089-3163, USA

Hudson, Brett (Actor, Producer, Writer)
c/o Staff Member *WME|IMG*
9601 Wilshire Blvd
Beverly Hills, CA 90210-5213, USA

Hudson, C B Jr (Business Person)
Torchmark Corp
2001 3rd Ave S
Birmingham, AL 35233-2115, USA

Hudson, Charles (Athlete, Baseball Player)
810 N Breckenridge St
Ennis, TX 75119-3106, USA

Hudson, Charles (Charlie) (Athlete, Baseball Player)
32 W Hooker Ave
Coalgate, OK 74538, USA

Hudson, Chris (Athlete, Football Player)
6361 Moondance Cv
Olive Branch, MS 38654-9060, USA

Hudson, Dave (Athlete, Hockey Player)
5204 Briar Tree Dr
Dallas, TX 75248-6032, USA

Hudson, Dawn (Actor, Business Person)
c/o Staff Member *Academy of Motion Pictures Arts & Sciences*
8949 Wilshire Blvd
Academy Foundation
Beverly Hills, CA 90211-1972, USA

Hudson, Emie (Actor)
14721 Summit Oaks Dr
Burnsville, MN 55337-4161, USA

Hudson, Ernie (Actor, Producer)
c/o Darryl Marshak *Marshak/Zachary Company, The*
8840 Wilshire Blvd Fl 1
Beverly Hills, CA 90211-2606, USA

Hudson, Garth (Music Group, Musician)
Skyline Music
32 Clayton St
Portland, ME 04103-2250, USA

Hudson, Gary (Actor)
c/o Staff Member *Origin Talent Agency*
4705 Laurel Canyon Blvd Ste 306
Studio City, CA 91607-5940, USA

Hudson, Gordon (Athlete, Football Player)
12498 S Falls Creek Rd
Riverton, UT 84065-1915, USA

Hudson, Hal (Athlete, Baseball Player)
422 Sandpiper Dr Apt C
Fort Pierce, FL 34982-5112, USA

Hudson, Haley (Actor)

Hudson, Harry (Musician)
c/o Kate Rosen *The Lede Company*
401 Broadway Ste 206
New York, NY 10013-3033, USA

Hudson, Hugh (Director)
c/o Staff Member *ICM Partners*
10250 Constellation Blvd Fl 7
Los Angeles, CA 90067-6207, USA

Hudson, Jennifer (Actor, Musician)
c/o Allison Statter *Blended Strategy Group*
1100 Glendon Ave Ste 1000
Los Angeles, CA 90024-3514, USA

Hudson, Jesse (Athlete, Baseball Player)
341 Albert Lewis Way
Mansfield, LA 71052-5723, USA

Hudson, Joe (Athlete, Baseball Player)
109 Pine Valley Dr
Medford, NJ 08055-9210, USA

Hudson, John (Athlete, Football Player)
3320 Highway 77
Paris, TN 38242-5495, USA

Hudson, Kate (Actor)
c/o Brad Cafarelli *PMK/BNC Public Relations*
1840 Century Park E Ste 1400
Los Angeles, CA 90067-2115, USA

Hudson, Lex (Athlete, Hockey Player)
General Delivery
Flat Rock, NL ADA 3LO, Canada

Hudson, Lucy-Jo (Actor)
Granada Television
Quay St
Manchester M60 9EA, ENGLAND

Hudson, Luke (Athlete, Baseball Player)
9912 Aster Cir
Fountain Valley, CA 92708-2309, USA

Hudson, Marvin (Athlete, Baseball Player)
698 Metasville Rd
Washington, GA 30673-2605, USA

Hudson, Mike (Athlete, Hockey Player)
1856 Knox Rd
Vancouver, BC V6T 1S3, Canada

Hudson, Oliver (Actor, Producer)
c/o David Seltzer *Management 360*
9111 Wilshire Blvd
Beverly Hills, CA 90210-5508, USA

Hudson, Orlando (Athlete, Baseball Player)
1416 Pocket Rd
Darlington, SC 29532-8416, USA

Hudson, Ray (Coach, Soccer Player)
DC United
14120 Newbrook Dr
Chantilly, VA 20151-2273, USA

Hudson, Rex (Athlete, Baseball Player)
12451 Cartwright Trl
Ponder, TX 76259-5220, USA

Hudson, Richard S (Athlete, Football Player)
Henry County High School
315 S Wilson St
Attn: Assistant Principal
Paris, TN 38242-5053, USA

Hudson, Robert W (Athlete, Football Player)
6122 Magnolia Ln
Rowlett, TX 75089-3163, USA

Hudson, Rodney (Athlete, Football Player)
c/o Joe Linta *JL Sports*
1204 Main St Ste 179
Branford, CT 06405-3787, USA

Hudson, Sally (Skier)
PO Box 2343
Olympic Valley, CA 96146-2343, USA

Hudson, Tim (Athlete, Baseball Player)
901 Rocky Hills Dr
Auburn, AL 36830-7222, USA

Hudson, Troy (Athlete, Baseball Player)
6040 Earle Brown Dr Ste 4S0
Minneapolis, MN 55430-2514, USA

Hudspeth, Tommy (Athlete, Football Coach, Football Player)
3522 E 71st Pl
Tulsa, OK 74136-5962, USA

Huebel, Rob (Actor)
c/o Matthew Labov *Forefront Media*
1669 Virginia Rd
Los Angeles, CA 90019-5935, USA

Huelskamp, Tim (Congressman, Politician)
126 Cannon Hob
Washington, DC 20515-5401, USA

Huerta, Carlos (Athlete, Football Player)
3060 E Post Rd Ste 110
Las Vegas, NV 89120-4449, USA

Huertas, Jon (Actor, Producer)
c/o Staff Member *WestSide Stories Entertainment*
11812 San Vicente Blvd Ste 200
Los Angeles, CA 90049-6622, USA

Hues, Matthias (Actor)
Lou Records
32 rue des Je??neurs
Paris 75002, FRANCE

Huet, Cristobal (Athlete, Hockey Player)
Sports Consulting Group
65 Monroe Ave Ste D
Pittsford, NY 14534-1318, USA

Huff, Aubrey (Athlete, Baseball Player)
741 S Cedros Ave
Solana Beach, CA 92075-1926, USA

Huff, Brent (Actor)
c/o Erik Seastrand *WME|IMG*
9601 Wilshire Blvd
Beverly Hills, CA 90210-5213, USA

Huff, Dann (Musician, Producer)
Dann Huff Productions
10 Music Cir S Fl 2
Nashville, TN 37203-3176, USA

Huff, Gary E (Athlete, Football Player)
3387 Shady Rest Rd
Havana, FL 32333-4869, USA

Huff, Josh (Athlete, Football Player)
c/o Sean Kiernan *Impact Sports (LA)*
12429 Ventura Ct
Studio City, CA 91604-2417, USA

Huff, Kenneth W (Ken) (Athlete, Football Player)
75402 Rowan
Chapel Hill, NC 27517-8577, USA

Huff, Marqueston (Athlete, Football Player)

Huff, Marty (Athlete, Football Player)
6700 Keithcrest Dr
Temperance, MI 48182-1231, USA

Huff, Mike (Athlete, Baseball Player)
5500 S Madison St Apt 18
Hinsdale, IL 60521-8115, USA

Huff, Orlando (Athlete, Football Player)
14623 196th Ave SE
Renton, WA 98059-8120, USA

Huff, Sam (Athlete, Football Player, Sportscaster)
Billie Van Pay
PO Box 963
Middleburg, VA 20118-0963, USA

Huff, Tanya (Writer)
c/o Staff Member *JABberwocky Literary Agency*
PO Box 4558
Sunnyside, NY 11104-0558, USA

Huffine, Candice (Model)
c/o Staff Member *IMG Models (NY)*
304 Park Ave S PH N
New York, NY 10010-4303, USA

Huffington, Arianna (Journalist, Writer)
Thrive Global
100 Crosby St Rm 308
New York, NY 10012-4716, USA

Huffington, Michael (Politician, Producer)

Huffins, Chris (Athlete, Decathlon Athlete, Olympic Athlete)
1319 Wildcliff Pkwy NE
Atlanta, GA 30329-3465, USA

Huffman, Felicity (Actor)
c/o Annett Wolf *Wolf-Kasteler Public Relations*
6255 W Sunset Blvd Ste 1111
Los Angeles, CA 90028-7426, USA

Huffman, Kerry (Athlete, Hockey Player)
5557 Sea Forest Dr Apt 215
New Port Richey, FL 34652-3213, USA

Huffman, Logan (Actor)
c/o Emily Taylor *Persona Public Relations*
6255 W Sunset Blvd Ste 705
Hollywood, CA 90028-7408, USA

Huffman, Phil (Athlete, Baseball Player)
194 Paxton Rd
Rochester, NY 14617-4657, USA

Huffman, Tim (Athlete, Football Player)
5426 Hidalgo Ct
Garland, TX 75043-5516, USA

Hufnagel, John (Athlete, Football Player)
1608 Maritime Oak Dr
Atlantic Beach, FL 32233-7333, USA

Hufsey, Billy (Actor)
15415 Muskingum Blvd
Brook Park, OH 44142-2327, USA

Hug, Steve (Athlete, Gymnast, Olympic Athlete)

Hugasian, Harry (Athlete, Football Player)
Arcadia Gardens
720 W Camino Real Ave
Arcadia, CA 91007-7839, USA

Huggins, Bob (Athlete, Basketball Player, Coach)
207 Beecher Hall
Cincinnati, OH 45221-0001, USA

Hughes, Abby (Athlete, Olympic Athlete, Skier)
c/o Gigi Rock *Heraea Marketing*
10905 E Pear Tree Dr
Cornville, AZ 86325-5523, USA

Hughes, Albert (Director, Producer, Writer)
c/o David Wirtschafter *WME|IMG*
9601 Wilshire Blvd
Beverly Hills, CA 90210-5213, USA

Hughes, Alfredrick (Athlete, Basketball Player)
5024 S Kildare Ave
Chicago, IL 60632-4543, USA

Hughes, Allen (Director, Producer, Writer)
c/o David Wirtschafter *WME|IMG*
9601 Wilshire Blvd
Beverly Hills, CA 90210-5213, USA

Hughes, Bobby (Athlete, Baseball Player)
114 Montreal St
Playa Del Rey, CA 90293-7608, USA

Hughes, Bradley (Athlete, Golfer)
204 Easton Ct
Simpsonville, SC 29680-7627, USA

Hughes, Brent (Athlete, Hockey Player)
1641 Nile Dr Apt 824
Corpus Christi, TX 78412-4981, USA

Hughes, Brent (Athlete, Hockey Player)
2016 Sweetgum Dr
Hoover, AL 35244-1628, USA

Hughes, Catherine L (Business Person)
Radio One
1010 Wayne Ave Ste 1400
Silver Spring, MD 20910-5652, USA

Hughes, Danan (Athlete, Football Player)
278 SE Sumpter Ct
Lees Summit, MO 64063-3669, USA

Hughes, Dave (Hughesy) (Comedian)
c/o Staff Member *Westside Talent*
44 Watton St
1st Floor
Werribee, Victoria 03030, Australia

Hughes, David (Athlete, Football Player)
2101 SE 2nd Pl
Renton, WA 98056-8864, USA

Hughes, Dennis (Athlete, Football Player)
360 Beechwood Dr
Athens, GA 30606-4010, USA

Hughes, Dustin (Athlete, Baseball Player)
5226 Savannah Pkwy
Southaven, MS 38672-7513, USA

Hughes, Eddie (Athlete, Basketball Player)
4253 Deerfield Hills Rd
Colorado Springs, CO 80916-3506, USA

Hughes, Ernie (Athlete, Football Player)
2116 Camino Brazos
Pleasanton, CA 94566-5811, USA

Hughes, Finola (Actor)
c/o Steven Jensen *Independent Group, The*
6363 Wilshire Blvd Ste 115
Los Angeles, CA 90048-5734, USA

Hughes, Frank (Athlete, Hockey Player)
PO Box 1856
Sparwood, BC V0B 2G0, Canada

Hughes, Frank John (Actor)
c/o Dan Baron *Agency for the Performing Arts (APA)*
405 S Beverly Dr Ste 500
Beverly Hills, CA 90212-4425, USA

Hughes, Glenn (Musician)
6671 W Sunset Blvd Ste 1585-114
Los Angeles, CA 90028-7116, USA

Hughes, Harry (Politician)
24788 Woods Dr
Denton, MD 21629-2323, USA

Hughes, Howie (Athlete, Hockey Player)
3711 27th Pl W Apt 205
Seattle, WA 98199-2062, USA

Hughes, Jack (Athlete, Hockey Player)
Beanpot Financial
54 Canal St Ste 350
Boston, MA 02114-2015, USA

Hughes, Jerry (Athlete, Football Player)
c/o Tom Condon *Creative Artists Agency (CAA)*
401 Commerce St PH
Nashville, TN 37219-2516, USA

Hughes, Jim (Athlete, Baseball Player)
530 S Londerry Ln
Anaheim, CA 92807-4654, USA

Hughes, John (Athlete, Hockey Player)
68 Sarah Janes Ln
Cornwall, PE C0A 1H0, CANADA

Hughes, Kate (Athlete, Golfer)
275 Merlot Ln
Saint Albans, MO 63073-1214, USA

Hughes, Kathleen (Actor)
8818 Rising Glen Pl
Los Angeles, CA 90069-1222, USA

Hughes, Keith (Athlete, Baseball Player)
176 Sycamore Rd
Havertown, PA 19083-3508, USA

Hughes, Kim (Athlete, Basketball Player)
123 NW 12th Ave Apt 244
Portland, OR 97209-4144, USA

Hughes, Larry (Athlete, Basketball Player)
3 Hanna Ct
Cleveland, OH 44108-1162, USA

Hughes, Macon (Athlete, Football Player)
6141 Avery Dr APT 7105
Fort Worth, TX 76132-5317, USA

Hughes, Mark (Coach)
c/o Staff Member *Blackburn Rovers Football Club*
Ewood Park
Blackburn
Lancashire BB2 4JF, UNITED KINGDOM

Hughes, Miko (Actor)
Jamieson Assoc
53 Sunrise Road
Superior, MT 59872, USA

Hughes, Montori (Athlete, Football Player)
c/o Joby Branion *Vanguard Sports Group*
23091 Mill Creek Dr
Laguna Hills, CA 92653-1258, USA

Hughes, Pat (Athlete, Football Player)
4 Woodside Dr
Stratham, NH 03885-6549, USA

Hughes, Pat (Athlete, Hockey Player)
8388 Webster Hills Rd
Dexter, MI 48130-9365, USA

Hughes, Pat (Commentator)
13 Fox Trl
Lincolnshire, IL 60069-4010, USA

Hughes, Phil (Athlete, Baseball Player)
c/o Team Member *New York Yankees*
161st St & River Ave
Yankee Stadium
Bronx, NY 10451, USA

Hughes, Randy (Athlete, Football Player)
17608 Cedar Creek Canyon Dr
Dallas, TX 75252-4966, USA

Hughes, Richard H (Dick) (Athlete, Baseball Player)
PO Box 598
Stephens, AR 71764-0598, USA

Hughes, Ryan (Athlete, Hockey Player)
21 Palmerston Pl
Basking Ridge, NJ 07920-2513, USA

Hughes, Sarah (Athlete, Figure Skater, Olympic Athlete)
John Hughes
12 Channel Dr
Great Neck, NY 11024-1212, USA

Hughes, Suzan (Actor)
c/o Staff Member *ICM Partners*
10250 Constellation Blvd Fl 7
Los Angeles, CA 90067-6207, USA

Hughes, Terry (Athlete, Baseball Player)
107 Woodcreek Dr
Spartanburg, SC 29303-1949, USA

Hughes, Tom (Athlete, Baseball Player)
610 Kimswick Ct
Deer Park, TX 77536-6139, USA

Hughes, Tyrone C (Athlete, Football Player)
4758 Eunice St
New Orleans, LA 70127-3420, USA

Hughes-Fulford, Millie (Astronaut)
Veterans Affairs Dept
4150 Clement St
Medical Center
San Francisco, CA 94121-1563, USA

Hughes-Fulford, Millie (Astronaut)
218 Reed Cir
Mill Valley, CA 94941-2514, USA

Hughley, DL (Actor, Comedian)
c/o Staff Member *Five Timz Productions*
22817 Ventura Blvd Ste 872
Woodland Hills, CA 91364-1202, USA

Hugo, Chad (Musician)
c/o Scott Vener *MGMT Entertainment (The Schiff Company)*
9220 W Sunset Blvd Ste 106
W Hollywood, CA 90069-3500, USA

Hugo Boss (Designer, Fashion Designer)
Hugo Boss AG
Dieselstrabe 12
Metzingen 72555, Germany

Hugstedt, Petter (Skier)
Kongsberg 03600, NORWAY

Hui, Tammy (Actor)
c/o Lisa King *King Talent*
36 Tiverton Ave
Toronto, ON M4M 2L9, Canada

Huisman, Justin (Athlete, Baseball Player)
10302 Pickett Way
Cedar Lake, IN 46303-7292, USA

Huisman, Michiel (Actor)
c/o John Grant *Conway van Gelder Grant*
8-12 Broadwick St
London W1F 8HW, UNITED KINGDOM

Huisman, Rick (Athlete, Baseball Player)
17W025 Oak Ln
Bensenville, IL 60106-2860, USA

Huismann, Mark (Athlete, Baseball Player)
5751 NW Plantation Ln
Lees Summit, MO 64064-1686, USA

Huizenga, Bill (Congressman, Politician)
1217 Longworth Hob
Washington, DC 20515-4901, USA

Hulbert, Mike (Athlete, Golfer)
7770 Apple Tree Cir
Orlando, FL 32819-4686, USA

Hulbig, Joe (Athlete, Hockey Player)
17 Apple Blossom Ln
Stow, MA 01775-1380, USA

Hulce, Tom (Actor)
2305 Stanley Hills Dr
Los Angeles, CA 90046-1533, USA

Hulett, Tim (Athlete, Baseball Player)
799 Dumaine Dr
Bossier City, LA 71111-6273, USA

Hull, Bobby (Athlete, Hockey Player)
6916 Lennox Pl
University Park, FL 34201-2256, USA

Hull, Brett (Athlete, Hockey Player, Olympic Athlete)
3520 Eben Way
Stillwater, MN 55082-8102, USA

Hull, Dennis W (Athlete, Hockey Player)
11642 County Road 29
Roseneath, ON K0K 2X0, Canada

Hull, Eric (Athlete, Baseball Player)
280 Covey Run
Selah, WA 98942-9605, USA

Hull, Gina (Athlete, Golfer)
264 Costado St
Saint Augustine, FL 32086-7019, USA

Hull, Jody (Athlete, Coach, Hockey Player)
c/o Staff Member *Peterborough Petes*
151 Lansdowne St W
Peterborough, ON K9J 1Y4, Canada

Hull, Mike (Athlete, Football Player)
3809 Vista Azul
San Clemente, CA 92672-4543, USA

Hullet, Jamie (Athlete, Golfer)
1153 Lakeview Dr
Mesquite, TX 75149-5813, USA

Hulme, Denis (Race Car Driver)
Cl-6
RDTE Puke
Bay of Plenny, NEW ZEALAND

Hulme, Keri (Writer)
Hodder & Stoughton
338 Euston Road
London NW1 3BH, UNITED KINGDOM (UK)

Hulse, Cale (Athlete, Hockey Player)
c/o Art Breeze *Pro-Rep Entertainment Consulting*
113-276 Midpark Gdns SE
Calgary, AB T2X 1T3, Canada

Hulse, Chuck (Race Car Driver)
7341 Spruce Cir
La Palma, CA 90623-1324, USA

Hulse, David (Athlete, Baseball Player)
1301 Kenwood Dr
San Angelo, TX 76903-7261, USA

Hultgren, Randy (Congressman, Politician)
427 Cannon Hob
Washington, DC 20515-5301, USA

Hultz, Don (Athlete, Football Player)
5078 Pleasant Ridge Rd
Millington, TN 38053-7752, USA

Hultzen, Danny (Athlete, Baseball Player)
c/o Staff Member *Chicago Cubs*
1060 W Addison St
Wrigley Field
Chicago, IL 60613-4397, USA

Human League (Music Group)
c/o Staff Member *Performers of the World*
5657 Wilshire Blvd Ste 280
Los Angeles, CA 90036-3755, USA

Human Nature (Music Group)
c/o Staff Member *Caplice Management*
PO Box 381
Darlinghurst, NSW 01300, Australia

Humber, Philip (Athlete, Baseball Player)
PO Box 130788
Tyler, TX 75713-0788, USA

Humbert, Richard (Athlete, Football Player)
12112 Ashton Park Dr
Glen Allen, VA 23059-7129, USA

Hume, Brit (Television Host)
c/o Staff Member *Fox News (DC)*
5151 Wisconsin Ave NW Fl 1
Washington, DC 20016-4132, USA

Hume, Kirsty (Model)
c/o Staff Member *LA Talent*
7700 W Sunset Blvd Ste 203
Los Angeles, CA 90046-3913, USA

Hume, Tom (Athlete, Baseball Player)
2102 7th St W
Palmetto, FL 34221-4218, USA

Humenik, Ed (Athlete, Golfer)
4746 SW Hammock Creek Dr
Palm City, FL 34990-7936, USA

Humes, Edward (Journalist)
Simon & Schuster
1230 Avenue of the Americas Fl CONC1
New York, NY 10020-1586, USA

Humes, Mary-Margaret (Actor)
c/o Lisa Blumenthal *Momentum Talent Management*
13935 Burbank Blvd Apt 102
Valley Glen, CA 91401-5078, USA

Humiston, Mike (Athlete, Football Player)
311 N Richhill St
Waynesburg, PA 15370-1224, USA

Humm, David (Athlete, Football Player)
4301 Via Olivero Ave
Las Vegas, NV 89102-3799, USA

Hummel, Rick (Commentator)
PO Box 270056
Saint Louis, MO 63127-0056, USA

Hummel, Tim (Athlete, Baseball Player)
1550 Kerr Rd
Whiteford, MD 21160-1318, USA

Hummer, John (Athlete, Basketball Player)
80 E Roanoke St Unit 17
Seattle, WA 98102-3285, USA

Humperdinck, Engelbert (Actor, Musician, Producer)
c/o Arthur Andelson *Kismet Talent Agency*
3435 Ocean Park Blvd Ste 107
Santa Monica, CA 90405-3320, USA

Humphery, Bobby (Athlete, Football Player)
914 E Highland Blvd
San Antonio, TX 78210-3529, USA

Humphrey, Claude (Athlete, Football Player)
3399 Lord Dunmore Cv
Bartlett, TN 38134-3089, USA

Humphrey, Jay (Athlete, Football Player)
14109 Brookridge Cir
Dallas, TX 75254-2709, USA

Humphrey, Paul (Athlete, Football Player)
1120 E Davis Dr Apt 515
Terre Haute, IN 47802-4068, USA

Humphrey, Richard (Athlete, Baseball Player)
26 Player Green Pl
Spring, TX 77382-2021, USA

Humphrey, Richard (Baseball Player)
21 Midland Dr
Morristown, NJ 07960-5064, USA

Humphrey, Ryan (Basketball Player)
Memphis Grizzlies
175 Toyota Plz Ste 150
Memphis, TN 38103-6601, USA

Humphrey, Terry (Athlete, Baseball Player)
7 Oakmont
Trabuco Canyon, CA 92679-4728, USA

Humphreys, Bob (Athlete, Baseball Player)
1803 Oakwood St
Bedford, VA 24523-1217, USA

Humphreys, Mike (Athlete, Baseball Player)
1402 Lost Creek Dr
Desoto, TX 75115-3662, USA

Humphreys, Todd (Race Car Driver)
Humphrey's Race Team
Route #5
Elbridge, NY 13060, USA

Humphries, Barry (Actor)
5 Soho Square
London W1V 5DE, UNITED KINGDOM (UK)

Humphries, DJ (Athlete, Football Player)
c/o Brian Mackler *Sportstars Inc*
1370 Avenue of the Americas Fl 19
New York, NY 10019-4602, USA

Humphries, Jay (Athlete, Basketball Player)
PO Box 1387
Parker, CO 80134-1400, USA

Humphries, Kris (Athlete, Basketball Player)
c/o Liza Anderson *Anderson Group Public Relations*
8060 Melrose Ave Fl 4
Los Angeles, CA 90046-7038, USA

Humphries, Rusty (Radio Personality)
Rusty Humphries Show
225 NE Hillcrest Dr
Grants Pass, OR 97526-3547, USA

Humphries, Stan (Athlete, Football Player)
4100 Chauvin Ln
Monroe, LA 71201-2057, USA

Humphries, Stefan (Athlete, Football Player)
8708 E Redwood Ln
Spokane, WA 99217-9757, USA

Hundley, Mandisa (Musician)
c/o Staff Member *The M Collective*
PO Box 273
Franklin, TN 37065-0273, USA

Hundley, Randy (Athlete, Baseball Player)
Randy Hundley Baseball Camp
1935 S Plum Grove Rd # 5
Rd # 285
Palatine, IL 60067-7258, USA

Hundley, Todd (Athlete, Baseball Player)
830 Raleigh Rd
Glenview, IL 60025-4328, USA

Hundon, James (Athlete, Football Player)
92 Kenneth Ct
Bay Point, CA 94565-1545, USA

Hung, Sammo (Actor)
c/o Maani Golesorkhi *Bluestone Entertainment*
9000 W Sunset Blvd Ste 700
Los Angeles, CA 90069-5807, USA

Hung, William (Musician, Reality Star)
c/o Mike Esterman *Esterman.Com, LLC*
Prefers to be contacted via email
Baltimore, MD XXXXX, USA

Hunger, Daniela (Swimmer)
SV Preussen
Hansastr 190
Berlin 13088, GERMANY

Hunley, Con (Musician)
6406 Spring View Ln
Knoxville, TN 37918-1203, USA

Hunley, Ricky C (Athlete, Football Player)
9617 Stonemasters Dr
Loveland, OH 45140-6210, USA

Hunnam, Charlie (Actor)
c/o Cynthia Pett-Dante *Brillstein Entertainment Partners*
9150 Wilshire Blvd Ste 350
Beverly Hills, CA 90212-3453, USA

Hunnicutt, Gayle (Actor)
174 Regents Park Road
London NW1, UNITED KINGDOM (UK)

Hunphrey, Bobby (Athlete, Football Player)
4209 Woodbine Ln
Hoover, AL 35226-4122, USA

Hunsicker, Gerald (Commentator)
11914 Cobblestone Dr
Houston, TX 77024-5003, USA

Hunt, Bobby (Athlete, Football Player)
5928 Bentway Dr
Charlotte, NC 28226-8053, USA

Hunt, Bonnie (Actor, Director, Talk Show Host)
415 25th St
Santa Monica, CA 90402-3103, USA

Hunt, Bryan (Artist)
31 Great Jones St
New York, NY 10012-1178, USA

Hunt, Byron (Athlete, Football Player)
PO Box 281
Rutherford, NJ 07070-0281, USA

Hunt, Charlie (Athlete, Football Player)
8700 Nathans Cove Ct
Jacksonville, FL 32256-9536, USA

Hunt, Cletidus (Athlete, Football Player)
7246 Creek Bend Dr
Memphis, TN 38125-3018, USA

Hunt, Courtney (Director, Writer)
c/o Staff Member *WME/IMG*
9601 Wilshire Blvd
Beverly Hills, CA 90210-5213, USA

Hunt, Crystal (Actor)
c/o Scott Zimmerman *Scott Zimmerman Management*
901 N Highland Ave
Los Angeles, CA 90038-2412, USA

Hunt, Ella (Actor)
c/o Piers Nimmo *Piers Nimmo Management*
8 Coningsby Road
London N4 1EG, UNITED KINGDOM

Hunt, Francesca (Actor)
c/o Dallas Smith *United Agents*
12-26 Lexington St
London W1F OLE, UNITED KINGDOM

Hunt, George (Athlete, Football Player)
1327 Forestedge Blvd
Oldsmar, FL 34677-5119, USA

Hunt, Helen (Actor)
c/o Stephen Huvane *Slate PR*
901 N Highland Ave
W Hollywood, CA 90038-2412, USA

Hunt, James (Politician)
6653D Governor Hunt Rd # D
Lucama, NC 27851-9415, USA

Hunt, Jimmy (Actor)
2279 Lansdale Ct
Simi Valley, CA 93065-2530, USA

Hunt, John (Athlete, Football Player)
8 Ulverston Way
Blythewood, SC 29016-8941, USA

Hunt, John R (Religious Leader)
Evangelical Covenant Church
5101 N Francisco Ave
Chicago, IL 60625, USA

Hunt, Kareem (Athlete, Football Player)

Hunt, Kevin (Athlete, Football Player)
11 Royal Ln
Londonderry, NH 03053-2507, USA

Hunt, Lamar (Football Executive, Soccer Player, Tennis Player)
1601 Elm St # 2800
Thanksgiving Tower
Dallas, TX 75201-4701, USA

Hunt, Linda (Actor)
c/o Tim Curtis *WME/IMG*
9601 Wilshire Blvd
Beverly Hills, CA 90210-5213, USA

Hunt, Linda (Athlete, Golfer)
6436 Bella Cir Unit 1105
Boynton Beach, FL 33437-5566, USA

Hunt, Margus (Athlete, Football Player)

Hunt, Marsha (Actor)
13131 Magnolia Blvd
Van Nuys, CA 91423-1528, USA

Hunt, Marsha (Actor, Writer)
c/o Staff Member *D&M Publishers*
2323 Quebec St Suite 201
Vancouver, BC V5T 4S7, Canada

Hunt, Peter (Director, Producer)
c/o Dennis Aspland *Aspland Management*
245 W 55th St Ste 1102
New York, NY 10019-5231, USA

Hunt, Randy (Athlete, Baseball Player)
324 Holly Ridge Dr
Montgomery, AL 36109-3904, USA

Hunt, Ray (Business Person)
Hunt Oil Company
1900 N Akard St
Dallas, TX 75201-2300

Hunt, Ron (Athlete, Baseball Player)
2806 Jackson Rd
Wentzville, MO 63385-4205, USA

Hunt, Sam (Athlete, Football Player)
1708 Eliza St
Nacogdoches, TX 75961-5700, USA

Hunt, Sam (Musician)
c/o Brad Belanger *Red Light Management (TN)*
PO Box 159310
Nashville, TN 37215-9310, USA

Hunt, Van (Musician)
c/o Staff Member *Creative Artists Agency (CAA)*
2000 Avenue of the Stars Ste 100
Los Angeles, CA 90067-4705, USA

Hunt, Wendy (DJ)
c/o Staff Member *Diva Central Inc*
7510 W Sunset Blvd # 1445
Los Angeles, CA 90046-3408, USA

Hunter, Anthony (Athlete, Football Player)
3553 Edgeview Dr
Cincinnati, OH 45213-2024, USA

Hunter, Billy (Athlete, Baseball Player, Coach)
104 E Seminary Ave
Lutherville Timonium, MD 21093-6127, USA

Hunter, Brian (Athlete, Baseball Player)
12141 Centralia St Unit 219
Lakewood, CA 90715-1565, USA

Hunter, Brian (Athlete, Baseball Player)
1440 Kasten Dr
Dolton, IL 60419-2469, USA

Hunter, Buddy (Athlete, Baseball Player)
14467 Penny Dr
Plattsmouth, NE 68048-5121, USA

Hunter, Charlie (Music Group, Musician)
Figurehead Mgmt
3470 19th St
San Francisco, CA 94110-1740, USA

Hunter, Dale (Athlete, Hockey Player)
c/o Staff Member *London Knights*
99 Dundas St
London, ON N6A 6K1, Canada

Hunter, Daniel (Athlete, Football Player)
210 N Lakeview Dr
Farmerville, LA 71241-2504, USA

Hunter, Dave (Athlete, Hockey Player)
53350 Range Road 220
Ardrossan, AB T8E 2B5, Canada

Hunter, Dorothy (Baseball Player)
2607 Miller Ave NW
Grand Rapids, MI 49544-1948, USA

Hunter, Duncan (Congressman, Politician)
223 Cannon Hob
Washington, DC 20515-0003, USA

Hunter, Herman (Athlete, Football Player)
541 Rural Hill Rd
Nashville, TN 37217-4107, USA

Hunter, Holly (Actor)
c/o David Seltzer *Management 360*
9111 Wilshire Blvd
Beverly Hills, CA 90210-5508, USA

Hunter, Ian (Music Group, Musician, Songwriter, Writer)
Helter Skelter
Plaza
535 Kings Road
London SW10 0S, UNITED KINGDOM (UK)

Hunter, Jeff (Athlete, Football Player)
3492 Monte Carlo Dr
Augusta, GA 30906-5717, USA

Hunter, Jesse (Music Group, Musician)
Friedman & LaRosa
1334 Lexington Ave
New York, NY 10128, USA

hunter, Jim (Athlete, Baseball Player)
12939 Penshurst Ln
Windermere, FL 34786-6672, USA

Hunter, Jim (Commentator)
3010 Franklins Chance Dr
Fallston, MD 21047-1353, USA

Hunter, Jim (Skier)
Jungle Jim Hunter Mgmt
864 Woodpark Way SW
Calgary, AB T2W 2V8, CANADA

Hunter, Justin (Athlete, Football Player)
c/o Jimmy Sexton *CAA (Memphis)*
6060 Poplar Ave Ste 470
Memphis, TN 38119-0910, USA

Hunter, Kendall (Athlete, Football Player)
c/o Adisa P Bakari *Kelley Drye & Warren LLP*
3050 K St NW Ste 400
Washington, DC 20007-5100, USA

Hunter, Les (Athlete, Basketball Player)
8712 W 92nd St
Overland Park, KS 66212-3817, USA

Hunter, Mark (Athlete, Hockey Player)
c/o Staff Member *London Knights*
99 Dundas St
London, ON N6A 6K1, Canada

Hunter, Mellisa (Reality Star)
c/o Mike Esterman *Esterman.Com, LLC*
Prefers to be contacted via email
Baltimore, MD XXXXX, USA

Hunter, Montgomery (Athlete, Football Player)
411 Washington St
Dover, OH 44622-1938, USA

Hunter, Patrick (Athlete, Football Player)
880 N David Ct
Chandler, AZ 85226-1659, USA

Hunter, Rachel (Actor, Model)
c/o Chuck Binder *Binder & Associates*
1465 Lindacrest Dr
Beverly Hills, CA 90210-2519, USA

Hunter, Rich (Athlete, Baseball Player)
3820 Agave Ct
Perris, CA 92570-7192, USA

Hunter, Robert (Politician)
2201 C St NW Dept of
Washington, DC 20520-0099, USA

Hunter, Ronald (Actor)
c/o Barbara Price *Kings Highway Entertainment*
14538 Benefit St Unit 103
Sherman Oaks, CA 91403-5504, USA

Hunter, Scott (Athlete, Football Player)
4 Yacht Club Dr Apt 48
Daphne, AL 36526-7190, USA

Hunter, Stephen (Writer)
Washington Post
Editorial Dept
1150 15th St NW
Washington, DC 20071-0001, USA

Hunter, Steven (Basketball Player)
Orlando Magic
8701 Maitland Summit Blvd
Waterhouse Center
Orlando, FL 32810-5915, USA

Hunter, Tim (Athlete, Coach, Hockey Player)
c/o Staff Member *San Jose Sharks*
525 W Santa Clara St
San Jose, CA 95113-1500, USA

Hunter, Tim (Director)
c/o Staff Member *Gersh*
9465 Wilshire Blvd Ste 600
Beverly Hills, CA 90212-2605, USA

Hunter, Tommy (Musician)
c/o Staff Member *Rocklands Entertainment*
1135 Pasadena Ave S Ste 209
South Pasadena, FL 33707-2855, USA

Hunter, Torii (Athlete, Baseball Player)
PO Box 1357
Prosper, TX 75078-1357, USA

Hunter, Trent (Athlete, Hockey Player)
26 MacKay Way
Roslyn, NY 11576-2169, USA

Hunter, Willard (Athlete, Baseball Player)
2562 Poppleton Ave
Omaha, NE 68105-2303, USA

Hunter-Gault, Charlayne (Correspondent)
News Hour Show
2700 S Quincy St Ste 250
Arlington, VA 22206-2222, USA

Hunter-Reay, Ryan (Race Car Driver)
3200 NE 40th Ct
Fort Lauderdale, FL 33308-6416, USA

Huntington, Neal (Commentator)
332 Rye Gate St
Bay Village, OH 44140-1274, USA

Huntington, Sam (Actor)
c/o Logan Eisenberg *United Talent Agency (UTA)*
9336 Civic Center Dr
Beverly Hills, CA 90210-3604, USA

Huntington, Samuel P (Politician)
Harvard University
Olin Institute
Political Science Dept
Cambridge, MA 02138, USA

Huntington-Whiteley, Rosie (Actor, Model)
c/o Stephen Huvane *Slate PR*
901 N Highland Ave
W Hollywood, CA 90038-2412, USA

Huntley, Joni (Athlete, Olympic Athlete, Track Athlete)
7148 SW 4th Ave
Portland, OR 97219-2220, USA

Huntley, Noah (Actor)
c/o Lindy King *United Agents*
12-26 Lexington St
London W1F OLE, UNITED KINGDOM

Huntley, Richard (Athlete, Football Player)
6005 Williams Rd Apt A
Charlotte, NC 28215-3606, USA

Huntz, Steve (Athlete, Baseball Player)
3303 Linden Rd Apt 405
Rocky River, OH 44116-4105, USA

Hunwlck, Matt (Athlete, Hockey Player)
37242 Mariano Dr
Sterling Heights, MI 48312-2054, USA

Hunyadfi, Steven (Coach, Swimmer)
838 Ridgewood Dr Apt 12
Fort Wayne, IN 46805-5712, USA

Hunyady, Emese (Speed Skater)
Beim Spitzriegel 1/2/9
Baden 02500, AUSTRIA

Hunziker, Terry (Designer)
208 3rd Ave S
Seattle, WA 98104-2608, USA

Hupp, Jana Marie (Actor)
c/o Karen Forman *Domain Talent*
1880 Century Park E Ste 1100
Los Angeles, CA 90067-1608, USA

Huppert, Dave (Athlete, Baseball Player)
6732 Stephens Path
Zephyrhills, FL 33542-0652, USA

Huppert, Isabelle (Actor)
c/o Isabelle de la Patelliere *Voyez Mon Agent*
20 Avenue Rapp
Paris 75007, FRANCE

Huras, Larry (Athlete, Hockey Player)
RR 1 PO
Allenford, ON N0H 1A0, Canada

Hurd, Gale Anne (Producer)
c/o Staff Member *Valhalla Motion Pictures*
3201 Cahuenga Blvd W
Los Angeles, CA 90068-1301, USA

Hurd, Michelle (Actor)
1077 E Santa Anita Ave
Burbank, CA 91501-1509, USA

Hurdle, Clinton M (Clint) (Athlete, Baseball Player, Coach)
9068 Sturbridge Pl
Highlands Ranch, CO 80129-2236, USA

Hurlburt, Bob (Athlete, Hockey Player)
205-3169 Tillicum Rd
Victoria, BC V9A 2B4, Canada

Hurlbut, Linda (Athlete, Golfer)
24741 Calle Conejo
Calabasas, CA 91302-3009, USA

Hurlbut, Mike (Athlete, Hockey Player)
86 Cougar Pt
Massena, NY 13662-3176, USA

Hurley, Bob (Athlete, Basketball Player)
1410 Shoreline Way
Hollywood, FL 33019-5006, USA

Hurley, Chad (Business Person)
YouTube, Inc
901 Cherry Ave
San Bruno, CA 94066-2914, USA

Hurley, Craig (Actor)
c/o Sandie Schnarr *AVO Talent Agency*
5670 Wilshire Blvd Ste 1930
Los Angeles, CA 90036-5603, USA

Hurley, Douglas G (Astronaut)
700 Thomwood Dr
Friendswood, TX 77546, USA

Hurley, Douglas G Ltcol (Astronaut)
1848 Lake Landing Dr
League City, TX 77573-7781, USA

Hurley, Elizabeth (Actor, Model)
Elizabeth Hurley Beach
P.O. Box 16
Cirencester
Gloucestershire GL7 9GH, UNITED KINGDOM

Hurley, Eric (Athlete, Baseball Player)
2024 Sterling Trace Dr
Keller, TX 76248-9739, USA

Hurlic, Philip (Actor)
2696 E 56th Way Apt 9
Long Beach, CA 90805-5041, USA

Hurns, Allen (Athlete, Football Player)
c/o Drew Rosenhaus *Rosenhaus Sports Representation*
3921 Alton Rd # 440
Miami Beach, FL 33140-3852, USA

Hurran, Nick (Director, Producer)
c/o Geoff Morley *United Talent Agency (UTA)*
9336 Civic Center Dr
Beverly Hills, CA 90210-3604, USA

Hurst, Bill (Athlete, Baseball Player)
13625 SW 83rd Ave
Palmetto Bay, FL 33158-1017, USA

Hurst, Bruce (Athlete, Baseball Player)
1080 N Riata St
Gilbert, AZ 85234-3466, USA

Hurst, Geoff (Athlete, Football Player)
c/o Staff Member *The FA*
25 Soho Square
London W1D 4FA, United Kingdom

Hurst, Grady (Athlete, Football Player)
5810 S 40th St Apt 118
Phoenix, AZ 85040-3965, USA

Hurst, Jackson (Actor)
c/o Staff Member *Lee Peterson and Associates*
78 San Marcos St
Austin, TX 78702-5236, USA

Hurst, James (Athlete, Baseball Player)
221 Westridge Blvd
Greenwood, IN 46142-2136, USA

Hurst, Jimmy (Athlete, Baseball Player)
901 University Ln
Tuscaloosa, AL 35401-7134, USA

Hurst, Jonathan (Athlete, Baseball Player)
308 Woodburn Creek Rd
Spartanburg, SC 29302-4279, USA

Hurst, Maurice (Athlete, Football Player)
P.O. Box 431068
Dallas, TX 75343, USA

Hurst, Michael (Actor)
Bruce Ugly Agency
218 Richmond Road
Grey Lynn
Auckland 2, NEW ZEALAND

Hurst, Pat (Athlete, Golfer)
730 Camino Amigo
Danville, CA 94526-2204, USA

Hurst, Rick (Actor)
1230 Horn Ave Apt 401
West Hollywood, CA 90069-2120, USA

Hurst, Ron (Athlete, Hockey Player)
8 Snowberry Cres
Georgetown, ON L7G 6M4, Canada

Hurst, Ryan (Actor)
c/o Sally Piper *Piper Kaniecki Management*
13273 Ventura Blvd Ste 104
Studio City, CA 91604-1840, USA

Hurston, Chuck (Athlete, Football Player)
9360 Prestwick Club Dr
Duluth, GA 30097-2400, USA

Hurt, Mary Beth (Actor)
c/o Paul Martino *Martino Management*
149 W 72nd St Apt 1D
New York, NY 10023-3228, USA

Hurt, Robert (Congressman, Politician)
1516 Longworth Hob
Washington, DC 20515-0905, USA

Hurt, William (Actor)
35425 Calamity Creek Ln
Drewsey, OR 97904-5711, USA

Hurtado, Edwin (Athlete, Baseball Player)
Toronto Blue Jays
7219 134th Ct SE
Newcastle, WA 98059-3004, USA

Hurtado, Nikko (Artist, Designer)
Black Anchor Collective
13567 1/2 Main St
Hesperia, CA 92345-4678, USA

Hurtado Larrea, Oswaldo (President)
Suecia 277 y Av Los Shyris
Quito, ECUADOR

Hurwit, Bruce (Director)
c/o Staff Member *Morra Brezner Steinberg & Tenenbaum (MBST) Entertainment*
345 N Maple Dr Ste 200
Beverly Hills, CA 90210-5174, USA

Hurwitz, Emanuel H (Musician)
25 Dollis Ave
London N3 1DA, UNITED KINGDOM (UK)

Hurwitz, Gregg (Writer)
c/o Aaron Priest *Aaron M. Priest Literary Agency*
708 3rd Ave Rm 2301
New York, NY 10017-4212, USA

Hurwitz, Jon (Producer)
c/o Maria Herrera *PMK/BNC Public Relations*
1840 Century Park E Ste 1400
Los Angeles, CA 90067-2115, USA

Hurwitz, Justin (Musician)
c/o Albert Tello *Lisa Taback Consulting (LT-LA)*
429 N Larchmont Blvd # 201
Los Angeles, CA 90004-3043, USA

Hurwitz, Mitchell (Writer)
c/o Dan Rabinow *Creative Artists Agency (CAA)*
2000 Avenue of the Stars Ste 100
Los Angeles, CA 90067-4705, USA

Husain, Mishal (Journalist)
c/o Staff Member *BBC Artist Mail*
PO Box 1116
Belfast BT2 7AJ, United Kingdom

Husak, Todd (Athlete, Football Player)
100 N Pacific Coast Hwy
El Segundo, CA 90245-4359, USA

Husar, Lubomyr Cardinal (Religious Leader)
Ploscha Sviatoho Jura 5
Lviv 290000, UKRAINE

Huscroft, Jamie (Athlete, Hockey Player)
3024 38th St SE
Puyallup, WA 98374-1949, USA

Huselius, Kristian (Athlete, Hockey Player)
Newport Sports Management
400-201 City Centre Dr
Attn Don Meehan
Mississauga, ON L5B 2T4, Canada

Huska, Ryan (Athlete, Hockey Player)
421 Quilchena Dr
Kelowna, BC V1W 4T7, Canada

Huskey, Robert L (Butch) (Athlete, Baseball Player)
PO Box 996
Apache, OK 73006-0996, USA

Huskins, Kent (Athlete, Hockey Player)
Octagon Sports Management
66 Slater St
23rd F Attn Larry Kelly
Ottawa, ON K1P 5H1, Canada

Husmann, Ed (Athlete, Football Player)
903 Longmire Rd APT 107
Conroe, TX 77304, USA

Huson, Jeff (Athlete, Baseball Player)
10349 Rowlock Way
Parker, CO 80134-9580, USA

Huss, Adam (Actor)
c/o Wendi Niad *Niad Management*
15021 Ventura Blvd Ste 860
Sherman Oaks, CA 91403-2442, USA

Hussey, Matthew (Actor)
GTGUK Services Ltd
Church Rd
Acorn House
E Brent, Somerset TA9 4ZH, UNITED KINGDOM

Hussey, Olivia (Actor)
c/o Staff Member *Frozen Flame Entertainment*
8033 W Sunset Blvd Ste 247
Los Angeles, CA 90046-2401, USA

Husted, Wayne D (Artist)
Keep Homestead Museum
Ely Road
Monson, MA 01057, USA

Huston, Anjelica (Actor, Director)
c/o Ina Treciokas *Slate PR*
901 N Highland Ave
W Hollywood, CA 90038-2412, USA

Huston, Carol (Actor)
10100 Santa Monica Blvd Ste 2500
Los Angeles, CA 90067-4116

Huston, Danny (Actor, Director)
c/o Lisa Kasteler *Wolf-Kasteler Public Relations*
6255 W Sunset Blvd Ste 1111
Los Angeles, CA 90028-7426, USA

Huston, Geoff (Athlete, Basketball Player)
2619 Carambola Cir N
Coconut Creek, FL 33066-2431, USA

Huston, Jack (Actor)
c/o Todd Diener *Untitled Entertainment*
350 S Beverly Dr Ste 200
Beverly Hills, CA 90212-4819, USA

Huston, John (Athlete, Golfer)
1134 Skye Ln
Palm Harbor, FL 34683-1457, USA

Huston, Ron (Athlete, Hockey Player)
31-2025 Kokanee Dr N
Cranbrook, BC V1C 6J2, Canada

Hutch, Jesse (Actor)
c/o Staff Member *Pacific Artists Management*
112 3rd Ave E Suite 210
Vancouver, BC V5T 1C8, CANADA

Hutch, Willie (Athlete, Hockey Player)
225 W 57th St
5th Flr.
New York, NY 10019-2104, USA

Hutcherson, Josh (Actor)
c/o Staff Member *Turkeyfoot Productions*
11812 San Vicente Blvd
Los Angeles, CA 90049-5022, USA

Hutcheson, Kieren (Actor)
c/o Melisa Spamer *Domain Talent*
1880 Century Park E Ste 1100
Los Angeles, CA 90067-1608, USA

Hutchins, Jason (Athlete, Baseball Player)
2401 Stone Castle Cir
College Station, TX 77845-5494, USA

Hutchins, Paul (Athlete, Football Player)
8818 S Jeffery Blvd
Chicago, IL 60617-2909, USA

Hutchins, Will (Actor)
PO Box 371
Glen Head, NY 11545-0371, USA

Hutchinson, Andrew (Athlete, Hockey Player)
5860 Printemp Dr
East Lansing, MI 48823-9778, USA

Hutchinson, Anthony (Athlete, Football Player)
124 Bellaire Ct
Bellaire, TX 77401-4219, USA

Hutchinson, Asa (Politician)
1501 N Pierce St Ste 102
Little Rock, AR 72207-5222, USA

Hutchinson, Chad (Athlete, Baseball Player)
915 Millie Ave
Menlo Park, CA 94025-4419, USA

Hutchinson, Ron (Athlete, Hockey Player)
213 Merlin Crt
Kelowna, BC V1V 1N2, Canada

Hutchinson, Scott (Athlete, Football Player)
726 Forest Glen Ct
Maitland, FL 32751-5109, USA

Hutchinson, Steven (Athlete, Football Player)
404 W Brookfield Ave
Nashville, TN 37205-4408, USA

Hutchinson, Tim (Politician)
1825 I St NW Attn
FL1200PUBPLCY&LAWDEPT
Washington, DC 20006-5403, USA

Hutchison, Dave (Athlete, Hockey Player)
Re/Max Centre City Realty Inc
3922 Hamilton Rd
Dorchester, ON N0L 1G2, Canada

Hutchison, Doug (Actor)
c/o Charles Lago *DTLA Entertainment Group*
400 S Main St Unit 804
Los Angeles, CA 90013-1325, USA

Hutchison, Kay Bailey (Politician)
25 Downs Lake Cir
Dallas, TX 75230-1900, USA

Huther, Bruce (Athlete, Football Player)
1156 N Bonnie Brae St
Denton, TX 76201-2421, USA

Hutson, Brian (Athlete, Football Player)
6077 Arboretum Dr
Frisco, TX 75034-7270, USA

Hutson, Candace (Actor)
3500 W Olive Ave Ste 920
Burbank, CA 91505-5514

Hutson, Herb (Athlete, Baseball Player)
7203 W Sugar Tree Ct
Savannah, GA 31410-2414, USA

Hutson, Tracy (Actor, Reality Star)

Hutt, Donald (Athlete, Football Player)
3167 S Hudspeth Ave
Meridian, ID 83642-4816, USA

Hutter, Mark (Race Car Driver)
Team Rensi Motorsports
6804 Hobson Valley Dr Ste 118
Woodridge, IL 60517-1448, USA

Huttlestone, Daniel (Actor)
c/o Josh Pearl *Creative Artists Agency (CAA)*
2000 Avenue of the Stars Ste 100
Los Angeles, CA 90067-4705, USA

Hutto, Jim (Athlete, Baseball Player)
1317 John Carroll Dr
Pensacola, FL 32504-7114, USA

Hutton, Anthony (Reality Star)

Hutton, Danny (Music Group, Musician)
2437 Horse Shoe Canyon Rd
Los Angeles, CA 90046-1539, USA

Hutton, Gunilla (Actor)
607 N La Cumbre Rd
Santa Barbara, CA 93110-2509, USA

Hutton, Lauren (Actor, Model)
382 Lafayette St Apt 6
New York, NY 10003-6945, USA

Hutton, Mark (Athlete, Baseball Player)
6 Corfu Court
Westlakes Adelaide, AU 05021, Australia

Hutton, Pascale (Actor)
c/o Ben Levine *LINK Entertainment*
11872 La Grange Ave
Los Angeles, CA 90025-5282, USA

Hutton, Ralph (Swimmer)
Vancouver Police Department
312 Main St
Vancouver, BC V6A 2T2, CANADA

Hutton, Rif (Actor)
c/o Staff Member *Momentum Talent and Literary Agency*
3500 W Olive Ave Ste 300
Burbank, CA 91505-4647, USA

Hutton, Timothy (Actor)
c/o Nikola Barisic *Untitled Entertainment (NY)*
215 Park Ave S Fl 8
New York, NY 10003-1622, USA

Hutton, Tommy (Athlete, Baseball Player)
Los Angeles Dodgers
18 Huntly Dr
Palm Beach Gardens, FL 33418-6812, USA

Hutton, Tommy (Athlete, Baseball Player)
18 Huntly Dr
Palm Beach Gardens, FL 33418-6812, USA

Hutzler, Brody (Actor)
c/o Staff Member *Pakula/King & Associates*
9229 W Sunset Blvd Ste 315
Los Angeles, CA 90069-3403, USA

Huvane, Kevin (Business Person)
16030 Ventura Blvd Ste 240
Encino, CA 91436-4487, USA

Huxhold, Ken (Athlete, Football Player)
8524 Stone Harbor Ave
Las Vegas, NV 89145-5704, USA

Huyck, Willard (Director)
875 Comstock Ave Apt 17D
Los Angeles, CA 90024-7515, USA

Hwang, David Henry (Writer)
c/o Scott Henderson *WME/IMG*
9601 Wilshire Blvd
Beverly Hills, CA 90210-5213, USA

Hyams, Peter (Director)
83 Ditmar Blvd
Whitehouse Station, NJ 08889-3739, USA

Hyatt, Fred (Athlete, Football Player)
19350 SE 52nd Pl
Morriston, FL 32668-3968, USA

Hyche, Heath (Comedian)
c/o Staff Member *Brillstein Entertainment Partners*
9150 Wilshire Blvd Ste 350
Beverly Hills, CA 90212-3453, USA

Hyche, Steve (Athlete, Football Player)
2801 Five Oaks Ln
Vestavia, AL 35243-2621, USA

Hyde, Allan (Actor)
c/o Rose Parkinson *Lisa Richards Agency (UK)*
33 Old Compton St
London W1D 5JU, UNITED KINGDOM

Hyde, Brandon (Athlete, Baseball Player)
203 Foresteria Dr
West Palm Beach, FL 33403-3413, USA

Hyde, Carlos (Athlete, Football Player)
c/o Eugene Parker *Independent Sports & Entertainment (ISE-IN)*
6435 W Jefferson Blvd # 197
Fort Wayne, IN 46804-6203, USA

Hyde, Dick (Athlete, Baseball Player)
1506 Cambridge Dr
Champaign, IL 61821-4957, USA

Hyde, Jonathan (Actor)
c/o Jeff Kolodny *Paradigm*
8942 Wilshire Blvd
Beverly Hills, CA 90211-1908, USA

Hyde, Micah (Athlete, Football Player)

Hyder, Greg (Athlete, Basketball Player)
16228 Wato Rd Apt A
Apple Valley, CA 92307-7813, USA

Hyde-White, Alex (Actor)
Borinstein Oreck Bogart
3172 Dona Susana Dr
Studio City, CA 91604-4356, USA

Hyers, Tim (Athlete, Baseball Player)
241 Ridge Rd
Covington, GA 30016-5138, USA

Hyland, Brian (Musician)
Stone Buffalo
PO Box 101
Helendale, CA 92342-0101, USA

Hyland, Robert (Athlete, Football Player)
30 Colonial Rd
White Plains, NY 10605-2212, USA

Hyland, Sarah (Actor)
c/o Katie Greenthal *The Lede Company*
9701 Wilshire Blvd # 930
Beverly Hills, CA 90212-2020, USA

Hylton, Thomas J (Journalist)
Pottstown Mercury
Editorial Dept
Hanover & Kings Sts
Pottstown, PA 19464, USA

Hyman, Dick (Musician)
223 1/2 E 48th St
New York, NY 10017, USA

Hyman, Fracaswell (Producer)
c/o Staff Member *WME/IMG*
9601 Wilshire Blvd
Beverly Hills, CA 90210-5213, USA

Hyman, Misty (Athlete, Swimmer)
3826 E Lupine Ave
Phoenix, AZ 85028-2125, USA

Hyman, Misty (Swimmer)
3826 E Lupine Ave
Phoenix, AZ 85028-2125, USA

Hymes, Randy (Athlete, Football Player)
9015 Blue Crab Dr
Texas City, TX 77591-9229, USA

Hymowitz, Kay S. (Writer)
Manhattan Institute For Policy Research
52 Vanderbilt Ave Fl 2
New York, NY 10017-3808, USA

Hynde, Chrissie (Actor, Musician)
c/o Gail Colson *Gailforce Management Ltd*
55 Fulham High St
London SW6 3JJ, UK

Hyndman, Mike (Athlete, Hockey Player)
2 Lighthouse Ln Apt 867
Hilton Head Island, SC 29928-7252

Hynes, Dave (Athlete, Hockey Player)
10 Trinity Ct
Wellesley Hills, MA 02481-2505, USA

Hynes, Garry (Director)
Druid Theater Co
Chapel Lane
Galway, IRELAND

Hynes, Louis (Actor)
c/o Oliver Slinger *Independent Talent Group*
40 Whitfield St
London W1T 2RH, UNITED KINGDOM

Hynes, Samuel (Writer)
130 Moore St
130 Moore St
Princeton, NJ 08540-3359, USA

Hynes, Tyler (Actor)
202-201 Laurier Ave E
Ottawa, ON K1N 6P1, CANADA

Hynoski, Henry (Athlete, Football Player)
PO Box 257
Elysburg, PA 17824-0257, USA

Hyre, John (Business Person)
870 High St Ste 104
Worthington, OH 43085-4141, USA

Hysong, Nick (Athlete, Track Athlete)
2822 E Cholla St
Phoenix, AZ 85028-1935, USA

Hytner, Nicholas R (Director)
National Theatre
South Bank
London SE1 9PX, UNITED KINGDOM (UK)

Hyzdu, Adam (Athlete, Baseball Player)
3530 N Hawes Rd Unit 2
Mesa, AZ 85207-1008, USA

Iacavazzi, Cosmo (Athlete, Football Player)
90 Vine St
Taylor, PA 18517-1225, USA

Iacocca, Lee (Business Person)
The Iacocca Foundation
867 Boylston St Fl 6
Boston, MA 02116-2774, USA

Iaconio, Frank (Race Car Driver)
250 US Highway 206
Flanders, NJ 07836-9071, USA

Iacono, Paul (Actor)
c/o Isaac Dunham *Schreck Rose Dapello Adams Berlin & Dunham*
888 7th Ave Fl 19
New York, NY 10106-2599, USA

Iafrate, Al A (Athlete, Hockey Player)
6990 Spring Meadow Ln
Plymouth, MI 48170-5838, USA

Iakovas, Primate Archbishop (Religious Leader)
31 Park Dr
South Rye, NY 10021, USA

Ian, Janis (Musician)
c/o Jo-Ann Geffen *JAG Entertainment*
4605 Lankershim Blvd Ste 807
North Hollywood, CA 91602-1879, 91505

Iannucci, Armando (Director)
c/o Chris Simonian *Creative Artists Agency (CAA)*
2000 Avenue of the Stars Ste 100
Los Angeles, CA 90067-4705, USA

Iaquaniello, Mike (Athlete, Football Player)
49105 Plum Tree Dr
Plymouth, MI 48170-3263, USA

Iassonga, Dan (Athlete, Baseball Player)
1501 Bailey Farm Ct SW
Marietta, GA 30064-5281, USA

Iassonga, Daniel (Baseball Player)
5950 N 78th St Unit 159
Scottsdale, AZ 85250-6183, USA

Iavaroni, Marcus (Athlete, Basketball Player)
6308 Starfish Ave
North Port, FL 34291-4525, USA

Ibaka, Serge (Athlete, Basketball Player)
c/o Staff Member *U1st Sports SL*
Calle Genova, 10 5
Madrid 28004, Spain

Ibanez, Raul (Athlete, Baseball Player)
12961 SW 143rd Ter
Miami, FL 33186-8943, USA

Ibiam, Francis A (Religious Leader)
Ganymede Unwana
PO Box 240 Afikpo
Imo State, NIGERIA

Ibrahimovic, Zlatan (Athlete, Soccer Player)
Paris Saint-Germain Football Club
24 Rue Du Commandant Guilbaud
Cedex 16
Paris 75781, France

Icahn, Carl (Business Person)
Icahn Co
445 Hamilton Ave Ste 1210
White Plains, NY 10601-1833, USA

Ice, Vanilla (Musician)
c/o Tommy Quon *TQ Management Agency*
2412 Piedra Dr
Plano, TX 75023-5329, USA

Ice-T (Actor, Musician, Producer, Reality Star)
c/o Soulgee McQueen *Trio Entertainment*
2014 Morris Ave Apt 3C
Bronx, NY 10453-4234, USA

Ichaso, Leon (Director)
c/o Michael Pio *Innovative Artists*
1505 10th St
Santa Monica, CA 90401-2805, USA

Ickes, Harold (Politician)
6215 Tally Ho Ln
Alexandria, VA 22307-1014, USA

Ickx, Jacky (Race Car Driver)
171 Chaussee de la Hulpe
Brussels 01170, BELGIUM

Icona Pop (Music Group)
c/o Staff Member *High Rise PR*
600 Luton Dr
Glendale, CA 91206-2626, USA

Iconic Boyz (Dancer)
14 Wilson Ave Ste 5
Englishtown, NJ 07726-1577, USA

Idle, Eric (Actor, Comedian)
Python Productions
6 Cambridge Gate
London NW1 4JR, UNITED KINGDOM

Idol, Billy (Musician, Songwriter)
c/o Tony Dimitriades *East End Management*
15260 Ventura Blvd Ste 2100
Sherman Oaks, CA 91403-5360, USA

Iduarte Foucher, Andres (Writer)
Calle Edimburgo 3
Colonia del Valle
Mexico City, DF 00012, MEXICO

Ifans, Rhys (Actor)
c/o Pip Gill *Pip Gill Publicity*
124 Brondesbury Rd
The Coach House
London NW6 6SB, UNITED KINGDOM

Ifeachor, Tracy (Actor)
c/o Nicolas Bernheim *NB Management*
1157 S Beverly Dr Fl 2
Los Angeles, CA 90035-1119, USA

Ifeanyi, Israel (Athlete, Football Player)
44733 Ruthron Ave
Lancaster, CA 93536-1431, USA

Iger, Robert A (Business Person)
Walt Disney Co
500 S Buena Vista St
Burbank, CA 91521-0007, USA

Iginia, J. (Athlete, Hockey Player)
PO Box 1540 Stn M
Sta. M
Calgary, AB T2P 3B9, CANADA

Iginla, Jarome (Athlete, Hockey Player)
c/o Donald Meehan *Newport Sports Management*
201 City Centre Dr
Suite 400
Mississauga, ON L58 2T4, CANADA

Iglesias, Enrique (Musician)
c/o Kim Estlund *Baker Winokur Ryder Public Relations*
9100 Wilshire Blvd
W Tower #500
Beverly Hills, CA 90212-3415, USA

Iglesias, Gabriel (Actor)
c/o Ann Gurrola *Marleah Leslie & Associates*
1645 Vine St Apt 712
Los Angeles, CA 90028-8812, USA

Iglesias, Julio (Musician)
c/o Jorge Iglesias *IAG International*
901 Surfside Blvd
Surfside, FL 33154-3107, USA

Iglesias, Melanie (Model)
c/o Siri Garber *Platform PR*
2666 N Beachwood Dr
Los Angeles, CA 90068-2308, USA

Iglesias, Tuaquin (Athlete, Football Player)
c/o Chad Speck *Allegiant Athletic Agency*
35 Market Sq Ste 201
Knoxville, TN 37902-1420, USA

Ignasiak, Gary (Athlete, Baseball Player)
1679 S Riverside Ave
Saint Clair, MI 48079-5142, USA

Ignasiak, Mike (Athlete, Baseball Player)
5821 Saline Ann Arbor Rd
Saline, MI 48176-9566, USA

Ignatius Zakka I Iwas, Patriarch (Religious Leader)
Syrian Orthodox Patriarchate
Bab Toma
PB 22260
Damascus, SYRIA

Iguchi, Tadahito (Athlete, Baseball Player)
Chiba Lotte Marines 1 Mihama
Mihama-ku, Chiba-shi
Chiba, IL 2618581, JAPAN

Iguodala, Andre (Athlete, Basketball Player)
910 S Michigan Ave Apt 1315
Chicago, IL 60605-2285, USA

Igwebuike, Donald (Athlete, Football Player)
14231 Angelton Ter
Burtonsville, MD 20866-2077, USA

Iha, James (Music Group, Musician)
1245 W Glenlake Ave
Chicago, IL 60660-2503, USA

Ihara, Michio (Artist)
125 Green St
Canton, MA 02021-1032, USA

Ihedigbo, James (Athlete, Football Player)

Ihenacho, Carl ""Duke"" (Athlete, Football Player)
c/o Frank Bauer *Sun West Sports*
7883 N Pershing Ave
Stockton, CA 95207-1749, USA

Ihnacak, Peter (Athlete, Hockey Player)
c/o Staff Member *Toronto Maple Leafs*
Air Canada Centre
400-40 Bay St
Toronto, ON M5J 2X2, CANADA

Ilkin, Tunch (Athlete, Football Player)
2610 Cedarvue Dr
Pittsburgh, PA 15241-2912, USA

Ijalana, Ben (Athlete, Football Player)
c/o Anthony J. Agnone *Eastern Athletic Services*
11350 McCormick Rd
Suite 800 - Executive Plaza
Hunt Valley, MD 21031-1002, USA

Ike, Reverend (Religious Leader)
4140 Broadway
New York, NY 10033-3701, USA

Ikeda, Daisaku (Religious Leader)
Soka Gokkai
32 Shinanomachi
Shinjuku
Tokyo 160-8583, JAPAN

Ikeuchi, Hiroyuki (Actor)
c/o Staff Member *LesPros Entertainment*
1-8-1-10F Shimo Meguro
Meguro
Tokyo 153-0064, Japan

Ikola, Willard (Athlete, Hockey Player, Olympic Athlete)
5697 Green Circle Dr Apt 316
Hopkins, MN 55343-9650, USA

Ikwuakor, Eme (Actor)
c/o Jason Priluck *Priluck Company*
24045 Sylvan St
Woodland Hills, CA 91367-1248, USA

Il Divo (Music Group, Musician)
c/o Meredith Plant *Octagon*
Octagon House
81-83 Fulham High St
London SW6 3JW, UK

Iler, Robert (Actor)
J Mitchell Management
70 W 36th St Ste 1006
C/O Maggie Schuster
New York, NY 10018-8007, USA

Iley, Barbara (Actor)
Paradigm Agency
10100 Santa Monica Blvd Ste 2500
Los Angeles, CA 90067-4116, USA

Ilg, Ray (Athlete, Football Player)
252 Shindagan Rd
Wilmot, NH 03287-4651, USA

Ilgauskas, Zydrunas (Athlete, Basketball Player)
32654 Lake Road
Avon Lake, OH 44012, USA

Ilgenfritz, Mark (Athlete, Football Player)
742 Sharp Mountain Crk SE
Marietta, GA 30067-5168, USA

Iliescu, Ion (President)
President's Office
Calea Victoriei 59-53
Bucharest, ROMANIA

Ilkin, Tunch (Athlete, Football Player)
2610 Cedarvue Dr
Pittsburgh, PA 15241-2912, USA

Illsley, John (Musician)
Damage Mgmt
16 Lambton Place
London W11 2SH, UNITED KINGDOM (UK)

Iloilo, Ratu Josefa (President)
President's Office
PO Box 2513
Suva
Viti Levu, FIJI

Iloka, George (Athlete, Football Player)

Ilsley, Blaise (Athlete, Baseball Player)
175 Toyota Plz Ste 300
Memphis, TN 38103-2697, USA

Imada, Ryuji (Athlete, Golfer)
2202 N Lois Ave Apt 3430
Tampa, FL 33607-2588, USA

Imagine Dragons (Music Group)
c/o Hillary Siskind *Interscope Records*
1755 Broadway Fl 6
New York, NY 10019-3768, USA

Imai, Nobuko (Musician)
Irene Witmer Mgmt
Kerkstrat 97
Amsterdam, GD 01017, NETHERLANDS

Iman (Actor, Model)
285 Lafayette St # 7DE
New York, NY 10012-3367, USA

Iman, Chanel (Model)
c/o Lisa Benson *IMG Models (NY)*
304 Park Ave S PH N
New York, NY 10010-4303, USA

Imbruglia, Natalie (Actor, Musician)
c/o Joanna Milosz *Jm Agency*
143A Chapel St
Prahran VIC 3181, Australia

Imhoff, Darrell (Athlete)
20183 Firerock Rd
Bend, OR 97703-9020

Imhoff, Gary (Actor)
Samantha Group
300 S Raymond Ave
Pasadena, CA 91105-2620, USA

Imhoff, Martin (Athlete, Football Player)
11224 Corte Playa Azteca
San Diego, CA 92124-4135, USA

Immelman, Trevor (Athlete, Golfer)
9536 Tavistock Rd
Orlando, FL 32827-7007, USA

Immelt, Jeffrey (Business Person)
General Electric Co
3135 Easton Tpke
Fairfield, CT 06828-0001, USA

Immerfall, Daniel (Dan) (Speed Skater)
1418 NW 3rd Ave APT 307
Gainesville, FL 32603-1994, USA

Impemba, Mario (Athlete, Baseball Player)
19945 Gallahad Dr
Macomb, MI 48044-1756, USA

Imperato, Carlo (Actor)
21940 Scallion Dr
Santa Clarita, CA 91350-1636, USA

Imperioli, Michael (Actor)
c/o Alexandra Crotin *The Lede Company*
9701 Wilshire Blvd # 930
Beverly Hills, CA 90212-2020, USA

Imus, Don (Radio Personality)
c/o Staff Member *ICM Partners*
10250 Constellation Blvd Fl 7
Los Angeles, CA 90067-6207, USA

IMX (Music Group)
c/o Staff Member *Pyramid Entertainment Group*
377 Rector Pl Apt 21A
New York, NY 10280-1439, USA

Inaba, Carrie Ann (Actor, Dancer)
c/o Staff Member *CBS Productions*
7800 Beverly Blvd
Los Angeles, CA 90036-2112, USA

Inamori, Kazuo (Business Person)
KDDI Corp
3-22 Nishi-Shinjuku
Shinjuku
Tokyo 163-8003, JAPAN

Inarritu, Alejandro (Actor)
c/o Staff Member *Anonymous Content*
3532 Hayden Ave
Culver City, CA 90232-2413, USA

Inarritu, Alejandro Gonzalez (Director)
c/o Kelly Bush Novak *ID Public Relations*
7060 Hollywood Blvd Fl 8th
Los Angeles, CA 90028-6021, USA

Incandella, Sal (Race Car Driver)
Indy Racing Regency
5811 W 73rd St
Indianapolis, IN 46278-1743, USA

Incaviglia, Peter J (Pete) (Athlete, Baseball Player)
PO Box 1047
Argyle, TX 76226-1047, USA

Inclan, Rafael (Actor)
c/o Staff Member *Televisa*
Blvd Adolfo Lopez Mateos 232
Colonia San Angel INN
DF CP 01060, MEXICO

Incognito, Richie (Athlete, Football Player)
7340 W Montgomery Rd
Peoria, AZ 85383-5301, USA

Incubus (Music Group)
c/o Steve Rennie *Ren Management Corporation*
1125 Coldwater Canyon Dr
Beverly Hills, CA 90210-2402, USA

Indelicato, Mark (Actor)
Brownstein & Associates
101 W End Ave Apt 11U # 209
New York, NY 10023-6321, USA

Indigo Girls (Music Group)
c/o Staff Member *High Road Touring*
751 Bridgeway Fl 2
Sausalito, CA 94965-2174, USA

Indurain, Miguel (Athlete, Cycler)
Avendia Villava
Pamplona (Navarra) E-31013, Spain

Infamous Stringdusters, The (Music Group, Musician)
c/o Michael Allenby *The Artist Farm*
100 W South St Ste 1A
Charlottesville, VA 22902-5099, USA

Infante, To??o (Actor)
c/o Staff Member *Televisa*
Blvd Adolfo Lopez Mateos 232
Colonia San Angel INN
DF CP 01060, MEXICO

Infected Mushroom (Music Group)
4373 Irvine Ave
Studio City, CA 91604-2705, USA

ing, Peter (Athlete, Hockey Player)
Fan-Tastic Sports
21021 Heron Way Ste 104
Lakeville, MN 55044-8085, USA

Ing, Peter (Athlete, Hockey Player)
Casino Niagara
PO Box 300 Stn Main
Stn Main
Niagara Falls, ON L2E 6T3, Canada

Ingarfield Jr, Earl (Athlete, Hockey Player)
619 Mourning Dove Dr
Sarasota, FL 34236-1903, USA

Ingarfield Sr, Earl (Athlete, Hockey Player)
1715 Lakehill Cres S
Lethbridge, AB T1K 3R2, Canada

Inge, Brandon (Athlete, Baseball Player)
5035 Fox Ridge Ct
Ann Arbor, MI 48103-9601, USA

Ingelsby, Tom (Athlete, Basketball Player)
1507 Canterbury Ln
Berwyn, PA 19312-1915, USA

Ingle, Doug (Music Group, Musician)
Entertainment Services Int'l
6400 Pleasant Park Dr
Chanhassen, MN 55317-8804, USA

Inglebright, Jim (Race Car Driver)
Roadrunner Motorsports
4984 Peabody Rd
Fairfield, CA 94533-6552, USA

inglett, joe (Athlete, Baseball Player)
3874 Gardiner Run
Copley, OH 44321-3160, USA

Inglis, Bill (Athlete, Hockey Player)
5709 Ozark Dr
Fort Worth, TX 76131-4004, USA

Inglis, Tim (Athlete, Football Player)
105 Crafton Park Ln
Cary, NC 27519-5575, USA

Ingraham, Laura (Correspondent, Radio Personality)
c/o Thomas Repicci *Octagon Entertainment*
1840 Century Park E Ste 200
Los Angeles, CA 90067-2114, USA

Ingram, Andre (Athlete, Basketball Player)
c/o Brad Slater *WME/IMG*
9601 Wilshire Blvd
Beverly Hills, CA 90210-5213, USA

Ingram, Brian (Athlete, Football Player)
4805 White Oak Path
Stone Mountain, GA 30088-3016, USA

Ingram, Clint (Athlete, Football Player)
7812 Chase Meadows Dr E
Jacksonville, FL 32256-4641, USA

Ingram, Garey (Athlete, Baseball Player)
PO Box 97389
Pearl, MS 39288-7389, USA

Ingram, Jack (Musician)
16001 Pontevedra Pl
Austin, TX 78738-6031, USA

Ingram, Jack (Race Car Driver)
699 Brevard Rd
Asheville, NC 28806-2229, USA

Ingram, McKoy (Athlete, Basketball Player)
2301 33rd St
Gulfport, MS 39501-6541, USA

Ingram, Melvin (Athlete, Football Player)
c/o David Dunn *Athletes First*
23091 Mill Creek Dr
Laguna Hills, CA 92653-1258, USA

Ingram, Preston (Baseball Player)
Negro Baseball Leagues
174 Douglas St SE
Atlanta, GA 30317-2626, USA

Ingram, Riccardo (Athlete, Baseball Player)
5720 Martin Grove Dr NW
Lilburn, GA 30047-6078, USA

Ingram Jr, Mark (Athlete, Football Player)
c/o Peter Raskin *TLA Worldwide (The Legacy Agency)*
1500 Broadway Ste 2501
New York, NY 10036-4082, USA

Ingrassia, Frank (Horse Racer)
39 Imlaystown Hightstown Rd
Allentown, NJ 08501-2104, USA

Ingrassia, Jacqueline (Horse Racer)
39 Imlaystown Hightstown Rd
Allentown, NJ 08501-2104, USA

Ingrassia, Paul J (Journalist)
111 Division Ave
New Providence, NJ 07974, USA

Inkster, Juli Simpson (Athlete, Golfer)
23140 Mora Glen Dr
Los Altos, CA 94024-6620, USA

Inman, Dale (Race Car Driver)
142 Holder Inman Rd
Randleman, NC 27317-8044, USA

Inman, Jerry (Athlete, Football Player)
PO Box 1113
Battle Ground, WA 98604-1113, USA

Inman, Joe (Athlete, Golfer)
3599 Tuckers Farm SE
Marietta, GA 30067-5182, USA

Inman, John (Athlete, Golfer)
2210 Chase St
Durham, NC 27707-2228, USA

Inmon, Earl (Athlete, Football Player)
3560 Creek Run Ln
Eustis, FL 32736-2515, USA

Innauer, Anton (Toni) (Coach, Skier)
Steinbruckstr 8/11
Innsbruck 06024, AUSTRIA

Innes, Laura (Actor)
2324 La Mesa Dr
Santa Monica, CA 90402-2331, USA

Inness, Gary (Athlete, Hockey Player)
7 Gowan Rd
Shanty Bay, ON L0L 2L0, Canada

Inniger Jr, Ervin (Athlete, Basketball Player)
311 11th Ave S Apt 101
Fargo, ND 58103-2856, USA

Innis (Musician)
c/o Staff Member *Paradigm*
8942 Wilshire Blvd
Beverly Hills, CA 90211-1908, USA

Innis, Jeff (Athlete, Baseball Player)
4920 Woodlong Ln
Cumming, GA 30040-5275, USA

Inoue, Yuichi (Artist)
Ohkamiyashiki 2475-2 Kurami
Samakawamachi 253-01 Kozagun
Kam, JAPAN

Inouye, Lisa (Actor)
c/o Nick Terzian *NTA Talent Agency*
1445 N Stanley Ave Fl 2
Los Angeles, CA 90046-4015, USA

Insane Clown Posse (Music Group, Musician)
c/o Staff Member *WME/IMG*
9601 Wilshire Blvd
Beverly Hills, CA 90210-5213, USA

Insko, Delmer M (Del) (Horse Racer)
2360 Fischer Rd
South Beloit, IL 61080-9728, USA

Inslee, Jay (Congressman, Politician)
2329 Rayburn Hob
Washington, DC 20515-3218, USA

Insley, Will (Artist)
231 Bowery Apt 6
New York, NY 10002-1237, USA

Insolo, Jimmy (Race Car Driver)
19636 Ermitie St.
Canyon Country, CA 91351, USA

Internet, The (Music Group)
c/o Caroline Yim *Creative Artists Agency (CAA)*
2000 Avenue of the Stars Ste 100
Los Angeles, CA 90067-4705, USA

Interpol (Music Group)
c/o Angus Baskerville *13 Artists (UK)*
11-14 Kensington St
Brighton BN1 4AJ, UNITED KINGDOM

In This Moment (Music Group)
c/o Staff Member *Mercenary Management*
8491 W Sunset Blvd Ste 179
West Hollywood, CA 90069-1911, USA

Inzaghi, Filippo (Soccer Player)
c/o Team Member *AC Milan*
Via Turati 3
Washington, DC 20221-0001, Italy

Iommi, Tony (Musician)
c/o Equator Music Ltd
17 Hereford Mansions
Hereford Rd
London W2 5BA, UNITED KINGDOM

Iorg, Dane (Athlete, Baseball Player)
5358 W Evergreen Cir
Highland, UT 84003-9476, USA

Iorg, Garth (Athlete, Baseball Player)
1 Brewers Way Stop 4
Milwaukee, WI 53214-3655, USA

Iovine, Jimmy (Business Person, Musician, Producer)
c/o Staff Member *Interscope Records (LA) - Main*
2220 Colorado Ave
Santa Monica, CA 90404-3506, USA

Iqbal Rashid, Ian (Director)
c/o Staff Member *United Talent Agency (UTA)*
9336 Civic Center Dr
Beverly Hills, CA 90210-3604, USA

Iraheta, Allison (Musician)
c/o Simon Fuller *XIX Entertainment (UK)*
32/33 Ransomes Dock
London SW11 4NP, UNITED KINGDOM (UK)

Irani, Ray R (Business Person)
Occidental Petroleum
10889 Wilshire Blvd Fl 10
Los Angeles, CA 90024-4213, USA

Irbe, Arturs (Athlete, Hockey Player)
6337 Georgetown Pike
McLean, VA 22101-2209, USA

Ireland, Dan (Director, Producer, Writer)
c/o Staff Member *Gersh*
9465 Wilshire Blvd Ste 600
Beverly Hills, CA 90212-2605, USA

Ireland, Kathy (Business Person, Model)
Kathy Ireland Worldwide
PO Box 1410
Rancho Mirage, CA 92270-1052, USA

Ireland, Marin (Actor)
c/o Emily Gerson Saines *Brookside Artists Management*
250 W 57th St Ste 1820
New York, NY 10107-1802, USA

Ireland, Rich (Baseball Player)
181 Glen Dr
Grants Pass, OR 97526-9018, USA

Ireland, Tim (Athlete, Baseball Player)
21001 San Ramon Valley Blvd Ste A4
San Ramon, CA 94583-3454, USA

Irie, Saaya (Actor)
c/o Staff Member *Ace Deuce Code*
2-20-1-701 Tomigaya
Shibuya
Tokyo 151-0063, Japan

Iris, Donnie (Music Group, Musician, Songwriter, Writer)
807 Darlington Rd
Beaver Falls, PA 15010-2817, USA

Irizarry, Vincent (Actor)
c/o Staff Member *Bret Adams Agency*
448 W 44th St
New York, NY 10036-5220, USA

Iron & Wine (Music Group, Musician)
c/o Rob Challice *Coda Music Agency (UK)*
56 Compton St
Clerkenwell
London EC1V 0ET, UNITED KINGDOM

Iron Maiden (Music Group)
c/o Staff Member *BMG Chrysalis US*
29 Music Sq E
Nashville, TN 37203-4322, USA

Irons, Gerald (Athlete, Football Player)
30010 E Legends Trail Ct
Spring, TX 77386-2998, USA

Irons, Grant (Athlete, Football Player)
30010 E Legends Trail Ct
Spring, TX 77386-2998, USA

Irons, Jack (Musician)
3460 Decker Canyon Rd
Malibu, CA 90265-2325, USA

Irons, Jeremy (Actor)
c/o Sally Fisher *Sally Fischer Public Relations*
330 W 58th St
New York, NY 10019-1827, USA

Irons, Max (Actor)
c/o Romilly Bowlby *DDA Public Relations*
192-198 Vauxhall Bridge Rd
London SW1V 1DX, UNITED KINGDOM

Irons, Nicholas (Actor)
Emptage Hallett
c/o Michael Emptage
24 Poland St
London W1F 8QL, UNITED KINGDOM

Irons, Robbie (Athlete, Hockey Player)
4227 Cordell Cv
Fort Wayne, IN 46845-8864, USA

Ironside, Michael (Actor, Producer)
c/o David Ginsberg *Insight*
5358 Melrose Ave # 200W
Los Angeles, CA 90038-5117, USA

Irrera, Dom (Actor, Comedian)
c/o Jamie Masada *Laugh Factory Management Company*
8001 W Sunset Blvd
West Hollywood, CA 90046-2401, USA

Irsay, Jim (Business Person, Football Executive)
1711 W 116th St
Carmel, IN 46032-6984, USA

Irvan, Ernie (Race Car Driver)
5111 Selkirk Plantation Rd
Wadmalow Island, SC 29847, USA

Irvin, Byron (Athlete, Basketball Player)
10940 S Parnell Ave
Chicago, IL 60628-3232, USA

Irvin, Daryl (Athlete, Baseball Player)
815 Confederacy Dr
Penn Laird, VA 22846-9633, USA

Irvin, John (Director)
c/o Jack Gilardi *ICM Partners*
10250 Constellation Blvd Fl 7
Los Angeles, CA 90067-6207, USA

Irvin, Ken (Athlete, Football Player)
8151 Nesbit Ferry Rd
Atlanta, GA 30350-1009, USA

Irvin, Michael (Athlete, Football Player)
2339 Aberdeen Bnd
Carrollton, TX 75007-2040, USA

Irvin, Moe (Actor)
c/o Danielle Lenniger *Luber Roklin Management*
5815 W Sunset Blvd Ste 208
Los Angeles, CA 90028-6481, USA

Irvin, Monte (Athlete, Baseball Player)
1815 Enclave Pkwy Apt 6111
Houston, TX 77077-3668, USA

Irvine, Daryl (Athlete, Baseball Player)
815 Confederacy Dr
Penn Laird, VA 22846-9633, USA

Irvine, Eddie (Race Car Driver)
Ferrari SpA
Casella Postale 589
Modena 41100, ITALY

Irvine, George (Athlete, Basketball Player)
339 NE 180th St
Shoreline, WA 98155-3550, USA

Irvine, Jeremy (Actor)
c/o Jessica Kolstad *Relevant*
400 S Beverly Dr Ste 220
Beverly Hills, CA 90212-4404, USA

Irvine, Paula (Actor)
PO Box 195
23852 Pacific Coast Hwy
Malibu, CA 90265, USA

Irvine, Ted (Athlete, Hockey Player)
5-2727 Portage Ave
Winnipeg, MB R3J 0R2, Canada

Irving, Amy (Actor)
c/o Gina Rugolo *Rugolo Entertainment*
195 S Beverly Dr Ste 400
Beverly Hills, CA 90212-3044, USA

Irving, John (Writer)
c/o Joseph (Joe) Veltre *Gersh*
41 Madison Ave Ste 3301
New York, NY 10010-2210, USA

Irving, Kyrie (Athlete, Basketball Player)
27 Ridgeview Ave
West Orange, NJ 07052-4315, USA

Irving, Nate (Athlete, Football Player)
c/o Fletcher Smith *Revolution Sports*
270 17th St NW Unit 3001
Atlanta, GA 30363-1261, USA

Irving, Stu (Athlete, Hockey Player, Olympic Athlete)
93 Hart St
Beverly, MA 01915-2162, USA

Irving, Terry (Athlete, Football Player)
3205 Avenue R 1/2 Apt 2
Galveston, TX 77550-9651, USA

Irvin Jr, LeRoy (Athlete, Football Player)
2905 Ruby Dr Apt C
Fullerton, CA 92831-3249, USA

Irwin, Ashton (Musician)
c/o Matt Emsell *Wonder Management*
10-16 Scrutton St
Level 4
London EC2A 4RU, UNITED KINGDOM

Irwin, Bill (Actor, Writer)
6 W 20th St Fl 10
New York, NY 10011-9263, USA

Irwin, Bindi (Actor)
Australia Zoo
Glass House Mountains Tourist Route
Beerwah, Queensland 04519, AUSTRALIA

Irwin, Glen (Athlete, Hockey Player)
4024 Chesapeake Ave
Hampton, VA 23669-4632

Irwin, Hale (Athlete, Golfer)
5720 N Saguaro Rd
Paradise Valley, AZ 85253-5237, USA

Irwin, Haley (Athlete, Hockey Player, Olympic Athlete)
440 Marquette St
Thunder Bay, ON P7E ST8 Canada, USA

Irwin, Heath (Athlete, Football Player)
5530 N 115th St
Longmont, CO 80504-8434, USA

Irwin, Ivan (Athlete, Hockey Player)
485 Maple Ave
Ajax, ON L1S 1E4, Canada

Irwin, Jennifer (Actor)
c/o Gayle Abrams *Oscars Abrams Zimel & Associates*
438 Queen St E
Toronto, ON M5A 1T4, CANADA

Irwin, Lou (Athlete, Hockey Player)
485 Maple Ave
Ajax, ON L1S 1E4, Canada

Irwin, Robert W (Artist)
Pace Gallery
32 E 57th St Fl 4
New York, NY 10022-2530, USA

Irwin, Steven (Athlete, Soccer Player)
Liverpool Football Club
Anfield Road
Liverpool
Merseyside L4 0TH, UK

Irwin, Tim (Athlete, Football Player)
Law Office Of Tim Irwin
PO Box 2186
Knoxville, TN 37901-2186, USA

Irwin, Tom (Actor)
PO Box 5617
Beverly Hills, CA 90209-5617, USA

Irwin, Tommy (Race Car Driver)
1724 Handley Ave
Winchester, VA 22601-3224, USA

Irwin-Mellencamp, Elaine (Model)
John Caugar Mellencamp
5072 Stevens Rd
Nashville, IN 47448-9484, USA

Isaac, Oscar (Actor, Musician)
c/o Amanda Silverman *The Lede Company*
401 Broadway Ste 206
New York, NY 10013-3033, USA

Isaacs, Jason (Actor)
c/o Jeff Golenberg *Silver Lining Entertainment*
421 S Beverly Dr Fl 7
Beverly Hills, CA 90212-4408, USA

Isaacs, Jeremy I (Director)
Royal Opera House
Covent Garden Bow St
London WC1 7Q4, UNITED KINGDOM (UK)

Isaacs, Susan (Writer)
Harper Collins Publishers
10 E 53rd St
New York, NY 10022-5244, USA

Isaacson, Walter (Journalist)
c/o Amanda Urban *ICM Partners (NY)*
730 5th Ave
New York, NY 10019-4105, USA

Isaak, Chris (Musician, Songwriter)
c/o Craig Fruin *CSM Management*
12711 Ventura Blvd Ste 350
Studio City, CA 91604-2400, USA

Isaak, Russell (Business Person)
CPI Corp
1706 Washington Ave
Saint Louis, MO 63103-1711, USA

Isabel, Margarita (Actor)
c/o Staff Member *TV Azteca*
Periferico Sur 4121
Colonia Fuentes del Pedregal
DF CP 14141, Mexico

Isabelle, Katharine (Actor)
c/o Wendy Murphey *LBI Entertainment*
2000 Avenue of the Stars
N Tower Fl 3
Los Angeles, CA 90067-4700, USA

Isabelle, Katherine (Actor)
c/o Jennifer Goldhar *Characters Talent Agency (Toronto)*
8 Elm St Fl 2
Toronto, ON M5G 1G7, CANADA

Isacksen, Peter (Actor)
c/o Staff Member *JWTwo Entertainment*
2425 Olympic Blvd # 200
East Tower
Santa Monica, CA 90404-4030, USA

Isaksson, Irma Sara (Musician, Songwriter, Writer)
United Stage Artists
PO Box 11026
Stockholm 100 61, SWEDEN

Isales, Orlando (Athlete, Baseball Player)
14710 SW 106th Ave
Miami, FL 33176-7791, USA

Isbell, Joe Bob (Athlete, Football Player)
1606 Nest Pl
Plano, TX 75093-6030, USA

Isbin, Sharon (Musician)
Columbia Artists Mgmt Inc
165 W 57th St
New York, NY 10019-2201, USA

Iscove, Robert (Director)
16045 Royal Oak Rd
Encino, CA 91436-3913, USA

Isdell, E Neville (Business Person)
Coca-Cola Co
1 Coca Cola Plz NW
310 North Ave NW
Atlanta, GA 30313-2499, USA

Iseman, Matt (Reality Star)
c/o Kyell Thomas *Octagon Entertainment*
1840 Century Park E Ste 200
Los Angeles, CA 90067-2114, USA

Isenbarger, John (Athlete, Football Player)
7808 Somerset Bay Apt C
Indianapolis, IN 46240-3329, USA

Isenhour, Tripp (Athlete, Golfer)
10012 N Fulton Ct
Orlando, FL 32836-3708, USA

Ishibashi, Kanichiro (Business Person)
1 Nagasakacho Azabu
Minatoku
Tokyo, JAPAN

Ishida, Jim (Actor)
871 N Vail Ave
Montebello, CA 90640-2432, USA

Ishiguro, Kazuo (Writer)
Rogers Coleridge White
20 Powis Mews
London W11 1JN, UNITED KINGDOM

Ishii, Linda (Athlete, Golfer)
2607 E 3rd St
Los Angeles, CA 90033-4124, USA

Ishikawa, Travis (Athlete, Baseball Player)
Ed Smith Stadium
2700 12th St
Sarasota, FL 34237-3000, USA

Ishmael, Kemel (Athlete, Football Player)
c/o Drew Rosenhaus *Rosenhaus Sports Representation*
3921 Alton Rd # 440
Miami Beach, FL 33140-3852, USA

Isikoff, Michael (Writer)
6209 Meadowbrook Ln
Chevy Chase, MD 20815, USA

Isitt, Debbie (Director)
c/o Nick Marston *Curtis Brown Ltd*
28-29 Hay Market
Hay Market House
London SW1Y 4SP, UNITED KINGDOM

Iskander, Fazil A (Writer)
Krasnoarmeiskaya Str 23 #104
Moscow 125319, RUSSIA

Islas, Claudia (Actor)
c/o Staff Member *TV Azteca*
Periferico Sur 4121
Colonia Fuentes del Pedregal
DF CP 14141, Mexico

Islas, Mauricio (Actor)
c/o Staff Member *Televisa*
Blvd Adolfo Lopez Mateos 232
Colonia San Angel INN
DF CP 01060, MEXICO

Isler, Samantha (Actor)
c/o Lauren Williams *Echo Lake Management*
421 S Beverly Dr Fl 8
Beverly Hills, CA 90212-4408, USA

Isley, Ernie (Musician)
403 Sheffield Estate Dr
Saint Louis, MO 63141-8523, USA

Isley, Ronald (Musician)
300 Wyndmoor Terrace Ct
Saint Louis, MO 63141-8021, USA

Isley Brothers (Music Group)
c/o Jeff Epstein *M.A.G./Universal Attractions*
15 W 36th St Fl 8
New York, NY 10018-7927, USA

Ismail, Qadry (Athlete, Football Player)
1506 Sunningdale Way
Bel Air, MD 21015-2101, USA

Ismail, Raghib R (Rocket) (Athlete, Football Player)
7423 Marigold Dr
Irving, TX 75063-5505, USA

Isner, John (Athlete, Tennis Player)
3514 Lindenwood Ave
Dallas, TX 75205-3230, USA

Ison, Christopher J (Journalist)
Minneapolis-Saint Paul Star Tribune
425 Portland Ave
Minneapolis, MN 55488-1511, USA

Israel, Alex (Artist, Designer)
c/o Staff Member *Creative Artists Agency (CAA)*
2000 Avenue of the Stars Ste 100
Los Angeles, CA 90067-4705, USA

Israel, Steve (Congressman, Politician)
2457 Rayburn Hob
Washington, DC 20515-4313, USA

Israelson, Larry (Athlete, Hockey Player)
PO Box 17 Site 17 RR 1
Didsbury, AB T0M 0W0, Canada

Isringhausen, Jason (Athlete, Baseball Player)
7060 N State Route 159
Moro, IL 62067-1622, USA

Issel, Dan (Athlete, Basketball Player, Coach)
325 E Palace Ave
Santa Fe, NM 87501-2275, USA

Isserlis, Steven (Musician)
Harrison/Parrott
12 Penzance Place
London W11 4PA, UNITED KINGDOM (UK)

Ito, Lance (Judge)
Los Angeles Superior Court
210 W Temple St Ste M6
Los Angeles, CA 90012-3267, USA

Ito, Robert (Actor)
843 N Sycamore Ave
Los Angeles, CA 90038-3316, USA

Itzin, Gregory (Actor)
c/o Brenda Feldman *Feldman PR*
13636 Ventura Blvd # 440
Sherman Oaks, CA 91423-3700, USA

Iuzzolino, Mike (Athlete, Basketball Player)
1048 New London Dr
Greensburg, PA 15601-1144, USA

Ivanisevic, Goran (Tennis Player)
Alijnoviceva 28
Split 58000, SERBIA & MONTENEGRO

Ivanov, Kalina (Actor, Designer)
c/o Sandra Marsh *Sandra Marsh Management*
9150 Wilshire Blvd Ste 220
Beverly Hills, CA 90212-3429, USA

Ivanovic, Ana (Athlete, Tennis Player)
DH-Management AG
Holeestrasse 86
Basel 04054, Switzerland

Ivens, Teri (Actor)
c/o Stephen Rice *Pantheon Talent*
1801 Century Park E Ste 1910
Los Angeles, CA 90067-2321, USA

Ivens, Terri (Actor)
c/o Staff Member *The Kohner Agency*
9300 Wilshire Blvd Ste 555
Beverly Hills, CA 90212-3211, USA

Iverson, Allen (Athlete, Basketball Player)
2010 Westbourne Way
Alpharetta, GA 30022-3112, USA

Iverson, Duke (Athlete, Football Player)
2908 Carissa Ct
Santa Rosa, CA 95405-7934, USA

Iverson, Portia (Religious Leader)
11312 Highway 75
Plattsmouth, NE 68048-8268, USA

Iverson, Willie (Athlete, Basketball Player)
14789 Rosemary St
Detroit, MI 48213-1539, USA

Iver (Vernon), Bon (Justin) (Music Group, Musician)
c/o Carrie Tolles *Shore Fire Media*
32 Court St Fl 16
Brooklyn, NY 11201-4441, USA

Ivery, Eddie Lee (Athlete, Football Player)
1080 Wrightsboro Rd
Thomson, GA 30824-7500, USA

Ives, J Atwood (Business Person)
Eastern Enterprises
201 Rivermoor St
West Roxbury, MA 02132-4905, USA

Ivey, Dana (Actor)
Paradigm Agency
10100 Santa Monica Blvd Ste 2500
Los Angeles, CA 90067-4116, USA

Ivey, Judith (Actor)
c/o Richard Fisher *Abrams Artists Agency*
275 7th Ave Fl 26
New York, NY 10001-6708, USA

Ivey, Royal (Athlete, Basketball Player)
6080 Indian Wood Cir SE
Mableton, GA 30126-2969, USA

Ivie, Mike (Athlete, Baseball Player)
PO Box 1565
Loganville, GA 30052-0035, USA

Ivins, Marsha S (Astronaut)
2811 Timber Briar Cir
Houston, TX 77059-2904, USA

Ivlow, John (Athlete, Football Player)
15238 S Poppy Ln
Plainfield, IL 60544-9201, USA

Ivo, Tommy (Race Car Driver)
247 S Orchard Dr
Burbank, CA 91506-2441

Ivory, Chris (Athlete, Football Player)

Ivory, Elvin (Athlete, Basketball Player)
306 Marathon Rd
Altadena, CA 91001-4427, USA

Ivory, Horace O (Athlete, Football Player)
5321 Diaz Ave
Fort Worth, TX 76107-5903, USA

Ivory, James (Athlete, Baseball Player)
3026 Wenonah Park Rd SW
Birmingham, AL 35211-5846, USA

Ivory, James (Director, Producer)
c/o Staff Member *Merchant Ivory Productions*
PO Box 338
New York, NY 10276-0338, USA

Iwanowski, Mark (Athlete, Football Player)
45 Keen Rd
Spring City, PA 19475-2724, USA

Iwatani, Toru (Designer)
Tokyo Polytechnic University
1583 Iiyama
Atsugi, Kanagawa 243 0297, JAPAN

Iwerks, Donald W (Business Person)
Iwerks Entertainment
4520 W Valerio St
Burbank, CA 91505-1046, USA

Iwerks, Leslie (Director, Producer)
c/o Scott Agostini *WME|IMG*
9601 Wilshire Blvd
Beverly Hills, CA 90210-5213, USA

Iwuh, Brian (Athlete, Football Player)
c/o Brian E. Overstreet *E.O. Sports Management*
1314 Texas St Ste 1212
Houston, TX 77002-3525, USA

Izibor, Laura (Musician)
c/o Staff Member *Paradigm (Monterey)*
404 W Franklin St
Monterey, CA 93940-2303, USA

Izo, George (Athlete, Football Player)
PO Box 325
Alexandria, VA 22313-0325, USA

Izquierdo, Hank (Athlete, Baseball Player)
6426 Emerald Dunes Dr Apt 105
West Palm Beach, FL 33411-2765, USA

Izquierdo, Hansel (Athlete, Baseball Player)
15470 SW 176th Ln
Miami, FL 33187-1622, USA

Izturis, Cesar (Athlete, Baseball Player)
375 S 3rd St
Burbank, CA 91502-1364, USA

Izzard, Eddie (Actor, Comedian)
c/o Nicola Van Gelder *Conway van Gelder Grant*
8-12 Broadwick St
London W1F 8HW, UNITED KINGDOM

Izzo, Larry (Athlete, Football Player)
1 Snowbird Pl
The Woodlands, TX 77381-4153, USA

Izzo, Tom (Athlete, Basketball Coach, Basketball Player, Coach)
Michigan State University
Berkowitz Complex, Suite 150
East Lansing, MI 48824, USA

J, Jessie (Musician)
Crown Music
91 Peterborough Rd
Matrix Complex
London SW6 3BU, UNITED KINGDOM

J, Ray (Actor, Musician)
c/o Sonja Norwood *Norwood & Norwood, Inc.*
22817 Ventura Blvd Ste 432
Woodland Hills, CA 91364-1202, USA

Jaa, Tony (Actor)
c/o Staff Member *BA Services*
PO Box 041
Choa Chu Kang Central Post Office
Singapore 916832, SINGAPORE

Jablonski, Henryk (President)
Ul Filtrowa 61 m 4
Warsaw 02-056, POLAND

Jablonski, Pat (Athlete, Hockey Player)
18726 Avenue Biarritz
Lutz, FL 33558-5307, USA

Jablonsky, Steve (Musician)
c/o Jeff Sanderson *Chasen & Company*
8560 W Sunset Blvd Ste 210
Los Angeles, CA 90069-2345, USA

Jabs, Matthias (Musician)
c/o Staff Member *UTA/The Agency Group*
888 7th Ave Fl 7
New York, NY 10106-0700, USA

Jace, Michael (Actor)
c/o Craig Dorfman *Frontline Management*
5670 Wilshire Blvd Ste 1370
Los Angeles, CA 90036-5649, USA

Jack, Eric (Athlete, Football Player)
4206 W Ross Ave
Glendale, AZ 85308-4701, USA

Jack, Jarrett (Athlete, Basketball Player)
c/o Jeff Schwartz *Excel Sports Management*
1700 Broadway Fl 29
New York, NY 10019-6559, USA

Jacke, Chris (Athlete, Football Player)
1631 Shallow Creek Ct
Green Bay, WI 54313-3963, USA

Jacke, Christoper L (Chris) (Athlete, Football Player)
PO Box 888
Phoenix, AZ 85001-0888, USA

Jacklin, Tony (Athlete, Golfer)
5070 18th Ave W
Bradenton, FL 34209-5125, USA

Jackman, Barret (Athlete, Hockey Player)
4924 Pershing Pl
Saint Louis, MO 63108-1202, USA

Jackman, Hugh (Actor)
c/o Michele Schweitzer *Rogers & Cowan*
909 3rd Ave Fl 9
New York, NY 10022-4752, USA

Jacks, Wayne (Race Car Driver)
Wayne Jacks Motorsports
2755 N Lamont St
Las Vegas, NV 89115-4517, USA

Jacks Mannequin (Musician)
c/o Staff Member *Maverick Recording Co (LA)*
3300 Warner Blvd
Burbank, CA 91505-4632, USA

Jackson, Al (Baseball Player)
Pittsburgh Pirates
3221 SE Morningside Blvd
Port Saint Lucie, FL 34952-5919, USA

Jackson, Alan (Musician, Songwriter)
Alan Jackson Fan Club
PO Box 1955
Brentwood, TN 37024-1955, USA

Jackson, Alfonza (Athlete, Football Player)
2701 Godwin Ln
Pensacola, FL 32526-9047, USA

Jackson, Alfred (Athlete, Football Player)
1811 Kirby Dr
Houston, TX 77019-3415, USA

Jackson, Alvin N (Al) (Athlete, Baseball Player)
3221 SE Morningside Blvd
Port Saint Lucie, FL 34952-5919, USA

Jackson, Andrew (Athlete, Football Player)

Jackson, Asa (Athlete, Football Player)
c/o Ken Zuckerman *Priority Sports & Entertainment - (LA)*
15233 Ventura Blvd Ste 718
Sherman Oaks, CA 91403-2237, USA

Jackson, Betty (Designer, Fashion Designer)
Betty Jackson Ltd
1 Netherwood Place
London W14 0BW, UNITED KINGDOM (UK)

Jackson, Bo (Athlete, Baseball Player, Football Player)
100 Oak Ridge Dr W
Burr Ridge, IL 60527-6870, USA

Jackson, Bob (Athlete, Football Player)
30608 Salem Dr
Bay Village, OH 44140-1127, USA

Jackson, Bobby (Basketball Player)
Sacramento Kings
1 Sports Pkwy
Arco Arena
Sacramento, CA 95834-2301, USA

Jackson, Bobby (Athlete, Football Player)
47 Tippin Dr
Huntington Station, NY 11746-2130, USA

Jackson, Brandon T (Actor, Producer)
c/o Michael Kives *Creative Artists Agency (CAA)*
2000 Avenue of the Stars Ste 100
Los Angeles, CA 90067-4705, USA

Jackson, Brett (Athlete, Baseball Player)

Jackson, Brian (Athlete, Football Player)
c/o Jordan Woy *Willis & Woy Management*
4890 Alpha Rd Ste 200
Dallas, TX 75244-4639, USA

Jackson, Calvin (Athlete, Football Player)
250 SW 28th Ter
Fort Lauderdale, FL 33312-1285, USA

Jackson, Charles (Athlete, Football Player)
PO Box 888285
Atlanta, GA 30356-0285, USA

Jackson, Cheyenne (Actor)
c/o Chelsea Hayes *Slate PR (NY)*
307 7th Ave Rm 2401
New York, NY 10001-6019, USA

Jackson, Chuck (Athlete, Baseball Player)
15821 SE 175th Pl
Renton, WA 98058-9122, USA

Jackson, Chuck (Musician)
Universal Attractions
225 W 57th St # 500
New York, NY 10019-2104, USA

Jackson, Clarence (Athlete, Football Player)
5251 Appleleaf Ct
North Chesterfield, VA 23234-2801, USA

Jackson, Conor (Athlete, Baseball Player)
7301 E 3rd Ave Unit 313
Scottsdale, AZ 85251-4461, USA

Jackson, Curtis (50 Cent) (Musician)
50 Poplar Hill Dr
Farmington, CT 06032-2419, USA

Jackson, Dallas (Producer, Writer)
c/o Staff Member *DJ Classicz*
150 S Barrington Pl
Los Angeles, CA 90049-3306, USA

Jackson, Damian (Athlete, Baseball Player)
2525 Cranston Dr Unit 3
Escondido, CA 92025-7381, USA

Jackson, Dane (Athlete, Hockey Player)
5887 Pinehurst Ct
Grand Forks, ND 58201-2813, USA

Jackson, Danny (Athlete, Baseball Player)
16421 Monrovia St
Overland Park, KS 66221-7941, USA

Jackson, Darrell (Athlete, Baseball Player)
PO Box 4424
Downey, CA 90241-1424, USA

Jackson, Darrell (Athlete, Football Player)
12727 SE 38th St
Bellevue, WA 98006-1235, USA

Jackson, Darrin (Athlete, Baseball Player)
333 W 35th St Attn Dept
Chicago, IL 60616-3621, USA

Jackson, Deanna (Basketball Player)
Indiana Fever
125 S Pennsylvania St
Conseco Fieldhouse
Indianapolis, IN 46204-3610, USA

Jackson, DeSean (Athlete, Football Player)
c/o Denise White *EAG Sports Management*
909 N Pacific Coast Hwy Ste 360
El Segundo, CA 90245-3864, USA

Jackson, Don (Athlete, Hockey Player)
13709 W Montecito Ln
Wichita, KS 67235-3450, USA

Jackson, Doris (Musician)
Nationwide Entertainment
2756 N Green Valley Pkwy
Henderson, NV 89014-2120, USA

Jackson, D'Qwell (Athlete, Football Player)

Jackson, Earnest (Athlete, Football Player)
915 Cole Ave Apt 2003
Rosenberg, TX 77471-3962, USA

Jackson, Edwin (Athlete, Baseball Player)
PO Box 6272
Columbus, GA 31917-6272, USA

Jackson, Ernie (Athlete, Football Player)
938 Pisgah N
Eads, TN 38028-9799, USA

Jackson, Frank (Athlete, Football Player)
5904 Gregory Ln
Allen, TX 75002-6710, USA

Jackson, Fred (Athlete, Football Player)

Jackson, Freddie (Actor)
c/o Carlos Keyes *Red Entertainment Agency*
3537 36th St Ste 2
Astoria, NY 11106-1347, USA

Jackson, Gildart (Actor)
c/o Chuck Binder *Binder & Associates*
1465 Lindacrest Dr
Beverly Hills, CA 90210-2519, USA

Jackson, Glenda (Actor)
c/o Lionel Larner *Lionel Larner Ltd*
119 W 57th St
New York, NY 10019-2303, USA

Jackson, Grady (Athlete, Football Player)
PO Box 841
Braselton, GA 30517-0015, USA

Jackson, Grant (Athlete, Baseball Player)
212 Mesa Cir
Pittsburgh, PA 15241-1721, USA

Jackson, Harold (Athlete, Coach, Football Player)
6144 Flight Ave
Los Angeles, CA 90056-1510, USA

Jackson, Harold (Journalist)
Birmingham News
2200 4th Ave N
Editorial Dept
Birmingham, AL 35203-3802, USA

Jackson, Honor (Athlete, Football Player)
384 Wren Dr
Santa Rosa, CA 95401-5852, USA

Jackson, Jack (Athlete, Hockey Player)
401 W 123rd Ter
Kansas City, MO 64145-1173, USA

Jackson, James A (Jim) (Athlete, Basketball Player)
17827 Windflower Way Unit 101
Dallas, TX 75252-5226, USA

Jackson, Janet (Actor, Dancer, Musician)
c/o Rona Menashe *Guttman Associates Public Relations*
118 S Beverly Dr Ste 201
Beverly Hills, CA 90212-3016, USA

Jackson, Jaren (Athlete, Basketball Player)
2940 S Germantown Rd
Germantown, TN 38138-7011, USA

Jackson, Jarious (Athlete, Football Player)
7423 Marigold Dr
Irving, TX 75063-5505, USA

Jackson, Jeff (Athlete, Hockey Player)
c/o Staff Member *Toronto Maple Leafs*
Air Canada Centre
400-40 Bay St
Toronto, ON M5J 2X2, CANADA

Jackson, Jeff (Athlete, Baseball Player)
853 S Kingsley Dr Apt D
Los Angeles, CA 90005-4367, USA

Jackson, Jeff (Athlete, Football Player)
1119 Parkview Dr
Griffin, GA 30224-4738, USA

Jackson, Jeremy (Actor, Producer)
c/o James J. Jones *Premier Talent Group*
4370 Tujunga Ave Ste 110
Studio City, CA 91604-2753, USA

Jackson, Jermaine (Basketball Player)
Atlanta Hawks
190 Marietta St NW Ste 405
Atlanta, GA 30303-2717, USA

Jackson, Jermaine (Musician, Songwriter)
4641 Hayvenhurst Ave
Encino, CA 91436-3251, USA

Jackson, Jesse (Activist, Politician, Religious Leader)
Operation Push
930 E 50th St
Chicago, IL 60615-2799, USA

Jackson, john (Athlete, Baseball Player)
PO Box 898
Hodge, LA 71247-0898, USA

Jackson, John (Athlete, Football Player)
8183 Alpine Aster Ct
Liberty Township, OH 45044-1904, USA

Jackson, John David (Boxer)
1022 S State St
Tacoma, WA 98405-3042, USA

Jackson, John (Fabolous) (Musician)
c/o Tammy Brook *FYI Public Relations*
174 5th Ave Ste 404
New York, NY 10010-5964, USA

Jackson, John M (Actor)
JAG
5555 Melrose Ave
Clara Bow #204
Los Angeles, CA 90038-3989, USA

Jackson, Jonathan (Actor)
c/o Graciella Sanchez *Echo Lake Management*
421 S Beverly Dr Fl 8
Beverly Hills, CA 90212-4408, USA

Jackson, Joshua (Actor)
c/o Doug Wald *Anonymous Content*
3532 Hayden Ave
Culver City, CA 90232-2413, USA

Jackson, Kareem (Athlete, Football Player)
c/o Sean Kiernan *Impact Sports (LA)*
12429 Ventura Ct
Studio City, CA 91604-2417, USA

Jackson, Kate (Actor)
c/o Staff Member *WME/IMG*
9601 Wilshire Blvd
Beverly Hills, CA 90210-5213, USA

Jackson, Keith (Athlete, Football Player)
1801 Champlin Dr Apt 1707
Little Rock, AR 72223-3987, USA

Jackson, Keith (Race Car Driver)
8941 W Jewell Pl
Lakewood, CO 80227-2388, USA

Jackson, Keith J (Athlete, Football Player)
PO Box 241695
Little Rock, AR 72223-0012, USA

Jackson, Ken (Athlete, Baseball Player)
PO Box 869
Waskom, TX 75692-0869, USA

Jackson, Kenny (Athlete, Football Player)
1319 Linn St
State College, PA 16803-3026, USA

Jackson, Kirby (Athlete, Football Player)
373 Vista Lake Ter
Suwanee, GA 30024-7418, USA

Jackson, Kwame (Business Person, Reality Star)
c/o Dan Klores *Dan Klores Communications (DKC)*
261 5th Ave Fl 2
New York, NY 10016-7601, USA

Jackson, Lamar (Athlete, Football Player)
University of Louisville
2301 S 3rd St
Athletic Dept
Louisville, KY 40292-2001, USA

Jackson, Larron (Athlete, Football Player)
20000 Mitchell Pl Unit 56
Denver, CO 80249-7231, USA

Jackson, La Toya (Model, Musician)
c/o Juliette Harris *It Girl Public Relations*
3763 Eddingham Ave
Calabasas, CA 91302-5835, USA

Jackson, Lauren (Basketball Player)
Seattle Storm
351 Elliott Ave W Ste 500
Key Arena
Seattle, WA 98119-4153, USA

Jackson, Lenzie (Athlete, Football Player)
4524 E La Puente Ave
Phoenix, AZ 85044-1421, USA

Jackson, Leo (Race Car Driver)
PO Box 726
191 Airport Road
Arden, NC 28704-0726, USA

Jackson, Leshon (Athlete, Football Player)
PO Box 957
Haskell, OK 74436-0957, USA

Jackson, Lillian (Baseball Player)
1050 W Camino Velasquez
Green Valley, AZ 85622-4527, USA

Jackson, Luke (Athlete, Basketball Player, Olympic Athlete)
7711 County Road 511
Rosharon, TX 77583-7286, USA

Jackson, Malik (Athlete)

Jackson, Mannie (Athlete, Basketball Player)
Harlem Globetrotters
5445 Triangle Pkwy Ste 300
Peachtree Corners, GA 30092-2568, USA

Jackson, Mark A (Athlete, Basketball Player, Sportscaster)
17 Winmere Pl
Dix Hills, NY 11746-6553, USA

Jackson, Mark A (Athlete, Football Player)
1480 Lloyd Ct
Wheaton, IL 60189-7368, USA

Jackson, Mel (Actor)
c/o Staff Member *Artists & Representatives (Stone Manners Salners)*
6100 Wilshire Blvd Ste 1500
Los Angeles, CA 90048-5110, USA

Jackson, Melvin (Athlete, Football Player)
4345 Enoro Dr
View Park, CA 90008-4870, USA

Jackson, Mervin (Athlete, Basketball Player)
16638 Kildare Ct
Tinley Park, IL 60477-1579, USA

Jackson, Michael (Athlete, Football Player)
14207 128th Pl NE
Kirkland, WA 98034-1575, USA

Jackson, Mick (Director)
1349 Berea Pl
Pacific Palisades, CA 90272-2602, USA

Jackson, Mike (Athlete, Baseball Player)
805 11th Ave Apt 2H
Paterson, NJ 07514-1012, USA

Jackson, Mike (Athlete, Baseball Player)
17214 Oak Dale Dr
Spring, TX 77379-8846, USA

Jackson, Milt (Athlete, Football Player)
100 McMindes Ct
Roseville, CA 95747-5853, USA

Jackson, Monte C (Athlete, Football Player)
11010 W Ocean Air Dr Apt 363
San Diego, CA 92130-4629, USA

Jackson, Nate (Athlete, Football Player)
11968 E Lake Cir
Greenwood Village, CO 80111-5245, USA

Jackson, Neil (Actor)
c/o Amy Slomovits *Haven Entertainment*
8111 Beverly Blvd Ste 201
Los Angeles, CA 90048-4531, USA

Jackson, Noah (Athlete, Football Player)
1640 Millburne Rd
Lake Forest, IL 60045-4106, USA

Jackson, Paris (Actor)
c/o Arnold Stiefel *Stiefel Entertainment*
21731 Ventura Blvd Ste 300
Woodland Hills, CA 91364-1851, USA

Jackson, Peter (Director)
c/o Staff Member *Weta Digital*
9-11 Manuka St
Miramar, Wellington, New Zealand

Jackson, Phil (Athlete, Basketball Coach, Basketball Player, Coach)
18942 Medicine Rock Ln
Lakeside, MT 59922-9514, USA

Jackson, Phillip (Actor)
c/o Pippa Markham *Markham & Froggatt*
4 Windmill St
London W1T 1HZ, UNITED KINGDOM

Jackson, Quinton (Rampage) (Athlete, Wrestler)
c/o Staff Member *ROAR (LA)*
9701 Wilshire Blvd Fl 8
Beverly Hills, CA 90212-2008, USA

Jackson, Ralph (Athlete, Basketball Player)
3235 W 111th Pl
Inglewood, CA 90303-2316, USA

Jackson, Randy (Musician, Reality Star)
Dream Merchant 21
1741 Ivar Ave
Los Angeles, CA 90028-5105, USA

Jackson, Randy B (Athlete, Football Player)
747 Musago Run
Lake Mary, FL 32746-2209, USA

Jackson, Ransom (Baseball Player)
Chicago Cubs
4990 Mars Hill Rd
Bogart, GA 30622-2042, USA

Jackson, Rebbie (Music Group, Musician, Songwriter, Writer)
4641 Hayvenhurst Ave
Encino, CA 91436-3251, USA

Jackson, Reggie (Athlete, Baseball Player)
c/o Staff Member *Doubleday/ RandomHouse*
1745 Broadway
New York, NY 10019-4640, USA

Jackson, Richard A (Religious Leader)
North Phoenix Baptist Church
5757 N Central Ave
Phoenix, AZ 85012-1397, USA

Jackson, Richard S (Richie) (Athlete, Football Player)
6000 Kingston Ct
New Orleans, LA 70131-5557, USA

Jackson, Rickey (Athlete, Football Player)
3015 Aspin Dr
Harvey, LA 70058-2175, USA

Jackson, Rickey A (Athlete, Football Player)
325 S Barfield Hwy
Pahokee, FL 33476-1929, USA

Jackson, Ron (Athlete, Baseball Player)
515 White Rd
Fayetteville, GA 30214-1211, USA

Jackson, Roy Lee (Athlete, Baseball Player)
8269 Lee Road 54
Auburn, AL 36830-8222, USA

Jackson, Russ (Athlete, Football Player)
4153 Vermont Cres
Burlington, ON L7M 4A9, Canada

Jackson, Ryan (Athlete, Baseball Player)
4065 S Lockwood Ridge Rd
Sarasota, FL 34231-7637, USA

Jackson, Samuel L (Actor)
c/o Staff Member *Uppity Films*
3532 Hayden Ave
Culver City, CA 90232-2413, USA

Jackson, Sasha (Actor)
c/o Richard Beddingfield *Beddingfield Company, The*
13600 Ventura Blvd Ste B
Sherman Oaks, CA 91423-5050, USA

Jackson, Shar (Actor)
c/o Phillip Christian *Phillip Christian Public Relations*
30 E 20th St
New York, NY 10003-1310, USA

Jackson, Sheldon (Athlete, Football Player)
4466 Teresita Ct
Chino, CA 91710-3929, USA

Jackson, Sherry (Actor)
800 N Lucia Ave # A
Redondo Beach, CA 90277-2233, USA

Jackson, Skai (Actor)
c/o Nicole Perna *Imprint PR*
6121 W Sunset Blvd
Neuehouse
Los Angeles, CA 90028-6442, USA

Jackson, Sonny (Athlete, Baseball Player)
117 Palm Bay Dr Apt B
Palm Beach Gardens, FL 33418-5790, USA

Jackson, Stephen (Athlete, Basketball Player)
6945 Brazos Ave
Port Arthur, TX 77642-6581, USA

Jackson, Steve (Athlete, Football Player)
43752 Lees Mill Sq
Leesburg, VA 20176-3821, USA

Jackson, Steve (Athlete, Football Player)
1153 Bergen Pkwy Ste M
Evergreen, CO 80439-9501, USA

Jackson, Steven (Athlete, Football Player)
c/o Ashley Smith Becker *Relativity Sports*
2029 Century Park E Ste 1550
Century City, CA 90067-3000, USA

Jackson, Stonewall (Musician, Songwriter)
6007 Cloverland Dr
Brentwood, TN 37027-7607, USA

Jackson, Stoney (Actor)
3151 Cahuenga Blvd W Ste 310
Los Angeles, CA 90068-1768, USA

Jackson, Tanard (Athlete, Football Player)
c/o Peter Schaffer *Authentic Athletix*
400 S Steele St Unit 47
Denver, CO 80209-3535, USA

Jackson, Tarvaris (Athlete, Football Player)
c/o Joel Segal *Lagardere Unlimited (NY)*
456 Washington St Apt 9L
New York, NY 10013-1555, USA

Jackson, Tim (Athlete, Football Player)
6501 White Oak Dr
Rowlett, TX 75089-7441, USA

Jackson, Tito (Musician)
c/o Chrissy Johnston *Intrigue Management*
83 Ducie St
Manchester M1 2JQ, UNITED KINGDOM

Jackson, Tom (Athlete, Football Player, Sportscaster)
7475 Brill Rd
Cincinnati, OH 45243-3525, USA

Jackson, Tracy (Athlete, Basketball Player)
10588 Spotted Horse Ln
Columbia, MD 21044-2214, USA

Jackson, Tre (Athlete, Football Player)
680 Harrison Ave
Peekskill, NY 10566-2219, USA

Jackson, Trevor (Actor)
c/o Beau Swayze *Management 360*
9111 Wilshire Blvd
Beverly Hills, CA 90210-5508, USA

Jackson, Trina (Athlete, Olympic Athlete, Swimmer)
9271 Saltwater Way
Jacksonville, FL 32256-9606, USA

Jackson, Tyoka (Athlete, Football Player)
2005 Weber Dr
District Heights, MD 20747-1242, USA

Jackson, Tyson (Athlete, Football Player)
c/o Ashley Smith Becker *Relativity Sports*
2029 Century Park E Ste 1550
Century City, CA 90067-3000, USA

Jackson, Verdell (Baseball Player)
Memphis Red Sox
413 Lincoln St
Venice, IL 62090-1117, USA

Jackson, Vernell (Athlete, Baseball Player)
413 Lincoln St
Venice, IL 62090-1117, USA

Jackson, Vestee (Athlete, Football Player)
6554 Eagle Creek Ln
Las Vegas, NV 89156-5945, USA

Jackson, Victoria (Actor, Comedian)
c/o Rebecca Shrager *People Store*
645 Lambert Dr NE
Atlanta, GA 30324-4125, USA

Jackson, Vincent E (Bo) (Athlete, Baseball Player, Football Player)
PO Box 158
Mobile, AL 36601-0158, USA

Jackson, Wanda (Musician)
Wanda Jackson Enterprises
8200 S Pennsylvania Ave
Oklahoma City, OK 73159-5202, USA

Jackson, Wardell (Athlete, Basketball Player)
185 Hamilton Ave
Columbus, OH 43203-1478, USA

Jackson, Waverly (Athlete, Football Player)
1231 Halifax St
South Hill, VA 23970-2319, USA

Jackson, Wilbur (Athlete, Football Player)
PO Box 1571
Ozark, AL 36361-1571, USA

Jackson, Willie (Athlete, Football Player)
PO Box 12627
Gainesville, FL 32604-0627, USA

Jackson, Zach (Athlete, Baseball Player)
7620 Menler Dr
Austin, TX 78735-1809, USA

Jackson Hoye, Rose (Actor)
c/o Staff Member *Haldeman Business Management*
1137 2nd St Ste 119
Santa Monica, CA 90403-5073, USA

Jackson Lee, Sheila (Congressman, Politician)
2160 Rayburn Hob
Washington, DC 20515-0918, USA

Jacob, Irene (Actor)
Nicole Cann
1 Rue Alfred du Vigny
Paris 75008, FRANCE

Jacob, Katerina (Actor)
Agentur Doris Mattes
Merzstr 14
Munich 81679, USA

Jacob, Ralph (Actor)
c/o Staff Member *Britto Agency PR*
277 Broadway Ste 110
New York, NY 10007-2072, USA

Jacobellis, Lindsey (Athlete, Olympic Athlete, Speed Skater)
30684 E Ski Bowl Way
Government Camp, OR 97028-0345, USA

Jacobi, Derek G (Actor)
c/o Staff Member *ICM Partners*
10250 Constellation Blvd Fl 7
Los Angeles, CA 90067-6207, USA

Jacobs, Allen (Athlete, Football Player)
3050 E Tolcate Ln
Salt Lake City, UT 84121-1545, USA

Jacobs, Ben (Athlete, Football Player)
c/o Derrick Fox *Derrick Fox Management*
Prefers to be contacted by telephone
CA, USA

Jacobs, Brandon (Athlete, Football Player)
2 Seven Trails Ln
Wayne, NJ 07470-2008, USA

Jacobs, Cam (Athlete, Football Player)
5420 Atlantic Vw
Saint Augustine, FL 32080-7148, USA

Jacobs, Chuck (Athlete, Football Player)

Jacobs, Dave (Athlete, Football Player)
8388 Glen Eagle Dr
Manlius, NY 13104-9445, USA

Jacobs, Gillian (Actor)
c/o Jill Kaplan *Authentic Talent and Literary Management (NY)*
20 Jay St Ste M17
Brooklyn, NY 11201-8300, USA

Jacobs, Glenn (Kane) (Athlete, Wrestler)
790 Locket Ln
Jefferson City, TN 37760-3462, USA

Jacobs, Harry (Athlete, Football Player)
6145 McKinley Pkwy Unit 22
Hamburg, NY 14075-5408, USA

Jacobs, Irwin M (Business Person)
Qualcomm Inc
5775 Morehouse Dr
San Diego, CA 92121-1714, USA

Jacobs, Jeremy (Business Person)
1300 N Davis Rd
East Aurora, NY 14052-9473, USA

Jacobs, John (Athlete, Golfer)

Jacobs, Katie (Producer, Writer)
c/o Tony Etz *Creative Artists Agency (CAA)*
2000 Avenue of the Stars Ste 100
Los Angeles, CA 90067-4705, USA

Jacobs, Lawrence-Hilton (Actor)
c/o Theo Caesar *90210 Talent Agency*
16430 Ventura Blvd Ste 200
Encino, CA 91436-2135, USA

Jacobs, Marc (Designer, Fashion Designer)
72 Spring St # 202
New York, NY 10012-4019, USA

Jacobs, Mike (Athlete, Baseball Player)
1583 Hikers Trail Dr
Chula Vista, CA 91915-1826, USA

Jacobs, Proverb (Athlete, Football Player)
4369 Detroit Ave
Oakland, CA 94619-1603, USA

Jacobs, Ray (Athlete, Football Player)
2402 W 5th Ave
Corsicana, TX 75110-4047, USA

Jacobs, Regina (Athlete, Olympic Athlete, Track Athlete)
3209 Wisconsin St
Oakland, CA 94602-4029, USA

Jacobs, Tim (Athlete, Football Player)
7306 Finns Ln
Lanham, MD 20706-1214, USA

Jacobs, Tim (Athlete, Hockey Player)
6516 County Road 301
Parachute, CO 81635-9122, USA

Jacobsen, Bucky (Athlete, Baseball Player)
1546 Boalch Ave NW
North Bend, WA 98045-8127, USA

Jacobsen, Casey (Athlete, Basketball Player)
Phoenix Suns
201 E Jefferson St
Phoenix, AZ 85004-2412, USA

Jacobsen, Peter (Athlete, Golfer)
27771 Marina Pointe Dr
Bonita Springs, FL 34134-0762, USA

Jacobsen, Peter (Athlete, Golfer)
9600 SW Barnes Rd Ste 175
Portland, OR 97225-6618, USA

Jacobsen, Stephanie (Actor)
c/o Andrew Edwards *Zero Gravity Management*
11110 Ohio Ave Ste 100
Los Angeles, CA 90025-3329, USA

Jacobs-Murk, Janet (Athlete, Baseball Player, Commentator)
899 Olentangy Rd
Franklin Lakes, NJ 07417-2811, USA

Jacobson, Abbi (Actor, Comedian)
c/o Rhett Usry *ID Public Relations (NY)*
40 Wall St Fl 51
New York, NY 10005-1385, USA

Jacobson, Peter (Actor)
c/o Elizabeth Much *East 2 West Collective*
11022 Santa Monica Blvd Ste 350
Los Angeles, CA 90025-7532, USA

Jacobson, Scott (Actor)

Jacoby, Brook (Athlete, Baseball Player)
100 Joe Nuxhall Way
Cincinnati, OH 45202-4109, USA

Jacoby, Joe (Athlete, Football Player)
2730 Willow Dr
Vienna, VA 22181-5347, USA

Jacoby, Scott (Actor)
PO Box 461100
Los Angeles, CA 90046-9100, USA

Jacome, Jason (Athlete, Baseball Player)
5115 N Camino Esplendora
Tucson, AZ 85718-6226, USA

Jacot, Christopher (Actor)
c/o Ted Schachter *Schachter Entertainment*
1157 S Beverly Dr Fl 2
Los Angeles, CA 90035-1119, USA

Jacot, Michele (Skier)
Residence du Brevent
74 Chamonix, FRANCE

Jacott, Carlos (Actor)
c/o JB Roberts *Thruline Entertainment*
9250 Wilshire Blvd Fl Ground
Beverly Hills, CA 90212-3352, USA

Jacox, Kendyl (Athlete, Football Player)
50 Schubach Dr
Sugar Land, TX 77479-5727, USA

Jacques, Jeff (Athlete, Hockey Player)
PO Box 107
Niagara On The Lake, ON L0S 1J0, Canada

Jacques, Jennie (Actor)
c/o Andrew Braidford *BWH Agency*
35 Soho Sq
Fl 5
London W1D 3QX, UNITED KINGDOM

Jacques, Reeves (Athlete, Football Player)
9135 Buffalo Speedway
Houston, TX 77025-4426, USA

Jacques, Russell (Artist)
48701 Shady View Dr
Palm Desert, CA 92260-6730, USA

Jacquez, Pat (Athlete, Baseball Player)
4430 Annandale Dr
Stockton, CA 95219-1782, USA

Jacquez, Thomas (Tom) (Athlete, Baseball Player)
4430 Annandale Dr
Stockton, CA 95219-1782, USA

Jacuzzi, Roy (Business Person)
Jacuzzi Whirlpool Bath
2121 N California Blvd
Walnut Creek, CA 94596-3572, USA

Jadagrace (Actor, Musician)
c/o Monique Moss *Integrated PR*
9025 Wilshire Blvd Ste 400
Beverly Hills, CA 90211-1828, USA

Jadakiss (Artist, Music Group, Musician)
c/o Drew Elliot *Artist International*
333 E 43rd St Apt 115
New York, NY 10017-4822, USA

Jade, Samantha (Musician)
c/o Staff Member *Jive Records*
550 Madison Ave Frnt 1
New York, NY 10022-3211, USA

Jadot, Jean L O (Religious Leader)
Ave de l'Atlantique 71-B-12
Brussels 01150, BELGIUM

Jaeckel, Barry (Athlete, Golfer)
210 Falcon Cv
Brandon, MS 39047-7733, USA

Jaeckel, Paul (Athlete, Baseball Player)
328 W 7th St
Claremont, CA 91711-4313, USA

Jaeckin, Just (Director)
8 Villa Mequillet
Neuilly/Seine 92200, FRANCE

Jaeger, Andrea (Athlete, Tennis Player)
256 Rancho Milagro Way
Silver Lining Ranch
Hesperus, CO 81326-8750, USA

Jaeger, Jeff T (Athlete, Football Player)
3026 Sahalee Dr W
Sammamish, WA 98074-6304, USA

Jaeger, Sam (Actor)
c/o Steve Dontanville *Circle of Confusion (NY)*
270 Lafayette St Ste 402
New York, NY 10012-3327, USA

Jaffe, Marielle (Actor)
c/o Staff Member *Inphenate*
9701 Wilshire Blvd Fl 10
Beverly Hills, CA 90212-2010, USA

Jaffe, Stanley R (Director, Producer)
Lean Building
10202 Washington Blvd
Culver City, CA 90232-3119, USA

Jaffrey, Raza (Actor)
c/o Larry Taube *Principal Entertainment*
9255 W Sunset Blvd Ste 500
Los Angeles, CA 90069-3301, USA

Jaffrey, Sakina (Actor)

Jagannathan, Poorna (Actor)
c/o Staff Member *Smith Talent Group*
77 Gold St
Brooklyn, NY 11201-1228, USA

Jager, Thomas (Tom) (Athlete, Olympic Athlete, Swimmer)
198 Creekside Ct
Glenwood Springs, CO 81601-2542, USA

Jagge, Finn Christian (Skier)
Michelets Vei 108
Stabekk 01320, NORWAY

Jagged Edge (Music Group)
c/o Nancy Josephson *WME|IMG*
9601 Wilshire Blvd
Beverly Hills, CA 90210-5213, USA

Jagger, Bianca (Actor, Model)
Bianca Jagger Human Rights Foundation
272 Kensington High St
#246
London W8 6ND, UNITED KINGDOM

Jagger, Dean (Actor)
c/o Staff Member *StarTree Productions*
9107 Wilshire Blvd Ste 450
Beverly Hills, CA 90210-5535, USA

Jagger, Jade (Business Person)
16th West 19th LLC
752 Pacific St
Brooklyn, NY 11238, USA

Jagger, James (Actor)
c/o Allan Mindel *Framework Entertainment*
9057 Nemo St # C
W Hollywood, CA 90069-5511, USA

Jagger, Mick (Musician)
116 Richmond Hill
Richmond
Greater London TW10 6, UNITED KINGDOM

Jaglom, Henry (Director)
9165 W Sunset Blvd Ste 300
Los Angeles, CA 90069-3195, USA

Jagr, Jaromir (Athlete, Hockey Player)
c/o J P Barry *CAA Hockey*
Prefers to be contacted by email or phone.
Los Angeles, CA NA, USA

Jaguares (Music Group)
c/o Staff Member *BMG*
1540 Broadway
New York, NY 10036-4039, USA

Jaha, John (Athlete, Baseball Player)
12776 SE Geneva Way
Happy Valley, OR 97086-6182, USA

Jahan, Marine (Actor, Dancer)
Media Artists Group
6300 Wilshire Blvd Ste 1470
Los Angeles, CA 90048-5200, USA

Jaheim (Musician)
Diane Mill
100 Evergreen Point #402
East Orange, NJ 07018, USA

Jaitley, Celina (Actor, Beauty Pageant Winner)
c/o Staff Member *Brillstein Entertainment Partners*
9150 Wilshire Blvd Ste 350
Beverly Hills, CA 90212-3453, USA

Jake Locker, Jake (Athlete, Football Player)
c/o David Dunn *Athletes First*
23091 Mill Creek Dr
Laguna Hills, CA 92653-1258, USA

Jakeman, Seth (Musician)
c/o Staff Member *Paradigm (Monterey)*
404 W Franklin St
Monterey, CA 93940-2303, USA

Jakes, John (Writer)
445 Meadow Lark Dr
Sarasota, FL 34236-1901, USA

Jakes, TD (Musician, Religious Leader, Writer)
T.D. Jakes Ministries
PO Box 763518
Dallas, TX 75376-3518, USA

Jakes, Van (Athlete, Football Player)
1147 Chateau Ter
McDonough, GA 30253-4653, USA

Jakl, Kelley (Actor, Musician)
c/o Colleen Schlegel *Schlegel Entertainment*
2934 1/2 N Beverly Glen Cir # 284
Los Angeles, CA 90077-1724, USA

Jakobs, Marco (Athlete)
Oststr 1B
Unna 59427, GERMANY

Jakobson, Maggie (Actor)
c/o Kesha Williams *KW Entertainment*
3727 W Magnolia Blvd Ste 430
Burbank, CA 91505-2818, USA

Jakopin, John (Athlete, Hockey Player)
1235 Adams St
Hollywood, FL 33019-1802, USA

Jakovac, JJ (Athlete, Golfer)
c/o Jim Lehrman *Medalist Management Inc*
36855 W Main St Ste 200
Purcellville, VA 20132-3561, USA

Jakowenko, George (Athlete, Football Player)
2520 Northside Dr APT 105
San Diego, CA 92108-2796, USA

Jakub, Lisa (Actor)
c/o Nancy LeFeaver *LeFeaver Talent Management Ltd*
202-2 College St
Toronto, ON M5G 1K3, CANADA

Jakubenko, Aaron (Actor)
c/o Christopher Burbidge *Fourward*
9701 Wilshire Blvd Fl 8
Beverly Hills, CA 90212-2008, USA

Jakubo, Mike (Athlete, Hockey Player)
1164 Maureen Cres
Sudbury, ON P3A 3K5, Canada

Jal, Emmanuel (Musician, Writer)
c/o Staff Member *Sonic360, Inc.*
Top Floor East
33 Riding House St.
London W1W 7DZ, UK

Jalbert, Pierre (Actor)
2642 N Beverly Glen Blvd
Los Angeles, CA 90077-2528, USA

Jam, Nicky (Musician)
c/o Greg Cortez *42West*
600 3rd Ave Fl 23
New York, NY 10016-1914, USA

Jamal, Ahmad (Music Group, Musician)
Brad Simon Organization
122 E 57th St # 300
New York, NY 10022-2623, USA

Jambor, Agi (Music Group, Musician)
1616 Bolton St
Baltimore, MD 21217-4316, USA

Jamerson, Dave (Athlete, Basketball Player)
13960 Salsbury Creek Dr
Carmel, IN 46032-8541, USA

James, Aaron (Athlete, Basketball Player)
3057 Orrin Ave
Youngstown, OH 44505-4436, USA

James, Alex (Musician)
c/o Staff Member *Parlophone Records*
EMI House
43 Brook Green
London W6 7EF, United Kingdom

James, Angela (Athlete, Hockey Player)
Seneca College York Campus 70 the Pond Rd
Attn: Sports Coordinator Seneca College York Campuscoordinator
North York, ON M3J 3M6, Canada

James, Anthony (Actor)
CNA Assoc
1875 Century Park E Ste 2250
Los Angeles, CA 90067-2563, USA

James, Art (Athlete, Baseball Player)
4520 Parkview Sq
Atlanta, GA 30349-9408, USA

James, Bill (Athlete, Baseball Player, Writer)
625 Ohio St
Lawrence, KS 66044-2357, USA

James, Bill (Sportscaster)
445 Tennessee St
Lawrence, KS 66044-1376, USA

James, Billy (Athlete, Basketball Player)
12 S Sunset Dr
Lexington, IN 47138-8935, USA

James, Bob (Athlete, Baseball Player)
15844 Cindy Ct
Canyon Country, CA 91387-1881, USA

James, Boney (Musician)
c/o Staff Member *Paradigm (Monterey)*
404 W Franklin St
Monterey, CA 93940-2303, USA

James, Bradie (Athlete, Football Player)
2509 Silver Table Dr
Lewisville, TX 75056-5680, USA

James, Bradley (Actor)
c/o Ruth Young *United Agents*
12-26 Lexington St
London W1F OLE, UNITED KINGDOM

James, Bryton (Actor)
2212 Scholarship
Irvine, CA 92612-5681, USA

James, Casey (Musician)
Casey James Cougar Club
350 Rice Ln
Millsap, TX 76066-2426, USA

James, Charlie (Athlete, Baseball Player)
3303 Tanglewood Way
Fulton, MO 65251-3981, USA

James, Cheryl (Salt) (Musician)
c/o Chrissy Johnston *Intrigue Management*
83 Ducie St
Manchester M1 2JQ, UNITED KINGDOM

James, Chris (Athlete, Baseball Player)
1040 Countv Road 2707
Alto, TX 75925-5915, USA

James, Chuck (Athlete, Baseball Player)
4840 Golden Drive SW
Mableton, GA 30126, USA

James, Claudis (Athlete, Football Player)
6767 Presidential Dr
Jackson, MS 39213-2427, USA

James, Cleo (Athlete, Baseball Player)
1631 Mesa Ave
Colorado Springs, CO 80906-2917, USA

James, Craig (Athlete, Football Player)
12714 W FM 455
Celina, TX 75009-3959, USA

James, Danielle (Actor)
c/o Roger Carey *Roger Carey Associates*
Suite 909, The Old House
Shepperton Film Studios, Studios Road
Shepperton, Mddx TW17 0QD, UNITED KINGDOM

James, Delvin (Athlete, Baseball Player)
13355 FM 1878
Nacogdoches, TX 75961-1039, USA

James, Dion (Athlete, Baseball Player)
5213 Creekside Trl
Sarasota, FL 34243-3890, USA

James, Don (Coach, Football Coach)
7047 Chanticleer Ave SE
Snoqualmie, WA 98065-9785, USA

James, Donald M (Business Person)
Vulcan Materials Co
1200 Urban Center Dr
Vestavia, AL 35242-2545, USA

James, Duncan (Musician)
c/o Staff Member *Concorde Intl Artists Ltd*
101 Shepherds Bush Rd
London W6 7LP, UNITED KINGDOM (UK)

James, Duncan (Musician)
c/o Staff Member *BMG (UK)*
Bedford House
6979 Fulham High Street
London SW6 3JW, United Kingdom

James, Edgerrin (Athlete, Football Player)
c/o Drew Rosenhaus *Rosenhaus Sports Representation*
3921 Alton Rd # 440
Miami Beach, FL 33140-3852, USA

James, E L (Erika Leonard) (Writer)
c/o Valerie Hoskins *Valerie Hoskins Associates*
20 Charlotte St
London W1T 2NA, UNITED KINGDOM (UK)

James, Forrest (Politician)
21911vy Creek Church Rd
Rutledge, AL 36071-3913, USA

James, Geraldine (Actor)
Julian Belfarge
46 Albermarle St
London W1X 4PP, UNITED KINGDOM (UK)

James, Gerry (Athlete, Hockey Player)
3674 Dolphin Dr
Nanoose Bay, BC V9P 9H1, Canada

James, G Larry (Athlete, Track Athlete)
Stockton State College
Atheletic Dept
Pomona, NJ 08240, USA

James, Godfrey (Actor)
The Shack Western Rd. Pevensey Bay
E. Sussex, ENGLAND

James, Hannah (Actor)
c/o Brett Ruttenberg *Imprint PR*
6121 W Sunset Blvd
Neuehouse
Los Angeles, CA 90028-6442, USA

James, Henry (Athlete, Basketball Player)
527 E Leith St
Fort Wayne, IN 46806-1118, USA

James, Ja'Wuan (Athlete, Football Player)
c/o Bill Johnson *SportsTrust Advisors*
3340 Peachtree Rd NE Fl 16
Atlanta, GA 30326-1000, USA

James, Jesse (Actor)
West Coast Choppers
718 W Anaheim St
Long Beach, CA 90813-2820, USA

James, John (Actor)
129 Leland Rd
Summertown, TN 38483-5111, USA

James, Johnny (Athlete, Baseball Player)
6037 E Larkspur Dr
Scottsdale, AZ 85254-4444, USA

James, John W (Athlete, Football Player)
23108 NE 69th Ave
Melrose, FL 32666-6330, USA

James, Joni (Music Group, Musician)
PO Box 7027
Westchester, IL 60154, USA

James, Joshua (Musician)
c/o Brittany Pearce *Fresh and Clean Media*
8820 Wilshire Blvd Ste 300
Beverly Hills, CA 90211-2619, USA

James, Kate (Model)
Men/Women Model Inc
199 Lafayette St Fl 7
New York, NY 10012-4281, USA

James, Kerry (Actor)
c/o Carrie Wheeler *Carrie Wheeler Management*
101-1001 Broadway W
Suite 338
Vancouver, BC V6H 4E4, CANADA

James, Kevin (Actor, Comedian)
c/o Jennifer Allen *Viewpoint Inc*
8820 Wilshire Blvd Ste 220
Beverly Hills, CA 90211-2622, USA

James, Larry D (Astronaut)
AFELM
USS Space Command
Peterson Air Force Base, CP 80914, USA

James, LeBron (Athlete, Basketball Player)
4157 Idlebrook Dr
Akron, OH 44333-1723, USA

James, Leela (Musician)
c/o Stephanie Mahler *Creative Artists Agency (CAA)*
405 Lexington Ave Fl 19
New York, NY 10174-1800, USA

James, Lennie (Actor)
Castaway Voice Overs
15 Broad Ct Ste 3
London WC2B 5QN, UNITED KINGDOM

James, Lily (Actor)
c/o Clair Dobbs *CLD Communications*
4 Broadway Ct
The Broadway
London SW191RG, UNITED KINGDOM

James, Lionel (Athlete, Football Player)
199 Woodbury Dr
Sterrett, AL 35147-8144, USA

James, Michael Raymond (Actor)
c/o Jeffrey Chassen *Imprint PR*
6121 W Sunset Blvd
Neuehouse
Los Angeles, CA 90028-6442, USA

James, Mickie (Athlete, Wrestler)
9504 Hungary Woods Dr
Glen Allen, VA 23060-3297, USA

James, Mike (Athlete, Baseball Player)
115 Austin Ct
Mary Esther, FL 32569-1396, USA

James, Oliver (Actor, Musician)
c/o Mary Putnam Greene *MPG Management*
7162 Beverly Blvd Ste 332
Los Angeles, CA 90036-2547, USA

James, Paul (Actor, Producer)
c/o Staff Member *HGTV*
9721 Sherrill Blvd
Knoxville, TN 37932-3330, USA

James, P D (Writer)
37-A Gold hawk Road
London W12 8QQ, England

James, Po (Athlete, Football Player)
1421 Sherman St
Hammond, IN 46320-2208, USA

James, Rick (Athlete, Baseball Player)
102 Stoney Creek Dr
Florence, AL 35633-1581, USA

James, Robert (Athlete, Football Player)
1511 N Highland Ave
Murfreesboro, TN 37130-2204, USA

James, Robert (Bob) (Music Group, Musician, Songwriter, Writer)
Monterey International
72 W Adams St # 1000
Chicago, IL 60603-5107, USA

James, Roland (Athlete, Football Player)
19 Spring Ln
Sharon, MA 02067-2240, USA

James, Sheila (Actor)
3201 Pearl St
Santa Monica, CA 90405-3106, USA

James, Sheryl (Journalist)
Saint Petersburg Times
490 1st Ave S
Editorial Dept
Saint Petersburg, FL 33701-4223, USA

James, Skip (Athlete, Baseball Player)
14429 Windsor St
Overland Park, KS 66224-3669, USA

James, Stephan (Actor)
c/o Norbert Abrams *Noble Caplan Abrams*
1260 Yonge St Fl 2
Toronto, ON M4T 1W5, CANADA

James, Steve (Director, Producer, Writer)
c/o Paul Canterna *Seven Summits Pictures & Management*
8906 W Olympic Blvd
Beverly Hills, CA 90211-3550, USA

James, Theo (Actor)
c/o Luke Windsor *Prosper PR (UK)*
535 Kings Rd
Suite 313 Plaza
London SW10 0SZ, UNITED KINGDOM

James, Tommy (Music Group, Musician)
Aura Entertainment
PO Box 4354
Clifton, NJ 07012-8354, USA

James, Toran (Athlete, Football Player)
RR 3 Box 14-13
Ahoskie, NC 27910, USA

James, Val (Athlete, Hockey Player)
105 S 32nd St
Wyandanch, NY 11798-2613, USA

James-Collier, Rob (Actor)
c/o Kate Buckley *42 Management (UK)*
8 Flitcroft St
London WC2H 8DL, UNITED KINGDOM

James Henrie, Lorenzo (Actor)
c/o Chris Rossi *Status PR*
PO Box 6191
Westlake Village, CA 91359-6191, USA

James of Holland Park, Phyllis D (Writer)
Elaine Green Ltd
37A Goldhawk Road
London W12 SQQ, UNITED KINGDOM (UK)

Jameson, Jenna (Adult Film Star, Model)
c/o Staff Member *Alley Katz Enterprises*
9899 Santa Monica Blvd # 606
Beverly Hills, CA 90212-1604, USA

Jamieson, Janet (Athlete, Baseball Player, Commentator)
25938 160th Ave SE
Covington, WA 98042-8239, USA

Jamil, Jameela (Actor)
c/o Jennifer Abel *PMK/BNC Public Relations*
1840 Century Park E Ste 1400
Los Angeles, CA 90067-2115, USA

Jamiroquai (Music Group)
c/o Staff Member *Nettwerk Management (LA)*
1545 Wilcox Ace
Suite 200
Los Angeles, CA 90028, USA

Jamison, Antawn (Athlete, Basketball Player)
Dallas Mavericks
6041 Providence Country Club Dr
Charlotte, NC 28277-2631, USA

Jamison, Jimi (Musician)
4002 Glendale Dr
Memphis, TN 38128-2408, USA

Jamison, Mikki (Actor)
1501 S Latawah St
Spokane, WA 99203-2252, USA

Jamison, Tim (Athlete, Football Player)
c/o David Dunn *Athletes First*
23091 Mill Creek Dr
Laguna Hills, CA 92653-1258, USA

Jammer, Quentin (Athlete, Football Player)
4020 Murphy Canyon Rd
San Diego, CA 92123-4407, USA

Jampolsky, Gerald (Writer)
Celestial Arts
PO Box 7123
Berkeley, CA 94707-0123

Janaszak, Steve (Athlete, Hockey Player, Olympic Athlete)
81 Bittersweet Hl
Wethersfield, CT 06109-3512, USA

Jance, J A (Writer)
Avon/William Morrow
1350 Avenue of the Americas
New York, NY 10019-4702, USA

Janda, Krystyna (Actor)
Teatr Powszechny
Ul Zamoyskiego 20
Warsaw, POLAND

Jande, Marine (Actor)
Gilla Roos
16 W 22nd St Fl 3
New York, NY 10010-5803

Jane, Jesse (Actor, Adult Film Star, Model)
c/o Staff Member *Media Artists Group*
8222 Melrose Ave Ste 304
Los Angeles, CA 90046-6839, USA

Jane, Thomas (Actor)
c/o Hannah Tenenbaum *Paradigm*
8942 Wilshire Blvd
Beverly Hills, CA 90211-1908, USA

Janecyk, Bob (Athlete, Hockey Player)
6445 Gran Via Dr NE
Rockford, MI 49341-9687, USA

Janecyl, Bob (Athlete, Hockey Player)
5973 Pheasant View Dr NE
Ada, MI 49301-8648, USA

Jane's Addiction (Music Group)
c/o Staff Member *WME|IMG*
9601 Wilshire Blvd
Beverly Hills, CA 90210-5213, USA

Janeski, Jerry (Athlete, Baseball Player)
28901 Via Buena Vis
San Juan Capistrano, CA 92675-5554, USA

Janet, Ernest (Athlete, Football Player)
21838 SE 275th St
Maple Valley, WA 98038-3249, USA

Jang, Jeong (Athlete, Golfer)
7769 Apple Tree Cir
Orlando, FL 32819-4682, USA

Janik, Doug (Athlete, Hockey Player)
51 Senator Ave
Agawam, MA 01001-2129, USA

Janikowski, Bruce (Athlete, Football Player)
2716 W 112th St
Shawnee Mission, KS 66211-3084, USA

Janikowski, Sebastian (Athlete, Football Player)

Janis, Conrad (Actor, Music Group, Musician)
1434 N Genesee Ave
Los Angeles, CA 90046-3930, USA

Janis, Elizabeth (Actor)
c/o Michael Greenwald *Endorse Management Group*
9854 National Blvd # 454
Los Angeles, CA 90034-2713, USA

Janis, Jeff (Athlete, Football Player)
c/o Jim Ivler *Sportstars Inc*
1370 Avenue of the Americas Fl 19
New York, NY 10019-4602, USA

Janish, Paul (Athlete, Baseball Player)
269 County Road 157b
Hallettsville, TX 77964-5267, USA

Janitz, John A (Business Person)
Textron Inc
40 Westminster St Ste 500
Providence, RI 02903-2503, USA

Jankins, Corey (Baseball Player)
Bowman
456 S Church St Apt J1
Lexington, SC 29072-3342, USA

Jankowska-Cieslak, Jadwiga (Actor)
Film Polski
Ul Mazewiecka 6/8
Warsaw 00-950, POLAND

Jankowski, Gene F (Television Host)
American Film Institute
901 15th St NW Ste 700
Washington, DC 20005-2361, USA

Jankowski, Peter (Producer)
c/o Staff Member *Wolf Films Inc (LA)*
260 S Los Robles Ave Ste 309
Pasadena, CA 91101-2897, USA

Jannazzo, Izzy (Boxer)
6924 62nd Ave
Flushing, NY 11379-1120, USA

Janney, Allison (Actor)
c/o Ina Treciokas *Slate PR*
901 N Highland Ave
W Hollywood, CA 90038-2412, USA

Janney, Craig H (Athlete, Hockey Player)
525 Fulton St
Geneva, IL 60134-2650, USA

Janotta, Howard (Athlete, Basketball Player)
18118 Brookwood Frst
San Antonio, TX 78258-4474, USA

Janowicz, Josh (Actor)
c/o Darren Goldberg *Global Creative*
1051 Cole Ave # B
Los Angeles, CA 90038-2601, USA

Janowitz, Will (Actor)
c/o David Ginsberg *Insight*
5358 Melrose Ave # 200W
Los Angeles, CA 90038-5117, USA

Janseen, Daniel (Business Person)
Solvay & Cie
33 Rue du Prince Albert
Brussels 01050, BELGIUM

Jansen, Dan (Athlete, Olympic Athlete, Speed Skater)
PO Box 3354
Mooresville, NC 28117-3354, USA

Jansen, Jim (Actor)
c/o Martin Gage *BRS / Gage Talent Agency (LA)*
6300 Wilshire Blvd Ste 1430
Los Angeles, CA 90048-5216, USA

Jansen, J.J. (Athlete, Football Player)

Jansen, Mallory (Actor)
c/o Tracey Silvester *Independent Management Company*
87-103 Epsom Rd
#15
Rosebery NSW 2018, AUSTRALIA

Janson, Chris (Musician)
c/o Jensen Sussman *Sweet Talk PR*
700 12th Ave S Unit 201
Nashville, TN 37203-3329, USA

Janssen, Cam (Athlete, Hockey Player)
313 Forest Run Dr
Eureka, MO 63025-2119, USA

Janssen, Casey (Athlete, Baseball Player)
232 24th St
Manhattan Beach, CA 90266-4300, USA

Janssen, Famke (Actor)
c/o Cheryl Maisel *PMK/BNC Public Relations*
1840 Century Park E Ste 1400
Los Angeles, CA 90067-2115, USA

Janssen, Frances (Athlete, Baseball Player)
4311 Mayflower Dr
Lafayette, IN 47909-3473, USA

Janssen, Tom (Cartoonist)
Prinsengract 304, 1016 HW
Amsterdam, Netherlands

Janssens, Mark (Athlete, Hockey Player)
115 Central Park W Apt 17A
New York, NY 10023-4295, USA

January, Don (Athlete, Golfer)
5006 Village Pl
Dallas, TX 75248-6029, USA

January, Don (Golfer)
4139 Sicily Dr
Frisco, TX 75034-6659, USA

January, Lois (Actor)
PO Box 1233
Beverly Hills, CA 90213-1233, USA

Jany, Alexandre (Alex) (Swimmer)
104 Blvd Livon
Marseille 13007, FRANCE

Janzen, Edmund (Religious Leader)
General Conference of Mennonite Brethren
8000 W 21st St N
Wichita, KS 67205-1744, USA

Janzen, Henry (Athlete, Football Player)
Sport Manitoba
200 Main St Suite 100
Winnipeg, MB R3C lA8, Canada

Janzen, Lee (Athlete, Golfer)
7512 Dr Phillips Blvd Ste 50-906
Orlando, FL 32819-5420, USA

Janzen, Marty (Athlete, Baseball Player)
650 N Prince St Attn Coachingstaff
Lancaster, PA 17603-3025, USA

Jaqua, Jon (Athlete, Football Player)
34320 McKenzie View Dr
Eugene, OR 97408-9205, USA

Jaquess, Pete (Athlete, Football Player)
631 Cunningham Ln
El Cajon, CA 92019-3504, USA

Jaramillo, Jason (Athlete, Baseball Player)
6111 Madeline Ln
Caledonia, WI 53108-9557, USA

Jaramillo, Rudy (Athlete, Baseball Player)
3855 Echo Brook Ln
Dallas, TX 75229-5222, USA

Jardine, Al (Musician)
PO Box 36
Big Sur, CA 93920-0036, USA

Jarecki, Andrew (Director, Musician, Producer)
c/o Staff Member *Hit the Ground Running Films*
200 W 57th St # 1304
New York, NY 10019-3211, USA

Jarecki, Eugene (Director, Producer)
c/o Staff Member *Charlotte Street Films*
145 Avenue of the Americas Fl 7
New York, NY 10013-1548, USA

Jarman Jr, Claude (Actor)
16 Tamal Vista Ln
Axminster
Kentfield, CA 94904-1006, USA

Jarmusch, Jim (Director)
c/o Bart Walker *ICM Partners*
10250 Constellation Blvd Fl 7
Los Angeles, CA 90067-6207, USA

Jaroncyk, Ryan (Baseball Player)
Bowman
2923 Roseann Ave
Escondido, CA 92027-5306, USA

Jarostchuk, Ilia (Athlete, Football Player)
4 MacArthur Rd
Wellesley, MA 02482-4422, USA

Jarrett, Dale (Race Car Driver)
1510 46th Ave NE
Hickory, NC 28601-8421, USA

Jarrett, Gary (Athlete, Hockey Player)
17716 E Silver Sage Ln
Rio Verde, AZ 85263-5283, USA

Jarrett, Jaiquawn (Athlete, Football Player)
c/o Adisa P Bakari *Kelley Drye & Warren LLP*
3050 K St NW Ste 400
Washington, DC 20007-5100, USA

Jarrett, Jason (Race Car Driver)
Jarrett-Favre Motorsports
2025 Evans St. NE
Box 465
Conover, NC 28613, USA

Jarrett, Morgan Grace (Actor)
c/o Brian Steinberg *Artists First (NY)*
261 Madison Ave Fl 9
New York, NY 10016-2311, USA

Jarrett, Ned (Race Car Driver)
3182 Ninth Tee Dr
Newton, NC 28658-8725, USA

Jarriel, Thomas E (Tom) (Correspondent)
ABC-TV
77 W 66th St
News Dept
New York, NY 10023-6201, USA

Jarrin, Jaime (Athlete, Baseball Player)
725 La Mirada Ave
San Marino, CA 91108-1729, USA

Jarry, Pierre (Athlete, Hockey Player)
4141 Av Pierre-De-Coubertin
Montreal, QC H1V 3N7, Canada

Jarryd, Anders (Tennis Player)
Maaneskoldsgatan 37
Lidkoping 531 00, SWEDEN

Jars of Clay (Music Group)
c/o Mike Snider *WME (Nashville)*
1201 Demonbreun St
Nashville, TN 37203-3140, USA

Ja Rule (Actor, Musician)
10 Lookout Dr
Saddle River, NJ 07458-3314, USA

Jaru the Damaja (Musician)
William Morris Agency
1325 Avenue of the Americas
New York, NY 10019-6026, USA

Jarvis, Bruce (Athlete, Football Player)
22601 SE 20th St
Sammamish, WA 98075-7140, USA

Jarvis, Curtis (Athlete, Football Player)
401 Albert Dr
Gardendale, AL 35071-2588, USA

Jarvis, Doug (Athlete, Coach, Hockey Player)
c/o Staff Member *Montreal Canadiens*
1275 Rue Saint-Antoine O
Montreal, QC H3C 5L2, Canada

Jarvis, James (Athlete, Basketball Player)
2921 NW Elmwood Dr
Corvallis, OR 97330-1237, USA

Jarvis, Katie (Actor)
c/o Billy Lazarus *United Talent Agency (UTA)*
9336 Civic Center Dr
Beverly Hills, CA 90210-3604, USA

Jarvis, Kevin (Athlete, Baseball Player)
1613 Whispering Hills Dr
Franklin, TN 37069-7242, USA

Jarvis, Pat (Athlete, Baseball Player)
4201 Providence Ln
Tucker, GA 30084-2630, USA

Jarvis, Ray (Athlete, Baseball Player)
15 Higgins St Apt 106
Smithfield, RI 02917-4033, USA

Jarvis, Ray (Athlete, Football Player)
315 Kristin Ct W
Brookfield, WI 53045-3585, USA

Jarvis, Wes (Athlete, Hockey Player)
National Training Risks
1155 Stellar Dr
Newmarket, ON L3Y 7B8, Canada

Jaso, John (Athlete, Baseball Player)
494 Weldon St
Redding, CA 96001-3642, USA

Jason, David (Actor)
c/o Staff Member *Lynda Ronan Personal Management*
Hunters House
1 Redcliffe Road
London SW20 9NR, UK

Jason, Dunn (Athlete, Football Player)
2201 Sweetleaf Ct
Lexington, KY 40513-1376, USA

Jason, Peter (Actor)
c/o Staff Member *Diverse Talent Group*
1875 Century Park E Ste 2250
Los Angeles, CA 90067-2563, USA

Jason, Sybil (Actor)
19200 Salt Lake Pl # Pi
Northridge, CA 91326-2345, USA

Jason & deMarco (Music Group)
c/o Staff Member *RJN Music!*
8033 W Sunset Blvd # 574
Los Angeles, CA 90046-2401, USA

Jasontek, Rebecca (Athlete, Olympic Athlete, Swimmer)
1201 Retswood Dr
Loveland, OH 45140-8701, USA

Jasper, Edward (Athlete, Football Player)
110 N Price St
Troup, TX 75789-1429, USA

Jaster, Larry (Athlete, Baseball Player)
1130 Sand Drift Way Apt A
West Palm Beach, FL 33411-5136, USA

Jastremski, Chet (Athlete, Olympic Athlete, Swimmer)
927 S Baldwin Dr
Bloomington, IN 47401-4813, USA

Jastrow, Terry L (Director)
13201 Old Oak Ln
Los Angeles, CA 90049-2501, USA

Jastrow II, Kenneth M (Business Person)
Temple-Inland Inc
303 S Temple Dr
Diboll, TX 75941-2419, USA

Jata, Paul (Athlete, Baseball Player)
5972 Quartz Valley Dr
Newport, KY 41076-7129, USA

Jauch, Ray (Athlete, Football Player)
5306 Harkey Rd
Waxhaw, NC 28173-8461, USA

Jauron, Dick M (Athlete, Coach, Football Coach, Football Player)
602 Wharton Dr
Lake Forest, IL 60045-4827, USA

Jauss, Dave (Athlete, Baseball Player)
3820 13th Ave SW
Naples, FL 34117-5330, USA

Javerbaum, David (Writer)
c/o Staff Member *3 Arts Entertainment*
9460 Wilshire Blvd Fl 7
Beverly Hills, CA 90212-2713, USA

Javier, Julian (Athlete, Baseball Player)
P.O. Box 71
San Francisco de Macoris, USA

Javier, Stan (Athlete, Baseball Player)
11544 NW 43rd Ter
Doral, FL 33178-4235, USA

Javier Galvan Y Fama (Music Group)
c/o Staff Member *Sony Music (Miami)*
404 Washington Ave Ste 700
Miami Beach, FL 33139-6615, USA

Javierre Ortas, Antonio M Cardinal (Religious Leader)
Via Rusticucci 13
Rome 00193, ITALY

Jaworski, Marian Cardinal (Religious Leader)
Mytropolycha Kuria Latynskoho
Ploscha Katedraina 1
29008, UKRAINE

Jaworski, Ronald V (Ron) (Athlete, Football Player, Sportscaster)
18 Brookwood Dr
Medford, NJ 08055-8178, USA

Jax, Garth (Athlete, Football Player)
5335 S Valentia Way Apt 137
Greenwood Village, CO 80111-3106, USA

Jay, Bob (Athlete, Hockey Player)
9 Sunnyside Ave
Burlington, MA 01803-4752, USA

Jay, Joey (Athlete, Baseball Player)
7209 Battenwood Ct
Tampa, FL 33615-2023, USA

Jay, Jon (Athlete, Baseball Player)
c/o Nez Balelo *CAA Sports*
2000 Avenue of the Stars Ste 100
Los Angeles, CA 90067-4705, USA

Jay, Ken (Musician)
Andy Gould Mgmt
9100 Wilshire Blvd Ste 400W
Beverly Hills, CA 90212-3464, USA

Jay, Riemersma (Athlete, Football Player)
3067 Regency Pkwy
Zeeland, MI 49464-6852, USA

Jay, Tony (Actor)
c/o Staff Member *Pakula/King & Associates*
9229 W Sunset Blvd Ste 315
Los Angeles, CA 90069-3403, USA

Jayne (Girardi), Erika (Musician, Reality Star)
c/o Jack Ketsoyan *EMC / Bowery*
8356 Fountain Ave Apt E1
W Hollywood, CA 90069-2968, USA

Jayston, Michael (Actor)
Michael Whitehall
125 Gloucester Road
London SW7 4TE, UNITED KINGDOM (UK)

Jay-Z (Musician, Producer)
c/o Staff Member *Roc Nation*
1411 Broadway Fl 38
New York, NY 10018-3409, USA

Jazz Crusaders, The (Music Group)
Universal
225 W 57th St Fl 5
New York, NY 10019-2104

JazzyFatNastees (Music Group)
c/o Stephanie Mahler *Creative Artists Agency (CAA)*
405 Lexington Ave Fl 19
New York, NY 10174-1800, USA

JB & The Moonshine Band (Music Group)
c/o Lex Lipsitz *LEX Music Group LLC*
1914 Bransford Ave
Nashville, TN 37204-2306, USA

Jbara, Gregory (Actor)
c/o Marilyn Szatmary *SMS Talent*
8383 Wilshire Blvd Ste 230
Beverly Hills, CA 90211-2436, USA

JBJ (Musician)
Q Prime
729 7th Ave Ste 1600
New York, NY 10019-6880, USA

J-Bolt (Producer)
Lightning Bolt Entertainment
3342 S Sandhill Rd Ste 9
Las Vegas, NV 89121-3455, USA

J. Duncan Jr., John (Congressman, Politician)
2207 Rayburn Hob
Washington, DC 20515-2003, USA

Jeager, Andrea (Athlete, Tennis Player)
3137 Devin Dr
Grand Junction, CO 81504-6057, USA

Jean, Norma (Musician)
22 Skyline Dr
Kimberling City, MO 65686-9658, USA

Jean, Wyclef (Musician)
c/o Cara Lewis *Cara Lewis Group*
7 W 18th St Fl 3
New York, NY 10011-4663, USA

Jean-Baptiste, Marianne (Actor)
c/o Elise Konialian *Untitled Entertainment (NY)*
215 Park Ave S Fl 8
New York, NY 10003-1622, USA

Jean-Baptiste, Stanley (Athlete, Football Player)

Jean-Louis, Jimmy (Actor)
c/o Marie Y LeMelle *Platinum Star Public Relations*
343 Pioneer Dr Unit 1705
Glendale, CA 91203-2740, USA

Jeannotte, Dan (Actor)
c/o Daniel Abrams *Oscars Abrams Zimel & Associates*
438 Queen St E
Toronto, ON M5A 1T4, CANADA

Jeanrenaud, Joan (Musician)
Kronos Quartet
1235 9th Ave
San Francisco, CA 94122-2306, USA

Jecha, Ralph (Athlete, Football Player)
717 Vinewood Ave
Willow Springs, IL 60480-1523, USA

Jee, Elizabeth (Actor)
Commercials Unlimited
8383 Wilshire Blvd Ste 850
Beverly Hills, CA 90211-2443, USA

Jee, Rupert (Business Person)
Hello Deli
213 W 53rd St
New York, NY 10019-5805

Jeelani, Abdul (Athlete, Basketball Player)
W525 State Road 59
Palmyra, WI 53156-9741, USA

Jeff, Reinke (Athlete, Football Player)
13821 320th St
New Prague, MN 56071-4126, USA

Jeffcoat, Don (Actor)
c/o Staff Member *The House of Representatives*
3118 Wilshire Blvd Ste D
Santa Monica, CA 90403-2345, USA

Jeffcoat, James W (Jim) (Athlete, Football Player)
5135 Summit Hill Dr
Dallas, TX 75287-7537, USA

Jeffcoat, Mike (Athlete, Baseball Player)
8609 Tuscan Way
Godley, TX 76044-3395, USA

Jefferies, Gregg (Athlete, Baseball Player)
7806 Bernal Ave
Pleasanton, CA 94588-7050, USA

Jefferies, Jim (Comedian)
c/o John Sacks *United Talent Agency (UTA)*
9336 Civic Center Dr
Beverly Hills, CA 90210-3604, USA

Jeffers, Patrick (Athlete, Football Player)
1509 Easy St
Austin, TX 78746-7406, USA

Jeffers, Rusty (Athlete)
PO Box 30081
Phoenix, AZ 85046-0081

Jefferson, Al (Athlete, Basketball Player)
c/o Jeff Schwartz *Excel Sports Management*
1700 Broadway Fl 29
New York, NY 10019-6559, USA

Jefferson, D.C. (Athlete, Football Player)

Jefferson, James (Athlete, Football Player)
11220 NE 53rd St
Kirkland, WA 98033-7505, USA

Jefferson, Jeff (Race Car Driver)
752 State Route 410
Naches, WA 98937-9400, USA

Jefferson, John L (Athlete, Football Player)
43590 Merchant Mill Ter
Leesburg, VA 20176-8228, USA

Jefferson, Reggie (Athlete, Baseball Player)
1881 Raymond Tucker Rd
Tallahassee, FL 32311-8793, USA

Jefferson, Richard (Basketball Player)
New Jersey Nets
390 Murray Hill Pkwy
East Rutherford, NJ 07073-2109, USA

Jefferson, Roy (Athlete, Football Player)
PO Box 182
Annandale, VA 22003-0182, USA

Jefferson, Shawn (Athlete, Football Player)
9607 Versailles Ct
Brentwood, TN 37027-3827, USA

Jefferson, Stan (Athlete, Baseball Player)
801 S Olive Ave UNIT 1522
West Palm Bch, FL 33401-6181, USA

Jefferson, Thad (Athlete, Football Player)
PO Box 1552
Rialto, CA 92377-1552, USA

Jefferson, Tony (Athlete, Football Player)

Jefferson Starship (Music Group)
c/o Staff Member *Fat City Artists*
1906 Chet Atkins Pl Apt 502
Nashville, TN 37212-2122, USA

Jeffery, Aaron (Actor)
c/o Robert Marsala *Wishlab*
195 S Beverly Dr Ste 414
Beverly Hills, CA 90212-3044, USA

Jeffery, Alshon (Athlete, Football Player)
c/o Ashley Smith Becker *Relativity Sports*
2029 Century Park E Ste 1550
Century City, CA 90067-3000, USA

Jeffires, Haywood (Athlete, Football Player)
3818 Hanberry Ln
Pearland, TX 77584-4951, USA

Jeffre, Justin (Musician)
DAS Communications
83 Riverside Dr
New York, NY 10024-5713, USA

Jeffress, Jeremy (Athlete, Baseball Player)
6901 Marlowe Rd
Richmond, VA 23225-4295, USA

Jeffrey, Larry (Athlete, Hockey Player)
35392 Blyth Rd RR 5
Goderich, ON N7A 3Y2, Canada

Jeffries, Chantel (Actor)
c/o Trixie Richter *Rogers & Cowan*
1840 Century Park E Fl 18
Los Angeles, CA 90067-2101, USA

Jeffries, Chris (Basketball Player)
Toronto Raptors
40 Bay St
Air Canada Center
Toronto, ON M5J 2X2, CANADA

Jeffries, Doug (Adult Film Star)
c/o Staff Member *Diva Central Inc*
7510 W Sunset Blvd # 1445
Los Angeles, CA 90046-3408, USA

Jeffries, Jared (Basketball Player)
Washington Wizards
601 F St NW
Washington, DC 20004-1605, USA

Jeffries, Willie (Athlete, Football Coach)
c/o Staff Member *College Football Hall Of Fame*
111 Saint Joseph St S
South Bend, IN 46601-1939, USA

Jelen, Ben (Musician)
c/o Staff Member *Maverick Recording Co (LA)*
3300 Warner Blvd
Burbank, CA 91505-4632, USA

Jelesky, Tom (Athlete, Football Player)
9556 W 1160 N
Demotte, IN 46310-9634, USA

Jelic, Chris (Athlete, Baseball Player)
33 Allegheny Ave Apt 5
Cuddy, PA 15031-9763, USA

Jelinek, Tomas (Athlete, Hockey Player)
c/o Staff Member *Calgary Flames*
PO Box 1540 Stn M
Stn M
Calgary, AB T2P 3B9, Canada

Jelks, Greg (Athlete, Baseball Player)
Slippery Rock Sliders
PO Box 501
Attn: Managers Office
Slippery Rock, PA 16057-0501, USA

Jelley, Thomas (Athlete, Football Player)
200 Tabernacle Rd
Black Mountain, NC 28711-7733, USA

Jells, Dietrich (Athlete, Football Player)
2264 Hideaway Pointe Dr
Little Elm, TX 75068-5983, USA

Jeltz, Steve (Athlete, Baseball Player)
606 W 28th Pl
Lawrence, KS 66046-4620, USA

Jem (Musician)
c/o Seth Friedman *Red Light Management*
5800 Bristol Pkwy Ste 400
Culver City, CA 90230-6898, USA

Jemison, Antawn (Athlete, Basketball Player)
Washington Wizards
601 F St NW
Washington, DC 20004-1605, USA

Jemison, Eddie (Actor)
c/o Gabrielle Krengel *Domain Talent*
1880 Century Park E Ste 1100
Los Angeles, CA 90067-1608, USA

Jemison, Mae C (Astronaut, Doctor)
Jemison Group
PO Box 591455
Houston, TX 77259-1455, USA

Jendresen, Erik (Producer, Writer)
c/o Scott Seidel *WME/IMG*
9601 Wilshire Blvd
Beverly Hills, CA 90210-5213, USA

Jendrick, Megan (Athlete, Olympic Athlete, Swimmer)
USA Swimming
PO Box 8844
Tacoma, WA 98419-0844, USA

Jeni, Richard (Comedian)
c/o Staff Member *Agency for the Performing Arts (APA)*
405 S Beverly Dr Ste 500
Beverly Hills, CA 90212-4425, USA

Jenke, Noel (Athlete, Football Player)
17665 Bonnie Ln
Brookfield, WI 53045-7800, USA

Jenkins, AJ (Athlete, Football Player)
c/o Alan Herman *Sportstars Inc*
1370 Avenue of the Americas Fl 19
New York, NY 10019-4602, USA

Jenkins, Andrew (Actor)
c/o Jon Simmons *Simmons & Scott Entertainment*
7942 Mulholland Dr
Los Angeles, CA 90046-1225, USA

Jenkins, Carter (Actor)
c/o Steven Nossokoff *Untitled Entertainment*
350 S Beverly Dr Ste 200
Beverly Hills, CA 90212-4819, USA

Jenkins, Charlie (Athlete, Olympic Athlete, Track Athlete)
12826 Forest Creek Ct
Sykesville, MD 21784-5526

Jenkins, Cullen (Athlete, Football Player)
4018 S Parker Way
De Pere, WI 54115-1696, USA

Jenkins, Daniel (Actor)
S M S Talent
8730 W Sunset Blvd Ste 440
Los Angeles, CA 90069-2277, USA

Jenkins, David W (Athlete, Figure Skater, Olympic Athlete)
5947 S Atlanta Ave
Tulsa, OK 74105-7545, USA

Jenkins, Dean (Athlete, Hockey Player)
244 Fairmount St
Lowell, MA 01852-3708, USA

Jenkins, Don (Athlete, Football Player)
49 W Main St
Frostburg, MD 21532-1640, USA

Jenkins, Ed (Athlete, Football Player)
1750 Washington St Ste B1
Boston, MA 02118-1831, USA

Jenkins, Ferguson (Athlete, Baseball Player)
Ferguson Jenkins Foundation
PO Box 664
Lewiston, NY 14092-0664, USA

Jenkins, Fletcher (Athlete, Football Player)
2347 S J St
Tacoma, WA 98405-3831, USA

Jenkins, Geoff (Athlete, Baseball Player)
5161 E Pasadena Ave
Phoenix, AZ 85018-1914, USA

Jenkins, George (Designer, Director)
2402 4th St Apt 10
Santa Monica, CA 90405-3668, USA

Jenkins, Hayes Alan (Athlete, Figure Skater, Olympic Athlete)
3183 Regency Pl
Westlake, OH 44145-6735, USA

Jenkins, Izel (Athlete, Football Player)
5106 Masters Ln N
Wilson, NC 27896-9136, USA

Jenkins, James (Baseball Player)
Cincinnati Indianapolis Clowns
630 Malcolm X Blvd
New York, NY 10037-1247, USA

Jenkins, Janoris (Athlete, Football Player)
c/o Malik Hafeez Shareef *Dimensional Sports, Inc.*
3148 Circle Dr SW
Roanoke, VA 24018-2110, USA

Jenkins, Jarvis (Athlete, Football Player)
c/o Joe Flanagan *BTI Sports Advisors*
615 South Blvd Apt C
Oak Park, IL 60302-4606, USA

Jenkins, Jelani (Athlete, Football Player)
c/o Joby Branion *Vanguard Sports Group*
23091 Mill Creek Dr
Laguna Hills, CA 92653-1258, USA

Jenkins, Jerry B (Writer)
Tyndale House Publishers
PO Box 80
351 Executive Dr
Wheaton, IL 60187-0080, USA

Jenkins, John (Athlete, Football Player)

Jenkins, Jolie (Actor)
c/o Staff Member *TalentWorks*
3500 W Olive Ave Ste 1400
Burbank, CA 91505-5512, USA

Jenkins, Kackie (Butch) (Actor)
PO Box 541G
Fairview, NC 28730, USA

Jenkins, Kaitlyn (Actor)
c/o Kim Matuka *Schuller Talent (LA)*
332 S Beverly Dr Ste 100
Beverly Hills, CA 90212-4812, USA

Jenkins, Katherine (Musician)
c/o Staff Member *Nettwerk Management (LA)*
1545 Wilcox Ace
Suite 200
Los Angeles, CA 90028, USA

Jenkins, Ken (Actor)
c/o Chris Schmidt *Paradigm*
8942 Wilshire Blvd
Beverly Hills, CA 90211-1908, USA

Jenkins, Kerry (Athlete, Football Player)
5492 Scout Trace Ln
Hoover, AL 35244-3912, USA

Jenkins, Kris (Athlete, Football Player)
309 E Morehead St Apt 622
Charlotte, NC 28202-2310, USA

Jenkins, Loren (Journalist)
Washington Post
Editorial Dept
1150 15th St NW
Washington, DC 20071-0001, USA

Jenkins, Lynn (Congressman, Politician)
1122 Longworth Hob
Washington, DC 20515-3209, USA

Jenkins, Malcolm (Athlete, Football Player)
c/o Tom Condon *Creative Artists Agency (CAA)*
401 Commerce St PH
Nashville, TN 37219-2516, USA

Jenkins, Marilyn (Athlete, Baseball Player, Commentator)
1511 Van Auken St SE
Grand Rapids, MI 49508-2511, USA

Jenkins, Mark (Writer)
c/o Staff Member *HarperCollins Publishers*
195 Broadway Fl 2
New York, NY 10007-3132, USA

Jenkins, MarTay (Athlete, Football Player)
3998 N 149th Ave
Goodyear, AZ 85395-8228, USA

Jenkins, Maxwell (Actor)
c/o Chase Lehner *Slate PR*
901 N Highland Ave
W Hollywood, CA 90038-2412, USA

Jenkins, Mike (Athlete, Football Player)
c/o Ashley Smith Becker *Relativity Sports*
2029 Century Park E Ste 1550
Century City, CA 90067-3000, USA

Jenkins, Patty (Director, Writer)
c/o Michael Sugar *Anonymous Content*
3532 Hayden Ave
Culver City, CA 90232-2413, USA

Jenkins, Richard (Actor)
c/o Rhonda Price *Gersh*
41 Madison Ave Ste 3301
New York, NY 10010-2210, USA

Jenkins, Robert (Athlete, Football Player)
2878 Fieldview Ter
San Ramon, CA 94583-1900, USA

Jenkins, Stephan (Music Group, Musician)
c/o Eric Godtland *Eric Godtland Management*
1040 Mariposa St Ste 200
San Francisco, CA 94107-2520, USA

Jenkins, Terrence (Actor)
c/o Liza Anderson *Anderson Group Public Relations*
8060 Melrose Ave Fl 4
Los Angeles, CA 90046-7038, USA

Jenkins, Tom (Athlete, Golfer)
107 Ranch Road 620 S
Lakeway, TX 78734-3942, USA

Jenkins, Walt (Athlete, Football Player)
22570 Thorncliffe St
Southfield, MI 48033-3426, USA

Jenks, Bobby (Athlete, Baseball Player)
3958 E Northridge Cir
Mesa, AZ 85215-1080, USA

Jenner, Blake (Actor)
c/o David (Dave) Fleming *Atlas Artists*
9220 W Sunset Blvd Ste 225
Los Angeles, CA 90069-3513, USA

Jenner, Brody (Reality Star)
6171 Latigo Canyon Rd
Malibu, CA 90265-2820, USA

Jenner, Caitlyn (Activist, Athlete, Decathlon Athlete, Olympic Athlete, Reality Star)
c/o Dollie Lucero *Boulevard Management*
21731 Ventura Blvd Ste 300
Woodland Hills, CA 91364-1851, USA

Jenner, Kendall (Model, Reality Star)
c/o Angela Ford *Boulevard Management*
21731 Ventura Blvd Ste 300
Woodland Hills, CA 91364-1851, USA

Jenner, Kris (Business Person, Reality Star)
c/o Angela Ford *Boulevard Management*
21731 Ventura Blvd Ste 300
Woodland Hills, CA 91364-1851, USA

Jenner, Kylie (Actor, Model)
c/o Katie Greenthal *The Lede Company*
9701 Wilshire Blvd # 930
Beverly Hills, CA 90212-2020, USA

Jennings, Adam (Athlete, Football Player)
330 Suwanee Ave
Suwanee, GA 30024-6768, USA

Jennings, Brandon (Athlete, Basketball Player)
c/o Bill Duffy *BDA Sports Management*
700 Ygnacio Valley Rd Ste 330
Walnut Creek, CA 94596-3838, USA

Jennings, Doug (Athlete, Baseball Player)
PO Box 812692
Boca Raton, FL 33481-2692, USA

Jennings, Garth (Director)
c/o Frank Wuliger *Gersh*
9465 Wilshire Blvd Ste 600
Beverly Hills, CA 90212-2605, USA

Jennings, Grant (Athlete, Hockey Player)
PO Box 190434
Anchorage, AK 99519-0434, USA

Jennings, Greg (Athlete, Football Player)
977 Green Ridge Dr
De Pere, WI 54115-7656, USA

Jennings, Jason (Athlete, Baseball Player)
6316 Caroline Dr
Frisco, TX 75034-4838, USA

Jennings, Jonas (Athlete, Football Player)
123 Davis Rd
Fayetteville, GA 30215-4912, USA

Jennings, Keith (Athlete, Basketball Player)
695 Holly Crest Dr
Culpeper, VA 22701-3071, USA

Jennings, Keith (Athlete, Football Player)
119 Axtell Dr
Summerville, SC 29485-3403, USA

Jennings, Ken (Actor)

Jennings, Lynn (Athlete, Olympic Athlete, Track Athlete)
PO Box 153
Weld, ME 04285-0153, USA

Jennings, Rashad (Athlete, Football Player)
c/o Adam Heller *Vantage Management Group*
518 Reamer Dr
Carnegie, PA 15106-1845, USA

Jennings, Richard (Athlete, Football Player)
975 Cobble Shores Dr
Sacramento, CA 95831-4318, USA

Jennings, Rick (Athlete, Football Player)
442 Sterling Pl Apt 12
Brooklyn, NY 11238-4536, USA

Jennings, Robin (Athlete, Baseball Player)
6052 Kingsford Ave
Park City, UT 84098-6316, USA

Jennings, Shooter (Musician)
c/o Michael Moses *Baker Winokur Ryder Public Relations*
9100 Wilshire Blvd
W Tower #500
Beverly Hills, CA 90212-3415, USA

Jennings, Stanford (Athlete, Football Player)
403 G St
Beckley, WV 25801-6613, USA

Jennings, Will (Musician, Songwriter)
c/o Staff Member *Gorfaine/Schwartz Agency Inc*
4111 W Alameda Ave Ste 509
Burbank, CA 91505-4171, USA

Jennings Desmond, Desmond (Athlete, Baseball Player)
2482 Vera Cruz Dr
Birmingham, AL 35235-2233, USA

Jenrette, Richard H (Business Person)
67 E 93rd St
New York, NY 10128-1331, USA

Jenrette, Rita (Writer)
9270 Alden Dr
Beverly Hills, CA 90210, USA

Jens, Salome (Actor)
Badgley Connor Talent
9229 W Sunset Blvd Ste 311
Los Angeles, CA 90069-3403, USA

Jens, Walter (Writer)
Sonnenstr 5
Tubingen, GERMANY

Jensen, Al (Athlete, Hockey Player)
NHL Scouting Service
50 Bay St 11th Fl
Toronto, ON M5J 3A5, Canada

Jensen, Bob (Athlete, Football Player)
566 Pineway Cir
Bloomfield Hills, MI 48302-2130, USA

Jensen, Chris (Athlete, Hockey Player)
20310 Enright Way
Farmington, MN 55024-2022, USA

Jensen, David (Athlete, Hockey Player)
65 Cheryl Ln
Holliston, MA 01746-1234, USA

Jensen, Derrick (Athlete, Football Player)
4423 Luke Ave
Destin, FL 32541-3585, USA

Jensen, Erik (Actor)
2419 Outpost Dr
Los Angeles, CA 90068-2644, USA

Jensen, Flemming (Athlete, Football Player)
9775 S Deer Brook Cir
Sandy, UT 84092-6035, USA

Jensen, Jerry (Athlete, Football Player)
2714 86th St SE
Everett, WA 98208-3548, USA

Jensen, Jim (Athlete, Football Player)
9821 NW 18th Ct
Plantation, FL 33322-5694, USA

Jensen, Jim D (Athlete, Football Player)
239 Habitat Cir
Windsor, CO 80550-6197, USA

Jensen, Karen (Actor)
9363 Wilshire Blvd
#212
Beverly Hills, CA 90210, USA

Jensen, Luke (Athlete, Tennis Player)
370 Ferry Lndg
Atlanta, GA 30328-3539, USA

Jensen, Marcus (Athlete, Baseball Player, Olympic Athlete)
19550 N Grayhawk Dr Unit 1134
Scottsdale, AZ 85255-3987, USA

Jensen, Maren (Actor)
Kessler Schneider Co
15260 Ventura Blvd Ste 1040
Sherman Oaks, CA 91403-5345

Jensen, Ryan (Athlete, Football Player)
c/o Michael McCartney *Priority Sports & Entertainment (Chicago)*
325 N La Salle Dr Ste 650
Chicago, IL 60654-8182, USA

Jensen, Ryan (Athlete, Baseball Player)
3059 S Larkspur St
Gilbert, AZ 85295-2034, USA

Jensen, Steve (Athlete, Hockey Player)
24921 Arena Dr
Deerwood, MN 56444-8780, USA

Jent, Chris (Athlete, Basketball Player)
445 Retreat Ln W
Powell, OH 43065-9768, USA

Jeong, Ken (Actor)
c/o Michelle Benson Margolis *The Lede Company*
9701 Wilshire Blvd # 930
Beverly Hills, CA 90212-2020, USA

Jeosen, Kevin (Athlete, Baseball Player)
4533 E County Down Dr
Chandler, AZ 85249-7339, USA

Jepsen, Carly Rae (Musician)
c/o Scooter Braun *SB Management*
755 N Bonhill Rd
Los Angeles, CA 90049-2303, USA

Jepsen, Les (Athlete, Basketball Player)
8075 9th Street Way N
Saint Paul, MN 55128-5360, USA

Jepsen, Roger (Politician)
3542 Pennyroyal Rd
Port Charlotte, FL 33953-4606, USA

Jeray, Nicole (Athlete, Golfer)
3728 Ridgeland Ave
Berwyn, IL 60402-4020, USA

Jeremiah (Musician)
c/o Staff Member *Siri Music Entertainment*
1324 Lexington Ave
New York, NY 10128-1145, USA

Jeremih (Musician)
c/o James Cruz *Combs Enterprises*
1440 Broadway Frnt 3
New York, NY 10018-2301, USA

Jeremy, Ron (Actor, Adult Film Star)
c/o Mike Esterman *Esterman.Com, LLC*
Prefers to be contacted via email
Baltimore, MD XXXXX, USA

Jericho, Chris (Athlete, Wrestler)
c/o Michael Braverman *Braverman Bloom Company*
14320 Ventura Blvd Ste 632
Sherman Oaks, CA 91423-2717, USA

Jermann, David (Artist)
2 Union St
Sparkill, NY 10976-1214

Jernigan, Jerrel (Athlete, Football Player)
c/o Hadley Engelhard *Enter-Sports Management*
6000 Lake Forrest Dr Ste 370
Atlanta, GA 30328-5902, USA

Jernigan, Tamara E (Tammy) (Astronaut)
4268 Brindisi Pl
Pleasanton, CA 94566-2238, USA

Jernigan, Timmy (Athlete, Football Player)

Jerod-Eddie, Tony (Athlete, Football Player)
c/o David Dunn *Athletes First*
23091 Mill Creek Dr
Laguna Hills, CA 92653-1258, USA

Jerry, John (Athlete, Football Player)
c/o Drew Rosenhaus *Rosenhaus Sports Representation*
3921 Alton Rd # 440
Miami Beach, FL 33140-3852, USA

Jerry, Reichow (Athlete, Football Player)
9 Meredith Drive
Santa Fe, NM 87506, USA

Jervey, Travis (Athlete, Football Player)
22 Sand Dollar Dr
Isle Of Palms, SC 29451-2647, USA

Jerzembeck, Mike (Athlete, Baseball Player)
10625 S Hall Dr
Charlotte, NC 28270-0285, USA

Jeselnik, Anthony (Actor, Comedian)
c/o Christie Smith *Rise Management*
6338 Wilshire Blvd
Los Angeles, CA 90048-5002, USA

Jessamy, Charles (Athlete, Football Player)
1836 S Shenandoah St
Los Angeles, CA 90035-4327, USA

Jessen, Ruth (Athlete, Golfer)
2823 NE Meadow Pl
Lake Forest Park, WA 98155-5348, USA

Jessie, Tim (Athlete, Football Player)
300 Cherry St APT 1
Shepherdsvlle, KY 40165-5971, USA

Jessiman, Hugh (Athlete, Hockey Player)
480 Hollow Tree Ridge Rd
Darien, CT 06820-3032, USA

Jessup, Bill (Athlete, Football Player)
13901 Sherwood St
Dr Unit 137D
Westminster, CA 92683-9502, USA

Jessup, Connor (Actor)
c/o Pam Winter *Gary Goddard Agency (GGA)*
304-250 The Esplanade
Toronto, ON M5A 1J2, CANADA

Jestadt, Garry (Athlete, Baseball Player)
9875 E Larkspur Dr
Scottsdale, AZ 85260-5145, USA

Jester, Virgil (Athlete, Baseball Player)
8130 Raleigh Pl
Westminster, CO 80031-4317, USA

Jet (Actor)
c/o Staff Member *Creative Artists Agency (CAA)*
2000 Avenue of the Stars Ste 100
Los Angeles, CA 90067-4705, USA

Jeter, Brad (Race Car Driver)
PO Box 6541
Greenville, SC 29606-6541, USA

Jeter, Derek (Athlete, Baseball Player)
c/o Staff Member *Miami Marlins*
501 Marlins Way
Miami, FL 33125-1121, USA

Jeter, Gene (Athlete, Football Player)
4854 Delray Rd
Montgomery, AL 36116-3502, USA

Jeter, John (Athlete, Baseball Player)
1012 N 5th St
Monroe, LA 71201-5531, USA

Jeter, Perry (Athlete, Football Player)
772 Lincoln Blvd
Steubenville, OH 43952-3256, USA

Jeter, Shawn (Athlete, Baseball Player)
4287 Walford St
Columbus, OH 43224-2342, USA

Jeter, Tommy (Athlete, Football Player)
14 Slate Path Dr
Spring, TX 77382-2009, USA

Jeter, Tony (Athlete, Football Player)
71 S Orange Ave
South Orange, NJ 07079-1715, USA

Jethro Tull (Music Group)
c/o Staff Member *WME|IMG*
9601 Wilshire Blvd
Beverly Hills, CA 90210-5213, USA

Jetsons (Music Group)
Signature Entertainment
5727 Topanga Canyon Blvd Apt 3
Woodland Hills, CA 91367-4847

Jett, Brent W (Astronaut)
5509 Crawford St
Houston, TX 77004-7119, USA

Jett, Jack E (Television Host)
c/o Collin Reno *WME|IMG*
9601 Wilshire Blvd
Beverly Hills, CA 90210-5213, USA

Jett, James (Athlete, Football Player)
PO Box 430
Kearneysville, WV 25430-0430, USA

Jett, Joan (Musician)
c/o Erica Gerard *PMK/BNC Public Relations*
622 3rd Ave Fl 8
New York, NY 10017-6707, USA

Jett, John (Athlete, Football Player)
9279 Courthouse Rd
Lancaster, VA 22503-2116, USA

Jetton, Paul (Athlete, Football Player)
1062 Harmon Hills Rd
Dripping Springs, TX 78620-3642, USA

Jevanord, Oystein (Musician)
Bandana Mgmt
11 Elvaston Place
#300
London SW7 5QC, UNITED KINGDOM (UK)

Jewel (Musician, Songwriter)
c/o Erica Gerard *PMK/BNC Public Relations*
622 3rd Ave Fl 8
New York, NY 10017-6707, USA

Jewell, Buddy (Musician)
c/o Staff Member *WME (Nashville)*
1201 Demonbreun St
Nashville, TN 37203-3140, USA

Jewell, Geri (Actor)

Jewett, Bob (Athlete, Football Player)
991 N Shore Dr
Springport, MI 49284-9414, USA

Jewett, Robert (Athlete, Football Player)
991 N Shore Dr
Springport, MI 49284-9414, USA

Jewett, Trent (Athlete, Baseball Player)
330 Sullivan Rd
Glen Morgan, WV 25813-7604, USA

Jewett-Beckett, Christine (Athlete, Baseball Player, Commentator)
PO Box 126
Stewart Valley, SK S0N 2P0, Canada

Jewison, Norman (Actor, Director, Producer)
c/o Staff Member *Yorktown Productions Ltd*
18 Gloucester Ln
Floor 5
Toronto ON M4Y 1L5, CANADA

Jewitt-Beckett, Christine (Baseball Player)
PO Box 126
Stewart Valley, SK S0N 2P0, CANADA

J. Fleischmann, Charles (Congressman, Politician)
511 Cannon Hob
Washington, DC 20515-0607, USA

J. Forbes, Randy (Congressman, Politician)
2438 Rayburn Hob
Washington, DC 20515-3518, USA

J. Heck, Joseph (Congressman, Politician)
132 Cannon Hob
Washington, DC 20515-1006, USA

Jiang, Tian (Musician)
Columbia Artists Mgmt Inc
165 W 57th St
New York, NY 10019-2201, USA

Jiang, Tiefeng (Artist)
Fingerhut Gallery
690 Bridgeway
Sausalito, CA 94965-2251, USA

Jiang, Zemin (President)
Central Military Commitee
Zhonganahai
Beijing, CHINA

Jibawi, Anwar (Actor, Comedian, Internet Star)
c/o Joe Izzi *WME|IMG*
9601 Wilshire Blvd
Beverly Hills, CA 90210-5213, USA

Jiles, Dwayne (Athlete, Football Player)
3712 Churchill Ct
Plano, TX 75075-6119, USA

Jiles, Pam (Athlete, Track Athlete)
2623 Wisteria St
New Orleans, LA 70122-6041

Jiles, Pamela (Pam) (Athlete, Track Athlete)
2623 Wisteria St
New Orleans, LA 70122-6041, USA

Jillette, Penn (Comedian)
c/o Peter Golden *Golden Entertainment West*
5328 Alhama Dr
Woodland Hills, CA 91364-2013, USA

Jillian, Ann (Actor)
PO Box 57739
Sherman Oaks, CA 91413-2739, USA

Jillson, Jeff (Athlete, Hockey Player)
14 Lincoln Dr
North Smithfield, RI 02896-6955, USA

Jim, Ridlon (Athlete, Football Player)
4468 E Lake Rd
Cazenovia, NY 13035-9214, USA

Jimenez, Carla (Actor)
c/o Liza Anderson *Anderson Group Public Relations*
8060 Melrose Ave Fl 4
Los Angeles, CA 90046-7038, USA

Jimenez, Joe (Athlete, Golfer)
PO Box 1737
Boerne, TX 78006-6737, USA

Jimenez, Manny (Baseball Player)
Kansas City A's
24003 Colmar Ln
Murrieta, CA 92562-1978, USA

Jimenez, Miguel Angel (Athlete, Golfer)
Advantage International
1751 Pinnacle Dr Ste 1500
Mc Lean, VA 22102-3833, USA

Jimenez, Nicario (Artist)
3841 29th Ave SW
Naples, FL 34117-8429, USA

Jimenez, Ubaldo (Athlete, Baseball Player)
c/o Pat Rooney *SFX Baseball*
676 N Michigan Ave Ste 3000
Chicago, IL 60611-2860, USA

Jimenez Pons, Eduardo (Writer)
c/o Gabriel Blanco *Gabriel Blanco Iglesias (Mexico)*
Rio Balsas 35-32
Colonia Cuauhtemoc
DF 06500, Mexico

Jimerson, Charlton (Athlete, Baseball Player)
22048 Betlen Way
Castro Valley, CA 94546-6504, USA

Jiminez, Cedric (Director)
c/o Lionel Ament *Film Talents*
36 Rue Du Louvre
Paris 07500, FRANCE

Jiminez, Houston (Athlete, Baseball Player)
Asheville Tourists
30 Buchanan Pl
Attn: Coaching Staff
Asheville, NC 28801-4243, USA

Jiminez, Miguel (Athlete, Baseball Player)
128 Post Ave Apt 5O
New York, NY 10034-3439, USA

Jimmy, Keyes (Athlete, Football Player)
5338 Southlake Dr
Milton, FL 32571-7000, USA

Jimmy, Richards (Athlete, Football Player)
733 Vanderbilt Ave
Virginia Beach, VA 23451-3632, USA

Jimmy Eat World (Music Group)
21 W Berridge Ln
Phoenix, AZ 85013-1509, USA

Jimoh, Ade (Athlete, Football Player)
4725 S Kaitlyn Ann Cir
Salt Lake City, UT 84123-3472, USA

Jin, Svoboda (Director)
Na Balkane 120
Prague 3, CZECH REPUBLIC

Jindal, Bobby (Politician)

Jindrak, Mark (Wrestler)
2355 Reyer Rd
Auburn, NY 13021

Jinks, Dan (Actor, Producer)

Jirsa, Ron (Coach)
University of Georgia
Athletic Dept
Athens, GA 30613, USA

Jirschele, Mike (Athlete, Baseball Player)
186 Robert St
Clintonville, WI 54929-1153, USA

JJ Grey and Mofro (Music Group)
c/o Jesse Aratow *Madison House*
1401 Walnut St Ste 500
Boulder, CO 80302-5332, USA

J. Kucinich, Dennis (Congressman, Politician)
2445 Rayburn Hob
Washington, DC 20515-0907, USA

J-Kwon (Musician)
c/o Staff Member *So So Def Recordings Inc*
1350 Spring St NW Ste 750
Atlanta, GA 30309-2870, USA

JLS (Music Group, Musician)
c/o Staff Member *Modest! Management*
91A Peterborough Rd
London SW6 3BU, UNITED KINGDOM

J. Markey, Edward (Congressman, Politician)
2108 Rayburn Hob
Washington, DC 20515-2107, USA

Joannou, Dakis (Business Person)
Deste Foundation Centre For Contemporary Art
Filellinon 11 & Em. Pappa street
Athens 142 34, Greece

Joanou, Phil (Actor, Director)
c/o Staff Member *United Talent Agency (UTA)*
9336 Civic Center Dr
Beverly Hills, CA 90210-3604, USA

Job, Brian (Swimmer)
PO Box 70427
Sunnyvale, CA 94086-0427, USA

Jobe, Brandt (Athlete, Golfer)
2433 NW Grand Cir
Oklahoma City, OK 73116-4123, USA

Jobert, Marlene (Actor)
c/o Staff Member *ArtMedia*
8 rue Danielle Casanova
Paris 75002, FRANCE

Jobko, William (Athlete, Football Player)
770 Fawn Ct
Loganville, GA 30052-3270, USA

Jobrani, Maz (Actor)
c/o Elizabeth Much *East 2 West Collective*
11022 Santa Monica Blvd Ste 350
Los Angeles, CA 90025-7532, USA

Joc, Yung (Musician)
100 Rock Creek Trl
Fayetteville, GA 30214-5355, USA

Jochum, Betsy (Athlete, Baseball Player, Commentator)
22997 Brick Rd
South Bend, IN 46628-9719, USA

Jocketty, Walt (Commentator)
520 N and South Rd # AQT304
Saint Louis, MO 63130-3826, USA

Jodat, Jim (Athlete, Football Player)
9687 Kensington Dr
Huntington Beach, CA 92646-4018, USA

Jodie, Brett (Athlete, Baseball Player)
1359 Corley Mill Rd
Lexington, SC 29072-7635, USA

Jodorowsky, Alejandro (Actor, Director)
3 Allee Marie Laurent
Paris F-75 020, France

Jodzio, Rick (Athlete, Hockey Player)
31202 Boca Raton Pl
Laguna Niguel, CA 92677-2484

Joe (Musician)
c/o Staff Member *Jive Records*
550 Madison Ave Frnt 1
New York, NY 10022-3211, USA

Joe, Billy (Athlete, Football Player)
3964 Butler Springs Way
Hoover, AL 35226-6234, USA

Joe, Devlin ' (Athlete, Football Player)
3715 Schintzius Rd
Eden, NY 14057-9790, USA

Joe, Leon (Athlete, Football Player)
5250 Grand Ave Ste 14
Gurnee, IL 60031-1877, USA

Joe, Reliford (Athlete, Baseball Player)
PO Box 1007
Douglas, GA 31534-1007, USA

Joe, William (Billy) (Football Player)
Florida A&M University
Athletic Dept
Tallahassee, FL 32307-0001, USA

Joeckel, Luke (Athlete, Football Player)
c/o Ben Dogra *Relativity Sports*
2029 Century Park E Ste 1550
Century City, CA 90067-3000, USA

Joel, Alexa Ray (Musician)
c/o Pete Pappalardo *Artist Group International (NY)*
150 E 58th St Fl 19
New York, NY 10155-1900, USA

Joel, Billy (Musician, Songwriter)
211 Elizabeth St Apt 3N
New York, NY 10012-4290, USA

Joel, Phil (Musician)
245 4th Ave S
Franklin, TN 37064-2623, USA

Joel, Piñeiro (Athlete, Baseball Player)
3410 Poinciana Ave
Miami, FL 33133-6525, USA

Joelson, Tsianina (Actor)
c/o Patti Felker *Felker, Toczek, Gellman, Suddleson*
10880 Wilshire Blvd Ste 2080
Los Angeles, CA 90024-4120, USA

Joens, Michael (Writer)
c/o Natasha Kern *Natasha Kern Literary Agency*
PO Box 1069
White Salmon, WA 98672-1069, USA

Joerger, David (Athlete, Basketball Coach, Basketball Player, Coach)
c/o Warren LeGarie *Warren LeGarie Sports Management*
1108 Masonic Ave
San Francisco, CA 94117-2915, USA

Joey+Rory (Music Group)
c/o Aaron Carnahan *Aaron Carnahan Management*
Prefers to be contacted by telephone or email
USA

Joffee, Roland (Director, Producer)
Lightmotive
662 N Robertson Blvd
W Hollywood, CA 90069-5022, USA

Jofre, Eder (Boxer)
Alamo de Ministero Rocha
Azevedo 373 C Cesar 21-15
Sao Paulo, BRAZIL

Jogia, Avan (Actor)
c/o Ben Levine *LINK Entertainment*
11872 La Grange Ave
Los Angeles, CA 90025-5282, USA

Jogis, Chris (Athlete)
7 Birch Rd
Larchmont, NY 10538-1526

Johannesen, Glenn (Athlete, Hockey Player)
10 Granby Ct
Derwood, MD 20855-1406, USA

Johannesen, Lena (Athlete)
PO Box 325
Culver City, CA 90232-0325

Johanns, Michael (Politician)
4597 S Atlantic Ave Bldg B
Port Orange, FL 32127-6983, USA

Johannsen, Jake (Actor, Comedian)
c/o Pam Ellis *Ellis Talent Group*
4705 Laurel Canyon Blvd Ste 300
Valley Village, CA 91607-5901, USA

Johannson, John (Athlete, Hockey Player)
3408 Zenith Ave S
Minneapolis, MN 55416-4622, USA

Johansen, David (Musician)
c/o Nina Nisenholtz *N2N Entertainment*
610 Harbor St Apt 3
Venice, CA 90291-5516, USA

Johansen, Iris (Writer)
c/o Author Mail *Bantam-Dell Publishing (NY)*
1745 Broadway
New York, NY 10019-4640, USA

Johansen, Trevor (Athlete, Hockey Player)
6741 N Placita Acebo
Tucson, AZ 85750-1049, USA

Johanson, Erika (Writer)
c/o Gabriel Blanco *Gabriel Blanco Iglesias (Mexico)*
Rio Balsas 35-32
Colonia Cuauhtemoc
DF 06500, Mexico

Johanson, Sue (Talk Show Host)
42 Parade Sq
Toronto, ON M1C 3T6, CANADA

Johansson, Bjorn (Athlete, Hockey Player)
Stenkulla
Odensbacken S-71593, Sweden

Johansson, Calle (Athlete, Hockey Player)
1708 Mayfair Pl
Crofton, MD 21114-2625, USA

Johansson, Mathias (Athlete, Hockey Player)
Ringgatan 17 A
Karlstad S-65349, SWEDEN

Johansson, Ove (Athlete, Football Player)
3511 Goodfellow Ln
Amarillo, TX 79121-1613, USA

Johansson, Paul (Actor)
c/o Gordon Gilbertson *Gilbertson Management*
1334 3rd Street Promenade Ste 201
Santa Monica, CA 90401-1320, USA

Johansson, Per-Ulrik (Athlete, Golfer)
19489 Harbor Rd
Jupiter, FL 33469-2345, USA

Johansson, Roger (Athlete, Hockey Player)
Fridemsgatan 9
Karlstad S-65461, Sweden

Johansson, Scarlett (Actor)
c/o CeCe Yorke *True Public Relations*
3575 Cahuenga Blvd W Ste 360
Los Angeles, CA 90068-1361, USA

Johjima, Kenji (Athlete, Baseball Player)
2412 109th Ave SE
Bellevue, WA 98004-7332, USA

John, Charles (Politician)
131 S Walnut St
Starke, FL 32091-3954, USA

John, Daymond (Business Person, Designer, Reality Star)
The Shark Group
214 W 39th St Ph B
New York, NY 10018-5498, USA

John, Elton (Musician, Songwriter)
c/o Staff Member *Rocket Music Management*
1 Blythe Rd
London W14 0HG, UNITED KINGDOM

John, Gottfried (Actor)
Elisabethweg 4
Utting, GERMANY D-86919

John, John (Politician)
95 Hill Top Dr
East Greenwich, RI 02818-4024, USA

John, Rienstra (Athlete, Football Player)
5056 Briscoglen Dr
Colorado Springs, CO 80906-8612, USA

John, Tommy (Athlete, Baseball Player)
c/o Kim Berger
760 Shoreline Dr
Cicero, IN 46034-9651, USA

John, Tylyn (Model)
813 Harbor Blvd # 133
W Sacramento, CA 95691-2201

Johncock, Gordon (Race Car Driver)
8740 Wickert Rd
South Branch, MI 48761-9626, USA

John-Kamen, Hannah (Actor)
c/o Romilly Bowlby *DDA Public Relations*
192-198 Vauxhall Bridge Rd
London SW1V 1DX, UNITED KINGDOM

Johns, Bibi (Actor)
D-82049
Pullach, Germany

Johns, Cindy (Actor)
PO Box 369
Arlington, TX 76004-0369

Johns, Daniel (Musician)
John Watson Mgmt
PO Box 281
Sunny Hills, NSW 02010, AUSTRALIA

Johns, Doug (Athlete, Baseball Player)
1131 SW 72nd Ave
Plantation, FL 33317-4125, USA

Johns, Freeman (Athlete, Football Player)
906 Sally Cir
Wichita Falls, TX 76301-7230, USA

Johns, Geoff (Producer)
c/o Staff Member *DC Entertainment*
1700 Broadway Frnt 7
New York, NY 10019-5934, USA

Johns, Glynis (Actor)
11645 Gorham Ave Apt 309
Los Angeles, CA 90049-4758, USA

Johns, Jasper (Artist)
PO Box 642
Sharon, CT 06069-0642, USA

Johns, Keith (Athlete, Baseball Player)
Arkansas Travelers
PO Box 55066
Attn: Coaching Staff
Little Rock, AR 72215-5066, USA

Johns, Lori (Race Car Driver)
PO Box 3667
Corpus Christi, TX 78463-3667, USA

Johns, Marcus (Actor)
c/o Sharon Lane *Lane Management Group*
4370 Tujunga Ave Ste 130
Studio City, CA 91604-2769, USA

Johns, Milton (Actor)
78 Temple Sheen Rd
London SW14 7RJ, ENGLAND

Johnson, Aaron (Athlete, Hockey Player)
4798 Chatelaine Dr
Dublin, OH 43017-2169, USA

Johnson, Abigail (Business Person)
Fidelity Investments
82 Devonshire St # V8C
Boston, MA 02109-3605, USA

Johnson, Adam (Athlete, Baseball Player)
7335 Heritage Palms Estates Dr
Fort Myers, FL 33966-5724, USA

Johnson, Addison (Cartoonist)
c/o Staff Member *King Features Syndication*
300 W 57th St Fl 15
New York, NY 10019-5238, USA

Johnson, Adrian (Athlete, Baseball Player)
8102 Meadville St
Houston, TX 77061-3111, USA

Johnson, Albert (Athlete, Football Player)
3506 Mahejan Dr
Pearland, TX 77584-5501, USA

Johnson, Allen (Athlete, Track Athlete)
Octagon
1751 Pinnacle Dr Ste 1500
McLean, VA 22102-3833, USA

Johnson, Allen (Race Car Driver)
PO Box 926
Greeneville, TN 37744-0926, USA

Johnson, Alonzo (Athlete, Football Player)
PO Box 134
Stanley, NC 28164-0134, USA

Johnson, Amy Jo (Actor)
c/o Joannie Burstein *Burstein Company*
15304 W Sunset Blvd Ste 208
Pacific Palisades, CA 90272-3656, USA

Johnson, Andre (Athlete, Football Player)
c/o Kennard McGuire *MS World LLC*
1270 Crabb River Rd Ste 600 PMB 104
Richmond, TX 77469-5635, USA

Johnson, Andreas (Musician)
c/o Staff Member *United Stage Artist*
Box 11029
Stockholm S-10061, Sweden

Johnson, Andy (Athlete, Football Player)
PO Box 6828
Athens, GA 30604-6828, USA

Johnson, Anjelah (Actor)
c/o Dave Rath *Generate Management*
8750 Wilshire Blvd Ste 200
Beverly Hills, CA 90211-2707, USA

Johnson, Anne-Marie (Actor)
2522 Silver Lake Ter
Los Angeles, CA 90039-2608, USA

Johnson, Anthony (Athlete, Basketball Player)
6428 Asbury Ct
Mableton, GA 30126-7751, USA

Johnson, Anthony (Athlete, Football Player)
534 Magnolia Ave
Saint Johns, FL 32259-9018, USA

Johnson, Arte (Actor, Comedian)
2725 Bottlebrush Dr
Los Angeles, CA 90077-2009, USA

Johnson, Ashley (Actor)
c/o Doreen Wilcox Little *Anonymous Content*
3532 Hayden Ave
Culver City, CA 90232-2413, USA

Johnson, Austin (Athlete, Football Player)

Johnson, Avery (Athlete, Basketball Coach, Basketball Player, Coach)
23 Grand Colonial Dr
Spring, TX 77382-2071

Johnson, Barry (Athlete, Football Player)
1103 Northwind Dr
Reston, VA 20194-1009, USA

Johnson, Bart (Actor)
c/o Matt Luber *Luber Roklin Management*
5815 W Sunset Blvd Ste 208
Los Angeles, CA 90028-6481, USA

Johnson, Bart (Athlete, Baseball Player)
1929 N Newland Ave
Chicago, IL 60707-3308, USA

Johnson, Batsey L (Designer, Fashion Designer)
Betsey Johnson Co
127 E 9th St Ste 703
Los Angeles, CA 90015-1737, USA

Johnson, Ben (Athlete, Baseball Player)
112 Locksley Dr
Greenwood, SC 29649-9185, USA

Johnson, Bethel (Athlete, Football Player)
817 Paisley Ln
Red Oak, TX 75154-8868, USA

Johnson, Betsey (Designer, Fashion Designer)
Betsey Johnson Co
498 Fashion Ave Rm 2103
New York, NY 10018-6735, USA

Johnson, Beverly (Actor, Model)
2711 Angelo Dr
Los Angeles, CA 90077-2142, USA

Johnson, Bill (Actor)
c/o Mike Pruitt *Actors Clearinghouse*
501 N 1H35
Austin, TX 78702, USA

Johnson, Bill (Athlete, Baseball Player)
14 Rankin Rd
Newark, DE 19711-4851, USA

Johnson, Bill (Congressman, Politician)
317 Cannon Hob
Washington, DC 20515-3602, USA

Johnson, Bob (Athlete, Football Player)
165 Magnolia Ave
Cincinnati, OH 45246-4506, USA

Johnson, Bob (Athlete, Hockey Player)
32361 Hearthstone Rd
Farmington Hills, MI 48334-3438

Johnson, Bob D (Athlete, Baseball Player)
650 Caves Hwy
Cave Junction, OR 97523-9820, USA

Johnson, Bob W (Athlete, Baseball Player)
1474 Barclay St
Saint Paul, MN 55106-1406, USA

Johnson, Brad (Athlete, Football Player)
1911 Nellie Gray Ct
Athens, GA 30606-8605, USA

Johnson, Brandon (Athlete, Football Player)
1541 W Coquina Dr
Gilbert, AZ 85233-7007, USA

Johnson, Brent (Athlete, Hockey Player)
808 N Florida St
Arlington, VA 22205-1153, USA

Johnson, Brian (Musician)
c/o Christopher Dalston *Creative Artists Agency (CAA)*
2000 Avenue of the Stars Ste 100
Los Angeles, CA 90067-4705, USA

Johnson, Brian (Athlete, Baseball Player)
7595 E Placita Vista Del Bosque
Tucson, AZ 85715-3651, USA

Johnson, Brooks (Coach)
Stanford University
Athletic Dept
Stanford, CA 94305, USA

Johnson, Bryant (Athlete, Football Player)
2963 Springbluff Ln
Buford, GA 30519-4195, USA

Johnson, Bryce (Actor)
c/o Staff Member *Artists Production Group (APG)*
9348 Civic Center Dr Fl 2
Beverly Hills, CA 90210-3610, USA

Johnson, Buck (Athlete, Basketball Player)
1132 Hardwood Cove Rd
Birmingham, AL 35242-7032, USA

Johnson, Butch (Athlete, Football Player)
9719 Red Oakes Dr
Highlands Ranch, CO 80126-3595, USA

Johnson, Calvin (Athlete, Football Player)
c/o Bus Cook *Bus Cook Sports, Inc*
1 Willow Bend Dr
Hattiesburg, MS 39402-8552, USA

Johnson, Cam (Athlete, Football Player)
c/o Adisa P Bakari *Kelley Drye & Warren LLP*
3050 K St NW Ste 400
Washington, DC 20007-5100, USA

Johnson, Carl (Athlete, Football Player)
3420 S Camellia Pl
Chandler, AZ 85248-3866, USA

Johnson, Carolyn Dawn (Musician, Songwriter)
c/o Staff Member *Creative Artists Agency (CAA)*
401 Commerce St PH
Nashville, TN 37219-2516, USA

Johnson, Cassie (Athlete, Olympic Athlete)
412 Birchwood Ct
Saint Paul, MN 55110-1805, USA

Johnson, Cecil (Athlete, Football Player)
1481 NW 103rd St Apt 260
Miami, FL 33147-1409, USA

Johnson, Chad (Athlete, Football Player)
2899 Juniper Ln
Davie, FL 33330-1349, USA

Johnson, Charles (Athlete, Baseball Player, Olympic Athlete)
12301 NW 7th St
Plantation, FL 33325-1729, USA

Johnson, Charles L (Charley) (Athlete, Football Player)
c/o Drew Rosenhaus *Rosenhaus Sports Representation*
3921 Alton Rd # 440
Miami Beach, FL 33140-3852, USA

Johnson, Charles R (Writer)
University of Washington
English Dept
Seattle, WA 98105, USA

Johnson, Charlie W (Athlete, Football Player)
1400 Willow Ave
Louisville, KY 40204-2506, USA

Johnson, Chris (Actor)
c/o Lindsay Whitaker *Haven Entertainment*
8111 Beverly Blvd Ste 201
Los Angeles, CA 90048-4531, USA

Johnson, Chris (Athlete, Football Player)
c/o Denise White *EAG Sports Management*
909 N Pacific Coast Hwy Ste 360
El Segundo, CA 90245-3864, USA

Johnson, Chris (Athlete, Golfer)
6210 W Sunset Rd
Tucson, AZ 85743-9581, USA

Johnson, Chuck (Athlete, Football Player)
1203 N Avenue M
Freeport, TX 77541-3611, USA

Johnson, Clark (Actor)
9560 Wilshire Blvd # 516
Beverly Hills, CA 90212-2427, USA

Johnson, Clay (Athlete, Basketball Player)
9414 NW 86th Ter
Kansas City, MO 64153-1491, USA

Johnson, Clemon (Athlete, Basketball Player)
3574 Four Oaks Blvd
Tallahassee, FL 32311-3308, USA

Johnson, Cliff (Athlete, Baseball Player)
9618 Mediator Pass
Converse, TX 78109-1925, USA

Johnson, Cornelius (Athlete, Football Player)
603 Dale St
Highland Springs, VA 23075-1611, USA

Johnson, Craig (Athlete, Hockey Player)
26 Golden Eagle
Irvine, CA 92603-0309, USA

Johnson, Curtis (Athlete, Football Player)
PO Box 70608
Toledo, OH 43607-0608, USA

Johnson, Curtis (Baseball Player)
Kansas City Monarchs
PO Box B-188
St Rose, LA 70087, USA

Johnson, Dakota (Actor)
c/o Robin Baum *Slate PR*
901 N Highland Ave
W Hollywood, CA 90038-2412, USA

Johnson, Dale (Actor)

Johnson, Damaris (Athlete, Football Player)

Johnson, Dane (Athlete, Baseball Player)
521 Island Ct
Palm Harbor, FL 34683-4607, USA

Johnson, Darius (Athlete, Football Player)
c/o Kennard McGuire *MS World LLC*
1270 Crabb River Rd Ste 600 PMB 104
Richmond, TX 77469-5635, USA

Johnson, Darrius (Athlete, Football Player)
402 Thomas St
Terrell, TX 75160-3832, USA

Johnson, Dave (Athlete, Baseball Player)
3202 Woodhollow Cir
Abilene, TX 79606-4211, USA

Johnson, Dave (Athlete, Baseball Player)
7101 Mount Vista Rd
Kingsville, MD 21087-1728, USA

Johnson, Davey (Athlete, Baseball Player, Coach)
1064 Howell Branch Rd
Winter Park, FL 32789-1004, USA

Johnson, David (Dave) (Athlete, Track Athlete)
Azusa Pacific University
PO Box 2713
Azusa, CA 91702, USA

Johnson, Demetrios (Athlete, Football Player)
840 Garonne Dr
Manchester, MO 63021-5656, USA

Johnson, Dennis (Athlete, Football Player)
PO Box 467
Hawthorne, NJ 07507-0467, USA

Johnson, DerMarr (Basketball Player)
Phoenix Suns
143 Basswood Cir
Ft Wright, KY 41011, USA

Johnson, Derrick (Athlete, Football Player)
c/o W Vann McElroy *Select Sports Group*
2700 Post Oak Blvd Ste 1450
Houston, TX 77056-5785, USA

Johnson, Dick (Athlete, Baseball Player)
5001 E Main St Lot 762
Mesa, AZ 85205-8172, USA

Johnson, D J (Athlete, Football Player)
3814 Kingsbury Dr
Louisville, KY 40207-4443, USA

Johnson, Don (Actor)
Don Johnson Productions
9633 Santa Monica Blvd # 278
Beverly Hills, CA 90210-4401, USA

Johnson, Don (Athlete, Baseball Player)
3935 King Pl
Cincinnati, OH 45223-2407, USA

Johnson, Donnell (Athlete, Football Player)
1792 Temple Ave Apt 1
Atlanta, GA 30337-2723, USA

Johnson, Dwayne (The Rock) (Actor, Athlete, Football Player)
c/o Melissa Kates *Viewpoint Inc*
8820 Wilshire Blvd Ste 220
Beverly Hills, CA 90211-2622, USA

Johnson, Dwight (Athlete, Football Player)
1812 King Cole Dr
Waco, TX 76705-2753, USA

Johnson, Earl (Athlete, Football Player)
340 S Keech St
Daytona Beach, FL 32114-4622, USA

Johnson, Ed (Athlete, Basketball Player)
196 Adobe Ln
Mount Airy, NC 27030-5658, USA

Johnson, Eddie (Athlete, Basketball Player)
Santa Rosa Correctional Institution
5850 E Milton Rd
Milton, FL 32583-7914, USA

Johnson, EJ (Reality Star)
c/o Diandra Escamilla *PMK/BNC Public Relations*
1840 Century Park E Ste 1400
Los Angeles, CA 90067-2115, USA

Johnson, Elliot (Athlete, Baseball Player)
11 Pee:ram Ct
Durham, NC 27703-7970, USA

Johnson, Eric (Actor)
c/o Darryl Mork *Darryl Mork Talent Management*
12012-133A Ave
Edmonton T5E 1GB, CANADA

Johnson, Eric (Athlete, Golfer)
893 Chateau Meadows Dr
Eugene, OR 97401-7046, USA

Johnson, Eric (Musician)
Joe Priesnitz Artist Mgmt
PO Box 5249
Austin, TX 78763-5249, USA

Johnson, Erik (Athlete, Baseball Player)
155 Carondelet Plaza
#505
St.Louis, MO 94583-7989, USA

Johnson, Ervin (Athlete, Basketball Player)
Minnesota Timberwolves
5340 Newport St
Englewood, CO 80111-1659, USA

Johnson, Essex (Athlete, Football Player)
1633 E Dimondale Dr
Carson, CA 90746-2914, USA

Johnson, Ezra (Athlete, Football Player)
402 Carriage Oaks Dr
Tyrone, GA 30290-1530, USA

Johnson, Footer (Athlete, Baseball Player)
5001 E Main St
Mesa, AZ 85205-8008, USA

Johnson, Frank (Athlete, Baseball Player)
1151 Cypress Hill Ln
Stockton, CA 95206-6245, USA

Johnson, Frank (Athlete, Basketball Player, Coach)
4320 N 40th St
Phoenix, AZ 85018-4105, USA

Johnson, Gary (Athlete, Baseball Player)
125 Willow Rd Ste 100
Menlo Park, CA 94025-2799, USA

Johnson, Gary L (Athlete, Football Player)
450 Oliver Rd
Haughton, LA 71037-8942, USA

Johnson, George (Athlete, Football Player)
c/o Brian Levy *Goal Line Football Management*
1025 Kane Concourse Ste 207
Bay Harbor Islands, FL 33154-2118, USA

Johnson, George (Athlete, Golfer)
285 Monarch Village Way
Stockbridge, GA 30281-7764, USA

Johnson, George T (Athlete, Basketball Player)
630 Highland Overlook
Atlanta, GA 30349-3919, USA

Johnson, Graham R (Musician)
83 Fordwych Road
London NW2 3TL, UNITED KINGDOM (UK)

Johnson, Greg (Athlete, Hockey Player)
1058 Runyon Rd
Rochester Hills, MI 48306-4522, USA

Johnson, Gregory (Astronaut)
134 NASA Research Center
2100 Brookpark Rd
Attn: Chief - External Programs Division
Cleveland, OH 44135-3191, USA

Johnson, Hailey Noelle (Actor)
c/o Staff Member *TalentWorks*
3500 W Olive Ave Ste 1400
Burbank, CA 91505-5512, USA

Johnson, Haylie (Actor)
c/o Lin Bickelmann *Encore Artists Management*
3815 W Olive Ave Ste 101
Burbank, CA 91505-4674, USA

Johnson, Holly (Musician)
Lustig Talent
PO Box 770850
Orlando, FL 32877-0850, USA

Johnson, Howard (Athlete, Baseball Player)
8597 SE Coconut St
Hobe Sound, FL 33455-2914, USA

Johnson, Jack (Musician)
59-524 Opae Rd
Haleiwa, HI 96712-8646, USA

Johnson, Jake (Actor, Comedian)
c/o Greg Walter *3 Arts Entertainment*
9460 Wilshire Blvd Fl 7
Beverly Hills, CA 90212-2713, USA

Johnson, Jamey (Musician)
c/o Staff Member *WME (Nashville)*
1201 Demonbreun St
Nashville, TN 37203-3140, USA

Johnson, Jannette (Skier)
PO Box 901
Sun Valley, ID 83353-0901, USA

Johnson, Jarit (Race Car Driver)
PO Box 3876
Mooresville, NC 28117-3876, USA

Johnson, Jarret (Athlete, Football Player)
78 Bensmill Ct
Reisterstown, MD 21136-6461, USA

Johnson, Jason (Athlete, Baseball Player)
18122 Emerald Bay St
Tampa, FL 33647-3315, USA

Johnson, Jason (Athlete, Football Player)
4713 Arabian Run
Indianapolis, IN 46228-7004, USA

Johnson, Jay (Actor, Comedian)
c/o Staff Member *WME/IMG*
9601 Wilshire Blvd Ste 800
Beverly Hills, CA 90210-5210, USA

Johnson, Jay Kenneth (Actor)
c/o Ryan Daly *Zero Gravity Management*
11110 Ohio Ave Ste 100
Los Angeles, CA 90025-3329, USA

Johnson, Jeff (Athlete, Baseball Player)
424 N Hardee St
Durham, NC 27703-2254, USA

Johnson, Jenna (Coach, Swimmer)
University of Tennessee
PO Box 15016
Athletic Dept
Knoxville, TN 37901-5016, USA

Johnson, Jeron (Athlete, Football Player)
c/o Joe Flanagan *BTI Sports Advisors*
615 South Blvd Apt C
Oak Park, IL 60302-4606, USA

Johnson, Jerry (Athlete, Baseball Player)
22054 Saddle Ct
Canyon Lake, CA 92587-7607, USA

Johnson, Jerry (Athlete, Football Player)
3740 Dove Hollow Ln
College Station, TX 77845-6056, USA

Johnson, Jesse (Athlete, Football Player)
102 Rosegill Rd
North Chesterfield, VA 23236-2748, USA

Johnson, Jim (Athlete, Hockey Player)
Interactive Coaching LLC
354 Edward Ave W
Winnipeg, MB R2C 2H8, Canada

Johnson, Jimmie (Race Car Driver)
Jimmie Johnson Fan Club
152 Woodfield Dr
Statesville, NC 28677-2619, USA

Johnson, Jimmy (Cartoonist)
United Feature Syndicate
200 Madison Ave
New York, NY 10016-3903, USA

Johnson, Jimmy (Athlete, Football Coach, Football Player)
656 Amaranth Blvd
Mill Valley, CA 94941-2605, USA

Johnson, Joanna (Actor)
c/o Staff Member *WME/IMG*
9601 Wilshire Blvd Ste 800
Beverly Hills, CA 90210-5210, USA

Johnson, Joe (Athlete, Baseball Player)
14 Evergreen Rd
Plainville, MA 02762-1902, USA

Johnson, Joe (Athlete, Basketball Player)
2704 Wolf Lake Dr SW
Atlanta, GA 30349-8772, USA

Johnson, Johari (Actor)
H W A Talent
3500 W Olive Ave Ste 1400
Burbank, CA 91505-5512, USA

Johnson, John (Athlete, Basketball Player)
4751 N 18th St
Milwaukee, WI 53209-6430, USA

Johnson, John (Athlete, Football Player)
133 Plymouth Dr
Lagrange, GA 30240-8537, USA

Johnson, John (Athlete, Golfer)
236 E Hemlock St
Oxnard, CA 93033-3619, USA

Johnson, John Henrv (Athlete, Baseball Player)
3345 Delna Dr
Sparks, NV 89431-1408, USA

Johnson, John Henry (Athlete, Baseball Player)
3345 Delna Dr
Sparks, NV 89431-1408, USA

Johnson, Johnny (Athlete, Football Player)
929 Delaware Ave
Santa Cruz, CA 95060-6403, USA

Johnson, Jonathan (Athlete, Baseball Player)
7 Alverston Ct
Irmo, SC 29063-8262, USA

Johnson, Joseph (Athlete, Football Player)
166 Homestead Hills Cir
Winston Salem, NC 27103-6446, USA

Johnson, Josh (Athlete, Football Player)
c/o Adam Heller *Vantage Management Group*
518 Reamer Dr
Carnegie, PA 15106-1845, USA

Johnson, J Seward (Artist)
Sculpture Foundation
2525 Michigan Ave Ste A6
Santa Monica, CA 90404-4031, USA

Johnson, Junior (Race Car Driver)
5022 Fairlawn Crescent Ct
Charlotte, NC 28226-3322, USA

Johnson, Kandee (Designer, Internet Star)
c/o Rachel Hunt *ID Public Relations*
7060 Hollywood Blvd Fl 8th
Los Angeles, CA 90028-6021, USA

Johnson, Keean (Actor)
c/o Brett Ruttenberg *Imprint PR*
6121 W Sunset Blvd
Neuehouse
Los Angeles, CA 90028-6442, USA

Johnson, Keith (Athlete, Baseball Player)
PO Box 4122
Park City, UT 84060-4122, USA

Johnson, Kenneth (Athlete, Basketball Player)
1401 N Wheeler Ave
Portland, OR 97227-1831, USA

Johnson, Kenneth (Athlete, Football Player)
536 E 169th St
Carson, CA 90746-1105, USA

Johnson, Kenneth (Athlete, Football Player)
1334 NW 42nd St
Miami, FL 33142-4812, USA

Johnson, Kenny (Actor)
c/o Josh Katz *United Talent Agency (UTA)*
9336 Civic Center Dr
Beverly Hills, CA 90210-3604, USA

Johnson, Kermit (Athlete, Football Player)
3259 Lincoln Ave
Altadena, CA 91001-4141, USA

Johnson, Kerryon (Athlete, Football Player)
c/o Drew Rosenhaus *Rosenhaus Sports Representation*
3921 Alton Rd # 440
Miami Beach, FL 33140-3852, USA

Johnson, Kevin (Baseball Player, Sportscaster)
NBC-TV
30 Rockefeller Plz
Sports Dept
New York, NY 10112-0015, USA

Johnson, Kevin (Athlete, Football Player)
c/o David Belenzon *David Belenzon Management, Inc.*
PO Box 5000
Rancho Santa Fe, CA 92067-5000, USA

Johnson, Keyshawn (Athlete, Football Player)
19232 Northfleet Way
Tarzana, CA 91356-5807, USA

Johnson, Lamar (Actor)
c/o Matt Shelton *Stride Management*
750 N San Vicente Blvd # 800W
W Hollywood, CA 90069-5788, USA

Johnson, Lamar (Athlete, Baseball Player)
4105 Sangre Trl
Arlington, TX 76016-2972, USA

Johnson, Lance (Athlete, Baseball Player)
5712 Foxfire Rd
Mobile, AL 36618-2653, USA

Johnson, Landon (Athlete, Football Player)
1915 Mountain Trail Dr
Charlotte, NC 28214-5429, USA

Johnson, Lane (Athlete, Football Player)

Johnson, Larry (Athlete, Baseball Player)
7417 Terrace River Dr
Temple Terrace, FL 33637-7924, USA

Johnson, Larry (Athlete, Football Player)
340 Glengarry Ln
State College, PA 16801-7092, USA

Johnson, Larry D (Basketball Player)
c/o Staff Member *Kansas City Chiefs*
1 Arrowhead Dr
Kansas City, MO 64129-1651, USA

Johnson, Lee (Athlete, Football Player)
1173 E McDaniel Cir
Alpine, UT 84004-1231, USA

Johnson, Leon (Athlete, Football Player)
813 Vine Arden Rd
Morganton, NC 28655-2758, USA

Johnson, Leonard (Athlete, Football Player)

Johnson, Leshon (Athlete, Football Player)
15102 Beverly St
Overland Park, KS 66223-3200, USA

Johnson, Levi (Athlete, Football Player)
1202 Craig Dr
Westland, MI 48186-5504, USA

Johnson, Lonnie (Athlete, Football Player)
8500 Amber Ridge Ct
Sanford, FL 32771-8325, USA

Johnson, Lou (Athlete, Baseball Player)
4532 Valley Ridge Ave
View Park, CA 90008-4827, USA

Johnson, Luci Baines (Politician)
170 Crescent Rd
Toronto, ON M4W 1V2, Canada

Johnson, Luther (Guitar Jr) (Musician)
c/o Staff Member *Concerted Efforts*
PO Box 440326
Somerville, MA 02144-0004, USA

Johnson, Lynn-Holly (Actor)
Cavaleri
178 S Victory Blvd Ste 205
Burbank, CA 91502-2881, USA

Johnson, Magic (Athlete, Basketball Player, Olympic Athlete)
12 Beverly Park
Beverly Hills, CA 90210-1540, USA

Johnson, Manny (Athlete, Football Player)
c/o Chad Speck *Allegiant Athletic Agency*
35 Market Sq Ste 201
Knoxville, TN 37902-1420, USA

Johnson, Marc (Musician)
A Train Mgmt
PO Box 29242
Oakland, CA 94604-9242, USA

Johnson, Margaret (Athlete, Baseball Player)
825 Country Club Dr SE Apt 1D
Rio Rancho, NM 87124-2265, USA

Johnson, Mark (Athlete, Hockey Player)
1609 Hidden Hill Dr
Verona, WI 53593-7971, USA

Johnson, Mark (Athlete, Baseball Player)
21 Baldwin Farms S
Greenwich, CT 06831-3308, USA

Johnson, Mark (Athlete, Baseball Player)
109 Mossy Lake Rd
Perry, GA 31069-9217, USA

Johnson, Mark (Athlete, Golfer)
PO Box 2945
Soldotna, AK 99669-2945, USA

Johnson, Mark (Athlete, Hockey Player, Olympic Athlete)
1609 Hidden Hill Dr
Verona, WI 53593-7971, USA

Johnson, Mark (Boxer)
1204 Howison Pl SW
Washington, DC 20024-4132, USA

Johnson, Mark Steven (Director, Writer)

Johnson, Marques (Athlete, Basketball Player)
5133 Dawn View Pl
Los Angeles, CA 90043-2006, USA

Johnson, Marvin (Boxer)
5452 Turfway Cir
Indianapolis, IN 46228-2094, USA

Johnson, Maurice (Athlete, Football Player)
112 Mountainview Rd
Mount Laurel, NJ 08054-4729, USA

Johnson, Michael (Musician)
Buddy Lee
665 Whyte Ave
Roseville, CA 95661-5240, USA

Johnson, Michael (Athlete, Track Athlete)
Michael Johnson Performance
6051 Alma Rd
McKinney, TX 75070-2139, USA

Johnson, Mickey (Athlete, Basketball Player)
3642 W Grenshaw St
Chicago, IL 60624-4207, USA

Johnson, Mike (Athlete, Football Player)
c/o Pat Dye Jr *SportsTrust Advisors*
3340 Peachtree Rd NE Fl 16
Atlanta, GA 30326-1000, USA

Johnson, Mike (Athlete, Hockey Player)
300 Portage Ave
Attn: Broadcast Dept Winnipeg Jets
Winnipeg, MB R3C 5S4, Canada

Johnson, Mike (Athlete, Baseball Player)
20251 State Highway 34
Pelican Rapids, MN 56572-7005, USA

Johnson, Mike (Athlete, Baseball Player)
124 Isle Verde Way
Palm Beach Gardens, FL 33418-1708, USA

Johnson, Mitchell (Athlete, Football Player)
2764 Unicorn Ln NW
Washington, DC 20015-2234, USA

Johnson, Monica (Writer)
Innovative Artists
1505 10th St
Santa Monica, CA 90401-2805, USA

Johnson, Monte (Athlete, Football Player)
425 Laurel Chase Ct
Atlanta, GA 30327-4655, USA

Johnson, Neil (Athlete, Basketball Player)
821 Plymouth Ln
Virginia Beach, VA 23451-5926, USA

Johnson, Nelson (Writer)
c/o Staff Member *Plexus Publishing, Inc*
143 Old Marlton Pike
Medford, NJ 08055-8750, USA

Johnson, Nic (Race Car Driver)
PTG Racing
441 Victory Rd
Winchester, VA 22602-4567, USA

Johnson, Nick (Athlete, Baseball Player)
8008 Sacramento St
Fair Oaks, CA 95628-7527, USA

Johnson, Norm (Athlete, Football Player)
400 Peachtree Industrial Blvd Apt 1615
Suwanee, GA 30024-6989, USA

Johnson, Norm (Athlete, Football Player)
10397 Owl Hollow Pl NW
Silverdale, WA 98383-7559, USA

Johnson, Norman (Musician)
Paramount Entertainment
PO Box 12
Far Hills, NJ 07931-0012, USA

Johnson, Ollie (Athlete, Basketball Player)
15 Shelburne St
Burlington, NJ 08016-4308, USA

Johnson, Ora J (Religious Leader)
General Assn of General Baptists
100 Stinson Dr
Poplar Bluff, MO 63901-8746, USA

Johnson, Paul (Football Coach)
Georgia Tech Athletic Association
150 Bobby Dodd Way NW
Atlanta, GA 30332-2501, USA

Johnson, Penny (Actor)
c/o Mitchell Stubbs *Mitchell K Stubbs & Assoc*
8675 Washington Blvd Ste 203
Culver City, CA 90232-7486, USA

Johnson, Pepper (Athlete, Football Player)
PO Box 1133
Russells Point, OH 43348-1133, USA

Johnson, Pete (Athlete, Football Player)
6304 Misty Cove Ln # in
Columbus, OH 43231-1689, USA

Johnson, Rafer L (Actor, Athlete, Decathlon Athlete)
4217 Woodcliff Rd
Sherman Oaks, CA 91403-4339, USA

Johnson, Ralph (Athlete, Baseball Player)
5703 E 30th Ave
Tampa, FL 33619-1525, USA

Johnson, Randell (Athlete, Football Player)

Johnson, Randy (Athlete, Baseball Player)
13509 Sundance Rd
Valley Center, CA 92082-4157, USA

Johnson, Rashad (Athlete, Football Player)
c/o Joel Segal *Lagardere Unlimited (NY)*
456 Washington St Apt 9L
New York, NY 10013-1555, USA

Johnson, Raylee (Athlete, Football Player)
2010 Black Fox Dr NE
Atlanta, GA 30345-4123, USA

Johnson, Ray William (Actor, Comedian, Internet Star, Producer)
c/o Todd Christopher *Gersh*
9465 Wilshire Blvd Ste 600
Beverly Hills, CA 90212-2605, USA

Johnson, Rebekka (Actor)
c/o Jennie Cooper-Church *Haven Entertainment*
8111 Beverly Blvd Ste 201
Los Angeles, CA 90048-4531, USA

Johnson, Reed (Athlete, Baseball Player)
30137 Mira Loma Dr
Temecula, CA 92592-2127, USA

Johnson, Reggie (Athlete, Football Player)
17907 Souter Ln
Land O Lakes, FL 34638-7887, USA

Johnson, Rian (Director, Writer)
c/o Brian Dreyfuss *Featured Artists Agency*
1880 Century Park E Ste 1402
Los Angeles, CA 90067-1630, USA

Johnson, Rob (Athlete, Football Player)
26635 Aracena Dr
Mission Viejo, CA 92691-5105, USA

Johnson, Ron (Athlete, Baseball Player)
428 S Maie Ave
Compton, CA 90220-2805, USA

Johnson, Rondin (Athlete, Baseball Player)
PO Box 1233
Hoodsport, WA 98548-1233, USA

Johnson, Rontrez (Athlete, Baseball Player)
1426 NE 18th Pl
Cape Coral, FL 33909-1612, USA

Johnson, Russ (Athlete, Baseball Player, Olympic Athlete)
3542 Russell Rd
Green Cove Springs, FL 32043-9498, USA

Johnson, Sam (Congressman, Politician)
1211 Longworth Hob
Washington, DC 20515-4303, USA

Johnson, Sammy (Athlete, Football Player)
142 Old Mill Rd Apt B
High Point, NC 27265-1283, USA

Johnson, Sam-Taylor (Actor)
c/o Ciara Parkes *Public Eye Communications*
535 Kings Rd
#313 Plaza
London SW10 0SZ, UNITED KINGDOM

Johnson, Scarlett (Actor)
c/o Duncan Millership *WME|IMG*
9601 Wilshire Blvd Ste 800
Beverly Hills, CA 90210-5210, USA

Johnson, Shannon (Basketball Player)
Connecticut Sun
Mohegan Sun Arena
Uncasville, CT 06382, USA

Johnson, Shawn (Athlete, Gymnast, Olympic Athlete)
c/o Rebecca Malzahn *ICON PR*
8961 W Sunset Blvd Ste 1C
W Hollywood, CA 90069-1886, USA

Johnson, Sheila (Business Person)
Washington Mystics
401 9th St NW
Washington, DC 20004-2128, USA

Johnson, Steffond (Athlete, Basketball Player)
10525 Marsh Ln
Dallas, TX 75229-5142, USA

Johnson, Steve (Athlete, Basketball Player)
9715 SW Quail Post Rd
Portland, OR 97219-6363, USA

Johnson, Steve (Race Car Driver)
3760 Mountain View Ln
Vestavia, AL 35223-2227, USA

Johnson, Syl (Musician, Songwriter, Writer)
Blue Sky Artists
761 Washington Ave N
Minneapolis, MN 55401-1101, USA

Johnson, Ted (Athlete, Football Player)
42 Plain Rd
Wayland, MA 01778-2312, USA

Johnson, Terry (Athlete, Hockey Player)
Endev Energy Inc
400-777 8 Ave SW
Attn Vice President Land
Calgary, AB T2P 3R5, Canada

Johnson, Teyo (Athlete, Football Player)
2222 Oak Rd
Lynnwood, WA 98087-6321, USA

Johnson, Thomas (Athlete, Baseball Player)
15107 Interlachen Dr Apt 324
Silver Spring, MD 20906-5629, USA

Johnson, Tim (Athlete, Baseball Player, Coach)
2700 Van Dorn St
Lincoln, NE 68502-4256, USA

Johnson, Tim (Athlete, Football Player)
21300 Redskin Park Dr
Ashburn, VA 20147-6100, USA

Johnson, Tim (Athlete, Football Player)
2839 Dorell Ave
Orlando, FL 32814-6757, USA

Johnson, T.J. (Athlete, Football Player)

Johnson, Tom (Athlete, Baseball Player)
2700 Knox Ave N
Minneapolis, MN 55411-1246, USA

Johnson, Tom (Athlete, Football Player)

Johnson, Tre (Athlete, Football Player)
680 Harrison Ave
Peekskill, NY 10566-2219, USA

Johnson, Trumaine (Athlete, Football Player)
c/o Joel Segal *Lagardere Unlimited (NY)*
456 Washington St Apt 9L
New York, NY 10013-1555, USA

Johnson, Tyrell (Athlete, Football Player)

Johnson, Undra (Athlete, Football Player)
1550 Cost Ave Apt 29
Clarksburg, WV 26301-4883, USA

Johnson, Vance (Athlete, Football Player)
2791 W Wagon Wheel Dr
Tucson, AZ 85745-3536, USA

Johnson, Vaughan (Athlete, Football Player)
4915 Arendell St Apt 253
Morehead City, NC 28557-2659, USA

Johnson, Vaughan M (Athlete, Football Player)
5800 Airline Dr
Metairie, LA 70003-3876, USA

Johnson, Vickie (Basketball Player)
c/o Staff Member *New York Liberty*
2 Penn Plz Fl 15
New York, NY 10121-1700, USA

Johnson, Vinnie (Athlete, Basketball Player)
5236 Elmgate Dr
Orchard Lake, MI 48324-3017, USA

Johnson, Wallace (Athlete, Baseball Player)
PO Box 64618
Gary, IN 46401-0618, USA

Johnson, Warren (Race Car Driver)
WJ Enterprises
700 N Price Rd
Sugar Hill, GA 30518-4724, USA

Johnson, Wendy (Race Car Driver)
445 Airpark Dr
Mooresville, NC 28115-6969, USA

Johnson, Wesley (Athlete, Basketball Player)
c/o Jeff Austin *Octagon Home Office*
7950 Jones Branch Dr # 700N
Mc Lean, VA 22107-0002, USA

Johnson, William A (Billy White Shoes) (Athlete, Football Player)
3701 Whitney Pl
Duluth, GA 30096-3170, USA

Johnson, William B (Business Person)
Ritz-Carlton Hotels
4445 Willard Ave Ste 800
Chevy Chase, MD 20815-3699, USA

Johnson, William H (Athlete, Football Player)
522 E Pleasant Grove Rd
Montgomery, AL 36105-6110, USA

Johnson, William R (Business Person)
H J Heinz Co
PO Box 57
Pittsburgh, PA 15230-0057, USA

Johnson, William W (Athlete, Football Player)
20 Mohawk Rd
Canton, MA 02021-1254, USA

Johnson, Woody (Business Person, Football Executive)
1195 Lamington Rd
Bedminster, NJ 07921-2764, USA

Johnson, Zach (Athlete, Golfer)
PO Box 2336
Cedar Rapids, IA 52406-2336, USA

Johnson Herjavec, Kym (Dancer)
c/o Penny Vizcarra *PV Public Relations*
121 N Almont Dr Apt 203
Beverly Hills, CA 90211-1860, USA

Johnson III, Edward (Business Person)
Fidelity Investments
82 Devonshire St # V8C
Boston, MA 02109-3605, USA

Johnson Jr, Benjamin S (ben) (Athlete, Track Athlete)
Ed Futerman
2 Saint Clair Ave E
#1500
Toronto, ON M4T 2R1, CANADA

Johnson Jr, Ernie (Sportscaster)
TNT-TV
1050 Techwood Dr NW
Sports Department
Atlanta, GA 30318-5604, USA

Johnson Jr, Johnnie (Athlete, Football Player)
PO Box 114
La Grange, TX 78945-0114, USA

Johnson, Jr., Tommy (Race Car Driver)
493 Southpoint Cir
Brownsburg, IN 46112-2203, USA

Johnson Pucci, Gail (Swimmer)
2132 Ward Dr
Walnut Creek, CA 94596-5731, USA

Johnsson, Kim (Athlete, Hockey Player)
5308 Oaklawn Ave
Minneapolis, MN 55424-1309, USA

Johnston, Allen H (Religious Leader)
Bishop's House
3 Wymer Terrace
PO Box 21
Hamilton, NEW ZELAND

Johnston, Amy (Actor)
c/o Roger Pliakas *Roger A. Pliakas, ESQ*
9720 Wilshire Blvd Ste 200
Beverly Hills, CA 90212-2006, USA

Johnston, Bernie (Athlete, Hockey Player)
715 Central Park Blvd
Port Orange, FL 32127-7555, USA

Johnston, Brian (Athlete, Football Player)
236 Hideaway Ln
Mooresville, NC 28117-8402, USA

Johnston, Bruce (Musician)
International Creative Mgmt
8942 Wilshire Blvd # 219
Beverly Hills, CA 90211-1908, USA

Johnston, Daryl (Moose) (Athlete, Football Player)
4414 Woodfin Dr
Dallas, TX 75220-6420, USA

Johnston, Ed (Athlete, Hockey Player)
c/o Staff Member *Pittsburgh Penguins*
1001 5th Ave
Pittsburgh, PA 15219-6201, USA

Johnston, Freedy (Musician, Songwriter, Writer)
Morebarn Music
30 Hillcrest Ave
Morristown, NJ 07960-5090, USA

Johnston, Greg (Athlete, Hockey Player)
c/o Staff Member *Toronto Maple Leafs*
Air Canada Centre
400-40 Bay St
Toronto, ON M5J 2X2, CANADA

Johnston, Jamie (Actor)
c/o Norbert Abrams *Noble Caplan Abrams*
1260 Yonge St Fl 2
Toronto, ON M4T 1W5, CANADA

Johnston, J Bennett (Politician)
1330 Connecticut Ave NW Ste 1C
Washington, DC 20036-1724, USA

Johnston, Jimmy (Athlete, Golfer)
Pro's Inc
9 S 12th St Fl 3
Richmond, VA 23219-4032, USA

Johnston, Joe (Director)
c/o Adam Kanter *Paradigm*
8942 Wilshire Blvd
Beverly Hills, CA 90211-1908, USA

Johnston, Joel (Athlete, Baseball Player)
1479 Sweetwater Way
Pottstown, PA 19464-1940, USA

Johnston, Joey (Athlete, Hockey Player)
RR 4
Station Delivery Ctr
Peterborough, ON K9J 6X5, Canada

Johnston, John Dennis (Actor)
S D B Partners
1801 Ave of Stars
#902
Los Angeles, CA 90067, USA

Johnston, Kristen (Actor)
c/o Laura Berwick *Berwick & Kovacik*
6230 Wilshire Blvd
Los Angeles, CA 90048-5126, USA

Johnston, Larry (Athlete, Hockey Player)
904 E Liberty St
Milford, MI 48381-2081, USA

Johnston, Levi (Reality Star)
c/o David Weintraub *DWE Talent*
Prefers to be contacted by email or phone.
Los Angeles, CA 90069, USA

Johnston, Lynn (Cartoonist)
Universal Press Syndicate
4520 Main St Ste 340
Kansas City, MO 64111-7705, USA

Johnston, Mark (Athlete, Football Player)
5604 Southwest Pkwy Apt 3535
Austin, TX 78735-6278, USA

Johnston, Marshall (Athlete, Hockey Player)
3933 Waville Rd NE
Bemidji, MN 56601-8987, USA

Johnston, Nate (Athlete, Basketball Player)
8870 Fontainebleau Blvd Apt 301
Miami, FL 33172-4427, USA

Johnston, Rex D (Athlete, Baseball Player, Football Player)
15117 Illinois Ave
Paramount, CA 90723-4106, USA

Johnston, Shaun (Actor)
Heartland
PO Box 2640 Stn M
Calgary, AB T2P 2M7, CANADA

Johnston, Tom (Musician)
PO Box 359
Sonoma, CA 95476-0359

Johnstone, Jay (Athlete, Baseball Player)
853 Chapea Rd
Pasadena, CA 91107-5656, USA

Johnstone, John (Athlete, Baseball Player)
5281 Villa Ridge Ct
Baldwinsville, NY 13027-8974, USA

Johnstone, Parker (Race Car Driver)
541 Division St
Campbell, CA 95008-6905, USA

Johnstone, Tony (Athlete, Golfer)
Proserv
5335 Wisconsin Ave NW Ste 850
Washington, DC 20015-2052, USA

Johnstone Jr, John W (Business Person)
2526 W 430 Rd
Adair, OK 74330-2877, USA

Johnston-Forbes, Cathy (Athlete, Golfer)
5104 Lunar Dr
Kitty Hawk, NC 27949-3958, USA

Johnston Jr, S K (Business Person)
Coca-Cola Enterprises
2500 Windy Ridge Pkwy SE Ste 700
Atlanta, GA 30339-8429, USA

Joiner, Rusty (Actor, Athlete, Model)
c/o Tom Parziale *Visionary Management*
1558 N Stanley Ave
Los Angeles, CA 90046-2711, USA

Jokinen, Olli (Athlete, Hockey Player)
4401 N Federal Hwy Ste 201
Boca Raton, FL 33431-5164, USA

Joli, France (Musician)
c/o Staff Member *Diva Central Inc*
7510 W Sunset Blvd # 1445
Los Angeles, CA 90046-3408, USA

Joliceur, David (Musician)
Famous Artists Agency
250 W 57th St
New York, NY 10107-0001, USA

Jolie, Angelina (Actor)
c/o Geyer Kosinski *Media Talent Group*
9200 W Sunset Blvd Ste 550
Los Angeles, CA 90069-3611, USA

Jolitz, Evan (Athlete, Football Player)
15 Old Kimball Rd
Brooklyn, CT 06234-1414, USA

Jolley, Gordon (Athlete, Football Player)
1380 N Chancey Ln
Midway, UT 84049-6963, USA

Jolley, Lewis (Athlete, Football Player)
2715 Rosegate Ln
Charlotte, NC 28270-0764, USA

Jolley, Willie (Writer)
PO Box 55459
Washington, DC 20040-5459, USA

Jolliff, Howie (Athlete, Basketball Player)
1394 Fox Creek Ln
Mount Pleasant, SC 29466-7536, USA

Jolly, Ken (Athlete, Football Player)
159 Bon Aire Dr
Dallas, TX 75218-1034, USA

Jolovitz, Jenna (Actor, Writer)
c/o Staff Member *Creative Artists Agency (CAA)*
2000 Avenue of the Stars Ste 100
Los Angeles, CA 90067-4705, USA

Joly, Greg (Athlete, Hockey Player)
21 McDonald Dr
Queensbury, NY 12804-6426, USA

Joly, Yvan (Athlete, Hockey Player)
16 Hwy 3
Wainfleet, ON L0S 1V0, Canada

Jomdt, L daniel (Business Person)
Walgreen Co
200 Wilmot Rd
Deerfield, IL 60015-4681, USA

Jomphe, Jean-Francois (Athlete, Hockey Player)
6440 Sky Pointe Dr Ste 140
Las Vegas, NV 89131-4048, USA

Jonas, Don (Athlete, Football Player)
1831 Seneca Blvd
Winter Springs, FL 32708-5534, USA

Jonas, Joe (Musician)
c/o Robert Mickelson *Creative Artists Agency (CAA)*
2000 Avenue of the Stars Ste 100
Los Angeles, CA 90067-4705, USA

Jonas, Kevin (Musician)
The Jonas Group
10153 1/5 Riverside Dr.
Toluca Lake, CA 91602, USA

Jonas, Nick (Actor, Musician)
c/o Marisa Martins *The Lede Company*
401 Broadway Ste 206
New York, NY 10013-3033, USA

Jonathan, Stan (Athlete, Hockey Player)
RR 1
Ohsweken, ON N0A 1M0, Canada

Jonathan, Wesley (Actor)
c/o Lynn Jeter *Lynn Jeter & Associates*
3699 Wilshire Blvd Ste 850
Los Angeles, CA 90010-2737, USA

Jones, Aaron (Athlete, Football Player)
PO Box 1403
Apopka, FL 32704-1403, USA

Jones, Adam (Athlete, Baseball Player)
c/o Staff Member *Baltimore Orioles*
333 W Camden St Ste 1
Baltimore, MD 21201-2476, USA

Jones, Adam (Athlete, Football Player)
c/o Peter Schaffer *Authentic Athletix*
400 S Steele St Unit 47
Denver, CO 80209-3535, USA

Jones, Al (Athlete, Baseball Player)
1339 Brussels St
San Francisco, CA 94134-2224, USA

Jones, Alex E (Journalist, Radio Personality)
PO Box 19549
Austin, TX 78760-9549, USA

Jones, Alfred (Boxer)
19303 Patton St
Detroit, MI 48219-2530, USA

Jones, Allen (Artist)
41 Charterhouse Square
London EC1M 6EA, UNITED KINGDOM (UK)

Jones, Andruw (Athlete, Baseball Player)
1204 Suncast Ln Ste 2
El Dorado Hills, CA 95762-9665, USA

Jones, Angus (Actor)
c/o Wendi Green *Paradigm*
8942 Wilshire Blvd
Beverly Hills, CA 90211-1908, USA

Jones, Anthony (Athlete, Basketball Player)
44 Hempstead Dr
Newark, DE 19702-7711, USA

Jones, Antonia (Actor)
Buzz Halliday
8899 Beverly Blvd Ste 620
Los Angeles, CA 90048-2428, USA

Jones, Arthur (Athlete, Football Player)
c/o Joe Panos *Athletes First*
23091 Mill Creek Dr
Laguna Hills, CA 92653-1258, USA

Jones, Ashthon (Musician)
c/o Simon Fuller *XIX Entertainment (UK)*
32/33 Ransomes Dock
London SW11 4NP, UNITED KINGDOM (UK)

Jones, Asjha (Basketball Player)
Connecticut Sun
Mohegan Sun Arena
Uncasville, CT 06382, USA

Jones, Askia (Athlete, Basketball Player)
3160 SW 132nd Ave
Miramar, FL 33027-3868, USA

Jones, Barry (Athlete, Baseball Player)
411 S Morton Ave
Centerville, IN 47330-1429, USA

Jones, Ben (Athlete, Baseball Player)
1323 Tewkesbury Pl NW
Washington, DC 20012-2921, USA

Jones, Ben (Athlete, Football Player)

Jones, Bert (Athlete, Football Player)
1492 Madera St
Ruston, LA 71270-2063, USA

Jones, Bertram H (Bert) (Athlete, Football Player)
PO Box 248
Simsboro, LA 71275-0248, USA

Jones, Bob (Bobby) (Athlete, Baseball Player)
32 Elm St
Rutherford, NJ 07070-1263, USA

Jones, Bobby (Athlete, Baseball Player)
7809 S Oxford Ave
Tulsa, OK 74136-8524, USA

Jones, Bobby (Athlete, Baseball Player)
10222 N Whitney Ave
Fresno, CA 93730-4742, USA

Jones, Bobby (Athlete, Basketball Player, Olympic Athlete)
Charlotte Christian School
7301 Sardis Rd
Charlotte, NC 28270-6063, USA

Jones, Bobby (Athlete, Football Player)
6824 Stewart Sharon Rd
Brookfield, OH 44403-9789, USA

Jones, Booker T (Actor, Musician)
c/o Staff Member *Concerted Efforts*
PO Box 440326
Somerville, MA 02144-0004, USA

Jones, Brad (Athlete, Football Player)

Jones, Brad (Athlete, Hockey Player)
c/o Staff Member *International Hockey League*
117 W 4th St
Rochester, MI 48307-2025, USA

Jones, Brandon (Athlete, Football Player)
1070 Randall Rd
Texarkana, TX 75501-2102, USA

Jones, Brent M (Athlete, Football Player, Sportscaster)
1540 Keller Pkwy
Keller, TX 76248-3686, USA

Jones, Brian (Athlete, Football Player)
84 Hackensack Ave APT 1
Weehawken, NJ 07086-6777, USA

Jones, Buckshot (Race Car Driver)
Buckshot Racing
182 Belue Cir
Spartanburg, SC 29316-5900, USA

Jones, Byron (Athlete, Football Player)
c/o Jared Fox *Sportstars Inc*
1370 Avenue of the Americas Fl 19
New York, NY 10019-4602, USA

Jones, Caleb Landry (Actor)
c/o Annett Wolf *Wolf-Kasteler Public Relations*
6255 W Sunset Blvd Ste 1111
Los Angeles, CA 90028-7426, USA

Jones, Calvin (Athlete, Baseball Player)
2815 Butterfield Stage Rd
Lewisville, TX 75077-3181, USA

Jones, Calvin (Athlete, Football Player)
25 Sierra St Apt E306
San Francisco, CA 94107-2855, USA

Jones, Carnetta (Actor)
CunninghamEscottDipene
10635 Santa Monica Blvd Ste 130
Los Angeles, CA 90025-8306, USA

Jones, Cedric (Athlete, Football Player)
48B Rodwell Ave Unit B
Greenwich, CT 06830-6121, USA

Jones, Chandler (Athlete, Football Player)
c/o Joe Panos *Athletes First*
23091 Mill Creek Dr
Laguna Hills, CA 92653-1258, USA

Jones, Charles (Athlete, Basketball Player)
2315 Windsor Ave
Baltimore, MD 21216-3227, USA

Jones, Charles A (Athlete, Basketball Player)
304 Chestnut St
Elizabethtown, KY 42701-9431, USA

Jones, Charlie (Sportscaster)
5 Daisy Ln
Menlo Park, CA 94025-3943, USA

Jones, Cherry (Actor)
c/o David Kalodner *WME/IMG (NY)*
11 Madison Ave Fl 18
New York, NY 10010-3669, USA

Jones, Chipper (Athlete, Baseball Player, Olympic Athlete)
5015 Heatherwood Ct
Roswell, GA 30075-2285, USA

Jones, Chris (Athlete, Baseball Player)
1821 Westward Ho Cir
El Cajon, CA 92021-3721, USA

Jones, Chris (Athlete, Baseball Player)
1371 N Santa Anna Ct
Chandler, AZ 85224-8570, USA

Jones, Chris T (Athlete, Football Player)
2372 Treasure Isle Dr
West Palm Beach, FL 33410-1312, USA

Jones, Clarence (Athlete, Baseball Player)
2641 Club Dr
Greensboro, GA 30642-3476, USA

Jones, Cleon (Athlete, Baseball Player)
751 Edwards St
Mobile, AL 36610-3334, USA

Jones, Clinton (Athlete, Football Player)
7559 McLaren Ave
West Hills, CA 91307-1525, USA

Jones, Cobi (Athlete, Soccer Player)
501 N Edinburgh Ave
Los Angeles, CA 90048-2309, USA

Jones, Coco (Actor)
c/o Jonathan Shank *Red Light Management*
5800 Bristol Pkwy Ste 400
Culver City, CA 90230-6898, USA

Jones, Colin (Athlete, Football Player)

Jones, Collis (Athlete, Basketball Player)
1217 Argyle Ave
Baltimore, MD 21217-2928, USA

Jones, Connor (Athlete, Baseball Player)

Jones, Courtney J L (Figure Skater)
National Skating Assn
15-27 Gee St
London EC1V 3RE, UNITED KINGDOM (UK)

Jones, Cullen (Athlete, Olympic Athlete, Swimmer)
12322 Aquitaine St
Charlotte, NC 28277-3266, USA

Jones, Dahntay (Athlete, Basketball Player)
3247 Wedge Hill Cv
Memphis, TN 38125-8891, USA

Jones, Dale (Athlete, Football Player)
PO Box 2716
Boone, NC 28607-2716, USA

Jones, Dalton (Athlete, Baseball Player)
4688 S Dixon Ln
Liberty, MS 39645-6117, USA

Jones, Damon (Athlete, Basketball Player)
c/o Staff Member *Mark Termini Associates*
Prefers to be contacted via telephone
Cleveland, OH, USA

Jones, Damon (Athlete, Football Player)
12690 Copper Springs Rd
Jacksonville, FL 32246-5143, USA

Jones, Dan (Athlete, Football Player)
5150 SW 20th St
Plantation, FL 33317-5410, USA

Jones, Daniel (Writer)
c/o Staff Member *New York Times*
229 W 43rd St
New York, NY 10036-3982, USA

Jones, Dante (Athlete, Football Player)
326 Partridge Run Dr
Duncanville, TX 75137-3133, USA

Jones, DaQuan (Athlete, Football Player)
c/o Jim Ivler *Sportstars Inc*
1370 Avenue of the Americas Fl 19
New York, NY 10019-4602, USA

Jones, Darryl (Athlete, Baseball Player)
15628 Kings Dr
Meadville, PA 16335-6546, USA

Jones, Darryl (Musician)
Rascoff/Zysblat
110 W 57th St # 300
New York, NY 10019-3319, USA

Jones, Daryl (Politician)
3517 Del Mar Ave
Davie, FL 33328-1340, USA

Jones, Daryll (Athlete, Football Player)
581 N Oakley Dr
Columbus, GA 31906-4369, USA

Jones, Datone (Athlete, Football Player)
c/o Sean Kiernan *Impact Sports (LA)*
12429 Ventura Ct
Studio City, CA 91604-2417, USA

Jones, David D (Athlete, Football Player)
3549 Asbury St
Dallas, TX 75205-1846, USA

Jones, Davy (Race Car Driver)
TRW Racing
1397 330th St
Adair, IA 50002-8581, USA

Jones, Dax (Athlete, Baseball Player)
10021 W Suddard Pl
Beach Park, IL 60087-1717, USA

Jones, Dhani (Athlete, Football Player)
10300 Gary Rd
Potomac, MD 20854-4155, USA

Jones, Don (Athlete, Football Player)
8446 Wren Creek Dr
Charlotte, NC 28269-6176, USA

Jones, Donell (Musician)
c/o Ra-Fael Blanco *2R's Entertainment & Media*
601 W 135th St Apt 6E
New York, NY 10031-8304, USA

Jones, Donnie (Athlete, Football Player)
c/o Drew Rosenhaus *Rosenhaus Sports Representation*
3921 Alton Rd # 440
Miami Beach, FL 33140-3852, USA

Jones, Donta (Athlete, Football Player)
4495 Jimmy Greens Pl # Pi
La Plata, MD 20646-5852, USA

Jones, Dot-Marie (Actor)
c/o Bryan deCastro *East 2 West Collective*
11022 Santa Monica Blvd Ste 350
Los Angeles, CA 90025-7532, USA

Jones, Doug (Actor)
c/o John Zander *Zander Magic*
9068 Priscilla St
Downey, CA 90242-4627, USA

Jones, Doug (Athlete, Baseball Player)
129 E Navilla Pl
Covina, CA 91723-3023, USA

Jones, Dub (Athlete, Football Player)
904 Glendale Dr
Ruston, LA 71270-2346, USA

Jones, Earl (Athlete, Basketball Player)
8402 Belding Ct
Brandywine, MD 20613-7107, USA

Jones, Earl (Athlete, Football Player)
14918 Landmark Dr
Louisville, KY 40245-6525, USA

Jones, Earl (Athlete, Track Athlete)
15114 Petoskey Ave
Detroit, MI 48238-2064, USA

Jones, Ed (Athlete, Football Player)
c/o Ladd Biro *Champion Management*
15455 Dallas Pkwy Ste 1350
Addison, TX 75001-6933, USA

Jones, Eddie (Actor)
Gage Group
14724 Ventura Blvd Ste 505
Sherman Oaks, CA 91403-3505, USA

Jones, Eddie (Athlete, Basketball Player)
3400 Paddock Rd
Weston, FL 33331-3520, USA

Jones, E Edward (Religious Leader)
Baptist Convention of America
777 S R L Thornton Fwy
Dallas, TX 75203-2901, USA

Jones, Elvin R (Musician)
DL Media
PO Box 2728
Bala Cynwyd, PA 19004-6728, USA

Jones, Ernest (Athlete, Football Player)
17410 SW 109th Ave
Miami, FL 33157-4042, USA

Jones, Evan (Actor)
c/o Jay Schachter *Abrams Artists Agency*
750 N San Vicente Blvd
E Tower Fl 11
Los Angeles, CA 90069-5788, USA

Jones, Felicity (Actor)
c/o Claire Maroussas *Independent Talent Group*
40 Whitfield St
London W1T 2RH, UNITED KINGDOM

Jones, Felix (Athlete, Football Player)
c/o Eugene Parker *Independent Sports & Entertainment (ISE-IN)*
6435 W Jefferson Blvd # 197
Fort Wayne, IN 46804-6203, USA

Jones, Finn (Actor)
c/o Sarah Spear *Curtis Brown Ltd*
28-29 Hay Market
Hay Market House
London SW1Y 4SP, UNITED KINGDOM

Jones, Freddie (Actor)
c/o Staff Member *Diamond Management*
31 Percy St
London W1T 2DD, UNITED KINGDOM

Jones, Freddie (Athlete, Football Player)
120 Word Ln
Harvest, AL 35749-8800, USA

Jones, Garrett (Athlete, Baseball Player)
670 W Wayman St Apt 1306
Chicago, IL 60661-1702, USA

Jones, Gary (Athlete, Baseball Player)
475 S Westridge Cir
Anaheim, CA 92807-3733, USA

Jones, Gary (Athlete, Football Player)
1410 Ten Mile Dr
Cedar Hill, TX 75104-6239, USA

Jones, Gemma (Actor)
Conway Van Gelder Robinson
18-21 Jermyn St
London SW1Y 6NB, UNITED KINGDOM (UK)

Jones, Glenn (Musician)
Universal Attractions
145 W 57th St # 1500
New York, NY 10019-2220, USA

Jones, Gordon (Athlete, Football Player)
18919 Fishermans Bend Dr
Lutz, FL 33558-9756, USA

Jones, Grace (Actor, Model, Musician)
c/o Staff Member *The Society Management*
156 5th Ave Ste 800
New York, NY 10010-7702, USA

Jones, Greg (Athlete, Baseball Player)
14260 Passage Way
Seminole, FL 33776-1001, USA

Jones, Greg (Athlete, Football Player)
2331 S Fenton Dr
Lakewood, CO 80227-3975, USA

Jones, Greg (Skier)
PO Box 500
Tahoe City, CA 96145-0500, USA

Jones, Gregory M (Athlete, Football Player)
3203 Kirby Ln
Walnut Creek, CA 94598-3908, USA

Jones, Griff Rhys (Actor, Producer, Writer)
c/o Staff Member *TalkBack Management*
20-21 Newman St
London W1T 1PG, UNITED KINGDOM (UK)

Jones, Grover (Deacon) (Athlete, Baseball Player)
1015 Goldfinch Ave
Sugar Land, TX 77478-3452, USA

Jones, Hal (Athlete, Baseball Player)
17700 Avalon Blvd Spc 67
Carson, CA 90746-0231, USA

Jones, Hassan (Athlete, Football Player)
1105 Folkstone Dr
McDonough, GA 30253-3927, USA

Jones, Hayes W (Athlete, Olympic Athlete, Track Athlete)
1040 James K Blvd
Pontiac, MI 48341-1826, USA

Jones, Henry (Hank) (Musician)
Joel Chriss
300 Mercer St Apt 3J
New York, NY 10003-6732, USA

Jones, Homer C (Athlete, Football Player)
416 S Texas St
Pittsburg, TX 75686-1538, USA

Jones, Horace (Athlete, Football Player)
7925 Hobart Ave
Pensacola, FL 32534-4030, USA

Jones, Jack (Musician)
c/o Staff Member *International Ventures*
25115 Avenue Stanford Ste 102
Valencia, CA 91355-4777, USA

Jones, Jacoby (Athlete, Football Player)
c/o Harold C Lewis *National Sports Agency*
12181 Prichard Farm Rd
Maryland Heights, MO 63043-4203, USA

Jones, Jacque (Athlete, Baseball Player, Olympic Athlete)
347 Saint Rita Ct
San Diego, CA 92113-2092, USA

Jones, James (Athlete, Football Player)

Jones, James (Athlete, Football Player)
1009 Hunters Creek Dr
Carrollton, TX 75007-1111, USA

Jones, James (Athlete, Football Player)
PO Box 22694
Kansas City, MO 64113-0694, USA

Jones, James (Athlete, Football Player)
9481 Highland Oak Dr Unit 1815
Tampa, FL 33647-2518, USA

Jones, James C (Athlete, Football Player)
2 Odyssey Dr
Tinley Park, IL 60477-4842, USA

Jones, James Earl (Actor)
PO Box 616
Pawling, NY 12564, USA

Jones, James (Jimmy) (Athlete, Basketball Player)
14700 Marvin Ln
Southwest Ranches, FL 33330-3404, USA

Jones, Jamie (Musician)
MPI Talent
9255 W Sunset Blvd Ste 407
Los Angeles, CA 90069-3302, USA

Jones, Janet (Actor)
9100 Wilshire Blvd Ste 1000W
Beverly Hills, CA 90212-3463, USA

Jones, January (Actor)
21017 Mendenhall Ct
Topanga, CA 90290-4484, USA

Jones, Jarvis (Athlete, Football Player)
c/o Joel Segal *Lagardere Unlimited (NY)*
456 Washington St Apt 9L
New York, NY 10013-1555, USA

Jones, Jasmine Cephas (Actor)
c/o Melissa Raubvogel *Imprint PR*
375 Hudson St
New York, NY 10014-3658, USA

Jones, Jason (Actor)
c/o Jay Gassner *United Talent Agency (UTA)*
9336 Civic Center Dr
Beverly Hills, CA 90210-3604, USA

Jones, Jason (Athlete, Football Player)
c/o Michael McCartney *Priority Sports & Entertainment (Chicago)*
325 N La Salle Dr Ste 650
Chicago, IL 60654-8182, USA

Jones, Jason (Athlete, Baseball Player)
1125 Oakview Dr SE
Smyrna, GA 30080-7917, USA

Jones, Jeff (Coach)
University of Virginia
Athletic Dept
Charlottesville, VA 22903, USA

Jones, Jeff (Athlete, Baseball Player)
51 Emmons Ct
Wyandotte, MI 48192-2553, USA

Jones, Jeff (Athlete, Baseball Player)
311 White Horse Pike
Haddon Heights, NJ 08035-1704, USA

Jones, Jeffrey (Actor)
7336 Santa Monica Blvd # 691
West Hollywood, CA 90046-6670, USA

Jones, Jenny (Comedian)
c/o Gail Stocker *Gail Stocker Presents*
1025 N Kings Rd Apt 113
Los Angeles, CA 90069-6007, USA

Jones, Jermaine (Athlete, Soccer Player)
c/o Richard Motzkin *Wasserman Media Group*
10960 Wilshire Blvd Ste 1200
Los Angeles, CA 90024-3714, USA

Jones, Jermaine (Musician)
c/o Staff Member *19 Entertainment*
401 Wilshire Blvd Ste 1070
Santa Monica, CA 90401-1428, USA

Jones, Jermaine (Athlete, Football Player)
1522 Victor II Blvd
Morgan City, LA 70380-2120, USA

Jones, Jerry (Business Person, Football Executive)
4400 Preston Rd
Dallas, TX 75205-3722, USA

Jones, Jill Marie (Actor)
c/o Liza Anderson *Anderson Group Public Relations*
8060 Melrose Ave Fl 4
Los Angeles, CA 90046-7038, USA

Jones, Jim (Musician)
c/o Gordon MacDonald *Buchwald*
5900 Wilshire Blvd Ste 3100
Los Angeles, CA 90036-5030, USA

Jones, Jimmie (Athlete, Football Player)
2658 Unicorn Ct
Herndon, VA 20171-2425, USA

Jones, Jimmie (Athlete, Football Player)
1205 Frenchmans Dr
Desoto, TX 75115-7764, USA

Jones, Jimmy (Athlete, Baseball Player)
3054 Newcastle Dr
Dallas, TX 75220-1636, USA

Jones, Jimmy (Athlete, Hockey Player)
12 Aspen Leaf Crt
Aurora, ON L4G 7T3, Canada

Jones, joe (Athlete, Baseball Player)
2411 Carlisle Pl
Sarasota, FL 34231-7013, USA

Jones, Joe (Athlete, Football Player)
1413 Scott Ct
Irving, TX 75060-3703, USA

Jones, Joey (Athlete, Football Player)
4032 Royal Oak Cir
Mountain Brk, AL 35243-5831, USA

Jones, John E (Athlete, Football Player)
19610 100th Ave NE
Bothell, WA 98011-2318, USA

Jones, John Marshall (Actor)
c/o Liza Anderson *Anderson Group Public Relations*
8060 Melrose Ave Fl 4
Los Angeles, CA 90046-7038, USA

Jones, John Paul (Musician)
Opium Arts
49 Portland Road
London W11 4LJ, UNITED KINGDOM (UK)

Jones, Jon (Athlete, Mixed Martial Arts)
c/o Tammy Brook *FYI Public Relations*
174 5th Ave Ste 404
New York, NY 10010-5964, USA

Jones, Julia (Actor)
c/o Ruth Bernstein *Viewpoint Inc*
8820 Wilshire Blvd Ste 220
Beverly Hills, CA 90211-2622, USA

Jones, Julio (Athlete, Football Player)
c/o Jimmy Sexton *CAA (Memphis)*
6060 Poplar Ave Ste 470
Memphis, TN 38119-0910, USA

Jones, Julius (Athlete, Football Player)
2765 NE 14th St Unit 41
Fort Lauderdale, FL 33304-1651, USA

Jones, June S (Athlete, Coach, Football Coach, Football Player)
6024 Airline Road
Dallas, TX 75205, USA

Jones, KC (Athlete, Basketball Player)
Basketball Hall of Fame
1000 Hall of Fame Ave Ste 100
Springfield, MA 01105-2545, USA

Jones, K C (Athlete, Basketball Player, Olympic Athlete)
Basketball Hall of Fame 1000 Hall of Fame Ave
1000 Hall of Fame Ave Ste 100
Springfield, MA 01105-2545, USA

Jones, K C (Athlete, Football Player)
102 N Atlantic Dr
Lantana, FL 33462-1914, USA

Jones, Keith (Athlete, Hockey Player)
Philadelphia Flyers
3601 S Broad St Ste 2
Attn Broadcast Dept
Philadelphia, PA 19148-5297, USA

Jones, Keith (Athlete, Hockey Player)
c/o Staff Member *Versus Network*
281 Tresser Blvd Fl 9
Stamford, CT 06901-3238, USA

Jones, Kelly (Musician)
Marsupial Mgmt
Home Farm
Welfor Newbury
Berkshire RG20 8HR, UNITED KINGDOM (UK)

Jones, Ken (Athlete, Football Player)
4455 Porter Rd
Niagara Falls, NY 14305-3309, USA

Jones, Kenneth V (Actor)
PRS
29/33 Berners St
London W1P 4AA, ENGLAND

Jones, Kent (Athlete, Golfer)
813 Los Prados De Guadalupe Dr NW
Los Ranchos, NM 87107-6671, USA

Jones, Kim (Athlete, Football Player)
1396 Madison Ave Apt 150
Loveland, CO 80537-3218, USA

Jones, Kimberly (Commentator)
20 Sherry Ln
Saddle Brook, NJ 07663-5935, USA

Jones, Larry (Athlete, Basketball Player)
1442 Cottingham Ct W
Columbus, OH 43209-3144, USA

Jones, Leroy (Athlete, Football Player)
347 Kantor Blvd
Casselberry, FL 32707-5760, USA

Jones, Leslie (Actor, Comedian)
c/o Josh Pearl *Creative Artists Agency (CAA)*
2000 Avenue of the Stars Ste 100
Los Angeles, CA 90067-4705, USA

Jones, Levi (Athlete, Football Player)
379 S Melba St
Gilbert, AZ 85233-5306, USA

Jones, Lolo (Athlete, Olympic Athlete, Track Athlete)
Lolo Jones Management
PO Box 82226
C/O Angelia Jefferson
Baton Rouge, LA 70884-2226, USA

Jones, L Q (Actor)
2144 1/2 N Cahuenga Blvd
Los Angeles, CA 90068-2708, USA

Jones, Luka (Actor)
c/o David (Dave) Becky *3 Arts Entertainment*
9460 Wilshire Blvd Fl 7
Beverly Hills, CA 90212-2713, USA

Jones, Lynn (Athlete, Baseball Player)
9959 Dicksonburg Rd
Conneautville, PA 16406-1817, USA

Jones, Maggie Elizabeth (Actor)
c/o Cindy Osbrink *Osbrink Talent Agency*
4343 Lankershim Blvd # 100
North Hollywood, CA 91602-2705, USA

Jones, Major (Athlete, Basketball Player)
2475 Brandy Mill Rd
Houston, TX 77067-1275, USA

Jones, Malia (Actor, Athlete)
c/o Michelle Henderson *Henderson Represents*
11846 Ventura Blvd Ste 302
Studio City, CA 91604-2620, USA

Jones, Mandana (Actor)
CAM
19 Denmark Street
London WC2H 8NA, England

Jones, Marcus (Athlete, Baseball Player)
20375 Longbay Dr
Yorba Linda, CA 92887-3250, USA

Jones, Marcus (Athlete, Football Player)
18701 Pepper Pike
Lutz, FL 33558-5315, USA

Jones, Marilyn (Actor)
Kaplan-Stahler Agency
8383 Wilshire Blvd Ste 923
Beverly Hills, CA 90211-2443, USA

Jones, Mark (Commentator, Sportscaster)
c/o Staff Member *ESPN (Main)*
935 Middle St
Espn Plaza
Bristol, CT 06010-1000, USA

Jones, Marvin (Athlete, Baseball Player)
4134 12th St
Ecorse, MI 48229-1224, USA

Jones, Marvin (Athlete, Football Player)
536 N Biscayne River Dr
Miami, FL 33169-6632, USA

Jones, Marvin M (Athlete, Football Player)
8891 NW 193rd St
Miami, FL 33157, USA

Jones, Matt (Actor)
c/o Brian Ferrantino *Ferrantino Entertainment*
139 S Beverly Dr Ste 312
Beverly Hills, CA 90212-3070, USA

Jones, Matt (Athlete, Football Player)
13838 Bella Riva Ln
Jacksonville, FL 32225-5434, USA

Jones, Maxine (Musician)
East West Records
75 Rockefeller Plz Ste 1200
New York, NY 10019-7849, USA

Jones, Merlakia (Basketball Player)
Cleveland Rockers
1 Center Ct
Gund Arena
Cleveland, OH 44115-4001, USA

Jones, Mick (Musician)
c/o Staff Member *Sanctuary Artist Management (UK)*
Sanctuary House
45-53 Sinclair Road
London W14 0NS, UNITED KINGDOM

Jones, Mick (Musician)
Hard to Handle Mgmt
16501 Ventura Blvd Ste 602
Encino, CA 91436-2072, USA

Jones, Mike (Athlete, Baseball Player)

Jones, Mike (Musician)
c/o Staff Member *Warner Bros*
4000 Warner Blvd # 16
Burbank, CA 91522-0002, USA

Jones, Mike A (Athlete, Football Player)
422 Davis Rd
Lebanon, TN 37087-0901, USA

Jones, Nasir (NAS) (Musician)
c/o Brian Edelman *WME/IMG*
9601 Wilshire Blvd
Beverly Hills, CA 90210-5213, USA

Jones, Nasir (Nas) (Actor, Musician)
c/o Staff Member *SMC Europe*
14 Bowling Green Ln
Clerkenwell
London EC1R OBD, UK

Jones, Nathan (Actor)
c/o Rick Bassman *Cunningham Escott Slevin & Doherty (CESD)*
10635 Santa Monica Blvd Ste 130
Los Angeles, CA 90025-8306, USA

Jones, Norah (Musician)
172 Pacific St
Brooklyn, NY 11201-6214, USA

Jones, Odell (Athlete, Baseball Player)
5831 Opal Ave
Palmdale, CA 93552-3967, USA

Jones, Orlando (Actor)
Illumina Productions
PO Box 769
N Hollywood, CA 91603-0769, USA

Jones, Ozell (Athlete, Basketball Player)
2220 Chestnut Ave Apt 1
Long Beach, CA 90806-4258, USA

Jones, Parnelli (Race Car Driver)
PO Box W
Torrance, CA 90508-0329, USA

Jones, Patrick (Actor)
c/o Staff Member *Martin Weiss Management*
PO Box 5656
Santa Monica, CA 90409-5656, USA

Jones, Peter (Business Person)
Peter Jones TV
Palliser House, Palliser Rd
West Kensington
London W14 9EB, UK

Jones, P. J. (Race Car Driver)
2334 S Broadway # 2186
Santa Ana, CA 92707-3250, USA

Jones, PJ (Race Car Driver)
Patrick Racing
8431 Georgetown Rd
Indianapolis, IN 46268-5628, USA

Jones, Preston (Actor)
c/o Alan Iezman *Shelter Entertainment*
9255 W Sunset Blvd Ste 300
Los Angeles, CA 90069-3313, USA

Jones, Preston (Athlete, Football Player)
116 Hamilton Dr
Anderson, SC 29621-1558, USA

Jones, Quincy (Actor, Musician, Producer)
Quincy Jones Music Publishing
6671 W Sunset Blvd Ste 1574A
Los Angeles, CA 90028-7123, USA

Jones, Randy (Musician)
c/o Lee Runchey *Chrome PR*
9107 Wilshire Blvd Ste 450
Beverly Hills, CA 90210-5535, USA

Jones, Randy (Athlete, Baseball Player)
7668 El Camino Real Ste 104 PMB 435
Carlsbad, CA 92009-7932, USA

Jones, Randy (Athlete, Hockey Player)
7 Red Fox Trl
Sicklerville, NJ 08081-3709, USA

Jones, Rashida (Actor, Musician)
c/o Jillian Roscoe *ID Public Relations*
7060 Hollywood Blvd Fl 8th
Los Angeles, CA 90028-6021, USA

Jones, Rebecca (Actor)
c/o Gabriel Blanco *Gabriel Blanco Iglesias (Mexico)*
Rio Balsas 35-32
Colonia Cuauhtemoc
DF 06500, Mexico

Jones, Rees (Athlete, Golfer)
10 Belleclaire Pl
Verona, NJ 07044-5106, USA

Jones, Renee (Actor)
c/o Pearl Wexler *The Kohner Agency*
9300 Wilshire Blvd Ste 555
Beverly Hills, CA 90212-3211, USA

Jones, Reshad (Athlete, Football Player)
c/o Joel Segal *Lagardere Unlimited (NY)*
456 Washington St Apt 9L
New York, NY 10013-1555, USA

Jones, Rich (Athlete, Basketball Player)
101 Luna Way Apt 232
Las Vegas, NV 89145-0187, USA

Jones, Richard T (Actor)
c/o Michael McConnell *Zero Gravity Management (II)*
5660 Silver Valley Ave
Agoura Hills, CA 91301-4000, USA

Jones, Rick (Athlete, Baseball Player)
PO Box 440981
Jacksonville, FL 32222-0010, USA

Jones, Rickie Lee (Musician, Songwriter)
c/o Bruce Solar *Agency for the Performing Arts (APA)*
405 S Beverly Dr Ste 500
Beverly Hills, CA 90212-4425, USA

Jones, Ricky (Athlete, Baseball Player)
PO Box 440981
Jacksonville, FL 32222-0010, USA

Jones, Robert (Athlete, Football Player)
728 Barton Creek Blvd
Austin, TX 78746-4142, USA

Jones, Robert (K C) (Athlete, Basketball Player, Coach)
c/o Staff Member *Naismith Memorial Basketball Hall of Fame*
1000 W Columbus Ave
Springfield, MA 01105-2518, USA

Jones, Robin (Athlete, Basketball Player)
16640 Cynthia Ct
Tinley Park, IL 60477-8209, USA

Jones, Rod (Athlete, Football Player)
1121 Angie Ln
Desoto, TX 75115-3873, USA

Jones, Roger (Athlete, Football Player)
712 Trebor Dr
Goodlettsville, TN 37072-2935, USA

Jones, Ron (Athlete, Hockey Player)
301 Brock St
Coppell, TX 75019-3937, USA

Jones, Ronald (Popeye) (Athlete, Basketball Player)
108 E North St
Dresden, TN 38225-1160, USA

Jones, Rondell (Athlete, Football Player)
421 Competition Rd
Raleigh, NC 27603-1962, USA

Jones, Rosie (Athlete, Golfer)
4895 High Point Rd
Atlanta, GA 30342-2340, USA

Jones, Ross (Athlete, Baseball Player)
4135 Eastridge Cir
Pompano Beach, FL 33064-1847, USA

Jones, Rulon K (Athlete, Football Player)
4003 N 3775 E
Eden, UT 84310, USA

Jones, Ruppert (Athlete, Baseball Player)
7668 El Camino Real Ste 104 PMB 435
Carlsbad, CA 92009-7932, USA

Jones, Rushen (Athlete, Football Player)
3386 E Tiffany Ct
Gilbert, AZ 85298-0842, USA

Jones, Sarah (Actor)
c/o Siri Garber *Platform PR*
2666 N Beachwood Dr
Los Angeles, CA 90068-2308, USA

Jones, Sean (Athlete, Football Player)
4602 McKeever Ln
Missouri City, TX 77459-6310, USA

Jones, Selwyn (Athlete, Football Player)
11216 Grimes Ave
Pearland, TX 77584-5524, USA

Jones, Shelton (Athlete, Basketball Player)
8112 Lockman Ln
Charlotte, NC 28269-5192, USA

Jones, Shirley (Actor, Musician)
8530 Wilshire Blvd Ste 200
Beverly Hills, CA 90211-3130, USA

Jones, Simon (Actor)
Innovative Artists
1505 10th St
Santa Monica, CA 90401-2805, USA

Jones, Spike (Athlete, Football Player)
3612 Club Dr NW
Kennesaw, GA 30144-2019, USA

Jones, Stacy (Athlete, Baseball Player)
1777 Ponderosa Rd
Attalla, AL 35954-5653, USA

Jones, Star (Actor, Producer, Talk Show Host)
c/o Tamara Houston *Round Table Entertainment*
509 N Fairfax Ave Ste 200
Los Angeles, CA 90036-1733, USA

Jones, Stephen J M (Designer, Fashion Designer)
36 Great Queen St
London WC1E 6BT, UNITED KINGDOM (UK)

Jones, Sterling (Actor)
c/o Katie Mason Stern *Luber Roklin Management*
5815 W Sunset Blvd Ste 208
Los Angeles, CA 90028-6481, USA

Jones, Steve (Musician)
Solo Agency
55 Fulham High St
London SW6 3JJ, UNITED KINGDOM (UK)

Jones, Steve (Athlete, Baseball Player)
8116 Kingsdale Dr
Knoxville, TN 37919-7005, USA

Jones, Steve (Athlete, Basketball Player)
3355 N Sutton Sq
Stafford, TX 77477-4722, USA

Jones, Steve (Football Player)
12774 Fee Fee Rd
Saint Louis, MO 63146-4402, USA

Jones, Taiwan (Athlete, Football Player)
c/o Doug Hendrickson *Relativity Sports*
2029 Century Park E Ste 1550
Century City, CA 90067-3000, USA

Jones, Tamala (Actor)
c/o Danielle Allman-Del *D2 Management*
10351 Santa Monica Blvd Ste 210
Los Angeles, CA 90025-6937, USA

Jones, Ta'rhonda (Actor, Musician)
c/o Marisa Paonessa *Paonessa Talent Agency*
1512 N Fremont St Ste 105
Chicago, IL 60642-2567, USA

Jones, Taylor (Cartoonist)
Times-Mirror Syndicate
Times-Mirror Square
Los Angeles, CA 90053, USA

Jones, Tebucky (Athlete, Football Player)
77 Ely Rd
Farmington, CT 06032-1706, USA

Jones, Terry (Actor, Director, Writer)
Python Pictures
34 Thistlewaite Rd
London E5 QQQ, UNITED KINGDOM

Jones, Thomas (Athlete, Football Player)
2742 Clinch Haven Rd
Big Stone Gap, VA 24219-4158, USA

Jones, Thomas D (Astronaut)
c/o Staff Member *NASA-JSC*
2101 Nasa Pkwy # 1
Astronaut Office - Mail Code Cb
Houston, TX 77058-3607, USA

Jones, Thomas F (Athlete, Baseball Player)
13846 Atlantic Blvd Apt 509
Jacksonville, FL 32225-3286, USA

Jones, Tim (Athlete, Baseball Player)
30 Chicot Dr
Maumelle, AR 72113-5801, USA

Jones, Tim (Athlete, Baseball Player)
7711 Greenback Ln Apt 62
Citrus Heights, CA 95610-5807, USA

Jones, Toby (Actor)
c/o Billy Lazarus *United Talent Agency (UTA)*
9336 Civic Center Dr
Beverly Hills, CA 90210-3604, USA

Jones, Todd B G (Athlete, Baseball Player)
421 Eagle Pointe Dr
Pell City, AL 35128-7266, USA

Jones, Tom (Musician)
c/o Staff Member *Hall OR Nothing Independent Publicity*
35-37 Parkgate Rd
Unit 4A Ransomes Dock
London SW11 4NP, UNITED KINGDOM

Jones, Tommy Lee (Actor)
PO Box 966
San Saba, TX 76877-0966, USA

Jones, Tony (Athlete, Football Player)
1820 N Brown Rd Ste 40
Lawrenceville, GA 30043-1800, USA

Jones, Tracy (Athlete, Baseball Player)
101 Harbor Green Dr Apt 602
Bellevue, KY 41073-1155, USA

Jones, Ty (Athlete, Hockey Player)
11803 E 20th Ave
Spokane Valley, WA 99206-7002, USA

Jones, Tyler Patrick (Actor)
c/o Barbara Buky *Cosden Morgan Agency*
7080 Hollywood Blvd Ste 1009
Hollywood, CA 90028-6937, USA

Jones, Van (Commentator)
c/o Staff Member *CNN (NY)*
10 Columbus Cir
Time Warner Center
New York, NY 10019-1158, USA

Jones, Victor (Athlete, Football Player)
17727 Sedona Way
Cornelius, NC 28031-8766, USA

Jones, Victor T (Athlete, Football Player)
PO Box 132241
Dallas, TX 75313-2241, USA

Jones, Vinnie (Actor, Producer)
c/o Melissa Kates *Viewpoint Inc*
8820 Wilshire Blvd Ste 220
Beverly Hills, CA 90211-2622, USA

Jones, Wali (Athlete, Basketball Player)
3160 SW 132nd Ave
Miramar, FL 33027-3868, USA

Jones, Wallace (Athlete, Basketball Player, Olympic Athlete)
512 Chinoe Rd
Lexington, KY 40502-2402, USA

Jones, Walter (Athlete, Football Player)
520 Raymond Pl NW
Renton, WA 98057-3432, USA

Jones, Walter Emanuel (Actor)
K & K Entertainment
1498 W Sunset Blvd
Los Angeles, CA 90026-3471, USA

Jones, Wayne (Actor, Comedian)
Smooth Man Productions
206 Belmont Dr
Palatka, FL 32177-6402, USA

Jones, Wilbert (Athlete, Basketball Player)
3360 Idlecreek Way
Decatur, GA 30034-4916, USA

Jones, William A (Dub) (Athlete, Football Player)
904 Glendale Dr
Ruston, LA 71270-2346, USA

Jones, Willie D (Athlete, Football Player)
4440 Hidden Orchard Ln
Indianapolis, IN 46228-3023, USA

Jones Cox, Vena (Business Person)
Real Life Real Estate
PO Box 58279
Cincinnati, OH 45258-0279, USA

Jones-Doxey, Marilyn (Athlete, Baseball Player, Commentator)
5058 Red Oak Pl
Bradenton, FL 34207-2245, USA

Jones-Drew, Maurice (Athlete, Football Player)
c/o Adisa P Bakari *Kelley Drye & Warren LLP*
3050 K St NW Ste 400
Washington, DC 20007-5100, USA

Jones III, Samuel L (Actor)
c/o Staff Member *Abrams Artists Agency*
750 N San Vicente Blvd
E Tower Fl 11
Los Angeles, CA 90069-5788, USA

Jones Jr, Robert Trent (Athlete, Golfer)
1900 S Ocean Dr Apt 1612
Fort Lauderdale, FL 33316-3715, USA

Jones Jr, Roy (Actor, Boxer, Producer, Sportscaster)
c/o Darren Prince *Prince Marketing Group*
18 Seneca Trl
Sparta, NJ 07871-1514, USA

Jones-Thompson, Marion (Athlete, Olympic Athlete, Track Athlete)

Jong, Erica (Writer)
121 Davis Hill Rd
Weston, CT 06883-2015, USA

Jonigkeit, Evan (Actor)
c/o Christopher Highland *Industry Entertainment Partners*
1133 Broadway Ste 630
New York, NY 10010-8072, USA

Jon-Jules, Danny (Actor)
BBC Information - Artist Mail
PO Box 1116
Belfast B3Z 7AJ, UK

Jonrowe, Dee Dee (Athlete)
PO Box 272
Willow, AK 99688-0272, USA

Jonson, Johnny (Athlete, Football Player)
PO Box 4283
Mooresville, NC 28117-4283, USA

Jonsson, Hans (Athlete, Hockey Player)
Lakasund 1S9
Bonassund, Sweden 891 78, USA

Jonsson, Jorgen (Athlete, Hockey Player)
2000 E Gene Autry Way
Anaheim, CA 92806-6143, USA

Jonsson, Ulrika (Actor)
c/o Jon Fowler *Curtis Brown Ltd*
28-29 Hay Market
Hay Market House
London SW1Y 4SP, UNITED KINGDOM

Jonze, Spike (Actor, Director)
c/o Staff Member *Dickhouse Productions*
5555 Melrose Ave Rm 110
Los Angeles, CA 90038-3993, USA

Joon-ho, Bong (Director)
c/o Mike Simpson *WME|IMG*
9601 Wilshire Blvd
Beverly Hills, CA 90210-5213, USA

Joop, Wolfgang (Designer, Fashion Designer)
Joop
Harvestehuder Weg 22
Ashburn, VA 20149-0001, GERMANY

Joost, Henry (Director)
c/o Rowena Arguelles *Creative Artists Agency (CAA)*
2000 Avenue of the Stars Ste 100
Los Angeles, CA 90067-4705, USA

Joplin, Josh (Musician)
c/o Staff Member *MCT Management*
520 8th Ave Rm 2205
New York, NY 10018-4160, USA

Jopling, Jay (Business Person)
White Cube
144 - 152 Bermondsey St
London SE1 3TQ, UK

Jordan, Anthony (Athlete, Football Player)
38 Albemarle St
Rochester, NY 14613-1402, USA

Jordan, Brian (Athlete, Baseball Player)
Brian Jordan Foundation
PO Box 43345
Atlanta, GA 30336-0345, USA

Jordan, Brian (Athlete, Football Player)
320 Chason Wood Way
Roswell, GA 30076-3996, USA

Jordan, Buford (Athlete, Football Player)
11 Acadia St
Kenner, LA 70065-1001, USA

Jordan, Cameron (Cam) (Football Player)
c/o Doug Hendrickson *Relativity Sports*
2029 Century Park E Ste 1550
Century City, CA 90067-3000, USA

Jordan, Claudia (Actor, Reality Star)
c/o Anthony Turk *Turk Entertainment Public Relations & Productions*
358 S Cochran Ave Apt 103
Los Angeles, CA 90036-3349, USA

Jordan, Curtis (Athlete, Football Player)
629 Surfside Ave
Virginia Beach, VA 23451-3658, USA

Jordan, Darin (Athlete, Football Player)
44 Connell Dr
Stoughton, MA 02072-3708, USA

Jordan, Dion (Athlete, Football Player)
c/o Doug Hendrickson *Relativity Sports*
2029 Century Park E Ste 1550
Century City, CA 90067-3000, USA

Jordan, Don (Boxer)
5100 2nd Ave
Los Angeles, CA 90043-1951, USA

Jordan, Don D (Business Person)
Reliant Energy
1111 Louisiana St
Houston, TX 77002-5230, USA

Jordan, Eddie (Athlete, Basketball Player)
158 Monroe Ave
Belle Mead, NJ 08502-4632, USA

Jordan, Glenn (Director)
9401 Wilshire Blvd Ste 700
Beverly Hills, CA 90212-2944, USA

Jordan, Hamilton (Actor)
The Harry Walker Agency Inc
355 Lexington Ave Fl 21
New York, NY 10017-6603, USA

Jordan, Jeremy (Actor, Musician)
c/o Ted Schachter *Schachter Entertainment*
1157 S Beverly Dr Fl 2
Los Angeles, CA 90035-1119, USA

Jordan, Jim (Congressman, Politician)
1524 Longworth Hob
Washington, DC 20515-2702, USA

Jordan, Kathy (Tennis Player)
114 Walter Hays Dr
Palo Alto, CA 94303-2923, USA

Jordan, Kevin (Athlete, Baseball Player)
127 Ney St
San Francisco, CA 94112-1642, USA

Jordan, Lamont (Athlete, Football Player)
1407 Alberta Dr
Forestville, MD 20747-1902, USA

Jordan, Larry (Athlete, Football Player)
4780 Kirk Rd
Youngstown, OH 44515-5403, USA

Jordan, Laura (Actor)
c/o Matthew Lesher *Insight*
5358 Melrose Ave # 200W
Los Angeles, CA 90038-5117, USA

Jordan, Leander (Athlete, Football Player)
1661 Peachtree Cir N
Jacksonville, FL 32207-6423, USA

Jordan, Lee Roy (Athlete, Football Player)
7710 Caruth Blvd
Dallas, TX 75225-8103, USA

Jordan, Leslie (Actor)
c/o Billy Miller *Billy Miller Management*
8322 Ridpath Dr
Los Angeles, CA 90046-7710, USA

Jordan, Mary (Journalist)
Washington Post
Editorial Dept
1150 15th St NW
Washington, DC 20071-0001, USA

Jordan, Michael (Athlete, Basketball Player, Olympic Athlete)
172 Bears Club Dr
Jupiter, FL 33477-4203, USA

Jordan, Michael B (Actor)
c/o Staff Member *Outlier Society*
1661 Lincoln Blvd Fl 4
Santa Monica, CA 90404-3731, USA

Jordan, Montell (Musician)
c/o Staff Member *Richard De La Font Agency*
3808 W South Park Blvd
Broken Arrow, OK 74011-1261, USA

Jordan, Neil (Director, Writer)
c/o Staff Member *WME|IMG*
9601 Wilshire Blvd
Beverly Hills, CA 90210-5213, USA

Jordan, Neil P (Director)
6 Sorrento Terrace
Dalkey
County Dublin, IRELAND

Jordan, Patty (Athlete, Golfer)
4372 Twilight Ln
Hamburg, NY 14075-1526, USA

Jordan, Randy (Athlete, Football Player)
2220 Rockingham Loop
College Station, TX 77845-4854, USA

Jordan, Ricardo (Athlete, Baseball Player)
Arcadia Road Prison 13617 SE Highway 70 # B04316
Arcadia, FL 34266-7800, USA

Jordan, Ricky (Athlete, Baseball Player)
965 Moonlit Way
Folsom, CA 95630-7506, USA

Jordan, Scott (Athlete)
1530 Carroll Dr NW Ste 103
Atlanta, GA 30318-3600, USA

Jordan, Scott (Athlete, Baseball Player)
265 Great Oak Dr
Athens, GA 30605-4504, USA

Jordan, Shelby (Athlete, Football Player)
29208 Posey Way
Rancho Palos Verdes, CA 90275-4629, USA

Jordan, Stanley (Musician)
SJ Productions
16845 N 29th Ave # 2000
Phoenix, AZ 85053-3053, USA

Jordan, Steve (Athlete, Football Player)
1762 Magnolia Cir
Pleasanton, CA 94566-4764, USA

Jordan, Steven (Stevie J) (Musician)
c/o Devin Mann *WME|IMG*
9601 Wilshire Blvd
Beverly Hills, CA 90210-5213, USA

Jordan, Tom (Athlete, Baseball Player)
15 Dulce Rd
Santa Fe, NM 87508-8284, USA

Jordan, Tony (Athlete, Football Player)
38 Albemarle St
Rochester, NY 14613-1402, USA

Jordanaires, The (Music Group)
PO Box 1381
C/O Ray Walker
Goodlettsville, TN 37070-1381, USA

Jordanova, Vera (Actor, Model)
c/o Jessie Blackhall *Cunningham Escott Slevin & Doherty (CESD)*
333 7th Ave Ste 1102
New York, NY 10001-5111, USA

Jorden, Tim (Athlete, Football Player)
11402 N 26th Pl
Scottsdale, AZ 85260, USA

Jordison, Joey (Musician)
c/o Staff Member *Gersh*
41 Madison Ave Ste 3301
New York, NY 10010-2210, USA

Jorgensen, Bodil (Actor)
c/o Lene Seested *Panorama Agency (Denmark)*
Ryesgade 103B
CopenHagen DK-2100, DENMARK

Jorgensen, Mike (Athlete, Baseball Player, Coach)
12523 Ridgefield Dr
Saint Louis, MO 63131-3622, USA

Jorgensen, Roger (Athlete, Basketball Player)
642 Woodcrest Dr
Pittsburgh, PA 15205-1520, USA

Jorgensen, Ryan (Athlete, Baseball Player)
5 Links Ct
Kingwood, TX 77339-5326, USA

Jorgensen, Terry (Athlete, Baseball Player)
1493 S Sugar Bush Rd
Luxemburg, WI 54217-9311, USA

Jorginho (Soccer Player)
Rua Levi Carreiro 420
Barra de Tijuca, BRAZIL

Jose, Felix (Athlete, Baseball Player)
6814 W Calumet Cir
Lake Worth, FL 33467-7007, USA

Jose, Jose (Musician)
Fanny Schatz Mgmt
Melchor Ocampo 309
Mexico City, DF CP 11590, MEXICO

Jose, Lind (Baseball Player)
Pittsburgh Pirates
18 Villa Santa
Dorado, PR 00646-5770, USA

Josef, Diego (Actor)
c/o Penny Vizcarra *PV Public Relations*
121 N Almont Dr Apt 203
Beverly Hills, CA 90211-1860, USA

Josef Liefers, Jan (Actor)
c/o Martina Jansen *Players Agentur Management*
Sophienstrasse 21
Berlin 10178, GERMANY

Josefowicz, Leila (Musician)
I M G Artists
420 W 45th St
New York, NY 10036-3501, USA

Joseph, Aubrey (Actor)
c/o Liz York *Principal Entertainment*
9255 W Sunset Blvd Ste 500
Los Angeles, CA 90069-3301, USA

Joseph, Chris (Athlete, Hockey Player)
17 L'Hirondelle Crt St
Albert
Edmonton, AB T8N SX9, Canada

Joseph, Cory (Athlete, Basketball Player)
c/o Leon Rose *CAA Basketball*
405 Lexington Ave Fl 19
New York, NY 10174-1800, USA

Joseph, Curtis (Athlete, Hockey Player)
c/o Donald Meehan *Newport Sports Management*
201 City Centre Dr
Suite 400
Mississauga, ON L58 2T4, CANADA

Joseph, Daryl J (Astronaut)
615 Peachtree Ct
Campbell, CA 95008-6353, USA

Joseph, Davin (Athlete, Football Player)
17912 Bimini Isle Ct
Tampa, FL 33647-2782, USA

Joseph, James (Athlete, Football Player)
8942 Stoneridge Pl
Montgomery, AL 36117-8876, USA

Joseph, Jonathan (Athlete, Football Player)

Joseph, Kevin (Athlete, Baseball Player)
8826 Lacrosse Dr
Dallas, TX 75231-4826, USA

Joseph, Linval (Athlete, Football Player)
c/o Bill Johnson *SportsTrust Advisors*
3340 Peachtree Rd NE Fl 16
Atlanta, GA 30326-1000, USA

Joseph, Vance (Athlete, Football Player)
6416 Sherman Peak Ct
Castle Rock, CO 80108-9492, USA

Joseph, William (Musician)
c/o Staff Member *MCT Management*
520 8th Ave Rm 2205
New York, NY 10018-4160, USA

Joseph, William (Athlete, Football Player)
1071 NE 107th St
Miami, FL 33161-7353, USA

Josephine, Charlotte (Royalty)
Grand Ducal Palace
Luxembourg, LUXEMBOURG

Josephson, Karen (Swimmer)
2630 San Carlos Dr
Walnut Creek, CA 94598-3112, USA

Josephson, Lester (Josey) (Athlete, Football Player)
5388 N Genernatas Dr
Tucson, AZ 85704, USA

Josephson, Sarah (Swimmer)
2630 San Carlos Dr
Walnut Creek, CA 94598-3112, USA

Joshi, Indira (Actor)
c/o Staff Member *BBC Artist Mail*
PO Box 1116
Belfast BT2 7AJ, United Kingdom

Joshua, Larry (Actor)
c/o Judy Orbach *Judy O Productions*
6136 Glen Holly St
Hollywood, CA 90068-2338, USA

Joshua, Von (Athlete, Baseball Player)
57449 Windmill Pt
New Hudson, MI 48165-8123, USA

Jossa, Jacqueline (Actor)
c/o Peter Brooks *Creative Artists Management (CAM-UK)*
55-59 Shaftesbury Ave.
London W1D 6LD, UNITED KINGDOM

Jost, Mike (Athlete, Baseball Player)
339 W Woodward St
Vail, AZ 85641-2826, USA

Jostyn, Jennifer (Actor)
c/o Staff Member *Abrams Artists Agency*
750 N San Vicente Blvd
E Tower Fl 11
Los Angeles, CA 90069-5788, USA

Josue, Steve (Athlete, Football Player)
18711 NE 3rd Ct Apt 215
Miami, FL 33179-3808, USA

Joswick, Bob (Athlete, Football Player)
5829 W Orlando Cir
Broken Arrow, OK 74011-1153, USA

Joswick, Robert (Athlete, Football Player)
10902 Wilson Ave
Alta Loma, CA 91737-2438, USA

Joubert, Brian (Figure Skater)
Federation Francaise des Sports De Glace
35 rue Felicien David
Paris 75016, FRANCE

Jourdain Jr, Michel (Race Car Driver)
Team Rahal
4601 Lyman Dr
Hilliard, OH 43026-1249, USA

Journell, Jimmy (Athlete, Baseball Player)
1511 Eastgate Rd
Springfield, OH 45503-2427, USA

Journey (Music Group)
c/o Peter Grosslight *WME|IMG*
9601 Wilshire Blvd
Beverly Hills, CA 90210-5213, USA

Jovanovski, Ed (Athlete, Hockey Player)
528 E Alexander Palm Rd
Boca Raton, FL 33432-7985, USA

Jovovich, Milla (Actor, Model, Musician)
c/o Jason Weinberg *Untitled Entertainment*
350 S Beverly Dr Ste 200
Beverly Hills, CA 90212-4819, USA

Jow, Malese (Actor)
c/o Angela Mach *Platform PR*
2666 N Beachwood Dr
Los Angeles, CA 90068-2308, USA

Joy, Megan (Musician)
Prefers to be contacted by email.

Joy, Mike (Race Car Driver)
111 Mystic Lake Loop
Mooresville, NC 28117-6000, USA

Joy, Robert (Actor)
c/o Donna Massetti *SMS Talent*
8383 Wilshire Blvd Ste 230
Beverly Hills, CA 90211-2436, USA

Joy, Vance (Musician)
c/o Chelsey Northern *Atlantic Records*
3400 W Olive Ave Fl 2
Burbank, CA 91505-5538, USA

Joyal, Eddie (Athlete, Hockey Player)
6469 Wandermere Dr
San Diego, CA 92120-3214, USA

Joyce, Andrea (Correspondent, Sportscaster)
c/o Staff Member *NBC Sports (NY)*
30 Rockefeller Plz
New York, NY 10112-0015, USA

Joyce, Delvin (Athlete, Football Player)
355 Trott Cir
Martinsville, VA 24112-7659, USA

Joyce, Duane (Athlete, Hockey Player)
143 W Elm St
Pembroke, MA 02359-2136, USA

Joyce, Elaine (Actor)
724 N Roxbury Dr
Beverly Hills, CA 90210-3212, USA

Joyce, James (Athlete, Baseball Player)
9785 SW 167th Pl
Beaverton, OR 97007-8705, USA

Joyce, James (Baseball Player)
9785 SW 167th Pl
Beaverton, OR 97007-8705, USA

Joyce, Jim (Athlete, Baseball Player)
9785 SW 167th Pl # Pi
Beaverton, OR 97007-8705, USA

Joyce, Joan (Athlete, Golfer)
20024 Back Nine Dr
Boca Raton, FL 33498-4707, USA

Joyce, Kara Lynn (Athlete, Olympic Athlete, Swimmer)
1778 Fairoaks Pl
Decatur, GA 30033-1449, USA

Joyce, Kevin (Athlete, Basketball Player, Olympic Athlete)
420 W Olive St Apt 9
Long Beach, NY 11561-3128, USA

Joyce, Lisa (Actor)
c/o Leslee Dart *42West*
600 3rd Ave Fl 23
New York, NY 10016-1914, USA

Joyce, Matt (Athlete, Football Player)
6330 E Wilshire Dr
Scottsdale, AZ 85257-1122, USA

Joyce, Matt (Athlete, Football Player)
3804 Villas Del Sol Ct
Tampa, FL 33609-4440, USA

Joyce, Mike (Athlete, Baseball Player)
1 Mission Ct # 122
Winfield, IL 60190-2068, USA

Joyce, Tom (Artist)
21 Likely Rd # A
Santa Fe, NM 87508-5963, USA

Joyce, William (Artist, Writer)
c/o Michael Siegel *Siegel Sports & Entertainment*
1149 3rd St Fl 3
Santa Monica, CA 90403-7201, USA

Joyce, William H (Business Person)
Union Carbide
10 Riverview Dr
Danbury, CT 06810-6268, USA

Joy Lenz, Bethany (Actor)
c/o Cheryl McLean *Creative Public Relations*
3385 Oak Glen Dr
Los Angeles, CA 90068-1311, USA

Joyner, Alrederick (Al) (Athlete, Track Athlete)
CMG World Wide
8560 W Sunset Blvd PH
West Hollywood, CA 90069-2311, USA

Joyner, Harry (Athlete, Basketball Player)
1100 N Alyssa Cir
Payson, AZ 85541-3371, USA

Joyner, Lisa (Television Host)
c/o Karen Samfilippo *IMPR*
1158 26th St # 548
Santa Monica, CA 90403-4698, USA

Joyner, Michelle (Actor)
Paradigm Agency
10100 Santa Monica Blvd Ste 2500
Los Angeles, CA 90067-4116, USA

Joyner, Seth (Athlete, Football Player)
5138 N 79th Pl
Scottsdale, AZ 85250-7209, USA

Joyner, Tom (Radio Personality)
PO Box 630495
Irving, TX 75063-0128

Joyner, Wally (Athlete, Baseball Player)
516 E 2800 S
Mapleton, UT 84664-4850, USA

Joyner-Kersee, Jacqueline (Jackie) (Athlete, Olympic Athlete, Track Athlete)
Women's Sports Foundation
1049 Bristol Manor Dr
Ballwin, MO 63011-5106, USA

Jozwiak, Brian J (Athlete, Coach, Football Coach, Football Player)
203 Ruby Lake Ln
Winter Haven, FL 33884-3267, USA

J. Rahall II, Nick (Congressman, Politician)
2307 Rayburn Hob
Washington, DC 20515-4803, USA

J. Ribble, Reid (Congressman, Politician)
1513 Longworth Hob
Washington, DC 20515-2506, USA

J. Rogers, Mike (Congressman, Politician)
133 Cannon Hob
Washington, DC 20515-2208, USa

J. Rooney, Thomas (Congressman, Politician)
1529!-QN.9WQRTH Hqb
Washington, DC 20515-0001, USA

J. Roskam, Peter (Congressman, Politician)
227 Ca,Rtn<M Hob
Washington, DC 20515-0001, USA

J. Tiberi, Patrick (Congressman, Politician)
106 Cannon Hob
Washington, DC 20515-3204, USA

Ju, Ming (Artist)
28 Lane 460
Chih Shan Road Section 2
Taipei, TAIWAN

Juanes (Musician)
PO Box 370648
Miami, FL 33137-0648, USA

Juantorena Danger, Alberto (Athlete, Track Athlete)
National Institute for Sports
Sports City
Havana, CUBA

Juarez, Ricardo (Rocky) (Athlete, Boxer, Olympic Athlete)
3916 Weems St
Houston, TX 77009-4747, USA

Juchheim, Alwin (Politician)
939 Ave of Pines St
Grenada, MS 38901-4609, USA

Judd, Ashley (Actor)
PO Box 1569
Franklin, TN 37065-1569, USA

Judd, Cris (Actor, Dancer)
c/o Monica Barkett *Global Artists Agency*
6253 Hollywood Blvd Apt 508
Los Angeles, CA 90028-8251, USA

Judd, Jackie (Correspondent)
ABC-TV
77 W 66th St
News Dept
New York, NY 10023-6201, USA

Judd, Mike (Athlete, Baseball Player)
9805 Shadow Rd
La Mesa, CA 91941-4154, USA

Judd, Naomi (Musician)
c/o Julie Colbert *WME/IMG*
9601 Wilshire Blvd
Beverly Hills, CA 90210-5213, USA

Judd, Wynonna (Musician)
5601 Pinewood Rd
Franklin, TN 37064-9306, USA

Juden, Jeff (Athlete, Baseball Player)
29 Ingalls Ter Apt 1
Swampscott, MA 01907-5200, USA

Judge, Christopher (Actor, Writer)
c/o Melanie Marquez *M4 Publicity*
11684 Ventura Blvd # 213
Studio City, CA 91604-2699, USA

Judge, Mike (Actor, Animator, Producer, Writer)
c/o Staff Member *Ternion Pictures*
1010 W Martin Luther King Jr Blvd
Austin, TX 78701-1070, USA

Judges, Gordon (Athlete, Football Player)
1782 Meadowview Ave
Pickering, ON L1V 3G8, Canada

Judkins, Jeff (Athlete, Basketball Player)
3471 S 3570 E
Salt Lake City, UT 84109-3243, USA

Judson, Howie (Athlete, Baseball Player)
239 Fairway Cir
Winter Haven, FL 33881-8742, USA

Judson, William (Athlete, Football Player)
652 Sinclair Way
Jonesboro, GA 30238-7962, USA

Jue, Bhawoh (Athlete, Football Player)
21048 Lowry Park Ter APT 402
Ashburn, VA 20147-6435, USA

Juenger, David (Athlete, Football Player)
790 Cliffside Dr
Chillicothe, OH 45601-2902, USA

Juergensen, Heather (Actor)
c/o Staff Member *Generate Management*
8750 Wilshire Blvd Ste 200
Beverly Hills, CA 90211-2707, USA

Juhl, Finn (Designer)
Kratvaenget 15
Chartottenlund 02920, DENMARK

Juicy J (Musician)
411 N Oakhurst Dr Unit 402
Beverly Hills, CA 90210-5607, USA

Jules, Gary (Musician)
c/o Staff Member *Paradigm (Monterey)*
404 W Franklin St
Monterey, CA 93940-2303, USA

Julian, Fred (Athlete, Football Player)
730 Strawberry Valley Ave NW
Comstock Park, MI 49321-9600, USA

Julian, Janet (Actor)
Borinstein Oreck Bogart
3172 Dona Susana Dr
Studio City, CA 91604-4356, USA

Julian, Jonathan (Actor)
c/o Susan Nathe *Nathe & Associates*
8281 Melrose Ave Ste 200
Los Angeles, CA 90046-6823, USA

Julian II, Alexander (Designer, Fashion Designer)
Alexander Julian Inc
PO Box 60
Georgetown, CT 06829-0060, USA

Julich, Bobby (Athlete, Cycler, Olympic Athlete)
998 Brush Creek Ln
Glenwood Springs, CO 81601-4502, USA

Julien, Claire (Actor)
c/o Jamie Harhay Skinner *Baker Winokur Ryder Public Relations*
9100 Wilshire Blvd
W Tower #500
Beverly Hills, CA 90212-3415, USA

Julien, Claude (Athlete, Coach, Hockey Player)
c/o Staff Member *Boston Bruins*
100 Legends Way Ste 250
Td Banknorth Garden
Boston, MA 02114-1389, USA

Julien, Claude (Athlete, Hockey Player)
Boston Bruins
100 Legends Way Ste 250
Attn: Coaching Staff
Boston, MA 02114-1389, USA

Julien, Max (Actor)
3580 Avenida Del Sol
Studio City, CA 91604-4018, USA

Julio, Jorge (Athlete, Baseball Player)
3957 San Simeon Ln
Weston, FL 33331-5059, USA

Jullen, Claude (Coach)
Montreal Canadiens
1260 de la Gauchetiere W
Montreal, QC H3B 5E8, CANADA

Juma, Kevin (Athlete, Football Player)
1120 Cliff Ave Apt 501
Tacoma, WA 98402-5132, USA

June, Cato (Athlete, Football Player)
13500 Van Brady Rd
Upper Marlboro, MD 20772-7905, USA

Juneau, Joe (Athlete, Hockey Player)
Harfan Technologies Inc
100-2 rue de Jardin
Attn: VIce President's Office
Port-Rouge, QC G3H 3R7, Canada

Jung, Ernst (Writer)
8815 Lagenensligen/Wiltingen
GERMANY

Jung, Jessica (Musician)
c/o Darren Boghosian *United Talent Agency (UTA)*
9336 Civic Center Dr
Beverly Hills, CA 90210-3604, USA

Jung, Ji-Hoon (Rain) (Actor)
c/o Cho Dong Won *J.tune Entertainment*
2F, M Building 221-5
NonHyunDong GangNamGu
Seoul 135010, Korea

Junge, Eric (Athlete, Baseball Player)
89 Clinton St Apt 2R
New York, NY 10002-3889, USA

Junger, Gil (Director, Producer)
c/o Staff Member *Creative Artists Agency (CAA)*
2000 Avenue of the Stars Ste 100
Los Angeles, CA 90067-4705, USA

Junger, Sebastian (Writer)
c/o Cathy Saypol *CSPR Inc*
PO Box 689
Stone Ridge, NY 12484-0689, USA

Jungman, Eric (Actor)
c/o Staff Member *Leslie Allan-Rice Management*
1007 Maybrook Dr
Beverly Hills, CA 90210-2715, USA

Jungueira, Bruno (Race Car Driver)
2127 Brickell Ave Apt 3105
Miami, FL 33129-2105, USA

Junior, Ester J (E J) (Athlete, Football Player)
911 W Summit St
Bolivar, MO 65613-1021, USA

Junior Varsity (Music Group)
Victory Records
346 N Justine St Ste 504
Chicago, IL 60607-1021, USA

Junker, Steve (Athlete, Football Player)
17S6 Thrums Rd
Castlegar, BC VlN 4N4, Canada

Junkin, Abner (Athlete, Football Player)
5 Lakeside Ln
Newport, AR 72112-3948, USA

Junkin, Trey (Athlete, Football Player)
300 Wren St
Winnfield, LA 71483-2662, USA

Junqueira, Bruno (Race Car Driver)
721 Crandon Blvd Apt 308
Key Biscayne, FL 33149-2565, USA

Juppe, Alain (Politician)
57 rue de Varenne
Paris, FRANCE F-75007

Jurak, Ed (Athlete, Baseball Player)
3650 S Walker Ave
San Pedro, CA 90731-6046, USA

Juran, Nathan (Director, Writer)
197 Desert Lakes Dr
Rancho Mirage, CA 92270-4053, USA

Jurasik, Peter (Actor)
969 1/2 Manzanita St
Los Angeles, CA 90029-3009, USA

Jurasin, Bobby (Athlete, Football Player)
160 Huron Woods Dr
Marquette, MI 49855-9699, USA

Jurek, Scott (Athlete)
c/o Zach Rosenfield *Stan Rosenfield & Associates*
2029 Century Park E Ste 1190
Los Angeles, CA 90067-2931, USA

Jurevicius, Joe (Athlete, Football Player)
1779 Berkshire Rd
Gates Mills, OH 44040-9747, USA

Jurewicz, Mike (Athlete, Baseball Player)
13804 Evergreen Ct
Saint Paul, MN 55124-9257, USA

Jurgens, Dan (Cartoonist)
5033 Green Farms Rd
Edina, MN 55436-1091, USA

Jurgensen, Sonny (Athlete, Football Player)
6963 Greentree Dr
Naples, FL 34108-8528, USA

Jurgensmeier-Carroll, Margaret (Athlete, Baseball Player, Commentator)
5245 Rowena Dr
Roscoe, IL 61073-7221, USA

Jurich, Tom (Athlete, Football Player)
11 San Marco St Apt 601
Clearwater Beach, FL 33767-2060, USA

Juriga, James (Athlete, Football Player)
3001 Easton Pl
Saint Charles, IL 60175-5610, USA

Juriga, Jim (Athlete, Football Player)
3001 Easton Pl
Saint Charles, IL 60175-5610, USA

Jurkovic, John (Athlete, Football Player)
2212 June Dr
Schererville, IN 46375-3079, USA

Jurkovic, Mirko (Athlete, Football Player)
68520 Garver Lake Rd
Edwardsburg, MI 49112-9404, USA

Jury, Bob (Athlete, Football Player)
2 Sassafras Ln
Greensburg, PA 15601-9023, USA

Just, Ward S (Writer)
36 Ave Junot
Paris, FRANCE

Juster, Norton (Writer)
55 Kellogg Ave
Amherst, MA 01002-2138, USA

Justice, David (Athlete, Baseball Player)
18570 Old Coach Way
Poway, CA 92064-6651, USA

Justice, Donald R (Writer)
338 Rocky Shore Dr
Iowa City, IA 52246-3836, USA

Justice, Victoria (Actor)
c/o Meghan Prophet *PMK/BNC Public Relations*
1840 Century Park E Ste 1400
Los Angeles, CA 90067-2115, USA

Justin, Dan (Athlete, Hockey Player)
53 Beaufort Rd
Toronto, ON M4E 1M8, Canada

Justin, Kerry (Athlete, Football Player)
13331 W Marlette Ct
Litchfield Park, AZ 85340-5377, USA

Justin, Paul (Athlete, Football Player)
2529 W Via Perugia
Phoenix, AZ 85086-6631, USA

Just Jinger (Music Group)
c/o Staff Member *Paradigm (Monterey)*
404 W Franklin St
Monterey, CA 93940-2303, USA

Justman, Seth (Musician)
Nick Ben-Meir
2850 Ocean Park Blvd Ste 300
Santa Monica, CA 90405-6216, USA

Juszczyk, Kyle (Athlete, Football Player)
c/o Joe Linta *JL Sports*
1204 Main St Ste 179
Branford, CT 06405-3787, USA

Jutze, Skip (Athlete, Baseball Player)
3395 Zephyr Ct
Wheat Ridge, CO 80033-5967, USA

Juvenile (Musician)
c/o Staff Member *ICM Partners*
10250 Constellation Blvd Fl 7
Los Angeles, CA 90067-6207, USA

J. Visclosky, Peter (Congressman, Politician)
2256 Rayburn Hob
Washington, DC 20515-4324, USA

J W, Pirtle (Athlete, Baseball Player)
1205 Carver Dr
Champaign, IL 61820-2412, USA

J. Walz, Timothy (Congressman, Politician)
1722 Longworth Hob
Washington, DC 20515-3008, USA

K

Kaake, Jeff (Actor)
2533 N Carson St # 3105
Carson City, NV 89706-0242, USA

Kaas, Carmen (Model)
Men/Women Model Inc
199 Lafayette St Fl 7
New York, NY 10012-4281, USA

Kaas, Patrica (Musician)
Talent Sorcier
3 Rue des Petites-Ecuries
Paris 75010, FRANCE

Kaat, Jim (Athlete, Baseball Player)
PO Box 1130
Port Salerno, FL 34992-1130, USA

Kab, Vyto (Athlete, Football Player)
18 Grissing Ct
Cedar Grove, NJ 07009-1916, USA

Kaba, Agim (Actor, Producer)
c/o Adam Griffin *LINK Entertainment*
11872 La Grange Ave
Los Angeles, CA 90025-5282, USA

Kabakov, Ilya (Artist)
Gladstone Gallery
525 W 52nd St
New York, NY 10019-5074, USA

Kabat-Zinn, Jon (Writer)
Sounds True, Inc
413 S Arthur Ave
Louisville, CO 80027-3013, USA

Kaberle, Frantisek (Athlete, Hockey Player)
Belehradska 2213
Kladno 272 01, CZECH REPUBLIC

Kabua, Imata (President)
President's Office
Cabinet Building
PO Box 2
Majuro, MARSHALL ISLANDS

Kacherski, John (Athlete, Football Player)
5477 Gordon Way
Dublin, OH 43017-8870, USA

Kachowski, Mark (Athlete, Hockey Player)
113 Pine Creek Dr
Venetia, PA 15367-1330, USA

Kaci (Musician)
c/o Staff Member *Curb Records (LA)*
3907 W Alameda Ave Ste 104
Burbank, CA 91505-4359

Kacyvenski, Isaiah (Athlete, Football Player)
1081 Beacon St # 8
Brookline, MA 02446-5610, USA

Kaczmarek, Jane (Actor)
c/o Melissa Kates *Viewpoint Inc*
8820 Wilshire Blvd Ste 220
Beverly Hills, CA 90211-2622, USA

Kaczur, Nick (Athlete, Football Player)
17 K Marie Dr
Attleboro, MA 02703-6730, USA

Kadare, Ismael (Writer)
63 Blvd Saint-Michel
Paris 75005, FRANCE

Kadela, Dave (Athlete, Football Player)
3 Marshwinds
Hilton Head Island, SC 29926-1106, USA

Kadish, Lawrence (Horse Racer)
135 Jericho Tpke
Old Westbury, NY 11568-1508, USA

Kadish, Michael S (Mike) (Athlete, Football Player)
7941 Sudbury Ln SE
Ada, MI 49301-9356, USA

Kadison, Joshua (Musician, Songwriter, Writer)
Nick Bode
1265 Electric Ave
Venice, CA 90291-3397, USA

Kadziel, Ron (Athlete, Football Player)
2492 Creek Dr
Park City, UT 84060-6866, USA

Kaeding, Nate (Athlete, Football Player)
1528 1st Ave Unit A
Coralville, IA 52241-1100, USA

Kae-Kazim, Hakeem (Actor)
c/o Laura Gibson *Generate Management*
8750 Wilshire Blvd Ste 200
Beverly Hills, CA 90211-2707, USA

Kaelin, Kato (Actor)
c/o Nicole St. John *elev8*
489 S Robertson Blvd Ste 206
Beverly Hills, CA 90211-3637, USA

Kaepernick, Colin (Athlete, Football Player)
c/o Jeff Nalley *Select Sports Group*
2700 Post Oak Blvd Ste 1450
Houston, TX 77056-5785, USA

Kaese, Trent (Athlete, Hockey Player)
Cottonwood Golf Course
197S Haslam Rd
Nanaimo, BC V9X ITl, Canada

Kaeser, Joe (Business Person)
Siemens Aktiengesellschaft
Wittelsbacherplatz 2
Munich 80333, Germany

Kaesviharn, Kevin (Athlete, Football Player)
6334 Merrimac Ln N
Osseo, MN 55311-3835, USA

Kafentzis, Kurt (Athlete, Football Player)
1305 Perkins Ave
Richland, WA 99354-3106, USA

Kafentzis, Mark (Athlete, Football Player)
15912 134th Avenue Ct E
Puyallup, WA 98374-9647, USA

Kafka, Mike (Athlete, Football Player)
c/o Michael McCartney *Priority Sports & Entertainment (Chicago)*
325 N La Salle Dr Ste 650
Chicago, IL 60654-8182, USA

Kaftan, George (Athlete, Basketball Player)
2591 Lantern Light Way
Manasquan, NJ 08736-2247, USA

Kagan, Daryn (Correspondent)
Cable News Network
1050 Techwood Dr NW
News Dept
Atlanta, GA 30318-5695, USA

Kagan, Daryn (Correspondent)
1579 Monroe Dr NE Ste F PMB 134
Atlanta, GA 30324-5034, USA

Kagan, Jeremy Paul (Director)
2024 N Curson Ave
Los Angeles, CA 90046-2210, USA

Kagasoff, Daren (Actor)
c/o John Carrabino *John Carrabino Management*
5900 Wilshire Blvd Ste 740
Los Angeles, CA 90036-5032, USA

Kagen, David (Actor)
c/o Staff Member *Coast to Coast Talent Group*
3350 Barham Blvd
Los Angeles, CA 90068-1404, USA

Kagge, Erling (Skier)
Munkedamsveien 86
Oslo 00270, NORWAY

Kahan, Richard (Actor)
c/o Elena Kirschner *Red Management*
415 Esplanade W Box 3
North Vancouver, BC V7M 1A6, CANADA

Kahane, Jeffrey (Musician)
I M G Artists
420 W 45th St
New York, NY 10036-3501, USA

Kahler, Bob (Athlete, Football Player)
5500 Salem Square Dr N
Palm Harbor, FL 34685-1146, USA

Kahler, Robert (Athlete, Football Player)
5500 Salem Square Dr N
Palm Harbor, FL 34685-1146, USA

Kahn, Joseph (Director, Writer)
c/o Staff Member *HSI Entertainment*
3630 Eastham Dr
Culver City, CA 90232-2411, USA

Kahn, Roger (Commentator)
PO Box 556
Stone Ridge, NY 12484-0556, USA

Kahn, Roger (Writer)
280 Marcotte Rd
Kingston, NY 12401-8318, USA

Kahn, Shahid (Business Person)
Flex-N-Gate
1306 E University Ave
Urbana, IL 61802-2093, USA

Kahne, Kasey (Race Car Driver)
PO Box 1749
Davidson, NC 28036-1749, USA

Kai, Teanna (Adult Film Star)
c/o Staff Member *Atlas Multimedia Inc*
9005 Eton Ave Ste C
Canoga Park, CA 91304-6533, USA

Kaif, Katrina (Actor)
c/o Staff Member *Badaparda*
PO Box 1981
Chandigarh, Punjab 160003, INDIA

Kaige, Chen (Director)
c/o John Campisi *Creative Artists Agency (CAA)*
2000 Avenue of the Stars Ste 100
Los Angeles, CA 90067-4705, USA

Kaimer, Karl (Athlete, Football Player)
3 Kerr Ave
Lavallette, NJ 08735-2138, USA

Kain, Karin A (Dancer)
National Ballet of Canada
470 Queens Quay W
Toronto, ON M5V 3K4, CANADA

Kain, Khalil (Actor)
c/o Staff Member *Envision Entertainment*
8840 Wilshire Blvd Fl 3
Beverly Hills, CA 90211-2606, USA

Kaine, Tim (Politician)
222 Central Park Ave Ste 120
Virginia Beach, VA 23462-3023, USA

Kainer, Don (Athlete, Baseball Player)
1923 Sieber Dr
Houston, TX 77017-6201, USA

Kaiser, Bob (Athlete, Baseball Player)
8 Independence Way
Southampton, NJ 08088-9047, USA

Kaiser, Don (Athlete, Baseball Player)
2901 E 12th St
Ada, OK 74820-7259, USA

Kaiser, George B (Business Person)
BOK Financial Corporation
Bank of Oklahoma Tower
PO Box 2300
Tulsa, OK 74192-0001, USA

Kaiser, Jason (Athlete, Football Player)
3885 Cheyenne Pl
Sedalia, CO 80135-8931, USA

Kaiser, Jeff (Athlete, Baseball Player)
26227 James Dr
Grosse Ile, MI 48138-2172, USA

Kaiser, Natasha (Athlete, Track Athlete)
2601 Hickman Rd
Des Moines, IA 50310-6101, USA

Kaiser, Suki (Actor)
c/o Pam Winter *Gary Goddard Agency (GGA)*
304-250 The Esplanade
Toronto, ON M5A 1J2, CANADA

Kaiser, Tim (Producer)
c/o Scott Schwartz *Vision Art Management*
750 N San Vicente Blvd Ste R800
West Hollywood, CA 90069-5778, USA

Kaiser Chiefs (Music Group)
c/o Staff Member *Helter Skelter (UK)*
535 Kings Rd
The Plaza
London SW10 0SZ, UNITED KINGDOM (UK)

Kaiserman, William (Designer, Fashion Designer)
29 W 56th St
New York, NY 10019-3986, USA

Kajlich, Bianca (Actor)
c/o Chris Henze *Thruline Entertainment*
9250 Wilshire Blvd Fl Ground
Beverly Hills, CA 90212-3352, USA

Kaka (Athlete, Soccer Player)
c/o Staff Member *Real Madrid*
Avenida De Concha Espina, 1
Estadio Santiago Bernabéu
Madrid 28036, Spain

Kaku, Michio (Writer)
c/o Robert Holtz *Kaku Media Inc*
848 N Rainbow Blvd # 3311
Las Vegas, NV 89107-1103, USA

Kalafat, Ed (Athlete, Basketball Player)
2323 Kingfish Rd
Naples, FL 34102-1539, USA

Kalanick, Travis (Business Person)
565 Broome St PH
New York, NY 10013-1530, USA

Kalas, Harry (Sportscaster)
Philadelphia Phillies
3308 Chatham Pl
Media, PA 19063-4313, USA

Kalas, Todd (Commentator)
9417 Cavendish Dr Apt 108
Tampa, FL 33626-5173, USA

Kalem, Toni (Actor)
c/o Erin Junkin *WME|IMG (NY)*
11 Madison Ave Fl 18
New York, NY 10010-3669, USA

Kalember, Patricia (Actor)
Innovative Artists
1505 10th St
Santa Monica, CA 90401-2805, USA

Kaler, Jamie (Actor)
955 2nd St Apt 9
Santa Monica, CA 90403-2448

Kaleta, Patrick (Athlete, Hockey Player)
3011 Cloverbank Rd Unit 39
Hamburg, NY 14075-3460, USA

Kalichstein, Joseph (Musician)
I C M Artists
40 W 57th St
New York, NY 10019-4001, USA

Kalidas, Preeya (Actor)
c/o Oliver Thomson *Cole Kitchenn Personal Management*
ROAR House
46 Charlotte St
London W1T 2GS, UNITED KINGDOM

Kalil, Matt (Athlete, Football Player)
c/o Tom Condon *Creative Artists Agency (CAA)*
401 Commerce St PH
Nashville, TN 37219-2516, USA

Kalil, Ryan (Athlete, Football Player)
c/o Tom Condon *Creative Artists Agency (CAA)*
401 Commerce St PH
Nashville, TN 37219-2516, USA

kalina, Richard (Artist)
44 King St
New York, NY 10014-4960, USA

Kaline, Al (Athlete, Baseball Player)
3613 York Ct
Bloomfield Hills, MI 48301-2058, USA

Kaline, Albert W (Al) (Athlete, Baseball Player)
3613 York Ct
Bloomfield Hills, MI 48301-2058, USA

Kaling, Mindy (Actor, Comedian)
c/o Katie Greenthal *The Lede Company*
9701 Wilshire Blvd # 930
Beverly Hills, CA 90212-2020, USA

Kalinin, Dmitri (Athlete, Hockey Player)
Puckagency LLC
555 Pleasantville Rd Ste 210N
Attn Jay Grossman
Briarcliff Manor, NY 10510-1900, USA

Kalis, Todd A (Athlete, Football Player)
900 Bayview Ct
Cranberry Township, PA 16066-3424, USA

Kalish, Ryan (Athlete, Baseball Player)
37 Obre Pl
Shrewsbury, NJ 07702-4123, USA

Kalitta, Connie (Race Car Driver)
American International Airways
1010 James L Hart Pkwy
Ypsilanti, MI 48197-9790, USA

Kalitta, Doug (Race Car Driver)
Kalitta Motorsports
1010 James L Hart Pkwy
Ypsilanti, MI 48197-9790, USA

Kallaugher, Kevin (Kall) (Cartoonist)
Baltimore Sun
501 N Calvert St
Editorial Dept
Baltimore, MD 21278-1000, USA

Kallir, Lilian (Musician)
Columbia Artists Mgmt Inc
165 W 57th St
New York, NY 10019-2201, USA

Kallur, Anders (Athlete, Hockey Player)
Utsiktsvagen 14
Falun S-79131, Sweden

Kalmanir, Thomas (Athlete, Football Player)
425 E Shelldrake Cir
Fresno, CA 93730-1230, USA

Kalogridis, Laeta (Producer)
c/o Adriana Alberghetti *WME|IMG*
9601 Wilshire Blvd
Beverly Hills, CA 90210-5213, USA

Kalplan, Deborah (Director, Writer)
c/o Staff Member *WME|IMG*
9601 Wilshire Blvd
Beverly Hills, CA 90210-5213, USA

Kalu, N D (Athlete, Football Player)
3719 Poplar Springs Dr
Missouri City, TX 77459-6722, USA

Kalu, Ndukwe (Athlete, Football Player)
1910 Quail Hollow Dr
Fresno, TX 77545, USA

Kalule, Ayub (Boxer)
Palle Skjulet
Bagsvaert 12
Copenhagen 02880, DENMARK

Kaluuya, Daniel (Actor)
c/o Conor McCaughan *Troika*
10A Christina St.
London EC2A 4PA, UNITED KINGDOM

Kalyagin, Aleksander A (Actor)
1905 Goda Str 3
#91
Moscow 123100, RUSSIA

Kalyan, Adhir (Actor)
1714 Sunset Plaza Dr
Los Angeles, CA 90069-1312, USA

Kamal, Gray (Musician)
William Morris Agency
1325 Avenue of the Americas
New York, NY 10019-6026, USA

Kamali, Norma (Designer, Fashion Designer)
OMO Norma Kamali
11 W 56th St
New York, NY 10019-3902, USA

Kaman, Chris (Athlete, Basketball Player)
300 N Dianthus St
Manhattan Beach, CA 90266-6717, USA

Kamana III, John (Athlete, Football Player)
2319 Kapahu St
Honolulu, HI 96813-1433, USA

Kamano, Stacy (Actor)
c/o Staff Member *AKA Talent Agency*
325 N Larchmont Blvd
Los Angeles, CA 90004-3011, USA

Kamanu, Lew (Athlete, Football Player)
1822 Alewa Dr
Honolulu, HI 96817-1212, USA

Kamara, Alvin (Athlete, Football Player)
c/o Damarius Bilbo *Revolution Sports*
270 17th St NW Unit 3001
Atlanta, GA 30363-1261, USA

Kamensky, Valeri (Athlete, Hockey Player)
5 Stonehedge Dr S
Greenwich, CT 06831-3219, USA

Kamieniecki, Scott (Athlete, Baseball Player)
9286 Sand Hill Dr
Grand Blanc, MI 48439-2692, USA

Kaminir, Lisa (Actor)
Ellis Talent Group
14241 N Maple Dr
#207
Sherman Oaks, CA 01423, USA

Kaminski, Kevin (Athlete, Hockey Player)
4560 Venture Dr
Southaven, MS 38671-9719, USA

Kaminski, Larry (Athlete, Football Player)
31423 State Highway 3 NE
Poulsbo, WA 98370-9373, USA

Kaminsky, Yan (Athlete, Hockey Player)
4842 Wildrose Ct NW
Kennesaw, GA 30152-7752, USA

Kamm, Brian (Athlete, Golfer)
479 Barnette Rd
Bluff City, TN 37618-4143, USA

Kammerer, Carl (Athlete, Football Player)
6941 Brooks Rd
Highland, MD 20777-9540, USA

Kamoze, Ini (Musician)
Famous Artists Agency
250 W 57th St
New York, NY 10107-0001, USA

Kampa, Bob (Athlete, Football Player)
2001 Jennifer Dr
Aptos, CA 95003-2840, USA

Kampa, Robert (Athlete, Football Player)
2001 Jennifer Dr
Aptos, CA 95003-2840, USA

Kampman, Aaron (Athlete, Football Player)
2887 Moose Creek Trl
Suamico, WI 54313-3260, USA

Kampouris, Elena (Actor)
c/o Melissa Raubvogel *Imprint PR*
375 Hudson St
New York, NY 10014-3658, USA

Kanaan, Tony (Race Car Driver)
Andretti Green Racing
7615 Zionsville Rd
Indianapolis, IN 46268-2174, USA

Kanakaredes, Melina (Actor)
Tria-Greek Kuzina
230 W Olentangy St
Powell, OH 43065-8433, USA

Kanal, Tony (Musician, Songwriter, Writer)
Rebel Waltz Inc
PO Box 9215
Laguna Beach, CA 92652-7212, USA

Kanaly, Steve (Actor)
4663 Grand Ave
Ojai, CA 93023-9309, USA

Kane, Adelaide (Actor)
c/o Vivian Poulton *Frog Management*
120 Lake St
Unit 11
Northbridge, WA 06865, AUSTRALIA

Kane, Andy (Handy Andy) (Actor)
c/o Staff Member *David Anthony Promotions*
PO Box 286
Warrington
Cheshire WA2 8GA, UNITED KINGDOM

Kane, Big Daddy (Musician)
c/o Jeff Epstein *M.A.G./Universal Attractions*
15 W 36th St Fl 8
New York, NY 10018-7927, USA

Kane, Brad (Actor, Producer)
c/o Daniel (Danny) Greenberg *WME/IMG*
9601 Wilshire Blvd Ste 1
Beverly Hills, CA 90210-5213, USA

Kane, Carol (Actor)
c/o Annick Muller *Wolf-Kasteler Public Relations*
40 Exchange Pl Ste 704
New York, NY 10005-2778, USA

Kane, Chelsea (Actor, Musician)
c/o Meghan Prophet *PMK/BNC Public Relations*
1840 Century Park E Ste 1400
Los Angeles, CA 90067-2115, USA

Kane, Christian (Actor, Musician)
c/o Jeff Golenberg *Silver Lining Entertainment*
421 S Beverly Dr Fl 7
Beverly Hills, CA 90212-4408, USA

Kane, John C (Business Person)
Cardinal Health
7000 Cardinal Pl
Dublin, OH 43017-1091, USA

Kane, Jonny (Race Car Driver)
7615 Zionsville Rd
Indianapolis, IN 46268-2174, USA

Kane, Khalil (Actor)
c/o Staff Member *Envision Entertainment*
8840 Wilshire Blvd Fl 3
Beverly Hills, CA 90211-2606, USA

Kane, Lorie (Athlete, Golfer)
101-5397 Eglinton Ave W
Etobicoke, ON M9C 5K6, Canada

Kane, Nick (Musician)
AstroMedia
1620 16th Ave S
Nashville, TN 37212-2908, USA

Kane, Patrick (Athlete, Hockey Player)
c/o Pat Brisson *Creative Artists Agency (CAA)*
2000 Avenue of the Stars Ste 100
Los Angeles, CA 90067-4705, USA

Kane, Patrick (Athlete, Hockey Player)
401 N Wabash Ave Unit 33J
Chicago, IL 60611-3637, USA

Kane, Richard (Athlete, Football Player)
2525 Greensboro Pt
Reno, NV 89509-5708, USA

Kane Elson, Marion (Swimmer)
4669 Badger Rd
Santa Rosa, CA 95409-2632, USA

Kanell, Danny (Athlete, Football Player)
6167 NW 23rd Way
Boca Raton, FL 33496-3609, USA

Kanellis, Maria (Actor, Wrestler)
c/o Jessica Cohen *JCPR*
9903 Santa Monica Blvd # 983
Beverly Hills, CA 90212-1671, USA

Kaneshiro, Takeshi (Actor)
c/o Staff Member *WME/IMG*
9601 Wilshire Blvd
Beverly Hills, CA 90210-5213, USA

Kanew, Jeffery R (Director)
c/o Staff Member *Directors Guild of America*
7920 W Sunset Blvd Ste 600
Los Angeles, CA 90046-3347, USA

Kang, Dong-Suk (Musician)
Clarion/Seven Muses
47 Whitehall Park
London N19 3TW, UNITED KINGDOM (UK)

Kang, Jimin (Athlete, Golfer)
8245 E Bell Rd Unit 209
Scottsdale, AZ 85260-1025, USA

Kang, Sung (Actor)
c/o Scott Schachter *United Talent Agency (UTA)*
9336 Civic Center Dr
Beverly Hills, CA 90210-3604, USA

Kang, Tim (Actor)
c/o Anna Liza Recto *Bold Management & Production*
8228 W Sunset Blvd # 106
West Hollywood, CA 90046-2414, USA

Kangas-Brody, Jennifer (Athlete, Golfer)
6275 Knob Bend Dr
Grand Blanc, MI 48439-7459, USA

Kanicki, James (Athlete, Football Player)
4590 Schramling Rd
Pierpont, OH 44082-9712, USA

Kanievska, Marek (Director)
International Creative Mgmt
8942 Wilshire Blvd # 219
Beverly Hills, CA 90211-1908, USA

Kannegiesser, Gordon (Athlete, Hockey Player)
Knox Insurance
705 Cassells St
North Bay, ON P1B 4A3, Canada

Kannegiesser, Sheldon (Athlete, Hockey Player)
Knox Insurance
70S Cassells St
North Bay, ON PlB 4A3, Canada

Kannenberg, Bernd (Athlete, Track Athlete)
Sportschule
Sonthofen/Aligau 87527, GERMANY

Kanouse, Lyle (Actor)
c/o Staff Member *The Gage Group*
5757 Wilshire Blvd Ste 659
Los Angeles, CA 90036-3682, USA

Kansas (Music Group)
c/o Staff Member *Creative Artists Agency (CAA)*
2000 Avenue of the Stars Ste 100
Los Angeles, CA 90067-4705, USA

Kansch, Heather (Artist)
Knowle
Rundlerohy Newton Abbot
Devon TQ12 2PJ, UNITED KINGDOM (UK)

Kanter, Paul (Musician)
Ron Rainey Mgmt
315 S Beverly Dr Ste 407
Beverly Hills, CA 90212-4301, USA

Kao, Archie (Actor)
c/o Tim Kwok *Convergence Entertainment*
9150 Wilshire Blvd Ste 247
Beverly Hills, CA 90212-3429, USA

Kapadia, Asif (Actor, Director, Writer)
c/o Robert (Bob) Bookman *Paradigm*
8942 Wilshire Blvd
Beverly Hills, CA 90211-1908, USA

Kapanen, Sami (Athlete, Hockey Player)
Kalpa Hockey
Sairaalakatu I5
Attn: Owners Office
Kuopio 70110, Finland

Kapele, John (Athlete, Football Player)
45-543 Paleka Rd Apt A
Kaneohe, HI 96744-3413, USA

Kapelos, John (Actor)
c/o Staff Member *McCabe Group*
3211 Cahuenga Blvd W Ste 104
Los Angeles, CA 90068-1372, USA

Kapicic, Stefan (Actor)
c/o Paul Little *PAL Public Relations*
Prefers to be contacted by email or phone.
Los Angeles, CA NA, USA

Kapinos, Tom (Producer, Writer)
15960 Alcima Ave
Pacific Palisades, CA 90272-2404, USA

Kapioitas, John (Business Person)
ITT Sheraton Corp
1111 Westchester Ave
West Harrison, NY 10604-3525, USA

Kaplan, Jonathan S (Director)
4323 Ben Ave
Studio City, CA 91604-1704, USA

Kaplan, Ken (Athlete, Football Player)
8313 N Fremont Ave
Tampa, FL 33604-2707, USA

Kaplan, Steven (Actor)
c/o Ellen Gilbert *Abrams Artists Agency*
750 N San Vicente Blvd
E Tower Fl 11
Los Angeles, CA 90069-5788, USA

Kapler, Gabe (Athlete, Baseball Player)
PO Box 246
Frazier Park, CA 93225-0246, USA

Kaplon, Al (Actor)
2899 Agoura Rd Ste 172
Westlake Village, CA 91361-3218, USA

Kapnek, Emily (Actor)
c/o Rachael Reiss *PMK/BNC Public Relations*
1840 Century Park E Ste 1400
Los Angeles, CA 90067-2115, USA

Kapono, Jason (Athlete, Basketball Player)
22 Benevolo Dr
Henderson, NV 89011-3134, USA

Kapoor, Anish (Artist)
33 Coleherne Road
London SW10, UNITED KINGDOM (UK)

Kapoor, Kareena (Actor)
Sominate International
12 Horsham Ave
N Finchley
London N12 9BE, UNITED KINGDOM

Kapoor, Ravi (Actor)
c/o Matthew Lesher *Insight*
5358 Melrose Ave # 200W
Los Angeles, CA 90038-5117, USA

Kapp, Joseph (Joe) (Athlete, Football Player)
PO Box 1973
Los Gatos, CA 95031-1973, USA

Kapp Horner, Alex (Actor, Producer)
c/o Staff Member *T&A Pictures*
15233 Ventura Blvd Fl 9
Sherman Oaks, CA 91403-2250, USA

Kaprisky, Valerie (Actor)
Artmedia
20 Ave Rapp
Paris 75007, FRANCE

Kaptur, Marcy (Congressman, Politician)
2186 Rayburn Hob
Washington, DC 20515-1502, USA

Kapture, Mitzi (Actor)
c/o Rod Baron *Baron Entertainment*
13848 Ventura Blvd Ste A
Sherman Oaks, CA 91423-3654

Kapur, Steve (Apache Indian) (Musician)
c/o Staff Member *Mission Control Artists Agency*
Unit 3 City Business Centre
St Olav's Court, Lower Road
London SE16 2XB, UNITED KINGDOM (UK)

Karabin, Ladislav (Athlete, Hockey Player)
8907 Russo Rd.
Ft. Pierce, FL 349S1-3826, USA

Karamatic, George (Athlete, Football Player)
982 Donald Way
Santa Maria, CA 93455-5019, USA

Karan, Amara (Actor)
c/o Alexa Pearson *Beaumont Communications*
189-190 Shoreditch High St
Unit 2
London E1 6HU, UNITED KINGDOM

Karan, Donna (Designer, Fashion Designer)
Donna Karan
550 Seventh Ave
NY 10018, USA

Karaszewski, Larry (Director, Producer)
c/o David Kopple *Creative Artists Agency (CAA)*
2000 Avenue of the Stars Ste 100
Los Angeles, CA 90067-4705, USA

Karath, Kym (Actor)
40 Halsey Dr
Old Greenwich, CT 06870-1226, USA

Karatz, Bruce E (Business Person)
Kaufman & Broad Home
10990 Wilshire Blvd Fl 5
Los Angeles, CA 90024-3902, USA

Karcher, Ken (Athlete, Football Player)
373 Freemantle Ct
Saline, MI 48176-9155, USA

Karchner, Matt (Athlete, Baseball Player)
401 E 2nd St
Berwick, PA 18603-4801, USA

Kardashian, Khloe (Actor)
c/o Dollie Lucero *Boulevard Management*
21731 Ventura Blvd Ste 300
Woodland Hills, CA 91364-1851, USA

Kardashian, Kourtney (Reality Star)
c/o Noelle Keshishian *Jenner Communications*
Prefers to be contacted by email.
Woodland Hills, CA NA, USA

Kardashian, Rob (Actor, Reality Star)
c/o Lance Klein *WME/IMG*
9601 Wilshire Blvd
Beverly Hills, CA 90210-5213, USA

Kardashian West, Kim (Actor, Model, Reality Star)
c/o Ina Treciokas *Slate PR*
901 N Highland Ave
W Hollywood, CA 90038-2412, USA

Karim, Reef (Actor)
c/o Staff Member *Daris Hatch Management*
10027 Rossbury Pl
Los Angeles, CA 90064-4825, USA

Karin, Anna (Actor)
c/o Jacqueline Stander *Scott Stander & Associates*
4533 Van Nuys Blvd Ste 401
Sherman Oaks, CA 91403-2950, USA

Karina, Anna (Actor)
Artmedia
20 Ave Rapp
Paris 75007, FRANCE

Kariya, Paul (Athlete, Hockey Player)
2493 Aquasanta
Tustin, CA 92782-1104, CANADA

Karkovice, Ron (Athlete, Baseball Player)
272 Celebration Blvd
Kissimmee, FL 34747-5082, USA

Karl, George (Athlete, Basketball Player)
1411 El Nido Way
Sacramento, CA 95864-2903, USA

Karl, George (Coach)
10936 N Port Washington Rd
Mequon, WI 53092-5031, USA

Karl, Scott (Athlete, Baseball Player)
6446 Lilium Ln
Carlsbad, CA 92011-2793, USA

Karlander, Al (Athlete, Hockey Player)
4940 Deer Ridge Dr N
Carmel, IN 46033-8904, USA

Karlander, Al (Athlete, Hockey Player)
249 W Admiral Way S
Carmel, IN 46032-5152, USA

Karlen, John (Actor)
PO Box 1195
Santa Monica, CA 90406-1195, USA

Karlin, Ben (Producer, Writer)
c/o Staff Member *3 Arts Entertainment*
9460 Wilshire Blvd Fl 7
Beverly Hills, CA 90212-2713, USA

Karlis, Rich (Athlete, Football Player)

Karlsson, Lena (Musician)
MOB Agency
6404 Wilshire Blvd Ste 505
Los Angeles, CA 90048-5507, USA

Karlstad, Geir (Speed Skater)
Hamarveien 5A
Fjellhamar 01472, NORWAY

Karlzen, Mary (Musician, Songwriter, Writer)
Little Big Man
155 Avenue of the Americas Rm 700
New York, NY 10013-1507, USA

Karmanos Jr, Peter (Business Person)
Compuware Corp
1 Campus Martius
Detroit, MI 48226-5099, USA

Karn, Richard (Actor)
c/o Christopher Wright *Wright Entertainment*
14724 Ventura Blvd Ste 1201
Sherman Oaks, CA 91403-3512, USA

Karnes, Jay (Actor)
c/o Jonathan Howard *Innovative Artists*
1505 10th St
Santa Monica, CA 90401-2805, USA

Karns, Christine (Race Car Driver)
Karns Racing
24 Grieson Rd
Honey Brook, PA 19344-9757, USA

Karnuth, Jason (Athlete, Baseball Player)
2822 Helding Park Ct
Katy, TX 77494-8522, USA

Karol, Scott (Producer)
c/o Staff Member *Cinelou Films*
844 Seward St
Los Angeles, CA 90038-3602, USA

Karolyi, Bela (Athlete, Coach, Olympic Athlete)
454 Forest Service 200 Rd
Huntsville, TX 77340-2686, USA

Karon, Jan (Writer)
7060 Esmont Farm
Esmont, VA 22937-1818, USA

Karp, Ryan (Athlete, Baseball Player)
8 Fox Run Rd
Medway, MA 02053-2242, USA

Karpa, Dave (Athlete, Hockey Player)
18 Jupiter Hills Dr
Newport Beach, CA 92660-9206

Karpinski, Keith (Athlete, Football Player)
1803 Sycamore Ave
Royal Oak, MI 48073-5020, USA

Karpluk, Erin (Actor)
c/o Staff Member *ROAR (LA)*
9701 Wilshire Blvd Fl 8
Beverly Hills, CA 90212-2008, USA

Karpovsky, Alex (Actor)
c/o Douglas Lucterhand *WME/IMG*
9601 Wilshire Blvd
Beverly Hills, CA 90210-5213, USA

Karpowich, Ed (Athlete, Football Player)
PO Box 177
Fallon, NV 89407-0177, USA

Karr, Mary (Writer)
Syracuse University
English Ofc Bldg
Syracuse, NY 13244-0001, USA

Karras, Louis (Athlete, Football Player)
904 Tulip Cir
Weston, FL 33327-2450, USA

Karras, Ted (Athlete, Football Player)
1122 N Shelby St
Gary, IN 46403-1447, USA

Karros, Eric P (Athlete, Baseball Player)
PO Box 2380
Manhattan Beach, CA 90267-2380, USA

Karsay, Steve (Athlete, Baseball Player)
20244 N 102nd Pl # 1213
Scottsdale, AZ 85255-7151, USA

Karstens, Jeff (Athlete, Baseball Player)
7280 Jamacha Rd
San Diego, CA 92114-3013, USA

Kartheiser, Vincent (Actor)
c/o Craig Schneider *Pinnacle Public Relations*
8721 Santa Monica Blvd # 133
W Hollywood, CA 90069-4507, USA

Kartz, Keith (Athlete, Football Player)
19232 E Hinsdale Ln
Centennial, CO 80016-2147, USA

Karusseit, Ursula (Actor)
Volksbunne
Rasa Luxemburg Platz
Berlin 10178, GERMANY

Karvan, Claudia (Actor, Musician)
c/o Robyn Gardiner *RGM Artists*
8-12 Ann St
Surry Hills, NSW 02010, AUSTRALIA

Kar-Wai, Wong (Director)
Jet Tone Production
21/F Park Commercial Centre
No. 180 Tung Lo Wan Rd.
Hong Kong, China

Karyo, Tcheky (Actor)
c/o Staff Member *Current Entertainment*
9378 Wilshire Blvd Ste 210
Beverly Hills, CA 90212-3167, USA

Kasa, Nick (Athlete, Football Player)
c/o Bruce Tollner *REP 1 Sports Group*
80 Technology Dr
Irvine, CA 92618-2301, USA

Kasabian (Music Group)
c/o Mike Dewdney *International Talent Booking*
9 Kingsway
Fl 6
London WC2B 6XF, UNITED KINGDOM

Kasabian, Kamera (Musician)
c/o Staff Member *Paradigm (Monterey)*
404 W Franklin St
Monterey, CA 93940-2303, USA

Kasabov, Anton (Actor)
c/o Scott Karp *The Syndicate*
10203 Santa Monica Blvd Fl 5
Los Angeles, CA 90067-6416, USA

Kasatonov, Alexei (Athlete, Hockey Player)
153 Eagle Rock Way
Montclair, NJ 07042-1621, USA

Kasay, John (Athlete, Football Player)
8812 Covey Rise Ct
Charlotte, NC 28226-2649, USA

Kasch, Cody (Actor)
c/o Staff Member *ICM Partners*
10250 Constellation Blvd Fl 7
Los Angeles, CA 90067-6207, USA

Kasch, Max (Actor)
c/o Staff Member *Abrams Artists Agency*
750 N San Vicente Blvd
E Tower Fl 11
Los Angeles, CA 90069-5788, USA

Kasdan, Lawrence (Actor, Director, Producer)
c/o Staff Member *Kasdan Pictures*
PO Box 17578
Beverly Hills, CA 90209-3578, USA

Kaselowski, Brian (Race Car Driver)
K Auto Motorsports
2790 Auburn Rd
Auburn Hills, MI 48326-3180, USA

Kasem, Jean (Actor)
138 N Mapleton Dr
Los Angeles, CA 90077-3536, USA

Kasem, Kerri (Actor)
c/o Steve Rohr *Lexicon Public Relations*
1049 Havenhurst Dr # 365
West Hollywood, CA 90046-6002, USA

Kash, Daniel (Actor, Director)
c/o Staff Member *Coolwaters Productions*
10061 Riverside Dr # 531
Toluca Lake, CA 91602-2560, USA

Kasher, Moshe (Comedian)
c/o Josh Lieberman *3 Arts Entertainment*
9460 Wilshire Blvd Fl 7
Beverly Hills, CA 90212-2713, USA

Ka Shing, Li (Business Person)
Li Ka Shing Foundation
7/F Cheung Kong Center
2 Queens Road Central
HONG KONG

Ka-shing, Li (Business Person)
Computershare Hong Kong Investor Services Limited
Rooms 1712 - 1716, 17th Floor,
Hopewell Centre
183 Queen
Hong Kong, HONG KONG

Kashkashian, Kim (Musician)
c/o Staff Member *Musicians Corporate Management*
PO Box 825
Highland, NY 12528-0825, USA

Kashner, Sam (Writer)
c/o Staff Member *Simon & Schuster*
1230 Avenue of the Americas Fl CONC1
New York, NY 10020-1586, USA

Kasich, John (Politician)
Kasich for America
4679 Winterset Dr
Columbus, OH 43220-8113, USA

Kaskade (DJ, Musician)
c/o Jay Brown *Roc Nation*
9348 Civic Center Dr
Beverly Hills, CA 90210-3624, USA

Kaskey, Raymond J (Artist)
Kaskey Studio Inc
3804 38th St
Brentwood, MD 20722-1707, USA

Kasko, Eddie (Athlete, Baseball Player, Coach)
32 Major Ginter Ct
Richmond, VA 23227-3349, USA

Kasl, Dr. Charlotte (Writer)
Many Roads, One Journey
PO Box 1302
Lolo, MT 59847-1302, USA

Kason, Corinne (Actor)
Lovell Assoc
7095 Hollywood Blvd Ste 1006
Los Angeles, CA 90028-8912, USA

Kasovitz, Mathieu (Actor)
Cineart
36 Rue de Ponthieu
Paris, FRANCE 75008

Kasparaitis, Darius (Athlete, Hockey Player)
16400 NE 30th Ave
N Miami Beach, FL 33160-4133, USA

Kasparov, Garry (Athlete)
Kasparov Agency
3114 45th St Ste 8
West Palm Beach, FL 33407-1945, USA

Kasper, Kevin (Athlete, Football Player)
4564 E Collinwood Dr
Gilbert, AZ 85298-4009, USA

Kasper, Len (Commentator)
445 Drexel Ave
Glencoe, IL 60022-2102, USA

Kasper, Steve (Athlete, Coach, Hockey Player)
6 Swan Ln
Andover, MA 01810-2844, USA

Kasper, Walter Cardinal (Religious Leader)
Via dell Erba 1
Rome 00193, ITALY

Kasperek, Dick (Athlete, Football Player)
824 S County Line Rd
Hinsdale, IL 60521-4554, USA

Kass, Carmen (Model)
City Models
Rue Jean Mermoz
Paris 75008, FRANCE

Kass, Danny (Skier)
PO Box 8549
Mammoth Lakes, CA 93546-8549, USA

Kassell, Brad (Athlete, Football Player)
20117 Rancho Cielo Ct
Lago Vista, TX 78645-6046, USA

Kassim, Yasmin (Actor)
c/o Brandi George *Advantage PR*
3900 W Alameda Ave Ste 1200
Burbank, CA 91505-4317, USA

Kassir, John (Actor)
c/o Nic de Armendi *JLA Talent Agency*
9151 W Sunset Blvd
West Hollywood, CA 90069-3106, USA

Kassovitz, Mathieu (Actor, Director, Producer)
MNP Entreprise
18 Rue Du Fbg Du Temple
Paris 75011, France

Kastelic, Ed (Athlete, Hockey Player)
1839 W Muirwood Dr
Phoenix, AZ 85045-1773

Kasten, Robert (Politician)
1683 31st St NW
Washington, DC 20007-2968, USA

Kaster, Deena (Athlete, Olympic Athlete, Track Athlete)
1208 Majestic Pines Drive
Mammoth Lakes, CA 93546, USA

Kastor, Deena (Olympic Athlete, Track Athlete)
PO Box 5068
Mammoth Lakes, CA 93546-5068, USA

Kaszycki, Mike (Athlete, Hockey Player)
9 Shore Blvd
St Catharines, ON L2N 5T9, Canada

Kata, Matt (Athlete, Baseball Player)
1711 Westend Pl
Round Rock, TX 78681-2252, USA

Katchor, Ben (Cartoonist)
Little Brown
3 Center Plz
Boston, MA 02108-2003, USA

Kate, Lauren (Writer)
PO Box 461514
Los Angeles, CA 90046-9514, USA

Kates, Kimberley (Actor)
David Talent
116 S Gardner St
Los Angeles, CA 90036-2718, USA

Katic, Stana (Actor)
c/o Larry Taube *Principal Entertainment*
9255 W Sunset Blvd Ste 500
Los Angeles, CA 90069-3301, USA

Katims, Jason (Producer)
c/o Staff Member *Creative Artists Agency (CAA)*
2000 Avenue of the Stars Ste 100
Los Angeles, CA 90067-4705, USA

Katin, Peter R (Musician)
Maureen Lunn
Top Farm Parish Lane
Hedgerley
Bucks SL2 3JH, UNITED KINGDOM (UK)

Katkaveck, Leo (Athlete, Basketball Player)
1408 Jeremy Ln
Rocky Mount, NC 27803-1516, USA

Katolin, Mike (Athlete, Football Player)

Katona, Kerry (Actor)
c/o Mark Thomas *TM Media*
45 Circus Rd
London NW8 9JH, UNITED KINGDOM

Kats, Justin (Fearitself) (Internet Star)
c/o Staff Member *Abrams Artists Agency*
750 N San Vicente Blvd
E Tower Fl 11
Los Angeles, CA 90069-5788, USA

Katsav, Moshe (Politician, President)
President's Office
3 Hanassi
Jerusalem 92188, ISRAEL

Katsoudas, Stella (Musician, Songwriter, Writer)
Ashley Talent
2002 Hogback Rd Ste 20
Ann Arbor, MI 48105-9736, USA

Katt, Nicky (Actor)
c/o John Carrabino *John Carrabino Management*
5900 Wilshire Blvd Ste 740
Los Angeles, CA 90036-5032, USA

Katt, William (Actor)
5860 Le Sage Ave
Woodland Hills, CA 91367-5902, USA

Kattan, Chris (Actor, Comedian)
c/o Evan Hainey *Untitled Entertainment*
350 S Beverly Dr Ste 200
Beverly Hills, CA 90212-4819, USA

Kattus, Eric (Athlete, Football Player)
854 Adams Rd
Loveland, OH 45140-7242, USA

Katula, Matt (Athlete, Football Player)
1765 Horsham Trl
Alpharetta, GA 30004-3563, USA

Katy B (Musician)
c/o Tom Schroeder *Coda Music Agency (UK)*
56 Compton St
Clerkenwell
London EC1V 0ET, UNITED KINGDOM

Katz, Alex (Artist)
435 W Broadway Fl 5
New York, NY 10012-5902, USA

Katz, Hilda (Artist)
915 W End Ave # 5D
New York, NY 10025-3535, USA

Katz, Jonathan (Actor, Animator, Comedian, Producer)
c/o Bonnie Burns *Burns & Burns Management*
10523 Mars Ln
Los Angeles, CA 90077-3109, USA

Katz, Omri (Actor)
c/o Harry Gold *TalentWorks*
3500 W Olive Ave Ste 1400
Burbank, CA 91505-5512, USA

Katz, Richard (Actor)
c/o Kirsten Wright *Amanda Howard Associates*
74 Clerkenwell Rd
London EC1M 5QA, UNITED KINGDOM (UK)

Katz, Ross (Producer)
c/o Staff Member *United Talent Agency (UTA)*
9336 Civic Center Dr
Beverly Hills, CA 90210-3604, USA

Katz, Simon (Musician)
Searles
Chapel
26A Munster St
London SW6 4EN, UNITED KINGDOM (UK)

Katz, Sky (Musician)
c/o Kelly-Marie Smith *Status PR*
PO Box 6191
Westlake Village, CA 91359-6191, USA

Katzenberg, Jeffrey (Business Person)
1025 Loma Vista Dr
Beverly Hills, CA 90210-2620, USA

Katzenmayer, Travis (Baseball Player)
562 N Overland
Mesa, AZ 85207-6670, USA

Katzenmeier, Travis (Athlete, Baseball Player)
1128 N Mountain Rd
Mesa, AZ 85207-2408, USA

Katzenmoyer, Andy (Athlete, Football Player)
5764 Salem Dr
Westerville, OH 43082-8186, USA

Katzur, Klaus (Swimmer)
Robert-Siewart-Str 76
Chemnitz 00912, GERMANY

kauffman, bob (Athlete, Basketball Player)
1677 Rivermist Dr SW
Lilburn, GA 30047-2451, USA

Kauffman, Joel (Race Car Driver)
Kitzbradshaw Racing
114 Meadow Hill Cir
Mooresville, NC 28117-8089, USA

Kauffman, Marta (Producer, Writer)
c/o Staff Member *Bright Kauffman Crane Productions*
4000 Warner Blvd Bldg 750
Burbank, CA 91522-0001

Kaufman, Adam (Actor)
c/o Steven Levy *Framework Entertainment*
9057 Nemo St # C
W Hollywood, CA 90069-5511, USA

Kaufman, Avy (Actor)
c/o Rick Kurtzman *Creative Artists Agency (CAA)*
2000 Avenue of the Stars Ste 100
Los Angeles, CA 90067-4705, USA

Kaufman, Bob (Ajax) (Athlete, Basketball Player)
1677 Rivermist Dr SW
Lilburn, GA 30047-2451, USA

Kaufman, Charlie (Writer)
c/o Sharon Jackson *WME/IMG*
9601 Wilshire Blvd
Beverly Hills, CA 90210-5213, USA

Kaufman, Curt (Athlete, Baseball Player)
308 Hillway Dr
Glenwood, IA 51534-1210, USA

Kaufman, Donald (Writer)
c/o Staff Member *United Talent Agency (UTA)*
9336 Civic Center Dr
Beverly Hills, CA 90210-3604, USA

Kaufman, Joan (Athlete, Baseball Player, Commentator)
1111 Crystal Spg
San Antonio, TX 78258-6909, USA

Kaufman, Napolean (Athlete, Football Player)
72 Incline Green Ln
Alamo, CA 94507-2334, USA

Kaufman, Napoleon (Athlete, Football Player)
1913 Via Di Salemo
Pleasanton, CA 94566, USA

Kaufman, Tim (Race Car Driver)
Kaufman Racing
8201 Meade Ave
Burbank, IL 60459-1944, USA

Kaufusi, Steve (Athlete, Football Player)
3018 Comanche Ln
Provo, UT 84604-4344, USA

Kaulitz, Bill (Musician)
c/o Staff Member *Universal Music Deutschland*
Stralauer Allee 1
Berlin 10245, Germany

Kauth, Kathleen (Athlete, Hockey Player, Olympic Athlete)
13 Hillcrest Ln
Saratoga Springs, NY 12866-8528, USA

Kavana (Musician)
Tony Denton Promotions
19 S Molton Ln
Mayfair
London, England W1K 5LE

Kavanagh, Brad (Actor)
c/o Jeff Golenberg *Silver Lining Entertainment*
421 S Beverly Dr Fl 7
Beverly Hills, CA 90212-4408, USA

Kavanaugh, Ryan (Producer)
c/o Staff Member *Proxima Media*
2121 Avenue of the Stars Ste 2320
Los Angeles, CA 90067-0016, USA

Kavandi, Janet L (Astronaut)
3907 Park Circle Way
Houston, TX 77059-3019, USA

Kavelaars, Ingrid (Actor)

Kavner, Julie (Actor)
c/o Paul Martino *Martino Management*
149 W 72nd St Apt 1D
New York, NY 10023-3228, USA

Kavovit, Andrew (Actor)
c/o Staff Member *TalentWorks*
3500 W Olive Ave Ste 1400
Burbank, CA 91505-5512, USA

Kawakubo, Rei (Designer, Fashion Designer)
Comme des Garcons
5-11-5 Minamiaoyana
Minatoku
Tokyo, JAPAN

Kawalerowicz, Jersy (Director, Writer)
Ul Marconich 5m 21
Warsaw 02-954, POLAND

Kawasaki, Guy (Business Person, Writer)
c/o Staff Member *Keynote Speakers*
2686 Middlefield Rd Ste F
Redwood City, CA 94063-3481, USA

Kay, Bill (Athlete, Football Player)
4266 Waterston Courtyard
Evans, GA 30809-5036, USA

Kay, Dianne (Actor)
1565 Calle Del Estribo
Pacific Palisades, CA 90272-2009, USA

Kay, Jason (Jay) (Musician)
c/o Staff Member *WME/IMG*
9601 Wilshire Blvd Ste 1
Beverly Hills, CA 90210-5213, USA

Kay, John (Musician)
Elite Management Corp
2211 Norfolk St Ste 760
Houston, TX 77098-4033, USA

Kay, Lisa (Actor)
c/o Jeremy Conway *Conway van Gelder Grant*
8-12 Broadwick St
London W1F 8HW, UNITED KINGDOM

Kay, Michael (Athlete, Baseball Player)
58 Dingletown Rd
Greenwich, CT 06830-3539, USA

Kay, Michael (Commentator)
58 Dingletown Rd
Greenwich, CT 06830-3539, USA

Kay, Michael (Athlete, Baseball Player)
58 Dingletown Rd
Greenwich, CT 06830-3539, USA

Kay, Peter (Actor)
c/o Staff Member *McIntyre Management Ltd*
35 Soho Sq
2nd Floor
London W1D 3QX, UK

Kay, Robbie (Actor)
c/o Melanie Greene *Affirmative Entertainment*
6525 W Sunset Blvd # 7
Los Angeles, CA 90028-7212, USA

Kay, Vanessa (Actor)
c/o Staff Member *Comedy Central (LA)*
2049 Century Park E # 4170
Los Angeles, CA 90067-3101, USA

Kay, William H (Athlete, Football Player)
4266 Waterston Courtyard
Evans, GA 30809-5036, USA

Kaye, David (Actor)
10443 Kling St
Toluca Lake, CA 91602-1529, USA

Kaye, Jonathan (Athlete, Golfer)
328 W El Camino Dr
Phoenix, AZ 85021-5525, USA

Kaye, Judy (Actor, Musician)
Bret Adams
448 W 44th St
New York, NY 10036-5220, USA

Kaye, Justin (Athlete, Baseball Player)
3591 Arville St Unit 302B
Las Vegas, NV 89103-1679, USA

Kaye, Thorsten (Actor)
c/o Staff Member *ICM Partners*
10250 Constellation Blvd Fl 7
Los Angeles, CA 90067-6207, USA

Kayleigh, Layla (Actor, Television Host)
c/o Staff Member *United Talent Agency (UTA)*
9336 Civic Center Dr
Beverly Hills, CA 90210-3604, USA

Kayser, Allan (Actor)

Kaz (Artist)
c/o Staff Member *Fantagraphics Books*
7563 Lake City Way NE
Seattle, WA 98115-4218, USA

Kazan, Lainie (Actor, Musician)
9903 Santa Monica Blvd # 283
Beverly Hills, CA 90212-1671, USA

Kazan, Zoe (Actor)
c/o Jennifer Konawal *Washington Square Arts (NY)*
310 Bowery Fl 2
New York, NY 10012-2861, USA

Kazankina, Tatyana (Athlete, Track Athlete)
Hoshimina St
111211
Saint Petersburg, RUSSIA

Kazanski, Ted (Athlete, Baseball Player)
1544 Dormie Dr
Gladwin, MI 48624-8104, USA

Kazee, Steve (Actor)
c/o Staff Member *D2 Management*
10351 Santa Monica Blvd Ste 210
Los Angeles, CA 90025-6937, USA

Kazinsky, Robert (Actor)
c/o Sammy Boyd *Creative Artists Management (CAM-UK)*
55-59 Shaftesbury Ave.
London W1D 6LD, UNITED KINGDOM

Kazmir, Scott (Athlete, Baseball Player)
16619 Rose Bay Trl
Cypress, TX 77429-4935, USA

KC & The Sunshine Band (Music Group)
c/o Danny Nozell *CTK Management*
2817 W End Ave
PO Box 389
Nashville, TN 37203-1453, USA

K-Ci & JoJo (Music Group)
c/o Carlos Keyes *Red Entertainment Agency*
3537 36th St Ste 2
Astoria, NY 11106-1347, USA

K D, Dunn (Athlete, Football Player)
2264 Colleen Ct
Decatur, GA 30032-7153, USA

K. Davis, Danny (Congressman, Politician)
2159 Rayburn Hob
Washington, DC 20515-2307, USa

Kea, Clarence (Athlete, Basketball Player)
9175 Jennifer St
Beaumont, TX 77707-2727, USA

Keach, James (Actor)
c/o Staff Member *Catfish Productions*
23852 Pacific Coast Hwy Ste 313
Malibu, CA 90265-4876, USA

Keach, Stacy (Actor)
101 N Robertson Blvd Ste 200
Beverly Hills, CA 90211-2191, USA

Keady, Gene (Coach)
Purdue University
Mackey Arena
West Lafayette, IN 47907, USA

Keagan, Carrie (Television Host)
c/o Staff Member *No Good TV (NGTV)*
9944 Santa Monica Blvd
Beverly Hills, CA 90212-1607, USA

Keaggy, Ian (Musician)
7049 Asberry Dr
Nashville, TN 37221-4305, USA

Keaggy, Phil (Musician)
c/o Staff Member *Street Level Artists Agency*
1832 S Briarwood Dr
Warsaw, IN 46580-4140, USA

Keagle, Greg (Athlete, Baseball Player)
11 Wolcott Dr
Horseheads, NY 14845-1012, USA

Kealey, Steve (Athlete, Baseball Player)
1080 1700 Ave
Abilene, KS 67410-6321, USA

Kean, Laurel (Athlete, Golfer)
25280 Ojibway Ct
Punta Gorda, FL 33983-6069, USA

Keanan, Staci (Actor)
c/o David Shapira *David Shapira & Associates*
193 N Robertson Blvd
Beverly Hills, CA 90211-2103, USA

Keane (Musician)
c/o Staff Member *Everybodys*
53 Corsica St
Highbury N5 1JT, UNITED KINGDOM

Keane, Dolores (Musician)
D K Entertainments
Caherlistrane, Galway, IRELAND

Keane, Glen (Animator)
c/o Staff Member *Disney Animation (LA)*
500 S Buena Vista St
Burbank, CA 91521-9500, USA

Keane, Jeff (Cartoonist)
c/o Claudia Smith *King Features Syndication*
300 W 57th St Fl 15
New York, NY 10019-5238, USA

Keane, Katie Amanda (Actor)
c/o Paul Bennett *PB Management*
6523 W 6th St
Los Angeles, CA 90048-4715, USA

Keane, Kerrie (Actor)
S D B Partners
1801 Ave of Stars
#902
Los Angeles, CA 90067, USA

Keane, Mike (Athlete, Hockey Player)
91 Lowson Cres
THE RINK
Winnipeg, MB R3P 0T3, Canada

Keane, Roy M (Soccer Player)
Sunderland FC
Sunderland
Stadium Park
Manchester, Tyne & Wear SR5 1SU, UNITED KINGDOM (UK)

Keans, Doug (Athlete, Hockey Player)
8352 Manatee Bay Dr
Tampa, FL 33635-9503

Kearney, Bob (Athlete, Baseball Player)
4155 Elizabeth Dr
Stevensville, MI 49127-9530, USA

Kearney, Jim (Athlete, Football Player)
Washington High School
1817 E 59th St
Kansas City, MO 64130-3329, USA

Kearney, Mat (Musician)
c/o Scott Clayton *WME (Nashville)*
1201 Demonbreun St
Nashville, TN 37203-3140, USA

Kearney, Tim (Athlete, Football Player)
2144 Dartmouth Gate Ct
Wildwood, MO 63011-5436, USA

Kearns, Austin (Athlete, Baseball Player)
719 Haverhill Dr
Lexington, KY 40503-3426, USA

Kearns, Dennis (Athlete, Hockey Player)
1292 Esquimalt Ave
West Vancouver, BC V7T 1K3, CANADA

Kearns, Michael (Athlete, Basketball Player)
PO Box 263
Monroe, NC 28111-0263, USA

Kearns, Thomas (Athlete, Basketball Player)
1 Kensett Ln
Darien, CT 06820-2438, USA

Kearse, Frank (Athlete, Football Player)

Kearse, Jermaine (Athlete, Football Player)
c/o Gary Uberstine *PSE Management*
1500 Rosecrans Ave Ste 500
Manhattan Beach, CA 90266-3771, USA

Kearse, Jevon (Athlete, Football Player)
5919 NW 59th Ave
Parkland, FL 33067-4428, USA

Keaser, Lloyd (Athlete, Olympic Athlete, Wrestler)
43960 Tavern Dr
Ashburn, VA 20147-3905, USA

Keathley, George (Director)
Missouri Repertory Theater
4949 Cherry St
Kansas City, MO 64110-2229, USA

Keating, Bill (Athlete, Football Player)
2552 E Alameda Ave Unit 14
Denver, CO 80209-3324, USA

Keating, Chris (Athlete, Football Player)
741 Canton Ave
Milton, MA 02186-3121, USA

Keating, Dominic (Actor)
c/o Luc Chaudhary *International Artists Management*
25-27 Heath St.
Hamstead NW3 6TR, UNITED KINGDOM

Keating, Paul (Royalty)
31 Bligh St Level 2
Sydney 02000, AUSTRALIA

Keating, Ronan (Musician)
c/o Staff Member *The Artists Partnership*
101 Finsbury Pavement
London EC2A 1RS, UNITED KINGDOM

Keating, Ronan (Musician)
Carol Assoc-War Mgmt
Bushy Park Rd
57 Meadowbank
Dublin, IRELAND

Keating, Thomas A (Athlete, Football Player)
3725 W St NW
Washington, DC 20007-1714, USA

Keatley, Greg (Athlete, Baseball Player)
140 Rockridge Ct
Lexington, SC 29072-7970, USA

Keaton, Curtis (Athlete, Football Player)
246 Briarcliff Dr
Kannapolis, NC 28081-7155, USA

Keaton, Diane (Actor, Director, Producer)
c/o Jessica Kovacevic *WME|IMG*
9601 Wilshire Blvd
Beverly Hills, CA 90210-5213, USA

Keaton, Josh (Actor)
c/o Brian Wilkins *LINK Entertainment*
11872 La Grange Ave
Los Angeles, CA 90025-5282, USA

Keaton, Michael (Actor, Director, Producer)
c/o Mara Buxbaum *ID Public Relations*
7060 Hollywood Blvd Fl 8th
Los Angeles, CA 90028-6021, USA

Keats, Ele (Actor)
c/o Rob D'Avola *Rob DAvola & Associates*
9107 Wilshire Blvd # 405
Beverly Hills, CA 90210-5531, USA

Kebbel, Arielle (Actor)
c/o Ruth Bernstein *Viewpoint Inc*
8820 Wilshire Blvd Ste 220
Beverly Hills, CA 90211-2622, USA

Kebbell, Toby (Actor)
c/o Samantha Mast *Rogers & Cowan*
1840 Century Park E Fl 18
Los Angeles, CA 90067-2101, USA

Kebede, Liya (Model)
c/o Staff Member *IMG Models (NY)*
304 Park Ave S PH N
New York, NY 10010-4303, USA

Keb Mo (Musician, Songwriter, Writer)
Monterey International
72 W Adams St # 1000
Chicago, IL 60603-5107, USA

Keckin, Val (Athlete, Football Player)
8918 Montrose Way
San Diego, CA 92122, USA

Kecman, Dan (Athlete, Football Player)
16413 Fox Valley Ter
Rockville, MD 20853-3220, USA

Keczmer, Dan (Athlete, Olympic Athlete)
8303 Bridle Pl
Brentwood, TN 37027-8128, USA

Keczmer, Don (Athlete, Hockey Player)
8303 Bridle Pl
Brentwood, TN 37027-8128, USA

Keddie, Asher (Actor)

Kedes, Maureen (Actor)
Tisherman Agency
6767 Forest Lawn Dr # 101
Los Angeles, CA 90068-1027, USA

Kee, Lee Shau (Business Person)
Henderson Land Development Company Limited
72-76/F, Two International Finance Centre
8 Finance Street, Central
Hong Kong

Keeble, Jerry (Athlete, Football Player)
PO Box 367
Dunnigan, CA 95937-0367, USA

Keeble, John (Musician)
International Talent Group
729 7th Ave Ste 1600
New York, NY 10019-6880, USA

Keedy, Pat (Athlete, Baseball Player)
6308 Mountainview Cir
Gardendale, AL 35071-2088, USA

Keefe, Adam (Athlete, Basketball Player)
15933 Alcima Ave
Pacific Palisades, CA 90272-2405, USA

Keefe, Mike (Cartoonist)
Denver Post
5990 Washington St
Editorial Dept
Denver, CO 80216-1349, USA

Keefe, Sheldon (Athlete, Hockey Player)
c/o Staff Member *Pembroke Lumber Kings*
PO Box 92 Stn Main
Stn Main
Pembroke, ON K8A 6X1, Canada

Keegan, Andrew (Actor)
c/o Barry McPherson *Agency for the Performing Arts*
135 W 50th St Fl 17
New York, NY 10020-1201, USA

Keegan, Kari (Actor)
2042 S Oxford Ave
Los Angeles, CA 90018-1529, USA

Keegan, Michelle (Actor)
c/o Ruth Young *United Agents*
12-26 Lexington St
London W1F OLE, UNITED KINGDOM

Keehne, Virginya (Actor)
Craig Mgmt
125 S Sycamore Ave
Los Angeles, CA 90036-2938, USA

Keeling, Charles D (Musician)
Scripps Oceanography Institute
Ritler Hall
9500 Gilman Dr
La Jolla, CA 92093-0001, USA

Keeling, Harold (Athlete, Basketball Player)
6707 Broad Oaks Dr
Richmond, TX 77406-7629, USA

Keelor, Greg (Musician)
c/o Staff Member *ArtistDirect*
9046 Lindblade St
Culver City, CA 90232-2513, USA

Keen, Dafne (Actor)
c/o Natalie Day *Independent Talent Group*
40 Whitfield St
London W1T 2RH, UNITED KINGDOM

Keen, Robert Earl (Musician, Songwriter)
Rosetta
PO Box 2186
Bandera, TX 78003-2186, USA

Keen, Sam (Writer)
16331 Norrbom Rd
Sonoma, CA 95476-4783, USA

Keena, Monica (Actor)
c/o Kieran Maguire *The Arlook Group*
11663 Gorham Ave Apt 5
Los Angeles, CA 90049-4749, USA

Keenan, Larry (Athlete, Hockey Player)
132 Gordon Dr
North Bay, ON P1B 8B2, Canada

Keenan, Maynard James (Musician)
c/o Staff Member *Virgin Records (NY)*
150 5th Ave Fl 7
New York, NY 10011-4372, USA

Keene, Larry (Athlete, Hockey Player)
1232 Gordon Dr.
North Bay, ON P1B 8B2, CANADA

Keene, Phillip P (Actor)
c/o Liza Anderson *Anderson Group Public Relations*
8060 Melrose Ave Fl 4
Los Angeles, CA 90046-7038, USA

Keene, Tommy (Musician, Songwriter, Writer)
Black Park Mgmt
PO Box 107
Sunbury, NC 27979-0107, USA

Keene Cherot, Kyera (Actor)

Keener, Catherine (Actor)
c/o Leslie Siebert *Gersh*
9465 Wilshire Blvd Ste 600
Beverly Hills, CA 90212-2605, USA

Keener, Jeff (Athlete, Baseball Player)
2107 Dewey St
Murphysboro, IL 62966-2451, USA

Keener, Joe (Athlete, Baseball Player)
16915 Glendower Ave
Edwards, CA 93523-3515, USA

Keenum, Case (Athlete, Football Player)
c/o Jeff Nalley *Select Sports Group*
2700 Post Oak Blvd Ste 1450
Houston, TX 77056-5785, USA

Keery, Joe (Actor)
c/o Lindsey Ludwig-Rahm *Viewpoint Inc*
89 5th Ave Ste 402
New York, NY 10003-3020, USA

Keeslar, Matt (Actor)
c/o Amy Pham *Aquarius Public Relations*
5320 Sylmar Ave
Sherman Oaks, CA 91401-5612, USA

Keesling, Barbara (Writer)
c/o Staff Member *Random House Publicity*
1745 Broadway Frnt 3
New York, NY 10019-4343, USA

Keeton, Durwood (Athlete, Football Player)
1372 Diamond Gate Pl
El Paso, TX 79936-7841, USA

Keeton, Rickey (Athlete, Baseball Player)
3433 Stathem Ave
Cincinnati, OH 45211-5723, USA

Keflezighi, Meb (Athlete, Olympic Athlete, Track Athlete)
Mammoth Track Club
PO Box 7552
Mammoth Lakes, CA 93546-7552, USA

Kegel, Oliver (Athlete)
Am Bogen 23
Berlin 13589, GERMANY

Keggi, Caroline (Athlete, Golfer)
9228 E Happy Hollow Dr
Scottsdale, AZ 85262-2575, USA

Kehlani (Musician)
c/o Ariana White *Atlantic Records*
3400 W Olive Ave Fl 2
Burbank, CA 91505-5538, USA

Kehoe, Rick (Athlete, Hockey Player)
1027 Highland Dr
Canonsburg, PA 15317-5227

Keibler, Stacy (Actor, Wrestler)
c/o Nicole Perez-Krueger *PMK/BNC Public Relations*
1840 Century Park E Ste 1400
Los Angeles, CA 90067-2115, USA

Keillor, Garrison (Correspondent, Writer)
A Prairie Home Companion
480 Cedar St
Saint Paul, MN 55101-2217, USA

Keim, Jenny (Swimmer)
R O'Brien
1 Hall of Fame Dr
Swimming Hall of Fame
Fort Lauderdale, FL 33316-1611, USA

Keisel, Brett (Athlete, Football Player)
c/o Eric Metz *Lock Metz Milanovic LLC*
6900 E Camelback Rd Ste 600
Scottsdale, AZ 85251-8044, USA

Keisler, Randy (Athlete, Baseball Player)
6842 Durango Creek Dr
Magnolia, TX 77354-2749, USA

Keitel, Harvey (Actor)
c/o Dorothee Grosjean *Cineart*
28 Rue Mogador
Paris F-75009, FRANCE

Keith, David (Actor, Director)
4815 Kingston Pike Ste 166
Knoxville, TN 37919-5110, USA

Keith, Duncan (Athlete, Hockey Player)
1700 W Melrose St
Chicago, IL 60657-1004, USA

Keith, Embray (Athlete, Football Player)
1232 Sunnymede Ave
South Bend, IN 46615-1016, USA

Keith, Penelope (Actor)
66 Berkeley House
Hay Hill
London SW3, UNITED KINGDOM (UK)

Keith, Sarah (Actor)
c/o Ashley Partington *Abrams Artists Agency*
750 N San Vicente Blvd
E Tower Fl 11
Los Angeles, CA 90069-5788, USA

Keith, Toby (Musician)
PO Box 8739
Rockford, IL 61126-8739, USA

Keithley, Gary (Athlete, Football Player)
1801 W Westhill Dr
Cleburne, TX 76033-5952, USA

Keith Rennie, Callum (Actor)
c/o Elizabeth Hodgson *Elizabeth Hodgson Management Group*
405-1688 Cypress St
Vancouver, BC V6J 5J1, CANADA

Kekalainen, Jarmo (Athlete, Hockey Player)
Jokerit Helsinki Areenakuja 1
Helsinki, SF 00240, Finland

Kekich, Mike (Athlete, Baseball Player)
5314 Canada Vista Pl NW
Albuquerque, NM 87120-2412, USA

Kelce, Jason (Athlete, Football Player)
c/o Scott Smith *XAM Sports*
3509 Ice Age Dr
Madison, WI 53719-5409, USA

Kelce, Travis (Athlete, Football Player)
c/o Adam Heller *Vantage Management Group*
518 Reamer Dr
Carnegie, PA 15106-1845, USA

Kelcher, Louie (Athlete, Football Player)
10239 Twin Lake Loop
Dripping Springs, TX 78620-2629, USA

Kelemete, Senio (Athlete, Football Player)

Kelis (Chef, Musician)
c/o Dana Meyerson *Biz 3 Publicity*
1321 N Milwaukee Ave # 452
Chicago, IL 60622-9151, USA

Kelker-Kelly, Robert (Actor)
4704 Whitsett Ave
Studio City, CA 91604-1140, USA

Kell, Ayla (Actor)
c/o Scott Zimmerman *Scott Zimmerman Management*
901 N Highland Ave
Los Angeles, CA 90038-2412, USA

Kell, Everett (Skeeter) (Athlete, Baseball Player)
PO Box 10113
Conway, AR 72034-0001, USA

kell, Everett ""Skeeter"" (Athlete, Baseball Player)
PO Box 10113
Conway, AR 72034-0001, USA

Kellar, Mark (Athlete, Football Player)
5514 Oak Gln
Minneapolis, MN 55439-1944, USA

Kelleher, Mick (Athlete, Baseball Player)
1451 Alamo Pintado Rd
Solvang, CA 93463-9757, USA

Keller, Bill (Athlete, Basketball Player)
7901 40th Ave N Lot 84
Saint Petersburg, FL 33709-4250, USA

Keller, Cord (Producer)
c/o Staff Member *Innovative Artists*
1505 10th St
Santa Monica, CA 90401-2805, USA

Keller, Dave (Athlete, Baseball Player)
4403 Marchmont Blvd
Land O Lakes, FL 34638-7760, USA

Keller, Dustin (Athlete, Football Player)
c/o Roosevelt Barnes *Independent Sports & Entertainment (ISE-IN)*
6435 W Jefferson Blvd # 197
Fort Wayne, IN 46804-6203, USA

Keller, Gary (Athlete, Basketball Player)
1365 Snell Isle Blvd NE Apt 5D
Saint Petersburg, FL 33704-2403, USA

Keller, Jason (Race Car Driver)
Progressive Motorsports
201 Rolling Hill Rd
Mooresville, NC 28117-6845, USA

Keller, Joyce (Television Host)
11.6 Lake Ter Apt 207
Boynton Beach, FL 33426-4231, USA

Keller, Kalyn (Athlete, Olympic Athlete, Swimmer)
11830 Federalist Way Apt 34
Fairfax, VA 22030-7893, USA

Keller, Klete (Athlete, Olympic Athlete, Swimmer)
13649 Cotesworth Ct
Huntersville, NC 28078-5661, USA

Keller, Kris (Athlete, Baseball Player)
2496 Oakview Dr
Jacksonville, FL 32246-2462, USA

Keller, Larry (Athlete, Football Player)
2933 Five Oaks Ln
Brenham, TX 77833-0089, USA

Keller, Martha (Actor)
Lemonstr 9
Munich 81679, GERMANY

Keller, Marthe (Actor)
c/o Laurent Gregoire *Agence Adequat*
21 Rue D'Uzes
Paris 75002, FRANCE

Keller, Mary Page (Actor)
c/o Staff Member *SMS Talent*
8383 Wilshire Blvd Ste 230
Beverly Hills, CA 90211-2436, USA

Keller, Melissa (Actor)

Keller, Rachel (Actor)
c/o Roger Karshan *Suskin Management*
2 Charlton St Apt 5K
New York, NY 10014-4970, USA

Keller, Rita (Baseball Player)
6410 Westchester St
Portage, MI 49024-3276, USA

Keller, Ron (Athlete, Baseball Player)
PO Box 3267
Cashiers, NC 28717-3267, USA

Keller, Thomas (Chef)
French Laundry
6540 Washington St
Yountville, CA 94599-1315, USA

Kellerman, Ernie (Athlete, Football Player)
408 Fairway Vw
Chagrin Falls, OH 44023-6718, USA

Kellerman, Faye (Writer)
Karpfinger Agency
357 W 20th St Apt A
New York, NY 10011-4960, USA

Kellerman, Jonathan (Writer)
c/o Brian Pike *Creative Artists Agency (CAA)*
2000 Avenue of the Stars Ste 100
Los Angeles, CA 90067-4705, USA

Kellerman, Max (Actor, Sportscaster)

Kellerman, Sally (Actor)
c/o Staff Member *Artists & Representatives (Stone Manners Salners)*
6100 Wilshire Blvd Ste 1500
Los Angeles, CA 90048-5110, USA

Kellermann, Ernie (Athlete, Football Player)
90 Glenview Dr
Aurora, OH 44202-8219, USA

Kellermeyer, Doug (Athlete, Football Player)
111 N Parliman Rd
Lagrangeville, NY 12540-6218, USA

Kelley, Bill (Athlete, Football Player)
6446 US Highway 69 S
Lone Oak, TX 75453-2242, USA

Kelley, Brian (Athlete, Football Player)
98 Constitution Way
Basking Ridge, NJ 07920-2961, USA

Kelley, David E (Producer, Writer)
c/o Staff Member *David E Kelley Productions*
1600 Rosecrans Ave Bldg 4B
Manhattan Beach, CA 90266-3708, USA

Kelley, Dean (Athlete, Basketball Player)
5900 Longleaf Dr
Lawrence, KS 66049-5801, USA

Kelley, Devin (Actor)
c/o Dan Baron *Agency for the Performing Arts (APA)*
405 S Beverly Dr Ste 500
Beverly Hills, CA 90212-4425, USA

Kelley, Dwight (Athlete, Football Player)
1006 Clubview Blvd N
Columbus, OH 43235-1222, USA

Kelley, Earl A (Athlete, Basketball Player)
5900 Longleaf Dr
Lawrence, KS 66049-5801, USA

Kelley, Gaynor N (Business Person)
Perkin-Elmer Corp
710 Bridgeport Ave
Shelton, CT 06484-4794, USA

Kelley, Gordon (Athlete, Football Player)
3101 S Ocean Blvd Apt 126
Highland Beach, FL 33487-2573, USA

Kelley, Ike (Athlete, Football Player)
1006 Clubview Blvd N
Columbus, OH 43235-1222, USA

Kelley, Jon (Television Host)

Kelley, Josh (Musician)

Kelley, Kevin (Athlete, Baseball Player)
1311 Quarterpath Ct
Richmond, TX 77406-6502, USA

Kelley, Kitty (Writer)
1228 Eton Ct NW
Washington, DC 20007-3240, USA

Kelley, Malcolm David (Actor)
c/o Mark Smith *Savage Agency*
1041 N Formosa Ave
West Hollywood, CA 90046-6703, USA

Kelley, Manon (Adult Film Star)
PO Box 315
Bellmore, NY 11710-0315, USA

Kelley, Mike (Producer, Writer)
c/o Sonya Rosenfeld *Creative Artists Agency (CAA)*
2000 Avenue of the Stars Ste 100
Los Angeles, CA 90067-4705, USA

Kelley, Nathalie (Actor)
c/o Megan Silverman *WME|IMG*
9601 Wilshire Blvd
Beverly Hills, CA 90210-5213, USA

Kelley, Rich (Athlete, Basketball Player)
314 Raymundo Dr
Woodside, CA 94062-4129, USA

Kelley, Ryan (Actor)
c/o Kevin Derkash *East 2 West Collective*
11022 Santa Monica Blvd Ste 350
Los Angeles, CA 90025-7532, USA

Kelley, Shawn (Athlete, Baseball Player)
10051 Meadowstone Dr
Apison, TN 37302-7603, USA

Kelley, Sheila (Actor, Producer)
524 Lorraine Blvd
Los Angeles, CA 90020-4732, USA

Kelley, Shelia (Actor)
524 Lorraine Blvd
Los Angeles, CA 90020-4732, USA

Kelley, Steve (Cartoonist)
San Diego Union
600 B St Ste 1201
Editorial Dept
San Diego, CA 92101-4505, USA

Kelley, Tom (Athlete, Baseball Player)
710 11th Ave S
North Myrtle Beach, SC 29582-3754, USA

Kelley, William G (Business Person)
Consolidated Stores
1105 N Market St
Wilmington, DE 19801-1216, USA

Kellgren, Christer (Athlete, Hockey Player)
Rothlinsvag 41
Saro 42942, Sweden

Kellin, Kevin (Athlete, Football Player)
12500 Capri Cir N Apt 302
Treasure Island, FL 33706-4972, USA

Kellman, Barnet (Director)
c/o Staff Member *Jackoway Tyerman Wertheimer Austen Mandelbaum Morris & Klein*
1925 Century Park E Fl 22
Los Angeles, CA 90067-2701, USA

Kellner, Catherine (Actor)
c/o Michael Lazo *Untitled Entertainment*
350 S Beverly Dr Ste 200
Beverly Hills, CA 90212-4819, USA

Kellner, Deborah (Actor)
c/o Jessica (Pilch) Samuel *Sanders Armstrong Caserta*
4111 W Alameda Ave Ste 505
Burbank, CA 91505-4163, USA

Kellogg, Clark (Athlete, Basketball Player)
4155 Palmer Park Cir W APT 208
New Albany, OH 43054-1177, USA

Kellogg, Jeffrey (Athlete, Baseball Player)
22900 Cherry Hill Ct
Mattawan, MI 49071-9562, USA

Kellogg, Jeffrey (Baseball Player)
22900 Cherry Hill Ct
Mattawan, MI 49071-9562, USA

Kellogg, Mike (Athlete, Football Player)
7497 Tabor St
Arvada, CO 80005-3283, USA

Kellogg, William S (Business Person)
Kohl's Corp
N56W17000 Ridgewood Dr
Menomonee Falls, WI 53051-7096, USA

Kellum, Echo (Actor)
c/o Nilda Carrazana *Status PR*
PO Box 6191
Westlake Village, CA 91359-6191, USA

Kellum, Marv (Athlete, Football Player)
115 Oakmont Dr
Pittsburgh, PA 15229-2903, USA

Kelly, Aaron (Musician)
c/o Simon Fuller *XIX Entertainment (UK)*
32/33 Ransomes Dock
London SW11 4NP, UNITED KINGDOM (UK)

Kelly, Arvesta (Athlete, Basketball Player)
1040 Oxford St N
Saint Paul, MN 55103-1246, USA

Kelly, Bob (Athlete, Baseball Player)
6 Mohawk Dr
Niantic, CT 06357-2812, USA

Kelly, Bob (Athlete, Hockey Player)
10 Peyton Ct
Marlton, NJ 08053-4700, USA

Kelly, Brendan (Actor)
c/o Staff Member *Allman/Rea Management*
141 Barrington Walk
#E
Los Angeles, CA 90049, USA

Kelly, Brian (Athlete, Football Player)
2517 Cozumel Dr
Tampa, FL 33618-1901, USA

Kelly, Bryan (Athlete, Baseball Player)
5400 Cub Lake Dr
Apopka, FL 32703-1946, USA

Kelly, Dale (Baseball Player)
Toronto Blue Jays
425 Tupelo Ct
Santa Maria, CA 93454-6238, USA

Kelly, Dan (Athlete, Hockey Player)
165 Mulberry St.
Newark, NY 17102, USA

Kelly, Daniel (Actor)
c/o Staff Member *Can Public Relations (CPR)*
1 Yonge St Suite 1801
Toronto, ON M5E 1W7, Canada

Kelly, Daniel-Hugh (Actor)
Innovative Artists
1505 10th St
Santa Monica, CA 90401-2805, USA

Kelly, David Patrick (Actor)
c/o Staff Member *Paradigm*
8942 Wilshire Blvd
Beverly Hills, CA 90211-1908, USA

Kelly, Dean Lennox (Actor)
c/o Staff Member *Scott Marshall Partners Ltd*
49/50 Eagle Wharf Road
Holborn Studios
London N1 7ED, UNITED KINGDOM

Kelly, Dennis (Athlete, Football Player)

Kelly, Diva Kelly (Athlete, Wrestler)
c/o Staff Member *World Wrestling Entertainment (WWE)*
1241 E Main St
Stamford, CT 06902-3520, USA

Kelly, Don (Athlete, Baseball Player)
216 Cliffside Dr
Mars, PA 16046-4802, USA

Kelly, Elisworth (Artist)
PO Box 1708
Chatham, NY 12037, USA

Kelly, Ellison (Athlete, Football Player)
146 Manning Ave
Hamilton, ON L9A 3E9, Canada

kelly, Ellsworth (Artist)
PO Box 151
Spencertown, NY 12165-0151, USA

Kelly, Greg (Correspondent)
Fox News Channel
1211 Avenue of the Americas Lowr C31
New York, NY 10036-8799, USA

Kelly, Harold (Horse Racer)
440 Tennent Rd
Manalapan, NJ 07726-3410, USA

Kelly, James M (Astronaut)

Kelly, Jean Louisa (Actor)
c/o Adam Levine *Industry Entertainment Partners*
955 Carrillo Dr Ste 300
Los Angeles, CA 90048-5400, USA

Kelly, Jeff (Athlete, Football Player)
6437 Munke Rd
La Grange, TX 78945-5836, USA

Kelly, Jerry (Athlete, Golfer)
723 Wilder Dr
Madison, WI 53704-6011, USA

Kelly, Jim (Athlete, Football Player)
c/o Steve Kauffman *Kauffman Sports Management Group*
Prefers to be contacted by telephone
Malibu, CA, USA

Kelly, Joanne (Actor)
c/o Joannie Burstein *Burstein Company*
15304 W Sunset Blvd Ste 208
Pacific Palisades, CA 90272-3656, USA

Kelly, John (Musician)
EMI America Records
6920 W Sunset Blvd
Los Angeles, CA 90028-7010, USA

Kelly, John D (Athlete, Football Player)
816 NE 18th Ave Apt 4
Fort Lauderdale, FL 33304-3005, USA

Kelly, John Paul (Athlete, Hockey Player)
PO Box 10416 RPO 10
Lloydminster, AB T9V 3A5, Canada

Kelly, Justin (Actor)
c/o Brad Stokes *LINK Entertainment*
11872 La Grange Ave
Los Angeles, CA 90025-5282, USA

Kelly, Kenny (Athlete, Baseball Player)
1318 Louisiana St
Plant City, FL 33563-5828, USA

Kelly, Kevin (Baseball Player)
1311 Quarterpath Ct
Richmond, TX 77406-6502, USA

Kelly, Leonard P (Red) (Athlete, Hockey Player)
30 Dunvegan Rd
Toronto, ON M4V 2P6, Canada

Kelly, Leroy (Athlete, Football Player)
91 Club House Dr
Willingboro, NJ 08046-3418, USA

Kelly, Malcolm (Athlete, Football Player)
c/o Chad Speck *Allegiant Athletic Agency*
35 Market Sq Ste 201
Knoxville, TN 37902-1420, USA

Kelly, Mark E (Astronaut)
2121 Barrington Dr
League City, TX 77573-6690, USA

Kelly, Megyn (Correspondent, Television Host)
c/o Bryan Freedman *Freedman & Taitelman*
1901 Avenue of the Stars Ste 500
Los Angeles, CA 90067-6027, USA

Kelly, Michael (Actor)
c/o Alexandra Kahn *Relevant (NY)*
333 Hudson St Rm 502
New York, NY 10013-1033, USA

Kelly, Mike (Athlete, Baseball Player)
8490 S Maple Ave
Tempe, AZ 85284-2244, USA

Kelly, Mike (Athlete, Football Player)
7941 David Kenney Farm Rd
Huntersville, NC 28078-8730, USA

Kelly, Mike (Congressman, Politician)
515 Cannon Hob
Washington, DC 20515-1309, USA

Kelly, Minka (Actor)
c/o Todd Diener *Untitled Entertainment*
350 S Beverly Dr Ste 200
Beverly Hills, CA 90212-4819, USA

Kelly, Moira (Actor)
c/o Troy Nankin *Wishlab*
195 S Beverly Dr Ste 414
Beverly Hills, CA 90212-3044, USA

Kelly, Morgan (Actor)
c/o Tina Petro *Epic Talent*
3451 St. Laurent #400
Montreal QC H2X 2T6, Canada

Kelly, Pat (Athlete, Baseball Player)
1131 Howertown Rd
Catasauqua, PA 18032-1512, USA

Kelly, Paul (Musician, Songwriter)
c/o Staff Member *Paradigm (Monterey)*
404 W Franklin St
Monterey, CA 93940-2303, USA

Kelly, R (Musician, Songwriter)
c/o Chris Chambers *The Chamber Group*
75 Broad St Rm 708
New York, NY 10004-3244, USA

Kelly, Richard (Director)
c/o Staff Member *Darko Entertainment*
120 S Gardner St
Los Angeles, CA 90036-2718, USA

Kelly, Robert (Athlete, Football Player)
5380 N 750 E
Hamlet, IN 46532-9531, USA

Kelly, Roberto (Athlete, Baseball Player)
Augusta Greenjackets
510 Franklin Dr
Arlington, TX 76011-2244, USA

Kelly, Roz (Actor)
5161 Riverton Ave Apt 105
North Hollywood, CA 91601-3943

Kelly, Ryan (Athlete, Basketball Player)
c/o Chris Emens *Octagon (AZ)*
16055 N Dial Blvd Ste 8
Scottsdale, AZ 85260-1642, USA

Kelly, Ryan (Actor)
c/o Staff Member *Ambition Talent*
439 Wellington St W Suite 204
Toronto, ON M5V 1E7, Canada

Kelly, Scott J (Astronaut)
2121 Barrington Dr
League City, TX 77058-3607, USA

Kelly, Thomas (Athlete, Basketball Player)
2117 Forge Rd
Santa Barbara, CA 93108-2238, USA

Kelly, Thomas (Athlete, Football Player)
14524 La Mesa Dr
La Mirada, CA 90638-4026, USA

Kelly, Todd (Athlete, Football Player)
237 Gwinhurst Rd
Knoxville, TN 37934-4535, USA

Kelly, Tom (Athlete, Baseball Player, Coach)
1643 Currie St N
Saint Paul, MN 55119-7160, USA

Kelly, Tori (Musician)
c/o Staff Member *Stoked PR*
118 Commercial St
#202
London E1 6NF, UNITED KINGDOM

Kelly, Van (Athlete, Baseball Player)
11 Beauregard Dr
Spencer, NC 28159-1957, USA

Kelly III, Thomas J (Journalist)
PO Box 2208
Sanatoga Branch
Pottstown, PA 19464, USA

Kelly-Sordelet, Collin (Actor)
c/o Jason Gutman *Gersh*
41 Madison Ave Ste 3301
New York, NY 10010-2210, USA

Kelm, Larry (Athlete, Football Player)
67 Driftoak Cir
The Woodlands, TX 77381-6632, USA

Kelman, James (Writer)
Weidenfeld-Nicolson
Upper Saint Martin's Lane
London WC2H 9EA, UNITED KINGDOM (UK)

Kelsay, Chris (Athlete, Football Player)
29 Peppermill Ln
Orchard Park, NY 14127-4532, USA

Kelser, Gregory (Athlete, Basketball Player)
30400 Forest Dr
Franklin, MI 48025-1598, USA

Kelsey, David (Actor)
c/o Dee Dee Shaughnessy *JE Talent*
155 Montgomery St Ste 805
San Francisco, CA 94104-4113, USA

Kelso, Ben (Athlete, Basketball Player)
1877 Midchester Dr
West Bloomfield, MI 48324-1138, USA

Kelso, Bill (Athlete, Baseball Player)
136 NE Briarcliff Rd
Kansas City, MO 64116-4512, USA

Kelso, Mark (Athlete, Football Player)
897 Luther Rd
East Aurora, NY 14052-9764, USA

Kelton, David (Athlete, Baseball Player)
515 Riverside Dr
Lagrange, GA 30240-9635, USA

Keltz, Jonathan (Actor)
c/o Craig Schneider *Pinnacle Public Relations*
8721 Santa Monica Blvd # 133
W Hollywood, CA 90069-4507, USA

Kem (Music Group)
c/o Staff Member *Paradigm (Monterey)*
404 W Franklin St
Monterey, CA 93940-2303, USA

Kemal, Yashar (Writer)
PK14 Basinkoy
Istanbul, TURKEY

Kemmerer, Beatrice (Athlete, Baseball Player, Commentator)
8437 Carter St
Bremen, IN 46506-9201, USA

Kemmerer, Russ (Athlete, Baseball Player)
6335 Colebrook Dr
Indianapolis, IN 46220-4205, USA

Kemp, Gary (Musician)
International Talent Group
729 7th Ave Ste 1600
New York, NY 10019-6880, USA

Kemp, Jeff (Athlete, Football Player)
22101 NE 66th Pl
Redmond, WA 98053-2337, USA

Kemp, Jeremy (Actor)
Marina Martin
12/13 Poland St
London W1V 3DE, UNITED KINGDOM (UK)

Kemp, Martin (Musician)
Mission Control
Business Center
Lower Road
London SE16 2XB, UNITED KINGDOM (UK)

Kemp, Matt (Athlete, Baseball Player)
c/o Staff Member *Los Angeles Dodgers*
1000 Elysian Park Ave
Los Angeles, CA 90012, USA

Kemp, Perry (Athlete, Football Player)
PO Box 78
Westland, PA 15378-0078, USA

Kemp, Ross (Actor)
EastEnders
BBC Elstree Centre
Clarendon Road
Borehamwood, Herts UK WD6 1JF

Kemp, Shawn (Athlete, Basketball Player)
18237 Belding Ct
Brandywine, MD 20613-7107, USA

Kemp, Steve (Athlete, Baseball Player)
436 Fernleaf Ave
Corona Del Mar, CA 92625-2111, USA

Kempainen, Robert (Athlete, Olympic Athlete, Track Athlete)
1753 Princeton Ave
Saint Paul, MN 55105-1915, USA

Kemper, Ellie (Actor)
c/o Michael Lasker *Mosaic Media Group*
407 N Maple Dr # 100
Beverly Hills, CA 90210-3818, USA

Kempf, Florian (Athlete, Football Player)
8039 Pine Rd Apt 1
Philadelphia, PA 19111-1808, USA

Kempinska, Charles (Athlete, Football Player)
925 State St
Natchez, MS 39120-3577, USA

Kempner, Patty (Athlete, Olympic Athlete, Swimmer)
5295 E 45th St
Yuma, AZ 85365-7616, USA

Kemppel, Nina (Athlete, Olympic Athlete, Track Athlete)
2819 McCollie Ave
Anchorage, AK 99517-1221, USA

Kempthorne, Dirk (Politician)
PO Box 1508
Eagle, ID 83616-9101, USA

Kempton, Tim (Athlete, Basketball Player)
4131 N 43rd St
Phoenix, AZ 85018-4211, USA

Kempton, tin (Athlete, Basketball Player)
16223 W Cambridge Ave
Goodyear, AZ 85395-2084, USA

Kemsley, Dorit (Designer, Reality Star)
Beverly Beach by Dorit
14515 Alondra Blvd
La Mirada, CA 90638-5602, USA

Ken, Baird (Athlete, Hockey Player)
Lot 4 Berry Bay
White Lake, MB R0B 1M0, Canada

Kenady, Chris (Athlete, Hockey Player)
5042 Tuxedo Blvd
Mound, MN 55364-9254

Kendal, Felicity (Actor)
Chatto & Linnit
Prince of Wales Coventry St
London W1V 7FE, UNITED KINGDOM (UK)

Kendall, Donald M (Business Person)
PepsiCo Inc
Anderson Hill Road
Purchase, NY 10577, USA

Kendall, Fred (Athlete, Baseball Player)
57575 Johnston Rd
Anza, CA 92539-9646, USA

Kendall, Jason (Athlete, Baseball Player)
11730 Stonehenge Ln
Los Angeles, CA 90077-1302, USA

Kendall, Jeannie (Musician)
Joe Taylor Artist Agency
2802 Columbine Pl
Nashville, TN 37204-3104, USA

Kendall, Pete (Athlete, Football Player)
PO Box 888
Phoenix, AZ 85001-0888, USA

Kendall, Skip (Athlete, Golfer)
8406 Kemper Ln
Windermere, FL 34786-5318, USA

Kendall, Tom (Race Car Driver)
International Motor Sports Assn
1394 Broadway Ave
Braselton, GA 30517-2909, USA

Kenders, Al (Athlete, Baseball Player)
8744 Matilija Ave
Panorama City, CA 91402-3320, USA

Kendrena, Ken (Baseball Player)
4235 Stone Mountain Dr
Chino Hills, CA 91709-6155, USA

Kendrick, Alex (Producer)
c/o Staff Member *Sherwood Pictures*
2201 Whispering Pines Rd
Albany, GA 31707-2421, USA

Kendrick, Anna (Actor)
c/o Mick Sullivan *Creative Artists Agency (CAA)*
2000 Avenue of the Stars Ste 100
Los Angeles, CA 90067-4705, USA

Kendrick, Darren (Actor)
c/o Albert Giannelli *Omnium Entertainment Group*
444 N Larchmont Blvd Ste 108
Los Angeles, CA 90004-3030, USA

Kendrick, Frank (Athlete, Basketball Player)
8355 Providence Dr
Fishers, IN 46038-5233, USA

Kendrick, Howard (Athlete, Baseball Player)
8650 E Joshua Tree Ln
Scottsdale, AZ 85250-4923, USA

Kendrick, Kyle (Athlete, Baseball Player)
7475 Wisconsin Ave Ste 600
Bethesda, MD 20814-3492, USA

Kendrick E G, ""Ken"" (Athlete, Baseball Player)
3964 E Paradise View Dr
Paradise Valley, AZ 85253-3800, USA

Kendricks, Lance (Athlete, Football Player)
c/o Neil Cornrich *NC Sports, LLC*
best to contact via email
Columbus, OH 43201, USA

Kendricks, Mychal (Athlete, Football Player)
c/o Doug Hendrickson *Relativity Sports*
2029 Century Park E Ste 1550
Century City, CA 90067-3000, USA

Keneally, Thomas M (Writer)
24 Serpentine
Bilgola Beach, NSW 02107, AUSTRALIA

Keneley, Matt (Athlete, Football Player)
25142 Sandia Ct
Laguna Hills, CA 92653-5606, USA

Kener, Kira (Adult Film Star)
Vivid Entertainment
1933 N Bronson Ave Apt 209
Los Angeles, CA 90068-5632, USA

Kenichi, Chen (Chef)
Akasaka Shisen Hanten 2-5-5 Hiragacho
Zenkoku Ryokan Kaikan
Chiyoda-ku, Tokyo, japan

Kenmore, Joan (Actor)
33106 Ocean Rdg
Dana Point, CA 92629-1084, USA

Kenn, Michael L (Mike) (Athlete, Football Player)
360 Bardolier
Alpharetta, GA 30022-5129, USA

Kenna, E Douglas (Doug) (Athlete, Business Person, Football Player)
111 Saint Joseph St S
South Bend, IN 46601-1939, USA

Kennan, Brian (Musician)
PO Box 770850
Lustig Talent
Orlando, FL 32877-0850, USA

Kennard, Derek (Athlete, Football Player)
15849 S 35th Way
Phoenix, AZ 85048-7278, USA

Kennard, Devon (Athlete, Football Player)

Kennard, Trevor (Athlete, Football Player)
TKM Inc
207 Oxford St
Winnipeg, MB R3M 3H8, USA

Kennedy, Adam (Athlete, Baseball Player)
5025 Windhill Dr
Riverside, CA 92507-0615, USA

Kennedy, Alan D (Business Person)
Tupperware Corp
PO Box 2353
Orlando, FL 32802-2353, USA

Kennedy, Courtney (Athlete, Hockey Player, Olympic Athlete)
13 Whispering Hill Rd
Woburn, MA 01801-4781, USA

Kennedy, Dan (Business Person, Writer)
Kennedy Inner Circle Inc
5818 N 7th St # 103
Phoenix, AZ 85014-5806, USA

Kennedy, Dean (Athlete, Hockey Player)
GD
Pincher Creek, AB T0K 1W0, Canada

Kennedy, D James (Religious Leader)
Coral Ridge Presbyterian Church
5554 N Federal Hwy
Fort Lauderdale, FL 33308-3209, USA

Kennedy, Douglas (Writer)
c/o Staff Member *LIESERLAW*
91 Rue De L'University
Paris 75007, FRANCE

Kennedy, Dwayne (Comedian)
c/o Rick Messina *Messina Baker Entertainment*
8033 W Sunset Blvd
West Hollywood, CA 90046-2401, USA

Kennedy, Ethel (Politician)
PO Box 328
Hyannis Port, MA 02647-0328, USA

Kennedy, Eugene (Athlete, Basketball Player)
8218 Westrock Dr
Dallas, TX 75243-6524, USA

Kennedy, Forbes (Athlete, Hockey Player)
20 Oakland Dr
Charlottetown, PE C1C 1P4, Canada

Kennedy, Ian (Athlete, Baseball Player)
c/o Team Member *New York Yankees*
161st St & River Ave
Yankee Stadium
Bronx, NY 10451, USA

Kennedy, James C (Business Person)
Cox Enterprises
1400 Lake Hearn Dr NE
Brookhaven, GA 30319-1418, USA

Kennedy, Jamie (Actor, Producer)
c/o Staff Member *Jamie Kennedy Entertainment*
2508 N Vermont Ave
Los Angeles, CA 90027-1243, USA

Kennedy, Jason (Television Host)
c/o Staff Member *Fifteen Minutes*
5670 Wilshire Blvd Ste 830
Los Angeles, CA 90036-5684, USA

Kennedy, Jim (Athlete, Baseball Player)
13940 SW Lisa Ln
Beaverton, OR 97005-4315, USA

Kennedy, Jimmy (Athlete, Football Player)
901 N Broadway
Saint Louis, MO 63101-2800, USA

Kennedy, Joe (Athlete, Basketball Player)
201 43rd St
Virginia Beach, VA 23451-2503, USA

Kennedy, Joey D (Joe) Jr (Journalist)
1635 11th Pl S
Birmingham, AL 35205-5907, USA

Kennedy, John (Athlete, Baseball Player)
10 Hill Dr
Topsham, ME 04086-1484, USA

Kennedy, John Milton (Actor)
5711 Reseda Blvd # 204
Tarzana, CA 91356-2201, USA

Kennedy, Junior (Athlete, Baseball Player)
6006 Lassen Ridge Rd
Bakersfield, CA 93306-7773, USA

Kennedy, Kathleen (Producer)
c/o Staff Member *United Talent Agency (UTA)*
9336 Civic Center Dr
Beverly Hills, CA 90210-3604, USA

Kennedy, Ken (Wrestler)
c/o Kerry Rodgerson *World Wrestling Entertainment (WWE)*
1241 E Main St
Stamford, CT 06902-3520, USA

Kennedy, Kenoy (Athlete, Football Player)
16275 O Conner Ave
Forney, TX 75126-7572, USA

Kennedy, Kevin (Athlete, Baseball Player, Coach, Television Host)
c/o Staff Member *Fox Sports (NY)*
1211 Avenue of the Americas Ste 302
New York, NY 10036-8799, USA

Kennedy, Lan (Athlete, Baseball Player)
2405 Brockton Way
Henderson, NV 89074-5471, USA

Kennedy, Lee (Business Person)
Equifax Inc
1550 Peachtree St NW
Atlanta, GA 30309-2468, USA

Kennedy, Leon Isaac (Actor)
859 N Hollywood Way # 384
Burbank, CA 91505-2814, USA

Kennedy, Lincoln (Athlete, Football Player)
2027 E Minton St
Mesa, AZ 85213-1438, USA

Kennedy, Mike (Athlete, Hockey Player)
DTZ Barnicke
900-50 Burnhamthorpe Rd W
Mississauga, ON L5B 3C2, Canada

Kennedy, Mimi (Actor)
c/o Todd Justice *Justice & Ponder*
PO Box 480033
Los Angeles, CA 90048-1033, USA

Kennedy, M Peter (Figure Skater)
7650 SE 41st St
Mercer Island, WA 98040-3437, USA

Kennedy, Nigel (Musician)
Russels
Regency House
1-4 Warwick St
London W1R 5WB, UNITED KINGDOM (UK)

Kennedy, Page (Actor)
c/o Dominic Friesen *Bridge and Tunnel Communications*
8149 Santa Monica Blvd # 407
West Hollywood, CA 90046-4912, USA

Kennedy, Patrick (Actor)
c/o Staff Member *ICM (London)*
76 Oxford St
London W1D 1BS, UNITED KINGDOM

Kennedy, Ray F (Business Person)
Masco Corp
17450 College Pkwy
Livonia, MI 48152-2300, USA

Kennedy, Robert F Jr (Attorney)
Pace Environmental Litigation Clinic
78 N Broadway
Pace University School of Law
White Plains, NY 10603-3710, USA

Kennedy, Robert H (Athlete, Football Player)
4906 N 76th Pl
Scottsdale, AZ 85251-1507, USA

Kennedy, Rory (Director, Producer)
7238 Birdview Ave
Malibu, CA 90265-4111, USA

Kennedy, Ryan (Actor)
c/o Lesa Kirk *Kirk Talent Agencies Inc*
196 3rd Ave W Suite 102
Vancouver, BC V5Y 1E9, CANADA

Kennedy, Sheldon (Athlete, Hockey Player)
Sheldon Kennedy Child Advisory Center
400-3820 24 Ave NW
Calgary, AB T3B 2X9, CANADA

Kennedy, Ted (Athlete, Hockey Player)
Physically unable to sign autographs

Kennedy, Terrence E (Terry) (Athlete, Baseball Player)
333 N Pennington Dr Unit 23
Chandler, AZ 85224-8266, USA

Kennedy, T Lincoln (Athlete, Football Player)
3917 Spring Garden Pl
Apt 1
Spring Valley, CA 91977, USA

Kennedy, William (Athlete, Basketball Player)
9927 Galleon Dr
West Palm Beach, FL 33411-1807, USA

Kennedy, William J (Athlete, Football Player)
16383 Ronnie Ln
Livonia, MI 48154-2249, USA

Kennedy, William J (Writer)
New York State Writers Institute
Washington Ave
Albany, NY 12222-0001, USA

Kennedy, X Joseph (X J) (Writer)
22 Revere St
Lexington, MA 02420-4424, USA

Kennedy Schlossberg, Caroline (Writer)
ESI Design
111 5th Ave Fl 12
New York, NY 10003-1005, USA

Kenner, Ellen (Radio Personality, Talk Show Host)
PO Box 440
North Scituate, RI 02857-0440, USA

kenner, Kevin (Musician)
Columbia Artists Mgmt Inc
165 W 57th St
New York, NY 10019-2201, USA

Kennerd, Trevor (Athlete, Football Player)
207 Oxford St
TKM INC
Winnipeg, MB R3M 3H8, Canada

Kenney, Bill (Athlete, Football Player)
4481 SW Bowsprit Dr
Lees Summit, MO 64082-4713, USA

Kenney, Emma (Actor)
c/o Staff Member *Carsey-Werner Company*
16027 Ventura Blvd Ste 600
Encino, CA 91436-2798, USA

Kenney, Jerry (Athlete, Baseball Player)
926 E Windfield Ct
Beloit, WI 53511-6547, USA

Kenney, Stephen F (Steve) (Athlete, Football Player)
1105 Silver Oaks Ct
Raleigh, NC 27614-9359, USA

Kenney, William P (Athlete, Football Player)
2808 SW Arthur Dr
Lees Summit, MO 64082-4062, USA

Kennibrew, Dee Dee (Musician)
Superstars Unlimited
PO Box 371371
Las Vegas, NV 89137-1371, USA

Kennington, DJ (Race Car Driver)
10206 Ford Rd
St Thomas, ON N5P 3T1, CANADA

Kennison, Eddie (Athlete, Football Player)
26339 Richwood Oaks Dr
Katy, TX 77494-0310, USA

Kenny, Brian (Sportscaster)
c/o Nick Khan *Creative Artists Agency (CAA)*
2000 Avenue of the Stars Ste 100
Los Angeles, CA 90067-4705, USA

Kenny, Shannon (Actor)
c/o Joannie Burstein *Burstein Company*
15304 W Sunset Blvd Ste 208
Pacific Palisades, CA 90272-3656, USA

Kenny, Tom (Actor, Musician, Writer)
c/o Kara Welker *Generate Management*
8750 Wilshire Blvd Ste 200
Beverly Hills, CA 90211-2707, USA

Kenon, Larry (Athlete, Basketball Player)
25057 Toutant Beauregard Rd
San Antonio, TX 78255-3402, USA

Kenseth, Matt (Race Car Driver)
Joe Gibbs Racing
13415 Reese Blvd W
Huntersville, NC 28078-7933, USA

Kensing, Logan (Athlete, Baseball Player)
208 E Bandera Rd
Boerne, TX 78006-2902, USA

Kensit, Patsy (Actor, Musician)
14 Lambton Place Nottinghill
London W11 2SH, UNITED KINGDOM (UK)

Kent, Arthur (Correspondent)
2184 Torringford St
Torrington, CT 06790-2540, USA

Kent, Jean (Actor)
London Mgmt
2-4 Noel St
London W1V 3RB, UNITED KINGDOM (UK)

Kent, Jeff (Athlete, Baseball Player)
5513 Foxfield Ln
Austin, TX 78738-7702, USA

Kent, Joey (Athlete, Football Player)
6409 Eric St NW
Huntsville, AL 35810-1605, USA

Kent, Jonathan (Director)
International Creative Mgmt
76 Oxford St
London W1N 0AX, UNITED KINGDOM (UK)

Kent, Steve (Athlete, Baseball Player)
3118 Minthorn Dr
Killeen, TX 76542-1932, USA

Kentner, Louis (Musician)
1 Mallord St
London SW3, UNITED KINGDOM (UK)

Kenty, Hilmer (Boxer)
Escot Boxing
19260 Bretton Dr
Detroit, MI 48223-1364, USA

Kenville, Bill (Athlete, Basketball Player)
59 Crary Ave
Binghamton, NY 13905-3828, USA

Kenworthy, Dick (Athlete, Baseball Player)
5551 Rue Royale Apt D
Indianapolis, IN 46227-1960, USA

Kenworthy, Gus (Olympic Athlete, Skier)
US Ski And Snowboard Association
1 Victory Ln # 100
Park City, UT 84060-7463, USA

Kenya, Wendi (Actor)
Michael Forman Management
607 N Bedford Dr
Beverly Hills, CA 90210-3215, USA

Kenyon, Mel (Race Car Driver)
4645 S. 25 West
Lebanon, IN 46052, USA

Kenzle, Leila (Actor)
c/o Staff Member *Agency for the Performing Arts (APA)*
405 S Beverly Dr Ste 500
Beverly Hills, CA 90212-4425, USA

Kenzo (Designer, Fashion Designer)
3 Place des Victories
Paris 75001, FRANCE

Keo, Shiloh (Athlete, Football Player)
c/o Michael McCartney *Priority Sports & Entertainment (Chicago)*
325 N La Salle Dr Ste 650
Chicago, IL 60654-8182, USA

Keogan, Murray (Athlete, Hockey Player)
5631 E Superior St
Duluth, MN 55804-2530

Keoghan, Barry (Actor)
c/o Sam Fox *Troika*
10A Christina St.
London EC2A 4PA, UNITED KINGDOM

Keoghan, Phil (Television Host)
c/o Staff Member *ICM Partners*
10250 Constellation Blvd Fl 7
Los Angeles, CA 90067-6207, USA

Keoke, Kimo (Actor)
612 1/2 N Spaulding Ave
Los Angeles, CA 90036-1838, USA

Keon, David M (Dave) (Athlete, Hockey Player)
115 Brackenwood Rd
Palm Beach Gardens, FL 33418-9065, USA

Keough, Joe (Athlete, Baseball Player)
606 Belmark Ct
San Antonio, TX 78258-2503, USA

Keough, Lainey (Designer, Fashion Designer)
42 Dawson St
Dublin 00002, IRELAND

Keough, Marty (Athlete, Baseball Player)
6874 E Nightingale Star Cir
Scottsdale, AZ 85266-7044, USA

Keough, Matt (Athlete, Baseball Player)
31142 Via Colinas
Trabuco Canyon, CA 92679-4005, USA

Keough, Riley (Actor)
c/o Maha Dakhil *Creative Artists Agency (CAA)*
2000 Avenue of the Stars Ste 100
Los Angeles, CA 90067-4705, USA

Kepcher, Carolyn (Reality Star)

keppel, Bobby (Athlete, Baseball Player)
1297 Stephenridge Ct
Saint Charles, MO 63304-3405, USA

Keppinger, Jeff (Athlete, Baseball Player)
1578 Cordillo Ct
Dacula, GA 30019-7750, USA

Kepshire, Kurt (Athlete, Baseball Player)
4 Stonebridge Rd
Oxford, CT 06478-1164, USA

Ke Quan, Jonathan (Actor)

Ker, Crawford (Athlete, Football Player)
214 Harbor View Ln
Largo, FL 33770-4007, USA

Ker, Joshua (Athlete, Football Player)
2927 Lakeshore Dr
Muskegon, MI 49441, USA

Kerbow, Randall (Athlete, Football Player)
10122 Lost Hollow Ln
Missouri City, TX 77459-2494, USA

Kerbow, Randy (Athlete, Football Player)
3803 Crystal Falls Dr
Missouri City, TX 77459-4249, USA

Kercher, Dick (Athlete, Football Player)
2396 Manzano Loop NE
Rio Rancho, NM 87144-7529, USA

Kercheval, Ken (Actor)
Stephany Hurkos
11935 Kling St Apt 10
Valley Village, CA 91607-5406, USA

Kercheval, Ralph (Athlete, Football Player)
1220 Richmond Rd
Lexington, KY 40502-1614, USA

Kerdyk, Tracy (Athlete, Golfer)
441 Valencia Ave Apt 401
Coral Gables, FL 33134-5782, USA

Keresztury, Bill (Athlete, Football Player)
16845 FM 32
Blanco, TX 78606-5443, USA

Kerfeld, Charlie (Athlete, Baseball Player)
15402 66th Avenue Ct NW
Gig Harbor, WA 98332-8736, USA

Kerkovich, Rob (Actor)
c/o Lorraine Berglund *Lorraine Berglund Management*
11537 Hesby St
North Hollywood, CA 91601-3618, USA

Kerley, Jeremy (Athlete, Football Player)

Kern, Bill (Athlete, Baseball Player)
625 W Green St
Allentown, PA 18102-1601, USA

Kern, Jim (Athlete, Baseball Player)
9560 Mitchell Bend Ct
Granbury, TX 76048-7708, USA

Kern, Joey (Actor)
c/o Staff Member *Paradigm*
8942 Wilshire Blvd
Beverly Hills, CA 90211-1908, USA

Kern, Rex W (Athlete, Football Player)
12 Canon Dr
Greenwood Village, CO 80111-3210, USA

Kernaghan, Lee (Musician)
c/o Stephen White *Stephen White Management*
7 Kingslangley Rd
Greenwich, NSW 02065, Australia

Kernan, Joseph (Politician)
200 W Washington St Ste 226
Indianapolis, IN 46204-2728, USA

Kernek, George (Athlete, Baseball Player)
16423 Cotton Gin Ave
Wayne, OK 73095-3172, USA

Kerner, Gabriele (Nena) (Musician)
C/O EAS
Beethofenstrasse, 53
Hamburg D-22083, Germany

Kerner, Ian (Writer)
c/o Staff Member *HarperCollins Publishers*
195 Broadway Fl 2
New York, NY 10007-3132, USA

Kerns, Joanna (Actor)
c/o Sean Freidin *ICM Partners*
10250 Constellation Blvd Fl 7
Los Angeles, CA 90067-6207, USA

Kerns, Sandra (Actor)
620 Resolano Dr
Pacific Palisades, CA 90272-3032, USA

Kerr, Alan (Athlete, Hockey Player)
Okanagan Hockey School
201-853 Eckhardt Ave W
Penticton, BC V2A 9C4, Canada

Kerr, Allen (Musician)
419 Carrington St
Adelaide, SA 05000, AUSTRALIA

Kerr, Brook (Actor)
c/o Martin (Marty) Berneman *Precision Entertainment*
6338 Wilshire Blvd
Los Angeles, CA 90048-5002, USA

Kerr, Cristie (Athlete, Golfer)
20010 N 103rd St
Scottsdale, AZ 85255-3304, USA

Kerr, Edward (Actor)
c/o Arlene Glucksman-Jones *Commercial Talent*
12711 Ventura Blvd Ste 285
Studio City, CA 91604-2487, USA

Kerr, Graham (Chef, Writer)
Kerr Corp
1020 N Sunset Dr
Camano Island, WA 98282-6665, USA

Kerr, Judy (Actor)
4139 Tujunga Ave
Studio City, CA 91604-3065, USA

Kerr, Kristen (Actor)
c/o Steven Jensen *Independent Group, The*
6363 Wilshire Blvd Ste 115
Los Angeles, CA 90048-5734, USA

Kerr, Miranda (Model)
c/o Aleen Keshishian *Lighthouse Management and Media*
9000 W Sunset Blvd Ste 1520
Los Angeles, CA 90069-5815, USA

Kerr, Pat (Designer, Fashion Designer)
Pat Kerr Inc
200 Wagner Pl PH 2
Memphis, TN 38103-3670, USA

Kerr, Reg (Athlete, Hockey Player)
424 Fox Meadow Dr
Northfield, IL 60093-4301, USA

Kerr, Steve (Athlete, Basketball Player)
PO Box 1964
Rancho Santa Fe, CA 92067-1964, USA

Kerr, Tim (Athlete, Coach, Hockey Player)
157 Fellswood Dr
Moorestown, NJ 08057-4015, USA

Kerr, William T (Business Person)
Meredith Corp
1716 Locust St
Des Moines, IA 50309-3023, USA

Kerrigan, Joseph T (Joe) (Athlete, Baseball Player, Coach)
578 Farmdale Cir
Blue Bell, PA 19422-1369, USA

Kerrigan, Marguerite (Athlete, Baseball Player, Commentator)
7218 10th St N
Saint Petersburg, FL 33702-5710, USA

Kerrigan, Nancy (Athlete, Figure Skater, Olympic Athlete)
7 Cedar Ave
Stoneham, MA 02180-2420, USA

Kerrigan, Pamela (Athlete, Golfer)
3205 Tuckers Ln
Hingham, MA 02043-1567, USA

Kerrigan, Ryan (Football Player)
c/o David Dunn *Athletes First*
23091 Mill Creek Dr
Laguna Hills, CA 92653-1258, USA

Kerry, Alexandra (Actor)
c/o Staff Member *TalentWorks*
3500 W Olive Ave Ste 1400
Burbank, CA 91505-5512, USA

Kerry, John (Politician)
19 Louisburg Sq
Boston, MA 02108-1202, USA

Kersey, Merritt (Athlete, Football Player)
17 Ballance Mill Rd
Nottingham, PA 19362-9507, USA

Kersey, Paul (Actor)
c/o Staff Member *TalentWorks*
3500 W Olive Ave Ste 1400
Burbank, CA 91505-5512, USA

Kersh, David (Musician)
Mark Hybner Entertainment
PO Box 223
Shiner, TX 77984-0223, USA

Kershaw, Clayton (Athlete, Baseball Player)
c/o Staff Member *Los Angeles Dodgers*
1000 Elysian Park Ave
Los Angeles, CA 90012, USA

Kershaw, Doug (Musician)
RR 1 Box 34285
Weld County Road 47
Eaton, CO 80615, USA

Kershaw, Sammy (Musician)
c/o Richard De La Font *Richard De La Font Agency*
3808 W South Park Blvd
Broken Arrow, OK 74011-1261, USA

Kershaw, Sammy (Race Car Driver)
111 Kay Dr.
Easley, 29640 SC, USA

Kershenbaum, David (Musician, Producer)
19021 Devonport Ln
Tarzana, CA 91356-5800, USA

kerslake, Doug (Athlete, Hockey Player)
5427 Pine Grove Ave
Norfolk, VA 23502-4924

Kerson, Chris (Actor)
c/o Gail Parenteau *Parenteau Guidance*
132 E 35th St # J
New York, NY 10016-3892, USA

Kersten, Wally (Athlete, Football Player)
4604 Longfellow Ave
Minneapolis, MN 55407-3638, USA

Kertesz, Daniella (Actor)
c/o Zohar Ya'kobson *Zohar Yakobson Representation*
136 Ben Yehuda St.
Tel Aviv 65271, ISRAEL

Kerwin, Brian (Actor)
c/o Staff Member *Paradigm*
8942 Wilshire Blvd
Beverly Hills, CA 90211-1908, USA

Kerwin, Irene (Athlete, Baseball Player, Commentator)
610 W Albany Ave
Peoria, IL 61604-1506, USA

Kerwin, Joseph P (Astronaut)
10411 River Rd
College Station, TX 77845-6719, USA

Kerwin, Lance (Actor)
PO Box 1708
Kapaa, HI 96746-5708, USA

Kerwin, Tom (Athlete, Basketball Player)
283 Salter Path Rd Unit 114
Atlantic Beach, NC 28512-6178, USA

Keseday, Robert (Athlete, Football Player)
57 Linden Ave
Park Ridge, NJ 07656-1254, USA

Keselowski, Brad (Race Car Driver)
c/o Staff Member *Penske Racing South*
200 Penske Way
Mooresville, NC 28115-8022, USA

Keser, Dean (Athlete, Football Player)
202 Rod Cir
Middletown, MD 21769-7826, USA

Kesha (Musician)
c/o Nicki Loranger *Vector Management*
1100 Glendon Ave Ste 2000
Los Angeles, CA 90024-3524, USA

Keshishian, Alek (Director, Writer)
c/o Aleen Keshishian *Lighthouse Management and Media*
9000 W Sunset Blvd Ste 1520
Los Angeles, CA 90069-5815, USA

Kesler, Ryan (Athlete, Hockey Player)
5982 Pontiac Trl
West Bloomfield, MI 48323-2225

Kessel Jr, Phil (Athlete, Hockey Player)
Newport Sports Management
400-201 City Centre Dr
Attn Wade Arnott
Mississauga, ON L5B 2T4, Canada

Kessell, Rick (Athlete, Hockey Player)
60 Underhill Dr
North York, ON M3A 2J7, Canada

Kessell, Simone (Actor)
c/o Staff Member *Status PR (NY)*
59 Chelsea Piers
Level 3
New York, NY 10011-1008, USA

Kessinger, Donald E (Don) (Athlete, Baseball Player, Coach)
108 Waterstone Dr
Oxford, MS 38655-0009, USA

Kessinger, Keith (Athlete, Baseball Player)
12004 Water Ridge Dr
Oxford, MS 38655-6019, USA

Kessinger, Ted (Athlete, Football Player)
612 N Washington St
Lindsborg, KS 67456-1516, USA

Kessler, Glenn (Producer, Writer)
c/o Staff Member *Creative Artists Agency (CAA)*
2000 Avenue of the Stars Ste 100
Los Angeles, CA 90067-4705, USA

Kessler, Ron (Writer)
c/o Staff Member *Trident Media Group LLC*
41 Madison Ave Fl 36
New York, NY 10010-2257, USA

Kessler, Todd (Producer, Writer)
c/o Staff Member *Creative Artists Agency (CAA)*
2000 Avenue of the Stars Ste 100
Los Angeles, CA 90067-4705, USA

Kester, Rick (Athlete, Baseball Player)
PO Box 623
Gardnerville, NV 89410-0623, USA

Kestner, Boyd (Actor)
Mirisch Agency
1801 Century Park E Ste 1801
Los Angeles, CA 90067-2320, USA

Kesy, Jack (Actor)
c/o Lena Roklin *Luber Roklin Management*
5815 W Sunset Blvd Ste 208
Los Angeles, CA 90028-6481, USA

Ketchum, Hal (Musician)
602 Wayside Dr
Wimberley, TX 78676-0020

Ketchum, Rai (Musician, Songwriter, Writer)
602 Wayside Dr
Wimberley, TX 78676-0020, USA

Ketola, Veli-Pekka (Athlete, Hockey Player)
Talikkalankuja 6
Pori 28300, Finland

Ketola-Lacamera, Helen (Athlete, Baseball Player, Commentator)
907 New York St
Edgewater, FL 32132-2373, USA

Ketter, Kerry (Athlete, Hockey Player)
3259 Majestic Dr
Courtenay, BC V9N 9X4, Canada

Kettle, Roger (Cartoonist)
c/o Staff Member *King Features Syndication*
300 W 57th St Fl 15
New York, NY 10019-5238, USA

Key, Jimmy (Athlete, Baseball Player)
138 Viera Dr
Palm Beach Gardens, FL 33418-1741, USA

Key, Keegan Michael (Actor)
c/o Joel Zadak *Artists First*
9465 Wilshire Blvd Ste 900
Beverly Hills, CA 90212-2608, USA

Key, Larry (Athlete, Football Player)
9661 60th St N
Attn: Church Administrations
Pinellas Park, FL 33782-3206, USA

Key, Sean (Athlete, Football Player)
4637 Chapel Creek Dr
Plano, TX 75024-6852, USA

Key, Ted (Cartoonist)
1694 Glenhardie Rd
Wayne, PA 19087-1004, USA

Key, Wade (Athlete, Football Player)
104 Cool Rock
Boerne, TX 78006-2998, USA

Keyes, Alan (Politician)
Loyalty to Liberty
PO Box 83759
Gaithersburg, MD 20883-3759, USA

Keyes, Leroy (Athlete, Football Player)
6156 Pleasant Ave
Pennsauken, NJ 08110-3537, USA

Keymah, T'Keyah Crystal (Actor)
121 N San Vicente Blvd
Beverly Hills, CA 90211-2303, USA

Keynes, Skander (Actor)
c/o Christian Hodell *Hamilton Hodell Ltd*
20 Golden Sq
Fl 5
London W1F 9JL, UNITED KINGDOM

Keys, Alicia (Musician, Songwriter)
c/o Patrick Whitesell *WME/IMG*
9601 Wilshire Blvd
Beverly Hills, CA 90210-5213, USA

Keys, Brady (Athlete, Football Player)
2931 Banchory Rd
Winter Park, FL 32792-4501, USA

Keys, Rudy (Athlete, Basketball Player)
4308 Ludi Mae Ct
Charlotte, NC 28227-6638, USA

Keys, Tyrone (Athlete, Football Player)
5708 Clouds Peak Dr
Lutz, FL 33558-4974, USA

Keyser, Brian (Athlete, Baseball Player)
11983 Cypress Links Dr
Fort Myers, FL 33913-8404, USA

Keyser, Richard L (Business Person)
WW Grainger Inc
100 Grainger Pkwy
Lake Forest, IL 60045-5202, USA

Keyworth, Jon (Athlete, Football Player)

Khabibulin, Nikolai (Athlete, Hockey Player)
Puckagency LLC
555 Pleasantville Rd Ste 210N
Attn Jay Grossman
Briarcliff Manor, NY 10510-1900, USA

Khajag, Barsamian (Religious Leader)
Armenian Church of America
630 2nd Ave
Eastern Diocese
New York, NY 10016-4806, USA

Khaled, DJ (Musician)
c/o Tammy Brook *FYI Public Relations*
174 5th Ave Ste 404
New York, NY 10010-5964, USA

Khali, Simbi (Actor)
Innovative Artists
1505 10th St
Santa Monica, CA 90401-2805, USA

Khalid (Musician)
c/o Cara Lewis *Cara Lewis Group*
7 W 18th St Fl 3
New York, NY 10011-4663, USA

Khalifa, Sam (Athlete, Baseball Player)
1050 N Camino Seco Apt 1044
Tucson, AZ 85710-1770, USA

Khalifa, Wiz (Musician)
c/o Constance Schwartz *SMAC Entertainment*
13456 Beach Ave
Marina Del Rey, CA 90292-5624, USA

Khalil, Christel (Actor)
c/o Meredith Fine *Coast to Coast Talent Group*
3350 Barham Blvd
Los Angeles, CA 90068-1404, USA

Khalil, Cristel (Actor)

Khamenei, Hojatolislam Sayyed Ali (President)
Religious Leader's Office
Teheran, IRAN

Khan, Aamir (Actor)
Aamir Khan Productions
Flat No 601, 6th Fl
Dhairya Residency, 12th Rd
Mumbai, Maharashta, INDIA

Khan, Alia (Designer)
Asian Andaz Inc
40 E 34th St Rm 1719
New York, NY 10016-4504, USA

Khan, Amir (Athlete, Boxer)
Khan Boxing Ltd.
Premier House
Prince St
Bolton BL1 2NP, UNITED KINGDOM

Khan, Chaka (Actor, Musician)
1128 S Point View St
Los Angeles, CA 90035-2619, USA

Khan, Inamullah (Religious Leader)
Muslim Congress
D26 Block 8
Gulshan-E_Iqbal
Karachi 75300, PAKISTAN

Khan, Jemima (Journalist, Writer)
c/o Staff Member *AP Watt Ltd*
20 John St
London WC1N 2DR, UNITED KINGDOM

Khan, Salman (Actor, Musician)

Khanh, Emanuelle (Designer, Fashion Designer)
Emanuelle Khanh International
45 Ave Victor Hugo
Paris 75116, FRANCE

Kharin, Sergei (Athlete, Hockey Player)
PO Box 3532
Ann Arbor, MI 48106, USA

Khatami, Mohammad (Politician, President)
President's Office
Dr Ali Shariati Ave
Teheran, IRAN

Khayat, Edward (Eddie) (Athlete, Coach, Football Coach, Football Player)
7813 Haydenberry Cv
Nashville, TN 37221-4675, USA

Khayat, Nadir (RedOne) (Producer)
c/o Alan Melina *New Heights Entertainment*
PO Box 8489
Calabasas, CA 91372-8489, USA

Khayat, Robert (Athlete, Football Player)
PO Box 667
Oxford, MS 38655-0667, USA

Kheng Hua, Tan (Actor)
c/o Claudia Greene *Mayhem Entertainment Public Relations*
3107 E Discovery St
Ontario, CA 91762-7239, USA

Kher, Anupam (Actor)
402 Marina
Juhu Tara Road
Juhu Beach Mumbai, MS 400049, INDIA

K. Hirono, Mazie (Congressman, Politician)
1410 Longworth Hob
Washington, DC 20515-3821, USA

Khmylev, Yuri (Athlete, Hockey Player)
8236 Oakway Ln
Buffalo, NY 14221-2871

Khokhlov, Boris (Dancer)
Myaskovsky St 11-13
#102
Moscow 121019, USA

Khondji, Darius (Director)
c/o Sue Greenleaves *Independent Talent Group*
40 Whitfield St
London W1T 2RH, UNITED KINGDOM

Khorkina, Svetlana (Gymnast, Olympic Athlete)
Russian Gymnastics Federation
Lujnetskaya Nabereynaya 8
Moscow 119270, RUSSIA

Khotan (Musician)
c/o Gabriel Blanco *Gabriel Blanco Iglesias (Mexico)*
Rio Balsas 35-32
Colonia Cuauhtemoc
DF 06500, Mexico

Khouri, Callie (Director)
c/o Staff Member *United Talent Agency (UTA)*
9336 Civic Center Dr
Beverly Hills, CA 90210-3604, USA

Khristich, Dmitri (Athlete, Hockey Player)
5002 N Convent Ln Apt E
Apt E
Philadelphia, PA 19114-3125

Khruschev, Sergei (Misc)
Watson Institute
Brown University
Box 1970
Providence, RI 02912-0001, USA

Kibaki, Mwai (President)
President's Office
Harambee House
Harambee Ave
Nairobi, KENYA

Kiberd, James (Actor)
c/o Gary Epstein *Phoenix Artists*
330 W 38th St Rm 607
New York, NY 10018-2908, USA

Kibler, John (Athlete, Baseball Player)
2701 El Camino Real # 205
Palo Alto, CA 94306-1713, USA

Kibrick, Sidney (Actor)
10449 Ashton Ave Apt 101
Los Angeles, CA 90024-5185, USA

Kickinger, Roland (Actor)
c/o Staff Member *Coralie Jr Theatrical Agency*
907 S Victory Blvd
Burbank, CA 91502-2430, USA

Kidd, Carl (Athlete, Football Player)
2317 Peach Tree Dr
Little Rock, AR 72211-4331, USA

Kidd, Dylan (Director)
c/o Staff Member *Creative Artists Agency (CAA)*
2000 Avenue of the Stars Ste 100
Los Angeles, CA 90067-4705, USA

Kidd, Glenna Sue (Athlete, Baseball Player, Commentator)
51 17th St
Logansport, IN 46947-2842, USA

Kidd, Ian (Athlete, Hockey Player)
2512 E 7th St
Duluth, MN 55812-1406, USA

Kidd, Jason (Athlete, Basketball Player, Olympic Athlete)
c/o Jeff Schwartz *Excel Sports Management*
1700 Broadway Fl 29
New York, NY 10019-6559, USA

Kidd, Jodie (Model)
c/o Staff Member *IMG*
304 Park Ave S Fl 12
New York, NY 10010-4314, USA

Kidd, John (Athlete, Football Player)
4204 Moorland Dr
Midland, MI 48640-1906, USA

Kidd, Sue (Baseball Player)
51 17th St
Logansport, IN 46947-2842, USA

Kidd, Warren (Athlete, Basketball Player)
313 River Rd
Harpersville, AL 35078-7014, USA

Kidd, William W (Billy) (Athlete, Olympic Athlete, Skier)
Billy Kidd Racing
2305 Mount Werner Cir
Steamboat Springs, CO 80487-9023, USA

Kidder, Molly (Actor)
c/o Jill Witterschein *Innovative Artists*
1505 10th St
Santa Monica, CA 90401-2805, USA

Kid Ink (Musician)
c/o Mitch Blackman *ICM Partners (NY)*
730 5th Ave
New York, NY 10019-4105, USA

Kidjo, Angelique (Musician)
c/o Staff Member *Red Light Management*
5800 Bristol Pkwy Ste 400
Culver City, CA 90230-6898, USA

Kidman, Nicole (Actor)
c/o Morgan Pesante *42West*
1840 Century Park E Ste 700
Los Angeles, CA 90067-2122, USA

Kid Rock (Musician)
PO Box 1230
Clarkston, MI 48347-1230, USA

Kiecker, Dana (Athlete, Baseball Player)
4104 Prairie Ridge Rd
Saint Paul, MN 55123-1625, USA

Kiedis, Anthony (Musician)
c/o Laura Rister *Untitled Entertainment*
350 S Beverly Dr Ste 200
Beverly Hills, CA 90212-4819, USA

Kiefel, Ron (Athlete, Cycler, Olympic Athlete)
3893 Field Dr
Wheat Ridge, CO 80033-4372, USA

Kiefer, Mark (Athlete, Baseball Player)
11822 Old Fashion Way
Garden Grove, CA 92840-2117, USA

Kiefer, Nicolas (Athlete, Tennis Player)
c/o Staff Member *ATP Tour*
201 Atp Tour Blvd
Ponte Vedra Beach, FL 32082-3211, USA

Kiefer, Steve (Athlete, Baseball Player)
38324 Divot Dr
Beaumont, CA 92223-8093, USA

Kiehl, Marina (Skier)
Hermie-Bland Str 11
Munich 81545, GERMANY

Kiel, John (Athlete, Football Player)
12100 Pebblepointe Pass
Carmel, IN 46033-9678, USA

Kielty, Bob (Bobby) (Athlete, Baseball Player)
21504 Appaloosa Ct
Canyon Lake, CA 92587-7628, USA

Kiely, John (Athlete, Baseball Player)
84 Brown St
Brockton, MA 02301-1006, USA

Kieper, John (Race Car Driver)
15643 NE Siskiyou Ct
Portland, OR 97230-5151, USA

Kier, Miss Lady (Musician)
P.O. Box 32805
London, England N1 5WP, United Kingdom

Kier, Udo (Actor)
c/o Richard Schwartz *Richard Schwartz Management*
2934 1/2 N Beverly Glen Cir # 107
Los Angeles, CA 90077-1724, USA

Kieschnick, Brook (Baseball Player)
Chicago Cubs
201 Evans Ave
San Antonio, TX 78209-3721, USA

Kieschnick, Brooks (Athlete, Baseball Player)
107 Dover Rd
San Antonio, TX 78209-6169, USA

Kiesel, Theresia (Athlete, Track Athlete)
Stifterstr 24
Truan 04050, AUSTRIA

Kiesza (Musician)
c/o Sam Kirby *WME/IMG (NY)*
11 Madison Ave Fl 18
New York, NY 10010-3669, USA

Kiewel, Jeff (Athlete, Football Player)
9923 E Karst Pl
Tucson, AZ 85748-4566, USA

Kiffin, Irv (Athlete, Basketball Player)
1703 Whitehall Dr Apt 204
Davie, FL 33324-6908, USA

Kiffin, Lane (Athlete, Football Player)
906 9th St
Manhattan Beach, CA 90266-5953, USA

Kiffin, Monte (Athlete, Football Player)
6005 Williamsburg Cv
Jonesboro, AR 72404-9636, USA

Kiggens, Lisa (Athlete, Golfer)
1504 Club View Dr
Bakersfield, CA 93309-3541, USA

Kight, Kelvin (Athlete, Football Player)
3748 Bramblevine Cir
Lithonia, GA 30038-2920, USA

Kightlinger, Laura (Actor, Comedian, Producer, Writer)
c/o David Martin *Avalon Management*
9171 Wilshire Blvd Ste 320
Beverly Hills, CA 90210-5516, USA

Kihn, Greg (Musician)
Riot Mgmt
55 Santa Clara Ave Ste 120
Oakland, CA 94610-1375, USA

Kiick, Jim (Athlete, Football Player)
1532 SE 12th St PH 1
Ft Lauderdale, FL 33316-1434, USA

Kiindarius, Cosmos (Producer)
c/o Staff Member *In Motion Pictures*
10785 W Twain Ave Ste 210
Las Vegas, NV 89135-3028, USA

Kikuchi, Rinko (Actor)
c/o Staff Member *Creative Artists Agency (CAA)*
2000 Avenue of the Stars Ste 100
Los Angeles, CA 90067-4705, USA

Kilbey, Steven (Musician)
Globeshine
101 Chamberlayne Road
London NW10 3ND, UNITED KINGDOM (UK)

Kilborn, Craig (Talk Show Host)
c/o Shani Rosenzweig *United Talent Agency (UTA)*
9336 Civic Center Dr
Beverly Hills, CA 90210-3604, USA

Kilbourne, Wendy (Actor)
9300 Wilshire Blvd Ste 410
Beverly Hills, CA 90212-3228, USA

Kilburn, Terry (Actor)
Meadowbrook Theatre
Oakland University
Walton & Squirrel
Rochester, MI 48063, USA

Kilcher, Q'Orianka (Actor)
c/o Jordyn Palos *Persona Public Relations*
6255 W Sunset Blvd Ste 705
Hollywood, CA 90028-7408, USA

Kilcullen, Bob (Athlete, Football Player)
400 E Division St
Pilot Point, TX 76258-4510, USA

Kilger, Chad (Athlete, Hockey Player)
1351 Second St E
Cornwall, ON K6H 2B6, Canada

Kilgore, Al (Cartoonist)
21655 113th Dr
Queens Village, NY 11429-2617, USA

Kilgore, Jon (Athlete, Football Player)
2422 Glen Oaks Ct NE
Atlanta, GA 30345-3928, USA

Kilgus, Paul (Athlete, Baseball Player)
1088 Saint Andrews Cir
Bowling Green, KY 42103-2461, USA

Kilian, Thomas J (Business Person)
Conseco Inc
PO Box 1957
Carmel, IN 46082-1957, USA

Kilius, Marika (Figure Skater)
Postfach 201151
Dreieich 63271, GERMANY

Kilkenny, Mike (Athlete, Baseball Player)
10665 NE 153rd St
Fort Mc Coy, FL 32134-4916, USA

Killam, Taran (Actor)
c/o Joel Zadak *Artists First*
9465 Wilshire Blvd Ste 900
Beverly Hills, CA 90212-2608, USA

Killeen, Denise (Athlete, Golfer)
803 Golden Wood Trce
Canton, GA 30114-6572, USA

Killeen, Evans (Athlete, Baseball Player)
137 Main St
Westhampton Beach, NY 11978-2607, USA

Killens, Terry (Athlete, Football Player)
5665 Water Spring Way
Mason, OH 45040-7319, USA

Killett, Charlie (Athlete, Football Player)
114 Forrest Heights Rd
Paris, TN 38242-5749, USA

Kill Hannah (Music Group)
c/o Staff Member *In De Goot Entertainment*
119 W 23rd St Ste 609
New York, NY 10011-2594, USA

Killmer, Kara (Actor)
c/o Sheva Cohen *Agency for the Performing Arts (APA)*
405 S Beverly Dr Ste 500
Beverly Hills, CA 90212-4425, USA

Killorin, Pat (Athlete, Football Player)
8304 Partridgeberry Dr
Baldwinsville, NY 13027-8946, USA

Kills, Natalia (Musician)
c/o Staff Member *High Rise PR*
600 Luton Dr
Glendale, CA 91206-2626, USA

Killum, Ernie (Athlete, Basketball Player)
PO Box 370832
Decatur, GA 30037, USA

Killy, Jean-Claude (Skier)
Villa Les 13 Chemin Bellefontaine
Cologny-GE 01223, SWITZERLAND

Kilmer, Jack (Actor)
c/o Kami Putnam-Heist *Anonymous Content*
3532 Hayden Ave
Culver City, CA 90232-2413, USA

Kilmer, Val (Actor)
PO Box 364
Rowe, NM 87562-0364, USA

Kilmer, William O (Billy) (Athlete, Football Player)
1853 Monte Carlo Way Apt 36
Coral Springs, FL 33071-7829, USA

Kilmore, Chris (Musician)
c/o Staff Member *ArtistDirect*
9046 Lindblade St
Culver City, CA 90232-2513, USA

Kilner, Kevin (Actor)
Innovative Artists
1505 10th St
Santa Monica, CA 90401-2805, USA

Kilpatrick, Carl (Athlete, Basketball Player)
10517 23rd Street Ct E
Edgewood, WA 98372-1595, USA

Kilpatrick, Kwame (Politician)
Mayor's Office
2 Woodward Ave Rm 1126
City-County Building
Detroit, MI 48226-3453, USA

Kilrea, Brian (Athlete, Coach, Hockey Player)
2192 Saunderson Dr
Ottawa, ON K1G 2G4, Canada

Kilts, James M (Business Person)
Centerview Partners
31 W 52nd St Fl 21
New York, NY 10019-6396, USA

Kilzer, Louis C (Lon) (Journalist)
Minneapolis-Saint Paul Star-Tribune
425 Portland Ave
Minneapolis, MN 55488-1511, USA

Kim, Anthony (Athlete, Golfer)
c/o Clarke Jones *IMG (Cleveland)*
1360 E 9th St Ste 100
Cleveland, OH 44114-1730, USA

Kim, Chloe (Athlete, Skier)
Mammoth Mountain Ski & Snowboard Team
10001 Minaret Rd
Mammoth Lakes, CA 93546, USA

Kim, Claudia (Actor)
c/o Staff Member *United Talent Agency (UTA)*
9336 Civic Center Dr
Beverly Hills, CA 90210-3604, USA

Kim, Daniel Dae (Actor)
PO Box 10151
Honolulu, HI 96816-0151, USA

Kim, Jacqueline (Actor)
Innovative Artists
1505 10th St
Santa Monica, CA 90401-2805, USA

Kim, Lil' (Musician)
c/o Michael Schweiger *Central Entertainment Group*
250 W 40th St Fl 12
New York, NY 10018-4601, USA

Kim, Nelli V (Gymnast)
2480 Cobblehill
#A Alocove
Woodbury, MN 55125, USA

Kim, Yoon-jin (Actor)
c/o Staff Member *WME|IMG*
9601 Wilshire Blvd
Beverly Hills, CA 90210-5213, USA

Kim, Young Sam (President)
Sangdo-dong 7-6
Tongjakku
Seoul, SOUTH KOREA

Kim, Young Uck (Musician)
Columbia Artists Mgmt Inc
165 W 57th St
New York, NY 10019-2201, USA

Kim, Yuna (Athlete, Figure Skater)
Korea Skating Union
Room #607, Olympic Center
88 Bangyee-Dong
Songpa-Gu, Seoul 138-749, Korea

Kim, Yunjin (Actor)
c/o Alex Chaice *Global Creative*
1051 Cole Ave # B
Los Angeles, CA 90038-2601, USA

Kimball, Bobby (Musician)
World Entertainment Assoc
297101 Kinderkamack Road
#128
Oradell, NJ 07649, USA

Kimball, Bruce (Athlete, Football Player)
41 Spring Rd
Rye, NH 03870-2449, USA

Kimball, Cheyenne (Musician)

Kimball, Dick (Coach)
1540 Waltham Dr
Ann Arbor, MI 48103-5631, USA

Kimball, Shawn (Athlete, Baseball Player)
75 Black Stream Dr
Levant, ME 04456-4427, USA

Kimball, Toby (Athlete, Basketball Player)
6859 Avenida Ave
La Jolla, CA 92037-6407, USA

Kimball-Purdham, Mary Ellen (Athlete, Baseball Player, Commentator)
15299 S 18th St
Vicksburg, MI 49097-9738, USA

Kimber, Bill (Athlete, Football Player)
7801 Point Meadows Dr Unit 3102
Jacksonville, FL 32256-9145, USA

Kimber, William (Athlete, Football Player)
7801 Point Meadows Dr Unit 3102
Jacksonville, FL 32256-9145, USA

Kimble, Bo (Athlete, Basketball Player)
100 Poe Ct
North Wales, PA 19454-4430, USA

Kimble, Darin (Athlete, Hockey Player)
1202 27th St
Granite City, IL 62040-3431, USA

Kimble, Gregory "Bo" (Athlete, Basketball Player)
100 Poe Ct Unit 83
North Wales, PA 19454-4430, USA

Kimble, Warren (Artist)
RR 3Box 1038
Brandon, VT 05733, USA

Kimbra (Musician)
c/o Dave Tamaroff *WME|IMG*
9601 Wilshire Blvd
Beverly Hills, CA 90210-5213, USA

Kimbrough, Charles (Actor, Musician)
255 Amalfi Dr
Santa Monica, CA 90402-1125, USA

Kimbrough, Elbert (Athlete, Football Player)
886 W 2nd St
Galesburg, IL 61401-5711, USA

Kimbrough, John (Athlete, Football Player)
2016 Fleming Dr
McKinney, TX 75072-3986, USA

Kimbrough, Stan (Athlete, Basketball Player)
3922 Elm Ave
Cincinnati, OH 45236-3908, USA

Kimbrough, Tony (Athlete, Football Player)
4726 Sharp Rd
Sturgis, MS 39769-8939, USA

Kimbrough, Will (Musician)
Cedar Creek Music
164 Dove Creek Rd
Frankfort, KY 40601-8945, USA

Kimm, Bruce (Athlete, Baseball Player, Coach)
3168 121st St
Amana, IA 52203-8046, USA

Kimmel, Frank (Race Car Driver)
KFPI/Amber Estes
102 Brookshire Dr
Danville, KY 40422-3200, USA

Kimmel, Jerry (Athlete, Football Player)
1411 Colesville Rd
Harpursville, NY 13787-1430, USA

Kimmel, Jimmy (Comedian, Television Host)
Jimmy Kimmel Live
6834 Hollywood Blvd Ste 600
Hollywood, CA 90028-6135, USA

Kimmell, Dana (Actor)

Kimmins, Kenneth (Actor)
c/o Joannie Burstein *Burstein Company*
15304 W Sunset Blvd Ste 208
Pacific Palisades, CA 90272-3656, USA

Kims of Comedy (Comedian)
c/o Staff Member *Paradigm (Monterey)*
404 W Franklin St
Monterey, CA 93940-2303, USA

Kimura, Kazuo (Designer)
Japan Design Foundation
2-2 Cenba Chuo
Higashiku
Osaka 00541, JAPAN

Kinard, Billy (Athlete, Football Player)
41 Vail Ln
Watchung, NJ 07069-6149, USA

Kinard, Terry (Athlete, Football Player)
PO Box 1780
Conyers, GA 30012-7954, USA

Kinberg, Simon (Director, Producer, Writer)
c/o Staff Member *Genre Films*
10201 W Pico Blvd Bldg 49
Los Angeles, CA 90064-2606, USA

Kincade, Keylon (Athlete, Football Player)
1344 Gayle St
Burleson, TX 76028-8628, USA

Kincaid, Jamaica (Writer)
College Road
North Bennington, VT 05257, USA

Kincaid, Jim (Athlete, Football Player)
401 Tryon Dr
Goldsboro, NC 27530-9149, USA

Kinchen, Brian (Athlete, Football Player)
19052 E Pinnacle Cir
Baton Rouge, LA 70810-7996, USA

Kinchen, Todd W (Athlete, Football Player)
247 Guava Dr
Baton Rouge, LA 70808-5031, USA

Kinchla, Chan (Musician)
c/o Staff Member *ArtistDirect*
9046 Lindblade St
Culver City, CA 90232-2513, USA

Kind, Danielle (Actor)
C/O Micheline Watson
Take One Talent Management Inc
PO Box 20019 Rpo Nelson
Ottawa, ON K1N 9N5, CANADA

Kind, Richard (Actor)
c/o Arlene Forster *Forster Entertainment*
12533 Woodgreen St
Los Angeles, CA 90066-2723, USA

Kind, Ron (Congressman, Politician)
1406 Longworth Hob
Washington, DC 20515-4903, USA

Kind, Roslyn (Actor, Musician)
Scott Stander
13707 Riverside Dr
#201
Sherman Oaks, CA 91423, USA

Kindall, Jerry (Athlete, Baseball Player)
7220 E Grey Fox Ln
Tucson, AZ 85750-1377, USA

Kinder, Melvyn (Writer)
c/o Staff Member *Random House*
1540 Broadway
New York, NY 10036-4039, USA

Kinder, Richard D (Business Person)
Kinder and Morgan
500 Dallas St Ste 1000
Houston, TX 77002-4718, USA

Kinderman, Keith (Athlete, Football Player)
5837 Bradfordville Rd
Tallahassee, FL 32309-6613, USA

Kindig, Howard (Athlete, Football Player)
18115 Langkawi Ln
Houston, TX 77044-1629, USA

Kindle, Greg (Athlete, Football Player)
7606 Heron Park Ct
Humble, TX 77396-2222, USA

Kindrachuk, Orest (Athlete, Hockey Player)
14044th Ave
Asbury Park, NJ 07712-4944, USA

Kindred, David A (Writer)
Atlanta Constitution
72 Marietta St NW
Editorial Dept
Atlanta, GA 30303-2804, USA

Kindricks, Bill (Athlete, Football Player)
1466 Alma Loop
San Jose, CA 95125-1731, USA

Kiner, Steve (Athlete, Football Player)
4660 Hitching Post Trl
Atlanta, GA 30342-2816, USA

King, Adrienne (Actor)
c/o Aine Leicht *Horror & Hilarity*
Prefers to be contacted by email or phone.
Los Angeles, CA 90067, USA

King, Aja Naomi (Actor)
c/o Jill McGrath *Door24*
115 W 29th St Rm 1102
New York, NY 10001-5106, USA

King, Albert (Athlete, Basketball Player)
88 Sturbridge Cir
Wayne, NJ 07470-8402, USA

King, Alton (Athlete, Baseball Player)
8226 Esper St
Detroit, MI 48204-3120, USA

King, Angelo (Athlete, Football Player)
2922 W Royal Ln Apt 2090
Irving, TX 75063-6235, USA

King, Benjamin (Actor)
c/o Elizabeth Much *East 2 West Collective*
11022 Santa Monica Blvd Ste 350
Los Angeles, CA 90025-7532, USA

King, Bernard (Athlete, Basketball Player)
307 Jupiter Hills Dr
Duluth, GA 30097-5900, USA

King, Bernard (Athlete, Football Player)
Hollywood Christian School
1708 N State Road 7
Attn: Athletic Dept
Hollywood, FL 33021-4507, USA

King, Billie Jean (Athlete, Tennis Player)
101 W 79th St PH 1B
New York, NY 10024-6495, USA

King, Candice (Actor)
c/o CeCe Yorke *True Public Relations*
3575 Cahuenga Blvd W Ste 360
Los Angeles, CA 90068-1361, USA

King, Candie (Athlete, Golfer)
2673 Saleroso Dr
Rowland Heights, CA 91748-4364, USA

King, Carlos (Athlete, Football Player)
107 S Corncrib Ct
Cary, NC 27513-5407, USA

King, Carole (Musician)
11684 Ventura Blvd # 273
Studio City, CA 91604-2699, USA

King, Cheryl (Actor)
CLInc Talent
843 N Sycamore Ave
Los Angeles, CA 90038-3316, USA

King, Clyde E (Athlete, Baseball Player, Coach)
103 Stratford Rd
Goldsboro, NC 27534-8971, USA

King, Colbert (Journalist)
Washington Post
Editorial Dept
1150 15th St NW
Washington, DC 20071-0001, USA

King, Curtis (Athlete, Baseball Player)
2538 Beechwood Dr
Vineland, NJ 08361-2932, USA

King, Dan (Athlete, Basketball Player)
4803 Grand Dell Dr
Crestwood, KY 40014-9794, USA

King, Dana (Correspondent)
CBS-TV
524 W 57th St
News Dept
New York, NY 10019-2924, USA

King, Dave (Athlete, Hockey Player)
7748 E Clinton St
Scottsdale, AZ 85260-5582, USA

King, David J (Athlete, Football Player)
4365 Riverstone Shls
Ellenwood, GA 30294-6550, USA

King, Dennis (Artist)
3857 26th St
San Francisco, CA 94131-2007, USA

King, Derek (Athlete, Hockey Player)
100 Princes Blvd
Toronto, ON M6K 3C3, CANADA

King, Diana (Musician)
c/o Stephen Ford *Diva Central Inc*
7510 W Sunset Blvd # 1445
Los Angeles, CA 90046-3408, USA

King, Don (Business Person)
Don King Promotions
3300 Las Vegas Blvd S PH
Treasure Island Casino
Las Vegas, NV 89109-8916, USA

King, Donald W (Athlete, Football Player)
1621 Fox Hall Rd
Savannah, GA 31406-5005, USA

King, Ed (Athlete, Football Player)
9903 North Blvd
Cleveland, OH 44108-3429, USA

King, Elle (Musician)
c/o Marty Diamond *Paradigm*
140 Broadway Ste 2600
New York, NY 10005-1011, USA

King, Eric (Athlete, Baseball Player)
1063 Stanford Dr
Simi Valley, CA 93065-4952, USA

King, Erik (Actor)
c/o Joannie Burstein *Burstein Company*
15304 W Sunset Blvd Ste 208
Pacific Palisades, CA 90272-3656, USA

King, Evelyn (Champagne) (Musician)
c/o Stephen Ford *Diva Central Inc*
7510 W Sunset Blvd # 1445
Los Angeles, CA 90046-3408, USA

King, Ezell (Athlete, Baseball Player)
PO Box 321154
Houston, TX 77221-1154, USA

King, Frank (Baseball Player)
Negro Baseball Leagues
4950 Governors Dr Apt 2326
Forest Park, GA 30297-6167, USA

King, Gayle (Correspondent, Television Host)
c/o Staff Member *CBS News (NY)*
524 W 57th St Fl 8
New York, NY 10019-2930, USA

King, Gordon (Athlete, Football Player)
2641 Highwood Dr
Roseville, CA 95661-7916, USA

King, Gordon D (Athlete, Football Player)
2641 Highwood Dr
Roseville, CA 95661-7916, USA

King, Graham (Producer)
c/o Staff Member *Initial Entertainment Group*
5555 Melrose Ave Bldg 100
Los Angeles, CA 90038-3991, USA

King, G Stephen (Athlete, Football Player)
45 Chipping Stone Rd
North Attleboro, MA 02760-4485, USA

King, Hal (Athlete, Baseball Player)
828 Geneva Dr
Oviedo, FL 32765-9503, USA

King, Hogue Maxine (Mick) (Swimmer)
US Air Force Academy
PO Box 155
Usaf Academy, CO 80840-0155, USA

King, Horace (Athlete, Football Player)
884 Fairburn Rd NW
Atlanta, GA 30331-3341, USA

King, Jaime (Actor)
1612 Schuyler Rd
Beverly Hills, CA 90210-2543, USA

King, Jeff (Athlete, Baseball Player)
6201 Farm Terrace St
Alvarado, TX 76009-6304, USA

King, Jim (Athlete, Baseball Player)
720 Stokenbury Rd
Elkins, AR 72727-3214, USA

King, Joe (Athlete, Football Player)
373 Boyd Rd
Hallsville, TX 75650-7003, USA

King, Joey (Actor)
c/o Jillian Roscoe *ID Public Relations*
7060 Hollywood Blvd Fl 8th
Los Angeles, CA 90028-6021, USA

King, John (Correspondent, Television Host)
5003 Belt Rd NW
Washington, DC 20016-4234, USA

King, Kaki (Musician)
c/o Staff Member *Paradigm (Monterey)*
404 W Franklin St
Monterey, CA 93940-2303, USA

King, Kathryn (Katie) (Athlete, Hockey Player, Olympic Athlete)
140 Commonwealth Ave
Attn Womens Ice Hockey Coach
Chestnut Hill, MA 02467-3800, USA

King, Kenny (Athlete, Football Player)
1184 Verde Oaks Ln
Fort Worth, TX 76135-9034, USA

King, Kent Masters (Actor)
c/o Richard Schwartz *Richard Schwartz Management*
2934 1/2 N Beverly Glen Cir # 107
Los Angeles, CA 90077-1724, USA

King, Kevin (Athlete, Baseball Player)
9071 S 105th St E
Braggs, OK 74423-5091, USA

King, Kris (Athlete, Hockey Player)
c/o Staff Member *National Hockey League (NHL)*
50 Bay St 11th Fl
Toronto, ON M5J 2X8, Canada

King, Lamar (Athlete, Football Player)
4523 Golden Meadow Dr
Perry Hall, MD 21128-9037, USA

King, Lamnar (Athlete, Football Player)
4523 Golden Meadow Dr
Perry Hall, MD 21128-9037, USA

King, Larry (Journalist, Talk Show Host)
Larry King Enterprises
PO Box 600157
Newtonville, MA 02460-0002, USA

King, Linden (Athlete, Football Player)
727 W 7th St APT 607
Los Angeles, CA 90017-3755, USA

King, Loyd (Athlete, Basketball Player)
118 Wilde Brook Dr
Asheville, NC 28806-1052, USA

King, Mark (Musician)
P.O. Box 23
Sandown PO36 9QL, UK

King, Michael Patrick (Producer, Writer)
c/o Simon Halls *Slate PR*
901 N Highland Ave
W Hollywood, CA 90038-2412, USA

King, Michelle (Producer)
c/o Andy Patman *Paradigm*
8942 Wilshire Blvd
Beverly Hills, CA 90211-1908, USA

King, Nellie (Athlete, Baseball Player)
3890 Bigelow Blvd Apt 405
Pittsburgh, PA 15213-1158, USA

King, Perry (Actor)
3647 Wrightwood Dr
Studio City, CA 91604-3947, USA

King, Phillip (Artist)
Bernard Jackson Gallery
14A Clifford St
London W1X 1RF, UNITED KINGDOM (UK)

King, Ray (Athlete, Baseball Player)
4220 N 161st Ave
Goodyear, AZ 85395-6437, USA

King, Ray (Athlete, Baseball Player)
14870 W Encanto Blvd Unit 1046
Goodyear, AZ 85395-6605, USA

King, Reggie (Athlete, Basketball Player)
PO Box 860021
Shawnee, KS 66286-0021, USA

King, Regina (Actor)
c/o Marcel Pariseau *True Public Relations*
3575 Cahuenga Blvd W Ste 360
Los Angeles, CA 90068-1361, USA

King, Richard L (Business Person)
Albertson's Inc
250 E Parkcenter Blvd
Boise, ID 83706-3999, USA

King, Robert (Producer)
c/o Andy Patman *Paradigm*
8942 Wilshire Blvd
Beverly Hills, CA 90211-1908, USA

King, R Stacey (Athlete, Basketball Player)
5340 RFD
Long Grove, IL 60047-9744, USA

King, Scott (Athlete, Hockey Player)
203 Maple Ave
Hershey, PA 17033-1549, USA

King, Shaun (Athlete, Football Player)
1646 41st St S
Saint Petersburg, FL 33711-2710, USA

King, Shaun (Business Person)
Upfront Media Group, Inc
135 W 29th St Rm 1101
New York, NY 10001-5159, USA

King, Shawn Southwick (Actor)
c/o Staff Member *WME|IMG*
9601 Wilshire Blvd
Beverly Hills, CA 90210-5213, USA

King, Stephen (Writer)
49 Florida Ave
Bangor, ME 04401-3005, USA

King, Steve (Athlete, Hockey Player)
2200 Buttonbush Cres
Mississauga, ON L5L 1C5, Canada

King, Steve (Congressman, Politician)
1131 Longworth Hob
Washington, DC 20515-1008, USA

King, Steven (Athlete, Hockey Player)
55 Chestnut Dr
East Greenwich, RI 02818-2102, USA

King, Tavarres (Athlete, Football Player)
c/o Alan Herman *Sportstars Inc*
1370 Avenue of the Americas Fl 19
New York, NY 10019-4602, USA

King, Ted (Actor, Musician)
c/o Staff Member *Paradigm*
8942 Wilshire Blvd
Beverly Hills, CA 90211-1908, USA

King, Thea (Musician)
16 Milverton Road
London NW6 7AS, UNITED KINGDOM (UK)

King, Tom (Athlete, Basketball Player)
4930 Sea Watch Dr
Fernandina Beach, FL 32034-5741, USA

King, Vania (Athlete, Tennis Player)
c/o Staff Member *Lagardere Unlimited (DC)*
5335 Wisconsin Ave NW Ste 850
Washington, DC 20015-2052, USA

King, Vick (Athlete, Football Player)
255 E 23rd St
Larose, LA 70373-2136, USA

King, Wayne (Athlete, Hockey Player)
129 Seventh St
Midland, ON L4R 3Y9, Canada

King, W David (Coach)
Calgary Flames
PO Box 1540 Stn M
Station M
Calgary, AB T2P 3B9, CANADA

King, Zach (Actor, Internet Star)
c/o Staff Member *Fullscreen Media (LA)*
12180 Millennium Ste 100
Los Angeles, CA 90094-2951, USA

Kingdom, Roger (Athlete, Track Athlete)
146 S Fairmount St Apt 1
Pittsburgh, PA 15206-3580, USA

Kingery, Ellsworth (Athlete, Football Player)
501 Auburn Ave
Monroe, LA 71201-5303, USA

Kingery, Mike (Athlete, Baseball Player)
51923 298th St
Grove City, MN 56243-4305, USA

Kingery, Wayne (Athlete, Football Player)
1045 Walters St Apt 411
Lake Charles, LA 70607-4686, USA

King III, Martin Luther (Activist)
Martin Luther King Jr. Center
449 Auburn Ave NE
Atlanta, GA 30312-1503, USA

King Jr, Woodie (Producer)
417 Convent Ave
New York, NY 10031-4213, USA

Kinglsey, Ben (Actor)
International Creative Mgmt
76 Oxford St
London W1N 0AX, UNITED KINGDOM (UK)

Kingman, Brian (Athlete, Baseball Player)
1258 E Charleston Ave
Phoenix, AZ 85022-1249, USA

Kingman, Dave (Athlete, Baseball Player)
PO Box 209
Glenbrook, NV 89413-0209, USA

Kingrea, Richard O (Athlete, Football Player)
102 N Bayview St
Fairhope, AL 36532-2505, USA

Kingrea, Rick (Athlete, Football Player)
102 N Bayview St
Fairhope, AL 36532-2505, USA

Kingsale, Gene (Athlete, Baseball Player)
105 Angelfish Ln
Jupiter, FL 33477-7227, USA

Kingsley, Ben (Actor)
c/o Staff Member *Lavender Pictures*
124 Finchley Rd
Regina House
London NW3 5JS, UNITED KINGDOM

Kingsley, Patricia (Business Person)
371 Alma Real Dr
Pacific Palisades, CA 90272-4416, USA

Kings of Convenience (Music Group)
c/o Staff Member *Paradigm (Monterey)*
404 W Franklin St
Monterey, CA 93940-2303, USA

Kings of Leon (Music Group)
c/o Andy Mendelsohn *Vector Management*
276 5th Ave Rm 604
New York, NY 10001-4527, USA

Kingsriter, Doug (Athlete, Football Player)
3118 Saint Johns Dr
Dallas, TX 75205-2938, USA

Kingston, Alex (Actor)
c/o Larry Taube *Principal Entertainment*
9255 W Sunset Blvd Ste 500
Los Angeles, CA 90069-3301, USA

Kingston, George (Athlete, Hockey Player)
235 W Camino Descanso
Palm Springs, CA 92264-8323, USA

Kingston, Jack (Congressman, Politician)
2372 Rayburn Hob
Washington, DC 20515-0605, USA

Kingston, Maxine Hong (Writer)
University of California
English # 603
Berkeley, CA 94720-0001, USA

Kingston, Sean (Musician)
c/o Robert Gibbs *ICM Partners*
10250 Constellation Blvd Fl 7
Los Angeles, CA 90067-6207, USA

Kinkade, Mike (Athlete, Baseball Player)
3802 Broadway
Attn: Coaching Staff
Everett, WA 98201-5032, USA

Kinkade, Mike (Athlete, Baseball Player, Olympic Athlete)
14413 W Las Brizas Ln
Sun City West, AZ 85375-2703, USA

Kinley, Heather (Musician)
Epic Records
1211 S Highland Ave
Los Angeles, CA 90019-1734, USA

Kinley, Jennifer (Musician)
Epic Records
1211 S Highland Ave
Los Angeles, CA 90019-1734, USA

Kinleys (Music Group)
PO Box 128501
Nashville, TN 37212-8501, USA

Kinmont, Kathleen (Actor)
9929 Sunset Blvd
#310
Los Angeles, CA 90069, USA

Kinnaman, Joel (Actor)
c/o Jared Ceizler *Magnolia Entertainment*
9595 Wilshire Blvd Ste 601
Beverly Hills, CA 90212-2506, USA

Kinnaman, Melanie (Actor)
1354 N Curson Ave
Los Angeles, CA 90046-4004, USA

Kinnear, Dominic (Coach)
San Jose Earthquakes
3550 Stevens Creek Blvd Ste 200
San Jose, CA 95117-1031, USA

Kinnear, Geordie (Athlete, Hockey Player)
81 Benedict Ter
Longmeadow, MA 01106-1103, USA

Kinnear, Geordie (Athlete, Hockey Player)
Charlotte Checkers
210 E Trade St Ste E480
Attn: Coaching Staff
Charlotte, NC 28202-0130, USA

Kinnear, Greg (Actor, Comedian)
c/o Stephanie Ritz *WME|IMG*
9601 Wilshire Blvd
Beverly Hills, CA 90210-5213, USA

Kinnear III, James W (Business Person)
Ten Standard Forum
PO Box 120
Stamford, CT 06904-0120, USA

Kinnebrew, Larry (Athlete, Football Player)
216 Kingston Ave NE
Rome, GA 30161-5628, USA

Kinney, Dallas (Journalist, Photographer)
13010 Silver Sands Dr
Fort Myers, FL 33913-6934, USA

Kinney, Dennis (Athlete, Baseball Player)
PO Box 304
Schnecksville, PA 18078-0304, USA

Kinney, Emily (Actor)
c/o Annick Oppenheim *Wolf-Kasteler Public Relations*
6255 W Sunset Blvd Ste 1111
Los Angeles, CA 90028-7426, USA

Kinney, Erron (Athlete, Football Player)
3112 Natoma Cir
Thompsons Stn, TN 37179-9605, USA

Kinney, Jeff (Athlete, Football Player)
2720 W 161st Ter
Stilwell, KS 66085-7818, USA

Kinney, Jeff (Writer)
c/o Keith Fleer *Keith Fleer, A Professional Corp*
401 Wilshire Blvd Ste 1200
Santa Monica, CA 90401-1456, USA

Kinney, Josh (Athlete, Baseball Player)
588 Uoper Portage Rd
Port Allegany, PA 16743-3230, USA

Kinney, Kathy (Actor)
c/o Billy Miller *Billy Miller Management*
8322 Ridpath Dr
Los Angeles, CA 90046-7710, USA

Kinney, Matt (Athlete, Baseball Player)
12 Owens Way
Hermon, ME 04401-0878, USA

Kinney, Steve (Athlete, Football Player)
1714 Merrill Loop
San Jose, CA 95124-5814, USA

Kinney, Taylor (Actor)
264 Mount Hope School Rd
Willow Street, PA 17584-9754, USA

Kinney, Terry (Actor)
c/o Staff Member *Steppenwolf Films*
8163 Gaffield Pl
Evanston, IL 60201, USA

Kinnunen, Mike (Athlete, Baseball Player)
5818 McKinley Pl N
Seattle, WA 98103-5711, USA

Kinsella, Brian (Athlete, Hockey Player)
1750 Fern Trail Dr
Lancaster, OH 43130-8118, USA

Kinsella, John P (Swimmer)
PO Box 3067
Sumas, WA 98295-3067, USA

Kinsella, Sophie (Writer)
Transworld Publishers
61-63 Uxbridge Rd
London W5 5SA, UNITED KINGDOM

Kinsella, Thomas (Writer)
Killalane
Laragh
County Wicklow, IRELAND

Kinser, Mark (Race Car Driver)
Mark Kinser Racing
11 Vista Dr
GENERAL DELIVERY
Oolitic, IN 47451-3036, USA

Kinser, Steve (Race Car Driver)
Steve Kinser Racing
280 E Smithville Rd
Bloomington, IN 47401-9251, USA

Kinsey, Angela (Actor)
c/o Jenny Delaney *Jenny Delaney Management*
10636 Wilshire Blvd Apt 207
Los Angeles, CA 90024-7326, USA

Kinsey, Tarence (Athlete, Basketball Player)
11328 Grand Winthrop Ave
Riverview, FL 33578-4279, USA

Kinshofer-Guthlein, Christa (Skier)
Munchnerstr 44
Rosenheim 83026, GERMANY

Kinski, Nastassja (Actor, Model)
c/o Staff Member *Agent Agitateur*
147 Rue Saint Martin
Paris 75003, FRANCE

Kinsler, Ian (Athlete, Baseball Player)
401 N Carroll Ave
Southlake, TX 76092-6407, USA

Kinsman, Brent (Actor)
c/o Staff Member *AKA Talent Agency*
325 N Larchmont Blvd
Los Angeles, CA 90004-3011, USA

Kinsman, Shane (Actor)
c/o Staff Member *AKA Talent Agency*
325 N Larchmont Blvd
Los Angeles, CA 90004-3011, USA

Kinzer, Matt (Athlete, Baseball Player)
16409 E Domiano Ln
Hammond, LA 70401-6858, USA

Kinzer, Matt (Athlete, Football Player)
16409 E Domiano Ln
Hammond, LA 70401-6858, USA

Kinzinger, Adam (Congressman, Politician)
1218 Longworth Hob
Washington, DC 20515-2901, USA

KioKio (DJ)
c/o Staff Member *Diva Central Inc*
7510 W Sunset Blvd # 1445
Los Angeles, CA 90046-3408, USA

Kiper Jr, Mel (Sportscaster)
ESPN-TV
935 Middle St
Sports Dept Espn Plaza
Bristol, CT 06010-1000, USA

Kipketer, Wilson (Athlete, Track Athlete)
Atletik Forbund Idraettens Hus
Brondby Stadion 20
Brondby 02605, DENMARK

Kipp, Fred (Athlete, Baseball Player)
6613 W 126th Ter
Leawood, KS 66209-2599, USA

Kipper, Bob (Athlete, Baseball Player)
PO Box 636
Attn Coaching Staff
Portland, ME 04104-0636, USA

Kipper, Bob (Athlete, Baseball Player)
117 Tuscany Way
Greer, SC 29650-4070, USA

Kipper, Thornton (Athlete, Baseball Player)
4680 W Geronimo St
Chandler, AZ 85226-5306, USA

Kiprusoff, Miikka (Athlete, Hockey Player)
c/o Staff Member *Octagon Hockey*
510 Marquette Ave Fl 13
Minneapolis, MN 55402-1102, USA

Kiraly, Charles F (Karch) (Athlete, Coach, Olympic Athlete, Volleyball Player)
c/o Staff Member *Simon & Schuster*
1230 Avenue of the Americas Fl CONC1
New York, NY 10020-1586, USA

Kirby, Bruce (Actor)
629 N Orlando Ave Apt 3
West Hollywood, CA 90048-2193, USA

Kirby, Durwood (Writer)
PO Box 3454
Fort Myers, FL 33918-3454, USA

Kirby, Jim (Athlete, Baseball Player)
520 Lohman Rd
Mount Juliet, TN 37122-4005, USA

Kirby, John (Athlete, Football Player)
586 A St
David City, NE 68632-1939, USA

Kirby, Luke (Actor)
c/o Kish Iqbal *Gary Goddard Agency (GGA)*
304-250 The Esplanade
Toronto, ON M5A 1J2, CANADA

Kirby, Malachi (Actor)
c/o Staff Member *Public Eye Communications*
535 Kings Rd
#313 Plaza
London SW10 0SZ, UNITED KINGDOM

Kirby, Stuart (Race Car Driver)
832 Broadway Ave
Bowling Green, KY 42101-2538, USA

Kirby, Terry (Athlete, Football Player)
744 Michelle Dr
Newport News, VA 23601-4626, USA

Kirby, Vanessa (Actor)
c/o Megan Moss *Narrative*
1601 Vine St Fl 6
Los Angeles, CA 90028-8802, USA

Kirby, Wayne (Athlete, Baseball Player)
333 W Camden St
Attn: Coaching Staff
Baltimore, MD 21201-2496, USA

Kirby, Wayne (Athlete, Baseball Player)
320 Kenya Rd
Las Vegas, NV 89123-1169, USA

Kirby, Will (Doctor, Reality Star)
LaserWay Hermosa Beach
307 S Robertson Blvd
Beverly Hills, CA 90211-3602, USA

Kirchbach, Gunar (Athlete)
Georgi-Dobrowoiski-Ste 10
Furstenwalde 15517, GERMANY

Kirchiro, Bill (Athlete, Football Player)
9889 Fleming Ave
Bethesda, MD 20814-2145, USA

Kirchner, Jamie Lee (Actor)
c/o Maani Golesorkhi *Bluestone Entertainment*
9000 W Sunset Blvd Ste 700
Los Angeles, CA 90069-5807, USA

Kirchner, Mark (Athlete)
Haruptstr 74A
Scheibe-Alsbach 98749, GERMANY

Kirchner, Mark (Athlete, Football Player)
1522 Palmer St
Houston, TX 77003-4622, USA

Kircus, David (Athlete, Football Player)
3880 Banyan Grove Ln APT 301
Virginia Bch, VA 23462-7478, USA

Kirgo, George (Actor, Writer)
178 N Carmelina Ave
Los Angeles, CA 90049-2737, USA

Kiriazis, Nick (Actor)
c/o Staff Member *Pakula/King & Associates*
9229 W Sunset Blvd Ste 315
Los Angeles, CA 90069-3403, USA

Kirilenko, Andrei (Athlete, Basketball Player)
1406 E Perrys Hollow Rd
Salt Lake City, UT 84103-4249, USA

Kirilenko, Maria (Tennis Player)
c/o Staff Member *Women's Tennis Association (WTA-US)*
1 Progress Plz Ste 1500
St Petersburg, FL 33701-4335, USA

Kirk, Bill (Athlete, Baseball Player)
16 Timber Villa
Elizabethtown, PA 17022-9424, USA

Kirk, Gavin (Athlete, Hockey Player)
33 Carlingview Dr
MOLSON CANADA
Toronto, ON M9W 5E4, Canada

Kirk, James (Actor)
c/o Tyman Stewart *Characters Talent Agency*
200-1505 2nd Ave W
Vancouver, BC V6H 3Y4, CANADA

Kirk, Justin (Actor)
c/o Lainie Sorkin Becky *Management 360*
9111 Wilshire Blvd
Beverly Hills, CA 90210-5508, USA

Kirk, Rahsaan Roland (Musician)
Atlantic Records
9229 W Sunset Blvd Ste 900
Los Angeles, CA 90069-3410, USA

Kirk, Tammy Jo (Race Car Driver)
732 Peek Road
Dalton, GA 30721

Kirk, Tara (Athlete, Olympic Athlete, Swimmer)
15 W Montgomery St
Baltimore, MD 21230-3844, USA

Kirk, Walt (Athlete, Basketball Player)
3730 Pennsylvania Ave Apt 302
Dubuque, IA 52002-3785, USA

Kirkby, Emma (Musician)
Consort of Music
54A Leamington Road Villas
London W11 1HT, UNITED KINGDOM (UK)

Kirke, Jemima (Actor)
c/o Ruth Bernstein *Viewpoint Inc*
8820 Wilshire Blvd Ste 220
Beverly Hills, CA 90211-2622, USA

Kirkland, Levon (Athlete, Football Player)
308 Saint Helena Ct
Greenville, SC 29607-5988, USA

Kirkland, Lori (Producer)
c/o Staff Member *Luber Roklin Management*
5815 W Sunset Blvd Ste 208
Los Angeles, CA 90028-6481, USA

Kirkland, Mike (Musician)
Bob Flick Productions
300 Vine St Ste 14
Seattle, WA 98121-1465, USA

Kirkland, Mike (Athlete, Football Player)
3350 N Sassafras Hill Rd
Fayetteville, AR 72703-9640, USA

Kirkland, Niatia (Lil Mama) (Musician)
c/o Laura Pallas *Pallas Management*
4536 Greenbush Ave
Sherman Oaks, CA 91423-3112, US

Kirkland, Sally (Actor)

Kirkland, Wilber (Athlete, Basketball Player)
127 Kimberwick Cir
Glenmoore, PA 19343-1124, USA

Kirkland, Willie (Athlete, Baseball Player)
19374 Northrop St
Detroit, MI 48219-5500, USA

Kirkman, Jen (Actor, Comedian)
c/o Kara Baker *Avalon Management*
9171 Wilshire Blvd Ste 320
Beverly Hills, CA 90210-5516, USA

Kirkman, Michael (Athlete, Baseball Player)
171 SW Tina Gin
Lake City, FL 32024-4898, USA

Kirkman, Rick (Cartoonist)
c/o Staff Member *King Features Syndication*
300 W 57th St Fl 15
New York, NY 10019-5238, USA

Kirkman, Robert (Writer)
c/o David Alpert *Circle of Confusion*
8931 Ellis Ave
Los Angeles, CA 90034-3336, USA

Kirkpatrick, Chris (Actor, Musician)
c/o Staff Member *Good Guy Entertainment*
555 Esplanade Apt 316
Redondo Beach, CA 90277-4085, USA

Kirkpatrick, David (Director, Producer)
c/o Staff Member *Plymouth Rock Studios*
36 Cordage Park Cir Ste 305
Plymouth, MA 02360-7332, USA

Kirkpatrick, Dre (Athlete, Football Player)
c/o Brian E. Overstreet *E.O. Sports Management*
1314 Texas St Ste 1212
Houston, TX 77002-3525, USA

Kirkpatrick, Ed (Athlete, Baseball Player)
24791 Via Larga
Laguna Niguel, CA 92677-1933, USA

Kirkpatrick, Maggie (Actor)
Shanahan Mgmt
PO Box 1509
Darlinghurst, NSW 01300, AUSTRALIA

Kirkpatrick, Ralph (Musician)
Old Quarry
Guilford, CT 06437, USA

Kirkreit, Daron (Athlete, Baseball Player, Olympic Athlete)
1669 Utica Trl
Lake Mary, FL 32746-7662, USA

Kirksey, Christian (Athlete, Football Player)

Kirksey, Roy (Athlete, Football Player)
204 Williams St
Taylors, SC 29687-2056, USA

Kirkup, James (Writer)
British Monomarks
BM-Box 2780
London WC1V 6XX, UNITED KINGDOM (UK)

Kirkwood, Craig (Actor)
c/o Staff Member *Levine Management*
8549 Wilshire Blvd # 212
Beverly Hills, CA 90211-3104, USA

Kirkwood, Don (Athlete, Baseball Player)
455 W Elmwood Ave
Clawson, MI 48017-1231, USA

Kirllenko, Andrei (Basketball Player)
Utah Jazz
301 W South Temple
Delta Center
Salt Lake City, UT 84101-1219, USA

Kirner, Gary (Athlete, Football Player)
3507 Senasac Ave
Long Beach, CA 90808-2847, USA

Kirouac, Lou (Athlete, Football Player)
3630 Chattahoochee Ct
Duluth, GA 30096-3210, USA

Kirrene, Joe (Athlete, Baseball Player)
2557 Kilpatrick Ct
San Ramon, CA 94583-1726, USA

Kirschke, Travis (Athlete, Football Player)
10196 Crooked Stick Trl
Lone Tree, CO 80124-8510, USA

kirschner, David (Actor)
c/o Staff Member *WME/IMG*
9601 Wilshire Blvd
Beverly Hills, CA 90210-5213, USA

Kirsebom, Vendela (Model)
c/o Staff Member *TR Management Group*
11740 Wilshire Blvd Apt A2109
Los Angeles, CA 90025-6530, USA

Kirshbaum, Ralph (Musician)
Columbia Artists Mgmt Inc
165 W 57th St
New York, NY 10019-2201, USA

Kirshner, Mia (Actor)
c/o Ronda Cooper *Characters Talent Agency*
200-1505 2nd Ave W
Vancouver, BC V6H 3Y4, CANADA

Kirtman, David (Athlete, Football Player)
PO Box 50743
Bellevue, WA 98015-0743, USA

Kirton, Mark (Athlete, Hockey Player)
251 North Service Rd W
Oakville, ON L6M 3E7, Canada

Kisabaka, Lisa (Athlete, Track Athlete)
Franz-Hitze-Str 22
Leverkusen 51372, GERMANY

Kiselak, Mike (Athlete, Football Player)
234 Churchill Loop
Grapevine, TX 76051-8002, USA

Kiser, Garland (Athlete, Baseball Player)
267 Carr Dr
Blountville, TN 37617-4608, USA

Kiser, Terry (Actor)
Innovative Artists
1505 10th St
Santa Monica, CA 90401-2805, USA

Kisio, Kelly (Athlete, Hockey Player)
c/o Staff Member *Calgary Hitmen*
P.O. Box 1420
Stn Main
Calgary, AB T2P 3B9, Canada

Kisor, Henry (Writer)
2800 Harrison St
Evanston, IL 60201-1218, USA

KISS (Music Group)
c/o Kristen Foster *PMK/BNC Public Relations*
1840 Century Park E Ste 1400
Los Angeles, CA 90067-2115, USA

Kissane, James (Athlete, Basketball Player)
6 Mellen Ln
Wayland, MA 01778-2015, USA

Kissane, Jim (Athlete, Basketball Player)
6 Mellen Ln
Wayland, MA 01778-2015, USA

Kissell, Ed (Athlete, Football Player)
150 Wallace Rd
Bedford, NH 03110-5139, USA

Kissell, Larry (Congressman, Politician)
1632 Longworth Hob
Washington, DC 20515-2007, USA

Kissel-Lafser, Audrey (Athlete, Baseball Player, Commentator)
9506 Port Dr
Affton, MO 63123-6530, USA

Kissin, Evgeni I (Musician)
Harold Holt
31 Sinclair Rd
London W14 0NS, UNITED KINGDOM (UK)

Kissinger, Henry A (Politician)
350 Park Ave Fl 26
New York, NY 10022-6045, USA

Kissling, Conny (Skier)
Hubel
Messen 03254, SWITZERLAND

Kitaen, Tawny (Actor)
Talent Group
5670 Wilshire Blvd Ste 820
Los Angeles, CA 90036-5613, USA

Kitaj, R B (Artist)
Marlborough Fine Art
6 Albermarle St
London W1, UNITED KINGDOM (UK)

Kitano, Takeshi (Actor, Director)
Office Kitano
5-4-14 Akasaka Minataku
Tokyo 107-0052, JAPAN

Kitbunchu, M Michael Cardinal (Religious Leader)
122 Soi Naaksuwan
Thanon Nonsi Yannawa
Bangkok 10120, THAILAND

Kitchen, Curtis (Athlete, Basketball Player)
343 19th Ave
Seattle, WA 98122-5735, USA

Kitchen, Michael (Actor)
International Creative Mgmt
76 Oxford St
London W1N 0AX, UNITED KINGDOM (UK)

Kitchen, Mike (Athlete, Coach, Hockey Player)
c/o Staff Member *Florida Panthers*
1 Panther Pkwy
Sunrise, FL 33323-5315, USA

Kitchens, Jimmy (Race Car Driver)
Moy Racing
486 Withrow Rd
Forest City, NC 28043-9693, USA

Kite, Greg (Athlete, Basketball Player)
3060 Seigneury Dr
Windermere, FL 34786-8353, USA

Kite, Jimmy (Race Car Driver)
Blueprint Racing
6800 W 73rd St
Bedford Park, IL 60638-6024, USA

Kite, Tom (Athlete, Golfer)
907 Terrace Mountain Dr
West Lake Hills, TX 78746-2730, USA

Kitna, Jon (Athlete, Football Player)
18898 Bella Vista Ct
Northville, MI 48168-3534, USA

Kitsch, Taylor (Actor)
c/o Stephanie Simon *Untitled Entertainment*
350 S Beverly Dr Ste 200
Beverly Hills, CA 90212-4819, USA

Kitsis, Edward (Eddy) (Producer)
c/o Philip Raskind *WME/IMG*
9601 Wilshire Blvd
Beverly Hills, CA 90210-5213, USA

Kitson, Syd (Athlete, Football Player)
3 Frost Ln
New Providence, NJ 07974-1246, USA

Kitt, A J (Skier)
2437 N Franklin Ave
Louisville, CO 80027-1216, USA

Kitt, Tom (Musician, Writer)
c/o John Buzzetti *WME/IMG (NY)*
11 Madison Ave Fl 18
New York, NY 10010-3669, USA

Kittle, Ron (Athlete, Baseball Player)
PO Box 1998
Valparaiso, IN 46384-1998, USA

Kittles, Kerry (Athlete, Basketball Player)
PO Box 233
New Vernon, NJ 07976-0233, USA

Kittles, Tory (Actor)
c/o Matt Luber *Luber Roklin Management*
5815 W Sunset Blvd Ste 208
Los Angeles, CA 90028-6481, USA

Kiwanuka, Mathias (Athlete, Football Player)
c/o Tom Condon *Creative Artists Agency (CAA)*
401 Commerce St PH
Nashville, TN 37219-2516, USA

Kiyoko, Hayley (Actor)
c/o Staff Member *AKA Talent Agency*
325 N Larchmont Blvd
Los Angeles, CA 90004-3011, USA

Kiyosaki, Kim (Business Person, Writer)
CASHFLOW Technologies Inc
4330 N Civic Center Plz Ste 100
Scottsdale, AZ 85251-3529, USA

Kiyosaki, Robert (Business Person, Writer)
The Rich Dad Company
4330 N Civic Center Plz Ste 100
Scottsdale, AZ 85251-3529, USA

Kizer, DeShone (Athlete, Football Player)
c/o Brian Murphy *Athletes First*
23091 Mill Creek Dr
Laguna Hills, CA 92653-1258, USA

Kjell, Adrien (Athlete, Hockey Player)
Norumsgarde ISI
Goteborg 41743, SWEDEN

Kjellberg, Felix (PewDiePie) (Internet Star)
c/o Staff Member *Maker Studios*
3515 Eastham Dr
Culver City, CA 90232-2440, USA

Kjer, Bodil (Actor)
Vestre Pavilion Frydenlund
Frydenlund Alle 19
Vedbaek 02950, DENMARK

Kjus, Lasse (Athlete, Skier)
LK International AG
Gewerbestr. 11
Cham 06330, Switzerland

Klabunde, Charles S (Artist)
68 W 3rd St
New York, NY 10012-1029, USA

Klages, Fred (Athlete, Baseball Player)
2813 Crossvine Cir
Spring, TX 77380-1396, USA

Klammer, Franz (Skier)
Mooswald 22
Fresach/Ktn 09712, AUSTRIA

Klaplisch, Cedric (Director)
Cineart
36 Rue de Ponthieu
Paris 75008, FRANCE

Klasnic, John (Athlete, Football Player)
924 Highland Ave
McKeesport, PA 15133-3920, USA

Klass, Beverly (Athlete, Golfer)
PO Box 244364
Boynton Beach, FL 33424-4364, USA

Klassen, Danny (Athlete, Baseball Player)
5680 SW Pomegranate Way
Palm City, FL 34990-8627, USA

Klassen, Ralph (Athlete, Hockey Player)
826 Avenue C N
Saskatoon, SK S7L 1J8, Canada

Klatt, Trent (Athlete, Hockey Player)
New York Islanders
200 Merrick Ave
Attn Player Development Dept
East Meadow, NY 11554-1596, USA

Klatt, Trent (Athlete, Hockey Player)
29951 Thistle Ln
New Hudson, MI 48165-9844, USA

Klattenhoff, Diego (Actor)
c/o Francis Okwu *Zero Gravity Management*
11110 Ohio Ave Ste 100
Los Angeles, CA 90025-3329, USA

Klaus, Bobby (Athlete, Baseball Player)
10661 Gabacho Dr
San Diego, CA 92124-1404, USA

Klaus, Deita (Actor)
c/o Staff Member *Digigraphics/Dream Girl World*
4650 Libbit Ave
Encino, CA 91436-2122, USA

Klaus, Vaclav (Politician, President)
c/o Staff Member *Kancelar Prezidenta Republiky (Czech Republic)*
Hradecek
Prague 1 119 08, Czech Republic

Klausing, Chuck (Coach, Football Coach)
2115 Lazor St
Indiana, PA 15701-3463, USA

Klawitter, Tom (Athlete, Baseball Player)
3220 Dover Ct
Janesville, WI 53546-1956, USA

Klaxons (Music Group)
c/o Staff Member *Paradigm (Monterey)*
404 W Franklin St
Monterey, CA 93940-2303, USA

Klebba, Martin (Actor)
c/o Staff Member *The Stevens Group*
14011 Ventura Blvd Ste 200W
Sherman Oaks, CA 91423-5218, USA

Klecko, Joseph E (Joe) (Athlete, Football Player)
105 Stella Ln
Aston, PA 19014-2741, USA

Klee, Ken (Athlete, Hockey Player)
8487 W Quarles Pl
Littleton, CO 80128-8910, USA

Klein, AJ (Athlete, Football Player)
c/o Scott Smith *XAM Sports*
3509 Ice Age Dr
Madison, WI 53719-5409, USA

Klein, Calvin (Designer, Fashion Designer)
c/o Staff Member *Calvin Klein Inc*
200 Madison Ave
New York, NY 10016-3903, USA

Klein, Chris (Actor)
c/o Cynthia Pett-Dante *Brillstein Entertainment Partners*
9150 Wilshire Blvd Ste 350
Beverly Hills, CA 90212-3453, USA

Klein, Danny (Musician)
Nick Ben-Meir
2850 Ocean Park Blvd Ste 300
Santa Monica, CA 90405-6216, USA

Klein, Emilee (Athlete, Golfer)
7660 Beverly Blvd Apt 315
Los Angeles, CA 90036-2743, USA

Klein, Jennifer (Producer)
c/o Carlos Goodman *Bloom Hergott Diemer Rosenthal Laviolette Feldman Schenkman & Goodman*
150 S Rodeo Dr Fl 3
Beverly Hills, CA 90212-2410, USA

Klein, Jess (Musician, Songwriter, Writer)
Drake Assoc
177 Woodland Ave
Westwood, NJ 07675-3218, USA

Klein, Joe (Journalist, Writer)
Newsweek Magazine
251 W 57th St
Editorial Dept
New York, NY 10019-1802, USA

Klein, Jonathan (Business Person)
c/o Staff Member *CNN (NY)*
10 Columbus Cir
Time Warner Center
New York, NY 10019-1158, USA

Klein, Marci (Director, Producer, Writer)
c/o Jeff Jacobs *Creative Artists Agency (CAA)*
2000 Avenue of the Stars Ste 100
Los Angeles, CA 90067-4705, USA

Klein, Marty (Writer)
2439 Birch St Ste 2
Palo Alto, CA 94306-1946, USA

Klein, Naomi (Producer, Writer)
c/o Staff Member *American Program Bureau*
1 Gateway Ctr Ste 751
Newton, MA 02458-2817, USA

Klein, Perry (Athlete, Football Player)
30760 Broad Beach Rd
Malibu, CA 90265-2613, USA

Klein, Richard J (Athlete, Football Player)
609 E 2nd St
Pana, IL 62557-1446, USA

Klein, Robert (Actor, Musician)
c/o Rory Rosegarten *Conversation Company*
1044 Northern Blvd Ste 304
Roslyn, NY 11576-1589, USA

Klein, Robert O (Bob) (Athlete, Football Player)
15933 Alcima Ave
Pacific Palisades, CA 90272-2405, USA

Klein Borkow, Dana (Producer)
c/o Staff Member *WME|IMG*
9601 Wilshire Blvd
Beverly Hills, CA 90210-5213, USA

Kleine, Joe (Athlete, Basketball Player, Olympic Athlete)
53 Hickory Hills Cir
Little Rock, AR 72212-2766, USA

Kleine, Joseph (Joe) (Baseball Player)
Cornwall Community Police
PO Box 87 Stn Main
Cornwall, ON K6H 5R9, Canada

Kleinendorst, Kurt (Athlete, Hockey Player)
7049 S Village Commons Way
Midvale, UT 84047-4638, USA

Kleinendorst, Scot (Athlete, Hockey Player)
35387 Lake St
Cohasset, MN 55721-2160, USA

Kleiner, Jeremy (Producer)
c/o Staff Member *Plan B Entertainment*
9150 Wilshire Blvd Ste 350
Beverly Hills, CA 90212-3453, USA

Kleinsasser, Jim (Athlete, Football Player)
6835 Cardinal Cove Dr
Mound, MN 55364-9535, USA

Kleinsmith, Bruce (Cartoonist)
PO Box 1083
San Juan Bautista, CA 95045-1083, USA

Kleiser, Randal (Director)
3050 Runyon Canyon Rd
Los Angeles, CA 90046-1347, USA

Kleisinger, Terry (Athlete, Hockey Player)
37 Elisia Dr
Moose Jaw, SK S6J 1G9, Canada

Klementieff, Pom (Actor)
c/o Megan Moss *Narrative*
1601 Vine St Fl 6
Los Angeles, CA 90028-8802, USA

Klemm, Adrian (Athlete, Football Player)
900 W Olympic Blvd UNIT 43D
Los Angeles, CA 90015-1395, USA

Klemm, Jay (Athlete, Baseball Player)
11 June Rd
North Salem, NY 10560-2319, USA

Klemm, Jay (Athlete, Baseball Player)
1605 Airy Hill Ct Unit D
Crofton, MD 21114-2723, USA

Klemm, Jon (Athlete, Hockey Player)
400 61st St
Willowbrook, IL 60527-1806, USA

Klemm, Jon (Athlete, Hockey Player)
Spokane Chiefs
700 W Mallon Ave
Attn: Coaching Staff
Spokane, WA 99201-2134, USA

Klemmer, John (Musician)
Boardman
10548 Clearwood Ct
Los Angeles, CA 90077-2019, USA

Kleon, Austin (Writer)
19885 Detroit Rd # 222
Rocky River, OH 44116-1815, USA

Klepper, Jordan (Comedian, Television Host)
c/o Fred Hashagen *United Talent Agency (UTA)*
888 7th Ave Fl 7
New York, NY 10106-0700, USA

Klesko, Ryan (Athlete, Baseball Player)
c/o Staff Member *San Diego Padres*
100 Park Blvd
San Diego, CA 92101-7405, USA

Klesla, Rostislav (Athlete, Hockey Player)
9425 E Desert Village Dr
Scottsdale, AZ 85255-6095, USA

Klesla, Rotislav (Athlete, Hockey Player)
200 W Nationwide Blvd
Columbus, OH 43215-2561, USA

Klett, Peter (Musician)
11410 NE 124th St # 627
Kirkland, WA 98034-4399, USA

Klever, Rocky (Athlete, Football Player)
407 W Edgewood Ave
Linwood, NJ 08221-1709, USA

Klick, Jim (Athlete, Football Player)
4001 E Lake Estates Dr
Davie, FL 33328-3072, USA

Klicullen, Bob (Athlete, Football Player)
400 E Division St
Pilot Point, TX 76258-4510, USA

Klieman, Rikki (Attorney, Commentator)
5683 Holly Oak Dr
Los Angeles, CA 90068-2521, USA

Klim, Michael (Swimmer)
177 Bridge Road
Richmond, VIC 03121, AUSTRALIA

Klima, Petr (Athlete, Hockey Player)
1000 Forest Ln
Bloomfield Hills, MI 48301-4112, USA

Klimchock, Lou (Athlete, Baseball Player)
8876 S Myrtle Ave
Tempe, AZ 85284-3178, USA

Kline, Bobby (Athlete, Baseball Player)
6656 31st Way S
Saint Petersburg, FL 33712-5404, USA

Kline, Jeff (Producer, Writer)
c/o Staff Member *WME|IMG*
9601 Wilshire Blvd Ste 750
Beverly Hills, CA 90210-5228, USA

Kline, John (Congressman, Politician)
2439 Rayburn Hob
Washington, DC 20515-3001, USA

Kline, Kevin (Actor)
26 Wing and Wing
Garrison, NY 10524, USA

Kline, Owen (Actor)
c/o Staff Member *WME|IMG*
9601 Wilshire Blvd Ste 750
Beverly Hills, CA 90210-5228, USA

Kline, Richard (Actor)
c/o Harry Gold *TalentWorks*
3500 W Olive Ave Ste 1400
Burbank, CA 91505-5512, USA

Kline, Steve (Athlete, Baseball Player)
78 Milledge Rd
Attn: Coaching Staff
Augusta, GA 30904-3022, USA

Kline, Steve (Athlete, Baseball Player)
5500 SW 182nd Ave
Beaverton, OR 97078-3858, USA

Kline, Steve (Athlete, Baseball Player)
258 Trutt Rd
Winfield, PA 17889-9304, USA

Kline-Randall, Maxine (Athlete, Baseball Player, Commentator)
3751 Milnes Rd
Hillsdale, MI 49242-9313, USA

Klingbeil, Chuck (Athlete, Football Player)
PO Box 237
Hancock, MI 49930-0237, USA

Klingenbeck, Scott (Athlete, Baseball Player)
6230 Kincora Ct
Cincinnati, OH 45233-4458, USA

Klingler, David (Athlete, Football Player)
Dallas Theological Seminary
7100 Regency Square Blvd Ste 100
Houston, TX 77036-3247, USA

Klingman, Lynzee (Actor)
c/o Staff Member *United Talent Agency (UTA)*
9336 Civic Center Dr
Beverly Hills, CA 90210-3604, USA

Klink, Joe (Athlete, Baseball Player)
119 Green Heron Ct
Daytona Beach, FL 32119-1303, USA

Klinsmann, Jurgen (Soccer Player)
3419 Via Lido # 600
Newport Beach, CA 92663-3908, USA

Klitbo, Cynthia (Actor)
c/o Staff Member *Televisa*
Blvd Adolfo Lopez Mateos 232
Colonia San Angel INN
DF CP 01060, MEXICO

Klitschko, Wladimir (Actor, Athlete, Boxer)
Klitschko Management Group
Borselstr.28
Haus I
Hamburg 22765, Germany

Klosowski, Dolores (Baseball Player)
14254 Farnsworth Dr
Sterling Heights, MI 48312-4352, USA

Kloss, Ilana (Athlete, Tennis Player)
World TeamTennis
2100 Palomar Airport Rd Ste 208
Carlsbad, CA 92011-4404, USA

Kloss, Karlie (Model)
c/o Andrea Hackett *Derris & Company*
48 W 25th St Fl 11
New York, NY 10010-2719, USA

Klosterman, Bruce (Athlete, Football Player)
14194 Deerfield Ct
Dubuque, IA 52003-9414, USA

Klosterman, Chuck (Writer)
c/o Dan Greenberg *Levine Greenberg Literary Agency*
307 7th Ave Rm 2407
New York, NY 10001-6062, USA

Klotz, H Louis (Red) (Athlete, Basketball Player, Coach)
114 S Osborne Ave
Margate City, NJ 08402-2530, USA

Klotz, Jack (Athlete, Football Player)
17 Pickwick Ln
Newtown Square, PA 19073-4607, USA

Klotz, John S (Athlete, Football Player)
17 Pickwick Ln
Newtown Square, PA 19073-4607, USA

Klous, Patricia (Actor)
2539 Benedict Canyon Dr
Beverly Hills, CA 90210-1020, USA

Kloves, Steve (Director, Writer)
c/o David O'Connor *Creative Artists Agency (CAA)*
2000 Avenue of the Stars Ste 100
Los Angeles, CA 90067-4705, USA

Kluber, Corey (Athlete, Baseball Player)
c/o BB Abbott *Jeter Sports Management*
PO Box 1388
Solana Beach, CA 92075-7388, USA

Klueh, Duane (Athlete, Basketball Player)
252 Francis Avenue Ct
Terre Haute, IN 47804-5101, USA

Kluer, Duane (Athlete, Basketball Player, Coach)
252 Francis Avenue Ct
Terre Haute, IN 47804-5101, USA

Klug, Karl (Athlete, Football Player)
c/o Neil Cornrich *NC Sports, LLC*
best to contact via email
Columbus, OH 43201, USA

Kluger, Richard (Writer)
c/o Staff Member *Random House Publicity*
1745 Broadway Frnt 3
New York, NY 10019-4343, USA

Klugh, Earl (Musician)
c/o Staff Member *Richard De La Font Agency*
3808 W South Park Blvd
Broken Arrow, OK 74011-1261, USA

Klum, Heidi (Model, Producer, Television Host)
568 Broadway Rm 603
New York, NY 10012-3260, USA

Klutts, Mickey (Athlete, Baseball Player)
6136 Maple Ave
Lake Isabella, CA 93240-9706, USA

Kluttz, Lonnie (Athlete, Basketball Player)
183 Greenwing Ln
Saint Matthews, SC 29135-8168, USA

Kluwe, Chris (Athlete, Football Player)
6686 Montford Dr
Huntington Beach, CA 92648-6625, USA

Kluzak, Gord (Athlete, Hockey Player)
Boston Bruins
100 Legends Way Ste 250
Attn: Broadcast Dept
Boston, MA 02114-1389, USA

Kluzak, Gord (Athlete, Hockey Player)
770 Boylston St Apt 27C
Boston, MA 02199-7724, USA

Klymaxx (Music Group)
c/o Staff Member *Diva Central Inc*
7510 W Sunset Blvd # 1445
Los Angeles, CA 90046-3408, USA

Klymkiw, Julius (Athlete, Hockey Player)
66 Buttercup Ave
Winnipeg, MB R2V 2S5, Canada

Kmak, Joe (Athlete, Baseball Player)
1021 Hatteras Ct
Foster City, CA 94404-3546, USA

K'naan (Musician)
c/o Aaron Schubert *Paquin Entertainment Agency (Winnipeg)*
468 Stradbrook Ave
Winnipeg MB M6K 3J1, CANADA

Knackert, Brent (Athlete, Baseball Player)
16802 Leafwood Cir
Huntington Beach, CA 92647-4851, USA

Knafelc, Gary (Athlete, Football Player)
2147 Burley Ave
Clermont, FL 34711-5744, USA

Knafelc, Greg (Athlete, Football Player)
1243 Prairie Falcon Trl
Green Bay, WI 54313-7177, USA

Knape, Lindberg Ulrike (Swimmer)
Drostvagen 7
Karlskoga 691 33, SWEDEN

Knapp, Alexis (Actor)
c/o Emma Lewis *Paradigm*
8942 Wilshire Blvd
Beverly Hills, CA 90211-1908, USA

Knapp, Beau (Actor)
c/o Heidi Lopata *Narrative*
1601 Vine St Fl 6
Los Angeles, CA 90028-8802, USA

Knapp, Chris (Athlete, Baseball Player)
788 Rich Dr
Oviedo, FL 32765-6447, USA

Knapp, Jennifer (Musician)
c/o Staff Member *Creative Artists Agency (CAA)*
401 Commerce St PH
Nashville, TN 37219-2516, USA

Knapp, Lindsay (Athlete, Football Player)
5018 Bruce Ave
Minneapolis, MN 55424-1318, USA

Knapp, Rick (Athlete, Baseball Player)
23427 Garrett Ave
Port Charlotte, FL 33954-2534, USA

Knapp, Sebastian (Actor)
c/o Lorraine Berglund *Lorraine Berglund Management*
11537 Hesby St
North Hollywood, CA 91601-3618, USA

Knapp, Stefan (Artist)
Sandhills
Godalming
Surrey, UNITED KINGDOM (UK)

Knappett, Jessica (Actor)
c/o Will Wood *Multitude Media*
32 Bloomsbury St
London WC1B 3QJ, UNITED KINGDOM

Knapple, Jeff (Athlete, Football Player)
10025 Toluca Lake Ave
Toluca Lake, CA 91602-2923, USA

Knauss, Hans (Skier)
Fastenberg 60
Schladming 08970, AUSTRIA

Kneale, R Bryan C (Artist)
10A Muswell Road
London N10 2BG, UNITED KINGDOM (UK)

Knebel, John A (Politician)
1418 Labumum St
McLean, VA 22101-2523, USA

Knechtel, Dave (Athlete, Football Player)
14 Ambroise Lane
Winnipeg, MB R2M 5P2, Canada

Kneifel, Chris (Race Car Driver)
6 Timberline Ln
Riverwoods, IL 60015-2443, USA

Knepper, Bob (Athlete, Baseball Player)
20410 Silver Horn Ln
Monument, CO 80132-8092, USA

Knepper, Robert (Actor)
c/o Adam Griffin *LINK Entertainment*
11872 La Grange Ave
Los Angeles, CA 90025-5282, USA

Knibbs, Darrel (Athlete, Hockey Player)
2236 Surfwood Dr
Muskegon, MI 49441-1162

Knicely, Alan (Athlete, Baseball Player)
700 Three Leagues Rd
McGaheysville, VA 22840-2680, USA

Knickle, Rick (Athlete, Hockey Player)
192 Martinwood Way NE
Calgary, AB T3J 3H8, Canada

Knickman, Clarence Roy (Athlete, Cycler, Olympic Athlete)
436 Fallbrook Ave
Newbury Park, CA 91320-4929, USA

Knief, Gayle (Athlete, Football Player)
1825 SE Birchwood Cir
Waukee, IA 50263-8194, USA

Knight, Aramis (Actor)
c/o Brett Ruttenberg *Imprint PR*
6121 W Sunset Blvd
Neuehouse
Los Angeles, CA 90028-6442, USA

Knight, Beverley (Musician)
c/o Staff Member *DWL Management*
53 Goodge St #200
London W1T 1TG, UNITED KINGDOM

Knight, Billy (Athlete, Basketball Player)
1051 Bluffhaven Way NE
Brookhaven, GA 30319-4818, USA

Knight, Brandon (Athlete, Baseball Player)
New York Yankees
PO Box 1685
Ventura, CA 93002-1685, USA

Knight, Brevin (Athlete, Basketball Player)
3226 Bedford Ln
Germantown, TN 38139-8043, USA

Knight, Brian (Baseball Player)
1123 Stuart St
Helena, MT 59601-2138, USA

Knight, Brian (Athlete, Baseball Player)
1123 Stuart St
Helena, MT 59601-2138, USA

Knight, Carlos (Actor)
c/o Ford Englerth *Redrock Entertainment Development*
149 E Santa Anita Ave
Burbank, CA 91502-1926, USA

Knight, Charles F (Business Person)
Emerson Electric Co
8000 W Florissant Ave # 41000
Saint Louis, MO 63136-1414, USA

Knight, Chris (Musician, Songwriter, Writer)
Rick Alter Mgmt
1018 17th Ave S Ste 12
Nashville, TN 37212-2219, USA

Knight, Christopher (Actor)
1600 Monterey Blvd
Hermosa Beach, CA 90254-2901, USA

Knight, Curt (Athlete, Football Player)
7230 Rio Flora Pl
Downey, CA 90241-2030, USA

Knight, David (Athlete, Football Player)
2600 Farm Rd
Alexandria, VA 22302-2821, USA

Knight, Gladys (Musician)
c/o Staff Member *Shakeji*
3175 E Warm Springs Rd Ste 115
Las Vegas, NV 89120-3138, USA

Knight, Jean (Musician)
Ken Keene Artists
PO Box 1875
Gretna, LA 70054-1875, USA

Knight, Jonathan (Musician)
20 Chase St Apt 2
Danvers, MA 01923-3225, USA

Knight, Jordan (Musician)
c/o Tracy Nguyen *Industry Public Relations*
6600 W Sunset Blvd Ste 200
Los Angeles, CA 90028-7162, USA

Knight, Keltie (Actor)
c/o Susan (Sue) Madore *Guttman Associates Public Relations*
118 S Beverly Dr Ste 201
Beverly Hills, CA 90212-3016, USA

Knight, Marcus (Athlete, Football Player)
326 Threatt Ln
Sylacauga, AL 35150-8635, USA

Knight, Matthew (Actor)
c/o Dani De Lio *Creative Drive Artists*
20 Minowan Miikan Lane
Toronto, ON M6J 0E5, CANADA

Knight, Negele (Athlete, Basketball Player)
18624 N 4th Ave
Phoenix, AZ 85027-5665, USA

Knight, Paul (Producer)
c/o Anthony Jones *United Agents*
12-26 Lexington St
London W1F OLE, UNITED KINGDOM

Knight, Phil (Business Person)
Nike Inc
1 SW Bowerman Dr
Beaverton, OR 97005-0979, USA

Knight, Ray (Athlete, Baseball Player)
1500 S Capitol St SE
Attn: Broadcast Dept
Washington, DC 20003-3599, USA

Knight, Ray (Athlete, Baseball Player)
PO Box 129
Auburn, AL 36831-0129, USA

Knight, Robert M (Bobby) (Athlete, Basketball Player, Coach)
8003 County Road 6910
Lubbock, TX 79407-5760, USA

Knight, Roger (Athlete, Football Player)
705 W Queen Creek Rd Unit 2212
Chandler, AZ 85248-3430, USA

Knight, Ron (Athlete, Basketball Player)
1426 Ellsmere Ave
Los Angeles, CA 90019-3800, USA

Knight, Sandra (Actor)
626 Kaimalino St
Kailua, HI 96734-1613, USA

Knight, Shawn (Athlete, Football Player)
13090 Welcome Way
Reno, NV 89511-8688, USA

Knight, Shirley (Actor)
c/o Martin Gage *BRS / Gage Talent Agency (LA)*
6300 Wilshire Blvd Ste 1430
Los Angeles, CA 90048-5216, USA

Knight, Sterling (Actor)
c/o Ruth Bernstein *Viewpoint Inc*
8820 Wilshire Blvd Ste 220
Beverly Hills, CA 90211-2622, USA

Knight, Steve (Writer)
c/o Staff Member *Creative Artists Agency (CAA)*
2000 Avenue of the Stars Ste 100
Los Angeles, CA 90067-4705, USA

Knight, Steve (Athlete, Football Player)
4503 Bevington Ln Apt A
Indianapolis, IN 46240-4478, USA

Knight, Steven (Director)
c/o Natasha Galloway *The Rights House (UK)*
Drury House
34-43 Russell St
London WC2B 5HA, UNITED KINGDOM

Knight, Suge (Actor, Musician, Producer)

Knight, Toby (Athlete, Basketball Player)
106 Claywood Dr
Brentwood, NY 11717-5724, USA

Knight, Tom (Athlete, Football Player)
PO Box 888
Phoenix, AZ 85001-0888, USA

Knight, T.R. (Actor)
c/o Ashley Franklin *Thruline Entertainment*
9250 Wilshire Blvd Fl Ground
Beverly Hills, CA 90212-3352, USA

Knight, Travis (Athlete, Basketball Player)
3159 Millcreek Rd
Pleasant Grove, UT 84062-8790, USA

Knight, Travis (Director, Producer)
c/o Staff Member *Laika Entertainment*
6750 NE Bennett St
Hillsboro, OR 97124-5973, USA

Knight, Trevor (Adult Film Star)
c/o Staff Member *Diva Central Inc*
7510 W Sunset Blvd # 1445
Los Angeles, CA 90046-3408, USA

Knight, Wayne (Actor)
c/o Ryan Martin *Buchwald*
5900 Wilshire Blvd Ste 3100
Los Angeles, CA 90036-5030, USA

Knight, Wendi (Adult Film Star)
c/o Staff Member *Atlas Multimedia Inc*
9005 Eton Ave Ste C
Canoga Park, CA 91304-6533, USA

Knightley, Keira (Actor)
c/o Adam Isaacs *MGMT Entertainment (The Schiff Company)*
9220 W Sunset Blvd Ste 106
W Hollywood, CA 90069-3500, USA

Knightlinger, Lauren (Actor)
c/o Peter Principato *Artists First*
9465 Wilshire Blvd Ste 900
Beverly Hills, CA 90212-2608, USA

Knighton, Terrance (Athlete, Football Player)
c/o Mitchell Frankel *Impact Sports (FL)*
2799 NW 2nd Ave Ste 203
Boca Raton, FL 33431-6709, USA

Knighton, Zachary (Actor)
c/o Nick Frenkel *3 Arts Entertainment*
9460 Wilshire Blvd Fl 7
Beverly Hills, CA 90212-2713, USA

Knights, Dave (Musician)
195 Sandycombe Road
Kew TW9 2EW, UNITED KINGDOM (UK)

Knipscheer, Fred (Athlete, Hockey Player)
13404 Macaw Pl
Carmel, IN 46033-8964, USA

Knisley, Sam (Athlete, Basketball Player)
14808 Hanover Pike
Upperco, MD 21155-9735, USA

Knoblauch, Chuck (Athlete, Baseball Player)
11702 Forest Glen St
Houston, TX 77024-6414, USA

Knoedler, Justin (Athlete, Baseball Player)
315 Eagle Ridge Dr # D
Chatham, IL 62629-2037, USA

Knoff, Kurt (Athlete, Football Player)
11121 Bluestem Ln
Eden Prairie, MN 55347-4732, USA

Knoop, Bobby (Athlete, Baseball Player)
2543 E Mountain Sky Ave
Phoenix, AZ 85048-9516, USA

Knopf, Sascha (Actor, Model)
c/o Bradley Frank *Platform PR*
2666 N Beachwood Dr
Los Angeles, CA 90068-2308, USA

Knopfler, David (Musician)
Damage Mgmt
16 Lambton Place
London W11 2SH, UNITED KINGDOM (UK)

Knopfler, Mark (Musician)
Paul Crockford Mgmt
37 Ruston Mews
London W11 1RB, UNITED KINGDOM (UK)

Knopper, Steve (Writer)
3445 W Moncrieff Pl
Denver, CO 80211-3161, USA

Knorr, Micah (Athlete, Football Player)
10391 Whitecrown Cir
Corona, CA 92883-9267, USA

Knorr, Randy (Athlete, Baseball Player)
10310 Greenhedges Dr
Tampa, FL 33626-1729, USA

Knorr, Randy (Athlete, Baseball Player)
Syracuse Chiefs 1 Tex Simone Dr
Attn: Managers Office
Syracuse, NY 13208-1274, USA

Knostman, Richard (Dick) (Athlete, Basketball Player)
346 Crestone Ave
Salida, CO 81201-1521, USA

Knott, Eric (Athlete, Baseball Player)
1906 Dog Leg Dr
Sebring, FL 33872-3838, USA

Knott, Jon (Athlete, Baseball Player)
4250 Vicenza Dr Unit A
Venice, FL 34293-0714, USA

Knotts, Gary (Athlete, Baseball Player)
18 Covey St
Decatur, AL 35603-6021, USA

Knowles, Beyonce (Actor, Musician)
c/o Andrea Nelson-Meigs *ICM Partners*
10250 Constellation Blvd Fl 7
Los Angeles, CA 90067-6207, USA

Knowles, Darold (Athlete, Baseball Player)
1369 Curlew Rd
Dunedin, FL 34698-1924, USA

Knowles, Darold (Athlete, Baseball Player)
373 Douglas Ave
Attn: Coaching Staff
Dunedin, FL 34698-7913, USA

Knowles, Harry (Internet Star)
PO Box 180011
Austin, TX 78718-0011, USA

Knowles, Matthew (Actor)
c/o Troy Zien *3 Arts Entertainment*
9460 Wilshire Blvd Fl 7
Beverly Hills, CA 90212-2713, USA

Knowles, Nick (Television Host)
c/o Staff Member *Hilary Knight Management*
Grange Farm
Church Lane
Old Northampton NN6 9QZ, UK

Knowles, Rodney (Athlete, Basketball Player)
3592 Island Dr
N Topsail Beach, NC 28460-8202, USA

Knowles, Solange (Actor, Musician)
c/o Marty Diamond *Paradigm*
140 Broadway Ste 2600
New York, NY 10005-1011, USA

Knowles, Tony (Politician)
1146 S St
Anchorage, AK 99501-4230, USA

Knowlton, Steve R (Skier)
Palmer Yeager Assoc
6600 E Hampden Ave # 210
Denver, CO 80224-3045, USA

Knox, Bill (Athlete, Football Player)
7836 Forest Ave
Gary, IN 46403-2139, USA

Knox, Chuck (Athlete, Football Player)
48711 San Vicente St
La Quinta, CA 92253-2220, USA

Knox, John (Athlete, Baseball Player)
3701 W Oak Shores Dr
Crossroads, TX 76227-2606, USA

Knox, Kenny (Athlete, Golfer)
3813 Dills Rd
Monticello, FL 32344-4699, USA

Knox, Kevin (Athlete, Basketball Player)
c/o Aaron Turner *Verus Management Team*
6009 Landerhaven Dr Ste D
Cleveland, OH 44124-4192, USA

Knox, Terence (Actor)
c/o Lin Bickelmann *Encore Artists Management*
3815 W Olive Ave Ste 101
Burbank, CA 91505-4674, USA

Knoxville, Johnny (Actor)
c/o Staff Member *Dickhouse Productions*
5555 Melrose Ave
Los Angeles, CA 90038-3989, USA

Knuble, Mike (Athlete, Hockey Player, Olympic Athlete)
K 0 Sports
501 S Cherry St Ste 580
Attn Kurt Overhardt
Denver, CO 80246-1327, USA

Knudsen, Arthur G (Skier)
5111 Wright Ave Apt 104
Racine, WI 53406-4530, USA

Knudsen, Erik (Actor)
c/o Joannie Burstein *Burstein Company*
15304 W Sunset Blvd Ste 208
Pacific Palisades, CA 90272-3656, USA

Knudsen, Kurt (Athlete, Baseball Player)
5155 Patti Jo Dr
Carmichael, CA 95608-0968, USA

Knudson, Mark (Athlete, Baseball Player)
881 W 100th Ave
Northglenn, CO 80260-6255, USA

Knudson, Thomas J (Journalist)
Sacramento Bee
Editorial Dept
21st & Q Sts
Sacramento, CA 95852, USA

Knutson, Zak (Actor, Director, Producer)
c/o Cris Dennis *Film Artists Associates*
21044 Ventura Blvd Ste 215
Woodland Hills, CA 91364-6501, USA

Ko, Lydia (Athlete, Golfer)
c/o Jay Burton *IMG (Cleveland)*
1360 E 9th St Ste 100
Cleveland, OH 44114-1730, USA

Koalska, Matt (Athlete, Hockey Player)
95 RoseAveW
Saint Paul, MN 55117-4927, USA

Koart, Matt (Athlete, Football Player)
122 Sonora Ave
Danville, CA 94526-3834, USA

Koback, Nick (Athlete, Baseball Player)
76 Hedgehog Ln
West Simsbury, CT 06092-2104, USA

Kobasew, Chuck (Athlete, Hockey Player)
12 Chardonnay Crt
Osoyoos, BC V0H 1V6, CANADA

Kobe, Katsuhiko (Chef)
Ristorante Massa
1-23-11 Ebisu
Shibuya-ku, Tokyo, Japan

Kobel, Kevin (Athlete, Baseball Player)
7650 E Williams Dr Unit 1072
Scottsdale, AZ 85255-4810, USA

Kober, Jeff (Actor)
4544 Ethel Ave
Studio City, CA 91604-1002, USA

Koblitz, Karen (Artist)
2919 Tilden Ave
Los Angeles, CA 90064-4013, USA

Kobza, Jerry (Race Car Driver)
Shenandoah Valley Motorsports
11 S Oak Ln
Waynesboro, VA 22980-5269, USA

Koch, Aaron (Athlete, Football Player)
9 Garnet Dr
Franklin, MA 02038-4625, USA

Koch, Alan (Athlete, Baseball Player)
1714 Pebble Creek Dr
Prattville, AL 36066-7206, USA

Koch, Alexander (Actor)
c/o Michael Samonte *Sunshine Sachs*
720 Cole Ave
Los Angeles, CA 90038-3606, USA

Koch, Bill (Business Person)
Oxbow Corp
1601 Forum Pl Ste 1001
West Palm Beach, FL 33401-8105, USA

Koch, Billy (Athlete, Baseball Player, Olympic Athlete)
353 S McMullen Booth Rd Apt 136
Clearwater, FL 33759-4526, USA

Koch, Carin (Athlete, Golfer)
5231 E Herrera Dr
Phoenix, AZ 85054-7183, USA

Koch, Charles (Business Person)
Charles Koch Institute
1320 N Courthouse Rd Ste 500
Arlington, VA 22201-2598, USA

Koch, David (Business Person)
Koch Industries
PO Box 2256
Wichita, KS 67201-2256, USA

Koch, Desmond (Des) (Athlete, Football Player, Track Athlete)
23296 Gilmore St
Canoga Park, CA 91307-3426, USA

Koch, Ed (Artist)
PO Box 33515
Juneau, AK 99803-3515, USA

Koch, Gary (Athlete, Golfer)
2934 W Lawn Ave
Tampa, FL 33611-1647, USA

Koch, Gregory M (Greg) (Athlete, Football Player)
34 Valley Oaks Cir
Spring, TX 77382-1722, USA

Koch, Pete (Athlete, Football Player)
866 W 16th St
Newport Beach, CA 92663-2802, USA

Koch, Peter (Actor)
c/o Staff Member *Fly Trap, The*
900 E 1st St
Los Angeles, CA 90012-4032, USA

Koch, William (Bill) (Athlete, Olympic Athlete, Skier)
PO Box 115
Ashland, OR 97520-0004, USA

Kochan, Dieter (Athlete, Hockey Player)
2005 Spruce Ln
Houghton, MI 49931-2721, USA

Koch Jr, Howard (Producer)
Producers Guild of America
8530 Wilshire Blvd Ste 450
Beverly Hills, CA 90211-3115, USA

Kochman, Roger (Athlete, Football Player)
521 Beverly Blvd
Upper Darby, PA 19082-3615, USA

Kocourek, Dave (Athlete, Football Player)
206 Waterway Ct Unit 101
Marco Island, FL 34145-3547, USA

Kocur, Joe (Athlete, Hockey Player)
c/o Staff Member *Detroit Red Wings*
2645 Woodward Ave
Joe Luis Arena
Detroit, MI 48201-3028, USA

Kodes, Jan (Tennis Player)
Na Berance 18
Prague 6/Dejvioe 160 00, CZECH REPUBLIC

Kodjoe, Boris (Actor, Model)
c/o Evan Hainey *Untitled Entertainment*
350 S Beverly Dr Ste 200
Beverly Hills, CA 90212-4819, USA

Koecher, Dick (Athlete, Baseball Player)
3310 Grand Cypress Dr Apt 102
Naples, FL 34119-7979, USA

Koechner, David (Actor, Writer)
c/o John Elliott *Mosaic Media Group*
407 N Maple Dr # 100
Beverly Hills, CA 90210-3818, USA

Koegel, Pete (Athlete, Baseball Player)
301 the Birches
Saugerties, NY 12477-5249, USA

Koegel, Warren (Athlete, Football Player)
Coastal Carolina University
1273 N Fraser St
Georgetown, SC 29440-2853, USA

Koelling, Brian (Athlete, Baseball Player)
20230 Augusta Dr
Lawrenceburg, IN 47025-7370, USA

Koen, Karleen (Writer)
Random House
1745 Broadway Frnt 3 # B1
New York, NY 10019-4343, USA

Koenen, Michael (Athlete, Football Player)
c/o Michael McCartney *Priority Sports & Entertainment (Chicago)*
325 N La Salle Dr Ste 650
Chicago, IL 60654-8182, USA

Koenig, Walter (Actor)
PO Box 4395
North Hollywood, CA 91617-0395, USA

Koepfer, Karl (Athlete, Football Player)
2017 Waters Edge Dr
Westlake, OH 44145-6603, USA

Koepp, David (Director, Writer)
c/o Richard Lovett *Creative Artists Agency (CAA)*
2000 Avenue of the Stars Ste 100
Los Angeles, CA 90067-4705, USA

Koetter, Dirk (Coach, Football Coach)
Arizona State University
Athletic Dept
Tempe, AZ 85287-0001, USA

Koffler, Pamela (Producer)
c/o Staff Member *Killer Films (US)*
526 W 26th St Rm 715
New York, NY 10001-5524, USA

Kofoed, Bart (Athlete, Basketball Player)
10161 Foxhall Dr
Charlotte, NC 28210-7846, USA

Kogan, Theo (Actor, Musician)
Wilhelmina Creative Mgmt
300 Park Ave S # 200
New York, NY 10010-5313, USA

Kogen, Jay (Producer, Writer)
433 Bellagio Ter
Los Angeles, CA 90049-1707, USA

Koger, Gene (Athlete, Baseball Player)
285 Koger Rd
Reidsville, NC 27320-9555, USA

Kogut, Charles (Athlete, Football Player)
210 W 22nd St Ste 110
Oak Brook, IL 60523-4035, USA

Koh, Janice (Actor)
c/o Lim Hui Ling *Fly Entertainment*
213 Henderson Rd
Henderson Industrial Park #03-10
Singapore 159553, SINGAPORE

Kohan, David (Producer)
c/o Staff Member *KoMut Entertainment*
300 Television Plaza
Burbank, CA 91505, USA

Kohan, Jenji (Director, Producer)
c/o Joe Cohen *Creative Artists Agency (CAA)*
2000 Avenue of the Stars Ste 100
Los Angeles, CA 90067-4705, USA

Koharski, Don (Athlete, Hockey Player)
6946 Old Pasco Rd # 275
Wesley Chapel, FL 33544-3504, USA

Kohde-Kilsch, Claudia (Tennis Player)
Elsa-Brandstrom-Str 22
Saarbrucken 66119, GERMANY

Kohl, Ernest (Musician)
c/o Staff Member *Diva Central Inc*
7510 W Sunset Blvd # 1445
Los Angeles, CA 90046-3408, USA

Kohl, Herbert (Politician)
929 N Astor St Unit 2708
Milwaukee, WI 53202-3491, USA

Kohlbrand, Joe (Athlete, Football Player)
3709 Indian River Dr
Cocoa, FL 32926-8705, USA

Kohler, Jurgen (Soccer Player)
Borussia Dortmund
Postfach 100509
Dortmund 44005, GERMANY

Kohlhaas, Jeannette (Athlete, Golfer)
24247 Purple Finch Dr
Aldie, VA 20105-5913, USA

Kohli, Virat (Athlete)
c/o Bunty Sajdeh *Cornerstone Sport and Entertainment Pvt Ltd*
H1, Heliopolis, 157 A
Colaba Rd
Mumbai Maharashtra 400005, INDIA

Kohlmeier, Ryan (Athlete, Baseball Player)
301 Vine St
Cottonwood Falls, KS 66845-9812, USA

Kohlsaat, Peter (Cartoonist)
5536 Richmond Curv
Minneapolis, MN 55410-2534, USA

Kohn, Alfie (Writer)
c/o Staff Member *Houghton Mifflin Company (Trade Division)*
222 Berkeley St Ste 8
Boston, MA 02116-3753, USA

Kohrs, Bob (Athlete, Football Player)
521 W Palm Ln
Phoenix, AZ 85003-1129, USA

Koib, Thomas Claudia A (Coach, Swimmer)
Stanford University
Athletic Dept
Stanford, CA 94305, USA

Koiv, Kerli (Musician)
c/o Staff Member *Island Def Jam Group*
825 8th Ave Fl 28
New York, NY 10019-7416, USA

Koivu, Mikko (Athlete, Hockey Player)
5500 Halifax Ln
Minneapolis, MN 55424-1439, USA

Koivu, Saku (Athlete, Hockey Player)
Thompson, Dorfman, Sweatman
PO Box 639 Stn Main
Attn: Donald Baizley
Winnipeg, MB R3C 2K6, Canada

Kojac, George (Swimmer)
33 Arboles Del Norte
Fort Pierce, FL 34951-2877, USA

Kojis, Don (Athlete, Basketball Player)
8186 Commercial St
La Mesa, CA 91942-2926, USA

Kok, Willem (Politician)
Binnenhof 20
The Hague, EA 02500, Netherlands

Koker, Danny (Musician, Reality Star)
c/o Jenni Levine *WME|IMG*
9601 Wilshire Blvd
Beverly Hills, CA 90210-5213, USA

Kokkonen, Elissa Lee (Musician)
Columbia Artists Mgmt Inc
165 W 57th St
New York, NY 10019-2201, USA

Kokosalaki, Sophia (Designer, Fashion Designer)
c/o Staff Member *Sophia Kokosalaki*
3/138 Long Acre
Convent Garden
London, England, United Kingdom

Kok Oudegeest, Mary (Swimmer)
Escuela Nacional de Natacion
Izarra
Alava, SPAIN

Kolanko, Mary Lou (Baseball Player)
3109 W Henry Ave
Tampa, FL 33614-5924, USA

Kolanos, Krys (Athlete, Hockey Player)
3407 Underhill Dr NW
Calgary, AB T2N 4E9, Canada

Kolat, Cary (Athlete, Olympic Athlete, Wrestler)
160 Durham Eubanks Rd
Pittsboro, NC 27312-6408, USA

Kolb, Brandon (Athlete, Baseball Player)
2043 Pin Oak Pl
Danville, CA 94506-2119, USA

Kolb, Dan (Athlete, Baseball Player)
PO Box 700
Walnut, IL 61376-0700, USA

Kolb, Danny (Athlete, Baseball Player)
1601 51st Dr
Union Grove, WI 53182-9548, USA

Kolb, Gary (Athlete, Baseball Player)
5143 Hopewell Dr
Charleston, WV 25313-1784, USA

Kolb, Jon (Athlete, Football Player)
32 Lee Ave
Grove City, PA 16127-4648, USA

Kolb, Kevin (Athlete, Football Player)
4711 Steepleridge Trl
Granbury, TX 76048-5001, USA

Kolber, Suzy (Sportscaster)
ESPN-TV
Sports Dept
ESPN Plaza 935 Middle St
Bristol, CT 06010, USA

Kole, Warren (Actor)
c/o Staff Member *D/F Management*
8609 Washington Blvd # 8607
Culver City, CA 90232-7441, USA

Kolehmainen, Mikko (Athlete)
Poppelitie 18
Mikkeli 50130, FINLAND

Kolen, Mike (Athlete, Football Player)
1735 Vaughn Ln
Montgomery, AL 36106-2617, USA

Kolesar, Robert (Athlete, Football Player)
5003 Lincoln Ave
Cleveland, OH 44134-1866, USA

Kolinsky, Sue (Producer)
c/o Staff Member *Innovative Artists*
1505 10th St
Santa Monica, CA 90401-2805, USA

Kollar, Bill (Athlete, Football Player)
4899 Montrose Blvd Apt 605
Houston, TX 77006-6165, USA

Kolnik, Juraj (Athlete, Hockey Player)
HC Geneve-Servette Chemin de la Graviere 4
Les Acasias CH-1227, Switzerland

Kolodziej, Ross (Athlete, Football Player)
4869 Pine Cone Cir
Middleton, WI 53562-4056, USA

Kolodziewjski, Chris (Athlete, Football Player)
1123 Sandalwood Dr
Lawrenceville, GA 30043-4621, USA

Kolstad, Dean (Athlete, Hockey Player)
15492 Brooklodge Rd
Hickory Corners, MI 49060-9740, USA

Kolstad, Hal (Athlete, Baseball Player)
15149 Bel Escou Dr
San Jose, CA 95124-5032, USA

Kolsti, Paul (Cartoonist)
Dallas News
Editorial Dept
Communications Center
Dallas, TX 75265, USA

Koltsov, Konstantin (Athlete, Hockey Player)
1135 Park Overlook Dr NE
Atlanta, GA 30324-5683, USA

Kolvenbach, Peter-Hans (Religious Leader)
Borgo Santo Spirito 5
CP 6139
Rome 00195, ITALY

Kolzig, Olaf (Athlete, Hockey Player)
Pro-Rep Group
201-280 Midpark Way SE
Attn Art Breeze
Calgary, AB T2X 1J6, Canada

Komadoski, Neil (Athlete, Hockey Player)
876 Judson Manor Dr
Saint Louis, MO 63141-6057, USA

Komal (Royalty)
Royal Palace
Narayanhiti
Durbag Marg
Kathmandu, NEPAL

Koman, Bill (Athlete, Football Player)
5 Upper Ladue Rd
Saint Louis, MO 63124-1677, USA

Koman, Michael (Writer)
c/o Staff Member *ICM Partners*
10250 Constellation Blvd Fl 7
Los Angeles, CA 90067-6207, USA

Komarniski, Zenith (Athlete, Hockey Player)
1590 37B Ave NW
Edmonton, AB T6T 0E2, CANADA

Komenich, Nadia (Gymnast)
The Bart Conner Gymnastics Academy
PO Box 720217
Norman, OK 73070-4166, USA

Kometani, Pam (Athlete, Golfer)
4342 Kilauea Ave
Honolulu, HI 96816-5113, USA

Komine, Shane (Athlete, Baseball Player)
641 8th Ave
Honolulu, HI 96816-2109, USA

Komisarek, Mike (Athlete, Hockey Player)
Olympic Sports Management
9 Alden Rd
Wellesley, MA 02481-6702, USA

Komisarz, Rachel (Athlete, Olympic Athlete, Swimmer)
9402 Magnolia Ridge Dr Unit 201
Louisville, KY 40291-6756, USA

Komlos, Peter (Musician)
Torokvesz Ulca 94
Budapest 01025, HUNGARY

Komminsk, Brad (Athlete, Baseball Player)
150 Park Ave
Attn Coaching Staff
Norfolk, VA 23510-2712, USA

Komminsk, Brad (Athlete, Baseball Player)
688 Fallside Ln
Westerville, OH 43081-5003, USA

Kompara, John (Athlete, Football Player)
13030 Coldwater Loop
Clermont, FL 34711-8014, USA

Komunyakaa, Yusef (Writer)
900 W State St
Trenton, NJ 08618-5328, USA

Konare, Alpha Oumar (President)
President's Office
BP
Bamako, MALI

Koncak, Jon (Athlete, Basketball Player, Olympic Athlete)
PO Box 10040
Jackson, WY 83002-0040, USA

Koncar, Mark (Athlete, Football Player)
447 N Alpine Blvd
Alpine, UT 84004-1264, USA

Konchalovsky, Andrei (Director, Producer, Writer)

Kondakova, Elena V (Astronaut)
Russian Space Agency
42 Shchapkinst
Moscow 129857, Russia

Kondia, Tom (Athlete, Basketball Player)
3517 Cleveland Ave
Brookfield, IL 60513-1103, USA

Kondracki, Larysa (Director, Producer)
c/o Cassandra Vargas *PMK/BNC Public Relations*
1840 Century Park E Ste 1400
Los Angeles, CA 90067-2115, USA

Konefal, Victoria (Actor)
c/o Jessica Katz *Katz Public Relations*
14527 Dickens St
Sherman Oaks, CA 91403-3756, USA

Konerko, Paul (Athlete, Baseball Player)
8053 E Leaning Rock Rd
Scottsdale, AZ 85266-1645, USA

Koneski, Jr., Walter (Race Car Driver)
Koneski Racing
368 Broezel Ave
Lancaster, NY 14086-1322, USA

Kongos (Music Group)
c/o Corrie Christopher Martin *Paradigm*
8942 Wilshire Blvd
Beverly Hills, CA 90211-1908, USA

Konieczny, Doug (Athlete, Baseball Player)
9503 Dundalk St
Spring, TX 77379-4314, USA

Konitz, Lee (Musician)
Bennett Morgan
1282 RR 376
Wappingers Falls, NY 12590, USA

Konner, Jennifer (Jenni) (Producer)
c/o Tom Lassally *3 Arts Entertainment*
9460 Wilshire Blvd Fl 7
Beverly Hills, CA 90212-2713, USA

Konopasek, Ed (Athlete, Football Player)
2336 Meadowledge Ct
De Pere, WI 54115-8690, USA

Konowalchuk, Steve (Athlete, Hockey Player)
2628 S Adams St
Denver, CO 80210-6232, USA

Konowalchuk, Steve (Athlete, Hockey Player)
Seattle Thunderbirds
625 W James St
Attn: Coaching Staff
Kent, WA 98032-4406, USA

Konrad, John H (Astronaut)
Hughes Space-Communications Group
PO Box 92919
Los Angeles, CA 90009-2919, USA

Konrad, Rob (Athlete, Football Player)
11884 Windmill Lake Dr
Boynton Beach, FL 33473-7846, USA

Konroyd, Steve (Athlete, Hockey Player)
Chicago Blackhawks
1901 W Madison St
Attn: Broadcast Dept
Chicago, IL 60612-2459, USA

Konroyd, Steve (Athlete, Hockey Player)
317 S Park Ave
Hinsdale, IL 60521-4638, USA

Konstantinov, Vladimir (Athlete, Hockey Player)
6782 Enclave
West Bloomfield, MI 48322-1399, USA

Kontos, Chris (Athlete, Hockey Player)
40 Beck Blvd
Penetanguishene, ON L9M 1E1, Canada

Konuszewski, Dennis (Athlete, Baseball Player)
3054 Yorkshire Dr
Bay City, MI 48706-9244, USA

Konz, Peter (Athlete, Football Player)
c/o Joe Flanagan *BTI Sports Advisors*
615 South Blvd Apt C
Oak Park, IL 60302-4606, USA

Kooistra, Scott (Athlete, Football Player)
106 Overlook Dr
Loveland, OH 45140-6689, USA

Kook, Shannon (Actor)
c/o Jordyn Palos *Persona Public Relations*
6255 W Sunset Blvd Ste 705
Hollywood, CA 90028-7408, USA

Kooks, The (Music Group)
c/o Jonny Kaps *+1 Management and PR*
242 Wythe Ave
Studio 6
Brooklyn, NY 11249-3149, USA

Kool & The Gang (Music Group)
Gang Touring
50 Church St Ste L011
Montclair, NJ 07042-2745, USA

Koolhoven, Martin (Director)
c/o Daniel Koefoed *Montecatini Management*
Teerketelsteeg 1
Amsterdam 1012 TB, The Netherlands

Koonce, George (Athlete, Football Player)
925 E Wells St Apt 217
Milwaukee, WI 53202-3953, USA

Koonce, Graham (Athlete, Baseball Player)
2474 Pimlico Pl
Alpine, CA 91901-3952, USA

Koons, Jeff (Artist)
600 Broadway
New York, NY 10012-3206, USA

Koontz, Dean (Writer)
PO Box 9529
Newport Beach, CA 92658-9529, USA

Koontz, Ed (Athlete, Football Player)
2860 Blackshear Ave
Pensacola, FL 32503-4874, USA

Kooper, Al (Musician)
Legacy Records
550 Madison Ave Frnt 1
New York, NY 10022-3211, USA

Koopmans-Kint, Cor (Swimmer)
Pacific Sands C'Van Park
Nambucca Heads, NSW 02448, AUSTRALIA

Koos, Torin (Athlete, Olympic Athlete, Skier)
1510 Madison St
Wenatchee, WA 98801-1731, USA

Kooser, Ted (Writer)
1820 Branched Oak Rd
Garland, NE 68360-9303, USA

Koosman, Jerry (Athlete, Baseball Player)
2483 State Road 35
Osceola, WI 54020-2205, USA

Kopacz, George (Athlete, Baseball Player)
14150 Somerset Ct
Orland Park, IL 60467-1142, USA

Kopas, Jack (Horse Racer)
PO Box 249
Ilderton, ON N0M 2A0, Canada

Kopay, Dave (Athlete, Football Player)
2035 Ridgeview Ave
Los Angeles, CA 90041-3018, USA

Kopecky, Tomas (Athlete, Hockey Player)
4401 N Federal Hwy Ste 201
Boca Raton, FL 33431-5164, USA

Kopell, Bernie (Actor)
19413 Olivos Dr
Tarzana, CA 91356-4403, USA

Kopeloff, Eric (Director)
c/o Staff Member *WME/IMG*
9601 Wilshire Blvd
Beverly Hills, CA 90210-5213, USA

Koper, Herbert (Athlete, Basketball Player)
11707 Rushmore
Oklahoma City, OK 73162-1636, USA

Kopervas, Gary (Cartoonist)
c/o Staff Member *King Features Syndication*
300 W 57th St Fl 15
New York, NY 10019-5238, USA

Kopicki, Joe (Athlete, Basketball Player)
47608 Cheryl Ct
Shelby Township, MI 48315-4708, USA

Kopins, Karen (Actor)
Sutton Barth Vennari
122 Old Mountain Tom Rd
Bantam, CT 06750, USA

Kopit, Arthur (Writer)
240 W 98th St Apt 11B
New York, NY 10025-5516, USA

Kopitar, Anze (Athlete, Hockey Player)
c/o Staff Member *Los Angeles Kings*
1111 S Figueroa St Ste 3100
Los Angeles, CA 90015-1333, USA

Koplitz, Lynne (Actor)
c/o Staff Member *Paradigm (Monterey)*
404 W Franklin St
Monterey, CA 93940-2303, USA

Koplove, Mike (Athlete, Baseball Player)
3235 Chaucer St
Philadelphia, PA 19145-5841, USA

Kopp, David (Actor)
c/o Deb Dillistone *Red Management*
415 Esplanade W Box 3
North Vancouver, BC V7M 1A6, CANADA

Kopp, Jeff (Athlete, Football Player)
9409 Hannahs Mill Dr Apt 403
Owings Mills, MD 21117-6855, USA

Kopp, Larry (Race Car Driver)
Lary Kopp Racing
5511 McCormick Ave.
Baltimore, MS 31206, USA

Koppel, Ted (Correspondent, Journalist)
c/o Staff Member *ABC TV (NY)*
44th St & Broadway
New York, NY 10112, USA

Koppelman, Chaim (Artist)
498 Broome St
New York, NY 10013-2672, USA

Koppelman, Charles (Business Person)

Koppen, Dan (Athlete, Football Player)

Koppes, Peter (Musician)
Globeshine
101 Chamberlayne Road
London NW10 3ND, UNITED KINGDOM (UK)

Koppikar, Isha (Actor)
c/o Staff Member *Canyon Entertainment*
PO Box 256
Palm Springs, CA 92263-0256, USA

Kopple, Barbara J (Director)
Cabin Creek Films
155 Avenue of the Americas
New York, NY 10013-1507, USA

Kopra, Timothy L (Astronaut)
2518 Lakeside Dr
Seabrook, TX 77586-3392, USA

Kopra, Timothy L Lt Colonel (Astronaut)
4912 Cross Creek Ln
League City, TX 77573-6267, USA

Korab, Jerry (Athlete, Hockey Player)
Korab Inc
213 Maison Ct
Palm Beach Gardens, FL 33410-2215, USA

Korach, Ken (Commentator)
1963 Troon Dr
Henderson, NV 89074-1040, USA

Korbut, Olga (Athlete, Gymnast, Olympic Athlete)
Olga Korbut Foundation
1124 Columbia St
Seattle, WA 98104-2026, USA

Korcheck, Steve (Athlete, Baseball Player)
2807 Saint Cloud Oaks Dr
Valrico, FL 33594-3840, USA

Korda, Petr (Athlete, Tennis Player)
4909 61st Avenue Dr W
Bradenton, FL 34210-4041, USA

Korec Jan, Chryzostom Cardinal (Religious Leader)
Biskupstvo Nitra
PP 46A
Nitra 95050, SLOVAKIA

Koreeda, Hirokazu (Director)
Directors' Guild of Japan
3-2 5F
Maruyamacho
Shibuya, Tokyo 150-0044, JAPAN

Koren, Edward B (Cartoonist)
New Yorker Magazine
4 Times Sq
Editorial Dept
New York, NY 10036-6518, USA

Koren, Steve (Producer, Writer)
c/o Staff Member *Creative Artists Agency (CAA)*
2000 Avenue of the Stars Ste 100
Los Angeles, CA 90067-4705, USA

Korf, Mia (Actor)
Paradigm Agency
10100 Santa Monica Blvd Ste 2500
Los Angeles, CA 90067-4116, USA

Korince, George (Athlete, Baseball Player)
3033 Townline Rd
Stevensville, ON L0S 1S1, Canada

Korjus, Tapio (Athlete, Track Athlete)
General Delivery
Lapua, FINLAND

Korloff, Sara (Actor)
Boris Karloff Enterprises
PO Box 2424
Rancho Mirage, CA 92270-1087, USA

Kormann, Peter (Athlete, Gymnast)
c/o Sheryl Shade *Shade Global*
171 W 57th St Apt 8A
New York, NY 10019-2222, USA

Korn (Music Group)
c/o Rod MacSween *International Talent Booking*
9 Kingsway
Fl 6
London WC2B 6XF, UNITED KINGDOM

Korn, Jim (Athlete, Hockey Player)
19670 Sweetwater Curv
Excelsior, MN 55331-8113, USA

Kornberg, Hannah (Actor)
c/o Holly Williams *Williams Unlimited*
5010 Buffalo Ave
Sherman Oaks, CA 91423-1414

Kornet, Frank (Athlete, Basketball Player)
9580 Stanton Rd
Lantana, TX 76226-7304, USA

Korney, Mike (Athlete, Hockey Player)
2565 Departure Bay Rd
Nanaimo, BC V9S 3W2, Canada

Kornheiser, Tony (Sportscaster, Writer)
Washington Post
Editorial Dept
1150 15th St NW
Washington, DC 20071-0001, USA

Korokoro, Florence (Actor)
c/o Belinda Foster *B&M Creative Artists*
8350 Wilshire Blvd
Suite 200
Los Angeles, CA 90048, USA

Koroll, Cliff (Athlete, Hockey Player)
23W569 Glendale Ter
Roselle, IL 60172-3541, USA

Koromzay, Alix (Actor)
334 Vernon Ave
Venice, CA 90291-2637, USA

Koronka, John (Athlete, Baseball Player)
1403 lOth St
Clermont, FL 34711-2808, USA

Korpan, Richard (Business Person)
Florida Progress Corp
100 Central Ave
Saint Petersburg, FL 33701-3324, USA

Kors, Michael (Designer, Fashion Designer)
Michael Kors Inc
11 W 42nd St Fl 28
New York, NY 10036-8002, USA

Kors, R J (Athlete, Football Player)
956 Gardenia Way
Corona Del Mar, CA 92625-1546, USA

Korsantiya, Alexander (Musician)
Columbia Artists Mgmt Inc
165 W 57th St
New York, NY 10019-2201, USA

Korsh, Aaron (Producer, Writer)
c/o Dennis Kim *Storied Media Group*
2866 Colorado Ave
Santa Monica, CA 90404-3637, USA

Korson, Adam (Actor)
c/o Marni Rosenzweig *The Rosenzweig Group*
8840 Wilshire Blvd # 111
Beverly Hills, CA 90211-2606, USA

Kortas, Ken (Athlete, Football Player)
466 Brooks Ln
Simpsonville, KY 40067-7419, USA

Korte, Steve (Athlete, Football Player)
5640 Oslo Ln
Park City, UT 84098-7708, USA

Korver, Kelvin (Athlete, Football Player)
16934 Pella Rd
Adams, NE 68301-7790, USA

Korver, Kyle (Athlete, Basketball Player)
c/o Jeff Schwartz *Excel Sports Management*
1700 Broadway Fl 29
New York, NY 10019-6559, USA

Kosarin, Kira (Actor, Musician)
c/o Stella Alex *Savage Agency*
1041 N Formosa Ave
West Hollywood, CA 90046-6703, USA

Kosar Jr, Bernie (Athlete, Football Player)
PO Box 8
Nashport, OH 43830-0008, USA

Kosberg, Robert (Producer, Writer)
Robert Kosberg Productions
1438 N Gower St Ste 10
Hollywood, CA 90028-8306, USA

Kosc, Greg (Baseball Player)
3465 Hunting Run Rd
Medina, OH 44256-8200, USA

Kosc, Greg (Athlete, Baseball Player)
3465 Hunting Run Rd
Medina, OH 44256-8200, USA

Kosco, Andy (Athlete, Baseball Player)
10324 Springfield Rd
Youngstown, OH 44514-3158, USA

Koshalek, Richard (Director)
Museum of Contemporary Art
250 S Grand Ave
Los Angeles, CA 90012-3021, USA

Koshansky, Joe (Athlete, Baseball Player)
13314 Point Pleasant Dr
Fairfax, VA 22033-3507, USA

Koshiro IV, Matsumoto (Actor, Dancer)
Kabukiza Theatre
12-15-4 Ginza
Chuoku, Tokyo 00104, JAPAN

Koshy, Liza (Actor)
c/o Katie Greenthal *The Lede Company*
9701 Wilshire Blvd # 930
Beverly Hills, CA 90212-2020, USA

Kosier, Kyle (Athlete, Football Player)
PO Box 93946
Southlake, TX 76092-0119, USA

Kosins, Gary (Athlete, Football Player)
13895 Ruffner Ln
Sebastian, FL 32958-3418, USA

Kosinski, Joseph (Director)
c/o Bryan Besser *Verve Talent & Literary Agency*
6310 San Vicente Blvd Ste 100
Los Angeles, CA 90048-5498, USA

Koski, Tony (Athlete, Basketball Player)
143 King James Dr
South Dennis, MA 02660, USA

Koskie, Corey (Athlete, Baseball Player)
161 Primrose Ln
Hamel, MN 55340-3603, USA

Koskoff, Sarah (Actor)
c/o Cliff Roberts *WME|IMG*
9601 Wilshire Blvd
Beverly Hills, CA 90210-5213, USA

Koslofski, Kevin (Athlete, Baseball Player)
1910 Shore Oak Dr
Decatur, IL 62521-5563, USA

Koslow, Lauren (Actor)
c/o John Crosby *John Crosby Management*
1357 N Spaulding Ave
Los Angeles, CA 90046-4009, USA

Kosmalski, Len (Athlete, Basketball Player)
404 Washington Ave PH 8
Miami Beach, FL 33139-6606, USA

Koss, Johann Olav (Speed Skater)
Dagaliveien 21
Oslo 00387, NORWAY

Koss, Stein (Athlete, Football Player)
5219 N Casa Blanca Dr Apt 31
Paradise Valley, AZ 85253-6201, USA

Kosser, Ted (Writer)
1820 Branched Oak Rd
Garland, NE 68360-9303, USA

Kostadinova, Stefka (Athlete, Track Athlete)
Rue Anghel Kantchev 4
Sofia 01000, BULGARIA

Kostelic, Janica (Skier)
Ski Association
Trg Sportova 11
Zagreb 01000, CROATIA

Kostiuk, Mike (Athlete, Football Player)
24663 Beierman Ave
Warren, MI 48091-1716, USA

Kostner, Isolde (Skier)
General Delivery
Hortisei BZ, ITALY

Kostopoulos, Tom (Athlete, Hockey Player)
8336 Wheatstone Ln
Raleigh, NC 27613-1479, USA

Kostro, Frank (Athlete, Baseball Player)
16876 E Weaver Pl
Aurora, CO 80016-5042, USA

Kosugi, Kane (Actor)
c/o Lou Pitt *The Pitt Group*
275 Homewood Rd
Los Angeles, CA 90049-2709, USA

Kosuth, Joseph (Artist)
591 Broadway
New York, NY 10012-3211, USA

Koszelak, Stanley N (Astronaut)
1125 Mendocino Way
Redlands, CA 92374-4975, USA

Kotalik, Ales (Athlete, Hockey Player)
Octagon Sports Management
66 Slater St 23rd Fl
Attn Larry Kelly
Ottawa, ON K1P 5H1, Canada

Kotarski, Mike (Athlete, Baseball Player)
31 Grove St
Lexington, MA 02420-1623, USA

Kotb, Hoda (Television Host)
c/o Staff Member *The Today Show*
30 Rockefeller Plz
New York, NY 10112-0015, USA

Kotcheff, W Theodore (Ted) (Director)
Ted Kotcheff Productions
13451 Firth Dr
Beverly Hills, CA 90210-1118, USA

Kotchman, Casey (Athlete, Baseball Player)
8442 125th Ct
Seminole, FL 33776-3200, USA

Koteas, Elias (Actor)
c/o Perri Kipperman *Kipperman Management*
345 7th Ave Rm 503
New York, NY 10001-5054, USA

Koterba, Jeff (Cartoonist)
Omaha World Herald
Editorial Dept
14th & Dodge St Wichita
Omaha, NE 68102, USA

Kotero, Apollonia (Actor, Model)
c/o Staff Member *Mary Grady Agency (MGA)*
4400 Coldwater Canyon Ave Ste 135
the Landmark Bldg
Studio City, CA 91604-5038, USA

Kotil, Ariene (Baseball Player)
2801 W Jefferson St
Joliet, IL 60435-5299, USA

Kotil, Arlene (Athlete, Baseball Player, Commentator)
2801 W Jefferson St
Joliet, IL 60435-5299, USA

Kotite, Richard E (Rich) (Athlete, Coach, Football Coach, Football Player)
2119 Via Palma Dr
North Myrtle Beach, SC 29582-7803, USA

Kotlarek, Gene (Skier)
4910 Walking Horse Pt
Colorado Springs, CO 80923-1110, USA

Kotlarek, George (Skier)
330 N Arlington Ave Apt 512
Duluth, MN 55811-5127, USA

Kotsay, Mark (Athlete, Baseball Player)
6659 Calle Ponte Bella
Rancho Santa Fe, CA 92091-0208, USA

Kotsonis, Ieronymous (Religious Leader)
Archdiocese of Athens
Hatzichristou 8
Athens 402, Greece 53212, USA

Kotsopoulos, Chris (Athlete, Hockey Player)
1713 Midnight Ln
Stroudsburg, PA 18360-7771, USA

Kottaras, George (Athlete, Baseball Player)
11677 E Del Timbre Dr
Scottsdale, AZ 85259-5908, USA

Kottke, Leo (Musician, Songwriter)
c/o Staff Member *Paradigm (Monterey)*
404 W Franklin St
Monterey, CA 93940-2303, USA

Kotto, Yaphet F (Actor)
c/o Larry Goldhar *Characters Talent Agency (Toronto)*
8 Elm St Fl 2
Toronto, ON M5G 1G7, CANADA

Kotzky, Alex S (Cartoonist)
20317 56th Ave
Oakland Gardens, NY 11364-1641, USA

Kouandjio, Cyrus (Athlete, Football Player)
c/o Bus Cook *Bus Cook Sports, Inc*
1 Willow Bend Dr
Hattiesburg, MS 39402-8552, USA

Koufax, Sandy (Athlete, Baseball Player)
c/o Harlan Werner *Sports Placement Service*
330 W 11th St Apt 105
Los Angeles, CA 90015-3200, USA

Kounen, Jan (Actor, Director, Producer, Writer)
c/o Robert Newman *WME|IMG*
9601 Wilshire Blvd
Beverly Hills, CA 90210-5213, USA

Kournikova, Anna (Athlete, Tennis Player)
c/o Teal Cannaday *Teal Entertainment*
2708 Wilshire Blvd
Santa Monica, CA 90403-4706, USA

Koutouvides, Niko (Athlete, Football Player)
129 9th Ln
Kirkland, WA 98033-3992, USA

Kouzmanoff, Kevin (Athlete, Baseball Player)
28606 Evergreen Manor Dr
Evergreen, CO 80439-8387, USA

Kovac, Ed (Athlete, Football Player)
2654 Gracewood Ave
Cincinnati, OH 45239-7240, USA

Kovacic, Ernst (Musician)
Ingpen & Williams
14 Kensington Court
London W8 5DN, UNITED KINGDOM (UK)

Kovack, Nancy (Actor)
270 Oakmont Dr
Los Angeles, CA 90049, USA

Kovacs, Andras (Director)
Magyar Jakobinusok Ter 2/3
Budapest 01122, HUNGARY

Kovacs, Denes (Musician)
Iranyi Utca 12
Budapest V, HUNGARY

Kovacs, Mijou (Actor)
c/o Staff Member *JFPM*
11 rue Chanez
Paris Cedex 16
Paris 75781, FRANCE

Kovalchick-Roark, Dorothy (Athlete, Commentator, Golfer)
112 Maridale Dr
West Monroe, LA 71291-2350, USA

Kovalchuk, Ilya (Athlete, Hockey Player)
8 Frick Dr
Alpine, NJ 07620, USA

Kovalenko, Alexei (Athlete, Hockey Player)
1 Trimont Ln Apt 2000A
Pittsburgh, PA 15211-1279, USA

Kovalev, Alexei (Athlete, Hockey Player)
Eclipse Sports Management
331 Madison Ave Fl 3
New York, NY 10017-5116, USA

Kovalev, Sergey (Athlete, Boxer)
c/o Egis Klimas *Egis Klimas*
Prefers to be contacted by telephone or email
Edmond, WA, USA

Kove, Martin (Actor)
c/o Deb Bailey *Janette Anderson Entertainment*
9682 Via Torino
Burbank, CA 91504-1410, USA

Kovic, Ron (Writer)
507 N Lucia Ave
Redondo Beach, CA 90277-3009, USA

Kowalczyk, Ed (Musician)
Freedman & Smith
350 W End Ave Apt 1
New York, NY 10024-6818, USA

Kowalczyk, Jozef (Religious Leader)
Nuncjatura Apostolska
Al Ch Szucha 12
#163
Warsaw 00-582, POLAND

Kowalczyk, Walt (Athlete, Football Player)
144 W Maryknoll Rd
Rochester Hills, MI 48309-1938, USA

Kowalkowski, Robert (Athlete, Football Player)
2410 Correll Dr
Lake Orion, MI 48360-2258, USA

Kowalkowski, Scott (Athlete, Football Player)
3995 Kelsey Rd
Lake Orion, MI 48360-2516, USA

Kowalski, Ted (Musician)
GEMS
PO Box 1031
Montrose, CA 91021-1031, USA

Kowitz, Brian (Athlete, Baseball Player)
1657 Bullock Cir
Owings Mills, MD 21117-1609, USA

Koy, Ernie (Athlete, Football Player)
PO Box 6
Kenney, TX 77452-0006, USA

Koy, Jo (Comedian)
c/o Joe Meloche *Arsonhouse Entertainment*
11150 W Olympic Blvd Ste 1140
Los Angeles, CA 90064-1800, USA

Koy, Ted (Athlete, Football Player)
1225 County Road 155
Georgetown, TX 78626-1937, USA

Koyama, Debbie (Athlete, Golfer)
118 Tranquila Dr
Camarillo, CA 93012-5174, USA

Koz, Dave (Musician)
c/o Staff Member *Agency for the Performing Arts (APA)*
405 S Beverly Dr Ste 500
Beverly Hills, CA 90212-4425, USA

Kozak, Don (Athlete, Hockey Player)
1510 E Beacon Dr
Gilbert, AZ 85234-2674, USA

Kozak, Harley Jane (Actor)
21336 Colina Dr
Topanga, CA 90290, USA

Kozak, Julie (Journalist)
Extra c/o Warner Bros
4000 Warner Blvd
Burbank, CA 91522-0002, USA

Kozak, Les (Athlete, Hockey Player)
1072 Kimbro Dr
Baton Rouge, LA 70808-6042, USA

Kozak, Scott (Athlete, Football Player)
18617 S Grasle Rd
Oregon City, OR 97045-8898, USA

Kozelko, Tom (Athlete, Basketball Player)
6200 Peninsula Dr
Traverse City, MI 49686-1916, USA

Kozer, Sarah (Actor)
8383 Wilshire Blvd Ste 510
C/O Ric Tanner
Beverly Hills, CA 90211-2406, USA

Kozerski, Bruce (Athlete, Football Player)
3088 Waterbury Ct
Edgewood, KY 41017-8124, USA

Kozlicki, Ron (Athlete, Basketball Player)
5002 Hidden Branches Dr
Atlanta, GA 30338-3910, USA

Kozlov, Viktor (Athlete, Hockey Player)
106 W 74th St
Attn Paul Theofanous
New York, NY 10023-2334, USA

Kozlov, Vyacheslav (Athlete, Hockey Player)
4240 Irma Ct
Atlanta, GA 30327-3713, USA

Kozlova, Anna (Athlete, Olympic Athlete, Swimmer)
c/o Staff Member *Premier Management Group (PMG Sports)*
700 Evanvale Ct
Cary, NC 27518-2806, USA

Kozlowski, Ben (Athlete, Baseball Player)
9083 Briarwood Dr
Seminole, FL 33772-2810, USA

Kozlowski, Brian (Athlete, Football Player)
210 Via Ithaca
Newport Beach, CA 92663-4908, USA

Kozlowski, Christine (Beauty Pageant Winner)
PO Box 742
Vicksburg, MS 39181-0742, USA

Kozlowski, Glen (Athlete, Football Player)
455 Belmont Pl Unit 262
Provo, UT 84606-7612, USA

Kozlowski, Linda (Actor)
7022 Grasswood Ave
Malibu, CA 90265-4247, USA

Kozlowski, Mike (Athlete, Football Player)
563 N 2430 W
Provo, UT 84601-7278, USA

Koznick, Kristina (Athlete, Olympic Athlete, Skier)
PO Box 85
Wolcott, CO 81655-0085, USA

Kozol, Jonathan (Writer)
16 Lowell St
Cambridge, MA 02138-4741, USA

Kraatz, Victor (Figure Skater)
Connecticut Skating Center
300 Alumni Rd
Newington, CT 06111-1868, USA

Kraayeveld, Dave (Athlete, Football Player)
10515 124th Ave NE
Kirkland, WA 98033-4628, USA

Krabbe, Jeroen (Actor)
Van Eeghaustraat 107
Amsterdam, EZ 01071, NETHERLANDS

Krabbe, Katrin (Athlete, Olympic Athlete)
JahnstraBe 6
Neubrandenburg D-17033, Germany

Krabbe-Zimmermann, Katrin (Athlete, Track Athlete)
Dorfstr 9
Pinnow 17091, GERMANY

Krackow, Jurgen (Business Person)
Schumannstr 100
Dusseldorf 40237, GERMANY

Kraemer, Joe (Athlete, Baseball Player)
3212 NE 401st Cir
La Center, WA 98629-5241, USA

Kraft, Craig A (Artist)
1239 Good Hope Rd SE
Washington, DC 20020-6907, USA

Kraft, Greg (Athlete, Golfer)
331 Cleveland St Apt 655
Clearwater, FL 33755-4027, USA

Kraft, Jonathan (Business Person, Football Executive)
27 Woodland Rd
Chestnut Hill, MA 02467-2318, USA

Kraft, Lindsey (Actor)
c/o Dominique Appel *Imprint PR*
6121 W Sunset Blvd
Neuehouse
Los Angeles, CA 90028-6442, USA

Kraft, Robert (Musician)
Kraftbox Entertainment
1416 N La Brea Ave
C/O Henson Studios
Hollywood, CA 90028-7506, USA

Kraft, Robert (Business Person, Football Executive)
260 Heath St
Chestnut Hill, MA 02467-2823, USA

Kraft, Ryan (Athlete, Hockey Player)
16219 Hawthorn Path
Lakeville, MN 55044-7573, USA

Kragen, Greg (Athlete, Football Player)
601 47th St
Sacramento, CA 95819-3141, USA

Kragen, Ken (Director, Producer)
c/o Staff Member *Kragen & Company*
2103 Ridge Dr
Los Angeles, CA 90049-1153, USA

Krahl, Jim (Athlete, Football Player)
514 Rolling Mill Dr
Sugar Land, TX 77498-3072, USA

Krainin, Julian (President)
Krainin Productions
25211 Summerhill Ln
Stevenson Ranch, CA 91381-2262, USA

Krajicek, Lukas (Athlete, Hockey Player)
5319 Fishersound Ln
Apollo Beach, FL 33572-3344, USA

Krajicek, Richard (Tennis Player)
Octagon
1751 Pinnacle Dr Ste 1500
McLean, VA 22102-3833, USA

Krakau, Merv (Athlete, Football Player)
706 Prairie St
Guthrie Center, IA 50115-1711, USA

Krakauer, Jon (Writer)
c/o Joseph (Joe) Veltre *Gersh*
41 Madison Ave Ste 3301
New York, NY 10010-2210, USA

Krake, Skip (Athlete, Hockey Player)
5401 37 St
Lloydminster, AB T9V 1T8, Canada

Krakoski, Joe (Athlete, Football Player)
1359 Garden Wall Cir
Reston, VA 20194-1979, USA

Krakow, Erin (Actor)
c/o Naisha Arnold *Untitled Entertainment*
350 S Beverly Dr Ste 200
Beverly Hills, CA 90212-4819, USA

Krakowski, Jane (Actor, Musician)
c/o Lauren Auslander *LUNA*
116 Nassau St # 615
New York, NY 10038-2402, USA

Krall, Diana (Musician)
c/o Sam Feldman *Feldman Agency (Toronto)*
200-1505 2nd Ave W
Vancouver, BC V6H 3Y4, CANADA

Krall, Gerald (Athlete, Football Player)
9236 Mandell Rd
Perrysburg, OH 43551-3913, USA

Kraly, Steve (Athlete, Baseball Player)
15 Boland Rd
Apalachin, NY 13732-4120, USA

Kramarsky, David (Director, Producer)
1630 Berkeley St Apt 1
Santa Monica, CA 90404-4134, USA

Kramer, Barry (Athlete, Basketball Player)
101 Deanna Ct
Schenectady, NY 12309-1333, USA

Kramer, Billy J (Musician)
Mars Talent
27 L Ambiance Ct
Bardonia, NY 10954-1421, USA

Kramer, Brad (Horse Racer)
11295 E Lytle Rd
Lennon, MI 48449-9512, USA

Kramer, Chris (Actor)
c/o Deb Dillistone *Red Management*
415 Esplanade W Box 3
North Vancouver, BC V7M 1A6, CANADA

Kramer, Clare (Actor)
c/o Staff Member *GN Media*
13709 Burbank Blvd
Van Nuys, CA 91401-5040, USA

Kramer, Eric Allen (Actor)
c/o Steve Rodriguez *McGowan Management*
170 S Beverly Dr Ste 304
Beverly Hills, CA 90212-3000, USA

Kramer, Erik (Athlete, Football Player)
5950 Kingham Ct
Agoura Hills, CA 91301-4436, USA

Kramer, Gerald L (Jerry) (Athlete, Football Player)
11768 Chinden Blvd
Boise, ID 83714, USA

Kramer, Jana (Actor, Musician)
c/o Nicole Perez-Krueger *PMK/BNC Public Relations*
1840 Century Park E Ste 1400
Los Angeles, CA 90067-2115, USA

Kramer, Jim (Writer)
c/o Staff Member *3 Arts Entertainment*
9460 Wilshire Blvd Fl 7
Beverly Hills, CA 90212-2713, USA

Kramer, Joel (Athlete, Basketball Player)
3817 E Highland Ave
Phoenix, AZ 85018-3619, USA

Kramer, Joey (Musician)
28202 Canyon Vw
Magnolia, TX 77355-3054, USA

Kramer, John A (Jack) (Tennis Player)
231 Glenroy Pl
Los Angeles, CA 90049-2419, USA

Kramer, Kent (Athlete, Football Player)
200 Troon Rd
McKinney, TX 75072-6783, USA

Kramer, Kyle (Athlete, Football Player)
2170 Little Miami Dr
Spring Valley, OH 45370-9789, USA

Kramer, Larry (Activist, Writer)
Gay Men's Health Crisis
119 W 24th St Lbby 1
New York, NY 10011-1913, USA

Kramer, Randy (Athlete, Baseball Player)
143 Camino Pacifico
Aptos, CA 95003-5886, USA

Kramer, Stepfanie (Actor, Director)
c/o Susan Patricola *Patricola Public Relations*
369 S Doheny Dr # 1408
Beverly Hills, CA 90211-3508, USA

Kramer, Thomas (Tommy) (Athlete, Football Player)
130 Canteen
Canyon Lake, TX 78133-4335, USA

Kramer, Tom (Athlete, Baseball Player)
10665 Hamilton Ave
Cincinnati, OH 45231-1703, USA

Kramer, Wayne (Musician)
Performers of the World
8901 Melrose Ave # 200
West Hollywood, CA 90069-5605, USA

Kramer-Hartman, Ruth (Athlete, Baseball Player, Commentator)
PO Box 38
Limekiln, PA 19535-0038, USA

Kranchick, Matt (Athlete, Football Player)
579 Crossroad School Rd
Carlisle, PA 17015-9433, USA

Kranepool, Ed (Athlete, Baseball Player)
177 High Pond Dr
Jericho, NY 11753-2806, USA

Kranitz, Rick (Athlete, Baseball Player)
35481 N 87th Pl
Scottsdale, AZ 85266-1096, USA

Krantz, Judith (Writer)
166 Groverton Pl
Los Angeles, CA 90077-3732, USA

Kranz, Fran (Actor)
245 Strada Corta Rd
Los Angeles, CA 90077-3726, USA

Kranz, Ken (Athlete, Football Player)
N57W24143 N Sycamore Cir
Sussex, WI 53089-5160, USA

Krapek, Karl (Business Person)
United Technologies Corp
United Technologies Building
Hartford, CT 06101, USA

Krasinski, John (Actor)
c/o Molly Kawachi *ID Public Relations (NY)*
40 Wall St Fl 51
New York, NY 10005-1385, USA

Krasniqi, Luan (Boxer)
Oschlewg 10
Rottweil 78628, GERMANY

Krasnoff, Eric (Business Person)
Pall Corp
2200 Northem Blvd
Greenvale, NY 11548, USA

Krasny, Yuri (Artist)
Sloane Gallery
1612 17th St
Oxford Office Building
Denver, CO 80202-1204, USA

Kratch, Bob (Athlete, Football Player)
1640 Waterbury
Waconia, MN 55387-1244, USA

Kratka, Paul (Actor)

Kratochvilova, Jarmila (Athlete, Track Athlete)
Goleuv Jenikov
582 82, CZECH REPUBLIC

Kratz, Erik (Athlete, Baseball Player)
1840 Manor Dr
Harrisonburg, VA 22801-7625, USA

Kratzert, Bill (Athlete, Golfer)
7470 Founders Way
Ponte Vedra Beach, FL 32082-1914, USA

Kraulis, Andrew (Actor)
c/o Amanda Rosenthal *Amanda Rosenthal Talent Agency*
315 Harbord St
Toronto, ON M6G 1G9, CANADA

Kraus, Daniel (Athlete, Basketball Player)
2525 Pot Spring Rd Unit S233
Lutherville Timonium, MD 21093-2890, USA

Kraus, Peter (Actor)
Kaiserplatz 7
Munich D-80803, Germany

Krause, Alison (Musician)
Grand Ole Opry
2804 Opryland Dr
Nashville, TN 37214-1209, USA

Krause, Brian (Actor)
c/o Andi Schecter *Jonas Public Relations*
1327 Ocean Ave Ste F
Santa Monica, CA 90401-1024, USA

Krause, Dieter (Athlete)
Karl-Marx-Allee 21
Berlin 01017, GERMANY

Krause, Larry (Athlete, Football Player)
N9169 Mill Rd
Summit Lake, WI 54485-9717, USA

Krause, Louisa (Actor)
c/o Jennifer Konawal *Washington Square Arts (NY)*
310 Bowery Fl 2
New York, NY 10012-2861, USA

Krause, Nick (Actor)
c/o Rebecca Many Rosenberg *Artists First*
9465 Wilshire Blvd Ste 900
Beverly Hills, CA 90212-2608, USA

Krause, Paul J (Athlete, Football Player)
18099 Judicial Way N
Lakeville, MN 55044-7105, USA

Krause, Peter (Actor)
c/o Kimberly Christman *42West*
1840 Century Park E Ste 700
Los Angeles, CA 90067-2122, USA

Krause, Ryan (Football Player)
14508 Jefferson St
Omaha, NE 68137-3968, USA

Kraushaar, Sitke (Athlete)
Friedr-Ludwig-Jahn-Str 34
Sonneberg 02692, GERMANY

Krauss, Alison (Musician)
3700 Richland Ave
Nashville, TN 37205-2438, USA

Krauss, Barry (Athlete, Football Player)
753 Whitehall Pl
Carmel, IN 46033-3064, USA

Krausse, Lew (Athlete, Baseball Player)
12811 NE 186th St
Holt, MO 64048-8956, USA

Krausse, Stefan (Athlete)
Kart-Zink-Str 2
Ilmenau 96883, GERMANY

Kravchuk, Igor (Athlete, Hockey Player)
300 Ch de la Riviere Rouge
Harrington, QC J8G 2S7, Canada

Kravec, Ken (Athlete, Baseball Player)
6752 Taeda Dr
Sarasota, FL 34241-9152, USA

Kravits, Jason (Actor)
6310 San Vicente Blvd Ste 520
Los Angeles, CA 90048-5421, USA

Kravitz, Danny (Athlete, Baseball Player)
8810 Route 487
Dushore, PA 18614-8040, USA

Kravitz, Lenny (Musician, Songwriter)
Kravitz Design
13 Crosby St Rm 401
New York, NY 10013-3145, USA

Kravitz, Zoe (Actor)
c/o Jillian Neal *Untitled Entertainment*
350 S Beverly Dr Ste 200
Beverly Hills, CA 90212-4819, USA

Krawczyk, Ray (Athlete, Baseball Player)
67 Cloudcrest
Aliso Viejo, CA 92656-1323, USA

Krayzelburg, Lenny (Athlete, Olympic Athlete, Swimmer)
c/o Peter Carlisle *Octagon Olympics & Action Sports*
7 Ocean St Ste 2
South Portland, ME 04106-2800, USA

Krebbs, John (Race Car Driver)
3232 Amoruso Way
Diamond Ridge
Roseville, CA 95747-9786, USA

Krebs, Art (Race Car Driver)
327 31st St
Gulfport, MS 39507-2341, USA

Krebs, Robert D (Business Person)
Burlington North/Santa Fe
2650 Lou Menk Dr
Fort Worth, TX 76131-2830, USA

Krebs, Susan (Actor)
4704 Tobias Ave
Sherman Oaks, CA 91403-2825, USA

Kredel, Elmar Maria (Religious Leader)
Obere Karolinenstra 5
Bamber 96033, GERMANY

Kregel, Kevin R (Astronaut)
360 Bluff Ridge Trl
Blanco, TX 78606-5893, USA

Krehbiel, Frederick A (Business Person)
Molex Inc
2222 Wellington Ct
Lisle, IL 60532-1682, USA

Krehbiel, John Hammond (Business Person)
Molex Inc.
2222 Wellington Ct
Lisle, IL 60532-1682, USA

Kreider, Dan (Athlete, Football Player)
102 Fawn Hl
Millersville, PA 17551-9758, USA

Kreider, Steve (Athlete, Football Player)
350 Harrow Ln
Blue Bell, PA 19422-3110, USA

Kreiling, Melia (Actor)
c/o Pip Gill *Pip Gill Publicity*
124 Brondesbury Rd
The Coach House
London NW6 6SB, UNITED KINGDOM

Kreischer, Bert (Comedian, Television Host)
c/o Matt Schuler *Levity Entertainment Group (LEG)*
6701 Center Dr W Ste 300
Los Angeles, CA 90045-2482, USA

Kreitling, Richard (Athlete, Football Player)
301 Ramsey St Apt 303
Hastings, MN 55033-1241, USA

Krejci, David (Athlete, Hockey Player)
c/o Staff Member *Boston Bruins*
100 Legends Way Ste 250
Td Banknorth Garden
Boston, MA 02114-1389, USA

Kreklow, Wayne (Athlete, Basketball Player)
4001 S Old Mill Creek Rd
Columbia, MO 65203-9635, USA

krels, Jason (Soccer Player)
Dallas Burn
14800 Quorum Dr Ste 300
Dallas, TX 75254-1408, USA

Kremer, Andrea (Sportscaster)
ESPN-TV
Sports Dept
ESPN Plaza 935 Middle St
Bristol, CT 06010, USA

Kremer, Gidon (Musician)
I C M Artists
40 W 57th St
New York, NY 10019-4001, USA

Kremer, Howard (Comedian)
c/o Staff Member *ICM Partners*
10250 Constellation Blvd Fl 7
Los Angeles, CA 90067-6207, USA

Kremer, Ken (Athlete, Football Player)
6116 Double Eagle Ct
Kansas City, MO 64152-4970, USA

Kremers, Jimmy (Athlete, Baseball Player)
11601 S 109th East Ave
Bixby, OK 74008-2803, USA

Kremmel, Jim (Athlete, Baseball Player)
524 W 18th Ave
Spokane, WA 99203-2011, USA

Kremser, Karl (Athlete, Football Player)
301 W Glenview Dr
Salisbury, NC 28147-7227, USA

Krenchicki, Wayne (Athlete, Baseball Player)
19256 430th St
Pittsfield, IL 62363-3234, USA

Krenk, Mitch (Athlete, Football Player)
218 N 11th St
Nebraska City, NE 68410-2030, USA

Krentz, Dale (Athlete, Hockey Player)
71 Lodge Pl
Sylvan Lake, AB T4S 2N2, Canada

Krenzel, Craig (Athlete, Football Player)
10174 Jerome Rd
Dublin, OH 43017-7606, USA

Krepfle, Keith (Athlete, Football Player)
82 E Butler Dr
Drums, PA 18222-2603, USA

Krerowicz, Mark (Athlete, Football Player)
1425 Luscombe Dr
Toledo, OH 43614-2618, USA

Kresa, Kent (Business Person)
Northrop Grumman Corp
1840 Century Park E
Los Angeles, CA 90067-2101, USA

Kresge, Chris (Athlete, Golfer)
834 Trailwood Dr
Apopka, FL 32712-3217, USA

Kresge, Cliff (Athlete, Golfer)
c/o Jim Lehrman *Medalist Management Inc*
36855 W Main St Ste 200
Purcellville, VA 20132-3561, USA

Kress, Nathan (Actor)
PO Box 2289
Pasadena, CA 91102-2289, USA

Kressley, Carson (Reality Star, Television Host)
c/o Penny Vizcarra *PV Public Relations*
121 N Almont Dr Apt 203
Beverly Hills, CA 90211-1860, USA

Kretschmann, Thomas (Director)
c/o Jim Osborne *Agency for the Performing Arts (APA)*
405 S Beverly Dr Ste 500
Beverly Hills, CA 90212-4425, USA

Kreuger, Rick (Athlete, Baseball Player)
4664 Sheldon Ct
Hudsonville, MI 49426-7810, USA

Kreuk, Kristin (Actor)
c/o Russ Mortensen *Pacific Artists Management*
112 3rd Ave E Suite 210
Vancouver, BC V5T 1C8, CANADA

Kreuter, Chad (Athlete, Baseball Player)
5800 SW 85th St
Miami, FL 33143-8224, USA

Kreutz, Olin (Athlete, Football Player)
1886 Hilltop Ln
Bannockburn, IL 60015-1522, USA

Kreutzer, Frank (Athlete, Baseball Player)
1937 SW Palm City Rd Apt I
Stuart, FL 34994-4334, USA

Kreutzmann, Bill (Musician)
PO Box 1073
San Rafael, CA 94915-1073, USA

Kreviazuk, Chantal (Musician, Songwriter)
c/o Staff Member *Paradigm (Monterey)*
404 W Franklin St
Monterey, CA 93940-2303, USA

Krevis, Al (Athlete, Football Player)

Krewella (Music Group)
c/o Jason Pinyan *Innovative Artists*
1505 10th St
Santa Monica, CA 90401-2805, USA

Kribel, Joel (Athlete, Golfer)
26254 N 46th St
Phoenix, AZ 85050-8510, USA

Kricfalusi, John (Animator)
c/o Staff Member *Rough Draft Korea*
Kyejin B/D, 425-7
Togok-dong, Kannam-Gu
Seoul 135-270, KOREA

Krick, Jaynie (Athlete, Baseball Player, Commentator)
911 Glen Eagle Ln
Fort Wayne, IN 46845-9501, USA

Krickstein, Aaron (Tennis Player)
7559 Fairmont Ct
Boca Raton, FL 33496-5902, USA

Krieg, Dave (Athlete, Football Player)
2439 E Desert Willow Dr
Phoenix, AZ 85048-9007, USA

Krieg, Jim (Athlete, Football Player)
76690 Lark Ln
Indian Wells, CA 92210-8984, USA

Krieger, Ali (Athlete, Soccer Player)
c/o Dan Levy *Wasserman Media Group (NC)*
4208 Six Forks Rd Ste 1020
Raleigh, NC 27609-5738, USA

Krieger, Robbie (Musician, Songwriter, Writer)
3011 Ledgewood Dr
Los Angeles, CA 90068-1959, USA

Krieger, Robby (Musician)
c/o Mike Monterulo *The Kirby Organization (TKO-LA)*
9200 W Sunset Blvd Ste 600
Los Angeles, CA 90069-3196, USA

Krieps, Vicky (Actor)
c/o Katja Szigat *Players Agentur Management*
Sophienstrasse 21
Berlin 10178, GERMANY

Kriewald, Doug (Athlete, Football Player)
5031 Snow Mesa Dr
Fort Collins, CO 80528-8590, USA

Kriewaldt, Clint (Athlete, Football Player)
320 E Fernwood Ln
Appleton, WI 54913-7651, USA

Krige, Alice (Actor)
c/o Mel McKeon *McKeon-Myones Management*
3500 W Olive Ave Ste 770
Burbank, CA 91505-5527, USA

Krimm, John (Athlete, Football Player)
2565 Abington Rd
Upper Arlington, OH 43221-3003, USA

Kring, Tim (Writer)
c/o Staff Member *Imperative Entertainment*
1663 18th St Fl 2
Santa Monica, CA 90404-3807, USA

Kripke, Eric (Writer)
Kripke Enterprises
1880 Century Park E Ste 950
Los Angeles, CA 90067-1612, USA

Krisher, Bill (Athlete, Football Player)
5915 Over Downs Dr
Dallas, TX 75230-4044, USA

Kristen, Marta (Actor)
c/o Albert Esquivel *AE Talent Management*
500 S Westmoreland Ave
Los Angeles, CA 90020-1529, USA

Kristiansen, Ingrid (Athlete, Track Athlete)
Nils Collett Vogts Vei 51B
Oslo, 765, NORWAY

Kristina Sisco, Kristina (Actor)
c/o Staff Member *Cohen/Thomas Agency*
1888 N Crescent Heights Blvd
Los Angeles, CA 90069-1647, USA

Kristof, Kathy M (Writer)
Los Angeles Times
2300 E Imperial Hwy
Editorial Dept
El Segundo, CA 90245-2813, USA

Kristofferson, Kris (Actor, Musician)
3179 Sumac Ridge Rd
Malibu, CA 90265-5127, USA

Krivda, Rick (Athlete, Baseball Player)
101 Bree Way
Jeannette, PA 15644-5406, USA

Krivokrasov, Sergei (Athlete, Hockey Player)
8505 E Alameda Ave Unit 3329
Denver, CO 80230-6070, USA

Krivsky, Wayne (Commentator)
3841 Gregory Ln
Erlanger, KY 41018-3819, USA

Kriwet, Heinz (Business Person)
Thyssen AG
August-Thyssen-Str 1
Dusseldorf 40211, GERMANY

Krizmanich, Jack (Actor)
c/o Mara Santino *Luber Roklin Management*
5815 W Sunset Blvd Ste 208
Los Angeles, CA 90028-6481, USA

Kroeger, Chad (Musician, Songwriter)
408 Monarch Pl
Lahaina, HI 96761-9070, USA

Kroeger, Josh (Athlete, Baseball Player)
13477 N 87th Ln
Peoria, AZ 85381-6114

Kroeger, Mike (Musician)
408 Monarch Pl
Lahaina, HI 96761-9070, USA

Kroell, Ronnie (Actor, Model)
c/o Dino May *Dino May Management*
13223 Bloomfield St
Sherman Oaks, CA 91423-3207, USA

Kroenke, Zach (Athlete, Baseball Player)
Double Diamond Sports Management
7640 NW 79th Ave Apt L8
Tamarac, FL 33321-2868, USA

Kroes, Doutzen (Model)
c/o Staff Member *Paparazzi Model Management*
Singel 512-2
AZ 01017, THE NETHERLANDS

Krofft, Marty (Actor, Producer)
Sid & Marty Krofft Pictures
4024 Radford Ave Studio Cocbscenter
Studio City, CA 91604-2101, USA

Kroft, Steve (Correspondent)

Krohn, Jonathan (Writer)
15335 Little Stone Way
Alpharetta, GA 30004-6901, USA

Kroll, Alex (Athlete, Football Player)
581 Whalley Rd
Charlotte, VT 05445-9531, USA

Kroll, Bob (Athlete, Football Player)
1120 N Orlando Ave
Maitland, FL 32751-4446, USA

Kroll, Gary (Athlete, Baseball Player)
9038 E 40th St
Tulsa, OK 74145-3713, USA

Kroll, Robert L (Athlete, Football Player)
P.O. Box 8563
Maitland, FL 32751, USA

Krom, Tommy (Athlete, Basketball Player)
519 Briar Hill Rd
Louisville, KY 40206-3009, USA

Kromm, Richard (Rich) (Athlete, Coach, Hockey Player)
1935 Cheyenne Dr
Evansville, IN 47715-7044, USA

Kronberger, Petra (Skier)
Ellmautal 37
Pfarrwerfen 05452, AUSTRIA

Krone, Julie (Horse Racer)
7305 Marine Pl
Carlsbad, CA 92011-4684, USA

Kroner, Gary (Athlete, Football Player)
7330 Buckingham Ct
Boulder, CO 80301-6409, USA

Kronwall, Niklas (Athlete, Hockey Player)
22235 Picadilly Cir
Novi, MI 48375-4796, USA

Krook, Kevin (Athlete, Hockey Player)
216 20 St
Cold Lake, AB T9M 1E2, Canada

Kroon, Marc (Athlete, Baseball Player)
12617 N 56th Pl
Scottsdale, AZ 85254-4259, USA

Kropfelder, Nicholas (Soccer Player)
13803 Lighthouse Ave
Ocean City, MD 21842-4565, USA

Kropog, Troy (Athlete, Football Player)
c/o Ken Zuckerman *Priority Sports & Entertainment - (LA)*
15233 Ventura Blvd Ste 718
Sherman Oaks, CA 91403-2237, USA

Kropp, Tom (Athlete, Basketball Player)
1811 W 41st St
Kearney, NE 68845-8286, USA

Krosney, Alexandra (Actor)

Kross, David (Actor)
c/o Staff Member *Julian Belfrage & Associates*
9 Argyll St Fl 3
London W1F 7TG, UNITED KINGDOM

Kross, Kayden (Adult Film Star, Model)
c/o Drew Elliot *Artist International*
333 E 43rd St Apt 115
New York, NY 10017-4822, USA

Krough, Jeff (Race Car Driver)
PO Box 602
Kamiah, ID 83536-0602, USA

Krsnich, Rocky (Athlete, Baseball Player)
5701 W 92nd St
Overland Park, KS 66207-2442, USA

KRS-One (Musician)
c/o Staff Member *JL Entertainment*
18653 Ventura Blvd # 340
Tarzana, CA 91356-4103, USA

Krstic, Nenad (Basketball Player)
New Jersy Nets
390 Murray Hill Pkwy
East Rutherford, NJ 07073-2109, USA

Kruckei, Marie (Baseball Player)
52128 Woodridge Dr
South Bend, IN 46635-1053, USA

Kruckel, Marie (Athlete, Baseball Player, Commentator)
52128 Woodridge Dr
South Bend, IN 46635-1053, USA

Kruczek, Mike (Athlete, Football Player)
4028 Gilder Rose Pl
Winter Park, FL 32792-9416, USA

Krueger, Bill (Athlete, Baseball Player)
30132 SE Redmond Fall City Rd
Fall City, WA 98024-7104, USA

Krueger, Charlie (Athlete, Football Player)
44 Regency Dr
Clayton, CA 94517-1729, USA

Krueger, Phil (Race Car Driver)
8662 Houston Rd
Freetown, IN 47235-9624, USA

Krueger, Rolf (Athlete, Football Player)
PO Box 638
Wallis, TX 77485-0638, USA

Krug, Chris (Athlete, Baseball Player)
PO Box 1350
Wildomar, CA 92595-1350, USA

Krug, Gene (Athlete, Baseball Player)
1327 Baylor Dr
Colorado Springs, CO 80909-3301, USA

Krug, Manfred (Actor)
Rankestr. 9
Berlin D-10789, Germany

Kruger, Diane (Actor, Model)
c/o Heidi Lopata *Narrative*
1601 Vine St Fl 6
Los Angeles, CA 90028-8802, USA

Kruger, Hardy (Actor)
PO Box 2450
Palm Springs, CA 92263-2450, USA

Kruger, Lon (Athlete, Basketball Coach, Basketball Player, Coach)
University of Oklahoma
Athletic Dept
Norman, OK 73019-0001, USA

Kruger, Paul (Athlete, Football Player)
c/o Joe Panos *Athletes First*
23091 Mill Creek Dr
Laguna Hills, CA 92653-1258, USA

Kruger, Pit (Actor)
Geleitstr 10
Frankfurt/Main 60599, GERMANY

Kruk, John (Athlete, Baseball Player)
PO Box 7847
Naples, FL 34101-7847, USA

Krukow, Mike (Athlete, Baseball Player)
PO Box 34001
Reno, NV 89533-4001, USA

Krulicki, Jim (Athlete, Hockey Player)
PO Box 35 Stn C
58 Boiler Beach Rd RR 1 Stn Main
Kitchener, ON N2G 3W9, Canada

Krulwich, Robert (Correspondent)
CBS-TV
524 W 57th St
News Dept
New York, NY 10019-2924, USA

Krumholtz, David (Actor)
c/o Hilary Hansen *Vision PR*
2 Penn Plz Rm 2601
New York, NY 10121-0001, USA

Krumrie, Tim (Athlete, Football Player)
c/o Staff Member *Kansas City Chiefs*
1 Arrowhead Dr
Kansas City, MO 64129-1651, USA

Krupa, Joanna (Model, Reality Star)
c/o Jennifer Hebert *Brilliant Talent*
PO Box 58003
Sherman Oaks, CA 91413-3003, USA

Krupa, Marta (Actor)
c/o Jennifer Hebert *Brilliant Talent*
PO Box 58003
Sherman Oaks, CA 91413-3003, USA

Krupicka, Jarda (Athlete, Hockey Player)
Budweiser Import GmbH
Lindenstrasse 20
Kloten 08302, Switzerland

Krupp, Uwe (Athlete, Hockey Player)
2465 Ala Wai Blvd Apt 1204
Honolulu, HI 96815-3453, USA

Kruscschev, Sergei Dr (Writer)
Brown University
PO Box 1970
Providence, RI 02912-0001, USA

Kruse, Martin (Religious Leader)
Prinz-Friedrrich-Leopold-Str 14
Berlin 14219, GERMANY

Krushelnyski, Mike (Athlete, Hockey Player)
PO Box 834
Cohoes, NY 12047-0834, USA

Krusiec, Michelle (Actor)
c/o Jennifer Wiley-Stockton *JWS Entertainment*
Prefers to be contacted by email.
New York, NY NA, USA

Krutko, Larry (Athlete, Football Player)
1565 6th St
Waynesburg, PA 15370-1653, USA

Krygier, Todd (Athlete, Hockey Player)
23946 Wintergreen Cir Apt 13
Novi, MI 48374-3681, USA

Krynzel, Dave (Athlete, Baseball Player)
951 Derringer Ln
Henderson, NV 89014-2595, USA

Krypreos, Nick (Athlete, Hockey Player)
9209 Copenhaver Dr
Potomac, MD 20854-3016, USA

Kryskow, Dave (Athlete, Hockey Player)
58 Sandstone Ridge Cres
Okotoks, AB T1S 1P9, Canada

Krystkowiak, Larry (Athlete, Basketball Player)
1937 E Siesta Dr
Sandy, UT 84093-6239, USA

Krzysztof, Oliwa (Athlete, Hockey Player)
707 Derzee Ct
Delmar, NY 12054-9645, USA

Krzyzewski, Mike (Athlete, Basketball Player, Coach)
4406 W Cornwallis Rd
Durham, NC 27705-8126, USA

K. Simpson, Michael (Congressman, Politician)
2312 Rayburn Hob
Washington, DC 20515-0102, USA

KT Tunstall (Musician)
c/o Simon Banks *SB Management*
755 N Bonhill Rd
Los Angeles, CA 90049-2303, USA

Kuba, Filip (Athlete, Hockey Player)
4914 Carranza Ct
Tampa, FL 33616-1412, USA

Kubala, Ray (Athlete, Football Player)
3433 Alexandrite Way
Round Rock, TX 78681-2436, USA

Kuban, Bob (Musician)
17626 Lasiandra Dr
Wildwood, MO 63005-4912, USA

Kubek, Tony (Athlete, Baseball Player, Sportscaster)
121 E Water St Apt 120
Appleton, WI 54911-5775, USA

Kubel, Jason (Athlete, Baseball Player)
21031 Ventura Blvd Ste 1000
Woodland Hills, CA 91364-2227, USA

Kubenka, Jeff (Athlete, Baseball Player)
9706 Endcliff
San Antonio, TX 78250-3426, USA

Kuberski, Bob (Athlete, Football Player)
11301 Elam Dr
Glen Mills, PA 19342-2358, USA

Kuberski, Robert (Athlete, Football Player)
11301 Elam Dr
Glen Mills, PA 19342-2358, USA

Kuberski, Steve (Athlete, Basketball Player)
1056 Sand Castle Rd
Sanibel, FL 33957-3615, USA

Kubiak, Gary (Athlete, Coach, Football Coach, Football Player)
PO Box 350
Plantersville, TX 77363-0350, USA

Kubiak, Leo (Athlete, Basketball Player)
2638 N Prestwick Way
Lecanto, FL 34461-6902, USA

Kubiak, Ted (Athlete, Baseball Player)
11956 Bernardo Plaza Dr
San Diego, CA 92128-2538, USA

Kubik, Brad (Athlete, Football Player)
3025 W Oakhaven Ln
Springfield, MO 65810-1948, USA

Kubin, Larry (Athlete, Football Player)
315 Cannery Ln
Forest Hill, MD 21050-3066, USA

Kubina, Pavel (Athlete, Hockey Player)
1145 81st St S
Saint Petersburg, FL 33707-2726, USA

Kubinski, Tim (Athlete, Baseball Player)
4852 Caballeros Ave
Sn Luis Obisp, CA 93401-7964, USA

Kubiszvn, Jack (Athlete, Baseball Player)
2306 University Blvd Ste A
Tuscaloosa, AL 35401-1581, USA

Kubski, Gil (Athlete, Baseball Player)
4542 Scenario Dr
Huntington Beach, CA 92649-2221, USA

Kubski, Gill (Athlete, Baseball Player)
4542 Scenario Dr
Huntington Beach, CA 92649-2221, USA

Kucek, Jack (Athlete, Baseball Player)
8220 Blue Heron Ln
Canfield, OH 44406-9134, USA

Kucera, Frantisek (Athlete, Hockey Player)
Sportovni Centrum Letnany Tupolevova ul. 699
Praha Letnany 00009, Czech Republic

Kuchar, Matt (Athlete, Golfer)
121 Plantation Cir
Ponte Vedra Beach, FL 32082-3921, USA

Kuchma, Leonid D (President)
President's Office
Bankova Str 11
Kiev 252011, UKRAINE

Kuchta, Frank (Athlete, Football Player)
5021 Fairlawn Rd
Lyndhurst, OH 44124-1124, USA

Kuczenski, Bruce (Athlete, Basketball Player)
135 Southshire Dr
Southington, CT 06489-4224, USA

Kudelski, Bob (Athlete, Hockey Player)
PO Box 351
Midway, UT 84049-0351, USA

Kuder, Mary (Artist)
Kuder Art Studio
539 Navahopi Rd
Sedona, AZ 86336-4007, USA

Kudlow, Lawrence (Television Host)
Kudlow & Company
900 Sylvan Ave
CNBC
Englewood Cliffs, NJ 07632-3312, USA

Kudoh, Youki (Actor, Musician)
Hirata Office
2-8-15-404 Akasaka
Minato
Tokyo, JAPAN

Kudrave, David (Race Car Driver)
7918 Zionsville Rd
Indianapolis, IN 46268-1649, USA

Kudrna, Julius (Athlete)
Sekaninova 36
Prague 2 120 00, CZECH REPUBLIC

Kudrow, Lisa (Actor)
c/o Staff Member *Is or Isn't Entertainment*
8391 Beverly Blvd Ste 125
Los Angeles, CA 90048-2633, USA

Kuechenberg, Rudy (Athlete, Football Player)
2841 N 73rd Ave
Hollywood, FL 33024-2733, USA

Kuechly, Luke (Athlete, Football Player)
c/o Ben Dogra *Relativity Sports*
2029 Century Park E Ste 1550
Century City, CA 90067-3000, USA

Kuehl, Ryan (Athlete, Football Player)
10409 Masters Ter
Potomac, MD 20854-3862, USA

Kuehn, Art (Athlete, Football Player)
19510 NE 185th St
Woodinville, WA 98077-5403, USA

Kuehn, Enrico (Athlete)
BSD
An der Schiessstatte 4
Berchtesgaden 83471, GERMANY

Kuehne, Hank (Athlete, Golfer)
9480 Stanton Rd
Lantana, TX 76226-7303, USA

Kuehne, Kelli (Athlete, Golfer)
7211 Oakbluff Dr
Dallas, TX 75254-2736, USA

Kuerten, Gustavo (Tennis Player)
Octagon
1751 Pinnacle Dr Ste 1500
McLean, VA 22102-3833, USA

Kuester, John (Athlete, Basketball Player)
105 Carnoustie Way
Media, PA 19063-1858, USA

Kufeldt, James (Business Person)
Winn-Dixie Stores
5050 Edgewood Ct
Jacksonville, FL 32254-3699, USA

Kufuor, John Agyekum (President)
Chairman's Office
Castle
PO Box 1627
Accra, GHANA

Kugbila, Edmund (Athlete, Football Player)
c/o Hadley Engelhard *Enter-Sports Management*
6000 Lake Forrest Dr Ste 370
Atlanta, GA 30328-5902, USA

Kugler, Pete (Athlete, Football Player)
9984 Whitetail Ln
Littleton, CO 80127-6104, USA

Kuhaulua, Fred (Athlete, Baseball Player)
89-203 Ualakahiki Pl
Waianae, HI 96792-3937, USA

Kuhaulua, Jesse (Wrestler)
Azumazeki Stable
4-6-4 Higashi Komagata
Ryogoku
Tokyo, JAPAN

Kuhlemann, Bill (Race Car Driver)
Summit Racing
PO Box 535
Richfield, OH 44286-0535, USA

Kuhlman, Ron (Actor)
5738 Willis Ave
Van Nuys, CA 91411-3327, USA

Kuhn, Markus (Athlete, Football Player)
c/o Neil Cornrich *NC Sports, LLC*
best to contact via email
Columbus, OH 43201, USA

Kuiper, Duane (Athlete, Baseball Player)
3665 Deer Trail Dr
Danville, CA 94506-6021, USA

Kuiper, Glen (Commentator)
321 Sequoia Ter
Danville, CA 94506-4545, USA

Kuipers, Andre Dr (Astronaut)
European Space Centre
8-10 rue Mario Nikis
Paris Cedex F-75738, France

Kukkonen, Lasse (Athlete, Hockey Player)
Puckagency LLC
555 Pleasantville Rd Ste 210N
210N Attn Jay Grossman
Briarcliff Manor, NY 10510-1900, USA

Kukoc, Toni (Athlete, Basketball Player)
1830 Hybernia Dr
Highland Park, IL 60035-5500, USA

Kukulowicz, Adolph (Athlete, Hockey Player)
1342 Sea Lovers Lane RR 5
Gabriola, BC V0R 1X5, Canada

Kulak, Stu (Athlete, Hockey Player)
113 Sunglo Dr
Penticton, BC V2A 8X6, Canada

Kulbacki, Joe (Football Player)
PO Box 97
Colden, NY 14033-0097, USA

Kulbacki, Joseph (Athlete, Football Player)
9419 S Hill Rd
Boston, NY 14025, USA

Kuleshov, Valery (Musician)
c/o Staff Member *Musicians Corporate Management*
PO Box 825
Highland, NY 12528-0825, USA

Kulich, Vladimir (Actor)
c/o Lesa Kirk *Open Entertainment*
1051 Cole Ave
Los Angeles, CA 90038-2601, USA

Kulka, Konstanty A (Musician)
Filharmonia Narodowa
Ul Jasna 5
Warsaw 00-007, POLAND

Kulongoski, Theodore (Politician)
4232 NE Couch St
Portland, OR 97213-1630, USA

Kulpa, Ronald (Athlete, Baseball Player)
1958 Parkland Woods Dr
Maryland Heights, MO 63043-4701, USA

Kumar, Sanjay (Business Person)
Computer Associates Int'l
1 CA Plz
Islandia, NY 11749-7001, USA

Kumaratunga, Chandrika B (President)
President's Office
Republic Square
Sri Jayewardenepura Kotte
SRI LANKA

Kumbernuss, Astrid (Athlete, Track Athlete)
Neubrandenburg Jahnstadion
Schwedenstr 25
Neubrandenburg 17033, GERMANY

Kumble, Roger (Actor, Director, Writer)
c/o Jonathan Berry *3 Arts Entertainment*
9460 Wilshire Blvd Fl 7
Beverly Hills, CA 90212-2713, USA

Kume, Mike (Athlete, Baseball Player)
6810 Woodard Rd
Andover, OH 44003-9638, USA

Kumerow, Eric (Athlete, Football Player)
736 Fairview Ln
Bartlett, IL 60103-4566, USA

Kummer, Glenn F (Business Person)
Fleetwood Enterprises
3125 Myers St
Riverside, CA 92503-5527, USA

Kumpel, Mark (Athlete, Hockey Player, Olympic Athlete)
22 Oceanwood Dr
Scarborough, ME 04074-8755, USA

Kundera, Milan (Writer)
Gallimard
5 Rue Sebastien-Bottin
Paris 75007, FRANCE

Kunerth, Mark J (Producer, Writer)
c/o Ted Chervin *ICM Partners*
10250 Constellation Blvd Fl 7
Los Angeles, CA 90067-6207, USA

Kuney, Eva Lee (Actor)
8962 Shale Valley St
Las Vegas, NV 89123-3271, USA

Kunin, Madeleine (Politician)
900 Wake Robin Dr
Shelburne, VT 05482-7583, USA

Kunis, Mila (Actor)
c/o Susan Curtis *Curtis Talent Management*
9607 Arby Dr
Beverly Hills, CA 90210-1202, USA

Kunitz, Matt (Producer)
c/o Staff Member *WME|IMG*
9601 Wilshire Blvd
Beverly Hills, CA 90210-5213, USA

Kunkel, Jeff (Athlete, Baseball Player)
905 Heatherglen Ct
Lewisville, TX 75077-3145, USA

Kunkel-Huff, Anna (Baseball Player)
9220 E Fairway Blvd Apt C136
Sun Lakes, AZ 85248-6579, USA

Kunnert, Kevin (Athlete, Basketball Player)
8286 SW Wilderland Ct
Portland, OR 97224-7646, USA

Kunstler, Mort (Artist)
137 Cove Neck Rd
Oyster Bay, NY 11771-1824, USA

Kuntar, Les (Athlete, Hockey Player)
9721 SW 89th Loop
Ocala, FL 34481-5577, USA

Kuntz, Murray (Athlete, Hockey Player)
4571 Sugar Maple Dr
Gloucester, ON K1V 1R7, Canada

Kuntz, Rusty (Athlete, Baseball Player)
2112 W 125th St
Leawood, KS 66209-1382, USA

Kunz, Eddie (Athlete, Baseball Player)
22312 SW Sequoia Ter
Sherwood, OR 97140-7321, USA

Kunz, George J (Athlete, Football Player)
8215 Bermuda Rd
Las Vegas, NV 89123-2213, USA

Kunz, Lee (Athlete, Football Player)
4096 Youngfield St
Wheat Ridge, CO 80033-3862, USA

Kunze, Terry (Athlete, Basketball Player)
6931 Halifax Ave N
Minneapolis, MN 55429-1373, USA

Kunzu, Hari (Writer)
EP Dutton
375 Hudson St
New York, NY 10014-3658, USA

Kuok Hock Nien, Robert (Business Person)
Kuok Limited
No.1 Kim Seng Promenade
#07-01 Great World City
237994, Singapore

Kupchak, Mitch (Athlete, Basketball Player, Olympic Athlete)
361 Fordyce Rd
Los Angeles, CA 90049-2009, USA

Kupcinet, Kari (Actor)
1660 Mill Trl
Highland Park, IL 60035-1502, USA

Kupec, C J (Athlete, Basketball Player)
6448 River Run
Columbia, MD 21044-6022, USA

Kupets, Courtney (Athlete, Gymnast, Olympic Athlete)
133 Falling Shoals Dr
Athens, GA 30605-5740, USA

Kupfer, Harry (Director)
Komische Oper
Behrenstr 55-57
New York, NY 10117-0001, GERMANY

Kupp, Cooper (Athlete, Football Player)
c/o Ryan Tollner *REP 1 Sports Group*
80 Technology Dr
Irvine, CA 92618-2301, USA

Kupp, Craig (Athlete, Football Player)
609 S 31st Ave
Yakima, WA 98902-4009, USA

Kupp, Jacob (Jake) (Athlete, Football Player)
4801 Snowmountain Rd
Yakima, WA 98908-2848, USA

Kupperman, Joel (Actor)
PO Box 672
Mansfield Center, CT 06250-0672, USA

Kurasov, Georgy (Artist)
4/2 Inzenernaja St
Saint Petersburg 191011, RUSSIA

Kureishi, Hanif (Writer)
81 Comeragh Road
London W14 9HS, UNITED KINGDOM (UK)

Kurek, Ralph (Athlete, Football Player)
2373 Lime Pond Rd
South Royalton, VT 05068-4411, USA

Kurisko, Jamie (Athlete, Football Player)
3270 Aldrich Dr
Cumming, GA 30040-5378, USA

Kuriyama, Chiaki (Actor)
c/o Staff Member *Space Craft Group*
2-6-18 Minami Aoyama
Shibuya
Tokyo 107-0062, JAPAN

Kurkova, Karolina (Model)
c/o Michelle Schwartz *Rogers & Cowan*
909 3rd Ave Fl 9
New York, NY 10022-4752, USA

Kurnick, Howie (Athlete, Football Player)
2339 Bretton Dr
Cincinnati, OH 45244-3729, USA

Kurosaki, Ryan (Athlete, Baseball Player)
2024 Fairmont Dr
Benton, AR 72015-3163, USA

Kurosawa, Takuya (Race Car Driver)
Dale Coyne Racing
13400 S Budler Rd
Plainfield, IL 60544-9493, USA

Kurpeikis, Justin (Athlete, Football Player)
1108 Longfellow Ln
State College, PA 16803-2414, USA

Kurrasch, David B (Business Person)
The Monkey Hook, LLC
25672 Raintree Rd
Laguna Hills, CA 92653-7528, USA

Kurrasch, Roy (Athlete, Football Player)
803 Levering Ave Apt 4
Los Angeles, CA 90024-2754, USA

Kurrat, Kiaus-Dieter (Athlete, Track Athlete)
Am Hochwald 30
28460
Klemmachow 01453, GERMANY

Kurri, Jari (Athlete, Hockey Player)
Hockey Hall of Fame Brookfield Place
30 Yonge St
Toronto, ON M5E 1X8, Canada

Kurri, Jarri (Athlete, Hockey Player)
c/o Staff Member *Hockey Hall of Fame* Brookfield Place
30 Yonge St
Toronto, ON M5E 1X8, CANADA

Kursinski, Anne (Athlete, Horse Racer, Olympic Athlete)
107 Spring Hill Rd
Frenchtown, NJ 08825-3019, USA

Kurt, Gary (Athlete, Hockey Player)
Waterloo Regional Police
11 Wasaga Woods Cir
Wasaga Beach, ON L9Z 2N1, Canada

Kurtenbach, Orland J (Athlete, Hockey Player)
14066 29A Ave
Surrey, BC V4P 2J8, Canada

Kurth, Wallace (Wally) (Actor, Musician)
2143 N Valley Dr
Manhattan Beach, CA 90266-2247, USA

Kurtis, Bill (Television Host)

Kurtis, Dalene (Actor, Model)
c/o Juliette Harris *It Girl Public Relations*
3763 Eddingham Ave
Calabasas, CA 91302-5835, USA

Kurtz, Hal (Athlete, Baseball Player)
511 Flat Iron Square Rd
Church Hill, MD 21623-1269, USA

Kurtz, Howard (Television Host)
c/o Staff Member *Fox News*
1211 Avenue of the Americas Lowr C1
New York, NY 10036-8705, USA

Kurtz, Swoosie (Actor)
c/o Konrad Leh *Creative Talent Group*
1900 Avenue of the Stars Ste 2475
Los Angeles, CA 90067-4512, USA

Kurtzman, Alex (Producer)
c/o BeBe Lerner *ID Public Relations*
7060 Hollywood Blvd Fl 8th
Los Angeles, CA 90028-6021, USA

Kurtzman, Katy (Actor, Director)
c/o Staff Member *Lynn Production & Mgmt*
20411 Chapter Dr
Woodland Hills, CA 91364-5612, USA

Kurvers, Tom (Athlete, Hockey Player)
15128 Glen Oak St
Minnetonka, MN 55345-5722, USA

Kurylenko, Olga (Actor)
c/o Romilly Bowlby *DDA Public Relations*
192-198 Vauxhall Bridge Rd
London SW1V 1DX, UNITED KINGDOM

Kuryluk, Merve (Athlete, Hockey Player)
63 Alexandra Ave
Yorkton, SK S3N 2J6, Canada

Kusama, Karyn (Director)
Endeavor Talent Agency
9701 Wilshire Blvd Ste 1000
Beverly Hills, CA 90212-2010, USA

Kusatsu, Clyde (Actor)
Paradign Agency
10100 Santa Monica Blvd Ste 2500
Los Angeles, CA 90067-4116, USA

Kush, Rod (Athlete, Football Player)
45 Willow Point Dr
Ashland, NE 68003-9408, USA

Kushell, Bob (Producer, Writer)
c/o Barry Kotler *Creative Artists Agency (CAA)*
2000 Avenue of the Stars Ste 100
Los Angeles, CA 90067-4705, USA

Kushell, Lisa (Actor)
c/o Staff Member *Abrams Artists Agency*
750 N San Vicente Blvd
E Tower Fl 11
Los Angeles, CA 90069-5788, USA

Kushner, Dale (Athlete, Hockey Player)
202-1260 Wally Rd
Comox, BC V9M 3N9, CANADA

Kushner, Dave (Musician)
4234 Babcock Ave
Studio City, CA 91604-1509, USA

Kushner, Harold S (Religious Leader, Writer)
Temple Israel
145 Hartford St
Natick, MA 01760-3199, USA

Kushner, Jared (Business Person)
Kushner Companies
666 5th Ave
New York, NY 10103-0001, USA

Kushner, Robert E (Artist)
DC Moore Gallery
724 5th Ave
New York, NY 10019-4106, USA

Kushner, Tony (Writer)
c/o Joyce Ketay *Gersh*
41 Madison Ave Ste 3301
New York, NY 10010-2210, USA

Kuske, Kevin (Athlete)
BSD
An der Schlessstatte 4
Berchtesgaden 83471, GERMANY

Kusnitz, Jared (Actor)
c/o Staff Member *DBA Impact*
PO Box 2514
Toluca Lake, CA 91610-0514, USA

Kusnyer, Art (Athlete, Baseball Player)
6598 Taeda Dr
Sarasota, FL 34241-9145, USA

Kusturica, Emir (Actor, Director, Musician, Writer)
Fondazione Culturale Edison
Largo VIII Marzo, 9
Parma 43100, ITALY

Kutcher, Ashton (Actor, Producer)
c/o Kathleen Flaherty *K21 Communications*
6806 Lexington Ave
Los Angeles, CA 90038-1106, USA

Kutcher, Randy (Athlete, Baseball Player)
3016 Purple Sage Ln
Palmdale, CA 93550-7972, USA

Kuti, Fela (Musician)
Rosebud Agency
650 Delancey St Apt 309
San Francisco, CA 94107-2084, USA

Kutless (Musician)
c/o Staff Member *WME (Nashville)*
1201 Demonbreun St
Nashville, TN 37203-3140, USA

Kutner, Rob (Writer)
c/o Staff Member *Kaplan-Stahler Agency*
8383 Wilshire Blvd Ste 923
Beverly Hills, CA 90211-2443, USA

Kutsuna, Shiolo (Actor)
c/o Hilary Hansen *Vision PR*
2 Penn Plz Rm 2601
New York, NY 10121-0001, USA

Kuttner, Robert (Writer)
c/o Staff Member *Chelsea Green Publishing*
85 N Main St Ste 120
White River Junction, VT 05001-7135, USA

Kutyna, Marty (Athlete, Baseball Player)
2255 NW 14th St
Delray Beach, FL 33445-2610, USA

Kutzler, Jerry (Athlete, Baseball Player)
8415 27th Ave
Kenosha, WI 53143-6232, USA

Kuykendall, Fulton (Athlete, Football Player)
1497 Rucker Cir
Woodstock, GA 30188-2133, USA

Kuzava, Bob (Athlete, Baseball Player)
1118 Vinewood St
Wyandotte, MI 48192-4945, USA

Kuziel, Bob (Athlete, Football Player)
PO Box 822
Venice, FL 34284-0822, USA

Kuzmic, Kristina (Chef, Internet Star)
c/o Staff Member *Westport Entertainment Associates*
1120 W State Route 89A Ste B1
Sedona, AZ 86336-5763, USA

Kuzmicz, George (Athlete, Hockey Player)
12 Devonridge Cres
Scarborough, ON M1C 5A5, Canada

Kuznetsoff, Alexel (Musician)
Columbia Artists Mgmt Inc
165 W 57th St
New York, NY 10019-2201, USA

Kuzyk, Mimi (Actor)
Artists Agency
1180 S Beverly Dr Ste 301
Los Angeles, CA 90035-1154, USA

Kvapil, Travis (Race Car Driver)
Roush Fenway Racing
122 Knob Hill Rd
Mooresville, NC 28117-6847, USA

Kvasha, Oleg (Athlete, Hockey Player)
22 Bluff Rd
Glen Cove, NY 11542-1778, USA

Kvitova, Petra (Athlete, Tennis Player)
c/o Staff Member *Women's Tennis Association (WTA (UK))*
Palliser House
Palliser Rd
London W149EB, UK

Kwalick, Thaddeus J (Ted) (Athlete, Football Player)
755 Purdue Ct
Santa Clara, CA 95051-5527, USA

Kwan, Jennie (Actor)
Innovative Artists
1505 10th St
Santa Monica, CA 90401-2805, USA

Kwan, Michelle (Athlete, Figure Skater, Olympic Athlete)
140 N Thurston Ave
Los Angeles, CA 90049-2422, USA

Kwan, Nancy (Actor)
Marlin
252 7th Ave Apt 9P
New York, NY 10001-7340, USA

Kwanten, Ryan (Actor)
c/o Ben Levine *LINK Entertainment*
11872 La Grange Ave
Los Angeles, CA 90025-5282, USA

Kwapis, Ken (Comedian, Director, Producer)
c/o Staff Member *In Cahoots*
4024 Radford Ave
Editorial Bldg 2 #7
Studio City, CA 91604-2101, USA

Kwasniewski, Aleksander (President)
Kancelaria Prezydenta RP
Ul Wiejska 4/8
Warsaw 00-902, POLAND

Kweli, Talib (Musician)
c/o Steve Levine *ICM Partners*
10250 Constellation Blvd Fl 7
Los Angeles, CA 90067-6207, USA

Kweller, Ben (Musician)
c/o Ken Weinstein *Big Hassle Media*
40 Exchange Pl Ste 1900
New York, NY 10005-2714, USA

Kwiatkowski, Joel (Athlete, Hockey Player)
1481 Tenby Ct NE
Grand Rapids, MI 49505-5745, USA

Kwon, Boa (Musician)
c/o Staff Member *Creative Artists Agency (CAA)*
2000 Avenue of the Stars Ste 100
Los Angeles, CA 90067-4705, USA

Kwong, Norman Honorable (Athlete, Football Player)
178 Oakbriar Close SW
Calgary, AB T2V 5G6, Canada

Kwouk, Burt (Actor)
Diamond Mgmt
31 Percey St
London W1T 2DD, UNITED KINGDOM (UK)

Kygo (DJ, Musician)
c/o Alexandra Baker *High Rise PR*
600 Luton Dr
Glendale, CA 91206-2626, USA

Kyl, Jon (Politician)
4442 E Camelback Rd
Unit 160, Phoenix AZ, 85018-2838

Kyle, Aaron (Athlete, Football Player)
8544 Townley Rd Apt 2M
Huntersville, NC 28078-1868, USA

Kyle, David L (Business Person)
ONEOK Inc
100 W 5th St Ste Ll
PO Box 871
Tulsa, OK 74103-4298, USA

Kyle, Gary (Musician)
c/o Brandy Reed *RPR Media*
Prefers to be contacted by email or phone.
Nashville, TN NA, USA

Kyle, Jason (Athlete, Football Player)
16801 Jetton Rd
Cornelius, NC 28031-7445, USA

Kyle, Richardson (Athlete, Football Player)
3516 Balmar Mews Rd
Baltimore, MD 21211-1471, USA

Kyle, Taya (Activist, Writer)
Chris Kyle Frog Foundation
PO Box 1337
Midlothian, TX 76065-1337, USA

Kyles, Cedric (Cedric The Entertainer) (Actor, Comedian, Producer)
c/o Dollie Lucero *Boulevard Management*
21731 Ventura Blvd Ste 300
Woodland Hills, CA 91364-1851, USA

Kyles, Stan (Athlete, Baseball Player)
827 Old Wynd Ct
Spartanburg, SC 29301-4231, USA

Kylian, Jiri (Dancer)
Dance Theatre
Scheldeldoekshaven 60
Gravenhage, EN 02511, NETHERLANDS

Kyo, Machiko (Actor)
Olimpia Copu
6-35 JinguMae
Shibuyaku
Tokyo, JAPAN

Kypreos, Nick (Athlete, Hockey Player)
c/o Staff Member *Rogers Sportsnet (Toronto)*
9 Channel Nine Crt
Scarborough, ON M1S 4B5, Canada

Kysar, Jeff (Athlete, Football Player)
570 June St
Rialto, CA 92376-5729, USA

Kyte, Jim (Athlete, Hockey Player)
226 Sherwood Dr
Ottawa, ON K1Y 3V8, Canada

Laaksonen, Antti (Athlete, Hockey Player)
9225 Red Oak Dr
Victoria, MN 55386-4515, USA

Laaveg, Paul (Athlete, Football Player)
PO Box 131
Moneta, VA 24121-0131, USA

Labandeira, Josh (Athlete, Baseball Player)
2166 W Cricklewood Ct
Porterville, CA 93257-6270, USA

L'Abbe, Moe (Athlete, Hockey Player)
4520 Golden Triangle Blvd
Fort Worth, TX 76244-6316, USA

Labeaux, Sandy (Athlete, Football Player)
PO Box 3132
San Ramon, CA 94583-8132, USA

LaBeef, Sleepy (Musician)
14469 E Highway 264
Lowell, AR 72745-9212, USA

LaBelle, Patti (Musician)
c/o Staff Member *W&W Public Relations*
476 Union Ave # 200
Middlesex, NJ 08846-1968, USA

Labelle, Rob (Actor)
c/o Staff Member *Elizabeth Hodgson Management Group*
405-1688 Cypress St
Vancouver, BC V6J 5J1, CANADA

LaBeouf, Shia (Actor)
c/o John Crosby *John Crosby Management*
1357 N Spaulding Ave
Los Angeles, CA 90046-4009, USA

Labeque, Katia (Musician)
Columbia Artists Mgmt Inc
165 W 57th St
New York, NY 10019-2201, USA

Labeque, Marielle (Musician)
Columbia Artists Mgmt Inc
165 W 57th St
New York, NY 10019-2201, USA

Labine, Tyler (Actor)
c/o Tyman Stewart *Characters Talent Agency*
200-1505 2nd Ave W
Vancouver, BC V6H 3Y4, CANADA

Labiosa, David (Actor)
c/o JR Dibbs *Malaky International*
205 S Beverly Dr Ste 211
Beverly Hills, CA 90212-3893, USA

Labonte, Bobby (Race Car Driver)
Bobby Labonte Racing
PO Box 358
Trinity, NC 27370-0358, USA

Labonte, Justin (Race Car Driver)
PO Box 843
Trinity, NC 27370-0843, USA

Labonte, Terry (Race Car Driver)
1100 Clodfelter Rd
Winston Salem, NC 27107-8806, USA

Laborde, Alden J (Business Person)
63 Oriole St
New Orleans, LA 70124-4517, USA

Labossiere, Gord (Athlete, Hockey Player)
114 Rue du Faubourg RR 5
Saint-Ferreol-Les-Neiges, QC G0A 3R0, Canada

Labounty, Matt (Athlete, Football Player)
360 W 17th Ave
Eugene, OR 97401-3859, USA

Labounty_, Matt (Athlete, Football Player)
360 W 17th Ave
Eugene, OR 97401-3859, USA

Laboy, Travis (Athlete, Football Player)
1567 E Prescott Ct
Chandler, AZ 85249-4798, USA

Labraaten, Dan (Athlete, Hockey Player)
Byrviken 303
Leksand S-79392, Sweden

Labrador, Honey (Actor, Television Host)
c/o Staff Member *Last Bastion Entertainment*
459 S Sycamore Ave
Los Angeles, CA 90036-3505, USA

Labrava, David (Actor)
c/o Alex Czuleger *The Green Room*
7080 Hollywood Blvd Ste 1100
Los Angeles, CA 90028-6938, USA

Labre, Yvon (Athlete, Hockey Player)
7812 Tilmont Ave
Parkville, MD 21234-5539, USA

Labrinth (Music Group)
c/o Staff Member *WME|IMG (UK)*
103 New Oxford St WMA
Centrepoint
London WC1A 1DD, UNITED KINGDOM

LaBute, Neil (Director, Writer)
c/o Brad Gross *Brad Gross Agency, The*
161 S Arden Blvd
Los Angeles, CA 90004-3716, USA

Labyorteaux, Matthew (Actor)
2531 Page Dr
Altadena, CA 91001-2633, USA

Labyorteaux, Patrick (Actor)
c/o Kim Dorr *Defining Artists Agency*
8721 W Sunset Blvd Ste 209
W Hollywood, CA 90069-2272, USA

Lacasse, Ryan (Athlete, Football Player)
3 Gaslight Ln
North Easton, MA 02356-2721, USA

Lacefield, Reggie (Athlete, Basketball Player)
674 Old School House Rd
Middletown, DE 19709-9690, USA

Lacey, Bob (Athlete, Baseball Player)
7623 E Decatur St
Mesa, AZ 85207-5728, USA

Lacey, Chonn (Athlete, Football Player)
1314 W Ontario St
Philadelphia, PA 19140-5220, USA

Lacey, Deborah (Actor)
1801 Ave of Stars #1250
Los Angeles, CA 90067, USA

Lacey, Jeff (Boxer)
Gary Shaw Productions LLC
33 Divan Way
Wayne, NJ 07470-5201, USA

Lachance, Michael (Mike) (Race Car Driver)
183 Sweetmans Lane
Englishtown, NJ 07726, USA

Lachance, Michel (Horse Racer)
81 Agress Rd
Millstone Township, NJ 08535-1121, USA

Lachance, Scott (Athlete, Hockey Player, Olympic Athlete)
15 Meadow View Ln
Andover, MA 01810-4759, USA

LaChapelle, David (Artist, Photographer)
c/o Steven Pranica *Creative Exchange Agency*
545 W 25th St Fl 19
New York, NY 10001-5501, USA

Lachapelle, Sean (Athlete, Football Player)
9860 Izilda Ct
Sacramento, CA 95829-8167, USA

LaChappelle, Sean P (Athlete, Football Player)
8724 Lodestone Cir
Elk Grove, CA 95624-2520, USA

Lachemann, Bill (Athlete, Baseball Player)
208 Riverview Ln
Great Falls, MT 59404-1523, USA

Lachemann, Marcel E (Athlete, Baseball Player, Coach)
PO Box 587
Penryn, CA 95663-0587, USA

Lachemann, Rene G (Athlete, Baseball Player, Coach)
7500 E Boulders Pkwy Unit 66
Scottsdale, AZ 85266-1212, USA

Lacher, Blaine (Athlete, Hockey Player)
29 Shannon Cres SE
Medicine Hat, AB T1B 4C2, Canada

Lachey, Drew (Musician, Television Host)
3831 Encino Verde Pl
Encino, CA 91436-3800, USA

Lachey, James M (Jim) (Athlete, Football Player)
1445 Roxbury Rd Apt G
Columbus, OH 43212-3211, USA

Lachey, Nick (Musician, Television Host)
3831 Encino Verde Pl
Encino, CA 91436-3800, USA

Lachman, Dichen (Actor)
c/o Laura Myones *McKeon-Myones Management*
3500 W Olive Ave Ste 770
Burbank, CA 91505-5527, USA

Lachowicz, Al (Athlete, Baseball Player)
1000 Sunset Bay Ct
Granbury, TX 76048-1239, USA

Lachowicz, Al (Athlete, Baseball Player)
1000 Sunset Bay Ct
Granbury, TX 76048-1239, USA

Lacina, Corbin (Athlete, Football Player)
1550 Skyline Ct
Saint Paul, MN 55121-1148, USA

Lackey, Brad (Race Car Driver)
Badco
35 Monument Plaza
Pleasant Hill, CA 94523, USA

Lackey, John (Athlete, Baseball Player)
c/o Steve Hilliard *Octagon Home Office*
7950 Jones Branch Dr # 700N
Mc Lean, VA 22107-0002, USA

Lackey, Mercedes (Writer)
c/o Staff Member *JABberwocky Literary Agency*
PO Box 4558
Sunnyside, NY 11104-0558, USA

Laclotte, Michel R (Director)
10 Bis Rue du Pre-aux-Clerc
Paris 75007, FRANCE

Lacock, Pete (Athlete, Baseball Player)
13609 S 37th Pl
Phoenix, AZ 85044-4562, USA

Lacorte, Frank (Athlete, Baseball Player)
1667 El Dorado Dr
Gilroy, CA 95020-3754, USA

Lacoss, Mike (Athlete, Baseball Player)
145 County Road 816
Higdon, AL 35979-9126, USA

Lacoste, Catherine (Golfer)
Calle B6
#4 El Soto de la Moraleja Alcobendas
Madrid, SPAIN

La Coste??a, Banda (Music Group)
c/o Staff Member *BMG*
1540 Broadway
New York, NY 10036-4039, USA

Lacroix, Andre J (Athlete, Hockey Player)
115 S Franklin St
Chagrin Falls, OH 44022-3214, USA

Lacroix, Christian M (Designer, Fashion Designer)
XCLX
51 Rue De Bretagne
Paris F-75 003, France

lacroix, Eric (Athlete, Hockey Player)
Colorado Avalanche
1000 Chopper Cir
Denver, CO 80204-5805

Lacrosse, Dave (Athlete, Football Player)
1712 Harmon Rd
Conshohocken, PA 19428-1205, USA

Lacy, Alan (Business Person)
Sears Roebuck Co
3333 Beverly Blvd
Hoffman Estates, IL 60179-0002, USA

Lacy, Eddie (Athlete, Football Player)
c/o Pat Dye Jr *SportsTrust Advisors*
3340 Peachtree Rd NE Fl 16
Atlanta, GA 30326-1000, USA

Lacy, Jake (Actor)
c/o Carrie Gordon *The Lede Company*
401 Broadway Ste 206
New York, NY 10013-3033, USA

Lacy, Kerry (Athlete, Baseball Player)
145 County Road 816
Higdon, AL 35979-9126, USA

Lacy, Lee (Athlete, Baseball Player)
Lee Lacy Baseball Academy
6310 Neveda Ave
Apt E420
Woodland Hills, CA 91367-3437, USA

Lacy, Raymon (Athlete, Baseball Player)
2860 State Highway 63 W
Wiergate, TX 75977-9783, USA

Lacy Clay Jr., William (Congressman, Politician)
2418 Rayburn Hob
Washington, DC 20515-1702, USA

Ladd, Andrew (Athlete, Hockey Player)
16821 Crystal Ct
Tinley Park, IL 60477-2779

Ladd, Cheryl (Actor)
c/o Jay Schwartz *Jay D Schwartz & Associates*
6767 Forest Lawn Dr Ste 211
Los Angeles, CA 90068-1051, USA

Ladd, David (Actor)
3761 Benedict Canyon Ln
Sherman Oaks, CA 91423-4670, USA

Ladd, Diane (Actor)
c/o Scott Hart *Scott Hart Entertainment*
14622 Ventura Blvd # 746
Sherman Oaks, CA 91403-3600, USA

Ladd, Jim (Radio Personality, Writer)
3321 S La Cienega Blvd
Los Angeles, CA 90016-3114, USA

Ladd, Jordan (Actor)
c/o Craig Schneider *Pinnacle Public Relations*
8721 Santa Monica Blvd # 133
W Hollywood, CA 90069-4507, USA

Ladd, Margaret (Actor)
c/o Staff Member *Abrams Artists Agency*
750 N San Vicente Blvd
E Tower Fl 11
Los Angeles, CA 90069-5788, USA

Ladd, Pete (Athlete, Baseball Player)
239 Town Farm Rd
New Gloucester, ME 04260-4438, USA

Ladin, Eric (Actor)
c/o Staff Member *Main Title Entertainment*
8383 Wilshire Blvd Ste 408
Beverly Hills, CA 90211-2435, USA

Ladler, Kenny (Athlete, Football Player)
c/o Scott Smith *XAM Sports*
3509 Ice Age Dr
Madison, WI 53719-5409, USA

Ladouceur, L P (Athlete, Football Player)
3807 Prescott Ave Unit B
Dallas, TX 75219-2238, USA

Ladouceur, Randy (Athlete, Hockey Player)
12116 Mabledon Ct
Raleigh, NC 27613-5520, CANADA

Lady Antebellum (Music Group)
c/o Coran Capshaw *Red Light Management*
455 2nd St NE
#500
Charlottesville, VA 22902-5791, USA

Ladygo, Pete (Athlete, Football Player)
124 Orchard St
Keyser, WV 26726-3153, USA

Ladysmith Black Mambazo (Musician)
326 Ridge Rd Unit D
Cedar Grove, NJ 07009-1636, USA

Laettner, Christian (Athlete, Basketball Player, Olympic Athlete)
1225 Church Rd
Angola, NY 14006-8831, USA

LaFell, Brandon (Athlete, Football Player)
c/o Neil Schwartz *Schwartz & Feinsod*
4 Hillandale Rd
Rye Brook, NY 10573-1705, USA

Laferriere, Rick (Athlete, Hockey Player)
RE/MAX Chay Realty
152 Bayfield St
Barrie, ON L4M 3B5, Canada

Lafferty, James (Actor)
c/o Whitney Tancred *42West*
1840 Century Park E Ste 700
Los Angeles, CA 90067-2122, USA

Laffey, Aaron (Athlete, Baseball Player)
32301 Monaco Pl
Avon Lake, OH 44012-2567, USA

Laffite, Jacques (Race Car Driver)
Soci??t?? Internationale De Communication Sport Et Loisir
30 Rue Athime Rue
Garches F-92 380, France

LaFleur, Art (Actor)
c/o Joel King *Pakula/King & Associates*
9229 W Sunset Blvd Ste 315
Los Angeles, CA 90069-3403, USA

Lafleur, David (Athlete, Football Player)
3900 Thompson Rd
Sulphur, LA 70665-8901, USA

Lafleur, Greg (Athlete, Football Player)
12527 50th Dr SE
Everett, WA 98208-9627, USA

La Fleur, Guy (Athlete, Hockey Player)
14 Place du Moulin
L'Ile-Bizard, QC H9E 1N2, CANADA

Lafleur, Guy (Athlete, Hockey Player)
Montreal Canadiens
0-1275 Rue Saint-Antoine O
Montreal, QC H3C 5L2, Canada

Lafleur, Guy D (Athlete, Hockey Player)
14 Place du Moulin
L'Ile-Bizard, QC H9E 1N2, Canada

Lafley, Alan G (Business Person)
Procter & Gamble Co
1 Procter and Gamble Plz
Cincinnati, OH 45202-3393, USA

LaFontaine, Patrick (Pat) (Athlete, Hockey Player, Olympic Athlete)
Companions in Courage
PO Box 768
Huntington, NY 11743-0768

Laforest, Pete (Athlete, Baseball Player)
2212 Lansing Ave
Portage, MI 49002-3630, USA

LaForge, Claude (Athlete, Hockey Player)
122-1975 Ch du Fer A Cheval
Ste-Julie, QC J3E 0B7, CANADA

Lafrancois, Roger (Athlete, Baseball Player)
64 Aspinook St
Jewett City, CT 06351-1802, USA

Lafrate, Al (Athlete, Hockey Player)
7975 Five Mile Rd.
Livonia, MI 48154, USA

La Frenais, Ian (Director, Producer, Writer)
c/o Bruce Kaufman *ICM Partners*
10250 Constellation Blvd Fl 7
Los Angeles, CA 90067-6207, USA

Lafreniere, Jason (Athlete, Hockey Player)
261 Front Rd W RR 1
1 L'Orignal, ON KOB IKO, Canada

LaFrentz, Raef (Athlete, Basketball Player)
PO Box 220
Adel, IA 50003-0220, USA

Lafton, James D (Athlete, Football Player)
15487 Mesquite Tree Trl
Poway, CA 92064-2286, USA

Laga, Mike (Athlete, Baseball Player)
148 Maple Ridge Rd
Florence, MA 01062-9749, USA

Laga'aia, Jay (Actor)
Karen Kay Management
PO Box 446
Auckland, NEW ZEALAND

Lagace, Jean-Guy (Athlete, Hockey Player)
6420 Ziklag Cir
Birmingham, AL 35235-2160

Lagace, Pierre (Athlete, Hockey Player)
2403 Brooksboro Dr
Erie, PA 16510-4053

Lagana, Jr., Bobby (Race Car Driver)
72 Woodruff Ave
Scarsdale, NY 10583-5126, USA

Lagana, Sr., Bobby (Race Car Driver)
72 Woodruff Ave
Scarsdale, NY 10583-5126, USA

Lagarde, Tom (Athlete, Basketball Player, Olympic Athlete)
3809 E Greensboro Chapel Hill Rd
Snow Camp, NC 27349-9841, USA

Lagares, Juan (Athlete, Baseball Player)
c/o Sam Levinson *ACES*
188 Montague St Fl 6
Brooklyn, NY 11201-3609, USA

Lagasse, Emeril (Chef)
Nola Restaurant
534 Saint Louis St
New Orleans, LA 70130-2118, USA

Lagasse, Jr., Scott (Race Car Driver)
JTG Racing
7201 Caldwell Rd
Harrisburg, NC 28075-7480, USA

Lagatd, Bernar (Athlete, Olympic Athlete, Track Athlete)
9121 E Cottonwood Ct
Tucson, AZ 85749-9783, USA

Lagattuta, Bill (Correspondent)
CBS-TV
7800 Beverly Blvd
News Dept
Los Angeles, CA 90036-2112, USA

Lagedrost, Kelly (Athlete, Golfer)
10011 Kimbrough Dr
Brooksville, FL 34601-5260, USA

Lageman, Jeff (Athlete, Football Player)
2907 Forest Cir
Jacksonville, FL 32257-5617, USA

Lagerberg, Bengt (Musician)
Motor SE
Gotabergs Gatan 2
Gothenburg 400 14, SWEDEN

Lagerfelt, Caroline (Actor)
8730 W Sunset Blvd Ste 480
Los Angeles, CA 90069-2277, USA

Laghi, Pio Cardinal (Religious Leader)
Catholic Education Congregation
Piazza Pio XII 3
Rome 00193, ITALY

Lago, David Scott (Actor)
c/o Marv Dauer *Marv Dauer Management*
11661 San Vicente Blvd Ste 104
Los Angeles, CA 90049-5150, USA

Lagod, Chet (Athlete, Football Player)
7016 Rocky Trl
Chattanooga, TN 37421-5213, USA

Lagos, Richard (President)
President's Office
Palacio de la Monedo
Santiago, CHILE

Lagrand, Morris (Athlete, Football Player)
4419 Ellenwood Ave
Saint Louis, MO 63116-1521, USA

LaGravenese, Richard (Director, Producer, Writer)
c/o Erwin Stoff *3 Arts Entertainment*
9460 Wilshire Blvd Fl 7
Beverly Hills, CA 90212-2713, USA

Lagrone, John (Athlete, Football Player)
PO Box 428
Fritch, TX 79036-0428, USA

Lagrossa, Stephanie (Reality Star)
c/o Jamie Lopez
3400 Beacon Ave S
the Actors Group
Seattle, WA 98144-6702, USA

Lagrow, Lerrin (Athlete, Baseball Player)
12271 E Turquoise Ave
Scottsdale, AZ 85259-5105, USA

Laguardia, Ernesto (Actor)
c/o Gabriel Blanco *Gabriel Blanco Iglesias (Mexico)*
Rio Balsas 35-32
Colonia Cuauhtemoc
DF 06500, Mexico

Laguna, Ismael (Boxer)
Panama Zona 6
Entrega General
PANAMA

Lahache, Floyd (Athlete, Hockey Player)
Kahnawake
Kahnawake, QC JOL 1BO, Canada

Lahaie, Dick (Race Car Driver)
Drag Racing HOF
13700 SW 16th Ave
Ocala, FL 34473-3970, USA

Lahair, Bryan (Athlete, Baseball Player)
13712 W Country Gables Dr
Surprise, AZ 85379-8335, USA

Lahana, Emma (Actor)
c/o Graciella Sanchez *Echo Lake Management*
421 S Beverly Dr Fl 8
Beverly Hills, CA 90212-4408, USA

La Havas, Lianne (Musician)
c/o Alex Hardee *Coda Music Agency (UK)*
56 Compton St
Clerkenwell
London EC1V 0ET, UNITED KINGDOM

Lahbib, Simone (Actor)
c/o Staff Member *Ken McReddie Ltd*
101 Finsbury Pavement
London EC2A 1RS, UK

Lahgenbrunner, Jamie (Athlete, Hockey Player)
94233 Warloe Shore Ln
Moose Lake, MN 55767-6713, USA

Lahiri, Jhumpa (Writer)
Houghton Mifflin
222 Berkeley St Ste 700
Boston, MA 02116-3777, USA

Lahood, Mike (Athlete, Football Player)
23816 S Bronze Dr
Sun Lakes, AZ 85248-0851, USA

Lahoud, Joe (Athlete, Baseball Player)
90 Tinker Hill Rd
New Preston Marble Dale, CT 06777-1415, USA

Lahould, Emile (President)
Presidential Palace
Baabda
Beirut, LEBANON

Lahren, Tomi (Journalist, Television Host)
c/o Staff Member *TheBlaze*
PO Box 143189
Irving, TX 75014-3189, USA

Lahti, Christine (Actor, Director)
126 Wadsworth Ave
Santa Monica, CA 90405-3510, USA

Lahti, Jeff (Athlete, Baseball Player)
4632 Tyler Dr
Hood River, OR 97031-9742, USA

Laich, Brooks (Athlete, Hockey Player)
PO Box 471
Wawota, SK S0G 5A0, Canada

Laidlaw, Scott (Athlete, Football Player)
209 Peyton Leann Pt
La Vergne, TN 37086-3293, USA

Laidlaw, Tom (Athlete, Hockey Player)
Laidlaw Sports Management
6 Putnam Grn Apt F
Greenwich, CT 06830-6031

Lail, Elizabeth (Actor)
c/o Bob Glennon *Authentic Talent and Literary Management (NY)*
20 Jay St Ste M17
Brooklyn, NY 11201-8300, USA

Lail, Leah (Actor)
c/o Staff Member *Commercial Talent*
12711 Ventura Blvd Ste 285
Studio City, CA 91604-2487, USA

Laimbeer, Bill (Athlete, Basketball Player)
470 Gray Ct
Marco Island, FL 34145-1939, USA

Laine, Cleo (Musician)
Acker's Int'l Jazz
53 Cambridge Mansions
London SW11 4RX, UNITED KINGDOM (UK)

Laine, Skylar (Musician)
c/o Staff Member *19 Entertainment*
401 Wilshire Blvd Ste 1070
Santa Monica, CA 90401-1428, USA

Laing, Bill (Athlete, Hockey Player)
PO Box 88
Harris, SK S0L 1K0, Canada

Laing, Quintin (Athlete, Hockey Player)
PO Box 88
Harris, SK S0L 1K0, Canada

Laird, Bruce (Athlete, Football Player)
20 Stoneridge Ct
Baltimore, MD 21239-1339, USA

Laird, Gerald (Athlete, Baseball Player)
18245 N Pima Rd Apt 2072
Scottsdale, AZ 85255-6370, USA

Laird, Peter (Cartoonist)
351 Pleasant St Ste B
Northampton, MA 01060-3998, USA

Laird, Ron (Athlete, Olympic Athlete, Track Athlete)
4706 Diane Dr
Ashtabula, OH 44004-4636, USA

Laird, Ronald (Ron) (Athlete, Track Athlete)
4706 Diane Dr
Ashtabula, OH 44004-4636, USA

Laitman, Jeffrey (Misc)
Mount Sinai Medical Center
Anatomy Dept
1 Lavy Place
New York, NY 10029, USA

Lajeunesse, Serge (Athlete, Hockey Player)
33 Rue Larocque E
Sainte-Agathe-Des-Monts, QC J8C 1H8, Canada

LaJoie, Jon (Comedian)
c/o Trevor Engelson *Underground Management*
1180 S Beverly Dr Ste 509
Los Angeles, CA 90035-1157, USA

LaJoie, Randy (Race Car Driver)
PO Box 3478
Westport, CT 06880-8478, USA

Lajole, Bill (Baseball Player)
Detroit Tigers
456 Yacht Harbor Dr
Osprey, FL 34229-9744, USA

Lake, Antwan (Athlete, Football Player)
1032 Bluebell Dr
Dacula, GA 30019-7855, USA

Lake, Carnell A (Athlete, Football Player)
PO Box 55048
Irvine, CA 92619-5048, USA

Lake, Don (Actor, Writer)
c/o Gayle Divine *Divine Management*
3822 Latrobe St
Los Angeles, CA 90031-1446

Lake, Julie (Actor)
c/o Dennis Gonzalez *Detail PR*
750 Lexington Ave Fl 9
New York, NY 10022-9847, USA

Lake, Oliver E (Musician)
DL Media
PO Box 2728
Bala Cynwyd, PA 19004-6728, USA

Lake, Ricki (Actor, Talk Show Host)
c/o Nancy Josephson *WME|IMG*
9601 Wilshire Blvd
Beverly Hills, CA 90210-5213, USA

Lake, Sanoe (Actor)
c/o Staff Member *Luber Roklin Management*
5815 W Sunset Blvd Ste 208
Los Angeles, CA 90028-6481, USA

Lake, Steve (Athlete, Baseball Player)
7402 N 177th Ave
Waddell, AZ 85355-9320, USA

Laker, Fredrick A (Business Person)
Princess Tower West Sunrise
Box F207 Freeport
Grand Bahamas, BAHAMAS

Laker, Tim (Athlete, Baseball Player)
325 Spring Breeze Ct
Simi Valley, CA 93065-6719, USA

Lakin, Christine (Actor)
c/o Amy Slomovits *Haven Entertainment*
8111 Beverly Blvd Ste 201
Los Angeles, CA 90048-4531, USA

Lakshmi, Padma (Actor, Television Host)
c/o Christina Papadopoulos *Baker Winokur Ryder Public Relations*
200 5th Ave Fl 5
New York, NY 10010-3307, USA

Lalaine (Actor, Musician)
c/o Peter Young *Sovereign Talent Group*
1642 Westwood Blvd Ste 202
Los Angeles, CA 90024-5609, USA

La Lanne, Jack (Athlete)
430 Quintana Rd
Morro Bay, CA 93442-1937, USA

Lalas, Alexi (Athlete, Soccer Player)
1641 8th St
Manhattan Beach, CA 90266-6352, USA

La Ley (Music Group)
c/o Staff Member *United Talent Agency (UTA)*
9336 Civic Center Dr
Beverly Hills, CA 90210-3604, USA

Laliberte, Guy (Astronaut, Business Person)
Cirque de Soleil
8400 2e Av
Montreal, QC H1Z 4M6, CANADA

LaLiberte, Nicole (Actor)
c/o Bianca Bianconi *42West*
600 3rd Ave Fl 23
New York, NY 10016-1914, USA

Laliberte-Bourque, Andree (Director)
Musee du Quebec
1 Av Wolfe-Montcalm
Quebec, QC G1R 5H3, CANADA

Lalime, Patrick (Athlete, Hockey Player)
Pulver Sports
479 Bedford Park Ave
Attn Ian Pulver
Toronto, ON M5M 1K2, Canada

Lalive, Caroline (Athlete, Olympic Athlete, Skier)
30 Blue Sage Cir Steamboat
Springs, CO 80487-3024, USA

Lally, Bob (Athlete, Football Player)
2716 182nd St
Redondo Beach, CA 90278-3931, USA

Lalonde, Bobby (Athlete, Hockey Player)
523 Broadgreen St
Pickering, ON L1W 3E8, Canada

Lalonde, Larry (Musician)
Figurehead Mgmt
3470 19th St
San Francisco, CA 94110-1740, USA

Lalonde, Ron (Athlete, Hockey Player)
5 Forest Trail
RR 1
Gormley, ON L4A 2E6, Canada

Lalor, Mike (Athlete, Hockey Player)
51 Meadowbrook Rd
Needham, MA 02492-1913

Lam, Derek (Designer)
Derek Lam
764 Madison Ave Frnt 1
New York, NY 10065-6550, USA

Lamar, Chuck (Commentator)
2250 Kent Pl
Clearwater, FL 33764-6623, USA

Lamar, Dwight (Bo) (Athlete, Basketball Player)
103 Claire St
Lafayette, LA 70507-4803, USA

Lamar, Kendrick (Musician)
c/o Zach Iser *Creative Artists Agency (CAA)*
405 Lexington Ave Fl 19
New York, NY 10174-1800, USA

LaMarr, Phil (Actor, Comedian)
c/o Staff Member *Sanders Armstrong Caserta*
4111 W Alameda Ave Ste 505
Burbank, CA 91505-4163, USA

Lamas, AJ (Actor)
c/o Ryan Daly *Zero Gravity Management*
11110 Ohio Ave Ste 100
Los Angeles, CA 90025-3329, USA

Lamb, Ben (Actor)
c/o Deborah Willey *Independent Talent Group*
40 Whitfield St
London W1T 2RH, UNITED KINGDOM

Lamb, Brad (Athlete, Football Player)
2901 Macintosh Ln Apt H
Maineville, OH 45039-9346, USA

Lamb, David (Athlete, Baseball Player)
603 Hampshire Rd Apt 465
Westlake Village, CA 91361-2307, USA

Lamb, John (Athlete, Baseball Player)
PO Box 2
Sharon, CT 06069-0002, USA

Lamb, Mike (Athlete, Baseball Player)
17 Meadow Wood Dr
Trabuco Canyon, CA 92679-4737, USA

Lamb, Ray (Athlete, Baseball Player)
3 Corte Tallista
San Clemente, CA 92673-6863, USA

Lamb, Wally (Writer)
c/o Staff Member *HarperCollins Publishers*
195 Broadway Fl 2
New York, NY 10007-3132, USA

Lamberg, Adam (Actor)
c/o Stephanie Davis *Wet Dog Entertainment*
2458 Crest View Dr
Los Angeles, CA 90046-1407, USA

Lambert, Adam (Musician)
c/o Dvora Vener Englefield *The Lede Company*
9701 Wilshire Blvd # 930
Beverly Hills, CA 90212-2020, USA

Lambert, Chris (Athlete, Baseball Player)
1072 Cilley Rd
Manchester, NH 03103-2908, USA

Lambert, Christopher (Actor, Producer)
c/o Staff Member *McKeon-Myones Management*
3500 W Olive Ave Ste 770
Burbank, CA 91505-5527, USA

Lambert, Dan (Athlete, Hockey Player)
7375 E Wingspan Way
Scottsdale, AZ 85255-4758

Lambert, Dion (Athlete, Football Player)
11249 Wheatland Ave
Sylmar, CA 91342-7033, USA

Lambert, Frank (Athlete, Football Player)
2550 Yeager Rd Apt 16-12
West Lafayette, IN 47906-4002, USA

Lambert, Gordon (Athlete, Football Player)
PO Box 11
Pageton, WV 24871-0011, USA

Lambert, Jack (Athlete, Football Player)
c/o Staff Member *Pittsburgh Steelers*
3400 S Water St
Pittsburgh, PA 15203-2358, USA

Lambert, John (Athlete, Basketball Player)
260 Clear Ridge Dr
Healdsburg, CA 95448-7057, USA

Lambert, Lane (Athlete, Hockey Player)
Nashville Predators
501 Broadway
Nashville, TN 37203-3980

Lambert, Mary (Musician)
c/o JD Sobol *Almond Talent Management*
8217 Beverly Blvd Ste 8
W Hollywood, CA 90048-4534, USA

Lambert, Miranda (Musician)
c/o Staff Member *Shopkeeper Management*
1200 Villa Pl Ste 407
Nashville, TN 37212-3045, USA

Lambert, Sheila (Basketball Player)
Charlotte Sting
100 Hive Dr
Charlotte, NC 28217, USA

Lamberti, Pasquale (Athlete, Football Player)
8 Wellington Ave
Everett, MA 02149-1818, USA

Lambiel, Stephane (Figure Skater)
c/o Staff Member *Art on Ice Production*
Siewerdtstrasse 95
Zurich CH-8050, SWITZERLAND

Lamb Of God (Music Group)
c/o Tim Borror *Sound Talent Group*
1870 Joe Crosson Dr
Hangar 111
El Cajon, CA 92020-1271, USA

Lamborn, Doug (Congressman, Politician)
437 Cannon Hob
Washington, DC 20515-1902, USA

Lamby, Dick (Athlete, Hockey Player, Olympic Athlete)
3 Ocean Ave
Salem, MA 01970-5456

Lamelin, Stephanie (Actor)
c/o Katie Mason Stern *Luber Roklin Management*
5815 W Sunset Blvd Ste 208
Los Angeles, CA 90028-6481, USA

Lamkin, Kathy (Actor)
c/o Linda McAlister *Linda McAlister Talent*
30 N Raymond Ave Ste 213
Pasadena, CA 91103-3997, USA

Lamm, Richard D (Politician)
University of Denver
W Center Ave For Public Policy
Denver, CO 80219, USA

Lamm, Robert (Musician)
Air Tight Mgmt
115 West Rd
Winchester Center, CT 06098-2301, USA

Lammens, Hank (Athlete, Hockey Player)
11 Hilltop Rd
Norwalk, CT 06854-5001

Lammers, Esmee (Director, Writer)
Features Creative Mgmt
Entrepotdok 76A
Amsterdam, AD 00101, NETHERLANDS

Lammons, Pete (Athlete, Football Player)
5006 E Fallen Bough Dr
Houston, TX 77041-7887, USA

Lamonica, Darryl (Athlete, Football Player)
8796 N 6th St
Fresno, CA 93720-1711, USA

Lamonica, Daryle (Athlete, Football Player)
8796 N 6th St
Fresno, CA 93720-1711, USA

Lamonica, Roberto de (Artist)
Rua Anibal de Mendanca 180
AP 202
Rio De Janeiro, RJ ZC-37, BRAZIL

Lamont, Gene W (Athlete, Baseball Player, Coach)
5349 Carmilfra Dr
Sarasota, FL 34231-4264, USA

LaMontagne, Ray (Musician)
c/o Staff Member *Paradigm (Monterey)*
404 W Franklin St
Monterey, CA 93940-2303, USA

Lamoriello, Lou (Athlete, Hockey Player)
6D Cove Ln N # D
North Bergen, NJ 07047-6237

LaMorte, Robia (Actor)
c/o Rob D'Avola *Rob DAvola & Associates*
9107 Wilshire Blvd # 405
Beverly Hills, CA 90210-5531, USA

Lamothe, Marc (Athlete, Hockey Player)
248 Bruyere St
Ottawa, ON K1N 5E6, Canada

Lamott, Anne (Writer)
c/o Steven Barclay *Steven Barclay Agency*
12 Western Ave
Petaluma, CA 94952-2907, USA

Lamp, Dennis (Athlete, Baseball Player)
30824 La Miranda Unit 228
Rancho Santa Margarita, CA 92688-5812, USA

Lamp, Jeff (Athlete, Basketball Player)
4971 Credit River Dr
Savage, MN 55378-4610, USA

Lampanelli, Lisa (Comedian)
1053 Fairfield Beach Rd
Fairfield, CT 06824-6561, USA

Lampard, Frank (Athlete, Soccer Player)
Chelsea Football Club
Stamford Bridge
Fulham Road
London SW6 1HS, UNITED KINGDOM

Lampard, Keith (Athlete, Baseball Player)
6124 Highway 6 N
Houston, TX 77084-1304, USA

Lamparski, Richard (Writer)
4202 Calle Real Apt 245
Santa Barbara, CA 93110-4081, USA

Lampert, Zohra (Actor)
Don Buchwald
5900 Wilshire Blvd Ste 3100
Los Angeles, CA 90036-5030, USA

Lamphear, Dan (Athlete, Football Player)
669 Bent Ridge Ln
Barrington, IL 60010-6604, USA

Lampkin, Tom (Athlete, Baseball Player)
19307 NE Davis Rd
Brush Prairie, WA 98606-8777, USA

Lampley, Jim (Sportscaster)
3325 Caminito Daniella
Del Mar, CA 92014-4155, USA

Lamplugh, Ian (Baseball Player)
1830 Fairburn Dr
Victoria, BC V8N 1P9, CANADA

Lamplugh, Ian (Athlete, Baseball Player)
1830 Fairburn Dr
Victoria, BC V8N 1P9, Canada

Lamplugh, Ian (Athlete, Baseball Player)
1830 Fairburn Dr
Victoria BC, V8N 1P9 Canada, USA

Lampman, Bryce (Athlete, Hockey Player)
1568 Redwood Ln SW
Rochester, MN 55902-1688

Lampman, Mike (Athlete, Hockey Player)
7007 Hawaii Kai Dr Apt D22
Honolulu, HI 96825-3141

Lampton, Michael (Astronaut)
University of California
Space Science Laboratory # 407
Berkeley, CA 94720-0001, USA

Lanasa, Katherine (Actor, Dancer)
c/o Wendy Murphey *LBI Entertainment*
2000 Avenue of the Stars
N Tower Fl 3
Los Angeles, CA 90067-4700, USA

Lancaster, Les (Athlete, Baseball Player)
PO Box 1105
Dothan, AL 36302-1105, USA

Lancaster, Mark (Horse Racer)
195 Mill Ln W
Columbus, NJ 08022-1941, USA

Lancaster, Neal (Athlete, Golfer)
6 Quail Run
Smithfield, NC 27577, USA

Lancaster, Penny (Actor)
c/o Staff Member *Special Artists Agency*
9200 W Sunset Blvd Ste 410
W Hollywood, CA 90069-3506, USA

Lancaster, Sarah (Actor)
c/o Robert (Rob) Gomez *Precision Entertainment*
6338 Wilshire Blvd
Los Angeles, CA 90048-5002, USA

Lance, Dirk (Musician)
c/o Staff Member *ArtistDirect*
9046 Lindblade St
Culver City, CA 90232-2513, USA

Lance, Gary (Athlete, Baseball Player)
212 Sunset Cir
Prosperity, SC 29127-8426, USA

Lance, Leonard (Congressman, Politician)
426 Cannon Hob
Washington, DC 20515-3813, USA

Lancellotti, Rick (Athlete, Baseball Player)
5190 Thompson Rd
Clarence, NY 14031-1127, USA

Lancelotti, Rick (Athlete, Baseball Player)
5190 Thompson Rd
Clarence, NY 14031-1127, USA

Landaker, Dave (Baseball Player)
Topps
3593 Buffum St
Simi Valley, CA 93063-3215, USA

Landau, Jacob (Artist)
2 Pine Dr
Roosevelt, NJ 08555-7011, USA

Landau, Jon (Director, Producer, Writer)
c/o Staff Member *LightStorm Entertainment*
919 Santa Monica Blvd
Santa Monica, CA 90401-2704, USA

Landau, Juliet (Actor)
Miss Juliet Productions
PO Box 2792
Hollywood, CA 90078-2792

Landeau, Aleksia (Actor)
c/o Staff Member *Metropolitan (MTA)*
4526 Wilshire Blvd
Los Angeles, CA 90010-3801, USA

Landecker, Amy (Actor)
c/o Lisa Sharon Goldberg *Lisa Sharon Goldberg*
88 Leonard St Apt 607
New York, NY 10013-3495, USA

Lander, David L (Actor)
c/o Staff Member *Arlene Thornton & Associates*
12711 Ventura Blvd Ste 490
Studio City, CA 91604-2477, USA

Lander, Natalie (Actor)
c/o Scott Zimmerman *Scott Zimmerman Management*
1644 Courtney Ave
Los Angeles, CA 90046-2708, USA

Landers, Amy (Actor)
c/o Staff Member *Badgley-Connor-King*
9229 W Sunset Blvd Ste 311
Los Angeles, CA 90069-3403, USA

Landers, Andy (Coach)
University of Georgia
Athletic Dept
Athens, GA 30602-0001, USA

Landers, Audrey (Actor, Musician)
688 Eagle Watch Ln
Osprey, FL 34229-9356, USA

Landers, Judy (Actor)
3933 Losillias Dr
Sarasota, FL 34238-4537, USA

Landers, Kristy (Actor)
c/o Gregory (Greg) Redlitz *Robert Thorne Company*
9654 Heather Rd
Beverly Hills, CA 90210-1757, USA

Landers, Robert (Athlete, Golfer)
PO Box 497
Azle, TX 76098-0497, USA

Landes, Michael (Actor)
c/o Jason Weinberg *Untitled Entertainment*
350 S Beverly Dr Ste 200
Beverly Hills, CA 90212-4819, USA

Landesberg, Sylven (Athlete, Basketball Player)
c/o Jeff Schwartz *Excel Sports Management*
1700 Broadway Fl 29
New York, NY 10019-6559, USA

Landesman, Peter (Producer)
c/o Amanda Lundberg *42West*
600 3rd Ave Fl 23
New York, NY 10016-1914, USA

Landestoy, Rafael (Athlete, Baseball Player)
13564 SW 177th Ter
Miami, FL 33177-7777, USA

Landeta, Sean (Athlete, Football Player)
PO Box 422
Manhasset, NY 11030-0422, USA

Landey, Nina (Actor)
c/o Staff Member *Bauman Redanty & Shaul Agency*
5757 Wilshire Blvd
Suite 473
Beverly Hills, CA 90212, USA

Landham, Sonny (Actor)

Landi, Alex (Actor)
c/o Jessica Katz *Katz Public Relations*
14527 Dickens St
Sherman Oaks, CA 91403-3756, USA

Landi, Sal (Actor)
c/o Craig Mobbs *AKA Talent Agency*
325 N Larchmont Blvd
Los Angeles, CA 90004-3011, USA

Landis, Bill (Athlete, Baseball Player)
525 E Sycamore Dr
Hanford, CA 93230-1443, USA

Landis, Floyd (Athlete)
Ouch Pro Cycling Team
3530 Grand Ave Ste 4
Oakland, CA 94610-2036, USA

Landis, John (Director)
c/o Staff Member *Levitsky Productions*
9701 Wilshire Blvd Ste 800
Beverly Hills, CA 90212-2033, USA

Lando, Joe (Actor)
c/o Staff Member *GVA Talent Agency Inc*
193 N Robertson Blvd
Beverly Hills, CA 90211-2103, USA

Landon, Bruce (Athlete, Hockey Player)
250 Dewey St
West Springfield, MA 01089-1606

Landon, Jennifer (Actor)
c/o Jamie Freed *Paris Hilton Entertainment*
2934 1/2 N Beverly Glen Cir # 383
Los Angeles, CA 90077-1724, USA

Landon, Larry (Athlete, Hockey Player)
Pro Hockey Players Association
3964 Portage Rd
Niagara Falls, ON L2J 2K9, Canada

Landon, R Kirk (Business Person)
Lennar
700 NW 107th Ave Ste 300
Miami, FL 33172-3139, USA

Landon Jr, Michael (Actor, Director, Producer)
9595 Wilshire Blvd Ste 711
Beverly Hills, CA 90212-2514, USA

Landreaux, Ken (Athlete, Baseball Player)
JD Legends Promotions
10808 Foothill Blvd Ste 160 PMB 454
Rancho Cucamonga, CA 91730-0601, USA

Landreth, Larry (Athlete, Baseball Player)
116 St Vincent St S
Stratford, ON N5A 2W8, Canada

Landri, Derek (Athlete, Football Player)
5142 Donnington Rd
Clarence, NY 14031-1501, USA

Landrieu, Mary (Politician)
405 E Capitol St SE
Washington, DC 20003-3810, USA

Landrieu, Moon (Politician)
4301 S Prieur St
New Orleans, LA 70125-5125, USA

Landrith, Hobie (Athlete, Baseball Player)
1462 Nome Ct
Sunnyvale, CA 94087-4264, USA

Landrum, Bill (Athlete, Baseball Player)
840 Silverpoint Rd
Chapin, SC 29036-7963, USA

Landrum, Ced (Athlete, Baseball Player)
2425 Hillview Dr
Fort Worth, TX 76119-2722, USA

Landrum, Joe (Athlete, Baseball Player)
840 Silverpoint Rd
Chapin, SC 29036-7963, USA

Landrum, Mike (Athlete, Football Player)
88 Raybourn Rd
Sumrall, MS 39482-3926, USA

Landrum, Tito (Athlete, Baseball Player)
428 E 58th St Apt Grd
New York, NY 10022-2362, USA

Landry, Ali (Actor, Model)
c/o Staff Member *Reel Talent Management*
PO Box 491035
Los Angeles, CA 90049-9035, USA

Landry, Damarius (Athlete, Football Player)

Landry, Dawan (Athlete, Football Player)
309 Kennedy St
Ama, LA 70031, USA

Landry, Gregory P (Greg) (Athlete, Coach, Football Coach, Football Player)
133 Melanie Ln
Troy, MI 48098-1707, USA

Landry, Jarvis (Athlete, Football Player)
c/o Damarius Bilbo *Revolution Sports*
270 17th St NW Unit 3001
Atlanta, GA 30363-1261, USA

Landry, Troy (Reality Star)
Choot Em Enterprises
506 Renwick Blvd
Berwick, LA 70342-3212, USA

Landsberger, Mark (Athlete, Basketball Player)
1702 8th Ave SE
Saint Cloud, MN 56304-2104, USA

Landsburg, Valerie (Actor)
31 Talbot Ave
Rockland, ME 04841-2922, USA

Landsee, Bob (Athlete, Football Player)
PO Box 628128
Middleton, WI 53562-8128, USA

Landsee, Robert (Athlete, Football Player)
PO Box 628128
Middleton, WI 53562-8128, USA

Landy, Leonard (Actor)
78229 Kistler Way
Palm Desert, CA 92211-2725, USA

Lane, Abbe (Actor, Musician)
500 Bel Air Rd
Los Angeles, CA 90077-3817, USA

Lane, Barry (Athlete, Golfer)
I M G
1360 E 9th St Ste 100
Cleveland, OH 44114-1730, USA

Lane, Cristy (Musician)
PO Box 654
Madison, TN 37116-0654, USA

Lane, Diane (Actor)
DaLane Productions
9903 Santa Monica Blvd # 1037
Beverly Hills, CA 90212-1671, USA

Lane, Dick (Athlete, Baseball Player)
642 25th St
Hermosa Beach, CA 90254-2210, USA

Lane, Garcia (Athlete, Football Player)
5128 Stone Ridge Rd S Apt I
Columbus, OH 43213-4141, USA

Lane, Gord (Athlete, Hockey Player)
5656 Vantage Point Rd
Columbia, MD 21044-2613

Lane, Jason (Athlete, Baseball Player)
8930 Oak Grove Ave
Sebastopol, CA 95472-2460, USA

Lane, Jerome (Athlete, Basketball Player)
1500 Marion Ave Apt 509
Akron, OH 44313-7628, USA

Lane, John R (Jack) (Misc)
San Francisco Museum of Modem Art
151 3rd St
San Francisco, CA 94103-3107, USA

Lane, Lilas (Actor)
c/o Peter Himberger *Impact Artists Group LLC*
42 Hamilton Ter
New York, NY 10031-6403, USA

Lane, MacArthur (Athlete, Football Player)
3238 Knowland Ave
Oakland, CA 94619-2630, USA

Lane, Malcolm D (Misc)
5607 Roxbury Pl
Baltimore, MD 21209-4501, USA

Lane, Marvin (Marv) (Athlete, Baseball Player)
40164 Gulliver Dr
Sterling Heights, MI 48310-1729, USA

Lane, Max (Athlete, Football Player)
16 Strong St
Newburyport, MA 01950-2411, USA

Lane, Mike (Cartoonist)
Baltimore Sun
501 N Calvert St
Editorial Dept
Baltimore, MD 21278-1000, USA

Lane, Nathan (Actor, Musician)
c/o Simon Halls *Slate PR*
901 N Highland Ave
W Hollywood, CA 90038-2412, USA

Lane, Sasha (Actor)

Lane, Skip (Athlete, Business Person, Football Player)
14 Roosevelt Rd
Westport, CT 06880-6840, USA

Lane, Tory (Actor, Adult Film Star, Model)
c/o Staff Member *LA Direct Models*
3599 Cahuenga Blvd W Ste 4D
Los Angeles, CA 90068-1596, USA

Lanegan, Mark (Musician)
Helter Skelter Plaza
535 Kings Road
London SW1O 0S, UNITED KINGDOM (UK)

Laneuville, Eric (Actor)
5140 W Slauson Ave
Los Angeles, CA 90056-1641, USA

Lang, Andrew (Athlete, Basketball Player)
1048 Woodruff Plantation Pkwy SE
Marietta, GA 30067-9106, USA

Lang, Antonio (Athlete, Basketball Player)
2255 Barretts Ln
Mobile, AL 36617-2734, USA

Lang, Belinda (Actor)
Ken McReddie
91 Regent St
London W1R 7TB, UNITED KINGDOM (UK)

Lang, Chip (Athlete, Baseball Player)
132 Westminster Dr
Pittsburgh, PA 15229-3165, USA

Lang, Gene (Athlete, Football Player)
11526 Azalea Trce
Gulfport, MS 39503-8398, USA

Lang, Helmut (Designer, Fashion Designer)
Helmut Lang New York
819 Washington St
New York, NY 10014-1405, USA

Lang, Jack (Writer)
4 Barry Dr
E Northport, NY 11731-1307, USA

Lang, Jonny (Musician)
Blue Sky Artists
761 Washington Ave N
Minneapolis, MN 55401-1101, USA

Lang, June (Actor)
12756 Kahlenberg Ln
North Hollywood, CA 91607-2919, USA

Lang, Katherine Kelly (Actor, Model)
""The Bold and The Beautiful""
7800 Beverly Blvd Ste 3371
Bell-Phillip Television Productions Inc
Los Angeles, CA 90036-2112, USA

Lang, KD (Actor, Musician)
1314 NW Irving St Apt 713 # 714
Portland, OR 97209-2728, USA

Lang, Kenard (Athlete, Football Player)
1781 Oakbrook Dr
Longwood, FL 32779-3168, USA

Lang, Lang (Musician)
c/o Staff Member *Columbia Artists Mgmt Inc*
1790 Broadway Fl 6
New York, NY 10019-1537, USA

Lang, Le-Lo (Athlete, Football Player)
19436 E Maplewood Pl
Aurora, CO 80016-3868, USA

Lang, Stephen (Actor)
c/o Staff Member *The Actors Studio*
432 W 44th St
New York, NY 10036-5205, USA

Lang, T.J. (Athlete, Football Player)
c/o Michael McCartney *Priority Sports & Entertainment (Chicago)*
325 N La Salle Dr Ste 650
Chicago, IL 60654-8182, USA

Langdon, Darren (Athlete, Hockey Player)
1 Oake's Rd
Deer Lake, NL A8A 1X5, Canada

Langdon, Sue Ane (Actor)
4618 Park Mirasol
Calabasas, CA 91302-1731, USA

Langdon, Sue Ann (Actor)
4618 Park Mirasol
Calabasas, CA 91302-1731, USA

Lange, Andre (Athlete)
BSD
An der Schiessstatte 4
Berchtesgaden 83471, GERMANY

Lange, Artie (Actor)
c/o Rich Super *Gersh*
9465 Wilshire Blvd Ste 600
Beverly Hills, CA 90212-2605, USA

Lange, Dick (Athlete, Baseball Player)
39744 Salvatore Dr
Sterling Heights, MI 48313-5165, USA

Lange, Eric (Actor)
c/o Michael Geiser *Jill Fritzo Public Relations*
208 E 51st St # 305
New York, NY 10022-6557, USA

Lange, Jessica (Actor)
c/o Jason Weinberg *Untitled Entertainment*
350 S Beverly Dr Ste 200
Beverly Hills, CA 90212-4819, USA

Lange, Niklaus (Actor)
c/o Staff Member *AKA Talent Agency*
325 N Larchmont Blvd
Los Angeles, CA 90004-3011, USA

Lange, Ted (Actor)
c/o Joy Pervis *J Pervis Talent Agency*
3050 Amwiler Rd Ste 200
Atlanta, GA 30360-2807, USA

Lange, Thomas (Athlete)
ratzeburger Ruderclub
Domhof 57
Farmville, VA 23909-0001, GERMANY

Langehorne, Reggie (Athlete, Football Player)
12260 Smiths Neck Rd
Carrollton, VA 23314-3802, USA

Langella, Frank (Actor)
c/o Frank Frattaroli *Circle of Confusion*
8931 Ellis Ave
Los Angeles, CA 90034-3336, USA

Langen, Christoph (Athlete)
BC Onterhaching
Ottobrunner Str 16
Unterhaching 82008, GERMANY

Langenbrunner, Jamie (Athlete, Hockey Player, Olympic Athlete)
2 Maywood Ct
Caldwell, NJ 07006-4316

Langencamp, Reather (Actor)
156 F St SE
Washington, DC 20003-2603, USA

Langenkamp, Heather (Actor)
c/o Staff Member *AFX Studios*
14734 Arminta St
Panorama City, CA 91402-5904, USA

Langer, AJ (Actor)
c/o Michael Valeo *Valeo Entertainment*
8581 Santa Monica Blvd Ste 570
West Hollywood, CA 90069-4120, USA

Langer, Bernhard (Athlete, Golfer)
3667 Princeton Pl
Boca Raton, FL 33496-2711, USA

Langer, James J (Jim) (Athlete, Football Player)
14280 Wolfram St NW
Ramsey, MN 55303-4563, USA

Langerhans, Ryan (Athlete, Baseball Player)
18911 Angel Mountain Dr
Leander, TX 78641-3805, USA

Langevin, Dave (Athlete, Hockey Player)
6506 Gleason Ct
Minneapolis, MN 55436-1850

Langevin, Jim (Politician)
Jim Langevin for Congress
181 Knight St Ste A
Warwick, RI 02886-1296, USA

Langfeld, Josh (Athlete, Hockey Player)
13050 Linnet St NW
Minneapolis, MN 55448-7078

Langford, Jevon (Athlete, Football Player)
1 Paul Brown Stadium
Cincinnati, OH 45202-3418, USA

Langford, Katherine (Actor)
c/o Jeff Golenberg *Silver Lining Entertainment*
421 S Beverly Dr Fl 7
Beverly Hills, CA 90212-4408, USA

Langford, Kendall (Athlete, Football Player)
c/o Adisa P Bakari *Kelley Drye & Warren LLP*
3050 K St NW Ste 400
Washington, DC 20007-5100, USA

Langford, Rick (Athlete, Baseball Player)
611 Riviera Dunes Way Apt 101
Palmetto, FL 34221-7151, USA

Langham, C Antonio (Athlete, Football Player)
PO Box 232
Town Creek, AL 35672-0232, USA

Langham, Franklin (Athlete, Golfer)
PO Box 3428
Peachtree City, GA 30269-7428, USA

Langham, Wallace (Actor)
c/o Kristin Nava *Abrams Artists Agency*
750 N San Vicente Blvd
E Tower Fl 11
Los Angeles, CA 90069-5788, USA

Langham, Wally (Actor)
c/o Josh Katz *United Talent Agency (UTA)*
9336 Civic Center Dr
Beverly Hills, CA 90210-3604, USA

Langhorne, Reggie (Athlete, Football Player)
12260 Smiths Neck Rd
Carrollton, VA 23314-3802, USA

Langkow, Daymond (Athlete, Hockey Player)
7940 E Quill Ln
Scottsdale, AZ 85255-6428

Langley, Neva (Beauty Pageant Winner)
6300 Rivoli Dr
Macon, GA 31210-1459, USA

Langley, Roger (Skier)
Broad St
Barre, MA 01005, USA

Langlois, Lisa (Actor)
c/o Staff Member *Leavitt Talent Group*
11500 W Olympic Blvd Ste 400
Los Angeles, CA 90064-1525, USA

Langlois, Paul (Musician)
Management Trust
309B-219 Dufferin St
Toronto, ON M6K 3J1, CANADA

Langlois Jr, Albert (Athlete, Hockey Player)
2473 Crest View Dr
Los Angeles, CA 90046-1406

Langmann, Thomas (Producer)
La Petite Reine
20, rue de Saint-Petersbourg
Paris F-75008, France

Langone, Kenneth (Business Person)
Invemed Associates
375 Park Ave Ste 2205
New York, NY 10152-0189, USA

Langone, Stefano (Musician)
c/o Simon Fuller *XIX Entertainment (UK)*
32/33 Ransomes Dock
London SW11 4NP, UNITED KINGDOM (UK)

Langston, Mark E (Athlete, Baseball Player)
56 Golden Eagle
Irvine, CA 92603-0309, USA

Langston, Murray (Actor, Comedian)
Entertainment Alliance
PO Box 4734
Santa Rosa, CA 95402-4734, USA

Langton, Brooke (Actor)
Rigberg Roberts Rugolo
1180 S Beverly Dr Ste 601
Los Angeles, CA 90035-1158, USA

Langton, Brooke (Actor)
c/o Mark Measures *Kazarian, Measures, Ruskin & Associates*
5200 Lankershim Blvd Ste 820
N Hollywood, CA 91601-3194, USA

Langway, Rod (Athlete, Hockey Player)
Brookfield Place
30 Yonge St
Toronto, ON M5E 1X8, CANADA

Lanier, Bob (Athlete, Basketball Player, Coach)
Bob Lanier Enterprises Inc.
N93W14575 Whittaker Way
Menomonee Falls, WI 53051-1652, USA

Lanier, Chris (Artist)
c/o Staff Member *Fantagraphics Books*
7563 Lake City Way NE
Seattle, WA 98115-4218, USA

Lanier, Harold C (Hal) (Athlete, Baseball Player, Coach)
3270 Countryside View Dr
Saint Cloud, FL 34772-7050, USA

Lanier, Ken (Athlete, Football Player)
21923 E Ridge Trail Cir
Aurora, CO 80016-2665, USA

Lanier, Lorenzo (Rimp) (Athlete, Baseball Player)
4515 E Frontenac Dr
Cleveland, OH 44128-5004, USA

Lanier, Lorenzo ""Rimp"" (Athlete, Baseball Player)
4515 E Frontenac Dr
Cleveland, OH 44128-5004, USA

Lanier, Willie E (Athlete, Football Player)
2911 E Brigstock Rd
Midlothian, VA 23113-3905, USA

Lankford, Frank (Athlete, Baseball Player)
104 Lakeview Ave NE
Atlanta, GA 30305-3725, USA

Lankford, James (Congressman)
509 Cannon Hob
Washington, DC 20515-4207, USA

Lankford, Kim (Actor)
6071 US 64
Bloomfield, NM 87413-9551, USA

Lankford, Paul (Athlete, Football Player)
3838 Biggin Church Rd W
Jacksonville, FL 32224-7984, USA

Lankford, Ray (Athlete, Baseball Player)
1520 Lake Whitney Dr
Windermere, FL 34786-6041, USA

Lannan, John (Athlete, Baseball Player)
2515 W Edgewood Rd
Tampa, FL 33609-5300, USA

Lannetta, Chris (Athlete, Baseball Player)
Jack Winery
PO Box 6048
Napa, CA 94581-1048, USA

Lanois, Daniel (Actor, Musician)
c/o Staff Member *Paradigm (Monterey)*
404 W Franklin St
Monterey, CA 93940-2303, USA

lanotta, Howard (Athlete, Basketball Player)
18118 Brookwood Frst
San Antonio, TX 78258-4474, USA

Lanphear, Dan (Athlete, Football Player)
669 Bent Ridge Ln
Barrington, IL 60010-6604, USA

LanSala, James (Misc)
Amalgamated Transit Union
10000 New Hampshire Ave
Silver Spring, MD 20903-1706, USA

Lansanah, Danny (Athlete, Football Player)
c/o Ed Wasielewski *EMG Sports - PA*
PO Box 2
Richboro, PA 18954-0002, USA

Lansbury, Angela (Actor, Musician)
635 N Bonhill Rd
Los Angeles, CA 90049-2301, USA

Lansbury, David (Actor)
Don Buchwald
5900 Wilshire Blvd Ste 3100
Los Angeles, CA 90036-5030, USA

Lansford, Alex (Athlete, Football Player)
PO Box 905
Lampasas, TX 76550-0007, USA

Lansford, Carney (Athlete, Baseball Player)
43736 Pocahontas Rd
Baker City, OR 97814-8173, USA

Lansford, Jody (Athlete, Baseball Player)
5730 San Lorenzo Dr
San Jose, CA 95123-2967, USA

Lansford, Mike (Athlete, Football Player)
6200 E Canyon Rim Rd Ste 205
Anaheim, CA 92807-4340, USA

Lansing, Mike (Athlete, Baseball Player)
9691 Sun Meadow St
Highlands Ranch, CO 80129-6925, USA

Lansing, Sherry (Producer)
10741 Levico Way
Los Angeles, CA 90077-1918, USA

Lanter, Matt (Actor)
c/o Whitney Tancred *42West*
1840 Century Park E Ste 700
Los Angeles, CA 90067-2122, USA

Lantz, Stu (Athlete, Basketball Player)
5270 Mount Burnham Dr
San Diego, CA 92111-3948, USA

Lanus, Valentino (Actor)
c/o Angel Hidalgo *Angel Hidalgo Management*
Gral Mendez #3 Int. C001
Col Ampliacion Daniel Garza
Mexico City 11830, MEXICO

Lanvin, Bernard (Designer, Fashion Designer)
22 Rue du Faubourg Saint Honore
Paris 70008, FRANCE

Lanz, David (Musician)
c/o Narada
4650 N Port Washington Rd
Milwaukee, WI 53212-1077, USA

Lanz, Rick (Athlete, Hockey Player)
18962 20 Ave
Surrey, BC V3Z 9V2, Canada

Lanza, Charles (Athlete, Football Player)
19 Snowberry Ct
Cockeysville, MD 21030-1954, USA

La Oreja de Van Gogh (Music Group)
c/o Staff Member *Sony Music (Miami)*
404 Washington Ave Ste 700
Miami Beach, FL 33139-6615, USA

Laoretti, Larry (Athlete, Golfer)
712 Baytree Dr
Titusville, FL 32780-2310, USA

LaPaglia, Anthony (Actor)
c/o Jennifer Allen *Viewpoint Inc*
8820 Wilshire Blvd Ste 220
Beverly Hills, CA 90211-2622, USA

LaPaglia, Jonathan (Actor)
c/o Evan Hainey *Untitled Entertainment*
350 S Beverly Dr Ste 200
Beverly Hills, CA 90212-4819, USA

Lapaine, Daniel (Actor)
c/o Robert Marsala *Wishlab*
195 S Beverly Dr Ste 414
Beverly Hills, CA 90212-3044, USA

Laperriere, Ian (Athlete, Hockey Player)
C A A Sports
2000 Avenue of the Stars Fl 3
Los Angeles, CA 90067-4704, USA

Laperrlere, Jacques (Athlete, Hockey Player)
New Jersey Devils
165 Mulberry St
Newark, NJ 07102-3607

Lapham, Bill (Athlete, Football Player)
136 S 52nd St
West Des Moines, IA 50265-2895, USA

Lapham, Dave (Athlete, Football Player)
8254 Sunfish Ln
Maineville, OH 45039-8978, USA

Lapidus, Edmond (Ted) (Designer, Fashion Designer)
66 Blvd Maurice-Barres
Neuilly-sur-Seine 92200, FRANCE

Lapin, Nicole (Business Person, Commentator, Television Host)
c/o Jaime Cassavechia *EJ Media Group*
349 5th Ave Fl 3
New York, NY 10016-5021, USA

Lapine, James E (Director, Writer)
c/o Staff Member *Judi Farkas Management*
116 N Mansfield Ave
Los Angeles, CA 90036-3021, USA

Lapira, Liza (Actor)
c/o Jack Ketsoyan *EMC / Bowery*
8356 Fountain Ave Apt E1
W Hollywood, CA 90069-2968, USA

Lapka, Myron (Athlete, Football Player)
3982 Hemway Ct
Simi Valley, CA 93063-2848, USA

Lapkus, Lauren (Actor)
c/o Naomi Odenkirk *Odenkirk Provissiero Entertainment*
1936 N Bronson Ave
Raleigh Studios
Los Angeles, CA 90068-5602, USA

La Placa, Alison (Actor)
c/o Staff Member *Marshak/Zachary Company, The*
8840 Wilshire Blvd Fl 1
Beverly Hills, CA 90211-2606, USA

LaPlaca, Alison (Actor)
1614 Argyle Ave
Hollywood, CA 90028-6408, USA

LaPlanche, Rosemary (Actor)
13914 Hartsook St
Sherman Oaks, CA 91423-1210, USA

La Plante, Lynda (Writer)
c/o Nigel Stoneman *La Plante Global*
5-11 Regent St
Charles House
London SW1Y4LR, UNITED KINGDOM

Lapoint, Dave (Athlete, Baseball Player)
11704 Stonewood Gate Dr
Riverview, FL 33579-4025, USA

Lapointe, Claude (Athlete, Hockey Player)
400 S Orange St Apt 214
Media, PA 19063-3655

Lapointe, Martin (Athlete, Hockey Player)
317 Washington St
Saint Paul, MN 55102-1609

Lapointe, Ron (Athlete, Football Player)
940 E Haverford Rd
Bryn Mawr, PA 19010-3845, USA

Laport, Osvaldo (Actor)
c/o Staff Member *Telefe (Argentina)*
Pavon 2444
Buenos Aires C1248AAT, ARGENTINA

LaPorte, Danny (Race Car Driver)
949 Via Del Monte
Palos Verdes Estates, CA 90274-1615, USA

Lapotaire, Jane (Actor)
92 Oxford Gardens
#C
London W10, UNITED KINGDOM (UK)

Lappalainen, Markku (Musician)
Island Def Jam Records
8920 W Sunset Blvd # 200
Los Angeles, CA 90069-1832, USA

Lappas, Steve (Coach)
Villanova University
Athletic Dept
Villanova, PA 19085, USA

Lappe, Frances Moore (Writer)
989 Market St
San Francisco, CA 94103-1708, USA

Lappin, Peter (Athlete, Hockey Player)
1258 Meadows Rd
Geneva, IL 60134-3214

La Prada, Edgar (Athlete, Hockey Player)
12 Shuniah St
Thunder Bay, ON P7A 2Y8, CANADA

LaPraed, Ronald (Ron) (Musician)
Management Assoc
1920 Benson Ave
Saint Paul, MN 55116-3214, USA

Lara, Joe (Actor)
15301 Ventura Blvd # 345
Sherman Oaks, CA 91403-3102, USA

Laraway, Jack (Athlete, Football Player)
278 Breezewood Dr
Bay Village, OH 44140-1279, USA

Lardner Jr, George (Journalist)
Washington Post
Editorial Dept
1150 15th St NW
Washington, DC 20071-0001, USA

Lardon, Brad (Athlete, Golfer)
324 Cordova Ln
Santa Fe, NM 87505-0617, USA

Lardy, Henry A (Misc)
3902 Meyer Ave
Madison, WI 53711-1617, USA

Laredo, Jaime (Musician)
Harold Holt
31 Sinclair Road
London W14 0NS, UNITED KINGDOM (UK)

Laredo, Ruth (Musician)
I C M Artists
40 W 57th St
New York, NY 10019-4001, USA

Larena, John (Designer)
c/o Staff Member *Mirisch Agency*
8840 Wilshire Blvd Ste 100
Beverly Hills, CA 90211-2606, USA

Laresca, Vincent (Actor)
c/o Brandy Gold *TalentWorks*
3500 W Olive Ave Ste 1400
Burbank, CA 91505-5512, USA

Larese, York (Athlete, Basketball Player)
22 Grove Pl Unit 15
Winchester, MA 01890-3863, USA

Large, Storm (Musician)
The Dowd Agency
444 Park Ave S PH
New York, NY 10016-7536, USA

Largent, Steve (Athlete, Football Player, Politician)
2914 E 44th Pl
Tulsa, OK 74105-5229, USA

Larian, Isaac (Business Person)
c/o Staff Member *MGA Entertainment*
16380 Roscoe Blvd Ste 150
Van Nuys, CA 91406-1221, USA

Larionov, Igor (Athlete, Hockey Player)
2363 Tilbury Pl
Bloomfield Hills, MI 48301-2732

Larish, Jeff (Baseball Player)
5229 E Baker Dr
Cave Creek, AZ 85331-2458

Lariviere, Garry (Athlete, Hockey Player)
44 Royal Oak Dr
St Catharines, ON L2N 6K7, Canada

Lark, Maria (Actor)
c/o Staff Member *Frontier Booking International*
165 W 46th St Ste 1110
New York, NY 10036-2516, USA

Larkin, Andy (Athlete, Baseball Player)
2844 E Flower St
Gilbert, AZ 85298-5754, USA

Larkin, Barry (Athlete, Baseball Player)
5410 Osprey Isle Ln
Orlando, FL 32819-4015, USA

Larkin, Barry L (Athlete, Baseball Player, Olympic Athlete)
5410 Osprey Isle Ln
Orlando, FL 32819-4015, USA

Larkin, Gene (Athlete, Baseball Player)
9495 Abbott Ct
Eden Prairie, MN 55347, USA

Larkin, Pat (Athlete, Baseball Player)
23400 Canzonet St
Woodland Hills, CA 91367-6013, USA

Larkin, Patty (Musician, Songwriter, Writer)
SRO Artists
6629 University Ave Ste 206
Middleton, WI 53562-3037, USA

Larkin, Stephen (Athlete, Baseball Player)
9178 Solon Dr
Cincinnati, OH 45242-4616, USA

Larmer, Jeff (Athlete, Hockey Player)
27 Donald Ave RR 1
Nottawa, ON L0M 1P0, Canada

Larmer, Steve (Athlete, Hockey Player)
1664 Poplar Point Rd RR 4
Peterborough, ON K9J GXS, Canada

Larocca, Greg (Athlete, Baseball Player)
14 Tinker Rd
Bedford, NH 03110-4429, USA

Laroche, Adam (Athlete, Baseball Player)
2535 Poplar Rd
Fort Scott, KS 66701-8111, USA

Laroche, Dave (Athlete, Baseball Player)
815 W 18th St
Fort Scott, KS 66701-3400, USA

LaRoche, Philippe (Skier)
Club de Ski Acrobatique
Lac Beauport, QC G0A 2OQ, CANADA

Laroque, Michele (Actor)
Artmedia
20 Ave Rapp
Paris 75007, FRANCE

Larose, Chad (Athlete, Hockey Player)
Newport Sports Management
400-201 City Centre Dr
Attn Patrick Morris
Mississauga, ON L5B 2T4, Canada

Larose, Claude (Athlete, Hockey Player)
Sher-Wood 2745 Rue de la Sherwood
Sherbrooke, QC JIK 1E1, Canada

Larose, Claude (Athlete, Hockey Player)
5060 NW 54th St
Coconut Creek, FL 33073-3713, USA

Larose, Dan (Athlete, Football Player)
4873 N Raymond Rd
Luther, MI 49656-9503, USA

Larose, Guy (Athlete, Hockey Player)
5 Tip Cart Rd
Sutton, MA 01590-4801

Larose, John (Athlete, Baseball Player)
99 Roland St
Cumberland, RI 02864-5515, USA

Larose, Paul (Athlete, Hockey Player)
170 Rue Taschereau
Trois-Rivieres, QC G8W 1G9, Canada

Larose, Vic (Athlete, Baseball Player)
2908 E Sylvia St
Phoenix, AZ 85032-7135, USA

Larouche, Pierre (Athlete, Hockey Player)
112 Vanderbilt Dr
Pittsburgh, PA 15243-1323

LaRouche Jr, Lyndon H (Politician)
18520 Round Top Ln
Round Hill, VA 20141-2052, USA

La Roux (Musician)
c/o Marty Diamond *Paradigm*
140 Broadway Ste 2600
New York, NY 10005-1011, USA

Larracuente, Brandon (Actor)
c/o Abe Hoch *A Management Company*
16633 Ventura Blvd Ste 1450
Encino, CA 91436-1887, USA

Larrieux, Amel (Musician)
Bliss Life
2114 Pico Blvd # B
Santa Monica, CA 90405-1718, USA

Larroquette, John (Actor)
1220 Main St Ste 400
Vancouver, WA 98660-2963, USA

Larry, Rentz (Athlete, Football Player)
2 Grove Isle Dr Apt 1504
Miami, FL 33133-4112, USA

Larry, Wendy (Coach)
Old Dominion University
Athletic Dept
Norfolk, VA 23529-0001, USA

Larry Sanitsky, Larry Sanitsky (Producer)
c/o Nancy Josephson *WME|IMG*
9601 Wilshire Blvd
Beverly Hills, CA 90210-5213, USA

Larsen, Blaine (Musician)
c/o Dale Morris *Morris Artists Management*
2001 Blair Blvd
Nashville, TN 37212-5007, USA

Larsen, Don (Athlete, Baseball Player)
PO Box 2863
Hayden Lake, ID 83835-2863, USA

Larsen, Gary L (Athlete, Football Player)
4317 San Juan St NE
Lacey, WA 98516-6277, USA

Larsen, Larry (Actor)
PO Box 189
Rico, CO 81332-0189, USA

Larsen, Paul E (Religious Leader)
Evangelical Convenant Church
5101 N Francisco Ave
Chicago, IL 60625, USA

Larson, Bill (Athlete, Football Player)
1365 Redwood Dr
Windsor, CO 80550-4603, USA

Larson, Brandon (Athlete, Baseball Player)
8922 Rich Way
San Antonio, TX 78251-2971, USA

Larson, Brie (Actor)
c/o Anne Woodward *Authentic Talent & Literary Management*
3615 Eastham Dr # 650
Culver City, CA 90232-2410, USA

Larson, Bruce (Race Car Driver)
PO Box 71
Dauphin, PA 17018-0071, USA

Larson, Dan (Athlete, Baseball Player)
797 Oxen St
Paso Robles, CA 93446-4656, USA

Larson, Gary (Cartoonist)
Universal Press Syndicate
4520 Main St Ste 340
Kansas City, MO 64111-7705, USA

Larson, Gerald (Jerry Lacy) (Actor)
c/o Staff Member *Sutton Barth & Vennari Inc*
5900 Wilshire Blvd Ste 700
Los Angeles, CA 90036-5009, USA

Larson, Greg (Athlete, Football Player)
PO Box 393
Nisswa, MN 56468-0393, USA

Larson, Jack (Actor)
1205 Coast Village Rd
Santa Barbara, CA 93108-2718, USA

Larson, Jay (Musician)
c/o Staff Member *Paradigm (Monterey)*
404 W Franklin St
Monterey, CA 93940-2303, USA

Larson, Jill (Actor)
Innovative Artists
1505 10th St
Santa Monica, CA 90401-2805, USA

Larson, Kent (Adult Film Star)
c/o Staff Member *Diva Central Inc*
7510 W Sunset Blvd # 1445
Los Angeles, CA 90046-3408, USA

Larson, Kurt (Athlete, Football Player)
N66W35796 W Spring Hollow Cir
Oconomowoc, WI 53066-6211, USA

Larson, Kyle (Athlete, Football Player)
5203 I Ave
Kearney, NE 68847-8461, USA

Larson, Lance (Athlete, Olympic Athlete, Swimmer)
16636 Treetop Ln
Riverside, CA 92503-9709, USA

Larson, Lyndon (Athlete, Football Player)
4117 E Encanto St
Mesa, AZ 85205-5121, USA

Larson, Lynn (Athlete, Football Player)
12209 N 66th St
Scottsdale, AZ 85254-4521, USA

Larson, Paul (Athlete, Football Player)
3718 W Harding Rd
Turlock, CA 95380-9217, USA

Larson, Pete (Athlete, Football Player)
8136 Regents Ct
University Park, FL 34201-2233, USA

Larson, Peter N (Business Person)
Brunswick Corp
26125 N Riverwoods Blvd
Mettawa, IL 60045-3420, USA

Larson, Reed (Athlete, Hockey Player)
5241 Viking Dr Ste 200
Minneapolis, MN 55435-5312

Larson, Rick (Congressman, Politician)
108 Cannon Hob
Washington, DC 20515-0914, USA

Larson, Sarah (Model)
c/o Kenya Knight *Nous Model Management*
117 N Robertson Blvd
Los Angeles, CA 90048-3101, USA

Larson, Shana (Producer, Writer)
c/o Lucy Stille *Agency for the Performing Arts*
135 W 50th St Fl 17
New York, NY 10020-1201, USA

Larson, Ted (Athlete, Football Player)
c/o Anthony J. Agnone *Eastern Athletic Services*
11350 McCormick Rd
Suite 800 - Executive Plaza
Hunt Valley, MD 21031-1002, USA

Larson, William H (Athlete, Football Player)
1365 Redwood Dr
Windsor, CO 80550-4603, USA

Larson, Wolf (Actor)
10600 Holman Ave Apt 1
Los Angeles, CA 90024-5931, USA

Larson-Pessolano, Becky (Athlete, Golfer)
121 Manor Ct
Springfield, MA 01118-2449, USA

Larsson, Curt (Athlete, Hockey Player)
Nygatan 9
Sodertalje 15173, Sweden

Larsson, Dean (Athlete, Golfer)
Advantage International
1751 Pinnacle Dr Ste 1500
Mc Lean, VA 22102-3833, USA

Larter, Ali (Actor)
c/o Alissa Vradenburg *Untitled Entertainment*
350 S Beverly Dr Ste 200
Beverly Hills, CA 90212-4819, USA

LaRue, Chi Chi (Director, DJ)
c/o Staff Member *Diva Central Inc*
7510 W Sunset Blvd # 1445
Los Angeles, CA 90046-3408, USA

LaRue, Eva (Actor, Television Host)
c/o Anthony Turk *Turk Entertainment Public Relations & Productions*
358 S Cochran Ave Apt 103
Los Angeles, CA 90036-3349, USA

LaRue, Florence (Actor, Musician)
c/o Konrad Leh *Creative Talent Group*
1900 Avenue of the Stars Ste 2475
Los Angeles, CA 90067-4512, USA

Larue, Jason (Athlete, Baseball Player)
30020 Twin Ridge Dr
Bulverde, TX 78163-2400, USA

Larue, Renee (Adult Film Star)
c/o Staff Member *Atlas Multimedia Inc*
9005 Eton Ave Ste C
Canoga Park, CA 91304-6533, USA

Larussa, Tonv (Baseball Player)
338 Golden Meadow Pl # Pi
Alamo, CA 94507-2711

LaRussa, Tony (Athlete, Baseball Player, Coach)
Tony LaRussa's Animal Rescue Foundation
2890 Mitchell Dr
Walnut Creek, CA 94598-1635, USA

Larv, Frank (Baseball Player)
11813 Baseball Dr
Northport, AL 35475-4908

LaSalle, Eriq (Actor, Director)
PO Box 69646
W Hollywood, CA 90069, USA

Lasardo, Robert (Actor)
c/o Charles Lago *DTLA Entertainment Group*
301 N Palm Canyon Dr Ste A
Palm Springs, CA 92262-5672, USA

La Scala, Nancy (Actor)
c/o Victor Kruglov *Kruglov & Associates*
6565 W Sunset Blvd Ste 280
Los Angeles, CA 90028-7219, USA

Lascher, David (Actor)
c/o Staff Member *Vanguard Management Group*
8060 Melrose Ave Fl 4
Los Angeles, CA 90046-7038, USA

LaScola, Judith (Artist)
Compositions Gallery
317 Sutter St
San Francisco, CA 94108-4301, USA

Lash, Bill (Skier)
17438 Bothell Way NE Unit C305
Bothell, WA 98011-1965, USA

Lash, Jim (Athlete, Football Player)
597 Van Everett Ave
Akron, OH 44306-2418, USA

Lashar, Tim (Athlete, Football Player)
4056 Nicole Pl
Norman, OK 73072-1758, USA

Lasher, Fred (Athlete, Baseball Player)
N9596 County Road K
Merrillan, WI 54754-8038, USA

Lashley, Nick (Musician)
1034 Garfield Ave
Venice, CA 90291-4935, USA

Lasker, Deedee (Athlete, Golfer)
1665 Chamisal Ct
Carlsbad, CA 92011-5031, USA

Lasker, Greg (Athlete, Football Player)
2521 Yeoman Ln
West Lafayette, IN 47906-0617, USA

Las Ketchup (Music Group)
c/o Staff Member *Sony Music (Spain)*
Paseo de la Castellana 93
Madrid 28046, SPAIN

Laskey, Bill (Athlete, Baseball Player)
PO Box 1556
Burlingame, CA 94011-1556, USA

Laskey, Frank (Athlete, Football Player)
584 Battle Branch Vista Dr
Franklin, NC 28734-8548, USA

Laskoski, Gary (Athlete, Hockey Player)
10 Summit Vw
Goshen, NY 10924-5713

Laskowski, John (Athlete, Basketball Player)
216 E Lakewood Dr
Bloomington, IN 47408-1040, USA

Lasky, Scott (Sportscaster)
c/o Staff Member *Maxx Sports & Entertainment*
546 5th Ave Fl 6
New York, NY 10036-5000, USA

Laslavic, Jim (Athlete, Football Player)
648 A Ave
Coronado, CA 92118-2205, USA

Lasorda, Tommy (Athlete, Baseball Player, Coach)
1473 W Maxzim Ave
Fullerton, CA 92833-4611, USA

Lasowski, Elisa (Actor)
c/o Ed Smith *Sherpa Management*
Valiant House
Vicarage Crescent
London SW11 3LX, UNITED KINGDOM

Lasse, Dick (Athlete, Football Player)
111 Windcrest Ct
Beaver Falls, PA 15010-1178, USA

Lasse, Richard S (Athlete, Football Player)
111 Windcrest Ct
Beaver Falls, PA 15010-1178, USA

Lasser, Louise (Actor, Comedian)
200 E 71st St Apt 20C
New York, NY 10021-0472, USA

Lasseter, John (Animator, Director)
c/o Staff Member *Pixar Animation Studios*
1200 Park Ave
Emeryville, CA 94608-3677, USA

Lassetter, Don (Athlete, Baseball Player)
PO Box 326
Lyon, MS 38645-0326, USA

Lassez, Sarah (Actor)
Innovative Artists
1505 10th St
Santa Monica, CA 90401-2805, USA

Lassic, Derrick (Athlete, Football Player)
3320 Lee St SE
Smyrna, GA 30080-4438, USA

Lassiter, Amanda (Basketball Player)
Minnesota Lunx
600 1st Ave N Ste Sky
Target Center
Minneapolis, MN 55403-1400, USA

Lassiter, Ike (Athlete, Football Player)
4760 Matterhorn Way
Antioch, CA 94531-8317, USA

Lassiter, Isaac (Athlete, Football Player)
4760 Matterhorn Way
Antioch, CA 94531-8317, USA

Lassiter, James (Producer)
c/o Staff Member *Creative Artists Agency (CAA)*
2000 Avenue of the Stars Ste 100
Los Angeles, CA 90067-4705, USA

Lassiter, Kwamie (Athlete, Football Player)
2820 S Alma School Rd Ste 18
Chandler, AZ 85286-4394, USA

Last Vegas (Music Group)
c/o Ben Epand *10th Street Entertainment*
700 N San Vicente Blvd # G410
W Hollywood, CA 90069-5060, USA

Laswell, Greg (Musician)
c/o Anthony Paolercio *UTA/The Agency Group*
888 7th Ave Fl 7
New York, NY 10106-0700, USA

Latarte, Steve (Race Car Driver)
18420 Nantz Rd
Cornelius, NC 28031-8614, USA

Lateef the Truthspeaker (Musician)
c/o Staff Member *Madison House*
1401 Walnut St Ste 500
Boulder, CO 80302-5332, USA

Latham, Bill (Athlete, Baseball Player)
211 Magnolia St
Trussville, AL 35173-1307, USA

Latham, Chris (Athlete, Baseball Player)
6331 Buzz Aldrin Dr
Las Vegas, NV 89149-1389, USA

Latham, Jody (Actor)
c/o Lindy King *United Agents*
12-26 Lexington St
London W1F OLE, UNITED KINGDOM

Latham, Louise (Actor)
300 Hot Springs Rd
Santa Barbara, CA 93108-2037, USA

Latham, Tom (Congressman, Politician)
2217 Rayburn Hob
Washington, DC 20515-4904, USA

Lathan, Sanaa (Actor)
c/o Philip Grenz *ICM Partners*
10250 Constellation Blvd Fl 7
Los Angeles, CA 90067-6207, USA

Lathan, Stan (Director, Producer, Writer)
c/o Staff Member *Simmons Lathan Media Group*
6100 Wilshire Blvd Ste 1111
Los Angeles, CA 90048-5198, USA

Lathon, Lamar L (Athlete, Football Player)
23 Westpoint Dr
Missouri City, TX 77459-6331, USA

Latifah, Queen (Actor, Musician)
c/o Shakim Compere *Flavor Unit Entertainment*
8484 Wilshire Blvd Ste 850
Beverly Hills, CA 90211-3217, USA

Latimer, Alivia (Actor)
c/o Joan Green *Joan Green Management*
1836 Courtney Ter
Los Angeles, CA 90046-2106, USA

Latimer, Cody (Athlete, Football Player)
c/o Ed Wasielewski *EMG Sports - PA*
PO Box 2
Richboro, PA 18954-0002, USA

Latimer, Don (Athlete, Football Player)
562 S Kalispell Way
Aurora, CO 80017-2112, USA

Latimore (Musician)
Rodgers Redding
1048 Tattnall St
Macon, GA 31201-1537, USA

Latimore, Joseph (Actor)
1505 10th St
Santa Monica, CA 90401-2805, USA

Latin, Jerry (Athlete, Football Player)
2312 Clover Ave
Rockford, IL 61102-3412, USA

Latman, Barry (Athlete, Baseball Player)
2726 Shelter Island Dr
P.O. Box 519
San Diego, CA 92106-2731, USA

Laton, Gary (Race Car Driver)
Gary Laton Motorsports
4011 Hands Mill Hwy
York, SC 29745-9647, USA

Latos, Jim (Athlete, Hockey Player)
1026 Whitewood Cres
Saskatoon, SK S7J 4L1, Canada

Latourelle, Ron (Athlete, Football Player)
2366 Portage Ave Suite 4A
Winnipeg, MB R3J 0N4, Canada

Latreille, Phil (Athlete, Hockey Player)
2905 Fox Run
Appleton, WI 54914-8741

Latta, David (Athlete, Hockey Player)
1419 Moodie St E
Thunder Bay, ON P7E 4Y8, Canada

Lattanzi, Chloe (Musician)
c/o Staff Member *Innovative Artists*
235 Park Ave S Fl 7
New York, NY 10003-1405, USA

Lattimore, Brian (Athlete, Football Player)
1790 Santa Blas Walk Apt 503
Saint Louis, MO 63138-1989, USA

Lattimore, Jamari (Athlete, Football Player)
c/o Anthony J. Agnone *Eastern Athletic Services*
11350 McCormick Rd
Suite 800 - Executive Plaza
Hunt Valley, MD 21031-1002, USA

Lattimore, Kenny (Actor)
c/o Sara Ramaker *Paradigm*
8942 Wilshire Blvd
Beverly Hills, CA 90211-1908, USA

Lattin, David (Athlete, Basketball Player)
8230 Twin Tree Ln
Houston, TX 77071-2918, USA

Lattisaw, Stacy (Musician)
9537 Fort Foote Rd
Ft Washington, MD 20744-5726, USA

Lattlmore, Kenny (Musician)
Rhythm Jazz Entertainment Group
4465 Don Milagro Dr
Los Angeles, CA 90008-2831, USA

Latzke, Paul (Athlete, Football Player)
1123 Escalona Dr
Santa Cruz, CA 95060-3303, USA

Lau, Andy (Actor, Producer)
c/o Staff Member *Focus Films*
18/F, Futura Plaza
111-113 How Ming St
Kwun Tong, Kowloon, Hong Kong

Lau, Constance (Actor)
c/o Lim Hui Ling *Fly Entertainment*
213 Henderson Rd
Henderson Industrial Park #03-10
Singapore 159553, SINGAPORE

Lauda, Andreas-Nikolaus (Niki) (Race Car Driver)
San Costa de Baix
Santa Eulalia
Ibiza, SPAIN

Laude, Bill (Athlete, Baseball Player)
662 Franklin Ave
Frankfort, IL 60423-1206, USA

Lauder, Leonard A (Business Person)
Estee Lauder Companies
767 5th Ave Fl CONC6
New York, NY 10153-0003, USA

Lauder, Ronald (Business Person)
Estee Lauder Companies
767 5th Ave Fl CONC6
New York, NY 10153-0003, USA

Laudner, Tim (Athlete, Baseball Player)
1114 Hollybrook Dr
Wayzata, MN 55391-1370, USA

Lauen, Michel (Athlete, Hockey Player)
4535 W 56th St
Minneapolis, MN 55424-1556, USA

Lauer, Andrew (Actor)
3018 3rd St
Santa Monica, CA 90405-5410, USA

Lauer, Andy (Actor)
c/o Andrea Pett-Joseph *Brillstein Entertainment Partners*
9150 Wilshire Blvd Ste 350
Beverly Hills, CA 90212-3453, USA

Lauer, Bonnie (Athlete, Golfer)
525 Via Laguna Vis
San Luis Obispo, CA 93405-4757, USA

Lauer, Brad (Athlete, Hockey Player)
10 Deer Moss Trail
Stittsville, ON K2S 1C9, CANADA

Lauer, Martin (Athlete, Track Athlete)
Hardstr 41
Lauf 77886, GERMANY

Lauer, Matt (Correspondent)
c/o Ken Lindner *Ken Lindner & Associates*
1901 Avenue Of The Stars Ste 1010
Los Angeles, CA 90067-6012, USA

Laufenberg, Brandon (Athlete, Football Player)
5712 Orchid Ln
Dallas, TX 75230-4022, USA

Laughlin, Craig (Athlete, Hockey Player)
Washington Capitals
627 N Glebe Rd Ste 850
Arlington, VA 22203-2129

Laughlin, Craig (Athlete, Hockey Player)
2217 Mount Tabor Rd
Gambrills, MD 21054-1801

Laughlin, John (Actor)
Laughlin Enterprises
13116 Albers St
Sherman Oaks, CA 91401-6002, USA

Laughlin, Teresa (TC) (Actor, Designer)
TC Laughlin Design Group Inc
8 Larchmont Ave
Larchmont, NY 10538-4220, USA

Laughlin, Jr., Mike (Race Car Driver)
Laughlin Racing
114 Pride Dr
Simpsonville, SC 29681-3298, USA

Laukkanen, Janne (Athlete, Hockey Player)
401 Channelside Dr
Tampa, FL 33602-5400, USA

Laundry, LaRon (Athlete, Football Player)
c/o Joel Segal *Lagardere Unlimited (NY)*
456 Washington St Apt 9L
New York, NY 10013-1555, USA

Lauper, Cyndi (Musician, Songwriter)
c/o Lisa Barbaris *So What Management*
890 W End Ave Apt 1A
New York, NY 10025-3520, USA

Laurance, Ashley (Actor)
c/o James D. Boyle *Atherton Group Talent, The (TAG)*
1310 E University Ave
Georgetown, TX 78626-6115, USA

Laurance, Dale (Business Person)
Occidental Petroleum
10889 Wilshire Blvd Fl 10
Los Angeles, CA 90024-4213, USA

Laurance, Matthew (Actor)
1951 Hillcrest Rd
Los Angeles, CA 90068-3116, USA

Laure, Carole (Actor, Musician)
Cineart
36 Rue de Ponthieu
Paris 75008, FRANCE

Laurel, Rich (Athlete, Basketball Player)
706 Antelope Way
Kissimmee, FL 34759-4212, USA

Lauren, Carly (Model)
Playboy Promotions
9346 Civic Center Dr Ste 200
Beverly Hills, CA 90210-3604, USA

Lauren, Dylan (Business Person)
Dylan's Candy Bar
1011 3rd Ave
New York, NY 10065-8501, USA

Lauren, Joy (Actor)
c/o Mary Sanders *inMomentum Management*
14622 Ventura Blvd # 778
Sherman Oaks, CA 91403-3600, USA

Lauren, Lauren Bush (Activist, Model)
FEED
420 W 14th St Ste 6NE
New York, NY 10014-1017, USA

Lauren, Ralph (Designer, Fashion Designer)
Polo Ralph Lauren Corp
867 Madison Ave
New York, NY 10021-4103, USA

Lauren, Tammy (Actor)
Gage Group
14724 Ventura Blvd Ste 505
Sherman Oaks, CA 91403-3505, USA

Laurent, Melanie (Actor, Writer)
c/o Cecile Felsenberg *UBBA*
6 rue de Braque
Paris 75003, FRANCE

Laurente, Dennis (Boxer)
c/o Staff Member *Top Rank Inc.*
3908 Howard Hughes Pkwy
#580
Las Vegas, NV 89109, USA

Laurents, Arthur (Writer)
608 Northville Tpke
Riverhead, NY 11901-4717, USA

Lauria, Dan (Actor)
c/o Harry Gold *TalentWorks*
3500 W Olive Ave Ste 1400
Burbank, CA 91505-5512, USA

Lauria, Matt (Actor)
c/o Jillian Roscoe *ID Public Relations*
7060 Hollywood Blvd Fl 8th
Los Angeles, CA 90028-6021, USA

Laurie, Greg (Religious Leader)
Harvest Christian Fellowship Church
6115 Arlington Ave
Riverside, CA 92504-1999, USA

Laurie, Harry (Athlete, Basketball Player)
540 Bramhall Ave Apt 3
Jersey City, NJ 07304-2323, USA

Laurie, Hugh (Actor, Comedian)
c/o Ina Treciokas *Slate PR*
901 N Highland Ave
W Hollywood, CA 90038-2412, USA

Laurie, Piper (Actor)
c/o Deborah Miller *Shelter Entertainment*
9255 W Sunset Blvd Ste 300
Los Angeles, CA 90069-3313, USA

Laurinaitis, James (Athlete, Football Player)
345 Ridgeway Dr
Metairie, LA 70001-3044, USA

Laurita, Jacqueline (Reality Star)
322 Water View Dr
Franklin Lakes, NJ 07417-2954, USA

Lauro, Lindore (Athlete, Football Player)
111 Scott Dr
New Castle, PA 16105-3101, USA

Laus, Paul (Athlete, Hockey Player)
44 Chardonnay Pl
Grimsby, ON L3M SSG, Canada

Laut, David (Athlete, Olympic Athlete)
421 Eastwood Dr
Oxnard, CA 93030-4014, USA

Lautenschlaeger, Fred (Athlete, Football Player)
612 Breton Pl
Arnold, MD 21012-1536, USA

Lauterstein, Alex (DJ)
c/o Staff Member *Diva Central Inc*
7510 W Sunset Blvd # 1445
Los Angeles, CA 90046-3408, USA

Lautner, Taylor (Actor)
c/o Alan Nierob *Rogers & Cowan*
1840 Century Park E Fl 18
Los Angeles, CA 90067-2101, USA

Lauvao, Shawn (Athlete, Football Player)
c/o David Dunn *Athletes First*
23091 Mill Creek Dr
Laguna Hills, CA 92653-1258, USA

Lauzerique, George (Athlete, Baseball Player)
601 Oleaster Ave
Wellington, FL 33414-8197, USA

Lavalais, Chad (Athlete, Football Player)
3460 Tupelo Trl
Auburn, GA 30011-4601, USA

Lavallee, Kevin (Athlete, Hockey Player)
1210 Butterfly Ct
Marco Island, FL 34145-2308

Lavalliere, Mike (Athlete, Baseball Player)
4550 Pinebrook Cir Apt 603
Bradenton, FL 34209-8017, USA

Lavelle, Gary (Athlete, Baseball Player)
122 Tranquility Trce
Chesapeake, VA 23320-4088, USA

Lavelle, James (DJ, Musician)
c/o Joel Zimmerman *WME/IMG (NY)*
11 Madison Ave Fl 18
New York, NY 10010-3669, USA

Lavender, Brian (Athlete, Hockey Player)
11585 Decatur St Apt C
Denver, CO 80234-3567

Lavender, Jay (Producer)
c/o Staff Member *Artists First*
9465 Wilshire Blvd Ste 900
Beverly Hills, CA 90212-2608, USA

Lavender, Jody (Race Car Driver)
Jody Lavender Racing
PO Box 1527
Hartsville, SC 29551-1527, USA

Lavender, Joseph (Athlete, Football Player)
1215 Alma St
Glendale, CA 91202-2014, USA

Laventhol, Henry L (Hank) (Artist)
445 Heritage Hls Unit F
Somers, NY 10589-1941, USA

Laver, Rod (Tennis Player)
3009 Via Conquistador
Carlsbad, CA 92009-3025, USA

Lavi, Inbar (Actor)
c/o Jeffrey Chassen *Imprint PR*
6121 W Sunset Blvd
Neuehouse
Los Angeles, CA 90028-6442, USA

Lavigne, Avril (Musician, Songwriter)
c/o Kristen Foster *PMK/BNC Public Relations*
1840 Century Park E Ste 1400
Los Angeles, CA 90067-2115, USA

Lavin, Bernice E (Business Person)
Alberto-Culver
2525 Armitage Ave
Melrose Park, IL 60160-1125, USA

Lavin, Leonard H (Business Person)
Alberto-Culver
2525 Armitage Ave
Melrose Park, IL 60160-1125, USA

Lavin, Linda (Actor, Musician)
c/o Bill Veloric *Innovative Artists*
235 Park Ave S Fl 7
New York, NY 10003-1405, USA

Lavin, TJ (Athlete, Television Host)
c/o Staff Member *Dragon Talent*
8444 Wilshire Blvd PH
Beverly Hills, CA 90211-3200, USA

Laviolette, Peter (Athlete, Coach, Hockey Player, Olympic Athlete)
7000 Firehouse Rd
Longboat Key, FL 34228-1138

Lavoie, Dominic (Athlete, Hockey Player)
5081 Garlenda Dr
El Dorado Hills, CA 95762-5456

Lavoine, Marc (Actor)
c/o Staff Member *ArtMedia*
8 rue Danielle Casanova
Paris 75002, FRANCE

Lavon, Peaches (Musician)
c/o Janice Gaffney *Butterscotch Castle*
535 Geary St Apt 612
San Francisco, CA 94102-1635, USA

LaVoo, George (Director, Producer, Writer)
c/o Jon Rubinstein *Authentic Talent and Literary Management (NY)*
20 Jay St Ste M17
Brooklyn, NY 11201-8300, USA

LaVorgna, Adam (Actor)

Lavoy, Robert (Athlete, Basketball Player)
613 Wood Rd
Seffner, FL 33584-5446, USA

Lavrov, Kyrill Y (Actor)
Michurinskaya 1
#36
Saint Petersburg 197046, RUSSIA

Law, Andrew (Actor)
c/o Fred Hashagen *United Talent Agency (UTA)*
888 7th Ave Fl 7
New York, NY 10106-0700, USA

Law, Jude (Actor)
c/o Pippa Beng *Premier PR*
2-4 Bucknall St
London WC2H 8LA, UNITED KINGDOM

Law, Ron (Baseball Player)
Cleveland Indians
3 Mountainview Rd
Greenwood Village, CO 80111-1736, USA

Law, Rudy (Athlete, Baseball Player)
JD Legends Promotions
3663 S Valley View Blvd Apt 211
Las Vegas, NV 89103-1819, USA

Law, Ty (Athlete, Football Player)
10862 Hawks Vista St
Plantation, FL 33324-8206, USA

Law, Vance (Athlete, Baseball Player)
1682 N 1950 W
Provo, UT 84604-1177, USA

Law, Vern (Athlete, Baseball Player)
1718 N 1050 W
Provo, UT 84604-1159, USA

Lawanson, Ruth (Athlete, Olympic Athlete, Volleyball Player)
490 Arthur Rd
Martinez, CA 94553-1402, USA

Lawler, Jerry (Athlete, Wrestler)
415 Saint Nick Dr
Memphis, TN 38117-4115, USA

Lawler, Kate (Reality Star)
c/o Staff Member *Channel 4 Television Corporation*
124 Horseferry Road
London SW1P 2

Lawler, Steve (DJ, Musician)
c/o Joel Zimmerman *WME|IMG (NY)*
11 Madison Ave Fl 18
New York, NY 10010-3669, USA

Lawless, Burton (Athlete, Football Player)
2035 Oak Glen Dr
Mc Gregor, TX 76657-3455, USA

Lawless, Lucy (Actor)
Lawlessinc
16030 Ventura Blvd Ste 380
Encino, CA 91436-2778, USA

Lawless, Renee (Actor)
c/o Siri Garber *Platform PR*
2666 N Beachwood Dr
Los Angeles, CA 90068-2308, USA

Lawless, Tom (Athlete, Baseball Player)
734 E Port Ave Attn Managersofc
Corpus Christi, TX 78401-1006, USA

Lawley, Kian (Internet Star)
c/o Lisa Filipelli *Select Management Group*
6100 Wilshire Blvd Ste 400
Los Angeles, CA 90048-5109, USA

Lawrence, Andrew (Actor)
c/o Staff Member *Kass Management*
1011 Euclid St Unit B
Santa Monica, CA 90403-4296, USA

Lawrence, Bill (Writer)
c/o Staff Member *Broder Webb Chervin Silbermann Agency, The (BWCS)*
10250 Constellation Blvd
Los Angeles, CA 90067-6200, USA

Lawrence, Braxton Janice (Basketball Player)
Cleveland Rockers
1 Center Ct
Gund Arena
Cleveland, OH 44115-4001, USA

Lawrence, Brian (Athlete, Baseball Player)
3379 County Road 1132
Linden, TX 75563-7375, USA

Lawrence, Carol (Actor)
160 Riverside Blvd Apt 4F
New York, NY 10069-0702, USA

Lawrence, Demarcus (Athlete, Football Player)

Lawrence, Don (Athlete, Football Player)
12620 Cedar St
Shawnee Mission, KS 66209-3167, USA

Lawrence, Francis (Actor)
c/o Gretchen Rush *Hansen, Jacobson, Teller, Hoberman, Newman, Warren & Richman*
450 N Roxbury Dr Fl 8
Beverly Hills, CA 90210-4222, USA

Lawrence, Francis (Director)
c/o Erwin Stoff *3 Arts Entertainment*
9460 Wilshire Blvd Fl 7
Beverly Hills, CA 90212-2713, USA

Lawrence, Henry (Athlete, Football Player)
2110 2nd Ave E
Palmetto, FL 34221-3310, USA

Lawrence, James (Loz) (Musician)
PO Box 33
Pontypool, Gwent NP4 6YU, UNITED KINGDOM (UK)

Lawrence, Jennifer (Actor)
Jennifer Lawrence Foundation
4350 Brownsboro Rd Ste 110
Louisville, KY 40207-1681, USA

Lawrence, Jim (Athlete, Baseball Player)
225 Haddington St
Caledonia, ON N3W 1G1, Canada

Lawrence, Joe (Athlete, Baseball Player)
4358 Poydras St
Lake Charles, LA 70605-4400, USA

Lawrence, Joey (Actor)
c/o Mark Rousso *Industry Entertainment Partners*
955 Carrillo Dr Ste 300
Los Angeles, CA 90048-5400, USA

Lawrence, Kent (Athlete, Football Player)
150 Charter Ct
Athens, GA 30605-4628, USA

Lawrence, Mark (Athlete, Hockey Player)
41844 E Bayshore Dr
Paw Paw, MI 49079-9758

Lawrence, Martin (Actor, Comedian)
15999 High Knoll Rd
Encino, CA 91436-3426, USA

Lawrence, Matthew (Actor)
c/o Greg Wapnick *Luber Roklin Management*
5815 W Sunset Blvd Ste 208
Los Angeles, CA 90028-6481, USA

Lawrence, Nigel (Musician)
c/o Staff Member *Paradigm (Monterey)*
404 W Franklin St
Monterey, CA 93940-2303, USA

Lawrence, Rolland (Athlete, Football Player)
317 Sugarcreek Dr
Franklin, PA 16323-5641, USA

Lawrence, Russell (Actor)
7800 Beverly Blvd # 3305
Los Angeles, CA 90036-2112, USA

Lawrence, Sean (Athlete, Baseball Player)
336 S Poplar Ave
Elmhurst, IL 60126-3565, USA

Lawrence, Sharon (Actor, Producer)
c/o Joshua Pasch *Authentic Talent & Literary Management*
3615 Eastham Dr # 650
Culver City, CA 90232-2410, USA

Lawrence, Steve (Musician)
c/o Howard Bragman *LaBrea Media*
8306 Wilshire Blvd # 4002
Beverly Hills, CA 90211-2304, USA

Lawrence, Tracy (Musician, Songwriter)
c/o Greg Oswald *WME (Nashville)*
1201 Demonbreun St Ste 1460
Nashville, TN 37203-5079, USA

Lawrence, Vicki (Actor, Musician)
6000 Lido Ln
Long Beach, CA 90803-4105, USA

Lawrence, Wendy B (Astronaut)
National Reconnaissance Office
14675 Lee Rd
Chantilly, VA 20151-1715, USA

Lawrence, Wendy B Captain (Astronaut)
6225 Argyle St
Ferndale, WA 98248-8995, USA

Laws, Hubert (Musician)
1078 S Ogden Dr
Los Angeles, CA 90019-6501, USA

Laws, Ronnie (Musician)
c/o Staff Member *Pyramid Entertainment Group*
377 Rector Pl Apt 21A
New York, NY 10280-1439, USA

Lawson, Ana Maria (Beauty Pageant Winner)
PO Box 59064
Potomac, MD 20859-9064, USA

Lawson, Ben (Actor)
c/o Jamie Harhay Skinner *Baker Winokur Ryder Public Relations*
9100 Wilshire Blvd
W Tower #500
Beverly Hills, CA 90212-3415, USA

Lawson, Bianca (Actor)
c/o Nicki Fioravante *Viewpoint Inc*
8820 Wilshire Blvd Ste 220
Beverly Hills, CA 90211-2622, USA

Lawson, Danny (Athlete, Hockey Player)

Lawson, Denis (Actor, Director)
c/o Staff Member *Yakety Yak*
25 D'Arblay St
London W1F 8EJ, UNITED KINGDOM (UK)

Lawson, Doyle (Musician)
c/o Staff Member *Paradigm (Monterey)*
404 W Franklin St
Monterey, CA 93940-2303, USA

Lawson, Josh (Actor)
c/o Lisa Mann *Lisa Mann Creative Management*
19-25 Cope St
Redfern NSW 02016, AUSTRALIA

Lawson, Kara (Basketball Player)
c/o Staff Member *Sacramento Monarchs*
1 Sports Pkwy
Arco Arena
Sacramento, CA 95834-2300, USA

Lawson, Ken (Ken L) (Actor)
c/o Staff Member *Agency West Entertainment*
6255 W Sunset Blvd Ste 908
Hollywood, CA 90028-7410, USA

Lawson, Leigh (Actor)
P F D Drury House
34-43 Russell St
London WC2B 5HA, UNITED KINGDOM (UK)

Lawson, Maggie (Actor)
2401 Canyon Dr
Los Angeles, CA 90068-2413, USA

Lawson, Manny (Athlete, Football Player)
c/o Neil Schwartz *Schwartz & Feinsod*
4 Hillandale Rd
Rye Brook, NY 10573-1705, USA

Lawson, Nevin (Athlete, Football Player)
c/o Jordan Woy *Willis & Woy Management*
4890 Alpha Rd Ste 200
Dallas, TX 75244-4639, USA

Lawson, Nigella (Chef)
c/o Staff Member *Uitgeverij Contact*
Portbus 218
Amsterdam 1000 AE, The Netherlands

Lawson, Richard (Actor)
8840 Wilshire Blvd # 200
Beverly Hills, CA 90211-2606, USA

Lawson, Steve (Athlete, Baseball Player)
PO Box 5630
Brookings, OR 97415-0120, USA

Lawson, Twiggy (Actor, Model)
c/o Maureen Vincent *United Agents*
12-26 Lexington St
London W1F OLE, UNITED KINGDOM

Lawson, Ty (Athlete, Football Player)
c/o Ashley Smith Becker *Relativity Sports*
2029 Century Park E Ste 1550
Century City, CA 90067-3000, USA

Lawson, William (Baseball Player)
8800 E McClellan St
Tucson, AZ 85710-4419, USA

Lawson, William (Athlete, Baseball Player)
8800 E McClellan St
Tucson, AZ 85710-4419, USA

Lawston, Marlene (Actor)
c/o Victoria Kress *Abrams Artists Agency*
275 7th Ave Fl 26
New York, NY 10001-6708, USA

Lawton, Brian (Athlete, Hockey Player)
5012 Oak Bend Ln
Minneapolis, MN 55436-1167

Lawton, Jonathan (J.F.) (Writer)
c/o Sara Bottfeld *Industry Entertainment Partners*
955 Carrillo Dr Ste 300
Los Angeles, CA 90048-5400, USA

Lawton, Liam (Musician)
GM Publicity
86 Haddington Rd
Ballsbridge, Dublin 4
IRELAND

Lawton, Marcus (Athlete, Baseball Player)
15354 Dellwood Cv
Gulfport, MS 39503-2718, USA

Lawton, Mary (Cartoonist)
Chronicle Features
901 Mission St
San Francisco, CA 94103-3052, USA

Lawton, Matthew (Matt) (Athlete, Baseball Player)
27264 Bethel Rd
Saucier, MS 39574-9020, USA

Lax, John (Athlete, Hockey Player)
3 Greendale Ln
Harwich, MA 02645, USA

Laxton, Bill (Athlete, Baseball Player)
261 Mansion Ave
Audubon, NJ 08106-1529, USA

Laxton, Brett (Athlete, Baseball Player)
13216 Montrose South Dr
Denham Springs, LA 70726-7447, USA

Laxton, Gordie (Athlete, Hockey Player)
2843 Big Timber Dr NE
Grand Rapids, MI 49525-3018

Layden, Frank (Basketball Coach, Coach)
241 N Vine St Apt 1204W
Salt Lake City, UT 84103-1938, USA

Layevska, Anna (Actor)
c/o Staff Member *Cesar Carrera*
C/ Isabel Serrano, 12
Madrid 28029, Spain

Layman, Jason (Athlete, Football Player)
163 New Center Rd
Sevierville, TN 37876-2167, USA

Layne, Jerry (Baseball Player)
2323 Cypress Gardens Blvd
Winter Haven, FL 33884-2120, USA

Layne, Jerry (Athlete, Baseball Player)
2323 Cypress Gardens Blvd
Winter Haven, FL 33884-2120, USA

Layne, KiKi (Actor)
c/o Cara Tripicchio *Shelter PR*
5670 Wilshire Blvd Ste 1200
Los Angeles, CA 90036-5621, USA

Layne, Shontelle (Musician)
c/o Carl Sturken *SRC - Street Records Corporation*
Universal - Motown
1755 Broadway New Media
New York, NY 10019, USA

Layton, Dennis (Athlete, Basketball Player)
872 S 14th St
Newark, NJ 07108-1320, USA

Lazar, Danny (Athlete, Baseball Player)
8444 Oakwood Ave
Munster, IN 46321-1915, USA

Lazar, Laurence (Religious Leader)
Romanian Orthodox Episcopate
2522 Grey Tower Rd
Jackson, MI 49201-9120, USA

Lazard, Justin (Actor)
9350 Wilshire Blvd Ste 324
Beverly Hills, CA 90212-3206, USA

Lazaro, Jeff (Athlete, Hockey Player)
5831 Bancroft Dr
New Orleans, LA 70122-1315

Lazarus, Mell (Cartoonist)
Creators Syndicate
5777 W Century Blvd # 700
Los Angeles, CA 90045-5600, USA

Lazarus, Shelly (Business Person)
Ogilvy & Mather Worldwide
309 W 49th St
New York, NY 10019-7316, USA

Lazenby, George (Actor)
c/o Charles Sherman *Charles Sherman Public Relations*
8306 Wilshire Blvd Ste 2017
Beverly Hills, CA 90211-2304, USA

Lazetich, Bill (Athlete, Football Player)
3840 Rimrock Rd Apt 2100
Billings, MT 59102-0153, USA

Lazetich, Pete (Athlete, Football Player)
185 Martin St
Reno, NV 89509-2827, USA

Lazier, Buddy (Race Car Driver)
Dreyer & Reinbold Racing
9375 Whitley Dr
Indianapolis, IN 46240-1349, USA

Lazier, Jacques (Race Car Driver)
PO Box 8055
Rch Cucamonga, CA 91701-0055, USA

Lazier, Robert (Buddy) (Race Car Driver)
130 Gasoline Aly
Indianapolis, IN 46222-3965, USA

Lazlo, Viktor (Actor, Musician)
56 rue de Lisbonne
Paris F-75008, France

Lazorko, Jack (Athlete, Baseball Player)
1360 Meandering Way
Rockwall, TX 75087-2309, USA

Lazure, Gabrielle (Actor)
Cineart
36 Rue de Ponthieu
Paris 75008, FRANCE

Lazzarato, Gigi (Gorgeous) (Internet Star, Model)
c/o Laura Ackerman *Advantage PR*
3900 W Alameda Ave Ste 1200
Burbank, CA 91505-4317, USA

L. Berman, Howard (Congressman, Politician)
2221 Rayburn Hob
Washington, DC 20515-0528, USA

L. Braley, Bruce (Congressman, Politician)
1727 Longworth Hob
Washington, DC 20515-1007, USA

Icahn, Carl (Misc)
767 5th Ave Ste 4700
New York, NY 10153-0108, USA

L. Delauro, Rosa (Congressman, Politician)
2413 Rayburn Hob
Washington, DC 20515-0512, USA

Le, Cung (Actor)
c/o Scott Karp *The Syndicate*
10203 Santa Monica Blvd Fl 5
Los Angeles, CA 90067-6416, USA

Lea, Nicholas (Actor)
c/o Monica Barkett *Global Artists Agency*
6253 Hollywood Blvd Apt 508
Los Angeles, CA 90028-8251, USA

Leabu, Tristan Lake (Actor)
LA Talent
7700 W Sunset Blvd Ste 203
C/O Tracy Dwyer
Los Angeles, CA 90046-3913, USA

Leach, Jalal (Athlete, Baseball Player)
3718 Phillip Island Rd
West Sacramento, CA 95691-5939, USA

Leach, Jamie (Athlete, Hockey Player)
100 Youville St
ST BONIFACE GOLF CLUB
Winnipeg, MB R2H 2S1, Canada

Leach, Mike (Athlete, Football Player)

Leach, Penelope (Misc)
3 Tanza Lane
London NW3 2UA, UNITED KINGDOM (UK)

Leach, Reggie (Athlete, Hockey Player)
906 Clydesdale Dr
Bear, DE 19701-2205

Leach, Rick (Athlete, Baseball Player)
593 Layman Creek Cir
Grand Blanc, MI 48439-1384, USA

Leach, Rosemary (Actor)
Felix de Wolfe
51 Maida Vale
London W9 1SD, UNITED KINGDOM (UK)

Leach, Sheryl (Animator)
SL Productions
4226 Lupton Ct
High Point, NC 27262-8393, USA

Leach, Steve (Athlete, Hockey Player, Olympic Athlete)
435 N Main St
Wolfeboro, NH 03894-4313

Leach, Terry (Athlete, Baseball Player)
2135 SW Locks Rd
Stuart, FL 34997-7011, USA

Leachman, Cloris (Actor)
c/o Juliet Green *Juliet Green Management*
9025 Wilshire Blvd Ste 400
Beverly Hills, CA 90211-1828, USA

Leadbetter, Kelly (Athlete, Golfer)
9606 Tavistock Ct
Orlando, FL 32827-7018, USA

Leadon, Bernie (Musician)
2000 Glen Echo Rd Ste 105
Nashville, TN 37215-2857, USA

Leaf, Ryan (Athlete, Football Player)
1510 1st Ave S
Great Falls, MT 59401-3805, USA

League, Brandon (Athlete, Baseball Player)
72385 Lake Heather Heights Ct
Dunedin, FL 34698-5649, USA

Leah, Rachelle (Actor, Athlete)
c/o Ivo Fischer *WME|IMG*
9601 Wilshire Blvd
Beverly Hills, CA 90210-5213, USA

Leahy, Bob (Athlete, Football Player)
1975 Padova Pt
Edmond, OK 73034-2149, USA

Leahy, Gerry (Athlete, Football Player)
5129 Oakridge Dr
Beaverton, MI 48612-8591, USA

Leahy, Pat (Athlete, Hockey Player)
1 Bristol Dr
Duxbury, MA 02332-4117

Leahy, Patrick (Politician, Senator)
31 Green Acres Dr
Burlington, VT 05408-2415, USA

Leak, Jennifer (Actor)
James D'Auria Associates
PO Box 2219
Amagansett, NY 11930-2219, USA

Leak, Justice (Actor)
c/o Staff Member *People Store*
645 Lambert Dr NE
Atlanta, GA 30324-4125, USA

Leake, Brett (Comedian)
3561 Leatherwood Ln
Maidens, VA 23102-2025, USA

Leakes, NeNe (Actor, Reality Star)
c/o Steven Grossman *Untitled Entertainment*
350 S Beverly Dr Ste 200
Beverly Hills, CA 90212-4819, USA

Leaks, Manny (Athlete, Basketball Player)
9912 North Blvd
Cleveland, OH 44108-3430, USA

Leaks Jr, Roosevelt (Athlete, Football Player)
11525 Glen Falloch Ct
Austin, TX 78754-5807, USA

Leal, Sharon (Actor, Musician)
c/o Anne Woodward *Authentic Talent & Literary Management*
3615 Eastham Dr # 650
Culver City, CA 90232-2410, USA

LeAnn, Summer (Actor)
c/o Jana Luker *Jana Luker Agency*
20501 Ventura Blvd Ste 115
Woodland Hills, CA 91364-6288, USA

Lear, Harold (Athlete, Basketball Player)
8960 E Gail Rd
Scottsdale, AZ 85260-6146, USA

Lear, Norman (Director, Producer, Writer)
c/o Staff Member *Act III Communications*
100 N Crescent Dr Ste 250
Beverly Hills, CA 90210-5451, USA

Learn, Ed (Athlete, Football Player)
1154 Lakeshore Rd W RR 3
St Catharines, ON L2R 6P9, Canada

Learned, Michael (Actor)
1600 N Beverly Dr
Beverly Hills, CA 90210-2316, USA

Leary, Denis (Actor, Comedian, Producer)
c/o Staff Member *Apostle Pictures*
568 Broadway Rm 301
New York, NY 10012-3271, USA

Leary, Ronald (Athlete, Football Player)
c/o Adisa P Bakari *Kelley Drye & Warren LLP*
3050 K St NW Ste 400
Washington, DC 20007-5100, USA

Leary, Tim (Athlete, Baseball Player)
2461 Santa Monica Blvd
Santa Monica, CA 90404-2138, USA

Leatherdale, Douglas W (Business Person)
Saint Paul Companies
385 Washington St
Saint Paul, MN 55102-1396, USA

Leaud, Jean-Pierre (Actor)
c/o Francois-Xavier Molin *ArtMedia*
8 rue Danielle Casanova
Paris 75002, FRANCE

Leavell, Allen (Athlete, Basketball Player)
7007 Windy Pines Dr
Spring, TX 77379-4733, USA

Leavell, Chuck (Musician)
Charlane Plantation
665 Charlane Dr
Dry Branch, GA 31020-5256, USA

Leavenworth, Scotty (Actor)
c/o Susan Curtis *Curtis Talent Management*
9607 Arby Dr
Beverly Hills, CA 90210-1202, USA

Leaves (Music Group)
c/o Staff Member *Paradigm (Monterey)*
404 W Franklin St
Monterey, CA 93940-2303, USA

Leavitt, Allan (Athlete, Football Player)
2261 Royal Fern Ln S
Jacksonville, FL 32223-1875, USA

Leavitt, Phil (Musician)
c/o Richard Lustig *Lustig Talent Enterprises Inc*
PO Box 770850
Orlando, FL 32877-0850, USA

Leavy, Jon (Race Car Driver)
Leavy Racing Enterprises
7700 NW 37th Ave
Miami, FL 33147-4423, USA

Lebadang (Artist)
Circle Gallery
303 E Wacker Dr
Chicago, IL 60601-5212, USA

Lebda, Brett (Athlete, Hockey Player)
557 Chatham Cir
Buffalo Grove, IL 60089-3343

LeBeau, C Richard (Dick) (Athlete, Coach, Football Player)
10405 Stone Ct
Montgomery, OH 45242-5128, USA

LeBeauf, Sabrina (Actor)
735 Kappock St Apt 6F
Bronx, NY 10463-4629, USA

LeBel, B Harper (Athlete, Football Player)
3379 Scadlock Ln
Sherman Oaks, CA 91403-4914, USA

LeBel, Robert (Bob) (Misc)
25 Rue Saint Pierre
Cite De Chambly, QC J3L 1L7, CANADA

Leber, Ben (Athlete, Football Player)
5 Bridge Ln
Minneapolis, MN 55424-1224, USA

LeBlanc, Christian LeBlanc (Actor)

LeBlanc, Jean-Paul (Athlete, Hockey Player)
120 Gadwall Ln
Manlius, NY 13104-9679

LeBlanc, Matt (Actor)
c/o Troy Zien *3 Arts Entertainment*
9460 Wilshire Blvd Fl 7
Beverly Hills, CA 90212-2713, USA

Leblanc, Ray (Athlete, Hockey Player)
3070 19th Pl SW
Largo, FL 33774-1437

LeBlanc, Wade (Baseball Player)
3035 Henderson Bayou Rd
Lake Charles, LA 70605-2247

Lebo, Jeff (Athlete, Basketball Player)
500 Hidden Lake Way
Santa Rosa Beach, FL 32459-0200, USA

Leboeuf, Laurence (Actor)
KL Benzakein Talent
c/o Karen Benzakein
1445 Lambert Closse
Montreal H3H 1Z5, CANADA

LeBoeuf, Raymond W (Business Person)
PPG Industries
1 Ppg Pl Ste 800
Pittsburgh, PA 15222-5432, USA

Le Bon, Charlotte (Actor)
c/o Ali Benmohamed *United Talent Agency (UTA)*
9336 Civic Center Dr
Beverly Hills, CA 90210-3604, USA

LeBon, Simon (Musician, Songwriter, Writer)
c/o Staff Member *DD Productions*
122 Av. Des Champs-Élysées
Paris 75008, FRANCE

Leboutillier, Peter (Athlete, Hockey Player)
2203 Pot Spring Rd
Luthvle Timon, MD 21093-2723

Lebowitz, Fran (Writer)
Random House
1745 Broadway Frnt 3 # B1
New York, NY 10019-4343, USA

LeBrock, Kelly (Actor, Model)
Bartels Co
PO Box 57593
Sherman Oaks, CA 91413-2593, USA

Lebron, Juan (Baseball Player)
Bowman
PO Box 242
Arroyo, PR 00714-0242, USA

LeBrun, Christopher M (Artist)
Marlborough Fine Art
6 Albermarle St
London W1X 4BY, UNITED KINGDOM (UK)

Lecaine, Bill (Athlete, Hockey Player)
10484 Tracewood Cir
Highlands Ranch, CO 80130-8893

LeCarre, John (Writer)
9 Gainsborough Gardens
London NW3 1BJ, UK

Lecause, Carl (Horse Racer)
4120 Via Aragon
North Fort Myers, FL 33903-1391, USA

LeCavalier, Vincent (Athlete, Hockey Player)
c/o Staff Member *MFIVE Sports Offices*
2500 Rue Trolley
Saint-Lazare, QC J7T 2B1, Canada

Lechler, Shane (Athlete, Football Player)
2115 Countryshire Ln
Richmond, TX 77406-3192, USA

Lechner, Ed (Athlete, Football Player)
6716 W 82nd St
Minneapolis, MN 55438-1235, USA

Lechter, Sharon L (Writer)
Cashflow Technologies
4330 N Civic Center Plz Ste 100
Scottsdale, AZ 85251-3529, USA

Leckey, Nick (Athlete, Football Player)
1056 E Windsor Dr
Gilbert, AZ 85296-4254, USA

Leckner, Eric (Athlete, Basketball Player)
4436 Parview Dr N
Charlotte, NC 28226-3419, USA

Leckonby, William (Athlete, Football Player)
1311 Santee Mill Rd
Bethlehem, PA 18017-1111, USA

LeClair, James M (Jim) (Athlete, Football Player)
214 1st Ave NW
Mayville, ND 58257-1116, USA

Leclair, Jim (Athlete, Football Player)
600 Plymouth Way
Burlingame, CA 94010-2733, USA

Le Clair, John (Athlete, Hockey Player)
208 Turnbridge Circle
Haverford, PA 19041, USA

Leclair, John (Athlete, Hockey Player, Olympic Athlete)
108 Tunbridge Cir
Haverford, PA 19041-1058

Leclaire, Pascal (Athlete, Hockey Player)
250 Daniel Burnham Sq
Square #250
Columbus, OH 43215-2689, USA

LeClerc, Jean (Actor)
19 W 44th St Ste 1500
New York, NY 10036-6101, USA

Leclerc, Katie (Actor)
c/o Liza Anderson *Anderson Group Public Relations*
8060 Melrose Ave Fl 4
Los Angeles, CA 90046-7038, USA

Leclerc, Mike (Athlete, Hockey Player)
473 Abbie Way
Costa Mesa, CA 92627-3162

Leclerc, Rene (Athlete, Hockey Player)
4265 Av Laurin
Quebec, QC G1P 1T6, Canada

Leclerc, Roger (Athlete, Football Player)
257 Elm St
Agawam, MA 01001-2444, USA

LeClezio, Jean-Marie (Writer)
Editions Gallimard
5 Rue Sebastien-Bottin
Paris 75007, USA

Lecomte, Benoit (Swimmer)
Cross Atlantic Swimming Challenge
3005 S Lamar Blvd Ste D109 PMB 353
Austin, TX 78704-4785, USA

Leconte, Henri (Tennis Player)
IMG
Pier House
Strand-on-Green
Chiswick, London W4 3NN, UNITED KINGDOM (UK)

Leconte, Patrice (Director)
c/o Staff Member *ArtMedia*
8 rue Danielle Casanova
Paris 75002, FRANCE

Le Corre, Erwan (Misc)
21 rue du pere chevrier
Lyon 75020, France

Lecount, Terry (Athlete, Football Player)
1288 Branchfield Ct
Riverdale, GA 30296-2148, USA

Lecroy, Matt (Athlete, Baseball Player, Olympic Athlete)
PO Box 2148
Woodbridge, VA 22195-2148, USA

Lecuyer, Doug (Athlete, Hockey Player)
9203 210 St NW
Edmonton, AB T5T 6X2, Canada

Ledbetter, Monte (Athlete, Football Player)
340 Sawgrass Dr
Valdosta, GA 31602-1477, USA

Ledecky, Katie (Athlete, Olympic Athlete, Swimmer)
5395 Elliott Rd
Bethesda, MD 20816, USA

Ledee, Ricky (Athlete, Baseball Player)
10 Broomsedge Ct
Hilton Head Island, SC 29926-1707, USA

Leder, Mimi (Director)
c/o Sara Bottfeld *Industry Entertainment Partners*
955 Carrillo Dr Ste 300
Los Angeles, CA 90048-5400, USA

Ledesma, Aaron (Athlete, Baseball Player)
13820 Cherry Creek Dr
Charleston, SC ?941 '1-0R, USA

Ledet, Joshua (Musician)
c/o Staff Member *19 Entertainment*
401 Wilshire Blvd Ste 1070
Santa Monica, CA 90401-1428, USA

Ledford, Brandy (Actor)
c/o Pam Ellis *Ellis Talent Group*
4705 Laurel Canyon Blvd Ste 300
Valley Village, CA 91607-5901, USA

Ledingham, Walt (Athlete, Hockey Player)
5421 Glenwood St
Duluth, MN 55804-1333, USA

Ledoyen, Virginie (Actor, Model)
c/o Beatrice Hall *ArtMedia*
8 rue Danielle Casanova
Paris 75002, FRANCE

Leduc, Bob (Athlete, Hockey Player)
385 Buxton St
Harrisville, RI 02830-1704

Ledyard, Courtney (Athlete, Football Player)
419 Miller Ave
Freeport, NY 11520-6112, USA

Ledyard, Grant (Athlete, Hockey Player)
112 Old Meadow Dr
East Amherst, NY 14051-2402

Lee, AJ (Athlete, Wrestler)
c/o Staff Member *World Wrestling Entertainment (WWE)*
1241 E Main St
Stamford, CT 06902-3520, USA

Lee, Alexondra (Actor)
c/o Staff Member *Loeb & Loeb (Office 1)*
10100 Santa Monica Blvd Ste 2200
Century City, CA 90067-4120, USA

Lee, Amy (Musician)
135 Joralemon St
Brooklyn, NY 11201-4007, USA

Lee, Andy (Radio Personality, Television Host)
2DayFM Studios
Level 15
50 Goulburn St
Sidney, NSW 02000, Australia

Lee, Andy Scott (Musician)
c/o Staff Member *DCM International & Dance Crazy Management*
Suite 3, 294-296 Nether St
Finchley
London N3 1RJ, UK

Lee, Ang (Director, Producer)
206 Hommocks Rd
Larchmont, NY 10538-3915, USA

Lee, Anthonia W (Amp) (Athlete, Football Player)
990 Brickyard Rd
Chipley, FL 32428-4346, USA

Lee, Barbara (Congressman, Politician)
2267 Rayburn Hob
Washington, DC 20515-4202, USA

Lee, Beverly (Musician)
Bevi Corp
PO Box 100
Clifton, NJ 07015-0100, USA

Lee, Bill (Athlete, Baseball Player)
305 Common View Dr
Craftsbury, VT 05826-9779, USA

Lee, Blake (Actor)
c/o Eric Kranzler *Management 360*
9111 Wilshire Blvd
Beverly Hills, CA 90210-5508, USA

Lee, Bobby (Actor)
c/o Staff Member *Gersh*
9465 Wilshire Blvd Ste 600
Beverly Hills, CA 90212-2605, USA

Lee, Bracken (Politician)
PO Box 58371
Salt Lake City, UT 84158-0371, USA

Lee, Brandon (Adult Film Star)
c/o Staff Member *Diva Central Inc*
7510 W Sunset Blvd # 1445
Los Angeles, CA 90046-3408, USA

Lee, Brenda (Musician)
Brenda Lee Management
PO Box 101188
Nashville, TN 37224-1188, USA

Lee, Briana (Adult Film Star)
8033 W Sunset Blvd # 851
W Hollywood, CA 90046-2401, USA

Lee, Butch (Athlete, Basketball Player)
6616 Bluestone Ct
Charlotte, NC 28212-6431, USA

Lee, Byung-Hun (Actor)
c/o Ame Vanlden *Vanlden Public Relations*
4070 Wilson Pike
Franklin, TN 37067-8126, USA

Lee, Carl (Athlete, Football Player)
1 Stonegate Dr
Hurricane, WV 25526-9217, USA

Lee, Carlos (Athlete, Baseball Player)
1400 N 11th Ave
Melrose Park, IL 60160-3524, USA

Lee, Casey (Actor)
c/o Theo Caesar *90210 Talent Agency*
16430 Ventura Blvd Ste 200
Encino, CA 91436-2135, USA

Lee, Caspar (Internet Star)
c/o Carolyn Moneta *WME|IMG*
9601 Wilshire Blvd
Beverly Hills, CA 90210-5213, USA

Lee, Catherine J (Artist)
PO Box 132
Condon, OR 97823-0132, USA

Lee, Chang-Rae (Writer)
International Creative Mgmt
40 W 57th St Ste 1800
New York, NY 10019-4033, USA

Lee, Charles R (Business Person)
GTE Corp
1255 Corporate Dr
Irving, TX 75038-2562, USA

Lee, Claudia (Actor)
c/o Adam Griffin *LINK Entertainment*
11872 La Grange Ave
Los Angeles, CA 90025-5282, USA

Lee, Cliff (Athlete, Baseball Player)
c/o Darek Braunecker *Frontline Athlete Management (AR)*
PO Box 2612
Palm City, FL 34991-2612, USA

Lee, Clyde (Athlete, Basketball Player)
1439 Summer Glow Ave
Henderson, NV 89012-4456, USA

Lee, Corey (Athlete, Baseball Player)
278 Lancashire Run
Smithfield, NC 27577-8025, USA

Lee, C.S. (Actor, Director)
c/o Andrew Tetenbaum *ATA Management (NY)*
85 Broad St Fl 18
New York, NY 10004-2783, USA

Lee, David (Athlete, Basketball Player)
c/o Mark Bartelstein *Priority Sports & Entertainment (Chicago)*
325 N La Salle Dr Ste 650
Chicago, IL 60654-8182, USA

Lee, David (Actor)
c/o Paula Rosenberg *ICA Talent Management*
1112 Montana Ave Ste 520
Santa Monica, CA 90403-7236, USA

Lee, David (Athlete, Baseball Player)
56 Terrace Dr
Pittsburgh, PA 15205-4312, USA

Lee, David A (Athlete, Football Player)
2518 N Waverly Dr
Bossier City, LA 71111-5940, USA

Lee, Debra (Business Person, Producer)
c/o Staff Member *BET - Black EntertainmentTelevision (DC)*
1235 W St NE
One Bet Plaza
Washington, DC 20018-1211, USA

Lee, Denise (Actor)

Lee, Derek (Athlete, Baseball Player)
741 Birchwood Rd
Frankfort, IL 60423-1031, USA

Lee, Derek (Athlete, Baseball Player)
3576 Brittany Way
El Dorado Hills, CA 95762-3952, USA

Lee, Dickey (Musician)
Mars Talent
27 L Ambiance Ct
Bardonia, NY 10954-1421, USA

Lee, Don (Athlete, Baseball Player)
9101 E Palm Tree Dr
Tucson, AZ 85710-8626, USA

Lee, Doug (Athlete, Basketball Player)
10770 Procyon St
Las Vegas, NV 89141-8844, USA

Lee, Dwight (Athlete, Football Player)
69250 Beebe St Apt 37
Richmond, MI 48062-1504, USA

Lee, Ed (Athlete, Hockey Player)
6 Normand St Apt D
Bristol, RI 02809-4719

Lee, Edward (Athlete, Football Player)
1781 Verbena St NW
Washington, DC 20012-1048, USA

Lee, Edward (Writer)
Necro Publications/Bedlam Press
PO Box 540298
Orlando, FL 32854-0298, USA

Lee, Eugene (Actor)
c/o Heather Collier *Collier Talent Agency*
2313 Lake Austin Blvd Ste 103
Austin, TX 78703-4545, USA

Lee, Eunice (Musician)
Columbia Artists Mgmt Inc
165 W 57th St
New York, NY 10019-2201, USA

Lee, Francis (Actor)
c/o Charlotte Knight *Knight Hall Agency*
7 Mallow St
Lower Ground Fl
London EC1Y 8RQ, UNITED KINGDOM

Lee, Geddy (Musician)
Macklam Feldman Mgmt
200-1505 2nd Ave W
Vancouver, BC V6H 3Y4, CANADA

Lee, Grandma (Actor, Comedian)
Lee Strong
626 Staffordshire Dr
Jacksonville, FL 32225, USA

Lee, Gregory (Athlete, Basketball Player)
8077 Wild Flower Way
San Diego, CA 92120-1622, USA

Lee, Greta (Actor)
c/o Mackenzie Condon Roussos *United Talent Agency (UTA)*
888 7th Ave Fl 7
New York, NY 10106-0700, USA

Lee, Hana Mae (Actor)
c/o Dominique Appel *Imprint PR*
6121 W Sunset Blvd
Neuehouse
Los Angeles, CA 90028-6442, USA

Lee, J (Actor)
c/o Beau Swayze *Management 360*
9111 Wilshire Blvd
Beverly Hills, CA 90210-5508, USA

Lee, Jackie (Musician)
c/o Andrew Cohen *Suit Management*
33 Music Sq W Ste 100B
Nashville, TN 37203-6606, USA

Lee, Jack R (Athlete, Football Player)
6306 Mid Pines Dr
Houston, TX 77069-1346, USA

Lee, Jacky (Athlete, Football Player)
6306 Mid Pines Dr
Houston, TX 77069-1346, USA

Lee, James Kyson (Actor)
c/o Staff Member *Kass Management*
1011 Euclid St Unit B
Santa Monica, CA 90403-4296, USA

Lee, Jared B (Cartoonist)
Jared B Lee Studio
2942 Hamilton Rd
Lebanon, OH 45036-8857, USA

Lee, Jason (Actor, Producer)
c/o Nancy Iannios *Core Public PR*
1875 Century Park E Ste 930
Los Angeles, CA 90067-2540, USA

Lee, Jason Scott (Actor)
c/o Cynthia Shelton-Droke *Sweet Mud Group*
648 Broadway # 1002
New York, NY 10012-2348, USA

Lee, Jennifer (Writer)
c/o Rich Freeman *Code Entertainment*
280 S Beverly Dr Ste 513
Beverly Hills, CA 90212-3908, USA

Lee, Jennifer Nicole (Fitness Expert, Model)
c/o Jon Orlando *Exposure Marketing Group*
348 Hauser Blvd Apt 414
Los Angeles, CA 90036-5590, USA

Lee, Jenny (Athlete, Golfer)
c/o Staff Member *Ladies Pro Golf Association (LPGA)*
100 International Golf Dr
Daytona Beach, FL 32124-1092, USA

Lee, Jim (Business Person)
c/o Staff Member *DC Comics*
1700 Broadway Frnt 7
New York, NY 10019-5934, USA

Lee, Joe (Business Person)
Darden Restaurants
5900 Lake Ellenor Dr
Orlando, FL 32809-4618, USA

Lee, Jon (Actor, Musician)
c/o Staff Member *McLean-Williams Management*
Chester House Unit 3:06
Kennington Park 1-3 Brixton Road
London SW9 6DE, UNITED KINGDOM

Lee, Jonna (Actor)
8721 W Sunset Blvd Ste 103
Los Angeles, CA 90069-2271, USA

Lee, Julia (Actor)
c/o Staff Member *Privilege Talent Agency*
PO Box 260860
Encino, CA 91426-0860, USA

Lee, Katie (Chef, Television Host)
c/o Jonathan Rosen *WME|IMG (NY)*
11 Madison Ave Fl 18
New York, NY 10010-3669, USA

Lee, Keith (Athlete, Basketball Player)
11653 Metz Pl
Eads, TN 38028-6912, USA

Lee, Ki Hong (Actor)
c/o Sarah Shyn *3 Arts Entertainment*
9460 Wilshire Blvd Fl 7
Beverly Hills, CA 90212-2713, USA

Lee, Kurk (Athlete, Basketball Player)
2745 Scarborough Cir
Windsor Mill, MD 21244-8024, USA

Lee, Larry (Athlete, Football Player)
PO Box 3889
Highland Park, MI 48203-0889, USA

Lee, Laurie Ann (Athlete, Baseball Player, Commentator)
19528 Cohasset St
Reseda, CA 91335-2436, USA

Lee, Lela (Actor)
c/o Marilyn Szatmary *SMS Talent*
8383 Wilshire Blvd Ste 230
Beverly Hills, CA 90211-2436, USA

Lee, Leron (Athlete, Baseball Player)
8150 Warren Ct
Granite Bay, CA 95746-9576, USA

Lee, Lloyd (Athlete, Football Player)
635 Homewood Ave
Highland Park, IL 60035-2420, USA

Lee, London (Actor)
1650 Broadway Ste 1410
New York, NY 10019-6957

Lee, Malcolm D (Actor, Director, Writer)
c/o Adam Kanter *Paradigm*
8942 Wilshire Blvd
Beverly Hills, CA 90211-1908, USA

Lee, Mark (Athlete, Baseball Player)
130 N Rosemont St
Amarillo, TX 79106-5214, USA

Lee, Mark (Athlete, Baseball Player)
3580 Brunswick Dr
Colorado Springs, CO 80920-7338, USA

Lee, Mark (Athlete, Football Player)
14120 NE 183rd St Unit 233
Woodinville, WA 98072-7073, USA

Lee, Mark C (Astronaut)
4574 Bishops Ct
Middleton, WI 53562-2326, USA

Lee, Mark C Colonel (Astronaut)
79 S Player Crest Cir
Spring, TX 77382-1809, USA

Lee, Marqise (Athlete, Football Player)
c/o Andrew Kessler *Athletes First*
23091 Mill Creek Dr
Laguna Hills, CA 92653-1258, USA

Lee, Michele (Actor)
Michele Lee Productions
16030 Ventura Blvd Ste 240
Encino, CA 91436-4487, USA

Lee, Michelle (Actor)
141 N Gunston Dr
Los Angeles, CA 90049-2012, USA

Lee, Mike (Athlete, Baseball Player)
1790 Calmin Dr
Fallbrook, CA 92028-4303, USA

Lee, Min-ho (Actor)
c/o Staff Member *Starhaus Entertainment*
L#601 Hill B/D
563-4 Shinsa-dong, Kangnam-gu
Seoul, Korea

Lee, Natasha (Actor, Dancer, Model)

Lee, Reggie (Actor)
c/o Jamie Harhay Skinner *Baker Winokur Ryder Public Relations*
9100 Wilshire Blvd Ste 655
W Tower #500
Beverly Hills, CA 90212-3491, USA

Lee, Rex (Actor)
c/o Marc Hamou *Thruline Entertainment*
9250 Wilshire Blvd Fl Ground
Beverly Hills, CA 90212-3352, USA

Lee, Robert M (Athlete, Football Player)
363 Parker Ave
San Francisco, CA 94118-4235, USA

Lee, Robinne (Actor)
c/o Darren Goldberg *Global Creative*
1051 Cole Ave # B
Los Angeles, CA 90038-2601, USA

Lee, Rock (Athlete, Basketball Player)
4616 Blackfoot Ave
San Diego, CA 92117-6230, USA

Lee, Ron (Athlete, Basketball Player)
65 Pine St
Woburn, MA 01801-3225, USA

Lee, Ronnie (Athlete, Football Player)
139 Shady Trl
Mc Gregor, TX 76657-3768, USA

Lee, Russell (Athlete, Basketball Player)
1457 Smokehouse Ln
Stone Mountain, GA 30088-3312, USA

Lee, Ruta (Actor)
2623 Laurel Canyon Blvd
Los Angeles, CA 90046-1106, USA

Lee, Samuel (Sammy) (Coach)
16537 Harbour Ln
Huntington Beach, CA 92649-2105, USA

Lee, Sandra (Chef, Television Host)
c/o Staff Member *The Food Network.com*
1180 Avenue of the Americas Fl 14
New York, NY 10036-8401, USA

Lee, Sean (Athlete, Football Player)
c/o Michael McCartney *Priority Sports & Entertainment (Chicago)*
325 N La Salle Dr Ste 650
Chicago, IL 60654-8182, USA

Lee, Shannon (Actor)
c/o Steven Younger *Myman Greenspan Fineman Fox Rosenberg & Light*
11601 Wilshire Blvd Ste 2200
Los Angeles, CA 90025-1758, USA

Lee, Sheryl (Actor)
c/o Daniel (Danny) Sussman *Brillstein Entertainment Partners*
9150 Wilshire Blvd Ste 350
Beverly Hills, CA 90212-3453, USA

Lee, Spike (Director, Producer)
c/o Staff Member *40 Acres & A Mule Filmworks Inc (NY)*
75 S Elliott Pl
Brooklyn, NY 11217-1207, USA

Lee, Steven (Television Host)
c/o Staff Member *Travel Channel*
1 Discovery Pl
Silver Spring, MD 20910-3354, USA

Lee, Sung Hi (Actor)
c/o Staff Member *TalentWorks*
3500 W Olive Ave Ste 1400
Burbank, CA 91505-5512, USA

Lee, Terry (Athlete, Baseball Player)
2611 Cascara Dr
Eugene, OR 97403-2562, USA

Lee, Tommy (Musician)
c/o David Weise *David Weise and Associates*
16000 Ventura Blvd Ste 600
Encino, CA 91436-2753, USA

Lee, Tony (Actor)
c/o Dave Phillips *Edmonds Management*
1635 N Cahuenga Blvd Fl 5
Los Angeles, CA 90028-6201, USA

Lee, Travis (Athlete, Baseball Player, Olympic Athlete)
PO Box 1572
Rancho Santa Fe, CA 92067-1572, USA

Lee, Vernon R (Religious Leader)
Wyatt Baptist Church
3863 W Hillsboro St
El Dorado, AR 71730-6752, USA

Lee, Vincent (Baseball Player)
Baltimore Black Sox
3228 Avondale Ave
Baltimore, MD 21215-4702, USA

Lee, William Gregory (Actor)
c/o Jeff Witjas *Agency for the Performing Arts (APA)*
405 S Beverly Dr Ste 500
Beverly Hills, CA 90212-4425, USA

Lee, Willie James (Athlete, Baseball Player)
233 Star Dust Cir
Birmingham, AL 35214-3719, USA

Lee, Zeph (Athlete, Football Player)
7417 1/2 S Normandie Ave
Los Angeles, CA 90044-2468, USA

Leech, Allen (Actor)
c/o Ciara Parkes *Public Eye Communications*
535 Kings Rd
#313 Plaza
London SW10 0SZ, UNITED KINGDOM

Leech, Beverly (Actor)
9150 Wilshire Blvd Ste 175
Beverly Hills, CA 90212-3450, USA

Leede, Ed (Athlete, Basketball Player)
6400 S Fiddlers Green Cir Ste 2100
Greenwood Village, CO 80111-4938, USA

Lee Fincher, Stephen (Congressman, Politician)
1118 Longworth Hob
Washington, DC 20515-1011, USA

Lee-Harmon, Annabelle (Baseball Player)
960 Senate St
Costa Mesa, CA 92627-3332, USA

Lee-Hom, Wang (Actor)
c/o Bryan Lourd *Creative Artists Agency (CAA)*
2000 Avenue of the Stars Ste 100
Los Angeles, CA 90067-4705, USA

Leek, Gene (Athlete, Baseball Player)
4055 Hamilton St Apt 5
San Diego, CA 92104-6108, USA

Leeman, Gary (Athlete, Hockey Player)
12-1027 Old Bridge Rd RR 2
Port Carling, ON P0B 1J0, Canada

Leen, Bill (Musician)
William Morris Agency
2100 W End Ave Ste 1000
Nashville, TN 37203-5240, USA

Leeper, Dave (Athlete, Baseball Player)
23997 Kaleb Dr
Corona, CA 92883-9385, USA

Leerhsen, Erica (Actor)
c/o Brian Wilkins *LINK Entertainment*
11872 La Grange Ave
Los Angeles, CA 90025-5282, USA

Leese, Howard (Musician)
219 2st Ave N
#333
Seattle, WA 98109, USA

Leestma, David C (Astronaut)
4314 Lake Grove Dr
Seabrook, TX 77586-4114, USA

Leestma, David C Captain (Astronaut)
4314 Lake Grove Dr
Seabrook, TX 77586-4114, USA

Leetch, Brian (Athlete, Hockey Player)
40 Battery St PH 12
Boston, MA 02109-1907

Leetch, Brian J (Athlete, Hockey Player, Olympic Athlete)
c/o Staff Member *PuckAgency LLC*
555 Pleasantville Rd Ste 210N
North Building, Suite 210
Briarcliff Manor, NY 10510-1900, USA

Leetzow, Max (Athlete, Football Player)
4744 E Caley Pl
Centennial, CO 80121-3202, USA

Leeuwenburg, Jay (Athlete, Football Player)
8042 S Cook Way
Centennial, CO 80122-3608, USA

Leeves, Jane (Actor)
c/o Molly Madden *3 Arts Entertainment*
9460 Wilshire Blvd Fl 7
Beverly Hills, CA 90212-2713, USA

Lefcourt, Peter (Actor)
c/o Staff Member *Creative Artists Agency (CAA)*
2000 Avenue of the Stars Ste 100
Los Angeles, CA 90067-4705, USA

Lefebvre, Jim (Athlete, Baseball Player, Coach)
10375 N 101st St
Scottsdale, AZ 85258-4829, USA

Lefebvre, Joe (Athlete, Baseball Player)
11 Lottie Ln
Chichester, NH 03258-6556, USA

Lefebvre, Ryan (Commentator)
13620 S Pebblebrook Ln
Greenwood, MO 64034-8957, USA

Lefebvre, Sylvain (Athlete, Hockey Player)
7833 Vallagio Ln
Englewood, CO 80112-5872

Lefevre, Rachelle (Actor)
c/o Britney Ross *42West*
1840 Century Park E Ste 700
Los Angeles, CA 90067-2122, USA

Lefferts, Craig (Athlete, Baseball Player)
Stockton Ports 404 W Fremont St Attn: Coaching Staff
Stockton, CA 95203-2806, USA

Lefkowitz, Louis (Politician)
575 Park Ave
New York, NY 10065-7332, USA

Lefley, Chuck (Athlete, Hockey Player)
PO Box 65
Grosse Isle, MB R0C 1G0, Canada

Leflore, Ron (Athlete, Baseball Player)
6263 93rd Ter N Apt 4206
Pinellas Park, FL 33782-4640, USA

LeFrak, Richard (Business Person)
LeFrak
40 W 57th St Fl 23
New York, NY 10019-4011, USA

Leftwich, Byron (Athlete, Football Player)
1725 Catherine Fran Dr
Accokeek, MD 20607-3231, USA

Leftwich, Phil (Athlete, Baseball Player)
16046 S 13th Ave
Phoenix, AZ 85045-0608, USA

Legace, Jean-Guy (Athlete, Hockey Player)
126 Casa Grande Ln
Santa Rosa Beach, FL 32459-3162, USA

Legace, Manny (Athlete, Hockey Player)
40708 Village Oaks
Novi, MI 48375-4464

Legend, John (Actor, Musician)
c/o Dvora Vener Englefield *The Lede Company*
9701 Wilshire Blvd # 930
Beverly Hills, CA 90212-2020, USA

Legette, Burnie (Athlete, Football Player)
1118 Doyle Pl
Colorado Springs, CO 80915-2327, USA

Legette, Tyrone (Athlete, Football Player)
1304 Hancock St
Columbia, SC 29205-4850, USA

Legg, Greg (Athlete, Baseball Player)
2 Stadium Way
Lakewood, NJ 08701-4536, USA

Leggat, Ashley (Actor)
c/o Staff Member *Walt Disney Co, The (Buena Vista Motion Picture Group)*
500 S Buena Vista St
Burbank, CA 91521-0007

Leggatt, Ian (Athlete, Golfer)
9726 E Mountain Spring Rd
Scottsdale, AZ 85255-6640, USA

Legge, Barry (Athlete, Hockey Player)
Division 12 Police Station 210 Lyje St
Winnipeg, MB R3J 2Cl, Canada

Legge, Katherine (Race Car Driver)
307 Park Ave
Chardon, OH 44024-1311, USA

Legge, Michael (Actor)
c/o Staff Member *Independent Talent Group*
40 Whitfield St
London W1T 2RH, UNITED KINGDOM

Legge, Randy (Athlete, Hockey Player)
322 Primrose Lane
Newmarket, ON L3Y 5Z2, CANADA

Leggero, Natasha (Actor)
c/o Jennifer Sims *Imprint PR*
375 Hudson St
New York, NY 10014-3658, USA

Legien, Waldemar (Athlete)
Ul Grottgera 10
Bytom 41-902, POLAND

Legler, Tim (Athlete, Basketball Player)
275 82nd St
Stone Harbor, NJ 08247-1707, USA

Legrande, Larry (Athlete, Baseball Player)
1331 Leon St NW
Roanoke, VA 24017-6011, USA

Legree, Lance (Athlete, Football Player)
25 Ardmore Ave
Clifton, NJ 07012-1807, USA

LeGros, James (Actor)
c/o David Lillard *Industry Entertainment Partners*
955 Carrillo Dr Ste 300
Los Angeles, CA 90048-5400, USA

Leguizamo, John (Actor, Comedian, Producer)
c/o Jeff Golenberg *Silver Lining Entertainment*
421 S Beverly Dr Fl 7
Beverly Hills, CA 90212-4408, USA

Legursky, Doug (Athlete, Football Player)

Legwand, David (Athlete, Hockey Player)
37700 Lakeshore Dr
Harrison Twp, MI 48045-2849, USA

Lehan, Michael (Athlete, Football Player)
418 Madison Ave S
Hopkins, MN 55343-8469, USA

Lehane, Dennis (Writer)
341 Kerrville South Dr
Kerrville, TX 78028-8770, USA

Lehew, Jim (Athlete, Baseball Player)
3086 Fairview Rd
Grantsville, MD 21536-2239, USA

Lehman, Kristen (Actor)

Lehman, Manny (DJ, Musician)
c/o Len Evans *Project Publicity*
540 W 43rd St
New York, NY 10036, USA

Lehman, Tom (Athlete, Golfer)
9820 E Thompson Peak Pkwy Unit 704
Scottsdale, AZ 85255-6656, USA

Lehmann, Edie (Actor)
24844 Malibu Rd
Malibu, CA 90265-4617, USA

Lehmann, Erich L (Misc)
Research Statistics Group
Education Testing Service
Princeton, NJ 08541-0001, USA

Lehmann, Michael (Director, Producer)
c/o Staff Member *Industry Entertainment Partners*
955 Carrillo Dr Ste 300
Los Angeles, CA 90048-5400, USA

Lehmkuhl, Reichen (Model, Reality Star, Writer)
c/o Staff Member *Models International Agency*
1800 Century Park E Fl 6
Los Angeles, CA 90067-1501, USA

Lehne, Fredric (Actor)
c/o Staff Member *Bauman Redanty & Shaul Agency*
5757 Wilshire Blvd
Suite 473
Beverly Hills, CA 90212, USA

Lehninger, Albert L (Misc)
15020 Tanyard Rd
Sparks, MD 21152-9752, USA

Lehr, John (Actor, Producer, Writer)
c/o Staff Member *WME/IMG*
9601 Wilshire Blvd
Beverly Hills, CA 90210-5213, USA

Lehr, Justin (Athlete, Baseball Player)
107 S Millport Cir
Spring, TX 77382-4017, USA

Lehr, Zella (Musician)
1961 NE 31st St
Lighthouse Point, FL 33064-7643, USA

Lehrer, Jim (Journalist, Television Host, Writer)
c/o Jim Griffin *Paradigm*
140 Broadway Ste 2600
New York, NY 10005-1011, USA

Lehtinen, Jere (Athlete, Hockey Player)
622 Stratford Ln
Coppell, TX 75019-6129, USA

Lehto, JJ (Race Car Driver)
Hogan Racing LLC
3473 Rider Trl S
Earth City, MO 63045-1110, USA

Lehtonen, Kari (Athlete, Hockey Player)
4036 Lively Ln
Dallas, TX 75220-1872

Lehuep, John (Athlete, Football Player)
205 Bud Nalley Dr
Easley, SC 29642-3578, USA

Lehvonen, Hank (Athlete, Hockey Player)
4000 N Federal Hwy Ste 207
Boca Raton, FL 33431-4527, USA

Lei, Kaylani (Actor, Adult Film Star, Model)
c/o Gina Rodriguez *GiToni Productions*
Prefers to be contacted via telephone or email
Tarzana, CA 91335, USA

Leibel, Rudolph (Misc)
464 Riverside Dr # 95
New York, NY 10027-6822, USA

Leibman, Ron (Actor)
22 Kinnicutt Rd
Pound Ridge, NY 10576-1800, USA

Leibovitz, Annie (Artist, Photographer)
Annie Leibovitz Photography
405 W 14th St FRNT 1
New York, NY 10014-1071, USA

Leibowitz, Barry (Athlete, Basketball Player)
10670 NW 17th Pl
Plantation, FL 33322-6454, USA

Leibrandt, Charlie (Athlete, Baseball Player)
1235 Stuart Rdg
Alpharetta, GA 30022-6364, USA

Leicester, Jon (Athlete, Baseball Player)
17151 Corbina Ln Apt 112
Huntington Beach, CA 92649-5168, USA

Leick, Hudson (Actor)
c/o Staff Member *Imperium 7 Talent Agency*
5455 Wilshire Blvd Ste 1706
Los Angeles, CA 90036-4217, USA

Leier, Ed (Athlete, Hockey Player)
2250 Christopherson Rd Suite 10
Surrey, BC V4A 3L3, Canada

Leifer, Carol (Actor, Comedian)
c/o Lori Jonas *Jonas Public Relations*
1327 Ocean Ave Ste F
Santa Monica, CA 90401-1024, USA

Leifheit, Sylvia (Model)
Agentur Reed
Treppendorfer Weg 13
Berlin 12527, GERMANY

Leigeb, Brian (Football Player)
c/o Team Member *Oakland Raiders*
1220 Harbor Bay Pkwy
Alameda, CA 94502-6570, USA

Leigh, Barbara (Actor)
PO Box 244
Los Angeles, CA 90078-0244, USA

Leigh, Cherami (Actor)
c/o Staff Member *Venture IAB*
3211 Cahuenga Blvd W Ste 104
Los Angeles, CA 90068-1372, USA

Leigh, Chyler (Actor)
c/o Joannie Burstein *Burstein Company*
15304 W Sunset Blvd Ste 208
Pacific Palisades, CA 90272-3656, USA

Leigh, Danni (Musician)
c/o Bridget Bauer *Bismeaux Productions*
PO Box 463
Austin, TX 78767-0463, USA

Leigh, Jennifer Jason (Actor)
c/o Jason Weinberg *Untitled Entertainment*
350 S Beverly Dr Ste 200
Beverly Hills, CA 90212-4819, USA

Leigh, Katie (Actor)
c/o Staff Member *Social Stars Web*
PO Box 999
Powder Springs, GA 30127-0999, USA

Leigh, Makenzie (Actor)
c/o Emily Gerson Saines *Brookside Artists Management*
250 W 57th St Ste 1820
New York, NY 10107-1802, USA

Leigh, Mike (Director)
Thin Man Films
9 Greek St
Soho
London W1D 4DQ, UNITED KINGDOM (UK)

Leigh, Nikki (Actor)
c/o Nilda Carrazana *Status PR*
PO Box 6191
Westlake Village, CA 91359-6191, USA

Leigh, Regina (Musician)
Bobby Roberts
909 Meadowlark Ln
Goodlettsville, TN 37072-2309, USA

Leighton, Amanda (Actor)
c/o Laura Ackerman *Advantage PR*
3900 W Alameda Ave Ste 1200
Burbank, CA 91505-4317, USA

Leighton, Brad (Race Car Driver)
c/o Staff Member *NASCAR*
1801 W Speedway Blvd
Daytona Beach, FL 32114-1243, USA

Leighton, GB (Musician)
c/o Staff Member *Paradigm (Monterey)*
404 W Franklin St
Monterey, CA 93940-2303, USA

Leighton, Laura (Actor)
c/o Staci Wolfe *Polaris PR*
8135 W 4th St Fl 2
Los Angeles, CA 90048-4415, USA

Leija, James (Jesse) (Athlete, Boxer)
PO Box 14058
San Antonio, TX 78214-0058, USA

Leiker, Tony (Athlete, Football Player)
411 E 21st St
Hays, KS 67601-2805, USA

Leimkuehler, Paul (Business Person, Skier)
351 Darbys Run
Bay Village, OH 44140-2968, USA

Leinart, Matt (Athlete, Football Player, Heisman Trophy Winner)
6966 Turf Dr
Huntington Beach, CA 92648-1546, USA

Leinonen, Mikko (Athlete, Hockey Player)
Tappara Tampere Liiga-Tapparan Toimisto
Kissanmaankatu 9
Tampere, SF 33520, Finland

Leiper, Dave (Athlete, Baseball Player)
13082 N 103rd St
Scottsdale, AZ 85260-7272, USA

Leipheimer, Levi (Athlete, Cycler, Olympic Athlete)

Leister, John (Athlete, Baseball Player)
304 Devon Dr
Saint Louis, MI 48880-9427, USA

Leisure, David (Actor)
PO Box 684267
Park City, UT 84068-4267, USA

Leitch, David (Actor, Director)
c/o Staff Member *87Eleven*
8711 Aviation Blvd
Inglewood, CA 90301-2003, USA

Leitch, Matthew (Actor)
c/o Colleen Schlegel *Schlegel Entertainment*
1119 Colorado Ave Ste 12
Santa Monica, CA 90401-3009, USA

Leiter, Al (Athlete, Baseball Player)
106 Prospect St
Summit, NJ 07901-2472, USA

Leiter, Bob (Athlete, Hockey Player)
1921 Shore point Village
Gimli, MB ROC 1BO, Canada

Leiter, Ken (Athlete, Hockey Player)
30098 Warley Ct
Novi, MI 48377-2191, USA

Leiter, Mark (Athlete, Baseball Player)
1959 Vermont Ave
Toms River, NJ 08755-1340, USA

Leith, Virginia (Actor)
2120 N Cardillo Ave
Palm Springs, CA 92262-2810, USA

Leitner, Patric-Fritz (Athlete)
BSD
An der Schiessstatte 4
Berchtesgaden 83471, GERMANY

Leitner, Ted (Commentator)
PO Box 232248
Encinitas, CA 92023-2248, USA

Leitso, Tyron (Actor)
c/o Deb Dillistone *Red Management*
415 Esplanade W Box 3
North Vancouver, BC V7M 1A6, CANADA

Leius, Scott (Athlete, Baseball Player)
12620 42nd Pl N
Minneapolis, MN 55442-2344, USA

Lekakis, Paul (Musician)
c/o Staff Member *Diva Central Inc*
7510 W Sunset Blvd # 1445
Los Angeles, CA 90046-3408, USA

Lekang, Anton (Skier)
47 Pratt St
Winsted, CT 06098-2025, USA

Lelbrandt, Charlie (Athlete, Baseball Player)
Cincinnati Reds
1235 Stuart Rdg
Alpharetta, GA 30022-6364, USA

Lelliott, Jeremy (Actor)
c/o Joan Green *Joan Green Management*
1836 Courtney Ter
Los Angeles, CA 90046-2106, USA

L. Ellmers, Renee (Congressman, Politician)
1533 Longworth Hob
Washington, DC 20515-3302

LeLouch, Claude (Director)
15 Ave Hoche
Paris 75008, FRANCE

Lemaire, Jacques (Athlete, Hockey Player)
803 Riviera Dunes Way
Palmetto, FL 34221-7125

Lemaire, Jacques G (Athlete, Coach, Hockey Player)
803 Riviera Dunes Way
Palmetto, FL 34221-7125, USA

Lemanczyk, Dave (Athlete, Baseball Player)
24 Lehigh Ct
Rockville Centre, NY 11570-2016, USA

Lemaster, Dennv (Athlete, Baseball Player)
4833 Carlene Way SW
Lilburn, GA 30047-4705, USA

Lemaster, Denny (Athlete, Baseball Player)
4833 Carlene Way SW
Lilburn, GA 30047-4705, USA

Lemaster, Frank (Athlete, Football Player)
PO Box 159
Birchrunville, PA 19421-0159, USA

Lemaster, Johnnie (Athlete, Baseball Player)
317 4th St
Paintsville, KY 41240-1153, USA

Lemaster, Jr., Ron (Race Car Driver)
3705 Brandon Rd
Huntington, WV 25704-1107, USA

Le Mat, Paul (Actor)
6300 Wilshire Blvd Ste 1460
Los Angeles, CA 90048-5200, USA

Lemay, Moe (Athlete, Hockey Player)
6296 Lanark St
Chilliwack, BC V2R 3G9, Canada

Le May Doan, Catriona (Speed Skater)
Landmark Sport Group
1 City Centre Dr Suite 301
Mississauga, ON L5B 1M2, CANADA

LeMay-Doan, Michelle (Speed Skater)
Landmark Sport Group
277 Richmond St W
Toronto, ON M5V 1X1, CANADA

Lembeck, Michael (Actor, Director)
23852 Pacific Coast Hwy # 355
Malibu, CA 90265-4876, USA

Lemche, Kris (Actor)
c/o Brian Wilkins *LINK Entertainment*
11872 La Grange Ave
Los Angeles, CA 90025-5282, USA

Lemelin, Jacques (Athlete, Hockey Player)
1301 Av Mathieu-Choret
Quebec, QC G2L 1V1, Canada

Lemelin, Reggie (Athlete, Hockey Player)
10 Benevento Cir
Peabody, MA 01960-1268

LeMesurier, John (Actor)
56 Barron's Keep
London W14, UNITED KINGDOM (UK)

Lemieux, Alain (Athlete, Hockey Player)
202 Drake St
Kissimmee, FL 34747-5021

Lemieux, Claude (Athlete, Hockey Player)
420 De Sola Ter
Corona Dl Mar, CA 92625-2650

Lemieux, Jean (Athlete, Hockey Player)
202 Drake St
Kissimmee, FL 34747-5021

Lemieux, Jocelyn (Athlete, Hockey Player)
15 Rue de Montauban
Blainville, QC J7B 1T4, Canada

Lemieux, Joseph H (Business Person)
Owens-Illinois Inc
1 Seagate
Toledo, OH 43604-1558, USA

LeMieux, Kathryn (Cartoonist)
c/o Staff Member *King Features Syndication*
300 W 57th St Fl 15
New York, NY 10019-5238, USA

Lemieux, Mario (Athlete, Hockey Player)
Mario Lemieux Foundation
816 5th Ave Fl 6
Pittsburgh, PA 15219-4765, USA

Lemieux, Raymond U (Misc)
7602 119 St NW
Edmonton, AB T6G 1W3, CANADA

Lemke, Anthony (Actor)
c/o Jennifer Goldhar *Characters Talent Agency (Toronto)*
8 Elm St Fl 2
Toronto, ON M5G 1G7, CANADA

Lemke, Cheryl (Television Host)
WOWT-TV
3501 Farnam St
Omaha, NE 68131-3301, USA

Lemke, Mark (Athlete, Baseball Player)
3 Olena Dr
Whitesboro, NY 13492-2103, USA

Lemme, Steve (Comedian)
Broken Lizard Industries
PO Box 642809
Los Angeles, CA 90064-8279, USA

Lemmerman, Bruce (Athlete, Football Player)
621 Silverado Way
Eagle Point, OR 97524-9011, USA

Lemmon, Chris (Actor)
80 Murray Dr
South Glastonbury, CT 06073-2435, USA

Lemmon, Christopher (Actor)
80 Murray Dr
S Glastonbury, CT 06073-2435, USA

Lemmons, Kasi (Actor, Director)
c/o Frank Wuliger *Gersh*
9465 Wilshire Blvd Ste 600
Beverly Hills, CA 90212-2605, USA

Lemon, Chet (Athlete, Baseball Player)
38150 Timberlane Dr
Umatilla, FL 32784-9302, USA

Lemon, Cleo (Athlete, Football Player)
1525 Harrington Park Dr
Jacksonville, FL 32225-4919, USA

Lemon, Don (Correspondent, Journalist)
c/o Staff Member *N.S. Bienstock*
888 7th Ave Fl 7
New York, NY 10106-0700, USA

Lemon, Mike (Athlete, Football Player)
455 Whitree Ln
Chesterfield, MO 63017-2450, USA

Lemond, Greg (Athlete, Cycler, Olympic Athlete)
2175 Appleby Rd
Greenback, TN 37742-2328, USA

Lemonds, Dave (Athlete, Baseball Player)
3080 Arches Bluff Cir
Lancaster, SC 29720-0091, USA

Lemongelio, Mark (Baseball Player)
Houston Astros
4986 Bostonian Loop
New Prt Rchy, FL 34655-1472, USA

Lemongello, Mark (Athlete, Baseball Player)
4986 Bostonian Loop
New Prt Rchy, FL 34655-1472, USA

Lemonier, Corey (Athlete, Football Player)
c/o Eric Metz *Lock Metz Milanovic LLC*
6900 E Camelback Rd Ste 600
Scottsdale, AZ 85251-8044, USA

Lemonis, Marcus (Business Person, Reality Star)
c/o Staff Member *CNBC (Main)*
900 Sylvan Ave
Englewood Cliffs, NJ 07632-3312, USA

Lemon Jelly (Music Group)
c/o Staff Member *Paradigm (Monterey)*
404 W Franklin St
Monterey, CA 93940-2303, USA

Lemos, Richie (Boxer)
18658 Klum Pl
Rowland Heights, CA 91748-4850, USA

Lemper, Ute (Actor, Dancer, Musician)
Les Visiteurs du Soir
40 Rue de la Folie Regnault
Paris 75011, FRANCE

Lenard, Voshon (Athlete, Basketball Player)
27946 Pebblebrook St
Southfield, MI 48034-1504, USA

Lenardon, Tim (Athlete, Hockey Player)
1435 Appleridge Rd
Kelowna, BC V1W 3A6, Canada

Lenarduzzl, Mlke (Athlete, Hockey Player)
18165 Pine Ridge Dr
Prairieville, LA 70769-3455

Lendeborg Jr, Jorge (Actor)
c/o Nicole Perna *Imprint PR*
6121 W Sunset Blvd
Neuehouse
Los Angeles, CA 90028-6442, USA

Lendl, Ivan (Athlete, Tennis Player)
400 5 1/2 Mile Rd
Goshen, CT 06756-1032, USA

Lenehan, Nancy (Actor)
c/o Meghan Schumacher *Meghan Schumacher Management*
13351D Riverside Dr Ste 387
Sherman Oaks, CA 91423-2508, USA

L. Engel, Eliot (Congressman, Politician)
2161 Rayburn Hob
Washington, DC 20515-2206, USA

Lengies, Vanessa (Actor)
c/o John Carrabino *John Carrabino Management*
5900 Wilshire Blvd Ste 740
Los Angeles, CA 90036-5032, USA

Lenk, Maria (Swimmer)
Rua Cupertino Durao 16
Leblon
Rio de Janeiro 22441, BRAZIL

Lenk, Thomas (Artist)
Gemeinde Braunsbach
Schloss Tierberg 07176, GERMANY

Lenk, Tom (Actor)
c/o Bernard Kira *BMK-ENT*
8060 Melrose Ave Fl 4
Los Angeles, CA 90046-7038, USA

Lenkaitis, Bill (Athlete, Football Player)
10 Longwood Dr Unit 143
Westwood, MA 02090-1137, USA

Lenkaitis, William E (Athlete, Football Player)
10 Longwood Dr Unit 143
Westwood, MA 02090-1137, USA

Lennix, Harry (Actor)
c/o Andrew Freedman *Andrew Freedman Public Relations*
35 E 84th St
New York, NY 10028-0871, USA

Lennon, Diane (Musician)
1984 State Highway 165
Branson, MO 65616-8936, USA

Lennon, Janet (Musician)
223 Devonshire Dr
Branson, MO 65616-3489, USA

Lennon, Julian (Musician, Songwriter)
Man from Another Room
20 Bulstrode St
London W1M 5FR, UNITED KINGDOM

Lennon, Kathy (Musician)
Overlook Dr
#10
Branson, MO 65616, USA

Lennon, Patrick (Athlete, Baseball Player)
60 Meister Blvd
Freeport, NY 11520-5938, USA

Lennon, Peggy (Musician)
1984 State Highway 165
Branson, MO 65616-8936, USA

Lennon, Richard G (Religious Leader)
Archdiocese of Boston
2121 Commonwealth Ave
Boston, MA 02135-3101, USA

Lennon, Sean (Musician)
Dakota Hotel
1 W 72nd St
New York, NY 10023-3486, USA

Lennon, Thomas (Actor, Producer)
c/o Peter Principato *Artists First*
9465 Wilshire Blvd Ste 900
Beverly Hills, CA 90212-2608, USA

Lennox, Annie (Musician)
c/o Staff Member *19 Entertainment*
35-37 Parkgate Rd #32/33
#32/33 Ransomes Dock
London SW11 4NP, UNITED KINGDOM

Lennox, Kai (Actor)
c/o Gabrielle Allabashi *Ellis Talent Group*
4705 Laurel Canyon Blvd Ste 300
Valley Village, CA 91607-5901, USA

Lenny, Rick H. (Business Person)
Hershey Foods
100 Crystal A Dr Unit 8
Hershey, PA 17033-9702, USA

Leno, Jay (Actor, Comedian, Talk Show Host)
c/o Dick Guttman *Guttman Associates Public Relations*
118 S Beverly Dr Ste 201
Beverly Hills, CA 90212-3016, USA

Lenon, Paris (Athlete, Football Player)
1505 Taylor St
Lynchburg, VA 24504-3437, USA

Lenox, Adriane (Actor)
c/o Staff Member *Leading Artists*
145 W 45th St Rm 1000
New York, NY 10036-4032, USA

Lenska, Rula (Actor, Model)
David Daley Assoc
586A Kings Road
London SW6 2DX, UNITED KINGDOM (UK)

Lentine, Jim (Athlete, Baseball Player)
1066 Calle Del Cerro Unit 1411
San Clemente, CA 92672-6075, USA

Lentinen, Jere (Athlete, Hockey Player)
2601 Avenue of the Stars
Frisco, TX 75034-9015, USA

Lenton, Lisbeth (Athlete, Olympic Athlete)
Australian Swimming Inc
Unit 12/7 Beissel Street
Canberra, Belconnen 02617, AUSTRALIA

Lentz, Jack (Athlete, Football Player)
1035 Park Ave # 5B
New York, NY 10028-0912, USA

Lentz, Leary (Athlete, Basketball Player)
1309 Whispering Pines Dr
Houston, TX 77055-6854, USA

Lenz, Kay (Actor)
5916 Filaree Hts
Malibu, CA 90265-3721, USA

Lenz, Kim (Musician, Songwriter, Writer)
Mark Pucia Media
5000 Oak Bluff Ct
Atlanta, GA 30350-1069, USA

Lenz, Nicole (Actor)
c/o Victor Del Toro *Elite Model Management (LA)*
518 N La Cienega Blvd
West Hollywood, CA 90048-2002, USA

Lenz, Rick (Actor)
12955 Calvert St
Van Nuys, CA 91401-3206, USA

Leo, Jim (Athlete, Hockey Player)
201 Old Oak Pl
Thurmont, MD 21788-1854, USA

Leo, Melissa (Actor)
c/o Alex Spieller *Baker Winokur Ryder Public Relations*
200 5th Ave Fl 5
New York, NY 10010-3307, USA

Leo Bwarie, Joseph (Actor, Musician)
c/o Gail Parenteau *Parenteau Guidance*
132 E 35th St # J
New York, NY 10016-3892, USA

Leon, Eddie (Athlete, Baseball Player)
5285 N Strada De Rubino
Tucson, AZ 85750-6043, USA

Leon, Kenny (Actor, Director, Producer)
True Colors Theatre Company
659 Auburn Ave NE Apt 257
Atlanta, GA 30312-1981, USA

Leon, Lourdes (Actor, Designer)

Leon, Valerie (Actor)
Essanay Ltd
2 Conduit St
London, W1R 9TG, UNITED KINGDOM (UK)

Leonard, Bob (Slick) (Athlete, Basketball Player, Coach)
3744 Abney Point Dr
Zionsville, IN 46077-7706, USA

Leonard, Brian (Athlete, Football Player)
49 W Shore Rd
Gouverneur, NY 13642-4520, USA

Leonard, Dennis (Athlete, Baseball Player)
4102 SW Evergreen St
Blue Springs, MO 64015-9713, USA

Leonard, Franklin (Producer)
c/o Harvey Gettleson *Gettleson Witzer & OConnor*
16000 Ventura Blvd
Encino, CA 91436-2744, USA

Leonard, Gary (Athlete, Basketball Player)
2406 Ridgefield Rd
Columbia, MO 65203-1532, USA

Leonard, James (Athlete, Football Player)
RR 332 Box 349
Mullica Hill, NY 10862, USA

Leonard, Jeffrey (Athlete, Baseball Player)
1071 Stoney Creek Dr
San Ramon, CA 94582-5637, USA

Leonard, Jim (Athlete, Football Player)
119 Cress Rd
Santa Cruz, CA 95060-1001, USA

Leonard, Joshua (Actor)
c/o Elizabeth Much *East 2 West Collective*
11022 Santa Monica Blvd Ste 350
Los Angeles, CA 90025-7532, USA

Leonard, Justin (Athlete, Golfer)
c/o Barry Hyde *Wasserman Media Group*
10960 Wilshire Blvd Ste 1200
Los Angeles, CA 90024-3714, USA

Leonard, Lydia (Actor)
c/o Jane Berliner *Authentic Talent and Literary Management (NY)*
20 Jay St Ste M17
Brooklyn, NY 11201-8300, USA

Leonard, Mark (Athlete, Baseball Player)
1371 Chestnut Hill Dr
Manteca, CA 95336-5187, USA

Leonard, Robert Sean (Actor)
c/o Scott Henderson *WME|IMG*
9601 Wilshire Blvd
Beverly Hills, CA 90210-5213, USA

Leonard, Robert (Slick) (Athlete, Basketball Coach, Basketball Player, Coach)
5398 Baltimore Ct
Carmel, IN 46033-8882, USA

Leonard, Sugar Ray (Athlete, Boxer, Olympic Athlete)
c/o Meghan Prophet *PMK/BNC Public Relations*
1840 Century Park E Ste 1400
Los Angeles, CA 90067-2115, USA

Leonard, Wayne (Business Person)
Entergy Corp
10055 Grogans Mill Rd Ste 150
The Woodlands, TX 77380-1048, USA

Leonard-Linehan, Rhoda (Athlete, Baseball Player, Commentator)
84 Bruce Rd
Norwood, MA 02062-3103, USA

Leone, Justin (Athlete, Baseball Player)
5605 Dawnbreak Dr
Las Vegas, NV 89149-5137, USA

Leone, Sunny (Adult Film Star)
Sun Lust Pictures
14622 Ventura Blvd Ste 102 # 1022
Sherman Oaks, CA 91403-3662, USA

Leonetti, Jean-Baptiste (Director)
c/o Jerome Duboz *WME|IMG*
9601 Wilshire Blvd
Beverly Hills, CA 90210-5213, USA

Leong, Page (Actor)
C N A Assoc
1925 Century Park E Ste 750
Los Angeles, CA 90067-2708, USA

Leonhard, Dave (Athlete, Baseball Player)
87 Corning St
Beverly, MA 01915-3732, USA

Leonhard, Jim (Athlete, Football Player)
c/o Scott Smith *XAM Sports*
3509 Ice Age Dr
Madison, WI 53719-5409, USA

Leoni, Tea (Actor, Producer)
c/o Staff Member *And Then Productions*
120 Broadway Ste 200
Santa Monica, CA 90401-2385, USA

Leonidas, Stephanie (Actor)
c/o Andrew Rogers *ICM Partners*
10250 Constellation Blvd Fl 7
Los Angeles, CA 90067-6207, USA

Leonskaja, Elisabeth (Musician)
Columbia Artists Mgmt Inc
165 W 57th St
New York, NY 10019-2201, USA

Leopold, Bobby (Athlete, Football Player)
801 Beckleymeade Ave Apt 1116
Dallas, TX 75232-5225, USA

Leopold, Jordan (Athlete, Hockey Player, Olympic Athlete)
Octagon Athlete Representation
8000 Norman Center Dr
Dr Ste 400
Minneapolis, MN 55437-1178, USA

Leopold, Tom (Comedian)
c/o Staff Member *Gersh*
9465 Wilshire Blvd Ste 600
Beverly Hills, CA 90212-2605, USA

Lepage, Kevin (Race Car Driver)
618 Rice Hill Rd
Franklin, VT 05457-9821, USA

Lepchenko, Varvara (Athlete, Tennis Player)
1362 Doe Trail Rd
Allentown, PA 18104-2053, USA

Lepcio, Ted (Athlete, Baseball Player)
263 Greenlodge St
Dedham, MA 02026-6400, USA

Lepley, Tyler (Actor)
c/o Siri Garber *Platform PR*
2666 N Beachwood Dr
Los Angeles, CA 90068-2308, USA

Lepore, Amanda (Actor, Model)
c/o Bill Coleman *Peace Bisquit*
963 Kent Ave Bldg E
Brooklyn, NY 11205-4461, USA

Lepperd, Thomas (Athlete, Baseball Player)
8943 Greenway Dr
West Des Moines, IA 50266-8547, USA

Lepperd, Thomas (Baseball Player)
8943 Greenway Dr
West Des Moines, IA 50266-8547, USA

Leppert, Don (Athlete, Baseball Player)
9226 Rami Ave
Columbus, OH 43240-2158, USA

Leppert, Don (Athlete, Baseball Player)
6630 Crumpler Blvd Apt 201
Olive Branch, MS 38654-1985, USA

Lepsis, Matt (Athlete, Football Player)
6787 Trailing Oaks Dr
Frisco, TX 75034-5883, USA

Lequia-Barker, Joan (Athlete, Baseball Player, Commentator)
3236 34th St SW
Grandville, MI 49418-1905, USA

Lerch, Randy (Athlete, Baseball Player)
19490 Monterey St
Morgan Hill, CA 95037-2606, USA

Lerche, Sondre (Musician)
c/o Staff Member *Paradigm (Monterey)*
404 W Franklin St
Monterey, CA 93940-2303, USA

Lerew, Anthony (Athlete, Baseball Player)
139 Battle Rd
Hurtsboro, AL 36860-2807, USA

LeRibeus, Josh (Athlete, Football Player)
c/o Jordan Woy *Willis & Woy Management*
4890 Alpha Rd Ste 200
Dallas, TX 75244-4639, USA

Lerman, Logan (Actor)
c/o Kami Putnam-Heist *Anonymous Content*
3532 Hayden Ave
Culver City, CA 90232-2413, USA

Lerner, Harriet (Writer)
c/o Staff Member *HarperCollins Publishers*
195 Broadway Fl 2
New York, NY 10007-3132, USA

Lerner, Michael (Actor)
Innovative Artists
1505 10th St
Santa Monica, CA 90401-2805, USA

Le Rosa, Stefan (Actor)
c/o Staff Member *Nickelodeon UK*
PO Box 6425
LONDON W1A 6UR, UNITED KINGDOM

Leroux, Nicolette (Athlete, Golfer)
4786 Orchard Ln
Delray Beach, FL 33445-5306, USA

Leroux, Sydney (Athlete, Soccer Player)
c/o Dan Levy *Wasserman Media Group (NC)*
4208 Six Forks Rd Ste 1020
Raleigh, NC 27609-5738, USA

Leroy, Emarlos (Athlete, Football Player)
10135 Gate Pkwy N Apt 712
Jacksonville, FL 32246-8260, USA

LeRoy, Gloria (Actor)
Shelly & Pierce
13775A Mono Way # 220
Sonora, CA 95370-8813, USA

Les, Jim (Athlete, Basketball Player)
4030 Shadvbrooke Ct
Granite Bay, CA 95746-8839, USA

Les, Jim (Athlete, Basketball Player)
3221 W Summerbend Ct
Peoria, IL 61615-8893, USA

Lesane, Jimmy (Athlete, Football Player)
3629 Coronado Rd
Baltimore, MD 21244-3848, USA

Lesar, David (Business Person)
Halliburton Co
500 N Akard St
Lincoln Plaza
Dallas, TX 75201-3302, USA

Leschin, Luisa (Producer, Writer)
c/o Staff Member *WME|IMG*
9601 Wilshire Blvd
Beverly Hills, CA 90210-5213, USA

Lesh, Phil (Musician)
c/o Jonathan Levine *Paradigm (Nashville)*
222 2nd Ave S Ste 1600
Nashville, TN 37201-2375, USA

Lesher, Brian (Athlete, Baseball Player)
217 Vassar Dr
Newark, DE 19711-3158, USA

LeSieur, Michael (Writer)
c/o Sean Perrone *Kaplan/Perrone Entertainment*
9171 Wilshire Blvd Ste 350
Beverly Hills, CA 90210-5523, USA

Leskanic, Curt (Athlete, Baseball Player)
2032 Alaqua Dr
Longwood, FL 32779-3116, USA

Leskanich, Katrina (& the Waves) (Music Group, Musician)
c/o Staff Member *International Artists Holland*
PO Box 32
West Wardsboro, VT 05360-0032, The Netherlands

Lesko, Matthew (Writer)
HiRise Promotions Inc
1555 N Dearborn Pkwy Fl 25
C/O Kim McCoy
Chicago, IL 60610-1448, USA

Lesley, Brad (Athlete, Baseball Player)
5235 Kester Ave Apt 207
Sherman Oaks, CA 91411-4076, USA

Leslie, Conor (Actor)
c/o Katie Rhodes *Untitled Entertainment*
350 S Beverly Dr Ste 200
Beverly Hills, CA 90212-4819, USA

Leslie, Ed (Actor, Wrestler)
c/o Nick Cordasco *Prince Marketing Group*
18 Seneca Trl
Sparta, NJ 07871-1514, USA

Leslie, Fred W (Astronaut)
2038 Springhouse Rd SE
Huntsville, AL 35802-1890, USA

Leslie, Lisa (Athlete, Basketball Player, Model, Olympic Athlete)
PO Box 452447
Los Angeles, CA 90045-8533, USA

Leslie, Robbie (DJ)
c/o Staff Member *Diva Central Inc*
7510 W Sunset Blvd # 1445
Los Angeles, CA 90046-3408, USA

Leslie, Rose (Actor)
c/o Heather Nunn *Anonymous Content*
3532 Hayden Ave
Culver City, CA 90232-2413, USA

Leslie, Ryan (Musician)
c/o Chris Chambers *The Chamber Group*
75 Broad St Rm 708
New York, NY 10004-3244, USA

Lesnar, Brock (Athlete, Wrestler)
c/o Drew Elliot *Artist International*
333 E 43rd St Apt 115
New York, NY 10017-4822, USA

Lesniak, John (Race Car Driver)
47 Industrial Park Access Rd # 198
Middlefield, CT 06455-1263, USA

Lessard, Rick (Athlete, Hockey Player)
125 Chocolay River Trl
Marquette, MI 49855-9589

Lessard, Stefan (Musician)
2001 Rim Rock Canyon Rd
Laguna Beach, CA 92651-2843, USA

Lesseos, Mimi (Actor, Athlete)
2484 Vista Del Monte Dr
Acton, CA 93510-1899, USA

Lester, Adrian (Actor)
c/o William Baylock *Seven Summits Pictures & Management*
8906 W Olympic Blvd
Beverly Hills, CA 90211-3550, USA

Lester, Bill (Race Car Driver)
6224 View Crest Dr
Oakland, CA 94619-3717, USA

Lester, Jon (Athlete, Baseball Player)
3575 Ridgewood Rd NW
Atlanta, GA 30327-2419, USA

Lester, Ketty (Actor, Musician)
5118 W 20th St Apt 4
Los Angeles, CA 90016-1319, USA

Lester, Mark (Actor)
Carlton Clinic
1 Carlton St
Cheltenham
Glou GLS2 6AG, UNITED KINGDOM (UK)

Lester, Mark L (Director)
17268 Camino Yatasto
Pacific Palisades, CA 90272, USA

Lester, Richard (Dick) (Director)
c/o Staff Member *Creative Artists Agency (CAA)*
2000 Avenue of the Stars Ste 100
Los Angeles, CA 90067-4705, USA

Lester, Robert (Athlete, Football Player)
c/o Pat Dye Jr *SportsTrust Advisors*
3340 Peachtree Rd NE Fl 16
Atlanta, GA 30326-1000, USA

Lester, Ronnie (Athlete, Basketball Player)
2530 Coco Palm Cir
Wesley Chapel, FL 33543-4028, USA

Lester, Tim (Athlete, Football Player)
1160 Bream Dr
Alpharetta, GA 30004-4411, USA

Lesueur, Emily (Athlete, Olympic Athlete, Swimmer)
2208 E Nora St
Mesa, AZ 85213-1562, USA

Lesuk, Bill (Athlete, Hockey Player)
40 Bracken Ave
East St Paul, MB R2E 0K2, Canada

Lesure, James (Actor)
c/o Lisa Chance *Kyle Avery Public Relations*
1107 Fair Oaks Ave # 321
S Pasadena, CA 91030-3311, USA

Letbetter, R Steve (Business Person)
Reliant Energy
1111 Louisiana St
Houston, TX 77002-5230, USA

Leterrier, Louis (Director)
c/o Guymon Casady *Management 360*
9111 Wilshire Blvd
Beverly Hills, CA 90210-5508, USA

Letho, JJ (Race Car Driver)
Champion Racing
2901 Center Port Cir
Pompano Beach, FL 33064-2105, USA

Le Tigre (Music Group)
Esther Creative Group
27 W 24th St Ste 404
C/O Tom Sarig
New York, NY 10010-3289, USA

Letlow, W R (Russ) (Athlete, Football Player)
1876 Thelma Dr
San Luis Obispo, CA 93405-6238, USA

Letner, Robert (Athlete, Football Player)
6515 Patty Ln
Harrison, TN 37341-6987, USA

Leto, Jared (Actor, Musician)
c/o Robin Baum *Slate PR*
901 N Highland Ave
W Hollywood, CA 90038-2412, USA

Letowski, Trevor (Athlete, Hockey Player)
3612 Lion Ridge Ct
Raleigh, NC 27612-4235, USA

Letowskl, Trevor (Athlete, Hockey Player)
1457 London Rd
Isarnia Sting, ON N7S 6K4, Canada

Letscher, Brian (Actor)
c/o Carolyn Govers *Anonymous Content*
3532 Hayden Ave
Culver City, CA 90232-2413, USA

Letscher, Matt (Actor)
c/o Nancy Sanders *Sanders Armstrong Caserta*
4111 W Alameda Ave Ste 505
Burbank, CA 91505-4163, USA

Lett, Clifford (Athlete, Basketball Player)
7067 Rampart Way
Pensacola, FL 32505-3478, USA

Lett, Jim (Athlete, Baseball Player)
5751 State Route 34
Winfield, WV 25213-9323, USA

Lett, Leon (Athlete, Football Coach, Football Player)
ULM Athletics
308 Warhawk Way
Monroe, LA 71209-0001, USA

Letterle, Daniel (Actor)
c/o Geordie Frey *GEF Entertainment*
533 N Las Palmas Ave
Los Angeles, CA 90004-1017, USA

Letterman, David (Comedian, Talk Show Host)
c/o Stephen (Steve) Rubenstein *Rubenstein Communications*
1345 Avenue of the Americas Fl 30
New York, NY 10105-0109, USA

Letts, Tracy (Actor, Writer)
c/o Staff Member *Dewalt & Musik Management*
623 N Parish Pl
Burbank, CA 91506-1701, USA

Leung, Ken (Actor)
c/o Paul Hilepo *PH Entertainment Group*
2728 Thomson Ave
Long Island City, NY 11101-2922, USA

Levandowski, Leo (Athlete, Football Player)
1823 Twin House Rd
Oxford, PA 19363-3918, USA

Levang, Neil (Actor)
15630 Condor Ridge Rd
Canyon Country, CA 91387-3979, USA

Levangie, Gigi (Writer)
c/o Stephanie Davis *Wet Dog Entertainment*
2458 Crest View Dr
Los Angeles, CA 90046-1407, USA

Levasseur, Louis (Athlete, Hockey Player)
499 Av Murdoch
Rouyn-Noranda, QC J9X 1H3, Canada

Level 42 (Music Group, Musician)
c/o Guy Richard *UTA Music/The Agency Group*
9336 Civic Center Dr
Beverly Hills, CA 90210-3604, USA

Levellers (Music Group)
c/o Staff Member *Paradigm (Monterey)*
404 W Franklin St
Monterey, CA 93940-2303, USA

Levels, Dwayne (Athlete, Football Player)
3614 Colonial Ave
Dallas, TX 75215-3640, USA

Leven, Jeremy (Writer)
c/o Staff Member *Paradigm*
8942 Wilshire Blvd
Beverly Hills, CA 90211-1908, USA

Levendis, George (Business Person)
c/o Staff Member *Syco Entertainment*
9830 Wilshire Blvd Fl 3
Beverly Hills, CA 90212-1804, USA

Levene, Ben (Artist)
Royal Academy of Arts
Piccadilly
London W1V 2LP, UNITED KINGDOM (UK)

Levene, Keith (Musician)
c/o Staff Member *Taang! Records*
3830 5th Ave
San Diego, CA 92103-3141, USA

Levenick, Dave (Athlete, Football Player)
1749 SE Hondo Ave
Port Saint Lucie, FL 34952-5743, USA

Levens, Dorsey (Athlete, Football Player)
4249 Olde Mill Ln NE
Atlanta, GA 30342-3400, USA

Levenseller, Mike (Athlete, Football Player)
1533 S Wilton Rd
Tacoma, WA 98465-1032, USA

Levenstein, John (Comedian)
c/o Staff Member *ICM Partners*
10250 Constellation Blvd Fl 7
Los Angeles, CA 90067-6207, USA

Leveque, Michel (Politician)
Minister of State's Office
BP 522
Monaco Cedex 98015, MONACO

Lever, Don (Athlete, Hockey Player)
247 Quail Hollow Ln
East Amherst, NY 14051-1633

Lever, Lafayette (Athlete, Basketball Player)
1702 W Lynx Way
Chandler, AZ 85248-5425, USA

Leverette, Otis (Athlete, Football Player)
716 N Lee St
Americus, GA 31719-3093, USA

Levering, Kate (Actor)
c/o Connie Tavel *Forward Entertainment*
1880 Century Park E Ste 1405
Los Angeles, CA 90067-1630, USA

Leveritt, Mara (Writer)
c/o Staff Member *St Martins Press*
175 5th Ave
Publicity Dept
New York, NY 10010-7703, USA

Levert, Eddie (Musician)
c/o Staff Member *Associated Booking Corp*
PO Box 2055
New York, NY 10021-0051, USA

Levesque, Joanna (Jojo) (Musician)
c/o Diana Levesque *Momma D's Management*
151 Lafayette St Rm 6
New York, NY 10013-3617, USA

Levesque, Paul (Triple H) (Athlete, Wrestler)
c/o Kerry Rodgerson *World Wrestling Entertainment (WWE)*
1241 E Main St
Stamford, CT 06902-3520, USA

Levet, Thomas (Athlete, Golfer)
108 Via Quantera
Palm Beach Gardens, FL 33418-6217, USA

Levi, Alan J. (Actor)
c/o Debbee Klein *Paradigm*
8942 Wilshire Blvd
Beverly Hills, CA 90211-1908, USA

Levi, Mica (Musician)
c/o Liz Hart *Miss Management*
244 5th Ave # R233
New York, NY 10001-7604, USA

Levi, Wayne (Athlete, Golfer)
17 Ironwood Rd
New Hartford, NY 13413-3902, USA

Levi, Zachary (Actor)
c/o Staff Member *Middle Man Productions*
11271 Ventura Blvd Ste 434
Studio City, CA 91604-3136, USA

LeVias, Jerry (Athlete, Football Player)
3322 Chris Dr
Houston, TX 77063-6230, USA

Levie, Craig (Athlete, Hockey Player)
44 Rockyvalley Villas NW
Calgary, AB T3G 5X3, Canada

Levien, David (Director, Producer, Writer)
c/o Warren Zavala *WME/IMG*
9601 Wilshire Blvd Ste 800
Beverly Hills, CA 90210-5210, USA

Levieva, Margarita (Actor)
c/o Alexandra Crotin *The Lede Company*
9701 Wilshire Blvd # 930
Beverly Hills, CA 90212-2020, USA

Levin, Carl (Politician)
1300 E Lafayette St Apt 1806
Detroit, MI 48207-2922, USA

Levin, Drake (Musician)
Paradise Artists
108 E Matilija St
Ojai, CA 93023-2639, USA

Levin, Harvey (Journalist, Television Host)
TMZ
4000 Warner Blvd
Burbank, CA 91522-0001, USA

Levin, Mark (Radio Personality, Talk Show Host)
WPLJ-FM Radio
2 Pennsylvania Plz #1700
New York, NY 10121, USA

Levine, Adam (Musician)
c/o Sara Newkirk Simon *WME/IMG*
9601 Wilshire Blvd Ste 800
Beverly Hills, CA 90210-5210, USA

Levine, Alan (Athlete, Baseball Player)
10916 E Paradise Dr
Scottsdale, AZ 85259-7007, USA

Levine, Anthony (Athlete, Football Player)

Levine, Chloe (Actor)
c/o Devin Sauschuck *42West*
600 3rd Ave Fl 23
New York, NY 10016-1914, USA

Levine, Irene (Writer)
Chicago Tribune
160 N Stetson Ave
C/O Travel
Chicago, IL 60601-6707, USA

Levine, Jack (Artist)
68 Morton St
New York, NY 10014-4021, USA

Levine, Jerry (Actor, Director)
c/o Staff Member *Rain Management Group*
11162 La Grange Ave
Los Angeles, CA 90025-5632, USA

Levine, Jonathan (Director)
c/o Ragna Nervik *The Ragna Nervik Company*
Prefers to be contacted via telephone
Los Angeles, CA, USA

Levine, Ken (Writer)
c/o Staff Member *Broder Webb Chervin Silbermann Agency, The (BWCS)*
10250 Constellation Blvd Fl 17
Los Angeles, CA 90067-6217, USA

Levine, Rachmiel (Misc)
614 Walnut St
Newton, MA 02460-2462, USA

Levine, Samm (Actor, Producer)
c/o Melanie Marquez *M4 Publicity*
11684 Ventura Blvd # 213
Studio City, CA 91604-2699, USA

Levine, Samuel A (Actor)
c/o Staff Member *Badgley-Connor-King*
9229 W Sunset Blvd Ste 311
Los Angeles, CA 90069-3403, USA

Levine, S Robert (Business Person)
Cabletron Systems
PO Box 5005
Rochester, NH 03866, USA

Levine, Ted (Actor)
c/o Robbie Kass *Kass Management*
1011 Euclid St Unit B
Santa Monica, CA 90403-4296, USA

Levingston, Cliff (Basketball Player)
Denver Nuggets
1000 Chopper Cir
Pepsi Center
Denver, CO 80204-5805, USA

Levinlra, Ira (Writer)
40 E 49th St
New York, NY 10017, USA

Levins, Scott (Athlete, Hockey Player)
815 Covered Bridge Dr
Delaware, OH 43015-3193, USA

Levinsohn, Gary (Producer)
c/o Staff Member *Mutual Film Company*
3535 Hayden Ave Ste 340
Culver City, CA 90232-2462, USA

Levinson, Barry (Actor, Director, Producer, Writer)
104 Wooster St Apt 2N
New York, NY 10012-3870, USA

Levinson, Chris (Writer)
c/o Staff Member *WME/IMG*
9601 Wilshire Blvd
Beverly Hills, CA 90210-5213, USA

Levis, Jesse (Athlete, Baseball Player)
1219 Highland Ave
Fort Washington, PA 19034-1605, USA

Levis, Patrick (Actor, Musician)
c/o Kim Dorr *Defining Artists Agency*
8721 W Sunset Blvd Ste 209
W Hollywood, CA 90069-2272, USA

Levi-Strauss, Claude (Misc)
2 Rue des Marronniers
Paris 75016, FRANCE

Levitan, Steve (Producer)
c/o Jay Sures *United Talent Agency (UTA)*
9336 Civic Center Dr
Beverly Hills, CA 90210-3604, USA

Levitas, Andrew (Actor)
c/o Samantha Mast *Rogers & Cowan*
1840 Century Park E Fl 18
Los Angeles, CA 90067-2101, USA

Levitre, Andy (Athlete, Football Player)
c/o David Dunn *Athletes First*
23091 Mill Creek Dr
Laguna Hills, CA 92653-1258, USA

Levitt, Chad (Athlete, Football Player)
104 Towanda Ave
Melrose Park, PA 19027-2932, USA

Levitt, George (Misc)
82 Via Del Corso
Palm Beach Gardens, FL 33418-3773, USA

LeVox, Gary (Musician)
c/o Jake Basden *Big Machine Records*
1219 16th Ave S
Nashville, TN 37212-2901, USA

Levrault, Allen (Athlete, Baseball Player)
PO Box 1316
Westport, MA 02790-0694, USA

Levy, Dan (Actor, Producer)
c/o Alex Schack *Slate PR*
901 N Highland Ave
W Hollywood, CA 90038-2412, USA

Levy, DeAndre (Athlete, Football Player)

Levy, Eugene (Actor, Director)
c/o Drew MacKenzie *Great North Artists Management*
350 Dupont St
Toronto, ON M5R 1V9, CANADA

Levy, Jane (Actor)
c/o Ruth Bernstein *Viewpoint Inc*
8820 Wilshire Blvd Ste 220
Beverly Hills, CA 90211-2622, USA

Levy, Kenneth (Business Person)
KLA-Tencor Corp
160 Rio Robles
San Jose, CA 95134-1813, USA

Levy, Mariana (Actor)
c/o Staff Member *Televisa*
Blvd Adolfo Lopez Mateos 232
Colonia San Angel INN
DF CP 01060, MEXICO

Levy, Marv (Coach, Football Coach, Football Player)
2550 N Lakeview Ave Unit N1101
Chicago, IL 60614-8191, USA

Levy, Mary (Athlete, Football Player)
2800 N Lake Shore Dr Apt 1516
Chicago, IL 60657-6269, USA

Levy, Shawn (Actor, Director)
c/o Staff Member *21 Laps Entertainment*
10201 W Pico Blvd Bldg 41 # 400
Los Angeles, CA 90064-2606, USA

Levy, William (Actor, Model)
c/o Anjelica Cohn *Creative Artists Agency (CAA)*
2000 Avenue of the Stars Ste 100
Los Angeles, CA 90067-4705, USA

Levya, Danell (Athlete, Gymnast, Olympic Athlete)
Universal Gymnastics
13439 SW 131st St
Miami, FL 33186-5818, USA

Lewallyn, Dennis (Athlete, Baseball Player)
2900 Breckenridge Dr
Pensacola, FL 32526-2903, USA

Lewan, Taylor (Athlete, Football Player)
c/o Tom Condon *Creative Artists Agency (CAA)*
401 Commerce St PH
Nashville, TN 37219-2516, USA

Lewin, Josh (Commentator)
1081 W Winding Creek Dr
Grapevine, TX 76051-7837, USA

Lewinsky, Monica (Activist)
c/o Dini Von Mueffling *HvM Communications*
1133 Broadway Ste 332
New York, NY 10010-7969, USA

Lewis, Aaron (Musician)
Staind/Elektra Records
75 Rockefeller Plz
New York, NY 10019-6908

Lewis, Albert R (Athlete, Football Player)
3532 Macedonia Rd
Centreville, MS 39631-3634, USA

Lewis, Al (Grandpa) (Actor)
PO Box 277
New York, NY 10044-0205, USA

Lewis, Allan (Athlete, Baseball Player)
Urb La Florida R-15
David Chiriqui, Panama, USA

Lewis, Ananda (Actor)
c/o Marvet Britto *Britto Agency PR*
277 Broadway Ste 110
New York, NY 10007-2072, USA

Lewis, Ashton (Race Car Driver)
Lewis Motorsports
4317 Triple Crown Dr SW
Concord, NC 28027-8978, USA

Lewis, Barbara (Musician)
Hello Stranger Productions
PO Box 300488
Fern Park, FL 32730-0488, USA

Lewis, Bill (Coach, Football Coach)
Georgia Institute of Technology
8701 S Hardy Dr
Tempe, AZ 85284-2800, USA

Lewis, Bob (Athlete, Basketball Player)
63910 E Squash Blossom Ln
Tucson, AZ 85739-1264, USA

Lewis, Bobby (Musician)
Lustig Talent
PO Box 770850
Orlando, FL 32877-0850, USA

Lewis, Brooke (Actor)
c/o Staff Member *Coolwaters Productions*
10061 Riverside Dr # 531
Toluca Lake, CA 91602-2560, USA

Lewis, Bubba (Actor)
c/o Ryan Daly *Zero Gravity Management*
11110 Ohio Ave Ste 100
Los Angeles, CA 90025-3329, USA

Lewis, Carl (Actor, Athlete, Olympic Athlete, Track Athlete)
528 Palisades Dr
Pacific Palisades, CA 90272-2844, USA

Lewis, Chad (Athlete, Football Player)
4529 N 100 W
Provo, UT 84604-5511, USA

Lewis, Charlotte (Athlete, Basketball Player, Olympic Athlete)
2814 N Sheridan Rd
Peoria, IL 61604-2716, USA

Lewis, Clea (Actor)
1659 S Highland Ave
Los Angeles, CA 90019-5540, USA

Lewis, Colby (Athlete, Baseball Player)
15200 Merlot Cellars Dr
Bakersfield, CA 93314-4733, USA

Lewis, Crystal (Musician)
Proper Mgmt
PO Box 68
Franklin, TN 37065-0068, USA

Lewis, Damian (Actor)
Markham & Froggalt
Julian House
4 Windmill St
London W1P 1HF, UNITED KINGDOM (UK)

Lewis, Damione (Athlete, Football Player)
411 Walden Trl
Waxhaw, NC 28173-8542, USA

Lewis, Dan (Athlete, Football Player)
460 S Park St
Detroit, MI 48215-4108, USA

Lewis, Darren (Athlete, Football Player)
1810 Olympus Dr
Lancaster, TX 75134-4195, USA

Lewis, Darryll (Athlete, Football Player)
2441 S Nadine St Apt 1
West Covina, CA 91792-3562, USA

Lewis, Dave (Athlete, Hockey Player)
Carolina Hurricanes
1400 Edwards Mill Rd
Raleigh, NC 27607-3624

Lewis, Dave (Athlete, Coach, Hockey Player)
2040 Ranch Rd
Holly, MI 48442-8027

Lewis, Dave (Athlete, Football Player)
14015 Tahiti Way Apt 111
Marina Del Rey, CA 90292-6507, USA

Lewis, David Levering (Writer)
Rutgers University
History Dept
East Rutherford, NJ 08903, USA

Lewis, David R (Athlete, Football Player)
37357 Shelter Dr
Selbyville, DE 19975-3807, USA

Lewis, Dawnn (Actor)
c/o Staff Member *The Gage Group*
5757 Wilshire Blvd Ste 659
Los Angeles, CA 90036-3682, USA

Lewis, D D (Athlete, Football Player)
1624 Northcrest Dr
Plano, TX 75075-8749, USA

Lewis, D D (Athlete, Football Player)
2530 Dolly Wright St
Houston, TX 77088-7528, USA

Lewis, Dion (Athlete, Football Player)
10 Twiller St
Albany, NY 12209-2128, USA

Lewis, Emmanuel (Actor)
859 Highway 92 N
Fayetteville, GA 30214-1364, USA

Lewis, Fiona (Actor)
210 Palisades Ave
Santa Monica, CA 90402-2734, USA

Lewis, Frank (Athlete, Football Player)
118 Presque Isle Dr
Houma, LA 70363-3828, USA

Lewis, Freddie (Athlete, Basketball Player)
4122 Illinois Ave NW
Washington, DC 20011-5950, USA

Lewis, Garry (Athlete, Football Player)
1000 Alcorn Dr Apt 737
Lorman, MS 39096-7500, USA

Lewis, Gary (Athlete, Football Player)
4652 S Cooper St
Seattle, WA 98118-5647, USA

Lewis, Gary (Athlete, Football Player)
PO Box 8321
Fort Worth, TX 76124, USA

Lewis, Glenn (Musician)
c/o Staff Member *Creative Artists Agency (CAA)*
2000 Avenue of the Stars Ste 100
Los Angeles, CA 90067-4705, USA

Lewis, Grady (Athlete, Basketball Player)
8926 W Topeka Dr
Peoria, AZ 85382-8590

Lewis, Huey (Actor, Musician)
c/o Bob Brown *Bob Brown Management*
PO Box 779
Mill Valley, CA 94942-0779, USA

Lewis, Jamal (Athlete, Football Player)
75 Summit Ave
Newark, NJ 07112-1210, USA

Lewis, James (Little JJ) (Actor, Comedian)
c/o Staff Member *Gill Talent Group*
800 Forrest St NW
Atlanta, GA 30318-7620, USA

Lewis, Jason (Actor)
c/o Ruth Bernstein *Viewpoint Inc*
8820 Wilshire Blvd Ste 220
Beverly Hills, CA 90211-2622, USA

Lewis, Jeff (Designer, Reality Star)
c/o Nicole Perez-Krueger *PMK/BNC Public Relations*
1840 Century Park E Ste 1400
Los Angeles, CA 90067-2115, USA

Lewis, Jeff (Athlete, Football Player)
230 N 2nd St Trlr 6
Berthoud, CO 80513-1327, USA

Lewis, Jenifer (Actor)
PO Box 5617
Beverly Hills, CA 90209-5617, USA

Lewis, Jenna (Reality Star)
c/o Juliette Harris *It Girl Public Relations*
3763 Eddingham Ave
Calabasas, CA 91302-5835, USA

Lewis, Jensen (Athlete, Baseball Player)
5311 Salem Rd
Cincinnati, OH 45230-1327, USA

Lewis, Jermaine (Athlete, Football Player)
4919 Pleasant Grove Rd
Reisterstown, MD 21136-3913, USA

Lewis, Jerry Lee (Musician)
Jerry Lee Lewis
PO Box 384
Nesbit, MS 38651-0384, USA

Lewis, Jim (Athlete, Baseball Player)
5311 Hansel Ave Apt D12
Orlando, FL 32809-3415, USA

Lewis, Jim (Athlete, Baseball Player)
676 Sparks St
Jackson, MI 49202-2027, USA

Lewis, J L (Athlete, Golfer)
2504 Orleans Dr
Cedar Park, TX 78613-4727, USA

Lewis, John (Congressman, Politician)
343 Cannon Hob
Washington, DC 20515-1005, USA

Lewis, John (Race Car Driver)
524 El Cerrito Ave
Hillsborough, CA 94010-6822, USA

Lewis, Johnny (Athlete, Baseball Player)
810 Tara Cir
Cantonment, FL 32533-9700, USA

Lewis, Jon Peter (Musician, Reality Star)
PO Box 533
Newbury Park, CA 91319-0533, USA

Lewis, Judah (Actor)
c/o Nils Larsen *Management 360*
9465 Wilshire Blvd Ste 900
Beverly Hills, CA 90212-2608, USA

Lewis, Juliette (Actor)
c/o Carleen Donovan *Donovan Public Relations*
30 E 20th St Ste 2FE
New York, NY 10003-1310, USA

Lewis, Karen (Writer)
c/o James Sarnoff *The Sarnoff Company Inc*
10 Universal City Plz #2000
Universal City, CA 91608, USA

Lewis, Keenan (Athlete, Football Player)
c/o Brian E. Overstreet *E.O. Sports Management*
1314 Texas St Ste 1212
Houston, TX 77002-3525, USA

Lewis, Kendrick (Athlete, Football Player)
c/o Bus Cook *Bus Cook Sports, Inc*
1 Willow Bend Dr
Hattiesburg, MS 39402-8552, USA

Lewis, Kevin (Athlete, Football Player)
4417 Roy St
Orlando, FL 32812-7350, USA

Lewis, Lennox (Boxer)
XS Promotions
57 Fonthill Road
Aberdeen AB11 6UQ, UNITED STATES

Lewis, Leona (Actor, Musician)
c/o Dvora Vener Englefield *The Lede Company*
9701 Wilshire Blvd # 930
Beverly Hills, CA 90212-2020, USA

Lewis, Leslie (Actor)
c/o Gail Parenteau *Parenteau Guidance*
132 E 35th St # J
New York, NY 10016-3892, USA

Lewis, Marcedes (Athlete, Football Player)
3725 Bouton Dr
Lakewood, CA 90712-3822, USA

Lewis, Mark (Athlete, Baseball Player)
591 Hermay Dr
Hamilton, OH 45013-1415, USA

Lewis, Mark (Athlete, Football Player)
PO Box 11021
Spring, TX 77391-1021, USA

Lewis, Marvin (Coach, Football Coach)
Cincinnati Bengals
10040 E Happy Valley Rd Unit 596
Scottsdale, AZ 85255-2300, USA

Lewis, Mary (Christianni Brand) (Writer)
88 Maida Vale
London W9, UNITED KINGDOM (UK)

Lewis, Matthew (Actor)
c/o Sarah Spear *Curtis Brown Ltd*
28-29 Hay Market
Hay Market House
London SW1Y 4SP, UNITED KINGDOM

Lewis, Michael (Writer)
c/o Matthew Snyder *Creative Artists Agency (CAA)*
2000 Avenue of the Stars Ste 100
Los Angeles, CA 90067-4705, USA

Lewis, Mike (Athlete, Basketball Player)
490 Windsor Park Rd
Kernersville, NC 27284-7013, USA

Lewis, Mike (Athlete, Football Player)
3350 Blodgett St
Houston, TX 77004-6305, USA

Lewis, Mo (Athlete, Baseball Player)
2212 Rosemount Ln
San Ramon, CA 94582-5719, USA

Lewis, Mo (Athlete, Football Player)
3280 Northside Pkwy NW Apt 314
Atlanta, GA 30327-2260, USA

Lewis, Nate (Athlete, Football Player)
3374 Brooksong Way
Dacula, GA 30019-1199, USA

Lewis, Norm (Actor)
c/o Jeremy Katz *Katz Company, The*
1674 Broadway Fl 7
New York, NY 10019-5838, USA

Lewis, Phill (Actor)
c/o Gregg A Klein *AKA Talent Agency*
325 N Larchmont Blvd
Los Angeles, CA 90004-3011, USA

Lewis, Ralph (Athlete, Basketball Player)
3004 Maryannes Ct
North Wales, PA 19454-2024, USA

Lewis, Ramsey (Musician)
c/o Ted Kurland *Ted Kurland Associates*
173 Brighton Ave
Boston, MA 02134-2003, USA

Lewis, Rashard (Basketball Player)
Seattle SuperSonics
351 Elliott Ave W Ste 500
Seattle, WA 98119-4153, USA

Lewis, Ray (Athlete, Football Player)
c/o Matt Kramer *CAA Sports (Atlanta)*
3560 Lenox Rd NE Ste 1525
Atlanta, GA 30326-4338, USA

Lewis, Richard (Actor, Comedian)
c/o Mike Eistenstadt *Amsel, Eisenstadt & Frazier Talent Agency (AEF)*
5055 Wilshire Blvd Ste 860
Los Angeles, CA 90036-6108, USA

Lewis, Richard J (Producer)
c/o Carel Cutler *ICM Partners*
10250 Constellation Blvd Fl 7
Los Angeles, CA 90067-6207, USA

Lewis, Richie (Athlete, Baseball Player)
13209 E County Road 700 S
Losantville, IN 47354-9514, USA

Lewis, Robert (Athlete, Basketball Player)
3656 Bay Dr
Edgewater, MD 21037-4143, USA

Lewis, Rommie (Athlete, Basketball Player)
5511 Mountville Rd
Adamstown, MD 21710-9612, USA

Lewis, Ron (Athlete, Football Player)
12821 Haverford Rd W Apt 1
Jacksonville, FL 32218-4879, USA

Lewis, Russell Dennis (Actor)
c/o Stephen Belden *More/Medavoy Management*
10203 Santa Monica Blvd # 400
Los Angeles, CA 90067-6405, USA

Lewis, Scott (Athlete, Baseball Player)
2584 Fairway Dr
Costa Mesa, CA 92627-1312, USA

Lewis, Shane (Race Car Driver)
209 Ridge Rd
Jupiter, FL 33477-9660, USA

Lewis, Shaznay (Musician)
c/o Staff Member *Concorde Intl Artists Ltd*
101 Shepherds Bush Rd
London W6 7LP, UNITED KINGDOM (UK)

Lewis, Sherman (Athlete, Football Player)
45822 Bristol Cir
Novi, MI 48377-3900, USA

Lewis, Thaddaeus (Athlete, Football Player)
c/o Drew Rosenhaus *Rosenhaus Sports Representation*
3921 Alton Rd # 440
Miami Beach, FL 33140-3852, USA

Lewis, Thomas (Athlete, Football Player)
1545 E Villa Theresa Dr
Phoenix, AZ 85022-1282, USA

Lewis, Tim (Athlete, Football Player)
120 Serenity Ct
Alpharetta, GA 30022-4898, USA

Lewis, Travis (Athlete, Football Player)
c/o Erik Burkhardt *Select Sports Group*
2700 Post Oak Blvd Ste 1450
Houston, TX 77056-5785, USA

Lewis, Vaughan A (Prime Minister)
United Workers Party
1 Riverside Road
Castries, SAINT LUCIA

Lewis, Vicki (Actor, Comedian)
c/o Jim Mannino *Jim Mannino PR*
27 W 76th St Apt 1C
New York, NY 10023-1554, USA

Lewis, Will (Athlete, Football Player)
1980 Seattle Seahawks
Sammamish, WA 98074-3473, USA

Lewis, W Paul (Race Car Driver)
3408 Bristol Hwy
Johnson City, TN 37601-1320, USA

Lewis III, Leo (Athlete, Football Player)
1400 N Countryshire Dr
Columbia, MO 65202-9769, USA

Lewis III, Randy (Race Car Driver)
4101 Big Ranch Rd
Napa, CA 94558-1406, USA

Lewis-Moore, Kapron (Athlete, Football Player)
c/o David Lee *Players Rep Sports Management*
34208 Aurora Rd
#250
Cleveland, OH 44139, USA

Ley, Rick (Athlete, Hockey Player)
18 Stonehaven Rd
Dunnville, ON N1A 2W6, Canada

Ley, Terry (Athlete, Baseball Player)
2955 SE Custer Rd
Prineville, OR 97754-9424, USA

Leyden, Paul (Actor)
c/o Rhonda Price *Gersh*
41 Madison Ave Ste 3301
New York, NY 10010-2210, USA

Leygue, Louis Georges (Artist)
6 Rue de Docteur Blanche
Paris 75016, FRANCE

Leyland, Jim (Athlete, Baseball Player, Coach)
261 Tech Rd
Pittsburgh, PA 15205-1734, USA

Leyritz, Jim (Athlete, Baseball Player)
10773 SW 14th Pl
Davie, FL 33324-7126, USA

Leyton, John (Actor, Musician)
53 Keyes House
Dolphin Square
London SW1V 3NA, UNITED KINGDOM (UK)

Leyva, Nick (Athlete, Baseball Player, Coach)
3845 E Menlo St
Mesa, AZ 85215-1716, USA

Leyva, Victor (Athlete, Football Player)
17690 Road 320
Springville, CA 93265-9635, USA

Lezak, Jason (Athlete, Olympic Athlete, Swimmer)
c/o Evan Morgenstein *Premier Management Group (PMG Sports)*
700 Evanvale Ct
Cary, NC 27518-2806, USA

Lezcano, Carlos (Athlete, Baseball Player)
3870 S Dew Drop Ln
Gilbert, AZ 85297-8033, USA

Lezcano, Sixto (Athlete, Baseball Player)
7828 Bardmoor Hill Cir
Orlando, FL 32835-8158, USA

LFO (Musician)
Evolution Talent Agency
1776 Broadway Fl 15
New York, NY 10019-2002

L. Fudge, Marcia (Congressman, Politician)
1019 Longworth Hob
Washington, DC 20515-3012, USA

Ignasiak, Gary (Athlete, Baseball Player)
3084 Angelus Dr
Waterford, MI 48329-2506, USA

L. Hanna, Richard (Congressman, Politician)
319 Cajimon Hob
Washington, DC 20515-0001, USA

L. Hastings, Alcee (Congressman, Politician)
2353 Rayburn Hob
Washington, DC 20515-3811, USA

L'Hermitte, Thierry (Actor)
ICE 3
13 Rue Yves-Toudic
Paris 75010, France

Li, Gong (Actor, Model)
c/o Julie Moore *The J-Line Group Inc*
8671 Wilshire Blvd Fl 4
Beverly Hills, CA 90211-2926, USA

Li, Jet (Actor)
c/o Steve Chasman *Current Entertainment*
9378 Wilshire Blvd Ste 210
Beverly Hills, CA 90212-3167, USA

Li, Keyu (Designer, Fashion Designer)
21 Gong-Jian Hutong
Di An-Men
Beijing 100009, CHINA

Li, Richard (Business Person)
38th Floor, Citibank Tower. Citibank Plaza
3 Garden Road
Central, Hong Kong, Hong Kong

Li, Yiyun (Writer)

Liaklev, Reidar (Speed Skater)
2770 Jaren
NORWAY

Liars (Music Group)
c/o David T Viecelli *The Billions Corporation*
PO Box 47710
Chicago, IL 60647-7212, USA

Liars Inc (Music Group)
c/o Staff Member *Foodchain Records*
6464 W Sunset Blvd Ste 920
Los Angeles, CA 90028-8011, USA

Libby, Jeff (Athlete, Hockey Player)
24 Foxwell Dr
Scarborough, ME 04074-7608

Liber, Jon (Baseball Player)
Pittsburgh Pirates
2805 Churchbell Ct
Mobile, AL 36695-2528, USA

Liberato, Liana (Actor)
c/o Michelle Benson Margolis *The Lede Company*
9701 Wilshire Blvd # 930
Beverly Hills, CA 90212-2020, USA

Libertini, Richard (Actor)
215 Euclid Ave Apt 205
Long Beach, CA 90803-6025, USA

Liberty, Marcus (Athlete, Basketball Player)
3923 N Drake Ave
Chicago, IL 60618-3205, USA

Libett, Nick (Athlete, Hockey Player)
4272 N McNay Ct
West Bloomfield, MI 48323-2839

Liboiron, Landon (Actor)
c/o Kimberlin Belloni *Artists First*
9465 Wilshire Blvd Ste 900
Beverly Hills, CA 90212-2608, USA

Libran, Frankie (Athlete, Baseball Player)
PO Box 312
Mayaguez, PR 00681-0312, USA

Liburd, Melanie (Actor)
c/o Femi Oguns *Identity Agency Group (UK)*
95 Grays Inn Rd
London WC1X 8TX, UNITED KINGDOM

Licad, Cecile (Musician)
Columbia Artists Mgmt Inc
165 W 57th St
New York, NY 10019-2201, USA

Licht, Jeremy (Actor)
4355 Clybourn Ave
Toluca Lake, CA 91602-2906, USA

Lichtenberg, Byron K (Astronaut)
5701 Impala South Rd
Athens, TX 75752-6053, USA

Lichtenberg, Byron K Dr (Astronaut)
570llmpala South Rd
Athens, TX 75752-6053, USA

Lichtenberger, H W (Business Person)
Praxair Inc
39 Old Ridgebury Rd Ste 7
Danbury, CT 06810-5100, USA

Lichtensteiger, Kory (Athlete, Football Player)

Lichti, Todd (Athlete, Basketball Player)
2331 Holly View Dr
Martinez, CA 94553-3375, USA

Lick, Dennis A (Athlete, Football Player)
7625 W Arquilla Dr Apt 1B
Palos Heights, IL 60463-2643, USA

Lickert, John (Athlete, Baseball Player)
PO Box 279
North Scituate, RI 02857-0279, USA

Lickliter, Frank (Athlete, Golfer)
846 S Main St
Franklin, OH 45005-2731, USA

Licon, Jeffrey (Actor)
c/o Katie Mason Stern *Luber Roklin Management*
5815 W Sunset Blvd Ste 208
Los Angeles, CA 90028-6481, USA

Lidback, Jenny (Athlete, Golfer)
25628 N Abajo Dr
Rio Verde, AZ 85263-7215, USA

Liddell, Chuck (Iceman) (Athlete, Wrestler)
c/o Heidi Liddell *WS Entertaintment*
15300 Ventura Blvd
Sherman Oaks, CA 91403-3103, USA

Liddell, Dave (Athlete, Baseball Player)
2631 Preakness Way
Norco, CA 92860-4201, USA

Liddington, Bob (Athlete, Hockey Player)
2538 E Sahuaro Dr
Phoenix, AZ 85028-2538

Liddle, Steve (Athlete, Basketball Player)
437 Heath Pl
Smyrna, TN 37167-2636, USA

Liddy, Edward M (Business Person)
Allstate Corp
2775 Sanders Rd
Allstate Plaza
Northbrook, IL 60062-6110, USA

Liddy, G Gordon (Actor)
9112 Riverside Dr
Fort Washington, MD 20744-6863, USA

Liddy, G Gordon (Politician)
9112 Riverside Dr
Fort Washington, MD 20744-6863, USA

Lidge, Brad (Athlete, Baseball Player)
447 N Gate Stone
Houston, TX 77007-8341, USA

Lidov, Arthur (Artist)
Pleasant Ridge Rd
Poughquag, NY 12570, USA

Lidster, Doug (Athlete, Hockey Player)
770 Taylor St
Chelsea, MI 48118-1443

Lidstrom, Nicklas (Athlete, Hockey Player)
Newport Sports Management
400-201 City Centre Dr
Attn Don Meehan
Mississauga, ON L5B 2T4, Canada

Lidstrom, Niklas (Attorney, Hockey Player)
47725 Bellagio Dr
Northville, MI 48167-9803

Liebenstein, Todd (Athlete, Football Player)
4486 Chain 0 Lakes Rd
Eagle River, WI 54521-8856, USA

Liebensteuin, Todd (Athlete, Football Player)
4486 Chain O Lakes Rd
Eagle River, WI 54521-8856, USA

Lieber, Jon (Athlete, Baseball Player)
3060 Isle of Palms Dr W
Mobile, AL 36695-2576, USA

Lieber, Larry (Cartoonist)
c/o Staff Member *King Features Syndication*
300 W 57th St Fl 15
New York, NY 10019-5238, USA

Lieber, Paul (Actor)
c/o Margrit Polak *Margrit Polak Management*
1920 Hillhurst Ave Ste 405
Los Angeles, CA 90027-2712, USA

Lieber, Rob (Writer)
c/o Staff Member *ICM Partners*
10250 Constellation Blvd Fl 7
Los Angeles, CA 90067-6207, USA

Lieberher, Jaeden (Actor)
c/o Staff Member *Dayton-Milrad Cho*
8899 Beverly Blvd Ste 918
Los Angeles, CA 90048-2427, USA

Lieberman, Joe (Politician, Senator)

Lieberman, Nancy (Athlete, Basketball Player, Olympic Athlete)
5756 Quebec Ln
Plano, TX 75024-2904, USA

Liebert, Ottmar (Musician)
Jones & O'Malley
10123 Camarillo St
Toluca Lake, CA 91602-1601, USA

Lieberthal, Michael S (Mike) (Athlete, Baseball Player)
3926 Avenida Verano
Thousand Oaks, CA 91360-6903, USA

Liebesman, Jonathan (Director)
617 N Fuller Ave
Los Angeles, CA 90036-1938, USA

Liebman, David (Musician)
2206 Brislin Road
Stroudsberg, PA 18360, USA

Liebrich, Barbara (Athlete, Baseball Player)
16608 N 51st St
Scottsdale, AZ 85254-1063, USA

Liefeld, Bob (Cartoonist)
3845 Welsh Pony Ln
Yorba Linda, CA 92886-7929, USA

Liefeld, Rob (Artist, Cartoonist, Producer)
c/o Phillip Christian *Phillip Christian Public Relations*
30 E 20th St
New York, NY 10003-1310, USA

Liefer, Jeff (Athlete, Baseball Player)
1116 W Bay Ave
Newport Beach, CA 92661-1017, USA

Lien, Jennifer (Actor)
9932 Lemon Ave
Alta Loma, CA 91737-3621, USA

Lienhard, Bill (Athlete, Basketball Player, Olympic Athlete)
1320 Lawrence Ave
Lawrence, KS 66049-2938, USA

Lifehouse (Music Group)
c/o Dave Klein *Creative Artists Agency (CAA)*
2000 Avenue of the Stars Ste 100
Los Angeles, CA 90067-4705, USA

Life On Repeat (Music Group, Musician)
c/o Steve Taylor *Anthem Artist Management*
9048 Woodland Trl
Alpharetta, GA 30009-8758, USA

Lifeson, Alex (Musician)
Macklam Feldman Mgmt
200-1505 2nd Ave W
Vancouver, BC V6H 3Y4, CANADA

Lifford, Tina (Actor)
c/o Nancy Sanders *Sanders Armstrong Caserta*
4111 W Alameda Ave Ste 505
Burbank, CA 91505-4163, USA

Ligarde, Sebastian (Actor)
c/o Staff Member *Televisa*
Blvd Adolfo Lopez Mateos 232
Colonia San Angel INN
DF CP 01060, MEXICO

Light, John (Actor)
c/o Arlene Forster *Forster Entertainment*
12533 Woodgreen St
Los Angeles, CA 90066-2723, USA

Light, Judith (Actor)
c/o Staff Member *Tao Management*
2934 N Beverly Glen Cir Ste 392
Los Angeles, CA 90077-1724, USA

Light, Matt (Athlete, Football Player)
261 East St
Foxboro, MA 02035-3023, USA

Lightfoot, Gordon (Musician, Songwriter, Writer)
c/o Staff Member *Early Morning Productions, Inc.*
1365 Yonge St Suite 207
Toronto, ON M4T 2P7, Canada

Ligon, Bill (Athlete, Basketball Player)
PO Box 1432
Gallatin, TN 37066-1432, USA

Ligtenberg, Kerry (Athlete, Baseball Player)
9274 Albright Ct
Inver Grove Heights, MN 55077-4546, USA

Lil' Cease (Musician)
Famous Artists Agency
250 W 57th St Ste 615
New York, NY 10107-0605, USA

Lil Dicky (Musician)
c/o Jules Ferree *Scooter Braun Projects*
1755 Broadway
New York, NY 10019-3743, USA

Liles, John-Michael (Athlete, Hockey Player)
Top Shelf Sports Management
21 Hopperton Dr
Attn Joseph Resnick
North York, ON M2L 2S5, Canada

Liles, Kevin (Business Person)
75 Rockefeller Plz Fl 32
New York, NY 10019-6908, USA

Lil' Flip (Musician)
Clover G Music
PO Box 111356
Tacoma, WA 98411-1356, USA

Lil' J (Actor, Musician, Television Host)
c/o Staff Member *Thruline Entertainment*
9250 Wilshire Blvd Fl Ground
Beverly Hills, CA 90212-3352, USA

Lilja, Andreas (Athlete, Hockey Player)
6501 N Federal Hwy Ste 2
Boca Raton, FL 33487-3137

Lilja, George (Athlete, Football Player)
335 Breeze Point Cir
Warren, PA 16365-2548, USA

Liljeberg, Rebecka (Actor)
Kolbäcksgränd 33
Bagarmossen 12846, Sweden

Lil Jon (Musician)
c/o David Wirtschafter *WME|IMG*
9601 Wilshire Blvd
Beverly Hills, CA 90210-5213, USA

Lill, John R (Musician)
Harold Holt
31 Sinclair Road
London W14 0NS, UNITED KINGDOM (UK)

Lillard, Damian (Athlete, Basketball Player)
c/o Aaron Goodwin *Goodwin Sports Management*
121 Lakeside Ave Ste B
Seattle, WA 98122-6599, USA

Lillard, Matthew (Actor, Producer)
c/o Sam Maydew *Silver Lining Entertainment*
421 S Beverly Dr Fl 7
Beverly Hills, CA 90212-4408, USA

Lilley, Chris (Actor)
RGM Associates
c/o Sharne MacDonald
PO Box 128
Surry Hills NSW 2010, AUSTRALIA

Lilley, John (Athlete, Hockey Player)
25 Curtis St
Wakefield, MA 01880-5109, USA

Lillibridge, Brent (Athlete, Baseball Player)
14631 43rd Dr SE
Snohomish, WA 98296-6993, USA

Lillien, Lisa (Writer)
c/o Bill Stankey *Westport Entertainment Associates*
1120 W State Route 89A Ste B1
Sedona, AZ 86336-5763, USA

Lilliquist, Derek (Athlete, Baseball Player)
2235 Atlantis Dr
Vero Beach, FL 32963-3140, USA

Lillis, Bob (Athlete, Baseball Player, Coach)
5107 Cherry Tree Ln
Orlando, FL 32819-3848, USA

Lillis, Charles M (Business Person)
MediaOne Group
188 Inverness Dr W
Englewood, CO 80112-5205, USA

Lillix (Music Group)
c/o Staff Member *Bruce Allen Talent*
425 Carrall St
Suite 400
Vancouver, BC V6B 6E3, CANADA

Lilly, Bob (Athlete, Football Player)
721 Caudle Ln
Savannah, TX 76227-7928, USA

Lilly, Evangeline (Actor)
c/o Jennifer Allen *Viewpoint Inc*
8820 Wilshire Blvd Ste 220
Beverly Hills, CA 90211-2622, USA

Lilly, Ted (Athlete, Baseball Player)
1305 W Waveland Ave
Chicago, IL 60613-3720, USA

Lilly, Theodore (Baseball Player)
Montreal Expos
PO Box 257
Bass Lake, CA 93604-0257, USA

Lilly, Tony (Athlete, Football Player)
13815 Holly Forest Dr
Manassas, VA 20112-3864, USA

Lilly-Heavey, Kristine (Athlete, Olympic Athlete, Soccer Player)
11100 Twisted Elm Dr
Austin, TX 78726-2371, USA

Lillywhite, Verl (Athlete, Football Player)
1828 N Barkley
Mesa, AZ 85203-2702, USA

Lil Twist (Musician)
c/o Cortez Bryant *Maverick Management*
9350 Civic Center Dr Ste 100
Beverly Hills, CA 90210-3629, USA

Lil Wayne (Musician)
c/o Derek Sherron *The Chamber Group*
75 Broad St Rm 708
New York, NY 10004-3244, USA

Lily, Morgan (Actor)
c/o Casey Crawford *Origin Talent Agency*
4705 Laurel Canyon Blvd Ste 306
Studio City, CA 91607-5940, USA

Lilyholm, Len (Athlete, Hockey Player, Olympic Athlete)
4376 Thielen Ave
Minneapolis, MN 55436-1523, USA

Lim, Phillip (Designer)
Phillip Lim Retail LLC
304 Hudson St Fl 8N
New York, NY 10013-1015, USA

Lim, Siew-Ai (Athlete, Golfer)
304 Morning Sun Dr
Birmingham, AL 35242-2912, USA

Lima, Adriana (Actor, Model)
c/o Jesse Stowell *Full Picture Management (NY)*
915 Broadway Fl 20
New York, NY 10010-7131, USA

Lima, Floriana (Actor)
c/o Adam Levine *Industry Entertainment Partners*
955 Carrillo Dr Ste 300
Los Angeles, CA 90048-5400, USA

Liman, Doug (Director, Producer, Writer)
c/o Adam Kanter *Paradigm*
8942 Wilshire Blvd
Beverly Hills, CA 90211-1908, USA

Limbaugh, Rush (Politician)
PO Box 2795
Palm Beach, FL 33480-2795, USA

Limbrick, Garrett (Athlete, Football Player)
PO Box 472
Hempstead, TX 77445-0472, USA

Lime, Yvonne (Actor)
Fedderson
6135 E McDonald Dr
Paradise Valley, AZ 85253-5222, USA

Limos, Tiffany (Actor)
c/o Staff Member *Paradigm*
8942 Wilshire Blvd
Beverly Hills, CA 90211-1908, USA

Lin, Bridget (Actor)
8 Fei Ngo Shan Road
Kowloon
Hong Kong, CHINA

Lin, Brigitte (Actor)
Taiwan Cinema-Drama Assn
196 Chunghua Rd
#10/F Section 1
Taipei, TAIWAN

Lin, Ching-Hsia (Actor)
Taiwan Cinema-Drama Assn
196 Chunghua Road
10/F Sec 1
Taipei, TAIWAN

Lin, Cho-Liang (Musician)
5404 John Dreaper Dr
Houston, TX 77056-4231, USA

Lin, Jeremy (Linsanity) (Athlete, Basketball Player)
c/o Roger Montgomery *Montgomery Sports Group*
19141 Stone Oak Pkwy
San Antonio, TX 78258-3366, USA

Lin, Justin (Director)
c/o Staff Member *Perfect Storm Entertainment*
1850 Industrial St Apt 703
Los Angeles, CA 90021-1265, USA

Lin, Mei (Chef, Reality Star)
c/o Joy Limanon *Peridot*
1112 Montana Ave Ste 295
Santa Monica, CA 90403-1652, USA

Lin, Yu Ping (Athlete, Golfer)
1000 S Romney Dr
Walnut, CA 91789-4804, USA

Linares, Julio (Athlete, Baseball Player)
PO Box 62
San Pedro De Macoris, Dominican Republic

Lincecum, Tim (Athlete, Baseball Player)
16062 SE 4th St
Bellevue, WA 98008-4809, USA

Lincicome, Brittany (Athlete, Golfer)
7971 Idlewild Ln
Seminole, FL 33777-3108, USA

Lincoln, Andrew (Actor)
c/o Chelsea Hayes *Slate PR (NY)*
307 7th Ave Rm 2401
New York, NY 10001-6019, USA

Lincoln, Blanche (Politician)
3942 27th Rd N
Arlington, VA 22207-5242, USA

Lincoln, Brad (Athlete, Baseball Player)
331 S Shanks St
Clute, TX 77531-4622, USA

Lincoln, Howard (Commentator)
Seattle Mariners
6 Holly Hill Dr
Mercer Island, WA 98040-5326, USA

Lincoln, Jeremy (Athlete, Football Player)
71 Broadway Apt 20A
New York, NY 10006-2612, USA

Lincoln, Keith P (Athlete, Football Player)
550 SE Crestview St
Pullman, WA 99163-2257, USA

Lincoln, Michael (Mike) (Athlete, Baseball Player)
8269 Moss Oak Ave
Citrus Heights, CA 95610-0763, USA

Lind, Adam (Athlete, Baseball Player)
6520 Turf Way
Anderson, IN 46013-9588, USA

Lind, Don L (Astronaut)
51 N 376 E
Smithfield, UT 84335-1111, USA

Lind, Don L Dr (Astronaut)
51 N 376 E
Smithfield, UT 84335-1111, USA

Lind, Emily Alyn (Actor)
c/o Alex Schack *Slate PR*
901 N Highland Ave
W Hollywood, CA 90038-2412, USA

Lind, Jack (Athlete, Baseball Player)
6132 E Redmont Dr
Mesa, AZ 85215-0878, USA

Lind, Jose (Athlete, Baseball Player)
18 Brisas Del Plata
Dorado, PR 00646-5123, USA

Lind, Juha (Athlete, Hockey Player)
1260 de la Gauchetiere W
Montreal, QC H3B 5E8, Canada

Lind, Natalie Alyn (Actor)
c/o Alex Schack *Slate PR*
901 N Highland Ave
W Hollywood, CA 90038-2412, USA

Lind, Sarah (Actor)
c/o Staff Member *Lucas Talent Inc*
1238 Homer St Suite 6
Vancouver, BC V6B 2Y5, CANADA

Lindahl, David (Business Person)
PHP Inc
75 Old High St
Whitman, MA 02382-1143

Lindahl, George III (Business Person)
Union Pacific Resources
PO Box 1330
Houston, TX 77251-1330, USA

Lindberg, Chad (Actor)
c/o Staff Member *Michael Black Management*
9701 Wilshire Blvd Fl 10
Beverly Hills, CA 90212-2010, USA

Lindbergh, Reeve (Writer)
839 Tripp Ln
St Johnsbury, VT 05819-8507, USA

Lindbom, Johan (Athlete, Hockey Player)
Torplyckevagen 7
Bankeryd 564 34, Sweden

Lindelind, Liv (Model)
PO Box 1029
Frazier Park, CA 93225-1029, USA

Lindell, Heather (Actor)

Lindell, Rian (Athlete, Football Player)
45 Stoughton Ln
Orchard Park, NY 14127-2083, USA

Lindelof, Damon (Producer)
c/o Cassandra Vargas *PMK/BNC Public Relations*
1840 Century Park E Ste 1400
Los Angeles, CA 90067-2115, USA

Lindeman, Jim (Athlete, Baseball Player)
2278 S Scott St
Des Plaines, IL 60018-3147, USA

Lindemann, Maggie (Musician)
c/o Daniel Kim *Creative Artists Agency (CAA)*
2000 Avenue of the Stars Ste 100
Los Angeles, CA 90067-4705, USA

Lindemulder, Janine (Adult Film Star)
c/o Staff Member *Vivid Entertainment*
1933 N Bronson Ave Apt 209
Los Angeles, CA 90068-5632, USA

Linden, Eric (Athlete, Hockey Player)
1 Pattison Pl.
Philadelphia, PA 19148, USA

Linden, Hal (Actor, Musician)
c/o Staff Member *Stone Manners Talent & Literary (NY)*
900 Broadway Ste 803
New York, NY 10003-1229, USA

Linden, Todd (Athlete, Baseball Player)
10786 Wayward Pl NW
Silverdale, WA 98383-9965, USA

Linder, Brandon (Athlete, Football Player)
c/o Alan Herman *Sportstars Inc*
1370 Avenue of the Americas Fl 19
New York, NY 10019-4602, USA

Linder, Kate (Actor)
c/o Brenda Feldman *Feldman PR*
13636 Ventura Blvd # 440
Sherman Oaks, CA 91423-3700, USA

Lindes, Hal (Musician)
Damage Mgmt
16 Lambton Place
London W11 2SH, UNITED KINGDOM (UK)

Lindh, Hilary (Skier)
PO Box 33036
Juneau, AK 99803-3036, USA

Lindholm, Mikael (Athlete, Hockey Player)
Norra Abyggebyvagen 44
Gavle, 805 98 Sweden

Lindhome, Riki (Actor, Director, Writer)
c/o Mary Ellen Mulcahy *Framework Entertainment*
9057 Nemo St # C
W Hollywood, CA 90069-5511, USA

Lindig, Bill M (Business Person)
Sysco Corp
1390 Enclave Pkwy
Houston, TX 77077-2099, USA

Lindland, Matt (Athlete, Olympic Athlete, Wrestler)
26501 SE Mattson Ln
Eagle Creek, OR 97022-9606, USA

Lindley, Christina (Model)
Lindley Enterprises
114 Rhine Dr
Madison, TN 37115-3561, USA

Lindley, Leta (Athlete, Golfer)
104 Alegria Way
Palm Beach Gardens, FL 33418-1722, USA

Lindley, Ryan (Athlete, Football Player)
c/o Bruce Tollner *REP 1 Sports Group*
80 Technology Dr
Irvine, CA 92618-2301, USA

Lindner, William G (Misc)
Transport Workers Union
80 W End Ave
New York, NY 10023-6301, USA

Lindo, Delroy (Actor)
c/o Brian Swardstrom *United Talent Agency (UTA)*
888 7th Ave Fl 7
New York, NY 10106-0700, USA

Lindon, Vincent (Actor)
Artmedia
20 Ave Rapp
Paris 75007, FRANCE

Lindros, Brett (Athlete, Hockey Player)
85 Crescent Rd
Toronto, ON M4W 1T7, Canada

Lindros, Eric (Athlete, Hockey Player)
411 Glencairn Ave
Toronto, ON M5N 1V4, Canada

Lindroth, Eric (Misc)
13151 Dufresne Pl
San Diego, CA 92129-2383, USA

Lindsay, Bill (Athlete, Hockey Player)
Florida Panthers
1 Panther Pkwy
Sunrise, FL 33323-5315

Lindsay, Bill (Athlete, Hockey Player)
700 NW 7th Ave
Boca Raton, FL 33486-3518

Lindsay, Everett (Athlete, Football Player)
101 Wildwood Beach Rd Apt 13.101
Wildwood Beach Rd Apt 13.
Saint Paul, MN 55115-1684, USA

Lindsay, Jack (Writer)
56 Maids Causeway
Cambridge, UNITED KINGDOM (UK)

Lindsay, Robert (Actor, Musician)
c/o Christian Hodell *Hamilton Hodell Ltd*
20 Golden Sq
Fl 5
London W1F 9JL, UNITED KINGDOM

Lindsey, Bill (Athlete, Baseball Player)
1317 Winterberry Dr
Reidsville, NC 27320-7154, USA

Lindsey, Brady (Actor)
c/o Adam Park *Park Noack Agency*
10866 Wilshire Blvd Ste 400
Los Angeles, CA 90024-4338, USA

Lindsey, Dale (Athlete, Football Player)
4020 Murphy Canyon Rd
San Diego, CA 92123-4407, USA

Lindsey, Doug (Athlete, Baseball Player)
2410 Silver Spur Ln
Leander, TX 78641-7883, USA

Lindsey, Hub (Athlete, Football Player)
1320 Frebis Ave
Columbus, OH 43206-3717, USA

Lindsey, James E (Athlete, Football Player)
1165 E Joyce Blvd
Fayetteville, AR 72703-5183, USA

Lindsey, Meredith (Actor)
c/o Staff Member *Polygon Group, The*
9723 Glenoaks Blvd
Sun Valley, CA 91352-1520, USA

Lindsey, Rodney (Rod) (Athlete, Baseball Player)
610 Comanchee Dr Lot 43
Opelika, AL 36804-6500, USA

Lindsey, Steven (Astronaut)
3217 W Yarrow Cir
Superior, CO 80027-6021, USA

Lindsey, Steven W (Athlete, Football Player)
1327 County Road 123
Water Valley, MS 38965-6114, USA

Lindsey, Terry (Athlete, Football Player)
324 W Brookdale Pl
Fullerton, CA 92832-1426, USA

Lindsley, Blake (Actor)
Gold Marshak Liedtke
3500 W Olive Ave Ste 1400
Burbank, CA 91505-5512, USA

Lindstrand, Per (Misc)
Thunder & Colt
Maesbury Road
Oswestry, Shropshire SY10 8HA, UNITED KINGDOM (UK)

Lindstrom, Charlie (Chuck) (Athlete, Baseball Player)
PO Box 486
Atlanta, IL 61723-0486, USA

Lindstrom, Chris (Athlete, Football Player)
70 Dudley Hill Rd
Dudley, MA 01571-5924, USA

Lindstrom, David (Dave) (Athlete, Football Player)
13209 Woodson St
Overland Park, KS 66209-3817, USA

Lindstrom, Jack (Cartoonist)
United Feature Syndicate
200 Madison Ave
New York, NY 10016-3903, USA

Lindstrom, Jon (Actor)
c/o Staff Member *Gilbertson Management*
1334 3rd Street Promenade Ste 201
Santa Monica, CA 90401-1320, USA

Lindstrom, Matt (Athlete, Baseball Player)
316 Mohawk Ave
Rexburg, ID 83440-2227, USA

Lindstrom, Pia (Journalist)
30 Rockefeller Plz Ste 700
New York, NY 10112-0015, USA

Lindstrom, Willy (Athlete, Hockey Player)
Verkebrovagan 40
Galve 80591, SWEDEN

Lindvall, Angela (Actor, Model)
c/o Siri Garber *Platform PR*
2666 N Beachwood Dr
Los Angeles, CA 90068-2308, USA

Line, Bill (Athlete, Football Player)
1010 Skyview Cir
Gillette, WY 82716-5015, USA

Line, Lorie (Musician)
PO Box 400
Mound, MN 55364-0400, USA

Linebrink, Scott (Athlete, Baseball Player)
2100 County Road 156
Granger, TX 76530-5328, USA

Lineger, Jerry (Astronaut)
c/o Staff Member *Washington Speakers Bureau*
1663 Prince St
Alexandria, VA 22314-2818, USA

Linehan, Scott (Athlete, Football Player)
6315 Westchester Dr
Dallas, TX 75205-1668, USA

Lineker, Gary (Athlete, Soccer Player)
c/o Diana van Bunnens *Jon Holmes Media Ltd*
Holborn Gate 26 Floor 5
Southampton Buildings
London WC2A 1PQ, UNITED KINGDOM

Linenger, Jerry M (Astronaut)
550 S Stony Point Rd
Suttons Bay, MI 49682-9575, USA

Linenger, Jerry M Dr (Astronaut)
550 S Stony Point Rd
Suttons Bay, MI 49682-9575, USA

Lines, Dick (Athlete, Baseball Player)
1716 Pebble Beach Ln
Lady Lake, FL 32159-2238, USA

Liney, John (Cartoonist)
c/o Staff Member *King Features Syndication*
300 W 57th St Fl 15
New York, NY 10019-5238, USA

Ling (Model)
I M G Models
304 Park Ave S # 1200
New York, NY 10010-4301, USA

Ling, Bai (Actor)
c/o Gary Reichman *Media Artists Group*
8222 Melrose Ave Ste 304
Los Angeles, CA 90046-6839, USA

Ling, David (Athlete, Hockey Player)
53 Green Rd
I
Sydney, NS B1P 3E4, Canada

Ling, Julia (Actor)
c/o Mike Liotta *True Public Relations*
3575 Cahuenga Blvd W Ste 360
Los Angeles, CA 90068-1361, USA

Ling, Lisa (Correspondent, Journalist)
c/o Henry Reisch *WME/IMG (NY)*
11 Madison Ave Fl 18
New York, NY 10010-3669, USA

Lingenfelter, Bob (Athlete, Football Player)
Cleveland Browns
53144 865 Rd
Plainview, NE 68769-2505, USA

Lingenfelter, John (Race Car Driver)
Summit Racing
PO Box 535
Richfield, OH 44286-0535, USA

Lingenfelter, Steve (Athlete, Basketball Player)
17378 Ithaca Ct
Lakeville, MN 55044-8742, USA

Lingle, Linda (Politician)
201 E Adams St APT 3A
Springfield, IL 62701-1110, USA

Lingmerth, Goran (Athlete, Football Player)
624 Enfield Ct
Delray Beach, FL 33444-1749, USA

Lingner, Adam (Athlete, Football Player)
70 Stoughton Ln
Orchard Park, NY 14127-2084, USA

Linhart, Anton (Athlete, Football Player)
13 Summer Run Ct
Timonium, MD 21093-4346, USA

Linhart, Carl (Athlete, Baseball Player)
2647 Delmar Ave
Granite City, IL 62040-3439, USA

Linhart, Toni (Athlete, Football Player)
13 Summer Run Ct
Lutherville Timonium, MD 21093-4346, USA

Liniak, Cole (Athlete, Baseball Player)
PO Box 235625
Encinitas, CA 92023-5625, USA

Linke, Lisa (Actor, Comedian)
c/o Lesley Kahn *Lesly Kahn & Company*
1720 N La Brea Ave
Los Angeles, CA 90046-3010, USA

Linke, Paul (Actor)
c/o Staff Member *Flick Commercials*
9057 Nemo St # A
W Hollywood, CA 90069-5511, USA

Linkert, Lo (Artist, Cartoonist)
9541 Lenore Dr
Garden Grove, CA 92841-4925, USA

Linkin Park (Music Group)
c/o Michael Arfin *Artist Group International (NY)*
150 E 58th St Fl 19
New York, NY 10155-1900, USA

Linklater, Hamish (Actor)
c/o Peg Donegan *Framework Entertainment*
9057 Nemo St # C
W Hollywood, CA 90069-5511, USA

Linklater, Lorelei (Actor)
c/o Alex Czuleger *The Green Room*
7080 Hollywood Blvd Ste 1100
Los Angeles, CA 90028-6938, USA

Linklater, Richard (Director, Producer, Writer)
Detour Filmproduction
PO Box 13351
Austin, TX 78711-3351, USA

Linkletter, Nicole (Model)
c/o Staff Member *Elite Model Management (NY)*
245 5th Ave Fl 24
New York, NY 10016-8728, USA

Linley, Cody (Actor)
c/o Scott Appel *Scott Appel Public Relations*
13547 Ventura Blvd # 203
Sherman Oaks, CA 91423-3825, USA

Linn, Jack (Athlete, Football Player)
8418 Trillium Rd
Fort Myers, FL 33967-3486, USA

Linn, Rex (Actor)
c/o Shannon Barr *Rogers & Cowan*
1840 Century Park E Fl 18
Los Angeles, CA 90067-2101, USA

Linn, Teri Ann (Actor)
Sutton Barth Vennari
145 S Fairfax Ave Ste 310
Los Angeles, CA 90036-2176, USA

Linn-Baker, Mark (Actor)
27702 Fairweather St
Canyon Country, CA 91351-2925, USA

Linne, Aubrey (Athlete, Football Player)
4606 Lanham St
Midland, TX 79705-3213, USA

Linne, Larry (Athlete, Football Player)

Linneha, Richard M Dr (Astronaut)
16802 Hartwood Way
Houston, 77058-2305 TX, USA

Linnehan, Richard M (Astronaut)
16802 Hartwood Way
Houston, TX 77058-2305, USA

Linney, Laura (Actor)
c/o Jennifer Plante *Slate PR (NY)*
307 7th Ave Rm 2401
New York, NY 10001-6019, USA

Linnin, Chris (Athlete, Football Player)
1037 Purple Sage Loop
Castle Rock, CO 80104-7846, USA

Linsalata, Joe (Baseball Player)
4017 Washington St
Hollywood, FL 33021-7349, USA

Linsalata, Joe (Athlete, Baseball Player)
4017 Washington St
Hollywood, FL 33021-7349, USA

Linseman, Ken (Athlete, Hockey Player)
1070 Ocean Blvd
Hampton, NH 03842-1500

Linskey, Mike (Baseball Player)
Bowman
18826 Polo Meadow Dr
Humble, TX 77346-8121, USA

Linson, Art (Director, Producer)
Art Linson Productions
Warner Bros
4000 Warner Blvd
Burbank, CA 91522-0001, USA

Lintel, Michelle (Actor)
c/o John Paradise *The Paradise Group*
PO Box 69451
West Hollywood, CA 90069-0451, USA

Linteris, Gregory T (Astronaut)
US Commerce Dept
Fire Science Division
Gaithersburg, MD 20899-0001, USA

Linteris, Gregory T Dr (Astronaut)
15325 Turkey Foot Rd
Gaithersburg, MD 20878-3640, USA

Linton, Doug (Athlete, Baseball Player)
PO Box 23464
Rochester, NY 14692-3464, USA

Lintz, Larry (Athlete, Baseball Player)
8529 Sun Sprite Way
Elk Grove, CA 95624-3816, USA

Lintz, Madison (Actor)
c/o Brad Stokes *LINK Entertainment*
11872 La Grange Ave
Los Angeles, CA 90025-5282, USA

Linville, Joanne (Actor)
345 N Maple Dr # 302
Beverly Hills, CA 90210-3869, USA

Linz, Alex D (Actor)
Innovative Artists
1505 10th St
Santa Monica, CA 90401-2805, USA

Linz, Phil (Athlete, Baseball Player)
404 Catoctin Cir SW
Leesburg, VA 20175-2508, USA

Linzy, Frank (Athlete, Baseball Player)
38947 E 151st St S
Coweta, OK 74429-8550, USA

Lioeanjie, Rene (Misc)
National Maritime Union
1150 17th St NW
Washington, DC 20036-4603, USA

Liotta, Ray (Actor)
c/o Brooks Butterfield *PMK/BNC Public Relations*
1840 Century Park E Ste 1400
Los Angeles, CA 90067-2115, USA

Lioutas, Tommy (Actor)
c/o Norbert Abrams *Noble Caplan Abrams*
1260 Yonge St Fl 2
Toronto, ON M4T 1W5, CANADA

Lipa, Dua (Musician)
c/o Sam Kirby *WME|IMG (NY)*
11 Madison Ave Fl 18
New York, NY 10010-3669, USA

Lipa, Elisabeta (Athlete)
Str Reconstructiei 1
#78
Bucharest, ROMANIA

Lipetri, Angelo (Athlete, Baseball Player)
150 Yoakum Ave
Farmingdale, NY 11735-5034, USA

Lipinski, Ann Marie (Journalist)
Chicago Tribune
160 N Stetson Ave
Editorial Dept
Chicago, IL 60601-6707, USA

Lipinski, Daniel (Congressman, Politician)
1717 Longworth Hob
Washington, DC 20515-1901, USA

Lipinski, Tara (Actor, Athlete, Figure Skater, Olympic Athlete)
c/o Jeff Raymond *Rogers & Cowan*
1840 Century Park E Fl 18
Los Angeles, CA 90067-2101, USA

Lipman, Maureen (Actor)
c/o Staff Member *Talking Concepts*
74 Albert Promenade
Loughborough
Leicestershire WS13 6PW, UNITED KINGDOM

Lipnicki, Jonathan (Actor)
c/o Danielle Bilodeau *Cue Agency*
560 Beatty St Suite L100
Vancouver, BC V6B 2L3, CANADA

Lippard, Stephen J (Misc)
2425 L St NW Apt 440
Washington, DC 20037-2424, USA

Lipper, David (Actor)
c/o Samantha Waranch *JAG Entertainment*
4605 Lankershim Blvd Ste 807
North Hollywood, CA 91602-1879, 91505

Lippett, Ronnie (Athlete, Football Player)
610 Foundry St
South Easton, MA 02375-1318, USA

Lippincott, Philip E (Business Person)
Campbell Soup Co
Campbell Place
Cemden, NJ 08103, USA

Lipps, Lisa (Adult Film Star)
Moonlite Bunny Ranch
69 Moonlight Rd
Mound House, NV 89706-7048, USA

Lipps, Louis (Athlete, Football Player)
132 Ruth St
Pittsburgh, PA 15211-2308, USA

Lipset, Seymour M (Misc)
900 N Stafford St Apt 2131
Arlington, VA 22203-1850, USA

Lipshutz, Bruce H (Misc)
University of California
Chemistry Dept
Santa Barbara, CA 93106-0001, USA

Lipski, Bob (Athlete, Baseball Player)
1 Snook St
Scranton, PA 18505-2865, USA

Lipton, Holly (Musician)
c/o Staff Member *Charles Rapp Enterprises Inc*
88 Pine St Ste 1701
New York, NY 10005-1849, USA

Lipton, James (Actor, Producer, Television Host)
c/o Staff Member *James Lipton Productions*
120A E 23rd St Fl 3A
New York, NY 10010-4516, USA

Lipton, Peggy (Actor, Model)
c/o Belle Zwerdling *Progressive Artists Agency*
1041 N Formosa Ave
West Hollywood, CA 90046-6703, USA

Lipton, Robert (Actor)
c/o Staff Member *Judy Fox Personal Talent Management*
Prefers to be contacted via telephone
Los Angeles, CA 90069, USA

Lipuma, Chris (Athlete, Hockey Player)
16032 Crystal Creek Dr Apt 1B
Orland Park, IL 60462-5355

Liquor, Shirley Q (Comedian)
c/o Stephen Ford *Diva Central Inc*
7510 W Sunset Blvd # 1445
Los Angeles, CA 90046-3408, USA

Liquori, Martin (Marty) (Athlete, Olympic Athlete, Sportscaster, Track Athlete)
2915 NW 58th Blvd
Gainesville, FL 32606-8517, USA

Liriano, Francisco (Athlete, Baseball Player)
c/o Greg Genske *The Legacy Agency*
500 Newport Center Dr Ste 800
Newport Beach, CA 92660-7008, USA

Liriano, Nelson (Athlete, Baseball Player)
Burlington Royals
PO Box 1143
Burlington, NC 27216-1143, USA

Lisbon, Don (Athlete, Football Player)
1707 5th Ave APT 22
Youngstown, OH 44504-1866, USA

Lisch, Russell (Athlete, Football Player)
206 Country Club Ln
Belleville, IL 62223-1910, USA

Lisch, Rusty (Athlete, Football Player)
206 Country Club Ln
Belleville, IL 62223-1910, USA

Liscio, Patti (Golfer)
7803 Glenneagle Dr
Dallas, TX 75248-2335, USA

Liscio, Tony (Athlete, Football Player)
10348 Trailcliff Dr
Dallas, TX 75238-1556, USA

Lisi, Rick (Athlete, Baseball Player)
143 Pinto Rd
Rogers, AR 72756-7148, USA

Lisin, Vladimir (Business Person)
Novolipstek Steel
2, pl. Metallurgov
Lipetsk 398040, Russia

Lisitsa, Valentina (Musician)
Columbia Artists Mgmt Inc
165 W 57th St
New York, NY 10019-2201, USA

Liska, Stephen (Actor)
c/o Larry Metzger *Grant Savic Kopaloff & Associates*
4929 Wilshire Blvd Ste 259
Los Angeles, CA 90010-3816, USA

Liske, Pete (Athlete, Football Player)
116 E Mountain Brook Ln
Wenatchee, WA 98801-9159, USA

Liss, Joe (Actor)
c/o Scott Howard *Howard Entertainment*
16530 Ventura Blvd Ste 305
Encino, CA 91436-4594, USA

Lissemore, Sean (Athlete, Football Player)

Lissie (Musician)
c/o Staff Member *Paradigm (Monterey)*
404 W Franklin St
Monterey, CA 93940-2303, USA

Lissing, Daniel (Actor)
c/o Rob Woodburn *Woodburn Sweitzer Management*
Level 19, 2 Market Street
Sydney NSW 2000, Australia

List, Peyton (Actor)
c/o Erica Plotkin *SLASH-PR*
32 Union Sq E Ste 1008
New York, NY 10003-3209, USA

List, Robert (Politician)
50 W Liberty St # 210
Reno, NV 89501-1940, USA

List, Spencer (Actor)
c/o Erica Gianchetti *SLASH-PR*
32 Union Sq E Ste 1008
New York, NY 10003-3209, USA

Listach, Pat (Athlete, Baseball Player)
Chicago Cubs
1060 W Addison St Ste 1
Chicago, IL 60613-4398

Listach, Pat (Athlete, Baseball Player)
6030 Durande Dr
Baton Rouge, LA 70820-5421, USA

Lister, Alton (Athlete, Basketball Player)
5413 Kirkridge Pl
Garland, TX 75044-4633, USA

Lister, Tommy (Actor)
c/o Staff Member *Cindy Cowan Entertainment*
8265 W Sunset Blvd Ste 205
West Hollywood, CA 90046-2470, USA

Listopad, Ed (Athlete, Football Player)
6719 Roberts Ave
Dundalk, MD 21222-1053, USA

Lit (Music Group)
c/o Ruta Seopetys *Sepetys Entertainment Group*
5543 Edmondson Pike Ste 8A
Nashville, TN 37211-5808, USA

Lithgow, John (Actor)
c/o Mandi Warren *Viewpoint Inc*
89 5th Ave Ste 402
New York, NY 10003-3020, USA

Litsch, Jesse (Athlete, Baseball Player)
134 21st Ave N
St Petersburg, FL 33704-3428, USA

Littell, Mark (Athlete, Baseball Player)
27358 N 88th Ln
Peoria, AZ 85383-4853, USA

Little, Bernie (Race Car Driver)
PO Box 194
Novi, MI 48376-0194, USA

Little, Bryan (Athlete, Baseball Player)
4766 Tiffany Park Cir
Bryan, TX 77802-5822, USA

Little, Chad (Race Car Driver)
8718 Statesville Rd
Charlotte, NC 28269-2622, USA

Little, Dwight H (Director)
c/o Robert Lazar *Resolution (LA)*
1801 Century Park E
Los Angeles, CA 90067-2302, USA

Little, Floyd D (Athlete, Football Player)
33207 Pacific Hwy S
Federal Way, WA 98003-6442, USA

Little, George (Athlete, Football Player)
1805 Powers St
McKeesport, PA 15132-5150, USA

Little, Grady (Athlete, Baseball Player)
13115 Odell Hejg_hts Dr
Mint Hill, NC 28227-4390, USA

Little, Jack (Athlete, Football Player)
PO Box 23528
Waco, TX 76702-3528, USA

Little, Jeff (Athlete, Baseball Player)
5711 W Camper Rd
Genoa, OH 43430-9300, USA

Little, Larry C (Athlete, Coach, Football Player)
14761 SW 169th Ln
Miami, FL 33187-1745, USA

Little, Leonard (Athlete, Football Player)
c/o Chad Speck *Allegiant Athletic Agency*
35 Market Sq Ste 201
Knoxville, TN 37902-1420, USA

Little, Mark (Athlete, Baseball Player)
28014 Moss Fern Dr
Katy, TX 77494-3240, USA

Little, Milton (Musician)
Camil Productions
6606 Solitary Ave
Las Vegas, NV 89110, USA

Little, Rich (Actor, Comedian)
2809 Coast Line Ct
Las Vegas, NV 89117-3523, USA

Little, Robert A (Chef)
49 Firth St
London W1V 5TE, UNITED KINGDOM (UK)

Little, Sally (Athlete, Golfer)
3210 S Ocean Blvd Apt 702
Highland Beach, FL 33487-2597, USA

Little, Scott (Athlete, Baseball Player)
1321 Rosebud Dr
Jackson, MO 63755-1086, USA

Little, Steve (Actor)
c/o Naomi Odenkirk *Odenkirk Provissiero Entertainment*
1936 N Bronson Ave
Raleigh Studios
Los Angeles, CA 90068-5602, USA

Little, Steven (Musician)
Premier Talent
3 E 54th St # 1100
New York, NY 10022-3108, USA

Little, Tasmin E (Musician)
harold Holt
31 Sinclair Road
London W14 0NS, UNITED KINGDOM (UK)

Little, W Grady (Athlete, Baseball Player, Coach)
10608 Fortuna Ct
Matthews, NC 28105-4824, USA

Little, William (Athlete, Baseball Player)
7161 Chevy Chase
Memphis, TN 38125-2610, USA

Little Big Town (Music Group)
c/o Jason Owen *Sandbox Entertainment*
3810 Bedford Ave Ste 200
Nashville, TN 37215-2555, USA

Littlefield, David (Commentator)
3 Morningside Ln
Casco, ME 04015-4255, USA

Littlefield, John (Actor)
c/o Judy Orbach *Judy O Productions*
6136 Glen Holly St
Hollywood, CA 90068-2338, USA

Littlefield, John (Athlete, Baseball Player)
1935 Ramar Rd
Bullhead City, AZ 86442-6949, USA

Littlefield, Warren (Producer)
815 Brooktree Rd
Pacific Palisades, CA 90272-3904, USA

Littleford, Beth (Actor)
c/o Karen Forman *Karen Forman Management*
17547 Ventura Blvd Ste 102
Encino, CA 91316-5164, USA

Littlejohn, Dennis (Athlete, Baseball Player)
222 Port Logan Dr
Bakersfield, CA 93312-7087, USA

Little Man Tate (Music Group)
c/o Staff Member *Paradigm (Monterey)*
404 W Franklin St
Monterey, CA 93940-2303, USA

Little Ones, The (Music Group)
c/o Jason Colton *Red Light Management*
455 2nd St NE
#500
Charlottesville, VA 22902-5791, USA

Littler, Gene (Athlete, Golfer)
PO Box 1949
Rancho Santa Fe, CA 92067-1949, USA

Little Richard (Musician)
c/o William (Bill) Sobel *Edelstein Laird & Sobel*
9255 W Sunset Blvd Ste 800
Los Angeles, CA 90069-3320, USA

Littles, Gene (Athlete, Basketball Player)
6421 E Beck Ln
Scottsdale, AZ 85254-2005, USA

Littleton, Larry (Athlete, Baseball Player)
1076 Dunbarton Trce NE
Brookhaven, GA 30319-2674, USA

Littleton, Wes (Athlete, Baseball Player)
14770 W Laurel Ln
Surprise, AZ 85379-6309, USA

Littman, David (Athlete, Hockey Player)
3761 Spring House Ct SE
Marietta, GA 30067-4929

Littman, Jonathan (Producer)
c/o Staff Member *Jerry Bruckheimer Films / Television*
1631 10th St
Santa Monica, CA 90404-3705, USA

Litton, Bruce (Race Car Driver)
Bruce Litton Racing
PO Box 34174
Indianapolis, IN 46234-0174, USA

Litton, Greg (Athlete, Baseball Player)
22 Hillbrook Way
Pensacola, FL 32503-2850, USA

Littrell, Brian (Musician)
c/o John Marx *WME/IMG*
9601 Wilshire Blvd
Beverly Hills, CA 90210-5213, USA

Liu, Lucy (Actor)
c/o Mary Ellen Mulcahy *Framework Entertainment*
9057 Nemo St # C
W Hollywood, CA 90069-5511, USA

Liu, Simu (Actor)
c/o Chris Lee *Authentic Talent & Literary Management*
3615 Eastham Dr # 650
Culver City, CA 90232-2410, USA

Liuget, Corey (Athlete, Football Player)
c/o Tony Fleming *Impact Sports (LA)*
12429 Ventura Ct
Studio City, CA 91604-2417, USA

Liukin, Nastia (Athlete, Gymnast, Olympic Athlete)
c/o Joann Mignano *Krupp Kommunications*
59 W 19th St Rm 4C
New York, NY 10011-4228, USA

Liut, Mike (Athlete, Hockey Player)
26011 German Mill Rd
Franklin, MI 48025-1139

Livage, Jacques (Misc)
College de France
11 Place M Berthelot
Paris Cedex 05 75231, FRANCE

Live (Music Group)
c/o Staff Member *Paradigm (Monterey)*
404 W Franklin St
Monterey, CA 93940-2303, USA

Lively, Blake (Actor)
c/o Leslie Sloane *Vision PR*
2 Penn Plz Rm 2601
New York, NY 10121-0001, USA

Lively, Bud (Athlete, Baseball Player)
8605 Esslinger Ct SE
Huntsville, AL 35802-3640, USA

Lively, Eric (Actor)
c/o Ben Press *Primary Wave Entertainment*
10850 Wilshire Blvd Fl 6
Los Angeles, CA 90024-4319, USA

Lively, Penelope M (Writer)
c/o David Higham Associates
5-8 Lower John Street
London W1R 4HA, UNINTED KINGDOM

Lively, Robyn (Actor)
c/o Justin Grey Stone *Management 360*
9111 Wilshire Blvd
Beverly Hills, CA 90210-5508, USA

Livers, Virgil (Athlete, Football Player)
234 Johnson Ct
Tulare, CA 93274-3199, USA

Livingston, Andy (Athlete, Football Player)
650 E Century Ave
Gilbert, AZ 85296-1118, USA

Livingston, Barry (Actor)
11310 Blix St
North Hollywood, CA 91602-1209, USA

Livingston, Bruce (Athlete, Football Player)
511 25th Ave W
Bradenton, FL 34205-8264, USA

Livingston, Mike (Athlete, Football Player)
8181 Monrovia St
Shawnee Mission, KS 66215-2728, USA

Livingston, Robert L Jr (Politician)
Livingston Group
PO Box 1246
San Sebastian, PR 00685-1246, USA

Livingston, Ron (Actor)
Rigberg Roberts Rugolo
1180 S Beverly Dr Ste 601
Los Angeles, CA 90035-1158, USA

Livingston, Shaun (Basketball Player)
Los Angeles Clippers
1111 S Figueroa St
Staples Center
Los Angeles, CA 90015-1300, USA

Livingston, Stanley (Actor)
PO Box 1782
Studio City, CA 91614-0782, USA

Livingston, Warren (Athlete, Football Player)
308 E Malibu Dr
Tempe, AZ 85282-5304, USA

Livingstone, Bob (Athlete, Football Player)
1625 Bluebird Ln
Munster, IN 46321-3322, USA

Livingstone, Scott (Athlete, Baseball Player)
1303 Pecos Dr
Southlake, TX 76092-5915, USA

Lizalde, Enrique (Actor)
c/o Staff Member *Televisa*
Blvd Adolfo Lopez Mateos 232
Colonia San Angel INN
DF CP 01060, MEXICO

Lizarazo, Carolina (Actor)
c/o Gabriel Blanco *Gabriel Blanco Iglesias (Mexico)*
Rio Balsas 35-32
Colonia Cuauhtemoc
DF 06500, Mexico

Lizaso, Saul (Actor)
c/o Staff Member *Televisa*
Blvd Adolfo Lopez Mateos 232
Colonia San Angel INN
DF CP 01060, MEXICO

Lizzo (Musician)

Ljungberg, Fredrik (Model, Soccer Player)
c/o Noelle Keshishian *Jenner Communications*
Prefers to be contacted by email.
Woodland Hills, CA NA, USA

Llaca, Patricia (Actor)
c/o Staff Member *TV Azteca*
Periferico Sur 4121
Colonia Fuentes del Pedregal
DF CP 14141, Mexico

Llamosa, Carlos (Soccer Player)
New England Revolution
1 Patriot Pl
Cmgi Field
Foxboro, MA 02035-1388, USA

LL Cool J (Actor, Musician)
LL COOL J Inc.
6311 Romaine St
Los Angeles, CA 90038-2617, USA

Llenas, Winston (Athlete, Baseball Player)
Apartado #92
Santiago, Dominican Republic

Llewellyn, John A (Astronaut)
University of South Florida
4202 E Fowler Ave
Tampa, FL 33620-9951, USA

Llewellyn, John Dr (Astronaut)
141140th Ave E
Madeira Beach, FL 33708-2204, USA

Llewellyn, Robert (Actor, Writer)
c/o Maureen Vincent *United Agents*
12-26 Lexington St
London W1F OLE, UNITED KINGDOM

Llewelyn, Doug (Actor)
8075 W 3rd St # 303
Los Angeles, CA 90048-4318, USA

Llewelyn-Bowen, Laurence (Actor, Designer)
c/o Staff Member *Fresh Partners LTD*
Centre Square
Hardwicks Way
Wandsworth SW18 4AW, UK

Llitch, Michael (Misc)
c/o Staff Member *Detriot Tigers*
2100 Woodward Ave
Comerica Park
Detroit, MI 48201-3474, USA

Llosa, Mario Vargas (Writer)
Las Magnolias 295
6 Piso
Barranco, Lima 00004, PERU

Lloyd, Arroyn (Actor)
c/o Michael Bircumshaw *Water Street Anthem Entertainment*
5225 Wilshire Blvd Ste 615
Los Angeles, CA 90036-4350, USA

Lloyd, Brandon (Athlete, Football Player)
21109 E 50th Street Ct S
Blue Springs, MO 64015-2254, USA

Lloyd, Carli (Athlete, Soccer Player)
c/o Josh Weil *WME/IMG*
9601 Wilshire Blvd
Beverly Hills, CA 90210-5213, USA

LLoyd, Cher (Musician)
c/o Staff Member *Hackford Jones PR*
19 Nassau St
London W1W 7AF, UK

Lloyd, Christopher (Actor)
c/o Bob Gersh *Gersh*
9465 Wilshire Blvd Ste 600
Beverly Hills, CA 90212-2605, USA

Lloyd, Danny (Athlete, Football Player)
2572 Wakefield Ct
Brentwood, CA 94513-5067, USA

Lloyd, Dave (Athlete, Football Player)
24432 County Road 3107
Gladewater, TX 75647-8842, USA

Lloyd, Emily Ann (Actor)
c/o Staff Member *United Talent Agency (UTA)*
9336 Civic Center Dr
Beverly Hills, CA 90210-3604, USA

Lloyd, Eric (Actor)
c/o Alicia Gelernt *Noble Media Management*
330 W 38th St Rm 405
New York, NY 10018-2942, USA

Lloyd, Gary (Race Car Driver)
Thee Dixon Racing
410 Marly Dr
Durham, NC 27703-5641, USA

Lloyd, Geoffrey E R (Misc)
2 Prospect Row
Cambridge CB1 1DU, UNITED KINGDOM (UK)

Lloyd, Georgina (Writer)
Bantam Books
1540 Broadway
New York, NY 10036-4039, USA

Lloyd, Graeme (Athlete, Baseball Player)
455 Oceanview Ave
Palm Harbor, FL 34683-1816, USA

Lloyd, Greg (Athlete, Football Player)
144 Memory Ln
Stockbridge, GA 30281-6263, USA

Lloyd, Jake (Actor)
Osbrink Talent
4343 Lankershim Blvd # 100
North Hollywood, CA 91602-2705, USA

Lloyd, Madison (Actor)
Osbrink Talent
4343 Lankershim Blvd # 100
North Hollywood, CA 91602-2705, USA

Lloyd, Norman (Actor)
c/o Staff Member *The Marion Rosenberg Office*
8428 Melrose Pl Ste B
Los Angeles, CA 90069-5300, USA

Lloyd, Sabrina (Actor)
c/o Julia Buchwald *Buchwald*
5900 Wilshire Blvd Ste 3100
Los Angeles, CA 90036-5030, USA

Lloyd, Sam (Actor)
c/o Staff Member *Heidi Rotbart Management*
1810 Malcolm Ave Apt 207
Los Angeles, CA 90025-7610, USA

Lloyd, Scott (Athlete, Basketball Player)
7545 E Northwest Hwy Apt 143
Dallas, TX 75238-4216, USA

Lloyd, Tony (Athlete, Baseball Player)
6536 Cherokee Dr
Fairfield, AL 35064-1703, USA

Llyod, Tony (Baseball Player)
Birmingham Black Barons
6536 Cherokee Dr
Fairfield, AL 35064-1703, USA

LMFAO (Music Group)
c/o Johnny Maroney *Moodswing 360*
135 W 26th St Fl 12
New York, NY 10001-6872, USA

L. Mica, John (Congressman, Politician)
2187 Rayburn Hob
Washington, DC 20515-4609, USA

Immerfall, Dan (Athlete, Olympic Athlete, Speed Skater)
5421 Trempealeau Trl
Madison, WI 53705-4662, USA

Impe, Ed Van (Athlete, Hockey Player)
Philadelphia Flyers
3601 S Broad St Ste 2
Philadelphia, PA 19148-5297

Impemba, Mario (Commentator)
19945 Gallahad Dr
Macomb, MI 48044-1756, USA

Imus, Don (Journalist)
16 West Ave
Darien, CT 06820-4401, USA

Inhofe, James (Politician)
117 4th St SE
Washington, DC 20003-1002, USA

L. Noem, Kristi (Congressman, Politician)
226 Cannon Hob
Washington, DC 20515-3818, USA

Lo, Ismael (Musician)
Mad Minute Music
5-7 Rue Paul Bert
Saint Ouen 93400, FRANCE

Lo, Tove (Musician)
c/o Staff Member *High Rise PR*
600 Luton Dr
Glendale, CA 91206-2626, USA

Loach, Ken C (Director)
c/o Staff Member *Sixteen Films*
187 Wardour St
Floor 2
London W1F 8ZB, ENGLAND

Loach, Kenneth (Ken) (Director)
Parallax Pictures
7 Denmark St
London WC2H 8LS, UNITED KINGDOM (UK)

Loach, Lonnie (Athlete, Hockey Player)
125 Dixon Ave
New Liskeard, ON P0J 1P0, CANADA

Loaiza, Esteban (Athlete, Baseball Player)
1404 Lands End Ct
Southlake, TX 76092-4224, USA

Loar, John (Producer)
c/o Staff Member *Red Bird Cinema*
PO Box 826
166 Montair Dr
Danville, CA 94526-0826, USA

Lobdell, Erinn (Reality Star)
2472 N Bremen St
Milwaukee, WI 53212-3036, USA

Lobdell, Frank (Artist)
Pier 70
San Francisco, CA 94102, USA

Lobe, Jasmine (Actor, Writer)
c/o Lee Stollman *Gotham Group*
1041 N Formosa Ave # 200
West Hollywood, CA 90046-6703, USA

Lobenstein, Bill (Athlete, Football Player)
584 Juedes Ln
Marshall, WI 53559-8864, USA

Lobenstein, William (Athlete, Football Player)
584 Juedes Ln
Marshall, WI 53559-8864, USA

Lo Bianco, Tony (Actor)
c/o Staff Member *Artists Only Management*
10203 Santa Monica Blvd
Los Angeles, CA 90067-6405, USA

LoBiondo, Frank (Congressman, Politician)
2427 Rayburn Hob
Washington, DC 20515-0524, USA

Lobkowicz, Nicholas (Misc)
Katholische Universitat
Eichstatt 85071, GERMANY

Lobo, Rebecca (Athlete, Basketball Player, Olympic Athlete)
PO Box 734
Granby, CT 06035-0734, USA

Loc, Tone (Music Group)
c/o Staff Member *M.A.G./Universal Attractions*
15 W 36th St Fl 8
New York, NY 10018-7927, USA

Locane, Amy (Actor)
c/o Staff Member *Buchwald*
5900 Wilshire Blvd Ste 3100
Los Angeles, CA 90036-5030, USA

Locas, Jacques (Athlete, Hockey Player)

Loceff, Michael (Producer)
c/o Staff Member *Luber Roklin Management*
5815 W Sunset Blvd Ste 208
Los Angeles, CA 90028-6481, USA

Lochead, Bill (Athlete, Hockey Player)
Fauerbacher Str 16
Ober-Morlen D-61239, Germany

Lochhead, Kenneth C (Artist)
35 Wilton Cres
Ottawa, ON K1S 2T4, CANADA

Lochmueller, Robert (Athlete, Basketball Player)
18 William Tell Blvd
Tell City, IN 47586-2030, USA

Lochte, Ryan (Athlete, Olympic Athlete, Swimmer)
Daytona Beach Swimming
4701 City Center Pkwy
Gainesville, FL 32605, USA

LoCicero, Lisa (Actor)
c/o Staff Member *Pakula/King & Associates*
9229 W Sunset Blvd Ste 315
Los Angeles, CA 90069-3403, USA

Lock, Don (Athlete, Baseball Player)
11725 W Alderny Ct Unit 42
Wichita, KS 67212-6510, USA

Lockbaum, Gordie (Athlete, Football Player)
35 Brookshire Rd
Worcester, MA 01609-1251, USA

Locke, Bobby (Athlete, Baseball Player)
194 Eighty Acres Rd
Dunbar, PA 15431-2274, USA

Locke, Bruce (Actor)
5670 Wilshire Blvd Ste 820
Los Angeles, CA 90036-5613

Locke, Chuck (Athlete, Baseball Player)
2525 Brownwood Ct
Poplar Bluff, MO 63901-2657, USA

Locke, Gary (Politician)
Unit 7300 Box 10
DPO, AP 96521-0010, USA

Locke, Kimberley (Actor, Musician)
c/o Mark Measures *Kazarian, Measures, Ruskin & Associates*
5200 Lankershim Blvd Ste 820
N Hollywood, CA 91601-3194, USA

Locke, Larry (Baseball Player)
Cleveland Indians
155 Eighty Acres Rd Apt 2
Dunbar, PA 15431-2275, USA

Locke, Ron (Athlete, Baseball Player)
11140 Caravel Cir Apt 102
Fort Myers, FL 33908-3996, USA

Locke, Spencer (Actor)
c/o Sharon Lane *Lane Management Group*
4370 Tujunga Ave Ste 130
Studio City, CA 91604-2769, USA

Locke, Tembi (Actor)
c/o Bob McGowan *McGowan Management*
170 S Beverly Dr Ste 304
Beverly Hills, CA 90212-3000, USA

Locker, Bob (Athlete, Baseball Player)
1705 Durston Rd
Bozeman, MT 59715-2734, USA

Lockett, Frank (Athlete, Football Player)
2705 Cerritas Via
Harvey, LA 70058-2936, USA

Lockett, Ken (Athlete, Hockey Player)
89 Germorda Dr
Oakville, ON L6H 2P9, Canada

Lockett, Kevin (Athlete, Football Player)
1319 W Xyler St
Tulsa, OK 74127-2717, USA

Lockhart, Anne (Actor)
c/o Linda McAlister *Linda McAlister Talent*
30 N Raymond Ave Ste 213
Pasadena, CA 91103-3997, USA

Lockhart, Eugene (Athlete, Football Player)
2215 High Country Dr
Carrollton, TX 75007-1701, USA

Lockhart, Ian (Athlete, Basketball Player)
Q25 Calle Excelsa
Yauco, PR 00698-3172, USA

Lockhart, June (Actor)
c/o Staff Member *Agency for the Performing Arts (APA)*
405 S Beverly Dr Ste 500
Beverly Hills, CA 90212-4425, USA

Lockhart, Keith (Athlete, Baseball Player)
3330 McKinley Point Dr
Dacula, GA 30019-1599, USA

Lockhart, Paul S (Astronaut)
3142 Pleasant Cove Ct
Houston, TX 77059-3232, USA

Lockhart, Paul S Lt Colonel (Astronaut)
PSC 802 Box 74
Apo, AE 09607, USA

Locklear, Gene (Athlete, Baseball Player)
1811 Penasco Rd
El Cajon, CA 92019-3708, USA

Locklear, Heather (Actor)
c/o CeCe Yorke *True Public Relations*
3575 Cahuenga Blvd W Ste 360
Los Angeles, CA 90068-1361, USA

Locklear, Sean (Athlete, Football Player)
26235 235th Ave SE
Maple Valley, WA 98038-4705, USA

Locklin, Kerry (Athlete, Football Player)
2087 E Emilie Ave
Fresno, CA 93730-4731, USA

Locklin, Stu (Athlete, Baseball Player)
532 Carfax Pl SW
Albuquerque, NM 87121-2273, USA

Lockwood, Gary (Actor)
1065 E Loma Alta Dr
Altadena, CA 91001-1507, USA

Lockwood, Scott (Athlete, Football Player)
870 West Ln
Estes Park, CO 80517-9624, USA

Lockwood, Skip (Athlete, Baseball Player)
PO Box 872
Wrentham, MA 02093-0872, USA

Locorriere, Dennis (Musician)
P.O. Box 4444
Worthing BN11 3WJ, SUSSEX

Lodboa, Dan (Athlete, Hockey Player)
1 Garden St
Thorold, ON L2V 3H9, Canada

Loder, Anne Marie (Actor)
c/o Jamie Levitt *Lauren Levitt & Associates Inc*
1525 W 8th Ave Fl 3
Vancouver BC V6J 1T5, CANADA

Loder, Kevin (Athlete, Basketball Player)
505 W 4th St
Mishawaka, IN 46544-1818, USA

Loder, Kurt (Journalist, Television Host)

Lodge, David John (Writer)
University of Birmingham
English Dept
Birmingham B15 2TT, UNITED KINGDOM (UK)

Lodish, Mike (Athlete, Football Player)
1150 Trailwood Path
Bloomfield Hills, MI 48301-1742, USA

Loduca, Paul (Athlete, Baseball Player)
3227 Medaris Ln
San Antonio
San Antonio, TX 78258-1624, USA

Lodwick, Todd (Athlete, Olympic Athlete, Skier)
Winter Sports Club
845 Howelsen Hill Pkwy
Steamboat Springs, CO 84077, USA

Loe, Kameron (Athlete, Baseball Player)
2323 N Houston St Apt 312
Dallas, TX 75219-7623, USA

Loeb, Jerome T (Business Person)
May Department Stores
611 Olive St
Saint Louis, MO 63101-1702, USA

Loeb, Lisa (Musician, Songwriter)
c/o Monique Moss *Integrated PR*
9025 Wilshire Blvd Ste 400
Beverly Hills, CA 90211-1828, USA

Loeber, Jerry (Athlete, Baseball Player)
578 Bayville Rd
Locust Valley, NY 11560-1211, USA

Loebsak, David (Congressman, Politician)
1527 Longworth Hob
Washington, DC 20515-4316, USA

Loeffler, Cullen (Athlete, Football Player)

Loehr, Bet (Actor)
c/o Staff Member *Coast to Coast Talent Group*
3350 Barham Blvd
Los Angeles, CA 90068-1404, USA

Loehr, Bret (Actor)
c/o Staff Member *Coast to Coast Talent Group*
3350 Barham Blvd
Los Angeles, CA 90068-1404, USA

Loewen, Adam (Athlete, Baseball Player)
7252 E Whispering Wind Dr
Scottsdale, AZ 85255-2716, USA

Loewen, Darcy (Athlete, Hockey Player)
10611 Kearney Mountain Ave
Las Vegas, NV 89166-5042

Loewer, Carlton (Athlete, Baseball Player)
PO Box 3590
Alpine, WY 83128-0590, USA

Lofgren, Nils (Musician, Songwriter, Writer)
Vision Music
PO Box 2439
Ellicott City, MD 21041-2439, USA

Lofgren, Zoe (Congressman, Politician)
1401 Longworth Hob
Washington, DC 20515-4005, USA

Lofthouse, Mark (Athlete, Hockey Player)
Mark Lofthouse
Surrey, BC V3S 8K4, Canada

Loftin, Lennie (Actor)
c/o Scott Zimmerman *Scott Zimmerman Management*
901 N Highland Ave
Los Angeles, CA 90038-2412, USA

Lofton, Cirroc (Actor)
c/o Staff Member *Innovative Artists*
1505 10th St
Santa Monica, CA 90401-2805, USA

Lofton, Curtis (Athlete, Football Player)

Lofton, Fred C (Religious Leader)
Progressive National Baptist Convention
601 50th St NE
Washington, DC 20019-5498, USA

Lofton, James (Athlete, Baseball Player)
14103 Cerise Ave Apt 18
Hawthorne, CA 90250-8843, USA

Lofton, James D (Athlete, Football Player)
13177 Via Mesa Dr
San Diego, CA 92129-2287, USA

Lofton, Kenny (Athlete, Baseball Player)
PO Box 68473
Tucson, AZ 85737-8473, USA

Lofton, Oscar (Athlete, Football Player)
10612 Hillbrook Ave
Baton Rouge, LA 70810-7747, USA

Logan, Bennie (Athlete, Football Player)
c/o Todd France *Creative Artists Agency (CAA) Sports*
3500 Lenox Rd NE
Atlanta, GA 30326-4228, USA

logan, bob (Athlete, Hockey Player)
11 White Pine Rd
Amherst, MA 01002-3467

Logan, Chuck (Athlete, Football Player)
2526 Lawndale Ave
Evanston, IL 60201-1158, USA

Logan, Daniel (Actor)
c/o Staff Member *Entertainment Legends Management*
360 E 1st St Ste 66
Tustin, CA 92780-3211, USA

Logan, Dave (Athlete, Hockey Player)
142 Acorn Ln
Shelburne, VT 05482-7330

Logan, Dick (Athlete, Football Player)
1144 S Main St
North Canton, OH 44720-4274, USA

Logan, Ernie (Athlete, Football Player)
609 Francis Ct
Spring Lake, NC 28390-3006, USA

Logan, Exavier (Nook) (Athlete, Baseball Player)
19410 Creek Bend Dr
Spring, TX 77388-3095, USA

Logan, Jack (Musician)
William Morris Agency
1325 Avenue of the Americas
New York, NY 10019-6026, USA

Logan, James K (Athlete, Football Player)
US Court of Appeals
301 Danley Ave
Opp, AL 36467-3204, USA

Logan, Jerry (Athlete, Football Player)
1624 Hillcrest Dr
Graham, TX 76450-4702, USA

Logan, John (Producer, Writer)
c/o David O'Connor *Creative Artists Agency (CAA)*
2000 Avenue of the Stars Ste 100
Los Angeles, CA 90067-4705, USA

Logan, Johnny (Athlete, Baseball Player)
6115 W Cleveland Ave
Milwaukee, WI 53219-2653, USA

Logan, Lara (Television Host)
c/o Carole Cooper *N.S. Bienstock*
888 7th Ave Fl 7
New York, NY 10106-0700, USA

Logan, Marc (Athlete, Football Player)
PO Box 11886
Lexington, KY 40578-1886, USA

Logan, Melissa (Musician)
K Records
924 Jefferson St SE
#101
Olympia, WA 98501, USA

Logan, Phyllis (Actor)
47 Courtfield Rd. #9
London SW7 4DB, UK

Logan, Randy (Athlete, Football Player)
330 W Fornance St
Norristown, PA 19401-2906, USA

Logan, Samantha (Actor)
c/o Courtney Miller *Innovative Artists*
1505 10th St
Santa Monica, CA 90401-2805, USA

Logan, Tom (Director)
PO Box 10547
Costa Mesa, CA 92627-0190, USA

Logano, Joey (Race Car Driver)
Joey Logano Racing
9911 Rose Commons Dr Ste 15
Huntersville, NC 28078-0323, USA

Loggins, Kenny (Musician, Songwriter)
1418 Shoreline Dr
Santa Barbara, CA 93109-2071, USA

Logic (Musician)
c/o Robert Mickelson *Creative Artists Agency (CAA)*
2000 Avenue of the Stars Ste 100
Los Angeles, CA 90067-4705, USA

Logue, Donal (Actor)
c/o Perri Kipperman *Kipperman Management*
345 7th Ave Rm 503
New York, NY 10001-5054, USA

Logue, Karina (Actor)
c/o Justin Evans *The Independent Group*
6363 Wilshire Blvd Ste 115
Los Angeles, CA 90048-5734, USA

Lohan, Ali (Actor)
c/o Glenn Gulino *G2 Entertainment LLC*
1 Columbus Pl Apt S25E
New York, NY 10019-8208, USA

Lohan, Dina (Reality Star)
c/o Gina Rodriguez *GiToni Productions*
Prefers to be contacted via telephone or email
Tarzana, CA 91335, USA

Lohan, Lindsay (Actor)
c/o Scott Simpson *Agency for the Performing Arts (APA)*
405 S Beverly Dr Ste 500
Beverly Hills, CA 90212-4425, USA

Lohan, Michael (Reality Star)
c/o Gina Rodriguez *GiToni Productions*
Prefers to be contacted via telephone or email
Tarzana, CA 91335, USA

Lohan, Sinead (Musician, Songwriter, Writer)
Pat Egan Sound
Merchant's Court
24 Merchant's Quay
Dublin, IRELAND

Lohaus, Brad (Athlete, Basketball Player)
55 Tartan Dr
North Liberty, IA 52317-8002, USA

Lohman, Alison (Actor)
c/o Jennifer Rawlings *Omni Artists*
9465 Wilshire Blvd Ste 900
Beverly Hills, CA 90212-2608, USA

Lohmann, Katie (Actor)
c/o Jon Orlando *Exposure Marketing Group*
348 Hauser Blvd Apt 414
Los Angeles, CA 90036-5590, USA

Lohmeyer, Eddie (Horse Racer)
63 Red Valley Rd
Cream Ridge, NJ 08514-2007, USA

Lohmiller, Chip (Athlete, Football Player)
PO Box 810
Crosslake, MN 56442-0810, USA

Lohr, Aaron (Actor)
c/o Robert Stein *Robert Stein Management*
PO Box 3797
Beverly Hills, CA 90212-0797, USA

Lohr, Bob (Athlete, Golfer)
8221 Sorbas Ct
Orlando, FL 32836-8716, USA

Lohrke, Jack (Athlete, Baseball Player)
2817 Lucena Dr
San Jose, CA 95132-2244, USA

Lohse, Kyle (Athlete, Baseball Player)
9820 E Thompson Peak Pkwy Unit 726
Scottsdale, AZ 85255-6657, USA

Loiola, Jose (Athlete, Volleyball Player)
3521 Maple Ave
Manhattan Beach, CA 90266-3509, USA

Loiseau, Shawn (Athlete, Football Player)
c/o Adam Heller *Vantage Management Group*
518 Reamer Dr
Carnegie, PA 15106-1845, USA

Loiselle, Claude (Athlete, Hockey Player)
Toronto Maple Leafs
400-40 Bay St
Toronto, ON M5J 2X2, Canada

Loiselle, Claude (Athlete, Hockey Player)
7 Orchard Dr
Queensbury, NY 12804-6206

Loiselle, Rich (Athlete, Baseball Player)
200 Clover Chase Cir
Woodstock, IL 60098-4197, USA

Loken, Kristanna (Actor)
c/o Staff Member *ICM Partners*
10250 Constellation Blvd Fl 7
Los Angeles, CA 90067-6207, USA

Lokey, Lorey (Business Person)
Business Wire
44 Montgomery St Fl 39
San Francisco, CA 94104-4602, USA

Lolich, Mickey (Athlete, Baseball Player)
6252 Robin Hl
Washington, MI 48094-2186, USA

Lolich, Ron (Athlete, Baseball Player)
7055 SW Dogwood Pl
Portland, OR 97225-1571, USA

Lollar, Tim (Athlete, Baseball Player)
PO Box 166
Red Feather Lakes, CO 80545-0166, USA

Lollobrigida, Gina (Actor)
Via Appia Antica 223
Rome 00178, ITALY

Loman, Doug (Athlete, Baseball Player)
25 Lincoln St
Bakersfield, CA 93305-3412, USA

Lomas, Mark (Athlete, Football Player)
PO Box 17781
Irvine, CA 92623-7781, USA

Lomasney, Steve (Athlete, Baseball Player)
7 Arnold Rd
Peabody, MA 01960-5203, USA

Lomax, Neil V (Athlete, Football Player)
13090 Knaus Rd
Lake Oswego, OR 97034-1551, USA

Lombard, George (Athlete, Baseball Player)
2275 Rhinehill Rd SE
Atlanta, GA 30315-7413, USA

Lombard, Karina (Actor, Model)
EOS Entertainment Corporation
1209 N Orange St
Wilmington, DE 19801-1120, USA

Lombard, Louise (Actor)
c/o Lena Roklin *Luber Roklin Management*
5815 W Sunset Blvd Ste 208
Los Angeles, CA 90028-6481, USA

Lombardi, Leigh (Actor)
c/o Staff Member *Abrams Artists Agency*
275 7th Ave Fl 26
New York, NY 10001-6708, USA

Lombardi, Louis (Actor)
c/o Erik Kritzer *LINK Entertainment*
11872 La Grange Ave
Los Angeles, CA 90025-5282, USA

Lombardi, Phil (Athlete, Baseball Player)
26440 Brooks Cir
Stevenson Ranch, CA 91381-1417, USA

Lombardo, John (Musician)
Agency for Performing Arts
9200 W Sunset Blvd Ste 900
Los Angeles, CA 90069-3604, USA

Lombardozzi, Domenick (Actor)
c/o Michael Garnett *Leverage Management*
3030 Pennsylvania Ave
Santa Monica, CA 90404-4112, USA

Lombardozzi, Steve (Athlete, Baseball Player)
12404 Hall Shop Rd
Fulton, MD 20759-9746, USA

Lomenda, Mark (Athlete, Hockey Player)
52 Everwoods Close SW
Calgary, AB T2Y 5A6, Canada

Lomenda, Michael (Actor)
c/o Siri Garber *Platform PR*
2666 N Beachwood Dr
Los Angeles, CA 90068-2308, USA

Lommi, Tony (Musician)
Red Light Communications
3305 Lobban Pl
Charlottesville, VA 22903-7069, USA

Lomon, Kevin (Athlete, Baseball Player)
13397 Morris Loop
Cameron, OK 74932-2173, USA

Lonborg, Jim (Athlete, Baseball Player)
498 First Parish Rd
Scituate, MA 02066-3201, USA

London, Antonio (Athlete, Football Player)
108 Oak Forest Way
Pelham, AL 35124-2516, USA

London, Carolyn (Producer)
c/o Staff Member *Bankable Productions*
226 W 26th St Fl 4
New York, NY 10001-6700, USA

London, Jason (Actor)
c/o Dominic Friesen *Bridge and Tunnel Communications*
8149 Santa Monica Blvd # 407
West Hollywood, CA 90046-4912, USA

London, Jeremy (Actor, Director, Producer)
c/o Jean-Pierre (JP) Henraux *Henraux Management*
Prefers to be contacted by telephone
CA, USA

London, Lauren (Actor)
c/o Troy Zien *3 Arts Entertainment*
9460 Wilshire Blvd Fl 7
Beverly Hills, CA 90212-2713, USA

London, Lisa (Actor, Model)
8949 W Sunset Blvd Ste 201
Los Angeles, CA 90069-1806, USA

London, Michael (Producer)
c/o Staff Member *Groundswell Productions / Michael Landon Productions*
9350 Wilshire Blvd Ste 324
Beverly Hills, CA 90212-3206, USA

London, Rick (Cartoonist)
c/o Staff Member *Artistic Licensing Agency*
240 Central Ave Apt 224
Hot Springs, AR 71901-3541, USA

London, Stacy (Reality Star, Television Host)
c/o Staff Member *TLC*
1 Discovery Pl
Silver Spring, MD 20910-3354, USA

London, Theophilus (Musician)
c/o Daniel Kim *Creative Artists Agency (CAA)*
2000 Avenue of the Stars Ste 100
Los Angeles, CA 90067-4705, USA

Loneker, Keith (Athlete, Football Player)
56 W Lincoln Ave
Roselle Park, NJ 07204-1358, USA

Lonergan, Kenneth (Director, Writer)
c/o John Buzzetti *WME|IMG (NY)*
11 Madison Ave Fl 18
New York, NY 10010-3669, USA

Lonergan, Kenneth (Writer)
c/o Staff Member *WME|IMG*
9601 Wilshire Blvd
Beverly Hills, CA 90210-5213, USA

Lonestar (Music Group)
c/o Gary Borman *Moir/Borman Entertainment*
9461 Charleville Blvd
Beverly Hills, CA 90212-3017, USA

Lonetto, Sarah (Baseball Player)
26560 Burg Rd Apt 132
Warren, MI 48089-3594, USA

Loney, James (Athlete, Baseball Player)
c/o Joe Urbon *Creative Artists Agency (CAA)*
405 Lexington Ave Fl 19
New York, NY 10174-1800, USA

Loney, Troy (Athlete, Hockey Player)
4245 Glasgow Rd
Valencia, PA 16059-1729

Long, Bill (Athlete, Baseball Player)
7699 Dimmick Rd
West Chester, OH 45241-1166, USA

Long, Billy (Congressman, Politician)
1541 Longworth Hob
Washington, DC 20515-3806, USA

Long, Bob (Athlete, Baseball Player)
3646 Willow Lake Cir
Chattanooga, TN 37419-1459, USA

Long, Bob (Athlete, Football Player)
630 N 4th St Unit 614
Milwaukee, WI 53203-2809, USA

Long, Bob (Athlete, Football Player)
1749 W Sonoran View Dr
Green Valley, AZ 85622-5822, USA

Long, Bob (Athlete, Football Player)
PO Box 245
Ashland, PA 17921-0245, USA

Long, Bobby (Musician)
c/o John Salter *Red Light Management*
5800 Bristol Pkwy Ste 400
Culver City, CA 90230-6898, USA

Long, Carl (Athlete, Baseball Player)
401 Duggins Dr
Kinston, NC 28501-8211, USA

Long, Carson (Athlete, Football Player)
1618 Walnut St
Ashland, PA 17921-1724, USA

Long, Charles F (Chuck) II (Athlete, Football Player)
2425 N MacArthur Blvd
Oklahoma City, OK 73127-1605, USA

Long, Chris (Athlete, Football Player)
c/o Steve Rosner *16W Marketing LLC*
75 Union Ave Ste 2
Rutherford, NJ 07070-1212, USA

Long, Chuck (Athlete, Football Coach, Football Player)
1651 Naismith Dr
Lawrence, KS 66045-4069, USA

Long, Dallas (Athlete, Olympic Athlete, Track Athlete)
PO Box 355
Whitefish, MT 59937-0355, USA

Long, Dave (Athlete, Football Player)
309 16th St
Marion, IA 52302-4356, USA

Long, Dennis (Denny) (Soccer Player)
RR 5
Poplar Bluff, MO 63901, USA

Long, Don (Athlete, Baseball Player)
747 Puget Ln
Edmonds, WA 98020-2643, USA

Long, Elizabeth Valk (Business Person)
J.M. Smucker Co
1 Strawberry Ln
Orrville, OH 44667-1298, USA

Long, Grant (Athlete, Basketball Player)
8501 Morton Taylor Rd
Van Buren Twp, MI 48111-5313, USA

Long, Howie (Actor, Football Player, Sportscaster)
c/o Jack Gilardi *ICM Partners*
10250 Constellation Blvd Fl 7
Los Angeles, CA 90067-6207, USA

Long, Jackie (Actor)
c/o Tammy Brook *FYI Public Relations*
174 5th Ave Ste 404
New York, NY 10010-5964, USA

Long, Jake (Athlete, Football Player)
c/o Tom Condon *Creative Artists Agency (CAA)*
401 Commerce St PH
Nashville, TN 37219-2516, USA

Long, Jeoff (Athlete, Baseball Player)
11 Flower Ct
Lakeside Park, KY 41017-2102, USA

Long, Jessica (Athlete, Swimmer)
c/o Peter Carlisle *Octagon Olympics & Action Sports*
7 Ocean St Ste 2
South Portland, ME 04106-2800, USA

Long, Joan D (Producer)
La Burrage Place
Lindfield, NSW 02070, AUSTRALIA

Long, Joey (Athlete, Baseball Player)
5541 Kiser Lake Rd
Conover, OH 45317-9643, USA

Long, John (Athlete, Basketball Player)
11976 Hunt St
Romulus, MI 48174-3830, USA

Long, Justin (Actor)
8436 W 3rd St # 640
Los Angeles, CA 90048-4163, USA

Long, Kevin (Athlete, Baseball Player)
6 Southpine Ct
Columbia, SC 29212-2918, USA

Long, Kevin (Athlete, Baseball Player)
8540 E Via Montoya
Scottsdale, AZ 85255-4936, USA

Long, Khari (Athlete, Football Player)
4405 Call Field Rd
Wichita Falls, TX 76308-2445, USA

Long, Kyle (Athlete, Football Player)
c/o Marvin Demoff *Morris Yorn Barnes Levine Krintzman Rubenstein Kohner & Gellman*
2000 Avenue of the Stars Ste 300N
Tower N Fl 3
Los Angeles, CA 90067-4704, USA

Long, Mark (Reality Star)
c/o Staff Member *MTV Networks (LA)*
1575 N Gower St Ste 100
Los Angeles, CA 90028-6488, USA

Long, Matt (Actor)
c/o Robert Glennon *Authentic Talent and Literary Management (NY)*
20 Jay St Ste M17
Brooklyn, NY 11201-8300, USA

Long, Mel (Athlete, Football Player)
837 Imani Cir
Toledo, OH 43604-8425, USA

Long, Nia (Actor)
c/o Amanda Silverman *The Lede Company*
401 Broadway Ste 206
New York, NY 10013-3033, USA

Long, Richard (Artist)
Old School
Lower Failand
Bristol BS8 3SL, UNITED KINGDOM (UK)

Long, Rien (Athlete, Football Player)
460 Great Circle Rd
Nashville, TN 37228-1404, USA

Long, Rob (Producer)
c/o Brett Loncar *Creative Artists Agency (CAA)*
2000 Avenue of the Stars Ste 100
Los Angeles, CA 90067-4705, USA

Long, Robert (Misc)
University of California
Paleontology Museum # 101
Berkeley, CA 94720-0001, USA

Long, Robert M (Business Person)
Longs Drug Stores
141 N Civic Dr
Walnut Creek, CA 94596-3815, USA

Long, Rocky (Athlete, Football Player)
San Dego State University
5500 Campanile Dr
San Diego, CA 92182-0003, USA

Long, Ryan (Athlete, Baseball Player)
3102 Winchester Ranch Trl
Katy, TX 77493-4400, USA

Long, Scott (Actor, Reality Star)

Long, Shelley (Actor)
c/o Bobby Moses *Mavrick Artists Agency*
8447 Wilshire Blvd Ste 301
Beverly Hills, CA 90211-3206, USA

Long, Tanisha (Actor, Model)
c/o Siri Garber *Platform PR*
2666 N Beachwood Dr
Los Angeles, CA 90068-2308, USA

Long, Ted (Athlete, Hockey Player)
188 Abbott Pl
Woodstock, ON N4S 8J7, Canada

Long, Terrance (Athlete, Baseball Player)
3433 Cross Creek Dr
Montgomery, AL 36116-3648, USA

Long, Tim (Athlete, Football Player)
10028 Casa Nuestra Dr
Charlotte, NC 28214-2378, USA

Long, Trevor (Actor)
c/o Jade Wiselogle *Persona Public Relations*
6255 W Sunset Blvd Ste 705
Hollywood, CA 90028-7408, USA

Long, William Ivey (Designer)
International Creative Mgmt
40 W 57th St Ste 1800
New York, NY 10019-4033, USA

Longet, Claudine (Actor)
Ronald D Austin
6000 E Hopkins
Aspen, CO 81611, USA

Longfield, William (Business Person)
CR Bard Inc
1 Becton Dr
Franklin Lakes, NJ 07417-1815, USA

Longley, Clint (Athlete, Football Player)
13602 Camino De Oro Ct
Corpus Christi, TX 78418-6910, USA

Longley, Luc (Athlete, Basketball Player)
Basketball Australia Hall of Fame
PO Box 7141 Alexandria, NSW 2015
Australi< 87102, USA

Longmire, Sam (Athlete, Football Player)
4513 N Via Entrada Apt 163
Tucson, AZ 85718-7610, USA

Longmire, Tony (Athlete, Baseball Player)
419 Fleming Ave E
Vallejo, CA 94591-4030, USA

Longmuir, Derek (Musician)
27 Preston Grange
Preston Pans E
Lothian, SCOTLAND

Longo, Cody (Actor)
c/o Greg Clark *Untitled Entertainment*
350 S Beverly Dr Ste 200
Beverly Hills, CA 90212-4819, USA

Longo, Lenny (Musician)
Texas Sounds
PO Box 1644
Dickinson, TX 77539-1644, USA

Longo, Robert (Artist)
Longo Studio
224 Centre St Rm 601
New York, NY 10013-3619, USA

Longo, Tom (Athlete, Football Player)
2 Donna Ln
Wayne, NJ 07470-2711, USA

Longo, Tony (Actor)
24 Westwind St
Marina Del Rey, CA 90292-7135

Longoria, Eva (Actor, Producer)
c/o Staff Member *Unbelievable Entertainment*
7095 Hollywood Blvd Ste 797
Hollywood, CA 90028-8912, USA

Longoria, Evan (Athlete, Baseball Player)
c/o Staff Member *Tampa Bay Devil Rays*
1 Tropicana Dr
Tropicana Field
Saint Petersburg, FL 33705-1703, USA

Long-View (Music Group)
c/o Staff Member *Paradigm (Monterey)*
404 W Franklin St
Monterey, CA 93940-2303, USA

Longwell, Ryan (Athlete, Football Player)
9507 Sloane St
Orlando, FL 32827-7046, USA

Lonneke (Model)
Pauline's Talent Corp
379 W Broadway # 502
New York, NY 10012-5121, USA

Lonow, Claudia (Comedian)
c/o Staff Member *ICM Partners*
10250 Constellation Blvd Fl 7
Los Angeles, CA 90067-6207, USA

Lonsberry, Ross (Athlete, Hockey Player)
32610 Big Springs Rd
Acton, CA 93510-1501, USA

Lonsbrough, Porter Anita (Swimmer)
6 Rivendell Gardens
Tettendall
Wolverhampton WV6 8SY, UNITED KINGDOM (UK)

Lonsdale, Keiynan (Actor)
c/o Staff Member *Silver Lining Entertainment*
421 S Beverly Dr Fl 7
Beverly Hills, CA 90212-4408, USA

Lonsdale, Laurie (Writer)
49 Lighthouse St
Whitby, ON L1N 9R9, CANADA

Lonsdale, Michael (Actor)
25 rue de General-Foy
Paris, FRANCE F-75008

Loob, Hakan (Athlete, Hockey Player)
Farjestads BK Box 318
Karlstad S-65108, Sweden

Loob, Peter (Athlete, Hockey Player)
Nadendalsvagen 5
Vadstena S-59232, SWEDEN

Look, Bruce (Athlete, Baseball Player)
4298 Maitland Rd
Williamsburg, MI 49690-9575, USA

Look, Dean (Athlete, Baseball Player)
80 Victorian Hills Dr
Okemos, MI 48864-3160, USA

Look, Dean Z (Athlete, Football Player)
80 Victorian Hills Dr
Okemos, MI 48864-3160, USA

Looker, Dane (Athlete, Football Player)
7213 41st Avenue Ct E
Tacoma, WA 98443-1811, USA

Lookinland, Mike (Actor)
PO Box 9968
Salt Lake City, UT 84109-0968, USA

Loomis, Robbie (Race Car Driver)
Hendrick Racing
4414 Pappa Joe Hendrtck Blvd.
Charlotte, NC 28262, USA

Loomis, Rod (Actor)
5114 Vineland Ave
North Hollywood, CA 91601-3814

Looney, Brian (Athlete, Baseball Player)
188 Romulus Rd
Cheshire, CT 06410-3535, USA

Looney, Don (Athlete, Football Player)
6529 Turnberry Dr
Fort Worth, TX 76132-4514

Looney, Joe (Athlete, Football Player)
c/o Andy Ross *Select Sports Group*
2700 Post Oak Blvd Ste 1450
Houston, TX 77056-5785, USA

Looney, Shelley (Athlete, Hockey Player, Olympic Athlete)
PO Box 170
New Vernon, NJ 07976-0170, USA

Looper, Aaron (Athlete, Baseball Player)
1405 Manchester Dr
Shawnee, OK 74804-2327, USA

Looper, Braden (Athlete, Baseball Player, Olympic Athlete)
442 Shadow Creek Dr
Palos Heights, IL 60463-2912, USA

Loose, John W (Business Person)
Coming Corp
Houghton Park
Corning, NY 14831-0001, USA

Lopasky, Bill (Athlete, Football Player)
16 Masonic Dr
Dallas, PA 18612-9192, USA

Lopasky, William (Athlete, Football Player)
Huntsville Ceasetown Rd
Dallas, PA 18612, USA

Lopata, Stan (Athlete, Baseball Player)
2239 Leisure World
Mesa, AZ 85206-5384, USA

Loper, Daniel (Athlete, Football Player)
115 Stillwater Trl
Hendersonville, TN 37075-4305, USA

Lopert, Tanya (Actor)
Cineart
36 Rue de Pnthieu
Paris 75008, FRANCE

Lopes, Davey (Athlete, Baseball Player)
309 San Elijo St
San Diego, CA 92106-3455, USA

Lopes, Davey (Athlete, Baseball Player)
Los Angeles Dodgers
1000 Elysian Park Ave Attn Coachingstaff
Los Angeles, CA 90090-1112, USA

Lopez, Adamari (Actor)
c/o Staff Member *Telemundo*
2470 W 8th Ave
Hialeah, FL 33010-2000, USA

Lopez, Albie (Athlete, Baseball Player)
1019 S Roles Dr
Gilbert, AZ 85296-8606, USA

Lopez, Arturo (Athlete, Baseball Player)
PO Box 770908
Orlando, FL 32877-0908, USA

Lopez, Colby (Seth Rollins) (Athlete, Wrestler)
c/o Staff Member *World Wrestling Entertainment (WWE)*
1241 E Main St
Stamford, CT 06902-3520, USA

Lopez, Danny (Little Red) (Boxer)
16531 Aquamarine Ct
Chino Hills, CA 91709-4644, USA

Lopez, Feliciano (Athlete, Tennis Player)
IMG Center
1360 E 9th St Ste 100
Cleveland, OH 44114-1730, USA

Lopez, Felipe (Athlete, Baseball Player)
11171 Sun Center Dr Ste 290
Rancho Cordova, CA 95670-6190, USA

Lopez, George (Actor, Comedian, Producer, Talk Show Host)
c/o Staff Member *George Lopez Presents*
4000 Warner Blvd Bldg 9
Burbank, CA 91522-0001, USA

Lopez, Hector (Athlete, Baseball Player)
11415 Faldo Ct
Hudson, FL 34667-8540, USA

Lopez, Israel (Cachao) (Musician)
c/o Staff Member *Paradigm (Monterey)*
404 W Franklin St
Monterey, CA 93940-2303, USA

Lopez, Javier (Athlete, Baseball Player)
c/o Barry Meister *Meister Sports Management*
770 Lake Cook Rd Ste 300
Deerfield, IL 60015-4920, USA

Lopez, Javy (Athlete, Baseball Player)
32262 Paseo Candela
San Juan Capistrano, CA 92675-3230, USA

Lopez, Jennifer (Actor, Musician)
c/o Chantal Artur *Sunshine Sachs*
720 Cole Ave
Los Angeles, CA 90038-3606, USA

Lopez, Juan (Athlete, Baseball Player)
1451 Lavilla Ct
Deltona, FL 32725-4759, USA

Lopez, Luis (Athlete, Baseball Player)
1701 Pleasant Run Rd
Carrollton, TX 75006-7537, USA

Lopez, Luis (Athlete, Baseball Player)
Greenville Drive
945 S Main St Attn Coachingstaff
Greenville, SC 29601-3334, USA

Lopez, Luis (Athlete, Baseball Player)
636 40th St
Brooklyn, NY 11232-3108, USA

Lopez, Lynda (Television Host)
c/o Staff Member *Arlene Thornton & Associates*
12711 Ventura Blvd Ste 490
Studio City, CA 91604-2477, USA

Lopez, Marga (Actor)
c/o Staff Member *Televisa*
Blvd Adolfo Lopez Mateos 232
Colonia San Angel INN
DF CP 01060, MEXICO

Lopez, Mario (Actor, Television Host)
c/o Lisa Perkins *Baker Winokur Ryder Public Relations*
9100 Wilshire Blvd
W Tower #500
Beverly Hills, CA 90212-3415, USA

Lopez, Mickey (Athlete, Baseball Player)
17430 SW 117th Ave
Miami, FL 33177-2203, USA

Lopez, Raul (Basketball Player)
Utah Jazz
301 W South Temple
Delta Center
Salt Lake City, UT 84101-1219, USA

Lopez, Robert (Musician)
c/o John Buzzetti *WME/IMG (NY)*
11 Madison Ave Fl 18
New York, NY 10010-3669, USA

Lopez, Rodrigo (Baseball Player)
Baltimore Orioles
333 W Camden St Ste 1
Oriole Park
Baltimore, MD 21201-2476, USA

Lopez, Sal (Actor, Musician)
c/o Ivan De Paz *DePaz Management*
2011 N Vermont Ave
Los Angeles, CA 90027-1931, USA

Lopez, Sergi (Actor)
c/o Staff Member *ICM Partners*
10250 Constellation Blvd Fl 7
Los Angeles, CA 90067-6207, USA

Lopez, Steven (Athlete)
P.O. Bix 678
Sugarland, TX 77487, USA

Lopez, Trini (Actor, Musician)
1139 Abrigo Rd
Palm Springs, CA 92262-4101, USA

Lopez-Garcia, Antonio (Artist)
Marlborough Fine Art
6 Albermarle St
London W1, UNITED KINGDOM (UK)

Lopez Tarso, Ignacio (Actor)
c/o Staff Member *Televisa*
Blvd Adolfo Lopez Mateos 232
Colonia San Angel INN
DF CP 01060, MEXICO

Lopez Trujillo, Alfonso Cardinal (Religious Leader)
Arzobispado
Calle 57 N 48-28
Medellin, COLUMBIA

Lopienski, Tom (Athlete, Football Player)
128 Blackberry Dr
Hudson, OH 44236-4701, USA

Lopitalier, Phil (Athlete, Baseball Player)
231 N Kings Ave
Massapequa, NY 11758-3325, USA

Lopresti, Pete (Athlete, Hockey Player)
5100 Tifton Dr
Minneapolis, MN 55439-1457

Loquasto, Santo (Designer)
Paradigm Agency
10100 Santa Monica Blvd Ste 2500
Los Angeles, CA 90067-4116, USA

Lorca, Valeria (Actor)
c/o Staff Member *Telefe (Argentina)*
Pavon 2444
Buenos Aires C1248AAT, ARGENTINA

Lorch, Karl (Athlete, Football Player)
92-861 Palailai St
Kapolei, HI 96707-1239, USA

Lord, Albert L (Business Person)
SLM Holding Corp
11600 American Dream Way
Reston, VA 20190-4758, USA

Lord, Jammal (Athlete, Football Player)
3110 Travis Creek Way
Fresno, TX 77545-7079, USA

Lord, Peter (Animator, Director)
c/o Staff Member *Aardman Animations*
Gas Ferry Road
Bristol BS1 6UN, UNITED KINGDOM

Lord, Phil (Director, Producer)
c/o Staff Member *Lord Miller*
10201 W Pico Blvd Bldg 3
Los Angeles, CA 90064-2606, USA

Lorde (Musician)
c/o Jonathan Daniel *Crush Music Management*
60-62 E 11th St
Fl 7
New York, NY 10003, USA

Lords, Traci (Actor, Adult Film Star)
c/o Juliet Green *Juliet Green Management*
9025 Wilshire Blvd Ste 400
Beverly Hills, CA 90211-1828, USA

Loree, Brad (Actor)
c/o Brenda Wong *TalentCo*
111 Water St #308
Vancouver BC V6B 1A7, CANADA

Loren, Josie (Actor)
c/o Ellen Meyer *Ellen Meyer Management*
315 S Beverly Dr Ste 202
Beverly Hills, CA 90212-4310, USA

Loren, Lela (Actor)
c/o Amanda Silverman *The Lede Company*
401 Broadway Ste 206
New York, NY 10013-3033, USA

Loren, Sophia (Actor)
Casa Postale 430
Geneva 12 01211, SWITZERLAND

Loren, Veronica (Actor)
c/o Staff Member *International Artists PR & Talent Management*
3010 Wilshire Blvd # 594
Los Angeles, CA 90010-1103, USA

Lorentz, Jim (Athlete, Hockey Player)
2555 Staley Rd
Grand Island, NY 14072-2040

Lorenz, Danny (Athlete, Hockey Player)
Kent Valley Ice Centre 6015 S 240th St
Kent, WA 98032-3406

Lorenz, Lee (Cartoonist)
PO Box 131
Easton, CT 06612-0131, USA

Lorenzen, Fred (Race Car Driver)
64 E Elm St Apt 4
Chicago, IL 60611-1019, USA

Lorenzo, Blas (Actor)
PO Box 2127
Los Angeles, CA 90078-2127

Lorenzo, Francisco (Boxer)
c/o Staff Member *Top Rank Inc.*
3908 Howard Hughes Pkwy
#580
Las Vegas, NV 89109, USA

Lorenzoni, Andrea (Astronaut)
Via B Vergine del Carmelo 168
Rome 00144, ITALY

Loretta, Mark (Athlete, Baseball Player)
PO Box 9505
Rancho Santa Fe, CA 92067-4505, USA

Lorey, Dean (Writer)
c/o Rob Carlson *United Talent Agency (UTA)*
9336 Civic Center Dr
Beverly Hills, CA 90210-3604, USA

Loria, Christopher (Astronaut)
c/o Staff Member *NASA-JSC*
2101 Nasa Pkwy # 1
Astronaut Office - Mail Code Cb
Houston, TX 77058-3607, USA

Loria, Jeffrey (Baseball Player)
Florida Marlins
44 Cocoanut Row Unit 407-B
Palm Beach, FL 33480-4069, USA

Loria, Jeffrey (Commentator)
19 E 72nd St Apt 14C
New York, NY 10021-4193, USA

Lorick, Tony (Athlete, Football Player)
PO Box 2403
Fredericksburg, TX 78624-1906, USA

Lorig, Khatuna (Athlete, Olympic Athlete)
c/o Staff Member *USA Archery*
1 Olympic Plz
Colorado Springs, CO 80909-5780, USA

Lorimer, Bob (Athlete, Hockey Player)
24 Cranberry Lane
Aurora, ON L4G 5Y3, Canada

Loring, Gloria (Actor, Musician)
PO Box 1243
Cedar Glen, CA 92321-1243, USA

Loring, John R (Artist)
621 Avon Rd
West Palm Bch, FL 33401-7803, USA

Loring, Lisa (Actor)
c/o Staff Member *Genesis Creations*
1815 Via Capri
Chula Vista, CA 91913-1523, USA

Loring, Lynn (Actor)
22205 Ryan Ridge Way
Woodland Hills, CA 91367-4484, USA

Lorraine, Andrew (Athlete, Baseball Player)
10436 E Acoma Dr
Scottsdale, AZ 85255-1711, USA

Lorraine, Andrew (Athlete, Baseball Player)
Everett Aquasox
3802 Broadway Attn Coachingstaff
Everett, WA 98201-5032, USA

Lorre, Chuck (Producer, Writer)
1880 Century Park E Ste 950
Los Angeles, CA 90067-1612, USA

Lorscheider, Aloisio Cardinal (Religious Leader)
Guna Metropolitana
CP 05 Tone Basilica
Aparecida, SP 12570-000, BRAZIL

Lorthridge, Ryan (Athlete, Basketball Player)
PO Box 68693
Jackson, MS 39286-8693, USA

Lortie, Louis (Musician)
Cramer/Marder Artists
3436 Springhill Rd
Lafayette, CA 94549-2535, USA

Los, Marinus (Misc)
American Cyanamid Corp
4201 Quakerbridge Rd
Princeton Junction, NJ 08550-5205, USA

Losier, Michael (Writer)
605-827 Fairfield Rd
Victoria, BC V8V 5B2, Canada

Los Lagos, Banda (Music Group)
c/o Staff Member *Sony Music (Miami)*
404 Washington Ave Ste 700
Miami Beach, FL 33139-6615, USA

Los Lobos (Music Group)
c/o Staff Member *Paradigm (Monterey)*
404 W Franklin St
Monterey, CA 93940-2303, USA

Los Lonely Boys (Music Group)
Los Lonely Boys
403 Ridgewood Rd
Austin, TX 78746-5786, USA

Losman, J P (Athlete, Football Player)
70 Oakland Pl
Buffalo, NY 14222-2040, USA

Los Mauricios (Writer)
c/o Staff Member *Gabriel Blanco Iglesias (Colombia)*
Dg 127A #20-36
Conjunto Plenitud, Apto 132
Bogota, Colombia

Los Rabanes (Music Group)
c/o Staff Member *Sony Music (Miami)*
404 Washington Ave Ste 700
Miami Beach, FL 33139-6615, USA

Los Sementales de Nuevo Leon (Music Group)
c/o Staff Member *Sony Music (Miami)*
404 Washington Ave Ste 700
Miami Beach, FL 33139-6615, USA

Los Super Reyes (Music Group, Musician)
c/o Staff Member *Warner Music (NY)*
75 Rockefeller Plz
New York, NY 10019-6908, USA

Lothamer, Ed (Athlete, Football Player)
10534 Riggs Dr
Overland Park, KS 66212-1888, USA

Lo Truglio, Joe (Actor)
c/o Andy Corren *Andy Corren Management*
PO Box 5955
Sherman Oaks, CA 91413-5955, USA

Lott, John (Athlete, Football Player)
26242 Hitching Rail Rd
Laguna Hills, CA 92653-6300, USA

Lott, Phil (Producer)
c/o Staff Member *ICM Partners*
10250 Constellation Blvd Fl 7
Los Angeles, CA 90067-6207, USA

Lott, Pixie (Musician)
c/o Staff Member *Mercury Records (NY)*
810 7th Ave
New York, NY 10019-5818, USA

Lott, Ronald M (Ronnie) (Sportscaster)
Fox-TV
PO Box 900
Sports Dept
Beverly Hills, CA 90213-0900, USA

Lott, Ronnie (Athlete, Football Player)
11342 Canyon View Cir
Cupertino, CA 95014-4838, USA

Lott, Thomas (Athlete, Football Player)
3617 Sailmaker Ln
Plano, TX 75023-3712, USA

Lott, Trent (Politician, Senator)
2401 Pennsylvania Ave NW Apt 806
Washington, DC 20037-1735, USA

Lotti, Helmut (Musician)
c/o Staff Member *Piet Roelen Talent Agency*
Antwerpsesteenweg 16
Vosselaar BE 02350, Belgium

Lotulelei, Star (Athlete, Football Player)
c/o Bruce Tollner *REP 1 Sports Group*
80 Technology Dr
Irvine, CA 92618-2301, USA

Lotz, Anne Graham (Religious Leader)
AnGel Ministries
3246 Lewis Farm Rd
Raleigh, NC 27607-6723, USA

Lotz, Caity (Actor)
c/o David (Dave) Fleming *Atlas Artists*
9220 W Sunset Blvd Ste 225
Los Angeles, CA 90069-3513, USA

Louboutin, Christian (Designer)
Christian Louboutin
306 W 38th St Fl 12
New York, NY 10018-8404, USA

Louchiey, Corey (Athlete, Football Player)
8 Misty Creek Ln
Greenville, SC 29611-7718, USA

Loucks, Scott (Athlete, Baseball Player)
1801 Viola Dr
Sierra Vista, AZ 85635-2149, USA

Loucks, Vernon R Jr (Business Person)
Baxter International
1 Baxter Pkwy
Deerfield, IL 60015-4658, USA

Louden, Stephanie (Athlete, Golfer)
621 Verbena Ln
Frisco, TX 75036-8849, USA

Louderback, Tom (Athlete, Football Player)
PO Box 6879
Oakland, CA 94603-0879, USA

Louganis, Greg (Athlete, Swimmer)
c/o Greg Sims *Arya Artist Management*
555 W 5th St Ste 3100
Los Angeles, CA 90013-1018, USA

Loughery, Kevin (Athlete, Basketball Player, Coach)
4474 Club Dr NE
Atlanta, GA 30319-1122, USA

Loughlin, Lori (Actor)
c/o Elizabeth Much *East 2 West Collective*
11022 Santa Monica Blvd Ste 350
Los Angeles, CA 90025-7532, USA

Loughlin, Mary Anne (Correspondent)
WTBS-TV News Dept
1050 Techwood Dr NW
Atlanta, GA 30318-5695, USA

Louis, Jin Luxian (Religious Leader)
Shesshan Catholic Seminary
Beijing, CHINA

Louis, Lance (Athlete, Football Player)
c/o Ryan Tollner *REP 1 Sports Group*
80 Technology Dr
Irvine, CA 92618-2301, USA

Louisa, Maria (Model)
Next Model Mgmt
23 Watts St
New York, NY 10013, USA

Louis-Dreyfus, Julia (Actor, Comedian)
c/o Lindsay Krug *ID Public Relations*
7060 Hollywood Blvd Fl 8th
Los Angeles, CA 90028-6021, USA

Louise, Tina (Actor, Musician)
310 E 46th St Apt 24G
New York, NY 10017-3031, USA

Louiso, Todd (Actor)
S M S Talent
8730 W Sunset Blvd Ste 440
Los Angeles, CA 90069-2277, USA

Loukas, Angelo (Athlete, Football Player)
1535 Robin Rd
Bannockburn, IL 60015-1852, USA

Loun, Don (Athlete, Baseball Player)
9095 Wexford Dr
Vienna, VA 22182-2152, USA

Lourd, Billie Catherine (Actor)
c/o Megan Senior *Slate PR*
901 N Highland Ave
W Hollywood, CA 90038-2412, USA

Louris, Gary (Musician, Songwriter, Writer)
Sussman Assoc
1222 16th Ave S Ste 300
Nashville, TN 37212-2920, USA

Lousma, Jack R (Astronaut)
2722 Roseland Dr
Ann Arbor, MI 48103-2137, USA

Lousma, Jack R Colonel (Astronaut)
2722 Roseland Dr
Ann Arbor, MI 48103-2137, USA

Loustel, Ron (Athlete, Hockey Player)
7-116 Wellington Cres
Winnipeg, MB R3M 0A9, Canada

Loutty, All (Prime Minister)
29 Ahmed Hesmat St
Zamalek
Cairo, EGYPT

Loux, Shane (Athlete, Baseball Player)
5965 Secluded Ct
Sylvania, OH 43560-9218, USA

Lovato, Demi (Actor)
c/o Cara Hutchison *The Lede Company*
401 Broadway Ste 206
New York, NY 10013-3033, USA

Love, Ben H (Misc)
1327 Anna Ct
Boy Scouts of America
Cedar Park, TX 78613-4022, USA

Love, Courtney (Musician, Songwriter)
c/o Jen Appel *Grandstand Media*
138 W 25th St Fl 9
New York, NY 10001-7405, USA

Love, Darlene (Actor, Musician)
c/o Len Evans *Project Publicity*
540 W 43rd St
New York, NY 10036, USA

Love, Duval (Athlete, Football Player)
c/o Steve Feldman *Paragon Sports & Entertainment*
30100 Town Center Dr # 196
Laguna Niguel, CA 92677-2064, USA

Love, Faizon (Actor)
c/o Paula Rosenberg *ICA Talent Management*
1112 Montana Ave Ste 520
Santa Monica, CA 90403-7236, USA

Love, Ian (Musician)
c/o Staff Member *Paradigm (Monterey)*
404 W Franklin St
Monterey, CA 93940-2303, USA

Love, Kevin (Athlete, Basketball Player)
c/o Staff Member *Cleveland Cavaliers*
1 Center Ct
Cleveland, OH 44115-4001, USA

Love, Loni (Actor, Comedian)
c/o Bryan deCastro *East 2 West Collective*
11022 Santa Monica Blvd Ste 350
Los Angeles, CA 90025-7532, USA

Love, Mike (Musician)
c/o Elliott Lott *Boulder Creek Entertainment*
PO Box 91002
San Diego, CA 92169-3002, USA

Love, Patricia (Writer)
c/o Author Mail *Bantam-Dell Publishing (NY)*
1745 Broadway
New York, NY 10019-4640, USA

Love, Randy (Athlete, Football Player)
2202 Fairlands Dr
Garland, TX 75040-1158, USA

Love, Sean (Athlete, Football Player)
121 Hunter St
Tamaqua, PA 18252-2405, USA

Love, Stan (Athlete, Basketball Player)
1950 Egan Way
Lake Oswego, OR 97034-2728, USA

Love, Stanley G (Astronaut)
4315 Indian Sunrise Ct
Houston, TX 77059-5582, USA

Love, Stanley G Dr (Astronaut)
4315 Indian Sunrise Ct
Houston, TX 77059-5582, USA

Love & Rockets (Music Group)
4 The Lakes Bushey
Hertfordshire WD2 1HS, UK

Love III, Davis (Athlete, Golfer)
Love Golf Design
100 Retreat Rd
Saint Simons Island, GA 31522-2491, USA

Lovejoy, Deirdre (Actor)
c/o Kelli M Jones *Status PR (NY)*
59 Chelsea Piers
Level 3
New York, NY 10011-1008, USA

Lovelace, Alan (Astronaut)
440 S Babcock St
Melbourne, FL 32901-1276, USA

Lovelace, Vance (Athlete, Baseball Player)
5608 12th Ave S
Tampa, FL 33619-3756, USA

Lovelady, Edwin (Athlete, Football Player)
2707 Glenwood Pkwy # B
Chattanooga, TN 37404-1712, USA

Loveless, Patty (Musician, Songwriter)
c/o Staff Member *WME|IMG*
9601 Wilshire Blvd
Beverly Hills, CA 90210-5213, USA

Lovell, James A Captain (Astronaut)
964 Lake Rd
Lake Forest, IL 60045-2223, USA

Lovell, James A, Jr (Astronaut)
Lovell Communications
PO Box 49
Lake Forest, IL 60045-0049, USA

Lovell, Jaqueline (Sara Saint James) (Actor, Adult Film Star)
c/o Staff Member *Martin and Donalds*
2131 Hollywood Blvd Ste 308
Hollywood, FL 33020-6751, USA

Lovell, Jim (Astronaut)
Lovell Communications
PO Box 49
Lake Forest, IL 60045-0049, USA

Lovell, Vella (Actor)
c/o Mona Loring *Status PR*
PO Box 6191
Westlake Village, CA 91359-6191, USA

Lovemark, Jaime (Athlete, Golfer)
16449 La Via Feliz
Rancho Santa Fe, CA 92067, USA

Lovering, David (Musician)
PO Box 373
Los Olivos, CA 93441-0373, USA

Loverne, David (Athlete, Football Player)
2307 Amber Falls Dr
Rocklin, CA 95765-4200, USA

Lovetere, John (Athlete, Football Player)
445 Old Statesville Rd
Watertown, TN 37184-4827, USA

Lovett, Lyie (Musician, Songwriter, Writer)
Haber Corp
1016 17th Ave S # 1
Nashville, TN 37212-2202, USA

Lovett, Lyle (Musician)
c/o Ken Levitan *Vector Management*
PO Box 120479
Nashville, TN 37212-0479, USA

Lovett, Ruby (Musician)
Myers Media
PO Box 378
Canton, NY 13617, USA

Lovett, Steve (Actor)
c/o Steve Lovett *Lovett Management*
1327 Brinkley Ave
Los Angeles, CA 90049-3619, USA

Lovibond, Ophelia (Actor)
c/o Brantley Brown *Authentic Talent & Literary Management*
3615 Eastham Dr # 650
Culver City, CA 90232-2410, USA

Loviglio, Jay (Athlete, Baseball Player)
23 3rd Ave
East Islip, NY 11730-2015, USA

Loville, Derek (Athlete, Football Player)
3020 E Camelback Rd Ste 213
Phoenix, AZ 85016-4423, USA

Lovitt, Hayley (Actor)
c/o Bill Perlman *Foundation Media Partners*
23679 Calabasas Rd # 625
Calabasas, CA 91302-1502, USA

Lovitz, Jon (Actor, Comedian, Producer, Writer)
c/o Chuck Binder *Binder & Associates*
1465 Lindacrest Dr
Beverly Hills, CA 90210-2519, USA

Lovrich, Pete (Athlete, Baseball Player)
19119 Weber Rd Apt 3
Mokena, IL 60448-1034, USA

Lovsin, Ken (Athlete, Hockey Player)
Freson Bros 114-440148 St
Stonv Plain, AB T7Z 1N3, Canada

Lovullo, Torey (Athlete, Baseball Player)
32108 Sailview Ln
Westlake Village, CA 91361-3619, USA

Lovuolo, Frank (Athlete, Football Player)
6 Pleasant Ct
Binghamton, NY 13905-1516, USA

Low, Reed (Athlete, Hockey Player)
1869 Pomme Rd
Arnold, MO 63010-2453

Lowder, Kyle (Actor)
c/o Michael P Levine *Levine Management*
8549 Wilshire Blvd # 212
Beverly Hills, CA 90211-3104, USA

Lowdermilk, Dwayne (Athlete, Hockey Player)
National Training Rink
110-20740 Mufford Cres
Langley, BC V2Y 1N9, Canada

Lowdermilk, R Kirk (Athlete, Football Player)
8080 Apollo Rd NE
Kensington, OH 44427-9626, USA

Lowe, Chad (Actor)
c/o David Rose *Innovative Artists*
1505 10th St
Santa Monica, CA 90401-2805, USA

Lowe, Cortland (Athlete, Golfer)
713 Taylor Ridge Rd
Winston Salem, NC 27106-5075, USA

Lowe, Crystal (Actor, Model)
c/o Tyman Stewart *Characters Talent Agency*
200-1505 2nd Ave W
Vancouver, BC V6H 3Y4, CANADA

Lowe, Darren (Athlete, Hockey Player)
55 Harbord St
UNIVERSITY OF TORONTO
Toronto, ON M5S 2W6, Canada

Lowe, Derek (Athlete, Baseball Player)
12711 Terabella Way
Fort Myers, FL 33912-0910, USA

Lowe, Gary (Athlete, Football Player)
2671 Tift Way NW
Kennesaw, GA 30152-6002, USA

Lowe, Kevin (Athlete, Coach, Hockey Player)
Edmonton Oilers
11230 110 St NW
Edmonton, AB T5G 3H7, Canada

Lowe, Lloyd (Athlete, Football Player)
8805 Deerwood Dr
Rowlett, TX 75088-4809, USA

Lowe, Nick (Musician, Songwriter)
c/o Paul Charles *Asgard Promotions*
125 Parkway
London NW1 7PS, UNITED KINGDOM

Lowe, Norman Odie (Athlete, Hockey Player)
137-5484 25 Ave
Vernon, BC V1T 7A8, Canada

Lowe, Paul (Athlete, Football Player)
5134 Logan Ave
San Diego, CA 92114-6221, USA

Lowe, Rob (Actor)
PO Box 5038
Santa Barbara, CA 93150-5038, USA

Lowe, Sean (Athlete, Baseball Player)
802 Oak Dr
Mesquite, TX 75149-4028, USA

Lowe, Sidney (Athlete, Basketball Player, Coach)
2631 Wallingford Rd
Winston Salem, NC 27101-1923, USA

Lowe, Stephanie (Athlete, Golfer)
2004 Delancey Dr
Norman, OK 73071-3872, USA

Lowe, Woodrow (Athlete, Coach, Football Player)
Jackson-Olin High School
282 Grande View Pkwy
Maylene, AL 35114-6073, USA

Loweecey, Alice (Writer)
c/o Staff Member *Midnight Ink*
2143 Wooddale Dr
Woodbury, MN 55125-2989, USA

Lowell, Carey (Actor)
c/o Sue Leibman *Barking Dog Entertainment*
Prefers to be contacted by email or phone.
New York, NY 10014, USA

Lowell, Charlie (Musician)
Flood Burnstead McCready McCarthy
1700 Hayes St Ste 304
Nashville, TN 37203-3593, USA

Lowell, Christopher (Designer, Television Host)
The Christopher Lowell Show
2800 Olympic Blvd Fl 2
Santa Monica, CA 90404-4101, USA

Lowell, Mike (Athlete, Baseball Player)
620 Santurce Ave
Coral Gables, FL 33143-6360, USA

L. Owens, William (Congressman, Politician)
431 Cannon Hob
Washington, DC 20515-1603, USA

Lowenstein, Evan (Actor, Musician)
c/o Ruthanne Secunda *ICM Partners*
10250 Constellation Blvd Fl 7
Los Angeles, CA 90067-6207, USA

Lowenstein, Jaron (Actor, Musician)
c/o Ruthanne Secunda *ICM Partners*
10250 Constellation Blvd Fl 7
Los Angeles, CA 90067-6207, USA

Lowenstein, John (Athlete, Baseball Player)
7017 Via Locanda Ave
Las Vegas, NV 89131-0114, USA

Lower, Britt (Actor)
c/o Fred Hashagen *United Talent Agency (UTA)*
888 7th Ave Fl 7
New York, NY 10106-0700, USA

Lowery, David (Director, Producer)
c/o Craig Kestel *WME|IMG*
9601 Wilshire Blvd
Beverly Hills, CA 90210-5213, USA

Lowery, Devon (Baseball Player)
112 E Catawba St
Belmont, NC 28012-3306, USA

Lowery, Dwight (Athlete, Football Player)
c/o Frank Bauer *Sun West Sports*
7883 N Pershing Ave
Stockton, CA 95207-1749, USA

Lowery, Nick (Athlete, Football Player)
8416 E Via De Jardin
Scottsdale, AZ 85258-3207, USA

Lowery, Steve (Athlete, Golfer)
52265 Via Castile
La Quinta, CA 92253-7817, USA

Lowery, Terrell (Athlete, Baseball Player)
3565 Antigua Pl
West Sacramento, CA 95691-5822, USA

Lowes, Katie (Actor)
c/o Alexandra Crotin *The Lede Company*
9701 Wilshire Blvd # 930
Beverly Hills, CA 90212-2020, USA

Lown, Turk (Athlete, Baseball Player)
1106 Van Buren St
Pueblo, CO 81004-2832, USA

Lowndes, Jessica (Actor)
c/o Adam Goldworm *Aperture Entertainment*
7620 Lexington Ave
West Hollywood, CA 90046-5410, USA

Lowry, Calvin (Athlete, Football Player)
3500 N Capital of Texas Hwy Apt 1211
Austin, TX 78746-3385, USA

Lowry, Dave (Athlete, Hockey Player)
PO Box 1540 Stn M
Calgary, AB T2P 3B9, Canada

Lowry, Lois (Writer)
205 Brattle St
Cambridge, MA 02138-3345, USA

Lowry, Noah (Athlete, Baseball Player)
4631 Thomas Lake Harris Dr Unit 230
Santa Rosa, CA 95403-0194, USA

Lowry, Shanti (Actor)

Low Stars (Music Group)
c/o Staff Member *Paradigm (Monterey)*
404 W Franklin St
Monterey, CA 93940-2303, USA

Loy, Frank E (Misc)
Marshall German Fund
11 Dupont Cir NW Ste 400
Washington, DC 20036-1226, USA

Loynd, Mike (Athlete, Baseball Player)
16652 Benton Taylor Dr
Chesterfield, MO 63005-4861, USA

Lozada, Evelyn (Actor, Reality Star)
c/o Matt Kirschner *Talent Resources*
124 E 36th St Ste A
New York, NY 10016-3402, USA

Lozada, Johnny (Actor)
c/o Staff Member *Televisa*
Blvd Adolfo Lopez Mateos 232
Colonia San Angel INN
DF CP 01060, MEXICO

Lozado, Willie (Athlete, Baseball Player)
1555 Edwardsville Galena Rd
Georgetown, IN 47122-8702, USA

Lozano, Conrad (Musician)
Gold Mountain
3575 Cahuenga Blvd W Ste 450
Los Angeles, CA 90068-1364, USA

Lozano, Karyme (Actor)
c/o Ivan De Paz *DePaz Management*
2011 N Vermont Ave
Los Angeles, CA 90027-1931, USA

Lozano Barragan, Javier Cardinal (Religious Leader)
Health Care Workers Assistance
Via Conciliazione 3
Rome 00193, ITALY

L. Richmond, Cedric (Congressman, Politician)
415 Cannon Hob
Washington, DC 20515-2211, USA

L. Rush, Bobby (Congressman, Politician)
2268 Rayburn Hob
Washington, DC 20515-0502, USA

Ishinabe, Yutaka (Chef)
Queen Alice GuestHouse 3-2-33 Nishi Azabu
Minato-ku, Tokyo, Japan

Isikoff, Michael (Writer)
123 Main St # A
Irvington, NY 10533-1718, USA

Lu, Edward T (Ed) (Astronaut)
12332 Kosich Pl
Saratoga, CA 95070-3575, USA

Lu, Lisa (Actor)
c/o Andrew Ooi *Echelon Talent Management*
2915 Argo Pl
Burnaby, BC V3J 7G4, CANADA

Lu, Qihui (Artist)
100-301
398 Xin-Pei Road
Xin-Zuan, Shanghai, CHINA

Lubich, Bronko (Wrestler)
3146 Whitemarsh Cir
Dallas, TX 75234-2239, USA

Lubich, Silvia Chiara (Misc)
Focolare Movement
306 Via di Frascati
Rocca Di Papa, RM 00040, ITALY

Lubin, Steven (Musician)
State University of New York
School of Arts
Purchase, NY 10577, USA

Lubischer, Steve (Athlete, Football Player)
6 Fiore Ct
Oceanport, NJ 07757-1405, USA

Lublin, Nancy (Business Person)
Do Something
19 W 21st St Fl 8
New York, NY 10010-6853, USA

Lubotsky, Mark (Musician)
Overtoom 329 III
Amsterdam, JM 01054, NETHERLANDS

Lubratich, Steve (Athlete, Baseball Player)
24 Sackett Rd
Lee, NH 03861-6616, USA

Luc, Tone (Actor, Musician)
Headline Talent
1650 Broadway Ste 508
New York, NY 10019-6833, USA

Lucado, Max (Religious Leader, Writer)
Oak Hills Church of Christ
6929 Camp Bullis Rd
San Antonio, TX 78256-2334, USA

Lucas, Craig (Director, Producer, Writer)
c/o Staff Member *Gersh*
9465 Wilshire Blvd Ste 600
Beverly Hills, CA 90212-2605, USA

Lucas, Dan (Athlete, Hockey Player)
609 Forest Ave
Portland, ME 04101-1515

Lucas, Dave (Athlete, Hockey Player)
15 Peels Lane
Lindsay, ON K9V 2X8, CANADA

Lucas, Dick (Athlete, Football Player)
1231 Spring Valley Ln
West Chester, PA 19380-5111, USA

Lucas, Erin (Actor, Reality Star)
c/o Staff Member *Creative Management Entertainment Group (CMEG)*
2050 S Bundy Dr Ste 280
Los Angeles, CA 90025-6128, USA

Lucas, Gary (Athlete, Baseball Player)
1511 High St
Rice Lake, WI 54868-1874, USA

Lucas, George (Director, Producer)
3270 Kerner Blvd # 2009
San Rafael, CA 94901-4840, USA

Lucas, Geralyn (Writer)
1349 Lexington Ave Apt 4D
New York, NY 10128-1514, USA

Lucas, Isabel (Actor)
c/o Oren Segal *Management Production Entertainment (MPE)*
9229 W Sunset Blvd Ste 301
W Hollywood, CA 90069-3417, USA

Lucas, Jerry (Athlete, Basketball Player, Olympic Athlete)
Dr Memorabilia
231 E 2nd St
Chillicothe, OH 45601-2612, USA

Lucas, Jessica (Actor)
c/o Staff Member *Thruline Entertainment*
9250 Wilshire Blvd Fl Ground
Beverly Hills, CA 90212-3352, USA

Lucas, John (Athlete, Basketball Player)
21 Pin Oak Estates Ct
Bellaire, TX 77401-4225, USA

Lucas, Josh (Actor)
8459 Ridpath Dr
Los Angeles, CA 90046-7711, USA

Lucas, Ken (Athlete, Football Player)
1108 Stamps Cv
Cleveland, MS 38732-4014, USA

Lucas, Matt (Actor, Producer, Writer)
c/o Kevin McLaughlin *Main Stage Public Relations*
Prefers to be contacted by email or phone.
New York, NY NA, USA

Lucas, Michael (Adult Film Star, Director)
Lucas Entertainment
208 W 30th St Rm 501
New York, NY 10001-0582, USA

Lucas, Ray (Athlete, Football Player)
44 Harrison Ave # 2
Harrison, NJ 07029-1331, USA

Lucas, Richard J (Richie) (Athlete, Football Player)
1238 Old Boalsburg Rd
State College, PA 16801-6152, USA

Lucas, Tim (Athlete, Football Player)
5081 S Florence Dr
Greenwood Village, CO 80111-3613, USA

Lucca, Lou (Baseball Player)
Topps
10211 Willow Bend Cir Apt 1B
Charlotte, NC 28210-8424, USA

Luccardi, Olivia (Actor)
c/o Anthony Aiello *One Entertainment (NY)*
347 5th Ave Rm 1404
New York, NY 10016-5034, USA

Lucchesi, Frank (Athlete, Baseball Player, Coach)
4703 Mill Creek Dr
Colleyville, TX 76034-3646, USA

Lucchesini, Andrea (Musician)
Arts Management Group
1133 Broadway Ste 1025
New York, NY 10010-7985, USA

Lucci, Mike (Athlete, Football Player)
3184 Middlebelt Rd
West Bloomfield, MI 48323-1937, USA

Lucci, Susan (Actor)
c/o Fran Curtis *Rogers & Cowan*
909 3rd Ave Fl 9
New York, NY 10022-4752, USA

Luce, Derrel (Athlete, Football Player)
4112 Green Oak Dr
Waco, TX 76710-1440, USA

Luce, Lew (Athlete, Football Player)
850 Symphony Isles Blvd
Ruskin, FL 33572-2764, USA

Luce, R Duncan (Misc)
20 Whitman Ct
Irvine, CA 92617-4057, USA

Luce, William (Bill) (Writer)
1400 NE 2nd Ave APT 1009
Portland, OR 97232-1144, USA

Lucebert (Artist, Writer)
Boendermakerhof 10
Bergen N-H, TB 01861, NETHERLANDS

Lucero (Musician)
c/o Staff Member *Sony Music (Miami)*
404 Washington Ave Ste 700
Miami Beach, FL 33139-6615, USA

Luchento, Tom (Horse Racer)
3 Hedge Row Ct
Columbus, NJ 08022-1129, USA

Luchko, Klara S (Actor)
Kotelmicheskaya Nab 1/15 Korp B #308
Moscow 109240, RUSSIA

Luchsinger, Susie (Musician)
Psalms Ministries
PO Box 990
Atoka, OK 74525-0990, USA

Lucic, Milan (Athlete, Hockey Player)
50 Fleet St Ste 301
Boston, MA 02109-1129, USA

Lucid, Shannon W Dr (Astronaut)
1622 Gunwale Rd
Houston, TX 77062-4538, USA

Lucie, Milan (Athlete, Hockey Player)
6256 Brooks St
Vancouver, BC V5S 3J1, Canada

Lucier, Lou (Athlete, Baseball Player)
7 Jaclyn Rae Dr
Millbury, MA 01527-3372, USA

Lucier, Wayne (Athlete, Football Player)
13 Jana Rd
Salem, NH 03079-2261, USA

Lucio, Shannon (Actor)
c/o Justin Grey Stone *Management 360*
9111 Wilshire Blvd
Beverly Hills, CA 90210-5508, USA

Luck, Andrew (Athlete, Football Player)
PO Box 441191
Indianapolis, IN 46244-1191, USA

Luck, Oliver (Athlete, Football Player)
PO Box 441191
Indianapolis, IN 46244-1191, USA

Luck, Terry (Athlete, Football Player)
920 Forrest View Ct
Canton, GA 30114-4466, USA

Luckett, Letoya (Actor)
c/o Everly Lee *Zero Gravity Management*
11110 Ohio Ave Ste 100
Los Angeles, CA 90025-3329, USA

Luckhurst, Mick (Athlete, Football Player)
103 Pierrepont Isle
Duluth, GA 30097-5908, USA

Luckinbill, Laurence (Actor)
RR 3 Flintlock Ridge Rd
Katonah, NY 10536, USA

Luckinbill, Lawrence (Actor)
PO Box 330
Georgetown, CT 06829-0330, USA

Luckinbill, Thad (Actor)
c/o Staff Member *Black Label Media*
9150 Wilshire Blvd Ste 155
Beverly Hills, CA 90212-3428, USA

Lucking, William (Actor)
c/o Staff Member *Twentieth Century Artists*
15760 Ventura Blvd Ste 700
Encino, CA 91436-3016, USA

Lucky, Lillian (Baseball Player)
243 Owens St
Niles, MI 49120-4150, USA

Lucky, Mike (Athlete, Football Player)
4156 N Morning Dove Cir
Mesa, AZ 85207-1194, USA

Lucroy, Jonathan (Athlete, Baseball Player)
9 Huntington Rd Apt 10-E
Scarsdale, NY 10583-2039, USA

Lucy, Donny (Athlete, Baseball Player)
3674 Oak Cliff Dr
Fallbrook, CA 92028-9413, USA

Lucy, Jemma (Model)
c/o Suzy Kilshaw *SuperConnector*
31 Basendale
Whetstone N20 0EG, UNITED KINGDOM

Luczo, Stephen J (Business Person)
Seagate Technology
920 Disc Dr
Scotts Valley, CA 95066-4544, USA

Ludacris (Actor, Musician, Producer)
c/o Chaka Zulu *Disturbing Tha Peace*
1451 Woodmont Ln NW
Atlanta, GA 30318-2866, USA

Ludaker, Dave (Baseball Player)
3593 Buffum St
Simi Valley, CA 93063-3215, USA

Luddington, Camilla (Actor)
c/o Tracy Steinsapir *Main Title Entertainment*
8383 Wilshire Blvd Ste 408
Beverly Hills, CA 90211-2435, USA

Luding-Rothenburger, Christa (Speed Skater)
Dresdener Eisspot-Club
Pieschener Allee 1
Dresden 01067, GERMANY

Ludington, Ronald (Athlete, Figure Skater, Olympic Athlete)
611 Thompson Station Rd
Newark, DE 19711-7505, USA

Ludlow, Elizabeth (Actor)
c/o Mitchell Gossett *Industry Entertainment Partners*
955 Carrillo Dr Ste 300
Los Angeles, CA 90048-5400, USA

Ludlum, Robert (Actor)
c/o Ben Smith *ICM Partners*
10250 Constellation Blvd Fl 7
Los Angeles, CA 90067-6207, USA

Ludwick, Eric (Athlete, Baseball Player)
7146 Madarang Ave
Las Vegas, NV 89178-8002, USA

Ludwick, Ryan (Athlete, Baseball Player)
115 Roberts Cir
Georgetown, TX 78633-1960, USA

Ludwig, Alexander (Actor)
c/o Jason Weinberg *Untitled Entertainment*
350 S Beverly Dr Ste 200
Beverly Hills, CA 90212-4819, USA

Ludwig, Craig (Athlete, Hockey Player)
8401 Albritton Dr
Frisco, TX 75036-7702, USA

Ludwig, Ken (Writer)
c/o Peter Franklin *WME|IMG (NY)*
11 Madison Ave Fl 18
New York, NY 10010-3669, USA

Ludzik, Steve (Athlete, Hockey Player)
2508 Silvan St
Niagara Falls, ON L2J 4K5, Canada

Luebber, Steve (Athlete, Baseball Player)
3302 Moorhead Dr
Joplin, MO 64804-5323, USA

Luebbers, Larry (Athlete, Baseball Player)
2045 Timberwyck Ln
Burlington, KY 41005-2500, USA

Luebke, Cory (Athlete, Baseball Player)
5077 Native Pony Trl
College Grove, TN 37046-1408, USA

Lueck, Bill (Athlete, Football Player)
4801 N Hidden Ter
Litchfield Park, AZ 85340-5066, USA

Luecken, Rick (Athlete, Baseball Player)
2902 Fontana Dr
Houston, TX 77043-1305, USA

Luetkemeyer, Blaine (Congressman, Politician)
1740 Longworth Hob
Washington, DC 20515-3503, USA

Luft, Joey (Actor)
108 E Matilija St
Ojai, CA 93023-2639

Luft, Lorna (Actor, Musician)
c/o Victoria Varela *Varela Media*
45 Rockefeller Plz Fl 20
New York, NY 10111-3193, USA

Lugar, Richard (Politician, Senator)
7841 Old Dominion Dr
McLean, VA 22102-2425, USA

Lugavere, Max (Television Host)
c/o Marcel Pariseau *True Public Relations*
3575 Cahuenga Blvd W Ste 360
Los Angeles, CA 90068-1361, USA

Lugbill, Jon (Athlete, Olympic Athlete)
American Cance Assn
2422 Grove Ave
Richmond, VA 23220-4416, USA

Luger, Lex (Athlete, Wrestler)
c/o Staff Member *World Wrestling Entertainment (WWE)*
1241 E Main St
Stamford, CT 06902-3520, USA

Lugner, Richard (Actor)
Lugner Einkaufszentrum
Lugner City Gablenzgasse 5-13
Vienna 01150, Austria

Lugo, Julio (Athlete, Baseball Player)
1555 Gants Cir
Kissimmee, FL 34744-6459, USA

Lugo, Ruddy (Athlete, Baseball Player)
1555 Gants Cir
Kissimmee, FL 34744-6459, USA

Luhrmann, Baz (Director, Producer)
c/o Staff Member *Bazmark Inq (AUS)*
PO Box 430
Kings Cross
NSW 02011, AUSTRALIA

luis, isaac (Athlete, Baseball Player)
PO Box 1167
Carolina, PR 00986-1167, USA

Luisi, Caesar (Actor)
c/o Christopher Smith *Paradigm*
8942 Wilshire Blvd
Beverly Hills, CA 90211-1908, USA

Lujack, Johnny (Athlete, Football Player, Heisman Trophy Winner)
6321 Crow Valley Dr
Bettendorf, IA 52722-6219, USA

Lujan, Ben Ray (Congressman, Politician)
330 Cannon Hob
Washington, DC 20515-4302, USA

Lujan, Fernando (Actor)
c/o Staff Member *TV Azteca*
Periferico Sur 4121
Colonia Fuentes del Pedregal
DF CP 14141, Mexico

Lukachyk, Rob (Athlete, Baseball Player)
100 High St
Woodbridge, NJ 07095-3018, USA

Lukacs, John (Writer)
c/o Staff Member *Simon & Schuster*
1230 Avenue of the Americas Fl CONC1
New York, NY 10020-1586, USA

Lukas, D Wayne (Coach)
5242 Katella Ave # 103
Los Alamitos, CA 90720-2820, USA

Lukas, DWayne (Horse Racer)
1034 Oak Canyon Ln
Glendora, CA 91741-2256, USA

Lukas, D Wayne (Race Car Driver)
5699 Happy Canyon Rd
Santa Ynez, CA 93460-9741, USA

Lukashenko, Aleksandr (President)
President's Office
JK Marks St 38
Minsk 220016, BELARUS

Lukasiak, Chloe (Dancer, Reality Star)
c/o Trixie Richter *Rogers & Cowan*
1840 Century Park E Fl 18
Los Angeles, CA 90067-2101, USA

Lukasiewicz, Mark (Athlete, Baseball Player)
4771 Lynnville Way
Clay, NY 13041-8986, USA

Lukather, Steve (Musician)
Fitzgerald-Hartley
34 N Palm St Ste 100
Ventura, CA 93001-2610, USA

Luke, Derek (Actor)
c/o Alex Spieller *Baker Winokur Ryder Public Relations*
200 5th Ave Fl 5
New York, NY 10010-3307, USA

Luke, John (Reality Star)
c/o Karen Patmas *National Talent LA*
5670 Wilshire Blvd # 1867
Los Angeles, CA 90036-5679, USA

Luke, Matt (Athlete, Baseball Player)
5262 Eucalyptus Hill Rd
Yorba Linda, CA 92886-4209, USA

Luke, Steve (Athlete, Football Player)
812 Bluffview Dr
Columbus, OH 43235-1728, USA

Luke, Tommy (Athlete, Football Player)
116 W Shore Dr
Saltillo, MS 38866-5745

Luke, Triandos (Athlete, Football Player)
PO Box 324
Phoenixville, PA 19460-0324, USA

Luken, Tom (Athlete, Football Player)
4708 Virginia Ln
Minneapolis, MN 55424-1763, USA

Luker, Rebecca (Actor)
c/o Sarah Fargo *Paradigm*
140 Broadway Ste 2600
New York, NY 10005-1011, USA

Luketic, Robert (Actor)
c/o Amanda Lundberg *42West*
600 3rd Ave Fl 23
New York, NY 10016-1914, USA

Lukin, Matt (Musician)
Legends of 21st Century
7 Trinity Row
Florence, MA 01062-1931, USA

Lukkarinen, Marjut (Skier)
Lohja Ski Team
Lohja, FINLAND

Lukowich, Bernie (Athlete, Hockey Player)
833 Gannet Crt
Victoria, BC V9B 6V6, Canada

Lukowich, Brad (Athlete, Hockey Player)
2402 Arroyo Grande
Leander, TX 78641-8885

Lukowich, Morris (Athlete, Hockey Player)
212 Scimitar Bay NW
Calgary, AB T3L 1L7, CANADA

Luksa, Chuck (Athlete, Hockey Player)
362 Kirby Cres
Newmarket, ON L3X 1G8, Canada

Lula da Silva, Luis Ignacio (President)
Palacio do Planotto
Praca dos 3 Poderas
Brasilia, DF 70 150, BRAZIL

lulo, Ken (Horse Racer)
165 Prospect St Fl 2
Passaic, NJ 07055-5160, USA

Lulu (Actor, Musician)
CIA
101 Shepherds Bush
Concorde House
London W6 7LP, UNITED KINGDOM (UK)

Lum, Mike (Athlete, Baseball Player)
3476 Cochise Dr SE
Atlanta, GA 30339-4324, USA

Lumbly, Carl (Actor)
c/o Karen Forman *Domain Talent*
1880 Century Park E Ste 1100
Los Angeles, CA 90067-1608, USA

Lumenti, Ralph (Athlete, Baseball Player)
9 Tomaso Rd
Milford, MA 01757-2224, USA

Lumley, Dave (Athlete, Hockey Player)
PO Box 610
Murfreesboro, AR 71958-0610

Lumley, Joanna (Actor)
18 Albert Square
London SW8 1BS, UNITED KINGDOM

Lumme, Jyrki (Athlete, Hockey Player)
40 Bay St
Toronto, ON M5J 2K2, Canada

Lumpkin, Sean (Athlete, Football Player)
5608 Highland Rd
Minneapolis, MN 55436-2538, USA

Luna, Barbara (Actor)
18026 Rodarte Way
Encino, CA 91316-4370, USA

Luna, Diego (Actor)
c/o Staff Member *Canana Films*
Zacatecas 142-A
Colonia Roma
Mexico City 06700, MEXICO

Luna, Gabriel (Actor)
c/o Cindy Guagenti *Baker Winokur Ryder Public Relations*
9100 Wilshire Blvd
W Tower #500
Beverly Hills, CA 90212-3415, USA

Luna-Hill, Betty (Baseball Player)
19887 Red Feather Rd
Apple Valley, CA 92307-5514, USA

Lunar, Fernando (Athlete, Baseball Player)
2147 Cielo Grande Ct
Alamogordo, NM 88310-7827, USA

Lunatics, St (Musician)
c/o Staff Member *Team Lunatics (MO)*
4246 Forest Park Ave Ste 2C
Saint Louis, MO 63108-2811, USA

Lund, Gordy (Athlete, Baseball Player)
1602 S Harvard Ave
Arlington Heights, IL 60005-3517, USA

Lund, Katia (Director)
c/o Sandra Lucchesi *Gersh*
9465 Wilshire Blvd Ste 600
Beverly Hills, CA 90212-2605, USA

Lund, Larry (Athlete, Hockey Player)
101-4593 Lakeside Rd
Penticton, BC V2A 8W4, Canada

Lunday, James (Actor)
c/o Staff Member *TLC*
1 Discovery Pl
Silver Spring, MD 20910-3354, USA

Lunday, Kenneth (Athlete, Football Player)
1419 W Locust St
Durant, OK 74701-3458, USA

Lundberg, Anders (Misc)
Goteberg University
Physiology Dept
Box 33033
Goteborg 40 033, SWEDEN

Lundberg, Brian (Athlete, Hockey Player)
7284 Walton
Lake Cowichan, BC VOR 2GO, Canada

Lunde, Martin (Arn Anderson) (Athlete, Wrestler)
10520 Wynyates Ln
Charlotte, NC 28270-2504, USA

Lundeen, George (Artist)
328 E 4th St
Loveland, CO 80537, USA

Lunden, Joan (Correspondent)
32 Orchard Hill Ln
Greenwich, CT 06831-3626, USA

Lundgren, Dolph (Actor)
c/o Craig Baumgarten *Zero Gravity Management*
11110 Ohio Ave Ste 100
Los Angeles, CA 90025-3329, USA

Lundgren, Terry (Business Person)
Federated Department Stores
151 W 34th St
New York, NY 10001-2101, USA

Lundholm, Bengt (Athlete, Hockey Player)
Ovre Gruvriset
Falun 79161, Sweden

Lundholm, Mark (Actor, Comedian)
c/o Staff Member *WME|IMG*
9601 Wilshire Blvd
Beverly Hills, CA 90210-5213, USA

Lundquist, Dave (Athlete, Baseball Player)
714 12th Ave NE
Hickory, NC 28601-2707, USA

Lundquist, David (Athlete, Baseball Player)
Hickory Crawdads
PO Box 1268
Attn: Coaching Staff
Hickory, NC 28603-1268, USA

Lundquist, Steve (Athlete, Olympic Athlete, Swimmer)
246 Northwind Dr
Stockbridge, GA 30281-6216, USA

Lundquist, Verne (Sportscaster)
NBC-TV
1710 Natches Way Unit 2
Steamboat Springs, CO 80487-9056, USA

Lundqvist, Alex (Model)
c/o Sean Patterson *SAM Worldwide*
92 Laight St Apt 9B
New York, NY 10013-2025, USA

Lundqvist, Henrik (Athlete, Hockey Player)
c/o Tony Godsick *Team 8 Global*
30650 Pinetree Rd Ste 1
Pepper Pike, OH 44124-5920, USA

Lundstedt, Tom (Athlete, Baseball Player)
PO Box 269
Ephraim, WI 54211-0269, USA

Lundstrom, Tord (Athlete, Hockey Player)
Bryn as Bygg_nads AB
Gavle 80133, Sweden

Lundy, Carmen (Musician)
Abby Hoffer
223 1/2 E 48th St
New York, NY 10017, USA

Lundy, Jessica (Actor)
c/o Staff Member *Metropolitan (MTA)*
4526 Wilshire Blvd
Los Angeles, CA 90010-3801, USA

Lundy-Paine, Brigette (Actor)
c/o Ruth Bernstein *Viewpoint Inc*
8820 Wilshire Blvd Ste 220
Beverly Hills, CA 90211-2622, USA

Luner, Jaime (Actor)
Martin Hurwitz
427 N Canon Dr Ste 215
Beverly Hills, CA 90210-4840, USA

Luner, Jamie (Actor)
c/o Jason Priluck *Priluck Company*
24045 Sylvan St
Woodland Hills, CA 91367-1248, USA

Lunghi, Cherie (Actor)
Yakety Yak
8A Bloomsbury Square
London WC1A 2NE, UNITED KINGDOM

Lunka, Zoltan (Boxer)
Weinheimer Str 2
Schriesheim 69198, GERMANY

Lunke, Hilary (Athlete, Golfer)
11701 Broad Oaks Dr
Austin, TX 78759-3713, USA

Lunn, Bob (Athlete, Golfer)
PO Box 1495
Woodbridge, CA 95258-1495, USA

Lunsford, Scott (Actor)
c/o Staff Member *Avalon Artists Group*
5455 Wilshire Blvd Ste 900
Los Angeles, CA 90036-4250, USA

Lunsford, Stephen (Actor)
c/o Bonnie Liedtke *Authentic Talent & Literary Management*
3615 Eastham Dr # 650
Culver City, CA 90232-2410, USA

Lunsford, Trey (Athlete, Baseball Player)
3955 Nail Rd
Southaven, MS 38672-6739, USA

Luongo, Chris (Athlete, Hockey Player)
103 Arabian Dr
Madison, AL 35758-6634, USA

Luongo, Roberto (Athlete, Hockey Player)
7280 Lemon Grass Dr
Parkland, FL 33076-3950, USA

Lupaschek, Ross (Athlete, Hockey Player)
11347164 Ave NW
Edmonton, AB TSX 3W1, Canada

Lupati, Mike (Athlete, Football Player)
c/o Ryan Tollner *REP 1 Sports Group*
80 Technology Dr
Irvine, CA 92618-2301, USA

Lupberger, Edwin A (Business Person)
Entergy Corp
10055 Grogans Mill Rd Ste 150
The Woodlands, TX 77380-1048, USA

Lupe, Justine (Actor)
c/o Jill McGrath *Door24*
115 W 29th St Rm 1102
New York, NY 10001-5106, USA

Lupica, Mike (Writer)
4 Issacs Path
East Hampton, NY 11937-1897, USA

Lupien, Gilles (Athlete, Hockey Player)
77 Rue de Bleury
SPORT PROSPECTS INC
Rosemere, QC J7A 4L9, Canada

Luplow, Al (Baseball Player)
4250 E Lakecress Dr
Saginaw, MI 48603-1687, USA

Luplow, Al (Athlete, Baseball Player)
4250 E Lakecress Dr
Saginaw, MI 48603-1687, USA

Lupo, Benedetto (Musician)
Gerhild Baron Mgmt
Dombacher Str 41/III/3
Vienna 01170, AUSTRIA

Lupo, Frank (Producer, Writer)
c/o Staff Member *Rain Management Group*
11162 La Grange Ave
Los Angeles, CA 90025-5632, USA

LuPone, Patti (Actor, Musician)
c/o Iris Grossman *Echo Lake Management*
421 S Beverly Dr Fl 8
Beverly Hills, CA 90212-4408, USA

Lupu, Radu (Musician)
Terry Harrison Mgmt
3 Clarendon Court
Charlbury, Oxon 0X7 3PS, UNITED KINGDOM (UK)

Lupul, Jaffrey (Athlete, Hockey Player)
600 1/2 36th St
Newport Beach, CA 92663-6203, USA

Lupus, Peter (Actor)
Revolucion World Wide, LLC.
10617 E Vivid Ave
Mesa, AZ 85212-8060, USA

Lurie, Alison (Writer)
159 Sapsucker Woods Rd
Ithaca, NY 14850-1923, USA

Lurie, Alison (Writer)
Cornell University
English Dept
Ithaca, NY 14850, USA

Lurie, Jeffrey (Business Person, Football Executive)
312 Llanfair Rd
Wynnewood, PA 19096-1216, USA

Lurie, Rod (Director)
4333 Bellingham Ave
Studio City, CA 91604-1606, USA

Lurtsema, Bob (Athlete, Football Player)
17025 Kings Pl
Lakeville, MN 55044-7137, USA

Lusader, Scott (Athlete, Baseball Player)
4169 Bold Mdws
Oakland Township, MI 48306-4701, USA

Lusby, Vaughn (Athlete, Football Player)
4011 N Belt Line Rd Apt 928
Irving, TX 75038-8419, USA

Luscinski, Jim (Athlete, Football Player)
24 Crescent St # 1
Kingston, MA 02364-2254, USA

Luse, Bernadette (Athlete, Golfer)
2528 Reading Dr
Orlando, FL 32804-4938, USA

Lush, Mike (Athlete, Football Player)
910 Rebecca Ln
Orefield, PA 18069-8842, USA

Lusha, Masiela (Actor, Producer)
Illuminary Films
7046 Hollywood Blvd
Los Angeles, CA 90028-6008, USA

Lusi, Jing (Actor)
c/o Romilly Bowlby *DDA Public Relations*
192-198 Vauxhall Bridge Rd
London SW1V 1DX, UNITED KINGDOM

Lusis, Janis (Athlete, Track Athlete)
Vesetas 8-3
Riga, 1013, LATVIA

Lusk, Herbert (Athlete, Football Player)
71 Palomar Real
Campbell, CA 95008-4206, USA

Lusk, Jacob (Musician)
c/o Simon Fuller *XIX Entertainment (UK)*
32/33 Ransomes Dock
London SW11 4NP, UNITED KINGDOM (UK)

Lussier, Patrick (Director)
c/o Adriana Alberghetti *WME|IMG*
9601 Wilshire Blvd
Beverly Hills, CA 90210-5213, USA

Lustig, Aaron (Actor)
525 S Niagara St
Burbank, CA 91505-4719, USA

Lustig, William (Producer)
15016 Marble Dr
Sherman Oaks, CA 91403-4521, USA

Lustiger, Jean-Marie Cardinal (Religious Leader)
Maison Dioceine
8 Rue de la Ville-l'Eveque
Paris 75008, FRANCE

Lutes, Eric (Actor)
c/o Kate Edwards *Grand View Management*
578 Washington Blvd # 688
Marina Del Rey, CA 90292-5442, USA

Luther, Bobbi Sue (Actor, Model)
c/o Staff Member *Paradigm*
8942 Wilshire Blvd
Beverly Hills, CA 90211-1908, USA

Luther, Ed (Athlete, Football Player)
30486 Le Prt
Laguna Niguel, CA 92677-5537, USA

Luttrell, Marcus (Writer)
c/o Don Epstein *Greater Talent Network Inc*
437 5th Ave Ste 8A
New York, NY 10016-2205, USA

Luttrell, Rachel (Actor)
c/o Staff Member *SMS Talent*
8383 Wilshire Blvd Ste 230
Beverly Hills, CA 90211-2436, USA

Lutui, Taitusi ""Deuce"" (Athlete, Football Player)
4514 E Mountain Sage Dr
Phoenix, AZ 85044-6086, USA

Lutz, Bob (Athlete, Tennis Player)
101 Via Ensueno
San Clemente, CA 92672-2456, USA

Lutz, Bob (Business Person)
3966 Pleasant Lake Rd
Ann Arbor, MI 48103-9628, USA

Lutz, Joleen (Actor)
8019 1/2 Melrose Ave Ste 3
Los Angeles, CA 90046-7032, USA

Lutz, Kellan (Actor)
c/o Ryan Daly *Zero Gravity Management*
11110 Ohio Ave Ste 100
Los Angeles, CA 90025-3329, USA

Lutz, Mark (Actor)
c/o Nancy LeFeaver *LeFeaver Talent Management Ltd*
202-2 College St
Toronto, ON M5G 1K3, CANADA

Lutz, Matilda (Actor)
c/o Cara Tripicchio *Shelter PR*
5670 Wilshire Blvd Ste 1200
Los Angeles, CA 90036-5621, USA

Luu, Chan (Designer)
818 S Broadway Fl 6
Los Angeles, CA 90014-3224, USA

Luuloa, Keith (Athlete, Baseball Player)
30905 Young Dove St
Menifee, CA 92584-8358, USA

LuValle, James (Athlete, Track Athlete)
1174 Los Altos Ave Apt 160
Los Altos, CA 94022-1062, USA

Luvana, Carmen (Adult Film Star)
c/o Adam & Eve Productions
9445 De Soto Ave
Chatsworth, CA 91311-4920, USA

Lüvland, Rolf (Musician)
c/o Staff Member *Continental Artist Management AS*
Sandakerveien 24 D, F2
Oslo N-0473, Norway

Luyties, Ricci (Athlete, Olympic Athlete, Volleyball Player)
University of California - San Diego
2215 Hartford St San
Diego, CA 92110-2336, USA

Lu Yu, Chen (Talk Show Host, Television Host)
c/o Staff Member *Phoenix TV / HongKong Shenzhen*
No. 2-6 Dai King St
Tai Po Industrial Estate
Tai Po, N. T. Hong Kong

Luzhkov, Yuri M (Politician)
Government of Moscow
Tverskaya Str 13
Moscow 103032, RUSSIA

Luzi, Mario (Writer)
Via Belle Riva 20
Florence 50136, ITALY

Luzinski, Greg (Athlete, Baseball Player)
25680 Streamlet Ct
Bonita Springs, FL 34135-7829, USA

Luzinski, Ryan (Athlete, Baseball Player)
25680 Streamlet Ct
Bonita Springs, FL 34135-7829, USA

Ivey, James (Cartoonist)
5840 Dahlia Dr Apt 7
Orlando, FL 32807-3251, USA

Iwamura, Akinori (Athlete, Baseball Player)
623 Saxony Blvd
Saint Petersburg, FL 33716-1297, USA

L. Watt, Melvin (Congressman, Politician)
2304 Rayburn Hob
Washington, DC 20515-4206, USA

Lydecker, Libby Hudson (Actor)
c/o Paul Greenstone *Paul Greenstone Entertainment*
1400 California Ave Apt 201
Santa Monica, CA 90403-4395, USA

Lyden, Mitch (Athlete, Baseball Player)
6055 NW 72nd Ct
Parkland, FL 33067-2441, USA

Lydman, Toni (Athlete, Hockey Player)
6035 Corinne Ln
Clarence Center, NY 14032-9510, USA

Lydon, James (Jimmy) (Actor)
3538 Lomacitas Ln
Bonita, CA 91902-1105, USA

Lydon, John (Johnny Rotten) (Musician)
31962 Pacific Coast Hwy
Malibu, CA 90265-2506, USA

Lydon, Malcolm (Astronaut)
684 E Pelham Rd NE
Atlanta, GA 30324-5202, USA

Lydy, Scott (Athlete, Baseball Player)
4278 S Leoma Ln
Chandler, AZ 85249-4782, USA

Lye, Mark (Athlete, Golfer)
6230 Lightbourn Way
Naples, FL 34113-8386, USA

Lyght, Todd (Athlete, Football Player)
1598 Martingale St
Eugene, OR 97401-6964, USA

Lyle, Garry (Athlete, Football Player)
222 Beach Dr NE
Saint Petersburg, FL 33701-3414, USA

Lyle, George (Athlete, Hockey Player)
33754 N 69th St
Scottsdale, AZ 85266-7014, USA

Lyle, Kami (Musician, Songwriter, Writer)
DS Mgmt
2814 12th Ave S Ste 202
Nashville, TN 37204-2513, USA

Lyle, Keith (Athlete, Football Player)
9615 Maypan Pl
Seminole, FL 33777-4906, USA

Lyle, Sandy (Athlete, Golfer)
4905 Duck Creek Ln
Ponte Vedra Beach, FL 32082-3023, USA

Lyle, Sparky (Athlete, Baseball Player)
2906 Santa Maria Dr
Gilbertsville, PA 19525-9322, USA

Lyles, Lester (Athlete, Football Player)
6315 14th St NW
Washington, DC 20011-8003, USA

Lyles, Robert (Athlete, Football Player)
PO Box 1075
Jackson, MS 39215, USA

Lyman, Dorothy (Actor)
Alan Vizuary Co
8909 W Olympic Blvd Ste 200
Beverly Hills, CA 90211-3543, USA

Lyman, Dustin (Athlete, Football Player)
10529 Dacre Pl
Lone Tree, CO 80124-9788

Lynch, Arthur (Athlete, Football Player)

Lynch, Cynthia (Athlete, Wrestler)
4205 Bridlepath Pl
Louisville, KY 40245-1971, USA

Lynch, David (Director)
David Lynch Foundation
216 E 45th St Fl 12
New York, NY 10017-3304, USA

Lynch, Dustin (Musician)
c/o Staff Member *WME (Nashville)*
1201 Demonbreun St
Nashville, TN 37203-3140, USA

Lynch, Ed (Athlete, Baseball Player)
27600 N 66th Way
Scottsdale, AZ 85266-6756, USA

Lynch, Edele (Musician)
Clintons
55 Drury Lane
Covent Garden
London WC2B 5SQ, UNITED KINGDOM (UK)

Lynch, Evanna (Actor)
c/o Ricky Rollins *Hyphenate Creative Management*
8149 Santa Monica Blvd # 111
West Hollywood, CA 90046-4912, USA

Lynch, Fran (Athlete, Football Player)
2553 Lake Vista Dr
Broomfield, CO 80023-4528, USA

Lynch, George (Basketball Player)
5930 Royal Ln
Dallas, TX 75230-3849, USA

Lynch, Holly (Actor)
c/o Scott Karp *The Syndicate*
8265 W Sunset Blvd Ste 205
West Hollywood, CA 90046-2470, USA

Lynch, Jack (Athlete, Hockey Player)
23 Cynthia Crt
Barrie, ON L4M 2X3, Canada

Lynch, Jair (Athlete, Gymnast, Olympic Athlete)
9207 Three Oaks Dr
Silver Spring, MD 20901-3363, USA

Lynch, Jane (Actor)
8610 Lookout Mountain Ave
Los Angeles, CA 90046-1816, USA

Lynch, Jennifer (Director, Producer)
c/o Ross Fineman *Fineman Entertainment*
4370 Tujunga Ave Ste 235
Studio City, CA 91604-2779, USA

Lynch, Jessica (Beauty Pageant Winner)
c/o Staff Member *Miss New York City Scholarship Organization*
35 E 19th St Fl 2
New York, NY 10003-1313, USA

Lynch, Jim (Athlete, Football Player)
1717 W 91st Pl
Kansas City, MO 64114-3237, USA

Lynch, John (Athlete, Football Player)
831 NE 72nd St
Boca Raton, FL 33487-2439, USA

Lynch, John Carroll (Actor)
c/o James Suskin *Suskin Management*
2 Charlton St Apt 5K
New York, NY 10014-4970, USA

Lynch, Keavy (Musician)
Clintons
55 Drury Lane
Covent Garden
London WC2B 5SQ, UNITED KINGDOM (UK)

Lynch, Kelly (Actor, Model)
c/o Mark Temple *Law Offices of Mark Temple, The*
10880 Wilshire Blvd Ste 2070
Los Angeles, CA 90024-4118, USA

Lynch, Lashana (Actor)
c/o Danielle Robinson *Alan Siegel Entertainment*
9200 W Sunset Blvd Ste 804
West Hollywood, CA 90069-3603, USA

Lynch, Lorenzo (Athlete, Football Player)
864 Bentwater Pkwy
Cedar Hill, TX 75104-8287, USA

Lynch, Marshawn (Athlete, Football Player)
c/o Doug Hendrickson *Relativity Sports*
2029 Century Park E Ste 1550
Century City, CA 90067-3000, USA

Lynch, Richard (Actor)
Richard Sindell
1910 Holmby Ave Apt 1
Los Angeles, CA 90025-5936, USA

Lynch, Ross (Actor)
c/o Stella Alex *Savage Agency*
1041 N Formosa Ave
West Hollywood, CA 90046-6703, USA

Lynch, Shane (Musician)
Carol Assoc-War Mgmt
Bushy Park Road
57 Meadowbank
Dublin, IRELAND

Lynche, Michael (Musician)
c/o Simon Fuller *XIX Entertainment (UK)*
32/33 Ransomes Dock
London SW11 4NP, UNITED KINGDOM (UK)

Lynde, Janice (Actor)
c/o David Moore *Moore Artist's Management*
310 Washington Blvd Ste 117
Marina Del Rey, CA 90292-5149, USA

Lyndon, Frank (Musician)
Paramount Entertainment
PO Box 12
Far Hills, NJ 07931-0012, USA

Lyne, Adrian (Director)
9876 Beverly Grove Dr
Beverly Hills, CA 90210-2120, USA

Lynette, Lady (Actor)
11979 Rochester Ave Apt 6
Los Angeles, CA 90025-2136, USA

Lyngstad, Anni-Frida (Musician, Songwriter, Writer)
Mono Music
Sodra Brobaeken 41A
Skeppsholmen
Stockholm 111 49, Sweden

Lynley, Carol (Actor)
Don gerler
3349 Cahuenga Blvd W Ste 1
Los Angeles, CA 90068-1379, USA

Lynn, Anthony (Athlete, Football Player)
1508 Brook Ln
Celina, TX 75009-2279, USA

Lynn, Betty (Actor)
The Surry Arts Council
PO Box 141
218 Rockford St
Mount Airy, NC 27030-0141, USA

Lynn, Cheryl (Actor, Musician)
c/o Jeff Epstein *M.A.G./Universal Attractions*
15 W 36th St Fl 8
New York, NY 10018-7927, USA

Lynn, Eleanor (Actor)
136 Lonford Dr S
San Francisco, CA 94080, USA

Lynn, Fred (Athlete, Baseball Player)
7336 El Fuerte St
Carlsbad, CA 92009-6409, USA

Lynn, Janet (Athlete, Olympic Athlete, Speed Skater)
4215 Marsh Ave
Rockford, IL 61114-6143, USA

Lynn, Johnnie (Athlete, Football Player)
5 Woodvalley Ct
Reisterstown, MD 21136-4629, USA

Lynn, Johnny (Athlete, Football Player)
238 Hidden Dr
Blackwood, NJ 08012-4432, USA

Lynn, Jonathan (Director)
c/o Mike Marcus *Echo Lake Management*
421 S Beverly Dr Fl 8
Beverly Hills, CA 90212-4408, USA

Lynn, Keith (Race Car Driver)
Schnitz Racing
222 N 3rd St
Decatur, IN 46733-1377, USA

Lynn, Loretta (Musician, Songwriter)
44 Hurricane Mills Rd
Hurricane Mills, TN 37078-2147, USA

Lynn, Meredith Scott (Actor)
Rigberg Roberts Rugolo
1180 S Beverly Dr Ste 601
Los Angeles, CA 90035-1158, USA

Lynn, Na'im (Comedian)
c/o Jeff Witjas *Agency for the Performing Arts (APA)*
405 S Beverly Dr Ste 500
Beverly Hills, CA 90212-4425, USA

Lynn, Salomon Janet (Figure Skater)
2193 Tollisontown Rd
Sparta, TN 38583-6572, USA

Lynn, Vera (Actor, Musician)
Hampers Croft Common Ln
Ditchling, East Sussex BN6 8TH, UNITED KINGDOM

Lynn Allen, Ginger (Actor, Adult Film Star, Model)
5965 Nora Lynn Dr
Woodland Hills, CA 91367-1056, USA

Lynn Chadwick, Aimee (Actor)
c/o Melanie Sharp *Sharp Talent*
117 N Orlando Ave
Los Angeles, CA 90048-3403, USA

Lynne, Jeff (Musician)
c/o Staff Member *Gallissas*
Wielandstrasse 17
Berlin 10629, Germany

Lynne, Shelby (Musician, Songwriter, Writer)
c/o Staff Member *WME/IMG*
9601 Wilshire Blvd
Beverly Hills, CA 90210-5213, USA

Lynskey, Melanie (Actor)
c/o Imogen Johnson *Johnson and Laird Management*
P.O. Box 78340
Grey Lynn Auckland 01245, NEW ZEALAND

Lynyrd Skynyrd (Music Group)
c/o Staff Member *Vector Management*
PO Box 120479
Nashville, TN 37212-0479, USA

Lyn-Z (Musician)
3820 San Rafael Ave
Los Angeles, CA 90065-3225, USA

Lyon, Brandon (Athlete, Baseball Player)
526 W 8th S
Preston, ID 83263-1459, USA

Lyon, Sue (Actor)
1244 Havenhurst Dr
West Hollywood, CA 90046-4911, USA

Lyonne, Natasha (Actor, Producer)
c/o Sara Planco *Viewpoint Inc*
89 5th Ave Ste 402
New York, NY 10003-3020, USA

Lyons, Barry (Athlete, Baseball Player)
1079 Frank P Corso St
Biloxi, MS 39530-1922, USA

Lyons, Bill (Athlete, Baseball Player)
811 Tomahawk
Heyworth, IL 61745-9309, USA

Lyons, Brooke (Actor)
c/o Staff Member *Burstein Company*
15304 W Sunset Blvd Ste 208
Pacific Palisades, CA 90272-3656, USA

Lyons, Curt (Athlete, Baseball Player)
124 Virginia Dr
Richmond, KY 40475-8631, USA

Lyons, David (Actor)
c/o Annabelle Sheehan *RGM Artists*
8-12 Ann St
Surry Hills, NSW 02010, AUSTRALIA

Lyons, Elena (Actor)
c/o Brian McCabe *Venture IAB*
3211 Cahuenga Blvd W Ste 104
Los Angeles, CA 90068-1372, USA

Lyons, Jeffrey (Journalist)
205 W 57th St Apt 5DD
New York, NY 10019-2112, USA

Lyons, Jennifer (Actor)
c/o Carlos Martinez *Scribe Services Public Relations*
4445 Cartwright Ave Apt 102
Toluca Lake, CA 91602-2326, USA

Lyons, Lamar (Athlete, Football Player)
3726 Bluff Pl
San Pedro, CA 90731-7006, USA

Lyons, Marty (Athlete, Football Player)
8 White Pine Ct
Smithtown, NY 11787-1199, USA

Lyons, Mitchell W (Mitch) (Athlete, Football Player)
8080 Myers Lake Ave NE
Rockford, MI 49341-8406, USA

Lyons, Robert F (Actor)
1801 Ave of Stars
#1250
Los Angeles, CA 90067, USA

Lyons, Steve (Athlete, Baseball Player)
JD Legends Promotions
3012nd St
Hermosa Beach, CA 90254-4662, USA

Lyons, Thomas L (Athlete, Football Player)
2814 Drummond Pt SE
Atlanta, GA 30339-5332, USA

Lysacek, Evan (Figure Skater)
Toyota Sports Center
555 N Nash St
El Segundo, CA 90245-2818, USA

Lysander, Rick (Athlete, Baseball Player)
12667 Gaillon Ct
San Diego, CA 92128-6179, USA

Lyte, MC (Musician)
c/o Judy Page *Mitchell K Stubbs & Assoc*
8675 Washington Blvd Ste 203
Culver City, CA 90232-7486, USA

Lythgoe, Nigel (Producer)
Nigel Lythgoe Productions
9000 W Sunset Blvd Ste 1560
West Hollywood, CA 90069-5817, USA

Lytle, Matt (Athlete, Football Player)
4602 Irish Creek Rd
Bernville, PA 19506-8346, USA

Lytle, Roland (Athlete, Football Player)
902 Press St
Houston, TX 77020-8646, USA

Lyttle, Jim (Athlete, Baseball Player)
751 Camino Lakes Cir
Boca Raton, FL 33486-6961, USA

Lytton, Louisa (Actor)
Milton Keynes Theatre
Marlborough Gate
Central Milton Keynes MK9 3NZ, United Kingdom

Lyubimov, Alexey B (Musician)
Klimentovskiy Per 9
#12
Moscow, RUSSIA

Lyubshin, Stanislav A (Actor)
Vernadskogo Prosp 123
#171
Moscow 117571, RUSSIA

Izauierdo, Hansel (Athlete, Baseball Player)
10003 NW 9th Street Cir Apt 9
Miami, FL 33172-5120, USA

Izturis, Cesar (Athlete, Baseball Player)
7901 Hispanola Ave Apt 607
North Bay Village, FL 33141-4153, USA

M

M2M (Music Group)
c/o Staff Member *Creative Artists Agency (CAA)*
2000 Avenue of the Stars Ste 100
Los Angeles, CA 90067-4705, USA

Ma, Remy (Musician)
c/o Drew Elliot *Artist International*
333 E 43rd St Apt 115
New York, NY 10017-4822, USA

Ma, Tzi (Actor)
Greene & Associates
526 N Larchmont Blvd # 201
Los Angeles, CA 90004-1300

Ma, Yo-Yo (Musician)
54 Highland St
Cambridge, MA 02138-3332, USA

Maarleveld, John (Athlete, Football Player)
42 Carlton Pl
Rutherford, NJ 07070-1120, USA

Maas, Bill (Athlete, Football Player)
653 NE Shoreline Dr
Lees Summit, MO 64064-1382, USA

Maas, Kevin (Athlete, Baseball Player)
17672 Hillside Ct
Castro Valley, CA 94546-1403, USA

Maas, William T (Bill) (Athlete, Football Player)
PO Box 2175
Lees Summit, MO 64063-7175, USA

Mabe, Manabu (Artist)
Rua das Canjeranas 321
Jabaquara
Sao Paulo, SP, BRAZIL

Maberly, Kate (Actor)
c/o Staff Member *Hetherwood Productions*
450 S Beverly Dr
Beverly Hills, CA 90210, USA

Mabeus, Chris (Athlete, Baseball Player)
311 Doe Run Cir
Henderson, NV 89012-2705, USA

Mabius, Eric (Actor)
c/o Geordie Frey *GEF Entertainment*
533 N Las Palmas Ave
Los Angeles, CA 90004-1017, USA

Mably, Luke (Actor)
c/o Stephanie Ritz *WME|IMG*
9601 Wilshire Blvd
Beverly Hills, CA 90210-5213, USA

Mabon, Lee (Athlete, Baseball Player)
948 N Barksdale St
Memphis, TN 38107-3101, USA

Mabra, Ron (Athlete, Football Player)
155 Thornton Ct
Fayetteville, GA 30214-3830, USA

Mabrey, Sunny (Actor)
c/o Amy Slomovits *Haven Entertainment*
8111 Beverly Blvd Ste 201
Los Angeles, CA 90048-4531, USA

Mabry, John (Athlete, Baseball Player)
715 Bellerive Manor Dr
Saint Louis, MO 63141-6084, USA

Mabus, Raymond (Politician)
4004 Carson Pl
Alexandria, VA 22304-1745, USA

Mac, Fleetwood (Music Group)
c/o Carl Stubner *Sanctuary Music Management*
15301 Arizona Ave
Bldg B #400
Santa Monica, CA 91403, USA

Macadam, AL (Athlete, Hockey Player)
PO Box 232
Morell, PE C0A 1S0, Canada

MacAfee Sr, Ken (Athlete, Football Player)
26 W Elm Ter
Brockton, MA 02301-3629, USA

Macallan, Jes (Actor)
c/o Allison Garman *Rogers & Cowan*
1840 Century Park E Fl 18
Los Angeles, CA 90067-2101, USA

Macaluso, mike (Basketball Player)
9373 E Hidden Hill Ct
Lone Tree, CO 80124-5417, USA

Macapagal-Arroyo, Gloria (President)
Malacanang Palace
JP Laurel St
Metro Manila 00100, PHILIPPINES

MacArthur, Hayes (Actor)
c/o Sean Grumman *WME|IMG*
9601 Wilshire Blvd
Beverly Hills, CA 90210-5213, USA

MacArthur, Robb (Reality Star)

Macc, Willie (Actor)
Charles Belk Management
8939 S Sepulveda Blvd Ste 110 PMB 240
C/O Charles Belk
Los Angeles, CA 90045-3632, USA

Maccarone, Sam (Director)
c/o David Krintzman *Morris Yorn Barnes Levine Krintzman Rubenstein Kohner & Gellman*
2000 Avenue of the Stars Ste 300N
Tower N Fl 3
Los Angeles, CA 90067-4704, USA

Macchio, Ralph (Actor)
c/o Jill Fritzo *Jill Fritzo Public Relations*
208 E 51st St # 305
New York, NY 10022-6557, USA

Maccormack, Frank (Athlete, Baseball Player)
2 Schmidts Pl
Secaucus, NJ 07094-4110, USA

Macdermid, Paul (Athlete, Hockey Player)
1900 3rd Ave E
Attn: Owners Office Owen Sound Attack
Owen Sound, ON N4K 2M6, Canada

MacDermid, Paul (Athlete, Hockey Player)
81 Lakeland Dr
Sauble Beach, ON N0H 2G0, Canada

Macdissi, Peter (Actor)
c/o Louise Spinner Ward *United Talent Agency (UTA)*
9336 Civic Center Dr
Beverly Hills, CA 90210-3604, USA

MacDonald, Adam (Actor)
c/o Staff Member *Characters Talent Agency*
200-1505 2nd Ave W
Vancouver, BC V6H 3Y4, CANADA

MacDonald, Andrew (Athlete, Hockey Player)
c/o Staff Member *Cooney Management Company*
Four Seasons Place
Suite 1202
Boston, MA 02116, USA

Macdonald, Andrew (Producer)
c/o Staff Member *DNA Films*
10 Amwell St
London EC1R 1UQ, UNITED KINGDOM

MacDonald, Ann-Marie (Writer)
c/o Staff Member *Simon & Schuster*
1230 Avenue of the Americas Fl CONC1
New York, NY 10020-1586, USA

Macdonald, Bob (Athlete, Baseball Player)
18 Secretariat Dr
Hendersonville, NC 28792-8551, USA

MacDonald, Danielle (Actor)
c/o Siri Garber *Platform PR*
2666 N Beachwood Dr
Los Angeles, CA 90068-2308, USA

MacDonald, Iain B (Director, Producer)

MacDonald, Jeffrey (Athlete, Football Player)
9334 Cody Dr
Broomfield, CO 80021-5325, USA

MacDonald, Julien (Designer, Fashion Designer)
c/o Staff Member *Julien MacDonald*
Haydens Place
247A Portobello Road
London, England W11 1LT, United Kingdom

MacDonald, Kelly (Actor)
c/o Claire Maroussas *Independent Talent Group*
40 Whitfield St
London W1T 2RH, UNITED KINGDOM

MacDonald, Lowell (Athlete, Hockey Player)
178 Amblewood Ln
Naples, FL 34105-7147, USA

MacDonald, Mark (Athlete, Football Player)
25377 Eureka Ave
Wyoming, MN 55092-9090, USA

Macdonald, Norm (Actor, Comedian)
c/o Marc Gurvitz *Brillstein Entertainment Partners*
9150 Wilshire Blvd Ste 350
Beverly Hills, CA 90212-3453, USA

MacDonald, Paul (Athlete, Hockey Player)
81 Lakeland Dr
Sauble Beach, ON N0H 2G0, CANADA

Macdougal, Mike (Athlete, Baseball Player)
2429 N Travis
Mesa, AZ 85207-2539, USA

MacDowell, Andie (Actor)
c/o Alex Spieller *Baker Winokur Ryder Public Relations*
200 5th Ave Fl 5
New York, NY 10010-3307, USA

Macek, Don (Athlete, Football Player)
3615 Monte Real
Escondido, CA 92029-7911, USA

Macfadyen, Angus (Actor)
c/o Bradley Kramer *Kramer Management*
Prefers to be contacted by email or phone.
Na, CA NA, USA

Macfadyen, Matthew (Actor)
c/o Hylda Queally *Creative Artists Agency (CAA)*
2000 Avenue of the Stars Ste 100
Los Angeles, CA 90067-4705, USA

MacFarlane, Luke (Actor)
c/o Bonnie Bernstein *ICM Partners (NY)*
730 5th Ave
New York, NY 10019-4105, USA

Macfarlane, Mike (Athlete, Baseball Player)
14909 Alhambra St
Overland Park, KS 66224-3905, USA

MacFarlane, Rachael (Director)
c/o Joy Fehily *PMK/BNC Public Relations*
1840 Century Park E Ste 1400
Los Angeles, CA 90067-2115, USA

MacFarlane, Seth (Actor, Director)
c/o Staff Member *Fuzzy Door Productions*
9944 Santa Monica Blvd
Beverly Hills, CA 90212-1607, USA

MacGowan, Shane (Musician)
Free Trade Agency
Chapel Place
Rivington St
London EC2A 3DQ, UNITED KINGDOM (UK)

MacGraw, Ali (Actor)
c/o Alan Nevins *Renaissance Literary & Talent*
PO Box 17379
Beverly Hills, CA 90209-3379, USA

MacGregor, Bruce (Athlete, Hockey Player)
8112 NW l33rd St.
Edmonton, AB TSR OBl, CANADA

MacGregor, Jeff (Actor, Writer)
c/o Katherine Herring *HarperCollins Publishers*
195 Broadway Fl 2
New York, NY 10007-3132, USA

MacGregor, Joanna C (Musician)
Columbia Artists Mgmt Inc
165 W 57th St
New York, NY 10019-2201, USA

Macgregor, Randy (Athlete, Hockey Player)
701 Torrance Ave
Vestal, NY 13850-1338, Canada

MacGuigan, Garth (Athlete, Hockey Player)
3600 Hoya Dr APT 223
Arlington, TX 76015-3429, USA

Mach, Brian (Athlete, Hockey Player)
8715 Osprey Ln
Chanhassen, MN 55317-8565, USA

Macha, Ken (Athlete, Baseball Player, Coach)
1118 Winnie Way
Latrobe, PA 15650-9080, USA

Macha, Mike (Athlete, Baseball Player)
PO Box 865
Port O Connor, TX 77982-0865, USA

Machado, J P (Athlete, Football Player)
710 Butterfly Ln
Weldon Spring, MO 63304-7899, USA

Machado, Justina (Actor)
c/o Brit Reece *PMK/BNC Public Relations*
1840 Century Park E Ste 1400
Los Angeles, CA 90067-2115, USA

Machado, Robert (Athlete, Baseball Player)
c/o Derek Reynolds *Doyle & McKean*
530 Wilshire Blvd Ste 280
Santa Monica, CA 90401-1423, USA

Machado-Van Sant, Helene (Athlete, Baseball Player, Commentator)
1221 Marion Ave
San Bernardino, CA 92407-1217, USA

Macharski, Franciszak Cardinal (Religious Leader)
Metropolita Krakowski
Ul Franciszkanska 3
Krakow 31-004, POLAND

Machemehl, Chuck (Baseball Player)
809 Charlotte Dr
McKinney, TX 75071-6081, USA

Machemer, Dave (Athlete, Baseball Player)
222 Morning Walk Path
Benton Harbor, MI 49022-3471, USA

Machida, Lyoto (Athlete, Boxer)
c/o Staff Member *UFC*
PO Box 26959
Las Vegas, NV 89126-0959, USA

Machine Head (Music Group)
c/o Richard De La Font *Richard De La Font Agency*
3808 W South Park Blvd
Broken Arrow, OK 74011-1261, USA

Macht, Gabriel (Actor)
c/o Lindsay Krug *ID Public Relations*
7060 Hollywood Blvd Fl 8th
Los Angeles, CA 90028-6021, USA

Macht, Stephen (Actor)
248 S Rodeo Dr
Beverly Hills, CA 90212-3804, USA

Machurek, Mike (Athlete, Football Player)
686 N Senita Way
Eagle, ID 83616-6890, ID

Macias, Eduardo R (Director)
c/o Gabriel Blanco *Gabriel Blanco Iglesias (Mexico)*
Rio Balsas 35-32
Colonia Cuauhtemoc
DF 06500, Mexico

Macias, Jose (Athlete, Baseball Player)
c/o Staff Member *Stockton Ports*
404 W Fremont St
Banner Island Ballpark
Stockton, CA 95203-2806, USA

Macias, Julio (Actor)
c/o Penny Vizcarra *PV Public Relations*
121 N Almont Dr Apt 203
Beverly Hills, CA 90211-1860, USA

macieod, Bill (Athlete, Baseball Player)
14 Heritage Way
Marblehead, MA 01945-2332, USA

MacInnes Wood, Jacqueline (Actor)
c/o Janice Lee *Rogers & Cowan*
1840 Century Park E Fl 18
Los Angeles, CA 90067-2101, USA

Macinnis, Allan (Athlete, Hockey Player)
401 Wythe House Ct
Saint Louis, MO 63141-8179, USA

MacIntosh, Craig (Cartoonist)
3403 W 28th St
Minneapolis, MN 55416-4302, USA

MacIntyre, Colin (Musician)
c/o Staff Member *Paradigm (Monterey)*
404 W Franklin St
Monterey, CA 93940-2303, USA

Macintyre, Marguerite (Actor)

MacIntyre, Scott (Musician)

Macio (Musician)
c/o Staff Member *Paradigm (Monterey)*
404 W Franklin St
Monterey, CA 93940-2303, USA

Maciver, Norm (Athlete, Hockey Player)
2119 Ponderosa Cir
Duluth, MN 55811-1960, USA

Mack, Alex (Athlete, Football Player)
c/o Marvin Demoff *Morris Yorn Barnes Levine Krintzman Rubenstein Kohner & Gellman*
2000 Avenue of the Stars Ste 300N
Tower N Fl 3
Los Angeles, CA 90067-4704, USA

Mack, Allison (Actor)
c/o Michelle Bega *Rogers & Cowan*
1840 Century Park E Fl 18
Los Angeles, CA 90067-2101, USA

Mack, Bill (Athlete, Football Player)
51910 N Shoreham Ct
South Bend, IN 46637-1357, USA

Mack, Bill (Radio Personality)
Bill Mack Country, Inc.
PO Box 8777
Fort Worth, TX 76124-0777, USA

Mack, Cedric (Athlete, Football Player)
116 Chestnut St
Lake Jackson, TX 77566-5526, USA

Mack, Elbert (Athlete, Football Player)
c/o Brian Levy *Goal Line Football Management*
1025 Kane Concourse Ste 207
Bay Harbor Islands, FL 33154-2118, USA

Mack, J Kevin (Athlete, Football Player)
29359 Hummingbird Cir
Westlake, OH 44145-5287, USA

Mack, Khalil (Athlete, Football Player)
c/o Joel Segal *Lagardere Unlimited (NY)*
456 Washington St Apt 9L
New York, NY 10013-1555, USA

Mack, Quinn (Athlete, Baseball Player)
35324 Marsh Ln
Wildomar, CA 92595-9019, USA

Mack, Rico (Athlete, Football Player)
1200 R D Mack Rd
Statham, GA 30666-3140, USA

Mack, Sam (Athlete, Basketball Player)
8142S S Prairie Park Pl
Chicago, IL 60619-4800, USA

Mack, Shane (Athlete, Baseball Player, Olympic Athlete)
35324 Marsh Ln
Wildomar, CA 92595-9019, USA

Mack, Stacey (Athlete, Football Player)
1431 19th St
Orlando, FL 32805-4415, USA

Mack, Thomas (Tom) (Athlete, Football Player)
52 Grand Miramar Dr
Henderson, NV 89011-2202, USA

Mack, Tony (Baseball Player)
California Angels
431 Rogers Rd Apt 18
Lexington, KY 40505-1932, USA

Mack, Tremain (Athlete, Football Player)
3604 Rock Creek Dr
Tyler, TX 75707-1634, USA

Mack, Warner (Musician)
National Talent Agency
2260 E Apple Ave
Muskegon, MI 49442-4369, USA

Mack, William (Athlete, Football Player)
51910 N Shoreham Ct
South Bend, IN 46637-1357, USA

Mackall, Michelle (Athlete, Golfer)
2057 Oxford Ave
Cardiff By The Sea, CA 92007-1719, USA

Mackanin, Pete (Athlete, Baseball Player, Coach)
16630 N 65th St
Scottsdale, AZ 85254-1419, USA

MacKasey, Blair (Athlete, Hockey Player)
317 Washington St
Attn Dir Player Personnel
Saint Paul, MN 55102-1609, USA

Mackasey, Blair (Athlete, Hockey Player)
188 Centennial Ave
Beaconsfield, QC H9W 2J7, Canada

Mackay, David (Director)
Gersh Agency
232 N Canon Dr
Beverly Hills, CA 90210-5302, USA

Mackay, David William Donald (Astronaut)
Pear Tree Cottage
Road Winterburne Dauntsey Salisbury
Wiltshire SP46EW, UK

Mackay, Harvey (Business Person, Writer)
Mackay Envelope Corp
2100 Elm St SE
Minneapolis, MN 55414-2597, USA

Macken, Eoin (Actor)
c/o Annick Oppenheim *Wolf-Kasteler Public Relations*
6255 W Sunset Blvd Ste 1111
Los Angeles, CA 90028-7426, USA

Mackenroth, Jack (Designer, Reality Star)
c/o Steve Glick *Glick Agency*
1321 7th St Ste 203
Santa Monica, CA 90401-1631, USA

MacKenzie, Aaron (Athlete, Hockey Player)
775 Deer Meadow Dr
Loveland, CO 80537-2417, USA

Mackenzie, Barry (Athlete, Hockey Player)
562 Summerhill Cres
Sudbury, ON P3A 4Y6, Canada

MacKenzie, Benjamin (Actor)
c/o Staff Member *Management 360*
9111 Wilshire Blvd
Beverly Hills, CA 90210-5508, USA

Mackenzie, Brock (Athlete, Golfer)
c/o Jim Lehrman *Medalist Management Inc*
36855 W Main St Ste 200
Purcellville, VA 20132-3561, USA

MacKenzie, Eric (Athlete, Baseball Player)
2002 James St E
Bright's Grove, ON N0N 1C0, Canada

Mackenzie, Gordy (Athlete, Baseball Player)
PO Box 86
Fruitland Park, FL 34731-0086, USA

Mackenzie, Ken (Athlete, Baseball Player)
15 Fair St
Guilford, CT 06437-2601, USA

MacKenzie, Peter (Actor)
c/o Joel King *Pakula/King & Associates*
9229 W Sunset Blvd Ste 315
Los Angeles, CA 90069-3403, USA

Mackenzie, Warren (Artist)
8695 68th St N
Stillwater, MN 55082-7310, USA

Mackenzie, Will (Athlete, Golfer)
35 Laurel Oaks Cir
Jupiter, FL 33469-2757, USA

Mackey, Cindy (Athlete, Golfer)
1190 Millstone Run
Bogart, GA 30622-3062, USA

Mackey, John (Business Person)
Whole Foods Market
550 Bowie St
Austin, TX 78703-4644, USA

Mackey, Kyle (Athlete, Football Player)
2516 Pine Park Dr
Silsbee, TX 77656-8086, USA

Mackey, Louis (Athlete, Football Player)
7002 Winter Blossom Dr
Humble, TX 77346-3387, USA

Mackey, Malcolm (Athlete, Basketball Player)
2479 Peachtree Rd NE Apt 1101
Atlanta, GA 30305-4133, USA

Mackey, Rick (Misc)
5938 Four Mile Rd
Nanana, AK 99760, USA

Mackie, Anthony (Actor)
c/o Jason Spire *Inspire Entertainment (LA)*
2332 Cotner Ave Ste 302
Los Angeles, CA 90064-1848, USA

Mackie, Bob (Fashion Designer)
Bob Mackie Design Group, Ltd
230 Park Ave Rm 446
New York, NY 10169-0499, USA

Mackintosh, Cameron A (Producer)
Cameron Mackintosh Ltd
1 Bedford Sq
London WC1B 3RA, UNITED KINGDOM (UK)

Mackintosh, Steven (Actor)
c/o Staff Member *Yakety Yak*
25 D'Arblay St
London W1F 8EJ, UNITED KINGDOM (UK)

Macklemore (Musician)
1935 10th Ave E
Seattle, WA 98102-4252, USA

Macklin, David (Athlete, Football Player)
16042 S 14th Dr
Phoenix, AZ 85045-0613, USA

Macklin, Rudy (Athlete, Basketball Player)
10749 Hillgate Ave
Baton Rouge, LA 70810-7067, USA

Macknowski, John (Athlete, Basketball Player)
1920 Garnet Ln
Dandridge, TN 37725-4428, USA

Mackovic, John (Athlete, Football Coach, Football Player)
79295 Rancho La Quinta Dr
La Quinta, CA 92253-6217, USA

Mackowiak, Rob (Athlete, Baseball Player)
4419 Ortona Ln
Wesley Chapel, FL 33543-6439, USA

Mackrides, Bill (Athlete, Football Player)
23 Roberts Rd
Newtown Square, PA 19073-2011, USA

Mackrides, William (Athlete, Football Player)
23 Roberts Rd
Newtown Square, PA 19073-2011, USA

MacLachlan, Kyle (Actor)
c/o Alexandra Kahn *Relevant (NY)*
333 Hudson St Rm 502
New York, NY 10013-1033, USA

Maclachlan, Patricia (Writer)
21 Unquomonk Rd
Williamsburg, MA 01096-9718, USA

MacLachlan, Patricia (Writer)
21 Unquomonk Rd
Williamsburg, MA 01096-9718, USA

MacLaine, Shirley (Actor, Writer)
Maclaine Enterprises
PO Box 33950
Santa Fe, NM 87594-3950, USA

MacLean, Bonnie (Artist)
PO Box 103
Buckingham, PA 18912-0103, USA

MacLean, Don (Athlete, Basketball Player)
216 Los Padres Dr
Thousand Oaks, CA 91361-1333, USA

Maclean, Doug (Athlete, Hockey Player)
466 Notre Dame St
Summerside, PE C1N 1T3, Canada

MacLean, Doug (Coach)
330 Tucker Dr
Worthington, OH 43085-3030, USA

MacLean, John (Athlete, Coach, Hockey Player)
52 Maple Ave
Morristown, NJ 07960-5218, USA

Maclean, John (Athlete, Hockey Player)
52 Maple Ave
Morristown, NJ 07960-5218, USA

MacLean, Paul (Athlete, Hockey Player)
110-1000 Palladium Dr
Attn: Coaching Staff Ottawa Senators
Ottawa, ON K2V 1A5, Canada

Maclean, Paul (Athlete, Hockey Player)
41544 Glade Rd
Canton, MI 48187-3770, USA

MacLean, Steven G (Astronaut)
Astronaut Program
6767 Rte de L'Aeroport
Saint-Hubert, QC J3Y 8Y9, CANADA

Maclean, Steven G Dr (Astronaut)
President, Canadian Space Agency
Saint-Hubert, QC BY 8Y9, Canada

Macleay, Lachlan (Astronaut)
2520 International Cir Apt 115
Colorado Springs, CO 80910-3192, USA

Maclellan, Brian (Athlete, Hockey Player)
627 N Glebe Rd Ste 850
Attn Dir Player Personnel
Arlington, VA 22203-2129, USA

Macleod, Bill (Athlete, Baseball Player)
14 Heritage Way
Marblehead, MA 01945-2332, USA

MacLeod, Gavin (Actor)
PO Box 2608
4222 Rancho Las Palmas Dr
Rancho Mirage, CA 92270-1097, USA

MacLeod, John (Basketball Coach, Coach)
4610 E Fanfol Dr
Phoenix, AZ 85028-5206, USA

MacLeod, Lewis (Actor)
c/o Staff Member *Hobsons International*
2 Dukes Gate
London W4 5DX, UNITED KINGDOM

Macleod, Pat (Athlete, Hockey Player)
7467 Ivy Hills Pl
Cincinnati, OH 45244-3041, USA

Macleod, Tom (Athlete, Football Player)
15412 N Hazard Rd
Spokane, WA 99208-8289, USA

Maclin, Jeremy (Athlete, Football Player)
c/o Ben Dogra *Relativity Sports*
2029 Century Park E Ste 1550
Century City, CA 90067-3000, USA

Maclin, Lonnie (Athlete, Baseball Player)
9635 Meeks Blvd
Saint Louis, MO 63132-1507, USA

MacMahon, Brian (Misc)
89 Warren St
Needham, MA 02492-3115, USA

MacMahon, Julian (Actor)

MacManus, Tristan (Dancer)
c/o Josh Sabarra *Breaking News PR*
9601 Wilshire Blvd Ste 1106
Beverly Hills, CA 90210-5213, USA

Macmillan, Bill (Athlete, Hockey Player)
Upper Meadowbank Rd RR 2
Cornwall, PE COA IHO, Canada

Macmillan, Bob (Athlete, Hockey Player)
The Sport Page Club 236 Kent St
Charlottetown PE ClA 1P3, Canada

Macmillan, Duncan L. (Business Person)
Bloomberg L.P.
731 Lexington Ave Fl LL2
New York, NY 10022-1346, USA

MacMillan, John (Athlete, Hockey Player)
2672 W Conifer Dr
Eagle, ID 83616-4667, USA

MacMillan, Shannon (Soccer Player)
Portland University
Athletic Dept
Portland, OR 97203, USA

Macneil, AL (Athlete, Hockey Player)
151 Parkview Way SE
Calgary, AB T2J 4N3, Canada

MacNeil, Bernie (Athlete, Hockey Player)
1014 Cunningham Rd
Kingston, ON K7L 4V3, Canada

MacNeil, Karen (Writer)
Karen MacNeil & Company
1335 Main St Ste 109
Saint Helena, CA 94574-1940, USA

MacNeil, Robert (Correspondent, Writer)
c/o Staff Member *Penguin Press HC*
375 Hudson St Bsmt 3
New York, NY 10014-7465, USA

Macneil, Robert (Journalist)
2700 S Quincy St
Arlington, VA 22206-2242, USA

MacNichol, Peter (Actor)
International Creative Mgmt
8942 Wilshire Blvd # 219
Beverly Hills, CA 90211-1908, USA

MacNicol, Peter (Actor)
c/o Ron West *Thruline Entertainment*
9250 Wilshire Blvd Fl Ground
Beverly Hills, CA 90212-3352, USA

Macoherson, Harry (Athlete, Baseball Player)
971 Bay Vista Blvd
Englewood, FL 34223-2405, USA

Macomber, Debbie (Writer)
c/o Irene Goodman *Irene Goodman Literary Agency*
27 W 24th St Ste 700B
New York, NY 10010-4105, USA

Macomber, George B H (Skier)
1 Design Center Pl Ste 600
Boston, MA 02210-2349, USA

Macon, Eddie (Athlete, Football Player)
140 Westmoor Ave
Daly City, CA 94015-3842, USA

Macosko, Anna (Athlete, Golfer)
1315 Tanglewood Dr
Commerce, TX 75428-3835, USA

MacPhail, Andy (Baseball Player)
Chicago Cubs
1080 Sunset Rd
Winnetka, IL 60093-3625, USA

Macphail, Andy (Commentator)
12403 Hunters Gin
Owings Mills, MD 21117-1040, USA

Macpherson, Daniel (Actor)
c/o Danica Smith *Kovert Creative*
506 Santa Monica Blvd Ste 400
Santa Monica, CA 90401-2412, USA

Macpherson, Elle (Model)
c/o Michael McConnell *Zero Gravity Management (II)*
5660 Silver Valley Ave
Agoura Hills, CA 91301-4000, USA

Macpherson, Harry (Athlete, Baseball Player)
971 Bay Vista Blvd
Englewood, FL 34223-2405, USA

Mac Quayle (DJ)
c/o Staff Member *Diva Central Inc*
7510 W Sunset Blvd # 1445
Los Angeles, CA 90046-3408, USA

Macrae, Scott (Athlete, Baseball Player)
1164 Forest Brook Ct
Marietta, GA 30068-2827, USA

MacSweyn, Ralph (Athlete, Hockey Player)

MacTavish, Craig (Athlete, Coach, Hockey Player)
2301 Ravine Way
Attn: Coaching Staff
Glenview, IL 60025-7627, USA

Maculan, Tim (Actor)
c/o Christopher Black *Opus Entertainment*
5225 Wilshire Blvd Ste 905
Los Angeles, CA 90036-4353, USA

Macwhorter, Keith (Athlete, Baseball Player)
PO Box 323
Swansea, MA 02777-0323, USA

Macy, Kyle (Athlete, Basketball Player)
3308 Nantucket Dr
Lexington, KY 40502-3205, USA

Macy, William H (Actor)
c/o Staff Member *The Actors Studio*
432 W 44th St
New York, NY 10036-5205, USA

Madball (Music Group)
c/o Paul Gourlie *UTA Music/The Agency Group*
9336 Civic Center Dr
Beverly Hills, CA 90210-3604, USA

Maddalena, Julie (Actor)
c/o Staff Member *Tisherman Gilbert Motley Drozdoski Talent Agency (TGMD)*
6767 Forest Lawn Dr # 101
Los Angeles, CA 90068-1027, USA

Maddaloni, Martin J (Misc)
Plumbing & Pipe Fitting Union
901 Massachusetts Ave NW
Washington, DC 20001-4307, USA

Madden, Beezie (Athlete, Horse Racer, Olympic Athlete)
3980 Stone Bridge Rd
Cazenovia, NY 13035-9535, USA

Madden, Benji (Musician)
c/o Lori Sale *Artist & Brand Management*
9320 Wilshire Blvd Ste 212
Beverly Hills, CA 90212-3217, USA

Madden, David (Writer)
Louisiana State University
US Civil War Center
Baton Rouge, LA 70803-0001, USA

Madden, Diane (Dancer)
Trisha Brown Dance Co
211 W 61st St
New York, NY 10023-7832, USA

Madden, D S (Religious Leader)
American Baptist Assn
4605 N State Line Ave
Texarkana, TX 75503-2916, USA

Madden, Joe (Athlete, Baseball Player)
2515 S Ysabella Ave
Tampa, FL 33629-6238, USA

Madden, Joel (Musician)
c/o Staff Member *Fein Music*
81 Pondfield Rd Ste 236
Bronxville, NY 10708-3818, USA

Madden, John (Director)
c/o Jenne Casarotto *Casarotto Ramsay & Associates Ltd (UK)*
Waverley House
7-12 Noel St
London W1F 8GQ, UNITED KINGDOM

Madden, John (Athlete, Football Coach, Football Player, Sportscaster)
c/o Sandy Montag *The Montag Group*
7 Renaissance Sq Fl 2
White Plains, NY 10601-3039, USA

Madden, John (Athlete, Hockey Player)
115 NW 7th St
Boca Raton, FL 33432-2623, USA

Madden, John P (Director)
William Morris Agency
52/53 Poland Place
London W1F 7LX, UNITED KINGDOM (UK)

Madden, Mike (Athlete, Baseball Player)
4733 Frankfort Way
Denver, CO 80239-5922, USA

Madden, Morris (Athlete, Baseball Player)
105 Jennings St
Laurens, SC 29360-3317, USA

Madden, Richard (Actor)
c/o Conor McCaughan *Troika*
10A Christina St.
London EC2A 4PA, UNITED KINGDOM

Madden, Steve (Designer)
Steve Madden Ltd
5216 Barnett Ave
Long Island City, NY 11104-1018, USA

Maddie & Tae (Music Group)
c/o Jake Basden *Big Machine Records*
1219 16th Ave S
Nashville, TN 37212-2901, USA

Maddix, Raydell (Athlete, Baseball Player)
4108 Oak Knoll Ct APT 39
Tampa, FL 33610-2462, USA

Maddock, Robert (Athlete, Football Player)
3541 Geranium Ave
Corona Del Mar, CA 92625-1673, USA

Maddon, Joe (Athlete, Baseball Player, Coach)
2153 E Inca St
Mesa, AZ 85213-3419, USA

Maddow, Rachel (Journalist, Radio Personality)
c/o Staff Member *MSNBC*
30 Rockefeller Plz
New York, NY 10112-0015, USA

Maddox, Bob (Athlete, Football Player)
7612 Colson Dr
Louisville, KY 40220-3358, USA

Maddox, Elliott (Athlete, Baseball Player)
34006 Pickford Ct
Wesley Chapel, FL 33545-4859, USA

Maddox, Garry (Athlete, Baseball Player)
312 Wynne Ln
Penn Valley, PA 19072-1338, USA

Maddox, Jerry (Athlete, Baseball Player)
20647 Thundersky Cir
Riverside, CA 92508-3177, USA

Maddox, Mark (Athlete, Football Player)
PO Box 3922
Chandler, AZ 85244-3922, USA

Maddox, Robert (Athlete, Football Player)
7612 Colson Dr
Louisville, KY 40220-3358, USA

Maddox, Tommy (Athlete, Football Player)
265 Wild Wood Dr
Decatur, TX 76234-4791, USA

Maddux, Greg (Athlete, Baseball Player)
20 Painted Feather Way
Las Vegas, NV 89135-7855, USA

Maddux, Mike (Athlete, Baseball Player)
PO Box 90111
Arlington, TX 76004-3111, USA

Maddy, Penelope Jo (Misc)
University of California
Philosophy Dept
Irvine, CA 92717, USA

Madekwe, Ashley (Actor)
c/o Christina Gualazzi *Silver Lining Entertainment*
421 S Beverly Dr Fl 7
Beverly Hills, CA 90212-4408, USA

Madeley, Darrin (Athlete, Hockey Player)
Lake Forest Academy 1500 W Kennedy Rd
Lake Forest, IL 60045-1047, USA

Mader, Rebecca (Actor)
c/o Allan Grifka *Alchemy Entertainment*
7024 Melrose Ave Ste 420
Los Angeles, CA 90038-3394, USA

Maderos, George (Athlete, Football Player)
12 Spinnaker Way
Chico, CA 95926-1627, USA

Madi, Ferenc (President)
Egyetem Ter 1-3
Budapest 01364, HUNGARY

Madigan, Amy (Actor)
c/o Staff Member *Industry Entertainment Partners*
955 Carrillo Dr Ste 300
Los Angeles, CA 90048-5400, USA

Madigan, Connie (Athlete, Hockey Player)
7655 NE Alameda St
Portland, OR 97213-5931, USA

Madigan, Kathleen (Comedian)
c/o Michael O'Brien *Michael OBrien Entertainment*
Prefers to be contacted by telephone or email
New York, NY 10012, USA

Madigan, Sam (Athlete, Football Player)
3685 Heron Ridge Ln
Weston, FL 33331-3711, USA

Madill, Jeff (Athlete, Hockey Player)
6812 NW 104th St
Kansas City, MO 64154-1882, USA

Madio, James (Actor)
c/o Steve Maihack *44 West Entertainment*
151 Petaluma Blvd S Apt 311
Petaluma, CA 94952-5185, USA

Madise, Adrian (Athlete, Football Player)
1561 Drury Dr
Dallas, TX 75232-1939, USA

Madison, Bailee (Actor)
c/o Annick Oppenheim *Wolf-Kasteler Public Relations*
6255 W Sunset Blvd Ste 1111
Los Angeles, CA 90028-7426, USA

Madison, Dora (Actor)
c/o Mia Hansen *Portrait PR*
5320 Sylmar Ave
Sherman Oaks, CA 91401-5612, USA

Madison, Holly (Model, Reality Star)
817 N Orange Dr
Los Angeles, CA 90038-3325, USA

Madison, Martha (Actor)
c/o Jason Egenberg *Authentic Talent & Literary Management*
3615 Eastham Dr # 650
Culver City, CA 90232-2410, USA

Madison, Sam (Athlete, Football Player)
13153 SW 25th Pl # Pi
Davie, FL 33325-5140, USA

Madison, Scotti (Athlete, Baseball Player)
5397 Thornapple Ln NW
Acworth, GA 30101-7886, USA

Madison, Scotty (Athlete, Baseball Player)
5397 Thornapple Ln NW
Acworth, GA 30101-7886, USA

Madkins, Gerald (Athlete, Basketball Player)
528 W 8th St
Merced, CA 95341-6023, USA

Madlock, Bill (Athlete, Baseball Player)
104 Prairie Ave Apt 1
Highwood, IL 60040-1714, USA

Madoff, Bernard (Bernie) (Business Person)
Butner Low FCI
PO Box 999
Butner, NC 27509-0999, USA

Madonna (Actor, Dancer, Musician, Songwriter)
c/o Guy Oseary *Maverick Management*
9350 Civic Center Dr Ste 100
Beverly Hills, CA 90210-3629, USA

Madore, Joe (Race Car Driver)
Jam Motorsports
400 S Vermont Ave Ste 125
Oklahoma City, OK 73108-1025, USA

Madrid, Alex (Athlete, Baseball Player)
PO Box 1974
Saint Johns, AZ 85936-1974, USA

Madrigal, Al (Actor, Comedian)
c/o Geoff Cheddy *Brillstein Entertainment Partners*
9150 Wilshire Blvd Ste 350
Beverly Hills, CA 90212-3453, USA

Madritsch, Bobby (Athlete, Baseball Player)
8628 Linder Ave
Burbank, IL 60459-2928, USA

Madrugada (Music Group)
c/o Staff Member *Paradigm (Monterey)*
404 W Franklin St
Monterey, CA 93940-2303, USA

Madsen, Loren (Artist)
426 Broome St
New York, NY 10013-3251, USA

Madsen, Mark (Basketball Player)
10132 Gristmill Rdg
Eden Prairie, MN 55347-4760, USA

Madsen, Michael (Actor)
c/o Chuck Binder *Binder & Associates*
1465 Lindacrest Dr
Beverly Hills, CA 90210-2519, USA

Madsen, Virginia (Actor)
PO Box 5370
Sherman Oaks, CA 91413-5370, USA

Madson, Michael (Actor)
The Firm
9100 Wilshire Blvd Ste 100W
Beverly Hills, CA 90212-3435, USA

Madson, Ryan (Athlete, Baseball Player)
16 Thomas Rd
Ladera Ranch, CA 92694-1544, USA

Maduro, Calvin (Athlete, Baseball Player)
793 Springdale Dr
Millersville, MD 21108-1435, USA

Mae, Vanessa (Actor, Musician)
c/o Staff Member *UTA Music/The Agency Group (UK)*
361-373 City Rd
London EC1V 1PQ, UNITED KINGDOM

Maegle, Dick (Athlete, Football Player)
4207 Deforest Ridge Cir
Katy, TX 77494-4444, USA

Maehl, Jeff (Athlete, Football Player)

Maese, Joe (Athlete, Football Player)
3202 Murray Rd
Finksburg, MD 21048-2408, USA

Maestro, Mia (Actor)
c/o Pamela Kohl *3 Arts Entertainment*
9460 Wilshire Blvd Fl 7
Beverly Hills, CA 90212-2713, USA

Maffay, Peter (Actor)
Klenzestr. 1
Tutzing, GERMANY D-82327

Maffett, Debra Sue (Debbie) (Beauty Pageant Winner)
1525 McGavock St
Nashville, TN 37203, USA

Maffia, Roma (Actor)
c/o Staff Member *Artists & Representatives (Stone Manners Salners)*
6100 Wilshire Blvd Ste 1500
Los Angeles, CA 90048-5110, USA

Maga, Mickey (Actor)
123 Jasper St Spc 24
Encinitas, CA 92024-2069, USA

Magadan, Dave (Athlete, Baseball Player)
3733 Johnathon Ave
Palm Harbor, FL 34685-3605, USA

Magallanes, Ever (Athlete, Baseball Player)
834 Governor St
Costa Mesa, CA 92627-3342, USA

Magee, Alex (Athlete, Football Player)
c/o Roosevelt Barnes *Independent Sports & Entertainment (ISE-IN)*
6435 W Jefferson Blvd # 197
Fort Wayne, IN 46804-6203, USA

Magee, Andrew (Andy) (Athlete, Golfer)
6100 E Huntress Dr
Paradise Valley, AZ 85253-4217, USA

Magee, Brandon (Athlete, Football Player)
c/o Blake Baratz *The Institute for Athletes*
3600 Minnesota Dr Ste 550
Edina, MN 55435-7925, USA

Magee, Calvin (Athlete, Football Player)
1985 2320 Comanche Trl
Grand Prairie, TX 75052-8595, USA

Magee, Dave (Race Car Driver)
9398 N Meridian Rd
Fortville, IN 46040-9733, USA

Magee, Dave (Horse Racer)
9398 N Meridian Rd
Fortville, IN 46040-9733, USA

Magee, Wendell (Athlete, Baseball Player)
6500 Muskogee Cv
Leeds, AL 35094-3868, USA

Maggard, Dave (Athlete, Track Athlete)
University of Houston
Athletic Dept
Houston, TX 77204-0001, USA

Maggart, Brandon (Actor)
8730 W Sunset Blvd Ste 480
Los Angeles, CA 90069-2277

Maggart, Garett (Actor)
c/o Staff Member *SDB Partners Inc*
315 S Beverly Dr Ste 411
Beverly Hills, CA 90212-4301, USA

Maggert, Jeff (Athlete, Golfer)
62 W Bracebridge Cir
Spring, TX 77382-2539, USA

Maggette, Corey (Basketball Player)
Los Angeles Clippers
1111 S Figueroa St
Staples Center
Los Angeles, CA 90015-1300, USA

Maggs, Darryl (Athlete, Hockey Player)
20902 E US Highway 24
Woodland Park, CO 80863-9018, USA

Maggs, Don (Athlete, Football Player)
38335 Tamarac Blvd Apt 212
Willoughby, OH 44094-8193, USA

Magic Numbers, The (Music Group)
c/o Dan Moore *SuperVision Management Group*
Zeppelin Building
59-61 Farringdon Rd
London EC1M 3JB, UK

Magilton, Gerald E (Jerry) (Astronaut)
Marlin Marietta Astro Space
100 Campus Dr
Newtown, PA 18940-1784, USA

Magilton, Gerard (Astronaut)
Martin Marietta Astro Space
100 Campus Dr
Newtown, PA 18940-1784, USA

Maginnes, John (Athlete, Golfer)
612 Topwater Ln
Greensboro, NC 27455-3458, USA

Magliozzi, Ray (Television Host)

Magnante, Mike (Athlete, Baseball Player)
5305 Via Quinto
Newbury Park, CA 91320-6937, USA

Magnus, Edie (Correspondent)
NBC-TV
30 Rockefeller Plz
News Dept
New York, NY 10112-0015, USA

Magnus, Johnny (Actor)
c/o Staff Member *Cassell-Levy Inc*
843 N Sycamore Ave
Los Angeles, CA 90038-3316, USA

Magnus, Sandra H (Sandy) (Astronaut)
2010 Legend Grove Ct
Houston, TX 77062-8046, USA

Magnus, Siobhan (Musician)
c/o Simon Fuller *XIX Entertainment (UK)*
32/33 Ransomes Dock
London SW11 4NP, UNITED KINGDOM (UK)

Magnussen, Jan (Race Car Driver)
5294 Winder Hwy
Braselton, GA 30517-1709, USA

Magoon, Bob (Misc)
1688 Meridian Ave
Miami Beach, FL 33139-2710, USA

Magrane, Joe (Athlete, Baseball Player)
221 S Rome Ave APT 116
Tampa, FL 33606-1866, USA

Magrane, Shannon (Musician)
c/o Staff Member *19 Entertainment*
401 Wilshire Blvd Ste 1070
Santa Monica, CA 90401-1428, USA

Magrann, Tom (Athlete, Baseball Player)
910 N 31st Ct
Hollywood, FL 33021-5509, USA

Magrath, Kelly (Race Car Driver)
Jim Dunn Racing
840 Kallin Ave
Long Beach, CA 90815-5004, USA

Magri, Charles G (Charlie) (Boxer)
345 Bethnal Green Road
Bethnal Green
London E2 6LG, UNITED KINGDOM (UK)

Magrini, Pete (Athlete, Baseball Player)
2402 Rancho Cabeza Dr
Santa Rosa, CA 95404-2326, USA

Magro, Ronnie (Reality Star)
c/o Matt Cohen *IAG Entertainment & Sports*
5189 Argonne Ct
San Diego, CA 92117-1054, USA

Magruder, Chris (Athlete, Baseball Player)
1740 Leisure Ln
Yakima, WA 98908-9224, USA

Magsamen, Sandra (Artist, Writer)
Orchard Books/Scholastic
557 Broadway
New York, NY 10012-3962, USA

Maguire, Gregory (Writer)
HarperCollins Children's Books
1350 Avenue of the Americas
New York, NY 10019-4702, USA

Maguire, Kevin (Athlete, Hockey Player)
Toronto Maple Leafs
400-40 Bay St
Alumni Association President
Toronto, ON M5J 2X2, CANADA

Maguire, Les (Musician)
Barry Collins
21A Cliftown Road
Southend-on-Sea
Essex SS1 1AB, UNITED KINGDOM (UK)

Maguire, Paul L (Athlete, Football Player, Sportscaster)
707 Ocean Blvd
Isle Of Palms, SC 29451-2136, USA

Maguire, Sean (Actor)
c/o Liz York *Principal Entertainment*
9255 W Sunset Blvd Ste 500
Los Angeles, CA 90069-3301, USA

Maguire, Tobey (Actor)
Maguire Entertainment
9220 W Sunset Blvd Ste 300
Los Angeles, CA 90069-3503, USA

Magyar, Derek (Actor)
c/o Staff Member *Wilkins Management*
12200 W Olympic Blvd Ste 400
Los Angeles, CA 90064-1047, USA

Mahaffey, Art (Athlete, Baseball Player)
3140 W Tilghman St
PO Box 261
Allentown, PA 18104-4222, USA

Mahaffey, John (Athlete, Golfer)
594 Sawdust Rd Unit 229
Spring, TX 77380-2215, USA

Mahaffey, Randy (Athlete, Basketball Player)
25 Berkeley Rd
Avondale Estates, GA 30002-1468, USA

Mahaffey, Valerie (Actor)
c/o Steven Muller *Innovative Artists*
1505 10th St
Santa Monica, CA 90401-2805, USA

Mahal, Taj (Musician, Songwriter, Writer)
c/o Staff Member *Red Light Management*
5800 Bristol Pkwy Ste 400
Culver City, CA 90230-6898, USA

Mahalic, Drew (Athlete, Football Player)
2114 SW Sunset Dr
Portland, OR 97239-2066, USA

Mahan, Hunter (Athlete, Golfer)
3316 Snowmass Ln
McKinney, TX 75070-6007, USA

Mahar, kevin (Baseball Player)
2506 E Wheeler St
Midland, MI 48642-3178, USA

Maharidge, Date D (Writer)
Stanford University
Communications Dept
Stanford, CA 94305, USA

Maharis, George (Actor)
9100 Wilshire Blvd Ste 333E
Beverly Hills, CA 90212-3405, USA

Mahay, Ron (Athlete, Baseball Player)
1825 N Rose St
Burbank, CA 91505-1317, USA

Mahe, Reno (Athlete, Football Player)
2619 Knollbrook Ln
Spring, TX 77373-9130, USA

Mahendru, Annet (Actor)
c/o Susan Ferris *Bohemia Group*
1680 Vine St Ste 518
Los Angeles, CA 90028-8833, USA

Maher, Bill (Talk Show Host)
c/o CeCe Yorke *True Public Relations*
3575 Cahuenga Blvd W Ste 360
Los Angeles, CA 90068-1361, USA

Mahfouz, Robbie (Athlete, Football Player)
181 Belle Terre Blvd
Covington, LA 70433-4734, USA

Mahlberg, Greg (Athlete, Baseball Player)
5100 N Placita Del Lazo
Tucson, AZ 85750-1535, USA

Mahler, Mickey (Athlete, Baseball Player)
7911 Quirt St
San Antonio, TX 78227-2636, USA

Mahlum, Eric (Athlete, Football Player)
17794 NW Solano Ct
Portland, OR 97229-2210, USA

Maholm, Paul (Athlete, Baseball Player)
135 Wild Mdws
Hattiesburg, MS 39402-8108, USA

Mahomes, Pat (Baseball Player)
Minnesota Twins
3110 Oleander Dr
Tyler, TX 75707-2000, USA

Mahon, Sean (Actor)
c/o Staff Member *McCabe Group*
3211 Cahuenga Blvd W Ste 104
Los Angeles, CA 90068-1372, USA

Mahone, Austin (Musician)
PO Box 409009
Fort Lauderdale, FL 33340-9009, USA

Mahoney, Brian (Athlete, Basketball Player)
96 Greystone Rd
Rockville Centre, NY 11570-4515, USA

Mahoney, Dan (Writer)
13 Swan Ln
Levittown, NY 11756-3921, USA

Mahoney, David L (Business Person)
McKesson HBOX Inc
1 Post St Ste 107
San Francisco, CA 94104-5203, USA

Mahoney, Jim (Athlete, Baseball Player)
345 Hawthorne Ave # 2
Apt R19
Hawthorne, NJ 07506-1244, USA

Mahoney, Marie (Athlete, Baseball Player, Commentator)
2121 Pinegate Dr
Houston, TX 77008-1388, USA

Mahoney, Marle (Baseball Player)
2218 Saxon Dr
Houston, TX 77018-4640, USA

Mahoney, Mike (Athlete, Baseball Player)
4412 98th St
Urbandale, IA 50322-1362, USA

Mahony, Cardinal Roger (Religious Leader)
3424 Wilshire Blvd
Los Angeles, CA 90010-2263, USA

Mahood, Beverley (Musician)
c/o Staff Member *Paquin Entertainment Agency (Winnipeg)*
468 Stradbrook Ave
Winnipeg MB M6K 3J1, CANADA

Mahorn, Rick (Athlete, Basketball Player)
3091 Mapleridge Ct
Rochester Hills, MI 48309-4505, USA

Mahovlich, Francis W (Frank) (Athlete, Hockey Player)
The Senate of Canada 908 Victoria Bldg
Room 908-VB
Ottawa, ON K1A OA4, Canada

Mahovlich, Peter (Athlete, Hockey Player)
116 Farr Ln
Queensbury, NY 12804-1989, USA

Mahre, Phil (Athlete, Olympic Athlete, Skier)
Mahre Training Center
PO Box 739
Deer Valley Resort
Park City, UT 84060-0739, USA

Mahre, Steve (Athlete, Olympic Athlete, Skier)
7610 W Chestnut Ave
Yakima, WA 98908-1553, USA

Maiava, Kaluka (Athlete, Football Player)
c/o Ken Zuckerman *Priority Sports & Entertainment - (LA)*
15233 Ventura Blvd Ste 718
Sherman Oaks, CA 91403-2237, USA

Maida, Adam J Cardinal (Religious Leader)
Archdiocese of Detroit
1234 Washington Blvd Ste 1
Detroit, MI 48226-1894, USA

Maida, Raine (Musician)
c/o Staff Member *Paradigm (Monterey)*
404 W Franklin St
Monterey, CA 93940-2303, USA

Maidlow, Steve (Athlete, Football Player)
1311 Garfield Ave
Springfield, OH 45504-1430, USA

Maier, Hermann (Athlete, Skier)
Im 8 ErJet
Unterbergasse
Flachau 05542, Austria

Maier, Mitch (Baseball Player)
19142 Hadley St
Stilwell, KS 66085-9442, USA

Maier, Sepp (Soccer Player)
Parkstr 62
Anzing 84405, GERMANY

Maietta, Mike (Race Car Driver)
154 Pleasant Hill Rd Ste 5
Scarborough, ME 04074-7119, USA

Mailhot, Jacques (Athlete, Hockey Player)
2303 Canyon Springs Dr
Belton, TX 76513-1055

Mailhouse, Robert (Actor)
1623 N Dillon St
Los Angeles, CA 90026-1203, USA

Maillard, Carol (Musician)
Sweet Honey Agency
PO Box 600099
Newtonville, MA 02460-0001, USA

Maine, John (Athlete, Baseball Player)
16332 Autumn Cove Ln
Huntersville, NC 28078-1327, USA

Maine, Scott (Baseball Player)
470 Bella Vista Ct N
Jupiter, FL 33477-5560, USA

Maines, Natalie (Musician)
c/o Erica Gerard *PMK/BNC Public Relations*
622 3rd Ave Fl 8
New York, NY 10017-6707, USA

Maines, Nicole (Actor)
c/o Dede Binder-Goldsmith *Defining Artists Agency*
8721 W Sunset Blvd Ste 209
W Hollywood, CA 90069-2272, USA

Mair, Adam (Athlete, Hockey Player)
25 San Fernando Ln
East Amherst, NY 14051-2235, USA

Mairena, Oswaldo (Athlete, Baseball Player)
160 E Athletics Way # Pi
Mesa, AZ 85201-5068, USA

Maisel, Lucian (Actor)
c/o Marc Hamou *Thruline Entertainment*
9250 Wilshire Blvd Fl Ground
Beverly Hills, CA 90212-3352, USA

Maisenberg, Olega (Musician)
In Der Gugl 9
Klostemeuburg, AUSTRIA

Maisky, Mischa M (Musician)
Columbia Artists Mgmt Inc
165 W 57th St
New York, NY 10019-2201, USA

Maisonneuve, Brian (Soccer Player)
Columbus Crew
2121 Volman Ave
Columbus, OH 43211, USA

Maitland, Jack (Athlete, Football Player)
3079 N Palm Aire Dr
Pompano Beach, FL 33069-3457, USA

Maitreya, Sananda (Musician)
Sananda Records
Sempione 38
Milan 20154, ITALY

Majerle, Dan (Athlete, Basketball Player, Olympic Athlete)
Maherle's Sports Bar
24 N 2nd St
Phoenix, AZ 85004-2319, USA

Majewski, Gary (Athlete, Baseball Player)
1103 Chamboard Ln
Houston, TX 77018-3212, USA

Majewski, Val (Athlete, Baseball Player)
890 Oakley Dr
Freehold, NJ 07728-8237, USA

Majkowski, Don (Athlete, Football Player)
1593 Bayhill Dr
Duluth, GA 30097-5980, USA

Majoli, Iva (Tennis Player)
27 Framingham Ln
Pittsford, NY 14534-1047, USA

Major, Clarence L (Writer)
University of California
English Dept
Voorhies Hall
Davis, CA 95616, USA

Major, John (Politician)
House of Commons
London, England

Majorino, Tina (Actor)
c/o Abby Bluestone *Innovative Artists*
1505 10th St
Santa Monica, CA 90401-2805, USA

Major Lazer (Musician)
c/o Dana Meyerson *Biz 3 Publicity*
1321 N Milwaukee Ave # 452
Chicago, IL 60622-9151, USA

Majors, Bobby (Athlete, Football Player)
9631 Pecan Springs Cir
Chattanooga, TN 37421-4722, USA

Majors, Faith (Actor)
c/o David Shapira *David Shapira & Associates*
193 N Robertson Blvd
Beverly Hills, CA 90211-2103, USA

Majors, John I (Johnny) (Athlete, Coach, Football Coach, Football Player)
4207 Beechwood Rd
Knoxville, TN 37920-6011, USA

Majors, Jonathan (Actor)
c/o Carrie Gordon *The Lede Company*
401 Broadway Ste 206
New York, NY 10013-3033, USA

Majors, Lee (Actor)
1831 Rocking Horse Dr
Simi Valley, CA 93065-5913, USA

Majtyka, Roy (Baseball Player)
2082 Orangeside Rd
Palm Harbor, FL 34683-3340, USA

Majumder, Shaun (Actor, Comedian, Musician)
c/o Chris Schmidt *Paradigm*
8942 Wilshire Blvd
Beverly Hills, CA 90211-1908, USA

Makar, Jimmy (Race Car Driver)
131 Ridgecliff Dr
Statesville, NC 28677-9000, USA

Makarov, Askold A (Dancer)
Plutalova Str 18-4
Saint Petersburg 197136, RUSSIA

Makarov, Sergei (Athlete, Hockey Player)
190 12th Ave
Santa Cruz, CA 95062-4802, USA

Makarova, Inna V (Actor)
Ukrainian Blvd 11
Moscow 121059, RUSSIA

Makatsch, Heike (Actor)
c/o Sybille Breitbach *Wasted Management*
Dieffenbachstrasse 33
Berlin D-10967, Germany

Make Good Your Escape (Music Group)
c/o Staff Member *Paradigm (Monterey)*
404 W Franklin St
Monterey, CA 93940-2303, USA

Makela, Mikko (Athlete, Hockey Player)
27 Rivermont Cres W
MIKKO MAKELA'S DEVELPMENTAL HOCKEY
Lethbridge, AB T1K 8A4, Canada

Maker, Marvin (Horse Racer)
RR 1 Box 201
Pemberton, NJ 08068, USA

Maki, Ally (Actor)
c/o Carly Morgan *Kovert Creative*
506 Santa Monica Blvd Ste 400
Santa Monica, CA 90401-2412, USA

Makings, Elizabeth (Athlete, Golfer)
10063 E San Bernardo Dr
Scottsdale, AZ 85258-5665, USA

Makinson, Jessica (Comedian)
c/o Staff Member *Berwick & Kovacik*
6230 Wilshire Blvd
Los Angeles, CA 90048-5126, USA

Makkena, Wendy (Actor)
c/o Jeanne Nicolosi *Nicolosi & Company*
150 W 25th St Rm 1200
New York, NY 10001-7404, USA

Mako (Actor)
6477 Peppertree Ln
Somis, CA 93066-9758, USA

Makowski, Tom (Athlete, Baseball Player)
6686 Omphalius Rd
Colden, NY 14033-9763, USA

Makowsky, Bruce (Designer)
77 Beverly Park Ln
Beverly Hills, CA 90210-1571, USA

Maksudian, Mike (Athlete, Baseball Player)
12148 E San Simeon Dr
Scottsdale, AZ 85259-6049, USA

Malahide, Patrick (Actor)
International Creative Mgmt
76 Oxford St
London W1N 0AX, UNITED KINGDOM (UK)

Malakar, Sanjaya (Musician, Reality Star)
c/o Staff Member *SUM Company*
10736 Jefferson Blvd # 140
Culver City, CA 90230-4933, USA

Malakhov, Vladimir (Athlete, Hockey Player)
PO Box 420536
Kissimmee, FL 34742-0536, USA

Malakian, Daron (Musician)
Velvet Hammer
9911 W Pico Blvd # 350
Los Angeles, CA 90035-2703, USA

Malamala, Siupeli (Athlete, Football Player)
122 110th Ave SE
Bellevue, WA 98004-6332, USA

Malandrino, Catherine (Designer, Fashion Designer)
468 Broome St
New York, NY 10013-2611, USA

Malandro, Kristina (Actor)
2518 Cardigan Ct
Los Angeles, CA 90077-1337, USA

Malanowski-Marlowe, Jean (Baseball Player)
100 Smallacombe Dr # 205-24
Scranton, PA 18508-2650, USA

Malarchuk, Clint (Athlete, Hockey Player)
PO Box 1540 Stn M
Attn: Coaching Staff
Calgary, AB T2P 3B9, Canada

Malarchuk, Clint (Athlete, Hockey Player)
1308 Myers Dr
Gardnerville, NV 89410-6166, USA

Malarkey, Michael (Actor)
c/o Matt Goldman *Silver Lining Entertainment*
421 S Beverly Dr Fl 7
Beverly Hills, CA 90212-4408, USA

Malaska, Mark (Athlete, Baseball Player)
3823 Cumberland Dr
Youngstown, OH 44515-4610, USA

Malave, Omar (Athlete, Baseball Player)
1511 Talisker Dr
Clearwater, FL 33755-1347, FL

Malchow, Tom (Athlete, Olympic Athlete, Swimmer)
10220 NW Edgewood Dr
Portland, OR 97229-7617, USA

Malco, Romany (Actor)
c/o Staff Member *Mosaic Media Group*
407 N Maple Dr # 100
Beverly Hills, CA 90210-3818, USA

Malcolm, George J (Musician)
99 Wimbledon Hill Road
London SW19 4BE, UNITED KINGDOM (UK)

Malcomson, Paula (Actor, Producer)
c/o Heidi Lopata *Narrative*
1601 Vine St Fl 6
Los Angeles, CA 90028-8802, USA

Maldini, Paolo (Coach, Soccer Player)
AC Milan
Via Turati 3
Washington, DC 20221-0001, ITALY

Maldonado, Candy (Athlete, Baseball Player)
HC 2 Box 16800
Arecibo, PR 00612-9396, USA

Maleeva, Katerina (Tennis Player)
Mladostr 1 #45
NH 14
Sofia 01174, BULGARIA

Maleeva-Fragniere, Manuela (Tennis Player)
Bourg-Dessous 28
La Tour de Peitz 01814, SWITZERLAND

Malek, Rami (Actor)
c/o Marisa Martins *The Lede Company*
401 Broadway Ste 206
New York, NY 10013-3033, USA

Maler, Jim (Athlete, Baseball Player)
5132 SW 129th Ter
Miramar, FL 33027-5839, USA

Malerba, Dr Franco (Astronaut)
Atlantis Via Cantore 14/2
Genova, Italy

Malerba, Franco E (Astronaut)
Via Cantore 10
Genova 16149, ITALY

Maley, David (Athlete, Hockey Player)
45 Pleasant Ave
Excelsior, MN 55331-8583, USA

Malgunas, Stewart (Athlete, Hockey Player)
6784 Westmount Cres
Prince George, BC V2N 6R3, Canada

Malick, Terrence (Director, Producer)
c/o Chris Donnelly *LBI Entertainment*
2000 Avenue of the Stars
N Tower Fl 3
Los Angeles, CA 90067-4700, USA

Malick, Wendie (Actor)
c/o Nevin Dolcefino *Innovative Artists*
1505 10th St
Santa Monica, CA 90401-2805, USA

Malicki-Sanchez, Keram (Actor)
c/o Fred Toczek *Felker, Toczek, Gellman, Suddleson*
10880 Wilshire Blvd Ste 2080
Los Angeles, CA 90024-4120, USA

Malielegaoi, Tuilaepa Sailele (Prime Minister)
Prime Minister's Office
PO Box L1861
Vailima, Apia, SAMOA

Malik, Art (Actor)
18 Sydney Mews
London SW3 6HL, UNITED KINGDOM (UK)

Malik, Marek (Athlete, Hockey Player)
919 Anchorage Rd
Tampa, FL 33602-5755, USA

Malik, Zayn (Musician)
c/o Richard Griffiths *Modest! Management*
91A Peterborough Rd
London SW6 3BU, UNITED KINGDOM

Malil, Shelley (Actor)
c/o Mark Measures *Kazarian, Measures, Ruskin & Associates*
5200 Lankershim Blvd Ste 820
N Hollywood, CA 91601-3194, USA

Malina, Joshua (Actor, Producer)
c/o Craig Schneider *Pinnacle Public Relations*
8721 Santa Monica Blvd # 133
W Hollywood, CA 90069-4507, USA

Malinchak, Bill (Athlete, Football Executive)
16824 Pierre Cir
Delray Beach, FL 33446-3692, USA

Malinin, Mike (Musician)
c/o John Branigan *WME/IMG*
9601 Wilshire Blvd
Beverly Hills, CA 90210-5213, USA

Malinowski, Merlin (Athlete, Hockey Player)
PO Box 42 Stn Main
MARYS LINCOLNS
St Marys, ON N4X 1A9, Canada

Malizia, Mike (Athlete, Golfer)
570 SE Southwood Trl
Stuart, FL 34997-6367, USA

Malkin, Evgenl (Athlete, Hockey Player)
66 Mario Lemieux Pl
Pittsburgh, PA 15219-3504, USA

Malkin, Laurence (Writer)
c/o Josh Kesselman *Thruline Entertainment*
9250 Wilshire Blvd Fl Ground
Beverly Hills, CA 90212-3352, USA

Malkin, Michelle (Correspondent)
445C E Cheyenne Mountain Blvd # 415
Colorado Springs, CO 80906-4506, USA

Malkmus, Bobby (Athlete, Baseball Player)
400 Wallingford Ter
Union, NJ 07083-7328, USA

Malkmus, Stephen (Actor, Musician)
3535 E Burnside St
Portland, OR 97214-2052, USA

Malkovich, John (Actor)
c/o Staff Member *Mr Mudd*
137 N Larchmont Blvd # 113
Los Angeles, CA 90004-3704, USA

Mallard, Josh (Athlete, Football Player)
175 International Dr
Athens, GA 30605-6617, USA

Mallard, Wesly (Athlete, Football Player)
6073 SW 67th Pl
Portland, OR 97223-7613, USA

Mallary, Robert (Artist)
PO Box 97
Conway, MA 01341-0097, USA

Mallea, Eduardo (Writer)
Posadas 1120
Buenos Aires, ARGENTINA

Mallee, John (Athlete, Baseball Player)
7426 Hamlin St
Schererville, IN 46375-3454, USA

Mallet, Jeff (Horse Racer)
210 Woodingham Trl
Venice, FL 34292-3931, USA

Mallett, Jerry (Athlete, Baseball Player)
4070 Cascade Trl
Mc Gregor, TX 76657-4102, USA

Mallett, Ronnie (Athlete, Football Player)
22113 Liberty Cemetery Rd
Jennings, LA 70546-8804, USA

Mallett, Ryan (Athlete, Football Player)
c/o David Dunn *Athletes First*
23091 Mill Creek Dr
Laguna Hills, CA 92653-1258, USA

Mallette, Brian (Athlete, Baseball Player)
1179 Lowery Fire House Rd
Glenwood, GA 30428-2214, USA

Mallette, Troy (Athlete, Hockey Player)
1550 Bum Rd
PO Box 764
Levack, ON P0M 2C0, CANADA

Mallick, Dan (Misc)
42045 Tilton Dr
Quartz Hill, CA 93536-7321, USA

Mallick, Fran (Athlete, Football Player)
42 Republic Dr Apt 135
Bloomfield, CT 06002-5462, USA

Mallicoat, Rob (Athlete, Baseball Player)
6205 214th Ave NE
Redmond, WA 98053-2310, USA

Mallinger, John (Athlete, Golfer)

Mallon, Meg (Athlete, Golfer)
5105 N Ocean Blvd Apt C
Ocean Ridge, FL 33435-7087, USA

Mallon, Thomas (Writer)
801 25th St NW
Washington, DC 20037-2209, USA

Mallory, Carole (Writer)
c/o Staff Member *Simon & Schuster*
1230 Avenue of the Americas Fl CONC1
New York, NY 10020-1586, USA

Mallory, Irvin (Athlete, Football Player)
3 Paula Ln
Waterford, CT 06385-1521, USA

Mallory, John (Athlete, Football Player)
151B Mountain Ave
Summit, NJ 07901-4172, USA

Mallory, Larry (Athlete, Football Player)
1911 Stonebrook Dr
Arlington, TX 76012-5707, USA

Mallory, Rick (Athlete, Football Player)
920 W Emerson St
Seattle, WA 98119-1419, USA

Mallory, Sheldon (Athlete, Baseball Player)
21353 Old North Church Rd
Frankfort, IL 60423-3016, USA

Malloy, Bob (Athlete, Baseball Player)
1904 San Carlos Ave
Allen, TX 75002-2626, USA

Malloy, Marty (Athlete, Baseball Player)
PO Box 1644
Chiefland, FL 32644-1644, USA

Malloy, Matt (Actor)
c/o Mark A. Schlegel *Cornerstone Talent Agency*
37 W 20th St Ste 1007
New York, NY 10011-3714, USA

Malloy, Robert (Pete Hamil) (Actor, Writer)
c/o Staff Member *ICM Partners*
10250 Constellation Blvd Fl 7
Los Angeles, CA 90067-6207, USA

Malloys, The (Music Group)
c/o Staff Member *Creative Artists Agency (CAA)*
2000 Avenue of the Stars Ste 100
Los Angeles, CA 90067-4705, USA

Malmsteen, Yngwie (Musician)
Polygram Records
825 8th Ave
New York, NY 10019-7416, USA

Malo, Raul (Musician, Songwriter, Writer)

Maloff, Sam (Designer)
PO Box 8051
Rancho Cucamonga, CA 91701-0051, USA

Malone, Beverly L (Misc)
American Nurses Assn
Maryland Ave SW
Washington, DC 20002, USA

Malone, Brendan (Coach)
Indiana Pacers
125 S Pennsylvania St
Conseco Fieldhouse
Indianapolis, IN 46204-3610, USA

Malone, Chuck (Athlete, Baseball Player)
310 Liberty St
Marked Tree, AR 72365-2209, USA

Malone, Greg (Athlete, Hockey Player)
1771 Waterford Ct
Pittsburgh, PA 15241-3150, USA

Malone, Jeff (Athlete, Basketball Player)
415 Lee Road 313
Smiths Station, AL 36877-3168, USA

Malone, Jena (Actor)
c/o Allison Band *Gersh*
9465 Wilshire Blvd Ste 600
Beverly Hills, CA 90212-2605, USA

Malone, John (Business Person)
Liberty Media
12300 Liberty Blvd
Englewood, CO 80112-7009

Malone, Karl (Athlete, Basketball Player, Olympic Athlete)
Karl Malone Foundation For Kids
PO Box 429
Bountiful, UT 84011-0429, USA

Malone, Kevin (Commentator)
21345 Placerita Canyon Rd
Newhall, CA 91321-1845, USA

Malone, Maicel (Athlete, Olympic Athlete, Track Athlete)
111 Frances Dr
Havana, FL 32333-8635, USA

Malone, Mike (Athlete, Basketball Coach, Basketball Player, Coach)
c/o Staff Member *Sacramento Kings*
1 Sports Pkwy
Sacramento, CA 95834-2301, USA

Malone, Patricia (Business Person)
c/o Staff Member *Gucci America*
50 Hartz Way
Secaucus, NJ 07094-2420, USA

Malone, Ryan (Athlete, Hockey Player)
Octagon Sports Management
1751 Pinnacle Dr Ste 1500
McLean, VA 22102-3833, USA

Malone, Shannon (Actor, Television Host)
c/o Jerry Shandrew *Shandrew Public Relations*
1050 S Stanley Ave
Los Angeles, CA 90019-6634, USA

Malone, Van (Athlete, Football Player)
4762 S 203rd East Ave
Broken Arrow, OK 74014-8820, USA

Maloney, Dave (Athlete, Hockey Player)
22 Glen Rd
Greenwich, CT 06830-4632, USA

Maloney, Don (Athlete, Hockey Player)
21 Guilford Ln
Greenwich, CT 06831-4121, USA

Maloney, Jim (Athlete, Baseball Player)
9722 Groffs Mill Dr Ste 107
Unit 102
Owings Mills, MD 21117-6341, USA

Maloney, Phil (Athlete, Hockey Player)
3626 Yellowpoint Rd
RR 3
Ladysmith, BC V9G 1E8, CANADA

Maloney, Sean (Athlete, Baseball Player)
244 Pheasant Run
Saunderstown, RI 02874-2033, USA

Maloof, Adrienne (Business Person, Reality Star)
c/o Staff Member *Maloof Motion Pictures*
523 Commercial St NE
Albuquerque, NM 87102-2338, USA

Maloof, Gavin (Business Person)
c/o Staff Member *Sacramento Kings*
1 Sports Pkwy
Sacramento, CA 95834-2301, USA

Maloof, Mary Lou Metzger (Musician)
5100 Stern Ave
Sherman Oaks, CA 91423-1244, USA

Maloof Jr, George (Business Person)
Palms Casino Resort
4321 W Flamingo Rd
Las Vegas, NV 89103-3903, USA

Maloog, Jack (Athlete, Baseball Player)
3140 S Vista Dr
Chandler, AZ 85248-3728, USA

Malrena, Oswaldo (Baseball Player)
Chicago Cubs
160 E Athletics Way
Mesa, AZ 85201-5068, USA

Maltais, Steve (Athlete, Hockey Player)
646 Country Club Dr
Itasca, IL 60143-1681, USA

Maltbie, Roger (Athlete, Golfer)
179 Longmeadow Dr
Los Gatos, CA 95032-5655, USA

Maltby, Kirk (Athlete, Hockey Player)
58 Putnam Pl
Grosse Pointe Shores, MI 48236-1224, USA

Malthe, Natassia (Actor)
c/o Trina Allen *Play Management*
220-807 Powell St
Vancouver, BC V6A 1H7, CANADA

Maltin, Leonard (Correspondent)
10424 Whipple St
Toluca Lake, CA 91602-2809, USA

Malubay, Ramiele (Musician)

Maluma (Musician)
c/o Frank Salzano *Salzano, Jackson & Lampert*
275 Madison Ave Fl 35
New York, NY 10016-1133, USA

Maly, Arturo (Actor)
c/o Staff Member *Telefe (Argentina)*
Pavon 2444
Buenos Aires C1248AAT, ARGENTINA

Mambo, Kevin (Actor)
c/o Hannah Roth *Buchwald*
5900 Wilshire Blvd Ste 3100
Los Angeles, CA 90036-5030, USA

Mamet, David (Writer)
2 Northfield Plz Ste 200
Northfield, IL 60093-1272, USA

Mamet, Zosia (Actor)
c/o Sarah Shyn *3 Arts Entertainment*
9460 Wilshire Blvd Fl 7
Beverly Hills, CA 90212-2713, USA

Mana (Music Group)
c/o Staff Member *Creative Artists Agency (CAA)*
2000 Avenue of the Stars Ste 100
Los Angeles, CA 90067-4705, USA

Manafort, Jason (Race Car Driver)
414 New Britain Ave
Plainville, CT 06062-2065, USA

Manahan, Austin (Athlete, Baseball Player)
2150 W Alameda Rd UNIT 1101
Phoenix, AZ 85085-1948, USA

Manca, Massimo (Athlete, Football Player)
3867 Miriam Dr
Doylestown, PA 18902-9176, USA

Manchester, Melissa (Musician)
c/o Peter Varano *AVO Talent Agency*
5670 Wilshire Blvd Ste 1930
Los Angeles, CA 90036-5603, USA

Mancina, Mark (Actor)
c/o Staff Member *Gorfaine/Schwartz Agency Inc*
4111 W Alameda Ave Ste 509
Burbank, CA 91505-4171, USA

Mancuso, Gail (Director, Producer)
c/o Matthew Labov *Forefront Media*
1669 Virginia Rd
Los Angeles, CA 90019-5935, USA

Mancuso, Nick (Actor)

Mancuso, Rudy (Actor, Comedian, Internet Star, Musician)
c/o Avi Gilbert *3 Arts Entertainment*
9460 Wilshire Blvd Fl 7
Beverly Hills, CA 90212-2713, USA

Mancuso Jr, Frank (Producer)
c/o Staff Member *FGM Entertainment*
201 N Canon Dr # 328
Beverly Hills, CA 90210-5301

Mandarich, Tony (Athlete, Football Player)
12767 E Altadena Dr
Scottsdale, AZ 85259-3418, USA

Mandel, Howie (Comedian, Game Show Host, Television Host)
c/o Lewis Kay *Kovert Creative*
506 Santa Monica Blvd Ste 400
Santa Monica, CA 90401-2412, USA

Mandel, Johnny (Composer)
28946 Cliffside Dr
Malibu, CA 90265-4212

Mandelbaum, Michael (Writer)
Basic Books
387 Park Ave S
New York, NY 10016-8810, USA

Manderson, Stephen Paul (Professor Green) (Musician)
c/o Andy Duggan *Primary Talent International (UK)*
10-11 Jockeys Fields
The Primary Bldg
London WC1R 4BN, UNITED KINGDOM

Mandich, Dan (Athlete, Hockey Player)
9075 Hyland Creek Cir
Minneapolis, MN 55437-1907, USA

Mandley, Pete (Athlete, Football Player)
103 E Smoke Tree Rd
Gilbert, AZ 85296-2250, USA

Mando, Michael (Actor)
c/o Kami Putnam-Heist *Anonymous Content*
3532 Hayden Ave
Culver City, CA 90232-2413, USA

Mandrell, Barbara (Musician)
PO Box 620
Hendersonville, TN 37077-0620, USA

Mandrell, Louise (Actor)
Mandrell Inc
1101 Hunters Ln
Ashland City, TN 37015-2829, USA

Mandvi, Aasif (Actor)
c/o Christina Papadopoulos *Baker Winokur Ryder Public Relations*
200 5th Ave Fl 5
New York, NY 10010-3307, USA

Mandylor, Costas (Actor)
c/o Matt Luber *Luber Roklin Management*
5815 W Sunset Blvd Ste 208
Los Angeles, CA 90028-6481, USA

Mandylor, Louis (Actor)
c/o Erik Kritzer *LINK Entertainment*
11872 La Grange Ave
Los Angeles, CA 90025-5282, USA

Mane, Gucci (Musician)
c/o Ashley Kalmanowitz *Atlantic Records*
1290 Avenue of the Americas Fl 28
New York, NY 10104-0106, USA

Mane, Tyler (Actor)
c/o Lesa Kirk *Open Entertainment*
1051 Cole Ave
Los Angeles, CA 90038-2601, USA

Manell, George (Race Car Driver)
5455 Polaris Ave
Las Vegas, NV 89118-2421, USA

Maneluk, george (Athlete, Hockey Player)
39 Weeping Willow Dr
Winnipeg, MB R2M 4H9, Canada

Manery, Kris (Athlete, Hockey Player)
48568 Quail Run Dr S
Plymouth, MI 48170-5717, USA

Manery, Randy (Athlete, Hockey Player)
6587 Garrett Rd
Buford, GA 30518-1109

Maness, James (Athlete, Football Player)
1001 Jarvis Ln
Azle, TX 76020-3321, USA

Manetti, Larry (Actor)
4615 Winnetka
Woodland Hills, CA 91364

Manfra, Fred (Commentator)
1104 S Dunbar Ave
Tampa, FL 33629-4247, USA

Manganiello, Joe (Actor)
c/o Staff Member *3:59 Productions*
3401 Coy Dr
Sherman Oaks, CA 91423-4529, USA

Mangano, Joy (Business Person)
Joy Mangano Foundation
334 Martin Luther King Jr Dr
Rising Tide Capital
Jersey City, NJ 07305-3618, USA

Manges, Mark (Athlete, Football Player)
701 White Ave
Cumberland, MD 21502-3816, USA

Mangieri, Dino (Athlete, Football Player)
108 Lamport Blvd Apt 3C
Staten Island, NY 10305-3629, USA

Mangini, Eric (Athlete, Football Player)
59 Moss ln
Brewster, MA 02631-2618, USA

Mangione, Chuck (Musician)
476 Hampton Blvd
Rochester, NY 14612-4227

Mangold, James Allen (Director, Producer)
c/o Staff Member *Tree Line Films*
1708 Berkeley St
Santa Monica, CA 90404-4105, USA

Mangold, Nick (Athlete, Football Player)
33 Crescent Rd
Madison, NJ 07940-2519, USA

Mangual, Angel (Baseball Player)
Pittsburgh Pirates
1406 R Del Valle
Ponce, PR 00728, USA

Mangual, Pepe (Athlete, Baseball Player)
2325 Calle Tabonuco
Urb Los Caobos
Ponce, PR 00716-2712, USA

Mangum, John (Athlete, Football Player)
150 Summerwood Dr
Pearl, MS 39208-9074, USA

Mangum, Jonathan (Actor)
c/o Staff Member *Shapiro/West & Associates*
141 El Camino Dr Ste 205
Beverly Hills, CA 90212-2786, USA

Mangum, Kris (Athlete, Football Player)
16720 Krishna Ln
Charlotte, NC 28277-1638, USA

Manheim, Camryn (Actor, Producer)
c/o Peg Donegan *Framework Entertainment*
9057 Nemo St # C
W Hollywood, CA 90069-5511, USA

Manheim, Milo (Actor)
c/o Meghan Prophet *PMK/BNC Public Relations*
1840 Century Park E Ste 1400
Los Angeles, CA 90067-2115, USA

Maniaci, Joe (Athlete, Football Player)
3215 Rankin Ave
Windsor, ON N9E 3C2, Canada

Maniago, Cesare (Athlete, Hockey Player)
19-788 Citadel Dr
Port Coquitlam, BC V3C 6G9, CANADA

Manic Street Preachers (Music Group)
c/o Staff Member *Paradigm (Monterey)*
404 W Franklin St
Monterey, CA 93940-2303, USA

Manigault-Newman, Omarosa (Commentator, Reality Star)
c/o John Seitzer *Agency for the Performing Arts (APA)*
405 S Beverly Dr Ste 500
Beverly Hills, CA 90212-4425, USA

Manilow, Barry (Musician)
c/o Victoria Varela *Varela Media*
45 Rockefeller Plz Fl 20
New York, NY 10111-3193, USA

Manis, Randy (Producer)
c/o Staff Member *Killer Films (US)*
526 W 26th St Rm 715
New York, NY 10001-5524, USA

Maniscalco, Sebastian (Comedian)
c/o Rachel Williams *Levity Entertainment Group (LEG)*
6701 Center Dr W Ste 300
Los Angeles, CA 90045-2482, USA

Mankell, Henning (Writer)
c/o Staff Member *Leopard förlag AB*
S:t Paulsgatan 11
Stockholm 118 46, Sweden

Mankins, Logan (Athlete, Football Player)
1 Mockingbird Ln
North Attleboro, MA 02760-2775, USA

Mankowski, Phil (Athlete, Baseball Player)
2280 Southwestern Blvd
Buffalo, NY 14224-4423, USA

Manley, Dexter (Athlete, Football Player)
PO Box 25049
Washington, DC 20027-8049, USA

Manley, Elizabeth (Figure Skater)
Marco Enterprises
74830 Velie Way Ste A
Palm Desert, CA 92260-7954, USA

Manley, Joe (Athlete, Football Player)
3365 County Road 92
Rogersville, AL 35652-2736, USA

Manley, Leon (Athlete, Football Player)
1207 Knollpark Cir
Austin, TX 78758-3815, USA

Mann, Aimee (Musician)
Girlie Action Media And Marketing
59 W 19th St Ste 4A
New York, NY 10011-4228, USA

Mann, Almee (Musician, Songwriter, Writer)
Michael Hausman Mgmt
511 Avenue of the Americas Unit 197
New York, NY 10011-8436, USA

Mann, Art (Producer, Television Host)
HDNet Films
122 Hudson St Fl 5
New York, NY 10013-2355, USA

Mann, Brad (Actor)
c/o Michelle Gauvin *Performers Management*
5-636 Clyde Ave
West Vancouver, BC V7T 1E1, CANADA

Mann, Charles (Athlete, Football Player)
20603 Holyoke Dr
Ashburn, VA 20147-3233, USA

Mann, David W (Religious Leader)
6311 Donna Dr
Fort Wayne, IN 46819-1203, USA

Mann, Demi (Actor)
c/o Staff Member *Creative Artists Agency (CAA)*
2000 Avenue of the Stars Ste 100
Los Angeles, CA 90067-4705, USA

Mann, Errol (Athlete, Football Player)
5521 Bonanza Pl
Missoula, MT 59808-9386, USA

Mann, Gabriel (Actor)
c/o Whitney Tancred *42West*
1840 Century Park E Ste 700
Los Angeles, CA 90067-2122, USA

Mann, Garbriel (Actor)
United Talent Agency
9336 Civic Center Dr
Beverly Hills, CA 90210-3604, USA

Mann, H Thompson (Athlete, Swimmer)
23 Pleasant St Apt 501
Newburyport, MA 01950-2634, USA

Mann, Jason (Director, Reality Star)
c/o Staff Member *WME|IMG*
9601 Wilshire Blvd
Beverly Hills, CA 90210-5213, USA

Mann, Jim (Athlete, Baseball Player)
197 N Franklin St Apt 1
Holbrook, MA 02343-1111, USA

Mann, Jimmy (Athlete, Hockey Player)
1538 Scio Ridge Rd
Ann Arbor, MI 48103-8991

Mann, Leslie (Actor)
c/o Brad Cafarelli *PMK/BNC Public Relations*
1840 Century Park E Ste 1400
Los Angeles, CA 90067-2115, USA

Mann, Manfred (Misc)
EMI Records
43 Brook Green
London W6 7EF, UNITED KINGDOM (UK)

Mann, Marvin L (Business Person)
Lexmark International
740 W New Circle Rd
Lexington, KY 40511-1876, USA

Mann, Michael (Director, Producer)
c/o Staff Member *Forward Pass Inc*
12233 W Olympic Blvd Ste 340
Los Angeles, CA 90064-1092, USA

Mann, Monroe (Actor, Producer, Writer)
c/o Staff Member *Loco Dawn Films, LLC*
499 Seventh Avenue
12th Floor North
New York, NY 10018, USA

Mann, Robert (Athlete, Football Player)
515 SW Hampton Ct
Port Saint Lucie, FL 34986-2022, USA

Mann, Shelley I (Swimmer)
1301 S Scott St # 638S
Arlington, VA 22204-6205, USA

Mann, Tamela (Actor, Musician)

Mann, Terrence V (Actor)
c/o Steve Stone *Cornerstone Talent Agency*
37 W 20th St Ste 1007
New York, NY 10011-3714, USA

Mann, Thomas (Actor)
c/o Michael Hepburn *Industry Entertainment Partners*
955 Carrillo Dr Ste 300
Los Angeles, CA 90048-5400, USA

Mannelly, Patrick (Athlete, Football Player)
1128 Kildare Ave
Libertyville, IL 60048-1203, USA

Mannheim Steamroller (Music Group)
9120 Mormon Bridge Rd
Omaha, NE 68152-1937, USA

Manning, Aaron (Athlete, Football Player)
6906 27th Ave
Kenosha, WI 53143-5214, USA

Manning, Archie (Athlete, Football Player)
1420 1st St
New Orleans, LA 70130-5713, USA

Manning, Charlie (Athlete, Baseball Player)
PO Box 532
Pulaski, TN 38478-0532, USA

Manning, Danieal (Athlete, Football Player)

Manning, Danny (Athlete, Basketball Player, Olympic Athlete)
5134 Ballincourt Ln
Winston Salem, NC 27104-5056, USA

Manning, Eli (Athlete, Football Player)
c/o Team Member *New York Giants*
Giants Stadium
E Rutherford, NJ 07073, USA

Manning, Jim (Athlete, Baseball Player)
41 Fox Run Dr
Weaverville, NC 28787-8307, USA

Manning, Peyton (Athlete, Football Player)
Peyton Manning Foundation
PO Box 3367
Englewood, CO 80155-3367, USA

Manning, Rick (Athlete, Baseball Player)
22447 N 49th Pl # Pi
Phoenix, AZ 85054-7102, USA

Manning, Taryn (Actor, Musician)
c/o Oren Segal *Management Production Entertainment (MPE)*
9229 W Sunset Blvd Ste 301
W Hollywood, CA 90069-3417, USA

Manning, Wade (Athlete, Football Player)
5133 Malaya St
Denver, CO 80249-8548, USA

Manningham, Mario (Athlete, Football Player)
c/o Drew Rosenhaus *Rosenhaus Sports Representation*
3921 Alton Rd # 440
Miami Beach, FL 33140-3852, USA

Mannion, Pace (Athlete, Basketball Player)
4190 S Achilles Dr
Salt Lake City, UT 84124-3266, USA

Mannix, Ernie (Musician)
c/o Staff Member *Greenspan Artist Management*
8760 W Sunset Blvd
West Hollywood, CA 90069-2206, USA

Manno, Bob (Athlete, Hockey Player)
5643 Peer St
Niagara Falls, ON L2G 1W8, Canada

Manoa, Tim (Athlete, Football Player)
1285 Boardman Canfield Rd
Youngstown, OH 44512-4058, USA

Manoff, Dinah (Actor)
Innovative Artists
1505 10th St
Santa Monica, CA 90401-2805, USA

Manon, Julio (Athlete, Baseball Player)
4726 15th Ave S
Saint Petersburg, FL 33711-2328, USA

Manor, Brison (Athlete, Football Player)
285 Spruce St
Bridgeton, NJ 08302-3347, USA

Manos, Sam (Athlete, Football Player)
1424 E Normandy Blvd
Deltona, FL 32725-8408, USA

Manoukian, Don (Athlete, Football Player)
5405 Mae Anne Ave
Reno, NV 89523-1813, USA

Manowar (Music Group)
Prefers to be contacted via email

Manrique, Fred (Baseball Player)
Toronto Blue Jays
1775 SW 2nd Ave
Boca Raton, FL 33432-7230, USA

Mansell, Kevin (Business Person)
Kohl's Corp
N56W17000 Ridgewood Dr
Menomonee Falls, WI 53051-7096, USA

Mansell, Nigel (Race Car Driver)
Nigel Mansell Racing
Brands Hatch
Longfield, Kent DA3 8NG, UNITED KINGDOM (UK)

Mansfield, Von (Athlete, Football Player)
3530 194th St
Homewood, IL 60430-4325, USA

Mansfield-Kelley, Marie (Athlete, Baseball Player, Commentator)
9 Eastland Rd
Jamaica Plain, MA 02130-4616, USA

Mansolino, Doug (Athlete, Baseball Player)
106 Santee Way
Loudon, TN 37774-2123, USA

Manson, Amy (Actor)
c/o Tom Spriggs *Coronel Group*
1100 Glendon Ave Fl 17
Los Angeles, CA 90024-3588, USA

Manson, Dave (Athlete, Hockey Player)
211 Cowboys Pkwy
Irving, TX 75063-5931, USA

Manson, Marilyn (Musician)
c/o Carrie Tolles *Shore Fire Media*
32 Court St Fl 16
Brooklyn, NY 11201-4441, USA

Manson, Shirley (Musician)
c/o Staff Member *Untitled Entertainment*
350 S Beverly Dr Ste 200
Beverly Hills, CA 90212-4819, USA

Mansour, Nicole (Actor)

Mant, Cathy (Athlete, Golfer)
326 Broadmoor Way
McDonough, GA 30253-4291, USA

Mantador, Steve (Athlete, Hockey Player)
6301 Osprey Ter
Coconut Creek, FL 33073-2624, USA

Mantegna, Gia (Actor)
c/o Lauren Williams *Echo Lake Management*
421 S Beverly Dr Fl 8
Beverly Hills, CA 90212-4408, USA

Mantegna, Joe (Actor, Producer, Writer)
c/o Jack Gilardi *ICM Partners*
10250 Constellation Blvd Fl 7
Los Angeles, CA 90067-6207, USA

Mantei, Matt (Athlete, Baseball Player)
4709 Chicago Path
Stevensville, MI 49127-9356, USA

Mantel, Hilary (Writer)
A W Heath
79 St Martin's Ln
London WC2N 4AA, UNTED KINGDOM (UK)

Mantel, Hillary M (Writer)
AM Heath
79 Saint Martin's Lane
London WC2N 4AA, UNITED KINGDOM (UK)

Mantello, Joe (Actor, Director)

Mantha, Moe (Athlete, Hockey Player, Olympic Athlete)
1538 Scio Ridge Rd
Ann Arbor, MI 48103-8991, USA

Manthey, Jerri (Actor)
PO Box 801507
Valencia, CA 91380-1507

Mantilla, Felix (Athlete, Baseball Player)
6973 N Tacoma St
Milwaukee, WI 53224-4759, USA

Mantis, Nick (Athlete, Basketball Player)
2344 Autumn Dr
Crown Point, IN 46307-9668, USA

Manto, Jeff (Athlete, Baseball Player)
725 Radcliffe St
Bristol, PA 19007-5223, USA

Mantooth, Randolph (Actor)
c/o Staff Member *Artists & Representatives (Stone Manners Salners)*
6100 Wilshire Blvd Ste 1500
Los Angeles, CA 90048-5110, USA

Mantranga, Jonah (Musician)
c/o Staff Member *Paradigm (Monterey)*
404 W Franklin St
Monterey, CA 93940-2303, USA

Mantz, Michael R (Astronaut)
1940 Elanita Dr
San Pedro, CA 90732-4430, USA

Mantzoukas, Jason (Actor)
c/o Christie Smith *Rise Management*
6338 Wilshire Blvd
Los Angeles, CA 90048-5002, USA

Manucci, Dan (Athlete, Football Player)
1208 W Sand Dune Dr
Gilbert, AZ 85233-5615, USA

Manuel, Barry (Athlete, Baseball Player)
805 Oak St
Mamou, LA 70554-2715, USA

Manuel, Charles F (Chuck) (Baseball Player)
2931 Plantation Rd
Winter Haven, FL 33884-1233, USA

Manuel, Charlie (Athlete, Baseball Player, Coach)
2931 Plantation Rd
Winter Haven, FL 33884-1233, USA

Manuel, E J (Athlete, Football Player)
c/o Malik Hafeez Shareef *Dimensional Sports, Inc.*
3148 Circle Dr SW
Roanoke, VA 24018-2110, USA

Manuel, Jay (Reality Star, Television Host)
c/o Lisa Shotland *CAA (London)*
3 Shortlands, Hammersmith
Fl 5
London W6 8DA, UNITED KINGDOM

Manuel, Jerry (Athlete, Baseball Player, Coach)
5556 Ridge Park Dr
Loomis, CA 95650-9400, USA

Manuel, Lionel (Athlete, Football Player)
827 E Cedar Dr
Chandler, AZ 85249-3319, USA

Manuel, Marquand (Athlete, Football Player)
3672 Churchill Downs Dr
Davie, FL 33328-1307, USA

Manuel, Robert (Actor)
La Maison du Buisson
22-26 Rue Jules Regnier
Plaisir 78370, FRANCE

Manuelidis, Laura (Misc)
Yale University Medical School
Neuropathology Dept
New Haven, CT 06520, USA

Manumaleuna, Brandon (Athlete, Football Player)
1218 Koleeta Dr
Harbor City, CA 90710-1824, USA

Manusky, Greg (Athlete, Football Player)
4939 Eastbourne Ct
San Jose, CA 95138-2124, USA

Manville, Dick (Athlete, Baseball Player)
1436 Lake Francis Dr
Apopka, FL 32712-2007, USA

Manville, Lesley (Actor)
c/o Nathan Fuller *Public Eye Communications*
535 Kings Rd
#313 Plaza
London SW10 0SZ, UNITED KINGDOM

Manwaring, Kirt (Athlete, Baseball Player)
18690 SE Lakeside Way
Jupiter, FL 33469-8111, USA

Manz, Wolfgang (Musician)
Pasteuralle 55
Hanover 30655, GERMANY

Manzanero, Armando (Musician)
Pro Art
Paz Soidan 170
Of 903
San Isidro, Lima 00027, PERU

Manzanillo, Josias (Athlete, Baseball Player)
274 Kennebec St
Mattapan, MA 02126-1106, USA

Manzella, Tommy (Athlete, Baseball Player)
3213 Veronica Dr
Chalmette, LA 70043-3555, USA

Manzi, Catello (Horse Racer)
1 Hickory Ln
Freehold, NJ 07728-1588, USA

Manzi, Louis (Horse Racer)
4036 Grace Ave
Bronx, NY 10466-2210, USA

Manzi, Rocco (Horse Racer)
112 Willow Meadow Way
Oneida, NY 13421-1852, USA

Manziel, Johnny (Athlete, Football Player)
c/o Team Member *Cleveland Browns*
76 Lou Groza Blvd
Berea, OH 44017-1269, USA

Manzo, Caroline (Business Person, Reality Star)
c/o Staff Member *Bravo TV (NY)*
30 Rockefeller Plz
New York, NY 10112-0015, USA

Manzo, Dina (Business Person, Reality Star)
705 Ewing Ave
Franklin Lakes, NJ 07417-2228, USA

Manzullo, Donald (Congressman, Politician)
2228 Rayburn Hob
Washington, DC 20515-1316, USA

Mapa, Alec (Actor)
c/o Stephen Ford *Diva Central Inc*
7510 W Sunset Blvd # 1445
Los Angeles, CA 90046-3408, USA

Maple, Eddie (Race Car Driver)
420 Fair Hill Dr # 1
Elkton, MD 21921-2573, USA

Maple, Eddie (Horse Racer)
25 Spartina Cres
Bluffton, SC 29910-4702, USA

Maples, Marla (Actor, Model)
1976 S La Cienega Blvd Ste C PMB 805
Los Angeles, CA 90034-1627, USA

Maponga, Stansly (Athlete, Football Player)
c/o Bus Cook *Bus Cook Sports, Inc*
1 Willow Bend Dr
Hattiesburg, MS 39402-8552, USA

Mapother, William (Actor)
c/o Brian Medavoy *More/Medavoy Management*
10203 Santa Monica Blvd # 400
Los Angeles, CA 90067-6405, USA

Maps and Atlases (Music Group)
c/o Ed Thompson *13 Artists (UK)*
11-14 Kensington St
Brighton BN1 4AJ, UNITED KINGDOM

Mar, Marcela (Actor)
c/o Luis Balaguer *Latin World Entertainment (LA)*
9777 Wilshire Blvd Ste 915
Beverly Hills, CA 90212-1902, USA

Mara, Kate (Actor)
c/o Jennifer Allen *Viewpoint Inc*
8820 Wilshire Blvd Ste 220
Beverly Hills, CA 90211-2622, USA

Mara, Ratu Sir Kamisese K T (President)
11 Ballery Road
Suva, FIJI

Mara, Rooney (Actor)
c/o Christine Tripicchio *Shelter PR*
5670 Wilshire Blvd Ste 1200
Los Angeles, CA 90036-5621, USA

Maradona, Diego (Athlete, Soccer Player)
Brandsen 805
Capital Federal 01161, ARGENTINA

Maragos, Chris (Athlete, Football Player)
c/o Scott Smith *XAM Sports*
3509 Ice Age Dr
Madison, WI 53719-5409, USA

Marak, Paul (Athlete, Baseball Player)
1211 Comanche Trl
Alamogordo, NM 88310-4010, USA

Maran, Josie (Actor)
Josie Maran Cosmetics
12236 Sherman Way
N Hollywood, CA 91605-5503, USA

Marangi, Gary (Athlete, Football Player)
26 Morton St
Port Jefferson Station, NY 11776-4013, USA

Maraniss, David (Journalist)
Washington Post
Editorial Dept
1150 15th St NW
Washington, DC 20071-0001, USA

Marano, Laura (Actor)
c/o Staff Member *Marano Entertainment*
21650 Oxnard St Ste 350
Woodland Hills, CA 91367-7855, USA

Marano, Vanessa (Actor)
c/o Mona Loring *Status PR*
PO Box 6191
Westlake Village, CA 91359-6191, USA

Maratos, Terry (Actor)
c/o Staff Member *Cage Group, The*
14724 Ventura Blvd Ste 505
Sherman Oaks, CA 91403-3505

Marber, Patrick (Writer)
Judy Daish
2 Saint Charles Place
London W10 6EG, UNITED KINGDOM (UK)

Marbles, Jenna (Internet Star)
16030 Ventura Blvd Ste 240
Encino, CA 91436-4487, USA

Marbley, Harlan (Athlete, Boxer, Olympic Athlete)
6113 Parkview Ln
Clinton, MD 20735-3850, USA

Marbury, Joseph (Athlete, Baseball Player)
1472 21st St N
Birmingham, AL 35234-2708, USA

Marbury, Kerry (Athlete, Football Player)
1201 Locust Ave
Fairmont, WV 26554-2451, USA

Marbury, Rendon (Athlete, Baseball Player)
1472 21st St N
Birmingham, AL 35234-2708, USA

Marbury, Stephan (Athlete, Basketball Coach, Olympic Athlete)
2940 W 31st St Apt 4G
Brooklyn, NY 11224-1734, USA

Marbury, Stephon (Athlete, Basketball Player, Olympic Athlete)
2940 W 31st St Apt 4G
Brooklyn, NY 11224-1734, USA

Marceau, Sophie (Actor)
c/o Staff Member *Orbis Media*
27 Rue Cardinet
Paris 75017, USA

March, Forbes (Actor)
c/o Staff Member *Innovative Artists*
1505 10th St
Santa Monica, CA 90401-2805, USA

March, Jane (Actor, Model)
c/o Camilla Storey *Camilla Storey Management*
14 Kinnerton Pl S
Kinnerton St
London SW1X 8EH, UNITED KINGDOM

March, Little Peggy (Musician)
Cape Entertainment
1161 NW 76th Ave
Plantation, FL 33322-5120, USA

March, Stephanie (Actor)
c/o Erica Tarin *ID Public Relations*
7060 Hollywood Blvd Fl 8th
Los Angeles, CA 90028-6021, USA

Marchant, Kenny (Congressman, Politician)
1110 Longworth Hob
Washington, DC 20515-3401, USA

Marchant, Todd (Athlete, Hockey Player, Olympic Athlete)
10448 Caribou Way
Tustin, CA 92782-1470, USA

Marchetti, Gino J (Athlete, Football Player)
324 Devon Way
West Chester, PA 19380-6825, USA

Marchetti, Leo V (Misc)
Fraternal Order of Police
5615 Belair Rd
Baltimore, MD 21206-3619, USA

Marchinko, Jhoni (Producer)
c/o Staff Member *United Talent Agency (UTA)*
9336 Civic Center Dr
Beverly Hills, CA 90210-3604, USA

Marchiol, Ken (Athlete, Football Player)
6489 S Olathe St # 5
Centennial, CO 80016-1052, USA

Marchisano, Francesco Cardinal (Religious Leader)
Cancelleria Apostolica Palazzo
Plazza Cancelleria 1
Rome 00186, ITALY

Marchlewski, Frank (Athlete, Football Player)
428 Toledo Dr
Lower Burrell, PA 15068-3315, USA

Marciano, David (Actor)
c/o Staff Member *Buchwald*
5900 Wilshire Blvd Ste 3100
Los Angeles, CA 90036-5030, USA

Marciano, Rob (Television Host)
c/o Brian Dubin *Artist Brand Alliance*
11 E 86th St Fl 9
New York, NY 10028-0501, USA

Marcil, Vanessa (Actor)
c/o Steve Small *aTa Management (LA)*
2508 N Vermont Ave # 702
Los Angeles, CA 90027-1243, USA

Marcille, Eva (Actor, Model, Reality Star)
c/o Joseph Babineaux *Perspective Public Relations*
9107 Wilshire Blvd Ste 450
Beverly Hills, CA 90210-5535, USA

Marciniak, Ron (Athlete, Football Player)
2222 Hopespring Loop
The Villages, FL 32162-7044, USA

Marcinkevicius, Iustinus M (Writer)
Mildos Str 33
#6
Vilnius 232055, LITHUANIA

Marcinko, Richard (Writer)
c/o Kimberly Witherspoon *Inkwell Management*
521 5th Ave
New York, NY 10175-0003, USA

Marcinyshyn, Dave (Athlete, Hockey Player)
36 Doucette Pl
St. Albert, AB T8N 6S6, Canada

Marcis, Dave (Race Car Driver)
Marcis Auto Racing
10 Greenleaf Road
Arden, NC 28704, USA

Marciulionis, Sarunas (Athlete, Basketball Player)
Hotel Sarunas
Hotel Sarunas Raitininku Street 4 Attn
Vilnius 02051, Lithuania

Marco, Gian (Musician)
c/o Staff Member *Creative Artists Agency (CAA)*
2000 Avenue of the Stars Ste 100
Los Angeles, CA 90067-4705, USA

Marcol, Czeslaw C (Chester) (Athlete, Football Player)
PO Box 466
Dollar Bay, MI 49922-0466, USA

Marcon, Lou (Athlete, Hockey Player)
927 Mountdale Ave
Thunder Bay, ON P7E 2Z8, Canada

Marcontell, Ed (Athlete, Football Player)
PO Box 884
Rusk, TX 75785-0884, USA

Marcos (Musician)
East West America Records
75 Rockefeller Plz
New York, NY 10019-6908, USA

Marcotte, Don (Athlete, Hockey Player)
12 Cote St
Amesbury, MA 01913-3804, USA

Marcovicci, Andrea (Actor, Musician)
Donald Smith Promotions
1640 E 48th St
#14U
New York, NY 10017, USA

Marcum, Art (Writer)
c/o Matt Rosen *Grandview*
7122 Beverly Blvd Ste F
Los Angeles, CA 90036-2572, USA

Marcum, Shaun (Athlete, Baseball Player)
1413 Jill Ln
Excelsior Springs, MO 64024-9790, USA

Marcus, Bernard (Business Person)
Marcus Foundation
2455 Paces Ferry Rd SE Bldg C
Atlanta, GA 30339-6444, USA

Marcus, John (Race Car Driver)
PO Box 1018
Talladega, AL 35161-1018, USA

Marcus, Sparky (Actor)
910 Arlene Ct
Yreka, CA 96097-2744, USA

Marcus, Trula M (Actor)
The Agency
1800 Avenue of the Stars Ste 400
Los Angeles, CA 90067-4206, USA

Marden, Brice (Artist)
6 Saint Lukes Pl
New York, NY 10014-3974, USA

Marderian, Greg (Athlete, Football Player)
1400 Barton Rd Apt 1701
Redlands, CA 92373-1404, USA

Mardones, Benny (Musician)
Tony Cee
PO Box 410
Utica, NY 13503-0410, USA

Mare, Olindo (Athlete, Football Player)
5 Serenity Dr
Mandeville, LA 70471-6764, USA

Maree, Sydney (Athlete, Track Athlete)
2 Braxton Rd
Bryn Mawr, PA 19010-1029, USA

Marek, Marcus (Athlete, Football Player)
26 Nora Ct
New Ipswich, NH 03071-3504, USA

Maren, Elizabeth (Actor)
3126 Oakcrest Dr
Los Angeles, CA 90068-1856, USA

Margal, Albert M (Prime Minister)
8 Hornsey Rise Gardens
London N19, UNITED KINGDOM (UK)

Margalit, Israela (Musician)
Columbia Artists Mgmt Inc
165 W 57th St
New York, NY 10019-2201, USA

Margarita, Henry R (Athlete, Football Player)
4 Drury Ln
Stoneham, MA 02180-3205, USA

Margavage, Dave (Athlete, Football Player)
474 Woodview Dr
Lexington, KY 40515-5945, USA

Margeot, Jean Cardinal (Religious Leader)
Bonne Terre
Vacoas, MAURITIUS

Margera, Bam (Actor, Producer, Writer)
PO Box 671
Westtown, PA 19395-0671, USA

Margerum, Ken (Athlete, Football Player)
300 Plum St Spc 109
Capitola, CA 95010-2224, USA

Margo, Philip (Musician)
American Mgmt
19948 Mayall St
Chatsworth, CA 91311-3522, USA

Margolin, Phillip (Writer)
c/o Jean V Naggar *Jean Naggar Literary Agency*
216 E 75th St Ste 1E
New York, NY 10021-2921, USA

Margolin, Stuart (Actor)
Three Owl Productions
PO Box 478 Stn Ganges
Salt Spring Island, BC V8K 2W1, CANADA

Margolis, Cindy (Actor, Model)
c/o Glenn Gulino *G2 Entertainment LLC*
1 Columbus Pl Apt S25E
New York, NY 10019-8208, USA

Margolis, Mark (Actor)
c/o Van Johnson *Van Johnson Company*
9595 Wilshire Blvd Ste 900
Beverly Hills, CA 90212-2509, USA

Margolyes, Miriam (Actor)
c/o Staff Member *The Rights House (UK)*
Drury House
34-43 Russell St
London WC2B 5HA, UNITED KINGDOM

Margoneri, Joe (Athlete, Baseball Player)
341 Turkeytown Rd
West Newton, PA 15089-1850, USA

Margot, Sandra (Athlete, Wrestler)
PO Box 1168
Studio City, CA 91614-0168, USA

Margoyles, Miriam (Actor)
P F D Drury House
34-43 Russell St
London WC2B 5HA, UNITED KINGDOM (UK)

Margret, Ann (Actor, Dancer, Musician)
2707 Benedict Canyon Dr
Beverly Hills, CA 90210-1024, USA

Margrethe II (Royalty)
Amalienborg Palace
Copenhgen K 01257, DENMARK

Margulies, Donald (Writer)
Yale University
English Dept
New Haven, CT 06520, USA

Margulies, Julianna (Actor)
c/o Michelle Bohan *WME|IMG*
9601 Wilshire Blvd
Beverly Hills, CA 90210-5213, USA

Mari, Teairra (Musician)
c/o Armah David *Undertaker Entertainment*
1901 N Buena Vista St
Empire Center
Burbank, CA 91504-5005, USA

Mariam, Mengistu Haile (President)
PO Box 1536
Gunhill Enclave
Harare, ZIMBABWE

Mariano, Jarah (Model)
c/o Staff Member *IMG Models (NY)*
304 Park Ave S PH N
New York, NY 10010-4303, USA

Marichal, Juan (Athlete, Baseball Player)
9458 NW 54th Doral Circle Ln
Doral, FL 33178-2048, USA

Marie, Ann (Actor)
1608 N Cahuenga Blvd # 354
Hollywood, CA 90028-6202, USA

Marie, Aurelius J B L (President)
Zicack
Portsmouth, DOMINICA

Marie, Constance (Actor)
c/o Robbie Kass *Kass Management*
1011 Euclid St Unit B
Santa Monica, CA 90403-4296, USA

Marie, Lisa (Actor, Model)
c/o Chris Forberg *LA Models*
555 W 25th St
New York, NY 10001-5542, USA

Marie, Princess (Royalty)
Schloss Vaduz
Vaduz 09490, LIECHTENSTEIN

Marie, Scheana (Actor, Reality Star)
c/o Mark Modesitt *MODE Public Relations*
3450 Cahuenga Blvd W Apt 907
Los Angeles, CA 90068-1594, USA

Marienthal, Eli (Actor)
c/o Lisa Gallant *Gallant Management*
1112 Montana Ave # 454
Santa Monica, CA 90403-1652, USA

Marienthal, Eric (Musician)
15030 Ventura Blvd # 710
Sherman Oaks, CA 91403-5470, USA

Marillion (Musician)
c/o Staff Member *Paradigm (Monterey)*
404 W Franklin St
Monterey, CA 93940-2303, USA

Marimow, William K (Journalist)
1942 Panama St
Philadelphia, PA 19103-6610, USA

Marin, Cheech (Actor, Comedian)
Chicano Collection
923 E 3rd St Apt 203
Los Angeles, CA 90013-1846, USA

Marin, Jack (Athlete, Basketball Player)
3909 Regent Rd
Durham, NC 27707-5311, USA

Marin, Mindy (Director)
c/o Jeremy Plager *Creative Artists Agency (CAA)*
2000 Avenue of the Stars Ste 100
Los Angeles, CA 90067-4705, USA

Marina and the Diamonds (Music Group)
c/o Marty Diamond *Paradigm*
140 Broadway Ste 2600
New York, NY 10005-1011, USA

Marinaro, Ed (Actor, Athlete, Football Player)
Atlas Entertainment
6100 Wilshire Blvd Ste 1170
Los Angeles, CA 90048-5116, USA

Marinca, Anamarie (Actor)
c/o Annabelle Karouby *Plan A*
15 Rue Martel
Paris 65020, FRANCE

Marinelli, Rod (Athlete, Football Player)
1981 W Southmeadow Ln
Lake Forest, IL 60045-4831, USA

Marini, Gilles (Actor, Model)
PO Box 1505
Studio City, CA 91614-0505, USA

Marini, Hector (Athlete, Hockey Player)
4534 Gatineau Ave
Mississauga, ON L4Z 2X6, Canada

Marinin, Maxim (Figure Skater)
c/o Staff Member *Champions on Ice*
3500 American Blvd W Ste 190
Minneapolis, MN 55431-4431, USA

Marino, Cathy (Athlete, Golfer)
6313 Willowdale Dr
Plano, TX 75093-7802, USA

Marino, Dan (Football Player)
1647 Passion Vine Cir
Weston, FL 33326-3661, USA

Marino, Ken (Actor)
c/o David Gardner *Artists First*
9465 Wilshire Blvd Ste 900
Beverly Hills, CA 90212-2608, USA

Marino, Stephen (Athlete, Golfer)
203 Evergrene Pkwy Unit 18-B
Palm Beach Gardens, FL 33410-1508, USA

Marino, Tom (Congressman, Politician)
410 Cannon Hob
Washington, DC 20515-4402, USA

Marinovich, Marv (Athlete, Football Player)
1/2 Santa Margarita Pkwy
Rancho Santa Margarita, CA 92688, USA

Marinovich, Todd (Athlete, Football Player)
132 E Balboa Blvd
Newport Beach, CA 92661-1118, USA

Marinucci, Chris (Athlete, Hockey Player)
30300 Laplant Rd
Grand Rapids, MN 55744-6062

Mario (Musician)
c/o Staff Member *J Erving Group*
555 Whitehall St SW Apt N
Atlanta, GA 30303-3715, USA

Mario, Ernest (Business Person)
ALZA Corp
1950 Charleston Rd
Mountain View, CA 94043-1247, USA

Marion, Brock (Athlete, Football Player)
24051 Schultz Rd NE
Aurora, OR 97002-9652, USA

Marion, Frank (Athlete, Football Player)
15920 SW 99th Ct
Miami, FL 33157-1615, USA

Marion, Fred (Athlete, Football Player)
4956 Cypress Hammock Dr
Saint Cloud, FL 34771-8922, USA

Marion, Jerry (Athlete, Football Player)
12411 Riverfront Park Dr
Bakersfield, CA 93311-5112, USA

Marion, Shawn (Athlete, Basketball Player)
Best
303 E Main St
#200
Louisville, KY 40202, USA

Mariota, Marcus (Athlete, Football Player)
c/o Ryan Tollner *REP 1 Sports Group*
80 Technology Dr
Irvine, CA 92618-2301, USA

Mariucci, Steve (Athlete, Football Player)
15940 Romita Ct
Monte Sereno, CA 95030-3092, USA

Mariye, Lily (Director, Writer)
c/o Staff Member *Bauman Redanty & Shaul Agency*
5757 Wilshire Blvd
Suite 473
Beverly Hills, CA 90212, USA

Mark, Albert J (Beauty Pageant Winner)
Miss American Pageant
1325 Broadway
Atlantic City, NJ 08401, USA

Mark, Greg (Athlete, Football Player)
4060 El Prado Blvd
Miami, FL 33133-6310, USA

Mark, Reed (Athlete, Football Player)
3724 Falcon Way
Saint Paul, MN 55123-2491, USA

Mark, Reuben (Business Person)
Colgate-Palmolive Co
300 Park Ave Fl 3
New York, NY 10022-7499, USA

Markakis, Nick (Athlete, Baseball Player)
14324A Cuba Rd
Cockeysville, MD 21030-1008, USA

Markbreit, Jerry (Athlete, Football Player)
9739 Keystone Ave
Skokie, IL 60076-1136, USA

Marker, Steve (Musician)
Borman Entertainment
1250 6th St Ste 401
Santa Monica, CA 90401-1638, USA

Markey, Lucille P (Misc)
18 La Gorce Circle Lane
La Gorce Island
Miami Beach, FL 33141, USA

Markgraf-Sobrero, Kathryn (Athlete, Olympic Athlete, Soccer Player)
5858 N Maitland Ct
Milwaukee, WI 53217-4630, USA

Markham, Dale (Athlete, Football Player)
1832 Valley Dr
Bismarck, ND 58503-0195, USA

Markham, Monte (Actor)
PO Box 607
Malibu, CA 90265-0607, USA

Markie, Biz (Actor, Musician)
c/o Stephanie Mahler *Creative Artists Agency (CAA)*
405 Lexington Ave Fl 19
New York, NY 10174-1800, USA

Markland, Jeff (Athlete, Football Player)
1135 Thornfield Ln
Las Vegas, NV 89123-0828, USA

Markle, Meghan (Actor)
Frogmore House
Windsor SL4 2JG, UNITED KINGDOM

Markle, Paul (Athlete, Football Player)
413 Beresford Ave
Toronto, ON M6S 3B6, Canada

Markle, Peter F (Director)
7510 W Sunset Blvd # 509
Los Angeles, CA 90046-3408, USA

Markopolos, Harry (Writer)
c/o Staff Member *American Program Bureau*
1 Gateway Ctr Ste 751
Newton, MA 02458-2817, USA

Markov, Danny (Athlete, Hockey Player)
17875 Collins Ave Apt 3402
Sunny Isles Beach, FL 33160-2718, USA

Markovich, Mark (Athlete, Football Player)
400 W Thousand Oaks Dr
Peoria, IL 61615-1394, USA

Markowitz, Michael (Artist)
23rd Street Gallery
3747 23rd St
San Francisco, CA 94114-3407, USA

Markowitz, Robert (Director, Producer)
11521 Amanda Dr
Studio City, CA 91604-4144, USA

Marks, John (Athlete, Hockey Player)
3421 Bay Ridge Way
Port Charlotte, FL 33953-4612

Marks, Sen'Derrick (Athlete, Football Player)
c/o Hadley Engelhard *Enter-Sports Management*
6000 Lake Forrest Dr Ste 370
Atlanta, GA 30328-5902, USA

Markwart, Nevin (Athlete, Hockey Player)
PO Box 4
Hanover, MA 02339-0004

Marlatt, Harvey (Athlete, Basketball Player)
10145 Lakeview Dr
Atlanta, MI 49709-9224, USA

Marleau, Patrick (Athlete, Hockey Player)
12021 Magnolia Ct
Saratoga, CA 95070-5386

Marley, Damian (Musician)
Headline Entertainment
8 Haughton Ave
Kingston 00010, JAMAICA

Marley, Julian (Musician)
c/o Staff Member *Ghetto Youths International*
16115 SW 117th Ave Ste A21
Miami, FL 33177-1615, USA

Marley, Skip (Musician)
c/o Emma Banks *CAA (London)*
3 Shortlands, Hammersmith
Fl 5
London W6 8DA, UNITED KINGDOM

Marley, Stephen (Musician)
c/o Patrick McAuliff *Monterey International (Chicago)*
72 W Adams St # 1000
Chicago, IL 60603-5107, USA

Marley, Ziggy (Musician, Songwriter)
Ziggy Marley Management
269 S Beverly Dr # 175
Beverly Hills, CA 90212-3851, USA

Marlin, Sterling (Race Car Driver)
RR 2 Box 162
Ronda, NC 28670, USA

Marling, Brit (Actor)
c/o Michael Sugar *Anonymous Content*
3532 Hayden Ave
Culver City, CA 90232-2413, USA

Marling, Laura (Musician)
c/o Linda Carbone *Press Here Publicity*
138 W 25th St Ste 900
New York, NY 10001-7470, USA

Marlohe, Berenice (Actor)
c/o Andy Coleman *LINK Entertainment*
11872 La Grange Ave
Los Angeles, CA 90025-5282, USA

Marlowe, Andrew (Producer)
c/o Scott Greenberg *Creative Artists Agency (CAA)*
2000 Avenue of the Stars Ste 100
Los Angeles, CA 90067-4705, USA

Marlowe, Marion (Actor)
6790 E Calle La Paz
Tucson, AZ 85715-9000, USA

Marmol, Carlos (Athlete, Baseball Player)
3786 W Pippin St
Chicago, IL 60652-1347, USA

Marnay, Audrey (Actor)
c/o Elisabeth Simpson *Agence Elisabeth Simpson*
62 Boulevard Du Montparnasse
Paris 75015, FRANCE

Marnie, Larry (Coach, Football Coach)
Arizona State University
Athletic Dept
Tempe, AZ 85287-0001, USA

Marohn, James (Horse Racer)
700 Birchwood Dr
Westbury, NY 11590-5807, USA

Marohn, William D (Business Person)
Whirlpool Corp
2000 N State St
RR 63
Benton Harbor, MI 49022, USA

Marois, Daniel (Athlete, Hockey Player)
Hockey Specific Training
19 51e Ave
Notre-Dame-De-L'Ile-Perrot, QC J7V 7L8, CANADA

Marolewski, Fred (Athlete, Baseball Player)
15705 W Waterford Ln
Manhattan, IL 60442-8160, USA

Maron, Marc (Actor, Comedian, Horse Racer, Talk Show Host)
c/o Britney Ross *42West*
1840 Century Park E Ste 700
Los Angeles, CA 90067-2122, USA

Marone, Lou (Athlete, Baseball Player)
10851 Carbet Pl
San Diego, CA 92124-2042, USA

Maroney, Daniel V Jr (Misc)
Amalgamated Transil Union
10000 New Hampshire Ave
Silver Spring, MD 20903-1706, USA

Maroney, Kelli (Actor, Producer)
c/o Staff Member *Bohemia Group*
1680 Vine St Ste 518
Los Angeles, CA 90028-8833, USA

Maroney, Laurence (Athlete, Football Player)
PO Box 11302
Saint Louis, MO 63105-0102, USA

Maroney, McKayla (Athlete, Gymnast)
c/o Staff Member *WME/IMG*
9601 Wilshire Blvd
Beverly Hills, CA 90210-5213, USA

Maroon 5 (Music Group)
c/o Carleen Donovan *Donovan Public Relations*
30 E 20th St Ste 2FE
New York, NY 10003-1310, USA

Maroth, Mike (Athlete, Baseball Player)
909 Johns Point Dr
Oakland, FL 34787-8953, USA

Maroto, Enrique (Athlete, Baseball Player)
701 NW 136th Ave
Miami, FL 33182-2291, USA

Marotte, Gilles (Athlete, Hockey Player)

Maroulis, Constantine (Musician)
c/o Erin Grush *Cunningham Escott Slevin & Doherty (CESD)*
333 7th Ave Ste 1102
New York, NY 10001-5111, USA

Marquardt, Bridget (Model, Reality Star)
c/o Jonathan Stone *SW PR Shop*
142 S Crescent Dr
Beverly Hills, CA 90212-3102, USA

Marques, Tarso (Race Car Driver)
Payton-Coyne Racing
13400 S Budler Rd
Plainfield, IL 60544-9493, USA

Marquette, Chris (Actor)
c/o Jason Cunningham *Paradigm*
8942 Wilshire Blvd
Beverly Hills, CA 90211-1908, USA

Marquez, Alfonso (Athlete, Baseball Player)
PO Box 413
Arbuckle, CA 95912-0413, USA

Marquez, Alfonso (Baseball Player)
4102 S Skyline Ct
Gilbert, AZ 85297-9668, USA

Marquez, Gonzalez Felipe (Politician)
Secretario General
PSOE
Madrid 28023, SPAIN

Marquez, Jeff (Athlete, Baseball Player)
801 Rio Grande Dr
Vacaville, CA 95687-4343, USA

Marquez, Jeffrey (Athlete, Baseball Player)
801 Rio Grande Dr
Vacaville, CA 95687-4343, USA

Marquez, Juan Manuel (Athlete, Boxer)
961 Everett St
Los Angeles, CA 90026-4408, USA

Marquis, Jason (Athlete, Baseball Player)
300 Vogel Ave
Staten Island, NY 10309-2905, USA

Marraccini, Matt (Actor)

Marrero, Eli (Athlete, Baseball Player)
10230 SW 64th St
Miami, FL 33173-2807, USA

Marrero, Mariale (Internet Star)
c/o Kimberly Perplies *James Grant Group Ltd*
94 Strand On the Green
Chiswick
London W4 3NN, UNITED KINGDOM

Marrin, Pete (Athlete, Hockey Player)
1276 Mapleridge Cres
Oakville, ON L6M 2G9, Canada

Marriott, Craig (Actor)
c/o Staff Member *Nickelodeon UK*
PO Box 6425
LONDON W1A 6UR, UNITED KINGDOM

Marriott, J Willard Jr (Business Person)
Marriott International
10400 Fernwood Rd
Bethesda, MD 20817-1102, USA

Marriott, Richard E (Business Person)
Host Marriott Corp
10400 Fernwood Rd
Bethesda, MD 20817-1118, USA

Marrone, Doug (Athlete, Football Player)
Georgia Tech
6100 Waitsfield Dr S
Jamesville, NY 13078-9306, USA

Mars, Bruno (Musician)
c/o Dvora Vener Englefield *The Lede Company*
9701 Wilshire Blvd # 930
Beverly Hills, CA 90212-2020, USA

Mars, Jacqueline (Business Person)
Mars Inc
6885 Elm St Ste 1
McLean, VA 22101-6038, USA

Mars, John (Business Person)
Mars Inc
6885 Elm St Ste 1
McLean, VA 22101-6038, USA

Mars, Mick (Musician)
9229 W Sunset Blvd Ste 718
Los Angeles, CA 90069-3407, USA

Marsalis, Branford (Musician)
Wilkins Mgmt
323 Broadway
Cambridge, MA 02139-1801, USA

Marsalis, James (Athlete, Football Player)
101 Royal Oak Ln
Kathleen, GA 31047-2149, USA

Marsalis, Wynton (Musician)
c/o Staff Member *Creative Artists Agency (CAA)*
2000 Avenue of the Stars Ste 100
Los Angeles, CA 90067-4705, USA

Marsan, Eddie (Actor)
c/o Staff Member *Independent Talent Group*
40 Whitfield St
London W1T 2RH, UNITED KINGDOM

Marschall, Marita (Actor)
Agentur Alexander
Lamontstr 9
Munich 81679, GERMANY

Marsden, Bernie (Musician)
Int'l Talent Booking
27A Floral St
#300
London WC2E 9DQ, UNITED KINGDOM (UK)

Marsden, Freddie (Musician)
Barry Collins
21A Cliftown Road
Southend-on-Sea
Essex SS1 1AB, UNITED KINGDOM (UK)

Marsden, Gerald (Gerry) (Musician)
Barry Collins
21A Cliftown Rd
Southend-on-Sea
Essex SS1 1AB, UNITED KINGDOM (UK)

Marsden, James (Actor)
4218 Warner Blvd
Burbank, CA 91505-4041, USA

Marsden, Jason (Actor)

Marsden, Matthew (Actor)
c/o Paul Nelson *Mosaic Media Group*
407 N Maple Dr # 100
Beverly Hills, CA 90210-3818, USA

Marsden, Roy (Actor)
London Mgmt
2-4 Noel St
London W1V 3RB, UNITED KINGDOM (UK)

Marsh, Brad (Athlete, Hockey Player)
1000 Palladium Dr
Kanata, ON K2V 1A4, Canada

Marsh, Doug (Athlete, Football Player)
629 Forest Ave
Saint Louis, MO 63135-2050, USA

Marsh, Frank (Athlete, Baseball Player)
304 Bay Shore Ave Apt 426
Mobile, AL 36607-2059, USA

Marsh, Gary (Athlete, Hockey Player)
1871 Cardiff Cres
Courtenay, BC V9N 3Z5, Canada

Marsh, Graham (Athlete, Golfer)
Graham Marsh Golf Design
29 Commerce Drive
P.O. Box 300
Rogina, Queensland 04226, Australia

Marsh, Graham (Golfer)
112 Pga Tour Blvd
Ponte Vedra Beach, FL 32082-3046, USA

Marsh, Henry (Athlete, Track Athlete)
General Delivery
Bountiful, UT 84010, USA

Marsh, James (Director)
c/o Duncan Heath *Independent Talent Group*
40 Whitfield St
London W1T 2RH, UNITED KINGDOM

Marsh, Jean (Actor)
c/o Staff Member *Diamond Management*
31 Percy St
London W1T 2DD, UNITED KINGDOM

Marsh, Jodie (Fitness Expert, Model)

Marsh, Julian (DJ)
c/o Staff Member *Diva Central Inc*
7510 W Sunset Blvd # 1445
Los Angeles, CA 90046-3408, USA

Marsh, Kym (Musician)
c/o Staff Member *Safe Management*
111 Guildford Rd
Lightwater
Surrey GU18 5RA, UNITED KINGDOM (UK)

Marsh, Linda (Actor)
170 W End Ave Apt 22P
New York, NY 10023-5414, USA

Marsh, Marian (Actor)
PO Box 1
Palm Desert, CA 92261-0001, USA

Marsh, Michael (Mike) (Athlete, Track Athlete)
2425 Holly Hall St Apt 152
Houston, TX 77054-3996, USA

Marsh, Miles L (Business Person)
Fort James Corp
1919 S Broadway
Green Bay, WI 54304-4905, USA

Marsh, Peter (Athlete, Hockey Player)
210 Coe Rd
Clarendon Hills, IL 60514-1002, USA

Marsh, Randy (Baseball Player)
3023 Winterbourne Rd
Edgewood, KY 41017-9683, USA

Marsh, Randy (Athlete, Baseball Player)
3023 Winterbourne Rd
Edgewood, KY 41017-9683, USA

Marsh, Thomas (Tom) (Athlete, Baseball Player)
9140 Summerfield Rd
Temperance, MI 48182-9757, USA

Marshall, Albert L (Ben) (Athlete, Hockey Player)
9603 166th Street Ct E
Puyallup, WA 98375-2203, USA

Marshall, Amanda (Actor)
Macklam Feldman Mgmt
200-1505 2nd Ave W
Vancouver, BC V6H 3Y4, CANADA

Marshall, Amanda (Musician)
c/o Staff Member *Creative Artists Agency (CAA)*
2000 Avenue of the Stars Ste 100
Los Angeles, CA 90067-4705, USA

Marshall, Amanda (Musician)
c/o Rob Light *Creative Artists Agency (CAA)*
2000 Avenue of the Stars Ste 100
Los Angeles, CA 90067-4705, USA

Marshall, Amber (Actor)
PO Box 5040 Stn Main
High River, AB T1V 1M3, CANADA

Marshall, Arthur (Athlete, Football Player)
4821 Rocky Shoals Cir
Evans, GA 30809-7042, USA

Marshall, Brandon (Athlete, Football Player)
c/o Denise White *EAG Sports Management*
909 N Pacific Coast Hwy Ste 360
El Segundo, CA 90245-3864, USA

Marshall, Brian (Musician)
Agency Group
1776 Broadway Ste 430
New York, NY 10019-2002, USA

Marshall, Burchard (Athlete, Baseball Player)
60 Crouch Ave Apt C12B
Norwich, CT 06360-7329, USA

Marshall, Chan (Cat Power) (Actor, Musician)
c/o Oren Segal *Management Production Entertainment (MPE)*
9229 W Sunset Blvd Ste 301
W Hollywood, CA 90069-3417, USA

Marshall, Chan (Cat Power) (Musician)
c/o Staff Member *Matador Records (NY)*
304 Hudson St Fl 7
New York, NY 10013-1012, USA

Marshall, Charles (Athlete, Football Player)
4605 Preston Bend Dr
Arlington, TX 76016-1970, USA

Marshall, Chuck (Athlete, Football Player)
11215 Ponderosa Ln
Franktown, CO 80116-9306, USA

Marshall, Dave (Athlete, Baseball Player)
4802 E Centralia St
Long Beach, CA 90808-1312, USA

Marshall, David (Athlete, Football Player)
2740 Towne Village Dr
Duluth, GA 30097-7614, USA

Marshall, Donny (Athlete, Basketball Player)
410 N 63rd St
Seattle, WA 98103-5526, USA

Marshall, Donyell (Athlete, Basketball Player)
55 Ridgecreek Trl
Chagrin Falls, OH 44022-2379, USA

Marshall, Ed (Athlete, Football Player)
7010 Monarch St
Corpus Christi, TX 78413-4328, USA

Marshall, Elaine (Politician)
North Carolina Secretary Of State
PO Box 25128
Raleigh, NC 27611-5128, USA

Marshall, Frank (Director, Producer)
c/o Staff Member *Kennedy/Marshall Company*
619 Arizona Ave # 2
Santa Monica, CA 90401-1609, USA

Marshall, F Ray (Politician)
PO Box Y
Austin, TX 78713-8925, USA

Marshall, Grant (Athlete, Hockey Player)
29 Garside Ave
Wayne, NJ 07470-2410

Marshall, James (Actor)
1833 Rutgers Dr
Thousand Oaks, CA 91360-5021, USA

Marshall, James (Horse Racer)
700 Anderson Rd
Jackson, NJ 08527-5340, USA

Marshall, James L (Jim) (Athlete, Football Player)
15150 Blanco Rd Apt 19208
San Antonio, TX 78232-3365, USA

Marshall, Jim (Athlete, Baseball Player, Coach)
19700 N 76th St Apt 1119
Scottsdale, AZ 85255-4787, USA

Marshall, Jim (Athlete, Football Player)
4241 Basswood Rd
Minneapolis, MN 55416-3848, USA

Marshall, Johnston (Athlete, Hockey Player)
Carolina Hurricanes
1400 Edwards Mill Rd
Attn Dir Pro Scouting
Raleigh, NC 27607-3624, USA

Marshall, Keith (Athlete, Baseball Player)
334 Beckwith Rd
Pine City, NY 14871, USA

Marshall, Ken (Actor)
Marshall Artists
345 N Maple Dr # 302
Beverly Hills, CA 90210-3869, USA

Marshall, Kris (Actor)
c/o Claire Maroussas *Independent Talent Group*
40 Whitfield St
London W1T 2RH, UNITED KINGDOM

Marshall, Larry (Athlete, Football Player)
4605 SW Hickory Ln
Blue Springs, MO 64015-4524, USA

Marshall, Leonard (Athlete, Football Player)
PO Box 272016
Boca Raton, FL 33427-2016, USA

Marshall, Michael G (Mike) (Athlete, Baseball Player)
38324 Jendral Ave
Zephyrhills, FL 33542-7830, USA

Marshall, Mike (Athlete, Baseball Player)
6505 Amposta Dr
El Paso, TX 79912-2422, USA

Marshall, Neil (Director)
c/o David Gardner *Artists First*
9465 Wilshire Blvd Ste 900
Beverly Hills, CA 90212-2608, USA

Marshall, Paula (Actor)
6361 Innsdale Dr
Los Angeles, CA 90068-1623, USA

Marshall, Peter (Television Host)
16714 Oak View Dr
Encino, CA 91436-3238, USA

Marshall, Richard (Athlete, Football Player)
c/o Drew Rosenhaus *Rosenhaus Sports Representation*
3921 Alton Rd # 440
Miami Beach, FL 33140-3852, USA

Marshall, Rob (Director)
Moxie Pictures
2644 30th St Ste 100
Santa Monica, CA 90405-3051, USA

Marshall, Scott (Actor, Director)

Marshall, Sean (Athlete, Baseball Player)
6515 N Kilbourn Ave
Lincolnwood, IL 60712-3436, USA

Marshall, Theda (Athlete, Baseball Player)
708 E Phillips Dr N
Littleton, CO 80122-2864, USA

Marshall, Thurgood (Politician)
6546 28th St N
Arlington, VA 22213-1207, USA

Marshall, Tom (Athlete, Basketball Player)
9548 Mariners Cove Ln
Fort Myers, FL 33919-4592, USA

Marshall, Vester (Athlete, Basketball Player)
2204 1st Ave Apt 201
Seattle, WA 98121-1600, USA

Marshall, Warren (Athlete, Football Player)
10108 Clairbourne Pl
Raleigh, NC 27615-1323, USA

Marshall, Whit (Athlete, Football Player)
497 King Rd NW
Atlanta, GA 30342-4046, USA

Marshall, Wilber B (Athlete, Football Player)
4553 Sir Page Ln
Titusville, FL 32796-1444, USA

Marshall, Willie (Athlete, Hockey Player)
2110 Acorn Ct
Lebanon, PA 17042-5769

Marshall-Green, Logan (Actor)
c/o Christine Tripicchio *Shelter PR*
5670 Wilshire Blvd Ste 1200
Los Angeles, CA 90036-5621, USA

Marshall Tucker Band (Music Group)
c/o Ron Rainey *Ron Rainey Management Inc.*
8500 Wilshire Blvd Ste 525
Beverly Hills, CA 90211-3111, USA

Marshburn, Thomas H Dr (Astronaut)
11810 Shoal Landing St
Pearland, TX 77584-8751, USA

Marshmello (Musician)
c/o Staff Member *UTA Music/The Agency Group*
9336 Civic Center Dr
Beverly Hills, CA 90210-3604, USA

Marsilii, Bill (Writer)
c/o Rich Green *ICM Partners*
10250 Constellation Blvd Fl 7
Los Angeles, CA 90067-6207, USA

Marson, Lou (Athlete, Baseball Player)
1680 Glendola Rd
Wall Township, NJ 07719-4506, USA

Marsonek, Sam (Athlete, Baseball Player)
712 Welton Rd
Lutz, FL 33548-5039, USA

Marsters, James (Actor)
c/o Jenni Weinman *The Current Co. PR*
8671 Wilshire Blvd Ste 400
Beverly Hills, CA 90211-2912, USA

Marston, Joshua (Director, Writer)
c/o Cliff Roberts *WME|IMG*
9601 Wilshire Blvd
Beverly Hills, CA 90210-5213, USA

Marston, Natalie Elizabeth (Actor)
c/o Shepard Smith *Luber Roklin Management*
5815 W Sunset Blvd Ste 208
Los Angeles, CA 90028-6481, USA

Marta, Lynn (Actor)
c/o Staff Member *Bobby Ball Talent Agency*
4342 Lankershim Blvd
Universal City, CA 91602, USA

Marte, Judy (Actor)
c/o Michael Cooper *Creative Artists Agency (CAA)*
2000 Avenue of the Stars Ste 100
Los Angeles, CA 90067-4705, USA

Martel, Arlene (Actor)
2109 S Wilbur Ave
Walla Walla, WA 99362-9048, USA

Martemucci, Anna (Director)
c/o Chad Hamilton *Anonymous Content*
3532 Hayden Ave
Culver City, CA 90232-2413, USA

Martha, Paul (Athlete, Football Player)
5008 Starfish Way
San Diego, CA 92154-8420, USA

Marti, Benita (Actor)
c/o Staff Member *Select Artists Ltd (CA-Valley Office)*
PO Box 4359
Burbank, CA 91503-4359, USA

Martika (Musician)
Entertainment Artists
2409 21st Ave S Ste 100
Nashville, TN 37212-5317, USA

Martin, Aaron (Athlete, Football Player)
3605 Seth Ct
Springdale, MD 20774-5408, USA

Martin, Agnes B (Artist)
414 Placilas Road
Taos, NM 87571, USA

Martin, Al (Athlete, Baseball Player)
11000 N 77th Pl Unit 1005
Scottsdale, AZ 85260-5599, USA

Martin, Al (Athlete, Baseball Player)
15251 S 50th St Apt 2054
Phoenix, AZ 85044-9117, USA

Martin, Amos (Athlete, Football Player)
11824 Duane Point Cir Apt 201
Louisville, KY 40243-2725, USA

Martin, Andrea (Actor, Comedian)
c/o Steve Tellez *Innovative Artists*
1505 10th St
Santa Monica, CA 90401-2805, USA

Martin, Ann (Correspondent)
KCBS-TV
6121 W Sunset Blvd
Los Angeles, CA 90028-6442, USA

Martin, Ann M (Writer)
c/o Staff Member *Scholastic Entertainment*
557 Broadway
New York, NY 10012-3962, USA

Martin, Ariel (Baby Ariel) (Internet Star, Musician)
Charlotte Towne, P.A.
29 S Federal Hwy
Dania, FL 33004-3604, USA

Martin, Babe (Athlete, Baseball Player)
114 N Holloway Rd
Ballwin, MO 63011-3205, USA

Martin, Billy (Musician)
c/o Brian Greenbaum *Creative Artists Agency (CAA)*
2000 Avenue of the Stars Ste 100
Los Angeles, CA 90067-4705, USA

Martin, Billy (Athlete, Football Player)

Martin, Blanche (Athlete, Football Player)
1621 Stoney Point Dr
Lansing, MI 48917-1409, USA

Martin, Bob (Athlete, Basketball Player)
5812 44th Ave S
Minneapolis, MN 55417-3017, USA

Martin, Bob (Athlete, Football Player)
14200 N 27th St
Davey, NE 68336-3638, USA

Martin, Boris '"Babe"' (Athlete, Baseball Player)
5660 N Kolb Rd Apt 150
Tucson, AZ 85750-3204

Martin, Brian (Athlete)
777 San Antonio Rd Apt 132
Palo Alto, CA 94303-4858, USA

Martin, Casey (Athlete, Golfer)
University of Oregon
2727 Leo Harris Pkwy
Attn: Athletic Dept
Eugene, OR 97401-8835, USA

Martin, Chris (Actor)
c/o Barry McPherson *Agency for the Performing Arts*
135 W 50th St Fl 17
New York, NY 10020-1201, USA

Martin, Chris (Athlete, Football Player)
c/o Jeff Lynch *Sports Management Worldwide*
1100 NW Glisan St Ste 2B
Portland, OR 97209-3064, USA

Martin, Chris (Musician)
c/o Estelle Wilkinson *Propaganda Management*
14 Percy St
London W1T 1DR, UNITED KINGDOM

Martin, Christy (Boxer)
1203 Foxtree Trl
Apopka, FL 32712-3030, USA

Martin, Cuonzo (Athlete, Basketball Player)
4315 Thistlewood Way
Knoxville, TN 37919-7884, USA

Martin, Curtis (Athlete, Football Player)
100 Hilton Ave Apt PH-1
Garden City, NY 11530-1564, USA

Martin, Dave (Athlete, Football Player)
9306 E Berry Ave
Greenwood Village, CO 80111-3509, USA

Martin, Dave (Chef)
c/o Staff Member *Magical Elves Inc*
453 S Spring St
Los Angeles, CA 90013-2013, USA

Martin, David (Correspondent)
CBS-TV
2020 M St NW
News Dept
Washington, DC 20036-3368, USA

Martin, Deana (Actor)
c/o Staff Member *Studio A Productions*
3000 Green Mountain Dr Ste 107
Branson, MO 65616-4011, USA

Martin, Demetri (Actor, Comedian)
c/o Staff Member *Society Group, The*
2 Hyde Park Sq
London W2 2NW, UNITED KINGDOM

Martin, Don (Athlete, Football Player)
1003 Hilltop Dr
Carrollton, MO 64633-1909, USA

Martin, Doug (Athlete, Football Player)
c/o David Dunn *Athletes First*
23091 Mill Creek Dr
Laguna Hills, CA 92653-1258, USA

Martin, Doug (Athlete, Golfer)
1406 Meadowlake Way
Union, KY 41091-7118, USA

Martin, Duane (Actor)
22401 S Summit Ridge Cir
Chatsworth, CA 91311-2682, USA

Martin, Ed (Baseball Player)
Philadelphia Stars
6666 Brookmont Ter Apt 407
Nashville, TN 37205-4622, USA

Martin, Ed F (Actor)
c/o Steven Neibert *Imperium 7 Talent Agency*
5455 Wilshire Blvd Ste 1706
Los Angeles, CA 90036-4217, USA

Martin, Eric (Athlete, Football Player)
111 Windfall Pl
Clinton, MS 39056-6072, USA

Martin, Gene (Athlete, Baseball Player)
133 Winchester Dr
Leesburg, GA 31763-5064, USA

Martin, George (Athlete, Football Player)
6101 Ravenna Way
Elk Grove, CA 95757-2812, USA

Martin, George R R (Writer)
103 San Salvador Ln
Santa Fe, NM 87501-1739, USA

Martin, Graham Patrick (Actor)
c/o Jessica Katz *Katz Public Relations*
14527 Dickens St
Sherman Oaks, CA 91403-3756, USA

Martin, Greg (Musician)
Mitchell Fox Mgmt
212 3rd Ave N # 301
Nashville, TN 37201-1604, USA

Martin, Henry R (Cartoonist)
1382 Newtown Langhorne Rd # G206
Newtown, PA 18940-2418, USA

Martin, Ingle (Athlete, Football Player)
320 Red Feather Ln
Brentwood, TN 37027-4771, USA

Martin, Jacques (Athlete, Coach, Hockey Player)
Florida Panthers
0-1275 Rue Saint-Antoine O
Montreal, QC H3C 5L2, Canada

Martin, J C (Athlete, Baseball Player)
616 Birch View Dr Apt 36
Matthews, NC 28105-0019, USA

Martin, Jerry (Athlete, Baseball Player)
109 Chelton Ct
Columbia, SC 29212-8522, USA

Martin, Jesse L (Actor)
c/o Bob McGowan *McGowan Management*
170 S Beverly Dr Ste 304
Beverly Hills, CA 90212-3000, USA

Martin, Joe (Cartoonist)
Weederman Grafix
C/O Neatly Chiseled Features
1870 Loramoor Lane
Lake Geneva, WI 53147, USA

Martin, John (Athlete, Baseball Player)
2037 SW Stratford Way
Palm City, FL 34990-2033, USA

Martin, Jonathan (Athlete, Football Player)
c/o Ken Zuckerman *Priority Sports & Entertainment - (LA)*
15233 Ventura Blvd Ste 718
Sherman Oaks, CA 91403-2237, USA

Martin, Judith (Miss Manners) (Journalist)
1651 Harvard St NW
Washington, DC 20009-3702, USA

Martin, Justin (Actor)
c/o Laura Ackerman *Advantage PR*
3900 W Alameda Ave Ste 1200
Burbank, CA 91505-4317, USA

Martin, Kellie (Actor)
c/o William (Willie) Mercer *Thruline Entertainment*
9250 Wilshire Blvd Fl Ground
Beverly Hills, CA 90212-3352, USA

Martin, Kelvin (Athlete, Football Player)
608 Guadalupe Rd
Keller, TX 76248-7337, USA

Martin, Kenyon (Athlete, Basketball Player)
924 Bentwater Pkwy
Cedar Hill, TX 75104-8269, USA

Martin, Keshawn (Athlete, Football Player)
c/o Bruce Tollner *REP 1 Sports Group*
80 Technology Dr
Irvine, CA 92618-2301, USA

Martin, Kevin (Athlete, Basketball Player)
c/o Dan Fegan *Relativity Sports*
2029 Century Park E Ste 1550
Century City, CA 90067-3000, USA

Martin, Larue (Athlete, Basketball Player)
6033 N Sheridan Rd Apt 30E
Chicago, IL 60660-3047, USA

Martin, Madeleine (Actor)
c/o Jill Fritzo *Jill Fritzo Public Relations*
208 E 51st St # 305
New York, NY 10022-6557, USA

Martin, Marcus (Athlete, Football Player)
c/o Joe Panos *Athletes First*
23091 Mill Creek Dr
Laguna Hills, CA 92653-1258, USA

Martin, Maria (Actor)
c/o Staff Member *Select Artists Ltd (CA-Valley Office)*
PO Box 4359
Burbank, CA 91503-4359, USA

Martin, Mark (Race Car Driver)
c/o Staff Member *Hendrick Motorsports*
4400 Papa Joe Hendrick Blvd
Charlotte, NC 28262-5703, USA

Martin, Mark (Athlete, Hockey Player)
5887 SE Riverboat Dr
Stuart, FL 34997-1511, USA

Martin, Marsai (Actor)
c/o Alex Schack *Slate PR*
901 N Highland Ave
W Hollywood, CA 90038-2412, USA

Martin, Max (Producer)
882 N Doheny Dr
West Hollywood, CA 90069-4821, USA

Martin, Meaghan (Actor)
c/o Nick Errington *Grantham-Hazeldine*
162-168 Regent St
#427
London W1B 5TE, UNITED KINGDOM

Martin, Medeski (Musician)
c/o Staff Member *Paradigm (Monterey)*
404 W Franklin St
Monterey, CA 93940-2303, USA

Martin, Mike (Athlete, Baseball Player)
10745 Irving Park Ave
Las Vegas, NV 89166-6032, USA

Martin, Mike (Athlete, Football Player)

Martin, Millicent (Actor, Musician)
London Mgmt
2-4 Noel St
London W1V 3RB, UNITED KINGDOM (UK)

Martin, Norberto (Athlete, Baseball Player)
5905 Ricker Rd
Raleigh, NC 27610-4271, USA

Martin, Ray (Athlete, Baseball Player)
383 Adams St
Quincy, MA 02169-1703, USA

Martin, R Bruce (Misc)
University of Virginia
Chemistry Dept
Charlottesville, VA 22903, USA

Martin, Renie (Athlete, Baseball Player)
509 Little Eagle Ct
Valrico, FL 33594-3973, USA

Martin, Ricky (Actor, Dancer, Musician)
c/o Karynne Tencer *Tencer and Associates*
411 N Oakhurst Dr
Beverly Hills, CA 90210-4037, USA

Martin, Rod (Athlete, Football Player)
PO Box 23
Manhattan Beach, CA 90267-0023, USA

Martin, Roland (Correspondent)

Martin, Rudolf (Actor)
c/o Georg Georgi *Das Imperium*
Torstrasse 129
Berlin 10119, GERMANY

Martin, Rudolph (Actor)
c/o Staff Member *Treusch/Erickson Associates*
8955 Norma Pl
Los Angeles, CA 90069-4818, USA

Martin, Sammy (Athlete, Football Player)
114 Summit Dr
Carriere, MS 39426-7665, USA

Martin, Sandy (Actor)
CNA Assoc
1875 Century Park E Ste 2250
Los Angeles, CA 90067-2563, USA

Martin, Sherrod (Athlete, Football Player)
c/o Hadley Engelhard *Enter-Sports Management*
6000 Lake Forrest Dr Ste 370
Atlanta, GA 30328-5902, USA

Martin, Stacy (Actor)
c/o Jessica Kovacevic *WME/IMG*
9601 Wilshire Blvd Ste 800
Beverly Hills, CA 90210-5210, USA

Martin, Steve (Actor, Comedian, Producer, Writer)
LA Films
PO Box 929
Beverly Hills, CA 90213-0929, USA

Martin, Terry (Athlete, Hockey Player)
185 Hampton Hill Dr
Williamsville, NY 14221-5842, USA

Martin, Todd (Athlete, Olympic Athlete, Tennis Player)
21 Kay St # 5
Newport, RI 02840-2941, USA

Martin, Tom (Athlete, Baseball Player)
8001 Surf Dr
Panama City, FL 32408-8530, USA

Martin, Tony (Athlete, Football Player)
28 Tall Timbers Rd
Thomasville, GA 31757-4808, USA

Martin, Victor Hugo (Actor)
c/o Staff Member *TV Azteca*
Periferico Sur 4121
Colonia Fuentes del Pedregal
DF CP 14141, Mexico

Martin, Wayne (Athlete, Football Player)
PO Box 4
Cherry Valley, AR 72324-0004, USA

Martin, Zack (Athlete, Football Player)
c/o Tom Condon *Creative Artists Agency (CAA)*
401 Commerce St PH
Nashville, TN 37219-2516, USA

Martin Chase, Deborah (Debra) (Producer)
c/o Staff Member *WME/IMG*
9601 Wilshire Blvd
Beverly Hills, CA 90210-5213, USA

Martindale, Margo (Actor)
c/o Andrew Freedman *Andrew Freedman Public Relations*
35 E 84th St
New York, NY 10028-0871, USA

Martindale, Wink (DJ, Television Host)
5744 Newcastle Ln
Calabasas, CA 91302-3117, USA

Martinek, Radek (Athlete, Hockey Player)
64 Hope Dr
Plainview, NY 11803-5650, USA

Martines, Alessandra (Actor)
c/o Francois-Xavier Molin *ArtMedia*
8 rue Danielle Casanova
Paris 75002, FRANCE

Martinez, A (Actor)
PO Box 6387
Malibu, CA 90264-6387, USA

Martinez, Alfredo (Athlete, Baseball Player)
2346 Thomas St
Los Angeles, CA 90031-2820, USA

Martinez, Anais (Musician)
Univision Music Group
5820 Canoga Ave Ste 300
Woodland Hills, CA 91367-6533, USA

Martinez, Angela (Actor)
c/o Ben Scantlin *Imagination 9 Entertainment*
1520 Hauser Blvd
Los Angeles, CA 90019-3970, USA

Martinez, Angie (Musician)
c/o Nadja Rangel *Roc Nation*
1411 Broadway Fl 38
New York, NY 10018-3409, USA

Martinez, Benito (Actor)
c/o Ro Diamond *SDB Partners Inc*
315 S Beverly Dr Ste 411
Beverly Hills, CA 90212-4301, USA

Martinez, Billy Joe (Actor)
c/o Linda McAlister *Linda McAlister Talent*
30 N Raymond Ave Ste 213
Pasadena, CA 91103-3997, USA

Martinez, Buck (Athlete, Baseball Player, Coach)
10315 Long Beach Blvd
Long Beach Township, NJ 08008-3135, USA

Martinez, Carmelo (Athlete, Baseball Player)
32 Brisas Del Plata
Dorado, PR 00646-5118, USA

Martinez, Chito (Athlete, Baseball Player)
100 Legacy Barn Dr Apt 101
Dr Apt 101
Collierville, TN 38017-8726, USA

Martinez, Cliff (Musician)
2400 Summit To Summit Mtrwy
Topanga, CA 90290-4134, USA

Martinez, Constantino (Tino) (Athlete, Baseball Player)
324 Blanca Ave
Tampa, FL 33606-3630, USA

Martinez, Daniel J (Artist)
University of California
Studio Art Dept
Irvine, CA 92717, USA

Martinez, Dave (Athlete, Baseball Player)
3315 Enterprise Rd E
Safety Harbor, FL 34695-5307, USA

Martinez, Edgar (Athlete, Baseball Player)
3036 249th Ave SE
Sammamish, WA 98075-9421, USA

Martinez, Flora (Actor, Musician)
c/o Fernan Martinez *Fernan Martinez Communications*
4141 NE 2nd Ave Ste 106C
Miami, FL 33137-3500, USA

Martinez, Fred (Baseball Player)
California Angels
2346 Thomas St
Los Angeles, CA 90031-2820, USA

Martinez, Greg (Athlete, Baseball Player)
1596 Palora Ave
Las Vegas, NV 89169-2504, USA

Martinez, J Dennis (Athlete, Baseball Player)
9400 SW 63rd Ct
Miami, FL 33156-1817, USA

Martinez, Jorge (Actor)
c/o Staff Member *Telefe (Argentina)*
Pavon 2444
Buenos Aires C1248AAT, ARGENTINA

Martinez, Jose (Athlete, Baseball Player)
14601 SW 33rd Ct
Miramar, FL 33027-3729, USA

Martinez, JR (Actor, Reality Star)
c/o Monique Moss *Integrated PR*
9025 Wilshire Blvd Ste 400
Beverly Hills, CA 90211-1828, USA

Martinez, Mel (Politician)
140 W Fawsett Rd
Winter Park, FL 32789-6016, USA

Martinez, Natalie (Actor)
c/o Jamie Harhay Skinner *Baker Winokur Ryder Public Relations*
9100 Wilshire Blvd
W Tower #500
Beverly Hills, CA 90212-3415, USA

Martinez, Olivier (Actor)
c/o Antonio Rubial *A6 Cinema*
Conde De Xiquena 13
#3D
Madrid 28004, SPAIN

Martinez, Patrice (Actor)
c/o Staff Member *Select Artists Ltd (CA-Valley Office)*
PO Box 4359
Burbank, CA 91503-4359, USA

Martinez, Pedro (Athlete, Baseball Player)
3029 Birkdale
Weston, FL 33332-1813, USA

Martinez, Pedro A (Baseball Player)
186 Fairmount Ave
Hyde Park, MA 02136-3506, USA

Martinez, Ramon J (Athlete, Baseball Player)
Dominican Repubic
Bo San Miguel #9
Managuayaba Santo, Domingo, USA

Martinez, Silvio (Athlete, Baseball Player)
4914 103rd St Fl 2
Corona, NY 11368-3121, USA

Martinez, Tino (Athlete, Baseball Player, Olympic Athlete)
324 Blanca Ave
Tampa, FL 33606-3630, USA

Martinez, Tippy (Athlete, Baseball Player)
1524 Dellsway Rd
Towson, MD 21286-5901, USA

martinez, Victor (Athlete, Baseball Player)
10157 Tavistock Rd
Orlando, FL 32827-7054, USA

Martinez Somalo, Eduardo Cardinal (Religious Leader)
Palazzo delle Congregazioni
Piazza Pio XII 3
Rome 00193, ITALY

Martin-Green, Sonequa (Actor)
c/o Brianna Smith *ID Public Relations*
7060 Hollywood Blvd Fl 8th
Los Angeles, CA 90028-6021, USA

Martini, Max (Actor, Director)
c/o Andrea Britton *Characters Talent Agency (Toronto)*
8 Elm St Fl 2
Toronto, ON M5G 1G7, CANADA

Martinkovic, John (Athlete, Football Player)
1269 April Ln
Green Bay, WI 54304-4038, USA

Martino, Frank D (Misc)
Chemical Workers Union
1655 W Market St
Akron, OH 44313-7004, USA

Martino, Renato R Cardinal (Religious Leader)
Justice & Peace Curia
Piazzo S Calisto 16
Vatican City 00120, VATICAN CITY

Martins, Joao Carlos (Musician)
c/o Staff Member *Musicians Corporate Management*
PO Box 825
Highland, NY 12528-0825, USA

Martins, Steve (Athlete, Hockey Player)
22475 N Linden Dr
Lake Barrington, IL 60010-5956

Martinson, Lestie H (Director)
2288 Coldwater Canyon Dr
Beverly Hills, CA 90210-1756, USA

Martinson, Steve (Athlete, Hockey Player)
1160 Montgomery Blvd Apt 1116
Allen, TX 75013-2717

Martlin, Marlee (Actor)
1723 Cloverfield Blvd
Santa Monica, CA 90404-4007, USA

Marton, Katalin (Kati) (Writer)
c/o Amanda Urban *ICM Partners (NY)*
730 5th Ave
New York, NY 10019-4105, USA

Martone, Lino (Musician)
c/o Gabriel Blanco *Gabriel Blanco Iglesias (Mexico)*
Rio Balsas 35-32
Colonia Cuauhtemoc
DF 06500, Mexico

Marts, Lonnie (Athlete, Football Player)
13650 Bromley Point Dr
Jacksonville, FL 32225-2635, USA

Marty, Martin E (Religious Leader)
175 E Delaware Pl Apt 8508
Chicago, IL 60611-7750, USA

Marty, Mike (Coach, Football Coach)
Saint Louis Rams
29899 Agoura Rd Ste 200
Agoura Hills, CA 91301-2497, USA

Martyn, Bob (Athlete, Baseball Player)
9984 NW Leahy Rd
Portland, OR 97229-6350, USA

Martz, Gary (Athlete, Baseball Player)
188 Lillian Ct SE
Salem, OR 97306, USA

Martz, Mike (Athlete, Football Coach, Football Player)
222 Republic Dr
Allen Park, MI 48101-3650, USA

Martz, Randy (Athlete, Baseball Player)
211 HI Pointe Pl
East Alton, IL 62024-1641, USA

Martzke, Rudy (Writer)
USA Today
1000 Wilson Blvd
Editorial Dept
Arlington, VA 22209-3927, USA

Maruk, Dennis (Athlete, Hockey Player)
15 Berry Creek Dr
Etobicoke, ON M9W 4A1, Canada

Maruyama, Karen (Actor)
c/o Staff Member *Halpern Management*
PO Box 5042
Santa Monica, CA 90409-5042, USA

Maruyama, Shigeki (Athlete, Golfer)
4551 Dempsey Ave
Encino, CA 91436-3136, USA

Marvaso, Tommy (Athlete, Football Player)
PO Box 400
Bethany Beach, DE 19930-0400, USA

Marve, Eugene (Athlete, Football Player)
4516 W Lamb Ave
Tampa, FL 33629-6530, USA

Marvel, Elizabeth (Actor)
c/o Annick Muller *Wolf-Kasteler Public Relations*
40 Exchange Pl Ste 704
New York, NY 10005-2778, USA

Marvelettes, The (Music Group)
9936 Majorca Pl
Boca Raton, FL 33434-3714, USA

Marx, Gilda (Designer, Fashion Designer)
Gilda Marx Industries
11755 Exposition Blvd
Los Angeles, CA 90064-1338, USA

Marx, Greg (Athlete, Football Player)
18721 Jamestown Cir
Northville, MI 48168-3532, USA

Marx, Jeffrey A (Journalist)
Lexington Herald-Leader
Editorial Dept
Main & Midland
Lexington, KY 40507, USA

Marx, Richard (Musician, Songwriter)
27856 Winding Way
Malibu, CA 90265-4457, USA

Marx, Timothy (Producer)
c/o Staff Member *ICM Partners*
10250 Constellation Blvd Fl 7
Los Angeles, CA 90067-6207, USA

Maryland, Russell (Athlete, Football Player)
1330 Eagle Bnd
Southlake, TX 76092-9406, USA

Mary Mary (Music Group)
c/o Richard De La Font *Richard De La Font Agency*
3808 W South Park Blvd
Broken Arrow, OK 74011-1261, USA

Marzoli, Andrea (Misc)
Berkeley Geochronolgoy Center
2455 Ridge Rd
Berkeley, CA 94709-1211, USA

Mas, Adrian (Actor)
c/o Gabriel Blanco *Gabriel Blanco Iglesias (Mexico)*
Rio Balsas 35-32
Colonia Cuauhtemoc
DF 06500, Mexico

Masak, Ron (Actor)
5440 Shirley Ave
Tarzana, CA 91356-2941, USA

Masakayan, Liz (Athlete, Volleyball Player)
2864 Palomino Cir
La Jolla, CA 92037-7066, USA

Masako, Princess (Royalty)
Imperial Palace
1-1 Chiyoda-ku
Tokyo, JAPAN

Masaoka, Onan (Athlete, Baseball Player)
1323 Auwae Rd
Hilo, HI 96720-6906, USA

Mase (Musician)
c/o Staff Member *Combs Enterprises*
1440 Broadway Frnt 3
New York, NY 10018-2301, USA

Masekela, Hugh (Musician)
c/o Staff Member *Opus 3 Artists (LA)*
5670 Wilshire Blvd Ste 1790
Los Angeles, CA 90036-5627, USA

Masekela, Sal (Television Host)
c/o Staff Member *ROAR (LA)*
9701 Wilshire Blvd Fl 8
Beverly Hills, CA 90212-2008, USA

MaShay, Pepper (Actor, Musician)
c/o Staff Member *Diva Central Inc*
7510 W Sunset Blvd # 1445
Los Angeles, CA 90046-3408, USA

Mashburn, Jamal (Athlete, Basketball Player)
5625 Pine Tree Dr
Miami Beach, FL 33140-2149, USA

Mashburn, Jesse (Athlete, Track Athlete)
13549 Borgata Ln
Oklahoma City, OK 73170-2056, USA

Mashkov, Vladimir L (Actor)
Oleg Tabakov Theater
Chaokygina Str 12A
Moscow, RUSSIA

Mashore, Clyde (Athlete, Baseball Player)
590 Valmore Pl
Brentwood, CA 94513-6909, USA

Mashore, Damon (Athlete, Baseball Player)
1538 W Rush Rd
Eagle, ID 83616-3630, USA

Masiello, Tony (Politician)
Mayor's Office
65 Niagara Sq
City Hall
Buffalo, NY 14202-3313, USA

Maske, Henry (Boxer)
Sauerland Promotion
Hochstadenstr 1-3
Cologne 50674, GERMANY

Maslany, Tatiana (Actor)
c/o Sarah Yorke *Baker Winokur Ryder Public Relations*
200 5th Ave Fl 5
New York, NY 10010-3307, USA

Maslow, James (Actor, Musician)
c/o Ed Solorzano *The Brand Partners*
6404 Wilshire Blvd Ste 500
Los Angeles, CA 90048-5507, USA

Maslowski, Matt (Athlete, Football Player)
22281 Destello
Mission Viejo, CA 92691-1525, USA

Masnick, Paul (Athlete, Hockey Player)
303-155 Hillcrest Ave
Cooksville, ON L5B 3Z2, Canada

Mason, Bob (Athlete, Hockey Player)
Minnesota Wild
317 Washington St
Saint Paul, MN 55102-1667

Mason, Bob (Athlete, Hockey Player, Olympic Athlete)
9549 Yukon AveS
Minneapolis, MN 55438-1651, USA

Mason, Bobbie Ann (Writer)
PO Box 518
Lawrenceburg, KY 40342-0518, USA

Mason, Chris (Athlete, Hockey Player)
450 Beauchamp Cir
Franklin, TN 37067-6443, USA

Mason, Dave (Athlete, Football Player)
37 Jackson Ave
Winchester, VA 22601-4933, USA

Mason, Dave (Musician, Songwriter)
3396 Bernese Ct
Carson City, NV 89705-7013, USA

Mason, Derrick (Athlete, Football Player)
8665 Ritchboro Rd
District Heights, MD 20747-2658, USA

Mason, Don (Athlete, Baseball Player)
55 Gunwale Way
Yarmouth Port, MA 02675-2029, USA

Mason, Glen (Coach, Football Coach)
University of Minnesota
Athletic Dept
Minneapolis, MN 55455, USA

Mason, Hank (Athlete, Baseball Player)
5004 W Leyburn Ct Apt 102
Henrico, VA 23228-4852, USA

Mason, Jackie (Actor, Comedian)
World According to Me
146 W 57th St Apt 68D
New York, NY 10019-0079, USA

Mason, Jim (Athlete, Baseball Player)
11410 Queens Way
Theodore, AL 36582-8312, USA

Mason, Laurence (Actor)
c/o Mara Santino *Luber Roklin Management*
5815 W Sunset Blvd Ste 208
Los Angeles, CA 90028-6481, USA

Mason, Lindsey (Athlete, Football Player)
3 Elwell Ct
Randallstown, MD 21133-4307, USA

Mason, Marlyn (Actor, Musician)
27 Glen Oak Ct
Medford, OR 97504-7671, USA

Mason, Marsha (Actor)
c/o Alexa Pagonas *Michael Black Management*
9701 Wilshire Blvd Fl 10
Beverly Hills, CA 90212-2010, USA

Mason, Marty (Athlete, Baseball Player)
8255 SE Angelina Ct
Hobe Sound, FL 33455-8948, USA

Mason, Mercedes (Actor)
c/o Alex Spieller *Baker Winokur Ryder Public Relations*
200 5th Ave Fl 5
New York, NY 10010-3307, USA

Mason, Mike (Athlete, Baseball Player)
723 Wildflower Ln
Chanhassen, MN 55317-3523, USA

Mason, Nick (Musician)
Agency Group
370 City Road
London EC1V 2QA, UNITED KINGDOM (UK)

Mason, Roger (Athlete, Baseball Player)
4587 Stover Rd
Bellaire, MI 49615-9046, USA

Mason, Ron (Coach)
Michigan State University
Athletic Dept
East Lansing, MI 48224, USA

Mason, Stephen (Musician, Songwriter)
c/o Janet Weir *Red Light Management*
5800 Bristol Pkwy Ste 400
Culver City, CA 90230-6898, USA

Mason, Steve (Musician)
Agency Group Ltd
370 City Road
London EC1V 2QA, UNITED KINGDOM (UK)

Mason, Tom (Actor)
870 Heights Pl
Oyster Bay, NY 11771-1122, USA

Mason, Vince (Musician)
Famous Artists Agency
250 W 57th St
New York, NY 10107-0001, USA

Mason, Willy (Musician)
c/o Staff Member *Paradigm (Monterey)*
404 W Franklin St
Monterey, CA 93940-2303, USA

Mason, Zachary (Producer, Writer)
c/o Staff Member *Farrar, Straus and Giroux*
175 Varick St Fl 9
New York, NY 10014-7407, USA

Mass, Jochen (Race Car Driver)
RTL-Sportredaktion
Cologne 50570, GERMANY

Mass, Wayne (Athlete, Football Player)
71 Eagle View Dr
Durango, CO 81303-6686, USA

Massa, Felipe (Race Car Driver)
c/o Staff Member *Jaguar Racing Ltd*
Bradbourne Drive
Tilbrook
Milton Keynes MK7 8BJ, United Kingdom

Massa, Gordon (Athlete, Baseball Player)
12312 The Gates Dr
Raleigh, NC 27614-7323, USA

Massaquoi, Jonathan (Athlete, Football Player)
c/o Bus Cook *Bus Cook Sports, Inc*
1 Willow Bend Dr
Hattiesburg, MS 39402-8552, USA

Massaro, Ashley (Wrestler)
c/o Kerry Rodgerson *World Wrestling Entertainment (WWE)*
1241 E Main St
Stamford, CT 06902-3520, USA

Masse, Bill (Baseball Player)
US Olympic Team
2501 Amherst Ct Apt 25A
Boynton Beach, FL 33436-9017, USA

Massenburg, Tony (Athlete, Basketball Player)
13265 Tony Ln
Stony Creek, VA 23882-3209, USA

Masset, Nick (Athlete, Baseball Player)
14575 W Mountain View Blvd Unit 11107
Surprise, AZ 85374-8674, USA

Massey, Athena (Actor)
8383 Wilshire Blvd # 954
Beverly Hills, CA 90211-2425, USA

Massey, Debbie (Athlete, Golfer)
PO Box 1220
Indian River, MI 49749-1220, USA

Massey, Kyle (Actor)
Boy-O-Boy Entertainment
Creekmoor Ln POB 6811
Riverdale, GA 30296, USA

Massey, Robert (Athlete, Football Player)
6746 Terry Ln
Charlotte, NC 28215-3672, USA

Massey, Vincent (Misc)
University of Michigan
Biochemistry Dept
Ann Arbor, MI 48109, USA

Massiah, Corinne (Actor)
c/o Judy Landis *Judy Landis Management*
Prefers to be contacted by telephone or email
Westlake Village, CA 91362, USA

Massie, Bobby (Athlete, Football Player)
c/o Neil Schwartz *Schwartz & Feinsod*
4 Hillandale Rd
Rye Brook, NY 10573-1705, USA

Massie, Giddeon (Athlete, Cycler, Olympic Athlete)
PO Box 31
Zionhill, PA 18981-0031, USA

Massie, Rick (Athlete, Football Player)
238 Doyle Ave
Paris, KY 40361-1223, USA

Massie, Robert K (Writer)
52 W Clinton Ave
Irvington, NY 10533-2130, USA

Massie, Toby (Race Car Driver)
Massie Flying Hillbilly Racing
3862 N 2450 East Rd
Le Roy, IL 61752-9498, USA

Massimino, Michael J (Astronaut)
15814 Elk Park Ln
Houston, TX 77062-4775, USA

Massive Attack (Music Group)
c/o Perri Cohen *Nasty Little Man*
285 W Broadway Rm 310
New York, NY 10013-2257, USA

Massoglia, Chris (Actor)
c/o Sandra Chang *Anonymous Content*
3532 Hayden Ave
Culver City, CA 90232-2413, USA

Massoud, Mena (Actor)
c/o Amira de Vera *Project Four Public Relations*
2604-125 Western Battery Rd
Toronto, ON M6K 3R8, CANADA

Mast, Dick (Athlete, Golfer)
15831 Tower View Dr
Clermont, FL 34711-9381, USA

Mast, Rick (Race Car Driver)
4909 Stough Rd SW
Concord, NC 28027-8969, USA

Mastanddrea, Katlin (Actor)
c/o DebraLynn Findon *Discover Management (LA)*
11425 Moorpark St
Studio City, CA 91602-2009, USA

Masteller, Dan (Athlete, Baseball Player)
1530 Bay Laurel Dr
Menlo Park, CA 94025-5808, USA

Masters, Ben (Actor)
c/o Staff Member *SMS Talent*
8383 Wilshire Blvd Ste 230
Beverly Hills, CA 90211-2436, USA

Masters, Billy (Athlete, Football Player)
501 SW Silverspur Cir
Lees Summit, MO 64081-2482, USA

Masters, Geoff (Tennis Player)
De Lorain St
Wavell Heights, QLD 04012, AUSTRALIA

Masters, Jamie (Athlete, Hockey Player)
178 Clitheroe Rd
Grafton, ON KOK 2GO, Canada

Masters, Margie (Athlete, Golfer)
8440 E Hazeltine Ln
Tucson, AZ 85710-7161, USA

Masterson, Alanna (Actor)
c/o Brett Ruttenberg *Imprint PR*
6121 W Sunset Blvd
Neuehouse
Los Angeles, CA 90028-6442, USA

Masterson, Chase (Actor)
c/o Bob McGowan *McGowan Management*
170 S Beverly Dr Ste 304
Beverly Hills, CA 90212-3000, USA

Masterson, Christopher (Chris) Kennedy (Actor)
c/o Staff Member *United Talent Agency (UTA)*
9336 Civic Center Dr
Beverly Hills, CA 90210-3604, USA

Masterson, Connie (Athlete, Golfer)
4004 Island Bay Cir
Sanford, FL 32771-6344, USA

Masterson, Danny (Actor, Producer)
c/o Carol Masterson *Masterson Management*
1566 Hillcrest Ave
Glendale, CA 91202-1238, USA

Masterson, Fay (Actor)
c/o Adam Levine *Industry Entertainment Partners*
955 Carrillo Dr Ste 300
Los Angeles, CA 90048-5400, USA

Masterson, Justin (Athlete, Baseball Player)
8550 W Covington Bradford Rd
Covington, OH 45318-8934, USA

Masterson, Lisa (Talk Show Host)
Masterson MD
1333 Ocean Ave Ste A
Santa Monica, CA 90401-1001, USA

Masterson, Mary Stuart (Actor)
c/o John Carrabino *John Carrabino Management*
5900 Wilshire Blvd Ste 740
Los Angeles, CA 90036-5032, USA

Masterson, Sean (Actor, Writer)
c/o Melanie Truhett *Truhett / Garcia Management*
8033 W Sunset Blvd
West Hollywood, CA 90046-2401, USA

Mastny, Tom (Athlete, Baseball Player)
302 Lochleven Ct
Grovetown, GA 30813-5830, USA

Mastodon (Music Group, Musician)
c/o Jon Goldwater *Pinnacle Entertainment*
30 Glenn St
White Plains, NY 10603-3254, USA

Maston, Le'shai (Athlete, Football Player)
7856 Overridge Dr
Dallas, TX 75232-4316, USA

Mastracchio, Richard A (Rick) (Astronaut)
1423 Roden Blvd Sheppard Afb
Houston, TX 76311-1378, USA

Mastrantonio, Mary Elizabeth (Actor, Musician)
c/o Gary Gersh *Innovative Artists*
235 Park Ave S Fl 7
New York, NY 10003-1405, USA

Mastrogiacomo, Gina (Actor)
Pakula/King
9229 W Sunset Blvd Ste 315
Los Angeles, CA 90069-3403, USA

Mastroianni, Chiara (Actor)
P F D Drury House
34-43 Russell St
London WC2B 5HA, UNITED KINGDOM (UK)

Mastroianni, Darin (Athlete, Baseball Player)
4248 Yosemite Ave S
Minneapolis, MN 55416-3125, USA

Mastronardi, Alessandra (Actor)
c/o Angharad Wood *Tavistock Wood Management*
45 Conduit St
London W1S 2YN, UNITED KINGDOM

Mastrov, Mark (Sportscaster)
c/o Staff Member *WME|IMG*
9601 Wilshire Blvd
Beverly Hills, CA 90210-5213, USA

Masur, Andy (Commentator)
8558 E Kettle Pl
Centennial, CO 80112-2709, USA

Masur, Richard (Actor)
10340 Santa Monica Blvd
Los Angeles, CA 90025-6904, USA

Mata, Victor (Athlete, Baseball Player)
Juan Pablo Pina
#16 Alto
Santo Domingo, Dominican Republic, USA

Mata'aho (Royalty)
Royal Palace
PO Box 6
Nuku'alofa, TONGA

Matalin, Mary (Journalist, Talk Show Host, Writer)
Gaslight Inc
325 Fishers Rd
Maurertown, VA 22644-2760, USA

Matan, Bill (Athlete, Football Player)
1660 Peachtree St NW Apt 6109
Atlanta, GA 30309-2485, USA

Matarazzo, Gaten (Actor)
c/o Peggy Sherwin Becker *Parkside Talent*
454 Penns Way
Basking Ridge, NJ 07920-3071, USA

Matarazzo, Heather (Actor)
c/o Kieran Maguire *The Arlook Group*
11663 Gorham Ave Apt 5
Los Angeles, CA 90049-4749, USA

Matarazzo, Len (Athlete, Baseball Player)
464 Deer Run
New Castle, PA 16105-1448, USA

Matchbox Twenty (Music Group)
c/o Michael Lippman *Lippman Entertainment*
23586 Calabasas Rd Ste 208
Calabasas, CA 91302-1361, USA

Matchett, Kari (Actor)
806 Woodlawn Ave
Venice, CA 90291-4915, USA

Matchick, Tom (Athlete, Baseball Player)
7700 Pilliod Rd
Holland, OH 43528-8077, USA

Matenopoulos, Debbie (Actor, Producer)
c/o Staff Member *Fifteen Minutes*
5670 Wilshire Blvd Ste 830
Los Angeles, CA 90036-5684, USA

Matesa, Zlatko (Prime Minister)
Prime Minister's Office
Jordanovac 71
Zagreb 41000, CROATIA

Mateschitz, Dietrich (Business Person)
Red Bull
Am Brunnen 1
Fuschl am See 05330, Austria

Matheny, Jim (Athlete, Football Player)
6850 N Pira Ave
Meridian, ID 83646-4953, USA

Matheny, Mike (Athlete, Baseball Player)
c/o John Boggs *John Boggs & Associates*
6265 Greenwich Dr Ste 240
San Diego, CA 92122-5921, USA

Mathers, Jerry (Actor)
23965 Via Aranda
Valencia, CA 91355-3112, USA

Matheson, 1Tim (Actor, Director)
c/o Mike Liotta *True Public Relations*
3575 Cahuenga Blvd W Ste 360
Los Angeles, CA 90068-1361, USA

Matheson, Chris (Writer)
c/o Rima Greer *Above the Line Agency*
468 N Camden Dr Ste 200
Beverly Hills, CA 90210-4507, USA

Matheson, Jim (Congressman, Politician)
2434 Rayburn Hob
Washington, DC 20515-0305, USA

Mathews, Byron (Baseball Player)
557 Golfwood Dr
Ballwin, MO 63021-6316, USA

Mathews, Carole (Actor)
39668 Old Spring Rd
Murrieta, CA 92563-5550, USA

Mathews, Greg (Athlete, Baseball Player)
4007 Layang Layang Cir
Cir Apt H
Carlsbad, CA 92008-4166, USA

Mathews, Harlan (Senator)
420 Hunt Club Rd
Nashville, TN 37221-4310, USA

Mathews, Nelson (Athlete, Baseball Player)
211 E Crestview Dr
Columbia, IL 62236-1203, USA

Mathews, Ray (Athlete, Football Player)
PO Box 108
Harrisville, PA 16038-0108, USA

Mathews, Rick (Athlete, Baseball Player)
837 Drake Ave
Centerville, IA 52544-2524, USA

Mathews, Ross (Comedian, Correspondent, Television Host)
c/o Staff Member *E! Entertainment Television (LA)*
5750 Wilshire Blvd
Los Angeles, CA 90036-3697, USA

Mathews, Ryan (Athlete, Football Player)
c/o Frank Bauer *Sun West Sports*
7883 N Pershing Ave
Stockton, CA 95207-1749, USA

Mathews, Thom (Actor)
c/o Annie Schmidt *Untitled Entertainment (NY)*
215 Park Ave S Fl 8
New York, NY 10003-1622, USA

Mathews, T J (Athlete, Baseball Player)
211 E Crestview Dr
Columbia, IL 62236-1203, USA

Mathias, Buster Jr (Boxer)
4409 Carol Ave SW
Wyoming, MI 49519-4519, USA

Mathias, Carl (Athlete, Baseball Player)
567 Long Ln
Oley, PA 19547-9009, USA

Mathias, Ric (Athlete, Football Player)
13753 Cardinal Point Trl
Verona, WI 53593-8152

Mathieson, Jim (Athlete, Hockey Player)
88 Shaws Mill Rd
Gorham, ME 04038-2231

Mathieson, John (Director)
c/o Spyros Skouras *The Skouras Agency*
1149 3rd St Ste 300
Santa Monica, CA 90403-7201, USA

Mathieu, Marquis (Athlete)
113 W Lake Shore Dr
Hallandale, FL 33009-6026

Mathieu, Mireille (Actor, Musician)
Info Stelle Deutschland
<Gérrestr.13
Fulda D - 36041, Germany

Mathieu, Philip (Musician)
Lindy S MArtin Mgmt
5 Loblolly Ct
Executive Suite
Pinehurst, NC 28374-9349, USA

Mathieu, Tyrann (Athlete, Football Player)

Mathilde, Princess (Royalty)
Koninklijk Palace
Rue de Brederode
Brussels 01000, BELGIUM

Mathis, Alonzo (Gorilla Zoe) (Musician)
c/o Staff Member *Atlantic Records*
1290 Avenue of the Americas Fl 28
New York, NY 10104-0106, USA

Mathis, Bill (Athlete, Football Player)
43 West Paces Dr NW
Atlanta, GA 30327, USA

Mathis, Clint (Soccer Player)
c/o Lyle Yorks *James Grant Sports Ltd (USA)*
3233 M St NW
Washington, DC 20007-3556, USA

Mathis, Evan (Athlete, Football Player)
c/o Drew Rosenhaus *Rosenhaus Sports Representation*
3921 Alton Rd # 440
Miami Beach, FL 33140-3852, USA

Mathis, Greg (Judge)
1962 Stradella Rd
Los Angeles, CA 90077-2321, USA

Mathis, Jeff (Athlete, Baseball Player)
4420 Spring Valley Dr
Marianna, FL 32448-5414, USA

Mathis, Johnny (Musician)
PO Box 2066
Burbank, CA 91507-2066, USA

Mathis, Rashean (Athlete, Football Player)
26200 Marsh Landing Pkwy
Ponte Vedra Beach, FL 32082-1224, USA

Mathis, Robert (Athlete, Football Player)
c/o Hadley Engelhard *Enter-Sports Management*
6000 Lake Forrest Dr Ste 370
Atlanta, GA 30328-5902, USA

Mathis, Ron (Athlete, Baseball Player)
1441 Wagner St
Houston, TX 77007-3721, USA

Mathis, Samantha (Actor)
c/o Courtney Kivowitz *MGMT Entertainment (The Schiff Company)*
9220 W Sunset Blvd Ste 106
W Hollywood, CA 90069-3500, USA

Mathis, Terance (Athlete, Football Player)
3415 Camellia Ln
Suwanee, GA 30024-5348, USA

Mathison, Bruce (Athlete, Football Player)
1228 E Squawbush Pl
Phoenix, AZ 85048-4450, USA

Mathison, Cameron (Actor)
c/o Staff Member *Innovative Artists*
1505 10th St
Santa Monica, CA 90401-2805, USA

Mathison, Camerson (Actor)
c/o Staff Member *Innovative Artists*
1505 10th St
Santa Monica, CA 90401-2805, USA

Mathison, Melissa (Writer)
655 Macculloch Dr
Los Angeles, CA 90049-2024, USA

Matias, John (Athlete, Baseball Player)
98-1616 Hoolauae St
Aiea, HI 96701-1801, USA

Matiko, Marie (Actor)
c/o Staff Member *Sovereign Talent Group*
1642 Westwood Blvd Ste 202
Los Angeles, CA 90024-5609, USA

Matisyahu (Musician)
c/o Carla Sacks *Sacks and Co*
119 W 57th St PH North
New York, NY 10019-2401, USA

Matkevich, Mark (Actor)
c/o Staff Member *Glasser/Black Management*
283 Cedarhurst Ave
Cedarhurst, NY 11516-1671, USA

Matlack, Jon (Athlete, Baseball Player)
2495 Sawdust Rd
Aot 1101
Spring, TX 77380-3354, USA

Matlack-Sagrati, Ruth (Athlete, Baseball Player, Commentator)
1086 Bristol Pike Apt 312
Bensalem, PA 19020-5664, USA

Matlin, Marlee (Actor, Producer)
c/o Staff Member *Solo One Productions*
8149 Santa Monica Blvd # 279
West Hollywood, CA 90046-4912, USA

Matlock, Glen (Musician)
Solo Agency
55 Fulham High St
London SW6 3JJ, UNITED KINGDOM (UK)

Matola, Sharon (Misc)
Belize Zoo & Tropical Education Center
PO Box 1787
Belize City, BELIZE

Matos, Francisco (Athlete, Baseball Player)
Arkansas Travelers
PO Box 55066
Coaching Staff
Little Rock, AR 72215-5066, USA

Matos, Julius (Athlete, Baseball Player)
12823 Valimar Rd
New Port Richey, FL 34654-4815, USA

Matranga, Dave (Athlete, Baseball Player)
303 N Park Ln
Orange, CA 92867-7640, USA

Matricaria, Ronald (Business Person)
Saint Jude Medical Inc
1 Lillehei Plz
Saint Paul, MN 55117-1799, USA

Matsik, George A (Business Person)
Ball Corp
10 Longs Peak Dr
Broomfield, CO 80021-2510, USA

Matson, April (Actor)
c/o Jennifer Millar *Paradigm*
8942 Wilshire Blvd
Beverly Hills, CA 90211-1908, USA

Matson, J Randel (Randy) (Athlete, Track Athlete)
1002 Park Pl
College Station, TX 77840-3008, USA

Matson, Pat (Athlete, Football Player)
987 Village Circle Dr
Greenwood, IN 46143-8465, USA

Matson, Randy (Athlete, Olympic Athlete, Track Athlete)
1002 Park Pl
College Station, TX 77840-3008, USA

Matsos, Arch (Athlete, Football Player)
1410 Coventry Close St
East Lansing, MI 48823-2419, USA

Matsos, Archie (Athlete, Football Player)
1410 Coventry Close St
East Lansing, MI 48823-2419, USA

Matsuda, Naomi (Actor)
c/o Staff Member *AKA Talent Agency*
325 N Larchmont Blvd
Los Angeles, CA 90004-3011, USA

Matsuda, Seiko (Actor, Musician)
Propaganda Films Mgmt
1741 Ivar Ave
Los Angeles, CA 90028-5105, USA

Matsui, Hideki (Athlete, Baseball Player)
845 United Nations Plz Apt 52C
New York, NY 10017-3536, USA

Matsui, Kaz (Athlete, Baseball Player)
229 N Almont Dr
Beverly Hills, CA 90211-1615, USA

Matsui, Keiko (Musician)
Ted Kurland
173 Brighton Ave
Boston, MA 02134-2003, USA

Matsui, Kosei (Artist)
Ibaraki-ken
Kasama-shi
Kasama 00350, JAPAN

Matsukisa, Nobuyaki (Nobu) (Chef)
c/o Staff Member *Verve Entertainment*
5900 Wilshire Blvd # 1720
Los Angeles, CA 90036-5013, USA

Matsumoto, Shigeharu (Writer)
International House of Japan
11-16 Roppongi
Minatuku
Tokyo, JAPAN

Matsushita, Hiro (Race Car Driver)
1600 Avenida Salvador
San Clemente, CA 92672-3265, USA

Matsuzaka, Daisuke (Athlete, Baseball Player)
c/o Scott Boras *Boras Corporation*
18 Corporate Plaza Dr
Newport Beach, CA 92660-7901, USA

Matt, Morris (Athlete, Hockey Player)
9 Elmdale Blvd
Brandon, MB R7B 1B5, Canada

Matta, del Meskin (Religious Leader)
Deir el Makarios Monastery
Cairo, EGYPT

Matt and Kim (Music Group)
c/o Staff Member *Right On PR*
4010 Cherrywood Rd
Austin, TX 78722-1222, USA

Matte, Thomas R (Tom) (Athlete, Football Player)
11309 Old Carriage Rd
Glen Arm, MD 21057-9422, USA

Mattea, Kathy (Actor, Musician)
Kathy Mattea Fan Club
866 Sage Dr
Pleasant Grove, UT 84062-2019, USA

Mattei, Frank (Musician)
Joe Taylor Mgmt
PO Box 1017
Turnersville, NJ 08012-0837, USA

Mattek-Sands, Bethanie (Athlete, Tennis Player)
c/o Staff Member *CMPR*
1600 Rosecrans Ave Bldg 3
Manhattan Beach, CA 90266-3708, USA

Matter, Niall (Actor)
c/o Trina Allen *Play Management*
220-807 Powell St
Vancouver, BC V6A 1H7, CANADA

Mattes, Eva (Actor)
Agentur Carola Studlar
Neurieder Str
#1C
San Diego, CA 92152-0001, GERMANY

Mattes, Ron (Athlete, Football Player)
1718 Moreland Wood Trl NW
Concord, NC 28027-8093, USA

Mattes, Troy (Athlete, Baseball Player)
2932 Lexington St
Sarasota, FL 34231-6118, USA

Mattesich, Rudi (Skier)
General Delivery
Troy, VT 05868, USA

Matteson, Troy (Athlete, Golfer)
6518 Old Shadburn Ferry Rd
Buford, GA 30518-1138, USA

Matteucci, Matt (Athlete, Hockey Player)
4282 W Timberwood Dr
Traverse City, MI 49686-3844

Matthes, Roland (Swimmer)
Luitpoldstr 35A
Marktheidenfeld 97828, GERMANY

Matthes, Ulrich (Actor)
Kuno-Fischer-Str 14
Berlin 14057, GERMANY

Matthew, Catriona (Athlete, Golfer)
I M G
Pler House Strand on the Green
Chiswick
London W4 3NN, United Kingdom

Matthews, Al (Athlete, Football Player)
2880 Donnell Dr Unit 1901
Round Rock, TX 78664-2348, USA

Matthews, Aubrey (Athlete, Football Player)
15 St Charles Pl
Madison, MS 39110-9593, USA

Matthews, Bill (Athlete, Football Player)
32 Olde Farm Rd
South Easton, MA 02375-1438, USA

Matthews, Bo (Athlete, Football Player)
PO Box 17167
Huntsville, AL 35810-7167, USA

Matthews, Bruce R (Athlete, Football Player)
6423 Oilfield Rd
Sugar Land, TX 77479-9603, USA

Matthews, Casey (Athlete, Football Player)
c/o David Dunn *Athletes First*
23091 Mill Creek Dr
Laguna Hills, CA 92653-1258, USA

Matthews, Cerys (Musician)
c/o Staff Member *UTA Music/The Agency Group (UK)*
361-373 City Rd
London EC1V 1PQ, UNITED KINGDOM

Matthews, Chris (Television Host)
c/o Staff Member *MSNBC*
30 Rockefeller Plz
New York, NY 10112-0015, USA

Matthews, Clay (Athlete, Football Player)
6068 Canterbury Dr
Agoura Hills, CA 91301-4131, USA

Matthews, Cliff (Athlete, Football Player)

Matthews, Dakin (Actor)
c/o Staff Member *McCabe Group*
3211 Cahuenga Blvd W Ste 104
Los Angeles, CA 90068-1372, USA

Matthews, Dave (Musician, Songwriter)
c/o Wendy Murphey *LBI Entertainment*
2000 Avenue of the Stars
N Tower Fl 3
Los Angeles, CA 90067-4700, USA

Matthews, DeLane (Actor)
Don Buchwald
5500 Wilshire Blvd # 2200
Los Angeles, CA 90036-3802, USA

Matthews, Denny (Commentator)
11816 Norwood Dr
Leawood, KS 66211-3006, USA

Matthews, Gary N (Athlete, Baseball Player)
1542 W Jackson Blvd
Chicago, IL 60607-5304, USA

Matthews, Ian (Musician)
Geoffrey Blumenauer
11846 Balboa Blvd # 204
Granada Hills, CA 91344-2753, USA

Matthews, Jake (Athlete, Football Player)

Matthews, Kevin (Athlete, Football Player)
c/o David Dunn *Athletes First*
23091 Mill Creek Dr
Laguna Hills, CA 92653-1258, USA

Matthews, Liesel (Actor)
c/o Staff Member *Creative Artists Agency (CAA)*
2000 Avenue of the Stars Ste 100
Los Angeles, CA 90067-4705, USA

Matthews, Mike (Athlete, Baseball Player)
14326 Bakerwood Pl
Haymarket, VA 20169-2638, USA

Matthews, Pat Stanley (Actor)
210 Stanton St
Walla Walla, WA 99362-2058, USA

Matthews, Rishard (Athlete, Football Player)
c/o Kennard McGuire *MS World LLC*
1270 Crabb River Rd Ste 600 PMB 104
Richmond, TX 77469-5635, USA

Matthews, Shane (Athlete, Football Player)
848 NW 136th St
Newberry, FL 32669-3329, USA

Matthews, Steve (Athlete, Football Player)
342 Short Springs Rd
Tullahoma, TN 37388-5234, USA

Matthews, Vincent (Vince) (Athlete, Track Athlete)
6755 193rd Lane
Fresh Meadows, NY 11365, USA

Matthews Jr, Gary (Athlete, Baseball Player)
4721 Dorchester Rd
Corona Del Mar, CA 92625-2717, USA

Matthias, Shawn (Athlete, Hockey Player)
Newport Sports Management
400-201 City Centre Dr
Attn Don Meehan
Mississauga, ON L5B 2T4, Canada

Matthies, Nina (Athlete, Coach, Volleyball Player)
Pepperdine University
24255 Pacific Coast Hwy
Athletic Dept
Malibu, CA 90263-3999, USA

Matthiesen, David H Dr (Astronaut)
3770 E Surrey Ct
Rocky River, OH 44116-4206, USA

Mattiace, Len (Athlete, Golfer)
12803 Hunt Club Rd N
Jacksonville, FL 32224-7654, USA

Mattingly, Don (Athlete, Baseball Player)
7601 Newburgh Rd
Evansville, IN 47715-4527, USA

Mattingly, Mack F (Politician, Senator)
4315 10th St
East Beach
Saint Simons Island, GA 31522-3004, USA

Mattingly, Thomas K Radm (Astronaut)
1500 Quail St Spc 103
Newport Beach, CA 92660-2732, USA

Mattiussi, Dick (Athlete, Hockey Player)
6 Varley Cres
Brantford, ON N3R 7Z3, Canada

Mattos, Grant (Athlete, Football Player)
1392 Miller Pl
Los Angeles, CA 90069-1423, USA

Mattson, Riley (Athlete, Football Player)
12 Coconut Grove Ln
Lahaina, HI 96761-8735, USA

Mattson, Robin (Actor)
Stan Kamens Mgmt
7772 Torreyson Dr
Los Angeles, CA 90046-1227, USA

Mattson-Baumgart, Jacqueline (Athlete, Baseball Player, Commentator)
4814 W Fillmore Dr
Milwaukee, WI 53219-2364, USA

Mattsson, Helena (Actor)
c/o Liza Anderson *Anderson Group Public Relations*
8060 Melrose Ave Fl 4
Los Angeles, CA 90046-7038, USA

mattsson, Markus (Athlete, Hockey Player)
Instrumentointi-OY Sarankulmankatu 20
Tampere, SF 33900, Finland

Matula, Rick (Athlete, Baseball Player)
1817 Chapel Heights Dr
Wharton, TX 77488-4459, USA

Matusz, Brian (Athlete, Baseball Player)
4748 E White Dr
Paradise Vly, AZ 85253-2416, USA

Matuszek, Len (Athlete, Baseball Player)
10326 Deerfield Rd
Cincinnati, OH 45242-5105, USA

Matvichuk, Richard (Athlete, Hockey Player)
8 Chapel Hill Ct
Cedar Grove, NJ 07009-1302, USA

Matz, Johanna (Actor)
Opernring 4
Vienna 01010, Austria

Matzdorf, Pat (Athlete, Track Athlete)
1252 Bainbridge Dr
Naperville, IL 60563-2065, USA

Maualuga, Rey (Athlete, Football Player)

Mauban, Maria (Actor)
4 sq. Vitruve
Paris 75020, France

Mauch, Billy (Bill) (Actor)
538 W Northwest Hwy Unit C
Palatine, IL 60067-8695, USA

Mauck, Carl (Athlete, Football Player)
2129 Winthrop Hill Rd
Argyle, TX 76226-2103, USA

Mauck, Matt (Athlete, Football Player)
3 Coral Pl
Greenwood Village, CO 80111-3457, USA

Mauer, Joe (Athlete, Baseball Player)
c/o Ron Shapiro *Shapiro Sher Guinot & Sandler*
36 S Charles St Ste 2000
Baltimore, MD 21201-3104, USA

Mauga, Josh (Athlete, Football Player)

Maugham, R H (Religious Leader)
Christian & Missionary Alliance
8595 Explorer Dr
Colorado Springs, CO 80920-1012, USA

Maulden, Jerry L (Business Person)
Entergy Corp
10055 Grogans Mill Rd Ste 150
The Woodlands, TX 77380-1048, USA

Mauldin, Greg (Athlete, Hockey Player)
69 Zain Cir
Milford, MA 01757-2831

Mauldin, William H (Cartoonist)
Loomis-Watkins Agency
150 E 35th St
New York, NY 10016-4102

Maule, Brad (Actor)
c/o Hank Hedland *Opus Entertainment*
5225 Wilshire Blvd Ste 905
Los Angeles, CA 90036-4353, USA

Maumenee, Alfred E (Misc)
1700 Hillside Rd
Stevenson, MD 21153-0662, USA

Maura, Carmen (Actor)
GRPC SL
Calle Fuencarral 17
Madrid 28004, SPAIN

Maurer, Andy (Athlete, Football Player)
30 Perrydale Ave
Medford, OR 97501-2037, USA

Maurer, Dave (Athlete, Baseball Player)
18761 Heathcote Dr
Wayzata, MN 55391-3670, USA

Maurer, Rob (Athlete, Baseball Player)
3114 E Gum St
Evansville, IN 47714-2614, USA

Mauresmo, Amelie (Amy) (Tennis Player)
Athleteline
2 rue du chemin vert
Clichy 92110, FRANCE

Maurey, Nicole (Actor)
Residence Les Tuilerie
6 Square De Caustiglione
BP 9005
Le Chesnay F-78150, FRANCE

Mauriac, Claude (Writer)
24 Quai de Bethune
Paris 75004, FRANCE

Maurice, Ann (Actor)
c/o Lucy Inskip *House Doctor Network*
Gladstone Forge, Gladstone Ln
Cold Ash
Berkshire RG18 9PR, UK

Maurice, Paul (Athlete, Hockey Player)
3032 Cone Manor Ln
Raleigh, NC 27613-6604

Mauriello, Julianna Rose (Actor)
c/o Nancy Carson *Carson-Adler Agency*
250 W 57th St Ste 2128
New York, NY 10107-2104, USA

Mauriello, Ralph (Athlete, Baseball Player)
4241 Persimmon St
Moorpark, CA 93021-3515, USA

Maurin, Laurence (Skier)
PO Box 1980
West Bend, WI 53095-7980, USA

Mauro, Jeff (Television Host)
c/o Scott Feldman *Two Twelve Management*
PO Box 2305
New York, NY 10021-0056, USA

Maurstad, Toralv (Actor, Director)
National Theatre
Storlingsgt 15
Osto 00001, NORWAY

Maury, Duncan (Athlete, Football Player)
1554 Fallbrook Ave
Clovis, CA 93611-7348, USA

Mauser, Tim (Athlete, Baseball Player)
114 Shadow Creek Ln
Aledo, TX 76008-3111, USA

Mauti, Michael (Athlete, Football Player)
c/o Michael McCartney *Priority Sports & Entertainment (Chicago)*
325 N La Salle Dr Ste 650
Chicago, IL 60654-8182, USA

Mauti, Rich (Athlete, Football Player)
304 Plantation Dr
Mandeville, LA 70471-1502, USA

Mavericks, The (Music Group)
c/o Jake Basden *Big Machine Records*
1219 16th Ave S
Nashville, TN 37212-2901, USA

Mavety, Larry (Athlete, Hockey Player)
243 Olympus Ave
Kingston, ON K7M 5S3, Canada

Mawae, Kevin J (Athlete, Football Player)
3704A Estes Rd
Nashville, TN 37215-1729, USA

Mawby, Russell G (Misc)
WK Kellogg FOundation
1 Michigan Ave E
Battle Creek, MI 49017-4012, USA

Max, Peter (Artist)
PeterMax.com
118 Riverside Dr
New York, NY 10024-3708, USA

Max, Tucker (Writer)
815A Brazos St # 220
Austin, TX 78701-2502, USA

Maxa, Rudy (Radio Personality, Television Host)
SavTrav Productions, Inc.
P.O. Box 65066
St. Paul, MN 55165-0066, USA

Maxcy, Brian (Athlete, Baseball Player)
1037 Eagle Valley Dr
Birmingham, AL 35242-6962, USA

Maxey, Caty (Designer)
c/o Staff Member *Mirisch Agency*
8840 Wilshire Blvd Ste 100
Beverly Hills, CA 90211-2606, USA

Maxey, Marlon (Athlete, Basketball Player)
109 E 59th St # 2
Chicago, IL 60637-2103, USA

Maxie, Brett (Athlete, Football Player)
1610 Fair Oaks Dr
Westlake, TX 76262-8209, USA

Maxie, Larry (Athlete, Baseball Player)
296 Verdugo Way
Upland, CA 91786-7138, USA

Maxson, Alvin (Athlete, Football Player)
17377 E Adriatic Pl Apt S302
Aurora, CO 80013-5130, USA

Maxvill, Dal (Athlete, Baseball Player, Commentator)
1115 Eagle Creek Rd
Wildwood, MO 63005-6606, USA

Maxwell (Musician)
c/o Marilyn Laverty *Shore Fire Media*
32 Court St Fl 16
Brooklyn, NY 11201-4441, USA

Maxwell, Brad (Athlete, Hockey Player)
27285 Natchez Ave
Elko, MN 55020-9563

Maxwell, Cedric (Athlete, Basketball Player)
151 Tremont St Apt 25R
Apt 25R
Boston, MA 02111-1123, USA

Maxwell, Charlie (Athlete, Baseball Player)
730 Mapleview Dr
Paw Paw, MI 49079-1185, USA

Maxwell, Dobie (Comedian)
333 W North Ave # 343
Chicago, IL 60610-1293, USA

Maxwell, Frank (Politician)
Federation of TV-Radio Artists
260 Madison Ave
New York, NY 10016-2400, USA

Maxwell, Jacqui (Actor)
c/o Karen Goldberg *Inphenate*
9701 Wilshire Blvd Fl 10
Beverly Hills, CA 90212-2010, USA

Maxwell, Jason (Athlete, Baseball Player)
608 Summit Oaks Ct
Nashville, TN 37221-4447, USA

Maxwell, John (Business Person, Writer)
The John Maxwell Company
2170 Satellite Blvd Ste 195
Duluth, GA 30097-4971, USA

Maxwell, Julie (Writer)
c/o Staff Member *Rogers, Coleridge & White Ltd.*
20 Powis Mews
London W11 1JN, UK

Maxwell, Justin (Athlete, Baseball Player)

Maxwell, Kevin (Athlete, Hockey Player)
16 Morton Ln
West Hartford, CT 06117-1427

Maxwell, Monica (Athlete, Basketball Player)
5864 Augusta Meadows Dr
Indianapolis, IN 46254-7055, USA

Maxwell, Ronald F (Director, Writer)
c/o Staff Member *Phoenix Organization, The*
540 San Vicente Blvd Apt 21
Santa Monica, CA 90402-1865, USA

Maxwell, Stella (Model)
c/o Katie Rhodes *Untitled Entertainment*
350 S Beverly Dr Ste 200
Beverly Hills, CA 90212-4819, USA

Maxwell, Tommy (Athlete, Football Player)
2502 Herons Nest Dr
Granbury, TX 76048-1206, USA

Maxwell, Vernon (Athlete, Basketball Player)
2601 NW 23rd Blvd Apt 170
Gainesville, FL 32605-5954, USA

Maxwell, Vernon (Athlete, Football Player)
1955 E Citation Ln
Tempe, AZ 85284-4708, USA

May, Alan (Athlete, Hockey Player)
c/o Staff Member *Boston Bruins*
100 Legends Way Ste 250
Td Banknorth Garden
Boston, MA 02114-1389, USA

May, Alan (Athlete, Hockey Player)
Washington Capitals
627 N Glebe Rd Ste 850
Arlington, VA 22203-2129

May, Bob (Athlete, Golfer)
420 Grand Augusta Ln
Las Vegas, NV 89144-4300, USA

May, Brad (Athlete, Hockey Player)
9167 E Mountain Spring Rd
Scottsdale, AZ 85255-9151

May, Brian (Musician, Songwriter)
Old Bakehouse
16A High St Barnes
London SW13, UNITED KINGDOM (UK)

May, Carlos (Athlete, Baseball Player)
6102 Amherst Pl
Matteson, IL 60443-1988, USA

May, Chad (Athlete, Football Player)
1300 S Jesse St
Chandler, AZ 85286-1142, USA

May, Darrell (Athlete, Baseball Player)
3315 Windsor Rd
Austin, TX 78703-2263, USA

May, David (Actor)
c/o Staff Member *Cunningham Escott Slevin & Doherty (CESD)*
10635 Santa Monica Blvd Ste 130
Los Angeles, CA 90025-8306, USA

May, Dean (Athlete, Football Player)
7487 Alhambra Ct
Spring Hill, FL 34606-6602, USA

May, Deborah (Actor)
Artists Agency
1180 S Beverly Dr Ste 301
Los Angeles, CA 90035-1154, USA

May, Deems (Athlete, Football Player)
3932 Beresford Rd
Charlotte, NC 28211-3716, USA

May, Derrick (Athlete, Baseball Player)
2 Jaymar Blvd
Newark, DE 19702-2877, USA

May, Don (Athlete, Basketball Player)
1128 Colwick Dr
Dayton, OH 45420-2206, USA

May, Don (Athlete, Basketball Player)
PO Box 331
Lake Ariel, PA 18436-0331, USA

May, Elaine (Actor, Comedian, Director, Writer)
146 Central Park W Apt SD
New York, NY 10023-6297, USA

May, Isabel (Actor)
c/o Leanne Coronel *Coronel Group*
1100 Glendon Ave Fl 17
Los Angeles, CA 90024-3588, USA

May, Mark E (Football Player, Sportscaster)
c/o Staff Member *ESPN (Main)*
935 Middle St
Espn Plaza
Bristol, CT 06010-1000, USA

May, Mathilda (Actor)
Artmedia
20 Ave Rapp
Paris 75007, FRANCE

May, Milt (Athlete, Baseball Player)
2200 Manatee Ave W
Bradenton, FL 34205-5430, USA

May, Ray (Athlete, Football Player)
1921 Wellington Rd
Los Angeles, CA 90016-1822, USA

May, Robert (Producer)
c/o Staff Member *SenArt Films*
555 W 25th St Fl 4
New York, NY 10001-5542, USA

May, Rudy (Athlete, Baseball Player)
1231 Brickhouse Point Rd
Elizabeth City, NC 27909-6070, USA

may, Scott (Athlete, Baseball Player)
1630 Raven Cir Unit H
Estes Park, CO 80517-9477, USA

May, Scott (Athlete, Basketball Player, Olympic Athlete)
2001 E Hillside Dr Lot 1
Bloomington, IN 47401-6692, USA

May, Suzanne (Actor)
c/o Staff Member *Frontline Management*
5670 Wilshire Blvd Ste 1370
Los Angeles, CA 90036-5649, USA

May, Torsten (Boxer)
Sauerland Promotion
Hans-Bockler-Str 163
Hurth 50354, GERMANY

Mayaki, Ibrahim Hassane (Prime Minister)
Prime Minister's Office
State House
Niamey, NIGER

Mayall, Rik (Actor, Comedian)
Brunskill Mgmt
169 Queen's Gale
London SW7 5HE, UNITED KINGDOM (UK)

Mayasich, John (Athlete, Hockey Player)
801 McKinley Ave Apt 304
Eveleth, MN 55734-1485

Maybank, Anthuan (Athlete, Olympic Athlete, Track Athlete)
171 N Porter St
Elgin, IL 60120-4476, USA

Mayberry, Doug (Athlete, Football Player)
PO Box 1390
Williams, CA 95987-1390, USA

Mayberry, Jermane (Athlete, Football Player)
201 Town Center Ln APT 1402
Keller, TX 76248-2162, USA

Mayberry, John C (Athlete, Baseball Player)
11115 W 121st Ter
Overland Park, KS 66213-1945, USA

Mayberry, Lee (Athlete, Basketball Player)
4115 E 36th St N
Tulsa, OK 74115-1709, USA

Mayberry, Tony (Athlete, Football Player)
15704 Cochester Rd
Tampa, FL 33647-1100, USA

Mayberry, Jr., John (Athlete, Baseball Player)
11115 W 121st Ter
Overland Park, KS 66213-1945, USA

Maybin, Cameron (Athlete, Baseball Player)
85 Brompton Rd
Arden, NC 28704-8607, USA

Maybury, John (Director)
c/o Staff Member *WME|IMG*
9601 Wilshire Blvd
Beverly Hills, CA 90210-5213, USA

Mayer, Christian (Skier)
Siedlerweg 18
Finkelstein 09884, AUSTRIA

Mayer, Ed (Athlete, Baseball Player)
440 Oakland Ave
Corte Madera, CA 94925-1524, USA

Mayer, Gene (Tennis Player)
115 South St
Glen Dale, MD 20769, USA

Mayer, John (Musician, Songwriter)
c/o Larry Solters *Scoop Marketing*
12754 Ventura Blvd Ste C
Studio City, CA 91604-2441, USA

Mayer, Marissa (Business Person)
Yahoo! Inc.
701 First Ave
Sunnyvale, CA 94089-1019, USA

Mayer, P Augustin Cardinal (Religious Leader)
Ecclesia Dei
Vatican City 00120, VATICAN CITY

Mayer, Shawn (Athlete, Football Player)
15 Neptune Dr
Joppa, MD 21085-4519, USA

Mayer, Travis (Athlete, Olympic Athlete, Skier)

Mayers, Jamal (Athlete, Hockey Player)
9800 Countryshire Pl
Saint Louis, MO 63141-7914, USA

Mayes, Alonzo (Athlete, Football Player)
3000 SE 56th St
Oklahoma City, OK 73135-1620, USA

Mayes, David (Athlete, Football Player)
3018 Kingsley Rd
Shaker Heights, OH 44122-2816, USA

Mayes, Derrick (Athlete, Football Player)
3335 N Keystone Ave
Indianapolis, IN 46218-2075, USA

Mayes, Rob (Actor)
c/o Christina Gualazzi *Silver Lining Entertainment*
421 S Beverly Dr Fl 7
Beverly Hills, CA 90212-4408, USA

Mayes, Rueben (Athlete, Football Player)
2953 Lord Byron Pl
Eugene, OR 97408-4638, USA

Mayfair, Billy (Athlete, Golfer)
PO Box 25490
Scottsdale, AZ 85255-0108, USA

Mayfield, Baker (Athlete, Football Player)
c/o Jack Mills *Capital Sports Advisors*
1919 14th St # 410
Boulder, CO 80302-5310, USA

Mayfield, Corey (Athlete, Football Player)
3009 Guadalupe Dr
Forney, TX 75126-6944, USA

Mayhew, Lauren (Actor)
c/o David Eisenberg *Protege Entertainment*
710 E Angeleno Ave
Burbank, CA 91501-2213, USA

Mayhew, Martin (Athlete, Football Player)
4035 Sonnet Dr
Tallahassee, FL 32303-2225, USA

Mayhew, Peter (Actor)
c/o Staff Member *Entertainment Legends Management*
360 E 1st St Ste 66
Tustin, CA 92780-3211, USA

Maynard, Aaron (Race Car Driver)
33 Lake Rd
Milton, VT 05468-3513

Maynard, Andrew (Boxer)
Mike Trainer
3922 Fairmont Ave
Bethesda, MD 20814, USA

Maynard, Brad (Athlete, Football Player)
4915 Sage Ln
Long Grove, IL 60047-5275, USA

Maynard, Don (Athlete, Football Player)

Maynard, Emily (Reality Star)
c/o Liza Anderson *Anderson Group Public Relations*
8060 Melrose Ave Fl 4
Los Angeles, CA 90046-7038, USA

Maynard, Emily (Reality Star)
3025 Greystone Dr
Morgantown, WV 26508-8600, USA

Maynard, Mimi (Actor)
c/o Staff Member *Illuminata Pictures*
11217 Ventura Blvd
#417
Studio City, CA 91604, USA

Maynard, Mujaahid (Athlete, Olympic Athlete, Wrestler)
471 N Jackson Gap Way
Aurora, CO 80018-1695, USA

Mayne, Brent (Athlete, Baseball Player)
1863 Parkglen Cir
Costa Mesa, CA 92627-4506, USA

Mayne, Kenny (Sportscaster)
ESPN-TV
935 Middle St
Sports Dept Espn Plaza
Bristol, CT 06010-1000, USA

Mayne, Lew (Athlete, Football Player)
PO Box 701
Daingerfield, TX 75638-0701, USA

Mayne, Roy (Race Car Driver)
24 Reynolds Rd
Sumter, SC 29150-3221, USA

Maynor, Stephanie (Athlete, Golfer)
6213 Three Apple Downs
Columbia, MD 21045-7419, USA

Mayo, Jackie (Athlete, Baseball Player)
94 7 AUIWSta Dr
Youngstown, OH 44512-7923, USA

Mayo, Miranda (Actor)
c/o Steve Rohr *Lexicon Public Relations*
1049 Havenhurst Dr # 365
West Hollywood, CA 90046-6002, USA

Mayo, Ron (Athlete, Football Player)
7515 Buchanan St Apt 231
Hyattsville, MD 20784-6307, USA

Mayock, Michael (Athlete, Football Player)
607 Georges Ln
Ardmore, PA 19003-1905, USA

Mayock, Mike (Athlete, Football Player)
607 Georges Ln
Ardmore, PA 19003-1905, USA

Mayotte, Tim (Athlete, Olympic Athlete, Tennis Player)
2430 Beacon St UNIT 201
Chestnut Hill, MA 02467-1466, USA

Mayotte, Tim (Athlete, Tennis Player)
2430 Beacon St UNIT 201
Chestnut Hill, MA 02467-1466, USA

Mayowa, Benson (Athlete, Football Player)

Mayron, Melanie (Actor, Director)
1435 N Ogden Dr
Los Angeles, CA 90046-3906, USA

Mays, Alvoid (Athlete, Football Player)
3903 Cape Vista Dr
Bradenton, FL 34209-6725, USA

Mays, Damon (Athlete, Football Player)
5711 W Arrowhead Lakes Dr
Glendale, AZ 85308-6222, USA

Mays, David (Business Person)
2690 Cobb Pkwy SE Ste A-5 PMB 304
Smyrna, GA 30080-3005, USA

Mays, Jayma (Actor)
c/o Ruth Bernstein *Viewpoint Inc*
8820 Wilshire Blvd Ste 220
Beverly Hills, CA 90211-2622, USA

Mays, Jeryn (Actor)
360 W Avenue 26 Apt 126
Los Angeles, CA 90031-1477, USA

Mays, Joe (Athlete, Baseball Player)
7620 205th St E
Bradenton, FL 34202-8304, USA

Mays, Joe (Athlete, Football Player)

Mays, Lyle (Musician)
Ted Kurland
173 Brighton Ave
Boston, MA 02134-2003, USA

Mays, Malcolm (Actor)
c/o Alexandra Crotin *The Lede Company*
9701 Wilshire Blvd # 930
Beverly Hills, CA 90212-2020, USA

Mays, Melinda (Race Car Driver)
2221 Peachtree Rd NE Ste D PMB 440
Atlanta, GA 30309-1133, USA

Mays, Rueben (Athlete, Football Player)
7306 172nd St SW
Edmonds, WA 98026-5121, USA

Mays, Stafford (Athlete, Football Player)
2235 W Viewmont Way W
Seattle, WA 98199-3951, USA

Mays, Taylor (Athlete, Football Player)
c/o David Dunn *Athletes First*
23091 Mill Creek Dr
Laguna Hills, CA 92653-1258, USA

Mays, Tristin (Actor)
c/o Jeff Morrone *Atlas Artists*
9220 W Sunset Blvd Ste 225
Los Angeles, CA 90069-3513, USA

Mays, Willie (Athlete, Baseball Player)
51 Mount Vernon Ln
Atherton, CA 94027-3036, USA

Maysey, Matt (Athlete, Baseball Player)
10190 Katy Fwy Ste 350
Houston, TX 77043-5239, USA

May-Treanor, Misty (Athlete, Olympic Athlete, Volleyball Player)
2892 N Bellflower Blvd Ste 482
Long Beach, CA 90815-1125, USA

Mayweather Jr, Floyd (Athlete, Boxer)
Prince Boxing Gym
3030 Jensen Dr
Houston, TX 77026-5511, USA

Mazar, Debi (Actor)
c/o Peg Donegan *Framework Entertainment*
9057 Nemo St # C
W Hollywood, CA 90069-5511, USA

Mazarella, Jacqueline (Actor)
c/o Tony Martinez *Kazarian, Measures, Ruskin & Associates*
5200 Lankershim Blvd Ste 820
N Hollywood, CA 91601-3194, USA

Mazaroski, William S (Bill) (Baseball Player)
RR 6 Box 130
Greensburg, PA 15601, USA

Maze, Krista (Race Car Driver)
PO Box 7791
Huntington Beach, CA 92615-7791, USA

Mazeroski, Bill (Athlete, Baseball Player)
281 Walton Tea Room Rd
Greensburg, PA 15601-6406, USA

Mazouz, David (Actor)
c/o Jeffrey Chassen *Imprint PR*
6121 W Sunset Blvd
Neuehouse
Los Angeles, CA 90028-6442, USA

Mazur, Heather (Actor)
c/o Hannah Roth *Buchwald*
5900 Wilshire Blvd Ste 3100
Los Angeles, CA 90036-5030, USA

Mazur, Jay (Athlete, Hockey Player)
148 Elderberry Dr
South Portland, ME 04106-6890

Mazur, John (Athlete, Football Coach, Football Player)
672 Cornwallis Dr
Mount Laurel, NJ 08054-3217, USA

Mazur, Monet (Actor)
c/o Bianca Bianconi *42West*
600 3rd Ave Fl 23
New York, NY 10016-1914, USA

Mazurek, Fred (Athlete, Football Player)
79340 Citrus
La Quinta, CA 92253-8520, USA

Mazza, Valeria (Model)
Riccardo Ga
8/10 Via Revere
Milan 20123, ITALY

Mazzanti, Geno (Athlete, Football Player)
4188 E Highway 82
Lake Village, AR 71653-6057, USA

Mazzanti, Jerry (Athlete, Football Player)
1712 S Lakeshore Dr
Lake Village, AR 71653-1573, USA

Mazzara, Glen (Producer)
c/o Staff Member *Creative Artists Agency (CAA)*
2000 Avenue of the Stars Ste 100
Los Angeles, CA 90067-4705, USA

Mazzarello, Marcelo (Actor)
c/o Staff Member *Telefe (Argentina)*
Pavon 2444
Buenos Aires C1248AAT, ARGENTINA

Mazzaro, Vin (Athlete, Baseball Player)
48 Avalon Way
Waretown, NJ 08758-2698, USA

Mazzello, Joseph (Joe) (Actor)
c/o Brett Ruttenberg *Imprint PR*
6121 W Sunset Blvd
Neuehouse
Los Angeles, CA 90028-6442, USA

Mazzetti, Tim (Athlete, Football Player)
2 N La Salle St Ste 800
Chicago, IL 60602-3785, USA

Mazzilli, Lee L (Athlete, Baseball Player, Coach)
67 Stonehedge Dr S
Greenwich, CT 06831-3220, USA

Mazzone, Leo (Athlete, Baseball Player)
4518 Mystique WayNE
Roswell, GA 30075-2087, USA

Mbatha-Raw, Gugu (Actor)
c/o Pandora Weldon *Public Eye Communications*
535 Kings Rd
#313 Plaza
London SW10 0SZ, UNITED KINGDOM

Mbeki, Thabo (President)
President's Office
Union Buildings
Pretoria 00001, SOUTH AFRICA

Mbenga, D J (Athlete, Basketball Player)
6112 Winton St
Dallas, TX 75214-2636, USA

M. Bilirakis, Gus (Congressman, Politician)
407 Cannon Hob
Washington, DC 20515-3901, USA

McAdams, Bob (Athlete, Football Player)
4 Vineyard Pl
Asheville, NC 28804-3621, USA

McAdams, Carl (Athlete, Football Player)
206 E Main St
Antlers, OK 74523-3256, USA

McAdams, Carl (Athlete, Football Player)
HC 82 Box 526
Atoka, OK 74525, USA

McAdams, Rachel (Actor)
c/o Shelley Browning *Magnolia Entertainment*
9595 Wilshire Blvd Ste 601
Beverly Hills, CA 90212-2506, USA

McAddley, Jason (Athlete, Football Player)
3600 S Tower Ave
Chandler, AZ 85286-2692, USA

McAdoo, Bob (Athlete, Basketball Player, Coach)
20970 Via Alamanda Apt 1
Boca Raton, FL 33428-1335, USA

McAfee, John (Business Person)
McAfee Inc
2821 Mission College Blvd
Santa Clara, CA 95054-1838, USA

McAfee, Pat (Athlete, Football Player)
c/o Roosevelt Barnes *Independent Sports & Entertainment (ISE-IN)*
6435 W Jefferson Blvd # 197
Fort Wayne, IN 46804-6203, USA

McAillister-Morton, Susie (Athlete, Golfer)
40241 Club View Dr
Rancho Mirage, CA 92270-3527, USA

McAleese, Mary P (Politician, President)
President's Office
Office of the President Upper Marion Street Government Complex
Dublin 2, IRELAND

McAleese, Peter (Producer)
c/o Lisa Helsing Lenhoff *Lenhoff & Lenhoff*
324 S Beverly Dr
Beverly Hills, CA 90212-4801

McAleney, Ed (Athlete, Football Player)
981 Shore Rd
Cape Elizabeth, ME 04107-1908, USA

McAlister, Chris (Athlete, Football Player)
8206 Pumpkin Hill Ct
Pikesville, MD 21208-1872, USA

McAlister, James E (Athlete, Football Player, Track Athlete)
155 Glorieta St
Pasadena, CA 91103-3018, USA

McAllister, Chris (Athlete, Hockey Player)
162 Eastlawn St
Fairfield, CT 06824-6480

McAllister, Deuce (Athlete, Football Player)
c/o Staff Member *Philadelphia Eagles*
1 Novacare Way
Philadelphia, PA 19145-5996, USA

McAlpine, Chris (Athlete, Hockey Player)
199 Oakhill Dr
Saint Paul, MN 55126-4835

McAnally, Ernie (Athlete, Baseball Player)
PO Box 492
Mt Pleasant, TX 75456-0492, USA

McAnally, Mac (Musician, Songwriter)
c/o Staff Member *Paradigm (Monterey)*
404 W Franklin St
Monterey, CA 93940-2303, USA

McAnally, Ron (Race Car Driver)
Motorsports HOF
191 Union Ave
Saratoga Springs, NY 12866-3513, USA

McAnany, Jim (Athlete, Baseball Player)
6725 Sasparilla Dr
Simi Valley, CA 93063-5813, USA

McAndrew, James (Race Car Driver)
Team Matthew Inc
420-A S First St
Bangor, PA 18013, USA

McAndrew, Jamie (Athlete, Baseball Player)
120 W Kaler Dr
Phoenix, AZ 85021-7239, USA

McAndrew, Jim (Athlete, Baseball Player)
16540 E El Lago Blvd Unit 41
Fountain Hills, AZ 85268-4732, USA

McAndrew, Tracey (Nell) (Actor, Model)
c/o Staff Member *Adult Model SEM Group*
98 Cockfosters Rd
Barnet
Hertfordshirt EN4 0DP, UNITED KINGDOM

McAneeley, Bob (Athlete, Hockey Player)
40 Flagstone Cres
St. Albert, AB T8N 1R3, Canada

McAneeley, Ted (Athlete, Hockey Player)
234 Aikane St
Kailua, HI 96734-1603, USA

McAnulty, Paul (Athlete, Baseball Player)
921 Palomar Way
Oxnard, CA 93033-5111, USA

McArdle, Andrea (Actor, Musician)
Edd Kalehoff
14 Shady Glen Ct
New Rochelle, NY 10805-1806, USA

McArdle, John (Athlete, Baseball Player)
6640 Lynford St
Philadelphia, PA 19149-2124, USA

McArthur, Alex (Actor)
2421 Carnegie Ln Frnt House
Redondo Beach, CA 90278-3589, USA

McArthur, Kevin (Athlete, Football Player)
3817 Meredith Ln
Mesquite, TX 75180-5017, USA

McArthur, K Megan (Astronaut)
103 Harborcrest Dr
Seabrook, TX 77586-4601, USA

McArthur, William S (Bill) (Astronaut)
2512 Mountain Falls Ct
Friendswood, TX 77546-5592, USA

McAuley, Alphonso (Actor)
c/o David (Dave) Fleming *Atlas Artists*
9220 W Sunset Blvd Ste 225
Los Angeles, CA 90069-3513, USA

McAuley, Jordan (Business Person, Writer)
Contact Any Celebrity
8721 Santa Monica Blvd # 431
Los Angeles, CA 90069-4507, USA

McAuliffe, Callan (Actor)
c/o Nicholas Bogner *Affirmative Entertainment*
6525 W Sunset Blvd # 7
Los Angeles, CA 90028-7212, USA

McAvoy, James (Actor)
c/o Ruth Young *United Agents*
12-26 Lexington St
London W1F OLE, UNITED KINGDOM

McBain, Andrew (Athlete, Hockey Player)
87 Balsam Ave
Toronto, ON M4E 3B8, Canada

McBain, Diane (Actor)
20185 Canyon View Dr # 1
Canyon Country, CA 91351-5734, USA

McBain, Jason (Athlete, Hockey Player)
PO Box 221
Eastport, ID 83826-0221

McBath, Mike (Athlete, Football Player)
5044 Sailwind Cir
Orlando, FL 32810-1839, USA

McBean, Al (Athlete, Baseball Player)
PO Box 4475
St Thomas, VI 00801, USA

McBean, Wayne (Athlete, Hockey Player)
555 Lakeside Greens Dr
Chestermere, AB T1X 1C5, Canada

McBee, Rives (Athlete, Golfer)
1504 Canyon Oaks Dr
Irving, TX 75061-2116, USA

McBeth, Marcus (Athlete, Baseball Player)
4719 E Mountain Sage Dr
Phoenix, AZ 85044-6204, USA

McBrain, Nicko (Musician)
c/o Staff Member *Phantom Music Management*
36 Bridle Ln
Bridle House
London W1F 9BZ, UNITED KINGDOM

McBratney, Sam (Writer)
c/o Staff Member *HarperCollins Publishers*
195 Broadway Fl 2
New York, NY 10007-3132, USA

McBriar, Mat (Athlete, Football Player)
4020 Buena Vista St
Dallas, TX 75204-7804, USA

McBride, Bake (Athlete, Baseball Player)
4077 Reliant Cir
Owensboro, KY 42301-0024, USA

McBride, Chi (Actor)
c/o Sam Maydew *Silver Lining Entertainment*
421 S Beverly Dr Fl 7
Beverly Hills, CA 90212-4408, USA

McBride, Danny (Actor)
c/o Matthew Labov *Forefront Media*
1669 Virginia Rd
Los Angeles, CA 90019-5935, USA

McBride, Jeff (Magician)
McBride Magin
3132 Shadowridge Ave
Las Vegas, NV 89120-3467, USA

McBride, Jon A (Astronaut)
Image Development Group
1018 Kanawha Blvd E Ste 901
Charleston, WV 25301-2800, USA

McBride, Jon A Captain (Astronaut)
2705 N Indian River Dr
Cocoa, FL 32922-7075, USA

McBride, Justin (Misc)
PBR
101 W Riverwalk
Pueblo, CO 81003-3243, USA

McBride, Ken (Athlete, Baseball Player)
3446 Cypress Cir
Westlake, OH 44145-4409, USA

McBride, Macay (Athlete, Baseball Player)
608 McDonald Rd
Sylvania, GA 30467-5718, USA

McBride, Martina (Musician)
c/o Tracy Weaver, Director of Fan Relations
P.O. Box 391627
Nashville, TN 37229, USA

McBride, Melissa (Actor)
c/o Nigel Meiojas *United Talent Agency (UTA)*
9336 Civic Center Dr
Beverly Hills, CA 90210-3604, USA

McBride, Oscar (Athlete, Football Player)
11 Algerwood
Ladera Ranch, CA 92694-0313, USA

Mcbride, Susan (Writer)
8712 Garden Ct
Brentwood, MO 63144-1830, USA

McBride, Trumaine (Athlete, Football Player)

McBride, Turk (Athlete, Football Player)
c/o Eugene Parker *Independent Sports & Entertainment (ISE-IN)*
6435 W Jefferson Blvd # 197
Fort Wayne, IN 46804-6203, USA

McBroom, Amanda (Musician, Songwriter, Writer)
167 Fairview Rd
Ojai, CA 93023-9537, USA

McBurney, Jim (Athlete, Hockey Player)
161 Louise Ave
Sault Ste. Marie, ON P6A 5X1, Canada

McCabe, Bryan (Athlete, Hockey Player)
c/o Staff Member *Toronto Maple Leafs*
Air Canada Centre
400-40 Bay St
Toronto, ON M5J 2X2, CANADA

McCabe, Frank (Athlete, Basketball Player, Olympic Athlete)
3415 N Sheridan Rd
Peoria, IL 61604-1430, USA

McCabe, Joe (Athlete, Baseball Player)
3003 Gardens Blvd
Naples, FL 34105-6647, USA

McCabe, John (Musician)
Novello Co
8/9 Firth St
London W1V 5TZ, UNITED KINGDOM (UK)

McCabe, Marcia (Actor)
1990 Broadway Box 417 Ansonia Sta
. New York, NY 10023

McCabe, Patrick (Writer)
Picador
Macmillan Books
25 Eckeston Place
London SW1W 9NF, UNITED KINGDOM (UK)

McCabe, Zia (Musician)
Mongui Mgmt
PO Box 5908
Portland, OR 97228-5908, USA

McCafferty, Donald F (Don) Jr (Coach, Football Coach)
167 E Shore Rd
Halesite, NY 11743-1128, USA

McCaffrey, Christian (Athlete, Football Player)
c/o Ira Stahlberger *IMG (Cleveland)*
1360 E 9th St Ste 100
Cleveland, OH 44114-1730, USA

McCaffrey, Mike (Athlete, Football Player)
6040 N Nantucket Ave
Fresno, CA 93704-1620, USA

McCahill, John (Athlete, Hockey Player)
1547 Henley Cres
Sarnia, ON N7S 5Z7, Canada

McCain, Brice (Athlete, Football Player)

McCain, Edwin (Songwriter, Writer)
c/o Cass Scripps *UTA Music*
209 10th Ave S Ste 511
Nashville, TN 37203-0795, USA

McCain, Meghan (Politician)
c/o Staff Member *The View*
57 W 66th St
New York, NY 10023-6201, USA

McCall, Brian (Athlete, Baseball Player)
550 Tremont Ave
Greensburg, PA 15601-4263, USA

McCall, Davina (Actor)
c/o Staff Member *John Noel Management*
10A Belmont St
Floor 2
London NW1 8HH, UNITED KINGDOM (UK)

McCall, Don (Athlete, Football Player)
16830 Kingsbury St Apt 131
Granada Hills, CA 91344-6465, USA

McCall, Joe (Athlete, Football Player)
2944 Falconhill Dr
Apopka, FL 32712-2495, USA

McCall, John (Windy) (Athlete, Baseball Player)
32 N Stone Ave # 4
Tucson, AZ 85701-1458, USA

McCall, Larry (Athlete, Baseball Player)
354 Justice Ridge Rd
Candler, NC 28715-9576, USA

McCall, Mitzi (Actor)
c/o Staff Member *Cunningham Escott Slevin & Doherty (CESD)*
10635 Santa Monica Blvd Ste 130
Los Angeles, CA 90025-8306, USA

McCall, Reese (Athlete, Football Player)
1311 1st Ave N
Bessemer, AL 35020-5602, USA

McCallany, Holt (Actor)
c/o Lauren Auslander *LUNA*
116 Nassau St # 615
New York, NY 10038-2402, USA

McCallister, Blaine (Athlete, Golfer)
1878 Epping Forest Way S
Jacksonville, FL 32217-2670, USA

McCall Smith, Alexander (Writer)
c/o Staff Member *Random House*
1540 Broadway
New York, NY 10036-4039, USA

McCallum, David (Actor)
c/o Abe Hoch *A Management Company*
16633 Ventura Blvd Ste 1450
Encino, CA 91436-1887, USA

McCallum, Dunc (Athlete, Hockey Player)

McCallum, Napoleon (Athlete, Football Player)
314 Doe Run Cir
Henderson, NV 89012-2700, USA

McCambridge, Mercedes (Astronaut)
210932 Pleasant Park Dr
Conifer, CO 80433, USA

McCament, Randy (Athlete, Baseball Player)
17338 N Del Webb Blvd
Sun City, AZ 85373-1951, USA

McCammon, Bob (Athlete, Hockey Player)
200-322 Water St
Vancouver, BC V6B 1B6, Canada

McCanlies, Tim (Director, Producer, Writer)
c/o Lindsay Williams *Gotham Group*
1041 N Formosa Ave # 200
West Hollywood, CA 90046-6703, USA

McCann, Brendan (Athlete, Basketball Player)
1201 SW 141st Ave Apt 304
Pembroke Pines, FL 33027-3571, USA

McCann, Brian (Athlete, Baseball Player)
5706 Kennedy Rd
Suwanee, GA 30024-7696, USA

McCann, Lila (Musician)
c/o Rick Shipp *WME (Nashville)*
1201 Demonbreun St
Nashville, TN 37203-3140, USA

McCann, Rory (Actor)
c/o Michael Emptage *Emptage Hallett*
34-35 Eastcastle St
Fl 3
London W1W 8DW, UNITED KINGDOM (UK)

McCann, Tim (Director)
c/o Jennifer Konawal *Washington Square Arts (NY)*
310 Bowery Fl 2
New York, NY 10012-2861, USA

McCants, Darnerien (Athlete, Football Player)
43847 Chadwick Ter
Ashburn, VA 20148-3154, USA

McCants, Keith (Athlete, Football Player)
919 Selma Smith Ct Apt D
Tampa, FL 33605-4952, USA

McCants, Matt (Athlete, Football Player)
c/o Alan Herman *Sportstars Inc*
1370 Avenue of the Americas Fl 19
New York, NY 10019-4602, USA

McCants, Mel (Athlete, Basketball Player)
6404 Somis Way
Sacramento, CA 95828-1523, USA

McCants, Rashad (Athlete, Basketball Player)
c/o Jeff Schwartz *Excel Sports Management*
1700 Broadway Fl 29
New York, NY 10019-6559, USA

McCardell, Keenan (Athlete, Football Player)
PO Box 1262
Fresno, TX 77545-1262, USA

McCareins, Justin (Athlete, Football Player)
4118 Fallbrook Dr
Frisco, TX 75033-2855, USA

McCarren, Larry (Athlete, Football Player)
520 W Chickadee Ln
Green Bay, WI 54313-5039, USA

McCarrick, Theodore E Cardinal (Religious Leader)
Archdiocesan Pastoral Center
5001 Eastern Ave
Washington, DC 20017, USA

McCarroll, Jay (Fashion Designer, Reality Star)
c/o Nancy Kane *Kane & Associates*
Prefers to be contacted by email.
Venice, CA 90291, USA

McCarron, AJ (Athlete, Football Player)
c/o Todd France *Creative Artists Agency (CAA) Sports*
3500 Lenox Rd NE
Atlanta, GA 30326-4228, USA

McCarron, Chris (Horse Racer)
2840 Kearney Creek Ln
Lexington, KY 40511-8688, USA

McCarron, Scott (Athlete, Golfer)
PO Box 1894
La Quinta, CA 92247-1894, USA

McCartan, Jack (Athlete, Hockey Player, Olympic Athlete)
15504 Almond Ln
Eden Prairie, MN 55347-2554, USA

McCarter, Andre (Athlete, Basketball Player)
505 S Beverly Dr
#862
Beverly Hills, CA 90212, USA

McCarter, Willie (Athlete, Basketball Player)
5925 Campfield St
Jackson, MI 49201-8355, USA

McCarthy, Andrew (Actor)
c/o Brian Liebman *Liebman Entertainment*
29 W 46th St Fl 5
New York, NY 10036-4104, USA

McCarthy, Bill (Athlete, Football Player)
1640 Walnut Ave
Winter Park, FL 32789-2036, USA

McCarthy, Brandon (Athlete, Baseball Player)
34457 N Legend Trail Pkwy Unit 1018
Pkwv Unit 1018
Scottsdale, AZ 85262-4428, USA

McCarthy, Carolyn (Congressman, Politician)
2346 Rayburn Hob
Washington, DC 20515-3507, USA

McCarthy, Colin (Athlete, Football Player)
c/o Drew Rosenhaus *Rosenhaus Sports Representation*
3921 Alton Rd # 440
Miami Beach, FL 33140-3852, USA

McCarthy, Cormac (Writer)
c/o Amanda Urban *ICM Partners (NY)*
730 5th Ave
New York, NY 10019-4105, USA

McCarthy, Dan (Athlete, Hockey Player)
1346 Wolf Hill Rd
Cheshire, CT 06410-1739

McCarthy, Emilia (Actor)
c/o Shari Quallenberg *AMI Artist Management*
464 King St E
Toronto, ON M5A 1L7, CANADA

McCarthy, Greg (Athlete, Baseball Player)
56 Wakelee Avenue Ext
Shelton, CT 06484-3954, USA

McCarthy, Jenny (Actor, Model, Television Host)
c/o Brad Cafarelli *PMK/BNC Public Relations*
1840 Century Park E Ste 1400
Los Angeles, CA 90067-2115, USA

McCarthy, Joey (Race Car Driver)
McCarthy/Pritchard Motorsports
PO Box 1494
Dover, NJ 07802-1494, USA

McCarthy, John (Athlete, Basketball Player)
1350 Union Rd Apt 2F
Apt 2F
West Seneca, NY 14224-2940, USA

McCarthy, Julianna (Actor)
Stone Manners
6500 Wilshire Blvd # 550
Los Angeles, CA 90048-4920, USA

McCarthy, Kevin (Athlete, Hockey Player)
Philadelphia Flyers
3601 S Broad St Ste 2
Philadelphia, PA 19148-5297

McCarthy, Kevin (Athlete, Hockey Player)
1139 Warf Rd
Lexington, NC 27292-1929, USA

McCarthy, Kevin (Congressman, Politician)
326 Cannon Hob
Washington, DC 20515-0529, USA

McCarthy, Melissa (Actor)
c/o Dominique Appel *Imprint PR*
6121 W Sunset Blvd
Neuehouse
Los Angeles, CA 90028-6442, USA

McCarthy, Sandy (Athlete, Hockey Player)
1826 Quantz Cres
Innisfil, ON L9S 1X2, Canada

McCarthy, Shawn (Athlete, Football Player)
300 N Lakeshore Rd
Payson, AZ 85541-6220, USA

McCarthy, Timothy J (Misc)
Orland Park Police Department
15100 S Ravinia Ave
Orland Park, IL 60462-3745, USA

McCarthy, Tom (Director)
c/o Rhonda Price *Gersh*
41 Madison Ave Ste 3301
New York, NY 10010-2210, USA

McCarthy, Tom (Athlete, Baseball Player)
PO Box 38
Limington, ME 04049-0038, USA

McCarthy, Tom (Athlete, Hockey Player)
Huntsville Muskoka Otters
20 Park Dr
Huntsville, ON P1H 1P5, Canada

McCarthy, Tom (Commentator)
2229 Union Blvd
Allentown, PA 18109, USA

McCarthy, Tony (Songwriter, Writer)
29/33 Berners Road
London W1P 4AA, UNITED KINGDOM (UK)

McCarthy-Miller, Beth (Director, Producer)
c/o Dan Rabinow *Creative Artists Agency (CAA)*
2000 Avenue of the Stars Ste 100
Los Angeles, CA 90067-4705, USA

McCartney, Jesse (Musician)
c/o Sherry Kondor *Good Noize Entertainment*
11684 Ventura Blvd Ste 273
Studio City, CA 91604-2699, USA

McCartney, Paul (Musician, Songwriter)
Waterfall Estate
Starvecrow Lane
Peasmarsh Rye TN31 6XN, UNITED KINGDOM

McCartney, Ron (Athlete, Football Player)
10722 Bell Valley Dr
Knoxville, TN 37934-5098, USA

McCartney, Stella (Designer, Fashion Designer)
The Larches, Farm Hill
Furze Road
Bishampton, Pershore WR10 2NA, UNITED KINGDOM (UK)

McCarty, Darren (Athlete)
c/o Staff Member *Detroit Red Wings*
2645 Woodward Ave
Joe Luis Arena
Detroit, MI 48201-3028, USA

McCarty, David (Athlete, Baseball Player)
PO Box 11608
Oakland, CA 94611-0608, USA

McCarty, Mary (Baseball Player)
9455 N Genesee Rd
Mount Morris, MI 48458-9734, USA

McCarty, Walter (Athlete, Basketball Player)
7525 Pine Valley Ln
Indianapolis, IN 46250-2379, USA

McCarver, J Timothy (Tim) (Athlete, Baseball Player, Sportscaster)
5825 Riegels Harbor Rd
Sarasota, FL 34242-1779, USA

McCarver, Tim (Athlete, Baseball Player)
San Francisco Giants
5825 Riegels Harbor Rd
Sarasota, FL 34242-1779, USA

McCary, Michael (Musician)
Southpaw Entertainment
10675 Santa Monica Blvd
Los Angeles, CA 90025-4807, USA

McCashin, Constance (Actor)
66 Fountain St
West Newton, MA 02465-3023, USA

McCaskill, Kirk E (Athlete, Baseball Player)
1738 Oxford Ave
Cardiff By The Sea, CA 92007-1633, USA

McCatty, Steve (Athlete, Baseball Player)
1075 Woodbriar Dr
Oxford, MI 48371-6069, USA

McCauley, Alyn (Athlete, Hockey Player)
Newport Sports Management
400-201 City Centre Dr
Mississauga, ON L5B 2T4, Canada

McCauley, Don (Athlete, Football Player)
1005 Tuscany Dr
Hillsborough, NC 27278-7690, USA

McCauley, Herb (Horse Racer)
69 Horseshoe Ct
Oceanport, NJ 07757-1170, USA

McCauley, Wes (Athlete, Hockey Player)
251 Elderberry Dr
South Portland, ME 04106-7810

McChesney, Robert (Bob) (Writer)
1103 S Douglas Ave
Urbana, IL 61801-4934, USA

McCkorkle, Kevin (Actor)
c/o Peter Himberger *Impact Artists Group LLC*
42 Hamilton Ter
New York, NY 10031-6403, USA

McClain, Antoine (Athlete, Football Player)
c/o Joe Linta *JL Sports*
1204 Main St Ste 179
Branford, CT 06405-3787, USA

McClain, Cady (Actor)
c/o Marnie Sparer *Power Entertainment Group*
1505 10th St
Santa Monica, CA 90401-2805, USA

McClain, Charly (Musician)
John Lentz
PO Box 198888
Nashville, TN 37219-8888, USA

McClain, China Anne (Actor)
c/o Staff Member *Our Brand*
18565 Soledad Canyon Rd # 238
Canyon Country, CA 91351-3700, USA

McClain, Dewey (Athlete, Football Player)
1032 Flagg Way
Lawrenceville, GA 30044-3354, USA

McClain, Eugene (Athlete, Baseball Player)
828 W 8th St
Chester, PA 19013-3712, USA

McClain, Jameel (Athlete, Football Player)
c/o Sean Howard *Octagon Football*
600 Battery St Fl 2
San Francisco, CA 94111-1820, USA

McClain, Joe (Athlete, Baseball Player)
1370 Milligan Hwy
Johnson City, TN 37601-5518, USA

McClain, Katrina (Athlete, Basketball Player, Olympic Athlete)
Naismith HOF
PO Box 40893
North Charleston, SC 29423-0893, USA

McClain, Robert (Athlete, Football Player)
c/o Ed Wasielewski *EMG Sports - PA*
PO Box 2
Richboro, PA 18954-0002, USA

McClain, Rolando (Athlete, Football Player)
c/o Pat Dye Jr *SportsTrust Advisors*
3340 Peachtree Rd NE Fl 16
Atlanta, GA 30326-1000, USA

McClain, Scott (Athlete, Baseball Player)
660 Golden Gate Pt Apt 61
Sarasota, FL 34236-6645, USA

McClain, Sierra (Actor)
c/o Staff Member *Our Brand*
18565 Soledad Canyon Rd # 238
Canyon Country, CA 91351-3700, USA

McClain, Ted (Athlete, Basketball Player)
104 Eaton Ct
Nashville, TN 37218-1003, USA

McClain, Terrell (Athlete, Football Player)

McClairen, Jack (Athlete, Football Player)
1337 Idlewild Dr
Daytona Beach, FL 32114-1614, USA

McClairen, Jack (Cy) (Coach, Football Coach)
Pittsburgh Steelers
1337 Idlewild Dr
Daytona Beach, FL 32114-1614, USA

McClanahan, Brent (Athlete, Football Player)
1100 Sayword Ct
Bakersfield, CA 93312-5750, USA

McClanahan, Randy (Athlete, Football Player)
8107 W Via Del Sol
Peoria, AZ 85383-2142, USA

McClanahan, Rob (Athlete, Hockey Player, Olympic Athlete)
125 Chevy Chase Dr
Wayzata, MN 55391-1053, USA

McClard, Bill (Athlete, Football Player)
149 N Pleasant Ridge Dr
Rogers, AR 72756-0702, USA

McClarnon, Zahn (Actor)
c/o Gloria Hinojosa *Amsel, Eisenstadt & Frazier Talent Agency (AEF)*
5055 Wilshire Blvd Ste 860
Los Angeles, CA 90036-6108, USA

McClary, Thomas (Tom) (Athlete, Football Player)
Management Assoc
PO Box 701341
Dallas, TX 75370-1341, USA

McCleary, Norris (Athlete, Football Player)
115 Ferguson Dr
Kings Mountain, NC 28086-9727, USA

McCleary, Trent (Athlete, Hockey Player)
442 Curry Cres
Swift Current, SK S9H 4X4, Canada

McClellan, Kyle (Athlete, Baseball Player)
253 Fox Haven Dr
O Fallon, MO 63368-6584, USA

McClellan, Lloyd (Athlete, Baseball Player)
1082 Mission Hills Ct
Chesterton, IN 46304-9605, USA

McClellan, Paul (Athlete, Baseball Player)
PO Box 5184
Napa, CA 94581-0184, USA

McClellan, Zach (Athlete, Baseball Player)
931 Parkside Dr
Columbus, IN 47203-1324, USA

McClelland, Dave (Race Car Driver)
980 Eilinita Ave
Glendale, CA 91208-1128, USA

McClelland, Kevin (Athlete, Hockey Player)
2886 Keeley Cv
Southaven, MS 38671-7520, USA

McClelland, Melissa (Musician)
c/o Staff Member *Paradigm (Monterey)*
404 W Franklin St
Monterey, CA 93940-2303, USA

McClelland, Tim (Baseball Player)
5405 Woodland Ave
West Des Moines, IA 50266-7259, USA

McClelland, Tim (Athlete, Baseball Player)
5405 Woodland Ave
West Des Moines, IA 50266-7259, USA

McClellin, Shea (Athlete, Football Player)
c/o Bruce Tollner *REP 1 Sports Group*
80 Technology Dr
Irvine, CA 92618-2301, USA

McClenathan, Cory (Race Car Driver)
PO Box 1602
Lake Havasu City, AZ 86405-1602, USA

McClendon, Jacques (Athlete, Football Player)
c/o Tony Paige *Dream Point Sports*
1455 Pennsylvania Ave NW Ste 225
Washington, DC 20004-1026, USA

McClendon, Lloyd (Athlete, Baseball Player, Coach)
c/o Staff Member *Athlete Connection LLC*
PO Box 380135
Clinton Township, MI 48038-0060, USA

McClendon, Reiley (Actor)
c/o Abby Bluestone *Innovative Artists*
1505 10th St
Santa Monica, CA 90401-2805, USA

McClendon, Skip (Athlete, Football Player)
1456 E Pecos Rd Apt 3063
Gilbert, AZ 85295-1790, USA

McClendon, Willie (Athlete, Football Player)
575 Cativo Dr SW
Atlanta, GA 30311-2107, USA

McCleon, Dexter (Athlete, Football Player)
1901 Post Oak Blvd Apt 509
Houston, TX 77056-3926, USA

McClintock, Eddie (Actor)
c/o Richard Beddingfield *Beddingfield Company, The*
13600 Ventura Blvd Ste B
Sherman Oaks, CA 91423-5050, USA

McClintock, Jessica (Designer, Fashion Designer)
Jessica McClintock Co
2307 Broadway St
San Francisco, CA 94115-1291, USA

McClintock, Tom (Congressman, Politician)
428 Cannon Hob
Washington, DC 20515-4308, USA

McClinton, Curtis (Athlete, Football Player)
354 Matlock Rd Apt 234
McClinton Development Company
Mansfield, TX 76063-2232, USA

McClinton, Delbert (Musician)
c/o Staff Member *Alligator Records*
PO Box 60234
Chicago, IL 60660-0234, USA

McCloskey, Jack (Basketball Player)
Minnesota Timberwolves
600 1st Ave N
Target Center
Minneapolis, MN 55403-1400, USA

McCloskey, J Michael (Misc)
Sierra Club
85 2ns St
#200
San Francisco, CA 94105, USA

McCloskey, Leigh J (Actor)
6032 Philip Ave
Malibu, CA 90265-3747, USA

McCloskey, Mike (Athlete, Football Player)
108 Summer Ridge Dr
Lansdale, PA 19446-6707, USA

McCloskey, Pete (Politician)
2200 Geng Rd
Palo Alto, CA 94303-3358, USA

McCloskey, Rep (Politician)
580 Mountain Home Rd
Woodside, CA 94062-2515

McCloskey-Rogers, Gloria (Athlete, Baseball Player, Commentator)
PO Box 512
Macon, MO 63552-0512, USA

McCloud, George (Athlete, Basketball Player)
19501 W Country Club Dr # AT1603
Aventura, FL 33180-2471, USA

McCloud, Tyrus (Athlete, Football Player)
2850 NW 8th St
Pompano Beach, FL 33069-2139, USA

McCloughan, Dave (Athlete, Football Player)
2501 W 36th St
Loveland, CO 80538-5334, USA

McCloughan, Kent (Athlete, Football Player)
2241 Woody Creek Cir
Loveland, CO 80538-5333, USA

McClover, Darrell (Athlete, Football Player)
6120 SW 19th St
Pompano Beach, FL 33068-4911, USA

McClover, Stanley (Athlete, Football Player)
4720 Buckminister Ct
Charlotte, NC 28269-8173, USA

McClung, Seth (Athlete, Baseball Player)
9693 50th Ave N
Saint Petersburg, FL 33708-3600, USA

McClure, Bob (Athlete, Baseball Player)
3834 SE Fairway E
Stuart, FL 34997-6120, USA

McClure, Bryton (Actor)
c/o Jeff Witjas *Agency for the Performing Arts (APA)*
405 S Beverly Dr Ste 500
Beverly Hills, CA 90212-4425, USA

McClure, Donald S (Misc)
13 Green St
Princeton, NJ 08542-3715, USA

McClure, Eric (Race Car Driver)
Rensi Hamilton Racing
4011 Hands Mill Hwy
York, SC 29745-9647, USA

McClure, Kandyse (Actor)
c/o Richard Lucas *Lucas Talent Inc*
1238 Homer St Suite 6
Vancouver, BC V6B 2Y5, CANADA

McClure, Larry (Race Car Driver)
Morgan-McClure Racing
26502 Newbanks Rd
Abingdon, VA 24210-7500, USA

McClure, Tane (Actor)
Don Gerler
3349 Cahuenga Blvd W Ste 1
Los Angeles, CA 90068-1379, USA

McClurkin, Donnie (Musician)
c/o Staff Member *The Alliance Agency*
1035 Bates Ct
Hendersonville, TN 37075-8864, USA

McCluskey, David (Athlete, Football Player)
22 Tannassee Ln NW Apt E8
Rome, GA 30165, USA

McCluster, Dexter (Athlete, Football Player)

McCole Bartusiak, Skye (Actor)
c/o Mara Glauberg *Cunningham Escott Slevin & Doherty (CESD)*
333 7th Ave Ste 1102
New York, NY 10001-5111, USA

McColl, Bill (Football Player)
Chicago Bears
5166 Chelsea St
La Jolla, CA 92037-7908, USA

McColl, Peggy (Writer)
Dynamic Destinies, Inc
PO Box 179 Stn Main
Manotick, ON K4M 1A3, Canada

McCollough, David (Writer)
445 Park Ave
New York, NY 10022-2606, USA

McCollum, Andy (Athlete, Football Player)
3933 Autumn Farms Dr
Wildwood, MO 63069-2519, USA

McCollum, Betty (Congressman, Politician)
1714 Longworth Hob
Washington, DC 20515-2203, USA

McColm, Matt (Actor)
c/o Bob Read *ReBar Management*
10061 Riverside Dr # 722
Toluca Lake, CA 91602-2560

McColms, Matt (Actor)
c/o Staff Member *Agency for the Performing Arts (APA)*
405 S Beverly Dr Ste 500
Beverly Hills, CA 90212-4425, USA

McComas, Brian (Musician)
c/o Staff Member *Leon Medica Management*
187 Hidden Lake Rd
Hendersonville, TN 37075-5528, USA

McComb, Heather (Actor)
c/o Kathy McComb *Kathy McComb Management*
10630 1/2 Landale St
Toluca Lake, CA 91602-2317, USA

McComb, Jeremy (Musician)
c/o Staff Member *Paradigm (Monterey)*
404 W Franklin St
Monterey, CA 93940-2303, USA

McComb, Joanne (Athlete, Baseball Player, Commentator)
105 Nottingham Rd
Bloomsburg, PA 17815-3021, USA

McCombs, BIUy Joe (Misc)
755 E Mulberry Ave Ste 600
San Antonio, TX 78212-6013, USA

McCombs, Red (Business Person, Football Executive)
825 Contour Dr
San Antonio, TX 78212-1700, USA

McConathy, John (Athlete, Basketball Player)
2320 Belmont Blvd
Bossier City, LA 71111-2427, USA

McConaughey, Matthew (Actor)
J.K. Livin'
PO Box 596
Zachary, LA 70791-0596, USA

McConkey, Phil (Athlete, Football Player)
1856 Viking Way
La Jolla, CA 92037-3354, USA

McConneii-Serio, Suzie (Athlete, Basketball Player, Olympic Athlete)
2590 Rossmoor Dr
Pittsburgh, PA 15241-2584, USA

McConnell, Dave (Race Car Driver)
Dave McConnell Racing
101 Lantern Cir
McMurray, PA 15317-3654, USA

McConnell, Harden M (Misc)
Stanford University
Chemistry Dept
Stanford, CA 94305, USA

McConnell, John P (Business Person)
Worthington Industries
1205 Dearborn Dr
Columbus, OH 43085-4769, USA

McConnell, Mitch (Politician)
2318 Dundee Rd
Louisville, KY 40205-2070, USA

McConnell, Page (Musician)
c/o Staff Member *Paradigm (Monterey)*
404 W Franklin St
Monterey, CA 93940-2303, USA

McConnell, Robert M G (Rob) (Musician)
Thomas Cassidy
11761 E Speedway Blvd
Tucson, AZ 85748-2017, USA

McConnell, Sam (Athlete, Baseball Player)
301 McKinley St
Middletown, OH 45042-3256, USA

McConnell-Serio, Suzie (Athlete, Basketball Player)
2590 Rossmoor Dr
Pittsburgh, PA 15241-2584, USA

McConville, Frank (Misc)
Union of Plant Guard Workers of America
25510 Kelly Rd
Roseville, MI 48066-4994, USA

McCoo, Marilyn (Actor, Musician)
PO Box 7905
Beverly Hills, CA 90212-7905, USA

McCook, John (Actor)
10245 Briarwood Dr
Los Angeles, CA 90077-2521, USA

McCool, Bill (Athlete, Baseball Player)
9250 SE 121st Loop
Summerfield, FL 34491-9477, USA

McCool, Michelle (Wrestler)
c/o Kerry Rodgerson *World Wrestling Entertainment (WWE)*
1241 E Main St
Stamford, CT 06902-3520, USA

McCord, Alex (Reality Star)
c/o Staff Member *Bravo TV (NY)*
30 Rockefeller Plz
New York, NY 10112-0015, USA

McCord, AnnaLynne (Actor)
c/o Gary Mantoosh *Baker Winokur Ryder Public Relations*
9100 Wilshire Blvd
W Tower #500
Beverly Hills, CA 90212-3415, USA

McCord, Clinton (Athlete, Baseball Player)
1821 Knowles St
Nashville, TN 37208-2438, USA

McCord, Darris (Athlete, Football Player)
6160 W Surrey Rd
Bloomfield Hills, MI 48301-1661, USA

McCord, Gary (Athlete, Golfer)
15215 N Kierland Blvd Unit 738
Scottsdale, AZ 85254-8224, USA

McCord, Keith (Athlete, Basketball Player)
1609 Five Acre Rd
Dolomite, AL 35061-1036, USA

McCord, Kent (Actor)
c/o John Crowther *Marshak/Zachary Company, The*
8840 Wilshire Blvd Fl 1
Beverly Hills, CA 90211-2606, USA

McCord, Mack (Race Car Driver)
Gorilla AA/FA
PO Box 2608
Phoenix, AZ 85002-2608, USA

McCord, Quentin (Athlete, Football Player)
4194 Berwick Farm Dr
Duluth, GA 30096-2597, USA

McCord, Susie (Race Car Driver)
Gorilla AA/FA
PO Box 2608
Phoenix, AZ 85002-2608, USA

McCorkle, Kevin (Actor)
c/o Peter Kluge *Impact Artist Group LLC (LA)*
244 N California St
Fl 1
Burbank, CA 91505-3505, USA

McCormack, Catherine (Actor)

McCormack, Don (Athlete, Baseball Player)
866 Glenfield Dr
Palm Harbor, FL 34684-3218, USA

McCormack, Eric (Actor)
c/o Leanne Coronel *Coronel Group*
1100 Glendon Ave Fl 17
Los Angeles, CA 90024-3588, USA

McCormack, Mary (Actor)
c/o Dannielle Thomas *Untitled Entertainment*
350 S Beverly Dr Ste 200
Beverly Hills, CA 90212-4819, USA

McCormack, Patty (Actor)
c/o Kurt Patino *Patino Management Company*
10201 Riverside Dr Ste 207
Toluca Lake, CA 91602-2538, USA

McCormack, Will (Actor)
c/o Greg Clark *Untitled Entertainment*
350 S Beverly Dr Ste 200
Beverly Hills, CA 90212-4819, USA

McCormick, Carolyn (Actor)
Bresler Kelly Assoc
11500 W Olympic Blvd Ste 510
Los Angeles, CA 90064-1527, USA

McCormick, Len (Athlete, Football Player)
514 Bolton Pl
Houston, TX 77024-4601, USA

McCormick, Maureen (Actor, Musician)
c/o Alan Somers *Pure Arts Entertainment/ Rose Group*
9925 Jefferson Blvd
Culver City, CA 90232-3505, USA

McCormick, Mike (Athlete, Baseball Player)
McCormick Realty
10 Sawgrass Pl
Pinehurst, NC 28374-7114, USA

McCormick, Sierra (Actor)
c/o Oren Segal *Management Production Entertainment (MPE)*
9229 W Sunset Blvd Ste 301
W Hollywood, CA 90069-3417, USA

McCormick, Tim (Athlete, Basketball Player)
2S00 Leroy Ln
West Bloomfield, MI 48324-2234, USA

McCormick, Tom (Athlete, Football Player)
397 Wehmeyer Loop
Mountain Home, AR 72653-6656, USA

McCornack, Bill (Race Car Driver)
McCornack Racing
PO Box 12265
Lexington, KY 40582-2265, USA

McCorvey, Kez (Athlete, Football Player)
3704 Randall St
Tallahassee, FL 32309-3029, USA

McCosh, Shawn (Athlete, Hockey Player)
18992 N 74th Dr
Glendale, AZ 85308-5668

McCourt, Dale (Athlete, Hockey Player)
1341 West Bay Rd
Garson, ON P3L 1V3, Canada

McCourt, Frank (Business Person)
22426 Pacific Coast Hwy
Malibu, CA 90265-5033, USA

McCourt, James (Actor, Television Host)
c/o Staff Member *Princess Productions*
Newcombe House
45 Notting Hill Gate
London W11 3LQ, UNITED KINGDOM

McCourt, Malachy (Actor, Writer)
c/o Marc Bass *Beacon Talent Agency*
170 Apple Ridge Rd
Woodcliff Lk, NJ 07677-8149, USA

McCourty, Devin (Athlete, Football Player)

McCourty, Jason (Athlete, Football Player)

McCoury, Del (Musician)
c/o Staff Member *Paradigm (Monterey)*
404 W Franklin St
Monterey, CA 93940-2303, USA

McCovey, Willie (Athlete, Baseball Player)
PO Box 620342
Redwood City, CA 94062-0342, USA

McCown, Josh (Athlete, Football Player)
1312 Lookout Cir
Waxhaw, NC 28173-7224, USA

McCown, Luke (Athlete, Football Player)
30963 US Highway 69 N
Rusk, TX 75785-1720, USA

McCoy, Anthony (Athlete, Football Player)
c/o Ken Zuckerman *Priority Sports & Entertainment - (LA)*
15233 Ventura Blvd Ste 718
Sherman Oaks, CA 91403-2237, USA

McCoy, Charlie (Musician)
PO Box 50455
Nashville, TN 37205-0455, USA

McCoy, Colt (Athlete, Football Player)
c/o David Dunn *Athletes First*
23091 Mill Creek Dr
Laguna Hills, CA 92653-1258, USA

McCoy, Dave (Misc)
Mammoth Mountain Chairlifts
PO Box 24
Mammoth Lakes, CA 93546-0024, USA

McCoy, Gerald (Athlete, Football Player)
c/o Kelli Masters *Kelli Masters Management*
100 N Broadway Ave Ste 1700
Oklahoma City, OK 73102-8805, USA

McCoy, Larry (Athlete, Baseball Player)
5758 Highway 139
Greenway AR, 72430-7045 USA, USA

McCoy, Larry (Baseball Player)
5758 Highway 139
Greenway, AR 72430-7045, USA

McCoy, LeRon (Athlete, Football Player)
761 Cattail Dr
Harrisburg, PA 17111-3395, USA

McCoy, Matt (Actor)
c/o Staff Member *SMS Talent*
8383 Wilshire Blvd Ste 230
Beverly Hills, CA 90211-2436, USA

McCoy, Mike (Athlete, Football Player)
PO Box 3472
Ponte Vedra Beach, FL 32004-3472, USA

McCoy, Neal (Musician)

McCoy, Sandra (Actor)
c/o Cole Harris *Pantheon Talent*
1801 Century Park E Ste 1910
Los Angeles, CA 90067-2321, USA

McCoy, Tony (Athlete, Football Player)
9200 Oak Island Ln
Clermont, FL 34711-7304, USA

McCoy-Misick, LisaRaye (Actor)
c/o Pamela Sharp *Sharp & Associates*
1516 N Fairfax Ave
Los Angeles, CA 90046-2608, USA

McCracken, Paul (Athlete, Basketball Player)
914 Westwood Blvd Apt 256
Los Angeles, CA 90024-2905, USA

McCracken, Quinton (Athlete, Baseball Player)
11308 E Autumn Sage Dr
Scottsdale, AZ 85255-8949, USA

McCrane, Paul (Actor)
VOX
5670 Wilshire Blvd Ste 820
Los Angeles, CA 90036-5613, USA

McCraney, Tarell Alvin (Writer)
c/o Dan Halsted *Manage-ment*
1103 1/2 Glendon Ave
Los Angeles, CA 90024-3501, USA

McCrary, Bill (Athlete, Baseball Player)
121 Cortez Rd APT 17
Hot Springs, AR 71909-6130, USA

McCrary, Darius (Actor)
19518 Branding Iron Rd
Walnut, CA 91789-4212, USA

McCrary, Fred (Athlete, Football Player)
1525 River Oak Dr
Roswell, GA 30075-2508, USA

McCrary, Joel (Actor)
c/o Christopher Black *Opus Entertainment*
5225 Wilshire Blvd Ste 905
Los Angeles, CA 90036-4353, USA

McCrary, Michael (Athlete, Football Player)
12234 Eagles Landing Way
Boynton Beach, FL 33437-6020, USA

McCrary, Prentice (Athlete, Football Player)
5414 E Dolphin Cir
Mesa, AZ 85206-2225, USA

McCraw, Tommy (Athlete, Baseball Player)
3142 SE Monte Vista Ct
Port Saint Lucie, FL 34952-6062, USA

McCray, Bobby (Athlete, Football Player)
c/o Staff Member *EAG Sports Management*
909 N Pacific Coast Hwy Ste 360
El Segundo, CA 90245-3864, USA

McCray, Danny (Athlete, Football Player)
c/o Brian E. Overstreet *E.O. Sports Management*
1314 Texas St Ste 1212
Houston, TX 77002-3525, USA

McCray, Demetrius (Athlete, Football Player)

McCray, Kelcie (Athlete, Football Player)
c/o Pat Dye Jr *SportsTrust Advisors*
3340 Peachtree Rd NE Fl 16
Atlanta, GA 30326-1000, USA

McCray, Lerentee (Athlete, Football Player)

McCray, Nikki (Athlete, Basketball Player, Olympic Athlete)
4278 Fox Hills Dr
Louisville, TN 37777-5105, USA

McCray, Prentice (Athlete, Football Player)
2109 N Argonaut St
Stockton, CA 95204-6201, USA

McCray, Rick (Race Car Driver)
McCray Racing
28746 Glenheather Dr
Highland, CA 92346-5357, USA

McCray, Rodney (Athlete, Baseball Player)
45365 Horseshoe Cir
Canton, MI 48187-5042, USA

McCray, Rodney (Athlete, Basketball Player)
505 E Lincoln Ave Apt 404
Mount Vernon, NY 10552-3514, USA

McCreary, Bill (Athlete, Hockey Player)
4318 Highcrest Dr Apt 1
Brighton, MI 48116-9798

McCreary, Bob (Athlete, Football Player)
1473 Knolls Dr
Newton, NC 28658-9452, USA

McCreary, Sr., Bill (Athlete, Hockey Player)
3979 Broadmoor Ct
Howell, MI 48843-7464

McCree, Marlon (Athlete, Football Player)
15590 Camden Pl
San Diego, CA 92131-4318, USA

McCreery, Scotty (Musician)
c/o Ebie McFarland *EB Media*
21 Music Sq W
Nashville, TN 37203-3203, USA

McCrills, John W (Writer)
McCrillis & Eldredge Insurance
17 Depot St
Newport, NH 03773-1533, USA

McCrimmon, Jim (Athlete, Hockey Player)
2369 Bayside Rd SW
Airdrie, AB T4B 3E3, CANADA

McCrlmmon, jim (Athlete, Hockey Player)
734 Adelaide St
Pincher Creek, AB TOK 1 WO, Canada

McCrory, Bob (Athlete, Baseball Player)
511 Coal Town Rd
Purvis, MS 39475-3955, USA

McCrory, Glenn (Boxer)
Holborn 35 Station Road
County Durham, UNITED KINGDOM (UK)

McCrory, Helen (Actor)
c/o Clair Dobbs *CLD Communications*
4 Broadway Ct
The Broadway
London SW191RG, UNITED KINGDOM

McCrory, Milton (Milt) (Boxer)
Escot Boxing Enterprises
19244 Bretton Dr
Detroit, MI 48223-1364, USA

McCrudden, Ian (Actor)
Epiphany Pictures
10625 Esther Ave
Los Angeles, CA 90064-3202, USA

McCullers, Dale (Athlete, Football Player)
1613 Tupelo Dr
Waycross, GA 31501-5054, USA

McCullers, Daniel (Athlete, Football Player)
c/o Chad Speck *Allegiant Athletic Agency*
35 Market Sq Ste 201
Knoxville, TN 37902-1420, USA

McCullers, Lance (Athlete, Baseball Player)
3309 Hoedt Rd
Tampa, FL 33618-1611, USA

McCulley, Michael J (Astronaut)
100 Yacht Haven Dr
Cocoa Beach, FL 32931-2627, USA

McCulley, Michael J Captain (Astronaut)
100 Yacht Haven Dr
Cocoa Beach, FL 32931-2627, USA

McCulloch, Ed (Race Car Driver)
Schumacher Racing
1397 Cherry Tree Rd
Avon, IN 46123-7103, USA

McCulloch, Ian (Musician)
c/o Elinor Burns *Casarotto Ramsay & Associates Ltd (UK)*
Waverley House
7-12 Noel St
London W1F 8GQ, UNITED KINGDOM

McCulloch (McCullough), Bruce (Actor)

McCullouch, Earl (Athlete, Football Player)
2108 Santa Fe Ave Apt 15
Long Beach, CA 90810-3546, USA

McCullough, Bob (Athlete, Football Player)
2225 Deerfield Ln
Helena, MT 59601-8643, USA

McCullough, David (Actor)
c/o Staff Member *Creative Artists Agency (CAA)*
2000 Avenue of the Stars Ste 100
Los Angeles, CA 90067-4705, USA

McCullough, David (Writer)
Janklow & Nesbit Assoc
285 Madison Ave Fl 21
New York, NY 10017-6427, USA

McCullough, Earl (Athlete, Football Player, Track Athlete)
2108 Santa Fe Ave
Long Beach, CA 90810-3546, USA

McCullough, Julian (Musician)
c/o Staff Member *Paradigm (Monterey)*
404 W Franklin St
Monterey, CA 93940-2303, USA

McCullough, Julie (Actor, Comedian)
c/o Hillard Elkins *Elkins Entertainment*
8306 Wilshire Blvd # 438
Beverly Hills, CA 90211-2304, USA

McCullough, Mike (Athlete, Golfer)
6334 E Evening Glow Dr
Scottsdale, AZ 85266-7339, USA

McCullough, Rich (Athlete, Football Player)
910 Cypress Station Dr Apt 506
Houston, TX 77090-1516, USA

McCullough, Wayne (Athlete, Boxer)
9972 Shady Glade Ct
Las Vegas, NV 89148-1687, USA

McCullum, Sam (Athlete, Football Player)
7701 88th Pl SE
Mercer Island, WA 98040-5746, USA

McCumber, Josh (Athlete, Golfer)
2121 Sea Hawk Dr
Ponte Vedra Beach, FL 32082-1683, USA

McCumber, Mark (Athlete, Golfer, Sportscaster)
527 Le Master Dr
Ponte Vedra Beach, FL 32082-2312, USA

McCune, Lisa (Actor)
c/o Staff Member *RGM Artists*
8-12 Ann St
Surry Hills, NSW 02010, AUSTRALIA

McCurdy, Cindy (Golfer)
18 Cottage Dr
Newnan, GA 30265-5513, USA

McCurdy, Jennette (Actor)
c/o Mia Hansen *Portrait PR*
5320 Sylmar Ave
Sherman Oaks, CA 91401-5612, USA

McCurry, Jeff (Athlete, Baseball Player)
9015 Linkmeadow Ln
Houston, TX 77025-4122, USA

McCurry, Mike (Journalist, Politician)
Cable News Network
1050 Techwood Dr NW
News Dept
Atlanta, GA 30318-5695, USA

McCusker, Jim (Athlete, Football Player)
209 N Main St
Jamestown, NY 14701-5209, USA

McCutchen, Andrew (Athlete, Baseball Player)
6895 Bushnell Dr
Lakeland, FL 33813-3738, USA

McCutchen, Daniel (Athlete, Baseball Player)
723 Deer Run Way
New Braunfels, TX 78132-4194, USA

McCutcheon, Brian (Athlete, Hockey Player)
133 Iradell Rd
Ithaca, NY 14850-9265

McCutcheon, Darwin (Athlete, Hockey Player)
PO Box 5556
Vail, CO 81658-5556, USA

McCutcheon, Daylon (Athlete, Football Player)
4393 Hiwassee
Claremont, CA 91711-8320, USA

McCutcheon, Dayton (Athlete, Football Player)
901 Golden Springs Dr # F-G
Diamond Bar, CA 91765-1181, USA

McCutcheon, Lawrence (Athlete, Football Player)
16721 Sims Ln Apt C
Huntington Beach, CA 92649-3360, USA

McCutcheon, Martine (Actor, Musician)
c/o Staff Member *JJB Creative Ltd*
47-57 Marylebone Lane
1st Floor
London W1U 2NT, UK

McDaniel, Ed (Athlete, Football Player)
13111 Brenwood Trl
Hopkins, MN 55343-6801, USA

McDaniel, James (Actor)
c/o Craig Shapiro *ICM Partners*
10250 Constellation Blvd Fl 7
Los Angeles, CA 90067-6207, USA

McDaniel, Jeremy (Athlete, Football Player)
309 Rocky Run Rd
New Bern, NC 28562-8867, USA

McDaniel, John (Athlete, Football Player)
586 Janney Rd
Ohatchee, AL 36271-5213, USA

McDaniel, Lecharls (Athlete, Football Player)
12844 Starwood Ln
San Diego, CA 92131-4210, USA

McDaniel, Lindy (Athlete, Baseball Player)
8225 Chappel Ln
Lavon, TX 75166-1721, USA

McDaniel, Orlando (Athlete, Football Player)
1012 N Goos Blvd
Lake Charles, LA 70601-1866, USA

McDaniel, Randall C (Athlete, Football Player)
20405 Manor Rd
Excelsior, MN 55331-9470, USA

McDaniel, Terry (Athlete, Baseball Player)
1441 E 75th St
Kansas City, MO 64131-1867, USA

McDaniel, Terry (Athlete, Football Player)
730 Shenandoah
Cedar Hill, TX 75104-1242, USA

McDaniel, Tony (Athlete, Football Player)
c/o Drew Rosenhaus *Rosenhaus Sports Representation*
3921 Alton Rd # 440
Miami Beach, FL 33140-3852, USA

McDaniel, Xavier (Athlete, Basketball Player)
2 Oakmist Ct
Blythewood, SC 29016-8707, USA

McDaniels, Darryl (Darryl M) (Music Group, Musician)
Entertainment Artists
2409 21st Ave S Ste 100
Nashville, TN 37212-5317, USA

McDaniels, Josh (Coach, Football Coach)
c/o Staff Member *New England Patriots*
1 Patriot Pl
Foxboro, MA 02035-1388, USA

McDaniels, Pellom (Athlete, Football Player)
333 W Meyer Blvd Apt 608
Kansas City, MO 64113-1743, USA

McDavid, Ray (Athlete, Baseball Player)
1245 Market St Apt 1348
San Diego, CA 92101-7358, USA

McDermott, Alice (Writer)
Farrar Straus Giroux
19 Union Sq W
New York, NY 10003-3304, USA

McDermott, Charlie (Actor)
c/o Adam Griffin *LINK Entertainment*
11872 La Grange Ave
Los Angeles, CA 90025-5282, USA

McDermott, Dean (Actor)
c/o Patrick Havern *The Green Room*
7080 Hollywood Blvd Ste 1100
Los Angeles, CA 90028-6938, USA

McDermott, Doug (Athlete, Baseball Player)
c/o Mark Bartelstein *Priority Sports & Entertainment (Chicago)*
325 N La Salle Dr Ste 650
Chicago, IL 60654-8182, USA

McDermott, Dylan (Actor, Director)
c/o Geyer Kosinski *Media Talent Group*
9200 W Sunset Blvd Ste 550
Los Angeles, CA 90069-3611, USA

McDermott, Jim (Congressman, Politician)
1035 Longworth Hob
Washington, DC 20515-4707, USA

McDermott, R Terrance (Terry) (Speed Skater)
5078 Chain Bridge Rd
Bloomfield Hills, MI 48304-3727, USA

McDermott, Terry (Athlete, Baseball Player)
5051 Justin Dr NW
Albuquerque, NM 87114-4312, USA

McDiarmid, Ian (Actor)
Wood Lane
London W12 7RJ, UNITED KINGDOM (UK)

McDill, Allen (Athlete, Baseball Player)
213 N Park Dr
Arkadelphia, AR 71923-3506, USA

McDivitt, James A Brig Gen (Astronaut)
3530 E Calle Puerta De Acero
Tucson, AZ 85718-6000, USA

McDole, Ron (Athlete, Football Player)
2083 Lockes Mill Rd
Berryville, VA 22611-3931, USA

McDonagh, Bill (Athlete, Hockey Player)
11 Market St PO Box 284
Copper Cliff, ON P0M 1N0, Canada

McDonagh, John Michael (Director, Writer)
c/o Jeremy Barber *United Talent Agency (UTA)*
9336 Civic Center Dr
Beverly Hills, CA 90210-3604, USA

McDonagh, Martin (Director)
c/o Charlotte Knight *Knight Hall Agency*
7 Mallow St
Lower Ground Fl
London EC1Y 8RQ, UNITED KINGDOM

McDonald, Andrew (Athlete, Football Player)

McDonald, Audra (Actor, Musician)
c/o Sean Michael Gross *21C Media Group*
200 W 57th St Ste 403
New York, NY 10019-3269, USA

McDonald, Ben (Athlete, Baseball Player, Olympic Athlete)
8780 Henderson Rd
Denham Springs, LA 70726-6705, USA

McDonald, Bruce (Director, Producer)
c/o Bill Douglass *Paradigm*
8942 Wilshire Blvd
Beverly Hills, CA 90211-1908, USA

McDonald, Clinton (Athlete, Football Player)
c/o Jonathan Feinsod *Schwartz & Feinsod*
4 Hillandale Rd
Rye Brook, NY 10573-1705, USA

McDonald, Country Joe (Musician)
PO Box 7054
Berkeley, CA 94707-0054, USA

McDonald, Darnell (Athlete, Baseball Player)
542 W Windsor Ave Frnt
Phoenix, AZ 85003-1062, USA

McDonald, Darnell (Athlete, Football Player)
13551 Bentley Cir
Woodbridge, VA 22192-4336, USA

McDonald, Dave (Athlete, Baseball Player)
2545 SE 3rd St
Pompano Beach, FL 33062-5401, USA

McDonald, Devon (Athlete, Football Player)
10812 Green Meadow Pl # Pi
Indianapolis, IN 46229-3530, USA

McDonald, Donzell (Athlete, Baseball Player)
3225 Scranton St
Aurora, CO 80011-1827, USA

McDonald, Glenn (Athlete, Basketball Player)
2135 Vuelta Grande Ave
Long Beach, CA 90815-3562, USA

McDonald, Heather (Actor)
c/o Elizabeth Much *East 2 West Collective*
11022 Santa Monica Blvd Ste 350
Los Angeles, CA 90025-7532, USA

McDonald, Jiggs (Sportscaster)
8331 Arborfield Ct
Fort Myers, FL 33912-4684, USA

McDonald, John (Athlete, Baseball Player)
411 Tilden Rd
Scituate, MA 02066-2124, USA

McDonald, Keith (Athlete, Baseball Player)
5162 E Greensboro Ln
Anaheim, CA 92807-4612, USA

McDonald, Kevin Hamilton (Actor, Writer)

McDonald, Lanny (Athlete, Hockey Player)
23 Springside St
Calgary, AB T3Z 3M1, Canada

McDonald, Michael (Actor, Comedian, Director)
c/o Alison Leslie *Marleah Leslie & Associates*
1645 Vine St Apt 712
Los Angeles, CA 90028-8812, USA

McDonald, Michael (Musician, Songwriter)
64 Wai Kulu Pl
Lahaina, HI 96761-5713, USA

McDonald, Mike (Athlete, Football Player)
1067 E Angeleno Ave
Burbank, CA 91501-1420, USA

McDonald, Miriam (Actor)
c/o Brantley Brown *Authentic Talent & Literary Management*
3615 Eastham Dr # 650
Culver City, CA 90232-2410, USA

McDonald, Paul (Athlete, Football Player)
703 Orchid Ave
Corona Del Mar, CA 92625-2428, USA

McDonald, Ramos (Athlete, Football Player)
11620 Audelia Rd Apt 715
Dallas, TX 75243-5686, USA

McDonald, Ray (Athlete, Football Player)
c/o Tom Condon *Creative Artists Agency (CAA)*
401 Commerce St PH
Nashville, TN 37219-2516, USA

McDonald, Ricardo (Athlete, Football Player)
425 E 25th St
Paterson, NJ 07514-2306, USA

McDonald, Richie (Musician)
PO Box 128648
Nashville, TN 37212, USA

McDonald, Tim (Athlete, Attorney, Football Player)
10851 N Maple Ave
Fresno, CA 93730-3501, USA

McDonald, Vance (Athlete, Football Player)
c/o Erik Burkhardt *Select Sports Group*
2700 Post Oak Blvd Ste 1450
Houston, TX 77056-5785, USA

McDonell, Thomas (Actor)
c/o Annabel Gualazzi *WME|IMG*
9601 Wilshire Blvd
Beverly Hills, CA 90210-5213, USA

McDonnell, Joe (Athlete, Hockey Player)
Detroit Red Wings
2645 Woodward Ave
Detroit, MI 48201-3028

McDonnell, Mary (Actor)
c/o Kami Putnam-Heist *Anonymous Content*
3532 Hayden Ave
Culver City, CA 90232-2413, USA

McDonnell, Patrick (Cartoonist)
c/o Staff Member *King Features Syndication*
300 W 57th St Fl 15
New York, NY 10019-5238, USA

McDonnell, Stephen (Business Person)
Applegate
750 US Highway 202 Ste 300
Bridgewater, NJ 08807-5530, USA

McDonough, Al (Athlete, Hockey Player)
288 Edgewater Cres
Kitchener, ON N2A 4M1, Canada

McDonough, Hubie (Athlete, Hockey Player)
1152 Hayward St
Manchester, NH 03103-2817, USA

McDonough, Hubie (Athlete, Hockey Player)
Manchester Monarchs
555 Elm St Ste 3
Manchester, NH 03101-2535

McDonough, Mary (Actor)
6858 Cantaloupe Ave
Van Nuys, CA 91405-4148, USA

McDonough, Neal (Actor)
179 S Plymouth Blvd
Los Angeles, CA 90004-3835, USA

McDonough, Neil (Actor)
Rigberg Robert Rugolo
1180 S Beverly Dr Ste 601
Los Angeles, CA 90035-1158, USA

McDonough, Patrick (Athlete, Cycler, Olympic Athlete)
64 Myrtle St Apt 2
Boston, MA 02114-4577, USA

McDonough, Sean (Sportscaster)
ABC-TV
77 W 66th St
Sports Dept
New York, NY 10023-6201, USA

McDorman, Jake (Actor)
c/o Elissa Leeds-Fickman *Reel Talent Management*
PO Box 491035
Los Angeles, CA 90049-9035, USA

McDormand, Frances (Actor)
c/o Simon Halls *Slate PR*
901 N Highland Ave
W Hollywood, CA 90038-2412, USA

McDougal, Karen (Actor, Fitness Expert, Model)
c/o Jeff Cohen *International Talent Agency (ITA)*
9701 Wilshire Blvd Ste 1000
Beverly Hills, CA 90212-2010, USA

McDougal, Mike (Athlete, Hockey Player)
1973 Emerson Rd
Wales, MI 48027-2120

McDougale, Stockar (Athlete, Football Player)
15 Bradford Ct
Dearborn, MI 48126-4170, USA

McDougall, Charles (Writer)
c/o Staff Member *Industry Entertainment Partners*
955 Carrillo Dr Ste 300
Los Angeles, CA 90048-5400, USA

McDougall, Ian (Producer)
c/o Staff Member *Gersh*
9465 Wilshire Blvd Ste 600
Beverly Hills, CA 90212-2605, USA

McDougall, Marshall (Athlete, Baseball Player)
213 Bell Branch Ln
Saint Johns, FL 32259-4438, USA

McDougle, Dexter (Athlete, Football Player)

McDowel, Michael (Race Car Driver)
20310 Chartwell Center Dr
Cornelius, NC 28031-5253, USA

McDowell, Bubba (Athlete, Football Player)
6353 Richmond Ave
Houston, TX 77057-5964, USA

McDowell, Dagen (Correspondent)
c/o Staff Member *Fox Business Network (NY)*
1211 Avenue of the Americas Fl 15
New York, NY 10036-8705, USA

McDowell, Jack (Athlete, Baseball Player)
2875 Calle Rancho Vis
Encinitas, CA 92024-6672, USA

McDowell, Malcolm (Actor)
c/o Staff Member *Dontanville/Frattaroli (D/F)*
270 Lafayette St Ste 402
New York, NY 10012-3327, USA

McDowell, Michael (Race Car Driver)
Michael Waltrip Racing
PO Box 70
Sherrills Ford, NC 28673-0070, USA

McDowell, Oddibe (Athlete, Baseball Player)
5240 SW 18th St
West Park, FL 33023-3157, USA

McDowell, Roger (Athlete, Baseball Player)
2690 Pete Shaw Rd
Marietta, GA 30066-2224, USA

McDowell, Ronnie (Musician)
PO Box 53
Portland, TN 37148-0053, USA

McDowell, Sam (Athlete, Baseball Player)
2538 Jessup St
The Villages, FL 32162-5126, USA

McDsyes, Antonio (Athlete, Basketball Player)
979 County Road 473
Meridian, MS 39301-9636, USA

McDuffe, Peter (Athlete, Hockey Player)
85 Mill St
Milton, ON L9T 1R8, Canada

McDuffie, George (Athlete, Football Player)
819 Independence Rd
Toledo, OH 43607-2529, USA

McDuffie, Otis J (O J) (Athlete, Football Player)
1333 NW 121st Ave
Plantation, FL 33323-2438, USA

McDuffie, Robert (Musician)
Columbia Artists Mgmt Inc
165 W 57th St
New York, NY 10019-2201, USA

McDyess, Antonio (Athlete, Basketball Player, Olympic Athlete)
979 County Road 473
Meridian, MS 39301-9636, USA

McEachern, Shawn (Athlete, Hockey Player, Olympic Athlete)
71 Beach St
Marblehead, MA 01945-2957, USA

McElderry, Joe (Musician)
c/o Staff Member *Touchstone Media Ltd*
77 Oxford St
London W1D 2ES, UK

McEldowney, Brooke (Cartoonist)
United Feature Syndicate
200 Madison Ave
New York, NY 10016-3903, USA

McElhenney, Rob (Actor)
c/o Nick Frenkel *3 Arts Entertainment*
9460 Wilshire Blvd Fl 7
Beverly Hills, CA 90212-2713, USA

McElhenny, Hugh (Athlete, Football Player)
3013 Via Venezia
Henderson, NV 89052-3802, USA

McElhone, Natascha (Actor)
c/o Annalisa Gordon *The Artists Partnership*
101 Finsbury Pavement
London EC2A 1RS, UNITED KINGDOM

McElhorne, Natascha (Artist)
c/o Staff Member *ICM Partners*
10250 Constellation Blvd Fl 7
Los Angeles, CA 90067-6207, USA

McElligott, Sarah (Actor)
c/o Monica Barkett *Global Artists Agency*
6253 Hollywood Blvd Apt 508
Los Angeles, CA 90028-8251, USA

McElman, Andy (Athlete, Hockey Player)
260 Beach Dr
Algonquin, IL 60102-2502

McElmury, Jim (Athlete, Hockey Player, Olympic Athlete)
PO Box 25737
Woodbury, MN 55125-0737, USA

McElroy, Chuck (Athlete, Baseball Player)
1049 Nederland Ave
Port Arthur, TX 77640-4338, USA

McElroy, Hugh (Athlete, Football Player)
3899 Fonville Ave
Beaumont, TX 77705-2207, USA

McElroy, Leeland (Athlete, Football Player)
8301 Hartford Dr
Rowlett, TX 75089-8832, USA

McElroy, Reggie (Athlete, Football Player)
Route 1 Box 109A
Preston, MO 65732, USA

McElroy, Vann (Athlete, Football Player)
HC 34 Box 1011
Uvalde, TX 78801, USA

McElwain, Jason (Sportscaster)
c/o Staff Member *WME|IMG*
9601 Wilshire Blvd
Beverly Hills, CA 90210-5213, USA

McEnaney, Will (Athlete, Baseball Player)
169 Roycourt Cir
Royal Palm Beach, FL 33411-8295, USA

McEnery, Peter (Actor)
International Creative Agency
76 Oxford St
London W1N 0AX, UNITED KINGDOM (UK)

McEnroe, John (Athlete, Tennis Player)
McEnroe Tennis Academy
1 Randalls Is Frnt 10
New York, NY 10035-5197, USA

McEntee, Gerald W (Politician)
State County Municipal Employees Union
1625 L St NW
Washington, DC 20036-5665, USA

McEntire, Reba (Actor, Musician)
c/o Jake Basden *Big Machine Records*
1219 16th Ave S
Nashville, TN 37212-2901, USA

McEvoy, Thomas (Misc)
9651 Gisborn Dr
Las Vegas, NV 89147-8215, USA

McEwen, Craig (Athlete, Football Player)
1610 Hilton Head Ct Apt 1265
El Cajon, CA 92019-4578, USA

McEwen, Mark (Correspondent)
CBS TV
51 W 52nd St
News Dept
New York, NY 10019-6119, USA

McEwen, Tom (Race Car Driver)
Motorsports HOF
PO Box 194
Novi, MI 48376-0194, USA

McEwen, Tom (Writer)
Tampa Tribune
PO Box 31101
Editorial Dept
Saint Petersburg, FL 33731-1107, USA

McEwing, Joe (Athlete, Baseball Player)
630 Deerbrook Dr
Yardley, PA 19067-4537, USA

McFadden, Cynthia (Correspondent, Journalist, Television Host)
ABC News / 20/20
147 Columbus Ave
New York, NY 10023-5999, USA

McFadden, Darren (Athlete, Football Player)
c/o Ed Wasielewski *EMG Sports - PA*
PO Box 2
Richboro, PA 18954-0002, USA

McFadden, Davenia (Actor)
c/o Felicia Sager *Sager Management*
260 S Beverly Dr Ste 205
Beverly Hills, CA 90212-3812, USA

McFadden, Gates (Actor)
c/o Staff Member *SMS Talent*
8383 Wilshire Blvd Ste 230
Beverly Hills, CA 90211-2436, USA

McFadden, Leon (Athlete, Baseball Player)
8617 S 10th Ave
Inglewood, CA 90305-2346, USA

McFadden, Paul (Athlete, Football Player)
7395 Christopher Dr
Youngstown, OH 44514-2563, USA

McFall, Dan (Athlete, Hockey Player)
475 N Williston Rd
Williston, VT 05495-9572

McFarland, Anthony (Athlete, Football Player)
7733 Still Lakes Dr
Odessa, FL 33556-2262, USA

McFarland, Jim (Athlete, Football Player)
4917 Pine St
Omaha, NE 68106-2451, USA

McFarland, Kay (Athlete, Football Player)
7394 S Monaco St
Centennial, CO 80112-1528, USA

McFarland, Kirsten (Writer)
c/o Staff Member *ICM Partners*
10250 Constellation Blvd Fl 7
Los Angeles, CA 90067-6207, USA

McFarland, Mike (Race Car Driver)
PO Box 330
Mooresville, NC 28115-0330, USA

McFarlane, Andrew (Actor)
c/o Staff Member *Jeff Morrone Entertainment*
9350 Wilshire Blvd Ste 224
Beverly Hills, CA 90212-3204, USA

McFarlane, Todd (Cartoonist)
Todd McFarlane Entertainment
1711 W Greentree Dr Ste 208
Tempe, AZ 85284-2717, USA

McFayden, Brian (Actor)
c/o Babette Perry *Innovative Artists*
1505 10th St
Santa Monica, CA 90401-2805, USA

McFerrin, Bobby (Actor, Songwriter, Writer)
Original Artists
826 Broadway # 400
New York, NY 10003-4826, USA

Mcfly (Music Group)
c/o Staff Member *Universal Music Group*
100 Universal City Plz
Universal City, CA 91608-1002, USA

McG (Director, Producer)
c/o Staff Member *Wonderland Sound and Vision*
8739 W Sunset Blvd
W Hollywood, CA 90069-2205, USA

McGaffigan, Andy (Athlete, Baseball Player)
6243 Forestwood Dr E
Lakeland, FL 33811-2402, USA

McGahee, Willis (Athlete, Football Player)
1 Bills Dr
Orchard Park, NY 14127-2237, USA

McGahern, John (Writer)
Faber & Faber
3 Queen Square
London WC1N 3AU, UNITED KINGDOM (UK)

McGahey, Kathleen (Athlete, Hockey Player, Olympic Athlete)
7427 W 81st St
Los Angeles, CA 90045-2303, USA

McGann, Michelle (Athlete, Golfer)
1200 Singer Dr
Riviera Beach, FL 33404-2765, USA

McGann, Paul (Actor)
Marina Martin
12/13 Poland St
London W1V 3DE, UNITED KINGDOM (UK)

McGarity, Wane (Athlete, Football Player)
PO Box 202226
San Antonio, TX 78220-9226, USA

McGarrahan, Scott (Athlete, Football Player)
6636 W William Cannon Dr
Austin, TX 78735-8529, USA

McGarrigle, Anne (Musician)
c/o Staff Member *Concerted Efforts*
PO Box 440326
Somerville, MA 02144-0004, USA

McGarry, John (Athlete, Football Player)
5725 S Woodlawn Ave
Chicago, IL 60637-1602, USA

McGarry, Steve (Cartoonist)
United feature Syndicate
200 Madison Ave
New York, NY 10016-3903, USA

McGaughey, Shug (Horse Racer)
20941 NE 38th Ave
Miami, FL 33180-3783, USA

McGaw, Patrick (Actor)
Banner Entertainment
8265 W Sunset Blvd Ste 200
West Hollywood, CA 90046-2470, USA

McGeary, Jack (Athlete, Baseball Player)

McGee, Ben (Athlete, Football Player)
35 Castle Cv
Jackson, MS 39212-3448, USA

McGee, Herb (Athlete, Basketball Player)
PO Box 67
Southeastern, PA 19399-0067, USA

McGee, Jack (Actor)
c/o Karen Semler *Semler Entertainment*
13636 Ventura Blvd # 510
Sherman Oaks, CA 91423-3700, USA

McGee, Jake (Athlete, Baseball Player)
3323 W Sevilla Cir
Tampa, FL 33629-8319, USA

McGee, Michael B (Mike) (Athlete, Football Player)
University Of South California
2 Medical Park Rd Ste 502
Columbia, SC 29203-6876, USA

McGee, Pamela (Pam) (Basketball Player)
Los Angeles Sparks
1111 S Figueroa St
Staples Center
Los Angeles, CA 90015-1300, USA

McGee, Stacy (Athlete, Football Player)
c/o Peter Schaffer *Authentic Athletix*
400 S Steele St Unit 47
Denver, CO 80209-3535, USA

McGee, Stephen (Athlete, Football Player)
c/o Staff Member *Dallas Cowboys*
1 Cowboys Way Ste 100
Frisco, TX 75034-1977, USA

McGee, Tim (Athlete, Football Player)
4226 Maxwell Dr
Mason, OH 45040-6504, USA

McGee, Tony (Athlete, Football Player)
170 Tana Dr
Fayetteville, GA 30214-7539, USA

McGee, Trina (Actor)
c/o Stephen Rice *Pantheon Talent*
1801 Century Park E Ste 1910
Los Angeles, CA 90067-2321, USA

McGee, Willie (Athlete, Baseball Player)
2081 Lupine Rd
Hercules, CA 94547-1104, USA

McGeever, John (Athlete, Football Player)
1128 Glen Manor Dr
Birmingham, AL 35243-2012, USA

McGehee, Kevin (Athlete, Baseball Player)
8639 Rid11emont Dr
Pineville, LA 71360-2629, USA

McGehee, Robby (Race Car Driver)
16 Lynnbrook Rd
Saint Louis, MO 63131-2925, USA

McGeorge, Missie (Athlete, Golfer)
515 Asheville Ln
Roanoke, TX 76262-1420, USA

McGeorge, Rich (Athlete, Football Player)
2200 Trail Wood Dr
Durham, NC 27705-1305, USA

McGhee, Carla (Athlete, Basketball Player, Olympic Athlete)
986 Pembroke Pl
Auburn, AL 36830-3374, USa

McGhee-Anderson, Kathleen (Producer)
c/o Staff Member *Creative Artists Agency (CAA)*
2000 Avenue of the Stars Ste 100
Los Angeles, CA 90067-4705, USA

McGiffin, Carol (Actor, Talk Show Host)
c/o Staff Member *ITV Network*
200 Gray's Inn Rd
London, CA WC1X 8HF, United Kingdom

McGiinchy, Kevin (Athlete, Baseball Player)
388 Medford St
Malden, MA 02148-7209, USA

McGilberry, Randy (Athlete, Baseball Player)
825 Bayshore Dr Apt 507
Pensacola, FL 32507-3463, USA

McGill, Billy (Athlete, Basketball Player)
5129 W 58th Pl
Los Angeles, CA 90056-1601, USA

McGill, Bob (Athlete, Hockey Player)
Toronto Maple Leafs
400-40 Bay St
Toronto, ON M5J 2X2

McGill, Bob (Athlete, Hockey Player)
116 Oriole Dr
Holland Landing, ON L9N 1H1, Canada

McGill, Bruce (Actor)
c/o Scott Manners *Artists & Representatives (Stone Manners Salners)*
6100 Wilshire Blvd Ste 1500
Los Angeles, CA 90048-5110, USA

McGill, Bryant (Writer)
11C Lower Dorset St
Dubline 00001, IRELAND

McGill, Everett (Actor)
c/o Staff Member *WME|IMG*
9601 Wilshire Blvd
Beverly Hills, CA 90210-5213, USA

McGill, Jill (Athlete, Golfer)
6756 Inverness Ln
Dallas, TX 75214-2518, USA

McGill, Karmeeleyah (Athlete, Football Player)
1626 N Greenwood Ave
Clearwater, FL 33755, USA

McGill, Keith (Athlete, Football Player)

McGill, Mike (Athlete, Football Player)
8930 Louis Ct
Saint John, IN 46373-9708, USA

McGill, Paul (Actor)
c/o Jill Fritzo *Jill Fritzo Public Relations*
208 E 51st St # 305
New York, NY 10022-6557, USA

McGill, Ryan (Athlete, Hockey Player)
958 Yoeman Hall Rd
Kalispell, MT 59901-7610

McGillin, Howard (Actor)
c/o Staff Member *Cunningham Escott Slevin & Doherty (CESD)*
10635 Santa Monica Blvd Ste 130
Los Angeles, CA 90025-8306, USA

McGillion, Paul (Actor)
c/o Josh Weil *WME|IMG*
9601 Wilshire Blvd
Beverly Hills, CA 90210-5213, USA

McGillis, Kelly (Actor, Producer)
c/o David Williams *David Williams Management*
269 S Beverly Dr # 1408
Beverly Hills, CA 90212-3851, USA

McGillivray, Scott (Television Host)
c/o Staff Member *HGTV*
9721 Sherrill Blvd
Knoxville, TN 37932-3330, USA

McGinest, Willie (Athlete, Football Player)
25231 Prado Del Grandioso
Calabasas, CA 91302-3655, USA

McGinley, John C (Actor)
c/o Nancy Iannios *Core Public PR*
1875 Century Park E Ste 930
Los Angeles, CA 90067-2540, USA

McGinley, Ted (Actor)
c/o Cynthia Snyder *Cynthia Snyder Public Relations*
5739 Colfax Ave
N Hollywood, CA 91601-1636, USA

McGinn, Bernard J (Misc)
5702 Kenwood Ave
Chicago, IL 60637, USA

McGinn, Brian (Director)
c/o David Karp *WME|IMG*
9601 Wilshire Blvd
Beverly Hills, CA 90210-5213, USA

McGinn, Dan (Athlete, Baseball Player)
1309 S 189th Ct
Omaha, NE 68130-2842, USA

McGinnis, Dave (Athlete, Coach, Football Coach, Football Player)
Arizona Cardinals
PO Box 888
Phoenix, AZ 85001-0888, USA

McGinnis, George (Athlete, Basketball Player)
811e Bounty Ct
Indianapolis, IN 46236-8941, USA

McGinnis, Joe (Writer)
Janklow & Nesbit
285 Madison Ave Lbby
New York, NY 10017-6418, USA

McGinnis, Russ (Athlete, Baseball Player)
10368 Craftsman Way Apt 101
San Diego, CA 92127-3523, USA

McGinty, Damian (Actor)
c/o Paul Lyttle *Twenty Four Seven PR*
Prefers to be contacted via telephone or email
Los Angeles, CA, USA

McGirt, James (Buddy) (Boxer)
195 Suffolk Ave
Brentwood, NY 11717-4205, USA

McGiver, Boris (Actor)
c/o Staff Member *Harden-Curtis Associates*
214 W 29th St Rm 1203
New York, NY 10001-5754, USA

McGlinchy, Kevin (Athlete, Baseball Player)
10 West St
Malden, MA 02148-5311, USA

McGlockin, Jon (Athlete, Basketball Player)
5281 State Road
#83
Heartland, WI 53029, USA

McGloin, Matt (Athlete, Football Player)
c/o Jordan Woy *Willis & Woy Management*
4890 Alpha Rd Ste 200
Dallas, TX 75244-4639, USA

McGlothin, Pat (Athlete, Baseball Player)
1454 Kenesaw Ave
Knoxville, TN 37919-7749, USA

McGlynn, Dennis (Race Car Driver)
Dover Downs Speedway
PO Box 843
Dover, DE 19903-0843, USA

McGlynn, Dick (Athlete, Hockey Player)
38 Rock Glen Rd
Medford, MA 02155-1946, USA

McGlynn, Dick (Athlete, Hockey Player, Olympic Athlete)
38 Rock Glen Rd
Medford, MA 02155-1946, USA

McGlynn, Mike (Athlete, Football Player)
c/o Michael Perrett *Element Sports Group*
3340 Peachtree Rd NE Fl 16
Atlanta, GA 30326-1000, USA

McGlynn, Pat (Musician)
27 Preston Grange
Preston Pans E
Lothian, SCOTLAND

McGlynn, Ryan (Race Car Driver)
Raynard McGlynn Motorsports
1246 Sans Souci Pkwy
Hanover Township, PA 18706-5230, USA

McGorry, Matt (Actor)
c/o Meg Mortimer *Authentic Talent and Literary Management (NY)*
20 Jay St Ste M17
Brooklyn, NY 11201-8300, USA

McGovern, Elizabeth (Actor)
c/o Staff Member *Anonymous Content*
3532 Hayden Ave
Culver City, CA 90232-2413, USA

McGovern, Jim (Athlete, Golfer)
384 Francis Ct
Oradell, NJ 07649-1308, USA

McGovern, Jonny (Comedian, Musician)
c/o Len Evans *Project Publicity*
540 W 43rd St
New York, NY 10036, USA

McGovern, Maureen (Actor, Musician)
MM Productions Inc
12087 Evergreen St NW
C/O Jennifer Howe
Minneapolis, MN 55448-2433, USA

McGovern, Rob (Athlete, Football Player)
419 E 57th St Apt 2D
New York, NY 10022-3176, USA

McGowan, Alistair (Actor)
c/o Oriana Elia *Curtis Brown Ltd*
28-29 Hay Market
Hay Market House
London SW1Y 4SP, UNITED KINGDOM

McGowan, Dustin (Athlete, Baseball Player)
PO Box 1281
Ludowici, GA 31316-1281, USA

McGowan, Michael (Director)
c/o Bill Douglass *Paradigm*
8942 Wilshire Blvd
Beverly Hills, CA 90211-1908, USA

McGowan, Pat (Athlete, Golfer)
PO Box 88
Southern Pines, NC 28388-0088, USA

McGowan, Rose (Actor)
c/o Adam Kersh *Brigade Marketing*
116 W 23rd St Fl 5
New York, NY 10011-2599, USA

McGowan, Zach (Actor)
c/o Mike Gillespie *Primary Wave Entertainment*
10850 Wilshire Blvd Fl 6
Los Angeles, CA 90024-4319, USA

McGrady, Michael (Actor)
c/o Staff Member *Main Title Entertainment*
8383 Wilshire Blvd Ste 408
Beverly Hills, CA 90211-2435, USA

McGrady, Tracy (Athlete, Basketball Player)
23 Beacon Hl
Sugar Land, TX 77479-2551, USA

McGrath, Alister (Writer)
c/o Staff Member *HarperCollins Publishers*
195 Broadway Fl 2
New York, NY 10007-3132, USA

McGrath, Doug (Director)
c/o Staff Member *ICM Partners*
10250 Constellation Blvd Fl 7
Los Angeles, CA 90067-6207, USA

McGrath, Douglas (Actor, Director, Writer)
c/o Staff Member *Creative Artists Agency (CAA)*
2000 Avenue of the Stars Ste 100
Los Angeles, CA 90067-4705, USA

McGrath, Eugene R (Business Person)
Consolidated Edison
4 Irving Pl
New York, NY 10003-3502, USA

McGrath, Jeremy (Athlete, Motorcycle Racer)
JR Motorsports
801 SW Ordnance Rd
Ankeny, IA 50023-2823, USA

McGrath, Katie (Actor)
c/o Romilly Bowlby *DDA Public Relations*
192-198 Vauxhall Bridge Rd
London SW1V 1DX, UNITED KINGDOM

McGrath, Mark (Musician, Television Host)
c/o John Marx *WME|IMG*
9601 Wilshire Blvd
Beverly Hills, CA 90210-5213, USA

McGratton, Tom (Athlete, Hockey Player)
919-690 Regency Crt
Burlington, ON L7N 3H1, Canada

McGraw, Doctor (Dr) Phil (Doctor, Talk Show Host, Writer)
c/o Terri Corigliano *CBS Paramount Network Television*
4024 Radford Ave
Cbs Studios
Studio City, CA 91604-2190, USA

McGraw, Jay (Writer)

McGraw, Melinda (Actor)
c/o Staff Member *McKeon-Myones Management*
3500 W Olive Ave Ste 770
Burbank, CA 91505-5527, USA

McGraw, Mike (Athlete, Football Player)
P.O. Box 529
Medicine Bow, WY 82328, USA

McGraw, Robin (Writer)
c/o Staff Member *The Dr. Phil Foundation*
137 N Larchmont Blvd # 705
Los Angeles, CA 90004-3704, USA

McGraw, Tim (Musician)
c/o Rodney Essig *Creative Artists Agency (CAA)*
401 Commerce St PH
Nashville, TN 37219-2516, USA

McGraw, Tom (Athlete, Baseball Player)
11300 NE 379th St
La Center, WA 98629-4307, USA

McGreevey, James (Politician)
109A Green St
Woodbridge, NJ 07095-2910, USA

McGregor, Conor (Athlete, Mixed Martial Arts)
Straight Blast Gym Ireland
1A Concorde Industrial Estate
Naas Road
Dublin 00012, IRELAND

McGregor, Ewan (Actor)
c/o Lindy King *United Agents*
12-26 Lexington St
London W1F OLE, UNITED KINGDOM

McGregor, Gilbert (Athlete, Basketball Player)
3700 Orleans Ave Apt 4411
New Orleans, LA 70119-4854, USA

McGregor, Scott (Athlete, Baseball Player)
1514 Providence Rd
Towson, MD 21286-1523, USA

McGrew, Reggie (Athlete, Football Player)
1247 Lakeside Dr Apt 2039
Sunnyvale, CA 94085-1008, USA

McGriff, Elton (Athlete, Basketball Player)
4011 Shoreline Dr
Dallas, TX 75233-3709, USA

McGriff, Fred (Athlete, Baseball Player)
16314 Millan De Avila
Tampa, FL 33613-1089, USA

McGriff, Hershel (Race Car Driver)
General Delivery
Green Valley, AZ 85622, USA

McGriff, Lee (Athlete, Football Player)
3501 W University Ave Ste A
Gainesville, FL 32607-2465, USA

McGriff, Terry (Athlete, Baseball Player)
2905 Langston Dr
Fort Pierce, FL 34946-1180, USA

McGriff, Tery (Athlete, Baseball Player)
2905 Langston Dr
Fort Pierce, FL 34946-1180, USA

McGriff, Travis (Athlete, Football Player)
5910 NW 19th Pl
Gainesville, FL 32605-3246, USA

McGriggs, Lamar (Athlete, Football Player)
1209-115 Main St E
Hamilton, ON L8N 1G5, Canada

McGruder, Aaron (Cartoonist)
Universal Press Syndicate
4520 Main St Ste 340
Kansas City, MO 64111-7705, USA

McGuane III, Thomas F (Writer)
410 S 3rd Ave
Bozeman, MT 59715-5251, USA

McGuigan, Frank (Athlete, Football Player)
2715 Willits Rd
Philadelphia, PA 19114-3410, USA

McGuinn, Roger (Musician)
c/o Staff Member *Shore Fire Media*
32 Court St Fl 16
Brooklyn, NY 11201-4441, USA

McGuire, Betty (Actor)
H David Moss
6063 Vineland Ave Apt B
North Hollywood, CA 91606-4986, USA

McGuire, Bill (Athlete, Baseball Player)
17209 I St
Omaha, NE 68135-3626, USA

McGuire, Christine (Musician)
100 Rancho Cir
Las Vegas, NV 89107-4600, USA

McGuire, Kevin E (Athlete, Basketball Player)
20 Blue Jay Ln
North Oaks, MN 55127-2015, USA

McGuire, Marcy (Actor)
681 Red Arrow Trl
Palm Desert, CA 92211-7427, USA

McGuire, Mickey (Athlete, Baseball Player)
1521 Middle Park Dr
Dayton, OH 45414-1500, USA

McGuire, Phyllis (Musician)
7373 N Scottsdale Rd Ste A130
Scottsdale, AZ 85253-3522, USA

McGuire, Ryan (Athlete, Baseball Player)
10 Atwater
Irvine, CA 92602-2028, USA

McGuire, Walter E (Gene) (Athlete, Football Player)
3229 Country Club Dr
Lynn Haven, FL 32444-5125, USA

McGuire, Willard H (Misc)
National Education Assn
1201 16th St NW
Washington, DC 20036-3290, USA

McGuire, William Biff (Actor)
McKenrick
1443 Pandora Ave
Los Angeles, CA 90024-5164, USA

McGuire, William W (Business Person)
United HealthCare Corp
9900 Bren Rd E Ste 300W
Opus Center
Minnetonka, MN 55343-4402, USA

McGuire-Leveque, Sarah (Athlete, Golfer)
2433 S 15th St
Springfield, IL 62703-3644, USA

McGuire Sisters (Music Group)
c/o Stan Scottland *Stan Scottland Entertainment*
157 E 57th St Apt 18B
New York, NY 10022-2115, USA

McGwire, Mark (Athlete, Baseball Player, Olympic Athlete)
c/o Harlan Werner *Sports Placement Service*
330 W 11th St Apt 105
Los Angeles, CA 90015-3200, USA

McHale, Christina (Athlete, Tennis Player)
c/o Staff Member *Women's Tennis Association (WTA-US)*
1 Progress Plz Ste 1500
St Petersburg, FL 33701-4335, USA

McHale, Joel (Actor, Television Host)
c/o Lewis Kay *Kovert Creative*
506 Santa Monica Blvd Ste 400
Santa Monica, CA 90401-2412, USA

McHale, Kevin (Actor)
c/o Ashton Lunceford *Portrait PR*
5320 Sylmar Ave
Sherman Oaks, CA 91401-5612, USA

McHale, Kevin (Athlete, Basketball Player)
20 Blue Jay Ln
North Oaks, MN 55127-2015, USA

McHattie, Stephen (Actor)
c/o Ronda Cooper *Characters Talent Agency*
200-1505 2nd Ave W
Vancouver, BC V6H 3Y4, CANADA

McHattle, Stephen (Actor)
Macklam Feldman Mgmt
200-1505 2nd Ave W
Vancouver, BC V6H 3Y4, CANADA

McHenry, Vance (Athlete, Baseball Player)
2396 Brown St
Durham, CA 95938-9620, USA

M. Christensen, Donna (Congressman, Politician)
1510 Longworth Hob
Washington, DC 20515-5501, USA

McHugh, Heather (Writer)
University of Washington
English Dept
PO Box 35330
Seattle, WA 98195-0001, USA

McHugh, Mike (Athlete, Hockey Player)
945 Parish Pl
Hummelstown, PA 17036-8986

Mcilhargey, Jack (Athlete, Hockey Player)
2120 Birch St
Point Roberts, WA 98281-9507

McIlhenny, Don (Athlete, Football Player)
5855 Milton St Apt 109
Dallas, TX 75206-0036, USA

Mcilravy, Lincoln (Athlete, Olympic Athlete)
4220 210th St NE
Solon, IA 52333-9657, USA

McIlroy, Rory (Athlete, Golfer)
Holywood Golf Club
Nuns Walk
Demesne Rd
Holywood, County Down BT18 9LE, NORTHERN IRELAND

McIlvaine, Jim (Athlete, Basketball Player)
Camp Anokijig
Camp Anokijig W5639 Anokijig Ln
Plymouth, WI 53e73-2879, USA

Mcilvaine, Joe (Commentator)
106 Stoney Brook Blvd
Newtown Square, PA 19073-3974, USA

McInerney, Jay (Actor, Writer)
c/o Doug MacLaren *ICM Partners*
10250 Constellation Blvd Fl 7
Los Angeles, CA 90067-6207, USA

McInnis, Hugh (Athlete, Football Player)
290 Rockwell Church Rd NE
Winder, GA 30680-3039, USA

Mcinnis, Jeffrey (Athlete, Basketball Player)
34e4 Lazy Day Ln
Charlotte, NC 28269-e144, USA

McInnis, Marty (Athlete, Hockey Player, Olympic Athlete)
21 Peter Hobart Dr
Hingham, MA 02043-3751, USA

McIntosh, Bill (Athlete, Golfer)
226 Village Green Blvd APT 205
Ann Arbor, MI 48105-3602, USA

Mcintosh, Bradley (Actor, Musician)
c/o Becky Thompson *Action Talent International*
Moray House
23 - 31 Great Titchfield Street
London W1W 7PA, United Kingdom

McIntosh, Chris (Athlete, Football Player)
102 N Jefferson St
Verona, WI 53593-1213, USA

McIntosh, Damion (Athlete, Football Player)
1340 NW 93rd Ter
Plantation, FL 33322-4328, USA

McIntosh, Joe (Athlete, Baseball Player)
9120 SE 54th St
Mercer Island, WA 98040-5148, USA

McIntosh, Pollyanna (Actor)
c/o Angela Mach *Platform PR*
2666 N Beachwood Dr
Los Angeles, CA 90068-2308, USA

McIntosh, Tim (Athlete, Baseball Player)
1815 S Talbott Pl
Waynesboro, VA 22980-2250, USA

McIntyre, Guy (Athlete, Football Player)
257 Arrowhead Way
Hayward, CA 94544-6649, USA

McIntyre, Joe (Actor)
c/o Gina Rugolo *Rugolo Entertainment*
195 S Beverly Dr Ste 400
Beverly Hills, CA 90212-3044, USA

McIntyre, Joey (Musician)
c/o Jason Gutman *Gersh*
41 Madison Ave Ste 3301
New York, NY 10010-2210, USA

Mcintyre, Larry (Athlete, Hockey Player)
9420 E 116th St S
Bixby, OK 74008-1733

McIntyre, Melissa (Actor)
Creative Drive Artists
123-20 Carlton St
c/o Dani De Lio
Toronto, ON M5B 2H5, CANADA

McIntyre, Mike (Congressman, Politician)
2133 Rayburn Hob
Washington, DC 20515-2102, USA

McIntyre, Secedrick (Athlete, Football Player)
4801 Tannery Ave
Tampa, FL 33624-4533, USA

Mcintyre, Vonda (Writer)
PO Box 31041
Seattle, WA 98103-1041, USA

McIver, Everett (Athlete, Football Player)
1205 Avignon Dr SW
Conyers, GA 30094-8406, USA

McIver, Rose (Actor)
c/o Kimberlin Belloni *Artists First*
9465 Wilshire Blvd Ste 900
Beverly Hills, CA 90212-2608, USA

McIver Ewing, Blake (Actor)
c/o Clint Morris *October Coast PR*
2100 W Magnolia Blvd Ste 4
Burbank, CA 91506-1700, USA

McIvor, Richard (Athlete, Football Player)
4114 Huntington Ln
San Angelo, TX 76904-5916, USA

Mc.Julien, Paul (Athlete, Football Player)
12111 Gibbens Rd
Baton Rouge, LA 70807-1602, USA

McJulien, Paul (Athlete, Football Player)
20300 SE Morrison Ter # H
Gresham, OR 97030-2233, USA

McKagan, Duff (Musician)
c/o Ian Sales *International Talent Booking*
9 Kingsway
Fl 6
London WC2B 6XF, UNITED KINGDOM

McKay, Adam (Director)
c/o Staff Member *Gary Sanchez Productions*
1041 N Formosa Ave
West Hollywood, CA 90046-6703, USA

McKay, Bob (Athlete, Football Player)
4110 Bluffridge Dr
Austin, TX 78759-7354, USA

McKay, Cody (Athlete, Baseball Player)
5 Village Ct
Littleton, CO 80123-6640, USA

McKay, Dave (Athlete, Baseball Player)
9702 E La Posada Cir
Scottsdale, AZ 85255-3716, USA

McKay, Gardner (Actor, Director, Writer)
1040 Lunalilo St PH 2
Honolulu, HI 96822-5712, USA

McKay, Heather (Athlete)
48 Nesbitt Dr
East York, ON M4W 2G3, CANADA

McKay, John (Athlete, Football Player)
16601 Calle Haleigh
Pacific Palisades, CA 90272-1968, USA

McKay, Mhairi (Athlete, Golfer)
898 W Ashbourne Dr
Eagle, ID 83616-6433, USA

McKay, Nellie (Actor)
c/o Staff Member *Brookside Artists Management*
250 W 57th St Ste 1820
New York, NY 10107-1802, USA

McKay, Peggy (Actor)
8811 Wonderland Ave
Los Angeles, CA 90046-1851, USA

McKay, Randy (Athlete, Hockey Player)
44640 US Highway 41
Chassell, MI 49916-9102

McKay, Ray (Athlete, Hockey Player)
PO Box 182
Ilderton, ON N0M 2A0, Canada

McKay, Ross (Athlete, Hockey Player)
1401 Thornwood Dr
Downers Grove, IL 60516-1224

McKay, Tom (Actor)
c/o Staff Member *Independent Talent Group*
40 Whitfield St
London W1T 2RH, UNITED KINGDOM

McKean, Eddy (Race Car Driver)
Enerjetix Motors
20520 E 1st Ave
Greenacres, WA 99016-8617, USA

McKean, Jim (Athlete, Baseball Player)
740 Sand Pine Dr NE
Saint Petersburg, FL 33703-3181, USA

McKean, Michael (Actor, Comedian)
3202 Club Dr
Los Angeles, CA 90064-4812, USA

McKechnie, Walt (Athlete, Hockey Player)
McKeck's Place
PO Box 752
Haliburton, ON K0M 1S0, CANADA

McKee, Bonnie (Musician)
15353 SE 49th Pl
Bellevue, WA 98006-3652, USA

McKee, Frank S (Misc)
United Steelworkers Union
5 gateway Center
Pittsburgh, PA 15222, USA

McKee, Gina (Actor)
Rozane Vacca
8 Silver Place
London W1R 3LJ, UNITED KINGDOM (UK)

McKee, Jay (Athlete, Hockey Player)
Rochester Americans
1 War Memorial Sq Ste 228
Rochester, NY 14614-2192

McKee, Jay (Athlete, Hockey Player)
32 Hidden Meadow Xing
Lancaster, NY 14086-3279

McKee, Lonette (Actor)
c/o Drew Elliot *Artist International*
333 E 43rd St Apt 115
New York, NY 10017-4822, USA

McKee, Lucky (Director)
9300 Wilshire Blvd Ste 555
Beverly Hills, CA 90212-3211, USA

McKee, Maria (Musician)
Eleven Thirty
449 Trollingwood Rd # A
Haw River, NC 27258-8750, USA

McKee, Mike (Athlete, Hockey Player)
6 Linden Point Rd
Branford, CT 06405-5709

McKee, Roxanne (Actor)
c/o Gary Mantoosh *Baker Winokur Ryder Public Relations*
9100 Wilshire Blvd
W Tower #500
Beverly Hills, CA 90212-3415, USA

McKee, Todd (Actor)
611 N Flores St Apt 2
West Hollywood, CA 90048-2134, USA

McKeel, Walt (Athlete, Baseball Player)
7669 NC Highway 58 N
Stantonsburg, NC 27883-8635, USA

McKeen, Summer (Internet Star)
c/o Kyle Santillo *Scale Management*
6300 Wilshire Blvd
Los Angeles, CA 90048-5204, USA

McKeever, Vito (Athlete, Football Player)
6823 Coral Reef St
Lake Worth, FL 33467-7635, USA

McKellar, Danica (Actor)
c/o Matt Sherman *Matt Sherman Management*
8840 Wilshire Blvd # 109
Beverly Hills, CA 90211-2606, USA

McKellen, Ian (Actor)
c/o Chris Andrews *Creative Artists Agency (CAA)*
2000 Avenue of the Stars Ste 100
Los Angeles, CA 90067-4705, USA

McKeller, Keith (Athlete, Football Player)
1972 Waccamaw Path
Winston Salem, NC 27127-9433, USA

McKelvey, Rob (Athlete, Golfer)
1814 Duke Rd
Atlanta, GA 30341-4853, USA

McKelvin, Leodis (Athlete, Football Player)
c/o Hadley Engelhard *Enter-Sports Management*
6000 Lake Forrest Dr Ste 370
Atlanta, GA 30328-5902, USA

McKendry, Alex (Athlete, Hockey Player)
151 Courthouse Rd
Franklin Square, NY 11010-2913, USA

McKendry, Chris (Commentator, Journalist, Sportscaster)
57 Hermit Ln
Westport, CT 06880-1125, USA

McKenna, Alex (Actor)
c/o Staff Member *Grey Media Group*
16848 Charmel Ln
Pacific Palisades, CA 90272-2216, USA

McKenna, Aline Brosh (Writer)
c/o Todd Feldman *Creative Artists Agency (CAA)*
2000 Avenue of the Stars Ste 100
Los Angeles, CA 90067-4705, USA

McKenna, Andrew J (Business Person)
McDonald's Corp
1 McDonalds Dr
1 Kroc Dr
Oak Brook, IL 60523-1911, USA

McKenna, Chris (Director, Producer)
c/o Joy Fehily *PMK/BNC Public Relations*
1840 Century Park E Ste 1400
Los Angeles, CA 90067-2115, USA

McKenna, David (Dave) (Musician)
Thomas Cassidy
11761 E Speedway Blvd
Tucson, AZ 85748-2017, USA

McKenna, Kevin (Athlete, Basketball Player)
3068 Cimarron Pl
Eugene, OR 97405-1751, USA

McKenna, Paul (Writer)
c/o Staff Member *United Agents*
12-26 Lexington St
London W1F OLE, UNITED KINGDOM

McKenna, Virginia (Actor)
8 Buckfast Court
Runcorn, Cheshire WA7 1QJ, UNITED KINGDOM (UK)

McKenney, Donald H (Don) (Athlete, Hockey Player)
16 Edgewater Dr
Norton, MA 02766-2123

McKennitt, Loreena (Musician)
c/o Staff Member *Quinlan Road*
PO Box 933 Stn Main
Stratford, ON N5A 7M3, Canada

McKennitt, Lorena (Musician, Songwriter, Writer)
Quinlan Road
PO Box 933 Stn Main
Stratford, ON N5A 7M3, CANADA

McKennon, Keith R (Business Person)
5434 E Lincoln Dr
Paradise Vly, AZ 85253-4118, USA

McKenny, Jim (Athlete, Hockey Player)
City TV
299 Queen St W
Toronto, ON M5V 2Z5, Canada

McKenry, Michael (Athlete, Baseball Player)
8364 David Tippit Way
Knoxville, TN 37931-4478, USA

McKenzie, Andrew (Misc)
Leather Goods Plastics Novelty Union
265 W 14th St
New York, NY 10011-7103, USA

McKenzie, Benjamin (Actor)
c/o Jennifer Allen *Viewpoint Inc*
8820 Wilshire Blvd Ste 220
Beverly Hills, CA 90211-2622, USA

McKenzie, Bill (Athlete, Hockey Player)
2812 Harborside Way
Southport, NC 28461-8373

McKenzie, Bret (Actor, Comedian)
c/o Jason Heyman *United Talent Agency (UTA)*
9336 Civic Center Dr
Beverly Hills, CA 90210-3604, USA

McKenzie, Dan P (Misc)
Bullard Labs
Madingley Rise
Madingley Road
Cambridge CB3 0EZ, UNITED KINGDOM (UK)

McKenzie, Forrest (Athlete, Basketball Player)
2516 S Laurelwood
Santa Ana, CA 92704-5439, USA

McKenzie, Jacqueline (Actor)
c/o Brett Carella *Lab, The*
5540 Hollywood Blvd # 200
Hollywood, CA 90028-6808, USA

McKenzie, Jim (Athlete, Hockey Player)
9266 Chevoit Dr
Brentwood, TN 37027-6138

McKenzie, Kareem (Athlete, Football Player)
131 Desilvio Dr
Sicklerville, NJ 08081-3400, USA

McKenzie, Raleigh (Athlete, Football Player)
715 Huntsman Pl
Herndon, VA 20170-3160, USA

McKenzie, Reggie (Athlete, Football Player)
411 Carta Rd
Knoxville, TN 37914-3619, USA

McKenzie, Reginald (Reggie) (Athlete, Football Player)
13853 Trumbull St
Highland Park, MI 48203-3073, USA

McKenzie, Stan (Athlete, Basketball Player)
4927 Holly Tree Dr
Dallas, TX 75287-7239, USA

McKenzie, Thomasin (Actor)
c/o Mitchell Gossett *Industry Entertainment Partners*
955 Carrillo Dr Ste 300
Los Angeles, CA 90048-5400, USA

McKenzie, Vashti (Religious Leader)
Payne Memorial Church
1714 Madison Ave # 16
Baltimore, MD 21217-3750, USA

McKeon, Doug (Actor)
c/o Raymond Miller *Archetype*
1608 Argyle Ave
Los Angeles, CA 90028-6408, USA

McKeon, Jack (Athlete, Baseball Player, Coach)
1529 Charleigh Ct
Elon, NC 27244-9770, USA

McKeon, Joel (Athlete, Baseball Player)
1901 Pierce St Apt 7
Hollywood, FL 33020-4047, USA

McKeon, Lindsey (Actor)
c/o Robbie Kass *Kass Management*
1011 Euclid St Unit B
Santa Monica, CA 90403-4296, USA

McKeon, Matt (Soccer Player)
Kansas City Wizards
2 Arrowhead Dr
Kansas City, MO 64129, USA

McKeon, Nancy (Actor)
c/o Caitlin Green *Anderson Group Public Relations*
8060 Melrose Ave Fl 4
Los Angeles, CA 90046-7038, USA

McKeown, Bob (Correspondent)
CBS-TV
51 W 52nd St
News Dept
New York, NY 10019-6119, USA

McKeown, Leslie (Les) (Music Group, Musician)
Brian Gannon Mgmt
PO Box 106
Rochdale, OL 16 4HW, UNITED KINGDOM (UK)

McKey, Derrick (Athlete, Basketball Player)
8 Woodard Pl
Zionsville, IN 46077-8189, USA

McKibben, Bill (Writer)
c/o Staff Member *Simon & Schuster*
1230 Avenue of the Americas Fl CONC1
New York, NY 10020-1586, USA

McKibben, Mike (Athlete, Football Player)
2523 Forest Brook Dr
Pittsburgh, PA 15241-2586, USA

McKibbin, Nikki (Actor, Musician)
c/o JD Sobol *Almond Talent Management*
8217 Beverly Blvd Ste 8
W Hollywood, CA 90048-4534, USA

McKichan, Steve (Athlete, Hockey Player)
29830 Centre Rd
Strathroy, ON N7G 3H7, Canada

McKidd, Kevin (Actor)
c/o Cara Tripicchio *Shelter PR*
5670 Wilshire Blvd Ste 1200
Los Angeles, CA 90036-5621, USA

McKie, Aaron (Athlete, Basketball Player)
14ee Youngs Ford Rd
Gladwyne, PA 19035-1233, USA

McKie, Jason (Athlete, Football Player)
1008 Vineyard Dr
Gurnee, IL 60031-5100, USA

McKim, Peggy (Actor)
15801 Wyandotte St Unit 111
Van Nuys, CA 91406-3181, USA

McKinley, Alvin (Athlete, Football Player)
2792 Elkins Lake
Huntsville, TX 77340, USA

McKinley, Dennis (Athlete, Football Player)
150 McKinley Rd
Mc Cool, MS 39108-4220, USA

McKinley, Robin (Writer)
Writer's House
21 W 26th St Fl 1
New York, NY 10010-1003, USA

McKinley-Uselmann, Therese (Athlete, Baseball Player, Commentator)
1644 N Greenwood Ave
Park Ridge, IL 60068-1215, USA

McKinnely, Phil (Athlete, Football Player)
585 Edgehill Pl
Alpharetta, GA 30022-7006, USA

McKinney, Carlton (Athlete, Basketball Player)
310 E 4th Ave
Nixon, TX 78140-2939, USA

McKinney, Charlotte (Actor)
3862 S Orange Ave
Orlando, FL 32806-6218, USA

Mckinney, Frank (Business Person)
PO Box 388
Boynton Beach, FL 33425-0388, USA

McKinney, Gil (Actor)
c/o Steven Levy *Framework Entertainment*
9057 Nemo St # C
W Hollywood, CA 90069-5511, USA

McKinney, Jack (Basketball Coach, Coach)
St Joseph's University
5600 City Ave
Hawk's Hall of Fame
Philadelphia, PA 19131-1376, USA

McKinney, Mark (Actor)
c/o Staff Member *WME/IMG*
9601 Wilshire Blvd
Beverly Hills, CA 90210-5213, USA

McKinney, Odis (Athlete, Football Player)
23126 Collins St
Woodland Hills, CA 91367-4225, USA

McKinney, Rich (Athlete, Baseball Player)
2495 E Peterson Rd
Troy, OH 45373-7790, USA

McKinney, Royce (Athlete, Football Player)
1930 N Beech Daly Rd
Dearborn Heights, MI 48127-3462, USA

McKinney, Seth (Athlete, Football Player)
2403 Crown Ct
College Station, TX 77845-2006, USA

McKinney, Steve (Athlete, Football Player)
2403 Crown Ct
College Station, TX 77845-2006, USA

McKinney, Tamara (Athlete, Olympic Athlete, Skier)
4935 Parkers Mill Rd
Lexington, KY 40513-9760, USA

McKinnie, Bryant (Athlete, Football Player)
12535 Stoneway Ct
Davie, FL 33330-1215, USA

McKinnie, Silas (Athlete, Football Player)
22875 Summer House Ct Apt 205
Novi, MI 48375-4582, USA

McKinnis, Hugh (Athlete, Football Player)
4759 NW El Camino Blvd
Bremerton, WA 98312-1101, USA

McKinney, Kurt (Actor)
5003 Tilden Ave Unit 206
Sherman Oaks, CA 91423-1747, USA

McKinnney, Richard (Rick) (Athlete)
7659 Kavooras Dr
Sacramento, CA 95831-4207, USA

McKinnney, Tamara (Skier)
4935 Parkers Mill Rd
Lexington, KY 40513-9760, USA

McKinnon, Dan (Athlete, Hockey Player)
610 E River Dr
Warroad, MN 56763, USA

McKinnon, Dennis (Athlete, Football Player)
PO Box 47661
Chicago, IL 60647-7212, USA

McKinnon, Jerick (Athlete, Football Player)

McKinnon, Kate (Actor, Comedian)
c/o Fred Hashagen *United Talent Agency (UTA)*
888 7th Ave Fl 7
New York, NY 10106-0700, USA

McKinnon, Ray (Actor)
c/o Steve Rohr *Lexicon Public Relations*
1049 Havenhurst Dr # 365
West Hollywood, CA 90046-6002, USA

McKinnon, Ronald (Athlete, Football Player)
1063 Grand Oaks Dr
Bessemer, AL 35022-7237, USA

McKnight, Brian (Musician, Songwriter)
c/o Jack Ketsoyan *EMC / Bowery*
8356 Fountain Ave Apt E1
W Hollywood, CA 90069-2968, USA

McKnight, Ira (Athlete, Baseball Player)
8417 Laurel Valley Dr
Indianapolis, IN 46250-3906, USA

McKnight, James (Athlete, Football Player)
16705 Berkshire Ct
Southwest Ranches, FL 33331-1331, USA

McKnight, Jeff (Athlete, Baseball Player)
3296 Highway 92 W
Bee Branch, AR 72013-8937, USA

McKnight, Lauren (Actor)
c/o Mia Hansen *Portrait PR*
5320 Sylmar Ave
Sherman Oaks, CA 91401-5612, USA

McKnight, Scotty (Athlete, Football Player)
15 Manchester Ct
Coto De Caza, CA 92679-4724, USA

McKnight, Ted (Athlete, Football Player)
10236 Cedarbrooke Ln
Kansas City, MO 64131-4210, USA

McKnight, Tom (Athlete, Golfer)
78 Lexington Dr
Bluffton, SC 29910-4818, USA

McKnight, Tony (Athlete, Baseball Player)
406 Dundee Rd
Texarkana, AR 71854-9768, USA

McKoy, Bill (Athlete, Football Player)
4713 Legacy Cove Ln
Mableton, GA 30126-2580, USA

McKyer, Tim (Athlete, Football Player)
11201 Golden Dr
Charlotte, NC 28216-5624, USA

Mclachlan, Murray (Athlete, Hockey Player)
16 Oneida Ct
Chester Springs, PA 19425-2934

McLachlan, Sarah (Musician, Songwriter)
c/o Sam Feldman *Feldman Agency (Toronto)*
200-1505 2nd Ave W
Vancouver, BC V6H 3Y4, CANADA

McLain, Denny (Athlete, Baseball Player)
4432 Golf View Dr
Brighton, MI 48116-9187, USA

McLain, Kevin (Athlete, Football Player)
2551 State St Apt 222
Carlsbad, CA 92008-1624, USA

McLane, Drayton (Baseball Player, Commentator)
Houston Astros
100 N Apache Dr
Temple, TX 76504-2863, USA

McLane, James P (Jimmy) Jr (Swimmer)
85 Pinckney St
Boston, MA 02114-4303, USA

McLaren, John (Athlete, Baseball Player, Coach)
Seattle Mariners
7942 W Briden Ln
Peoria, AZ 85383-1016, USA

Mclaren, Kyle (Athlete, Hockey Player)
10744 Green Valley Dr
Gilroy, CA 95020-9333

McLaughlin, Bo (Athlete, Baseball Player)
536 N Grand
Mesa, AZ 85201-5031, USA

McLaughlin, Byron (Baseball Player)
Seattle Mariners
7030 Alamitos Ave
San Diego, CA 92154-4764, USA

McLaughlin, Caleb (Actor)
c/o Scott Braun *ID Public Relations (NY)*
40 Wall St Fl 51
New York, NY 10005-1385, USA

McLaughlin, Carol (Musician)
Columbia Artists Mgmt Inc
165 W 57th St
New York, NY 10019-2201, USA

Mclaughlin, Dan (Commentator)
12 Muirfield Ln
Saint Louis, MO 63141-7355, USA

McLaughlin, Jake (Actor)
c/o Miles Levy *Randy James Management*
12711 Ventura Blvd Ste 345
Studio City, CA 91604-2416, USA

McLaughlin, Joe (Athlete, Football Player)
65 Pells Fishing Rd
Brewster, MA 02631-2104, USA

McLaughlin, Joey (Athlete, Baseball Player)
1611 S Troost Ave
Tulsa, OK 74120-6615, USA

McLaughlin, John (Athlete, Football Player)
5415 Kansas St
Houston, TX 77007-1101, USA

McLaughlin, Madison (Actor)
c/o Matt Gogal *Abrams Artists Agency*
750 N San Vicente Blvd
E Tower Fl 11
Los Angeles, CA 90069-5788, USA

McLaughlin, Mike (Race Car Driver)
172 Lugnut Ln Ste B
Mooresville, NC 28117-9308, USA

McLean, AJ (Actor, Musician)
PO Box 618203
Orlando, FL 32861-8203, USA

McLean, Barney (Athlete, Skier)
9555 W 59th Ave Apt 303
Arvada, CO 80004-5396, USA

McLean, Don (Musician, Songwriter)
c/o Jim Lenz *Paradise Artists*
108 E Matilija St
Ojai, CA 93023-2639, USA

McLean, Greg (Director)
c/o Staff Member *WME|IMG*
9601 Wilshire Blvd
Beverly Hills, CA 90210-5213, USA

McLean, James (Athlete, Golfer)
c/o Jim Lehrman *Medalist Management Inc*
36855 W Main St Ste 200
Purcellville, VA 20132-3561, USA

Mclean, Jeff (Athlete, Hockey Player)
47 Iron Bottom Ln
Daniel Island, SC 29492-8415

McLean, Kirk (Athlete, Hockey Player)
Colorado Avalanche
1000 Chopper Cir
Denver, CO 80204-5805

McLean, Rene (Musician)
Brad Simon Organization
122 E 57th St # 300
New York, NY 10022-2623, USA

McLean, Ron (Athlete, Football Player)
761 Fairmont Ave
Santa Maria, CA 93455-3250, USA

McLean, Sally (Actor, Producer)
c/o Staff Member *Salmac Management*
PO Box 526
Mt Martha VIC 3934, AUSTRALIA

McLean, Scott (Athlete, Football Player)
375 Bear Ln
Lake Placid, FL 33852-4411, USA

McLeary, Marty (Athlete, Baseball Player)
2120 Long Meadow Dr
Spring Hill, TN 37174-7129, USA

McLeavy, Robin (Actor)
c/o Iris Grossman *Echo Lake Management*
421 S Beverly Dr Fl 8
Beverly Hills, CA 90212-4408, USA

Mclellan, Todd (Athlete, Hockey Player)
San Jose Sharks
525 W Santa Clara St
San Jose, CA 95113-1500

Mclellan, Zoe (Actor)
c/o Mandi Warren *Viewpoint Inc*
89 5th Ave Ste 402
New York, NY 10003-3020, USA

Mclelland, Dave (Athlete, Hockey Player)
714 Westminster Ave E
Penticton, BC V2A 1J3, Canada

McLemore, Dana (Athlete, Football Player)
125 Seagate Dr
San Mateo, CA 94403-4930, USA

McLemore, LaMonte (Musician)
Sterling/Winters
10877 Wilshire Blvd # 15
Los Angeles, CA 90024-4341, USA

McLemore, Mark (Athlete, Baseball Player)
533 S White Chapel Blvd
Southlake, TX 76092-7316, USA

McLemore, Mark (Athlete, Baseball Player)
7965 Eagle View Ln
Granite Bay, CA 95746-7333, USA

McLendon, Steve (Athlete, Football Player)

McLendon-Covey, Wendi (Actor)
c/o John Carrabino *John Carrabino Management*
5900 Wilshire Blvd Ste 740
Los Angeles, CA 90036-5032, USA

Mcleod, Al (Athlete, Hockey Player)
8021 N 14th Ave
Phoenix, AZ 85021-5631

McLeod, George (Athlete, Basketball Player)
834 Greenpark Dr
Houston, TX 77079-4502, USA

Mcleod, Jack (Athlete, Hockey Player)
13 John Hair Cres
Saskatoon, SK S7J 2K6, Canada

McLeod, Jimmy (Athlete, Hockey Player)
6404 SE 23rd Ave Apt 413
Portland, OR 97202-5458, USA

McLeod, Robert D (Athlete, Football Player)
2305 S Day St
Brenham, TX 77833-5516, USA

McLerran, Joshua (Actor)
c/o Staff Member *The Craze Agency*
9176 S 300 W Ste 3
Sandy, UT 84070-2564, USA

Mcllwain, Dave (Athlete, Hockey Player)
Yacht Club Woods
Grand Bend, ON NOM lTO, Canada

Mclnally, Pat (Athlete, Football Player)
19321 Ocean Heights Ln
Huntington Beach, CA 92648-7514, USA

McLouth, Nate (Athlete, Baseball Player)
2244 Wedgewood Dr
Asbury, IA 52002-9307, USA

Mclvor, Rick (Athlete, Football Player)
PO Box 148
Fort Davis, TX 79734-0148, USA

McMahan, Jack (Athlete, Baseball Player)
505 W Church St
Morrilton, AR 72110-3313, USA

McMahon, Art (Athlete, Football Player)
784 Providence Island Ct
Jacksonville, FL 32225-4946, USA

McMahon, Gerard (Actor, Musician)
c/o Tina Borek *Mitchell & Associates Talent*
18356 Oxnard St Ste 7
Tarzana, CA 91356-6712, USA

McMahon, James R (Jim) (Athlete, Football Player)
22431 N Violetta Dr
Scottsdale, AZ 85255-4428, USA

McMahon, Julian (Actor, Producer)
c/o Monique Moss *Integrated PR*
9025 Wilshire Blvd Ste 400
Beverly Hills, CA 90211-1828, USA

McMahon, Mike (Athlete, Football Player)
313 Oak Grove Ct
Wexford, PA 15090-9570

McMahon, Shane (Business Person, Wrestler)
c/o Staff Member *World Wrestling Entertainment (WWE)*
1241 E Main St
Stamford, CT 06902-3520, USA

McMahon, Stephanie (Wrestler)
c/o Kerry Rodgerson *World Wrestling Entertainment (WWE)*
1241 E Main St
Stamford, CT 06902-3520, USA

McMahon, Vince (Business Person)
c/o Staff Member *World Wrestling Entertainment (WWE)*
1241 E Main St
Stamford, CT 06902-3520, USA

McMakin, John (Athlete, Football Player)
PO Box 863
Anacortes, WA 98221-0863, USA

McManis, Sherrick (Athlete, Football Player)

McMann, Kennedy (Actor)
c/o Katie Britton *Buchwald*
5900 Wilshire Blvd Ste 3100
Los Angeles, CA 90036-5030, USA

McManus, Brandon (Athlete, Football Player)
c/o Drew Rosenhaus *Rosenhaus Sports Representation*
3921 Alton Rd # 440
Miami Beach, FL 33140-3852, USA

McManus, Don (Actor)
c/o Staff Member *Principal Entertainment*
9255 W Sunset Blvd Ste 500
Los Angeles, CA 90069-3301, USA

McManus, Doyle (Journalist)
LA Times
202 W 1st St Ste 500
Los Angeles, CA 90012-4401, USA

McManus, Jim (Athlete, Baseball Player)
2352 Hopkins Mill Rd
Duluth, GA 30096-4524, USA

McManus, Michaela (Actor)
1871 Talmadge St
Los Angeles, CA 90027-4540, USA

McManus, Michelle (Musician)

McManus, Rove (Actor, Talk Show Host)
c/o Kevin Whyte *Token*
1st Floor
274 Brunswick St
Fitzroy, Victoria 03065, AUSTRALIA

McMartin, John (Actor, Musician)
Artists Agency
1180 S Beverly Dr Ste 301
Los Angeles, CA 90035-1154, USA

McMath, Herb (Athlete, Football Player)
1515 E Glenn Ave
Springfield, IL 62703-3725, USA

McMath, Jimmy (Athlete, Baseball Player)
3321 22nd St
Tuscaloosa, AL 35401-5203, USA

McMenamin, Mark (Misc)
Mount Holyoke College
Geology Dept
South Hadley, MA 01075, USA

McMichael, Greg (Athlete, Baseball Player)
765 Crab Orchard Ct
Roswell, GA 30076-2373, USA

McMichael, Randy (Athlete, Football Player)
5503 Highland Preserve Dr
Mableton, GA 30126-7620, USA

McMichael, Steve (Athlete, Football Player)
644 Wild Indigo Ave
Romeoville, IL 60446-3973, USA

McMichen, Robert S (Misc)
International Typographical Union
PO Box 157
Colorado Springs, CO 80901-0157, USA

McMillan, Audray (Athlete, Football Player)
1230 Hahlo St
Houston, TX 77020-7340, USA

McMillan, Bob (Athlete, Hockey Player)
P.O Box 909
Sta. Central
Charlottetown, QC C1A BL9, CANADA

McMillan, Caroline (Athlete, Golfer)
5101 N Casa Blanca Dr Unit 206
Paradise Valley, AZ 85253-6987, USA

McMillan, Caroline (Athlete, Golfer)
7525 E Phantom Way
Scottsdale, AZ 85255-4622, USA

McMillan, Eddie (Athlete, Football Player)
6204 222nd St SW
Mountlake Terrace, WA 98043-2530, USA

McMillan, Erik (Athlete, Football Player)
17209 Chesterfield Airport Rd # 308
Chesterfield, MO 63005-1423, USA

McMillan, Ernie (Athlete, Football Player)
14816 Sycamore Manor Ct
Chesterfield, MO 63017-5535, USA

McMillan, Nate (Athlete, Basketball Player, Coach)
c/o Lonnie Cooper *Career Sports and Entertainment*
600 Galleria Pkwy SE Ste 1900
Atlanta, GA 30339-5990, USA

McMillan, Randy (Athlete, Football Player)
6832 Hayley Ridge Way Unit D
Baltimore, MD 21209-5206, USA

McMillan, Terry (Writer)
PO Box 2408
Danville, CA 94526-7408, USA

McMillan, Todd (Athlete, Football Player)
6113 W Spur Dr
Phoenix, AZ 85083-6531, USA

McMillan, Tommy (Athlete, Baseball Player)
712 Spring Lake Rd
Thomasville, GA 31792-8605, USA

McMillan, William (Bill) (Misc)
1930 Sandstone Vista Ln
Encinitas, CA 92024-4247, USA

McMillen, Robert (Athlete, Olympic Athlete, Track Athlete)
5708 Golden West Ave
Temple City, CA 91780-2503, USA

McMillen, Tom (Athlete, Basketball Player, Olympic Athlete)
1103 S Carolina Ave SE
Washington, DC 20003-2205, USA

McMillian, Audray G (Athlete, Football Player)
1230 Hahlo St
Houston, TX 77020-7340, USA

McMillian, Mark (Athlete, Football Player)
13820 S 44th St
Phoenix, AZ 85044-4849, USA

McMillian, Michael (Actor)
c/o Abby Bluestone *Innovative Artists*
1505 10th St
Santa Monica, CA 90401-2805, USA

McMillin, James R (Athlete, Football Player)
7985 Westview Dr
Lakewood, CO 80214-4541, USA

McMillon, Billy (Athlete, Baseball Player)
1516 Lost Creek Dr
Columbia, SC 29212-2859, USA

McMonagle, Donald R (Astronaut)
7737 E Shadow Vista Ct
Tucson, AZ 85750-0742, USA

McMonagle, Donald R Colonel (Astronaut)
7737 E Shadow Vista Ct
Tucson, AZ 85750-0742, USA

McMorris, Cathy (Congressman, Politician)
2421 Rayburn Hob
Washington, DC 20515-2902, USA

McMullen, Kathy (Athlete, Golfer)
526 Harrison St
Emmaus, PA 18049-2314, USA

McMullen, Ken (Athlete, Baseball Player)
10 Estaban Dr
Camarillo, CA 93010-1610, USA

McMullen, Kirk (Athlete, Football Player)
4108 County Line Rd
Macedon, NY 14502-9386, USA

McMurchy, Tom (Athlete, Hockey Player)
2060 Cape Horn Ave
Coquitlam, BC V3K 1J3, Canada

McMurray, Jamie (Race Car Driver)
Chip Ganassi Racing
7777 Woodland Dr
Indianapolis, IN 46278-1794, USA

McMurray, W Grant (Religious Leader)
Reorganized Church of Latter Day Saints
PO Box 1059
Independence, MO 64051-0559, USA

McMurtry, Craig (Athlete, Baseball Player)
2835 Bottoms East Rd
Troy, TX 76579-3013, USA

McMurtry, Greg (Athlete, Football Player)
755 Oak Point Ln
Madison Heights, MI 48071-1940, USA

McMurtry, James (Musician, Songwriter, Writer)
High Road
751 Bridgeway Fl 2
Sausalito, CA 94965-2174, USA

McMurtry, Larry (Writer)
PO Box 552
Archer City, TX 76351-0552, USA

McNab, Mercedes (Actor)
c/o Jason Egenberg *Authentic Talent & Literary Management*
3615 Eastham Dr # 650
Culver City, CA 90232-2410, USA

McNab, Peter (Athlete, Hockey Player)
Colorado Avalanche
1000 Chopper Cir
Denver, CO 80204-5805

McNab, Peter (Athlete, Hockey Player)
10311 Rancho Montecito Dr
Parker, CO 80138-7862

McNabb, Dexter (Athlete, Football Player)
300 Paddy Ct
Wrightstown, WI 54180-1087, USA

McNabb, Donovan (Athlete, Football Player)
c/o Mark Lepselter *Maxx Sports & Entertainment*
546 5th Ave Fl 6
New York, NY 10036-5000, USA

McNair, Kelly (Actor)
c/o Staff Member *GVA Talent Agency Inc*
193 N Robertson Blvd
Beverly Hills, CA 90211-2103, USA

McNairy, Mark (Designer)
c/o Jason Hodes *WME|IMG (NY)*
11 Madison Ave Fl 18
New York, NY 10010-3669, USA

McNairy, Scoot (Actor)
c/o Mia Hansen *Portrait PR*
5320 Sylmar Ave
Sherman Oaks, CA 91401-5612, USA

McNally, Kevin (Actor)
c/o Mark A. Schlegel *Cornerstone Talent Agency*
37 W 20th St Ste 1007
New York, NY 10011-3714, USA

McNally, Stephen (Ste) (Musician)
Day Time
Crown House
225 Kensington High St
London W8 8SA, UNITED KINGDOM (UK)

McNally, Terrence (Writer)
c/o Jonathan Lomma *WME|IMG*
9601 Wilshire Blvd
Beverly Hills, CA 90210-5213, USA

McNamara, Bob (Athlete, Football Player)
4909 Prescott Cir
Minneapolis, MN 55436-1011, USA

McNamara, Brian (Actor)
c/o Staff Member *Pathway Entertainment*
1739 Berkeley St # 110C
Santa Monica, CA 90404-4119, USA

McNamara, Eileen (Journalist)
Boston Globe
1 Exchange Pl Ste 201
Editorial Dept
Boston, MA 02109-2132, USA

McNamara, Jim (Baseball Player)
San Francisco Giants
15317 Surrey House Way
Centreville, VA 20120-1196, USA

McNamara, John (Athlete, Baseball Player, Coach)
1206 Beech Hill Rd
Brentwood, TN 37027-5530, USA

McNamara, John F (Athlete, Baseball Player)
15317 Surrey House Way
Centreville, VA 20120-1196, USA

McNamara, Julianne L (Actor, Gymnast)
Barry Axelrod
2236 Encinitas Blvd Ste A
Encinitas, CA 92024-4353, USA

McNamara, Julie (Business Person)
c/o Staff Member *CBS Paramount Network Television*
4024 Radford Ave
Cbs Studios
Studio City, CA 91604-2190, USA

McNamara, Katherine (Actor)
c/o Laura Ackerman *Advantage PR*
3900 W Alameda Ave Ste 1200
Burbank, CA 91505-4317, USA

McNamara, Melissa (Athlete, Golfer)
7715 S Quebec Ave
Tulsa, OK 74136-8104, USA

McNamara, William (Actor)
c/o Staff Member *TWB Productions*
1863 10th St Apt N
Santa Monica, CA 90404-4590, USA

McNamee, Peter (Athlete, Hockey Player)
47 Rolling Acres Dr
Whitby, ON L1R 2A1, Canada

McNanie, Sean (Athlete, Football Player)
14915 Rancho Real
Del Mar, CA 92014-4213, USA

McNaught, Erin (Beauty Pageant Winner)
c/o Ursula Hufnagl *Chic Management*
36 Jersey Road
Woollahra NSW 02025, AUSTRALIA

McNaught, Judith (Writer)
Pocket Books
1230 Avenue of the Americas Fl CONC1
New York, NY 10020-1586, USA

McNaughton, John D (Director)
1370 N Milwaukee Ave
Chicago, IL 60622-9107, USA

McNeal, Donald (Don) (Athlete, Football Player)
3311 Toledo Plz
Coral Gables, FL 33134-6483, USA

McNeal, Travis (Athlete, Football Player)
4707 40th Pl N
Birmingham, AL 35217, USA

McNealey, Christopher (Athlete, Basketball Player)

McNealy, Rusty (Athlete, Baseball Player)
3301 Bozeman St
Sacramento, CA 95838-4105, USA

McNeely, Jeff (Athlete, Baseball Player)
405 Everette St
Monroe, NC 28112-5622, USA

McNeely, Tom (Artist)
9 Blythwood Gdns
Toronto, ON M4N 3L2, Canada

McNeice, Ian (Actor)
c/o Renee Jennett *Renee Jennett Management*
5757 Wilshire Blvd Ste 473
Los Angeles, CA 90036-3632, USA

McNeil, Clifton (Athlete, Football Player)
1001 Westbury Dr
Mobile, AL 36609-3336, USA

McNeil, Emanuel (Athlete, Football Player)
2 University Ct Apt G17
Martin, TN 38237-4025, USA

McNeil, Frederick A (Fred) (Athlete, Football Player)
9667 W Olympic Blvd Apt 5
Beverly Hills, CA 90212-3745, USA

McNeil, Freeman (Athlete, Football Player)
52 Dunlop Rd
Huntington, NY 11743-3934, USA

McNeil, Gerald (Athlete, Football Player)
215 Haven Brook Ln
Richmond, TX 77406-3494, USA

McNeil, Kate (Actor)
1743 N Dillon St
Los Angeles, CA 90026-1113, USA

McNeil, Lori (Tennis Player)
Int'l Mgmt Group
1 Erieview Plz
1360 E 9th St #1300
Cleveland, OH 44114-1738, USA

McNeil, Mike (Athlete, Hockey Player)
1723 Bader Ave
South Bend, IN 46617-2521, USA

McNeil, Pat (Athlete, Football Player)
901 Marlin Dr
Mesquite, TX 75149-4961, USA

McNeil, Ryan (Athlete, Football Player)
4702 Avenue Q
Fort Pierce, FL 34947-7049, USA

McNeill, Bill (Athlete, Hockey Player)
8-1711 -l40th St.
Surrey, BC B4A 4H1, CANADA

McNeill, Mike (Athlete, Hockey Player)
52425 Spring Wood Ct
Granger, IN 46530-7438

McNeill, Robert (Athlete, Basketball Player)
1318 Wooded Way
Wayne, PA 19ele-1781, USA

McNeill, Rod (Athlete, Football Player)
1048 S Magnolia Ave
West Covina, CA 91791-3730, USA

McNeill, Stu (Athlete, Hockey Player)
1840 StDenis Pl
West Vancouver, BC V7V 3W7, Canada

McNeill, Tom (Athlete, Football Player)
31019 Torrey Rd
Waller, TX 77484-9354, USA

McNeill, W Donald (Don) (Tennis Player)
2165 15th Ave
Vero Beach, FL 32960-3435, USA

McNell, Rufus (Baseball Player)
Indianapolis Clowns
205 Heard St
Kinston, NC 28501-5850, USA

McNerney, Jerry (Congressman, Politician)
1210 Longworth Hob
Washington, DC 20515-1311, USA

McNertney, Jerry (Athlete, Baseball Player)
2404 NE 12th Ct
Ankeny, IA 50021-7443, USA

McNichol, Brian (Athlete, Baseball Player)
4343 N 21st St Apt 244
Phoenix, AZ 85016-0508, USA

McNichol, Kristy (Actor)
c/o Staff Member *Good Guy Entertainment*
555 Esplanade Apt 316
Redondo Beach, CA 90277-4085, USA

McNichols, Stephen (Politician)
6481 S Kearney Cir
Centennial, CO 80111-4315, USA

McNitt, Eliza (Director)
c/o Maha Dakhil *Creative Artists Agency (CAA)*
2000 Avenue of the Stars Ste 100
Los Angeles, CA 90067-4705, USA

McNorton, Bruce (Athlete, Football Player)
PO Box 672
Bloomfield Hills, MI 48303-0672, USA

McNown, Cade (Athlete, Football Player)
200 Lorraine Blvd
Los Angeles, CA 90004-3812, USA

McNulty, Bill (Athlete, Baseball Player)
32716 74th Avenue Ct E
Eatonville, WA 98328-8967, USA

McNulty, Carl (Athlete, Basketball Player)
212 Westmoreland Dr E
Kokomo, IN 46901-5155, USA

McNutt, Marvin (Athlete, Football Player)
c/o Adisa P Bakari *Kelley Drye & Warren LLP*
3050 K St NW Ste 400
Washington, DC 20007-5100, USA

McPartlin, Anthony (Television Host)
c/o Staff Member *Rabbit Vocal Management*
27 Poland St
Fl 3
London W1F 8QW, UNITED KINGDOM

McPartlin, Ryan (Actor)
c/o Miles Levy *Randy James Management*
12711 Ventura Blvd Ste 345
Studio City, CA 91604-2416, USA

McPartlnad, Marian M (Musician)
Abby Hoffer
223 1/2 E 48th St
New York, NY 10017, USA

McPeak, Holly (Athlete, Volleyball Player)
1400 the Strand
Manhattan Beach, CA 90266-4731, USA

McPhail, Coleman (Athlete, Football Player)
104 Flagstone Ct
Chapel Hill, NC 27517-8381, USA

McPhail, Jerris (Athlete, Football Player)
1820 Lake Glen Dr
Fuquay Varina, NC 27526-6951, USA

McPhee, George (Athlete, Hockey Player)
Washington Capitals
627 N Glebe Rd Ste 850
Arlington, VA 22203-2129

McPhee, George (Athlete, Hockey Player)
6723 Landon Ln
Bethesda, MD 20817-5639

McPhee, John (Writer)
475 Drakes Corner Rd
Princeton, NJ 08540-7516, USA

McPhee, Katharine (Musician)
c/o Carleen Donovan *Donovan Public Relations*
30 E 20th St Ste 2FE
New York, NY 10003-1310, USA

McPhee, Mike (Athlete, Hockey Player)
16 Brook Point Rd
Tantallon, NS B3Z 2R3, Canada

McPhee, Pernell (Athlete, Football Player)
c/o Bus Cook *Bus Cook Sports, Inc*
1 Willow Bend Dr
Hattiesburg, MS 39402-8552, USA

McPherson, Charles (Misc)
Joel Chriss
300 Mercer St Apt 3J
New York, NY 10003-6732, USA

McPherson, Dallas (Athlete, Baseball Player)
133 Shellbark Dr
McDonough, GA 30252-1622, USA

McPherson, Don (Athlete, Football Player)
1619 Station Way
Huntington Station, NY 11746-1978, USA

McPherson, John (Cartoonist)
Universal Press Syndicate
4520 Main St Ste 340
Kansas City, MO 64111-7705, USA

McPherson, Kristy (Athlete, Golfer)
c/o Staff Member *Gaylord Sports Management*
13845 N Northsight Blvd Ste 200
Scottsdale, AZ 85260-3609, USA

McPherson, Miles (Athlete, Football Player)
12088 Avenida Sivrita
San Diego, CA 92128-4546, USA

McQuagg, Sam (Race Car Driver)
8886 Hamilton Road
Midland, GA 31820, USA

McQuarrie, Christopher (Director, Producer)
Invisible Ink
9696 Culver Blvd Ste 203
Culver City, CA 90232-2754, USA

McQuarters, R W (Athlete, Football Player)
1548 E 54th St N
Tulsa, OK 74126-2811, USA

McQueen, Chad (Actor, Producer)
15260 Ventura Blvd Ste 1750
Sherman Oaks, CA 91403-5336, USA

McQueen, Cozell (Athlete, Basketball Player)
100 E Charing Cross
Cary, NC 27513-3024, USA

McQueen, Mike (Athlete, Baseball Player)
15018 Marlebone Ct
Houston, TX 77069-2022, USA

Mcqueen, Sam (Race Car Driver)
8866 Hamilton Rd
Midland, GA 31820, USA

McQueen, Steve (Director, Producer)
c/o Jodi Shields *Casarotto Ramsay & Associates Ltd (UK)*
Waverley House
7-12 Noel St
London W1F 8GQ, UNITED KINGDOM

McQueen, Steven R (Actor)
c/o Nicole Perna *Imprint PR*
6121 W Sunset Blvd
Neuehouse
Los Angeles, CA 90028-6442, USA

McQuilken, Kim (Athlete, Football Player)
801 Moore Rd
Newnan, GA 30263-5220, USA

McRae, Basil (Athlete, Hockey Player)
Basil McRae and Associates
759 Hyde Park Rd Suite 252
London, ON N6H 3S2, Canada

McRae, Bennie (Athlete, Football Player)
532 W 143rd St Apt 63
New York, NY 10031-6518, USA

McRae, Brian (Athlete, Baseball Player)
6721 W 121st St
Leawood, KS 66209-2003, USA

McRae, Charles (Athlete, Football Player)
601 Self Hollow Rd
Rockford, TN 37853-3411, USA

McRae, Frank (Actor)
Marshak/Zachary Company
5225 Wilshire Blvd Ste 501
Los Angeles, CA 90036-4349, USA

McRae, Gord (Athlete, Hockey Player)
8168 S Wabash Ct
Centennial, CO 80112-3329

McRae, Hal (Athlete, Baseball Player, Coach)
519 Sand Crane Ct
Bradenton, FL 34212-6203, USA

McRae, Jerrold (Athlete, Football Player)
208 Grovedale Trce
Antioch, TN 37013-1969, USA

McRae, Mo (Actor)
c/o Jordyn Palos *Persona Public Relations*
6255 W Sunset Blvd Ste 705
Hollywood, CA 90028-7408, USA

McRae, Shane (Actor)
c/o Jennifer Sims *Imprint PR*
375 Hudson St
New York, NY 10014-3658, USA

McRae, Tom (Musician)
c/o Staff Member *Paradigm (Monterey)*
404 W Franklin St
Monterey, CA 93940-2303, USA

McRaney, Gerald (Actor)
c/o Geoffrey Brandt *Course Management*
142 Porto Vecchio Way
Palm Beach Gardens, FL 33418-6223, USA

McReynolds, Jesse (Musician)
J&J Music
PO Box 1385
Gallatin, TN 37066-1385, USA

McReynolds, Kevin (Athlete, Baseball Player)
2 Country Pl
Roland, AR 72135-9763, USA

McReynolds, Larry (Race Car Driver)
123 Mystic Lake Loop
Mooresville, NC 28117-6000, USA

McReynolds, Madison (Actor)
c/o Bonnie Ventis *Clear Talent Group (LA)*
10950 Ventura Blvd
Studio City, CA 91604-3340, USA

McRoy, Spike (Athlete, Golfer)
15019 Collier Dr SE
Huntsville, AL 35803-3631, USA

McShane, Ian (Actor)
c/o Staff Member *McShane Productions*
New Bridge Street House
30 New Bridge St
London EC4V 6BJ, UNITED KINGDOM (UK)

McShane, Jamie (Actor)
c/o Staff Member *Select Artists Ltd (CA-Westside Office)*
1138 12th St Apt 1
Santa Monica, CA 90403-5459, USA

McShane, Jennifer (Jenny) (Actor)
c/o Laura Pallas *Pallas Management*
4536 Greenbush Ave
Sherman Oaks, CA 91423-3112, US

McShane, Michael (Actor)
c/o Maureen Vincent *United Agents*
12-26 Lexington St
London W1F OLE, UNITED KINGDOM

McShann, James C (Jay) (Musician)
Ozark Talent
718 Schwarz Rd
Lawrence, KS 66049-4506, USA

McSheffrey, Bryan (Athlete, Hockey Player)
PO Box 866 Stn Main
Renfrew, ON K7V 4H3, Canada

McShera, Sophie (Actor)
c/o Grant Parsons *Curtis Brown Ltd*
28-29 Hay Market
Hay Market House
London SW1Y 4SP, UNITED KINGDOM

McSorley, Gerard (Actor)
c/o Staff Member *Insight*
5358 Melrose Ave # 200W
Los Angeles, CA 90038-5117, USA

McSorley, Marty (Athlete, Hockey Player)
3301 the Strand
Hermosa Beach, CA 90254-2053

McSwain, Chuck (Athlete, Football Player)
PO Box 603
Caroleen, NC 28019-0603, USA

McSwain, Rod (Athlete, Football Player)
5393 Stonewood Dr
Hickory, NC 28602-5578, USA

McSween, Don (Athlete, Hockey Player)
4954 Glen Meadow Ct SE
Grand Rapids, MI 49546-7927

McSween, John (Athlete, Hockey Player)
4954 Glen Meadows Ct. St.
Grand Rapids, MI 49546, USA

McTaggart, Jim (Athlete, Hockey Player)
Seattle Thunderbirds
625 W James St
Kent, WA 98032-4406

McTavish, Gord (Athlete, Hockey Player)
McTavish Design
13 Nanaimo Dr
Ottawa, ON K2H 6X6, Canada

McTeer, Janet (Actor)
c/o Catherine Olim *PMK/BNC Public Relations*
1840 Century Park E Ste 1400
Los Angeles, CA 90067-2115, USA

McTeigue, James (Director)
c/o Lawrence Mattis *Circle of Confusion (NY)*
270 Lafayette St Ste 402
New York, NY 10012-3327, USA

McTiernan, John C (Director)
The Firm
9100 Wilshire Blvd Ste 100W
Beverly Hills, CA 90212-3435, USA

McVay, John (Athlete, Football Coach, Football Player)
7300 Sierra Dr
Granite Bay, CA 95746-6957, USA

McVeigh, John (Athlete, Football Player)
1404 W Beach Dr
Panama City, FL 32401-1927, USA

McVey, Robert (Athlete, Hockey Player, Olympic Athlete)
3333 NE 34th St Apt 1522
Fort Lauderdale, FL 33308-6914, USA

McVicar, Daniel (Actor)
1704 Oak St
Santa Monica, CA 90405-4804, USA

McVie, Christine (Actor, Musician)
c/o Staff Member *Sugaroo! LLC*
3650 Helms Ave
Culver City, CA 90232-2417, USA

McVie, John (Musician, Songwriter)
c/o Carl Stubner *Sanctuary Music Management*
15301 Arizona Ave
Bldg B #400
Santa Monica, CA 91403, USA

McVie, Tom (Athlete, Hockey Player)
3013 SE Spyglass Dr
Vancouver, WA 98683-3704

McWashington, Shawn (Athlete, Football Player)
3400 S King St
Seattle, WA 98144-2653, USA

McWatters, Bill (Athlete, Football Player)
3300 Thornway Dr
Columbus, OH 43231-6199, USA

McWilliam, Edward (Artist)
8A Holland Villas Road
London W14 8DP, UNITED KINGDOM (UK)

McWilliams, David (Football Executive, Football Player)
University of Texas
Athletic Dept
Austin, TX 78712, USA

McWilliams, Eric (Athlete, Basketball Player)
8632 Todd Allen Creek St
Las Vegas, NV 89178-2446, USA

McWilliams, John (Athlete, Football Player)
4540 E Blue Spruce Ln
Gilbert, AZ 85298-4637, USA

McWilliams, Larry (Athlete, Baseball Player)
4102 Beckley Ct
Colleyville, TX 76034-4670, USA

MDO (Music Group)
c/o Staff Member *Sony Music (Miami)*
404 Washington Ave Ste 700
Miami Beach, FL 33139-6615, USA

Meacham, Bobby (Athlete, Baseball Player)
20610 Prince Creek Dr
Katy, TX 77450-4908, USA

Meacham, Mildred (Athlete, Baseball Player, Commentator)
4027 Winedale Ln
Charlotte, NC 28205-4524, USA

Meacham, Rusty (Athlete, Baseball Player)
1906 Eden Glen Ln
Pearland, TX 77581-1700, USA

Meachem, Robert (Athlete, Football Player)

Mead, Amber (Actor)
c/o Courtney Kivowitz *MGMT Entertainment (The Schiff Company)*
9220 W Sunset Blvd Ste 106
W Hollywood, CA 90069-3500, USA

Mead, Charlie (Athlete, Baseball Player)
7482 Svl Box
Victorville, CA 92395-5157, USA

Mead, John (Athlete, Football Player)
401 Westwood Dr
Apt 2
Sister Bay, WI 54234, USA

Mead, Lee (Actor)
c/o Will Hollinshead *Independent Talent Group*
40 Whitfield St
London W1T 2RH, UNITED KINGDOM

Mead, Richelle (Writer)
c/o Staff Member *Kensington Publishing Corp.*
119 W 40th St Fl 21
New York, NY 10018-2522, USA

Mead, Shepherd (Writer)
53 Rivermead Court
London SW6 3RY, UNITED KINGDOM (UK)

Meade, Carl J (Astronaut)
5711 Bienveneda Ter
Palmdale, CA 93551-1189, USA

Meade, Carl J Colonel (Astronaut)
15013 Live Oak Springs Canyon Rd
Canyon Country, CA 91387-4804, USA

Meade, Emily (Actor)
c/o Carrie Gordon *The Lede Company*
401 Broadway Ste 206
New York, NY 10013-3033, USA

Meade, Glenn (Writer)
Saint Martin's Press
175 5th Ave Ste 400
New York, NY 10010-7848, USA

Meade, Robin (Television Host)
CNN Headline News
100 International Blvd NW
Atlanta, GA 30303, USA

Meaden, Deborah (Business Person, Talk Show Host)
c/o Staff Member *BBC Television Centre*
Incoming Mail
Wood Lane
London W12 7RJ, UNITED KINGDOM

Meaden, Levi (Actor)
c/o Carrie Wheeler *Carrie Wheeler Management*
101-1001 Broadway W
Suite 338
Vancouver, BC V6H 4E4, CANADA

Meador, Ed (Athlete, Football Player)
1135 Padgetts Hill Rd
Natural Bridge, VA 24578-4147, USA

Meadows, Bernard W (Artist)
34 Belsize Grove
London NW3, UNITED KINGDOM (UK)

Meadows, Brian (Athlete, Baseball Player)
218 Palos Verdes Dr
Troy, AL 36079-1701, USA

Meadows, Louie (Athlete, Baseball Player)
110 Heavens Ln
Maysville, NC 28555-9479, USA

Meadows, Stephen (Actor)
1760 Courtney Ave
Los Angeles, CA 90046-2103, USA

Meadows, Tim (Actor, Comedian)
c/o Geoff Cheddy *Brillstein Entertainment Partners*
9150 Wilshire Blvd Ste 350
Beverly Hills, CA 90212-3453, USA

Meads, Dave (Athlete, Baseball Player)
3220 Cypress Way
Santa Rosa, CA 95405-7512, USA

Meads, Johnny (Athlete, Football Player)
9419 Pine Lilly Ct
Navarre, FL 32566-2865, USA

Meagher, Mary T (Athlete, Olympic Athlete, Swimmer)
404 Vanderwall
Peachtree City, GA 30269-3335, USA

Meagher, Rick (Athlete, Hockey Player)
2698 Innisfil Rd
Mississauga, ON L5M 4J2, Canada

Mealey, Rondell (Athlete, Football Player)
2952 N Nobile St
Paulina, LA 70763-2523, USA

Meals, Gerald (Baseball Player)
2164 Shamrock Arbor Dr
Salem, OH 44460-7639, USA

Meals, Gerry (Athlete, Baseball Player)
2164 Shamrock Arbor Dr
Salem, OH 44460-7639, USA

Meamber, Tim (Athlete, Football Player)
3410 Grant St
Vancouver, WA 98660-1823, USA

Meaney, Colm (Actor)
11921 Laurel Hills Rd
Studio City, CA 91604-3726, USA

Means, Jimmy (Race Car Driver)
Jimmy Means Racing
102 Greenbriar Dr
Forest City, NC 28042, USA

Means, Marianne (Journalist)
2555 Pennsylvania Ave NW Apt 902
Washington, DC 20037-1637, USA

Means, Natrone J (Athlete, Football Player)
14602 Greenpoint Ln
Huntersville, NC 28078-2624, USA

Means, Winslow (Athlete, Basketball Player)
1336 Arch St
Zanesville, OH 43701-5714, USA

Meany, Charlie (Actor)

Meares, Pat (Athlete, Baseball Player)
8405 E Bridlewood St
Wichita, KS 67206-4408, USA

Mears, Casey (Race Car Driver)
c/o Staff Member *Valvoline*
PO Box 14000
Lexington, KY 40512-4000, USA

Mears, Clint (Race Car Driver)
Team Mears
416 Fairview Rd
Bakersfield, CA 93307-5516, USA

Mears, Derek (Actor)
c/o Steve Smith *Stagecoach Entertainment*
1990 S Bundy Dr Ste 645
Los Angeles, CA 90025-6365, USA

Mears, Gary (Musician)
12170 Country Road 215
Tyler, TX 75707, USA

Mears, Rick (Race Car Driver)
204 Spyglass Ln
Jupiter, FL 33477-4091, USA

Mears, Roger (Race Car Driver)
PO Box 520
Terrell, NC 28682-0520, USA

Mears, Walter R (Journalist)
Associated Press
2021 K St NW
Editorial Dept
Washington, DC 20006-1003, USA

Meat Loaf (Actor, Musician, Producer)
c/o Staff Member *TC Management*
10960 Wilshire Blvd Ste 1415
Los Angeles, CA 90024-3729, USA

Mebane, Brandon (Athlete, Football Player)
2310 SE 2nd Ct
Renton, WA 98056-8871, USA

Mecchi, Irene (Actor)
c/o Staff Member *WME|IMG*
9601 Wilshire Blvd
Beverly Hills, CA 90210-5213, USA

Mechalides, Louie (Race Car Driver)
8 Davis St
Tyngsboro, MA 01879-1606, USA

Meche, Gil (Athlete, Baseball Player)
112 Winged Foot Dr
Broussard, LA 70518-6158, USA

Mechlowicz, Scott (Actor)
c/o Eric Kranzler *Management 360*
9111 Wilshire Blvd
Beverly Hills, CA 90210-5508, USA

Mecir, Jim (Athlete, Baseball Player)
5517 Oak Grove Cir
Long Grove, IL 60047-5208, USA

Mecir, Miloslav (Tennis Player)
Julova 1
Bratislava 83101, CZECH REPUBLIC

Mecklenburg, Karl (Football Player)
7980 S Blackstone Pkwy
Aurora, CO 80016-7279, USA

Mecko, Joe (Athlete, Baseball Player)
2219 Templeton Dr
Arlington, TX 76006-5769, USA

Medak, Peter (Director)
1355 N Laurel Ave Apt 9
West Hollywood, CA 90046-4629, USA

Medavoy, Mike (Producer)
c/o Staff Member *Phoenix Pictures*
10203 Santa Monica Blvd Ste 400
Los Angeles, CA 90067-6405, USA

Medcalf, Kim (Actor)
London Mgmt
2-4 Noel St
London W1V 3RB, UNITED KINGDOM (UK)

Medders, Brandon (Athlete, Baseball Player)
500 Camille Ln
Tuscaloosa, AL 35405, USA

Meddick, Jim (Cartoonist)
United Feature Syndicate
200 Madison Ave
New York, NY 10016-3903, USA

Medearis, Angela Shelf (Chef, Writer)
c/o Staff Member *Diva Productions, Inc*
PO Box 91625
Austin, TX 78709-1625, USA

Medeiros, Glenn (Musician)
PO Box 8
Lawai, HI 96765-0008, USA

Mediate, Rocco (Athlete, Golfer)
c/o Staff Member *Lagardere Unlimited (AZ)*
13845 N Northsight Blvd Ste 200
Scottsdale, AZ 85260-3609, USA

Medich, George Doc (Athlete, Baseball Player)
3007 Woodfield Dr
Aliquippa, PA 15001-1163, USA

Medina, Luis (Athlete, Baseball Player)
16630 S Mountain Stone Trl
Phoenix, AZ 85048-2081, USA

Medina, Rafael (Athlete, Baseball Player)
Florida Marlins
2964 Peachtree Road Apt 330
Kissimmee, FL 33015-3423, USA

Medina Estevez, Jorge Arturo Cardinal (Religious Leader)
Congregation for Divine Worship
Vatican City 00120, VATICAN CITY

Medlen, Kris (Athlete, Baseball Player)
6633 Sutherland St
Abilene, TX 79606-1635, USA

Medley, Bill (Musician)
c/o Barry Rillera
9840 Hot Springs Dr
Huntington Beach, CA 92646, USA

Medley, Charles R O (Artist)
Charterhouse
Charterhouse Square
London EC1M 6AN, UNITED KINGDOM (UK)

Medlin, Dan (Athlete, Football Player)
712 Guilford Rd
Jamestown, NC 27282-9764, USA

Medlock, Mark (Musician)
Postfach 206143
Berlin 13537, GERMANY

Medlocke, Rickey (Musician)
15138 Portside Dr
Fort Myers, FL 33908-1893, USA

Medrano, Frank (Actor)
c/o Kate Ward *Ward Agency*
1617 N El Centro Ave Ste 15
Hollywood, CA 90028-6429, USA

Medress, Henry (Musician)
Brothers Mgmt
141 Dunbar Ave
Fords, NJ 08863-1551, USA

Medved, Aleksandr V (Wrestler)
Central Soviet Sports Federation
Skatertny p 4
Moscow, RUSSIA

Medved, David (Journalist)
8501 SE 82nd St
Mercer Island, WA 98040-5642, USA

Medved, Michael (Radio Personality, Writer)
c/o Staff Member *Greater Talent Network Inc*
437 5th Ave Ste 8A
New York, NY 10016-2205, USA

Medved, Ron (Athlete, Football Player)
6615 239th Ave E
Buckley, WA 98321-9422, USA

Medvedenko, Stanislav (Athlete, Basketball Player)
5721 S Crescent Park Apt 404
Playa Vista, CA 90094-4002, USA

Medvin, Scott (Athlete, Baseball Player)
673 Lynbrook Ave
Tonawanda, NY 14150-7309, USA

Medwin, Michael (Actor)
International Creative Mgmt
76 Oxford St
London W1N 0AX, UNITED KINGDOM (UK)

Mee, Darnell (Athlete, Basketball Player)
1742 Cave Mill Rd Apt B
Bowling Green, KY 42104-6370, USA

Meehan, Gerry (Athlete, Hockey Player)
2 Dafoe Crt
Aurora, ON L4G 7C8, Canada

Meehan, Greg (Athlete, Football Player)
1511 Verde Ridge Ln
Westlake Village, CA 91361-1546, USA

Meehan, Patrick (Congressman, Politician)
613 Cannon Hob
Washington, DC 20515-0003, USA

Meehl, Paul E (Misc)
1544 E River Ter
Minneapolis, MN 55414-3646, USA

Meek, Carrie (Politician)
6830 NW 28th Ave
Miami, FL 33147-6766, USA

Meek, Jeffrey (Actor)
c/o Joan Sittenfield *Joan Sittenfield Management*
1064 S Ogden Dr
Los Angeles, CA 90019-6501, USA

Meeke, Brent (Athlete, Hockey Player)
22456 E Sonoqui Blvd
Queen Creek, AZ 85142-5683

Meeker, Howie (Athlete, Hockey Player, Sportscaster)
979 Dickinson Way
Parksville, BC V9P 1Z7, Canada

Meeks, Aaron (Actor)
c/o Staff Member *Showtime Networks*
1041 N Formosa Ave # 300
West Hollywood, CA 90046-6703, USA

Meeks, Bob (Athlete, Football Player)
PO Box 5763
Denver, CO 80217-5763, USA

Meeks, Jeremy (Internet Star, Model)
c/o Jim Jordan *White Cross Productions*
26500 Agoura Rd Ste 525
Calabasas, CA 91302-1952, USA

Meeler, Phil (Athlete, Baseball Player)
102 Pine St
Knightdale, NC 27545-9443, USA

Meely, Cliff (Athlete, Basketball Player)
3240 Iris Ave Apt 204
Boulder, CO 80301-1969, USA

Meents, Scott (Athlete, Basketball Player)
4231 155th Pl SE
Bellevue, WA 98006-2579, USA

Meese (Music Group)
c/o Staff Member *Red Light Management*
5800 Bristol Pkwy Ste 400
Culver City, CA 90230-6898, USA

Meese, Edwin (Politician)
1075 Spring Hill Rd
Mc Lean, VA 22102-2304, USA

Meester, Brad (Athlete, Football Player)
61 Highway 1 S
Mount Vernon, IA 52314-9525, USA

Meester, Leighton (Actor)
c/o Kate Rosen *The Lede Company*
401 Broadway Ste 206
New York, NY 10013-3033, USA

Meeuwsen, Terry (Religious Leader, Television Host)
c/o 700 Club *Christian Broadcasting Network (CBN)*
977 Centerville Tpke
Virginia Beach, VA 23463-1001, USA

Me First And The Gimme Gimmes (Music Group)
c/o Staff Member *Fat Wreck Chords*
PO Box 193690
San Francisco, CA 94119-3690, USA

Megadeth (Music Group)
ESP Management
6310 San Vicente Blvd Ste 401
Los Angeles, CA 90048-5427, USA

Meger, Paul (Athlete, Hockey Player)
215-140 Letitia St
Barrie, ON L4N 1P5, CANADA

Meggett, Dave (Athlete, Football Player)
Lieber Correctional Institute
PO Box 205
SCDC ID: 00343610
Ridgeville, SC 29472-0205, USA

Meggysey, Dave (Athlete, Football Player)
2528 Benvenue Ave
Berkeley, CA 94704-3031, USA

Megrew, Mike (Athlete, Baseball Player)
25 Karen Dr
Hope Valley, RI 02832-1267, USA

Mehl, Lance A (Athlete, Football Player)
44920 Kacsmar Estates Dr
Saint Clairsville, OH 43950-9454, USA

Mehra, Smirti (Athlete, Golfer)
4038 Greystone Dr
Clermont, FL 34711-7197, USA

Mehta, Shailesh J (Business Person)
Providian Financial Corp
201 Mission St
San Francisco, CA 94105-1831, USA

Mehta, Ved (Writer)
139 E 79th St Fl 12
New York, NY 10075-0378, USA

Meier, Dave (Athlete, Baseball Player)
523 W Stuart Ave
Fresno, CA 93704-1430, USA

Meier, Richard A (Designer)
Richard Meier Partners
475 10th Ave Fl 6
New York, NY 10018-1179, USA

Meier, Shad (Athlete, Football Player)
6071 Bethany Blvd
Nashville, TN 37221-4314, USA

Meighan, Ron (Athlete, Hockey Player)
1692 Liberty Way
Orleans, ON K4A 4Y8, Canada

Meiias, Roman (Athlete, Baseball Player)
27325 Terrytown Rd
Sun City, CA 92586-5220, United States

Meijer, Doug (Business Person)
Meijer Inc
2929 Walker Ave NW
Grand Rapids, MI 49544-9428, USA

Meijer, Hank (Business Person)
Meijer Inc
2929 Walker Ave NW
Grand Rapids, MI 49544-9428, USA

Meiko (Musician)
c/o Allison Elbl *ID Public Relations*
7060 Hollywood Blvd Fl 8th
Los Angeles, CA 90028-6021, USA

Meilinger, Steve (Athlete, Football Player)
719 Camino Dr
Lexington, KY 40502-2776, USA

Meineke, Don (Athlete, Basketball Player)
1266 Westcliff Ct
Dayton, OH 45409-1144, USA

Meinhold, Carl (Athlete, Basketball Player)
5485 Perkiomen Ave
Reading, PA 19606-3676, USA

Meinwald, Jerrold (Misc)
Cornell University
Chemistry Dept
Ithaca, NY 14853, USA

Meira, Vitor (Race Car Driver)
Team Rahel
4601 Lyman Dr
Hilliard, OH 43026-1249, USA

Meirelles, Fernando (Director, Producer)
c/o Staff Member *WME|IMG*
9601 Wilshire Blvd
Beverly Hills, CA 90210-5213, USA

Meirelles, Priscilla (Model)
Carousel Productions, Inc
8 San Manuel St., Capitol
Pasig City, Metro Manila 01603, PHILIPPINES

Meisenhelder, Glen (Race Car Driver)
Glen-Ken
62 Chapin St
Feeding Hills, MA 01030-2302, USA

Meisner, Greg (Athlete, Football Player)
419 Glenmeade Rd
Greensburg, PA 15601-1170, USA

Meisner, Joachim Cardinal (Religious Leader)
Archbishop's Diocese
Marzellenstr 32
Cologne 50668, GERMANY

Meisner, Randy (Musician)
3706 Eureka Dr
Studio City, CA 91604-3104, USA

Meissner, Kimmie (Figure Skater)
Office of Public Relations
105 E Main St
the Academy Building
Newark, DE 19716-0799, USA

Meja (Musician)
Basic Music Mgmt
Norrtullsgatan 51
Stockholm 113 45, SWEDEN

Mejdani, Rexhep (President)
President's Office
Keshilli i Ministrave
Tirana, ALBANIA

Mejia, Hipolito (President)
Palacio Nacional
Calle Moises Garcia
Santo Domingo, DOMINICAN REPUBLIC

Mejia, Jorge Maria Cardinal (Religious Leader)
Biblioteca Apostolica Vaticina
Vatican City 00120, VATICAN CITY

Mejias, Roman (Athlete, Baseball Player)
27325 Terrytown Rd
Sun City, CA 92586-5220, USA

Mekka, Eddie (Actor)
Cosden Morgan
129 W Wilson St Ste 202
Costa Mesa, CA 92627-1586, USA

Mel, Renfro (Athlete, Football Player)
8211 Hunnicut Rd
Dallas, TX 75228-5930, USA

Melametsa, Anssl (Athlete, Hockey Player)
Kivirinne 8B
Esooo, 2760 Finland

Melamld, Aleksandr (Artist)
Ronald Freeman Fine Arts
31 Mercer St Frnt 1
New York, NY 10013-2595, USA

Melancon, Mei (Actor)
c/o Lena Roklin *Luber Roklin Management*
5815 W Sunset Blvd Ste 208
Los Angeles, CA 90028-6481, USA

Melander, Jon (Athlete, Football Player)
8255 Kelzer Pond Dr
Victoria, MN 55386-4500, USA

Melanie (Musician, Songwriter, Writer)
53 Baymont St # 5
Clearwater Beach, FL 33767-1705, USA

Melanson, Rollie (Athlete, Hockey Player)
728 Rue Pierre-Biard
Boucherville, QC J4B 7R3, CANADA

Melanson, Rollle (Athlete, Hockey Player)
728 Rue Pierre-Biard
Boucherville, QC J4B 7R3, Canada

Melanson, Rollle (Athlete, Hockey Player)
Vancouver Canucks
800 Griffiths Way
Vancouver, BC V6B 6G1, Canada

Melby, Russ (Athlete, Football Player)
8208 Spanish Meadows Ave
Las Vegas, NV 89131-1447, USA

Melchiondo, Mickey (Music Group, Musician)
4 Forrest Edge Dr
Titusville, NJ 08560-1313, USA

Melchionni, Bill (Athlete, Basketball Player)
ne Bay Tree Ct
Naples, FL 341e8-3429, USA

Melchionni, Gary (Athlete, Basketball Player)
1040 Grandview Blvd
Lancaster, PA 17601-5108, USA

Melchior, Ib (Writer)
424 W 119th St Apt 28
New York, NY 10027-7130, USA

Melek, Temara (Musician)
c/o Staff Member *Creative Artists Agency (CAA)*
2000 Avenue of the Stars Ste 100
Los Angeles, CA 90067-4705, USA

Melendez, A J (Musician)

Melendez, John (Actor, Writer)
c/o Staff Member *Chapter 2 Productions*
3500 W Olive Ave Ste 300
Burbank, CA 91505-4647, USA

Melendez, John (Musician)
c/o Staff Member *Paradigm (Monterey)*
404 W Franklin St
Monterey, CA 93940-2303, USA

Melendez, Kiki (Musician)
c/o Staff Member *Paradigm (Monterey)*
404 W Franklin St
Monterey, CA 93940-2303, USA

Melendez, Lisette (Musician)
Famous Artists Agency
250 W 57th St
New York, NY 10107-0001, USA

Meler, Dave (Baseball Player)
Minnesota Twins
523 W Stuart Ave
Fresno, CA 93704-1430, USA

Melhuse, Adam (Athlete, Baseball Player)
758 Center St
San Luis Obispo, CA 93405-2312, USA

Melikidze, Themo (Actor)
c/o Robert Stein *Robert Stein Management*
PO Box 3797
Beverly Hills, CA 90212-0797, USA

Melillo, Kevin (Athlete, Baseball Player)
5630 Fairway View Dr
Charlotte, NC 28277-2568, USA

Melinda (Artist)
M Entertainment
120 E Flamingo Rd
Las Vegas, NV 89109-4574, USA

Mellanby, Scott (Athlete, Hockey Player)
St Louis Blues
1401 Clark Ave
Saint Louis, MO 63103-2700

Mellanby, Scott (Athlete, Hockey Player)
2548 Town and Country Ln
Saint Louis, MO 63131-1121

Mellekas, John (Athlete, Football Player)
498 Broadway
Newport, RI 02840-1440, USA

Mellenby, Scott (Athlete, Hockey Player)
2548 Town and Country Ln
Saint Louis, MO 63131-1121, USA

Mellencamp, John (Musician, Songwriter)
PO Box 6777
Bloomington, IN 47407-6777, USA

Mellette, Aaron (Athlete, Football Player)
c/o Adisa P Bakari *Kelley Drye & Warren LLP*
3050 K St NW Ste 400
Washington, DC 20007-5100, USA

Melling, O R (Writer)
C/O Geraldine Whlean
26 Wolfe Tone Square E
Bray, Co Wicklow, IRELAND

Mello, Tamara (Actor)
c/o Brandy Gold *TalentWorks*
3500 W Olive Ave Ste 1400
Burbank, CA 91505-5512, USA

Mellons, Ken (Musician)
PO Box 8293
Hermitage, TN 37076-8293, USA

Mellor, Tom (Athlete, Hockey Player, Olympic Athlete)
794 Jerusalem Rd
Cohasset, MA 02025-1032

Melnick, Bruce E (Astronaut)
Boeing Aerospace
PO Box 21233
Kennedy Space Center, FL 32815-0233, USA

Melnick, Bruce E Cdr (Astronaut)
30 Captains Cove Rd
Inglis, FL 34449-9129, USa

Melnick, Daniel (Producer)
1123 Sunset Hills Rd
Los Angeles, CA 90069-1756, USA

Melniker, Benjamin (Producer)
Batfilm Productions
123 W 44th St # 10-K
New York, NY 10036-4089, USA

Melnyk, Larry (Athlete, Hockey Player)
1748 Sugarpine Crt
Coquitlam, BC V3E 3E4, Canada

Melnyk, Steve (Athlete, Golfer)
105 Virginia St
Saint Simons Island, GA 31522-5129, USA

Meloan, Jon (Athlete, Baseball Player)
8017 Lichtenauer Dr
Lenexa, KS 66219-2037, USA

Meloche, Gilles (Athlete, Hockey Player)
Pittsburgh Penguins
66 Mario Lemieux Pl Ste 2
Pittsburgh, PA 15219-3504

Meloche, Gilles (Athlete, Hockey Player)
401 Church Hill Rd
Venetia, PA 15367-1142

Melody (Musician)
c/o Staff Member *Sony Music (Miami)*
404 Washington Ave Ste 700
Miami Beach, FL 33139-6615, USA

Melody Depp, Lily-Rose (Actor)
c/o Robin Baum *Slate PR*
901 N Highland Ave
W Hollywood, CA 90038-2412, USA

Meloff, Chris (Athlete, Hockey Player)
8568 NW 52nd Pl
Coral Springs, FL 33067-2839, USA

Meloni, Christopher (Actor)
c/o Melissa Raubvogel *Imprint PR*
375 Hudson St
New York, NY 10014-3658, USA

Melrose, Barry J (Athlete, Coach, Hockey Player)
10 Windy Ridge Rd
Glens Falls, NY 12801-2473

Melroy, Pamela A (Astronaut)
3910 Valley Green Ct
Houston, TX 77059-5556, USA

Melroy, Pamela A Colonel (Astronaut)
920 N Barton St
Arlington, VA 22201-1910, USA

Melton, Bill (Athlete, Baseball Player)
9609 E Roadrunner Dr
Scottsdale, AZ 85262-1444, USA

Melton, Charles (Actor)
c/o Todd Diener *Untitled Entertainment*
350 S Beverly Dr Ste 200
Beverly Hills, CA 90212-4819, USA

Melton, Dave (Athlete, Baseball Player)
10253 Richwood Dr
Cupertino, CA 95014-3360, USA

Melton, Henry (Athlete, Football Player)
c/o Jordan Woy *Willis & Woy Management*
4890 Alpha Rd Ste 200
Dallas, TX 75244-4639, USA

Melua, Katie (Musician)
c/o Neil Warnock *UTA Music/The Agency Group (UK)*
361-373 City Rd
London EC1V 1PQ, UNITED KINGDOM

Meluskey, Mitch (Athlete, Baseball Player)
26 Meadowbrook Rd
Yakima, WA 98903-9505, USA

Melvill, Michael W (Astronaut)
24120 Jacaranda Dr
Tehachapi, CA 93561-8309, USA

Melvin, Bob (Athlete, Baseball Player, Coach)
5637 E. Canyon Ridge
Cave Creek, AZ 85331, USA

Melvin, Doug (Commentator)
4111 W Stonefield Rd
Mequon, WI 53092-2770, USA

Melvin, Leland D (Astronaut)
312 15th St NE
Washington, DC 20002-6502, USA

Melvin, Rachel (Actor)
c/o Anne Woodward *Authentic Talent & Literary Management*
3615 Eastham Dr # 650
Culver City, CA 90232-2410, USA

Melvin, Tre (Internet Star)
c/o Adam Wescott *Select Management Group*
6100 Wilshire Blvd Ste 400
Los Angeles, CA 90048-5109, USA

Melvoin, Wendy (Actor)
c/o Rick Jacobellis *First Artists Management*
4764 Park Granada Ste 110
Calabasas, CA 91302-3321, USA

Melzack, Ronald (Misc)
51 Banstead Ch
Montreal-Ouest, QC H4X 1P1, CANADA

Melzer, Jurgen (Athlete, Tennis Player)
Champ Events
Salmgasse 5/25
Wien 01030, Austria

Member, Tim (Athlete, Football Player)
3410 Grant St
Vancouver, WA 98660-1823, USA

Members, Swollen (Music Group, Musician)
c/o Staff Member *UTA Music/The Agency Group*
9336 Civic Center Dr
Beverly Hills, CA 90210-3604, USA

Memmel, Chellsie (Athlete, Gymnast, Olympic Athlete)
c/o Sheryl Shade *Shade Global*
171 W 57th St Apt 8A
New York, NY 10019-2222, USA

Men, Baha (Music Group)
Evolution Talent
1776 Broadway Fl 15
New York, NY 10019-2002

Menafee, Cornell (Athlete, Football Player)
403 Elm Ct
Opelika, AL 36801-6423, USA

Menard, Hillary ""Minnie"" (Athlete, Hockey Player)
8141 Wellington Blvd
Johnston, IA 50131-8740

Menard, Howie (Athlete, Hockey Player)
8 Springfield Lane
Courtice, ON L1E 1L9, Canada

Menard, Marc (Actor)
Infinite Artists
10-206 6th Ave E
Vancouver, BC V5T 1J8, CANADA

Menard, Paul (Race Car Driver)
136 Hanover Ln
Davidson, NC 28036-7795, USA

Menard, Renry W (Misc)
Scripps Institute of Oceanography
Geology Dept
La Jolla, CA 92093-0001, USA

Menard Jr, John (Business Person)
Menard Inc
4777 Menard Dr
Eau Claire, WI 54703-9604, USA

Mench, Kevin (Athlete, Baseball Player)
1305 Danbury Parks Dr
Keller, TX 76248-5271, USA

Menchaca, Marc (Actor)
c/o Ian Ames *TMT Entertainment Group*
648 Broadway # 1002
New York, NY 10012-2348, USA

Mencia, Carlos (Actor, Comedian)
c/o Yvette Shearer *Shearer Public Relations*
1356 Grandview Ave
Glendale, CA 91201-2224, USA

Mendelsohn, Ben (Actor)
c/o Lee-Anne Higgins *United Management*
Marlborough House
Ste 45, Level 4, 61 Marlborough St
Surry HillsNSW 02010, AUSTRALIA

Mendenhall, John (Athlete, Football Player)
PO Box 235
Cullen, LA 71021-0235, USA

Mendenhall, Ken (Athlete, Football Player)
1708 S Rankin St
Edmond, OK 73013-5128, USA

Mendes, Camila (Actor)
c/o Ruth Bernstein *Viewpoint Inc*
8820 Wilshire Blvd Ste 220
Beverly Hills, CA 90211-2622, USA

Mendes, Eva (Actor)
2341 E Live Oak Dr
Los Angeles, CA 90068-2525, USA

Mendes, Jonna (Athlete, Olympic Athlete, Track Athlete)
PO Box 92
Nixon, NV 89424-0092, USA

Mendes, Sam (Director)
532 W 22nd St Apt 5A
New York, NY 10011-1117, USA

Mendes, Shawn (Musician)
c/o Dvora Vener Englefield *The Lede Company*
9701 Wilshire Blvd # 930
Beverly Hills, CA 90212-2020, USA

Mendez, Carlos (Athlete, Baseball Player)
755 Braves Blvd NE
Rome, GA 30161-2983, USA

Mendez, Lazaro (DJ Laz) (Radio Personality)
Power 96
194 NW 187th St
Miami, FL 33169-4050, USA

Mendez, Lucia (Actor)
c/o Staff Member *TV Azteca*
Periferico Sur 4121
Colonia Fuentes del Pedregal
DF CP 14141, Mexico

Mendez, Luis Gerardo (Actor)
c/o Kenny Goodman *Goodmanagement*
137 N Larchmont Blvd
Los Angeles, CA 90004-3704, USA

Mendler, Bridgit (Actor, Musician)
c/o Alexander Yarosh *Gersh*
9465 Wilshire Blvd Ste 600
Beverly Hills, CA 90212-2605, USA

Mendoza, Dayana (Beauty Pageant Winner)
c/o Jessie Krysko *Cunningham Escott Slevin & Doherty (CESD)*
333 7th Ave Ste 1102
New York, NY 10001-5111, USA

Mendoza, Jessica (Athlete)
StantonShade
10 E 40th St Fl 4
New York, NY 10016-0200, USA

Mendoza, June (Artist)
34 Inner Park Road
London SW19 6DD, UNITED KINGDOM (UK)

Mendoza, Linda (Director)
c/o Staff Member *Creative Artists Agency (CAA)*
2000 Avenue of the Stars Ste 100
Los Angeles, CA 90067-4705, USA

Mendoza, Mike (Athlete, Baseball Player)
14207 S 20th St
Phoenix, AZ 85048-4519, USA

Mendoza, Minnie (Athlete, Baseball Player)
2866 Charlotte Dr
Murrells Inlet, SC 29576-8481, USA

Mendoza, Ramiro (Athlete, Baseball Player)
18706 Pepper Pike
Lutz, FL 33558-5303, USA

Mendoza, Reynol (Baseball Player)
2408 2nd St
Eagle Pass, TX 78852-4119, USA

Mendoza, Zuleyka Rivera (Beauty Pageant Winner)
c/o Richie Walls *FilmEngine*
9701 Wilshire Blvd
Beverly Hills, CA 90212-2020, USA

Menechino, Frank (Athlete, Baseball Player)
522 Arlene St
Staten Island, NY 10314-3818, USA

Menendez, Tony (Athlete, Baseball Player)
18730 NW 48th Ct
Miami Gardens, FL 33055-2536, USA

Meneses, Alex (Actor)
c/o Evan Hainey *Untitled Entertainment*
350 S Beverly Dr Ste 200
Beverly Hills, CA 90212-4819, USA

Meneses, Antonio (Musician)
Columbia Artists Mgmt Inc
165 W 57th St
New York, NY 10019-2201, USA

Menew (Music Group)
c/o Staff Member *REDCORE MUSIC GROUP*
520 8th Ave Rm 2001
New York, NY 10018-4166, USA

Mengelt, John (Athlete, Basketball Player)
2415 Moores Mill Rd Unit 265
Auburn, AL 36830-8484, USA

Menhart, Paul (Athlete, Baseball Player)
725 Kelsall Dr
Richmond Hill, GA 31324-7707, USA

Menheer-Zoromapal, Marie (Baseball Player)
8871 Lake Marion Creek Rd
Haines City, FL 33844-2004, USA

Menichetti, Roberto (Designer, Fashion Designer)
3 Loc Monteleto
Gubbio, ITALY

Menke, Denis (Athlete, Baseball Player)
1246 Berkshire Ln
Tarpon Springs, FL 34688-7626, USA

Mennea, Pietro (Athlete, Track Athlete)
Via Cassia 1041
Rome 00189, ITALY

Mennell, Laura (Actor)
c/o Craig Schneider *Pinnacle Public Relations*
8721 Santa Monica Blvd # 133
W Hollywood, CA 90069-4507, USA

Menninga, Chris (Race Car Driver)
Conquest Racing
5062 W 79th St
Indianapolis, IN 46268-1645, USA

Meno, Chorepiscopus John (Religious Leader)
263 Elm Ave
Teaneck, NJ 07666-2323, USA

Menon, Krishnan (Actor)
c/o Jai Khanna *Brillstein Entertainment Partners*
9150 Wilshire Blvd Ste 350
Beverly Hills, CA 90212-3453, USA

Menounos, Maria (Actor, Correspondent)
c/o Gary Mantoosh *Baker Winokur Ryder Public Relations*
9100 Wilshire Blvd
W Tower #500
Beverly Hills, CA 90212-3415, USA

Mensa, Vic (Musician)
c/o Jules Ferree *Scooter Braun Projects*
1755 Broadway
New York, NY 10019-3743, USA

Mensah, Peter (Actor)
c/o Staff Member *AVO Talent Agency*
5670 Wilshire Blvd Ste 1930
Los Angeles, CA 90036-5603, USA

Menshov, Vladimir V (Actor, Director)
3D Tverskaya-Yamskaya 52
Moscow 125047, RUSSIA

Mentez, Chris (Musician)
Arsisanian Assoc
6671 W Sunset Blvd Ste 1502
Los Angeles, CA 90028-7235, USA

Men Women & Children (Music Group)
c/o Staff Member *Paradigm (Monterey)*
404 W Franklin St
Monterey, CA 93940-2303, USA

Menzel, Idina (Actor, Musician)
c/o Kristen Foster *PMK/BNC Public Relations*
1840 Century Park E Ste 1400
Los Angeles, CA 90067-2115, USA

Menzel, Jiri (Director)
Studio 89
Kratky Film Jindrisska 34
Prague 1 112 07, CZECH REPUBLIC

Meola, Tony (Soccer Player)
488 Forest St # 1
Kearny, NJ 07032-3623, USA

Meoli, Christian (Actor)
c/o Brian McCabe *Venture IAB*
3211 Cahuenga Blvd W Ste 104
Los Angeles, CA 90068-1372, USA

Meoli, Rudy (Athlete, Baseball Player)
1211 San Gabriel Ave
Henderson, NV 89002-9402, USA

Meraz, Alex (Actor)
c/o Jeb Brandon *Corner Booth Entertainment*
11872 La Grange Ave Fl 1
Los Angeles, CA 90025-5283, USA

Merbold, Ulf (Astronaut)
Am Sonnenhang 4
Siegburg 53721, GERMANY

Merbold, Ulf D Dr (Astronaut)
Am Sonnenhang 4
Siegburg, Germany D-53721, USA

Mercado, Orlando (Athlete, Baseball Player)
5292 Bishop St Apt 10
Cypress, CA 90630-3082, USA

Mercado, Rosie (Journalist, Television Host)
c/o Katie Mason Stern *Luber Roklin Management*
5815 W Sunset Blvd Ste 208
Los Angeles, CA 90028-6481, USA

Mercado, Syesha (Musician)

Merced, Orlando (Athlete, Baseball Player)
PO Box 190494
San Juan, PR 00919-0494, USA

Mercein, Chuck (Athlete, Football Player)
59 Club Pointe Dr
White Plains, NY 10605-4466, USA

Mercer, Mark (Athlete, Baseball Player)
10607 Penn Ave S
Minneapolis, MN 55431-3445, USA

Mercer, Mike (Athlete, Football Player)
64463 McGrath Rd
Bend, OR 97701-8830, USA

Mercer, Ron (Athlete, Basketball Player)
San Antonio Spurs
1843 Glenhill Dr
Lexington, KY 40502-2817, USA

Mercer, Toby (Artist)
Mercer Studios
316 E Reserve Dr
Kalispell, MT 59901-6647, USA

Merchant, Andy (Athlete, Baseball Player)
PO Box 8
Malcolm, AL 36556-0008, USA

Merchant, Natalie (Musician, Songwriter)
c/o David Whitehead *Maine Road Management*
PO Box 1412
Woodstock, NY 12498-8412, USA

Merchant, Stephen (Actor, Director, Producer)
c/o Lewis Kay *Kovert Creative*
506 Santa Monica Blvd Ste 400
Santa Monica, CA 90401-2412, USA

Merchant, Tamzin (Actor)
c/o Camilla de La Moriniere *Tavistock Wood Management*
45 Conduit St
London W1S 2YN, UNITED KINGDOM

Mercier, Michele (Actor)
Residence Cape di Monte
Cannes 06400, FRANCE

Mercilus, Whitney (Athlete, Football Player)
c/o Sean Howard *Octagon Football*
600 Battery St Fl 2
San Francisco, CA 94111-1820, USA

Mercker, Kent (Athlete, Baseball Player)
5340 Muirfield Ct
Dublin, OH 43017-7629, USA

Merckx, Eddy (Athlete)
s'Herenweg 11
Meise 01860, Belgium

Mercredi, Vic (Athlete, Hockey Player)
GD
Fort Chipewyan, AB T0P 1B0, Canada

Mercredi, VIctor (Athlete, Hockey Player)
GD
Fort Chipewyan, AB T0P 1B0, Canada

Mercurio, Nicole (Actor)
Innovative Artists
1505 10th St
Santa Monica, CA 90401-2805, USA

Mercurio, Paul (Actor, Musician)
Beyond Films
53-55 Brisbane St Surreyhills
Sydney, NSW 02010, AUSTRALIA

Mercurio, Tara (Actor)
c/o Aaron Ray *Studio71*
8383 Wilshire Blvd Ste 1050
Beverly Hills, CA 90211-2415, USA

Mercy Me (Music Group, Musician)
c/o Scott Bickell *Brickhouse Entertainment*
106 Mission Ct Ste 1202
Franklin, TN 37067-6484, USA

Meredith, Cla (Athlete, Baseball Player)
8497 Mount Eagle Rd
Ashland, VA 23005-7827, USA

Meredith, Greg (Athlete, Hockey Player)
111 W 67th St Apt 36A
New York, NY 10023-5960

Meredith, james (Politician)
929 Meadowbrook Rd
Jackson, MS 39206-5945, USA

Meredith, James H (Misc)
929 Meadowbrook Rd
Jackson, MS 39206-5945, USA

Meredith, Jamon (Athlete, Football Player)
c/o Michael Perrett *Element Sports Group*
3340 Peachtree Rd NE Fl 16
Atlanta, GA 30326-1000, USA

Meredith, William (Writer)
Connecticut College
PO Box 1498
New London, CT 06320, USA

Merediz, Olga (Actor)
c/o Jed Abrahams *Kazarian, Measures, Ruskin & Associates (NYC)*
110 W 40th St Rm 2506
New York, NY 10018-3727, USA

Mereszczak, Laryssa (Athlete, Volleyball Player)
c/o Gigi Rock *Heraea Marketing*
10905 E Pear Tree Dr
Cornville, AZ 86325-5523, USA

Meridith, Ron (Athlete, Baseball Player)
308 Via Promesa
San Clemente, CA 92673-6820, USA

Merila, Mark (Athlete, Baseball Player)
11819 Westview Pkwy
San Diego, CA 92126-8540, USA

Meritano, Lorena (Actor)
c/o Gabriel Blanco *Gabriel Blanco Iglesias (Mexico)*
Rio Balsas 35-32
Colonia Cuauhtemoc
DF 06500, Mexico

Meriweather, Brandon (Athlete, Football Player)
c/o David Dunn *Athletes First*
23091 Mill Creek Dr
Laguna Hills, CA 92653-1258, USA

Meriwether, Chick (Baseball Player)
2409 Seifried St
Nashville, TN 37208-1344, USA

Meriwether, Chuck (Athlete, Baseball Player)
2409 Seifried St
Nashville, TN 37208-1344, USA

Meriwether, Lee (Actor)
Trish Harrison Business Management Inc.
19360 Rinaldi St Ste 517
Northridge, CA 91326-1607, USA

Meriwether, Porter (Athlete, Basketball Player)
8137 S Saint Lawrence Ave
Chicago, IL 60619-5007, USA

Merkens, Guido (Athlete, Football Player)
1238 Elkins Lk
Huntsville, TX 77340-7321, USA

Merkerson, S Epatha (Actor)
c/o Jillian Roscoe *ID Public Relations*
7060 Hollywood Blvd Fl 8th
Los Angeles, CA 90028-6021, USA

Merkin, Daphne (Writer)
c/o Staff Member *New York Times*
229 W 43rd St
New York, NY 10036-3982, USA

Merkosky, Glenn (Athlete, Hockey Player)
113 Farr Ln
Queensbury, NY 12804-1996

Merle, Carole (Skier)
Chalet La Calette
Super-Sauze 04400, FRANCE

Merlin, Jan (Actor)
347 N California St
Burbank, CA 91505-3508, USA

Merlo, James L (Athlete, Football Player)
1547 E Starpass Dr
Fresno, CA 93730-3448, USA

Merloni, Lou (Athlete, Baseball Player)
333 Ricciuti Dr Apt 1728
Quincy, MA 02169-6396, USA

Meron, Neil (Producer)
c/o Staff Member *Storyline Entertainment*
100 Universal City Plz
Universal City, CA 91608-1002, USA

Merovich, Pete (Soccer Player)
945 Spruce St
Pittsburgh, PA 15234-2127, USA

Merrells, Jason (Actor)
c/o Nicola Richardson *QVoice*
161 Drury Ln, Covent Garden
3rd Floor
London WC2B 5PN, UK

Merrick, Wayne (Athlete, Hockey Player)
68 Chesham Crt
London, ON N6G 3T4, CANADA

Merrill, Carl (Stump) (Athlete, Baseball Player, Coach)
18 Merrymeeting Dr
Topsham, ME 04086-1839, USA

Merrill, Casey (Athlete, Football Player)
78395 Avenue 41
Bermuda Dunes, CA 92203-1008, USA

Merrill, Catherine (Artist)
Old Church Pottery
1456 Florida St
San Francisco, CA 94110-4812, USA

Merrill, Mark (Athlete, Football Player)
2003 Costa Del Mar Rd Unit 690
Carlsbad, CA 92009-6815, USA

Merriman, Brent (Athlete, Baseball Player)
907 N Cobblestone St
Gilbert, AZ 85234-8742, USA

Merriman, Brett (Athlete, Baseball Player)
1725 S Coronado Rd Apt 3095
Gilbert, AZ 85295-0090, USA

Merriman, Ryan (Actor)
c/o Beth Holden-Garland *Untitled Entertainment*
350 S Beverly Dr Ste 200
Beverly Hills, CA 90212-4819, USA

Merriman, Shawne (Athlete, Football Player)
c/o David Dunn *Athletes First*
23091 Mill Creek Dr
Laguna Hills, CA 92653-1258, USA

Merritt, David (Athlete, Football Player)
479 Hartford Dr
Nutley, NJ 07110-3944, USA

Merritt, Jim (Athlete, Baseball Player)
2777 Blue Spruce Dr
Hemet, CA 92545-8701, USA

Merritt, Lloyd (Athlete, Baseball Player)
3201 Aspen Grove Dr APT K1
Apt 301
Franklin, TN 37067-4870, USA

Merritt, Tift (Musician)
c/o Staff Member *Red Light Management*
5800 Bristol Pkwy Ste 400
Culver City, CA 90230-6898, USA

Merriweather, Daniel (Musician)
c/o Staff Member *Allido*
19 Mercer St Apt 5
New York, NY 10013-2757, USA

Merriweather, Mike (Athlete, Football Player)
PO Box 8351
Stockton, CA 95208-0351, USA

Merrow, Susan (Misc)
Sierra Club
85 2nd St Ste 200
San Francisco, CA 94105-3488, USA

Merten, Lauri (Athlete, Golfer)
1010 Del Harbour Dr
Delray Beach, FL 33483-6510, USA

Mertens, Alan (Misc)
PacWest Racing Group
PO Box 1717
Bellevue, WA 98009-1717, USA

Mertens, Jerry (Athlete, Football Player)
465 Woodside Dr
Woodside, CA 94062-2375, USA

Mertz, Edwin T (Misc)
1504 Via Della Scala
Henderson, NV 89052-4128, USA

Mertzig, Jan (Athlete, Hockey Player)
Krokvagen 78
Huddinge 14131, Sweden

Meruelo, Alex (Business Person)
36 Indian Creek Island Rd
Indian Creek Village, FL 33154-2901, USA

Merullo, Matt (Athlete, Baseball Player)
8 Fox Run Rd
Madison, CT 06443-2052, USA

Merwin, William Stanley (Writer)
Farleigh Dickinson University Press
285 Madison Ave
Madison, NJ 07940-1099, USA

Merz, Curt (Athlete, Football Player)
1111 W Seminole St
Springfield, MO 65807-2551, USA

Merz, Sue (Athlete, Hockey Player, Olympic Athlete)
5 Douglas Dr
Greenwich, CT 06831-3612, USA

Mesa, Carlos (President)
President's Office
Palacio de Gobierno
Plaza Murilla
La Paz, BOLIVIA

Mesa, Jose (Athlete, Baseball Player)
2823 Santa Barbara Blvd
Cape Coral, FL 33914-4568, USA

Meschery, Tom (Athlete, Basketball Player)
1216 Versailles Ave
Alameda, CA 94501-5453, USA

Meselson, Matthew S (Misc)
Harvard University
Fairchild Biochemistry Laboratories
Cambridge, MA 02138, USA

Meseroll, Mark (Athlete, Football Player)
450 Roger Dr
Salisbury, NC 28147-8878, USA

Mesguich, Daniel (Actor, Director)
Agence Monita Derrieux
17-21 Rue Duret
Paris 75116, FRANCE

Mesic, Stipe (President)
Presidential Palace
Pantovcak 241
Zagreb 10000, CROATIA

Mesina Stanley, Dianne (Producer)
c/o Staff Member *United Talent Agency (UTA)*
9336 Civic Center Dr
Beverly Hills, CA 90210-3604, USA

Meskill, Thomas (Politician)
218 Stony Mill Ln
East Berlin, CT 06023-1042, USA

Mesler, Steve (Athlete)
c/o Lou Oppenheim *ICM Partners (NY)*
730 5th Ave
New York, NY 10019-4105, USA

Mesner, Bruce (Athlete, Football Player)
3178 NW 60th St
Boca Raton, FL 33496-3323, USA

Mesquida, Roxane (Actor)
c/o Elisabeth Simpson *Agence Elisabeth Simpson*
62 Boulevard Du Montparnasse
Paris 75015, FRANCE

Messager, Annette (Artist)
146 Blvd Camelinat
Colombier-Fontaine 92240, FRANCE

Messenger, Melinda (Model)
Arcadia Mgmt
2-3 Golden Square
London W1R 3AD, UNITED KINGDOM (UK)

Messenger, Randy (Athlete, Baseball Player)
455 Market St Ste 2240
San Francisco, CA 94105-2446, USA

Messer, Dale (Athlete, Football Player)
5449 N Brooks Ave
Fresno, CA 93711-2914, USA

Messerschmid, Ernst (Astronaut)
Universitat Stuttgart
Der Schone Weg 6
Reutlingen D-72766, GERMANY

Messerschmidt, J Alexander (Andy) (Baseball Player)
200 Lagunita Dr
Soquel, CA 95073-9594, USA

Messersmith, Andy (Athlete, Baseball Player)
200 Lagunita Dr
Soquel, CA 95073-9594, USA

Messi, Lionel (Leo) (Athlete, Soccer Player)
FC Barcelona
Aristides Maillo S/N
Barcelona 08028, SPAIN

Messick, Kevin (Producer)
c/o Staff Member *Gary Sanchez Productions*
1041 N Formosa Ave
West Hollywood, CA 90046-6703, USA

Messier, Joby (Athlete, Hockey Player)
PO Box 116
Wilcox, SK S0G 5E0, Canada

Messier, Mark (Athlete, Hockey Player)
Runaway Hill Club
Box EL 27031
Dunmore Town
Harbour Island, Bahamas

Messina, Chris (Actor)
c/o Chelsea Thomas *The Lede Company*
9701 Wilshire Blvd # 930
Beverly Hills, CA 90212-2020, USA

Messina, Jim (Musician)
c/o Staff Member *Agency for the Performing Arts (APA)*
405 S Beverly Dr Ste 500
Beverly Hills, CA 90212-4425, USA

Messina, Jo Dee (Musician, Songwriter)
PO Box 340020
Nashville, TN 37203-0020, USA

Messing, Debra (Actor)
c/o Molly Madden *3 Arts Entertainment*
9460 Wilshire Blvd Fl 7
Beverly Hills, CA 90212-2713, USA

Messner, Heinrich (Athlete, Skier)
Huebenweg 11
Hartford, CT 06150-0001, AUSTRIA

Messner, Johnny (Actor)
c/o Staff Member *McKeon-Myones Management*
3500 W Olive Ave Ste 770
Burbank, CA 91505-5527, USA

Mestnik, Frank (Athlete, Football Player)
730 Eagles Mere Ct
Alpharetta, GA 30005-4233, USA

Mestrik, Frank (Athlete, Football Player)
730 Eagles Mere Ct
Alpharetta, GA 30005-4233, USA

Meszaros, Andrej (Athlete, Hockey Player)
58 1/2 Martinique Ave
Tampa, FL 33606-4039

Meszaros, Maria (Director)
Malfilm Studio
Lumumba Utca 174
Budapest 01149, HUNGARY

Metallica (Music Group)
c/o Cliff Burnstein *Q Prime (NY)*
729 7th Ave Fl 16
New York, NY 10019-6831, USA

Metaxas, Eric (Writer)
c/o Staff Member *HarperCollins Publishers*
195 Broadway Fl 2
New York, NY 10007-3132, USA

Metcalf, Eric Q (Athlete, Football Player)
5112 S Fountain St
Seattle, WA 98178-2114, USA

Metcalf, John (Writer)
128 Lewis St
Ottawa, ON K2P 0S7, CANADA

Metcalf, Laurie (Actor)
Steppenwolf Theatre Company
1650 N Halsted St
Chicago, IL 60614-5518, USA

Metcalf, Mark (Actor)
c/o Staff Member *Peter Strain & Associates Inc (LA)*
10901 Whipple St Apt 322
N Hollywood, CA 91602-3245, USA

Metcalf, Shelby (Coach)
Texas A & M University
Athletic Dept
College Station, TX 77843-0001, USA

Metcalf, Terrance R (Terry) (Athlete, Football Player)
5112 S Fountain St
Seattle, WA 98178-2114, USA

Metcalf, Terrence (Athlete, Football Player)
37 County Road 253
Etta, MS 38627-9542, USA

Metcalf, Tom (Athlete, Baseball Player)
1390 Wisconsin River Dr
Port Edwards, WI 54469-1042, USA

Metcalf, Travis (Athlete, Baseball Player)
610 Tenna Lorna Ct
Dallas, TX 75208-3133, USA

Metcalfe, Jesse (Actor)
c/o Evan Hainey *Untitled Entertainment*
350 S Beverly Dr Ste 200
Beverly Hills, CA 90212-4819, USA

Metcalfe, Mike (Athlete, Baseball Player)
9 Cottage Pl
Ashland, NH 03217-4370, USA

Metcalfe, Scott (Athlete, Hockey Player)
36 Town Pump Cir
Spencerport, NY 14559-9734

Metcalf-Lindenburger, Dorothy M (Astronaut)
2235 Water Way
Seabrook, TX 77586-2814, USA

Metesh, Bernice (Athlete, Baseball Player, Commentator)
1210 Kelly Ave
Joliet, IL 60435-4251, USA

Metheny, Pat (Musician)
c/o Ted Kurland *Ted Kurland Associates*
173 Brighton Ave
Boston, MA 02134-2003, USA

Method Man (Musician, Television Host)
c/o Shauna Garr *Smart Girl Productions*
1041 N Formosa Ave
WR #302
West Hollywood, CA 90046-6703, USA

Metrano, Art (Actor)
131 N Croft Ave Apt 402
Los Angeles, CA 90048-3472, USA

Metric (Music Group)
c/o Staff Member *Paradigm (Monterey)*
404 W Franklin St
Monterey, CA 93940-2303, USA

Metrolis, Norma (Baseball Player)
175 Sea Dunes Dr
Melbourne Beach, FL 32951-3313, USA

Metropolit, Glen (Athlete, Hockey Player)
1070 Redwine Cove Rd SW
Dalton, GA 30720-4954

Metro Station (Music Group)
c/o Staff Member *Entertainment Fusion Group*
6420 Wilshire Blvd Ste 620
Los Angeles, CA 90048-5558, USA

Metta World Peace (Athlete, Basketball Player)
5617 Ridge Park Dr
Loomis, CA 95650-9487, USA

Mette-Marit, Princess (Royalty)
Det Kongelige
Slottet Drammensvein 1
Oslo 00010, NORWAY

Mettenberger, Zach (Athlete, Football Player)
c/o Joe Linta *JL Sports*
1204 Main St Ste 179
Branford, CT 06405-3787, USA

Metwally, Omar (Actor)
c/o James Suskin *Suskin Management*
2 Charlton St Apt 5K
New York, NY 10014-4970, USA

Metz, Chrissy (Actor)
c/o Lena Roklin *Luber Roklin Management*
5815 W Sunset Blvd Ste 208
Los Angeles, CA 90028-6481, USA

Metzelaars, Pete (Athlete, Football Player)
292 Point Carpenter Rd
Fort Mill, SC 29707-6875, USA

Metzenbaum, Howard M (Senator)
Consumer Federation of America
1424 16th St NW
Washington, DC 20036-2211, USA

Metzger, Butch (Athlete, Baseball Player)
641 Rivergate Way
Sacramento, CA 95831-3345, USA

Metzger, Clarence (Butch) (Athlete, Baseball Player)
641 Rivergate Way
Sacramento, CA 95831-3345, USA

Metzger, Henry (Misc)
35 Cummings Rd APT 366
Hanover, NH 03755-1338, USA

Metzger, Roger (Athlete, Baseball Player)
3560 Bluebonnet Blvd
Brenham, TX 77833-7180, USA

Metzig, Bill (Athlete, Baseball Player)
221 Chuck Wagon Rd
Lubbock, TX 79404-1903, USA

Meulens, Hensley (Athlete, Baseball Player)
Inidianapolis Indians
555 Mission Rock St
San Francisco, CA 94158-2119, USA

Meunier-Lebouc, Patricia (Athlete, Golfer)
152 Porto Vecchio Way
Palm Beach Gardens, FL 33418-6223, USA

Mewes, Jason (Actor)
c/o Gloria Hinojosa *Amsel, Eisenstadt & Frazier Talent Agency (AEF)*
5055 Wilshire Blvd Ste 860
Los Angeles, CA 90036-6108, USA

Mewhort, Jack (Athlete, Football Player)
c/o Michael McCartney *Priority Sports & Entertainment (Chicago)*
325 N La Salle Dr Ste 650
Chicago, IL 60654-8182, USA

Mey, Uwe-Jens (Speed Skater)
Vulkanstr 22
Berlin 10367, GERMANY

Meyer, Alejandra (Actor)
c/o Staff Member *Televisa*
Blvd Adolfo Lopez Mateos 232
Colonia San Angel INN
DF CP 01060, MEXICO

Meyer, Bob (Athlete, Baseball Player)
24446 Caswell Ct
Laguna Niguel, CA 92677-7008, USA

Meyer, Breckin (Actor)
c/o Ashley Franklin *Thruline Entertainment*
9250 Wilshire Blvd Fl Ground
Beverly Hills, CA 90212-3352, USA

Meyer, Brian (Athlete, Baseball Player)
33 Bank St
Medford, NJ 08055-2635, USA

Meyer, Carson (Actor)
c/o Zack Morgenroth *Lighthouse Management and Media*
9000 W Sunset Blvd Ste 1520
Los Angeles, CA 90069-5815, USA

Meyer, Dan (Athlete, Baseball Player)
11540 Marsh Creek Rd
Clayton, CA 94517-9759, USA

Meyer, Debbie (Athlete, Olympic Athlete, Swimmer)
Debbie Meyer Swim School
9675 Thesolious Ln
Reno, NV 89521-4455, USA

Meyer, Dina (Actor)
c/o Tiffany Kuzon *Mosaic Media Group*
407 N Maple Dr # 100
Beverly Hills, CA 90210-3818, USA

Meyer, Edgar (Musician)
c/o Staff Member *Studio Art Concert Agency*
Viale Della Resistenza 9
Suffield, CT 06080-0001, Italy

Meyer, Jerome J (Business Person)
Tektronix Inc
26600 SW Parkway Ave
Wilsonville, OR 97070-9232, USA

Meyer, Joey (Athlete, Baseball Player)
392 Kaimake Loop
Kailua, HI 96734-2019, USA

Meyer, John (Athlete, Football Player)
2085 Lost Dauphin Rd
De Pere, WI 54115-1605, USA

Meyer, Joyce (Religious Leader)
Joyce Meyers Ministries
PO Box 655
Fenton, MO 63026-0655, USA

Meyer, Karl H (Misc)
642 Wyndham Rd
Teaneck, NJ 07666-1825, USA

Meyer, Nicholas (Director, Producer, Writer)
c/o Alan Gasmer *Alan Gasmer Management Company*
10877 Wilshire Blvd Ste 603
Los Angeles, CA 90024-4348, USA

Meyer, Robert K (Misc)
3 Rawlings Place
Fadden, ACT 02904, AUSTRALIA

Meyer, Ron (Business Person, Producer)
c/o Staff Member *NBC Universal (LA)*
100 Universal City Plz
Universal City, CA 91608-1002, USA

Meyer, Ron (Athlete, Football Player)
628 18th St
Windom, MN 56101-1102, USA

Meyer, Scott (Athlete, Baseball Player)
6342 W Big Oak St
Phoenix, AZ 85083-7570, USA

Meyer, Stephenie (Writer)
c/o Jodi Reamer *Writers House*
21 W 26th St
New York, NY 10010-1083, USA

Meyer Maguire, Jennifer (Designer)
230 N Carmelina Ave
Los Angeles, CA 90049-2726, USA

Meyer-Petrovic, Anna (Athlete, Baseball Player, Commentator)
1125 N Nema Ave
Tucson, AZ 85712-4723, USA

Meyers, Anne Akiko (Musician)
ICM Artists
40 W 57th St
New York, NY 10019-4001, USA

Meyers, Ari (Actor)
c/o Holly Lebed *Holly Lebed Personal Management*
10535 Wilshire Blvd Apt 808
Los Angeles, CA 90024-4556, USA

Meyers, Augie (Musician)
Encore Talent
2137 Zercher Rd
San Antonio, TX 78209-1194, USA

Meyers, Chad (Athlete, Baseball Player)
816 Summit Ridge Dr
Papillion, NE 68046-8096, USA

Meyers, David (Dave) (Director)
c/o Ramses Ishak *United Talent Agency (UTA)*
9336 Civic Center Dr
Beverly Hills, CA 90210-3604, USA

Meyers, Josh (Comedian)
c/o April Lim *Global Artists Agency*
6253 Hollywood Blvd Apt 508
Los Angeles, CA 90028-8251, USA

Meyers, Krystal (Musician)
5902 Parham Rd
Franklin, TN 37064-9220, USA

Meyers, Nancy (Director)
c/o Jeff Berg *Resolution (LA)*
1801 Century Park E
Los Angeles, CA 90067-2302, USA

Meyers, Patricia (Athlete, Golfer)
113 Timberline Trl
Ormond Beach, FL 32174-4925, USA

Meyers, Seth (Actor, Comedian)
c/o Tim Sarkes *Brillstein Entertainment Partners*
9150 Wilshire Blvd Ste 350
Beverly Hills, CA 90212-3453, USA

Meyers-Drysdale, Ann (Athlete, Basketball Player, Olympic Athlete)
6621 Doral Dr
Huntington Beach, CA 92648-6129, USA

Meyers-Shyer, Hallie (Actor)
c/o Evelyn Karamanos *Relevant*
400 S Beverly Dr Ste 220
Beverly Hills, CA 90212-4404, USA

Meyfarth, Ulrike Nasse (Athlete, Olympic Athlete, Track Athlete)
SV Bayer 04 Leverkusen - Abt. Leichtathletik
Kalkstraße 46
Leverkusen 51377, GERMANY

Meyjes, Menno (Director, Producer, Writer)
c/o Jenne Casarotto *Casarotto Ramsay & Associates Ltd (UK)*
Waverley House
7-12 Noel St
London W1F 8GQ, UNITED KINGDOM

Mezei, Branislav (Athlete, Hockey Player)
8017 Laurel Ridge Ct
Delray Beach, FL 33446-9537

Mezzogiorno, Giovanna (Actor)
c/o Frederique Moidon *ArtMedia*
8 rue Danielle Casanova
Paris 75002, FRANCE

Mfume, Kweisi (Misc)
NAACP
PO Box 1557
President's Office
Baltimore, MD 21203-1557, USA

Mfume, Kweisi (Politician)
4805 Mount Hope Dr
Baltimore, MD 21215-3206, USA

MGK (Machine Gun Kelly) (Musician)
c/o Matt Galle *Paradigm*
140 Broadway Ste 2600
New York, NY 10005-1011, USA

MGMT (Music Group)
c/o Staff Member *Paradigm*
140 Broadway Ste 2600
New York, NY 10005-1011, USA

M. Grijalva, Raul (Congressman, Politician)
1511 Longworth Hob
Washington, DC 20515-4330, USA

M. Honda, Michael (Congressman, Politician)
1713 Longworth Hob
Washington, DC 20515-0515, USA

MIA (Musician)
c/o Todd Jacobs *WME|IMG*
9601 Wilshire Blvd
Beverly Hills, CA 90210-5213, USA

Mia, Pia (Musician)
c/o Michael Blumstein *Chase Entertainment*
7378 W Atlantic Blvd Ste 250
Margate, FL 33063-4214, USA

Miadich, Bart (Athlete, Baseball Player)
17841 Hillside Dr
Lake Oswego, OR 97034-7525, USA

Mialik, Larry (Athlete, Football Player)
100 Wisconsin Ave Apt 900
Madison, WI 53703-4169, USA

Miano, Rich (Athlete, Football Player)
Miano Sports Bar
7168 Makaa St
Honolulu, HI 96825-3103, USA

Micalef, Corrado (Athlete, Hockey Player)
P E I Rocket
46 Kensington Rd
Charlottetown, PE C1A 5H7, Canada

Micalef, Corrado (Athlete, Hockey Player)
12098 Av Camille-Tessier
Montreal, QC H1E 6A4, Canada

Micech, Phil (Athlete, Football Player)
3029 N 91st St
Milwaukee, WI 53222-4620, USA

Miceli, Dan (Athlete, Baseball Player)
1712 Cottonwood Creek Pl
Lake Mary, FL 32746-4407, USA

Micell, Justine (Actor)
Don Buchwald
5900 Wilshire Blvd Ste 3100
Los Angeles, CA 90036-5030, USA

Micelotta, Mickey (Athlete, Baseball Player)
3266 Jog Park Dr
Greenacres, FL 33467-2014, USA

Micelotta, Robert P ""Mickey"" (Athlete, Baseball Player)
2035 E Warm Springs Rd Unit 1007
Las Vegas, NV 89119-0454, USA

Michael, Archbishop (Religious Leader)
Antiochian Orthodox Christian Church
358 Mountain Rd
Englewood, NJ 07631-3798, USA

Michael, Bob (Politician)
1029 N Glenwood Ave
Peoria, IL 61606-1007

Michael, Kevin (Musician)
c/o Staff Member *Paradigm (Monterey)*
404 W Franklin St
Monterey, CA 93940-2303, USA

Michael, Thomas (Actor, Producer, Writer)
Peeping Tom Films

Michael Carroll, Jason (Musician)
c/o Staff Member *Creative Artists Agency (CAA)*
401 Commerce St PH
Nashville, TN 37219-2516, USA

Michael E Captain, Lopez-Aiegria (Astronaut)
_1_8715 Point Lookout Dr
Houston, TX 77058-4030, USA

Michaels, Al (Commentator)
401 S Bristol Ave
Los Angeles, CA 90049-3820, USA

Michaels, Alan R (Al) (Sportscaster)
c/o Josh Pyatt *WME|IMG*
9601 Wilshire Blvd
Beverly Hills, CA 90210-5213, USA

Michaels, Bret (Musician, Reality Star)
c/o Joann Mignano *Krupp Kommunications*
59 W 19th St Rm 4C
New York, NY 10011-4228, USA

Michaels, Chad (Impersonator)
c/o Stephen Ford *Diva Central Inc*
7510 W Sunset Blvd # 1445
Los Angeles, CA 90046-3408, USA

Michaels, Fern (Writer)
1006 S Main St
Summerville, SC 29483-4231, USA

Michaels, Gianna (Adult Film Star)
Look North Promotions
7 - 9 Clifford St
Unit 101
York, Yorkshire YO1 9RA, UK

Michaels, Jason (Athlete, Baseball Player, Coach)
10317 Carroll Cove Pl
Tampa, FL 33612-6508, USA

Michaels, Jillian (Fitness Expert, Reality Star)
c/o Giancarlo Chersich *Empowered Media*
9100 Wilshire Blvd Ste 520E
Beverly Hills, CA 90212-3455, USA

Michaels, Julia (Musician)
c/o Mike Greek *CAA (London)*
3 Shortlands, Hammersmith
Fl 5
London W6 8DA, UNITED KINGDOM

Michaels, Lorne (Producer, Writer)
Broadway Video
1619 Broadway Fl 10 # 900
New York, NY 10019-7463, USA

Michaels, Mia (Dancer)
c/o Tim O'Brien *Clear Talent Group (LA)*
10950 Ventura Blvd
Studio City, CA 91604-3340, USA

Michaels, Shawn (Athlete, Wrestler)
c/o Chris Stuart *Encore Sports and Entertainment*
4405 Manchester Ave Ste 205
Encinitas, CA 92024-7902, USA

Michaels, Tammy Lynn (Actor)
c/o Marcel Pariseau *True Public Relations*
3575 Cahuenga Blvd W Ste 360
Los Angeles, CA 90068-1361, USA

Michaels, Walter (Walt) (Athlete, Coach, Football Coach, Football Player)
282 Michaels Rd
Shickshinny, PA 18655-4142, USA

Michaelsen, Kari (Actor)
Kazarian/Spencer
11365 Ventura Blvd Ste 100
Studio City, CA 91604-3148, USA

Michaelson, Ingrid (Musician)
c/o Patrick Confrey *Derris & Company*
48 W 25th St Fl 11
New York, NY 10010-2719, USA

Michalak, Chris (Athlete, Baseball Player)
1108 Mockingbird Ln
Keller, TX 76248-2903, USA

Michaleczewski, Dariusz (Boxer)
Universum Box-Promotion
Am Stadtrand 27
Hamburg 22047, GERMANY

Michalek, Zbynek (Athlete, Hockey Player)
21455 N 81st St
Scottsdale, AZ 85255-6479, USA

Michalik, Art (Athlete, Football Player)
33400 Gafford Rd
Wildomar, CA 92595-8293, USA

Michalka, AJ (Actor)
c/o Ruth Bernstein *Viewpoint Inc*
8820 Wilshire Blvd Ste 220
Beverly Hills, CA 90211-2622, USA

Michalka, Aly (Actor, Musician)
c/o Britney Ross *42West*
1840 Century Park E Ste 700
Los Angeles, CA 90067-2122, USA

Michalka, Amanda (Musician)
c/o Stephanie Durning *42West*
1840 Century Park E Ste 700
Los Angeles, CA 90067-2122, USA

Michaud, Olivier (Athlete, Hockey Player)
289 Rue Saint-Jean-Baptiste
Beloeil, QC J3G 2V7, Canada

Michayluk, Dave (Athlete, Hockey Player)
Farm
Wakaw, SK SDK 4PO, Canada

Micheals, Rip (Comedian, Reality Star)
c/o Medjyn Chery *Medjynchery PR*
Prefers to be contacted by email or phone.
New York, NY NA, USA

Micheaux, Larry (Athlete, Basketball Player)
2914 Calender Lake Dr
Missouri City, TX 77459-3920, USA

Micheaux, Nicki (Actor)
c/o Michael Greenwald *Endorse Management Group*
9854 National Blvd # 454
Los Angeles, CA 90034-2713, USA

Micheel, Shaun (Athlete, Golfer)
1267 Dubray Lake Cir
Collierville, TN 38017-3952, USA

Michel, Alex (Reality Star)
PO Box 46605
Los Angeles, CA 90046-0605, USA

Michel, F Curtis (Astronaut)
2101 University Blvd
Houston, TX 77030-1218, USA

Michel, F Curtis Dr (Astronaut)
2101 University Blvd
Houston, TX 77030-1218, USA

Michel, Mike (Athlete, Football Player)
378 Drexel Ave
Ventura, CA 93003-2329, USA

Michel, Sony (Athlete, Football Player)
c/o Ben Renzin *Creative Artists Agency (CAA)*
405 Lexington Ave Fl 19
New York, NY 10174-1800, USA

Michele, Chrisette (Musician)
c/o Mark Siegel *ICM Partners*
10250 Constellation Blvd Fl 7
Los Angeles, CA 90067-6207, USA

Michele, Draya (Reality Star)
c/o Marcus Blassingame *TSD Agency*
Prefers to be contacted by telephone or email
USA

Michele, Lea (Actor, Musician)
c/o Jason Weinberg *Untitled Entertainment*
350 S Beverly Dr Ste 200
Beverly Hills, CA 90212-4819, USA

Michele, Michael (Actor)

Micheler, Elisabeth (Athlete)
Gruntenstr 45
Augsburg 86163, GERMANY

Micheletti, Joe (Athlete, Hockey Player)
New York Rangers
2 Penn Plz Fl 22
New York, NY 10121-2299

Micheletti, Joe (Athlete, Hockey Player)
143 Rolling Hills Rd
Thornwood, NY 10594-1821

Micheletti, Pat (Athlete, Hockey Player)
832 Ivy Ln
Saint Paul, MN 55123-2425

Michell, Keith (Actor)
Chatto & Linnit
Prince of Wales
Coventry St
London W1V 7FE, UNITED KINGDOM (UK)

Michell, Roger (Director)
Duncan Heath
Paramount House
162 Wardour
London, W1V 3AT, UNITED KINGDOM (UK)

Michelle, Ava (Actor)
c/o Matt Fletcher *TalentWorks*
3500 W Olive Ave Ste 1400
Burbank, CA 91505-5512, USA

Michelle, Candice (Actor, Model)
c/o Jerry Donato *Abraxas Talent Agency*
907 E 7th St Apt 209
Los Angeles, CA 90021-1431, USA

Michelle, Sheley (Actor)
c/o Mike Simpson *WME|IMG*
9601 Wilshire Blvd
Beverly Hills, CA 90210-5213, USA

Michelmore, Guy (Composer)
72 Goldsmith Ave.
London, ENGLAND W3 6HN

Michels, John (Athlete, Football Player)
4544 Alveo Rd
La Canada Flintridge, CA 91011-3703, USA

Michels, John (Athlete, Football Player)
832 Colonial Heights Rd Apt 2
Kingsport, TN 37663-2155, USA

Michels, Rinus (Coach, Football Coach)
Hotel Breitenbacher Hof
H-Heine-Allee 36
Dusseldorf 40213, GERMANY

Michener, Charles D (Misc)
1865 N 500th Rd
Baldwin City, KS 66006-7315, USA

Michiba, Rokusaburo (Chef)
Ginza Rokusan-Tei 8-8-7 Ginza Dai San
Sowaredo Building Chyuo-ku
Tokyo, Japan, USA

Michibata, Jessica (Model)
c/o Staff Member *The Tanabe Agency*
2-21-4 Aobadai
Meguro
Tokyo 153-0042, JAPAN

Michiko (Royalty)
Imperial Palace
1-1 Chiyoda-ku
Tokyo 00100, JAPAN

Michner, Andy (Race Car Driver)
PO Box 24697
Indianapolis, IN 46224-0697, USA

Mickell, Darren (Athlete, Football Player)
930 SW 88th Ter
Pembroke Pines, FL 33025-1466, USA

Mickelson, Ed (Athlete, Baseball Player)
1532 Charlemont Dr
Chesterfield, MO 63017-4604, USA

Mickelson, Phil (Athlete, Golfer)
Phil Mickelson Design
7077 E Marilyn Rd Ste 140
Scottsdale, AZ 85254-2782, USA

Mickens, Glenn (Athlete, Baseball Player)
5920 Kini Pl
Kapaa, HI 96746-8938, USA

Mickey, Joey (Athlete, Football Player)
6213 Canyon Dr
Oklahoma City, OK 73105-6415, USA

Mickolio, Kam (Athlete, Baseball Player)
1036 N 15th Ave
Bozeman, MT 59715-3265, USA

Micucci, Kate (Actor)
c/o Christie Smith *Rise Management*
6338 Wilshire Blvd
Los Angeles, CA 90048-5002, USA

Middendorf, Dave (Athlete, Football Player)
PO Box 525
Port Orchard, WA 98366-0525, USA

Middendorf, Max (Athlete, Hockey Player)
7791 E San Fernando Dr
Scottsdale, AZ 85255-4020

Middendorf, Tracy (Actor)
7880 Highway 290 W Apt 11101
Austin, TX 78736-3256, USA

Middlebrook, Jason (Athlete, Baseball Player)
3309 Glenview Ave
Austin, TX 78703-1446, USA

Middlebrook, Lindsay (Athlete, Hockey Player)
2060 Flamingo Dr
Florissant, MO 63031-3516

Middlebrooks, Charley (Athlete, Baseball Player)
Indianapolis Clowns
528 Rigby St NE
Marietta, GA 30060-1703, USA

Middlebrooks, Willie (Athlete, Football Player)
18775 SW 78th Ct
Cutler Bay, FL 33157-7404, USA

Middleditch, Thomas (Actor)
c/o Jodi Gottlieb *Independent Public Relations*
9601 Wilshire Blvd Ste 750
Beverly Hills, CA 90210-5228, USA

Middle of the Road (Music Group)
c/o Staff Member *Lyon & Partners Group*
Industrieweg 10
AR Groesbeek 06562, The Netherlands

Middleton, Mike (Model)
Louisa Models
Ebersberger Str 9
Munich 81679, GERMANY

Middleton, Rick (Athlete, Hockey Player)
PO Box 1161
Hampton, NH 03843-1161

Middleton, Terdell (Athlete, Football Player)
1893 Prospect St
Memphis, TN 38106-7645, USA

Middleton (Duchess of Cambridge), Kate (Catherine) (Royalty)
St James Palace
London SW1A 1BS, UNITED KINGDOM

Middleton-Gentry, Ruth (Baseball Player)
28 Grandview Heights
Hamilton, IN 46742, USA

Midkiff, Dale (Actor)
c/o John Frazier *Amsel, Eisenstadt & Frazier Talent Agency (AEF)*
5055 Wilshire Blvd Ste 860
Los Angeles, CA 90036-6108, USA

Midler, Bette (Actor, Musician)
Miss M Productions
1125 5th Ave # 15R
New York, NY 10128-0143, USA

Midon, Raul (Musician)
c/o Kathleen Kausch *Zot Management*
12100 Wilshire Blvd Ste 1540
Los Angeles, CA 90025-7139, USA

Midori (Musician)
Midori Foundation
850 7th Ave Ste 705
New York, NY 10019-5438, USA

Midthunder, Amber (Actor)
c/o Mona Loring *Status PR*
PO Box 6191
Westlake Village, CA 91359-6191, USA

Miechur, Thomas F (Misc)
Cement & Allied Workers Union
2500 Brickvale Dr
Elk Grove Village, IL 60007-6800, USA

Mieczko, A J (Athlete, Hockey Player)
295 Central Park W Apt 9G
New York, NY 10024-3023, USA

Mieczko, AJ (Athlete, Hockey Player, Olympic Athlete)
3 Hinckley Ln
Nantucket, MA 02554-2006, USA

Miehm, Kevin (Athlete, Hockey Player)
722 Elizabeth St
Kitchener, ON N2H 6H3, CANADA

Mielke, Gary (Athlete, Baseball Player)
1718 Orchid Dr S
North Mankato, MN 56003-1435, USA

Mientkiewicz, Doug (Athlete, Baseball Player, Olympic Athlete)
125 Bawiew Isle Dr
Islamorada, FL 33036-3308, USA

Mierkowicz, Ed (Athlete, Baseball Player)
7530 Macomb St Apt 1A
Grosse Ile, MI 48138-1522, USA

Mieske, Matt (Athlete, Baseball Player)
2199 E Bombay Rd
Midland, MI 48642-8351, USA

Mieto, Juha (Skier)
General Delivery
Mieto, FINLAND

Miggins, Larry (Athlete, Baseball Player)
2405 Kingston St
Houston, TX 77019-6603, USA

Mighty Clouds of Joy (Music Group)
c/o Staff Member *EMI Recorded Music (UK)*
27 Wrights Lane
London W8 5SW, UK

Mighty Mighty Bosstones (Music Group)
c/o Tobbe Lorentz *The Agency Group (Sweden)*
Ängelholmsgatan 3A 214 22
Malmo 214 22, SWEDEN

Migliazzo, Paul (Athlete, Football Player)
605 W 68th Ter
Kansas City, MO 64113-1954, USA

Migliore, Richard (Race Car Driver)
420 Fair Hill Dr # 1
Elkton, MD 21921-2573, USA

Migliore, Richard (Horse Racer)
48 Killearn Rd
Millbrook, NY 12545-6216, USA

Mignola, Mike (Cartoonist)
c/o Staff Member *Dark Horse Entertainment*
1438 N Gower St Ste 23
Hollywood, CA 90028-8306, USA

Mignonga, Vic (Actor)
7810 Pickford Knolls Ct
Houston, TX 77041-1274, USA

Migos (Musician)
c/o Pierre Thomas *Quality Control Music*
1479 Metropolitan Pkwy SW
Atlanta, GA 30310-4453, USA

Miguel (Musician)
c/o Troy Carter *Atom Factory/Coalition Media Group*
PO Box 927
Culver City, CA 90232-0927, USA

Miguel, Luis (Musician)
Ventura Productions
PO Box 978
Pico Rivera, CA 90660-0978, USA

Mihm, Chris (Athlete, Basketball Player)
Celeland Cavallers
47e8 Peace Pipe Path
Austin, TX 78746-24e9, USA

Mihok, Dash (Actor)
c/o Jamie Harhay Skinner *Baker Winokur Ryder Public Relations*
9100 Wilshire Blvd
W Tower #500
Beverly Hills, CA 90212-3415, USA

Mikan, Larry (Athlete, Basketball Player)
891 Carmona Ct
Chula Vista, CA 91910-8012, USA

Mikawos, Stan (Athlete, Football Player)
8 John Huyda Dr
Winnipeg, MB R2G 4C9, Canada

Mike, Dennery (Athlete, Football Player)
6419 Oakley St
Philadelphia, PA 19111-5218, USA

Mikel, Liz (Actor)
c/o Mary Collins *Mary Collins Agency*
2909 Cole Ave Ste 250
Dallas, TX 75204-1321, USA

Mike-Mayer, Istvan (Steve) (Athlete, Football Player)
681 Lincoln Ave
Glen Rock, NJ 07452-2519, USA

Mike-Mayer, Nicholas (Nick) (Athlete, Football Player)
681 Lincoln Ave
Glen Rock, NJ 07452-2519, USA

Mike Rizzo, Mike (DJ)
c/o Staff Member *Diva Central Inc*
7510 W Sunset Blvd # 1445
Los Angeles, CA 90046-3408, USA

Mikeska, Russ (Athlete, Football Player)
148 Phoenix Dr
Eatonton, GA 31024-5635, USA

Mike Will Made It (Musician)
c/o Vinny Kumar *Keniley Kumar Law*
5425 Peachtree Pkwy
Peachtree Corners, GA 30092-6536, USA

Mikhalkov, Nikita (Director)
Maly Kozikhinksy Per 4
#16-17
Moscow 103001, RUSSIA

Mikhalkov-Konchalovsky, Andrei S (Director)
Malaya Gruzinskaya 28 #130
Moscow 123557, RUSSIA

Mikita, Valerie (Actor)
c/o Staff Member *The Stevens Group*
14011 Ventura Blvd Ste 200W
Sherman Oaks, CA 91423-5218, USA

Mikkelsen, Mads (Actor)
c/o Theresa Peters *United Talent Agency (UTA)*
9336 Civic Center Dr
Beverly Hills, CA 90210-3604, USA

Mikkelson, Bill (Athlete, Hockey Player)
47 Glen Meadow Cres
St. Albert, AB T8N 3A2, Canada

Miklich, William (Athlete, Football Player)
Highway 106
Dousman, WI 53118, USA

Miko, Izabella (Actor)
c/o Kesha Williams *KW Entertainment*
3727 W Magnolia Blvd Ste 430
Burbank, CA 91505-2818, USA

Mikolajczyk, Ron (Athlete, Football Player)
18323 Oakde Rd
Odessa, FL 33556-4918, USA

Mikolajewski, Pete (Athlete, Football Player)
2520 Singing Vista Way
El Cajon, CA 92019-2740, USA

Miksis, Al (Athlete, Basketball Player)
10618 E Cedar Waxwing Dr
Sun Lakes, AZ 85248-7764, USA

Mikulski, Barbara (Politician)
3704 N Charles St Unit 1003
Baltimore, MD 21218-2325, USA

Mikulski, Barbara (Senator)
212 W Main St Ste 200
Salisbury, MD 21801-5106, USA

Mikvy, Bill (Athlete, Basketball Player)
586 Linton Hill Rd
Newtown, PA 18940-1204, USA

Milacki, Bob (Athlete, Baseball Player)
PO Box 15050
Reading, PA 19612-5050, USA

Milan, Don (Athlete, Football Player)
PO Box 126
Gardnerville, NV 89410-0126, USA

Milani, Denise (Model)

Milani, Tom (Athlete, Hockey Player)

Milano, Alyssa (Actor)
c/o Sarah Fuller *True Public Relations*
3575 Cahuenga Blvd W Ste 360
Los Angeles, CA 90068-1361, USA

Milbourne, Larry (Athlete, Baseball Player)
821 N Main Rd Apt 24B
Vineland, NJ 08360-8208, USA

Milbrett, Tiffeny (Athlete, Olympic Athlete, Soccer Player)
1902 SW Broadleaf Dr
Portland, OR 97219-6375, USA

Milburn, Darryl (Athlete, Football Player)
270 E Harding St
Baton Rouge, LA 70802-7323, USA

Milburn, Glyn (Athlete, Football Player)
11900 Courtleigh Dr APT 505
Los Angeles, CA 90066, USA

Milbury, Mike (Athlete, Hockey Player)
Boston Bruins
100 Legends Way Ste 250
Boston, MA 02114-1389

Milbury, Mike (Athlete, Coach, Hockey Player)
61 Edwardel Rd
Needham, MA 02492-4001

Milchan, Arnon (Producer)
c/o Staff Member *New Regency Pictures*
10201 W Pico Blvd Bldg 12
Los Angeles, CA 90064-2606, USA

Milchin, Mike (Athlete, Baseball Player, Olympic Athlete)
13651 Glynshel Dr
Winter Garden, FL 34787-5001, USA

Milem, John (Athlete, Football Player)
PO Box 5236
Salisbury, NC 28147, USA

Miles, Aaron (Athlete, Baseball Player)
1716 San Jose Dr
Antioch, CA 94509-4217, USA

Miles, Carl (Athlete, Baseball Player)
3710 S Lenoir St
Columbia, MO 65201-5463, USA

Miles, Darius (Athlete, Basketball Player)
1149 Lilac Dr
Belleville, IL 62220-3337, USA

Miles, Don (Athlete, Baseball Player)
400 Central Ave
Palacios, TX 77465-2000, USA

Miles, Eddie (Athlete, Football Player)
960 NW 48th Ave
Coconut Creek, FL 33063-4631, USA

Miles, Jeromy (Athlete, Football Player)
c/o Joe Linta *JL Sports*
1204 Main St Ste 179
Branford, CT 06405-3787, USA

Miles, Jeromy (Athlete, Football Player)

Miles, Jim (Athlete, Baseball Player)
134 Moores Creek Rd
Maben, MS 39750-5532, USA

Miles, Joanna (Actor)
2062 Vine St Apt 5
Los Angeles, CA 90068-3928, USA

Miles, John (Baseball Player)
Chicago American Giants
4130 Treehouse Dr
San Antonio, TX 78222-3510, USA

Miles, John R (Jack) (Writer)
3568 Mountain View Ave
Pasadena, CA 91107-4616, USA

Miles, Les (Football Coach)
c/o Staff Member *AAI Sports Inc.*
16000 Dallas Pkwy Ste 300
Dallas, TX 75248-6609, USA

Miles, Mark (Athlete, Tennis Player)
Assn of Tennis Pros
200 Tournament Players Road
Ponte Vedra Beach, FL 32082, USA

Miles, Ostell (Athlete, Football Player)
9400 W 11th Ave
Lakewood, CO 80215-3001, USA

Miles, Paige (Musician)
c/o Simon Fuller *XIX Entertainment (UK)*
32/33 Ransomes Dock
London SW11 4NP, UNITED KINGDOM (UK)

Miles, Sarah (Actor)
Chithurst Manor
Trotton near Petersfield
Hants GU31 5EU, UNITED KINGDOM (UK)

Miles, Sylvia (Actor)
c/o Staff Member *Agency for the Performing Arts (APA)*
405 S Beverly Dr Ste 500
Beverly Hills, CA 90212-4425, USA

Miles, Vera (Actor)
PO Box 1599
Palm Desert, CA 92261-1599, USA

Miles-Clark, Jearl (Athlete, Track Athlete)
J J Clark
University of Florida
Athletic Dept
Gainsville, FL 32604, USA

Miley, Dave (Athlete, Baseball Player, Coach)
235 Montage Mountain Rd
Moosic, PA 18507-1765, USA

Milgliore, Richard (Race Car Driver)
420 Fair Hill Dr # 1
Elkton, MD 21921-2573, USA

Milhoan, Michael (Actor)
c/o Staff Member *Sanders Armstrong Caserta*
4111 W Alameda Ave Ste 505
Burbank, CA 91505-4163, USA

Mili, Itula (Athlete, Football Player)
4468 W Glenmoor Hills Dr
South Jordan, UT 84009-9188, USA

Milian, Christina (Actor)
c/o Robyn Santiago *Illumination PR*
6 Rye Ridge Plz
Rye Brook, NY 10573-2820, USA

Milicevic, Ivana (Actor, Model)
c/o Graciella Sanchez *Echo Lake Management*
421 S Beverly Dr Fl 8
Beverly Hills, CA 90212-4408, USA

Milinchik, Joe (Athlete, Football Player)
9329 Barker Rd
New Hill, NC 27562-9795, USA

Milinichik, Joe (Athlete, Football Player)
4101 Tiber Falls Dr
Ellicott City, MD 21043-7170, USA

Militano, Mark (Athlete, Figure Skater, Olympic Athlete)
10940 Johnson St NE
Minneapolis, MN 55434-3777, USA

Militello, Sam (Athlete, Baseball Player)
3217 W Saint John St
Tampa, FL 33607-2127, USA

Milius, John F (Director, Writer)
888 Linda Flora Dr
Los Angeles, CA 90049-1629, USA

Mill, Andy (Athlete, Olympic Athlete, Skier)
798 Azalea St
Boca Raton, FL 33486-3513, USA

Mill, Meek (Musician)
c/o Greg Cortez *42West*
600 3rd Ave Fl 23
New York, NY 10016-1914, USA

Milla, Roger (Soccer Player)
Federation Camerounaise de Football
BP 1116
Yaounde, CAMEROON

Millan, Cesar (Television Host)
Cesar Millan Pack Project
PO Box 802888
Santa Clarita, CA 91380-2888, USA

Millan, Felix (Athlete, Baseball Player)
G16 Calle Camarero
Carolina, PR 00987-8523, USA

Millar, Jeff (Cartoonist)
24611 E Kingscrest Cir
Spring, TX 77389-4925, USA

Millar, Kevin (Athlete, Baseball Player)
40 Hartz Way Ste 10
Secaucus, NJ 07094-2403, USA

Millar, Miles (Producer, Writer)
c/o Staff Member *Millar/Gough Ink*
3800 Barham Blvd Ste 503
Los Angeles, CA 90068-1042, USA

Millard, Bryan (Athlete, Football Player)
2520 Bluebonnet Ln UNIT 15
Austin, TX 78704-4854, USA

Millard, Candice (Writer)
c/o Suzanne Gluck *WME|IMG (NY)*
11 Madison Ave Fl 18
New York, NY 10010-3669, USA

Millard, Keith (Athlete, Football Player)
3739 Oakhurst Way
Dublin, CA 94568-8834, USA

Millbern, David (Actor)
c/o Staff Member *Regent Entertainment*
10940 Wilshire Blvd Ste 1600
Los Angeles, CA 90024-3910, USA

Millcic, Darko (Basketball Player)
Detroit Pistons
2 Championship Dr
Palace
Auburn Hills, MI 48326-1753, USA

Milledge, Lastings (Athlete, Baseball Player)
11114 Sailbrooke Dr
Riverview, FL 33579-7074, USA

Millegan, Eric (Actor)
c/o Peter Young *Sovereign Talent Group*
1642 Westwood Blvd Ste 202
Los Angeles, CA 90024-5609, USA

Millen, Corey (Athlete, Hockey Player, Olympic Athlete)
1206 Doddridge Ave
Cloquet, MN 55720-2323, USA

Millen, Greg (Athlete, Hockey Player)
Toronto Maple Leafs
400-40 Bay St
Toronto, ON M5J 2X2, Canada

Millen, Greg (Athlete, Hockey Player)
980 Orch
Bridgenorth, ON KOL lHO, Canada

Millen, Hugh (Athlete, Football Player)
6836 Cascade Ave SE
Snoqualmie, WA 98065-9725, USA

Millen, Matt (Athlete, Football Player)
PO Box 196
Durham, PA 18039-0196, USA

Miller, Aaron (Athlete, Hockey Player, Olympic Athlete)
147 Appletree Point Rd
Burlington, VT 05408-2446

Miller, Aaron David (Writer)
c/o Staff Member *Random House*
1540 Broadway
New York, NY 10036-4039, USA

Miller, Abby Lee (Dancer, Reality Star)
ALDC Shoppe
11316 Santa Monica Blvd
Los Angeles, CA 90025-3119, USA

Miller, Alan (Journalist)
Los Angeles Times
2300 E Imperial Hwy
Editorial Dept
El Segundo, CA 90245-2813, USA

Miller, Alan (Athlete, Football Player)
3118 Erie Dr
Orchard Lake, MI 48324-1512, USA

Miller, Alice (Athlete, Golfer)
2 Log Church Rd
Wilmington, DE 19807-1724, USA

Miller, Allan (Actor)
Douglas Gorman Rothacker Wilhelm
33 W 46th St Ste 851
New York, NY 10036-4103, USA

Miller, Allison (Actor)
c/o William (Willie) Mercer *Thruline Entertainment*
9250 Wilshire Blvd Fl Ground
Beverly Hills, CA 90212-3352, USA

Miller, Amiah (Actor)
c/o Beau Swayze *Management 360*
9111 Wilshire Blvd
Beverly Hills, CA 90210-5508, USA

Miller, Andre (Basketball Player)
Denver Nuggets
1000 Chopper Cir
Pepsi Center
Denver, CO 80204-5805, USA

Miller, Andrew (Athlete, Baseball Player)
Detroit Tigers Foundation
417 SW 129th Ter
Newberry, FL 32669-2761, USA

Miller, Anthony (Athlete, Basketball Player)
1083 Superior St
Benton Harbor, MI 49022-5310, USA

Miller, Anthony (Athlete, Football Player)
325 S San Dimas Canyon Rd Apt 108
San Dimas, CA 91773-3064, USA

Miller, Beatrice (Actor, Musician)
c/o Rachel Altman *Paradigm*
140 Broadway Ste 2600
New York, NY 10005-1011, USA

Miller, Ben (Actor, Producer)
c/o Staff Member *Independent Talent Group*
40 Whitfield St
London W1T 2RH, UNITED KINGDOM

Miller, Bennett (Director)
c/o Leslee Dart *42West*
600 3rd Ave Fl 23
New York, NY 10016-1914, USA

Miller, Bill (Athlete, Baseball Player)
PO Box 2681
Aptos, CA 95001-2681, USA

Miller, Bill (Race Car Driver)
4895 Convair Dr
Carson City, NV 89706-0492, USA

Miller, Billy (Actor)
c/o Staff Member *Randy James Management*
12711 Ventura Blvd Ste 345
Studio City, CA 91604-2416, USA

Miller, Billy (Athlete, Football Player)
465 Cosmos Ct
Westlake, CA 91362, USA

Miller, Billy (Athlete, Football Player)
13745 Elkton Ct
Moorpark, CA 93021-5008, USA

Miller, Bob (Athlete, Baseball Player)
3133 Coventry Dr
Waterford, MI 48329-3213, USA

Miller, Bob (Athlete, Baseball Player)
17397 Glenmore
Redford, MI 48240-2127, USA

Miller, Bob (Athlete, Hockey Player)
1429 Main St
Marshfield, MA 02050-2072

Miller, Bode (Athlete, Olympic Athlete, Skier)
53 Augusta
Trabuco Canyon, CA 92679-4829, USA

Miller, Brad (Athlete, Basketball Player)
Sacramento Kings
5960 Via De La Rosa
Granite Bay, CA 95746-9040, USA

Miller, Brad (Congressman, Politician)
1127 Longworth Hob
Washington, DC 20515-3219, USA

Miller, Brandon (Race Car Driver)
Childress Racing
PO Box 1189
236 Industrial Dr.
Welcome, NC 27374-1189, USA

Miller, Bruce (Athlete, Baseball Player)
2126 Parkland Dr
Fort Wayne, IN 46825-3929, USA

Miller, Bruce (Athlete, Football Player)

Miller, Buddy (Musician)
Mark Pucci Media
5000 Oak Bluff Ct
Atlanta, GA 30350-1069, USA

Miller, Calvin (Athlete, Football Player)
1602 Fairfield Dr
Stillwater, OK 74074-2331, USA

Miller, Carl (Athlete, Football Player)
PO Box 773
Crowley, TX 76036-0773, USA

Miller, Charles D (Business Person)
Avery Dennison Corp
150 N Orange Grove Blvd
Pasadena, CA 91103-3534, USA

Miller, Cheryl (Athlete, Basketball Player, Olympic Athlete)
Tishman Agency
6767 Forest Lawn Dr Ste 206
Los Angeles, CA 90068-1051, USA

Miller, Chris (Director)
c/o Staff Member *Lord Miller*
10201 W Pico Blvd Bldg 3
Los Angeles, CA 90064-2606, USA

Miller, Chris (Athlete, Football Player)
2114 Elkhorn Dr
Eugene, OR 97408-1203, USA

Miller, Christa (Actor)
c/o Gary Mantoosh *Baker Winokur Ryder Public Relations*
9100 Wilshire Blvd Ste 400W
W Tower #500
Beverly Hills, CA 90212-3464, USA

Miller, Chryste Gaines (Athlete, Olympic Athlete, Track Athlete)
5408 E Saddleridge Ln
Lithonia, GA 30038-3976, USA

Miller, Coco (Basketball Player)
Washington Mystics
601 F St NW
Mcl Center
Washington, DC 20004-1605, USA

Miller, Corey (Athlete, Football Player)
2528 Crofton Way
Columbia, SC 29223-2299, USA

Miller, Corky (Athlete, Baseball Player)
1115 7th St
Calimesa, CA 92320-1013, USA

Miller, C Ray (Religious Leader)
United Brethren in Christ
302 Lake St
Huntington, IN 46750-9711, USA

Miller, Cymphonique (Dancer, Musician)
c/o Shannon Barr *Rogers & Cowan*
1840 Century Park E Fl 18
Los Angeles, CA 90067-2101, USA

Miller, Damian (Athlete, Baseball Player)
N1276 Wuensch Rd
La Crosse, WI 54601-2655, USA

Miller, Dan (Musician)
Trans Continental Records
7380 W Sand Lake Rd # 350
Orlando, FL 32819-5248, USA

Miller, Danny (Actor)
c/o Staff Member *Celeb Agents*
77 Oxford St
London ON W1D 2ES, UNITED KINGDOM (UK)

Miller, Darrell (Athlete, Baseball Player)
21159 Via Alisa
Yorba Linda, CA 92887-2510, USA

Miller, Dave (Cartoonist)
813 Timber Ridge Rd
Edmond, OK 73034-4918, USA

Miller, David Wiley (Artist, Cartoonist)
Back 40 Design
PO Box 7985
Back 40 Design
Edmond, OK 73083-7985, USA

Miller, Denise (Actor, Producer)
c/o Richard Sindell *Bob Waters Agency*
9301 Wilshire Blvd Ste 300
Beverly Hills, CA 90210-6119, USA

Miller, Dennis (Actor, Comedian)
c/o Lori Jonas *Jonas Public Relations*
1327 Ocean Ave Ste F
Santa Monica, CA 90401-1024, USA

Miller, Denny (Actor)
32252 Shadow Lake Ln
Castaic, CA 91384-4116, USA

Miller, Dyar (Athlete, Baseball Player)
8816 Admirals Bay Dr
Indianapolis, IN 46236-9292, USA

Miller, Eddie (Athlete, Baseball Player)
1819 Alfreda Blvd
San Pablo, CA 94806-4715, USA

Miller, Eddie (Athlete, Football Player)
1503 Summerwood Dr
Clarkston, GA 30021-3096, USA

Miller, Ezra (Actor)
c/o Liz Mahoney *Narrative*
1601 Vine St Fl 6
Los Angeles, CA 90028-8802, USA

Miller, Frank (Actor, Writer)
c/o Brooke Blumberg *Sunshine Sachs*
720 Cole Ave
Los Angeles, CA 90038-3606, USA

Miller, Frank (Cartoonist)
Dark House Publishing
10956 SE Main St
Milwaukie, OR 97222-7644, USA

Miller, Fred (Athlete, Football Player)
7143 Sawmill Trl
Houston, TX 77040-1830, USA

Miller, Fred D (Athlete, Football Player)
4535 Black Rock Rd
Upperco, MD 21155-9544, USA

Miller, Gabrielle (Actor)

Miller, George (Congressman, Politician)
2205 Rayburn Hob
Washington, DC 20515-0507, USA

Miller, George (Director, Producer)
Kennedy Miller Productions
30 Orwell St
King's Cross
Sydney, NSW 02011, AUSTRALIA

Miller, Heath (Athlete, Football Player)
c/o Tom Condon *Creative Artists Agency (CAA)*
401 Commerce St PH
Nashville, TN 37219-2516, USA

Miller, Jack (Politician)
11507 Orilla Del Rio Pl
Temple Terrace, FL 33617-2624, USA

Miller, Jack (Race Car Driver)
Arizona Motorsports
30 Gasoline Aly Ste F
Indianapolis, IN 46222-3900, USA

Miller, Jamir (Athlete, Football Player)
331 Grenadine Way
Hercules, CA 94547-2048, USA

Miller, Jason (Writer)
10000 Santa Monica Blvd PH 305
Los Angeles, CA 90067-7037, USA

Miller, Jason (Mayhem) (Athlete)
c/o Jeff Sussman *Jeff Sussman Management*
Prefers to be contacted by email or phone.
Sherman Oaks, CA 91403, USA

Miller, Jay (Athlete, Hockey Player)
175 Chester St
North Falmouth, MA 02556-2302

Miller, Jeff (Congressman, Politician)
2416 Rayburn Hob
Washington, DC 20515-1301, USA

Miller, Jeremy (Actor)
5255 Vesper Ave
Sherman Oaks, CA 91411-4011, USA

Miller, Jim (Athlete, Football Player)
PO Box 863
Ripley, MS 38663-0863, USA

Miller, Jody (Musician)
PO Box 413
Blanchard, OK 73010-0413, USA

Miller, Joel McKinnon (Actor)
c/o Michael Greene *Greene & Associates*
1901 Avenue of the Stars Ste 130
Los Angeles, CA 90067-6030, USA

Miller, Joey (Race Car Driver)
Country Joe Racing
22222 Dodd Blvd
Lakeville, MN 55044-8553, USA

Miller, John (Correspondent)
ABC-TV
77 W 66th St
News Dept
New York, NY 10023-6201, USA

Miller, John (Athlete, Baseball Player)
5105 River Ave Apt A
Newport Beach, CA 92663-2415, USA

Miller, John (Athlete, Baseball Player)
13443 Old Annapolis Rd
Mount Airy, MD 21771-7732, USA

Miller, Johnny (Athlete, Football Player)
94 Beach St
Revere, MA 02151-5006, USA

Miller, Johnny (Athlete, Golfer)
PO Box 970488
Orem, UT 84097-0488, USA

Miller, Jon (Baseball Player, Commentator, Sportscaster)
San Francisco Giants
401 Nevada Ave
Moss Beach, CA 94038-9643, USA

Miller, Jonathan (Director)
63 Gloucester Crescent
London NW1, UNITED KINGDOM (UK)

Miller, Jonny Lee (Actor)
c/o Ina Treciokas *Slate PR*
901 N Highland Ave
W Hollywood, CA 90038-2412, USA

Miller, Josh (Athlete, Football Player)
16 Summer Heights Dr
Franklin, MA 02038-2365, USA

Miller, Joyce D (Misc)
Amalgamated Clothing & Textile Workers
1710 Broadway Frnt 3
New York, NY 10019-5254, USA

Miller, J Ronald (Religious Leader)
Int'l Community Churches Council
21116 Washington Pkwy
Frankfort, IL 60423-3112, USA

Miller, Julie (Musician, Songwriter)
c/o Staff Member *Vector Management*
PO Box 120479
Nashville, TN 37212-0479, USA

Miller, Justin (Athlete, Football Player)
c/o Eugene Parker *Independent Sports & Entertainment (ISE-IN)*
6435 W Jefferson Blvd # 197
Fort Wayne, IN 46804-6203, USA

Miller, Justin (Athlete, Baseball Player)
2087 Bonnie Ave
Palm Harbor, FL 34683-5059, USA

Miller, Keith (Athlete, Baseball Player)
30082 Braeburn
New Hudson, MI 48165-8131, USA

Miller, Keith (Athlete, Baseball Player)
1831 W Alamosa Dr
Terrell, TX 75160-0811, USA

Miller, Keith (Politician)
3705 Arctic Blvd
Anchorage, AK 99503-5774, USA

Miller, Kelly (Athlete, Hockey Player)
3783 Chippendale Cir
Okemos, MI 48864-3861

Miller, Kelly (Basketball Player)
Indiana Fever
3763 Chippendale Circle
Okemos, MI 48864, USA

Miller, Kevin (Athlete, Hockey Player, Olympic Athlete)
4243 Redbud Trl
Williamston, MI 48895-9103

Miller, Kip (Athlete, Hockey Player)
1933 Birch Bluff Dr
Okemos, MI 48864-5915

Miller, Kristen (Actor)
Lighthouse
409 N Camden Dr Ste 202
Beverly Hills, CA 90210-4423, USA

Miller, Lamar (Athlete, Football Player)
c/o Drew Rosenhaus *Rosenhaus Sports Representation*
3921 Alton Rd # 440
Miami Beach, FL 33140-3852, USA

Miller, Larry (Actor, Comedian)
c/o Staff Member *Brillstein Entertainment Partners*
9150 Wilshire Blvd Ste 350
Beverly Hills, CA 90212-3453, USA

Miller, Larry (Athlete, Baseball Player)
3205 E Desert Cove Ave
Phoenix, AZ 85028-2735, USA

Miller, Larry (Athlete, Football Player)
3 Cour De La Reine
Palos Hills, IL 60465-2405, USA

Miller, Lemmie (Athlete, Baseball Player)
Rockford Riverhawks
4503 Interstate Blvd
Attn: Coaching Staff
Loves Park, IL 61111-5700, USA

Miller, Lennox (Athlete, Track Athlete)
2120 Pinecrest Dr
Altadena, CA 91001-2121, USA

Miller, Lenore (Misc)
Retail/Wholesale/Department Store Union
30 E 29th St
New York, NY 10016, USA

Miller, Levi (Actor)
c/o Mark Eaton *EATON Management*
90 Bourke Rd Alexandria
Suite 204
Sydney 02015, AUSTRALIA

Miller, Logan (Actor)
c/o Jamie Harhay Skinner *Baker Winokur Ryder Public Relations*
9100 Wilshire Blvd Ste 400W
W Tower #500
Beverly Hills, CA 90212-3464, USA

Miller, LW (Race Car Driver)
Miller Racing
206 Performance Rd
Mooresville, NC 28115-9591, USA

Miller, Marci (Actor, Model)
c/o Gary Ousdahl *Advanced Management*
8033 W Sunset Blvd # 935
Los Angeles, CA 90046-2401, USA

Miller, Marisa (Actor, Model)
5870 Melrose Ave Ste 3 PMB 665
Los Angeles, CA 90038-3738, USA

Miller, Mark (Musician)
Sawyer Brown Inc
5200 Old Harding Rd
Franklin, TN 37064-9406, USA

Miller, Mark (Athlete, Football Player)
2080 Crestwood St
Alliance, OH 44601-5741, USA

Miller, Matt (Athlete, Baseball Player)
3203 61st St
Lubbock, TX 79413-5519, USA

Miller, Matt (Athlete, Football Player)
15 Highgate Cir
Ithaca, NY 14850-1429, USA

Miller, McKaley (Actor)
c/o Emily Urbani *Osbrink Talent Agency*
4343 Lankershim Blvd # 100
North Hollywood, CA 91602-2705, USA

Miller, Michael (Athlete, Football Player)
116 E McClellan St
Flint, MI 48505-4224, USA

Miller, Mike (Athlete, Basketball Player)
2308 Bay Dr
Pompano Beach, FL 33062-2915, USA

Miller, Nancy (Writer)
c/o Nancy Josephson *WME|IMG*
9601 Wilshire Blvd
Beverly Hills, CA 90210-5213, USA

Miller, Nate (Boxer)
1214 Allengrove St
Philadelphia, PA 19124-2904, USA

Miller, Nicole J (Designer, Fashion Designer)
780 Madison Ave
New York, NY 10065-6108, USA

Miller, Norm (Athlete, Baseball Player)
43 Columbia Crest Pl
Spring, TX 77382-1331, USA

Miller, Oliver (Athlete, Basketball Player)
2912 S Meadow Dr
Fort Worth, TX 76133-7214, USA

Miller, Omar Benson (Actor)
c/o Stephen Tenenbaum *Morra Brezner Steinberg & Tenenbaum (MBST) Entertainment*
345 N Maple Dr Ste 200
Beverly Hills, CA 90210-5174, USA

Miller, Patina (Actor)
c/o Jennifer Sims *Imprint PR*
375 Hudson St
New York, NY 10014-3658, USA

Miller, Paul (Athlete, Baseball Player)
252 Redbud Ln
Batavia, IL 60510-3623, USA

Miller, Paul (Athlete, Hockey Player)
5 Celtic Ave
Billerica, MA 01821-1203

Miller, Penelope Ann (Actor)
c/o Oren Segal *Management Production Entertainment (MPE)*
9229 W Sunset Blvd Ste 301
W Hollywood, CA 90069-3417, USA

Miller, Perry (Athlete, Hockey Player)
471 McNaughton Ave
Winnipeg, MB R3L 1S5, Canada

Miller, Peter North (Business Person)
Dawson House
5 Jewry St
London EC3N 2EX, UNITED KINGDOM (UK)

Miller, Randy (Athlete, Baseball Player)
22523 Oak Mist Ln
Katy, TX 77494-2256, USA

Miller, Raymond (Ray) (Athlete, Baseball Player, Coach)
PO Box 41
New Athens, OH 43981-0041, USA

Miller, Rebecca (Actor)
c/o Leslee Dart *42West*
600 3rd Ave Fl 23
New York, NY 10016-1914, USA

Miller, Reggie (Athlete, Basketball Player, Olympic Athlete)
14301 E 113th St
Fishers, IN 46040-9660, USA

Miller, Reginald W (Reggie) (Athlete, Basketball Player)
3785 Puerco Canyon Rd
Malibu, CA 90265-4551, USA

Miller, Rhett (Musician)
c/o Ken Weinstein *Big Hassle Media*
40 Exchange Pl Ste 1900
New York, NY 10005-2714, USA

Miller, Rick (Athlete, Baseball Player)
12790 Silverthorn Ct
Bonita Springs, FL 34135-2452, USA

Miller, Robert M (Athlete, Football Player)
8475 Knox Rd
Clarkston, MI 48348-1721, USA

Miller, Robin (Chef)
c/o Staff Member *The Food Network.com*
1180 Avenue of the Americas Fl 14
New York, NY 10036-8401, USA

Miller, Rod (Athlete, Baseball Player)
413 Cabarton Rd
Cascade, ID 83611-5004, USA

Miller, Romeo (Musician)
6255 W Sunset Blvd Ste 908
Los Angeles, CA 90028-7410, USA

Miller, Roy (Athlete, Football Player)
c/o Michael McCartney *Priority Sports & Entertainment (Chicago)*
325 N La Salle Dr Ste 650
Chicago, IL 60654-8182, USA

Miller, Ryan (Athlete, Hockey Player)
700 Walbert Dr.
East Lansing, MI 48823-2176

Miller, Scott (Athlete, Football Player)
26432 Charford Way
Lake Forest, CA 92630-6520, USA

Miller, Shannon (Athlete, Gymnast, Olympic Athlete)
Shannon Miller Lifestyle
4311 Salisbury Rd
Jacksonville, FL 32216-6123, USA

Miller, Shauna (Writer)
c/o Jordyn Palos *Persona Public Relations*
6255 W Sunset Blvd Ste 705
Hollywood, CA 90028-7408, USA

Miller, Shawn (Athlete, Football Player)
PO Box 696
Oakley, UT 84055-0696, USA

Miller, Sienna (Actor)
c/o Mara Buxbaum *ID Public Relations*
7060 Hollywood Blvd Fl 8th
Los Angeles, CA 90028-6021, USA

Miller, Stanley L (Misc)
University of California
Chemistry Dept
La Jolla, CA 92093-0001, USA

Miller, Stephanie (Comedian, Television Host)
KTLK AM 1150
3400 W Olive Ave Ste 550
Burbank, CA 91505-5544, USA

Miller, Tangi (Actor)
c/o Adam Robinson *Southfield Village*
8228 W Sunset Blvd # 190
West Hollywood, CA 90046-2414, USA

Miller, Terry (Athlete, Football Player)
9015 W 2nd Ave
Stillwater, OK 74074-6775, USA

Miller, TJ (Actor, Comedian)
c/o David (Dave) Becky *3 Arts Entertainment*
9460 Wilshire Blvd Fl 7
Beverly Hills, CA 90212-2713, USA

Miller, Travis (Athlete, Baseball Player)
51 Whisper Way
Eaton, OH 45320-9597, USA

Miller, Trever (Athlete, Baseball Player)
24155 Hideout Trl
Land O Lakes, FL 34639-8111, USA

Miller, Ty (Actor)
c/o Staff Member *Tedesco Management*
Prefers to be contacted via telephone
Los Angeles, CA 90069, USA

Miller, Von (Athlete, Football Player)
c/o David Dunn *Athletes First*
23091 Mill Creek Dr
Laguna Hills, CA 92653-1258, USA

Miller, Wade (Athlete, Baseball Player)
12 Woods Way
Reading, PA 19610-1199, USA

Miller, Warren (Athlete, Hockey Player)
937 21st Ave N
South Saint Paul, MN 55075-1316, USA

Miller, Wentworth (Actor)
c/o Jennifer Allen *Viewpoint Inc*
8820 Wilshire Blvd Ste 220
Beverly Hills, CA 90211-2622, USA

Miller, William (Athlete, Baseball Player)
PO Box 2681
Aptos, CA 95001-2681, USA

Miller, Willie T (Athlete, Football Player)
308 Martin Dr
Birmingham, AL 35215-1180, USA

Miller, Zach (Athlete, Football Player)
c/o Ben Dogra *Relativity Sports*
2029 Century Park E Ste 1550
Century City, CA 90067-3000, USA

Millette, Joe (Athlete, Baseball Player)
759 Solana Dr
Lafayette, CA 94549-5206, USA

Millhauser, Steven (Writer)
235 Caroline St
Saratoga Springs, NY 12866-3505, USA

Milliard, Ralph (Baseball Player)
101 Runaway Bay Dr Apt 304
Virginia Beach, VA 23452-8157

Milligan, Dustin (Actor)
c/o Deb Dillistone *Red Management*
415 Esplanade W Box 3
North Vancouver, BC V7M 1A6, CANADA

Milligan, Randy (Athlete, Baseball Player)
6905 Real Princess Ln
Gwynn Oak, MD 21207-4577, USA

Millikan, Joe (Race Car Driver)
4671 Bull Creek Rd
Franklinville, NC 27248, USA

Milliken, William (Politician)
6103 Peninsula Dr
Traverse City, MI 49686-1913, USA

Milliner, Dee (Athlete, Football Player)
c/o Pat Dye Jr *SportsTrust Advisors*
3340 Peachtree Rd NE Fl 16
Atlanta, GA 30326-1000, USA

Millionaire, Tony (Artist)
c/o Staff Member *Fantagraphics Books*
7563 Lake City Way NE
Seattle, WA 98115-4218, USA

Millionaires (Music Group)
c/o Jonathan Daniel *Crush Music Management*
60-62 E 11th St
Fl 7
New York, NY 10003, USA

Millman, Dan (Writer)
PO Box 6148
San Rafael, CA 94903-0148, USA

Millns, James (Athlete, Figure Skater, Olympic Athlete)
210 She Crab Ct
Summerville, SC 29486-5440, USA

Millns, Jim (Athlete, Figure Skater, Olympic Athlete)
210 She Crab Ct
Summerville, SC 29486-5440, USA

Milloy, Lawyer (Athlete, Football Player)
1 Bills Dr
Orchard Park, NY 14127-2237, USA

Mills, Alan (Athlete, Baseball Player)
1811 Bellgrove St
Lakeland, FL 33805-2523, USA

Mills, Alley (Actor)
444 Carroll Canal
Venice, CA 90291-4682, USA

Mills, Bill (Athlete, Baseball Player)
2431 NW 41st St Apt 5305
Gainesville, FL 32606-7411, USA

Mills, Billy (Athlete, Olympic Athlete, Track Athlete)
c/o Staff Member *Billy Mills Speakers Bureau, The*
7760 Winding Way # 723
Fair Oaks, CA 95628-5735, USA

Mills, Brad (Athlete, Baseball Player)
723 N 22nd Pl
Mesa, AZ 85213-6706, USA

Mills, Chris (Athlete, Basketball Player)
2223 Camden Ave
Los Angeles, CA 90064-1905, USA

Mills, Curtis (Athlete, Track Athlete)
328 Lake St
Lufkin, TX 75904, USA

Mills, Dick (Athlete, Baseball Player)
10345 E Desert Cove Ave
Scottsdale, AZ 85260-6304, USA

Mills, Donna (Actor)
c/o Darryl Marshak *Marshak/Zachary Company, The*
8840 Wilshire Blvd Fl 1
Beverly Hills, CA 90211-2606, USA

Mills, Eddie (Actor)
c/o Staff Member *Peter Strain & Associates Inc (LA)*
10901 Whipple St Apt 322
N Hollywood, CA 91602-3245, USA

Mills, Ernie (Athlete, Football Player)
21246 SW Plantation St
Dunnellon, FL 34431-3482, USA

Mills, Hayley (Actor)
c/o Alan Willig *Buchwald (NY)*
10 E 44th St
New York, NY 10017-3601, USA

Mills, Heather (Activist)
VBites
14 East St
Brighton
East Sussex BN1 1HP, UK

Mills, John Henry (Athlete, Football Player)
755 Bahia Cir
Ocala, FL 34472-8831, USA

Mills, Jordan (Athlete, Football Player)
6500 Wilshire Blvd Ste 2200
Los Angeles, CA 90048-4942

Mills, Judson (Actor)
c/o Dino May *Dino May Management*
13223 Bloomfield St
Sherman Oaks, CA 91423-3207, USA

Mills, Juliet (Actor, Writer)
5252 Lennox Ave
Sherman Oaks, CA 91401-5606, USA

Mills, Kyle (Writer)
c/o Staff Member *Vanguard Press*
387 Park Ave S Fl 12
New York, NY 10016-8810, USA

Mills, Leigh Ann (Athlete, Golfer)
1919 W Carmen St
Tampa, FL 33606-1225, USA

Mills, Mary (Athlete, Golfer)
310 S Ocean Blvd Apt 106
Boca Raton, FL 33432-6207, USA

Mills, Mike (Director)
c/o Blair Kohan *United Talent Agency (UTA)*
9336 Civic Center Dr
Beverly Hills, CA 90210-3604, USA

Mills, Noah (Actor, Model)
c/o Staff Member *Anonymous Content*
3532 Hayden Ave
Culver City, CA 90232-2413, USA

Mills, Pete (Football Player)
Buffalo Bills
27 Langfield Dr
Buffalo, NY 14215-3321, USA

Mills, Stephanie (Actor, Musician)
Associated Booking Corp
1995 Broadway # 501
New York, NY 10023-5882, USA

Mills, Terry (Athlete, Basketball Player)
Indiana Pacers
43786 Cherry Grove Ct E
Canton, MI 48188-5268, USA

Mills, William M (Billy) (Athlete, Track Athlete)
7760 Winding Way
Fair Oaks, CA 95628-5735, USA

Mills, Zach (Actor)
c/o Judy Savage *Savage Agency*
1041 N Formosa Ave
West Hollywood, CA 90046-6703, USA

Millwood, Kevin A (Athlete, Baseball Player)
330 Las Colinas Blvd E Apt 1722
Irving, TX 75039-5819, USA

Milmoe, Caroline (Actor)
Nigel Martin-Smith
41 S King St
Manchester M2 6DE, UNITED KINGDOM (UK)

Milner, Brian (Athlete, Baseball Player)
11825 Elko Ln
Fort Worth, TX 76108-4783, USA

Milner, Eddie (Athlete, Baseball Player)
491 Stambaugh Ave
Columbus, OH 43207-2565, USA

Milonakis, Andy (Actor)
c/o Jason Cunningham *Paradigm*
8942 Wilshire Blvd
Beverly Hills, CA 90211-1908, USA

Milos, Sofia (Actor)
c/o Monique Moss *Integrated PR*
9025 Wilshire Blvd Ste 400
Beverly Hills, CA 90211-1828, USA

Milow, Keith (Artist)
32 W 20th St
New York, NY 10011-4207, USA

Milsap, Ronnie (Musician, Songwriter)
806 N Curtiswood Ln
Nashville, TN 37204-4314, USA

Milstead, Charles (Football Player)
Houston Oilers
150 W Sam Houston Pkwy N APT 1301
Houston, TX 77024-4757, USA

Milstead, Rod (Athlete, Football Player)
11815 Brookeville Landing Ct
Bowie, MD 20721-4502, USA

Milteer, Lee (Business Person, Writer)
Lee Milteer Inc.
2100 Thoroughgood Rd
Virginia Beach, VA 23455-4015, USA

Milton, DeLisha (Basketball Player)
Los Angeles Sparks
1111 S Figueroa St
Staples Center
Los Angeles, CA 90015-1300, USA

Milton, Eric (Athlete, Baseball Player)
1133 Asquith Dr
Arnold, MD 21012-2153, USA

Mimbs, Michael (Athlete, Baseball Player)
2761 Mimbs Rd
Alamo, GA 30411-2502, USA

Mimbs, Mike (Basketball Player)
950 Huntcliffe Ct
Macon, GA 31210-7553, USA

Mimbs, Robert (Athlete, Football Player)
115 Hastings Cres
Regina, SK S4T 7N6, Canada

Mims (Musician)

Mims, Madeline Manning (Athlete, Track Athlete)
7477 E 48th St # 83-4
Tulsa, OK 74145-6679, USA

Min, Gao (Misc)
Olympic Committee
9 Tuyuguan
Beijing, CHINA

Minaj, Nicki (Musician)
c/o Gee Roberson *Blueprint Group*
9348 Civic Center Dr
Beverly Hills, CA 90210-3624, USA

Minarcin, Rudy (Athlete, Baseball Player)
1037 1st St
Vandergrift, PA 15690-1007, USA

Minarik, Henry (Athlete, Football Player)
1001 N Linda Ln Apt A
Lake City, MI 49651-9227, USA

Minaya, Omar (Athlete, Baseball Player, Commentator)
c/o Staff Member *San Diego Padres*
100 Park Blvd
San Diego, CA 92101-7405, USA

Minchey, Nate (Athlete, Baseball Player)
1212 Ramble Creek Dr
Pflugerville, TX 78660-2155, USA

Minchin, Tim (Actor, Comedian)
c/o Max Burgos *Agency for the Performing Arts (APA)*
405 S Beverly Dr Ste 500
Beverly Hills, CA 90212-4425, USA

Mincy, Charles (Athlete, Football Player)
1142 W 79th St
Los Angeles, CA 90044-3508, USA

Mincy, Purnell (Baseball Player)
Philadelphia Stars
127 W 96th St Apt 160
New York, NY 10025-6427, USA

Mindell, Earl (Writer)
Hay House
PO Box 5100
Carlsbad, CA 92018-5100

Mindless Behavior (Music Group)
c/o Troy Carter *Atom Factory/Coalition Media Group*
PO Box 927
Culver City, CA 90232-0927, USA

Minds, Simple (Music Group)
c/o Staff Member *Solo Agency Ltd (UK)*
53-55 Fulham High St
Fl 2
London SW6 3JJ, UNITED KINGDOM

Minear, Tim (Director, Writer)
c/o Lawrence Shuman *Shuman Company*
3815 Hughes Ave Fl 4
Culver City, CA 90232-2715, USA

Mineo, Gordon (Race Car Driver)
Flash Gordon Racing
214 Windy Ln
Rockwall, TX 75087-8005, USA

Miner, Harold (Athlete, Basketball Player)
PO Box 536
Redondo Beach, CA 90277-0536, USA

Miner, Steve (Director)
1137 2nd St Ste 103
Santa Monica, CA 90403-5069, USA

Miner, Zack (Baseball Player)
159 Rudder Cay Way
Jupiter, FL 33458-1612

Minervini, Craig (Athlete, Baseball Player)
229 Cameron Dr
Weston, FL 33326-3515, USA

Minetto, Craig (Athlete, Baseball Player)
1809 Lakeshore Dr
Lodi, CA 95242-4230, USA

Ming, Tsai (Chef)
Food Network
1180 Avenue of the Americas Ste 1220 # 1200
New York, NY 10036-8406, USA

Ming, Yao (Athlete, Basketball Player)
430 Thamer Ln
Houston, TX 77024-6946, USA

Mingenbach, Louise (Designer)
c/o Wayne Fitterman *United Talent Agency (UTA)*
9336 Civic Center Dr
Beverly Hills, CA 90210-3604, USA

Minghella, Max (Actor)
c/o Amanda Silverman *The Lede Company*
401 Broadway Ste 206
New York, NY 10013-3033, USA

Mingo, Barkevious (Athlete, Football Player)

Mingo, Gene (Athlete, Football Player)
5701 E Colorado Ave
Denver, CO 80224-2102, USA

Mingori, Steve (Athlete, Baseball Player)
8841 N Congress Ave Apt 637
Kansas City, MO 64153-1914, USA

Ming Wang, Chien (Athlete, Baseball Player)
c/o Team Member *New York Yankees*
161st St & River Ave
Yankee Stadium
Bronx, NY 10451, USA

Minhaj, Hasan (Comedian, Talk Show Host)
c/o Jennifer Sims *Imprint PR*
375 Hudson St
New York, NY 10014-3658, USA

Miniefield, Kevin (Athlete, Football Player)
1030 Lakehurst Dr
Waukegan, IL 60085-8232, USA

Mink, Rep (Politician)
PO Box 50144
Honolulu, HI 96850-5544

Minka (Adult Film Star)
USP Entertainment Inc
8635 W Sahara Ave # 564
Las Vegas, NV 89117-5858, USA

Minkoff, Rob (Director, Producer)
c/o Lindsay Williams *Gotham Group*
1041 N Formosa Ave # 200
West Hollywood, CA 90046-6703, USA

Minnelli, Liza (Actor, Musician, Producer)
PO Box 50129
Studio City, CA 91614-5013, USA

Minnette, Dylan (Actor)
c/o Jessie Greene *Monster Talent Management*
6333 W 3rd St Ste 912
Los Angeles, CA 90036-3176, USA

Minnick, Don (Athlete, Baseball Player)
1923 Blenheim Rd SW
Roanoke, VA 24015-2902, USA

Minniear, Randy (Athlete, Football Player)
739 Westport Rd
Easton, CT 06612-1537, USA

Minniefield, Dick (Athlete, Basketball Player)
10902 Little Gap Ct
Sugar Land, TX 77498-0946, USA

Minnifield, Chase (Athlete, Football Player)
c/o Brad Blank *Brad Blank & Associates*
1800 Sunset Harbour Dr
#2402
Miami Beach, FL 33139, USA

Minnifield, Frank (Athlete, Football Player)
4809 Chaffey Ln
Lexington, KY 40515-1166, USA

Minnillo Lachey, Vanessa (Actor, Television Host)
c/o Brett Ruttenberg *Imprint PR*
6121 W Sunset Blvd
Neuehouse
Los Angeles, CA 90028-6442, USA

Minogue, Dannii (Actor, Musician)
PO Box 46824
London SW11 3WS, UNITED KINGDOM

Minogue, Kylie (Dancer, Musician)
c/o Terry Blamey *Terry Blamey Management*
PO Box 13196
London SW6 4WF, UNITED KINGDOM (UK)

Minor, Blas (Athlete, Baseball Player)
7139 Dean St
Winton, CA 95388-9766, USA

Minor, Claudie (Athlete, Football Player)
730 17th St Ste 520
Denver, CO 80202-3539, USA

Minor, Damon (Athlete, Baseball Player)
6000 Airline Dr
Metairie, LA 70003-4373, USA

Minor, Gerry (Athlete, Hockey Player)
6516 Jackson Dr
San Diego, CA 92119-3309

Minor, Greg (Athlete, Basketball Player)
6543 Merrick Landing Blvd
Blvd
Windermere, FL 34786-7351, USA

Minor, Jerry (Comedian)
c/o Jennie Cooper-Church *Haven Entertainment*
8111 Beverly Blvd Ste 201
Los Angeles, CA 90048-4531, USA

Minor, Kory (Athlete, Football Player)
1402 W Farlington St
West Covina, CA 91790-3354, USA

Minor, Larry (Race Car Driver)
PO Box 398
San Jacinto, CA 92581-0398, USA

Minor, Lincoln (Athlete, Football Player)
5036 Coldwater Canyon Ave Apt 104
Sherman Oaks, CA 91423-1603, USA

Minor, Mark (Athlete, Basketball Player)
5693 Muldoon Ct
Dublin, OH 43016-4334, USA

Minor, Mike (Baseball Player)
4036 Cottonwood Ct
Lewisburg, TN 37091-6693

Minor, Rickey (Musician)
c/o Staff Member *WME/IMG*
9601 Wilshire Blvd
Beverly Hills, CA 90210-5213, USA

Minor, Ryan (Athlete, Baseball Player)
PO Box 1557
Salisbury, MD 21802-1557, USA

Minor, Shane (Musician)
ESP Mgmt
838 N Doheny Dr Apt 302
West Hollywood, CA 90069-4849, USA

Minor, Travis (Athlete, Football Player)
PO Box 1635
Hallandale, FL 33008-1635, USA

Minoso, Joe (Actor)
c/o Betsy Shepard *Connected Communications*
671 W Division St
Chicago, IL 60610-3533, USA

Minoso, Minnle (Athlete, Baseball Player)
3700 N Lake Shore Dr Apt 303
Chicago, IL 60613-4244, USA

Minow, Newton (Journalist)
375 Palos Rd
Glencoe, IL 60022-1951, USA

Minshall, Jim (Athlete, Baseball Player)
225 Marv Ingles Hwv
Melbourne, KY 41059-8217, USA

Minshew, Alicia (Actor)
c/o Seth Greenky *Green Key Mgmt (NY)*
251 W 89th St Ste 4-A
New York, NY 10024-1712, USA

Mint Condition (Music Group)
c/o Michael Paran *P Music Group*
11511 Vimy Rd
Granada Hills, CA 91344-2138, USA

Minter, Barry (Athlete, Football Player)
2626 Garcitas Crk
Richmond, TX 77406-1961, USA

Minter, Cedric (Athlete, Football Player)
5653 E Bay Trail Ct
Boise, ID 83716-7031, USA

Minter, Kelly (Actor)
c/o John Ly *John Ly Agency*
1601 N Gower St Ste 202
Hollywood, CA 90028-7598, USA

Minter, Kevin (Athlete, Football Player)
c/o Joel Segal *Lagardere Unlimited (NY)*
456 Washington St Apt 9L
New York, NY 10013-1555, USA

Minter, Kristin (Actor)
c/o Joshua Edwards *E Cubed Management*
928 S Broadway Apt 545
Los Angeles, CA 90015-4568, USA

Minter, Mike (Athlete, Football Player)
3661 Richwood Cir
Kannapolis, NC 28081-6704, USA

Minton, Greg (Athlete, Baseball Player)
4614 E Monte Way
Phoenix, AZ 85044-5597, USA

Mintz, Shiomo (Musician)
I C M Artists
40 W 57th St
New York, NY 10019-4001, USA

Mintz, Steve (Athlete, Baseball Player)
Fort Myers Miracle 14400 Six Mile Cypress Pkwy A
Fort Myers, FL 33912-4326, USA

Mintz-Plasse, Christopher (Actor)
c/o Peter Principato *Artists First*
9465 Wilshire Blvd Ste 900
Beverly Hills, CA 90212-2608, USA

Minus the Bear (Music Group)
c/o Craig Mogil *WME/IMG*
9601 Wilshire Blvd
Beverly Hills, CA 90210-5213, USA

Minutelli, Gino (Athlete, Baseball Player)
3305 Foxtrot Ct
Spring Hill, TN 37174-7116, USA

Mio, Eddie (Athlete, Hockey Player)
PO Box 252745
West Bloomfield, MI 48325-2745

Miou-Miou (Actor)
VMA
20 Ave Rapp
Paris 75008, FRANCE

Mir, Isabelle (Athlete, Skier)
Saint-Lary 65170, France

Mira, George (Athlete, Football Player)
19225 SW 128th Ct
Miami, FL 33177-4222, USA

Mirabella, Erin (Athlete, Cycler, Olympic Athlete)
914 N Idaho St
La Habra, CA 90631, USA

Mirabella, Paul (Athlete, Baseball Player)
125 Jenks Rd
Morristown, NJ 07960-8701, USA

Mirabelli, Doug (Athlete, Baseball Player)
9788 Edgewood Ave
Traverse City, MI 49685-8173, USA

Miraldi, Dean (Athlete, Football Player)
14015 Live Oak Ln
Grass Valley, CA 95945-9509, USA

Miranda, Christianne (Musician, Songwriter, Writer)
c/o Staff Member *Kult Records*
38 W 36th St Fl 3
New York, NY 10018-8078, USA

Miranda, Lin-Manuel (Actor, Dancer, Musician, Producer)
The Drama Book Shop Inc
213 W 40th St Fl 4
New York, NY 10018-1680, USA

Miranda, Patricia (Wrestler)
Stanford Wrestling - Department of Athletics
Stanford University
Arrillaga Family Sports Center
Stanford, CA 94305-6150, USA

Miranda, Paula (Actor)
c/o Paul Greenstone *Paul Greenstone Entertainment*
1400 California Ave Apt 201
Santa Monica, CA 90403-4395, USA

Mirchoff, Beau (Actor)
c/o Jessica Katz *Katz Public Relations*
14527 Dickens St
Sherman Oaks, CA 91403-3756, USA

Mirer, Rick (Athlete, Football Player)
PO Box 3422
Rancho Santa Fe, CA 92067-3422, USA

Mirich, Rex (Athlete, Football Player)
PO Box 645
Oracle, AZ 85623-0645, USA

Mirikitani, Janice (Writer)
Glide Memorial United Methodist Church
330 Ellis St
San Francisco, CA 94102-2735, USA

Mirisch, Walter M (Producer)
647 Warner Ave
Los Angeles, CA 90024-2566, USA

Mirkerevic, Dragen (Prime Minister)
Premier's Office
Vojvode Putnkia 3
Sarajevo 71000, BOSNIA & HERZEGOVINA

Mirkin, David (Actor, Director)
c/o David Gersh *Gersh*
9465 Wilshire Blvd Ste 600
Beverly Hills, CA 90212-2605, USA

Mirman, Eugene (Actor, Comedian)
c/o David Martin *Avalon Management*
9171 Wilshire Blvd Ste 320
Beverly Hills, CA 90210-5516, USA

Mirnyi, Max (Athlete, Tennis Player)
c/o Staff Member *ATP Tour*
201 Atp Tour Blvd
Ponte Vedra Beach, FL 32082-3211, USA

Mironov, Boris (Athlete, Hockey Player)
110 E Parsonage Way
Manalapan, NJ 07726-7949

Mironov, Dmitri (Athlete, Hockey Player)
2911 Bayview Ave
North York, ON M2K 1E8, Canada

Mironov, Yevgeniy V (Actor)
Oleg Tabajiv Theater
Chaokygina Str 12A
Moscow, RUSSIA

Miroslav, Frycer (Athlete)
Frycer Sports Agency Pelclova 5
Ostrava 702 00, Czech Republic

Mirra, Dave (Athlete)
Wasserman Media Group, LLC
12100 W Olympic Blvd Ste 400
Los Angeles, CA 90064-1052, USA

Mirren, Helen (Actor, Director, Producer)
c/o Katie Feldman *Stan Rosenfield & Associates*
2029 Century Park E Ste 1190
Los Angeles, CA 90067-2931, USA

Mirzoev, Akbar (Prime Minister)
Prime Minister's Office
Dushaube, TAJIKISTAN

Misaka, Walt (Athlete, Basketball Player)
173 W Aruba Dr
Saratoga Springs, UT 84045-5115, USA

Misaka, Wataru (Athlete, Basketball Player)
288 E 2450 S
Bountiful, UT 84010-5638, USA

Misch, Patrick (Athlete, Baseball Player)
725 N Dobson Rd Apt 255
Chandler, AZ 85224-9110, USA

Mischak, Bob (Athlete, Football Player)
73 Brookwood Rd Unit 12
Orinda, CA 94563-3310, USA

Mischke, Carl H (Religious Leader)
1034 Buena Vista Dr
Sun Prairie, WI 53590-2031, USA

Misersky, Antje (Athlete)
Grenzgraben 3A
Stutzerbach 98714, GERMANY

Misi, Koa (Athlete, Football Player)
c/o Ken Zuckerman *Priority Sports & Entertainment - (LA)*
15233 Ventura Blvd Ste 718
Sherman Oaks, CA 91403-2237, USA

Misiano, Christopher (Director)
c/o Staff Member *Creative Artists Agency (CAA)*
2000 Avenue of the Stars Ste 100
Los Angeles, CA 90067-4705, USA

Misiano, Vincent (Director)
c/o Staff Member *Creative Artists Agency (CAA)*
2000 Avenue of the Stars Ste 100
Los Angeles, CA 90067-4705, USA

Misko, John (Athlete, Football Player)
33252 Tule Oak Dr
Springville, CA 93265-9636, USA

Misner, Ivan (Business Person)
BNI
11525 N Community House Rd Ste 475
Charlotte, NC 28277-0776, USA

Mison, Tom (Actor)
c/o Staff Member *42 Management (UK)*
8 Flitcroft St
London WC2H 8DL, UNITED KINGDOM

Missick, Dorian (Actor)
c/o Myrna Jacoby *MJ Management*
130 W 57th St Apt 11A
New York, NY 10019-3311, USA

Missick, Simone (Actor)
c/o Jessica Cohen *JCPR*
9903 Santa Monica Blvd # 983
Beverly Hills, CA 90212-1671, USA

Mistler, John (Athlete, Football Player)
3111 E Desert Flower Ln
Phoenix, AZ 85048-8331, USA

Mistral, Fernanda (Actor)
c/o Staff Member *Telefe (Argentina)*
Pavon 2444
Buenos Aires C1248AAT, ARGENTINA

Mistry, Jimi (Actor)
c/o Staff Member *WME|IMG*
9601 Wilshire Blvd
Beverly Hills, CA 90210-5213, USA

Misuraca, Mike (Athlete, Baseball Player)
250 N College Park Dr Apt F26
Upland, CA 91786-9467, USA

Miszuk, John (Athlete, Hockey Player)
4 Willowglen Crt
Dundas, ON L9H 6Z9, CANADA

Mitchell, Aaron (Athlete, Football Player)
3613 Frankford Rd Apt 738
Dallas, TX 75287-6142, USA

Mitchell, Andrea (Correspondent, Journalist)
2710 Chain Bridge Rd NW
Washington, DC 20016-3404, USA

Mitchell, Basil (Athlete, Football Player)
806 Baker Ave
Mount Pleasant, TX 75455-4846, USA

Mitchell, Betsy (Athlete, Olympic Athlete, Swimmer)
Laurel High School
1 Lyman Cir Ofc Athletic
Beachwood, OH 44122-2110, USA

Mitchell, Beverley (Actor)
c/o Nicki Fioravante *Viewpoint Inc*
8820 Wilshire Blvd Ste 220
Beverly Hills, CA 90211-2622, USA

Mitchell, Bobby (Athlete, Baseball Player)
8697 Tiogawoods Dr
Sacramento, CA 95828-5116, USA

Mitchell, Bobby (Athlete, Baseball Player)
13887 Torrey Bella Ct
San Diego, CA 92129-4628, USA

Mitchell, Bobby (Athlete, Football Player)
450 Blue Beech Way
Chesapeake, VA 23320-3812, USA

Mitchell, Bobby (Athlete, Golfer)
435 Wimbish Dr
Danville, VA 24541-5823, USA

Mitchell, Brandon (Athlete, Football Player)
806 Schlessinger St
Abbeville, LA 70510-7050, USA

Mitchell, Brian (Actor)
5307B Wilkinson Ave Unit 20
Valley Village, CA 91607-2464, USA

Mitchell, Brian (Athlete, Football Player)
5435 Chandley Farm Cir
Centreville, VA 20120-1240, USA

Mitchell, Brian (Athlete, Football Player)
1205 Addison Ct
Winterville, NC 28590-9641, USA

Mitchell, Brian Stokes (Actor, Musician)
243 W 98th St Apt 5C
New York, NY 10025-5566, USA

Mitchell, Charlie (Athlete, Baseball Player)
5017 Hasty Dr
Nashville, TN 37211-5345, USA

Mitchell, Charlie (Athlete, Football Player)
6300 Seward Park Ave S
Seattle, WA 98118-3055, USA

Mitchell, Craig (Athlete, Baseball Player)
PO Box 174
Elk, CA 95432-0174, USA

Mitchell, Dale (Athlete, Football Player)
1837 Tanner Ave SW
Canton, OH 44706-2623, USA

Mitchell, Daryl (Chill) (Actor)
c/o Danica Smith *Kovert Creative*
506 Santa Monica Blvd Ste 400
Santa Monica, CA 90401-2412, USA

Mitchell, David (Actor)
c/o Michele Milburn *Milburn Browning Associates*
91, Brick Lane
The Old Truman Brewery
London E1 6QL, UNITED KINGDOM

Mitchell, David Robert (Actor)
c/o Maha Dakhil *Creative Artists Agency (CAA)*
2000 Avenue of the Stars Ste 100
Los Angeles, CA 90067-4705, USA

Mitchell, Donald (Athlete, Football Player)
5620 Minner Dr
Beaumont, TX 77708-4515, USA

Mitchell, Earl (Athlete, Football Player)
c/o Brad Leshnock *BTI Sports Advisors*
615 South Blvd Apt C
Oak Park, IL 60302-4606, USA

Mitchell, Elizabeth (Actor)
c/o Ben Levine *LINK Entertainment*
11872 La Grange Ave
Los Angeles, CA 90025-5282, USA

Mitchell, Elvis (Producer, Radio Personality, Writer)
KCRW
1900 Pico Blvd
Santa Monica, CA 90405-1628, USA

Mitchell, Freddie (Athlete, Football Player)
606 N Brunnell Pkwy
Lakeland, FL 33815-1258, USA

Mitchell, George (Politician)
151 Crandon Blvd Apt 110
Key Biscayne, FL 33149-1529, USA

Mitchell, George J (Politician, Senator)
DLA Piper Rudnick Gray Cary
1251 Avenue of the Americas Ste C2-75
New York, NY 10020-0073, USA

Mitchell, Jason (Actor)
c/o Allison Garman *Rogers & Cowan*
1840 Century Park E Fl 18
Los Angeles, CA 90067-2101, USA

Mitchell, Jeff (Athlete, Football Player)
12151 Roseland Dr
New Port Richey, FL 34654-6323, USA

Mitchell, Jeff (Athlete, Hockey Player)
Suburban Hockey Schools
23995 Freeway Park Dr Ste 200
Farmington Hills, MI 48335-2829

Mitchell, Jessie (Baseball Player)
Birmingham Black Barons
124 Dugan Ave Apt A
Birmingham, AL 35214-5182, USA

Mitchell, Jim H (Athlete, Football Player)
120 Twin Creek Ter
Forest, VA 24551-1328, USA

Mitchell, John (Athlete, Baseball Player)
5017 Hasty Dr
Nashville, TN 37211-5345, USA

mitchell, John (Athlete, Basketball Player)
1708 Castleberry Way
Birmingham, AL 35214-4826, USA

Mitchell, John Cameron (Actor, Director)
c/o Craig Gering *Creative Artists Agency (CAA)*
2000 Avenue of the Stars Ste 100
Los Angeles, CA 90067-4705, USA

Mitchell, Johnny (Athlete, Football Player)
8721 S Normal Ave
Chicago, IL 60620-2119, USA

Mitchell, Joni (Musician)
c/o Alisse Kingsley *Muse Media*
115 1/2 N Larchmont Blvd
Los Angeles, CA 90004-3704, USA

Mitchell, Kawika (Athlete, Football Player)
971 N Lake Sybelia Dr
Maitland, FL 32751-4811, USA

Mitchell, Keith (Athlete, Baseball Player)
731 S 42nd St
San Diego, CA 92113-1813, USA

Mitchell, Keith C (Prime Minister)
Ministerial Complex 6th Fl
Botanical Gardens
Saint George's, GRENADA

Mitchell, Kel (Actor)
c/o Caitlin Scott *PMK/BNC Public Relations*
1840 Century Park E Ste 1400
Los Angeles, CA 90067-2115, USA

Mitchell, Ken (Athlete, Football Player)
504 Clifton Rd
Crescent City, FL 32112-5404, USA

Mitchell, Kenneth (Actor)

Mitchell, Kevin (Athlete, Baseball Player)
3869 Ocean View Blvd
San Diego, CA 92113-1736, USA

Mitchell, Kim (Musician)
41 Britain St.
#305
Toronto, ON M5A 1R7, Canada

Mitchell, Kirsty (Actor)
c/o Tracy Curtis *Grit Artists*
3770 Highland Ave Ste 201
Manhattan Beach, CA 90266-3279, USA

Mitchell, Larry (Athlete, Baseball Player)
1040 Preston Ave
Charlottesville, VA 22903-2109, USA

Mitchell, Leroy (Athlete, Football Player)
6598 Pinewood Dr
Parker, CO 80134-6356, USA

Mitchell, Luke (Actor)
c/o Gabriel Cohen *Management 360*
9111 Wilshire Blvd
Beverly Hills, CA 90210-5508, USA

Mitchell, Lydell D (Athlete, Football Player)
702 Reservoir St
Baltimore, MD 21217-4632, USA

Mitchell, Mack (Athlete, Football Player)
1200 Maynard St
Diboll, TX 75941-2602, USA

Mitchell, Maia (Actor, Musician)
c/o Peter McGrath *Echo Lake Management*
421 S Beverly Dr Fl 8
Beverly Hills, CA 90212-4408, USA

Mitchell, Michael (Actor)

Mitchell, Mike (Director)
c/o Gregory McKnight *United Talent Agency (UTA)*
9336 Civic Center Dr
Beverly Hills, CA 90210-3604, USA

Mitchell, Murray (Athlete, Basketball Player)
401 Northshore Blvd Apt 905
Portland, TX 78374-3807, USA

Mitchell, Paul (Athlete, Baseball Player)
23 Carr Rd
Berlin, MA 01503-1116, USA

Mitchell, Penelope (Actor)
c/o Stacy O'Neil *Brillstein Entertainment Partners*
9150 Wilshire Blvd Ste 350
Beverly Hills, CA 90212-3453, USA

Mitchell, Pete (Athlete, Football Player)
100 Paddock Pl
Ponte Vedra Beach, FL 32082-3957, USA

Mitchell, Radha (Actor)
c/o Staff Member *Summit Business Management Inc*
16255 Ventura Blvd Ste 625
Encino, CA 91436-2307, USA

Mitchell, Rick (DJ)
c/o Staff Member *Diva Central Inc*
7510 W Sunset Blvd # 1445
Los Angeles, CA 90046-3408, USA

Mitchell, Robert (Athlete, Baseball Player)
Cleveland Buckeyes
2009 Elmwood Ave
Tampa, FL 33605-6625, USA

Mitchell, Roger (Director, Producer)
c/o Beth Swofford *Creative Artists Agency (CAA)*
2000 Avenue of the Stars Ste 100
Los Angeles, CA 90067-4705, USA

Mitchell, Roger (Athlete, Football Player)
Chaminade-Madonna College Prep
500 E Chaminade Dr
Hollywood, FL 33021-5853, USA

Mitchell, Roland (Athlete, Football Player)
PO Box 5701
Lake Charles, LA 70606-5701, USA

Mitchell, Roy (Athlete, Hockey Player)
4844 N Tredwell Way
Boise, ID 83703-2779

Mitchell, Russ (Correspondent, Television Host)
c/o Staff Member *CBS News (NY)*
524 W 57th St Fl 8
New York, NY 10019-2930, USA

Mitchell, Sam (Athlete, Basketball Player, Coach)
2349 Rugby Ave
Atlanta, GA 30337-1020, USA

Mitchell, Sasha (Actor)
c/o Kathy McComb *Kathy McComb Management*
10630 1/2 Landale St
Toluca Lake, CA 91602-2317, USA

Mitchell, Scott (Athlete, Football Player)
5060 Franklin Rd
Bloomfield Hills, MI 48302-2614, USA

Mitchell, Shareen (Actor)
J Michael Bloom
9255 W Sunset Blvd Ste 710
Los Angeles, CA 90069-3304, USA

Mitchell, Shay (Actor)
c/o Michael Geiser *Jill Fritzo Public Relations*
208 E 51st St # 305
New York, NY 10022-6557, USA

Mitchell, Silas Weir (Actor)
2340 Ronda Vista Dr
Los Angeles, CA 90027-4644, USA

Mitchell, Steve (Actor)
c/o Staff Member *Select Artists Ltd (CA-Westside Office)*
1138 12th St Apt 1
Santa Monica, CA 90403-5459, USA

Mitchell, Susan (Writer)
Florida Atlantic University
English Dept
Boca Raton, FL 33431, USA

Mitchell, Todd (Athlete, Basketball Player)
8000 Quarry Rd
Maumee, OH 43537-9472, USA

Mitchell, Tom (Athlete, Football Player)
1421 SW 49th Ter
Cape Coral, FL 33914-6934, USA

Mitchell, Vernessa (Musician)
c/o Staff Member *Diva Central Inc*
7510 W Sunset Blvd # 1445
Los Angeles, CA 90046-3408, USA

Mitchum, Carrie (Actor)
Camden ITG Talent
1501 Main St Ste 204
Venice, CA 90291-3699, USA

Mitichyan, Roman (Athlete, Mixed Martial Arts, Wrestler)
c/o Noelle Kim *National Talent LA*
7041 Yolanda Ave
Reseda, CA 91335-4014, USA

Mitra, Rhona (Actor)
c/o Jason Weinberg *Untitled Entertainment*
350 S Beverly Dr Ste 200
Beverly Hills, CA 90212-4819, USA

Mitre, Santiago (Director)
c/o Nick Shumaker *United Talent Agency (UTA)*
888 7th Ave Fl 7
New York, NY 10106-0700, USA

Mitre, Sergio (Athlete, Baseball Player)
1707 Summer Sky St
Chula Vista, CA 91915-1846, USA

Mitrione, Matt (Athlete, Football Player)
729 Toddsbury Ln
Richmond, IN 47374-7152, USA

Mitsotakis, Constantine (Prime Minister)
1 Aravantinou St
Athens 106 74, GREECE

Mitsoula, Jana (Actor)
Collingwood Management Inc
300-100 Pender St E
c/o Dylan Thomas Collingwood #
Vancouver, BC V6A 1T3, CANADA

Mitta, Aleksander N (Director)
Malaya Gruzinskaya Str 28
#105
Moscow 123557, RUSSIA

Mittal, Lakshmi (Business Person)
LNM Group
15th Floor
Hofplein 20
Rotterdam 03032, NETHERLANDS

Mitte, RJ (Actor)
c/o Liza Anderson *Anderson Group Public Relations*
8060 Melrose Ave Fl 4
Los Angeles, CA 90046-7038, USA

Mittermaier-Neureuther, Rosi (Skier)
Winkelmoosalm
Reit Im Winkel 83242, GERMANY

Mittermayer, Tatjana (Skier)
Bucha 2A
Lenggries, GERMANY

Mitterwald, George (Athlete, Baseball Player)
5314 Kenyon Rd
Orlando, FL 32810-1714, USA

Mitts, Heather (Soccer Player)
US Soccer/ Heather Mitts
18400 Avalon Blvd Ste 500
Carson, CA 90746-2183, USA

Mitz, Alonzo (Athlete, Football Player)
2609 NE 4th St Apt 216
Renton, WA 98056-4053, USA

Mitzelfeld, Jim (Journalist)
969 N Lebanon St
Arlington, VA 22205-1455, USA

Mix, Bryant (Athlete, Football Player)
37 Greenwood Plantation Rd
Natchez, MS 39120-8946, USA

Mix, Ronald J (Ron) (Athlete, Football Player)
2317 Caminito Recodo
San Diego, CA 92107-1529, USA

Mix, Steve (Athlete, Basketball Player)
508 N Valencia Cir SW
Vero Beach, FL 32968-6009, USA

Mix Master Mike (DJ)
c/o Staff Member *UTA Music/The Agency Group (UK)*
361-373 City Rd
London EC1V 1PQ, UNITED KINGDOM

Mixon, Joe (Athlete, Football Player)
c/o Peter Schaffer *Authentic Athletix*
400 S Steele St Unit 47
Denver, CO 80209-3535, USA

Mixon, Katy (Actor)
c/o Larry Taube *Principal Entertainment*
9255 W Sunset Blvd Ste 500
Los Angeles, CA 90069-3301, USA

Mixon, Ken (Athlete, Football Player)
12741 Kapok Ln
Davie, FL 33330-5201, USA

Mixon, Wayne (Politician)
2219 Demeron Rd
Tallahassee, FL 32308-0943, USA

Miyavi (Actor, Musician)
c/o Christine Tripicchio *Shelter PR*
5670 Wilshire Blvd Ste 1200
Los Angeles, CA 90036-5621, USA

Miyazaki, Hayao (Animator)
c/o Staff Member *Studio Ghibli*
1-4-25 Kajino-cho
Koganei-shi
Tokyo 184-0002, JAPAN

Miyazawa, Kiichi (Prime Minister)
6-34-1 Jingu-Mae
Shibuyaku
Tokyo 00150, JAPAN

Mize, Larry (Athlete, Golfer)
106 Graystone Ct
Columbus, GA 31904-4300, USA

Mizerock, John (Athlete, Baseball Player, Coach)
2297 Juneau Rd
Punxsutawney, PA 15767-9428, USA

Mizrahi, Isaac (Fashion Designer, Television Host)
Isaac Mizrahi Studio
475 10th Ave Fl 4
New York, NY 10018-1120, USA

Mizrahie, Barbara (Athlete, Golfer)
6440 Park Lake Cir
Boynton Beach, FL 33437-3228, USA

Mizuno, Sonoya (Actor)
c/o Ciara Parkes *Public Eye Communications*
535 Kings Rd
#313 Plaza
London SW10 0SZ, UNITED KINGDOM

Mkapa, Benjamin William (President)
President's Office
State House
PO Box 9120
Dar es Salaam, TANZANIA

Mlambo, Sibongile (Actor)
c/o Laura Gibson *Generate Management*
8750 Wilshire Blvd Ste 200
Beverly Hills, CA 90211-2707, USA

M. Landry, Jeffrey (Congressman, Politician)
206 Cannon Hob
Washington, DC 20515-3801, USA

M. Levin, Sander (Congressman, Politician)
1236 Longworth Hob
Washington, DC 20515-2503, USA

Mlicki, Dave (Athlete, Baseball Player)
8100 Tillinghast Dr
Dublin, OH 43017-8843, USA

Mlkvy, Bill (Athlete, Basketball Player)
586 Linton Hill Rd
Newtown, PA 18940-1204, USA

Mlneta, Norman (Politician)
1631 Cliff Dr
Edgewater, MD 21037-4922, USA

Mlnner, Ruth (Politician)
1056 Church Hill Rd
Milford, DE 19963-5539, USA

M. Lowey, Nita (Congressman, Politician)
2365 Rayburn Hob
Washington, DC 20515-2308, USA

M. Lumis, Cynthia (Congressman, Politician)
113 Cannon Hob
Washington, DC 20515-3512, USA

Mmahat, Kevin (Athlete, Baseball Player)
5500 Erlanger Rd
Kenner, LA 70065-1534, USA

Mnouchkine, Ariane (Director)
Theater du Soleil
Cartoucherie
Paris 75012, FRANCE

Moaddi, Peyman (Actor)
c/o Shelley Browning *Magnolia Entertainment*
9595 Wilshire Blvd Ste 601
Beverly Hills, CA 90212-2506, USA

Moakler, Shanna (Actor, Model, Reality Star)
c/o Carlos Martinez *Scribe Services Public Relations*
4445 Cartwright Ave Apt 102
Toluca Lake, CA 91602-2326, USA

Moates, Dave (Athlete, Baseball Player)
1215 30th St W
Bradenton, FL 34205-3259, USA

Moats, Arthur (Athlete, Football Player)
c/o Drew Rosenhaus *Rosenhaus Sports Representation*
3921 Alton Rd # 440
Miami Beach, FL 33140-3852, USA

Moats, David (Journalist)
Rutland Herald
PO Box 668
Editorial Dept
Rutland, VT 05702-0668, USA

Mobb Deep (Music Group)
c/o Staff Member *Interscope Records*
1755 Broadway Fl 6
New York, NY 10019-3768, USA

Mobley, Cuttino (Athlete, Basketball Player)
11706 Empress Oaks Ct
Houston, TX 77082-6842, USA

Mobley, Singor (Athlete, Football Player)
2123 US Highway 80 E
Mesquite, TX 75150-5549, USA

Moby (Musician)
Deutsch-Ebgkuscge Freundschaft
51 Lonsdale Rd
London NW6 6RA, UNITED KINGDOM

Moceanu, Dominique (Gymnast)
211 Walden Ridge Dr
Hinckley, OH 44233-9001, USA

Mochrie, Colin (Actor)
c/o Staff Member *Jeff Andrews Entertainment*
50 Rosehill Ave Suite 1811
Toronto, ON M4T 1G6, CANADA

Mochrie, Dottie (Athlete, Golfer)
15 Blazing Star Trl
Landrum, SC 29356-3305, USA

Mock, Garrett (Athlete, Baseball Player)
13850 Maisemore Rd
Houston, TX 77015-2303, USA

Mock, Janet (Writer)
c/o Michael Cohen *PMK/BNC Public Relations*
622 3rd Ave Fl 8
New York, NY 10017-6707, USA

Mockett, Cathy (Athlete, Golfer)
3143 Madeira Ave
Costa Mesa, CA 92626-2323, USA

Mocumbi, Pascoal (Prime Minister)
Prime Minister's Office
Avenida Julius Nyerere 1780
Maputo, MOZAMBIQUE

Moczynski, Betty (Athlete, Baseball Player, Commentator)
4912 S 19th St Apt B
Milwaukee, WI 53221-2830, USA

Modano, Mike (Athlete, Hockey Player, Olympic Athlete)
10114 E Hualapai Dr
Scottsdale, AZ 85255-7167, USA

Modean, Jayne (Actor)
6145 Estates Dr
Piedmont, CA 94611-3117, USA

Modin, Fredrik (Athlete, Hockey Player)
8955 Dunn Ct
Dublin, OH 43017-8880, USA

Modine, Matthew (Actor, Director, Producer)
420 W 25th St Apt 9C
New York, NY 10001-6554, USA

Modrow, Hans (Prime Minister)
Frankfurter Tor 6
Berlin 10243, GERMANY

Modry, Jaroslav (Athlete, Hockey Player)
7 Castle Ct
Albany, NY 12211-1910

Moe (Music Group)
c/o Staff Member *Paradigm (Monterey)*
404 W Franklin St
Monterey, CA 93940-2303, USA

moe. (Music Group)
45 Hadlock Rd
Falmouth, ME 04105-2559, USA

Moe, Douglas E (Doug) (Athlete, Basketball Player)
13 Arnold Palmer
San Antonio, TX 78257-1722, USA

Moeaki, Tony (Athlete, Football Player)

Moegle, Dickey (Athlete, Football Player)
4207 Deforest Ridge Cir
Katy, TX 77494-4444, USA

Moehler, Brian (Athlete, Baseball Player)
4492 Belvedere Pl SE
Marietta, GA 30067-4066, USA

Moe-Humphreys, Karen (Swimmer)
505 Augusta Dr
Moraga, CA 94556-3004, USA

Moeller, Chad (Athlete, Baseball Player)
11058 E Raintree Dr
Scottsdale, AZ 85255-1809, USA

Moeller, Dennis (Athlete, Baseball Player)
2324 Ridgemont Dr
Birmingham, AL 35244-1219, USA

Moeller, Edward (Athlete, Basketball Player)
5301 Creedmoor Rd Apt 502
Raleigh, NC 27612-3833, USA

Moeller, Joe (Athlete, Baseball Player)
1505 Avenida De Nogales
San Clemente, CA 92672-9464, USA

Moeller, Ron (Athlete, Baseball Player)
7355 Appleridge Ct
Cincinnati, OH 45247-5055, USA

Moen, Travis (Athlete, Hockey Player)
Newport Sports Management
400-201 City Centre Dr
Attn Don Meehan
Mississauga, ON L5B 2T4, Canada

Moennig, Katherine (Actor)
c/o Peg Donegan *Framework Entertainment*
9057 Nemo St # C
W Hollywood, CA 90069-5511, USA

Moers, Walter (Writer)
c/o Staff Member *The Overlook Press*
195 Broadway Fl 9
New York, NY 10007-3122, USA

Moesta-Anderson, Rebecca (Writer)
Anderzone
PO Box 767
Monument, CO 80132-0767, USA

Moffat, Alex (Comedian)
c/o Marisa Paonessa *Paonessa Talent Agency*
1512 N Fremont St Ste 105
Chicago, IL 60642-2567, USA

Moffat, Katherine (Kitty) (Actor)
Henderson/Hogan
8285 W Sunset Blvd Ste 1
West Hollywood, CA 90046-2420, USA

Moffat, Lyle (Athlete, Hockey Player)
111-1027 Pandora Ave
Victoria, BC V8V 3P6, Canada

Moffat, Mike (Athlete, Hockey Player)
17 Riverbend Rd
Markham, ON L3R 1K4

Moffat, Steven (Writer)
c/o Charles (Charlie) Ferraro *United Talent Agency (UTA)*
9336 Civic Center Dr
Beverly Hills, CA 90210-3604, USA

Moffatt, Katy (Musician, Songwriter)
7 Ryan Cir
Lebanon, IL 62254-1948, USA

Moffet, Jane (Athlete, Baseball Player, Commentator)
2737 Lime Bluff Rd
Muncy, PA 17756-7801, USA

Moffett, D W (Actor)
Three Arts Entertainment
9460 Wilshire Blvd Ste 700
Beverly Hills, CA 90212-2713, USA

Moffett, James R (Business Person)
Freeport-McMoRan Inc
1615 Poydras St Ste 1746
New Orleans, LA 70112-1280, USA

Moffett, Tim (Athlete, Football Player)
115 County Road 213
Oxford, MS 38655-8855, USA

Moffitt, Randy (Athlete, Baseball Player)
1725 Baltic Ave
Prescott, AZ 86301-6501, USA

Mofford, Ian (Athlete, Football Player)
PO Box 1158
Waitsfield, VT 05673-1158, USA

Mogae, Festus G (President)
President's Office
State House
Private Bag 001
Gaborone, BOTSWANA

Mogenburg, Dietmar (Athlete, Track Athlete)
Alter Garfen 34
Leverkusen 51371, GERMANY

Moger, Sandy (Athlete, Hockey Player)
Vernon Minor Hockey Association
PO Box 1894 Stn Main
Vernon, BC V1T 8Z7, Canada

Mogilevsky, Evgeny (Musician)
Columbia Artists Mgmt Inc
165 W 57th St
New York, NY 10019-2201, USA

Mogilny, Alexander (Athlete, Hockey Player)
27543 Pacific Coast Hwy
Malibu, CA 90265-4339, USA

MoHair (Music Group)
c/o Staff Member *Paradigm (Monterey)*
404 W Franklin St
Monterey, CA 93940-2303, USA

Mohamed, Mike (Athlete, Football Player)
c/o Doug Hendrickson *Relativity Sports*
2029 Century Park E Ste 1550
Century City, CA 90067-3000, USA

Mohler, Mike (Athlete, Baseball Player)
1627 S Shirley Ave
Gonzales, LA 70737-3917, USA

Mohoney, John (Actor)
International Creative Mgmt
8942 Wilshire Blvd # 219
Beverly Hills, CA 90211-1908, USA

Mohoney, Roger (Cartoonist)
c/o Staff Member *King Features Syndication*
300 W 57th St Fl 15
New York, NY 10019-5238, USA

Mohony, Roger Cardinal (Religious Leader)
Archdiocese of Los Angeles
3424 Wilshire Blvd
Los Angeles, CA 90010-2241, USA

Mohorcic, Dale (Athlete, Baseball Player)
15501 Rockside Rd
Maple Heights, OH 44137-3948, USA

Mohoric, Dale (Athlete, Baseball Player)
250 S Ogden St
Buffalo, NY 14206-3523, USA

Mohr, Chris (Athlete, Football Player)
PO Box 1232
Thomson, GA 30824-1232, USA

Mohr, Dustan (Athlete, Baseball Player)
103 Parkwood Dr
Hattiesburg, MS 39402-2217, USA

Mohr, Jay (Actor, Comedian)
c/o Staff Member *Giraffe Productions*
225 W 34th St Ste 2000
New York, NY 10122-2000, USA

Mohr, Todd (Musician)
Morris Bliessner
1658 York St
Denver, CO 80206-1410, USA

Mohri, Dr Mamoru (Astronaut)
NASDA, Tsukuba Space Center 2-1-1, Sengen, Tububa-shi General Manager's Office
Ibaraki, Japar 00305, USA

Mohri, Mamoru (Astronaut)
NASDA
2-1-2 Sengen
Tukubashi
Ibaraki 00305, JAPAN

Moiler, Randy (Athlete, Hockey Player)
3950 NW 23rd Ter
Boca Raton, FL 33431-5405

Moine, Marc Forne (President)
President's Office
Casa de la Valle
Andorra la Vella, ANDORRA

Moir, Richard (Actor)
Shanahan Mgmt
PO Box 1509
Darlinghurst, NSW 01300, AUSTRALIA

Moisan, Bill (Athlete, Baseball Player)
PO Box 41
Newton, NH 03858-0041, USA

Moise, Patty (Race Car Driver)
Atkins Motorsports
222 Raceway Dr
Mooresville, NC 28117-6510, USA

Moiseyev, Jack (Horse Racer)
499 Scotland Dr
Jackson, NJ 08527-1188, USA

Mojsiejenko, Ralf (Athlete, Football Player)
11334 Baldwin Rd
Bridgman, MI 49106-9727, USA

Mojslejenko, Ralf (Athlete, Football Player)
11334 Baldwin Rd
Bridgman, MI 49106-9727, USA

Mok, Karen (Actor)
c/o Staff Member *Creative Artists Agency (CAA)*
2000 Avenue of the Stars Ste 100
Los Angeles, CA 90067-4705, USA

Mok, Ken (Director, Producer)
c/o Steve Wohl *Paradigm*
8942 Wilshire Blvd
Beverly Hills, CA 90211-1908, USA

Mokeski, Paul (Athlete, Basketball Player)
4004 Crestwood Dr
Carrollton, TX 75007-1645, USA

Mokosak, Carl (Athlete, Hockey Player)
2815 Central Park Way NE APT 201
Grand Rapids, MI 49505-3485

Mol, Gretchen (Actor)
c/o John Carrabino *John Carrabino Management*
5900 Wilshire Blvd Ste 740
Los Angeles, CA 90036-5032, USA

Molale, Brandon (Actor)
c/o Staff Member *DDC Entertainment*
1129 2nd St
Hermosa Beach, CA 90254-5336, USA

Molden, Alex (Athlete, Football Player)
2083 Wellington Dr
West Linn, OR 97068-3663, USA

Mole, Fenton (Athlete, Baseball Player)
2741 Diamond St
San Francisco, CA 94131-3003, USA

Moler, Jason (Athlete, Baseball Player, Olympic Athlete)
2918 Ranch Road 620 N Unit 281
Austin, TX 78734-2269, USA

Molfentcer, Henning (Producer)
c/o Staff Member *Babelsberg Film*
August-Bebelstr. 26-53
Potsdam 14482, Germany

Molin, Lars (Athlete, Hockey Player)
Ostra Prinsgatan 30A
Umea 90322, Sweden

Molina, Alfred (Actor)
c/o Joan Hyler *Hyler Management*
20 Ocean Park Blvd Unit 25
Santa Monica, CA 90405-3590, USA

Molina, Beniie (Athlete, Baseball Player)
6475 E Crabtree Pl
Yuma, AZ 85365-1115, USA

Molina, Gabe (Athlete, Baseball Player)
5531 E 118th Ave
Thornton, CO 80233-1855, USA

Molina, Islay (Izzy) (Athlete, Baseball Player)
369 Atwater St
Port Charlotte, FL 33954-2904, USA

Molina, Jose (Athlete, Baseball Player)
c/o Team Member *New York Yankees*
161st St & River Ave
Yankee Stadium
Bronx, NY 10451, USA

Molina, Izzy (Athlete, Baseball Player)
18132 NW 19th St
Pembroke Pines, FL 33029-3026, USA

Molina, Yadier (Athlete, Baseball Player)
6431 River Pointe Way
Jupiter, FL 33458-1819, USA

Molinari, Susan (Politician)
3 Friendship Dr Unit A-3
West Bridgewater, MA 02379-1266, USA

Molinaro, Bob (Athlete, Baseball Player)
1 Harbourside Dr Apt 2312
Delray Beach, FL 33483-5170, USA

Molitor, Paul L (Athlete, Baseball Player, Coach)
c/o Staff Member *John Boggs & Associates*
6265 Greenwich Dr Ste 240
San Diego, CA 92122-5921, USA

Molk, David (Athlete, Football Player)

Molko, Brian (Musician)
c/o Rod MacSween *International Talent Booking*
9 Kingsway
Fl 6
London WC2B 6XF, UNITED KINGDOM

Moll, Richard (Actor)
Mountain Bluebird Inc
PO Box 2286
Big Bear City, CA 92314-2286, USA

Molla, Jordi (Actor, Director)
Kuranda Movies SL
Calle Segre 14
Madrid 28002, SPAIN

Mollen, Jenny (Actor)
2515 Benedict Canyon Dr
Beverly Hills, CA 90210-1020, USA

Moller, Andreas (Soccer Player)
Borussia Dortmund
Postfach 100509
Dortmund 44005, GERMANY

Moller, Frank (Athlete)
Sportclub Berlin
Weissenseer Weg 51-55
Berlin 13051, GERMANY

Moller, Hans (Artist)
2207 W Allen St
Allentown, PA 18104-4327, USA

Moller, Mike (Athlete, Hockey Player)
70 Oaklands Cres
Red Deer, AB T4P 0C4, Canada

Moller, Ralf (Actor)
c/o Pamela Fischer *Fischer & Partner*
Oranienstraße 9
Berlin 10978, GERMANY

Moller, Randy (Athlete, Hockey Player)
Florida Panthers
1 Panther Pkwy
Sunrise, FL 33323-5315

Moller-Gladisch, Silke (Athlete, Track Athlete)
Lange Str 6
Rostock 18055, GERMANY

Molloy, Matt (Musician)
Macklam Feldman Mgmt
200-1505 2nd Ave W
Vancouver, BC V6H 3Y4, CANADA

Moloney, Janel (Actor)
c/o Staff Member *Gersh*
9465 Wilshire Blvd Ste 600
Beverly Hills, CA 90212-2605, USA

Moloney, Michael (Actor, Reality Star)

Moloney, Paddy (Musician)
Macklam Feldman Mgmt
200-1505 2nd Ave W
Vancouver, BC V6H 3Y4, CANADA

Moloney, Rich (Athlete, Baseball Player)
125 Mallard Way
Waltham, MA 02452-8117, USA

Momaday, N scott (Writer)
1600E Univ Dept 1600E
Tucson, AZ 85721-0001, USA

Momaday, N Scott (Writer)
University of Arizona
English Dept
Tucson, AZ 85721-0001, USA

Momesso, Sergio (Athlete, Hockey Player)
Momesso Caffe
1850 Rue des Loisirs
Saint-Lazare, QC J7T 3B4, CANADA

Momoa, Jason (Actor)
c/o Meredith Wechter *WME/IMG*
9601 Wilshire Blvd
Beverly Hills, CA 90210-5213, USA

Momolu-Briggs, Korto (Fashion Designer)
Art Scene and Art Market
200 E 3rd St
Little Rock, AR 72201-1608, USA

Mom Rajawong, Sirikit Kitiyarara (Royalty)
Royal Residence
Chirtalad a Villa
Bangkok, Thailand

Momsen, Robert (Athlete, Football Player)
4730 Glendale Ave Apt 102
Toledo, OH 43614-1974, USA

Momsen, Taylor (Actor, Musician)
c/o John Stratton *DAS Communications*
83 Riverside Dr
New York, NY 10024-5713, USA

Monaco, Kelly (Actor)
c/o Alejandra Cristina *Ace PR*
4122 Sunnyslope Ave
Sherman Oaks, CA 91423-4308, USA

Monae, Janelle (Musician)
Bad Boy Entertainment
1440 Broadway Fl 16
New York, NY 10018-2320, USA

Monaghan, Cameron (Actor, Musician)
c/o Brandi George *Advantage PR*
3900 W Alameda Ave Ste 1200
Burbank, CA 91505-4317, USA

Monaghan, Dominic (Actor)
c/o Jeff Raymond *Rogers & Cowan*
1840 Century Park E Fl 18
Los Angeles, CA 90067-2101, USA

Monaghan, Kris (Athlete, Golfer)
54 Golf Course Dr
Ranchos De Taos, NM 87557-7914, USA

Monaghan, Michelle (Actor)
c/o Frank Frattaroli *Circle of Confusion*
8931 Ellis Ave
Los Angeles, CA 90034-3336, USA

Monaghan, Thomas (Misc)
3001 Earhart Rd
Ann Arbor, MI 48105, USA

Monaghan, Tom (Business Person)
The Ave Maria Foundation
PO Box 373
One Ave Maria Dr
Ann Arbor, MI 48106-0373, USA

Monahan, Dan (Actor)
c/o Helene Sokol *Cuzzins Management*
499 N Canon Dr
Beverly Hills, CA 90210-4887, USA

Monahan, David (Actor, Director)
c/o Pam Braverman *The House of Representatives*
3118 Wilshire Blvd Ste D
Santa Monica, CA 90403-2345, USA

monahan, Garry (Athlete, Hockey Player)
4665 Piccadilly North
West Vancouver, BC V7W 1E3, Canada

Monahan, Hartland (Athlete, Hockey Player)
47 Shelter Cove Ln Apt 235
Hilton Head Island, SC 29928-3567

Monahan, Patrick (Musician)
c/o Susan Novak *Dan Klores Communications (DKC)*
261 5th Ave Fl 2
New York, NY 10016-7601, USA

Monahan, Shane (Athlete, Baseball Player)
47 Shelter Cove Ln Apt 235
Hilton Head Island, SC 29928-3567, USA

Mon&raln, Bob (Athlete, Hockey Player)
55 Stonehaven Cres
Dartmouth, NS B2V 2S7, Canada

Monbouauette, Bill (Athlete, Baseball Player)
46 Doonan St
Medford, MA 02155-1333, USA

Monchak, Alex (Al) (Athlete, Baseball Player)
7414 8th Ave W
Bradenton, FL 34209-3425, USA

Moncrief, Donte (Athlete, Football Player)
c/o Joel Segal *Lagardere Unlimited (NY)*
456 Washington St Apt 9L
New York, NY 10013-1555, USA

Moncrief, Sidney (Athlete, Basketball Player)
2019 Wilson Rd # A
Little Rock, AR 72205-7043, USA

Moncrieff, Karen (Actor)
c/o Brad Gross *Brad Gross Agency, The*
161 S Arden Blvd
Los Angeles, CA 90004-3716, USA

Mondale, Walter (Politician)
600 S 2nd St Apt 405
Minneapolis, MN 55401-2162, USA

Mondale, Walter (Politician)
50 S 6th St Ste 1500
Minneapolis, MN 55402-1498, USA

Monday, Kenny (Athlete, Olympic Athlete, Wrestler)
4119 W Deer Crossing Dr
Stillwater, OK 74074-2192, USA

Monday, Rick (Athlete, Baseball Player)
811 Gayfeather Ln
Vero Beach, FL 32963-2048, USA

Monday, Robert J (Rick) (Baseball Player, Sportscaster)
811 Gayfeather Ln
Vero Beach, FL 32963-2048, USA

Mondesi, Raul (Athlete, Baseball Player)
Los Angeles Dodgers
1169 Old Phillips Rd
Glendale, CA 91207-1153, USA

Mondou, Pierre (Athlete, Hockey Player)
239 Rue Wildor-Larochelle
Sorel-Tracy, QC J3P 6R2, CANADA

Monds, Wonderful (Athlete, Baseball Player)
665 NW Fairhaven Dr
Port St Lucie, FL 34983-1079, USA

Monduzzi, Dino Cardinal (Religious Leader)
Via Monfe della Farina 64
Rome 00186, ITALY

Moner, Isabela (Actor)
c/o Meghan Prophet *PMK/BNC Public Relations*
1840 Century Park E Ste 1400
Los Angeles, CA 90067-2115, USA

Monet, Daniella (Actor)
c/o Kasey Kitchen *ICON PR*
8961 W Sunset Blvd Ste 1C
W Hollywood, CA 90069-1886, USA

Money, Don (Athlete, Baseball Player)
282 Old Forest Rd
Vineland, NJ 08360-1667, USA

Money, Eddie (Musician)
c/o Josh Humiston *Agency for the Performing Arts (APA)*
405 S Beverly Dr Ste 500
Beverly Hills, CA 90212-4425, USA

Money, Eric (Athlete, Basketball Player)
457 S Harvard Ave
Tucson, AZ 85710-4630, USA

Money, John W (Misc)
2104 E Madison St
Baltimore, MD 21205-2337, USA

Money, Ken (Astronaut)
DCIEM
2000-1133 Sheppard Ave W
Downsview, ON M3K 2C9, CANADA

Moneyham, Bill (Baseball Player)
Oakland A's
5731 White Crane Rd
Merced, CA 95340-8573, USA

Moneymaker, Chris (Misc)
11910 Hidden Acres
Byhalia, MS 38611-9538, USA

Monfort, Charles (Athlete, Baseball Player)
PO Box G
Greeley, CO 80632, USA

Monge, Sid (Athlete, Baseball Player)
10 Lilah Ln
Reading, MA 01867-1075, USA

Monger, Matt (Athlete, Football Player)
1306 N Douglas Dr
Claremore, OK 74017-4623, USA

Monheit, Jane (Musician)
c/o Cynthia B. Herbst *American International Artists*
356 Pine Valley Rd
Hoosick Falls, NY 12090-3859, USA

Monica (Musician)
MonDeenise Productions
4305 Melanie Ln
College Park, GA 30349-2848, USA

Monin, Clarence V (President)
Locomotive Engineers Brotherhood
7061 E Pleasant Valley Rd
Independence, OH 44131-5543, USA

Mo'Nique (Actor, Comedian, Television Host)
c/o Ricky Anderson *Anderson & Smith P.C.*
7322 Southwest Fwy Ste 2010
1 Arena Pl
Houston, TX 77074-2077, USA

Moniz, Wendy (Actor)
c/o Nancy Sanders *Sanders Armstrong Caserta*
4111 W Alameda Ave Ste 505
Burbank, CA 91505-4163, USA

Monk, Arthur (Art) (Athlete, Football Player, Sportscaster)
900 American Rose Pkwy
Orlando, FL 32825-8278, USA

Monk, Debra (Actor)
Gage Group
315 W 57th St Frnt 4H
New York, NY 10019-3158, USA

Monk, Quincy (Athlete, Football Player)
104 White Oak Blvd Apt 104
Jacksonville, NC 28546-4539, USA

Monk, Sophie (Actor)
c/o Jack Ketsoyan *EMC / Bowery*
8356 Fountain Ave Apt E1
W Hollywood, CA 90069-2968, USA

Monkees, The (Music Group)
c/o Staff Member *UTA Music/The Agency Group (UK)*
361-373 City Rd
London EC1V 1PQ, UNITED KINGDOM

Monroe, A L (Mike) (Misc)
International Brotherhood pf Painters
1750 New York Ave NW
Washington, DC 20006-5301, USA

Monroe, Asher Book (Actor)
c/o Bryan Leder *Authentic Talent & Literary Management*
3615 Eastham Dr # 650
Culver City, CA 90232-2410, USA

Monroe, Ashley (Musician)
c/o Staff Member *Crush Music Management*
60-62 E 11th St
Fl 7
New York, NY 10003, USA

Monroe, Betty (Actor)
c/o Staff Member *TV Azteca*
Periferico Sur 4121
Colonia Fuentes del Pedregal
DF CP 14141, Mexico

Monroe, Craig (Athlete, Baseball Player)
4123 Lynn Dr
Texarkana, TX 75503-2816, USA

Monroe, Earl (Athlete, Basketball Player)
1925 Adam Clayton Powell Jr Blvd Apt 6D
Jr Blvd Apt 60
New York, NY 10026-2214, USA

Monroe, Eugene (Athlete, Football Player)

Monroe, Larry (Athlete, Baseball Player)
451 W Center Rd
Palatine, IL 60074-1017, USA

Monroe, Lola (Model, Musician)
c/o Staff Member *New Era Agency, The*
Prefers to be contacted via telephone or email
Atlanta, GA, USA

Monroe, Maika (Actor)
c/o Nicole Perna *Imprint PR*
6121 W Sunset Blvd
Neuehouse
Los Angeles, CA 90028-6442, USA

Monroe, Meredith (Musician)
c/o Evan Miller *Abrams Artists Agency*
750 N San Vicente Blvd
E Tower Fl 11
Los Angeles, CA 90069-5788, USA

Monroe, Mircea (Actor)
c/o Brian Wilkins *LINK Entertainment*
11872 La Grange Ave
Los Angeles, CA 90025-5282, USA

Monroe, Rodney (Athlete, Basketball Player)
892 Forest Glen Ln
Wellington, FL 33414-6328, USA

Monroe, Zach (Athlete, Baseball Player)
1 Sandalwood Ln
Bartonville, IL 61607-2145, USA

Monsilovich, Larry (Athlete, Football Player)
35 Alice Ln
Oxford, PA 19363-1025, USA

Monson, Dan (Basketball Player, Coach)
University of Minnesota
Bierman Athletic Building
Minneapolis, MN 55455, USA

Monsters, The (Music Group)
c/o Staff Member *Paradigm (Monterey)*
404 W Franklin St
Monterey, CA 93940-2303, USA

Mont, Tommy (Athlete, Football Player)
19303 N New Tradition Rd APT 222
Sun City West, AZ 85375-3851, USA

Montag, Holly (Reality Star)
c/o Jennifer Hebert *Brilliant Talent*
PO Box 58003
Sherman Oaks, CA 91413-3003, USA

Montague, Ed (Athlete, Baseball Player)
1521 Cherrywood Dr
San Mateo, CA 94403-3903, USA

Montague, John (Athlete, Baseball Player)
6001 Vineyard Ln
Montgomery, AL 36117-5003, USA

Montague, Lee (Actor)
Conway Van Gelder Robinson
18-21 Jermyn St
London SW1Y 6NB, UNITED KINGDOM (UK)

Montalban, Paolo (Actor)
c/o Staff Member *Innovative Artists*
1505 10th St
Santa Monica, CA 90401-2805, USA

Montalbano, Chuck (Athlete, Golfer)
4725 Farmdale Ave
North Hollywood, CA 91602-1109, USA

Montalvo, Rafael (Athlete)
Hudson Valley Renegades
PO Box 661
Attn: Coaching Staff
Fishkill, NY 12524-0661, USA

Montana, Claude (Designer, Fashion Designer)
131 Rue Saint-Denis
Paris 75001, FRANCE

Montana, French (Musician)
c/o Staff Member *FYI Public Relations*
174 5th Ave Ste 404
New York, NY 10010-5964, USA

Montana, Joe (Athlete, Football Player)
1823 Morley Way
Santa Rosa, CA 95404-3648, USA

Montana, Manny (Actor)
c/o Mona Loring *Status PR*
PO Box 6191
Westlake Village, CA 91359-6191, USA

Montaner, Megan (Actor)
c/o Marco Labrador *Kailash*
4 - 5º D
Plaza De Callao
Madrid 28013, SPAIN

Montanez, Luis (Athlete, Baseball Player)
5745 SW 34th St
Miami, FL 33155-4912, USA

Montanez, Willie (Athlete, Baseball Player)
HC 5 Box 52020
Caguas, PR 00725-9201, USA

Montano, Sumalee (Actor)
c/o Paolo Andres *Rothman/Andres Entertainment*
4400 Coldwater Canyon Ave Ste 235
Studio City, CA 91604-5065, USA

Montefusco, John (Athlete, Baseball Player)
1 Oakdale Dr Apt 3D
Middletown, NJ 07748-2124, USA

Monteiro, Antonio M (President)
President's Office
Cia de la Republica
Sao Tiago Praia, CAPE VERDE

Monteith, Hank (Athlete, Hockey Player)
PO Box 1598 Stn Main
St Marys, ON N4X 1B9, CANADA

Monteith, Kelly (Comedian)
293 Bellino Dr
Pacific Palisades, CA 90272-3102, USA

Monteleone, Rich (Athlete, Baseball Player)
441 Lucerne Ace
Tampa, FL 33606-3838, USA

Montermini, Andrea (Race Car Driver)
434 E Main St
Brownsburg, IN 46112-1419, USA

Montero, Agustin (Athlete, Baseball Player)
4600 Parkview Dr
McCullom Lake, IL 60050-2455, USA

Montero, Gabriela (Musician)
c/o Staff Member *Paradigm (Monterey)*
404 W Franklin St
Monterey, CA 93940-2303, USA

Montero, Miguel (Athlete, Baseball Player)

Montero, Pablo (Actor)
c/o Staff Member *Televisa*
Blvd Adolfo Lopez Mateos 232
Colonia San Angel INN
DF CP 01060, MEXICO

Monterola, Pablo (Musician)
c/o Staff Member *BMG*
1540 Broadway
New York, NY 10036-4039, USA

Montgomerie, Colin (Athlete, Golfer)
c/o Staff Member *IMG (UK)*
McCormack House, Hogarth Business Park
Burlington Ln
Chiswick London W4 2TH, UNITED KINGDOM

Montgomerv, Jeff (Athlete, Baseball Player)
11717 Canterbury Ct
Leawood, KS 66211-2940, USA

Montgomery, Alton (Athlete, Football Player)
925 Meriwether St Apt B
Griffin, GA 30224-4025, USA

Montgomery, Anthony (Actor)
c/o Jerry Shandrew *Shandrew Public Relations*
1050 S Stanley Ave
Los Angeles, CA 90019-6634, USA

Montgomery, Belinda (Actor)
Epstein-Wyckoff
280 S Beverly Dr Ste 400
Beverly Hills, CA 90212-3904, USA

Montgomery, Bob (Athlete, Baseball Player)
2 Parkway Dr
Saugus, MA 01906-1957, USA

Montgomery, Chase (Race Car Driver)
Tomar Motorsports
232 Main St.
Box 68
Peterson, IA 51047, USA

Montgomery, Chuck (Actor)
c/o Staff Member *Buchwald*
5900 Wilshire Blvd Ste 3100
Los Angeles, CA 90036-5030, USA

Montgomery, Cleo (Athlete, Football Player)
860 Hebron Pkwy Ste 753
Lewisville, TX 75057-5145, USA

MontgomerY, David (Athlete, Baseball Player)
8525 Ardmore Ave
Glenside, PA 19038-8454, USA

Montgomery, Delmonico (Athlete, Football Player)
3011 Pecan Way Ct
Richmond, TX 77406-6902, USA

Montgomery, Eddie (Musician)
c/o Staff Member *Hallmark Direction Company*
713 18th Ave S
Nashville, TN 37203-3214, USA

Montgomery, James P (Jim) (Athlete, Olympic Athlete, Swimmer)
1537 Bella Vista Dr
Dallas, TX 75218-3510, USA

Montgomery, Janet (Actor)
c/o Christopher Farrar *Hamilton Hodell Ltd*
20 Golden Sq
Fl 5
London W1F 9JL, UNITED KINGDOM

Montgomery, Jeff (Athlete, Baseball Player)
2713 W 116th St
Leawood, KS 66211-3025, USA

Montgomery, Jim (Athlete, Hockey Player)
PO Box 357
Dubuque, IA 52004-0357, USA

Montgomery, John Michael (Musician)
PO Box 37
Goodlettsville, TN 37070-0037, USA

Montgomery, Lisa Kennedy (Actor)
Game Show Network
10202 Washington Blvd
Culver City, CA 90232-3119, USA

Montgomery, Marv (Athlete, Football Player)
1509 S Macon St
Aurora, CO 80012-5140, USA

Montgomery, Melba (Musician)
Joe Taylor Artist Agency
2802 Columbine Pl
Nashville, TN 37204-3104, USA

Montgomery, Mike (Athlete, Football Player)
4224 High Star Ln
Dallas, TX 75287-6624, USA

Montgomery, Mike (Basketball Player, Coach)
Golden State Warriors
1001 Broadway
Oakland, CA 94607-4019, USA

Montgomery, Monty (Athlete, Baseball Player)
807 Corn Tassel Trl
Martinsville, VA 24112-5601, USA

Montgomery, Poppy (Actor)
c/o Christina Papadopoulos *Baker Winokur Ryder Public Relations*
200 5th Ave Fl 5
New York, NY 10010-3307, USA

Montgomery, Ray (Athlete, Baseball Player)
3107 S Webber Ct
Pearland, TX 77584-9418, USA

Montgomery, Ryan (Royce da 5'9) (Musician)
c/o Peter Schwartz *WME|IMG (NY)*
11 Madison Ave Fl 18
New York, NY 10010-3669, USA

Montgomery, Steve (Athlete, Baseball Player)
13731 Mercado Dr
Del Mar, CA 92014-3415, USA

Montgomery, Wilbert (Athlete, Football Player)
45990 Tournament Dr
Northville, MI 48168-8498, USA

Montgomery, Will (Athlete, Football Player)

Montgomery Jr, Dan (Actor)
c/o Karyn Spencer *Peter Strain & Associates Inc (LA)*
10901 Whipple St Apt 322
N Hollywood, CA 91602-3245, USA

Montiel, Fernando (Boxer)
c/o Staff Member *Top Rank Inc.*
3908 Howard Hughes Pkwy
#580
Las Vegas, NV 89109, USA

Montler, Mike (Athlete, Football Player)
479 Tiara Vista Dr
Grand Junction, CO 81507-8716, USA

montovo, Charlie (Athlete, Baseball Player)
202 Stoneridge Dr
Duson, LA 70529-3951, USA

Montoya, Al (Athlete, Hockey Player)
2410 Indian Ridge Dr
Glenview, IL 60026-1030, USA

Montoya, Al (Athlete, Hockey Player)
2 Penn Plz
New York, NY 10121-0101, USA

Montoya, Juan Pablo (Race Car Driver)
Ganassi Racing
8500 Westmoreland Dr NW
Concord, NC 28027-7571, USA

Montoya, Rebeka (Actor)
c/o Alan Iezman *Shelter Entertainment*
9255 W Sunset Blvd Ste 300
Los Angeles, CA 90069-3313, USA

Montoyo, Jose Carlos (Charlie) (Athlete, Baseball Player)
438 Summer Sails Dr
Valrico, FL 33594-8021, USA

Montreuil, Allan (Athlete, Baseball Player)
2016 Laurel Ave
Gretna, LA 70056-5232, USA

Montross, Eric (Athlete, Basketball Player)
4668 S NC Highway 150
Lexington, NC 27295-8026, USA

Montsho, Este (Musician)
William Morris Agency
1325 Avenue of the Americas
New York, NY 10019-6026, USA

Montville, Leigh (Writer)
Boston Globe
Editorial Dept
135 WT Morrissey Blvd
Dorchester, MA 02125, USA

Monty Q (DJ)
c/o Staff Member *Diva Central Inc*
7510 W Sunset Blvd # 1445
Los Angeles, CA 90046-3408, USA

Monye, Ugo (Athlete, Rugby Player)
c/o Dominie Bradshaw *Mint Event Management*
21 Baring Road
Beaconsfield
Bucks HP9 2NB, UNITED KINGDOM

Monzikova, Anya (Actor)
c/o Ryan Daly *Zero Gravity Management*
11110 Ohio Ave Ste 100
Los Angeles, CA 90025-3329, USA

Moock, Joe (Athlete, Baseball Player)
12432 Pecos Ave
Greenwell Springs, LA 70739-3039, USA

Moodie, Janice (Athlete, Golfer)
10746 Woodchase Cir
Orlando, FL 32836-5870, USA

Moody, Eric (Athlete, Baseball Player)
336 Gleneagle Cir
Irmo, SC 29063-8432, USA

Moody, Keith M (Athlete, Football Player)
4632 Riverview Ct
Tracy, CA 95377-8288, USA

Moody, Lynne (Actor)
8708 Skyline Dr
Los Angeles, CA 90046-1422, USA

Moody, Micky (Musician)
Int'l Talent Booking
27A Floral St #300
London WC2E 9DQ, UNITED KINGDOM (UK)

Moody, Nick (Athlete, Football Player)
c/o Tony Paige *Dream Point Sports*
1455 Pennsylvania Ave NW Ste 225
Washington, DC 20004-1026, USA

Moody, Orville (Athlete, Golfer)
9221 Chesapeake Ln
McKinney, TX 75071-6039, USA

Moody, Ritchie (Baseball Player)
7920 Graceland St
Dayton, OH 45459-3835, USA

Moody-Luckhurst, Terri (Athlete, Golfer)
103 Pierrepont Isle
Duluth, GA 30097-5908, USA

Moodysson, Lukas (Director)
Hantverkaregatan 12
Malmo 21155, Sweden

Moog, Andy (Athlete, Hockey Player)
109 Sunrise Dr
Coppell, TX 75019-3691, USA

Moomaw, Donn D (Athlete, Football Player)
3124 Corda Dr
Los Angeles, CA 90049-1104, USA

Moon, Warren (Athlete, Football Player)
4900 SE 2nd Pl
Renton, WA 98059-4959, USA

Mooney, Debra (Actor)
c/o Mike Smith *Principal Entertainment*
9255 W Sunset Blvd Ste 500
Los Angeles, CA 90069-3301, USA

Mooney, Ed (Athlete, Football Player)
4105 63rd St
Lubbock, TX 79413-5023, USA

Mooney, John (Musician)
Intrepid Artists
1300 Baxter St # 405
Midtown Plaza
Charlotte, NC 28204-3053, USA

Mooney, Kyle (Actor, Comedian)
c/o Dan McManus *Mosaic Media Group*
407 N Maple Dr # 100
Beverly Hills, CA 90210-3818, USA

Mooney, Paul (Actor)
c/o Staff Member *Simon & Schuster*
1230 Avenue of the Americas Fl CONC1
New York, NY 10020-1586, USA

Mooney, Peter (Actor)
c/o Pam Winter *Gary Goddard Agency (GGA)*
304-250 The Esplanade
Toronto, ON M5A 1J2, CANADA

Mooneyham, Bill (Athlete, Baseball Player)
5731 White Crane Rd
Atwater, CA 95301-8573, USA

Mooneyhan, Bill (Athlete, Baseball Player)
5731 White Crane Rd
Atwater, CA 95301-8573, USA

Moonves, Leslie (Business Person, Producer)
Moon Rise Unlimited
9000 W Sunset Blvd Fl 10
W Hollywood, CA 90069-5801, USA

Moon Zombie, Sherrie (Actor, Model)
8491 W Sunset Blvd # 215
West Hollywood, CA 90069-1911, USA

Moordyukova, Nonna V (Actor)
Rublevskoye Shosse 34
Korp 2 #549
Moscow 121609, RUSSIA

Moore, Abra (Musician)
Haber Corp
15821 Ventura Blvd Ste 270
Encino, CA 91436-4775, USA

Moore, Adam (Athlete, Baseball Player)
2030 Countv Road 2260
Mineola, TX 75773-6448, USA

Moore, Andre (Athlete, Basketball Player)
12137 S Justine St
Chicago, IL 60643-5443, USA

Moore, Archie (Athlete, Baseball Player)
201 Courtland Rd
Indiana, PA 15701-3202, USA

Moore, Arthur (Misc)
Sheet Metal Workers Int'l Assn
1750 New York Ave NW Ste 600
Washington, DC 20006-5386, USA

Moore, Balor (Athlete, Baseball Player)
901 W Viejo Dr
Friendswood, TX 77546-5836, USA

Moore, Barry (Athlete, Baseball Player)
6702 Conifer Cir
Indian Trail, NC 28079-7588, USA

Moore, Ben (Bobby Purify) (Musician)
c/o Staff Member *Proper Music*
The New Powerhouse, Gateway Business Centre
Kangley Bridge Road
London SE26 5AN, UK

Moore, Benjamin (Artist)
3123 39th Place S
Seattle, WA 98144, USA

Moore, Bill (Billy) (Athlete, Baseball Player)
10849 Mirador Dr
Rancho Cucamonga, CA 91737-6991, USA

Moore, Billie (Athlete, Basketball Player, Coach)
2247 Meadow Ln
Fullerton, CA 92831-2122, USA

Moore, Bob (Athlete, Baseball Player)
2500 Wellington Rd
Los Angeles, CA 90016-3034, USA

Moore, Bobby (Athlete, Baseball Player)
3703 Hyde Park Ave
Cincinnati, OH 45209-2321, USA

Moore, Brad (Athlete, Baseball Player)
3135 Challenger Point Dr
Loveland, CO 80538-7222, USA

Moore, Brandon (Athlete, Football Player)
15010 S 47th St
Phoenix, AZ 85044-6889, USA

Moore, Brent (Athlete, Football Player)
137 Wild Horse Valley Dr
Novato, CA 94947-3615, USA

Moore, Bud (Race Car Driver)
PO Box 2916
Spartanburg, SC 29304-2916, USA

Moore, Bud (Race Car Driver)
315 Old Canaan Rd
Spartanburg, SC 29306-6226, USA

Moore, Chante (Musician, Songwriter)
c/o Staff Member *Shanachie Entertainment*
37 E Clinton St
Newton, NJ 07860-1870, USA

Moore, Charlie (Athlete, Baseball Player)
342 County Road 276
Cullman, AL 35057-4976, USA

Moore, Chris (Producer)
c/o Staff Member *LivePlanet*
11150 Santa Monica Blvd Ste 1200
Los Angeles, CA 90025-3386, USA

Moore, Christina (Actor)
c/o Paul Rosicker *Gersh*
9465 Wilshire Blvd Ste 600
Beverly Hills, CA 90212-2605, USA

Moore, Christopher (Chris) (Director, Producer)
c/o Staff Member *WME|IMG*
9601 Wilshire Blvd
Beverly Hills, CA 90210-5213, USA

Moore, Christy (Musician)
c/o Paul Charles *Asgard Promotions*
125 Parkway
London NW1 7PS, UNITED KINGDOM

Moore, Corwin (Writer)
c/o Staff Member *Creative Artists Agency (CAA)*
2000 Avenue of the Stars Ste 100
Los Angeles, CA 90067-4705, USA

Moore, Damontre (Athlete, Football Player)
c/o Joby Branion *Vanguard Sports Group*
23091 Mill Creek Dr
Laguna Hills, CA 92653-1258, USA

Moore, Darla (Business Person)
Rainwater, Inc
777 Main St Ste 2250
Fort Worth, TX 76102-5308, USA

Moore, Darryl (Athlete, Football Player)
503 High St
Minden, LA 71055-3698, USA

Moore, Dave (Football Player)
c/o Team Member *Tampa Bay Buccaneers*
1 Buccaneer Pl
Tampa, FL 33607-5701, USA

Moore, Dayton (Athlete, Baseball Player)
2508 W 118th St
Leawood, KS 66211-3032, USA

Moore, Demi (Actor)
c/o Meredith O'Sullivan Wasson *The Lede Company*
9701 Wilshire Blvd # 930
Beverly Hills, CA 90212-2020, USA

Moore, Denarius (Athlete, Football Player)

Moore, Derland P (Athlete, Football Player)
1917 Madison St
Mandeville, LA 70448-5840, USA

Moore, Derrick (Athlete, Football Player)
966 Mount Tabor Rd
Oxford, GA 30054-4500, USA

Moore, Dick (Cartoonist)
Dick Moore Assoc
1560 Broadway
New York, NY 10036-1537, USA

Moore, DJ (Athlete, Football Player)
c/o Damarius Bilbo *Revolution Sports*
270 17th St NW Unit 3001
Atlanta, GA 30363-1261, USA

Moore, Dominic (Athlete, Hockey Player)

Moore, Dorothy (Musician)
Sirius Entertainment
13531 Clairmont Way Unit 8
Oregon City, OR 97045-4249, USA

Moore, Dylan (Actor)
c/o David Guc *Vanguard Management Group*
8060 Melrose Ave Fl 4
Los Angeles, CA 90046-7038, USA

Moore, Eric P (Athlete, Football Player)
2225 Lindsay Ln
Florissant, MO 63031-5626, USA

Moore, Gary (Athlete, Baseball Player)
7985 Roundrock Rd
Dallas, TX 75248-5341, USA

Moore, Gwen (Congressman, Politician)
2245 Rayburn Hob
Washington, DC 20515-2001, USA

Moore, Henry (Athlete, Football Player)
2200 Pleasure Dr
Bryant, AR 72019-6365, USA

Moore, Herman J (Athlete, Football Player)
4840 N Adams Rd Ste 503
Rochester Hills, MI 48306-1415, USA

Moore, Indya (Actor, Model)
c/o Alyx Carr *42West*
600 3rd Ave Fl 23
New York, NY 10016-1914, USA

Moore, Jackie (Musician)
T-Best Talent Agency
508 Honey Lake Ct
Danville, CA 94506-1237, USA

Moore, Jackie (Athlete, Basketball Player)
2721 Laurel Valley Ln
Arlington, TX 76006-4019, USA

Moore, Jacqueline (Wrestler)
15030 Ventura Blvd Ste 525
Sherman Oaks, CA 91403-5470, USA

Moore, Jeffrey B (Athlete, Football Player)
2090 Dogwood Estates Cv
Germantown, TN 38139-5620, USA

Moore, Jerald (Athlete, Football Player)
1806 Sabine Ln
Richmond, TX 77406-7940, USA

Moore, Jerry (Athlete, Football Player)
401 Ivory Dr
Little Rock, AR 72205-2640, USA

Moore, Joel David (Actor)
Coattails Entertainment
11271 Ventura Blvd Ste 434
Studio City, CA 91604-3136, USA

Moore, John (Director, Producer, Writer)
c/o Rowena Arguelles *Creative Artists Agency (CAA)*
2000 Avenue of the Stars Ste 100
Los Angeles, CA 90067-4705, USA

Moore, Julianne (Actor)
c/o Evelyn O'Neill *Management 360*
9111 Wilshire Blvd
Beverly Hills, CA 90210-5508, USA

Moore, Junior (Athlete, Baseball Player)
3728 Wall Ave
Richmond, CA 94804-3346, USA

Moore, Justin (Musician)
c/o Jake Basden *Big Machine Records*
1219 16th Ave S
Nashville, TN 37212-2901, USA

Moore, Kellen (Athlete, Football Player)
c/o David Dunn *Athletes First*
23091 Mill Creek Dr
Laguna Hills, CA 92653-1258, USA

Moore, Kelly (Race Car Driver)
8 Ginn Rd
Scarborough, ME 04074-9567, USA

Moore, Kelvin (Athlete, Baseball Player)
75 Stoney Point Ter
Covington, GA 30014-7070, USA

Moore, Kelvin (Athlete, Football Player)
1564 W 110th Pl
Los Angeles, CA 90047-4915, USA

Moore, Kenya (Beauty Pageant Winner, Reality Star)
c/o Gloria Hinojosa *Amsel, Eisenstadt & Frazier Talent Agency (AEF)*
5055 Wilshire Blvd Ste 860
Los Angeles, CA 90036-6108, USA

Moore, Kerwin (Athlete, Baseball Player)
18137 Goddard St
Detroit, MI 48234-4404, USA

Moore, Kip (Musician)
c/o Shawn McSpadden *Red Light Management (TN)*
PO Box 159310
Nashville, TN 37215-9310, USA

Moore, Lance (Athlete, Football Player)
c/o Dave Butz *Sportstars Inc*
1370 Avenue of the Americas Fl 19
New York, NY 10019-4602, USA

Moore, Leonard E (Lenny) (Athlete, Football Player)
8815 Stonehaven Rd
Randallstown, MD 21133-4223, USA

Moore, Leroy (Athlete, Football Player)
842 Golf Dr Apt 201
Pontiac, MI 48341-2385, USA

Moore, Lloyd (Race Car Driver)
152 Frew Run Rd
Frewsburg, NY 14738-9791, USA

Moore, Lorrie (Writer)
University of Wisconsin
English Dept
Madison, WI 53706, USA

Moore, Mandy (Actor, Musician)
c/o Jillian Roscoe *ID Public Relations*
7060 Hollywood Blvd Fl 8th
Los Angeles, CA 90028-6021, USA

Moore, Mandy (Choreographer, Dancer)
c/o Brendan Filuk *Bloc Talent Agency (LA)*
1680 Vine St Ste 600
Los Angeles, CA 90028-8800, USA

Moore, Manfred (Athlete, Football Player)
1672 Buckingham Rd
Los Angeles, CA 90019-5903, USA

Moore, Marcus (Athlete, Baseball Player)
2931 Florida Ave
Richmond, CA 94804-3107, USA

Moore, Mary (Athlete, Baseball Player)
4225 Lake Grove Ct
White Lake, MI 48383-1528, USA

Moore, Matt (Athlete, Football Player)
c/o G. Lynn Lashbrook *Sports Management Worldwide*
1100 NW Glisan St Ste 2B
Portland, OR 97209-3064, USA

Moore, McNeil (Athlete, Football Player)
1212 Woodlawn Dr
Center, TX 75935-3030, USA

Moore, Melba (Actor, Musician)
Artist Services Inc
1017 O St NW # B
Washington, DC 20001-4229, USA

Moore, Melissa Anne (Actor)
PO Box 55
Versailles, KY 40383-0055, USA

Moore, Michael (Director)
Dog Eat Dog Films
430 W 14th St Ste 401
New York, NY 10014-1037, USA

Moore, Mike (Athlete, Baseball Player)
2101 Stratta Dr
Weatherford, OK 73096-1069, USA

Moore, Mindy (Athlete, Golfer)
36 Black Hickory Way
Ormond Beach, FL 32174-5704, USA

Moore, Moulty (Athlete, Football Player)
5781 S Sable Cir
Margate, FL 33063-5697, USA

Moore, Nathanlel (Nat) (Athlete, Football Player)
20041 E Oakmont Dr
Hialeah, FL 33015-2048, USA

Moore, Otis (Baseball Player)
Pittsburgh Pirates
2923 178th Dr Apt 3
Hammond, IN 46323-3245, USA

Moore, Patrick (Athlete, Golfer)
4638 E Dartmouth St
Mesa, AZ 85205-6324, USA

Moore, Rahim (Athlete, Football Player)
c/o Sean Kiernan *Impact Sports (LA)*
12429 Ventura Ct
Studio City, CA 91604-2417, USA

Moore, Ralph (Musician)
Denon Records
135 W 50th St # 1915
New York, NY 10020-1201, USA

Moore, Richard (Actor)
c/o Michael Emptage *Emptage Hallett*
34-35 Eastcastle St
Fl 3
London W1W 8DW, UNITED KINGDOM (UK)

Moore, Rob (Athlete, Football Player)
825 E Sagittarius Pl
Chandler, AZ 85249-3650, USA

Moore, Robert A (Athlete, Football Player)
1906 E Gate Dr
Stone Mountain, GA 30087-1947, USA

Moore, Robert R (Athlete, Football Player)
20 Sally Ann Rd
Orinda, CA 94563-3525, USA

Moore, Ron (Athlete, Football Player)
5730 Oakwood St
Spencer, OK 73084, USA

Moore, Ronald D (Producer, Writer)
c/o Brett Loncar *Creative Artists Agency (CAA)*
2000 Avenue of the Stars Ste 100
Los Angeles, CA 90067-4705, USA

Moore, Sam (Musician)
I'ma Da Wife Enterprises
7119 E Shea Blvd Ste 109-436
#109-436
Scottsdale, AZ 85254-6224, USA

Moore, Scott (Athlete, Baseball Player)
3503 Orange Ave
Long Beach, CA 90807-4828, USA

Moore, Shameik (Actor)
c/o Siri Garber *Platform PR*
2666 N Beachwood Dr
Los Angeles, CA 90068-2308, USA

Moore, Shawn (Athlete, Football Player)
573 Brookfield Dr
Centreville, MD 21617-2397, USA

Moore, Shemar (Actor)
727 Esplanade Unit 102
Redondo Beach, CA 90277-4638, USA

Moore, Sio (Athlete, Football Player)

Moore, Stephen (Actor)
Lyttelton
Royal National Theatre
South Bank
London SE1 9PX, UK

Moore, Sterling (Athlete, Football Player)
c/o Jordan Woy *Willis & Woy Management*
4890 Alpha Rd Ste 200
Dallas, TX 75244-4639, USA

Moore, Terry (Actor)
c/o Budd Burton Moss *Burton Moss*
10533 Strathmore Dr
Los Angeles, CA 90024-2540, USA

Moore, Toby (Actor)
c/o Staff Member *Sanders Armstrong Caserta*
4111 W Alameda Ave Ste 505
Burbank, CA 91505-4163, USA

Moore, Toby Leonard (Actor)
c/o Jennifer Sims *Imprint PR*
375 Hudson St
New York, NY 10014-3658, USA

Moore, Tom (Athlete, Football Player)
1038 Forest Harbor Dr
Hendersonville, TN 37075-9649, USA

Moore, Tommy (Athlete, Baseball Player)
PO Box 336
Pioneertown, CA 92268-0336, USA

Moore, Tracy (Athlete, Basketball Player)
12116 E 37th Pl
Tulsa, OK 74146-3104, USA

Moore, Trey (Athlete, Baseball Player)
5128 Bellerive Bend Dr
College Station, TX 77845-4477, USA

Moore, William (Athlete, Football Player)
c/o Ken Landphere *Octagon Football*
600 Battery St Fl 2
San Francisco, CA 94111-1820, USA

Moore, Zach (Athlete, Football Player)
c/o Blake Baratz *The Institute for Athletes*
3600 Minnesota Dr Ste 550
Edina, MN 55435-7925, USA

Moore, Zeke (Athlete, Football Player)
3422 Prudence Dr
Houston, TX 77045-5718, USA

Moore Capito, Shelley (Congressman, Politician)
2443 Rayburn Hob
Washington, DC 20515-4705, United States

Moorehead, Emery (Athlete, Football Player)
1005 Sussex Dr
Northbrook, IL 60062-3328, USA

Moore Jr, Charles (Athlete, Track Athlete)
10 Barclay St
New York, NY 10007-2708, USA

Moore (Paxson), Melanie Deanne (Actor)
c/o Melisa Spamer *Domain Talent*
1880 Century Park E Ste 1100
Los Angeles, CA 90067-1608, USA

Moorer, Allison (Actor, Musician, Songwriter, Writer)
TKO Artist Mgmt
1107 17th Ave S
Nashville, TN 37212-2203, USA

Moores, John (Athlete, Baseball Player)
8022 Oxfordshire Dr
Spring, TX 77379-4665, USA

Moore-Warner, Eleanor (Athlete, Baseball Player)
2172 Kinney Ave NW
Grand Rapids, MI 49534-1160, USA

Moore-Watkins, Pauline (Actor)
4077 Sunset Dr Apt 202
Lake Oswego, OR 97035-4391, USA

Mooring, John (Athlete, Football Player)
1901 Pat Booker Rd
Universal City, TX 78148-3438, USA

Moorman, Brian (Athlete, Football Player)

Moorman, Mo (Athlete, Football Player)
9641 Shelbyville Rd
Simpsonville, KY 40067-6506, USA

Moorse, Kiki (Musician)
K Records
924 Jefferson St SE
#101
Olympia, WA 98501, USA

MOP (Music Group)
c/o Staff Member *Interscope Records*
1755 Broadway Fl 6
New York, NY 10019-3768, USA

Mora, Danny (Actor)

Mora, Gene (Cartoonist)
United Feature Syndicate
200 Madison Ave
New York, NY 10016-3903, USA

Mora, Jim L (Coach, Football Coach)
c/o Bob LaMonte *Professional Sports Representation*
2425 Manzanita Ln
Reno, NV 89509-7027, USA

Mora, Melvin (Athlete, Baseball Player)
2316 Willow Vale Dr
Fallston, MD 21047-1502, USA

Mora, Philippe (Director)
Altman Co
9255 W Sunset Blvd Ste 901
Los Angeles, CA 90069-3306, USA

Mora, Sergio (Reality Star)

Morabito, Rocky (Journalist, Photographer)
3036 Gilmore St
Jacksonville, FL 32205, USA

Morabito, Tim (Athlete, Football Player)
PO Box 152
Garnerville, NY 10923-0152, USA

Moraga, David (Athlete, Baseball Player)
608 Peach Ct
Fairfield, CA 94534-1522, USA

Morales, Esai (Actor)
c/o Jasmin Espada *Espada PR*
925 N La Brea Ave Ste 14118
West Hollywood, CA 90038-2321, USA

Morales, Esal (Actor)
7527 Woodrow Wilson Dr
Los Angeles, CA 90046-1324, USA

Morales, Jerry (Athlete, Baseball Player, Coach)
Washington Nationals
2400 E Capitol St NE
Attn: Coaching Staff
Washington, DC 20003-1734, USA

Morales, Jose M (Athlete, Baseball Player)
17411 Fosgate Rd
Montverde, FL 34756-3002, USA

Morales, Kendry (Athlete, Baseball Player)
c/o Staff Member *Los Angeles Dodgers*
1000 Elysian Park Ave
Los Angeles, CA 90012, USA

Morales, Natalie (Actor)
c/o Vincent Nastri *Bleecker Street Entertainment*
853 Broadway Ste 1214
New York, NY 10003-4717, USA

Morales, Natalie (Chef, Correspondent)
c/o Staff Member *NBC News (NY)*
30 Rockefeller Plz
New York, NY 10112-0015, USA

Morales, Pedro (Athlete, Wrestler)
118 Willry St
Woodbridge, NJ 07095-2414, USA

Morales, P Pablo (Swimmer)
University of Nebraska
Athletic Dept
Lincoln, NE 68588, USA

Morales, Rich (Athlete, Baseball Player)
1650 Rosita Rd
Pacifica, CA 94044-4431, USA

Morales, Willie (Athlete, Baseball Player)
4866 W Willow Vista Ct
Tucson, AZ 85741-3962, USA

Moran, Al (Athlete, Baseball Player)
34134 Banbury St
Farmington Hills, MI 48331-2216, USA

Moran, Al (Athlete, Baseball Player)
34134 Banbury St
Farmington Hills, MI 48331-2216, USA

Moran, Bill (Athlete, Baseball Player)
200 Shore Dr
Portsmouth, VA 23701-1241, USA

Moran, Billy (Athlete, Baseball Player)
107 Emerling Ln
Peachtree City, GA 30269-3220, USA

Moran, Carl (Baseball Player)
Chicago White Sox
200 Shore Dr
Portsmouth, VA 23701-1241, USA

Moran, Dylan (Actor, Comedian)
c/o Staff Member *PBJ Management*
22 Rathbone St
London W1T 1LA, UNITED KINGDOM

Moran, Ian (Athlete, Hockey Player)
84 S Station St
Duxbury, MA 02332-4535, USA

Moran, John (Religious Leader)
Missionary Church
PO Box 9127
Fort Wayne, IN 46899-9127, USA

Moran, Ian (Athlete, Hockey Player)
427 Bay Rd
Duxbury, MA 02332-5228, USA

Moran, Nick (Actor)
c/o Staff Member *Diverse Talent Group*
1875 Century Park E Ste 2250
Los Angeles, CA 90067-2563, USA

Moran, Richard J (Rich) (Athlete, Football Player)
7252 Mimosa Dr
Carlsbad, CA 92011-5149, USA

Moran, Sean (Athlete, Football Player)
13577 W 84th Dr
Arvada, CO 80005-5825, USA

Moran, Tommy (Actor)

Moran, Tony (DJ, Musician)
c/o Len Evans *Project Publicity*
540 W 43rd St
New York, NY 10036, USA

Morandini, Mickey (Athlete, Baseball Player, Olympic Athlete)
1045 Walker Pass
Chesterton, IN 46304-3473, USA

Moranis, Rick (Actor)
c/o Troy Bailey *Bailey Brand Management*
1017 Ocean Ave Apt G
Santa Monica, CA 90403-3526, USA

Morante, Laura (Actor)
Carol Levi Co
Via Giuseppe Pisanelli
Rome 00196, ITALY

Morasca, Jenna (Reality Star)
M Morasca
6027 Belle Terre Ct
Bridgeville, PA 15017-3459, USA

Morast, Daniel J (Misc)
International Wildlife Coalition
634 N Falmouth Hwy
North Falmouth, MA 02556-3314, USA

Morath, Max (Musician)
Producers Inc
1186 N 56th St
Tampa, FL 33617, USA

Morauta, Mekere (Prime Minister)
Premier's Office
Marea Haus
Walgani
Port Moresby, PAPUA NEW GUINEA

Morceli, Noureddine (Athlete, Track Athlete)
Youth & Sports Minitry
3 Rue Mohamed Belouizdad
Algiers, ALGERIA

Morcott, Southwood J (Business Person)
Dana Corp
PO Box 1000
Toledo, OH 43697-1000, USA

Mordashov, Alexei (Business Person)
2/3 Klara Tsetkin St
Moscow RU-127299, Russia

Mordecai, Mike (Athlete, Baseball Player)
10 Cross Creek Ln
Dothan, AL 36303-9320, USA

Mordillo, Guillermo (Cartoonist)
Haye Top Present
Oberweg 8
Unterhacing 82008, GERMANY

Mordkovitch, Lydia (Musician)
25B Belsize Ave
London NW3 3BL, UNITED KINGDOM (UK)

More, Camilla (Actor)
Sharon Kemp
477 S Robertson Blvd
#204
Beverly Hills, CA 90211, USA

More, Jayson (Athlete, Hockey Player)
9532 Thoroughbred Way
Brentwood, TN 37027-8922, USA

Moreau, Doug (Athlete, Football Player)
5875 Highland Rd
Baton Rouge, LA 70808-6559, USA

Moreau, Marguerite (Actor)
c/o Graciella Sanchez *Echo Lake Management*
421 S Beverly Dr Fl 8
Beverly Hills, CA 90212-4408, USA

Morehead, Dave (Athlete, Baseball Player)
13872 Glenmere Dr
Santa Ana, CA 92705-2812, USA

Moreino, Joe (Athlete, Football Player)
25 Gemini Dr
East Providence, RI 02914-4081, USA

Moreira, Airto (Musician)
A Train Mgmt
PO Box 29242
Oakland, CA 94604-9242, USA

Morejon, Dan (Athlete, Baseball Player)
22625 SW 207th Ave
Miami, FL 33170-4846, USA

Moreland, Keith (Athlete, Baseball Player)
4209 Hidden Canyon Cv
Austin, TX 78746-1256, USA

Morelli, Oscar (Actor)
c/o Staff Member *Televisa*
Blvd Adolfo Lopez Mateos 232
Colonia San Angel INN
DF CP 01060, MEXICO

Morello, Tom (Musician)
GAS Entertainment
8935 Lindblade St
Culver City, CA 90232-2438, USA

Morelos, Lisette (Actor)
c/o Staff Member *Televisa*
Blvd Adolfo Lopez Mateos 232
Colonia San Angel INN
DF CP 01060, MEXICO

Moreno, Arturo "Arte" (Business Person)
c/o Staff Member *Los Angeles Angels Of Anaheim*
2000 E Gene Autry Way
Angels Stadium of Anaheim
Anaheim, CA 92806-6143, USA

Moreno, Azucar (Music Group)
c/o Staff Member *Sony Music (Miami)*
404 Washington Ave Ste 700
Miami Beach, FL 33139-6615, USA

Moreno, Catalina Sandino (Actor)
c/o Estelle Lasher *Lasher Group*
1133 Avenue of the Americas Fl 27
New York, NY 10036-6710, USA

Moreno, Isabel (Actor)
c/o Gabriel Blanco *Gabriel Blanco Iglesias (Mexico)*
Rio Balsas 35-32
Colonia Cuauhtemoc
DF 06500, Mexico

Moreno, Jaime (Musician)
New York/New Jersey Mtrostars
1 Harmon Plz Ste 300
Secaucus, NJ 07094-2800, USA

Moreno, Jaime (Race Car Driver)
252 Montclaire Circle
Weston, FL 33326, USA

Moreno, Jose Elias (Actor)
c/o Staff Member *Televisa*
Blvd Adolfo Lopez Mateos 232
Colonia San Angel INN
DF CP 01060, MEXICO

Moreno, Knowshon (Athlete, Football Player)
c/o Ben Dogra *Relativity Sports*
2029 Century Park E Ste 1550
Century City, CA 90067-3000, USA

Moreno, Lea (Actor)
c/o Steven Neibert *Imperium 7 Talent Agency*
5455 Wilshire Blvd Ste 1706
Los Angeles, CA 90036-4217, USA

Moreno, Moses (Athlete, Football Player)
11627 Lakeside Ave
Lakeside, CA 92040-1614, USA

Moreno, Orber (Athlete, Baseball Player)
5250 Los Palma Vista Dr
Orlando, FL 32837-4604, USA

Moreno, Rita (Actor)
c/o Judy Katz *Judy Katz Public Relations*
1345 Avenue Of The Americas Fl 2
New York, NY 10105-0014, USA

Moreno, Roberto (Race Car Driver)
Herdez Competition
57 Gasoline Aly Ste A
Indianapolis, IN 46222-5932, USA

Moresco, Robert (Actor, Director, Producer, Writer)
c/o Chris Silbermann *ICM Partners*
10250 Constellation Blvd Fl 7
Los Angeles, CA 90067-6207, USA

Moresco, Tim (Athlete, Football Player)
118 Parkside West Ct
Norcross, GA 30071-1529, USA

Moret, Rogelio (Roger) (Athlete, Baseball Player)
HC 1 P.O. Box 5225
Guaynabo, PR 00971, USA

Moretti, Fabrizio (Musician)
114 E 13th St Apt 8C
New York, NY 10003-5354, USA

Moretz, Chloe Grace (Actor)
c/o Megan Moss *Narrative*
1601 Vine St Fl 6
Los Angeles, CA 90028-8802, USA

Morey, Bill (Actor)
Kazarian/Spencer
11365 Ventura Blvd Ste 100
Studio City, CA 91604-3148, USA

Morgado, Arnold (Athlete, Football Player)
1750 Kaahumanu St
Apt 53-C
Pearl City, HI 96782, USA

Morgado, Diogo (Actor)
c/o Liza Anderson *Anderson Group Public Relations*
8060 Melrose Ave Fl 4
Los Angeles, CA 90046-7038, USA

Morgado, Doris (Actor)
c/o Jasmin Espada *Espada PR*
925 N La Brea Ave Ste 14118
West Hollywood, CA 90038-2321, USA

Morgan, Aaron (Athlete, Football Player)

Morgan, Alex (Athlete, Soccer Player)
c/o Dan Levy *Wasserman Media Group (NC)*
4208 Six Forks Rd Ste 1020
Raleigh, NC 27609-5738, USA

Morgan, Angelique (Reality Star)
c/o Anthony Embry *AE Entertainment Public Relations*
124 Evening Shade Dr
Charleston, SC 29414-9144, USA

Morgan, Barbara R (Astronaut)
2996 S Rookery Ln
Boise, ID 83706-5484, USA

Morgan, Bill (Writer)
c/o Staff Member *Da Capo Press*
11 Cambridge Ctr
Cambridge, MA 02142-1400, USA

Morgan, Bobbv (Athlete, Baseball Player)
3004 Stonybrook Rd
Oklahoma City, OK 73120-5716, USA

Morgan, Bobby (Athlete, Baseball Player)
3004 Stonybrook Rd
Oklahoma City, OK 73120-5716, USA

Morgan, Brit (Actor)
c/o Jessica Cohen *JCPR*
9903 Santa Monica Blvd # 983
Beverly Hills, CA 90212-1671, USA

Morgan, Chad (Actor)
c/o Staff Member *SMS Talent*
8383 Wilshire Blvd Ste 230
Beverly Hills, CA 90211-2436, USA

Morgan, Cindy (Actor, Comedian)
PO Box 677
Boynton Beach, FL 33425-0677, USA

Morgan, Colin (Actor)
c/o Ruth Young *United Agents*
12-26 Lexington St
London W1F OLE, UNITED KINGDOM

Morgan, Craig (Musician)
c/o Staff Member *WME (Nashville)*
1201 Demonbreun St Ste 1280
Nashville, TN 37203-5078, USA

Morgan, Dan (Athlete, Football Player)
1915 Funny Cide Dr
Waxhaw, NC 28173-8299, USA

Morgan, Debbi (Actor)
c/o Paul Hilepo *PH Entertainment Group*
2728 Thomson Ave
Long Island City, NY 11101-2922, USA

Morgan, Debelah (Musician)
DAS Communications
83 Riverside Dr
New York, NY 10024-5713, USA

Morgan, Derrick (Athlete, Football Player)
26826 Morgan Run
Westlake, OH 44145-7404, USA

Morgan, Frank (Musician)
Integrity Talent
PO Box 961
Burlington, MA 01803-5961, USA

Morgan, Gil (Athlete, Golfer)
PO Box 806
Edmond, OK 73083-0806, USA

Morgan, Glen (Director, Producer, Writer)
c/o Staff Member *WME/IMG*
9601 Wilshire Blvd
Beverly Hills, CA 90210-5213, USA

Morgan, James C (Business Person)
Applied Materials
3050 Bowers Ave
Santa Clara, CA 95054-3298, USA

Morgan, Jane (Musician)
64 North St
Kennebunkport, ME 04046-6019, USA

Morgan, Jaye P (Actor, Musician)
1185 La Grange Ave
Newbury Park, CA 91320-5316, USA

Morgan, Jeffrey Dean (Actor)
97 W Pine Rd
Staatsburg, NY 12580-5405, USA

Morgan, Joe (Athlete, Football Player)
c/o Brian E. Overstreet *E.O. Sports Management*
1314 Texas St Ste 1212
Houston, TX 77002-3525, USA

Morgan, Joe (Athlete, Baseball Player)
1988 MGR: Boston Red Sox
Walpole, MA 02081-2713, USA

Morgan, Joe (Athlete, Baseball Player, Coach)
15 Oak Hill Dr
Walpole, MA 02081-2713, USA

Morgan, Joseph (Actor)
c/o Richard Konigsberg *RKM*
400 N Mansfield Ave
Los Angeles, CA 90036-2622, USA

Morgan, Josh (Athlete, Football Player)
c/o Joel Segal *Lagardere Unlimited (NY)*
456 Washington St Apt 9L
New York, NY 10013-1555, USA

Morgan, Kevin (Athlete, Baseball Player)
205 Yearling Rd Lot 10
Duson, LA 70529-3118, USA

Morgan, Larry (Race Car Driver)
5399 Horn's Hill Rd.
Newark, OH 43055, USA

Morgan, Lindsey (Actor)
c/o Tim Taylor *Luber Roklin Management*
5815 W Sunset Blvd Ste 208
Los Angeles, CA 90028-6481, USA

Morgan, Lorrie (Actor, Musician)

Morgan, Marabel (Writer)
Total Woman Inc
1300 NW 167th St
Miami, FL 33169-5787, USA

Morgan, Michelle (Actor)
c/o Penny Noble *Noble Caplan Abrams*
1260 Yonge St Fl 2
Toronto, ON M4T 1W5, CANADA

Morgan, Mike (Athlete, Baseball Player)
PO Box 681130
Park City, UT 84068-1130, USA

Morgan, Mike (Athlete, Football Player)

Morgan, Mike (Cartoonist)
Creators Syndicate
5777 W Century Blvd Ste 1700
Los Angeles, CA 90045-5671, USA

Morgan, Munden (Athlete, Basketball Player)
149 Windrush Rd
Winston Salem, NC 27106-2593, USA

Morgan, Peter (Director, Producer)
c/o Greg Hunt *Independent Talent Group*
40 Whitfield St
London W1T 2RH, UNITED KINGDOM

Morgan, Piers (Journalist, Television Host)
c/o Tracey Chapman *James Grant Group Ltd*
94 Strand On the Green
Chiswick
London W4 3NN, UNITED KINGDOM

Morgan, Quincy (Athlete, Football Player)
4654 N Jupiter Rd Apt 1411
Garland, TX 75044-8820, USA

Morgan, Rob (Actor)
c/o Nancy Curtis *Harden-Curtis Associates*
850 7th Ave Ste 903
New York, NY 10019-5438, USA

Morgan, Shelly Taylor (Actor)
Pakula/King
9229 W Sunset Blvd Ste 315
Los Angeles, CA 90069-3403, USA

Morgan, Sonja (Reality Star)
c/o Michael Schweiger *Central Entertainment Group*
250 W 40th St Fl 12
New York, NY 10018-4601, USA

Morgan, Stanley D (Athlete, Football Player)
PO Box 383048
Germantown, TN 38183-3048, USA

Morgan, Tracy (Actor, Comedian)
c/o Lewis Kay *Kovert Creative*
506 Santa Monica Blvd Ste 400
Santa Monica, CA 90401-2412, USA

Morgan, Trevor (Actor)
c/o David Lillard *Industry Entertainment Partners*
955 Carrillo Dr Ste 300
Los Angeles, CA 90048-5400, USA

Morgan, Vanessa (Actor)
c/o Christina Lazzaro *Sharp & Associates*
1516 N Fairfax Ave
Los Angeles, CA 90046-2608, USA

Morgan, Walter (Athlete, Golfer)
15536 Fishermans Rest Ct
Cornelius, NC 28031-7646, USA

Morgan, Walter T J (Misc)
57 Woodbury Dr
Sutton
Surrey, UNITED KINGDOM (UK)

Morgan, W Jason (Misc)
Princton University
Geophysic Dept
Princeton, NJ 08544-0001, USA

Morgenstern, Maia (Actor)
c/o Catherine Davray *Catherine Davray Agency*
16 bis rue de l'Abbe de l'Epee
Paris 75005, FRANCE

Morgenstern, Thomas (Athlete, Skier)
Eichenweg 15
Lieserbrucke 09851, Austria

Morgenthau, Robert (Politician)
1 Hogan Pl
New York, NY 10013-4311, USA

Morgridge, John P (Business Person)
Cisco Systems
170 W Tasman Dr
San Jose, CA 95134-1706, USA

Morhardt, Moe (Athlete, Baseball Player)
219 Spencer Hill Rd
Winsted, CT 06098-2214, USA

Mori, Barbara (Actor)
c/o Eric Rovner *WME/IMG*
9601 Wilshire Blvd
Beverly Hills, CA 90210-5213, USA

Mori, Hanae (Designer, Fashion Designer)
Hanae Mori Haute Couture
17-19 Ave Montaigne
Paris, 75008, FRANCE

Mori, Yoshiro (Prime Minister)
Prime Minister's Office
1-6-1 Nagatoicho
Chiyodaku
Tokyo 00100, JAPAN

Moriarty, Cathy (Actor)
c/o Brian Liebman *Liebman Entertainment*
29 W 46th St Fl 5
New York, NY 10036-4104, USA

Moriarty, Michael (Actor)
200 W 58th St Apt 3B
New York, NY 10019-1477, USA

Moriarty, Mike (Athlete, Baseball Player)
5 E Oleander Dr
Mount Laurel, NJ 08054-3601, USA

Moriarty, Tom (Athlete, Football Player)
28800 Fairmount Blvd
Cleveland, OH 44124-4542, USA

Morimoto, Masaharu (Chef)
88 10th Ave Lbby L2
New York, NY 10011-4760, USA

Morin, Alan (Athlete, Golfer)
139 Jay Ct
Royal Palm Beach, FL 33411-1723, USA

Morin, Brent (Comedian)
c/o Josh Lieberman *3 Arts Entertainment*
9460 Wilshire Blvd Fl 7
Beverly Hills, CA 90212-2713, USA

Morin, Lee M Captain (Astronaut)
10 Marys Creek Ln
Friendswood, TX 77546-3492, USA

Morin, Lee M E (Astronaut)
10 Marys Creek Ln
Friendswood, TX 77546-3492, USA

Morissette, Alanis (Musician, Songwriter)
c/o Dvora Vener Englefield *The Lede Company*
9701 Wilshire Blvd # 930
Beverly Hills, CA 90212-2020, USA

Morissette, Dave (Athlete, Hockey Player)
6565 Rue Champetre
Saint-Hyacinthe, QC J2R 1B1, Canada

Moritz, Brett (Athlete, Football Player)
613 Cameron Ridge Ct
Parkton, MD 21120-8906, USA

Moritz, Louisa (Actor)
405 S Cliffwood Ave
Los Angeles, CA 90049-3827

Moritz, Neal (Producer)
1606 N Beverly Dr
Beverly Hills, CA 90210-2316, USA

Mork, Truis (Musician)
Harrison/Parrott
12 Penzance Place
London W11 4PA, UNITED KINGDOM (UK)

Morkis, Dorothy (Athlete, Horse Racer, Olympic Athlete)
17 Farm St
Dover, MA 02030-2303, USA

Morlan, John (Athlete, Baseball Player)
3290 Belgreen Dr
Grove City, OH 43123-8297, USA

Morland, David (Athlete, Golfer)
5531 Oxford Moor Blvd
Windermere, FL 34786-7012, USA

Morley, Joanne (Athlete, Golfer)
I M G
Pier House Strand on the Ocean
Chiswick
London W4 3NN, United Kingdom

Morman, Alvin (Athlete, Baseball Player)
117 Philadelphia Dr
Rockingham, NC 28379-8607, USA

Morman, Russ (Athlete, Baseball Player)
1800 Tulare St
Fresno, CA 93721-2505, USA

Mormon, Russ (Athlete, Baseball Player)
1200 SW Stonecreek Dr
Blue Springs, MO 64015-8806, USA

Morneau, Justin (Athlete, Baseball Player)
2705 Willow Dr
Hamel, MN 55340-5300, USA

Mornhinweg, Marty (Athlete, Football Coach, Football Player)
3507 Trevi Ct
Philadelphia, PA 19145-5759, USA

Morning After Girls, The (Music Group)
c/o Staff Member *Paradigm (Monterey)*
404 W Franklin St
Monterey, CA 93940-2303, USA

Morningstar, Darren (Athlete, Basketball Player)
1515 W Ingomar Rd
Pittsburgh, PA 15237-1644, USA

Morningwood (Music Group)
Anton Brooks
Bad Moon PR
19 B All Saints Rd
London W11 1HE, UNITED KINGDOM

Morogiello, Dan (Athlete, Baseball Player)
99 Distillery Rd
Whitehouse Station, NJ 08889-3005, USA

Moronko, Jeff (Athlete, Baseball Player)
3903 Bartons Ct
Sugar Land, TX 77479-1941, USA

Moroski, Mike (Athlete, Football Player)
1214 Pine Ln
Davis, CA 95616-1700, USA

Morozov, Aleksey (Athlete, Hockey Player)
c/o Staff Member *Pittsburgh Penguins*
1001 5th Ave
Pittsburgh, PA 15219-6201, USA

Morrell, David (Writer)
c/o Staff Member *Vanguard Press*
387 Park Ave S Fl 12
New York, NY 10016-8810, USA

Morretti, Tobias (Actor)
ZBF Agentur
Ordensmeisterstr 15-16
Berling 12099, GERMANY

Morrin, Wayne (Athlete, Hockey Player)
12 Carpenter Dr
Quispamsis, NB E2E 1T4, Canada

Morris, Alfred (Athlete, Football Player)
c/o Staff Member *Dallas Cowboys*
1 Cowboys Way Ste 100
Frisco, TX 75034-1977, USA

Morris, Ashley Austin (Actor)
c/o Rob Kolker *Red Letter Entertainment*
550 W 45th St Apt 501
New York, NY 10036-3779, USA

Morris, Byron (Bam) (Athlete, Football Player)
251 NE 4th St
Cooper, TX 75432-1833, USA

Morris, Charles R. (Writer)
The Century Foundation
2040 S St NW # 2
Washington, DC 20009-7124, USA

Morris, Chris (Athlete, Basketball Player)
3097 Milford Chase SW
Marietta, GA 30008-6883, USA

Morris, Danny (Athlete, Baseball Player)
802 E Main St
Petersburg, IN 47567-1232, USA

Morris, Darius (Athlete, Basketball Player)
c/o Brian Dyke *Shibumi Sports*
4771 Sweetwater Blvd # 228
Sugar Land, TX 77479-3121, USA

Morris, Derek (Athlete, Hockey Player)
Thunder Creek Management
453-230 22nd St E
Attn Brad Devine
Saskatoon, SK S7K 0E9, Canada

Morris, Dick (Misc)
64 Twin Lakes Rd
South Salem, NY 10590-1009, USA

Morris, Donnie Joe (Athlete, Football Player)
1414 NW 13th Ave
Amarillo, TX 79107-1604, USA

Morris, Doug (Business Person)
c/o Staff Member *Universal Music Group*
100 Universal City Plz
Universal City, CA 91608-1002, USA

Morris, Dwaine (Athlete, Football Player)
4002 Kilkenny Dr
Baton Rouge, LA 70814-7525, USA

Morris, Errol (Director)
c/o Staff Member *Block-Korenbrot Public Relations*
6100 Wilshire Blvd Ste 170
Los Angeles, CA 90048-5109, USA

Morris, Eugene (Athlete, Football Player)
11315 SW 243rd Ter
Homestead, FL 33032-7125, USA

Morris, Garrett (Actor, Comedian)
12067 Guerin St Unit 201
Studio City, CA 91604-4764, USA

Morris, Gary (Musician)
Gary Morris Productions
PO Box 176
Chromo, CO 81128-0176, USA

Morris, Hal (Athlete, Baseball Player)
2000 E Gene Autry Way
Anaheim, CA 92806-6143, USA

Morris, Heather (Actor)
c/o Jennifer Merlino *Untitled Entertainment*
350 S Beverly Dr Ste 200
Beverly Hills, CA 90212-4819, USA

Morris, Isaiah (Athlete, Basketball Player)
4308 W Cermak Rd
Chicago, IL 60623-2901, USA

Morris, Jack (Athlete, Baseball Player)
1 Twins Way Attn Dept
Minneapolis, MN 55403-1418, USA

Morris, Jan (Writer)
Trefan Morys
Llanystumdwy
Criccieth, Gwymedd, WALES

Morris, Jason (Athlete, Olympic Athlete)
575 Swaggertown Rd
Schenectady, NY 12302-9628, USA

Morris, Jenny (Musician)
Artist & Event Mgmt
PO Box 537
Randwick, NSW 02031, AUSTRALIA

Morris, Jim (Athlete, Baseball Player)
2216 Rock Creek Dr
Kerrville, TX 78028-6502, USA

Morris, John (Athlete, Baseball Player)
5538 E Paradise Ln
Scottsdale, AZ 85254-1165, USA

Morris, John (Athlete, Baseball Player)
2645 Elm Dr
North Bellmore, NY 11710-1303, USA

Morris, Johnny (Athlete, Football Player)
753 Shoreline Rd
Lake Barrington, IL 60010-3825, USA

Morris, Jon (Athlete, Hockey Player)
16 Gail St
Chelmsford, MA 01824-3510, USA

Morris, Jon (Athlete, Football Player)
16 Gail St
Chelmsford, MA 01824-3510, USA

Morris, Julian (Actor)
c/o Pandora Weldon *Public Eye Communications*
535 Kings Rd
#313 Plaza
London SW10 0SZ, UNITED KINGDOM

Morris, Kathryn (Actor)
c/o David (Dave) Fleming *Atlas Artists*
9220 W Sunset Blvd Ste 225
Los Angeles, CA 90069-3513, USA

Morris, Keith (Musician)
International Creative Mgmt
8942 Wilshire Blvd # 219
Beverly Hills, CA 90211-1908, USA

Morris, Lamorne (Actor)
c/o Peter Principato *Artists First*
9465 Wilshire Blvd Ste 900
Beverly Hills, CA 90212-2608, USA

Morris, Larry (Artist)
105 N Union St # 4
Alexandria, VA 22314-3217, USA

Morris, Maren (Musician)
c/o Staff Member *Red Light Management (TN)*
PO Box 159310
Nashville, TN 37215-9310, USA

Morris, Marianne (Athlete, Golfer)
39 Holly Dr
Franklin, OH 45005-1594, USA

Morris, Matt (Musician)
c/o Staff Member *WME/IMG*
9601 Wilshire Blvd
Beverly Hills, CA 90210-5213, USA

Morris, Matt (Athlete, Baseball Player)
397 Old Jupiter Beach Rd
Jupiter, FL 33477-5034, USA

Morris, Mitch (Actor)
c/o Benjamin Tappan *Tappan Entertainment*
8324 Fountain Ave Apt C
Los Angeles, CA 90069-2916, USA

Morris, Nathan (Musician)
c/o Staff Member *Southpaw Entertainment*
1710 N Fuller Ave Apt 323
Los Angeles, CA 90046-3064, USA

Morris, Phil (Actor)
704 Strand
Manhattan Beach, CA 90266, USA

Morris, Phil (Race Car Driver)
Blue RidgeMotorsports
32 E Side Hwy
Waynesboro, VA 22980-7011, USA

Morris, Ron (Athlete, Olympic Athlete, Track Athlete)
330 S Reese Pl
Burbank, CA 91506-2724, USA

Morris, Sarah Ann (Actor)
c/o Staff Member *TalentWorks*
3500 W Olive Ave Ste 1400
Burbank, CA 91505-5512, USA

Morris, Sarah Jane (Actor)
c/o Connie Tavel *Forward Entertainment*
1880 Century Park E Ste 1405
Los Angeles, CA 90067-1630, USA

Morris, Wanya (Musician)
c/o Joe Mulvihill *LiveWire Entertainment (FL)*
7575 Dr Phillips Blvd Ste 255
Orlando, FL 32819-7220, USA

Morris, Warren (Athlete, Baseball Player, Olympic Athlete)
1215 Wilshire Dr
Alexandria, LA 71303-3141, USA

Morris, Wayna (Musician)
c/o Staff Member *Southpaw Entertainment*
1710 N Fuller Ave Apt 323
Los Angeles, CA 90046-3064, USA

Morris, Wayne (Athlete, Football Player)
5715 Old Ox Rd
Dallas, TX 75241-2118, USA

Morris, Wingerter Pam (Swimmer)
PO Box 14381
New Bern, NC 28561-4381, USA

Morrison, Adam (Athlete, Basketball Player)
309 W Brierwood Ave
Spokane, WA 99218-2507, USA

Morrison, Allan E (Athlete, Football Player)
2303 Reading Hills Ave
Henderson, NV 89052-5836, USA

Morrison, Amy (Actor)
c/o Linda Bridges *Talent Banque*
661 Dominion Rd Balmoral
Auckland 01334, New Zealand

Morrison, Christopher (Mink) (Director)
c/o Staff Member *ICM Partners*
10250 Constellation Blvd Fl 7
Los Angeles, CA 90067-6207, USA

Morrison, Dan (Athlete, Baseball Player)
7069 Key Haven Rd Apt 401
Seminole, FL 33777-3856, USA

Morrison, Darryl (Athlete, Football Player)
703 Brigadier Ct SE
Leesburg, VA 20175-4450, USA

Morrison, Don (Athlete, Football Player)
9741 County Road 2434
Royse City, TX 75189-4609, USA

Morrison, Doug (Athlete, Hockey Player)
2112 Shannon Woods Way
Westbank, BC V4T 2R5, Canada

Morrison, Dwight (Athlete, Basketball Player)
6112 E Singletree St
Apache Junction, AZ 85119-9548, USA

Morrison, Felton (Baseball Player)
Philadelphia Stars
3860 N Bouvier St
Philadelphia, PA 19140-3528, USA

Morrison, Fred (Athlete, Football Player)
38189 Greywalls Dr
Murrieta, CA 92562-3058, USA

Morrison, Ian (Scotty) (Misc)
Kennisis Lake
PO Box 314
Haliburton, ON K0M 1S0, CANADA

Morrison, James (Actor)
c/o Mitch Clem *Mitch Clem Management*
7080 Hollywood Blvd Ste 1100
Hollywood, CA 90028-6938, USA

Morrison, James (Musician)
c/o Bill Silva *Bill Silva Management*
8255 Santa Monica Blvd
W Hollywood, CA 90046-5912, USA

Morrison, Jennifer (Actor)
c/o John Carrabino *John Carrabino Management*
5900 Wilshire Blvd Ste 740
Los Angeles, CA 90036-5032, USA

Morrison, Jim (Athlete, Baseball Player)
Philadelphia Phillies
2300 El Jobean Rd
Port Charlotte, FL 33948-1109, USA

Morrison, Jim (Athlete, Hockey Player)
1 Potts Lane
Port Hope, ON L1A 0A4, Canada

Morrison, Kevin (Athlete, Hockey Player)
671 George St
Sydney, NS B1P 1L2, Canada

Morrison, Kirk (Athlete, Football Player)
c/o Staff Member *EAG Sports Management*
909 N Pacific Coast Hwy Ste 360
El Segundo, CA 90245-3864, USA

Morrison, Lew (Athlete, Hockey Player)
406 Souris St.
Hartney, MB R0M 0Z0, CANADA

Morrison, Mark (Musician)
Atlantic Records
1290 Avenue of the Americas Fl CONC4
New York, NY 10104-0106, USA

Morrison, Matthew (Actor)
c/o Evelyn Karamanos *Relevant*
400 S Beverly Dr Ste 220
Beverly Hills, CA 90212-4404, USA

Morrison, Mike (Athlete, Basketball Player)
113 Rivanna Ln
Greenville, SC 29607-5488, USA

Morrison, Patricia (Musician)
1100 Alta Loma Rd Apt 16A
West Hollywood, CA 90069-2441, USA

Morrison, Scotty (Athlete, Hockey Player)
1017 Land Rd RR 1
Haliburton, ON K0M 1S0, Canada

Morrison, Shelley (Actor)
1209 S Alfred St
Los Angeles, CA 90035-2569, USA

Morrison, Temuera (Actor)
c/o Staff Member *Abrams Artists Agency*
750 N San Vicente Blvd
E Tower Fl 11
Los Angeles, CA 90069-5788, USA

Morrison, Temuera (Actor)
c/o Joseph (Joe) Rice *JR Talent Group*
Prefers to be contacted by email or phone.
Los Angeles, CA NA, USA

Morrison, Toni (Writer)
Princeton University
Dickinson Hall
Princeton, NJ 08544-0001, USA

Morrison, Van (Musician, Songwriter)
Exile Productions Ltd
88-90 Baker St
Fl 2
London W1U 6TQ, UNITED KINGDOM

Morrison-Gamberdella, Ester (Baseball Player)
3179 Pleasant Creek Rd
Rogue River, OR 97537-9803, USA

Morrison-Gamberdella, Esther (Athlete, Baseball Player)
3179 Pleasant Creek Rd
Rogue River, OR 97537-9803, USA

Morriss, Guy (Athlete, Football Player)
2013 Creekview Dr
Commerce, TX 75428-3946, USA

Morrissette, Billy (Actor, Director, Writer)
c/o Brian Inerfeld *Protocol Entertainment (LA)*
8899 Beverly Blvd # 600
Los Angeles, CA 90048-2412, USA

Morrissey (Musician)
c/o Jeremy Rosen *Selverne & Co.*
650 Rose Ave Apt 2
Venice, CA 90291-2777, USA

Morrissey, David (Actor)
c/o Laura Symons *Premier PR*
2-4 Bucknall St
London WC2H 8LA, UNITED KINGDOM

Morrissey, Jim (Athlete, Football Player)
48 Fox Trl
Lincolnshire, IL 60069-4012, USA

Morrow, Bobby (Athlete, Olympic Athlete, Track Athlete)
2022 Elmwood Dr
Harlingen, TX 78550-8078, USA

Morrow, Bobby Joe (Athlete, Track Athlete)
PO Box 9
Beeville, TX 78104-0009, USA

Morrow, Brandon (Athlete, Baseball Player)
3638 N 51st Dr
Phoenix, AZ 85033-4604, USA

Morrow, Brenden (Athlete, Hockey Player)
3528 Centenary Ave
Dallas, TX 75225-5013, USA

Morrow, Bruce (Cousin Brucie) (Radio Personality)
c/o Staff Member *Sirius/XM Satellite Radio*
1221 Avenue of the Americas Fl 19
New York, NY 10020-1001, USA

Morrow, Harold (Athlete, Football Player)
3390 US Highway 82
Maplesville, AL 36750-5112, USA

Morrow, Jo (Actor)
17000 Ramsey Rd
White City, OR 97503-8525, USA

Morrow, Joshua (Actor)
c/o Marv Dauer *Marv Dauer Management*
11661 San Vicente Blvd Ste 104
Los Angeles, CA 90049-5150, USA

Morrow, Ken (Athlete, Hockey Player)
1255 Hempstead Tpke
Attn Dir Pro Scouting
Uniondale, NY 11553-1260, USA

Morrow, Ken (Athlete, Hockey Player, Olympic Athlete)
6732 r-bnticello Dr.
Kansas City, MO 64152, USA

Morrow, Mari (Actor)
c/o David Ziff *Cunningham Escott Slevin & Doherty (CESD)*
10635 Santa Monica Blvd Ste 130
Los Angeles, CA 90025-8306, USA

Morrow, Rob (Actor)
c/o Stephanie Comer *Magnolia Entertainment*
9595 Wilshire Blvd Ste 601
Beverly Hills, CA 90212-2506, USA

Morse, Cathy (Athlete, Golfer)
6228 Celadon Cir
West Palm Beach, FL 33418-1436, USA

Morse, David (Musician)
Agency for Performing Arts
9200 W Sunset Blvd Ste 900
Los Angeles, CA 90069-3604, USA

Morse, David (Actor)
Yvette Bikoff
1040 1st Ave # 1126
New York, NY 10022-2991, USA

Morse, Helen (Actor)
147 King St #A
Sydney, NSW 02000, AUSTRALIA

Morse, John (Athlete, Golfer)
9291 17 Mile Rd
Marshall, MI 49068-9755, USA

Morse, Mike (Athlete, Baseball Player)
417 NW 97th Ave
Plantation, FL 33324-7075, USA

Morse, Natalie (Actor)
William Morris Agency
52/53 Poland Place
London W1F 7LX, UNITED KINGDOM (UK)

Morse, Robert (Actor)
13830 Davana Ter
Sherman Oaks, CA 91423-4216, USA

Morse, Steve (Athlete, Football Player)
32743 Weybridge St
Fulshear, TX 77441-4132, USA

Morshower, Glenn (Actor)
c/o Melanie Marquez *M4 Publicity*
11684 Ventura Blvd # 213
Studio City, CA 91604-2699, USA

Morstead, Thomas (Athlete, Football Player)
c/o W Vann McElroy *Select Sports Group*
2700 Post Oak Blvd Ste 1450
Houston, TX 77056-5785, USA

Mortensen, Chris (Sportscaster)
ESPN-TV
935 Middle St
Sports Dept Espn Plaza
Bristol, CT 06010-1000, USA

Mortensen, Clayton (Athlete, Baseball Player)
1340 Fairview Ave
Rexburg, ID 83440-5078, USA

Mortensen, Viggo (Actor)
c/o Lynn Rawlins *Rawlins Company*
97 Greenmeadow Ave
Newbury Park, CA 91320-4145, USA

Mortimer, Barrett Angela (Tennis Player)
Oaks
Coombe Hill
Kingston-on-Thames, Surrey, UNITED KINGDOM (UK)

Mortimer, Emily (Actor)
c/o Greg Hunt *Independent Talent Group*
40 Whitfield St
London W1T 2RH, UNITED KINGDOM

Mortimer, Tinsley (Reality Star)
c/o Staff Member *Bravo TV (NY)*
30 Rockefeller Plz
New York, NY 10112-0015, USA

Mortita, Pat (Noriyuki) (Actor)
6399 Wilshire Blvd # 444
Los Angeles, CA 90048-5703, USA

Morton, Alicia (Actor)
c/o Staff Member *WME/IMG*
9601 Wilshire Blvd
Beverly Hills, CA 90210-5213, USA

Morton, Charie (Athlete, Baseball Player)
5122 Sea Forest Dr
Johns Island, SC 29455-5450, USA

Morton, Charlie (Athlete, Baseball Player)
8422 Broadstone Ct
Bradenton, FL 34202-4627, USA

Morton, Craig (Athlete, Football Player)
9850 N 73rd St Unit 2037
Scottsdale, AZ 85258-1032, USA

Morton, Euan (Actor)
c/o Kim Correro *Nancy Seltzer & Associates*
6220 Del Valle Dr
Los Angeles, CA 90048-5306, USA

Morton, Genevieve (Model)
c/o Lisa Benson *IMG Models (NY)*
304 Park Ave S PH N
New York, NY 10010-4303, USA

Morton, Guy (Athlete, Baseball Player)
567 Femdale Ave
Vermilion, OH 44089-2437, USA

Morton, Joe (Actor)
c/o Staff Member *Vanguard Management Group*
8060 Melrose Ave Fl 4
Los Angeles, CA 90046-7038, USA

Morton, John (Athlete, Football Player)
39991 Purmice Dr
Cassel, CA 96016, USA

Morton, Johnnie (Athlete, Football Player)
2911 Oakwood Ln
Torrance, CA 90505-7121, USA

Morton, Kevin (Athlete, Baseball Player)
12 Glen Pines Ln
Norwalk, CT 06850-1800, USA

Morton, Kristopher (Colt) (Athlete, Baseball Player)
3245 Santa Barbara Dr
Wellington, FL 33414-7267, USA

Morton, Richard (Athlete, Basketball Player)
1111 Gilman Ave
San Francisco, CA 94124-3622, USA

Morton, Samantha (Actor)
c/o Troy Nankin *Wishlab*
195 S Beverly Dr Ste 414
Beverly Hills, CA 90212-3044, USA

Mortson, Cleland (Athlete, Hockey Player)

Mosca, Angelo (Athlete, Football Player)
PO Box 144
Niagara On The Lake, ON L0S 1J0, Canada

Moschen, Michael (Artist)
PO Box 178
Cornwall Bridge, CT 06754-0178, USA

Moschitto, Ross (Athlete, Baseball Player)
1200 Warburton Ave Apt 47
Yonkers, NY 10701-1062, USA

Moscoso, Guillermo (Athlete, Baseball Player)
3667 Victoria Manor Dr Apt 103
Lakeland, FL 33805-2989, USA

Moscow, David (Actor)
c/o Christina Papadopoulos *Baker Winokur Ryder Public Relations*
200 5th Ave Fl 5
New York, NY 10010-3307, USA

Mosebar, Donald H (Don) (Athlete, Football Player)
1713 Walnut Ave
Manhattan Beach, CA 90266-5016, USA

Moseby, Lloyd (Athlete, Baseball Player)
9140 Los Lagos Cir S
Granite Bay, CA 95746-5842, USA

Mosel, Tad (Writer)
149 E Side Dr Apt 26-B
Concord, NH 03301-5410, USA

Moseley, Bill (Actor)
c/o Doug Ely *AKA Talent Agency*
325 N Larchmont Blvd
Los Angeles, CA 90004-3011, USA

Moseley, Dustin (Athlete, Baseball Player)
6013 Timberwood Ln
Texarkana, AR 71854-8170, USA

Moseley, John (Athlete, Football Player)
408 Manor Dr
Columbia, MO 65203-1734, USA

Moseley, Jonny (Athlete, Olympic Athlete, Skier)
167 Trinidad Dr
Belvedere Tiburon, CA 94920-1037, USA

Moseley, Mark (Athlete, Football Player)
7250 Middle Rd
Middletown, VA 22645-2121, USA

Moseley, William (Actor)
c/o Siri Garber *Platform PR*
2666 N Beachwood Dr
Los Angeles, CA 90068-2308, USA

Moselle, Dominic (Athlete, Football Player)
2019 Hammond Ave
Superior, WI 54880-2751, USA

Moser, Barry (Misc)
115 Pantry Rd
North Hatfield, MA 01066, USA

Moser, Casey (Athlete, Baseball Player)
9013 FM 368 N
Iowa Park, TX 76367-5341, USA

Moser, Rick (Athlete, Football Player)
1616 Esplanada Ave
Apt 10
Redondo Beach, CA 90277, USA

Moser-Proll, Annemarie (Skier)
Moser Cafe-Bar
#92
Kleinari 115 05602, AUSTRIA

Moses, Christina Marie (Actor)
c/o Amanda Nesbitt *The Lede Company*
9701 Wilshire Blvd # 930
Beverly Hills, CA 90212-2020, USA

Moses, Dezman (Athlete, Football Player)
c/o Blake Baratz *The Institute for Athletes*
3600 Minnesota Dr Ste 550
Edina, MN 55435-7925, USA

Moses, Ed (Athlete, Olympic Athlete, Swimmer)
c/o Staff Member *Premier Management Group (PMG Sports)*
700 Evanvale Ct
Cary, NC 27518-2806, USA

Moses, Edwin (Athlete, Olympic Athlete, Track Athlete)
1184 Daventry Way NE
Brookhaven, GA 30319-4547, USA

Moses, Haven C (Athlete, Football Player)
1140 Cherokee St Unit 640
Denver, CO 80204-3684, USA

Moses, Jerry (Athlete, Baseball Player)
9 Court Ln
Ipswich, MA 01938-3027, USA

Moses, John (Athlete, Baseball Player)
734 E Port Ave Attn Coachingstaff
Corpus Christi, TX 78401-1006, USA

Moses, Kim (Producer)
c/o Staff Member *WME|IMG*
9601 Wilshire Blvd
Beverly Hills, CA 90210-5213, USA

Moses, Mark (Actor)
c/o Leanne Coronel *Coronel Group*
1100 Glendon Ave Fl 17
Los Angeles, CA 90024-3588, USA

Moses, Morgan (Athlete, Football Player)
c/o Andy Ross *Select Sports Group*
2700 Post Oak Blvd Ste 1450
Houston, TX 77056-5785, USA

Moses, Rick (Actor, Musician)
Calder Agency
19919 Redwing St
Woodland Hills, CA 91364-2620, USA

Moses, William R (Actor, Producer)
c/o Steven Siebert *Lighthouse Entertainment Group*
9229 W Sunset Blvd Ste 630
W Hollywood, CA 90069-3419, USA

Mosher, Gregory D (Director, Producer)
c/o Patrick Herold *Helen Merrill Ltd*
295 Lafayette St Ste 915
New York, NY 10012-2700, USA

Mosimann, Anton (Chef)
Mosimann's
11B W Halkin St
London SW1X 8JL, UNITED KINGDOM (UK)

Mosisilli, Pakalitha (Prime Minister)
Chairman's Office
Military Council
PO Box 527
Maseru 00100, LESOTHO

Moskau, Paul (Athlete, Baseball Player)
27843 N Makena Pl
Peoria, AZ 85383-3918, USA

Moskovitz, Dustin (Business Person)
Asana
1550 Bryant St Ste 200
San Francisco, CA 94103-4853, USA

Moskowitz, Robert (Artist)
81 Leonard St Apt 5
New York, NY 10013-3436, USA

Mosler, John (Athlete, Football Player)
12604 Cambridge Rd
Leawood, KS 66209-1327, USA

Mosley, Brandon (Athlete, Football Player)
c/o Todd France *Creative Artists Agency (CAA) Sports*
3500 Lenox Rd NE
Atlanta, GA 30326-4228, USA

Mosley, Brian (Actor)
After Dinner
Saga Court
S Heath G Missenden
Bucks HP16 9QQ, UNITED KINGDOM (UK)

Mosley, C.J. (Athlete, Football Player)
c/o Jimmy Sexton *CAA (Memphis)*
6060 Poplar Ave Ste 470
Memphis, TN 38119-0910, USA

Mosley, J Brooke (Religious Leader)
1604 Foulkeways
Gwynedd, PA 19436-1033, USA

Mosley, Max R (Race Car Driver)
Int'l Automobile Fed
2 Chermin Blandonnet
Geneva 01215, SWITZERLAND

Mosley, Michael (Actor)
c/o Laurie Smith *Smith Talent Group*
77 Gold St
Brooklyn, NY 11201-1228, USA

Mosley, Mike (Athlete, Football Player)
109 Heritage Hill Rd
Wimberley, TX 78676-5632, USA

Mosley, Roger E (Actor)
4470 W Sunset Blvd Ste 107 PMB 342
Los Angeles, CA 90027-6309, USA

Mosley, Sugar Shane (Boxer)
c/o Larry O. Williams Jr. *Williams Talent Agency*
1438 N Gower St Ste 43
Hollywood, CA 90028-8362, USA

Mosley, Timothy (Timbaland) (Musician, Producer)
c/o Richard Weitz *WME|IMG*
9601 Wilshire Blvd
Beverly Hills, CA 90210-5213, USA

Mosley, Walter (Writer)
c/o Bruce Miller *Washington Square Arts (NY)*
310 Bowery Fl 2
New York, NY 10012-2861, USA

Mosquera, Julio (Athlete, Baseball Player)
1419 Stone Creek Dr
Tarpon Springs, FL 34689-3045, USA

Moss, Carrie-Anne (Actor)
c/o Elizabeth Hodgson *Elizabeth Hodgson Management Group*
405-1688 Cypress St
Vancouver, BC V6J 5J1, CANADA

Moss, Cynthia (Misc)
African Wildlife Foundation
Mara Road
PO Box 48177
Nairobi, KENYA

Moss, Damian (Athlete, Baseball Player)
1877 GA Highway 19 S
Dublin, GA 31021-1480, USA

Moss, Eddie (Athlete, Football Player)
15404 Eagle Estates Ln
Florissant, MO 63034-1616, USA

Moss, Elisabeth (Actor)
c/o Gay Ribisi *Ribisi Entertainment*
3278 Wilshire Blvd Apt 702
Los Angeles, CA 90010-1425, USA

Moss, Elza (Religious Leader)
Primitive Advent Christian Church
273 Frame Road
Elkview, WV 25071, USA

Moss, Geoffrey (Cartoonist)
315 E 68th St
New York, NY 10065-5692, USA

Moss, Kate (Model)
Kate Moss Agency (KMA)
37 Tile Yard Studios
Tile Yard Road N7 9AH, UNITED KINGDOM

Moss, Lance (Race Car Driver)
Moss Motorsports
100 West First St.
Dallas, NC 29021, USA

Moss, Les (Athlete, Baseball Player, Coach)
420 Tullis Ave
Longwood, FL 32750-5535, USA

Moss, Lottie (Model)
c/o Staff Member *The Society Management*
156 5th Ave Ste 800
New York, NY 10010-7702, USA

Moss, Paige (Actor)
c/o Staff Member *Marshak/Zachary Company, The*
8840 Wilshire Blvd Fl 1
Beverly Hills, CA 90211-2606, USA

Moss, P Buckley (Artist)
1 Poplar Grove Ln
Mathews, VA 23109, USA

Moss, Perry (Athlete, Basketball Player)
165 Columbia Dr
Amherst, MA 01002-3107, USA

Moss, Perry (Athlete, Football Player, Golfer)
5660 S Lakeshore Dr Apt 505
Shreveport, LA 71119-4038, USA

Moss, Randy (Athlete, Football Player)
4100 Carmel Rd
Charlotte, NC 28226-6150, USA

Moss, Roland (Athlete, Football Player)
411 Camelot Dr
Salisbury, NC 28144-9416, USA

Moss, Ronn (Actor)
2401 Nottingham Ave
Los Angeles, CA 90027-1036, USA

Moss, Santana (Athlete, Football Player)
18619 SW 50th Ct
Miramar, FL 33029-6245, USA

Moss, Shirley (Artist)
Moss Studios
PO Box 18104
Anaheim, CA 92817-8104, USA

Moss, Sterling (Race Car Driver)
46 Shepherd St.
Mayfair
London W1Y 8JN, UNITED KINGDOM

Moss, Stirling (Race Car Driver)
Stirling Moss Ltd
46 Shephard St
London W1Y 8JN, UNITED KINGDOM (UK)

Moss, Tegan (Actor)
c/o Tyman Stewart *Characters Talent Agency*
200-1505 2nd Ave W
Vancouver, BC V6H 3Y4, CANADA

Moss, Zefross (Athlete, Football Player)
126 Kensington Dr
Madison, AL 35758-7844, USA

Moss-Bachrach, Ebon (Actor)
c/o Brian Nossokoff *United Talent Agency (UTA)*
9336 Civic Center Dr
Beverly Hills, CA 90210-3604, USA

Mosser, Jonell (Musician)
Phil Mayo Co
PO Box 304
Bomoseen, VT 05732-0304, USA

Mossi, Don (Athlete, Baseball Player)
23250 Canyon Ln
Caldwell, ID 83607-7709, USA

Most, Don (Actor)
c/o Marina Anderson *Media Hound PR*
PO Box 261939
Encino, CA 91426-1939, USA

Mostardo, Rich (Athlete, Football Player)
3376 Summit Rd
Ravenna, OH 44266-9015, USA

Mostert, Dutch (Artist)
93696 Mallard Ln
North Bend, OR 97459-8407, USA

Mostow, Jonathan (Director)
Creative Artists Agency
9830 Wilshire Blvd
Beverly Hills, CA 90212-1804, USA

Mota, Andres (Athlete, Baseball Player)
PO Box 2820
Toluca Lake, CA 91610-0820, USA

Mota, Andy (Athlete, Baseball Player)
9068 NW 50th Ct
Coral Springs, FL 33067-1933, USA

Mota, Bethany (Internet Star)
c/o Jon Teiber *Creative Artists Agency (CAA)*
2000 Avenue of the Stars Ste 100
Los Angeles, CA 90067-4705, USA

Mota, Guillermo (Athlete, Baseball Player)
c/o Staff Member *Los Angeles Dodgers*
1000 Elysian Park Ave
Los Angeles, CA 90012, USA

Mota, Jose (Athlete, Baseball Player)
19058 E La Crosse St
Glendora, CA 91741-1918, USA

Mota, Manny (Athlete, Baseball Player)
1000 Vin Scully Ave
Los Angeles, CA 90090-1112, USA

Mota, Ross (Athlete, Track Athlete)
R Teatro 194 4 Esq
Porto 04100, PORTUGAL

Mote, Kelley (Athlete, Football Player)
41121 Ocean View Dr
Avon, NC 27915, USA

Moten, Mike (Athlete, Football Player)
706 Loomis Ave
Daytona Beach, FL 32114-4724, USA

Mother Mother (Music Group)
c/o Staff Member *Paradigm (Monterey)*
404 W Franklin St
Monterey, CA 93940-2303, USA

Mothersbaugh, Mark (Musician)
8766 Appian Way
Los Angeles, CA 90046-7733, USA

Motion, Andrew (Writer)
Campaign to Protect Rural England
5-11 Lavington St
London SE1 0NZ, UK

Motion City Soundtrack (Music Group)
Asquared Management
2336 W Belmont Ave
Chicago, IL 60618-6423, USA

Motley, Darryl (Athlete, Baseball Player)
10800 W 65th St
Shawnee, KS 66203-3810, USA

Motley Crue (Music Group)
c/o Frank Cimler *10th Street Entertainment*
700 N San Vicente Blvd # G410
W Hollywood, CA 90069-5060, USA

Motorhead (Music Group)
c/o Neil Warnock *UTA Music/The Agency Group (UK)*
361-373 City Rd
London EC1V 1PQ, UNITED KINGDOM

Motsepe, Keo (Dancer)
c/o Courtney Tunney *Management 360*
9111 Wilshire Blvd
Beverly Hills, CA 90210-5508, USA

Motsepe, Patrice (Business Person)
ARM - African Rainbow Minerals
PO Box 786136
Sandton 02196, South Africa

Mott, Darwin (Athlete, Hockey Player)
3078 Cranbourn Cres
Regina, SK S4V 3B3, Canada

Mott, John C (Athlete, Football Player)
215 Thistledown Ln
Hamilton, MT 59840-9153, USA

Mott, Morris (Athlete, Hockey Player)
9 Elmdale Blvd
Brandon, MB R7B 1B5, Canada

Mott, Steve (Athlete, Football Player)
7018 N Highfield Dr
Birmingham, AL 35242-7239, USA

Mott, Stewart R (Politician)
515 Madison Ave
New York, NY 10022-5403, USA

Motta, Dick (Basketball Coach, Coach)
423 Highway 89
Fish Haven, ID 83287-5109, USA

Motta, Zeke (Athlete, Football Player)
c/o Joe Flanagan *BTI Sports Advisors*
615 South Blvd Apt C
Oak Park, IL 60302-4606, USA

Mottau, Mike (Athlete, Hockey Player)
154 Cove Neck Rd
Oyster Bay, NY 11771-1826, USA

Mottola, Chad (Athlete, Baseball Player)
6479 Lake Pembroke Pl
Orlando, FL 32829-7620, USA

Mottola, Greg (Director, Writer)
c/o Staff Member *United Talent Agency (UTA)*
9336 Civic Center Dr
Beverly Hills, CA 90210-3604, USA

Mottola, Tommy (Business Person, Producer)
The Mottola Company
745 5th Ave Ste 800
New York, NY 10151-0099, USA

Motton, Curt (Athlete, Baseball Player)
8990 Carls Ct Apt A
Ellicott City, MD 21043-5163, USA

Mouawad, Jerry (Director)
Imago Theater
17 SE 8th Ave
Portland, OR 97214-1239, USA

Mouchawar, Alan (Athlete, Olympic Athlete, Water Polo Player)
1943 Port Trinity Pl
Newport Beach, CA 92660-7127, USA

Mould, Bob (Musician, Songwriter)
c/o Perri Cohen *Nasty Little Man*
285 W Broadway Rm 310
New York, NY 10013-2257, USA

Moulton, Sara (Chef, Television Host)
c/o Staff Member *Grand Productions*
2811 Champion Rd
Naperville, IL 60564-4958, USA

Mounce, Tony (Athlete, Baseball Player)
3901 W 46th Ave
Kennewick, WA 99337-2781, USA

Mounsey, Tara (Athlete, Hockey Player, Olympic Athlete)
22 Forge Pond Unit B
Canton, MA 02021-2990, USA

Mount, Anson (Actor)
c/o Emily Gerson Saines *Brookside Artists Management*
250 W 57th St Ste 1820
New York, NY 10107-1802, USA

Mount, Rick (Athlete, Basketball Player)
904 Hopkins Rd
Lebanon, IN 46052-1436, USA

Mount, Thomas H (Tom) (Producer)
c/o Staff Member *Mount Film Company*
9245 Cordell Dr
Los Angeles, CA 90069-1753, USA

Mountain, Danny (Adult Film Star)
c/o Staff Member *LA Direct Models*
3599 Cahuenga Blvd W Ste 4D
Los Angeles, CA 90068-1596, USA

Moura, Wagner (Actor)
c/o Brent Travers *Ascend Entertainment (LA)*
950 10th St Apt A
Santa Monica, CA 90403-2987, USA

Mourinho, Jose (Athlete, Football Executive, Football Player)
c/o Staff Member *Creative Artists Agency (CAA)*
2000 Avenue of the Stars Ste 100
Los Angeles, CA 90067-4705, USA

Mourning, Alonzo (Athlete, Basketball Player, Olympic Athlete)
Mourning Family Foundation
100 S Biscayne Blvd Fl 3
Miami, FL 33131-2038, USA

Mouser, Mary (Actor)
c/o Siri Garber *Platform PR*
2666 N Beachwood Dr
Los Angeles, CA 90068-2308, USA

Mouskouri, Nana (Musician, Songwriter)
Les Visiteurs du Soir
40 Rue de la Folie Regnault
Paris 75011, FRANCE

Moussier, Sabine (Actor)
c/o Staff Member *Televisa*
Blvd Adolfo Lopez Mateos 232
Colonia San Angel INN
DF CP 01060, MEXICO

Mouton, James (Athlete, Baseball Player)
4710 Lakeside Meadow Ct
Missouri City, TX 77459-1630, USA

Mouton, Lyle (Athlete, Baseball Player)
3073 Branch Dr
Clearwater, FL 33760-1741, USA

Moverman, Oren (Director)
c/o Staff Member *WME|IMG*
9601 Wilshire Blvd
Beverly Hills, CA 90210-5213, USA

Movessian, Victoria (Viki) (Athlete, Hockey Player)
17 Webb St
Lexington, MA 02420-2219, USA

Movsessian, Vicki (Athlete, Hockey Player, Olympic Athlete)
17 Webb St
Lexington, MA 02420-2219, USA

Mowatt, Ezekial (Athlete, Football Player)
245 Prospect Ave Apt 2B
Hackensack, NJ 07601-2571, USA

Mower, Patrick (Actor)
c/o Staff Member *Burnett Granger & Assoc*
Prince of Wales Theatre
31 Coventy St
London W1D 6AS, UNITED KINGDOM (UK)

Mowers, Mark (Athlete, Hockey Player)
10 Pollock Dr
Middleton, MA 01949-1747, USA

Mowerson, Robert (Swimmer)
2601 Kenzie Ter Apt 324
Minneapolis, MN 55418-4239, USA

Mowrey, Caitlin (Actor)

Mowrey, Dude (Musician)
Joe Taylor Artist Agency
2802 Columbine Pl
Nashville, TN 37204-3104, USA

Mowry, Tahj (Actor)
c/o Jason Egenberg *Authentic Talent & Literary Management*
3615 Eastham Dr # 650
Culver City, CA 90232-2410, USA

Mowry, Tamera (Actor, Producer)
c/o Whitney Tancred *42West*
1840 Century Park E Ste 700
Los Angeles, CA 90067-2122, USA

Mowry-Hardrict, Tia (Actor)
c/o Adam Griffin *LINK Entertainment*
11872 La Grange Ave
Los Angeles, CA 90025-5282, USA

Moxey, Jim (Athlete, Hockey Player)
7 Blue Heron Dr
Orangeville, ON L9W 5K6, Canada

Moxness, Barbara (Athlete, Golfer)
5512 Mirror Lakes Dr
Minneapolis, MN 55436-2037, USA

Moyer, Jamie (Athlete, Baseball Player)
2426 32nd Ave W
Seattle, WA 98199-3202, USA

Moyer, Ken (Athlete, Football Player)
1714 Meadow Creek Ct
Dayton, OH 45458-1132, USA

Moyer, Paul (Correspondent)
12742 Highwood St
Los Angeles, CA 90049-2624, USA

Moyer, Stephen (Actor)
c/o Alexandra Crotin *The Lede Company*
9701 Wilshire Blvd # 930
Beverly Hills, CA 90212-2020, USA

Moyers, Bill (Journalist)
151 Central Park W Apt Sn
New York, NY 10023-1577, USA

Moyers, Bill D (Correspondent)
c/o Staff Member *HarperCollins Publishers*
195 Broadway Fl 2
New York, NY 10007-3132, USA

Moyet, Alison (Musician)
Primary Talent
2-12 Petonville Road
London N1 9PL, UNITED KINGDOM (UK)

Moylan, Peter (Athlete, Baseball Player)
285 Red Gate Dr
Canton, GA 30115-7502, USA

Moyle, Allan (Director, Writer)
c/o Staff Member *Wisdom Literary*
287 S Robertson Blvd Ste 258
Beverly Hills, CA 90211-2810, USA

Moynahan, Bridget (Actor, Model)
c/o Christina Papadopoulos *Baker Winokur Ryder Public Relations*
200 5th Ave Fl 5
New York, NY 10010-3307, USA

Moynihan, Bobby (Actor, Comedian)
c/o Naomi Odenkirk *Odenkirk Provissiero Entertainment*
1936 N Bronson Ave
Raleigh Studios
Los Angeles, CA 90068-5602, USA

Moynihan, Christopher (Actor)
c/o Ron West *Thruline Entertainment*
9250 Wilshire Blvd Fl Ground
Beverly Hills, CA 90212-3352, USA

Mozeliak, John (Athlete, Baseball Player)
5 Maryhill Dr
Saint Louis, MO 63124-1368, USA

Mozo, Rebecca (Actor)
c/o Staff Member *Insight*
5358 Melrose Ave # 200W
Los Angeles, CA 90038-5117, USA

M. Palazzo, Steven (Congressman, Politician)
331 Cannon Hob
Washington, DC 20515-0901, USA

Mraz, Jason (Musician, Songwriter)
PO Box 69A36
Los Angeles, CA 90069-0047, USA

Mrazek, Jerome (Athlete, Hockey Player)
673 8th St E
Prince Albert, SK S6V 0W8, Canada

Mrazovich, Chuck (Athlete, Basketball Player)
7260 W 12th Ave
Hialeah, FL 33014-4618, USA

Mr Big (Music Group)
c/o Staff Member *Premier Talent*
3 E 54th St # 1100
New York, NY 10022-3108, USA

Mrosko, Robert (Athlete, Football Player)
2874 Coleridge Rd
Cleveland, OH 44118-3544, USA

Mroudjae, Ali (Prime Minister)
BP 58 Rond Point Gobadjou
Moroni, COMOROS

Msuya, Cleopa D (Prime Minister)
Prime Minister's Office
PO Box 980
Dodoma, TANZANIA

Mu'all, Sheikh Rashid bin Ahmed al (Politician)
Ruler's Place
Umm Al Quwain
UNITED ARAB EMIRATES

Muccino, Gabriele (Director)
c/o Jason Weinberg *Untitled Entertainment*
350 S Beverly Dr Ste 200
Beverly Hills, CA 90212-4819, USA

Mucha, Barb (Athlete, Golfer)
5922 Crystal View Dr
Orlando, FL 32819-4207, USA

Muchlinski, Mike (Athlete, Baseball Player)
3908 243rd Pl SE Unit Q301
Bothell, WA 98021-6918, USA

Muckalt, Bill (Athlete, Hockey Player)
3800 Portage Cv
Houghton, MI 49931-2904, USA

Mucke, Manuela (Athlete)
Charlottenstr 13
Berlin 10315, GERMANY

Muckensturm, Jerry (Athlete, Football Player)
4209 Hickory Ln
Jonesboro, AR 72401-8430, USA

Muckier, John (Athlete, Hockey Player)
387 Wood Acres Dr
East Amherst, NY 14051-1660, USA

Muckler, John (Coach)
Ottawa Senators
1000 Palladium Dr
Kanata, ON K2V 1A4, CANADA

Mudcrutch (Music Group)
c/o Staff Member *Warner Bros Records (LA)*
PO Box 6868
Burbank, CA 91510-6868, USA

Mudd, Howard E (Athlete, Coach, Football Player)
311 W Walnut St
Indianapolis, IN 46202-3163, USA

Mudd, Jodie (Athlete, Golfer)
3512 Mildred Dr
Louisville, KY 40216-4341, USA

Mudd, Roger (Journalist)
7167 Old Dominion Dr
Mc Lean, VA 22101-2705, USA

Mudd, Roger H (Correspondent)
7167 Old Dominion Dr
McLean, VA 22101-2705, USA

Mudge, Nancy (Athlete, Baseball Player)
23019 County Road 1
Elk River, MN 55330-9437, USA

Mudiay, Emmanuel (Athlete, Basketball Player)
c/o Dwon Clifton *Rival Sports Group*
9464 Wilshire Blvd
Beverly Hills, CA 90212-2707, USA

Mudra, Darrell (Coach, Football Coach)
424 Tiger Hammock Rd
Crawfordville, FL 32327-1470, USA

Mudrock, Phil (Athlete, Baseball Player)
2548 E 6600 S
Salt Lake City, UT 84121-2346, USA

Mudvayne (Music Group)
c/o Mike Monterulo *The Kirby Organization (TKO-LA)*
9200 W Sunset Blvd Ste 600
Los Angeles, CA 90069-3196, USA

Muelhaupt Jr, Chuck (Athlete, Football Player)
4111 Tonawanda Dr
Des Moines, IA 50312-2911, USA

Muelier, Charles W (Business Person)
Ameren Corp
1901 Chouteau Ave
Saint Louis, MO 63103-3085, USA

Mueller, Bill (Athlete, Baseball Player)
570 W Canvon Wav
Chandler, AZ 85248-5123, USA

Mueller, Brooke (Actor)
c/o Steve Honig *Honig Company, The*
4804 Laurel Canyon Blvd # 828
Studio City, CA 91607-3717, USA

Mueller, Jessie (Actor, Musician)
c/o Paula Muzik *Innovative Artists*
235 Park Ave S Fl 7
New York, NY 10003-1405, USA

Mueller, Les (Athlete, Baseball Player)
PO Box 294
Millstadt, IL 62260-0294, USA

Mueller, Vance (Athlete, Football Player)
7900 Stony Creek Rd
Jackson, CA 95642-8900, USA

Mueller, Willard (Willie) (Athlete, Baseball Player)
2320 Tolbert Ln
West Bend, WI 53090-1234, USA

Mueller-Bajda, Dolores (Baseball Player)
2913 N Linder Ave
Chicago, IL 60641-4812, USA

Mueller-Stahl, Armin (Actor)
c/o ZBF
Ordensmeisterstr. 15-16
Berlin, GERMANY D-12099

Muellner, William (Athlete, Football Player)
727 Sherwood Rd
La Grange Park, IL 60526-1545, USA

Muetterties, Earl L (Misc)
University of California
Chemistry Dept
Berkeley, CA 94720-0001, USA

Muetzelfeldt, Bruno (Religious Leader)
Lutheran World Federation
150 Rt de Femey
Geneva 20 01211, SWITZERLAND

Mugabe, Robert G (President)
President's Office
Munhumutapa Bldg
Samora Machel Ave
Harare, ZIMBABWE

Mugler, Thierry (Designer, Fashion Designer)
c/o Patrick Alaux
4 Rue Faubourg
Saint Honore
Paris 75008, FRANCE

Muhammad, Muhsin (Athlete, Football Player)
c/o Staff Member *Golden Peak Sports & Entertainment LLC*
11352 Haswell Dr
Parker, CO 80134-7548, USA

Muhammad, Wallace D (Religious Leader)
American Muslim Mission
7351 S Stony Island Ave
Chicago, IL 60649-3106, USA

Muhlbach, Don (Athlete, Football Player)
c/o David Dunn *Athletes First*
23091 Mill Creek Dr
Laguna Hills, CA 92653-1258, USA

Muir, David (Correspondent, Television Host)
c/o Carole Cooper *N.S. Bienstock*
888 7th Ave Fl 7
New York, NY 10106-0700, USA

Muir DeGraad, Karen (Swimmer)
Applebosch State Hospital
Ozwatini
Natal, SOUTH AFRICA

Muise, Andi (Model)
c/o Staff Member *Premier Model Management*
40-42 Parker St
London WC2B 5PQ, UK

Muise, Andi (Model)

Mujica, Aylin (Actor)
c/o Staff Member *TV Azteca*
Periferico Sur 4121
Colonia Fuentes del Pedregal
DF CP 14141, Mexico

Mukaddam, Ali (Actor)
c/o Yanick Landry *Edward G Agency*
19 Isabella St
Toronto, ON M4Y 1M7, CANADA

Mukai, Chiaki Naito (Astronaut)

Mulaney, John (Actor, Comedian)
c/o David (Dave) Becky *3 Arts Entertainment*
9460 Wilshire Blvd Fl 7
Beverly Hills, CA 90212-2713, USA

Mulari, Tarja (Speed Skater)
Motion Oy
Vanhan Mankkaantie 33
Espoo 02180, FINDLAND

Mularkey, Mike (Athlete, Football Coach, Football Player)
1719 Beach Ave
Atlantic Beach, FL 32233-5838, USA

Mulcahy, J Patrick (Business Person)
Raiston Purina Co
Checkerboard Square
Saint Louis, MO 63164-0001, USA

Mulcahy, Russell (Director)
c/o Staff Member *Agency for the Performing Arts (APA)*
405 S Beverly Dr Ste 500
Beverly Hills, CA 90212-4425, USA

Muldaur, Maria (Musician, Songwriter, Writer)
Piedmont Talent
3157 Whitson Rd
Gastonia, NC 28054-3901, USA

Mulder, Karen (Model)
c/o Staff Member *Metropolitan Modeling Agency*
5 Union Sq W Ste 500
New York, NY 10003-3306, USA

Mulder, Mark (Athlete, Baseball Player)
10295 E Cholla St
Scottsdale, AZ 85260-6038, USA

Muldoon, Patrick (Actor, Model)
Eclectic Pictures
7119 W Sunset Blvd # 375
Los Angeles, CA 90046-4411, USA

Muldoon, Paul B (Writer)
Princeton University
Creative Writing Program
Princeton, NJ 08544-0001, USA

Mulgrew, Kate (Actor)
c/o Lisa Loosemore *Viking Entertainment*
445 W 23rd St Ste 1A
New York, NY 10011-1445, USA

Mulhern, Matt (Actor)
Gold Marshak Liedtke
3500 W Olive Ave Ste 1400
Burbank, CA 91505-5512, USA

Mulhern, Richard (Athlete, Hockey Player)
397 Walpole Ave
Beaconsfield, QC H9W 2G6, Canada

Mulhern, Ryan (Athlete, Hockey Player)
19 Beachview Ter
Middletown, RI 02842-5904, USA

Mulholland, Terry (Athlete, Baseball Player)
Dirty Dogg Saloon
10409 N Scottsdale Rd
Scottsdale, AZ 85253-1428, USA

Mulitalo, Edwin (Athlete, Football Player)
110 Santa Barbara Ave
Daly City, CA 94014-1045, USA

Mulkerin, Ted (Writer)
c/o Staff Member *WME|IMG*
9601 Wilshire Blvd
Beverly Hills, CA 90210-5213, USA

Mulkey, Chris (Actor)
Paradigm Agency
10100 Santa Monica Blvd Ste 2500
Los Angeles, CA 90067-4116, USA

Mulkey-Robertson, Kim (Basketball Player, Coach)
Baylor University
Athletic Dept
Waco, TX 76798, USA

Mull, Brandon (Writer)
c/o Andrea Smith *Simon & Schuster*
1230 Avenue of the Americas Fl CONC1
New York, NY 10020-1586, USA

Mull, Clay (Athlete, Olympic Athlete, Speed Skater)
4344 S New Hope Rd
Gastonia, NC 28056-8454, USA

Mull, Martin (Actor)
338 S Chadbourne Ave
Los Angeles, CA 90049-3709, USA

Mullady, Tom (Athlete, Football Player)
2855 Crooked Oak Dr
Germantown, TN 38138-7614, USA

Mullally, Megan (Actor, Musician)
c/o Heidi Lopata *Narrative*
1601 Vine St Fl 6
Los Angeles, CA 90028-8802, USA

Mullan, Peter (Writer)
c/o Staff Member *ICM Partners*
10250 Constellation Blvd Fl 7
Los Angeles, CA 90067-6207, USA

Mullane, Richard M Colonel (Astronaut)
1301 Las Lomas Rd NE
Albuquerque, NM 87106-4527, USA

Mullane, Richard M (Mike) (Astronaut)
1301 Las Lomas Rd NE
Albuquerque, NM 87106-4527, USA

Mullaney, Mark (Athlete, Football Player)
9000 Harrow Way
Eden Prairie, MN 55347-2300, USA

Mullavey, Greg (Actor)
1818 Thayer Ave Apt 303
Los Angeles, CA 90025-4965, USA

Mullen, Brian (Athlete, Hockey Player)
124 Berkeley Cir
Basking Ridge, NJ 07920-2023, USA

Mullen, Ford (Moon) (Athlete, Baseball Player)
20505 Marine Dr Unit 3
Stanwood, WA 98292-7852, USA

Mullen, Joe (Athlete, Hockey Player)
3601 S Broad St Ste 2
Attn Coaching Staff
Philadelphia, PA 19148-5250, USA

Mullen, Josep P (Joey) (Athlete, Hockey Player)
36 Friends Ln
South Dennis, MA 02660-2549, USA

Mullen, Nicole (Musician)
c/o Staff Member *Word Records*
25 Music Sq W
Nashville, TN 37203-3205, USa

Mullen, Rodney (Athlete, Skateboarder)
Almost Skateboards
225 S Aviation Blvd
El Segundo, CA 90245-4604, USA

Mullen, Scott (Athlete, Baseball Player)
73 Walling Grove Rd
Beaufort, SC 29907-1067, USA

Mullen, Tom (Athlete, Football Player)
107 Greenbriar Ridge Ct
Saint Louis, MO 63122-3355, USA

Mullen, Tony (Race Car Driver)
11825 Upper Manatee River Rd
Bradenton, FL 34212-9434, USA

Mullen Jr, Larry (Musician)
Principle Mgmt
30-32 Sir John Rogerson Quay
Dublin 2, IRELAND

Muller, Gerd (Soccer Player)
Neuestr 21
Munich 81479, GERMANY

Muller, Herta (Writer)
c/o Staff Member *Henry Holt & Company*
175 5th Ave Ste 400
New York, NY 10010-7726, USA

Muller, Jorg (Race Car Driver)
Insert Motorsport
Fassoldshof 1
Mainleus 95336, GERMANY

Muller, Kirk (Athlete, Hockey Player)
1001 N 4th St Ste 3
Attn: Coaching Staff
Milwaukee, WI 53203-1314, USA

Muller, Lisel (Writer)
LSU Press
PO Box 25053
Baton Rouge, LA 70894, USA

Muller, Marcia (Writer)
Mysterious Press
1271 Avenue of the Americas
Warner Books
New York, NY 10020-1300, USA

Muller, Michel (Actor, Writer)
c/o Celine Kamina *UBBA*
6 rue de Braque
Paris 75003, FRANCE

Muller, Peter (Skier)
Haldenstr 18
Adliswil 08134, SWITZERLAND

Muller-Stahl, Armin (Actor)
Gartenweg 31
Sierksdorf 23730, GERMANY

Mulligan, Carey (Actor)
c/o Jessica Kolstad *Relevant*
400 S Beverly Dr Ste 220
Beverly Hills, CA 90212-4404, USA

Mulligan, Gerry (Writer)
c/o Staff Member *3 Arts Entertainment*
9460 Wilshire Blvd Fl 7
Beverly Hills, CA 90212-2713, USA

Mulligan, Sean (Athlete, Baseball Player)
24474 Eastgate Dr
Diamond Bar, CA 91765-4626, USA

Mulligan, Wayne (Athlete, Football Player)
2410 the Haul Over
Johns Island, SC 29455-6103, USA

Mullin, Chris (Athlete, Basketball Player, Olympic Athlete)
Saint John's University
8000 Utopia Pkwy
Athletic Dept
Jamaica, NY 11439-9000, USA

Mullin, J Stanley (Skier)
Sheppard Mullin Richter Hampton
333 S Hope St
Los Angeles, CA 90071-1406, USA

Mulliniks, Rance (Athlete, Baseball Player)
2614 S Peppertree St
Visalia, CA 93277-5507, USA

Mullins, Eric (Athlete, Football Player)
3249 Parkwood Dr
Houston, TX 77021-1136, USA

Mullins, Fran (Athlete, Baseball Player)
4316 Coolidge Ave
Minneapolis, MN 55424-1018, USA

Mullins, Gerry (Athlete, Football Player)
PO Box 523
Saxonburg, PA 16056-0523, USA

Mullins, Greg (Athlete, Baseball Player)
PO Box 443
Florahome, FL 32140-0443, USA

Mullins, Jeff (Athlete, Basketball Player, Olympic Athlete)
8770 W Orchid Island Cir
Vero Beach, FL 32963-4149, USA

Mullins, Shawn (Musician, Songwriter, Writer)
High Road
751 Bridgeway Fl 2
Sausalito, CA 94965-2174, USA

Mullins, Terry (Race Car Driver)
105 Artesia Dr
Oak Ridge, TN 37830-7818, USA

Mullova, Viktoria Y (Musician)
Askonas Holt Ltd
27 Chancery Lane
London WC2A 1PF, UNITED KINGDOM (UK)

Mulloy, Gardner (Tennis Player)
800 NW 9th Ave
Miami, FL 33136-3006, USA

Muloin, Wayne (Athlete, Hockey Player)
2991 Hayes St
Avon, OH 44011-2178, USA

Mulroney, Dermot (Actor)
c/o Stephen Huvane *Slate PR*
901 N Highland Ave
W Hollywood, CA 90038-2412, USA

Muluzi, Bakili (President)
President's Office
Private Bag 301
Capitol City
Lilongwe 00003, MALAWI

Mulvaney, Mick (Congressman, Politician)
1004 Longworth Hob
Washington, DC 20515-1703, USA

Mulvenna, Glenn (Athlete, Hockey Player)
1480 Kilrush Dr
Ormond Beach, FL 32174-2882, USA

Mulvey, Grant (Athlete, Hockey Player)
491 S Hampshire Ave
Elmhurst, IL 60126-4105, USA

Mulvey, Kevin (Athlete, Baseball Player)
8149 Mulligan Cir
Port Saint Lucie, FL 34986-3310, USA

Mulvey, Paul (Athlete, Hockey Player)
8009 Oak Hollow Ln
Fairfax Station, VA 22039-2651, USA

Mulvey, Peter (Musician)
c/o Staff Member *Young / Hunter Management*
350 Massachusetts Ave # 230
Arlington, MA 02474-6713, USA

Mumba, Samantha (Actor, Musician)
c/o Jane Owen *Jane Owen PR*
408 N Doheny Dr
West Hollywood, CA 90048-1747, USA

Mumford & Sons (Music Group)
White House Pictures
21-22 Great Castle St
London W1G 0HY, UNITED KINGDOM

Mumley, Nick (Athlete, Football Player)
1432 Audubon Dr
Columbus, IN 47203-1432, USA

Mumphord, Lloyd (Athlete, Football Player)
625 Glen St
Opelousas, LA 70570-6738, USA

Mumphrey, Jerry (Athlete, Baseball Player)
7709 FM 850
Tyler, TX 75705-2135, USA

Mumy, Bill (Actor)
c/o Staff Member *Sutton Barth & Vennari Inc*
5900 Wilshire Blvd Ste 700
Los Angeles, CA 90036-5009, USA

Mumy, Liliana (Actor)
c/o Meredith Fine *Coast to Coast Talent Group*
3350 Barham Blvd
Los Angeles, CA 90068-1404, USA

Muna, Solomon Tandeng (Prime Minister)
PO Box 15 Mbengwi
Mono Division
North West Province, CAMEROON

Munchak, Michael A (Mike) (Athlete, Football Player)
9155 Saddlebow Dr
Brentwood, TN 37027-6060, USA

Muncrief, Kevin (Athlete, Golfer)
939 S Flood Ave
Norman, OK 73069-4504, USA

Mundae, Misty (Actor)
PO Box 447
Ringwood, NJ 07456-0447

Mundie, Craig (Business Person)
3 Centerpointe Dr Ste 300
Waggener Edstrom Worldwide - Rapid Response Team
Lake Oswego, OR 97035-8663

Muni, Craig (Athlete, Hockey Player)
9291 Via Cimato Dr
Clarence Center, NY 14032-9152, USA

Muniz, Frankie (Actor)
c/o Jeff Kolodny *Paradigm*
8942 Wilshire Blvd
Beverly Hills, CA 90211-1908, USA

Muniz, Manuel (Athlete, Baseball Player)
PO Box 6301
Caguas, PR 00726-6301, USA

Munk, Chris (Athlete, Basketball Player)
14 Hillview Ct
San Francisco, CA 94124-2487, USA

Munn, Allison (Actor)
c/o David Lederman *Innovative Artists*
1505 10th St
Santa Monica, CA 90401-2805, USA

Munn, Jeff (Athlete, Baseball Player)
901 E Van Buren St Apt 3012
Phoenix, AZ 85006-4039, USA

Munn, Olivia (Actor, Talk Show Host)
c/o David (Dave) Fleming *Atlas Artists*
9220 W Sunset Blvd Ste 225
Los Angeles, CA 90069-3513, USA

Munnerlyn, Captain (Athlete, Football Player)
c/o Hadley Engelhard *Enter-Sports Management*
6000 Lake Forrest Dr Ste 370
Atlanta, GA 30328-5902, USA

Munninghoff, Scott (Athlete, Baseball Player)
866 Laverty Ln
Cincinnati, OH 45230-3558, USA

Munos, Maria (Television Host)

Munoz, Anthony (Athlete, Football Player, Sportscaster)
6529 Irwin Simpson Rd
Mason, OH 45040-9285, USA

Munoz, Bobby (Athlete, Baseball Player)
9040 NW 20th St
Pembroke Pines, FL 33024-3211, USA

Munoz, Mike (Athlete, Baseball Player)
1000 Carroll Meadows Ct
Southlake, TX 76092-3830, USA

Munoz, Oscar (Athlete, Baseball Player)
14161 Leaning Pine Dr
Miami Lakes, FL 33014-2512, USA

Munro, Alice (Writer)
PO Box 1133
Clinton, ON N0M 1L0, CANADA

Munro, Lochlyn (Actor)
c/o Angie Edgar *Alchemy Entertainment*
7024 Melrose Ave Ste 420
Los Angeles, CA 90038-3394, USA

Munro, Peter (Athlete, Baseball Player)
2557 Army Pl
Bellmore, NY 11710-4806, USA

Munroe, George (Athlete, Basketball Player)
870 United Nations Plz Apt 13E
New York, NY 10017-1824, USA

Munson, Eric (Athlete, Baseball Player)
5550 Wilshire Blvd Apt 314
Los Angeles, CA 90036-4858, USA

Munson, John (Musician)
Monterey Peninsula Artists
509 Hartnell St
Monterey, CA 93940-2825, USA

Munter, Leilani (Race Car Driver)
Maia Motorsports
PO Box 3355
Mooresville, NC 38117, USA

Munter, Scott (Athlete, Baseball Player)
1851 W Pelican Dr
Chandler, AZ 85286-5164, USA

Mura, Steve (Athlete, Baseball Player)
31892 Old Oak Rd
Trabuco Canyon, CA 92679-3245, USA

Murai, Hiro (Director, Producer)
c/o Danielle Hinde *Doomsday Entertainment*
1641 Ivar Ave
Los Angeles, CA 90028-6304, USA

Murakami, Haruki (Writer)
c/o Amanda Urban *ICM Partners (NY)*
730 5th Ave
New York, NY 10019-4105, USA

Murakami, Masanori (Athlete, Baseball Player)
1-4-15-1506 Nisho Ohi Shinagawa-Ku
Tokyo 140-0015, Japan

Murakami, Ryu (Writer)
Kodansha Books
2-12-21 Otowa
Bunkyoku
Tokyo 112-8001, JAPAN

Muraliyev, Amangeldy (Prime Minister)
Prime Minister's Office
Ul Perromayskaya 57
Bishkek, KYRGYZSTAN

Muransky, Ed (Athlete, Football Player)
8144 N Lima Rd
Youngstown, OH 44514-2720, USA

Muratova, Kira G (Director)
Proletarsjy Blvd 14B
#15
Odessa 270015, RUSSIA

Murayama, Tomiichi (Politician, Prime Minister)
Sorifu 1-6-1 Nagatacho Chiyada-ku
Oita, Tokyo 00100, JAPAN

Murchison, Ira (Athlete, Track Athlete)
10113 S Sangamon St
Chicago, IL 60643-2228, USA

Murchison, Lee (Athlete, Football Player)
2429 W Euclid Ave
Stockton, CA 95204-2734, USA

Murciano, Jr, Enrique (Actor)
c/o Karynne Tencer *Tencer and Associates*
411 N Oakhurst Dr
Beverly Hills, CA 90210-4037, USA

Murdoch, Don (Athlete, Hockey Player)
Hockey In The Rockies School
PO Box 383 Stn Main
Attn Owners Office
Cranbrook, BC V1C 4H9, Canada

Murdoch, Robert J (Bob) (Athlete, Coach, Hockey Player)
410 11th Ave S
Cranbrook, BC V1C 2P9, Canada

Murdoch, Rupert (Business Person)
23 E 22nd St FRNT 1
New York, NY 10010-5347, USA

Murdoch, Sarah (Actor)
c/o Staff Member *WME|IMG*
9601 Wilshire Blvd
Beverly Hills, CA 90210-5213, USA

Murdoch, Stuart (Musician, Songwriter, Writer)
Legends of 21st Century
7 Trinity Row
Florence, MA 01062-1931, USA

Murdock, David H (Business Person)
Dole Food Company
PO Box 5700
Thousand Oaks, CA 91359-5700, USA

Murdock, Guy (Athlete, Football Player)
106 Medinah Ln
Tower Lakes, IL 60010-1350, USA

Murdock, Shirley (Musician)
Millennium Entertainment Group
1319 5th Ave N
Nashville, TN 37208-2725, USA

Muresan, Georghe (Actor, Basketball Player)
New Jersey Nets
390 Murray Hill Pkwy
East Rutherford, NJ 07073-2109, USA

Murgatroyd, Peta (Dancer)
c/o Liza Anderson *Anderson Group Public Relations*
8060 Melrose Ave Fl 4
Los Angeles, CA 90046-7038, USA

Murkowsk, Frank (Politician)
PO Box 70049
Fairbanks, AK 99707-0049, USA

Murkowski, Lisa (Politician)
232 S Carolina Ave SE
Washington, DC 20003-1940, USA

Murley, Matt (Athlete, Hockey Player)
32 Hialeah Dr
Troy, NY 12182-9770, USA

Murphey, Michael Martin (Musician, Songwriter)
c/o Lance Cowan *LCMedia*
PO Box 965
Cane Ridge, TN 37013, USA

Murphy, Ben (Actor)
2690 Rambla Pacifico
Malibu, CA 90265-3423, USA

Murphy, Bill (Athlete, Football Player)
Excel Communications
6411 SW 25th St
Miramar, FL 33023-2829, USA

Murphy, Billy (Athlete, Baseball Player)
5309 66th Avenue Ct W
University Place, WA 98467-2231, USA

Murphy, Bob (Athlete, Golfer)
11910 N Lake Dr
Boynton Beach, FL 33436-5556, USA

Murphy, Bob (Baseball Player, Sportscaster)
New York Mets
35 The Falls Dr
Vestavia Hills, AL 35216-3112, USA

Murphy, Carolyn (Model)
c/o Staff Member *IMG World*
200 5th Ave Fl 7
New York, NY 10010-3307, USA

Murphy, Charles Q (Actor)
c/o Lorrie Bartlett *ICM Partners*
10250 Constellation Blvd Fl 7
Los Angeles, CA 90067-6207, USA

Murphy, Cillian (Actor)
c/o Craig Bankey *Main Stage Public Relations*
Prefers to be contacted by phone or email.
Los Angeles, CA NA, USA

Murphy, Dale (Athlete, Baseball Player)
467 Aspen Ridge Ln
Alpine, UT 84004-1223, USA

Murphy, Dan (Athlete, Baseball Player)
19661 Symeron Rd
Apple Valley, CA 92307-4736, USA

Murphy, Danny (Actor)
c/o Staff Member *Kazarian, Measures, Ruskin & Associates*
5200 Lankershim Blvd Ste 820
N Hollywood, CA 91601-3194, USA

Murphy, Danny (Athlete, Baseball Player)
120 N Ocean Blvd Aot S-4
Delray Beach, FL 33483-7013, USA

Murphy, David (Athlete, Baseball Player)
3508 Rolling Oaks Dr
Flower Mound, TX 75022-2907, USA

Murphy, David Lee (Musician)
c/o Staff Member *Agency for the Performing Arts (APA)*
405 S Beverly Dr Ste 500
Beverly Hills, CA 90212-4425, USA

Murphy, Dennis A (Athlete, Hockey Player)
22790 Kentfield St
Grand Terrace, CA 92313-5763, USA

Murphy, Dick (Athlete, Baseball Player)
6890 Connie Dr
Avon, IN 46123-8532, USA

Murphy, Donna (Actor, Musician)
c/o Jonathan Howard *Innovative Artists*
1505 10th St
Santa Monica, CA 90401-2805, USA

Murphy, Donnie (Athlete, Baseball Player)
7272 E Gainey Ranch Rd Unit 53
Scottsdale, AZ 85258-1508, USA

Murphy, Dwayne (Athlete, Baseball Player)
1811 S Karen Dr
Chandler, AZ 85286-6350, USA

Murphy, Ed (Basketball Player, Coach)
University of Mississippi
Smith Coliseum
University, MS 38677, USA

Murphy, Eddie (Actor, Comedian)
c/o Arnold Robinson *Rogers & Cowan*
1840 Century Park E Fl 18
Los Angeles, CA 90067-2101, USA

Murphy, Erin (Actor)
c/o Staff Member *Randy James Management*
12711 Ventura Blvd Ste 345
Studio City, CA 91604-2416, USA

Murphy, Gord (Athlete, Hockey Player)
Florida Panthers
1 Panther Pkwy
Attn: Coaching Staff
Sunrise, FL 33323-5315, USA

Murphy, Gord (Athlete, Hockey Player)
10041 Cartgate Ct
Dublin, OH 43017-8865, USA

Murphy, James (Athlete, Football Player)
1-1420 Clarence Ave
Winnipeg, MB R3T 1T6, Canada

Murphy, Joe (Athlete, Hockey Player)
10292 Horton Rd
Goodrich, MI 48438-9473, USA

Murphy, Larry (Athlete, Hockey Player)
1167 Connaught Dr
Ennismore, ON K0L 1T0, Canada

Murphy, Lawrence T (Larry) (Athlete, Hockey Player)
Detroit Red Wings
2645 Woodward Ave
Detroit, MI 48201-3028, USA

Murphy, Louis (Athlete, Football Player)
c/o Drew Rosenhaus *Rosenhaus Sports Representation*
3921 Alton Rd # 440
Miami Beach, FL 33140-3852, USA

Murphy, Marc (Chef)
c/o Scott Feldman *Two Twelve Management*
PO Box 2305
New York, NY 10021-0056, USA

Murphy, Mark (Athlete, Football Player)
736 Michigan Ave
Evanston, IL 60202-2512, USA

Murphy, Mark S (Athlete, Football Player)
1020 Ruby St NW
Hartville, OH 44632-9651, USA

Murphy, Mary (Dancer, Reality Star)
c/o Harry Gold *TalentWorks*
3500 W Olive Ave Ste 1400
Burbank, CA 91505-5512, USA

Murphy, Mary (Athlete, Golfer)
1069 Meda St
Memphis, TN 38104-5819, USA

Murphy, Mike (Athlete, Coach, Hockey Player)
National Hockey League
50 Bay St 11th Fl
Attn: Hockev Operations Deot
Toronto, ON M5J 3A5, Canada

Murphy, Peter (Musician)

Murphy, Rob (Athlete, Baseball Player)
44 S Sewalls Point Rd
Stuart, FL 34996-6728, USA

Murphy, Rob (Athlete, Hockey Player)
Hockey Stall Inc
35 Mika St
Stittsville, ON K2S 1K8, Canada

Murphy, Roisin (Musician)
c/o Staff Member *Spectrum Talent*
9107 Wilshire Blvd Ste 450
Beverly Hills, CA 90210-5535, USA

Murphy, Rosemary (Actor)
220 E 73rd St
New York, NY 10021-4319, USA

Murphy, Ryan (Producer)
c/o Staff Member *Ryan Murphy Productions*
10201 W Pico Blvd
Los Angeles, CA 90064-2606, USA

Murphy, Sean (Athlete, Golfer)
1004 June Pl
Lovington, NM 88260-4521, USA

Murphy, Terry (Journalist)
77 W 66th St
New York, NY 10023-6201, USA

Murphy, Tim (Congressman, Politician)
322 Cannon Hob
Washington, DC 20515-4602, USA

Murphy, Timothy V (Actor)
c/o Staff Member *The Actors Studio*
432 W 44th St
New York, NY 10036-5205, USA

Murphy, Tod (Athlete, Basketball Player)
23 Parsons Hill Rd
Wenham, MA 01984-1823, USA

Murphy, Tom (Athlete, Baseball Player)
26561 Via Sacramento
Capistrano Beach, CA 92624-1337, USA

Murphy, Tommy (Athlete, Baseball Player)
1824 Dunsford Rd
Jacksonville, FL 32207-4206, USA

Murphy, Trent (Athlete, Football Player)
c/o Tom Condon *Creative Artists Agency (CAA)*
401 Commerce St PH
Nashville, TN 37219-2516, USA

Murphy, Troy (Athlete, Basketball Player)

Murphy-O'Connor, Cormac Cardinal (Religious Leader)
Archbishop's House
Ambrosden Ave
London SW1P 1QJ, UNITED KINGDOM (UK)

Murray, Aaron (Athlete, Football Player)
c/o Pat Dye Jr *SportsTrust Advisors*
3340 Peachtree Rd NE Fl 16
Atlanta, GA 30326-1000, USA

Murray, Aj (Athlete, Baseball Player)
2154 E 4500 S
Vernal, UT 84078-9207, USA

Murray, Andy (Athlete, Tennis Player)
c/o Staff Member *77 Management*
81-83 Fulham High St
Chester House/Fulham Green
London SW6 3JA, UNITED KINGDOM

Murray, Anne (Musician)
12 St. Clair Ave E Box 69030
Toronto, ON M4T 1L7, CANADA

Murray, Ashleigh (Actor)
c/o Jaime Misher *Innovative Artists*
235 Park Ave S Fl 7
New York, NY 10003-1405, USA

Murray, Bill (Actor, Comedian)
c/o Staff Member *Broadway Publicity*
1745 Broadway
New York, NY 10019-4640, USA

Murray, Bob (Athlete, Hockey Player)
Anaheim Ducks
2695 E Katella Ave
Attn: General Manager
Anaheim, CA 92806-5904, USA

Murray, Bob (Athlete, Hockey Player)
445 S Bridge View Dr
Anaheim, CA 92808-1346, USA

Murray, Bob (Athlete, Hockey Player)
3137 Beacon Dr
Coquitlam, BC V3C 3W7, Canada

Murray, Brain Doyle (Actor)
Abrams Artists
9200 W Sunset Blvd Ste 1125
Los Angeles, CA 90069-3610, USA

Murray, Calvin (Athlete, Baseball Player, Olympic Athlete)
17434 Courtney Pine Cir
Spring, TX 77379-8505, USA

Murray, Chad Michael (Actor)
c/o Jeffrey Chassen *Imprint PR*
6121 W Sunset Blvd
Neuehouse
Los Angeles, CA 90028-6442, USA

Murray, Chris (Misc)
IBM T J Watson Research Center
PO Box 218
Yorktown Heights, NY 10598-0218, USA

Murray, Dale (Athlete, Baseball Player)
5695 FM 2718
Yorktown, TX 78164-1939, USA

Murray, Dan (Athlete, Baseball Player)
4312 W 78th St
Prairie Village, KS 66208-4352, USA

Murray, Dan (Athlete, Football Player)
9 Washington Rd
Ogdensburg, NJ 07439-1036, USA

Murray, Dave (Musician)
Sanctuary Music Mgmt
82 Bishop's Bridge Road
London W2 6BB, UNITED KINGDOM (UK)

Murray, David K (Musician)
Joel Chriss
300 Mercer St Apt 3J
New York, NY 10003-6732, USA

Murray, DeMarco (Athlete, Football Player)
c/o Pat Dye Jr *SportsTrust Advisors*
3340 Peachtree Rd NE Fl 16
Atlanta, GA 30326-1000, USA

Murray, Don (Actor)
1201 La Patera Canyon Rd
Goleta, CA 93117-1548, USA

Murray, Doug (Cartoonist)
Marvel Comic Group
10 E 40th St # 900
New York, NY 10016-0200, USA

Murray, Eddie C (Athlete, Baseball Player)
15609 Bronco Dr
Canyon Country, CA 91387-4717, USA

Murray, Edward P (Eddie) (Athlete, Football Player)
1070 Forest Bay Dr
Waterford, MI 48328-4284, USA

Murray, Glen (Athlete, Hockey Player)
1320 lOth St
Manhattan Beach, CA 90266-6036, USA

Murray, Glenn (Athlete, Baseball Player)
2 Spalding St
Nashua, NH 03060-4737, USA

Murray, Hannah (Actor)
c/o Romilly Bowlby *DDA Public Relations*
192-198 Vauxhall Bridge Rd
London SW1V 1DX, UNITED KINGDOM

Murray, Heath (Athlete, Baseball Player)
249 Riverside Dr
Troy, OH 45373-1411, USA

Murray, Jaime (Actor)
c/o Jamie Harhay Skinner *Baker Winokur Ryder Public Relations*
9100 Wilshire Blvd
W Tower #500
Beverly Hills, CA 90212-3415, USA

Murray, James (Actor, Director, Producer)
c/o Dexter Scott *Vector Management*
276 5th Ave Rm 604
New York, NY 10001-4527, USA

Murray, Jasmine (Musician)

Murray, Jillian (Actor)
c/o Samir Karar *LINK Entertainment*
11872 La Grange Ave
Los Angeles, CA 90025-5282, USA

Murray, Jim (Athlete, Hockey Player)
37 Viceroy Cres
Brandon, MB R7B 3R7, Canada

Murray, Joe (Athlete, Football Player)
26982 Falling Leaf Dr
Laguna Hills, CA 92653-7539, USA

Murray, Jonathan (Producer)
c/o Staff Member *Bunim/Murray Productions*
1015 Grandview Ave
Glendale, CA 91201-2205, USA

Murray, Keith (Artist, Musician)
Famous Artists Agency
250 W 57th St
New York, NY 10107-0001, USA

Murray, Larry (Athlete, Baseball Player)
3200 Round Hill Dr
Hayward, CA 94542-2122, USA

Murray, Latavius (Athlete, Football Player)
c/o Bruce Tollner *REP 1 Sports Group*
80 Technology Dr
Irvine, CA 92618-2301, USA

Murray, Margaret (Baseball Player)
1320 S Desert Meadows Cir Apt 3109
Green Valley, AZ 85614-1832, USA

Murray, Marty (Athlete, Hockey Player)
1301 34th Ave SW
Minot, ND 58701-7221, USA

Murray, Matt (Athlete, Baseball Player)
109 Greenwood Ave
Swampscott, MA 01907-2124, USA

Murray, Michael (Musician)
4436 Zeller Rd
Columbus, OH 43214-2620, USA

Murray, Mike (Athlete, Hockey Player)
1916 Mobley Way Apt 408
Knoxville, TN 37922-2278, USA

Murray, Neil (Musician)
Int'l Talent Booking
27A Floral St
#300
London WC2E 9DQ, UNITED KINGDOM (UK)

Murray, Patrick (Athlete, Football Player)
c/o Jonathan Feinsod *Schwartz & Feinsod*
4 Hillandale Rd
Rye Brook, NY 10573-1705, USA

Murray, Patty (Politician)
2419 8th Ave N Apt 301
Seattle, WA 98109-2285, USA

Murray, Peg (Actor)
800 Lighthouse Rd
Southold, NY 11971-2301, USA

Murray, Randy (Athlete, Hockey Player)
1016 68 Ave SW Suite 200
Calgary, AB T2V 4J2

Murray, Rem (Athlete, Hockey Player)
60593 Balmoral Way
Rochester, MI 48306-2064, USA

Murray, Rich (Athlete, Baseball Player)
435 E 108th St
Los Angeles, CA 90061-2507, USA

Murray, Rob (Athlete, Hockey Player)
Alaska Aces
724 E 15th Ave
Attn: Coaching Staff
Anchorage, AK 99501-5462, USA

Murray, Sean (Actor)
c/o Al Onorato *Unified Management*
PO Box 101
Sunland, CA 91041-0101, USA

Murray, Terence R (Terry) (Athlete, Hockey Player)
11 Kirkwood Rd
Scarborough, ME 04074-9456, USA

Murray, terry (Athlete, Hockey Player)
Los Angeles Kings
1111 S Figueroa St Ste 3100
Attn Coaching Staff
Los Angeles, CA 90015-1333, USA

Murray, Tracy (Athlete, Basketball Player)
25519 Brassie Ln
La Verne, CA 91750-5918, USA

Murray, Troy (Athlete, Hockey Player)
Chicago Blackhawks
1901 W Madison St
Attn: Broadcast Dept
Chicago, IL 60612-2459, USA

Murray, Troy (Athlete, Hockey Player)
409 6th Ave
La Grange, IL 60525-2439, USA

Murray-Leslie, Alex (Musician)
K Records
924 Jefferson St SE
#101
Olympia, WA 98501, USA

Murray of Epping Forest, Lionel (Len) (Misc)
29 Crescent
Loughton
Essex 1G10 4PY, UNITED KINGDOM (UK)

Murrey, Dorie (Athlete, Basketball Player)
407 N 182nd Ct
Shoreline, WA 98133-4310, USA

Murro, Noam (Director)
c/o Staff Member *Management 360*
9111 Wilshire Blvd
Beverly Hills, CA 90210-5508, USA

Murs, Olly (Musician)
c/o Harry Magee *Modest! Management*
91A Peterborough Rd
London SW6 3BU, UNITED KINGDOM

Murton, Matt (Athlete, Baseball Player)
2304 Silver Palm Dr Apt 302
Kissimmee, FL 34747-2738, USA

Murukarni, Masanori (Baseball Player)
1-4-15-1506 Nisho Ohi Shinagawaku
Tokyo 140-0015, JAPAN

Murzyn, Dana (Athlete, Hockey Player)
41 Sunset Way SE
Calgary, AB T2X 3H6, Canada

Musa, Said (Prime Minister)
Prime Minister's Office
East Bloc
Belmopan, BELIZE

Musburger, Brent (Sportscaster)
286 Locha Dr
Jupiter, FL 33458-7733, USA

Muse (Music Group)
c/o Cliff Burnstein *Q Prime (NY)*
729 7th Ave Fl 16
New York, NY 10019-6831, USA

Muser, Tony (Athlete, Baseball Player, Coach)
11222 Martha Ann Dr
Los Alamitos, CA 90720-2956, USA

Musgrave, Bill (Athlete, Football Player)
4062 Leprechan Way
Duluth, GA 30097-8147, USA

Musgrave, F Story (Astronaut)
8572 Sweetwater Trl
Kissimmee, FL 34747-1519, USA

Musgrave, F Story Dr (Astronaut)
8572 Sweetwater Trl
Kissimmee, FL 34747-1519, USA

Musgrave, Mandy (Actor)
c/o Shannon Barr *Rogers & Cowan*
1840 Century Park E Fl 18
Los Angeles, CA 90067-2101, USA

Musgrave, Spain (Athlete, Football Player)
9727 Mount Pisgah Rd Apt 811
Silver Spring, MD 20903-2011, USA

Musgrave, Ted (Race Car Driver)
175 Lakeside Dr E
Port Orange, FL 32128-6620, USA

Musgraves, Dennis (Athlete, Baseball Player)
17100 N Highway 124
Centralia, MO 65240-3830, USA

Musgraves, Kacey (Musician)
c/o Marc Dennis *Creative Artists Agency (CAA)*
401 Commerce St PH
Nashville, TN 37219-2516, USA

Musgrove, Spain (Athlete, Football Player)
2350 Deckman Ln
Silver Spring, MD 20906-2266, USA

Musharraf, Parvez (President)
President's Office
Aiwan-e-Sadr
Mall & Mayo Roads
Islamabad, PAKISTAN

Mushok, Mike (Musician)
c/o Staff Member *UTA Music/The Agency Group (UK)*
361-373 City Rd
London EC1V 1PQ, UNITED KINGDOM

Music, The (Music Group)
c/o Staff Member *Paradigm (Monterey)*
404 W Franklin St
Monterey, CA 93940-2303, USA

Musil, Frank (Athlete, Hockey Player)
1606-4769 Hazel St
Burnaby, BC V5H 1S7, Canada

Musiol, Bogdan (Athlete)
Fitness-Studio
Talstr 50
Zella-Mehlis 98544, GERMANY

Musiq (Musician)
Def Soul Records
825 8th Ave # 2700
New York, NY 10019-7416, USA

Musiq Soulchild (Music Group)
c/o Staff Member *Paradigm (Monterey)*
404 W Franklin St
Monterey, CA 93940-2303, USA

Musk, Elon (Business Person)
Tesla Motors
3500 Deer Creek Rd
Palo Alto, CA 94304-1317, USA

Musk, Maye (Model)
c/o Ivan Bart *IMG Models (NY)*
304 Park Ave S PH N
New York, NY 10010-4303, USA

Musker, John (Animator, Director)
c/o Staff Member *Creative Artists Agency (CAA)*
2000 Avenue of the Stars Ste 100
Los Angeles, CA 90067-4705, USA

Musonge, Pater Mafani (Prime Minister)
Prime Minister's Office
Yaounde, BP 01057, CAMEROON

Musselman, Jeff (Athlete, Baseball Player)
1842 Port Tiffin Pl
Newport Beach, CA 92660-7121, USA

Musselman, Ron (Athlete, Baseball Player)
5313 Autumn Dr
Wilmington, NC 28409-5701, USA

Musselwhite, Charlie (Musician)
c/o Kevin Morrow *Morrow Management*
5003 Westpark Dr Unit 102
Valley Village, CA 91601-3612, USA

Musser, Neal (Athlete, Baseball Player)
9050 Carlton Rd
Port Saint Lucie, FL 34987-3215, USA

Mussill, Barney (Athlete, Baseball Player)
912 Moorland Dr
Grosse Pointe Woods, MI 48236-1131, USA

Mussina, Mike (Athlete, Baseball Player)
737 White Church Rd
Muncy, PA 17756-8004, USA

Musso, John (Athlete, Football Player)
242 E 3rd St
Hinsdale, IL 60521-4221, USA

Musso, Mitchel (Actor)
c/o Elissa Leeds-Fickman *Reel Talent Management*
PO Box 491035
Los Angeles, CA 90049-9035, USA

Musson, Ron (Race Car Driver)
Motorsports HOF
PO Box 194
Novi, MI 48376-0194, USA

Mustaf, Jerrod (Athlete, Basketball Player)
7724 Hanover Pkwy Apt 302
Greenbelt, MD 20770-2625, USA

Mustafa, Isaiah (Actor)
c/o Kasey Kitchen *ICON PR*
8961 W Sunset Blvd Ste 1C
W Hollywood, CA 90069-1886, USA

Mustaine, Dave (Musician)
ESP Mgmt
838 N Doheny Dr Apt 302
West Hollywood, CA 90069-4849, USA

Muster, Brad (Athlete, Football Player)
167 San Andreas Dr
Novato, CA 94945-1654, USA

Muster, Thomas (Tennis Player)
370 Felter Ave
Hewlett, NY 11557-1132, USA

Musto, Michael (Writer)
Village Voice
36 Cooper Sq Frnt 1
New York, NY 10003-7118

Mutchnick, Max (Producer)
c/o Staff Member *KoMut Entertainment*
300 Television Plaza
Burbank, CA 91505, USA

Muth, Ellen (Actor)
Muth Fans Inc
25 Parkland Pl
Milford, CT 06460-7723, USA

Muth, Rene (Coach)
Pennsylvania State University
Athletic Dept
University Park, PA 16802, USA

Muti, Ornella (Actor)
c/o Staff Member *Agentur Reuter*
Feldbrunnenstr. 50
Hamburg 20148, Germany

Mutis, Jeff (Athlete, Baseball Player)
630 E Wyoming St
C/O Thomas Mutis
Allentown, PA 18103-3536, USA

Mutombo, Dikembe (Athlete, Basketball Player)
4787 Northside Dr
Atlanta, GA 30327-4551, USA

Mutter, Anne-Sophie (Musician)
Effnerstr 48
Munich 81925, GERMANY

Muxworthy, Jake (Actor)
c/o Staff Member *United Talent Agency (UTA)*
9336 Civic Center Dr
Beverly Hills, CA 90210-3604, USA

Muzzatti, Jason (Athlete, Hockey Player)
4581 Dunmorrow Dr
Okemos, MI 48864-1256, USA

M. Velazquez, Nydia (Congressman, Politician)
2302 Rayburn Hob
Washington, DC 20515-4801, USA

Mwine, Ntare (Actor)
c/o August Kammer *TalentWorks*
3500 W Olive Ave Ste 1400
Burbank, CA 91505-5512, USA

Mwinyi, Ali Hassam (President)
President's Office
State House
PO Box 9120
Dar es Salaam, TANZANIA

Mya (Actor, Musician)
c/o Chelsea Brandon *Core Public PR*
1875 Century Park E Ste 930
Los Angeles, CA 90067-2540, USA

My Bloody Valentine (Music Group)
c/o Mick Griffiths *Asgard Promotions*
125 Parkway
London NW1 7PS, UNITED KINGDOM

My Chemical Romance (Music Group)
c/o Matt Galle *Paradigm*
140 Broadway Ste 2600
New York, NY 10005-1011, USA

Mycoskie, Blake (Business Person)
c/o Liz Dalling *Special Artists Agency*
9200 W Sunset Blvd Ste 410
W Hollywood, CA 90069-3506, USA

Myer, Steve (Athlete, Football Player)
423 E Mead Dr
Chandler, AZ 85249-5331, USA

Myers, A Maurice (Business Person)
Waste Management Inc
1001 Fannin St Ste 3900
Houston, TX 77002-6717, USA

Myers, Anne M (Religious Leader)
Church of the Brethren
1451 Dundee Ave
Elgin, IL 60120-1694, USA

Myers, Brett (Athlete, Baseball Player)
312 S Pimlico St
Saint Augustine, FL 32092-3003, USA

Myers, Chris (Athlete, Football Player)
c/o Drew Rosenhaus *Rosenhaus Sports Representation*
3921 Alton Rd # 440
Miami Beach, FL 33140-3852, USA

Myers, Danny (Race Car Driver)
Childress Racing
PO Box 1189
Industrial Dr
Welcome, NC 27374-1189, USA

Myers, Dave (Athlete, Baseball Player)
4221 71st Avenue Ct NW
Gig Harbor, WA 98335-6517, USA

Myers, Dee Dee (Actor, Writer)
c/o Ari Greenburg *WME/IMG*
9601 Wilshire Blvd Ste 200
Beverly Hills, CA 90210-5205, USA

Myers, Frank (Athlete, Football Player)
3874 Woodhollow Dr Apt 410
Euless, TX 76040-7473, USA

Myers, Greg (Athlete, Baseball Player)
38 Princeton Dr
Rancho Mirage, CA 92270-3159, USA

Myers, Hap (Athlete, Hockey Player)
604 Wolf Willow Rd NW
Edmonton, AB T5T 1E6, Canada

Myers, Jack (Athlete, Football Player)
18408 Paseo Olivos Ct
Saratoga, CA 95070-3643, USA

Myers, Jimmy (Athlete, Baseball Player)
1312 NW 14th Pl
Moore, OK 73170-1461, USA

Myers, Lisa (Correspondent)
NBC-TV
4001 Nebraska Ave NW
News Dept
Washington, DC 20016-2795, USA

Myers, Mike (Actor, Comedian)
c/o Ina Treciokas *Slate PR*
901 N Highland Ave
W Hollywood, CA 90038-2412, USA

Myers, Mike (Athlete, Baseball Player)
337 High Ridge Way
Castle Pines, CO 80108-3422, USA

Myers, Pete (Athlete, Basketball Player)
19W011 13th St
Lombard, IL 60148-4758, USA

Myers, Randy (Athlete, Baseball Player)
16722 NE Caples Rd
Battle Ground, WA 98604-9236, USA

Myers, Robert (Bob) (Athlete)
c/o Staff Member *SFX Sports Management*
5335 Wisconsin Ave NW Ste 850
Washington, DC 20015-2052, USA

Myers, Rochelle (Writer)
3827 California St
San Francisco, CA 94118-1501, USA

Myers, Roderick (Rod) (Athlete, Baseball Player)
1816 S 3rd St
Conroe, TX 77301-5131, USA

Myers, Rodney (Rod) (Athlete, Baseball Player)
5801 E Wildcat Dr
Cave Creek, AZ 85331-3064, USA

Myers, Russell (Cartoonist)
Tribune Media Services
435 N Michigan Ave Ste 1500
Chicago, IL 60611-4012, USA

Myers, Tikalsky Linda (Skier)
RR 5 Box 2651
Santa Fe, NM 87506, USA

Myers, Tom (Athlete, Football Player)
6015 Rapid Creek Ct
Kingwood, TX 77345-1954, USA

Myers, Wil (Athlete, Baseball Player)
c/o Jeff Berry *Creative Artists Agency (CAA)*
405 Lexington Ave Fl 19
New York, NY 10174-1800, USA

Myette, Aaron (Athlete, Baseball Player)
5138 236 St
Langley, BC V2Z 2P5, Canada

Myhres, Brantt (Athlete, Hockey Player)
The Sports Corporation
2735-10088 102 Ave NW
Edmonton, AB T5J 2Z1, Canada

Myles, Alannah (Musician)
Miracle Prestige
1 Water Lane
Camden Town
London NW1 8N2, UNITED KINGDOM (UK)

Myles, Eve (Actor)
c/o Torchwood Production Office
BBC Television Centre
Cardiff, Wales, UNITED KINGDOM

Myles, Sophia (Actor)
c/o Lindy King *United Agents*
12-26 Lexington St
London W1F OLE, UNITED KINGDOM

Mylnlkov, Sergel (Athlete, Hockey Player)
Kuzkin Cup Hockey
ul Talalikhin vi 28
Moscow 109029, Russia

Myrah, Don (Athlete, Cycler, Olympic Athlete)
5291 Kentfield Dr
San Jose, CA 95124-5524, USA

Myre, Philippe (Phil) (Athlete, Hockey Player)
101 Rue Dugas
Joliette, QC J6E 4G7, Canada

Myrick, Daniel (Director)
Artisan Entertainment
2700 Colorado Ave
Santa Monica, CA 90404-3553, USA

Myrin, Arden (Actor)
c/o Staff Member *Paradigm*
8942 Wilshire Blvd
Beverly Hills, CA 90211-1908, USA

Myron, Vicki (Writer)
c/o Staff Member *Grand Central Publishing*
237 Park Ave
C/O Author Mail: (Author's Name)
New York, NY 10017-3140, USA

Myrow, Brian (Athlete, Baseball Player)
2500 Prairie Ridge Ct
Fort Worth, TX 76179-5537, USA

Myrtle, Chip (Athlete, Football Player)
6010 S Lima Way
Englewood, CO 80111-5813, USA

Mysen, Bjorn O (Misc)
Camegie Institution
5221 Broad Branch Road
Washington, DC 20015, USA

Myslinski, Tom (Athlete, Football Player)
1347 Marsh Harbor Dr
Jacksonville, FL 32225-2644, USA

Myss, Caroline (Writer)
Transworld Publishers
61-63 Uxbridge Road
London W5 5SA, UNITED KINGDOM

Mystic (Music Group, Musician)
c/o Staff Member *General Entertainment*
1409 East Blvd Ste 231
Charlotte, NC 28203-5817, USA

Mystikal (Musician)
c/o Staff Member *ICM Partners*
10250 Constellation Blvd Fl 7
Los Angeles, CA 90067-6207, USA

N

Na, Li (Athlete, Tennis Player)
c/o Max Eisenbud *IMG World*
200 5th Ave Fl 7
New York, NY 10010-3307, USA

Nabe, Ricky (Actor)
c/o Staff Member *Envision Entertainment*
8840 Wilshire Blvd Fl 3
Beverly Hills, CA 90211-2606, USA

Naber, Jofin P (Swimmer)
PO Box 50107
Pasadena, CA 91115-0107, USA

Naber, John (Athlete, Olympic Athlete, Swimmer)
PNaber And Associates Inc PO Box 50107 O Box 50107
Pasadena, CA 91115-0107, USA

Nabers, Drayton Jr (Business Person)
Protective Life Corp
2801 Highway 280 S Ofc
Birmingham, AL 35223-2488, USA

Nabholz, Chris (Athlete, Baseball Player)
2030 W Market St
Pottsville, PA 17901-1917, USA

Nabokov, Evgeni (Athlete, Hockey Player)
5763 Poppy Hills Pl # Pi
San Jose, CA 95138-2243, USA

Nabors, Richard (Athlete, Football Player)
1625 Brighton Ct
Beaumont, TX 77706-3220, USA

Naccarato, Vin (Musician)
Paramount Entertainment
PO Box 12
Far Hills, NJ 07931-0012, USA

Nachamkin, Boris (Athlete, Basketball Player)
350 E 62nd St Apt 5J
New York, NY 10065-8261, USA

Nachbaur, Don (Athlete, Hockey Player)
671 Clermont Dr
Richland, WA 99352-9519, USA

Nachmanoff, Jeffrey (Director)
1963 Canyon Dr
Los Angeles, CA 90068-3604, USA

Nachmansohn, David (Misc)
560 Riverside Dr
New York, NY 10027-3202, USA

Nacincik, John (Athlete, Basketball Player)
2815 Garrett Rd
White Hall, MD 21161-9737, USA

Nadal, Rafael (Athlete, Tennis Player)
Rafa Nadal Foundation
Ave Diagonal 618
#50A
Palma de Mallorca 08021, SPAIN

Nada Surf (Music Group)
c/o Staff Member *Paradigm (Monterey)*
404 W Franklin St
Monterey, CA 93940-2303, USA

Nadeau, Jerry (Race Car Driver)
192 Apple Hill Rd
Troutman, NC 28166-9570, USA

Nadel, Barbara (Writer)
c/o Staff Member *St Martins Press*
175 5th Ave
Publicity Dept
New York, NY 10010-7703, USA

Nadel, Eric (Sportscaster)
10612 De Bercy Ct
Dallas, TX 75229-5331, USA

Nader, Michael (Actor)
28 E 10th St Apt 7K
New York, NY 10003-6212, USA

Nader, Ralph (Activist, Writer)
53 Hillside Ave
Winsted, CT 06098-1531, USA

Nadler, Jerrold (Congressman, Politician)
2334 Rayburn Hob
Washington, DC 20515-3208, USA

Nadon, Branden (Actor)
PMG Management
228-1118 Homer St
Vancouver, BC V6B 6L5, CANADA

Nady, Xavier (Athlete, Baseball Player)
15671 Via Santa Pradera
San Diego, CA 92131-4314, USA

Naegle, Sue (Business Person)
HBO Entertainment
2500 Broadway Ste 400
Santa Monica, CA 90404-3176, USA

Naehring, Tim (Athlete, Baseball Player)
7300 Pinehurst Dr
Cincinnati, OH 45244-3272, USA

Naeole, Chris (Athlete, Football Player)
1314 Charter Ct E
Jacksonville, FL 32225-2658, USA

Nafziger, Dana A (Athlete, Football Player)
251 El Dorado Way
Pismo Beach, CA 93449-1535, USA

Nagahama, Kazu (Actor)
c/o Staff Member *Ology Entertainment*
9151 W Sunset Blvd
West Hollywood, CA 90069-3106, USA

Nagakura, Saburo (Misc)
2-7-13 Higashicho
Kichijoji
Musashino, Tokyo 1800002, JAPAN

Nagao, Tomoaki (Nigo) (Business Person, Producer)
Nowhere Co, Ltd
2-9-9 Sendagaya
Shibuyaku
Tokyo 151-0051, Japan

Nagashima, Shigeo (Baseball Player)
3-29-19 Denenchofu
Ohtaku
Tokyo 00145, JAPAN

Nagel, Craig (Athlete, Football Player)
303 Kingsway Ct
Cold Spring, KY 41076-3510, USA

Nagel, Steven R (Astronaut)
3801 Eagle View Ct
Columbia, MO 65203-1064, USA

Nagel, Thomas (Misc)
New York University
40 Washington Sq S Frnt 1
Law School
New York, NY 10012-1099, USA

Nagelson, Russ (Rusty) (Athlete, Baseball Player)
4 Carriage Ct
Little Rock, AR 72211-2280, USA

Nageotte, Clint (Athlete, Baseball Player)
4700 Morningside Dr
Cleveland, OH 44109-4560, USA

Nagl, Miriam (Athlete, Golfer)
2120 Harbourside Dr Unit 616
Longboat Key, FL 34228-4261, USA

Nagle, Browning (Athlete, Football Player)
8990 Grovelawn Dr
Germantown, TN 38139-5698, USA

Nagler, Gern (Athlete, Football Player)
73595 Agave Ln
Palm Desert, CA 92260-6685, USA

Nagobads, George (Athlete, Hockey Player)
5180 Circle Dr
Minneapolis, MN 55439-1401, USA

Nagra, Parminder (Actor)
c/o Oriana Elia *Curtis Brown Ltd*
28-29 Hay Market
Hay Market House
London SW1Y 4SP, UNITED KINGDOM

Nagy, Charles (Athlete, Baseball Player, Olympic Athlete)
60 Robin Rd
Westbury, NY 11590-1104, USA

Nagy, Ladislav (Athlete, Hockey Player)
7801 N 54th St
Paradise Valley, AZ 85253-3003, USA

Nagy, Mike (Athlete, Baseball Player)
24 Nial@ra Ln
West Yarmouth, MA 02673-5039, USA

Nagy, Steve (Athlete, Baseball Player)
2205 NE Ridgewood Dr
Poulsbo, WA 98370-8529, USA

Nahan, Stu (Sportscaster)
11274 Canton Dr
Studio City, CA 91604-4154, USA

Nahorodny, Bill (Athlete, Baseball Player)
1948 Rainbow Dr
Clearwater, FL 33765-3564, USA

Nahrgang, Jim (Athlete, Hockey Player)
18283 Parkshore Dr
Northville, MI 48168-8591, USA

Naifeh, Steven W (Writer)
335 Sumter St SE
Aiken, SC 29801-4661, USA

Nail, David (Musician)
411 Forrest St
Franklin, TN 37064-3316, USA

Nailon, Lee (Athlete, Basketball Player)
10013 W Bella Vista St
Wichita, KS 67212-6783, USA

Naimoli, Vincent (Baseball Player)
Tampa Bay Devil Rays
18440 Exciting Idlewild Blvd # 100
Lutz, FL 33548-4573, USA

Nair, Mira (Director)
c/o Staff Member *Mirabai Films*
27 W 24th St Ste 403
New York, NY 10010-3287, USA

Nair, Staz (Actor, Musician)
c/o Marnie Briskin *Circle of Confusion (NY)*
270 Lafayette St Ste 402
New York, NY 10012-3327, USA

Naisbitt, John (Writer)
Spittelauer Platz 5A3A
Vienna 01090, AUSTRIA

Naish, Bronwen (Musician)
Moelfre Xwm Pennant
Gamdolbenmaen
Gwunedd
North Wales LL5 9AX, WALES

Najafi, Babak (Director)
c/o Shelley Browning *Magnolia Entertainment*
9595 Wilshire Blvd Ste 601
Beverly Hills, CA 90212-2506, USA

Najee (Musician)
Associated booking Corp
1995 Broadway # 501
New York, NY 10023-5882, USA

Najera, Eduardo (Basketball Player)
c/o Staff Member *Dallas Mavericks*
1333 N Stemmons Fwy Ste 105
Dallas, TX 75207-3722, USA

Najera, Rick (Actor)
c/o Michelle Grant *Grant Management*
1158 26th St # 414
Santa Monica, CA 90403-4698, USA

Najimy, Kathy (Actor, Comedian)
c/o Richard Fisher *Abrams Artists Agency*
275 7th Ave Fl 26
New York, NY 10001-6708, USA

Nakajima, Tommy (Athlete, Golfer)
c/o Staff Member *IMG (Tokyo)*
8-18 Moto-Akasaka
1-chome, Minato-ku
Tokyo 00107, JAPAN

Nakama, Keo (Swimmer)
1344 9th Ave
Honolulu, HI 96816-2615, USA

Nakano, Shinji (Race Car Driver)
Fernandez Racing
6950 Guion Rd # 51
Indianapolis, IN 46268-2576, USA

Naked, Bif (Musician)
Crazed Mgmt
PO Box 779
New Hope, PA 18938-0779, USA

Naked and Famous, The (Music Group)
c/o Staff Member *CRS Music Management*
PO Box 41-434
St Lukes, Auckland 01346, New Zealand

Nalder, Eric C (Journalist)
Seattle Times
1120 John St
Editorial Dept
Seattle, WA 98109-5321, USA

Nalen, Tom (Athlete, Football Player)
3146 S Clayton St
Denver, CO 80210-6808, USA

Nalick, Anna (Musician)
c/o Jesse Nicita *RPMedia*
Prefers to be contacted by email or phone.
Los Angeles, CA NA, USA

Nall, Benita Krista (Actor)
c/o Staff Member *Main Title Entertainment*
8383 Wilshire Blvd Ste 408
Beverly Hills, CA 90211-2435, USA

Nall, N Anita (Swimmer)
PO Box 872505
Tempe, AZ 85287-2505, USA

Nalle, Karen Dotrice (Actor)
501 Sadie Rd
Topanga, CA 90290-3432, USA

Nam, Leonardo (Actor)
c/o Sharon Paz *Abrams Artists Agency*
750 N San Vicente Blvd
E Tower Fl 11
Los Angeles, CA 90069-5788, USA

Namaliu, Rabbie L (Prime Minister)
PO Box 6655
National Capital District
Boroko, PAPUA NEW GUINEA

Namath, Joe (Actor, Athlete, Football Player)
Namanco Productions
300 E 51st St Apt 7D
New York, NY 10022-7810, USA

Namestnikov, Evgeny (Athlete, Hockey Player)
1302 Lakeview Dr
Wolverine Lake, MI 48390-2233, USA

Nance, John J (Writer)
4512 S 8th St
Tacoma, WA 98405-1208, USA

Nance, Shane (Athlete, Baseball Player)
3403 Harbour Breeze Ln
Pearland, TX 77584-7958, USA

Nance, Todd (Musician)
Brown Cat Inc
400 Foundry St
Athens, GA 30601-2623, USA

Nance Jr, Larry (Athlete, Basketball Player)
c/o Mark Bartelstein *Priority Sports & Entertainment (Chicago)*
325 N La Salle Dr Ste 650
Chicago, IL 60654-8182, USA

Nandi, Ivo (Actor)
c/o Beth Stein *Beth Stein and Associates*
925 N La Brea Ave # 4
West Hollywood, CA 90038-2321, USA

Nanjiani, Kumail (Actor, Comedian)
4470 W Sunset Blvd Ste 536
Los Angeles, CA 90027-6050, USA

Nanne, Lou (Athlete, Hockey Player, Olympic Athlete)
6982 Tupa Dr
Minneapolis, MN 55439-1641, USA

Nantais, Rich (Athlete, Hockey Player)
9585 Rue Jourdain
Quebec, QC G2K 1K5, Canada

Nantz, Jim (Sportscaster)
c/o Alan Zucker *Excel Sports Management*
1700 Broadway Fl 29
New York, NY 10019-6559, USA

Napier, James (Actor)
c/o Grahame Dunster *Auckland Actors*
PO Box 56-460
Dominion Road
Auckland 00003, NEW ZEALAND

Napier, John (Designer)
MLR Douglas House
16-18 Douglas St
London SW1P 4PB, UNITED KINGDOM (UK)

Napier, Mark (Athlete, Hockey Player)
NHL Alumni Assocation
400 Kipling Ave 2nd Fl
Attn Executive Director
Etobicoke, ON M8V 3L1, Canada

Napier, Neil (Actor)
c/o Mona Loring *Status PR*
PO Box 6191
Westlake Village, CA 91359-6191, USA

Napier, Wilfrid F Cardinal (Religious Leader)
Archbishop's House
154 Gordon Road
Greyville 04023, SOUTH AFRICA

Naples, Al (Athlete, Baseball Player)
99 Nickerson Rd
Orleans, MA 02653-3314, USA

Napoleon, Ed (Athlete, Baseball Player)
1312 73rd St NW
Bradenton, FL 34209-1155, USA

Napoles, Jose (Boxer)
Cerrada De Tizapan 9-303 Ediciov
Codigo Postel
Suffield, CT 06080-0001, MEXICO

Napoli, Mike (Athlete, Baseball Player)
c/o Staff Member *Los Angeles Dodgers*
1000 Elysian Park Ave
Los Angeles, CA 90012, USA

Naponic, Robert (Athlete, Football Player)
10807 Timberglen Dr
Houston, TX 77024-6808, USA

Naragon, Hal (Athlete, Baseball Player)
1521 Hagey Dr
Barberton, OH 44203-7724, USA

Narain, Nicole (Actor)
8033 W Sunset Blvd # 224
Los Angeles, CA 90046-2401, USA

Naranjo, Monica (Musician)
c/o Staff Member *Sony Music (Miami)*
404 Washington Ave Ste 700
Miami Beach, FL 33139-6615, USA

Nardelli, Michael (Actor)
2615 N Vermont Ave
Los Angeles, CA 90027-1244, USA

Nardini, Thomas (Tom) (Actor)
139 Beach Ave
Madison, CT 06443-2854, USA

Narducci, Tim (Musician)
Artists Group International
9560 Wilshire Blvd Ste 400
Beverly Hills, CA 90212-2442, USA

Narizzano, Silvio (Cas) (Director)
Al Parker
55 Park Lane
London W1Y 3DD, UNITED KINGDOM (UK)

Narron, Jerry (Athlete, Baseball Player, Coach)
100 Harding Pl
Goldsboro, NC 27534-9100, USA

Narron, Sam (Athlete, Baseball Player)
101 Mill Pl
Goldsboro, NC 27534-8933, USA

Naruhito (Royalty)
Imperial Palaca
1-1 Chiyoda
Chiyoda-ku
Tokyo, JAPAN

Narveson, Chris (Athlete, Baseball Player)
5525 E Thomas Rd Unit Hl
Phoenix, AZ 85018-8126, USA

Narz, Jack (Television Host)
1906 Beverly Place
Beverly Hills, CA 90210, USA

Nas (Musician)
30 Vintage Ct
McDonough, GA 30253-4246, USA

Nasclemento, Milton (Musician, Songwriter, Writer)
Tribo Producoes
Av A Lombardi 800
Rio de Janeiro 22 640-000, BRAZIL

Nash, Amber (Actor)
c/o Jessica Katz *Katz Public Relations*
14527 Dickens St
Sherman Oaks, CA 91403-3756, USA

Nash, Charles F (Cotton) (Athlete, Basketball Player)
600 Summershade Cir
Lexington, KY 40502-2723, USA

Nash, David (Artist)
Capel Rhiw Blanau
Flestiniog
Gwynedd Wales LL41 3NT, WALES

Nash, Dick (Musician)
EMI Music
1750 Vine St
Capital Records
Hollywood, CA 90028-5209, USA

Nash, Graham (Musician, Songwriter)
c/o Brent Smith *WME|IMG*
9601 Wilshire Blvd
Beverly Hills, CA 90210-5213, USA

Nash, Jamia Simone (Actor, Musician)
c/o Nancy Carson *Carson-Adler Agency*
250 W 57th St Ste 2128
New York, NY 10107-2104, USA

Nash, Jim (Athlete, Baseball Player)
1722 Stone Bridge Ct
Marietta, GA 30064-4765, USA

Nash, Joe (Athlete, Football Player)
29 Vermont St
West Roxbury, MA 02132-2336, USA

Nash, Joy (Actor)
c/o Melissa Raubvogel *Imprint PR*
375 Hudson St
New York, NY 10014-3658, USA

Nash, Kate (Musician)
c/o Margrit Polak *Margrit Polak Management*
1920 Hillhurst Ave Ste 405
Los Angeles, CA 90027-2712, USA

Nash, Kevin (Wrestler)
c/o Andrew Stawiarski *ADS Management*
269 S Beverly Dr Ste 441
Beverly Hills, CA 90212-3851, USA

Nash, Leigh (Musician)
c/o Staff Member *Paradigm (Monterey)*
404 W Franklin St
Monterey, CA 93940-2303, USA

Nash, Niecy (Actor, Television Host)
17821 Lassen St Apt 108
Northridge, CA 91325-4703, USA

Nash, Noreen (Actor)
719 N Maple Dr
Beverly Hills, CA 90210-3480, USA

Nash, Rick (Athlete, Hockey Player)
c/o Staff Member *Columbus Blue Jackets*
200 W Nationwide Blvd Ste Level
Nationwide Arena
Columbus, OH 43215-2564, USA

Nash, Robert (Athlete, Basketball Player)
659 Kahiau Loop
Honolulu, HI 96821-2539, USA

Nash, Steve (Athlete, Basketball Player)
2903 Manhattan Ave
Manhattan Beach, CA 90266-2050, USA

Nash, Ted (Composer, Musician)
c/o Jud Friedman *4 Entertainment*
101 S Topanga Canyon Blvd Unit 665
Topanga, CA 90290-2030, USA

Nash, Terius (The-Dream) (Musician)
c/o Mitch Blackman *ICM Partners (NY)*
730 5th Ave
New York, NY 10019-4105, USA

Nash, Tyson (Athlete, Hockey Player)
Phoenix Coyotes
6751 N Sunset Blvd Ste 200
Attn: Broadcast Dept
Glendale, AZ 85305-3162, USA

Nash, Tyson (Athlete, Hockey Player)
17751 N 92nd Way
Scottsdale, AZ 85255-6025, USA

Nash, Wyatt (Actor)
c/o Atil Singh *Principal Entertainment*
9255 W Sunset Blvd Ste 500
Los Angeles, CA 90069-3301, USA

Nasland, Markus (Athlete, Hockey Player)
808 Griffiths Way
Vancouver, BC V68 6G1, USA

Naslund, Markus (Athlete, Hockey Player)
Mik
154 Earl St
Kingston, ON K7L 2H2, Canada

Naslund, Mats (Athlete, Hockey Player)
6963 Progressona
Switzerland

Naslund, Ron (Athlete, Hockey Player, Olympic Athlete)
2600 Cheyenne Cir
Hopkins, MN 55305-2309, USA

Nasr, Seyyed Hossein (Misc)
George Washington University
Gelman Library
Washington, DC 20052-0001, USA

Nasreddine, Alain (Athlete, Hockey Player)
35 Brians Pl
Wilkes Barre, PA 18702-7864, USA

Nasser, Jack (Producer)
c/o Staff Member *Nasser Entertainment Group*
11350 Ventura Blvd Ste 101
Studio City, CA 91604-3140, USA

Nasser, Jacques A (Business Person)
One Equity Partners
1st National Plaza
Chicago, IL 60607, USA

Nassetta, Christopher (Business Person)
10410 Bellagio Rd
Los Angeles, CA 90077-3819, USA

Nassib, Ryan (Athlete, Football Player)
c/o Todd France *Creative Artists Agency (CAA) Sports*
3500 Lenox Rd NE
Atlanta, GA 30326-4228, USA

Nassif, Paul (Doctor, Reality Star)
Spalding Drive Cosmetic Surgery & Dermatology
120 S Spalding Dr Ste 301
Beverly Hills, CA 90212-1841, USA

Nastase, Ilie (Tennis Player)
Calea Plevnei 14
Bucarest, HUNGARY

Nastu, Phil (Athlete, Baseball Player)
52 Stratfield Pl
Bridgeport, CT 06606-4002, USA

Nat, Marie-Jose (Actor)
c/o Laurent Gregoire *Agence Adequat*
21 Rue D'Uzes
Paris 75002, FRANCE

Natal, Bob (Athlete, Baseball Player)
3913 Cockrill Dr
McKinney, TX 75072-2413, USA

Natali, Vincenzo (Director)
c/o Philip Raskind *WME|IMG*
9601 Wilshire Blvd
Beverly Hills, CA 90210-5213, USA

Nater, Swen (Athlete, Basketball Player)
Costco Wholesale Corp
999 Lake Dr
Issaquah, WA 98027-8990, USA

Nathan, Joe (Athlete, Baseball Player)
1880 Farmstead Cir
Eden Praire, MN 55347, USA

Nathan, Joseph A (Business Person)
Compuware Corp
1 Campus Martius
Detroit, MI 48226-5099, USA

Nathan, Tony C (Athlete, Coach, Football Coach, Football Player)
15110 Dunbarton Pl
Miami Lakes, FL 33016-1415, USA

Nathaniel (Popp), Bishop (Religious Leader)
Romanian Orthodox Episcopate
2522 Grey Tower Rd
Jackson, MI 49201-9120, USA

Nathanson, Jeff (Writer)
c/o Staff Member *United Talent Agency (UTA)*
9336 Civic Center Dr
Beverly Hills, CA 90210-3604, USA

Nathanson, Matt (Musician)
70 Nebraska St
San Francisco, CA 94110-5719, USA

Nathanson, Michael (Actor)
c/o Kelli M Jones *Status PR (NY)*
59 Chelsea Piers
Level 3
New York, NY 10011-1008, USA

Nathanson, Roy (Musician)
Brad Simon Organization
122 E 57th St # 300
New York, NY 10022-2623, USA

Nation, Joey (Athlete, Baseball Player)
2125 N Roff Ave
Oklahoma City, OK 73107-2749, USA

Natividad, Kitten (Actor)
PO Box 48938
Los Angeles, CA 90048, USA

Natowich, Andrew (Athlete, Football Player)
24 Lexington Ave
Brattleboro, VT 05301-6626, USA

Natt, Calvin (Athlete, Basketball Player)
25201 E Indore Dr
Aurora, CO 80016-2189, USA

Nattiel, Ricky (Athlete, Football Player)
835 NW 119th St
Gainesville, FL 32606-0449, USA

Nattress, Ric (Athlete, Hockey Player)
Stoney Creek Warriors
467 Charlton Ave E
Attn Coaching Staff
Hamilton, ON L8N 1Z4, Canada

Natural (Musician)
Official International Fan Club
PO Box 5097
Bellingham, WA 98227-5097, USA

Natyshak, Mike (Athlete, Hockey Player)
2005 Mount Vernon Ave
Toledo, OH 43607-1545, USA

Naude, C F Beyers (Religious Leader)
26 Hoylake Road
Greenside 02193, SOUTH AFRICA

Naudet, Jules (Producer)
c/o Staff Member *WME|IMG*
9601 Wilshire Blvd
Beverly Hills, CA 90210-5213, USA

Nauert, Paul (Baseball Player)
1201 Steeple Run
Lawrenceville, GA 30043-6354, USA

Nauert, Paul (Athlete, Baseball Player)
1201 Steeple Run
Lawrenceville, GA 30043-6354, USA

Naughton, David (Actor)
4 Via Las Colinas Apt 8
Rancho Mirage, CA 92270-6020, USA

Naughton, James (Actor)
127 Valley Forge Rd
Weston, CT 06883-1914, USA

Naughton, Laurie (Actor)
c/o Bruce Smith *OmniPop Talent Group*
4605 Lankershim Blvd Ste 201
Toluca Lake, CA 91602-1874, USA

Naughton, Naturi (Musician)
c/o Kerry Smalls *The Chamber Group*
75 Broad St Rm 708
New York, NY 10004-3244, USA

Naulis, Willie (Basketball Player)
Chuck & Willie's Auto Agency
13900 Hawthome Blvd
Hawthome, CA 90250, USA

Naulty, Dan (Athlete, Baseball Player)
23705 Via Del Rio
Yorba Linda, CA 92887-2717, USA

Nauman, Bruce L (Artist)
4630 Rising Hill Rd
Altadena, CA 91001-3748, USA

Naumenko, Gregg (Athlete, Hockey Player)
101 Iroquois Trl
Wood Dale, IL 60191-2222, USA

Naumoff, Paul (Athlete, Football Player)
932 Mohawk St
Columbus, OH 43206-2633, USA

Nause, Martha (Athlete, Golfer)
13206 Patterson Trl
Minocqua, WI 54548, USA

Nauta, Kate (Actor)
c/o Ben Press *Primary Wave Entertainment*
10850 Wilshire Blvd Fl 6
Los Angeles, CA 90024-4319, USA

Nava, Daniel (Athlete, Baseball Player)
315 t Francis St
Redwood City, CA 94062-2215, USA

Nava, Gregory (Director)
International Creative Mgmt
8942 Wilshire Blvd
Beverly Hills, CA 90211-1908, USA

Navarez, Alfred (Musician)
MPI Talent
9255 W Sunset Blvd Ste 407
Los Angeles, CA 90069-3302, USA

Navarro, Christian (Actor)
c/o Laurina Spencer *Slate PR*
901 N Highland Ave
W Hollywood, CA 90038-2412, USA

Navarro, Dave (Musician)
c/o Joy Fehily *PMK/BNC Public Relations*
1840 Century Park E Ste 1400
Los Angeles, CA 90067-2115, USA

Navarro, Dioner (Athlete, Baseball Player)
9930 Jonas Salk Dr Apt 314
Riverview, FL 33578-7445, USA

Navarro, Jaime (Athlete, Baseball Player)
4213 Reaves Rd
Kissimmee, FL 34746-3427, USA

Navarro, Juan Carlos (Athlete, Basketball Player)
10545 Ashglen Cir S
Collierville, TN 38017-3660, USA

Navarro, Julio (Athlete, Baseball Player)
10-32 Calle 3
Santa Rosa
Bayamon, PR 00959-6612, USA

Navarro, Tito (Athlete, Baseball Player)
556 Calle Creuz
San Juan, PR 00923-1826, USA

Navas, Bibiana (Actor)
c/o Gabriel Blanco *Gabriel Blanco Iglesias (Mexico)*
Rio Balsas 35-32
Colonia Cuauhtemoc
DF 06500, Mexico

Navayne, Kevin (Actor)
c/o Kennedy Diaz *Sessions Public Relations*
601 S Figueroa St
Los Angeles, CA 90017-5704, USA

Navedo, Andrea (Actor, Musician)
c/o Michael Geiser *Jill Fritzo Public Relations*
208 E 51st St # 305
New York, NY 10022-6557, USA

Navies, Hannibal (Athlete, Football Player)
2891 Grey Moss Pass
Duluth, GA 30097-6272, USA

Navis, Hannibal (Athlete, Football Player)
4616 Rustling Woods Dr
Denver, NC 28037-5600, USA

Navon, Itzhak (President)
Education & Culture Ministry
Hakiria
Jerusalem, ISRAEL

Navratilova, Martina (Athlete, Tennis Player)
Martina Enterprises Inc
2555 Collins Ave Apt 1711
Miami Beach, FL 33140-4777, USA

Nay, Jonas (Actor)
c/o Sara Puro-Steele *Independent Talent Group*
40 Whitfield St
London W1T 2RH, UNITED KINGDOM

Naymenko, Gregg (Athlete)
2695 E Katella Ave
Anaheim, CA 92806-5904

Nayyar, Kunal (Actor)
c/o Jason Kim *Lovett Management*
1327 Brinkley Ave
Los Angeles, CA 90049-3619, USA

Nazarian, Sam (Business Person)
SBE
5900 Wilshire Blvd Ste 3100
Los Angeles, CA 90036-5030, USA

N. Cicilline, David (Congressman, Politician)
128 Cannon Hob
Washington, DC 20515-1102, USA

Ndayizeye, Domitien (President)
President's Office
Bujumbura, BURUNDI

Ndegeocello, Me'Shell (Musician)
Monetary Peninsula Artists
509 Hartnell St
Monterey, CA 93940-2825, USA

Ndegeocello, Michelle (Musician)
c/o Staff Member *Paradigm (Monterey)*
404 W Franklin St
Monterey, CA 93940-2303, USA

Ndimira, Pascal Firmin (Prime Minister)
Prime Minister's Office
Bujumbura, BURUNDI

N'Dour, Youssou (Musician)
Konzertagentur Berthold Seliger
Nonnengasse 15
Fulda 36037, GERMANY

N'Dour, Youssou (Musician)
c/o Staff Member *Nonesuch Records*
75 Rockefeller Plz Fl 8
New York, NY 10019-6908, USA

Neagle, Denny (Athlete, Baseball Player)
16254 Sandstone Dr
Morrison, CO 80465-2163, USA

Neal, Blaine (Athlete, Baseball Player)
256 Dowdy Dr
Gibbstown, NJ 08027-1175, USA

Neal, Craig (Athlete, Basketball Player)
122 Wellesley Dr NE
Albuquerque, NM 87106-2129, USA

Neal, Curley (Athlete, Basketball Player)
1275 Regency Pl
Lake Mary, FL 32746-4339, USA

Neal, Diane (Actor)

Neal, Dylan (Actor)
c/o Lena Lees *Play Management*
220-807 Powell St
Vancouver, BC V6A 1H7, CANADA

Neal, Edwin (Actor)
501 W Powell Ln
Austin, TX 78753-5978, USA

Neal, Elise (Actor)
c/o Pamela Sharp *Sharp & Associates*
1516 N Fairfax Ave
Los Angeles, CA 90046-2608, USA

Neal, Fred (Curly) (Basketball Player)
PO Box 915415
Longwood, FL 32791-5415, USA

Neal, Lia (Athlete, Olympic Athlete, Swimmer)
Rome K Neal
43 N Oxford St # 2
Brooklyn, NY 11205-1006, USA

Neal, Lloyd (Athlete, Basketball Player)
905 NE Mariners Loop
Portland, OR 97211-1574, USA

Neal, Lorenzo (Athlete, Football Player)
10520 Waterbury Dr
Stockton, CA 95209-4204, USA

Neal, Mike (Athlete, Football Player)
c/o Ashley Smith Becker *Relativity Sports*
2029 Century Park E Ste 1550
Century City, CA 90067-3000, USA

Neal, Scott (Actor)

Neal, T Daniel (Dan) (Athlete, Football Player)
3200 Shoal Lake Dr
Lexington, KY 40515-5415, USA

Neale, Gary L (Business Person)
Northern Indiana Service
801 E 86th Ave
Merrillville, IN 46410-6271, USA

Neale, Harry (Athlete, Hockey Player)
224 Quail Hollow Ln
East Amherst, NY 14051-1634, USA

Nealon, Kevin (Actor, Comedian)
16105 Northfield St
Pacific Palisades, CA 90272-4263, USA

Nealy, Eddie (Athlete, Basketball Player)
702 Lightstone Dr
San Antonio, TX 78258-2305, USA

Neame, Christopher (Actor)
Borinstein Oreck Bogart
3172 Dona Susana Dr
Studio City, CA 91604-4356, USA

Near, Holly (Actor, Musician, Songwriter, Writer)
PO Box 236
Ukiah, CA 95482-0236, USA

Nearing, Merna (Baseball Player)
21079 W Good Hope Rd Apt D-1
Lannon, WI 53046-9770, USA

Neary, Martin G J (Musician)
2 Little Cloister
Westminster Abbey
London SW1P 3PL, UNITED KINGDOM (UK)

Neary, Robert (Actor, Director)
c/o Lin Bickelmann *Encore Artists Management*
3815 W Olive Ave Ste 101
Burbank, CA 91505-4674, USA

Neaton, Pat (Athlete, Hockey Player)
3519 Olde Dominion Dr # 2
Brighton, MI 48114-4942, USA

Nebel, Dorothy Hoyt (Skier)
5340 Balfor Dr
Virginia Beach, VA 23464-2441, USA

Nebout, Claire (Actor)
Artmedia
20 Ave Rapp
Paris 75007, FRANCE

Necciai, Ron (Athlete, Baseball Player)
6261 Overlook Ln
Rostraver Township, PA 15012-3928, USA

Nechaev, Victor (Athlete, Hockey Player)
435 Wenham Rd
Pasadena, CA 91107-5223, USA

Neck, Tommy (Athlete, Football Player)
2107 Marie Pl
Monroe, LA 71201-3413, USA

Neckar, Stanislav (Athlete, Hockey Player)
10255 Waterside Oaks Dr
Tampa, FL 33647-3194, USA

Ned, Derrick (Athlete, Football Player)
430 Charles St
Eunice, LA 70535-4904, USA

Nedeljakova, Barbara (Actor)
Beverly Hecht Agency
3500 W Olive Ave Ste 1180
C/O Robert Depp
Burbank, CA 91505-4651, USA

Nedney, Joe (Athlete, Football Player)
121 Lauren Cir
Scotts Valley, CA 95066-3836, USA

Nedomansky, Vaclav (Athlete, Hockey Player)
6600 Beachview Dr Apt 204
Rancho Palos Verdes, CA 90275-5840, USA

Nedorost, Vaclav (Athlete, Hockey Player)
1 Panther Pkwy
Sunrise, FL 33323-5315, USA

Nedved, Petr (Athlete, Hockey Player)
11230 110 St NW
Edmonton, AB T5G 3H7, Canada

Needham, Col (Business Person)
Internet Movie Database
410 Terry Ave N
Seattle, WA 98109-5210, USA

Needham, Connie (Actor)
2000 Corporate Dr Apt 202
Ladera Ranch, CA 92694-1109, USA

Needham, James J (Business Person)
97 Coopers Farm Rd Unit 1
Southampton, NY 11968-4066, USA

Needham, Tracey (Actor)
c/o Tony Chargin *Ovation Management*
12028 National Blvd
Los Angeles, CA 90064-3542, USA

Needleman, Jacob (Misc)
841 Wawona Ave
Oakland, CA 94610-1250, USA

Neel, Roy (Politician)
3307 Northampton St NW
Washington, DC 20015-1652, USA

Neel, Troy (Athlete, Baseball Player)
PO Box 1582
El Campo, TX 77437-1582, USA

Neely, Bob (Athlete, Hockey Player)
72 Squire Bakers Lane
Markham, ON L3P 3H2, CANADA

Neely, Cam (Athlete, Hockey Player)
100 Legends Way Ste 250
Attn Office of the President
Boston, MA 02114-1390, United States

Neely, Cam (Athlete, Hockey Player)
76 Davison Dr
Lincoln, MA 01773-2216, USA

Neely, Gina (Chef, Television Host)
c/o Staff Member *The Food Network.com*
1180 Avenue of the Americas Fl 14
New York, NY 10036-8401, USA

Neely, Pat (Chef, Television Host)
533 Lower Glass Bridge Rd
Lagrange, GA 30240-8713, USA

Neely, Ralph E (Athlete, Football Player)
6943 Sperry St
Dallas, TX 75214-2855, USA

Neely, Rumy (Fashion Designer, Internet Star, Writer)
c/o Lori Sale *Artist & Brand Management*
9320 Wilshire Blvd Ste 212
Beverly Hills, CA 90212-3217, USA

Neeman, Cal (Athlete, Baseball Player)
93 Champagne Dr
Lake Saint Louis, MO 63367-1604, USA

Neeson, Liam (Actor)
c/o Staff Member *Artists Rights Group (ARG)*
4A Exmoor St
London W10 6BD, UNITED KINGDOM

Nef, Sonia (Skier)
Halten 345
Grub 09035, SWITZERLAND

Neff, Bob (Athlete, Football Player)
2 Crestview
Athens, TX 75751-2932, USA

Neff, Lucas (Actor)
c/o Jason Weinberg *Untitled Entertainment*
350 S Beverly Dr Ste 200
Beverly Hills, CA 90212-4819, USA

Negga, Ruth (Actor)
c/o Jonty Brook *Markham & Froggatt*
4 Windmill St
London W1T 1HZ, UNITED KINGDOM

Negoesco, Stephen (Coach)
University of San Francisco
Athletic Dept
San Francisco, CA 94117, USA

Negray, Ron (Athlete, Baseball Player)
4502 Lahm Dr
New Franklin, OH 44319-3418, USA

Negreanu, Daniel (Actor)
PO Box 416
2251 North Rampart Blvd
Las Vegas, NV 89125-0416, USA

Negron, Chuck (Musician)
J-Bird Entertainment
248 W Park Ave # 180
Long Beach, NY 11561-3212, USA

Nehamas, Alexander (Misc)
Princeton University
Philosophy Dept
Princeton, NJ 08544-0001, USA

Nehemiah, Renaldo (Athlete, Football Player)
15515 Owens Glen Ter
North Potomac, MD 20878-2369, USA

Nehmer, Meinhard (Athlete)
Vamkevitz
Altenkirchen 18556, GERMANY

Neibauer, Gary (Athlete, Baseball Player)
4005 19th St NE LOT 520
Bismarck, ND 58503-5484, USA

Neibhors, William (Athlete, Football Player)
1904 Chippendale Dr SE
Huntsville, AL 35801-1309, USA

Neid, Silvia (Soccer Player)
Betramstr 18
Frankfurt/Main 60320, GERMANY

Neidert, John (Athlete, Football Player)
4731 Placid Cir
Sarasota, FL 34231-6486, USA

Neidich, Charles (Musician)
Colbert Artists
111 W 57th St
New York, NY 10019-2211, USA

Neidlinger, Jim (Athlete, Baseball Player)
139 Sunset Dr
Burlington, VT 05408-1910, USA

Neiger, Al (Athlete, Baseball Player)
1517 Rockland Rd Apt 103
Wilmington, DE 19803-3621, USA

Neil, Hildegarde (Actor)
Vernon Conway
5 Spring St
London W2 3RA, UNITED KINGDOM (UK)

Neil, Ray (Baseball Player)
Ethiopian Clowns
250 N Wells Ave Apt 511
Benton Harbor, MI 49022-7735, USA

Neil, Vince (Musician)
9103 Alta Dr Unit 601
Las Vegas, NV 89145-8552, USA

Neill, Mary Gardner (Director)
Seattle Art Museum
Volunteer Park
Seattle, WA 98112, USA

Neill, Mike (Athlete, Baseball Player, Olympic Athlete)
17 Cape May Pt
Greensboro, NC 27455-1363, USA

Neill, Sam (Actor)
c/o Ann Churchill-Brown *Shanahan Management*
Level 3 Berman House
Surry Hills 02010, AUSTRALIA

Neill, William M (Athlete, Football Player)
34 Gibbs Dr
Wayne, NJ 07470-4103, USA

Neils, Steve (Athlete, Football Player)
1329 Waterford Rd
Woodbury, MN 55125-2366, USA

Neilson, Jim (Athlete, Hockey Player)
907-525 St Mary Ave
Winnipeg, MB R3C 3X3, Canada

Neilson-Bell, Sandra (Swimmer)
3101 Mistyglen Cir
Austin, TX 78746-7811, USA

Neinas, Charles M (Chuck) (Misc)
5344 Westridge Dr
Boulder, CO 80301-6501, USA

Neis, Reagan Dale (Actor)
c/o Susan Curtis *Curtis Talent Management*
9607 Arby Dr
Beverly Hills, CA 90210-1202, USA

Neison, Chuck (Athlete, Baseball Player)
8681 Carriage Hill Draw
Savage, MN 55378-2366, USA

Neistat, Casey (Internet Star, Television Host)
c/o Staff Member *CNN (NY)*
10 Columbus Cir
Time Warner Center
New York, NY 10019-1158, USA

Neitling, Marissa (Actor)
c/o Andrew Edwards *Zero Gravity Management*
11110 Ohio Ave Ste 100
Los Angeles, CA 90025-3329, USA

Nelkin, Stacey (Actor)
2770 Hutton Dr
Beverly Hills, CA 90210-1216

Nelligan, Kate (Actor)
c/o Gary Gersh *Innovative Artists*
235 Park Ave S Fl 7
New York, NY 10003-1405, USA

Nelly (Musician)
c/o Juliette Harris *It Girl Public Relations*
3763 Eddingham Ave
Calabasas, CA 91302-5835, USA

Nelms, Michael (Mike) (Athlete, Football Player)
11331 Fawn Lake Pkwy
Spotsylvania, VA 22551-4665, USA

Nelsen, Bill (Athlete, Football Player)
13512 Dornoch Dr
Orlando, FL 32828-8802, USA

Nelson, Al (Athlete, Football Player)
660 Boas St Apt 918
Harrisburg, PA 17102-1323, USA

Nelson, Andy (Athlete, Football Player)
12251 Manor Rd
Glen Arm, MD 21057-9542, USA

Nelson, Ben (Politician)
9738 Fieldcrest Dr
Omaha, NE 68114-4933, USA

Nelson, Bob (Baseball Player)
Baltimore Orioles
10830 Wallbrook Dr
Dallas, TX 75238-2943, USA

Nelson, Brad (Athlete, Baseball Player)
1405 210th St
Algona, IA 50511-7076, USA

Nelson, Bry (Athlete, Baseball Player)
11 Campden Hill Rd
Sherwood, AR 72120-6536, USA

Nelson, Charles L (Athlete, Football Player)
3028 162nd Pl SE
Mill Creek, WA 98012-7848, USA

Nelson, Charlie (Athlete, Baseball Player, Olympic Athlete)
11205 Kinsley St
Eden Prairie, MN 55344-1826, USA

Nelson, Cindy (Athlete, Olympic Athlete, Skier)
PO Box 1699
0171 Larkspur Lane
Vail, CO 81658-1699, USA

Nelson, Colette (Fitness Expert, Model)
PO Box 1122
Seaford, NY 11783-0078, USA

Nelson, Cordner (Misc)
USA Track & Field
4341 Starlight Dr
Indianapolis, IN 46239-1473, USA

Nelson, Craig T (Actor)
c/o Cynthia Snyder *Cynthia Snyder Public Relations*
5739 Colfax Ave
N Hollywood, CA 91601-1636, USA

Nelson, Darrin (Athlete, Football Player)
215 Marianne Ct
Mountain View, CA 94040-3283, USA

Nelson, Dave (Athlete, Baseball Player)
12213 Clubhouse Dr
Lakewood Ranch, FL 34202-2098, USA

Nelson, Deborah (Journalist)
Seattle Times
1120 John St
Editorial Dept
Seattle, WA 98109-5321, USA

Nelson, Dennis (Athlete, Football Player)
6098 E 2370 St
Kewanee, IL 61443-8529, USA

Nelson, Derrie (Athlete, Football Player)
7790 S Marian Rd
Hastings, NE 68901-7564, USA

Nelson, Diane (Horse Racer)
147 Main St Ste B
Cold Spring Harbor, NY 11724-1425, USA

Nelson, Dick (Athlete, Baseball Player)
102 N Maple St
Enfield, CT 06082-3958, USA

Nelson, Donald A (Nellie) (Basketball Player, Coach)
Dallas Mavericks
1333 N Stemmons Fwy Ste 105
Dallas, TX 75207-3722, USA

Nelson, Drew (Actor)
c/o Staff Member *Select Artists Ltd (CA-Westside Office)*
1138 12th St Apt 1
Santa Monica, CA 90403-5459, USA

Nelson, Ed (Athlete, Football Player)
7647 Westlake Rd
Sterlington, LA 71280-3231, USA

Nelson, Gene (Athlete, Baseball Player)
36131 Pine Bluff Loop
Dade City, FL 33525-9527, USA

Nelson, George D (Astronaut)
AAAS Project
1200 New York Ave NW Ste 100
Washington, DC 20005-3929, USA

Nelson, George D Dr (Astronaut)
1543 Toledo Ct
Bellingham, WA 98229-5375, USA

Nelson, Gunnar (Musician)
c/o John Ferriter *The Alternative Company*
2980 N Beverly Glen Cir Ste 302
Los Angeles, CA 90077-1703, USA

Nelson, Haywood ""Butch"" (Athlete, Football Player)
697 Salter Rd
Luverne, AL 36049-5749, USA

Nelson, Jameer (Athlete, Basketball Player)
c/o Staff Member *Cornerstone Management*
944 County Line Rd
Bryn Mawr, PA 19010-2502, USA

Nelson, James E (Religious Leader)
Baha i Faith
536 Sheridan Rd
Wilmette, IL 60091-2891, USA

Nelson, Jamie (Athlete, Baseball Player)
3422 Kildare Dr
Hoover, AL 35226-2120, USA

Nelson, Jeff (Athlete, Baseball Player)
5846 Pine Brook Farm Rd
Sykesville, MD 21784-8679, USA

Nelson, Jeff (Athlete, Baseball Player)
323 289th Pl NE
Carnation, WA 98014-9640, USA

Nelson, Jeff (Athlete, Hockey Player)
249 Simon Rd
Waldoboro, ME 04572-5716, USA

Nelson, Joe (Athlete, Baseball Player)
7979 SE Hidden Bridge Ct
Jupiter, FL 33458-1057, USA

Nelson, John Allen (Actor)

Nelson, John R (Misc)
1111 Hermann Dr Unit 19A
Houston, TX 77004-6930, USA

Nelson, Jordy (Athlete, Football Player)
9471 Fairview Church Rd
Riley, KS 66531-9677, USA

Nelson, Judd (Actor)
c/o Jeff Goldberg *Jeff Goldberg Management*
817 Monte Leon Dr
Beverly Hills, CA 90210-2629, USA

Nelson, Karl (Athlete, Football Player)
58 Woodland Rd
Montvale, NJ 07645-1333, USA

Nelson, Kent C (Business Person)
United Parcel Service
55 Glenlake Pkwy
Atlanta, GA 30328-3498, USA

Nelson, Kirsten (Actor)
5237 Bluebell Ave
Valley Village, CA 91607-2339, USA

Nelson, Larry (Athlete, Golfer)
438 Langley Oaks Dr SE
Marietta, GA 30067-4981, USA

Nelson, Lee (Athlete, Football Player)
4178 Summit Way
Marietta, GA 30066-2364, USA

Nelson, Lori (Actor)
19558 Pine Valley Ave
Northridge, CA 91326-1408, USA

Nelson, Marilyn Carison (Business Person)
Carlson Companies
PO Box 59159
Carlson Parkway
Minneapolis, MN 55459-8200, USA

Nelson, Mary (Athlete, Baseball Player)
320 Wagon Xing
Universal City, TX 78148-3634, USA

Nelson, Matthew (Musician)
205 Saddlebridge Ln
Franklin, TN 37069-4316, USA

Nelson, Mel (Athlete, Baseball Player)
27420 Fisher St
Highland, CA 92346-3251, USA

Nelson, Ralph A (Misc)
Carle Foundation Hospital
611 W Park St
Urbana, IL 61801-2512, USA

Nelson, Richard (Baseball Player)
104 Montgomery Ln
Perryville, AR 72126-8114, USA

Nelson, Ricky (Baseball Player)
Seattle Mariners
4627 E Shomi St
Phoenix, AZ 85044-4012, USA

Nelson, Rob (Athlete, Baseball Player)
1605 Mayflower Ave
Arcadia, CA 91006-5016, USA

Nelson, Roger (Athlete, Baseball Player)
4113 Limerick Dr
Lake Wales, FL 33859-5748, USA

Nelson, Ron (Athlete, Basketball Player)
1550 Eagle Ridge Ln NE
Albuquerque, NM 87122-1187, USA

Nelson, Scott (Baseball Player)
811 Overlook Dr
Coshocton, OH 43812-9107, USA

Nelson, Scott (Athlete, Baseball Player)
811 Overlook Dr
Coshocton, OH 43812-9107, USA

Nelson, Shane (Athlete, Football Player)
559 Carmel Dr
Sandia, TX 78383-5678, USA

Nelson, Terry (Athlete, Football Player)
3393 Highway 51 N
Arkadelphia, AR 71923-8584, USA

Nelson, Tim Blake (Actor, Director)
c/o Amy Guenther *Gateway Management Company Inc*
860 Via De La Paz Ste F10
Pacific Palisades, CA 90272-3631, USA

Nelson, Todd (Athlete, Hockey Player)
Oklahoma City Barons
501 N Walker Ave Ste 140
Attn Coaching Staff
Oklahoma City, OK 73102-1233, USA

Nelson, Tracy (Actor)
Piedmont Talent
3157 Whitson Rd
Gastonia, NC 28054-3901, USA

Nelson, William (Bill) (Politician)
3000 Rocky Point Rd
Malabar, FL 32950-4613, USA

Nelson, Willie (Musician, Songwriter)
12400 W Highway 71 Ste 350
Bee Cave, TX 78738-6500, USA

Nelson Jr, J Bryon (Golfer)
Fairway Ranch
RR 2 Box 5 Litsey Road
Roanoke, TX 76262, USA

Nelson-Walker, Doris (Baseball Player)
7887 N 16th St Unit 129
Phoenix, AZ 85020-4453, USA

Nemchinov, Sergei (Athlete, Hockey Player)
53 Walker Ave
Rye, NY 10580-1219, USA

Nemcova, Petra (Model)
c/o Michael Samonte *Sunshine Sachs*
720 Cole Ave
Los Angeles, CA 90038-3606, USA

Nemec, Corin (Actor)
859 N Hollywood Way # 104
Burbank, CA 91505-2814, USA

Nemechek, Joe (Race Car Driver)
Ginn Racing
128 S Iredell Industrial Park Rd
Mooresville, NC 28115-7128, USA

Nemechek, III, Joseph Frank (Race Car Driver)
128 S Iredell Industrial Park Rd
Mooresville, NC 28115-7128, USA

Nemelka, Richard (Athlete, Basketball Player)
6108 S 1300 E
Salt Lake City, UT 84121, USA

Nemeth, Miklos (Prime Minister)
European Reconstruction Bank
1 Exchange Square
London EC2A 2EH, UNITED KINGDOM (UK)

Nemov, Alexei (Gymnast)
Gymnastics Federation
Lujnetskaya Nabereynaya 8
Moscow 119270, RUSSIA

Nen, Dick (Athlete, Baseball Player)
48 Via Barcaza
Trabuco Canyon, CA 92679-4831, USA

Nen, Robb (Athlete, Baseball Player)
JD Legends Promotions
10808 Foothill Blvd Ste 160 PMB 454
Rancho Cucamonga, CA 91730-0601, USA

Nenez, Clemente (Baseball Player)
6433 Blackberry Pl
Riverside, CA 92505-2205, USA

Nenninger, Eric (Actor)

Neon Trees (Music Group)
c/o Staff Member *In De Goot Entertainment*
119 W 23rd St Ste 609
New York, NY 10011-2594, USA

N*E*R*D (Music Group)
c/o Staff Member *Paradigm (Monterey)*
404 W Franklin St
Monterey, CA 93940-2303, USA

Neri, Francesca (Actor)
c/o Philip Button *WME|IMG*
9601 Wilshire Blvd
Beverly Hills, CA 90210-5213, USA

Neri Vela, Rodolfo Dr (Astronaut)
Playa Copacabana 131
Col Militar Marte, DF 08830, Mexico

Nerl, Manuel (Artist)
greg Kucera Gallery
212 3rd Ave S
Seattle, WA 98104-2608, USA

Nerl Vela, Rodolfo (Astronaut)
Playa Copacabana 131
Col Marte
Mexico City, DF 08830, MEXICO

Nerman, Maxens (Actor)
Continent II
62, Rue des Grands Champs
75020, PARIS

Nero, Franco (Actor)
c/o Camilla Fluxman-Pines *Muse Management*
1541 Ocean Ave Ste 200
Santa Monica, CA 90401-2104, USA

Nero, Haley (Actor)
c/o Staff Member *Charlie's Talent Agency*
1350 Old Skokie Rd Ste 202
Highland Park, IL 60035-3058, USA

Nero, Peter (Musician)
668 Viking Pl
The Villages, FL 32163-4278, USA

Nershi, Bill (Musician)
1002 County Road 99
Nederland, CO 80466, USA

Nesbit, Jamar (Athlete, Football Player)
4083 Richmond Park Dr E
Jacksonville, FL 32224-2223, USA

Nesbitt, James (Actor)
c/o Ian Johnson *Ian Johnson Publicity*
8 Flitcroft St
London WC2H 8DL, UNITED KINGDOM

Nesbitt-Wisham, Mary (Athlete, Baseball Player)
PO Box 194
Hollister, FL 32147-0194, USA

Nesbo, Jo (Writer)
c/o Keith Fleer *Keith Fleer, A Professional Corp*
401 Wilshire Blvd Ste 1200
Santa Monica, CA 90401-1456, USA

Neserovic, Radoslav (Basketball Player)
San Antonio Spurs
1 at and T Center Pkwy
Alamodome
San Antonio, TX 78219-3604, USA

Neshek, Pat (Athlete, Baseball Player)
471 Spoonbill Ln
Melbourne Beach, FL 32951-3269, USA

Nesher, Avi (Director)
Gersh Agency
232 N Canon Dr
Beverly Hills, CA 90210-5302, USA

Nesic, Alex (Actor)
c/o Staff Member *Artists First*
9465 Wilshire Blvd Ste 900
Beverly Hills, CA 90212-2608, USA

Nesmith, Michael (Musician)
13 Sleepy Hollow Dr
Carmel Valley, CA 93924-9017, USA

Nespoli, Paolo (Astronaut)
2011 Dawn Crest Ct
League City, TX 77573-3931, USA

Nespral, Jackie (Correspondent)
NBC-TV
30 Rockefeller Plz
News Dept
New York, NY 10112-0015, USA

Ness, Rick (Musician)
Metropolitan Entertainment Group
2 Penn Plz Rm 1549
New York, NY 10121-1704, USA

Nessen, Ronald H (Ron) (Politician)
1835 K St NW Ste 805
Washington, DC 20006-1203, USA

Nesterenko, Eric (Athlete, Hockey Player)
PO Box 1025
Vail, CO 81658-1025, USA

Nestorowicz, Victoria (Actor)
c/o Staff Member *Noble Caplan Abrams*
1260 Yonge St 2nd Fl
Toronto, ON M4T 1W5, CANADA

Netanyahu, Benjamin (Politician)
38 Rehou King George
Tel Aviv 61231, Israel

Netherland, Joseph H (Business Person)
FMC Corp
200 E Randolph St
Chicago, IL 60601-6436, USA

Netolicky, Bob (Athlete, Basketball Player)
PO Box 531
Carmel, IN 46082-0531, USA

Netter, Gil (Producer)
c/o Staff Member *Netter Productions*
2454 Glyndon Ave
Venice, CA 90291-5005, USA

Nettles, Doug (Athlete, Football Player)
15311 Pine Orchard Dr Apt 2H
Silver Spring, MD 20906-8330, USA

Nettles, Graig (Athlete, Baseball Player)
4255 Parris Dr
Lenoir City, TN 37772-3947, USA

Nettles, Jennifer (Musician)
c/o Jason Owen *Sandbox Entertainment*
3810 Bedford Ave Ste 200
Nashville, TN 37215-2555, USA

Nettles, Jim (Athlete, Baseball Player)
4632 N Darien Dr
Tacoma, WA 98407-1212, USA

Nettles, Jim (Athlete, Football Player)
3817 Mandeville Canyon Rd
Los Angeles, CA 90049-1027, USA

Nettles, John (Actor)
Saraband Assoc
265 Liverpool Road
London N1 1LX, UNITED KINGDOM (UK)

Nettles, Morris (Athlete, Baseball Player)
551 1/2 San Juan Ave
Venice, CA 90291-5643, USA

Neu, Mike (Athlete, Baseball Player)
406 Fraga Ct
Martinez, CA 94553-6812, USA

Neubeck, Francis G (Astronaut)
133 N Bay Ct
Lynn Haven, FL 32444-3058, USA

Neubert, Keith (Actor, Athlete, Football Player)
c/o Karen Wang-Lavelle *Ken Lindner & Associates*
1901 Avenue Of The Stars Ste 1010
Los Angeles, CA 90067-6012, USA

Neufeld, Ray (Athlete, Hockey Player)
3919 Henderson Hwy
Winnipeg, MB R2G 1P4, Canada

Neufeld, Ryan (Athlete, Football Player)
625 Spring Hill Dr
Morgan Hill, CA 95037-4814, USA

Neugebauer, Nick (Athlete, Baseball Player)
1231 W Breckenridge Ave
Gilbert, AZ 85233-3603, USA

Neugebauer, Randy (Congressman, Politician)
1424 Kibgwirth Hob
Washington, DC 20515-0001, USA

Neuheisel, Rick (Athlete, Coach, Football Coach, Football Player)
3601 Winding Creek Rd
Sacramento, CA 95864-1530, USA

Neumann, Liselotte (Athlete, Golfer)
11003 Muirfield Dr
Rancho Mirage, CA 92270-1431, USA

Neumann, Peter (Athlete, Football Player)
31 Frederick St
St Catharines, ON L2S 2S5, Canada

Neumeier, Dan (Athlete, Baseball Player)
N2635 County Road V
Lodi, WI 53555-1568, USA

Neuner, Doris (Athlete)
6024 Innsbruck
AUSTRIA

Neustadt, Richard (Politician)
1010 Memorial Dr
Cambridge, MA 02138-4859, USA

Neustaedter, Alex (Actor)
c/o Mona Loring *Status PR*
PO Box 6191
Westlake Village, CA 91359-6191, USA

Neuwelt, Edward A (Misc)
Oregon Health Sciences University
Neurology Dept
Portland, OR 97201, USA

Neuwirth, Bebe (Actor)
c/o Adam Schweitzer *ICM Partners (NY)*
730 5th Ave
New York, NY 10019-4105, USA

Neverett, Tim (Sportscaster)
111 Coburn Ave # 119
Nashua, NH 03063-2807, USA

Nevett, Elijah (Athlete, Football Player)
931 30th St N
Bessemer, AL 35020-3565, USA

Neville, Aaron (Musician)
c/o Marc Allen *Red Light Management*
455 2nd St NE
#500
Charlottesville, VA 22902-5791, USA

Neville, Arthel (Correspondent, Television Host)
1840 Victory Blvd
Glendale, CA 91201-2558, USA

Neville, Bill (Cartoonist)
506 Oakdale Rd
Jamestown, NC 27282-9214, USA

Neville, Cyril (Musician)
9321 Notches Dr
Austin, TX 78748-5051, USA

Neville, David (Designer)
Rag & Bone
425 W 13th St Fl 3
New York, NY 10014-1123, USA

Neville, John (Actor, Director)
139 Winnett Ave
Toronto, ON M6C 3L7, CANADA

Neville, Katherine (Writer)
PO Box 788
Warrenton, VA 20188-0788, USA

Neville, Robert C (Misc)
Boston University
Theology School
Boston, MA 02215, USA

Neville, Thomas O (Athlete, Football Player)
PO Box 11175
Montgomery, AL 36111-0175, USA

Nevin, Bob (Athlete, Hockey Player)
Soupy's Tavern
376 Dundas St E
SOUPY'S TAVERN
Toronto, ON M5A 2A5, Canada

Nevin, Brooke (Actor)
c/o Suzanne (Sue) Wohl *TalentWorks*
3500 W Olive Ave Ste 1400
Burbank, CA 91505-5512, USA

Nevin, Kaleigh (Actor)
3SG Talent Management
LL7-45 Charles St E
c/o Mary Swinton
Toronto, ON M4Y 0B8, CANADA

Nevin, Phil (Athlete, Baseball Player, Olympic Athlete)
18795 Heritage Dr
Poway, CA 92064-6643, USA

Nevins, Claudette (Actor)
Gold Marshak Liedtke
3500 W Olive Ave Ste 1400
Burbank, CA 91505-5512, USA

Nevins, Sheila (Business Person, Producer)
c/o Staff Member *Home Box Office (HBO-LA)*
2500 Broadway Ste 400
Santa Monica, CA 90404-3176, USA

Nevis, Drake (Athlete, Football Player)
c/o Pat Dye Jr *SportsTrust Advisors*
3340 Peachtree Rd NE Fl 16
Atlanta, GA 30326-1000, USA

Nevitt, Chuck (Athlete, Basketball Player)
3124 Cartwright Dr
Raleigh, NC 27612-2113, USA

New, Hannah (Actor)
c/o Caryn Leeds *Wolf-Kasteler Public Relations*
6255 W Sunset Blvd Ste 1111
Los Angeles, CA 90028-7426, USA

Newark, Samantha (Musician)
c/o Arlene Thornton *Arlene Thornton & Associates*
12711 Ventura Blvd Ste 490
Studio City, CA 91604-2477, USA

Newbern, George (Actor)
c/o Staff Member *Leslie Allan-Rice Management*
1007 Maybrook Dr
Beverly Hills, CA 90210-2715, USA

Newberry, Bob (Race Car Driver)
key Prts Racing
5835 Mariaville Rd
Schenectady, NY 12306, USA

Newberry, Jeremy (Athlete, Football Player)
2525 Sunset Rd
Brentwood, CA 94513-2895, USA

Newberry, Thomas (Tom) (Athlete, Football Player)
224 Tarpon St
Tavernier, FL 33070-2534, USA

Newbill, Ivano (Athlete, Basketball Player)
4147 4th Ave
Los Angeles, CA 90008-3901, USA

Newbrough, Ashley (Actor)
c/o William (Willie) Mercer *Thruline Entertainment*
9250 Wilshire Blvd Fl Ground
Beverly Hills, CA 90212-3352, USA

Newcomb, Gerry (Artist)
7029 17th Ave NW
Seattle, WA 98117-5551, USA

Newcomb, Mike (Radio Personality)
OnSecondThought
4927 E Palo Brea Ln
Cave Creek, AZ 85331-5995, USA

Newcombe, John (Athlete, Tennis Player)
325 Mission Valley Rd
New Braunfels, TX 78132-3629, USA

Newcomer, Carrie (Musician)
PO Box 5653
Bloomington, IN 47407-5653, USA

New Edition (Music Group)
c/o Amy Malone *GIC Public Relations*
Prefers to be contacted via email or telephone
Los Angeles, CA 90069, USA

Newell, Alex (Actor, Musician)
c/o Jordyn Palos *Persona Public Relations*
6255 W Sunset Blvd Ste 705
Hollywood, CA 90028-7408, USA

Newell, Mike (Actor, Director, Producer)
c/o Staff Member *50 Cannon Entertainment*
Oxford House
76 Oxford St
London W1D 1BS, UNITED KINGDOM (UK)

Newell, Rick (Athlete, Hockey Player)
5223 N 24th St
Phoenix, AZ 85016-3590, USA

Newell, Tom (Athlete, Baseball Player)
9525 Cordoba Blvd
Sparks, NV 89441-5569, USA

Newfield, Heidi (Musician)
c/o Staff Member *McGhee Entertainment (TN)*
21 Music Sq W
Nashville, TN 37203-3203, USA

Newfield, Marc (Athlete, Baseball Player)
1717 N Los Robles Ave
Pasadena, CA 91104-1051, USA

Newgard, Christopher (Misc)
Southwestern Medical Center
Biochemistry Dept
Dallas, TX 75237, USA

Newhan, David (Athlete, Baseball Player)
2125 Walnut Ln
Vista, CA 92084-7716, USA

Newhan, Ross (Sportscaster)
2678 Harvest Crest Ln
Corona, CA 92881-3572, USA

Newhart, Bob (Actor, Comedian)
c/o Staff Member *Monarch Entertainment Group*
3120 W Empire Ave
Burbank, CA 91504-3107, USA

Newhauser, Don (Athlete, Baseball Player)
321 Sheryl Dr
Deltona, FL 32738-8441, USA

Newhouse, Fredrick (Fred) (Athlete, Track Athlete)
3003 Pine Lake Trl
Houston, TX 77068-1435, USA

Newhouse, Marshall (Athlete, Football Player)
c/o Jordan Woy *Willis & Woy Management*
4890 Alpha Rd Ste 200
Dallas, TX 75244-4639, USA

New Kids on the Block (NKOTB) (Music Group)
c/o Erica Gerard *PMK/BNC Public Relations*
622 3rd Ave Fl 8
New York, NY 10017-6707, USA

Newkirk, Ingrid (Activist)
PETA
501 Front St
Norfolk, VA 23510-1009, USA

Newland, Bob (Athlete, Football Player)
3895 Vine Maple St
Eugene, OR 97405-4494, USA

Newlin, Mike (Athlete, Basketball Player)
1414 Horseshoe Dr
Sugar Land, TX 77478-3464, USA

Newman, Al (Athlete, Baseball Player)
Newmie's Rewards
15240 Fairlawn Shores Trl SE
Prior Lake, MN 55372-1940, USA

Newman, Alan (Athlete, Baseball Player)
24 Rice Ln
Dry Prong, LA 71423-8742, USA

Newman, Alec (Actor)
c/o Laina Cohn *Cohn / Torgan Management*
Prefers to be contacted by telephone or email
Los Angeles, CA, USA

Newman, Ali (Brother Ali) (Musician)
c/o James Rubin *WME|IMG (NY)*
11 Madison Ave Fl 18
New York, NY 10010-3669, USA

Newman, Barry (Actor)
c/o Tom Chasin *Chasin Agency, The*
8281 Melrose Ave Ste 202
Los Angeles, CA 90046-6890, USA

Newman, Dan (Athlete, Hockey Player)
192 E County Road
27 RR 1
Cottam, ON NOR 1BO, Canada

Newman, Edward K (Ed) (Athlete, Football Player)
10100 SW 140th St
Miami, FL 33176-6685, USA

Newman, James H (Astronaut)
Naval Post Graduate School
1 University Cir
Attn Nasa Visiting Professor
Monterey, CA 93943-5098, USA

Newman, Jeff (Athlete, Baseball Player, Coach)
10133 N 103rd St
Scottsdale, AZ 85258-4953, USA

Newman, John (Musician)
c/o Ryan Lofthouse *Closer Artists (UK)*
91 Peterborough Rd
Matrix Complex
London SW6 3BU, UNITED KINGDOM

Newman, Johnny (Athlete, Basketball Player)
Dallas Mavericks
206 W Broad St
Richmond, VA 23220-4217, USA

Newman, Josh (Athlete, Baseball Player)
5909 Canyon Creek Dr
Dublin, OH 43016-7419, USA

Newman, Kevin (Correspondent)
ABC-TV
77 W 66th St
News Dept
New York, NY 10023-6201, USA

Newman, Kyle (Director)
c/o Staff Member *Fire Thief Films*
13801 Ventura Blvd
Sherman Oaks, CA 91423-3603, USA

Newman, Laraine (Actor, Comedian)
1617 S Beverly Glen Blvd Apt 108
Los Angeles, CA 90024-6183, USA

Newman, Loraine (Comedian)
c/o Staff Member *TalentWorks*
3500 W Olive Ave Ste 1400
Burbank, CA 91505-5512, USA

Newman, Nanette (Actor)
Seven Pines Wentworth
Surrey GU25 4QP, UNITED KINGDOM (UK)

Newman, Nell (Business Person)
Newman's Own Organics
246 Post Rd E
Westport, CT 06880-3615, USA

Newman, Phyllis (Actor, Musician)
c/o Judy Katz *Judy Katz Public Relations*
1345 Avenue Of The Americas Fl 2
New York, NY 10105-0014, USA

Newman, Randy (Musician, Songwriter)
1610 San Remo Dr
Pacific Palisades, CA 90272-2741, USA

Newman, Ray (Athlete, Baseball Player)
584 Vista Dr
Murrells Inlet, SC 29576-9029, USA

Newman, Ryan (Actor)
c/o Gladys Gonzalez *John Carrabino Management*
5900 Wilshire Blvd Ste 740
Los Angeles, CA 90036-5032, USA

Newman, Ryan (Race Car Driver)
298/318 Jennings Rd
Statesville, NC 28625, USA

Newman, Terence (Athlete, Football Player)
1 Cowboys Pkwy
Irving, TX 75063-4924, USA

Newman, Thomas (Musician)
c/o Michael Gorfaine *Gorfaine/Schwartz Agency Inc*
4111 W Alameda Ave Ste 509
Burbank, CA 91505-4171, USA

Newmar, Julie (Actor)
c/o Harlan Boll *Davidson & Choy Publicity*
4311 Wilshire Blvd Ste 515
Los Angeles, CA 90010-3708, USA

Newmark, Dave (Athlete, Basketball Player)
545 Pierce St Apt 2301
Albany, CA 94706-1065, USA

New Order (Music Group, Musician)
c/o Staff Member *Warner Bros Records (NY)*
75 Rockefeller Plz
New York, NY 10019-6908, USA

Newsboys (Music Group)
Sparrow Records
PO Box 5010
Brentwood, TN 37024-5010, USA

Newsom, David (Actor)
Innovative Artists
1505 10th St
Santa Monica, CA 90401-2805, USA

Newsom, Gavin (Politician)
Deane & Company
1787 Tribute Rd Ste K
Sacramento, CA 95815-4404, USA

Newsom, Joanna (Actor)
c/o Molly Kawachi *ID Public Relations (NY)*
40 Wall St Fl 51
New York, NY 10005-1385, USA

Newsome, Billy (Athlete, Football Player)
17404 Meridian E # 115
Puyallup, WA 98375-6234, USA

Newsome, Harry (Athlete, Football Player)
531 Manor Rd
Cheraw, SC 29520, USA

Newsome, Jonathan (Athlete, Football Player)

Newsome, Ozzie (Athlete, Football Player)
6 Padonia Woods Ct
Cockeysville, MD 21030-1744, USA

Newsome, Paula (Actor)
15044 Martha St
Van Nuys, CA 91411-3223, USA

Newsome, Timothy A (Athlete, Football Player)
7005 Quartermile Ln
Dallas, TX 75248-1447, USA

Newsome, Vince (Athlete, Football Player)

Newson, Warren (Athlete, Baseball Player)
13232 Padre Ave
Fort Worth, TX 76244-4326, USA

New Song (Music Group)
c/o Staff Member *VanLiere-Wilcox*
251 2nd Ave S
Franklin, TN 37064-2659, USA

Newsted, Jason (Musician)
205 Alamo View Pl
Walnut Creek, CA 94595-2600, USA

Newton, Becki (Actor)
c/o Ruth Bernstein *Viewpoint Inc*
8820 Wilshire Blvd Ste 220
Beverly Hills, CA 90211-2622, USA

Newton, Ben (Actor)
c/o Staff Member *Sasha Leslie Management*
34 Pember Rd
London NW10 5LS, UNITED KINGDOM

Newton, Bill (Athlete, Basketball Player)
2902 Manitou Park Dr
Rochester, IN 46975-8936, USA

Newton, Cam (Athlete, Football Player, Heisman Trophy Winner)
c/o Bus Cook *Bus Cook Sports, Inc*
1 Willow Bend Dr
Hattiesburg, MS 39402-8552, USA

Newton, Christopher (Director)
22 Prideaux St
Niagara-On-The-Lake, ON L0S 1J0, CANADA

Newton, C M (Athlete, Basketball Player, Coach)
9160 Enterprise Ave NE
Tuscaloosa, AL 35406-1042, USA

Newton, Derek (Athlete, Football Player)

Newton, John Haymes (Actor)
c/o Staff Member *Pakula/King & Associates*
9229 W Sunset Blvd Ste 315
Los Angeles, CA 90069-3403, USA

Newton, Juice (Musician, Songwriter)
PO Box 2158
Santa Monica, CA 90407-2158, USA

Newton, Nate (Athlete, Football Player)
1921 White Oak Clearing
Southlake, TX 76092-6929, USA

Newton, Robert L (Athlete, Football Player)
11500 NE 76th St Apt A-353
Vancouver, WA 98662-3901, USA

Newton, Thandie (Actor)
c/o Sally Long-Innes *Independent Talent Group*
40 Whitfield St
London W1T 2RH, UNITED KINGDOM

Newton, Tom (Athlete, Football Player)
169 Park Rd
Rochester, NY 14622-1217, USA

Newton, Wayne (Actor, Musician)
3945 E Patrick Ln Ste B
Las Vegas, NV 89120-3958, USA

Newton-John, Olivia (Actor, Musician, Producer)
c/o Mark Hartley *Fitzgerald-Hartley Co (Ventura)*
34 N Palm St Ste 100
Ventura, CA 93001-2610, USA

Neyelova, Marina M (Actor)
Potapovsky Per 12
Moscow 117333, RUSSIA

Ne-Yo (Musician)
c/o Reynell (Tango) Hay *Compound Entertainment*
1755 Broadway
New York, NY 10019-3743, USA

Neyra, Gianella (Actor)
c/o Staff Member *Telefe (Argentina)*
Pavon 2444
Buenos Aires C1248AAT, ARGENTINA

Nezelek, Andy (Athlete, Baseball Player)
5707 Long Cove Rd
Midlothian, VA 23112-2450, USA

Nezhat, Camran (Misc)
Fertility/Endocrinology Ctr
5555 Peachtree Dunwoody Rd
Atlanta, GA 30342-1703, USA

Ngata, Haloti (Athlete, Football Player)
c/o Michael McCartney *Priority Sports & Entertainment (Chicago)*
325 N La Salle Dr Ste 650
Chicago, IL 60654-8182, USA

Ngata, Haoti (Athlete, Football Player)
c/o Staff Member *Baltimore Ravens*
6 Rod Cir
Middletown, MD 21769-7868, USA

Nguema, Tedoro Obiang (President)
President's Office
Malabo
EQUATORIAL GUINEA

Nguyen, Dat (Athlete, Football Player)
3610 Spears Rd
Houston, TX 77066-4117, USA

Nguyen, Dustin (Actor)
c/o Andrew Ooi *Echelon Talent Management*
2915 Argo Pl
Burnaby, BC V3J 7G4, CANADA

Nguyen, Navia (Actor)
c/o Michael Greenwald *Endorse Management Group*
9854 National Blvd # 454
Los Angeles, CA 90034-2713, USA

Nguyen, Scotty (Misc)
c/o Staff Member *Poker Royalty, LLC*
10789 W Twain Ave Ste 200
Las Vegas, NV 89135-3030, USA

Niccol, Andrew (Director, Producer, Writer)
c/o Todd Feldman *Creative Artists Agency (CAA)*
2000 Avenue of the Stars Ste 100
Los Angeles, CA 90067-4705, USA

Nichol, Joseph McGinty (McG) (Musician, Producer, Writer)
c/o Staff Member *Wonderland Sound and Vision*
8739 W Sunset Blvd
W Hollywood, CA 90069-2205, USA

Nichol, Scott (Athlete, Hockey Player)
9696 Garnet Ct
Brentwood, TN 37027-2231, USA

Nicholas, Alison (Athlete, Golfer)
Pat Darby The Flat
Badgar Farm House
Badgar near Wolverhampton WV6 7IS, United Kingdom

Nicholas, Denise (Actor)
932 S Longwood Ave
Los Angeles, CA 90019-1752, USA

Nicholas, Eric (Writer)
c/o Staff Member *Gersh*
9465 Wilshire Blvd Ste 600
Beverly Hills, CA 90212-2605, USA

Nicholas, Henry (Misc)
Hospital & Health Care Union
330 W 42nd St Ste 1905
New York, NY 10036-6902, USA

Nicholas, J D (Musician)
Management Assoc
1920 Benson Ave
Saint Paul, MN 55116-3214, USA

Nicholas, Peter M (Business Person)
Boston Scientific Corp
1 Boston Scientific Pl
Natick, MA 01760-1537, USA

Nicholas, Stephen (Football Player)
c/o Chad Speck *Allegiant Athletic Agency*
35 Market Sq Ste 201
Knoxville, TN 37902-1420, USA

Nicholas, Thomas Ian (Actor)
c/o Staff Member *Red Compass Media*
2930 Westwood Blvd
Los Angeles, CA 90064-4137, USA

Nicholas(Smisko), Bishop (Religious Leader)
American Carpatho
312 Garfield St
Johnstown, PA 15906-2122, USA

Nicholls, Bernie (Athlete, Hockey Player)
17101 Planters Row
Addison, TX 75001-5039, USA

Nicholls, Craig (Musician)
Winterman-Goldstein
17 Holdsworth St
Newton, NSW 02042, AUSTRALIA

Nicholls, Paul (Actor)
c/o Staff Member *IFA Talent Agency*
8730 W Sunset Blvd Ste 490
Los Angeles, CA 90069-2210, USA

Nichols, Austin (Actor)
c/o Joan Green *Joan Green Management*
1836 Courtney Ter
Los Angeles, CA 90046-2106, USA

Nichols, Bobby (Athlete, Golfer)
8681 Glenlyon Ct
Fort Myers, FL 33912-2408, USA

Nichols, Carl (Athlete, Baseball Player)
901 E Artesia Blvd
Compton, CA 90221-5356, USA

Nichols, Dr. Michael (Writer)
c/o Staff Member *Guilford Press*
72 Spring St Fl 4
New York, NY 10012-4068, USA

Nichols, Hamilton J (Athlete, Football Player)
11015 Kirkmead Dr
Houston, TX 77089-3116, USA

Nichols, Jeff (Director, Producer)
c/o Dan McManus *Mosaic Media Group*
407 N Maple Dr # 100
Beverly Hills, CA 90210-3818, USA

Nichols, Joe (Musician)
c/o George Couri *Triple 8 Management*
1611 W 6th St
Austin, TX 78703-5059, USA

Nichols, John (Writer)
c/o Staff Member *The New Press*
120 Wall St Fl 31
New York, NY 10005-4007, USA

Nichols, Kenwood C (Business Person)
Champion Int'l Corp
1 Champion Plaza
Stamford, CT 06921, USA

Nichols, Larry (Designer)
Moleculon Research Corp
139 Main St
Cambridge, MA 02142-1530, USA

Nichols, Marisol (Actor)
c/o Siri Garber *Platform PR*
2666 N Beachwood Dr
Los Angeles, CA 90068-2308, USA

Nichols, Mark (Race Car Driver)
Henderson Motosports
532 E Main St
Abingdon, VA 24210-3410, USA

Nichols, Mark (Athlete, Football Player)
21659 Lucas Ct
Santa Clarita, CA 91390-5268, USA

Nichols, Nichelle (Actor)
c/o Staff Member *GB Entertainment*
PO Box 1083
Studio City, CA 91614-0083, USA

Nichols, Nicole (Business Person)
c/o Staff Member *OWN: The Oprah Winfrey Network*
Prefers to be contacted by email or phone.
W Hollywood, CA 90046, USA

Nichols, Peter R (Writer)
Alan Brodie
211 Piccadilly
London W1V 9LD, UNITED KINGDOM (UK)

Nichols, Rachel (Actor)
c/o Peter Kiernan *Free Association*
10202 Washington Blvd
Robert Young Bldg Suite 3200
Culver City, CA 90232-3119, USA

Nichols, Reid (Athlete, Baseball Player)
Milwaukee Brewers
17547 W East Wind Ave
Goodyear, AZ 85338-5840, USA

Nichols, Rod (Athlete, Baseball Player)
1570 Elk Trail Dr
Helena, MT 59601-9633, USA

Nichols, Stephen (Actor)
11664 National Blvd # 116
Los Angeles, CA 90064-3802, USA

Nicholson, Dave (Athlete, Baseball Player)
15316 Lakepoint Dr
Benton, IL 62812-4676, USA

Nicholson, Don (Dyno) (Race Car Driver)
604 E Vista Del Playa Ave
Orange, CA 92865-3436, USA

Nicholson, Jack (Actor)
12758 Mulholland Dr
Beverly Hills, CA 90210-1329, USA

Nicholson, Jim (Athlete, Football Player)
91-845 Kauwili St
Ewa Beach, HI 96706-2854, USA

Nicholson, Julianne (Actor)
c/o Karen Samfilippo *IMPR*
1158 26th St # 548
Santa Monica, CA 90403-4698, USA

Nichting, Chris (Athlete, Baseball Player)
7151 Gracely Dr
Cincinnati, OH 45233-1019, USA

Nickelback (Music Group)
c/o Bryan Coleman *Union Entertainment Group*
4952 Warner Ave
Huntington Beach, CA 92649-4479, USA

Nickel Creek (Music Group)
Sugar Hill Records
PO Box 120897
Nashville, TN 37212-0897, USA

Nickells, Bruce (Horse Racer)
PO Box 5009
Lighthouse Point, FL 33074-5009, USA

Nickens, David (Race Car Driver)
604 E Vista Del Playa Ave
Orange, CA 92865-3436, USA

Nickerson, Denise (Actor)
4294 S Salida Way Unit 1
Aurora, CO 80013-3291, USA

Nickerson, Hardy O (Athlete, Football Player)
8716 Longview Club Dr
Waxhaw, NC 28173-6696, USA

Nickerson Jr, Donald A (Religious Leader)
Episcopal Church
815 2nd Ave Bsmt
New York, NY 10017-4594, USA

Nickla, Ed (Athlete, Football Player)
21 Ida Ln
North Babylon, NY 11703-1403, USA

Nicklaus, Jack (Athlete, Golfer)
The Nicklaus Companies
3801 Pga Blvd Ste 565
Palm Beach Gardens, FL 33410-2760, USA

Nickle, Doug (Athlete, Baseball Player)
PO Box 190
Eagle, ID 83616-0190, USA

Nickles, Don (Politician)
903 Centrillion Dr
Mc Lean, VA 22102-1443, USA

Nicks, Carl (Athlete, Basketball Player)
10200 Yosemite Ln
Indianapolis, IN 46234-9821, USA

Nicks, Hakeem (Athlete, Football Player)
c/o Tom Condon *Creative Artists Agency (CAA)*
401 Commerce St PH
Nashville, TN 37219-2516, USA

Nicks, Orlando (Athlete, Basketball Player)
10200 Yosemite Ln
Indianapolis, IN 46234-9821, USA

Nicks, Regina (Musician)
Bobby Roberts
909 Meadowlark Ln
Goodlettsville, TN 37072-2309, USA

Nicks, Stevie (Musician)
PO Box 112083
Carrollton, TX 75011-2083, USA

Nickson, Julia (Actor)
Elkins Entertainment
8306 Wilshire Blvd # 438
Beverly Hills, CA 90211-2304, USA

Nickulas, Eric (Athlete, Hockey Player)
616 Huckins Neck Rd
Centerville, MA 02632-1440, USA

Nico & Vinz (Music Group)
c/o Keith Sarkisian *WME/IMG*
9601 Wilshire Blvd
Beverly Hills, CA 90210-5213, USA

Nicol, Lesley (Actor)
c/o Paul Pearson *London Theatrical*
18 Leamore St
London W6 0JZ, UNITED KINGDOM

Nicol, Steve (Coach, Football Coach)
New England Revolution
1 Patriot Pl
Cmgi Field
Foxboro, MA 02035-1388, USA

Nicolaou, Kyriacos Costa (Misc)
Scripps Research Institute
10550 N Torrey Pines Rd
La Jolla, CA 92037-1000, USA

Nicole, Britt (Musician)
c/o Amy Fogleman *Creative Trust, Inc.*
5141 Virginia Way Ste 320
Brentwood, TN 37027-2317, USA

Nicole, Jasika (Actor)
c/o John Essay *Essay Management*
364 W 46th St
New York, NY 10036-3919, USA

Nicole Heimann, Nadine (Actor)
c/o Mark Schumacher *Schumacher Management*
Prefers to be contacted by email or phone.
Los Angeles, CA 90064, USA

Nicolet, Aurele (Musician)
Hans Ulrich Schmid
Postfach 1617
Hanover 30016, GERMANY

Nicolet, Danielle (Actor)
c/o Elizabeth Much *East 2 West Collective*
11022 Santa Monica Blvd Ste 350
Los Angeles, CA 90025-7532, USA

Nicol-Fox, Helen (Athlete, Baseball Player)
432 E Cornell Dr
Tempe, AZ 85283-1908, USA

Nicollier, Claude (Astronaut)
20 Leeward Ln
Houston, TX 77058-4212, USA

Nicolson, Graeme (Athlete, Hockey Player)
Village Animal Hospital
PO Box 779
Lakefield, ON K0L 2H0, Canada

Nicolucci, Guy (Writer)
c/o Staff Member *Gersh*
9465 Wilshire Blvd Ste 600
Beverly Hills, CA 90212-2605, USA

Nicora, Attilio Cardinal (Religious Leader)
Patrimony of Apostolic See
Palazzo Apostolico
00120, VATICAN CITY

Nicosia, Steve (Athlete, Baseball Player)
5601 Black Iron Trl
Powder Springs, GA 30127-6324, USA

Nieberg, Lars (Misc)
Gestit Waldershausen
Homberg 35315, GERMANY

Nied, David (Athlete, Baseball Player)
211 Masters Ln
Midlothian, TX 76065-7209, USA

Niedenfuer, Tom (Athlete, Baseball Player)
3933 Losillias Dr
Sarasota, FL 34238-4537, USA

Nieder, William H (Bill) (Athlete, Track Athlete)
PO Box 310
Mountain Ranch, CA 95246-0310, USA

Niederhoffer, Victor (Misc)
Niederhoffer Cross Zeckhauser
757 3rd Ave
New York, NY 10017-2013, USA

Niedermayer, Rob (Athlete, Hockey Player)
Titan Sports Management
1105-1009 Expo Blvd
Attn Kevin Epp
Vancouver, BC V6Z 2V9, Canada

Niedermayer, Scott (Athlete, Hockey Player)
Titan Sports Management
1105-1009 Expo Blvd
Attn Kevin Epp
Vancouver, BC V6Z 2V9, Canada

Niedernhuber, Barbara (Athlete)
Schwarzeckstr 58
Ramsau 83486, GERMANY

Niederpruem, Clare (Actor)
c/o Staff Member *Luber Roklin Management*
5815 W Sunset Blvd Ste 208
Los Angeles, CA 90028-6481, USA

Niehaus, Dave (Sportscaster)
Seattle Mariners
PO Box 4100
Safeco Field
Seattle, WA 98194-0100, USA

Niehaus, David (Athlete, Baseball Player)
18406 NW Montreux Dr
Issaquah, WA 98027-7817, USA

Niehaus, Ralph (Athlete, Football Player)
114 Siebenthaler Ave
Cincinnati, OH 45215-3716, USA

Niehaus, Steve (Athlete, Football Player)
114 Siebenthaler Ave
Cincinnati, OH 45215-3716, USA

Niekamp, Jim (Athlete, Hockey Player)
3511 E Cochise Dr
Phoenix, AZ 85028-3924, USA

Niekamp, Ted (Athlete, Hockey Player)
3511 E Cochise Dr
Phoenix, AZ 85028-3924, USA

Niekro, Lance (Athlete, Baseball Player)
817 Woodmont Ln
Lakeland, FL 33813-1267, USA

Niekro, Phil (Athlete, Baseball Player)
6382 Nichols Rd
Flowery Branch, GA 30542-2619, USA

Niel, Steve (Actor)
c/o Laura Walsh *Central Artists*
1023 N Hollywood Way Ste 102
Burbank, CA 91505-2554, USA

Nielsen, Brigitte (Actor, Model)
c/o Tanya Kleckner *Henderson Represents*
11846 Ventura Blvd Ste 302
Studio City, CA 91604-2620, USA

Nielsen, Connie (Actor)
c/o Estelle Lasher *Lasher Group*
1133 Avenue of the Americas Fl 27
New York, NY 10036-6710, USA

Nielsen, Gifford (Athlete, Football Player)
10 Sarahs Cv
Sugar Land, TX 77479-2449, USA

Nielsen, Jeff (Athlete, Hockey Player)
5233 France Ave S
Minneapolis, MN 55410-2038, USA

Nielsen, Jerry (Athlete, Baseball Player)
7747 Woodchuck Way
Citrus Heights, CA 95610-2543, USA

Nielsen, Lonnie (Athlete, Golfer)
15 Redbrick Rd
Orchard Park, NY 14127-3940, USA

Nielsen, Rick (Musician)
4 Jacoby Pl
Rockford, IL 61107-1817, USA

Nielsen, Scott (Athlete, Baseball Player)
2898 E Valley View Ave
Salt Lake City, UT 84117-5550, USA

Niemann, Jeff (Athlete, Baseball Player)
5922 Jason St
Houston, TX 77074-7742, USA

Niemann, Randy (Athlete, Baseball Player)
7743 Greenbrier Cir
Port Saint Lucie, FL 34986-3300, USA

Niemann, Richard (Athlete, Basketball Player)
7911 Stanford Ave
Saint Louis, MO 63130-3613, USA

Niemann-Stirnemann, Gunda (Speed Skater)
Postfach 503
Erfurt 99010, GERMANY

Niemi, Lisa (Actor)
c/o Staff Member *Atria Books*
1230 Avenue of the Americas
New York, NY 10020-1513, USA

Niemiec-Konwinski, Dolly (Athlete, Baseball Player)
1821 Spring Meadow Ct SE
Caledonia, MI 49316-9154, USA

Nieminen, Toni (Skier)
Landen Kanava 99
vesijarvenkatu 74
Lahti 15140, FINLAND

Nierman, Leonardo (Artist)
Amsterdam 43 PH
Mexico City 11 DF, MEXICO

Nies, Eric (Model, Reality Star)
c/o John Edmonds-Kozma *Bang Productions (NY)*
122 W 27th St Fl 8
New York, NY 10001-6227, USA

Nieson, Chuck (Athlete, Baseball Player)
31923 Trails End Rd
Clinton, MN 56225-5163, USA

Nieto, Adriana (Actor)
c/o Staff Member *Televisa*
Blvd Adolfo Lopez Mateos 232
Colonia San Angel INN
DF CP 01060, MEXICO

Nieto, Tom (Athlete, Baseball Player)
5812 16th St
Zephyrhills, FL 33542-3762, USA

Nieuwendyk, Joe (Athlete, Hockey Player)
2601 Avenue of the Stars Ste 100
Attn: General Manager
Frisco, TX 75034-9016, USA

Nieuwendyk, Joe (Athlete, Hockey Player)
3204 Drexel Dr
Dallas, TX 75205-2913, USA

Nieves, Juan (Athlete, Baseball Player, Coach)
Chicago White Sox
333 W 35th St
Attn: Coaching Staff
Chicago, IL 60616-3621, USA

Nieves, Melvin (Athlete, Baseball Player)
120 Wilderness Ct
West End, NC 27376, USA

Nigam, Anjul (Actor)
c/o Lisa DiSante-Frank *DiSante Frank & Company*
10061 Riverside Dr Ste 377
Toluca Lake, CA 91602-2560, USA

Nigam, Sonu (Musician)
c/o Linda Jones *The Mass Appeal*
11607 Burbank Blvd Ste A
N Hollywood, CA 91601-2345, USA

Nighswander, Nicholas (Athlete, Football Player)
PO Box 46
Burgoon, OH 43407-0046, USA

Nightingale, Maxine (Musician)
c/o Stephen Ford *Diva Central Inc*
7510 W Sunset Blvd # 1445
Los Angeles, CA 90046-3408, USA

Nighy, Bill (Actor)
c/o Pippa Markham *Markham & Froggatt*
4 Windmill St
London W1T 1HZ, UNITED KINGDOM

Nigro, Frank (Athlete, Hockey Player)
45 Princeton Terr
Brampton, ON L6S 3S4, CANADA

Niinimaa, Janne (Athlete, Hockey Player)
Thompson, Dorfman, Sweatman
PO Box 639 Stn Main
Attn: Donald Baizley
Winnipeg, MB R3C 2K6, Canada

Niittymaki, Antero (Athlete, Hockey Player)
1184 Nevada Ave
San Jose, CA 95125-3327, USA

Nikkanen, Kurt (Musician)
Columbia Artists Mgmt Inc
165 W 57th St
New York, NY 10019-2201, USA

Niklas, Jan (Actor)
Konigsberger Str. 20
Munich, GERMANY D-81927

Nikolishin, Andrei (Athlete, Hockey Player)
105 Bloomfield Ave
Hartford, CT 06105-1007, USA

Nilan, Chris (Athlete, Hockey Player)
577 Adams St Unit D
Milton, MA 02186-5636, USA

Niland, John H (Athlete, Football Player)
16058 Chalfont Ct
Dallas, TX 75248-3547, USA

Niles, Prescott (Musician)
Artists & Audience Entertainment
PO Box 35
Pawling, NY 12564-0035, USA

Nill, Jim (Athlete, Hockey Player)
20847 Dundee Dr.
Novi, MI 48375, USA

Nill, Jim (Athlete, Hockey Player)
Detroit Red Wings 600 Civic Center Dr
Attn: Asst General Manager
Novi, MI 48375, USA

Nilsmark, Catrin (Athlete, Golfer)
187 Commodore Dr
Jupiter, FL 33477-4007, USA

Nilsson, Dave (Athlete, Baseball Player)
34 Lawnhill Road
Neiang, Queensland, AU 04211, Australia

Nilsson, Inger (Actor)
Box 12710
Stockholm 11294, SWEDEN

Nilsson, Kent (Athlete, Hockey Player)
9034 Crichton Wood Dr
Orlando, FL 32819-4836, USA

Nilsson, Nils (Athlete, Hockey Player)
Vattugatan 8
Forshaga 667 32, SWEDEN

Nilsson, Ulf (Athlete, Hockey Player)
QBrick AB Sodra Hamnvagen 22
Stockholm S-11541, Sweden

Nimmo, Brandon (Athlete, Baseball Player)
c/o Ryan Hamill *Creative Artists Agency (CAA)*
2000 Avenue of the Stars Ste 100
Los Angeles, CA 90067-4705, USA

Nimmo, Dirk (Actor)
Michael Whitehall
125 Gloucester Road
London SW7 4TE, UNITED KINGDOM (UK)

Nimmons, Ernest (Baseball Player)
Indianapolis Clowns
1509 Paine St
Lorain, OH 44052-3253, USA

Nimphius, Kurt (Athlete, Basketball Player)
750 Dry Creek Rd
Sedona, AZ 86336-3621, USA

Nimri, Najwa (Actor, Musician)
c/o Staff Member *Kuranda Management*
Isla De Oza, 30
Madrid 28035, SPAIN

Nimziki, Joe (Director)
Paradigm Agency
10100 Santa Monica Blvd Ste 2500
Los Angeles, CA 90067-4116, USA

Nine (9) Inch Nails (Music Group)
c/o Jim Guerinot *Rebel Waltz Inc*
PO Box 9215
Laguna Beach, CA 92652-7212, USA

Nine Black Alps (Music Group)
c/o William Hann *13 Artists (UK)*
11-14 Kensington St
Brighton BN1 4AJ, UNITED KINGDOM

Ninedays (Music Group)
c/o Staff Member *Epic Records Group*
550 Madison Ave Fl 22
New York, NY 10022-3211, USA

Nininger, Harvey H (Misc)
PO Box 420
Sedona, AZ 86339-0420, USA

Ninkovich, Rob (Athlete, Football Player)

Ninowski, Jim (Athlete, Football Player)
2715 Melcombe Cir Apt 302
Troy, MI 48084-3453, USA

Nipar, Yvette (Actor)
Irv Schechter
9300 Wilshire Blvd Ste 410
Beverly Hills, CA 90212-3228, USA

Nipp, Maury (Athlete, Football Player)
631 E Michelle St
West Covina, CA 91790-5146, USA

Nipper, Al (Athlete, Baseball Player)
401 White Birch Valley Ct
Chesterfield, MO 63017-2457, USA

Nippert, Dustin (Athlete, Baseball Player)
PO Box 8540
Stockton, CA 95208-0540, USA

Nippert, Merlin (Athlete, Baseball Player)
1015 N Michigan Ave
Mangum, OK 73554-1820, USA

Nischwitz, Ron (Athlete, Baseball Player)
6790 Garber Rd
Dayton, OH 45415-1504, USA

Nish, Wayne (Chef)
405 E 58th St
New York, NY 10022-2302, USA

Nishikori, Kei (Athlete, Tennis Player)
5618 Title Row Dr
Bradenton, FL 34210-4072, USA

Nishilori, Kei (Athlete, Tennis Player)
5618 Title Row Dr
Bradenton, FL 34210-4072, USA

Nishimura, Mayumi (Chef)
Clearspring Ltd
19A Acton Park Estate
London W3 7QE, UK

Nishkian, Byron (Skier)
150 4th St PH
San Francisco, CA 94130-2201, USA

Nispel, Marcus (Director)
2125 Rockledge Rd
Los Angeles, CA 90068-3135, USA

Nissalke, Tom (Basketball Coach, Coach)
3075 E Kennedy Dr Apt 406
Salt Lake City, UT 84108-2200, USA

Nistico, Lou (Athlete, Hockey Player)
404 Westbury Cres
Thunder Bay, ON P7C 4N4, Canada

Nitkowski, C J (Athlete, Baseball Player)
205 Townsend Ln
Alpharetta, GA 30004-2553, USA

Nittmann, David (Artist)
PO Box 19065
Boulder, CO 80308-2065, USA

Nittmo, Bjorn (Athlete, Football Player)
201 E Jefferson St
Phoenix, AZ 85004-2412, USA

Nitty Gritty Dirt Band (Music Group)
c/o Staff Member *Paradigm (Monterey)*
404 W Franklin St
Monterey, CA 93940-2303, USA

Nitz, Leonard (Athlete, Cycler, Olympic Athlete)
5515 Ruhkala Rd
Rocklin, CA 95677-3117, USA

Nitzkowski, Monte (Athlete, Olympic Athlete, Swimmer)
7041 Seal Cir
Huntington Beach, CA 92648-3035, USA

Niven, Kip (Actor)
8109 Sagamore Rd
Leawood, KS 66206-1232, USA

Niven, Laurence (Larry) (Writer)
136 El Camino Dr
Beverly Hills, CA 90212-2705, USA

Niven Jr, David (Actor, Producer)
10701 Wilshire Blvd Apt 1506
Los Angeles, CA 90024-4441, USA

Nivola, Alessandro (Actor)
c/o Alexandra Crotin *The Lede Company*
9701 Wilshire Blvd # 930
Beverly Hills, CA 90212-2020, USA

Niwa, Gail (Musician)
Siegel Artist Mgmt
18 Amherst Ave
Wilkes Barre, PA 18702-1607, USA

Niwano, Nikkyo (Religious Leader)
Rissho Kosel-Kai
2-11-1 Wada Suginamiku
Tokyo 00166, JAPAN

Nix, Garth (Writer)
Harper Collins
77 - 85 Fulham palace road
London W12 8ER, UNITED KINGDOM

Nix, Jimmy (Race Car Driver)
520 SE 30th St Ste 6
Oklahoma City, OK 73129-4900, USA

Nix, John L (Athlete, Football Player)
2278 Lindsey Ct
Fallbrook, CA 92028-5304, USA

Nix, Kent (Athlete, Football Player)
2732 Colonial Pkwy
Fort Worth, TX 76109-1211, USA

Nix, Laynce (Athlete, Baseball Player)
1506 Princeton Ave
Midland, TX 79701-5762, USA

Nix, Matt (Writer)
c/o Staff Member *WME|IMG*
9601 Wilshire Blvd
Beverly Hills, CA 90210-5213, USA

Nixey, Troy (Director)
c/o Gary Ungar *Exile Entertainment*
732 El Medio Ave
Pacific Palisades, CA 90272-3451, USA

Nix III, Louis (Athlete, Football Player)
c/o Todd France *Creative Artists Agency (CAA) Sports*
3500 Lenox Rd NE
Atlanta, GA 30326-4228, USA

Nixon, Cynthia (Actor)
10 Bleecker St Apt 3B
New York, NY 10012-2436, USA

Nixon, Derek Lee (Actor, Producer, Writer)
c/o Staff Member *Aristar Entertainment*
27335 Lasso Bnd Fl 1
San Antonio, TX 78260-2633, USA

Nixon, Donell (Athlete, Baseball Player)
Seattle Mariners
2681 Mount Olive Rd
Whiteville, NC 28472-6863, USA

Nixon, Jeff (Athlete, Football Player)
549 Linwood Ave
Buffalo, NY 14209-1403, USA

Nixon, Kimberley (Actor)
c/o Larry Taube *Principal Entertainment*
9255 W Sunset Blvd Ste 500
Los Angeles, CA 90069-3301, USA

Nixon, Norm (Athlete, Basketball Player)
Nixon and Associates
607 Marguerita Ave
Santa Monica, CA 90402-1919, USA

Nixon, Otis (Athlete, Baseball Player)
1000 Montage Way Apt 1814
Atlanta, GA 30341-6071, USA

Nixon, Russ (Athlete, Baseball Player)
4265 N Tee Pee Ln
Las Vegas, NV 89129-2628, USA

Nixon, Sam (Musician, Television Host)
c/o Staff Member *CBBC*
PO Box 9989
Salford M5 0DP, UK

Nixon, Torran (Athlete, Football Player)
3265 Thorn St
San Diego, CA 92104-4754, USA

Nixon, Trot (Athlete, Baseball Player)
1023 Ocean Ridge Dr
Wilmington, NC 28405-5287, USA

Nixon-Eisenhower, Julie (Politician)
255 Foxall Ln
Berwyn, PA 19312-1843, USA

Niyazov, Saparmurad (President)
President's Office
Karl Marx Str 24
Ashkabad 744017, TURKMENISTAN

Niziolek, Robert (Athlete, Football Player)
206 Brome Ave
Lafayette, CO 80026-1738, USA

Niznik, Stephanie (Actor)
15263 Mulholland Dr
Los Angeles, CA 90077-1620, USA

Noah, Joakim (Athlete, Basketball Player)
c/o Bill Duffy *BDA Sports Management*
700 Ygnacio Valley Rd Ste 330
Walnut Creek, CA 94596-3838, USA

Noah, Joakim (Athlete, Basketball Player)
5 Bannockburn Ct
Bannockburn, IL 60015-1818, USA

Noah, Trevor (Comedian, Talk Show Host, Television Host)
The Daily Show with Trevor Noah
733 11th Ave
New York, NY 10019-5051, USA

Noah, Yannick (Athlete, Coach, Musician, Tennis Player)
230 Central Park S
New York, NY 10019-1409, USA

Noakes, Michael (Artist)
146 Hamilton Terrace
Saint John's Wood
London NW8 9UX, UNITED KINGDOM (UK)

Nobel, Ben (Actor)
c/o Bella Grundy *King Talent (Toronto)*
36 Tiverton Ave
Toronto ON M4M, Canada

Nobilo, Frank (Athlete, Golfer)
10209 Atterbury Ct
Orlando, FL 32827-7041, USA

Noble, Adrian K (Director)
Royal Shakespeare Co
Barbican Theater
London EC2Y 8BQ, UNITED KINGDOM (UK)

Noble, Brandon (Athlete, Football Player)
2154 Ferncroft Ln
Chester Springs, PA 19425-3846, USA

Noble, Brian (Athlete, Football Player)
2400 Luberon Dr
Henderson, NV 89044-0360, USA

Noble, John (Actor)
c/o Nicolas Bernheim *NB Management*
8906 W Olympic Blvd
Beverly Hills, CA 90211-3550, USA

Noble, Karen (Athlete, Golfer)
36 Edgewood Rd
Chatham, NJ 07928-2002, USA

Noble, Reginald (Redman) (Musician)
c/o Peter Schwartz *WME|IMG (NY)*
11 Madison Ave Fl 18
New York, NY 10010-3669, USA

Noble, Ross (Actor, Comedian)
c/o Staff Member *Real Talent Management (UK)*
24 Goodge St
London W1T 2QF, UNITED KINGDOM

Noble, Samantha (Actor)
c/o David Rudy *Armada Partners*
815 Moraga Dr
Los Angeles, CA 90049-1633, USA

Noblitt, Niles L (Business Person)
Biomet Inc
PO Box 587
Airport Industrial Park
Warsaw, IN 46581-0587, USA

Noboa, Junior (Athlete, Baseball Player)
Arizona Diamondbacks
PO Box 2095
Attn: Director, Latin American Ops
Phoenix, AZ 85001-2095, USA

Noce, Paul (Athlete, Baseball Player)
942 W Maumee St
Adrian, MI 49221-1916, USA

Nock, George (Athlete, Football Player)
1025 Nine North Dr Ste H
Alpharetta, GA 30004-3951, USA

Nodell, Mart (Cartoonist)
117 Lake Irene Dr
West Palm Beach, FL 33411-2266, USA

No Doubt (Music Group)
c/o Irving Azoff *Azoff Music Management*
1100 Glendon Ave Ste 2000
Los Angeles, CA 90024-3524, USA

Noel, Alyson (Writer)
14 Monarch Bay Plz # 186
Monarch Beach, CA 92629-3467, USA

Noel, Chris (Actor)
6815 Lake Ave
West Palm Beach, FL 33405-4525, USA

Noel, Claude (Athlete, Hockey Player)
300 Portage Ave
Attn: Coaching Staff Winnipeg Jets
Winnipeg, MB R3C 5S4, Canada

Noel, Claude (Athlete, Hockey Player)
4361 Bridgeside Pl
New Albany, OH 43054-7053, USA

Noel, Don (Race Car Driver)
PO Box 2757
Lake Isabella, CA 93240-2757, USA

Noel, Nerlens (Athlete, Basketball Player)
c/o Andy Miller *ASM Sports*
450 Fashion Ave Ste 1700
New York, NY 10123-1700, USA

Noel, Philip W (Politician)
20403 Wildcat Run Dr
Estero, FL 33928-2014, USA

Noel, Sydelle (Actor)
c/o Alexandra Crotin *The Lede Company*
9701 Wilshire Blvd # 930
Beverly Hills, CA 90212-2020, USA

Noel, Y'lan (Actor)
c/o Jillian Roscoe *ID Public Relations*
7060 Hollywood Blvd Fl 8th
Los Angeles, CA 90028-6021, USA

Nogle, Donald (Athlete, Football Player)
1248 Calle Christopher
Encinitas, CA 92024-5519, United States

Noguchi, Soichi (Astronaut)
c/o Staff Member *NASA-JSC*
2101 Nasa Pkwy # 1
Astronaut Office - Mail Code Cb
Houston, TX 77058-3607, USA

Nogueira, Ana (Actor)
c/o Jaime Misher *Innovative Artists*
235 Park Ave S Fl 7
New York, NY 10003-1405, USA

Nogulich, Natalia (Actor)
11841 Kiowa Ave Apt 7
Los Angeles, CA 90049-6016

Nogulich, Natalija (Actor)
11841 Kiowa Ave Apt 7
Los Angeles, CA 90049-6016, USA

Noji, Minae (Actor)
c/o Shepard Smith *Luber Roklin Management*
5815 W Sunset Blvd Ste 208
Los Angeles, CA 90028-6481, USA

Nojima, Minoru (Musician)
John Gingrich Mgmt
PO Box 515
New York, NY 10028-0005, USA

Nokelainen, Petteri (Athlete, Hockey Player)
c/o Staff Member *Boston Bruins*
100 Legends Way Ste 250
Td Banknorth Garden
Boston, MA 02114-1389, USA

Nokes, Matt (Athlete, Baseball Player)
22S5 Oxford Ave
Cardiff By The Sea, CA 92007-1915, USA

Nolan, Christopher (Director, Writer)
c/o Staff Member *Syncopy Films*
4000 Warner Blvd Bldg 203
Burbank, CA 91522-0001, USA

Nolan, Coleen (Actor)
c/o Staff Member *Urban Associates*
Prefers to be contacted via email or telephone
London, UK

Nolan, Deanna (Basketball Player)
Detroit Shock
2 Championship Dr
Palace
Auburn Hills, MI 48326-1753, USA

Nolan, Gary (Athlete, Baseball Player)
97 Acacia Ave
Oroville, CA 95966-3658, USA

Nolan, Graham (Cartoonist)
162 Godfrey Ter
East Aurora, NY 14052-2040, USA

Nolan, Joe (Athlete, Baseball Player)
9515 Alix Dr
Saint Louis, MO 63123-7101, USA

Nolan, Jonathan (Director, Producer)
Kilter Films
150 S Rodeo Dr
Beverly Hills, CA 90212-2408, USA

Nolan, Kathleen (Actor)
c/o Staff Member *The House of Representatives*
3118 Wilshire Blvd Ste D
Santa Monica, CA 90403-2345, USA

Nolan, Katie (Correspondent, Television Host)
c/o Meghan Mackenzie *WME|IMG*
9601 Wilshire Blvd
Beverly Hills, CA 90210-5213, USA

Nolan, Nolan (Athlete, Football Player)
1400 Zillock Rd Ofc
San Benito, TX 78586-9730, USA

Nolan, Owen (Athlete, Hockey Player)
17110 Cooper Hill Dr.
Morgan Hill, CA 95017, USA

Nolan, Simon (Athlete, Hockey Player)
1342 Rue des Grandes-Marees
Quebec, QC G1Y 2T1, CANADA

Nolan, Ted (Athlete, Coach, Hockey Player)
269 Queen St E
Sault Ste. Marie, ON P6A 1Y9, Canada

Nolasco, Amaury (Actor)
c/o Evan Hainey *Untitled Entertainment*
350 S Beverly Dr Ste 200
Beverly Hills, CA 90212-4819, USA

Nolasco, Elvis (Actor)
c/o Matt Goldman *Silver Lining Entertainment*
421 S Beverly Dr Fl 7
Beverly Hills, CA 90212-4408, USA

Nolasco, Ricky (Athlete, Baseball Player)
3370 NE 190th St Apt 1812
Miami, FL 33180-2417, USA

Nold, Dick (Athlete, Baseball Player)
715 Athens St
San Francisco, CA 94112-3513, USA

Nolen, Paul (Athlete, Basketball Player)
480 Pecan Dr
Burleson, TX 76028-6308, USA

Noles, Dickie (Athlete, Baseball Player)
15 Hidden Valley Rd
Aston, PA 19014-2513, USA

Nolet, Simon (Athlete, Hockey Player)
1342 Rue des Grandes-Marees
Quebec, QC G1Y 2T1, Canada

Nolfi, George (Director)
c/o David Wirtschafter *WME|IMG*
9601 Wilshire Blvd
Beverly Hills, CA 90210-5213, USA

Nolin, Gena Lee (Actor)
c/o Jerry Shandrew *Shandrew Public Relations*
1050 S Stanley Ave
Los Angeles, CA 90019-6634, USA

Nolte, Eric (Athlete, Baseball Player)
2388S Noelle Ave
Murrieta, CA 92544-2258, USA

Nolte, Nick (Actor, Producer)
c/o Arnold Robinson *Rogers & Cowan*
1840 Century Park E Fl 18
Los Angeles, CA 90067-2101, USA

Nolting, Paul F (Religious Leader)
Church of Lutheran Confession
620 E 50th St
Loveland, CO 80538-1838, USA

Nomina, Tom (Athlete, Football Player)
731 N Namaqua Ave
Loveland, CO 80537-4401, USA

Nomo, Hideo (Athlete, Baseball Player)
11746 Stonehenge Ln
Los Angeles, CA 90077-1302, USA

Nool, Erki (Athlete, Track Athlete)
Regati 1
Tallinn 11911, ESTONIA

Noonan, Brian (Athlete, Hockey Player)
262 W Eggleston Ave Apt F
Elmhurst, IL 60126-3885, USA

Noonan, Chris (Director)
c/o Craig Gering *Creative Artists Agency (CAA)*
2000 Avenue of the Stars Ste 100
Los Angeles, CA 90067-4705, USA

Noonan, Danny (Athlete, Football Player)
1 Cowboys Pkwy
Irving, TX 75063-4924, USA

Noonan, Karl (Athlete, Football Player)
7149 Oxford Hunt Dr
Stanley, NC 28164-6803, USA

Noonan, Katie (Musician)
c/o Staff Member *The Harbour Agency*
135 Forbes St
Woolloomooloo NSW 2011, Australia

Noonan, Patrick F (Misc)
3553 Hamlet Pl
Chevy Chase, MD 20815-4822, USA

Noonan, Peggy (Writer)
Reagan Books
10 E 53rd St
New York, NY 10022-5244, USA

Noone, Kathleen (Actor)
130 W 42nd St Ste 1804
New York, NY 10036-7902, USA

Noone, Nora Jane (Actor)
c/o Staff Member *Independent Talent Group*
40 Whitfield St
London W1T 2RH, UNITED KINGDOM

Noone, Peter (Actor, Musician)
Robert Thomas Agency
42350 Niagara Dr
Sterling Heights, MI 48313-2927, USA

Noor Al-Hussein (Royalty)
Royal Palace
Amman, JORDAN

Nordbrook, Tim (Athlete, Baseball Player)
7 Shelbys Path Apt E
Sparks Glencoe, MD 21152-9276, USA

Norden, Tommy (Actor)
34 Bal Bay Dr
Bal Harbour, FL 33154-1349, USA

Nordgren, Fred (Athlete, Football Player)
1385 Ranier Loop NW
Salem, OR 97304-2081, USA

Nordhagen, Wayne (Athlete, Baseball Player)
2S896 Ramillo Way
Valencia, CA 91355-1925, USA

Nordlander, Mattias (Musician)
MOB Agency
6404 Wilshire Blvd Ste 505
Los Angeles, CA 90048-5507, USA

Nordling, Jeffrey (Actor)
245 Spencer St
Glendale, CA 91202-1813, USA

Nordmann, Robert (Athlete, Basketball Player)
631 E Sherwood Rd
Williamston, MI 48895-9436, USA

Nordquist, Helen (Athlete, Baseball Player)
PO Box 474
Alton, NH 03809-0474, USA

Nordquist, Mark (Athlete, Football Player)
3495 Seacrest Dr
Carlsbad, CA 92008-2039, USA

Nordsieck, Kenneth H (Astronaut)
2807 Ridge Rd
Madison, WI 53705-5223, USA

Noren, Irv (Athlete, Baseball Player)
3154 Camino Crest Dr
Oceanside, CA 92056-3613, USA

Noren, Lars (Writer)
Ostermalmsgatan 33
Stockholm 11426, SWEDEN

Norgaard, Chloe (Model)
c/o Staff Member *One Management*
42 Bond St Fl 2
New York, NY 10012-2768, USA

Norgard, Erik C (Athlete, Football Player)
404 Winterthur Way
Highlands Ranch, CO 80129-5662, USA

Noriander, John (Basketball Player)
801 9th St N Apt 102
Virginia, MN 55792-2393, USA

Norick, Lance (Race Car Driver)
6306 S Macdill Ave Apt 1724
Tampa, FL 33611-5059, USA

Noriega, Carlos I (Astronaut)
4630 Silhouette Dr
Katy, TX 77493-8099, USA

Noriega, Carlos L Lt Colonel (Astronaut)
4630 Silhouette Dr
Katy, TX 77493-8099, USA

Noriega, Danny (Musician, Reality Star)

Noriega, Victor (Actor)
c/o Staff Member *Televisa*
Blvd Adolfo Lopez Mateos 232
Colonia San Angel INN
DF CP 01060, MEXICO

Noris, Joe (Athlete, Hockey Player)
1111 Via Carolina
La Jolla, CA 92037-6254, USA

Norman, Chris (Musician)
Denis Vaughan Mgmt
PO Box 28286
London N21 3WT, UNITED KINGDOM (UK)

Norman, Dan (Athlete, Baseball Player)
7701 W Saint John Rd Apt 2041
Glendale, AZ 85308-8630, USA

Norman, Fred (Athlete, Baseball Player)
5921 Monnett Rd
Julian, NC 27283-9187, USA

Norman, Greg (Athlete, Golfer)
328 S Beach Rd
Hobe Sound, FL 33455-2606, USA

Norman, Jessye (Musician)
Jessye Norman School of the Arts
739 Greene St
Augusta, GA 30901-2322, USA

Norman, Joe (Athlete, Football Player)
1526 Saunders Dr
Wooster, OH 44691-1558, USA

Norman, Josh (Athlete, Football Player)

Norman, Ken (Athlete, Basketball Player)
19020 Kedzie Ave
Homewood, IL 60430-4359, USA

Norman, Les (Athlete, Baseball Player)
1401 Dogwood Dr
Greenwood, MO 64034-8671, USA

Norman, Marsha (Writer)
375 Greenwich St # 700
New York, NY 10013-2376, USA

Norman, Nelson (Athlete, Baseball Player)
3282 Fairfax Ave NE
Palm Bay, FL 32905-5915, USA

Norman, Pettis (Athlete, Football Player)
1430 Bar Harbor Cir
Dallas, TX 75232-3010, USA

Norman, Steve (Musician)
International Talent Group
729 7th Ave Ste 1600
New York, NY 10019-6880, USA

Norman, Tim (Reality Star)
Sweetie Pie's
3643 Delmar Blvd
Saint Louis, MO 63108-3617, USA

Norman, Todd (Athlete, Football Player)
27517 Via Montoya
San Juan Capistrano, CA 92675-5364, USA

Norona, David (Actor)
c/o Staff Member *The Kohner Agency*
9300 Wilshire Blvd Ste 555
Beverly Hills, CA 90212-3211, USA

Noronen, Mika (Athlete, Hockey Player)
65 S Autumn Dr
Rochester, NY 14626, USA

Norrena, Fredrik (Athlete, Hockey Player)
1751 Barrington Rd
Columbus, OH 43221-3838, USA

Norris, Aaron (Director, Producer)
c/o Staff Member *Holmes Weinberg, PC*
30765 Pacific Coast Hwy Ste 411
Malibu, CA 90265-3646, USA

Norris, Chuck (Actor, Producer)
PO Box 872
Navasota, TX 77868-0872, USA

Norris, Daran (Actor)
c/o Dede Binder-Goldsmith *Defining Artists Agency*
8721 W Sunset Blvd Ste 209
W Hollywood, CA 90069-2272, USA

Norris, Darran (Actor)
c/o Staff Member *ICM Partners*
10250 Constellation Blvd Fl 7
Los Angeles, CA 90067-6207, USA

Norris, David Owen (Musician)
Aughton Rise
Collingbourne
Kingston Wilts SN8 3SA, UNITED KINGDOM (UK)

Norris, Dean (Actor)
c/o Keith Addis *Industry Entertainment Partners*
955 Carrillo Dr Ste 300
Los Angeles, CA 90048-5400, USA

Norris, Dwayne (Athlete, Hockey Player)
850 Eastlake Ct
Oxford, MI 48371-6802, USA

Norris, Jack (Athlete, Hockey Player)
PO Box 323
Delisle, SK S0L 0P0, CANADA

Norris, Jim (Athlete, Baseball Player)
611 Falls Creek Ct
Burleson, TX 76028-7664, USA

Norris, John (Journalist, Television Host)

Norris, Martyn (Athlete, Basketball Player)
18943 Crescent Bay Dr
Houston, TX 77094-3329, USA

Norris, Michele (Correspondent)
ABC-TV
5010 Creston St
News Dept
Hyattsville, MD 20781-1216, USA

Norris, Mike (Athlete, Baseball Player)
735 Watson Canyon Ct Apt 218
San Ramon, CA 94582-4948, USA

Norris, Paul J (Business Person)
WR Grace Co
7500 Grace Dr
Columbia, MD 21044-4029, USA

Norris, Terry (Boxer)
Don King Productions
968 Pinehurst Dr
Las Vegas, NV 89109-1569, USA

Norris, Tim (Athlete, Golfer)
1604 Little Kitten Ave
Manhattan, KS 66503-7500, USA

Norrish, Rod (Athlete, Hockey Player)
3516 Amherst Ave
Dallas, TX 75225-7419, USA

Norseth, Mike (Athlete, Football Player)
9774 S Jameson Point Cv
Sandy, UT 84092-4200, USA

North, Andy (Athlete, Golfer)
3289 High Point Rd
Madison, WI 53719, USA

North, Billy (Athlete, Baseball Player)
5523 106th Ave NE
Kirkland, WA 98033-7413, USA

North, Chandra (Model)
c/o Staff Member *Storm Model Management*
5 Jubilee Pl
1st Floor
London SW3 3TD, UK

North, Heather (Actor)
12996 Galewood St
Studio City, CA 91604-4045, USA

North, Jay (Actor)
290 NE 1st Ave
Lake Butler, FL 32054-1202, USA

North, Oliver L (Politician)
c/o Staff Member *Fox News*
1211 Avenue of the Americas Lowr C1
New York, NY 10036-8705, USA

North, Peter (Adult Film Star)
c/o Staff Member *Vivid Entertainment*
1933 N Bronson Ave Apt 209
Los Angeles, CA 90068-5632, USA

Northam, Jeremy (Actor)
c/o Chris Andrews *Creative Artists Agency (CAA)*
2000 Avenue of the Stars Ste 100
Los Angeles, CA 90067-4705, USA

Northcutt, Dennis (Athlete, Football Player)
13761 Saxon Lake Dr S
Jacksonville, FL 32225-2680, USA

Northey, Scott (Athlete, Baseball Player)
9920 Bankside Dr
Roswell, GA 30076-3735, USA

Northrop, Wayne (Actor)
37900 Road 800
Raymond, CA 93653-9714, USA

Northrup, MD, Christiane (Writer)
Empowering Women's Wisdom
PO Box 199
Yarmouth, ME 04096-0199, USA

Northway, Douglas (Doug) (Swimmer)
3239 E 3rd St
Tucson, AZ 85716-4231, USA

Norton, Brad (Athlete, Hockey Player)
21310 Castillo St
Woodland Hills, CA 91364-4420, USA

Norton, Bryan (Athlete, Golfer)
4001 W 105th St APT 244
Overland Park, KS 66207, USA

Norton, Corin (Actor)
c/o Staff Member *Bruce Heller and Associates*
3272 Motor Ave
Los Angeles, CA 90034-3772, USA

Norton, Edward (Actor)
360 N Martel Ave
Los Angeles, CA 90036-2516, USA

Norton, Gale (Politician)
6645 S Quemoy Cir
Aurora, CO 80016-2686, USA

Norton, Graham (Actor)
c/o Melanie Rockcliffe *Troika*
10A Christina St.
London EC2A 4PA, UNITED KINGDOM

Norton, Greg (Athlete, Baseball Player)
11130 Eliot Ct
Denver, CO 80234-4682, USA

Norton, James (Actor)
c/o Emma Jackson *Premier PR*
2-4 Bucknall St
London WC2H 8LA, UNITED KINGDOM

Norton, James A (Athlete, Football Player)
2550 S Ellsworth Rd Unit 13
Mesa, AZ 85209-1198, USA

Norton, James C (Athlete, Football Player)
PO Box 495997
Garland, TX 75049-5997, USA

Norton, Jeff (Athlete, Hockey Player, Olympic Athlete)
PO Box 323
Duxbury, MA 02331-0323, USA

Norton, Jerry (Athlete, Football Player)
6901 Chevy Chase Ave
Dallas, TX 75225-2416, USA

Norton, Jim (Actor, Comedian)
c/o Jonathan Brandstein *Morra Brezner Steinberg & Tenenbaum (MBST) Entertainment*
345 N Maple Dr Ste 200
Beverly Hills, CA 90210-5174, USA

Norton, Judy (Actor)
c/o Karen Renna *Karen Renna & Associates*
PO Box 4227
Burbank, CA 91503-4227, USA

Norton, Peter (Designer)
225 Arizona Ave # 200W
Santa Monica, CA 90401-1243, USA

Norton, Phil (Athlete, Baseball Player)
677 County Road 3772
Queen City, TX 75572-7947, USA

Norton, Richard (Actor)
c/o Ray Cavaleri *Cavaleri & Associates*
3500 W Olive Ave Ste 300
Burbank, CA 91505-4647, USA

Norton, Rick (Athlete, Football Player)
901 W Mahoney St
Plant City, FL 33563-4435, USA

Norton, Tom (Athlete, Baseball Player)
4900 Southwood Dr
Sheffield Lake, OH 44054-1559, USA

Norton Jr, Ken (Athlete, Coach, Football Coach, Football Player)
Seattle Seahawks
800 Occidental Ave S Ste 200
Coaching Staff
Seattle, WA 98134-1200, USA

Norvell, Jay (Athlete, Football Player)
2166 Clinton Ave
Alameda, CA 94501-4945, USA

Norvill, Eryn Jean (Actor)
c/o Lisa Mann *Lisa Mann Creative Management*
19-25 Cope St
Redfern NSW 02016, AUSTRALIA

Norville, Deborah (Journalist)
c/o Rick Hersh *Celebrity Consultants LLC*
3340 Ocean Park Blvd Ste 1005
Santa Monica, CA 90405-3255, USA

Norvind, Nailea (Actor)
c/o Staff Member *Televisa*
Blvd Adolfo Lopez Mateos 232
Colonia San Angel INN
DF CP 01060, MEXICO

Norwell, Andrew (Athlete, Football Player)
c/o Adam Heller *Vantage Management Group*
518 Reamer Dr
Carnegie, PA 15106-1845, USA

Norwich, Craig (Athlete, Hockey Player)
66 9th St E Unit 2711
Saint Paul, MN 55101-2282, USA

Norwood, Brandy (Actor, Musician)
Norwood Kids Foundation
928 Summit St
McComb, MS 39648-3154, USA

Norwood, Jerious (Football Player)
c/o Staff Member *Atlanta Falcons*
4400 Falcon Pkwy
Flowery Branch, GA 30542-3176, USA

Norwood, Jordan (Athlete, Football Player)
c/o Peter Schaffer *Authentic Athletix*
400 S Steele St Unit 47
Denver, CO 80209-3535, USA

Norwood, Lee (Athlete, Hockey Player)
28876 Olson St
Livonia, MI 48150-4038, USA

Norwood, Ray J (Actor, Musician)
c/o Kim Dorr *Defining Artists Agency*
8721 W Sunset Blvd Ste 209
W Hollywood, CA 90069-2272, USA

Norwood, Robin (Writer)
c/o Staff Member *Simon & Schuster*
1230 Avenue of the Americas Fl CONC1
New York, NY 10020-1586, USA

Norwood, Scott (Athlete, Football Player)
42923 Shelbourne Sq
Chantilly, VA 20152-2097, USA

Norwood, Willie (Athlete, Baseball Player)
225 Gunsmoke Dr
Diamond Bar, CA 91765-1257, USA

Norwood, Willie (Athlete, Basketball Player)
414 W 122nd St Apt B
Los Angeles, CA 90061-1314, USA

Nosek, Randy (Athlete, Baseball Player)
15485 Knobhill Dr
Linden, MI 48451-8716, USA

Noseworthy, Jack (Actor)
c/o Lori Jonas *Jonas Public Relations*
1327 Ocean Ave Ste F
Santa Monica, CA 90401-1024, USA

Nosseck, Noel (Director)
10490 Wilshire Blvd Apt 904
Los Angeles, CA 90024-4667, USA

Nossek, Joe (Athlete, Baseball Player)
630 Sunrise Dr
Amherst, OH 44001-1659, USA

Noszka, Matthew (Actor, Model)
c/o Katie Greenthal *The Lede Company*
9701 Wilshire Blvd # 930
Beverly Hills, CA 90212-2020, USA

Notaro, Tig (Actor, Comedian)
c/o Hunter Seidman *Integral Entertainment*
Prefers to be contacted by email or phone.
Santa Monica, CA 90403, USA

Noth, Chris (Actor)
13656 Oak Canyon Ave
Sherman Oaks, CA 91423-4723, USA

Nothing More (Music Group)
c/o Nick Storch *ICM Partners (NY)*
730 5th Ave
New York, NY 10019-4105, USA

Nothstein, Marty (Athlete, Cycler, Olympic Athlete)
1019 Village Round
Allentown, PA 18106-9779, USA

Notley, Alice (Writer)
c/o Staff Member *Wesleyan University Press*
215 Long Ln
Middletown, CT 06457-4073, USA

Noto, Lucio A (Business Person)
Mobil Corp
3225 Gallows Rd
Fairfax, VA 22037-0003, USA

Nott, Tara (Athlete, Olympic Athlete, Weightlifter)
9516 Hayes St
Overland Park, KS 66212-5029, USA

Nottebohm, Andreas (Artist)
Mentzstr 44
Mulheim An Der Ruhr, GERMANY

Nottingham, Don (Athlete, Football Player)
PO Box 459
Belleview, FL 34421-0459, USA

Nottle, Ed (Athlete, Baseball Player)
7527 Midway Dr
Evansville, IN 47711-6300, USA

Nouri, Michael (Actor)
c/o Joannie Burstein *Burstein Company*
15304 W Sunset Blvd Ste 208
Pacific Palisades, CA 90272-3656, USA

Nova, Nikki (Actor)
4331 E Baseline Rd Ste B105
PO Box 431
Gilbert, AZ 85234-2960, USA

Novack, K J (Business Person)
America Online
22000 Aol Way
Dulles, VA 20166-9302, USA

Novak, BJ (Actor, Comedian)
c/o Jodi Gottlieb *Independent Public Relations*
9601 Wilshire Blvd Ste 750
Beverly Hills, CA 90210-5228, USA

Novak, David C (Business Person)
Tricon Global Restaurants
PO Box 436569
Louisville, KY 40253-6569, USA

Novak, Jack (Athlete, Football Player)
308 River Chase Ct
Georgetown, TX 78628-5314, USA

Novak, Kim (Actor)
13777 Agate Rd
Eagle Point, OR 97524-6567, USA

Novak, Nick (Athlete, Football Player)
c/o Chad Wiestling *Integrated Sports Management*
2120 Texas St Apt 2204
Houston, TX 77003-3054, USA

Novak, Pablo (Actor)
c/o Staff Member *Telefe (Argentina)*
Pavon 2444
Buenos Aires C1248AAT, ARGENTINA

Novak, Popper Ilona (Swimmer)
Il Orso Utca 23
Budapest, HUNGARY

Novakovic, Bojana (Actor)
c/o Staff Member *Shanahan Management*
Level 3 Berman House
Surry Hills 02010, AUSTRALIA

Novelli, William (Misc)
American Association of Retired Persons
601 E St NW
Washington, DC 20049-0001, USA

Novello, Antonia C (Misc)
2700 Virginia Ave NW # 501
Washington, DC 20037-1909, USA

Novello, Antonia Dr (Politician)
1616 Foss Ave
Orlando, FL 32814-6732, USA

Novello, Don (Fr Guido Sarducci) (Actor, Comedian)
Elizabeth Rush Agency
82 Cumberland Ave
Verona, NJ 07044-2105, USA

Noveskey, Matt (Musician)
Ashley Talent
2002 Hogback Rd Ste 20
Ann Arbor, MI 48105-9736, USA

Novoa, Rafael (Actor)
c/o Staff Member *TV Caracol*
Calle 76 #11 - 35
Piso 10AA
Bogota DC 26484, COLOMBIA

Novoa, Rafael (Athlete, Baseball Player)
3420 N 47th Way
Phoenix, AZ 85018-6014, USA

Novoselic, Krist (Activist, Musician)
3105 S Lucile St
Seattle, WA 98108-3032, USA

Novoselsky, Brent (Athlete, Football Player)
405 Marvins Way
Buffalo Grove, IL 60089-6419, USA

Novotny, Dave (Musician)
Helter Skelter Plaza
535 Kings Road
London SW10 0S, UNITED KINGDOM (UK)

Nowak, Lisa M (Astronaut)
17123 Parsley Hawthome Court
Houston, TX 77059, USA

Nowak, Lisa M Cdr (Astronaut)
17123 Parsley Hawthorne Ct
Houston, TX 77059-3231, USA

Nowak, Peter (Coach, Soccer Player)
DC United
14120 Newbrook Dr
Chantilly, VA 20151-2273, USA

Nowak, Tim (Athlete, Hockey Player)
8060 Easton Village Dr
Easton, MD 21601-7457, USA

Nowatzke, Tom (Athlete, Football Player)
4335 Diuble Rd
Ann Arbor, MI 48103-9606, USA

Nowicki, Tom (Actor)
c/o Staff Member *Davis Management*
4111 Lankershim Blvd
Studio City, CA 91602-2828

Nowitzki, Dirk (Athlete, Basketball Player)
10735 Strait Ln
Dallas, TX 75229-5428, USA

Nowra, Louis (Writer)
Level 18 Plaza 11
500 Oxford St
Bondi Junction, NSW 02011, AUSTRALIA

Nowrasteh, Cyrus (Director)
c/o Stephanie Davis *Wet Dog Entertainment*
2458 Crest View Dr
Los Angeles, CA 90046-1407, USA

Noxon, Marti (Writer)
c/o Staff Member *WME|IMG*
9601 Wilshire Blvd
Beverly Hills, CA 90210-5213, USA

Noyce, Phillip (Director)
6666 Whitley Ter
Los Angeles, CA 90068-3221, USA

Noyd, R Allen (Religious Leader)
General Council
1294 Rutledge Rd
Christian Church
Transfer, PA 16154-2226, USA

Noyes, Albert Jr (Misc)
5102 Fairview Dr
Austin, TX 78731-5426, USA

Nri, Cyril (Actor)
Bosun House
1 Deer Park Road
Merton
London SW19 3TL, UK

Nsengiyremeye, Dismas (Prime Minister)
Prime Minister's Office
Kigali, RWANDA

Ntombi (Royalty)
Royal Residence
PO Box 1
Lobamba, SWAZILAND

Ntoutoume, Jean-Francois (Prime Minister)
Prime Minister's Office
BP 546
Libreville, GABON

Nucci, Danny (Actor)
6361 Innsdale Dr
Los Angeles, CA 90068-1623, USA

Nugent, Kevin (Athlete, Hockey Player)
7 Hearthstone Ln
Farmington, CT 06032-2480, USA

Nugent, Mike (Athlete, Football Player)
c/o Ken Harris *Optimum Sports Management*
3225 S Macdill Ave Ste 330
Tampa, FL 33629-8171, USA

Nugent, Nelle (Producer)
Foxboro Entertainment
234 W 44th St Ste 1005
New York, NY 10036-3909, USA

Nugent, Ted (Musician)
2424 Coopers Crossing Rd
China Spring, TX 76633-3121, USA

Nujoma, Sam S (President)
President's Office
State House
Mugabe Ave
Windhoek 09000, NAMIBIA

Numan, Gary (Musician, Songwriter, Writer)
86 Staines Road
Wraysbury
N Staines, Middlesex TW19 5A, UNITED KINGDOM (UK)

Numeroff, Laura Joffe (Writer)
c/o Staff Member *HarperCollins Publishers*
195 Broadway Fl 2
New York, NY 10007-3132, USA

Numminen, Teppo (Athlete, Hockey Player)
Buffalo Sabres 1 Seymour H Knox Ill Plz Ste 1
Attn: Coaching Staff
Buffalo, NY 14203-3096, USA

Numminen, Teppo (Athlete, Hockey Player)
5975 Tipperary Mnr
Clarence Center, NY 14032-9509, USA

Nunes, Constance (Actor, Model)
c/o Gabrielle Terzian *NTA Talent Agency*
1445 N Stanley Ave Fl 2
Los Angeles, CA 90046-4015, USA

Nunes, Devin (Congressman, Politician)
1013 Longworth Hob
Washington, DC 20515-0004, USA

Nunez, Abraham (Athlete, Baseball Player)
Pittsburgh Pirates
2863 Post Rock Dr
Tarpon Springs, FL 34688-7311, USA

Nunez, Chris (Reality Star)
c/o Elizabeth Much *East 2 West Collective*
11022 Santa Monica Blvd Ste 350
Los Angeles, CA 90025-7532, USA

Nunez, Edwin (Athlete, Baseball Player)
2015 E Minton St
Mesa, AZ 85213-1442, USA

Nunez, Jorge (Musician)

Nunez, Oscar (Actor)
c/o Bruce Smith *OmniPop Talent Group*
4605 Lankershim Blvd Ste 201
Toluca Lake, CA 91602-1874, USA

Nunez, Victor (Director)
Paul Kohner
9300 Wilshire Blvd Ste 555
Beverly Hills, CA 90212-3211, USA

Nunez, Vladimir (Athlete, Baseball Player)
2597 Pierce Brennen Ct
Lawrenceville, GA 30043-1323, USA

Nunez Jr, Miguel A (Actor)
PO Box 570516
Tarzana, CA 91357-0516, USA

Nunley, Frank (Athlete, Football Player)
2131 Mulberry Cir
San Jose, CA 95125-4647, USA

Nunley, Jeremy (Athlete, Football Player)
908 Franklin Heights Dr
Winchester, TN 37398-4689, USA

Nunn, Samuel A (Sam) (Politician)
781 Marietta St NW
Atlanta, GA 30318-5750, USA

Nunn, Teri (Musician)
MOB Agency
6404 Wilshire Blvd Ste 505
Los Angeles, CA 90048-5507, USA

Nunn, Terri (Actor)
5503 Hartglen Pl
Agoura Hills, CA 91301-4036, USA

Nunn, Trevor R (Director)
Royal National Theater
South Bank
London SE1 9PX, UNITED KINGDOM (UK)

Nunnally, Jon (Athlete, Baseball Player)
13516 W Solano Dr
Litchfield Park, AZ 85340-4084, USA

Nunnari, Talmadge (Athlete, Baseball Player)
7101 Joy St Apt A8
Pensacola, FL 32504-6480, USA

Nunnery, R B (Athlete, Football Player)
3276 Claude Smith Rd
Magnolia, MS 39652-9534, USA

Nurding, Louise (Actor)
42 Colwith Road
London, ENGLAND W6 9EY

Nussbaum, Danny (Actor)
Conway Van Gelder RObinson
18-21 Jermyn St
London SW1Y 6NB, UNITED KINGDOM (UK)

Nussbaum, Joe (Actor, Director)
29002 Via Patina
Valencia, CA 91354-3050, USA

Nussbaum, Karen (Misc)
9-5 National Working Women Assn
231 W Wisconsin Ave Apt 900
Milwaukee, WI 53203-2306, USA

Nussbaum, Martha C (Misc)
University of Chicago
111 E 60th St
Law School
Chicago, IL 60637-2105, USA

Nussmeier, Doug (Athlete, Football Player)
28493 SW Meadows Loop
Wilsonville, OR 97070-6779, USA

Nutini, Paolo (Musician)
Atlantic Records UK
Electric Lighting Station
46 Kensington Ct
Londo W8 5DA, UNITED KINGDOM

Nutt, Dennis (Athlete, Basketball Player)
704 Magnolia Dr
Arkadelphia, AR 71923-4109, USA

Nutt, Jim (Artist)
1035 Greenwood Ave
Wilmette, IL 60091-1753, USA

Nutter, Alice (Musician)
Doug Smith Assoc
PO Box 1151
London W3 8ZJ, UNITED KINGDOM (UK)

Nutter, David (Director)
911 El Medio Ave
Pacific Palisades, CA 90272-2418, USA

Nutting, Ed (Athlete, Football Player)
100 Abernathy Road NE
#600
Atlanta, GA 30328, USA

Nutting, Robert (Sportscaster)
366 Oglebay Dr
Wheeling, WV 26003-1624, USA

Nutzie, Futzie (Artist, Cartoonist)
PO Box 325
Aromas, CA 95004-0325, USA

Nuveman, Stacey (Athlete, Olympic Athlete, Softball Player)
2801 NE 50th St # Usa
Oklahoma City, OK 73111-7203, USA

Nuwer, Hank (Journalist, Writer)
PO Box 31
Fairland, IN 46126-0031, USA

Nuyen, France (Actor)
c/o Budd Burton Moss *Burton Moss*
10533 Strathmore Dr
Los Angeles, CA 90024-2540, USA

Nuzorewa, Abel Tendekayi (Prime Minister)
United African National Council
40 Charter Road
Harare, ZIMBABWE

Nwosu, Julius (Athlete, Basketball Player)
12436 Park Regency P1
Rd Apt 1122
San Antonio, TX 78230-5992, USA

Nyad, Diana (Athlete, Olympic Athlete, Swimmer)
c/o Rachel Karten *ID Public Relations*
7060 Hollywood Blvd Fl 8th
Los Angeles, CA 90028-6021, USA

Nyberg, Frederik (Skier)
Kaptensgatan 2C
Froson 832 00, SWEDEN

Nyberg, Karen L (Astronaut)
2518 Lakeside Lndg
Seabrook, TX 77586-8313, USA

Nyberg, Karen L Dr (Astronaut)
1848 Lake Landing Dr
League City, TX 77573-7781, USA

Nye, Bill (The Science Guy) (Reality Star, Television Host)
3826 Mound View Ave
Studio City, CA 91604-3630, USA

Nye, Blaine (Athlete, Football Player)
1200 Bay Laurel Dr
Menlo Park, CA 94025-5871, USA

Nye, Erie (Business Person)
Texas Utilities Co
1601 Bryan St
Energy Plaza
Dallas, TX 75201-3431, USA

Nye, Naomi Shihab (Writer)
c/o Staff Member *HarperCollins Children's Books*
1350 Avenue of the Americas
New York, NY 10019-4702, USA

Nye, Rich (Athlete, Baseball Player)
40W2S7 Seavey Rd
Batavia, IL 60510-9420, USA

Nye, Ryan (Athlete, Baseball Player)
3319 Golf Course Dr
Alma, AR 72921-8601, USA

Nyers, Dick (Athlete, Football Player)
4055 N Riverside Dr
Columbus, IN 47203-1118, USA

Nykoluk, Mike (Athlete, Hockey Player)
47 Bennington Dr Apt 2
Naples, FL 34104-6553, USA

Nylander, Michael (Athlete, Hockey Player)
726 S Monroe St
Hinsdale, IL 60521-4320, USA

Nylund, Gary (Athlete, Hockey Player)
10-15255 36 Ave
Surrey, BC V3Z 0Y4, Canada

Nyman, Chris (Athlete, Baseball Player)
1700 Happy Creek Rd
Front Royal, VA 22630-6438, USA

Nyman, Jerry (Athlete, Baseball Player)
114 N Parkwood Ln
Payson, AZ 85541-4357, USA

Nyman, Michael L (Composer, Musician)
Michael Nyman Ltd
PO Box 430
High Wycombe HP13 5QT, UNITED KINGDOM (UK)

Nyman, Nyls (Athlete, Baseball Player)
PO Box 236
Susanville, CA 96130-0236, USA

Nyong'o, Lupita (Actor)
c/o Rebecca Sides Capellan *ID Public Relations (NY)*
40 Wall St Fl 51
New York, NY 10005-1385, USA

Nyquist, Ryan (Athlete)
c/o Steven Astephen *Wasserman Media Group - Carlsbad*
2251 Faraday Ave # 200
Carlsbad, CA 92008-7209, USA

Nystrom, Bob (Athlete, Hockey Player)
475 Berry Hill Rd.
Oyster Bay, NY 11771, USA

Nystrom, Eric (Athlete, Hockey Player)
475 Berry Hill Rd.
Oyster Bay, NY 11771, USA

Nystrom, Joakim (Tennis Player)
Torsgatan 194
Skellefteaa 931 00, SWEDEN

Nystrom, Lee (Athlete, Football Player)
18411 Priory Ave
Minnetonka, MN 55345-2459, USA

Nystrom (Nystr??m), Lene (Actor)
c/o Staff Member *Lindberg Management*
Lavendelstaede 5-7
Baghuset, 4. Sal
Copenhagen K 1462, DENMARK

Nyvell, Vic (Athlete, Football Player)
P.O. Box 159C
Kilgore, TX 75663, USA

O, Karen (Musician)
Yeah Yeah Yeahs
249 Metropolitan Ave
Brooklyn, NY 11211-4009, USA

Oakenfold, Paul (DJ, Musician)
6901 Oporto Dr
Los Angeles, CA 90068-2638, USA

Oakes, Don (Athlete, Football Player)
4448 Pheasant Ridge Rd Apt 305
Roanoke, VA 24014-5206, USA

Oakes, Summer Rayne (Model)
59 Grand St
Brooklyn, NY 11249-4110, USA

Oakley, Charles (Athlete, Basketball Player)
700 Park Regency p1
NE Apt 1105
Antlanta, GA 30326-4211, USA

Oakley, Tyler (Internet Star)
c/o Laura Ackerman *Advantage PR*
3900 W Alameda Ave Ste 1200
Burbank, CA 91505-4317, USA

Oak Ridge Boys (Music Group)
Oak Ridge Boys Inc
88 New Shackle Island Rd
Hendersonville, TN 37075-2393, USA

O.A.R. (Music Group)
c/o Dave Roberge *Red Light Management*
10 E 40th St Fl 22
New York, NY 10016-0201, USA

Oates, Adam (Athlete, Hockey Player)
165 Mulberry St
Attn Coaching Staff
Newark, NJ 07102-3607, USA

Oates, Adam R (Athlete, Hockey Player)
114 Lighthouse Dr
Jupiter, FL 33469, USA

Oates, Bart S (Athlete, Football Player, Sportscaster)
2 Silverbrook Rd
Morristown, NJ 07960-8016, USA

Oates, John (Musician)
c/o Jonathan Wolfson *Wolfson Entertainment*
2659 Townsgate Rd Ste 119
Westlake Village, CA 91361-2767, USA

Oates, Joyce Carol (Writer)
Princeton University
English Dept
Princeton, NJ 08540, USA

Oats, Carleton (Athlete, Football Player)
10605 E Coralbell Ave
Mesa, AZ 85208-7442, USA

Obama, Barack (Politician, President)
1250 24th St NW
Washington, DC 20037-1124, USA

Obama, Michelle (Politician)
PO Box 91000
Washington, DC 20090-1000, USA

Obando, Sherman (Athlete, Baseball Player)
7037 Coral Cove Dr
Orlando, FL 32818-2866, USA

O'Bannon, Dan (Director)
c/o Staff Member *Agency for the Performing Arts (APA)*
405 S Beverly Dr Ste 500
Beverly Hills, CA 90212-4425, USA

O'Bannon, Ed (Athlete, Basketball Player)
1387 Minuet St
Henderson, NV 89052-6454, USA

O'Bannon, Ed (Basketball Player)
11930 Agnes St
Cerritos, CA 90703-6902, USA

O'Bard, Ronnie (Athlete, Football Player)
27121 Puerta Del Oro
Mission Viejo, CA 92691-4421, USA

Obee, Duncan (Athlete, Football Player)
4488 283rd St
Toledo, OH 43611-1864, USA

Obeid, Atef (Prime Minister)
Prime Minister's Office
PO Box 191
1 Majlis El-Shaab St
Cairo, EGYPT

Obeidallah, Dean (Comedian)
338 E 70th St Apt 3A
New York, NY 10021-8682, USA

Obeidat, Ahmad Abdul-Majeed (Prime Minister)
Law & Arbitration Center
PO Box 926544
Amman, JORDAN

Oben, Roman (Athlete, Football Player)
11476 Creekstone Ln
San Diego, CA 92128-6325, USA

Oberding, Mark (Basketball Player)
4131 Cliff Oaks St
San Antonio, TX 78229-3536, USA

Oberer, Angela (Actor, Producer)
PO Box 4122
Los Angeles, CA 90078-4122, USA

Oberg, Margo (Misc)
RR 1 Box 73
Koloa
Kaui, HI 96756, USA

Oberg, Tom (Athlete, Football Player)
280 Avery St
Ashland, OR 97520-2202, USA

Oberholser, Arron (Golfer)
c/o Staff Member *Pro Golfers Association (PGA)*
112 TPC Blvd
Ponte Vedra Beach, FL 32082, USA

Oberkfell, Ken (Athlete, Baseball Player)
403 Line Drive Cir
Lincoln, NE 68508-4010, USA

Obermeyer, Klaus F (Designer, Fashion Designer)
Sport Obermeyer
115 Aspen Airport Business Ctr
Aspen, CO 81611-2502, USA

Obermueller, Wes (Athlete, Baseball Player)
7031 27th Ave
Newhall, IA 52315-9600, USA

O'Berry, Mike (Athlete, Baseball Player)
5977 S Fork Dr
Hoover, AL 35244-5466, USA

Oberst, Conor (Actor, Musician)
c/o Chloe Walsh *Grandstand Media*
39 W 32nd St Rm 1603
New York, NY 10001-3839, USA

Oberto, Fabricio (Athlete, Basketball Player)
8135 Monticello Ave
Skokie, IL 60076-3325, USA

O'Boyle, Maureen (Television Host)
WBTV News 3
1 Julian Price Pl
Charlotte, NC 28208-5211, USA

Obradors, Jacqueline (Actor)
c/o Todd Eisner *Abrams Artists Agency*
750 N San Vicente Blvd
E Tower Fl 11
Los Angeles, CA 90069-5788, USA

O'Bradovich, Ed (Athlete, Football Player)
235 N Smith St Apt 207
Palatine, IL 60067-8503, USA

Obregon, Alejandro (Artist)
Apartado Aereo 37
Barranquilla, COLOMBIA

Obregon, Ana (Actor)
Paul Kohner
9300 Wilshire Blvd Ste 555
Beverly Hills, CA 90212-3211, USA

O'Brian, Richard (Actor)
Jonathan Alparas
27 Floral St
London C2E 9DP, UNITED KINGDOM (UK)

O'Brian-Cooke, Penny (Baseball Player)
307-1335 East 27th St
North Vancouver, BC V7J 1S6, CANADA

O'Brien, Austin (Actor)
c/o Trice Koopman *Koopman Management*
851 Oreo Pl
Pacific Palisades, CA 90272-2457, USA

O'Brien, Bob (Athlete, Baseball Player)
1425 El Paso Ave
Clovis, CA 93611-7396, USA

O'Brien, Cathy (Athlete, Track Athlete)
19 Foss Farm Rd
Durham, NH 03824-2927, USA

O'Brien, Charlie (Athlete, Baseball Player)
4932 E 38th Pl
Tulsa, OK 74135-5529, USA

O'Brien, Clay (Actor)
652 Larkspur Ln
Gardnerville, NV 89460-7579, USA

O'Brien, Conan (Comedian, Talk Show Host)
Conaco
4000 Warner Blvd Bldg 2
Burbank, CA 91522-0001, USA

O'Brien, Dan (Athlete, Baseball Player)
4240 Wells Rd
Petersburg, MI 49270-9532, USA

O'Brien, Dan (Athlete, Decathlon Athlete, Olympic Athlete)
PO Box 4128
Scottsdale, AZ 85261-4128, USA

O'Brien, David (Athlete, Football Player)
66 Emerson Rd
Watertown, MA 02472-1606, USA

O'Brien, Dylan (Actor)
c/o Liz York *Principal Entertainment*
9255 W Sunset Blvd Ste 500
Los Angeles, CA 90069-3301, USA

OBrien, Dylan (Actor)
c/o Liz York *Principal Entertainment*
9255 W Sunset Blvd Ste 500
Los Angeles, CA 90069-3301, USA

O'Brien, Ed (Musician)
Nasty Little Man
72 Spring St # 1100
New York, NY 10012-4019, USA

O'Brien, Edna (Writer)
Wylie Agency
52 Knightsbridge
London SW1X 7JP, UNITED KINGDOM (UK)

O'Brien, Emily (Actor)
c/o Joseph Le *Joseph Le Talent Agency*
3500 W Olive Ave Ste 300
Burbank, CA 91505-4647, USA

O'Brien, G Dennis (Athlete, Hockey Player)
31 Hope St N
Port Hope, ON L1A 2N4, Canada

O'Brien, Jim (Athlete, Football Player)
413 Bethany St
Thousand Oaks, CA 91360-2025, USA

O'Brien, Jim (Basketball Player, Coach)
Philadelphia 76er's
55 Harbour Blvd
1 Union Center
Camden, NJ 08103-1056, USA

O'Brien, John (Writer)
2 Columbine Pl
Delran, NJ 08075-2860, USA

O'Brien, Johnny (Athlete, Baseball Player)
2405 N 75th St
Seattle, WA 98103-4959, USA

O'Brien, Kenneth J (Ken) Jr (Athlete, Football Player)
201 Manhattan Ave
Manhattan Beach, CA 90266-6439, USA

O'Brien, Margaret (Actor)
1250 La Peresa Dr
Thousand Oaks, CA 91362-2229, USA

O'Brien, Mark (Business Person)
Pulte Corp
33 Bloomfield Hills Pkwy
Bloomfield Hills, MI 48304-2944, USA

O'Brien, Maureen (Actor)
Kate Feast
Primrose Hill Studios
Fitzroy Road
London NW1 8TR, UNITED KINGDOM (UK)

O'Brien, Miles (Television Host)
c/o Staff Member *CNN (NY)*
10 Columbus Cir
Time Warner Center
New York, NY 10019-1158, USA

O'Brien, M Vincent (Coach, Horse Racer)
Ballydoyle House
Cashel
County Tipperary, IRELAND

O'Brien, Pat (Sportscaster, Television Host)
c/o Bruce Kaufman *ICM Partners*
10250 Constellation Blvd Fl 7
Los Angeles, CA 90067-6207, USA

O'Brien, Pete (Athlete, Baseball Player)
5509 Montclair Dr
Colleyville, TX 76034-5028, USA

O'Brien, Ron (Coach)
3002 Morning Glory Dr
Lake Placid, FL 33852-8456, USA

O'Brien, Scott (Athlete, Football Player)
12690 Overlook Mountain Dr
Charlotte, NC 28216-6726, USA

O'Brien, Soledad (Correspondent, Television Host)
Starfish Media Group
134 W 26th St Rm 1150
New York, NY 10001-6971, USA

O'Brien, Syd (Athlete, Baseball Player)
10189 Hemlock St
Rancho Cucamonga, CA 91730-3023, USA

O'Brien, Tim (Athlete, Track Athlete)
17 Partride Lane
Boxford, MA 01921, USA

O'Brien, Tim (Musician)
3629 Robin Rd
Nashville, TN 37204-3824, USA

O'Brien, Tina (Actor)
c/o Martin Spencer *Paradigm*
8942 Wilshire Blvd
Beverly Hills, CA 90211-1908, USA

O'Brien, Trever (Actor)
c/o Faras Rabadi *Emerald Talent Group*
3500 W Olive Ave Ste 300
Burbank, CA 91505-4647, USA

O'Brien, Trevor (Actor)
c/o Staff Member *Abrams Artists Agency*
750 N San Vicente Blvd
E Tower Fl 11
Los Angeles, CA 90069-5788, USA

O'Bryan, Sean (Actor)
c/o Staff Member *Alan Siegel Entertainment*
9200 W Sunset Blvd Ste 804
West Hollywood, CA 90069-3603, USA

Obst, Lynda (Producer)
c/o Staff Member *Lynda Obst Productions*
5555 Melrose Ave Rm 210
Los Angeles, CA 90038-3996

O'Byrne, Ryan (Athlete, Hockey Player)
1262 Beach Dr
Victoria, BC V8S 2N3, Canada

O'Callahan, Jack (Athlete, Hockey Player, Olympic Athlete)
101 Linden Ave
Glencoe, IL 60022-2144, USA

O'Callahan, John (Athlete, Football Player)
361 La Perle Ln Apt A
Costa Mesa, CA 92627-9553, USA

O'Caroll, Sinead (Musician)
Clintons
55 Drury Lane
Covent Garden
London WC2B 5SQ, UNITED KINGDOM (UK)

Ocasek, Ric (Musician, Songwriter)
75 Altamont Rd
Millbrook, NY 12545-6149, USA

Occhipinti, Andrea (Actor)
Carol Levi Co
Via Giuseppe Pisanelli
Rome 00196, ITALY

Ocean, Billy (Musician)
Laura Jay Enterprises
32 Willesden Lane
London NW6 7ST, UNITED KINGDOM (UK)

Ocean, Frank (Musician)
c/o Mara Buxbaum *ID Public Relations*
7060 Hollywood Blvd Fl 8th
Los Angeles, CA 90028-6021, USA

Ocean Colour Scene (Music Group)
c/o Staff Member *Paradigm (Monterey)*
404 W Franklin St
Monterey, CA 93940-2303, USA

Oceansize (Music Group)
c/o Staff Member *Paradigm (Monterey)*
404 W Franklin St
Monterey, CA 93940-2303, USA

Ochirbat, Punsalmaagiyn (President)
Tengeriin Tsag Co
Olympic St 14
Ulan Bator, MONGOLIA

Ochoa, Alex (Athlete, Baseball Player)
14526 NW 83rd Psge
Hialeah, FL 33016-5726, USA

Ochoa, Ellen (Astronaut)
150 S Villa Pl
Boise, ID 83712-8361, USA

Ochoa, Ellen Dr (Astronaut)
150 S Villa Pl
Boise, ID 83712-8361, USA

Ochoa, Lorena (Golfer)
c/o Staff Member *Ladies Pro Golf Association (LPGA)*
100 International Golf Dr
Daytona Beach, FL 32124-1092, USA

Ochoa, Raymond (Actor)
c/o Robin Spitzer *Origin Talent Agency*
4705 Laurel Canyon Blvd Ste 306
Studio City, CA 91607-5940, USA

Ochoa, Ryan (Actor)
c/o Staff Member *Innovative Artists*
1505 10th St
Santa Monica, CA 90401-2805, USA

Ochocinco, Chad (Athlete, Football Player)
c/o Drew Rosenhaus *Rosenhaus Sports Representation*
3921 Alton Rd # 440
Miami Beach, FL 33140-3852, USA

Ochowicz, Elli (Athlete, Olympic Athlete, Speed Skater)
5895 Dakota Trl
Park City, UT 84098-6396, USA

Ochowicz, James (Athlete, Cycler, Olympic Athlete)
5895 Dakota Trl
Park City, UT 84098-6396, USA

Ochowicz, Sheila Young (Athlete, Olympic Athlete, Speed Skater)
5895 Dakota Trl
Park City, UT 84098-6396, USA

Ochse, Alyshia (Actor)
c/o Yoni Ovadia *Generate Management*
8750 Wilshire Blvd Ste 200
Beverly Hills, CA 90211-2707, USA

Ockels, Wubbo (Astronaut)
ESTEC
Postbus 299
Noordwijk, AG 02200, NETHERLANDS

Ockels, Wubbo J Dr (Astronaut)
ESTEC Postbus 299
Code ADM-RE
Noordwijk, NL-2200 Netherlands, USA

O'Connell, Aaron (Actor, Model)
c/o Staff Member *Gilbertson Management*
1334 3rd Street Promenade Ste 201
Santa Monica, CA 90401-1320, USA

O'Connell, Charlie (Actor)
c/o Staff Member *Artistry Management*
340 N Camden Dr Ste 302
Beverly Hills, CA 90210-5116, USA

O'Connell, Jack (Actor)
c/o Lisa Kasteler *Wolf-Kasteler Public Relations*
6255 W Sunset Blvd Ste 1111
Los Angeles, CA 90028-7426, USA

O'Connell, Jerry (Actor)
23062 Mulholland Hwy
Calabasas, CA 91302-2050, USA

O'Connell, Maura (Musician)
Maura O'Connell Mgmt
4222 Lindawood Dr
Nashville, TN 37215-3208, USA

O'Connell, Mike (Athlete, Hockey Player)
17 Border St
Cohasset, MA 02025-2020, USA

O'Connell, William (Actor)
5835 Mineral Spring Rd
Suffolk, VA 23438-9462, USA

O'Connolly, James (Astronaut)
1305 Lafayette Dr
Alexandria, VA 22308-1107, USA

O'Connolly, James (Director)
61 Edith Grove
London SW10, UNITED KINGDOM (UK)

O'Connor, Bill (Athlete, Football Player)
1905-40 Richview Rd
Toronto, ON M9A 5C1, Canada

O'Connor, Brian (Athlete, Baseball Player)
3054 Inwood Dr
Cincinnati, OH 45241-3101, USA

O'Connor, Bryan D Colonel (Astronaut)
1305 Lafayette Dr
Alexandria, VA 22308-1107, USA

O'Connor, Derrick (Actor)
c/o Staff Member *Markham & Froggatt*
4 Windmill St
London W1T 1HZ, UNITED KINGDOM

O'Connor, Frances (Actor)
c/o Staff Member *Creative Artists Agency (CAA)*
2000 Avenue of the Stars Ste 100
Los Angeles, CA 90067-4705, USA

O'Connor, Gavin (Director)
c/o Simon Halls *Slate PR*
901 N Highland Ave
W Hollywood, CA 90038-2412, USA

O'Connor, Glynnis (Actor)
c/o Staff Member *Bauman Redanty & Shaul Agency*
5757 Wilshire Blvd
Suite 473
Beverly Hills, CA 90212, USA

O'Connor, Jack (Athlete, Baseball Player)
PO Box 430
Yucca Valley, CA 92286-0430, USA

O'Connor, Josh (Actor)
c/o Clair Dobbs *CLD Communications*
4 Broadway Ct
The Broadway
London SW191RG, UNITED KINGDOM

O'Connor, Mark (Musician)
CM Mgmt
5749 Lanyan Dr
Woodland Hills, CA 91367, USA

O'Connor, Martin J (Religious Leader)
Palazzo San Carlo
Vatican City 00120, VATICAN CITY

O'Connor, Mary (Athlete, Basketball Player, Olympic Athlete)
60 Romanock Pl
Fairfield, CT 06825-7240, USA

O'Connor, Maryanne (Basketball Player)
60 Romanock Pl
Fairfield, CT 06825-7240, USA

O'Connor, Michael (Athlete, Baseball Player)
c/o Staff Member *Washington Nationals*
1500 S Capitol St SE
Washington, DC 20003-3599, USA

O'Connor, Myles (Athlete, Hockey Player)
O'Connors Fine Footwear
1415 1 St SW
Calgary, AB T2R 0V9, Canada

O'Connor, Patrick (Actor)
c/o Staff Member *Select Artists Ltd (CA-Westside Office)*
1138 12th St Apt 1
Santa Monica, CA 90403-5459, USA

O'Connor, Patrick D (Pat) (Director)
International Creative Mgmt
76 Oxford St
London W1N 0AX, UNITED KINGDOM (UK)

O'Connor, Renee (Actor)
c/o Staff Member *Grant Management*
1158 26th St # 414
Santa Monica, CA 90403-4698, USA

O'Connor, Sandra Day (Attorney)
United States Supreme Court
11th St NE
PO Box 8795
Washington, DC 20543-0001, USA

O'Connor, Sinead (Musician, Songwriter)
c/o Staff Member *Purple PR*
27-29 Glasshouse St
London W1B 5DF, UK

O'Connor, Thom (Artist)
Moss Road
Voorheesville, NY 12186, USA

O'Connor, Zeke (Athlete, Football Player)
Sir Edmund Hillary Foundation
222 Jarvis St
Toronto, ON M7A 0B6, Canada

O'Conor, John (Musician)
Columbia Artists Mgmt Inc
165 W 57th St
New York, NY 10019-2201, USA

O'Day, Aubrey (Musician)
c/o Steven Grossman *Untitled Entertainment*
350 S Beverly Dr Ste 200
Beverly Hills, CA 90212-4819, USA

O'Day, Darren (Athlete, Baseball Player)
4395 Oakdale Vinii¥KS Cir SE
Smyrna, GA 30080-6982, USA

ODB (Musician)
Famous Artists Agency
250 W 57th St
New York, NY 10107-0001, USA

Oddlelfson, Chris (Athlete, Hockey Player)
PO Box 604
Brackendale, BC V0N 1H0, Canada

Oddsson, David (Prime Minister)
Prime Minister's Office
Stjo'maaroshusio
Reykjavik 00150, ICELAND

O'Dea, Judith (Actor)
PO Box 3566
Flagstaff, AZ 86003-3566, USA

Odegard, Vickie (Golfer)
112 Ashford Dr
Bridgeport, WV 26330-1138, USA

Odelein, Lyle (Athlete, Hockey Player)
1020 Cherrywood Trl
Coppell, TX 75019-6372, USA

Odelein, Selmar (Athlete, Hockey Player)
Farm
Quill Lake, SK SOA 3WO, Canada

Odeleln, Lyle (Athlete, Hockey Player)
12569 Winding Hollow Ln
Frisco, TX 75033-3497

O'Dell, Billy (Athlete, Baseball Player)
225 Odell Rd
Newberry, SC 29108-9250, USA

Odell, Bob H (Athlete, Coach, Football Coach, Football Player)
911 Stenton Pl
Ocean City, NJ 08226-4343, USA

Odell, Deborah (Actor)
c/o Staff Member *Characters Talent Agency*
200-1505 2nd Ave W
Vancouver, BC V6H 3Y4, CANADA

O'Dell, Jennifer (Actor)
c/o Scott Hart *Scott Hart Entertainment*
14622 Ventura Blvd # 746
Sherman Oaks, CA 91403-3600, USA

O'Dell, Nancy (Television Host)
c/o Thomas Repicci *Octagon Entertainment*
1840 Century Park E Ste 200
Los Angeles, CA 90067-2114, USA

O'Dell, Stewart (Athlete, Football Player)
3532 State Road 144
Mooresville, IN 46158, USA

O'Dell, Tawni (Writer)
Viking Press
375 Hudson St
New York, NY 10014-3658, USA

Odell, Tom (Musician)
c/o Marty Diamond *Paradigm*
140 Broadway Ste 2600
New York, NY 10005-1011, USA

Oden, Beverly (Athlete, Olympic Athlete, Volleyball Player)
4631 Lockhaven Cir
Irvine, CA 92604-2336, USA

Oden, Derrick (Athlete, Football Player)
1805 S Barkley Dr
Mobile, AL 36606-1151, USA

Oden, Songul (Actor)
c/o Gaye Sokmen *Gaye Sökmen Talent Agency*
Karanfil Caddesi Yolal Sokak Ic
Levent No:3
Istanbul 34330, Turkey

Odenkirk, Bob (Actor)
c/o Staff Member *Bob Industries*
1313 5th St
Santa Monica, CA 90401-1414, USA

Odessa, Devon (Actor)
c/o Staff Member *McCabe Group*
3211 Cahuenga Blvd W Ste 104
Los Angeles, CA 90068-1372, USA

Odgers, Jeff (Athlete, Hockey Player)
The Farm
Spy Hill, SK 50A 3WO, Canada

Odjig, Daphne (Artist)
102 Foresbrook Place
Penticton, BC V2A 7N4, CANADA

Odjlck, Gino (Athlete, Hockey Player)
Musquem Golf Academy
3904 51st Ave W
Vancouver, BC V6N 3W1, Canada

Odom, Cliff (Athlete, Football Player)
6708 Marthas Vineyard Dr
Arlington, TX 76001-5508, USA

Odom, Jason (Athlete, Football Player)
11506 Joshuas Bend Dr
Tampa, FL 33612-5071, USA

Odom, John Lee (Blue Moon) (Athlete, Baseball Player)
853 S Verde St
Anaheim, CA 92805-5443, USA

Odom, Lamar (Athlete, Basketball Player)
c/o Dollie Lucero *Boulevard Management*
21731 Ventura Blvd Ste 300
Woodland Hills, CA 91364-1851, USA

Odom, Steve (Athlete, Football Player)
971 Marina Way S Ste B
Richmond, CA 94804-3749, USA

Odomes, Nathaniel B (Nate) (Athlete, Football Player)
900 Quail Creek Dr
Columbus, GA 31907-6536, USA

Odom Jr, Leslie (Actor, Musician)
c/o Carleen Donovan *Donovan Public Relations*
30 E 20th St Ste 2FE
New York, NY 10003-1310, USA

Odoms, Riley M (Athlete, Football Player)
834 1/2 Staffordshire Rd
Stafford, TX 77477, USA

O'Donahue, Pat (Athlete, Football Player)
1524 Wheeler Rd Unit D
Madison, WI 53704-7048, USA

O'Donis, Colby (Musician)
c/o Juliette Harris *It Girl Public Relations*
3763 Eddingham Ave
Calabasas, CA 91302-5835, USA

O'Donnell, Andrew (Athlete, Basketball Player)
3310 Lincoln Ave
Allentown, PA 18103-7917, USA

O'Donnell, Annie (Actor)
Capital Artists
6404 Wilshire Blvd Ste 950
Los Angeles, CA 90048-5529, USA

O'Donnell, Chris (Actor)
c/o Jason Weinberg *Untitled Entertainment*
350 S Beverly Dr Ste 200
Beverly Hills, CA 90212-4819, USA

O'Donnell, Daniel (Musician)
Daniel O'Donnell Visitor Centre
Main Street
County Donegal, Ireland

O'Donnell, Fred (Athlete, Hockey Player)
690 Carnaby St
Kingston, ON K7M 5M7, CANADA

O'Donnell, George (Athlete, Baseball Player)
70 Crusaders Rd
Springfield, IL 62704-5207, USA

O'Donnell, Jake (Athlete, Basketball Player)
8682 SE Soundings Pl
Hobe Sound, FL 33455-4231, USA

O'Donnell, James Michael (Baseball Player)
204 N Diamond St
Clifton Heights, PA 19018-1507, USA

O'Donnell, Joe (Athlete, Football Player)
447 Bodley Cres
Milan, MI 48160-1206, USA

O'Donnell, John J (Misc)
Air Line Pilots Assn
1625 Massachusetts Ave NW Ste 800
Washington, DC 20036-2204, USA

O'Donnell, Keir (Actor)
c/o Tom Parziale *Visionary Management*
1558 N Stanley Ave
Los Angeles, CA 90046-2711, USA

O'Donnell, Lawrence (Television Host)
c/o Ari Emanuel *WME/IMG*
9601 Wilshire Blvd
Beverly Hills, CA 90210-5213, USA

O'Donnell, Neil K (Athlete, Football Player)
PO Box 403
New Vernon, NJ 07976-0403, USA

O'Donnell, Pat (Athlete, Football Player)
c/o Drew Rosenhaus *Rosenhaus Sports Representation*
3921 Alton Rd # 440
Miami Beach, FL 33140-3852, USA

O'Donnell, Rosie (Actor, Comedian, Talk Show Host)
c/o Cindi Berger *PMK/BNC Public Relations*
622 3rd Ave Fl 8
New York, NY 10017-6707, USA

O'Donnell, William (Bill) (Horse Racer)
569 Penn Estate
East Stroudsburg, PA 18301, USA

O'Donoghue, Colin (Actor)
c/o Allan Grifka *Alchemy Entertainment*
7024 Melrose Ave Ste 420
Los Angeles, CA 90038-3394, USA

O'Donoghue, Don (Athlete, Hockey Player)

O'Donoghue, John (Athlete, Baseball Player)
5246 Far Oak Cir
Sarasota, FL 34238-3304, USA

O'Donoghue, John (Athlete, Baseball Player)
10107 Summerfield Dr
Denham Springs, LA 70726-1583, USA

O'Donoghue, Neil (Athlete, Football Player)
1118 Flushing Ave
Clearwater, FL 33764-4906, USA

O'Donohue, Jessica (Actor)
c/o Dan Cotoia *Letnom Management*
1776 Broadway Fl 9
New York, NY 10019-2002, USA

O'Dowd, Anna Mae (Athlete, Baseball Player)
1179 Pelzer Ave
The Villages, FL 32162-8691, USA

O'Dowd, Chris (Actor)
c/o Nick Frenkel *3 Arts Entertainment*
9460 Wilshire Blvd Fl 7
Beverly Hills, CA 90212-2713, USA

Odrick, Jared (Athlete, Football Player)
c/o Eugene Parker *Independent Sports & Entertainment (ISE-IN)*
6435 W Jefferson Blvd # 197
Fort Wayne, IN 46804-6203, USA

O'Driscoll, Martha (Actor)
22 Indian Creek Island Rd
Indian Creek Village, FL 33154-2904, USA

Odrowski, Gerry (Athlete, Hockey Player)
PO Box 126
Trout Creek, ON P0I I 2L0, Canada

Oduber, Nelson O (Prime Minister)
Movimienti Electoral di Pueblo
Curnana 84
Oranjestad, ARUBA

Oduya, Johnny (Athlete, Hockey Player)
Newport Sports Management
400-201 City Centre Dr
Attn Don Meehan
Mississauga, ON L5B 2T4, Canada

Oduye, Adepero (Actor)
c/o Katherine Atkinson *Washington Square Films*
310 Bowery Fl 2
New York, NY 10012-2861, USA

Oedekerk, Steve (Actor, Director, Producer)
O Entertainment
31878 Camino Capistrano Ste 101
San Juan Capistrano, CA 92675-3221, USA

Oëë, Tommy (Director)
c/o Staff Member *WME/IMG*
9601 Wilshire Blvd
Beverly Hills, CA 90210-5213, USA

Oefelein, William A (Astronaut)
1205 Hawkhill Dr
Friendswood, TX 77546-7811, USA

Oefelein, William A Cdr (Astronaut)
Adventure Write
PO Box 113074
Anchorage, AK 99511-3074, USA

Oelkers, Bryan (Athlete, Baseball Player)
3404 Taylor Ave
Bridgeton, MO 63044-3055, USA

Oerlemans, Reinout (Actor)
c/o Staff Member *3 Ball Entertainment*
3650 Redondo Beach Ave
Redondo Beach, CA 90278-1107, USA

Oester, Ron (Athlete, Baseball Player)
3776 9 Mile Tobasco Rd
Cincinnati, OH 45255-5232, USA

O'Farrill, Orlando (Baseball Player)
Philadelphia Stars
Villa Rafaela Herrera Casa A-30
Managua, NICARAGUA

Offerdahl, John A (Athlete, Football Player)
2749 NE 37th Dr
Fort Lauderdale, FL 33308-6326, USA

Offerman, Jose (Athlete, Baseball Player)
10720 Moorpark St
North Hollywood, CA 91602-2723, USA

Offerman, Nick (Actor)
c/o Heidi Lopata *Narrative*
1601 Vine St Fl 6
Los Angeles, CA 90028-8802, USA

Office, Rowland (Athlete, Baseball Player)
1028 Lake Glen Way
Sacramento, CA 95822-3224, USA

Offishall, Kardinal (Musician)
c/o Staff Member *MCA Records (LA)*
2220 Colorado Ave
Santa Monica, CA 90404-3506, USA

Offspring, The (Music Group)
c/o Jim Guerinot *Rebel Waltz Inc*
PO Box 9215
Laguna Beach, CA 92652-7212, USA

of Kent, Prince Michael (Royalty)

of Kent, Prince Michael (Royalty)
Kensington Palace
London W8 5AF, UK

of Kent, Princess Michael (Designer, Royalty, Writer)
Kensington Palace
London W8 5AF, UK

O'Flaherty, Eric (Athlete, Baseball Player)
1100 106th Ave NE Apt 507
Bellevue, WA 98004-4387, USA

O'Flaherty, Gerry (Athlete, Hockey Player)
5446 Cortez Cres
North Vancouver, BC V7R 4R4, Canada

Of Mice and Men (Music Group)
c/o Eric Rushing *The Artery Foundation*
PO Box 160451
Sacramento, CA 95816-0451, USA

Of Monaco, Prince Albert II (Politician)
Palouis De Monaco
Boite Postal 518
Monte Carlo 98015, Monaco

Of Monaco, Princess Stephanie (Royalty)
Palais Grimaldi
2 Boulevard De Moulins
Monte Carlo 98015, Monaco

of Wales, Prince Charles (Royalty)
St. James' Palace
London SW1, UK

of Wessex, HRH Prince Edward (Royalty)
Bagshot Park
Bagshot
Surrey GU19 5PN, UK

Ogbuehi, Cedric (Athlete, Football Player)
c/o Ryan Williams *Athletes First*
23091 Mill Creek Dr
Laguna Hills, CA 92653-1258, USA

Ogden, Bud (Athlete, Basketball Player)
3324 S 4th St
Springfield, IL 62703-4619, USA

Ogden, Joanne (Baseball Player)
200 1/2 W Cypress St
Glendale, CA 91204-2660, USA

Ogden, Jonathan (Athlete, Football Player)
14 Corral De Tierra Pl
Henderson, NV 89052-6705, USA

Ogden, Margaret (Writer)
7102 Harts Lake Rd S
Roy, WA 98580-9241, USA

Ogden, Ray (Athlete, Football Player)
188 Anderson Dr
Brunswick, GA 31520-1610, USA

Ogea, Chad (Athlete, Baseball Player)
3233 Plantation Ct
Baton Rouge, LA 70820-5753, USA

Ogg, Steven (Actor)
c/o Warren Binder *MGMT Entertainment (The Schiff Company)*
9220 W Sunset Blvd Ste 106
W Hollywood, CA 90069-3500, USA

Ogi, Adolf (President)
Bundesiause-Nord
Kochergasse 10
Berne 03003, SWITZERLAND

Ogier, Bulle (Actor)
Artmedia
20 Ave Rapp
Paris 75007, FRANCE

Ogilvie, Brian (Athlete, Hockey Player)
3 MacEwan Meadow Rise NW
Calgary, AB T3K 3K1, Canada

Ogilvie, Lana (Model)

Ogilvy, Geoff (Golfer)
c/o Staff Member *Pro Golfers Association (PGA)*
112 TPC Blvd
Ponte Vedra Beach, FL 32082, USA

Ogilvy, Ian (Actor)
Julian Belfarge
46 Albermarle St
London W1X 4PP, UNITED KINGDOM (UK)

Ogilvy, Ian (Athlete, Hockey Player)
14 New Burlington St.
London W1S 3B, UK

Ogle, Brett (Golfer)
Advantage International
1751 Pinnacle Dr Ste 1500
Mc Lean, VA 22102-3833, USA

Oglesby, Randy (Actor)

Oglive, Benjamin A (Ben) (Athlete, Baseball Player)
1012 E Sandpiper Dr
Tempe, AZ 85283-2021, USA

Oglivie, Ben (Athlete, Baseball Player)
1012 E Sandpiper Dr
Tempe, AZ 85283-2021, USA

O'Grady, Brittany (Actor, Musician)
c/o Ruth Bernstein *Viewpoint Inc*
8820 Wilshire Blvd Ste 220
Beverly Hills, CA 90211-2622, USA

O'Grady, Gail (Actor)
c/o Alan Iezman *Shelter Entertainment*
9255 W Sunset Blvd Ste 300
Los Angeles, CA 90069-3313, USA

O'Grady, Paul (Comedian)
c/o Robin Morgan *Useful TV*
19-21 Crawford St
London W1H 2JG, UNITED KINGDOM

O'Grady, Sean (Boxer)
Adoreable Promotions
PO Box 9
Bay City, MI 48707-0009, USA

Ogrin, David (Athlete, Golfer)
1074 Running Riv
New Braunfels, TX 78130-2429, USA

Ogrodnick, John (Athlete, Hockey Player)
37034 Aldgate Ct
Farmington Hills, MI 48335-5402, USA

Ogunleye, Adewale (Athlete, Football Player)
19113 NW 23rd Ct
Pembroke Pines, FL 33029-5336, USA

Oh, Sadaharu (Baseball Player)
Fukuoka Dorne Daiei Hawks
6F 2-2-2 Jigyohama
Chuo-Ku Fukouka 00810, JAPAN

Oh, Sandra (Actor)
c/o Marsha McManus *Principal Entertainment*
9255 W Sunset Blvd Ste 500
Los Angeles, CA 90069-3301, USA

Oh, Soon-Tek (Actor)
8002 Hollywood Way
Sun Valley, CA 91352-4225, USA

O'Hair, Sean (Athlete, Golfer)
c/o Staff Member *Pro Golfers Association (PGA)*
112 TPC Blvd
Ponte Vedra Beach, FL 32082, USA

O'Halloran, Greg (Athlete, Baseball Player)
1021 Hedge Dr
Mississauga, ON L4Y 1G3, Canada

O'Hanlon, Bill (Writer)
c/o Staff Member *Loretta Barrett Books, Inc.*
101 5th Ave Fl 11
New York, NY 10003-1008, USA

O'Hanlon, Francis (Athlete, Basketball Player)
27 W Wayne Ave
Easton, PA 18042-1662, USA

O'Hara, Catherine (Actor)
575 Hanley Ave
Los Angeles, CA 90049-1922, USA

O'Hara, David (Actor)
c/o Tammy Rosen *Sanders Armstrong Caserta*
4111 W Alameda Ave Ste 505
Burbank, CA 91505-4163, USA

O'Hara, Jenny (Actor)
8663 Wonderland Ave
Los Angeles, CA 90046-1452, USA

O'Hara, Kelli (Actor)
c/o Jennifer Plante *Slate PR (NY)*
307 7th Ave Rm 2401
New York, NY 10001-6019, USA

O'Hara, Paige (Actor)
c/o Staff Member *Douglas Gorman Rothacker & Wilhelm Inc*
33 W 46th St Ste 801
New York, NY 10036-4103, USA

O'Hara, Shaun (Athlete, Football Player)
c/o Anthony J. Agnone *Eastern Athletic Services*
11350 McCormick Rd
Suite 800 - Executive Plaza
Hunt Valley, MD 21031-1002, USA

O'Hara, Terrence J (Director)
Armstrong/Hirsch
1888 Century Park E Ste 1800
Los Angeles, CA 90067-1722, USA

O'Hare, Denis (Actor)
c/o Gary Gersh *Innovative Artists*
235 Park Ave S Fl 7
New York, NY 10003-1405, USA

O'Heir, Jim (Actor, Comedian)
c/o Lynda Bensky *Bensky Entertainment*
15021 Ventura Blvd # 343
Sherman Oaks, CA 91403-2442, USA

Oher, Michael (Athlete, Football Player)
c/o Raphael Berko *Media Artists Group*
8222 Melrose Ave Ste 304
Los Angeles, CA 90046-6839, USA

Ohl, Don (Athlete, Basketball Player)
2 E Lockhaven Ct
Edwardsville, IL 62025-3703, USA

Ohlendorf, Ross (Athlete, Baseball Player)
2300 Barton Creek Blvd Apt 40
Austin, TX 78735-1687, USA

Ohlsson, Garrick (Musician)
International Creative Mgmt
8942 Wilshire Blvd # 219
Beverly Hills, CA 90211-1908, USA

Ohlund, Mattias (Athlete, Hockey Player)
C A A Hockey
204-822 11 Ave SW
Attn J P Barry
Calgary, AB T2R 0E5, Canada

Ohman, Will (Athlete, Baseball Player)
4346 N Desert Oasis Cir
Mesa, AZ 85207-7246, USA

Ohme, Kevin (Athlete, Baseball Player)
1005 Whitehurst Rd LOT 84
Plant City, FL 33563-2870, USA

Ohno, Apolo (Athlete, Olympic Athlete, Speed Skater)
2201 Century Hl
Los Angeles, CA 90067-3536, USA

Ohoven, Ute-Henriette (Misc)
c/o Staff Member *United Nations Educational, Scientific and Cultural Organization (UNESCO)*
7, place de Fontenoy
75352
Paris 07 SP, France

Ohrnberger, Rich (Athlete, Football Player)
c/o Eric Metz *Lock Metz Milanovic LLC*
6900 E Camelback Rd Ste 600
Scottsdale, AZ 85251-8044, USA

Ohtani, Shohei (Athlete, Baseball Player)
c/o Nez Balelo *CAA Sports*
2000 Avenue of the Stars Ste 100
Los Angeles, CA 90067-4705, USA

O'Hurley, John (Actor)
1710 Monte Cielo Ct
Beverly Hills, CA 90210-2422, USA

Oimeon, Casper (Skier)
540 S Mountain Ave
Ashland, OR 97520-3242, USA

Oistrakh, Igor D (Musician)
Novolesnaya Str 3
Korp 2 #10
Moscow, RUSSIA

Oiter, Bailey (President)
President's Office
Palikia
Pohnepei FM
Kolonia 96941, MICRONESIA

Oja, Kim (Actor)
c/o Staff Member *The Gage Group*
5757 Wilshire Blvd Ste 659
Los Angeles, CA 90036-3682, USA

Ojala, Kirt (Athlete, Baseball Player)
1902 Forest Lake Dr SE
Grand Rapids, MI 49546-8234, USA

O'Jays, The (Music Group, Musician)

Ojeda, Augie (Athlete, Baseball Player)
5351 W Morgan Pl
Chandler, AZ 85226-8613, USA

Ojeda, Augle (Athlete, Baseball Player)
9402 Dorothy Ave
South Gate, CA 90280-5106, USA

Ojeda, Bob (Athlete, Baseball Player)
20 Somerset Dr
Rumson, NJ 07760-1101, USA

Ojeda, Miguel (Baseball Player)
c/o Staff Member *San Diego Padres*
100 Park Blvd
San Diego, CA 92101-7405, USA

Ojinnaka, Quinn (Athlete, Football Player)
c/o Brian E. Overstreet *E.O. Sports Management*
1314 Texas St Ste 1212
Houston, TX 77002-3525, USA

Oka, Masi (Actor, Writer)
c/o Matt Luber *Luber Roklin Management*
5815 W Sunset Blvd Ste 208
Los Angeles, CA 90028-6481, USA

Okafor, Alex (Athlete, Football Player)
c/o Andrew Kessler *Athletes First*
23091 Mill Creek Dr
Laguna Hills, CA 92653-1258, USA

Okafor, Emeka (Athlete, Basketball Player)
c/o Jeff Schwartz *Excel Sports Management*
1700 Broadway Fl 29
New York, NY 10019-6559, USA

Okafor, Jahlil (Athlete, Basketball Player)
c/o Bill Duffy *BDA Sports Management*
700 Ygnacio Valley Rd Ste 330
Walnut Creek, CA 94596-3838, USA

Okajima, Hideki (Athlete, Baseball Player)
4 Liberty St
Framingham, MA 01702-8435, USA

Okamoto, Ayako (Golfer)
22627 Ladeene Ave
Torrance, CA 90505-3438, USA

Okamura, Arthur (Artist)
210 Kale Rd
Bolinas, CA 94924, USA

Okano, Lyrica (Actor)
c/o Kelli M Jones *Status PR (NY)*
59 Chelsea Piers
Level 3
New York, NY 10011-1008, USA

Okazake, Kenji (Race Car Driver)
840 Kallin Ave
Long Beach, CA 90815-5004, USA

O'Keefe, Jodie Lyn (Actor)
c/o Pamela Sharp *Sharp & Associates*
1516 N Fairfax Ave
Los Angeles, CA 90046-2608, USA

O'Keefe, Michael (Actor)
c/o Staff Member *Paradigm*
8942 Wilshire Blvd
Beverly Hills, CA 90211-1908, USA

O'Keefe, Miles (Actor)
c/o Alexandra Karrys *Divine Management*
117 N Orlando Ave
Los Angeles, CA 90048-3403, USA

O'Keefe, Richard (Athlete, Basketball Player)
31 Corte Ortega Apt 7
Greenbrae, CA 94904-1992, USA

O'Keefe, Stuart (Chef)
c/o Jason Pinyan *Innovative Artists*
1505 10th St
Santa Monica, CA 90401-2805, USA

O'Keefe, Tommy (Athlete, Basketball Player)
1000 Potomac Ln
Alexandria, VA 22308-2638, USA

O'Keeffe, Miles (Actor)
c/o Staff Member *Momentum Talent and Literary Agency*
3500 W Olive Ave Ste 300
Burbank, CA 91505-4647, USA

O'Kelley, Tricia (Actor)
c/o Staff Member *T&A Pictures*
15233 Ventura Blvd Fl 9
Sherman Oaks, CA 91403-2250, USA

Okeniyi, Dayo (Actor)
c/o Jamie Harhay Skinner *Baker Winokur Ryder Public Relations*
9100 Wilshire Blvd
W Tower #500
Beverly Hills, CA 90212-3415, USA

Okerlund, Todd (Athlete, Hockey Player, Olympic Athlete)
2950 Dean Pkwy Apt 1104
Minneapolis, MN 55416-4321, USA

Okobi, Chukky (Athlete, Football Player)
22506 W 76th Ter
Shawnee, KS 66227-2138, USA

Okogie, Anthony Olubunmi Cardinal (Religious Leader)
Archdiocese
PO Box 8
19 Catholic Mission St
Lagos, NIGERIA

Okogwu Jr, Patrick (Tinie Tempah) (Musician)
c/o Staff Member *Parlophone Records*
EMI House
43 Brook Green
London W6 7EF, United Kingdom

Okolowicz, Jeff (Musician)
Living Eye Productions
PO Box 12956
Rochester, NY 14612-0956, USA

Okolowicz, Ted (Musician)
Living Eye Productions
PO Box 12956
Rochester, NY 14612-0956, USA

Okonedo, Sophie (Actor)
c/o Luke Windsor *Prosper PR (UK)*
Prefers to be contacted by email.
NA NA, UNITED KINGDOM

Okoniewski, Steve (Athlete, Football Player)
2691 Hillside Heights Dr
Green Bay, WI 54311-6774, USA

Okonkwo, Chike (Actor)
c/o Lou Coulson *Lou Coulson Agency*
37 Berwick St
1st Floor
London W1F 8RS, UNITED KINGDOM (UK)

Okonma, Tyler (The Creator) (Musician)
Diystro, Llc
165 S La Brea Ave
Los Angeles, CA 90036-2909, USA

O'Koren, Mike (Athlete, Basketball Player)
109 Quaker Rd
Mickleton, NJ 08056-1304, USA

Okorn, Mitja (Actor)
c/o Donata Rojewska *High Spot Talent Agency*
Rozbrat 44A
Warsaw 00-419, POLAND

Okoye, Amobi (Athlete, Football Player)
4230 Leaflock Ln
Katy, TX 77450-8249, USA

Okoye, Christian E (Athlete, Football Player)
10082 Big Pine Dr
Alta Loma, CA 91737-4247, USA

Okposo, Kyle (Athlete, Hockey Player)
4442 Derrymoor Ct
Rosemount, MN 55068-4387

Okrent, Daniel (Sportscaster)
645 W End Ave Apt 12F
New York, NY 10025-7354, USA

Okrie, Len (Athlete, Baseball Player)
2636 Burke Ln
Fayetteville, NC 28306-2629, USA

Okuda, Amy (Actor)
c/o Joshua Pasch *Authentic Talent & Literary Management*
3615 Eastham Dr # 650
Culver City, CA 90232-2410, USA

Okuda, Hiroshi (Business Person)
Toyota Motor Corp
1 Toyotacho
Toyota City
Aichi Prefecture 00471, JAPAN

Okumura, Tomohiro (Musician)
Jecklin Assoc
2717 Nichols Ln
Davenport, IA 52803-3620, USA

Okung, Russell (Athlete, Football Player)
c/o Lamont Smith *All Pro Sports and Entertainment*
50 S Steele St Ste 480
Denver, CO 80209-2836, USA

Okungbowa, Tony (DJ)
1863 Preston Ave
Los Angeles, CA 90026-1825, USA

Okur, Mehmet (Athlete, Basketball Player)
1387 E Perrys Hollow Rd
Salt Lake City, UT 84103-4263, USA

O'Lachlan, Alex (Actor)
c/o Staff Member *June Cann Management*
73 Jersey Rd
Woollahra 02025, AUSTRALIA

Oladipo, Victor (Athlete, Basketball Player)
9221 Bayway Dr
Orlando, FL 32819-4087, USA

Olajuwon, Hakeem (Athlete, Basketball Player, Olympic Athlete)
1305 N Horseshoe Dr
Sugar Land, TX 77478-3428, USA

Olander, Jim (Athlete, Baseball Player)
10769 S Grey Mist Ct
Vail, AZ 85641-6452, USA

Olander, Jimmy (Musician)
3020 Jubilee Ridge Rd
Franklin, TN 37069-4777, USA

Olandt, Ken (Actor)
Gold Marshak Liedtke
3500 W Olive Ave Ste 1400
Burbank, CA 91505-5512, USA

Olay, Ruth (Musician)
PO Box 10311
Eugene, OR 97440-2311, USA

Olazabel, Jose Maria (Golfer)
Sergio Gomez
Apartado 26
San Sebastian E-20080, SPAIN

Olberding, Mark (Athlete, Basketball Player)
4131 Cliff Oaks St
San Antonio, TX 78229-3536, USA

Olberman, Bob (Athlete, Football Player)
4486 Dobbs Xing
Marietta, GA 30068-2714, USA

Olbermann, Keith (Sportscaster, Television Host)
c/o Joseph (Joe) Veltre *Gersh*
41 Madison Ave Ste 3301
New York, NY 10010-2210, USA

Olczyk, Eddie (Athlete, Hockey Player)
4581 Pamela Ct
Long Grove, IL 60047-5271

Old Crow Medicine Show (Music Group)
c/o Staff Member *Paradigm (Monterey)*
404 W Franklin St
Monterey, CA 93940-2303, USA

Old Dominion (Music Group)
c/o Clint Higham *Morris Artists Management*
2001 Blair Blvd
Nashville, TN 37212-5007, USA

Olde, Jeff (Director, Producer)
c/o Staff Member *VH1 Television*
1515 Broadway
New York, NY 10036-8901, USA

Oldenburg, Claes T (Artist)
556 Broome St
New York, NY 10013-1517, USA

Oldenburg, Richard E (Director)
447 E 57th St Apt 9A
New York, NY 10022-3172, USA

Olderman, Murray (Sportscaster)
72750 Country Club Dr Apt 122
Rancho Mirage, CA 92270-4085, USA

Oldershaw, Kelsey (Actor)
c/o Darren Goldberg *Global Creative*
1051 Cole Ave # B
Los Angeles, CA 90038-2601, USA

Oldfield, Bruce (Designer, Fashion Designer)
27 Beauchamp Place
London SW3, UNITED KINGDOM(UK)

Oldfield, Sally (Musician)
Global Artists Mgmt
Willy-Brandt-Str 39
Erftstadt 50374, GERMANY

Oldham, John (Athlete, Baseball Player)
1845 Anne Way
San Jose, CA 95124-6137, USA

Oldham, John (Athlete, Basketball Player)
915 Nutwood St
Bowling Green, KY 42103-4929, USA

Oldham, Tasha (Director)
c/o Jerry Shandrew *Shandrew Public Relations*
1050 S Stanley Ave
Los Angeles, CA 90019-6634, USA

Oldham, Todd (Designer, Fashion Designer)
c/o Staff Member *Creative Artists Agency (CAA)*
2000 Avenue of the Stars Ste 100
Los Angeles, CA 90067-4705, USA

Oldis, Bob (Athlete, Baseball Player)
5420 S Marigold Way
Gilbert, AZ 85298-8679, USA

Oldman, Gary (Actor, Director, Producer)
c/o Douglas Urbanski *Douglas Management Group*
PO Box 691763
West Hollywood, CA 90069-9763, USA

Olds, Bill (Athlete, Football Player)
7414 Pohick Rd
Lorton, VA 22079-1518, USA

Olds, Gabriel (Actor)
c/o Darryl Marshak *Marshak/Zachary Company, The*
8840 Wilshire Blvd Fl 1
Beverly Hills, CA 90211-2606, USA

Olds, Sharon (Writer)
New York University
58 W 10th St Ste 303
Attn: English Department
New York, NY 10011-8702, USA

Olds, Wally (Athlete, Hockey Player, Olympic Athlete)
7343 Colfax Ave S
Minneapolis, MN 55423-3022, USA

Oleander, Amanda (Internet Star)
c/o Staff Member *United Talent Agency (UTA)*
9336 Civic Center Dr
Beverly Hills, CA 90210-3604, USA

Oleary, Dan (Athlete, Football Player)
3300 W 159th St
Cleveland, OH 44111-1946, USA

O'Leary, George (Coach, Football Coach)
Central Florida University
Athletic Dept
Orlando, FL 32918, USA

O'Leary, John (Actor)
Gage Group
14724 Ventura Blvd Ste 505
Sherman Oaks, CA 91403-3505, USA

O'Leary, John (Athlete, Football Player)
4819 N 160th St
Omaha, NE 68116-8038, USA

O'Leary, Kevin (Business Person, Reality Star)
c/o Staff Member *United Talent Agency (UTA)*
9336 Civic Center Dr
Beverly Hills, CA 90210-3604, USA

O'Leary, Marrissa (Actor)
c/o Staff Member *Select Artists Ltd (CA-Valley Office)*
PO Box 4359
Burbank, CA 91503-4359, USA

O'Leary, Matthew (Actor)
c/o Brian Swardstrom *United Talent Agency (UTA)*
888 7th Ave Fl 7
New York, NY 10106-0700, USA

O'Leary, Michael (Actor)
123 Grove St Apt 10
Clifton, NJ 07013-1584, USA

O'Leary, Troy (Athlete, Baseball Player)
1060 W Norwood St
Rialto, CA 92377-8220, USA

O'Leary, William (Actor)
c/o Staff Member *Coast to Coast Talent Group*
3350 Barham Blvd
Los Angeles, CA 90068-1404, USA

Oleg, Deripaska (Business Person)
Basic Element Company
30 Rochdelskaya St
Moscow 123022, Russia

Olejnik, Craig (Actor)
c/o Robert Stein *Robert Stein Management*
PO Box 3797
Beverly Hills, CA 90212-0797, USA

Oleksy, Jozef (Prime Minister)
Ul Wiktorii Wiedenskiej 5 M 4
Warsaw 02-954, POLAND

Olerich, Dave (Athlete, Football Player)
2138 Wellesley St
Palo Alto, CA 94306-1335, USA

Olerud, John (Athlete, Baseball Player)
PO Box 606
Medina, WA 98039-0606, USA

Oleschuk, Bill (Athlete, Hockey Player)
132 Sanderling Rise NW
Calgary, AB T3K 3M7, Canada

Olesz, Rostislav (Athlete, Hockey Player)
201 N Westshore Dr Apt 2801
Chicago, IL 60601-7278

Olevsky, Julian (Musician)
68 Blue Hills Rd
Amherst, MA 01002-2220, USA

Oleynick, Frank (Athlete, Basketball Player)
1164 Brooklawn Ave
Bridgeport, CT 06604-1206, USA

Oleynik, Larisa (Actor)
216 San Juan Ave
Venice, CA 90291-3730, USA

Oliceira, Ana Cristina (Actor)
c/o Clifford Gilbert-Lurie *Ziffren Brittenham*
1801 Century Park W Fl 7
Los Angeles, CA 90067-6406, USA

Olin, Ken (Producer)
c/o David Stone *WME/IMG*
9601 Wilshire Blvd
Beverly Hills, CA 90210-5213, USA

Olin, Lena (Actor)
c/o Michael Lazo *Untitled Entertainment*
350 S Beverly Dr Ste 200
Beverly Hills, CA 90212-4819, USA

Olin, Lina (Actor)
c/o Staff Member *Industry Entertainment Partners*
955 Carrillo Dr Ste 300
Los Angeles, CA 90048-5400, USA

Olin, Roxy (Actor)
c/o Katie Mason Stern *Luber Roklin Management*
5815 W Sunset Blvd Ste 208
Los Angeles, CA 90028-6481, USA

Olinger, Marilyn (Baseball Player)
6451 Far Hills Ave
Dayton, OH 45459-2725, USA

Olinski, Harry (Athlete, Football Player)
3205 Furman Blvd
Louisville, KY 40220-1949, USA

Oliphant, Patrick B (Cartoonist)
Universal Press Syndicate
4520 Main St Ste 340
Kansas City, MO 64111-7705, USA

Oliphant, Randall (Business Person)
Barrick Gold Corp
200 Bay St
Toronto, ON M5J 2J3, CANADA

Olitski, Jules (Artist)
PO Box 440
Marlboro, VT 05344-0440, USA

Oliu, Ingrid (Actor)
c/o Staff Member *Cunningham Escott Slevin & Doherty (CESD)*
10635 Santa Monica Blvd Ste 130
Los Angeles, CA 90025-8306, USA

Oliva, Sergio (Misc)
Oliva's Gym
7383 Rogers Ave
Chicago, IL 60626, USA

Oliva, Tony (Athlete, Baseball Player)
1 Twins Way
Attn Alumni Association
Minneapolis, MN 55403-1418, USA

Olivares, Ed (Athlete, Baseball Player)
HC 2 Box 12887
San German, PR 00683, USA

Olivares, Omar (Athlete, Baseball Player)
PO Box 1328
San German, PR 00683-1328, USA

Olivares, Ruben (Boxer)
Geno Productions
PO Box 113
Montebello, CA 90640-0113, USA

Olivas, John D (Astronaut)
595 36th St
Manhattan Beach, CA 90266-3409, USA

Olivas, John D Dr (Astronaut)
595 36th St
Manhattan Beach, CA 90266-3409, USA

Olive, Jason (Actor, Model)
c/o Cory Richman *Liebman Entertainment*
29 W 46th St Fl 5
New York, NY 10036-4104, USA

Olive, John (Athlete, Basketball Player)
8652 Harjoan Ave
San Diego, CA 92123-3445, USA

Oliveira, Elmar (Musician)
Cramer/Marder Artists
3436 Springhill Rd
Lafayette, CA 94549-2535, USA

Oliver, Al (Athlete, Baseball Player)
PO Box 1466
Portsmouth, OH 45662-1466, USA

Oliver, Albert (Al) (Athlete, Baseball Player)
PO Box 1466
Portsmouth, OH 45662-1466, USA

Oliver, Bob (Athlete, Baseball Player)
1716 G St
Rio Linda, CA 95673-4534, USA

Oliver, Christian (Actor)
7211 Mulholland Dr
Los Angeles, CA 90068-2031, USA

Oliver, Clancy (Athlete, Football Player)
233 Springview
Irvine, CA 92620-1970, USA

Oliver, Darren (Athlete, Baseball Player)
1804 Larkspur Ct
Southlake, TX 76092-3572, USA

Oliver, Dave (Athlete, Baseball Player)
1709 Timberlake Cir
Lodi, CA 95242-4283, USA

Oliver, Dean (Race Car Driver)
21386 Notus Rd
Greenleaf, ID 83626-8940, USA

Oliver, Hubie (Athlete, Football Player)
136 Blake St
Elyria, OH 44035-5422, USA

Oliver, Jamie (Chef)
Jamie's Kitchen
15 The Brambles
Bishops Storford
Herts CM23 4PX, UNITED KINGDOM

Oliver, Joe (Athlete, Baseball Player)
4137 Bounce Dr
Orlando, FL 32812-8147, USA

Oliver, John (Comedian, Television Host)
c/o David Martin *Avalon Management*
9171 Wilshire Blvd Ste 320
Beverly Hills, CA 90210-5516, USA

Oliver, Kristine (Musician)
349 Stable Rd
Franklin, TN 37069-4527, USA

Oliver, Louis (Athlete, Football Player)
5082 SW 167th Ave
Miramar, FL 33027-4910, USA

Oliver, Nate (Athlete, Baseball Player)
4403 Oak Hill Rd
Oakland, CA 94605-4632, USA

Oliver, Pam (Sportscaster)
Fox-TV
205 E 67th St
Sports Dept
New York, NY 10065-6089, USA

Oliver, Ron (Director, Writer)
c/o Mark Itkin *WME/IMG*
9601 Wilshire Blvd Ste GF1
Beverly Hills, CA 90210-5231, USA

Oliver, Winslow (Athlete, Football Player)
2027 Summerall Ct
Richmond, TX 77406-6737, USA

Oliveras, Mako (Athlete, Baseball Player)
PO Box 8717
Bayamon, PR 00960-8717, USA

Oliveres, Rubin (Actor)
PO Box 113
Montebello, CA 90640-0113

Olivia (Musician)
c/o Staff Member *Interscope Records (LA) - Main*
2220 Colorado Ave
Santa Monica, CA 90404-3506, USA

Olivieri, Dawn (Actor)
c/o David (Dave) Fleming *Atlas Artists*
9220 W Sunset Blvd Ste 225
Los Angeles, CA 90069-3513, USA

Olivo, America (Actor)
PO Box 54228
Cincinnati, OH 45254-0228, USA

Olivo, Joey (Boxer)
9628 Poinciana St
Pico Rivera, CA 90660-4242, USA

Olivo, Karen (Actor)
c/o Brian Liebman *Liebman Entertainment*
29 W 46th St Fl 5
New York, NY 10036-4104, USA

Olivo, Miguel (Athlete, Baseball Player)
10004 Plaza De Oro Dr
Oakdale, CA 95361-9235, USA

Olivor, Jane (Music Group, Musician)
Ed Keane
32 Saint Edward Rd
Boston, MA 02128-1263, USA

Olkewicz, Neal (Athlete, Football Player)
17717 Crystal Spring Ter
Ashton, MD 20861-3605, USA

Olkewicz, Walter (Actor)
Gold Marshak Liedtke
3500 W Olive Ave Ste 1400
Burbank, CA 91505-5512, USA

Oller, Tony (Actor, Musician)
c/o Rebecca Many Rosenberg *Artists First*
9465 Wilshire Blvd Ste 900
Beverly Hills, CA 90212-2608, USA

Ollie, Kevin (Athlete, Basketball Player)
5106 Flanagan Dr
Glastonbury, CT 06033-3293, USA

Ollie, mack (Athlete, Basketball Player)
4023 N Grandview Dr
Peoria, IL 61614-6624, USA

Ollom, Jim (Athlete, Baseball Player)
10916 27th Ave SE
Everett, WA 98208-7807, USA

Olmedo, Alex (Tennis Player)
5067 Woodley Ave
Encino, CA 91436-1472, USA

Olmos, Edward James (Actor)
c/o Staff Member *Olmos Productions Inc*
500 S Buena Vista St
Old Animation Bldg 3A-6, Mail Code 1803
Burbank, CA 91521-0001, USA

Olmstead, Chris Von Saltza (Athlete, Olympic Athlete, Swimmer)
520 Crocker Rd
Sacramento, CA 95864-5608, USA

Olmstead, Matt (Producer)
c/o Staff Member *ICM Partners*
10250 Constellation Blvd Fl 7
Los Angeles, CA 90067-6207, USA

Olmsted, Al (Athlete, Baseball Player)
1008 Pinecone Trl
Florissant, MO 63031-7436, USA

Olmsted, Al (Athlete, Baseball Player)
1008 Pinecone Trl
Florissant, MO 63031-7436, USA

O'Loughlin, Alex (Actor, Producer, Writer)
c/o Sarah Linsten *Linsten Morris Management*
3 Gladstone St
Suite 301
Newtown, NSW 02042, AUSTRALIA

O'Loughlin, Gerald S (Actor)
23388 Mulholland Dr # 204
Woodland Hills, CA 91364-2733, USA

Olowaonkandi, Michael (Basketball Player)
c/o Staff Member *Los Angeles Clippers*
1111 S Figueroa St
Los Angeles, CA 90015-1300, USA

Olowokandi, Michael (Athlete, Basketball Player)
Minnesota Timberwolves
10061 SW 60th Ct
Miami, FL 33156-1980, USA

Olsavsky, Bill (Athlete, Football Player)
132 Walnut Ave
Saint Clairsville, OH 43950-1702, USA

Olsavsky, Jerry (Athlete, Football Player)
92 Lake Shore Dr
Youngstown, OH 44511-3552, USA

Olsen, Andrew (Baseball Player)
555 4th St N
St Petersburg, FL 33701, USA

Olsen, Ashley (Actor)
The Row
609 Greenwich St Fl 3
New York, NY 10014-3610, USA

Olsen, Bud (Athlete, Basketball Player)
1602 Gardiner Ln Apt 130
Louisville, KY 40205-2761, USA

Olsen, Darryl (Athlete, Hockey Player)
3517 S Helen Dr
Magna, UT 84044-2769

Olsen, Elizabeth (Actor)
c/o Marla Farrell *Shelter PR*
928 Broadway Ste 505
New York, NY 10010-8143, USA

Olsen, Eric Christian (Actor)
c/o Theresa Peters *United Talent Agency (UTA)*
9336 Civic Center Dr
Beverly Hills, CA 90210-3604, USA

Olsen, Greg (Athlete, Football Player)
c/o Drew Rosenhaus *Rosenhaus Sports Representation*
3921 Alton Rd # 440
Miami Beach, FL 33140-3852, USA

Olsen, Gregory (Astronaut, Business Person)
Sensors Unlimited
3490 US Highway 1 Ste 12
Princeton, NJ 08540-5920, USA

Olsen, Kevin (Athlete, Baseball Player)
3353 Dales Dr
Norco, CA 92860-2281, USA

Olsen, Mary-Kate (Actor, Designer)
The Row
609 Greenwich St Fl 3
New York, NY 10014-3610, USA

Olsen, Mike (Race Car Driver)
PO Box 427
Main St.
North Haverhill, NH 03774-0427, USA

Olsen, Phil (Athlete, Football Player)
112 Hitching Post Rd
Bozeman, MT 59715-8027, USA

Olsen, Scott (Athlete, Baseball Player)
2991 NE 185th St Apt 1701
Aventura, FL 33180-2904, USA

Olshansky, Igor (Athlete, Football Player)
PO Box 5000
Rancho Santa Fe, CA 92067-5000, USA

Olson, Allen (Politician)
631 Broken Arrow Rd
Chanhassen, MN 55317-9569, USA

Olson, Benji (Athlete, Football Player)
126 Gardengate Dr
Franklin, TN 37069-4024, USA

Olson, Bree (Actor, Adult Film Star, Model)
c/o Staff Member *Central Entertainment Group*
250 W 40th St Fl 12
New York, NY 10018-4601, USA

Olson, Candice (Designer)
Divine Design
2760 Mornington Dr NW
Atlanta, GA 30327-1216, USA

Olson, Dennis (Athlete, Hockey Player)
521 First Ave S
Kenora, ON P9N 1W6, Canada

Olson, Greg (Athlete, Baseball Player)
18592 Saint Mellion Pl
Eden Prairie, MN 55347-3487, USA

Olson, Gregg (Athlete, Baseball Player)
2728 Carrington Ct
Auburn, AL 36830-6480, USA

Olson, Harold (Athlete, Football Player)
511 Crested Hawk Rdg
Canton, GA 30114-5111, USA

Olson, Jake (Athlete, Football Player)
c/o Staff Member *United Talent Agency (UTA)*
9336 Civic Center Dr
Beverly Hills, CA 90210-3604, USA

Olson, James (Actor)
250 W 57th St Ste 803
New York, NY 10107-0800, USA

Olson, Kaitlin (Actor)
c/o Amy Slomovits *Haven Entertainment*
8111 Beverly Blvd Ste 201
Los Angeles, CA 90048-4531, USA

Olson, Karl (Athlete, Baseball Player)
PO Box 1897
Zephyr Cove, NV 89448-1897, USA

Olson, Lute (Athlete, Basketball Player, Coach)
5831 E Finisterra
Tucson, AZ 85750-1008, USA

Olson, Lynne (Writer)
c/o Staff Member *Ross Yoon Literary Agency*
1666 Connecticut Ave NW Ste 500
Washington, DC 20009-1039, USA

Olson, Mark (Musician, Songwriter, Writer)
Sussman Assoc
1222 16th Ave S Ste 300
Nashville, TN 37212-2920, USA

Olson, Nancy (Actor)
c/o Tom Monjack *Tom Monjack Celebrity Enterprises*
28650 Avenida Maravilla # A
Cathedral City, CA 92234-8115, USA

Olson, Peter (Congressman, Politician)
312 Cannon Hob
Washington, DC 20515-3207, USA

Olson, Richard E (Business Person)
Champion Int'l Corp
1 Champion Plaza
Stamford, CT 06921, USA

Olson, Tim (Athlete, Baseball Player)
7506 S Telluride Ct
Centennial, CO 80016-1649, USA

Olson, Weldon (Athlete, Hockey Player, Olympic Athlete)
2039 Bluestone Dr
Findlay, OH 45840-7337, USA

Olssen, Lance (Athlete, Football Player)
5222 E Timberwood Dr
Newburgh, IN 47630-3014, USA

Olstead, Renee (Musician)
c/o Jessica Katz *Katz Public Relations*
14527 Dickens St
Sherman Oaks, CA 91403-3756, USA

Olszewski, Jan F (Prime Minister)
Biuro Poselskie
Al Ujazdowskie 13
Warsaw 00-567, POLAND

Olwine, Ed (Athlete, Baseball Player)
3419 Jacona Pl
The Villages, FL 32162-6681, USA

Olympia (Music Group, Musician)
c/o Staff Member *Equal Vision Records*
PO Box 38202
Albany, NY 12203-8202, USA

Olyphant, Timothy (Actor)
c/o Cara Tripicchio *Shelter PR*
5670 Wilshire Blvd Ste 1200
Los Angeles, CA 90036-5621, USA

O'Malley, Bryan Lee (Writer)
c/o Staff Member *Oni Press*
1319 SE M L King Blvd Ste 240
Portland, OR 97214-4187, USA

O'Malley, Jim (Athlete, Football Player)
12491 Longmire Lakeview
Conroe, TX 77304-1087, USA

O'Malley, Joe (Athlete, Football Player)
656 Sugar Creek Trl SE
Conyers, GA 30094-3808, USA

O'Malley, Martin (Politician)
1501 Saint Paul St Ste 115
Baltimore, MD 21202-2808, USA

O'Malley, Mike (Actor, Director, Writer)
c/o Michael Nilon *Stride Management*
750 N San Vicente Blvd # 800W
W Hollywood, CA 90069-5788, USA

O'Malley, Peter (Baseball Player)
326 S Hudson Ave
Los Angeles, CA 90020-4804, USA

O'Malley, Rory (Actor)
c/o Lauren Auslander *LUNA*
116 Nassau St # 615
New York, NY 10038-2402, USA

O'Malley, Sean Patrick (Religious Leader)
Archdiocese of Boston
2121 Commonwealth Ave
Brighton, MA 02135-3101, USA

O'Malley, Susan (Misc)
Washington Wizards
601 F St NW
Washington, DC 20004-1605, USA

O'Malley, Thomas D (Business Person)
Tosco Corp
1700 E Putnam Ave Ste 500
Old Greenwich, CT 06870-1380, USA

O'Malley, Tom (Athlete, Baseball Player)
89 Carriage S.Cl
Montoursville, PA 17754-9112, USA

Omameh, Patrick (Athlete, Football Player)
c/o Neil Schwartz *Schwartz & Feinsod*
4 Hillandale Rd
Rye Brook, NY 10573-1705, USA

Omar, Chamassi Said (Prime Minister)
Prime Minister's Office
BP 421
Moroni, COMOROS

Omar, Don (Musician)
45 Ann Arbor Pl
Closter, NJ 07624-1538, USA

O'Mara, Jason (Actor)
c/o Michael (Mike) Jelline *United Talent Agency (UTA)*
9336 Civic Center Dr
Beverly Hills, CA 90210-3604, USA

O'Mara, Mark (Horse Racer)
7746 Ivydale Dr APT B
Indianapolis, IN 46250, USA

Omarion (Actor)
c/o Staff Member *Pyramid Entertainment Group*
377 Rector Pl Apt 21A
New York, NY 10280-1439, USA

Omartian, Stormie (Writer)
c/o Staff Member *Harvest House Publisher*
PO Box 41210
Eugene, OR 97404-0322, USA

O. Matsui, Doris (Congressman, Politician)
222 Cannon Hob
Washington, DC 20515-3517, USA

O'Meara, Jo (Actor, Musician)

O'Meara, Mark (Athlete, Golfer)
2000 Auburn Dr Ste 330
Beachwood, OH 44122-4327, USA

O'Meara, Peter (Actor)
c/o Staff Member *ROAR (LA)*
9701 Wilshire Blvd Fl 8
Beverly Hills, CA 90212-2008, USA

OMG Girlz (Music Group, Musician)
c/o Staff Member *Interscope Records (LA) - Main*
2220 Colorado Ave
Santa Monica, CA 90404-3506, USA

Omidyar, Pierre (Business Person)
eBay
2145 Hamilton Ave
San Jose, CA 95125-5905, USA

Ommanney, Catherine (Reality Star)
c/o Staff Member *Bravo TV (NY)*
30 Rockefeller Plz
New York, NY 10112-0015, USA

Omundson, Timothy (Actor)
c/o Michael Bircumshaw *Water Street Anthem Entertainment*
5225 Wilshire Blvd Ste 615
Los Angeles, CA 90036-4350, USA

On, Richard (Music Group)
c/o Sid Craig *Craig Management*
2240 Miramonte Cir E Unit C
Palm Springs, CA 92264-5734, USA

Onanian, Edward (Religious Leader)
Diocese of Armenian Church
630 2nd Ave
New York, NY 10016-4806, USA

Onarati, Peter (Actor)
Liberman Zerman
252 N Larchmont Blvd Ste 200
Los Angeles, CA 90004-3754, USA

Ondaatje, Michael (Writer)
Glendon College
English Dept
2275 Bayview
Toronto, ON M4N 3M6, CANADA

Ondrasik, John (Musician, Songwriter)
c/o Staff Member *Paradigm*
140 Broadway Ste 2600
New York, NY 10005-1011, USA

ONeal, Alexander (Musician)
c/o Eminence Leisure
18-24 John St
Luton LU1 2JE, UNITED KINGDOM

O'neal, Blair (Athlete, Golfer)
c/o Eddie Smith *Gaylord Sports Management*
13845 N Northsight Blvd Ste 200
Scottsdale, AZ 85260-3609, USA

O'Neal, Griffin (Actor)
21368 Pacific Coast Hwy
Malibu, CA 90265-5203, USA

O'Neal, Jamie (Musician)
c/o Staff Member *Creative Artists Agency (CAA)*
2000 Avenue of the Stars Ste 100
Los Angeles, CA 90067-4705, USA

O'Neal, Jermaine (Athlete, Basketball Player)
c/o Arn Tellem *Wasserman Media Group*
10960 Wilshire Blvd Ste 1200
Los Angeles, CA 90024-3714, USA

O'Neal, Leslie C (Athlete, Football Player)
5617 Adobe Falls Rd Unit A
San Diego, CA 92120-4654, USA

O'Neal, Randy (Athlete, Baseball Player)
10015 Honey Tree Ct
Orlando, FL 32836-5937, USA

O'Neal, Ryan (Actor)
c/o Scott Zimmerman *Scott Zimmerman Management*
1644 Courtney Ave
Los Angeles, CA 90046-2708, USA

O'Neal, Shaquille (Athlete, Basketball Player, Olympic Athlete)
New Jersey Legends
1415 Constitution Rd SE
Blackhall Studios
Atlanta, GA 30316-4606, USA

O'Neal, Shaunie (Actor, Reality Star)
c/o Staff Member *DB Agency/Mogul Media Group*
6129 Saint Clair Ave
North Hollywood, CA 91606-4631, USA

O'Neal, Steve (Athlete, Football Player)
2914 Coronado Dr
College Station, TX 77845-7716, USA

O'Neal, Tatum (Actor)
c/o Miles Levy *Randy James Management*
12711 Ventura Blvd Ste 345
Studio City, CA 91604-2416, USA

One Direction (Music Group)
c/o Harry Magee *Modest! Management*
91A Peterborough Rd
London SW6 3BU, UNITED KINGDOM

One Eskimo (Music Group)
c/o Nick Matthews *Coda Music Agency (UK)*
56 Compton St
Clerkenwell
London EC1V 0ET, UNITED KINGDOM

O'Neil, Edward W (Athlete, Football Player)
6691 Aiken Rd
Lockport, NY 14094-9648, USA

O'Neil, Lawrence (Director)
International Creative Mgmt
8942 Wilshire Blvd # 219
Beverly Hills, CA 90211-1908, USA

O'Neil, Melissa (Actor, Musician)
c/o Daniel Birnbaum *Talent House (Toronto)*
204-A St George St
Toronto, ON M5R 2N6, CANADA

O'Neil, Susie (Athlete, Swimmer)
177 Bridge Road
Richmond, Vic 03121, Australia

O'Neil, Tricia (Actor)

O'Neill, Brian (Athlete, Hockey Player)
2600-1800 Av McGill College
Montreal, QC H3A 3J6, Canada

O'Neill, Ed (Actor)
c/o Alexander Yarosh *Gersh*
9465 Wilshire Blvd Ste 600
Beverly Hills, CA 90212-2605, USA

O'Neill, Jennifer (Actor, Model)
Jennifer O'Neill Ministries
1811 Beech Ave
Nashville, TN 37203-5415, USA

O'Neill, Kevin (Athlete, Football Player)
1363 Masters Dr
Metamora, MI 48455-8701, USA

O'Neill, Michael (Actor)
c/o Staff Member *Mitchell K Stubbs & Assoc*
8675 Washington Blvd Ste 203
Culver City, CA 90232-7486, USA

O'Neill, Paul (Athlete, Baseball Player)
7785 Hartford Hill Ln
Montgomery, OH 45242-4347, USA

O'Neill, Paul H (Politician)
3 Vonlent Pl
Pittsburgh, PA 15232-1444, USA

O'Neill, Susan (Susie) (Swimmer)
207 Kent St
#1800
Sydney, NSW 02000, AUSTRALIA

O'Neill, Willa (Actor)
c/o Staff Member *Auckland Actors*
PO Box 56-460
Dominion Road
Auckland 00003, NEW ZEALAND

OneRepublic (Music Group)
c/o Jeff Frasco *Creative Artists Agency (CAA)*
2000 Avenue of the Stars Ste 100
Los Angeles, CA 90067-4705, USA

Onesti, Larry (Athlete, Football Player)
5476 E James Rd
Bloomington, IN 47408-9402, USA

Onetto, Victoria (Actor)
c/o Staff Member *Telefe (Argentina)*
Pavon 2444
Buenos Aires C1248AAT, ARGENTINA

Onkotz, Dennis (Athlete, Football Player)
551 Brush Valley Rd
Boalsburg, PA 16827-1018, USA

Ono, Yoko (Artist)
c/o Chloe Walsh *Grandstand Media*
138 W 25th St Fl 9
New York, NY 10001-7405, USA

Onobun, Fendi (Athlete, Football Player)

Onodi, Henrietta (Gymnast)
Gymnastic Federation
Magyar Toma Szovetseg
Budapest 01143, HUNGARY

O'Nora, Brian (Athlete, Baseball Player)
5265 Nashua Dr
Youngstown, OH 44515-5174, USA

O'Nora, Brian (Baseball Player)
4294 Maureen Dr
Youngstown, OH 44511-1014, USA

Ontiveros, Steve (Athlete, Baseball Player)
6349 N 78th St Unit 126
Scottsdale, AZ 85250-4771, USA

Ontiveros, Steve (Athlete, Baseball Player)
18061 N 87th Dr Unit 2127
Peoria, AZ 85382-3073, USA

Ontkean, Michael (Actor)
PO Box 51
Kilauea, HI 96754-0051, USA

Onufriyenko, Yuri I (Astronaut, Misc)
Potchta Kosmonavtov
Moskovskoi Oblasti
Syvisdny Goroduk 141160, RUSSIA

oOoOO (DJ)
c/o Jason Edwards *13 Artists (UK)*
11-14 Kensington St
Brighton BN1 4AJ, UNITED KINGDOM

Oosterhouse, Carter (Television Host)
c/o Howard Bragman *LaBrea Media*
8306 Wilshire Blvd # 4002
Beverly Hills, CA 90211-2304, USA

Opalinski-Harrer, Janice (Athlete, Volleyball Player)
Women's Pro Volleyball Assn
3653 Diamond Head Cir
Honolulu, HI 96815-4430, USA

Opasik, Jim (Artist)
1914 Beverly Rd
Baltimore, MD 21228-4227, USA

Operator (Music Group)
c/o Staff Member *UTA Music/The Agency Group*
9336 Civic Center Dr
Beverly Hills, CA 90210-3604, USA

Opie, John D (Business Person)
General Electric Co
3135 Easton Tpke
Fairfield, CT 06828-0001, USA

Oppegard, Peter (Athlete, Figure Skater, Olympic Athlete)
432 Enclave Cir Apt 305
Costa Mesa, CA 92626-7077, USA

Oppenheimer, Allan (Actor)
1207 Beverly Green Dr
Beverly Hills, CA 90212-4105, USA

Oppenheimer, Deborah (Producer)
c/o Staff Member *United Talent Agency (UTA)*
9336 Civic Center Dr
Beverly Hills, CA 90210-3604, USA

Oppewal, Jeannine (Misc)
c/o Barbara Halperin *Gersh*
9465 Wilshire Blvd Ste 600
Beverly Hills, CA 90212-2605, USA

O'Pry, Sean (Model)
c/o Staff Member *VNY Model Management*
928 Broadway Ste 800
New York, NY 10010-8123, USA

Oquendo, Jose (Athlete, Baseball Player)
357 SE Ashley Oaks Way
Stuart, FL 34997-2806, USA

O'Quinn, Danny (Race Car Driver)
O'Quinn Motorsports
PO Box 1342
Coeburn, VA 24230-1342, USA

O'Quinn, Terry (Actor)
Innovative Artists
1505 10th St
Santa Monica, CA 90401-2805, USA

Oquist, Mike (Athlete, Baseball Player)
1910 Raton Ave
La Junta, CO 81050-3427, USA

Ora, Rita (Musician)
c/o Staff Member *First Access Entertainment*
Prefers to be contacted by email or phone.
Los Angeles, CA NA, USA

Orakpo, Brian (Athlete, Football Player)
c/o Ben Dogra *Relativity Sports*
2029 Century Park E Ste 1550
Century City, CA 90067-3000, USA

Orange, Walter (Clyde) (Music Group, Musician)
Management Assoc
1920 Benson Ave
Saint Paul, MN 55116-3214, USA

Orban, Bill (Athlete, Hockey Player)
4 Binscarth Cres
Kanata, ON K2L 1S1, Canada

Orbit, William (Musician)
c/o Staff Member *Creative Artists Agency (CAA)*
2000 Avenue of the Stars Ste 100
Los Angeles, CA 90067-4705, USA

Orci, Roberto (Producer)
c/o Staff Member *Kurtzman/Orci*
100 Universal Plaza
Bldg. 5171
Universal City, CA 91608, USA

Ordaz, Luis (Athlete, Baseball Player)
130 N Division St
Attn: Coaching Staff
Auburn, NY 13021-1707, USA

Ordonez, Magglio (Athlete, Baseball Player)
3101 S Ocean Dr Apt 2703
Hollywood, FL 33019-2892, USA

Ordonez, Rey (Athlete, Baseball Player)
1000 SE 9th Ave
Hialeah, FL 33010-5810, USA

Orduna, Joe (Athlete, Football Player)
15 Grant
Irvine, CA 92620-3354, USA

O'Ree, William E (Willie) (Athlete, Hockey Player)
7961 Anders Cir
La Mesa, CA 91942-2304, USA

O'Regan, Tom (Athlete, Hockey Player)
19 Homestead Park
Needham Heights, MA 02494-1517

O'Reilly, Bill (Television Host)
c/o Evan Bell *Bell & Co*
535 5th Ave
New York, NY 10017-3620, USA

O'Reilly, Cyril (Actor)
Stone Manners
6500 Wilshire Blvd # 550
Los Angeles, CA 90048-4920, USA

O'Reilly, Sir Anthony J.F. (Business Person)
The O'Reilly Foundation
2 Fitzwilliam Sq
Dublin 00002, Ireland

O'Reilly, Terry (Athlete, Coach, Hockey Player)
PO Box 5544
Salisbury, MA 01952-0544, USA

Oremans, Miriam (Tennis Player)
Octagon
1751 Pinnacle Dr Ste 1500
McLean, VA 22102-3833, USA

Orenstein, Andrew (Producer)
c/o Staff Member *United Talent Agency (UTA)*
9336 Civic Center Dr
Beverly Hills, CA 90210-3604, USA

Oreskaband (Music Group)
c/o Staff Member *Paradigm (Monterey)*
404 W Franklin St
Monterey, CA 93940-2303, USA

Orgad, Ben-Zion (Composer)
14 Bloch St
Tel-Aviv 64161, ISRAEL

Organ, H Bryan (Artist)
Stables
Marston Trussel near Market Harborough
Leics LE16 9TX, UNITED KINGDOM (UK)

Orgy (Music Group)
c/o Staff Member *Creative Artists Agency (CAA)*
2000 Avenue of the Stars Ste 100
Los Angeles, CA 90067-4705, USA

Oriard, Michael (Athlete, Football Player)
3010 NW McKinley Dr
Corvallis, OR 97330-1138, USA

Orie, Kevin (Athlete, Baseball Player)
6 Ppg Pl
Pi Ste 600
Pittsburgh, PA 15222-5425, USA

Origliasso, Jessica (Actor)
c/o Staff Member *The Harbour Agency*
135 Forbes St
Woolloomooloo NSW 2011, Australia

Origliasso, Lisa (Actor)
c/o Staff Member *The Harbour Agency*
135 Forbes St
Woolloomooloo NSW 2011, Australia

Orji, Yvonne (Actor)
c/o Norman Aladjem *Mainstay Entertainment*
9250 Beverly Blvd Fl 3
Beverly Hills, CA 90210-3710, USA

Orlandi, Oluchi (Model)
c/o Staff Member *Model Africa*
Paramount Place
105 Main Road
Green Point, Cape Town 08001, South Africa

Orlando, Bo (Athlete, Football Player)
1360 Armstrong Rd
Bethlehem, PA 18017-1002, USA

Orlando, Gates (Athlete, Hockey Player)
252 Bennington Hills Ct
West Henrietta, NY 14586-9765

Orlando, Geoarge J (Misc)
Distillery Wine & Allied Workers
219 Paterson Ave
Little Falls, NJ 07424-1657, USA

Orlando, Tony (Musician)
c/o David Brokaw *Brokaw Company*
PO Box 462
Culver City, CA 90232-0462, USA

Orleans, Joan (Musician)
PO Box 2596
New York, NY 10163-2596, USA

Orlenko, Oksana (Actor)
c/o Staff Member *Sharp Entertainment*
1515 Broadway
New York, NY 10036-8901, USA

Orlich, Dan (Athlete, Football Player)
1030 Porter Cir
Reno, NV 89509-2349, USA

Orlovsky, Dan (Athlete, Football Player)
c/o David Dunn *Athletes First*
23091 Mill Creek Dr
Laguna Hills, CA 92653-1258, USA

Orman, Suze (Business Person, Television Host)
Suze Orman Financial Group
2000 Powell St Ste 1605
Emeryville, CA 94608-1861, USA

Ormond, Julia (Actor)
c/o Leslie Siebert *Gersh*
9465 Wilshire Blvd Ste 600
Beverly Hills, CA 90212-2605, USA

Ormond, Paul (Business Person)
Manor Care Inc
333 N Summit St
Toledo, OH 43604-1531, USA

Orms, Barry (Athlete, Basketball Player)
500 N Rossmore Ave Apt 403
Los Angeles, CA 90004-2437, USA

Orndorff, Paul (Athlete, Wrestler)
135 Pamela Ct
Fayetteville, GA 30214-4309, USA

Ornish, Dean (Doctor, Writer)
Preventative Medicine Research Insitute
900 Bridgeway Ste 2
Sausalito, CA 94965-2100, USA

Ornstein, Michael (Actor)
c/o Marsha McManus *Principal Entertainment*
9255 W Sunset Blvd Ste 500
Los Angeles, CA 90069-3301, USA

Ornston, David E. (Producer)
Salvatore/Ornston Productions
5650 Camellia Ave
North Hollywood, CA 91601-1710, USA

Oropesa, Eddie (Athlete, Baseball Player)
15757 SW 102nd St
Miami, FL 33196-5420, USA

Orosco, Jesse (Athlete, Baseball Player)
16242 Winecreek Rd
San Diego, CA 92127-3733, USA

Orosz, Tom (Athlete, Football Player)
425 1/2 5th St
Fairport Harbor, OH 44077-5629, USA

O'Rourke, Beto (Politician)
PO Box 3628
El Paso, TX 79923-3628, USA

O'Rourke, Charles C (Athlete, Football Player)
220 Bedford St Apt 7A
Bridgewater, MA 02324-3123, USA

O'Rourke, Charlie (Athlete, Baseball Player)
15612 N Little Spokane Dr
Spokane, WA 99208-8527, USA

O'Rourke, PJ (Actor)
c/o Missy Malkin *Brillstein Entertainment Partners*
9150 Wilshire Blvd Ste 350
Beverly Hills, CA 90212-3453, USA

O'Rourke, P.J. (Athlete, Hockey Player)
1 Cherry Ln
Georgetown, MA 01833-1112, USA

Orpik, Brooks (Athlete, Hockey Player)
Sports Management
51 Nathaniel Pl
Englewood, NJ 07631-2736, USA

Orr, Bobby (Athlete, Hockey Player)
6413 Mullin St
Jupiter, FL 33458-6666, USA

Orr, Christopher (Actor)
c/o Staff Member *3 Arts Entertainment*
9460 Wilshire Blvd Fl 7
Beverly Hills, CA 90212-2713, USA

Orr, David A (Business Person)
Home Farm House Shackleford
Godalming
Surrey GU8 6AH, UNITED KINGDOM (UK)

Orr, Gregory (Writer)
University Of Virginia
PO Box 400121
Charlottesville, VA 22904-4121, USA

Orr, James E (Athlete, Football Player)
3104 Glynn Ave
Brunswick, GA 31520, USA

Orr, Kay (Politician)
1610 Brent Blvd
Lincoln, NE 68506-1866, USA

Orr, Louis (Athlete, Basketball Player, Coach)
6915 Wilson Ln
Bethesda, MD 20817-4923, USA

Orr, Pete (Athlete, Baseball Player)
400 Rannie Rd
Newmarket, ON L3X 2N3, Canada

Orr, Terrence S (Dancer)
American Ballet Theatre
890 Broadway Fl 3
New York, NY 10003-1278, USA

Orr, Terry (Athlete, Football Player)
2710 Kellogg Ave
Dallas, TX 75216-3250, USA

Orrall, Robert Ellis (Musician)
3 E 54th St # 1400
New York, NY 10022-3108, USA

Orr-Cahall, Christina (Director)
Norton Gallery of Art
1450 S Dixie Hwy
West Palm Beach, FL 33401-7198, USA

Orr-Ewing, Hamish (Business Person)
Fox Mill
Purton near Swindon
Wilts SN5 9EF, UNITED KINGDOM (UK)

Orrico, Stacie (Musician)
c/o Staff Member *Creative Artists Agency (CAA)*
2000 Avenue of the Stars Ste 100
Los Angeles, CA 90067-4705, USA

Orr III, James E (Business Person)
UNUMProvident Corp
2211 Congress St
Portland, ME 04122-0003, USA

Orr Jr, James E (Jim) (Athlete, Football Player)
3104 Glynn Ave
Brunswick, GA 31520, USA

Orser, Brian (Figure Skater)
Toronto, Cricket, Skating & Curling Club
141 Wilson Ave
Toronto, ON M5M 3A3, Canada

Orser, Leland (Actor)
c/o Kami Putnam-Heist *Anonymous Content*
3532 Hayden Ave
Culver City, CA 90232-2413, USA

Orsin, Raymond (Cartoonist)
Cleveland Plain Dealer
1801 Superior Ave E
Cleveland, OH 44114-2198, USA

Orsini, Myrna J (Artist)
Orsini Studios
4411 N 7th St
Tacoma, WA 98406-3507, USA

Orsino, John (Athlete, Baseball Player)
6141 Terra Mere Cir
Boynton Beach, FL 33437-4920, USA

Orsulak, Joe (Athlete, Baseball Player)
29 Keansburg Rd
Parsippany, NJ 07054-3508, USA

Orta, Jorge (Athlete, Baseball Player)
1201 Heather Hill Cres
Flossmoor, IL 60422-1425, USA

Ortega, Amancio (Business Person)
Edificio Inditex
Industria de Diseno Textil
Avenida de la Diputacion
La Coruna, Arteixo 15142, SPAIN

Ortega, Bill (Athlete, Baseball Player)
4635 NW 95th Ave
Doral, FL 33178-2091, USA

Ortega, Jeannie (Musician)
Hollywood Records
500 S Buena Vista St
Burbank, CA 91521-0002, USA

Ortega, Jenna (Actor)
c/o Gary Mantoosh *Baker Winokur Ryder Public Relations*
9100 Wilshire Blvd
W Tower #500
Beverly Hills, CA 90212-3415, USA

Ortega, Keith (Athlete, Football Player)
142 Lucille St
Lake Charles, LA 70601-8423, USA

Ortega, Kenny (Actor, Director, Producer)
c/o Andy Patman *Paradigm*
8942 Wilshire Blvd
Beverly Hills, CA 90211-1908, USA

Ortega, Manuel (Actor)
c/o Staff Member *Telefe (Argentina)*
Pavon 2444
Buenos Aires C1248AAT, ARGENTINA

Ortega, Phil (Athlete, Baseball Player)
307 Leighton Dr
Ventura, CA 93001-1556, USA

Ortega, Phil (Athlete, Baseball Player)
3200 S Litzler Dr Apt 3-211
Flagstaff, AZ 86005-8913, USA

Ortega, Ralph (Athlete, Football Player)
10465 SW 124th St
Miami, FL 33176-4721, USA

Ortega Saavedra, Daniel (President)
Frente Sandinista de Liberacion National
Managua, NICARAGUA

Ortega y Alamino, Jaime Cardinal (Religious Leader)
Apartado 594
Calle Habana 152
Havana 10100, CUBA

Ortenzio, Frank (Athlete, Baseball Player)
2357 Oak Forest Dr
Jacksonville Beach, FL 32250-2942, USA

Ortiz, Adalberto (Junior) (Athlete, Baseball Player)
161 Kinchafoonee Creek Rd
Leesburg, GA 31763-4903, USA

Ortiz, Alejo (Actor)
c/o Staff Member *Telefe (Argentina)*
Pavon 2444
Buenos Aires C1248AAT, ARGENTINA

Ortiz, Ana (Actor)
c/o Bob Gersh *Gersh*
9465 Wilshire Blvd Ste 600
Beverly Hills, CA 90212-2605, USA

Ortiz, Cristina (Musician)
Harrison/Parrott
12 Penzance Place
London W11 4PA, UNITED KINGDOM (UK)

Ortiz, David (Athlete, Baseball Player)
BigPapiShop
114 Brookline Ave
Boston, MA 02215, USA

Ortiz, Domingo (Misc)
Brown Cat Inc
400 Foundry St
Athens, GA 30601-2623, USA

Ortiz, Jaina Lee (Actor)
c/o Kate Rosen *The Lede Company*
401 Broadway Ste 206
New York, NY 10013-3033, USA

Ortiz, Javier (Athlete, Baseball Player)
19520 SW 39th Ct
Miramar, FL 33029-2736, USA

Ortiz, John (Actor)
c/o Jason Gutman *Gersh*
41 Madison Ave Ste 3301
New York, NY 10010-2210, USA

Ortiz, Louis (Baseball Player)
1683 La Verde Dr
San Marcos, CA 92078-5223, USA

Ortiz, Luis (Athlete, Baseball Player)
6408 Rogers Dr
North Richland Hills, TX 76182-4807, USA

Ortiz, Russ (Athlete, Baseball Player)

Ortiz, Shalim (Actor)
c/o Irene Marie *Irene Marie Management Group*
728 Ocean Dr
Miami Beach, FL 33139-6220, USA

Ortiz, Tito (Athlete, Boxer)
c/o Staff Member *John Lewis Entertainment Group*
3071 S Valley View Blvd
Las Vegas, NV 89102-7889, USA

Ortiz, Victor (Athlete, Boxer)

Ortlieb, Patrick (Skier)
Hotel Montana
Obertech
Lech 06764, AUSTRIA

Ortmann, Charles (Athlete, Football Player)
4 River Birch Ln
Savannah, GA 31411-2847, USA

Ortmeier, Dan (Athlete, Baseball Player)
2121 Fairmont Dr
Flower Mound, TX 75028-4606, USA

Orton, Beth (Musician)
c/o Beth Holden-Garland *Untitled Entertainment*
350 S Beverly Dr Ste 200
Beverly Hills, CA 90212-4819, USA

Orton, John (Athlete, Baseball Player)
2929 E Dublin St
Gilbert, AZ 85295-0403, USA

Orton, Kyle (Football Player)
c/o Staff Member *Chicago Bears*
1000 Football Dr
Lake Forest, IL 60045, USA

Orton, Randy (Athlete, Wrestler)
c/o Kerry Rodgerson *World Wrestling Entertainment (WWE)*
1241 E Main St
Stamford, CT 06902-3520, USA

Oruche, Phina (Actor)
c/o Staff Member *Bauman Redanty & Shaul Agency*
5757 Wilshire Blvd
Suite 473
Beverly Hills, CA 90212, USA

O'Russell, David (Producer)
c/o Susan Ciccone *42West*
1840 Century Park E Ste 700
Los Angeles, CA 90067-2122, USA

Orvella, Chad (Athlete, Baseball Player)
1205 N 27th Pl
Renton, WA 98056-1472, USA

Orvick, George M (Religious Leader)
Evangelical Lutheran Synod
6 Browns Ct
Mankato, MN 56001-6121, USA

Orvis, Herb (Athlete, Football Player)
14175 W Indian School Rd Ste B4
Goodyear, AZ 85395-8494, USA

Ory, Meghan (Actor)
c/o Russ Mortensen *Pacific Artists Management*
112 3rd Ave E Suite 210
Vancouver, BC V5T 1C8, CANADA

O'Sadnick, Craig (Athlete, Football Player)
10 Huntington Forest Ct E
Saint Charles, MO 63301-0490, USA

Osawa, Maria (Actor, Adult Film Star, Model)
c/o Staff Member *T-Powers*
4-6-1-5F Naka Meguro
Meguro, Tokyo 153-0061, JAPAN

Osborn, Dan (Ozzie) (Athlete, Baseball Player)
5061 W 73rd Ave
Westminster, CO 80030-5122, USA

Osborn, David V (Dave) (Athlete, Football Player)
18067 Judicial Way S
Lakeville, MN 55044-8895, USA

Osborn, Jim (Athlete, Football Player)
4 Canyon Ct
Algonquin, IL 60102-6306, USA

Osborn, John Jay (Writer)
14 Fair Oaks St
San Francisco, CA 94110-2209, USA

Osborn, Kassidy (Musician)
LGB Media
1228 Pineview Ln
Nashville, TN 37211-7422, USA

Osborn, Kelsi (Musician)
LGB Media
1228 Pineview Ln
Nashville, TN 37211-7422, USA

Osborn, Kristyn (Musician, Songwriter, Writer)
LGB Media
1228 Pineview Ln
Nashville, TN 37211-7422, USA

Osborne, Barrie M (Director, Producer)
c/o Staff Member *Emerald City Productions*
9 Glen Dr
Mill Valley, CA 94941-1252, United States

Osborne, Burl (Religious Leader)
Salvation Army
799 Bloomfield Ave
Verona, NJ 07044-1367, USA

Osborne, Dan (Model, Reality Star)
c/o Staff Member *Force 1 Management*
5 St Johns Ln
London EC1M 4BH, UNITED KINGDOM

Osborne, Donovan (Athlete, Baseball Player)
1651 Brightstone Ct
Reno, NV 89521-4049, USA

Osborne, Jeffrey (Musician, Songwriter, Writer)
Entertainment Artists
2409 21st Ave S Ste 100
Nashville, TN 37212-5317, USA

Osborne, Joan (Musician, Songwriter)
c/o Staff Member *Paradigm (Monterey)*
404 W Franklin St
Monterey, CA 93940-2303, USA

Osborne, Mark (Athlete, Hockey Player)
28 Princess Anne Cres
Etobicoke, ON M9A 2P1, Canada

Osborne, Mary Pope (Writer)
c/o Matthew Snyder *Creative Artists Agency (CAA)*
2000 Avenue of the Stars Ste 100
Los Angeles, CA 90067-4705, USA

Osborne, Richard (Athlete, Football Player)
3720 S Loop 1604 E
San Antonio, TX 78264-9512, USA

Osborne, Tom (Athlete, Football Coach, Football Player)
5400 Trotter Rd
Lincoln, NE 68516-3419, USA

Osbourne, Jack (Reality Star)
c/o Staff Member *Schweet Entertainment*
1040 N Las Palmas Ave Bldg 10
Los Angeles, CA 90038-2409, USA

Osbourne, Kelly (Musician)
c/o Marcel Pariseau *True Public Relations*
3575 Cahuenga Blvd W Ste 360
Los Angeles, CA 90068-1361, USA

Osbourne, Ozzy (Musician, Songwriter)
c/o Sharon Osbourne *Sharon Osbourne Management*
1 Pratt Mews
Regent House
London NW1 0AD, UNITED KINGDOM

Osbourne, Sharon (Business Person, Reality Star, Talk Show Host)
c/o Staff Member *CBS Paramount Network Television*
4024 Radford Ave
Cbs Studios
Studio City, CA 91604-2190, USA

Osburn, Pat (Athlete, Baseball Player)
208 64th Street Ct NW
Bradenton, FL 34209-1625, USA

Osby, Greg (Musician)
Bridge Agency
35 Clark St Apt A5
Brooklyn Heights, NY 11201-2374, USA

Oseary, Guy (Business Person, Producer)
c/o Guy Oseary *Maverick Management*
9350 Civic Center Dr Ste 100
Beverly Hills, CA 90210-3629, USA

Osemele, Kelechi (Athlete, Football Player)
c/o David Dunn *Athletes First*
23091 Mill Creek Dr
Laguna Hills, CA 92653-1258, USA

Osgood, Chris (Athlete, Hockey Player)
1445 Penniman Ave
Plymouth, MI 48170-1036, USA

Osgood, Kassim (Athlete, Football Player)
c/o Drew Rosenhaus *Rosenhaus Sports Representation*
3921 Alton Rd # 440
Miami Beach, FL 33140-3852, USA

O'Shea, Danny (Athlete, Hockey Player)
7343 Colfax Ave S
Minneapolis, MN 55423-3022

O'Shea, Kevin (Athlete, Hockey Player)

O'Shea, Terry (Athlete, Football Player)
1034 Quincy Dr
Greensburg, PA 15601-1128, USA

Osher, John (Business Person)
Maltz Jupiter Theatre
1001 E Indiantown Rd
Board of Directors
Jupiter, FL 33477-5110, USA

Oshima, Nagisa (Director)
Oshima Productions
2-15-7 Arasaka
Minatoku
Tokyo, JAPAN

Oshodin, Willie (Athlete, Football Player)
8134 Murray Hill Dr
Fort Washington, MD 20744-4416, USA

Oshry, Claudia (Internet Star)
c/o Seth Jacobs *Brillstein Entertainment Partners*
9150 Wilshire Blvd Ste 350
Beverly Hills, CA 90212-3453, USA

Osiecki, Mark (Athlete, Hockey Player)
7482 New Albany Links Dr
New Albany, OH 43054-6012

Osiecki, Sandy (Athlete, Football Player)
11 Bryan Cir
Seymour, CT 06483-3676, USA

Osik, Keith (Athlete, Baseball Player)
5 Pal Ct
Shoreham, NY 11786-2352, USA

Osinski, Dan (Athlete, Baseball Player)
9723 W Amber Trl
Sun City, AZ 85351-1346, USA

Oslin, K T (Musician)
Moress-Nanas-Hart
704 18th Ave S
Nashville, TN 37203-3215, USA

Osman, Mat (Musician)
Interceptor Enterprises
98 White Lion St
London N1 9PF, UNITED KINGDOM (UK)

Osmar, Dean (Misc)
PO Box 32
Clam Gulch, AK 99568-0032, USA

Osment, Emily (Actor)
c/o Eric Kranzler *Management 360*
9111 Wilshire Blvd
Beverly Hills, CA 90210-5508, USA

Osment, Haley Joel (Actor)
c/o Kristin Konig *MGMT Entertainment (The Schiff Company)*
9220 W Sunset Blvd Ste 106
W Hollywood, CA 90069-3500, USA

Osmond, Cliff (Actor, Director)
15515 W Sunset Blvd UNIT 210
Pacific Plsds, CA 90272-3530, USA

Osmond, Donny (Actor, Musician, Producer)
Donny Osmond Entertainment
1329 S 800 E
Orem, UT 84097-7737, USA

Osmond, Ken (Actor)
9863 Wornom Ave
Sunland, CA 91040-1535, USA

Osmond, Marie (Actor, Musician)
1391 Quiet River Ave
Henderson, NV 89012-7219, USA

Osorio, Jorge Federico (Musician)
Columbia Artists Mgmt Inc
165 W 57th St
New York, NY 10019-2201, USA

Osrin, Raymond H (Cartoonist)
Cleveland Plain Dealer
1801 Superior Ave E
Cleveland, OH 44114-2198, USA

Oss, Arnold (Athlete, Hockey Player, Olympic Athlete)
25601 N Abajo Dr
Rio Verde, AZ 85263-7219, USA

Ossana, Diana (Producer, Writer)
c/o Amanda Lundberg *42West*
600 3rd Ave Fl 23
New York, NY 10016-1914, USA

Ostaseski, Frank (Director)
Zen Hospice Project
1161 Mission St Fl 1
San Francisco, CA 94103-1571, USA

Osteen, Claude W (Athlete, Baseball Player)
2313 Duncan Perry Rd
Grand Prairie, TX 75050-2039, USA

Osteen, Darrell (Athlete, Baseball Player)
73901 Cezanne Dr
Palm Desert, CA 92211-4512, USA

Osteen, Joel (Religious Leader, Writer)
Lakewood Church
3700 Southwest Fwy
Houston, TX 77027-7514, USA

Oster, Bill (Athlete, Baseball Player)
56 Little Neck Rd
Centerport, NY 11721-1617, USA

Osterhage, Jeff (Actor)
7309 Santa Barbara St
Carlsbad, CA 92011-4638, USA

Osteroth, Alexander (Actor)
Steinsdorfstr. 20
Munich, GERMANY 80538

Ostertag, Greg (Athlete, Basketball Player)
2803 County Road NE 2010
Mount Vernon, TX 75457-5840, USA

Osting, Jimmy (Athlete, Baseball Player)
4900 Higgins View Ln
Fisherville, KY 40023-9778, USA

Ostlund, Ruben (Director)
c/o Jerome Duboz *WME/IMG*
9601 Wilshire Blvd
Beverly Hills, CA 90210-5213, USA

Ostos, Javier (Swimmer)
FINA
Isabel La Catolica 13
Desp 401-2
Mexico City 1, DF, MEXICO

Ostrom, John H (Misc)
52 Hillhouse Rd
Goshen, CT 06756-1001, USA

Ostroski, Gerald (Athlete, Football Player)
6926 E 115th Pl S
Bixby, OK 74008-8248, USA

Ostrosky, David (Actor)
c/o Staff Member *Televisa*
Blvd Adolfo Lopez Mateos 232
Colonia San Angel INN
DF CP 01060, MEXICO

Ostrosser, Brian (Athlete, Baseball Player)
27 Chelsea Cres
Stoney Creek, ON L8E 5R7, Canada

Ostrovsky, Josh (The Fat Jew) (Comedian, Internet Star)
c/o Noah Rothman *Underground Management*
1180 S Beverly Dr Ste 509
Los Angeles, CA 90035-1157, USA

Ostrum, Peter (Actor)
6475 E Shore Rd
Glenfield, NY 13343-2303, USA

O'Sullevan, Peter J (Sportscaster, Writer)
37 Cranmer Court
London SW3 3HW, UNITED KINGDOM (UK)

O'Sullivan, Chris (Athlete, Hockey Player)
114 Elmer Rd
Dorchester Center, MA 02124-5034

O'Sullivan, Dan (Athlete, Basketball Player)
33 Crescent Ave
Summit, NJ 07901-1902, USA

O'Sullivan, Gilbert (Musician)
Park Promotions
PO Box 651
Park Road
Oxford OX2 9RB, UNITED KINGDOM (UK)

O'Sullivan, Richard (Actor)
Al Mitchell
5 Anglers Lane
Kentish Town
London NW5 3DG, UNITED KINGDOM (UK)

O'Sullivan, Sonia (Athlete, Track Athlete)
Kim McDonald
201 High St
Hampton Hill
Middx TW12 1NL, UNITED KINGDOM (UK)

O' Sullivan, Thaddeus (Director)
c/o Anthony Jones *United Agents*
12-26 Lexington St
London W1F OLE, UNITED KINGDOM

Osuna, Antonio (Athlete, Baseball Player)
10345 W Olympic Blvd
Los Angeles, CA 90064-2524, USA

Osvart, Andrea (Actor)
Amego Film
81 Vaci Utca
Budapest 01056, HUNGARY

Oswald, Mark (Race Car Driver)
Championship Quest Motorsports
237B N Hollywood Rd
Houma, LA 70364-2807, USA

Oswald, Paul (Athlete, Football Player)
521 Cambridge Ct
Alpharetta, GA 30005-4216, USA

Oswald, Stephen S (Astronaut)
NASA
2101 Nasa Pkwy Spc Johnsoncenter
Houston, TX 77058-3696, USA

Oswald, Stephen S Rear Admiral (Astronaut)
16806 Glenshannon Dr
Houston, TX 77059-5504, USA

Oswalt, Patton (Actor, Comedian)
c/o Dave Rath *Generate Management*
8750 Wilshire Blvd Ste 200
Beverly Hills, CA 90211-2707, USA

Oswalt, Roy (Athlete, Baseball Player, Olympic Athlete)
PO Box 8
Weir, MS 39772-0008, USA

Osweiler, Brock (Athlete, Football Player)
c/o Jimmy Sexton *CAA (Memphis)*
6060 Poplar Ave Ste 470
Memphis, TN 38119-0910, USA

Oszajca, John (Musician)
Interscope Records
2220 Colorado Ave
Santa Monica, CA 90404-3506, USA

Ota, Tadamichi (Chef)
Nakanobo Zuien 808 Arimamachi Kita-ku
Kobe-shi
Kyogo-ken, japan

Otanez, Willis (Athlete, Baseball Player)
7904 March Brown Ave
Las Vegas, NV 89149-5101, USA

Otellini, Paul (Business Person)
Intel Corp
2200 Mission College Blvd
Santa Clara, CA 95054-1549, USA

Otep (Musician)
c/o Staff Member *Zen Media Group*
272 Grand St Ste B
Brooklyn, NY 11211-4796, USA

Oteri, Cheri (Actor, Comedian)
c/o Lori Sale *Artist & Brand Management*
9320 Wilshire Blvd Ste 212
Beverly Hills, CA 90212-3217, USA

Otero, Ricky (Athlete, Baseball Player)
126 Calle Sorbona
Urb University Gardens
San Juan, PR 00927, USA

Othenin-Girard, Dominque (Director)
327 S Church Ln
Los Angeles, CA 90049-3057, USA

Othick, Trent (Producer)
c/o Staff Member *Creative Artists Agency (CAA)*
2000 Avenue of the Stars Ste 100
Los Angeles, CA 90067-4705, USA

Otis, Amos J (Athlete, Baseball Player)
8930 Tiger Shale Way
Las Vegas, NV 89123-3132, USA

Otis, Carre (Actor, Model)
c/o Staff Member *Storm Model Management*
5 Jubilee Pl
1st Floor
London SW3 3TD, UK

Otis, James L (Jim) (Athlete, Football Player)
14795 Greenleaf Valley Dr
Chesterfield, MO 63017-5542, USA

Otman, Assed Mohamed (Prime Minister)
Villa Rissani
Route Oued Akrach
Souissi, Rabat, MOROCCO

O'Toole, Annette (Actor)
3202 Club Dr
Los Angeles, CA 90064-4812, USA

O'Toole, Dennis (Denny) (Athlete, Baseball Player)
9105 Royal Oak Ln
Union, KY 41091-8806, USA

O-Town (Music Group)
c/o Mona Loring *Status PR*
PO Box 6191
Westlake Village, CA 91359-6191, USA

Otsuka, Akinori (Athlete, Baseball Player)
891 Fairway Dr
Boulder City, NV 89005-3609, USA

Otsuki, Tamayo (Actor)
Patterson Assoc
20318 Hiawatha St
Chatsworth, CA 91311-2553, USA

Ott, Billy (Athlete, Baseball Player)
132 W Nyack Way
West Nyack, NY 10994-2202, USA

Ott, Ed (Athlete, Baseball Player)
3164 New London Rd
Forest, VA 24551-1814, USA

Ott, Steve (Athlete, Hockey Player)
2758 StClair Rd
Pointe Aux Roches, ON NOR lNO, Canada

Otten, Jim (Athlete, Baseball Player)
1430 N Diane Cir
Mesa, AZ 85203-3845, USA

Otten, Mac (Athlete, Basketball Player)
2010 Burroughs Dr
Dayton, OH 45406-4420, USA

Ottey, Merlene (Athlete, Olympic Athlete, Track Athlete)
Jamaican Olympic Committee
PO Box 544
Kingston 00010, JAMAICA

Ottinger, LD (Race Car Driver)
1021 Scarlet Rd
Newport, TN 37821-7520, USA

Otto, August J (Gus) (Athlete, Football Player)
14411 Open Meadow Ct W
Chesterfield, MO 63017-9627, USA

Otto, Bob (Athlete, Football Player)
1713 Guthrie Dr
Las Vegas, NV 89117-9000, USA

Otto, Dave (Athlete, Baseball Player)
1383 Shady Ln
Wheaton, IL 60187-3722, USA

Otto, James (Musician)
c/o Dan Anderson *Red Light Management (TN)*
PO Box 159310
Nashville, TN 37215-9310, USA

Otto, James E (Jim) (Athlete, Football Player)
100 Estates Dr
Auburn, CA 95602, USA

Otto, Joel (Athlete, Hockey Player)
Calgary Hitmen
PO Box 1540 Stn M
Station M
Calgary, AB T2P 3B9, CANADA

Otto, Kristin (Swimmer)
ZDF Sportedaktion
Postfach 4040
Mainz 55100, GERMANY

Otto, Michael (Business Person)
Spiegel Inc
3500 Lacey Rd
Downers Grove, IL 60515-5422, USA

Otto, Miranda (Actor)
c/o Catherine Olim *PMK/BNC Public Relations*
1840 Century Park E Ste 1400
Los Angeles, CA 90067-2115, USA

Otto, Sylke (Athlete)
BSD
An der Schiessstatte 4
Berchtesgaden 83471, GERMANY

Otto Jr, A T (Misc)
Railroad Yardmasters Union
1411 Peterson Ave Ste 201
Park Ridge, IL 60068-5076, USA

Ouaido, Nassour Guelengdoussia (Prime Minister)
Prime Minister's Office
N'Djamena, CHAD

Oubre, Louis (Athlete, Football Player)
11008 Curran Blvd
New Orleans, LA 70127-1408, USA

Oudin, Melanie (Athlete, Tennis Player)
c/o Sam Duvall *Topnotch Management*
5335 Wisconsin Ave NW Ste 850
Washington, DC 20015-2052, USA

Ouedraogo, Gerard Kango (Prime Minister)
01 BP 347
Ouagadougou, BURKINA FASO

Ouedraogo, Kdre Desire (Prime Minister)
Prime Minister's Office
Parliament Building
Ouagadougou, BURKINA FASO

Ouellet, Joseph G N Cardinal (Religious Leader)
Archdiocese
34 Rue de l'Eveche E
CP 730 SUCC A
Rimouski, QC G5L 7C7, CANADA

Ouellet, Maryse (Athlete, Model, Wrestler)
c/o Staff Member *World Wrestling Entertainment (WWE)*
1241 E Main St
Stamford, CT 06902-3520, USA

Ouellette, Gerry (Athlete, Hockey Player)
352 Ch Portage
Grand-Sault/Grand Falls, NB E3Z 1M7, Canada

Ouellette, Phil (Athlete, Baseball Player)
7421 Poppy St
Corona, CA 92881-3739, USA

Ouimet, Ted (Athlete, Hockey Player)
580 Albert St
Strathroy, ON N7G 1W9, Canada

Oureiro, Natalia (Musician)
c/o Staff Member *BMG*
1540 Broadway
New York, NY 10036-4039, USA

Ourisson, Guy (Misc)
10 Rue Geiler
Strasbourg 67000, FRANCE

Our Lady Peace (Music Group)
c/o Eric Lawrence *Coalition Entertainment Management*
10271 Yonge St Suite 302
Richmond Hill, ON L4C 3B5, Canada

Ousland, Borge (Skier)
Axel Huitfeldts V5
Oslo 01170, NORWAY

Outkast (Music Group)
c/o Sara Newkirk Simon *WME/IMG*
9601 Wilshire Blvd
Beverly Hills, CA 90210-5213, USA

Outlar, Jesse (Sportscaster)
1252 Stephens St SW
Lilburn, GA 30047-4354, USA

Outlaw, Charles (Bo) (Athlete, Basketball Player)
7716 Belvoir Dr
Orlando, FL 32835-8185, USA

Outlaw, Travis (Athlete, Basketball Player)
c/o Bill Duffy *BDA Sports Management*
700 Ygnacio Valley Rd Ste 330
Walnut Creek, CA 94596-3838, USA

Outman, Josh (Athlete, Baseball Player)
4 Pueblo Cir
Festus, MO 63028-6215, USA

Outman, Tim (Artist)
57101 N Bank Rd
McKenzie Bridge, OR 97413-9629, USA

OV7 (Music Group)
c/o Staff Member *Sony Music (Miami)*
404 Washington Ave Ste 700
Miami Beach, FL 33139-6615, USA

Ovchinikov, Vladmir P (Musician)
Manygate
13 Cotswold Mews
30 Battersea Square
London SW11 3RA, UNITED KINGDOM (UK)

Ovechkin, Alexander (Athlete, Hockey Player)
4401 N Federal Hwy Ste 201
Boca Raton, FL 33431-5164, USA

Overall, Park (Actor)
1374 Ripley Island Rd
Afton, TN 37616-6102, USA

Overbay, Lyle (Athlete, Baseball Player)
107 Captain Ln
Centralia, WA 98531-1614, USA

Overbeck, Carla (Athlete, Olympic Athlete, Soccer Player)
205 Zapata Ln
Chapel Hill, NC 27517-7742, USA

Overbeek, Jan T G (Misc)
Zweerslaan 35
Bilthoven, HN 03723, NETHERLANDS

Overgard, Robert M (Religious Leader)
Church of Lutheran Brethren
PO Box 655
Fergus Falls, MN 56538-0655, USA

Overgard, William (Cartoonist)
United Feature Syndicate
200 Madison Ave
New York, NY 10016-3903, USA

Overhauser, Chad (Athlete, Football Player)
8303 N Mopac Expy Ste 425B
Austin, TX 78759-8322, USA

Overman, Ion (Actor)
c/o Staff Member *GVA Talent Agency Inc*
193 N Robertson Blvd
Beverly Hills, CA 90211-2103, USA

Overman, Larry E (Misc)
University of California
Chemistry Dept
Irvine, CA 92717, USA

Overmyer, Amanda (Musician)

Overmyer, Eric (Writer)
c/o Rob Kenneally *Creative Artists Agency (CAA)*
2000 Avenue of the Stars Ste 100
Los Angeles, CA 90067-4705, USA

Overstreet, Chord (Actor, Musician)
c/o Chelsea Thomas *The Lede Company*
9701 Wilshire Blvd # 930
Beverly Hills, CA 90212-2020, USA

Overstreet, Paul (Musician, Songwriter, Writer)
White Horse Enterprises
475 Annex Ave
Nashville, TN 37209-2747, USA

Overstreet, Tommy (Musician)

Overstreet, Will (Athlete, Football Player)
106 Avondale St
Jackson, MS 39216, USA

Overton, Kelly (Actor)
c/o Staff Member *Management 360*
9111 Wilshire Blvd
Beverly Hills, CA 90210-5508, USA

Overton, Rick (Actor)
c/o Staff Member *Sutton Barth & Vennari Inc*
5900 Wilshire Blvd Ste 700
Los Angeles, CA 90036-5009, USA

Overy, Mike (Athlete, Baseball Player)
3010 N 152nd Ln
Goodyear, AZ 85395-8636, USA

Ovitz, Michael S (Business Person)
457 N Rockingham Ave
Los Angeles, CA 90049-2637, USA

Owchar, Dennis (Athlete, Hockey Player)
32 Raeview Dr
Stouffville, ON L4A 3G7, Canada

Owchinko, Bob (Athlete, Baseball Player)
15111 N Hayden Rd Ste 160
Scottsdale, AZ 85260-2555, USA

Owen, Clive (Actor)
c/o Michelle Benson Margolis *The Lede Company*
9701 Wilshire Blvd # 930
Beverly Hills, CA 90212-2020, USA

Owen, Dave (Athlete, Baseball Player)
1921 FM 3136
Cleburne, TX 76031-8792, USA

Owen, Edwyn (Bob) (Athlete, Hockey Player)
3630 SW Stratford Rd
Topeka, KS 66604-2544, USA

Owen, Gary (Comedian)
c/o Chelsea Thomas *The Lede Company*
9701 Wilshire Blvd # 930
Beverly Hills, CA 90212-2020, USA

Owen, Jake (Musician)
c/o Jensen Sussman *Sweet Talk PR*
700 12th Ave S Unit 201
Nashville, TN 37203-3329, USA

Owen, Larry (Athlete, Baseball Player)
6170 Braymoore Dr
Galena, OH 43021-9082, USA

Owen, Michael (Athlete, Soccer Player)
c/o Staff Member *Liverpool FC Football Club*
69/71 Anfield Road
Liverpool L4 OTQ, UNITED KINGDOM

Owen, Randy (Musician)
PO Box 529
Fort Payne, AL 35968, USA

Owen, Rena (Actor, Model)
c/o Michael Greene *Greene & Associates*
1901 Avenue of the Stars Ste 130
Los Angeles, CA 90067-6030, USA

Owen, Spike (Athlete, Baseball Player)
11211 Musket Rim St
Austin, TX 78738-6613, USA

Owen, Tom (Athlete, Football Player)
PO Box 3
Albany, OK 74721-0003, USA

Owens, Al (Baseball Player)
Nashville Elite Giants
460 W Downer Pl Apt 3B
Aurora, IL 60506-5175, USA

Owens, Billy (Athlete, Basketball Player)
608 Canary Dr
Carlisle, PA 17013-8768, USA

Owens, Brig (Athlete, Football Player)
6902 Lupine Ln
Mc Lean, VA 22101-1578, USA

Owens, Buddy (Athlete, Baseball Player)
460 W Downer Pl Apt 3B
Aurora, IL 60506-5175, USA

Owens, Burgess (Athlete, Football Player)
1430 Telegraph Rd
West Chester, PA 19380-1621, USA

Owens, Charles W (Tinker) (Athlete, Football Player)
2547 McGee Dr
Norman, OK 73072-6704, USA

Owens, Chris (Athlete, Football Player)
c/o Frank Bauer *Sun West Sports*
7883 N Pershing Ave
Stockton, CA 95207-1749, USA

Owens, Chris (Actor)
TallGirl Public Relations
14531 Albers St Apt 3
Sherman Oaks, CA 91411-3784, USA

Owens, Cotton (Race Car Driver)
Cotton Owens Garage
116 Pinewood Rd
Pauline, SC 29374-2223, USA

Owens, Craig (Musician)
c/o Staff Member *Equal Vision Records*
PO Box 38202
Albany, NY 12203-8202, USA

Owens, Dan (Athlete, Football Player)
5547 Ashleigh Walk Dr
Suwanee, GA 30024-7684, USA

Owens, Darrick (Athlete, Football Player)
610 Cypress St
Raceland, LA 70394-2817, USA

Owens, Eric (Athlete, Baseball Player)
7351 E Vista Bonita Dr
Scottsdale, AZ 85255-4993, USA

Owens, Geoffrey (Actor)
c/o Karen Semler *Semler Entertainment*
13636 Ventura Blvd # 510
Sherman Oaks, CA 91423-3700, USA

Owens, Henry (Athlete, Baseball Player)
4944 SW 140th Ct
Miami, FL 33175-4806, USA

Owens, Jackson (Athlete, Baseball Player)
PO Box 6046
Decatur, IL 62524-6046, USA

Owens, Jayhawk (Athlete, Baseball Player)
7662 Piney Meadow Ln
Cincinnati, OH 45244-2980, USA

Owens, Jim (Athlete, Baseball Player)
1426 Ramada Dr
Houston, TX 77062-5908, USA

Owens, Joe (Athlete, Football Player)
2754 Highway 13 N
Columbia, MS 39429-8634, USA

Owens, Kem (Musician)
c/o Staff Member *The Paradise Group*
PO Box 69451
West Hollywood, CA 90069-0451, USA

Owens, Lorenzo (Musician)
c/o Staff Member *Paradigm (Monterey)*
404 W Franklin St
Monterey, CA 93940-2303, USA

Owens, Luke (Athlete, Football Player)
2970 Richmond Rd
Beachwood, OH 44122-3248, USA

Owens, Mel (Athlete, Football Player)
1230 Market St Apt 504
San Francisco, CA 94102-4801, USA

Owens, Montell (Athlete, Football Player)

Owens, Morris (Athlete, Football Player)
3010 W Yorkshire Dr Apt 1114
Phoenix, AZ 85027-3919, USA

Owens, Rawleigh C (R C) (Athlete, Football Player)
626 E Yosemite Ave
Manteca, CA 95336-5826, USA

Owens, Steve (Athlete, Football Player, Heisman Trophy Winner)
3700 W Robinson St Ste 230
Norman, OK 73072-3639, USA

Owens, Terrell (Athlete, Football Player)
c/o Alegra Kastens *NMA PR*
7916 Melrose Ave Ste 1
Los Angeles, CA 90046-7160, USA

Owens, Terry (Athlete, Football Player)
458 N 100 W
Saint George, UT 84770-2810, USA

Owens, Tom (Athlete, Basketball Coach)
19788 Wildwood Dr
West Linn, OR 97068-2252, USA

Owens, William (Politician)
14111 Vance Jackson Rd Apt 9306
San Antonio, TX 78249-1999, USA

Owensby, Earl (Actor)
1056 Old Springs Rd
Shelby, NC 28152, USA

Owings, Jim (Athlete, Football Player)
961 Chestnut St SE Ste 107
Gainesville, GA 30501-6902, USA

Owings, Micah (Athlete, Baseball Player)
2219 Sidney Drve Dr NE
Gainesville Ga 30506-1168,
GA 30506-1168, USA

Owl City (Music Group, Musician)
c/o Sonia Aneja *Stunt Company*
67 35th St Unit 51
Brooklyn, NY 11232-2218, USA

Ownbey, Rick (Athlete, Baseball Player)
2166 Via Monserate
Fallbrook, CA 92028-9335, USA

Owsley, Douglas (Misc)
Smithsonian Institute
17th & M Sts NW
Washington, DC 20036, USA

Oxenberg, Catherine (Actor)
c/o Howard Fishman *Hirsch Wallerstein Hayum Matlof & Fishman*
10100 Santa Monica Blvd Fl 23
Los Angeles, CA 90067-4003, USA

Oyakawa, Yoshi (Athlete, Swimmer)
4171 Hutchinson Rd
Cincinnati, OH 45248-2219, USA

Oye, Erlend (Musician)
c/o Staff Member *Paradigm (Monterey)*
404 W Franklin St
Monterey, CA 93940-2303, USA

Oyelowo, David (Actor)
c/o Christian Hodell *Hamilton Hodell Ltd*
20 Golden Sq
Fl 5
London W1F 9JL, UNITED KINGDOM

Oyelowo, Jessica (Actor)
6025 Calvin Ave
Tarzana, CA 91356-1114, USA

Oyeyemi, Helen (Writer)
c/o Staff Member *Allen & Unwin*
PO Box 8500
St Leonards, NSW 08500, Australia

Oz, Daphne (Television Host)
c/o Jill Fritzo *Jill Fritzo Public Relations*
208 E 51st St # 305
New York, NY 10022-6557, USA

Oz, Doctor (Dr) Mehmet (Doctor, Talk Show Host)
14 Edgewater Rd
Cliffside Park, NJ 07010-2805, USA

Oz, Frank (Director)
Oz Inc
32 Greenwood Ct
Orinda, CA 94563-3611, USA

Oz, Lisa (Writer)
14 Edgewater Rd
Cliffside Pk, NJ 07010-2805, USA

Ozaki, Masashi (Golfer)
Bridgestone Sports
14230 Lochridge Blvd Ste G
Covington, GA 30014-4953, USA

Ozbek, Rifat (Designer, Fashion Designer)
Ozbek Ltd
18 Haunch of Venison Yard
London W1Y 1AF, UNITED KINGDOM (UK)

Ozolinsh, Sandis (Athlete, Hockey Player)
701 Golf Club Dr
Castle Rock, CO 80108-8359

Ozomatli (Music Group)
c/o Amy Blackman *Tsunami Entertainment*
1600 E Desert Inn Rd Ste 270
Las Vegas, NV 89169-2576, USA

Ozougwu, Cheta (Athlete, Football Player)

Ozsan, Hal (Actor)
c/o Katie Mason Stern *Luber Roklin Management*
5815 W Sunset Blvd Ste 208
Los Angeles, CA 90028-6481, USA

Ozzie, Raymond (Ray) (Designer)
33 Harbor St
Manchester By The Sea, MA 01944-1461, USA

P

P, Master (Actor, Musician)
c/o Patrick Hughes *Foundation Media Partners*
23679 Calabasas Rd # 625
Calabasas, CA 91302-1502, USA

Paabo, Svante (Director)
Evolutionary Anthropology Inst
Deutscher Platz 6
Leipzig 04103, USA

Paak, Anderson (Musician)
c/o Zach Iser *Creative Artists Agency (CAA)*
405 Lexington Ave Fl 19
New York, NY 10174-1800, USA

Paavola, Rodney (Athlete, Hockey Player)
General Delivery
Hancock, MI 49930-9999, USA

Pablo, Petey (Musician)
c/o Richard Williams *Witz Communications*
555 Fayetteville St Ste 300
Raleigh, NC 27601-3066, USA

Pacar, Johnny (Actor)
c/o Matt Goldman *Silver Lining Entertainment*
421 S Beverly Dr Fl 7
Beverly Hills, CA 90212-4408, USA

Pace, Calvin (Athlete, Football Player)
c/o Pat Dye Jr *SportsTrust Advisors*
3340 Peachtree Rd NE Fl 16
Atlanta, GA 30326-1000, USA

Pace, Dominic (Actor)
c/o Budd Burton Moss *Burton Moss*
10533 Strathmore Dr
Los Angeles, CA 90024-2540, USA

Pace, Judy (Actor)
4139 S Cloverdale Ave
Los Angeles, CA 90008-1034, USA

Pace, Justin (Actor)
c/o Todd Justice *Justice & Ponder*
PO Box 480033
Los Angeles, CA 90048-1033, USA

Pace, Lee (Actor)
c/o David Kalodner *WME|IMG (NY)*
11 Madison Ave Fl 18
New York, NY 10010-3669, USA

Pace, Orlando (Athlete, Football Player)
969 Tucker Ln
St Louis, MO 63131, USA

Pacella, John (Athlete, Baseball Player)
1500 Abbotsford Green Dr
Powell, OH 43065-8938, USA

Pachal, Clayton (Athlete, Hockey Player)
230 Laycoe Cres
Saskatoon, SK S7S 1H5, Canada

Pacillo, Pat (Athlete, Baseball Player, Olympic Athlete)
107 20th Ave
Belmar, NJ 07719-2653, USA

Pacino, Al (Actor)
c/o Staff Member *The Actors Studio*
432 W 44th St
New York, NY 10036-5205, USA

Paciorek, Jim (Athlete, Baseball Player)
14007 E Troika St
Vail, AZ 85641-5971, USA

Paciorek, John (Athlete, Baseball Player)
8400 Huntington Dr
San Gabriel, CA 91775-1154, USA

Paciorek, Tom (Athlete, Baseball Player)
2389 Broad Creek Dr
Stone Mountain, GA 30087-3755, USA

Pacioretty, Max (Athlete, Hockey Player)
5340 NW 2nd Ave Apt 130
Boca Raton, FL 33487-3889

Packard, Kelly (Actor, Model)
c/o Michael Valeo *Valeo Entertainment*
8581 Santa Monica Blvd Ste 570
West Hollywood, CA 90069-4120, USA

Packard, Scott (Baseball Player)
135 Eastview Dr
Horseheads, NY 14845-2548, USA

Packard, Scott (Athlete, Baseball Player)
135 Eastview Dr
Horseheads, NY 14845-2548, USA

Packer, Billy (Sportscaster)
Bazel Group
115 Penn Warren Dr Ste 300
Brentwood, TN 37027-5054, USA

Packer, David (Actor)
c/o Staff Member *Creative Artists Agency (CAA)*
2000 Avenue of the Stars Ste 100
Los Angeles, CA 90067-4705, USA

Packer, Erica (Model, Musician)
11004 Bellagio Pl
Los Angeles, CA 90077-3217, USA

Packer, James (Business Person)
Consolidated Press Holdings
54 Park St
Sydney NSW 2000, AUSTRALIA

Packer, Will (Producer)
c/o Staff Member *Will Packer Productions*
6565 W Sunset Blvd Ste 425
Los Angeles, CA 90028-7242, USA

Pacquet, Fernand (Horse Racer)
7563 S State Road 7
Lake Worth, FL 33449-6701, USA

Pacquiao, Manny (Athlete, Boxer)
Wild Card Boxing Gym
1123 Vine St Ste 14A
Los Angeles, CA 90038-1670, USA

Pacula, Joanna (Actor)
c/o Chuck Binder *Binder & Associates*
1465 Lindacrest Dr
Beverly Hills, CA 90210-2519, USA

Padalecki, Jared (Actor)
c/o Jason Heyman *United Talent Agency (UTA)*
9336 Civic Center Dr
Beverly Hills, CA 90210-3604, USA

Paddio, Gerald (Athlete, Basketball Player)
2801 Crystal Bay Dr
Las Vegas, NV 89117-2235, USA

Paddock, John (Athlete, Hockey Player)
Philadelphia Flyers
3601 S Broad St Ste 2
Philadelphia, PA 19148-5297

Padilla, Anthony (Smosh) (Comedian, Internet Star, Producer)
c/o Laura Ackerman *Advantage PR*
3900 W Alameda Ave Ste 1200
Burbank, CA 91505-4317, USA

Padilla, Douglas (Doug) (Athlete, Track Athlete)
182 N 555 W
Orem, UT 84057-1937, USA

Padilla, Vicente (Athlete, Baseball Player)
1816 O Henry Ct
Arlington, TX 76006-2673, USA

Padjen, Gary (Athlete, Football Player)
9314 Tower Bridge Rd Apt B
Indianapolis, IN 46240-5434, USA

Padukone, Deepika (Actor)
c/o Danielle Robinson *Alan Siegel Entertainment*
9200 W Sunset Blvd Ste 804
West Hollywood, CA 90069-3603, USA

Paea, Stephen (Athlete, Football Player)
c/o David Dunn *Athletes First*
23091 Mill Creek Dr
Laguna Hills, CA 92653-1258, USA

Paek, Jim (Athlete, Hockey Player)
7396 Crystal View Dr SE
Caledonia, MI 49316-7981

Paek, Jim (Athlete, Hockey Player)
Grand Rapids Griffins
130 Fulton St W Ste 111
Grand Rapids, MI 49503-2682

Paepke, Dennis (Athlete, Baseball Player)
4560 Trieste Dr
Carlsbad, CA 92010-3741, USA

Paepke, Jack (Athlete, Baseball Player)
4560 Trieste Dr
Carlsbad, CA 92010-3741, USA

Paes, Leander (Athlete, Tennis Player)
c/o Staff Member *ATP Tour*
201 Atp Tour Blvd
Ponte Vedra Beach, FL 32082-3211, USA

Paetkau, David (Actor)
c/o Mia Hansen *Portrait PR*
5320 Sylmar Ave
Sherman Oaks, CA 91401-5612, USA

Paetsch, Nathan (Athlete, Hockey Player)
324 Tennyson Terrace
East Amherst, NY 14051

Paevey, Ryan (Actor, Model)
c/o Todd Justice *Justice & Ponder*
PO Box 480033
Los Angeles, CA 90048-1033, USA

Paez, Jorge (Maromero) (Boxer)
233 Paulin Ave
Calexico, CA 92231-2615, USA

Paffrath, Amy (Actor)
c/o Scott Karp *The Syndicate*
10203 Santa Monica Blvd Fl 5
Los Angeles, CA 90067-6416, USA

Pagac, Fred (Athlete, Football Player)
1 Bills Dr
Orchard Park, NY 14127-2237, USA

Pagan, Dave (Athlete, Baseball Player)
504 10th Ave W
Nipawin, SK S0E 1E0, Canada

Pagan, Jeoffrey (Athlete, Football Player)

Pagan, Reo (Baseball Player)
Negro Baseball Leagues
280 Creekview Trl
Fayetteville, GA 30214-7230, USA

Page, Bettle (Model)
JL Swanson
PO Box 56176
Chicago, IL 60656-0132, USA

Page, Corey (Actor)
Agency for Performing Arts
9200 W Sunset Blvd Ste 900
Los Angeles, CA 90069-3604, USA

Page, David (Artist)
3724 Greenmount Ave
Baltimore, MD 21218-1843, USA

Page, Ellen (Actor)
c/o Kristina Sorensen *Vie Entertainment*
8409 Santa Monica Blvd
West Hollywood, CA 90069-4209, USA

Page, Erika (Actor)
Progressive Artists Agency
400 S Beverly Dr Ste 216
Beverly Hills, CA 90212-4404, USA

Page, Genevieve (Actor)
52 Rue de Vaugirard
Paris 75006, FRANCE

Page, Greg (Boxer)
Don King Promotions
968 Pinehurst Dr
Las Vegas, NV 89109-1569, USA

Page, Harrison (Actor)
S D B Partners
1801 Ave of Stars
#902
Los Angeles, CA 90067, USA

Page, Jimmy (Musician)
29 Melbury Rd.
Kensington
London W14 8AB, UNITED KINGDOM

Page, Kimberly (Actor)
c/o Staff Member *The Paradise Group*
PO Box 69451
West Hollywood, CA 90069-0451, USA

Page, Larry (Business Person)
Google Inc
1600 Amphitheatre Pkwy
Mountain View, CA 94043-1351, USA

Page, Michael (Misc)
PO Box 229
North Salem, NY 10560-0229, USA

Page, Mike (Athlete, Baseball Player)
599 Briarcliff Dr
Woodruff, SC 29388-2326, USA

Page, Murriel (Basketball Player)
Washington Mystics
601 F St NW
Mcl Center
Washington, DC 20004-1605, USA

Page, Pierre (Athlete, Coach, Hockey Player)
2000 E Gene Autry Way
Anaheim, CA 92806-6143, USA

Page, Rege-Jean (Actor)
c/o Paul Nelson *Mosaic Media Group*
407 N Maple Dr # 100
Beverly Hills, CA 90210-3818, USA

Page, Sam (Actor)
c/o Lena Roklin *Luber Roklin Management*
5815 W Sunset Blvd Ste 208
Los Angeles, CA 90028-6481, USA

Page, Solomon (Athlete, Football Player)
9302 Vista Cir
Irving, TX 75063-5060, USA

Page, Steven (Musician)
c/o Larry Webman *Paradigm*
140 Broadway Ste 2600
New York, NY 10005-1011, USA

Page, Tim (Journalist)
Washington Post
Editorial Dept
1150 15th St NW
Washington, DC 20071-0001, USA

Pageau, Paul (Athlete, Hockey Player)
102 Glen Hollow Dr
Stoney Creek, ON L8J 3R4, Canada

Pagel, Karl (Athlete, Baseball Player)
2698 N Ellis St
Chandler, AZ 85224-1777, USA

Pagel, Mike (Athlete, Football Player)
11981 Coopers Run
Strongsville, OH 44149-9260, USA

Paget, Debra (Actor)
411 Kari Ct
Houston, TX 77024-6804, USA

Pagett, Dana (Athlete, Basketball Player)
120 Yale Ln
Seal Beach, CA 90740-2522, USA

Pagett, Nicola (Actor)
22 Victoria Road
Mortlake
London SW14, UNITED KINGDOM (UK)

Paggi, Nicole (Actor)
c/o Staff Member *McGowan Management*
170 S Beverly Dr Ste 304
Beverly Hills, CA 90212-3000, USA

Paglia, Camile (Writer)
c/o Staff Member *Random House Publicity*
1745 Broadway Frnt 3
New York, NY 10019-4343, USA

Paglia, Camille (Writer)
University of the Arts
320 S Broad St
Humanities Dept
Philadelphia, PA 19102-4994, USA

Pagliarulo, Michael T (Mike) (Athlete, Baseball Player)
11 Fieldstone Dr
Winchester, MA 01890-3257, USA

Pagliei, Joe (Athlete, Football Player)
7 Pine Ridge Ct
Sewell, NJ 08080-3648, USA

Pagnozzi, Matt (Athlete, Baseball Player)
1710 W Park Ave
Chandler, AZ 85224-9002, USA

Pagnozzi, Thomas A (Tom) (Athlete, Baseball Player)
3288 E Piper Gin
Fayetteville, AR 72703-4394, USA

Pagnucco, Chris (Athlete, Football Player)
937 W Belden Ave
Chicago, IL 60614-3239, USA

Pahang (Misc)
Istana Abu Bakar
Pekan
Pahang, MALAYSIA

Pahlsson, Samuel (Athlete, Hockey Player)
9429 Tartan Ridge Blvd
Dublin, OH 43017-8924

Pahukoa, Jeff (Athlete, Football Player)
20191 Cape Coral Ln
Huntington Beach, CA 92646-8514, USA

Paich, David (Musician)
Fitzgerald-Hartley
34 N Palm St Ste 100
Ventura, CA 93001-2610, USA

Paiement, Rosaire (Athlete, Hockey Player)
3351 S Palm Aire Dr Apt 301
Pompano Beach, FL 33069-4254

Paiement, Wilf (Athlete, Hockey Player)
1064 Streambank Dr
Mississauga, ON L5H 3Z1, Canada

Paige, Elaine (Actor, Musician)
c/o Lisa Sharon Goldberg *Lisa Sharon Goldberg*
88 Leonard St Apt 607
New York, NY 10013-3495, USA

Paige, Janis (Actor)
1700 Rising Glen Rd
Los Angeles, CA 90069-1230, USA

Paige, Peter (Actor)
c/o Suzanne (Sue) Wohl *TalentWorks*
3500 W Olive Ave Ste 1400
Burbank, CA 91505-5512, USA

Paige, Tarah (Actor)
c/o Michael Henderson *Heresun Management*
4119 W Burbank Blvd
Burbank, CA 91505-2122, USA

Paik, Kun Woo (Musician)
Worldwide Artists
12 Rosebery
Thomton Heath
Surrey CR7 8PT, UNITED KINGDOM (UK)

Pailes, William A (Astronaut)
4725 S Saint George Ct
Springfield, MO 65810-2457, USA

Paille, Daniel (Athlete, Hockey Player)
c/o Pat Brisson *Creative Artists Agency (CAA)*
2000 Avenue of the Stars Ste 100
Los Angeles, CA 90067-4705, USA

Paille, Marcel (Athlete, Hockey Player)

Paine, Horner (Athlete, Football Player)
1105 W York Ave
Enid, OK 73703-7104, USA

Paine, John (Musician)
Bob Flick Productions
300 Vine St Ste 14
Seattle, WA 98121-1465, USA

Painter, John Mark (Musician)
Michael Dixon Mgmt
119 Pebble Creek Rd
Franklin, TN 37064-5525, USA

Painter, Lance (Athlete, Baseball Player)
2683 E Pinto Dr
Gilbert, AZ 85296-8934, USA

Painter, Vinston (Athlete, Football Player)
c/o Neil Schwartz *Schwartz & Feinsod*
4 Hillandale Rd
Rye Brook, NY 10573-1705, USA

Pain White Ts (Music Group)
c/o Ken Fermaglich *UTA Music*
142 W 57th St Fl 6
New York, NY 10019-3300, USA

Paisley, Brad (Musician)
c/o Bill Simmons *Fitzgerald Hartley Co (Nashville)*
1908 Wedgewood Ave
Nashville, TN 37212-3733, USA

Pak, Se Ri (Golfer)
8836 Elliotts Ct
Orlando, FL 32836-5027, USA

Pakeledinaz, Martin (Designer)
Gersh Agency
232 N Canon Dr
Beverly Hills, CA 90210-5302, USA

Paksas, Rolandus (Prime Minister)
President's Office
Gediminas 53
Vilnius 232026, LITHUANIA

Palacios, Rey (Athlete, Baseball Player)
183 Kings Gate S
Rochester, NY 14617-5439, USA

Palahniuk, Chuck (Writer)
c/o Edward Hibbert *Donadio & Olson*
157 E 86th St
New York, NY 10028-2175, USA

Palance, Holly (Actor)
2224 Linda Flora Dr
Los Angeles, CA 90077-1411, USA

Palast, Greg (Musician)

Palatella, Lou (Athlete, Football Player)
1532 Kennewick Dr
Sunnyvale, CA 94087-4158, USA

Palau, Doug (Producer)
c/o Staff Member *WME|IMG*
9601 Wilshire Blvd
Beverly Hills, CA 90210-5213, USA

Palau, Luis (Misc)
1500 NW 167th Pl
Beaverton, OR 97006-7342, USA

Palazzari, Doug (Athlete, Hockey Player)
616 Michigan Ave W
Gilbert, MN 55741-5136, USA

Palazzi, Togo (Athlete, Basketball Player)
84 Framingham Rd
Southborough, MA 01772-1268, USA

Paldridge, Curt (Athlete, Football Player)
2820 Country Club Ln
Dekalb, IL 60115-4922, USA

Palelei, Lonnie (Athlete, Football Player)
1808 SW Chief Cir
Blue Springs, MO 64015-5420, USA

Palepoi, Tenny (Athlete, Football Player)

Palermo, Olivia (Reality Star)
c/o Barbara Saint-Aime *Platform PR*
2666 N Beachwood Dr
Los Angeles, CA 90068-2308, USA

Palesh, Shirley (Athlete, Baseball Player)
1829 El Segundo Ave
Schofield, WI 54476-3928, USA

Paleta, Ludwika (Actor)
c/o Staff Member *Televisa*
Blvd Adolfo Lopez Mateos 232
Colonia San Angel INN
DF CP 01060, MEXICO

Paley, Albert R (Artist)
Paley Studio
25 N Washington St
Rochester, NY 14614-1110, USA

Paley, Grace (Misc)
PO Box 112
Thetford, VT 05074-0112

Palffy, Zigmund (Athlete, Hockey Player)
HK 36 Skalica Clementisova SO
Skalica, 909 01 Slovakia

Palias, Cecile (Actor)
P F D
Drury House
34-43 Russell St
London WC2B 5HA, UNITED KINGDOM (UK)

Palicki, Adrianne (Actor)
c/o Michael Sugar *Anonymous Content*
3532 Hayden Ave
Culver City, CA 90232-2413, USA

Palin, Bristol (Reality Star)
BSMP
711 H St Ste 620
Anchorage, AK 99501-3454, USA

Palin, Michael (Actor, Writer)
Prominent Palin Productions Ltd.
34 Tavistock Street
London WC2E 7PB, UK

Palin, Sarah (Politician)
1140 W Parks Hwy
Wasilla, AK 99654-6910, USA

Pall, Donn (Athlete, Baseball Player)
155 Wellington Dr
Bloomingdale, IL 60108-3012, USA

Pall, Gloria (Actor, Model)
Showgirl Press
12814 Victory Blvd
North Hollywood, CA 91606-3013

Pall, Olga (Skier)
Fahrenweg 28
Absam 06060, AUSTRIA

Palladino, Eric (Actor)
2119 Lyans Dr
La Canada Flintridge, CA 91011-1540, USA

Palladino, Erik (Actor)
c/o Leanne Coronel *Coronel Group*
1100 Glendon Ave Fl 17
Los Angeles, CA 90024-3588, USA

Palladino, Vincent (Misc)
National Assn of Postal Supervisors
1727 King St
Alexandria, VA 22314-2700, USA

Palladio, Sam (Actor, Musician)
c/o Brantley Brown *Authentic Talent & Literary Management*
3615 Eastham Dr # 650
Culver City, CA 90232-2410, USA

Palli, Anne-Marie (Golfer)
4510 N Alta Hacienda Dr
Phoenix, AZ 85018-2004, USA

Pallone, Dave (Athlete, Baseball Player)
4420 Dickason Ave Apt 1135
Dallas, TX 75219-6642, USA

Pallone Jr., Frank (Congressman, Politician)
237 Cannon Hob
Washington, DC 20515-0526, USA

Pally, Adam (Actor)
c/o Lewis Kay *Kovert Creative*
506 Santa Monica Blvd Ste 400
Santa Monica, CA 90401-2412, USA

Palm, Cortney (Actor)
c/o James Cole *Primary Wave Entertainment*
10850 Wilshire Blvd Fl 6
Los Angeles, CA 90024-4319, USA

Palmas, Giorgia (Actor, Model)

Palmateer, Mike (Athlete, Hockey Player)
30 Simmons Cres
Aurora, ON L4G 6B5, CANADA

Palmeiro, Orlando (Athlete, Baseball Player)
11991 SW 103rd Ter
Miami, FL 33186-2654, USA

Palmeiro, Rafael C (Athlete, Baseball Player)
5216 Reims Ct
Colleyville, TX 76034-5574, USA

Palmer, Alisa (Actor)
c/o Staff Member *Catch Up Agentur*
Gorzer Strasse 35a
Munchen 81669, Germany

Palmer, Amanda (Musician)
c/o Staff Member *High Road Touring*
751 Bridgeway Fl 2
Sausalito, CA 94965-2174, USA

Palmer, Ashlee (Athlete, Football Player)
c/o Drew Rosenhaus *Rosenhaus Sports Representation*
3921 Alton Rd # 440
Miami Beach, FL 33140-3852, USA

Palmer, Brad (Athlete, Hockey Player)
PO Box 544
Lake Cowichan, BC V0R 2G0, CANADA

Palmer, Carl (Musician)
Asia
9 Hillgate St
London W8 7SP, UNITED KINGDOM (UK)

Palmer, Carson (Athlete, Football Player, Heisman Trophy Winner)
c/o David Dunn *Athletes First*
23091 Mill Creek Dr
Laguna Hills, CA 92653-1258, USA

Palmer, C R (Business Person)
Rowan Companies
2800 Post Oak Blvd
Transco Tower
Houston, TX 77056-6100, USA

Palmer, David (Athlete, Baseball Player)
5090 Oak Nut Ct
Stone Mountain, GA 30087-3290, USA

Palmer, David (Athlete, Football Player)
527 Carlton Pl
Birmingham, AL 35214-1331, USA

Palmer, Dean (Athlete, Baseball Player)
3907 W Millers Bridge Rd
Tallahassee, FL 32312-1054, USA

Palmer, Geoffrey (Actor)
c/o Liz Nelson *Conway van Gelder Grant*
8-12 Broadwick St
London W1F 8HW, UNITED KINGDOM

Palmer, Geoffrey W R (Prime Minister)
63 Roxburgh St
Mount Victoria
Wellington, NEW ZEALAND

Palmer, Gery (Athlete, Football Player)
6411 E Irish Pl
Centennial, CO 80112-2404, USA

Palmer, Gregg (Actor)
36927 Atka Ct
Palmdale, CA 93552-5456

Palmer, Jesse (Athlete, Football Player, Reality Star)
26749 Wyatt Ln
Stevenson Ranch, CA 91381-1001, USA

Palmer, Jim (Athlete, Baseball Player)
4 Route 385
Catskill, NY 12414-5028, USA

Palmer, Keke (Actor)
c/o Staff Member *Laron Entertainment*
1880 Century Park E
Los Angeles, CA 90067-1600, USA

Palmer, Lowell (Athlete, Baseball Player)
PO Box 5253
El Dorado Hills, CA 95762-0005, USA

Palmer, Matt (Athlete, Baseball Player)
c/o Staff Member *Los Angeles Dodgers*
1000 Elysian Park Ave
Los Angeles, CA 90012, USA

Palmer, Mitch (Athlete, Football Player)
14420 Cypress Pt
Poway, CA 92064-6600, USA

Palmer, Nate (Athlete, Football Player)

Palmer, Patsy (Actor)
c/o Staff Member *International Artistes*
Holborn Hall - 4th Floor
London WC1V 7BD, UK

Palmer, Peter (Actor)
216 Kingsway Dr
Temple Terrace, FL 33617-4823, USA

Palmer, Ralph (Baseball Player)
Chicago American Giants
844 48th St SE
Grand Rapids, MI 49508-4718, USA

Palmer, Richard H (Athlete, Football Player)
14420 Cypress Pt
Poway, CA 92064-6600, USA

Palmer, Rob (Athlete, Hockey Player)
3812 Sepulveda Blvd Ste 310
Torrance, CA 90505-2481

Palmer, Sandra (Athlete, Golfer)
52 Hilton Head Dr
Rancho Mirage, CA 92270-1607, USA

Palmer, Scott (Athlete, Football Player)
7408 Lady Suzannes Ct
Austin, TX 78729-7793, USA

Palmer, Teresa (Actor)
c/o Robin Baum *Slate PR*
901 N Highland Ave
W Hollywood, CA 90038-2412, USA

Palmer, Walter (Athlete, Basketball Player)
87 South St
Rockport, MA 01966-1924, USA

Palmeri, Tara (Correspondent)
c/o Bradley Singer *WME|IMG (NY)*
11 Madison Ave Fl 18
New York, NY 10010-3669, USA

Palmieri, Eddie (Musician)
Berkeley Agency
1311 Spruce St
Berkeley, CA 94709-1434, USA

Palmieri, Jennifer (Writer)
c/o Keith Urbahn *Javelin*
203 S Union St Ste 200
Alexandria, VA 22314-3356, USA

Palmieri, Paul (Religious Leader)
Church of Jesus Christ
6th & Lincoln Sts
Monongahela, PA 15063, USA

Palminteri, Chazz (Actor)
Neighborhood Films
PO Box 622
Bedford, NY 10506-0622, USA

Palomeque, Lincoln (Actor)
c/o Staff Member *TV Caracol*
Calle 76 #11 - 35
Piso 10AA
Bogota DC 26484, COLOMBIA

Palomino, Carlos (Boxer)
14242 Burbank Blvd # 8
Sherman Oaks, CA 91401-4937, USA

Palone, Dave (Horse Racer)
100 Quarry Rd
Washington, PA 15301-9563, USA

Paltrow, Gwyneth (Actor)
Goop Inc
212 26th St Ste 206
Santa Monica, CA 90402-2524, USA

Paltrow, Jake (Director)
c/o John Lesher *WME|IMG*
9601 Wilshire Blvd
Beverly Hills, CA 90210-5213, USA

Palumba, Joe (Athlete, Football Player)
927 Old Garth Rd
Charlottesville, VA 22901-1937, USA

Paly, Bar (Actor)
c/o David Gardner *Artists First*
9465 Wilshire Blvd Ste 900
Beverly Hills, CA 90212-2608, USA

Palys, Stan (Athlete, Baseball Player)
448 Center St
Covington Township, PA 18444-7824, USA

Pamphile, Kevin (Athlete, Football Player)

Pampling, Rod (Golfer)
4709 Rangewood Dr
Flower Mound, TX 75028-1695, USA

Panabaker, Danielle (Actor)
c/o John Carrabino *John Carrabino Management*
5900 Wilshire Blvd Ste 740
Los Angeles, CA 90036-5032, USA

Panabaker, Kay (Actor)
c/o Lena Roklin *Luber Roklin Management*
5815 W Sunset Blvd Ste 208
Los Angeles, CA 90028-6481, USA

Panafieu, Bernard L A Cardinal (Religious Leader)
Archdiocese
14 Place du Colonel-Edon
Marseille Cedex 07 13284, FRANCE

Panagaris, Orianthi (Musician)
c/o Sterling McIlwaine *19 Entertainment*
401 Wilshire Blvd Ste 1070
Santa Monica, CA 90401-1428, USA

Pancake, Sam (Actor)
c/o Joel King *Pakula/King & Associates*
9229 W Sunset Blvd Ste 315
Los Angeles, CA 90069-3403, USA

Panch, Marvin (Race Car Driver)
1648 Taylor Rd # 406
Port Orange, FL 32128-6753, USA

Pancholy, Maulik (Actor)
c/o Staff Member *ROAR (LA)*
9701 Wilshire Blvd Fl 8
Beverly Hills, CA 90212-2008, USA

Panday, Basdeo (Prime Minister)
Premier's Office
Eric Williams Plaza
Port of Spain, TRINIDAD & TOBAGO

Pandolfo, Jay (Athlete, Hockey Player)
Pro-Athletes Management
3 Meadowcroft Rd
Burlington, MA 01803-1019, USA

Panettiere, Hayden (Actor)
c/o Emily Gerson Saines *Brookside Artists Management*
250 W 57th St Ste 1820
New York, NY 10107-1802, USA

Pang, Chris (Actor)
c/o Wendy Powell *Active Artists Management*
43/38 Manchester Ln
Melbourne VIC 3000, AUSTRALIA

Pang, Darren (Athlete, Hockey Player)
1009 Mississippi Ave Unit G
Saint Louis, MO 63104-2474

Pang, Qing (Figure Skater)
c/o Staff Member *Champions on Ice*
3500 American Blvd W Ste 190
Minneapolis, MN 55431-4431, USA

Panhofer, Walter (Musician)
Erdbergstr 35/9
Vienna 01030, AUSTRIA

Panic, Milan (Business Person, Prime Minister)
1050 Arden Rd
Pasadena, CA 91106-4004, USA

Panic at the Disco (Music Group)
c/o Fueled by Ramen
PO Box 1803
Tampa, FL 33601-1803, USA

Panichas, George A (Writer)
PO Box AB
College Park, MD 20741-3025, USA

Panisello, Stephanie (Actor)
c/o Micaela Hicks *Atlas Talent Agency*
8721 W Sunset Blvd Ste 205
Los Angeles, CA 90069-2272, USA

Panish, Morton B (Misc)
52 Baldwin Rd
Freeport, ME 04032-6485, USA

Panjabi, Archie (Actor)
c/o Angelique ONeil *Angelique ONeil Enterprises*
200 Riverside Blvd
Suite 401 at Trump Place
New York, NY 10069-0901, USA

Pankewicz, Greg (Athlete, Hockey Player)
2171 Cape Hatteras Dr Unit 5
Windsor, CO 80550-7258

Pankey, Irv (Athlete, Football Player)
348 Walker St
Aberdeen, MD 21001-3543, USA

Pankin, Stuart (Actor)
1288 Bienevenda Ave
Pacific Palisades, CA 90272, USA

Pankovits, Jim (Athlete, Baseball Player)
1400 Shucker Cir Apt 208
Mount Pleasant, SC 29464-4897, USA

Pankow, James (Musician)
3874 Puerco Canyon Rd
Malibu, CA 90265-4504, USA

Pankow, John (Actor)
Gersh Agency
232 N Canon Dr
Beverly Hills, CA 90210-5302, USA

Panos, Joe (Athlete, Football Player)
31010 Chequamegon Dr
Hartland, WI 53029-8560, USA

Pansino, Rosanna (Chef, Internet Star)
c/o Tess Finkle *Metro Public Relations*
8671 Wilshire Blvd # 208
Beverly Hills, CA 90211-2926, USA

Panteleev, Grigori (Athlete, Hockey Player)
5 Commonwealth Rd
Natick, MA 01760-1526

Panther, Jim (Athlete, Baseball Player)
7936 Tiger Palm Way
Fort Myers, FL 33966-6447, USA

Pantoja, Arnie (Actor)
c/o Julie Balfour *AKA Talent Agency*
325 N Larchmont Blvd
Los Angeles, CA 90004-3011, USA

Pantoliano, Joe (Actor)
c/o Devon Jackson *Trademark Talent*
5900 Wilshire Blvd Ste 710
Los Angeles, CA 90036-5019, USA

Panza dl Blumo, Giuseppe (Misc)
PO Box 3183
Lugano 06901, SWITZERLAND

Paola (Royalty)
Koninklijk Palais
Rue de Brederode
Brussels 01000, BELGIUM

Paolini, Christopher (Writer)
c/o Matthew Sugarman *Weintraub Tobin*
10250 Constellation Blvd Ste 2900
Los Angeles, CA 90067-6229, USA

Paolo, Connor (Actor)
c/o Michael Gagliardo *PMK/BNC Public Relations*
622 3rd Ave Fl 8
New York, NY 10017-6707, USA

Paolozzi, Eduardo L (President)
107 Dovehouse
London SW3 6JZ, UNITED KINGDOM (UK)

Paopao, Joe (Athlete, Football Player)
200 University Ave W
Waterloo, ON N2L 3G1, Canada

Papa, Greg (Athlete, Baseball Player)
11 San Andreas Dr
Danville, CA 94506-2035, USA

Papa, John (Athlete, Baseball Player)
275 Mary Ave
Stratford, CT 06614-5329, USA

Papa, Tom (Actor, Comedian)
c/o David (Dave) Becky *3 Arts Entertainment*
9460 Wilshire Blvd Fl 7
Beverly Hills, CA 90212-2713, USA

Papach, George (Athlete, Football Player)
5454 Hohman Ave
Hammond, IN 46320-1931, USA

Papadopoulos, Tassos (President)
Presidential Palace
5 Ioannis Ceridos St
Nicosia, CYPRUS

Papajohn, Michael (Actor)
c/o Penny Vizcarra *PV Public Relations*
121 N Almont Dr Apt 203
Beverly Hills, CA 90211-1860, USA

Papale, Vince (Athlete, Football Player)
2219 S 15th St
Philadelphia, PA 19145-3920, USA

Papa Roach (Music Group)
c/o Andrew Goodfriend *The Kirby Organization (TKO-NY)*
141 Halstead Ave PH
Mamaroneck, NY 10543-2607, USA

Papas, Irene (Actor)
38 Xenokratous St
Athens 106 76, GREECE

Papathanassiou, Aspassia (Actor)
38 Xenokratous St
Athens 106 76, GREECE

Papazian, Marty (Actor)
c/o Lin Bickelmann *Encore Artists Management*
3815 W Olive Ave Ste 101
Burbank, CA 91505-4674, USA

Papazian, Robert (Producer)
c/o Gene Schwam *Hanson & Schwam Public Relations*
9350 Wilshire Blvd Ste 315
Beverly Hills, CA 90212-3206, USA

Pape, Ken (Athlete, Baseball Player)
73 Roseheart
San Antonio, TX 78259-2264, USA

Papelbon, Jonathan (Athlete, Baseball Player)
1200 Tices Ln Ste 101
East Brunswick, NJ 08816-1335, USA

Papi, Stan (Athlete, Baseball Player)
10673 N Inverary Ln
Fresno, CA 93730-3584, USA

Papis, Max (Race Car Driver)
Max Papis Racing
112 Byers Creek Rd
Mooresville, NC 28117-4376, USA

Papit, Johnny (Athlete, Football Player)
29 Sellers Ave
Lexington, VA 24450-1930, USA

Papoose (Musician)

Pappalardo, Salvatore Cardinal (Religious Leader)
Arcibescovado
Via Matteo Bonello 2
Los Angeles, CA 90134-0001, ITALY

Pappas, Brenden (Athlete, Golfer)
5770 SW 42nd Pl
Ocala, FL 34474-9516, USA

Pappas, Deane (Athlete, Golfer)
4409 Stoney Dr
Jonesboro, AR 72404-9571, USA

Pappas, Erik (Athlete, Baseball Player)
10248 S Seeley Ave
Chicago, IL 60643-2631, USA

Pappin, James J (Jim) (Athlete, Hockey Player)
44827 Oro Grande Cir
Indian Wells, CA 92210-7412, USA

Paquette, Craig (Athlete, Baseball Player)
16615 S 27th Ave # 5
Phoenix, AZ 85045-2202, USA

Paquin, Anna (Actor)
c/o JoAnne Colonna *Brillstein Entertainment Partners*
9150 Wilshire Blvd Ste 350
Beverly Hills, CA 90212-3453, USA

Paquin, Kit (Actor)
c/o Staff Member *Trilogy Talent*
13425 Ventura Blvd Fl 2
Sherman Oaks, CA 91423-3974, USA

Paradis, Vanessa (Actor, Model, Musician)
7760 Woodrow Wilson Dr
Los Angeles, CA 90046-1212, USA

Paradise, Bob (Athlete, Hockey Player, Olympic Athlete)
1303 Beechwood Pl
Saint Paul, MN 55116-2202, USA

Paradise, Dick (Athlete, Hockey Player)

Parado, Alejandra (Actor)
c/o Gabriel Blanco *Gabriel Blanco Iglesias (Mexico)*
Rio Balsas 35-32
Colonia Cuauhtemoc
DF 06500, Mexico

Parahia, Murray (Musician)
I M G Artists
420 W 45th St
New York, NY 10036-3501, USA

Paramore (Music Group)
c/o Ken Weinstein *Big Hassle Media*
40 Exchange Pl Ste 1900
New York, NY 10005-2714, USA

Parazaider, Walter (Musician)
Front Line Mgmt
8900 Wilshire Blvd Ste 300
Beverly Hills, CA 90211-1959, USA

Parazynski, Scott E (Astronaut)
2015 Wroxton Rd
Houston, TX 77005-1654, USA

Parcells, Bill (Athlete, Coach, Football Coach, Football Player)
c/o Staff Member *Miami Dolphins*
7500 SW 30th St
Davie, FL 33314-1020, USA

Parchem, Aaron (Athlete, Figure Skater, Olympic Athlete)
2128 Bordeaux St
West Bloomfield, MI 48323-3013, USA

Pardee, Arthur B (Misc)
3304 Great Meadow Rd
Dedham, MA 02026-4077, USA

Pardes, Herbert (Misc)
15 Claremont Ave # 93
New York, NY 10027-6809, USA

Pardo, Al (Athlete, Baseball Player)
908 Hillary Cir
Lutz, FL 33548-5052, USA

Pardo, JD (Actor)
c/o Nicki Fioravante *Viewpoint Inc*
8820 Wilshire Blvd Ste 220
Beverly Hills, CA 90211-2622, USA

Pardo, Jimmy (Comedian)
c/o Bruce Smith *OmniPop Talent Group*
4605 Lankershim Blvd Ste 201
Toluca Lake, CA 91602-1874, USA

Pardue, Kip (Actor)
c/o Staff Member *Main Title Entertainment*
8383 Wilshire Blvd Ste 408
Beverly Hills, CA 90211-2435, USA

Pardus, Dan (Race Car Driver)
Jim & Judie Motorsports
4345 Motorsports Dr SW
Concord, NC 28027-8977, USA

Pardy, Adam (Athlete, Hockey Player)
Octagon Sports Management
66 Slater St 23rd Fl
Attn Larry Kelly
Ottawa, ON K1P 5H1, Canada

Pare, Jessica (Actor)
c/o Dani De Lio *Creative Drive Artists*
20 Minowan Miikan Lane
Toronto, ON M6J 0E5, CANADA

Pare, Michael (Actor)
c/o John Ferriter *The Alternative Company*
2980 N Beverly Glen Cir Ste 302
Los Angeles, CA 90077-1703, USA

Paredes, Marisa (Actor)
Alsira Maroto Garcia
Gran Via 63
#3 Izda
Madrid 28013, SPAIN

Parekh, Kal (Actor)
c/o Jenn Lederer *AFST Management*
350 W 43rd St Apt 32G
New York, NY 10036-6476, USA

Parent, Bernie (Athlete, Hockey Player)
Offices of Bernie Parent
125 N Route 73
West Berlin, NJ 08091-9225, USA

Parent, Mark (Athlete, Baseball Player)
1959 Winsome Ln
Adams, TN 37010-8961, USA

Parent, Monique (Actor, Model)
PO Box 3458
Ventura, CA 93006-3458, USA

Parenteau, Pierre-Aiexandr (Athlete, Hockey Player)
158 Rue de Bresolettes
Boucherville, QC J4B 6M8, Canada

Paretsky, Sara N (Writer)
5831 S Blackstone Ave
Chicago, IL 60637-1855, USA

Pargo, Jannero (Athlete, Basketball Player)
3280 Timberwood Ln
Riverwoods, IL 60015-2418, USA

Parham, Gus (Athlete, Football Player)
Taylor Made Office Systems
4294 El Camino Real
Los Altos, CA 94022-1048, USA

Parilla, Jennifer (Athlete, Gymnast, Olympic Athlete)
21822 Rushford Dr
Lake Forest, CA 92630-6503, USA

Parilla, Lana (Actor)
c/o Liza Anderson *Anderson Group Public Relations*
8060 Melrose Ave Fl 4
Los Angeles, CA 90046-7038, USA

Parillaud, Anne (Actor)
c/o Elisabeth Tanner *Time-Art*
8 rue Danielle Casanova
Paris 75002, FRANCE

Paris, Bubba (Athlete, Football Player)
8474 Vine Ln
Tracy, CA 95304-8111, USA

Paris, Clarke (Race Car Driver)
Crave Racing
PO Box 972
Harvey, LA 70059-0972, USA

Paris, Kelly (Athlete, Baseball Player)
1515 Redwood Cir
Thousand Oaks, CA 91360-6336, USA

Paris, Twila (Musician, Songwriter, Writer)
Proper Mgmt
PO Box 68
Franklin, TN 37065-0068, USA

Parise, Louis (Misc)
National Maritime Union
1125 15th St NW
Washington, DC 20005-2702, USA

Parise, Robert L (Basketball Player)
20 Stonybrook Rd Apt 1
Framingham, MA 01702-5997, USA

Parise, Zach (Athlete, Hockey Player)
c/o Wade Arnott *Newport Sports Management*
201 City Centre Dr
Suite 400
Mississauga, ON L58 2T4, CANADA

Parish, Robert (Athlete, Basketball Player)
18730 Peninsula Club Dr
Cornelius, NC 28031-5114, USA

Parisot, Dean (Director)
c/o Staff Member *3 Arts Entertainment*
9460 Wilshire Blvd Fl 7
Beverly Hills, CA 90212-2713, USA

Parisse, Annie (Actor)
c/o Jill McGrath *Door24*
115 W 29th St Rm 1102
New York, NY 10001-5106, USA

Parizeau, Michel (Athlete, Hockey Player)
250 Rue Chauveau
Drummondville, QC J2C 6L2, Canada

Park, Alan (Actor)
c/o Lorne Perlmutar *Diamondfield Entertainment*
124 Portland St
Toronto, ON M5V 2N5, Canada

Park, Alyssa (Musician)
Columbia Artists Mgmt Inc
165 W 57th St
New York, NY 10019-2201, USA

Park, Chan Ho (Athlete, Baseball Player)
c/o Team Member *New York Yankees*
161st St & River Ave
Yankee Stadium
Bronx, NY 10451, USA

Park, D Bradford (Brad) (Athlete, Coach, Hockey Player)
100 Legends Way Ste 250
Boston, MA 02114-1390, USA

Park, Ernie (Athlete, Football Player)
3160 Private Road 1101
Clyde, TX 79510-4905, USA

Park, Grace (Actor)
c/o Tyman Stewart *Characters Talent Agency*
200-1505 2nd Ave W
Vancouver, BC V6H 3Y4, CANADA

Park, Jim (Athlete, Hockey Player)
33 Braeburn Dr
Thornhill, ON L3T 4V2, Canada

Park, Joon (Actor)
c/o Susan Yoo *Susan Yoo*
Prefers to be contacted via telephone
Los Angeles, CA, USA

Park, Linda (Actor)
c/o Ro Diamond *SDB Partners Inc*
315 S Beverly Dr Ste 411
Beverly Hills, CA 90212-4301, USA

Park, Maximo (Musician)
c/o Kirk Sommer *WME/IMG*
9601 Wilshire Blvd
Beverly Hills, CA 90210-5213, USA

Park, Megan (Actor)
c/o Dominique Appel *Imprint PR*
6121 W Sunset Blvd
Neuehouse
Los Angeles, CA 90028-6442, USA

Park, Nick (Animator, Director)
c/o Staff Member *Aardman Animations*
Gas Ferry Road
Bristol BS1 6UN, UNITED KINGDOM

Park, Patrick (Musician)
c/o Staff Member *Red Light Management*
5800 Bristol Pkwy Ste 400
Culver City, CA 90230-6898, USA

Park, Ray (Actor)
c/o Jason Priluck *Priluck Company*
24045 Sylvan St
Woodland Hills, CA 91367-1248, USA

Park, Richard (Athlete, Hockey Player)
6416 Vista Pacifica
Rancho Palos Verdes, CA 90275-5896

Park, Soo Joo (Actor, Model)
c/o Kylee Kilgore *LUNA*
116 Nassau St # 615
New York, NY 10038-2402, USA

Park, Steve (Race Car Driver)
261 Indian Trl
Mooresville, NC 28117-8968, USA

Parke, Evan Dexter (Actor)
c/o Staff Member *McCabe Group*
3211 Cahuenga Blvd W Ste 104
Los Angeles, CA 90068-1372, USA

Parkening, Christopher (Musician)
IMG Artists
420 W 45th St
New York, NY 10036-3501, USA

Parker, Alan (Director)
c/o Staff Member *Independent Talent Group*
40 Whitfield St
London W1T 2RH, UNITED KINGDOM

Parker, Andrea (Actor)
c/o Dan Baron *Agency for the Performing Arts (APA)*
405 S Beverly Dr Ste 500
Beverly Hills, CA 90212-4425, USA

Parker, Anthony (Basketball Player)
Orlando Magic
8701 Maitland Summit Blvd
Waterhouse Center
Orlando, FL 32810-5915, USA

Parker, Anthony (Athlete, Football Player)
1054 E Geneva Dr
Tempe, AZ 85282-3805, USA

Parker, Bob (Skier)
408 Camino Don Miguel
Santa Fe, NM 87505-5948, USA

Parker, Brant J (Cartoonist)
901 Glenwood Blvd
Waynesboro, VA 22980-3409, USA

Parker, Caryl Mack (Musician)
Scream Marketing
PO Box 120053
Nashville, TN 37212-0053, USA

Parker, Chris (Actor)
Elstree Centre
Clarendon Road
Borehamwood
Herts WD6 1JF, UK

Parker, Christian (Athlete, Baseball Player)
10101 Mesa Arriba Ave NE
Albuquerque, NM 87111-4962, USA

Parker, Christopher (Actor)
Shepherd Mgmt
13 Radnor Walk
London SW3 4BP, UNITED KINGDOM (UK)

Parker, Clay (Athlete, Baseball Player)
6614 Brickston St
Hixson, TN 37343-2593, USA

Parker, Corey (Actor)
c/o Marc Epstein *Marc Epstein Entertainment*
108 Breeze Ave
Venice, CA 90291-3360, USA

Parker, Craig (Actor)
c/o Joe Smith *ICM Partners*
10250 Constellation Blvd Fl 7
Los Angeles, CA 90067-6207, USA

Parker, Daniel T (Actor)
c/o Paul Greenstone *Paul Greenstone Entertainment*
1400 California Ave Apt 201
Santa Monica, CA 90403-4395, USA

Parker, Dave (Athlete, Baseball Player)
4038 Oak Tree Ct
Loveland, OH 45140-1090, USA

Parker, DeVante (Athlete, Football Player)

Parker, Franklin (Writer)
Western Carolina University
Education & Psychology Dept
Cullowhee, NC 28723, USA

Parker, George M (Misc)
Glass Workers Union
1440 S Byme Road
Toledo, OH 43614, USA

Parker, Georgie (Actor)
c/o Staff Member *Morrissey Management*
16 Princess Ave
Rosebery
Sydney NSW 02018, AUSTRALIA

Parker, Hank Jr (Race Car Driver)
MRO
5555 Concord Pkwy S Ste 405
Concord, NC 28027-4622, USA

Parker, Jabari (Athlete, Basketball Player)
c/o Arn Tellem *Wasserman Media Group*
10960 Wilshire Blvd Ste 1200
Los Angeles, CA 90024-3714, USA

Parker, Jack Jr (Horse Racer)
38 Lea Ct
Frederica, DE 19946-1985, USA

Parker, Jack Sr (Horse Racer)
127 Roosevelt Ave
Westwood, NJ 07675-2316, USA

Parker, Jameson (Actor)
1604 N Vista St
Los Angeles, CA 90046-2818, USA

Parker, Jeff (Athlete, Hockey Player)
2018 Riviera Ave S
Lakeland, MN 55043-9419

Parker, Lara (Actor)
PO Box 1254
Topanga, CA 90290-1254, USA

Parker, Larry (Athlete, Football Player)
4207 Boulder Pass Dr
Bakersfield, CA 93311-2833, USA

Parker, Maceo (Musician)
109 W Newark Ave
Wildwood, NJ 08260-1038

Parker, Mary-Louise (Actor)
c/o Jennifer Allen *Viewpoint Inc*
8820 Wilshire Blvd Ste 220
Beverly Hills, CA 90211-2622, USA

Parker, Molly (Actor)
c/o Murray Gibson *Red Management*
415 Esplanade W Box 3
North Vancouver, BC V7M 1A6, CANADA

Parker, Nate (Actor, Producer)
c/o Staff Member *Tiny Giant Entertainment*
1640 5th St Ste 118
Santa Monica, CA 90401-3384, USA

Parker, Nathaniel (Actor)
c/o Staff Member *Independent Talent Group*
40 Whitfield St
London W1T 2RH, UNITED KINGDOM

Parker, Nicole (Actor)
c/o Mark Rousso *Industry Entertainment Partners*
955 Carrillo Dr Ste 300
Los Angeles, CA 90048-5400, USA

Parker, Nicole Ari (Actor)
c/o Maani Golesorkhi *Bluestone Entertainment*
9000 W Sunset Blvd Ste 700
Los Angeles, CA 90069-5807, USA

Parker, Orlando (Athlete, Football Player)
4402 Chatham Pl
Montgomery, AL 36108-4902, USA

Parker, Paula Jai (Actor)
c/o Marie Y LeMelle *Platinum Star Public Relations*
343 Pioneer Dr Unit 1705
Glendale, CA 91203-2740, USA

Parker, Preston (Athlete, Football Player)

Parker, Rick (Athlete, Baseball Player)
2641 NE 74th St
Kansas City, MO 64119-5349, USA

Parker, Riddick (Athlete, Football Player)
11226 NE 68th St Apt 212-B
Kirkland, WA 98033-7181, USA

Parker, Robert (Astronaut)
NASA
2101 Nasa Pkwy Spc Johnsoncenter
Houston, TX 77058-3696, USA

Parker, Robert (Athlete, Basketball Player)
7947 S Chappel Ave
Chicago, IL 60617-1052, USA

Parker, Robert A (Astronaut)
5316 Godbey Dr
La Canada Flintridge, CA 91011-1833, USA

Parker, Ron (Athlete, Football Player)

Parker, Sarah Jessica (Actor, Producer)
c/o Staff Member *Pretty Matches Productions*
1100 Avenue of the Americas
G14, Suite 39
New York, NY 10036-6712, USA

Parker, Scott (Athlete, Hockey Player)
1950 W Wolfensberger Ct
Castle Rock, CO 80109-9699

Parker, Sean (Business Person)
45 W 18th St Fl 7
New York, NY 10011-4655, USA

Parker, T Jefferson (Writer)
c/o Staff Member *Trident Media Group LLC*
41 Madison Ave Fl 36
New York, NY 10010-2257, USA

Parker, Tony (Athlete, Basketball Player)
1210 Sloan St
Greensboro, NC 27401-3442, USA

Parker, Trey (Actor, Animator, Director, Producer)
311 N Rockingham Ave
Los Angeles, CA 90049-2635, USA

Parker, Vaughn (Athlete, Football Player)
2500 6th Ave Unit 107
San Diego, CA 92103-6629, USA

Parker, Wes (Athlete, Baseball Player)
Los Angeles Dodgers
1000 Elysian Park Ave
Attn: Community Relations Dept
Los Angeles, CA 90090-1112, USA

Parker, Willie (Athlete, Football Player)
9327 Kai Dr
Beach City, TX 77523-2333, USA

Parker-Bowles, Camilla (Royalty)
Clarence House
Stable Yard Gate
London SW1, UK

Parker Jr, Ray (Musician)
c/o Staff Member *Performers of the World*
5657 Wilshire Blvd Ste 280
Los Angeles, CA 90036-3755, USA

Parkey, Cody (Athlete, Football Player)

Parkhill, Barry (Athlete, Basketball Player)
3429 Cesford Grange
Keswick, VA 22947-9127, USA

Parkhurst, Heather Elizabeth (Actor)
8491 W Sunset Blvd # 440
West Hollywood, CA 90069-1911, USA

Parkinson, Bradford W (Business Person)
2780 Volley Cir
Meadow Vista, CA 95722-9530, USA

Parkinson, Katherine (Actor)
c/o Sarah McCormick *Curtis Brown Ltd*
28-29 Hay Market
Hay Market House
London SW1Y 4SP, UNITED KINGDOM

Parks, Catherine (Actor)
7141 Santa Monica Blvd Apt 528
West Hollywood, CA 90046-3471, USA

Parks, Cherokee (Athlete, Basketball Player)
5331 Kadena Garden Ct
North Las Vegas, NV 89031-6605, USA

Parks, Chris (Athlete, Wrestler)
c/o Staff Member *TNA Wrestling*
209 10th Ave S Ste 302
Nashville, TN 37203-0730, USA

Parks, Dallas (Athlete, Baseball Player)
3353 Pittman Grove Church Rd
Raeford, NC 28376-6012, USA

Parks, David W (Dave) (Athlete, Football Player)
6629 Southpoint Dr
Dallas, TX 75248-2221, USA

Parks, Derek (Athlete, Baseball Player)
7828 Day Creek Blvd
Act 1214
Rancho Cucamonga, CA 91739-8569, USA

Parks, Greg (Athlete, Hockey Player)
400 Campbell Rd 2nd Fl
ST ALBERT STEEL
St. Albert, AB T8N 0R8, Canada

Parks, Maxie (Athlete, Track Athlete)
4545 E Norwich Ave
Fresno, CA 93726-2726, USA

Parks, Phaedra (Attorney, Reality Star)
3070 Montclair Cir SE
Smyrna, GA 30080-3797, USA

Parks, Suzan-Lori (Actor, Writer)
c/o Staff Member *Creative Artists Agency (CAA)*
2000 Avenue of the Stars Ste 100
Los Angeles, CA 90067-4705, USA

Parks-Young, Barbara (Athlete, Baseball Player)
5078 Edinboro Ln
Wilmington, NC 28409-8518, USA

Parlavecchio, Chet (Athlete, Football Player)
211 Brooklake Rd
Florham Park, NJ 07932-2214, USA

Parlen, Megan (Actor)
c/o Staff Member *Cunningham Escott Slevin & Doherty (CESD)*
10635 Santa Monica Blvd Ste 130
Los Angeles, CA 90025-8306, USA

Parlow, Cindy (Athlete, Olympic Athlete, Soccer Player)
2611 English Hill Dr
Murfreesboro, TN 37130-1433, USA

Parmalee (Music Group)
c/o Kevin Neal *WME (Nashville)*
1201 Demonbreun St
Nashville, TN 37203-3140, USA

Parmalee, Bernie (Athlete, Football Player)
3160 Rock Manor Way
Buford, GA 30519-7698, USA

Parmele, Jalen (Athlete, Football Player)
c/o Bruce Tollner *REP 1 Sports Group*
80 Technology Dr
Irvine, CA 92618-2301, USA

Parmenter, Charles S (Misc)
Indiana University
Chemistry Dept
Bloomington, IN 47405, USA

Parmenter, Skip (Athlete, Football Player)
34881 Seagrass Plantation Ln34881
Seagrass Plantation Ln
Dagsboro, DE 19939-3398, USA

Parnell, Bobby (Athlete, Baseball Player)
2265 Barger Rd
Salisbury, NC 28146-5049, USA

Parnell, Chris (Actor)
2281 Moreno Dr
Los Angeles, CA 90039-3049, USA

Parnell, Lee Roy (Musician)
PO Box 23451
Nashville, TN 37202-3451, USA

Parnell, Peter (Writer)
c/o Staff Member *United Talent Agency (UTA)*
9336 Civic Center Dr
Beverly Hills, CA 90210-3604, USA

Parnevik, Jesper (Athlete, Golfer)
17553 SE Conch Bar Ave
Jupiter, FL 33469-1709, USA

Parodi, Starr (Musician)
c/o Staff Member *Evolution Music Partners*
1680 Vine St Ste 500
Hollywood, CA 90028-8800, USA

Paronto, Chad (Athlete, Baseball Player)
617 Benedict Rd
Pittsfield, MA 01201-2899, USA

Parque, jim (Athlete, Baseball Player)
3142 Halverson Way
Roseville, CA 95661-4038, USA

Parque, Jim (Athlete, Baseball Player, Olympic Athlete)
4109 Crystal Ridge Dr SE
Puyallup, WA 98372-5214, USA

Parr, Robert G (Misc)
616 Beechtree Ct
Chapel Hill, NC 27514-6702, USA

Parr, Todd (Writer)
c/o Staff Member *Suppertime Entertainment*
21300 Oxnard St Ste 100
Woodland Hills, CA 91367-5016, USA

Parra, Derek (Athlete, Olympic Athlete, Speed Skater)
US Speedskating
1895 E Oak Bend Dr
Draper, UT 84020-5510, USA

Parra, Manny (Athlete, Baseball Player)
c/o Joe Urbon *Creative Artists Agency (CAA)*
405 Lexington Ave Fl 19
New York, NY 10174-1800, USA

Parrack, Jim (Actor)
c/o Jamie Harhay Skinner *Baker Winokur Ryder Public Relations*
9100 Wilshire Blvd
W Tower #500
Beverly Hills, CA 90212-3415, USA

Parrella, John (Athlete, Football Player)
9401 Thornwood Dr
Lincoln, NE 68512-9401, USA

Parrett, Jeff (Athlete, Baseball Player)
722 Seattle Dr
Lexington, KY 40503-2127, USA

Parrett, William (Business Person)
Deloitte Touche Tohmatsu
433 Country Club Rd W
New Canaan, CT 06840-3604, USA

Parrilla, Lana (Actor)
c/o David Lillard *Industry Entertainment Partners*
955 Carrillo Dr Ste 300
Los Angeles, CA 90048-5400, USA

Parriott, James (Director)
c/o Jamie (James) Mandelbaum *Jackoway Tyerman Wertheimer Austen Mandelbaum Morris & Klein*
1925 Century Park E Fl 22
Los Angeles, CA 90067-2701, USA

Parris, Fred (Musician)
Paramount Entertainment
PO Box 12
Far Hills, NJ 07931-0012, USA

Parris, Gary (Athlete, Football Player)
5170 9th St
Vero Beach, FL 32966-2841, USA

Parris, Jonathan (Athlete, Baseball Player)
610 Madison Gdns
Old Bridge, NJ 08857-2832, USA

Parris, Steve (Athlete, Baseball Player)
2340 W Toledo Pl
Chandler, AZ 85224-4132, USA

Parris, Teyonah (Actor)
c/o Jenny Tversky *Shelter PR*
928 Broadway Ste 505
New York, NY 10010-8143, USA

Parrish, Bernie (Athlete, Football Player)
1419 Wilder Dr
Springfield, MO 65804-2565, USA

Parrish, Hunter (Actor)
c/o Lainie Sorkin Becky *Management 360*
9111 Wilshire Blvd
Beverly Hills, CA 90210-5508, USA

Parrish, Janel (Actor)
c/o Nicole Perez-Krueger *PMK/BNC Public Relations*
1840 Century Park E Ste 1400
Los Angeles, CA 90067-2115, USA

Parrish, John (Athlete, Baseball Player)
1110 Logan Ln
Narvon, PA 17555-9579, USA

Parrish, Lance M (Athlete, Baseball Player)
1750 Stony Creek Dr
Rochester, MI 48307-1785, USA

Parrish, Larry A (Athlete, Baseball Player, Coach)
1269 Blakely Hwy
Fort Gaines, GA 39851-4029, USA

Parrish, Lemar (Athlete, Football Player)
52 Brittany Way
Palmetto, GA 30268-8575, USA

Parrish, Mark (Athlete, Hockey Player, Olympic Athlete)
15525 51st Ave N
Minneapolis, MN 55446-2220, USA

Parro, Dave (Athlete, Hockey Player)
820 3rd Ave
Hershey, PA 17033-1903

Parros, George (Athlete, Hockey Player)
1105 Manhattan Ave
Hermosa Beach, CA 90254-3726, USA

Parros, Peter (Actor)
c/o Peter Kluge *Impact Artist Group LLC (LA)*
244 N California St
Fl 1
Burbank, CA 91505-3505, USA

Parrott, Mike (Athlete, Baseball Player)
PO Box 1264
Lyons, CO 80540-1264, USA

Parry, Craig (Golfer)
5139 Latrobe Dr
Windermere, FL 34786-8916, USA

Parry, Edward (Athlete, Basketball Player)
6152 Benoit Rd
Clay, MI 48001-3302, USA

Parry, Ken (Actor)
c/o Linda Kremer *Billy Marsh Drama Ltd*
20 Garrick St
London WC2E 9BT, UK

Parry-Okeden, Blair (Misc)
Cox Enterprises
6205 Peachtree Dunwoody Rd
Atlanta, GA 30328-4524, USA

Parseghian, Gregory (Business Person)
Federal Home Loan Mortgage
8200 Jones Branch Dr
McLean, VA 22102-3107, USA

Parshall, George W (Misc)
2401 Pennsylvania Ave Apt 714
Wilmington, DE 19806-1410, USA

Parsons, Alan (Musician)
c/o Marina Anderson *Media Hound PR*
PO Box 261939
Encino, CA 91426-1939, USA

Parsons, Bill (Athlete, Baseball Player)
322 Karen Ave Unit 3901
Las Vegas, NV 89109-0453, USA

Parsons, Bob (Athlete, Football Player)
1292 Thorndale Ln
Lake Zurich, IL 60047-2795, USA

Parsons, Casey (Athlete, Baseball Player)
17214 E Galactica Ct
Greenacres, WA 99016-7766, USA

Parsons, Craig (Athlete, Hockey Player)
30 Yonge St
Toronto, ON M5E 1X8, CANADA

Parsons, Estelle (Actor)
924 W End Ave Apt T5
New York, NY 10025-3543, USA

Parsons, Jim (Actor)
c/o Marsha McManus *Principal Entertainment*
9255 W Sunset Blvd Ste 500
Los Angeles, CA 90069-3301, USA

Parsons, Johnny (Race Car Driver)
Brian Bollinger CMG
10500 Crosspoint Blvd
Indianapolis, IN 46256-3331, USA

Parsons, Karyn (Actor)

Parsons, Lilah (DJ, Model, Television Host)
c/o Max Clifford *Max Clifford Associates*
Moss House
15-16 Brooks Mews
Mayfair, London W1K 4DS, UNITED KINGDOM

Parsons, Nathan (Actor)
c/o Siri Garber *Platform PR*
2666 N Beachwood Dr
Los Angeles, CA 90068-2308, USA

Parsons, Nicholas (Actor)
Susan Shaper
174/178 N Gower St
London NW1 2NB, UNITED KINGDOM (UK)

Parsons, Phil (Athlete, Race Car Driver)
18801 Coveside Ln
Cornelius, NC 28031-5250, USA

Parsons, Tom (Athlete, Baseball Player)
7106 Lorraine Ave NW
North Canton, OH 44720-8832, USA

Parsons-Zipay, Suzanne (Athlete, Baseball Player)
2310 Englewood Rd
Englewood, FL 34223-6333, USA

Partee, Dennis (Athlete, Football Player)
103 Denise Dr
Marshall, TX 75672-8403, USA

Parten, Ty (Athlete, Football Player)
41121 N Prosperity Way
Anthem, AZ 85086-1510, USA

Partlow, Hope (Musician)
c/o Staff Member *Virgin Records (NY)*
150 5th Ave Fl 7
New York, NY 10011-4372, USA

Parton, Dolly (Actor, Musician, Songwriter)
Dolly Parton Foundation
2700 Dollywood Parks Blvd
Pigeon Forge, TN 37863-4102, USA

Parton, Stella (Musician)
PO Box 120871
Nashville, TN 37212-0871, USA

Partridge, Rick (Athlete, Football Player)
707 Reeder Rd
Paramus, NJ 07652-3721, USA

PARTYNEXTDOOR (Musician)
c/o James Rubin *WME/IMG (NY)*
11 Madison Ave Fl 18
New York, NY 10010-3669, USA

Parvanov, Georgi (President)
President's Office
2 Dondukov Blvd
Sofia 01123, BULGARIA

Pasanella, Marco (Designer)
Pasanella Co
45 W 18th St
New York, NY 10011-4609, USA

Pasarell, Charles (Tennis Player)
78200 Miles Ave
Indian Wells, CA 92210-6803, USA

Pascal, Adam (Actor)
c/o Staff Member *Paradigm*
8942 Wilshire Blvd
Beverly Hills, CA 90211-1908, USA

Pascal, Amy (Business Person, Producer)
10960 Wilshire Blvd Fl 5
Los Angeles, CA 90024-3708, USA

Pascal, Pedro (Actor)
c/o Jason Weinberg *Untitled Entertainment*
350 S Beverly Dr Ste 200
Beverly Hills, CA 90212-4819, USA

Paschal, Doug (Athlete, Football Player)
4600 Coburn Ct
Charlotte, NC 28277-2553, USA

Paschall, Bill (Athlete, Baseball Player)
7926 Windspray Dr
Summerfield, NC 27358-9715, USA

Paschall, Jim (Race Car Driver)
RR 2 Box 450
Denton, NC 27239, USA

Paschke, Melanie (Athlete, Track Athlete)
Asseweg 2
Braunschweig 38124, GERMANY

Pasco, Richard (Actor)
Michael Whitehall
125 Gloucester Road
London SW7 4TE, UNITED KINGDOM (UK)

Pascoal, Hermeto (Musician)
Brasil Universo Prod
RVN Vitor Guisard 209
Rio de Janerio 21832, BRAZIL

Pascoe, Bear (Athlete, Football Player)

Pascrell Jr., Bill (Congressman, Politician)
2370 Rayburn Hob
Washington, DC 20515-0906, USA

Pascual, Camilo (Athlete, Baseball Player)
7741 SW 32nd St
Miami, FL 33155-2611, USA

Pascual, Luis (Director)
Theatre de l'Europe
1 Place Paul Claudel
Paris 75006, FRANCE

Pascucci, Val (Athlete, Baseball Player)
11163 James Pl
Cerritos, CA 90703-6450, USA

Pasdar, Adrian (Actor)
c/o Peter Varano *AVO Talent Agency*
5670 Wilshire Blvd Ste 1930
Los Angeles, CA 90036-5603, USA

Pashnick, Larry (Athlete, Baseball Player)
506 Highland St
Wyandotte, MI 48192-2433, USA

Pasian, Karina (Musician)
c/o Staff Member *Island Def Jam Group*
825 8th Ave Fl 28
New York, NY 10019-7416, USA

Pasik, Mario (Actor)
c/o Staff Member *Telefe (Argentina)*
Pavon 2444
Buenos Aires C1248AAT, ARGENTINA

Pasillas, Jose (Musician)
c/o Staff Member *ArtistDirect*
9046 Lindblade St
Culver City, CA 90232-2513, USA

Pasin, Dave (Athlete)
787 Holly Oak Dr
Palo Alto, CA 94303-4143

Paskai, Laszio Cardinal (Religious Leader)
Uri Utca 62
Budapest 01014, HUNGARY

Paslawski, Greg (Athlete, Hockey Player)
10 Topping Ln
Des Peres, MO 63131-1901, USA

Pasley, Kevin (Athlete, Baseball Player)
2701 Lancaster Dr
Sun City Center, FL 33573-6517, USA

Pasmore, E J Victor (Artist)
Dar Gamri
Gudja, MALTA

Pasmore, Scott (Sportscaster)
c/o Terry Bross *Turn 2 Sports Management LLC*
PO Box 27345
Scottsdale, AZ 85255-0139, USA

Pasqua, Dan (Athlete, Baseball Player)
10423 Capistrano
Moreno Vally, CA 92557-3036, USA

Pasquale, Edward (Athlete, Hockey Player)
101 Marietta St NW Ste 1900
Atlanta, GA 30303-2771, USA

Pasquale, Steven (Actor)
c/o Emily Gerson Saines *Brookside Artists Management*
250 W 57th St Ste 1820
New York, NY 10107-1802, USA

Pasqualini, Tony (Actor)
c/o Sandra Joseph *SLJ Management*
833 N Edinburgh Ave PH 11
Los Angeles, CA 90046-6999, USA

Pasqualino, Luke (Actor)
c/o Brantley Brown *Authentic Talent & Literary Management*
3615 Eastham Dr # 650
Culver City, CA 90232-2410, USA

Pasqualoni, Paul (Coach, Football Coach)
Syracuse University
Athletic Ofc Bldg
Syracuse, NY 13244-0001, USA

Pasquesi, Anthony (Athlete, Football Player)
463 N Clubview Ct
Addison, IL 60101-2998, USA

Pasquesi, David (Actor)
c/o Mark Teitelbaum *Teitelbaum Artists Group*
8840 Wilshire Blvd Fl 3
Beverly Hills, CA 90211-2606, USA

Pasquin, John (Director)
c/o Staff Member *Paradox Productions*
801 Tarcuto Way
Los Angeles, CA 90077-3216, USA

Pass, Patrick (Athlete, Football Player)
4 Spruce Pond Rd
Franklin, MA 02038-2500, USA

Passaglia, Martin (Athlete, Basketball Player)
7377 Capay Ave
Orland, CA 95963-9687, USA

Passante, Brandi (Actor)
c/o David Weintraub *DWE Talent*
Prefers to be contacted by email or phone.
Los Angeles, CA 90069, USA

Passarelli, Pasquale (Wrestler)
Ander Froschlache 23
Munster 04400, GERMANY

Passenger (Musician)
c/o Ari Millar *ie Music Ltd*
111 Frithville Gardens
Shepherds Bush
London W12 7JQ, UNITED KINGDOM (UK)

Passion Pit (Music Group)
c/o Staff Member *Foundations Artist Management*
55 Prospect St
Brooklyn, NY 11201-1497, USA

Passmore, Christi (Race Car Driver)
GAP Roofing
Rt. 3
Box 6870
Pryor, OK 74361, USA

Passmore, John A (Misc)
6 Jansz Crescent
Manuka, ACT 02603, AUSTRALIA

Passmore, Matt (Actor)
c/o Christopher Burbidge *Fourward*
10250 Constellation Blvd Ste 2710
Los Angeles, CA 90067-6227, USA

Passos, Rosa (Musician)
c/o Staff Member *Concord Music Group, Inc*
900 N Rohlwing Rd
Itasca, IL 60143-1161, USA

Pastan, Linda (Writer)
5610 Wisconsin Ave Apt 1102
Chevy Chase, MD 20815-4419, USA

Pasternak, Harley (Fitness Expert)
c/o Carmen Bonnici *Pacific Artists Management*
112 3rd Ave E Suite 210
Vancouver, BC V5T 1C8, CANADA

Pasternak, Michael (Actor)
c/o Craig Wyckoff *Epstein Wyckoff Corsa Ross (LA)*
11350 Ventura Blvd Ste 100
Studio City, CA 91604-3140, USA

Pasternak, Reagan (Actor)
c/o Staff Member *Noble Caplan Abrams*
1260 Yonge St Fl 2
Toronto, ON M4T 1W5, CANADA

Pastore, Frank (Athlete, Baseball Player)
1542 Francis Way
Upland, CA 91786-2353, USA

Pastore, Vincent (Actor)
PO Box 207
Bronx, NY 10464-0207, USA

Pastorini Jr, Darite A (Dan) (Athlete, Football Player)
1316 Stanford St
Houston, TX 77019-4327, USA

Pastornicky, Cliff (Athlete, Baseball Player)
4815 50th Ave W
Bradenton, FL 34210-4907, USA

Pastrana, Arango Andres (President)
Palacio de Narino
Plaza de Bolivar
Carrera 8A
Bogota, DE, COLUMBIA

Pastrana, Travis (Athlete)
Familie
1545 Faraday Ave
Carlsbad, CA 92008-7449, USA

Pat, Dunsmore (Athlete, Football Player)
21301 Whispering Dr
Lenexa, KS 66220-3212, USA

Pataki, Governor George E (Politician)
Chadbourne & Parke, LLP
1017 Route 9D
Garrison, NY 10524-3636, USA

Pataky, Elsa (Actor)
c/o Celine Kamina *UBBA*
6 rue de Braque
Paris 75003, FRANCE

Patat, Frederic (Misc)
Faculte de Medecine
2 Bis Blvd Tonnelle
Tours Cedex 37032, FRANCE

Patchett, Ann (Writer)
Parnassus Books
3900 Hillsboro Pike Ste 14
Nashville, TN 37215-2714, USA

Pate, Bob (Athlete, Baseball Player)
43724 Sentry Ln
Lancaster, CA 93536-5864, USA

Pate, Cynthia (Beauty Pageant Winner)
Future Productions
7907 Stafford Trl
Savage, MN 55378-4308, USA

Pate, Jerry (Golfer)
5 Hyde Park Rd
Pensacola, FL 32503-5830, USA

Pate, Rupert (Athlete, Football Player)
428 Shadowbrook Dr
Burlington, NC 27215-4775, USA

Pate, Steve (Golfer)
32023 Wallington Ct
Westlake Village, CA 91361-4136, USA

Patek, Freddie (Athlete, Baseball Player)
5408 NE Wedgewood Ln
LN
Lees Summit, MO 64064-1220, USA

Patel, Dev (Actor)
c/o Grace Clissold *Curtis Brown Ltd*
28-29 Hay Market
Hay Market House
London SW1Y 4SP, UNITED KINGDOM

Patera, Dennis (Athlete, Football Player)
61535 S Highway 97 Apt 9512
Bend, OR 97702-2154, USA

Patera, George (Athlete, Football Player)
7305 172nd St SW
Edmonds, WA 98026-5121, USA

Patera, John A (Jack) (Athlete, Coach, Football Coach, Football Player)
82 Osprey Dr
Cle Elum, WA 98922, USA

Patera, Ken (Athlete, Olympic Athlete, Weightlifter)
6932 Stratford Draw
Saint Paul, MN 55125-2413, USA

Patera, Pavel (Athlete, Hockey Player)
175 Kellogg Blvd W
Xcel Enegy Arena
Saint Paul, MN 55102-1206, USA

Paterra, Greg (Athlete, Football Player)
305 Douglas Ave
Elizabeth, PA 15037-1724, USA

Paterra, Herb (Athlete, Football Player)
3696 Woodmonte Dr
Rochester, MI 48306-4799, USA

Paterson, Bill (Actor)
Kerry Gardner
15 Kensington High St
London W8 5NP, UNITED KINGDOM (UK)

Paterson, Joe (Athlete, Hockey Player)
49 Sullivan Pl
Lake George, NY 12845-4334

Paterson, Joe (Athlete, Hockey Player)
Adirondack Phantoms
1 Civic Center Plz
Glens Falls, NY 12801-4532

Paterson, Katherine (Writer)
70 Wildersburg Cmn
Barre, VT 05641-9761, USA

Paterson, Rick (Athlete, Hockey Player)
2695 E Katella Ave
Anaheim, CA 92806-5904

Patey, Doug (Athlete, Hockey Player)
4177 Garnetwood Chase
Mississauga, ON L4W 2H2, Canada

Patey, Larry (Athlete, Hockey Player)
2713 Autumn Run Ct
Wildwood, MO 63005-7001

Pathon, Jerome (Athlete, Football Player)
4827 Eagles Watch Ln
Indianapolis, IN 46254-9531, USA

Patinkin, Mandy (Actor, Musician)
535 W 110th St Apt 12CE
New York, NY 10025-2086, USA

Patitz, Tatjana (Model)
c/o Gordon Rael *JV Entertainment*
5455 Wilshire Blvd Ste 2114
Los Angeles, CA 90036-4290, USA

Patrese, Ricardo (Race Car Driver)
Via Umberto 1
Padova 35100, ITALY

Patric, Jason (Actor, Producer)
c/o Michelle Bega *Rogers & Cowan*
1840 Century Park E Fl 18
Los Angeles, CA 90067-2101, USA

Patrick, Bronswell (Athlete, Baseball Player)
3202 Morton Ln
Greenville, NC 27834-4930, USA

Patrick, Craig (Athlete, Coach, Hockey Player)
113 Royston Rd
Pittsburgh, PA 15238-2311, USA

Patrick, Danica (Race Car Driver)
Danica Racing
12985 N 119th St
Scottsdale, AZ 85259-2735, USA

Patrick, Frank (Athlete, Football Player)
5689 SW 98th St
Denton, NE 68339-3346, USA

Patrick, Glenn (Athlete, Hockey Player)
14 Gordon Ave
Dallas, PA 18612-1113

Patrick, Ian (Actor)
c/o Monique Moss *Integrated PR*
9025 Wilshire Blvd Ste 400
Beverly Hills, CA 90211-1828, USA

Patrick, James (Athlete, Hockey Player)
Buffalo Sabres
1 Seymour H Knox III Plz Ste 1
Buffalo, NY 14203-3096

Patrick, James (Athlete, Hockey Player)
5024 Red Tail Run
Buffalo, NY 14221-4176

Patrick, John (Writer)
PO Box 2386 Fortuna Mill Estate
Charlotte Amalie, VI 00801, USA

Patrick, Marcus (Actor)
c/o Staff Member *Gar Lester Agency*
11026 Ventura Blvd Ste 10
Studio City, CA 91604-3598, USA

Patrick, Nicholas J M (Astronaut)
10811 Oak Creek St
Houston, TX 77024-3016, USA

Patrick, Pat (Misc)
Patrick Racing
8431 Green Town Road
#400
Indianapolis, IN 46234, USA

Patrick, Richard (Musician)
c/o Jamie Talbot *Sanctuary Artist Management*
8750 Wilshire Blvd Ste 200
Beverly Hills, CA 90211-2707, USA

Patrick, Robert (Actor, Producer)
c/o Leanne Coronel *Coronel Group*
1100 Glendon Ave Fl 17
Los Angeles, CA 90024-3588, USA

Patrick, Robert (Race Car Driver)
Patrick Racing
PO Box 3366
College Station
Fredericksburg, VA 22402-3366, USA

Patrick, Steve (Athlete, Hockey Player)
Patrick Realty Ltd
2003 Portage Ave
Winnipeg, MB R3J 0K3, Canada

Patrick, Tera (Adult Film Star)
c/o Jonathan Lipman *Identity One*
90 -96 Brewery Road
N7 9NT
London N7 9NT, UNITED KINGDOM

Patrick, Thomas M (Business Person)
Peoples Energy Corp
130 E Randolph St
Chicago, IL 60601-6207, USA

Patridge, Audrina (Actor, Reality Star)
c/o Kelsey Hertel *S/W PR Shop*
584 N Larchmont Blvd # B
Los Angeles, CA 90004-1306, USA

Patten, Joel (Athlete, Football Player)
13415 Marble Rock Dr
Chantilly, VA 20151-2482, USA

Patterson, Bob (Athlete, Baseball Player)
1093 7th Street Blvd SE
Hickory, NC 28602-4342, USA

Patterson, Carly (Athlete, Gymnast, Olympic Athlete)
PO Box 1280
Angel Fire, NM 87710-1280, USA

Patterson, Colin (Athlete, Hockey Player)
128-2100 13th St S
Cranbrook, BC V1C 7J5, Canada

Patterson, Cordarrelle (Athlete, Football Player)
c/o Joby Branion *Vanguard Sports Group*
23091 Mill Creek Dr
Laguna Hills, CA 92653-1258, USA

Patterson, Corey (Athlete, Baseball Player)
1115 Gordon Combs Rd NW
Marietta, GA 30064-1225, USA

Patterson, Danny (Athlete, Baseball Player)
13944 E Yucca St
Scottsdale, AZ 85259-4638, USA

Patterson, Daryl (Athlete, Baseball Player)
20145 Tollhouse Rd
Clovis, CA 93619-9760, USA

Patterson, Dave (Athlete, Baseball Player)
8425 Evanston Ave
Raytown, MO 64138-3346, USA

Patterson, Dennis (Athlete, Hockey Player)
903 Chase Way Blvd
Auburn Hills, MI 48326-3879

Patterson, Don (Athlete, Football Player)
1558 Halisport Lake Dr NW
Kennesaw, GA 30152-4072, USA

Patterson, Elvis V (Athlete, Football Player)
3939 Alberta St
Houston, TX 77021-4009, USA

Patterson, Gary (Cartoonist)
Patterson International
25208 Malibu Rd
Malibu, CA 90265-4635, USA

Patterson, Gil (Athlete, Baseball Player)
16124 Pebblebrook Dr
Tampa, FL 33624-1035, USA

Patterson, James (Business Person, Writer)
James Patterson Entertainment
710 S Ocean Blvd
Palm Beach, FL 33480-4813, USA

Patterson, Jarrod (Athlete, Baseball Player)
405 6th St N
Clanton, AL 35045-2823, USA

Patterson, Jeff (Athlete, Baseball Player)
292 Barnes Rd
Tustin, CA 92782-3748, USA

Patterson, John (Athlete, Baseball Player)
2659 E Jade Pl
Chandler, AZ 85286-2697, USA

Patterson, John (Athlete, Baseball Player)
2709 Country Club Dr
Orange, TX 77630-2142, USA

Patterson, Katerine (Writer)
70 Wildersburg Cmn
Barre, VT 05641-9761, USA

Patterson, Ken (Athlete, Baseball Player)
4921 N County Road 1147
Midland, TX 79705-9611, USA

Patterson, Lorna (Actor)
23852 Pacific Coast Hwy # 355
Malibu, CA 90265-4876, USA

Patterson, Marne (Actor)
c/o Matthew Lesher *Insight*
5358 Melrose Ave # 200W
Los Angeles, CA 90038-5117, USA

Patterson, Marnette (Actor)
c/o Matthew Lesher *Insight*
5358 Melrose Ave # 200W
Los Angeles, CA 90038-5117, USA

Patterson, Mike (Athlete, Baseball Player)
19306 Chamblee Ave
Cerritos, CA 90703-6751, USA

Patterson, Mike (Athlete, Football Player)

Patterson, Percival J (Prime Minister)
Prime Minister's Office
1 Devon Road
PO Box 272
Kingston 6, JAMAICA

Patterson, Reggie (Athlete, Baseball Player)
PO Box 401
Bessemer, AL 35021, USA

Patterson, Richard North (Writer)
c/o Fred Hill *Hill Nadell Literary Agency*
6442 Santa Monica Blvd Ste 201
Los Angeles, CA 90038-1530, USA

Patterson, Ross (Actor)
c/o Harris Hartman *Sloane, Offer, Weber and Dern*
10100 Santa Monica Blvd Ste 750
Los Angeles, CA 90067-4101, USA

Patterson, Scott (Actor)
c/o Gary Mantoosh *Baker Winokur Ryder Public Relations*
9100 Wilshire Blvd
W Tower #500
Beverly Hills, CA 90212-3415, USA

Patterson, Scott (Athlete, Baseball Player)
409 W Washington St Apt C
Freeburg, IL 62243-1335, USA

Patterson, Todd (Race Car Driver)
Todd Racing
PO Box 338
920 Industrial Rd.
Augusta, KS 67010-0338, USA

Patterson, Willie (Baseball Player)
New York Cubans
409 Tuscaloosa Ave SW Apt 7
Birmingham, AL 35211-1457, USA

Patterson, Worthy (Athlete, Basketball Player)
2091 Kerwood Ave
Los Angeles, CA 90025-6006, USA

Pattillo, Linda (Correspondent)
Cable News Network
820 1st St NE Ste 1000
News Dept
Washington, DC 20002-4363, USA

Pattin, Marty (Athlete, Baseball Player)
3401 Sweetgrass Ct
Lawrence, KS 66049-4245, USA

Pattinson, Robert (Actor)
c/o Nick Frenkel *3 Arts Entertainment*
9460 Wilshire Blvd Fl 7
Beverly Hills, CA 90212-2713, USA

Pattison, Jim (Business Person)
Jim Pattison Group, The
1067 Cordova St W Suite 1800
Vancouver, BC V6C 1C7, Canada

Pattison, Mark (Athlete, Football Player)
3828 48th Ave NE
Seattle, WA 98105-5227, USA

Patton, Candice (Actor)

Patton, Donovan (Actor)
c/o Staff Member *Glasser/Black Management*
283 Cedarhurst Ave
Cedarhurst, NY 11516-1671, USA

Patton, Eric (Athlete, Football Player)
23732 San Esteban Dr
Mission Viejo, CA 92691-3346, USA

Patton, Marvcus (Athlete, Football Player)
12994 Wyckland Dr
Clifton, VA 20124-2053, USA

Patton, Mel (Athlete, Olympic Athlete, Track Athlete)
2312 Via Del Aquacate
Fallbrook, CA 92028-9697, USA

Patton, Melvin (Mel) (Athlete, Track Athlete)
17200 Goldenwest St UNIT 227
Huntingtn Bch, CA 92647-9501, USA

Patton, Paula (Actor, Director)
c/o Oren Segal *Management Production Entertainment (MPE)*
9229 W Sunset Blvd Ste 301
W Hollywood, CA 90069-3417, USA

Patton, Quinton (Athlete, Football Player)
c/o Kevin Poston *Deal LLC*
28025 S Harwich Dr
Farmington Hills, MI 48334-4259, USA

Patton, Sean (Actor)
c/o Dave Rath *Generate Management*
8750 Wilshire Blvd Ste 200
Beverly Hills, CA 90211-2707, USA

Patton, Tom (Athlete, Baseball Player)
577 Daisy Dr
New Holland, PA 17557-8708, USA

Patton, Troy (Athlete, Baseball Player)
c/o Staff Member *Baltimore Orioles*
333 W Camden St Ste 1
Baltimore, MD 21201-2476, USA

Patton, Virginia (Actor)
2205 Melrose Ave
Ann Arbor, MI 48104-4069, USA

Patton, Will (Actor)
c/o Kate Edwards *Grand View Management*
578 Washington Blvd # 688
Marina Del Rey, CA 90292-5442, USA

Patty, J Edward (Budge) (Tennis Player)
La Mame
14 Ave de Jurigoz
Lausanne 01006, SWITZERLAND

Patty, Sandi (Musician)
5701 NW 163rd Ter
Edmond, OK 73013-9435, USA

Patu, Saul (Athlete, Football Player)
10234 Renton Ave S
Seattle, WA 98178-2347, USA

Patulski, Walter G (Walt) (Athlete, Football Player)
420 Kimber Rd
Syracuse, NY 13224-1836, USA

Patzaichin, Ivan (Athlete)
SC Sportiv Unirea Tricolor
Soseaua Stefan Cel Mare 9
Bucharest, ROMANIA

Pauk, Gyorgy (Musician)
27 Armitage Road
London NW11, UNITED KINGDOM (UK)

Paul, Aaron (Actor)
c/o Jennifer Allen *Viewpoint Inc*
8820 Wilshire Blvd Ste 220
Beverly Hills, CA 90211-2622, USA

Paul, Adrian (Actor, Director, Producer)
c/o Staff Member *Filmblips*
2911-4968 Yonge St
North York, ON M2N 7G9, CANADA

Paul, Alan (Music Group, Musician)
Columbia/CBS Records
1801 Century Park W
Los Angeles, CA 90067-6409, USA

Paul, Alexandra (Actor)
8475 Brier Dr
Los Angeles, CA 90046-1907, USA

Paul, Chris (Athlete, Basketball Player)
9111 Memorial Dr
Houston, TX 77024-5814, USA

Paul, Christi (Correspondent)
Cable News Network
1050 Techwood Dr NW
News Dept
Atlanta, GA 30318-5695, USA

Paul, Don Michael (Actor, Director)

Paul, Emily (Actor)
c/o Simon Millar *Rumble Media*
1620 Broadway Ste C
Santa Monica, CA 90404-2777, USA

Paul, Henry (Music Group, Musician)
Vector Mgmt
1607 17th Ave S
Nashville, TN 37212-2812, USA

Paul, Jake (Internet Star)
c/o Carolyn Moneta *WME|IMG*
9601 Wilshire Blvd
Beverly Hills, CA 90210-5213, USA

Paul, Jarrad (Actor)
c/o Michael Lasker *Mosaic Media Group*
407 N Maple Dr # 100
Beverly Hills, CA 90210-3818, USA

Paul, John Michael (Actor)

Paul, Josh (Athlete, Baseball Player)
28751 Windover St
Wesley Chapel, FL 33545-4378, USA

Paul, Logan (Internet Star)
c/o Gary Binkow *Studio71*
8383 Wilshire Blvd Ste 1050
Beverly Hills, CA 90211-2415, USA

Paul, Markus (Athlete, Football Player)
PO Box 423041
Kissimmee, FL 34742-3041, USA

Paul, Mike (Athlete, Baseball Player)
5121 N Circulo Sobrio
Tucson, AZ 85718-6037, USA

Paul, Rand (Politician)
PO Box 72598
Newport, KY 41072-0598, USA

Paul, Robert (Figure Skater)
10675 Rochester Ave
Los Angeles, CA 90024-5009, USA

Paul, Ron (Politician)
c/o Andrew Stuart *Stuart Agency, The*
1410 Broadway Fl 23
New York, NY 10018-5023, USA

Paul, Sean (Actor, Musician)
c/o Jeff Epstein *M.A.G./Universal Attractions*
15 W 36th St Fl 8
New York, NY 10018-7927, USA

Paul, Steven (Producer)
c/o Staff Member *Crystal Sky Pictures*
10203 Santa Monica Blvd Fl 5
Los Angeles, CA 90067-6416, USA

Paul, Whitney (Athlete, Football Player)
6802 Thornwild Rd
Missouri City, TX 77489-2649, USA

Paul, Wolfgang (Soccer Player)
Postfach 1324
Olsberg-Bigge 59939, GERMANY

Paul, Xavier (Athlete, Baseball Player)
2637 5th St
Slidell, LA 70458-4105, USA

Paula, Alejandro F (Jandi) (Prime Minister)
Primier's Office
Fort Amsterdam 17
Willemstad, NETHERLANDS ANTILLES

Paulauskas, Arturas (President)
President's Office
Gediminas 53
Vilnius 232026, LITHUANIA

Paulette, Pauley (Actor)
c/o Stephen Jaffe *Jaffe & Company Strategic Media*
9663 Santa Monica Blvd # 663
Beverly Hills, CA 90210-4303, USA

Pauley, David (Athlete, Baseball Player)
19839 N 45th Ave
Glendale, AZ 85308-7389, USA

Pauley, Jane (Journalist)
c/o Wayne Kabak *WSK Management*
1350 Avenue Of The Americas Fl 2
New York, NY 10019-4703, USA

Paulin, Scott (Actor)
c/o Staff Member *Artists & Representatives (Stone Manners Salners)*
6100 Wilshire Blvd Ste 1500
Los Angeles, CA 90048-5110, USA

Paulino, Felipe (Athlete, Baseball Player)
2400 Business Center Dr Apt 312
Pearland, TX 77584-2494, USA

Paulino, Ronny (Athlete, Baseball Player)
129 Cardinal Cir
Pittsburgh, PA 15237-1067, USA

Paul Jr, John (Race Car Driver)
44 Musdogee Rd.
Atlanta, GA 30305, USA

Paulk, Charlie (Athlete, Basketball Player)
5750 Friars Rd Apt 102
San Diego, CA 92110-1833, USA

Paulk, Jeff (Athlete, Football Player)
7751 S Bonarden Ln
Tempe, AZ 85284-1569, USA

Paulo (DJ)
c/o Staff Member *Diva Central Inc*
7510 W Sunset Blvd # 1445
Los Angeles, CA 90046-3408, USA

Paulsen, Erik (Congressman, Politician)
127 Cannon Hob
Washington, DC 20515-0904, USA

Paulsen, Logan (Athlete, Football Player)

Paulson, Brandon (Athlete, Olympic Athlete, Wrestler)
9062 Collins Dr NW
Anoka, MN 55303-7208, USA

Paulson, Carl (Golfer)
137 Royal Creek Dr
Lexington, SC 29072-7099, USA

Paulson, Dainard (Athlete, Football Player)
700 W Goodlander Rd
Selah, WA 98942-8740, USA

Paulson, Dennis (Golfer)
2795 Dove Tail Dr
San Marcos, CA 92078-0932, USA

Paulson, John (Business Person)
Paulson & CO
590 Madison Ave Fl 29
New York, NY 10022-2524, USA

Paulson, Richard L (Business Person)
Potlatch Corp
601 W Riverside Ave
Spokane, WA 99201-0621, USA

Paulson, Sarah (Actor)
c/o Alla Plotkin *ID Public Relations (NY)*
40 Wall St Fl 51
New York, NY 10005-1385, USA

Paultz, Billy (Athlete, Basketball Player)
1941 Waters Edge Ln
Seabrook, TX 77586-2599, USA

Paulusma, Polly (Musician)
c/o Staff Member *Paradigm (Monterey)*
404 W Franklin St
Monterey, CA 93940-2303, USA

Paup, Bryce E (Athlete, Football Player)
4300 Oak Ridge Cir
De Pere, WI 54115-8327, USA

Pausini, Laura (Musician)
c/o Staff Member *Creative Artists Agency (CAA)*
2000 Avenue of the Stars Ste 100
Los Angeles, CA 90067-4705, USA

Pavan, Marisa (Actor)
4 Allee des Brouillards
Paris 75018, FRANCE

Pavano, Carl (Athlete, Baseball Player)
120 Senate Ln
Fairfield, CT 06824-2082, USA

Pavelich, Mark (Athlete, Hockey Player, Olympic Athlete)
19 E Norwood Shores
Lutsen, MN 55612, USA

Pavelich, Marty (Athlete, Hockey Player)
PO Box 160448
Big Sky, MT 59716-0448

Pavelich, Matt (Athlete, Hockey Player)
3485 Everts Ave
Windsor, ON N9E 2V9, CANADA

Pavelka, Jake (Reality Star)
c/o Susan Haber *Haber Entertainment*
434 S Canon Dr Apt 204
Beverly Hills, CA 90212-4501, USA

Pavelski, Joe (Athlete, Hockey Player)
1486 Hicks Ave
San Jose, CA 95125-3821, USA

Paver, Michelle (Writer)
ILRM LLC
186 Bickenhall Mansions
London W1U 6BX, UNITED KINGDOM

Pavese, Jim (Athlete, Hockey Player)
65 Whittier Dr
Kings Park, NY 11754-2339

Pavia, Joe (Horse Racer)
1600 SW 3rd St
Pompano Beach, FL 33069-3102, USA

Pavin, Corey (Golfer)
3100 Harvard Ct
Plano, TX 75093-3450, USA

Pavlas, David (Dave) (Athlete, Baseball Player)
2825 Keenan Dr
Tyler, TX 75701-3706, USA

Pavletic, Viaiko (President)
Presidential Palace
Pantovcak 241
Zagreb 10000, CROATIA

Pavletich, Don (Athlete, Baseball Player)
13645 Adelaide Ln
Brookfield, WI 53005-4965, USA

Pavlick, Greg (Athlete, Baseball Player)
936 Pinellas Bavwav
S Unit TH8
Saint Petersburg, FL 33715-2158, USA

Pavlik, Kelly (Boxer)
Top Rank Inc
3908 Howard Hughes Pkwy #580
Las Vegas, NV 89109, USA

Pavlik, Roger (Athlete, Baseball Player)
622 Beaver Bend Rd
Houston, TX 77037-2004, USA

Pavlovic, Aleksandar (Basketball Player)
Utah Jazz
301 W South Temple
Delta Center
Salt Lake City, UT 84101-1219, USA

Pawelczyk, James A Dr (Astronaut)
2047 Pine Cliff Rd
State College, PA 16801-2405, USA

Pawelczyk, James A (Jim) (Astronaut)
NASA
2101 Nasa Pkwy Spc Johnsoncenter
Houston, TX 77058-3696, USA

Pawlenty, Tim (Politician)
4117 Countrvview Dr
Saint Paul, MN 55123-3948, USA

Pawloski, Stan (Athlete, Baseball Player)
11318 Shannondell Dr
Norristown, PA 19403-5601, USA

Pawlowski, John (Athlete, Baseball Player)
257 Mill Branch Way
North Augusta, SC 29860-8622, USA

Pawuk, Mark (Race Car Driver)
PO Box 535
Richfield, OH 44286-0535, USA

Paxon, L William (Bill) (Misc)
Akin Gump Strauss Hauer Feld
1333 New Hampshire Ave NW Ste 400
Washington, DC 20036-1564, USA

Paxson, Jim (Athlete, Basketball Player)
8500 N Sendero Tres M # M
Paradise Valley, AZ 85253-8116, USA

Paxson, Jim (Athlete, Basketball Player)
3225 Southdale Dr Apt 1
Dayton, OH 45409-1130, USA

Paxson, John (Athlete, Basketball Player, Misc)
125 Boardman Ct
Lake Bluff, IL 60044-2454, USA

Paxson, Melanie (Actor)

Paxton, Mike (Athlete, Baseball Player)
1145 S Indian Wells Dr
Collierville, TN 38017-3667, USA

Paxton, Sara (Actor)
c/o Alyx Carr *42West*
600 3rd Ave Fl 23
New York, NY 10016-1914, USA

Paxton, Tom (Music Group, Musician, Songwriter, Writer)
Fleming Tamulevich Assoc
733 N Main St
Ann Arbor, MI 48104-1030, USA

Payette, Jean (Athlete, Hockey Player)
512 Bathurst Ave
Ottawa, ON K1G 0X5, Canada

Payette, Julie (Astronaut)
Space Agency
12175 Shenandoah Rd
Middletown, CA 95461-7707, USA

Paymer, David (Actor)
c/o Matt Shelton *Stride Management*
750 N San Vicente Blvd # 800W
W Hollywood, CA 90069-5788, USA

Payne, Alexander (Actor, Director, Producer)
Ad Hominem
506 Santa Monica Blvd Ste 400
Santa Monica, CA 90401-2412, USA

Payne, Allen (Actor)
c/o Staff Member *Harrison Stokes*
8730 W Sunset Blvd Ste 270
West Hollywood, CA 90069-2247, USA

Payne, Barbara (Athlete, Baseball Player)
10603 Gainsborough Ct
Bakersfield, CA 93312-7042, USA

Payne, Bruce (Actor)
c/o Nigel Mikoski *Connekt Creative*
136-1020 Mainland St
Vancouver, BC V6B 2T5, CANADA

Payne, Davis (Athlete, Hockey Player)
16406 Wilson Creek Ct
Chesterfield, MO 63005-4566

Payne, Dougie (Musician)
Wildlife Entertainment
21 Heathmans Road
London SW6 4TJ, UNITED KINGDOM (UK)

Payne, Freda (Music Group, Musician)
c/o Staff Member *Diva Central Inc*
7510 W Sunset Blvd # 1445
Los Angeles, CA 90046-3408, USA

Payne, Greg (Model)
c/o Staff Member *Why Not Model Agency*
via Zenale 9
Milano 20123, Italy

Payne, Julie (Actor)
c/o Staff Member *Pakula/King & Associates*
9229 W Sunset Blvd Ste 315
Los Angeles, CA 90069-3403, USA

Payne, Kenny (Athlete, Basketball Player)
1968 General Warfield Way
Lexington, KY 40505-4836, USA

Payne, Kherington (Actor)
c/o Staff Member *Luber Roklin Management*
5815 W Sunset Blvd Ste 208
Los Angeles, CA 90028-6481, USA

Payne, Liam (Musician)
c/o Richard Griffiths *Modest! Management*
91A Peterborough Rd
London SW6 3BU, UNITED KINGDOM

Payne, Rod (Athlete, Football Player)
9622 Stonemasters Dr
Loveland, OH 45140-6209, USA

Payne, Seth (Athlete, Football Player)
5004 Chestnut St
Bellaire, TX 77401-3412, USA

Payne, Steve (Athlete, Hockey Player)
N6497 County Rd N
Beldenville, WI 54003-4903

Payne, Tom (Actor)
c/o Oriana Elia *Curtis Brown Ltd*
28-29 Hay Market
Hay Market House
London SW1Y 4SP, UNITED KINGDOM

Payne, Waylon (Actor, Musician)
c/o Ben Feigin *Anonymous Content*
3532 Hayden Ave
Culver City, CA 90232-2413, USA

Paynter, Kent (Athlete, Hockey Player)
RR 1
Richmond, PE COB 1 YO, Canada

Pays, Amanda (Actor)
11955 Addison St
Valley Village, CA 91607-3106, USA

Paysinger, Spencer (Athlete, Football Player)

Payton, Amanda (Actor)
c/o Mia Hansen *Portrait PR*
5320 Sylmar Ave
Sherman Oaks, CA 91401-5612, USA

Payton, Christian (Actor)
c/o Staff Member *WME|IMG*
9601 Wilshire Blvd
Beverly Hills, CA 90210-5213, USA

Payton, Eddie (Athlete, Football Player)
118 Woodland Hills Blvd
Madison, MS 39110-7820, USA

Payton, Elfrid (Athlete, Basketball Player)
c/o Ty Sullivan *CAA Sports*
2000 Avenue of the Stars Ste 100
Los Angeles, CA 90067-4705, USA

Payton, Gary (Astronaut)
1011 Old North Gate Rd
Colorado Springs, CO 80921-7100, USA

Payton, Gary (Athlete, Basketball Player, Olympic Athlete)
2745 S Monte Cristo Way
Las Vegas, NV 89117-2974, USA

Payton, James (Actor)
c/o Staff Member *Debbie Edler Management Ltd.*
Little Friars Cottage
Lombard St
Eynsham, Oxon OX29 4HT, UK

Payton, Jay (Athlete, Baseball Player)
2002 Wild Waters Dr
Raleigh, NC 27614-7636, USA

Payton, JoMarie (Actor)
c/o Gar Lester *Gar Lester Agency*
11026 Ventura Blvd Ste 10
Studio City, CA 91604-3598, USA

Payton, Khary (Actor)
c/o Theodore B Gekis *Gekis Management*
4217 Verdugo View Dr
Los Angeles, CA 90065-4317, USA

Payton, Nicholas (Musician)
Management Ark
116 Village Blvd Ste 200
Princeton, NJ 08540-5700, USA

Payton, Sean (Football Coach, Football Player)
c/o Jamie Fritz *Fritz Martin Management*
8550 W Charleston Blvd Ste 102 PMB 335
Las Vegas, NV 89117-9086, USA

Pazienza, Vinny (Boxer)
c/o Darren Prince *Prince Marketing Group*
18 Seneca Trl
Sparta, NJ 07871-1514, USA

Pazik, Mike (Athlete, Baseball Player)
8413 Comanche Ct
Bethesda, MD 20817-4533, USA

Pazsitzky, Christina (Comedian)
c/o Rob Greenwald *Rogers & Cowan*
1840 Century Park E Fl 18
Los Angeles, CA 90067-2101, USA

P. Bilbray, Brian (Congressman, Politician)
2410 Rayburn Hob
Washington, DC 20515-0504, USA

P. Duffy, Sean (Congressman, Politician)
1208 Longworth Hob
Washington, DC 20515-0604, USA

Peace, Terry (Actor)
PO Box 74
Allison Park, PA 15101-0074, USA

Peace, Warren (Baseball Player)
Newark Eagles
27921 NC 903
Robersonville, NC 27871-8904, USA

Peaches and Herb (Music Group)
c/o Staff Member *M.A.G./Universal Attractions*
15 W 36th St Fl 8
New York, NY 10018-7927, USA

Peacocke, Arthur R (Misc)
Society of Ordained Scientists
11 Summer St
St Mark's Rectory
Augusta, ME 04330-5128, USA

Peacosh, Gene (Athlete, Hockey Player)
915 9th St S
Cranbrook, BC V1C 1R8, Canada

Peake, Don (Musician)
c/o Mike Rosen *Working Artists Agency*
13525 Ventura Blvd
Sherman Oaks, CA 91423-3801

Peake, Pat (Athlete, Hockey Player)
327 Hecht Dr
Madison Heights, MI 48071-2890

Peaker, E J (Actor)
4935 Densmore Ave
Encino, CA 91436-1537, USA

Peaks, Pandora (Adult Film Star)
Photo Clubs
6011 Winterpointe Ln Apt 201
Raleigh, NC 27606-2278, USA

Pear, Dave (Athlete, Football Player)
3126 199th Ave SE
Sammamish, WA 98075-9652, USA

Pearce, Colby (Athlete, Cycler, Olympic Athlete)
755 Hawthorn Ave
Boulder, CO 80304-2139, USA

Pearce, Frank (Business Person)
Blizzard Entertainment
PO Box 18979
Irvine, CA 92623-8979, USA

Pearce, Guy (Actor)
c/o Ann Churchill-Brown *Shanahan Management*
Level 3 Berman House
Surry Hills 02010, AUSTRALIA

Pearce, Jacqueline (Actor)
Rhubarb Personal Mgmt
6 Langley St #41
London WC2H 9JA, UNITED KINGDOM (UK)

Pearce, Josh (Athlete, Baseball Player)
110 Fedderly Ln
Yakima, WA 98908-8014, USA

Pearce, Richard I (Director)
240 Bentley Cir
Los Angeles, CA 90049-2414, USA

Pearce, Stevan (Congressman, Politician)
2432 Rayburn Hob
Washington, DC 20515-2402, USA

Pearce, Steve (Athlete, Baseball Player)
4519 W Vasconia St
Tampa, FL 33629-8327, USA

Pearcy, James W (Athlete, Football Player)
PO Box 609
Cobbs Creek, VA 23035-0609, USA

Pearcy, Stephen (Musician)
c/o Staff Member *Top Fuel Records*
4804 Laurel Canyon Blvd Ste 504
Valley Village, CA 91607-3717, USA

Pearl, Barry (Actor)
c/o Staff Member *Coolwaters Productions*
10061 Riverside Dr # 531
Toluca Lake, CA 91602-2560, USA

Pearl, Bruce (Athlete, Basketball Coach)
Auburn University
Athletic Dept
Auburn, AL 36849-0001, USA

Pearl Jam (Music Group)
c/o Nicole Vandenberg *Vandenberg Communications*
1900 S Corgiat Dr
Seattle, WA 98108-2817, USA

Pearlman, Steve (Director, Producer)
c/o Sean Freidin *ICM Partners*
10250 Constellation Blvd Fl 7
Los Angeles, CA 90067-6207, USA

Pearlman, Zack (Actor)
c/o Staff Member *Anderson Group Public Relations*
8060 Melrose Ave Fl 4
Los Angeles, CA 90046-7038, USA

Pearlstein, Philip (Artist)
361 W 36th St Apt 6A
New York, NY 10018-6407, USA

Pearlstine, Norman (Writer)
c/o Lynn Nesbit *Janklow & Nesbit Associates*
285 Madison Ave Fl 21
New York, NY 10017-6427, USA

Pears, David F (Misc)
7 Sandford Road
Littlemore
Oxford OX4 4PU, UNITED KINGDOM (UK)

Pears, Erik (Athlete, Football Player)
c/o Jeff Sperbeck *The Novo Agency*
1537 Via Romero Ste 100
Alamo, CA 94507-1527, USA

Pearson, Albie (Athlete, Baseball Player)
49 Lambeth Dr
Bella Vista, AR 72714-3117, USA

Pearson, Barry (Athlete, Football Player)
85 Westledge Rd
West Simsbury, CT 06092-2327, USA

Pearson, Corey (Actor)
c/o Colton Gramm *Brillstein Entertainment Partners*
9150 Wilshire Blvd Ste 350
Beverly Hills, CA 90212-3453, USA

Pearson, David (Race Car Driver)
290 Burnett Rd
Spartanburg, SC 29316-5934, USA

Pearson, Drew (Athlete, Football Player)
3721 Mount Vernon Way
Plano, TX 75025-3729, USA

Pearson, Jack (Actor)
c/o Staff Member *Morrissey Management*
77 Glebe Point Road
Sydney NSW 2037, AUSTRALIA

Pearson, Jason (Athlete, Baseball Player)
2373 Sunset Dr
Freeport, IL 61032-8348, USA

Pearson, Jayice (Athlete, Football Player)
14500 Perry St
Overland Park, KS 66221-7542, USA

Pearson, Larry (Race Car Driver)
Buckshot Racing
182 Belue Cir
Spartanburg, SC 29316-5900, USA

Pearson, Mel (Athlete, Hockey Player)

Pearson, Preston (Athlete, Football Player)
9104 Moss Farm Ln
Dallas, TX 75243-7429, USA

Pearson, Rob (Athlete, Hockey Player)
15 Belleview Crt
Courtice, ON L1E 1J1, Canada

Pearson, Scott (Athlete, Hockey Player)
114 Lauren Ln
Brunswick, GA 31525-9579

Pearson, Terry (Athlete, Baseball Player)
3010 Wisteria Ln
Northport, AL 35473-8165, USA

Pearson-Tesseine, Dolly (Baseball Player)
1510A Canterbury Trl
Mount Pleasant, MI 48858-4002, USA

Peart, Neil (Musician)
c/o Staff Member *SL Feldman & Associates (Vancouver)*
200-1505 2nd Ave W
Vancouver, BC V6H 3Y4, CANADA

Pease, Patsy (Actor)
15432 Hartland St
Van Nuys, CA 91406-5216

Peasgood, Julie (Actor)
c/o Staff Member *NCI Management Ltd*
51 Queen Ann Street
Floor 2
London W1G 9HS, UNITED KINGDOM (UK)

Peat, Andrus (Football Player)
c/o Tom Condon *Creative Artists Agency (CAA)*
401 Commerce St PH
Nashville, TN 37219-2516, USA

Peatros, Maurice (Athlete, Baseball Player)
Homestead Grays
969 Peaceful Ln
San Jacinto, CA 92582-3167, USA

Peavy, Jake (Athlete, Baseball Player)
PO Box 346
Catherine, AL 36728-0346, USA

Peay, Francis (Athlete, Football Player)
7351 Overbrook Dr
Saint Louis, MO 63121-2533, USA

Peca, Michael (Athlete, Hockey Player)
46 Golden Pheasant Dr
Getzville, NY 14068-1461

Peca, Michael (Athlete, Hockey Player)
Buffalo Junior Sabres
1615 Amherst Manor Dr
Williamsville, NY 14221-2040

Peck, Austin (Actor)
c/o Robert Attermann *Abrams Artists Agency*
275 7th Ave Fl 26
New York, NY 10001-6708, USA

Peck, Ethan (Actor)
c/o Steven Grossman *Untitled Entertainment*
350 S Beverly Dr Ste 200
Beverly Hills, CA 90212-4819, USA

Peck, J Eddie (Actor)
c/o Kim Dorr *Defining Artists Agency*
8721 W Sunset Blvd Ste 209
W Hollywood, CA 90069-2272, USA

Peck, Josh (Actor)
c/o Sam Maydew *Silver Lining Entertainment*
421 S Beverly Dr Fl 7
Beverly Hills, CA 90212-4408, USA

Peck, Mizuo (Actor)
c/o Melissa Raubvogel *Imprint PR*
375 Hudson St
New York, NY 10014-3658, USA

Peck, Tom (Race Car Driver)
Peckie's Auto Body Repair
417 E North St
Mc Connellsburg, PA 17233-1141, USA

Pecota, Bill (Athlete, Baseball Player)
332 NE Warrington Ct
Lees Summit, MO 64064-1605, USA

Pedersen, Allen (Athlete, Hockey Player)
2261 Fieldcrest Dr
Colorado Springs, CO 80921-4000, USA

Pedersen, Jacob (Athlete, Football Player)

Pedersen, Monica (Designer, Television Host)
c/o Staff Member *HGTV*
9721 Sherrill Blvd
Knoxville, TN 37932-3330, USA

Pedersen, Tilly Scott (Actor)
c/o George Englund *George Englund Jr Management*
11661 San Vicente Blvd Ste 609
Los Angeles, CA 90049-5114, USA

Pederson, Barry (Athlete, Hockey Player)
Boston Bruins
100 Legends Way Ste 250
Boston, MA 02114-1389

Pederson, Barry (Athlete, Hockey Player)
16 Cutting Rd
Swampscott, MA 01907-1602, USA

Pederson, Denis (Athlete, Hockey Player)
PO Box 31721
Pitt Meadows, BC V3Y 2H1, Canada

Pederson, Mark (Athlete, Hockey Player)
PO Box 9531
Kalispell, MT 59904-2531

Pederson, Stu (Athlete, Baseball Player)
45 Alannah Ct
Palo Alto, CA 94303-3009, USA

Pederson, Tom (Athlete, Hockey Player)
3140 Bay Rd
Redwood City, CA 94063-3907

Pedrad, Nasim (Comedian)
c/o Michael Rotenberg *3 Arts Entertainment*
9460 Wilshire Blvd Fl 7
Beverly Hills, CA 90212-2713, USA

Pedre, Jorge (Athlete, Baseball Player)
7894 Bellflower Dr
Buena Park, CA 90620-2208, USA

Pedregon, Frank (Race Car Driver)
6174 Cabernet Pl
Alta Loma, CA 91737-6968, USA

Pedretti, Victoria (Actor)
c/o Jamie Arons *Rogers & Cowan*
1840 Century Park E Fl 18
Los Angeles, CA 90067-2101, USA

Pedriaue, Al (Athlete, Baseball Player)
10382 E Oakbrook St
Tucson, AZ 85747-5967, USA

Pedrigue, Al (Athlete, Baseball Player)
10382 E Oakbrook St
Tucson, AZ 85747-5967, USA

Pedrique, Al (Athlete, Baseball Player, Coach)
10382 E Oakbrook St
Tucson, AZ 85747-5967, USA

Pedroia, Dustin (Athlete, Baseball Player)
c/o Seth Levinson *ACES*
188 Montague St Fl 6
Brooklyn, NY 11201-3609, USA

Peebles, Danny (Athlete, Football Player)
12205 Fieldmist Dr
Raleigh, NC 27614-7539, USA

Peek, Richard (Athlete, Basketball Player)
15631 State Highway 31 W
Tyler, TX 75709-3335, USA

Peele, Jordan (Director)
c/o Staff Member *Sonar Entertainment*
2121 Avenue of the Stars Ste 2150
Los Angeles, CA 90067-5028, USA

Peeler, Anthony (Athlete, Basketball Player)
4502 E 48th St
Kansas City, MO 64130-2231, USA

Peeples, Aubrey (Actor)
c/o Domina Holbeck *Abrams Artists Agency*
750 N San Vicente Blvd
E Tower Fl 11
Los Angeles, CA 90069-5788, USA

Peeples, George (Athlete, Basketball Player)
1032 Loma Lisa Ln
Arcadia, CA 91006-2218, USA

Peeples, Nathaniel (Athlete, Baseball Player)
Kansas City Monarchs
536 Lipford St
Memphis, TN 38112-2934, USA

Peeples, Nia (Actor)
8000 Badura Ave Unit 1103
Las Vegas, NV 89113-2108, USA

Peet, Amanda (Actor)
1228 N Wetherly Dr
Los Angeles, CA 90069-1816, USA

Peet, Lizzie (Actor)
952 Maltman Ave Apt 108
Los Angeles, CA 90026-2754, USA

Peete, Rodney (Athlete, Football Player, Television Host)
5056 Chicopee Ave
Encino, CA 91316-2508, USA

Peeters, Pete (Athlete, Hockey Player)
2695 E Katella Ave
Anaheim, CA 92806-5904

Peeters, Pete (Athlete)
farm
Namao, AB TOA 2NO, Canada

Peets, Brian (Athlete, Football Player)
5361 Auburn Blvd
Sacramento, CA 95841-2805, USA

Pegg, Simon (Actor)
c/o Dawn Sedgwick *Dawn Sedgwick Management*
3 Goodwins Ct
Covent Garden
London WC2N 4LL, United Kingdom

Pegler, Luke (Actor)
c/o Staff Member *Independent Management Company*
87-103 Epsom Rd
#15
Rosebery NSW 2018, AUSTRALIA

Pegram, Erric (Athlete, Football Player)
2030 Chicopee Ave
Encino, CA 91316, USA

Peguero, Julio (Athlete, Baseball Player)
1500 State Road 1
Socorro, NM 87801-5093, USA

Pegues, Steve (Athlete, Baseball Player)
362 Presidents Dr
Pontotoc, MS 38863-2322, USA

Peguese, Willis (Athlete, Football Player)
Hialeah-Miami Lakes High School
7977 W 12th Ave
Hialeah, FL 33014-3595, USA

Peil, Mary Beth (Actor)
c/o Lindsay Porter *Gersh*
41 Madison Ave Ste 3301
New York, NY 10010-2210, USA

Peirce, Kimberly (Director, Producer, Writer)
c/o Gregory Shephard *Writ Large*
5815 W Sunset Blvd Ste 401
Los Angeles, CA 90028-6482, USA

Peirse, Sarah (Actor)
c/o Dallas Smith *United Agents*
12-26 Lexington St
London W1F OLE, UNITED KINGDOM

Peirsol, Aaron (Athlete, Olympic Athlete, Swimmer)
9412 Hazelbrook Dr
Huntington Beach, CA 92646-4747, USA

Peirson, John (Athlete, Hockey Player)
3 Steepletree Ln
Wayland, MA 01778-3912

Peizerat, Gwendal (Figure Skater)
c/o Staff Member *Champions on Ice*
3500 American Blvd W Ste 190
Minneapolis, MN 55431-4431, USA

Peko, Domata (Athlete, Football Player)

Pelaez, Alex (Athlete, Baseball Player)
1501 Oleander Ave
Chula Vista, CA 91911-5623, USA

Peldon, Ashley (Actor)
c/o Wendy Peldon *Caviar Entertainment*
2934 N Beverly Glen Cir # 115
Los Angeles, CA 90077-1724, USA

Peldon, Courtney (Actor)
c/o Steve Rodriguez *McGowan Management*
170 S Beverly Dr Ste 304
Beverly Hills, CA 90212-3000, USA

Pele (Athlete, Soccer Player)
Rua Riachuelo 121-3
Andar-Fones 34-1633/35
Santos SP, Brazil

Pelfrey, Mike (Athlete, Baseball Player)
2336 N Rosemont Cir
Wichita, KS 67228-8074, USA

Pelfrey, Raymond (Athlete, Football Player)
1301 Summit St
Portsmouth, OH 45662-3719, USA

Peli, Oren (Director)
c/o Michael (Mike) Esola *WME/IMG*
9601 Wilshire Blvd
Beverly Hills, CA 90210-5213, USA

Pelikan, Lisa (Actor)
c/o Jean Diamond *Diamond Management*
31 Percy St
London W1T 2DD, UNITED KINGDOM

Pellegrino, Mark (Actor)
c/o Mary Ellen Mulcahy *Framework Entertainment*
9057 Nemo St # C
W Hollywood, CA 90069-5511, USA

Pellerin, Scott (Athlete, Hockey Player)
10 Dunraven Rd
Windham, NH 03087-1263

Pelletier, Bronson (Actor)
c/o Staff Member *Carrier Talent Management*
705-1080 Howe St
Vancouver, BC V6Z 2T1, CANADA

Pelletier, Bruno (Musician)
c/o Staff Member *Agence Ginette Achim, Inc.*
1053 Av Laurier O
Outremont, QC H2V 2L2, Canada

Pelletier, Jean-Marc (Athlete, Hockey Player)
83 Canterbury Cir
East Longmeadow, MA 01028-5705

Pelley, Scott (Correspondent, Journalist)
120 Acker Rd
Kendalia, TX 78027-2021, USA

Pellington, Mark (Director, Producer)
c/o Staff Member *3 Arts Entertainment*
9460 Wilshire Blvd Fl 7
Beverly Hills, CA 90212-2713, USA

Pellow, Kit (Athlete, Baseball Player)
1229 W Bluegrass Rd
Nixa, MO 65714-8058, USA

Pellow, Marti (Musician)
c/o Staff Member *Chris Davis Management Ltd.*
Tenbury House
36 Teme St, Tenbury Wells
Worcestershire WR15 8AA, UK

Pelluer, Steve (Athlete, Football Player)
1306 177th Ave NE
Bellevue, WA 98008-3208, USA

Peloffy, Andre (Athlete, Hockey Player)
114 Fairway Dr E
Morehead City, NC 28557-9682

Pelosi, Nancy (Congressman, Politician)
235 Cannon Hob
Washington, DC 20515-1314, USA

Pelphrey, Tom (Actor)
c/o Cyrena Esposito *Red Letter Entertainment*
550 W 45th St Apt 501
New York, NY 10036-3779, USA

Peltier, Dan (Athlete, Baseball Player)
1643 Oak Hill Dr
Hastings, MN 55033-5000, USA

Peltier, Leonard (Writer)
c/o Staff Member *St Martins Press*
175 5th Ave
Publicity Dept
New York, NY 10010-7703, USA

Peltonen, Ville (Athlete, Hockey Player)
12210 NW 71st St
Parkland, FL 33076-4601, USA

Peltz, Nicola (Actor)
c/o Stephen Huvane *Slate PR*
901 N Highland Ave
W Hollywood, CA 90038-2412, USA

Peluce, Meeno (Actor)
2445 Metzler Dr
Los Angeles, CA 90031-2830, USA

Peluso, Mike (Athlete, Hockey Player)
6111 Magnolia Dr
Bismarck, ND 58503-9311

Peluso, Mike (Athlete, Hockey Player)
3616 W Fuller St
Edina, MN 55410-2362

Pelyk, Mike (Athlete, Hockey Player)
56-385 The East Mall
Toronto, ON M9B 6J4, Canada

Pelzer, Dave (Writer)
PO Box 1846
Rancho Mirage, CA 92270-1081

Pember, Dave (Athlete, Baseball Player)
1013 Sandy Springs Rd NW
Rd NW
Huntsville, AL 35806-2411, USA

Pemberton, Brock (Athlete, Baseball Player)
1402 N Elm St
Owasso, OK 74055-4926, USA

Pemberton, Johnny (Actor)
c/o Jennie Cooper-Church *Haven Entertainment*
8111 Beverly Blvd Ste 201
Los Angeles, CA 90048-4531, USA

Pemberton, Rudy (Athlete, Baseball Player)
PO Box 602
Imperial, PA 15126-0602, USA

Pena, Alejandro (Athlete, Baseball Player)
12635 Etris Rd
Roswell, GA 30075-1039, USA

Pena, Brayan (Athlete, Baseball Player)
14217 SW 102nd St
Miami, FL 33186-6970, USA

Pena, Carlos (Musician)
c/o Glenn Hughes III *Gem Entertainment Group*
10920 Wilshire Blvd Ste 150
Los Angeles, CA 90024-3990, USA

Pena, Carlos (Athlete, Baseball Player)
8157 Via Bella Notte
Orlando, FL 32836-7705, USA

Pena, Federico (Politician)
362 Detroit St Unit A
Denver, CO 80206-4377, USA

Pena, Geronimo (Athlete, Baseball Player)
Dominican Republic
KM 17 7 Pista Duarte
Los Alcarrizzos
USA

Pena, Hipolito (Athlete, Baseball Player)
11412 Park Blvd
Seminole, FL 33772-4620, USA

Pena, Jim (Athlete, Baseball Player)
3228 E Silverwood Dr
Phoenix, AZ 85048-7257, USA

Pena, Juan (Athlete, Baseball Player)
5356 SW 133rd Ave
Miramar, FL 33027-5442, USA

Pena, Michael (Actor)
c/o Danica Smith *Kovert Creative*
506 Santa Monica Blvd Ste 400
Santa Monica, CA 90401-2412, USA

Pena, Orlando (Athlete, Baseball Player)
1750 W 46th St Apt 416
Hialeah, FL 33012-2849, USA

Pena, Ramiro (Athlete, Baseball Player)
c/o Team Member *New York Yankees*
161st St & River Ave
Yankee Stadium
Bronx, NY 10451, USA

Pena, Robert (Athlete, Football Player)
77 John Parker Rd
East Falmouth, MA 02536-5116, USA

Pena, Tony (Athlete, Baseball Player, Coach)
New York Yankees
161st Street and River Avenue
Attn: Coaching Staff
Bronx, NY 10451-2100, USA

Pena, Willy Mo (Athlete, Baseball Player)
27520 Breakers Dr
Wesley Chapel, FL 33544-6667, USA

Pena, Wily Mo (Athlete, Baseball Player)
27520 Breakers Dr
Wesley Chapel, FL 33544-6667, USA

Penaranda, Jairo (Athlete, Football Player)
2023 Lloyd Ctr
Portland, OR 97232-1314, USA

PenaVega, Carlos (Actor)
c/o Michael Geiser *Jill Fritzo Public Relations*
208 E 51st St # 305
New York, NY 10022-6557, USA

Pence, Hunter (Athlete, Baseball Player)
c/o Jeff Borris *Beverly Hills Sports Council*
1666 20th St Ste 200A
Santa Monica, CA 90404-3828, USA

Pence, Josh (Actor)
c/o Sandra Chang *Anonymous Content*
3532 Hayden Ave
Culver City, CA 90232-2413, USA

Pence, Mike (Congressman, Politician)
100 Cannon Hob
Washington, DC 20515-2802, USA

Penchion, Bob (Athlete, Football Player)
315 County Road 266
Town Creek, AL 35672-3939, USA

Pender, Jerry Lee (Athlete, Basketball Player)
5126 Wildlife Dr
Rocky Mount, NC 27803-8916, USA

Pender, Mel (Athlete, Olympic Athlete, Track Athlete)
1212 Fawndale Dr NW
Kennesaw, GA 30152-3956, USA

Pendleton, Austin (Actor)
155 E 76th St
New York, NY 10021-2810, USA

Pendleton, Karen (Actor)
7328 N Fruit Ave
Fresno, CA 93711-0717, USA

Pendleton, Terry (Athlete, Baseball Player)
332 Grassmeade Way
Snellville, GA 30078-7782, USA

Penfold, James (Model)
c/o Staff Member *DNA Model Management*
555 W 25th St Fl 6
New York, NY 10001-5542, USA

Penghlis, Thaao (Actor)
c/o Christopher Barrett *Metropolitan (MTA)*
4526 Wilshire Blvd
Los Angeles, CA 90010-3801, USA

Pengilly, Kirk (Musician)
The Eye Foundation
94-98 Chalmers Street
Surry Hills, NSW 02010, Australia

Penguin Prison (Music Group)
c/o Staff Member *High Rise PR*
600 Luton Dr
Glendale, CA 91206-2626, USA

Penhaligon, Susan (Actor)
109 Jermyn St
London, ENGLAND SW1

Penhall, Bruce (Race Car Driver)
PO Box 5625
Norco, CA 92860-8021, USA

Peniche, Arturo (Actor)
c/o Staff Member *Televisa*
Blvd Adolfo Lopez Mateos 232
Colonia San Angel INN
DF CP 01060, MEXICO

Peniche, Kari Ann (Designer, Reality Star)
c/o Eileen Koch *Eileen Koch & Company*
9350 Wilshire Blvd Ste 323
Beverly Hills, CA 90212-3206, USA

Penick, Trevor (Musician)
Trans Continental Records
7380 W Sand Lake Rd # 350
Orlando, FL 32819-5248, USA

Penikett, Tahmoh (Actor)
c/o Robert Stein *Robert Stein Management*
PO Box 3797
Beverly Hills, CA 90212-0797, USA

Peniston, CeCe (Musician)
250 W 57th St # 821
New York, NY 10107-0001, USA

Penn, Chris (Athlete, Football Player)
PO Box 123
S Coffeyville, OK 74072-0123, USA

Penn, Dylan (Actor)
c/o Heather Nunn *Anonymous Content*
3532 Hayden Ave
Culver City, CA 90232-2413, USA

Penn, Hayden (Athlete, Baseball Player)
9150 Canyon Park Ter
Santee, CA 92071-4733, USA

Penn, Jesse (Athlete, Football Player)
8420 Wildcreek Dr
Plano, TX 75025-4150, USA

Penn, Kal (Actor, Producer)
c/o Daniel Spilo *Industry Entertainment Partners*
955 Carrillo Dr Ste 300
Los Angeles, CA 90048-5400, USA

Penn, Michael (Musician)
c/o Staff Member *Kraft-Engel Management*
15233 Ventura Blvd Ste 200
Sherman Oaks, CA 91403-2244, USA

Penn, Sean (Actor, Director)
28965 Grayfox St
Malibu, CA 90265-4254, USA

Penn, Shannon (Athlete, Baseball Player)
6922 Lois Dr
Cincinnati, OH 45239-4315, USA

Penn, Zak (Director, Producer)
Zak Pen's Co
6240 W 3rd St Apt 421
Los Angeles, CA 90036-7620, USA

Penna, Angel (Horse Racer)
17 Chestnut Hl # H
Roslyn, NY 11576-2821, USA

Pennacchio, Len A (Misc)
Stanford University
Human Genome Center
Stanford, CA 94305, USA

Penn & Teller (Comedian, Magician)
c/o Glenn Alai *Star Price Productions*
3555 W Reno Ave Ste L
Las Vegas, NV 89118-1609, USA

Pennebaker, Ed (Artist)
428 County Road 9351
Green Forest, AR 72638-9764, USA

Penner, Dustin (Athlete, Hockey Player)
The Sports Corporation
2735-10088 102 Ave NW
Attn Rich Winter
Edmonton, AB T5J 2Z1, Canada

Penner, Jonathan (Actor)
c/o Staff Member *Modus Entertainment*
8569 Holloway Dr Apt 1
West Hollywood, CA 90069-6918, USA

Penney, Steve (Athlete, Hockey Player)
155 Notre Dame St
Saint-Ferreol-Les-Neiges, QC G0A 3R0, CANADA

Penniman, Michael (Mika) (Musician)
c/o Jbeau Lewis *United Talent Agency (UTA)*
9336 Civic Center Dr
Beverly Hills, CA 90210-3604, USA

Pennington, Ann (Actor)
701 N Oakhurst Dr
Beverly Hills, CA 90210-3532, USA

Pennington, Art (Athlete, Baseball Player)
Chicago American Giants
922 5th St SE Apt E5
Cedar Rapids, IA 52401-2440, USA

Pennington, Brad (Athlete, Baseball Player)
202 Tucker St
Salem, IN 47167-1054, USA

Pennington, Chad (Athlete, Football Player)
c/o Tom Condon *Creative Artists Agency (CAA)*
401 Commerce St PH
Nashville, TN 37219-2516, USA

Pennington, Cliff (Athlete, Hockey Player)
9960 5th St N Apt 203
Saint Petersburg, FL 33702-2200

Pennington, Janice (Actor, Model)
PO Box 11402
Beverly Hills, CA 90213-4402, USA

Pennington, Julia (Actor)
PO Box 5617
Beverly Hills, CA 90209-5617, USA

Pennington, Michael (Actor)
Marmont Mgmt
Langham House
302/8 Regent St
London W1R 5AL, UNITED KINGDOM (UK)

Pennington, T Durwood (Athlete, Football Player)
480 Peninsula Rd
Gainesville, GA 30506-1705, USA

Pennington, Ty (Reality Star, Television Host)
c/o Staff Member *Agency SGH*
6525 W Sunset Blvd PH
Hollywood, CA 90028-7212, USA

Pennison, Jay (Athlete, Football Player)
2203 McKeever Rd
Rosharon, TX 77583-2635, USA

Pennock, Chris (Actor)
25150 1/2 Malibu Rd
Malibu, CA 90265-4639, USA

Pennock of Norton, Raymond (Business Person)
Morgan Grenfell Group
23 Great Winchester St
London EC2P 2AX, UNITED KINGDOM (UK)

Pennv, Brad (Athlete, Baseball Player)
25071 Abercrombie Ln
Calabasas, CA 91302-2360, USA

Penny, Brad (Athlete, Baseball Player)
25071 Abercrombie Ln
Calabasas, CA 91302-2360, USA

Penny, Joe (Actor)
PO Box 1551
Burbank, CA 91507-1551, USA

Penny, Rashaad (Athlete, Football Player)
c/o Brian Hannula *Alliance Sports (San Diego)*
2305 Historic Decatur Rd Ste 100
San Diego, CA 92106-6071, USA

Penny, Roger P (Business Person)
Bethlehem Steel
1170 8th Ave
Bethlehem, PA 18018-2255, USA

Penny, Sudney (Actor)
Baker/Winokur/Ryder
9100 Wilshire Blvd Ste 600
Beverly Hills, CA 90212-3494, USA

Penny, Sydney (Actor)
c/o Bob McGowan *McGowan Management*
170 S Beverly Dr Ste 304
Beverly Hills, CA 90212-3000, USA

Pennyfeather, Will (Athlete, Baseball Player)
333 Rector St Apt 6D
Perth Amboy, NJ 08861-4277, USA

Pennywell, Carlos (Athlete, Football Player)
3729 Clover Dr
Arcadia, LA 71001-3628, USA

Pennywell, Robert (Athlete, Football Player)
1523 Staring Ln
Baton Rouge, LA 70810-1458, USA

Penot, Jacques (Actor)
9 rue de l'Isly
Paris F-75008, France

Penrose, Craig R (Athlete, Football Player)
1609 Camino Way
Woodland, CA 95695-5517, USA

Penske, Roger (Race Car Driver)
Team Penske
200 Penske Way
Mooresville, NC 28115-8022, USA

Pensky, Robert (Writer)
236 Bay State Rd Attn Dept
Boston, MA 02215-1403, USA

Pentatonix (Music Group)
c/o Dvora Vener Englefield *The Lede Company*
9701 Wilshire Blvd # 930
Beverly Hills, CA 90212-2020, USA

Pentecost, Del (Actor)
c/o Staff Member *Paradigm*
8942 Wilshire Blvd
Beverly Hills, CA 90211-1908, USA

Pentland, Jeff (Athlete, Baseball Player)
1032 N Cherry
Mesa, AZ 85201-3208, USA

Pentz, Gene (Athlete, Baseball Player)
207 Rainbow Dr
Johnstown, PA 15904-2253, USA

People, Village (Music Group, Musician)
c/o Staff Member *WME|IMG*
9601 Wilshire Blvd
Beverly Hills, CA 90210-5213, USA

Pepaj, Niko (Actor)
c/o Brianne Watson *Vanguard Management Group*
8060 Melrose Ave Fl 4
Los Angeles, CA 90046-7038, USA

Pepe, Neil (Actor)
c/o John Buzzetti *WME|IMG (NY)*
11 Madison Ave Fl 18
New York, NY 10010-3669, USA

Pepin, Jacques (Chef)
214 Durham Rd
Madison, CT 06443-2451, USA

Pepitone, Joe (Athlete, Baseball Player)
32 Lois Ln
Farmingdale, NY 11735-6003, USA

Peplinski, Jim (Athlete, Hockey Player)
Peplinski's Leasemaster
212 Meridian Rd NE
Calgary, AB T2A 2N6, Canada

Peplowski, Mike (Athlete, Basketball Player)
4110 Harris Rd
Williamston, MI 48895-9204, USA

Peppas, June (Athlete, Baseball Player)
1700 NE Indian River Dr Apt 302
Jensen Beach, FL 34957-5860, USA

Pepper, Barry (Actor)
c/o Nancy Iannios *Core Public PR*
1875 Century Park E Ste 930
Los Angeles, CA 90067-2540, USA

Pepper, Cynthia (Actor)
219 Friendly Ct
Henderson, NV 89052-5660

Pepper, Don (Athlete, Baseball Player)
7 Beckenham Ln
Greenville, SC 29609-6023, USA

Pepper, Dottle (Golfer)
108 Micco Cir
Jupiter, FL 33458-7730, USA

Pepper, Laurin (Athlete, Baseball Player)
8932 Davis St
Ocean Springs, MS 39564-3633, USA

Peppers, Julius (Athlete, Football Player)
229 N Church St # 304E
Charlotte, NC 28202-2169, USA

Peppler, Mary Jo (Athlete, Volleyball Player)
Bridge Volleyball Club
2390 Boswell Rd Ste 400
Chula Vista, CA 91914-3541, USA

Perabo, Piper (Actor)
c/o Kate Rosen *The Lede Company*
401 Broadway Ste 206
New York, NY 10013-3033, USA

Peralta, Jhonny (Athlete, Baseball Player)
12970 Woodlark Ln
Saint Louis, MO 63131-1314, USA

Peralta, Ricardo (Astronaut)
Ingeneria Instituto
Ciudad Universitaria
Mexico City, DF 04510, MEXICO

Peralta, Wily (Athlete, Baseball Player)
c/o Peter Greenberg *TLA Worldwide (The Legacy Agency)*
1500 Broadway Ste 2501
New York, NY 10036-4082, USA

Peranoski, Ron (Baseball Player)
Los Angeles Dodgers
3805 Indian River Dr E
Vero Beach, FL 32963-1404, USA

Perayra, Marianela (Television Host)
c/o Mike Esterman *Esterman.Com, LLC*
Prefers to be contacted via email
Baltimore, MD XXXXX, USA

Percival, Lance (Actor)
PVA 2 High St
Westbury-on-Trim
Bristol BS9 3DU, UNITED KINGDOM (UK)

Percival, Mac (Athlete, Football Player)
7219 Timberlake Dr
Sugar Land, TX 77479-6309, USA

Percival, Troy E (Athlete, Baseball Player)
2127 Century Ave
Riverside, CA 92506-4653, USA

Perconte, Jack (Athlete, Baseball Player)
6197 Hinterlong Ct
Lisle, IL 60532-2818, USA

Perdomo, Chance (Actor)
c/o Staff Member *Scott Marshall Partners Ltd*
49/50 Eagle Wharf Road
Holborn Studios
London N1 7ED, UNITED KINGDOM

Perdue, Sonny (Politician)
217 Houston Dr
Bonaire, GA 31005, USA

Perdue, Will (Athlete, Basketball Player)
2500 Broadmeade Rd # 2
Louisville, KY 40205-2206, USA

Perec, Marie-Jose (Athlete, Track Athlete)
Federacion d'Athletisme
10 Rue du Fg Poissonniere
Paris 75480, FRANCE

Peregrym, Missy (Actor)
c/o Ame VanIden *VanIden Public Relations*
4070 Wilson Pike
Franklin, TN 37067-8126, USA

Perelman, Ronald O (Business Person)
MacAndrews & Forbes
35 E 62nd St
New York, NY 10065-8014, USA

Perelman, Vadim (Director)
c/o Simon Millar *Rumble Media*
1620 Broadway Ste C
Santa Monica, CA 90404-2777, USA

Perenyi, Miklos (Musician)
Erdoalja Utca 1/B
Budapest 01037, HUNGARY

Peretokin, Mark (Dancer)
Bolshoi Theater
Teatralnaya Pl 1
Moscow 103009, RUSSIA

Peretti, Jonah (Business Person)
BuzzFeed, Inc
111 E 18th St
New York, NY 10003-2107, USA

Perez, Atanasio (Athlete, Baseball Player)
1717 N Bayshore Dr
Miami, FL 33132-1180, USA

Perez, Chris (Musician)
Big FD Entertainment
301 Arizona Ave Ste 200
Santa Monica, CA 90401-1364, USA

Perez, Danny (Athlete, Baseball Player)
10511 Cuesta Brava Ln
El Paso, TX 79935-2210, USA

Perez, Dick (Artist)
PO Box 503
Wayne, PA 19087-0503, USA

Perez, Eddie (Athlete, Baseball Player)
615 Rose Creek Cir
Duluth, GA 30097-7895, USA

Perez, Eduardo (Athlete, Baseball Player)
113 Calle Las Flores
San Juan, PR 00911-2298, USA

Perez, George (Athlete, Baseball Player)
PO Box 414
Bandon, OR 97411-0414, USA

Perez, Hugo (Soccer Player)
22018 Newbridge Dr
Lake Forest, CA 92630-6511, USA

Perez, Luiz (Louie) (Musician)
Gold Mountain
3575 Cahuenga Blvd W Ste 450
Los Angeles, CA 90068-1364, USA

Perez, Manny (Actor, Producer)
c/o Scott Zimmerman *Scott Zimmerman Management*
1644 Courtney Ave
Los Angeles, CA 90046-2708, USA

Perez, Marty (Athlete, Baseball Player)
30 Willowick Dr
Lithonia, GA 30038-1722, USA

Perez, Melido (Athlete, Baseball Player)
Nigua KM 21 1/2
Santa Domingo, Dominican Republic

Perez, Mike (Athlete, Baseball Player)
10538 Hc 1
Penuelas, PR 00624-9890, USA

Perez, Neifi (Athlete, Baseball Player)
43515 Blacksmith Sq Apt 106
Ashburn, VA 20147-4637, USA

Perez, Odalis A (Baseball Player)
Los Angeles Dodgers
Stadium
1000 Elysian Park Ave
Los Angeles, CA 90012, USA

Perez, Oliver (Baseball Player)
c/o Scott Boras *Boras Corporation*
18 Corporate Plaza Dr
Newport Beach, CA 92660-7901, USA

Perez, Rosie (Actor, Producer)
c/o Sam Maydew *Silver Lining Entertainment*
421 S Beverly Dr Fl 7
Beverly Hills, CA 90212-4408, USA

Perez, Scott (Cartoonist)
DC Comics
2900 W Alameda Ave # 1
Burbank, CA 91505-4220, USA

Perez, Timothy Paul (Actor)
Badgley Connor Talent
9229 W Sunset Blvd Ste 311
Los Angeles, CA 90069-3403, USA

Perez, Tony (Athlete, Baseball Player, Coach)
1717 N Bayshore Dr # A-2735
Miami, FL 33132-1180, USA

Perez, Vincent (Actor)
c/o Staff Member *ArtMedia*
8 rue Danielle Casanova
Paris 75002, FRANCE

Perez, Yorkis (Athlete, Baseball Player)
3303 Potter St
Philadelphia, PA 19134-1404, USA

Perez-Brown, Maria (Producer)
c/o Staff Member *WME|IMG*
9601 Wilshire Blvd
Beverly Hills, CA 90210-5213, USA

Perezchica, Tony (Athlete, Baseball Player)
79220 Victoria Dr
La Quinta, CA 92253-4274, USA

Perez de Tagle, Anna Maria (Actor)
c/o Alejandra Cristina *Ace PR*
4122 Sunnyslope Ave
Sherman Oaks, CA 91423-4308, USA

Perez Limon, Iyari (Actor)
c/o Mitchell Stubbs *Mitchell K Stubbs & Assoc*
8675 Washington Blvd Ste 203
Culver City, CA 90232-7486, USA

Pergine, John (Athlete, Football Player)
5 Jody Dr
Plymouth Meeting, PA 19462-2625, USA

Perillo, Gregory (Artist)
2 Blackwell Rd
Nesconset, NY 11767-2802, USA

Perino, Dana (Television Host)
611 Pennsylvania Ave SE # 312
Washington, DC 20003-4303, USA

Perishers, The (Music Group)
c/o Staff Member *Paradigm (Monterey)*
404 W Franklin St
Monterey, CA 93940-2303, USA

Perisho, Matt (Athlete, Baseball Player)
1462 W Cardinal Way
Chandler, AZ 85286-4379, USA

Perkins, Broderick (Athlete, Baseball Player)
5367 San Vincente Blvd
Apt 237
Los Angeles, CA 91977-6509, USA

Perkins, Bruce (Athlete, Football Player)
19014 E Ryan Rd
Queen Creek, AZ 85142-6877, USA

Perkins, Cecil (Athlete, Baseball Player)
711 Cushwa Rd
Martinsburg, WV 25403-1228, USA

Perkins, Dan (Athlete, Baseball Player)
14621 SW 87th Ct
Palmetto Bay, FL 33176-8017, USA

Perkins, Desi (Designer, Internet Star)
c/o Eman Redwan *United Talent Agency (UTA)*
2000 Avenue of the Stars
Los Angeles, CA 90067-4700, USA

Perkins, Elivs (Musician)
c/o Staff Member *Paradigm (Monterey)*
404 W Franklin St
Monterey, CA 93940-2303, USA

Perkins, Elizabeth (Actor)
c/o Cynthia Pett-Dante *Brillstein Entertainment Partners*
9150 Wilshire Blvd Ste 350
Beverly Hills, CA 90212-3453, USA

Perkins, Emily (Actor)
c/o Tyman Stewart *Characters Talent Agency*
200-1505 2nd Ave W
Vancouver, BC V6H 3Y4, CANADA

Perkins, Glen (Athlete, Baseball Player)
18401 Lake Forest Dr
Lakeville, MN 55044-5282, USA

Perkins, John (Writer)
c/o Paul Fedorko *Trident Media Group LLC*
41 Madison Ave Fl 36
New York, NY 10010-2257, USA

Perkins, Kathleen Rose (Actor)
c/o Devon Jackson *Trademark Talent*
5900 Wilshire Blvd Ste 710
Los Angeles, CA 90036-5019, USA

Perkins, Kendrick (Athlete, Basketball Player)
8522 Haven Trl # 1
Tomball, TX 77375-2650, USA

Perkins, Lucian (Journalist, Photographer)
3103 17th St NW
Washington, DC 20010-2701, USA

Perkins, Millie (Actor)
2511 Canyon Dr
Los Angeles, CA 90068-2415, USA

Perkins, Ross (Athlete, Hockey Player)
4-400 Jim Common Dr
Sherwood Park, AB T8H 0K8, Canada

Perkins, Sam (Athlete, Basketball Player)
14901 Bellbrook Dr
Dallas, TX 75254-7673, USA

Perkins, Tex (Musician)
Stack/Polydor Records
70 Universal City Plz
Universal City, CA 91608-1011, USA

Perkins, Warren (Athlete, Basketball Player)
717 Fairfield Ave
Gretna, LA 70056-7625, USA

Perkins, W Ray (Athlete, Coach, Football Coach, Football Player)
5356 Anna Ln
Tuscaloosa, AL 35406-2876, USA

Perkowski, Harry (Athlete, Baseball Player)
211 McGinnis St
Beckley, WV 25801-5725, USA

Perks, Craig (Golfer)
321 Thibodeaux Dr
Lafayette, LA 70503-4444, USA

Perles, George (Athlete, Football Coach, Football Player)
6153 W Longview Dr
East Lansing, MI 48823-9739, USA

Perley, James (Misc)
American Assn of University Professors
1012 14th St NW
Washington, DC 20005-3403, USA

Perlich, Max (Actor)
c/o Staff Member *Metropolitan (MTA)*
4526 Wilshire Blvd
Los Angeles, CA 90010-3801, USA

Perlick-Keating, Edythe (Baseball Player)
3051 S Palm Aire Dr Bldg 34
Pompano Beach, FL 33069-4277, USA

Perlini, Fred (Athlete, Hockey Player)
409 Albert St W
Sault Ste. Marie, ON P6A 1C2, Canada

Perlman, Jon (Athlete, Baseball Player)
3225 Bryn Mawr Dr
Dallas, TX 75225-7646, USA

Perlman, Lawrence (Business Person)
Ceridian Corp
3311 E Old Shakopee Rd
Minneapolis, MN 55425-1640, USA

Perlman, Rhea (Actor, Producer)
c/o Melissa Sun *Stan Rosenfield & Associates*
2029 Century Park E Ste 1190
Los Angeles, CA 90067-2931, USA

Perlman, Ron (Actor)
c/o Patrick Carson *PC Social Media*
1521 Monterey Blvd # 2
Hermosa Beach, CA 90254-3677, USA

Perlmutter, Ed (Congressman, Politician)
1221 Longworth Hob
Washington, DC 20515-0517, USA

Perlozzo, Sam (Athlete, Baseball Player, Coach)
18101 Emerald Bay St
Tampa, FL 33647-3316, USA

Perls, Tom (Misc)
9 Beaver Pond Rd
Beverly, MA 01915-1202, USA

Pernandez, Mervyn (Athlete, Football Player)
1546 Morning Star Dr
Morgan Hill, CA 95037-9033, USA

Pernas, Sofia (Actor)
c/o Chris Rossi *Status PR*
PO Box 6191
Westlake Village, CA 91359-6191, USA

Perner, Wolfgang (Athlete)
Schildlehen 29
ramsau-D 08972, AUSTRIA

Pernice Jr, Tom (Golfer)
c/o Staff Member *Pro Golfers Association (PGA)*
112 TPC Blvd
Ponte Vedra Beach, FL 32082, USA

Peron, Isabelita Martinez de (President)
Moreto 3
Los Jeronimos
Madrid 28014, SPAIN

Perot, Henry Ross (Business Person)
c/o Staff Member *Perot Group*
2300 W Plano Pkwy
Plano, TX 75075-8427, USA

Perot, Pete (Athlete, Football Player)
2401 Hillside Rd
Ruston, LA 71270-2093, USA

Perot Jr, Henry Ross (Business Person)
c/o Staff Member *Perot Group*
2300 W Plano Pkwy
Plano, TX 75075-8427, USA

Perranoski, Ron (Athlete, Baseball Player)
4800 Highway A1a Apt 118
Vero Beach, FL 32963-1258, USA

Perreau, Gigi (Actor)
18411 Hatteras St Unit 120
Tarzana, CA 91356-1962, USA

Perreault, Bob (Athlete, Hockey Player)

Perreault, Gilbert (Athlete, Hockey Player)
4 Rue de la Serenite
Victoriaville, QC G6S 1J4, Canada

Perreault, Gilbert (Gil) (Athlete, Hockey Player)
Buffalo Sabres
1 Seymour H Knox III Plz Ste 1
Buffalo, NY 14203-3096

Perreault, Yanic (Athlete, Hockey Player)
1565 Rue Malouin
Sherbrooke, QC J1J 3C5, Canada

Perret, Craig (Horse Racer)
825 Antioch Rd
Shelbyville, KY 40065-9755, USA

Perretta, Ralph (Athlete, Football Player)
1305 Calle Scott
Encinitas, CA 92024-5532, USA

Perrette, Pauley (Actor)
c/o Stephen Jaffe *Jaffe & Company Strategic Media*
9663 Santa Monica Blvd # 663
Beverly Hills, CA 90210-4303, USA

Perri, Christina (Musician)
c/o Ryan Chisholm *Nettwerk Management (LA)*
1545 Wilcox Ace
Suite 200
Los Angeles, CA 90028, USA

Perrier, Mireille (Actor)
Cineart
36 Rue de Ponthieu
Paris 75008, FRANCE

Perriman, Breshad (Athlete, Football Player)
c/o Drew Rosenhaus *Rosenhaus Sports Representation*
3921 Alton Rd # 440
Miami Beach, FL 33140-3852, USA

Perriman, Brett (Athlete, Football Player)
PO Box 83337
Conyers, GA 30013-8019, USA

Perrin, Benny (Athlete, Football Player)
2509 Burningtree Dr SE
Decatur, AL 35603-5138, USA

Perrin, Eric (Athlete, Hockey Player)
408 Colemans Run
Woodstock, GA 30188-5328

Perrin, Lonnie (Athlete, Football Player)
2811 Pumpkin St
Clinton, MD 20735-1063, USA

Perrine, Valerie (Actor)
c/o Lynda Bensky *Bensky Entertainment*
15021 Ventura Blvd # 343
Sherman Oaks, CA 91403-2442, USA

Perrineau Jr, Harold (Actor, Producer)
c/o Stacy Abrams *Abrams Entertainment*
5225 Wilshire Blvd Ste 515
Los Angeles, CA 90036-4349, USA

Perron, Jean (Coach)
5 Thomas Mellon Cir
San Francisco, CA 94134-2501, USA

Perroni, Maite (Actor)
c/o Staff Member *Televisa S.A. de C.V.*
Av. Vasco de Quirroga 2000
DF 01210, Mexico

Perrotta, Tom (Writer)
Saint Martin's Press
175 5th Ave Ste 400
New York, NY 10010-7848, USA

Perry, Alex (Designer)
Alex Perry
Level 1, 60 Riley St
East Sydney NSW 2010, Australia

Perry, Alex Ross (Actor)
c/o Adam Kersh *Brigade Marketing*
116 W 23rd St Fl 5
New York, NY 10011-2599, USA

Perry, Anne (Writer)
Turn Vawr
Seafield Postmahomack
Rosshire IV20 1RE, SCOTLAND

Perry, Barry W (Business Person)
Engelhard Corp
101 Wood Ave S
Iselin, NJ 08830-2749, USA

Perry, Chan (Athlete, Baseball Player)
788 NE County Road 353
Mayo, FL 32066-5450, USA

Perry, Chris (Athlete, Football Player)
c/o Eugene Parker *Independent Sports & Entertainment (ISE-IN)*
6435 W Jefferson Blvd # 197
Fort Wayne, IN 46804-6203, USA

Perry, Chris (Athlete, Golfer)
170 Valley Run Dr
Powell, OH 43065-9454, USA

Perry, Darren (Athlete, Football Player)
6451 Pinehurst Ln
Mason, OH 45040-2051, USA

Perry, Ed (Athlete, Football Player)
1583 SW 161st Ave
Pembroke Pines, FL 33027-5140, USA

Perry, Elliott (Athlete, Basketball Player)
3306 Darby Dan Cv
Germantown, TN 38138-8260, USA

Perry, Felton (Actor)
PO Box 931359
Los Angeles, CA 90093-1359, USA

Perry, Gaylord (Athlete, Baseball Player)
PO Box 1180
Gaffney, SC 29342-1180, USA

Perry, Gerald (Athlete, Baseball Player)
5112 Kurt Ln SW
Conyers, GA 30094-4732, USA

Perry, Gerald (Athlete, Football Player)
2940 Dell Dr
Columbia, SC 29209-4906, USA

Perry, Gerald E (Athlete, Football Player)
336 5th St
Manhattan Beach, CA 90266-5712, USA

Perry, Herb (Athlete, Baseball Player)
978 N Fletcher Ave
Mayo, FL 32066-4506, USA

Perry, Jeff (Actor)
c/o Staff Member *Steppenwolf Films*
8163 Gaffield Pl
Evanston, IL 60201, USA

Perry, Jim (Athlete, Baseball Player)
155 Printers Ln
New London, NC 28127-8104, USA

Perry, Joe (Musician, Songwriter)
1405 Tremont St
Duxbury, MA 02332-3711, USA

Perry, John Bennett (Actor)
Judy Schoen
606 N Larchmont Blvd Ste 309
Los Angeles, CA 90004-1309, USA

Perry, Katy (Musician)
c/o Bradford Cobb *Direct Management Group*
8332 Melrose Ave
Los Angeles, CA 90069-5420, USA

Perry, Kenny (Golfer)
418 Quail Ridge Rd
Franklin, KY 42134-9650, USA

Perry, Kimberly (Musician)
c/o Jake Basden *Big Machine Records*
1219 16th Ave S
Nashville, TN 37212-2901, USA

Perry, Leon (Athlete, Football Player)
RR 1 Box 195A
Gloster, MS 39638, USA

Perry, Linda (Musician, Producer)
Custard Records
8939 1/2 Santa Monica Blvd
West Hollywood, CA 90069-4912, USa

Perry, Matthew (Actor)
c/o Lisa Kasteler *Wolf-Kasteler Public Relations*
6255 W Sunset Blvd Ste 1111
Los Angeles, CA 90028-7426, USA

Perry, Michael Dean (Athlete, Football Player)
PO Box 221771
Charlotte, NC 28222-1771, USA

Perry, Neil (Musician)
c/o Jake Basden *Big Machine Records*
1219 16th Ave S
Nashville, TN 37212-2901, USA

Perry, Nick (Athlete, Football Player)
c/o Joe Panos *Athletes First*
23091 Mill Creek Dr
Laguna Hills, CA 92653-1258, USA

Perry, Pat (Athlete, Baseball Player)
1115 W Franklin St
Taylorville, IL 62568-2037, USA

Perry, Rachel (Actor)
c/o Staff Member *Envision Entertainment*
8840 Wilshire Blvd Fl 3
Beverly Hills, CA 90211-2606, USA

Perry, Richard (Musician, Producer)
300 N Swall Dr Unit 208
Beverly Hills, CA 90211-4732, USA

Perry, Rick (Politician)
1010 Colorado St
Austin, TX 78701-2334, USA

Perry, Rod (Athlete, Football Player)
PO Box 532551
Indianapolis, IN 46253-2551, USA

Perry, Ruth (Prime Minister)
Prime Minister's Office
Capitol Hill
Monrovia, LIBERIA

Perry, Ryan (Athlete, Baseball Player)
PO Box 5937
Peoria, AZ 85385-5937, USA

Perry, Sarah (Actor)
c/o Samantha Dodd *Carey Dodd & Associates*
78 York St
London W1H 1DP, UNITED KINGDOM

Perry, Scott (Athlete, Football Player)
3708 S Dolphin St
San Pedro, CA 90731-6020, USA

Perry, Steve (Musician)
c/o Lee Phillips *Manatt Phelps & Phillips LLP*
11355 W Olympic Blvd Fl 2
Los Angeles, CA 90064-1656, USA

Perry, Todd (Athlete, Football Player)
625 Briars Bnd
Alpharetta, GA 30004-1177, USA

Perry, Tyler (Actor, Director, Producer)
c/o Staff Member *Tyler Perry Company*
3133 Continental Colony Pkwy SW
Atlanta, GA 30331-3109, USA

Perry, Vernon (Athlete, Football Player)
PO Box 3
Jackson, MS 39205-0003, USA

Perry, William (Politician)
620 Sand Hill Rd Apt 421E
Palo Alto, CA 94304-2079, USA

Perry, William (Refrigerator) (Athlete, Football Player)
349 Kershaw St NE
Aiken, SC 29801-4432, USA

Perry, Wilmont (Athlete, Football Player)
1757 W River Rd
Franklinton, NC 27525-8293, USA

Perry, Yvonne (Actor)
As World Turns Show
524 W 57th St
CBS-TV
New York, NY 10019-2930, USA

Perry, Zoe (Actor)
c/o Stephanie Nese *Levity Entertainment Group (LEG)*
6701 Center Dr W Ste 300
Los Angeles, CA 90045-2482, USA

Perryman, Jim (Athlete, Football Player)
2345 Southwood Dr
Pittsburgh, PA 15241-3344, USA

Perryman, Robert (Athlete, Football Player)
PO Box 8543
Haverhill, MA 01835-0985, USA

Persoff, Nahemiah (Actor)
5670 Moonstone Beach Dr
Cambria, CA 93428-2210, USA

Persoff, Nehemiah (Actor)
5670 Moonstone Beach Dr
Cambria, CA 93428-2210, USA

Person, Chuck (Athlete, Basketball Player)
2301 S Garfield Dr
Indianapolis, IN 46203-4218, USA

Person, Robert (Athlete, Baseball Player)
25 Bellerive Acres
Saint Louis, MO 63121-4328, USA

Person, Wesley (Athlete, Basketball Player)
PO Box 481
Brantley, AL 36009-0481, USA

Persons, Peter (Golfer)
1153 Saint Andrews Dr
Macon, GA 31210-4760, USA

Persson, Goeran (Prime Minister)
Statsradsberedningen
Rosenbad 4
Stockholm 103 33, SWEDEN

Persson, Nina (Musician)
Motor SE
Gotabergs Gatan 2
Gothenburg 400 14, SWEDEN

Persson, Ricard (Athlete, Hockey Player)
Thompson, Dorfman, Sweatman
PO Box 639 Stn Main
Attn: Donald Baizley
Winnipeg, MB R3C 2K6, Canada

Persson, Stefan (Business Person)
Sverige H & M Hennes & Mauritz AB
Sverigekontoret
Stockholm SE-106 38, SWEDEN

Pertucceli, Valeria (Actor)
c/o Staff Member *Telefe (Argentina)*
Pavon 2444
Buenos Aires C1248AAT, ARGENTINA

Pertwee, Sean (Actor)
c/o Annie Schmidt *Untitled Entertainment (NY)*
215 Park Ave S Fl 8
New York, NY 10003-1622, USA

Peruzovic, Josip (Actor, Wrestler)
c/o Nick Cordasco *Prince Marketing Group*
18 Seneca Trl
Sparta, NJ 07871-1514, USA

Pervical, Troy (Baseball Player)
California Angels
2127 Century Ave
Riverside, CA 92506-4653, USA

Perzanowski, Stan (Athlete, Baseball Player)
10908 Wheat Rd
New Park, PA 17352-9563, USA

Perzigian, Jerry (Producer, Writer)
c/o Joseph Cohen *Creative Artists Agency (CAA)*
2000 Avenue of the Stars Ste 100
Los Angeles, CA 90067-4705, USA

Pescatelli, Tammy (Actor)

Pesce, PJ (Director, Writer)
c/o Anne Damato *Rain Management Group*
11162 La Grange Ave
Los Angeles, CA 90025-5632, USA

Pesci, Joe (Actor)
Falu Productions
PO Box 6
Lavallette, NJ 08735-0006, USA

Pescow, Donna (Actor)
8267 Paseo Canyon Dr
Malibu, CA 90265, USA

Pesi, Gino Anthony (Actor)
Public Displays of Affection
PO Box 93909
Los Angeles, CA 90093-0909, USA

Pesonen, Richard (Athlete, Football Player)
765 Pine Hills Pl
The Villages, FL 32162-1617, USA

Pestana, Simon (Actor)
c/o Staff Member *Telefe (Argentina)*
Pavon 2444
Buenos Aires C1248AAT, ARGENTINA

Pestano, Vinnie (Athlete, Baseball Player)
6058 E Silverspur Trl
Anaheim, CA 92807-4728, USA

Pestova, Daniela (Actor)

Pesut, George (Athlete, Hockey Player)
1008-415 Michigan St
Victoria, BC V8V 1R8, Canada

Petagine, Roberto (Athlete, Baseball Player)
1098 Hunting Lodge Dr
Miami Springs, FL 33166-5754, USA

Petcka, Joe (Actor)
c/o Marta Michaud *Cinematic Management*
249 1/2 E 13th St
New York, NY 10003-5602, USA

Peter, Philipp (Race Car Driver)
Dorricott Racing
29103 Arnold Dr
Sonoma, CA 95476-9761, USA

Peterdi, Gabor (Artist)
108 Highland Ave
Norwalk, CT 06853-1315, USA

Peterek, Jeff (Athlete, Baseball Player)
8073 Elm Valley Rd
Three Oaks, MI 49128-9552, USA

Peterffy, Thomas (Business Person)
Interactive Brokers LLC
1 Pickwick Plz Ste 100
Greenwich, CT 06830-5531, USA

Peterman, Melissa (Actor, Television Host)
2609 Waverly Dr
Los Angeles, CA 90039-2724, USA

Peter Paul & Mary (Music Group, Musician)
121 Mount Hermon Way
Ocean Grove, NJ 07756-1443

Peters, Andrew (Athlete, Hockey Player)
4191 Main St
Buffalo, NY 14226-3436, USA

Peters, Andy (Television Host)
c/o Staff Member *BBC Artist Mail*
PO Box 1116
Belfast BT2 7AJ, United Kingdom

Peters, Anthony L (Tony) (Athlete, Football Player)
2402 Boston St
Muskogee, OK 74401-5233, USA

Peters, Barbara (Director)
1118 Magnolia Blvd
North Hollywood, CA 91601, USA

Peters, Bernadette (Actor, Musician)
c/o Judy Katz *Judy Katz Public Relations*
1345 Avenue Of The Americas Fl 2
New York, NY 10105-0014, USA

Peters, Bob (Coach)
Bernidji State University
Athletic Dept
Bernidji, MN 56601, USA

Peters, Caleigh (Musician)
c/o Siri Garber *Platform PR*
2666 N Beachwood Dr
Los Angeles, CA 90068-2308, USA

Peters, Charlie (Writer)
c/o Todd Feldman *Creative Artists Agency (CAA)*
2000 Avenue of the Stars Ste 100
Los Angeles, CA 90067-4705, USA

Peters, Chris (Athlete, Baseball Player)
613 Chessbriar Dr
Bethel Park, PA 15102-1531, USA

Peters, Clarke (Actor)
c/o Staff Member *Artists & Representatives (Stone Manners Salners)*
6100 Wilshire Blvd Ste 1500
Los Angeles, CA 90048-5110, USA

Peters, Corey (Athlete, Football Player)

Peters, Dan (Musician)
Legends of 21st Century
7 Trinity Row
Florence, MA 01062-1931, USA

Peters, Evan (Actor)
c/o Tim Taylor *Luber Roklin Management*
5815 W Sunset Blvd Ste 208
Los Angeles, CA 90028-6481, USA

Peters, Garry (Athlete, Hockey Player)
3020 Eastview
Saskatoon, SK S7J 3J2, Canada

Peters, Gary (Athlete, Baseball Player)
6120 Wilshire Cir
Sarasota, FL 34238-2563, USA

Peters, Gretchen (Musician, Songwriter, Writer)
Gretchen Peters Management
PO Box 331242
Nashville, TN 37203-7512, USA

Peters, Jason (Athlete, Football Player)
11611 Secretariat Dr
Walton, NE 68461-9804, USA

Peters, Jim (Athlete, Hockey Player)
60 Main St
Essex Jct, VT 05452-3145

Peters, Jon (Producer)
c/o Staff Member *Peters Entertainment*
21731 Ventura Blvd Ste 300
Woodland Hills, CA 91364-1851, USA

Peters, Marcus (Athlete, Football Player)
c/o Doug Hendrickson *Relativity Sports*
2029 Century Park E Ste 1550
Century City, CA 90067-3000, USA

Peters, Maria Liberia (Prime Minister)
Prime Minister's Office
Fort Amsterdam
Willemstad, NETHERLANDS ANTILLES

Peters, Marjorie (Athlete, Baseball Player)
4081 S 122nd St
Greenfield, WI 53228-1823, USA

Peters, Mary (Athlete, Track Athlete)
Willowtree Cottage
River Road
Dunmurray, Belfast, NORTHERN IRLAND

Peters, Mike (Cartoonist)
PO Box 957
Bradenton, FL 34206-0957, USA

Peters, Ralph (Writer)
c/o Scott Miller *Trident Media Group LLC*
41 Madison Ave Fl 36
New York, NY 10010-2257, USA

Peters, Ray (Athlete, Baseball Player)
11013 Southerland Dr
Denton, TX 76207-8687, USA

Peters, Rick (Actor)
c/o Patricia (Patty) Woo *Patty Woo Management*
8906 W Olympic Blvd
Beverly Hills, CA 90211-3550, USA

Peters, Rick (Athlete, Baseball Player)
43977 W Juniper Ave
Maricopa, AZ 85138-4072, USA

Peters, Russell (Actor)
c/o Leslie Sloane *Vision PR*
2 Penn Plz Rm 2601
New York, NY 10121-0001, USA

Peters, Steve (Athlete, Baseball Player)
12400 Ladonna Dr
Oklahoma City, OK 73170-1026, USA

Peters, Steve (Athlete, Hockey Player)
1021 Golfview Rd
Peterborough, ON K9J 7W2, Canada

Peters, Timothy (Race Car Driver)
BHR
PO Box 1708
Mount Juliet, TN 37121-1708, USA

Peters, Tom (Business Person)
PO Box 290058
466 Eaton Rd
Charlestown, MA 02129-0201, USA

Peters, Volney (Athlete, Football Player)
PO Box 1017
Blairsden Graeagle, CA 96103-1017, USA

Petersen, Chris (Athlete, Baseball Player)
242 Timberland Ave
Longwood, FL 32750-6159, USA

petersen, jim (Athlete, Basketball Player)
2622 W Lake St Apt 702
Minneapolis, MN 55416-5490, USA

Petersen, Kurt (Athlete, Football Player)
5520 Linmore Ln
Plano, TX 75093-7619, USA

Petersen, Loy (Athlete, Basketball Player)
475 NE Meadowlark Ln
Madras, OR 97741-9063, USA

Petersen, Patty (Actor)
60 Kennedy St
Camarillo, CA 93010, USA

Petersen, Ted (Athlete, Football Player)
323 Ridge Point Cir Apt 32A
Bridgeville, PA 15017-1566, USA

Petersen, Toby (Athlete, Hockey Player)
3105 Milton Ave
Dallas, TX 75205-1449

Petersen, William (Actor, Producer)
c/o Staff Member *High Horse Films*
100 Universal City Plz Bldg E
Universal City, CA 91608-1002, USA

Petersen, Wolfgang (Director)
c/o Staff Member *Radiant Productions*
914 Montana Ave Fl 2
Santa Monica, CA 90403-1505, USA

Petersmark, Brett (Athlete, Football Player)
2082 Pennsbury Ln
Hanover Park, IL 60133-6715, USA

Peterson, Adam (Athlete, Baseball Player)
5610 NE 33rd Ave
Vancouver, WA 98663-1414, USA

Peterson, Adrian (Athlete, Football Player)
c/o Ben Dogra *Relativity Sports*
2029 Century Park E Ste 1550
Century City, CA 90067-3000, USA

Peterson, Anthony (Boxer)
c/o Staff Member *Top Rank Inc.*
3908 Howard Hughes Pkwy
#580
Las Vegas, NV 89109, USA

Peterson, Anthony (Athlete, Football Player)
1974 Montrose Dr
Atlanta, GA 30344-3003, USA

Peterson, Ben (Athlete, Olympic Athlete, Wrestler)
205 Dewey Ave
Watertown, WI 53094-3915, USA

Peterson, Brent (Athlete, Hockey Player)
724 Glen Oaks Dr
Franklin, TN 37067-1345

Peterson, Buzz (Coach)
University of Tennessee
Athletic Dept
Knoxville, TN 37996-0001, USA

Peterson, Cal (Athlete, Football Player)
22646 Ingomar St
Canoga Park, CA 91304-4622, USA

Peterson, David C (Journalist, Photographer)
174 Rainbow Dr
Livingston, TX 77399-1074, USA

Peterson, Debbi (Musician)
Bangles Mall
1341 W Fullerton Ave # 180
Chicago, IL 60614-2362, USA

Peterson, Donald H Colonel (Astronaut)
220 Eagle Ct
Bedford, TX 76021-3216, USA

Peterson, Donald R (Astronaut)
Aerospace Operations Consultants
220 Eagle Ct
Bedford, TX 76021-3216, USA

Peterson, Forrest J (Misc)
17 Collins Meadow Dr
Georgetown, SC 29440, USA

Peterson, Fritz (Athlete, Baseball Player)
PO Box 454
Onalaska, WI 54650-0454, USA

Peterson, Harding (Hardy) (Athlete, Baseball Player)
2822 Sherbrooke Ln Apt C
Palm Harbor, FL 34684-2545, USA

Peterson, Jessie Lee (Radio Personality, Television Host)
PO Box 35090
Los Angeles, CA 90035-0090, USA

Peterson, John (Wrestler)
457 19th Ave
Comstock, WI 54826-9746, USA

Peterson, Jordan (Writer)
c/o Rob Greenwald *Rogers & Cowan*
1840 Century Park E Fl 18
Los Angeles, CA 90067-2101, USA

Peterson, Kyle (Athlete, Baseball Player)
13253 Hamilton St
Omaha, NE 68154-5293, USA

Peterson, Larry (Race Car Driver)
Bales Motorsports
PO Box 4098
107 Bennett St.
Sidney, OH 45365-4098, USA

Peterson, Loralyn (Actor)
c/o Jon Orlando *Exposure Marketing Group*
348 Hauser Blvd Apt 414
Los Angeles, CA 90036-5590, USA

Peterson, Michael (Athlete, Football Player)
PO Box 904
Alachua, FL 32616-0904, USA

Peterson, Morris (Athlete, Basketball Player)
909 Lafayette St Apt 12
New Orleans, LA 70113-1041, USA

Peterson, Patrick (Athlete, Football Player)
c/o Denise White *EAG Sports Management*
909 N Pacific Coast Hwy Ste 360
El Segundo, CA 90245-3864, USA

Peterson, Patrick (Athlete, Baseball Player)
c/o Patrick William Lawlor *Galaxy Sports*
811 E Hillsboro Blvd
Deerfield Beach, FL 33441-3521, USA

Peterson, Peter G (Politician)
345 Park Ave Bsmt LB4
New York, NY 10154-0004, USA

Peterson, Seth (Actor)
3424 Blair Dr
Los Angeles, CA 90068-1412, USA

Peterson, Todd (Athlete, Football Player)
3249 Chatham Rd NW
Atlanta, GA 30305-1101, USA

Peterson, Vicki (Musician)
Bangles Mall
1341 W Fullerton Ave # 180
Chicago, IL 60614-2362, USA

Peterson, William (Actor)
c/o Steve Dontanville *Circle of Confusion (NY)*
270 Lafayette St Ste 402
New York, NY 10012-3327, USA

Peterson, William W (Athlete, Football Player)
13536 Mijo Ln
Lakeside, CA 92040-4824, USA

Peterson-Fox, Betty Jean (Athlete, Baseball Player)
PO Box 280
110 E NORTH ST
Wyanet, IL 61379-0280, USA

Peterson-Parker, Katie (Golfer)
527 Henkel Cir
Winter Park, FL 32789-5127, USA

Pete Stark, Fortney (Congressman, Politician)
239 Cannon Hob
Washington, DC 20515-0513, USA

Petherbridge, Edward (Actor)
Jonathan Altaras
13 Shorts Gardens
London WC2H 9AT, UNITED KINGDOM (UK)

Petievich, Gerald (Producer, Writer)
c/o Brian Lipson *WME/IMG*
9601 Wilshire Blvd
Beverly Hills, CA 90210-5213, USA

Petit, Michel (Athlete, Hockey Player)
70 Wooded Park Pl
Spring, TX 77380-2490

Petit, Philippe (Misc)
Cathedral of Saint John the Devine
1047 Amsterdam Ave
New York, NY 10025-1747, USA

Petitbon, John (Athlete, Football Player)
3804 N Labarre Rd
Metairie, LA 70002-1817, USA

Petitbon, Richie (Athlete, Football Coach, Football Player)
9628 Percussion Way
Vienna, VA 22182-3334, USA

Petitgout, Luke (Athlete, Football Player)
267 Prospect St
Ridgewood, NJ 07450-5121, USA

Petke, Mike (Soccer Player)
DC United
14120 Newbrook Dr
Chantilly, VA 20151-2273, USA

Petkovic, Andrea (Athlete, Tennis Player)
c/o Staff Member *Women's Tennis Association (WTA-US)*
1 Progress Plz Ste 1500
St Petersburg, FL 33701-4335, USA

Petkovsek, Mark (Athlete, Baseball Player)
5575 Duff St
Beaumont, TX 77706-6307, USA

Peto, Richard (Misc)
Radcliffe Infirmary
Harkness Building
Oxford, ON OX2 6HE, UNITED KINGDOM (UK)

Petra, Yvon (Tennis Player)
Residence du Prieure
Saint Germain en Laye 78100, FRANCE

Petralli, Geno (Athlete, Baseball Player)
604 E Anderson St
Weatherford, TX 76086-5704, USA

Petras, Ernestine (Athlete, Baseball Player)
5 Greenwood Ave
Haskell, NJ 07420-1417, USA

Petree, Andy (Race Car Driver)
Petree Racing
PO Box 325
908 Upward Rd.
East Flat Rock, NC 28726-0325, USA

Petrenko, Victor (Figure Skater)
c/o Staff Member *Champions on Ice*
3500 American Blvd W Ste 190
Minneapolis, MN 55431-4431, USA

Petrenko, Viktor (Figure Skater)
International Skating Center
PO Box 577
Simsbury, CT 06070-0577, USA

Petrey, Dan (Athlete, Baseball Player)
The Athletic Connection
PO Box 380135
Clinton Township, MI 48038-0060, USA

Petri, Michala (Musician)
Nordskraenten 3
Kokkedal 02980, DENMARK

Petri, Nina (Actor)
Agentur Carola Studlar
Agnesstr 47
Munich 80798, GERMANY

Petrich, Bob (Athlete, Football Player)
1391 Silverberry Ct
El Cajon, CA 92019-2835, USA

Petrick, Ben (Athlete, Baseball Player)
1553 NE Jackson School Rd
Hillsboro, OR 97124-2425, USA

Petrick, Billy (Athlete, Baseball Player)
103 Hickory Ln
Morris, IL 60450-1627, USA

Petrie, Alistair (Actor, Musician)
c/o Roxane Vacca *Roxane Vacca Management*
61 Judd St
London WC1H 9QT, UNITED KINGDOM

Petrie, Donald (Director)
c/o Alan Gasmer *Alan Gasmer Management Company*
10877 Wilshire Blvd Ste 603
Los Angeles, CA 90024-4348, USA

Petrie, Geoff (Athlete, Basketball Player)
3675 Holly Hill Ln
Loomis, CA 95650-8818, USA

Petriw, Adrian (Actor)
c/o Michelle Gauvin *Performers Management*
5-636 Clyde Ave
West Vancouver, BC V7T 1E1, CANADA

Petrocelli, Americo P (Rico) (Athlete, Baseball Player)
37 Green Heron Ln
Nashua, NH 03062-2239, USA

Petrone, Shana (Musician)
c/o Staff Member *Creative Artists Agency (CAA)*
401 Commerce St PH
Nashville, TN 37219-2516, USA

Petrone, Shana (Musician)
Creative Artists Agency
3310 W End Ave Ste 500
Nashville, TN 37203-1087, USA

Petroni, Michael (Director)
United Talent Agency
9336 Civic Center Dr
Beverly Hills, CA 90210-3604, USA

Petroske, John (Athlete, Hockey Player)
705 17th St N Apt 206
Virginia, MN 55792-2182, USA

Petrovic, Tim (Golfer)
12708 Tradition Dr
Dade City, FL 33525-8240, USA

Petrovicky, Robert (Athlete, Hockey Player)
20944 Island Sound Cir Unit 106
Estero, FL 33928-8996

Petrovicky, Ronald (Athlete, Hockey Player)
4768 Strom Pl
Prince George, BC V2M 7E4, Canada

Petrucci, John (Musician)
c/o Staff Member *UTA Music/The Agency Group*
9336 Civic Center Dr
Beverly Hills, CA 90210-3604, USA

Petry, Dan (Athlete, Baseball Player)
The Athletic Connection
PO Box 380135
Clinton Township, MI 48038-0060, USA

Petsch, Madelaine (Actor)
c/o Siri Garber *Platform PR*
2666 N Beachwood Dr
Los Angeles, CA 90068-2308, USA

Pet Shop Boys (Music Group)
c/o Staff Member *Creative Artists Agency (CAA)*
2000 Avenue of the Stars Ste 100
Los Angeles, CA 90067-4705, USA

Petsko, Gregory A (Misc)
8 Jason Rd
Belmont, MA 02478-3129, USA

Pett, Joel (Cartoonist)
Lexington Herald-Leader
1010 W New Circle Rd
Lexington, KY 40511-1839, USA

Pettee, Roger (Athlete, Football Player)
627 Mirabay Blvd
Apollo Beach, FL 33572-3379, USA

Pettersson, Carl (Athlete, Golfer)
2208 Oak Lawn Way
Wake Forest, NC 27587-4700, USA

Pettibon, Raymond (Artist)
Michael Kohn Gallery
920 Colorado Ave
Santa Monica, CA 90401-2717, USA

Pettibon, Richard A (Richie) (Athlete, Football Player)
9628 Percussion Way
Vienna, VA 22182-3334, USA

Pettibone, Jay (Athlete, Baseball Player)
5112 Via Marcos
Yorba Linda, CA 92887-2530, USA

Pettie, Jim (Athlete, Hockey Player)
81 Kirk Rd
Rochester, NY 14612-3301

Petties, Neal (Athlete, Football Player)
767 Jewell Dr
San Diego, CA 92113-2731, USA

Pettiford, Valarie (Actor)
c/o Joel Dean *TalentWorks*
3500 W Olive Ave Ste 1400
Burbank, CA 91505-5512, USA

Pettigrew, Brandon (Athlete, Football Player)
c/o Sean Howard *Octagon Football*
600 Battery St Fl 2
San Francisco, CA 94111-1820, USA

Pettigrew, Gary (Athlete, Football Player)
1107 W 33rd Ave
Spokane, WA 99203-1403, USA

Pettijohn, Francis J (Misc)
11630 Glen Arm Rd # V51
Glen Arm, MD 21057-9403, USA

Pettinato, Rachelle (Actor)
c/o Staff Member *Select Artists Ltd (CA-Westside Office)*
1138 12th St Apt 1
Santa Monica, CA 90403-5459, USA

Pettinger, Matt (Athlete, Hockey Player)
3075 Eastdowne Rd
Victoria, BC V8R 5S1, Canada

Pettini, Joe (Athlete, Baseball Player)
112 Logan Ct
Bethany, WV 26032-2016, USA

Pettis, Austin (Athlete, Football Player)
c/o Bradley Cicala *Terra Firma Sports Management*
330 W Spring St Ste 355
Columbus, OH 43215-7305, USA

Pettis, Gary (Athlete, Baseball Player)
1871 Crispin Dr
Brentwood, CA 94513-2659, USA

Pettis, Madison (Actor)
c/o Alissa Vradenburg *Untitled Entertainment*
350 S Beverly Dr Ste 200
Beverly Hills, CA 90212-4819, USA

Pettis, Madison (Actor)
c/o Adam Griffin *LINK Entertainment*
11872 La Grange Ave
Los Angeles, CA 90025-5282, USA

Pettit, Bob (Athlete, Basketball Player)
7 Garden Ln
New Orleans, LA 70124-1024, USA

Pettit, Donald R (Astronaut)
2014 Country Ridge Dr
Houston, TX 77062-3636, USA

Pettit, Paul (Athlete, Baseball Player)
928 Sarazen St
Hemet, CA 92543-8057, USA

Pettit Jr, Robert L (Bob) (Basketball Player)
7 Garden Ln
New Orleans, LA 70124-1024, USA

Pettitte, Andy (Athlete, Baseball Player)
c/o Team Member *New York Yankees*
161st St & River Ave
Yankee Stadium
Bronx, NY 10451, USA

Pettway, Kenneth (Athlete, Football Player)
2631 Via Verona
Lancaster, CA 93535-2853, USA

Petty, Kyle (Race Car Driver)
Kyle Petty Charity Ride
125 Floyd Smith Dr
Suite 45
Charlotte, NC 28262, USA

Petty, Lori (Actor)
c/o Leslie Conliffe *Intellectual Property Group (IPG)*
12400 Wilshire Blvd Ste 500
Los Angeles, CA 90025-1055, USA

Petty, Maurice (Race Car Driver)
248 Branson Mill Rd
Randleman, NC 27317-8007, USA

Petty, Richard (Race Car Driver)
Richard Petty Museum
311 Branson Mill Rd
Randleman, NC 27317-8008, USA

Pettyfer, Alex (Actor)
c/o Simon Halls *Slate PR*
901 N Highland Ave
W Hollywood, CA 90038-2412, USA

Pettyiohn, Adam (Athlete, Baseball Player)
4626 W Addisyn Ct
Visalia, CA 93291-9150, USA

Pettyjohn, Adam (Athlete, Baseball Player)
717 Westwood Dr
Exeter, CA 93221-1438, USA

Pevec, Katja (Actor)
c/o Anne Woodward *Authentic Talent & Literary Management*
3615 Eastham Dr # 650
Culver City, CA 90232-2410, USA

Pevey, Marty (Athlete, Baseball Player)
158 Nightwind Trce
Acworth, GA 30101-5981, USA

Peviani, Bob (Athlete, Football Player)
25262 Northrup Dr
Laguna Hills, CA 92653-5223, USA

Peyroux, Madeline (Musician, Songwriter, Writer)
Bumstead Productions
PO Box 158 Stn E
Station E
Toronto, ON M6H 4E2, CANADA

Peyton, Brad (Director)
c/o Staff Member *ASAP Entertainment*
4205 Santa Monica Blvd
Los Angeles, CA 90029-3027, USA

Pezzano, Chuck (Writer)
27 Mountainside Ter
Clifton, NJ 07013-1107, USA

Pfaff, Judy (Artist)
Holly Solomon Gallery
175 E 79th St Apt 2B
New York, NY 10075-0565, USA

Pfann, George R (Athlete, Coach, Football Coach, Football Player)
120 Warwick Pl
Ithaca, NY 14850-1731, USA

Pfeiffer, Dedee (Actor, Model)
c/o David Rose *Innovative Artists*
1505 10th St
Santa Monica, CA 90401-2805, USA

Pfeiffer, Michelle (Actor)
c/o Lana Parilla
3737 W Magnolia Blvd.
Suite 300
Burbank, CA 91505, USA

Pfeil, Bobby (Athlete, Baseball Player)
2358 Pheasant Run Cir
Stockton, CA 95207-5210, USA

Pfeil, Mark (Golfer)
2565 Chelsea Rd
Palos Verdes Estates, CA 90274-4309, USA

Pfister, Dan (Athlete, Baseball Player)
1436 Nautilus Isle
Dania, FL 33004-2332, USA

Pflug, Jo Ann (Actor)
PO Box 3292
Jupiter, FL 33469-1004, USA

P. Frelinghuysen, Rodney (Congressman, Politician)
2369 Rayburn Hob
Washington, DC 20515-3225, USA

Pfund, Lee (Athlete, Baseball Player)
420 Columbine Ln
West Chicago, IL 60185-1753, USA

Pfund, Randy (Basketball Coach, Coach)
10000 Thrushgill Ln APT 10110
Apt 1206
Franklin, TN 37067-6647, USA

P. Gibson, Christopher (Chris) (Congressman, Politician)
502 Cannon Hob
Washington, DC 20515-1003, USA

Phair, Liz (Actor, Musician, Songwriter)
c/o Jason Weinberg *Untitled Entertainment*
350 S Beverly Dr Ste 200
Beverly Hills, CA 90212-4819, USA

Phair, Lyle (Athlete, Hockey Player)
16256 Winchester Dr
Northville, MI 48168-2347

Pham, Dorian Brown (Actor)
c/o Jamie Harhay Skinner *Baker Winokur Ryder Public Relations*
9100 Wilshire Blvd
W Tower #500
Beverly Hills, CA 90212-3415, USA

Pham Dinh Tung, Paul J Cardinal (Religious Leader)
Archdiocese
Toa Tong Giam Muc
Pho Nha Chung
Hanoi 00040, VIETNAM

Phan, Michelle (Business Person, Internet Star)
c/o Staff Member *United Talent Agency (UTA)*
9336 Civic Center Dr
Beverly Hills, CA 90210-3604, USA

Phaneuf, Al (Athlete, Football Player)
5376 Pepper Brush Cv
Apopka, FL 32703-1971, USA

Phaneuf, Dion (Athlete, Hockey Player)
Newport Sports Management
400-201 City Centre Dr
Attn Don Meehan
Mississauga, ON L5B 2T4, Canada

Phaneuf, Jean-Luc (Athlete, Hockey Player)
230 Rue Chagall
Repentigny, QC J5Z 4K1, Canada

Phantogram (Music Group)
c/o Mike Mori *Paradigm (Chicago)*
2209 W North Ave
Chicago, IL 60647-6084, USA

Pharris, Chrystee (Actor)
c/o Marleah Leslie *Marleah Leslie & Associates*
1645 Vine St Apt 712
Los Angeles, CA 90028-8812, USA

Phegley, Roger (Athlete, Basketball Player)
43 Timberlane Dr
Morton, IL 61550-1146, USA

Pheil, Anna (Actor)
c/o Scott Zimmerman *Scott Zimmerman Management*
1644 Courtney Ave
Los Angeles, CA 90046-2708, USA

Phelan, Jack (Athlete, Basketball Player)
5504 Country Lakes Trl
Sarasota, FL 34243-3813, USA

Phelan, Jim (Athlete, Basketball Player)
16579 Old Emmitsburg Rd
Emmitsburg, MD 21727-8927, USA

Phelos, Travis (Athlete, Baseball Player)
PO Box 336
Wheaton, MO 64874-0336, USA

Phelps, Brian (Actor)
1265 Coldwater Canyon Dr
Beverly Hills, CA 90210-2419, USA

Phelps, Doug (Musician)
Mitchell Fox Mgmt
212 3rd Ave N # 301
Nashville, TN 37201-1604, USA

Phelps, James (Actor)
JOP Project
PO Box 9765
Coldfield
Sutton B75 5XB, UNITED KINGDOM (UK)

Phelps, Jaycie (Athlete, Gymnast, Olympic Athlete)
Jaycie Phelps Athletic Center
3802A N 600 W
Greenfield, IN 46140-9642, USA

Phelps, Josh (Athlete, Baseball Player)
1503 Regal Mist Loop
Trinity, FL 34655-4974, USA

Phelps, Kelly Joe (Athlete, Football Player)
Fleming/Tamulevich Assoc
8782 Brooks Creek Dr Apt 1516
Cincinnati, OH 45249-3001, USA

Phelps, Ken (Athlete, Baseball Player)
6030 E Foothill Dr N
Paradise Valley, AZ 85253-3070, USA

Phelps, Michael (Athlete, Olympic Athlete, Swimmer)
Michael Phelps Foundation
7 Ocean St Ste 2
South Portland, ME 04106-2800, USA

Phelps, Oliver (Actor)
c/o Staff Member *JOP Project*
PO Box 9765
Sutton Coldfield B75 5XB, United Kingdom

Phelps, Richard (Athlete)
c/o Staff Member *ESPN (Main)*
935 Middle St
Espn Plaza
Bristol, CT 06010-1000, USA

Phelps, Richard F (Digger) (Coach)
ESPN-TV
Sports Dept
ESPN Plaza 935 Middle St
Bristol, CT 06010, USA

Phelps, Tommy (Athlete, Baseball Player)
4418 Pawnee Path
Valrico, FL 33594-5529, USA

Phelps, Travis (Athlete, Baseball Player)
PO Box 336
Wheaton, MO 64874-0336, USA

Phenix, Perry Lee (Athlete, Football Player)
4849 Frankford Rd Apt 715
Dallas, TX 75287-5309, USA

Pheto, Terry (Actor)
c/o Nick LoPiccolo *Paradigm*
8942 Wilshire Blvd
Beverly Hills, CA 90211-1908, USA

Phifer, Mekhi (Actor)
c/o Emily Gerson Saines *Brookside Artists Management*
250 W 57th St Ste 1820
New York, NY 10107-1802, USA

Phifer, Roman Z (Athlete, Football Player)
PO Box 83215
Los Angeles, CA 90083-0215, USA

Philaret, Patriarch (Religious Leader)
10 Osvobozdeniya St
Minsk 22004, BELARUS

Philbin, Gerry (Athlete, Football Player)
9976 Marsala Way
Delray Beach, FL 33446-9727, USA

Philbin, Regis (Television Host)
101 W 67th St Apt 51A
New York, NY 10023-5953, USA

Philbrick, Denise (Athlete, Golfer)

Philcox, Todd (Athlete, Football Player)
1201 1st St N Apt 703
Jacksonville Beach, FL 32250-8205, USA

Philip, Primate (Religious Leader)
Antiochian Orthodox Christian Church
358 Mountain Rd
Englewood, NJ 07631-3798, USA

Philipp, Stephanie (Model)
Agentur Margit de la Berg
Icking-Isartal 82057, GERMANY

Philippoussis, Mark (Tennis Player)
Octagon
1751 Pinnacle Dr Ste 1500
McLean, VA 22102-3833, USA

Philipps, Busy (Actor)
c/o Rachel Karten *ID Public Relations*
7060 Hollywood Blvd Fl 8th
Los Angeles, CA 90028-6021, USA

Philips, brandon (Athlete, Baseball Player)
586 Rowland Rd
Stone Mountain, GA 30083-4573, USA

Philips, Chuck (Journalist)
Los Angeles Times
2300 E Imperial Hwy
Editorial Dept
El Segundo, CA 90245-2813, USA

Philips, Emo (Actor)
c/o Staff Member *OmniPop Talent Group*
4605 Lankershim Blvd Ste 201
Toluca Lake, CA 91602-1874, USA

Philips, Gina (Actor)
c/o Erik Kritzer *LINK Entertainment*
11872 La Grange Ave
Los Angeles, CA 90025-5282, USA

Phillios, Jason (Athlete, Baseball Player)
7111 Defranzo Loop
Fort George G Meade, MD 20755-4053, USA

Phillipoff, Harold (Athlete, Hockey Player)
446 Harrison St
Sumas, WA 98295-9613, USA

Phillippe, Ryan (Actor)
c/o Nicole Perna *Imprint PR*
6121 W Sunset Blvd
Neuehouse
Los Angeles, CA 90028-6442, USA

Phillips, Anthony (Musician, Songwriter, Writer)
Solo Agency
55 Fulham High St
London SW6 3JJ, UNITED KINGDOM (UK)

Phillips, Bijou (Actor, Model, Musician)
2151 Hollyridge Dr
Los Angeles, CA 90068-3514, USA

Phillips, Bill (Writer)
High Point Media LLC
10100 Santa Monica Blvd Ste 1300
Los Angeles, CA 90067-4114, USA

Phillips, Bobbie (Actor)
The Kelly Agency
3001 Heavenly Ridge St
Thousand Oaks, CA 91362-1178, USA

Phillips, Brandon (Athlete, Baseball Player)
586 Rowland Rd
Stone Mountain, GA 30083-4573, USA

Phillips, Caryl (Writer)
Amherst College
English Dept
Amherst, MA 01002, USA

Phillips, Chris (Athlete, Hockey Player)
C A A Hockey
204-822 11 Ave SW
Attn J P Barry
Calgary, AB T2R 0E5, Canada

Phillips, Chynna (Actor, Musician)
1007 Montana Ave Apt 230
Santa Monica, CA 90403-1603, USA

Phillips, Connie Anne (Business Person)
Conde Nast
1 World Trade Ctr Fl 20
New York, NY 10007-0090, USA

Phillips, Damaris (Chef)
c/o Staff Member *The Food Network.com*
1180 Avenue of the Americas Fl 14
New York, NY 10036-8401, USA

Phillips, Davey (Baseball Player)
42 Lily Pond Ln
Weldon Spring, MO 63304-0542, USA

Phillips, Davey (Athlete, Baseball Player)
42 Lily Pond Ln
Weldon Spring, MO 63304-0542, USA

Phillips, David (Producer)
Corner of the Sky
1724 N Highland Ave Apt 328
Los Angeles, CA 90028-4417, USA

Phillips, Eddie (Athlete, Baseball Player)
1323 S Oak Run Pl
Springfield, MO 65809-2024, USA

Phillips, Eddie Lee (Athlete, Basketball Player)
800 McCary St SW
Birmingham, AL 35211-2944, USA

Phillips, Emo (Comedian)
Harbour Agency
63 William St # 300
Chicopee, MA 01020-2433, AUSTRALIA

Phillips, Ethan (Actor)
c/o Harry Gold *TalentWorks*
3500 W Olive Ave Ste 1400
Burbank, CA 91505-5512, USA

Phillips, Gary (Athlete, Basketball Player)
729 Country Club Dr
Kerrville, TX 78028-2781, USA

Phillips, Gene (Athlete, Basketball Player)
4630 Eldon Run
San Antonio, TX 78247-5520, USA

Phillips, Gersha (Designer)
c/o Staff Member *Paradigm*
8942 Wilshire Blvd
Beverly Hills, CA 90211-1908, USA

Phillips, Glasgow (Director)
c/o Brett Hansen *United Talent Agency (UTA)*
9336 Civic Center Dr
Beverly Hills, CA 90210-3604, USA

Phillips, Graham (Actor)
c/o Dannielle Thomas *Untitled Entertainment*
350 S Beverly Dr Ste 200
Beverly Hills, CA 90212-4819, USA

Phillips, Grant Lee (Musician)
c/o Staff Member *Paradigm (Monterey)*
404 W Franklin St
Monterey, CA 93940-2303, USA

Phillips, Jack (Athlete, Baseball Player)
721 May Rd
Potsdam, NY 13676-3244, USA

Phillips, James (Red) (Athlete, Football Player)
PO Box 1658
Alex City, AL 35011, USA

Phillips, Jason (Athlete, Football Player)
3001 N Boulevard
Richmond, VA 23230-4331, USA

Phillips, Jason (Athlete, Baseball Player)
265 Katie Ln
Montoursville, PA 17754-8275, USA

Phillips, Jason (Athlete, Baseball Player)
1777 Tara Way
San Marcos, CA 92078-1081, USA

Phillips, Jeff Daniel (Actor)
c/o Katie Mason Stern *Luber Roklin Management*
5815 W Sunset Blvd Ste 208
Los Angeles, CA 90028-6481, USA

Phillips, Jess (Athlete, Football Player)
2820 San Antonio St
Beaumont, TX 77701-8036, USA

Phillips, Jim (Athlete, Football Player)
832 Yorkshire Dr
Auburn, AL 36830-7564, USA

Phillips, Joe (Athlete, Football Player)
425 Barker Ave
Oregon City, OR 97045-3449, USA

Phillips, John (Athlete, Football Player)
c/o Jim Ivler *Sportstars Inc*
1370 Avenue of the Americas Fl 19
New York, NY 10019-4602, USA

Phillips, John (Coach)
University of Tulsa
Athletic Dept
Tulsa, OK 74104, USA

Phillips, John L (Astronaut)
154 Canoe Cove Ln
Sandpoint, ID 83864-7968, USA

Phillips, J R (Athlete, Baseball Player)
22410 N 74th Ln
Glendale, AZ 85310-5670, USA

Phillips, Julianne (Actor)
27727 Pacific Coast Hwy
Malibu, CA 90265-4344, 90265-4344

Phillips, Kevin (Actor)
c/o Todd Eisner *Abrams Artists Agency*
750 N San Vicente Blvd
E Tower Fl 11
Los Angeles, CA 90069-5788, USA

Phillips, Kirk (Athlete, Football Player)
2103 E Alma Ave
Sherman, TX 75090-4008, USA

Phillips, Leslie (Actor)
78 Maida Vale
London W9 1PR, UNITED KINGDOM

Phillips, Lou Diamond (Actor)
c/o JB Roberts *Thruline Entertainment*
9250 Wilshire Blvd Fl Ground
Beverly Hills, CA 90212-3352, USA

Phillips, Loyd (Athlete, Football Player)
General Delivery
Springdale, AR 72764-9999, USA

Phillips, Mackenzie (Actor)
PO Box 396
Minisink Hills, PA 18341, USA

Phillips, Mel (Athlete, Football Player)
6368 Milk Wagon Ln
Miami Lakes, FL 33014-6083, USA

Phillips, Michelie (Actor, Musician)
c/o Marc Chancer *Origin Talent Agency*
4705 Laurel Canyon Blvd Ste 306
Studio City, CA 91607-5940, USA

Phillips, Michelle (Actor)
c/o Merritt Blake *The Blake Agency*
23441 Malibu Colony Rd
Malibu, CA 90265-4640, USA

Phillips, Paul (Athlete, Baseball Player)
507 N Mine Ave
Demopolis, AL 36732-2021, USA

Phillips, Phillip (Musician)
c/o Brett Radin *19 Entertainment*
401 Wilshire Blvd Ste 1070
Santa Monica, CA 90401-1428, USA

Phillips, Princess Zara (Royalty)
Gatcombe Park
Minchinhampton
Stroud GL6 9AT, United Kingdom

Phillips, Scott (Musician)
Agency Group
1776 Broadway Ste 430
New York, NY 10019-2002, USA

Phillips, Shaun (Athlete, Football Player)
c/o Staff Member *EAG Sports Management*
909 N Pacific Coast Hwy Ste 360
El Segundo, CA 90245-3864, USA

Phillips, Sian (Actor)
8 Alexa Court
78 Lexham Gardens
London, ENGLAND W8 6JL, UNITED KINGDOM (UK)

Phillips, steve (Sportscaster)
148 Mather St
Wilton, CT 06897-5011, USA

Phillips, Stone (Correspondent)

Phillips, Stu (Musician)
654 Long Hollow Pike
Goodlettsville, TN 37072-3449, USA

Phillips, Tari (Basketball Player)
New York Liberty
2 Penn Plz Fl 15
Madison Square Garden
New York, NY 10121-1700, USA

Phillips, Taylor (Athlete, Baseball Player)
594 Mein Mitchell Rd
Hiram, GA 30141-5810, USA

Phillips, Ted (Business Person, Football Executive)
125 E Ellis Ave
Libertyville, IL 60048-1957, USA

Phillips, Teresa (Basketball Player, Coach)
Tennessee State University
Athletic Dept
Nashville, TN 37209, USA

Phillips, Todd (Actor, Director, Producer, Writer)
c/o Todd Feldman *Creative Artists Agency (CAA)*
2000 Avenue of the Stars Ste 100
Los Angeles, CA 90067-4705, USA

Phillips, Tony (Athlete, Baseball Player)
14850 N Scottsdale Rd Ste 500
Scottsdale, AZ 85254-3464, USA

Phillips, Wade (Athlete, Coach, Football Coach, Football Player)
c/o Gary O'Hagan *IMG Coaches*
601 Carlson Pkwy Ste 610
Minnetonka, MN 55305-5215, USA

Phillips-Bannister, Kristie (Gymnast)
KPAC Gymnastics
2809 Amity Hill Rd
Statesville, NC 28677-9744, USA

Phillips, Craig, and Dean (Musician)
c/o Staff Member *INO Records*
210 Jamestown Park Ste 100
Brentwood, TN 37027-7570, USA

Phillopusis, Mark (Tennis Player)
c/o Staff Member *Octagon (VA)*
7100 Forest Ave Ste 201
Richmond, VA 23226-3742, USA

Philyaw, Charles (Athlete, Football Player)
3929 Eileen Ln
Shreveport, LA 71109-1921, USA

Philyaw, Dino (Athlete, Football Player)
3164 Arrowhead St
Eugene, OR 97404-3858, USA

Phinney, Davis (Athlete, Cycler, Olympic Athlete)
4710 Holiday Dr Unit 302
Boulder, CO 80304-2361, USA

Phipps, Martin (Musician)
c/o Darrell Alexander *Cool Music Ltd*
1A Fishers Ln
Chiswick
London W4 1RX, England

Phipps, Michael E (Mike) (Athlete, Football Player)
2748 NE 25th St
Lighthouse Point, FL 33064-8308, USA

Phipps, Ogden M (Horse Racer)
1486 N Lake Way
Palm Beach, FL 33480-3031, USA

Phish (Music Group)
c/o Patrick Jordan *Red Light Management*
455 2nd St NE
#500
Charlottesville, VA 22902-5791, USA

Phoebus, Thomas H (Tom) (Athlete, Baseball Player)
2822 SW Lakemont Pl
Palm City, FL 34990-6094, USA

Phoenix, Beth (Wrestler)
c/o Kerry Rodgerson *World Wrestling Entertainment (WWE)*
1241 E Main St
Stamford, CT 06902-3520, USA

Phoenix, Joaquin (Actor)
c/o Susan Patricola *Patricola Public Relations*
369 S Doheny Dr # 1408
Beverly Hills, CA 90211-3508, USA

Phoenix, Nikki (Adult Film Star, Model)
c/o Staff Member *ATMLA*
22020 Clarendon St Ste 300
Woodland Hills, CA 91367-6333, USA

Phoenix, Rain (Actor)
PO Box 520
Royal Palm Beach, FL 33411, USA

Phoenix, Steve (Athlete, Baseball Player)
11212 Horizon Hills Dr
El Cajon, CA 92020-8231, USA

Phoenix, Summer (Actor)
2054 Laughlin Park Dr
Los Angeles, CA 90027-1712, USA

Physioc, Steve (Sportscaster)
32923 Brookseed Dr
Trabuco Canyon, CA 92679-4318, USA

Piatkowski, Eric (Athlete, Basketball Player)
9211 N 46th St
Phoenix, AZ 85028-5516, USA

Piatkowski, Walt (Athlete, Basketball Player)
2453 Broadmoor Ct
Rapid City, SD 57702-5312, USA

Piatt, Adam (Athlete, Baseball Player)
1808 SE 37th Ter
Cape Coral, FL 33904-5036, USA

Piatt, Doug (Athlete, Baseball Player)
29 L St
Beaver, PA 15009-1520, USA

Piazza, Mike (Athlete, Baseball Player)
1401 W 27th St
Miami Beach, FL 33140-4208, USA

Piazza, Vincent (Actor)
c/o Rhonda Price *Gersh*
41 Madison Ave Ste 3301
New York, NY 10010-2210, USA

Picard, Alexandre (Athlete, Hockey Player)
200 W Nationwide Blvd
ARENA
Columbus, OH 43215-2561, USA

Picard, Robert (Athlete, Hockey Player)
1410 Carambola Rd
West Palm Bch, FL 33406-5310

Picard, Roger (Athlete, Hockey Player)
733 Rue de Perce
Repentigny, QC J6A 7J5, Canada

Picardo, Robert (Actor)
c/o Peter Young *Sovereign Talent Group*
1642 Westwood Blvd Ste 202
Los Angeles, CA 90024-5609, USA

Picasso, Paloma (Actor, Designer)
Paloma Picasso & Cie.
41 Rue Martre
Clichy 92117, France

Picatto, Alexandra (Actor)
c/o Kari Estrin *Paradigm*
8942 Wilshire Blvd
Beverly Hills, CA 90211-1908, USA

Piccard, Bertrand (Misc)
Media Impact
Rue de Lausanne 42
Geneva 01201, SWITZERLAND

Picciolo, Rob (Athlete, Baseball Player)
11773 Invierno Dr
San Diego, CA 92124-2814, USA

Piccoli, Camille (Actor)
Cineart
36 Rue de Ponthieu
Paris 75008, FRANCE

Piccoli, Michel (Actor)
11 Rue des Lions Saint Paul
Paris 75004, FRANCE

Piccone, Lou (Athlete, Football Player)
49 S Youngs Rd
Williamsville, NY 14221-7024, USA

Piccone, Robin (Designer, Fashion Designer)
Piccone Apparel Corp
1424 Washington Blvd
Venice, CA 90291, USA

Pichardo, Hipolito (Athlete, Baseball Player)
21218 Saint Andrews Blvd Apt 305
Boca Raton, FL 33433-2435, USA

Pichette, Dave (Athlete, Hockey Player)
4751 Rue Escoffier
Quebec, QC G1Y 3J4, Canada

Pichler, Joseph A (Business Person)
Kroger Co
1014 Vine St Ste 2200
Cincinnati, OH 45202-1116, USA

Pichlikova, Lenka (Actor)
101 Knickerbocker Ave
Stamford, CT 06907-2520, USA

Pick, Amelie (Actor)
Artmedia
20 Ave Rapp
Paris 75007, FRANCE

Pickard, Nancy (Writer)
2225 Ashley River Rd APT 186
Charleston, SC 29414-4779, USA

Pickel, William (Bill) (Athlete, Football Player)
9 Autumn Ridge Rd
South Salem, NY 10590-1103, USA

Pickens, Bruce (Athlete, Football Player)
2644 Sardis Chase Ct
Buford, GA 30519-6007, USA

Pickens, Carl M (Athlete, Football Player)
623 Terrace Ave
Murphy, NC 28906, USA

Pickens, Madeleine (Business Person)
Saving America's Mustangs
2683 Via De La Valle # G313
Del Mar, CA 92014-1911, USA

Pickens, Robert (Athlete, Football Player)
6701 S Crandon Ave Apt 21B
Chicago, IL 60649-1274, USA

Pickens, T Boone (Business Person)
8117 Preston Rd Ste 260
Dallas, TX 75225-6321, USA

Pickens Jr, James (Actor)
c/o Lauren Tobin *Panther PR*
13351D Riverside Dr # 699
Sherman Oaks, CA 91423-2508, USA

Pickering, Byron (Artist)
6919 NE Highland Dr
Lincoln City, OR 97367, USA

Pickering, Calvin (Baseball Player)
Baltimore Orioles
201 Tanglewood Pl Apt 305
Tampa, FL 92604-2811, USA

Pickering, Jeff (Cartoonist)
c/o Staff Member *King Features Syndication*
300 W 57th St Fl 15
New York, NY 10019-5238, USA

Pickett, Cecil ""Ricky"" (Athlete, Baseball Player)
110 Wagon Wheel Rd
Willow Park, TX 76087-3135, USA

Pickett, Cindy (Actor)
c/o Andrew Howard *Shelter Entertainment*
9255 W Sunset Blvd Ste 300
Los Angeles, CA 90069-3313, USA

Pickett, Ricky (Athlete, Baseball Player)
1017 Wood Ridge Dr
Azle, TX 76020-3759, USA

Pickett, Ryan (Athlete, Football Player)
901 N Broadway
Saint Louis, MO 63101-2800, USA

Pickford, Kevin (Athlete, Baseball Player)
6006 N Harcourt Dr
Coeur D Alene, ID 83815-8473, USA

Pickler, Kellie (Musician)
c/o Larry Fitzgerald *Fitzgerald Hartley Co (Nashville)*
1908 Wedgewood Ave
Nashville, TN 37212-3733, USA

Pickles, Christina (Actor)
137 S Westgate Ave
Los Angeles, CA 90049-4222, USA

Pickren, Bradley (Actor)
c/o Philip Marcus *Clear Talent Group (LA)*
10950 Ventura Blvd
Studio City, CA 91604-3340, USA

Pickren, Spencer (Actor)
c/o Philip Marcus *Clear Talent Group (LA)*
10950 Ventura Blvd
Studio City, CA 91604-3340, USA

Pico, Jeff (Athlete, Baseball Player)
100 Penzance Ave APT 74
Chico, CA 95973-8258, USA

Picou, James (Horse Racer)
5826 SW 89th Ln
Cooper City, FL 33328-5172, USA

Picoult, Jodi (Writer)
38 Goodfellow Rd
Hanover, NH 03755-4800, USA

Pictor, Bruce (Musician)
Variety Artists
1111 Riverside Ave Ste 501
Paso Robles, CA 93446-2683, USA

Pidgeon, Rebecca (Actor)
Julian Belfarge
46 Albermarle St
London W1X 4PP, UNITED KINGDOM (UK)

Piech, Ferdinand (Business Person)
Volkswagenwerk AG
Braunschweiger Str 63
Schwulper 38179, GERMANY

Piedmont, Matt (Director, Producer)
c/o Gregory McKnight *United Talent Agency (UTA)*
9336 Civic Center Dr
Beverly Hills, CA 90210-3604, USA

Piedra, Jorge (Athlete, Baseball Player)
5608 Fairfax Dr
Frisco, TX 75034-5927, USA

Piekarski, Julie (Actor)
Phoenix Productions
301-100 Donwood Dr
Winnipeg, MB R2G 0W1, CANADA

Pienaar, Jacobus F (Misc)
Rugby Football Union
PO Box 99
Newlands, 7725, SOUTH AFRICA

Pierce, Adrienne (Musician)
c/o Staff Member *Paradigm (Monterey)*
404 W Franklin St
Monterey, CA 93940-2303, USA

Pierce, Antonio (Athlete, Football Player, Sportscaster)
c/o Andy Elkin *Creative Artists Agency (CAA)*
2000 Avenue of the Stars Ste 100
Los Angeles, CA 90067-4705, USA

Pierce, Bernard (Athlete, Football Player)

Pierce, Chonda (Comedian)
c/o Andrew Tetenbaum *ATA Management (NY)*
85 Broad St Fl 18
New York, NY 10004-2783, USA

Pierce, David Hyde (Actor)
c/o Chris Kanarick *ID Public Relations (NY)*
40 Wall St Fl 51
New York, NY 10005-1385, USA

Pierce, Ed (Athlete, Baseball Player)
543 Crestview Dr
Glendora, CA 91741-2942, USA

Pierce, Jack (Athlete, Baseball Player)
1002 Cortez St
Laredo, TX 78040-6237, USA

Pierce, Jeff (Athlete, Baseball Player)
1046 Lantern Ln
Circle Pines, MN 55014-1335, USA

Pierce, Jeffrey (Actor)
c/o Gary Pearl *Pearl Pictures & Management*
10956 Weyburn Ave Ste 200
Los Angeles, CA 90024-2835, USA

Pierce, Jill (Actor)
Extreme Team Productions
15941 Harlem Ave # 319
Tinley Park, IL 60477-1609, USA

Pierce, John (Musician)
c/o Staff Member *Paradigm (Monterey)*
404 W Franklin St
Monterey, CA 93940-2303, USA

Pierce, Jonathan (Musician)
Muse Assoc
330 Franklin Rd # 135-8
Brentwood, TN 37027-3280, USA

Pierce, Lincoln (Cartoonist)
United Feature Syndicate
200 Madison Ave
New York, NY 10016-3903, USA

Pierce, Paul (Athlete, Basketball Player)
c/o Jeff Schwartz *Excel Sports Management*
1700 Broadway Fl 29
New York, NY 10019-6559, USA

Pierce, Randy (Athlete, Hockey Player)
178 Five Arches Dr RR 3
Pakenham, ON K0A 2X0, Canada

Pierce, Ron (Horse Racer)
PO Box 361
Clarksburg, NJ 08510-0361, USA

Pierce, Stack (Actor)
Haeggstrom Office
11288 Ventura Blvd # 620
Studio City, CA 91604-3187, USA

Pierce, Tamora (Writer)
612 Westcott St
Syracuse, NY 13210-2536, USA

Pierce, Tony (Athlete, Baseball Player)
6119 Brittany Ct
Columbus, GA 31909-4247, USA

Pierce, Wendell (Actor)
c/o Donald Spradlin *Essential Talent Management*
7958 Beverly Blvd
Los Angeles, CA 90048-4511, USA

Pierces, The (Music Group)
c/o Staff Member *Paradigm (Monterey)*
404 W Franklin St
Monterey, CA 93940-2303, USA

Pierce The Veil (Music Group)
c/o Heather Gonzales *Fearless Records*
13772 Goldenwest St # 545
Westminster, CA 92683-3123, USA

Piercy, Marge (Writer)
PO Box 1473
Wellfleet, MA 02667-1473, USA

Pieri, Damon (Athlete, Football Player)
1120 W Tuckey Ln
Phoenix, AZ 85013-1049, USA

Pierpoint, Eric (Actor)
2199 Topanga Skyline Dr
Topanga, CA 90290-4050, USA

Pierre, Juan (Athlete, Baseball Player)
6148 NW 65th Ter
Parkland, FL 33067-1553, USA

Pierre-Paul, Jason (Athlete, Football Player)
c/o Eugene Parker *Independent Sports & Entertainment (ISE-IN)*
6435 W Jefferson Blvd # 197
Fort Wayne, IN 46804-6203, USA

Piers, Julie (Golfer)
5019 SW Hammock Creek Dr
Palm City, FL 34990-7909, USA

Piersoll, Chris (Athlete, Baseball Player)
4417 Groveland Ave
Sarasota, FL 34231-7557, USA

Pierson, Geoff (Actor)
c/o Paul Hemrend *Edna Talent Management*
318 Dundas St W
Toronto, ON M5T 1G5, CANADA

Pierson, John (Athlete, Hockey Player)
3 Steepletree Ln
Wayland, MA 01778-3912, USA

Pierson, Kate (Musician)
Direct Management Group
947 N La Cienega Blvd Ste G
Los Angeles, CA 90069-4700, USA

Pierson, Pete (Athlete, Football Player)
19130 Beckett Dr
Odessa, FL 33556-2274, USA

Pierzynski, Anthony J (AJ) (Athlete, Baseball Player)
2139 N Clifton Ave
Chicago, IL 60614-4115, USA

Pieterse, Sasha (Actor)
c/o Gary Mantoosh *Baker Winokur Ryder Public Relations*
9100 Wilshire Blvd
W Tower #500
Beverly Hills, CA 90212-3415, USA

Pietkiewicz, Stan (Athlete, Basketball Player)
2213 Venetian Way
Winter Park, FL 32789-1215, USA

Pietrangeli, Nicola (Tennis Player)
Via Eustachio Manfredi
Rome 00015, ITALY

Pietrangelo, Frank (Athlete, Hockey Player)
6371 Moretta Dr
Niagara Falls, ON L2J 4H7, Canada

Pietrus, Mickael (Basketball Player)
Golden State Warriors
1001 Broadway
Oakland, CA 94607-4019, USA

Pietrus, Mickael (Athlete, Basketball Player)
13420 Bonica Way
Windermere, FL 34786-5701, USA

Pietruski Jr, John M (Business Person)
27 Paddock Ln
Colts Neck, NJ 07722-1266, USA

Pietrzak, Jim (Athlete, Football Player)
9800 4th St N Ste 400
Saint Petersburg, FL 33702-2464, USA

Pietz, Amy (Actor)
c/o Scott Howard *Howard Entertainment*
16530 Ventura Blvd Ste 305
Encino, CA 91436-4594, USA

Pifferini, Bob Sr (Athlete, Football Player)
PO Box 1495
Twain Harte, CA 95383-1495, USA

Pignatano, Joe (Athlete, Baseball Player)
28111 Hiram St Unit 903
Bonita Springs, FL 34135-2513, USA

Pignatiello, Carmen (Athlete, Baseball Player)
4087 Milford Ln
Aurora, IL 60504-2059, USA

Pignatiellp, Carmen (Athlete, Baseball Player)
4087 Milford Ln
Aurora, IL 60504-2059, USA

Pi-Gonazalez, Amaury (Sportscaster)
4940 Adagio Ct
Fremont, CA 94538-3201, USA

Pigott, Mark C (Business Person)
PACCAR Inc
777 106th Ave NE
Bellevue, WA 98004-5027, USA

Pigott, Sebastian (Actor)
c/o Andrew Edwards *Zero Gravity Management*
11110 Ohio Ave Ste 100
Los Angeles, CA 90025-3329, USA

Pikaizen, Viktor A (Musician)
Chekhova Str 31/22
#37
Moscow, RUSSIA

Pike, Gary (Musician)
10031 Benares Pl
Sun Valley, CA 91352-4207, USA

Pike, Jim (Musician)
MPI Talent Agency
9255 W Sunset Blvd Ste 407
Los Angeles, CA 90069-3302, USA

Pike, Rosamund (Actor)
c/o Shelley Browning *Magnolia Entertainment*
9595 Wilshire Blvd Ste 601
Beverly Hills, CA 90212-2506, USA

Pikser, Jeremy (Actor)
c/o Margaret Riley *Lighthouse Management and Media*
9000 W Sunset Blvd Ste 1520
Los Angeles, CA 90069-5815, USA

Pilarczyk, Daniel E (Religious Leader)
100 E 8th St
Cincinnati, OH 45202-2129, USA

Pilares, Kealoha (Athlete, Football Player)
c/o Ryan Morgan *MAG Sports Agency*
8222 Melrose Ave Fl 2
Los Angeles, CA 90046-6825, USA

Pileggi, Mitch (Actor)
c/o Joel King *Pakula/King & Associates*
9229 W Sunset Blvd Ste 315
Los Angeles, CA 90069-3403, USA

Pilic, Nicki (Tennis Player)
DTB
Otto-Fleck-Schneise 8
Frankfurt/Maim 60528, GERMANY

Piligian, Craig (Producer)
c/o Staff Member *WME|IMG*
9601 Wilshire Blvd
Beverly Hills, CA 90210-5213, USA

Pilkey, Dav (Writer)
Scholastic Press
555 Broadway
New York, NY 10012-3919, USA

Pilkey, Dave (Writer)
7406 Summer Trail Dr
Sugar Land, TX 77479-6232, USA

Pill, Alison (Actor)
c/o Joannie Burstein *Burstein Company*
15304 W Sunset Blvd Ste 208
Pacific Palisades, CA 90272-3656, USA

Pilla, Anthony M (Religious Leader)
Catholic Bishops National Conference
3211 4th St NE
Washington, DC 20017-1104, USA

Pillath, Roger (Athlete, Football Player)
N3623 Lepinsky Rd
Peshtigo, WI 54157-9403, USA

Piller, Zach (Athlete, Football Player)
3907 Dunleer Ct
Tallahassee, FL 32309-2630, USA

Pillers, Lawrence (Athlete, Football Player)
4305 Hanging Moss Rd
Jackson, MS 39206-4719, USA

Pillow, Ray (Musician)
900 Harpeth Trace Dr
Nashville, TN 37221-3114, USA

Pilon, Rich (Athlete, Hockey Player)
RR 8 LCD Main
Saskatoon, SK S7K 1M2, Canada

Pilotdrift (Music Group)
c/o Staff Member *Paradigm (Monterey)*
404 W Franklin St
Monterey, CA 93940-2303, USA

Pimental, Nancy (Actor, Writer)
c/o Staff Member *WME|IMG*
9601 Wilshire Blvd
Beverly Hills, CA 90210-5213, USA

Pimentel, Jessica (Actor)
c/o Laurie Smith *Smith Talent Group*
77 Gold St
Brooklyn, NY 11201-1228, USA

Pimentel, Miguel (Musician)
c/o Mark Pitts *ByStorm Entertainment*
198 W 21st St # 721
New York, NY 10011-3202, USA

Pincay, Laffit (Horse Racer)
719 Carriage House Dr
Arcadia, CA 91006-2010, USA

Pinchak, Jimmy (Jax) (Actor)
c/o Staff Member *Agency for the Performing Arts (APA)*
405 S Beverly Dr Ste 500
Beverly Hills, CA 90212-4425, USA

Pinchot, Bronson (Actor)
c/o Susan Ferris *Bohemia Group*
1680 Vine St Ste 518
Los Angeles, CA 90028-8833, USA

Pinckney, Ed (Athlete, Basketball Player)
3350 SW 27th Ave Apt 1202
Miami, FL 33133-5326, USA

Pinckney, Sandra (Chef, Television Host)
c/o Staff Member *The Food Network.com*
1180 Avenue of the Americas Fl 14
New York, NY 10036-8401, USA

Pinder, Cyril (Athlete, Football Player)
290 174th St Apt 1409
Sunny Isles Beach, FL 33160-3252, USA

Pinder, Gary (Athlete, Hockey Player)
320 39 Ave SW
Calgary, AB T2S 0W7, Canada

Pinder, Gerry (Athlete, Hockey Player)
320 39 Ave SW
Calgary, AB T2S 0W7, Canada

Pinder, Michael (Mike) (Misc)
Moody Blues
53-55 High St
Cobham
Surrey KT11 3DP, UNITED KINGDOM (UK)

Pine, Chris (Actor)
c/o John Carrabino *John Carrabino Management*
5900 Wilshire Blvd Ste 740
Los Angeles, CA 90036-5032, USA

Pine, Courtney (Musician)
Elizabeth Rush Agency
100 Park St Apt 4
Montclair, NJ 07042-2996, USA

Pine, Phillip (Actor)
1101 S Jackson St
El Dorado Springs, MO 64744-1827, USA

Pine, Robert (Actor)
c/o Glenn Hughes III *Gem Entertainment Group*
10920 Wilshire Blvd Ste 150
Los Angeles, CA 90024-3990, USA

Pineau-Valencienne, Didler (Business Person)
Schneider
64/70 J Baptiste Clement
Boulogne-Billancourt 92646, FRANCE

Pineda, Allan (Apl. de. ap) (Musician)
c/o William Derella *DAS Communications*
83 Riverside Dr
New York, NY 10024-5713, USA

Pineda, Daniella (Actor)
c/o Nicole Perna *Imprint PR*
6121 W Sunset Blvd
Neuehouse
Los Angeles, CA 90028-6442, USA

Pineda, Salvador (Actor)
c/o Staff Member *TV Azteca*
Periferico Sur 4121
Colonia Fuentes del Pedregal
DF CP 14141, Mexico

Pinero, Joel (Athlete, Baseball Player)
9406 Lake Washington Blvd NE
Bellevue, WA 98004-5409, USA

Pines, Alexander (Misc)
University of California
Chemistry Dept
Hildebrand Hall
Berkeley, CA 94720-0001, USA

Pingel, John S (Athlete, Football Player)
80 Celestial Way Apt 203
Juno Beach, FL 33408-2314, USA

Pinger, Mark (Swimmer)
5201 Orduna Dr Apt 6
Coral Gables, FL 33146-2655, USA

Ping Lu, Kun (Misc)
Beth Israel Deaconess Medical Center
3300 Brookline Ave
Boston, MA 02215, USA

Pingree, Chellie (Congressman, Politician)
1318 Longworth Hob
Washington, DC 20515-4332, USA

Piniella, Louis V (Lou) (Athlete, Baseball Player, Coach)
1005 Taray De Avila
Tampa, FL 33613-1045, USA

Pink, Steve (Actor, Director)
c/o Gabrielle (Gaby) Morgerman *WME|IMG*
9601 Wilshire Blvd
Beverly Hills, CA 90210-5213, USA

Pinkel, Donald P (Misc)
275 Marlene Dr
San Luis Obispo, CA 93405-1023, USA

Pinkel, Gary (Coach, Football Coach)
University of Missouri
Athletic Dept
Columbia, MO 64211, USA

Pinker, Steven (Doctor, Writer)
Harvard University
Psychology Dept
Cambridge, MA 01238, USA

Pinkett, Allen (Athlete, Football Player)
2026 Tuam St
Houston, TX 77004-1349, USA

Pinkett Smith, Jada (Actor, Producer)
c/o Karynne Tencer *Tencer and Associates*
411 N Oakhurst Dr
Beverly Hills, CA 90210-4037, USA

Pink Floyd (Music Group, Musician)
370 City Rd. Islington
London EC1V 2QA, UK

Pinkham Jr, Daniel R (Composer)
150 Chilton St
Cambridge, MA 02138-1227, USA

Pinkins, Tonya (Actor)
Innovative Artists
1505 10th St
Santa Monica, CA 90401-2805, USA

Pink (P!nk) (Musician)
c/o Roger Davies *RDWM America*
1158 26th St Ste 564
Santa Monica, CA 90403-4698, USA

Pinkston, Rob (Actor)
c/o Randy James *Randy James Management*
12711 Ventura Blvd Ste 345
Studio City, CA 91604-2416, USA

Pinkston, Ryan (Actor)
c/o Staff Member *Morra Brezner Steinberg & Tenenbaum (MBST) Entertainment*
345 N Maple Dr Ste 200
Beverly Hills, CA 90210-5174, USA

Pinkston, Todd (Athlete, Football Player)
1 Novacare Way
Philadelphia, PA 19145-5900, USA

Pinmonkey (Music Group)
c/o Staff Member *WME (Nashville)*
1201 Demonbreun St
Nashville, TN 37203-3140, USA

Pinner, Artose (Athlete, Football Player)
102 Big Blue Ct
Hopkinsville, KY 42240-2600, USA

Pinney, Ray (Athlete, Football Player)
6529B NE Windermere Rd
Seattle, WA 98105-2057, USA

Pino, Danny (Actor)
c/o Geordie Frey *GEF Entertainment*
533 N Las Palmas Ave
Los Angeles, CA 90004-1017, USA

Pinol, Jacqueline (Actor)
c/o Tracy Quinn *Quinn Management*
17328 Ventura Blvd Ste 416
Encino, CA 91316-3904, USA

Pinone, John (Athlete, Basketball Player)
108 Riverview Rd
Glastonbury, CT 06033-3140, USA

Pinsent, Gordon (Actor)
c/o Steve Lovett *Lovett Management*
1327 Brinkley Ave
Los Angeles, CA 90049-3619, USA

Pinsky, Drew (Doctor, Radio Personality, Reality Star, Television Host)
Dr Drew Productions
14742 Ventura Blvd
#PH
Sherman Oaks, CA 91403, USA

Pinsky, Robert N (Writer)
Boston University
236 Bay State Rd Attn Dept
Boston, MA 02215-1403, USA

Pinson, Bobby (Musician)
c/o Susan Niles *Susan Niles Public Relations*
726 Bresslyn Rd
Nashville, TN 37205-2602, USA

Pinson, Julie (Actor)
13576 Cheltenham Dr
Sherman Oaks, CA 91423-4818, USA

Pintauro, Danny (Actor)
c/o Arnold M Preston *Preston Entertainment Inc*
8033 W Sunset Blvd # 7250
Los Angeles, CA 90046-2401

Pinto, Freida (Actor)
c/o Heidi Lopata *Narrative*
1601 Vine St Fl 6
Los Angeles, CA 90028-8802, USA

Pinto, Martina (Actor)
c/o Laura Ratchev *Numerochiuso Agency*
Viale Parioli 13
Rome 00197, Italy

Pintscher, Matthias (Composer)
Van Walsum Mgmt
4 Addison Bridge Place
London W14 8XP, UNITED KINGDOM (UK)

Piotrowski, Tom (Athlete, Basketball Player)
80 Clarks Landing Rd
Port Republic, NJ 08241-9741, USA

Piovanelli, Silvano Cardinal (Religious Leader)
Piazzi S Glovanni 3
Florence 50129, ITALY

Piper, Billie (Actor)
c/o Staff Member *Rights House, The*
Drury House
34-43 Russell St
London WC2B 5HA, UK

Piper, Jacki (Actor)
Lengford Assoc
17 Westfields Ave
Barnes
London SW13 0AT, UNITED KINGDOM (UK)

Pipes, Leah (Actor)
c/o Ruth Bernstein *Viewpoint Inc*
8820 Wilshire Blvd Ste 220
Beverly Hills, CA 90211-2622, USA

Pipettes, The (Music Group)
c/o Staff Member *Paradigm (Monterey)*
404 W Franklin St
Monterey, CA 93940-2303, USA

Pippen, Scottie (Athlete, Basketball Player, Olympic Athlete)
Scottie Pippen Youth Foundation
5125 Lee Ave
Little Rock, AR 72205-3642, USA

Pippig, Uta (Athlete, Olympic Athlete, Track Athlete)
Postfach 1249
Straus berg, D 15331, USA

Piques, Jon Paul (Comedian, Internet Star)
c/o Lion Shirdan *UPRISE Management*
2317 Mount Olympus Dr
Los Angeles, CA 90046-1639, USA

Piquet, Nelson (Race Car Driver)
Autodromo
SEN/CDPM
Rua da Gasolina #01
Brasilia, DF 7007-400, BRAZIL

Pirae, Marcus Jean (Actor)
c/o Tom Parziale *Visionary Management*
1558 N Stanley Ave
Los Angeles, CA 90046-2711, USA

Pirelli, Leopoldo (Business Person)
Via Gaetano Negri 10
Milan 20123, ITALY

Pires, Alexandre (Musician)
c/o Staff Member *BMG*
1540 Broadway
New York, NY 10036-4039, USA

Pires, Mary Joao (Musician)
Columbia Artists Mgmt Inc
165 W 57th St
New York, NY 10019-2201, USA

Pirkl, Greg (Athlete, Baseball Player)
6822 Emerald Bay Ln
Indianapolis, IN 46237-5063, USA

Pirner, Dave (Musician, Songwriter, Writer)
Monterey Peninsula Artists
509 Hartnell St
Monterey, CA 93940-2825, USA

Pirok, Pauline (Athlete, Baseball Player)
13636 86th Ave
Orland Park, IL 60462-1612, USA

Pirro, Jeanine (Judge, Television Host)
c/o Staff Member *Fox News*
1211 Avenue of the Americas Lowr C1
New York, NY 10036-8705, USA

Pirtle, Gerry (Athlete, Baseball Player)
602 S Maryland Ave
Claremore, OK 74017-8128, USA

Pirus, Alex (Athlete, Hockey Player)
15W222 Concord St
Elmhurst, IL 60126-5326

Pisarcik, Joe (Athlete, Football Player)
27 Compass Cir
Mount Laurel, NJ 08054-6106, USA

Pisarkiewicz, Steve (Athlete, Football Player)
2550 Citrus Tower Blvd Apt 10206
Clermont, FL 34711-6839, USA

Pischetsrider, Bernd (Business Person)
Bayerishe Motoren Werke
Petuelring 130
Munich 80788, GERMANY

Pisciotta, Marc (Athlete, Baseball Player)
867 Village Greene NW
Marietta, GA 30064-4749, USA

Piscopo, Joe (Actor, Comedian)
c/o Wendi Niad *Niad Management*
15021 Ventura Blvd Ste 860
Sherman Oaks, CA 91403-2442, USA

Piscotty, Stephen (Athlete, Baseball Player)

Piskula, Grace (Athlete, Baseball Player)
2411 Woodlake Ct
Naperville, IL 60564-8411, USA

Pistone, Tom (Race Car Driver)
7858 Old Concord Rd.
Charlotte, NC 28213, USA

Pistorius, Oscar (Athlete, Track Athlete)
c/o Kate Silvers *Fast Track Agency*
105 Victoria St Fl 6
London SW1E 6QT, UNITED KINGDOM

Pitbull (Musician)
c/o Staff Member *Latium Entertainment*
1635 N Cahuenga Blvd # 500
Los Angeles, CA 90028-6201, USA

Pitcock, Joan (Golfer)
341 E Lester Ave
Fresno, CA 93720-1615, USA

Pitillo, Maria (Actor)
c/o Jonathan Howard *Innovative Artists*
1505 10th St
Santa Monica, CA 90401-2805, USA

Pitino, Rick (Basketball Coach, Coach)
214 Mockingbird Gardens Dr
Louisville, KY 40207-5711, USA

Pitlick, Lance (Athlete, Hockey Player)
5010 Shenandoah Ln N
Minneapolis, MN 55446-2120

Pitlock, Skip (Athlete, Baseball Player)
215 Prospect St
Seguin, TX 78155-6018, USA

Pitman, Jennifer S (Race Car Driver)
Weathercock House
Upper Lamboum Hungerford
Berks RG17 8QT, UNITED KINGDOM (UK)

Pitoc, John Paul (Actor)
c/o Amy Slomovits *Haven Entertainment*
8111 Beverly Blvd Ste 201
Los Angeles, CA 90048-4531, USA

Pitoitua, Ropati (Athlete, Football Player)
c/o Brian Levy *Goal Line Football Management*
1025 Kane Concourse Ste 207
Bay Harbor Islands, FL 33154-2118, USA

Pitou Zimmerman, Penny (Skier)
560 Sanborn Rd
Sanbornton, NH 03269-2401, USA

Pitt, Brad (Actor, Producer)
c/o Staff Member *Plan B Entertainment*
9150 Wilshire Blvd Ste 350
Beverly Hills, CA 90212-3453, USA

Pitt, Michael (Actor)
c/o Chris Donnelly *LBI Entertainment*
2000 Avenue of the Stars
N Tower Fl 3
Los Angeles, CA 90067-4700, USA

Pitta, Dennis (Athlete, Football Player)
c/o David Dunn *Athletes First*
23091 Mill Creek Dr
Laguna Hills, CA 92653-1258, USA

Pittaro, Chris (Athlete, Baseball Player)
42 Pintinalli Dr
Trenton, NJ 08619-1558, USA

Pittis, Domenic (Athlete, Hockey Player)
5243 Barron Dr NW
Calgary, AB T2L 1T7, Canada

Pittman, Charles (Athlete, Basketball Player)
16286 N 29th Dr
Phoenix, AZ 85053-3004, USA

Pittman, Danny (Football Player)
New York Giants
University of Wyoming Attn: Alumni Association
Laramie, WY 82071, USA

Pittman, Sheldon (Race Car Driver)
Morgan McClure Racing
26502 Newbanks Rd
Abingdon, VA 24210-7500, USA

Pittman Jr, James A (Misc)
5 Ridge Dr
Mountain Brk, AL 35213-3631, USA

Pitts, Chester (Athlete, Football Player)
c/o Staff Member *EAG Sports Management*
909 N Pacific Coast Hwy Ste 360
El Segundo, CA 90245-3864, USA

Pitts, Frank (Athlete, Football Player)
8249 S Laredo Ave
Baton Rouge, LA 70811-4055, USA

Pitts, Gaylen (Athlete, Baseball Player)
214 Rocky Bluff Ln
Mountain Home, AR 72653-7186, USA

Pitts, Greg (Actor)
c/o Amy Slomovits *Haven Entertainment*
8111 Beverly Blvd Ste 201
Los Angeles, CA 90048-4531, USA

Pitts, Hugh (Athlete, Football Player)
3612 Short St
Greenville, TX 75401-3900, USA

Pitts, Jacob (Actor)
c/o Jonathan Mason *Buchwald (NY)*
10 E 44th St
New York, NY 10017-3601, USA

Pitts, John (Athlete, Football Player)
4899 W Tyson St
Chandler, AZ 85226-2909, USA

Pitts, Robert (R C) (Athlete, Basketball Player)
12655 E Millburn Ave
Baton Rouge, LA 70815-6827, USA

Pitts, Ron (Sportscaster)
Fox TV
205 E 67th St
Sports Dept
New York, NY 10065-6089, USA

Pitts, Ron (Athlete, Football Player)
3811 Davids Rd
Agoura Hills, CA 91301-3643, USA

Pitts, Tyrone S (Religious Leader)
Progressive National Baptist Convention
601 50th St NE
Washington, DC 20019-5498, USA

Pittsley, Jim (Athlete, Baseball Player)
102 Dixon Ave
Du Bois, PA 15801-1215, USA

Pivec, Dave (Athlete, Football Player)
1288 Fenwick Garth
Arnold, MD 21012-2107, USA

Piven, Jeremy (Actor)
c/o Jeff Golenberg *Silver Lining Entertainment*
421 S Beverly Dr Fl 7
Beverly Hills, CA 90212-4408, USA

Pivonka, Michal (Athlete, Hockey Player)
8312 Grand Estuary Trl Unit 102
Bradenton, FL 34212-4264

Pixies (Music Group, Musician)
c/o John Branigan *WME/IMG*
9601 Wilshire Blvd
Beverly Hills, CA 90210-5213, USA

Piza, Arthur Luiz de (Artist)
16 Rue Dauphine
Paris 75006, FRANCE

Pizarro, Artur (Musician)
c/o Staff Member *Musicians Corporate Management*
PO Box 825
Highland, NY 12528-0825, USA

Pizarro, Juan (Athlete, Baseball Player)
2262 Ave Borinquen
San Juan, PR 00915-4421, USA

Pizzarelli, John (Musician)
c/o Staff Member *Challenge Records International*
Noorderweg 68
Hilversum 1221 AB, The Netherlands

Pizzo, Angelo (Director, Producer)
2121 S High St
Bloomington, IN 47401-4311, USA

Pizzolatto, Nic (Director, Producer)
c/o Leslee Dart *42West*
600 3rd Ave Fl 23
New York, NY 10016-1914, USA

Place, Marcella (Athlete, Hockey Player, Olympic Athlete)
141 Meadow View Rd
Orinda, CA 94563-3250, USA

Place, Mary Kay (Actor)
c/o Staff Member *Gersh*
9465 Wilshire Blvd Ste 600
Beverly Hills, CA 90212-2605, USA

Placebo (Music Group)
Elevator Lady Ltd
4 South Street
Epsom
Surrey KT18 7PF, UNITED KINGDOM

Placido, Michele (Actor)
c/o Staff Member *C.D.A. Studio Di Nardo*
Via Cavour
Rome 00184, ITALY

Pladson, Gordon (Gordie) (Athlete, Baseball Player)
19087 87A Ave
Surrey, BC V4N 6E4, Canada

Plager, Bob (Athlete, Hockey Player)
St Louis Blues
1401 Clark Ave
Saint Louis, MO 63103-2700

Plager, Robert B (Bob) (Athlete, Coach, Hockey Player)
362 Branchport Dr
Chesterfield, MO 63017-2902

Plainic, Zoran (Basketball Player)
New Jersey Nets
390 Murray Hill Pkwy
East Rutherford, NJ 07073-2109, USA

Plain White T's (Music Group)
c/o Sharrin Summers *Hollywood Records*
500 S Buena Vista St
Burbank, CA 91521-0002, USA

Plakson, Suzie (Actor)
302 N La Brea Ave # 363
Los Angeles, CA 90036-2518, USA

plamondon, Gerry (Athlete, Hockey Player)
450 Rue de Montreal
Sherbrooke, QC J1H 1E5, Canada

Plana, Tony (Actor)
c/o Todd Eisner *Abrams Artists Agency*
750 N San Vicente Blvd
E Tower Fl 11
Los Angeles, CA 90069-5788, USA

Plan B (Music Group)
c/o Staff Member *Paradigm (Monterey)*
404 W Franklin St
Monterey, CA 93940-2303, USA

Planchon, Roger (Director, Writer)
Teatre National Populaire
8 Pl Lazare Goujon
Villeurbanne 69627, FRANCE

Plank, Doug (Athlete, Football Player)
12622 E Paradise Dr
Scottsdale, AZ 85259-3455, USA

Plank, Ed (Eddie) (Athlete, Baseball Player)
135 Winson Ave
Englewood, FL 34223-3135, USA

Plank, Kevin (Business Person)
Under Armour, Inc.
1020 Hull St Ste 300
Baltimore, MD 21230-5358, USA

Plant, Robert (Musician, Songwriter)
c/o Rod MacSween *International Talent Booking*
9 Kingsway
Fl 6
London WC2B 6XF, UNITED KINGDOM

Plante, Bruce (Cartoonist)
Chattanooga Times
100 E 11th St Ste 400
Editorial Dept
Chattanooga, TN 37402-4214, USA

Plante, Cam (Athlete, Hockey Player)
36 Frobisher Cres
Brandon, MB R7A 5B9, Canada

Plante, Dan (Athlete, Hockey Player)
5 Gillingham Ct
Algonquin, IL 60102-6285

Plante, Derek (Athlete, Hockey Player)
5325 Roosevelt Dr
Hermantown, MN 55811-3679

Plante, Jacques (Athlete, Hockey Player)

Plante, Pierre (Athlete, Hockey Player)
25 Rue Ewing
Salaberry-De-Valleyfield, QC J6S 2X8, Canada

Plante, Tyler (Athlete, Hockey Player)
36 Frobisher Cres
Brandon, MB R7A 5B9, Canada

Plante, William M (Correspondent)
CBS-TV
2020 M St NW
News Dept
Washington, DC 20036-3368, USA

Plantenberg, Erik (Athlete, Baseball Player)
1846 Creekside Dr NE
Owatonna, MN 55060-3973, USA

Plantery, Mark (Athlete, Hockey Player)
ON182 Alexander Dr
Geneva, IL 60134-6001

Plantier, Phil (Athlete, Baseball Player)
PO Box 122000
San Diego, CA 92112-2000, USA

Plantu (Cartoonist)
Le Monde
Editorial Dept
21 Bis Rue Claude Bernard
Paris 75005, FRANCE

Planutis, Jerry (Athlete, Football Player)
4741 Beechnut Dr
Saint Joseph, MI 49085-9321, USA

Plaskett, Thomas G (Business Person)
5215 N O Connor Blvd Ste 1070
Irving, TX 75039-3738, USA

Platinli, Michel (Soccer Player)
World Cup Organization
17-21 Ave Gen Mangin
Paris Cedex 75024, FRANCE

Platov, Yevgeni (Dancer)
Connecticut Skating Center
300 Alumni Rd
Newington, CT 06111-1868, USA

Platt, David (Soccer Player)
FourFourTwo
52 Victoria Street
McMahons Point NSW 2060, AUSTRALIA

Platt, Howard (Actor)
9200 W Sunset Blvd Ste 1130
Los Angeles, CA 90069-3606, USA

Platt, Lewis E (Lew) (Business Person)
Hewlett-Packard Co
3000 Hanover St
Palo Alto, CA 94304-1185, USA

Platt, Marc (Producer)
c/o Staff Member *Marc Platt Productions*
100 Universal City Plz
Bungalow 5163
Universal City, CA 91608-1002, USA

Platt, Oliver (Actor, Producer)
c/o Felicia Pollack *ID Public Relations (NY)*
40 Wall St Fl 51
New York, NY 10005-1385, USA

Platten, Rachel (Musician)
c/o Ben Singer *Silverberg Management Group (SMG)*
3030 Nebraska Ave Ste 201
Santa Monica, CA 90404-4140, USA

Platts, Todd (Congressman, Politician)
2455 Rayburn Hob
Washington, DC 20515-2401, USA

Plavinsky, Dmitri P (Artist)
Arbat Str 51
Kotp 2 #97
Moscow 121002, RUSSIA

Plavsic, Adrien (Athlete, Hockey Player)
Lausanne Hockey Club SA
Case Postale 171
Lausanne 01000, Switzerland

Player, Gary (Athlete, Golfer)
22 S Main St STE 100
Greenville, SC 29601-4873, SOUTH AFRICA

Player, Scott (Athlete, Football Player)
1583 W Saltsage Dr
Phoenix, AZ 85045-1712, USA

Playfair, Jim (Athlete, Hockey Player)
Phoenix Coyotes
6751 N Sunset Blvd Ste 200
Glendale, AZ 85305-3162

Playfair, Jim (Athlete, Hockey Player)
200-99 Station St
Saint John, NB E2L 4X4, Canada

Playfair, Larry (Athlete, Hockey Player)
Buffalo Sabres
1 Seymour H Knox III Plz Ste 1
Buffalo, NY 14203-3096

Playfair, Larry (Athlete, Hockey Player)
724 Ransom Rd
Grand Island, NY 14072-1464

Plaza, Aubrey (Actor)
c/o Courtney Kivowitz *MGMT Entertainment (The Schiff Company)*
9220 W Sunset Blvd Ste 106
W Hollywood, CA 90069-3500, USA

Pleasant, Anthony (Athlete, Football Player)
17249 Connor Quay Ct
Cornelius, NC 28031-6503, USA

Pleasant, Reggie (Athlete, Football Player)
8270 Milford Plantation Rd
Pinewood, SC 29125-9249, USA

Pleau, Larry (Athlete, Hockey Player)
St Louis Blues
1401 Clark Ave
Saint Louis, MO 63103-2700

Pleau, Larry (Athlete, Hockey Player, Olympic Athlete)
650 Spyglass Summit Dr
Chesterfield, MO 63017-2143

Plec, Julie (Producer)
c/o Kimberly Bialek *WME|IMG*
9601 Wilshire Blvd
Beverly Hills, CA 90210-5213, USA

Pleis, Bill (Athlete, Baseball Player)
11 Palomino Ridge Ct
Lake Saint Louis, MO 63367-2162, USA

Plemons, Jesse (Actor)
c/o Staff Member *Simmons & Scott Entertainment*
7942 Mulholland Dr
Los Angeles, CA 90046-1225, USA

Plesac, Dan (Athlete, Baseball Player)
40 Hartz Way Ste 1
Secaucus, NJ 07094-2403, USA

Pleshette, John (Actor)
2643 Creston Dr
Los Angeles, CA 90068-2207, USA

Pless, Rance (Athlete, Baseball Player)
5528 Asheville Hwy
Greeneville, TN 37743-2287, USA

Pletcher, Eidon (Cartoonist)
210 Canberra Ct
Slidell, LA 70458-1520, USA

Pletnev, Mikhail V (Musician)
Starpkonyushenny Per 33
#16
Moscow, RUSSIA

Plett, Willi (Athlete, Hockey Player)
125 Riding Trail Ct
Roswell, GA 30075-1759

Plimpton, Martha (Actor)
c/o Jill Littman *Impression Entertainment*
9229 W Sunset Blvd Ste 700
Los Angeles, CA 90069-3407, USA

Plodinec, Tim (Athlete, Baseball Player)
23251 Gilmore St
West Hills, CA 91307-3427, USA

Ploeger, Kurt (Athlete, Football Player)
937 1st Ave NW
Byron, MN 55920-1411, USA

Ploen, Ken (Athlete, Football Player)
178 Shoreline Dr
Winnipeg, MB R3P 2E8, Canada

Plotkin, Stanley A (Musician)
3940 Delancey St
Philadelphia, PA 19104-4107, USA

Plouffe, Trevor (Athlete, Baseball Player)
24915 John Fremont Rd
Hidden Hills, CA 91302-1134, USA

Plowright, Joan (Actor)
Malthouse
Horsham Road Ashurst Steying
West Sussex BN44 3AR, UNITED KINGDOM (UK)

Plum, Milton R (Milt) (Athlete, Football Player)
1104 Oakside Ct
Raleigh, NC 27609-3596, USA

Plum, Ted (Athlete, Football Player)
17 Laurel Hill Dr
Cherry Hill, NJ 08003-2658, USA

Plumb, Eve (Actor)
c/o Penny Vizcarra *PV Public Relations*
121 N Almont Dr Apt 203
Beverly Hills, CA 90211-1860, USA

plumb, Ron (Athlete, Hockey Player)
975 Auden Park Dr
Kingston, ON K7M 7T9, Canada

Plumer, Patricia (PattiSue) (Athlete, Track Athlete)
USA Track & Field
4341 Starlight Dr
Indianapolis, IN 46239-1473, USA

Plumlee, Mason (Athlete, Basketball Player)
c/o Mark Bartelstein *Priority Sports & Entertainment (Chicago)*
325 N La Salle Dr Ste 650
Chicago, IL 60654-8182, USA

Plummer, Amanda (Actor)

Plummer, Bill (Athlete, Baseball Player, Coach)
52171 Sageway Dr
Redding, CA 96003-9384, USA

Plummer, Christopher (Actor, Musician)
49 Wampum Hill Rd # 480
Weston, CT 06883-1228, USA

Plummer, Gary (Athlete, Basketball Player)
1220 Sixth Ave # G
Belmont, CA 94002-3899, USA

Plummer, Gary (Athlete, Football Player)
10374 Rue Chamberry
San Diego, CA 92131-2212, USA

Plummer, Glenn (Actor)
c/o Brian Wilkins *LINK Entertainment*
11872 La Grange Ave
Los Angeles, CA 90025-5282, USA

Plunk, Eric (Athlete, Baseball Player)
9520 Pats Point Dr
Corona, CA 92883-5068, USA

Plunkett, Jim (Athlete, Football Player, Heisman Trophy Winner)
51 Kilroy Way
Atherton, CA 94027-5405, USA

Plunkett, Warren (Athlete, Football Player)
25150 N Windy Walk Dr Unit 30
Scottsdale, AZ 85255-8106, USA

Plushenko, Evgeni (Figure Skater)
c/o Staff Member *Champions on Ice*
3500 American Blvd W Ste 190
Minneapolis, MN 55431-4431, USA

Plus One (Music Group)
c/o Teresa Davis *Paradigm (Nashville)*
222 2nd Ave S Ste 1600
Nashville, TN 37201-2375, USA

Ply, Bobby (Athlete, Football Player)
8616 Ash Ave
Raytown, MO 64138-3431, USA

Plympton, Jeff (Athlete, Baseball Player)
8 Robin St
Plainville, MA 02762-1522, USA

Plyushch, Ivan S (Misc)
Verkhovna Rada
M Hrushevskoho 5
Kiev 252019, UKRAINE

P. McGovern, James (Congressman, Politician)
438 Cannon Hob
Washington, DC 20515-0519, USA

P. McKeon, Howard H (Congressman, Politician)
2184 Rayburn Hob
Washington, DC 20515-2701, USA

PM Dawn (Music Group)
Raw Shack
857 Atlantic Ave # 5
Brooklyn, NY 11238-2797, USA

P. Moran, James (Congressman, Politician)
2239 Rayburn Hob
Washington, DC 20515-4608, USA

Png, Pierre (Actor)
c/o Angela Mach *Platform PR*
2666 N Beachwood Dr
Los Angeles, CA 90068-2308, USA

Pniowsky, Anna (Actor)
c/o Brett Ruttenberg *Imprint PR*
6121 W Sunset Blvd
Neuehouse
Los Angeles, CA 90028-6442, USA

Poapst, Steve (Athlete, Hockey Player)
208 E Washington St
Villa Park, IL 60181-3013

Poapst, Steve (Athlete, Hockey Player)
Rockford Icehogs
300 Elm St
Rockford, IL 61101-1238

Pochman, Owen (Athlete, Football Player)
7405 91st Ave SE
Mercer Island, WA 98040-5805, USA

Pochmara, Brian (Athlete, Hockey Player)
18854 Monica Dr
Clinton Township, MI 48036-4204

Pocklington, Peter H (Misc)
Edmonton Oilers
11230 110 St NW
Edmonton, AB T5G 3H7, CANADA

Pocoroba, Biff (Athlete, Baseball Player)
1989 Waterton Ct
Grayson, GA 30017-1184, USA

Pocza, Harvie (Athlete, Hockey Player)
135 Sun Harbour Close SE
Calgary, AB T2X 3C4, Canada

POD (Music Group)
c/o Staff Member *Paradigm (Monterey)*
404 W Franklin St
Monterey, CA 93940-2303, USA

Podein, Shjon (Athlete, Hockey Player)
4350 Browndale Ave
Minneapolis, MN 55424-1012

Podell, Eyal (Actor)
c/o Samantha Crisp *The Kohner Agency*
9300 Wilshire Blvd Ste 555
Beverly Hills, CA 90212-3211, USA

Podesta, Rossana (Actor)
Via Bartolomeo Ammanatti 8
Rome 00187, ITALY

Podeswa, Jeremy (Director, Writer)
c/o Staff Member *Rebelfilms Inc.*
317 Manning Ave
Toronto, ON M6J 2K8, CANADA

Podewell, Cathy (Actor)
17328 S Crest Dr
Los Angeles, CA 90035, USA

Podloski, Ray (Athlete, Hockey Player)
1622 Kerr Rd NW
Sumas, WA 98295-9613, USA

Podolak, Edward J (Ed) (Athlete, Football Player)
2227 Emma Rd
Basalt, CO 81621-8326, USA

Podollan, Jason (Athlete, Hockey Player)
430 Niblick Crt
Vernon, BC V1H 1V6, Canada

Podolski, Lukas (Soccer Player)
Norbert Pflippen
Heinz-Nixdorf-Straüe 33
Münchengladbach 41179, GERMANY

Podsednik, Scott (Athlete, Baseball Player)
c/o Staff Member *Chicago White Sox*
333 W 35th St
US Cellular Field
Chicago, IL 60616-3621, USA

Poe, Dontari (Athlete, Football Player)
c/o Jimmy Sexton *CAA (Memphis)*
6060 Poplar Ave Ste 470
Memphis, TN 38119-0910, USA

Poe, Gregory (Designer, Fashion Designer)
Dutch Courage
1950 S Santa Fe Ave
Los Angeles, CA 90021-2928, USA

Poe, Johnnie (Athlete, Football Player)
924 Donald F McHenry Pl
East Saint Louis, IL 62201-1046, USA

Poe, Ted (Congressman, Politician)
320 Cannon Hob
Washington, DC 20515-0603, USA

Poehler, Amy (Actor, Comedian)
c/o Staff Member *Paper Kite Productions*
4208 Overland Ave
Culver City, CA 90230-3736, USA

Poepping, Mike (Athlete, Baseball Player)
13047 230th Ave
Pierz, MN 56364-1563, USA

Poesy, Clemence (Actor)
c/o Laura Meerson *Agence Adequat*
21 Rue D'Uzes
Paris 75002, FRANCE

Poff, John (Athlete, Baseball Player)
2786 Mishler Rd
Mio, MI 48647-9505, USA

Pogorelich, Ivo (Musician)
Kantor Concert Mgmt
67 Teignmouth Road
London NW2 4EA, UNITED KINGDOM (UK)

Pogue, David (Correspondent)
c/o Staff Member *CNBC (Main)*
900 Sylvan Ave
Englewood Cliffs, NJ 07632-3312, USA

Pohl, Dan (Athlete, Golfer)
3424 E Suncrest Ct
Phoenix, AZ 85044-3506, USA

Pohl, Don (Golfer)
3424 E Suncrest Ct
Phoenix, AZ 85044-3506, USA

Pohl, Frederick (Writer)
855 S Harvard Dr
Palatine, IL 60067-7026, USA

Pohl, Johnny (Athlete, Hockey Player)
10812 Falling Water Ln Unit G
Saint Paul, MN 55129-5267

Pohlad, Carl (Baseball Player, Business Person)
c/o Staff Member *Minnesota Twins*
34 Kirby Punkett Pl
Metrodome
Minneapolis, MN 55412, USA

Poimboeuf, Lance (Athlete, Football Player)
309 Fairfield Dr
Thibodaux, LA 70301-3721, USA

Poindexter, Anthony (Athlete, Football Player)
RR 3 Box 128
Forest, VA 24551, USA

Poindexter, Buster (Musician)
c/o Nina Nisenholtz *N2N Entertainment*
610 Harbor St Apt 3
Venice, CA 90291-5516, USA

Poindexter, Christian H (Business Person)
Constellation Energy Group
39 W Lexington St
Baltimore, MD 21201-3910, USA

Pointer, Aaron (Athlete, Baseball Player)
4902 N Scenic View Ln
Tacoma, WA 98407-1365, USA

Pointer, Aaron (Baseball Player)
Houston Colt .45's
4902 N Scenic View Ln
Tacoma, WA 98407-1365, USA

Pointer, Anita (Musician)
12060 Crest Ct
Beverly Hills, CA 90210-1348, USA

Pointer, Bonnie (Musician)
T-Best Talent Agency
508 Honey Lake Ct
Danville, CA 94506-1237, USA

Pointer, Priscilla (Actor)
c/o Staff Member *WME|IMG*
9601 Wilshire Blvd
Beverly Hills, CA 90210-5213, USA

Pointer, Priscilla (Musician)
213 16th St
Santa Monica, CA 90402-2215, USA

Point of Grace (Music Group)
c/o David Breen *The Breen Agency*
25 Music Sq W
Nashville, TN 37203-3205, USA

Poirier, Mark (Writer)
c/o Rowena Arguelles *Creative Artists Agency (CAA)*
2000 Avenue of the Stars Ste 100
Los Angeles, CA 90067-4705, USA

Poison (Music Group)
c/o Adam Kornfeld *Artist Group International (NY)*
150 E 58th St Fl 19
New York, NY 10155-1900, USA

Poitier, Sidney (Actor)
1718 Angelo Dr
Beverly Hills, CA 90210-2722, USA

Polaha, Kristoffer (Actor)
c/o Paul Rosicker *Gersh*
9465 Wilshire Blvd Ste 600
Beverly Hills, CA 90212-2605, USA

Polamalu, Troy (Athlete, Football Player)
135 Windwood Dr
Wexford, PA 15090-8502, USA

Polanco, Dascha (Actor)
c/o Dave Mckeown *Shirley Grant Management*
PO Box 866
Teaneck, NJ 07666-0866, USA

Polanco, Placido (Athlete, Baseball Player)
8950 SW 63rd Ct
Miami, FL 33156-1830, USA

Polano, Nick (Athlete, Hockey Player)
16981 Birchwood Dr
Northville, MI 48168-4422, USA

Polanski, Roman (Director)
c/o Staff Member *Majorelle PR & Events*
19 Rue Du 4 Septembre
Paris 75002, FRANCE

Polansky, Mark (Astronaut)
15906 Meadowside Dr
Houston, TX 77062-4761, USA

Polcovich, Kevin (Athlete, Baseball Player)
3 Beardsley St
Auburn, NY 13021-2809, USA

Pole, Dick (Athlete, Baseball Player)
3790 Eagle Hammock Dr
Sarasota, FL 34240-8238, USA

Poledouris, Basil (Composer)
Kraft-Benjamin-Engel
15233 Ventura Blvd Ste 200
Sherman Oaks, CA 91403-2244, USA

Polee, Dwayne (Athlete, Basketball Player)
1169 E 60th St
Los Angeles, CA 90001-1117, USA

Poletiek, Noah (Actor)
c/o Staff Member *Protege Entertainment*
710 E Angeleno Ave
Burbank, CA 91501-2213, USA

Poletto, Severino Cardinal (Religious Leader)
Via Arcivescovado 12
Torino 10121, ITALY

Polic, Henry II (Actor)
Sutton Barth Vennari
145 S Fairfax Ave Ste 310
Los Angeles, CA 90036-2176, USA

Police, The (Music Group)
194 Kensington Park Rd.
London, ENGLAND W11 2ES, UNITED KINGDOM

Polich, Mike (Athlete, Hockey Player)
825 3rd St NE
Osseo, MN 55369-1409

Polish, Mark (Actor, Producer)
c/o Staff Member *Prohibition Pictures*
2658 Griffith Park Blvd # 738
Los Angeles, CA 90039-2520, USA

Polish, Michael (Director)
c/o John Garvey *Creative Artists Agency (CAA)*
2000 Avenue of the Stars Ste 100
Los Angeles, CA 90067-4705, USA

Polishchuk, Oleksiy (Figure Skater)
c/o Staff Member *Champions on Ice*
3500 American Blvd W Ste 190
Minneapolis, MN 55431-4431, USA

Politte, Cliff (Athlete, Baseball Player)
614 Castle Meadows Ct
Ballwin, MO 63021-4447, USA

Poliziani, Dan (Athlete, Hockey Player)
1325 E Victor Rd Apt 109
Victor, NY 14564-9535

Polizzi, Nicole (Snooki) (Reality Star)
13 Rohn St
East Hanover, NJ 07936-3651, USA

Polk, Chris (Athlete, Football Player)

Polke, Sigmar (Artist)
Michael Werner
4 E 77th St # 200
New York, NY 10075-1727, USA

Pollack, Andrea (Swimmer)
SSV
Postfach 420140
Kassel 34070, GERMANY

Pollack, Daniel (Musician)
University of Southern California
Music Dept
Los Angeles, CA 90089-0001, USA

Pollack, Frank (Athlete, Football Player)
6464 Kenwood Rd
Cincinnati, OH 45243-2314, USA

Pollack, Jim (Actor)
Ericka Wain
1418 N Highland Ave # 102
Los Angeles, CA 90028-7611, USA

Pollack, Sam (Misc)
6811 de Monkland Ave
Montreal, QC H4B 1J2, CANADA

Pollak, Kevin (Actor, Comedian)
c/o Staff Member *Red Bird Cinema*
11601 Wilshire Blvd Ste 2200
Los Angeles, CA 90025-1758, USA

Pollak, Mike (Athlete, Football Player)
c/o Ken Zuckerman *Priority Sports & Entertainment - (LA)*
15233 Ventura Blvd Ste 718
Sherman Oaks, CA 91403-2237, USA

Pollan, Michael (Writer)
c/o Steven Barclay *Steven Barclay Agency*
12 Western Ave
Petaluma, CA 94952-2907, USA

Pollan, Tracy (Actor)
c/o Bob Gersh *Gersh*
9465 Wilshire Blvd Ste 600
Beverly Hills, CA 90212-2605, USA

Pollard, Bob (Athlete, Football Player)
8987 Washington Blvd
Beaumont, TX 77707-2814, USA

Pollard, Frank (Athlete, Football Player)
1526 N 12th St
Waco, TX 76707-2320, USA

Pollard, Marcus (Athlete, Football Player)
2991 Cameo Dr
Carmel, IN 46032-9313, USA

Pollard, Michael J (Actor)
520 S Burnside Ave Apt 12A
Los Angeles, CA 90036-3956, USA

Pollard, Scot (Athlete, Basketball Player)
2378 Finchley Rd
Carmel, IN 46032-7353, USA

Pollard, Su (Actor)
c/o Staff Member *Noel Gay Artists*
2 Stephen St
London W1T 1AN, UNITED KINGDOM

Pollard, Tiffany (New York) (Actor, Reality Star)
c/o Chuck Binder *Binder & Associates*
1465 Lindacrest Dr
Beverly Hills, CA 90210-2519, USA

Pollari, Joey (Actor)
c/o Nancy Kremer *Nancy Kremer Management*
4545 Morse Ave
Studio City, CA 91604-1008, USA

Polle, David R (Misc)
Nashville Predators
501 Broadway
Nashville, TN 37203-3980, USA

Polle, Norman R (Bud) (Athlete, Coach, Hockey Player)
1509-2004 Fullerton Ave
North Vancouver, BC V7P 3G8, Canada

Pollen, Arabella R H (Designer, Fashion Designer)
Canham Mews
#8 Canham Road
London W3 7SR, UNITED KINGDOM (UK)

Polley, Dale (Athlete, Baseball Player)
107 Redding Rd
Georgetown, KY 40324-1078, USA

Polley, Sarah (Actor, Director)
c/o Frank Frattaroli *Circle of Confusion*
8931 Ellis Ave
Los Angeles, CA 90034-3336, USA

Pollini, Maurizio (Musician)
RESIA
Via Manzoni 31
Milan 20120, ITALY

Pollitt-Deschaine, Alice (Athlete, Baseball Player)
9140 Silver Strand Rd
Levering, MI 49755-9103, USA

Pollock, Alex J (Business Person)
Federal Home Loan Bank
111 E Wacker Dr
Chicago, IL 60601-3713, USA

Pollock, Tom (Director, Producer)
c/o Staff Member *Montecito Picture Company*
1482 E Valley Rd Ste 477
Montecito, CA 93108-1200, USA

Polo, Ana Maria (Actor)
c/o Staff Member *Telemundo*
2470 W 8th Ave
Hialeah, FL 33010-2000, USA

Polo, Teri (Actor)
c/o Bob McGowan *McGowan Management*
170 S Beverly Dr Ste 304
Beverly Hills, CA 90212-3000, USA

Polo, Terri (Actor)
c/o Staff Member *United Talent Agency (UTA)*
9336 Civic Center Dr
Beverly Hills, CA 90210-3604, USA

Polofsky, Gordon (Athlete, Football Player)
8815 Gatwick Dr
Concord, TN 37922-6098, USA

Polombus, Tyler (Athlete, Football Player)

Polone, Gavin (Producer)
c/o Staff Member *WME|IMG*
9601 Wilshire Blvd
Beverly Hills, CA 90210-5213, USA

Poloni, John (Athlete, Baseball Player)
1714 Polo Club Dr
Tarpon Springs, FL 34689-8013, USA

Polonich, Dennis (Athlete, Hockey Player)
70 Varsity Estates Close NW
Calgary, AB T3B 5J1, Canada

Polowski, Larry (Athlete, Football Player)
365 E Brookhollow Dr
Boise, ID 83706-6730, USA

Polozkova, Lidia P (Speed Skater)
Solianka Str 14/2
Moscow 109240, RUSSIA

Polson, John (Actor)
c/o Robyn Gardiner *RGM Artists*
8-12 Ann St
Surry Hills, NSW 02010, AUSTRALIA

Polson, Ralph (Athlete, Basketball Player)
3846 S Eagle Ln
Spokane Valley, WA 99206-6351, USA

Polynice, Olden (Athlete, Basketball Player)
PO Box 220339
Newhall, CA 91322-0339, USA

Polyphonic Spree, The (Music Group)
c/o Staff Member *Paradigm (Monterey)*
404 W Franklin St
Monterey, CA 93940-2303, USA

Pomers, Scarlett (Actor, Musician)
c/o Rhonda Boudreaux *Rhonda Boudreaux Publicity*
Prefers to be contacted via telephone
Oakland, CA 00900, USA

Pominville, Jason (Athlete, Hockey Player)
5373 Glenview Dr
Clarence, NY 14031-1843, USA

Pommier, Jean-Bernard (Musician)
2 Chemin des Cotes de Montmoiret
Lausanne 01012, SWITZERLAND

Pomodora, Arnaldo (Artist)
Via Vigevano 5
Milan 20144, ITALY

Pompedda, Mario Francesco Cardinal (Religious Leader)
Palazzo della Cancelleria
Plazza della Cancelleria 1
Rome 00186, ITALY

Pompeo, Ellen (Actor)
c/o Amanda Silverman *The Lede Company*
401 Broadway Ste 206
New York, NY 10013-3033, USA

Pompeo, Mike (Congressman, Politician)
107 Cannon Hob
Washington, DC 20515-0902, USA

Ponazecki, Joe (Actor)
Don Buchwald
10 E 44th St Frnt 1
New York, NY 10017-3654, USA

Ponce, Carlos (Musician)
c/o Staff Member *WME|IMG*
9601 Wilshire Blvd
Beverly Hills, CA 90210-5213, USA

Ponce, Carlos (Athlete, Baseball Player)
802 Sky Pine Way APT C2
Greenacres, FL 33415-9023, USA

Ponce, LuAnne (Actor)
Gold Marshak Liedtke
3500 W Olive Ave Ste 1400
Burbank, CA 91505-5512, USA

Ponce, Walter (Musician)
Columbia Artists Mgmt Inc
165 W 57th St
New York, NY 10019-2201, USA

Poncino, Larry (Baseball Player)
2954 N Calle Ladera
Tucson, AZ 85715-3202, USA

Poncino, Larry (Athlete, Baseball Player)
2954 N Calle Ladera
Tucson, AZ 85715-3202, USA

Pond, Lennie (Race Car Driver)
4301 Caronado Dr
Chester, VA 23831-4502, USA

Pond, Matt (Musician)
c/o Staff Member *Paradigm (Monterey)*
404 W Franklin St
Monterey, CA 93940-2303, USA

Ponder, Christian (Football Player)
c/o Jimmy Sexton *CAA (Memphis)*
6060 Poplar Ave Ste 470
Memphis, TN 38119-0910, USA

Ponder, Dave (Athlete, Football Player)
1818 Sandalwood Ln
Grapevine, TX 76051-7344, USA

Ponder, Samantha Steele (Sportscaster)
c/o Nick Khan *Creative Artists Agency (CAA)*
2000 Avenue of the Stars Ste 100
Los Angeles, CA 90067-4705, USA

Pondexter, Cliff (Athlete, Basketball Player)
1135 W Stuart Ave
Fresno, CA 93711-2040, USA

Ponikarovsky, Alexei (Athlete, Hockey Player)
645 29th St
Manhattan Beach, CA 90266-2232

Pons, B Stanley (Misc)
University of Utah
Chemistry Dept
Eyring Building
Salt Lake City, UT 84112, USA

Pons, Lele (Comedian, Internet Star)
c/o Diandra Escamilla *PMK/BNC Public Relations*
1840 Century Park E Ste 1400
Los Angeles, CA 90067-2115, USA

Ponsoldt, James (Director)
c/o Brad Petrigala *Brillstein Entertainment Partners*
9150 Wilshire Blvd Ste 350
Beverly Hills, CA 90212-3453, USA

Ponson, Sidney (Athlete, Baseball Player)
443 Hendricks Isle Slip 2
Fort Lauderdale, FL 33301-5740, USA

Pontes, Marcos (Astronaut)
16807 Soaring Forest Dr
Houston, TX 77059-4002, USA

Pontes, Marcos Major (Astronaut)
16807 Soaring Forest Dr
Houston, TX 77059-4002, USA

Ponti, Cario (Producer)
Palazzo Colonna
1 Piazza d'Ara Coell 1
Rome, ITALY

Ponti, Michael (Musician)
Heubergstr 32
Eschenlohe 83565, GERMANY

Pontius, Chris (Actor, Writer)
c/o Beth Holden-Garland *Untitled Entertainment*
350 S Beverly Dr Ste 200
Beverly Hills, CA 90212-4819, USA

Ponty, Jean-Luc (Musician)
10340 Santa Monica Blvd
Los Angeles, CA 90025-6904, USA

Ponzini, Anthony (Actor)
Gold Marshak Liedtke
3500 W Olive Ave Ste 1400
Burbank, CA 91505-5512, USA

Pook, Chris (Race Car Driver)
Championship Auto Racing
5350 Lakeview Parkway South Dr
Indianapolis, IN 46268-5129, USA

Pool, David (Athlete, Football Player)
460 Vista Glen Dr
Cincinnati, OH 45246-2366, USA

Poole, Bob (Athlete, Football Player)
7802 Shadyvilla Ln
Houston, TX 77055, USA

Poole, Brian (Musician)
67 Tower Drive
Neath Hill
Milton Keynes MK14 6JX, UNITED KINGDOM (UK)

Poole, David J (Artist)
Trinity Flint Bam
Weston Lane
Petersfield Hants GU32 3NN, UNITED KINGDOM (UK)

Poole, George B (Athlete, Football Player)
PO Box 278
Gloster, MS 39638-0278, USA

Poole, Jim (Athlete, Baseball Player)
605 Falls Lake Dr
Alpharetta, GA 30022-8059, USA

Poole, Keith (Athlete, Football Player)
2027 E Teakwood Pl
Chandler, AZ 85249-3508, USA

Poole, Larry (Athlete, Football Player)
15803 Sea Oats Pl
Tampa, FL 33624-1629, USA

Poole, Nathan (Athlete, Football Player)
8686 Longwood St
San Diego, CA 92126-3654, USA

Poole, Oliver (Athlete, Football Player)
PO Box 184
Gloster, MS 39638-0184, USA

Poole, Tyrone (Athlete, Football Player)
3415 Rivers Call Blvd
Atlanta, GA 30339-5662, USA

Pooley, Don (Athlete, Golfer)
5251 N Camino Sumo
Tucson, AZ 85718-6047, USA

Pooley, Paul (Athlete, Hockey Player)
51029 Broken Wood Ct
Granger, IN 46530-4816

Poons, Larry (Artist)
PO Box 115
Islamorada, FL 33036-0115, USA

Poots, Imogen (Actor)
c/o Samira Higham *Independent Talent Group*
40 Whitfield St
London W1T 2RH, UNITED KINGDOM

Pop, Iggy (Musician)
3579 Stewart Ave
Miami, FL 33133-6828, USA

Popcorn, Faith (Journalist)
Brain Reserve
1 Dag Hammarskjold Plz Fl 16
885 Second Avenue Fl 16
New York, NY 10017-2244, USA

Pope, Bucky (Athlete, Football Player)
7 Bunker Hill Dr
Washington Crossing, PA 18977-1415, USA

Pope, Carly (Actor, Producer)
c/o Ben Levine *LINK Entertainment*
11872 La Grange Ave
Los Angeles, CA 90025-5282, USA

Pope, Cassadee (Musician)
c/o Jake Basden *Big Machine Records*
1219 16th Ave S
Nashville, TN 37212-2901, USA

Pope, Eddie (Soccer Player)
New York/New Jersey MetroStars
1 Harmon Plz Ste 300
Secaucus, NJ 07094-2800, USA

Pope, Edwin (Sportscaster)
Miami Herald Editorial Dept
1 Herald Plz
Miami, FL 33132-1609, USA

Pope, Marquez (Athlete, Football Player)
110 Avila St
San Francisco, CA 94123-2010, USA

Pope, Monsanto (Athlete, Football Player)
312 13th St NW Apt 10
Charlottesville, VA 22903-2754, USA

Pope, Odeon (Musician)
Brad Simon Organization
122 E 57th St # 300
New York, NY 10022-2623, USA

Pope, Rosie (Reality Star)
Rosie Pope Maternity
18 E 41st St Rm 1702
New York, NY 10017-6231, USA

Pope, Willie (Baseball Player)
Homestead Grays
7616 Bennett St
Pittsburgh, PA 15208-1602, USA

Popeil, Ron (Business Person)
192 Monte Cielo Dr
Beverly Hills, CA 90210, USA

Popein, Larry (Athlete, Hockey Player)
80-650 Harrington Rd
Kamloops, BC V2B 6T7

popfinger, Bill (Horse Racer)
2395 NE 28th St
Lighthouse Point, FL 33064-8235, USA

popfinger, Frank (Horse Racer)
52 Cambridge Ave
Garden City, NY 11530-5125, USA

Popiel, Jan (Athlete, Hockey Player)
1074 Central Park Rd
Decatur, GA 30033-8800, USA

Popiel, Poul P (Athlete, Hockey Player)
2501 Peppermill Ridge Dr
Wildwood, MO 63005-6707

Popoff, A Jay (Musician)
Sepetys Entertainment
1223 Wilshire Blvd # 804
Santa Monica, CA 90403-5406, USA

Popoff, Frank P (Business Person)
Dow Chemical
2030 Dow Ctr
Midland, MI 48674-2030, USA

Popov, Aleksandr (Swimmer)
Swimming Assn
Sports House
Maitland Road #7
Hackett 02602, AUSTRALIA

Popov, Alexander (Athlete, Olympic Athlete, Swimmer)
International Olympic Committee
IOC Athletes Commission
Château De Vidy, Lausanne CH-1007, Switzerland

Popovac, Gwynn (Artist)
17270 Robin Rdg
Sonora, CA 95370-8108, USA

Popovic, Mark (Athlete, Hockey Player)
30 New Mountain Rd
Stoney Creek, ON L8G 2R7, Canada

Popovich, Gregg (Athlete, Basketball Coach, Basketball Player, Coach)
41 Vineyard Dr
San Antonio, TX 78257-1236, USA

Popovich, Milt (Athlete, Football Player)
810 N Hoback St
Helena, MT 59601-3883, USA

Popovich, Paul (Athlete, Baseball Player)
2604 Woodlawn Rd
Northbrook, IL 60062-5951, USA

Popowich, Paul (Actor)
c/o Paul Hemrend *Edna Talent Management*
318 Dundas St W
Toronto, ON M5T 1G5, CANADA

Popp, Nathaniel (Religious Leader)
Romanian Orthodox Episcopate
PO Box 309
Grass Lake, MI 49240-0309, USA

Popper, John (Musician)
c/o Staff Member *ArtistDirect*
9046 Lindblade St
Culver City, CA 90232-2513, USA

Popplewell, Anna (Actor)
c/o Staff Member *Sasha Leslie Management*
34 Pember Rd
London NW10 5LS, UNITED KINGDOM

Poppy (Internet Star, Musician)
c/o Brit Reece *PMK/BNC Public Relations*
1840 Century Park E Ste 1400
Los Angeles, CA 90067-2115, USA

Poppycock, Prince (Musician)
c/o Stephen Ford *Diva Central Inc*
7510 W Sunset Blvd # 1445
Los Angeles, CA 90046-3408, USA

Popson, Dave (Athlete, Basketball Player)
82 Fall St
Ashley, PA 18706-2709, USA

Poquette, Ben (Athlete, Basketball Player)
17917 N Shore Estates Rd
Spring Lake, MI 49456-9114, USA

Poquette, Tom (Athlete, Baseball Player)
3411 Ridgeway Dr
Eau Claire, WI 54701-8142, USA

Poquette, Tom (Baseball Player)
3411 Ridgeway Dr
Eau Claire, WI 54701-8142

Porcaro, Steve (Musician)
Fitzgeraid-Hartley
34 N Palm St
Ventura, CA 93001-2600, USA

Porcello, Rick (Baseball Player)
PO Box 27
Oldwick, NJ 08858-0027

Porch, Colleen (Actor)
c/o Staff Member *Metropolitan (MTA)*
4526 Wilshire Blvd
Los Angeles, CA 90010-3801, USA

Porcher, Robert (Athlete, Football Player)
PO Box 691464
Orlando, FL 32869-1464, USA

Porizkova, Paulina (Actor, Model)
c/o Meghan Prophet *PMK/BNC Public Relations*
1840 Century Park E Ste 1400
Los Angeles, CA 90067-2115, USA

Pork Tornado (Music Group)
c/o Staff Member *Paradigm (Monterey)*
404 W Franklin St
Monterey, CA 93940-2303, USA

Porras, German (Director)
c/o Staff Member *Gabriel Blanco Iglesias (Colombia)*
Dg 127A #20-36
Conjunto Plenitud, Apto 132
Bogota, Colombia

Porretta, Matthew (Actor)
Damage Mgmt
10 Southwick Mews
London W2, UNITED KINGDOM (UK)

Port, Chris (Athlete, Football Player)
452 Walnut St
New Orleans, LA 70118-4932, USA

Port, Michael (Sportscaster)
9465 Saint Andrews Dr
Santee, CA 92071-2449, USA

Port, Whitney (Reality Star)
c/o Kate Rosen *The Lede Company*
401 Broadway Ste 206
New York, NY 10013-3033, USA

Porter, Adina (Actor)
c/o Heidi Ifft *Bamboo Management*
17 Buccaneer St
Marina Del Rey, CA 90292-5103, USA

Porter, Alan (Athlete, Baseball Player)
993 Browning Pl
Warminster, PA 18974-3807, USA

Porter, Andrew (Athlete, Baseball Player)
4881 Linscott Pl Apt 1
Los Angeles, CA 90016-5422, USA

Porter, Billy (Musician)
c/o Staff Member *Gersh*
9465 Wilshire Blvd Ste 600
Beverly Hills, CA 90212-2605, USA

Porter, Bob (Athlete, Baseball Player)
771 Pueblo Ave
Napa, CA 94558-3546, USA

Porter, Chuck (Athlete, Baseball Player)
9321 Snyder Ln
Perry Hall, MD 21128-9414, USA

Porter, Colin (Athlete, Baseball Player)
245 E Sunburst Cir
Tucson, AZ 85704-7325, USA

Porter, Dan (Athlete, Baseball Player)
40275 Colony Dr
Murrieta, CA 92562-5514, USA

Porter, Daryl (Athlete, Football Player)
9053 W Sunrise Blvd
Plantation, FL 33322-5218, USA

Porter, Doug (Athlete, Football Player)
PO Box 588
Grambling, LA 71245-0588, USA

Porter, Gail (Actor)
c/o Staff Member *Yakety Yak*
25 D'Arblay St
London W1F 8EJ, UNITED KINGDOM (UK)

Porter, Gary (Misc)
c/o Staff Member *Feld Entertainment, Inc.*
8607 Westwood Center Dr Ste 500
Vienna, VA 22182-7501, USA

Porter, Gregory (Actor)
c/o Staff Member *Wehmann Models/ Talent Inc*
1128 Harmon Pl Ste 202
Minneapolis, MN 55403-2055, USA

Porter, Gregory (Musician)
c/o Paul Ewing *Wingsmusic Entertainment, Inc*
Prefers to be contacted via email or telephone
NY, USA

Porter, Jack (Athlete, Football Player)
1027 County Road 1530
Rush Springs, OK 73082-2416, USA

Porter, Jay (Athlete, Baseball Player)
9677 Heather Cir W
Palm Beach Gardens, FL 33410-5467, USA

Porter, Jody (Musician)
MOB Agency
6404 Wilshire Blvd Ste 505
Los Angeles, CA 90048-5507, USA

Porter, Joey (Athlete, Football Player)
c/o Staff Member *Pittsburgh Steelers*
3400 S Water St
Pittsburgh, PA 15203-2358, USA

Porter, Kalan (Musician, Reality Star)
c/o Joanne Setterington *BMG Canada Inc*
100-190 Liberty St
Toronto, ON M6K 3L5, CANADA

Porter, Lee (Athlete, Golfer)
1604 Birch Ln
Greensboro, NC 27408-6500, USA

Porter, Marina Oswald (Misc)
1850 WFM Rd. 550
Rockwall, TX 75087

Porter, Marquis (Bo) (Athlete, Baseball Player)
1500 S Capitol St SE Attn Coachr
Washington, DC 20003-3599, USA

Porter, Randy (Race Car Driver)
Laughlin Racing
113 Pride Dr.
Simpsonville, SC 29681-3241, USA

Porter, Rufus (Athlete, Football Player)
8 to 80
2555 Eldridge Pkwy #1321
Houston, TX 77077, USA

Porter, Scott (Actor)
c/o Staff Member *Brillstein Entertainment Partners*
9150 Wilshire Blvd Ste 350
Beverly Hills, CA 90212-3453, USA

Porter, Sean (Athlete, Football Player)
c/o Adisa P Bakari *Kelley Drye & Warren LLP*
3050 K St NW Ste 400
Washington, DC 20007-5100, USA

Porter, Terry (Basketball Player, Coach)
Milwaukee Bucks
1543 N 2nd St Fl 6
Bradley Center
Milwaukee, WI 53212-4036, USA

Porter, Tracy (Athlete, Football Player)
c/o Ashley Smith Becker *Relativity Sports*
2029 Century Park E Ste 1550
Century City, CA 90067-3000, USA

Porterfield, Ellary Hume (Actor)
c/o Marv Dauer *Marv Dauer Management*
11661 San Vicente Blvd Ste 104
Los Angeles, CA 90049-5150, USA

Porterfield, Garry (Athlete, Football Player)
7621 S Harvard Pl
Tulsa, OK 74136-8000, USA

Porter-King, Mary Bea (Golfer)
6412 Kalama Rd
Kapaa, HI 96746-8633, USA

Portilla, Jose (Athlete, Football Player)
3520 Mystic Dr
Buford, GA 30519-7060, USA

Portillo, Alfonso (President)
President's Office
Palacio Nacional
Guatemala City, GUATEMALA

Portis, Clinton (Athlete, Football Player)
7409 Georgetown Pike
McLean, VA 22102-2111, USA

Portisch, Lajos (Misc)
Chess Federation
Nephadsereg Utca 10
Budapest 01055, HUNGARY

Portishead (Music Group)
c/o Frank Riley *High Road Touring*
751 Bridgeway Fl 2
Sausalito, CA 94965-2174, USA

Portland, Rene (Coach)
Pennsylvania State University
Greenberg Complex
University Park, PA 16802, USA

Portman, Daniel (Actor)
c/o Staff Member *Hunwick Hughes*
Hudson House
8 Albany Street
Edinburgh EH1 1QB, UNITED KINGDOM

Portman, Natalie (Actor)
c/o Keleigh Thomas Morgan *Sunshine Sachs*
720 Cole Ave
Los Angeles, CA 90038-3606, USA

Portman, Robert (Athlete, Basketball Player)
2107 Cedar St
San Carlos, CA 94070-4753, USA

Portugal, Mark (Athlete, Baseball Player)
67 Serpentine Rd
Warren, RI 02885-1812, USA

Portugal. The Man (Music Group, Musician)
c/o Matt Hickey *High Road Touring*
751 Bridgeway Fl 2
Sausalito, CA 94965-2174, USA

Portwich, Ramona (Athlete)
KC Limmer
Stockhardweg 3
Hanover 30453, GERMANY

Porvari, Jukka (Athlete, Hockey Player)
Pohjola Vahinkovakuutus Oy Ostoreskontra
E1 Lapinmaentie 1
Pohjola FI-00013, Finland

Poryes, Michael (Producer, Writer)
c/o Debbee Klein *Paradigm*
8942 Wilshire Blvd
Beverly Hills, CA 90211-1908, USA

Porzingis, Kristaps (Athlete, Basketball Player)
c/o Andy Miller *ASM Sports*
450 Fashion Ave Ste 1700
New York, NY 10123-1700, USA

Porzio, Mike (Athlete, Baseball Player)
PO Box 2242
Westport, CT 06880-0242, USA

Posa, Victor (Athlete, Hockey Player)
8170 Burleigh Rd
Grand Blanc, MI 48439-9750, CANADA

Posada, Jorge (Athlete, Baseball Player)
300 E 77th St Apt 11B
New York, NY 10075-2484, USA

Posada, Jorge (Baseball Player)
9335 Balada St
Coral Gables, FL 33156-2333

Posada, Leo (Athlete, Baseball Player)
8200 Grand Canal Dr
Miami, FL 33144-3538, USA

Posavad, Mike (Athlete, Hockey Player)
Compass Flooring
6390 Kestrel Rd
Mississauga, ON L5T 1Z3, Canada

Poschl, Hanno (Actor)
Singerstr. 13/15
Vienna 01010, Austria

Pose, Scott (Athlete, Baseball Player)
1306 Rodessa Run
Raleigh, NC 27607-6011, USA

Posehn, Brian (Comedian)
c/o Dave Rath *Generate Management*
8750 Wilshire Blvd Ste 200
Beverly Hills, CA 90211-2707, USA

Posen, Zac (Designer, Reality Star)
c/o Susan Posen
115 Spring St
New York, NY 10012-3817, USA

Poses, Frederic M (Business Person)
AlliedSignal Inc
PO Box 4000
Morristown, NJ 07962, USA

Posey, Bill (Congressman, Politician)
120 Cannon Hob
Washington, DC 20515-2106, USA

Posey, Buster (Athlete, Baseball Player)
3985 N Peardale Dr
Lafayette, CA 94549-2819, USA

Posey, DeVier (Athlete, Football Player)
c/o Michael Perrett *Element Sports Group*
3340 Peachtree Rd NE Fl 16
Atlanta, GA 30326-1000, USA

Posey, James (Athlete, Basketball Player)
4671 E 153rd St
Cleveland, OH 44128-3014, USA

Posey, Parker (Actor)
c/o Meg Mortimer *Authentic Talent and Literary Management (NY)*
20 Jay St Ste M17
Brooklyn, NY 11201-8300, USA

Posey, Sam (Race Car Driver)
Low Road
Sharon, CT 06069, USA

Posey, Tyler (Actor)
c/o Sarah Shyn *3 Arts Entertainment*
9460 Wilshire Blvd Fl 7
Beverly Hills, CA 90212-2713, USA

Posluszny, Paul (Athlete, Football Player)
c/o Michael McCartney *Priority Sports & Entertainment (Chicago)*
325 N La Salle Dr Ste 650
Chicago, IL 60654-8182, USA

Posner, Mike (Musician)
c/o Jesse Kirschbaum *New Universal Entertainment Agency*
150 5th Ave
New York, NY 10011-4311, USA

Post, Avery D (Religious Leader)
39 Boothman Ln
Randolph, NH 03593-5101, USA

Post, Markie (Actor)
c/o Christopher Wright *Wright Entertainment*
14724 Ventura Blvd Ste 1201
Sherman Oaks, CA 91403-3512, USA

Post, Richard (Athlete, Football Player)
1812 Rickey Canyon Rd
Rice, WA 99167-9754, USA

Post, Sandra (Golfer)
Ladies Pro Golf Assn
100 International Golf Dr
Daytona Beach, FL 32124-1082, USA

Post, William (Business Person)
Pinnacle West Capital
400 E Van Buren St Ste 700
PO Box 52132
Phoenix, AZ 85004-2294, USA

Postaer, Staffan (Writer)
c/o David Krintzman *Morris Yorn Barnes Levine Krintzman Rubenstein Kohner & Gellman*
2000 Avenue of the Stars Ste 300N
Tower N Fl 3
Los Angeles, CA 90067-4704, USA

Postell, Lavor (Athlete, Basketball Player)
2008 Murray Hill Ln
Albany, GA 31707-3268, USA

Postema, Pam (Baseball Player)
171 Garver Rd
Mansfield, OH 44903-9056, USA

Post III, Glen F (Business Person)
Centurytel Inc
100 Century Park Dr
Monroe, LA 71203, USA

Postlewait, Kathy (Golfer)
111 Saint Johns Landing Dr
Winter Springs, FL 32708-6501, USA

Postrel, Virginia (Writer)
c/o Staff Member *Simon & Schuster*
1230 Avenue of the Americas Fl CONC1
New York, NY 10020-1586, USA

Pote, Lou (Athlete, Baseball Player)
10601 Orchard Ln
Chicago Ridge, IL 60415-1864, USA

Poteat, Hank (Athlete, Football Player)
23 Oxford Cir
Southampton, NJ 08088-3592, USA

Potente, Franka (Actor)
c/o Ashley Franklin *Thruline Entertainment*
9250 Wilshire Blvd Fl Ground
Beverly Hills, CA 90212-3352, USA

Pothier, Brian (Athlete, Hockey Player)
437 Neck Rd
Rochester, MA 02770-1709, USA

Poti, Tom (Athlete, Hockey Player, Olympic Athlete)
2 Honey Locust Ln
Sandwich, MA 02563-2700

Potter, Chris (Actor, Director)
c/o Gayle Abrams *Oscars Abrams Zimel & Associates*
438 Queen St E
Toronto, ON M5A 1T4, CANADA

Potter, Chris (Musician)
c/o Louise Holland *Vision Arts Management*
16 Clint Finger Rd
Saugerties, NY 12477-4360, USA

Potter, Cynthia (Cindy) (Sportscaster, Swimmer)
1188 Ragley Hall Rd NE
Brookhaven, GA 30319-2512, USA

Potter, Dan M (Religious Leader)
21 Forest Dr
Albany, NY 12205-2521, USA

Potter, Lauren (Actor)
c/o Patrick Welborn *Allegory Creative Management*
13261 Moorpark St Ste 103
Sherman Oaks, CA 91423-5156, USA

Potter, Mike (Athlete, Baseball Player)
21582 Archer Cir
Huntington Beach, CA 92646-8017, USA

Potter, Mike (Race Car Driver)
1318 E Lakeview Dr
Johnson City, TN 37601-2312, USA

Potter, Monica (Actor)
c/o Christian Donatelli *MGMT Entertainment (The Schiff Company)*
9220 W Sunset Blvd Ste 106
W Hollywood, CA 90069-3500, USA

Potter, Nate (Athlete, Football Player)

Potter, Philip A (Religious Leader)
3A York Castle Ave
Kingston 00006, JAMAICA

Potter, Ryan (Actor)
c/o Karen Renna *Karen Renna & Associates*
PO Box 4227
Burbank, CA 91503-4227, USA

Potter, Scott (Athlete, Baseball Player)
1637 Cordova Ave
Daytona Beach, FL 32117-1708, USA

Potter, Steve (Athlete, Football Player)
750 SE 7th Ave
Pompano Beach, FL 33060-9502, USA

Pottinger, Stanley (Writer)
c/o Staff Member *St Martins Press*
175 5th Ave
Publicity Dept
New York, NY 10010-7703, USA

Potts, Annie (Actor, Producer)
c/o Karen Samfilippo *IMPR*
1158 26th St # 548
Santa Monica, CA 90403-4698, USA

Potts, Cliff (Actor)
PO Box 131
Topanga, CA 90290-0131, USA

Potts, Mike (Athlete, Baseball Player)
60418th St
Butner, NC 27509-2001, USA

Potts, Roosevelt (Athlete, Football Player)
2800 Crystal St Apt J-4
Anderson, IN 46012-1446, USA

Potts, Sarah-Jane (Actor)
c/o Staff Member *Anonymous Content*
3532 Hayden Ave
Culver City, CA 90232-2413, USA

Potts, Tony (Television Host)
c/o Access Hollywood *KNBC (LA)*
3000 W Alameda Ave
Burbank, CA 91523-0002, USA

Potvin, Denis (Athlete, Hockey Player)
Ottawa Senators
110-1000 Palladium Dr
Ottawa, ON K2V 1A5, CANADA

Potvin, Felix (Athlete, Hockey Player)
40 Grove St Ste 430
Wellesley, MA 02482-7774, USA

Potvin, Jean R (Athlete, Hockey Player)
24 Longwood Dr
Huntingtn Sta, NY 11746-4716

Potvin, Nathaniel (Actor)
c/o Kasey Kitchen *ICON PR*
8961 W Sunset Blvd Ste 1C
W Hollywood, CA 90069-1886, USA

Poudrier, Daniel (Athlete, Hockey Player)
189 Sainte-Marguerite St N
Thetford Mines, QC G6H 4T6, Canada

Pough, Ernest (Athlete, Football Player)
2141 Buckman St
Jacksonville, FL 32206-4124, USA

Poul, Alan (Producer)
1544 N Sierra Bonita Ave
Los Angeles, CA 90046-2812, USA

Poulin, Dave (Athlete, Hockey Player)
Toronto Maple Leafs
400-40 Bay St
Toronto, ON M5J 2X2, Canada

Poulin, Dave (Athlete, Coach, Hockey Player)
16771 Orchard Ridge Ct
Granger, IN 46530-5916

Poulin, Rene (Horse Racer)
147 Alden St
Wallington, NJ 07057-1433, USA

Poullain, Frankie (Musician)
c/o Sue Whitehouse *Whitehouse Management*
PO Box 43829
London NW6 3PJ, UNITED KINGDOM

Poulsen, Ken (Athlete, Baseball Player)
PO Box 1699
Oakhurst, CA 93644-1699, USA

Poulson, Josh (Actor)
c/o Staff Member *WME|IMG*
9601 Wilshire Blvd
Beverly Hills, CA 90210-5213, USA

Poulter, Ian (Athlete, Golfer)
9791 Covent Garden Dr
Orlando, FL 32827-7066, USA

Pouncey, Mike (Football Player)
c/o Joel Segal *Lagardere Unlimited (NY)*
456 Washington St Apt 9L
New York, NY 10013-1555, USA

Pound, Richard W D (Misc)
87 Arlington Ave
Westmount, QC H3Y 2W5, CANADA

Pounder, CCH (Actor)
c/o Judy Page *Mitchell K Stubbs & Assoc*
8675 Washington Blvd Ste 203
Culver City, CA 90232-7486, USA

Poundstone, Paula (Actor, Comedian)
c/o Bonnie Burns *Burns & Burns Management*
10523 Mars Ln
Los Angeles, CA 90077-3109, USA

Poupard, Paul Cardinal (Religious Leader)
Pontificium Consilium Pro Dialogo
00120, VATICAN CITY

Pousette, Lena (Actor)
Atkins Assoc
8040 Ventura Canyon Ave
Panorama City, CA 91402-6313, USA

Povich, Maury (Journalist)
c/o Staff Member *MoPo Productions*
200 Park Ave S Ste 1320
New York, NY 10003-1510, USA

Povitsky, Esther (Actor, Comedian, Internet Star)
c/o Lee Kernis *Brillstein Entertainment Partners*
9150 Wilshire Blvd Ste 350
Beverly Hills, CA 90212-3453, USA

Powe, Jerrell (Athlete, Football Player)
c/o Bus Cook *Bus Cook Sports, Inc*
1 Willow Bend Dr
Hattiesburg, MS 39402-8552, USA

Powe, Karl (Athlete, Football Player)
PO Box 13293
Mobile, AL 36663-0293, USA

Powell, Alonzo (Athlete, Baseball Player)
2502 S Tyler St Attn Coachingstaff
Tacoma, WA 98405-1051, USA

Powell, Andre (Athlete, Football Player)
N50W16962 Maple Crest Ln
Menomonee Falls, WI 53051-6689, USA

Powell, Bilal (Athlete, Football Player)
c/o Joel Segal *Lagardere Unlimited (NY)*
456 Washington St Apt 9L
New York, NY 10013-1555, USA

Powell, Brittney (Actor, Model)
c/o Mike Eistenstadt *Amsel, Eisenstadt & Frazier Talent Agency (AEF)*
5055 Wilshire Blvd Ste 860
Los Angeles, CA 90036-6108, USA

Powell, Charley (Athlete, Football Player)
2 Char Bea Ln
Saint Louis, MO 63132-3607, USA

Powell, Cincy (Athlete, Basketball Player)
2541 Brookside Dr
Irving, TX 75063-3173, USA

Powell, Clifton (Actor)
c/o Christopher Black *Opus Entertainment*
5225 Wilshire Blvd Ste 905
Los Angeles, CA 90036-4353, USA

Powell, Colin (Politician)
1317 Ballantrae Farm Dr
McLean, VA 22101-3028, USA

Powell, Cristen (Race Car Driver)
3072 Patricia Ave
Los Angeles, CA 90064-4504, USA

Powell, Dante (Athlete, Baseball Player)
5715 E Walton St
Long Beach, CA 90815-1325, USA

Powell, Dennis (Athlete, Baseball Player)
1743 Eastgate Ave
Upland, CA 91784-9211, USA

Powell, Dick (Athlete, Baseball Player)
2864 Hunt Valley Dr
Glenwood, MD 21738-9639, USA

Powell, Drew (Actor)
c/o Billy Miller *Billy Miller Management*
8322 Ridpath Dr
Los Angeles, CA 90046-7710, USA

Powell, Dwane (Cartoonist)
PO Box 191
Raleigh, NC 27602-9150, USA

Powell, Glen (Actor)
c/o Gary Mantoosh *Baker Winokur Ryder Public Relations*
9100 Wilshire Blvd
W Tower #500
Beverly Hills, CA 90212-3415, USA

Powell, Hosken (Athlete, Baseball Player)
1289 Tamara Dr
Pensacola, FL 32504-6642, USA

Powell, Jane (Actor)
62 Cedar Rd
Wilton, CT 06897-3626, USA

Powell, Jay (Athlete, Baseball Player)
188 Green Glades
Ridgeland, MS 39157-8662, USA

Powell, Jeremy (Athlete, Baseball Player)
3022 W Summit Walk Ct
Anthem, AZ 85086-1012, USA

Powell, Jesse (Musician)
c/o Staff Member *Pyramid Entertainment Group*
377 Rector Pl Apt 21A
New York, NY 10280-1439, USA

Powell, John (Athlete, Olympic Athlete)
5545 Sobb Ave
Las Vegas, NV 89118-3422, USA

Powell, John G (Athlete, Track Athlete)
John Powell Assoc
10445 Mary Ave
Cupertino, CA 95014-1348, USA

Powell, John W (Boog) (Athlete, Baseball Player)
Boog's Barbeque
333 W Camden St
Baltimore, MD 21201-2496, USA

Powell, Landon (Athlete, Baseball Player)
104 Meyers Dr
Greenville, SC 29605-1923, USA

Powell, Leroy (Athlete, Baseball Player)
PO Box 4036
Muscle Shoals, AL 35662-4036, USA

Powell, Marvin (Athlete, Football Player)
10411 Harborbluff Way
Tampa, FL 33615-3658, USA

Powell, Michael (Mike) (Athlete, Track Athlete)
Team Powell
PO Box 8000-354
Alta Loma, CA 91701, USA

Powell, Monroe (Musician)
Personality Presents
880 E Sahara Ave # 101
Las Vegas, NV 89104-3002, USA

Powell, Nicole (Basketball Player)
Charlotte Sting
100 Hive Dr
Charlotte, NC 28217, USA

Powell, Paul (Athlete, Baseball Player)
5254 E Enrose St
Mesa, AZ 85205-5484, USA

Powell, Robert (Actor)
10 Pond Place
London W12 7RJ, UNITED KINGDOM (UK)

Powell, Ronald (Athlete, Football Player)

Powell, Ross (Athlete, Baseball Player)
605 Bristlewood Dr
McKinney, TX 75072-8361, USA

Powell, Sandy (Designer)
London Mgmt
2-4 Noel St
London W1V 3RB, UNITED KINGDOM (UK)

Powell, Susan (Actor)
4207 147th Street Ct NW
Gig Harbor, WA 98332-9041, USA

Powell, Ted (Athlete, Football Player)
308 Hodder Ln
Henrico, VA 23075-2510, USA

Powell, Ty (Athlete, Football Player)

Powell III, Earl A (Rusty) (Misc)
National Gallery of Art
Constitution Ave & 4th St NW
Washington, DC 20565-0001, USA

Powell Jobs, Laurene (Business Person)
2101 Waverley St
Palo Alto, CA 94301-3955, USA

Powell Jr, D Duane (Cartoonist)
215 S McDowell St
Raleigh, NC 27601-1331, USA

Power, Dave (Actor)
c/o Staff Member *Bauman Redanty & Shaul Agency*
5757 Wilshire Blvd
Suite 473
Beverly Hills, CA 90212, USA

Power, J D (Dave) (Business Person)
J D Power Associates
2625 Townsgate Rd Ste 100
Westlake Village, CA 91361-5737, USA

Power, Samantha (Activist, Writer)
US Mission
United Nations Plz
New York, NY 10017, USA

Power, Taryn (Actor)
522 1/2 S Main St
Viroqua, WI 54665-2058, USA

Power, Ted (Athlete, Baseball Player)
Louisville Bats 401 E Main St Attn: Coaching Staf
Louseville, K 40707-1110, USA

Powers, Alexandra (Actor)
United Talent Agency
9336 Civic Center Dr
Beverly Hills, CA 90210-3604, USA

Powers, Clyde (Athlete, Football Player)
17 S Point Ct
Bluffton, SC 29910-6132, USA

Powers, James B (Religious Leader)
American Baptist Assn
4605 N State Line Ave
Texarkana, TX 75503-2916, USA

Powers, Jeff (Athlete)
USA Water Polo
2124 Main St Ste 210
Huntington Beach, CA 92648-2405, USA

Powers, Jerraud (Athlete, Football Player)

Powers, Keith (Actor)
c/o Mara Santino *Luber Roklin Management*
5815 W Sunset Blvd Ste 208
Los Angeles, CA 90028-6481, USA

Powers, Ross (Athlete, Olympic Athlete, Snowboarder)
c/o Peter Carlisle *Octagon Olympics & Action Sports*
7 Ocean St Ste 2
South Portland, ME 04106-2800, USA

Powers, Stefanie (Actor)
c/o Staff Member *Douglas Gorman Rothacker & Wilhelm Inc*
33 W 46th St Ste 801
New York, NY 10036-4103, USA

Powers, Warren (Athlete, Football Player)
3909 Lausanne Rd
Randallstown, MD 21133-4511, USA

Powers, Warren A (Athlete, Football Player)
14742 Thornbird Manor Pkwy
Chesterfield, MO 63017-2497, USA

Powis, Lynn (Athlete, Hockey Player)
2669 S Columbine St
Denver, CO 80210-6441

Powis, Lynn (Athlete, Hockey Player)
23 Lombard Cres
St. Albert, AB T8N 3N1, Canada

Powley, Bel (Actor)
c/o Annick Oppenheim *Wolf-Kasteler Public Relations*
6255 W Sunset Blvd Ste 1111
Los Angeles, CA 90028-7426, USA

Powlus, Ron (Athlete, Football Player)
1012 Ruthann Dr
Berwick, PA 18603-2426, USA

Powter, Daniel (Musician)
c/o Staff Member *Paradigm (Monterey)*
404 W Franklin St
Monterey, CA 93940-2303, USA

Poyer, Jordan (Athlete, Football Player)
c/o Ryan Morgan *MAG Sports Agency*
8222 Melrose Ave Fl 2
Los Angeles, CA 90046-6825, USA

Poynter, Dougie (Musician)
c/o Staff Member *Universal Music Group*
100 Universal City Plz
Universal City, CA 91608-1002, USA

Poza, Jorge (Actor)
c/o Staff Member *Televisa*
Blvd Adolfo Lopez Mateos 232
Colonia San Angel INN
DF CP 01060, MEXICO

Pozderac, Phil (Athlete, Football Player)
2193 Carmel Dr
Carrollton, TX 75006-2814, USA

Pozdnykova, Tatyana (Athlete, Track Athlete)
4151 NW 43rd St
Gainesville, FL 32606-4582, USA

Prada, Aura Helena (Actor)
c/o Gabriel Blanco *Gabriel Blanco Iglesias (Mexico)*
Rio Balsas 35-32
Colonia Cuauhtemoc
DF 06500, Mexico

Prada, Miuccia (Designer, Fashion Designer)
Prada SPA
Via Andrea Maffei 2
Milan 20154, ITALY

Prado, Edgar (Horse Racer)
1519 Shoreline Way
Hollywood, FL 33019-5011, USA

Prady, Bill (Producer)
10063 Toluca Lake Ave
Toluca Lake, CA 91602-2941, USA

Prall, Willie (Athlete, Baseball Player)
3 Pheasant Run
Kinnelon, NJ 07405-3022, USA

Prance, Ghilean T (Misc)
Kew Royal Botanic Gardens
Richmond
Surrey TW9 3AE, UNITED KINGDOM (UK)

Prangley, Chris (Actor)
c/o Staff Member *Coast to Coast Talent Group*
3350 Barham Blvd
Los Angeles, CA 90068-1404, USA

Prappas, Ted (Race Car Driver)
3072 Patricia Ave
Los Angeles, CA 90064-4504, USA

Pras (Musician)
DAS Communications
83 Riverside Dr
New York, NY 10024-5713, USA

Prater, Shaun (Athlete, Football Player)

Prather, Joan (Actor)
31647 Sea Level Dr
Malibu, CA 90265-2633, USA

Pratiwi, Sudarmono (Astronaut)
Jalan Pegangsaan
Timur
Jakarta 00016, INDONESIA

Pratt, Andy (Athlete, Baseball Player)
9626 W Greenhurst Dr
Sun City, AZ 85351-2027, USA

Pratt, Awadagin (Musician)
Cramer/Marder Artists
3436 Springhill Rd
Lafayette, CA 94549-2535, USA

Pratt, Chris (Actor)
c/o Alan Nierob *Rogers & Cowan*
1840 Century Park E Fl 18
Los Angeles, CA 90067-2101, USA

Pratt, Deborah (Actor, Producer, Writer)
c/o Staff Member *Hirsch Wallerstein Hayum Matlof & Fishman*
10100 Santa Monica Blvd Fl 23
Los Angeles, CA 90067-4003, USA

Pratt, Heidi Montag (Musician, Reality Star)
c/o Kyell Thomas *Octagon Entertainment*
1840 Century Park E Ste 200
Los Angeles, CA 90067-2114, USA

Pratt, Kelly (Athlete, Hockey Player)
23 Lombard Cres
St. Albert, AB T8N 3N1, Canada

Pratt, Keri Lynn (Actor)
c/o Staff Member *Innovative Artists*
1505 10th St
Santa Monica, CA 90401-2805, USA

Pratt, Kyla (Actor)
c/o Ernest Dukes *The Nottingham Group*
1800 Century Park E Ste 210
Los Angeles, CA 90067-1505, USA

Pratt, Mary (Athlete, Baseball Player)
40 Greenleaf St Unit 401
Quincy, MA 02169-4468, USA

Pratt, Michael (Athlete, Basketball Player)
3211 Chipaway Ct
Floyds Knobs, IN 47119-9621, USA

Pratt, Nolan (Athlete, Hockey Player)
Springfield Falcons
594 North St
Windsor Locks, CT 06096-1147

Pratt, Robert (Athlete, Football Player)
320 Greenway Ln
Richmond, VA 23226-1632, USA

Pratt, Spencer (Reality Star)
c/o Kyell Thomas *Octagon Entertainment*
1840 Century Park E Ste 200
Los Angeles, CA 90067-2114, USA

Pratt, Stephanie (Reality Star)
c/o Leslie Allan-Rice *Leslie Allan-Rice Management*
1007 Maybrook Dr
Beverly Hills, CA 90210-2715, USA

Pratt, Susan C (Actor)
7 Old Pound Rd
Pound Ridge, NY 10576-1737, USA

Pratt, Todd (Athlete, Baseball Player)
219 Kramer St
Carrollton, GA 30117-3705, USA

Pratt, Tracy (Athlete, Hockey Player)
1705-15038 101 Ave
Surrey, BC V3R 0N2, Canada

Pratt, Victoria (Actor)
c/o Gordon Gilbertson *Gilbertson Management*
1334 3rd Street Promenade Ste 201
Santa Monica, CA 90401-1320, USA

Pratt, Victoria (Actor)
c/o Cheryl McLean *Creative Public Relations*
3385 Oak Glen Dr
Los Angeles, CA 90068-1311, USA

Prattes, Colt (Actor, Dancer)
c/o Gary Mantoosh *Baker Winokur Ryder Public Relations*
9100 Wilshire Blvd
W Tower #500
Beverly Hills, CA 90212-3415, USA

Prebola, Gene (Athlete, Football Player)
24 Hayward Rd
Sparta, NJ 07871-3119, USA

Precourt, Charles J (Astronaut)
1960 Shoshone Dr
Ogden, UT 84403-4655, USA

Precourt, Charles J Colonel (Astronaut)
1960 Shoshone Dr
Ogden, UT 84403-4655, USA

Preece, Steve (Athlete, Football Player)
1501 SE 78th Ave
Vancouver, WA 98664-1777, USA

Pregenzer, John (Athlete, Baseball Player)
6316 104th St E
Puyallup, WA 98373-4127, USA

Pregulman, Merv (Athlete, Football Player)
44 S Crest Rd
Chattanooga, TN 37404-4005, USA

Preissing, Tom (Athlete, Hockey Player)
1590 Little Raven St Unit 601
Denver, CO 80202-6183

Prejean, Helen Sister (Writer)
317 Bonnabel Blvd
Metairie, LA 70005-3740, USA

Prejean, Patrick (Actor)
B5 135 Poissonniere
Paris F-75002, France

Preki (Soccer Player)
Kansas City Wizards
2 Arrowhead Dr
Kansas City, MO 64129, USA

Prendergast, John (Writer)
c/o Joseph (Joe) Veltre *Gersh*
41 Madison Ave Ste 3301
New York, NY 10010-2210, USA

Prentice, Dean S (Athlete, Hockey Player)
350 Doon Valley Dr
Kitchener, ON N2P 2M9, Canada

Prentice, Justin (Actor)
c/o Siri Garber *Platform PR*
2666 N Beachwood Dr
Los Angeles, CA 90068-2308, USA

Prentiss, Paula (Actor, Comedian)
719 Foothill Rd
Beverly Hills, CA 90210-3437, USA

Prepon, Laura (Actor)
c/o Michael Geiser *Jill Fritzo Public Relations*
208 E 51st St # 305
New York, NY 10022-6557, USA

Prescott, Dak (Athlete, Football Player)
c/o Jeffrey Guerrerio *ProSource Sports Management*
2200 Forsythe Ave
Monroe, LA 71201-3613, USA

Prescott, Jon (Actor)
c/o Miles Levy *Randy James Management*
12711 Ventura Blvd Ste 345
Studio City, CA 91604-2416, USA

Presko, Joe (Athlete, Baseball Player)
1612 NE 77th Ter
Kansas City, MO 64118-1939, USA

Presle, Micheline (Actor)
6 Rue Antoine Dubois
Paris 75006, FRANCE

Presley, Alex (Baseball Player)
276 Turkey Creek Rd
Ruston, LA 71270-1649, USA

Presley, Brian (Actor)
c/o Nikki Joel *ICM Partners*
10250 Constellation Blvd Fl 7
Los Angeles, CA 90067-6207, USA

Presley, Jim (Athlete, Baseball Player)
333 W Camden St Attn Coaching
Baltimore, MD 21201-2496, USA

Presley, Lisa-Marie (Musician)
Elvis Presley Enterprises
3734 Elvis Presley Blvd
Graceland Corporate Offices
Memphis, TN 38116-4106, USA

Presley, Priscilla (Actor, Producer)
PO Box 17838
Beverly Hills, CA 90209-3838, USA

Presley, Richard (Musician)
c/o Staff Member *WME|IMG*
9601 Wilshire Blvd
Beverly Hills, CA 90210-5213, USA

Presley, Wayne (Athlete, Hockey Player)
1339 Kingsway Dr
Highland, MI 48356-1165

Press, Bill (Correspondent)
Bill Press Show
217 8th St SE
Washington, DC 20003-2108, USA

Pressel, Morgan (Athlete, Golfer)
c/o Chris Armstrong *Wasserman Media Group*
10960 Wilshire Blvd Ste 1200
Los Angeles, CA 90024-3714, USA

Pressey, Paul (Athlete, Basketball Player, Coach)
782 Haddonstone Cir
Lake Mary, FL 32746-5603, USA

Pressfield, Steven (Writer)
PO Box 2353
Springfield, VA 22152-0353, USA

Pressler, Larry L (Politician)
2812 Davis Ave
Alexandria, VA 22302-2507, USA

Pressler, Menahem M J (Musician)
Melvin Kaplan
1 Lawson Ln Ste 320
Burlington, VT 05401-8445, USA

Pressley, Dominic (Athlete, Basketball Player)
1406 Whooping Ct
Upper Marlboro, MD 20774-7086, USA

Pressley, Harold (Athlete, Basketball Player)
6470 Matheny Way
Citrus Heights, CA 95621-4839, USA

Pressley, Paul (Athlete, Basketball Player)
Pressliz Inc
600 County Road 4694
Timpson, TX 75975, USA

Pressley, Robert (Race Car Driver)
6 Forestdale Dr
Asheville, NC 28803-1811, USA

Pressly, Jaime (Actor)
6300 Canoga Ave Ste 1500
Woodland Hills, CA 91367-8015, USA

Pressman, Edward R (Producer)
Edward Pressman Films
130 El Camino Dr
Beverly Hills, CA 90212-2705, USA

Pressman, Lawrence (Actor)
c/o Deborah Miller *Shelter Entertainment*
9255 W Sunset Blvd Ste 300
Los Angeles, CA 90069-3313, USA

Pressman, Michael (Actor, Director, Producer)
c/o Staff Member *Gersh*
9465 Wilshire Blvd Ste 600
Beverly Hills, CA 90212-2605, USA

Pressman, Sally (Actor)
c/o Staff Member *Abrams Artists Agency*
750 N San Vicente Blvd
E Tower Fl 11
Los Angeles, CA 90069-5788, USA

Presswood, Hank (Athlete, Baseball Player)
1445 W 71st Pl
Chicago, IL 60636-3961, USA

Presswood, Henry (Baseball Player)
Cincinnati Buckeyes
1445 W 71st Pl
Chicago, IL 60636-3961, USA

Presta, Peter (DJ, Musician)
c/o Len Evans *Project Publicity*
540 W 43rd St
New York, NY 10036, USA

Prestel, Jim (Athlete, Football Player)
6150 Hurricane Ct
Parker, CO 80134-5704, USA

Preston, Carrie (Actor)
c/o Staff Member *Anderson Group Public Relations*
8060 Melrose Ave Fl 4
Los Angeles, CA 90046-7038, USA

Preston, Cynthia (Actor)
c/o Penny Vizcarra *PV Public Relations*
121 N Almont Dr Apt 203
Beverly Hills, CA 90211-1860, USA

Preston, Douglas (Writer)
c/o Staff Member *Tom Doherty Associates, LLC*
175 5th Ave
New York, NY 10010-7703, USA

Preston, J A (Actor)
Paradigm Agency
10100 Santa Monica Blvd Ste 2500
Los Angeles, CA 90067-4116, USA

Preston, Kelly (Actor)
735 N Bonhill Rd
Los Angeles, CA 90049-2303, USA

Preston, Ray (Athlete, Football Player)
1570 Chestnut Ct W
Palm Harbor, FL 34683-2115, USA

Preston, Simon J (Musician)
Little Hardwick
Langton Green Tunbridge Wells
Kent TN3 OEY, UNITED KINGDOM (UK)

Prestridge, Luke (Athlete, Football Player)
22803 State Highway 249
Tomball, TX 77375-8318, USA

Prettyman, Tristan (Musician)
c/o Staff Member *Paradigm (Monterey)*
404 W Franklin St
Monterey, CA 93940-2303, USA

Pretty Reckless, The (Music Group)
c/o John Stratton *DAS Communications*
83 Riverside Dr
New York, NY 10024-5713, USA

Pretty Ricky (Music Group)
c/o Staff Member *Atlantic Records*
1290 Avenue of the Americas Fl 28
New York, NY 10104-0106, USA

Preus, David W (Religious Leader)
2481 Como Ave
Saint Paul, MN 55108-1445, USA

Previte, Richard (Business Person)
Advanced Micro Devices
2485 Augustine Dr
PO Box 3453
Santa Clara, CA 95054-3002, USA

Prevost, Josette (Actor)
Tisherman Agency
6767 Forest Lawn Dr # 101
Los Angeles, CA 90068-1027, USA

Prew, Augustus (Actor)
c/o Brantley Brown *Authentic Talent & Literary Management*
3615 Eastham Dr # 650
Culver City, CA 90232-2410, USA

Pribilinec, Jozef (Athlete, Track Athlete)
Moyzesova 75
Lutila 966 22, SLOVAKIA

Price, AJ (Athlete, Basketball Player)
c/o Jeff Schwartz *Excel Sports Management*
1700 Broadway Fl 29
New York, NY 10019-6559, USA

Price, Alan (Musician, Songwriter, Writer)
Lustig Talent
PO Box 770850
Orlando, FL 32877-0850, USA

Price, Antony (Designer, Fashion Designer)
468 Kings Road
London SW1, UNITED KINGDOM (UK)

Price, Brent (Athlete, Basketball Player)
1111 W Wynona Ave
Enid, OK 73703-6909, USA

price, Bryan (Baseball Player, Coach)
10987 N 122nd Street
Scottsdale, AZ 85259

Price, Charles W (Athlete, Football Player)
3712 43rd St
Lubbock, TX 79413-3036, USA

Price, David (Baseball Player)
c/o Bo McKinnis *McKinnis Sports Management*
209 10th Ave S Ste 405
Nashville, TN 37203-0764, USA

Price, Elex (Athlete, Football Player)
2833 Newport St
Jackson, MS 39213-5335, USA

Price, Ferne (Baseball Player)
720 E Mary Ln
Terre Haute, IN 47802-4617, USA

Price, Frank (Misc)
Price Entertainment
2425 Olympic Blvd
Santa Monica, CA 90404-4030, USA

Price, Frederick K C (Religious Leader)
Crenshaw Christian Church
7901 S Vermont Ave
Los Angeles, CA 90044-3531, USA

Price, George C (Prime Minister)
House of Representatives
Belmopan, BELIZE

Price, Hillary (Cartoonist)
221 Pine St # 4G3
Florence, MA 01062-1267, USA

Price, Jim (Athlete, Baseball Player)
2100 Woodward Ave
Detroit, MI 48201-3470, USA

Price, Joe (Athlete, Baseball Player)
1874 Arabian Ct
Hebron, KY 41048-8436, USA

Price, Katie (Jordan) (Actor, Model)
Pricey Media
P.O. Box 5036
Argus House, Crowhurst Road
Brighton, East Sussex BN1 8AR, UK

Price, Kelly (Musician)
JL Ent
18653 Ventura Blvd # 340
Tarzana, CA 91356-4103, USA

Price, Lindsay (Actor)
c/o Stephanie Simon *Untitled Entertainment*
350 S Beverly Dr Ste 200
Beverly Hills, CA 90212-4819, USA

Price, Lloyd (Musician, Songwriter, Writer)
95 Horseshoe Hill Rd
Pound Ridge, NY 10576-1636, USA

Price, Lonny (Actor)
c/o Jack Tantleff *Paradigm*
140 Broadway Ste 2600
New York, NY 10005-1011, USA

Price, Marc (Actor)
8444 Magnolia Dr
Los Angeles, CA 90046-1932, USA

Price, Margo (Musician)
c/o Jonathan Levine *Paradigm (Nashville)*
222 2nd Ave S Ste 1600
Nashville, TN 37201-2375, USA

Price, Marvin (Athlete, Baseball Player)
Chicago American Giants
12136 S Princeton Ave
Chicago, IL 60628-6516, USA

Price, Megyn (Actor)
c/o Leslie Allan-Rice *Leslie Allan-Rice Management*
1007 Maybrook Dr
Beverly Hills, CA 90210-2715, USA

Price, MIke (Athlete, Basketball Player)
4415 Thornleigh Dr
Indianapolis, IN 46226-2165, USA

Price, Mike (Coach, Football Coach)
University of Texas
Athletic Dept
El Paso, TX 79968-0001, USA

Price, Mitchell (Athlete, Football Player)
3935 Thousand Oaks Dr Apt 1506
San Antonio, TX 78217-1877, USA

Price, Molly (Actor)
c/o Stephen Hirsch *Gersh*
41 Madison Ave Ste 3301
New York, NY 10010-2210, USA

Price, Nick (Golfer)
Nick Price Group Inc
900 S US Highway #1 Ste #5
Jupiter, FL 33477, USA

Price, Noel (Athlete, Hockey Player)
21 Windeyer Cres
Kanata, ON K2K 2P6, Canada

Price, Peerless (Athlete, Football Player)
3300 Moye Trl
Duluth, GA 30097-3780, USA

Price, Phoebe (Actor)
Pmodelmanagement
8109 Kirkwood Dr
Los Angeles, CA 90046-2001, USA

Price, Steven (Athlete, Hockey Player)
Stable 26 Inc
300-180 King St S
Waterloo, ON N2J 1P8, CANADA

Price, Terry (Athlete, Football Player)
59 Fieldstone Dr
South Glastonbury, CT 06073-3717, USA

Price, Tom (Congressman, Politician)
403 Cannon Hob
Washington, DC 20515-1807, USA

Price, W Mark (Basketball Player)
Georgia Institute of Technology
Athletic Dept
Atlanta, GA 30332-0001, USA

Price-Bunch, Ashil (Golfer)
1629 Country Club Dr
Morristown, TN 37814-3316, USA

Priddy, Bob (Athlete, Baseball Player)
136 Shingiss St Apt 214
Mc Kees Rocks, PA 15136-5500, USA

Priddy, Bob (Athlete, Basketball Player)
Lazy Arrow Ranch
PO Box 3169
Boys Ranch, TX 79010-3169, USA

Priddy, Nancy (Actor)
11223 Sunshine Ter
Studio City, CA 91604-3123, USA

Pride, Charley (Athlete, Baseball Player)
Memphis Red Sox
PO Box 670507
Dallas, TX 75367-0507, USA

Pride, Charlie (Musician)
CECCA Productions
PO Box 670507
Dallas, TX 75367-0507, USA

Pride, Curtis (Athlete, Baseball Player)
1310 Wood Dale Ter
Wellington, FL 33414-9028, USA

Pride, Dicky (Athlete, Golfer)
1214 Belleaire Cir
Orlando, FL 32804-6706, USA

Pride, Lynn (Basketball Player)
Minnesota Lynx
600 1st Ave N Ste Sky
Target Center
Minneapolis, MN 55403-9802, USA

Pride, Mack (Baseball Player)
Kansas City Monarchs
3305 Pierce St
Wheat Ridge, CO 80033-6333, USA

Pridemore, Tom (Athlete, Football Player)
3935 Poplar Springs Rd
Gainesville, GA 30507-8618, USA

Pridie, Jason (Baseball Player)
4475 E Campbell Ct
Gilbert, AZ 85234-7643

Pridy, Todd (Athlete, Baseball Player)
3430 Scenic Dr
Napa, CA 94558-4239, USA

Priesand, Sally J (Religious Leader)
10 Wedgewood Cir
Eatontown, NJ 07724-1203, USA

Priest, Eddie (Athlete, Baseball Player)
445 Ballard Rd
Altoona, AL 35952-6227, USA

Priest, Judas (Music Group)
c/o Lydia Kirschstein *Trinifold Management*
12 Oval Rd
Camden
London NW1 7DH, UNITED KINGDOM

Priest, Maxi (Musician)
Virgin Records
150 5th Ave Fl 7
New York, NY 10011-4372, USA

Priest, Steve (Musician)
DCM International
296 Nether St
Finchley
London N3 1RJ, UNITED KINGDOM (UK)

Priestlay, Ken (Athlete, Hockey Player)
5438 Crescent Dr
Delta, BC V4K 2C9, Canada

Priestley, Jason (Actor, Race Car Driver)
c/o JB Roberts *Thruline Entertainment*
9250 Wilshire Blvd Fl Ground
Beverly Hills, CA 90212-3352, USA

Priestley, Jr, Thomas (Director, Photographer)
c/o Jay Gilbert *Broder Webb Chervin Silbermann Agency, The (BWCS)*
10250 Constellation Blvd
Los Angeles, CA 90067-6200, USA

Prieto, Ariel (Athlete, Baseball Player)
Vermont Lake Monsters 1 King Street
Ferry Dock Attn
Burlimrton, VT 05401, USA

Prieto, Chris (Athlete, Baseball Player)
PO Box 10911
Eugene, OR 97440-2911, USA

Primatesta, Raul Francisco Cardinal (Religious Leader)
Arzobispado
Ave H Irigoyen 98
Cordoba 05000, ARGENTINA

Primeau, Keith (Athlete, Hockey Player)
508 N Union Ave
Margate City, NJ 08402-1236

Primeau, Wayne (Athlete, Hockey Player)
Durham Fury
595 Wentworth St E
Oshawa, ON LIH 3V8, Canada

Primrose, Neil (Musician)
Wildlife Entertainment
21 Heathmans Road
London SW6 4TJ, UNITED KINGDOM (UK)

Primus (Music Group)
c/o Ken Weinstein *Big Hassle Media*
40 Exchange Pl Ste 1900
New York, NY 10005-2714, USA

Primus, Barry (Actor)
2735 Creston Dr
Los Angeles, CA 90068-2209

Prince, Angel (Dancer)
Prince Dance
PO Box 1991
Honokaa, HI 96727-1832, USA

Prince, Brooklynn (Actor)
c/o Thor Bradwell *Thirty Three Management*
215 Thompson St # 282
New York, NY 10012-1360, USA

Prince, Don (Baseball Player)
11143 James B White Hwy S
Whiteville, NC 28472-6419, USA

Prince, Faith (Actor, Musician)
Innovative Artists
1505 10th St
Santa Monica, CA 90401-2805, USA

Prince, Harold S (Hal) (Director, Producer)
Harold Prince Organization
10 Rockefeller Plz Ste 816
New York, NY 10020-0052, USA

Prince, Jonathan (Actor)
333 S Roxbury Dr
Beverly Hills, CA 90212-3710, USA

Prince, Karim (Actor)
c/o Staff Member *Buchwald*
5900 Wilshire Blvd Ste 3100
Los Angeles, CA 90036-5030, USA

Prince, Larry L (Business Person)
Genuine Parts Co
2999 Wildwood Pkwy
Atlanta, GA 30339-8580, USA

Prince, Tayshaun (Athlete, Basketball Player)
5550 Leeds Ct
Oakland Township, MI 48306-4911, USA

Prince, Tom (Athlete, Baseball Player)
6816 10th Ave NW
Bradenton, FL 34209-1209, USA

Prince-Bythewood, Gina (Director, Producer, Writer)

Prince Harry (Royalty)
Frogmore House
Windsor SL4 2JG, UNITED KINGDOM

Princess Ann Claire (Actor, Musician, Royalty)

Princess Beatrice (Royalty)
Buckingham Palace
London SW1A 1AA, United Kingdom

Princess Eugenie (Royalty)
Buckingham Palace
London SW1A 1AA, United Kingdom

Principal, Victoria (Actor, Business Person, Producer)
c/o Staff Member *Victoria Principal Productions*
23852 Pacific Coast Hwy
Malibu, CA 90265-4876, USA

Principe, Dom (Athlete, Football Player)
300 N Highway A1A Apt E303
Jupiter, FL 33477-4542, USA

Principi, Anthony (Politician)
Veteran Affairs Department
24710 New Post Rd
Saint Michaels, MD 21663-2308, USA

Prine, Andrew (Actor)
3364 Longridge Ave
Sherman Oaks, CA 91423, USA

Prine, John (Musician, Songwriter, Writer)
Al Bunetta Mgmt
33 Music Sq W Ste 102B
Nashville, TN 37203-6607, USA

Pringle, Joan (Actor)
Gold Marshak Liedtke
3500 W Olive Ave Ste 1400
Burbank, CA 91505-5512, USA

Pringley, Mike (Athlete, Football Player)
6344 Mimosa Cir
Tucker, GA 30084-1946, USA

Prinosil, David (Athlete)
TC Wolfsberg
Am Schanzl 3
Amberg 92224, GERMANY

Prinsloo, Behati (Actor, Model)
c/o Simon Chambers *Storm Model Management*
5 Jubilee Pl
1st Floor
London SW3 3TD, UK

Prinz, Bret (Athlete, Baseball Player)
15471 N 88th Ave
Peoria, AZ 85382-3789, USA

Prinze Jr, Freddie (Actor)
2435 Mandeville Canyon Rd
Los Angeles, CA 90049-1235, USA

Prioleau, Pierson (Athlete, Football Player)
2221 Santee River Rd
Alvin, SC 29479-3844, USA

Prior, Anthony (Athlete, Football Player)
3861 Lofton Pl
Riverside, CA 92501-1809, USA

Prior, Maddy (Musician)
Park Promotions
PO Box 651
Park Road
Oxford OX2 9RB, UNITED KINGDOM (UK)

Prior, Mark (Athlete, Baseball Player)
4340 Altamirano Way
San Diego, CA 92103-1004, USA

Prior, Tom (Actor)
c/o Eric Podwall *Podwall Entertainment*
710 N Orlando Ave Apt 203
Loft 203
Los Angeles, CA 90069-5549, USA

Priory, Richard B (Business Person)
Duke Energy Co
526 S Church St
Charlotte, NC 28202-1802, USA

Pritchard, Barry (Musician)
Lustig Talent
PO Box 770850
Orlando, FL 32877-0850, USA

Pritchard, Buddy (Athlete, Baseball Player)
507 E Sunny Hills Rd
Fullerton, CA 92835-1357, USA

Pritchard, Kevin (Athlete, Basketball Player)
10492 Mission Park Ave
Las Vegas, NV 89135-1047, USA

Pritchard, Michael (Athlete, Football Player)
1041 Collingtree St
Las Vegas, NV 89145-8513, USA

Pritchard, Ron (Athlete, Football Player)
4210 S Pacific Dr
Chandler, AZ 85248-5200, USA

Pritchett, Chris (Athlete, Baseball Player)
959 Fir Tree Pl
Carlsbad, CA 92011-3926, USA

Pritchett, Kelvin (Athlete, Football Player)
4765 Guilford Forest Dr SW
Atlanta, GA 30331-7395, USA

Pritchett, Matt (Cartoonist)
London Daily Telegraph
181 Marsh Wall
London E14 9SR, UNITED KINGDOM (UK)

Pritchett, Stanley (Athlete, Football Player)
523 Monteagle Trce
Stone Mountain, GA 30087-4937, USA

Pritchett, Wes (Athlete, Football Player)
1194 Brookgate Way NE
Brookhaven, GA 30319-2877, USA

Pritikin, Greg (Director)
c/o Staff Member *Anonymous Content*
3532 Hayden Ave
Culver City, CA 90232-2413, USA

Pritko, Steve (Athlete, Football Player)
5813 Nicholson St
Pittsburgh, PA 15217-2309, USA

Probst, Jeff (Game Show Host, Reality Star, Television Host)
c/o James (Jamie) Feldman *Lichter Grossman Nichols Adler & Feldman Inc*
9200 W Sunset Blvd Ste 1200
Los Angeles, CA 90069-3607, USA

Proceviat, Dick (Athlete, Hockey Player)
56078 Rocky Plains Road
Whitemouth, MB ROE 2GO, Canada

Prochazka, Martin (Athlete, Hockey Player)
40 Bay St
Toronto, ON M5J 2K2, Canada

Prochnow, Jurgen (Actor)
c/o Staff Member *ICM Partners*
10250 Constellation Blvd Fl 7
Los Angeles, CA 90067-6207, USA

Prock, Markus (Athlete)
6142 Mieders
AUSTRIA

Proclaimers, The (Music Group)
c/o Staff Member *A.S.S. Concerts & Promotion GMBH*
Rahlstedter Str. 92 A
Hamburg 22149, Germany

Procter, Emily (Actor)
c/o Brad Slater *WME|IMG*
9601 Wilshire Blvd
Beverly Hills, CA 90210-5213, USA

Proctor, Bob (Writer)
LifeSuccess Productions, LLC
8900 E Pinnacle Peak Rd Ste D240
Scottsdale, AZ 85255-3651, USA

Proctor, Charles N (Skier)
100 Lockewood Ln Apt 238
Scotts Valley, CA 95066-3959, USA

Proctor, David (Baseball Player)
Bowman
5517 SW 23rd St
Topeka, KS 66614-1727, USA

Proctor, James (Jim) (Athlete, Baseball Player)
2 Westmoreland Pl
Saint Louis, MO 63108-1228, USA

Proctor, Scott (Athlete, Baseball Player)
428 NE Bavberrv Ln
Jensen Beach, FL 34957-4612, USA

Prodi, Romano (Prime Minister)
European Communities Commission
200 Rue de la Loi
Brussels, BELGIUM

P. Roe, David (Congressman, Politician)
419 Cannon Hob
Washington, DC 20515-0908, USA

Proehl, Ricky (Athlete, Football Player)
3504 Bromley Wood Ln
Greensboro, NC 27410-2181, USA

Professor, Griff (Actor, Musician)
c/o Staff Member *WME|IMG*
9601 Wilshire Blvd
Beverly Hills, CA 90210-5213, USA

Profit, Gene (Athlete, Football Player)
18 Loganwood Ct
Rockville, MD 20852-3413, USA

Profit, Mel (Athlete, Football Player)
PO Box 4155
Redondo Beach, CA 90277-1750, USA

Project 86 (Music Group)
c/o Staff Member *Paradigm (Monterey)*
404 W Franklin St
Monterey, CA 93940-2303, USA

Prokhorov, Mikhail (Business Person)
PO Box 55
Morrisonville, NY 12962-0055, RUSSIA

Prokop, Matt (Actor)
c/o Jillian Roscoe *ID Public Relations*
7060 Hollywood Blvd Fl 8th
Los Angeles, CA 90028-6021, USA

Prokopec, Luke (Athlete, Baseball Player)
178 18th St
Renmark, SA 05341, Australia

Proly, Mike (Athlete, Baseball Player)
112 Country Mist Dr
Greer, SC 29651-1919, USA

Pronger, Chris (Athlete, Hockey Player)
Newport Sports Management
400-201 City Centre Dr
Attn Don Meehan
Mississauga, ON L5B 2T4, Canada

Pronger, Sean (Athlete, Hockey Player)
290 Magnolia St
Costa Mesa, CA 92627

Pronovost, Claude (Athlete, Hockey Player)
268 388e Av
Saint-Hippolyte, QC J8A 3A2, Canada

Pronovost, Jean (Athlete, Hockey Player)
Hockey Ministries International
7-1100 Av des Canadiens-De-Montreal
Montreal, QC H3B 2S2, Canada

Proops, Greg (Actor)
c/o Lee Kernis *Brillstein Entertainment Partners*
9150 Wilshire Blvd Ste 350
Beverly Hills, CA 90212-3453, USA

Prophet, Billy (Musician)
Paramount Entertainment
PO Box 12
Far Hills, NJ 07931-0012, USA

Prophet, Elizabeth Clare (Religious Leader)
Church Universal & Triumphant
Box A
Livingston, MT 59047, USA

Prophet, Ronnie (Musician)
5970 Sailboat Ave
Tavares, FL 32778-9200, USA

Propp, Brian (Athlete, Hockey Player)
2320 Riverton Rd
Cinnaminson, NJ 08077-3719

Props, Rene (Actor)
Agency for Performing Arts
9200 W Sunset Blvd Ste 900
Los Angeles, CA 90069-3604, USA

Prosch, Jay (Athlete, Football Player)
c/o Bill Johnson *SportsTrust Advisors*
3340 Peachtree Rd NE Fl 16
Atlanta, GA 30326-1000, USA

Prospal, Vaclav (Athlete, Hockey Player)
17 S Treasure Dr
Tampa, FL 33609-3508, USA

Prospal, Vactav (Athlete, Hockey Player)
401 Channelside Dr
Ice Palace
Tampa, FL 33602-5400, USA

Prosper, Sandra (Actor)
c/o Staff Member *Mitchell K Stubbs & Assoc*
8675 Washington Blvd Ste 203
Culver City, CA 90232-7486, USA

Prosser, C Ladd (Misc)
101 W Windsor Rd # 2106
Urbana, IL 61802-6663, USA

Prosser, Robert (Religious Leader)
Cumberland Presbyterian Church
1978 Union Ave
Memphis, TN 38104-4134, USA

Prost, Alain M P (Race Car Driver)
Prost-Grand-Prix
7 Ave Eugene Freyssinet
Guyancourt 78286, FRANCE

Protopopov, Oleg (Figure Skater)
Chalet Hubel
Grindelwald 03818, SWITZERLAND

Proulx, Brooklynn (Actor)
c/o Jennifer Rawlings *Omni Artists*
6121 W Sunset Blvd
Los Angeles, CA 90028-6442, USA

Proulx, E Annie (Writer)
c/o Staff Member *The Sayle Literary Agency*
1 Petersfield
Cambridge CB1 1BB, UK

Prout, Bob (Athlete, Football Player)
23102 N Shepard Rd
Chillicothe, IL 61523-9035, USA

Prout, Brian (Musician)
Dreamcatcher Artists Mgmt
2908 Poston Ave
Nashville, TN 37203-1312, USA

Prout, Kirsten (Actor)
c/o Allan Grifka *Alchemy Entertainment*
7024 Melrose Ave Ste 420
Los Angeles, CA 90038-3394, USA

Proval, David (Actor)
c/o Andrew Howard *Shelter Entertainment*
9255 W Sunset Blvd Ste 300
Los Angeles, CA 90069-3313, USA

Provence, Andrew (Athlete, Football Player)
224 Providence Rd
Fayetteville, GA 30215-2844, USA

Provenza, Paul (Actor)
c/o Peter Golden *Golden Entertainment West*
5328 Alhama Dr
Woodland Hills, CA 91364-2013, USA

Provenzano, Chris (Director, Writer)
c/o David Ginsberg *Insight*
5358 Melrose Ave # 200W
Los Angeles, CA 90038-5117, USA

Provost, Jon (Actor)
Living Legends Ltd
PO Box 529
Santa Rosa, CA 95402-0529, USA

Provost, Michael (Actor)
c/o Brad Stokes *LINK Entertainment*
11872 La Grange Ave
Los Angeles, CA 90025-5282, USA

Prowse, David (Actor)
c/o Nick Cordasco *Prince Marketing Group*
18 Seneca Trl
Sparta, NJ 07871-1514, USA

Proyas, Alex (Director)
c/o Staff Member *Believe Media*
1455 Gordon St
Los Angeles, CA 90028-8408, USA

Prpic, Joel (Athlete, Hockey Player)
2586 South Shore Rd
Sudbury, ON P3G 1M3, Canada

Prudden, Bonnie (Misc)
PO Box 65240
Tucson, AZ 85728-5240, USA

Prudhomme, Don (Race Car Driver)
1232 Distribution Way
Vista, CA 92081-8816, USA

Pruett, Jeanne (Musician, Songwriter)
Joe Taylor Artists Agency
PO Box 279
Williamstown, NJ 08094-0279, USA

Pruett, Scott (Race Car Driver)
Rocket Sports
3400 West Rd
East Lansing, MI 48823-7309, USA

Pruitt, Gregory D (Greg) (Athlete, Football Player)
13851 Larchmere Blvd
Cleveland, OH 44120-1349, USA

Pruitt, James (Athlete, Football Player)
PO Box 244483
Boynton Beach, FL 33424-4483, USA

Pruitt, Jason (Baseball Player)
Topps
320 Clark Drive Apt 101
Summerfield, NC 27358, USA

Pruitt, Jordan (Musician)

Pruitt, Ron (Athlete, Baseball Player)
3632 Turnberry Dr
Medina, OH 44256-6827, USA

Prunskiene, Kazimiera (Politician)
Lithuanian-European Institute
Vilnius St 45-13
Vilnius 02001, LITHUANIA

Prust, Brandon (Athlete, Hockey Player)
Newport Sports Management
400-201 City Centre Dr
Attn Don Meehan
Mississauga, ON L5B 2T4, Canada

Pryce, Jonathan (Actor, Musician)
46 Albermarle St
London, ENGLAND W1X 4PP, UNITED KINGDOM

Pryce, Travor (Athlete, Football Player)
13655 Broncos Pkwy
Englewood, CO 80112-4150, USA

Prydz, Eric (DJ)
c/o Simon Clarkson *WME|IMG (UK)*
103 New Oxford St WMA
Centrepoint
London WC1A 1DD, UNITED KINGDOM

Pryor, Calvin (Athlete, Football Player)

Pryor, Chris (Athlete, Hockey Player)
Philadelphia Flyers
3601 S Broad St Ste 2
Philadelphia, PA 19148-5297

Pryor, Chris (Athlete, Hockey Player)
6877 Macbeth Ct
Saint Paul, MN 55125-2409

Pryor, David H (Politician)
712 S 6 1/2 St
Paragould, AR 72450-5005, USA

Pryor, Greg (Athlete, Baseball Player)
9726 W 115th Ter
Overland Park, KS 66210-2927, USA

Pryor, Kelli (Writer)
c/o Andrea Simon *Andrea Simon Entertainment*
6345 Balboa Blvd Ste 138
Encino, CA 91316-1510, USA

Pryor, Mark (Politician)
5511 Stonewall Rd
Little Rock, AR 72207-4527, USA

Pryor, Nicholas (Actor)
116 Inlet Ct
Hampstead, NC 28443-2558, USA

Pryor, Rain (Actor, Producer)
4509 Weitzel Ave
Baltimore, MD 21214-2856, USA

Przybilla, Joel (Athlete, Basketball Player)
104 Oakview Cir
Monticello, MN 55362-8973, USA

Psaltis, Jim (Athlete, Football Player)
910 Centre Court Dr
Tracy, CA 95376-4909, USA

P. Sarbanes, John (Congressman)
2444 Rayburn Hob
Washington, DC 20515-0903, USA

P-Square (Music Group)
c/o Jude Engees Okoye *Northside Entertainment Ltd*
Prefers to be contacted by email
Nigeria

PSY (Musician)
c/o Scooter Braun *SB Management*
755 N Bonhill Rd
Los Angeles, CA 90049-2303, USA

Psy (Musician)
10490 Wilshire Blvd Apt 403
Los Angeles, CA 90024-4647, USA

Psycho Les (Musician)
c/o Staff Member *UTA/The Agency Group*
888 7th Ave Fl 7
New York, NY 10106-0700, USA

Ptacek, Bob (Athlete, Football Player)
648 Deptford Ave
Dayton, OH 45429-5941, USA

Ptacek, Louis (Misc)
University of Utah
Howard Hughes Institute
Salt Lake City, UT 84112, USA

Ptak, Frank (Business Person)
Illinois Tool Works
3600 W Lake Ave
Glenview, IL 60026-1215, USA

Ptashne, Mark S (Misc)
Harvard University
Biochemistry Dept
Cambridge, MA 02138, USA

Public Enemy (Music Group, Musician)
c/o Walter F. Leaphart Jr *Creamworks*
8391 Beverly Blvd Ste 352
Los Angeles, CA 90048-2633, USA

Pucci, Ben (Athlete, Football Player)
8502 Timber West St
San Antonio, TX 78250-4209, USA

Puck, Wolfgang (Chef)
Spago Restaurant
176 N Canon Dr
Beverly Hills, CA 90210-5304, USA

Puckett, Gary (Musician, Songwriter, Writer)
10710 Seminole Blvd Ste 3
Largo, FL 33778-3316, USA

Pudi, Danny (Actor, Comedian)
2026 Rose Villa St
Pasadena, CA 91107-5043, USA

Puenzo, Luis A (Director)
Cinematografia Nacional Instituto
Lima 319
Buenos Aires 01073, ARGENTINA

Puett, Tommy (Actor)
16621 Cerulean Ct
Chino Hills, CA 91709-4690, USA

Puetz, Garry (Athlete, Football Player)
1779 Robinson Rd
Dahlonega, GA 30533-6119, USA

Puffer, Brandon (Athlete, Baseball Player)
1546 Haynie Bnd
Round Rock, TX 78665-1216, USA

Pugacheva, Alia B (Musician)
State Variety Theater
Bersenevskaya Nab 20/2
Moscow 109072, RUSSIA

Pugh, Daniel Patrick (Dan Patrick) (Sportscaster)
c/o Staff Member *Simon & Schuster*
1230 Avenue of the Americas Fl CONC1
New York, NY 10020-1586, USA

Pugh, Florence (Actor)
c/o Sophie Patterson *Tavistock Wood Management*
45 Conduit St
London W1S 2YN, UNITED KINGDOM

Pugh, Justin (Athlete, Football Player)
c/o Andy Ross *Select Sports Group*
2700 Post Oak Blvd Ste 1450
Houston, TX 77056-5785, USA

Pugh, Larry (Football Player)
RR 4
New Castle, PA 16101, USA

Pugh, Lewis Gordon (Sportscaster)
c/o Staff Member *WME|IMG*
9601 Wilshire Blvd
Beverly Hills, CA 90210-5213, USA

Pugh, Tim (Athlete, Baseball Player)
7906 N 125th East Cir
Owasso, OK 74055-3539, USA

Pugh, Willard E. (Actor)
c/o Shirley Wilson *Shirley Wilson Agency*
5410 Wilshire Blvd Ste 806
Los Angeles
Los Angeles, CA 90036-4267, USA

Pugliese, Charles (Producer)
c/o Staff Member *Killer Films (US)*
526 W 26th St Rm 715
New York, NY 10001-5524, USA

Pugsley, Don (Actor)
c/o Gar Lester *Gar Lester Agency*
11026 Ventura Blvd Ste 10
Studio City, CA 91604-3598, USA

Puhl, Terry (Athlete, Baseball Player)
918 Gondola St
Sugar Land, TX 77478-3414, USA

Puig, Rich (Athlete, Baseball Player)
4216 Mill Valle_yCt
Tampa, FL 33618-7430, USA

Puig, Yasiel (Athlete, Baseball Player)
c/o Dan Horwitz *Beverly Hills Sports Council*
1666 20th St Ste 200A
Santa Monica, CA 90404-3828, USA

Pujats, Janis Cardinal (Religious Leader)
Metropolijas Jurija
Maza Pils Iela 2/A
Riga 01050, LATVIA

Pujol I Soley, Jordi (Politician)
Generalitat Palau
Placa Sant Jaume S/N
Barcelona 00002, SPAIN

Pujols, Albert (Athlete, Baseball Player)
102 Grand Meridien Forest Dr
Wildwood, MO 63005-4980, USA

Pujols, Luis B (Athlete, Baseball Player, Coach)
2 Townsend St Apt 2-613
San Francisco, CA 94107-2061, USA

Pulcini, Robert (Director)
c/o Staff Member *Creative Artists Agency (CAA)*
2000 Avenue of the Stars Ste 100
Los Angeles, CA 90067-4705, USA

Puleo, Charlie (Athlete, Baseball Player)
3202 Miser Station Rd
Louisville, TN 37777-3604, USA

Pulford, Robert J (Bob) (Athlete, Hockey Player)
78 Coventry Rd
Northfield, IL 60093-3117

Pulido, Carlos (Athlete, Baseball Player)
55 SE 6th St Apt 2001
Miami, FL 33131-2564, USA

Puljic, Vinko Cardinal (Religious Leader)
Nadbiskupski Ordinarijat
Kaptol 7
Sarajevo 71000, BOSNIA HERZEGOVINA

Pulkkinen, David (Athlete, Hockey Player)
5095 Croatia Rd
Sudbury, ON P3G 1L5, Canada

Pullard, Anthony (Athlete, Basketball Player)
3518 Monroe St
Lake Charles, LA 70607-3204, USA

Pullen, Melanie Clark (Actor)
c/o Staff Member *Actors and Movers*
71 Strand Rd.
Auburn House
Bray, County Wicklow NA, IRELAND

Pulliam, Harvey (Athlete, Baseball Player)
1111 James Donlon Blvd Apt 2064
Antioch, CA 94509-7034, USA

Pulliam, Keshia Knight (Actor)
PO Box 866
Teaneck, NJ 07666-0866, USA

Pullman, Bill (Actor, Director)
c/o Tony Lipp *Anonymous Content*
3532 Hayden Ave
Culver City, CA 90232-2413, USA

Pullman, Philip (Writer)
24 Templar Road
Oxford OX2 8LT, UNITED KINGDOM (UK)

Pullos, Haley (Actor)
c/o Sean Reilly *The Brand Partners*
6404 Wilshire Blvd Ste 500
Los Angeles, CA 90048-5507, USA

Pulman, Bill (Actor, Director, Producer)
c/o Doreen Wilcox Little *Anonymous Content*
3532 Hayden Ave
Culver City, CA 90232-2413, USA

Pulos, Jenni (Reality Star)
c/o Alex Spieller *Baker Winokur Ryder Public Relations*
200 5th Ave Fl 5
New York, NY 10010-3307, USA

Pulp (Music Group)
c/o Staff Member *Paradigm (Monterey)*
404 W Franklin St
Monterey, CA 93940-2303, USA

Pulsford, Nigel (Musician)
c/o Michael Moses *Baker Winokur Ryder Public Relations*
9100 Wilshire Blvd
W Tower #500
Beverly Hills, CA 90212-3415, USA

Pulsipher, Bill (Athlete, Baseball Player)
10 Woodbine Ln
East Moriches, NY 11940-1413, USA

Pulsipher, Lindsay (Actor)
c/o Laura Myones *McKeon-Myones Management*
3500 W Olive Ave Ste 770
Burbank, CA 91505-5527, USA

Pulver, Liselotte (Actor)
Villa Bip
Kanton Vaudois
Perroy 01166, SWITZERLAND

Pump, Lil (Musician)
c/o Staff Member *Warner Bros Records (LA)*
PO Box 6868
Burbank, CA 91510-6868, USA

Pumpkins, Penelope (Adult Film Star)
1247 14th St #104
Santa Monica, CA 90404, USA

Pumple, Rich (Athlete, Hockey Player)
51 Monmouth Dr
Riverside, RI 02915-1467, USA

Punch, Lucy (Actor)
c/o Christian Donatelli *MGMT Entertainment (The Schiff Company)*
9220 W Sunset Blvd Ste 106
W Hollywood, CA 90069-3500, USA

Punsley, Bernard (Actor)
1415 Granvia Altemeia
Palos Verdes Estates, CA 90274, USA

Punto, Nick (Athlete, Baseball Player)
25 Friar Ln
Ladera Ranch, CA 92694-1431, USA

Puppa, Daren (Athlete, Hockey Player)
4526 Cheval Blvd
Lutz, FL 33558-5331

Pupunu, Alfred (Athlete, Football Player)
13343 S Akagi Ln
Draper, UT 84020-8216, USA

Purcell, Dominic (Actor)
c/o Beth Holden-Garland *Untitled Entertainment*
350 S Beverly Dr Ste 200
Beverly Hills, CA 90212-4819, USA

Purcell, Herman (Athlete, Baseball Player)
Cleveland Buckeyes
1031 Cass Ave SE
Grand Rapids, MI 49507-1119, USA

Purcell, Lee (Actor)
11101 Provence Ln
Tujunga, CA 91042-1263, USA

Purcell, Sarah (Actor)
6525 Esplanade
Playa Del Rey, CA 90293-7521, USA

Purcey, David (Athlete, Baseball Player)
4339 Highlander Dr
Dallas, TX 75287-6842, USA

Purdee, Nathan (Actor)
56 W 66th St
New York, NY 10023-6225, USA

Purdin, John (Athlete, Baseball Player)
4942 Southgate Pkwy
Myrtle Beach, SC 29579-4147, USA

Purdom, Edmund (Actor)
Via Isonzo 42/C
Rome 00198, ITALY

Purdy, Alfred (Writer)
Harbour Publishing
PO Box 219
Madeira Park, BC V0N 2H0, CANADA

Purdy, Amy (Athlete, Snowboarder)
Challenged Athletes Foundation
9591 Waples St
San Diego, CA 92121-2953, USA

Purdy, Jolene (Actor)
c/o Siri Garber *Platform PR*
2666 N Beachwood Dr
Los Angeles, CA 90068-2308, USA

Purdy, Roy (Musician)
c/o Avi Wasserman *Creative Artists Agency (CAA)*
2000 Avenue of the Stars Ste 100
Los Angeles, CA 90067-4705, USA

Purdy, Ted (Athlete, Golfer)
6040 N 22nd Pl
Phoenix, AZ 85016-2005, USA

Purefoy, James (Actor)
c/o JoAnne Colonna *Brillstein Entertainment Partners*
9150 Wilshire Blvd Ste 350
Beverly Hills, CA 90212-3453, USA

Pure Reason Revolution (Music Group)
c/o Staff Member *Paradigm (Monterey)*
404 W Franklin St
Monterey, CA 93940-2303, USA

Purim, Flora (Musician)
A Train Mgmt
PO Box 29242
Oakland, CA 94604-9242, USA

Purinton, Dale (Athlete, Hockey Player)
Cowichan Valley Capitals
2687 James St
Duncan, BC V9L 2X5, Canada

Purinton, Dale (Athlete, Hockey Player)
2045 Cowichan Bay Rd
Cowichan Bay, BC V0R 1N1, Canada

Purkey, Bob (Athlete, Baseball Player)
5559 Steeplechase Ct
Bethel Park, PA 15102-4501, USA

Purl, Linda (Actor)
c/o Peter Young *Sovereign Talent Group*
1642 Westwood Blvd Ste 202
Los Angeles, CA 90024-5609, USA

Purnell, Ella (Actor)
c/o Oriana Elia *Curtis Brown Ltd*
28-29 Hay Market
Hay Market House
London SW1Y 4SP, UNITED KINGDOM

Purpura, Tim (Baseball Player)
7033 Benjamin Way
Colleyville, TX 76034-1115, USA

Purser, Shannon (Actor)
c/o Mia Hansen *Portrait PR*
5320 Sylmar Ave
Sherman Oaks, CA 91401-5612, USA

Purtzer, Tom (Golfer)
9828 E Desert Cove Ave
Scottsdale, AZ 85260-6220, USA

Purvis, Jeff (Race Car Driver)
1157 Dunbar Cave Rd
Clarksville, TN 37043-2045, USA

Puryear, Martin (Artist)
Nancy Drysdale Gallery
700 New Hampshire Ave NW # 917
Washington, DC 20037-2407, USA

Pusha T (Musician)
c/o Tammy Brook *FYI Public Relations*
174 5th Ave Ste 404
New York, NY 10010-5964, USA

Pushelberg, Glenn (Designer)
Yabu Pushelberg
55 Booth Ave
Toronto, ON M4M 2M3, CANADA

Pushor, Jamie (Athlete, Hockey Player)
29 Jay Rd W
Lake George, NY 12845-4426

Puskaric, Joseph (Athlete, Baseball Player)
200 Westbrook Ct APT 155
Marshall, MI 49068-3126, USA

Puskarioc, Joseph (Baseball Player)
429 35th St
McKeesport, PA 15132-7226, USA

Pussycat Dolls (Music Group)
c/o Jack Ketsoyan *EMC / Bowery*
8356 Fountain Ave Apt E1
W Hollywood, CA 90069-2968, USA

Pustari, Rit (Race Car Driver)
Pustari-Goodrich Racing
4 Taft St # 82
Norwalk, CT 06854-4279, USA

Pustovyi, Yarolslav Dr (Astronaut)
2101 Nasa Pkwy Spc Centerbldg
Houston, TX 77058-3607, USA

Putch, John (Actor)
3972 Sunswept Dr
Studio City, CA 91604-2330, USA

Puth, Charlie (Musician)
c/o Troy Carter *Atom Factory/Coalition Media Group*
PO Box 927
Culver City, CA 90232-0927, USA

Putin, Vladimir (Politician)
The State
Office of the Prime Minister
Krelim
Moscow 103073, Russia

Putin, Vladimir V (President)
President's Office
Kremlin
Staraya Pl 4
Moscow 103132, RUSSIA

Putman, Earl (Athlete, Football Player)
9203 W Behrend Dr
Peoria, AZ 85382-0966, USA

Putman, Ed (Athlete, Baseball Player)
PO Box 3366
Mesquite, NV 89024-3366, USA

Putman, Pat (Baseball Player)
Texas Rangers
2311 Carrell Rd
Fort Myers, FL 33901-8012, USA

Putnam, David (Actor, Producer)
c/o Staff Member *Enigma Productions*
429 Santa Monica Blvd Ste 700
Santa Monica, CA 90401-3435, USA

Putnam, Duane (Athlete, Football Player)
1545 S Magnolia Ave
Ontario, CA 91762-5335, USA

Putnam, Pat (Athlete, Baseball Player)
4040 Staley Rd
Fort Myers, FL 33905-6410, USA

Putti, Frank (Athlete, Baseball Player)
1981 Downing Pl
Palm Harbor, FL 34683-5727, USA

Puttnam, David T (Producer)
Engima Productions
29A Tufton St
London SW1P 3QL, UNITED KINGDOM (UK)

Putz, JJ (Athlete, Baseball Player)
7818 N Sherri Ln
Paradise Valley, AZ 85253-2922, USA

Putzier, Jeb (Athlete, Football Player)
5305 Pocahontas St
Bellaire, TX 77401-4822, USA

Puz, Craig A (Astronaut)
S313 Devils Head Cir
Golden, CO 80403-2066, USA

Pyatt, Nelaon (Athlete, Hockey Player)
1680 Arthur St W
Thunder Bay, ON P7K 1A8, Canada

Pyburn, Jack (Athlete, Football Player)
1197 Peachtree St NE Ste 533A
Atlanta, GA 30361-3508, USA

Pye, Eddie (Athlete, Baseball Player)
307 Polk St
Columbia, TN 38401-4453, USA

Pye, William B (Artist)
43 Hambalt Road
Clapham
London SW4 9EQ, UNITED KINGDOM (UK)

Pyeatt, John (Johnny) (Athlete, Football Player)
18374 E Via De Palmas
Queen Creek, AZ 85242, USA

Pyecha, John (Athlete, Baseball Player)
107 Nottingham Dr
Chapel Hill, NC 27517-6569, USA

Pyfrom, Shawn (Actor)
c/o Eric Podwall *Podwall Entertainment*
710 N Orlando Ave Apt 203
Loft 203
Los Angeles, CA 90069-5549, USA

Pygram, Wayne (Actor)
c/o Bob Knotek *McCann - Knotek Associates*
8539 W Sunset Blvd Ste 4
Los Angeles, CA 90069-2350, USA

Pyle, Andy (Musician)
Larry Page
29 Ruston Mews
London W11 1RB, UNITED KINGDOM (UK)

Pyle, Missi (Actor)
c/o Staff Member *McKeon-Myones Management*
3500 W Olive Ave Ste 770
Burbank, CA 91505-5527, USA

Pyle, Missy (Actor)
Paradigm Agency
10100 Santa Monica Blvd Ste 2500
Los Angeles, CA 90067-4116, USA

Pyle, Palmer (Athlete, Football Player)
6337 W Beverly Ln
Glendale, AZ 85306-1631, USA

Pyne, George F (Athlete, Football Player)
123 Congress St
Milford, MA 01757-2006, USA

Pyne, Natasha (Actor)
Kate Feast
Primrose Hill Studios
Fitzroy Road
London NW1 8TR, UNITED KINGDOM (UK)

Pyott, David E I (Business Person)
Allergan Inc
2525 Dupont Dr
Irvine, CA 92612-1599, USA

Pyper-Ferguson, John (Actor)
c/o Tom Spriggs *Coronel Group*
1100 Glendon Ave Fl 17
Los Angeles, CA 90024-3588, USA

Pyznarski, Tim (Athlete, Baseball Player)
10716 Austin Ave
Chicago Ridge, IL 60415-2224, USA

Q, Maggie (Actor, Model)
c/o Evan Hainey *Untitled Entertainment*
350 S Beverly Dr Ste 200
Beverly Hills, CA 90212-4819, USA

Q, ScHoolboy (Musician)
c/o Caroline Yim *Creative Artists Agency (CAA)*
2000 Avenue of the Stars Ste 100
Los Angeles, CA 90067-4705, USA

Qaiyum, Gregory (GQ) (Actor)
c/o Sandra Joseph *SLJ Management*
833 N Edinburgh Ave PH 11
Los Angeles, CA 90046-6999, USA

Qarase, Laisenia (Prime Minister)
Prime Minister's Office
6 Berkeley Crescent
Suva
VITI LEVU, FIJI

Qasimi, Sheikh Saqr bin Muhammad al (President)
Ruler's Palace
Ras Al Khaimah
UNITED ARAB EMIRATES

Qasimi, Sheikh Sultan bin Muhammad al (President)
Ruler's Palace
Sharjah, UNITED ARAB EMIRATES

Qi, Shu (Actor)
c/o Herve Bougon *IMG Models (Paris)*
20 rue de la Baume
Fl 7
Paris 75008, FRANCE

Qin, Shaobo (Actor)
c/o Don Hughes *IAI Presentations*
PO Box 4
Pismo Beach, CA 93448-0004, USA

Q-Tip (Musician)
251 Marietta St
Englewood Cliffs, NJ 07632-1644, USA

Quackenbush, Max (Athlete, Hockey Player)
476 Lockview Rd
Fall River, NS B2T 1J1, Canada

Quade, John (Actor)
Alex Brewis
12429 Laurel Terrace Dr
Studio City, CA 91604-2402, USA

Quade, Mike (Athlete, Baseball Player)
7105 Fairway Bend Cir
Sarasota, FL 34243-3604, USA

Quaerna, Jerry (Athlete, Football Player)
1211 Pheasant Ct
Lake Geneva, WI 53147-1077, USA

Quaid, Dennis (Actor)
c/o Lisa Kasteler *Wolf-Kasteler Public Relations*
6255 W Sunset Blvd Ste 1111
Los Angeles, CA 90028-7426, USA

Quaid, Jack (Actor)
c/o Tony Lipp *Anonymous Content*
3532 Hayden Ave
Culver City, CA 90232-2413, USA

Quaid, Randy (Actor)
PO Box 12
Middlebury, VT 05753-0012, USA

Quaintance, Rachel (Comedian)
c/o Bruce Smith *OmniPop Talent Group*
4605 Lankershim Blvd Ste 201
Toluca Lake, CA 91602-1874, USA

Qualife, Pete (Musician)
Larry Page
29 Ruston Mews
London W11 1RB, UNITED KINGDOM (UK)

Qualley, Margaret (Actor)
c/o Evelyn Karamanos *Relevant*
400 S Beverly Dr Ste 220
Beverly Hills, CA 90212-4404, USA

Qualley, Rainey (Actor)
c/o Bianca Bianconi *42West*
600 3rd Ave Fl 23
New York, NY 10016-1914, USA

Qualls, Chad (Athlete, Baseball Player)
8416 Big View Dr
Austin, TX 78730-1534, USA

Qualls, DJ (Actor)
c/o Staff Member *Artists First*
9465 Wilshire Blvd Ste 900
Beverly Hills, CA 90212-2608, USA

Qualls, Jim (Athlete, Baseball Player)
410 N County Road 950
Sutter, IL 62373-5021, USA

Qualters, Tom (Athlete, Baseball Player)
235 Mallard Rd
Somerset, PA 15501-7023, USA

Quan, Samantha (Actor)

Quance, Kristine (Athlete, Olympic Athlete, Swimmer)
1320 Moncado Dr
Glendale, CA 91207-1832, USA

Quann, Megan (Athlete, Olympic Athlete, Swimmer)
3516 109th Street Ct NW
Gig Harbor, WA 98332-8991, USA

Quant, Mary (Designer, Fashion Designer)
Mary Quant Ltd
3 Ives St
London SW3 2NE, UNITED KINGDOM (UK)

Quantrill, Paul (Athlete, Baseball Player)
Inside Edge Baseball Academy
31619 N 20th Ave
Phoenix, AZ 85085-7068, USA

Quarashi (Musician)
c/o Staff Member *Creative Artists Agency (CAA)*
2000 Avenue of the Stars Ste 100
Los Angeles, CA 90067-4705, USA

Quaresma, Rhonda Lee (Misc)
PO Box 22033 RPO Cataraqui
Kingston, ON K7M 8S5, CANADA

Quarles, Kelcy (Athlete, Football Player)
c/o Eugene Parker *Independent Sports & Entertainment (ISE-IN)*
6435 W Jefferson Blvd # 197
Fort Wayne, IN 46804-6203, USA

Quarles, Shelton (Athlete, Football Player)
17019 Candeleda De Avila
Tampa, FL 33613-5213, USA

Quarless, Andrew (Athlete, Football Player)
c/o Peter Schaffer *Authentic Athletix*
400 S Steele St Unit 47
Denver, CO 80209-3535, USA

Quarrie, Donald (Don) (Athlete, Track Athlete)
Jamaican Amateur Athletic Assn
PO Box 272
Kingston 00005, JAMAICA

Quarshie, Hugh (Actor)
PO Box 20092
London NW2 6FJ, UNITED KINGDOM (UK)

Quarterman, Simon (Actor)
c/o Leanne Coronel *Coronel Group*
1100 Glendon Ave Fl 17
Los Angeles, CA 90024-3588, USA

Quasthoff, Thomas (Musician)
Cramer/Marser Artists
3436 Springhill Rd
Lafayette, CA 94549-2535, USA

Quatro, Suzi (Musician, Songwriter, Writer)
Jive
4 Pasteur Courtyard Whittle Road
Corby
Norths, FL NN17 5DX, UNITED KINGDOM (UK)

Quayle, Anna (Actor)
CDA
47 Courtfield Road
London, ENGLAND SW7 4DB, UNITED KINGDOM (UK)

Quayle, Dan (Politician)
c/o Laura Minter
6224 N 61st Pl # Pi
Paradise Valley, AZ 85253-4212, USA

Quayle, Jenny (Actor)
c/o Staff Member *Michelle Braidman Assoc*
Lower John St Fl 3 #10/11
London W1F 9EB, UNITED KINGDOM (UK)

Qubein, Nido (Business Person)
Creative Services Inc
PO Box 6008
806 Westchester Dr
High Point, NC 27262-6008, USA

Quddus (Television Host)
c/o Mike Esterman *Esterman.Com, LLC*
Prefers to be contacted via email
Baltimore, MD XXXXX, USA

Queen (Music Group, Musician)
16-A High Street Barnes
London SW13 9LW, UK

Queen, Ida (Musician)
Traditional Arts Services
16045 36th Ave NE
Lake Forest Park, WA 98155-6623, USA

Queen, Jeff (Athlete, Football Player)
1367 Temple Heights Dr
Oceanside, CA 92056-2210, USA

Queen, Konga (Actor, Wrestler)
PO Box 5050
Carson, CA 90749-5050, USA

Queen Elizabeth II (Royalty)
Buckingham Palace
London SW1A 1AA, UNITED KINGDOM (UK)

Queen Rania (Royalty)
Royal Palace
Amman, JORDAN

Queens of the Stone Age (Music Group)
c/o Michele Hug *Nasty Little Man*
285 W Broadway Rm 310
New York, NY 10013-2257, USA

Queensryche (Music Group)
c/o Staff Member *Monterey International (Chicago)*
72 W Adams St # 1000
Chicago, IL 60603-5107, USA

Queffelec, Anne (Musician)
15 Ave Corneille
Maisons-Laffittle 78600, FRANCE

Quellmatz, Udo (Athlete)
Friedhofstr 10
Omgolstandt 85049, GERMANY

Quenneville, Joel (Athlete, Hockey Player)
Chicago Blackhawks
1901 W Madison St
Chicago, IL 60612-2459

Quenneville, Joel (Athlete, Coach, Hockey Player)
650 S Oak St
Hinsdale, IL 60521-4634

Quentin, Carlos (Athlete, Baseball Player)
1223 Crestview Dr
Cardiff, CA 92007-1400, USA

Quenzrd, Nathalie (Actor)
Cineart
36 Rue de Ponthieu
Paris 75008, FRANCE

Querrey, Sam (Athlete, Tennis Player)
12607 Stanwood Pl
Los Angeles, CA 90066-1525, USA

Query, Jeff (Athlete, Football Player)
75 Anise Tree Pl
Spring, TX 77382-1700, USA

Quester, Hugues (Actor)
Cineart
36 Rue de Ponthieu
Paris 75008, FRANCE

Questlove (Musician)
c/o Carleen Donovan *Donovan Public Relations*
30 E 20th St Ste 2FE
New York, NY 10003-1310, USA

Questrom, Allen I (Business Person)
J C Penney Co
6501 Legacy Dr
Plano, TX 75024-3698, USA

Quezada, Steven Michael (Actor)
c/o Gloria Hinojosa *Amsel, Eisenstadt & Frazier Talent Agency (AEF)*
5055 Wilshire Blvd Ste 860
Los Angeles, CA 90036-6108, USA

Quick, Clarence E (Musician, Songwriter, Writer)
376 Quincy St
Brooklyn, NY 11216-1502, USA

Quick, Diana (Actor)
39 Seymour Walk
London SW10, UNITED KINGDOM (UK)

Quick, James E (Jim) (Actor)
PO Box 12760
Scottsdale, AZ 85267-2760, USA

Quick, Jim (Athlete, Baseball Player)
6061 Keeble Ln
Camino, CA 95709-9100, USA

Quick, Jonathan (Athlete, Hockey Player)
c/o Staff Member *Los Angeles Kings*
1111 S Figueroa St Ste 3100
Los Angeles, CA 90015-1333, USA

Quick, Matthew (Writer)
PO Box 808
Kill Devil Hills, NC 27948-0808, USA

Quick, Michael A (Mike) (Athlete, Football Player)
13 Slab Branch Ct
Marlton, NJ 08053-5407, USA

Quick, Rebecca (Talk Show Host)
900 Sylvan Ave
Squawk Box
Englewood Cliffs, NJ 07632-3312, USA

Quick, Richard (Coach, Swimmer)
Stanford University
Athletic Dept
Stanford, CA 94305, USA

Quicksilver (Music Group)
c/o Staff Member *Paradigm (Monterey)*
404 W Franklin St
Monterey, CA 93940-2303, USA

Quie, Al (Politician)
4209 Christy Ln
Minnetonka, MN 55345-3001, USA

Quigley, Dana (Athlete, Golfer)
900 Ocean Dr Apt 201
Juno Beach, FL 33408-1716, USA

Quigley, Linnea (Actor)
2608 N Ocean Blvd Ste 1 # 126
Pompano Beach, FL 33062-2955, USA

Quigley, Mary T (Actor)
Velvet Ears, Inc
11845 Kling St
Valley Village, CA 91607-4009, USA

Quigley, Mike (Congressman, Politician)
4345 N Milwaukee Ave
Chicago, IL 60641-1522, USA

Quigley, Philip J (Phil) (Business Person)
Pacific Telesis Group
130 Keamy St
San Francisco, CA 94108, USA

Quik, D J (Musician)
International Creative Mgmt
8942 Wilshire Blvd # 219
Beverly Hills, CA 90211-1908, USA

Quilici, Frank (Athlete, Baseball Player, Coach)
19475 N Grayhawk Dr Unit 1088
Scottsdale, AZ 85255-7420, USA

Quillan, Frederick (Fred) (Athlete, Football Player)
2924 Bailey Ln
Eugene, OR 97401-6926, USA

Quin, Glover (Athlete, Football Player)

Quinaz, Victor (Director)
c/o Chad Hamilton *Anonymous Content*
3532 Hayden Ave
Culver City, CA 90232-2413, USA

Quincey, Kyle (Athlete, Hockey Player)
c/o Pat Morris *Newport Sports Management*
201 City Centre Dr
Suite 400
Mississauga, ON L58 2T4, CANADA

Quindlen, Anna (Writer)
c/o Staff Member *Random House Publicity*
1745 Broadway Frnt 3
New York, NY 10019-4343, USA

Quinlan, Kathleen (Actor)
141 S Clark Dr Apt 214
West Hollywood, CA 90048-3242, USA

Quinlan, Maeve (Actor)
c/o Staff Member *Main Title Entertainment*
8383 Wilshire Blvd Ste 408
Beverly Hills, CA 90211-2435, USA

Quinlan, Robb (Athlete, Baseball Player)
5875 Upland Ln N
Minneapolis, MN 55446-4535, USA

Quinlan, Sally (Athlete, Golfer)
2621 Colina Vista Loop #A
Austin, TX 78750-8533, USA

Quinlan, Tom (Athlete, Baseball Player)
1061 Sterling St S
Saint Paul, MN 55119-5972, USA

Quinlan, William D (Bill) (Athlete, Football Player)
393 Mount Vernon St
Lawrence, MA 01843-3103, USA

Quinn, Abby (Actor)
c/o Erin Culley *Creative Artists Agency (CAA)*
2000 Avenue of the Stars Ste 100
Los Angeles, CA 90067-4705, USA

Quinn, Aidan (Actor)
c/o Nancy Gates *United Talent Agency (UTA)*
888 7th Ave Fl 7
New York, NY 10106-0700, USA

Quinn, Aileen (Actor)
c/o David Moss *David Moss Company*
6063 Vineland Ave Apt B
N Hollywood, CA 91606-4986, USA

Quinn, Brady (Athlete, Football Player)
c/o Team Member *Cleveland Browns*
76 Lou Groza Blvd
Berea, OH 44017-1269, USA

Quinn, Brandon (Actor)
c/o Ben Feigin *Anonymous Content*
3532 Hayden Ave
Culver City, CA 90232-2413, USA

Quinn, Brian (Actor, Producer)
c/o Dexter Scott *Vector Management*
276 5th Ave Rm 604
New York, NY 10001-4527, USA

Quinn, Brian (Coach, Soccer Player)
San Jose Earthquakes
3550 Stevens Creek Blvd Ste 200
San Jose, CA 95117-1031, USA

Quinn, Colin (Actor, Comedian)
c/o Staff Member *Agency for the Performing Arts (APA)*
405 S Beverly Dr Ste 500
Beverly Hills, CA 90212-4425, USA

Quinn, Colleen (Actor)
Bauman Assoc
5750 Wilshire Blvd # 473
Los Angeles, CA 90036-3697, USA

Quinn, Dan (Athlete, Hockey Player)
1816 Flower Dr
Palm Bch Gdns, FL 33410-1700

Quinn, Danny (Actor)
c/o Michael Greenwald *Endorse Management Group*
9854 National Blvd # 454
Los Angeles, CA 90034-2713, USA

Quinn, David W (Business Person)
Centex Corp
2728 N Harwood St Ste 200
Dallas, TX 75201-1579, USA

Quinn, Ed (Actor)
c/o Staff Member *Burstein Company*
15304 W Sunset Blvd Ste 208
Pacific Palisades, CA 90272-3656, USA

Quinn, Glenn (Actor)
Sanders Armstrong Management
4111 W Alameda Ave Ste 505
Burbank, CA 91505-4163, USA

Quinn, Jane Bryant (Journalist)
Newsweek Magazine
251 W 57th St
Editorial Dept
New York, NY 10019-1802, USA

Quinn, Jim (Misc)
675 S Sierra Ave Unit 32
Solana Beach, CA 92075-3232, USA

Quinn, Mark (Athlete, Baseball Player)
1013 S Dancove Dr
West Covina, CA 91791-3720, USA

Quinn, Martha (Actor, Model)
28890 Hampton Pl
Malibu, CA 90265-4235, USA

Quinn, Mike (Athlete, Football Player)
10703 Del Monte Dr
Houston, TX 77042-2326, USA

Quinn, Molly (Actor)
c/o John Carrabino *John Carrabino Management*
5900 Wilshire Blvd Ste 740
Los Angeles, CA 90036-5032, USA

Quinn, Patricia (Actor)
Jonathan Altaras Associates
11 Garrick Street
London WC2E 9AR, United Kingdom

Quinn, Robert (Athlete, Football Player)
c/o Carl Carey *Champion Pro Consulting Group*
3547 Ruth St
Houston, TX 77004-5515, USA

Quinn, Sally (Journalist)
3014 N St NW
Washington, DC 20007-3404, USA

Quinn, Stephen (Athlete, Football Player)
783 1375N Ave
Mount Sterling, IL 62353-1069, USA

Quinnett, Brian (Athlete, Basketball Player)
862 Indian Hills Dr
Moscow, ID 83843-9373, USA

Quinney, Ken (Athlete, Hockey Player)
3638 Starbright Ln
Las Vegas, NV 89147-6524

Quinones, John (Correspondent)
c/o Staff Member *ABC News*
77 W 66th St Fl 3
New York, NY 10023-6201, USA

Quinones, John (Television Host)
c/o Staff Member *ABC TV (NY)*
44th St & Broadway
New York, NY 10112, USA

Quinones, Luis (Athlete, Baseball Player)
5821 Calle San Bruno
Urb Santa Teresita
Ponce, PR 00730-4443, USA

Quinones, Rey (Athlete, Baseball Player)
216 Calle Ronda
San Juan, PR 00926-2351, USA

Quint, Deron (Athlete, Hockey Player)
23610 N 24th Ter
Phoenix, AZ 85024-5218

Quintal, Stephane (Athlete, Hockey Player)
1356A Rue la Fontaine
Montreal, QC H2L 1T5, Canada

Quintana, Chela (Golfer)
Ladies Pro Golf Assn
100 International Golf Dr
Daytona Beach, FL 32124-1082, USA

Quintanilla, Omar (Athlete, Baseball Player)
12457 Paseo De Arco Ct
El Paso, TX 79928-5669, USA

Quintin, J F (Athlete, Hockey Player)
6821 Oak St
Kansas City, MO 64113-2476

Quinto, Zachary (Actor)
c/o Alexandra Kahn *Relevant (NY)*
333 Hudson St Rm 502
New York, NY 10013-1033, USA

Quirico, Rafael (Athlete, Baseball Player)
2901 N Dale Mabry Hwy Apt 2103
Tampa, FL 33607-2483, USA

Quiring, Frederic (Actor)
Cineart
36 Rue de Ponthieu
Paris 75008, FRANCE

Quirk, Art (Athlete, Baseball Player)
2 Ensign Ln
Stonington, CT 06378-2944, USA

Quirk, Jamie (Athlete, Baseball Player)
310 W 123rd Ter
Kansas City, MO 64145-1186, USA

Quiroga, Elena (Writer)
Agencia Balcells
Diagonal 580
Barcelona 08021, SPAIN

Quiroga, Jorge (Tuto) (President)
President's Office
Palacio de Gobierno
Plaza Murllia
La Paz, BOLIVIA

Quist, Janet (Model)
13446 Poway Rd # 239
Poway, CA 92064-4714, USA

Quitones, John (Correspondent)
ABC-TV
77 W 66th St
News Dept
New York, NY 10023-6201, USA

Quivers, Robin (Radio Personality, Talk Show Host)
c/o Staff Member *Howard Stern Show*
1221 Avenue of the Americas
Sirius Satellite Radio
New York, NY 10020-1001, USA

Qulgley, Brett (Golfer)
127 Sandpiper Cir
Jupiter, FL 33477-8434, USA

Qulgley, Dana (Golfer)
2670 Tecumseh Dr
West Palm Beach, FL 33409-7421, USA

Quon, Di (Actor)
c/o Steve Maihack *44 West Entertainment*
151 Petaluma Blvd S Apt 311
Petaluma, CA 94952-5185, USA

Qureia, Ahmed (Prime Minister)
Prime Minister's Office
Gara City
Gaza Strip
Palestine, ISRAEL

R

R5 (Music Group, Musician)
c/o Stella Alex *Savage Agency*
1041 N Formosa Ave
West Hollywood, CA 90046-6703, USA

Raab, Chris (Actor)
c/o Staff Member *Haber Entertainment*
434 S Canon Dr Apt 204
Beverly Hills, CA 90212-4501, USA

Raab, Marc (Athlete, Football Player)
1211 Cuyamaca Ave
Spring Valley, CA 91977-4610, USA

Raab, Stefan (Musician)
c/o Staff Member *Allendorf Riehl GmbH*
Kaesenstrasse 17
Koeln D-50677, Germany

Raabe, Brian (Athlete, Baseball Player)
38760 Kost Trl
North Branch, MN 55056-6722, USA

Raaurn, Gustav (Skier)
PO Box 700
Mercer Island, WA 98040-0700, USA

Raba, Robert (Athlete, Football Player)
16066 Acre St
North Hills, CA 91343-4822, USA

Rabara, Shelby (Actor)
c/o Lucas Kosoglad *Innovative Artists*
1505 10th St
Santa Monica, CA 90401-2805, USA

Rabb, John (Athlete, Baseball Player)
8614 Hooper Ave
Los Angeles, CA 90002-1143, USA

Rabe, Charlie (Athlete, Baseball Player)
6059 E Sierra Blanca St
Mesa, AZ 85215-7753, USA

Rabe, Josh (Athlete, Baseball Player)
1800 College Ave
Attn: Mens Baseball Head Coa
Quincy, IL 62301-2670, USA

Rabe, Lily (Actor)
c/o Peg Donegan *Framework Entertainment*
9057 Nemo St # C
W Hollywood, CA 90069-5511, USA

Rabe, Pamela (Actor)
Shanahan Mgmt
PO Box 1509
Darlinghurst, NSW 01300, AUSTRALIA

Rabelo, Mike (Athlete, Baseball Player)
5813 N 17th St
Tampa, FL 33610-4308, USA

Rabin, Trevor (Composer)
Kraft-Benjamin-Engel
15233 Ventura Blvd Ste 200
Sherman Oaks, CA 91403-2244, USA

Rabinovitch, Benton S (Misc)
12530 42nd Ave NE
Seattle, WA 98125-4621, USA

Rabinowitz, Dorothy (Journalist)
Wall Street Journal
200 Liberty St
Editorial Dept
New York, NY 10281-1003, USA

Rabinowitz, Jesse C (Misc)
University of California
Molecular & Cell Biology Dept
Berkeley, CA 94720-0001, USA

Raburn, Ryan (Athlete, Baseball Player)
PO Box 304
Balm, FL 33503-0304, USA

Racan, Ivica (Prime Minister)
Prime Minister's Office
Jordanovac 71
Zagreb 41000, CROATIA

Rachal, Latorio (Athlete, Football Player)
3266 Golden Ave
Long Beach, CA 90806-1208, USA

Rachin, Julian (Musician)
Columbia Artists Mgmt Inc
165 W 57th St
New York, NY 10019-2201, USA

Rachins, Alan (Actor)
c/o Mark Teitelbaum *Teitelbaum Artists Group*
8840 Wilshire Blvd Fl 3
Beverly Hills, CA 90211-2606, USA

Racicot, Jody (Actor)
c/o Jamie Levitt *Lauren Levitt & Associates Inc*
1525 W 8th Ave Fl 3
Vancouver BC V6J 1T5, CANADA

Racicot, Marc F (Politician)
28013 Swan Cove Dr
Bigfork, MT 59911-7846, USA

Racicot, Pierre (Athlete, Hockey Player)
828 Hampton Ct
Weston, FL 33326-2917

Racine, Bruce (Athlete, Hockey Player)
35 S Ridge Meadows Ln
Troy, MO 63379-6306

Racine, Yves (Athlete, Hockey Player)
Arizona Capital Inc
1515 Av StJean Baptiste
Quebec, QC G2E 5E2, Canada

Rackers, Neil (Athlete, Football Player)
945 Shady Path Ct
Saint Peters, MO 63376-3898, USA

Rackley, David (Athlete, Baseball Player)
621 Circle Trace Rd
Monroe, NC 28110-7675, USA

Rackley, Derek (Athlete, Football Player)
5659 Legends Club Cir
Braselton, GA 30517-6029, USA

Rackley, Luther (Athlete, Basketball Player)
36 W 128th St Apt 2
New York, NY 10027-3100, USA

Rackley, Marv (Athlete, Baseball Player)
522 S Bibb St
Westminster, SC 29693-2134, USA

Raczka, Mike (Athlete, Baseball Player)
72 Foley Dr
Southington, CT 06489-4400, USA

Radachowsky, George (Athlete, Football Player)
87 Merrimac St
Danbury, CT 06810-6463, USA

Radcliff, Paula (Athlete, Track Athlete)
c/o Peter Carlisle *Octagon Olympics & Action Sports*
7 Ocean St Ste 2
South Portland, ME 04106-2800, USA

Radcliffe, Daniel (Actor)
c/o Scott Boute *Serge PR*
339 W 12th St
New York, NY 10014-1721, USA

Raddatz, Martha (Commentator, Journalist, Television Host)
c/o Staff Member *ABC News*
77 W 66th St Fl 3
New York, NY 10023-6201, USA

Rade, John (Athlete, Football Player)
1448 N Waterbrook Way
Star, ID 83669-5327, USA

Rademacher, Bill (Athlete, Football Player)
5409 Maple Rdg
Haslett, MI 48840-8651, USA

Rademacher, Ingo (Actor)
667 Santa Clara Ave
Venice, CA 90291-3445, USA

Rademacher, Pete (Athlete, Boxer, Olympic Athlete)
5585 River Styx Rd
Medina, OH 44256-8786, USA

Rademacher, T Peter (Pete) (Boxer)
5585 River Styx Rd
Medina, OH 44256-8786, USA

Rader, Dave (Athlete, Baseball Player)
2345 Summit Dr
Escondido, CA 92025-7513, USA

Rader, Douglas L (Doug) (Athlete, Baseball Player, Coach)
PO Box 2768
Stuart, FL 34995-2768, USA

Radford, Mark (Athlete, Basketball Player)
5160 NE Wistaria Dr
Portland, OR 97213-2557, USA

Radford, Michael (Director)
38 Rickering Mews
London W2 5AD, UNITED KINGDOM (UK)

Radford, Wayne (Athlete, Basketball Player)
3829 Steeplechase Dr
Carmel, IN 46032-8506, USA

Radigan, Terry (Musician, Songwriter)
Frank Callan Corp
209 10th Ave S Ste 322
Nashville, TN 37203-0744, USA

Radinsky, Scott (Athlete, Baseball Player)
1605 E Hillcrest Dr Unit B
Thousand Oaks, CA 91362-2647, USA

Radiohead (Music Group)
c/o Perri Cohen *Nasty Little Man*
285 W Broadway Rm 310
New York, NY 10013-2257, USA

Radisic, Zivko (President)
President's Office
Marsala Titz 7
Sarajevo 71000, BOSNIA & HERZEGOVINA

Radison, Dan (Athlete, Baseball Player)
116 SE 20th Ave
Deerfield Beach, FL 33441-4521, USA

Radke, Brad W (Athlete, Baseball Player)
125 18th St
Belleair Beach, FL 33786-3313, USA

Radko, Christopher (Artist)
PO Box 536
Elmsford, NY 10523-0536, USA

Radloff, Wayne (Athlete, Football Player)
106 Wedgefield Dr
Hilton Head Island, SC 29926-2260, USA

Radlosky, Rob (Athlete, Baseball Player)
151 Lake Susan Dr
West Palm Beach, FL 33411-9255, USA

Radmanovich, Ryan (Athlete, Baseball Player)
25 Ware Ave
West Hartford, CT 06119-1532, USA

Radnor, Josh (Actor)
c/o Jacob Fenton *United Talent Agency (UTA)*
9336 Civic Center Dr
Beverly Hills, CA 90210-3604, USA

Radojevic, Danilo (Dancer)
American Ballet Theatre
890 Broadway Fl 3
New York, NY 10003-1278, USA

Radosevich, George (Athlete, Football Player)
414 Shaffer Ave
Elizabeth, PA 15037-1840, USA

Radovich, Frank (Athlete, Basketball Player)
121 Lakewood Dr
Statesboro, GA 30458-9041, USA

Rady, Michael (Actor)
c/o Anne Woodward *Authentic Talent & Literary Management*
3615 Eastham Dr # 650
Culver City, CA 90232-2410, USA

Radziwill, Carole (Journalist, Reality Star, Writer)
c/o Lizzie Grubman *Lizzie Grubman Public Relations*
1201 Broadway Ste 810
New York, NY 10001-5656, USA

Radziwill, Lee (Actor, Business Person, Designer)
c/o Staff Member *Inkwell Management*
521 5th Ave
New York, NY 10175-0003, USA

Rae, Cassidy (Actor)
SDB Partners Inc
c/o Ro Diamond
1801 Avenue of the Stars #902
Los Angeles, CA 90067, USA

Rae, Emily (Actor)
c/o Pamela Kohl *3 Arts Entertainment*
9460 Wilshire Blvd Fl 7
Beverly Hills, CA 90212-2713, USA

Rae, Fiona (Artist)
The Royal Academy of Arts
Burlington House
Piccadilly
London W1J 0BD, UK

Rae, Issa (Actor)
c/o Jay Gassner *United Talent Agency (UTA)*
9336 Civic Center Dr
Beverly Hills, CA 90210-3604, USA

Rae, Mike (Athlete, Football Player)
18541 Auburn Ave
Santa Ana, CA 92705-2704, USA

Rae, Odessa (Actor)
c/o Brian Michael Brenner *LA Talent*
7700 W Sunset Blvd Ste 203
Los Angeles, CA 90046-3913, USA

Rae, Patricia (Actor)

Rae, Robert K (Bob) (Politician)
Goodman Phillips Vineberg
250 Yonge St
Toronto, ON M5B 2L7, CANADA

Raekwon (Musician)
c/o Drew Elliot *Artist International*
333 E 43rd St Apt 115
New York, NY 10017-4822, USA

Raether, Hal (Athlete, Baseball Player)
4501 Shoreline Dr APT 301
Spring Park, MN 55384-9501, USA

Rae Westley, Jennifer (Actor)
c/o Staff Member *da Vinci Talent*
919 Rue Marie Anne E
Montreal, QC H2J 2B2, CANADA

Rafalski, Brian (Athlete, Hockey Player, Olympic Athlete)
20 Holton Ln
Essex Fells, NJ 07021-1709, USA

Rafelson, Bob (Director)
1543 Dog Team Road
1022 Palm Ave. #3
New Haven, VT 05472, USA

Raffarin, Jean-Pierre (Prime Minister)
Sénat
15 Rue De Vaugirard
Cedex 06
Paris F-75291, FRANCE

Rafferty, Sarah (Actor)
c/o Mona Loring *Status PR*
PO Box 6191
Westlake Village, CA 91359-6191, USA

Rafferty, Tom (Athlete, Football Player)
1526 Mount Gilead Rd
Keller, TX 76262-7358, USA

Raffo, Al (Athlete, Baseball Player)
330 Pleasant View Cir
Jasper, TN 37347-7242, USA

Rafsanjani, Hojatoleslam H (President)
Expediency Council of Islamic Order
Majilis
Teheran, IRAN

Rafter, Patrick (Tennis Player)
PO Box 1235
North Sydney, NSW 02059, AUSTRALIA

Raftery, Erin (Actor)
c/o Matt Taylor *DDO Artist Agency (LA)*
4605 Lankershim Blvd Ste 340
N Hollywood, CA 91602-1876, USA

Raftery, S Frank (Misc)
Painters & Allied Trades Union
1750 New York Ave NW
Washington, DC 20006-5301, USA

Ragan, Dave (Athlete, Golfer)
Dave Ragan Inc
4001 Windy Rd
Concord, NC 28027-7441, USA

Ragan, David (Race Car Driver)
c/o Staff Member *NASCAR*
1801 W Speedway Blvd
Daytona Beach, FL 32114-1243, USA

Rage Against The Machine (Music Group)
c/o Don Muller *WME|IMG*
9601 Wilshire Blvd
Beverly Hills, CA 90210-5213, USA

Rager, Roger (Race Car Driver)
1680 64th St SW
Pequot Lakes, MN 56472-2068, USA

Raggi, Florencia (Actor)
c/o Staff Member *Telefe (Argentina)*
Pavon 2444
Buenos Aires C1248AAT, ARGENTINA

Raggio, Brady (Athlete, Baseball Player)
1650 Crater Ct
Reno, NV 89521-3030, USA

Raglan, Herb (Athlete, Hockey Player)
1206 Cabot St
Peterborough, ON K9H 6W9, CANADA

Ragland, Tom (Athlete, Baseball Player)
20201 Greenlawn St
Detroit, MI 48221-1187, USA

Raglin, Floyd (Athlete, Football Player)
2701 Alister Ave
Tustin, CA 92782-0934, USA

Ragnarsson, Marcus (Athlete, Hockey Player)
Hallonstigen 2
Bjorklinge, S-74030 Sweden

Rago, Pablo (Actor)
c/o Staff Member *Telefe (Argentina)*
Pavon 2444
Buenos Aires C1248AAT, ARGENTINA

Ragogna, Mike (Musician, Producer)
3975 Meier St Apt 201
Los Angeles, CA 90066-4187, USA

Ragsdale, William (Actor)
Innovative Artists
1505 10th St
Santa Monica, CA 90401-2805, USA

Rahal, Bashar (Actor)
c/o Victor Kruglov *Kruglov & Associates*
6565 W Sunset Blvd Ste 280
Los Angeles, CA 90028-7219, USA

Rahal, Robert W (Bobby) (Race Car Driver)
Team Rahal Racing
5 New Albany Farms Rd
New Albany, OH 43054-9000, USA

Rahane, Ajinkya (Athlete)
c/o Bunty Sajdeh *Cornerstone Sport and Entertainment Pvt Ltd*
H1, Heliopolis, 157 A
Colaba Rd
Mumbai Maharashtra 400005, INDIA

Rahim, Tahar (Actor)
c/o Gregory Weill *Agence Adequat*
21 Rue D'Uzes
Paris 75002, FRANCE

Rahlves, Daron (Athlete, Olympic Athlete, Skier)
PO Box 333
Truckee, CA 96160-0333, USA

Rahm, Kevin (Actor)
c/o Connie Tavel *Forward Entertainment*
1880 Century Park E Ste 1405
Los Angeles, CA 90067-1630, USA

Rahman Khan, Ataur (Prime Minister)
Bangladesh Jatiya League
500 A Dhanmondi R/A
Road 7
Dhaka, BANGLADESH

Rahner, Robert (Horse Racer)
2000 Boyle Rd APT 8D
Selden, NY 11784-1235, USA

Rahyel, Bobby (Race Car Driver)
934 Crescent Blvd
Glen Ellyn, IL 60137-4255, USA

Rahzel (Musician)
c/o Staff Member *UTA/The Agency Group*
888 7th Ave Fl 7
New York, NY 10106-0700, USA

Raible, Steve (Athlete, Football Player)
2721 1st Ave Unit 1002
Seattle, WA 98121-3521, USA

Raich, Benjamin (Athlete, Skier)
Ferienhof Raich
Leins 12
Arzl im Pitztal- Tirol A-6471, Austria

Raich, Eric (Athlete, Baseball Player)
3963 Edward Dr
Brunswick, OH 44212-1509, USA

Raider-Wexler, Victor (Actor)
c/o Lorraine Berglund *Lorraine Berglund Management*
11537 Hesby St
North Hollywood, CA 91601-3618, USA

Raiken, Sherwin (Athlete, Basketball Player)
2400 McClellan Ave Apt 120B
Pennsauken, NJ 08109-4609, USA

Raikkonen, Kimi (Race Car Driver)
c/o Staff Member *Formula Management Ltd*
PO Box 222
Borehamwood
Herts WD6 3FJ, United Kingdom

Railsback, Steve (Actor)
11684 Ventura Blvd # 581
Studio City, CA 91604-2699, USA

Raimi, Sam (Writer)
c/o Staff Member *Ghosthouse Underground*
2700 Colorado Ave Ste 200
Santa Monica, CA 90404-5502, USA

Raimi, Ted (Director, Producer)
c/o Steve Smith *Stagecoach Entertainment*
1990 S Bundy Dr Ste 645
Los Angeles, CA 90025-6365, USA

Raimondi, Ben (Athlete, Football Player)
5 Grandview Dr
Holmdel, NJ 07733-2007, USA

Rain, Steve (Athlete, Baseball Player)
20320 E Crestline Dr
Walnut, CA 91789-4605, USA

Raine, Craig A (Writer)
New College
English Dept
Oxford OX1 3BN, UNITED KINGDOM (UK)

Rainer, Luise (Actor)
54 Eaton Square
London SW1, UNITED KINGDOM (UK)

Rainer, Wali (Athlete, Football Player)
4715 Monaco Dr
Sandston, VA 23150-3205, USA

Raines, Mike (Athlete, Football Player)
112 Lupine Dr
Jacksonville, FL 32259-5406, USA

Raines, Tim (Athlete, Baseball Player)
1242 Saint Albans Loop
Lake Mary, FL 32746-1978, USA

Raines, Tony (Race Car Driver)
Front Row Motorsports
3536 Denver Dr
Denver, NC 28037-7217, USA

Rainey, Chuck (Athlete, Baseball Player)
6484 Del Cerro Blvd
San Diego, CA 92120-4804, USA

Rainey, Matt (Journalist)
Star-Ledger
1 Star Ledger Plz Ste 1
Editorial Dept
Newark, NJ 07102-1227, USA

Rains, Dan (Athlete, Football Player)
2509 Wigwam Rd
Aliquippa, PA 15001-4340, USA

Rains, Luce (Actor, Producer)
c/o Andrew Stawiarski *ADS Management*
269 S Beverly Dr Ste 441
Beverly Hills, CA 90212-3851, USA

Rainwater, G L (Business Person)
Ameren Corp
1901 Chouteau Ave
Saint Louis, MO 63103-3085, USA

Rainwater, Gregg (Actor)
PO Box 291836
Los Angeles, CA 90029-8836, USA

Raisa, Francia (Actor)
c/o Brett Ruttenberg *Imprint PR*
6121 W Sunset Blvd
Neuehouse
Los Angeles, CA 90028-6442, USA

Raisman, Alexandra (Athlete, Gymnast)
c/o Peter Carlisle *Octagon Olympics & Action Sports*
7 Ocean St Ste 2
South Portland, ME 04106-2800, USA

Raisman, Aly (Athlete, Gymnast, Olympic Athlete)
Brestyan's American Gymnastics Club
13 Ray Ave
Burlington, MA 01803-4720, USA

Raitt, Bonnie L (Musician, Songwriter, Writer)
PO Box 626
Los Angeles, CA 90078-0626, USA

Raji, B.J. (Athlete, Football Player)
c/o David Dunn *Athletes First*
23091 Mill Creek Dr
Laguna Hills, CA 92653-1258, USA

Rajisich, Dave (Athlete, Baseball Player)
1605 N Main St
Flagstaff, AZ 86004-4917, USA

Rajsich, Dave (Athlete, Baseball Player)
13378 W Cypress St
Goodyear, AZ 85395-3120, USA

Rajsich, Gary (Athlete, Baseball Player)
6510 Charleston Dr
Colleyville, TX 76034-5670, USA

Rajsich, Rhonda (Athlete)
c/o Gigi Rock *Heraea Marketing*
10905 E Pear Tree Dr
Cornville, AZ 86325-5523, USA

Rajskub, Mary Lynn (Actor, Writer)
c/o Christie Smith *Rise Management*
6338 Wilshire Blvd
Los Angeles, CA 90048-5002, USA

Rakers, Aaron (Athlete, Baseball Player)
553 W 3rd St
Trenton, IL 62293-1013, USA

Rakers, Jason (Athlete, Baseball Player)
547 Hickory Hollow Dr
Canfield, OH 44406-1052, USA

Rakestraw, Larry (Athlete, Football Player)
2462 Welford Ct
Suwanee, GA 30024-3130, USA

Rakestraw, Wilbur (Race Car Driver)
2609 Marietta Hwy.
Dallas, GA 39157, USA

Rakhmonov, Emomali (President)
President's Office
Supreme Soviet
Dushanbe, TAJIKISTAN

Raki, Laya (Actor)
Atkins Assoc
8040 Ventura Canyon Ave
Panorama City, CA 91402-6313, USA

Rakim (Musician)
c/o Ben Feigin *Anonymous Content*
3532 Hayden Ave
Culver City, CA 90232-2413, USA

Rakoczy, Gregg (Athlete, Football Player)
8709 Hidden Green Ln
Tampa, FL 33647-2271, USA

Rakos, Shawn (Athlete, Baseball Player)
23405 Fiske Road E
Orting, WA 98360, USA

Rakowski, Mieczyslaw F (Prime Minister)
Miesiecznik Dzis
Ul Poznanska 3
Warsaw 00-680, POLAND

Rales, Steven M (Business Person, Producer)
c/o Staff Member *Indian Paintbrush*
2308 Broadway
Santa Monica, CA 90404-2916, USA

Rall, Ted (Cartoonist)
Chronicle Features
901 Mission St
San Francisco, CA 94103-3052, USA

Rall, Tommy (Dancer)
777 Enchanted Way
Pacific Palisades, CA 90272-2819, USA

Ralph, Christopher (Actor)

Ralph, Jason (Actor)
c/o Sarah Fargo *Paradigm*
140 Broadway Ste 2600
New York, NY 10005-1011, USA

Ralph, Jim (Athlete, Hockey Player)
439 Hollandview Trail
Aurora, ON L4G 7M6, Canada

Ralston, Bob (Actor)
17027 Tennyson Pl
Granada Hills, CA 91344-1225

Ralston, Dennis (Tennis Player)
2005 San Vincente Dr
Concord, CA 94519-1018, USA

Ralston, John R (Athlete, Coach, Football Coach, Football Player)
1525 Highland Pines Ct
Reno, NV 89503-1653, USA

Ralston, Steve (Soccer Player)
New England Revolution
1 Patriot Pl
Cmgi Field
Foxboro, MA 02035-1388, USA

Ramage, Rob (Athlete, Hockey Player)
16127 Wilson Manor Dr
Chesterfield, MO 63005-4583, USA

Ramahata, Victor (Prime Minister)
PO Box 6004
Antanarivo 00101, MADAGASCAR

Ramamurthy, Sendhil (Actor)
c/o Roger Charteris *The Artists Partnership*
101 Finsbury Pavement
London EC2A 1RS, UNITED KINGDOM

Rama Rau, Santha (Writer)
496 Leedsville Rd
Amenia, NY 12501-5820, USA

Ramazzott, Eros (Musician)
c/o Staff Member *Universal Music Publishing Group (Latin)*
420 Lincoln Rd Ste 200
Miami Beach, FL 33139-3014, USA

Rambin, Leven (Actor)
c/o Kate Rosen *The Lede Company*
401 Broadway Ste 206
New York, NY 10013-3033, USA

Rambis, Kurt (Athlete, Basketball Player, Coach)
20 Chatham
Manhattan Beach, CA 90266-7225, USA

Rambis, Kurt (Athlete, Basketball Player)
20 Chatham
Manhattan Beach, CA 90266-7225, USA

Rambo, David (Religious Leader)
c/o Vanessa Livingston *Rothman Brecher Ehrich Livingston*
9250 Wilshire Blvd # Phb
Beverly Hills, CA 90212-3352, USA

Rambo, John (Athlete, Track Athlete)
1847 Myrtle Ave
Long Beach, CA 90806-5613, USA

Rambola, Tony (Musician)
c/o Staff Member *WME/IMG*
9601 Wilshire Blvd
Beverly Hills, CA 90210-5213, USA

Ramenofsky, Marilyn (Athlete, Olympic Athlete, Swimmer)
2909 Anza Ave
Davis, CA 95616-0215, USA

Ramey, Louis (Actor, Comedian)
Top Draw Entertainment
10839 Union Tpke
Forest Hills, NY 11375-6823, USA

Ramgoolam, Navinchandra (Prime Minister)
85 Sir Seewilsagur Ramgoolam St
Port Louis, MAURITIUS

Ramgoolam, Seewosagur (Prime Minister)
85 Desforges St
Port Louis, MAURITIUS

Ramini, TJ (Actor)
c/o Joel King *Pakula/King & Associates*
9229 W Sunset Blvd Ste 315
Los Angeles, CA 90069-3403, USA

Ramirez, Alex (Athlete, Baseball Player)
PO Box 880
Winter Haven, FL 33882-0880, USA

Ramirez, Allan (Athlete, Baseball Player)
8 Line Drive Rd
Victoria, TX 77905-5414, USA

Ramirez, Aramis (Athlete, Baseball Player)
1440 N Lake Shore Dr Apt 10EG
Chicago, IL 60610-1626, USA

Ramirez, Carolina (Actor)
c/o Gabriel Blanco *Gabriel Blanco Iglesias (Mexico)*
Rio Balsas 35-32
Colonia Cuauhtemoc
DF 06500, Mexico

Ramirez, Cierra (Actor)
c/o Thomas Richards *Corsa Agency, The*
11849 W Olympic Blvd Ste 100
Los Angeles, CA 90064-1164, USA

Ramirez, Dania (Actor, Producer)
c/o Jeff Morrone *Atlas Artists*
9220 W Sunset Blvd Ste 225
Los Angeles, CA 90069-3513, USA

Ramirez, Edgar (Actor)
c/o Jill Littman *Impression Entertainment*
9229 W Sunset Blvd Ste 700
Los Angeles, CA 90069-3407, USA

Ramirez, Efren (Actor)
c/o Staff Member *Randy James Management*
12711 Ventura Blvd Ste 345
Studio City, CA 91604-2416, USA

Ramirez, Erasmo (Athlete, Baseball Player)
3605 S Parton St
Santa Ana, CA 92707-4824, USA

Ramirez, Giovani Dos Santos (Athlete, Soccer Player)
c/o Staff Member *Villarreal CF SAD*
Camino Miralcamp s/n
Vila-real Castellon CP 12540, Spain

Ramirez, Hanley (Athlete, Baseball Player)
2430 N Shore Ter
Miami Beach, FL 33141-2448, USA

Ramirez, Horacio (Athlete, Baseball Player)
6424 Queens Court Trce
Mableton, GA 30126-7227, USA

Ramirez, Manny (Athlete, Baseball Player)
16101 Emerald Estates Dr Apt 156
Weston, FL 33331-6112, USA

Ramirez, Manny (Athlete, Football Player)

Ramirez, Mario (Athlete, Baseball Player)
HC 3 Box 14107
Yauco, PR 00698, USA

Ramirez, Michael P (Mike) (Cartoonist)
Los Angeles Times
2300 E Imperial Hwy
Editorial Dept
El Segundo, CA 90245-2813, USA

Ramirez, Milt (Athlete, Baseball Player)
7 Calle Tulio Larrinaga
Urb Ramirez De Arellano
Mayaguez, PR 00682-2447, USA

Ramirez, Rafael (Baseball Player)
5701 NW 3rd St
Miami, FL 33126-4705, USA

Ramirez, Raul (Tennis Player)
Avenida Ruiz
65 Sur Ensenada
Baja California, MEXICO

Ramirez, Sara (Actor)
c/o Haley Hileman (Urman) *Viewpoint Inc*
8820 Wilshire Blvd Ste 220
Beverly Hills, CA 90211-2622, USA

Ramm, Haley (Actor)
c/o Wendi Niad *Niad Management*
15021 Ventura Blvd Ste 860
Sherman Oaks, CA 91403-2442, USA

Rammstein (Music Group)
c/o Staff Member *Pilgrim Management*
Eichenstrasse, 62/63
Berlin 13156, GERMANY

Ramones, The (Music Group)
c/o Gary Kurfirst *Kurfirst/Blackwell Management*
601 W 26th St Fl 11
New York, NY 10001-1101

Ramon Gaspar, Henderson (Athlete, Baseball Player)
205 Cedar Run Dr
Douglassville, PA 19518-8707, USA

Ramos, Anthony (Actor)
c/o Jill McGrath *Door24*
115 W 29th St Rm 1102
New York, NY 10001-5106, USA

Ramos, Bobby (Athlete, Baseball Player)
15109 SW 62nd St
Miami, FL 33193-2735, USA

Ramos, Cesar (Athlete, Baseball Player)
8371 Tele11raoh Rd
Pico Rivera, CA 90660-4928, USA

Ramos, Constance (Connie) (Actor, Reality Star)

Ramos, Diego (Actor)
c/o Gabriel Blanco *Gabriel Blanco Iglesias (Mexico)*
Rio Balsas 35-32
Colonia Cuauhtemoc
DF 06500, Mexico

Ramos, Domingo (Athlete, Baseball Player)
Carr Duarte KM 8 1/2 Licey Al Medio
Santiago, Dominican Republic

Ramos, John (Athlete, Baseball Player)
4214 W Leona St
Tampa, FL 33629-7714, USA

Ramos, Jorge (Journalist, Television Host)
c/o Dario Brignole *Shine Entertainment Media*
5600 Collins Ave Apt 6J
Miami Beach, FL 33140-2406, USA

Ramos, Ken (Athlete, Baseball Player)
9 lronbrid11e Ln
Pueblo, CO 81001-1303, USA

Ramos, Mario (Athlete, Baseball Player)
1105 Clemson Cv
Pflugerville, TX 78660-4918, USA

Ramos, Mel (Artist)
5941 Ocean View Dr
Oakland, CA 94618-1842, USA

Ramos, Moises (Reality Star)
c/o Staff Member *Fly on the Wall*
12030 Riverside Dr
Valley Village, CA 91607-3749, USA

Ramos, Monica (Musician)
MNW Records Group
PO Box 535
Taby 183 25, SWEDEN

Ramos, Nathalia (Actor)
c/o Mia Hansen *Portrait PR*
5320 Sylmar Ave
Sherman Oaks, CA 91401-5612, USA

Ramos, Pedro (Athlete, Baseball Player)
6637 W 22nd Ln
Hialeah, FL 33016-3916, USA

Ramos, Sarah (Actor)
c/o Caryn Leeds *Wolf-Kasteler Public Relations*
6255 W Sunset Blvd Ste 1111
Los Angeles, CA 90028-7426, USA

Ramos, Tab (Athlete, Soccer Player)
Tab Ramos Soccer Programs
17 Blair Rd
Aberdeen, NJ 07747-1242, USA

Rampling, Charlotte (Actor)
c/o Elisabeth Tanner *Time-Art*
8 rue Danielle Casanova
Paris 75002, FRANCE

Rampone, Christie (Athlete, Soccer Player)
c/o Robert Raju *Axiom Sports & Entertainment*
340 Madison Ave Fl 19
New York, NY 10173-1921, USA

Ramsay, Anne (Actor)
c/o Todd Eisner *Abrams Artists Agency*
750 N San Vicente Blvd
E Tower Fl 11
Los Angeles, CA 90069-5788, USA

Ramsay, Bruce (Actor)
9150 Wilshire Blvd Ste 350
Beverly Hills, CA 90212-3453, USA

Ramsay, Craig (Athlete, Hockey Player)
Florida Panthers
1 Panther Pkwy
Sunrise, FL 33323-5315

Ramsay, Craig (Athlete, Coach, Hockey Player)
10602 Plantation Bay Dr
Tampa, FL 33647-3319

Ramsay, Gordon (Chef, Reality Star)
One Potato Two Potato
1950 Sawtelle Blvd Ste 346
Los Angeles, CA 90025-7072, USA

Ramsay, Laymon (Baseball Player)
Chicago American Giants
PO Box 26092
Birmingham, AL 35260-0092, USA

Ramsay, Robert (Athlete, Baseball Player)
6097 N La Rochelle Dr
Coeur D Alene, ID 83815-9802, USA

Ramsay, Tana (Chef, Writer)
c/o Staff Member *HarperCollins Publishers*
195 Broadway Fl 2
New York, NY 10007-3132, USA

Ramsay, Wayne (Athlete, Hockey Player)
Oak River, MB R0K 1T0, Canada

Ramsbottom, Nancy (Golfer)
2216 Parkers Hill Dr
Maidens, VA 23102-2243, USA

Ramsey, Bill (Athlete, Baseball Player)
6301 Village Grove Dr
Memphis, TN 38115-8119, USA

Ramsey, Boniface (Writer)
c/o Staff Member *New City Press*
202 Comforter Blvd
Hyde Park, NY 12538-2977, USA

Ramsey, Chuck (Athlete, Football Player)
17519 Martel Rd
Lenoir City, TN 37772-4235, USA

Ramsey, David (Actor)
c/o Mona Loring *Status PR*
PO Box 6191
Westlake Village, CA 91359-6191, USA

Ramsey, Derrick (Athlete, Football Player)
1801 Barwick Dr
Lexington, KY 40505-2546, USA

Ramsey, Fernando (Athlete, Baseball Player)
2501 Sandy Trl
Keller, TX 76248-8490, USA

Ramsey, Gerrard (Athlete, Football Player)
4102 US Highway 411 S
Maryville, TN 37801-9148, USA

Ramsey, John (Misc)
Campaign Headquarters
PO Box 243
Cheboygan, MI 49721-0243, USA

Ramsey, Laura (Actor)
c/o Mike Smith *Principal Entertainment*
9255 W Sunset Blvd Ste 500
Los Angeles, CA 90069-3301, USA

Ramsey, Marion (Actor)
c/o Aine Leicht *Horror & Hilarity*
Prefers to be contacted by email or phone.
Los Angeles, CA 90067, USA

Ramsey, Mary (Musician)
Agency for Performing Arts
9200 W Sunset Blvd Ste 900
Los Angeles, CA 90069-3604, USA

Ramsey, Mason (Musician)
c/o Michael Bryan *Creative Artists Agency (CAA)*
401 Commerce St PH
Nashville, TN 37219-2516, USA

Ramsey, Michael (Mike) (Athlete, Hockey Player)
445 W 79th St
Chanhassen, MN 55317-4505, USA

Ramsey, Mike (Athlete, Baseball Player)
PO Box 262
Harlem, GA 30814-0262, USA

Ramsey, Mike (Athlete, Baseball Player)
11564 92nd Way
Largo, FL 33773-4606, USA

Ramsey, Mike (Athlete, Hockey Player, Olympic Athlete)
6362 Oxbow Bnd
Chanhassen, MN 55317-9109

Ramsey, Nate (Athlete, Football Player)
1938 Cambridge St
Philadelphia, PA 19130-1508, USA

Ramsey, Ray (Athlete, Basketball Player)
1721 N Albany St
Springfield, IL 62702-3122, USA

Ramsey, Tom (Athlete, Football Player)
5435 E Otero Dr
Centennial, CO 80122-3875, USA

Ramsey, Wayne (Athlete, Hockey Player)
NW17-14-21
Oak River, MB ROK lTO, Canada

Ramsey, Wes (Actor)
c/o Robert Attermann *Abrams Artists Agency*
275 7th Ave Fl 26
New York, NY 10001-6708, USA

Ramson, Eason (Athlete, Football Player)
3526 Bayberry Dr
Walnut Creek, CA 94598-2718, USA

Rancic, Bill (Business Person, Reality Star)
c/o Carrie Simons *Triple 7 PR*
11693 San Vicente Blvd # 333
Los Angeles, CA 90049-5105, USA

Rancic, Giuliana (Reality Star, Television Host)
c/o Pamela Kohl *3 Arts Entertainment*
9460 Wilshire Blvd Fl 7
Beverly Hills, CA 90212-2713, USA

Rancid (Music Group)
c/o Stormy Shepherd *Leave Home Booking*
1400 S Foothill Dr Ste 34
Salt Lake City, UT 84108-2392, USA

Rand, Reese Mary (Athlete, Track Athlete)
6650 Los Gatos Rd
Atascadero, CA 93422-3608, USA

Randa, Joe (Athlete, Baseball Player)
6436 Ensley Ln
Mission Hills, KS 66208-1932, USA

Randall, Alice (Writer)
c/o Staff Member *Houghton Mifflin Company (Trade Division)*
222 Berkeley St Ste 8
Boston, MA 02116-3753, USA

Randall, Anne (Model)
10526 W Tropicana Cir
Sun City, AZ 85351-2218, USA

Randall, Bob (Athlete, Baseball Player)
2105 Hillview Dr
Manhattan, KS 66502-1942, USA

Randall, Claire (Religious Leader)
10015 W Royal Oak Rd Apt 1214
Sun City, AZ 85351-3164, USA

Randall, Damarious (Athlete, Football Player)
c/o Dave Butz *Sportstars Inc*
1370 Avenue of the Americas Fl 19
New York, NY 10019-4602, USA

Randall, Frankie (Boxer)
355 Fish Hatchery Road
#02
Morristown, TN 37813, USA

Randall, James (Sap) (Athlete, Baseball Player)
158 Heather Ln
Ruston, LA 71270-1165, USA

Randall, Jon (Musician)
Joe's Garage
4405 Belmont Park Ter
Nashville, TN 37215-3609, USA

Randall, Josh (Actor)
I F A Talent Agency
8730 W Sunset Blvd # 490
Los Angeles, CA 90069-2210, USA

Randall, Kikkan (Athlete, Olympic Athlete, Track Athlete)
8601 Pioneer Dr
Anchorage, AK 99504-4215, USA

Randall, Mark (Athlete, Basketball Player)
10476 Lynx Bay
Lone Tree, CO 80124-9549, USA

Randall, Maurice (Race Car Driver)
426 Sumpter St # 606
Charlotte, MI 48813-1120, USA

Randall, Rebel (Actor)
PO Box 1405
Riverside, CA 92502-1405, USA

Randall, Scott (Athlete, Baseball Player)
785 Grey Eagle Cir N
Colorado Springs, CO 80919-1605, USA

Randall, Tom (Athlete, Football Player)
2521 Park Vista Cir
Ames, IA 50014-4568, USA

Randall Johnson, Nicole (Actor)
c/o Paul Brown *Industry Entertainment Partners*
955 Carrillo Dr Ste 300
Los Angeles, CA 90048-5400, USA

Randazzo, Mike (Actor, Talk Show Host)
3469 W Stones Crossing Rd
C/O Mike Randazzo
Greenwood, IN 46143-8564, USA

Randazzo, Tony (Athlete, Baseball Player)
2462 Los Alamos Ct
Las Cruces, NM 88011-1657, USA

Randi, James (Misc)
2941 Fairview Park Dr Ste 105
Falls Church, VA 22042-4526, USA

Randie, John (Athlete, Football Player)
PO Box 489
Harrisonburg, VA 22803-0489, USA

Randle, Ervin (Athlete, Football Player)
2401 NE Meadowlark Ln
Lawton, OK 73507-5057, USA

Randle, John (Athlete, Football Player)
375 Calamus Cir
Hamel, MN 55340-9228, USA

Randle, Joseph (Athlete, Football Player)
c/o Erik Burkhardt *Select Sports Group*
2700 Post Oak Blvd Ste 1450
Houston, TX 77056-5785, USA

Randle, Julius (Athlete, Basketball Player)
c/o George A Bass Jr *AAI Sports Inc.*
16000 Dallas Pkwy Ste 300
Dallas, TX 75248-6609, USA

Randle, Kirk (Kirko Bangz) (Musician)
c/o Staff Member *Warner Bros Records (LA)*
PO Box 6868
Burbank, CA 91510-6868, USA

Randle, Lenny (Athlete, Baseball Player)
39461 Cozumel Ct
Murrieta, CA 92563-2552, USA

Randle, Lynda (Musician)
5565 NW Barry Rd
PO Box 236
Kansas City, MO 64154-1408, USA

Randle, Tate (Athlete, Football Player)
495 Koebig Rd
Seguin, TX 78155-0327, USA

Randle, Theresa (Actor)

Randle, Ulmo (Sonny) (Athlete, Football Player)
PO Box 487
Harrisonburg, VA 22803-0487, USA

Randolph, Alvin (Athlete, Football Player)
319 Roble Ave
Redwood City, CA 94061-3732, USA

Randolph, Carl (Musician)
David Levin Mgmt
200 W 57th St Ste 308
New York, NY 10019-3211, USA

Randolph, Jackson H (Business Person)
Cinergy Corp
139 E 4th St
Cincinnati, OH 45202-4003, USA

Randolph, Jay (Baseball Player)
12021 Charter Oak Pkwy
Saint Louis, MO 63146-5207, USA

Randolph, Joyce (Actor)
295 Central Park W Apt 18A
New York, NY 10024-3024

Randolph, Robert (Musician)
c/o Coran Capshaw *Red Light Management*
455 2nd St NE
#500
Charlottesville, VA 22902-5791, USA

Randolph, Sam (Golfer)
1305 Briar Ridge Dr
Keller, TX 76248-8376, USA

Randolph, Stephen (Athlete, Baseball Player)
3706 Apache Forest Dr
Austin, TX 78739-4418, USA

Randolph, Willie L (Athlete, Baseball Player, Coach)
715 Jenny Trl
Franklin Lakes, NJ 07417-2907, USA

Randolph, Zach (Athlete, Basketball Player)
c/o Staff Member *Memphis Grizzlies*
191 Beale St
Memphis, TN 38103-3715, USA

Randrup, Michael (Misc)
10 Fairlawn Road
Lythamst Annes
Lancashire FY8 5PT, UNITED KINGDOM (UK)

Rands, Bernard (Composer)
Harvard University
Music Dept
Cambridge, MA 02138, USA

Randy, Duncan (Athlete, Football Player)
4240 Foster Dr
Des Moines, IA 50312-2542, USA

Raney, Catherine (Athlete, Olympic Athlete, Speed Skater)
5800 Chaseview Rd
Nashville, TN 37221-4115, USA

Rangel, Charles B (Politician)
74 W 132nd St Apt 4A
New York, NY 10037-3313

Ranger, Bruce (Horse Racer)
1302 SW Patricia Ave
Port Saint Lucie, FL 34953-4901, USA

Ranger, Doug (Songwriter, Writer)
New Frontier Mgmt
1921 Broadway
Nashville, TN 37203-2719, USA

Ranger, Paul (Athlete, Hockey Player)
58 Henderson Dr
Whitby, ON L1N 7Y5, CANADA

Ranheim, Paul (Athlete, Hockey Player)
5228 Abbott Ave S
Minneapolis, MN 55410-2125, USA

Ranieri, George (Athlete, Hockey Player)
217 Wimpole St SS 1
Mitchell, ON N0K 1N0, Canada

Ranki, Dezso (Musician)
OrdogoromLejto 11/B
Budapest 01112, HUNGARY

Rankin, Chris (Actor)
c/o Staff Member *Ken McReddie Ltd*
101 Finsbury Pavement
London EC2A 1RS, UK

Rankin, Ian (Writer)
c/o Staff Member *Orion Publishing Group*
5 Upper Saint Martins Ln
London WC2H 9EA, UNITED KINGDOM

Rankin, Judy (Golfer)
2715 Racquet Club Dr
Midland, TX 79705-7432, USA

Rankin, Kenny (Musician, Songwriter)
c/o Staff Member *Variety Artists International Inc*
1111 Riverside Ave Ste 501
Paso Robles, CA 93446-2683, USA

Rankin, Kevin (Actor)
c/o Brady McKay *Haven Entertainment*
8111 Beverly Blvd Ste 201
Los Angeles, CA 90048-4531, USA

Rankin Jr, Alfred M (Business Person)
NACCO Industries
5875 Landerbrook Dr Ste 220
Mayfield Heights, OH 44124-6502, USA

Ranks, Shabba (Musician)
c/o Clifton Dillon *Shang Artist Management*
222 NE 27th St
Miami, FL 33137-4522, USA

Rannazzisi, Stephen (Actor)
c/o Rob Greenwald *Rogers & Cowan*
1840 Century Park E Fl 18
Los Angeles, CA 90067-2101, USA

Rannells, Andrew (Actor, Musician)
c/o Christie Smith *Rise Management*
6338 Wilshire Blvd
Los Angeles, CA 90048-5002, USA

Ransey, Kelvin (Athlete, Basketball Player)
3195 Monterey Dr
Tupelo, MS 38801-6817, USA

Ransom, Cody (Athlete, Baseball Player)
3146 E Boston St
Gilbert, AZ 85295-1458, USA

Ransom, Derrick (Athlete, Football Player)
6521 Sparrowood Ct
Indianapolis, IN 46236-8122, USA

Ransom, Jeff (Athlete, Baseball Player)
2131 Curtis St
Berkeley, CA 94702-1815, USA

Ransone, James (Actor)
c/o Kimberlin Belloni *Artists First*
9465 Wilshire Blvd Ste 900
Beverly Hills, CA 90212-2608, USA

Raoul, Dale (Actor)
c/o Staff Member *JC Robbins Management*
865 S Sherbourne Dr
Los Angeles, CA 90035-1809, USA

Rapace, Noomi (Actor)
c/o Shelley Browning *Magnolia Entertainment*
9595 Wilshire Blvd Ste 601
Beverly Hills, CA 90212-2506, USA

Rapada, Clay (Athlete, Baseball Player)
37224 Summerglen Ave
Murrieta, CA 92563-5070, USA

Rapaport, Michael (Actor)
c/o Daniel (Danny) Sussman *Brillstein Entertainment Partners*
9150 Wilshire Blvd Ste 350
Beverly Hills, CA 90212-3453, USA

Raper, Kenneth B (Misc)
602 N Segoe Rd Apt 501
Madison, WI 53705-3118, USA

Raphael (Actor)
Kaduri Agency
16125 NE 18th Ave
North Miami Beach, FL 33162-4749, USA

Raphael, June Diane (Actor)
c/o Jon Rubinstein *Authentic Talent and Literary Management (NY)*
20 Jay St Ste M17
Brooklyn, NY 11201-8300, USA

Raphael, Sally Jessy (Journalist)
616 Quaker Hill Rd
Pawling, NY 12564-3321, USA

Raposo, Greg (Actor, Musician)
PO Box 434
Glen Head, NY 11545-0434

Rapp, Anthony (Actor)
c/o Sarah Fargo *Paradigm*
140 Broadway Ste 2600
New York, NY 10005-1011, USA

Rapp, Pat (Athlete, Baseball Player)
175 Bluebird Ln
Burkeville, TX 75932-6417, USA

Rapp, Vern (Athlete, Baseball Player, Coach)
11150 Irving Dr Unit 330
Westminster, CO 80031-6879, USA

Rappaport, Jill (Correspondent)
c/o Staff Member *Simon & Schuster*
1230 Avenue of the Americas Fl CONC1
New York, NY 10020-1586, USA

Rappaport, Sheeri (Actor)
c/o Staff Member *McCabe Group*
3211 Cahuenga Blvd W Ste 104
Los Angeles, CA 90068-1372, USA

Rappeneau, Jean-Paul (Director)
24 Rue Henri Barbusse
Paris 75005, FRANCE

Rapuano, Ed (Baseball Player)
10815 Japonica Ct
Boca Raton, FL 33498-4839, USA

Rapuano, Ed (Athlete, Baseball Player)
10815 Japonica Ct
Boca Raton, FL 33498-4839, USA

Rare, Vanessa (Actor)
c/o Staff Member *Auckland Actors*
PO Box 56-460
Dominion Road
Auckland 00003, NEW ZEALAND

Rarick, Cindy (Golfer)
1625 N Via Dorado
Tucson, AZ 85715-4724, USA

Rasa Don (Musician)
William Morris Agency
1325 Avenue of the Americas
New York, NY 10019-6026, USA

Rasby, Walter (Athlete, Football Player)
1201 Jade Glen Dr
Charlotte, NC 28262-1621, USA

Rascal, Dizzee (Musician)
c/o Peter Elliot *Primary Talent International (UK)*
10-11 Jockeys Fields
The Primary Bldg
London WC1R 4BN, UNITED KINGDOM

Rascal Flatts (Music Group)
c/o Jake Basden *Big Machine Records*
1219 16th Ave S
Nashville, TN 37212-2901, USA

Rasche, David (Actor)
c/o Brian Liebman *Liebman Entertainment*
29 W 46th St Fl 5
New York, NY 10036-4104, USA

Rascoe, Robert (Bobby) (Athlete, Basketball Player)
523 Sumpter Ave
Bowling Green, KY 42101-3750, USA

Rash, Jim (Actor)
c/o Staff Member *B Story*
614 N La Peer Dr
West Hollywood, CA 90069-5602, USA

Rash, Steve (Director)
c/o Staff Member *Gersh*
9465 Wilshire Blvd Ste 600
Beverly Hills, CA 90212-2605, USA

Rashad, Ahmad (Athlete, Football Player)
6540 Eastpointe Pines St
West Palm Beach, FL 33418-6907, USA

Rashad, Condola (Actor)
c/o Emily Gerson Saines *Brookside Artists Management*
250 W 57th St Ste 1820
New York, NY 10107-1802, USA

Rashad, Phylicia (Actor)
c/o David Rose *Innovative Artists*
1505 10th St
Santa Monica, CA 90401-2805, USA

Rasheeda (Musician)
c/o Staff Member *ICM Partners*
10250 Constellation Blvd Fl 7
Los Angeles, CA 90067-6207, USA

Rashid, Karim (Designer)
357 W 17th St
New York, NY 10011-5060, USA

Rashnikov, Viktor (Business Person)
Magnitogorsk Iron and Steel Works
92 Kirov St
Magnitogorsk, Chelyabinsk region 455002, Russia

Rask, Tuuka (Athlete, Hockey Player)
19 Pier 7 Unit 19
Charlestown, MA 02129-4225

Raskin, Alex (Journalist)
Los Angeles Times
2300 E Imperial Hwy
Editorial Dept
El Segundo, CA 90245-2813, USA

Rasley, Rocky (Athlete, Football Player)
1918 S Mills Ave Apt 4
Lodi, CA 95242-4475, USA

Rasmus, Colby (Athlete, Baseball Player)
3110 Newsome Rd
Phenix City, AL 36870-2827, USA

Rasmussen, Anders Fogh (Prime Minister)
prins Jorgens Gard 11
Copenhagen K 02000, DENMARK

Rasmussen, Blair (Athlete, Basketball Player)
1581 30th Ave NE
Issaquah, WA 98029-7364, USA

Rasmussen, Dennis (Athlete, Baseball Player)
PO Box 547341
Orlando, FL 32854-7341, USA

Rasmussen, Eric (Athlete, Baseball Player)
237 SW 45th St
Cape Coral, FL 33914-5907, USA

Rasmussen, Erik (Athlete, Hockey Player)
16705 50th Ct N
Minneapolis, MN 55446-4532

Rasmussen, Gerry (Cartoonist)
9352 64 Ave NW
Edmonton, AB T6E 0H9, Canada

Rasmussen, Poul Nyrup (Prime Minister)
Aliegade 6A
Frederiksberg 02000, DENMARK

Rasmussen, Randy (Athlete, Football Player)
3990 114th Ln NW
Coon Rapids, MN 55433-2506, USA

Rasmussen, Randy (Athlete, Football Player)
512 Meadow Rd # 7
Ferguson, NC 28624-9017, USA

Rasmussen, Wayne (Athlete, Football Player)
9000 E Maple St
Brandon, SD 57005-1026, USA

Rasner, Darrell (Athlete, Baseball Player)
Tohoku Rakuten Golden Eagles 2-11-6 Miyagino
Miyagino-ku Sendai-shi
Mivagi-ken 983-0045, Japan

Rassas, Nick (Athlete, Football Player)
PO Box 227
Moose, WY 83012-0227, USA

Rasuk, Victor (Actor)
c/o Katherine Atkinson *Washington Square Films*
310 Bowery Fl 2
New York, NY 10012-2861, USA

Ratajkowski, Emily (Model)
c/o Evan Hainey *Untitled Entertainment*
350 S Beverly Dr Ste 200
Beverly Hills, CA 90212-4819, USA

Ratchford, Abigail (Actor, Model)
c/o Chrissy Johnston *Intrigue Management*
83 Ducie St
Manchester M1 2JQ, UNITED KINGDOM

Ratchford, Jeremy (Actor)
c/o Chip Hooley *AKA Talent Agency*
325 N Larchmont Blvd
Los Angeles, CA 90004-3011, USA

Ratchuk, Peter (Athlete, Hockey Player)
218 Ruskin Rd
Buffalo, NY 14226-4256

Ratelle, Jean (Athlete, Hockey Player)
1200 Salem St Apt 111
Lynnfield, MA 01940-1595

Rath, Fred (Athlete, Baseball Player)
7308 Pelican Island Dr
Tampa, FL 33634-7470, USA

Rath, Gary (Athlete, Baseball Player)
4745 Riva Ridge Dr
Tuscaloosa, AL 35406-4037, USA

Rath, Meaghan (Actor)
c/o Jim Hess *Silver Lining Entertainment*
421 S Beverly Dr Fl 7
Beverly Hills, CA 90212-4408, USA

Rathbone, Jackson (Actor)
c/o Samir Karar *LINK Entertainment*
11872 La Grange Ave
Los Angeles, CA 90025-5282, USA

Rather, Bo (Athlete, Football Player)
7728 La Jessica Cir
Kalamazoo, MI 49009-7542, USA

Rather, Dan (Journalist)
Dan Rather Reports
45 E 80th St Apt 26A
New York, NY 10075-0189, USA

Rathje, Mike (Athlete, Hockey Player)
14850 Blossom Hill Rd
Los Gatos, CA 95032-4901

Rathke, Henrich K M H (Religious Leader)
Schleifmuhlenweg 11
Schwering 19061, GERMANY

Rathman, Tom (Athlete, Football Player)
222 Republic Dr
Allen Park, MI 48101-3650, USA

Rathwell, Jake (Athlete, Hockey Player)
15 Outlook
Temiscaming, QC JOZ 3RO, Canada

Ratican, Tim (Race Car Driver)
TNT Motorsports
929 Jacaranda Dr
Lady Lake, FL 32159-5110, USA

Ratigan, Brian (Athlete, Football Player)
743 26th St
Manhattan Beach, CA 90266-2366, USA

Ratigan, Dylan (Television Host)
c/o Alan Berger *Creative Artists Agency (CAA)*
2000 Avenue of the Stars Ste 100
Los Angeles, CA 90067-4705, USA

Ratkowski, Ray (Athlete, Football Player)
PO Box 2736
Hyannis, MA 02601-7736, USA

Ratleff, Ed (Athlete, Basketball Player, Olympic Athlete)
4202 Paseo De Oro
Cypress, CA 90630-3420, USA

Ratliff, Don (Athlete, Football Player)
9048 Bay Hill Blvd
Orlando, FL 32819-4880, USA

Ratliff, Gene (Athlete, Baseball Player)
315 Southern Walk Cir
Gray, GA 31032-4528, USA

Ratliff, Jon (Athlete, Baseball Player)
289 Boughton Hill Rd
Honeoye Falls, NY 14472-9706, USA

Ratliff, Theo (Athlete, Basketball Player)
118e Mount Paran Rd NW
Atlanta, GA 30327-3702, USA

Ratliffe, Paul (Athlete, Baseball Player)
78 Campton Pl
Laguna Niguel, CA 92677-4734, USA

Ratner, Brett (Director)
c/o Staff Member *Rat Entertainment/Rat TV*
5555 Melrose Ave # 307
Los Angeles, CA 90038-3989, USA

Ratner, Ellen (Actor, Radio Personality)
c/o Judy Orbach *Judy O Productions*
6136 Glen Holly St
Hollywood, CA 90068-2338, USA

Ratner, Mark A (Misc)
615 Greenleaf Ave
Glencoe, IL 60022-1745, USA

Ratser, Dmitri (Musician)
Naxim Gershunoff
1401 NE 9th St Apt 38
Fort Lauderdale, FL 33304-4412, USA

Ratt (Music Group)
c/o Andrew Buck *Agency for the Performing Arts (APA)*
405 S Beverly Dr Ste 500
Beverly Hills, CA 90212-4425, USA

Ratushinskaya, Irina B (Writer)
Vargius Publishing House
Kuzakova Str 18
Moscow 107005, RUSSIA

Ratzenberger, John (Actor)
Shelter Entertainment
23901 Calabasas Rd Ste 2002
Calabasas, CA 91302-3303, USA

Ratzer, Steve (Athlete, Baseball Player)
5746 Deer Flag Dr
Lakeland, FL 33811-2001, USA

Ratzinger, Joseph A Cardinal (Religious Leader)
Palazzo del S Uffizio II
Rome 00193, ITALY

Rau, Doug (Athlete, Baseball Player)
1615 Treasure Oaks Dr
Katy, TX 77450-5088, USA

Rauch, Bob (Athlete, Baseball Player)
3350 W Pepperwood Loop
Tucson, AZ 85742-9389, USA

Rauch, Jon (Athlete, Baseball Player, Olympic Athlete)
14081 N Old Forest Trl
Oro Valley, AZ 85755-5789, USA

Rauch, Matthew (Actor)
c/o Diana Doussant *Leading Artists*
145 W 45th St Rm 1000
New York, NY 10036-4032, USA

Rauch, Melissa (Actor)
c/o Alissa Vradenburg *Untitled Entertainment*
350 S Beverly Dr Ste 200
Beverly Hills, CA 90212-4819, USA

Rauch, Siegfried (Actor)
c/o Gabriele Frederking *Alexander Agency*
Lamontstrasse 9
Munich D-81679, GERMANY

Raudman, Bob (Athlete, Baseball Player)
PO Box 8675
Jackson, WY 83002-8675, USA

Raudman, Craig (Race Car Driver)
Dave Reed Racing/AMI
6145 Northbelt Pkwy Ste F
Norcross, GA 30071-2972, USA

Rauner-Harrington, Helen (Baseball Player)
2027 Kentucky Ave
Fort Wayne, IN 46805-4442, USA

Rauschenberg, Robert (Artist)
381 Lafayette St
New York, NY 10003-7051, USA

Rausse, Errol (Athlete, Hockey Player)
338 Rosslare Dr
Arnold, MD 21012-3014

Rautins, Andy (Athlete, Basketball Player)
c/o Bill Duffy *BDA Sports Management*
700 Ygnacio Valley Rd Ste 330
Walnut Creek, CA 94596-3838, USA

Rautins, Leo (Athlete, Basketball Player)
2030 SE Madison St
Stuart, FL 34997-5858, USA

Rautzhan, Lance (Athlete, Baseball Player)
2472 Covington Dr
Myrtle Beach, SC 29579-3123, USA

Ravalec, Blanche (Actor)
Babette Pouget
6 Square Villaret de Joyeuse
Paris 75017, FRANCE

Ravalomanana, Marc (President)
President's Office
Iavoloha
Antananarivo, MADAGASCAR

Raven, Eddy (Musician, Songwriter, Writer)
Great American Talent
PO Box 2476
Hendersonville, TN 37077-2476, USA

Raven, Marion (Musician)
c/o Frank Cimler *10th Street Entertainment*
700 N San Vicente Blvd # G410
W Hollywood, CA 90069-5060, USA

Ravensberg, Robert (Athlete, Football Player)
636 Sherwood Dr
Saint Louis, MO 63119-3754, USA

Raver, Kim (Actor)
c/o David (Dave) Fleming *Atlas Artists*
9220 W Sunset Blvd Ste 225
Los Angeles, CA 90069-3513, USA

Raver-Lampman, Emmy (Actor)
c/o Alexandra Crotin *The Lede Company*
9701 Wilshire Blvd # 930
Beverly Hills, CA 90212-2020, USA

Ravlich, Matt (Athlete, Hockey Player)
15 Appletree Ln
Dalton, MA 01226-1351

Ravony, Francisque (Prime Minister)
Union des Forces Vivas Democratiques
Antananarivo, MADAGASCAR

Ravotti, Eric (Athlete, Football Player)
6000 Christopher Wren Dr Apt 117
Wexford, PA 15090-7364, USA

Rawat, Navi (Actor)
c/o Craig Schneider *Pinnacle Public Relations*
8721 Santa Monica Blvd # 133
W Hollywood, CA 90069-4507, USA

Rawi, Raad (Actor)
c/o Ken McReddie *Ken McReddie Ltd*
101 Finsbury Pavement
London EC2A 1RS, UK

Rawis, Betsy (Golfer)
501 Country Club Dr
Wilmington, DE 19803-2430, USA

Rawley, Shane (Athlete, Baseball Player)
4587 Cherrybark Ct
Sarasota, FL 34241-9213, USA

Rawlings, David (Musician)
2815 W Linden Ave
Nashville, TN 37212-4710, USA

Rawlings, Pat (Artist)
2200 Space Park Dr Ste 200
Houston, TX 77058-3678, USA

Rawlings, Richard (Business Person, Reality Star)
2330 Merrell Rd
Dallas, TX 75229-4405, USA

Rawlinson, Chris (Athlete, Olympic Athlete)
Trafford Athletic Club
Longford Park Stadium
Ryebank Road
Chorlton Cum Hardy, Manchester M21 9TA, UNITED KINGDOM

Rawls, Betsy (Athlete, Golfer)
501 Country Club Dr # Sr
Wilmington, DE 19803-2430, USA

Rawls, Elizabeth E (Betsy) (Golfer)
501 Country Club Dr
Wilmington, DE 19803-2430, USA

Rawls, Sam (Cartoonist)
c/o Staff Member *King Features Syndication*
300 W 57th St Fl 15
New York, NY 10019-5238, USA

Rawson, Anna (Athlete, Golfer, Model)
c/o Jeff Chilcoat *Sterling Sports Management, LLC*
7650 Rivers Edge Dr Ste 100
Columbus, OH 43235-1342, USA

Ray, Amy (Musician, Songwriter)
c/o Staff Member *High Road Touring*
751 Bridgeway Fl 2
Sausalito, CA 94965-2174, USA

Ray, Bobby (B.o.B.) (Musician)
2352 Old Ivey Walk
Stone Mountain, GA 30087-2757, USA

Ray, Chris (Athlete, Baseball Player)
7063 Daffodil Rd
Mechanicsville, VA 23111-5002, USA

Ray, Darrol (Athlete, Football Player)
13000 Doriath Way
Oklahoma City, OK 73170-2108, USA

Ray, David (Athlete, Football Player)
6962 Bridgewater Dr
Huntington Beach, CA 92647-4023, USA

Ray, Dipierro (Athlete, Football Player)
10542 Fremont Pike Apt 256
Perrysburg, OH 43551-3367, USA

Ray, Ear (Athlete, Basketball Player)
446 N Lowell St
Casper, WY 82601-2147, USA

Ray, Earl (Athlete, Basketball Player)
446 N Lowell St
Casper, WY 82601-2147, USA

Ray, Eddie (Athlete, Football Player)
5319 Avondale Dr
Sugar Land, TX 77479-3814, USA

Ray, Frankie (Actor)

Ray, Fred Olen (Director)
PO Box 3563
Van Nuys, CA 91407, USA

Ray, Greg (Race Car Driver)
Access Motorsports
8227 Northwest Blvd Ste 300
Indianapolis, IN 46278-1386, USA

Ray, James Arthur (Business Person)
James Ray International
5927 Balfour Ct Ste 104
Carlsbad, CA 92008-7376, USA

Ray, Jimmy (Musician)
Nineteen Music/Mgmt
35-37 Parkgate Road
London SW11 4NP, UNITED KINGDOM (UK)

Ray, John (Athlete, Football Player)
10 Ranger Ln
Charleston, WV 25309, USA

Ray, Johnny (Athlete, Baseball Player)
12470 S 432
Chouteau, OK 74337-6097, USA

Ray, Ken (Athlete, Baseball Player)
8952 W Electra Ln
Peoria, AZ 85383-1404, USA

Ray, Larry (Athlete, Baseball Player)
606 Lockwood Ln
Franklin, TN 37064-1539, USA

Ray, Lisa (Actor)
c/o Dannielle Thomas *Untitled Entertainment*
350 S Beverly Dr Ste 200
Beverly Hills, CA 90212-4819, USA

Ray, Marguerite (Actor)
1329 N Vista St Apt 106
Los Angeles, CA 90046-4833, USA

Ray, Rachael (Chef, Talk Show Host)
22 Costellos Dr
Lake Luzerne, NY 12846-3120, USA

Ray, Rob (Athlete, Hockey Player)
Buffalo Sabres
1 Seymour H Knox III Plz Ste 1
Buffalo, NY 14203-3096

Ray, Rob (Athlete, Hockey Player)
289 Sausalito Dr
East Amherst, NY 14051-1472

Ray, Shane (Athlete, Football Player)
c/o Tony Fleming *Impact Sports (LA)*
12429 Ventura Ct
Studio City, CA 91604-2417, USA

Ray, Sugar (Music Group)
c/o Staff Member *Pinnacle Entertainment*
30 Glenn St
White Plains, NY 10603-3254, USA

Ray, Terry (Athlete, Football Player)
42559 Angel Wing Way
Brambleton, VA 20148-5635, USA

Ray, Vanessa (Actor)
c/o Randi Goldstein *Gersh*
41 Madison Ave Ste 3301
New York, NY 10010-2210, USA

Raybon, Marty (Musician)
Hallmark Direction
15 Music Sq W
Nashville, TN 37203-6200, USA

Raycroft, Andrew (Hockey Player)
c/o Staff Member *Toronto Maple Leafs*
Air Canada Centre
400-40 Bay St
Toronto, ON M5J 2X2, CANADA

rayder, franki (Model)
Why Not
via Zenale, 9
Milano 20123, Italy

Raydon, Curt (Athlete, Baseball Player)
PO Box 5124
Jasper, TX 75951-7701, USA

Raye, Collin (Musician)
c/o Dave Fowler *Nashville Artist Management*
Prefers to be contacted via telephone
Nashville, TN, USA

Raye, Lisa (Actor)
c/o Susan Haber *Haber Entertainment*
434 S Canon Dr Apt 204
Beverly Hills, CA 90212-4501, USA

Rayford, Floyd (Athlete, Baseball Player)
11701 Pointe Circle Dr
Fort Myers, FL 33908-2161, USA

Rayl, James (Athlete, Basketball Player)
58 Rideout Rd
Hollis, NH 03049-6110, USA

Raymer, Cory (Athlete, Football Player)
46629 Hampshire Station Dr
Sterling, VA 20165-7395, USA

Raymer, Greg (Misc)
2624 Forest Shadows Ln
Raleigh, NC 27614-8073, USA

Raymo, Maureen (Misc)
Boston University
Geology Dept
Boston, MA 02215, USA

Raymond, Claude (Athlete, Baseball Player)
3 Rue de la Citiere
Saint-Jean-Sur-Richelieu, QC J2W 1B8, Canada

Raymond, Corey (Athlete, Football Player)
106 Carter St
New Iberia, LA 70560-6214, USA

Raymond, Craig (Athlete, Basketball Player)
4617 N 265 E
Provo, UT 84604-5403

Raymond, Gary (Actor)
c/o Staff Member *Sharkey & Co*
44 Lexington St
London W1F 0LP, UNITED KINGDOM

Raymond, Kenneth N (Misc)
University of California
Chemistry Dept
Berkeley, CA 94720-0001, USA

Raymond, Lisa (Tennis Player)
Octagon
1751 Pinnacle Dr Ste 1500
McLean, VA 22102-3833, USA

Raymond, Mason (Athlete, Hockey Player)
RR 2 LCD Main
Cochrane, AB T4C 1A2, Canada

Raymond, Mistral (Athlete, Football Player)
c/o Adam Heller *Vantage Management Group*
518 Reamer Dr
Carnegie, PA 15106-1845, USA

Raymond, Usher (Dancer, Musician)
c/o Scooter Braun *SB Management*
755 N Bonhill Rd
Los Angeles, CA 90049-2303, USA

Raymonde, Tania (Actor)
c/o Katie Rhodes *Untitled Entertainment*
350 S Beverly Dr Ste 200
Beverly Hills, CA 90212-4819, USA

Raymund, Monica (Actor)
c/o Jill McGrath *Door24*
115 W 29th St Rm 1102
New York, NY 10001-5106, USA

Rayner, Chuck (Actor)
c/o Laraine Golden *Main Line Models & Talent*
1215 W Baltimore Pike Ste 9
Media, PA 19063-5540, USA

Ray Newman, Jaime (Actor)
c/o Nicole Perna *Imprint PR*
6121 W Sunset Blvd
Neuehouse
Los Angeles, CA 90028-6442, USA

Raynis, Richard (Producer)
c/o Staff Member *Creative Artists Agency (CAA)*
2000 Avenue of the Stars Ste 100
Los Angeles, CA 90067-4705, USA

Raynor, Bruce (Politician)
Unite
275 7th Ave Rm 1504
New York, NY 10001-6860, USA

Raynr, David (Actor, Director, Producer)
c/o Simon Millar *Rumble Media*
1620 Broadway Ste C
Santa Monica, CA 90404-2777, USA

Raz, Kavi (Actor)
c/o Staff Member *Almond Talent Management*
8217 Beverly Blvd Ste 8
W Hollywood, CA 90048-4534, USA

Raz, Lior (Actor, Producer)
c/o Itay Reiss *Artists First*
9465 Wilshire Blvd Ste 900
Beverly Hills, CA 90212-2608, USA

Raza, S Atiq (Business Person)
Advanced Micro Devices
2485 Augustine Dr
Santa Clara, CA 95054-3002, USA

Razanamasy, Guy (Prime Minister)
Prime Minister's Office
Mahazoarivo
Antananarivo, MADAGASCAR

Raz B (Actor, Musician)
c/o Mike Esterman *Esterman.Com, LLC*
Prefers to be contacted via email
Baltimore, MD XXXXX, USA

Raziano, Barry (Athlete, Baseball Player)
1315 4th St
Kenner, LA 70062-7311, USA

Razorlight (Music Group)
Universal Music Operations
364-366 Kensington High St
London W14 8NS, UNITED KINGDOM

R. Carter, John (Congressman, Politician)
409 Cannon Hob
Washington, DC 20515-0911, USA

R. Conseco, Francisco (Congressman, Politician)
1339 Longworth Hob
Washington, DC 20515-1202, USA

Re, Glovanni Battsti Cardinal (Religious Leader)
Palazzo delle Congregazioni
Piazza Pio XII #10
Rome 00193, ITALY

Rea, Connie (Athlete, Basketball Player)
13 Marina Dr
Winter Haven, FL 33881-9710, USA

Rea, Stephen (Actor)
c/o Nick Forgacs *Independent Talent Group*
40 Whitfield St
London W1T 2RH, UNITED KINGDOM

Read, Amy (Athlete, Golfer)
7301 Barbaradale Cir
Las Vegas, NV 89146-5160, USA

Read, James (Actor)
c/o Staff Member *Pakula/King & Associates*
9229 W Sunset Blvd Ste 315
Los Angeles, CA 90069-3403, USA

Read, Nicolas (Actor)
c/o Marc Bass *Beacon Talent Agency*
170 Apple Ridge Rd
Woodcliff Lk, NJ 07677-8149, USA

Read, Richard (Journalist)
Portland Oregonian
1320 SW Broadway
Editorial Dept
Portland, OR 97201-3427, USA

Readdy, William F (Bill) (Astronaut)
NASA
2101 Nasa Pkwy Spc Johnsoncenter
Houston, TX 77058-3696, USA

Readdy, William F Captain (Astronaut)
1818 S Lynn St
Arlington, VA 22202-1619, USA

Reading, John (Musician)
14321 Draft Horse Ln
Wellington, FL 33414-1020, USA

Read-Martin, Dolly (Actor)
30765 Pacific Coast Hwy Ste 103
Malibu, CA 90265-3643

Ready, Randy (Athlete, Baseball Player)
5106 Willow Ln
Dallas, TX 75244-7611, USA

Reagan, Bernice Johnson (Musician)
American University
History Dept
Washington, DC 20016, USA

Reagan, Michael (Radio Personality, Writer)
c/o Staff Member *Premiere Speakers Bureau*
109 International Dr Ste 300
Franklin, TN 37067-1764, USA

Reagan, Ron (Journalist)
2612 28th Ave W
Seattle, WA 98199-3320, USA

Reagins, Tony (Baseball Player)
8220 E Blackwillow Cir APT 104
Anaheim, CA 92808-1904, USA

Reagor, Montae (Athlete, Football Player)
1511 Drexel Dr
Waxahachie, TX 75165-4409, USA

Real, Roxanne (Musician)
Headline Talent
1650 Broadway Ste 508
New York, NY 10019-6833, USA

Real, Terrence (Writer)
Real Relational Solutions
754 Massachusetts Ave
Arlington, MA 02476-4712, USA

Reali, Tony (Sportscaster, Television Host)
c/o Staff Member *CAA Sports*
2000 Avenue of the Stars Ste 100
Los Angeles, CA 90067-4705, USA

Reality, Maxim (Musician)
Midi Mgmt
Jenkins Lane
Great Hallinsbury
Essex CM22 7QL, UNITED KINGDOM (UK)

Ream, Charles (Athlete, Football Player)
1412 Snowmass Rd
Columbus, OH 43235-2130, USA

Reames, Britt (Athlete, Baseball Player)
806 Dalton Rd
Seneca, SC 29678-3722, USA

Reamon, Tommy (Athlete, Football Player)
709 Galahad Dr
Newport News, VA 23608-1807, USA

Reams, Leroy (Athlete, Baseball Player)
6140 E 17th St
Oakland, CA 94621-4108, USA

Reardon, Jeff (Athlete, Baseball Player)
5 Marlwood Ln
Palm Beach Gardens, FL 33418-6805, USA

Reardon, John (Actor)
c/o Courtney Kivowitz *MGMT Entertainment (The Schiff Company)*
9220 W Sunset Blvd Ste 106
W Hollywood, CA 90069-3500, USA

Reaser, Elizabeth (Actor)
c/o Nancy Gates *United Talent Agency (UTA)*
888 7th Ave Fl 7
New York, NY 10106-0700, USA

Reason, Rhodes (Actor)
PO Box 503
Gladstone, OR 97027-0503, USA

Reasoner, Marty (Athlete, Hockey Player)
5250 Winlane Dr
Bloomfield Hills, MI 48302-2960

Reasons, Gary P (Athlete, Football Player)
17029 Hardwood Pl
Edmond, OK 73012-9121, USA

Reaugh, Daryl (Athlete, Hockey Player)
Dallas Stars
2601 Avenue of the Stars Ste 100
Frisco, TX 75034-9016

reaugh, daryl (Athlete, Hockey Player)
3400 Saint Johns Dr
Dallas, TX 75205-2906

Reaume, Marc (Athlete, Hockey Player)
2991 Laurler Dr.
Windsor, ON N9J lL7, Canada

Reaves, Ken (Athlete, Football Player)
413 Oakside Dr SW
Atlanta, GA 30331-3724, USA

Reaves, Shawn (Actor)
c/o Diana Prano *Multimedia Talent Management (NY)*
25 W 43rd St Fl 16
New York, NY 10036-7410, USA

Reaves, Stephanie (Race Car Driver)
Rapid Motorsports Inc
PO Box 430
Awendaw, SC 29429-0430, USA

Reaves, Willard (Athlete, Football Player)
150 Wallingford Cres
Winnipeg, MB R3P 1L5, Canada

Reavis, Dave (Athlete, Football Player)
5495 S Newport Cir
Greenwood Village, CO 80111-1601, USA

Reavis, Phil (Athlete, Olympic Athlete)
41 School St
Somerville, MA 02143-1721, USA

Rebardo, Joe (Musician)
Billy Paul Mgmt
7816 Rising Sun Ave
Philadelphia, PA 19111-2601, USA

Rebekah (Musician)
Int'l Talent Booking
27A Floral St
#300
London WC2E 9DQ, UNITED KINGDOM (UK)

Rebel Emergency (Music Group)
c/o Staff Member *Paradigm (Monterey)*
404 W Franklin St
Monterey, CA 93940-2303, USA

Reberger, Frank (Athlete, Baseball Player)
439 Sunset View Ln
Hope, ID 83836-9845, USA

Reboulet, Jeff (Athlete, Baseball Player)
Horizon Wealth Management
8280 Ymca Plaza Dr Bldg 5
Baton Rouge, LA 70810-0927, USA

Rebowe, Rusty (Athlete, Football Player)
656 Pine St
Norco, LA 70079-2136, USA

Rebraca, Zeljko (Athlete, Basketball Player)
1550 8th St
Manhattan Beach, CA 90266-6351, USA

Recari, Beatriz (Athlete, Golfer)
c/o Staff Member *Ladies Pro Golf Association (LPGA)*
100 International Golf Dr
Daytona Beach, FL 32124-1092, USA

Recasner, Eldridge (Athlete, Basketball Player)
6159 164th Ave SE
Bellevue, WA 98006-5613, USA

Recchi, Mark (Athlete, Hockey Player)
The Orr Hockey Group
PO Box 290836
Charlestown, MA 02129-0215, USA

Recher, Dave (Athlete, Football Player)
970 E Devon Dr
Gilbert, AZ 85296-3620, USA

Rechichar, Albert (Bert) (Athlete, Football Player)
141 W McClain Rd
Rostraver Township, PA 15012-3507, USA

Reckell, Peter (Actor)
c/o Staff Member *Rebel Entertainment Partners*
5700 Wilshire Blvd Ste 470
Los Angeles, CA 90036-4379, USA

Reckless Kelly (Music Group)
c/o Staff Member *Paradigm (Monterey)*
404 W Franklin St
Monterey, CA 93940-2303, USA

Records, Max (Actor)
c/o Ara Keshishian *Creative Artists Agency (CAA)*
2000 Avenue of the Stars Ste 100
Los Angeles, CA 90067-4705, USA

Rector, Jeff (Actor)
10748 Aqua Vista St
North Hollywood, CA 91602-3207, USA

Rector, Milton G (Misc)
National Council on Crime & Delinquency
288 Monroe Ave
River Edge, NJ 07661-1316, USA

Red Alert, Kool DJ (Musician)

Redbone, Leon (Musician)
Red Shark Inc
146 N Church St
Doylestown, PA 18901-3742, USA

Redd, Michael (Athlete, Basketball Player)
2 Crescent Pond
New Albany, OH 43054-9081, USA

Redd, Silas (Athlete, Football Player)
c/o Jim Ivler *Sportstars Inc*
1370 Avenue of the Americas Fl 19
New York, NY 10019-4602, USA

Redden, Barry (Athlete, Football Player)
22503 Diamond Shore Ct
Katy, TX 77450-8053, USA

Redden, Wade (Athlete, Hockey Player)
Newport Sports Management
400-201 City Centre Dr
Attn Don Meehan
Mississauga, ON L5B 2T4, Canada

Reddick, Cat (Athlete, Olympic Athlete, Soccer Player)
2620 Altadena Rd
Vestavia, AL 35243-4500, USA

Reddick, Josh (Athlete, Baseball Player)
97 Drew Dr
Guyton, GA 31312-4867, USA

Reddick, Lance (Actor, Musician)
c/o Amy Brownstein *PRStudio USA*
1875 Century Park E Ste 930
Los Angeles, CA 90067-2540, USA

Reddick, Pokey (Athlete, Hockey Player)
7794 Briana Renee Way
Las Vegas, NV 89123-0447

Redding, Cory (Athlete, Football Player)
c/o Kennard McGuire *MS World LLC*
1270 Crabb River Rd Ste 600 PMB 104
Richmond, TX 77469-5635, USA

Redding, Tim (Athlete, Baseball Player)
8882 Squire Trl
Bellevue, MI 49021-9566, USA

Reddout, Frank (Athlete, Basketball Player)
379 Niblick Cir
Winter Haven, FL 33881-9572, USA

Reddy, Helen (Musician)
c/o Staff Member *T-Best Talent Agency*
508 Honey Lake Ct
Danville, CA 94506-1237, USA

Redfern, Pete (Athlete, Baseball Player)
12516 Haddon Ave
Sylmar, CA 91342-3636, USA

Redfield, James (Actor, Producer, Writer)
3584 Pelham Pkwy
Pelham, AL 35124-2034, USA

Redfield, Joe (Athlete, Baseball Player)
307 Glenview Cir
Woodway, TX 76712-3141, USA

Redfoo (Musician)
c/o Staff Member *United Talent Agency (UTA)*
9336 Civic Center Dr
Beverly Hills, CA 90210-3604, USA

Redford, Blair (Actor)
c/o Sheva Cohen *Agency for the Performing Arts (APA)*
405 S Beverly Dr Ste 500
Beverly Hills, CA 90212-4425, USA

Redford, Jamie (Producer)
c/o Jim Ehrich *Rothman Brecher Ehrich Livingston*
9250 Wilshire Blvd # Phb
Beverly Hills, CA 90212-3352, USA

Redford, Paul (Producer, Writer)
c/o Cori Wellins *WME/IMG*
9601 Wilshire Blvd
Beverly Hills, CA 90210-5213, USA

Redford, Robert (Actor, Director)
The Redford Center
PO Box 29144
San Francisco, CA 94129-0144, USA

Redgrave, Corin (Actor)
Kate Feast
Primrose Hill Studios
Fitzroy Road
London NW1 8TR, UNITED KINGDOM (UK)

Redgrave, Jemma (Actor)
Conway Van Gelder Robinson
18-21 Jermyn St
London SW1Y 6NB, UNITED KINGDOM (UK)

Redgrave, Vanessa (Actor)
c/o Joe Machota *Creative Artists Agency (CAA)*
405 Lexington Ave Fl 19
New York, NY 10174-1800, USA

Red-Horse, Valerie (Actor, Director, Producer, Writer)
c/o Staff Member *Suite A Management Talent & Literary Agency*
120 El Camino Dr Ste 202
Beverly Hills, CA 90212-2723, USA

Red Hot Chili Peppers (Music Group)
c/o Cliff Burnstein *Q Prime (NY)*
729 7th Ave Fl 16
New York, NY 10019-6831, USA

Redick, JJ (Athlete, Basketball Player)
315 E New England Ave Unit 13
Winter Park, FL 32789-4477, USA

Reding, Juli (Actor)
PO Box 1806
Beverly Hills, CA 90213-1806, USA

Redman, Amanda (Actor)
c/o Staff Member *Lip Service Casting Ltd*
60-66 Wardour St
London W1F 0TA, UK

Redman, Brian (Race Car Driver)
10945 Scott Mill Rd
Jacksonville, FL 32223-6514, USA

Redman, Joshua (Race Car Driver)
Wilkins Management
323 Broadway
Cambridge, MA 02139-1801, USA

Redman, Julian "Tike" (Athlete, Baseball Player)
W155N6984 Amberleigh Cir
Menomonee Falls, WI 53051-5088, USA

Redman, Magdalen (Athlete, Baseball Player)
N7780 Vicksburg Way Apt D
Oconomowoc, WI 53066-2016, USA

Redman, Mark (Athlete, Baseball Player)
4120 Sunnyhill Dr
Carlsbad, CA 92008-3644, USA

Redman, Michele (Golfer)
3410 Queensland Ln N
Minneapolis, MN 55447-1153, USA

Redman, Prentice (Athlete, Baseball Player)
1831 Boulder Springs Dr
Dr Apt K
Saint Louis, MO 63146-3953, USA

Redman, Susle (Golfer)
137 SW Saratoga Ave
Port Saint Lucie, FL 34953-5974, USA

Redmann, Teal (Actor)
c/o Amy Abell *BRS / Gage Talent Agency (LA)*
6300 Wilshire Blvd Ste 1430
Los Angeles, CA 90048-5216, USA

Redmayne, Eddie (Actor)
c/o Pippa Beng *Premier PR*
2-4 Bucknall St
London WC2H 8LA, UNITED KINGDOM

Redmon, Glenn (Athlete, Baseball Player)
PO Box 2171
Riverview, FL 33568-2171, USA

Redmond, Craig (Athlete, Hockey Player)
10332 McEachern St
Maple Ridge, BC V2W 0B2, Canada

Redmond, Derek (Athlete, Olympic Athlete, Track Athlete)
c/o Staff Member *Definitive Sports Management*
One Kingsway Greyfriars Rd
Cardiff CF10 3DS, UK

Redmond, Marge (Actor)
Abrams Artists
9200 W Sunset Blvd Ste 1125
Los Angeles, CA 90069-3610, USA

Redmond, Markus (Actor)
c/o Staff Member *Gersh*
9465 Wilshire Blvd Ste 600
Beverly Hills, CA 90212-2605, USA

Redmond, Marlon (Athlete, Basketball Player)

Redmond, Michael E (Mickey) (Athlete, Hockey Player)
30699 Harlincin Ct
Franklin, MI 48025-1521, USA

Redmond, Mickey (Athlete, Hockey Player)
Detroit Red Wings
2645 Woodward Ave
Detroit, MI 48201-3028

Redmond, Mike (Athlete, Baseball Player)
13506 S Bluegrouse Ln
Spokane, WA 99224-8523, USA

Redmond, Rudy (Athlete, Football Player)
2014 Woodside Xing
Savannah, GA 31405-8183, USA

Redmond, Wayne (Athlete, Baseball Player)
18061 Sussex St
Detroit, MI 48235-2835, USA

Rednikova, Yekaterina (Actor)
358 N Gardner St
C/O Larry Hummel
Los Angeles, CA 90036-5721, USA

Redquest, Greg (Athlete, Hockey Player)
16 Hall St RR 1
Phelpston, ON L0L 2K0, Canada

Redstone, Sumner (Business Person)
c/o Staff Member *Viacom Entertainment Group*
15456 Ventura Blvd Ste 301
Sherman Oaks, CA 91403-3082

Redus, Gary (Athlete, Baseball Player)
2202 Mallard Ln SE
Decatur, AL 35601-6759, USA

Redwine, Jarvis J (Athlete, Football Player)
2707 W 79th St
Inglewood, CA 90305-1033, USA

Reece, Beasley (Athlete, Football Player, Sportscaster)
5005 Open Water Way
Streetman, TX 75859-3314, USA

Reece, Bob (Athlete, Baseball Player)
PO Box 1337
West Yellowstone, MT 59758-1337, USA

Reece, Carmen (Musician)
c/o Mark Feist *Real MF Ltd*
22425 Ventura Blvd # 179
Woodland Hills, CA 91364-1524, USA

Reece, Daniel (Danny) (Athlete, Football Player)
5519 S Corning Ave
Los Angeles, CA 90056-1302, USA

Reece, Dave (Athlete, Hockey Player)
138 Peaked Rock Rd
Wakefield, RI 02879-2384

Reece, Gabrielle (Athlete, Model, Volleyball Player)
c/o Lisa Shotland *CAA (London)*
3 Shortlands, Hammersmith
Fl 5
London W6 8DA, UNITED KINGDOM

Reece, John (Athlete, Football Player)
5927 Cape Hatteras Dr
Houston, TX 77041-5911, USA

Reece, Marcel (Athlete, Football Player)

Reece, Maynard (Artist)
5315 Robertson Dr
Des Moines, IA 50312-2133, USA

Reece, Thomas L (Business Person)
Dover Corp
280 Park Ave
New York, NY 10017-1274, USA

Reed, Alvin (Athlete, Football Player)
3910 Abbeywood Dr
Pearland, TX 77584-4943, USA

Reed, Alyson (Actor)
c/o Christopher Black *Opus Entertainment*
5225 Wilshire Blvd Ste 905
Los Angeles, CA 90036-4353, USA

Reed, Andre D (Athlete, Football Player)
1058 America Way
Del Mar, CA 92014-3919, USA

Reed, Angel Boris (Actor)
c/o Staff Member *Acme Talent & Literary*
4727 Wilshire Blvd Ste 333
Los Angeles, CA 90010-3874, USA

Reed, Bob (Athlete, Baseball Player)
42519 Lake Hospitality Ln
Altoona, FL 32702-9584, USA

Reed, Brooks (Athlete, Football Player)
c/o Ken Zuckerman *Priority Sports & Entertainment - (LA)*
15233 Ventura Blvd Ste 718
Sherman Oaks, CA 91403-2237, USA

Reed, Bruce (Writer)
c/o Staff Member *Public Affairs Books*
1094 Flex Dr
Jackson, TN 38301-5070, USA

Reed, Chad (Athlete, Motorcycle Racer)
c/o Steven Astephen *Wasserman Media Group - Carlsbad*
2251 Faraday Ave # 200
Carlsbad, CA 92008-7209, USA

Reed, Crystal (Actor)
c/o Gary Mantoosh *Baker Winokur Ryder Public Relations*
9100 Wilshire Blvd
W Tower #500
Beverly Hills, CA 90212-3415, USA

Reed, Darren (Athlete, Baseball Player)
8101 Santa Ana Rd
Ventura, CA 93001-9723, USA

Reed, Dizzy (Musician)
c/o Ken Fermaglich *UTA Music*
142 W 57th St Fl 6
New York, NY 10019-3300, USA

Reed, Ed (Athlete, Football Player)
Ed Reed Foundation
10015 Old Columbia Rd Ste H125
Columbia, MD 21046-1746, USA

Reed, Ed (Athlete, Football Player)
1 Winning Dr
Owings Mills, MD 21117-4776, USA

Reed, Eddie (Athlete, Baseball Player)
Memphis Red Sox
708 8th Ave S
Great Falls, MT 59405-2052, USA

Reed, Ellie (Actor)
c/o Josh Glick *Grandview*
7122 Beverly Blvd Ste F
Los Angeles, CA 90036-2572, USA

Reed, Eric (Musician)
Joel Chriss
300 Mercer St Apt 3J
New York, NY 10003-6732, USA

Reed, Hub (Athlete, Basketball Player)
46601 Garretts Lake Rd
Shawnee, OK 74804-9494, USA

Reed, Jack (Athlete, Baseball Player)
PO Box 97
Silver City, MS 39166-0097, USA

Reed, Jeff (Athlete, Baseball Player)
17688 Sylvan Hill Road
Elizabethton, TN 37643, USA

Reed, Jeremy (Athlete, Baseball Player)
7100 E Lincoln Dr Unit 3107
Paradise Valley, AZ 85253-4449, USA

Reed, Jerry (Athlete, Baseball Player)
13964 106th Ave
Largo, FL 33774-4543, USA

Reed, Jillian Rose (Actor)
c/o Jessica Katz *Katz Public Relations*
14527 Dickens St
Sherman Oaks, CA 91403-3756, USA

Reed, Jim (Race Car Driver)
8 Cutler Ln
Garrison, NY 10524-3919, USA

Reed, Jody (Athlete, Baseball Player)
19153 E Briarwood Dr
Centennial, CO 80016-2161, USA

Reed, Joe (Athlete, Football Player)
201 S Lakeline Blvd Ste 902
Cedar Park, TX 78613-2419, USA

Reed, Johnny (Musician)
Jackson Artists
7251 Lowell Dr # 200
Overland Park, KS 66204-1840, USA

Reed, Jordan (Athlete, Football Player)
311 Titan Dr Apt B
Lafayette, LA 70508-5284, USA

Reed, Josh (Athlete, Football Player)

Reed, Keith (Athlete, Baseball Player)
513A S Main St
Rolesville, NC 27571-9666, USA

Reed, Nikki (Actor)
c/o Ken Stovitz *MGMT Entertainment (The Schiff Company)*
9220 W Sunset Blvd Ste 106
W Hollywood, CA 90069-3500, USA

Reed, Oscar (Athlete, Football Player)
700 Elizabeth Ln
Minneapolis, MN 55411-3340, USA

Reed, Pamela (Actor)
c/o Staff Member *Innovative Artists*
1505 10th St
Santa Monica, CA 90401-2805, USA

Reed, Peyton (Actor, Director, Producer)
c/o Staff Member *Moxie Pictures*
2644 30th St Ste 100
Santa Monica, CA 90405-3051, USA

Reed, Priscilla (Musician)
153 Rue De Grande
Brentwood, TN 37027-8011, USA

Reed, Rex (Journalist)
Dakota Hotel
1 W 72nd St Apt 86
New York, NY 10023-3425, USA

Reed, Richard A (Rick) (Baseball Player)
Pittsburgh Pirates
86 Township Road 1539
Proctorville, OH 45669-7914, USA

Reed, Richard J (Misc)
University of Washington
Atmospheric Sciences Dept
Seattle, WA 98195-0001, USA

Reed, Rick (Athlete, Baseball Player)
4938 Crestone Way
Rochester, MI 48306-1682, USA

Reed, Rick (Athlete, Baseball Player)
110 Private Drive 255
Chesapeake, OH 45619-8166, ISA

Reed, Robert (Athlete, Football Player)
21 Wells St Apt 412
Saratoga Springs, NY 12866-1214, USA

Reed, Ronald L (Ron) (Athlete, Baseball Player, Basketball Player)
2613 Cliffview Dr SW
Lilburn, GA 30047-4794, USA

Reed, Royce (Actor)
c/o Dominic Friesen *Bridge and Tunnel Communications*
8149 Santa Monica Blvd # 407
West Hollywood, CA 90046-4912, USA

Reed, Shanna (Actor)
1327 Brinkley Ave
Los Angeles, CA 90049-3619, USA

Reed, Steve (Athlete, Baseball Player)
5335 Pine Ridge Rd
Golden, CO 80403-8030, USA

Reed, Tom (Congressman, Politician)
1037 Longworth Hob
Washington, DC 20515-0542, USA

Reed, Tony (Athlete, Football Player)
PO Box 341
Odessa, MO 64076-0341, USA

Reed, Willis (Athlete, Basketball Player, Football Player)
PO Box 1779
Ruston, LA 71273-1779, USA

Reeds, Mark (Athlete, Hockey Player)
Ottawa Senators
110-1000 Palladium Dr
Ottawa, ON K2V 1A5, Canada

Reeds, Mark (Athlete, Hockey Player)
7823 Cardinal Ridge Ct
Saint Louis, MO 63119-5014, USA

Reedus, Norman (Actor)
c/o JoAnne Colonna *Brillstein Entertainment Partners*
9150 Wilshire Blvd Ste 350
Beverly Hills, CA 90212-3453, USA

Reehl, Robert (Race Car Driver)
13434 Lambert Rd
Whittier, CA 90605-2454, USA

Reekie, Joe (Athlete, Hockey Player)
5110 Rue Vendome
Lutz, FL 33558-2859

Reep, Jon (Actor, Comedian)
c/o Judi Brown *Levity Entertainment Group (LEG)*
6701 Center Dr W Ste 300
Los Angeles, CA 90045-2482, USA

Rees, Dai (Designer, Fashion Designer)
c/o Staff Member *Dai Rees*
6 Blackstock Mews
Blackstock Road
London, England N42BT, United Kingdom

Rees, Dee (Director)
c/o Lori Stonebraker *Anonymous Content*
3532 Hayden Ave
Culver City, CA 90232-2413, USA

Rees, Jed (Actor)
c/o Kim Edwards *Kirk Talent Agencies Inc*
196 3rd Ave W Suite 102
Vancouver, BC V5Y 1E9, CANADA

Rees, John (Musician)
TPA
PO Box 124
Round Corner, NSW 02158, USA

Reese, Brian Adrian (Cassidy) (Musician)
c/o Greg Cohen *Amalgam Management*
705 Town Blvd NE Apt 510
Brookhaven, GA 30319-3082, USA

Reese, Calvin (Pokey) (Athlete, Baseball Player)
12416 Sylvan Oak Way
Charlotte, NC 28273-4728, USA

Reese, Eddie (Coach, Swimmer)
University of Texas
Athletic Dept
Austin, TX 78712, USA

Reese, Guy (Athlete, Football Player)
2409 Cardinal Way
McKinney, TX 75072-5966, USA

Reese, Izell (Athlete, Football Player)
4037 Thessa Cv NE
Roswell, GA 30075-5750, USA

Reese, Jeff (Athlete, Hockey Player)
697 Maple Ave
Haddonfield, NJ 08033-1146

Reese, Kevin (Athlete, Baseball Player)
1221 Willow St
San Diego, CA 92106-2538, USA

Reese, Rich (Athlete, Baseball Player)
PO Box 2339
Carefree, AZ 85377-2339, USA

Reese, Steve (Athlete, Football Player)
1146 Parkwood Trce
Stone Mountain, GA 30083-2485, USA

Reeser, Autumn (Actor)
c/o Hilary Hansen *Vision PR*
2 Penn Plz Rm 2601
New York, NY 10121-0001, USA

Reeser, Robert (Horse Racer)
139 Barksdale Ct
Milford, DE 19963-4174, USA

Reeves, Bryant (Athlete, Basketball Player)
116458 S 4710 Rd
Muldrow, OK 74948-6882, USA

Reeves, Dan (Athlete, Football Player)
785 W Conway Dr NW
Atlanta, GA 30327-3633, USA

Reeves, Dianne (Musician)
PO Box 66
Englishtown, NJ 07726-0066, USA

Reeves, Keanu (Actor)
c/o Cheryl Maisel *PMK/BNC Public Relations*
1840 Century Park E Ste 1400
Los Angeles, CA 90067-2115, USA

Reeves, Khalid (Athlete, Basketball Player)
11519 140th St
Jamaica, NY 11436-1018, USA

Reeves, Martha (Musician)
1300 E Lafayette St Apt 1211
Detroit, MI 48207-2921, USA

Reeves, Matt (Actor, Director)
c/o Heidi Lopata *Narrative*
1601 Vine St Fl 6
Los Angeles, CA 90028-8802, USA

Reeves, Melissa (Actor)
6520 Platt Ave # 634
West Hills, CA 91307-3218, USA

Reeves, Perrey (Actor)
c/o Craig Schneider *Pinnacle Public Relations*
8721 Santa Monica Blvd # 133
W Hollywood, CA 90069-4507, USA

Reeves, Richard (Misc)
Universal Press Syndicate
4520 Main St Ste 340
Kansas City, MO 64111-7705, USA

Reeves, Ronna (Musician)
1705 Wright Meadow Ct
Mount Juliet, TN 37122-4576, USA

Reeves, Saskia (Actor)
c/o Louise Owen *Independent Talent Group*
40 Whitfield St
London W1T 2RH, UNITED KINGDOM

Reeves, Scott (Actor)
6520 Platt Ave # 634
West Hills, CA 91307-3218, USA

Reeves, Stevie (Race Car Driver)
CAA Performance Group
218 Chestnut Ave.
Kannapolis, NC 28081, USA

Reeves, Teri (Actor)
c/o Paul Brown *Industry Entertainment Partners*
955 Carrillo Dr Ste 300
Los Angeles, CA 90048-5400, USA

Reeves, Walter (Athlete, Football Player)
5013 Lincoln Oaks Dr S Apt 1805
Fort Worth, TX 76132-2250, USA

Refaeli, Bar (Actor, Model)
c/o Scott Lipps *One Management*
42 Bond St Fl 2
New York, NY 10012-2768, USA

Reffner, Bryan (Race Car Driver)
Phelon Motors
3980 Richland Ave W
Aiken, SC 29801-6320, USA

Regaibuto, Joe (Actor)
724 24th St
Santa Monica, CA 90402-3138, USA

Regalado, Rudy (Athlete, Baseball Player)
PO Box 475
Borrego Springs, CA 92004-0475, USA

Regan, Brian (Actor, Comedian)
c/o Rory Rosegarten *Conversation Company*
1044 Northern Blvd Ste 304
Roslyn, NY 11576-1589, USA

Regan, Bridget (Actor)
c/o Annick Oppenheim *Wolf-Kasteler Public Relations*
6255 W Sunset Blvd Ste 1111
Los Angeles, CA 90028-7426, USA

Regan, Chris (Writer)
c/o Staff Member *Gersh*
9465 Wilshire Blvd Ste 600
Beverly Hills, CA 90212-2605, USA

Regan, Judith (Business Person, Writer)
c/o Staff Member *Regan Arts*
9255 Doheny Rd Apt 1206
West Hollywood, CA 90069-3214, USA

Regan, Laura (Actor)
c/o Ethan Salter *Greene & Associates*
1901 Avenue of the Stars Ste 130
Los Angeles, CA 90067-6030, USA

Regan, Phil (Athlete, Baseball Player, Coach)
1687 SW Harbour Isles Cir # 6
Port St Lucie, FL 34986-3405, USA

Regazzoni, Clay (Race Car Driver)
Via Monzoni 13
Lugano 06900, SWITZERLAND

Regbo, Toby (Actor)
c/o Brantley Brown *Authentic Talent & Literary Management*
3615 Eastham Dr # 650
Culver City, CA 90232-2410, USA

Regeher, Robyn (Athlete, Football Player)
1721 Monterey Blvd
Hermosa Beach, CA 90254-2905, USA

Regehr, Duncan (Actor)
2501 Main St
Santa Monica, CA 90405, USA

Regen, Elizabeth (Actor)
c/o Mark Measures *Kazarian, Measures, Ruskin & Associates*
5200 Lankershim Blvd Ste 820
N Hollywood, CA 91601-3194, USA

Reger, John (Athlete, Football Player)
9919 SW 42nd Rd
Gainesville, FL 32608-7103, USA

Reger, Nate (Writer)
c/o Staff Member *ICM Partners*
10250 Constellation Blvd Fl 7
Los Angeles, CA 90067-6207, USA

Reggio, Godfrey (Director)
Regional Education Institute
PO Box 2404
Santa Fe, NM 87504-2404, USA

Reghi, Mike (Baseball Player)
9344 Saybrook Dr
North Ridgeville, OH 44039-8748, USA

Regier, Darcy (Athlete, Hockey Player)
11302 E Paradise Ln
Scottsdale, AZ 85255-8920

Regilio, Nick (Athlete, Baseball Player)
4239 Hidden Lake Dr
Port Orange, FL 32129-7531, USA

Regine (Business Person)
502 Park Ave
New York, NY 10022-1108, USA

Regis, John (Athlete, Track Athlete)
67 Fairby Road
London SE12, UNITED KINGDOM (UK)

Register, Steven (Athlete, Baseball Player)
698 Hunter Ct
Auburn, AL 36832-5403, USA

Regner, Tom (Athlete, Football Player)
951 Craigmont Dr
Reno, NV 89511-1356, USA

Rehberg, Denny (Congressman, Politician)
2448 Rayburn Hob
Washington, DC 20515-3227, USA

Rehberg, Scott (Athlete, Football Player)
1153 Thistle Ln
Lebanon, OH 45036-7788, USA

Rehder, Tom (Athlete, Football Player)
730 Monarch Ln
Nipomo, CA 93444-9418, USA

Rehm, Diane (Radio Personality)
c/o Staff Member *National Public Radio (NPR)*
635 Massachusetts Ave NW
Washington, DC 20001-3740, USA

Rehm, Fred (Athlete, Basketball Player)
19340A Stonehedge Dr
Brookfield, WI 53045-3665, USA

Rehr, Frank (Cartoonist)
United Feature Syndicate
200 Madison Ave
New York, NY 10016-3903, USA

Rehrer-Carteaux, Rita (Athlete, Baseball Player)
3210 Kenwood Ave
Fort Wayne, IN 46805-2932, USA

Reich, Frank M (Athlete, Football Player)
12551 Glendurgan Dr
Carmel, IN 46032-8314, USA

Reich, Jason (Writer)
c/o Staff Member *Kaplan-Stahler Agency*
8383 Wilshire Blvd Ste 923
Beverly Hills, CA 90211-2443, USA

Reich, John (Director)
724 Bohemia Pkwy
Sayville, NY 11782-3300, USA

Reich, Robert (Politician)
1230 Bonita Ave
Berkeley, CA 94709-1923, USA

Reichard, Daniel (Actor)

Reichardt, Rick (Athlete, Baseball Player)
2605 NW 90th Ter
Gainesville, FL 32606-6742, USA

Reichel, Robert (Athlete, Hockey Player)
Lesni 391
Litvinov, ON 436 01, Czech Republic

Reichenbach, Mike (Athlete, Football Player)
2230 Cloverly Cir
Jamison, PA 18929-1555, USA

Reichert, Bill (Race Car Driver)
Bar's Leak Racing
203 S Gould St
Owosso, MI 48867-3249, USA

Reichert, Dan (Athlete, Baseball Player)
6620 Glass Ridge Dr
Lincoln, NE 68526-9752, USA

Reichert, Jack F (Business Person)
580 Douglas Dr
Lake Forest, IL 60045-3342, USA

Reichert, Tanja (Actor)
Pacific Artists
1404-510 Hastings St W
Vancouver, BC V6B 1L8, CANADA

Reichman, Fred (Artist)
1235 Stanyan St
San Francisco, CA 94117-3816, USA

Reichow, Garet N (Athlete, Football Player)
PO Box 31339
Santa Fe, NM 87594-1339, USA

Reichs, Kathy (Writer)
c/o Jennifer Rudolph Walsh *WME/IMG (NY)*
11 Madison Ave Fl 18
New York, NY 10010-3669, USA

Reid, Andy (Coach)
c/o Bob LaMonte *Professional Sports Representation*
2425 Manzanita Ln
Reno, NV 89509-7027, USA

Reid, Antonio (L.A.) (Producer)
Kear Music, Carter Turner Co
9229 W Sunset Blvd
W Hollywood, CA 90069-3402, USA

Reid, Brandon (Athlete, Hockey Player)
21 Place du Champagne
Kirkland, QC H9H 5J4, Canada

Reid, Caraun (Athlete, Football Player)
c/o Michael McCartney *Priority Sports & Entertainment (Chicago)*
325 N La Salle Dr Ste 650
Chicago, IL 60654-8182, USA

Reid, Christopher (Actor)
c/o Rod Baron *Baron Entertainment*
13848 Ventura Blvd Ste A
Sherman Oaks, CA 91423-3654

Reid, Corbin (Actor)
c/o Ricky Rollins *Hyphenate Creative Management*
8149 Santa Monica Blvd # 111
West Hollywood, CA 90046-4912, USA

Reid, Daphne (Actor)
New Millenium
1704 Parkwood Ave
Richmond, VA 23220-5324, USA

Reid, Dave (Athlete, Hockey Player)
Peterborough Petes
151 Lansdowne St W
Peterborough, ON K9J 1Y4, Canada

Reid, Dave (Athlete, Hockey Player)
1522 Hawkswood Dr RR 1
Ennismore, ON K0L 1T0, Canada

Reid, Don S (Musician, Songwriter, Writer)
American Major Talent
8747 W Commerce St
Hernando, MS 38632-8445, USA

Reid, Dorice (Athlete, Baseball Player)
1165 Via Santa Paulo
Vista, CA 92081-6332, USA

Reid, Douglas (Race Car Driver)
Doug Reid Racing
1217 24th Ave
Hueytown, AL 35023-3667, USA

Reid, Harold (Musician, Songwriter, Writer)
1004 E Beverley St
Staunton, VA 24401-3503, USA

Reid, Harry (Politician)
1155 23rd St NW Apt 2E
Washington, DC 20037-3302, USA

Reid, Jah (Athlete, Football Player)
c/o Derrick Fox *Derrick Fox Management*
Prefers to be contacted by telephone
CA, USA

Reid, Jesse (Athlete, Baseball Player)
2641 Carey Station Rd
Greensboro, GA 30642-2625, USA

Reid, Joe (Athlete, Football Player)
651 Shady Hollow St
Houston, TX 77056-1635, USA

Reid, Joy-Ann (Correspondent)
NBCU
30 Rockefeller Plz Fl 2
New York, NY 10112-0037, USA

Reid, J R (Athlete, Basketball Player)
121 Cemetary St
Chester, SC 29706-1620, USA

Reid, Michael B (Mike) (Athlete, Football Player)
825 Overton Ln
Nashville, TN 37220-1515, USA

Reid, Michael Eric (Actor)
c/o Staff Member *CeSoir Publicity and Events*
105 W Alameda Ave Ste 205
Burbank, CA 91502-2254, USA

Reid, Mike (Athlete, Football Player)
PO Box 362
Pacolet, SC 29372-0362, USA

Reid, Mike (Golfer)
935 E 80 N
Orem, UT 84097-4978, USA

Reid, Norman R (Misc)
50 Brabourne Rise
Park Langley Beckenham
Kent, UNITED KINGDOM (UK)

Reid, Scott (Athlete, Baseball Player)
10827 S 26th Ave
Phoenix, AZ 85041-9630, USA

Reid, Storm (Actor)
c/o Amanda Nesbitt *The Lede Company*
9701 Wilshire Blvd # 930
Beverly Hills, CA 90212-2020, USA

Reid, Tara (Actor)
c/o Staff Member *Wonder Works Studios Entertainment Group*
1149 N Gower St Ste 275
Los Angeles, CA 90038-1801, USA

Reid, Tim (Actor, Director)
New Millennium Studios
29 S Market St
Petersburg, VA 23803-4215, USA

Reid, Tom (Athlete, Hockey Player)
317 Washington St
Saint Paul, MN 55102-1609

Reid, Tom (Athlete, Hockey Player)
9320 Abigail Ct
Inver Grove Heights, MN 55077-4218

Reid, William J (Athlete, Football Player)
315 Ramona St
Palo Alto, CA 94301-1440, USA

Reierson, Dave (Athlete, Hockey Player)
99 Grand Ave
Grand Haven, MI 49417-2408

Reiff, Riley (Athlete, Football Player)
c/o Neil Cornrich *NC Sports, LLC*
best to contact via email
Columbus, OH 43201, USA

Reifsnyder, Robert H (Bob) (Athlete, Football Player)
4 Helm Ct
Berlin, MD 21811-1836, USA

Reightler, Kenneth S Captain (Astronaut)
1602 Honeysuckle Ridge Ct
Annapolis, MD 21401-6425, USA

Reightler Jr, Kenneth S (Astronaut)
1602 Honeysuckle Ridge Ct
Annapolis, MD 21401-6425, USA

Reihner, George (Athlete, Football Player)
1801 N Washington Ave
Scranton, PA 18509-1744, USA

Reilly, Gabrielle (Model)
PO Box 3145
Shawnee, KS 66203-0145, USA

Reilly, John (Actor)
c/o Peter Young *Sovereign Talent Group*
1642 Westwood Blvd Ste 202
Los Angeles, CA 90024-5609, USA

Reilly, John C (Actor)
c/o Peg Donegan *Framework Entertainment*
9057 Nemo St # C
W Hollywood, CA 90069-5511, USA

Reilly, Kelly (Actor)
c/o Michael Duff *Troika*
10A Christina St.
London EC2A 4PA, UNITED KINGDOM

Reilly, Kevin (Athlete, Football Player)
Webster Farms
521 Rothbury Rd
Wilmington, DE 19803-2439, USA

Reilly, Mike (Athlete, Baseball Player)
131 Smithfield Rd
Battle Creek, MI 49015-3545, USA

Reilly, Mike (Athlete, Football Player)
708 Loretto Ct
Dubuque, IA 52003-7813, USA

Reilly, Rick (Writer)
236 Cook St
Denver, CO 80206-5305, USA

Reilly, Trevor (Athlete, Football Player)

Reilly II, James F (Astronaut)
15903 Lake Lodge Dr
Houston, TX 77062-4745, USA

Reimer, James (Athlete, Hockey Player)
PO Box 508
Arborg, MB R0C 0A0, Canada

Reimer, Kevin (Athlete, Baseball Player)
1797 W 28th Ave Apt 250
Apache Junction, AZ 85120-9504, USA

Reimer, Roland (Religious Leader)
mennonite Brethren Churches Conference
8000 W 21st St N
Wichita, KS 67205-1744, USA

Reimers, Bruce (Athlete, Football Player)
2206 W River Dr
Humboldt, IA 50548-2638, USA

Reimold, Nolan (Athlete, Baseball Player)
10 Callahan Rd
Greenville, PA 16125-9629, USA

Rein, Andrew (Athlete, Olympic Athlete, Wrestler)
5251 Loop Hts
Rhinelander, WI 54501-2181, United States

Rein, Andrew (Athlete, Olympic Athlete, Wrestler)
5251 Loop Hts
Rhinelander, WI 54501-2181, USA

Reina (Musician)
c/o Staff Member *Diva Central Inc*
7510 W Sunset Blvd # 1445
Los Angeles, CA 90046-3408, USA

Reineck, Thomas (Athlete)
Graf-Bernadotte-Str 4
Essen 45133, GERMANY

Reineke, Chad (Athlete, Baseball Player)
1904 Tanglewood Dr
Defiance, OH 43512-3638, USA

Reiner, Alysia (Actor)
c/o Melanie Greene *Affirmative Entertainment*
6525 W Sunset Blvd # 7
Los Angeles, CA 90028-7212, USA

Reiner, Carl (Actor, Director)
c/o Staff Member *Clear Productions*
9171 Wilshire Blvd Ste 350
Beverly Hills, CA 90210-5523, USA

Reiner, John (Cartoonist)
Parade Magazine
30 Nathan Hale Dr Apt 71B
Huntington, NY 11743-7034, USA

Reiner, Rob (Actor, Director)
c/o Staff Member *Reiner/Greisman*
11999 San Vicente Blvd Ste 220
Los Angeles, CA 90049-5130, USA

Reinfeldt, Mike (Athlete, Football Player)
1204 Waterstone Blvd
Franklin, TN 37069-7208, USA

Reinhard, Bill (Athlete, Football Player)
5302 E Daggett St
Long Beach, CA 90815-3032, USA

Reinhardt, Doug (Athlete, Baseball Player, Reality Star)
c/o Liza Anderson *Anderson Group Public Relations*
8060 Melrose Ave Fl 4
Los Angeles, CA 90046-7038, USA

Reinhart, Haley (Actor, Musician, Reality Star)
c/o Scott Mantell *ICM Partners*
10250 Constellation Blvd Fl 7
Los Angeles, CA 90067-6207, USA

Reinhart, Lili (Actor)
c/o Jeffrey Chassen *Imprint PR*
6121 W Sunset Blvd
Neuehouse
Los Angeles, CA 90028-6442, USA

Reinhart, Paul (Athlete, Hockey Player)
2911 Altamont Cres
West Vancouver, BC V7V 3B9, Canada

Reinhold, Judge (Actor, Director)
17 La Vega
Lamy, NM 87540-9768, USA

Reininger, Travis (Athlete, Baseball Player)
464 Hunter Ct
Brighton, CO 80601-4360, USA

Reinking, Ann (Actor, Dancer, Director)
International Creative Mgmt
40 W 57th St Ste 1800
New York, NY 10019-4033, USA

Reinprecht, Steven (Athlete, Hockey Player)
45 S Garfield St
Denver, CO 80209-3115

Reinsdorf, Jerry (Baseball Player)
Chicago White Sox
40 E Elm St
Chicago, IL 60611-1016, USA

Reirden, Todd (Athlete, Hockey Player)
45 S Garfield St
Denver, CO 80209-3115

Reirden, Todd (Athlete, Hockey Player)
Pittsburgh Penguins
66 Mario Lemieux Pl Ste 2
Pittsburgh, PA 15219-3504

Reis, Tommy (Athlete, Baseball Player)
15456 SW 15th Terrace Rd
Ocala, FL 34473-8862, USA

Reiser, Paul (Actor, Producer)
c/o Mark Rousso *Industry Entertainment Partners*
955 Carrillo Dr Ste 300
Los Angeles, CA 90048-5400, USA

Reiser, Robbie (Race Car Driver)
Reiser Motorsports
8347 Glacier Dr
Denver, NC 28037-8994, USA

Reiss, Howard (Misc)
2336 Spaulding Ave
Berkeley, CA 94703-1628, USA

Reist, Chelsey (Actor)
c/o Brandi George *Advantage PR*
3900 W Alameda Ave Ste 1200
Burbank, CA 91505-4317, USA

Reisz, Michael (Actor)
c/o Sara Bottfeld *Industry Entertainment Partners*
955 Carrillo Dr Ste 300
Los Angeles, CA 90048-5400, USA

Reitenour, Megan (Race Car Driver)
c/o Gigi Rock *Heraea Marketing*
10905 E Pear Tree Dr
Cornville, AZ 86325-5523, USA

Reiter, Mario (Skier)
Hauselweg 5
Rankweil 06830, AUSTRIA

Reiter, Thomas (Astronaut)
Europe Astronaut Center
European Space Centre I EAC Linder Hohe Postfach 90 60 96
Koln D-51147, GERMANY

Reith, Brian (Athlete, Baseball Player)
5830 Lexington Dr
Parrish, FL 34219-5806, USA

Reitman, Ivan (Director, Producer)
900 Cold Springs Rd
Montecito, CA 93108-1009, USA

Reitman, Jason (Director)
c/o BeBe Lerner *ID Public Relations*
7060 Hollywood Blvd Fl 8th
Los Angeles, CA 90028-6021, USA

Reitman, Joe (Actor)
c/o Suzanne (Sue) Wohl *TalentWorks*
3500 W Olive Ave Ste 1400
Burbank, CA 91505-5512, USA

Reitsma, Chris (Athlete, Baseball Player)
32 Howell Bluff Rd
Ponce De Leon, FL 32455-4632, USA

Reitz, Joe (Athlete, Football Player)

Reitz, Ken (Athlete, Baseball Player)
1704 Carbine Ln
Saint Charles, MO 63303-1104, USA

ReK (Artist)
Rek's World
7608 Bayshore Dr
Margate City, NJ 08402-2058, USA

Rekar, Bryan (Athlete, Baseball Player)
4326 Waterville Ave
Wesley Chapel, FL 33543-7037, USA

Reklow, Jesse (Cartoonist)
2415 College Ave Apt 20
Berkeley, CA 94704-2458, USA

Relaford, Desmond (Athlete, Baseball Player)
11334 Aston Hall Dr
Jacksonville, FL 32246-0646, USA

Relch, Steve (Baseball Player)
US Olympic Team
28 Scofield Hill Rd
Washington Depot, CT 06794-1012, USA

Reld, Andy (Athlete, Football Coach, Football Player)
1215 Page Ter
Villanova, PA 19085-2132, USA

Relient K (Music Group)
c/o Kevin Spellman *Vector Management*
1100 Glendon Ave Ste 2000
Los Angeles, CA 90024-3524, USA

Reliford, Charlie (Baseball Player)
1509 Cypress St
Ashland, KY 41101-3624, USA

Reliford, Charlie (Athlete, Baseball Player)
1509 Cypress St
Ashland, KY 41101-3624, USA

Rell, M Jodi (Politician)
18 Andover Ct
Brookfield, CT 06804-2715, USA

Rellford, Richard (Athlete, Basketball Player)
28 Balfour Rd W
Palm Beach Gardens, FL 33418-7090, USA

R.E.M. (Music Group)
170 College Ave
Athens, GA 30601-2805, US

Remar, James (Actor)
c/o Steven Siebert *Lighthouse Entertainment Group*
9229 W Sunset Blvd Ste 630
W Hollywood, CA 90069-3419, USA

Rembert, Johnny (Athlete, Football Player)
809 W Cumberland Ct
Saint Johns, FL 32259-4515, USA

Remington, Deborah W (Artist)
309 W Broadway Apt 6
New York, NY 10013-5327, USA

Remini, Leah (Actor)
PO Box 15669
N Hollywood, CA 91615-5669, USA

Remlinger, Mike (Athlete, Baseball Player)
18331 N 93rd Way
Scottsdale, AZ 85255-6048, USA

Remmen, Larry (Horse Racer)
144 Konner Ave
Pine Brook, NJ 07058-9431, USA

Remmen, Ray (Horse Racer)
144 Konner Ave
Pine Brook, NJ 07058-9431, USA

Remmerswaal, Win (Athlete, Baseball Player)
Doktor Van Praag St 16
Wassenaar, Holland

Remmert, Dennis (Athlete, Football Player)
3933 Briarwood Dr
Cedar Falls, IA 50613-7508, USA

Remnick, David (Writer)
c/o Robert (Bob) Bookman *Paradigm*
8942 Wilshire Blvd
Beverly Hills, CA 90211-1908, USA

Remy, Gerald P (Jerry) (Athlete, Baseball Player)
137 Fox Rd Unit 411
Waltham, MA 02451-0210, USA

Renard, Mercedes (Actor)
c/o Evan Hainey *Untitled Entertainment*
350 S Beverly Dr Ste 200
Beverly Hills, CA 90212-4819, USA

Renaud, Line (Musician)
5 Rue du Bois-de-Boulogne
Paris 75116, FRANCE

Renaud, Mark (Athlete, Hockey Player)
11788 Tecumseh Rd E
Windsor, ON N8N 1L7, Canada

Renault, Dennis (Cartoonist)
Sacramento Bee
Editorial Dept
21st & Q Sts
Sacramento, CA 95852, USA

Rencher, Terrence (Athlete, Basketball Player)
2001 S MO Pac Expy Apt 924
Austin, TX 78746-7579, USA

Rendall, Mark (Actor)
c/o Staff Member *Artist Management Inc*
464 King St E
Toronto, ON M5A 1L7, CANADA

Rendell, Edward (Politician)
6114 Creekside Dr
Flourtown, PA 19031-1407, USA

Render, Michael (Killer Mike) (Musician)
2129 Hosea L Williams Dr SE
Atlanta, GA 30317-2553, USA

Rendon, Chelsea (Actor)
c/o Alex Czuleger *The Green Room*
7080 Hollywood Blvd Ste 1100
Los Angeles, CA 90028-6938, USA

Rene, France-Albert (President)
President's Office
State House
Victoria
Mahe, SEYCHELLES

Renee, Ciara (Actor)
c/o Joshua Pasch *Authentic Talent & Literary Management*
3615 Eastham Dr # 650
Culver City, CA 90232-2410, USA

Renfree, Sean (Athlete, Football Player)
c/o Eric Metz *Lock Metz Milanovic LLC*
6900 E Camelback Rd Ste 600
Scottsdale, AZ 85251-8044, USA

Renfro, Leonard (Athlete, Football Player)
8893 E 24th Pl Unit 103
Denver, CO 80238-2839, USA

Renfro, Mike (Athlete, Football Player)
PO Box 93073
Southlake, TX 76092-1073, USA

Renfroe, Jay (Producer)
c/o Staff Member *Renegade 83 Entertainment*
12925 Riverside Dr Bldg 413
Sherman Oaks, CA 91423-5263, USA

Renfroe, Laddie (Athlete, Baseball Player)
236 Hickory Ln
Batesville, MS 38606-9339, USA

Rengel, Mike (Athlete, Football Player)
1782 Montane Dr E
Golden, CO 80401, USA

Renick, Rick (Athlete, Baseball Player)
7320 Hawkins Rd
Sarasota, FL 34241-9375, USA

Renier, Jeremie (Actor)
c/o Marc Hamou *Thruline Entertainment*
9250 Wilshire Blvd Fl Ground
Beverly Hills, CA 90212-3352, USA

Renis, Tony (Musician)
Ischia Global
501 Deep Valley Dr Fl 1
Rolling Hills Estates, CA 90274-7605, USA

Renk, Silke (Athlete, Track Athlete)
Erhard-Hubner-Str 13
Halle/S 06132, GERMANY

Renko, Steven (Steve) (Athlete, Baseball Player)
15812 W 136th St
Olathe, KS 66062-5310, USA

Renna, Eugene A (Business Person)
Mobil Corp
3225 Gallows Rd
Fairfax, VA 22037-0003, USA

Renna, Patrick (Actor)
c/o Staff Member *Karen Renna & Associates*
PO Box 4227
Burbank, CA 91503-4227, USA

Renne, Paul (Misc)
Berkeley Geochronology Center
2445 Ridge Road
Berkeley, CA 94709, USA

Rennebohm, J Fred (Religious Leader)
Congregational Christian Churches Assn
PO Box 1620
Oak Creek, MI 53154, USA

Rennebohm, J Fred (Misc)
Holbeinstr 58
Berlin 12203, GERMANY

Renner, Jeremy (Actor)
c/o Staff Member *The Combine*
1226 S Holt Ave
Los Angeles, CA 90035-2408, USA

Rennert, Dutch (Baseball Player)
4608 Peele St
Elkton, FL 32033-4015, USA

Rennert, Dutch (Athlete, Baseball Player)
4608 Peele St
Elkton, FL 32033-4015, USA

Renni, Gino (Actor)
c/o Staff Member *Telefe (Argentina)*
Pavon 2444
Buenos Aires C1248AAT, ARGENTINA

Reno, Jean (Actor)
c/o Alexandra Schamis *AS Talents*
101, Rue De Lille
Paris 75007, FRANCE

Renoth, Heldi (Skier)
Lercheckerweg 23
Berchtesgaden 83471, GERMANY

Rensberger, Scott (Journalist)
914 7th St NE
Washington, DC 20002-3612, USA

Renteria, Edgar (Athlete, Baseball Player)
6633 Allison Rd
Miami, FL 33141-4510, USA

Renteria, Rich (Athlete, Baseball Player)
41905 Chaparral Dr
Temecula, CA 92592-8897, USA

Renteria, Rick (Athlete, Baseball Player)
41905 Chaparral Dr
Temecula, CA 92592-8897, USA

Rentie, Caesar (Athlete, Football Player)
7614 Fallen Antler Pl
Arlington, TX 76002-4320, USA

Renton, Kristen (Actor, Model)
c/o Vera Kim *Boudoir Agency*
1600 Rosecrans Ave
Media Center Fl 4
Manhattan Beach, CA 90266-3708, USA

Rentzel, Lance (Athlete, Football Player)
12104 Monument Dr Apt 354
Fairfax, VA 22033-4053, USA

Rentzepis, Peter M (Misc)
University of California
Chemistry Dept
Irvine, CA 92717, USA

Renucci, Robin (Actor)
64 rue Condorcet
Paris, FRANCE 75009

Reo, Don (Producer)
c/o Debbee Klein *Paradigm*
8942 Wilshire Blvd
Beverly Hills, CA 90211-1908, USA

REO Speedwagon (Music Group)
c/o Staff Member *TC Management*
10960 Wilshire Blvd Ste 1415
Los Angeles, CA 90024-3729, USA

Repeta, Nina (Actor)
Gage Group
14724 Ventura Blvd Ste 505
Sherman Oaks, CA 91403-3505, USA

Repin, Vadim V (Musician)
Eckholdtweg 2A
Lubeck 23566, GERMANY

Repko, Jason (Athlete, Baseball Player)
3503 Mount Adams View Dr
West Richland, WA 99353-8760, USA

Repoz, Roger (Athlete, Baseball Player)
930 Whitewater Dr
Fullerton, CA 92833-2194, USA

Rerych, Stephen (Athlete, Olympic Athlete, Swimmer)
6 Holiday Dr
Arden, NC 28704-8816, USA

Resch, Alexander (Athlete)
BSD
An der Schiessstatte 4
Berchtesgaden 83471, GERMANY

Resch, Chico (Athlete, Hockey Player)
PO Box 207
1171 Dahler Ave
Emily, MN 56447-0207, USA

Resch, Glenn "'Chico'" (Athlete, Hockey Player)
New Jersey Devils
165 Mulberry St
Newark, NJ 07102-3607

Resch, Glenn "'Chico'" (Athlete, Hockey Player)
607 8th St
Lyndhurst, NJ 07071-3147

Rescher, Nicholas (Misc)
1033 Milton St
Pittsburgh, PA 15218-1228, USA

Resop, Chris (Athlete, Baseball Player)
257 Ridge Dr
Naples, FL 34108-2902, USA

Resor, Helen (Athlete, Hockey Player, Olympic Athlete)
22 N Stanwich Rd
Greenwich, CT 06831-2841, USA

Ressler, Glenn E (Athlete, Football Player)
1524 Woodcreek Dr
Mechanicsburg, PA 17055-6766, USA

Reston, James (Journalist)
4714 Hunt Ave
Chevy Chase, MD 20815-5423, USA

Restovich, Michael (Athlete, Baseball Player)
3245 Hill Ct SW
Rochester, MN 55902-6633, USA

Retherford, Dave (Athlete, Football Player)
6400 Blue Stone Rd Unit 3033
Atlanta, GA 30328-3956, USA

Retore, Guy (Director)
Theatre de l'Est Parislen
159 Ave Gambetta
Paris 75020, FRANCE

Retta (Actor, Comedian)
c/o Sam Maydew *Silver Lining Entertainment*
421 S Beverly Dr Fl 7
Beverly Hills, CA 90212-4408, USA

Rettenmund, Merv (Athlete, Baseball Player)
655 India St Unit 123
San Diego, CA 92101-6738, USA

Retton, Mary Lou (Athlete, Gymnast)
Michael Suttle Business Management
23427 Fairway Valley Ln
Katy, TX 77494-2021, USA

Rettondini, Francesca (Actor)
c/o Staff Member *C.D.A. Studio Di Nardo*
Via Cavour
Rome 00184, ITALY

Retzer, Ken (Athlete, Baseball Player)
8445 Las Vegas Blvd S Apt 1137
Las Vegas, NV 89123-1693, USA

Retzer, Otto W (Director)
Justinus-Kerner-Str 10
Munich 80686, GERMANY

Retzlaff, Palmer (Pete) (Athlete, Football Player)
669 New Rd
Gilbertsville, PA 19525-9613, USA

Reuben, Gloria (Actor)
c/o Gary Mantoosh *Baker Winokur Ryder Public Relations*
9100 Wilshire Blvd
W Tower #500
Beverly Hills, CA 90212-3415, USA

Reubens, Paul (Actor, Comedian)
PO Box 29373
Los Angeles, CA 90029-0373, USA

Reuschel, Paul (Athlete, Baseball Player)
1143 Stacy Ln
Macomb, IL 61455-2646, USA

Reuschel, Ricky E (Rick) (Athlete, Baseball Player)
PO Box 143
Renfrew, PA 16053-0143, USA

Reuss, Jerry (Athlete, Baseball Player)
c/o Staff Member *JD Legends Promotions*
10808 Foothill Blvd Ste 160 PMB 454
Rancho Cucamonga, CA 91730-0601, USA

Reuten, Thekla (Actor)
c/o Paula Rosenberg *ICA Talent Management*
1112 Montana Ave Ste 520
Santa Monica, CA 90403-7236, USA

Reuter, Edzard (Business Person)
Daimler-benz AG
Postfach 800230
Stuttgart 70546, GERMANY

Reutershan, Randy (Athlete, Football Player)
105 NE 11th St
Delray Beach, FL 33444-4051, USA

Reutimann, David (Race Car Driver)
6910 Wire Rd
Zephyrhills, FL 33542-1656, USA

Reveiz, Fuad (Athlete, Football Player)
2160 Lakeside Centre Way Ste 250
Knoxville, TN 37922-0201, USA

Revell, Graeme (Composer)
APRA
PO Box 567
Crow's Nest, NSW 02065, AUSTRALIA

Revenig, Todd (Athlete, Baseball Player)
2622 E Birchwood Pl
Chandler, AZ 85249-3520, USA

Revere, Ben (Athlete, Baseball Player)
108 White Oak Dr
Richmond, KY 40475-8619, USA

Reverho, Christine (Actor)
c/o Staff Member *ArtMedia*
8 rue Danielle Casanova
Paris 75002, FRANCE

Revering, Dave (Athlete, Baseball Player)
1063 Crows Wing Way
Ivins, UT 84738-6364, USA

Revill, Clive (Actor)
15029 Encanto Dr
Sherman Oaks, CA 91403-4409, USA

Revis, Darrelle (Athlete, Football Player)
c/o Neil Schwartz *Schwartz & Feinsod*
4 Hillandale Rd
Rye Brook, NY 10573-1705, USA

Revolori, Tony (Actor)
c/o Marnie Briskin *Circle of Confusion (NY)*
270 Lafayette St Ste 402
New York, NY 10012-3327, USA

Revolution Mother (Music Group, Musician)
c/o Staff Member *Velvet Hammer*
9014 Melrose Ave
Los Angeles, CA 90069-5610, USA

Revs, The (Music Group)
c/o Staff Member *Paradigm (Monterey)*
404 W Franklin St
Monterey, CA 93940-2303, USA

Rex (Musician)
Concrete Mgmt
361 W Broadway # 200
New York, NY 10013-2209, USA

Rex, Simon (Actor, Musician)
c/o Katie Mason Stern *Luber Roklin Management*
5815 W Sunset Blvd Ste 208
Los Angeles, CA 90028-6481, USA

Rexha, Bebe (Musician)
c/o Sarah Stennett *Turn First Artists (UK)*
Grove Studios Adie Road
London W6 0PW, UNITED KINGDOM

Rey, Paola (Actor)
c/o Gabriel Blanco *Gabriel Blanco Iglesias (Mexico)*
Rio Balsas 35-32
Colonia Cuauhtemoc
DF 06500, Mexico

Rey, Vincent (Athlete, Football Player)

Reyburn, Daniel (Athlete, Baseball Player)
7127 Old Franklin Rd
Fairview, TN 37062-9159, USA

Reyes, Anthony (Athlete, Baseball Player)
8929 Watson Ave
Whittier, CA 90605-2035, USA

Reyes, Carlos (Athlete, Baseball Player)
7205 N Cortez Ave
Tampa, FL 33614-2638, USA

reyes, Jo-Jo (Athlete, Baseball Player)
7539 Whitegate Ave
Riverside, CA 92506-5455, USA

Reyes, Jose (Athlete, Baseball Player)
24 Stone Hill Dr S
Manhasset, NY 11030-4426, USA

Reyes, Judy (Actor)
c/o Liza Anderson *Anderson Group Public Relations*
8060 Melrose Ave Fl 4
Los Angeles, CA 90046-7038, USA

Reyes, Kendall (Athlete, Football Player)
c/o Alan Herman *Sportstars Inc*
1370 Avenue of the Americas Fl 19
New York, NY 10019-4602, USA

Reyes, Lalo (Actor)
c/o Paul Uvanitte *ProActive Management Group (PMG)*
10944 Bluffside Dr Apt 213
Studio City, CA 91604-3362, USA

Reyes, Natalia (Actor)
c/o Liam Scholey *Vision Entertainment*
119 Hurricane St
Marina Del Rey, CA 90292-5974, USA

Reyes, Sandra (Actor)
c/o Staff Member *TV Caracol*
Calle 76 #11 - 35
Piso 10AA
Bogota DC 26484, COLOMBIA

Reyes, Senen (Sen Dog) (Actor, Composer, Musician)
c/o Randy Cabrera *Venture IAB*
3211 Cahuenga Blvd W Ste 104
Los Angeles, CA 90068-1372, USA

Reyes, Silvestre (Congressman, Politician)
2210 Rayburn Hob
Washington, DC 20515-3221, USA

Reymundo, Alex (Comedian)
c/o Robert (Bob) Wallerstein *Hirsch Wallerstein Hayum Matlof & Fishman*
10100 Santa Monica Blvd Fl 23
Los Angeles, CA 90067-4003, USA

Reynolds, Alastair (Writer)
P F D Drury House
34-43 Russell St
London WC2B 5HA, UNITED KINGDOM (UK)

Reynolds, Archie (Athlete, Baseball Player)
1828 Pinecrest Dr
Tyler, TX 75701-5006, USA

Reynolds, Bob (Athlete, Baseball Player)
PO Box 2529
Unit K1
Ocean Shores, WA 98569-2529, USA

Reynolds, Caleb (Reality Star)
c/o Staff Member *Cunningham Escott Slevin & Doherty (CESD)*
10635 Santa Monica Blvd Ste 130
Los Angeles, CA 90025-8306, USA

Reynolds, Craig (Athlete, Baseball Player)
4210 Hidden Links Ct
Kingwood, TX 77339-5308, USA

Reynolds, Dallas (Athlete, Football Player)
c/o Frank Bauer *Sun West Sports*
7883 N Pershing Ave
Stockton, CA 95207-1749, USA

Reynolds, Debbie (Actor, Musician)
6514 Lankershim Blvd
N Hollywood, CA 91606-2409, USA

Reynolds, Don (Athlete, Baseball Player)
6035 NE 35th Pl
Portland, OR 97211-7358, USA

Reynolds, Ed (Athlete, Football Player)
173 Moyer Rd
Stoneville, NC 27048-8462, USA

Reynolds, Garett (Athlete, Football Player)
c/o Chad Speck *Allegiant Athletic Agency*
35 Market Sq Ste 201
Knoxville, TN 37902-1420, USA

Reynolds, Gene (Actor, Producer)
2034 Castilian Dr
Los Angeles, CA 90068-2609, USA

Reynolds, Greg (Athlete, Baseball Player)

Reynolds, Harold (Athlete, Baseball Player)
2890 NW Angelica Dr
Corvallis, OR 97330-3619, USA

Reynolds, Harry (Butch) (Athlete, Track Athlete)
Advantage International
1025 Thomas Jefferson St NW # 450
Washington, DC 20007-5201, USA

Reynolds, Jack (Athlete, Football Player)
11480 SW 102nd St
Miami, FL 33176-2588, USA

Reynolds, Jamai (Athlete, Football Player)
PO Box 10628
Green Bay, WI 54307-0628, USA

Reynolds, Jamal (Athlete, Football Player)
31 Sellers Dr
Q
Crawfordville, FL 32327-0595, USA

Reynolds, James (Actor)
1925 Hanscom Dr
South Pasadena, CA 91030-4009, USA

Reynolds, James (Baseball Player)
708 Highpoint Dr
Rocky Hill, CT 06067-1088, USA

Reynolds, Jerry O (Coach)
Sacramento Kings
1 Sports Pkwy
Arco Arena
Sacramento, CA 95834-2301, USA

Reynolds, Jim (Athlete, Baseball Player)
708 Highpoint Dr
Rocky Hill, CT 06067-1088, USA

Reynolds, Ken (Athlete, Baseball Player)
182 Greenwood St
Marlborough, MA 01752-3307, USA

Reynolds, Kevin (Director, Writer)
c/o Mike Simpson *WME|IMG*
9601 Wilshire Blvd
Beverly Hills, CA 90210-5213, USA

Reynolds, Mark (Athlete, Baseball Player)
10960 Wilshire Blvd Fl 5
Los Angeles, CA 90024-3708, USA

Reynolds, Randolph N (Business Person)
Reynolds Metal Co
6601 W Broad St
PO Box 27003
Richmond, VA 23230-1723, USA

Reynolds, Ricky (Athlete, Football Player)
18032 Java Isle Dr
Tampa, FL 33647-2708, USA

Reynolds, Robert (Musician)
AristoMedia
1620 16th Ave S
Nashville, TN 37212-2908, USA

Reynolds, Ronn (Athlete, Baseball Player)
5900 E Mainsgate Rd Apt 501
Wichita, KS 67220-2723, USA

Reynolds, Roxy (Actor)
c/o Staff Member *Sosincere Entertainment*
2054 Nostrand Ave Apt 4F
Brooklyn, NY 11210-2526, USA

Reynolds, Ryan (Actor)
c/o Staff Member *Dark Trick Films*
PO Box 10605
Beverly Hills, CA 90213-3605, USA

Reynolds, Shane (Athlete, Baseball Player)
604 Merrill St
Houston, TX 77009-6206, USA

Reynolds, Sheldon (Musician)
Great Scott Productions
137 N Wetherly Dr Apt 403
Los Angeles, CA 90048-2866, USA

Reynolds, Tom (Athlete, Baseball Player)
640 Jinks Crossing Rd
Bainbridge, GA 39819-1334, USA

Reynolds Booth, Nancy (Skier)
3197 Padaro Ln
Carpinteria, CA 93013-1115, USA

Reynor, Jack (Actor)
c/o Derick Mulvey *Macfarlane Chard (Ireland)*
24 Adelaide St
Dun Laoghaire
Dublin NA, IRELAND

Reynoso, Armando (Athlete, Baseball Player)
PO Box 442
Scottsdale, AZ 85252-0442, USA

Reza, Yasmina (Actor, Writer)
Marta Andras
14 Rue des Sablons
Paris 75116, FRANCE

Rezendes, Dave (Race Car Driver)
3 Sammys Ln
Assonet, MA 02702-1101, USA

Reznor, Trent (Musician)
1707 Mandeville Ln
Los Angeles, CA 90049-2522, USA

Rhames, Ving (Actor)
c/o Steven Muller *Innovative Artists*
1505 10th St
Santa Monica, CA 90401-2805, USA

Rhea, Caroline (Actor, Comedian)
c/o Jonathan Howard *Innovative Artists*
1505 10th St
Santa Monica, CA 90401-2805, USA

Rheams, Leonta (Athlete, Football Player)
1712 W Jackson St
Tyler, TX 75701-1209, USA

Rheaume, Manon (Athlete, Hockey Player)
Manon Rheaume Foundation
PO Box 701816
Plymouth, MI 48170-0971

Rheinecker, John (Athlete, Baseball Player)
6125 Ll Rd
Waterloo, IL 62298-4013, USA

Rhett, Alicia (Actor)
PO Box 700
Charleston, SC 29402-0700, USA

Rhett, Errict (Athlete, Football Player)
6 NW 108th Ter
Plantation, FL 33324-1560, USA

Rhett, Thomas (Musician)
c/o Jake Basden *Big Machine Records*
1219 16th Ave S
Nashville, TN 37212-2901, USA

Rhimes, Shonda (Producer, Writer)
c/o Staff Member *Shondaland*
1905 Wilcox Ave # 307
Los Angeles, CA 90068-3813, USA

Rhind-Tutt, Julian (Actor)
c/o Staff Member *The Rights House (UK)*
Drury House
34-43 Russell St
London WC2B 5HA, UNITED KINGDOM

Rhine, Kendall (Athlete, Baseball Player)
624e State Route 127 N
Alto Pass, IL 629e5-323e, USA

Rhinehart, Coby (Athlete, Football Player)
3206 Walker Dr
Richardson, TX 75082-2451, USA

Rhine Sr, Kendall (Athlete, Basketball Player)
6240 State Route 127 N
Alto Pass, IL 62905-3230, USA

Rhiness, Brad (Athlete, Hockey Player)
4 St. Lawrence Pl
Cobourg, ON K9A 4G8, Canada

Rhino, Randy (Athlete, Football Player)
5750 Vinings Retreat Way SW
Mableton, GA 30126-2578, USA

Rhoads, George (Artist)
1478 Mecklenburg Rd
Ithaca, NY 14850-9301, USA

Rhoads, James B (Misc)
1300 Fox Run Trl
Platte City, MO 64079-7640, USA

Rhoda, Hilary (Model)
c/o Staff Member *IMG*
304 Park Ave S Fl 12
New York, NY 10010-4314, USA

Rhoden, Rick (Athlete, Baseball Player)
1253 Killarney Dr
Ormond Beach, FL 32174-2828, USA

Rhodes, Arthur (Athlete, Baseball Player)
14114 Phoenix Rd
Phoenix, MD 21131-1020, USA

Rhodes, Cody (Actor, Athlete, Wrestler)

Rhodes, Cynthia (Actor, Dancer)
15260 Ventura Blvd Ste 2100
Sherman Oaks, CA 91403-5360, USA

Rhodes, Damian (Athlete, Hockey Player)
22309 N 36th St
Phoenix, AZ 85050-7399

Rhodes, Eugene (Athlete, Basketball Player)
4501 Springdale Rd Apt 218
Louisville, KY 40241-6123, USA

Rhodes, Harry (Athlete, Baseball Player)
7207 S Evans Ave
Chicago, IL 60619-1224, USA

Rhodes, Karl (Athlete, Baseball Player)
8507 Hidden Hollow Ct
Missouri City, TX 77459-7514, USA

Rhodes, Kerry (Athlete, Football Player)
c/o Team Member *New York Jets*
1 Jets Dr
Florham Park, NJ 07932-1215, USA

Rhodes, Kim (Actor)
c/o Jason Zenowich *Abrams Artists Agency*
750 N San Vicente Blvd
E Tower Fl 11
Los Angeles, CA 90069-5788, USA

Rhodes, Lou (Musician)
c/o Staff Member *Paradigm (Monterey)*
404 W Franklin St
Monterey, CA 93940-2303, USA

Rhodes, Mark (Musician, Television Host)
c/o Staff Member *CBBC*
PO Box 9989
Salford M5 0DP, UK

Rhodes, Nick (Musician)
DD Productions
93A Westbourne Park Villas
London W2 5ED, UNITED KINGDOM

Rhodes, Philip (Musician)
William Morris Agency
2100 W End Ave Ste 1000
Nashville, TN 37203-5240, USA

Rhodes, Randi (Radio Personality)
c/o Myles Peterson *Premiere Radio Network*
1270 Avenue of the Americas Fl 9
New York, NY 10020-1702, USA

Rhodes, Ray (Athlete, Coach, Football Coach, Football Player)
1507 Juliet Dr
Allen, TX 75013-5816, USA

Rhodes, Richard L (Writer)
Janklow & Nesbit
285 Madison Ave Lbby
New York, NY 10017-6418, USA

Rhodes, Richard Lee (Writer)
c/o Staff Member *Simon & Schuster*
1230 Avenue of the Americas Fl CONC1
New York, NY 10020-1586, USA

Rhodes, Rodrick (Athlete, Basketball Player)
PO Box 17704
Sugar Land, TX 77496-7704, USA

Rhodes, Trevante (Actor)
c/o Carissa Stewart *GSA Entertainment*
575 Lexington Ave Fl 4
New York, NY 10022-6146, USA

Rhodes, Xavier (Athlete, Football Player)

Rhodes, Zandra (Designer, Fashion Designer)
79-85 Bermondsey St
London SE1 3XF, UNITED KINGDOM (UK)

Rhomberg, Kevin (Athlete, Baseball Player)
9545 Graystone Ln
Mentor, OH 44060-4537, USA

Rhome, Gerald B (Jerry) (Athlete, Coach, Football Coach, Football Player)
3883 Morning Meadow Ln
Buford, GA 30519-4383, USA

Rhone, Earriest C (Ernie) (Athlete, Football Player)
3603 Potomac Ave
Texarkana, TX 75503-3519, USA

Rhone, Sylvia (Business Person)
Elektra Entertainment Group
75 Rockefeller Plz Fl 15
New York, NY 10019-6908

Rhude, Kellan (Actor)
c/o Staff Member *Diverse Talent Group*
1875 Century Park E Ste 2250
Los Angeles, CA 90067-2563, USA

Rhyan, Dick (Golfer)
111 Camp Dr
Georgetown, TX 78633-4874, USA

Rhymer, Don (Writer)
c/o David Kramer *United Talent Agency (UTA)*
9336 Civic Center Dr
Beverly Hills, CA 90210-3604, USA

Rhymes, Busta (Musician)
c/o Peter Schwartz *WME|IMG (NY)*
11 Madison Ave Fl 18
New York, NY 10010-3669, USA

Rhymes, Buster (Athlete, Football Player)
17120 NW 37th Ave
Carol City, FL 33056-4112, USA

Rhymes, Will (Athlete, Baseball Player)
2738 Mustang Hill Ln
Katy, TX 77449-4830, USA

Rhys, Matthew (Actor)
c/o Ciara Parkes *Public Eye Communications*
535 Kings Rd
#313 Plaza
London SW10 0SZ, UNITED KINGDOM

Rhys, Paul (Actor)
c/o Pippa Markham *Markham & Froggatt*
4 Windmill St
London W1T 1HZ, UNITED KINGDOM

Rhys, Phillip (Actor)
c/o Andy Cohen *Grade A Entertainment*
149 S Barrington Ave # 719
Los Angeles, CA 90049-3310, USA

Rhys-Davies, John (Actor)
3428 Oak Glen Dr
Los Angeles, CA 90068-1314, USA

Rhys Meyers, Jonathan (Actor)
PO Box 30
Mellow, County Cork, IRELAND

Rial, Monica (Actor)
c/o Mary Collins *Mary Collins Agency*
2909 Cole Ave Ste 250
Dallas, TX 75204-1321, USA

Ribant, Dennis (Athlete, Baseball Player)
46 Sidra Cv
Newport Coast, CA 92657-2115, USA

Ribble, Pat (Athlete, Hockey Player)
23 Cheyenne Crt
Leamington, ON N8H 5E2, CANADA

Ribbs, Willy (Race Car Driver)
Craftsman
1801 W Speedway Blvd
Daytona Beach, FL 32114-1215, USA

Ribeiro, Alfonso (Actor)
c/o Konrad Leh *Creative Talent Group*
1900 Avenue of the Stars Ste 2475
Los Angeles, CA 90067-4512, USA

Ribeiro, Andre (Race Car Driver)
4192 Weaver Ct.
Hilliard, OH 43026, USA

Ribeiro, Ignacio (Designer, Fashion Designer)
Clements Ribejro Ltd
48 S Molton St
London W1X 1HE, UNITED KINGDOM (UK)

Ribeiro, Mike (Athlete, Hockey Player)
5609 Monterey Dr
Frisco, TX 75034-4076

Ribisi, Giovanni (Actor)
c/o Eric Kranzler *Management 360*
9111 Wilshire Blvd
Beverly Hills, CA 90210-5508, USA

Ribisi, Marissa (Actor)
4121 Wilshire Blvd Apt 415
Los Angeles, CA 90010-3525, USA

Ribot, Mark (Composer, Musician)
c/o Staff Member *Concerted Efforts*
PO Box 440326
Somerville, MA 02144-0004, USA

Ricamora, Conrad (Actor)
c/o Richard Fisher *Abrams Artists Agency*
275 7th Ave Fl 26
New York, NY 10001-6708, USA

Ricamora, Conrad (Actor)

Ricard, Alan (Athlete, Football Player)
10306 Ripple Lake Dr
Houston, TX 77065-4087, USA

Ricardo, Benny (Athlete, Football Player)
3012 Harding Way
Costa Mesa, CA 92626-2846, USA

Ricardo Y Alberto (Music Group)
c/o Staff Member *Sony Music (Miami)*
404 Washington Ave Ste 700
Miami Beach, FL 33139-6615, USA

Ricca, John (Athlete, Football Player)
4 Fairfax Ct Apt 22
Chevy Chase, MD 20815-6522, USA

Riccelli, Frank (Athlete, Baseball Player)
PO Box 2102
Syracuse, NY 13220-2102, USA

Ricci, Christina (Actor)
c/o Rebecca Sides Capellan *ID Public Relations (NY)*
40 Wall St Fl 51
New York, NY 10005-1385, USA

Ricci, Chuck (Athlete, Baseball Player)
110 Moonlight Dr
Greencastle, PA 17225-1059, USA

Ricci, Italia (Actor)
ProtTgT Entertainment
10 E Angeleno Ave
Burbank, CA 91501, USA

Ricci, Mike (Athlete, Hockey Player)
286 Mountain Laurel Ln
Los Gatos, CA 95032-5740

Rice, Alex (Actor)
c/o Staff Member *Artist Representation Company, The*
1147 Big Island Rd S RR 1
Demorestville, ON K0K 1W0, CANADA

Rice, Andy (Athlete, Football Player)
801 N Main St
Hallettsville, TX 77964-2321, USA

Rice, Angourie (Actor)
c/o Catherine Poulton *Catherine Poulton Management*
105 Rupert St
Collingwood
Melbourne, Victoria 03066, AUSTRALIA

Rice, Anne (Writer)
9 Monte Carlo Dr
Kenner, LA 70065-2028, USA

Rice, Buddy (Race Car Driver)
Team Rahal
4601 Lyman Dr
Hilliard, OH 43026-1249, USA

Rice, Chace (Musician)
c/o Amina Bryant *CAA (London)*
3 Shortlands, Hammersmith
Fl 5
London W6 8DA, UNITED KINGDOM

Rice, Christopher (Writer)
1239 1st St
New Orleans, LA 70130-5708, USA

Rice, Condoleezza (Politician)
Stanford University
616 Serra St # C100
Freeman Spogli Institute for International Studies
Stanford, CA 94305-6060, USA

Rice, Damien (Musician)
c/o Bernadette Barrett *Mondo Management*
26-32 Voltaire Rd #2D
London SW6 6DH, UNITED KINGDOM (UK)

Rice, Elizabeth (Actor)
c/o Steven Warren *Hansen, Jacobson, Teller, Hoberman, Newman, Warren & Richman*
450 N Roxbury Dr Fl 8
Beverly Hills, CA 90210-4222, USA

Rice, Gene D (Religious Leader)
Church of God
PO Box 2430
Cleveland, TN 37320-2430, USA

Rice, Gigi (Actor)
14951 Alva Dr
Pacific Palisades, CA 90272-4402, USA

Rice, Glen (Athlete, Basketball Player)
910 SW 65th Ave
Miami, FL 33144, USA

Rice, Glenn (Athlete, Basketball Player)
4835 SW 82nd St
Miami, FL 33143-8603, USA

Rice, James E (Jim) (Athlete, Baseball Player)
35 Bobby Jones Dr
Andover, MA 01810-2880, USA

Rice, John (Baseball Player)
2666 E 73rd St Apt 12W
Chicago, IL 60649-2732, USA

Rice, John (Athlete, Baseball Player)
2666 E 73rd St Apt 12W
Chicago, IL 60649-2732, USA

Rice, Ken (Athlete, Football Player)
10619 Big Canoe
Big Canoe, GA 30143-5130, USA

Rice, Larry (Race Car Driver)
1150 Forest
Brownsburg, IN 46112, USA

Rice, Norman B (Politician)
Mayor's Office
600 4th Ave
Municipal Building
Seattle, WA 98104-1850, USA

Rice, Pat (Athlete, Baseball Player)
4090 Zurich Dr
Colorado Springs, CO 80920-7521, USA

Rice, Ray (Athlete, Football Player)
c/o Deb Poquette *Prestige Lifestyle Management*
1300 Saint Michaels Rd
Mount Airy, MD 21771-3228, USA

Rice, Regina (Actor, Producer)
c/o Chani Williams *WE Management*
PO Box 3981
Palos Verdes Peninsula, CA 90274-9549, USA

Rice, Ron (Athlete, Football Player)
112 Lofty Heights Dr
Durham, NC 27713-5850, USA

Rice, Sidney (Athlete, Football Player)
c/o Drew Rosenhaus *Rosenhaus Sports Representation*
3921 Alton Rd # 440
Miami Beach, FL 33140-3852, USA

Rice, Simeon (Athlete, Football Player)
371 Channelside Walk Way Unit 401
Tampa, FL 33602-6767, USA

Rice, Stuart A (Misc)
5555 S Everett Ave Apt C17
Chicago, IL 60637-1924, USA

Rice, Tim (Musician)
Chiltens
France-Hill Dr Camberley
Surrey GU153-30A, UNITED KINGDOM (UK)

Rice, Tony (Athlete, Football Player)
PO Box 6455
South Bend, IN 46660-6455, USA

Rice Jr, Jerry (Athlete, Football Player)
c/o Adam Heller *Vantage Management Group*
518 Reamer Dr
Carnegie, PA 15106-1845, USA

Rich, Adam (Actor)
4814 Lemona Ave
Sherman Oaks, CA 91403-2010, USA

Rich, Allan (Actor)
225 E 57th St Apt 19D
New York, NY 10022-2862, USA

Rich, Christopher (Actor)
Bresler Kelly Assoc
11500 W Olympic Blvd Ste 510
Los Angeles, CA 90064-1527, USA

Rich, Denise (Musician)
c/o Marc Jacobson *Marc Jacobson Law*
440 E 79th St Apt 11D
New York, NY 10075-1401, USA

Rich, John (Musician)
c/o Dale Morris *Morris Artists Management*
2001 Blair Blvd
Nashville, TN 37212-5007, USA

Rich, Randy (Athlete, Baseball Player)
9421 Eagle Springs Ct
Roseville, CA 95747-6316, USA

Rich, Richie (Fashion Designer)
MAC Cosmetics
575 Broadway Fl 2
New York, NY 10012-3230, USA

Rich, Tony (Musician)
Prestige
220 E 23rd St Ste 303
New York, NY 10010-4676, USA

Richard, Chris (Athlete, Baseball Player)
11389 Ironwood Rd
San Diego, CA 92131-1916, USA

Richard, Clayton (Athlete, Baseball Player)
3551 Eisenhower Rd
Lafayette, IN 47905-4108, USA

Richard, Cliff (Musician)
SGO Music
PO Box 2015
Salisbury SP2 7WU, UNITED KINGDOM

Richard, Deb (Golfer)
201 Triunfo Canyon Rd Apt 160
Westlake Village, CA 91361-2100, USA

Richard, Henri (Athlete, Hockey Player)
Montreal Canadiens
1275 Rue Saint-Antoine 0
Montreal, QC H3C SL2, Canada

Richard, Henri (Athlete, Hockey Player)
905-4300 Place des Cageux
Laval, QC H7W 4Z3, Canada

Richard, James Rodney (J R) (Athlete, Baseball Player)
5615 Chimney Rock Rd Apt 338
Houston, TX 77081-1957, USA

Richard, J R (Athlete, Baseball Player)
Mary Olive Baptist Church
2804 McGowen St
Attn Associate Pastor
Houston, TX 77004-1658, USA

Richard, Lee (Athlete, Baseball Player)
1621 14th St
Port Arthur, TX 77640-4482, USA

Ri'Chard, Robert (Actor)
c/o Steven Simon *Landis-Simon Productions Talent Management*
625 E Thousand Oaks Blvd
#279
Thousand Oaks, CA 91362, USA

Richard, Ruth (Athlete, Baseball Player)
924 Juniper St
Quakertown, PA 18951-1514, USA

Richard III, Oliver G (Business Person)
Columbia Energy Group
200 Civic Center Dr
Columbus, OH 43215-7510, USA

Richards, Ariana (Actor)
Don Buchwald
5900 Wilshire Blvd Ste 3100
Los Angeles, CA 90036-5030, USA

Richards, Bob (Athlete, Olympic Athlete, Track Athlete)
PO Box 134
Santo, TX 76472-0134, USA

Richards, Bobby (Athlete, Football Player)
2881 Fairplay Rd
Rutledge, GA 30663-2000, USA

Richards, Brad (Athlete, Hockey Player)
201 Lewis St
Southampton, NY 11968

Richards, Charles (Writer)
c/o David Hahn *Planned Television Arts*
1110 2nd Ave
New York, NY 10022-2021, USA

Richards, Curvin (Athlete, Football Player)
11000 Gatesden Dr Apt 1311
Tomball, TX 77377-8706, USA

Richards, Dakota Blue (Actor)
c/o Sue Latimer *Artists Rights Group (ARG)*
4A Exmoor St
London W10 6BD, UNITED KINGDOM

Richards, David R (Athlete, Football Player)
4209 San Carlos St
Dallas, TX 75205-2049, USA

Richards, DeLeon (Actor, Musician)
c/o Staff Member *Britto Agency PR*
277 Broadway Ste 110
New York, NY 10007-2072, USA

Richards, Denise (Actor)
23726 Long Valley Rd
Hidden Hills, CA 91302-2408, USA

Richards, Duane (Athlete, Baseball Player)
PO Box 54
Palestine, OH 45352-0054, USA

Richards, Erin (Actor)
c/o Christina Papadopoulos *Baker Winokur Ryder Public Relations*
200 5th Ave Fl 5
New York, NY 10010-3307, USA

Richards, Fred (Athlete, Baseball Player)
3540 Lochwolde Ln
Snellville, GA 30039-8605, USA

Richards, Garrett (Athlete, Baseball Player)
c/o Adam Rosenthal *Octagon (Chicago)*
875 N Michigan Ave Ste 2700
Chicago, IL 60611-1822, USA

Richards, Gene (Athlete, Baseball Player)
1468 Normandy Dr
Chula Vista, CA 91913-3903, USA

Richards, Golden (Athlete, Football Player)
7274 S Winesap Ct
Salt Lake City, UT 84121-4439, USA

Richards, Howard (Athlete, Football Player)
PSC 98 Box 30
Apo, AE 09830, USA

Richards, James B (Athlete, Football Player)
733 Vanderbilt Ave
Virginia Beach, VA 23451-3632, USA

Richards, Jasmine (Actor)
c/o Staff Member *Noble Caplan Abrams*
1260 Yonge St 2nd Fl
Toronto, ON M4T 1W5, CANADA

Richards, J August (Actor)
PO Box 99
China Spring, TX 76633-0099, USA

Richards, Jen (Actor)
c/o Melissa Hirschenson *Innovative Artists*
1505 10th St
Santa Monica, CA 90401-2805, USA

Richards, J R (Musician)
William Morris Agency
1325 Avenue of the Americas
New York, NY 10019-6026, USA

Richards, Keith (Musician)
c/o Jane Rose *Raindrop Services*
584 Broadway Rm 1101
New York, NY 10012-5238, USA

Richards, Kim (Actor, Reality Star)
c/o Bette Smith *Bette Smith Management*
499 N Canon Dr
Beverly Hills, CA 90210-4887, USA

Richards, Kyle (Actor, Reality Star)
Kyle by Alene Too
455 E Palmetto Park Rd Apt 6E
Boca Raton, FL 33432-5134, USA

Richards, Lou (Actor)
2467 Brighton Dr
#2B
Valencia, CA 91355, USA

Richards, Mark (Misc)
755 Hunter St
Newcastle, NSW 02302, AUSTRALIA

Richards, Mary (Producer)
c/o Staff Member *McKinney, Macartney Management*
Gable House
18 - 24 Turnham Green Terrace
London W4 1QP, UK

Richards, Michael (Actor, Comedian)
c/o Elizabeth Much *East 2 West Collective*
11022 Santa Monica Blvd Ste 350
Los Angeles, CA 90025-7532, USA

Richards, Mike (Athlete, Hockey Player)
c/o Donald Meehan *Newport Sports Management*
201 City Centre Dr
Suite 400
Mississauga, ON L58 2T4, CANADA

Richards, Paul G (Misc)
Lamont-Doherty Geological Observatory
Palisades, NY 10964, USA

Richards, Paul W (Astronaut)
NASA
605 First St
Annapolis, MD 21403-3321, USA

Richards, Renee (Tennis Player)
1604 Union St
San Francisco, CA 94123-4507, USA

Richards, Rex E (Misc)
13 Woodstock Close
Oxford OX2 8DB, UNITED KINGDOM (UK)

Richards, Richard N (Astronaut)
NASA
2101 Nasa Pkwy Spc Johnsoncenter
Houston, TX 77058-3696, USA

Richards, Richard N Captain (Astronaut)
226 Park Laureate Dr
Houston, TX 77024-5637, USA

Richards, Robert E (Bob) (Athlete, Track Athlete)
1616 Estates Dr
Waco, TX 76712-2208, USA

Richards, Rusty (Athlete, Baseball Player)
2606 Thompson Crossing Dr
Richmond, TX 77406-6932, USA

Richards, Sanya (Athlete, Olympic Athlete)
c/o Lowell Taub *Creative Artists Agency (CAA)*
405 Lexington Ave Fl 19
New York, NY 10174-1800, USA

Richards, Stephanie (Actor)
H David Moss
6063 Vineland Ave Apt B
North Hollywood, CA 91606-4986, USA

Richards, Todd (Athlete, Hockey Player)
Columbus Blue Jackets
200 W Nationwide Blvd Unit 1
Columbus, OH 43215-2564

Richards, Todd (Athlete, Hockey Player)
5208 107th Ave N
Minneapolis, MN 55443-5902

Richardson, Al (Athlete, Football Player)
3003 Mary Ashley Ct SE
Conyers, GA 30013-6419, USA

Richardson, Antonio (Athlete, Football Player)
c/o Eugene Parker *Independent Sports & Entertainment (ISE-IN)*
6435 W Jefferson Blvd # 197
Fort Wayne, IN 46804-6203, USA

Richardson, Bill (Politician)
1058 Encantado Dr
Santa Fe, NM 87501-1086, USA

Richardson, Bucky (Athlete, Football Player)
9015 Stones Throw Ln
Missouri City, TX 77459-2990, USA

Richardson, Cameron (Actor)
c/o Staff Member *United Talent Agency (UTA)*
9336 Civic Center Dr
Beverly Hills, CA 90210-3604, USA

Richardson, Cheryl (Actor)
749 Fair Oaks Dr
Alamo, CA 94507-1457, USA

Richardson, Cliff (Athlete, Basketball Player)
6236 Radiance Blvd E # 2
Fife, WA 98424-3868, USA

Richardson, Clint (Athlete, Basketball Player)
12e7 9th Ave NW
Puyallup, WA 98371-4e25, USA

Richardson, Cyril (Athlete, Football Player)
c/o W Vann McElroy *Select Sports Group*
2700 Post Oak Blvd Ste 1450
Houston, TX 77056-5785, USA

Richardson, Damien (Athlete, Football Player)
1300 E Cromwell Ave Apt 102
Fresno, CA 93720-2628, USA

Richardson, Dan (Musician)
c/o Staff Member *UTA/The Agency Group*
888 7th Ave Fl 7
New York, NY 10106-0700, USA

Richardson, Dave (Athlete, Hockey Player)
62 Agassiz Dr
Winnipeg, MB R3T 2K7, CANADA

Richardson, Donna (Misc)
Anchor Bay Entertainment
500 Kirts Blvd
Troy, MI 48084-4134, USA

Richardson, Dot (Athlete, Olympic Athlete, Softball Player)
1264 Boone Hill Dr
Lynchburg, VA 24503-3846, USA

Richardson, Eric (Athlete, Football Player)
509 Ely Blvd S
Petaluma, CA 94954-3813, USA

Richardson, Gloster (Athlete, Football Player)
9143 S Euclid Ave
Chicago, IL 60617-3749, USA

Richardson, Gordie (Athlete, Baseball Player)
23 Saint Paul Church Rd
Colquitt, GA 39837-6829, USA

Richardson, Grady (Athlete, Football Player)
3633 Mentone Ave Apt 203
Los Angeles, CA 90034-5659, USA

Richardson, Greg (Boxer)
382 Camden Ave
Youngstown, OH 44505-4845, USA

Richardson, Haley Lu (Actor)
c/o Annett Wolf *Wolf-Kasteler Public Relations*
6255 W Sunset Blvd Ste 1111
Los Angeles, CA 90028-7426, USA

Richardson, Hamilton (Tennis Player)
870 United Nations Plz
New York, NY 10017-1807, USA

Richardson, Huey (Athlete, Football Player)
161 W 16th St Apt 17A
New York, NY 10011-6207, USA

Richardson, Jack (Artist)
12171 Sunset Ave
Grass Valley, CA 95945-8512, USA

Richardson, Jake (Actor)
c/o Meredith Fine *Coast to Coast Talent Group*
3350 Barham Blvd
Los Angeles, CA 90068-1404, USA

Richardson, Jason (Athlete, Basketball Player)
c/o Dan Fegan *Relativity Sports*
2029 Century Park E Ste 1550
Century City, CA 90067-3000, USA

Richardson, Jay (Athlete, Football Player)
c/o Eugene Parker *Independent Sports & Entertainment (ISE-IN)*
6435 W Jefferson Blvd # 197
Fort Wayne, IN 46804-6203, USA

Richardson, Jeff (Athlete, Baseball Player)
47 Kuester Lk
Grand Island, NE 68801-8609, USA

Richardson, Jeffrey (Jeff) (Athlete, Baseball Player)
11779 W Fordson Dr
Marana, AZ 85653-7722, USA

Richardson, Jerome (Pooh) (Athlete, Basketball Player)
23434 Sherman Way
West Hills, CA 91307-1426, USA

Richardson, Jerry (Business Person, Football Executive)
6245 N Shore Dr # A14
Nebo, NC 28761-8604, USA

Richardson, Joely (Actor)
c/o Charles Finch *Finch & Partners*
Top Floor
29-37 Heddon St
London W1B 4BR, UNITED KINGDOM

Richardson, John (Athlete, Football Player)
2838 Shoreview Cir
Westlake Village, CA 91361-3311, USA

Richardson, Ken (Athlete, Hockey Player)
Hockey Heritage North
PO Box 156 Stn Main
Kirkland Lake, ON P2N 3M6, Canada

Richardson, Kevin (Musician)
c/o John Marx *WME|IMG*
9601 Wilshire Blvd
Beverly Hills, CA 90210-5213, USA

Richardson, Kevin Michael (Actor)
c/o Anita Haeggstrom *The Haeggstrom Office*
433 N Camden Dr Ste 600
Beverly Hills, CA 90210-4416, USA

Richardson, Kristin (Actor)
c/o Brady McKay *Haven Entertainment*
8111 Beverly Blvd Ste 201
Los Angeles, CA 90048-4531, USA

Richardson, LaTanya (Actor, Producer)
c/o Staff Member *Paradigm*
8942 Wilshire Blvd
Beverly Hills, CA 90211-1908, USA

Richardson, Laura (Congressman, Politician)
1330 Longworth Hob
Washington, DC 20515-0402, USA

Richardson, Leo (Actor)
c/o Lou Coulson *Lou Coulson Agency*
37 Berwick St
1st Floor
London W1F 8RS, UNITED KINGDOM (UK)

Richardson, Luke (Athlete, Hockey Player)
Ottawa Senators
110-1000 Palladium Dr
Ottawa, ON K2V 1A5, Canada

Richardson, Marque (Actor)
c/o Lisa Wright *LINK Entertainment*
11872 La Grange Ave
Los Angeles, CA 90025-5282, USA

Richardson, Michael Ray (Athlete, Basketball Player)
121 N Elk Ct
Aurora, CO 80018-1599, USA

Richardson, Mike (Producer)
c/o Staff Member *Dark Horse Entertainment*
1438 N Gower St Ste 23
Hollywood, CA 90028-8306, USA

Richardson, Mike (Athlete, Football Player)
1619 W Caldwell St
Compton, CA 90220-4333, USA

Richardson, Mike (Athlete, Football Player)
7310 Covewood Dr
Garland, TX 75044-2624, USA

Richardson, Miranda (Actor)
Kerry Gardner Mgmt
7 Saint George's Square
London SW1V 2HX, UNITED KINGDOM (UK)

Richardson, Nolan (Coach)
2539 E Joyce Blvd
Fayetteville, AR 72703-4553, USA

Richardson, Patricia (Actor)
c/o Craig Dorfman *Frontline Management*
5670 Wilshire Blvd Ste 1370
Los Angeles, CA 90036-5649, USA

Richardson, Quentin (Basketball Player)
Los Angeles Clippers
1111 S Figueroa St
Staples Center
Los Angeles, CA 90015-1300, USA

Richardson, Robert (Race Car Driver)
R3 Motorsports
330 Aviation Dr
Statesville, NC 28677-2509, USA

Richardson, Robert C (Bobby) (Athlete, Baseball Player)
47 Adams Ave
Sumter, SC 29150-4037, USA

Richardson, Salli (Actor)
c/o Brian Medavoy *More/Medavoy Management*
10203 Santa Monica Blvd # 400
Los Angeles, CA 90067-6405, USA

Richardson, Sam (Actor)
4121 Sequoyah Rd
Oakland, CA 94605-4539, USA

Richardson, Sean (Athlete, Football Player)
c/o Ryan Tollner *REP 1 Sports Group*
80 Technology Dr
Irvine, CA 92618-2301, USA

Richardson, Shelson (Athlete, Football Player)
c/o Ben Dogra *Relativity Sports*
2029 Century Park E Ste 1550
Century City, CA 90067-3000, USA

Richardson, Terry (Artist, Director, Photographer)
c/o Giovanni Testino *Art Partner*
1 Dekalb Ave Ste 4
Brooklyn, NY 11201-5324, USA

Richardson, Terry (Athlete, Hockey Player)
3598 Rosemary Heights Cres
Surrey, BC V3Z 0P2, Canada

Richardson, Trent (Athlete, Football Player)
c/o Ben Dogra *Relativity Sports*
2029 Century Park E Ste 1550
Century City, CA 90067-3000, USA

Richardson, W Franklyn (Religious Leader)
National Baptist Convention
52 S 6th Ave
Mount Vernon, NY 10550-3005, USA

Richardt, Mike (Athlete, Baseball Player)
3236 W Western Ave
Fresno, CA 93722-4843, USA

Richelmy, Lorenzo (Actor)
c/o Andrew Cannava *United Talent Agency (UTA)*
9336 Civic Center Dr
Beverly Hills, CA 90210-3604, USA

Richer, Stephane (Athlete, Hockey Player)
Club de Golf Montpelier
440 Ch Stephane-Richer
Lac Simon, QC J0V 1M0, CANADA

Richert, Nate (Actor)
c/o Iris Burton *Iris Burton Agency*
10100 Santa Monica Blvd Ste 1300
Los Angeles, CA 90067-4114, USA

Richert, Pete (Athlete, Baseball Player)
80 La Cerra Dr
Rancho Mirage, CA 92270-3811, USA

Richeson, Ray (Athlete, Football Player)
1348 Willoughby Rd
Vestavia Hills, AL 35216-2906, USA

Richey, Cliff (Tennis Player)
2936 Cumberland Dr
San Angelo, TX 76904-6163, USA

Richey, Jennifer (Actor)
c/o Staff Member *Cunningham Escott Slevin & Doherty (CESD)*
10635 Santa Monica Blvd Ste 130
Los Angeles, CA 90025-8306, USA

Richey, Nancy (Tennis Player)
2936 Cumberland Dr
San Angelo, TX 76904-6163, USA

Richey, Wade (Athlete, Football Player)
PO Box 775
Carencro, LA 70520-0775, USA

Richie, Lionel (Musician, Songwriter)
Lionel Richie Productions, Inc.
2850 Ocean Park Blvd Ste 300
Santa Monica, CA 90405-6216, USA

Richie, Nicole (Designer, Reality Star)
c/o Michael Baum *Impression Entertainment*
9229 W Sunset Blvd Ste 700
Los Angeles, CA 90069-3407, USA

Richie, Rob (Athlete, Baseball Player)
1835 Meadowvale Way
Sparks, NV 89431-2949, USA

Richie, Shane (Actor)
c/o Phil Dale *Qdos Entertainment*
8 King St
Covent Garden
London WC2 8HN, UNITED KINGDOM

Richie, Sofia (Actor)
c/o Jeff Raymond *Rogers & Cowan*
1840 Century Park E Fl 18
Los Angeles, CA 90067-2101, USA

Richings, Julian (Actor)
c/o Pam Winter *Gary Goddard Agency (GGA)*
304-250 The Esplanade
Toronto, ON M5A 1J2, CANADA

Richman, Adam (Television Host)
c/o Eileen Stringer *Rain Management Group*
11162 La Grange Ave
Los Angeles, CA 90025-5632, USA

Richman, Caryn (Actor)
PO Box 944
Palos Verdes Estates, CA 90274-0944, USA

Richman, Jonathan (Actor, Musician)
High Road
751 Bridgeway Fl 2
Sausalito, CA 94965-2174, USA

Richman, Peter Mark (Actor)
5114 Del Moreno Dr
Woodland Hills, CA 91364-2426, USA

Richmond, Branscombe (Actor)
PO Box 881095
Pukalani, HI 96788-1095, USA

Richmond, Grady Lee (Actor)
c/o Scott Carlsen *Scott Carlsen Entertainment*
5328 Alhama Dr
Woodland Hills, CA 91364-2013, USA

Richmond, Mitch (Athlete, Basketball Player, Olympic Athlete)
207 Saddlebow Rd
Bell Canyon, CA 91307-1035, USA

Richmond, Steve (Athlete, Hockey Player)
21290 W Pepper Dr
Lake Zurich, IL 60047-8046

Richmond, Tequan (Actor, Musician)
c/o Temple Poteat *AMP Live Entertainment*
3727 W Magnolia Blvd # 446
Burbank, CA 91505-2818, USA

Richt, Mark (Coach, Football Coach)
University of Georgia
PO Box 1472
Athletic Dept
Athens, GA 30603-1472, USA

Richter, Al (Athlete, Baseball Player)
3810 Atlantic Ave Apt 703
Virginia Beach, VA 23451-2736, USA

Richter, Andy (Actor, Comedian)
315 S Beverly Dr Ste 216
Beverly Hills, CA 90212-4310, USA

Richter, Barry (Athlete, Hockey Player, Olympic Athlete)
PO Box 259408
Madison, WI 53725-9408, USA

Richter, Dave (Athlete, Hockey Player)
16910 Trenton Ln
Eden Prairie, MN 55347-3377

Richter, Frank (Athlete, Football Player)
1906 US Highway 84 W
Cairo, GA 39827-4226, USA

Richter, Gerhard (Artist)
Bismarckstr 50
Cologne 50672, GERMANY

Richter, James A (Jim) (Athlete, Football Player)
8620 Bournemouth Dr
Raleigh, NC 27615-2008, USA

Richter, Jason James (Actor)
United Talent Agency
9336 Civic Center Dr
Beverly Hills, CA 90210-3604, USA

Richter, Joey (Actor, Internet Star, Musician)
c/o Melissa Berger-Brennan *Cunningham Escott Slevin & Doherty (CESD)*
10635 Santa Monica Blvd Ste 130
Los Angeles, CA 90025-8306, USA

Richter, John (Athlete, Basketball Player)
2740 Narcissa Rd
Plymouth Meeting, PA 19462-1107, USA

Richter, Les (Race Car Driver)
c/o Staff Member *NASCAR*
1801 W Speedway Blvd
Daytona Beach, FL 32114-1243, USA

Richter, Mike (Athlete, Hockey Player, Olympic Athlete)
5 Sidney Lanier Ln
Greenwich, CT 06831-3735

Richter, Pat V (Athlete, Football Executive, Football Player)
833 Kings Way
Madison, WI 53704-6046, USA

Richter, Sonja (Actor)
c/o Toni Howard *ICM Partners*
10250 Constellation Blvd Fl 7
Los Angeles, CA 90067-6207, USA

Richwine, Maria (Actor)
Abrams-Rubaloff Lawrence
8075 W 3rd St # 303
Los Angeles, CA 90048-4318, USA

Rickards, Ashley (Actor)
c/o Adam Griffin *LINK Entertainment*
11872 La Grange Ave
Los Angeles, CA 90025-5282, USA

Rickards, Emily Bett (Actor)
c/o Allan Grifka *Alchemy Entertainment*
7024 Melrose Ave Ste 420
Los Angeles, CA 90038-3394, USA

Ricker, Robert S (Religious Leader)
Baptists Conference
2002 S Arlington Heights Rd
Arlington Heights, IL 60005-4102, USA

Ricketts, Dave (Athlete, Baseball Player)
12860 Polo Parc Dr
Saint Louis, MO 63146-1504, USA

Ricketts, Jeff (Actor)

Ricketts, Tom (Athlete, Football Player)
720 Warrendale Bayne Rd
Wexford, PA 15090-7492, USA

Rickey, Dixon (Athlete, Football Player)
908 Country Creek Ln
Red Oak, TX 75154-3902, USA

Ricks, Lawrence (Athlete, Football Player)
6417 Timbermill Way
Reynoldsburg, OH 43068-4327, USA

Ricks, Mikhael (Athlete, Football Player)
5024 Lincoln St
Hollywood, FL 33021-5256, USA

Rico, Alfredo (Fred) (Athlete, Baseball Player)
7720 Ensign Ave
Sun Valley, CA 91352-4451, USA

Ricoeur, Paul (Misc)
18 Rue Henri Marrou
Chatenay Malabry 92290, FRANCE

Rida, Flo (Musician)
c/o Cara Lewis *Cara Lewis Group*
7 W 18th St Fl 3
New York, NY 10011-4663, USA

Riddick, Louis (Sportscaster)
c/o Staff Member *ESPN (Main)*
935 Middle St
Espn Plaza
Bristol, CT 06010-1000, USA

Riddick, Steve (Athlete, Olympic Athlete, Track Athlete)
PO Box 1000
Petersburg, VA 23804-1000, USA

Riddick, Theo (Athlete, Football Player)
c/o Joe Flanagan *BTI Sports Advisors*
615 South Blvd Apt C
Oak Park, IL 60302-4606, USA

Riddleberger, Denny (Athlete, Baseball Player)
35785 Hunter Ave
Westland, MI 48185-6669, USA

Riddoch, Greg (Athlete, Baseball Player, Coach)
703 Windflower Dr
Longmont, CO 80504-2770, USA

Rider, Amy (Actor)
c/o Amy Slomovits *Haven Entertainment*
8111 Beverly Blvd Ste 201
Los Angeles, CA 90048-4531, USA

Rider, Isiah (J R) (Athlete, Basketball Player)
P.O. Box 121R
Montchanin, DE 19710, USA

Ridge, Houston (Athlete, Football Player)
7027 Benson Ave
San Diego, CA 92114-5908, USA

Ridge, Thomas (Politician)
6105 Kennedy Dr
Chevy Chase, MD 20815-6509, USA

Ridgeley, Andrew (Musician)
8800 W Sunset Blvd # 401
Los Angeles, CA 90069-2105, USA

Ridgeway, Angle (Golfer)
c/o Staff Member *Pro Golfers Association (PGA)*
112 TPC Blvd
Ponte Vedra Beach, FL 32082, USA

Ridgeway, Frank (Cartoonist)
c/o Staff Member *King Features Syndication*
300 W 57th St Fl 15
New York, NY 10019-5238, USA

Ridgle, Elston (Athlete, Football Player)
5317 Wilkinson Ave
Studio City, CA 91607-2412, USA

Ridgley, Bob (Actor)
20th Century Artists
4605 Lankershim Blvd Ste 305
North Hollywood, CA 91602-1875, USA

Ridgway, Dave (Athlete, Football Player)
5875 W State Highway 250
Paris Crossing, IN 47270-9785, USA

Ridgway, Jeff (Athlete, Baseball Player)
9041 Parlor Dr
Ladson, SC 29456-5528, USA

Ridings, Tag (Athlete, Golfer)
1036 Barbara Ln
Keller, TX 76248-2856, USA

Ridlehuber, Preston (Athlete, Football Player)
720 Serramonte Dr
Marietta, GA 30068-4674, USA

Ridley, Calvin (Athlete, Football Player)
c/o Ben Setas *SportsTrust Advisors*
3340 Peachtree Rd NE Fl 16
Atlanta, GA 30326-1000, USA

Ridley, Curt (Athlete, Hockey Player)
722 E Grubb Dr
Mesquite, TX 75149-7502

Ridley, Daisy (Actor)
c/o Jonathan Arun *Jonathan Arun Talent*
37 Pearman St
Waterloo
London SE1 7RB, UNITED KINGDOM

Ridley, John (Director, Producer)
c/o Missy Malkin *Brillstein Entertainment Partners*
9150 Wilshire Blvd Ste 350
Beverly Hills, CA 90212-3453, USA

Ridley, Mike (Athlete, Hockey Player)
Home Run Sports
20 de la Seigneurie Blvd
Winnipeg, MB R3X 0E9, CANADA

Ridley, Stephen (Athlete, Football Player)

Ridlon, James A (Athlete, Football Player)
8006 E Lake Rd
Cazenovia, NY 13035, USA

Ridnour, Luke (Basketball Player)
Seattle SuperSonics
351 Elliott Ave W Ste 500
Seattle, WA 98119-4153, USA

Ridzik, Steve (Athlete, Baseball Player)
1806 Winged Elm Pl
Winter Garden, FL 34787-4864, USA

Riedel, Lars (Athlete, Track Athlete)
LAC Chemnitz
Reichenhainer Str 154
Chemnitz 09125, GERMANY

Riedling, John (Athlete, Baseball Player)
2118 Homestead Ln
Franklin, TN 37064-1177, USA

Riegel, Eden (Actor, Musician)
c/o Lisa Gallant *Gallant Management*
1112 Montana Ave # 454
Santa Monica, CA 90403-1652, USA

Rieger, Max (Skier)
Innsbrucker Str 12
Mittenwald 82481, GERMANY

Riegert, Peter (Actor)
c/o John S Kelly *Bresler Kelly & Associates*
11500 W Olympic Blvd Ste 510
Los Angeles, CA 90064-1527, USA

Riegger, John (Golfer)
53 Old Orchard Rd
Metropolis, IL 62960-3118, USA

Riegle, Bruce (Horse Racer)
300 W Main St
Greenville, OH 45331-1432, USA

Riegle, Gene (Coach, Horse Racer)
818 Chestnut Cir
Greenville, OH 45331-1075, USA

Riehle, Richard (Actor)
c/o Christopher Wright *Wright Entertainment*
14724 Ventura Blvd Ste 1201
Sherman Oaks, CA 91403-3512, USA

Rieker, Rich (Athlete, Baseball Player)
1223 Grey Fox Run
Weldon Spring, MO 63304-0307, USA

Rieker, Richard (Baseball Player)
5337 Foxshire Ct
Orlando, FL 32819-3824, USA

Riemann, Katja (Actor)
c/o Peter Schulz *Schulze & Heyn Film PR*
Rosa-Luxemburg-Str. 17
Berlin 10178, GERMANY

Riemelt, Max (Actor)
c/o Brian DePersia *WME/IMG*
9601 Wilshire Blvd
Beverly Hills, CA 90210-5213, USA

Riendeau, Vincent (Athlete, Hockey Player)
6105 Suitor Ch
Waterville, QC J0B 3H0, Canada

Rienstra, John (Athlete, Football Player)
5056 Briscoglen Dr
Colorado Springs, CO 80906-8612, USA

Riepe, James S (Business Person)
T Rowe Price Assoc
100 E Pratt St Ste 310
Baltimore, MD 21202-1065, USA

Ries, Christopher D (Artist)
Keelersburg Road
Tunkhannock, PA 18657, USA

Riesch, Maria (Athlete, Skier)
Postfach 1728
Garmisch Partenkirschen 82457, Germany

Riesenberg, Doug (Athlete, Football Player)
7275 SW Deerhaven Dr
Corvallis, OR 97333-9314, USA

Riesgo, Nikco (Damon) (Athlete, Baseball Player)
29625 Bermuda Ln
Southfield, MI 48076-1663, USA

Riesgraf, Beth (Actor)
c/o Alex Spieller *Baker Winokur Ryder Public Relations*
200 5th Ave Fl 5
New York, NY 10010-3307, USA

Riessen, Marty (Tennis Player)
PO Box 5444
Santa Barbara, CA 93150-5444, USA

Ries-Zillmer, Ruth (Baseball Player)
133 Adeline St
Walworth, WI 53184-9522, USA

Rieu, Andre (Musician)
Andre Rieu Productions
Postfach 1329
Maastricht, BH 06201, NETHERLANDS

Rieves, Charles (Athlete, Football Player)
3107 Long Bay Ct
Houston, TX 77059-3720, USA

Rieves, Charley (Athlete, Football Player)
3107 Long Bay Ct
Houston, TX 77059-3720, USA

Rifkin, Adam (Actor, Director, Writer)
c/o Simon Millar *Rumble Media*
1620 Broadway Ste C
Santa Monica, CA 90404-2777, USA

Rifkin, Ron (Actor, Musician)
c/o Jonathan Howard *Innovative Artists*
1505 10th St
Santa Monica, CA 90401-2805, USA

Rigali, Justin F Cardinal (Religious Leader)
Archdiocese
222 N 17th St
Philadelphia, PA 19103-1295, USA

Rigazio, Donald (Athlete, Hockey Player, Olympic Athlete)
8514 Cheffield Dr
Louisville, KY 40222-5665, USA

Rigby, Amy (Musician, Songwriter, Writer)
Press Network
1229 17th Ave S
Nashville, TN 37212-2801, USA

Rigby, Brad (Athlete, Baseball Player)
1317 Ballentyne Pl
Apopka, FL 32703-6870, USA

Rigby, Cathy (Athlete, Gymnast, Olympic Athlete)
McCoy Rigby Dance Academy
22601 La Palma Ave Ste 105
Yorba Linda, CA 92887-6711, USA

Rigby, Paul (Cartoonist)
119 Monterey Pointe Dr
West Palm Beach, FL 33418-5811, USA

Rigdon, Paul (Athlete, Baseball Player)
9231 Coxwell Ct
Jacksonville, FL 32221-1378, USA

Rigg, Diana (Actor)
Chichester Festival Theatre
Oaklands Park
Chichester
West Sussex PO19 6AP, UNITED KINGDOM

Rigg, Rebecca (Actor)
June Cann Mgmt
110 Queen St
Woollahra, NSW 02025, AUSTRALIA

Riggan, Jerrod (Athlete, Baseball Player)
PO Box 1019
Brewster, WA 98812-1019, USA

Riggans, Shawn (Athlete, Baseball Player)
12618 NW 14th Pl
Sunrise, FL 33323-5123, USA

Riggen, Patricia (Director)
Kilovoltio
Benjamin Franklin 80-12
c/o Ricardo Lozano
Distrito Federal 11800, MEXICO

Riggin, Pat (Athlete, Hockey Player)
112 Fairlane Ave
London, ON N6K 3E6, Canada

Riggins, John (Athlete, Football Player)
Schulte Sports Marketing
7272 Wisconsin Ave Ste 300
Bethesda, MD 20814-4858, USA

Riggins, Mark (Athlete, Baseball Player)
101 Arbor Dr
Murray, KY 42071-6835, USA

Riggio, Dominic (Athlete, Football Player)
4621 Mandalay Ave
Royal Oak, MI 48073-1623, USA

Riggio, Leonard (Business Person)
Barnes & Noble Inc
122 5th Ave Fl 2
New York, NY 10011-5693, USA

Riggle, Bob (Athlete, Football Player)
55 Waynesburg Rd
Washington, PA 15301-3224, USA

Riggle, Rob (Actor)
c/o Peter Principato *Artists First*
9465 Wilshire Blvd Ste 900
Beverly Hills, CA 90212-2608, USA

Riggleman, James D (Jim) (Athlete, Baseball Player, Coach)
14950 Gulf Blvd Apt 1003
Madeira Beach, FL 33708-2047, USA

Riggs, Adam (Athlete, Baseball Player)
26 Pebble Hollow Ct
Spring, TX 77381-4803, USA

Riggs, Chandler (Actor)
c/o Joannie Burstein *Burstein Company*
15304 W Sunset Blvd Ste 208
Pacific Palisades, CA 90272-3656, USA

Riggs, Gerald (Athlete, Football Player)
1810 Verona Dr
Chattanooga, TN 37421-3064, USA

Riggs, Gerald (Athlete, Football Player)
2574 Bright Ct
Decatur, GA 30034-2245, USA

Riggs, Jim (Athlete, Football Player)
15 Dellany Ct
Greer, SC 29651-6857, USA

Riggs, Lorrin A (Misc)
6 Penn Rd Apt 104
Hanover, NH 03755-1286, USA

Riggs, Ransom (Writer)
c/o Staff Member *Heroes and Villains Entertainment*
1041 N Formosa Ave
Formosa Bldg, Suite 202
West Hollywood, CA 90046-6703, USA

Riggs, Scott (Race Car Driver)
MBV/MB2 Motorsports
7065 Zephr Pl NW
Concord, NC 29028, USA

Riggs, Thron (Athlete, Football Player)
2645 E Southern Ave Apt A496
Tempe, AZ 85282-7791, USA

Righetti, Amanda (Actor, Producer)
c/o Gary Mantoosh *Baker Winokur Ryder Public Relations*
9100 Wilshire Blvd Ste 1000W
W Tower #500
Beverly Hills, CA 90212-3463, USA

Righetti, David A (Dave) (Athlete, Baseball Player)
18705 Alta Ventura Ct
Morgan Hill, CA 95037-9087, USA

Righteous Bros (Music Group)
c/o Staff Member *WME|IMG*
9601 Wilshire Blvd
Beverly Hills, CA 90210-5213, USA

Rightnowar, Ron (Athlete, Baseball Player)
8926 Stonybrook Blvd
Sylvania, OH 43560-8906, USA

Rights, Graham H (Religious Leader)
Moravian Church Southern Province
459 S Church St
Winston Salem, NC 27101-5314, USA

Rigoli, Joe (Athlete, Baseball Player)
148 Wagon Wheel Ln
Edinburg, VA 22824-3721, USA

Rigsby, Donald (Musician)
Donald Rigsby Group, Inc
31959 Amberlea Rd
Dade City, FL 33523-6289, USA

Rihanna (Musician)
c/o Amanda Silverman *The Lede Company*
401 Broadway Ste 206
New York, NY 10013-3033, USA

Rijker, Lucia (Actor)
c/o Harlan Werner *Sports Placement Service*
330 W 11th St Apt 105
Los Angeles, CA 90015-3200, USA

Rijo, Jose (Athlete, Baseball Player)
2127 Brickell Ave Apt 2101
Miami, FL 33129-2146, USA

Rikaart, Greg (Actor)
c/o Kyle Fritz *Kyle Fritz Management*
6325 Heather Dr
Los Angeles, CA 90068-1633, USA

Riker, Albert J (Misc)
2760 E 8th St
Tucson, AZ 85716-4712, USA

Riker, Robin (Actor)
c/o Staff Member *Buchwald*
5900 Wilshire Blvd Ste 3100
Los Angeles, CA 90036-5030, USA

Riker, Tom (Athlete, Basketball Player)
PO Box 628
Kill Devil Hl, NC 27948-0628, USA

Riles, Ernest (Athlete, Baseball Player)
221 Asante Dr
Ellenwood, GA 30294-3187, USA

Riley, Amber (Actor)
c/o Scooter Braun *SB Management*
755 N Bonhill Rd
Los Angeles, CA 90049-2303, USA

Riley, Bill (Athlete, Hockey Player)
286 Buckingham Ave
Riverview, NB E1B 2P2, Canada

Riley, Boots (Musician)
c/o Mark Ankner *WME|IMG*
9601 Wilshire Blvd
Beverly Hills, CA 90210-5213, USA

Riley, Bridget L (Artist)
Mayor Rowan Gallery
31A Bruton Place
London W1X 7A8, UNITED KINGDOM (UK)

Riley, Charlotte (Actor)
c/o John Grant *Conway van Gelder Grant*
8-12 Broadwick St
London W1F 8HW, UNITED KINGDOM

Riley, Chris (Athlete, Golfer)
2343 Rivoli St
Henderson, NV 89044-0525, USA

Riley, Elaine (Actor)
405 N Bay Front
Newport Beach, CA 92662-1047, USA

Riley, Eric (Athlete, Basketball Player)
6601 Sands Point Dr Apt 4
Houston, TX 77074-3731, USA

Riley, Forbes (Actor)
c/o Staff Member *Cohen Entertainment*
964 Hancock Ave Apt 305
West Hollywood, CA 90069-4091, USA

Riley, George (Athlete, Baseball Player)
451 Basket Rd
Oley, PA 19547-9245, USA

Riley, H John Jr (Business Person)
Cooper Industries
600 Travis St Ste 5300
Houston, TX 77002-3092, USA

Riley, James (Athlete, Football Player)
2201 Cardinal Dr
Edmond, OK 73013-7635, USA

Riley, Jeannie (Musician)
1003 Lakeview Dr
Brenham, TX 77833-4755, USA

Riley, Ken (Athlete, Football Player)
1865 E Gibbons St
Bartow, FL 33830-6712, USA

Riley, Kevin (Alex Riley) (Actor, Athlete, Wrestler)
3808 Villas Del Sol Ct
Tampa, FL 33609-4440, USA

Riley, Madison (Actor)
c/o Mona Loring *Status PR*
PO Box 6191
Westlake Village, CA 91359-6191, USA

Riley, Matt (Athlete, Baseball Player)
6 Kirra Ct
Aliso Viejo, CA 92656-4276, USA

Riley, Mike (Coach, Football Coach)
Oregon State University
Athletic Dept
Corvallis, OR 97331, USA

Riley, Pat (Athlete, Basketball Coach, Basketball Player, Coach)
800 S Pointe Dr # B
Miami Beach, FL 33139-7163, USA

Riley, Perry (Athlete, Football Player)
c/o Joel Segal *Lagardere Unlimited (NY)*
456 Washington St Apt 9L
New York, NY 10013-1555, USA

Riley, Rachel (Television Host)
c/o Staff Member *KBJ Management*
22 Rathbone St
London W1T 1LG, UNITED KINGDOM

Riley, Raven (Actor)
Evil Motion Pictures
Prefers to be contacted via email
Phoenix, AZ 85066, USA

Riley, Richard D (Misc)
16 Boathouse Rd
Laconia, NH 03246-1949, USA

Riley, Robert (Politician)
742 County Road 5
Ashland, AL 36251-5533, USA

Riley, Ruth (Athlete)
3777 Lapeer Rd
Auburn Hills, MI 48326-1733

Riley, Sam (Actor)
c/o Angharad Wood *Tavistock Wood Management*
45 Conduit St
London W1S 2YN, UNITED KINGDOM

Riley, Steve (Athlete, Football Player)
PO Box 2327
Park City, UT 84060-2327, USA

Riley, Talulah (Actor)
c/o Laura Symons *Premier PR*
2-4 Bucknall St
London WC2H 8LA, UNITED KINGDOM

Riley, Teddy (Musician, Songwriter)
c/o Monica Anders *Monica Anders*
458 Highland Vw
Houlton, WI 54082-2408, USA

Riley, Victor (Athlete, Football Player)
136 Sandy Oak Ln
Gaston, SC 29053-8775, USA

Rimando, Nick (Soccer Player)
DC United
2400 E Capitol St NE Ste 1
Rfk Stadium
Washington, DC 20003-1738, USA

Rimer, Jeff (Sportscaster)
9916 Morris Dr
Dublin, OH 43017-8859, USA

Rimes, LeAnn (Musician)
c/o Christina Garvin *Schure Media Group*
16 Skyline Dr Unit 594
Montville, NJ 07045-7024, USA

Rimington, Dave (Athlete, Football Player)
222 Riverside Dr # 11-D
New York, NY 10025-6809, USA

Rimmel, James E (Religious Leader)
Evangetical Presbyterian Church
26049 5 Mile Rd
Detroit, MI 48239-3235, USA

Rinaldi, Kathy (Tennis Player)
Advantage International
1025 Thomas Jefferson St NW # 450
Washington, DC 20007-5201, USA

Rinaldi, Rich (Athlete, Basketball Player)
1117 Perry Ln
Collegeville, PA 19426-1067, USA

Rinaldo, Benjamin (Skier)
Ski World
2680 Buena Park Dr
North Hollywood, CA 91604, USA

Rincon, Andy (Athlete, Baseball Player)
6809 Broadway Ave
Whittier, CA 90606-1618, USA

Rincon, Juan (Athlete, Baseball Player)
5150 Lincoln Dr
Minneapolis, MN 55436-1010, USA

Rincon, Ricardo (Baseball Player)
c/o Staff Member *Oakland Athletics*
7000 Coliseum Way Ste 3
Oakland, CA 94621-1992, USA

Rinearson, Peter M (Journalist)
Seattle Times
1120 John St
Editorial Dept
Seattle, WA 98109-5321, USA

Rineer, Jeff (Athlete, Baseball Player)
325 W Charlotte St
Millersville, PA 17551-9515, USA

Rinehart, Chad (Athlete, Football Player)

Rinehart, Kenneth (Misc)
University of Illinois
Chemistry Dept
Urbana, IL 61801, USA

RIng, Royce (Athlete, Baseball Player)
19705 NE 191st St
Woodinville, WA 98077-8831, USA

Ringadoo, Veerasamy (President)
Corner of Farquhar & Sir Celicourt Antelme Sts
Quatre-Bornes, MAURITIUS

Ringer, Robert J (Writer)
c/o Staff Member *The Harry Walker Agency*
355 Lexington Ave Fl 21
New York, NY 10017-6603, USA

Ringolsby, Tracy (Baseball Player)
1526 Fox Chase Rd
Cheyenne, WY 82009-8396, USA

Ringwald, Molly (Actor)
8436 W 3rd St # 650
Los Angeles, CA 90048-4163, USA

Rini, Mary (Athlete, Baseball Player)
24031 Meadowbridge Dr
Clinton Township, MI 48035-3010, USA

Rinker, Larry (Golfer)
1615 Woodland Ave
Winter Park, FL 32789-2774, USA

Rinna, Lisa (Actor, Reality Star)
c/o Jill Fritzo *Jill Fritzo Public Relations*
208 E 51st St # 305
New York, NY 10022-6557, USA

Rinne, Pekka (Athlete, Hockey Player)
Puckagency LLC
555 Pleasantville Rd Ste 210N
Attn Jay Grossman
Briarcliff Manor, NY 10510-1900, USA

Rintoul, Steve (Golfer)
17506 Osprey Manor Way
Lithia, FL 33547-5044, USA

Riordan, Cory (Athlete, Baseball Player)

Riordan, Mike (Athlete, Basketball Player)
Riordan's Saloon
14e Inwood Rd
Stevensville, MD 21666-3969, USA

Riordan, Richard J (Politician)
Bingham McCutchen
355 S Grand Ave Ste 4400
Los Angeles, CA 90071-3106, USA

Rios, Alberto (Writer)
Arizona State University
English Dept
Tempe, AZ 85287-0001, USA

Rios, Alexis (Baseball Player)
Yale Field
252 Derby Ave
West Haven, CT 06516, USA

Rios, Armando (Athlete, Baseball Player)
790 Ridenhour Cir # I
Orlando, FL 32809-7158, USA

Rios, Brandon (Boxer)
c/o Staff Member *Top Rank Inc.*
3908 Howard Hughes Pkwy
#580
Las Vegas, NV 89109, USA

Rios, Danny (Athlete, Baseball Player)
2523 W 9th Ln
Hialeah, FL 33010-1225, USA

Rios, Emily (Actor)
c/o Staff Member *Kass Management*
1011 Euclid St Unit B
Santa Monica, CA 90403-4296, USA

Rios, Marcelo (Tennis Player)
Int'l Mgmt Group
Via Augusta 200
#400
Barcelona 08021, SPAIN

Rios, Osvaldo (Actor)
c/o Staff Member *TV Caracol*
Calle 76 #11 - 35
Piso 10AA
Bogota DC 26484, COLOMBIA

Riotta, Vincent (Actor)
c/o Staff Member *Scott Marshall Partners Ltd*
49/50 Eagle Wharf Road
Holborn Studios
London N1 7ED, UNITED KINGDOM

Rioux, Gerry (Athlete, Hockey Player)
213 Grosvenor
Iroquois Falls A, ON POK 1GO, Canada

Ripa, Kelly (Actor, Talk Show Host)
c/o Staff Member *Live with Kelly & Ryan*
7 Lincoln Sq
New York, NY 10023-7219, USA

Ripert, Eric (Chef)
Le Bernardin
787 7th Ave Fl CONC1
New York, NY 10019-8103, USA

Ripken, Billy (Athlete, Baseball Player)
Major League Basebal Network
900 Mount Soma Ct
Fallston, MD 21047-1935, USA

Ripken Jr, Cal (Athlete, Baseball Player)
Cal Ripken Foundation
1427 Clarkview Rd Ste 100
Baltimore, MD 21209-0030, USA

Ripley, Alexandra (Writer)
24 Ripley St
Newport News, VA 23603-1305, USA

Ripley, Alice (Actor, Musician)
c/o Staff Member *Douglas Gorman Rothacker & Wilhelm Inc*
33 W 46th St Ste 801
New York, NY 10036-4103, USA

Ripley, Allen (Athlete, Baseball Player)
50 Dunham St
Attleboro, MA 02703-3052, USA

Rippelmeyer, Ray (Athlete, Baseball Player)
104 Eagle Ct
Waterloo, IL 62298-3158, USA

Rippey, Rodney Allan (Actor)
3941 Veselich Ave # 4-251
Los Angeles, CA 90039-1461, USA

Rippley, Steve (Baseball Player)
3900 Galt Ocean Dr Apt 1406
Fort Lauderdale, FL 33308-6606, USA

Rippley, Steve (Athlete, Baseball Player)
3900 Galt Ocean Dr Apt 1406
Fort Lauderdale, FL 33308-6606, USA

Rippon, Adam (Athlete, Figure Skater, Olympic Athlete)
c/o David Baden *IMG World*
304 Park Ave S Fl 11
New York, NY 10010-4305, USA

Riseborough, Andrea (Actor)
c/o Clair Dobbs *CLD Communications*
4 Broadway Ct
The Broadway
London SW191RG, UNITED KINGDOM

Risebrough, Doug (Athlete, Coach, Hockey Player)
5809 Schaefer Rd
Minneapolis, MN 55436-1115

Risher, Alan (Athlete, Football Player)
10532 Oakley Trace Dr
Baton Rouge, LA 70809-3320, USA

Risien, Cody L (Athlete, Football Player)
12060 Lake Ave Apt 401
Lakewood, OH 44107-1865, USA

Risinger, Earlene (Baseball Player)
334 Aurora St SE
Grand Rapids, MI 49507-3124, USA

Riske, Alison (Athlete, Tennis Player)
c/o Staff Member *Women's Tennis Association (WTA-US)*
1 Progress Plz Ste 1500
St Petersburg, FL 33701-4335, USA

Riske, David (Athlete, Baseball Player)
2671 Boboli Ct
Henderson, NV 89052-3183, USA

Risley, Bill (Athlete, Baseball Player)
1160 Prim Rose Cir
Greenwood, AR 72936-3066, USA

Rispoli, Michael (Actor)
c/o Staff Member *Gersh*
9465 Wilshire Blvd Ste 600
Beverly Hills, CA 90212-2605, USA

Rissling, Gary (Athlete, Hockey Player)
717 Paige Cir
Bel Air, MD 21014-5258, USA

Rissmiller, Pat (Athlete, Hockey Player)
276 Brackett St Apt 2R
Portland, ME 04102-3239

Rissmiller, Ray (Athlete, Football Player)
114 Iken Cir
Goose Creek, SC 29445-7148, USA

Rist, Robbie (Actor)
c/o Marni Anhalt *Imperium 7 Talent Agency*
5455 Wilshire Blvd Ste 1706
Los Angeles, CA 90036-4217, USA

Ristorucci, Lisa (Actor)
Progressive Artists Agency
400 S Beverly Dr Ste 216
Beverly Hills, CA 90212-4404, USA

Ritch, Michael (Race Car Driver)
David & Wright Motorsports
2730 Zion Church Rd
Concord, NC 28025-7027, USA

Ritcher, James A (Jim) (Athlete, Football Player)
8620 Boumemouth Dr
Raleigh, NC 27615, USA

Ritchie, Guy (Director, Producer)
c/o Kate Lee *Freuds Communications*
1 Stephen St
London W1T 1AL, UNITED KINGDOM

Ritchie, Jay (Athlete, Baseball Player)
8275 Highway 52
Rockwell, NC 28138-8545, USA

Ritchie, Jill (Actor)
c/o Staff Member *Rugolo Entertainment*
195 S Beverly Dr Ste 400
Beverly Hills, CA 90212-3044, USA

Ritchie, Jim (Artist)
Mark Hotel
19 E 82nd St
New York, NY 10028-0302, USA

Ritchie, Jon (Athlete, Football Player)
c/o Staff Member *Philadelphia Eagles*
1 Novacare Way
Philadelphia, PA 19145-5996, USA

Ritchie, Todd (Athlete, Baseball Player)
114 Hulan Dr
Kerens, TX 75144-6046, USA

Ritchie, Wally (Athlete, Baseball Player)
417 Robert Cir
Santa Clara, UT 84765-5617, USA

Ritchson, Alan (Actor)
c/o Staff Member *AllyCat Entertainment*
168 Tradewinds Dr
Santa Rosa Beach, FL 32459-8126, USA

Rittenhouse, Lenore (Golfer)
295 Bellhaven Dr
Carthage, NC 28327-7133, USA

Rittenhouse, Rebecca (Actor)
c/o Marla Farrell *Shelter PR*
928 Broadway Ste 505
New York, NY 10010-8143, USA

Ritter, Huntley (Actor, Producer)
c/o Adam Rosen *Rosen Feig Conley & Lunn LLP*
9454 Wilshire Blvd Ste 850
Beverly Hills, CA 90212-2909, USA

Ritter, Jason (Actor)
c/o Joannie Burstein *Burstein Company*
15304 W Sunset Blvd Ste 208
Pacific Palisades, CA 90272-3656, USA

Ritter, Josh (Musician)
Concerted Efforts
PO Box 440326
Somerville, MA 02144-0004, USA

Ritter, Krysten (Actor)
c/o Nancy Sanders *Sanders Armstrong Caserta*
4111 W Alameda Ave Ste 505
Burbank, CA 91505-4163, USA

Ritter, Lawrence (Baseball Player)
424 W End Ave Apt 6D
New York, NY 10024-5777, USA

Ritter, Paul (Actor)
c/o Lou Coulson *Lou Coulson Agency*
37 Berwick St
1st Floor
London W1F 8RS, UNITED KINGDOM (UK)

Ritter, Reggie (Athlete, Baseball Player)
1564 Estep Rd
Donaldson, AR 71941-8987, USA

Ritter, Tyson (Musician)
c/o Andrea Pett-Joseph *Brillstein Entertainment Partners*
9150 Wilshire Blvd Ste 350
Beverly Hills, CA 90212-3453, USA

Ritts, Jim (Golfer, Television Host)
Ladies Pro Golf Assn
100 International Golf Dr
Daytona Beach, FL 32124-1082, USA

Rittwage, Jim (Athlete, Baseball Player)
23931 Columbus Rd
Bedford, OH 44146-2969, USA

Ritz, Kevin (Athlete, Baseball Player)
836 N 6th St
Cambridge, OH 43725-1400, USA

Ritzman, Alice (Golfer)
614 S Foys Lake Dr
Kalispell, MT 59901-7440, USA

Riva, Diana Maria (Actor)
c/o Amy Guenther *Gateway Management Company Inc*
860 Via De La Paz Ste F10
Pacific Palisades, CA 90272-3631, USA

Rivaldo (Soccer Player)
AC Milan
Via Turati 3
Washington, DC 20221-0001, ITALY

Rivard, Bob (Athlete, Hockey Player)
882 Chapel Rd
Peterborough, ON K9H 7M3, Canada

Rivas, Daniel Louis (Actor)
c/o Paul Santana *Agency for the Performing Arts (APA)*
405 S Beverly Dr Ste 500
Beverly Hills, CA 90212-4425, USA

Rivas, Gonzalo (Actor)
c/o Staff Member *Televisa*
Blvd Adolfo Lopez Mateos 232
Colonia San Angel INN
DF CP 01060, MEXICO

Rivas, Sara (Actor)
c/o Paul Greenstone *Paul Greenstone Entertainment*
1400 California Ave Apt 201
Santa Monica, CA 90403-4395, USA

Rivas Monta??o, Hanna (Actor)
c/o Staff Member *Televisa*
Blvd Adolfo Lopez Mateos 232
Colonia San Angel INN
DF CP 01060, MEXICO

Rivera, Alex (Baseball Player)
228 4th Ave N
Edmonds, WA 98020-3116, USA

Rivera, Ana Liz (Actor)
c/o Staff Member *Televisa*
Blvd Adolfo Lopez Mateos 232
Colonia San Angel INN
DF CP 01060, MEXICO

Rivera, Angelica (Actor)
c/o Staff Member *Televisa*
Blvd Adolfo Lopez Mateos 232
Colonia San Angel INN
DF CP 01060, MEXICO

Rivera, Chita (Actor, Dancer, Musician)
c/o David Kalodner *WME/IMG (NY)*
11 Madison Ave Fl 18
New York, NY 10010-3669, USA

Rivera, David (Congressman, Politician)
417 Cannon Hob
Washington, DC 20515-1013, USA

Rivera, Emilio (Actor)
4637 Willowcrest Ave
Toluca Lake, CA 91602-1464, USA

Rivera, Geraldo (Journalist, Television Host)
c/o Tony D. Burton *Buchwald (NY)*
10 E 44th St
New York, NY 10017-3601, USA

Rivera, Jerry (Musician)
c/o Staff Member *BMG*
1540 Broadway
New York, NY 10036-4039, USA

Rivera, Jim (Athlete, Baseball Player)
2311 Abbey Dr Apt 7
Fort Wayne, IN 46835-3150, USA

Rivera, Jose (Producer, Writer)
c/o Rick Berg *Code Entertainment*
280 S Beverly Dr Ste 513
Beverly Hills, CA 90212-3908, USA

Rivera, Juan (Athlete, Baseball Player)
c/o Staff Member *Los Angeles Dodgers*
1000 Elysian Park Ave
Los Angeles, CA 90012, USA

Rivera, Luis (Athlete, Baseball Player)
16 Calle Lazaro Ramos
Cidra, PR 00739-3424, USA

Rivera, Lupillo (Music Group)
c/o Staff Member *Sony Music (Miami)*
404 Washington Ave Ste 700
Miami Beach, FL 33139-6615, USA

Rivera, Mariano (Athlete, Baseball Player)
1 Brook View Ln
Rye, NY 10580-1942, USA

Rivera, Mike (Athlete, Baseball Player)
2814 Harwood Ct
Kissimmee, FL 34744-8416, USA

Rivera, Mychal (Athlete, Football Player)

Rivera, Naya (Actor)
3722 Effingham Pl
Los Angeles, CA 90027-1428, USA

Rivera, Ron (Athlete, Football Player)
14420 Rancho Del Prado Trl
San Diego, CA 92127-3866, USA

Rivera, Ximena Sarinana (Musician)
c/o Staff Member *Warner Music*
4000 Warner Blvd
Burbank, CA 91522-0002, USA

Rivera Carrera, Norberto Cardinal (Religious Leader)
Curia Arzobispal
Aptdo Postal 24-4-33
Mexico City, DF 06700, MEXICO

Rivero, Jorge (Actor)
c/o David Moss *David Moss Company*
6063 Vineland Ave Apt B
N Hollywood, CA 91606-4986, USA

Rivers, David (Athlete, Basketball Player)
10509 Greensprings Dr
Tampa, FL 33626-1724, USA

Rivers, Glenn (Doc) (Athlete, Basketball Coach, Basketball Player, Coach)
5 Isle of Sicily
Winter Park, FL 32789-1505, USA

Rivers, Jamie (Athlete, Football Player)
4006 Lindell Blvd
Saint Louis, MO 63108-3202, USA

Rivers, Jamie (Athlete, Hockey Player)
2754 Farriers Lane
Gloucester, ON K1T 1X8, Canada

Rivers, Johnny (Musician, Songwriter, Writer)
3141 Coldwater Canyon Ln
Beverly Hills, CA 90210-1250, USA

Rivers, Keith (Athlete, Football Player)
c/o David Dunn *Athletes First*
23091 Mill Creek Dr
Laguna Hills, CA 92653-1258, USA

Rivers, Marcellus (Athlete, Football Player)
12003 Eden Ln
Frisco, TX 75033-1146, USA

Rivers, Melissa (Talk Show Host)
c/o Howard Bragman *LaBrea Media*
8306 Wilshire Blvd # 4002
Beverly Hills, CA 90211-2304, USA

Rivers, Mickey (Athlete, Baseball Player)
M D M Sports Marketing
218 Washington Ave Apt C14
Attn: David Ratner
Cedarhurst, NY 11516-1510, USA

Rivers, Philip (Athlete, Football Player)
8396 Santaluz Village Grn E
Green E
San Diego, CA 92127-2523, USA

Rivers, Reggie (Athlete, Football Player)
5003 E Weaver Pl
Centennial, CO 80121-3520, USA

Rivers, Shawn (Athlete, Hockey Player)
1962 Queensdale Ave
Gloucester, ON K1T 1K1, Canada

Rivers, Wayne (Athlete, Hockey Player)
2821 San Ardo Way
Belmont, CA 94002-1341

Rives, Don (Athlete, Football Player)
603 E Garfield Ave
Morton, TX 79346-4106, USA

Rivet, Craig (Athlete, Hockey Player)
Newport Sports Management
400-201 City Centre Dr
Attn Don Meehan
Mississauga, ON L5B 2T4, Canada

Riviere, Marie (Actor, Director)
c/o Staff Member *Dominique Sarais Agence Artistique*
37 rue du Port a l'Anglais
Alfortville 94140, France

Rizzle Kicks (Music Group)
c/o Staff Member *Sony Music Entertainment Germany*
Neumarkter Str. 28
Muenchen 81673, Germany

Rizzo, Anthony (Athlete, Baseball Player)
Anthony Rizzo Family Foundation
6574 N State Road 7 # 201
Coconut Creek, FL 33073-3625, USA

Rizzo, Jack (Athlete, Football Player)
PO Box 325
New Vernon, NJ 07976-0325, USA

Rizzo, Jerry (Athlete, Basketball Player)
2548 126th St Apt 1
Flushing, NY 11354-1126, USA

Rizzo, Joe (Athlete, Football Player)
6131 Dorsett Pl
Wilmington, NC 28403-0128, USA

Rizzo, Joe (Horse Racer)
5 Berkshire Dr
Howell, NJ 07731-2355, USA

Rizzo, John (Writer)
Steptoe & Johnson LLP
1330 Connecticut Ave NW Ste 1C
Washington, DC 20036-1795, USA

Rizzo, John R (Athlete, Football Player)
PO Box 325
New Vernon, NJ 07976-0325, USA

Rizzo, Patti (Golfer)
2455 Provence Cir
Weston, FL 33327-1303, USA

Rizzo, Rob (Race Car Driver)
Rizzo Racing
700 Main St
East Greenwich, RI 02818-3541, USA

Rizzo, Todd (Athlete, Baseball Player)
7 Williamsburg Ct
Sewell, NJ 08080-3230, USA

Rizzo-Depardon, Patti (Golfer)
1008 SE 5th Ct
Ft Lauderdale, FL 33301-3004, USA

Rizzotti, Jennifer (Basketball Player, Coach)
University of Hartford
Athletic Dept
West Hartford, CT 06117, USA

Rizzs, Rick (Sportscaster)
4008 243rd Pl SE
Issaauah, WA 98029-7586, USA

Rizzuto, Garth (Athlete, Hockey Player)
JO Ced(lr Bowl Cres RR 4
Fernie, BC VOB 1M4, Canada

R. Keating, William (Congressman, Politician)
315 Cannon Hob
Washington, DC 20515-0101, USA

R. Labrador, Raul (Congressman, Politician)
1523 Longworth Hob
Washington, DC 20515-4003, USA

R. Langevin, James (Congressman, Politician)
109 Cannon Hob
Washington, DC 20515-3902, USA

Roa, Joe (Athlete, Baseball Player)
677 E Brickley Ave
Hazel Park, MI 48030-1270, USA

Roa Bastos, Augusto (Writer)
Berutti 2828
Martinez
Buenos Aires, ARGENTINA

Roach, Andy (Athlete, Hockey Player)
PO Box 488
Mattawan, MI 49071-0488

Roach, Jason (Athlete, Baseball Player)
12295 SE Birkdale Run
Jupiter, FL 33469-1746, USA

Roach, Jay (Director, Producer, Writer)
c/o Staff Member *Everyman Pictures*
3000 Olympic Blvd Ste 1500
Santa Monica, CA 90404-5073, USA

Roach, John (Athlete, Football Player)
4101 San Carlos St
Dallas, TX 75205-2047, USA

Roach, Mel (Athlete, Baseball Player)
4131 Southaven Rd
Richmond, VA 23235-1026, USA

Roache, Linus (Actor)
c/o Staff Member *WME/IMG*
9601 Wilshire Blvd
Beverly Hills, CA 90210-5213, USA

Roaches, Carl (Athlete, Football Player)
1314 Twining Oaks Ln
Missouri City, TX 77489-2110, USA

Roaf, William L (Willie) (Athlete, Football Player)
1900 E 38th Ave
Pine Bluff, AR 71601-7280, USA

Roan, Michael (Athlete, Football Player)
11275 Green Valley Rd
Sebastopol, CA 95472-9771, USA

Roan, Oscar (Athlete, Football Player)
PO Box 1026
Rockwall, TX 75087-1026, USA

Roark, Anastasia (Actor)
c/o Steve Miller *Ford Models (LA)*
9200 W Sunset Blvd Ste 805
W Hollywood, CA 90069-3603, USA

Roarke, Mike (Athlete, Baseball Player)
97 Pawtuxet Ter
West Warwick, RI 02893-5242, USA

Roath, Stephen D (Business Person)
Longs Drug Stores
141 N Civic Dr
Walnut Creek, CA 94596-3815, USA

Robach, Amy (Correspondent)
c/o Henry Reisch *WME/IMG (NY)*
11 Madison Ave Fl 18
New York, NY 10010-3669, USA

Robards, Jake (Actor)
c/o Staff Member *Buchwald (NY)*
10 E 44th St
New York, NY 10017-3601, USA

Robards, Sam (Actor)
Rigberg Roberts Rugolo
1180 S Beverly Dr Ste 601
Los Angeles, CA 90035-1158, USA

Robb, AnnaSophia (Actor)
c/o Jill Fritzo *Jill Fritzo Public Relations*
208 E 51st St # 305
New York, NY 10022-6557, USA

Robb, Charles (Politician)
612 Chain Bridge Rd
Mc Lean, VA 22101-1810, USA

Robb, David (Actor)
c/o Michael Hallett *Emptage Hallett*
34-35 Eastcastle St
Fl 3
London W1W 8DW, UNITED KINGDOM (UK)

Robb, Doug (Musician)

Robb, Lynda Bird Johnson (Misc)
612 Chain Bridge Rd
McLean, VA 22101-1810, USA

Robb, Lynda Johnson (Politician)
612 Chain Bridge Rd
Mc Lean, VA 22101-1810, USA

Robb, Riddick (Athlete, Football Player)
101 Hearthstone Dr
Woodstock, GA 30189-5263, USA

Robbers on High Street (Music Group)
c/o Staff Member *Paradigm (Monterey)*
404 W Franklin St
Monterey, CA 93940-2303, USA

Robbie, Margot (Actor)
c/o Staff Member *LuckyChap Entertainment*
4000 Warner Blvd Bldg 144
Burbank, CA 91522-0001, USA

Robbie, Timothy J (Tim) (Football Executive)
Miami Dolphins
7500 SW 30th St
Davie, FL 33314-1020, USA

Robbins, Amy (Actor)
c/o Staff Member *Artists Rights Group (ARG)*
4A Exmoor St
London W10 6BD, UNITED KINGDOM

Robbins, Austin (Athlete, Football Player)
4627 Hilltop Ter SE
Washington, DC 20019-7837, USA

Robbins, Barret (Athlete, Football Player)
26186 Shadow Rock Ln
Valencia, CA 91381-0654, USA

Robbins, Brian (Director)
c/o Staff Member *Tollin/Robbins Management*
4130 Cahuenga Blvd Ste 305
Toluca Lake, CA 91602-2847, USA

Robbins, Bruce (Athlete, Baseball Player)
13023 E 239th St
Noblesville, IN 46060-6988, USA

Robbins, Deanna (Actor)
630 N Keystone St
Burbank, CA 91506-1922, USA

Robbins, Doug (Athlete, Baseball Player, Olympic Athlete)
7655 W Randolph County Line
Williamsburg, IN 47393-9500, USA

Robbins, Jacqueline (Actor)
c/o Jayson Marshall *Characters Talent Agency*
200-1505 2nd Ave W
Vancouver, BC V6H 3Y4, CANADA

Robbins, Jake (Athlete, Baseball Player)
14208 Castle Abbey Ln
Charlotte, NC 28277-1612, USA

Robbins, Jane (Actor)
Scott Marshall Mgmt
44 Perry Road
London W3 7NA, UNITED KINGDOM (UK)

Robbins, John (Writer)
c/o Staff Member *Red Wheel / Weiser /Conari*
65 Parker St Ste 7
Newburyport, MA 01950-4600, USA

Robbins, Kelly (Golfer)
1025 Lincoln Dr
Weidman, MI 48893-9365, USA

Robbins, Randy (Athlete, Football Player)
1131 E Valle Vista Dr
Nogales, AZ 85621-1229, USA

Robbins, Tim (Actor, Director)
c/o Staff Member *Actors Gang, The*
9070 Venice Blvd
Culver City, CA 90232-2305, USA

Robbins, Tom (Writer)
PO Box 338
La Conner, WA 98257-0338, USA

Robbins, Tony (Business Person, Writer)
Robbins Research International Inc
6160 Cornerstone Ct E Ste 200
San Diego, CA 92121-3720, USA

Robbins, Tootie (Athlete, Football Player)
6712 W Shannon St
Chandler, AZ 85226-1669, USA

Robelot, Jane (Correspondent)
CBS-TV
51 W 52nd St
News Dept
New York, NY 10019-6119, USA

Roberge, Bert (Athlete, Baseball Player)
267 Sunderland Dr
Auburn, ME 04210-9232, USA

Roberson, Antoinette (Musician)
c/o Staff Member *Diva Central Inc*
7510 W Sunset Blvd # 1445
Los Angeles, CA 90046-3408, USA

Roberson, Chris (Athlete, Baseball Player)
10626 Liberty Bell Dr
Tampa, FL 33647-3656, USA

Roberson, Irvin (Bo) (Athlete, Football Player, Track Athlete)
820 N Raymond Ave Apt 47
Pasadena, CA 91103-3151, USA

Roberson, James (Athlete, Football Player)
417 Labarre Ct
Saint Johns, FL 32259-4024, USA

Roberson, Kevin (Athlete, Baseball Player)
1565 E North Port Rd
Decatur, IL 62526-2823, USA

Roberson, Rick (Athlete, Basketball Player)
635 W West Ave
Fullerton, CA 92832-2120, USA

Roberson, Sid (Athlete, Baseball Player)
1859 Atlantic Beach Dr
Atlantic Bch, FL 32233-7346, USA

Robert, Rene (Athlete, Hockey Player)
90 Lord Byron Ln
Buffalo, NY 14221-1997, CANADA

Roberto, Phil (Athlete, Hockey Player)
5238 Ottawa Ave
Niagara Falls, ON L2E 4Y8, Canada

Roberts, Alfredo (Athlete, Football Player)
20406 Donegal Ln
Strongsville, OH 44149-0960, USA

Roberts, Andre (Athlete, Football Player)
c/o Scott Smith *XAM Sports*
3509 Ice Age Dr
Madison, WI 53719-5409, USA

Roberts, Ashley (Actor)
c/o Susan (Sue) Madore *Guttman Associates Public Relations*
118 S Beverly Dr Ste 201
Beverly Hills, CA 90212-3016, USA

Roberts, Bernard (Musician)
Uwchlaw'r Coed
Llanbedr
Gwynedd LL45 2NA, WALES

Roberts, Bert C Jr (Business Person)
MCI WorldCom Inc
500 Clinton Pkwy
Clinton, MS 39056-4032, USA

Roberts, Brad (Musician)
Macklam Feldman Mgmt
200-1505 2nd Ave W
Vancouver, BC V6H 3Y4, CANADA

Roberts, Bret (Actor)
c/o Scott Karp *The Syndicate*
8265 W Sunset Blvd Ste 205
West Hollywood, CA 90046-2470, USA

Roberts, Brian (Athlete, Baseball Player)
4712 Higel Ave
Sarasota, FL 34242-1208, USA

Roberts, Brian L (Business Person)
Comcast
1500 Market St Fl 11E
Philadelphia, PA 19102-2107, USA

Roberts, Bruce (Musician, Songwriter, Writer)
c/o Staff Member *Gorfaine/Schwartz Agency Inc*
4111 W Alameda Ave Ste 509
Burbank, CA 91505-4171, USA

Roberts, Cecil (Misc)
United Mine Workers
8315 Lee Hwy Ste 500
Fairfax, VA 22031-2242, USA

Roberts, Cokie (Correspondent, Journalist)
5315 Bradley Blvd
Bethesda, MD 20814-1244, USA

Roberts, Craig (Actor)
c/o Romilly Bowlby *DDA Public Relations*
192-198 Vauxhall Bridge Rd
London SW1V 1DX, UNITED KINGDOM

Roberts, Dale (Athlete, Baseball Player)
206 Berry Ave
Versailles, KY 40383-1457, USA

Roberts, Dallas (Actor)
c/o Marnie Briskin *Circle of Confusion (NY)*
270 Lafayette St Ste 402
New York, NY 10012-3327, USA

Roberts, Danny (Reality Star)
c/o Staff Member *Heffner Management*
80 Vine St Apt 203
Seattle, WA 98121-1369, USA

Roberts, Dave (Athlete, Baseball Player)
8109 Echo Hills Ct N
Benbrook, TX 76126-4730, USA

Roberts, Dave (Athlete, Baseball Player)
1208 Crestview Dr
Cardiff By The Sea, CA 92007-1400, USA

Roberts, Dave (Athlete, Baseball Player)
9705 Sam Bass Trl
Fort Worth, TX 76244-6092, USA

Roberts, David (Athlete, Hockey Player)
Telemus Capital Partners
110 Miller Ave Ste 300, ML 48104-1305

Roberts, David (Dave) (Athlete, Track Athlete)
14310 SW 73rd Ave
Archer, FL 32618-2914, USA

Roberts, Dee (Artist)
2012 N 19th St
Boise, ID 83702-0821, USA

Roberts, Doug (Athlete, Hockey Player)
PO Box 1011
Old Lyme, CT 06371-0999, USA

Roberts, Emma (Actor)
c/o David Sweeney *Sweeney Entertainment*
1601 Vine St # 6
Los Angeles, CA 90028-8802, USA

Roberts, Eric (Actor)
c/o Tom Monjack *Tom Monjack Celebrity Enterprises*
28650 Avenida Maravilla # A
Cathedral City, CA 92234-8115, USA

Roberts, Fred (Athlete, Basketball Player)
463 Knight Cir
Alpine, UT 84004-1259, USA

Roberts, Gary (Athlete, Hockey Player)
12348 NW 69th Ct
Parkland, FL 33076-3334

Roberts, Gordie (Athlete, Hockey Player)
3965 Yorktown Ln N
Minneapolis, MN 55441-1427, USA

Roberts, Grant (Athlete, Baseball Player)
1299 Vista Captain Dr
El Cajon, CA 92020-1343, USA

Roberts, Jake (Actor, Writer)
Box 3859
Stamford, CT 06905

Roberts, Jake (Athlete, Wrestler)
PO Box 1317
Gainesville, TX 76241-1317, USA

Roberts, J D (Athlete, Football Coach, Football Player)
6708 Trevi Ct
Oklahoma City, OK 73116-2604, USA

Roberts, Joe (Athlete, Basketball Player)
10975 Elvessa St
Oakland, CA 94605-5511, USA

Roberts, John (Director)
c/o Staff Member *Independent Talent Group*
40 Whitfield St
London W1T 2RH, UNITED KINGDOM

Roberts, John D (Misc)
California Institute of Technology
Chemistry Dept
Pasadena, CA 91125-0001, USA

Roberts, John D (J D) (Athlete, Coach, Football Player)
7700 W Hefner Rd Apt 88
Oklahoma City, OK 73162-4467, USA

Roberts, Julia (Actor)
c/o Marcy Engleman *Engelman & Company*
20 W 22nd St Ste 805
New York, NY 10010-5890, USA

Roberts, Julie (Musician)
c/o Staff Member *Creative Artists Agency (CAA)*
2000 Avenue of the Stars Ste 100
Los Angeles, CA 90067-4705, USA

Roberts, Larry (Race Car Driver)
MR Motorsports
PO Box 194
Novi, MI 48376-0194, USA

Roberts, Leon (Athlete, Baseball Player)
4711 Chapel Springs Ct
Arlington, TX 76017-1204, USA

Roberts, Leonard (Actor)
c/o Michael McConnell *Zero Gravity Management (II)*
5660 Silver Valley Ave
Agoura Hills, CA 91301-4000, USA

Roberts, Leonard (Athlete, Baseball Player)
1027 Waterford Dr
Dallas, TX 75218-2845, USA

Roberts, Leonard (Business Person)
Tandy Corp
100 Throckmorton St Ste 1600
Fort Worth, TX 76102-2846, USA

Roberts, Leon (Bip) (Athlete, Baseball Player)
2040 Canyon Woods Dr APT 296
San Ramon, CA 94582-4279, USA

Roberts, Loren (Athlete, Golfer)
8429 Orchard Hill Dr
Germantown, TN 38138-6297, USA

Roberts, Marcus (Musician)
Columbia Artists Mgmt Inc
165 W 57th St
New York, NY 10019-2201, USA

Roberts, Marvin (Athlete, Basketball Player)
5 S 500 W Unit 803
Salt Lake City, UT 84101-4124, USA

Roberts, M Brigitte (Writer)
Atkins & Stone
29 Fernshaw Road
London SW10 0TG, UNITED KINGDOM (UK)

Roberts, Mica (Musician)
c/o Curt Motley *Paradigm (Nashville)*
222 2nd Ave S Ste 1600
Nashville, TN 37201-2375, USA

Roberts, Michael D (Actor)
c/o Staff Member *Karen Renna & Associates*
PO Box 4227
Burbank, CA 91503-4227, USA

Roberts, Nora (Writer)
19239 Burnside Bridge Rd
Keedysville, MD 21756-1603, USA

Roberts, Pat (Politician)
2203 Whiteoaks Dr
Alexandria, VA 22306-2436, USA

Roberts, Rachel (Actor, Model)
c/o Deb Dillistone *Red Management*
415 Esplanade W Box 3
North Vancouver, BC V7M 1A6, CANADA

Roberts, Randy (Actor)
14220 Winterset Dr
Attn: Renee Amaireh
Greenwell Springs, LA 70739-3275, USA

Roberts, Randy (Actor)
14220 Winterset Dr
C/O Renee Amaireh
Greenwell Springs, LA 70739-3275, USA

Roberts, Randy (Actor)
Ryan Artists, Inc
239 NW 13th Ave Ste 215
C/O Mary Dangerfield
Portland, OR 97209-2927, USA

Roberts, Randy (Actor)
14220 Winterset Dr
Greenwell Springs, LA 70739-3275, USA

Roberts, Robin (Sportscaster, Television Host)
c/o Staff Member *Good Morning America (GMA)*
44th St & Broadway
New York, NY 10112, USA

Roberts, Rodney (Race Car Driver)
MR Motorsports
PO Box 92826
Lakeland, FL 33804-2826, USA

Roberts, Ryan (Athlete, Baseball Player)
6017 Avalon St
North Richland Hills, TX 76180-5593, USA

Roberts, Shawn (Actor)
c/o Mia Hansen *Portrait PR*
5320 Sylmar Ave
Sherman Oaks, CA 91401-5612, USA

Roberts, Stanley (Athlete, Basketball Player)
1192 Congaree Rd
Hopkins, SC 29061-9704, USA

Roberts, Tanya (Actor)
c/o Jay Schwartz *Jay D Schwartz & Associates*
6767 Forest Lawn Dr Ste 211
Los Angeles, CA 90068-1051, USA

Roberts, Thomas (Journalist, Television Host)
c/o Staff Member *MSNBC*
30 Rockefeller Plz
New York, NY 10112-0015, USA

Roberts, Tiffany (Athlete, Olympic Athlete, Soccer Player)
2772 Ascot Dr
San Ramon, CA 94583-2504, USA

Roberts, Tim (Athlete, Football Player)
3930 Minnow Rd
Rex, GA 30273-1536, USA

Roberts, Tony (Actor)
970 Park Ave # 8N
New York, NY 10028-0324, USA

Roberts, Trish (Athlete, Basketball Player, Olympic Athlete)
218 Carver Dr
Monroe, GA 30655-1814, USA

Roberts, Vicki (Actor)
c/o Arthur Andelson *Kismet Talent Agency*
3435 Ocean Park Blvd Ste 107
Santa Monica, CA 90405-3320, USA

Roberts, Walter (Athlete, Football Player)
268 Kenbrook Cir
San Jose, CA 95111-3262, USA

Roberts, William H (Athlete, Football Player)
18520 NW 67th Ave Apt 141
Hialeah, FL 33015-3302, USA

Roberts, Willie (Athlete, Baseball Player)
11476 Emuness Rd
Jacksonville, FL 32218, USA

Roberts, Willis (Athlete, Baseball Player)
11478 Vera Dr
Jacksonville, FL 32218-4064, USA

Roberts, Xavier (Business Person, Designer)
PO Box 1438
Cleveland, GA 30528-0027, USA

Robertson, Alvin (Athlete, Basketball Player, Olympic Athlete)
6515 Amber Oak
San Antonio, TX 78249-1586, USA

Robertson, Andre (Athlete, Baseball Player)
2229 Cross Ln
Orange, TX 77630-2561, USA

Robertson, Belinda (Designer, Fashion Designer)
BR Cashmere
22 Palmerston Place
Edinburgh EH12 5AL, SCOTLAND

Robertson, Bob (Athlete, Baseball Player)
10015 Shinnamon Dr SW
Cumberland, MD 21502-6149, USA

Robertson, Bob (Athlete, Football Player)
411 Belle Monti Ct
Aptos, CA 95003-5208, USA

Robertson, Britt (Actor)
c/o Francis Okwu *Zero Gravity Management*
11110 Ohio Ave Ste 100
Los Angeles, CA 90025-3329, USA

Robertson, Connor (Athlete, Baseball Player)
2201 Champions Cir
Franklin, TN 37064-2870, USA

Robertson, Craig (Athlete, Football Player)

Robertson, Daryl (Athlete, Baseball Player)
112 E Cranberry Hill Dr
Draper, UT 84020-9487, USA

Robertson, David (Athlete, Baseball Player)
c/o Team Member *New York Yankees*
161st St & River Ave
Yankee Stadium
Bronx, NY 10451, USA

Robertson, Davis (Dancer)
Joffrey Ballet
70 E Lake St Ste 1300
Chicago, IL 60601-7458, USA

Robertson, DeWayne (Athlete, Football Player)
1000 Fulton Ave
Hempstead, NY 11550-1030, USA

Robertson, Don (Athlete, Baseball Player)
5715 W Monte Vista Rd
Phoenix, AZ 85035-3626, USA

Robertson, Geordie (Athlete, Hockey Player)
1 Scarborough Park
Rochester, NY 14625-1363

Robertson, Gordon (Religious Leader, Television Host)
c/o 700 Club *Christian Broadcasting Network (CBN)*
977 Centerville Tpke
Virginia Beach, VA 23463-1001, USA

Robertson, Isiah (Athlete, Football Player)
PO Box 1405
Mabank, TX 75147-1405, USA

Robertson, Jason (Jase) (Reality Star)
Duck Commander
117 Kings Ln
West Monroe, LA 71292-9430, USA

Robertson, Jenny (Actor)
Shelter Entertainment
23901 Calabasas Rd Ste 2002
Calabasas, CA 91302-3303, USA

Robertson, Jerry (Race Car Driver)
Quick Time Motorsports
124 N 325 W # 58-6
Hurricane, UT 84737-2041, USA

Robertson, Jim (Athlete, Baseball Player)
2515 109th Ave SE
Bellevue, WA 98004-7331, USA

Robertson, Kathleen (Actor)
c/o Staff Member *Noble Caplan Abrams*
1260 Yonge St Fl 2
Toronto, ON M4T 1W5, CANADA

Robertson, Kimmy (Actor)
c/o Staff Member *AKA Talent Agency*
325 N Larchmont Blvd
Los Angeles, CA 90004-3011, USA

Robertson, Marcus A (Athlete, Football Player)
3218 Cypress Point Dr
Missouri City, TX 77459-3634, USA

Robertson, Mike (Athlete, Baseball Player)
2626 E Viking Rd
Las Vegas, NV 89121-4114, USA

Robertson, Nate (Athlete, Baseball Player)
7918 W 53rd St N
Maize, KS 67101-9185, USA

Robertson, Oscar (Athlete, Basketball Player, Olympic Athlete)
621 Tusculum Ave
Cincinnati, OH 45226-1771, USA

Robertson, Pat (Religious Leader, Television Host)
977 Centerville Tpke
Virginia Beach, VA 23463-1001, USA

Robertson, Phil (Reality Star)
Duck Commander
117 Kings Ln
West Monroe, LA 71292-9430, USA

Robertson, RIch (Athlete, Baseball Player)
32202 Sandwedge Dr
Waller, TX 77484-9017, USA

Robertson, Rich (Athlete, Baseball Player)
1201 Crescent Ter
Sunnyvale, CA 94087-2855, USA

Robertson, Robbie (Musician)
c/o Staff Member *Rebel Waltz Inc*
PO Box 9215
Laguna Beach, CA 92652-7212, USA

Robertson, Robble (Musician, Songwriter, Writer)
323 14th St
Santa Monica, CA 90402-2113, USA

Robertson, Sadie (Musician, Reality Star)
c/o Lee White *WME|IMG*
9601 Wilshire Blvd
Beverly Hills, CA 90210-5213, USA

Robertson, Si (Reality Star)
335 Philpot Rd
West Monroe, LA 71292-2649, USA

Robertson, Travian (Athlete, Football Player)

Robertson, Willie (Business Person, Reality Star)
Duck Commander
117 Kings Ln
West Monroe, LA 71292-9430, USA

Robes, Ernest C (Bill) (Skier)
3 Mile Road
Etna, NH 03750, USA

Robey, Nickell (Athlete, Football Player)
c/o Kelli Masters *Kelli Masters Management*
100 N Broadway Ave Ste 1700
Oklahoma City, OK 73102-8805, USA

Robey, Rick (Athlete, Basketball Player)
15129 Chestnut Ridge Cir
Louisville, KY 40245-5291, USA

Robichaud, Bernard (Actor)
c/o Karen Patmas *National Talent LA*
5670 Wilshire Blvd # 1867
Los Angeles, CA 90036-5679, USA

Robidas, Stephane (Athlete, Hockey Player)
3216 Wellshire Ct
Plano, TX 75093-3458

Robidoux, Billy Joe (Athlete, Baseball Player)
2 King George Dr
Ware, MA 01082-9799, USA

Robidoux, Florent (Athlete, Hockey Player)
5 Pearce Dr
Morden, MB R6M 1R2, CANADA

Robins, Oliver (Actor, Director)
c/o Dawn Goodson *Genius Talent Management*
342 1/2 N Genesee Ave
Los Angeles, CA 90036-2261, USA

Robinson, Adrien (Athlete, Football Player)
c/o Peter Schaffer *Authentic Athletix*
400 S Steele St Unit 47
Denver, CO 80209-3535, USA

Robinson, Aldrick (Athlete, Football Player)
c/o Jordan Woy *Willis & Woy Management*
4890 Alpha Rd Ste 200
Dallas, TX 75244-4639, USA

Robinson, Allen (Athlete, Football Player)
c/o Eugene Parker *Independent Sports & Entertainment (ISE-IN)*
6435 W Jefferson Blvd # 197
Fort Wayne, IN 46804-6203, USA

Robinson, Andrea (Actor)
c/o Alan Saffron *Saffron Management*
9171 Wilshire Blvd Ste 441
Beverly Hills, CA 90210-5516, USA

Robinson, Andrew (Actor)
2671 Byron Pl
Los Angeles, CA 90046-1021, USA

Robinson, Ann (Actor)
1357 Elysian Park Dr
Los Angeles, CA 90026-3407, USA

Robinson, Bo (Athlete, Football Player)
3712 Wosley Dr
Fort Worth, TX 76133-2013, USA

Robinson, Brooks (Athlete, Baseball Player)
PO Box 1168
Baltimore, MD 21203-1168, USA

Robinson, Bruce (Director)
c/o Rand Holston *Paradigm*
8942 Wilshire Blvd
Beverly Hills, CA 90211-1908, USA

Robinson, Bruce (Athlete, Baseball Player)
4641 Murphy Ave
San Diego, CA 92122-2720, USA

Robinson, Bumper (Actor)
c/o David Altman *Altman Greenfield & Selvaggi*
200 Park Ave S Ste 8
New York, NY 10003-1503, United States

Robinson, Chip (Race Car Driver)
PO Box 476
Oldwick, NJ 08858-0476, USA

Robinson, Chris (Director)
c/o Peter Safran *The Safran Company*
8748 Holloway Dr
Los Angeles, CA 90069-2327, USA

Robinson, Chris (Musician)
90 Altura Way
Greenbrae, CA 94904-1218, USA

Robinson, Christina (Actor)
c/o Jackie Lewis *LB Talent Agency*
3406 W Burbank Blvd
Burbank, CA 91505-2232, USA

Robinson, Claire (Chef)
c/o Staff Member *Brooks Group*
10 W 37th St Fl 5
New York, NY 10018-7396, USA

Robinson, Clarence (Arnie) (Athlete, Track Athlete)
2904 Ocean View Blvd
San Diego, CA 92113-1336, USA

Robinson, Cliff (Athlete, Basketball Player)
98 S Bardsbrook Cir
Spring, TX 77382-2858, USA

Robinson, Craig (Actor)
c/o Mark Schulman *3 Arts Entertainment*
9460 Wilshire Blvd Fl 7
Beverly Hills, CA 90212-2713, USA

Robinson, Craig (Athlete, Baseball Player)
3501 Champion Lake Blvd Apt 1603
Shreveport, LA 71105-3780, USA

Robinson, Daniel (Baseball Player)
10889 Dauphine St
Shreveport, LA 71106-8524, USA

Robinson, Dave (Athlete, Baseball Player)
6140 Camino Del Rincon
San Diego, CA 92120-3112, USA

Robinson, David (Athlete, Basketball Player)
Admiral Capital Group
52 Vanderbilt Ave Rm 1000
New York, NY 10017-3841, USA

Robinson, Denard (Athlete, Football Player)
c/o Michael Perrett *Element Sports Group*
3180 N Point Pkwy Ste 106
Alpharetta, GA 30005-4349, USA

Robinson, Dewey (Athlete, Baseball Player)
1388 Cottonwood Trl
Sarasota, FL 34232-3437, USA

Robinson, Don (Athlete, Baseball Player)
1215 86th Ct NW
Bradenton, FL 34209-9307, USA

Robinson, Doug (Athlete, Hockey Player)
6 Tiffany Crt
St Catharines, ON L2M 7N3, Canada

Robinson, Eddie (Athlete, Baseball Player)
6104 Cholla Dr
Fort Worth, TX 76112-1105, USA

Robinson, Emily (Actor)
c/o Shannon Barr *Rogers & Cowan*
1840 Century Park E Fl 18
Los Angeles, CA 90067-2101, USA

Robinson, Emily (Musician)
c/o Staff Member *Creative Artists Agency (CAA)*
2000 Avenue of the Stars Ste 100
Los Angeles, CA 90067-4705, USA

Robinson, Emily Erwin (Athlete, Football Player)
4400 Falcon Pkwy
Flowery Branch, GA 30542-3176, USA

Robinson, Floyd (Athlete, Baseball Player)
PO Box 152419
San Diego, CA 92195-2419, USA

Robinson, Frank (Athlete, Football Player)
15401 E Wyoming Dr Unit C
Aurora, CO 80017-4727, USA

Robinson, Gerald (Athlete, Football Player)
4708 Scarborough Pl
Stone Mountain, GA 30087-4104, USA

Robinson, Gerell (Athlete, Football Player)
c/o Michael McCartney *Priority Sports & Entertainment (Chicago)*
325 N La Salle Dr Ste 650
Chicago, IL 60654-8182, USA

Robinson, Glenn (Basketball Player, Coach)
Franklin & Marshall College
Athletic Dept
Lancaster, PA 17604, USA

Robinson, James (Baseball Player)
Philadelphia Stars
65 W 96th St Apt 22G
New York, NY 10025-6533, USA

Robinson, Janice (Musician)
c/o Staff Member *Diva Central Inc*
7510 W Sunset Blvd # 1445
Los Angeles, CA 90046-3408, USA

Robinson, Jay (Actor)
13757 Milbank St
Sherman Oaks, CA 91423-2966, USA

Robinson, Jeff (Athlete, Baseball Player)
27 Weber Ln
Trabuco Canyon, CA 92679-5235, USA

Robinson, Jeff (Athlete, Baseball Player)
5317 W 158th Pl
Overland Park, KS 66224-3616, USA

Robinson, Jerry (Athlete, Football Player)
2398 Julio Ln
Santa Rosa, CA 95401-5726, USA

Robinson, John (Actor)
c/o Oren Segal *Management Production Entertainment (MPE)*
9229 W Sunset Blvd Ste 301
W Hollywood, CA 90069-3417, USA

Robinson, John A (Athlete, Coach, Football Coach, Football Player)
6991 Goldstone Rd
Carlsbad, CA 92009-1711, USA

Robinson, Johnny N (Athlete, Football Player)
3209 S Grand St
Monroe, LA 71202-5225, USA

Robinson, Josh (Athlete, Football Player)
c/o Drew Rosenhaus *Rosenhaus Sports Representation*
3921 Alton Rd # 440
Miami Beach, FL 33140-3852, USA

Robinson, Julie Anne (Director)
c/o Jessica Sykes *Independent Talent Group*
40 Whitfield St
London W1T 2RH, UNITED KINGDOM

Robinson, Keenan (Athlete, Football Player)
c/o David Dunn *Athletes First*
23091 Mill Creek Dr
Laguna Hills, CA 92653-1258, USA

Robinson, Keith (Actor)
c/o Staff Member *Artists & Representatives (Stone Manners Salners)*
6100 Wilshire Blvd Ste 1500
Los Angeles, CA 90048-5110, USA

Robinson, Keith (Musician)
c/o Staff Member *Paradigm*
140 Broadway Ste 2600
New York, NY 10005-1011, USA

Robinson, Ken (Writer)
c/o Ken Hertz *Goldring, Hertz & Lichtenstein*
1800 Century Park E Fl 10
Los Angeles, CA 90067-1513, USA

Robinson, Kerry (Athlete, Baseball Player)
133 Vlasis Dr
Ballwin, MO 63011-3055, USA

Robinson, Khiry (Athlete, Football Player)
c/o Adam Heller *Vantage Management Group*
518 Reamer Dr
Carnegie, PA 15106-1845, USA

Robinson, Kim Stanley (Writer)
c/o Vince Gerardis *Grok! Studio*
Prefers to be contacted via email or telephone
Los Angeles, CA, USA

Robinson, Koren (Athlete, Football Player)
12 Henry Ave
Belmont, NC 28012-3930, USA

Robinson, Larry (Athlete, Hockey Player)
New Jersey Devils
165 Mulberry St
Newark, NJ 07102-3607

Robinson, Larry (Athlete, Coach, Hockey Player)
10709 Winding Stream Way
Bradenton, FL 34212-5255

Robinson, Laura (Actor)
Henderson/Hogan
8285 W Sunset Blvd Ste 1
West Hollywood, CA 90046-2420, USA

Robinson, Leon (Actor, Producer)
c/o Leo Bozzuto *Inphenate*
9701 Wilshire Blvd Fl 10
Beverly Hills, CA 90212-2010, USA

Robinson, Marcus (Athlete, Football Player)
PO Box 1924
Fort Valley, GA 31030-1924, USA

Robinson, Mark (Athlete, Football Player)
303 Pennsylvania Ave
Palm Harbor, FL 34683-5222, USA

Robinson, Marnia (Writer)
c/o Staff Member *North Atlantic Books*
2526 Martin Luther King Jr Way
Berkeley, CA 94704-2607, USA

Robinson, Matt (Athlete, Football Player)
12374 Mandarin Rd
Jacksonville, FL 32223-1892, USA

Robinson, Moe (Athlete, Hockey Player)
3811 Gregoire Rd
Russell, ON K4R 1E5, Canada

Robinson, Navia Ziraili (Actor)
c/o Mitchell Gossett *Industry Entertainment Partners*
955 Carrillo Dr Ste 300
Los Angeles, CA 90048-5400, USA

Robinson, Nichole (Actor, Model)
c/o PJ Shapiro *Ziffren Brittenham*
1801 Century Park W Fl 7
Los Angeles, CA 90067-6406, USA

Robinson, Nick (Actor)
c/o Cara Tripicchio *Shelter PR*
5670 Wilshire Blvd Ste 1200
Los Angeles, CA 90036-5621, USA

Robinson, Oliver (Athlete, Basketball Player)
9640 Eastpointe Cir
Birmingham, AL 35217-5202, USA

Robinson, Patrick (Athlete, Football Player)
Cincinnati Bengals
3775 N Advantage Way Dr Apt 105
Memphis, TN 38128-7209, USA

Robinson, Patrick (Designer, Fashion Designer)
Gap
1 Harrison St
San Francisco, CA 94105-1683, USA

Robinson, Paul (Athlete, Football Player)
1303 W 26th St
Safford, AZ 85546-3721, USA

Robinson, Rachel (Baseball Player)
The Jackie Robinson Foundation
75 Varick St Frnt 2
New York, NY 10013-1947

Robinson, Rachel (Misc)
75 Varick St Frnt
New York, NY 10013-1917, USA

Robinson, Rafael (Athlete, Football Player)
6203 Wynbrook Dr
Randolph, NJ 07869-1287, USA

Robinson, Rich (Musician)
c/o Staff Member *Paradigm (Monterey)*
404 W Franklin St
Monterey, CA 93940-2303, USA

Robinson, Richard D (Dave) (Athlete, Football Player)
406 S Rose Blvd
Akron, OH 44320-1308, USA

Robinson, Rob (Athlete, Hockey Player)
23466 Greening Dr
Novi, MI 48375-3225

Robinson, Robinson (Director)
c/o Peter Safran *The Safran Company*
8748 Holloway Dr
Los Angeles, CA 90069-2327, USA

Robinson, Ron (Athlete, Baseball Player)
3128 E Race Ave
Visalia, CA 93292-6858, USA

Robinson, Ronnie (Athlete, Basketball Player)
4169 S Germantown Rd
Memphis, TN 38125-2624, USA

Robinson, Rumeal (Athlete, Basketball Player)
3645 Brushy Wood Dr
Loganville, GA 30052-5481, USA

Robinson, Sam (Athlete, Basketball Player)
130 W Harcourt St
Long Beach, CA 90805-2124, USA

Robinson, Sammy (Athlete, Baseball Player)
Detroit Stars
503 Umatilla St SE
Grand Rapids, MI 49507-1218, USA

Robinson, Sandra Dee (Actor)
12400 W Highway 71 Ste 350 PMB 415
Bee Cave, TX 78738-6500, USA

Robinson, Shaun (Correspondent)
c/o Susan Haber *Haber Entertainment*
434 S Canon Dr Apt 204
Beverly Hills, CA 90212-4501, USA

Robinson, Shawna (Race Car Driver)
Shawna Robinson Racing
PO Box 1858
New Smyrna Beach, FL 32170-1858, USA

Robinson, Shelton (Athlete, Football Player)
18725 20th Dr SE
Bothell, WA 98012-8721, USA

Robinson, Smokey (Musician, Producer, Songwriter)
Smokey Robinson Foundation
385 S Lemon Ave Ste E181
Walnut, CA 91789-2727, USA

Robinson, Stephen (Astronaut)
286 Cottage Cir
Davis, CA 95616-4674, USA

Robinson, Ted (Sportscaster)
c/o Lou Oppenheim *ICM Partners (NY)*
730 5th Ave
New York, NY 10019-4105, USA

Robinson, Tony (Actor, Producer, Writer)
c/o Staff Member *Jeremy Hicks Associates*
3 Stedham Place
London WC1A 1HU, UK

Robinson, Trayvon (Athlete, Baseball Player)
1455 W 97th St
Los Angeles, CA 90047-3934, USA

Robinson, Trenton (Athlete, Football Player)
c/o Ryan Tollner *REP 1 Sports Group*
80 Technology Dr
Irvine, CA 92618-2301, USA

Robinson, V Gene (Religious Leader)
Saint Paul's Church
21 Centre St
Concord, NH 03301-6301, USA

Robinson, Wayne (Athlete, Football Player)
9550 Campo Rd Apt 45
Spring Valley, CA 91977-1244, USA

Robinson, Wendy Raquel (Actor)
c/o Patricia (Patty) Woo *Patty Woo Management*
8906 W Olympic Blvd
Beverly Hills, CA 90211-3550, USA

Robinson, Wilbert (Athlete, Basketball Player)
2124 Bedell Rd
Grand Island, NY 14072-1652, USA

Robinson, Zuleikha (Actor)
c/o Daniel Spilo *Industry Entertainment Partners*
955 Carrillo Dr Ste 300
Los Angeles, CA 90048-5400, USA

Robinson of Woolwich, John (Religious Leader)
Trinity College
Cambridge CB2 1TQ, UNITED KINGDOM (UK)

Robinson-Peete, Holly (Actor)
c/o Liza Anderson *Anderson Group Public Relations*
8060 Melrose Ave Fl 4
Los Angeles, CA 90046-7038, USA

Robisch, Dave (Athlete, Basketball Player)
16323 Meadowlands Ct
Westfield, IN 46074-8441, USA

Robiskie, Terry (Athlete, Football Player)
40 River Mountain Dr
Moreland Hills, OH 44022-2064, USA

Robison, Brian (Athlete, Football Player)
c/o W Vann McElroy *Select Sports Group*
2700 Post Oak Blvd Ste 1450
Houston, TX 77056-5785, USA

Robison, Bruce (Musician, Songwriter, Writer)
Artists Envoy Agency
1016 16th Ave S Apt 101
Nashville, TN 37212-2315, USA

Robison, Charlie (Musician, Songwriter)
c/o Staff Member *Paradigm (Monterey)*
404 W Franklin St
Monterey, CA 93940-2303, USA

Robison, Paula (Musician)
18 Allison Ave
Staten Island, NY 10306-2806, USA

Robison, Tommy (Athlete, Football Player)
30 Scotch Pine Ct
Crawfordville, FL 32327-1250, USA

Robitaille, Luc (Athlete, Hockey Player)
Los Angeles Kings
1111 S Figueroa St Ste 3100
Los Angeles, CA 90015-1333

Robitaille, Luc (Athlete, Hockey Player)
370 25th St
Santa Monica, CA 90402-2522

Robitaille, Mike (Athlete, Hockey Player)
Buffalo Sabres
1 Seymour H Knox III Plz Ste 1
Buffalo, NY 14203-3096

Robl, Harold (Athlete, Football Player)
W1089 County Road C
Gleason, WI 54435-9472, USA

Robles, Jorge (Actor)
c/o Staff Member *Televisa*
Blvd Adolfo Lopez Mateos 232
Colonia San Angel INN
DF CP 01060, MEXICO

Robles, Marisa (Musician)
38 Luttrll Ave
London SW15 6PE, UNITED KINGDOM (UK)

Robles, Mike (Producer)
ICM
8942 Wilshire Blvd
Beverly Hills, CA 90211-1908

Roboz, Zsuzsi (Artist)
6 Bryanston Court
George St
London W1H 7HA, UNITED KINGDOM (UK)

Robshaw, Chris (Athlete, Rugby Player)
c/o Stuart Peters *ABC Sports Management*
1 Hardwicks Square
Wandsworth
London SW18 4AW, UNITED KINGDOM

Robson, Ben (Actor)
c/o Jordan Berkus *United Talent Agency (UTA)*
9336 Civic Center Dr
Beverly Hills, CA 90210-3604, USA

Robson, Bryan (Soccer Player)
Middlesbrough FC
Riverside Stadium
Midds
Cleveland TS3 6RS, UNITED KINGDOM (UK)

Robson, Tom (Athlete, Baseball Player)
8902 E Hercules Ct
Sun Lakes, AZ 85248-9005, USA

Robson, Wade (Dancer)
c/o Andrew Jacobs *McDonald/Selznick Assoc (MSA)*
1611A N El Centro Ave
Hollywood, CA 90028, USA

Robuck, Nic (Actor)
c/o Jennifer Levy *Behr Abramson Levy*
9701 Wilshire Blvd Ste 800
Beverly Hills, CA 90212-2033, USA

Roby, Bradley (Athlete, Football Player)
c/o Michael Perrett *Element Sports Group*
3340 Peachtree Rd NE Fl 16
Atlanta, GA 30326-1000, USA

Roby, Courtney (Athlete, Football Player)
c/o Peter Schaffer *Authentic Athletix*
400 S Steele St Unit 47
Denver, CO 80209-3535, USA

Roby, Martha (Congressman, Politician)
414 Cannon Hob
Washington, DC 20515-1801, USA

Robyn (Musician)
c/o Eric Harle *DEF Management*
51 Lonsdale Road Queens Park
London NW6 6RA, UNITED KINGDOM

Rocca, Constantino (Golfer)
Golf Products International
30141 Agoura Rd Ste 102
Agoura Hills, CA 91301-4370, USA

Rocca, Costentino (Golfer)
Golf Projects International
30141 Agoura Rd Ste 102
Agoura Hills, CA 91301-4370, USA

Rocca, Mo (Correspondent)
c/o Jennifer Craig *Gersh*
9465 Wilshire Blvd Ste 600
Beverly Hills, CA 90212-2605, USA

Rocca, Peter (Swimmer)
534 Hazel Ave
San Bruno, CA 94066-4228, USA

Rocco, Rinaldo (Actor)
Carol Levi Co
Via Giuseppe Pisanelli
Rome 00196, ITALY

Rocha, Coco (Musician)
c/o Lauren Auslander *LUNA*
116 Nassau St # 615
New York, NY 10038-2402, USA

Rocha, Enrique (Actor)
c/o Staff Member *Televisa*
Blvd Adolfo Lopez Mateos 232
Colonia San Angel INN
DF CP 01060, MEXICO

Rocha, John (Designer, Fashion Designer)
12-13 Temple Ln
Dublin 00002, IRELAND

Rocha, Kali (Actor)
c/o Katie Rhodes *Untitled Entertainment*
350 S Beverly Dr Ste 200
Beverly Hills, CA 90212-4819, USA

Roche, Alden (Athlete, Football Player)
1082 Farragut St
New Orleans, LA 70114-2810, USA

Roche, Anthony D (Tony) (Tennis Player)
5 Kapiti St
Saint Ives, NSW 02075, AUSTRALIA

Roche, Brian (Athlete, Football Player)
1358 Oak Tree Cir
Chino Hills, CA 91709-2231, USA

Roche, John (Athlete, Basketball Player)
191 Clayton Ln Unit 303
Denver, CO 80206-5679, USA

Roche, Sebastian (Actor)
c/o Mary Ellen Mulcahy *Framework Entertainment*
9057 Nemo St # C
W Hollywood, CA 90069-5511, USA

Rochefort, Leon (Athlete, Hockey Player)
1661 Notre-Dame St E
Trois-Rivieres, QC G8T 4J9, Canada

Rochefort, Normand (Athlete, Hockey Player)
1530 Burgos Dr
Sarasota, FL 34238-2706

Rochester, Paul (Athlete, Football Player)
218 Evans Dr
Jacksonville, FL 32250-2631, USA

Rochford, Mike (Athlete, Baseball Player)
926 N 0 St
Lake Worth, FL 33460-2746, USA

Rochon, Debbie (Actor)
PO Box 1299
New York, NY 10009-8958

Rochon, Frank (Athlete, Hockey Player)
40 Colleen Cir
Downingtown, PA 19335-4935, USA

Rochon, Lela (Actor)
3332 Clerendon Rd
Beverly Hills, CA 90210-1059, USA

Rock (Actor, Wrestler)
World Wrestling Entertainment
1241 E Main St
Titan Towers
Stamford, CT 06902-3520, USA

Rock, Angela (Athlete, Volleyball Player)
University of California - SB
Athletic Dept
1210 Cheadle Hall
Santa Barbara, CA 93106-0001, USA

Rock, Chris (Actor, Comedian, Director, Producer)
c/o Jessica Pierson *Vision PR*
2 Penn Plz Rm 2601
New York, NY 10121-0001, USA

Rock, Tony (Comedian)
c/o April King *ICM Partners*
10250 Constellation Blvd Fl 7
Los Angeles, CA 90067-6207, USA

Rock, Walt (Athlete, Football Player)
1030 Highams Ct
Woodbridge, VA 22191-1445, USA

Rockburne, Dorothea G (Artist)
140 Grand St
New York, NY 10013-3104, USA

Rock City (Music Group)
c/o Noel Palm *Element Talent Agency*
2029 Verdugo Blvd # 203
Montrose, CA 91020-1626, USA

Rockefeller, Jay (Politician, Senator)
1515 Barberry Ln
Charleston, WV 25314-1901, USA

Rockefeller, Laurance S (Misc)
Rockefeller Bros Fund
30 Rockefeller Plz # 5600
New York, NY 10112-0015, USA

Rocker, David (Athlete, Football Player)
465 Belle Dr
Fayetteville, GA 30214-2703, USA

Rocker, John (Athlete, Baseball Player)

Rockett, Pat (Athlete, Baseball Player)
17107 Eagle Hollow Dr
San Antonio, TX 78248-1553, USA

Rockett, Rikki (Musician)
Randex Communications
906 Jonathan Ln
Marlton, NJ 08053-4517, USA

Rockford, Jim (Athlete, Football Player)
1829 Camden St
Springfield, IL 62702-3201, USA

Rockwell, Martha (Coach, Skier)
Dartmouth College
PO Box 9
Hanover, NH 03755-0009, USA

Rockwell, Nancy (Athlete, Baseball Player)
54658 County Road 101
Elkhart, IN 46514-8967, USA

Rockwell, Sam (Actor)
c/o Liz Mahoney *Narrative*
1601 Vine St Fl 6
Los Angeles, CA 90028-8802, USA

Rocky, A$AP (ASAP) (Musician)
c/o Theola Borden *RCA Records (NY)*
550 Madison Ave
New York, NY 10022-3211, USA

Roczen, Ken (Motorcycle Racer)
c/o Steven Astephen *Wasserman Media Group - Carlsbad*
2251 Faraday Ave # 200
Carlsbad, CA 92008-7209, USA

Rodan, Jay (Actor)
c/o Staff Member *WME/IMG*
9601 Wilshire Blvd
Beverly Hills, CA 90210-5213, USA

Rodas, Rich (Athlete, Baseball Player)
6877 Bergano Pl
Rancho Cucamonga, CA 91701-8606, USA

Roday, James (Actor, Writer)
16-20 W. 19th St.
Apt #8D
New York, NY 10011, USA

Rodberg, Agam (Actor)
c/o Hadas Mozes Lichtenstein *ADD Agency*
2 Raoul Wallenberg St
Ramat Hachayal
Tel Aviv 69719, Israel

Rodd, Marcia (Actor)
11738 Moorpark St Apt C
Studio City, CA 91604-2116, USA

Roddam, Franc (Director)
William Morris Agency
52/53 Poland Place
London W1F 7LX, UNITED KINGDOM (UK)

Roddick, Andy (Athlete, Tennis Player)
c/o Staff Member *Lagardere Unlimited (DC)*
5335 Wisconsin Ave NW Ste 850
Washington, DC 20015-2052, USA

Roden, Holland (Actor)
c/o Heather Nunn *Anonymous Content*
3532 Hayden Ave
Culver City, CA 90232-2413, USA

Rodenhauser, Mark (Athlete, Football Player)
1451 Charlotte Hwy
York, SC 29745-8947, USA

Rodenhiser, Dick (Athlete, Hockey Player, Olympic Athlete)
186 State St
Framingham, MA 01702-2462, USA

Roder, Mirro (Athlete, Football Player)
181 Herrick Rd
Riverside, IL 60546-2045, USA

Roderick, Brande (Actor, Model)
c/o Shannon Barr *Rogers & Cowan*
1840 Century Park E Fl 18
Los Angeles, CA 90067-2101, USA

Rodgers, Aaron (Athlete, Football Player)
PO Box 378
Suamico, WI 54173-0378, USA

Rodgers, Bill (Athlete, Olympic Athlete, Track Athlete)

Rodgers, Del (Athlete, Football Player)
3112 Yosemite Park Way
Elk Grove, CA 95758-4687, USA

Rodgers, Derrick (Athlete, Football Player)
5550 SW 192nd Ter
Southwest Ranches, FL 33332-3333, USA

Rodgers, Jacquizz (Athlete, Football Player)

Rodgers, Jimmie (Musician)
42230 Sandy Bay Rd
Bermuda Dunes, CA 92203-1394, USA

Rodgers, Jimmy (Basketball Coach, Coach)
9423 Greyhawk Trl
Naples, FL 34120-1890, USA

Rodgers, Johnny (Athlete, Football Player, Heisman Trophy Winner)
PO Box 11172
Omaha, NE 68111-0172, USA

Rodgers, Marion Elizabeth (Writer)
c/o Staff Member *Library of America, The*
14 E 60th St Ste 1101
New York, NY 10022-7115, USA

Rodgers, Michael (Actor)
c/o Staff Member *Metropolitan (MTA)*
4526 Wilshire Blvd
Los Angeles, CA 90010-3801, USA

Rodgers, Nile (Musician)
9 Covlee Dr
Westport, CT 06880-6406, USA

Rodgers, Paul (Musician)
Work Hard PR
19D Pinhold Road
London SW16 5GD, United Kingdom

Rodgers, Phil (Golfer)
Eddie Elias Enterprises
4067 N Shore Dr
Akron, OH 44333-8305, USA

Rodgers, Richard (Athlete, Football Player)
c/o Frank Bauer *Sun West Sports*
7883 N Pershing Ave
Stockton, CA 95207-1749, USA

Rodgers, Robert (Buck) (Athlete, Baseball Player, Coach)
5181 W Knoll Dr
Yorba Linda, CA 92886-4338, USA

Rodgers, Robert '"Buck'" (Athlete, Baseball Player)
5181 W Knoll Dr
Yorba Linda, CA 92886-4338, USA

Rodgers, Roscoe (Horse Racer)
7834 N Music Mountain Ln
Prescott Valley, AZ 86315-9085, USA

Rodgers-Cromartie, Dominique (Athlete, Football Player)
c/o Ashley Smith Becker *Relativity Sports*
2029 Century Park E Ste 1550
Century City, CA 90067-3000, USA

Rodina, Irina (Athlete)
13243 Fiji Way # 7
Marina Del Rey, CA 90292-7079, USA

Rodman, Dennis (Athlete, Basketball Player)
c/o Albert Morales *Nene Musik Productions LLC*
1406 SW Santiago Ave
Port St Lucie, FL 34953-4907, USA

Rodman, Judy (Musician, Songwriter)
308 Cody Hill Pl
Nashville, TN 37211-7927, USA

Rodrigue, George (Artist)
PO Box 51227
Lafayette, LA 70505-1227, USA

Rodrigues, Bienvenido (Athlete, Baseball Player)
PO Box 42
Santa Isabel, PR 00757-0042, USA

Rodrigues, Blenvenido (Baseball Player)
Chicago American Giants
PO Box 42
Santa Isabel, PR 00757-0042, USA

Rodrigues, Jordan (Actor, Musician)
c/o Stephen Harmon *The X Division*
30 Kingsway
#307
Cronulla NSW 02230, AUSTRALIA

Rodriguez, Adam (Actor)
c/o Lisa Perkins *Baker Winokur Ryder Public Relations*
9100 Wilshire Blvd
W Tower #500
Beverly Hills, CA 90212-3415, USA

Rodriguez, Alex (A-Rod) (Athlete, Baseball Player)
c/o Team Member *New York Yankees*
161st St & River Ave
Yankee Stadium
Bronx, NY 10451, USA

Rodriguez, Anthony (Golfer)
13602 Summer Glen Dr
San Antonio, TX 78247-3510, USA

Rodriguez, Carlos (Athlete, Baseball Player)
1270 Ginder Rd NW
Lancaster, OH 43130-8444, USA

Rodriguez, Eddie (Athlete, Baseball Player)
4320 N Elias St
Mesa, AZ 85215-7740, USA

Rodriguez, Eduardo (President)
President's Office
Palacio de Gobierno
Plaza Murilla
La Paz, BOLIVIA

Rodriguez, Edwin (Athlete, Baseball Player)
7901 30th Ave N
Saint Petersburg, FL 33710-1151, USA

Rodriguez, Elijah (Actor)
c/o Sean Reilly *The Brand Partners*
6404 Wilshire Blvd Ste 500
Los Angeles, CA 90048-5507, USA

Rodriguez, Ellie (Athlete, Baseball Player)
1787 Calle Astromelia
San Juan, PR 00926-7222, USA

Rodriguez, Evan (Athlete, Football Player)

Rodriguez, Francisco (Athlete, Baseball Player)
c/o Staff Member *New York Mets*
123-01 Roosevelt Avenue
Shea Stadium
Flushing, NY 11368-1699, USA

Rodriguez, Freddy (Actor)
c/o Robbie Kass *Kass Management*
1011 Euclid St Unit B
Santa Monica, CA 90403-4296, USA

Rodriguez, Genesis (Actor)
c/o Ivan De Paz *DePaz Management*
2011 N Vermont Ave
Los Angeles, CA 90027-1931, USA

Rodriguez, Gina (Actor)
c/o Staff Member *I Can & I Will Productions*
10850 Wilshire Blvd Ste 600
Los Angeles, CA 90024-4319, USA

Rodriguez, Henry (Athlete, Baseball Player)
295 Wadsworth Ave Apt 3F
New York, NY 10040-4416, USA

Rodriguez, Ivan (Pudge) (Athlete, Baseball Player)
15530 SW 70th Ter
Miami, FL 33193-2127, USA

Rodriguez, Jai (Actor, Television Host)
c/o Michael Einfeld *Michael Einfeld Management*
10630 Moorpark St Unit 101
Toluca Lake, CA 91602-2797, USA

Rodriguez, Javier (Actor)
c/o Staff Member *Select Artists Ltd (CA-Valley Office)*
PO Box 4359
Burbank, CA 91503-4359, USA

Rodriguez, Johnny (Actor)
c/o Staff Member *Central Artists*
1023 N Hollywood Way Ste 102
Burbank, CA 91505-2554, USA

Rodriguez, Jose Luis (El Puma) (Musician)
c/o Staff Member *BMG*
1540 Broadway
New York, NY 10036-4039, USA

Rodriguez, Juan (Chi Chi) (Athlete)
Eddie Elias Enterprises
3916 Clock Pointe Trl Ste 101
Stow, OH 44224-2932

Rodriguez, Krysta (Actor, Musician)
c/o Meg Mortimer *Authentic Talent and Literary Management (NY)*
20 Jay St Ste M17
Brooklyn, NY 11201-8300, USA

Rodriguez, Maggie (Television Host)
c/o Staff Member *CBS News (NY)*
524 W 57th St Fl 8
New York, NY 10019-2930, USA

Rodriguez, Mel (Actor)
c/o Lewis Kay *Kovert Creative*
506 Santa Monica Blvd Ste 400
Santa Monica, CA 90401-2412, USA

Rodriguez, Michelle (Actor)
c/o Jason Weinberg *Untitled Entertainment*
350 S Beverly Dr Ste 200
Beverly Hills, CA 90212-4819, USA

Rodriguez, MJ (Actor)
c/o Emily Rennert *Imprint PR*
375 Hudson St
New York, NY 10014-3658, USA

Rodriguez, Paul (Actor)
c/o Barry Katz *Barry Katz Entertainment*
10100 Santa Monica Blvd Ste 300
Los Angeles, CA 90067-4107, USA

Rodriguez, Raini (Actor)
c/o Susan Osser *Susan Osser Talent Company*
14617 Killion St
Sherman Oaks, CA 91411-3734, USA

Rodriguez, Ramon (Actor)
c/o Allan Grifka *Alchemy Entertainment*
7024 Melrose Ave Ste 420
Los Angeles, CA 90038-3394, USA

Rodriguez, Rich (Athlete, Baseball Player)
6250 Canoga Ave APT 503
Woodland Hls, CA 91367-8305, USA

Rodriguez, Rick (Athlete, Baseball Player)
7000 Coliseum Way Ste 3
Oakland, CA 94621-1917, USA

Rodriguez, Rico (Actor)
c/o Bonnie Ventis *Clear Talent Group (LA)*
10950 Ventura Blvd
Studio City, CA 91604-3340, USA

Rodriguez, Robert (Director, Producer)
c/o Staff Member *Los Hooligans Productions*
4900 Old Manor Rd
Austin, TX 78723-4522, USA

Rodriguez, Steve (Athlete, Baseball Player)
3071 Rockbridge Rd
Mc Gregor, TX 76657-3456, USA

Rodriguez, Valente (Actor)
c/o Suzanne (Sue) Wohl *TalentWorks*
3500 W Olive Ave Ste 1400
Burbank, CA 91505-5512, USA

Rodriguez, Vic (Athlete, Baseball Player)
2796 Via Piazza Loop
Fort Myers, FL 33905-5562, USA

Rodriguez, Wandy (Athlete, Baseball Player)
2795 Paddock Rd
Weston, FL 33331-3013, USA

Rodriquez, La Mala (Musician)
c/o Staff Member *Zona Bruta Discos S.L.*
C Clemente Fernandez 56 Local Izda
Madrid 28011, Spain

Rodriquez, Paul (Skateboarder)
Plan B Skateboards
121 Waterworks Way Ste 100
Irvine, CA 92618-7719, USA

Roe, Alex (Actor)
c/o Lena Roklin *Luber Roklin Management*
5815 W Sunset Blvd Ste 208
Los Angeles, CA 90028-6481, USA

Roe, Billy (Race Car Driver)
5450 E Deer Valley Dr Unit 1006
Phoenix, AZ 85054-8100, USA

Roe, Elwin (Preacher) (Athlete, Baseball Player)
204 Wildwood Ter
West Plains, MO 65775-2548, USA

Roe, Louise (Television Host)
c/o Staff Member *Liz Matthews PR*
8 Smokehouse Yard
44-46 St. John St
London EC1M 4DF, United Kingdom

Roe, Rocky (Athlete, Baseball Player)
2092 Appalachee Cir
Tavares, FL 32778-2014, USA

Roebuck, Daniel (Actor)
c/o Leslie Allan-Rice *Leslie Allan-Rice Management*
1007 Maybrook Dr
Beverly Hills, CA 90210-2715, USA

Roebuck, Ed (Athlete, Baseball Player)
103 Paseo De La Playa Apt 4
Redondo Beach, CA 90277-5348, USA

Roedel, Herb (Athlete, Football Player)
4810 201st St
Flushing, NY 11364-1012, USA

Roemer, Sarah (Actor, Model)
c/o Leslie Sloane *Vision PR*
2 Penn Plz Rm 2601
New York, NY 10121-0001, USA

Roenick, Jeremy (Athlete, Hockey Player, Olympic Athlete)
c/o Mark Lepselter *Maxx Sports & Entertainment*
546 5th Ave Fl 6
New York, NY 10036-5000, USA

Roenicke, Gary (Athlete, Baseball Player)
13625 Gold Country Dr
Penn Valley, CA 95946-9007, USA

Roenicke, Josh (Athlete, Baseball Player)
8130 Santa Rosa Ct
Sarasota, FL 34243-3000, USA

Roenicke, Ron (Athlete, Baseball Player)
787 Avenida Salvador
San Clemente, CA 92672-2369, USA

Roerig, Zach (Actor)
c/o Matt Shaffer *Innovative Artists*
1505 10th St
Santa Monica, CA 90401-2805, USA

Roesler, Mike (Athlete, Baseball Player)
12033 Fallen Leaf Ct
Fort Wayne, IN 46845-8992, USA

Roessler, Pat (Athlete, Baseball Player)
1210 Massachusetts Ave NW Apt 411
Washington, DC 20005-4517, USA

Roethlisberger, Ben (Athlete, Football Player)
Dreams Inc
2 S University Dr Ste 325
Plantation, FL 33324-3307, USA

Roethlisberger, Fred (Athlete, Gymnast, Olympic Athlete)
W9920 710th Ave
River Falls, WI 54022-4017, USA

Roffe-Barker, Melanie (Director)
c/o Staff Member *Don Capo Entertainment*
Ste 5 South Bank Terrace
Surbiton
Surrey KT6 6DG, UNITED KINGDOM (UK)

Roffe-Barker, Nigel (Director, Producer, Writer)
c/o Staff Member *Don Capo Entertainment*
Ste 5 South Bank Terrace
Surbiton
Surrey KT6 6DG, UNITED KINGDOM (UK)

Roffe-Steinrotter, Diann (Athlete, Olympic Athlete, Skier)
248 N 29th St
Camp Hill, PA 17011-2904, USA

Rogan, Joe (Comedian, Talk Show Host)
c/o Chandra Keyes *Jeff Sussman Management*
Prefers to be contacted by email or phone.
Sherman Oaks, CA 91403, USA

Rogan, Markus (Athlete, Swimmer)
Oesterreichischer Schwimmverband
Engerthstrasse 267-269
Wien 01020, Austria

Rogas, Dan (Athlete, Football Player)
2352 Evalon St
Beaumont, TX 77702-1310, USA

Rogen, Lauren Miller (Actor)
c/o Marsha McManus *Principal Entertainment*
9255 W Sunset Blvd Ste 500
Los Angeles, CA 90069-3301, USA

Rogen, Seth (Actor)
c/o Kaitlyn Horton *ID Public Relations*
7060 Hollywood Blvd Fl 8th
Los Angeles, CA 90028-6021, USA

Roger, Elena (Musician)
c/o Simon Beresford *Dalzell & Beresford Ltd*
55 Charterhouse St
The Paddock Suite, The Courtyard
London EC1M 6HA, UNITED KINGDOM (UK)

Rogers, Aaron (Director)

Rogers, Bill (Golfer)
710 Patterson Ave
San Antonio, TX 78209-5637, USA

Rogers, Brendan (Athlete, Football Player)
RBC Dominion Securities
800-1 Lombard Pi
Winnipeg, MB R3B 0X3, Canada

Rogers, Carlos (Athlete, Football Player)
c/o Todd France *Creative Artists Agency (CAA) Sports*
3500 Lenox Rd NE
Atlanta, GA 30326-4228, USA

Rogers, Chad (Business Person, Reality Star)
Hilton & Hyland
257 N Canon Dr
Beverly Hills, CA 90210-5301, USA

Rogers, Da'Rick (Athlete, Football Player)
c/o Joby Branion *Vanguard Sports Group*
23091 Mill Creek Dr
Laguna Hills, CA 92653-1258, USA

Rogers, Gene (Misc)
P.O. Box 3537
McAlester, OK 74502-3637, USA

Rogers, George (Athlete, Football Player, Heisman Trophy Winner)
589 Compass Rose Way
Irmo, SC 29063-7504, USA

Rogers, Graham (Actor)
c/o Sarah Shyn *3 Arts Entertainment*
9460 Wilshire Blvd Fl 7
Beverly Hills, CA 90212-2713, USA

Rogers, Greg (Writer)
614 Big Hill Cir
McAlester, OK 74501-2591, USA

Rogers, Harold (Congressman, Politician)
2406 Rayburn Hob
Washington, DC 20515-1705, USA

Rogers, Jackie (Race Car Driver)
5731 Camellia Ln
Wilmington, NC 28409-5801, USA

Rogers, Jamar (Musician)
c/o Stephen Ford *Diva Central Inc*
7510 W Sunset Blvd # 1445
Los Angeles, CA 90046-3408, USA

Rogers, Jimmy (Athlete, Baseball Player)
7235 S Janet St Trlr 10
Oklahoma City, OK 73150-7426, USA

Rogers, Kenny (Athlete, Baseball Player)
c/o Jim Mazza *Dreamcatcher Entertainment*
2910 Poston Ave
Nashville, TN 37203-1312, USA

Rogers, Kenny (Musician)
c/o Jim Mazza *Dreamcatcher Entertainment*
2910 Poston Ave
Nashville, TN 37203-1312, USA

Rogers, Kevin (Athlete, Baseball Player)
604 Douglas Ave
Cleveland, MS 38732-2026, USA

Rogers, Kylie (Actor)
c/o Nicole Perna *Imprint PR*
6121 W Sunset Blvd
Neuehouse
Los Angeles, CA 90028-6442, USA

Rogers, Lamarr (Baseball Player)
2931 W Park St
Phoenix, AZ 85041-6373, USA

Rogers, Melody (Actor)
2051 Nichols Canyon Rd
Los Angeles, CA 90046-1727, USA

Rogers, Mike (Athlete, Hockey Player)
Calgary Flames
PO Box 1540 Stn M
Calgary, AB T2P 3B9, Canada

Rogers, Mike (Athlete, Hockey Player)
63 Calling Horse Estate
Calgary, AB T3Z 1H4, Canada

Rogers, Mike (Congressman, Politician)
324 Cannon Hob
Washington, DC 20515-4301, USA

Rogers, Mimi (Actor)
c/o Jason Shapiro *Silver Lining Entertainment*
421 S Beverly Dr Fl 7
Beverly Hills, CA 90212-4408, USA

Rogers, Olan (Actor, Producer)
c/o Matt Shichtman *Gotham Group*
1041 N Formosa Ave # 200
West Hollywood, CA 90046-6703, USA

Rogers, Randy (Musician)
c/o Staff Member *HB Public Relations*
4611 Dakota Ave
Nashville, TN 37209-3525, USA

Rogers, Reg (Actor)
c/o Staff Member *Brookside Artists Management*
250 W 57th St Ste 1820
New York, NY 10107-1802, USA

Rogers, Sharon (Model)
4910 Ramblewood Ln SE
Olympia, WA 98513-9233, USA

Rogers, Stephen D (Steve) (Baseball Player)
3746 S Madison Ave
Tulsa, OK 74105-3016, USA

Rogers, Steve (Athlete, Baseball Player)
2 Lenape Ln
Princeton Junction, NJ 08550-1817, USA

Rogers, Suzanne (Actor)
11266 Canton Dr
Studio City, CA 91604-4154, USA

Rogers, Tracy (Athlete, Football Player)
1011 Tam O Shanter Dr
Bakersfield, CA 93309-2451, USA

Rogerson, Sean (Actor)
c/o Michelle Gauvin *Performers Management*
5-636 Clyde Ave
West Vancouver, BC V7T 1E1, CANADA

Roges, Al (Athlete, Basketball Player)
6217 Scenic Ave
Los Angeles, CA 90068-2914, USA

Rogge, Jacques (Misc)
Int'l Olympic Committee
Chateau de Vidy
Lausanne 01007, SWITZERLAND

Roggeman, Tom (Athlete, Football Player)
241 S 6th St Apt 2308
Philadelphia, PA 19106-3736, USA

Roggenburk, Garry (Athlete, Baseball Player)
33550 Streamview Dr
Avon, OH 44011-2597, USA

Roggin, Fred (Sportscaster)
NBC4 LOS ANGELES - KNBC
3000 W Alameda Ave
Burbank, CA 91523-0002

Rogodzinski, Mike (Athlete, Baseball Player)
227 Holborn Loop
Davenport, FL 33897-4624, USA

Rogoff, Ilan (Musician)
Apdo 1098
Palma de Mallorca 07080, SPAIN

Rogow, Stan (Producer)
c/o Staff Member *ICM Partners*
10250 Constellation Blvd Fl 7
Los Angeles, CA 90067-6207, USA

Rogowsky, Scott (Game Show Host)
c/o James Dixon *Dixon Talent*
375 Greenwich St Fl 5
New York, NY 10013-2376, USA

Rogue Wave (Music Group)
c/o Staff Member *Paradigm (Monterey)*
404 W Franklin St
Monterey, CA 93940-2303, USA

Roh, Craig (Athlete, Football Player)
c/o Blake Baratz *The Institute for Athletes*
3600 Minnesota Dr Ste 550
Edina, MN 55435-7925, USA

Rohde, Bruce (Business Person)
ConAgra Inc
1 Conagra Dr
Omaha, NE 68102-5003, USA

Rohde, Dave (Athlete, Baseball Player)
19191 Harvard Ave Apt 117B
Irvine, CA 92612-4646, USA

Rohde, David (Journalist)
229 W 43rd St
New York, NY 10036-3982, USA

Rohde, Kristen (Actor)
c/o Staff Member *Gersh*
9465 Wilshire Blvd Ste 600
Beverly Hills, CA 90212-2605, USA

Rohde, Len (Athlete, Football Player)
324 Alta Vista Ave
Los Altos, CA 94022-2103, USA

Rohlander, Uta (Athlete, Track Athlete)
Liebigstr 9
Leuna 06237, GERMANY

Rohlinger, Ryan (Athlete, Baseball Player)
2100 Canary St
West Bend, WI 53090-2764, USA

Rohloff, Jon (Athlete, Hockey Player)
40057 County Road 242
Cohasset, MN 55721-8819

Rohloff, Kenneth (Athlete, Basketball Player)
403 Jade Cv
Newport, NC 28570-5574, USA

Rohloff, Todd (Athlete, Hockey Player)
309 W Avenue C
Bismarck, ND 58501-3418

Rohm, Elisabeth (Actor)
c/o Michael McConnell *Zero Gravity Management (II)*
5660 Silver Valley Ave
Agoura Hills, CA 91301-4000, USA

Rohn, Dan (Athlete, Baseball Player)
2406 Arthur Ct
Traverse City, MI 49685-7411, USA

Rohner, Clayton (Actor)
6924 Treasure Trl
Los Angeles, CA 90068-1838, USA

Rohner, Georges (Artist)
Galerie Framond
3 Rue des Saints Peres
Paris 75006, FRANCE

Rohr, Bill (Athlete, Baseball Player)
67545 S Lae:una Dr
Cathedral Citv, CA 92234-7487, USA

Rohr, Les (Athlete, Baseball Player)
1508 Wicks Ln
Billings, MT 59105-4412, USA

Rohrbach, Kelly (Actor, Model)
c/o Ina Treciokas *Slate PR*
901 N Highland Ave
W Hollywood, CA 90038-2412, USA

Rohrbacher, Dana (Congressman, Politician)
2300 Rayburn Hob
Washington, DC 20515-2212, USA

Rohrer, Jeff (Athlete, Football Player)
3201 Executive Cir
Dallas, TX 75234-3764, USA

Rohrmeier, Dan (Athlete, Baseball Player)
1029 Ede:etree Ln
Cincinnati, OH 45238-4318, USA

Roig, Tony (Athlete, Baseball Player)
24125 E Lakeridge Dr
Liberty Lake, WA 99019-9612, USA

Roiland, Justin (Actor)
c/o Jay Gassner *United Talent Agency (UTA)*
9336 Civic Center Dr
Beverly Hills, CA 90210-3604, USA

Roiz, Sasha (Actor)
c/o Mona Loring *Status PR*
PO Box 6191
Westlake Village, CA 91359-6191, USA

Roizin, Dr Michael (Doctor)
Cleveland Clinic
2049 E 100th St
Cleveland, OH 44106-2104, USA

Rojas, Euky (Athlete, Baseball Player)
14777 SW 80th St
Miami, FL 33193-1515, USA

Rojas, Geoffrey (Prince Royce) (Musician)
c/o Miles Gidaly *WME/IMG (NY)*
11 Madison Ave Fl 18
New York, NY 10010-3669, USA

Rojas, Goffrey (Prince Royal) (Musician)
c/o Michael Vega *WME/IMG (Miami)*
119 Washington Ave Ste 400
Miami Beach, FL 33139-7202, USA

Rojas, Mel (Athlete, Baseball Player)
15645 Collins Ave Apt 802
North Miami Beach, FL 33160-4790, USA

Rojas, Nydia (Musician)
Silverlight Entertainment
9171 Wilshire Blvd Ste 426
Beverly Hills, CA 90210-5516, USA

Rojas, Octavio R (Cookie) (Athlete, Baseball Player, Coach)
19195 Mystic Pointe Dr Apt 3002
Aventura, FL 33180-4502, USA

Rojcewicz, Susan (Athlete, Basketball Player, Olympic Athlete)
30 Via Encina
Monterey, CA 93940-6112, USA

Rojeski, Shawn (Athlete, Olympic Athlete)
510 11th St NW
Chisholm, MN 55719-1157, USA

Rojo, Ana Patricia (Actor)
c/o Staff Member *Televisa*
Blvd Adolfo Lopez Mateos 232
Colonia San Angel INN
DF CP 01060, MEXICO

Rojo, Gustavo (Actor)
c/o Staff Member *Televisa*
Blvd Adolfo Lopez Mateos 232
Colonia San Angel INN
DF CP 01060, MEXICO

Roker, Al (Correspondent, Television Host)
Al Roker Productions
500 Fashion Ave Fl 8A
New York, NY 10018-0818, USA

Rokita, Todd (Congressman, Politician)
236 Cannon Hob
Washington, DC 20515-0503, USA

Rola (Model)
c/o Staff Member *Libera*
5-18 Maruyama-Cho
Dougenzaka Sq #404
Shibuya-Ku 150-0044, TOKYO

Roland, Ed (Musician, Songwriter, Writer)
Spivak Entertainment
11845 W Olympic Blvd Ste 1125
Los Angeles, CA 90064-5096, USA

Roland, Jim (Athlete, Baseball Player)
1802 Arbor Way Dr
Shelby, NC 28150-6166, USA

Roland, Johnny E (Athlete, Coach, Football Player)
8701 S Hardy Dr
Tempe, AZ 85284-2800, USA

Rolen, Scott (Athlete, Baseball Player)
721 Key Royale Dr
Holmes Beach, FL 34217-1231, USA

Roles-Williams, Barbara (Athlete, Figure Skater, Olympic Athlete)
3790 Leisure Ln
Las Vegas, NV 89103-2323, USA

Rolfe, Dale (Athlete, Hockey Player)
365 Hughson St
Gravenhurst, ON P1P 1G8, Canada

Rolison, Nathan (Nate) (Athlete, Baseball Player)
118 Countv Road 3709
Enterorise, MS 39330-7803, USA

Rolle, Antrel (Athlete, Football Player)
c/o Drew Rosenhaus *Rosenhaus Sports Representation*
3921 Alton Rd # 440
Miami Beach, FL 33140-3852, USA

Rolle, Butch (Athlete, Football Player)
17822 NW 15th St
Pembroke Pines, FL 33029-3134, USA

Roller, David E (Athlete, Football Player)
1404 Bristol Trce
Alpharetta, GA 30022-1080, USA

Rolling Stones (Music Group)
c/o Fran Curtis *Rogers & Cowan*
1840 Century Park E Fl 18
Los Angeles, CA 90067-2101, USA

Rollins, Henry (Musician, Songwriter)
c/o Richard Bishop *Red Light Management*
5800 Bristol Pkwy Ste 400
Culver City, CA 90230-6898, USA

Rollins, Jerry (Athlete, Hockey Player)
14062 Caminito Vistana
San Diego, CA 92130-3719, USA

Rollins, Jimmy (Athlete, Baseball Player)
120 Fox Chase Ct
Swedesboro, NJ 08085-3043, USA

Rollins, John (Golfer)
8703 Playground Ct
North Chesterfield, VA 23237-2378, USA

Rollins, Kenneth (Athlete, Basketball Player, Olympic Athlete)
1497 N County Road 175 W
Greencastle, IN 46135-9238, USA

Rollins, Phil (Athlete, Basketball Player)
221 Norbourne Blvd
Louisville, KY 40207-3922, USA

Rollins, Rich (Athlete, Baseball Player)
4146 Evergreen Ln
Richfield, OH 44286-9592, USA

Rollins, Rose (Actor)
c/o Jennifer Sims *Imprint PR*
375 Hudson St
New York, NY 10014-3658, USA

Rollins, Sonny (Composer, Musician)
c/o Ted Kurland *Ted Kurland Associates*
173 Brighton Ave
Boston, MA 02134-2003, USA

Rollins, Wayne (Tree) (Athlete, Basketball Player, Coach)
PO Box 1209
Apopka, FL 32704-1209, USA

Rolls, Damian (Athlete, Baseball Player)
11112 Shadybrook Dr
Tampa, FL 33625-5708, USA

Roloson, Dwayne (Athlete, Hockey Player)
Global Hockey Consultants
175 Federal St Ste 1325
Attn Mark Witkin
Boston, MA 02110-2221, USA

Rolston, Brian (Athlete, Hockey Player, Olympic Athlete)
Sports Consulting Group
65 Monroe Ave Ste D
Pittsford, NY 14534-1318, USA

Rolston, Holmes III (Misc)
Colorado State University
Philosophy Dept
Fort Collins, CO 80523-0001, USA

Roman, Bill (Athlete, Baseball Player)
1720 Yale Ct
Lake Forest, IL 60045-5117, USA

Roman, Dan (Baseball Player)
10313 Arran Ct
Huntersville, NC 28078-7021, USA

Roman, John (Athlete, Football Player)
13 Mendham Rd
Bernardsville, NJ 07924, USA

Roman, Joseph (Misc)
Glass & Ceramic Workers Union
556 E Town St
Columbus, OH 43215-4802, USA

Roman, Petre (Prime Minister)
Str Gogol 2
Sector 1
Bucharest, ROMANIA

Roman, Tami (Actor, Reality Star)
c/o Shakim Compere *Flavor Unit Entertainment*
8484 Wilshire Blvd Ste 850
Beverly Hills, CA 90211-3217, USA

Romanchych, Larry (Athlete, Hockey Player)
3989 206A St
Langley, BC V3A 7A8, Canada

Romanek, Mark (Director)
c/o Staff Member *Creative Artists Agency (CAA)*
2000 Avenue of the Stars Ste 100
Los Angeles, CA 90067-4705, USA

Romanetti, Ray (Horse Racer)
227 S Spring Valley Rd
Canonsburg, PA 15317-2823, USA

Romanick, Ron (Athlete, Baseball Player)
17108 E Kingstree Blvd Apt 1
Fountain Hills, AZ 85268-5556, USA

Romaniszyn, Jim (Athlete, Football Player)
619 Amy Lee Cir
Port Orange, FL 32127-7542, USA

Romano, Andy (Actor)
c/o Staff Member *Golan & Blumberg*
2761 E Woodbury Dr
Arlington Heights, IL 60004-7247, USA

Romano, Christy Carlson (Actor)
c/o Mark Modesitt *MODE Public Relations*
754 N Croft Ave
Los Angeles, CA 90069-5333, USA

Romano, Jason (Athlete, Baseball Player)
1411 Willow Oak Cir
Bradenton, FL 34209-7822, USA

Romano, John (Misc)
212 Valley Rd
Merion Station, PA 19066-1543, USA

Romano, Johnny (Athlete, Baseball Player)
160 W Pago Pago Dr
Naples, FL 34113-8616, USA

Romano, Larry (Actor)
Gold Marshak Liedtke
3500 W Olive Ave Ste 1400
Burbank, CA 91505-5512, USA

Romano, Mike (Athlete, Baseball Player)
PO Box 2761
Covington, LA 70434-2761, USA

Romano, Ray (Actor, Comedian, Producer, Writer)
5225 Encino Ave
Encino, CA 91316-2525, USA

Romano, Roberto (Athlete, Hockey Player)
S865 Rue Brossard
Saint-Leonard, QC HIT 3R6, Canada

Romano, Rocco (Athlete, Football Player)
Calgary Stampeders
1817 Crowchild Trail NW
Calgary, AB T2M 4R6, Canada

Romano, Tom (Athlete, Baseball Player)
1266 Penora St
Depew, NY 14043-4512, USA

Romano, Umberto (Artist)
162 E 83rd St
New York, NY 10028-1901, USA

Romanov, Stephanie (Actor)
c/o Staff Member *Diverse Talent Group*
1875 Century Park E Ste 2250
Los Angeles, CA 90067-2563, USA

Romanowski, Bill (Athlete, Football Player)
3706 Mt Diablo Blvd Ste 200
Lafayette, CA 94549-3638, USA

Romanus, Richard (Actor)
Chasin Agency
8899 Beverly Blvd Ste 716
Los Angeles, CA 90048-2449, USA

Romanus, Robert (Actor)
c/o Melanie Sharp *Sharp Talent*
117 N Orlando Ave
Los Angeles, CA 90048-3403, USA

Roman Waugh, Ric (Director)
2967 E 3rd St
Los Angeles, CA 90033-4108, USA

Romar, Lorenzo (Athlete, Basketball Player)
4408 164th Ln SE
Issaquah, WA 98027-9046, USA

Romario (Soccer Player)
Fluminense FC
Rua Alvaro Chaves 41
Rio de Janiero 22231-200, BRAZIL

Romby, Bob (Baseball Player)
Baltimore Elite Giants
38 Holman Mill Rd
Cumberland, VA 23040-2804, USA

Rome, Jim (Actor)
c/o Jeff Jacobs *Creative Artists Agency (CAA)*
2000 Avenue of the Stars Ste 100
Los Angeles, CA 90067-4705, USA

Rome, Jim (Sportscaster)
c/o Staff Member *Showtime Networks*
1041 N Formosa Ave # 300
West Hollywood, CA 90046-6703, USA

Rome, Stan (Athlete, Football Player)
4489 Green Island Rd
Valdosta, GA 31602-0870, USA

Romelfanger, Charles (Misc)
Pattern Makers League
4106 34th Ave
Moline, IL 61265-5501, USA

Romer, Suzanne F C (Prime Minister)
Prime Minister's Office
Willemstad, Curacao, NETHERLANDS ANTILLES

Romero, Celino (Musician)
Columbia Artists Mgmt Inc
165 W 57th St
New York, NY 10019-2201, USA

Romero, Danny Jr (Boxer)
800 Salida Sandia SW
Albuquerque, NM 87105-7607, USA

Romero, Ed (Athlete, Baseball Player)
1380 Wood Row Way
Wellington, FL 33414-9082, USA

Romero, J.C (Athlete, Baseball Player)
18172 S Section St Apt 1101
Fairhope, AL 36532-2246, USA

Romero, Mandy (Athlete, Baseball Player)
19280 SW 216th St
Miami, FL 33170-1214, USA

Romero, Ned (Actor)
19438 Lassen St
Northridge, CA 91324-1121, USA

Romero, Randy (Horse Racer)
1019 Kaliste Saloom Rd Apt 955
Lafayette, LA 70508-4936, USA

Romero, Richard (Actor)
c/o Staff Member *Select Artists Ltd (CA-Valley Office)*
PO Box 4359
Burbank, CA 91503-4359, USA

Romijn, Rebecca (Actor, Model)
c/o Lewis Kay *Kovert Creative*
506 Santa Monica Blvd Ste 400
Santa Monica, CA 90401-2412, USA

Romine, Alton (Athlete, Football Player)
286 Highway 79
Phil Campbell, AL 35581-6314, USA

Romine, Andrew (Athlete, Baseball Player)
22701 Fernwood St
Lake Forest, CA 92630-3612, USA

Romine, Austin (Athlete, Baseball Player)
22701 Fernwood St
Lake Forest, CA 92630-3612, USA

Romine, Kevin (Athlete, Baseball Player)
22701 Fernwood St
Lake Forest, CA 92630-3612, USA

Romine, Paul (Race Car Driver)
Aerolite Racing
3645 Developers Rd
Indianapolis, IN 46227-3521, United States

Rominger, Kent V (Astronaut)
2714 E Bridgeport Ave
Salt Lake City, UT 84121-5603, USA

Rominger, Kent V Captain (Astronaut)
2714 E Bridgeport Ave
Salt Lake City, UT 84121-5603, USA

Rominski, Dale (Athlete, Hockey Player)
32043 Staman Ct
Farmington Hills, MI 48336-1861

Romita Sr., John (Artist, Cartoonist)
11301 W Olympic Blvd # 587
Los Angeles, CA 90064-1653, USA

Romney, Ann (Politician)
311 Dunemere Dr
La Jolla, CA 92037-5312, USA

Romney, Mitt (Business Person, Politician)
2151 E 5340 S
Salt Lake City, UT 84117-7632, USA

Romo, Candice Crawford (Business Person)
Hawke + Sloane
2108 Dallas Pkwy Ste 214
Plano, TX 75093-4362, USA

Romo, Daniela (Actor)
c/o Staff Member *Televisa*
Blvd Adolfo Lopez Mateos 232
Colonia San Angel INN
DF CP 01060, MEXICO

Romo, Sergio (Athlete, Baseball Player)
c/o Barry Meister *Meister Sports Management*
770 Lake Cook Rd Ste 300
Deerfield, IL 60015-4920, USA

Romo, Tony (Athlete, Football Player)
c/o RJ Gonser *CAA (St. Louis)*
222 S Central Ave Ste 1008
Saint Louis, MO 63105-3509, USA

Ron, Duncan (Athlete, Football Player)
500 N Fountain Ave
Springfield, OH 45504-2539, USA

Ron, Moo-hyun (President)
President's Office
Chong Wa Dae
1 Sejong-no
Seoul, SOUTH KOREA

Ronaldinho (Athlete, Soccer Player)
Futbol Club Barcelona
Avenida Aristides Mailol
Barcelona 08028, SPAIN

Ronaldo, Cristiano (Athlete, Soccer Player)
FC Real Madrid
Avda Concha Espana 1
Madrid 28036, SPAIN

Ronan, Ed (Athlete, Hockey Player)
70 Jefferson Rd
Franklin, MA 02038-3363

Ronan, Len (Athlete, Hockey Player)
2006 SW Eastwood Ave
Gresham, OR 97080-5751, USA

Ronan, Marc (Athlete, Baseball Player)
5603 S Chadwick Dr
Rogers, AR 72758-8223, USA

Ronan, Saoirse (Actor)
c/o Derick Mulvey *Macfarlane Chard (Ireland)*
24 Adelaide St
Dun Laoghaire
Dublin NA, IRELAND

Rondeau, Pete (Race Car Driver)
PO Box 1918
Biddeford, ME 04005-1918, USA

Rondo, Rajon (Athlete, Basketball Player)
c/o Bill Duffy *BDA Sports Management*
700 Ygnacio Valley Rd Ste 330
Walnut Creek, CA 94596-3838, USA

Rondon, Gilberto (Gil) (Athlete, Baseball Player)
357 N Oak St Apt A
Orange, CA 92867-7737, USA

Roney, Matt (Athlete, Baseball Player)
1809 Nighthawk Ct
Edmond, OK 73034-6110, USA

Ronin, Costa (Actor)
c/o Alyx Carr *42West*
600 3rd Ave Fl 23
New York, NY 10016-1914, USA

Ronney, Paul D (Astronaut)
613 Ranchito Rd
Monrovia, CA 91016-3733, USA

Ronney, Paul D Dr (Astronaut)
613 Ranchito Rd
Monrovia, CA 91016-3733, USA

Ronning, Cliff (Athlete, Hockey Player)
317 Washington St
Saint Paul, MN 55102-1609, USA

Ronningen, Jon (Wrestler)
Mellomasveien 132
Trollasen 01414, NORWAY

Rono, Peter (Athlete, Track Athlete)
Mount Saint Mary's College
Athletic Dept
Emmitsburg, MD 21727, USA

Ronson, Mark (Musician)
c/o Chloe Walsh *Grandstand Media*
39 W 32nd St Rm 1603
New York, NY 10001-3839, USA

Ronson, Samantha (DJ, Musician)
3251 Descanso Dr
Los Angeles, CA 90026-6242, USA

Ronstadt, Linda (Musician)
Jess Morgan Co
5900 Wilshire Blvd Ste 2300
Los Angeles, CA 90036-5050, USA

Ronty, Paul (Athlete, Hockey Player)
2300 Commonwealth Ave Apt 3-4
Auburndale, MA 02466-1796

Roof, Gene (Athlete, Baseball Player)
175 Spring Valley Dr
Paducah, KY 42003-8894, USA

Roof, Michael (Actor)
c/o Staff Member *3 Arts Entertainment*
9460 Wilshire Blvd Fl 7
Beverly Hills, CA 90212-2713, USA

Roof, Phil (Athlete, Baseball Player)
1301 Pillar Chase
Paducah, KY 42001-6137, USA

Rook, Jerry (Athlete, Basketball Player)
Route 9 Box 124L
Jonesboro, AR 72404, USA

Rook, Susan (Correspondent)
Cable News Network
1050 Techwood Dr NW
News Dept
Atlanta, GA 30318-5695, USA

Rooker, Jim (Athlete, Baseball Player)
2378 Windchime Dr
Jacksonville, FL 32224-2016, USA

Rooker, Michael (Actor)
8330 McGroarty St
Sunland, CA 91040-3208, USA

Roomes, Rolando (Athlete, Baseball Player)
11520 E Pratt Ave
Mesa, AZ 85212-1949, USA

Roomful of Blues (Music Group, Musician)
c/o Staff Member *Concerted Efforts*
PO Box 440326
Somerville, MA 02144-0004, USA

Rooney, Art (Horse Racer)
1190 Washington Rd
Pittsburgh, PA 15228-1817, USA

Rooney, Jim (Soccer Player)
New England Revolution
1 Patriot Pl
Cmgi Field
Foxboro, MA 02035-1388, USA

Rooney, Joe Don (Musician)
Turner & Nichols
49 Music Sq W Ste 500
Nashville, TN 37203-3276, USA

Rooney, Kevin (Actor)
c/o Staff Member *Emptage Hallett*
34-35 Eastcastle St
Fl 3
London W1W 8DW, UNITED KINGDOM (UK)

Rooney, Pat (Athlete, Baseball Player)
4825 Lighthouse Dr
Racine, WI 53402-2666, USA

Rooney, Patrick W (Business Person)
Cooper Tire & Rubber Co
Lima & Western Aves
Findlay, OH 45840, USA

Rooney, Steve (Athlete, Hockey Player)
5 Helen Dr
Canton, MA 02021-2404

Rooney, Timothy (Horse Racer)
810 Central Park Ave
Yonkers, NY 10704, USA

Rooney, Wayne (Soccer Player)
c/o Staff Member *Ian Monk Associates*
2 Station Rd
Gerrards Cross
Buckinghamshire SL9 8EL, UK

Rooney II, Art (Business Person, Football Executive)
1300 Inverness Ave
Pittsburgh, PA 15217-1156, USA

Roop, Richard (Business Person)
Bottom Line Results Inc
743 Goldhills Pl S #239
Woodland Park, CO 80863-1101, USA

Roopenian, Mark (Athlete, Football Player)
358 Charles River Rd
Watertown, MA 02472-2737, USA

Rooper, Jemima (Actor)
c/o Staff Member *Conway van Gelder Grant*
8-12 Broadwick St
London W1F 8HW, UNITED KINGDOM

Roos, Don (Actor, Producer)
c/o Staff Member *Is or Isn't Entertainment*
8391 Beverly Blvd Ste 125
Los Angeles, CA 90048-2633, USA

Roos, Michael (Athlete, Football Player)

Roosevelt, Naaman (Athlete, Football Player)

Rooster (Music Group)
c/o Staff Member *BMG*
1540 Broadway
New York, NY 10036-4039, USA

Root, Bill (Athlete, Hockey Player)
33 Hamilton Hall Dr
Markham, ON L3P 3L5, Canada

Root, Bonnie (Actor)
c/o Tracy Steinsapir *Main Title Entertainment*
8383 Wilshire Blvd Ste 408
Beverly Hills, CA 90211-2435, USA

Root, Stephen (Actor)
c/o Chris Kanarick *ID Public Relations (NY)*
40 Wall St Fl 51
New York, NY 10005-1385, USA

Roots, The (Music Group)
c/o Carleen Donovan *Donovan Public Relations*
30 E 20th St Ste 2FE
New York, NY 10003-1310, USA

Roper, Dee Dee (Spinderella) (Musician)
Next Plateau Records
1650 Broadway Ste 1103
New York, NY 10019-6961, USA

Roper, John (Athlete, Baseball Player)
148 Wagon Wheel Ln
Edinburg, VA 22824-3721, USA

Roper, John (Athlete, Football Player)
4213 Alice St
Houston, TX 77021-4903, USA

Rorem, Ned (Composer, Writer)
PO Box 764
Nantucket, MA 02554-0764, USA

Rorty, Richard M (Misc)
402 Peacock Dr
Charlottesville, VA 22903-9725, USA

Rosa, Robi Draco (Composer, Musician, Producer)
Tanner Mainstain Assoc
10866 Wilshire Blvd # 10000
Los Angeles, CA 90024-4300, USA

Rosales, Adam (Athlete, Baseball Player)
1900 Woodland Ave
Park Ridge, IL 60068-1911, USA

Rosales, Jenny (Athlete, Golfer)
265 S Vine St
Anaheim, CA 92805-4128, USA

Rosario, Dante (Athlete, Football Player)

Rosario, Jimmy (Athlete, Baseball Player)
114 Calle Luna
Carolina, PR 00979-1609, USA

Rosario, Mel (Athlete, Baseball Player)
205 Round Tree Ct
Egg Harbor Township, NJ 08234-7910, USA

Rosario, Santiago (Athlete, Baseball Player)
Kansas City A's
PO Box 561238
Guayanilla, PR 00656-3238, USA

Rosas, Cesar (Musician, Songwriter, Writer)
Monterey International
72 W Adams St # 1000
Chicago, IL 60603-5107, USA

Rosato, Cristina (Actor)
c/o Sandy Martinez *Martinez Creative Management*
7012 St Laurent Blvd Suite 200
Montreal, QC H2S 3E2, Canada

Rosberg, Nico (Race Car Driver)
MERCEDES AMG PETRONAS Formula One Team
Operations Centre
Brackley, Northants NN13 7BD, UNITED KINGDOM

Rosburg, Bob (Golfer)
49425 Avenida Club La Quinta
La Quinta, CA 92253-2703, USA

Rose, Adam (Actor)
c/o Ashton Lunceford *Portrait PR*
5320 Sylmar Ave
Sherman Oaks, CA 91401-5612, USA

Rose, Amber (Actor)
30 Virginia Ln
Canonsburg, PA 15317-5802, USA

Rose, Anika Noni (Actor)
c/o David Williams *David Williams Management*
269 S Beverly Dr # 1408
Beverly Hills, CA 90212-3851, USA

Rose, Axl (Musician, Songwriter, Writer)
5055 Latigo Canyon Rd
Malibu, CA 90265-2812, USA

Rose, Barry (Athlete, Football Player)
1761 W White Ash Dr
Balsam Lake, WI 54810-2416, USA

Rose, Bernard (Director, Producer, Writer)
c/o Jenne Casarotto *Casarotto Ramsay & Associates Ltd (UK)*
Waverley House
7-12 Noel St
London W1F 8GQ, UNITED KINGDOM

Rose, Bobby (Athlete, Baseball Player)
292 Chamberlin Rd
Myrtle Beach, SC 29588-5422, USA

Rose, Brian (Athlete, Baseball Player)
5 Ashland St
South Dartmouth, MA 02748-3211, USA

Rose, Chaley (Actor)
c/o Rebecca Many Rosenberg *Artists First*
9465 Wilshire Blvd Ste 900
Beverly Hills, CA 90212-2608, USA

Rose, Charlie (Television Host)
Rose Communications
499 Park Ave # 1500
New York, NY 10022-1240, USA

Rose, Chris (Television Host)

Rose, Clarence (Golfer)
405 Walnut Creek Dr
Goldsboro, NC 27534-8995, USA

Rose, Cristine (Actor)
c/o Staff Member *SMS Talent*
8383 Wilshire Blvd Ste 230
Beverly Hills, CA 90211-2436, USA

Rose, Derrick (Athlete, Basketball Player)
c/o BJ Armstrong *Wasserman Media Group*
10960 Wilshire Blvd Ste 1200
Los Angeles, CA 90024-3714, USA

Rose, Don (Athlete, Baseball Player)
16254 Palomino Mesa Way
San Diego, CA 92127-4445, USA

Rose, Donovan (Athlete, Football Player)
103 Lenox Ct
Yorktown, VA 23693-5501, USA

Rose, Emily (Actor)
c/o Connie Tavel *Forward Entertainment*
1880 Century Park E Ste 1405
Los Angeles, CA 90067-1630, USA

Rose, Felipe (Musician)
1 Vanada Dr
Neptune, NJ 07753-2540, USA

Rose, George (Athlete, Football Player)
712 Indian Mound Rd
Brunswick, GA 31525-2124, USA

Rose, Howie (Baseball Player)
35 Woodland Dr
Roslyn, NY 11576-3036, USA

Rose, Jalen (Athlete, Basketball Player)
c/o Staff Member *ESPN (Main)*
935 Middle St
Espn Plaza
Bristol, CT 06010-1000, USA

Rose, Jamie (Actor)
c/o Staff Member *Marshak/Zachary Company, The*
8840 Wilshire Blvd Fl 1
Beverly Hills, CA 90211-2606, USA

Rose, Jessica Lee (Actor)
c/o Brad Marks *Blue Five Media*
9150 Wilshire Blvd Ste 103
Beverly Hills, CA 90212-3428, USA

Rose, Joe (Athlete, Football Player)
3293 SW 138th Way
Davie, FL 33330-4664, USA

Rose, John (Cartoonist)
95 Laurel St
Harrisonburg, VA 22801-2732, USA

Rose, Justin (Golfer)
c/o Staff Member *Pro Golfers Assoc of America (PGA)*
112 TPC Blvd
Ponte Vedra Beach, FL 32082-3077, USA

Rose, Katy (Musician)
c/o Staff Member *Paradigm (Monterey)*
404 W Franklin St
Monterey, CA 93940-2303, USA

Rose, Ken (Athlete, Football Player)
1080 Amberton Ln
Newbury Park, CA 91320-3515, USA

Rose, Lee (Director, Producer)
c/o Staff Member *Broder Webb Chervin Silbermann Agency, The (BWCS)*
10250 Constellation Blvd Ste 1700
Los Angeles, CA 90067-6253, USA

Rose, Lucy (Musician)
c/o Staff Member *ICM Partners*
10250 Constellation Blvd Fl 7
Los Angeles, CA 90067-6207, USA

Rose, Malik (Athlete, Basketball Player)
1318 Greystone Rdg
San Antonio, TX 78258-4406, USA

Rose, Marie (Actor)
6916 Chisholm Ave
Van Nuys, CA 91406-5111, USA

Rose, Mauri (Race Car Driver)
International Motorsports
PO Box 1018
Talladega, AL 35161-1018, USA

Rose, Molly Qerim (Sportscaster)
c/o Staff Member *ESPN (NY)*
77 W 66th St
New York, NY 10023-6201, USA

Rose, Pete (Athlete, Baseball Player, Coach)
c/o Charlie Hustle Inc
1018 Belle River Ct
Henderson, NV 89052-3898, USA

Rose, Peter H (Business Person)
Krytek Corp
2 Centennial Dr
Peabody, MA 01960-7911, USA

Rose, Ruby (Actor)
c/o Danica Smith *Kovert Creative*
506 Santa Monica Blvd Ste 400
Santa Monica, CA 90401-2412, USA

Rose, Shayna (Actor)
Rough Diamond Productions
1424 N Kings Rd
C/O Bill Kravitz
Los Angeles, CA 90069-1908, USA

Rose, Sherrie (Actor, Model)
1758 Laurel Canyon Blvd
Los Angeles, CA 90046-2134, USA

Rosecrans, James (Athlete, Football Player)
210 Houston Ave
Syracuse, NY 13224-1754, USA

Rosegarten, Rory (Producer)
c/o Staff Member *WME/IMG*
9601 Wilshire Blvd
Beverly Hills, CA 90210-5213, USA

Rose Jr, Pete (Athlete, Baseball Player)
3921 Legendary Ridge Ln
Cleves, OH 45002-2395, USA

Roselli, Bob (Athlete, Baseball Player)
100 Clydesdale Way
Roseville, CA 95678-6032, USA

Rosello, Dave (Athlete, Baseball Player)
160 Calle La Paz
Urb Bo Paris
Mayaguez, PR 00680-5441, USA

Rosema, Roger (Athlete, Football Player)
6081 Champagne Ct SE
Grand Rapids, MI 49546-6430, USA

Rosemont, Romy (Actor)
c/o Tracy Steinsapir *Main Title Entertainment*
8383 Wilshire Blvd Ste 408
Beverly Hills, CA 90211-2435, USA

Rosen, Andrew (Business Person)
Theory
38 Gansevoort St
New York, NY 10014-1502, USA

Rosen, Andrew (Producer)
c/o Staff Member *Aircraft Pictures*
147 Liberty St
Toronto, ON M6K 3G3, Canada

Rosen, Beatrice (Actor)
c/o Staff Member *Inspire Entertainment (NY)*
315 7th Ave Apt 17E
New York, NY 10001-6011, USA

Rosen, Hilary (Commentator)
c/o Staff Member *CNN (NY)*
10 Columbus Cir
Time Warner Center
New York, NY 10019-1158, USA

Rosen, Josh (Athlete, Football Player)
c/o Ryan Williams *Athletes First*
23091 Mill Creek Dr
Laguna Hills, CA 92653-1258, USA

Rosen, Nathaniel (Musician)
4555 Henry Hudson Pkwy Apt 1110
Bronx, NY 10471-3840, USA

Rosen, Sam (Actor)
c/o Staff Member *Brookside Artists Management*
250 W 57th St Ste 1820
New York, NY 10107-1802, USA

Rosenbaum, Michael (Actor)
c/o Staff Member *Rose and Bomb Productions*
1438 N Gower St
Hollywood, CA 90028-8383, USA

Rosenberg, Alan (Actor)
PO Box 5617
Beverly Hills, CA 90209-5617, USA

Rosenberg, Alyse (Producer)
c/o Staff Member *The Alpern Group*
15645 Royal Oak Rd
Encino, CA 91436-3905, USA

Rosenberg, Craig (Director, Writer)
c/o Staff Member *Firm, The*
2049 Century Park E Ste 2550
Los Angeles, CA 90067-3110, USA

Rosenberg, Howard (Misc)
5859 Larboard Ln
Agoura Hills, CA 91301-1422, USA

Rosenberg, Joel C (Writer)
Beverly Rykerd Public Relations
PO Box 88180
C/O Beverly Rykerd
Colorado Springs, CO 80908-8180, USA

Rosenberg, Michael (Producer)
c/o Staff Member *Imagine Films Entertainment*
9465 Wilshire Blvd
7th Floor
Los Angeles, CA 90067, USA

Rosenberg, Pierre M (Director)
Musee du Louvre
34-36 Quai du Louvre
Paris 75068, FRANCE

Rosenberg, Scott (Writer)
c/o David O'Connor *Creative Artists Agency (CAA)*
2000 Avenue of the Stars Ste 100
Los Angeles, CA 90067-4705, USA

Rosenberg, Steve (Athlete, Baseball Player)
2430 NE 35th St
Lighthouse Point, FL 33064-8155, USA

Rosenberg, Stuart (Director)
1984 Coldwater Canyon Dr
Beverly Hills, CA 90210-1731, USA

Rosenberg, Tina (Writer)
New School for Social Research
World Policy Institute
New York, NY 10011, USA

Rosenblatt, Dana (Boxer)
30 Cleveland Road
Chestnut Hill, MA 02467-1417, USA

Rosenbluth, Leonard (Lennie) (Athlete, Basketball Player)
123 Priestly Creek Dr
Chapel Hill, NC 27514-5432, USA

Rosenbohm, Jim (Baseball Player)
9513 Bedford Ave
Omaha, NE 68134-4607, USA

Rosendahl, Heidemarie (Heide) (Athlete, Track Athlete)
Burscheider Str 426
Leverkusen 51381, GERMANY

Rosende, Alberto (Actor)
c/o Michael Zecher *MZMGMTNY*
362 5th Ave Ste 809
New York, NY 10001-2210, USA

Rosenfels, Sage (Athlete, Football Player)
110 Ferndale St
Bellaire, TX 77401-5325, USA

Rosenfelt, David (Writer)
c/o Staff Member *St Martins Press*
175 5th Ave
Publicity Dept
New York, NY 10010-7703, USA

Rosengarten, David (Writer)
PO Box 20459
New York, NY 10025-1520, USA

Rosenman, Howard (Producer)
c/o Staff Member *Marshak/Zachary Company, The*
8840 Wilshire Blvd Fl 1
Beverly Hills, CA 90211-2606, USA

Rosenmeyer, Grant (Actor)
c/o Staff Member *DreamWorks SKG*
1000 Flower St
Glendale, CA 91201-3007, USA

Rosenthal, A M (Journalist)
229 W 43rd St Attn Dept
New York, NY 10036-3982, USA

Rosenthal, David S (Director, Writer)
1801 Century Park E Ste 2160
Los Angeles, CA 90067-2343

Rosenthal, Dick (Athlete, Basketball Player)
33108 Lake Forest Ct
Niles, MI 49120-7794, USA

Rosenthal, Gay (Producer)
c/o Mark Schulman *3 Arts Entertainment*
9460 Wilshire Blvd Fl 7
Beverly Hills, CA 90212-2713, USA

Rosenthal, Jane (Producer)
c/o Staff Member *Tribeca Productions*
375 Greenwich St Fl 7
New York, NY 10013-2379, USA

Rosenthal, Mark D (Writer)
c/o Tom Strickler *WME|IMG*
9601 Wilshire Blvd
Beverly Hills, CA 90210-5213, USA

Rosenthal, Mike (Athlete, Football Player)
6112 Every Sail Path
Clarksville, MD 21029-2904, USA

Rosenthal, Philip (Producer)
c/o Peter Nelson *Nelson Davis*
233 Wilshire Blvd Ste 900
Santa Monica, CA 90401-1211, USA

Rosenthal, Rick (Director, Producer)
c/o Staff Member *Whitewater Films*
11264 La Grange Ave
Los Angeles, CA 90025-5514, USA

Rosenthal, Sean (Athlete, Volleyball Player)
USA Volleyball
715 S Circle Dr
Colorado Springs, CO 80910-2324, USA

Rosenthal, Tony (Artist)
173 E 73rd St
New York, NY 10021-3510, USA

Rosenthal, Wayne (Athlete, Baseball Player)
10224 Allamanda Blvd
Palm Beach Gardens, FL 33410-5206, USA

Rosenzweig, Barney (Producer)
2311 Fisher Island Dr
Miami Beach, FL 33109-0086, USA

Rosenzweig, Mark R (Misc)
University of California
Psychology Dept
Tolman Hall
Berkeley, CA 94720-0001, USA

Rosewall, Ken (Tennis Player)
Turramurra
111 Pentacost Ave
Sydney, NSW 02074, AUSTRALIA

Rosewoman, Michele (Musician)
Abby Hoffer
223 1/2 E 48th St
New York, NY 10017, USA

Roshan, Hrithik (Actor)
c/o Staff Member *Carving Dreams Entertainment*
304-305, Oberoi Chambers II
B Wing, Off New Link Road, Andheri West
Mumbai 400053, INDIA

Rosin, Walter L (Religious Leader)
Lutheran Church Missouri Synod
1333 S Kirkwood Rd
Saint Louis, MO 63122-7295, USA

Roskos, John (Athlete, Baseball Player)
PO Box 45514
Rio Rancho, NM 87174-5514, USA

Ros-Lehtinen, Ileana (Congressman, Politician)
2206 Rayburn Hob
Washington, DC 20515-2504, USA

Rosman, Mackenzie (Actor)
c/o Kanica Suy *Sweeney Entertainment*
1601 Vine St # 6
Los Angeles, CA 90028-8802, USA

Rosnes, Renee (Musician)
Integrity Talent
PO Box 961
Burlington, MA 01803-5961, USA

Ross, Aaron (Athlete, Football Player)
c/o Denise White *EAG Sports Management*
909 N Pacific Coast Hwy Ste 360
El Segundo, CA 90245-3864, USA

Ross, Atticus (Composer, Musician)
c/o Sandy Robertson *World's End Inc*
183 N Martel Ave Ste 270
Los Angeles, CA 90036-2755, USA

Ross, Ben (Director)
United Talent Agency
9336 Civic Center Dr
Beverly Hills, CA 90210-3604, USA

Ross, Betsy (Sportscaster)
ESPN-TV
Sports Dept
ESPN Plaza 935 Middle St
Bristol, CT 06010, USA

Ross, Bob (Athlete, Baseball Player)
1071 Mountain View Dr
Hemet, CA 92545-1908, USA

Ross, Charlotte (Actor)
c/o Stephanie Simon *Untitled Entertainment*
350 S Beverly Dr Ste 200
Beverly Hills, CA 90212-4819, USA

Ross, Chelcie (Actor)
c/o Suzanne DeWalt *Dewalt & Musik Management*
623 N Parish Pl
Burbank, CA 91506-1701, USA

Ross, Cody (Athlete, Baseball Player)
21469 N 83rd St
Scottsdale, AZ 85255-6473, USA

Ross, Dave (Athlete, Baseball Player)
2604 Antietam Trl
Tallahassee, FL 32312-4841, USA

Ross, David (Athlete, Baseball Player)
2548 Halleck Ln
Tallahassee, FL 32312-7566, USA

Ross, David A (Director)
Whitney Museum of American Art
945 Madison Ave
New York, NY 10021-2764, USA

Ross, Dennis (Congressman, Politician)
404 Cannon Hob
Washington, DC 20515-2245, USA

Ross, Diana (Actor, Musician)
65 Meadow Wood Dr
Greenwich, CT 06830-7016, USA

Ross, Don (Athlete)
PO Box 981
Venice, CA 90294-0981, USA

Ross, Evan (Actor, Musician)
c/o Danica Smith *Kovert Creative*
506 Santa Monica Blvd Ste 400
Santa Monica, CA 90401-2412, USA

Ross, Fairbanks Anne (Swimmer)
10 Grandview Ave
Troy, NY 12180-2113, USA

Ross, Gary (Athlete, Baseball Player)
113 Shadow Moss Ln
Rockport, TX 78382-2002, USA

Ross, Gary (Director, Producer, Writer)
c/o Staff Member *Larger Than Life Productions*
100 Universal City Plz Bldg 5138
Universal City, CA 91608-1002

Ross, George (Business Person, Reality Star)

Ross, Heather (Musician)
HER Productions
6736 Breezy Palm Dr
Riverview, FL 33578-8802, USA

Ross, Jeffrey (Actor, Comedian)
c/o Amy Zvi *Thruline Entertainment*
9250 Wilshire Blvd Fl Ground
Beverly Hills, CA 90212-3352, USA

Ross, Jeremy (Athlete, Football Player)
c/o Joe Linta *JL Sports*
1204 Main St Ste 179
Branford, CT 06405-3787, USA

Ross, Jerry L (Astronaut)
NASA
2101 Nasa Pkwy Spc Johnsoncenter
Houston, TX 77058-3696, USA

Ross, Jerry L Colonel (Astronaut)
301 Gleneagles Dr
Friendswood, TX 77546-5634, USA

Ross, Jim (Athlete, Wrestler)
605 Shadow View Ct
Norman, OK 73072-4827, USA

Ross, John (Misc)
620 Sand Hill Rd Apt 405E
Palo Alto, CA 94304-2078, USA

Ross, Jonathan (Actor)
c/o Staff Member *Off The Kerb Productions*
Hammer House, 3rd Fl
113-117 Wardour St
London W1F 0UN, UK

Ross, Jonathon (Actor, Producer, Writer)
Talking Concepts
19 Bird Street
Lichfield, Staffordshire WS13 6PW, UNITED KINGDOM

Ross, Karie (Sportscaster)
ESPN-TV
Sports Dept
ESPN Plaza 935 Middle St
Bristol, CT 06010, USA

Ross, Katharine (Actor)
33050 Pacific Coast Hwy
Malibu, CA 90265-2300

Ross, Kevin (Athlete, Football Player)
146 High St
Woodbury, NJ 08096-2304, USA

Ross, Liberty (Actor, Model)
c/o Stephanie Simon *Untitled Entertainment*
350 S Beverly Dr Ste 200
Beverly Hills, CA 90212-4819, USA

Ross, Lonny (Actor)
c/o Ashley Franklin *Thruline Entertainment*
9250 Wilshire Blvd Fl Ground
Beverly Hills, CA 90212-3352, USA

Ross, Louis (Athlete, Football Player)
4283 Booker St
Orlando, FL 32811-4662, USA

Ross, Marion (Actor)
20929 Ventura Blvd Ste 47
PM 144
Woodland Hills, CA 91364-2334, USA

Ross, Mark (Athlete, Baseball Player)
2617 E Big View Dr
Oro Valley, AZ 85755-1938, USA

Ross, Mike (Congressman, Politician)
2436 Rayburn H(:)B
Washington, DC 20515-0001, USA

Ross, Rick (Musician)
c/o Kerry Smalls *The Chamber Group*
75 Broad St Rm 708
New York, NY 10004-3244, USA

Ross, Robert J (Bobby) (Coach, Football Coach)
US Millitary Academy
Athletic Dept
West Point, NY 10996, USA

Ross, Ryan (Actor, Musician)
c/o Staff Member *Jeff Ballard PR*
4814 Lemona Ave
Sherman Oaks, CA 91403-2010, USA

Ross, Scott (Athlete, Football Player)
303 Lake View Dr Unit D
Montgomery, TX 77356-5782, USA

Ross, Tracee Ellis (Actor)
c/o Rachel Karten *ID Public Relations*
7060 Hollywood Blvd Fl 8th
Los Angeles, CA 90028-6021, USA

Ross, Tyson (Athlete, Basketball Player)
c/o Joel Wolfe *Wasserman Media Group*
10960 Wilshire Blvd Ste 1200
Los Angeles, CA 90024-3714, USA

Ross, Willie (Athlete, Football Player)
1100 S Hamilton Ave
Chicago, IL 60612-4207, USA

Ross, Yolonda (Actor)
c/o Brian Liebman *Liebman Entertainment*
29 W 46th St Fl 5
New York, NY 10036-4104, USA

Rossdale, Gavin (Actor, Musician)
10900 Wilshire Blvd # 1230
Los Angeles, CA 90024-6501, USA

Rosselli, Joe (Athlete, Baseball Player)
6231 Le Sage Ave
Woodland Hills, CA 91367-1327, USA

Rossellini, Isabella (Actor)
555 W 59th St Apt 18A
New York, NY 10019-1240, USA

Rossen, Daniel (Musician)
c/o Sam Kirby *WME/IMG (NY)*
11 Madison Ave Fl 18
New York, NY 10010-3669, USA

Rosset, Ricardo (Race Car Driver)
Minardi Italia
Via Spallanzani 21
Faenza 48081, ITALY

Rossi, Gretchen (Reality Star)
c/o Jack Ketsoyan *EMC / Bowery*
8356 Fountain Ave Apt E1
W Hollywood, CA 90069-2968, USA

Rossi, Shorty (Actor)
c/o Staff Member *Shortywood Productions*
PO Box 431296
San Diego, CA 92143-1296, USA

Rossi, Theo (Actor)
c/o Beau Swayze *Management 360*
9111 Wilshire Blvd
Beverly Hills, CA 90210-5508, USA

Rossi, Tony (Ray) (Actor)
c/o Kristene Wallis *Wallis Agency*
210 N Pass Ave Ste 205
Burbank, CA 91505-3936, USA

Rossio, Terry (Writer)
c/o Brian Siberell *Creative Artists Agency (CAA)*
2000 Avenue of the Stars Ste 100
Los Angeles, CA 90067-4705, USA

Rossovich, Tim (Athlete, Football Player)
19895 Wildwood West Dr
Penn Valley, CA 95946-9547, USA

Rossum, Allen (Athlete, Football Player)
2520 Johnson Dr
Mesquite, TX 75181-4619, USA

Rossum, Emmy (Actor, Musician)
c/o Christian Donatelli *MGMT Entertainment (The Schiff Company)*
9220 W Sunset Blvd Ste 106
W Hollywood, CA 90069-3500, USA

Ross Williams, Roger (Director)
c/o Staff Member *Elevation Talent Agency*
119 W 23rd St Ste 409
New York, NY 10011-6374, USA

Rossy, Rico (Athlete, Baseball Player)
A7 Calle Atenas
Bayamon, PR 00959-4928, USA

Rostosky, Pete (Athlete, Football Player)
637 E McMurray Rd
Canonsburg, PA 15317-3430, USA

Rota, Darcy (Athlete, Hockey Player)
2510 Ashurst Ave
Coquitlam, BC V3K 5T4, Canada

Rota, Randy (Athlete, Hockey Player)
78 Bestwick Dr
Kamloops, BC V2C 6P7, Canada

Rotella, Pasquale (Business Person)
817 N Orange Dr
Los Angeles, CA 90038-3325, USA

Rotem, Jonathan (J.R.) (Producer)
c/o Zach Katz *Beluga Heights Management*
5225 Wilshire Blvd Ste 336
Los Angeles, CA 90036-4380, USA

Roth, Andrea (Actor)
c/o Susan (Sue) Madore *Guttman Associates Public Relations*
118 S Beverly Dr Ste 201
Beverly Hills, CA 90212-3016, USA

Roth, Arnold (Cartoonist)
9 Ebony Ct
Brooklyn, NY 11229-5939, USA

Roth, David Lee (Musician)
Maythelight Music
PO Box 495
Orleans, MA 02653-0495, USA

Roth, Doug (Athlete, Basketball Player)
9975 Spillway Cir Apt 201
Cordova, TN 38016-7152, USA

Roth, Ed (Race Car Driver)
The Rat Fink
377 E. 100th North
Manti, UT 84642, USA

Roth, Eli (Director, Producer)
c/o Dan Aloni *WME/IMG*
9601 Wilshire Blvd
Beverly Hills, CA 90210-5213, USA

Roth, Ellaine (Baseball Player)
872 Goguac St W
Springfield, MI 49015-1737, USA

Roth, Eric (Writer)
c/o Staff Member *Creative Artists Agency (CAA)*
2000 Avenue of the Stars Ste 100
Los Angeles, CA 90067-4705, USA

Roth, Rachel (Actor)
c/o Justine Hunt *Hines and Hunt Entertainment*
1213 W Magnolia Blvd
Burbank, CA 91506-1829, USA

Roth, Tim (Actor)
c/o Pippa Markham *Markham & Froggatt*
4 Windmill St
London W1T 1HZ, UNITED KINGDOM

Rothemund, Marc (Director)
c/o Daniel J Talbot *ICM Partners*
10250 Constellation Blvd Fl 7
Los Angeles, CA 90067-6207, USA

Rothenberg, Irv (Athlete, Basketball Player)
6600 Capistrano Beach Trl
Delray Beach, FL 33446-5664, USA

Rothery, Teryl (Actor)
c/o Staff Member *Twenty First Century Artists*
501-825 Granville St
Vancouver, BC V6Z 1K9, CANADA

Rothman, Les (Athlete, Basketball Player)
11854 Fountainside Cir
Boynton Beach, FL 33437-4923, USA

Rothrock, Ray (Business Person)
Venrock
3340 Hillview Ave
Palo Alto, CA 94304-1276, USA

Rothschild, Larry (Athlete, Baseball Player, Coach)
5115 S Nichol St
Tampa, FL 33611-4132, USA

Rothstein, Ron (Athlete, Basketball Coach, Basketball Player, Coach)
60 Edgewater Dr Apt 4E
Coral Gables, FL 33133-6971, USA

Rotimi (Actor, Dancer, Musician)
c/o Christopher Hart *United Talent Agency (UTA)*
9336 Civic Center Dr
Beverly Hills, CA 90210-3604, USA

Rottino, Vinny (Athlete, Baseball Player)
4939 Crystal Spg
Racine, WI 53406-1526, USA

Rouen, Amy Van Dyken (Athlete, Olympic Athlete, Swimmer)
20343 N Hayden Rd Ste 105
Scottsdale, AZ 85255-3876, USA

Rouen, Tom (Athlete, Football Player)
19947 N 84th St
Scottsdale, AZ 85255, USA

Roughan, Howard (Writer)
c/o Jennifer Rudolph Walsh *WME/IMG (NY)*
11 Madison Ave Fl 18
New York, NY 10010-3669, USA

Roulston, Tom (Athlete, Hockey Player)
5500 N Woodlawn St
Kechi, KS 67067-9052, USA

Roumel, Katie (Producer)
c/o Staff Member *Killer Films (US)*
526 W 26th St Rm 715
New York, NY 10001-5524, USA

Rounds, Lil (Musician)

Roundtree, Raleigh (Athlete, Football Player)
2001 Roosevelt Dr
Augusta, GA 30904-5021, USA

Roundtree, Richard (Actor)
7120 Hayvenhurst Ave Ste 409
Van Nuys, CA 91406-3813, USA

Rounsaville, Gene (Athlete, Baseball Player)
537 Red Rome Ln
Brentwood, CA 94513-2689, USA

Rountree, Mary (Athlete, Baseball Player)
8204 NW 80th St
Tamarac, FL 33321-1627, USA

Rourke, Jim (Athlete, Football Player)
466 Plymouth St
Abington, MA 02351-1842, USA

Rourke, Mickey (Actor)
c/o Staff Member *The Actors Studio*
432 W 44th St
New York, NY 10036-5205, USA

Rouse, Bob (Athlete, Hockey Player)
19135 74 Ave
RR 15
Surrey, BC V4N 6C3, CANADA

Rouse, Curtis (Athlete, Football Player)
301 Hampshire Ct
Clarksville, TN 37043-4661, USA

Rouse, Irving (Misc)
509 Rockavon Rd
Narberth, PA 19072-2318, USA

Rouse, Jeff (Athlete, Olympic Athlete, Swimmer)
993 Vernon Berry Ln
Tracy, CA 95376-6708, USA

Rouse, mike (Athlete, Baseball Player)
30055 Monteras St
Laguna Niguel, CA 92677-8822, USA

Rouse, Mitch (Actor)
c/o David (Dave) Becky *3 Arts Entertainment*
9460 Wilshire Blvd Fl 7
Beverly Hills, CA 90212-2713, USA

Rousey, Ronda (Athlete, Olympic Athlete, Wrestler)
c/o Brad Slater *WME/IMG*
9601 Wilshire Blvd
Beverly Hills, CA 90210-5213, USA

Roush, Jack (Race Car Driver)
c/o Randy Fuller *Roush Fenway Racing Team*
4202 Roush Pl NW
Concord, NC 28027-7112, USA

Rouson, Lee (Athlete, Football Player)
20 Main St
Flanders, NJ 07836-9112, USA

Rousseau, Bobby (Athlete, Hockey Player)
580 Ch du Golf
Louiseville, QC J5V 2L4, CANADA

Rousseau, Dune (Athlete, Hockey Player)
261 Stradford St
Winnipeg, MB R2Y 2E1, Canada

Roussel, Dominic (Athlete, Hockey Player)
Ecole De Hockey Co-Jean
58 Rue des Tourterelles Suite
Staff Coaching
Blainville, QC J7C 5T6, CANADA

Roussel, Tom (Athlete, Football Player)
882 S Corniche Du Lac
Covington, LA 70433-7226, USA

Rousset, Christophe (Musician)
Trawick Artists
1926 Broadway
New York, NY 10023-6915, USA

Routh, Brandon (Actor)
c/o Stewart Strunk *Main Title Entertainment*
8383 Wilshire Blvd Ste 408
Beverly Hills, CA 90211-2435, USA

Routledge, Alison (Actor)
Marmont Mgmt
Langham House
302/8 Regent St
London W1R 5AL, UNITED KINGDOM (UK)

Routledge, Patricia (Actor)
6 King George Gardens
Chichester
W Sussex PO19 6LB, UK

Roux, Albert H (Chef)
Le Gavroche
43 Upper Brook St
London W1Y 1PF, UNITED KINGDOM (UK)

Roux, Michel A (Chef)
Le Gavroche
43 Upper Brook St
London W1K 7QR, UK

Roux, Nick (Actor)
c/o Joe Montifiore *Rafterman Media*
4405 W Riverside Dr Ste 102
Burbank, CA 91505-4050, USA

Rovaris, Joy (Actor)
c/o Anne Massey *Fame Agency*
3525 Hessmer Ave Ste 305
Metairie, LA 70002-6407, USA

Rove, Karl (Politician)
1111 New Hampshire Ave NW #600
Washington, DC 20036-1532, USA

Roven, Charles (Producer)
c/o Mara Buxbaum *ID Public Relations*
7060 Hollywood Blvd Fl 8th
Los Angeles, CA 90028-6021, USA

Rowan, Kelly (Actor, Producer)
c/o Brit Reece *PMK/BNC Public Relations*
1840 Century Park E Ste 1400
Los Angeles, CA 90067-2115, USA

Rowand, Aaron (Athlete, Baseball Player)
34 Meadowhawk Ln
Las Vegas, NV 89135-5201, USA

Rowdon, Wade (Athlete, Baseball Player)
230 Crooked Tree Trl
Deland, FL 32724-3426, USA

Rowe, Bob (Athlete, Football Player)
222 Waterside Dr
Wildwood, MO 63040-1631, USA

Rowe, Brad (Actor, Producer, Writer)
1327 Brinkley Ave
Los Angeles, CA 90049-3619, USA

Rowe, Dave (Athlete, Football Player)
330 W Presnell St Apt 43
Asheboro, NC 27203-4700, USA

Rowe, John W (Business Person)
Unicom Corp
10 S Dearborn St
Chicago, IL 60603-2300, USA

Rowe, John W (Business Person)
Aetna Inc
151 Farmington Ave
Hartford, CT 06156-0002, USA

Rowe, Ken (Athlete, Baseball Player)
347 Princeton Dr
Dallas, GA 30157-0853, USA

Rowe, Kenny (Athlete, Football Player)

Rowe, Maggie (Comedian)
c/o Staff Member *ICM Partners*
10250 Constellation Blvd Fl 7
Los Angeles, CA 90067-6207, USA

Rowe, Mike (Television Host)
c/o Glenn Gulino *G2 Entertainment LLC*
1 Columbus Pl Apt S25E
New York, NY 10019-8208, USA

Rowe, Misty (Actor)
2193 River Rd
Egg Harbor City, NJ 08215-4745, USA

Rowe, Patrick (Athlete, Football Player)
6259 Alderley St
San Diego, CA 92114-6715, USA

Rowe, Ray (Athlete, Football Player)
11443 Westonhill Dr
San Diego, CA 92126-1450, USA

rowe, Tom (Athlete, Hockey Player)
38 Holly Hill Dr
Amherst, NH 03031-1627

Rowell, Victoria (Actor)

Rowland, Betty (Dancer)
125 N Barrington Ave Apt 103
Los Angeles, CA 90049-2949, USA

Rowland, Brad (Athlete, Football Player)
552 Rosebud Dr N
Lombard, IL 60148-6166, USA

Rowland, Derrick (Athlete, Basketball Player)
3 Island View Rd
Cohoes, NY 12047-4929, USA

Rowland, Gord (Athlete, Football Player)
198 Harris Blvd
Winnipeg, MB R3J 3P5, Canada

Rowland, J David (Business Person)
National Westminster Bank
41 Lothbury
London EC2P 2BP, UNITED KINGDOM (UK)

Rowland, John W (Misc)
Amalgamated Transit Union
10000 New Hampshire Ave
Silver Spring, MD 20903-1706, USA

Rowland, Justin (Athlete, Football Player)
1919 NW Loop 410 Ste 200
San Antonio, TX 78213-2325, USA

Rowland, Kelly (Musician)
c/o Matthew Knowles *Music World Entertainment*
PO Box 3727
Houston, TX 77253-3727, USA

Rowland, Landon H (Business Person)
Kansas City Southern
PO Box 219335
Kansas City, MO 64121-9335, USA

Rowland, Mike (Athlete, Baseball Player)
12104 E Mescal St
Scottsdale, AZ 85259-4230, USA

Rowland, Rich (Athlete, Baseball Player)
91 Clark Ave
Cloverdale, CA 95425-3918, USA

Rowland, Rodney (Actor, Model)
c/o Amy Abell-Rosenfield *BRS / Gage Talent Agency (LA)*
6300 Wilshire Blvd Ste 1430
Los Angeles, CA 90048-5216, USA

Rowland, Troy (Producer)
c/o Susan Curtis *Curtis Talent Management*
9607 Arby Dr
Beverly Hills, CA 90210-1202, USA

Rowlands, Gena (Actor)
c/o Lou Pitt *The Pitt Group*
275 Homewood Rd
Los Angeles, CA 90049-2709, USA

Rowley, Cynthia (Designer, Fashion Designer)
498 Fashion Ave
New York, NY 10018-6798, USA

Rowley, Elwood R (Athlete, Football Player)
712 Southwick Ave
Clayton, NC 27527-6666, USA

Rowling, JK (Writer)
PO Box 27036
Edinburgh EH10 5WB, SCOTLAND

Rowse, Darren (Internet Star)
PO BOX 1295
North Fitzroy, Victoria 03068, AUSTRALIA

Rowser, John (Athlete, Football Player)
17564 Alta Vista Dr
Southfield, MI 48075-1936, USA

Roxburgh, Melissa (Actor)
c/o Brad Pence *Atlas Artists*
9220 W Sunset Blvd Ste 225
Los Angeles, CA 90069-3513, USA

Roxburgh, Richard (Actor, Music Group)
c/o Sandra Chang *Anonymous Content*
3532 Hayden Ave
Culver City, CA 90232-2413, USA

Roxette (Music Group)
c/o Staff Member *D&D Management*
Drottning Gatan 55
Stockholm 11121, SWEDEN

Roy (Misc)
Beyond Belief
1639 Valley Dr
Las Vegas, NV 89108-2002, USA

Roy, Andre (Athlete, Hockey Player)
17352 Emerald Chase Dr
Tampa, FL 33647-3517, USA

Roy, Arundhati (Writer)
c/o Kimberly Witherspoon *Inkwell Management*
521 5th Ave Fl 36
New York, NY 10175-3699, USA

Roy, Brandon (Athlete, Basketball Player)
c/o Arn Tellem *Wasserman Media Group*
10960 Wilshire Blvd Ste 1200
Los Angeles, CA 90024-3714, USA

Roy, Deep (Actor)
c/o Victor Kruglov *Kruglov & Associates*
6565 W Sunset Blvd Ste 280
Los Angeles, CA 90028-7219, USA

Roy, Derek (Athlete, Hockey Player)
100 Rivermist Dr
Buffalo, NY 14202-4300

Roy, Drew (Actor)
c/o Jordan Berkus *United Talent Agency (UTA)*
9336 Civic Center Dr
Beverly Hills, CA 90210-3604, USA

Roy, Jean-Pierre (Athlete, Baseball Player)
407 Rue des Harfangs
Levis, QC G7A 3H4, Canada

Roy, John (Actor, Comedian)
c/o Gabrielle Krengel *Domain Talent*
1880 Century Park E Ste 1100
Los Angeles, CA 90067-1608, USA

Roy, Patricia (Athlete, Baseball Player)
5980 Prosperity Ln
Immokalee, FL 34142-9618, USA

Roy, Patrick (Athlete, Hockey Player)
201 Ch de la Plage-Saint-Laurent
Quebec, QC G1Y 1W6, Canada

Roy, Pierre (Athlete, Hockey Player)
120-145 King Edward St
Coquitlam, BC V3K 6M2, Canada

Roy, Rachel (Fashion Designer)
The Jones Group Inc
180 Rittenhouse Cir
Bristol, PA 19007-1618, USA

Roy, Stephane (Race Car Driver)
Hammerhead Racing
7026 E Aster Dr
Scottsdale, AZ 85254-5327, USA

Royal, Eddie (Athlete, Football Player)
c/o Todd France *Creative Artists Agency (CAA) Sports*
3500 Lenox Rd NE
Atlanta, GA 30326-4228, USA

Royal, Robert (Athlete, Football Player)
605 N Turnbull Dr
Metairie, LA 70001-4949, USA

Royale, Latrice (Impersonator, Reality Star)
c/o Len Evans *Project Publicity*
540 W 43rd St
New York, NY 10036, USA

Royals, Mark (Athlete, Football Player)
9921 Menander Wood Ct
Odessa, FL 33556-2449, USA

Royals, Reggie (Athlete, Basketball Player)
PO Box 742
Tulsa, OK 74101-0742, USA

Royal Underground (Music Group)
c/o Jill Siegel *10th Street Entertainment*
700 N San Vicente Blvd # G410
W Hollywood, CA 90069-5060, USA

Roybal-Allard, Lucille (Congressman, Politician)
2330 Rayburn Hob
Washington, DC 20515-0534, USA

Royce, Mike (Comedian)
c/o Staff Member *United Talent Agency (UTA)*
9336 Civic Center Dr
Beverly Hills, CA 90210-3604, USA

Roye, Orpheus (Athlete, Football Player)
26403 Primrose Ln
Westlake, OH 44145-5491, USA

Royer, Stan (Athlete, Baseball Player)
9301 Christopher Lake Dr
Columbia, IL 62236-3458, USA

Royo, Andre (Actor)
c/o Lisa Perkins *Baker Winokur Ryder Public Relations*
9100 Wilshire Blvd
W Tower #500
Beverly Hills, CA 90212-3415, USA

Royo, Sanchez Aristides (President)
Morgan & Morgan
PO Box 1824
Panama City 00001, PANAMA

Royster, Jeron K (Jerry) (Athlete, Baseball Player, Coach)
36000 Portofino Cir Apt 114
Palm Beach Gardens, FL 33418-1284, USA

Royster, Mazio (Athlete, Football Player)
7348 Crimson Dr
Highland, CA 92346-5316, USA

Royster, Willie (Athlete, Baseball Player)
229 55th St NE
Washington, DC 20019-6737, USA

Rozalla (Musician)
c/o Staff Member *Diva Central Inc*
7510 W Sunset Blvd # 1445
Los Angeles, CA 90046-3408, USA

Rozelle, Pete (Athlete, Football Player)
23800 Valley Oak Ct
Newhall, CA 91321-3746, USA

Rozema, Dave (Athlete, Baseball Player)
22411 Van St
Saint Clair Shores, MI 48081-2424, USA

Rozier, Clifford (Athlete, Basketball Player)
PO Box 1194
Palmetto, FL 34220-1194, USA

Rozier, Mike (Athlete, Football Player, Heisman Trophy Winner)
9 Hidden Hollow Ln
Sicklerville, NJ 08081-3910, USA

Roznovsky, Vic (Athlete, Baseball Player)
3342 W Alluvial Ave
Fresno, CA 93711-0207, USA

Rozon, Tim (Actor)
c/o Paul Hemrend *Edna Talent Management*
318 Dundas St W
Toronto, ON M5T 1G5, CANADA

Rozsival, Michal (Athlete, Hockey Player)
The Sports Corporation
2735-10088 102 Ave NW
Attn Rich Winter
Edmonton, AB T5J 2Z1, Canada

Rozumek, Dave (Athlete, Football Player)
17 Dearborn Ave # 1
Hampton, NH 03842-3320, USA

Rozzell, Aubrey (Athlete, Football Player)
PO Box 132
Quitman, MS 39355-0132, USA

R. Pierluisi, Pedro (Congressman, Politician)
1213 Longworth Hob
Washington, DC 20515-1313, USA

R. Pitts, Joseph (Congressman, Politician)
420 Carmon Hob
Washington, DC 20515-0001, USA

R. Rothman, Stevan (Congressman, Politician)
2303 Rayburn Hob
Washington, DC 20515-0920, USA

R. Rothman, Steven (Congressman, Politician)
2303 Rayburn Hob
Washington, DC 20515-0920, USA

R. Royce, Edward (Congressman, Politician)
2185 Rayburn Hob
Washington, DC 20515-1405, USA

R. Tipton, Scott (Congressman, Politician)
218 Cannon Hob
Washington, DC 20515-2803, USA

R. Turner, Michael (Congressman, Politician)
2454 Rayburn Hob
Washington, DC 20515-1312, USA

Ruah, Daniela (Actor)
c/o Samantha Hill *Wolf-Kasteler Public Relations*
6255 W Sunset Blvd Ste 1111
Los Angeles, CA 90028-7426, USA

Rubalcaba, Gonzalo (Musician)
Eardrums Music
5930 NW 201st St
Miami, FL 33105, USA

Rubel, Fran (Director, Producer)
c/o Staff Member *Kuzui Enterprises*
8225 Santa Monica Blvd
West Hollywood, CA 90046-5912, USA

Ruben, Joseph P (Joe) (Director)
250 W 57th St # 1905
New York, NY 10107-0001, USA

Rubens, Larry (Athlete, Football Player)
12213 Ansley Ct
Knoxville, TN 37934-1525, USA

Rubenstein, Ann (Correspondent)
NBC-TV
30 Rockefeller Plz
News Dept
New York, NY 10112-0015, USA

Rubenstein, David (Business Person)
Carlyle Group
1001 Pennsylvania Ave NW Ste 220S
Washington, DC 20004-2573, USA

Rubiano, Saenz Pedro Cardinal (Religious Leader)
Arzubispado
Carrera 7A N 10-20
Santafe de Bogota, DC 1, COLOMBIA

Rubick, Rob (Athlete, Football Player)
1571 Stonewood Dr
Lapeer, MI 48446-4200, USA

Rubin, Amy (Actor)
Hervey/Grimes
PO Box 64249
Los Angeles, CA 90064-0249, USA

Rubin, Chanda (Athlete, Olympic Athlete, Tennis Player)
708 S Saint Antoine St
Lafayette, LA 70501-5740, USA

Rubin, Chandra (Tennis Player)
708 S Saint Antoine St
Lafayette, LA 70501-5740, USA

Rubin, Leigh (Cartoonist)
Creators Syndicate
5777 W Century Blvd # 700
Los Angeles, CA 90045-5600, USA

Rubin, Rick (Musician, Producer)
c/o Staff Member *American Recordings*
3300 Warner Blvd
Burbank, CA 91505-4632, USA

Rubin, Vanessa (Musician)
Joel Chriss
300 Mercer St Apt 3J
New York, NY 10003-6732, USA

Rubin, William (Misc)
Museum of Modern Art
11 W 53rd St Lbby
New York, NY 10019-5497, USA

Rubinek, Saul (Actor)
c/o Rich Caplan *Noble Caplan Abrams*
1260 Yonge St 2nd Fl
Toronto, ON M4T 1W5, CANADA

Rubinoff, Marla (Actor)
c/o Staff Member *John Glenn Harding Management*
7004 Oakwood Ave
Los Angeles, CA 90036-2660, USA

Rubins, Kathleen Dr (Astronaut)
19220 Space Center Blvd Apt 623
Houston, TX 77058-3748, USA

Rubinstein, John (Actor)
4417 Leydon Ave
Woodland Hills, CA 91364-4847, USA

Rubinstein, Ronen (Actor)
c/o Oren Segal *Management Production Entertainment (MPE)*
9229 W Sunset Blvd Ste 301
W Hollywood, CA 90069-3417, USA

Rubinstein, Zeida (Actor)
The Agency
1800 Avenue of the Stars Ste 400
Los Angeles, CA 90067-4206, USA

Rubin-Vega, Daphne (Actor)
c/o Jeremy Katz *Katz Company, The*
1674 Broadway Fl 7
New York, NY 10019-5838, USA

Rubio, Marco (Politician, Senator)
PO Box 558701
Miami, FL 33255-8701, USA

Rubio, Nicole (Actor)
c/o Roger Neal *Neal Public Relations & Management*
3042 N Keystone St
Burbank, CA 91504-1621, USA

Rubio, Paulina (Musician)
c/o Carl Stubner *Sanctuary Music Management*
15301 Arizona Ave
Bldg B #400
Santa Monica, CA 91403, USA

Rubio, Ricky (Athlete, Basketball Player)
c/o Dan Fegan *Relativity Sports*
2029 Century Park E Ste 1550
Century City, CA 90067-3000, USA

Rucchin, Steve (Athlete, Hockey Player)
614 Acacia Ave
Corona Del Mar, CA 92625-1907

Rucci, Todd (Athlete, Football Player)
5 Southview Ln
Lititz, PA 17543-8205, USA

Ruccolo, Richard (Actor)
ER Talent
301 W 53rd St Apt 4K
New York, NY 10019-5768, USA

Rucinski, Mike (Athlete, Hockey Player)
5175 Pinetum Trl
Brighton, MI 48114-9076

Rucinski, Mike (Athlete, Hockey Player)
11980 Cape Cod Ln
Huntley, IL 60142-8168

Rucinsky, Martin (Athlete, Hockey Player)
800 Griffiths Way
Vancouver, BC V6B 6G1, Canada

Ruck, Alan (Actor)
c/o Lisa Lieberman *Innovative Artists*
235 Park Ave S Fl 7
New York, NY 10003-1405, USA

Rucka, Leo (Athlete, Football Player)
814 Crosby Dayton Rd
Crosby, TX 77532-5803, USA

Rucker, Anja (Athlete, Track Athlete)
TUS Jena
Wollnitzer Str 42
Jena 07749, GERMANY

Rucker, Darius (Musician)
c/o Ebie McFarland *EB Media*
21 Music Sq W
Nashville, TN 37203-3203, USA

Rucker, Dave (Athlete, Baseball Player)
18602 Piper Pl
Yorba Linda, CA 92886-2559, USA

Rucker, Frostee (Athlete, Football Player)

Rucker, Michael (Athlete, Football Player)
5971 Rolling Ridge Dr
Kannapolis, NC 28081-6705, USA

Rucker, Reggie (Athlete, Football Player)
26300 Village Ln Apt 303
Beachwood, OH 44122-8520, USA

Rucker, Reginald J (Reggie) (Athlete, Football Player)
3128 Richmond Rd
Beachwood, OH 44122-3249, USA

Rudd, Delaney (Athlete, Basketball Player)
422 Chesham Dr
Kernersville, NC 27284-7017, USA

Rudd, Dwayne (Athlete, Football Player)
PO Box 273309
Boca Raton, FL 33427-3309, USA

Rudd, John (Athlete, Basketball Player)
4440 Sweet Bay Dr
Lake Charles, LA 70611-3240, USA

Rudd, Kevin (Prime Minister)
Parliament House
Canberra ACT 2600, AUSTRALIA

Rudd, Paul (Actor)
c/o Jodi Gottlieb *Independent Public Relations*
9601 Wilshire Blvd Ste 750
Beverly Hills, CA 90210-5228, USA

Rudd, Ricky (Race Car Driver)
Virginia Sports Hall Of Fame
249 Central Park Ave Ste 230
PO Box 370
Virginia Beach, VA 23462-3174, USA

Rudd, Xavier (Musician)
c/o Staff Member *Paradigm (Monterey)*
404 W Franklin St
Monterey, CA 93940-2303, USA

Ruddock, Donovan (Razor) (Boxer)
7379 NW 34th St
Lauderhill, FL 33319-4962, USA

Ruddy, Albert (Producer)
1601 Clear View Dr
Beverly Hills, CA 90210-2010, USA

Ruddy, Tim (Athlete, Football Player)
3885 Vale View Ln
Mead, CO 80542-4500, USA

Rudelsky, Seth (Actor, Radio Personality)
On Broadway - Sirius
1221 Avenue of the Americas
New York, NY 10020-1001, USA

Rudi, Joseph O (Joe) (Athlete, Baseball Player)
PO Box 425
Baker City, OR 97814-0425, USA

Rudie, Evelyn (Actor)
Santa Monica Playhouse
7514 Hollywood Blvd
Los Angeles, CA 90046-2814, USA

Rudin, Scott (Producer)
c/o Staff Member *Scott Rudin Productions (NY)*
120 W 45th St Ste 1001
New York, NY 10036-4031, USA

Rudis-Bestudik, Mary (Baseball Player)
4333 Deeboyar Ave
Lakewood, CA 90712-3703, USA

Rudnay, Jack (Athlete, Football Player)
7219 Whipperwill Rd
Versailles, MO 65084-4033, USA

Rudner, Rita (Actor, Comedian)
331 Monarch Bay Dr
Dana Point, CA 92629-3408, USA

Rudnick, Paul (Writer)
c/o Robert (Bob) Bookman *Paradigm*
8942 Wilshire Blvd
Beverly Hills, CA 90211-1908, USA

Rudnick, Tim (Athlete, Football Player)
1516 Heather Ln
Des Plaines, IL 60018-1400, USA

Rudolph, Alan S (Director)
International Creative Mgmt
8942 Wilshire Blvd # 219
Beverly Hills, CA 90211-1908, USA

Rudolph, Ben (Athlete, Football Player)
561 E General Gorgas Dr
Mobile, AL 36617-3036, USA

Rudolph, Coleman (Athlete, Football Player)
412 Billings Farm Ln
Canton, GA 30115, USA

Rudolph, Council (Athlete, Football Player)
8310 Lago Vista Dr
Tampa, FL 33614-2769, USA

Rudolph, Ken (Athlete, Baseball Player)
1317 W Sands Ct
Gilbert, AZ 85233-6637, USA

Rudolph, Kyle (Athlete, Football Player)
c/o David Dunn *Athletes First*
23091 Mill Creek Dr
Laguna Hills, CA 92653-1258, USA

Rudolph, Maya (Actor)
c/o David (Dave) Becky *3 Arts Entertainment*
9460 Wilshire Blvd Fl 7
Beverly Hills, CA 90212-2713, USA

Rudometkin, John (Athlete, Basketball Player)
PO Box 136
Newcastle, CA 95658-0136, USA

Rudzinski, Paul (Athlete, Football Player)
3216 Delahaut St
Green Bay, WI 54301-1551, USA

Rue, Sara (Actor)
c/o Alan David *Alan David Management*
8840 Wilshire Blvd # 200
Beverly Hills, CA 90211-2606, USA

Ruebel, Matt (Athlete, Baseball Player)
7509 W Augusta Blvd
Yorktown, IN 47396-9354, USA

Ruegamer, Grey (Athlete, Football Player)
PO Box 70155
Las Vegas, NV 89170-0155, USA

Ruehl, Mercedes (Actor)
PO Box 178
Old Chelsea Station
New York, NY 10028-0002, USA

Ruelas, Gabriel (Gabe) (Athlete, Boxer)
1119 S Hudson Ave
Los Angeles, CA 90019-1807, USA

Ruell, Aaron (Actor, Director, Writer)
c/o Staff Member *Brillstein Entertainment Partners*
9150 Wilshire Blvd Ste 350
Beverly Hills, CA 90212-3453, USA

Rueter, Kirk (Athlete, Baseball Player)
46 Pheasant Ridge Ct
Nashville, IL 62263-5845, USA

Ruether, Mike (Athlete, Football Player)
23014 Gardner Dr
Alpharetta, GA 30009-2179, USA

Ruether, Rosemary R (Misc)
PO Box 930
Hermosa Beach, CA 90254-0930, USA

Ruettgers, Ken (Athlete, Football Player)
16897 Golden Stone Dr
Sisters, OR 97759-9696, USA

Ruettgers, Michael C (Business Person)
ECM Corp
35 Parkway Dr
Hopkinton, MA 01748, USA

Ruettiger, Rudy (Athlete, Football Player)
293 Goldstar St
Henderson, NV 89012-0104, USA

Ruff, Lindy (Athlete, Coach, Hockey Player)
5006 Winding Ln
Clarence, NY 14031-1500, USA

Ruffalo, Mark (Actor)
63 Kautz Rd
Callicoon, NY 12723-5308, USA

Ruffcorn, Scott (Athlete, Baseball Player)
2137 Barton Hills Dr
Austin, TX 78704-4659, USA

Ruffin, Bruce (Athlete, Baseball Player)
3410 Pawnee Pass S
Austin, TX 78738-1709, USA

Ruffin, Johnny (Athlete, Baseball Player)
4229 Trumpworth Ct
Valrico, FL 33596-8494, USA

Ruffner, Barry (Athlete, Football Player)
134 Frogtown Rd
New Alexandria, PA 15670-3080, USA

Ruffner, Paul (Athlete, Basketball Player)
4508 Brookshire Dr
Provo, UT 84604-5245, USA

Ruffo, Victoria (Actor)
c/o Staff Member *Televisa*
Blvd Adolfo Lopez Mateos 232
Colonia San Angel INN
DF CP 01060, MEXICO

Ruge, John A (Cartoonist)
240 Bronxville Rd Apt B4
Bronxville, NY 10708-2800, USA

Ruggiano, Justin (Athlete, Baseball Player)
2710 Capstone Way
Rockwall, TX 75032-6836, USA

Ruggiero, Adamo (Actor)
c/o Shari Quallenberg *AMI Artist Management*
464 King St E
Toronto, ON M5A 1L7, CANADA

Ruggiero, Angela (Athlete, Hockey Player, Olympic Athlete)
Shade Global
10 E 40th St Fl 48
New York, NY 10016-0301, USA

Ruhman, Chris (Athlete, Football Player)
13206 Vinery Ct
Cypress, TX 77429-5195, USA

Ruivivar, Anthony Michael (Actor)
c/o Nick Collins *Gersh*
9465 Wilshire Blvd Ste 600
Beverly Hills, CA 90212-2605, USA

Ruiz, Chico (Athlete, Baseball Player)
267 Calle Tapia
San Juan, PR 00912-4201, USA

Ruiz, John (Boxer)
John Ruiz Inc
PO Box 2581
Taunton, MA 02780-0980, USA

Ruiz, Jose Carlos (Actor)
c/o Staff Member *Televisa*
Blvd Adolfo Lopez Mateos 232
Colonia San Angel INN
DF CP 01060, MEXICO

Ruiz, Rodrigo (Actor)
c/o Staff Member *Televisa*
Blvd Adolfo Lopez Mateos 232
Colonia San Angel INN
DF CP 01060, MEXICO

Rukavina, Terry (Baseball Player)
6676 Washington Cir
Franklin, OH 45005-5521, USA

Ruklick, Joe (Athlete, Basketball Player)
1300 Central St Apt 302
Evanston, IL 60201-1678, USA

Ruland, Jeff (Athlete, Basketball Player)
38 Glen Lake Dr
Medford, NJ 08055-3104, USA

Rule, Bob (Athlete, Basketball Player)
4303 Kansas Ave
Riverside, CA 92507-5153, USA

Rule, Gordon (Athlete, Football Player)
716 Manchester Rd
Neenah, WI 54956-4910, USA

Rulin, Olesya (Actor)
c/o Christopher Burbidge *Fourward*
10250 Constellation Blvd Ste 2710
Los Angeles, CA 90067-6227, USA

Rulli, Sebastian (Actor)
c/o Mauricio Macias *m3*
174 Cronistas
P. O. Box 201
Satelite, Estado de Mexico 53100, Mexico

Rullo, Jerry (Athlete, Basketball Player)
3ee Brookline Blvd
Havertown, PA 19083-3923, USA

Rumble, Darren (Athlete, Hockey Player)
Seattle Thunderbirds
625 W James St
Kent, WA 98032-4406

Ruminer, Caleb (Actor)
c/o Staff Member *MTV Networks (LA)*
1575 N Gower St Ste 100
Los Angeles, CA 90028-6488, USA

Rummells, Dave (Golfer)
1820 Harbor Blvd
Kissimmee, FL 34744-6623, USA

Rumph, Donte (Athlete, Football Player)

Rumsey, Janet (Athlete, Baseball Player)
7830 W County Road 80 N
Greensburg, IN 47240-7910, USA

Rumsfeld, Donald (Business Person)
1718 M St NW # 366
Washington, DC 20036-4504, USA

Runager, Max (Athlete, Football Player)
PO Box 37971
Rock Hill, SC 29732-0534, USA

Runco, Mario Lt Cmdr (Astronaut)
207 Lakeshore Dr
Seabrook, TX 77586-6128, USA

Rundgren, Todd (Musician)
c/o Staff Member *UTA/The Agency Group*
888 7th Ave Fl 7
New York, NY 10106-0700, USA

Rundles, Rich (Athlete, Baseball Player)
2103 Creekside Way
Jefferson City, TN 37760-1707, USA

Run DMC (Music Group)
c/o Tracey Miller *Tracey Miller & Associates*
2610 Fire Rd
Egg Harbor Township, NJ 08234-9551, USA

Rundqvist, Thomas (Athlete, Hockey Player)
Slobacksvagen 3
Hammaro 66341, Sweden

Runga, Bic (Musician)
c/o Staff Member *Paradigm (Monterey)*
404 W Franklin St
Monterey, CA 93940-2303, USA

Runge, Brian (Athlete, Baseball Player)
1333 Via Isidro
Oceanside, CA 92056-5629, USA

Runge, Paul (Athlete, Baseball Player)
8225 E County Dr
El Cajon, CA 92021-8826, USA

Runge, Paul (Athlete, Baseball Player)
126 Diamante Way
Jupiter, FL 33477-5052, USA

Runnells, Tom (Athlete, Baseball Player, Coach)
6045 Settlers Ridge Cir
Sylvania, OH 43560-9474, USA

Runnels, Terri (Model, Wrestler)
11520 NW 8th Ln
Gainesville, FL 32606-0408, USA

RunningWolf, Myrton (Actor)
c/o Tracey Mapes *Imperium 7 Talent Agency*
5455 Wilshire Blvd Ste 1706
Los Angeles, CA 90036-4217, USA

Runrig (Music Group)
c/o Staff Member *Sony Music Entertainment Germany*
Neumarkter Str. 28
Muenchen 81673, Germany

Runte, Dan (Misc)
BIGFOOT 4x4, Inc.
2286 Rose Ln
Pacific, MO 63069-1163, USA

Runyan, Jon (Athlete, Football Player)
262 Mount Laurel Rd
Mount Laurel, NJ 08054, USA

Runyan, Jon (Congressman, Politician)
1239 Longworth Hob
Washington, DC 20515-3213, USA

Runyan, Marla (Athlete, Olympic Athlete, Track Athlete)
22 Robbins Rd
Watertown, MA 02472-3449, USA

Runyan, Sean (Athlete, Baseball Player)
1140 View Pointe Way
Lakeland, FL 33813-5625, USA

Runyon, Jennifer (Actor)
5922 SW Amberwood Ave
Corvallis, OR 97333-2702, USA

Ruotsalainen, Reijo (Athlete, Hockey Player)
Jukurit Mikkeli Raviradantie 1
Mikkeli 50100, Finland

RuPaul (Impersonator, Musician, Reality Star)
RuCo Inc
332 Bleecker St # F-22
New York, NY 10014-2980, USA

Rupe, Josh (Athlete, Baseball Player)
225 Arrowfield Rd
Virginia Beach, VA 23454-4300, USA

Rupe, Ryan (Athlete, Baseball Player)
5338 Pine Wood Hills Ct
Spring, TX 77386-3801, USA

Rupp, Debra Jo (Actor)
c/o Nancy Iannios *Core Public PR*
1875 Century Park E Ste 930
Los Angeles, CA 90067-2540, USA

Rupp, Duane (Athlete, Hockey Player)
2446 McMonagle Ave
Pittsburgh, PA 15216-2705, USA

Rupp, Michael (Athlete, Hockey Player)
1936 Medford Sq
Hilliard, OH 43026-2219

Ruppersberger, C. A. (Congressman, Politician)
2453 Rayburn Hob
Washington, DC 20515-3514, USA

Ruprecht, Tom (Writer)
c/o Staff Member *3 Arts Entertainment*
9460 Wilshire Blvd Fl 7
Beverly Hills, CA 90212-2713, USA

Rusch, Glendon (Athlete, Baseball Player)
3203 Hidden Springs Ln
Prospect, KY 40059-8574, USA

Rusch, Kristine Kathryn (Writer)
PO Box 479
Lincoln City, OR 97367-0479, USA

Ruscha, Edward (Artist)
1840 Carla Rdg
Beverly Hills, CA 90210-1914, USA

Rusedski, Greg (Tennis Player)
G-Force
PO Box 57
Caernarfon LL55 4WL, UNITED KINGDOM

Rush (Music Group)
c/o Ray Danniels *SRO Management*
189 Carlton St
Toronto, ON M5A 2K7, Canada

Rush, Barbara (Actor)
1709 Tropical Avenue
Beverly Hills, CA 90210, USA

Rush, Deborah (Actor)
c/o Rhonda Price *Gersh*
41 Madison Ave Ste 3301
New York, NY 10010-2210, USA

Rush, Geoffrey (Actor)
c/o Stan Rosenfield *Stan Rosenfield & Associates*
2029 Century Park E Ste 1190
Los Angeles, CA 90067-2931, USA

Rush, Ian (Athlete, Football Player)
McDonald's Sport Ambassadors
McDonald's Restaurants Ltd:
11 - 59 High Rd, East Finchley
London N2 8AW, UK

Rush, Jennifer (Musician)
c/o Staff Member *Armin Rahn Agency and Management*
Dreimuehlenstr. 7
Muenchen 80469, Germany

Rush, Jerry (Athlete, Football Player)
345 Sundown Way
Stone Mountain, GA 30087-6164, USA

Rush, Joshua (Actor)
c/o Susan Curtis *Curtis Talent Management*
9607 Arby Dr
Beverly Hills, CA 90210-1202, USA

Rush, Kareem (Athlete, Basketball Player)
2805 E 62nd St
Kansas City, MO 64130-3745, USA

Rush, Mathew (Adult Film Star)
c/o Staff Member *Diva Central Inc*
7510 W Sunset Blvd # 1445
Los Angeles, CA 90046-3408, USA

Rush, Matthew (Actor, Adult Film Star)
c/o Staff Member *Diva Central Inc*
7510 W Sunset Blvd # 1445
Los Angeles, CA 90046-3408, USA

Rush, Merrilee (Musician)
21458 NE Redmond Fall City Rd
Redmond, WA 98053-8227, USA

Rush, Odeya (Actor)
c/o Ruth Bernstein *Viewpoint Inc*
8820 Wilshire Blvd Ste 220
Beverly Hills, CA 90211-2622, USA

Rush, Robert J (Athlete, Football Player)
8201 Scruggs Dr
Germantown, TN 38138-6119, USA

Rush, Rudy (Comedian)
c/o Staff Member *ICM Partners*
10250 Constellation Blvd Fl 7
Los Angeles, CA 90067-6207, USA

Rush, Sarah (Actor)
c/o Staff Member *Acme Talent & Literary*
4727 Wilshire Blvd Ste 333
Los Angeles, CA 90010-3874, USA

Rush, Tom (Musician)
Maple Hill Productions Inc
PO Box 1570
Wilson, WY 83014-1570, USA

Rushdie, Salman (Writer)
c/o Andrew Wylie *The Wylie Agency*
250 W 57th St Ste 2114
New York, NY 10107-2114, USA

Rushen, Patrice (Musician)
PO Box 6278
Altadena, CA 91003-6278, USA

Rushford, Jim (Athlete, Baseball Player)
45 W Camino Presidio Quemado
Sahuarita, AZ 85629-8842, USA

Rushing, Marion (Athlete, Football Player)
358 Bathon Dr
Pinckneyville, IL 62274-3335, USA

Ruskin, Scott (Athlete, Baseball Player)
387 Saint Johns Golf Dr
Saint Augustine, FL 32092-1082, USA

Ruskowski, Terry (Athlete, Hockey Player)
2542 Silent Shore Ct
Richmond, TX 77406-1814, USA

Rusler, Robert (Actor)
c/o Daryn Simons *Acting Out Management*
Prefers to be contacted by telephone or email
Los Angeles, CA 90064, USA

Russ, Steve (Athlete, Football Player)
602 Charlesgate Cir
East Amherst, NY 14051-2428, USA

Russ, Tim (Actor, Director)
7336 Santa Monica Blvd # 711
West Hollywood, CA 90046-6670, USA

Russell, Adam (Athlete, Baseball Player)
627 Mariner Vlg
Huron, OH 44839-1004, USA

Russell, Andy (Athlete, Football Player)
625 Liberty Ave Ste 3100
Pittsburgh, PA 15222-3115, USA

Russell, Austin ""Chumlee"" (Reality Star)
24040 Camino Del Avion
A127
Monarch Beach, CA 92629-4005, USA

Russell, Betsy (Actor)
PO Box 1759
La Jolla, CA 92038-1759, USA

Russell, Bill (Athlete, Baseball Player, Coach)
27982 Red Pine Ct
Valencia, CA 91354-1888, USA

Russell, Bill (Athlete, Basketball Player, Olympic Athlete)
9415 SE 52nd St
Mercer Island, WA 98040-4723, USA

Russell, Bob (Athlete, Hockey Player)
World Hockey Centre
123-16715 Yonge St
Attn: Presidents Office
Newmarket, ON L3X 1X4, Canada

Russell, Brenda (Actor, Musician)
c/o Seth Keller *SKM Artist Management*
PO Box 25906
Los Angeles, CA 90025-0906, USA

Russell, Brian (Athlete, Football Player)
15310 SE 80th St
Newcastle, WA 98059-9242, USA

Russell, Cam (Athlete, Hockey Player)
Halifax Mooseheads
5284 Duke St
Halifax, NS B3J 3L2, Canada

Russell, Cameron (Model)
c/o Staff Member *Elite Model Management (UK)*
40-42 Parker St
London WC2B 5PQ, UNITED KINGDOM

Russell, Campy (Athlete, Basketball Player)
66 Earlmoor Blvd
Pontiac, MI 48341-2816, USA

Russell, Cazzie (Athlete, Basketball Player)
Savannah College of Art and Design
425 W Montgomery Xrd
Live Oak Community Church
Savannah, GA 31406-3310, USA

Russell, Chuck (Director)
c/o Robert Stein *Paradigm*
8942 Wilshire Blvd
Beverly Hills, CA 90211-1908, USA

Russell, D'Angelo (Athlete, Basketball Player)
c/o Aaron Mintz *CAA Sports*
2000 Avenue of the Stars Ste 100
Los Angeles, CA 90067-4705, USA

Russell, David O (Actor, Director, Producer)
c/o Nikki Weiss *Nikki Weiss & Co.*
754 N La Jolla Ave
Los Angeles, CA 90046-6808, USA

Russell, Fred (Sportscaster)
226 Ensworth Pl
Nashville, TN 37205-1922, USA

Russell, Henny (Actor)
c/o Alex Spieller *Baker Winokur Ryder Public Relations*
200 5th Ave Fl 5
New York, NY 10010-3307, USA

Russell, JaMarcus (Athlete, Football Player)
5230 Mossberg Dr E
Theodore, AL 36582-7332, USA

Russell, James (Athlete, Baseball Player)
6612 Cedar Crest Dr
North Richland Hills, TX 76182-4385, USA

Russell, Jeannie (Actor)
10912 Riverside Dr
N Hollywood, CA 91602-2210, USA

Russell, Jeff (Athlete, Baseball Player)
6612 Cedar Crest Dr
North Richland Hills, TX 76182-4385, USA

Russell, John (Athlete, Baseball Player, Coach)
7312 Emma Rd
Trl Unit 103
Bradenton, FL 34209-5874, USA

Russell, Johnny (Actor)
PO Box 740091
San Diego, CA 92174-0091, USA

Russell, Ken (Director)
c/o Staff Member *Independent Talent Group*
40 Whitfield St
London W1T 2RH, UNITED KINGDOM

Russell, Keri (Actor)
c/o Joannie Burstein *Burstein Company*
15304 W Sunset Blvd Ste 208
Pacific Palisades, CA 90272-3656, USA

Russell, Kimberly (Actor)
11617 Laurelwood Dr
Studio City, CA 91604-3818, USA

Russell, Kurt (Actor, Producer)
9200 W Sunset Blvd # PH22
West Hollywood, CA 90069-3502, USA

Russell, Leonard (Athlete, Football Player)
497 Saint Louis Ave Apt 102
Long Beach, CA 90814-3363, USA

Russell, Mark (Politician)
3201 33rd Pl NW
Washington, DC 20008-3304, USA

Russell, Phil (Athlete, Hockey Player)
590 Wind Drift Ln
Spring Lake, MI 49456-2168

Russell, Rubin (Athlete, Basketball Player)
P.O. Bix 542742
Grand Prairie, TX 75054-2742, USA

Russell, Taylor (Actor)
c/o Mary Falcon *Play Management*
220-807 Powell St
Vancouver, BC V6A 1H7, CANADA

Russell, Theresa (Actor)
c/o Scott Zimmerman *Scott Zimmerman Management*
1644 Courtney Ave
Los Angeles, CA 90046-2708, USA

Russell, Twan (Athlete, Football Player)
11201 NW 8th St
Plantation, FL 33325-1508, USA

Russell, Victoria (Actor)
c/o Staff Member *Wizzo and Company*
47 Beak St
London W1F 9SE, UK

Russell, William (Actor)
Kate Feast
Primrose Hill Studios
Fitzroy Road
London NW1 8TR, UNITED KINGDOM (UK)

Russell, Willy (Writer)
W R Ltd 43 Canning Street
London L87NN, England

Russert, Luke (Correspondent)

Russett, Andrea (Internet Star)
c/o Erin O'Brien *Fullscreen Media (LA)*
12180 Millennium Ste 100
Los Angeles, CA 90094-2951, USA

Russillo, Ryen (Commentator)
c/o Ted Chervin *ICM Partners*
10250 Constellation Blvd Fl 7
Los Angeles, CA 90067-6207, USA

Russo, Deanna (Actor)
c/o Jack Kingsrud *Zero Gravity Management*
11110 Ohio Ave Ste 100
Los Angeles, CA 90025-3329, USA

Russo, James (Actor)
c/o Staff Member *United Talent Agency (UTA)*
9336 Civic Center Dr
Beverly Hills, CA 90210-3604, USA

Russo, Joe (Director, Producer, Writer)
c/o Staff Member *United Talent Agency (UTA)*
9336 Civic Center Dr
Beverly Hills, CA 90210-3604, USA

Russo, Patricia (Business Person)
Lucent Technologies Inc
600 Mountain Ave
New Providence, NJ 07974-2008, USA

Russo, Rene (Actor, Model)
c/o John Crosby *John Crosby Management*
1357 N Spaulding Ave
Los Angeles, CA 90046-4009, USA

Rust, Paul (Actor)
c/o Christie Smith *Rise Management*
6338 Wilshire Blvd
Los Angeles, CA 90048-5002, USA

Rust, Rod (Athlete, Football Coach, Football Player)
1 W 13th St
Ocean City, NJ 08226-2945, USA

Rusteck, Dick (Athlete, Baseball Player)
6302 N 87th St
Scottsdale, AZ 85250-5712, USA

Rutan, Elbert L (Burt) (Designer)
14329 Rutan Rd
Mojave, CA 93501-2118, USA

Rutan, Richard G (Dick) (Designer)
2833 Delmar Ave
Mojave, CA 93501-1113, USA

Rutgens, Joe (Athlete, Football Player)
227 W Devlin St
Spring Valley, IL 61362-1923, USA

Ruth, Lauren (Cartoonist)
PO Box 200206
New Haven, CT 06520-0206, USA

Ruth, Mike (Athlete, Football Player)
85 Jenkins Rd
Andover, MA 01810-2318, USA

Rutherford, Jim (Athlete, Hockey Player)
2521 Sharon View Ln
Raleigh, NC 27614-6813, USA

Rutherford, Johnny (Athlete, Baseball Player)
765 Briar Hill Ln
Bloomfield Hills, MI 48304-1443, USA

Rutherford, Johnny (Race Car Driver)
4919 Black Oak Ln
River Oaks, TX 76114-2933

Rutherford, Kelly (Actor)
c/o Gavin Denton-Jones *Creative Artists Management (CAM-UK)*
55-59 Shaftesbury Ave.
London W1D 6LD, UNITED KINGDOM

Rutherford, Mike (Musician)
Solo Agency
55 Fulham High St
London SW6 3JJ, UNITED KINGDOM (UK)

Rutherfurd, Emily (Actor)
c/o Chris Schmidt *Paradigm*
8942 Wilshire Blvd
Beverly Hills, CA 90211-1908, USA

Ruthven, Dick (Athlete, Baseball Player)
13480 Providence Lake Dr
Alpharetta, GA 30004-7510, USA

Rutigliano, Sam (Athlete, Coach, Football Coach, Football Player)
9671 Metcalf Rd
Willoughby, OH 44094-9744, USA

Rutkowski, Ed (Athlete, Football Player)
47 Brenton Ln
Hamburg, NY 14075-4327, USA

Rutkowski, Ken (Business Person, Radio Personality)
Business Rockstars, LLC
604 Arizona Ave
Santa Monica, CA 90401-1610, USA

Rutland, Reggie (Athlete, Football Player)
4265 Jailette Rd
Atlanta, GA 30349-1881, USA

Rutledge, Jeffrey R (Jeff) (Athlete, Coach, Football Coach, Football Player)
6102 W Gary Dr
Chandler, AZ 85226-1193, USA

Rutledge, Johnny (Athlete, Football Player)
948 SW Avenue J
Belle Glade, FL 33430-4232, USA

Rutledge, Wayne (Athlete)

Rutschman, Adolph (Ad) (Coach, Football Coach)
2142 NW Pinehurst Dr
McMinnville, OR 97128-2426, USA

Ruttan, Susan (Actor)
c/o Christopher Black *Opus Entertainment*
5225 Wilshire Blvd Ste 905
Los Angeles, CA 90036-4353, USA

Rutten, Bas (Actor, Athlete, Wrestler)
c/o Chandra Keyes *Jeff Sussman Management*
Prefers to be contacted by email or phone.
Sherman Oaks, CA 91403, USA

Rutter, Artur (Chef)
Chez Sylvia 15-6-101 HiRashi Honcho
HiRashi Kurume-shi, Tokyo, japan

Rutting, Barbara (Actor)
Sommerholz 30
Neumarkt 05202, Austria

Ruttman, Joe (Race Car Driver)
c/o Staff Member *NASCAR*
1801 W Speedway Blvd
Daytona Beach, FL 32114-1243, USA

Ruud, Tom (Athlete, Football Player)
1821 S 33rd St
Lincoln, NE 68506-1905, USA

Ruuska, Percy Sylvia (Swimmer)
4216 College View Way
Carmichael, CA 95608, USA

Ruutel, Arnold (President)
Koidula Str 3-5
Tallinn 00010, ESTONIA

Ruzek, Roger (Athlete, Football Player)
921 Warwick St
Bedford, TX 76022-7856, USA

Ruzicka, Vladimir (Athlete, Hockey Player)
17 Highland Ct
Needham, MA 02492-3149, USA

R. Wolf, Frank (Congressman, Politician)
241 Cannon Hob
Washington, DC 20515-4610, USA

Ryal, Mark (Athlete, Baseball Player)
PO Box 291
Dewar, OK 74431-0291, USA

Ryal, Rusty (Athlete, Baseball Player)
204 E University Dr
Auburn, AL 36832-6703, USA

Ryan, Amy (Actor)
c/o Jason Gutman *Gersh*
41 Madison Ave Ste 3301
New York, NY 10010-2210, USA

Ryan, Arthur F (Business Person)
Prudential Insurance
751 Broad St
Prudential Plaza
Newark, NJ 07102-3754, USA

Ryan, B J (Athlete, Baseball Player)
4014 Wisteria Ln
Benton, LA 71006-9368, USA

Ryan, B J (Athlete, Baseball Player)
1211 Perdenalas Trl
Westlake, TX 76262-4820, USA

Ryan, Blanchard (Actor)
c/o Staff Member *Jeff Morrone Entertainment*
9350 Wilshire Blvd Ste 224
Beverly Hills, CA 90212-3204, USA

Ryan, Bobby (Athlete, Hockey Player)
c/o Donald Meehan *Newport Sports Management*
201 City Centre Dr
Suite 400
Mississauga, ON L58 2T4, CANADA

Ryan, Debble (Comedian)
University of Virginia
Athletic Dept
PO Box 3785
Charlottesville, VA 22903, USA

Ryan, Debby (Actor)
Shadowborn Productions
10100 Santa Monica Blvd Ste 1700
Los Angeles, CA 90067-4156, USA

Ryan, Dusty (Athlete, Baseball Player)
2770 Happy Valley Ave
Atwater, CA 95301-9452, USA

Ryan, Ed (Horse Racer)
PO Box 6249
Freehold, NJ 07728-6249, USA

Ryan, Frank (Athlete, Football Player)
PO Box 185
Grafton, VT 05146-0185, USA

Ryan, Jay (Actor)
c/o Karen Kay *Karen Kay Management*
2/25 Sale St
Freemans Bay, Auckland 01010, New Zealand

Ryan, Jay (Athlete, Baseball Player)
1232 Rocky River Rd W
Charlotte, NC 28213-5034, USA

Ryan, Jeri (Actor)
c/o Kyle Fritz *Kyle Fritz Management*
6325 Heather Dr
Los Angeles, CA 90068-1633, USA

Ryan, Katherine (Comedian)
c/o Kitty Laing *United Agents*
12-26 Lexington St
London W1F OLE, UNITED KINGDOM

Ryan, Ken (Athlete, Baseball Player)
45 Tanager Rd
Seekonk, MA 02771-2707, USA

Ryan, Ken (Athlete, Football Player)
45 Tanager Rd
Seekonk, MA 02771-2707, USA

Ryan, Lee (Actor)
c/o Jack Gilardi *ICM Partners*
10250 Constellation Blvd Fl 7
Los Angeles, CA 90067-6207, USA

Ryan, Lisa Dean (Actor)
c/o Staff Member *Pakula/King & Associates*
9229 W Sunset Blvd Ste 315
Los Angeles, CA 90069-3403, USA

Ryan, Logan (Athlete, Football Player)
c/o Neil Schwartz *Schwartz & Feinsod*
4 Hillandale Rd
Rye Brook, NY 10573-1705, USA

Ryan, Marisa (Actor)
c/o Bob McGowan *McGowan Management*
170 S Beverly Dr Ste 304
Beverly Hills, CA 90212-3000, USA

Ryan, Marja-Lewis (Actor)
c/o Josh Goldenberg *Kaplan/Perrone Entertainment*
9171 Wilshire Blvd Ste 350
Beverly Hills, CA 90210-5523, USA

Ryan, Mark (Actor)
c/o Staff Member *Starfish PR*
PO Box 7000-54
Redondo Beach, CA 90277, USA

Ryan, Matt (Actor)
c/o Staff Member *42 Management (UK)*
8 Flitcroft St
London WC2H 8DL, UNITED KINGDOM

Ryan, Matt (Athlete, Football Player)
c/o Staff Member *Atlanta Falcons*
4400 Falcon Pkwy
Flowery Branch, GA 30542-3176, USA

Ryan, Max (Actor)
c/o Erik Kritzer *LINK Entertainment*
11872 La Grange Ave
Los Angeles, CA 90025-5282, USA

Ryan, Meg (Actor)
c/o Stephen Huvane *Slate PR*
901 N Highland Ave
W Hollywood, CA 90038-2412, USA

Ryan, Michael (Athlete, Baseball Player)
521 Water St
Indiana, PA 15701-1927, USA

Ryan, Michelle (Actor)
c/o Claire Maroussas *Independent Talent Group*
40 Whitfield St
London W1T 2RH, UNITED KINGDOM

Ryan, Mike (Athlete, Baseball Player)
592 Stoneham Rd
Wolfeboro, NH 03894-4711, USA

Ryan, Mitchell (Actor)
30355 Mulholland Hwy
Cornell, CA 91301-3117, USA

Ryan, Nolan (Athlete, Baseball Player)
The Nolan Ryan Foundation
PO Box 6979
Round Rock, TX 78683-6979, USA

Ryan, Pat (Athlete, Football Player)
6930 Old Kent Dr
Knoxville, TN 37919-7472, USA

Ryan, Patrick G (Business Person)
Aon Corp
200 East Randolf St
Chicago, IL 60601, USA

Ryan, Paul (Congressman, Politician)
1233 Longworth Hob # B
Washington, DC 20515-0801, USA

Ryan, Rex (Athlete, Football Coach)
c/o Jimmy Sexton *CAA (Memphis)*
6060 Poplar Ave Ste 470
Memphis, TN 38119-0910, USA

Ryan, Rob (Athlete, Baseball Player)
12402 N Division St
Spokane, WA 99218-1930, USA

Ryan, Roz (Actor)
c/o Staff Member *The Gage Group*
5757 Wilshire Blvd Ste 659
Los Angeles, CA 90036-3682, USA

Ryan, Ryan (Actor)
c/o Staff Member *Warner Bros Television Production*
4000 Warner Blvd
Burbank, CA 91522-0002

Ryan, Shawn (Producer)
c/o Staff Member *ICM Partners*
10250 Constellation Blvd Fl 7
Los Angeles, CA 90067-6207, USA

Ryan, Thomas M (Business Person)
CVS Corp
1 Cvs Dr
Woonsocket, RI 02895-6195, USA

Ryan, Tim (Congressman, Politician)
1421 Longworth Hob
Washington, DC 20515-4703, USA

Ryan, Tim E (Athlete, Football Player)
1159 Calle Ventura
San Jose, CA 95120-5503, USA

Ryan, Timothy T (Tim) (Athlete, Football Player)
4901 Sugar Creek Dr
Evansville, IN 47715-7744, USA

Ryan, Tom K (Cartoonist)
North American Syndicate
235 E 45th St
New York, NY 10017-3305, USA

Ryans, DeMeco (Athlete, Football Player)
c/o Ben Dogra *Relativity Sports*
2029 Century Park E Ste 1550
Century City, CA 90067-3000, USA

Ryans, Larry (Athlete, Football Player)
110 Brookfield Dr
Greenwood, SC 29646-8501, USA

Ryazanov, Eldar A (Director)
Bolshoi Tishinski Per 12 #70
Moscow 123557, RUSSIA

Rybak, Alexander (Musician)
c/o Staff Member *Lionheart International AB*
P.O. Box 11108
Nytorgsgatan 40 A
Stockholm SE-10061, Sweden

Rybska, Agnieszka (Music Group, Musician)
RPM Music Productions
130 W 57th St Apt 9D
New York, NY 10019-3311, USA

Rychel, Warren (Athlete, Hockey Player)
Windsor Spitfires
8787 McHugh St
Windsor, ON N8S 0A1, Canada

Rychlec, Tom (Athlete, Football Player)
71 Round Hill Rd
Southington, CT 06489-3645, USA

Ryckman, Billy (Athlete, Football Player)
513 Doucet Rd
Lafayette, LA 70503-3557, USA

rycroft, Mark (Athlete, Hockey Player)
2746 S Grant St
Englewood, CO 80113-1611

Rycroft, Melissa (Actor)
c/o Susan (Sue) Madore *Guttman Associates Public Relations*
118 S Beverly Dr Ste 201
Beverly Hills, CA 90212-3016, USA

Ryczek, Dan (Athlete, Football Player)
3714 Monitor Pl
Olney, MD 20832-2248, USA

Ryczek, Paul (Athlete, Football Player)
9335 Scott Rd
Roswell, GA 30076-3416, USA

Rydal, Emma (Actor)
c/o Lucy Brazier *The Rights House (UK)*
Drury House
34-43 Russell St
London WC2B 5HA, UNITED KINGDOM

Rydalch, Ron (Athlete, Football Player)
500 E Durfee St
Grantsville, UT 84029-9781, USA

Rydell, Bobby (Actor, Music Group, Musician)
917 Bryn Mawr Ave
Penn Valley, PA 19072-1524, USA

Rydell, Christopher (Actor)
911 N Sweetzer Ave Apt C
Los Angeles, CA 90069-4368, USA

Rydell, Mark (Director)
Concourse Productions
3110 Main St Ste 220
Santa Monica, CA 90405-5353, USA

Ryder, JoJo (Actor, Producer, Writer)
c/o Staff Member *Untouchable J Productions*
9300 Civic Center Dr # 202
Beverly Hills, CA 90210-3604, USA

Ryder, Lisa (Actor)
c/o Deb Dillistone *Red Management*
415 Esplanade W Box 3
North Vancouver, BC V7M 1A6, CANADA

Ryder, Mark (Actor)
c/o Andrew Kurland *ICM Partners*
10250 Constellation Blvd Fl 7
Los Angeles, CA 90067-6207, USA

Ryder, Michael (Athlete, Hockey Player)
c/o Staff Member *Boston Bruins*
100 Legends Way Ste 250
Td Banknorth Garden
Boston, MA 02114-1389, USA

Ryder, Mitch (Music Group, Musician)
Entertainment Services Int'l
6400 Pleasant Park Dr
Chanhassen, MN 55317-8804, USA

Ryder, Nick (Athlete, Football Player)
14 Ridgeway
Goshen, NY 10924-1408, USA

Ryder, Winona (Actor)
c/o Michael Sugar *Anonymous Content*
3532 Hayden Ave
Culver City, CA 90232-2413, USA

Ryders, Ruff (Music Group)
c/o Staff Member *M.A.G./Universal Attractions*
15 W 36th St Fl 8
New York, NY 10018-7927, USA

Rydman, Blaine (Athlete, Hockey Player)
6880 Hanesbrook Cir
Clemmons, NC 27012-9651, USA

Ryerson, Gary (Athlete, Baseball Player)
1059 Terrace Crst
El Cajon, CA 92019-3129, USA

Rylan, Marcy (Emme) (Actor)
c/o Marnie Sparer *Power Entertainment Group*
1505 10th St
Santa Monica, CA 90401-2805, USA

Rylance, Mark (Actor, Director)
c/o Christian Hodell *Hamilton Hodell Ltd*
20 Golden Sq
Fl 5
London W1F 9JL, UNITED KINGDOM

Rymer, Charlie (Athlete, Golfer)
3851 Haws Ln
Orlando, FL 32814-6553, USA

Rymsha, Andy (Athlete, Hockey Player)
8124 Huntington Rd
Huntington Woods, MI 48070-1654

Rynkiewicz, Mariusz (Artist, Misc)
12401 Alexander Rd
Everett, WA 98204-4715, USA

Rypien, Mark (Race Car Driver)
8817 N Warren St
Spokane, WA 99208-4346, USA

Ryumin, Valery V (Astronaut)
Potchta Kosmonavtov
Moskovskoi Oblasti
Syvsdny Goroduk 141160, RUSSIA

Ryun, Jim (Athlete, Olympic Athlete, Track Athlete)
132 D St SE
Washington, DC 20003-1810, USA

Ryzhkov, Nikolai I (Misc)
State Duma
Okhotny Ryad 1
Moscow 103009, RUSSIA

RZA (Artist, Director, Musician)
c/o Staff Member *42West*
1840 Century Park E Ste 700
Los Angeles, CA 90067-2122, USA

Rzepczvnski, Marc (Athlete, Baseball Player)
5415 Christopher Dr
Yorba Linda, CA 92887-5851, USA

Rzeznik, Johnny (Musician)
c/o Staff Member *WME|IMG*
9601 Wilshire Blvd
Beverly Hills, CA 90210-5213, USA

S

s, Mel (Athlete, Baseball Player)
RR 1 Box 97
West Columbia, WV 25287-8692, USA

S, Robin (Musician)
c/o Stephen Ford *Diva Central Inc*
7510 W Sunset Blvd # 1445
Los Angeles, CA 90046-3408, USA

Saadiq, Raphael (Musician)
c/o Marty Diamond *Paradigm*
140 Broadway Ste 2600
New York, NY 10005-1011, USA

Saakashvili, Mikhail (President)
President's Office
Rustaveli Prosp 29
Tbilsi 380008, GEORGIA

Saalfeld, Kelly (Athlete, Football Player)
2003 S 19th St
Beatrice, NE 68310-5603, USA

Saar, Bettye (Artist)
8074 Willow Glen Rd
Los Angeles, CA 90046-1617, USA

Saari, Roy A (Swimmer)
PO Box 7086
Mammoth Lakes, CA 93546-7086, USA

Saarloos, Kirk (Athlete, Baseball Player)
8608 E Sunnywalk Ln
Anaheim, CA 92808-1689, USA

Saatchi, Charles (Business Person)
M&C Saatchi
36 Golden Square
London W1R 4EE, UNITED KINGDOM (UK)

Saatchi, Maurice (Business Person)
36 Golden Square
London W1R 4EE, UNITED KINGDOM (UK)

Saban, Haim (Business Person, Producer)
61 Beverly Park
Beverly Hills, CA 90210-1569, USA

Saban, Nick (Athlete, Football Coach, Football Player)
1549 Sharlo Ave
Baton Rouge, LA 70820-4553, USA

Sabara, Daryl (Actor)
c/o Katie Rhodes *Untitled Entertainment*
350 S Beverly Dr Ste 200
Beverly Hills, CA 90212-4819, USA

Sabathia, CC (Athlete, Baseball Player)
PO Box 30
Alpine, NJ 07620-0030, USA

Sabatini, Gabriela (Tennis Player)
151 Crandon Blvd Apt 1123
Key Biscayne, FL 33149-1566, USA

Sabatino, Joe (Actor)
c/o Melanie Sharp *Sharp Talent*
117 N Orlando Ave
Los Angeles, CA 90048-3403, USA

Sabatino, Michael (Actor)
13538 Valleyheart Dr N
Sherman Oaks, CA 91423-3124, USA

Sabato Jr, Antonio (Actor, Model)
c/o Tracy Steinsapir *Main Title Entertainment*
8383 Wilshire Blvd Ste 408
Beverly Hills, CA 90211-2435, USA

Sabb, Dwayne (Athlete, Football Player)
26 Marie Rd
Fords, NJ 08863-1306, USA

Sabbah, Michel (Religious Leader)
Latin Patriarch Office
PO Box 14152
Jerusalem, ISRAEL

Sabbatini, Rory (Athlete, Golfer)
9472 Sagrada Park
Fort Worth, TX 76126-1915, USA

Sabean, Brian (Baseball Player)
12 Solana Ct
Belmont, Cl\ 94nn2-36?, USA

Sabel, Erik (Athlete, Baseball Player)
3113 N 400 W
West Lafayette, IN 47906-5281, USA

Sabelle (Music Group, Musician, Songwriter, Writer)
Sarmast Entertainment
241 W 36th St Apt 2R
New York, NY 10018-7541, USA

Saberhagen, Bret W (Athlete, Baseball Player)
Make a Difference Foundation
22817 Ventura Blvd Ste 474
Woodland Hills, CA 91364-1202, USA

Sabihy, Kyle (Actor)
c/o Dino May *Dino May Management*
13223 Bloomfield St
Sherman Oaks, CA 91423-3207, USA

Sablan, Gregorio (Congressman, Politician)
423 Cannon Hob
Washington, DC 20515-4305, USA

Sabo, Christopher A (Chris) (Athlete, Baseball Player)
7455 Stonemeadow Ln
Montgomery, OH 45242-6305, USA

Sabo-Dusanko, Julie (Baseball Player)
7702 E Doubletree Ranch Rd Ste 150
Scottsdale, AZ 85258-2130, USA

Sabourin, Bob (Athlete, Hockey Player)
31 Jackson Ave
Ponte Vedra Beach, FL 32082-2808

Sabourin, Gary (Athlete, Hockey Player)
54 Holland Ave
Chatham, ON N7M 2C7, Canada

Sabuda, Robert (Writer)
155 W 72nd St Rm 401
New York, NY 10023-3250, USA

Saca, Elias Antonio (President)
Casa Presidencial Avda Cuba
Barrosan Jacinto
San Salvador, El SALVADOR

Sacca, Brian (Actor)
c/o Matt Smith *ICM Partners*
10250 Constellation Blvd Fl 7
Los Angeles, CA 90067-6207, USA

Sacchi, Robert (Actor)
203 N Gramercy Pl
Los Angeles, CA 90004-4021, USA

Sacco, David (Athlete, Hockey Player, Olympic Athlete)
3 Bishop Ln
Middleton, MA 01949-1697, USA

Sacco, Joe (Athlete, Hockey Player)
Colorado Avalanche
1000 Chopper Cir
Denver, CO 80204-5805

Sacco, Michael (Misc)
Seafarers International Union
5201 Auth Way
Suitland, MD 20746-4275, USA

Saccone, Viviana (Actor)
c/o Staff Member *Telefe (Argentina)*
Pavon 2444
Buenos Aires C1248AAT, ARGENTINA

Sachenbacher, Evi (Skier)
WSV Reit im Winkl
Rthausplatz 1
Reit im Winkl 83242, GERMANY

Sachs, William (Director)
3739 Montuso Pl
Encino, CA 91436-4001, USA

Sack, Kevin (Journalist)
Los Angeles Times
2300 E Imperial Hwy
Editorial Dept
El Segundo, CA 90245-2813, USA

Sack, Steve (Cartoonist)
Minneapolis Star-Tribune
425 Portland Ave
Minneapolis, MN 55488-1511, USA

Sackhoff, Katee (Actor)
c/o Brett Ruttenberg *Imprint PR*
6121 W Sunset Blvd
Neuehouse
Los Angeles, CA 90028-6442, USA

Sackinsky, Brian (Athlete, Baseball Player)
823 Kali Pl
Rocklin, CA 95765-6103, USA

Sacks, Greg (Race Car Driver)
6092 Sabal Creek Blvd
Port Orange, FL 32128-7131, USA

Sacks, Jonathan H (Religious Leader)
735 High Road
London N12 0US, UNITED KINGDOM (UK)

Sacramone, Alicia (Athlete, Gymnast, Olympic Athlete)
c/o Staff Member *USA Gymnastics*
130 E Washington St Ste 700
Indianapolis, IN 46204-4621, USA

Sacre, Robert (Athlete, Basketball Player)
c/o Keith Kreiter *Edge Sports International*
75 Tri State Intl Ste 180
Lincolnshire, IL 60069-4420, USA

Sade, Tanc (Actor)
c/o Tracey Silvester *Independent Management Company*
87-103 Epsom Rd
#15
Rosebery NSW 2018, AUSTRALIA

Sadecki, Raymond M (Ray) (Athlete, Baseball Player)
4237 E Clovis Ave
Mesa, AZ 85206-1945, USA

Sadek, Mike (Athlete, Baseball Player)
6741 Quartz Mine Rd
Mountain Ranch, CA 95246-9748, USA

Sadler, Billy (Athlete, Baseball Player)
236 Ilnverness Dr
Pensacola, FL 32503-5049, USA

Sadler, Carl (Athlete, Baseball Player)
2280 NW Bailey Grade Rd
Greenville, FL 32331-4500, USA

Sadler, Donnie (Athlete, Baseball Player)
802 Sadler Rd
Valley Mills, TX 76689-4499, USA

Sadler, Elliott (Race Car Driver)
108 Conway Ct
Mooresville, NC 28117-6052, USA

Sadler, Hermie (Race Car Driver)
PO Box 32
Emporia, VA 23847-0032, USA

Sadler, Ray (Athlete, Baseball Player)
4423 Lake Shore Villa Dr
Waco, TX 76710-1448, USA

Sadler, William (Actor)
10474 Santa Monica Blvd # 380
Los Angeles, CA 90025-6929, USA

Sadoski, Thomas (Actor)
c/o Sarah Clossey *United Talent Agency (UTA)*
9336 Civic Center Dr
Beverly Hills, CA 90210-3604, USA

Sadowski, Bob (Athlete, Baseball Player)
26 Barrington Ct
Sharpsburg, GA 30277-1849, USA

Sadowski, Bob (Athlete, Baseball Player)
351 Copper Lakes Blvd
Grover, MO 63040-1919, USA

Sadowski, Jim (Athlete, Baseball Player)
537 Fieldcrest Dr
Pittsburgh, PA 15209-1211, USA

Sadowski, Jonathan (Actor)
c/o Siri Garber *Platform PR*
2666 N Beachwood Dr
Los Angeles, CA 90068-2308, USA

Sadowsky, Clint (Athlete, Baseball Player)
2801 Tropicana Ave
Norman, OK 73071-1711, USA

Saenz, Chris (Athlete, Baseball Player)
7681 W August Moon Pl
Tucson, AZ 85743-5257, USA

Saferight, Harry (Baseball Player)
2321 Wadebridge Rd
Midlothian, VA 23113-3839, USA

Saffell, Tom (Athlete, Baseball Player)
1503 Clower Creek Dr Apt HA262
Sarasota, FL 34231-1911, USA

Saffold, Rodger (Athlete, Football Player)
c/o Alan Herman *Sportstars Inc*
1370 Avenue of the Americas Fl 19
New York, NY 10019-4602, USA

Safin, Marat (Tennis Player)
TC Weiden am Postkeller
Schirmitzer Weg
Weiden 92637, GERMANY

Safina, Dinara (Athlete, Tennis Player)
c/o Staff Member *Women's Tennis Association (WTA-US)*
1 Progress Plz Ste 1500
St Petersburg, FL 33701-4335, USA

Safka, Melanie (Musician)
Two Story Records, Inc
53 Baymont St
Clearwater, FL 33767-1705, USA

Safran Foer, Jonathan (Writer)
c/o Geoffrey Sanford *Anonymous Content*
3532 Hayden Ave
Culver City, CA 90232-2413, USA

Safuto, Dominick (Randy) (Music Group, Musician)
PO Box 656507
Fresh Meadows, NY 11365-6507, USA

Safuto, Frank (Music Group, Musician)
PO Box 656507
Fresh Meadows, NY 11365-6507, USA

Sagal, Jean (Actor)
Progressive Artists Agency
400 S Beverly Dr Ste 216
Beverly Hills, CA 90212-4404, USA

Sagal, Katey (Actor)
c/o Tom Monjack *Tom Monjack Celebrity Enterprises*
28650 Avenida Maravilla # A
Cathedral City, CA 92234-8115, USA

Sagal, Liz (Actor)
c/o Staff Member *Gersh*
9465 Wilshire Blvd Ste 600
Beverly Hills, CA 90212-2605, USA

Saganiuk, Rocky (Athlete, Hockey Player)
4024 Nightingale Dr
Valencia, PA 16059-1702

Sage, Bill (Actor)
c/o Sekka Scher *Ellipsis Entertainment Group*
175 Varick St Frnt 2
New York, NY 10014-4604, USA

Sage, Halston (Actor)
c/o Jason Weinberg *Untitled Entertainment*
350 S Beverly Dr Ste 200
Beverly Hills, CA 90212-4819, USA

Sage, William (Actor)
Gersh Agency
232 N Canon Dr
Beverly Hills, CA 90210-5302, USA

Sagebrecht, Marianne (Actor)
Kaulbachstr 61
Ruckgeb
Munich 80539, GERMANY

Sagely, Floyd (Athlete, Football Player)
362 Red Tail Rdg
Edwards, CO 81632-6407, USA

Sagemiller, Melissa (Actor)
c/o Leslie Siebert *Gersh*
9465 Wilshire Blvd Ste 600
Beverly Hills, CA 90212-2605, USA

Sager, A J (Athlete, Baseball Player)
10310 Belmont Meadows Ln
Perrysburg, OH 43551-6403, USA

Sager, Carole Bayer (Musician, Songwriter)
10761 Bellagio Rd
Los Angeles, CA 90077-3731, USA

Saget, Bob (Actor)
c/o Daniel (Danny) Sussman *Brillstein Entertainment Partners*
9150 Wilshire Blvd Ste 350
Beverly Hills, CA 90212-3453, USA

Saglio, Laura (Actor)
Cineart
36 Rue de Ponthieu
Paris 75008, FRANCE

Sagmoen, Marc (Athlete, Baseball Player)
3844 Happy Valley Rd
Sequim, WA 98382-7723, USA

Sagnier, Ludivine (Actor)
c/o Jon Rubinstein *Authentic Talent and Literary Management (NY)*
20 Jay St Ste M17
Brooklyn, NY 11201-8300, USA

Sagona, Katie (Actor)
Wilhelmina Creative Mgmt
300 Park Ave S # 200
New York, NY 10010-5313, USA

Sahagun, Elena (Actor)
Artists Agency
1180 S Beverly Dr Ste 301
Los Angeles, CA 90035-1154, USA

Sahara Hotnights (Music Group)
c/o Staff Member *Paradigm (Monterey)*
404 W Franklin St
Monterey, CA 93940-2303, USA

Sahgal, Ajay (Actor, Producer, Writer)
c/o Nicole Clemens *ICM Partners*
10250 Constellation Blvd Fl 7
Los Angeles, CA 90067-6207, USA

Sahl, Mort (Actor, Comedian)
1441 3rd Ave Apt 12C
New York, NY 10028-1976, USA

Sahm, Hans-Werner (Artist)
Zur Wasserburg 7
Bidingen
Schwab, GERMANY

Said, Boris (Race Car Driver)
32675 Schoolcraft Rd
Livonia, MI 48150-1604, USA

Said III, Boris (Race Car Driver)
441 Victory Rd
Winchester, VA 22602-4567, USA

Saidock, Tom (Athlete, Football Player)
20316 Old Colony Rd
Dearborn Heights, MI 48127-2758, USA

Sailer, Anton (Toni) (Skier)
Gundhabing 19
Kitzbuhl 06370, AUSTRIA

Saindon, Pat (Athlete, Football Player)
105 King Arthur Pl
Alabaster, AL 35007-9111, USA

Sainsbury of Preston Candover, John D (Business Person)
J Sainsbury PLC
Stamford House
Stamford St
London SE1 9LL, UNITED KINGDOM (UK)

Sainsbury of Turville, David J (Business Person)
4 Charterhouse Mews
Charterhouse Square
London EC1M 6BB, UNITED KINGDOM (UK)

Saint, Eva Marie (Actor)
10590 Wilshire Blvd Apt 408
Los Angeles, CA 90024-7333, USA

Saint, Silva (Adult Film Star)
c/o Staff Member *Atlas Multimedia Inc*
9005 Eton Ave Ste C
Canoga Park, CA 91304-6533, USA

Saint, Silvia (Adult Film Star)
Lange Nieuwstraat 157
Ijmuiden
North Holland 1972GH, The Netherlands

Sainte-Marie, Buffy (Musician, Songwriter)
RR 1 Box 368
Kapaa, HI 96746, USA

Saint James, Susan (Actor)

Sainz, Salvador (Actor, Director)
Ave Prat de la Riba 43
Reus (Tarragona) 43201, SPAIN

Saipe, Mike (Athlete, Baseball Player)
1386 Monitor Rd
San Diego, CA 92110-1543, USA

Sajak, Pat (Game Show Host)
The Wheel Of Fortune
10202 Washington Blvd
Robert Young Bldg #2000
Culver City, CA 90232-3119, USA

Sajko, Kristina (Model)
Karin Models
6 W 14th St Ste 3
New York, NY 10011-7506, USA

Sakai, Hiroyuki (Chef)
La Rochelle 2-15-1 Shibuya Toho
Seimei Building Shibuya-ku
Tokyo, USA

Sakamoto, Soichi (Coach, Swimmer)
768 McCully St
Honolulu, HI 96826-5908, USA

Sakata, Lenn (Athlete, Baseball Player)
San Jose Giants
6770 Hawaii Kai Dr Apt 609
Honolulu, HI 96825-1529, USA

Sakic, Joe (Athlete, Hockey Player)
Thompson, Dorfman, Sweatman
PO Box 639 Stn Main
Attn: Donald Baizley
Winnipeg, MB R3C 2K6, Canada

Sala, Edoardo (Actor)
Carol Levi Co
Via Giuseppe Pisanelli
Rome 00196, ITALY

Sala, Richard (Cartoonist)
3131 College Ave
Berkeley, CA 94705-2740, USA

Salaam, Abdul (Athlete, Football Player)
11153 Embassy Dr
Cincinnati, OH 45240-3005, USA

Salaam, Ephraim (Athlete, Football Player)
c/o Staff Member *EAG Sports Management*
909 N Pacific Coast Hwy Ste 360
El Segundo, CA 90245-3864, USA

Salad Hassan, Abdikassim (President)
President's Office
People's Palace
Mogadishu, SOMALIA

Salahi, Michaele (Reality Star)
c/o Staff Member *Bravo TV (NY)*
30 Rockefeller Plz
New York, NY 10112-0015, USA

Salamanca & Garcia (Writer)
c/o Gabriel Blanco *Gabriel Blanco Iglesias (Mexico)*
Rio Balsas 35-32
Colonia Cuauhtemoc
DF 06500, Mexico

Salas, Greg (Athlete, Football Player)
c/o Ken Zuckerman *Priority Sports & Entertainment - (LA)*
15233 Ventura Blvd Ste 718
Sherman Oaks, CA 91403-2237, USA

Salas, Mark (Athlete, Baseball Player)
2566 W Via Verde Dr
Rialto, CA 92377-2700, USA

Salata, Paul (Athlete, Football Player)
3723 Birch St Ste 11
Newport Beach, CA 92660-2614, USA

Salatin, Josh (Actor)
c/o Kyle Luker *Industry Entertainment Partners*
1133 Broadway Ste 630
New York, NY 10010-8072, USA

Salazar, Alberto (Athlete, Olympic Athlete, Track Athlete)
1 SW Bowerman Dr
Beaverton, OR 97005-0979, USA

Salazar, Arion (Musician)
Eric Godtland Mgmt
5715 Claremont Ave # C
Oakland, CA 94618-1279, USA

Salazar, Eliseo (Race Car Driver)
701 S Girls School Rd
Indianapolis, IN 46231-3132, USA

Salazar, Luis (Athlete, Baseball Player)
20808 Cabrillo Way
Boca Raton, FL 33428-1201, USA

Salazar, Rosa (Actor)
c/o Alex Schack *Slate PR*
901 N Highland Ave
W Hollywood, CA 90038-2412, USA

Saldana, Zoe (Actor)
8721 Santa Monica Blvd
West Hollywood, CA 90069-4507, USA

Saldanha, Carlos (Animator, Director)
c/o Staff Member *Blue Sky Studios*
1 American Ln Ste 210
Greenwich, CT 06831-2563, USA

Saldi, Jay (Athlete, Football Player)
303 Donley Ct
Southlake, TX 76092-5940, USA

Sale, Chris (Athlete, Basketball Player)
c/o BB Abbott *Jeter Sports Management*
PO Box 1388
Solana Beach, CA 92075-7388, USA

Sale, Jamie (Dancer)
12116 128 St NW
Edmonton, AB T5L 1C3, CANADA

Saleaumua, Dan (Athlete, Football Player)
8234 Marshall Dr
Overland Park, KS 66214-1537, USA

Saleen, Steve (Business Person, Race Car Driver)
Saleen Inc.
76 Fairbanks
Irvine, CA 92618-1602, USA

Salem (Music Group)
c/o Jason Edwards *13 Artists (UK)*
11-14 Kensington St
Brighton BN1 4AJ, UNITED KINGDOM

Salem, Dahlia (Actor)
c/o Robert (Rob) Gomez *Precision Entertainment*
6338 Wilshire Blvd
Los Angeles, CA 90048-5002, USA

Salem, Harvey (Athlete, Football Player)
25 Menlo Pl
Berkeley, CA 94707-1532, USA

Salem, Marc (Actor, Comedian)

Salem, Pamela (Actor)
c/o Tammy Green *The Green Agency*
2700 N Miami Ave
#301
Miami, FL 33154, USA

Salemi, Sam (Athlete, Football Player)
2971 Delaware Ave
Kenmore, NY 14217-2353, USA

Salenger, Meredith (Actor)
12700 Ventura Blvd Ste 100
Studio City, CA 91604-2469, USA

Salerno-Sonnenberg, Nadja (Musician)
c/o Staff Member *Columbia Artists Mgmt Inc*
1790 Broadway Fl 6
New York, NY 10019-1537, USA

Sales, Nykesha (Basketball Player)
Connecticut Sun
Mohegan Sun Arena
Uncasville, CT 06382, USA

Saleski, Don (Athlete, Hockey Player)
1800 N Ridley Creek Rd
Media, PA 19063-4529, USA

Salgado, Michael (Musician)
c/o Staff Member *Sony Music (Miami)*
404 Washington Ave Ste 700
Miami Beach, FL 33139-6615, USA

Saliba, Metropolitan Primate Philip (Religious Leader)
Antiochian Orthodox Christian Diocese
358 Mountain Rd
Englewood, NJ 07631-3798, USA

Saliers, Emily (Musician, Songwriter, Writer)
c/o Staff Member *Russell Carter Artist Management*
567 Ralph McGill Blvd NE
Atlanta, GA 30312-1110, USA

Salim, Salim Ahmed (Prime Minister)
Organization of African Unity
PO Box 3243
Addis Ababa, ETHIOPIA

Salinas, Carmen (Actor)
c/o Staff Member *Televisa*
Blvd Adolfo Lopez Mateos 232
Colonia San Angel INN
DF CP 01060, MEXICO

Salinas, Dixie Carter (Producer)
TNA Wrestling, LLC
209 10th Ave S Ste 302
Nashville, TN 37203-0730, USA

Salinas, Jorge (Actor)
c/o Staff Member *Televisa*
Blvd Adolfo Lopez Mateos 232
Colonia San Angel INN
DF CP 01060, MEXICO

Salinas, Maria Elena (Actor)
c/o Staff Member *Univision*
605 3rd Ave Fl 12
New York, NY 10158-0034, USA

Salinas, Nora (Actor)
c/o Staff Member *Televisa*
Blvd Adolfo Lopez Mateos 232
Colonia San Angel INN
DF CP 01060, MEXICO

Salinger, Diane (Actor)
c/o Robert Depp *Beverly Hecht Agency*
3500 W Olive Ave Ste 1180
Burbank, CA 91505-4651, USA

Salinger, Emmanuel (Actor)
Cineart
36 Rue de Ponthieu
Paris 75008, FRANCE

Salinger, Matt (Actor)
Bresler Kelly Assoc
11500 W Olympic Blvd Ste 510
Los Angeles, CA 90064-1527, USA

Salisbury, Benjamin (Actor)

Salisbury, Sean (Athlete, Football Player)
5823 Brushy Creek Trl
Dallas, TX 75252-2341, USA

Salise, Steve (Congressman, Politician)
429 Cannon Hob
Washington, DC 20515-3202, USA

Salkeld, Roger (Athlete, Baseball Player)
27824 Ridgegrove Dr
Santa Clarita, CA 91350-1747, USA

Salkind, Ilya (Producer)
Pinewood Studios
Iverheath
Iver
Bucks SL0 0NH, UNITED KINGDOM (UK)

Sall, John (Misc)
201 Vineyard Ln
Cary, NC 27513-3067, USA

Salle, David (Artist)
Larry Gagosian Gallery
980 Madison Ave PH
New York, NY 10075-1859, USA

Salles, Gualter (Race Car Driver)
Dale Coyne Racing
13400 S Budler Rd
Plainfield, IL 60544-9493, United States

Salles, Walter (Director, Producer)
c/o Staff Member *WME|IMG*
9601 Wilshire Blvd
Beverly Hills, CA 90210-5213, USA

Salley, John (Athlete, Basketball Player, Television Host)
Black Folk Entertainment
Salley Foundation
1ees2 Shana Way
Elk Grove, CA 95757-5956, USA

Sallinen, Aulis H (Composer)
Runneberginkatu 37A
Helsinki 10 00100, FINLAND

Sally, Jerome (Athlete, Football Player)
4107 Roxbury Ct
Columbia, MO 65203-6832, USA

Salming, Borje (Athlete, Hockey Player)
Borje SalminE and Company
Box 45438
Stockholm S-10431, Sweden

Salmon, Brad (Athlete, Baseball Player)
30832 Commander Ct
Daphne, AL 36527-3176, USA

Salmon, Colin (Actor)
c/o Sarah Spear *Curtis Brown Ltd*
28-29 Hay Market
Hay Market House
London SW1Y 4SP, UNITED KINGDOM

Salmon, Tim (Athlete, Baseball Player)
6061 E Sunnyside Dr
Scottsdale, AZ 85254-4977, USA

Salmons, John (Basketball Player)
Philadelphia 76ers
909 Waverly Rd
Bryn Mawr, PA 19010-1930, USA

Salo, Mika (Race Car Driver)
TWI Formula One
Leafield
Whitney
Oxon OX8 5PF, UNITED KINGDOM (UK)

Salo, Mike (Race Car Driver)
Sauber Racing
Wildbachstr. 9
Hinwil, SWITZERLAND

Salo, Ola (Musician)
c/o Staff Member *Live Nation*
Linnegatan 89
Box 21451
Stockholm 01041, SWEDEN

Salo, Tommy (Athlete, Hockey Player)
Leksands IF Ishockey
Box 118
Leksand, S-79323 Sweden

Salome, Angel (Athlete, Baseball Player)
2153 Amsterdam Ave Apt 15
New York, NY 10032-2530, USA

Salomon, Sandy (Actor)
Cineart
36 Rue de Ponthieu
Paris 75008, FRANCE

Salonen, Brian (Athlete, Football Player)
2801 S Russell St Ste 33
Missoula, MT 59801-7914, USA

Salonen, Esa-Pekka (Composer)
410 21st St
Santa Monica, CA 90402-2436, USA

Salonga, Lea (Actor, Musician)
c/o Staff Member *UTA Music/The Agency Group (UK)*
361-373 City Rd
London EC1V 1PQ, UNITED KINGDOM

Salopek, Paul (Journalist)
Chicago Tribune
160 N Stetson Ave
Editorial Dept
Chicago, IL 60601-6707, USA

Salt, Jennifer (Actor, Writer)
c/o Emily Rose *Mosaic Media Group*
407 N Maple Dr # 100
Beverly Hills, CA 90210-3818, USA

Saltalamacchia, Jarrod (Athlete, Baseball Player)
12688 Headwater Cir
Wellington, FL 33414-4908, USA

Salter, Bryant (Athlete, Football Player)
1073 Oswego Ln
The Villages, FL 32162-4040, USA

Salt-N-Pepa (Music Group)
c/o Stephen Ford *Diva Central Inc*
7510 W Sunset Blvd # 1445
Los Angeles, CA 90046-3408, USA

Saltpeter, Edwin E (Misc)
Comell University
Physical Sciences Dept
Ithaca, NJ 14853, USA

Saltykov, Aleksey A (Director)
Institute Mosfilmosvsky
Per 4A #104
Moscow 119285, RUSSIA

Salva, Victor (Director)
c/o Staff Member *Gersh*
9465 Wilshire Blvd Ste 600
Beverly Hills, CA 90212-2605, USA

Salvador, Bryce (Athlete, Hockey Player)
1059 Lawrence Ave
Westfield, NJ 07090-3740

Salvadori, Al (Athlete, Basketball Player)
787 Lindsay Rd
Carnegie, PA 15106-3845, USA

Salvail, Eve (DJ, Musician)
c/o Len Evans *Project Publicity*
540 W 43rd St
New York, NY 10036, USA

Salvatore, Adamo (Musician)
Tonight Music S.A.
Avenue Louise 522
Bruxelles 01050, BELGIUM

Salvatore, Chris (Actor)
c/o Stephen DeCayette *Prestige Talent Agency*
PO Box 33607
Granada Hills, CA 91394-3607, USA

Salvatore, Robert Anthony (R.A.) (Writer)
c/o Staff Member *Random House*
1540 Broadway
New York, NY 10036-4039, USA

Salvay, Bennett (Composer, Musician)
c/o Staff Member *Gorfaine/Schwartz Agency Inc*
4111 W Alameda Ave Ste 509
Burbank, CA 91505-4171, USA

Salvian, Dave (Athlete, Hockey Player)
4451 Breckongate Crt
Burlington, ON L7L 0B2, Canada

Sam, Michael (Athlete, Football Player)

Samaras, Lucas (Artist, Photographer)
Pace Gallery
32 E 57th St Fl 4
New York, NY 10022-2530, USA

Samardzija, Jeff (Athlete, Baseball Player)
c/o Adam Katz *Wasserman Media Group*
10960 Wilshire Blvd Ste 1200
Los Angeles, CA 90024-3714, USA

Samberg, Andy (Actor, Comedian)
c/o Molly Kawachi *ID Public Relations (NY)*
40 Wall St Fl 51
New York, NY 10005-1385, USA

Sambito, Joe (Athlete, Baseball Player)
23 Modesto
Irvine, CA 92602-0929, USA

Sambora, Richie (Musician, Songwriter)
c/o Staff Member *Bon Jovi Management*
PO Box 237040
New York, NY 10023-0028, USA

Samcoff, Ed (Athlete, Baseball Player)
49 Peter Ct
Campbell, CA 95008-2419, USA

Samford, Ron (Athlete, Baseball Player)
2174 Kessler Ct
Dallas, TX 75208-2948, USA

Samis, Phil (Athlete, Hockey Player)
1508-2111 Lakeshore Blvd W
Toronto, ON M8V 4B2, Canada

Sammartino, Bruno (Wrestler)
413 Goldsmith Rd
Pittsburgh, PA 15237-3723, USA

Sammel, Richard (Actor)
c/o Jennifer Abel *PMK/BNC Public Relations*
1840 Century Park E Ste 1400
Los Angeles, CA 90067-2115, USA

Sammie (Actor)
c/o Staff Member *Green Light Talent Agency*
24024 Saint Moritz Dr
Valencia, CA 91355-2033, USA

Sammons, Clint (Athlete, Baseball Player)
4500 Club House Dr
Marietta, GA 30066-2471, USA

Samms, Emma (Actor)
2934 1/2 N Beverly Glen Cir # 417
Los Angeles, CA 90077-1724, USA

Sammy, Sugar (Actor)
c/o Jodi Lieberman *Parallel Entertainment (LA)*
15025 Altata Dr
Pacific Palisades, CA 90272-4450, USA

Samotsvetov, Anatoly (Athlete, Hockey Player)
501 Broadway
Nashville, TN 37203-3980, USA

Sampaio, Jorge (President)
President's Office
Palacio de Belem
Lisbon 01300, PORTUGAL

Sampaio, Sara (Model)
c/o Staff Member *Oui Management*
20 Passage Dauphine
Paris 75006, FRANCE

Sampen, Bill (Athlete, Baseball Player)
11 Carnaby Ct
Brownsburg, IN 46112-8834, USA

Sample, Billy (Athlete, Baseball Player)
10 Pascack Rd
Township Of Washington,
NJ 07676-5116, USA

Samples, Keith (Director, Producer, Writer)
c/o Rob Kenneally *Creative Artists Agency (CAA)*
2000 Avenue of the Stars Ste 100
Los Angeles, CA 90067-4705, USA

Sampleton, Lawrence (Athlete, Football Player)
6500 Saint Stephens Dr
Austin, TX 78746-1716, USA

Sampras, Pete (Athlete, Olympic Athlete, Tennis Player)
2552 Via Anita
Palos Verdes Estates, CA 90274-1011

Sampson, Angus (Actor)
c/o Ellen Meyer *Ellen Meyer Management*
315 S Beverly Dr Ste 202
Beverly Hills, CA 90212-4310, USA

Sampson, Benj (Athlete, Baseball Player)
5912 Giverny
Flower Mound, TX 75022-5500, USA

Sampson, Chris (Athlete, Baseball Player)
13703 Elm Shores Dr
Houston, TX 77044-5615, USA

Sampson, Gary (Athlete, Hockey Player, Olympic Athlete)
PO Box 231985
Anchorage, AK 99523-1985, USA

Sampson, Greg (Athlete, Football Player)
3286 Highland Dr
Carlsbad, CA 92008-1918, USA

Sampson, Kelvin (Basketball Player, Coach)
University of Oklahoma
Lloyd Noble Complex
Norman, OK 73019-0001, USA

Sampson, Kendrick (Actor)
c/o Nicole Miller *NMA PR*
7916 Melrose Ave Ste 1
Los Angeles, CA 90046-7160, USA

Sampson, Ralph L Jr (Athlete, Basketball Player, Coach)
530 Myrtle St
Harrisonburg, VA 22802-4725, USA

Sampson, Robert (Actor)
20th Century Artists
4605 Lankershim Blvd Ste 305
North Hollywood, CA 91602-1875, USA

Sams, Dean (Musician)
c/o Staff Member *Borman Entertainment (TN)*
4322 Harding Pike Ste 429
Nashville, TN 37205-2661, USA

Sams, Jeffrey D (Actor)
c/o Toni Benson *Thirdhill Entertainment*
195 S Beverly Dr Ste 400
Beverly Hills, CA 90212-3044, USA

Sams, Judy (Golfer)
2603 Wells Ave
Sarasota, FL 34232-3954, USA

Sams, Russell (Actor)
c/o Jon Simmons *Simmons & Scott Entertainment*
7942 Mulholland Dr
Los Angeles, CA 90046-1225, USA

Samson, Savanna (Adult Film Star)
c/o Natalie Oliveras
118 Fullerton St #149
New York, NY 10038, USA

Samsonov, Sergei (Athlete, Hockey Player)
5363 Brookdale Rd
Bloomfield Hills, MI 48304-3617

Sam the Sham (Musician)
6123 Old Brunswick Rd
Arlington, TN 38002-5928, USA

Samuel, Amado (Athlete, Baseball Player)
1931 Yale Dr
Louisville, KY 40205-2038, USA

Samuel, Juan (Athlete, Baseball Player)
19712 Maddelena Cir
Estero, FL 33967-0537, USA

Samuel, Skinner (Politician)
111ndian Hill Rd
Winnetka, IL 60093-3923, USA

Samuel, Xavier (Actor)
c/o David Seltzer *Management 360*
9111 Wilshire Blvd
Beverly Hills, CA 90210-5508, USA

Samuels, Chris (Athlete, Football Player)
18303 Oakhampton Dr
Houston, TX 77084-3260, USA

Samuels, Dale (Athlete, Football Player)
7617 Highway X
Three Lakes, WI 54562-9224, USA

Samuels, Jack (Athlete, Baseball Player)
857 Hurst Pl
Brea, CA 92821-2362, USA

Samuels, Monique (Reality Star)
c/o Steve Honig *Honig Company, The*
4804 Laurel Canyon Blvd # 828
Studio City, CA 91607-3717, USA

Samuels, Roger (Athlete, Baseball Player)
4865 Tampico Way
San Jose, CA 95118-2348, USA

Samuels, Skyler (Actor)
c/o Aleen Keshishian *Lighthouse Management and Media*
9000 W Sunset Blvd Ste 1520
Los Angeles, CA 90069-5815, USA

Samuelson, Joan Benoit (Athlete, Olympic Athlete, Track Athlete)
95 Lower Flying Point Rd
Freeport, ME 04032-6305, USA

Samuelson, Kjell (Athlete, Hockey Player)
7 Knottingham Dr
Voorhees, NJ 08043-3930, USA

Samuelsson, Kjell (Athlete, Hockey Player)
10 Simsbury Dr
Voorhees, NJ 08043-3949, USA

Samuelsson, Marcus (Chef, Television Host)
c/o Andrew Chason *TLA Worldwide (The Legacy Agency)*
1500 Broadway Ste 2501
New York, NY 10036-4082, USA

Samuelsson, Mikael (Athlete, Hockey Player)
Puckagency LLC
555 Pleasantville Rd Ste 210N
Attn Rick Komarow
Briarcliff Manor, NY 10510-1900, USA

Samuelsson, Ulf (Athlete, Hockey Player)
19175 N 95th Pl
Scottsdale, AZ 85255-5573, USA

Samyn, Jean-Luc (Horse Racer)
57 Shore Rd
Manhasset, NY 11030-1323, USA

Sanabia, Olivia (Actor)
c/o Kelly-Marie Smith *Status PR*
PO Box 6191
Westlake Village, CA 91359-6191, USA

Sanabria, Marilyn (Actor)
c/o Laura Walsh *Central Artists*
1023 N Hollywood Way Ste 102
Burbank, CA 91505-2554, USA

Sanada, Hiroyuki (Actor)
Axon Entertainment
2-22-4-407, Minami-Aoyama
Minato-Ku
Tokyo 107-0062, JAPAN

San Basilio, Paloma (Music Group)
c/o Staff Member *Sony Music (Miami)*
404 Washington Ave Ste 700
Miami Beach, FL 33139-6615, USA

Sanborn, David (Musician)
c/o Patrick Rains *Patrick Rains & Assoc*
4825 Colfax Ave S
Minneapolis, MN 55419-5319, USA

Sanches, Brian (Athlete, Baseball Player)
903 N 31st St
Nederland, TX 77627-6706, USA

Sanchez, Aaron (Chef)
c/o Andrew Chason *TLA Worldwide (The Legacy Agency)*
1500 Broadway Ste 2501
New York, NY 10036-4082, USA

Sanchez, Alex (Athlete, Baseball Player)
1400 Mellissa Cir
Antioch, CA 94509-6301, USA

Sanchez, Antonio (Musician)
c/o Ray Costa *Costa Communications*
8265 W Sunset Blvd Ste 101
West Hollywood, CA 90046-2433, USA

Sanchez, Claudio (Musician)
2375 US-6
Wawayanda, NY 10940, USA

Sanchez, Duaner (Athlete, Baseball Player)
56748 Eastvue Dr
Osceola, IN 46561-9468, USA

Sanchez, Eduardo (Director)
c/o Staff Member *Elements Entertainment*
312 W 5th St Apt 815
Los Angeles, CA 90013-1750, USA

Sanchez, Elena (Actor)
c/o Siri Garber *Platform PR*
2666 N Beachwood Dr
Los Angeles, CA 90068-2308, USA

Sanchez, Emilio (Tennis Player)
Sabiono de Avena 28
Barcelona 46, SPAIN

Sanchez, Freddy (Athlete, Baseball Player)
2494 E Cloud Dr
Chandler, AZ 85249-3777, USA

Sanchez, Gaby (Athlete, Baseball Player)
5621 SW 130th Pl
Miami, FL 33183-1207, USA

Sanchez, Humberto (Athlete, Baseball Player)
3842 Beacon Ridge Way
Clermont, FL 34711-5344, USA

Sanchez, Israel (Athlete, Baseball Player)
5444 N Spaulding Ave Apt 2
Chicago, IL 60625-4608, USA

Sanchez, Jessica (Musician)
c/o Erin Culley *Creative Artists Agency (CAA)*
2000 Avenue of the Stars Ste 100
Los Angeles, CA 90067-4705, USA

Sanchez, Juan (Pepe) (Basketball Player)
c/o Staff Member *Detroit Pistons*
2 Championship Dr
Auburn Hills, MI 48326-1753, USA

Sanchez, Kiele (Actor)
c/o Daniel Spilo *Industry Entertainment Partners*
955 Carrillo Dr Ste 300
Los Angeles, CA 90048-5400, USA

Sanchez, Lauren (Actor)
c/o Janet Heng *WME|IMG*
9601 Wilshire Blvd
Beverly Hills, CA 90210-5213, USA

Sanchez, Linda (Congressman, Politician)
2423 Rayburn Hob
Washington, DC 20515-3812, USA

Sanchez, Loretta (Congressman, Politician)
1114 Longworth Hob
Washington, DC 20515-5001, USA

Sanchez, Lupe (Athlete, Football Player)
29070 Road 68
Visalia, CA 93277-9436, USA

Sanchez, Marco (Actor)
c/o Nancy Moon-Broadstreet *Sovereign Talent Group*
1642 Westwood Blvd Ste 202
Los Angeles, CA 90024-5609, USA

Sanchez, Mark (Athlete, Football Player)
c/o David Dunn *Athletes First*
23091 Mill Creek Dr
Laguna Hills, CA 92653-1258, USA

Sanchez, Monika (Actor)
c/o Gabriel Blanco *Gabriel Blanco Iglesias (Mexico)*
Rio Balsas 35-32
Colonia Cuauhtemoc
DF 06500, Mexico

Sanchez, Pepe (Director)
c/o Staff Member *Gabriel Blanco Iglesias (Colombia)*
Dg 127A #20-36
Conjunto Plenitud, Apto 132
Bogota, Colombia

Sanchez, Rey (Athlete, Baseball Player)
1831 Lyons Rd Apt 208
Coconut Creek, FL 33063-9273, USA

Sanchez, Rick (Correspondent, Journalist)

Sanchez, Roselyn (Actor)
c/o Lena Roklin *Luber Roklin Management*
5815 W Sunset Blvd Ste 208
Los Angeles, CA 90028-6481, USA

Sanchez Azuara, Rocio (Actor)
c/o Staff Member *TV Azteca*
Periferico Sur 4121
Colonia Fuentes del Pedregal
DF CP 14141, Mexico

Sanchez Gijon, Aitana (Actor)
Alsira Garcia Maroto
Gran Via 63 #3
Izda
Madrid 28013, SPAIN

Sanchez-Vicario, Arantxa (Tennis Player)
Sabino de Arana 28 #6-1A
Barcelona 08028, SPAIN

Sanctus Real (Music Group, Musician)
c/o Dan Spencer *Flat-Out Management*
1800 Blair Blvd
Nashville, TN 37212-5004, USA

Sand, Paul (Actor)
Paradigm Agency
10100 Santa Monica Blvd Ste 2500
Los Angeles, CA 90067-4116, USA

Sand, Shauna (Actor)
c/o David Weintraub *DWE Talent*
Prefers to be contacted by email or phone.
Los Angeles, CA 90069, USA

Sand, Todd (Figure Skater)
2973 Harbor Blvd # 468
Costa Mesa, CA 92626-3912, USA

Sanda, Dominique (Actor)
201 rue du Faubourg St. Honore
Paris, FRANCE F-75008

Sandbeck, Cal (Athlete, Hockey Player)
9590 Chicoria Ct
Trinidad, CO 81082-3976, USA

Sandberg, Jared (Athlete, Baseball Player)
4275 NE 125th St
Seattle, WA 98125-4635, USA

Sandberg, Ryne (Athlete, Baseball Player)
260 Shore Acres Cir
Lake Bluff, IL 60044-1345, USA

Sandberg, Sheryl (Business Person)
Facebook
1601 California Ave
Palo Alto, CA 94304-1111, USA

Sande, Emeli (Musician)
c/o Ambrosia Healy *The Fun Star*
8439 W Sunset Blvd Ste 2
Los Angeles, CA 90069-1925, USA

Sandelin, Scott (Athlete, Hockey Player)
4880 Adrian Ln
Hermantown, MN 55811-3904

Sandeno, Kaitlin (Athlete, Olympic Athlete, Swimmer)
c/o Staff Member *Premier Management Group (PMG Sports)*
700 Evanvale Ct
Cary, NC 27518-2806, USA

Sander, Casey (Actor)
c/o Jeffrey Leavitt *Leavitt Talent Group*
11500 W Olympic Blvd Ste 400
Los Angeles, CA 90064-1525, USA

Sander, Ian (Producer)
c/o Staff Member *WME|IMG*
9601 Wilshire Blvd
Beverly Hills, CA 90210-5213, USA

Sander, Mark (Athlete, Football Player)
4930 NW 83rd Ave
Lauderhill, FL 33351-5553, USA

Sanderman, Bill (Athlete, Football Player)
Tahoma Meadows Bed & Breakfast
PO Box 203
Homewood, CA 96141-0203, USA

Sanders, Ace (Athlete, Football Player)

Sanders, Anthony (Athlete, Baseball Player)
7881 E McGee Mountain Rd
Tucson, AZ 85750-7406, USA

Sanders, Ashton (Actor)
c/o Mia Hansen *Portrait PR*
5320 Sylmar Ave
Sherman Oaks, CA 91401-5612, USA

Sanders, Barry (Athlete, Football Player, Heisman Trophy Winner)
c/o Rhiannon Ellis *Moves Management*
25 Broad St # Ph-T
New York, NY 10004-2517, USA

Sanders, Bernie (Politician)
PO Box 905
Burlington, VT 05402-0905, USA

Sanders, Beverly (Actor)
12218 Morrison St
Valley Village, CA 91607-3627, USA

Sanders, Bill (Cartoonist)
PO Box 661
Milwaukee, WI 53201-0661, USA

Sanders, Bobby (Baseball Player)
Birmingham Black Barons
24799 Lake Shore Blvd Apt 712
Euclid, OH 44123-4246, USA

Sanders, Chris (Director)
c/o Rob Carlson *United Talent Agency (UTA)*
9336 Civic Center Dr
Beverly Hills, CA 90210-3604, USA

Sanders, Christoph (Actor)
c/o Laura Ackerman *Advantage PR*
3900 W Alameda Ave Ste 1200
Burbank, CA 91505-4317, USA

Sanders, Daryl (Athlete, Football Player)
9220 Shawnee Trl
Powell, OH 43065-5012, USA

Sanders, David (Athlete, Baseball Player)
10411 S Ellen St
Mulvane, KS 67110-9374, USA

Sanders, Deion (Athlete, Baseball Player)
1203 S Duncanville Rd
Cedar Hill, TX 75104-7600, USA

Sanders, Doug (Golfer)
1370 Afton St Apt 776
Houston, TX 77055-6989, USA

Sanders, Emmanuel (Athlete, Football Player)

Sanders, Eric D (Athlete, Football Player)
9325 Tailey Cir
Duluth, GA 30097-2451, USA

Sanders, Erin (Actor)
PO Box 2485
Toluca Lake, CA 91610-0485, USA

Sanders, James (Baseball Player)
Kansas City Monarchs
1001 43rd Place Ensley
Birmingham, AL 35208-1402, USA

Sanders, Jay O (Actor)
165 W 46th St # 409
New York, NY 10036-2501, USA

Sanders, Jeff (Athlete, Basketball Player)
PO Box 374
South Holland, IL 60473-0374, USA

Sanders, John (Athlete, Baseball Player)
3004 Cheshire Ct
Woodstock, GA 30189-6690, USA

Sanders, John M (Athlete, Football Player)
520 Old Whitfield Rd
Pearl, MS 39208-5512, USA

Sanders, Ken (Athlete, Baseball Player)
12141 Parkview Ln
Hales Corners, WI 53130-2341, USA

Sanders, Mariene (Correspondent)
WNET-TV
356 W 58th St
News Dept
New York, NY 10019-1804, USA

Sanders, Orban (Athlete, Football Player)
3520 NW Ferris Ave
Lawton, OK 73505-6104, USA

Sanders, Pharoah (Musician)
Joel Chriss
300 Mercer St Apt 3J
New York, NY 10003-6732, USA

Sanders, Pilar (Actor)
c/o Staff Member *Kim Dawson Agency, The*
1645 N Stemmons Fwy Ste B
Dallas, TX 75207-3444, USA

Sanders, Robert J (Athlete, Football Player)
412 Homestead Ave
Metairie, LA 70005-3208, USA

Sanders, Rupert (Director)
c/o Jack Thomas *Independent Talent Group*
40 Whitfield St
London W1T 2RH, UNITED KINGDOM

Sanders, Scott G (Athlete, Baseball Player)
315 Belmont Dr
Thibodaux, LA 70301-2908, USA

Sanders, Simone (Commentator)
c/o Staff Member *CNN (DC)*
820 1st St NE Ste 1100
Washington, DC 20002-4247, USA

Sanders, Summer (Athlete, Olympic Athlete, Swimmer)
731 Martingale Ln
Park City, UT 84098-7559, USA

Sanders, Terry Wayne (Homer Lee) (Actor)
PO Box 1570
Branson, MO 65615-1570, USA

Sanders, Thomas (Athlete, Football Player)
72 S Fiore Pkwy
Vernon Hills, IL 60061-3269, USA

Sanders, Thomas ""Satch"" (Athlete, Basketball Player, Misc)
PO Box 505
Sturbridge, MA 01566-0505, USA

Sanderson, Cael (Wrestler)
Steve Sanderson
1380 N Valley Hills Blvd
Heber City, UT 84032-1111, USA

Sanderson, Derek (Athlete, Hockey Player)
Howland Captital Management
75 Federal St Ste 1100
Boston, MA 02110-1911, USA

Sanderson, Geoff (Athlete, Hockey Player)
New York Islanders
200 Merrick Ave
East Meadow, NY 11554-1596, USA

Sanderson, Nikki (Actor)
c/o Coronation Sreet
Granada Studios, Quay St
Manchester M60 9EA, UNITED KINGDOM

Sanderson, Peter (Artist)
1105 Shell Gate Pl
Alameda, CA 94501-5949, USA

Sanderson, Reggie (Athlete, Football Player)
160 Mara Ave
Ventura, CA 93004-1513, USA

Sanderson, Scott (Athlete, Baseball Player)
945 Newcastle Dr
Lake Forest, IL 60045-4928, USA

Sanderson, Theresa (Tessa) (Athlete, Track Athlete)
Tee-Dee Promotion
Atles Center
Oxgate Lane
London NW2 7HU, UNITED KINGDOM (UK)

Sanderson, William (Actor)
c/o Lori DeWaal *Lori DeWaal & Associates PR*
14724 Ventura Blvd Ste 507
Sherman Oaks, CA 91403-3515, USA

Sandford, Ed (Athlete, Hockey Player)
18 Clearwater Rd
Winchester, MA 01890-4011

Sandgren, Linus (Cinematographer)
c/o Pontus Ronn *Talent Group (Sweden)*
Ängelholmsgatan 3A 214 22
Malmo 214 22, SWEDEN

Sandhu, Gia (Actor)
c/o Marni Rosenzweig *The Rosenzweig Group*
8840 Wilshire Blvd # 111
Beverly Hills, CA 90211-2606, USA

Sandiford, L Erskine (Prime Minister)
Hillvista
Porters
Saint James, BARBADOS

Sandit, Tom (Athlete)
540 S Ashland Ave
La Grange, IL 60525-2811

Sandlak, Jim (Athlete, Hockey Player)
74 Green Hedge Lane
London, ON N6H 5A6, Canada

Sandler, Adam (Actor, Comedian)
c/o Staff Member *Happy Madison Productions*
10202 Washington Blvd
Judy Garland Bldg
Culver City, CA 90232-3119, USA

Sandler, Elliott (Race Car Driver)
Cox Marketing
149-B Rolling Hills Rd.
Mooresville, NC 28117, USA

Sandlock, Mike (Athlete, Baseball Player)
81 Bible St
Cos Cob, CT 06807-2109, USA

Sandlund, Debra (Actor)
Innovative Artists
1505 10th St
Santa Monica, CA 90401-2805, USA

Sandoval, Arturo (Musician)
c/o Staff Member *Columbia Artists Mgmt Inc*
1790 Broadway Fl 6
New York, NY 10019-1537, USA

Sandoval, Hope (Music Group, Musician)
Rough Trade Mgmt
66 Golbarne Road
London W10 5PS, UNITED KINGDOM (UK)

Sandoval, Miguel (Actor)
Paradigm Agency
10100 Santa Monica Blvd Ste 2500
Los Angeles, CA 90067-4116, USA

Sandoval, Sonny (Musician)
East West America Records
75 Rockefeller Plz
New York, NY 10019-6908, USA

Sandoval Iniguez, Juan Cardinal (Religious Leader)
Morelos 244
San Pedro Tlaquepaque 45500, MEXICO

Sandow, Nick (Actor)
c/o Tina Thor *TMT Entertainment Group*
648 Broadway # 1002
New York, NY 10012-2348, USA

Sandre, Didier (Actor)
Agents Associes Beaume
201 Faubourg Saint Honore
Paris 75008, FRANCE

Sandrelli, Stefania (Actor)
TNA
Viale Parioli 41
Rome 00197, ITALY

Sandrich, Jay (Director)
c/o Staff Member *Creative Artists Agency (CAA)*
2000 Avenue of the Stars Ste 100
Los Angeles, CA 90067-4705, USA

Sands, Charlie (Athlete, Baseball Player)
4740 Stratford Ct Apt 1603
Naples, FL 34105-6689, USA

Sands, Jerry (Athlete, Baseball Player)
121 Christian St
Clayton, NC 27527-7519, USA

Sands, Julian (Actor)
c/o Kat Gosling *Troika*
10A Christina St.
London EC2A 4PA, UNITED KINGDOM

Sands, Tommy (Actor, Musician)
Green Linnet
916 19th Ave S
Nashville, TN 37212-2108, USA

Sands-Ferguson, Sarah Jane (Athlete, Baseball Player)
338 Rohrsburg Rd
Orangeville, PA 17859-9108, USA

Sandt, Tommy (Athlete, Baseball Player)
4207 Harvey Way
Lake Oswego, OR 97035-3412, USA

Sandusky, Alexander B (Alex) (Athlete, Football Player)
1946 Drane Ln
Eminence, KY 40019-7522, USA

Sandusky, Jerry (Football Coach)
SCI Greene Maximum Security Prison
175 Progress Dr
Waynesburg, PA 15370-8082, USA

Sandusky, Mike (Athlete, Football Player)
2786 Amberwood Ct
Naples, FL 34120-7520, USA

Sandvoss, Steve (Actor)
c/o Joan Hyler *Hyler Management*
20 Ocean Park Blvd Unit 25
Santa Monica, CA 90405-3590, USA

Sandy, Gary (Actor)
PO Box 818
Cynthiana, KY 41031-0818, USA

Sandy B (Musician)
Atlantic Entertainment Group
2922 Atlantic Ave Ste 200
Atlantic City, NJ 08401-6337, USA

Sandy Jr, Alomar (Baseball Player)
4635 Prestwick Xing
Westlake, OH 44145-5073, USA

Sanford, Chance (Athlete, Baseball Player)
15028 Bardwell Ln
Frisco, TX 75035-0412, USA

Sanford, Ed (Athlete, Hockey Player)
18 Clearwater Rd
Winchester, MA 01890-4011

Sanford, Jennifer S (Misc)
349 Cooper River Dr
Mt Pleasant, SC 29464-1815, USA

Sanford, Leo (Athlete, Football Player)
3044 Gorton Rd
Shreveport, LA 71119-3606, USA

Sanford, Lucius M (Athlete, Football Player)
8745 Carriage Hills Dr
Columbia, MD 21046, USA

Sanford, Mark (Politician)
800 Richland St
Columbia, SC 29201-2327, USA

Sanford, Meredith (Athlete)
8528 MS Highway 389
Starkville, MS 39759-6593

Sanford, Mo (Athlete, Baseball Player)
7716 Tylers Meadow Dr
West Chester, OH 45069-8500, USA

Sanford, Rick (Athlete, Football Player)
514 River Camp Dr
Lexington, SC 29072-8292, USA

Sanford, Ron (Athlete, Basketball Player)
3129 Santana Ln
Plano, TX 75023-3630, USA

Sangalo, Ivete (Musician)
Concerti e Produzioni S.r.l.
via Bonafous, 6
Torino 10123, Italy

Sangare, Oumou (Musician)
c/o Staff Member *Concerted Efforts*
PO Box 440326
Somerville, MA 02144-0004, USA

Sanger, David J (Musician)
Old Wesleyan Chapel
Embleton Near Cockermouth
Cumbria CA13 9YA, UNITED KINGDOM (UK)

Sanger, Stephan W (Business Person)
General Mills Inc
1 General Mills Blvd
PO Box 1113
Minneapolis, MN 55426-1348, USA

San Giacomo, Laura (Actor)
c/o Gina Rugolo *Rugolo Entertainment*
195 S Beverly Dr Ste 400
Beverly Hills, CA 90212-3044, USA

Sangster, Thomas (Actor)
c/o Duncan Millership *WME/IMG*
9601 Wilshire Blvd
Beverly Hills, CA 90210-5213, USA

Sangueli, Andrei (Prime Minister)
Parliament House
Prosp 105
Kishineau 277073, MOLDOVA

Sanguillen, Manny (Athlete, Baseball Player)
2838 SW 4th St
Boynton Beach, FL 33435-7902, USA

Sannes, Amy (Athlete, Olympic Athlete, Speed Skater)
143 W Pleasant Lake Rd
Saint Paul, MN 55127-2630, USA

Sano, Miguel (Athlete, Baseball Player)
c/o Kyle Thousand *Roc Nation*
1411 Broadway Fl 38
New York, NY 10018-3409, USA

Sano, Roya A (Religious Leader)
United Methodist Church
PO Box 320
Nashville, TN 37202-0320, USA

Sansom, Chip (Cartoonist)
PO Box 5610
Cincinnati, OH 45201-5610, USA

Sant, Alfred (Prime Minister)
National Labor Center
Mills End Road
Hannum, MALTA

Santamaria, Eduardo (Actor)
c/o Gabriel Blanco *Gabriel Blanco Iglesias (Mexico)*
Rio Balsas 35-32
Colonia Cuauhtemoc
DF 06500, Mexico

Santana, Ava (Actor)
c/o Claudia Speicher *New Orleans Talent Agency*
1347 Magazine St
New Orleans, LA 70130-4240, USA

Santana, Cara (Actor)
c/o Laurina Spencer *Slate PR*
901 N Highland Ave
W Hollywood, CA 90038-2412, USA

Santana, Carlos (Musician, Songwriter)
Santana Management
PO Box 10348
San Rafael, CA 94912-0348, USA

Santana, Johan (Athlete, Baseball Player)
10471 Via Lombardia Ct
Miromar Lakes, FL 33913-7782, USA

Santana, Juelz (Musician)
c/o Stephen J. Savva *Savva Entertainment*
546 5th Ave Fl 6
New York, NY 10036-5000, USA

Santana, Manuel (Tennis Player)
International Tennis Hall of Fame
194 Bellevue Ave
Newport, RI 02840-3586, USA

Santana, Rafael (Athlete, Baseball Player)
3220 SE 1st Ave
Cape Coral, FL 33904-4103, USA

Santana, Stella (Musician)
c/o Stephanie Durning *42West*
1840 Century Park E Ste 700
Los Angeles, CA 90067-2122, USA

Santangelo, F P (Athlete, Baseball Player)
3602 Rocky Ridge Way
El Dorado Hills, CA 95762-4432, USA

Santaolalla, Gustavo (Musician)
c/o Robert Messinger *Fortress Talent Management*
4764 Park Granada Ste 110
Calabasas, CA 91302-3321, USA

Santa Rosa, Gilberto (Musician)
c/o Staff Member *JL Entertainment*
18653 Ventura Blvd # 340
Tarzana, CA 91356-4103, USA

Santelmann, Tobias (Actor)
c/o Staff Member *Panorama Agency (Denmark)*
Ryesgade 103B
CopenHagen DK-2100, DENMARK

Santer, Jacques (Misc)
69 Rue J P Huberty
01742, LUXEMBOURG

Santerre, Andy (Race Car Driver)
5254 Pitt Rd. So.
Harrisburg, NC 28075, United States

Santiago, Benito R (Athlete, Baseball Player)
610 W Las Olas Blvd Apt 1212W
Fort Lauderdale, FL 33312-7129, USA

Santiago, Carlos (Baseball Player)
New York Cubans
7 Calle Archilla Cabrera
Mayaguez, PR 00680-3302, USA

Santiago, Daniel (Basketball Player)
c/o Staff Member *Phoenix Suns*
201 E Jefferson St
Phoenix, AZ 85004-2412, USA

Santiago, Eddie (Musician)
c/o Staff Member *Sony Music (Miami)*
404 Washington Ave Ste 700
Miami Beach, FL 33139-6615, USA

Santiago, Ellona (Musician)
c/o Mike Esterman *Esterman.Com, LLC*
Prefers to be contacted via email
Baltimore, MD XXXXX, USA

Santiago, Jose (Athlete, Baseball Player)
690 Calle Cesar Gonzalez Apt 2108
San Juan, PR 00918-3906, USA

Santiago, Ray (Actor)
c/o Mike Liotta *True Public Relations*
3575 Cahuenga Blvd W Ste 360
Los Angeles, CA 90068-1361, USA

Santiago, Rodiney (Model, Reality Star)
c/o Staff Member *Mega Model Management*
420 Lincoln Rd Ste 408
Suite #408
Miami Beach, FL 33139-3015, USA

Santiago, Tessie (Actor)
c/o Staff Member *Fireworks Entertainment*
421 S Beverly Dr
Beverly Hills, CA 90212-4400, USA

Santiago, Victor (Nore) (Musician)
c/o Don Buchwald *Buchwald (NY)*
10 E 44th St
New York, NY 10017-3601, USA

Santiago-Hudson, Ruben (Actor)
c/o Pamela Sharp *Sharp & Associates*
1516 N Fairfax Ave
Los Angeles, CA 90046-2608, USA

Santini, Geo (Director)
c/o Kieran Maguire *The Arlook Group*
11663 Gorham Ave Apt 5
Los Angeles, CA 90049-4749, USA

Santo Domingo, Rafael (Athlete, Baseball Player)
PO Box 21
Orocovis, PR 00720-0021, USA

Santorelli, Frank (Actor)
c/o Mitch Smelkinson *Stone, Meyer, Genow, Smelkinson and Binder*
9665 Wilshire Blvd Ste 500
Beverly Hills, CA 90212-2312, USA

Santorini, Al (Athlete, Baseball Player)
9 Daniele Dr
Ocean, NJ 07712-7910, USA

Santoro, Rodrigo (Actor)
c/o Kat Gosling *Troika*
10A Christina St.
London EC2A 4PA, UNITED KINGDOM

Santorum, Rick (Politician)
PO Box 609
Great Falls, VA 22066-0609, USA

Santos, Al (Actor)
c/o Staff Member *Buchwald*
5900 Wilshire Blvd Ste 3100
Los Angeles, CA 90036-5030, USA

Santos, Bruno (Model)
c/o Staff Member *Why Not Model Agency*
via Zenale 9
Milano 20123, Italy

Santos, Cairo (Athlete, Football Player)

Santos, Carlos (Comedian)
c/o Hugh Leon *Coast to Coast Talent Group*
3350 Barham Blvd
Los Angeles, CA 90068-1404, USA

Santos, Jose (Horse Racer)
1055 Papaya St
Hollywood, FL 33019-4842, USA

Santos, Nico (Actor)
c/o Hannah Donohue *42West*
600 3rd Ave Fl 23
New York, NY 10016-1914, USA

Santos, Omir (Athlete, Baseball Player)
2252 Viehman Trl
Kissimmee, FL 34746-2211, USA

Santos, Rey-Phillip (Actor)
c/o Staff Member *Dramatic Artists Agency*
103 W Alameda Ave Ste 139
Burbank, CA 91502-2253, USA

Santos, Rick (Race Car Driver)
S&S Automotive
14127 Washington Ave
San Leandro, CA 94578-3324, USA

Santos, Romeo (Musician)
c/o Edward Shapiro *Reed Smith*
599 Lexington Ave Fl 26
New York, NY 10022-7684, USA

Santos, Sergio (Athlete, Baseball Player)
746 Cienaga Dr
Fullerton, CA 92835-1224, USA

Santos de Oliveira, Alessandra (Basketball Player)
Washington Mystics
601 F St NW
Mcl Center
Washington, DC 20004-1605, USA

Santovenia, Nelson (Athlete, Baseball Player)
14642 SW 141st Ct
Miami, FL 33186-7260, USA

Sanu, Mohamed (Athlete, Football Player)
c/o Michael McCartney *Priority Sports & Entertainment (Chicago)*
325 N La Salle Dr Ste 650
Chicago, IL 60654-8182, USA

Sanz, Alejandro (Musician, Songwriter)
c/o Rosa Lagarrigue *RLM Productions*
Puerto de Santa Maria, 65
Madrid 28043, SPAIN

Sanz, Horatio (Actor)
c/o David (Dave) Becky *3 Arts Entertainment*
9460 Wilshire Blvd Fl 7
Beverly Hills, CA 90212-2713, USA

Sanzenbacher, Dane (Athlete, Football Player)
c/o Joe Flanagan *BTI Sports Advisors*
615 South Blvd Apt C
Oak Park, IL 60302-4606, USA

Saperstein, David (Director, Producer, Writer)
c/o Staff Member *Fran Saperstein Organization*
Marina del Rey, CA 90292, USA

Sapienza, Americo (Athlete, Football Player)
6 Forenza Rd
Peabody, MA 01960-3732, USA

Sapir, Tamir (Misc)
384 5th Ave Fl 7
New York, NY 10018-8166, USA

Saplenza, Al (Actor)
PO Box 691240
West Hollywood, CA 90069-9240, USA

Saporta, Gabe (Musician)
c/o Staff Member *Fueled By Ramen*
PO Box 1803
Tampa, FL 33601-1803, USA

Sapp, Bob (Actor)
c/o Blake Bandy *LINK Entertainment*
11872 La Grange Ave
Los Angeles, CA 90025-5282, USA

Sapp, Marvin (Musician)
c/o Staff Member *M.A.G./Universal Attractions*
15 W 36th St Fl 8
New York, NY 10018-7927, USA

Sapp, Ricky (Athlete, Football Player)
c/o Carl Carey *Champion Pro Consulting Group*
3547 Ruth St
Houston, TX 77004-5515, USA

Sapp, Theron (Athlete, Football Player)
892 N Belair Rd
Evans, GA 30809-4222, USA

Sapp, Warren (Athlete, Football Player)
c/o Drew Rosenhaus *Rosenhaus Sports Representation*
3921 Alton Rd # 440
Miami Beach, FL 33140-3852, USA

Sappleton, Wayne (Athlete, Basketball Player)
8040 N Nob Hill Rd Apt 205
Tamarac, FL 33321-7410, USA

Saprykin, Oleg (Athlete, Hockey Player)
15802 N 71st St Unit 301
Scottsdale, AZ 85254-7107

Sara, Mia (Actor)
c/o Lorrie Bartlett *ICM Partners*
10250 Constellation Blvd Fl 7
Los Angeles, CA 90067-6207, USA

Sarachan, Dave (Coach, Soccer Player)
Chicago Fire
980 N Michigan Ave Ste 1998
Chicago, IL 60611-7504, USA

Sarafian, Richard C (Actor, Director, Writer)
c/o Staff Member *Leavitt Talent Group*
11500 W Olympic Blvd Ste 400
Los Angeles, CA 90064-1525, USA

Sarafyan, Angela (Actor)
c/o Maria Herrera *PMK/BNC Public Relations*
1840 Century Park E Ste 1400
Los Angeles, CA 90067-2115, USA

Sarahyba, Daniella (Model)
c/o Staff Member *IMG Models (NY)*
304 Park Ave S PH N
New York, NY 10010-4303, USA

Saraiva Martins, Jose Cardinal (Religious Leader)
Via Pancrazio Pfeiffer 10
Rome 00193, ITALY

Saralegui, Cristina (Correspondent)
c/o Staff Member *Creative Artists Agency (CAA)*
2000 Avenue of the Stars Ste 100
Los Angeles, CA 90067-4705, USA

Sarandon, Chris (Actor)
c/o Miles Levy *Randy James Management*
12711 Ventura Blvd Ste 345
Studio City, CA 91604-2416, USA

Sarandon, Susan (Actor, Producer)
c/o Jim Berkus *United Talent Agency (UTA)*
9336 Civic Center Dr
Beverly Hills, CA 90210-3604, USA

Sarbanes, Paul (Politician)
830 W 40th St Apt 405
Baltimore, MD 21211-2126, USA

Sardarov, Yuriy (Actor)
c/o Michael Bircumshaw *Water Street Anthem Entertainment*
5225 Wilshire Blvd Ste 615
Los Angeles, CA 90036-4350, USA

Sardinha, Bronson (Athlete, Baseball Player)
156 Kuulei Rd
Kailua, HI 96734-2718, USA

Sardinha, Dane (Athlete, Baseball Player)
156 Kuulei Rd
Kailua, HI 96734-2718, USA

Sarfate, Dennis (Athlete, Baseball Player)
78 W Powell Way
Chandler, AZ 85248-5210, USA

Sargent, Gary (Athlete, Hockey Player)
9624 Power Dam Rd NE
Bemidji, MN 56601-7414

Sargent, Ronald L (Business Person)
Staples Inc
PO Box 9265
Framingham, MA 01701-9265, USA

Sargeson, Alan M (Misc)
National University
Chemistry Dept
Canberra, ACT 00200, AUSTRALIA

Sari, Gabriela (Actor)
c/o Staff Member *Telefe (Argentina)*
Pavon 2444
Buenos Aires C1248AAT, ARGENTINA

Sarich, Cory (Athlete, Hockey Player)
19322 Autumn Woods Ave
Tampa, FL 33647-3249, USA

Sarif, Shamim (Actor, Director, Writer)
Enlightenment Productions
77 Cheyne Court
London SW3 5TT, United Kingdom

Sark, Eari (Athlete, Football Player)
8656 W Bowling Green Ln NW
Lancaster, OH 43130-7857, USA

Sarkis, Inanna (Actor)
c/o Staff Member *WME/IMG*
9601 Wilshire Blvd
Beverly Hills, CA 90210-5213, USA

Sarkisian, Alex (Athlete, Football Player)
1604 E 142nd St
East Chicago, IN 46312-3008, USA

Sarkozy, Nicolas (President)
c/o UMP
55 Rue La Boetie
Paris 75384, FRANCE

Sarmiento, Manny (Athlete, Baseball Player)
14904 Southfork Dr
Tampa, FL 33624-2322, USA

Sarna, Craig (Athlete, Hockey Player)
1375 Brown Rd S
Wayzata, MN 55391-9316, USA

Sarne, Tanya (Designer, Fashion Designer)
Ghost
Chapel 263 Kensal Road
London W10 5DB, UNITED KINGDOM (UK)

Sarner, Craig (Athlete, Hockey Player, Olympic Athlete)
1375 Brown Rd S
Wayzata, MN 55391-9316, USA

Sarni, Vincent A (Baseball Player, Misc)
Pittsburgh Pirates
115 Federal St Ste 115B
Pnc Park
Pittsburgh, PA 15212-5740, USA

Sarnoff, Liz (Actor)

Sarosi, Imre (Coach, Swimmer)
1033 Bp Harrer Dal Utca 4
HUNGARY

Sarratt, Charles (Athlete, Football Player)
8943 E Shooting Star Dr
Gold Canyon, AZ 85118-2940, USA

Sarrazin, Dick (Athlete, Hockey Player)
3391 Ch des Grives
La Conception, QC J0T 1M0, Canada

Sarsgaard, Peter (Actor)
c/o Jon Rubinstein *Authentic Talent and Literary Management (NY)*
20 Jay St Ste M17
Brooklyn, NY 11201-8300, USA

Sartain, Gailard (Actor)
c/o Michael Livingston *Artists Agency Inc*
1180 S Beverly Dr Ste 301
Los Angeles, CA 90035-1154, USA

Sartorius, Jacob (Internet Star, Musician)
c/o Jbeau Lewis *United Talent Agency (UTA)*
9336 Civic Center Dr
Beverly Hills, CA 90210-3604, USA

Sartzetakis, Christos (President)
Presidential Palace
7 Vas Georgiou B
Odos Zalokosta 10
Athens, GREECE

Sarver, Bruce (Race Car Driver)
Bruce Sarver Racing
4550 Coffee Rd # 1-A
Bakersfield, CA 93308-5023, USA

Sarver, Michael (Musician)

Sasaki, Kazuhiro (Baseball Player)
Seattle Mariners
PO Box 4100
Safeco Field
Seattle, WA 98194-0100, USA

Sasaki, Norio (Coach)
Japan Football Association
3-10-15 Hongo
Bunkyo-ku
Tokyo 113-0033, Japan

Sasdy, Peter (Director)
Cleves
21 Matham Rd E
Molesey
Surrey KT8 0SX, ENGLAND

Saskamoose, Fred (Athlete, Hockey Player)
Sandy Lake Indian Res.
Canwood, SK SOJ OKO, CANADA

Sassano, C E (Business Person)
Bausch & Lomb
1 Bausch and Lomb Pl
Rochester, NY 14604-2799, USA

Sasse, Ben (Politician)
c/o Matthew Latimer *Javelin*
203 S Union St Ste 200
Alexandria, VA 22314-3356, USA

Sasser, Grant (Athlete, Hockey Player)
1949 SE Orient Dr Unit B
Gresham, OR 97080-7327

Sasser, Jason (Athlete, Basketball Player)
4211 Tiffany Trl
Grand Prairie, TX 75052-2823, USA

Sasser, Mackey (Athlete, Baseball Player)
19 Harrington Ln
Dothan, AL 36305-9732, USA

Sasser, Rob (Athlete, Baseball Player)
1004 Delta River Way
Knightdale, NC 27545-7326, USA

Sasso, Will (Actor, Comedian)
c/o Staff Member *Lord Mucker Entertainment*
839 E Orange Grove Ave
Burbank, CA 91501-1404, USA

Sassoon, David (Designer, Fashion Designer)
Bellville Sassoon
18 Culford Gardens
London SW3 2ST, UNITED KINGDOM (UK)

Sassou-Nguesso, Denis (President)
President's Office
Brazzaville, CONGO REPUBLIC

Sastre, Ines (Actor)
c/o Brad Schenck *ICM Partners*
10250 Constellation Blvd Fl 7
Los Angeles, CA 90067-6207, USA

Satan, Miroslav (Athlete, Hockey Player)
46 Kettlepond Rd
Jericho, NY 11753-1158

Satcher, David (Misc)
Kaiser Family Foundation
2400 Sand Hill Rd Ste 200
Menlo Park, CA 94025-6944, USA

Satcher, Leslie (Music Group, Musician, Songwriter, Writer)
Warner Bros Records
3300 Warner Blvd
Burbank, CA 91505-4694, USA

Satcher, Robert (Astronaut)
4813 Beech St
Bellaire, TX 77401-3403, USA

Satchwell, Brooke (Actor)
c/o Sarah Linsten *Linsten Morris Management*
3 Gladstone St
Suite 301
Newtown, NSW 02042, AUSTRALIA

Satele, Samson (Athlete, Football Player)

Sater, Steven (Writer)
c/o Rich Green *ICM Partners*
10250 Constellation Blvd Fl 7
Los Angeles, CA 90067-6207, USA

Sather, Glen (Athlete, Coach, Hockey Player)
77330 Vista Rosa
La Quinta, CA 92253-2586, USA

Satine, Elena (Actor)
c/o Paul Nelson *Mosaic Media Group*
407 N Maple Dr # 100
Beverly Hills, CA 90210-3818, USA

Satra, Sonia (Actor)
Innovative Artists
1505 10th St
Santa Monica, CA 90401-2805, USA

Satre, Philip G (Business Person)
Harrah's Entertainment
1023 Cherry Rd
Memphis, TN 38117-5423, USA

Satriani, Joe (Musician)
c/o Melissa Dragich-Cordero *Mad Ink PR*
NA
Los Angeles, CA NA, USA

Satriano, Tom (Athlete, Baseball Player)
5320 Otis Ave
Tarzana, CA 91356-4214, USA

Satterfield, Paul (Actor)
PO Box 6945
Beverly Hills, CA 90212-6945, USA

Satterwhite, Howard (Athlete, Football Player)
3418 Action Ln
San Antonio, TX 78210-3402, USA

Saturday, Jeff (Athlete, Football Player)
2437 Londonberry Blvd
Carmel, IN 46032-8219, USA

Saubert, Jean M (Skier)
147 Harbor Heights Blvd
Bigfork, MT 59911-3739, USA

Saucier, Frank (Athlete, Baseball Player)
1615 S Bryan St Apt 9
Amarillo, TX 79102-2326, USA

Saucier, Kevin (Athlete, Baseball Player)
10926 Country Ostrich Dr
Pensacola, FL 32534-9796, USA

Sauderbeck, Scott (Athlete, Baseball Player)
3919 Riverview Blvd
Bradenton, FL 34209-2000, USA

Sauer, Craig (Athlete, Football Player)
6926 Pagenkopf Rd
Maple Plain, MN 55359-8725, USA

Sauer, Kurt (Athlete, Hockey Player)
14945 63rd Pl N
Maple Grove, MN 55311-4103

Sauerbeck, Scott (Athlete, Baseball Player)
1904 8th St W
Palmetto, FL 34221-4346, USA

Sauers, Gene (Golfer)
9 Judsons Ct
Savannah, GA 31410-1060, USA

Saul, April (Journalist)
Philadelphia Inquirer
400 N Broad St
Editorial Dept
Philadelphia, PA 19130-4015, USA

Saul, Bernard (Misc)
1 Quincy St
Chevy Chase, MD 20815-4226, USA

Saul, Jim (Athlete, Baseball Player)
2405 Osborne St
Bristol, VA 24201-2322, USA

Saul, John (Writer)
c/o Staff Member *Grade A Entertainment*
149 S Barrington Ave # 719
Los Angeles, CA 90049-3310, USA

Saul, Mark (Actor)
c/o Adam Lazarus *BRS / Gage Talent Agency (LA)*
6300 Wilshire Blvd Ste 1430
Los Angeles, CA 90048-5216, USA

Saul, Ralph S (Business Person)
1400 Waverly Rd Apt B145
Gladwyne, PA 19035-1264, USA

Saul, Stephanie (Journalist)
Newsday
235 Pinelawn Rd
Editorial Dept
Melville, NY 11747-4250, USA

Sauli, Daniel (Actor)
c/o James Suskin *Suskin Management*
2 Charlton St Apt 5K
New York, NY 10014-4970, USA

Sauls, Don (Religious Leader)
Pentecostal Free Will Baptist Church
PO Box 1568
Dunn, NC 28335-1568, USA

Saulters, Glynn (Athlete, Basketball Player, Olympic Athlete)
240 Country Ln
Quitman, LA 71268-1226, USA

Saum, Sherri (Actor)
c/o Christian Donatelli *MGMT Entertainment (The Schiff Company)*
9220 W Sunset Blvd Ste 106
W Hollywood, CA 90069-3500, USA

Saunders, Bernie (Athlete, Hockey Player)
150 Pinecrest Dr Hastings On Hudson, NY 10706-3702

Saunders, Dennis (Athlete, Baseball Player)
2854 Rosewood St
Trenton, MI 48183-3602, USA

Saunders, Doug (Athlete, Baseball Player)
212 Crockett Rd
Cedar Park, TX 78613-3869, USA

Saunders, George (Writer)
Random House
1745 Broadway Frnt 3 # B1
New York, NY 10019-4343, USA

Saunders, Jennifer (Actor)
c/o Maureen Vincent *United Agents*
12-26 Lexington St
London W1F OLE, UNITED KINGDOM

Saunders, Joe (Athlete, Baseball Player)
6539 E Lafayette Blvd
Scottsdale, AZ 85251-3144, USA

Saunders, John (Cartoonist)
c/o Staff Member *King Features Syndication*
300 W 57th St Fl 15
New York, NY 10019-5238, USA

Saunders, John R (Race Car Driver)
Watkins Glen Speedway
PO Box 500F
Watkins Glen, NY 14891, USA

Saunders, Lori (Actor)
Lori's Friends
99 La Vuelta Rd
Santa Barbara, CA 93108-2621, USA

Saunders, Rachel (Beauty Pageant Winner)
203 Bocage Dr
Dothan, AL 36303-2944, USA

Saunders, Tony (Athlete, Baseball Player)
1067 Vena Ln
Pasadena, MD 21122-1861, USA

Saunders, Townsend (Athlete, Olympic Athlete, Wrestler)
733 Chantilly Dr
Sierra Vista, AZ 85635-4733, USA

Saura, Carlos (Director)
Antonio Duran
Calle Arturo Soria 52
#Edif 2 1-5A
Madrid 28027, SPAIN

Sauter, Jay (Race Car Driver)
4l5-D River Hwy
Box 278
Mooresville, NC 28115, USA

Sauter, Johnny (Race Car Driver)
PO Box 2218
Sandusky, OH 44871-2218, USA

Sauve, Robert (Bob) (Athlete, Hockey Player)
803-3080 Boul Le Carrefour
Laval, QC H7T 2R5, Canada

Sauveur, Rich (Athlete, Baseball Player)
3312 47th Ave E
Bradenton, FL 34203-3947, USA

Savage, Adam (Television Host)
Behr Abramson Kaller
9701 Wilshire Blvd Ste 800
Beverly Hills, CA 90212-2033, USA

Savage, Andrea (Actor, Producer, Writer)
c/o Julie Darmody *Rise Management*
6338 Wilshire Blvd
Los Angeles, CA 90048-5002, USA

Savage, Ann (Actor)
1541 N Hayworth Ave Apt 203
Los Angeles, CA 90046-3333, USA

Savage, Ben (Actor)
c/o Justin Baxter *Abrams Artists Agency*
750 N San Vicente Blvd
E Tower Fl 11
Los Angeles, CA 90069-5788, USA

Savage, Brian (Athlete, Hockey Player)
8030 E Whistling Wind Way
Scottsdale, AZ 85255-6480, USA

Savage, Chad (Adult Film Star)
c/o Staff Member *Diva Central Inc*
7510 W Sunset Blvd # 1445
Los Angeles, CA 90046-3408, USA

Savage, Chantay (Music Group, Musician)
Famous Artists Agency
250 W 57th St
New York, NY 10107-0001, USA

Savage, Dan (Writer)
The Stranger
1535 11th Ave Ste 300
Seattle, WA 98122-3933, USA

Savage, Don (Athlete, Basketball Player)
53 Park Edge # Le
Berkeley Heights, NJ 07922-1281, USA

Savage, Fred (Actor)
9100 Wilshire Blvd Ste 600W
Beverly Hills, CA 90212-3446, USA

Savage, Herschel (Adult Film Star)
c/o Staff Member *Vivid Entertainment*
1933 N Bronson Ave Apt 209
Los Angeles, CA 90068-5632, USA

Savage, Jack (Athlete, Baseball Player)
9920 White Blossom Blvd
Louisville, KY 40241-4163, USA

Savage, John (Actor)
5584 Bonneville Rd
Hidden Hills, CA 91302-1201, USA

Savage, Reggie (Athlete, Hockey Player)
2000 Harbour Gates Dr Apt 7
Annapolis, MD 21401-2286

Savage, Rick (Musician)
c/o Rod MacSween *International Talent Booking*
9 Kingsway
Fl 6
London WC2B 6XF, UNITED KINGDOM

Savage, Stephanie (Producer, Writer)
c/o Staff Member *Wonderland Sound and Vision*
8739 W Sunset Blvd
W Hollywood, CA 90069-2205, USA

Savage, Ted (Athlete, Baseball Player)
9424 Red Bud Tree Ln
Saint Louis, MO 63122-6572, USA

Savage, Tom (Athlete, Football Player)
c/o Neil Schwartz *Schwartz & Feinsod*
4 Hillandale Rd
Rye Brook, NY 10573-1705, USA

Savant, Doug (Actor)
c/o Kay Liberman *Liberman/Zerman Management*
252 N Larchmont Blvd Ste 200
Los Angeles, CA 90004-3754, USA

Savard, Denis (Athlete, Hockey Player)
8307 Regency Ct
Toronto, ON M5E 1X8, CANADA

Savard, Marc (Athlete, Hockey Player)
c/o Staff Member *Boston Bruins*
100 Legends Way Ste 250
Td Banknorth Garden
Boston, MA 02114-1389, USA

Savard, Serge A (Athlete, Hockey Player)
1790 Ch du Golf
RR 1
Saint Bruno, QC J3V 4P6, Canada

Savary, Jerome (Director)
Theatre National de Chaillot
1 Place du Trocadero
Paris 75116, FRANCE

Savchenko, Gleb (Dancer, Reality Star)
c/o Kate Edwards *Grand View Management*
578 Washington Blvd # 688
Marina Del Rey, CA 90292-5442, USA

Save Ferris (Music Group)
c/o Staff Member *Epic Records Group*
550 Madison Ave Fl 22
New York, NY 10022-3211, USA

Saverine, Bob (Athlete, Baseball Player)
228 Slice Dr
Stamford, CT 06907-1137, USA

Saverson, Henry (Baseball Player)
Detroit Stars
1726 Benjamin Ave NE
Grand Rapids, MI 49505-5434, USA

Saves the Day (Music Group)

Savident, John (Actor)
c/o Staff Member *Coronation Street*
Granada Television
Quay Street
Manchester M60 9EA, UNITED KINGDOM (UK)

Savidge, Jennifer (Actor)
c/o Staff Member *TalentWorks*
3500 W Olive Ave Ste 1400
Burbank, CA 91505-5512, USA

Saville, Curtis (Misc)
RFD Box 44
West Charleston, VT 05872, USA

Saville, Fleur (Actor)
c/o Staff Member *Auckland Actors*
PO Box 56-460
Dominion Road
Auckland 00003, NEW ZEALAND

Saville, Kathleen (Misc)
RFD Box 44
West Charleston, VT 05872, USA

Savinon, Dulce Maria (Actor, Musician)
c/o Mauricio Macias *m3*
174 Cronistas
P. O. Box 201
Satelite, Estado de Mexico 53100, Mexico

Savinykh, Viktor P (Misc)
Moscow State University
Gorochovskii 4
Moscow 103064, RUSSIA

Savitskaya, Svetalana Y (Misc)
Russian Association
Khovanskaya Str 3
Moscow 129515, RUSSIA

Savitt, Richard (Dick) (Tennis Player)
19 E 80th St Apt 11B
New York, NY 10075-0170, USA

Savoie, Matt (Athlete, Figure Skater, Olympic Athlete)
1026 N Maplewood Ave
Peoria, IL 61606-1034, USA

Savoretti, Jack (Musician)
c/o Michael Moses *Baker Winokur Ryder Public Relations*
9100 Wilshire Blvd
W Tower #500
Beverly Hills, CA 90212-3415, USA

Savoy, Guy (Chef)
101 Blvd Pereire
Paris 75017, FRANCE

Savoy, Nick (Business Person, Writer)
Love Systems
3900 San Fernando Rd Unit 2318
Glendale, CA 91204-2876, USA

Savransky, Moe (Athlete, Baseball Player)
128 Dorset D
Boca Raton, FL 33434-3076, USA

Savre, Danielle (Actor)
c/o Adam Griffin *LINK Entertainment*
11872 La Grange Ave
Los Angeles, CA 90025-5282, USA

Sawa, Devon (Actor)
23705 Park Belmonte
Calabasas, CA 91302-1606, USA

Sawalha, Julia (Actor)
P F D
Drury House
34-43 Russell St
London WC2B 5HA, UNITED KINGDOM (UK)

Sawalha, Nadia (Talk Show Host)
BBC
Broadcasting House
Portland Place
London W1A 1AA, UK

Sawyer, Alan (Athlete, Basketball Player)
117 San Juan Dr
Sequim, WA 98382-9326, USA

Sawyer, Amos (President)
President's Office
Executive Mansion
PO Box 9001
Monrovia, LIBERIA

Sawyer, Charles H (Misc)
466 Tuallitan Rd
Los Angeles, CA 90049-1941, USA

Sawyer, Daine (Correspondent)
147 Columbus Ave # 300
New York, NY 10023-6503, USA

Sawyer, Diane (Journalist)
c/o Staff Member *ABC News*
77 W 66th St Fl 3
New York, NY 10023-6201, USA

Sawyer, Elton (Race Car Driver)
Akins Motorsports
185 McKenzie Rd
Mooresville, NC 28115-7976, USA

Sawyer, Forrest (Correspondent)
NBC-TV
30 Rockefeller Plz
News Dept
New York, NY 10112-0015, USA

Sawyer, James L (Misc)
Leather Workers Union
11 Peabody Sq Ste 4
Peabody, MA 01960-5600, USA

Sawyer, John (Athlete, Football Player)
23637 Sunnyside Ln
Zachary, LA 70791-6118, USA

Sawyer, Ken (Athlete, Football Player)
40 S Quaker Ln
Hyde Park, NY 12538-2620, USA

Sawyer, Kevin (Athlete, Hockey Player)
519 S Lucille Ct
Spokane Valley, WA 99216-0827, USA

Sawyer, Paul (Race Car Driver)
Richmond International Raceway
PO Box 9257
Richmond, VA 23227-0257, USA

Sawyer, Rick (Athlete, Baseball Player)
1201 Calle Extrano
Bakersfield, CA 93309-7116, USA

Sawyer, Robert E (Religious Leader)
Moravian Church Southern Province
459 S Church St
Winston Salem, NC 27101-5314, USA

Sawyer, Talance (Athlete, Football Player)
6150 Brookhaven Dr
Bastrop, LA 71220-1878, USA

Sawyer Brown (Music Group)
c/o Staff Member *Paradigm (Nashville)*
222 2nd Ave S Ste 1600
Nashville, TN 37201-2375, USA

Sax, Dave (Athlete, Baseball Player)
3352 Eaton Dr
Roseville, CA 95661-7907, USA

Sax, Steve (Athlete, Baseball Player)
201 Wesley Ct
Roseville, CA 95661-7913, USA

Saxe, Adrian (Artist)
4835 N Figueroa St
Los Angeles, CA 90042-4408, USA

Saxon, Alex (Actor)
c/o Connie Tavel *Forward Entertainment*
1880 Century Park E Ste 1405
Los Angeles, CA 90067-1630, USA

Saxon, Edward (Producer)
c/o Staff Member *Creative Artists Agency (CAA)*
2000 Avenue of the Stars Ste 100
Los Angeles, CA 90067-4705, USA

Saxon, James E (Athlete, Football Player)
RR 3 Box 34X
Beaufort, SC 29906, USA

Saxon, James E (Jimmy) (Athlete, Football Player)
1 Mulberry Ln
West Lake Hills, TX 78746-4321, USA

Saxon, John (Actor)
203 Wheatfield Cir Apt 126
Brentwood, TN 37027-7706, USA

Saxon, Mike (Athlete, Football Player)
660 W Peninsula Dr
Coppell, TX 75019-6801, USA

Saxton, Brian (Athlete, Football Player)
3604 Tudor Dr
Pompton Plains, NJ 07444-1141, USA

Saxton, Jimmy (Athlete, Football Player)
1 Mulberry Ln
West Lake Hills, TX 78746-4321, USA

Saxton, Johnny (Boxer)
1710 4th Ave N
Crystal Palms
Lake Worth, FL 33460-2874, USA

Saxton, Shirley Childress (Music Group, Musician)
Sweet Honey Agency
PO Box 600099
Newtonville, MA 02460-0001, USA

Sayer, Leo (Music Group, Musician, Songwriter, Writer)
Mission Control
Business Center
Lower Road
London SE16 2XB, UNITED KINGDOM (UK)

Sayers, Gale (Athlete, Football Player)
1313 N Ritchie Ct Apt 407
Chicago, IL 60610-2153, USA

Saykally, Richard J (Misc)
University of California
Chemistry Dept
Latimer Hall
Berkeley, CA 94720-0001, USA

Sayles, John (Director)
210 13th St
Hoboken, NJ 07030-4435, USA

Saylor, Morgan (Actor)
c/o Rachel Karten *ID Public Relations*
7060 Hollywood Blvd Fl 8th
Los Angeles, CA 90028-6021, USA

Sbarge, Raphael (Actor)
c/o Staff Member *Main Title Entertainment*
8383 Wilshire Blvd Ste 408
Beverly Hills, CA 90211-2435, USA

Sbranti, Ron (Athlete, Football Player)
2925 Roosevelt Ln
Antioch, CA 94509-5040, USA

Scacchi, Greta (Actor)

Scaduto, Al (Cartoonist)
571 Swanson Cres
Milford, CT 06461-2735, USA

Scadyac, Tom (Director)
c/o Staff Member *Creative Artists Agency (CAA)*
2000 Avenue of the Stars Ste 100
Los Angeles, CA 90067-4705, USA

Scafa, Bob (Baseball Player)
US Olympic Team
2090 Milton Ave
Park Ridge, IL 60068-2320, USA

Scaggs, Boz (Musician, Songwriter)
c/o Craig Fruin *CSM Management*
12711 Ventura Blvd Ste 350
Studio City, CA 91604-2400, USA

Scagliotti-Smith, Allison (Actor)
c/o Samantha Crisp *The Kohner Agency*
9300 Wilshire Blvd Ste 555
Beverly Hills, CA 90212-3211, USA

Scalabrine, Brian (Athlete, Basketball Player)
6 Sterling Dr
Dover, MA 02030-2355, USA

Scales, Bobby (Athlete, Baseball Player)
3547 Archgate Ct
Alpharetta, GA 30004-0635, USA

Scales, Charlie (Athlete, Football Player)
4035 Vistaview St
West Mifflin, PA 15122-2134, USA

Scales, Dwight (Athlete, Football Player)
6112 Roosevelt Cir NW
Huntsville, AL 35810-1634, USA

Scales, Greg (Athlete, Football Player)
4118 Carnation Dr
Winston Salem, NC 27105-3219, USA

Scales, Hurles (Athlete, Football Player)
600 N Adams St
Amarillo, TX 79107-5068, USA

Scales, Prunella (Actor)
Conway Van Gelder Robinson
18-21 Jermyn St
London SW1Y 6NB, UNITED KINGDOM (UK)

Scalia, Jack (Actor)
6200 Kentland Ave
Woodland Hills, CA 91367-1721, USA

Scalians, Bret (Musician)
Media Five Entertainment
3005 Brodhead Rd Ste 170
Bethlehem, PA 18020-9426, USA

Scalzitti, Will (Baseball Player)
19321 SW 61st St
Ft Lauderdale, FL 33332-3354, USA

Scalzo, Tony (Musician)
c/o Staff Member *Russell Carter Artist Management*
567 Ralph McGill Blvd NE
Atlanta, GA 30312-1110, USA

Scaminace, Joseph M (Business Person)
Sherwin-Williams Co
101 W Prospect Ave Ste 1020
Cleveland, OH 44115-1027, USA

Scamurra, Peter (Athlete, Hockey Player)
15 Guinevere Ct
Getzville, NY 14068-1194

Scancarelli, Jim (Cartoonist)
Mark J Cohen
PO Box 1892
Santa Rosa, CA 95402-1892, USA

Scanga, Italo (Artist)
7127 Olivetas Ave
La Jolla, CA 92037-5332, USA

Scanlan, Bob (Athlete, Baseball Player)
12400 Montecito Rd Apt 315
Seal Beach, CA 90740-2733, USA

Scanlan, Hugh P S (Misc)
23 Seven Stones Dr
Broadstairs
Kent, UNITED KINGDOM (UK)

Scanlen, Eliza (Actor)
c/o Tracey Silvester *Independent Management Company*
87-103 Epsom Rd
#15
Rosebery NSW 2018, AUSTRALIA

Scanlon, Pat (Athlete, Baseball Player)
7400 Portland Ave
Minneapolis, MN 55423-4343, USA

Scapinello, Ray (Athlete, Hockey Player)
Hockey Hall of Fame
Brookfield Place 30 Yonge St
Toronto, ON M5E 1X8, Canada

Scarbath, John C (Jack) (Athlete, Football Player)
736 Calvert Rd
Rising Sun, MD 21911-2332, USA

Scarber, Sam (Athlete, Football Player)
12209 Crewe St
North Hollywood, CA 91605-5609, USA

Scarbery, Randy (Athlete, Baseball Player)
5010 E Lewis Ave
Fresno, CA 93727-2418, USA

Scarborough, Joe (Congressman, Journalist, Television Host)
c/o Staff Member *MSNBC*
30 Rockefeller Plz
New York, NY 10112-0015, USA

Scarbrough, W Carl (Misc)
Furniture Workers Union
1910 Air Lane Dr
Nashville, TN 37210-3810, USA

Scarce, Mac (Athlete, Baseball Player)
1010 Richmond Glen Cir
Alpharetta, GA 30004-8216, USA

Scardelletti, Robert A (Misc)
Transportation Communications Union
3 Research Pl
Rockville, MD 20850-3279, USA

Scardino, Albert J (Journalist)
19 Empire House
Thurloe Place
London SW7 2RU, UNITED KINGDOM (UK)

Scarf, Maggie (Writer)
c/o Camille McDuffie *Goldberg McDuffie Communications*
444 Madison Ave Ste 3300
New York, NY 10022-6922, USA

Scarface (Musician)
c/o Staff Member *American Talent Agency*
248 W 35th St Rm 501
New York, NY 10001-2505, USA

Scarfe, Gerald A (Cartoonist)
10 Cheyne Walk
London SW3, UNITED KINGDOM (UK)

Scargill, Arthur (Misc)
National Union of Mineworkers
2 Huddersfield Road
Bamsley, UNITED KINGDOM (UK)

Scarpati, Joseph H (Athlete, Football Player)
32 Lexington Cir
Marlton, NJ 08053-3860, USA

Scarpelli, Glenn (Actor)
PO Box 3903
Sedona, AZ 86340-3903, USA

Scarpitto, Bob (Athlete, Football Player)
123 White Oaks Ln
Carmel Valley, CA 93924-9650, USA

Scarry, Mike (Athlete, Football Player)
7430 Lake Breeze Dr Apt 104
Fort Myers, FL 33907-8058, USA

Scarsone, Steve (Athlete, Baseball Player)
10017 E South Bend Dr
Scottsdale, AZ 85255-2541, USA

Scarwid, Diana (Actor)
PO Box 3614
Savannah, GA 31414-3614, USA

Scatchard, Dave (Athlete, Hockey Player)
215 Orchard Valley Dr
Harriman, TN 37748-4698

Scates, Al (Coach, Volleyball Player)
UCLA
PO Box 24044
Athletic Dept - Volleyball
Los Angeles, CA 90024-0044, USA

Scattini, Monica (Actor)
Carol Levi Co
Via Giuseppe Pisanelli
Rome 00196, ITALY

Scelba-Shorte, Mercedes (Reality Star)
c/o Staff Member *Ty Ty Baby Productions*
8346 W 3rd St # 650
Los Angeles, CA 90048-4311, USA

Scelzi, Gary (Race Car Driver)
Alen Johnson Racing
2772 S Cherry Ave
Fresno, CA 93706-5424, USA

Scerbo, Cassie (Actor)
c/o Adam Griffin *LINK Entertainment*
11872 La Grange Ave
Los Angeles, CA 90025-5282, USA

Schaaf, Fred (Athlete, Baseball Player)
2782 Countryside Blvd Apt 3
Clearwater, FL 33761-3646, USA

Schaal, Kristen (Actor)
c/o Brittany Gilpin *Kovert Creative*
506 Santa Monica Blvd Ste 400
Santa Monica, CA 90401-2412, USA

Schaal, Paul (Athlete, Baseball Player)
PO Box 385143
Waikoloa, HI 96738-0143, USA

Schaal, Wendy (Actor)
c/o Adam Lazarus *BRS / Gage Talent Agency (LA)*
6300 Wilshire Blvd Ste 1430
Los Angeles, CA 90048-5216, USA

Schabarum, Pete (Athlete, Football Player)
46170 E Eldorado Dr
Indian Wells, CA 92210-8633, USA

Schacher, Mel (Musician)
Lustig Talent
PO Box 770850
Orlando, FL 32877-0850, USA

Schacht, Henry B (Business Person)
Lucent Technologies Inc
600 Mountain Ave
New Providence, NJ 07974-2008, USA

Schachter, Blanche (Baseball Player)
163 W 18th St Apt 3A
New York, NY 10011-4144, USA

Schachter, Steven (Director, Writer)
c/o Staff Member *Ken Gross Management*
11111 Santa Monica Blvd Ste 1700
Los Angeles, CA 90025-0449, USA

Schacker, Hal (Athlete, Baseball Player)
14044 Spoonbill Ln
Clearwater, FL 33762-4545, USA

Schade, Frank (Athlete, Basketball Player)
825 Nicolet Ave
Oshkosh, WI 54901-1635, USA

Schade, Molly (Actor)
c/o Devon Bratton *3 Arts Entertainment*
9460 Wilshire Blvd Fl 7
Beverly Hills, CA 90212-2713, USA

Schadler, Jay (Correspondent)

Schaech, Johnathon (Actor)
4906 Placidia Ave
N Hollywood, CA 91601-4834, USA

Schaefer, Bob (Athlete, Baseball Player, Coach)
9330 White Hickory Ln
Fort Myers, FL 33912-6856, USA

Schaefer, Don (Athlete, Football Player)
2033 Cool Springs Dr
Pittsburgh, PA 15234-2034, USA

Schaefer, Henry F III (Misc)
University of Georgia
Computational Quantum Chemistry Center
Athens, GA 30602-0001, USA

Schaefer, Jeff (Athlete, Baseball Player)
2110 Woodbend Trl
Fort Mill, SC 29708-8343, USA

Schaefer, Sara (Actor, Comedian)
c/o Rebecca Sides Capellan *ID Public Relations (NY)*
40 Wall St Fl 51
New York, NY 10005-1385, USA

Schaefer, Yvonne Maria (Actor, Producer)
YMC Films
343 E 76th St
New York, NY 10021-2404, USA

Schaeffer, Billy (Athlete, Basketball Player)
7 Ames Pl
Huntington Station, NY 11746-4701, USA

Schaeffer, Danny (Athlete, Baseball Player)
Round Rock Express
3400 E Palm Valley Blvd
Attn: Coaching Staff
Round Rock, TX 78665-3906, USA

Schaeffer, Eric (Actor, Director)
Signature Theater
4200 Campbell Ave
Arlington, VA 22206-3435, USA

Schaeffer, Leonard (Business Person)
Quintiles
4820 Emperor Blvd
Durham, NC 27703-8426, USA

Schaeffer, Mark (Athlete, Baseball Player)
18261 Parthenia St
Northridge, CA 91325-3303, USA

Schaefzel, John R (Writer)
2 Bay Tree Ln
Bethesda, MD 20816-1046, USA

Schafer, Edward (Politician)
4426 Carrie Rose Ln S
Fargo, ND 58104-6818, USA

Schafer, Jordan (Athlete, Baseball Player)
80 Pine Forest Dr
Haines City, FL 33844-9710, USA

Schaffel, Lewis (Basketball Player, Misc)
Miami Heat
601 Biscayne Blvd
American Airlines Arena
Miami, FL 33132-1801, USA

Schaffer, Eric (Music Group, Musician)
Kennedy Center for Performing Arts
Washington, DC 20011, USA

Schaffer, Jimmie (Athlete, Baseball Player)
655 Birch Ter
Coopersburg, PA 18036-2407, USA

Schaffermoth, Joe (Athlete, Baseball Player)
20 Marion Ave
Berkeley Heights, NJ 07922-1260, USA

Schaffernoth, Joe (Athlete, Baseball Player)
7 Stonewood Ct
Warren, NJ 07059-2701, USA

Schafrath, Dick (Athlete, Football Player)
704 Ashland Rd
Mansfield, OH 44905-2536, USA

Schalder, Ben (Athlete, Basketball Player)
808 Bauer Dr
San Carlos, CA 94070-3614, USA

Schall, Alvin A (Football Coach, Football Player)
US Appeals Court
717 Madison Pl NW
Washington, DC 20439-0001, USA

Schall, Benny (Athlete, Basketball Player)
4305 Robinhood Ln
Toledo, OH 43623-2537, USA

Schall, Gene (Athlete, Baseball Player)
1582 Bromley Dr
Harleysville, PA 19438-3056, USA

Schaller, Cliff (Athlete, Baseball Player)
1978 3847 Powner Rd
Cincinnati, OH 45248-2918, USA

Schaller, Willie (Soccer Player)
3283 S Indiana St
Lakewood, CO 80228-5499, USA

Schallock, Art (Athlete, Baseball Player)
749 Crocus Dr
Sonoma, CA 95476-8325, USA

Schamehorn, Kevin (Athlete, Hockey Player)
5536 Stoney Brook Rd
Kalamazoo, MI 49009-7703

Schankweiler, Scott (Athlete, Football Player)
1815 Wilson Point Rd
Middle River, MD 21220-5429, USA

Schanz, Heidi (Actor)
Gersh Agency
232 N Canon Dr
Beverly Hills, CA 90210-5302, USA

Schapansky, Glen (Athlete, Football Player)
PO Box 215
Woodlands, MB R0C 3H0, Canada

Schapker, Alison (Producer, Writer)
c/o Ilan Breil *Mosaic Media Group*
407 N Maple Dr # 100
Beverly Hills, CA 90210-3818, USA

Schapp, Dick (Sportscaster)
ESPN-TV
Sports Dept
ESPN Plaza 935 Middle St
Bristol, CT 06010, USA

Schar, Dwight (Business Person)
NVR Inc
7601 Lewinsville Rd Ste 300
McLean, VA 22102-2835, USA

Scharar, Erich (Athlete)
Grutstrasse 63
Herrliberg 08074, SWITZERLAND

Scharf, Ted (Athlete, Hockey Player)
50 Westmount Rd N
Waterloo, ON N2L 2R5, Canada

Schattinger, Jeff (Athlete, Baseball Player)
PO Box 134
Lake Arrowhead, CA 92352-0134, USA

Schatz, Donny (Race Car Driver)
Schatz Motorsports
4510 19th Ave S
Fargo, ND 58103-7700, USA

Schatzberg, Jerry N (Director)
c/o Staff Member *ICM Partners*
10250 Constellation Blvd Fl 7
Los Angeles, CA 90067-6207, USA

Schatzeder, Dan (Athlete, Baseball Player)
186 River Mist Dr
Oswego, IL 60543-8358, USA

Schaub, Matt (Athlete, Football Player)
c/o David Dunn *Athletes First*
23091 Mill Creek Dr
Laguna Hills, CA 92653-1258, USA

Schaudt, Martin (Athlete, Horse Racer)
Gerhardstr 10/2
Albstadt 72461, GERMANY

Schaum, Greg (Athlete, Football Player)
4303 Piney Park Rd
Perry Hall, MD 21128-9524, USA

Schauman, Wilhelm (Athlete, Golfer)
c/o Jim Lehrman *Medalist Management Inc*
36855 W Main St Ste 200
Purcellville, VA 20132-3561, USA

Schayes, Danny (Athlete, Basketball Player)
8582 E Cactus Wren Cir
Scottsdale, AZ 85266-1334, USA

Schechkter, Tomas (Race Car Driver)
5101 Decatur Blvd Ste P
Indianapolis, IN 46241-9529, USA

Scheckter, Jody D (Race Car Driver)
39 Ave Princess Grace
Monte Carlo, MONACO

Scheckter, Tomas (Race Car Driver)
11412 Divers Cove Ct
Indianapolis, IN 46236-8601, USA

Schecter, Leroy (Business Person)
12 Indian Creek Island Rd
Indian Creek Village, FL 33154-2903, USA

Schedeen, Anne (Actor)
c/o Tom Markley *Metropolitan Talent Agency*
7020 La Presa Dr
Los Angeles, CA 90068-3105, USA

Scheer-Demme, Amanda (Business Person, Producer)
c/o Staff Member *Thrive Music*
1024 N Orange Dr
Los Angeles, CA 90038-2336, USA

Scheff, Jerry (Musician)
Victoria Stone House
Duns Castle Estate
Duns, Berwickshire TD11 3NW, Scotland

Scheffer, Aaron (Athlete, Baseball Player)
1351 Sharon St
Westland, MI 48186-5044, USA

Scheffler, Israel (Misc)
Harvard University
Larsen Hall
Cambridge, MA 02138, USA

Scheffler, Tony (Football Player)
c/o Staff Member *Denver Broncos*
13655 Broncos Pkwy
Englewood, CO 80112-4151, USA

Schefft, Jen (Reality Star)
3650 N Magnolia Ave
Chicago, IL 60613-3821, USA

Scheid, Rich (Athlete, Baseball Player)
402 Grant Ave
Hightstown, NJ 08520-4100, USA

Scheinberg, Mark (Business Person)
Rational Group
Douglas Bay Complex, King Edward Rd
Onchan IM3 1DZ, Isle of Man

Scheinblum, Richie (Athlete, Baseball Player)
1308 Woodstock Dr
Palm Harbor, FL 34684-2246, USA

Schell, Catherine (Actor)
Postfach 800504
Cologne 51005, GERMANY

Schellen, Mark (Athlete, Football Player)
320 Shorewood Ln
Waterloo, NE 68069-9717, USA

Schellenbach, Kate (Musician)
Metropolitan Entertainment
2 Penn Plz # 2600
New York, NY 10121-0101, USA

Schellhase, Dave (Athlete, Basketball Player)
862 Walnut Rdg E
Logansport, IN 46947-3965, USA

Schellman, John A (Misc)
65 W 30th Ave # 508
Eugene, OR 97405-3485, USA

Schelmerding, Kirk (Race Car Driver)
Childress Racing
PO Box 1189
Industrial Dr
Welcome, NC 27374-1189, USA

Schembechler, Glenn E (Bo) Jr (Athlete, Coach, Football Player)
1904 Boulder Dr
Ann Arbor, MI 48104-4164, USA

Schenert, Turk (Athlete, Football Player)
239 Willow Ave
Pompton Lakes, NJ 07442-2443, USA

Schenk, Franziska (Speed Skater)
DSEG
Mensinger Str 68
Munich 80992, GERMANY

Schenkenberg, Markus (Actor, Model)
c/o Marta Michaud *Cinematic Management*
249 1/2 E 13th St
New York, NY 10003-5602, USA

Schenker, Dr Eran (Astronaut)
PO Box 4572
Jerusalem, USA

Schenker, Nathan (Athlete, Football Player)
26400 George Zeiger Dr Apt 116
Beachwood, OH 44122-7511, USA

Schenkkan, Robert F (Writer)
Dramatist Guild
1501 Broadway Ste 701
New York, NY 10036-5505, USA

Schenkman, Eric (Musician)
DAS Communications
84 Riverside Dr
New York, NY 10024-5723, USA

Schenn, Brayden (Athlete, Hockey Player)
c/o Donald Meehan *Newport Sports Management*
201 City Centre Dr
Suite 400
Mississauga, ON L58 2T4, CANADA

Schenn, Luke (Athlete, Hockey Player)
354 Thode Ave
Saskatoon, SK S7W 1B9, Canada

Schepisi, Fred (Director)
c/o Staff Member *WME/IMG*
9601 Wilshire Blvd
Beverly Hills, CA 90210-5213, USA

Schepisl, Frederic A (Director)
Film House
159 Eastern Road
South Melbourne, VIC 03205, AUSTRALIA

Scherbo, Vitali (Gymnast)
8308 Aqua Spray Ave
Las Vegas, NV 89128-7432, USA

Scherega, Harold A (Misc)
212 Homestead Ter
Ithaca, NY 14850-6220, USA

Scherer, Bernard (Athlete, Football Player)
PO Box 5201
Carmel By The Sea, CA 93921-5201, USA

Scherff, Brandon (Athlete, Football Player)
c/o Neil Cornrich *NC Sports, LLC*
best to contact via email
Columbus, OH 43201, USA

Scherfig, Lone (Director)
c/o Jodi Shields *Casarotto Ramsay & Associates Ltd (UK)*
Waverley House
7-12 Noel St
London W1F 8GQ, UNITED KINGDOM

Scherman, Fred (Athlete, Baseball Player)
7454 S Tipp Cowlesville Rd
Tipp City, OH 45371-8351, USA

Scherrer, Bill (Athlete, Baseball Player)
4155 E Rockledge Rd
Phoenix, AZ 85044-6770, USA

Scherzer, Max (Athlete, Baseball Player)
c/o Scott Boras *Boras Corporation*
18 Corporate Plaza Dr
Newport Beach, CA 92660-7901, USA

Scherzinger, Nicole (Actor, Musician)
c/o Ollie Ayling *First Access Entertainment (UK)*
Grove Studios, Adie Rd
London W6 0PW, UNITED KINGDOM

Scheuer, Paul J (Misc)
3271 Melemele Pl
Honolulu, HI 96822-1431, USA

Scheuring, Paul (Director)
c/o Chris Donnelly *LBI Entertainment*
2000 Avenue of the Stars
N Tower Fl 3
Los Angeles, CA 90067-4700, USA

Schevill, James (Writer)
1309 Oxford St
Berkeley, CA 94709-1424, USA

Schiebold, Hans (Artist)
13705 SW 118th Ct
Tigard, OR 97223-2857, USA

Schieffer, Bob (Journalist)
c/o Staff Member *CBS News (NY)*
524 W 57th St Fl 8
New York, NY 10019-2930, USA

Schierholtz, Nate (Athlete, Baseball Player)
c/o Damon Lapa *All Bases Covered Sports Management*
20669 N 101st St
Scottsdale, AZ 85255-3364, USA

Schiff, Andras (Musician)
Shirley Kirshbaum
711 W End Ave Apt 5KN
New York, NY 10025-0100, USA

Schiff, Mark (Actor, Comedian)
Gail Stocker Presents
1025 N Kings Rd Apt 113
Los Angeles, CA 90069-6007, USA

Schiff, Richard (Actor, Director)
c/o Michael Garnett *Leverage Management*
3030 Pennsylvania Ave
Santa Monica, CA 90404-4112, USA

Schiff, Robin (Writer)
c/o Staff Member *Broder Webb Chervin Silbermann Agency, The (BWCS)*
10250 Constellation Blvd
Los Angeles, CA 90067-6200, USA

Schiffer, Claudia (Model)
Aussenwall 94
Rheinberg 47495, GERMANY

Schiffer, Eric (Writer)
6965 El Camino Real Ste 105
PMB 517
Carlsbad, CA 92009-4101

Schiffer, Michael (Writer)
c/o Staff Member *Gotham Group*
1041 N Formosa Ave # 200
West Hollywood, CA 90046-6703, USA

Schiffner, Travis (Actor)
c/o Staff Member *Bohemia Group*
1680 Vine St Ste 518
Los Angeles, CA 90028-8833, USA

Schifrin, Lalo (Musician)
710 N Hillcrest Rd
Beverly Hills, CA 90210-3517, USA

schilebener, Andy (Athlete, Hockey Player)
1980 Silver Pines Cres
Orleans, ON K1W 1J7, Canada

Schiller, Harvey W (Misc)
Turner Sports
1050 Techwood Dr NW
Atlanta, GA 30318-5604, USA

Schiller, Lawrence J (Director, Writer)
353 Pineville Rd
Newtown, PA 18940-3111, USA

Schilling, Chuck (Athlete, Baseball Player)
907 Caroline Ct
New Bern, NC 28560-1804, USA

Schilling, Curt (Athlete, Baseball Player)
7 Woodridge Rd
Medfield, MA 02052-2526, USA

Schilling, Stehen (Athlete, Football Player)
c/o Doug Hendrickson *Relativity Sports*
2029 Century Park E Ste 1550
Century City, CA 90067-3000, USA

Schilling, Taylor (Actor)
c/o Marla Farrell *Shelter PR*
928 Broadway Ste 505
New York, NY 10010-8143, USA

Schimberg, Henry R (Business Person)
Coca-Cola Enterprises
2500 Windy Ridge Pkwy SE Ste 700
Atlanta, GA 30339-8429, USA

Schimberni, Mario (Business Person)
Armando Curcio Editore SpA
Via IV Novembre
Rome 00187, ITALY

Schindelholz, Lorenz (Athlete)
Hardstr 184
Herbetswil 04715, SWITZERLAND

Schindler, Steve (Athlete, Football Player)
6109 Willow Springs Dr
Morrison, CO 80465-2133, USA

Schinkel, Kenneth (Ken) (Athlete, Hockey Player)
19927 Beaulieu Ct
Fort Myers, FL 33908-4832, USA

Schino, Dominic (Producer)
c/o Staff Member *Magic Touch Records*
1215 36th Ave Apt 4E
#4-E
Long Island City, NY 11106-4736, USA

Schipper, Ron (Coach, Football Coach)
1088 Fountain View Cir Unit 1
Holland, MI 49423-5620, USA

Schiraldi, Calvin (Athlete, Baseball Player)
9108 Tweed Berwick Dr
Austin, TX 78750-3554, USA

Schirra, Heather (Model)
c/o Jon Orlando *Exposure Marketing Group*
348 Hauser Blvd Apt 414
Los Angeles, CA 90036-5590, USA

Schirripa, Steve (Actor)
c/o Robbie Kass *Kass Management*
1011 Euclid St Unit B
Santa Monica, CA 90403-4296, USA

Schisgal, Murray J (Writer)
International Creative Mgmt
40 W 57th St Ste 1800
New York, NY 10019-4033, USA

Schlag, Edward W (Misc)
Osterwaldstr 91
Munich 80805, GERMANY

Schlamme, Thomas (Actor)
c/o Rosalie Swedlin *Anonymous Content*
3532 Hayden Ave
Culver City, CA 90232-2413, USA

Schlatter, Charlie (Actor)
638 Lindero Canyon Rd # 322
Oak Park, CA 91377-5457, USA

Schleech, Russ (Misc)
21634 Paseo Maravia
Mission Viejo, CA 92692-4963, USA

Schlegel, Hans W (Astronaut)
European Astronaut Centre
Postfach 906058
Cologne 51140, GERMANY

Schleinzer, Markus (Director)
c/o Doug MacLaren *ICM Partners*
10250 Constellation Blvd Fl 7
Los Angeles, CA 90067-6207, USA

Schleinzer, Markus (Director)

Schleper, Sarah (Athlete, Olympic Athlete)
520 E Lionshead Cir Apt 301
Vail, CO 81657-5238, USA

Schlereth, Daniel (Athlete, Baseball Player)
9479 S Shadow Hill Cir
Lone Tree, CO 80124-5484, USA

Schlereth, Mark (Athlete, Football Player)
9479 S Shadow Hill Cir
Lone Tree, CO 80124-5484, USA

Schlesinger, Adam (Music Group, Musician, Songwriter, Writer)
MOB Agency
6404 Wilshire Blvd Ste 505
Los Angeles, CA 90048-5507, USA

Schlesinger, Bill (Athlete, Baseball Player)
4230 Glenway Ave Apt 2
Deer Park, OH 45236-3646, USA

Schlesinger, Cory (Athlete, Football Player)
24392 Parke Ln
Grosse Ile, MI 48138-1704, USA

Schlesinger, James (Politician)
7515 Colshire Dr Attn Ofc
the Mitre Corporation
McLean, VA 22102-7539, USA

Schlesinger, Rudy (Athlete, Baseball Player)
5708 Abelia Ct
Cincinnati, OH 45213-2434, USA

Schlessinger, Laura (Radio Personality, Writer)
PO Box 8120
Van Nuys, CA 91409-8120, USA

Schleyer, Paul Von R (Misc)
Frederich-Alexander-Universtat
Henkestr 41
Erlangen 91469, GERMANY

Schlichting, Travis (Athlete, Baseball Player)
2202 Parkland Cv
Round Rock, TX 78681-4086, USA

Schlitter, Brian (Athlete, Baseball Player)
912 S Greenwood Ave
Park Ridge, IL 60068-4544, USA

Schlondorff, Volker (Director)
Studio Babelsberg
Postfach 900361
Potsdam 14439, GERMANY

Schlopy, Erik (Athlete, Olympic Athlete, Skier)
731 Martingale Ln
Park City, UT 84098-7559, USA

Schloredt, Robert S (Bob) (Athlete, Football Player)
1827 N 167th St
Shoreline, WA 98133-5505, USA

Schlossberg, Edwin (Writer)
The John F Kennedy Presidential Library & Museum
Columbia Point
New York, NY 02125

Schlossberg, Katie (Actor)
Talent Group
6300 Wilshire Blvd Ste 2100
Los Angeles, CA 90048-5282, USA

Schlossberg, Katle (Actor)
Talent Group
5670 Wilshire Blvd Ste 820
Los Angeles, CA 90036-5613, USA

Schlosser, Eric (Writer)
c/o Staff Member *Houghton Mifflin*
3 Park Ave Rm 3618
New York, NY 10016-5902, USA

Schlueter, Dale (Athlete, Basketball Player)
16021 NE 101st Way
Vancouver, WA 98682-1860, USA

Schluter, Poul H (Politician)
Frederiksberg Allee 66
Frederiksberg C 01820, DENMARK

Schmack, Brian (Athlete, Baseball Player)
504 E Wye Mesa
Brookings, SD 57006-4534, USA

Schmautz, Bobby (Athlete, Hockey Player)
19866 N 90th Ave
Peoria, AZ 85382-8678, USA

Schmelz, Al (Athlete, Baseball Player)
7406 E Camino Rayo De Luz
Scottsdale, AZ 85266-4295, USA

Schmelz, Al (Athlete, Baseball Player)
7406 E Camino Rayo De Luz
Scottsdale, AZ 85266-4295, USA

Schmemann, Serge (Journalist)
229 W 43rd St
Attn Editorial Dept
New York, NY 10036-3982, USA

Schmich, Mary (Journalist)
Chicago Tribune
160 N Stetson Ave
Chicago, IL 60601-6707, USA

Schmid, Kyle (Actor)
c/o Lisa Perkins *Baker Winokur Ryder Public Relations*
9100 Wilshire Blvd
W Tower #500
Beverly Hills, CA 90212-3415, USA

Schmid, Rudi (Misc)
211 Woodland Rd
Kentfield, CA 94904-2631, USA

Schmidgall, Jennifer (Athlete, Hockey Player, Olympic Athlete)
3640 Wooddale Ave S Unit 103
Minneapolis, MN 55416-5157, USA

Schmidt, Bob (Athlete, Football Player)
10005 Sky View Way Apt 2106
Fort Myers, FL 33913-6606, USA

Schmidt, Curt (Athlete, Baseball Player)
1516 Mustang Valley Dr
Billings, MT 59105-5513, USA

Schmidt, Dave (Athlete, Baseball Player)
26636 Portales Ln
Mission Viejo, CA 92691-5122, USA

Schmidt, Dave (Athlete, Baseball Player)
7172 N Serenoa Dr
Sarasota, FL 34241-9270, USA

Schmidt, Eric (Business Person)
c/o Staff Member *Google Inc*
1600 Amphitheatre Pkwy
Mountain View, CA 94043-1351, USA

Schmidt, Freddy (Athlete, Baseball Player)
128 Constitution Ave
Wind Gap, PA 18091-1119, USA

Schmidt, Hank (Athlete, Football Player)
5800 Lake Murray Blvd Unit 11
La Mesa, CA 91942-2525, USA

Schmidt, Harald (Athlete, Track Athlete)
Schulstr 11
Hasselroth 63594, GERMANY

Schmidt, Jason (Athlete, Baseball Player)
6539 E Cheney Dr
Paradise Valley, AZ 85253-3511, USA

Schmidt, Jean (Congressman, Politician)
2464 Rayburn Hob
Washington, DC 20515-4603, USA

Schmidt, Jeff (Athlete, Baseball Player)
1028 Seminole Hwy
Madison, WI 53711-3021, USA

Schmidt, Joseph P (Joe) (Athlete, Football Coach, Football Player)
226 Norcliff Dr
Bloomfield Hills, MI 48302-1556, USA

Schmidt, Kathryn (Kate) (Athlete, Track Athlete)
1008 Dexter St
Los Angeles, CA 90042-2248, USA

Schmidt, Kendall (Musician)
c/o Ed Solorzano *The Brand Partners*
6404 Wilshire Blvd Ste 500
Los Angeles, CA 90048-5507, USA

Schmidt, Kenneth (Actor)
c/o Staff Member *Coast to Coast Talent Group*
3350 Barham Blvd
Los Angeles, CA 90068-1404, USA

Schmidt, Kevin (Actor)
c/o David Eisenberg *Protege Entertainment*
710 E Angeleno Ave
Burbank, CA 91501-2213, USA

Schmidt, Mike (Athlete, Baseball Player)
c/o Staff Member *National Baseball Hall of Fame*
25 Main St
Cooperstown, NY 13326-1300, USA

Schmidt, Roy (Athlete, Football Player)
106 Annas Walk
Athens, GA 30606-7450, USA

Schmidt, Sam (Race Car Driver)
Treadway Racing
6017 W. 7lst St.
Indianapolis, IN 46278, USA

Schmidt, Steve (Race Car Driver)
Schmidt Racing
8405 E 30th St
Indianapolis, IN 46219-1411, USA

Schmidt, Terry (Athlete, Football Player)
150 Price Rd
Erwin, TN 37650-6461, USA

Schmidt, William (Bill) (Athlete, Track Athlete)
1809 Devonwood Ct
Knoxville, TN 37922-6233, USA

Schmidt, Wolfgang (Athlete, Track Athlete)
Birkheckenstr 116B
Stuttgart 70599, GERMANY

Schmidt, Wrenn (Actor)
c/o Dale Davis *Davis Spylios Management*
244 W 54th St Ste 707
New York, NY 10019-5515, USA

Schmidt-Weitzman, Violet (Athlete, Baseball Player)
225 S Mill St
Mishawaka, IN 46544-2002, USA

Schmiesing, Joe (Athlete, Football Player)
410 Oak Street Cir S Apt 123
Sauk Centre, MN 56378-1272, USA

Schmit, Timothy B (Musician)
William Morris Agency
1325 Avenue of the Americas
New York, NY 10019-6026, USA

Schmitt, Dr H Harrison (Astronaut)
PO Box 90730
Albuquerque, NM 87199-0730, USA

Schmitt, John (Athlete, Football Player)
2 Mayflower Rd
Glen Head, NY 11545-3120, USA

Schmitt, Martin (Skier)
Muhleschweg 4
VA-Tannehim 78052, GERMANY

Schmitz, Toby (Actor)
c/o Staff Member *Shanahan Management*
Level 3 Berman House
Surry Hills 02010, AUSTRALIA

Schmock, Jonathan (Actor)
c/o Judy Orbach *Judy O Productions*
6136 Glen Holly St
Hollywood, CA 90068-2338, USA

Schmoeller, David (Director)
3910 Woodhill Ave
Las Vegas, NV 89121-6245, USA

Schmoll, Steve (Athlete, Baseball Player)
4029 Chastain Dr
Melbourne, FL 32940-1232, USA

Schnabel, Julian (Artist, Director)
c/o Maha Dakhil *Creative Artists Agency (CAA)*
2000 Avenue of the Stars Ste 100
Los Angeles, CA 90067-4705, USA

Schnabel, Marco (Director)
c/o Staff Member *3 Arts Entertainment*
9460 Wilshire Blvd Fl 7
Beverly Hills, CA 90212-2713, USA

Schnackenberg, Roy L (Artist)
1919 N Orchard St
Chicago, IL 60614-5159, USA

Schnapp, Noah (Actor)
c/o Charlie Roina *Jill Fritzo Public Relations*
208 E 51st St # 305
New York, NY 10022-6557, USA

Schnarch, David (Writer)
c/o Staff Member *HarperCollins Publishers*
195 Broadway Fl 2
New York, NY 10007-3132, USA

Schnarre, Monika (Actor, Model)
Alex Stevens
137 N Larchmont Blvd # 259
Los Angeles, CA 90004-3704, USA

Schneck, Dave (Athlete, Baseball Player)
3891 Lehigh Dr
Northampton, PA 18067-9771, USA

Schneck, Mike (Athlete, Football Player)
110 Three Degree Rd
Allison Park, PA 15101, USA

Schneider, Andrew (Journalist)
c/o Richard Weitz *WME|IMG*
9601 Wilshire Blvd
Beverly Hills, CA 90210-5213, USA

Schneider, Bernd (Race Car Driver)
Team AMG Mercedes
Daimlerstr 1
Affalterbach 71563, GERMANY

Schneider, Bob (Musician)
c/o Val Wolfe *UTA Music/The Agency Group*
9336 Civic Center Dr
Beverly Hills, CA 90210-3604, USA

Schneider, Brian (Athlete, Baseball Player)
458 Rudder Cay Way
Jupiter, FL 33458-1647, USA

Schneider, Cory (Athlete, Hockey Player)
12 Preston Ct
Swampscott, MA 01907-1650

Schneider, Dan (Producer, Writer)
c/o Staff Member *WME|IMG*
9601 Wilshire Blvd
Beverly Hills, CA 90210-5213, USA

Schneider, Dan (Athlete, Baseball Player)
PO Box 2421
Tubac, AZ 85646-2421, USA

Schneider, Fred (Musician, Songwriter)
c/o Staff Member *Direct Management Group*
8332 Melrose Ave
Los Angeles, CA 90069-5420, USA

Schneider, Helen (Musician)
c/o Staff Member *UD Promotion*
Uwe Darkow
Hauptstr. 64-66
Essen-Kettwig 45219, Germany

Schneider, Helge (Actor)
Helge Schneider Enterprises
Schloßstr. 33
Mülheim/Ruhr D-45468, Germany

Schneider, Howie (Cartoonist)
United Feature Syndicate
200 Madison Ave
New York, NY 10016-3903, USA

Schneider, Jeff (Athlete, Baseball Player)
268 Pin Oak Dr
Geneseo, IL 61254-1944, USA

Schneider, John (Actor, Musician)
709 Heritage Square Dr
Madison, TN 37115-5915, USA

Schneider, Kurt Hugo (Internet Star, Musician)
c/o Zachary Druker *WME|IMG*
9601 Wilshire Blvd
Beverly Hills, CA 90210-5213, USA

Schneider, Mathieu (Athlete, Hockey Player)
1311 6th St
Manhattan Beach, CA 90266-6041, USA

Schneider, Max (Actor)
c/o Jeff Golenberg *Silver Lining Entertainment*
421 S Beverly Dr Fl 7
Beverly Hills, CA 90212-4408, USA

Schneider, Paul (Actor)
c/o Jillian Roscoe *ID Public Relations*
7060 Hollywood Blvd Fl 8th
Los Angeles, CA 90028-6021, USA

Schneider, Rob (Actor, Comedian, Producer)
c/o Stan Rosenfield *Stan Rosenfield & Associates*
2029 Century Park E Ste 1190
Los Angeles, CA 90067-2931, USA

Schneider, Vreni (Skier)
Dorf
Elm 08767, SWITZERLAND

Schneider, William (Buzz) (Athlete, Hockey Player, Olympic Athlete)
5656 Turtle Lake Rd
Saint Paul, MN 55126-4769, USA

Schneider, William ""Buzz"" (Athlete, Hockey Player)
5656 Turtle Lake Rd
Saint Paul, MN 55126-4769, USA

Schneider, William G (Misc)
National Research Council
2-65 Whitemarl Dr
Ottawa, ON K1L 8J9, CANADA

Schneiderman, Leon (Musician)
The Alliance for Democracy
21 Main St Ste 4
Hudson, MA 01749-2164, USA

Schnelker, Bob (Coach)
Philadelphia Eagles
1825 NW 104th St
Vancouver, WA 98685-5044, USA

Schnelldorfer, Manfred (Figure Skater)
Seydlitzstr 55
Munich 80993, GERMANY

Schnellenberger, Howard (Athlete, Coach, Football Coach, Football Player)
5109 N Ocean Blvd Apt G
Ocean Ridge, FL 33435-7066, USA

Schnetzer, Ben (Actor)
c/o Rhonda Price *Gersh*
41 Madison Ave Ste 3301
New York, NY 10010-2210, USA

Schnetzer, Stephen (Actor)
c/o Matthew Sullivan *Sullivan Talent Group*
305 W 105th St Apt 3B
New York, NY 10025-9116, USA

Schnitker, Mike (Athlete, Football Player)
PO Box 1469
Grand Lake, CO 80447-1469, USA

Schnittker, Richard (Dick) (Athlete, Basketball Player)
203 E Las Granadas
Green Valley, AZ 85614-2233, USA

Schobel, Frank (Actor, Musician)
Wielandstrasse 6
Berlin D-12623, Germany

Schochet, Bob (Cartoonist)
6 Sunset Road
Highland Mills, NY 10930, USA

Schock, Aaron (Congressman, Politician)
328 Cannon Hob
Washington, DC 20515-0543, USA

Schock, Gina (Musician)
PO Box 720160
San Francisco, CA 94172-0160, USA

Schock, Ron (Athlete, Hockey Player)
1360 Whalen Rd
Penfield, NY 14526-1918, USA

Schoeffling, Michael (Actor)
413 Crestmont Dr
Newfoundland, PA 18445-5203, USA

Schoelen, Jill (Actor)
Gold Marshak Liedtke
3500 W Olive Ave Ste 1400
Burbank, CA 91505-5512, USA

Schoen, Gerry (Athlete, Baseball Player)
13 Santa Fe
Prescott, AZ 86305-5068, USA

Schoen, Tom (Athlete, Football Player)
437 W Belmont Ave Apt 13
Chicago, IL 60657-4756, USA

Schoenbaechler, Andreas (Skier)
Muhlrustistr 2
Affoltern a A 08910, SWITZERLAND

Schoenborn, Christoph Cardinal (Religious Leader)
Wollzeile 2
Vienna 01010, AUSTRIA

Schoene, Russ (Athlete, Basketball Player)
1136 205th Ave NE
Sammamish, WA 98074-6654, USA

Schoeneweis, Scott (Athlete, Baseball Player)
10863 N 139th St
Scottsdale, AZ 85259-5046, USA

Schoenfeld, Jim (Athlete, Hockey Player)
New York Rangers
2 Penn Plz Fl 22
New York, NY 10121-2299

Schoenfeld, Jim (Athlete, Coach, Hockey Player)
17702 N 95th St
Scottsdale, AZ 85255-6082

Schoenfield, Al (Athlete, Swimmer)
75 Santa Rosa St
San Luis Obispo, CA 93405-1819, USA

Schoenfield, Dana (Swimmer)
7734 E Lakeview Trl
Orange, CA 92869-2446, USA

Schoenke, Raymond F (Athlete, Football Player)
21151 Woodfield Rd
Laytonsville, MD 20882-4847, USA

Schoffer, Nicolas (Artist)
Villa Des Arts
15 Rue Hegesippe-Moreau
Paris 75018, FRANCE

Schofield, Annabel (Actor)
Special Artists Agency
345 N Maple Dr # 302
Beverly Hills, CA 90210-3869, USA

Schofield, Dick (Athlete, Baseball Player)
17703 Gardenview Place Ct
Glencoe, MO 63038-1495, USA

Schofield, Dwight (Athlete, Hockey Player)
9024 Cardinal Ter
Saint Louis, MO 63144-1103

Schofield, John (Actor, Producer)

Scholder, Fritz (Artist)
118 Cattletrack Road
Scottsdale, AZ 85251, USA

Scholes, Clarke (Athlete, Olympic Athlete, Swimmer)
20671 Wedgewood Dr
Grosse Pointe Woods, MI 48236-1560, USA

Schollander, Don (Athlete, Olympic Athlete, Swimmer)
3576 Lakeview Blvd
Lake Oswego, OR 97035-5544, USA

Schollander, Donald A (Don) (Swimmer)
3576 Lakeview Blvd
Lake Oswego, OR 97035-5544, USA

Scholten, Jim (Music Group, Musician)
Sawyer Brown Inc
5200 Old Harding Rd
Franklin, TN 37064-9406, USA

Scholtz, Bob (Athlete, Football Player)
6721 S 71st East Ave
Tulsa, OK 74133-1818, USA

Scholtz, Bruce (Athlete, Football Player)
6607 Cypress Pt N
Austin, TX 78746-7104, USA

Scholz, Tom (Musician)
c/o Gail Parenteau *Parenteau Guidance*
132 E 35th St # J
New York, NY 10016-3892, USA

Schomberg, A Thomas (Artist)
4923 Snowberry Ln
Evergreen, CO 80439-5622, USA

Schon, Kyra (Actor)
104 Evergreen Dr
Bedford, PA 15522-6510, USA

Schon, Neal (Musician)
c/o Larry Solters *Scoop Marketing*
12754 Ventura Blvd Ste C
Studio City, CA 91604-2441, USA

Schon, Neil (Musician)
c/o Staff Member *WME|IMG*
9601 Wilshire Blvd
Beverly Hills, CA 90210-5213, USA

Schoneberger, Barbara (Correspondent)
Kick Media AG
Eifelstrasse 31
Koln 50677, Germany

Schonhuber, Franz (Correspondent)
Europaburo
Fraunhoferstr 23
Munich 80469, GERMANY

Schoofs, Mark (Journalist)
Village Voice
32 Cooper Sq
Editorial Dept
New York, NY 10003-7117, USA

Schooler, Mike (Athlete, Baseball Player)
519 N Buttonwood St
Anaheim, CA 92805-2226, USA

Schools, Dave (Musician)
11230 Occidental Rd
Sebastopol, CA 95472-9650, USA

Schoon, Milton (Athlete, Basketball Player)
1218 Blaine Ave
Janesville, WI 53545-1834, USA

Schoonmaker, Jerry (Athlete, Baseball Player)
1432 Muirfield Dr
Dyer, IN 46311-1290, USA

Schorer, Jane (Journalist)
Des Moines Register
Editorial Dept
PO Box 957
Des Moines, IA 50304, USA

Schorr, Bill (Cartoonist)
United Feature Syndicate
200 Madison Ave
New York, NY 10016-3903, USA

Schott, Stephen (Baseball Player)
Oakland A's
12330 Hilltop Dr
Los Altos Hills, CA 94024-5218, USA

Schott, Steve (Baseball Player)
12330 Hilltop Dr
Los Altos Hills, CA 94024-5218

Schotte, Jan P Cardinal (Religious Leader)
Sinodo Dei Vescovi
00120, VATICAN CITY

Schottenheimer, Marty (Athlete, Football Coach, Football Player)
19825 N Cove Rd Ste B
Cornelius, NC 28031-0149, USA

Schourek, Pete (Athlete, Baseball Player)
14636 Lilva Dr
Centreville, VA 20120-1338, USA

Schrader, Ken (Race Car Driver)
Ken Schrader Racing Incorporated
PO Box 5430
Concord, NC 28027-1507, USA

Schrader, Kurt (Congressman, Politician)
314 Cannon Hob
Washington, DC 20515-0404, USA

Schrader, Maria (Actor)
c/o Joel Kleinman *Baier/Kleinman International*
3575 Cahuenga Blvd W Ste 500
Los Angeles, CA 90068-1344, USA

Schrader, Paul (Actor, Director, Writer)
c/o Frank Wuliger *Gersh*
9465 Wilshire Blvd Ste 600
Beverly Hills, CA 90212-2605, USA

Schrager, Ian (Business Person)
Ian Schrager Co
818 Greenwich St
New York, NY 10014-5134, USA

Schram, Bitty (Actor)
c/o David Williams *David Williams Management*
269 S Beverly Dr # 1408
Beverly Hills, CA 90212-3851, USA

Schram, Jessy (Actor)
c/o Mitchell Gossett *Industry Entertainment Partners*
955 Carrillo Dr Ste 300
Los Angeles, CA 90048-5400, USA

Schramka, Paul (Athlete, Baseball Player)
W180N7890 Town Hall Rd Apt A323
Menomonee Falls, WI 53051-4055, USA

Schramm, David (Actor)
3521 Berry Dr
Studio City, CA 91604-3882, USA

Schranz, Karl (Skier)
Hotel Garni
Saint Anton 06580, AUSTRIA

Schreck, Heidi (Actor, Writer)
c/o Gregory Shephard *Writ Large*
5815 W Sunset Blvd Ste 401
Los Angeles, CA 90028-6482, USA

Schreiber, Adam (Athlete, Football Player)
2520 River Summit Dr
Duluth, GA 30097-2255, USA

Schreiber, Larry (Athlete, Football Player)
388 Albion Ave
Woodside, CA 94062-3603, USA

Schreiber, Liev (Actor)
427 Washington St # 2EW
New York, NY 10013-1735, USA

Schreiber, Pablo (Actor)
c/o Frank Frattaroli *Circle of Confusion*
8931 Ellis Ave
Los Angeles, CA 90034-3336, USA

Schreiber, Ted (Athlete, Baseball Player)
116 Nantucket Is
Centerville, GA 31028-8547, USA

Schremmer, Patty (Golfer)
714 Siesta Key Cir
Sarasota, FL 34242-1250, USA

Schremp, Bob (Athlete, Football Player)
PO Box 584
Bellflower, CA 90707-0584, USA

Schremp, Rob (Athlete, Hockey Player)
303 Phillips St
Fulton, NY 13069-1514

Schrempf, Detlef (Athlete, Basketball Player, Olympic Athlete)
10700 NE 4th St Unit 3402
Bellevue, WA 98004-5946, USA

Schrempp, Jurgen E (Business Person)
Daimler-Chrysler AG
Plieningerstra
Stuttgart 70546, GERMANY

Schrenk, Steve (Athlete, Baseball Player)
2547 Oakboro Ln
Charlotte, NC 28214-6900, USA

Schreyer, Cindy (Golfer)
18 Cottage Dr
Newnan, GA 30265-5513, USA

Schrieber, Paul (Athlete, Baseball Player)
9715 E Gary Rd
Scottsdale, AZ 85260-6225, USA

Schriesheim, Alan (Misc)
1440 N Lake Shore Dr Apt 31AC
Chicago, IL 60610-5927, USA

Schroder, Bob (Athlete, Baseball Player)
2810 Jefferson Dr
Hattiesburg, MS 39402-2047, USA

Schroder, Chris (Athlete, Baseball Player)
2710 W Oklahoma Ave
Guthrie, OK 73044-6314, USA

Schroder, Jochen (Actor)
Postfach 10 23 46
Bochum D-44723, Germany

Schroder, Rick (Actor)
c/o Staff Member *Ricky Schroder Productions*
22603 Pacific Coast Hwy # 824
Malibu, CA 90265-5036, USA

Schroeder, Barbet (Director, Producer)
8033 W Sunset Blvd # 51
West Hollywood, CA 90046-2401, USA

Schroeder, Bill (Athlete, Baseball Player)
S75W17724 Harbor Cir
Muskego, WI 53150-9182, USA

Schroeder, Carly (Actor)
c/o Render Hocker *Play Management*
220-807 Powell St
Vancouver, BC V6A 1H7, CANADA

Schroeder, Dorsey (Race Car Driver)
PO Box 943
RR #1
Osage Beach, MO 65065-0943, USA

Schroeder, Gene (Athlete, Football Player)
10700 Park Pl UNIT 2312
Saint John, IN 46373-8671, USA

Schroeder, Gerhard (Misc)
Bundeskanzlerant
Willy-Brandt-Str 1
Berlin 10557, GERMANY

Schroeder, Jay (Athlete, Football Player)
1730 Stonebridge Dr Unit 21
Saint George, UT 84770-5099, USA

Schroeder, Jeret (Race Car Driver)
529 Old Mill Rd
Millersville, MD 21108-1327, USA

Schroeder, John (Athlete, Golfer)
PO Box 2768
Del Mar, CA 92014-5768, USA

Schroeder, Kenneth L (Business Person)
KLA-Tencor Corp
160 Rio Robles
San Jose, CA 95134-1813, USA

Schroeder, Patricia S (Politician)
c/o Staff Member *21st Century Speakers*
1352 Lake Ave
Gouldsboro, PA 18424, USA

Schroeder, Paul W (Writer)
University of Illinois
810 S Wright St Rm 119
History Dept
Urbana, IL 61801-3655, USA

Schroeder, Terry (Athlete, Coach)
4901 Lewis Rd
Agoura Hills, CA 91301-2453, USA

Schroll, William (Athlete, Football Player)
1640 Oakley Dr
Baton Rouge, LA 70806-8623, USA

Schrom, Ken (Athlete, Baseball Player)
1002 Black Diamond Ct
Portland, TX 78374-4162, USA

Schroy, Ken (Athlete, Football Player)
79 Russell Rd
Garden City, NY 11530-1933, USA

Schu, Rick (Athlete, Baseball Player)
2013 Driftwood Cir
El Dorado Hills, CA 95762-3744, USA

Schuba, Beatrice (Trixi) (Figure Skater)
Giorgengasse 2/1/8
Vienna 01190, AUSTRIA

Schubert, Eric (Athlete, Football Player)
722 Homestead Ave
Maybrook, NY 12543-1308, USA

Schubert, Mark (Coach, Swimmer)
PO Box 479
Surfside, CA 90743-0479, USA

Schubert, Steve (Athlete, Football Player)
7 Douglas Dr
Candia, NH 03034-2304, USA

Schuck, Anett (Athlete)
Defoestry 6A
Leipzig 04159, GERMANY

Schuck, John (Actor)
1501 Broadway Ste 703
New York, NY 10036-5501, USA

Schueler, Jon R (Artist)
40 W 22nd St
New York, NY 10010-5806, USA

Schueler, Ron (Athlete, Baseball Player)
7651 E Fledgling Dr
Scottsdale, AZ 85255-7710, USA

Schuenke, Donald J (Business Person)
Nortel Networks Corp
8200 Dixie Rd
Brampton, ON L6T 4B8, CANADA

Schuerholz, John (Baseball Player)
Atlanta Braves
1025 Royal Dr
Canonsburg, PA 15317-5004, USA

Schuessel, Wolfgang (Misc)
Chancellor's Office
Ballhausplatz 2
Vienna 01014, AUSTRIA

Schuessler, Jack (Business Person)
Wendy's International
4288 W Dublin Granville Rd
Dublin, OH 43017-2093, USA

Schuh, Harry F (Athlete, Football Player)
2309 Massey Rd
Memphis, TN 38119-6516, USA

Schuh, Jeff (Athlete, Football Player)
5550 Vagabond Ln N
Minneapolis, MN 55446-1323, USA

Schuhmacher, John (Athlete, Football Player)
6000 Reims Rd Apt 3006
Houston, TX 77036-3053, USA

Schul, Bob (Athlete, Olympic Athlete, Track Athlete)
320 Wisteria Dr
Oakwood, OH 45419-3553, USA

Schuldt, Travis (Actor)
c/o Robert Marsala *Wishlab*
195 S Beverly Dr Ste 414
Beverly Hills, CA 90212-3044, USA

Schule, Emilia (Actor)
c/o Harriet Long *Olivia Bell Management*
191 Wardour St.
London W1F 8ZE, UNITED KINGDOM

Schuler, Carolyn (Swimmer)
26552 Via Del Sol
Mission Viejo, CA 92691-6125, USA

Schuler, Dave (Athlete, Baseball Player)
3694 El Segundo Ct
Naples, FL 34109-1398, USA

Schulhofer, Scotty (Misc)
PO Box 1581
Waynesville, NC 28786-1581, USA

Schull, Amanda (Actor)
c/o Jessica Katz *Katz Public Relations*
14527 Dickens St
Sherman Oaks, CA 91403-3756, USA

Schull, Rebecca (Actor)
Writers & Artists
8383 Wilshire Blvd # 550
Beverly Hills, CA 90211-2425, USA

Schuller, Grete (Artist)
8 Barstow Rd Apt 7G
Great Neck, NY 11021-3547, USA

Schullstrom, Erik (Athlete, Baseball Player)
1425 Court St
Alameda, CA 94501-3145, USA

Schulman, Ariel (Director, Producer)
c/o Staff Member *Supermarche*
18 E 16th St Fl 4
New York, NY 10003-3111, USA

Schulman, Yaniv (Nev) (Producer)
c/o Charlotte Burke *ID Public Relations (NY)*
40 Wall St Fl 51
New York, NY 10005-1385, USA

Schult, Jurgen (Athlete, Track Athlete)
Drosselweg 6
Leuna 19069, GERMANY

Schulte, Greg (Baseball Player)
Arizona Diamondbacks
12927 W Fetlock Trl
Peoria, AZ 85383-3938, USA

Schulte, Paxton (Athlete, Hockey Player)
RR 1
Onoway, AB T0E 1V0, Canada

Schulte, Richard (Athlete, Football Player)
1216 N Kenneth Pl
Chandler, AZ 85226-7210, USA

Schulters, Lance (Athlete, Football Player)
594 Grant Ave
Roselle, NJ 07203-2911, USA

Schultz, Barney (Athlete, Baseball Player)
790 Woodlane Rd
Beverly, NJ 08010-1902, USA

Schultz, Bill (Athlete, Football Player)
10302 Lakeland Dr
Fishers, IN 46037-9323, USA

Schultz, Boomer (Race Car Driver)
Schultz Sports Marketing
PO Box 8648
South Lake Tahoe, CA 96158-1648, USA

Schultz, Buddy (Athlete, Baseball Player)
5629 E Thunderbird Rd
Scottsdale, AZ 85254-3741, USA

Schultz, Dave (Athlete, Hockey Player)
505 Alpine Ct
Mays Landing, NJ 08330-2213, USA

Schultz, Dave (Race Car Driver)
2365 Lazy River Ln
Fort Myers, FL 33905-2242, USA

Schultz, Dwight (Actor)
23210 Beaumont St
Valencia, CA 91354-2139, USA

Schultz, George (Athlete, Baseball Player)
400 Fern Brook Ln # 218
Mount Laurel, NJ 08054-9542, USA

Schultz, Howard (Business Person)
Starbucks Corp
2401 Utah Ave S Ste 1
Seattle, WA 98134-1498, USA

Schultz, John (Director)
c/o Staff Member *Creative Artists Agency (CAA)*
2000 Avenue of the Stars Ste 100
Los Angeles, CA 90067-4705, USA

Schultz, John (Athlete, Football Player)
503 Skyline Dr
Vestal, NY 13850-5321, USA

Schultz, Kurt (Athlete, Football Player)
5075 Rockledge Dr
Clarence, NY 14031-2426, USA

Schultz, Mark (Musician)
c/o Staff Member *Lucid Artist Management*
256 Seaboard Ln Ste C102
Franklin, TN 37067-2889, USA

Schultz, Michael A (Director)
Chrystalite Productions
PO Box 1940
Santa Monica, CA 90406-1940, USA

Schultz, Nick (Athlete, Hockey Player)
201 Downey St
Strasbourg, SK SOG 4VO, Canada

Schultz, Peter G (Misc)
Salk Research Institute
10550 N Torrey Pines Rd
La Jolla, CA 92037-1000, USA

Schulz, Axel (Athlete, Wrestler)
Zehmeplatz 10
Frankfurt/Oder D-15230, Germany

Schulz, Jeff (Athlete, Baseball Player)
1167 S Stockwell Rd
Evansville, IN 47714-0749, USA

Schulz, Jody (Athlete, Football Player)
222 Schulz Ln
Chester, MD 21619-2658, USA

Schulz, Kurt (Athlete, Football Player)
5075 Rockledge Dr
Clarence, NY 14031-2426, USA

Schulze, Don (Athlete, Baseball Player)
915 Myrtle Ave
Dixon, IL 61021-1429, USA

Schulze, Matt (Actor)
c/o David Gardner *Artists First*
9465 Wilshire Blvd Ste 900
Beverly Hills, CA 90212-2608, USA

Schulze, Paul (Actor)
c/o Staff Member *Kyle Fritz Management*
6325 Heather Dr
Los Angeles, CA 90068-1633, USA

Schulze, Richard (Business Person)
Best Buy Co
7601 Penn Ave S
Minneapolis, MN 55423-3683, USA

Schumacher, Gregg (Athlete, Football Player)
104 Surfview Dr Apt 2108
Palm Coast, FL 32137-2348, USA

Schumacher, Joel (Director)
Greenfield & Selvaggi
11766 Wilshire Blvd Ste 1610
Los Angeles, CA 90025-6565, USA

Schumacher, Kelly (Basketball Player)
Indiana Fever
125 S Pennsylvania St
Conseco Fieldhouse
Indianapolis, IN 46204-3610, USA

Schumacher, Kurt (Athlete, Football Player)
4533 Regency Crossing
Southport, NC 28461-8087, USA

Schumacher, Michael (Race Car Driver)
M S Office
Ave du Mont-Blanc 14B
Gland 01196, SWITZERLAND

Schumacher, Ralf (Race Car Driver)
Weber Mgmt
Wentage
Oxfordshire OX12.0DQ, UNITED KINGDOM (UK)

Schumacher, Tony (Race Car Driver)
PO Box 308
1134 Uufflems Le
Chateau, SWITZERLAND

Schumaker, Jared (Skip) (Athlete, Baseball Player)
6 Illuminata Ln
Ladera Ranch, CA 92694-1376, USA

Schuman, Allan L (Business Person)
Ecolab Inc
370 Wabasha St N Ste 1700
Ecolab Center
Saint Paul, MN 55102-1334, USA

Schuman, Melissa (Actor)
c/o Staff Member *Kazarian, Measures, Ruskin & Associates*
5200 Lankershim Blvd Ste 820
N Hollywood, CA 91601-3194, USA

Schuman, Tom (Musician)
PO Box 435
Highland Mills, NY 10930-0435, USA

Schumann, Ralf (Misc)
Steomach 22
Stockheim 97640, GERMANY

Schumer, Amy (Actor, Comedian)
c/o Amanda Silverman *The Lede Company*
401 Broadway Ste 206
New York, NY 10013-3033, USA

Schumer, Charles (Politician)
9 Prospect Park W Apt Lob
Brooklyn, NY 11215-1763, USA

Schur, Michael (Writer)
c/o Staff Member *3 Arts Entertainment*
9460 Wilshire Blvd Fl 7
Beverly Hills, CA 90212-2713, USA

Schurig, Roger (Athlete, Basketball Player)
1031 Brookside
Greensboro, GA 30642-6814, USA

Schurman, M F (Athlete, Hockey Player)
301 Beaver St
Summerside, PE C1N 2A2, Canada

Schurmann, Petra (Swimmer)
Max-Emanuel-Str 7
Starnberg 82319, GERMANY

Schurr, Wavne (Athlete, Baseball Player)
10030W 500 S
Hudson, IN 46747-9705, USA

Schurr, Wayne (Athlete, Baseball Player)
10030 W 500 S
Hudson, IN 46747-9705, USA

Schussler Florenza, Elisabeth (Writer)
Notre Dame University
Theology Dept
Notre Dame, IN 46556, USA

Schuster, Rudolf (President)
President's Office
Nam Slobody 1
Bratislava 91370, SLOVAKIA

Schutt, Rod (Athlete, Hockey Player)
1450 Gennings St
Sudbury, ON P3E 6J2, Canada

Schutz, Carl (Athlete, Baseball Player)
PO Box 162
French Settlement, LA 70733-0162, USA

Schutz, Stephen (Artist)
Blue Mountain Arts Inc
PO Box 4549
Boulder, CO 80306-4549, USA

Schutz, Susan Polis (Writer)
Blue Mountain Arts Inc
PO Box 4549
Boulder, CO 80306-4549, USA

Schuur, Diane (Music Group, Musician)
Paul Canter Enterprises
33042 Ocean Rdg
Dana Point, CA 92629-1078, USA

Schwab, Charles (Business Person)
PO Box 620070
Redwood City, CA 94062-0070, USA

Schwab, Corey (Athlete, Hockey Player)
San Jose Sharks
525 W Santa Clara St
San Jose, CA 95113-1500

Schwab, Corey (Athlete, Hockey Player)
20633 76th Ave SE
Snohomish, WA 98296-5169

Schwabe, Mike (Athlete, Baseball Player)
13341 Presidio Pl
Tustin, CA 92782-8608, USA

Schwall, Don (Athlete, Baseball Player)
741 Wolverine Rd
Mason, ML 15044-7425, USA

Schwantz, Jim (Athlete, Football Player)
1047 W Chatham Dr
Palatine, IL 60067-5817, USA

Schwarthoff, Florian (Athlete, Track Athlete)
Fischweiher 51
Heppenheim 64646, GERMANY

Schwartz, Ben (Actor)
c/o Staff Member *Haven Entertainment*
8111 Beverly Blvd Ste 201
Los Angeles, CA 90048-4531, USA

Schwartz, Don (Athlete, Football Player)
19410 NE Redmond Rd
Redmond, WA 98053, USA

Schwartz, Geoff (Athlete, Football Player)
c/o Michael McCartney *Priority Sports & Entertainment (Chicago)*
325 N La Salle Dr Ste 650
Chicago, IL 60654-8182, USA

Schwartz, Ivan E (Producer)
c/o Staff Member *Greater Cleveland Film Commission*
1301 E 9th St Ste 120
Cleveland, OH 44114-1800, USA

Schwartz, Josh (Producer, Writer)
c/o Greg Hodes *WME|IMG*
9601 Wilshire Blvd
Beverly Hills, CA 90210-5213, USA

Schwartz, Kevin (Race Car Driver)
606A Performance Rd
Mooresville, NC 28115-9595, USA

Schwartz, Lloyd (Journalist)
27 Pennsylvania Ave
Somerville, MA 02145-2217, USA

Schwartz, Maxime (Misc)
Institut Pasteur
25-28 Rue du Docteur-Roux
Paris Cedex 15 75724, FRANCE

Schwartz, Mitchell (Athlete, Football Player)

Schwartz, Neil J (Actor)
4757 Regalo Bello St
Las Vegas, NV 89135-2536, USA

Schwartz, Randy (Athlete, Baseball Player)
757 El Rancho Dr
El Cajon, CA 92019-1141, USA

Schwartz, Scott (Actor)
Baseball Cards, Movie Collectibles Etc
4619 Lakeview Canyon Rd
Westlake Village, CA 91361-4028, USA

Schwartz, Stephen L (Composer, Music Group, Musician, Songwriter, Writer)
Chaplin Entertainment
545 8th Ave # 14
New York, NY 10018-4307, USA

Schwartzman, Jason (Actor)
c/o Matthew Labov *Forefront Media*
1669 Virginia Rd
Los Angeles, CA 90019-5935, USA

Schwartzman, Robert (Actor)
c/o Joanne Roberts Wiles *ICM Partners*
10250 Constellation Blvd Fl 7
Los Angeles, CA 90067-6207, USA

Schwarz, Jeff (Athlete, Baseball Player)
912 Club Dr
Palm Beach Gardens, FL 33418-7065, USA

Schwarzenegger, Arnold (Actor, Politician)
PO Box 1234
Santa Monica, CA 90406-1234, USA

Schwarzenegger, Katherine (Writer)
c/o Hilary Williams *Digital Brand Architects*
750 N San Vicente Blvd Ste RE950
W Hollywood, CA 90069-5700, USA

Schwarzenegger, Patrick (Actor, Model)
c/o Christopher Hart *United Talent Agency (UTA)*
9336 Civic Center Dr
Beverly Hills, CA 90210-3604, USA

Schwarzman, Stephen (Steve) (Business Person)
The Blackstone Group
345 Park Ave Ste 1100
New York, NY 10154-1703, USA

Schwarzman, Steve (Business Person)
Blackstone Group
345 Park Ave Ste 1100
New York, NY 10154-1703, USA

Schwedes, Gerhard (Athlete, Football Player)
PO Box 570
Clayton, NY 13624-0570, USA

Schwedes, Scott (Athlete, Football Player)
6871 Claret Cir
Fayetteville, NY 13066-1048, USA

Schweickart, Rusty (Astronaut)
20 Sunnyside Ave Ste 427
Mill Valley, CA 94941-1933, USA

Schweig, Eric (Actor)
Prime Talent
PO Box 5163 Stn Terminal
Vancouver, BC V6B 4B2, CANADA

Schweiger, Til (Actor, Director, Producer)
c/o Staff Member *Barefoot Films*
Winsstr. 53
Berlin 10405, GERMANY

Schweighofer, Matthias (Actor)
c/o Martina Jansen *Players Agentur Management*
Sophienstrasse 21
Berlin 10178, GERMANY

Schweikert, David (Congressman, Politician)
1205 Longworth Hob
Washington, DC 20515-1704, USA

Schweikert, J E (Religious Leader)
Old Roman Catholic Church
4200 N Kedvale Ave
Chicago, IL 60641-2215, USA

Schweinsteiger, Bastian (Soccer Player)
FC Bayern Munich
Attention Bastian Schweinsteiger
Säbener Strasse 51
Munich 81547, GERMANY

Schweitz, John (Athlete, Basketball Player)
813 Smith Dr
Florence, SC 29501-5979, USA

Schwenke, Brian (Athlete, Football Player)
c/o Doug Hendrickson *Relativity Sports*
2029 Century Park E Ste 1550
Century City, CA 90067-3000, USA

Schwentke, Robert (Director)
c/o Fabian Haslob *Players Agentur Management*
Sophienstrasse 21
Berlin 10178, GERMANY

Schwertsik, Kurt (Composer)
Doblinger Music
Dorotheerhgasse 10
Vienna 01011, AUSTRIA

Schwery, Henry Cardinal (Religious Leader)
Bishoporic of Sion
CP 2068
Sion 2 01950, SWITZERLAND

Schwimmer, David (Actor)
c/o Ina Treciokas *Slate PR*
901 N Highland Ave
W Hollywood, CA 90038-2412, USA

Schwimmer, Lacey-Mae (Actor)
c/o Ben Russo *EMC / Bowery*
8356 Fountain Ave Apt E1
W Hollywood, CA 90069-2968, USA

Schygulla, Hanna (Actor)
ZBF Agentur
Leopoldstr 19
Munich 80802, GERMANY

Schypinski, Jerry (Athlete, Baseball Player)
28014 Shadowood Ln
Harrison Township, MI 48045-2246, USA

Scialfa, Patty (Music Group, Musician)
c/o Staff Member *Sony/BMG Music (NY)*
550 Madison Ave
New York, NY 10022-3211, USA

Sciambi, Jon (Baseball Player)
540 West Ave Apt 1813

Sciarra, John (Athlete, Football Player)
404 Morning Star Ln
Newport Beach, CA 92660-5711, USA

Scifres, Mike (Athlete, Football Player)
c/o Harold C Lewis *National Sports Agency*
12181 Prichard Farm Rd
Maryland Heights, MO 63043-4203, USA

Scifres, Steve (Athlete, Football Player)
2026 Northglen Dr
Colorado Springs, CO 80909-1629, USA

Sciole, Jennifer (Actor, Producer)
c/o Steve Honig *Honig Company, The*
4804 Laurel Canyon Blvd # 828
Studio City, CA 91607-3717, USA

Scioli, Brad (Football Player)
Indianapolis Colts
5433 Bay Harbor Dr
Indianapolis, IN 46254-4510, USA

Sciorra, Annabella (Actor)
c/o Chris Kanarick *ID Public Relations (NY)*
40 Wall St Fl 51
New York, NY 10005-1385, USA

Scioscia, Michael L (Mike) (Athlete, Baseball Player, Coach)
1915 Falling Star Ave
Westlake Village, CA 91362-5284, USA

Scissor Sisters (Music Group)
c/o Marty Diamond *Paradigm*
140 Broadway Ste 2600
New York, NY 10005-1011, USA

Sciutto, Nellie (Actor)
c/o Ted Schachter *Schachter Entertainment*
1157 S Beverly Dr Fl 2
Los Angeles, CA 90035-1119, USA

S Club 7 (Music Group)
c/o Staff Member *Creative Artists Agency (CAA)*
2000 Avenue of the Stars Ste 100
Los Angeles, CA 90067-4705, USA

Scobee, Josh (Athlete, Football Player)
c/o Ken Harris *Optimum Sports Management*
3225 S Macdill Ave Ste 330
Tampa, FL 33629-8171, USA

Scodelario, Kaya (Actor)
c/o Kate Staddon *Curtis Brown Ltd*
28-29 Hay Market
Hay Market House
London SW1Y 4SP, UNITED KINGDOM

Scofield, Dino (Actor)
3330 Barham Blvd Ste 103
Los Angeles, CA 90068-1476, USA

Scofield, John (Musician)
International Music Network
278 Main St
Gloucester, MA 01930-6022, USA

Scofield, Paul (Actor)
Gables
Balcombe
Sussex RH17 6ND, UNITED KINGDOM (UK)

Scoggins, Matt (Swimmer)
4900 Calhoun Canyon Loop
Austin, TX 78735-6417, USA

Scoggins, Tracy (Actor)
c/o Staff Member *Bette Smith Management*
499 N Canon Dr
Beverly Hills, CA 90210-4887, USA

Scola, Angelo Cardinal (Religious Leader)
Archdiocese
S Marco 320/A
Venezia 30124, ITALY

Scolari, Luiz Felipe (Football Coach)
FC Bunyodkor
3 Beruniy St
Shaykhontohur District
Tashkent, Uzbekistan

Scolari, Peter (Actor)
c/o Christopher Wright *Wright Entertainment*
14724 Ventura Blvd Ste 1201
Sherman Oaks, CA 91403-3512, USA

Scollay, Gabrielle (Actor)
c/o Fleur Griffin *Morrissey Management*
16 Princess Ave
Rosebery
Sydney NSW 02018, AUSTRALIA

Scolnik, Glenn (Athlete, Football Player)
301 Willowgate Dr
Indianapolis, IN 46260-1476, USA

Sconiers, Daryl (Athlete, Baseball Player)
15985 Hibiscus St
Fontana, CA 92335-4460, USA

Scorpions (Music Group)
c/o Steve Martin *Agency for the Performing Arts*
135 W 50th St Fl 17
New York, NY 10020-1201, USA

Scorsese, Martin (Director)
c/o Staff Member *Sikelia Productions*
110 W 57th St Fl 5
New York, NY 10019-3319, USA

Scorsese, Nicolette (Actor)
c/o Gregory (Greg) Mayo *Orange Grove Group, The*
12178 Ventura Blvd Ste 205
Studio City, CA 91604-2540, USA

Scorupco, Izabella (Actor)
c/o Anne Woodward *Authentic Talent & Literary Management*
3615 Eastham Dr # 650
Culver City, CA 90232-2410, USA

Scott, Adam (Actor)
c/o Christie Smith *Rise Management*
6338 Wilshire Blvd
Los Angeles, CA 90048-5002, USA

Scott, Adam (Athlete, Golfer)
The Adam Scott Company Pty Ltd.
PO Box 671
Auburn, ME 04212-0671, Australia

Scott, Alvin (Athlete, Basketball Player)
5786 W Townley Ave
Glendale, AZ 85302-4612, USA

Scott, Andrew (Actor)
c/o Clair Dobbs *CLD Communications*
4 Broadway Ct
The Broadway
London SW191RG, UNITED KINGDOM

Scott, Andy (Musician)
DCM International
296 Nether St
Finchley
London N3 1RJ, UNITED KINGDOM (UK)

Scott, Arthur (Athlete, Football Player)
209 Lincoln Ave
Conshohocken, PA 19428-2529, USA

Scott, Ashley (Actor)
c/o Peter Gallagher *Gallagher Management*
955 Carrillo Dr Ste 100
Los Angeles, CA 90048-5400, USA

Scott, Austin (Congressman, Politician)
516 Cannon Hob
Washington, DC 20515-2601, USA

Scott, Bo (Athlete, Football Player)
1301 Fountain Ln
Apt 1
Columbus, OH 43213, USA

Scott, Bobby (Athlete, Football Player)
9496 Whippoorwill Ln
Mason, OH 45040-9722, USA

Scott, Byron (Athlete, Basketball Player, Coach)
668 Euclid Ave Unit 527
Cleveland, OH 44114-3014, USA

Scott, Camilla (Actor)
23773 Via Canon Unit 201
Newhall, CA 91321-4632

Scott, Campbell (Actor)
6 Westwoods Road 1
Sharon, CT 06069-2225, USA

Scott, Captain E Winston (Astronaut)
150 W University Blvd Attn
Deancllgofaeronautics
Florida Institute of Technology
Melbourne, FL 32901-6982, USA

Scott, Carlos (Athlete, Football Player)
RR 1 Box 346
Hempstead, TX 77445, USA

Scott, Chad (Athlete, Football Player)
18526 Reliant Dr
Gaithersburg, MD 20879-5421, USA

Scott, Chris (Athlete, Football Player)
c/o Chad Speck *Allegiant Athletic Agency*
35 Market Sq Ste 201
Knoxville, TN 37902-1420, USA

Scott, Chuck (Athlete, Football Player)
875 Landover Xing
Suwanee, GA 30024-3045, USA

Scott, Clarence (Athlete, Football Player)
3-17-6 NishiAzabu Regency
Apt 202
Minato-ku, Tokyo, Japan

Scott, Clarence (Athlete, Football Player)
216 Sisson Ave NE
Atlanta, GA 30317-1422, USA

Scott, Clyde L (Smackover) (Athlete, Football Player, Track Athlete)
12840 Rivercrest Dr
Little Rock, AR 72212-1446, USA

Scott, Colonel David (Astronaut)
6033 W Century Blvd Ste 400
Scott Science and Technology Inc
Los Angeles, CA 90045-6416, USA

Scott, Dale (Athlete, Baseball Player)
1283 SW Cardinell Dr
Portland, OR 97201-3114, USA

Scott, Dale (Baseball Player)
1283 SW Cardinell Dr
Portland, OR 97201-3114, USA

Scott, Dale (Athlete, Baseball Player)
1283 SW Cardinell Dr
Portland, OR 97201-3114, USA

Scott, Darin (Actor, Director)
c/o Rich Freeman *Code Entertainment*
280 S Beverly Dr Ste 513
Beverly Hills, CA 90212-3908, USA

Scott, Darnay (Athlete, Football Player)
13151 Scabard Pl
San Diego, CA 92128-4055, USA

Scott, Darryl (Athlete, Baseball Player)
4026 E Hamblin Dr
Phoenix, AZ 85050-8712, USA

Scott, Dave (Athlete, Football Player)
3151 Robindale Rd
Decatur, GA 30034-4962, USA

Scott, David (Congressman, Politician)
225 Cannon Hob
Washington, DC 20515-3002, USA

Scott, David R (Astronaut)
Merces
30 Hackamore Ln Ste 1
Vc Johnson
Bell Canyon, CA 91307-1065, USA

Scott, Dennis (Athlete, Basketball Player)
9832 Laurel Valley Dr
Windermere, FL 34786-8911, USA

Scott, Dick (Athlete, Baseball Player)
166 Sunset Ln
Cairo, GA 39828-6737, USA

Scott, Dick (Athlete, Baseball Player)
7399 E Cortez Rd
Scottsdale, AZ 85260-5432, USA

Scott, Donna W (Actor)
c/o Steve Rohr *Lexicon Public Relations*
1049 Havenhurst Dr # 365
West Hollywood, CA 90046-6002, USA

Scott, Donnie (Athlete, Baseball Player)
6042 114th Ter N
Pinellas Park, FL 33782-2018, USA

Scott, Donovan (Actor)
Talent Group
6300 Wilshire Blvd Ste 2100
Los Angeles, CA 90048-5282, USA

Scott, Dougray (Actor)
c/o Staff Member *Dontanville/Frattaroli (D/F)*
270 Lafayette St Ste 402
New York, NY 10012-3327, USA

Scott, Dragos (Athlete, Football Player)
1750 Pacific Beach Dr
San Diego, CA 92109-6047, USA

Scott, Drew (Producer, Reality Star)
c/o Staff Member *Scott Brothers Entertainment*
8022 S Rainbow Blvd # 421
Las Vegas, NV 89139-6477, USA

Scott, Edward (Baseball Player)
Indianapolis Clowns
720 Kasserine Pass
Mobile, AL 36609-6430, USA

Scott, Edward (Politician)
4508 Greenbreeze Ln
Fuquay Varina, NC 27526-6864, USA

Scott, Emmet (Writer)
c/o Staff Member *New English Review*
PO Box 158397
Nashville, TN 37215-8397, USA

Scott, Freddie L (Athlete, Football Player)
PO Box 197
Coahoma, MS 38617-0197, USA

Scott, Gary (Athlete, Baseball Player)
36 Copper Beech Rd
Greenwich, CT 06830-4034, USA

Scott, Gavin (Writer)
c/o Jordan Bayer *Original Artists*
2801 Hyperion Ave Ste 104
Los Angeles, CA 90027-2571, USA

Scott, Herbert (Athlete, Football Player)
605 Rawhide Ct
Plano, TX 75023-4753, USA

Scott, H Lee Jr (Business Person)
Wal-Mart Stores
702 SW 8th St
Bentonville, AR 72712-6209, USA

Scott, Jack (Music Group, Musician, Songwriter, Writer)
34039 Coachwood Dr
Sterling Heights, MI 48312-5617, USA

Scott, Jake (Athlete, Football Player)
PO Box 857
Hanalei, HI 96714-0857, USA

Scott, Jake (Director, Producer)
PO Box 18106
Encino, CA 91416-8106, USA

Scott, James (Actor)
c/o Sandra Siegal *Siegal Company, The*
9025 Wilshire Blvd Ste 400
Beverly Hills, CA 90211-1828, USA

Scott, James (Athlete, Football Player)
10127 Chisholm Trl
Dallas, TX 75243-2511, USA

Scott, Jeremy (Designer)
c/o Staff Member *WME|IMG*
9601 Wilshire Blvd Ste 800
Beverly Hills, CA 90210-5210, USA

Scott, Jill (Actor, Musician)
c/o Chris Chambers *The Chamber Group*
75 Broad St Rm 708
New York, NY 10004-3244, USA

scott, joe b (Athlete, Baseball Player)
8241 Grayce Dr
Southaven, MS 38671-7052, USA

Scott, John (Athlete, Baseball Player)
917 S Pearl Ave
Compton, CA 90221-4320, USA

Scott, John (Athlete, Football Player)
1583 N Ellen Ave
Decatur, IL 62526, USA

Scott, Jonathan (Producer, Reality Star)
c/o Staff Member *Scott Brothers Entertainment*
8022 S Rainbow Blvd # 421
Las Vegas, NV 89139-6477, USA

Scott, Josey (Music Group, Musician)
Helter Skelter
Plaza
535 Kings Road
London SW10 0S, UNITED KINGDOM (UK)

Scott, Judson (Actor)
10000 Santa Monica Blvd PH 305
Los Angeles, CA 90067-7037

Scott, Kathryn Leigh (Actor)
3236 Bennett Dr
Los Angeles, CA 90068-1702, USA

Scott, Katrina (Fitness Expert)
Tone It Up LLC
703 Pier Ave Ste B # 806
Hermosa Beach, CA 90254-3943, USA

Scott, Kelsey (Actor)
c/o Lori Jonas *Jonas Public Relations*
1327 Ocean Ave Ste F
Santa Monica, CA 90401-1024, USA

Scott, Kevin B (Athlete, Football Player)
2335 Cascade St
Milpitas, CA 95035-7807, USA

Scott, Klea (Actor)
c/o Staff Member *Epstein Wyckoff Corsa Ross (LA)*
11350 Ventura Blvd Ste 100
Studio City, CA 91604-3140, USA

Scott, Lary R (Business Person)
Carolina Freight Corp
PO Box 1000
Cherryville, NC 28021-1000, USA

Scott, Lew (Athlete, Football Player)
4 Osprey Ct
Streamwood, IL 60107-2813, USA

Scott, Lindsay (Athlete, Football Player)
214 N Troup St
Valdosta, GA 31601-5738, USA

Scott, Lorna (Actor)
c/o Staff Member *Kjar and Associates*
10153 1/2 Riverside Dr
Toluca Lake, CA 91602-2561, USA

Scott, Luke (Athlete, Baseball Player)
1245 Arredondo Grant Rd
De Leon Springs, FL 32130-3719, USA

Scott, Melody Thomas (Actor)
12068 Crest Ct
Beverly Hills, CA 90210-1354, USA

Scott, Michael W (Mike) (Athlete, Baseball Player)
28355 Chat Dr
Laguna Niguel, CA 92677-1384, USA

Scott, Naomi (Actor)
c/o Peter McGrath *Echo Lake Management*
421 S Beverly Dr Fl 8
Beverly Hills, CA 90212-4408, USA

Scott, Patricia (Athlete, Baseball Player)
1901 Tanners Cove Rd
Hebron, KY 41048-8338, USA

Scott, Paul (Writer)
33 Drumsheugh Gardens
Edinburgh, SCOTLAND

Scott, Randy (Athlete, Football Player)
1440 Woodland Lake Dr
Snellville, GA 30078-2097, USA

Scott, Ray (Basketball Player, Coach)
Colonial Life Insurance
33200 Schoolcraft Rd
Livonia, MI 48150-1643, USA

Scott, Reid (Actor)
c/o Bridget Smith *Impression Entertainment*
9229 W Sunset Blvd Ste 700
Los Angeles, CA 90069-3407, USA

Scott, Reppert (Athlete, Football Player)
3133 N Bass Lake Rd
Eagle River, WI 54521-9150, USA

Scott, Richard U (Dick) (Athlete, Football Player)
3369 Upland Ct
Adamstown, MD 21710-9665, USA

Scott, Ridley (Director)
c/o Simon Halls *Slate PR*
901 N Highland Ave
W Hollywood, CA 90038-2412, USA

Scott, Robert (Baseball Player)
New York Black Yankees
236 W Grand St
Elizabeth, NJ 07202-1284, USA

Scott, Rodney (Athlete, Baseball Player)
4206 Priscilla Ave
Indianapolis, IN 46226-3334, USA

Scott, Ron (Athlete, Hockey Player)
8822 Madeleine Dr
Baldwinsville, NY 13027-8916

Scott, Sean (Athlete, Football Player)
3217 Boise St
Berkeley, CA 94702-2607, USA

Scott, Seann William (Actor, Producer)
Elephant Pictures
200 N Elizabeth St
#200C
Chicago, IL 60607, USA

Scott, Shelby (Misc)
American Federation of TV/Radio Artists
260 Madison Ave
New York, NY 10016-2400, USA

Scott, Stefanie (Actor)
c/o Mona Loring *Status PR*
PO Box 6191
Westlake Village, CA 91359-6191, USA

Scott, Stephen (Musician)
Bridge Agency
35 Clark St Apt A5
Brooklyn Heights, NY 11201-2374, USA

Scott, Steven M (Steve) (Athlete, Track Athlete)
700 Briggs Ave Spc 93
Pacific Grove, CA 93950-2265, USA

Scott, Suzanne (Business Person)
c/o Staff Member *Fox News*
1211 Avenue of the Americas Lowr C1
New York, NY 10036-8705, USA

Scott, Tighe (Race Car Driver)
RD #1 - Box 1847
First St.
Saylorsburg, PA 18353, United States

Scott, Tim (Athlete, Baseball Player)
956 W Julia Way
Hanford, CA 93230-8552, USA

Scott, Tim (Congressman, Politician)
1117 Longwortij Hob
Washington, DC 20515-0001, USA

Scott, TJ (Director)
c/o Michelle Czernin von Chudenitz *Popular Press Media Group (PPMG)*
468 N Camden Dr Ste 105A
Beverly Hills, CA 90210-4507, USA

Scott, Todd (Athlete, Football Player)
5605 Avenue P
Galveston, TX 77551-5028, USA

Scott, Tom (Musician)
Performers of the World
8901 Melrose Ave # 200
West Hollywood, CA 90069-5605, USA

Scott, Tom Everett (Actor)
c/o John Carrabino *John Carrabino Management*
5900 Wilshire Blvd Ste 740
Los Angeles, CA 90036-5032, USA

Scott, Tony (Athlete, Baseball Player)
156 Oakwood Ave
Spartanburg, SC 29302-1602, USA

Scott, Travis (Musician)
c/o Cara Lewis *Cara Lewis Group*
7 W 18th St Fl 3
New York, NY 10011-4663, USA

Scott, Trevor (Athlete, Football Player)
c/o Dave Butz *Sportstars Inc*
1370 Avenue of the Americas Fl 19
New York, NY 10019-4602, USA

Scott, Walter (Athlete, Football Player)
1991 Edgefield Rd
Trenton, SC 29847-2435, USA

Scott, Willard (Television Host)
10543 Carr Ln
Delaplane, VA 20144-1704, USA

Scott, William (Politician)
9229 Arlington Blvd Apt 250
Fairfax, VA 22031-2543, USA

Scott, William Lee (Actor)
c/o Daniel Spilo *Industry Entertainment Partners*
955 Carrillo Dr Ste 300
Los Angeles, CA 90048-5400, USA

Scott, Willie (Athlete, Football Player)
1123 Long St
Newberry, SC 29108-4231, USA

Scott, Winston E (Astronaut)
PO Box 1192
Cape Canaveral, FL 32920-1192, USA

Scott, W Richard (Misc)
940 Lathrop Pl
Stanford, CA 94305-1060, USA

Scotti, Benjamin (Athlete, Football Player)
715 N Beverly Dr
Beverly Hills, CA 90210-3321, USA

Scotti, Nick (Actor, Musician)
c/o Elise Konialian *Untitled Entertainment (NY)*
215 Park Ave S Fl 8
New York, NY 10003-1622, USA

Scott Kay, Dominic (Actor)
c/o Rich Hueners *Paradigm*
8942 Wilshire Blvd
Beverly Hills, CA 90211-1908, USA

Scotto, Rosanna (Correspondent)
WNYW TV
205 E 67th St
New York, NY 10065-6089, USA

Scottoline, Lisa (Writer)
Harper Collins Publishers
10 E 53rd St
New York, NY 10022-5244, USA

Scott Thomas, Kristin (Actor)
c/o Laurent Gregoire *Agence Adequat*
21 Rue D'Uzes
Paris 75002, FRANCE

Scotty K (DJ)
c/o Staff Member *Diva Central Inc*
7510 W Sunset Blvd # 1445
Los Angeles, CA 90046-3408, USA

Scott-Young, Mona (Producer)
c/o Mona Scott-Young *Monami Entertainment*
649 W 27th St
New York, NY 10001-1105, USA

Scovell, Nell (Producer)
c/o Staff Member *WME|IMG*
9601 Wilshire Blvd
Beverly Hills, CA 90210-5213, USA

Scoville, Darrel (Athlete, Hockey Player)
18 Landmark Rd
Scarborough, ME 04074-8482

Scowcroft, Brent (Politician)
350 Park Ave # 2600
New York, NY 10022-6022, USA

Scrafford, Kirk (Athlete, Football Player)
19400 US Highway 93 N
Florence, MT 59833-5914, USA

Scranton, Jim (Athlete, Baseball Player)
27519 Hammack Ave
Perris, CA 92570-7071, USA

Scranton, Nancy (Golfer)
15820 Sanctuary Dr
Tampa, FL 33647-1075, USA

Scratch (Artist, Musician)
William Morris Agency
1325 Avenue of the Americas
New York, NY 10019-6026, USA

Scremin, Claudio (Athlete, Hockey Player)
84 Littlebrook Ln
Eliot, ME 03903-1512

Scribner, Bucky (Athlete, Football Player)
512 Georgina Ave
Santa Monica, CA 90402, USA

Scribner, Marcus (Actor)
c/o Wendi Green *Paradigm*
8942 Wilshire Blvd
Beverly Hills, CA 90211-1908, USA

Scribner, Rick (Race Car Driver)
8904 Amerigo Ave
Orangevale, CA 95662-4612, USA

Scrimm, Angus (Actor)
PO Box 5193
North Hollywood, CA 91616-5193, USA

S. Critz, Mark (Congressman, Politician)
1022 Longworth Hob
Washington, DC 20515-4902, USA

Scrivener, Chuck (Athlete, Baseball Player)
1766 Hazel St
Birmingham, MI 48009-6892, USA

Scroggins, Tracy (Athlete, Football Player)
2026 Willow Leaf Dr
Rochester Hills, MI 48309-3730, USA

Scruggs, Eugene (Baseball Player)
Detroit Stars
618 Dawson Ter NW
Huntsville, AL 35811-1782, USA

Scruggs, Randy (Musician)
McLachlan Scruggs
2821 Bransford Ave
Nashville, TN 37204-3101, USA

Scruggs, Tony (Athlete, Baseball Player)
11621 Braddock Dr Apt 17
Culver City, CA 90230-5175, USA

Scudder, Scott (Athlete, Baseball Player)
943 Farm Road 1499
Paris, TX 75460-0602, USA

Scuderi, Rob (Athlete, Hockey Player)
Sports Consulting Group
65 Monroe Ave Ste D
Pittsford, NY 14534-1318, USA

Scudero, Joe (Athlete, Football Player)
11811 Mandy Ln
Manassas, VA 20112-3134, USA

Scully, James (Actor)
c/o Andrew Olson *Circle of Confusion*
8931 Ellis Ave
Los Angeles, CA 90034-3336, USA

Scully, John (Athlete, Football Player)
3500 Bankview Dr
Joliet, IL 60431-4804, USA

Scully, Sean P (Artist)
Timothy Taylor Gallery
1 Bruton Place
London W1X 7AB, UNITED KINGDOM (UK)

Scully, Vin (Sportscaster)
c/o Staff Member *Los Angeles Dodgers*
1000 Elysian Park Ave
Los Angeles, CA 90012, USA

Scully-Power, Paul D (Astronaut)
Civil Aviation Safety Authority
Box 2005
Canberra, ACT 02600, AUSTRALIA

Scurry, Briana (Athlete, Olympic Athlete, Soccer Player)
11610 137th Ave N
Dayton, MN 55327-9730, USA

Scurti, John (Actor)
c/o Jennifer Konawal *Washington Square Arts (NY)*
310 Bowery Fl 2
New York, NY 10012-2861, USA

Scutaro, Marco (Athlete, Baseball Player)
19877 E Country Club Dr Apt 3503
Miami, FL 33180-4812, USA

Sczurek, Stan (Athlete, Football Player)
689 Beaver Ridge Trl
Broadview Heights, OH 44147-1972, USA

Sea, Daniela (Actor)
c/o Staff Member *Morris Yorn Barnes Levine Krintzman Rubenstein Kohner & Gellman*
2000 Avenue of the Stars Ste 300N
Tower N Fl 3
Los Angeles, CA 90067-4704, USA

Seabol, Scott (Athlete, Baseball Player)
118 Belsar Rd
Elizabeth, PA 15037-2504, USA

Seabron, Malcolm (Athlete, Football Player)
10418 Cliffwood Dr
Houston, TX 77035-3702, USA

Seabrook, Andrea (Correspondent)
c/o Staff Member *National Public Radio (NPR)*
635 Massachusetts Ave NW
Washington, DC 20001-3740, USA

Seabrook, Brent (Athlete, Hockey Player)
3637 N Wayne Ave Apt 1
Chicago, IL 60613-5912

Seacrest, Ryan (Producer, Radio Personality, Television Host)
c/o Staff Member *Live with Kelly & Ryan*
7 Lincoln Sq
New York, NY 10023-7219, USA

Seaforth Hayes, Susan (Actor)
4528 Beck Ave
North Hollywood, CA 91602-1904, USA

Seaga, Edward P G (Prime Minister)
24-26 Grenada Crescent
New Kingston
Kingston 5, JAMAICA

Seagal, Steven (Actor)
c/o Adam Griffin *LINK Entertainment*
11872 La Grange Ave
Los Angeles, CA 90025-5282, USA

Seagrave, Jocelyn (Actor)

Seagraves, Ralph (Race Car Driver)
RR 10 Box 413
Winston Salem, NC 27127, USA

Seagren, Bob (Athlete, Olympic Athlete, Track Athlete)
200 S Capitol Ave # 1
Indianapolis, IN 46225-1052, USA

Seagrove, Jenny (Actor)
Marmont Mgmt
Langham House
302/8 Regent St
London W1R 5AL, UNITED KINGDOM (UK)

Seal (Musician)
c/o Mitch Rose *Creative Artists Agency (CAA)*
2000 Avenue of the Stars Ste 100
Los Angeles, CA 90067-4705, USA

Seal, Paul (Athlete, Football Player)
21599 Hidden Rivers Dr N
Southfield, MI 48075-6110, USA

Seale, Johnnie (Athlete, Baseball Player)
1941 County Road 207
Durango, CO 81301-7700, USA

Seale, Sam (Athlete, Football Player)
1818 Da Gama Ct
Escondido, CA 92026-1729, USA

Seales, Amanda (Actor, Comedian)
c/o April King *ICM Partners*
10250 Constellation Blvd Fl 7
Los Angeles, CA 90067-6207, USA

Sealey, Tom (Athlete, Basketball Player)
316 Fountain Ave
Brooklyn, NY 11208-4302, USA

Seals, Brady (Musician)
c/o Staff Member *Creative Artists Agency (CAA)*
2000 Avenue of the Stars Ste 100
Los Angeles, CA 90067-4705, USA

Seals, Bruce (Athlete, Basketball Player)
115 Prospect St
Ashland, MA 01721-2249, USA

Seals, George (Athlete, Football Player)
1101 1st St Unit 204
Coronado, CA 92118-1496, USA

Seals, Ray (Athlete, Football Player)
PO Box 3211
Lake City, FL 32056-3211, USA

Seals & Croft (Music Group)
c/o Staff Member *4STAR Entertainment LLC*
1675 York Ave Apt 32C
New York, NY 10128-6905, USA

Sealy, Tom (Athlete, Basketball Player)
387 Classon Ave
Brooklyn, NY 11238-1307, USA

Seaman, David (Soccer Player)
Arsenal London
Avenell Road
Highbury
London N5 1BU, UNITED KINGDOM (UK)

Seaman, Kim (Athlete, Baseball Player)
4900 Main St
Moss Point, MS 39563-2735, USA

Sean, Jay (Musician)
c/o Staff Member *Creative Artists Agency (CAA)*
2000 Avenue of the Stars Ste 100
Los Angeles, CA 90067-4705, USA

Sean, SeanMahan (Athlete, Football Player)
4202 E 116th Pl # Pi
Tulsa, OK 74137-6120, USA

Seanez, Rudy (Athlete, Baseball Player)
1422 McCabe Cove Rd
El Centro, CA 92243-9741, USA

Searage, Ray (Athlete, Baseball Player)
13537 Park Blvd
Seminole, FL 33776-3433, USA

Searcy, Leon (Athlete, Football Player)
3841 Biggin Church Rd W
Jacksonville, FL 32224-7985, USA

Searcy, Nick (Actor)
c/o Joseph (Joe) Rice *JR Talent Group*
Prefers to be contacted by email or phone.
Los Angeles, CA NA, USA

Searcy, Steve (Athlete, Baseball Player)
5112 Gouffon Rd
Knoxville, TN 37918-9319, USA

Searfoss, Richard (Astronaut)
24480 Silver Creek Way
Tehachapi, CA 93561-8399, USA

Searle, John R (Misc)
109 Yosemite Road
Berkeley, CA 94707, USA

Searles, Kyle (Actor)
c/o Michael McConnell *Zero Gravity Management (II)*
5660 Silver Valley Ave
Agoura Hills, CA 91301-4000, USA

Sears, Brian (Horse Racer)
83 Osprey Ct
Secaucus, NJ 07094-2934, USA

Sears, Jay (Horse Racer)
750 NW 30th Ave Apt A
Delray Beach, FL 33445-2077, USA

Sears, Ken (Athlete, Basketball Player)
40 Cutter Dr
Watsonville, CA 95076-2229, USA

Sears, Paul B (Misc)
17 Las Milpas
Taos, NM 87571, USA

Sears, Teddy (Actor)
c/o Sandy Erickson *Vic Ramos Management*
337 E 13th St Apt 6
New York, NY 10003-5852, USA

Sears, Todd (Athlete, Baseball Player)
513 NW Chapel Dr
Ankeny, IA 50023-1420, USA

Seastrunk, Lache (Athlete, Football Player)
c/o Brian E. Overstreet *E.O. Sports Management*
1314 Texas St Ste 1212
Houston, TX 77002-3525, USA

Seaver, Tom (Athlete, Baseball Player)
1761 Diamond Mountain Rd
Calistoga, CA 94515-9672, USA

Seaward, Tracey (Producer)
c/o Staff Member *ICM Partners*
10250 Constellation Blvd Fl 7
Los Angeles, CA 90067-6207, USA

Seaward, Tracy (Producer)
c/o Staff Member *Independent Talent Group*
40 Whitfield St
London W1T 2RH, UNITED KINGDOM

Seay, Bobby (Athlete, Baseball Player, Olympic Athlete)
2950 Viscaya Pl Unit 206
Sarasota, FL 34237-3695, USA

Seay, Laura (Actor)

Seay, Mark (Athlete, Football Player)
6 Via Palmieki Ct
Lake Elsinore, CA 92532-0146, USA

Seay, Virgil (Athlete, Football Player)
5611 Fort Corloran Dr
Burke, VA 22015-2112, USA

Sebaldt, Maria (Actor)
Geranienstr. 3
Grunwald, GERMANY D-82031

Sebastian, John (Musician)
11 Music Hill Rd
Woodstock, NY 12498-2238, USA

Sebastian, Toby (Actor)
c/o Bridget Smith *Impression Entertainment*
9229 W Sunset Blvd Ste 700
Los Angeles, CA 90069-3407, USA

Sebastiani, Sergio Cardinal (Religious Leader)
Palazzo delle Congregazioni
Lardo del Colonnato 3
Rome 00193, ITALY

Sebelius, Kathleen (Politician)
Health/Human Services Dept
200 Independence Ave SW
Washington, DC 20201-0007, USA

Sebesky, Don (Musician)
c/o Staff Member *Bennett Morgan & Associates*
1022 Route 376 Ste 4
Wappingers Falls, NY 12590-6372, USA

Sebestyen, Marta (Music Group, Musician)
Konzertgentur Berthold Seliger
Nonnengasse 15
Fulda 36037, GERMANY

Sebold, Alice (Writer)
c/o Steven Barclay *Steven Barclay Agency*
12 Western Ave
Petaluma, CA 94952-2907, USA

Sebra, Bob (Athlete, Baseball Player)
20 Misners Trl
Ormond Beach, FL 32174-8531, USA

Secada, Jon (Musician)
c/o Susan Haber *Haber Entertainment*
434 S Canon Dr Apt 204
Beverly Hills, CA 90212-4501, USA

Secor, Kyle (Actor)
Brillstein/Grey
9150 Wilshire Blvd Ste 350
Beverly Hills, CA 90212-3453, USA

Secord, Al (Athlete, Hockey Player)
950 Ginger Ct
Southlake, TX 76092-6063

Secord, John (Music Group, Musician)
Making Texas Music
PO Box 1013
Old Putnam Bank Building
Putnam, TX 76469-1013, USA

Secord, Richard (Politician)
Thermal Imaging
108 Windlake Ct
Niceville, FL 32578-4804, USA

Secrest, Charles (Baseball Player)
215 Orchard Grove Ave
Lewistown, PA 17044-7509, USA

Secret Machines (Music Group)
c/o Mike Luba *Madison House*
1401 Walnut St Ste 500
Boulder, CO 80302-5332, USA

Secrets, No (Music Group)
Official International Fan Club
PO Box 5247
Bellingham, WA 98227-5247, USA

Secrist, Don (Athlete, Baseball Player)
5851 Park Rd
Pinckneyville, IL 62274-2513, USA

Secules, Scott (Athlete, Football Player)
1007 Hawkins Wood Ln
Midlothian, VA 23114-4577, USA

Secunda, Andrew (Writer)
c/o Staff Member *United Talent Agency (UTA)*
9336 Civic Center Dr
Beverly Hills, CA 90210-3604, USA

Seda, Jon (Actor)
c/o Jeff Witjas *Agency for the Performing Arts (APA)*
405 S Beverly Dr Ste 500
Beverly Hills, CA 90212-4425, USA

Sedaka, Neil (Musician)
Sedaka Music
201 E 66th St Apt 3N
New York, NY 10065-6454, USA

Sedar, Ed (Athlete, Baseball Player)
8 S Lake Ave
Third Lake, IL 60030-8431, USA

Sedaris, Amy (Actor)
c/o Nancy Gates *United Talent Agency (UTA)*
888 7th Ave Fl 7
New York, NY 10106-0700, USA

Sedaris, David (Writer)
c/o Staff Member *Little, Brown & Co.*
1290 Avenue of the Americas
New York, NY 10104-0101, USA

Seddon, Dr Rhea M (Astronaut)
1709 Shagbark Trl
Murfreesboro, TN 37130-1136, USA

Seddon, Margaret Rhea (Astronaut)
1709 Shagbark Trl
Murfreesboro, TN 37130-1136, USA

Sedelmaier, Joe (Cartoonist)
Sedelmaier Film Productions
858 W Armitage Ave # 267
Chicago, IL 60614-4383, USA

Sedgwick, Bill (Race Car Driver)
33056 Acklins Ave
Acton, CA 93510-1747, USA

Sedgwick, Kyra (Actor)
c/o Annick Muller *Wolf-Kasteler Public Relations*
40 Exchange Pl Ste 704
New York, NY 10005-2778, USA

Sedin, Daniel (Athlete, Hockey Player)
C A A Hockey
204-822 11 Ave SW
Attn J P Barry
Calgary, AB T2R 0E5, Canada

Sedin, Henrik (Athlete, Hockey Player)
C A A Hockey
204-822 11 Ave SW
Attn J P Barry
Calgary, AB T2R 0E5, Canada

Sedlacek, Shawn (Athlete, Baseball Player)
11008 W 131st St
Overland Park, KS 66213-3659, USA

Sedlbauer, Ron (Athlete, Hockey Player)
3021 Woodland Park Dr
Burlington, ON L7N 1K8, Canada

Sedney, Jules (Prime Minister)
Maystreet 24
Paramaribo, SARINAME

Sedoris, Chris (Athlete, Football Player)
7500 Turner Ridge Rd
Crestwood, KY 40014-8951, USA

Seduction (Music Group)
c/o Staff Member *Diva Central Inc*
7510 W Sunset Blvd # 1445
Los Angeles, CA 90046-3408, USA

Sedykh, Yuri G (Athlete, Track Athlete)
Russian Light Athletics Federation
Luzhnetskaya Nab 8
Moscow, RUSSIA

See, Larry (Athlete, Baseball Player)
1913 W Remington Dr
Chandler, AZ 85286-6231, USA

See, Marshall (Athlete, Basketball Player)
1138 S Canal Cir
Camp Verde, AZ 86322-7014, USA

Seebold, Bill (Race Car Driver)
Motorsports HOF
PO Box 193
Novi, MI 48376-0193, USA

Seed, Huckleberry (Misc)
391 Crestview Dr
Mount Charleston, NV 89124-9229, USA

Seegal, Denise (Business Person)
Liz Claiborne Inc
1441 Broadway
New York, NY 10018-1905, USA

Seeger, Mike (Composer, Musician)
c/o Staff Member *Forklore Productions*
1671 Appian Way
Santa Monica, CA 90401-3258, USA

Seehorn, Rhea (Actor)
c/o Ruth Bernstein *Viewpoint Inc*
8820 Wilshire Blvd Ste 220
Beverly Hills, CA 90211-2622, USA

Seelbach, Chris (Athlete, Baseball Player)
347 Greenwood Dr
Hilton Head Island, SC 29928-4249, USA

Seelbach, Chuck (Athlete, Baseball Player)
13800 Fairhill Rd Apt 501
Cleveland, OH 44120-5510, USA

Seelenfreund, Alan (Business Person)
McKesson HBOC Inc
1 Post St Ste 107
San Francisco, CA 94104-5203, USA

Seeler, Uwe (Soccer Player)
HSV
Rothenbaumchaussee 125
Ashburn, VA 20149-0001, GERMANY

Seeley, Andrew (Actor, Musician)
c/o Jill Fritzo *Jill Fritzo Public Relations*
208 E 51st St # 305
New York, NY 10022-6557, USA

Seeley, Drew (Actor)
PO Box 250
Apopka, FL 32704-0250, USA

Seely, Jeannie (Musician, Songwriter)
c/o Staff Member *Tessier-Marsh Talent*
505 Canton Pass
Madison, TN 37115-5449, USA

Seerman, Jamie (Jaymay) (Musician)
c/o Lee Scheinbaum *Halfpipe Entertainment*
PO Box 10534
Beverly Hills, CA 90213-3534, USA

Seether (Music Group)
c/o Rick Smith *Wild Justice*
28411 Northwestern Hwy Ste 930
Southfield, MI 48034-5539, USA

Sefcik, Kevin (Athlete, Baseball Player)
16921 Steeplechase Pkwy
Orland Park, IL 60467-8769, USA

Seffrin, John R (Misc)
American Cancer Society
1599 Clifton Rd NE
Atlanta, GA 30322-4250, USA

Sefolosha, Thabo (Athlete, Basketball Player)
910 Colony Dr
Salisbury, MD 21804-8758, USA

Segal, Fred (Designer, Fashion Designer)
Fred Segal Jeans
8100 Melrose Ave
Los Angeles, CA 90046-7091, USA

Segal, George (Actor)
c/o Abe Hoch *A Management Company*
16633 Ventura Blvd Ste 1450
Encino, CA 91436-1887, USA

Segal, George (Horse Racer)
750 Michigan Ave
US Trotting Association
Columbus, OH 43215-1107, USA

Segal, Jonathan (Actor)
PO Box 3059
Tel Aviv 61030, ISRAEL

Segal, Peter (Director, Producer, Writer)
c/o Adam Kanter *Paradigm*
8942 Wilshire Blvd
Beverly Hills, CA 90211-1908, USA

Segall, Pamela (Actor)
c/o Staff Member *Meghan Schumacher Management*
13351D Riverside Dr Ste 387
Sherman Oaks, CA 91423-2508, USA

Seganti, Paolo (Actor)
PFD
Drury House
34-43 Russell St
London W8 7NA, UNITED KINGDOM (UK)

Ségara, Hélène (Musician)
c/o Staff Member *BG Productions*
10, rue Damré
Paris 75918, France

Segel, Jason (Actor, Producer)
c/o Jodi Gottlieb *Independent Public Relations*
9601 Wilshire Blvd Ste 750
Beverly Hills, CA 90210-5228, USA

Segelke, Herman (Athlete, Baseball Player)
1833 Kern Mountain Way
Antioch, CA 94531-7497, USA

Seger, Bob (Musician, Songwriter)
3841 Laplaya Ln
Orchard Lake, MI 48324-2940, USA

Seger, Shea (Music Group, Musician)
Helter Skelter
Plaza
535 Kings Road
London SW10 0S, UNITED KINGDOM (UK)

Segerstam, Leif S (Composer)
Garvey & Ivor
59 Lansdowne Place
Hove BN3 1FL, UNITED KINGDOM (UK)

Segreti, Donald (Politician)
387 Timber Ridge Dr
Bartlett, IL 60103-6605, USA

Segrist, Kal (Athlete, Baseball Player)
3813 55th St
Lubbock, TX 79413-4619, USA

Segui, David V (Athlete, Baseball Player)
2740 N 131st St
Kansas City, KS 66109-3365, USA

Segui, Diego P (Athlete, Baseball Player)
13421 Leavenworth Rd
Kansas City, KS 66109-3351, USA

Seguignol, Fernando (Athlete, Baseball Player)
3517 Turenne Way
Wellington, FL 33449-8061, USA

Seguin, Tyler (Athlete, Hockey Player)
17 Ferncastle Cres
Brampton, ON L7A 3P2, Canada

Segura, Tom (Comedian)
c/o Rob Greenwald *Rogers & Cowan*
1840 Century Park E Fl 18
Los Angeles, CA 90067-2101, USA

Seguso, Robert (Athlete, Olympic Athlete, Tennis Player)
3904 Bayside Ct
Bradenton, FL 34210-4107, USA

Sehorn, Jason (Athlete, Football Player)
PO Box 473880
Charlotte, NC 28247-3880, USA

Seibel, Phil (Athlete, Baseball Player)
351 Woodland Dr
Driftwood, TX 78619-4212, USA

Seibert, Kurt (Athlete, Baseball Player)
10914 Casetta Dr
Matthews, NC 28105-5918, USA

Seidel, Christiane (Actor)
c/o Maria Herrera *PMK/BNC Public Relations*
1840 Century Park E Ste 1400
Los Angeles, CA 90067-2115, USA

Seidel, Frederick (Writer)
c/o Staff Member *Farrar, Straus and Giroux*
175 Varick St Fl 9
New York, NY 10014-7407, USA

Seidel, Guenter (Athlete, Horse Racer, Olympic Athlete)
2108 Oxford Ave
Cardiff By The Sea, CA 92007-1820, USA

Seidel, Martie (Music Group, Musician)
Senior Mgmt
9465 Wilshire Blvd
Beverly Hills, CA 90212-2612, USA

Seidelman, Susan (Director)
Michael Shedler
225 W 34th St # 1012
New York, NY 10122-0049, USA

Seidenberg, Dennis (Athlete, Hockey Player)
20073 N 85th Pl
Scottsdale, AZ 85255-6301

Seidenberg, Ivan G (Business Person)
1095 Avenue of the Americas
Bell Atlantic Corp
New York, NY 10036-6797, USA

Seidler, David (Writer)
c/o Jeff Aghassi *Jeff Aghassi Management*
2810 S Bedford St
Los Angeles, CA 90034-2523, USA

Seifert, Bill (Race Car Driver)
16022 Lakeside Loop Ln
Cornelius, NC 28031-0379, United States

Seifert, George G (Athlete, Coach, Football Coach, Football Player, Sportscaster)
1276 Estate Dr
Los Altos, CA 94024-6100, USA

Seifert, Mike (Athlete, Football Player)
1605 E Bristlecone Dr
Hartland, WI 53029-8655, USA

Seifert, Mike (Athlete, Football Player)
N5610 Lac Verde Cir
Green Lake, WI 54941-9702, USA

Seigner, Emmanuelle (Actor)
c/o Gregory Weill *Agence Adequat*
21 Rue D'Uzes
Paris 75002, FRANCE

Seigner, Mathilde (Actor)
c/o Elisabeth Tanner *Time-Art*
8 rue Danielle Casanova
Paris 75002, FRANCE

Seignoret, Clarence H A (President)
24 Cork St
Roseau, DOMINICA

Seiheimer, Rick (Athlete, Baseball Player)
401 Hickory Hollow Ln
Brenham, TX 77833-9240, USA

Seikaly, Rony (Athlete, Basketball Player)
400 Alton Rd Apt 3201
Miami Beach, FL 33139-6756, USA

Seilheimer, Rick (Athlete, Baseball Player)
401 Hickory Hollow Ln
Brenham, TX 77833-9240, USA

Seiling, Ric (Athlete, Hockey Player)
71 Christina Dr
North Chili, NY 14514-9754

Seiling, Rod (Athlete, Hockey Player)
Ontario Racing Commission
400-10 Carlson Crt
Toronto, ON M9W 6L2, Canada

Seimetz, Amy (Actor)
c/o Adam Kersh *Brigade Marketing*
116 W 23rd St Fl 5
New York, NY 10011-2599, USA

Seinfeld, Evan (Actor, Adult Film Star, Musician)
14813 Huston St
Van Nuys, CA 91403-1608, USA

Seinfeld, Jerry (Actor, Comedian)
c/o Staff Member *Columbus 81 Productions*
1613 Chelsea Rd
San Marino, CA 91108-2419, USA

Seinfeld, Jessica (Chef)
2971 Bellmore Ave
Bellmore, NY 11710-4313, USA

Seiple, Larry (Athlete, Football Player)
1084 Alcove Loop
The Villages, FL 32162-4419, USA

Seisay, Mohammed (Athlete, Football Player)

Seitzer, Kevin (Athlete, Baseball Player)
Mac-N-Seitz
13705 Holmes Rd
Kansas City, MO 64145-1591, USA

Seixas, E Victor (Vic) Jr (Tennis Player)
8 Harbor Point Dr Apt 207
Mill Valley, CA 94941-3241, USA

Seizinger, Katja (Skier)
Rudolf-Epp-Str 48
Eberbach 69412, GERMANY

Sela, Rotem (Actor)
c/o Avivit Zlotogorsky *ADD Agency*
2 Raoul Wallenberg St
Ramat Hachayal
Tel Aviv 69719, Israel

Selanne, Teemu (Athlete, Hockey Player)
Thompson, Dorfman, Sweatman
PO Box 639 Stn Main
Attn: Donald Baizley
Winnipeg, MB R3C 2K6, Canada

Selby, Bill (Athlete, Baseball Player)
228 Eunice Bonner Rd
Waynesboro, MS 39367-9474, USA

Selby, Brit (Athlete, Hockey Player)
174 Divadale Dr
East York, ON M4G 2P6, Canada

Selby, David (Actor)
International Creative Mgmt
8942 Wilshire Blvd # 219
Beverly Hills, CA 90211-1908, USA

Selby, Philip (Composer)
Hill Cottage
Via 1 Maggio 93
Rignano Flaminio
Rome 00068, ITALY

Sele, Aaron (Athlete, Baseball Player)
4 Oak Tree Dr
Newport Beach, CA 92660-4290, USA

Seles, Monica (Athlete, Olympic Athlete, Tennis Player)
1 Fisher Rd
Pittsford, NY 14534-9502, USA

Seley, Jason (Artist)
Cornell University
Art Dept
Ithaca, NY 14853, USA

Self, Bill (Athlete, Basketball Player, Coach)
Bill Self's Assists Foundation
1651 Naismith Dr
Lawrence, KS 66045-4069, USA

Self, Steve (Athlete, Hockey Player)
744 River Rd S
Peterborough, ON K9J 1E8, Canada

Self, Todd (Athlete, Baseball Player)
10238 Cardiff Dr
Keithville, LA 71047-8980, USA

Selfridge, Andy (Athlete, Football Player)
5900 NE 7th Ave Apt 307N
Boca Raton, FL 33487-3996, USA

Selig, Bud (Athlete, Baseball Player)
Baseball Commissioner's Office
1480 E Standish Pl
Bayside, WI 53217-1958, USA

Selig-Prieb, Wendy (Baseball Player)
Milwaukee Brewers
6620 N Lake Dr
Milwaukee, WI 53217-4245, USA

Selivanov, Alexander (Athlete, Hockey Player)
1379 80th St S
Saint Petersburg, FL 33707-2722

Selleca, Connie (Actor)
c/o Chuck Binder *Binder & Associates*
1465 Lindacrest Dr
Beverly Hills, CA 90210-2519, USA

Selleck, Tom (Actor, Producer)
c/o Annett Wolf *Wolf-Kasteler Public Relations*
6255 W Sunset Blvd Ste 1111
Los Angeles, CA 90028-7426, USA

Seller, Peg (Coach, Swimmer)
72 Monkswood Cres
Newmarket, ON L3Y 2K1, CANADA

Sellers, Brad (Athlete, Basketball Player)
682 Arbor Way
Aurora, OH 44202-9113, USA

Sellers, Franklin (Religious Leader)
Reformed Episcopal Church
2001 Frederick Rd
Baltimore, MD 21228-5511, USA

Sellers, Goldie (Athlete, Football Player)
13425 Braun Rd
Golden, CO 80401-1646, USA

Sellers, Jeff (Athlete, Baseball Player)
833 S 224th Ln
Buckeye, AZ 85326-5593, USA

Sellers, Justin (Athlete, Baseball Player)
7640 NW 79th Ave Apt L8
Tamarac, FL 33321-2868, USA

Sellers, Larry (Actor)
c/o Vaughn Hart *Vaughn Hart & Associates*
12304 Santa Monica Blvd Ste 111
Los Angeles, CA 90025-2586, USA

Sellers, Michael (Actor, Producer, Writer)
c/o Staff Member *Quantum Entertainment*
209 E Alameda Ave Ste 203
Burbank, CA 91502-2674, USA

Sellers, Mike (Athlete, Football Player)
7526 Tottenham Dr
White Plains, MD 20695-4437, USA

Sellers, Robert (Writer)
c/o Staff Member *Pollinger Limited*
9 Staple Inn
Holborn
London WC1V 7QH, UK

Sellers, Ron F (Athlete, Football Player)
137 Via Paradisio
Palm Beach Gardens, FL 33418-6204, USA

Sellers, Shane (Horse Racer)
326 Orange Ave
Lake Arthur, LA 70549-4428, USA

Sellick, Phyllis (Musician)
Beverly House
29A Ranelagh Ave
Barnes SW13 0BN, UNITED KINGDOM (UK)

Sells, Dave (Athlete, Baseball Player)
700 Blue Ridge Ln
Vacaville, CA 95688-2023, USA

Selmon, Dewey W (Athlete, Football Player)
2725 S Berry Rd
Norman, OK 73072-6908, USA

Selmon, Lucious (Athlete, Coach, Football Player)
1 Alltel Stadium Pl
Jacksonville, FL 32202-1917, USA

Seltz, Rolland (Basketball Player)
3328 Oswego Heights Road
Shoreview, MN 55126, USA

Seltz, Rollie (Athlete, Basketball Player)
3328 Owasso Heights Rd
Saint Paul, MN 55126-4149, USA

Seltzer, David (Director, Producer, Writer)
c/o Dan Aloni *WME|IMG*
9601 Wilshire Blvd
Beverly Hills, CA 90210-5213, USA

Selverstone, Katy (Actor)

Selvie, George (Athlete, Football Player)
c/o Drew Rosenhaus *Rosenhaus Sports Representation*
3921 Alton Rd # 440
Miami Beach, FL 33140-3852, USA

Selvy, Frank (Athlete, Baseball Player)
125 Mount Vista Ave
Greenville, SC 29605-1120, USA

Selvy, Franklin D (Frank) (Athlete, Basketball Player)
18 Oglethorpe Ln
Hilton Head Island, SC 29926-4704, USA

Selway, Phil (Musician)
8017 Fareholm Dr
Los Angeles, CA 90046-2114, USA

Selwood, Brad (Athlete, Hockey Player)
77 Colonel Wayling Blvd
Sharon, ON L0G 1V0, Canada

Selwyn, Zach (Actor)
c/o Kenny Goodman *Goodmanagement*
9220 W Sunset Blvd Ste 106
W Hollywood, CA 90069-3500, USA

Selznick, Brian (Writer)
c/o Jason Dravis *Monteiro Rose Dravis Agency*
4370 Tujunga Ave Ste 145
Studio City, CA 91604-2788, USA

Semak, Alexander (Athlete, Hockey Player)
305 W 13th St Apt 1J
New York, NY 10014-1223

Sembello, Michael (Musician, Songwriter)
105 Shad Row Ste B
Piermont, NY 10968-3001, USA

Sember, Mike (Athlete, Baseball Player)
285 S Country Club Blvd
Boca Raton, FL 33487-2326, USA

Semchuk, Thomas ""Brandy"" (Athlete, Hockey Player)
1242 E Champlain Dr Apt 201
Fresno, CA 93720-5071

Semel, David (Director)
c/o Staff Member *3 Arts Entertainment*
9460 Wilshire Blvd Fl 7
Beverly Hills, CA 90212-2713, USA

Semel, Terry (Business Person)
Windsor Media Investments
10877 Wilshire Blvd Ste 1104
Los Angeles, CA 90024-4774, USA

Semenova, Juliana (Basketball Player)
Zalalela 4-35
Riga 01010, LATVIA

Semin, Alexander (Athlete, Hockey Player)
3133 N Piedmont St
Arlington, VA 22207-5330

Seminara, Frank (Athlete, Baseball Player)
8301 Ridge Blvd Apt 3C
Brooklyn, NY 11209-4352, USA

Semjonova, Uljana (Athlete, Basketball Player)
Zalaiela 4-35
Riga 01010, Latvia

Sempe, Jean-Jacques (Cartoonist)
4 rue de Moulin-Vert
Paris, France F-75014, USA

Sempe, Jean-Jacques (Cartoonist)
Editions Denoel
9 Rue du Cherche-Midi
Paris 75006, FRANCE

Semproch, Ray (Athlete, Baseball Player)
4220 Buechner Ave
Cleveland, OH 44109-5035, USA

Sena, Dominic (Director)
c/o Robert Newman *WME|IMG*
9601 Wilshire Blvd
Beverly Hills, CA 90210-5213, USA

Sendejo, Andrew (Athlete, Football Player)
c/o Erik Burkhardt *Select Sports Group*
2700 Post Oak Blvd Ste 1450
Houston, TX 77056-5785, USA

Sendel, Peter (Athlete)
Zallaer Str 9
Olympia, WA 98599-0001, GERMANY

Sendel, Sergio (Actor)
c/o Staff Member *Televisa*
Blvd Adolfo Lopez Mateos 232
Colonia San Angel INN
DF CP 01060, MEXICO

Sendlein, Lyle (Athlete, Football Player)
c/o Eric Metz *Lock Metz Milanovic LLC*
6900 E Camelback Rd Ste 600
Scottsdale, AZ 85251-8044, USA

Sendlein, Robin (Athlete, Football Player)
271 Emmie Ln
Fredericksburg, TX 78624-8062, USA

Senff, Dina (Nida) (Swimmer)
DW Coutuner-Senff
Praam 122
Amstelveen 1186 TL, NETERLANDS

Senior, Peter (Golfer)
c/o Staff Member *Pro Golfers Association (PGA)*
112 TPC Blvd
Ponte Vedra Beach, FL 32082, USA

Senn, Adam (Model)
c/o Staff Member *NEXT*
188 rue de Rivoli
Paris 75001, FRANCE

Senneker, Bob (Race Car Driver)
PO Box 140984
Grand Rapids, MI 49514-0984, USA

Sennett, Susan (Actor)
1201 Oak Ave
Manhattan Beach, CA 90266-5125, USA

Sensabaugh, Cody (Athlete, Football Player)

Senser, Joe (Athlete, Football Player)
Joe Senser's Sports Grill
4217 W 80th St
Bloomington, MN 55437, USA

Sensiba, Dave (Race Car Driver)
Throop Motorsports Racing
2775 Horseshoe Dr SW
Wyoming, MI 49418-9309, USA

Sensibaugh, Mike (Athlete, Football Player)
18414 Woodlands Terrace Dr
Glencoe, MO 63038-1829, USA

Senske, Sara (Race Car Driver)
Lynx Racing
5806 Saloma Ave
Van Nuys, CA 91411-3017, USA

Sensmeier, Martin (Actor)
c/o Justine Hunt *Hines and Hunt Entertainment*
1213 W Magnolia Blvd
Burbank, CA 91506-1829, USA

Senter, Marc (Actor)
c/o Jennifer Shoucair Weaver *S/W PR Shop*
584 N Larchmont Blvd # B
Los Angeles, CA 90004-1306, USA

Sentes, Rick (Athlete, Hockey Player)
2166 Abbott St
Kelowna, BC V1Y 1C7, Canada

Seoane, Manny (Athlete, Baseball Player)
8912 Southbay Dr
Tampa, FL 33615-2770, USA

Seow, Yit Kin (Musician)
8 North Terrace
London SW3 2BA, UNITED KINGDOM (UK)

Sepe, Crescenzio Cardinal (Religious Leader)
Piazza della Citta Leonina 9
Rome 00193, ITALY

Seper, Zeynep (Beauty Pageant Winner)
Rue de Dilbeeck 200
Brussels B-1082, BELGIUM

Seppa, Jyrki (Athlete, Hockey Player)
Vetiex Oy Silvolantie 3
Kerimaki, 58410, Finland

Septimus, Jake (Producer)
c/o Staff Member *Creative Artists Agency (CAA)*
2000 Avenue of the Stars Ste 100
Los Angeles, CA 90067-4705, USA

Sepulveda, Charlie (Musician)
Ralph Mercado Mgmt
568 Broadway # 608
New York, NY 10012-3225, USA

Serafin, Kim (Actor)
c/o Geoff Suddleson *United Talent Agency (UTA)*
9336 Civic Center Dr
Beverly Hills, CA 90210-3604, USA

Serafini, Dan (Athlete, Baseball Player)
1115 N Cantlon Ln
Reno, NV 89521-9694, USA

Serafini, Ron (Athlete, Hockey Player)
Morgan and Milzow Realty
25 S Main St
Clarkston, MI 48346-1525, USA

Serafinowitz, Peter (Actor, Producer, Writer)
c/o Peter Principato *Artists First*
9465 Wilshire Blvd Ste 900
Beverly Hills, CA 90212-2608, USA

Serano, Greg (Actor)
c/o Erik Kritzer *LINK Entertainment*
11872 La Grange Ave
Los Angeles, CA 90025-5282, USA

Seraphin, Oliver (Prime Minister)
44 Green's Lane
Goodwill, DOMINICA

Serayah (Musician)
c/o Staff Member *United Talent Agency (UTA)*
9336 Civic Center Dr
Beverly Hills, CA 90210-3604, USA

Serbedzija, Rade (Actor)
P F D
Drury House 34-43 Russell St
London WC2B 5HA, UNITED KINGDOM (UK)

Serebrier, Jose (Composer)
20 Queensgate Gardens
London SW7 5LZ, UNITED KINGDOM (UK)

Serebrov, Alexander A (Misc)
Potchta Kosmonavtov
Moskovskoi Oblasti
Syvisdny Goroduk 141160, RUSSIA

Serembus, John (Misc)
Upholsterers Union
25 N 4th St
Philadelphia, PA 19106-2104, USA

Serendipity Singers, The (Music Group)
349 S Main St
Wauconda, IL 60084-1966

Sergei, Ivan (Actor)
c/o Joannie Burstein *Burstein Company*
15304 W Sunset Blvd Ste 208
Pacific Palisades, CA 90272-3656, USA

Serhant, Ryan (Business Person, Reality Star)
c/o Staff Member *Bravo TV (NY)*
30 Rockefeller Plz
New York, NY 10112-0015, USA

Serig, Jennifer (Designer, Fashion Designer)
c/o Staff Member *Perception Public Relations LLC*
3940 Laurel Canyon Blvd Ste 169
Studio City, CA 91604-3709, USA

Serious, Yahoo (Actor)
12/33 E Crescent St
McMahons Point, NSW 02060, AUSTRALIA

Serkin, Peter A (Musician)
Manne Music College
55 W 13th St Bsmt
New York, NY 10011-7958, USA

Serkis, Andy (Actor)
c/o Jerry Schmitz *Grace PR*
260 S Beverly Dr Ste 205
Beverly Hills, CA 90212-3812, USA

Serlenga, Nikki (Athlete, Olympic Athlete, Soccer Player)
490 Myrtle Ave Apt 7M
Brooklyn, NY 11205-3077, USA

Serna, Assumpta (Actor)
c/o Alsira Garcia Maroto *Alsira Garcia-Maroto Talent Agency*
Calle De Los Invencibles 8
Bajo
Madrid 28019, SPAIN

Serna, Diego (Soccer Player)
Los Angeles Galaxy
1010 Rose Bowl Dr
Pasadena, CA 91103, USA

Serna, Paul (Athlete, Baseball Player)
32421 Outrigger Way
Laguna Niguel, CA 92677-4219, USA

Serna, Pepe (Actor)
40278 Rancho Palmeras
Rancho Mirage, CA 92270-3936, USA

Serota, Nicholas A (Director)
Tate Gallery
Millbank
London SW1P 4RG, UNITED KINGDOM (UK)

Serowik, Jeff (Athlete, Hockey Player)
371 Davisville Rd
East Falmouth, MA 02536-7085

Serra, Pablo (Writer)
c/o Gabriel Blanco *Gabriel Blanco Iglesias (Mexico)*
Rio Balsas 35-32
Colonia Cuauhtemoc
DF 06500, Mexico

Serra, Richard (Artist)
173 Duane St
New York, NY 10013-3334, USA

Serraiocco, Sara (Actor)
c/o Daniele Orazi *Officine Artistiche*
Via Luciano Manara 47
Rome 00-153, ITALY

Serrano, Jimmy (Athlete, Baseball Player)
2943 E Erika Ct
Grand Junction, CO 81504-6963, USA

Serrano, Juan (Musician)
Prince/SF Productions
1316 Oakmont Dr Apt 4
Walnut Creek, CA 94595-2434, USA

Serrano, Nestor (Actor)
c/o Danielle Galiana-Allman *InnerAct Entertainment*
141 S Barrington Ave Ste E
Los Angeles, CA 90049-3314, USA

Serratos, Christian (Actor)
c/o Christina Diamantas Karakasidis *Thruline Entertainment*
9250 Wilshire Blvd Fl Ground
Beverly Hills, CA 90212-3352, USA

Serreau, Coline (Director)
c/o Staff Member *ArtMedia*
8 rue Danielle Casanova
Paris 75002, FRANCE

Serricchio, Ignacio (Actor)
c/o Mary Putnam Greene *MPG Management*
7162 Beverly Blvd Ste 332
Los Angeles, CA 90036-2547, USA

Serum, Gary (Athlete, Baseball Player)
10525 Hidden Oaks Ln N
Champlin, MN 55316-3045, USA

Servais, Scott (Athlete, Baseball Player, Olympic Athlete)
4051 Williams Ave N
Renton, WA 98056-2118, USA

Servan-Schreiber, Jean-Claude (Journalist)
147 Bis Rue d'Alesia
Paris 75014, FRANCE

Server, Josh (Actor)
c/o Kacee Hudson *Shirley Hamilton*
333 E Ontario St Ste 302B
Chicago, IL 60611-4803, USA

Servia, Oriol (Race Car Driver)
PWR Racing
PO Box 1717
Bellevue, WA 98009-1717, USA

Service, Scott (Athlete, Baseball Player)
7959 Gaines Rd
Cincinnati, OH 45247-3419, USA

Serviss, Tom (Athlete, Hockey Player)
184 Comus Pl
Kelowna, BC V1V 1N2, Canada

Sessions, Jeff (Politician)
PO Box 39102
Washington, DC 20016, USA

Sessions, Pete (Congressman, Politician)
2233 Rayburn Hob
Washington, DC 20515-4501, USA

Sessions, Ronnie (Musician)
540 Gunson Ridge Rd
Cumberland City, TN 37050-4301, USA

Sessions, William (Politician)
2739 Cembalo Blvd Unit 210
San Antonio, TX 78230-3032, USA

Sestero, Greg (Actor, Director)
c/o Staff Member *Simon & Schuster*
1230 Avenue of the Americas Fl CONC1
New York, NY 10020-1586, USA

Setari, Robert (Actor)
c/o Patty Stevens *Vessel Entertainment*
10989 Bluffside Dr Apt 3210
Studio City, CA 91604-4407

Seter, Mordecai (Composer)
1 Kamy St
Ramat Aviv
Tel-Aviv, ISRAEL

Seth, Joshua (Actor)
c/o Staff Member *Sutton Barth & Vennari Inc*
5900 Wilshire Blvd Ste 700
Los Angeles, CA 90036-5009, USA

Seth, Vikram (Writer)
Phoenix House
Orion House
5 Upper St
London WC2H 9EA, UNITED KINGDOM (UK)

Sethu, Varada (Actor)
c/o Femi Oguns *Identity Agency Group (UK)*
95 Grays Inn Rd
London WC1X 8TX, UNITED KINGDOM

Settle, John (Athlete, Football Player)
2626 Placid St
Fitchburg, WI 53711-5427, USA

Settle, Keala (Actor, Musician)
c/o Morgan Pesante *42West*
1840 Century Park E Ste 700
Los Angeles, CA 90067-2122, USA

Settle, Matthew (Actor)
c/o Gary Mantoosh *Baker Winokur Ryder Public Relations*
9100 Wilshire Blvd
W Tower #500
Beverly Hills, CA 90212-3415, USA

Settles, Tawambi (Athlete, Football Player)
4204 Rogers Rd
Chattanooga, TN 37411-3244, USA

Setzer, Brian (Music Group, Musician)
c/o Staff Member *WME/IMG*
9601 Wilshire Blvd
Beverly Hills, CA 90210-5213, USA

Setzer, Dennis (Race Car Driver)
PO Box 665
Dawsonville, GA 30534-0013, USA

Setziol, LeRoy I (Roy) (Artist)
30450 SW Moriah Ln
Sheridan, OR 97378-9745, USA

Setzler, Steve (Athlete, Football Player)
1S767 Hemlock Ct
Saint Paul, MN 55124-7145, USA

Seubert, Rich (Athlete, Football Player)
122923 County Road C
Stratford, WI 54484-5231, USA

Seurer, Frank (Athlete, Football Player)
16168 S Brookfield St
Olathe, KS 66062-3927, USA

Sevani, Adam (Actor)
c/o Christian Donatelli *MGMT Entertainment (The Schiff Company)*
9220 W Sunset Blvd Ste 106
W Hollywood, CA 90069-3500, USA

Sevastyanov, Vitayi I (Misc)
Potchta Kosmonavtov
Moskovskoi Oblasti
Syvisdny Goroduk 141160, RUSSIA

Sevcik, Jaroslav (Athlete, Hockey Player)
New Bridge Academy
409 Glendale Dr
Attn Hockey Instructor
Lower Sackville, NS B4C 2T6, CANADA

Sevcik, John (Athlete, Baseball Player)
10107 Shinnecock Hills Dr
Austin, TX 78747-1318, USA

Sevendust (Music Group)
c/o Staff Member *In De Goot Entertainment*
119 W 23rd St Ste 609
New York, NY 10011-2594, USA

Severance, Joan (Actor)
PO Box 282
Carbondale, CO 81623-0282, USA

Severinsen, Al (Athlete, Baseball Player)
133 Warren Ave
Mystic, CT 06355-2136, USA

Severinsen, Carl H (Doc) (Musician)
11812 San Vicente Blvd Ste 200
Los Angeles, CA 90049-6622, USA

Severson, Jeff (Athlete, Football Player)
20625 Sierra Elena
Murrieta, CA 92562-8817, USA

Severson, Kimberly (Athlete, Horse Racer, Olympic Athlete)
631 Dobby Creek Rd
Scottsville, VA 24590-3026, USA

Severson, Rich (Athlete, Baseball Player)
5461 Sunset Falls Dr
Apollo Beach, FL 33572-3144, USA

Severyn, Brent (Athlete, Hockey Player)
4521 Avebury Dr
Plano, TX 75024-7358

Sevier, Corey (Actor)

Sevigny, Chloe (Actor)
c/o Frank Frattaroli *Circle of Confusion*
8931 Ellis Ave
Los Angeles, CA 90034-3336, USA

Sevsec, Pedro (Actor)
c/o Staff Member *Telemundo*
2470 W 8th Ave
Hialeah, FL 33010-2000, USA

Sevy, Jeff (Athlete, Football Player)
PO Box 2177
Loomis, CA 95650-2177, USA

Sewell, Rufus (Actor)
c/o Mara Buxbaum *ID Public Relations*
7060 Hollywood Blvd Fl 8th
Los Angeles, CA 90028-6021, USA

Sewell, Steve (Athlete, Football Player)
15918 E Crestridge Pl
Centennial, CO 80015-4219, USA

Sewell, Terri (Congressman, Politician)
1133 Longworth Hob
Washington, DC 20515-3201, USA

Seweryn, Andrzej (Actor)
Comedie Francaise
Place Colette
Paris 75001, FRANCE

Sexsmith, Ron (Musician)
c/o Staff Member *Paradigm (Monterey)*
404 W Franklin St
Monterey, CA 93940-2303, USA

Sexson, Richie (Athlete, Baseball Player)
23073 Canyon View Loop
Bend, OR 97701-0121, USA

Sexto, Camilo (Musician)
c/o Staff Member *BMG*
1540 Broadway
New York, NY 10036-4039, USA

Sexton, Brent (Actor)
c/o Staff Member *Greene & Associates*
1901 Avenue of the Stars Ste 130
Los Angeles, CA 90067-6030, USA

Sexton, Charlie (Musician)
Courage Artists
201-310 Water St
Vancouver, BC V6B 1B6, CANADA

Sexton, Chris (Athlete, Baseball Player)
6028 Squirrelwood Ct
Cincinnati, OH 45247-5972, USA

Sexton, Collin (Athlete, Baseball Player)
c/o Leon Rose *CAA Basketball*
308 Harper Dr Ste 210
Moorestown, NJ 08057-3245, USA

Sexton, Dan (Athlete, Hockey Player)
7683 133rd St W
Apple Valley, MN 55124-7617

Sexton, Jimmy (Athlete, Baseball Player)
2680 Baxter Rd # 1
Wilmer, AL 36587-8225, USA

Sexton III, Brendan (Actor)
c/o Staff Member *Gersh*
9465 Wilshire Blvd Ste 600
Beverly Hills, CA 90212-2605, USA

Seydoux, Lea (Actor)
c/o Dallas Smith *United Agents*
12-26 Lexington St
London W1F OLE, UNITED KINGDOM

Seyferth, Dietmar (Misc)
Massachusetts Institute of Technology
Chemistry Dept
Cambridge, MA 02139, USA

Seyfried, Amanda (Actor)
c/o Evelyn Karamanos *Relevant*
400 S Beverly Dr Ste 220
Beverly Hills, CA 90212-4404, USA

Seyfried, Gordon (Athlete, Baseball Player)
56428 Lowe Ave
Yucca Valley, CA 92284-1740, USA

Seymour, Cara (Actor)
c/o Vanessa Pereira *Artists Independent Management (LA)*
1522 2nd St
Santa Monica, CA 90401-2303, USA

Seymour, Carolyn (Actor)
c/o Jo Hole *Jo Hole Associates*
1 Long Ln
Uncommon
London SE1 4PG, UNITED KINGDOM

Seymour, Jane (Actor, Producer)
c/o Staff Member *PCH Film*
3380 Motor Ave
Los Angeles, CA 90034-3712, USA

Seymour, Paul (Athlete, Football Player)
4188 Shoals Dr
Okemos, MI 48864-3431, USA

Seymour, Paul C (Athlete, Football Player)
4188 Shoals Dr
Okemos, MI 48864-3431, USA

Seymour, Richard (Athlete, Football Player)
c/o Eugene Parker *Independent Sports & Entertainment (ISE-IN)*
6435 W Jefferson Blvd # 197
Fort Wayne, IN 46804-6203, USA

Seymour, Stephanie (Model)
c/o Staff Member *IMG Models (NY)*
304 Park Ave S PH N
New York, NY 10010-4303, USA

Seymour, Terri (Actor)
c/o Ivo Fischer *WME|IMG*
9601 Wilshire Blvd
Beverly Hills, CA 90210-5213, USA

Sezer, Ahmet Necdet (President)
President's Office
Cumhurbaskanlgl Kosku
Cankaya
Ankara, TURKEY

Sfar, Rachid (Prime Minister)
278 Ave de Tervuren
Brussels 01150, BELGIUM

Sgouros, Dimitris (Musician)
Tompazi 28 Str
Piraeus 18537, GREECE

Shaback, Nick (Athlete, Basketball Player)
3019 49th St Apt 2N
Astoria, NY 11103-1315, USA

Shabala, Adam (Athlete, Baseball Player)
6 M St
Streator, IL 61364-2613, USA

Shack, Edward S P (Eddie) (Athlete, Hockey Player)
508 Fairlawn Ave
North York, ON M5M 1V2, Canada

Shack, William A (Misc)
2597 Hilgard Ave
Berkeley, CA 94709-1104, USA

Shackelford, Brian (Athlete, Baseball Player)
2812 N Birch St
McAlester, OK 74501-2412, USA

Shackelford, Don (Athlete, Football Player)
P.O. Box 1468
Lansdale, PA 19446, USA

shackelford, ray (Athlete, Baseball Player)
716 El Toro Rd
Ojai, CA 93023-1756, USA

Shackelford, Ted (Actor)
4700 Placidia Ave
Toluca Lake, CA 91602-1544, USA

Shackleford, Brian (Athlete, Baseball Player)
2812 N Birch St
McAlester, OK 74501-2412, USA

Shackleford, Charles (Athlete, Basketball Player)
107 E Peyton Ave Apt 5H
Kinston, NC 28501-4375, USA

Shackleton, Simon (Elite Force) (Musician)
c/o Staff Member *Beatport*
2399 Blake St Ste 170
Denver, CO 80205-2187, USA

Shackouls, Bobby S (Business Person)
Burlington Resources
5051 Westheimer Rd
Houston, TX 77056-5622, USA

Shadic-Campbell, Lillian (Athlete, Baseball Player)
61 Bloody Hill Rd
Craryville, NY 12521-5101, USA

Shadow (DJ)
Quannum Projects LLC
690 5th St # 208
San Francisco, CA 94107-1517, USA

Shadows, M (Musician)
c/o Staff Member *World Audience Media Group*
11835 W Olympic Blvd Ste 135
Los Angeles, CA 90064-5047, USA

Shadyac, Tom (Director)
c/o Staff Member *Paradigm*
8942 Wilshire Blvd
Beverly Hills, CA 90211-1908, USA

Shafer, Martin (Business Person)
c/o Staff Member *Castle Rock Entertainment*
11999 San Vicente Blvd Ste 220
Los Angeles, CA 90049-5130, USA

Shafer, Matthew (Musician)
c/o Rick Roskin *Creative Artists Agency (CAA)*
2000 Avenue of the Stars Ste 100
Los Angeles, CA 90067-4705, USA

Shaffer, Akiva (Director, Writer)
c/o Staff Member *Mosaic Media Group*
407 N Maple Dr # 100
Beverly Hills, CA 90210-3818, USA

Shaffer, Atticus (Actor)
c/o Mitchell Gossett *Industry Entertainment Partners*
955 Carrillo Dr Ste 300
Los Angeles, CA 90048-5400, USA

Shaffer, Lee (Athlete, Basketball Player)
3822 Nottaway Rd
Durham, NC 27707-5421, USA

Shaffer, Paul (Musician)
Worldwide Pants
250 W 57th St Ste 1101
Ed Sullivan Theatre
New York, NY 10107-1101, USA

Shaggy (Radio Personality)
c/o Staff Member *WPKX*
1331 Main St Ste 4
Springfield, MA 01103-1621, USA

Shah, Idries (Writer)
AP Watt Ltd
26/28 Bedford Row
London WC1R 4HL, UNITED KINGDOM (UK)

Shah, Kiran (Actor)
c/o Michael Henderson *Heresun Management*
4119 W Burbank Blvd
Burbank, CA 91505-2122, USA

Shahan, Gil (Musician)
ICM Artists
40 W 57th St
New York, NY 10019-4001, USA

Shahans, Shirley Bridges (Race Car Driver)
1400 Colorado St
Boulder City, NV 89005-2489, USA

Shaheen, Jeanne (Politician)
73 Perkins Rd
Madbury, NH 03823-7612, USA

Shahi, Sarah (Actor)
c/o Laura Myones *McKeon-Myones Management*
3500 W Olive Ave Ste 770
Burbank, CA 91505-5527, USA

Shahidi, Yara (Actor)
c/o Liz York *Principal Entertainment*
9255 W Sunset Blvd Ste 500
Los Angeles, CA 90069-3301, USA

Shaiman, Marc (Composer)
38 W 26th St Apt 7B
New York, NY 10010-2014, USA

Shakar, Martin (Actor)
118 E 37th St
New York, NY 10016-3025, USA

Shake, Christi (Model)
c/o Mike Esterman *Esterman.Com, LLC*
Prefers to be contacted via email
Baltimore, MD XXXXX, USA

Shakes, Paul (Athlete, Hockey Player)
RR4
Stayner, ON LOM 1SO, Canada

Shakira (Musician)
c/o Dvora Vener Englefield *The Lede Company*
9701 Wilshire Blvd # 930
Beverly Hills, CA 90212-2020, USA

Shakurov, Sergei K (Actor)
Bibliotechnava Str 27
#94
Moscow 109544, RUSSIA

Shalala, Donna (Politician)
8565 Old Cutler Rd
Coral Gables, FL 33143-6217, USA

Shalets, Victoria (Actor)
c/o Angharad Wood *Tavistock Wood Management*
45 Conduit St
London W1S 2YN, UNITED KINGDOM

Shalhoub, Tony (Actor)
248 S Van Ness Ave
Los Angeles, CA 90004-3921, USA

Shalim (Musician)
c/o Staff Member *Sony Music (Miami)*
404 Washington Ave Ste 700
Miami Beach, FL 33139-6615, USA

Shallow, Parvati (Reality Star)
c/o Ken Jacobson *Ken Jacobson Management*
Preferred to be contacted by phone or email
Los Angeles, CA 91367, USA

Shamrock, Ken (Actor, Athlete, Wrestler)
c/o Staff Member *UFC*
PO Box 26959
Las Vegas, NV 89126-0959, USA

Shamsky, Art (Athlete, Baseball Player)
PO Box 1400
New York, NY 10163-1400, USA

Shanahan, Brendan (Athlete, Hockey Player)
47 Saquatucket Bluffs Rd
Harwich Port, MA 02646-2510

Shanahan, Greg (Athlete, Baseball Player)
3883 E St
Eureka, CA 95503-6026, USA

Shanahan, Mike (Athlete, Coach, Football Coach, Football Player)
20 Cherry Hills Farm Dr
Englewood, CO 80113-7165, USA

Shanahan, Sean (Athlete, Hockey Player)
121 Glen Rd
Toronto, ON M4W 2W1, Canada

Shand, David (Athlete, Hockey Player)
213 E Michigan Ave
Saline, MI 48176-1554

Shandrowsky, Alex (Misc)
Marine Engineer Beneficial Assn
444 N Capitol St NW
Washington, DC 20001-1512, USA

Shane, Bob (Music Group, Musician)
9410 S 46th St
Phoenix, AZ 85044-7512, USA

Shank, Harvey (Athlete, Baseball Player)
201 E Jefferson St
Phoenix, AZ 85004-2412, USA

Shank, Michael (Race Car Driver)
Michael Shank Racing
1386 Fields Ave
Columbus, OH 43211-2635, USA

Shankle, Joel (Athlete, Olympic Athlete, Track Athlete)
16181 Berryvale Ln
Culpeper, VA 22701-5530, USA

Shankley, Amelia (Actor)
c/o Staff Member *Natalie Hall Management*
621 Coronation Dr
Suite 3
Brisbane QLD 4066, AUSTRALIA

Shankman, Adam (Dancer, Director)
c/o BeBe Lerner *ID Public Relations*
7060 Hollywood Blvd Fl 8th
Los Angeles, CA 90028-6021, USA

Shanks, Michael (Actor, Director, Writer)
c/o Francis Okwu *Zero Gravity Management*
11110 Ohio Ave Ste 100
Los Angeles, CA 90025-3329, USA

Shan Kuo-Hsi, Paul Cardinal (Religious Leader)
Bishop's House
125 Szu-Wie 3rd Road
Kaohsiung 80203, TAIWAN

Shanley, Jim (Athlete, Football Player)
4 Brookside Dr
Apt D
Walla Walla, WA 99362, USA

Shanley, John Patrick (Director, Writer)
c/o Staff Member *Creative Artists Agency (CAA)*
2000 Avenue of the Stars Ste 100
Los Angeles, CA 90067-4705, USA

Shannon (Musician)
c/o Staff Member *Diva Central Inc*
7510 W Sunset Blvd # 1445
Los Angeles, CA 90046-3408, USA

Shannon (Music Group, Musician)
Big Mgmt
226 5th Ave
New York, NY 10001-7706, USA

Shannon, Carver (Athlete, Football Player)
6005 S La Cienega Blvd
Los Angeles, CA 90056-1523, USA

Shannon, Darrin (Athlete, Hockey Player)
Cia rica
23 Victoria St W
Alliston, ON L9R 1S9, Canada

Shannon, Darryl (Athlete, Hockey Player)
18 Landings Dr
Buffalo, NY 14228-1479

Shannon, June (Mama June) (Reality Star)
338 Kentwood Springs Dr
Hampton, GA 30228-5937, USA

Shannon, Mem (Musician, Songwriter)

Shannon, Michael (Actor)
c/o Byron Wetzel *Byron Wetzel Management*
200 Park Ave S Fl 8
New York, NY 10003-1526, USA

Shannon, Mike (Athlete, Baseball Player)
Mike Shannon's Steaks And Seafood
3104 Southwick Dr
Saint Charles, MO 63301-1191, USA

Shannon, Molly (Actor, Comedian)
c/o Steven Levy *Framework Entertainment*
9057 Nemo St # C
W Hollywood, CA 90069-5511, USA

Shannon, Polly (Actor)
c/o Rich Caplan *Noble Caplan Abrams*
1260 Yonge St 2nd Fl
Toronto, ON M4T 1W5, CANADA

Shannon, Randy (Athlete, Football Player)
7420 SW 107th Ave Apt 7-207
Miami, FL 33173-2970, USA

Shannon, Vicellous (Actor)
c/o Tony Chargin *Ovation Management*
12028 National Blvd
Los Angeles, CA 90064-3542, USA

Shantz, Robert C (Bobby) (Athlete, Baseball Player)
152 E Mount Pleasant Ave
Ambler, PA 19002-4209, USA

Shapiro, Dani (Writer)
Random House
1745 Broadway Frnt 3 # B1
New York, NY 10019-4343, USA

Shapiro, Debbie (Actor)
Agency for Performing Arts
9200 W Sunset Blvd Ste 900
Los Angeles, CA 90069-3604, USA

Shapiro, Jim (Actor)
Legislative Office Building Room 4028
Hartford, CT 06106 -159, USA

Shapiro, Joel E (Artist)
Pace Gallery
32 E 57th St Fl 4
New York, NY 10022-2530, USA

Shapiro, Karl (Writer)
211 W 106th St Apt 11C
New York, NY 10025-3688, USA

Shapiro, Mark (Commentator)
70 Winding River Trl
Chagrin Falls, OH 44022-3607, USA

Shapiro, Mel (Writer)
University of California
Theater Film/TV Dept
Los Angeles, CA 90024, USA

Shapiro, Neal (Horse Racer)
296 Sharon Rd
Trenton, NJ 08691-2313, USA

Shapiro, Rami (Rabbi) (Writer)
c/o Staff Member *SkyLight Paths Publishing*
PO Box 237
Woodstock, VT 05091-0237, USA

Shapiro, Robert (Attorney)
Christensen, Glaser, Fink, Jacobs, Glaser, Weil and Shapiro
10250 Constellation Blvd Fl 19
Los Angeles, CA 90067-6219, USA

Sharapova, Maria (Athlete, Tennis Player)
c/o Staff Member *IMG Academy*
5500 34th St W
Bradenton, FL 34210-3506, USA

Share, Charlie (Athlete, Baseball Player)
12922 Twin Meadows Ct
Saint Louis, MO 63146-1803, USA

Share, Charlie (Chuck) (Athlete, Basketball Player)
12922 Twin Meadows Ct
Saint Louis, MO 63146-1803, USA

Sharipov, Salizhan S (Astronaut)
Lyotchik Cosmonavt Yuri Gagarin
Cosmonaut Training Center 141160
Zvezdny Gorodok
Moskovskoi Oblasti Pot, Russia, USA

Sharkey, Ed (Athlete, Football Player)
3615 Russell Rd
Centralia, WA 98531-1666, USA

Sharkey, Jack (Writer)
39927 Chippewa Cir
Murrieta, CA 92562-4109, USA

Sharma, Barbara (Actor)
PO Box 29125
Los Angeles, CA 90029-0125, USA

Sharma, Chris (Athlete)
c/o Staff Member *Sanuk Climbing Team*
9600 Toledo Way
Irvine, CA 92618-1808, USA

Sharma, Rekha (Actor)
c/o Tim Emery *Seven Summits Pictures & Management*
8906 W Olympic Blvd
Beverly Hills, CA 90211-3550, USA

Sharma, Robin (Writer)
Sharma Leadership International
92B Scollard St.
2nd Floor
Toronto, ON M5R 1G2, Canada

Sharma, Suraj (Actor)
c/o Jennifer Plante *Slate PR (NY)*
307 7th Ave Rm 2401
New York, NY 10001-6019, USA

Sharman, Daniel (Actor)
c/o Leslie Sloane *Vision PR*
2 Penn Plz Rm 2601
New York, NY 10121-0001, USA

Sharman, Jim (Director)
M&L
49 Daringhurst St
Kings Cross, NSW 02100, AUSTRALIA

Sharockman, Ed (Athlete, Football Player)
9756 Russell Ave S
Minneapolis, MN 55431-2469, USA

Sharon, Dick (Athlete, Baseball Player)
1143 N 31st St
Billings, MT 59101-0132, USA

Sharp, Bill (Athlete, Baseball Player)
2244 Thornwood Ave
Wilmette, IL 60091-1454, USA

Sharp, Dee Dee (Musician)
William W Witherspoon Esq.
PO Box 7
C/O Dione Larue
Lakehurst, NJ 08733-0007, USA

Sharp, Kevin (Musician)
Rising Star
1415 River Landing Way
Woodstock, GA 30188-5345, USA

Sharp, Leslie (Actor)
International Creative Mgmt
8942 Wilshire Blvd # 219
Beverly Hills, CA 90211-1908, USA

Sharp, Linda K (Coach)
Phoenix Mercury
201 E Jefferson St
American West Arena
Phoenix, AZ 85004-2412, USA

Sharp, Marsha (Coach)
Texas Tech University
Athletic Dept
Lubbock, TX 79409, USA

Sharp, Nathan (Actor, Internet Star, Musician)
c/o Staff Member *Celebrity Talent Booking*
Prefers to be contacted by email.
NA NA, USA

Sharp, Preston (Actor, Reality Star)

Sharp, Scott (Race Car Driver)
Fernandez Racing
6950 Guion Rd # 51
Indianapolis, IN 46268-2576, United States

Sharpe, Luis (Athlete, Football Player)
Arizona State Prison
PO Box 3939
DOC #122301
Kingman, AZ 86402-3939, USA

Sharpe, Rochelle P (Journalist)
94 Dudley St # 2
Brookline, MA 02445-5937, USA

Sharpe, Shannon (Athlete, Football Player)
867 Carlton Rdg NE
Atlanta, GA 30342-4346, USA

Sharpe, Sterling (Athlete, Football Player)
81 Running Fox Rd
Columbia, SC 29223-3052, USA

Sharper, Darren (Athlete, Football Player)
11613 Heverley Ct
Glen Allen, VA 23059-4829, USA

Sharper, Jamie (Athlete, Football Player)
11613 Heverley Ct
Glen Allen, VA 23059-4829, USA

Sharples, Jeff (Athlete, Hockey Player)
2504 Mahaila Cir
Henderson, NV 89074-5909

Sharples, Scott (Athlete, Hockey Player)
50 Rockcliff Landng NW
Calgary, AB T3G 5Z6, Canada

sharpless, Josh (Athlete, Baseball Player)
206 Mountain Dr
Carnegie, PA 15106-2266, USA

Sharpley, Glen (Athlete, Hockey Player)
Sharpley Sports
536 Highland St
Haliburton, ON KOM 1SO, CANADA

Sharpton, Al (Activist, Religious Leader)
National Action Network
106 W 145th St Frnt
New York, NY 10039-4138, USA

Sharqi, Sheikh Hamad bin Muhammad al (President)
Royal Palace
Emiri Court
PO Box 1
Fujairah, UNITED ARAB EMIRATES

Shasky, John (Athlete, Basketball Player)
1755 S Benson Rd
Frankfort, KY 40601-7649, USA

Shatner, Melanie (Actor)
Henderson/Hogan
8285 W Sunset Blvd Ste 1
West Hollywood, CA 90046-2420, USA

Shatner, William (Actor)
c/o Staff Member *Le Big Boss Productions*
5555 Melrose Ave
Los Angeles, CA 90038-3989, USA

Shatraw, David (Actor)
c/o Staff Member *Artists & Representatives (Stone Manners Salners)*
6100 Wilshire Blvd Ste 1500
Los Angeles, CA 90048-5110, USA

Shattuck, Kim (Musician)
International Creative Mgmt
40 W 57th St Ste 1800
New York, NY 10019-4033, USA

Shattuck, Molly (Reality Star)
c/o Staff Member *Fox Broadasting Company*
PO Box 900
Beverly Hills, CA 90213-0900

Shattuck, Shari (Actor, Writer)
236 De Anza St
San Gabriel, CA 91776-1232

Shaud, Grant (Actor)
8738 Appian Way
Los Angeles, CA 90046-7733, USA

Shaughnessy, Charles (Actor)
c/o Staff Member *Marshak/Zachary Company, The*
8840 Wilshire Blvd Fl 1
Beverly Hills, CA 90211-2606, USA

Shaughnessy, Matt (Athlete, Football Player)

Shaunessy, Scott (Athlete, Hockey Player)
1 Treetop Ln
Duxbury, MA 02332-4123

Shave, Jon (Athlete, Baseball Player)
851 Parkview Pl W
Fernandina Beach, FL 32034-4633, USA

Shaver, Billy Joe (Musician, Songwriter)
c/o Staff Member *Class Act Entertainment*
PO Box 160236
Nashville, TN 37216-0236, USA

Shaver, Helen (Actor)
Innovative Artists
1505 10th St
Santa Monica, CA 90401-2805, USA

Shaver, Jeff (Athlete, Baseball Player)
9651 E Clinton St
Scottsdale, AZ 85260-6209, USA

Shavers, Ernie (Boxer)
30 Doreen Ave Moretown Wirral
Merseyside CH46 6DN, UNITED KINGDOM (UK)

Shavick, James (Actor, Director, Producer, Writer)

Shaw, Anthony (Director)
c/o Staff Member *Corymore Productions*
100 Universal City Plz # 2372A
Universal City, CA 91608-1002

Shaw, Bernard (Journalist)
7526 Heatherton Ln
Potomac, MD 20854-3222, USA

Shaw, Brad (Athlete, Hockey Player)
St Louis Blues
1401 Clark Ave
Saint Louis, MO 63103-2700

Shaw, Brad (Athlete, Hockey Player)
1866 Braumton Ct
Chesterfield, MO 63017-8027

Shaw, Brewster H Colonel (Astronaut)
3519 Rice Blvd
Houston, TX 77005-2937, USA

Shaw, Brian (Athlete, Basketball Coach, Basketball Player, Coach)
c/o Staff Member *Denver Nuggets*
1000 Chopper Cir
Denver, CO 80204-5805, USA

Shaw, Bryant (Athlete, Football Player)
13832 Far Hills Ln
Dallas, TX 75240-3737, USA

Shaw, Dennis (Athlete, Football Player)
14844 Priscilla St
San Diego, CA 92129-1525, USA

Shaw, Don (Athlete, Baseball Player)
857 Waterford Villas Dr
Lake Saint Louis, MO 63367-2574, USA

Shaw, Eric (Athlete, Football Player)
3450 Wallingford Ct
Lexington, KY 40503-4332, USA

Shaw, Fiona (Actor)
c/o Brian Swardstrom *United Talent Agency (UTA)*
888 7th Ave Fl 7
New York, NY 10106-0700, USA

Shaw, Frances (Actor)
c/o Justin Deanda *ICM Partners*
10250 Constellation Blvd Fl 7
Los Angeles, CA 90067-6207, USA

Shaw, Frankie (Actor)
c/o Katie Greenthal *The Lede Company*
9701 Wilshire Blvd # 930
Beverly Hills, CA 90212-2020, USA

Shaw, Jeffrey L (Jeff) (Athlete, Baseball Player)
4863 Saint Andrews Dr
Grove City, OH 43123-8198, USA

Shaw, Jim (Athlete, Hockey Player)
266 Churchill Dr
Saskatoon, SK S7K 3Y7, Canada

Shaw, Kim (Actor)
c/o Marilyn Glasser *Glasser/Black Management*
283 Cedarhurst Ave
Cedarhurst, NY 11516-1671, USA

Shaw, Lindsey (Actor)
c/o Evan Miller *Abrams Artists Agency*
750 N San Vicente Blvd
E Tower Fl 11
Los Angeles, CA 90069-5788, USA

Shaw, Mariena (Musician)
Berkeley Agency
1311 Spruce St
Berkeley, CA 94709-1434, USA

Shaw, Martin (Actor)
36 - 40 Glasshouse St
London W1B 5DL, UNITED KINGDOM (UK)

Shaw, Pete (Athlete, Football Player)
25052 Pappas Rd
Ramona, CA 92065-4920, USA

Shaw, Robert (Athlete, Football Player)
7154 Stonetrail Dr
Dallas, TX 75230-5403, USA

Shaw, Robert (Athlete, Football Player)
487 Old Coach Rd Apt D
Westerville, OH 43081-1392, USA

Shaw, Sandie (Musician)
c/o Staff Member *Shavian Enterprises*
14 Devonshire Place
London W1G 6HX, UNITED KINGDOM

Shaw, Scott (Journalist)
20771 Lake Rd
Cleveland, OH 44116-1335, USA

Shaw, Sedrick (Athlete, Football Player)
1007 Waller St
Austin, TX 78702-2632, USA

Shaw, Stan (Actor)
Innovative Artists
1505 10th St
Santa Monica, CA 90401-2805, USA

Shaw, Timothy A (Tim) (Swimmer)
5315 River Ave
Newport Beach, CA 92663-2208, USA

Shaw, Todd (Too Short) (Musician)
c/o Staff Member *Cunningham Escott Slevin & Doherty (CESD)*
10635 Santa Monica Blvd Ste 130
Los Angeles, CA 90025-8306, USA

Shaw, Victoria (Musician, Songwriter, Writer)
PO Box 58175
Nashville, TN 37205-8175, USA

Shaw, Vinessa (Actor)
8730 W Sunset Blvd # 490
W Hollywood, CA 90069-2210, USA

Shaw, Wayne (Athlete, Football Player)
625 12th St E
Saskatoon, SK S7N 0H3, Canada

Shaw, William L (Billy) (Athlete, Football Player)
3427 Old Rothell Rd
Toccoa, GA 30577, USA

Shaw Jr, Brewster H (Astronaut)
3519 Rice Blvd
Houston, TX 77005-2937, USA

Shawkat, Alia (Actor, Producer)
c/o Michelle Theodat *Kipperman Management*
345 7th Ave Rm 503
New York, NY 10001-5054, USA

Shawn, Wallace (Actor)
c/o Christopher Black *Opus Entertainment*
5225 Wilshire Blvd Ste 905
Los Angeles, CA 90036-4353, USA

Shay, Jerry (Athlete, Football Player)
81 E Shasta St
Chula Vista, CA 91910-6127, USA

Shaye, Lin (Actor)
Paul Kohner
9300 Wilshire Blvd Ste 555
Beverly Hills, CA 90212-3211, USA

Shaye, Skyler (Actor)
c/o Dorothy Koster Paul *Artists Only Management*
10203 Santa Monica Blvd Fl 5
Los Angeles, CA 90067-6416, USA

Shayk, Irina (Model)
c/o Ryan Brown *Brown Talent + PR*
133 W 13th St Apt 5
New York, NY 10011-7842, USA

Shazier, Ryan (Athlete, Football Player)
c/o Staff Member *Pittsburgh Steelers*
3400 S Water St
Pittsburgh, PA 15203-2358, USA

Shchedrin, Rodion K (Composer)
Tverskaya St
#31
Moscow 103050, RUSSIA

Shea, Charity (Actor)
c/o Scott Karp *The Syndicate*
10203 Santa Monica Blvd Fl 5
Los Angeles, CA 90067-6416, USA

Shea, Dan (Actor)
c/o Staff Member *Talent Plus*
1222 Lucas Ave Ste 300
Saint Louis, MO 63103-1937, USA

Shea, Eric (Actor)
27710 Jubilee Run Rd
Pearblossom, CA 93553-3439, USA

Shea, Jere (Actor)
SMS Talent
8730 W Sunset Blvd Ste 440
Los Angeles, CA 90069-2277, USA

Shea, John (Actor)
Mutant X
40 Carl Hall Road
Toronto, ON M3K 2B8, CANADA

Shea, Judith (Artist)
Barbara Krakow Gallery
10 Newbury St Ste 5
Boston, MA 02116-3223, USA

Shea, Katt (Actor)
International Creative Mgmt
8942 Wilshire Blvd # 219
Beverly Hills, CA 90211-1908, USA

Shea, Pat (Athlete, Football Player)
3315 Calle Del Sur
Carlsbad, CA 92009-8612, USA

Shea, Steve (Athlete, Baseball Player)
75 Hampton Mdws
Hampton, NH 03842-1815, USA

Shea, Terry (Coach, Football Coach)
San Jose State University
Athletic Dept
San Jose, CA 95192-0001, USA

Sheaffer, Danny (Athlete, Baseball Player)
165 Savannah Ln
Mount Airy, NC 27030-8688, USA

Shealy, Ryan (Athlete, Baseball Player)
2168 NE 63rd Ct
Fort Lauderdale, FL 33308-1335, USA

Shear, Jules (Actor, Musician, Songwriter, Writer)
c/o Staff Member *Concerted Efforts*
PO Box 440326
Somerville, MA 02144-0004, USA

Shear, Rhonda (Actor, Comedian, Model)
J Cast Productions
2550 Greenvalley Rd
Los Angeles, CA 90046-1438, USA

Sheard, Jabaal (Athlete, Football Player)
c/o Drew Rosenhaus *Rosenhaus Sports Representation*
3921 Alton Rd # 440
Miami Beach, FL 33140-3852, USA

Sheard, Kiera Kiki (Musician)
c/o Staff Member *EMI Gospel*
PO Box 5085
Brentwood, TN 37024-5085, USA

Shearer, Al (Actor, Reality Star)

Shearer, Alan (Soccer Player)
Newcastle United FC
Saint James Park
Newcastle-Tyne NE1 4ST, UNITED KINGDOM (UK)

Shearer, Bob (Golfer)
International Management Group
281 Clarence Street
2nd Floor
Sydney, NSW 02000, AUSTRALIA

Shearer, Harry (Actor, Comedian)
c/o Melanie Greene *Affirmative Entertainment*
6525 W Sunset Blvd # 7
Los Angeles, CA 90028-7212, USA

Shearer, S Bradford (Brad) (Athlete, Football Player)
1909B Lakeshore Dr Apt B
Austin, TX 78746-2904, USA

Shearin, Joe (Athlete, Football Player)
2508 State St Apt 6
Dallas, TX 75201-2044, USA

Shearmur, Edward (Ed) (Composer, Musician)
c/o Staff Member *Gorfaine/Schwartz Agency Inc*
4111 W Alameda Ave Ste 509
Burbank, CA 91505-4171, USA

Shearn, Tom (Athlete, Baseball Player)
PO Box 3586
Pflugerville, TX 78691-3586, USA

Shears, Jake (Musician)
c/o Marty Diamond *Paradigm*
140 Broadway Ste 2600
New York, NY 10005-1011, USA

Shears, Larry (Athlete, Football Player)
355 Cammel St
Mobile, AL 36610-3529, USA

Shearsmith, Reece (Actor)
c/o Emily Hargreaves *Multitude Media*
32 Bloomsbury St
London WC1B 3QJ, UNITED KINGDOM

Sheckler, Ryan (Actor, Skateboarder)
Etnies Skate Team
25422 Trabuco Rd Ste 105
Lake Forest, CA 92630-2796, USA

Shedd, Kenny (Athlete, Football Player)
342 Oleander St
Brentwood, CA 94513-6351, USA

Shedden, Doug (Athlete, Hockey Player)
7 E Main St
Stony Point, NY 10980-1615

Sheedy, Ally (Actor)
c/o Bill Veloric *Innovative Artists*
235 Park Ave S Fl 7
New York, NY 10003-1405, USA

Sheehan, Doug (Actor)
Innovative Artists
1505 10th St
Santa Monica, CA 90401-2805, USA

Sheehan, Jeremiah J (Business Person)
Reynolds Metals Co
6601 W Broad St
PO Box 27003
Richmond, VA 23230-1723, USA

Sheehan, Neil (Journalist)
4505 Klingle St NW
Washington, DC 20016-3580, USA

Sheehan, Patrick (Athlete, Golfer)
485 Graham Ave
Oviedo, FL 32765-8702, USA

Sheehan, Patty (Athlete, Golfer)
RLG ProImage
1568 La Vista Del Oceano
Santa Barbara, CA 93109-1739, USA

Sheehan, Robert (Actor)
c/o Ciara Parkes *Public Eye Communications*
535 Kings Rd
#313 Plaza
London SW10 0SZ, UNITED KINGDOM

Sheehan, Susan (Writer)
4505 Klingle St NW
Washington, DC 20016-3580, USA

Sheehy, Neil (Athlete, Hockey Player)
Sheehy Hockey LLC
900 2nd Ave S Ste 1650
Minneapolis, MN 55402-5359

Sheehy, Tim (Athlete, Hockey Player, Olympic Athlete)
4 Boswell Ln
Southborough, MA 01772-1763, USA

Sheen, Charlie (Actor)
c/o Staff Member *Estevez Sheen Productions*
99 S Raymond Ave Ste 601
Pasadena, CA 91105-2046, USA

Sheen, Martin (Actor)
c/o Staff Member *Estevez Sheen Productions*
99 S Raymond Ave Ste 601
Pasadena, CA 91105-2046, USA

Sheen, Michael (Actor, Producer)
c/o Tammy Rosen *Sanders Armstrong Caserta*
4111 W Alameda Ave Ste 505
Burbank, CA 91505-4163, USA

Sheeran, Ed (Musician)
c/o Stuart Camp *Grumpy Old Management*
41 Great Portland St
London W1W 7LA, UNITED KINGDOM

Sheerer, Gary (Athlete)
1557 Country Club Dr
Los Altos Hills, CA 94024-5908, USA

Sheets, Andy (Athlete, Baseball Player)
104 Villaggio Dr
Lafayette, LA 70508-6795, USA

Sheets, Ben (Athlete, Baseball Player, Olympic Athlete)
105 E Shore Rd
Monroe, LA 71203-8857, USA

Sheets, Kory (Athlete, Football Player)

Sheets, Larry (Athlete, Baseball Player)
1411 Chippendale Rd
Lutherville Timonium, MD 21093-1608, USA

Sheffer, Craig (Actor)
5699 Kanan Rd # 275
Agoura, CA 91301-3358, USA

Sheffield, Fred (Athlete, Basketball Player)
11664 McDougall
Tustin, CA 92782-3345, USA

Sheffield, Gary (Athlete, Baseball Player)
922 Anchorage Rd
Tampa, FL 33602-5754, USA

Sheffield, Lois (Athlete, Baseball Player)
49531 Peck Wadsworth Rd
Wellington, OH 44090-9778, USA

Sheffield, Tony (Baseball Player)
PO Box 164
Tullahoma, TN 37388-0164, USA

Shehee, Rashaan (Athlete, Football Player)
6120 Bay Club Ct
Bakersfield, CA 93312-6212, USA

Sheik, Duncan (Musician, Songwriter, Writer)
Nonesuch Records
75 Rockefeller Plz
New York, NY 10019-6908, USA

Sheila E (Musician)
Elevate Hope Foundation
4804 Laurel Canyon Blvd Ste 805
Valley Village, CA 91607-3717, USA

Sheindlin, Judith (Judge Judy) (Judge, Reality Star)
Big Ticket Television
5800 W Sunset Blvd
C/O Ktla Studios
Hollywood, CA 90028-6607, USA

Sheiner, David S (Actor)
1827 Veteran Ave Apt 19
Los Angeles, CA 90025-4567, USA

Sheinfeld, David (Composer)
112 Ash Way
San Rafael, CA 94903-2902, USA

Shelby, Derrick (Athlete, Football Player)

Shelby, John (Athlete, Baseball Player)
2232 Broadhead Pl
Lexington, KY 40515-1147, USA

Shelby, Mark (Composer, Musician)
Thomas Cassidy
11761 E Speedway Blvd
Tucson, AZ 85748-2017, USA

Shelby, Richard (Politician)
1414 High Forest Dr N
Tuscaloosa, AL 35406-2152, USA

Sheldon, Bob (Athlete, Baseball Player)
1161 Kienas Rd N
Kalispell, MT 59901-8181, USA

Sheldon, Jack (Musician)
PO Box 10398
Burbank, CA 91510-0398, USA

Sheldon, Rollie (Athlete, Baseball Player)
614 NE Coronado Ave
Lees Summit, MO 64063-2522, USA

Sheldon, Scott (Athlete, Baseball Player)
5202 Blue Cypress Ln
League City, TX 77573-6240, USA

Shell, Arthur (Art) (Athlete, Coach, Football Coach, Football Player)
Oakland, CA 94605, USA

Shell, Donnie (Athlete, Football Player)
2945 Shandon Rd
Rock Hill, SC 29730-9521, USA

Shell, Todd (Athlete, Football Player)
4222 E McLellan Cir Unit 15
Mesa, AZ 85205-3119, USA

Shellen, Stephen (Actor)
3655 St. Laurent
#205
Montreal, Quebec HX 2V5, Canada

Shellenback, Jim (Athlete, Baseball Player)
10627 Dreamy Ln
Parker, AZ 85344-7576, USA

Shellenbeck, Jim (Athlete, Baseball Player)
10627 Dreamy Ln
Parker, AZ 85344-7576, USA

Shellenberger, Michael (Activist, Writer)
The Breakthrough Institute
436 14th St Ste 820
Oakland, CA 94612-2726, USA

Shelley, Barbara (Actor)
c/o Staff Member *The Artists Partnership*
101 Finsbury Pavement
London EC2A 1RS, UNITED KINGDOM

Shelley, Jody (Athlete, Hockey Player)
211 Chestnut St
Haddonfield, NJ 08033-1814

Shelley, Rachel (Actor)
c/o Kesha Williams *KW Entertainment*
3727 W Magnolia Blvd Ste 430
Burbank, CA 91505-2818, USA

Shelly, Randy (Actor)
c/o Ellen Gilbert *Abrams Artists Agency*
750 N San Vicente Blvd
E Tower Fl 11
Los Angeles, CA 90069-5788, USA

Shelmerdine, Kirk (Race Car Driver)
Kirk Shelmerdine Racing
PO Box 1133
Welcome, NC 27374-1133, United States

Shelton, Angela (Frangela) (Actor, Comedian)
c/o Staff Member *Gekis Management*
4217 Verdugo View Dr
Los Angeles, CA 90065-4317, USA

Shelton, Ben (Athlete, Baseball Player)
1192 Clarence Ave Unit 11
Oak Park, IL 60304-2169, USA

Shelton, Blake (Musician)
c/o Narvel Blackstock *Starstruck Entertainment*
40 Music Sq W
Nashville, TN 37203-3206, USA

Shelton, Chris (Athlete, Baseball Player)
6382 S Shady Grove Cir
Salt Lake City, UT 84121-6508, USA

Shelton, Craig (Athlete, Basketball Player)
8618 Leslie Ave
Glenarden, MD 20706-1528, USA

Shelton, Danny (Athlete, Football Player)
c/o Jeff Sperbeck *The Novo Agency*
1537 Via Romero Ste 100
Alamo, CA 94507-1527, USA

Shelton, Deborah (Actor)
c/o Marc Bass *Beacon Talent Agency*
170 Apple Ridge Rd
Woodcliff Lk, NJ 07677-8149, USA

Shelton, Derek (Athlete, Baseball Player)
203 46th Ave St
Pete Beach, FL 33706-2575, USA

Shelton, L J (Athlete, Football Player)
650 Carrotwood Ter
Plantation, FL 33324-8240, USA

Shelton, Lonnie (Athlete, Basketball Player)
3883 Union Ave Apt 5
Bakersfield, CA 93305-2444, USA

Shelton, Marley (Actor)
c/o Stephanie Simon *Untitled Entertainment*
350 S Beverly Dr Ste 200
Beverly Hills, CA 90212-4819, USA

Shelton, Richard (Athlete, Football Player)
4083 Woodley Creek Rd
Jacksonville, FL 32218-9200, USA

Shelton, Ricky Van (Musician, Songwriter)

Shelton, Ronald W (Director)
c/o Staff Member *WME/IMG*
9601 Wilshire Blvd
Beverly Hills, CA 90210-5213, USA

Shelton, Samantha (Actor)
c/o Staff Member *Innovative Artists*
1505 10th St
Santa Monica, CA 90401-2805, USA

Shembo, Prince (Athlete, Football Player)
c/o Adisa P Bakari *Kelley Drye & Warren LLP*
3050 K St NW Ste 400
Washington, DC 20007-5100, USA

Shemin, Robert (Business Person, Writer)
Robert Shemin Inc
7965 S 700 E
C/O PREIG
Sandy, UT 84070-0256, USA

Shen, Parry (Actor)
c/o Staff Member *Lichtman/Salners Company*
12216 Moorpark St
Studio City, CA 91604-5228, USA

Shenandoh, Joanne (Musician, Songwriter, Writer)
Oneida Nation Territory
PO Box 450
Oneida, NY 13421-0450, USA

Shenkman, Ben (Actor)
2 Charlton St Apt 5K
New York, NY 10014-4970, USA

Shepard, Dax (Actor, Reality Star, Writer)
c/o David Palmer *Primate Pictures*
928 16th St
Santa Monica, CA 90403-3219, USA

Shepard, Devon (Producer, Writer)
c/o Staff Member *Agency for the Performing Arts (APA)*
405 S Beverly Dr Ste 500
Beverly Hills, CA 90212-4425, USA

Shepard, Judy (Activist)
The Matthew Shepard Foundation
301 Thelma Dr # 512
Casper, WY 82609-2325, USA

Shepard, Kenny Wayne (Musician)
c/o Emily Burton *Vector Management*
PO Box 120479
Nashville, TN 37212-0479, USA

Shepard, Kiki (Actor)
c/o Staff Member *Cunningham Escott Slevin & Doherty (CESD)*
10635 Santa Monica Blvd Ste 130
Los Angeles, CA 90025-8306, USA

Shepard, Sara (Writer)
c/o Andy McNicol *WME/IMG (NY)*
11 Madison Ave Fl 18
New York, NY 10010-3669, USA

Shepard, Vonda (Actor, Musician, Songwriter)
1114 Harvard St
Santa Monica, CA 90403-4710, USA

Sheperd, Ben (Musician)
9198 NE Hidden Cove Rd
Bainbridge Island, WA 98110-4106, USA

Sheperd, Elizabeth (Actor)
London Mgmt
2-4 Noel St
London W1V 3RB, UNITED KINGDOM (UK)

Sheperd, Morgan (Race Car Driver)
57 Rhody Creek Loop
Stuart, VA 24171-3011, USA

Shephard, Quinn (Actor)
c/o Stephanie Ritz *WME/IMG*
9601 Wilshire Blvd
Beverly Hills, CA 90210-5213, USA

Shepherd, Ashton (Musician)
c/o Nicole Zeller *P.L.A. Media*
1303 16th Ave S Ste A
Nashville, TN 37212-2929, USA

Shepherd, Chris (Director, Writer)
c/o Staff Member *Slinky Pictures*
Old Truman Brewery
91 Brick Ln
London E16 QN, UNITED KINGDOM (UK)

Shepherd, Cybill (Actor)
4355 Bergamo Dr
Encino, CA 91436-3303, USA

Shepherd, Gannon (Athlete, Football Player)
5818 Alvaton Ct
Norcross, GA 30092-3901, USA

Shepherd, Keith (Athlete, Baseball Player)
2201 Parnell Ave
Fort Wayne, IN 46805-3338, USA

Shepherd, Morgan (Race Car Driver)
PO Box 623
Conover, NC 28613-0623, USA

Shepherd, Ron (Athlete, Baseball Player)
5821 FM 349
Kilgore, TX 75662-6905, USA

Shepherd, Sherri (Actor, Comedian, Talk Show Host)
c/o Simone Smalls *Simone Smalls PR*
142 5th Ave # 1902
New York, NY 10011-4312, USA

Shepherd, William (Astronaut)
18623 Prince William Ln
Houston, TX 77058-4224, USA

Shepis, Tiffany (Actor)
c/o Michael J Roberts *D-Mentd Entertainment*
Prefers to be contact via email or telephone
Wilmington, NC, USA

Sheppard, Delia (Actor, Model)
c/o Cheryl Murphy *Spectrum Talent*
9107 Wilshire Blvd Ste 450
Beverly Hills, CA 90210-5535, USA

Sheppard, Gregg (Athlete, Hockey Player)
2521 Blue Jay Cres
North Battleford, SK S9A 3Z3, Canada

Sheppard, Jonathan (Misc)
287 Lamborntown Rd
West Grove, PA 19390-9237, USA

Sheppard, Julian (Comedian)
c/o Staff Member *Gersh*
9465 Wilshire Blvd Ste 600
Beverly Hills, CA 90212-2605, USA

Sheppard, Kelvin (Athlete, Football Player)
c/o Todd France *Creative Artists Agency (CAA) Sports*
3500 Lenox Rd NE
Atlanta, GA 30326-4228, USA

Sheppard, Mike (Coach, Football Coach)
University of New Mexico
Athletic Dept
Albuquerque, NM 87131-0001, USA

Sheppard, Ray (Athlete, Hockey Player)
Cornwall Colts
100 Water St E
Cornwall, ON K6H 6G4, Canada

Sheppard, Ray (Athlete, Hockey Player)
19110 Fox Landing Dr
Boca Raton, FL 33434-5156

Sheppard, William Morgan (Actor)
c/o Staff Member *SMS Talent*
8383 Wilshire Blvd Ste 230
Beverly Hills, CA 90211-2436, USA

Sher, Antony (Actor)
c/o Staff Member *Independent Talent Group*
40 Whitfield St
London W1T 2RH, UNITED KINGDOM

Sher, Eden (Actor)
c/o Adam Griffin *LINK Entertainment*
11872 La Grange Ave
Los Angeles, CA 90025-5282, USA

Sher, Stacey (Business Person, Producer)
3661 Alomar Dr
Sherman Oaks, CA 91423-4946, USA

Shera, Mark (Actor)
PO Box 15717
Beverly Hills, CA 90209-1717, USA

Sherba, John (Musician)
Kronos Quartet
1235 9th Ave
San Francisco, CA 94122-2306, USA

Sherbedgia, Rade (Actor)
Innovative Artists
1505 10th St
Santa Monica, CA 90401-2805, USA

Sherels, Marcus (Athlete, Football Player)

Sherer, Dave (Athlete, Football Player)
4212 Colgate Ave
Dallas, TX 75225-6603, USA

Sherffius, John (Cartoonist)
Saint Louis Post Dispatch
900 N Tucker Blvd
Editorial Dept
Saint Louis, MO 63101-1099, USA

Sheridan, Bonnie (Musician)
c/o Mike Eistenstadt *Amsel, Eisenstadt & Frazier Talent Agency (AEF)*
5055 Wilshire Blvd Ste 860
Los Angeles, CA 90036-6108, USA

Sheridan, Bonnie Bramlett (Actor, Musician)
18011 Martha St
Encino, CA 91316-1052, USA

Sheridan, Dave (Actor)
c/o Joy Pervis *J Pervis Talent Agency*
3050 Amwiler Rd Ste 200
Atlanta, GA 30360-2807, USA

Sheridan, Jamey (Actor)
c/o Steven Fisher *Underground Management*
1180 S Beverly Dr Ste 509
Los Angeles, CA 90035-1157, USA

Sheridan, Jim (Actor, Director, Producer, Writer)
Hell's Kitchen International Ltd.
21 Mespil Rd.
Dublin 00004, Ireland

Sheridan, Lisa (Actor)
c/o Mitch Clem *Mitch Clem Management*
7080 Hollywood Blvd Ste 1100
Hollywood, CA 90028-6938, USA

Sheridan, Liz (Actor)
11333 Moorpark St # 427
North Hollywood, CA 91602-2618

Sheridan, Neill (Athlete, Baseball Player)
150 Chaucer Ct
Pleasant Hill, CA 94523-4104, USA

Sheridan, Nicole (Adult Film Star)
c/o Staff Member *Atlas Multimedia Inc*
9005 Eton Ave Ste C
Canoga Park, CA 91304-6533, USA

Sheridan, Nicollette (Actor)
c/o Rick Genow *Stone, Meyer, Genow, Smelkinson and Binder*
9665 Wilshire Blvd Ste 500
Beverly Hills, CA 90212-2312, USA

Sheridan, Pat (Athlete, Baseball Player)
31654 Taft St
Wayne, MI 48184-2234, USA

Sheridan, Rondell (Actor)
Gail Stocker Presents
1025 N Kings Rd Apt 113
Los Angeles, CA 90069-6007, USA

Sheridan, Taylor (Actor)
c/o Alex Cole *Elevate Entertainment*
6300 Wilshire Blvd # 807
Los Angeles, CA 90048-5204, USA

Sheridan, Tye (Actor)
c/o Emily Rose *Mosaic Media Group*
407 N Maple Dr # 100
Beverly Hills, CA 90210-3818, USA

Sherk, Jerry M (Athlete, Football Player)
1819 Bel Air Ter
Encinitas, CA 92024-5502, USA

Sherk, Kathy (Golfer)
Canadian Golf Hall of Fame
1333 Dorval Dr
Oakville, ON L6M 4G2, CANADA

Sherk, Stefanie (Actor)
c/o Elizabeth Much *East 2 West Collective*
11022 Santa Monica Blvd Ste 350
Los Angeles, CA 90025-7532, USA

Sherlock, Glenn (Athlete, Baseball Player)
5905 E Beryl Ave
Paradise Valley, AZ 85253-1105, USA

Sherman, Anthony (Athlete, Football Player)
c/o Alan Herman *Sportstars Inc*
1370 Avenue of the Americas Fl 19
New York, NY 10019-4602, USA

Sherman, Bobby (Actor, Musician)
11611 San Vicente Blvd Ste 740
Los Angeles, CA 90049-6529, USA

Sherman, Brad (Congressman, Politician)
2242 Rayburn Hob
Washington, DC 20515-1001, USA

Sherman, Brent (Race Car Driver)
Atkins Motorsports
222 Raceway Dr
Mooresville, NC 28117-6510, USA

Sherman, Darrell (Athlete, Baseball Player)
5200 Chicago Ave APT U8
Riverside, CA 92507-5891, USA

Sherman, Edgar A (Coach, Football Coach)
681 Nancy Ln
Newark, OH 43055-4333, USA

Sherman, Heath (Athlete, Football Player)
2785 County Road 247
Wharton, TX 77488-5554, USA

Sherman, Mike (Athlete, Coach, Football Coach, Football Player)
3337 Arapaho Ridge Dr
College Station, TX 77845-4540, USA

Sherman, Richard (Athlete, Baseball Player)
c/o Ben Dogra *Relativity Sports*
2029 Century Park E Ste 1550
Century City, CA 90067-3000, USA

Sherman, Richard (Athlete, Football Player)
c/o Staff Member *San Francisco 49ers*
4949 Marie P Debartolo Way
Santa Clara, CA 95054-1156, USA

Sherman, Rod (Athlete, Football Player)
PO Box 4551
Incline Village, NV 89450-4551, USA

Sherman, Saul (Athlete, Football Player)
175 E Delaware Pl Apt 6410
Chicago, IL 60611-7730, USA

Sherman-Palladino, Amy (Director, Producer, Writer)
c/o Staff Member *Creative Artists Agency (CAA)*
2000 Avenue of the Stars Ste 100
Los Angeles, CA 90067-4705, USA

Sherod, Edmund (Athlete, Basketball Player)
519 Montvale Ave
Richmond, VA 23222-3020, USA

Sherr, Lynn (Correspondent)
c/o Staff Member *American Program Bureau*
1 Gateway Ctr Ste 751
Newton, MA 02458-2817, USA

Sherrard, Michael W (Mike) (Athlete, Football Player)
5661 Colodny Dr
Agoura Hills, CA 91301-2217, USA

Sherrill, Dennis (Athlete, Baseball Player)
1691 Tolley Ter SE
Palm Bay, FL 32909-8831, USA

Sherrill, George (Athlete, Baseball Player)
1442 E Vine Meadow Cir
Salt Lake City, UT 84121-1785, USA

Sherrill, Jackie W (Coach, Football Coach)
Mississippi State University
Athletic Dept
Mississippi State, MS 39762, USA

Sherrill, Tim (Athlete, Baseball Player)
PO Box 812
Harrison, AR 72602-0812, USA

Sherrin, Edward G (Ned) (Director)
4 Cornwall Mansions
Ashburnham Road
London SW10 0PE, UNITED KINGDOM (UK)

Sherrington, Georgina (Actor)
c/o Staff Member *JGM*
15 Lexham Mews
London W8 6JW, UNITED KINGDOM (UK)

Sherrit, Jim (Athlete, Hockey Player)
7 Dancy Dr
Orillia, ON L3V 7M1, Canada

Sherrod, Derek (Football Player)
c/o Adisa P Bakari *Kelley Drye & Warren LLP*
3050 K St NW Ste 400
Washington, DC 20007-5100, USA

Sherry, Norm (Athlete, Baseball Player, Coach)
141 Monte Vista
San Clemente, CA 92672-4829, USA

Sherry, Paul H (Religious Leader)
United Church of Christ
700 Prospect Ave E
Cleveland, OH 44115-1100, USA

Sherven, Gord (Athlete, Hockey Player)
184 Hampshire Grove NW
Calgary, AB T3A 5B3, Canada

Sherwin, Tim (Athlete, Football Player)
6 Mill Rd
Latham, NY 12110-1184, USA

Sherwood, Brad (Actor, Producer)
c/o Erik Kritzer *LINK Entertainment*
11872 La Grange Ave
Los Angeles, CA 90025-5282, USA

Sherwood, Dominic (Actor)
c/o Brett Ruttenberg *Imprint PR*
6121 W Sunset Blvd
Neuehouse
Los Angeles, CA 90028-6442, USA

Shesol, Jeff (Cartoonist)
Creators Syndicate
5777 W Century Blvd # 700
Los Angeles, CA 90045-5600, USA

Shestakova, Tatyana B (Actor)
Maly Drama Theatre
Rubinstein St 18
Saint Petersburgh, RUSSIA

Shetty, Reshma (Actor)
c/o Smith (Stevie) Stephanie *Station3 (LA)*
1051 Cole Ave Ste B
Los Angeles, CA 90038-2601, USA

Shevardnadze, eduard (Politician)
Plekhanova 103
Tbilisi 880064, Georgia

Shibutani, Alex (Athlete, Figure Skater, Olympic Athlete)
c/o Jay Ogden *IMG (LA)*
2049 Century Park E Ste 2460
Los Angeles, CA 90067-3126, USA

Shibutani, Maia (Athlete, Figure Skater, Olympic Athlete)
c/o Jay Ogden *IMG (LA)*
2049 Century Park E Ste 2460
Los Angeles, CA 90067-3126, USA

Shields, Ben (Actor)
10965 Fruitland Dr Apt 102
Studio City, CA 91604-4601, USA

Shields, Billy (Athlete, Football Player)
12701 Treeridge Ter
Poway, CA 92064-6426, USA

Shields, Brooke (Actor, Model)
c/o Jill Fritzo *Jill Fritzo Public Relations*
208 E 51st St # 305
New York, NY 10022-6557, USA

Shields, Carol (Writer)
103-407 Swift St
Victoria, BC V8W 1S2, Canada

Shields, James (Athlete, Baseball Player)
3042 Leanne Ct
Clearwater, FL 33759-1425, USA

Shields, Lebron (Athlete, Football Player)
1405 82nd Ave Lot 31
Vero Beach, FL 32966-8792, USA

Shields, Robert (Misc)
Robert Shields Designs
PO Box 10024
Sedona, AZ 86339-8024, USA

Shields, Sam (Athlete, Football Player)
c/o Drew Rosenhaus *Rosenhaus Sports Representation*
3921 Alton Rd # 440
Miami Beach, FL 33140-3852, USA

Shields, Samona (Samantha Strong) (Adult Film Star)
3324 Castle Heights Ave
Los Angeles, CA 90034-2729, USA

Shields, Scott (Athlete, Football Player)
16139 Pine Valley Dr
Northville, MI 48168-9655, USA

Shields, Steve (Athlete, Hockey Player)
Michigan Tech University Athletics
1400 Townsend Dr
Houghton, MI 49931-1295

Shields, Steve (Athlete, Baseball Player)
4969 Leonard Dr
Gadsden, AL 35903-4638, USA

Shields, Steve (Athlete, Hockey Player)
123 E Balboa Blvd
Newport Beach, CA 92661-1117

Shields, Tommy (Athlete, Baseball Player)
518 N Elm St
Lititz, PA 17543-1312, USA

Shields, Will H (Athlete, Football Player)
13125 W 127th Pl
Overland Park, KS 66213-3846, USA

Shields, Willow (Actor)
c/o Alexandra Heller *Advantage PR*
3900 W Alameda Ave Ste 1200
Burbank, CA 91505-4317, USA

Shiell, Jason (Athlete, Baseball Player)
301 Sting Ray Ct
Guyton, GA 31312-6592, USA

Shiely, John S (Business Person)
Briggs & Stratton
PO Box 702
Milwaukee, WI 53201-0702, USA

Shifflett, Garland (Athlete, Baseball Player)
1095 Cody St
Lakewood, CO 80215-4818, USA

Shifflett, Steve (Athlete, Baseball Player)
24004 E 172nd St
Pleasant Hill, MO 64080-7582, USA

Shifty, Shellshock (Musician)
Q Prime
729 7th Ave Ste 1600
New York, NY 10019-6880, USA

Shih, Wen Yann (Actor)
c/o Richie Walls *FilmEngine*
345 N Maple Dr Ste 222
Beverly Hills, CA 90210-5183, USA

Shikler, Aaron (Artist)
44 W 77th St
New York, NY 10024-5150, USA

Shiley, Newhouse Jean (Athlete, Track Athlete)
1100 Sunnybrae Ave
Chatsworth, CA 91311, USA

Shilling, Curt (Baseball Player)
c/o Staff Member *Boston Red Sox*
4 Jersey St
Boston, MA 02215-4148, USA

Shilton, Justin (Actor)

Shilton, Peter (Soccer Player)
Hubbards Cottage
Bentley Lane
Maxstoke near Coleshill B46 2QR, UNITED KINGDOM (UK)

Shimada, Yoko (Actor)
7245 Hillside Ave Apt 415
Los Angeles, CA 90046-2342, USA

Shimerman, Armin (Actor)
Innovative Artists
1505 10th St
Santa Monica, CA 90401-2805, USA

Shimkus, Joanna (Actor)
c/o Staff Member *Creative Artists Agency (CAA)*
2000 Avenue of the Stars Ste 100
Los Angeles, CA 90067-4705, USA

Shimkus, John (Congressman, Politician)
2452 Rayburn Hob
Washington, DC 20515-1009, USA

Shimmerman, Armin (Actor)
c/o Staff Member *Innovative Artists*
1505 10th St
Santa Monica, CA 90401-2805, USA

Shim'on, Rona-Lee (Actor)
c/o Estelle Lasher *Lasher Group*
1133 Avenue of the Americas Fl 27
New York, NY 10036-6710, USA

Shimono, Sab (Actor)
c/o Erin Connor *Connor Ankrum & Associates*
1680 Vine St Ste 1016
Los Angeles, CA 90028-8804, USA

Shinall, Zak (Athlete, Baseball Player)
16605 Sell Cir
Huntington Beach, CA 92649-3299, USA

Shinedown (Music Group)
c/o Staff Member *In De Goot Entertainment*
119 W 23rd St Ste 609
New York, NY 10011-2594, USA

Shinefield, Henry R (Misc)
2240 Hyde St # 2
San Francisco, CA 94109-1509, USA

Shiner, Dick (Athlete, Football Player)
19 Fox Trl
Gettysburg, PA 17325-7383, USA

Shines, Anthony (Razor) (Athlete, Baseball Player)
11508 Herb Cv
Austin, TX 78750-3671, USA

Shinn, Christopher (Comedian)
c/o Staff Member *Gersh*
9465 Wilshire Blvd Ste 600
Beverly Hills, CA 90212-2605, USA

Shinn, George (Business Person)
New Orleans/Oklahoma City Hornets
210 Park Ave Ste 1850
Oklahoma Tower
Oklahoma City, OK 73102-5636, USA

Shinners, John (Athlete, Football Player)
N120W1495 Freistadt Road
Germantown, WI 53022, USA

Shinoda, Mike (Musician)
Artist Group International
9560 Wilshire Blvd Ste 400
Beverly Hills, CA 90212-2442, USA

Shinske, Rich (Athlete, Hockey Player)
531 Pearkes Rd
Victoria, BC V9C 2L6, Canada

Shins, The (Music Group)
c/o Steve Martin *Nasty Little Man*
285 W Broadway Rm 310
New York, NY 10013-2257, USA

Shiny Toy Guns (Music Group)
c/o Staff Member *Paradigm (Monterey)*
404 W Franklin St
Monterey, CA 93940-2303, USA

Shipanoff, Dave (Athlete, Baseball Player)
3 Salina Dr
St. Albert, AB T8N 0L1, Canada

Shipka, Kiernan (Actor)
c/o Alexandra Crotin *The Lede Company*
9701 Wilshire Blvd # 930
Beverly Hills, CA 90212-2020, USA

Shipler, David K (Journalist)
4005 Thornapple St
Bethesda, MD 20815-5037, USA

Shipley, A.Q. (Athlete, Football Player)
c/o Eric Metz *Lock Metz Milanovic LLC*
6900 E Camelback Rd Ste 600
Scottsdale, AZ 85251-8044, USA

Shipley, Craig (Athlete, Baseball Player)
Boston Red Sox
4 Jersey St
Attn: V.P. Scouting Dept
Boston, MA 02215-4148, USA

Shipley, Jenny (Politician)
Parliament Buildings
Wellington, New Zealand

Shipley, Joe (Athlete, Baseball Player)
23 Park Dr
Saint Charles, MO 63303-3607

Shipley, Joe (Athlete, Baseball Player)
23 Park Dr
Saint Charles, MO 63303-3607, USA

Shipley, Julie (Race Car Driver)
M&S Management
13904 Fiji Way Apt 242
Marina Del Rey, CA 90292-6925, USA

Shipman, Claire (Correspondent)
ABC-TV
77 W 66th St
News Dept
New York, NY 10023-6201, USA

Shipman, Kim (Golfer)
239 Texas Dr
Hideaway, TX 75771-5030, USA

Shipp, Alexandra (Actor)
c/o Lisa Wright *LINK Entertainment*
11872 La Grange Ave
Los Angeles, CA 90025-5282, USA

Shipp, E R (Misc)
New York Daily News
220 E 42nd St
Editorial Dept
New York, NY 10017-5806, USA

Shipp, Jackie (Athlete, Football Player)
1664 N Virginia St
Reno, NV 89557-0001, USA

Shipp, Jerry (Athlete, Basketball Player, Olympic Athlete)
PO Box 370
Kingston, OK 73439-0370, USA

Shipp, John Wesley (Actor)
c/o Janette Anderson *Janette Anderson Entertainment*
9682 Via Torino
Burbank, CA 91504-1410, USA

Shipp, William (Athlete, Football Player)
3920 Camellia Dr
Mobile, AL 36693-2814, USA

Shipp Jr, Demetrius (Actor)
c/o Ariana Drummond *Kreative Approach Productions*
1710 W 38th St
Los Angeles, CA 90062-1044, USA

Shirayanagi, Peter Seiichi Cardinal (Religious Leader)
Archbishop's House
3-16-15 Sekiguchi
Bunkyoku
Tokyo 00112, JAPAN

Shire, David L (Composer)
19 Ludlow Ln
Palisades, NY 10964-1606, USA

Shire, Talia (Actor, Director)
c/o Peter Young *Sovereign Talent Group*
1642 Westwood Blvd Ste 202
Los Angeles, CA 90024-5609, USA

Shires, Jim (Athlete, Hockey Player)
24141 Fairway Ln
Trabuco Canyon, CA 92679-4184

Shirk, Gary (Athlete, Football Player)
5419 Silchester Ln
Charlotte, NC 28215-5307, USA

Shirley, Bart (Athlete, Baseball Player)
5757 S Staples St Apt 4208
Corpus Christi, TX 78413-3752, USA

Shirley, Bob (Athlete, Baseball Player)
13306 E 84th St N Apt 105
Owasso, OK 74055-8650, USA

Shirley, Steve (Athlete, Baseball Player)
9200 James Pl NE
Albuquerque, NM 87111-3323, USA

Shirton, Glen (Athlete, Hockey Player)
5 Ziraldo Rd
St Catharines, ON L2N 6S6, Canada

Shiver, Sanders (Athlete, Football Player)
9217 Christo Ct
Owings Mills, MD 21117-3596, USA

Shivers, Roy (Athlete, Football Player)
2067 Hidden Hollow Ln
Henderson, NV 89012-3203, USA

Shlesinger, Iliza (Comedian)
c/o Greg Longstreet *Polaris PR*
8135 W 4th St Fl 2
Los Angeles, CA 90048-4415, USA

Shlomi, Vince (Offer) (Director)
1680 Michigan Ave Ste 700
Miami Beach, FL 33139-2551, USA

Shmyr, John (Athlete, Hockey Player)
140 Nonquon Rd
Oshawa, ON L1G 3S5, Canada

Shoals, Roger (Athlete, Football Player)
365 Righters Mill Rd
Gladwyne, PA 19035-1542, USA

Shobert, Bubba (Race Car Driver)
8905 153rd St
Wolfforth, TX 79382-4305, USA

Shocked, Michelle (Musician)
Skyline Music
28 Union St
Whitefield, NH 03598-3503, USA

Shockey, Jeremy (Athlete, Football Player)
c/o Drew Rosenhaus *Rosenhaus Sports Representation*
3921 Alton Rd # 440
Miami Beach, FL 33140-3852, USA

Shockley, Costen (Athlete, Baseball Player)
403 Wilson St
Georgetown, DE 19947-2340, USA

Shockley, Jeremy (Football Player)
New York Giants
Giants Stadium
East Rutherford, NJ 07073, USA

Shockley, William (Actor)
6345 Balboa Blvd Ste 375
Encino, CA 91316-5238, USA

Shoebottom, Bruce (Athlete, Hockey Player)
40 Woodfield Dr
Scarborough, ME 04074-8437

Shoeffling, Michael (Actor)
PO Box 2563
Canyon Country, CA 91386-2563, USA

Shoemaker, Craig (Actor)
c/o Staff Member *Osbrink Talent Agency*
4343 Lankershim Blvd # 100
North Hollywood, CA 91602-2705, USA

Shoemaker, John (Race Car Driver)
American Eagle Racing
3305 Horseshoe Dr
Sacramento, CA 95821-1717, USA

Shoemaker, Sydney S (Misc)
104 Northway Rd
Ithaca, NY 14850-2241, USA

Shoemate, C Richard (Business Person)
Bestfoods
700 Sylvan Ave
International Plaza
Englewood Cliffs, NJ 07632-3150, USA

Shofner, Delbert M (Del) (Athlete, Football Player)
1665 Del Mar Ave
San Marino, CA 91108-2621, USA

Shofner, James (Jim) (Athlete, Football Coach, Football Player)
9620 Champions Dr
Granbury, TX 76049-4447, USA

Shoji, Dave (Coach)
University of Hawaii
Athletic Dept
Hilo, HI 96720, USA

Shonekan, Ernest A O (President)
12 Alexander Ave
Ikoyi
Lagos, NIGERIA

Shopay, Tom (Athlete, Baseball Player)
10145 NW 19th St
Doral, FL 33172-2529, USA

Shoppach, Kelly (Athlete, Baseball Player)
15358 Briarcrest Cir
Fort Myers, FL 33912-6359, USA

Shore, David (Producer, Writer)
c/o Lawrence Shuman *Shuman Company*
3815 Hughes Ave Fl 4
Culver City, CA 90232-2715, USA

Shore, Gary (Director)
c/o Staff Member *42 Management (UK)*
8 Flitcroft St
London WC2H 8DL, UNITED KINGDOM

Shore, Howard (Actor, Composer, Musician)
c/o Staff Member *Columbia Artists Mgmt Inc*
1790 Broadway Fl 6
New York, NY 10019-1537, USA

Shore, Pauly (Actor, Comedian)
c/o Staff Member *Landing Patch Productions*
8491 W Sunset Blvd Ste 700
West Hollywood, CA 90069-1911, USA

Shore, Roberta (Actor)
PO Box 71639
Salt Lake City, UT 84171-0639, USA

Shores, Del (Producer, Writer)
Del Shores Productions
8581 Santa Monica Blvd # 560
West Hollywood, CA 90069-4120, USA

Shorr, Lonnie (Actor, Comedian)
707 18th Ave S
Nashville, TN 37203-3214, USA

Short, Bill (Athlete, Baseball Player)
6 Magnolia Rd
Palm Coast, FL 32137, USA

Short, Brandon (Athlete, Football Player)
1717 Sumac St
McKeesport, PA 15132-5470, USA

Short, Columbus (Actor)
Great Picture Show
12400 Wilshire Blvd Ste 1275
Los Angeles, CA 90025-1078, USA

Short, Eugene (Athlete, Basketball Player)
8111 Fondren Lake Dr
Houston, TX 77071-3610, USA

Short, Kawann (Athlete, Football Player)
c/o Joel Segal *Lagardere Unlimited (NY)*
456 Washington St Apt 9L
New York, NY 10013-1555, USA

Short, Martin (Actor, Comedian)
15907 Alcima Ave
Pacific Palisades, CA 90272-2405, USA

Short, Nigel (Misc)
Daily Telegraph
Peterborough Court
Marsh Wall
London E14, UNITED KINGDOM (UK)

Short, Purvis (Athlete, Basketball Player)
8111 Fondren Lake Dr
Houston, TX 77071-3610, USA

Short, Richard (Actor)
c/o Staff Member *Innovative Artists*
1505 10th St
Santa Monica, CA 90401-2805, USA

Short, Rick (Athlete, Baseball Player)
3021 Forsythe Ct
Peoria, IL 61614-1119, USA

Short, Thomas C (Misc)
Theatrical Stage Employees Alliance
1515 Broadway
New York, NY 10036-8901, USA

Shorter, Frank (Athlete, Olympic Athlete, Track Athlete)
558 Utica Ct
Boulder, CO 80304-0773, USA

Shorter, Wayne (Composer, Musician)
International Music Network
278 Main St # 400
Gloucester, MA 01930-6022, USA

Shortland, Cate (Actor)
c/o Kate Richter *HLA Management*
PO Box 1536
Strawberry Hills 02012, AUSTRALIA

Shortridge, Stephen (Actor)
PO Box 3875
Coeur D Alene, ID 83816-2531, USA

Shortridge, Steve (Actor)
1707 Clear View Dr
Beverly Hills, CA 90210-2012, USA

Shorts, Cecil (Athlete, Football Player)
c/o Ryan Tollner *REP 1 Sports Group*
80 Technology Dr
Irvine, CA 92618-2301, USA

Shorts, Peter (Athlete, Football Player)
810 S Cedar Point Dr
Anaheim, CA 92808-1680, USA

Shostakovich, Maxim D (Musician)
PO Box 273
Jordanville, NY 13361-0273, USA

Shou, Robin (Actor)
Paradigm Agency
10100 Santa Monica Blvd Ste 2500
Los Angeles, CA 90067-4116, USA

Shouse, Brian (Athlete, Baseball Player)
1616 Magnolia
Washington, IL 61571-9266, USA

Shouse, Dexter (Athlete, Basketball Player)
4523 E Rhonda Dr
Phoenix, AZ 85018-7223, USA

Shout Out Louds (Music Group)
c/o Staff Member *Paradigm (Monterey)*
404 W Franklin St
Monterey, CA 93940-2303, USA

Show, Frida (Actor)
c/o Kim Matuka *Schuller Talent (LA)*
332 S Beverly Dr Ste 100
Beverly Hills, CA 90212-4812, USA

Show, Grant (Actor)
17 Jib St
Marina Del Rey, CA 90292-5908, USA

Showalter III, William N (Buck) (Athlete, Baseball Player, Coach)
9736 Hathaway St
Dallas, TX 75220-2114, USA

Showder, Lisa (Race Car Driver)
1650 E Golf Rd
Schaumburg, IL 60196-0001, USA

Shower, Kathy (Actor, Model)
Provenca 23 1-1
Barcelona, SPAIN

Shraner, Kim (Actor)
c/o Robyn Friedman *Artist Management Inc*
464 King St E
Toronto, ON M5A 1L7, CANADA

Shreve, Chasen (Athlete, Baseball Player)

Shreve, Susan R (Writer)
3506 35th St NW
Washington, DC 20016-3114, USA

Shribman, David M (Journalist)
Boston Globe
1130 Connecticut Ave NW Ste 520
Editorial Dept
Washington, DC 20036-3943, USA

Shrider, Richard (Athlete, Basketball Player)
6666 Morning Sun Rd
Oxford, OH 45056-8843, USA

Shrimpton, Jean (Actor, Model)
Abbey Hotel Penzance
Cornwall, UNITED KINGDOM (UK)

Shriner, Kin (Actor)
Don Buchwald
5900 Wilshire Blvd Ste 3100
Los Angeles, CA 90036-5030, USA

Shriner, Wil (Television Host)
5313 Quakertown Ave
Woodland Hills, CA 91364-3542, USA

Shriver, Lionel (Writer)
c/o Jenne Casarotto *Casarotto Ramsay & Associates Ltd (UK)*
Waverley House
7-12 Noel St
London W1F 8GQ, UNITED KINGDOM

Shriver, Loren J (Astronaut)
108 Charleston St
Friendswood, TX 77546-4928, USA

Shriver, Maria (Correspondent, Television Host)
11440 San Vicente Blvd Ste 300
Los Angeles, CA 90049-6217, USA

Shriver, Mark (Politician)
Save the Children
54 Wilton Rd
Westport, CT 06880-3108, USA

Shriver, Pam (Athlete, Olympic Athlete, Tennis Player)
Pam Shriver Tennis Challenge
14524 Dover Rd
Reisterstown, MD 21136-3877, USA

Shriver, Timothy (Business Person)
Special Olympics
1133 19th St NW Ste 1200
Washington, DC 20036-3645, USA

Shrontz, Frank A (Business Person)
2949 81st Pl SE # P
Mercer Island, WA 98040-3059, USA

Shroud, Johnathan (Writer)
Laura Cecil Literary Agency
17 Alwyne Villas
London N1 2HG, UNITED KINGDOM

Shroyer, Sonny (Actor)
301 E College St
Valdosta, GA 31602-3810, USA

Shtalenkov, Mikhail (Athlete, Hockey Player)
7 Faenza
Newport Coast, CA 92657-1602

Shuchuk, Gary (Athlete, Hockey Player)
5713 Lancashier Ct
Fitchburg, WI 53711-6504

Shue, Andrew (Actor)
c/o Jimmy Darmody *Creative Artists Agency (CAA)*
2000 Avenue of the Stars Ste 100
Los Angeles, CA 90067-4705, USA

Shue, Elisabeth (Actor)
c/o Stephen Huvane *Slate PR*
901 N Highland Ave
W Hollywood, CA 90038-2412, USA

Shue, Gene (Athlete, Basketball Player, Coach)
4338 Redwood Ave Unit 303
Marina Del Rey, CA 90292-7648, USA

Shuey, Paul (Athlete, Baseball Player)
5252 Mill Dam Rd
Wake Forest, NC 27587-6386, USA

Shugart, Clyde (Athlete, Football Player)
6368 Heronwalk Dr
Gulf Breeze, FL 32563-7024, USA

Shugarts, Bret (Athlete, Football Player)
18823 Forest Bend Creek Way
Spring, TX 77379-5510, USA

Shukovsky, Joel (Writer)
Shukovsky-English Ent
4024 Radford Ave
Studio City, CA 91604-2101, USA

Shula, David D (Dave) (Athlete, Coach, Football Coach, Football Player)
10805 Indian Trl
Cooper City, FL 33328-5509, USA

Shula, Don (Athlete, Coach, Football Coach, Football Player)
16 Indian Creek Island Rd
Indian Creek Village, FL 33154-2904, USA

Shula, Mike (Athlete, Coach, Football Coach, Football Player)
13754 Bromley Point Dr
Jacksonville, FL 32225-2634, USA

Shuler, Heath (Athlete, Football Player)
Shuler Real Estate
8550 Kingston Pike
Knoxville, TN 37919-5353, USA

Shuler, Joseph Heath (Congressman, Politician)
229 69,Non Hob
Washington, DC 20515-0001, USA

Shuler, Mickey C (Athlete, Football Player)
c/o Scott Smith *XAM Sports*
3509 Ice Age Dr
Madison, WI 53719-5409, USA

Shulock, John (Baseball Player)
4180 5th St SW
Vero Beach, FL 32968-3909, USA

Shulock, John (Athlete, Baseball Player)
4180 5th St SW
Vero Beach, FL 32968-3909, USA

Shultz, George (Politician)
776 Dolores St
Stanford, CA 94305-8428, USA

Shumaker, Anthony (Athlete, Baseball Player)
2213 Jefferson St
Paducah, KY 42001-3108, USA

Shuman-Juransinski, Amy (Baseball Player)
424 Douglass St
Wyomissing, PA 19610-2906, USA

Shumate, John (Athlete, Basketball Player, Coach)
16406 S 12th Pl
Phoenix, AZ 85048-4045, USA

Shumate, Rachel (Actor)
c/o Sean Fay *LINK Entertainment*
11872 La Grange Ave
Los Angeles, CA 90025-5282, USA

Shum Jr, Harry (Actor, Dancer, Musician)
c/o Nicole Perna *Imprint PR*
6121 W Sunset Blvd
Neuehouse
Los Angeles, CA 90028-6442, USA

Shumpert, Terry (Athlete, Baseball Player)
8432 Fairview Ct
Lone Tree, CO 80124-3181, USA

Shust, Aaron (Musician)
c/o Mitch White *Moose Management*
Prefers to be contacted via telephone
Nashville, TN, USA

Shuster, Bill (Congressman, Politician)
204 Cannon Hob
Washington, DC 20515-3816, USa

Shutan, Jan (Actor)
3115 Deep Canyon Dr
Beverly Hills, CA 90210-1035, USA

Shutt, Byron (Athlete, Hockey Player)
29723 Lake Rd
Bay Village, OH 44140-1277, USA

Shutt, Steve (Athlete, Coach, Hockey Player)
7814 Heritage Grand Pl
Bradenton, FL 34212-3261, USA

Shuttleworth, Mark (Astronaut)
HBD Ventura Capital
PO Box 1159
Durbanville 07551, SOUTH AFRICA

Shut Up Stella (Music Group)
c/o Staff Member *Paradigm (Monterey)*
404 W Franklin St
Monterey, CA 93940-2303, USA

Shy, Les (Athlete, Football Player)
1777 W Crystal Ln Unit 556
Mt Prospect, IL 60056-5437, USA

Shyamalan, M Night (Director, Producer)
c/o Staff Member *Night Chronicles*
1055 Westlakes Dr Ste 300
Berwyn, PA 19312-2410, USA

Shydner, Ritch (Comedian)
c/o Daniel Strone *Trident Media Group LLC*
41 Madison Ave Fl 36
New York, NY 10010-2257, USA

Shyer, Charles R (Director, Writer)
227 N Glenroy Ave
Los Angeles, CA 90049-2417, USA

Shys, The (Music Group)
c/o Staff Member *Paradigm (Monterey)*
404 W Franklin St
Monterey, CA 93940-2303, USA

Sia (Musician)
10265 Woodbridge St
Toluca Lake, CA 91602-2937, USA

Sia, Beau (Actor)
c/o Staff Member *Creative Artists Agency (CAA)*
2000 Avenue of the Stars Ste 100
Los Angeles, CA 90067-4705, USA

Sibbett, Jane (Actor)
c/o John Carrabino *John Carrabino Management*
5900 Wilshire Blvd Ste 740
Los Angeles, CA 90036-5032, USA

Siberry, Michael (Actor)
c/o Rob Kolker *Red Letter Entertainment*
550 W 45th St Apt 501
New York, NY 10036-3779, USA

Sibert, Sam (Athlete, Basketball Player)
PO Box 172491
Arlington, TX 76003-2491, USA

Sibley, David (Actor)
c/o Staff Member *Select Artists Ltd (CA-Westside Office)*
1138 12th St Apt 1
Santa Monica, CA 90403-5459, USA

Sibley, Mark (Athlete, Basketball Player)
41610 N Emerald Lake Dr
Anthem, AZ 85086-1039, USA

Sicard, Pedro (Actor)
c/o Gabriel Blanco *Gabriel Blanco Iglesias (Mexico)*
Rio Balsas 35-32
Colonia Cuauhtemoc
DF 06500, Mexico

Sichting, Jerry (Basketball Player)
3190 N Country Club Rd
Martinsville, IN 46151-7929, USA

Sicinski, Bob (Athlete, Hockey Player)
1741 Pengilley Pl
Mississauga, ON L5J 4R8, Canada

Siddall, Joe (Athlete, Baseball Player)
2785 Sierra Dr
Windsor, ON N9E 2Y9, Canada

Siddig, Alexander (Actor)

Siddiqui, Aamera (Actor)
c/o Staff Member *NUTS*
1500 Jackson St NE Ste 218
Minneapolis, MN 55413-2897, USA

Siddons, Anne (Writer)
175 N Plaza Ct
Mount Pleasant, SC 29464-6301, USA

Siddons, Anne R (Writer)
767 Vermont Road
Atlanta, GA 30319, USA

Siddons, Ann Rivers (Writer)
175 N Plaza Ct
Mount Pleasant, SC 29464-6301

Sidell, Devin (Actor)
c/o Angie Lucania *Entertainment Lab*
8447 Wilshire Blvd Ste 103
Beverly Hills, CA 90211-3244, USA

Sidewalk Prophets (Music Group, Musician)
c/o Scott Bickell *Brickhouse Entertainment*
106 Mission Ct Ste 1202
Franklin, TN 37067-6484, USA

Sidgmore, John (Business Person)
WorldCom
500 Clinton Center Dr Ste 2200
Clinton, MS 39056-5674, USA

Sidibe, Gabourey (Gabby) (Actor)
c/o Jill Kaplan *Authentic Talent and Literary Management (NY)*
20 Jay St Ste M17
Brooklyn, NY 11201-8300, USA

Sidime, Lamine (Prime Minister)
Prime Minister's Office
Conakry, GUINEA

Sidney, Dainon (Athlete, Football Player)
2537 Willowbranch Dr
Nashville, TN 37217-3807, USA

Sidorkiewicz, Peter (Athlete, Hockey Player)
1056 Swiss Hts
Oshawa, ON L1K 3B4, Canada

Sidran, Ben (Race Car Driver)
Go Jazz
PO Box 2023
Madison, WI 53701-2023, USA

Siebel Newsom, Jennifer (Actor, Producer)
c/o Staff Member *Girls' Club Hollywood*
30 Sir Francis Drake Blvd
PO Box 437
Ross, CA 94957-9601, USA

Sieber, Christopher (Actor)
c/o Richard Fisher *Abrams Artists Agency*
275 7th Ave Fl 26
New York, NY 10001-6708, USA

Siebern, Norm (Athlete, Baseball Player)
2006 Palo Alto Ave
Lady Lake, FL 32159-9211, USA

Siebert, Paul (Athlete, Baseball Player)
1711 Acker St
Orlando, FL 32837-6588, USA

Siebert, Wilfred C (Sonny) (Athlete, Baseball Player)
2555 Brush Creek Rd
Saint Louis, MO 63129-5601, USA

Siebler, Dwight (Athlete, Baseball Player)
4646 N 79th St
Ronkonkoma, NY 11779-4328, USA

Siega, Marcos (Director)
c/o Staff Member *WME|IMG*
9601 Wilshire Blvd
Beverly Hills, CA 90210-5213, USA

Siegal, Bernard (Writer)
61 0x Bow Ln
Woodbridge, CT 06525-1525

Siegal, Jay (Music Group, Musician)
Brothers Mgmt
141 Dunbar Ave
Fords, NJ 08863-1551, USA

Siegal, John (Football Player)
Chicago Bears
Harvey's Bt
Harveys Lake, PA 18618, USA

Siegel, Barry (Journalist)
Los Angeles Times
2300 E Imperial Hwy
Editorial Dept
El Segundo, CA 90245-2813, USA

Siegel, Bernie (Doctor, Writer)
61 Ox Bow Ln
Woodbridge, CT 06525-1525, USA

Siegel, Eric (Actor)
c/o Mickey Berman *United Talent Agency (UTA)*
9336 Civic Center Dr
Beverly Hills, CA 90210-3604, USA

Siegel, Herbert J (Business Person)
Chris-Craft Industries
767 5th Ave
New York, NY 10153-0023, USA

Siegel, Jake (Actor)
c/o Staff Member *JC Robbins Management*
865 S Sherbourne Dr
Los Angeles, CA 90035-1809, USA

Siegel, Janis (Musician)
International Creative Mgmt
40 W 57th St Ste 1800
New York, NY 10019-4033, USA

Siegel, L Pendleton (Business Person)
Potlatch Corp
601 W Riverside Ave
Spokane, WA 99201-0621, USA

Siegel, Norman (Attorney)
Committee for Norman Siegel
260 Madison Ave
New York, NY 10016-2400, USA

Siegel, Robert C (Correspondent)
c/o Gregory McKnight *United Talent Agency (UTA)*
9336 Civic Center Dr
Beverly Hills, CA 90210-3604, USA

Siegel, Ron (Chef)
Charles Nob Hill 1250 Jones St
San Francisco, CA 94109-4261, USA

Siemaszko, Casey (Actor)
Gersh Agency
232 N Canon Dr
Beverly Hills, CA 90210-5302, USA

Siemaszko, Nina (Actor)
c/o David Rose *Innovative Artists*
1505 10th St
Santa Monica, CA 90401-2805, USA

Sieminski, Chuck (Athlete, Football Player)
5000 Village Way Apt 204
Marcus Hook, PA 19061-6856, USA

Siemon, Jeffrey G (Jeff) (Athlete, Football Player)
5401 Londonderry Rd
Edina, MN 55436-1026, USA

Sienkiewicz, Troy (Athlete, Football Player)
186 Darcy Ave
Goose Creek, SC 29445-6664, USA

Sierchio, Tom (Actor, Writer)
c/o Alan Gasmer *Alan Gasmer Management Company*
10877 Wilshire Blvd Ste 603
Los Angeles, CA 90024-4348, USA

Siering, Lauri (Swimmer)
PO Box 1352
Tres Pinos, CA 95075-1352, USA

Sierota, Sydney (Musician)
c/o Jill Fritzo *Jill Fritzo Public Relations*
208 E 51st St # 305
New York, NY 10022-6557, USA

Sierra, Jessica (Musician)
c/o Network Solutions
PO Box 447
Herndon, VA 20172-0447, USA

Sierra, Karent (Reality Star)
4651 Ponce De Leon Blvd Ste 100
Coral Gables, FL 33146-2131, USA

Sierra, Pedro (Athlete, Baseball Player)
Indianapolis Clowns
3900 16th St NW APT 133
Washington, DC 20011-8302, USA

Sierra, Ruben A (Athlete, Baseball Player)
16361 SW 66th St
Miami, FL 33193-5600, USA

Sievers, Eric (Athlete, Football Player)
11550 Great Falls Way
Great Falls, VA 22066-1148, USA

Sievers, Gary (Actor)
c/o Staff Member *Dani's Agency*
434 E Southern Ave
Tempe, AZ 85282-5216, USA

Siff, Maggie (Actor)
c/o James Suskin *Suskin Management*
2 Charlton St Apt 5K
New York, NY 10014-4970, USA

Siffredi, Rocco (Adult Film Star)
14141 Covello St Ste 8C
Van Nuys, CA 91405-1400, USA

Sific, Mokdad (Prime Minister)
Prime Minister's Office
Government Palais
Al-Moradia
Algiers, ALGERIA

Sigalet, Jordan (Athlete, Hockey Player)
PO Box 3454 LCD LCD 1
Langley, BC V3A 4R8, Canada

Sigel, Beanie (Musician)
International Creative Mgmt
8942 Wilshire Blvd # 219
Beverly Hills, CA 90211-1908, USA

Sigel, Jay (Golfer)
1284 Farm Rd
Berwyn, PA 19312-2000, USA

Sigler, Jamie-Lynn (Actor)
c/o Glenn Gulino *G2 Entertainment LLC*
1 Columbus Pl Apt S25E
New York, NY 10019-8208, USA

Sigman, Stan (Business Person)
Cingular Creative Mgmt
5565 Glenridge Connector
Atlanta, GA 30342-4756, USA

Sigman, Stephanie (Actor)
c/o Ruth Bernstein *Viewpoint Inc*
8820 Wilshire Blvd Ste 220
Beverly Hills, CA 90211-2622, USA

Sigur Ros (Music Group)
c/o Staff Member *Paradigm (Monterey)*
404 W Franklin St
Monterey, CA 93940-2303, USA

Sikahema, Vai (Athlete, Football Player)
28 Abington Rd
Mount Laurel, NJ 08054-4720, USA

Sikes, Cynthia (Actor)
c/o Dede Binder-Goldsmith *Defining Artists Agency*
8721 W Sunset Blvd Ste 209
W Hollywood, CA 90069-2272, USA

Sikharulidze, Anton (Figure Skater)
Ice House Skating Rink
111 Midtown Bridge Approac
Hackensack, NJ 07601-7505, USA

Sikich, Mike P (Athlete, Football Player)
702 Tudor Dr
Janesville, WI 53546-2001, USA

Sikking, James B (Actor)
258 S Carmelina Ave
Los Angeles, CA 90049-3957, USA

Siklenka, Mike (Athlete, Hockey Player)
Farm
Meadow Lake, SK S9X 1 T8, Canada

Sikma, Jack (Athlete, Basketball Player)
10133 NE 64th St
Kirkland, WA 98033-6819, USA

Sikora, Joe (Actor)
c/o Myrna Jacoby *MJ Management*
130 W 57th St Apt 11A
New York, NY 10019-3311, USA

Sikora, Nicole (Athlete, Golfer)
Westchester Golf Range
701 Dobbs Ferry Rd
White Plains, NY 10607-1744, USA

Sikorski, Brian (Athlete, Baseball Player)
17930 Wexford St
Roseville, MI 48066-4630, USA

Silas, James (Athlete, Basketball Player)
6800 Thistle Hill Way
Austin, TX 78754-5800, USA

Silas, Paul (Athlete, Basketball Player, Coach)
2463 Peninsula Shores Ct
Denver, NC 28037-7655, USA

Silatolu, Amini (Athlete, Football Player)
c/o Bruce Tollner *REP 1 Sports Group*
80 Technology Dr
Irvine, CA 92618-2301, USA

Silatolu, Ratu Timoci (Prime Minister)
Prime Minister's Office
6 Berkeley Crescent
Suva
Viti Levu, FIJI

Silberling, Brad (Director, Producer)
c/o Paul Nelson *Mosaic Media Group*
407 N Maple Dr # 100
Beverly Hills, CA 90210-3818, USA

Silbermann, Jake (Actor)
c/o Robyn Ziegler *Robyn Ziegler Management*
143 W 29th St Ste 1103
New York, NY 10001-5134, USA

Silbey, Robert J (Misc)
Massachusetts Institute of Technology
Chemistry Dept
Cambridge, MA 02139, USA

Sileo, Dan (Athlete, Football Player)
43 Allison Way
East Haven, CT 06512-6003, USA

Silia, Felix (Actor)
8927 Snowden Ave
Arleta, CA 91331-6115, USA

Siliga, Sealver (Athlete, Football Player)

Silk (Artist, Musician)
c/o Staff Member *Faa*
250 W 57th St Ste 2203
New York, NY 10107-2204, USA

Silk, Anna (Actor)
c/o Abe Hoch *A Management Company*
16633 Ventura Blvd Ste 1450
Encino, CA 91436-1887, USA

Silk, Dave (Athlete, Hockey Player, Olympic Athlete)
PO Box 130
Minot, MA 02055-0130

Silla, Felix (Actor)
5313 Magenta Ct
Las Vegas, NV 89108-2305, USA

Sillas, Karen (Actor)
PO Box 725
Wading River, NY 11792-0725, USA

Siller, Eugenio (Actor)
c/o Bruno del Granado *CAA (Miami)*
1691 Michigan Ave Fl 5
Miami Beach, FL 33139-2520, USA

Silliman, Ron (Writer)
262 Orchard Rd
Paoli, PA 19301-1116, USA

Sillinger, Mike (Athlete, Hockey Player)
Edmonton Oilers
11230 110 St NW
Edmonton, AB T5G 3H7, Canada

Sillinger, Mike (Athlete, Hockey Player)
419-4009 Harbour Landing Dr
Regina, SK S4W 0E3, Canada

Sills, Douglas (Actor, Musician)
Gold Marshak Liedike
3500 W Olive Ave Ste 1400
Burbank, CA 91505-5512, USA

Siltala, Mike (Athlete, Hockey Player)
1693 Ruscombe Close
Mississauga, ON L5J 1Y4, Canada

Silva, Adele (Actor, Model)
c/o Staff Member *McLean-Williams Management*
Chester House Unit 3:06
Kennington Park 1-3 Brixton Road
London SW9 6DE, UNITED KINGDOM

Silva, Anderson (Athlete, Wrestler)
c/o Cheryl Lynch *Lynch Archer PR*
5115 Wilshire Blvd Apt 400
Los Angeles, CA 90036-4372, USA

Silva, Daniel (Writer)
3512 Winfield Ln NW
Washington, DC 20007-2344

Silva, Gilberto (Football Player)
Arsenal Stadium
Highbury
London N5 1BU, ENGLAND

Silva, Henry (Actor)
8747 Clifton Way Apt 305
Beverly Hills, CA 90211-2125, USA

Silva, Jackie (Athlete, Volleyball Player)
Jackie Sports and Marketing
Prefers to be contacted via email or telephone

Silva, Jason (Television Host)
c/o Marcel Pariseau *True Public Relations*
3575 Cahuenga Blvd W Ste 360
Los Angeles, CA 90068-1361, USA

Silva, Jose (Athlete, Baseball Player)
100 Cobblestone Ct
Oakdale, PA 15071-3852, USA

Silva, Zack (Actor)
Valeo Entertainment
8265 W Sunset Blvd Ste 103
C/O Michael Dean Valeo
West Hollywood, CA 90046-2433, USA

Silver, Edward J (Religious Leader)
Bible Way Church
5118 Clarendon Rd
Brooklyn, NY 11203-5329, USA

Silver, Harvey (Actor)
c/o Staff Member *Anonymous Content*
3532 Hayden Ave
Culver City, CA 90232-2413, USA

Silver, Jeffrey (Producer)
c/o Staff Member *Outlaw Productions*
9350 Civic Center Dr Ste 100
Beverly Hills, CA 90210-3629, USA

Silver, Joan Macklin (Director)
Silverfilm Productions
510 Park Ave Apt 9B
New York, NY 10022-6640, USA

Silver, Joel (Producer)
c/o Staff Member *Silver Pictures*
2434 Main St
Santa Monica, CA 90405-3516, USA

Silver, Michael B (Actor)
9229 W Sunset Blvd Ste 315
Los Angeles, CA 90069-3403, USA

Silvera, Charlie (Athlete, Baseball Player)
1240 Manzanita Dr
Millbrae, CA 94030-2934, USA

Silverberg, Robert (Writer)
c/o Tom Doherty Associates, LLC
175 5th Ave
New York, NY 10010-7703, USA

Silverbush, Lori (Actor)
c/o Brantley Brown *Authentic Talent & Literary Management*
3615 Eastham Dr # 650
Culver City, CA 90232-2410, USA

Silverio, Luis (Athlete, Baseball Player)
3130 NW 89th Ter
Kansas City, MO 64154-1835, USA

Silverman, Ben (Producer)
c/o Craig Jacobson *Hansen, Jacobson, Teller, Hoberman, Newman, Warren & Richman*
450 N Roxbury Dr Fl 8
Beverly Hills, CA 90210-4222, USA

Silverman, Henry R (Business Person)
Cendant Corp
9 W 57th St
New York, NY 10019-2701, USA

Silverman, Jerry (Horse Racer)
3888 Meadow Ln
Hollywood, FL 33021-2645, USA

Silverman, Jonathan (Actor)
c/o Jim Broutman *Broutman PR*
8225 Santa Monica Blvd
West Hollywood, CA 90046-5912, USA

Silverman, Sarah (Actor, Comedian)
c/o Lewis Kay *Kovert Creative*
506 Santa Monica Blvd Ste 400
Santa Monica, CA 90401-2412, USA

Silverstein, Elliott (Director)
Gersh Agency
232 N Canon Dr
Beverly Hills, CA 90210-5302, USA

Silverstone, Alicia (Actor)
c/o Jason Weinberg *Untitled Entertainment*
350 S Beverly Dr Ste 200
Beverly Hills, CA 90212-4819, USA

Silverstone, Ben (Actor)
c/o Staff Member *London Management*
2-4 Noel St
London W1V 3RB, UNITED KINGDOM (UK)

Silversun Pickups (Music Group)
c/o Cliff Burnstein *Q Prime (NY)*
729 7th Ave Fl 16
New York, NY 10019-6831, USA

Silvestre, Armando (Actor)
Cerro Macultepec 273Col. Campestre Churubusco
Mexico DF, MEXICO

Silvestri, Alan A (Composer, Musician)
c/o Staff Member *Gorfaine/Schwartz Agency Inc*
4111 W Alameda Ave Ste 509
Burbank, CA 91505-4171, USA

Silvestri, Dave (Athlete, Baseball Player, Olympic Athlete)
1888 Schoettler Valley Dr
Chesterfield, MO 63017-5141, USA

Silvestrini, Achille Cardinal (Religious Leader)
Oriental Churches Congregation
Via Conciliazione 34
Rome 00193, ITALY

Silvstedt, Victoria (Actor, Model)
c/o Liza Anderson *Anderson Group Public Relations*
8060 Melrose Ave Fl 4
Los Angeles, CA 90046-7038, USA

Sim, Gerald (Actor)
Associated Internationl Mgmt
7 Great Russell St
London W1D 1BS, UNITED KINGDOM (UK)

Sim, Jonathan (Athlete, Hockey Player)
104 Willow Ave
New Glasgow, NS B2H 1Z5, Canada

Simas, Bill (Athlete, Baseball Player)
2436 E Pryor Dr
Fresno, CA 93720-4408, USA

Simcoe, Anthony (Actor)
c/o Pauline Lee *International Casting Service & Associates*
2/218 Crown St (via Kings Lane)
Darlinghurst NSW 2010, Australia

Simeoni, Sara (Athlete, Track Athlete)
Via Castello Rivoli Veronese
Verona 37010, ITALY

Simhan, Meera (Actor)
Bamboo Management
17 Buccaneer St
C/O Heidi L Ifft
Marina Del Rey, CA 90292-5103, USA

Simic, Charles (Writer)
PO Box 192
Strafford, NH 03884-0192, USA

Simien, Tracy (Athlete, Football Player)
3219 Sumac Dr
Pearland, TX 77584-8069, USA

Simien, Wayne (Basketball Player)
c/o Staff Member *Miami Heat*
601 Biscayne Blvd
American Airlines Arena
Miami, FL 33132-1801, USA

Simkin, Margery (Misc)
CSA
606 N Larchmont Blvd Ste 4B
Los Angeles, CA 90004-1309, USA

Simkus, Arnold (Athlete, Football Player)
4248 Chicago Rd
Warren, MI 48092-1471, USA

Simmer, Charles (Athlete, Hockey Player)
70 Couplee View
SW
Calgary, AB T3H 5J7, Canada

Simmer, Charlie (Athlete, Hockey Player)
Calgary Flames
PO Box 1540 Stn M
Calgary, AB T2P 3B9, Canada

Simmer, Charlie (Athlete, Hockey Player)
70 Coulee View SW
Calgary, AB T3H 5J6, Canada

Simmonds, Ellie (Athlete, Olympic Athlete, Swimmer)
c/o Staff Member *Mission Sports Management*
11 Nortfields Prospect
London SW18 1PE, UK

Simmonds, Kennedy A (Prime Minister)
PO Box 167
Earle Mome Development
Basseterre, SAINT KITTS & NEVIS

Simmonds, Sara (Actor)
c/o Steven Jensen *Independent Group, The*
6363 Wilshire Blvd Ste 115
Los Angeles, CA 90048-5734, USA

Simmons, Angela (Reality Star)

Simmons, Arthur (Baseball Player)
Kansas City Monarchs
27 158th Pl Apt 2W
Calumet City, IL 60409-4945, USA

Simmons, Ben (Athlete, Basketball Player)
c/o Staff Member *Philadelphia 76ers*
3601 S Broad St Ste 4
Philadelphia, PA 19148-5250, USA

Simmons, Bill (Sportscaster, Talk Show Host)
c/o Lewis Kay *Kovert Creative*
506 Santa Monica Blvd Ste 400
Santa Monica, CA 90401-2412, USA

Simmons, Bob (Athlete, Football Player)
16040 Chalfont Cir
Dallas, TX 75248-3544, USA

Simmons, Brian (Athlete, Baseball Player)
226 Village Dr
Canonsburg, PA 15317-2367, USA

Simmons, Brian (Athlete, Football Player)
9240 Liberty Hill Ct
Cincinnati, OH 45242-4663, USA

Simmons, Canary (Athlete, Football Player)
13531 Lyndonville Dr
Houston, TX 77041-4804, USA

Simmons, Chelan (Actor)
c/o Staff Member *Pacific Artists Management*
112 3rd Ave E Suite 210
Vancouver, BC V5T 1C8, CANADA

Simmons, Curtis T (Curt) (Athlete, Baseball Player)
200 Park Rd
Ambler, PA 19002-1121, USA

Simmons, Dan (Writer)
c/o Michael Prevett *Gotham Group*
1041 N Formosa Ave # 200
West Hollywood, CA 90046-6703, USA

Simmons, Daniel (Diggy Simmons) (Musician)
c/o Daniel Kim *Creative Artists Agency (CAA)*
2000 Avenue of the Stars Ste 100
Los Angeles, CA 90067-4705, USA

Simmons, Earl (DMX) (Actor, Musician)
142 McLain St
Mount Kisco, NY 10549-4932, USA

Simmons, Ed (Athlete, Football Player)
PO Box 6632
Kennewick, WA 99336-0639, USA

Simmons, Gail (Reality Star)
c/o Ken Slotnick *AGI Entertainment*
150 E 58th St Fl 19
New York, NY 10155-1900, USA

Simmons, Gary (Athlete, Hockey Player)
2624 Inverness Dr
Lake Havasu City, AZ 86404-1373

Simmons, Gene (Business Person, Musician, Reality Star)
Gene Simmons Company
PO Box 16075
Beverly Hills, CA 90209-2075, USA

Simmons, Grant (Athlete, Basketball Player)
7274 E Costilla Pl
Centennial, CO 80112-1111, USA

Simmons, Henry (Actor)
c/o David Gardner *Artists First*
9465 Wilshire Blvd Ste 900
Beverly Hills, CA 90212-2608, USA

Simmons, Hubert (Baseball Player)
Baltimore Elite Giants
3247 Sonia Trl
Ellicott City, MD 21043-3273, USA

Simmons, Jaason (Actor)
Gilbertson & Kincaid Mgmt
1330 4th St
Santa Monica, CA 90401-1302, USA

Simmons, Jason (Athlete, Football Player)
2828 Spring St
Pittsburgh, PA 15210-2675, USA

Simmons, Jeff (Race Car Driver)
Team Green
7615 Zionsville Rd
Indianapolis, IN 46268-2174, USA

Simmons, Jerry (Athlete, Football Player)
2233 S King Dr
Chicago, IL 60616-1415, USA

Simmons, JK (Actor)
c/o Lisa Kasteler *Wolf-Kasteler Public Relations*
6255 W Sunset Blvd Ste 1111
Los Angeles, CA 90028-7426, USA

Simmons, Johnny (Actor)
c/o Ruth Bernstein *Viewpoint Inc*
8820 Wilshire Blvd Ste 220
Beverly Hills, CA 90211-2622, USA

Simmons, Joseph (Rev Run) (Actor, Producer)
Rush Philanthropic Arts Foundation
512 Seventh Ave
Fl 43
New York, NY 10018, USA

Simmons, Kimora Lee (Designer, Fashion Designer)
1055 Shadow Hill Way
Beverly Hills, CA 90210-2306, USA

Simmons, Lili (Actor)
c/o Kimberly Christman *42West*
1840 Century Park E Ste 700
Los Angeles, CA 90067-2122, USA

Simmons, Lionel (Athlete, Basketball Player)
406 Queen St # A
Philadelphia, PA 19147-3021, USA

Simmons, Lionel J (Athlete, Basketball Player)
406 Queen St # A
Philadelphia, PA 19147-3021, USA

Simmons, Lon (Sportscaster)
165 Pierce St APT 443
Daly City, CA 94015-1999, USA

Simmons, Nelson (Athlete)
4445 Rosebud Ln Apt B
La Mesa, CA 91941-6255, USA

Simmons, Richard (Fitness Expert)
Richard Simmons Inc
8899 Beverly Blvd Ste 811
Los Angeles, CA 90048-2452, USA

Simmons, Russell (Producer)
135 Madison Ave Fl 5
New York, NY 10016-6759, USA

Simmons, Stacey (Athlete, Football Player)
1780 Harbor Dr
Clearwater, FL 33755-1828, USA

Simmons, Ted L (Athlete, Baseball Player)
PO Box 26
Chesterfield, MO 63006-0026, USA

Simmons, Todd (Baseball Player)
26342 Meadow Creek Ln
Wildomar, CA 92595-4914, USA

Simmons, Tony (Athlete, Football Player)
366 Grand Ave Apt 319
Oakland, CA 94610-4840, USA

Simmons, Vanessa (Model)
c/o Staff Member *Ford Models (LA)*
9200 W Sunset Blvd Ste 805
W Hollywood, CA 90069-3603, USA

Simmons, Victor (Athlete, Football Player)
PO Box 2992
Chicago, IL 60690-2992, USA

Simms, Chris (Football Player)
c/o Team Member *Tampa Bay Buccaneers*
1 Buccaneer Pl
Tampa, FL 33607-5701, USA

Simms, Joan (Actor)
MGA
Southbank House
Black Prince Road
London SE1 7SJ, UNITED KINGDOM (UK)

Simms, Larry (Actor)
1043 Keeho Marina
Honolulu, HI 96819, USA

Simms, Mike (Athlete, Baseball Player)
118 Via Monte Picayo
San Clemente, CA 92673-6600, USA

Simms, Molly (Actor)
c/o Alissa Vradenburg *Untitled Entertainment*
350 S Beverly Dr Ste 200
Beverly Hills, CA 90212-4819, USA

Simms, Philip (Phil) (Athlete, Football Player, Sportscaster)
930 Old Mill Rd
Franklin Lakes, NJ 07417-1906, USA

Simms, Primate George Otto (Religious Leader)
62 Cypress Grove Road
Dublin 00006, IRELAND

Simo, Brian (Race Car Driver)
28033 Arnold Dr
EC-2
Sonoma, CA 95476-9710, USA

Simollardes, Drew (Musician)
David Levin Mgmt
200 W 57th St Ste 308
New York, NY 10019-3211, USA

Simon, Carly (Composer, Musician)
c/o Staff Member *Red Light Management*
10 E 40th St Fl 22
New York, NY 10016-0201, USA

Simon, Chris (Athlete, Hockey Player)
702 Foch Blvd
Williston Park, NY 11596-1010, Canada

Simon, Corey (Athlete, Football Player)
9010 Winged Foot Dr
Tallahassee, FL 32312-4000, USA

Simon, Daniella (Designer)
Daniella Fashions, Inc
315 W 70th St Apt 8I
New York, NY 10023-3512, USA

Simon, David (Actor, Producer, Writer)
c/o Staff Member *Creative Artists Agency (CAA)*
2000 Avenue of the Stars Ste 100
Los Angeles, CA 90067-4705, USA

Simon, Dick (Race Car Driver)
Dick Simon Racing
24896 Sea Crest Dr
Dana Point, CA 92629-1923, USA

Simon, George W (Astronaut)
PO Box 62
Sunspot, NM 88349-0062, USA

Simon, James (Athlete, Football Player)
8501 SW 103rd Ave
Gainesville, FL 32608-7206, USA

Simon, Jazmyn (Actor)
c/o Marisa Martins *The Lede Company*
401 Broadway Ste 206
New York, NY 10013-3033, USA

Simon, Josette (Actor)
Conway Van Gelder Robinson
18-21 Jermyn St
London SW1Y 6NB, UNITED KINGDOM (UK)

Simon, Paul (Musician, Songwriter)
82 Brookwood Ln
New Canaan, CT 06840-3101, USA

Simon, Roger M (Writer)
Baltimore Sun
1627 K St NW
Editorial Dept
Washington, DC 20006-1702, USA

Simon, Salem (Athlete, Football Player)
2245 Sheridan Rd
Evanston, IL 60201-2918, USA

Simon, Scott (Correspondent)
NBC-TV
30 Rockefeller Plz
News Dept
New York, NY 10112-0015, USA

Simon, Todd (Athlete, Hockey Player)
Morrell Wine Bar and Cafe
1 Rockefeller Plz
New York, NY 10020-2003

Simone, Hannah (Actor)
c/o Rachael Wesolowski *Independent Public Relations*
9601 Wilshire Blvd Ste 750
Beverly Hills, CA 90210-5228, USA

Simoneau, Mark (Athlete, Football Player)
17 Waterview Dr
Sicklerville, NJ 08081-1683, USA

Simoneau, Yves (Director, Producer)
c/o David Gersh *Gersh*
9465 Wilshire Blvd Ste 600
Beverly Hills, CA 90212-2605, USA

Simonetti, Frank (Athlete, Hockey Player)
33 Perkins St
Stoneham, MA 02180-4345

Simonini, Edward (Ed) (Athlete, Football Player)
3825 E 66th St
Tulsa, OK 74136-2820, USA

Simonis, Adrianus J Cardinal (Religious Leader)
Aartbisdom
BP 14019 Maliebaan
Utrecht, SB 03508, NETHERLANDS

Simons, Doug (Athlete, Baseball Player)
1988 Mount Olive Rd
Lookout Mountain, GA 30750-4746, USA

Simons, James (Producer)
c/o Staff Member *Paradigm*
8942 Wilshire Blvd
Beverly Hills, CA 90211-1908, USA

Simons, James (Business Person)
Renaissance Technologies
600 Route 25A
East Setauket, NY 11733-1235, USA

Simons, Timothy (Actor)
c/o Ben Curtis *Brillstein Entertainment Partners*
9150 Wilshire Blvd Ste 350
Beverly Hills, CA 90212-3453, USA

Simonsen, Rob (Composer, Musician)
c/o Neil Kohan *Greenspan Artist Management*
8760 W Sunset Blvd
West Hollywood, CA 90069-2206, USA

Simonson, Dave (Athlete, Football Player)
408 1st St SW
Austin, MN 55912-3254, USA

Simontacchi, Jason (Athlete, Baseball Player)
7300 Summer Manor Dr
Saint Louis, MO 63129-5700, USA

Simpkins, Dickey (Athlete, Basketball Player)
6104 St Andrews Way
Hixson, TN 37343-3284, USA

Simpkins, Ryan (Actor)
c/o Ashley Franklin *Thruline Entertainment*
9250 Wilshire Blvd Fl Ground
Beverly Hills, CA 90212-3352, USA

Simpkins, Ty (Actor)
c/o Lisa Perkins *Baker Winokur Ryder Public Relations*
9100 Wilshire Blvd
W Tower #500
Beverly Hills, CA 90212-3415, USA

Simple Kid (Music Group)
c/o Staff Member *Paradigm (Monterey)*
404 W Franklin St
Monterey, CA 93940-2303, USA

Simple Plan (Music Group)
c/o Staff Member *Creative Artists Agency (CAA)*
2000 Avenue of the Stars Ste 100
Los Angeles, CA 90067-4705, USA

Simpson, Alan (Politician)
1201 Sunshine Ave
Cody, WY 82414-4228, USA

Simpson, Bill (Athlete, Football Player)
5732 Huntley Ave
Garden Grove, CA 92845-2040, USA

Simpson, Carl (Athlete, Football Player)
12106 Parkview Ln
Alpharetta, GA 30005-5418, USA

Simpson, Carole (Correspondent)
ABC-TV
77 W 66th St
News Dept
New York, NY 10023-6201, USA

Simpson, Casey (Actor)
c/o Wendi Green *Paradigm*
8942 Wilshire Blvd
Beverly Hills, CA 90211-1908, USA

Simpson, Cody (Musician)
PO Box 1766
Studio City, CA 91614-0766, USA

Simpson, Craig (Athlete, Hockey Player)
CBC TV
PO Box 500 Stn A
Toronto, ON M5W 1E6, Canada

Simpson, Dick (Athlete, Baseball Player)
PO Box 3593
Culver City, CA 90231-3593, USA

Simpson, Duke (Athlete, Baseball Player)
3821 Park Dr
El Dorado Hills, CA 95762-4568, USA

Simpson, Herbert (Athlete, Baseball Player)
Birmingham Black Barons
1462 Farragut St
New Orleans, LA 70114-2818, USA

Simpson, Jessica (Designer, Musician)
5535 Dixon Trail Rd
Hidden Hills, CA 91302-1185, USA

Simpson, Jimmi (Actor)
c/o Jeffrey Chassen *Imprint PR*
6121 W Sunset Blvd
Neuehouse
Los Angeles, CA 90028-6442, USA

Simpson, Joe (Athlete, Baseball Player)
4681 Jefferson Township Ln
Marietta, GA 30066-1737, USA

Simpson, Joe (Producer)
21070 Las Flores Mesa Dr
Malibu, CA 90265-5231, USA

Simpson, John (Horse Racer)
51 High Rock Rd N
Hanover, PA 17331-9454, USA

Simpson, Juliene (Athlete, Basketball Player, Olympic Athlete)
31 Maple St
Bernardsville, NJ 07924-2738, USA

Simpson, Juliene Brazinski (Athlete, Basketball Player)
31 Maple St
Bernardsville, NJ 07924-2738, USA

Simpson, Keith (Athlete, Football Player)
20710 Castle Bend Dr
Katy, TX 77450-4911, USA

Simpson, OJ (Orenthal) (Athlete, Football Player)
c/o Staff Member *Glass Entertainment Group*
211 Rock Hill Rd
Bala Cynwyd, PA 19004-2052, USA

Simpson, Ralph (Athlete, Basketball Player)
Cerner Corp
2800 Rock Creek Pkwy
Kansas City, MO 64117-2521, USA

Simpson, Reid (Athlete, Hockey Player)
340 W Superior St Apt 1210
Chicago, IL 60654-6190

Simpson, Scott (Athlete, Golfer)
Cornerstone Sports
14646 N Kierland Blvd Ste 230
Scottsdale, AZ 85254-2765, USA

Simpson, Stern Carol (Misc)
American Assn of University Professors
1012 14th St NW
Washington, DC 20005-3403, USA

Simpson, Sturgill (Musician)
c/o Asha Goodman *Sacks and Co*
119 W 57th St PH North
New York, NY 10019-2401, USA

Simpson, Suzi (Actor, Model)
24338 El Toro Rd # E315
Laguna Woods, CA 92637-2776, USA

Simpson, Terry (Coach)
Anaheim Mighty Ducks
2000 E Gene Autry Way
Anaheim, CA 92806-6143, USA

Simpson, Todd (Athlete, Hockey Player)
Royal Lepage Kelowna
1-1890 Cooper Rd
Kelowna, BC V1Y 8B7, Canada

Simpson, Wayne K (Athlete, Baseball Player)
330 E Collamer Dr
Carson, CA 90746-1139, USA

Simpson, Webb (Athlete, Golfer)
c/o Thomas Parker *GPR Sports Management*
11715 Spinnaker Way
Hollywood, FL 33026-1233, USA

Simpson, William (Writer)
c/o Staff Member *HarperCollins Publishers*
195 Broadway Fl 2
New York, NY 10007-3132, USA

Simpson Sr, John F (Race Car Driver)
Mount Morris Star Route
Waynesburg, PA 15370, USA

Simpson-Wentz, Ashlee (Actor, Musician, Reality Star)
c/o Adam Griffin *LINK Entertainment*
11872 La Grange Ave
Los Angeles, CA 90025-5282, USA

Simpy Red (Music Group)
c/o Staff Member *Lee & Thompson*
4 Gee's Ct
St Christopher's Place
London W1U 1JD, UNITED KINGDOM

Sims, Al (Athlete, Hockey Player)
4215 Winding Way Dr
Fort Wayne, IN 46835-1466

Sims, Barry (Athlete, Football Player)
3578 Rosincress Dr
San Ramon, CA 94582-5077, USA

Sims, Billy R (Athlete, Football Player)
PO Box 3147
Coppell, TX 75019-7001, USA

Sims, Darryl (Athlete, Football Player)
PO Box 379
Mc Farland, WI 53558-0379, USA

Sims, Dion (Athlete, Football Player)
c/o Alan Herman *Sportstars Inc*
1370 Avenue of the Americas Fl 19
New York, NY 10019-4602, USA

Sims, Duane (Duke) (Athlete, Baseball Player)
10509 Shoalhaven Dr
Las Vegas, NV 89134-7425, USA

Sims, Duane ""Duke"" (Athlete, Baseball Player)
10509 Shoalhaven Dr
Las Vegas, NV 89134-7425, USA

Sims, Greg (Athlete, Baseball Player)
6700 Rancho Pico Way
Sacramento, CA 95828-1325, USA

Sims, Heath (Athlete, Olympic Athlete, Wrestler)
31167 Sunningdale Dr
Temecula, CA 92591-3967, USA

Sims, Jocko (Actor)
c/o Mike Liotta *True Public Relations*
3575 Cahuenga Blvd W Ste 360
Los Angeles, CA 90068-1361, USA

Sims, Keith (Athlete, Football Player)
2920 Luckie Rd
Weston, FL 33331-3005, USA

Sims, Ken (Athlete, Football Player)
4898 Converse Ave
East Saint Louis, IL 62207-2533, USA

Sims, Kenneth W (Athlete, Football Player)
PO Box 236
Kosse, TX 76653-0236, USA

Sims, Molly (Actor, Model)
c/o Alissa Vradenburg *Untitled Entertainment*
350 S Beverly Dr Ste 200
Beverly Hills, CA 90212-4819, USA

Sims, Pat (Athlete, Football Player)
c/o Todd France *Creative Artists Agency (CAA) Sports*
3500 Lenox Rd NE
Atlanta, GA 30326-4228, USA

Sims, Rob (Athlete, Football Player)
c/o Joel Segal *Lagardere Unlimited (NY)*
456 Washington St Apt 9L
New York, NY 10013-1555, USA

Sims, Robert (Athlete, Basketball Player)
915 Highland Ave Apt 3
Duarte, CA 91010-1935, USA

Simses, Kate (Actor)
c/o Ken Treusch *Bleecker Street Entertainment*
853 Broadway Ste 1214
New York, NY 10003-4717, USA

Sin, Jaime L Cardinal (Religious Leader)
121 Arzobispo St Entramuros
PO Box 132
Manila 10099, PHILIPPINES

Sinatro, Matt (Athlete, Baseball Player)
2619 239th Ave SE
Sammamish, WA 98075-9442, USA

Sinbad (Actor, Comedian)
c/o Jeff Greenberg *Gersh*
9465 Wilshire Blvd Ste 600
Beverly Hills, CA 90212-2605, USA

Sinceno, Kaseem (Athlete, Football Player)
168B Bradford Ct
Mount Laurel, NJ 08054-3705, USA

Sinclair, Adam (Actor)
c/o Mary Putnam Greene *MPG Management*
7162 Beverly Blvd Ste 332
Los Angeles, CA 90036-2547, USA

Sinclair, Ben (Actor, Director)
c/o Chelsea McKinnies *United Talent Agency (UTA)*
9336 Civic Center Dr
Beverly Hills, CA 90210-3604, USA

Sinclair, Bob (DJ, Musician)
c/o Mona Rennalls *Mona Rennalls Agency*
Paseo San Gervasio, 28 (1-1)
Barcelona E-08022, SPAIN

Sinclair, Harry (Director, Writer)
c/o Ken Kamins *ICM Partners*
10250 Constellation Blvd Fl 7
Los Angeles, CA 90067-6207, USA

Sinclair, Jaz (Actor)
c/o Louise Spinner Ward *United Talent Agency (UTA)*
9336 Civic Center Dr
Beverly Hills, CA 90210-3604, USA

Sinclair, Joshua (Actor, Director, Producer, Writer)
c/o Staff Member *Sun Gateway Entertainment*
Taubenheimstr 30
70372, GERMANY

Sinclair, Michael (Athlete, Football Player)
14215 Heidi Oaks Ln
Humble, TX 77396-3497, USA

Sindelar, Joan (Baseball Player)
504 W Sunland Ave
Phoenix, AZ 85041-4822, USA

Sindelar, Joey (Golfer)
18 Prospect Rdg
Horseheads, NY 14845-7988, USA

Sinden, Harry (Athlete, Hockey Player)
Boston Bruins
100 Legends Way Ste 250
Boston, MA 02114-1389

Sinden, Harry (Athlete, Hockey Player)
2449 Chesapeake Cir
West Palm Beach, FL 33409-7409

Sinegal, James (Business Person)
Costco Wholesale Corp
999 Lake Dr
Issaquah, WA 98027-8990, USA

Sing, Daniel (Actor)
c/o Kathryn Rawlings *Kathryn Rawlings Actors Agency*
4/28 Williamson Ave.
Grey Lynn
Auckland, New Zealand

Singer, Bryan (Director)
c/o Staff Member *Bad Hat Harry Productions*
1990 S Bundy Dr Ste 200
Los Angeles, CA 90025-5249, USA

Singer, Lori (Actor)
Chuck Binder
1465 Lindacrest Dr
Beverly Hills, CA 90210-2519, USA

Singer, Marc (Actor)
11218 Canton Dr
Studio City, CA 91604-4154, USA

Singer, Peter A D (Misc)
Princeton University
Human Values Center
Princeton, NJ 08544-0001, USA

Singer, Ramona (Designer, Reality Star)
c/o Staff Member *Central Entertainment Group*
250 W 40th St Fl 12
New York, NY 10018-4601, USA

Singer, William R (Bill) (Athlete, Baseball Player)
1119 Mallard Marsh Dr
Osprey, FL 34229-6810, USA

Singh, Lilly (Comedian, Dancer, Internet Star, Musician)
c/o Sarah Weichel *Anonymous Content*
2658 Griffith Park Blvd
PO Box 342
Los Angeles, CA 90039-2520, USA

Singh, Tjinder (Musician)
Legends of 21st Century
7 Trinity Row
Florence, MA 01062-1931, USA

Singh, Vijay (Golfer)
c/o Carlos Rodriguez *Impact Point*
Vorderhausstrasse 4A
Teufen CH-9053, SWITZERLAND

Singletary, Mike (Athlete, Coach, Football Coach, Football Player)
c/o Staff Member *Gil Scott Sports Management*
8901 Woodbine Ave Suite 228
Markham, ON L3R 9Y4, CANADA

Singletary, Tony (Director)
c/o Staff Member *Agency for the Performing Arts (APA)*
405 S Beverly Dr Ste 500
Beverly Hills, CA 90212-4425, USA

Singleton, Chris (Athlete, Baseball Player)
2038 Town Manor Ct
Dacula, GA 30019-3247, USA

Singleton, Chris (Athlete, Football Player)
42599 W Sunland Dr
Maricopa, AZ 85138-1632, USA

Singleton, Duane (Athlete, Baseball Player)
45 Samuel St
Ronkonkoma, NY 11779-4328, USA

Singleton, Isaac (Actor)
c/o Michael Greenwald *Endorse Management Group*
9854 National Blvd # 454
Los Angeles, CA 90034-2713, USA

Singleton, John (Director, Producer)
c/o Staff Member *New Deal Productions*
3343 W 43rd St
Los Angeles, CA 90008-4521, USA

Singleton, Kenneth (Kenny) (Athlete, Baseball Player)
10 Sparks Farm Rd
Sparks Glencoe, MD 21152-9300, USA

Singleton, Margie (Musician)
PO Box 567
Hendersonville, TN 37077-0567, USA

Sinisalo, Ilkka (Athlete, Hockey Player)
6221 Main St
Voorhees, NJ 08043-4629

Sinise, Gary (Actor)
Gary Sinise Foundation
PO Box 368
Woodland Hills, CA 91365-0368, USA

Sink, Sadie (Actor)
c/o Melissa Raubvogel *Imprint PR*
375 Hudson St
New York, NY 10014-3658, USA

Sinn, Pearl (Golfer)
132 21st Pl
Manhattan Beach, CA 90266-4402, USA

Sinner, George (Politician)
1013rd St N
Moorhead, MN 56560-1952, USA

Sinnott, John (Athlete, Football Player)
9 Primrose Ln
North Providence, RI 02904-3840, USA

Sinton, Nell (Artist)
484 Lake Park Ave # 189
Oakland, CA 94610-2730, USA

Siouzsie, Sioux (Musician)
Helter Skelter
Plaza
535 Kings Road
London SW10 0S, UNITED KINGDOM (UK)

Sipchen, Bob (Journalist)
Los Angeles Times
2300 E Imperial Hwy
Editorial Dept
El Segundo, CA 90245-2813, USA

Sipe, Brian W (Athlete, Football Player)
17 E H St
Encinitas, CA 92024-3616, USA

Sipin, John (Athlete, Baseball Player)
455 Ponza Ln
Soquel, CA 95073-9528, USA

Sipos, Shaun (Actor)
c/o Tyman Stewart *Characters Talent Agency*
200-1505 2nd Ave W
Vancouver, BC V6H 3Y4, CANADA

Sipp, Tony (Athlete, Baseball Player)
3976 River Pine Drive
Moss Point, MS 39563, USA

Sippy Cups, The (Music Group)
c/o Staff Member *Paradigm (Monterey)*
404 W Franklin St
Monterey, CA 93940-2303, USA

Siragusa, Tony (Athlete, Football Player)
349 Ashwood Ave
Kenilworth, NJ 07033-2056, USA

Sircar, Tiya (Actor, Musician)
c/o Lisa Perkins *Baker Winokur Ryder Public Relations*
9100 Wilshire Blvd
W Tower #500
Beverly Hills, CA 90212-3415, USA

Sires, Albin (Congressman, Politician)
2342 Rayburn Hob
Washington, DC 20515-3603, USA

Sirgo, Otto (Actor)
c/o Staff Member *Televisa*
Blvd Adolfo Lopez Mateos 232
Colonia San Angel INN
DF CP 01060, MEXICO

Siriano, Christian (Designer, Reality Star)
5 W 54th St
New York, NY 10019-5404, USA

Sirico, Tony (Actor)
c/o Bob McGowan *McGowan Management*
170 S Beverly Dr Ste 304
Beverly Hills, CA 90212-3000, USA

Sirikit (Royalty)
Chritrada Villa
Bangkok, THAILAND

Sir Mix-a-Lot (Musician)
16727 SE Lake Holm Rd
Auburn, WA 98092-5926, USA

Sirmon, Peter (Athlete, Football Player)
5255 McGavock Rd
Brentwood, TN 37027-5197, USA

Sirotka, Mike (Athlete, Baseball Player)
20704 N 90th Pl Unit 1005
Scottsdale, AZ 85255-9135, USA

Sirtis, Marina (Actor)
c/o Steve Rohr *Lexicon Public Relations*
1049 Havenhurst Dr # 365
West Hollywood, CA 90046-6002, USA

Sisco, Andrew (Athlete, Baseball Player)
25324 176th Ave SE
Covington, WA 98042-6709, USA

Sisco, Steve (Athlete, Baseball Player)
630 San Doval Pl
Thousand Oaks, CA 91360-1314, USA

Sisemore, Jerald G (Jerry) (Athlete, Football Player)
17301 Whippoorwill Trl
Lago Vista, TX 78645-9734, USA

Sisk, Bradford (Producer)
c/o Staff Member *Bankable Productions*
226 W 26th St Fl 4
New York, NY 10001-6700, USA

Sisk, Doug (Athlete, Baseball Player)
3610 42nd Ave NE
Tacoma, WA 98422-2480, USA

Sisk, John (Athlete, Football Player)
7814 W Wisconsin Ave
Wauwatosa, WI 53213-3420, USA

Sisk, Tommie (Athlete, Baseball Player)
110 E Carmel Dr
Meridian, ID 83646-3336, USA

Sisko, David (Race Car Driver)
2125 Linden Hwy
Hohenwald, TN 38462-2375, USA

Sislen, Myrna (Musician)
Lindy Martin Mgmt
5 Loblolly Ct
Pinehurst, NC 28374-9349, USA

Sisman, Adam (Writer)
c/o Staff Member *Penguin Press HC*
375 Hudson St Bsmt 3
New York, NY 10014-7465, USA

Sisman, Robyn (Writer)
c/o Staff Member *Curtis Brown Ltd*
28-29 Hay Market
Hay Market House
London SW1Y 4SP, UNITED KINGDOM

Sisqo (Musician)

Sissel (Musician)
Stageway Impressario
Skuteviksboder 11
Bergen 05035, NORWAY

Sissel, George A (Business Person)
Ball Corp
10 Longs Peak Dr
Broomfield, CO 80021-2510, USA

Sissi (Actor)
c/o Staff Member *Univision*
605 3rd Ave Fl 12
New York, NY 10158-0034, USA

Sisson, Doug (Athlete, Baseball Player)
1660 Durham Ct
Auburn, AL 36830-2191, USA

Sisson, Scott (Athlete, Football Player)
902 Ravenwood Way
Canton, GA 30115-6421, USA

Sissons, Kimber (Actor)
412 Amaz Dr
#204
Los Angeles, CA 90048, USA

Sister, Max (Designer, Fashion Designer)
Mount Everest Centre for Buddhist Studies
Kathmandu, NEPAL

Sister Hazel (Music Group)
c/o Staff Member *Sixthman*
83 Walton St NW
Atlanta, GA 30303-2179, USA

Sister Sledge (Music Group)
c/o Staff Member *Tony Denton Promotions Limited (UK)*
P.O. Box 2839
London W1K 5LE, United Kingdom

Sisto, Jeremy (Actor)
c/o Christina Papadopoulos *Baker Winokur Ryder Public Relations*
200 5th Ave Fl 5
New York, NY 10010-3307, USA

Sistrunk, Manny (Athlete, Football Player)
8318 Hitchcock Ln APT 716
Charlotte, NC 28262-5316, USA

Sistrunk, Otis (Athlete, Football Player)
PO Box 372
Dupont, WA 98327-0372, USA

Sites, Brian (Actor)
c/o Staff Member *Innovative Artists*
1505 10th St
Santa Monica, CA 90401-2805, USA

Sites, James W (Producer)
American Legion Magazine
700 N Pennsylvania St
Indianapolis, IN 46204-1172, USA

Sitkovetsky, Dmitry (Musician)
Columbia Artists Mgmt Inc
165 W 57th St
New York, NY 10019-2201, USA

Sitter, Charles R (Business Person)
Exxon Corp
5959 Las Colinas Blvd
Irving, TX 75039-2298, USA

Sittler, Darrell (Athlete, Hockey Player)
84 Buttonwood Ct
East Amherst, NY 14051-1644, USA

Sittler, Darryl (Athlete, Hockey Player)
Toronto Maple Leafs
400-40 Bay St
Toronto, ON M5J 2X2, Canada

Sittler, Darryl (Athlete, Hockey Player)
171 Glengarry Ave
Toronto, ON M5M 1E1, Canada

Sittler, Walter (Actor)
Agentur Heppeler
Seinstr 54
Munich 81667, GERMANY

Sitton, Charles (Athlete, Basketball Player)
3035 SW Homesteader Rd
West Linn, OR 97068-9612, USA

Sitton, Josh (Athlete, Football Player)

Sivad, Darryl (Actor)
c/o Staff Member *Leavitt Talent Group*
11500 W Olympic Blvd Ste 400
Los Angeles, CA 90064-1525, USA

Sivan, Troye (Musician)
c/o Rodrick Paul *Group III Management*
13914 Addison St
Sherman Oaks, CA 91423-1214, USA

Siwa, JoJo (Actor)

Siwy, Jim (Athlete, Baseball Player)
6919 April Wind Ave
Las Vegas, NV 89131-0119, USA

Sixthman (Music Group, Musician)
158 Moreland Ave SE
Atlanta, GA 30316-1676, USA

Sixx, Nikki (Musician)
4445 Deerhaven Ct
Westlake Village, CA 91362-5646, USA

Sizemore, Grady (Athlete, Baseball Player)
1951 W 26th St Apt 512
Cleveland, OH 44113-3467, USA

Sizemore, Matt (Adult Film Star)
c/o Staff Member *Diva Central Inc*
7510 W Sunset Blvd # 1445
Los Angeles, CA 90046-3408, USA

Sizemore, Ted (Athlete, Baseball Player)
14030 Conway Rd
Chesterfield, MO 63017-3402, USA

Sizemore, Tom (Actor)
c/o Mike Quinn *Silverstone Entertainment*
10 Universal City Plz
Fl 24
Universal City, CA 91608, USA

Sjoberg, Lars-Erik (Athlete, Hockey Player)

Sjoberg, Patrik (Athlete, Track Athlete)
Hokegatan 17
Goteberg 416 66, SWEDEN

Sjodin, Tommy (Athlete, Hockey Player)
Karlavagen 2
Gavle, 80266 Sweden

Sjostrom, Fredrik (Athlete, Hockey Player)
18362 N 94th Pl
Scottsdale, AZ 85255-6001

Skaalen, Jim (Athlete, Baseball Player)
2608 El Aguila Ln
Carlsbad, CA 92009-4332, USA

Skaggs, Dave (Athlete, Baseball Player)
11131 Arlington Ave
Riverside, CA 92505-2148, USA

Skaggs, Jim (Athlete, Football Player)
421 Falcon Ridge Rd
Ellensburg, WA 98926-5037, USA

Skaggs, Ricky (Actor, Musician)
c/o Bobby Cudd *Paradigm (Nashville)*
222 2nd Ave S Ste 1600
Nashville, TN 37201-2375, USA

Skah, Khalid (Athlete, Track Athlete)
Boite Postale 2577
Fez, MOROCCO

Skala, Brian T (Actor)
c/o Staff Member *Osbrink Talent Agency*
4343 Lankershim Blvd # 100
North Hollywood, CA 91602-2705, USA

Skalde, Jarrod (Athlete, Hockey Player)
5600 Cooper Rd
Cincinnati, OH 45242-7014, USA

Skalski, Joe (Athlete, Baseball Player)
15546 Drexel Ave
Dolton, IL 60419-2750, USA

Skarda, Randy (Athlete, Hockey Player)
26885 Noble Rd
Excelsior, MN 55331-8239

Skarsgard, Alexander (Actor)
c/o Liz Mahoney *Narrative*
1601 Vine St Fl 6
Los Angeles, CA 90028-8802, USA

Skarsgard, Bill (Actor)
c/o Shelley Browning *Magnolia Entertainment*
9595 Wilshire Blvd Ste 601
Beverly Hills, CA 90212-2506, USA

Skarsgard, Gustaf (Actor)
c/o Jim Dempsey *Paradigm*
8942 Wilshire Blvd
Beverly Hills, CA 90211-1908, USA

Skarsgard, Stellan (Actor)
Hogersgatan 40
Stockholm 118 26, SWEDEN

Skarsten, Rachel (Actor)
c/o Brad Pence *Atlas Artists*
9220 W Sunset Blvd Ste 225
Los Angeles, CA 90069-3513, USA

Skaugstad, Daryle (Athlete, Football Player)
17216 NE 195th St
Woodinville, WA 98072, USA

Skaugstad, Dave (Athlete, Baseball Player)
16222 Monterey Ln Spc 274
Huntington Beach, CA 92649-2248, USA

Skeels, Mark (Baseball Player)
12086 Calle Naranja
El Cajon, CA 92019-4814, USA

Skeen, Archie (Baseball Player)
2685 N 4275 W
Ogden, UT 84404-9074, USA

Skeet, DJ Skeet (DJ)
c/o Ron Laffitte *Red Light Management*
5800 Bristol Pkwy Ste 400
Culver City, CA 90230-6898, USA

Skeeters, The (Music Group)
c/o Staff Member *Paradigm (Monterey)*
404 W Franklin St
Monterey, CA 93940-2303, USA

Skeggs, Leonard T Jr (Misc)
10212 Blair Ln
Kirtland, OH 44094-9514, USA

Skeie, Andris (Prime Minister)
Prime Minister's Office
Brivibus Bulv 36
Riga, PDP 226170, LATVIA

Skelton, Mike (Writer)
c/o Jon Huddle *Fourth Wall Management*
9336 Civic Center Dr
Beverly Hills, CA 90210-3604, USA

Skerritt, Tom (Actor)
c/o Lou Pitt *The Pitt Group*
275 Homewood Rd
Los Angeles, CA 90049-2709, USA

Skibinski, Joe (Athlete, Football Player)
1912 Pine St
Peru, IL 61354-1828, USA

Skidmore, Paul (Athlete, Hockey Player)
469W 760 N
Santaquin, UT 84655-5545

Skidmore, Roe (Athlete, Baseball Player)
964 E Marlin Dr
Decatur, IL 62521-5549, USA

Skid Row (Music Group)
c/o John Domagall *ARM Entertainment*
1257 Arcade St
Saint Paul, MN 55106-2022, USA

Skiles, Scott (Athlete, Basketball Player)
26014 Estates Ridge Dr
Sorrento, FL 32776-7751, USA

Skillet (Music Group)
c/o Zach Kelm *Q Management Group*
PO Box 273
Franklin, TN 37065-0273, USA

Skinner, Al (Athlete, Basketball Player)
1266 Smithwell Pt NW
Kennesaw, GA 30152-4300, USA

Skinner, Emily (Actor)
c/o Bill Perlman *Foundation Media Partners*
23679 Calabasas Rd # 625
Calabasas, CA 91302-1502, USA

Skinner, Frank (Actor, Comedian)
P.O. Box 168
London, England W10 6WH, UK

Skinner, Jeff (Athlete, Hockey Player)
c/o Darren Ferris *Definitive Hockey Group*
200-65 International Blvd
Etobicoke, ON M9W 6L9, Canada

Skinner, Joel (Athlete, Baseball Player, Coach)
Charlotte Knights
324 S Mint St
Charlotte, NC 28202-1465, USA

Skinner, Jonty (Coach, Swimmer)
University of Alabama
Athletic Dept
Tuscaloosa, AL 35487-0001, USA

Skinner, Larry (Athlete, Hockey Player)
Nexient Learning
1600 Scott St Tower B 3rd Floor
Ottawa, ON KlY 4N7, Canada

Skinner, Mike (Race Car Driver)
Mike Skinner Enterprises
3685 Hwy
152 W
China Grove, NC 28023, USA

Skinner, Robert R (Bob) (Athlete, Baseball Player, Coach)
1576 Diamond St
San Diego, CA 92109-3050, USA

Skinner, Sonny (Golfer)
114 Northlake Dr
Sylvester, GA 31791-3909, USA

Skinner, Val (Golfer)
44 Bridge Ave
Bay Head, NJ 08742-4747, USA

Skinny Puppy (Music Group)
c/o Jeremy Holgersen *UTA/The Agency Group*
888 7th Ave Fl 7
New York, NY 10106-0700, USA

Skizas, Lou (Athlete, Baseball Player)
1125 Baytowne Dr APT 18
Champaign, IL 61822-6903, USA

Skjelbreid, Ann-Elen (Athlete)
5640 Eikelandsosen
NORWAY

Skladany, John (Athlete, Football Player)
541 Wilmington Cir
Oviedo, FL 32765-6988

Skladany, Thomas E (Tom) (Athlete, Football Player)
6666 Highland Lakes Pl
Westerville, OH 43082-8703, USA

Sklar, Jason (Comedian, Sportscaster)
8522 Edwin Dr
Los Angeles, CA 90046-1028, USA

Sklar, Randy (Comedian, Sportscaster)
2310 Kenilworth Ave
Los Angeles, CA 90039-3042, USA

Skok, Craig (Athlete, Baseball Player)
981 Slash Pine Way
Lawrenceville, GA 30043-3465, USA

Skolimowski, Jerzy (Director)
Film Polski
Ul Mazowiecka 6/8
Warsaw 00-048, POLAND

Skoll, Jeff (Business Person, Producer)
Skoll Foundation
250 University Ave Ste 200
Palo Alto, CA 94301-1738, USA

Skolnik, Michael (Business Person)
c/o Staff Member *Article 19 Films*
247 Centre St Fl 7
New York, NY 10013-3216, USA

Skoog, Meyer (Whitey) (Athlete, Basketball Player, Coach)
1545 Aspen Dr
Saint Peter, MN 56082-1586, USA

Skoog, Myer (Athlete, Baseball Player)
35689 398th Ln
Saint Peter, MN 56082-4333, USA

Skorodenski, Warren (Athlete, Hockey Player)
161 MacEwan Ridge Cir NW
Calgary, AB T3K 3W3, Canada

Skoronski, Bob (Athlete, Football Player)
8301 Old Sauk Rd Apt 108
Middleton, WI 53562-4391, USA

Skorupan, John P (Athlete, Football Player)
142 Crossing Ridge Trl
Cranberry Township, PA 16066-6512, USA

Skotheim, Robert A (Misc)
2120 Place Rd
Port Angeles, WA 98363-9664, USA

Skoula, Martin (Athlete, Hockey Player)
2441 Sheridan AveS
Minneapolis, MN 55405-2341

Skovbye, Tiera (Actor)
c/o Lena Lees *Play Management*
220-807 Powell St
Vancouver, BC V6A 1H7, CANADA

Skrein, Ed (Actor)
c/o Kate Buckley *42 Management (UK)*
8 Flitcroft St
London WC2H 8DL, UNITED KINGDOM

Skrepenak, Greg (Athlete, Football Player)
Hyders Total Fitnbess Center
400 Middle Rd
Nanticoke, PA 18634-3821, USA

Skribble (DJ, Musician)
c/o Len Evans *Project Publicity*
540 W 43rd St
New York, NY 10036, USA

Skriko, Petri (Athlete, Hockey Player)
Kirjatyontekijankatu 4 A 3
Helsinki, 170 Finland

Skrillex (DJ, Musician)
Big Dada HQ
PO Box 4296
London SE11 4WW, UNITED KINGDOM

Skrine, Buster (Athlete, Football Player)
c/o Alan Herman *Sportstars Inc*
1370 Avenue of the Americas Fl 19
New York, NY 10019-4602, USA

Skriver, Josephine (Model)
c/o Chris Gay *The Society Management*
156 5th Ave Ste 800
New York, NY 10010-7702, USA

Skrmetta, Matt (Athlete, Baseball Player)
527 Siena Ct
Satellite Beach, FL 32937-2991, USA

Skrovan, Steve (Comedian)
c/o Staff Member *WME|IMG*
9601 Wilshire Blvd
Beverly Hills, CA 90210-5213, USA

Skrudland, Brian (Athlete, Hockey Player)
Florida Panthers
1 Panther Pkwy
Sunrise, FL 33323-5315

Skrudland, Brian (Athlete, Hockey Player)
3225 7 St SW
Calgary, AB T2T 2X8, Canada

Skrypnk, Metropolitan Mstyslav S (Religious Leader)
Ukranian Orthodox Church
PO Box 445
South Bound Brook, NJ 08880-0445, USA

Skube, Bob (Athlete, Baseball Player)
4153 W Charlotte Dr
Glendale, AZ 85310-3214, USA

Skufca, Scott (Race Car Driver)
5903 Reynolds Rd
Mentor On The Lake, OH 44060-3033, USA

Skuta, Dan (Athlete, Football Player)
c/o Blake Baratz *The Institute for Athletes*
3600 Minnesota Dr Ste 550
Edina, MN 55435-7925, USA

Skuza, Dean (Race Car Driver)
650 Ken Mar Industrial Pkwy
Broadview Heights, OH 44147-2918, USA

Sky, Jennifer (Actor)
12533 Woodgreen St
Los Angeles, CA 90066-2723, USA

Sky, Nina (Music Group, Musician)
c/o Tammy Brook *FYI Public Relations*
174 5th Ave Ste 404
New York, NY 10010-5964, USA

Skye, Azura (Actor)
c/o Lisa Gallant *Gallant Management*
1112 Montana Ave # 454
Santa Monica, CA 90403-1652, USA

Skye, Ione (Actor)
c/o Mike Packenham *Concrete Entertainment*
468 N Camden Dr # 200
Beverly Hills, CA 90210-4507, USA

Skye, Justine (Actor, Model)
c/o Drew Hunter *One Management*
42 Bond St Fl 2
New York, NY 10012-2768, USA

Sky Eats Airplane (Music Group)
c/o Staff Member *Equal Vision Records*
PO Box 38202
Albany, NY 12203-8202, USA

Skyrms, Brian (Misc)
University of California
Philosophy Dept
Irvine, CA 92717, USA

Slaby, Lou (Athlete, Football Player)
6 Elder Pl
Denville, NJ 07834-9312, USA

Slack, Reggie (Athlete, Football Player)
5973 Queen St
Milton, FL 32570-3574, USA

Slade, Bernard N (Writer)
345 N Saltair Ave
Los Angeles, CA 90049-2914, USA

Slade, Chris (Athlete, Football Player)
4810 Ivy Rodge Dr SE
Unit 201
Smyrna, GA 30080, USA

Slade, Chris (Musician)
11 Leominster Road
Morden
Surrey SA4 6HN, UNITED KINGDOM (UK)

Slade, David (Director)
c/o Keith Redmon *Anonymous Content*
3532 Hayden Ave
Culver City, CA 90232-2413, USA

Slade, Jeff (Athlete, Basketball Player)
5354 Farmington Rd
Toledo, OH 43623-2636, USA

Slade, Mark (Actor)
38 Joppa Rd
Worcester, MA 01602-2230, USA

Slaggert, Mitchell (Actor, Model)
c/o Marisa Martins *The Lede Company*
401 Broadway Ste 206
New York, NY 10013-3033, USA

Slagle, Roger (Athlete, Baseball Player)
7560 George Nash Rd
White House, TN 37188-5101, USA

Slagle, Tim (Race Car Driver)
2824 Dorr Ave Ste E
Fairfax, VA 22031-1516, USA

Slaney, John (Athlete, Hockey Player)
10472 E Texas Sage Ln
Scottsdale, AZ 85255-8523

Slaney, John (Athlete, Hockey Player)
Portland Pirates
94 Free St
Portland, ME 04101-3920

Slaney, Mary Decker (Athlete, Olympic Athlete, Track Athlete)
87141 Kellmore St
Eugene, OR 97402-9128, USA

Slash (Musician)
c/o Staff Member *Slasher Films*
459 S Sycamore Ave
Los Angeles, CA 90036-3505, USA

Slate, Jenny (Actor)
c/o Jodi Gottlieb *Independent Public Relations*
9601 Wilshire Blvd Ste 750
Beverly Hills, CA 90210-5228, USA

Slaten, Doug (Athlete, Baseball Player)
8525 N Timberlane Dr
Scottsdale, AZ 85258-2009, USA

Slater, Bob (Baseball Player)
4322 Avenida Rio Del Oro
Yorba Linda, CA 92886-3011, USA

Slater, Christian (Actor)
c/o Alexandra Kahn *Relevant (NY)*
333 Hudson St Rm 502
New York, NY 10013-1033, USA

Slater, Helen (Actor)

Slater, Jackie (Athlete, Football Player)
PO Box 6411
Orange, CA 92863-6411, USA

Slater, Kelly (Actor, Athlete)
Slam Management
31652 2nd Ave
Laguna Beach, CA 92651-8244, USA

Slater, Mark (Athlete, Football Player)
10545 Rome Ave
Young America, MN 55397-9468, USA

Slater, Matthew (Athlete, Football Player)
c/o Ryan Tollner *REP 1 Sports Group*
80 Technology Dr
Irvine, CA 92618-2301, USA

Slaton, Jim (Athlete, Baseball Player)
4082 N Arbor Ln
Buckeye, AZ 85396-3603, USA

Slaton, Mike (Athlete, Football Player)
7691 Park Village Rd
San Diego, CA 92129-4514, USA

Slaton, Tony (Athlete, Football Player)
122 E Childs Ave Unit B
Merced, CA 95341-6346, USA

Slattery, John (Actor)
c/o Jillian Roscoe *ID Public Relations*
7060 Hollywood Blvd Fl 8th
Los Angeles, CA 90028-6021, USA

Slattvik, Simon (Athlete)
Bankgata 22
Lillehammer 02600, NORWAY

Slaught, Don (Athlete, Baseball Player)
27 Middleridge Ln S
Rolling Hills, CA 90274-4055, USA

Slaughter (Music Group)
c/o Staff Member *Artist Representation & Management*
1257 Arcade St
Saint Paul, MN 55106-2022

Slaughter, J Mack (Actor)
c/o Jeff Golenberg *Silver Lining Entertainment*
421 S Beverly Dr Fl 7
Beverly Hills, CA 90212-4408, USA

Slaughter, Karin (Writer)
c/o Victoria Sanders *Victoria Sanders & Assoc*
440 Buck Rd
Stone Ridge, NY 12484-5518, USA

Slaughter, Mickey (Athlete, Football Player)
1402 Mesa Ave
Ruston, LA 71270-2032, USA

Slaughter, Stering (Athlete, Baseball Player)
742 E Avenida Sierra Madre
Gilbert, AZ 85296-1108, USA

Slaughter, Sterling (Athlete, Baseball Player)
742 E Avenida Sierra Madre
Gilbert, AZ 85296-1108, USA

Slaughter, Webster (Athlete, Football Player)
3706 Rory Ct
Missouri City, TX 77459-6662, USA

Slauson, Matt (Athlete, Football Player)

Slavin, Jonathan (Actor)
c/o Mona Loring *Status PR*
PO Box 6191
Westlake Village, CA 91359-6191, USA

Slavin, Randall (Actor)
Gold Marshak Liedtke
3500 W Olive Ave Ste 1400
Burbank, CA 91505-5512, USA

Slavitt, David R (Writer)
35 West St Apt 5
Cambridge, MA 02139-1723, USA

Slay, Brandon (Wrestler)
6155 Lehman Dr
Colorado Springs, CO 80918-3456, USA

Slay, Darius (Athlete, Football Player)
c/o Ashley Smith Becker *Relativity Sports*
2029 Century Park E Ste 1550
Century City, CA 90067-3000, USA

Slayback, Bill (Athlete, Baseball Player)
25710 Armstrong Cir Unit E
Stevenson Ranch, CA 91381-2336, USA

Slayer (Musician)

Slayton, Bobby (Comedian)
c/o Sherry Marsh *Marsh Entertainment*
818 Warren Ave
Venice, CA 90291-2812, USA

Slayton, Natasha (Actor)
c/o Sherry Marsh *Marsh Entertainment*
818 Warren Ave
Venice, CA 90291-2812, USA

Sleater, Lou (Athlete, Baseball Player)
12246 Roundwood Rd Unit 710
Lutherville Timonium, MD 21093-3254, USA

Sledd, William L (Internet Star)
PO Box 3714
Paducah, KY 42002-3714, USA

Sledge, Kathy (Musician)

Sledge, Leroy (Athlete, Football Player)
6036 Golden Gate Cir
Dallas, TX 75241-5258, USA

Sledge, Termel (Athlete, Baseball Player)
30041 Medford Pl
Castaic, CA 91384-4565, USA

Sledge, Terrmel (Athlete, Baseball Player)
30041 Medford Pl
Castaic, CA 91384-4565, USA

Sleep, Mike (Athlete, Hockey Player)
249 Fairbank Cres
Thunder Bay, ON P7B 5M1, Canada

Sleepy Jackson, The (Music Group)
c/o Staff Member *Paradigm (Monterey)*
404 W Franklin St
Monterey, CA 93940-2303, USA

Slegr, Jiri (Athlete, Hockey Player)
U Cfsaskych lazni 7
Teplice 415 01, Czech Republic

Slegr, Jirl (Athlete, Hockey Player)
1 Fleet Center
Boston, MA 02114, USA

Sleigher, Louis (Athlete, Hockey Player)
250 Rte du President-Kennedy
Levis, QC G6V 9J6, Canada

Slezak, Erika (Actor)
International Creative Mgmt
40 W 57th St Ste 1800
New York, NY 10019-4033, USA

Slichter, Jacob (Musician)
Monterey Peninsula Artists
509 Hartnell St
Monterey, CA 93940-2825, USA

Slick, Grace (Musician, Songwriter)
5956 Kanan Dume Rd
Malibu, CA 90265-4027, USA

Slick, Rick (Musician)
Famous Artists Agency
250 W 57th St
New York, NY 10107-0001, USA

Slider, Rac (Athlete, Baseball Player)
123 Countv Road 3306
De Kalb, TX 75559-4342, USA

Slightly Stoopid (Music Group)
c/o Jon Phillips *Silverback Professional Artist Management*
9469 Jefferson Blvd Ste 101
Culver City, CA 90232-2915, USA

Slimane, Hedi (Designer)
10 avenue Hoche
Cedez 08
Paris 75381, USA

Slim Helu, Carlos (Business Person)
Telmex
Porque Via 198
Cuahtemoc CP
Mexico City, DF 06599, MEXICO

Slipknot (Musician)
c/o Ken Weinstein *Big Hassle Media*
40 Exchange Pl Ste 1900
New York, NY 10005-2714, USA

Sliwinska, Edyta (Dancer, Reality Star)
c/o Bob Knotek *McCann - Knotek Associates*
8539 W Sunset Blvd Ste 4
Los Angeles, CA 90069-2350, USA

Sloan (Music Group)
c/o Staff Member *Paradigm (Monterey)*
404 W Franklin St
Monterey, CA 93940-2303, USA

Sloan, Amy (Actor)
c/o Stephanie Nese *Levity Entertainment Group (LEG)*
6701 Center Dr W Ste 300
Los Angeles, CA 90045-2482, USA

Sloan, David (Athlete, Football Player)
10898 E Butherus Dr
Scottsdale, AZ 85255-1848, USA

Sloan, Ed (Musician)
216 Lincoln St
West Columbia, SC 29170-1812, USA

Sloan, Gerald E (Jerry) (Basketball Player, Coach)
300 S Washington St
Mc Leansboro, IL 62859-1141, USA

Sloan, Holly Goldberg (Director)
Sanford-Beckett-Skouras
1015 Gayley Ave Ste 300
Los Angeles, CA 90024-3440, USA

Sloan, Jerry (Athlete, Basketball Player)
5583 W 13680 S
Herriman, UT 84096-1713, USA

Sloan, Michael (Actor, Producer)

Sloan, P F (Musician, Songwriter, Writer)
All the Best
PO Box 164
Cedarhurst, NY 11516-0164, USA

Sloan, Stephen C (Steve) (Coach, Football Coach, Football Player)
University of Central Florida
Athletic Dept
Orlando, FL 32816-0001, USA

Sloane, Barry (Actor)
c/o Samantha Hill *Wolf-Kasteler Public Relations*
6255 W Sunset Blvd Ste 1111
Los Angeles, CA 90028-7426, USA

Sloane, Carol (Musician)
c/o Jerry Kravat *Park Avenue Talent*
165 W 46th St Ste 1100
New York, NY 10036-2516, USA

Sloane, Lindsay (Actor)
c/o Ron West *Thruline Entertainment*
9250 Wilshire Blvd Fl Ground
Beverly Hills, CA 90212-3352, USA

Sloat, Micah (Actor)
c/o Siri Garber *Platform PR*
2666 N Beachwood Dr
Los Angeles, CA 90068-2308, USA

Slobodyanik, Alexander (Musician)
Columbia Artists Mgmt Inc
165 W 57th St
New York, NY 10019-2201, USA

Slocum, Brian (Athlete, Baseball Player)
81 Rose Ave
Eastchester, NY 10709-3835, USA

Slocum, Heath (Golfer)
5640 Keystone Rd
Pensacola, FL 32504-8416, USA

Slocum, Ron (Athlete, Baseball Player)
35080 Chandler Ave Spc 28
Calimesa, CA 92320-1927, USA

Slocumb, Heathcliff (Heath) (Athlete, Baseball Player)
1045 Arthur St
Uniondale, NY 11553-3103, USA

Slonimsky, Sergey M (Composer)
9 Kanal Griboedova
#97
Saint Petersburg, RUSSIA

Slosburg, Phil (Athlete, Football Player)
201 Glen Ln
Elkins Park, PA 19027-1761, USA

Slotnick, Joey (Actor)
Gersh Agency
232 N Canon Dr
Beverly Hills, CA 90210-5302, USA

Slotnick, Mortimer H (Artist)
43 Amherst Dr
New Rochelle, NY 10804-1814, USA

Slovin, Eric (Writer)
c/o Staff Member *Artists First*
9465 Wilshire Blvd Ste 900
Beverly Hills, CA 90212-2608, USA

Slowes, Charles (Baseball Player, Sportscaster)
Tampa Bay Devil Rays
3936 Mimosa Pl
Palm Harbor, FL 34685-3674, USA

Slowey, Kevin (Athlete, Baseball Player)
1748 Quigg Dr
Pittsburgh, PA 15241-2023, USA

Sloyan, James (Actor)
920 Kagawa St
Pacific Palisades, CA 90272-3833, USA

Sluby, Tom (Athlete, Basketball Player)
39 Poplar St
Ramsey, NJ 07446-1535, USA

Sluman, Jeff (Golfer)
808 McKinley Ln
Hinsdale, IL 60521-4831, USA

Slusarski, Joe (Athlete, Baseball Player, Olympic Athlete)
11 Rodelle Woods Dr
Weldon Spring, MO 63304-7875, USA

Slutskaya, Irina (Figure Skater)
c/o Staff Member *Champions on Ice*
3500 American Blvd W Ste 190
Minneapolis, MN 55431-4431, USA

Slutsky, Lorie A (Misc)
New York Community Trust
2 Park Ave Fl 20
New York, NY 10016-9301, USA

Smaby, Matt (Athlete, Hockey Player)
5037 Newton AveS
Minneapolis, MN 55419-1027

Smagala, Stan (Athlete, Football Player)
13155 Meadow Hill Ln
Lemont, IL 60439-6743, USA

Smagorinsky, Joseph (Misc)
72 Gabriel Ct
Hillsborough, NJ 08844-1450, USA

Smail, Doug (Athlete, Hockey Player)
23550 Pondview Pl
Golden, CO 80401-9353

Smajstria, Craig (Athlete, Baseball Player)
4606 Honey Creek Ct
Pearland, TX 77584-1285, USA

Smajstrla, Craig (Athlete, Baseball Player)
4606 Honey Creek Ct
Pearland, TX 77584-1285, USA

Small, Aaron (Athlete, Baseball Player)
775 Loudon Rd
Loudon, TN 37774-6705, USA

Small, Jim (Athlete, Baseball Player)
7960 Island Ct
Stanwood, MI 49346-8920, USA

Small, Mark (Athlete, Baseball Player)
10605 229th Pl SW
Edmonds, WA 98020-6151, USA

Small, Marya (Actor)
CL Inc
843 N Sycamore Ave
Los Angeles, CA 90038-3316, USA

Small, Torrance (Athlete, Football Player)
66 Chateau Mouton Dr
Kenner, LA 70065-1903, USA

Smalley, Roy (Athlete, Baseball Player)
6319 Timber Trl
Minneapolis, MN 55439-1049, USA

Smalls, Joan (Model)
c/o Vanessa Gringer *IMG Models (NY)*
304 Park Ave S PH N
New York, NY 10010-4303, USA

Smallwood, Dwana (Dancer)
Alvin Ailey American Dance Foundation
211 W 61st St # 300
New York, NY 10023-7832, USA

Smallwood, Richard (Music Group, Musician)
Sierra Mgmt
1035 Bates Ct
Hendersonville, TN 37075-8864, USA

Smallwood, Yawin (Athlete, Football Player)

Smart, Amy (Actor)
3617 Woodcliff Rd
Sherman Oaks, CA 91403-5048, USA

Smart, Casper (Dancer)
c/o Cheryl Lynch *Lynch Archer PR*
5115 Wilshire Blvd Apt 400
Los Angeles, CA 90036-4372, USA

Smart, Elizabeth (Activist)
Elizabeth Smart Foundation Inc
1509 E Kristianna Cir
Salt Lake City, UT 84103-4224, USA

Smart, Erinn (Athlete, Olympic Athlete)
201 S 18th St Apt 301
Philadelphia, PA 19103-5920, USA

Smart, J D (Athlete, Baseball Player)
105 E Storey St
San Saba, TX 76877-5801, USA

Smart, Jean (Actor)
c/o Ame VanIden *VanIden Public Relations*
4070 Wilson Pike
Franklin, TN 37067-8126, USA

Smart, Keith (Athlete, Basketball Player, Coach)
5306 Asterwood Dr
Dublin, CA 94568-7718, USA

Smart, Marcus (Athlete, Basketball Player)
c/o Lee Melchionni *Wasserman Media Group*
10960 Wilshire Blvd Ste 1200
Los Angeles, CA 90024-3714, USA

Smashing Pumpkins (Music Group)
c/o Jbeau Lewis *United Talent Agency (UTA)*
9336 Civic Center Dr
Beverly Hills, CA 90210-3604, USA

Smash Mouth (Music Group, Musician)
c/o Staff Member *Creative Artists Agency (CAA)*
2000 Avenue of the Stars Ste 100
Los Angeles, CA 90067-4705, USA

Smear, Steve (Athlete, Football Player)
1701 Tree House Ct
Annapolis, MD 21401-6539, USA

Smedley, Geoffrey (Artist)
RR 3
Gambier Island
Gibsons, BC V0N 1V0, CANADA

Smedsmo, Dale (Athlete, Hockey Player)
609 3rd St NE
Roseau, MN 56751-1201, USA

Smeenge, Joel (Athlete, Football Player)
9148 Sugarland Dr
Jacksonville, FL 32256-9611, USA

Smehlik, Richard (Athlete, Hockey Player)
8824 Hearthstone Dr
East Amherst, NY 14051-2354

Smerek, Don (Athlete, Football Player)
1298 Valhalla Dr
Denver, NC 28037-5503, USA

Smerlas, Fred (Athlete, Football Player)
11 Saddle Ridge Rd
Sudbury, MA 01776-2770, USA

Smid, Ladislav (Athlete, Hockey Player)
2000 E Gene Autry Way
Anaheim, CA 92806-6143, USA

Smidt, Eric (Business Person)
60 Beverly Park
Beverly Hills, CA 90210-1544, USA

Smigel, Robert (Actor, Writer)
c/o Staff Member *Creative Artists Agency (CAA)*
2000 Avenue of the Stars Ste 100
Los Angeles, CA 90067-4705, USA

Smigelsky, Dave (Athlete, Football Player)
4332 Nesting Pl
Oakwood, GA 30566-3247, USA

Smiley, Don (Baseball Player)
10539 NW lOth St
Plantation, FL 33322-6546, USA

Smiley, Don (Baseball Player, President)
Florida Marlins
3233 Huntington
Weston, FL 33332-1820, USA

Smiley, Jane (Writer)
c/o Lynn Pleshette *Lynn Pleshette Literary Agency*
2700 N Beachwood Dr
Los Angeles, CA 90068-1922, USA

Smiley, Jane (Writer)
235 El Caminito Rd
Carmel Valley, CA 93924-9636, USA

Smiley, John (Athlete, Baseball Player)
1459 Laurel Dr
Sewickley, PA 15143-8865, USA

Smiley, Justin (Athlete, Football Player)
2771 Regatta Way
Tuscaloosa, AL 35406-4022, USA

Smiley, Rickey (Comedian)
c/o Staff Member *Breakwind Entertainment*
2633 McKinney Ave Ste 130
Dallas, TX 75204-8630, USA

Smiley, Tavis (Radio Personality, Television Host)
The Tavis Smiley Show
4401 W Sunset Blvd
Los Angeles, CA 90027-6017, USA

Smiley, Tommie B (Athlete, Football Player)
5340 Timberline Ln
Beaumont, TX 77706-7343, USA

S. Miller, Candice (Congressman, Politician)
1034 Longworth Hob
Washington, DC 20515-0510, USA

Smirnoff, Karina (Actor, Dancer, Reality Star)
c/o Jennifer Wentzo (Wilson) *CodedPR*
54 W 39th St Fl 10
New York, NY 10018-2066, USA

Smirnoff, Yakov (Actor, Comedian)
c/o Staff Member *Richard De La Font Agency*
3808 W South Park Blvd
Broken Arrow, OK 74011-1261, USA

Smith, Adam (Congressman, Politician)
2402 Rayburn Hob
Washington, DC 20515-0548, USa

Smith, Adrian (Athlete, Basketball Player, Olympic Athlete)
2829 Saddleback Dr
Cincinnati, OH 45244-3914, USA

Smith, Adrian (Congressman, Politician)
503 Canoonhob
Washington, DC 20515-0001, USA

Smith, Adrian (Musician)
Chipster Entertainment
1976 E High St Ste 101
Pottstown, PA 19464-3277, USA

Smith, Al (Athlete, Hockey Player)

Smith, Akili (Athlete, Football Player)
PO Box 95
Jamul, CA 91935-0095, USA

Smith, Al (Athlete, Basketball Player)
308 S Sterling Ave
Peoria, IL 61604-6063, USA

Smith, Al (Athlete, Football Player)
15 Pembroke St
Sugar Land, TX 77479-2929, USA

Smith, Al (Athlete, Football Player)
4061 Taggart Cay N Apt 108
Sarasota, FL 34233-4841, USA

Smith, Aldon (Athlete, Football Player)
c/o Ben Dogra *Relativity Sports*
2029 Century Park E Ste 1550
Century City, CA 90067-3000, USA

Smith, Alex (Athlete, Football Player)
420 Santa Rosa Dr
Los Gatos, CA 95032-5715, USA

Smith, Alex (Athlete, Football Player)

Smith, Alexis (Artist)
215 Windward Ave
Venice, CA 90291-3764, USA

Smith, Algee (Actor)
c/o Lisa Perkins *Baker Winokur Ryder Public Relations*
9100 Wilshire Blvd
W Tower #500
Beverly Hills, CA 90212-3415, USA

Smith, Alice (Musician)
c/o Staff Member *Paradigm (Monterey)*
404 W Franklin St
Monterey, CA 93940-2303, USA

Smith, Allison (Actor)
Innovative Artists
1505 10th St
Santa Monica, CA 90401-2805, USA

Smith, Amber (Actor, Model)
c/o Jerry Shandrew *Shandrew Public Relations*
1050 S Stanley Ave
Los Angeles, CA 90019-6634, USA

Smith, Andre (Athlete, Football Player)
c/o Ben Dogra *Relativity Sports*
2029 Century Park E Ste 1550
Century City, CA 90067-3000, USA

Smith, Ann (Athlete, Tennis Player)
3737 Cole Ave Apt 110
Dallas, TX 75204-1594, USA

Smith, Anna Deavere (Actor, Producer)
c/o Michael Samonte *Sunshine Sachs*
720 Cole Ave
Los Angeles, CA 90038-3606, USA

Smith, Anthony (Athlete, Football Player)
PO Box 573
Fontana, CA 92334-0573, USA

Smith, Antonio (Athlete, Football Player)
c/o Drew Rosenhaus *Rosenhaus Sports Representation*
3921 Alton Rd # 440
Miami Beach, FL 33140-3852, USA

Smith, Antowain (Athlete, Football Player)
2121 Hepburn St Apt 917
Houston, TX 77054-3221, USA

Smith, April (Writer)
427 7th St
Santa Monica, CA 90402-1907, USA

Smith, Art (Chef)
Southern Art & Bourbon Bar
3315 Peachtree Rd NE
Atlanta, GA 30326-1007, USA

Smith, Artie (Athlete, Football Player)
3809 W 68th St
Stillwater, OK 74074-2428, USA

Smith, Barbara (Business Person)
B. Smith Enterprises
1120 Avenue of the Americas Fl 4
New York, NY 10036-6700, USA

Smith, Barry (Athlete, Football Player)
2837 Voltz Ln
Knoxville, TN 37914-9796, USA

Smith, Barty (Athlete, Football Player)
2290 Dabney Rd
Richmond, VA 23230-3344, USA

Smith, Beau (Cartoonist)
PO Box 706
Ceredo, WV 25507-0706, USA

Smith, Ben (Cartoonist)
c/o Staff Member *King Features Syndication*
300 W 57th St Fl 15
New York, NY 10019-5238, USA

Smith, Ben (Athlete, Football Player)
1127 Riverbend Club Dr SE
Atlanta, GA 30339-2817, USA

Smith, Ben (Athlete, Hockey Player, Olympic Athlete)
47 Norwood Hts
Gloucester, MA 01930-1212, USA

Smith, Bennett W (Religious Leader)
Progressive National Baptist Convention
601 50th St NE
Washington, DC 20019-5498, USA

Smith, Bernie (Athlete, Baseball Player)
PO Box 513
Lutcher, LA 70071-0513, USA

Smith, Bevy (Business Person, Television Host)
c/o Ashley Mills *Creative Artists Agency (CAA)*
405 Lexington Ave Fl 19
New York, NY 10174-1800, USA

Smith, Bill (Athlete, Hockey Player)
New York Islanders
200 Merrick Ave
East Meadow, NY 11554-1596

Smith, Bill (Athlete, Football Player)
19 Woodcrest Dr
Lexington, NC 27295-1661, USA

Smith, Billy (Athlete, Baseball Player)
333 Rolling Hills Dr
Conroe, TX 77304-1280, USA

Smith, Billy (Athlete, Baseball Player)
5304 Vicksburg Dr
Arlington, TX 76017-4944, USA

Smith, Billy (Athlete, Hockey Player)
8356 Quail Meadow Way
West Palm Beach, FL 33412-1505, USA

Smith, Billy Ray Jr (Athlete, Football Player)
XX Sports Radio
6160 Cornerstone Ct E Ste 100
San Diego, CA 92121-3724, USA

Smith, Bob (Athlete, Baseball Player)
221 Hackberry Ln
Aiken, SC 29803-2733, USA

Smith, Bob (Golfer)
PO Box 6511
Ventura, CA 93006-6511, USA

Smith, Bobby (Athlete, Baseball Player)
2822 60th Ave
Oakland, CA 94605-1502, USA

Smith, Bobby (Athlete, Hockey Player)
10800 E Cactus Rd Unit 46
Scottsdale, AZ 85259-2505, USA

Smith, Bobby Gene (Athlete, Baseball Player)
1267 Tucker Rd Unit 15
Hood River, OR 97031-8601, USA

Smith, Brad (Athlete, Hockey Player)
Colorado Avalanche
1000 Chopper Cir
Denver, CO 80204-5805

Smith, Brad (Musician)
Shapiro Co
10990 Wilshire Blvd Fl 8
Los Angeles, CA 90024-3918, USA

Smith, Bradley (Brad) (Athlete, Football Player)
Brad Smith's True Foundation
1151 Mansell Dr
Youngstown, OH 44505-2242, USA

Smith, Brandon Mychal (Actor)
c/o Norman Aladjem *Mainstay Entertainment*
9250 Beverly Blvd Fl 3
Beverly Hills, CA 90210-3710, USA

Smith, Brent (Athlete, Football Player)
258 Ridgewood Dr
Pontotoc, MS 38863-3532, USA

Smith, Brian (Athlete, Baseball Player)
203 Bo Howard Rd
Toney, AL 35773-9235, USA

Smith, Brian D (Athlete, Hockey Player)

Smith, Brick (Athlete, Baseball Player)
6706 Easton Pl
Charlotte, NC 28212-5649, USA

Smith, Brooke (Actor)
c/o Christy Hall *Paradigm*
8942 Wilshire Blvd
Beverly Hills, CA 90211-1908, USA

Smith, Bruce W (Director)
c/o Staff Member *Jambalaya Studio*
111 N Artsakh St Ste 300
Glendale, CA 91206-4097, USA

Smith, Bryn (Athlete, Baseball Player)
1239 Highway 1
Santa Maria, CA 93455-5909, USA

Smith, Calvin (Athlete, Track Athlete)
16703 Sheffield Park Dr
Lutz, FL 33549-6833, USA

Smith, Chad (Musician)
c/o Peter Mensch *Q Prime (NY)*
729 7th Ave Fl 16
New York, NY 10019-6831, USA

Smith, Charles (Athlete, Basketball Player)
PO Box 433
Cedar Grove, NJ 07009-0433, USA

Smith, Charles Martin (Actor, Director)
c/o David Saunders *Agency for the Performing Arts (APA)*
405 S Beverly Dr Ste 500
Beverly Hills, CA 90212-4425, USA

Smith, Charlie E (Athlete, Football Player)
1906 Crescent Dr
Monroe, LA 71202-3024, USA

Smith, Charlie H (Athlete, Football Player)
14074 Skyline Blvd
Oakland, CA 94619-3622, USA

Smith, Chris (Athlete, Baseball Player)
4206 Dawn Ln
Oceanside, CA 92056-4716, USA

Smith, Chris (Golfer)
208 S Bellerive Dr
Peru, IN 46970-8060, USA

Smith, Chris M (Athlete, Football Player)
1424 Martway Cir Apt A
Olathe, KS 66061-5820, USA

Smith, Chuck (Athlete, Baseball Player)
1300 Saint Charles Pl Apt 810
Pembroke Pines, FL 33026-3340, USA

Smith, Chuck (Athlete, Football Player)
1155 Havenbrook Ct
Suwanee, GA 30024-2877, USA

Smith, Clinton J (Clint) (Athlete, Hockey Player)
501-1919 Bellevue Ave
West Vancouver, BC V7V 1B7, Canada

Smith, Colleen (Actor)
c/o Mark Scroggs *David Shapira & Associates*
193 N Robertson Blvd
Beverly Hills, CA 90211-2103, USA

Smith, Connie (Music Group, Musician)
Gurley Co
1204B Cedar Ln Apt B
Nashville, TN 37212-5910, USA

Smith, Corey (Athlete, Baseball Player)

Smith, Cory Michael (Actor)
c/o Scott Boute *Serge PR*
339 W 12th St
New York, NY 10014-1721, USA

Smith, Cotter (Actor)
15332 Antioch St # 800
Pacific Palisades, CA 90272-3628, USA

Smith, Dallas (Athlete, Hockey Player)
4154 N Potomac Dr
Florence, AZ 85132-6051

Smith, Dan (Athlete, Baseball Player)
715 N Carbon St
Girard, KS 66743-1025, USA

Smith, Daniel E. (Actor)
c/o Shannon McLaren *JKA Talent*
4324 Troost Ave Unit 206
Studio City, CA 91604-2886, USA

Smith, Danny (Actor)
c/o Lisa Harrison *WME|IMG*
9601 Wilshire Blvd
Beverly Hills, CA 90210-5213, USA

Smith, Dante (Mos Def) (Actor, Musician)
c/o Linda Carbone *Press Here Publicity*
138 W 25th St Ste 900
New York, NY 10001-7470, USA

Smith, D'Anthony (Athlete, Football Player)
c/o Bus Cook *Bus Cook Sports, Inc*
1 Willow Bend Dr
Hattiesburg, MS 39402-8552, USA

Smith, Darden (Music Group, Musician, Songwriter, Writer)
AGF Entertainment
30 W 21st St # 700
New York, NY 10010-6905, USA

Smith, Darrin (Athlete, Football Player)
7395 NW 19th Ct
Hollywood, FL 33024-1015, USA

Smith, Daryl (Athlete, Baseball Player)
3 Sunny Mills Ct
Randallstown, MD 21133-4449, USA

Smith, Daryl (Athlete, Football Player)
1636 Norton Hill Dr
Jacksonville, FL 32225-4937, USA

Smith, Dave (Athlete, Baseball Player)
16330 Jersey Dr
Jersey Village, TX 77040-2020, USA

Smith, Dave (Athlete, Football Player)
7906 W 116th Ter
Overland Park, KS 66210-2527, USA

Smith, Dave (Athlete, Football Player)
650 S 13th St Apt 123-20
Indiana, PA 15701-3566, USA

Smith, Delia (Actor, Chef, Writer)
Delia Online
PO Box 1124
Knaphill GU21 9AA, United Kingdom

Smith, Dennis (Athlete, Football Player)
2450 Achilles Dr
Los Angeles, CA 90046-1626, USA

Smith, Derek (Athlete, Football Player)
4949 Marie P Debartolo Way
Santa Clara, CA 95054-1156, USA

Smith, Derek (Athlete, Hockey Player)
201 Bramblewood Ln
East Amherst, NY 14051-2228

Smith, Dick (Athlete, Baseball Player)
1926 Norwood Ln
State College, PA 16803-1326, USA

Smith, Dick (Athlete, Baseball Player)
2615 Gates Rd
Lincolnton, NC 28092-7968, USA

Smith, Dick (Athlete, Baseball Player)
6850 Downing Rd Spc 35
Central Point, OR 97502-3418, USA

Smith, Dick (Athlete, Coach, Swimmer)
PO Box 1831
Dewey, AZ 86327-1831, USA

Smith, Dick (Athlete, Football Player)
5718 Chillum Pl NE
Washington, DC 20011-2528, USA

Smith, Dick (Business Person)
Dick Smith Foods
10 Cassola Pl
Penrith 02750, Australia

Smith, D.J. (Athlete, Football Player)
c/o Peter Schaffer *Authentic Athletix*
400 S Steele St Unit 47
Denver, CO 80209-3535, USA

Smith, D J (Athlete, Hockey Player)
Windsor Spitfires
8787 McHugh St
Windsor, ON N8S 0A1, Canada

Smith, Donald L (Athlete, Football Player)
3338 Pineview Dr
Holiday, FL 34691-9732, USA

Smith, Doug (Athlete, Basketball Player)
25482 Pennsylvania Ave
Novi, MI 48375-1785, USA

Smith, Doug (Athlete, Football Player)
25661 Pacific Crest Dr
Mission Viejo, CA 92692-5040, USA

Smith, Doug (Athlete, Hockey Player)
PO Box 276
Dunrobin, ON K0A 3M0, CANADA

Smith, Doug (Coach, Football Coach, Football Player)
University of Southern California
Heritage Hall
Los Angeles, CA 90089-0001, USA

Smith, Douglas (Actor)
c/o Mia Hansen *Portrait PR*
5320 Sylmar Ave
Sherman Oaks, CA 91401-5612, USA

Smith, Dwight (Athlete, Baseball Player)
PO Box 98
Varnville, SC 29944-0098, USA

Smith, Earl (Athlete, Baseball Player)
2764 N Leonard Ave
Fresno, CA 93737-9720, USA

Smith, Elliot (Athlete, Football Player)
1343 Cadillac Dr
Jackson, MS 39213-4811, USA

Smith, Elmore (Athlete, Basketball Player)
PO Box 24147S
Cleveland, OH 44124-847S, USA

Smith, Emmitt (Athlete, Football Player)
Pat & Emmitt Smith Charities
16000 Dallas Pkwy # 550N
Tollway Plaza North
Dallas, TX 75248-6607, USA

Smith, Eric (Race Car Driver)
Southtown Motorsports
1701 W Washington St
Bloomington, IL 61701-3701, USA

Smith, Eugene (Baseball Player)
Cincinnati Buckeyes
8337 Flora Ave
Saint Louis, MO 63114-6203, USA

Smith, F Dean (Athlete, Track Athlete)
PO Box 71
Breckenridge, TX 76424-0071, USA

Smith, Floyd (Athlete, Hockey Player)
138 Stonehenge Dr
Orchard Park, NY 14127-2845

Smith, Frankie (Athlete, Football Player)
620 N Grayson St
Groesbeck, TX 76642-1157, USA

Smith, Frederick W (Business Person)
FDX Corp
942 Shady Grove Rd S
Memphis, TN 38120-4117, USA

Smith, Garfield (Athlete, Basketball Player)
2006 Idylwild Ct
Richmond, KY 40475-3606, USA

Smith, Gary (Athlete, Hockey Player)
102-4451 Albert St
Villa Cortina
Burnaby, BC V5C 2G4, Canada

Smith, G Elaine (Religious Leader)
American Baptist Churches USA
PO Box 851
Valley Forge, PA 19482-0851, USA

Smith, Geno (Athlete, Football Player)
c/o Juan Perez *Roc Nation*
1411 Broadway Fl 38
New York, NY 10018-3409, USA

Smith, Geoff (Athlete, Hockey Player)
42-1525 Westside Rd S
Kelowna, BC V1Z 3Y3, Canada

Smith, George (Cartoonist)
Universal Press Syndicate
4520 Main St Ste 340
Kansas City, MO 64111-7705, USA

Smith, Gerald (Misc)
World Tennis Assn
133 1st St NE
Saint Petersburg, FL 33701-3307, USA

Smith, Gord (Athlete, Hockey Player)
78 Hampton Close
Orange, CT 06477-1933

Smith, Gordon (Politician)
8611 Country Club Dr
Bethesda, MD 20817-4579, USA

Smith, Greg (Athlete, Baseball Player)
27435 Hanes Rd E
Davenport, WA 99122-9443, USA

Smith, Greg (Athlete, Basketball Player)
9930 SW Lumbee Ln
Tualatin, OR 97062-7355, USA

Smith, Greg (Athlete, Hockey Player)
909 56th St W
Billings, MT 59106-2240

Smith, Gregory (Actor, Producer)
c/o Jennifer Goldhar *Characters Talent Agency (Toronto)*
8 Elm St Fl 2
Toronto, ON M5G 1G7, CANADA

Smith, Guy (Race Car Driver)
Tasman Motorsports
4192 Weaver Ct.
Hilliard, OH 43206, USA

Smith, Hal (Athlete, Football Player)
PO Box 939
Whittier, CA 90608-0939, USA

Smith, Harley Quinn (Actor)
c/o Heather Weiss-Besignano *ICON PR*
8961 W Sunset Blvd Ste 1C
W Hollywood, CA 90069-1886, USA

Smith, Harrison (Athlete, Football Player)

Smith, Harry (Correspondent)

Smith, Harry E (Black Jack) (Athlete, Coach, Football Coach, Football Player)
805 Leawood Ter
Columbia, MO 65203-2729, USA

Smith, Hedrick L (Journalist)
4204 Rosemary St
Chevy Chase, MD 20815-5218, USA

Smith, Helen (Athlete, Baseball Player)
1600 Westbrook Ave Apt 436
Richmond, VA 23227-3318, USA

Smith, Hunter (Athlete, Football Player)
320 W Cedar St
Zionsville, IN 46077-1301, USA

Smith, Huston (Writer)
c/o Staff Member *Red Wheel / Weiser /Conari*
65 Parker St Ste 7
Newburyport, MA 01950-4600, USA

Smith, Ian K (Doctor, Reality Star)
c/o Linda Shafran *Linda Shafran*
424 Wisconsin Ave Apt 1N
Oak Park, IL 60302-3678, USA

Smith, Jack (Athlete, Baseball Player)
250 Doubles Dr
Covington, GA 30016-1736, USA

Smith, Jackie L (Athlete, Football Player)
1566 Walpole Dr
Chesterfield, MO 63017-4615, USA

Smith, Jaclyn (Actor)
10398 W Sunset Blvd
Los Angeles, CA 90077-3613, USA

Smith, Jacob (Actor)
c/o Elaine Lively *LA Entertainment*
1375 S. San Fernando Blvd.
Suite 505
Burbank, CA 91504, USA

Smith, Jacquies (Athlete, Football Player)

Smith, Jaden (Actor, Musician)
c/o Kate Rosen *The Lede Company*
401 Broadway Ste 206
New York, NY 10013-3033, USA

Smith, James (Bonecrusher) (Boxer)
355 Keith Hills Road
Lillington, NC 27546, USA

Smith, Jamie Renee (Actor)
c/o Pam Grimes *Hervey/Grimes Talent Agency*
10561 Missouri Ave Apt 2
Los Angeles, CA 90025-5940, USA

Smith, Jason V (Athlete, Basketball Player)
c/o Mark Bartelstein *Priority Sports & Entertainment (Chicago)*
325 N La Salle Dr Ste 650
Chicago, IL 60654-8182, USA

Smith, J D (Athlete, Football Player)
1615 County Road 204
Richland Springs, TX 76871, USA

Smith, J D Jr (Athlete, Football Player)
3332 Florida St
Oakland, CA 94602-3808, USA

Smith, Jean (Baseball Player)
5351 S Lake Shore Dr
Harbor Springs, MI 49740-9109, USA

Smith, Jean Kennedy (Misc)
The Kennedy Center
2700 F St NW
Washington, DC 20566-0002, USA

Smith, Jennifer M (Prime Minister)
Premier's Office
Cabinet Building
105 Front St
Hamilton, HM 00012, BERMUDA

Smith, Jermaine (Athlete, Football Player)
1345 12th St
Augusta, GA 30901-3260, USA

Smith, Jim (Athlete, Baseball Player)
1730 S Arroyo Ln
Gilbert, AZ 85295-4815, USA

Smith, Jim (Athlete, Football Player)
2639 Round Table Blvd
Lewisville, TX 75056-5723, USA

Smith, Jim Field (Actor, Director)
c/o Trevor Engelson *Underground Management*
1180 S Beverly Dr Ste 509
Los Angeles, CA 90035-1157, USA

Smith, Jimmy (Athlete, Football Player)
c/o Drew Rosenhaus *Rosenhaus Sports Representation*
3921 Alton Rd # 440
Miami Beach, FL 33140-3852, USA

Smith, Jimmy Lee (Athlete, Football Player)
1302 Charter Ct E
Jacksonville, FL 32225-2658, USA

Smith, Jim Ray (Athlete, Football Player)
7049 Cliffbrook Dr
Dallas, TX 75254-7909, USA

Smith, Joe (Basketball Player)
7639 Leafwood Dr
Norfolk, VA 23518-4536, USA

Smith, John (Race Car Driver)
5611 Highway 81 N
Williamston, SC 29697-9742, USA

Smith, John L (Coach, Football Coach)
Michigan State University
Daugherty Field House
East Lansing, MI 48824, USA

Smith, John M (Athlete, Football Player)
184 Centre St
Dover, MA 02030-2413, USA

Smith, John W (Athlete, Wrestler)
5315 S Sangre Rd
Stillwater, OK 74074-2071, USA

Smith, Jordan (Musician)
c/o Staff Member *Feldman Agency (Toronto)*
200-1505 2nd Ave W
Vancouver, BC V6H 3Y4, CANADA

Smith, Jorja (Musician)
c/o Mike Greek *CAA (London)*
3 Shortlands, Hammersmith
Fl 5
London W6 8DA, UNITED KINGDOM

Smith, Josh (Athlete, Basketball Player)
c/o Brian Dyke *Shibumi Sports*
4771 Sweetwater Blvd # 228
Sugar Land, TX 77479-3121, USA

Smith, JR (Athlete, Basketball Player)
c/o Rich Paul *Klutch Sports Management*
Prefers to be contacted by telephone
Cleveland, OH, USA

Smith, J Robert (Athlete, Football Player)
6102 Timberlake Ct
Flower Mound, TX 75022-5627, USA

Smith, J T (Athlete, Football Player)
10110 Planters Row Dr
Frisco, TX 75033-0255, USA

Smith, Judy (Producer, Writer)
c/o Mark Itkin *WME|IMG*
9601 Wilshire Blvd
Beverly Hills, CA 90210-5213, USA

Smith, Justice (Actor)
c/o David Kohl *The Kohl Group*
12000 Riverside Dr Unit 219
Valley Village, CA 91607-6018, USA

Smith, Justin (Athlete, Football Player)
c/o Susan Patricola *Patricola Public Relations*
369 S Doheny Dr # 1408
Beverly Hills, CA 90211-3508, USA

Smith, Kathy (Misc)
PO Box 491433
Los Angeles, CA 90049-9433, USA

Smith, Katie (Athlete, Basketball Player, Olympic Athlete)
2494 Farleigh Rd
Columbus, OH 43221-2618, USA

Smith, Keith (Athlete, Baseball Player)
417 58th Ave E
Bradenton, FL 34203-6250, USA

Smith, Keith (Athlete, Baseball Player)
15711 Ada St
Canyon Country, CA 91387-1891, USA

Smith, Kellita (Actor)
c/o Norman Aladjem *Mainstay Entertainment*
9250 Beverly Blvd Fl 3
Beverly Hills, CA 90210-3710, USA

Smith, Ken (Athlete, Baseball Player)
Bluff City Jaguar 6335 Wheel Cv Attn Sales Dept
Memobis, TN 38119-8244, USA

Smith, Kenneth L (Athlete, Baseball Player, Football Player)
313 Ellen Dr
Deer Park, TX 77536-3534, USA

Smith, Kenny (Athlete, Basketball Player, Sportscaster)
c/o Staff Member *Turner Network Television (TNT)*
4000 Warner Blvd Bldg 160
Burbank, CA 91522-0001, USA

Smith, Kerr (Actor, Director)
1665 Eveningside Dr
Thousand Oaks, CA 91362-1247, USA

Smith, Kevin (Actor, Director, Producer, Writer)
c/o Staff Member *View Askew Productions Inc*
PO Box 400
Red Bank, NJ 07701-0400, USA

Smith, Kevin (Athlete, Football Player)
7001 Parkwood Blvd Apt 3204
Plano, TX 75024-7176, USA

Smith, Kim (Actor)
3116 Trails End Rd
Odessa, TX 79762-5035, USA

Smith, Kurtwood (Actor)
c/o Kelly Garner *Pop Art Management*
PO Box 55363
Sherman Oaks, CA 91413-0363, USA

Smith, Labradford (Athlete, Basketball Player)
410 Thompson Dr
Bay City, TX 77414-7910, USA

Smith, Lamar (Congressman, Politician)
2409 Rayburn Hob
Washington, DC 20515-4317, USA

Smith, Lance (Athlete, Football Player)
14907 Rocky Top Dr
Huntersville, NC 28078-2648, USA

Smith, Larry (Athlete, Basketball Player)
1767 Lakeside Dr
Vicksburg, MS 39180-9369, USA

Smith, Larry (Athlete, Football Player)
5020 Bayshore Blvd Apt 305
Tampa, FL 33611-3855, USA

Smith, Lauren Lee (Actor)
c/o Kathy Carpenter *KC Talent*
109-119 Pender St W
Vancouver, BC V6B 1S5, CANADA

Smith, Laverne (Athlete, Football Player)
2122 N Homestead St
Wichita, KS 67208-1872, USA

Smith, Lee (Athlete, Baseball Player)
PO Box 399
Castor, LA 71016-0399, USA

Smith, Lee A (Baseball Player)
Atlanta Braves
PO Box 174
Castor, LA 71016-0174, USA

Smith, Leonard P (Athlete, Football Player)
18053 Creek Hollow Rd
Baton Rouge, LA 70817-3304, USA

Smith, Lois (Actor)
c/o Steve Stone *Cornerstone Talent Agency*
37 W 20th St Ste 1007
New York, NY 10011-3714, USA

Smith, Lonnie (Athlete, Baseball Player)
145 Wesley Forest Dr
Fayetteville, GA 30214-1094, USA

Smith, Louise (Race Car Driver)
International Motorsports
PO Box 1018
Talladega, AL 35161-1018, USA

Smith, Lovie (Athlete, Coach, Football Coach, Football Player)
c/o Matthew Smith *IMG Coaches*
601 Carlson Pkwy Ste 610
Minnetonka, MN 55305-5215, USA

Smith, Lucky Blue (Model)
c/o Mimi Yapor-Cox *Next Model Management (LA)*
8447 Wilshire Blvd PH
Beverly Hills, CA 90211-1683, USA

Smith, Madeline (Actor)
Joan Gray
Sunbury Island
Sunbury on Thames
Middx, UNITED KINGDOM (UK)

Smith, Maggie (Actor)
c/o Paul Lyon-Maris *Independent Talent Group*
40 Whitfield St
London W1T 2RH, UNITED KINGDOM

Smith, Malcolm (Race Car Driver)
Motorsports HOF
PO Box 194
Novi, MI 48376-0194, USA

Smith, Malcolm (Athlete, Football Player)

Smith, Marcus (Athlete, Football Player)
c/o Todd France *Creative Artists Agency (CAA) Sports*
3500 Lenox Rd NE
Atlanta, GA 30326-4228, USA

Smith, Margaret (Producer, Writer)
c/o Gail Stocker *Gail Stocker Presents*
1025 N Kings Rd Apt 113
Los Angeles, CA 90069-6007, USA

Smith, Margo (Musician, Songwriter, Writer)
Tristar Enterprises Inc
PO Box 682064
Franklin, TN 37068-2064, USA

Smith, Marilynn (Golfer)
3784 N 162nd Ln
Goodyear, AZ 85395-8017, USA

Smith, Mark (Athlete, Baseball Player)
907 Forest Green Rd
Reedville, VA 22539-3577, USA

Smith, Mark (Athlete, Baseball Player)
1312 Elmhurst Ln
Flower Mound, TX 75028-3847, USA

Smith, Mark (Athlete, Hockey Player)
Ayla Boutique
381 E Campbell Ave
Campbell, CA 95008-2013

Smith, Marquis (Athlete, Football Player)
843 51st St
San Diego, CA 92114-1002, USA

Smith, Martha (Actor, Model)
9690 Heather Rd
Beverly Hills, CA 90210-1757, USA

Smith, Marty (Motorcycle Racer, Sportscaster)
c/o Matt Kramer *CAA Sports (Atlanta)*
3560 Lenox Rd NE Ste 1525
Atlanta, GA 30326-4338, USA

Smith, Marvel (Athlete, Football Player)
30 Waterfront Dr
Pittsburgh, PA 15222-4748, USA

Smith, Marvin (Smitty) (Musician)
Joel Chriss
300 Mercer St Apt 3J
New York, NY 10003-6732, USA

Smith, Matt (Actor)
c/o Michael Duff *Troika*
10A Christina St.
London EC2A 4PA, UNITED KINGDOM

Smith, Melanie (Actor)
Innovative Artists
1505 10th St
Santa Monica, CA 90401-2805, USA

Smith, Michael (Athlete, Basketball Player)
332 58th St NE
Washington, DC 20019-6953, USA

Smith, Michael Bailey (Actor)
c/o Alexandra Karrys *Divine Management*
117 N Orlando Ave
Los Angeles, CA 90048-3403, USA

Smith, Michael W (Musician, Songwriter)
c/o Steve Rohr *Lexicon Public Relations*
1049 Havenhurst Dr # 365
West Hollywood, CA 90046-6002, USA

Smith, Mike (Athlete, Baseball Player)
3226 Livingston Rd
Jackson, MS 39213-6106, USA

Smith, Mike (Athlete, Baseball Player)
6 Willett Pond Rd
Westwood, MA 02090-3417, USA

Smith, Mike (Athlete, Baseball Player)
7605 Antique Oak St
Live Oak, TX 78233-3102, USA

Smith, Mike (Athlete, Football Player)
619 Feamster Dr
Houston, TX 77022-2505, USA

Smith, Mike (Cartoonist)
Las Vegas Sun
2275 Corporate Cir Ste 300
Editorial Dept
Henderson, NV 89074-7745, USA

Smith, Mike (Horse Racer)
3445 NE 210th St
Miami, FL 33180-3587, USA

Smith, Mike (Race Car Driver)
Paul Smith Racing
800 NE 3rd St Ste 2
Boynton Beach, FL 33435-3194, USA

Smith, Mindy (Musician, Songwriter, Writer)
Vanguard Records
2700 Pennsylvania Ave Ste 1100
Santa Monica, CA 90404-4059, USA

Smith, Mitchell (Race Car Driver)
Mitchell Smith Racing
4834 W 200 S
Anderson, IN 46011-8749, USA

Smith, Moishe (Artist)
Utah State University
Art Dept
Logan, UT 84322-0001, USA

Smith, Monika (Actor)
c/o David Gardner *Artists First*
9465 Wilshire Blvd Ste 900
Beverly Hills, CA 90212-2608, USA

Smith, Myron (Athlete, Football Player)
6604 Sandgate Dr
Arlington, TX 76002-5549, USA

Smith, Nate (Athlete, Baseball Player)
6365 Tahoe Dr
Atlanta, GA 30349-4052, USA

Smith, Neil (Athlete, Football Player)
5366 W 95th St
Prairie Village, KS 66207-3204, USA

Smith, Nicholas (Actor)
Michelle Braidman
10/11 Lower John St
London, ENGLAND W1R 3PE, UNITED KINGDOM (UK)

Smith, Noland (Athlete, Football Player)
4338 Watkins Dr
Jackson, MS 39206-4450, USA

Smith, O Guinn (Athlete, Track Athlete)
1 Hawthorne Pl Apt 3P
Boston, MA 02114-2333, USA

Smith, Orin R (Business Person)
Engelhard Corp
425 33rd Ave SW
Vero Beach, FL 32968-3127, USA

Smith, Orlando (Tubby) (Coach)
University of Kentucky
Athletic Dept
Lexington, KY 40536-0001, USA

Smith, Otis (Athlete, Basketball Player)
6055 4 Mile Rd NE
Ada, MI 49301-9589, USA

Smith, Ozzie (Athlete, Baseball Player)
PO Box 251
Saint Albans, MO 63073-0251, USA

Smith, Patti (Musician, Songwriter)
Primary Talent International Ltd
2-12 Pentonville Road
5th Fl
Sausalito, London N1 9PL, UNITED KINGDOM

Smith, Paul (Athlete, Baseball Player)
711 Trevino Ln
Conroe, TX 77302-3835, USA

Smith, Paul B (Designer, Fashion Designer)
Paul Smith Ltd
41/44 Floral St
Covent Garden
London WC2E 9DG, UNITED KINGDOM (UK)

Smith, Pete (Athlete, Baseball Player)
5517 Kingsley Mnr
Cumming, GA 30041-6119, USA

Smith, Pete (Athlete, Baseball Player)
3512 Dixon Ln
The Villages, FL 32162-7150, USA

Smith, Phyllis (Actor)
c/o Gregg Gellman *Morris Yorn Barnes Levine Krintzman Rubenstein Kohner & Gellman*
2000 Avenue of the Stars Ste 300N
Tower N Fl 3
Los Angeles, CA 90067-4704, USA

Smith, Putter (Actor)
1414 Lyndon St
South Pasadena, CA 91030-3812, USA

Smith, Quanterus (Athlete, Football Player)
c/o Jordan Woy *Willis & Woy Management*
4890 Alpha Rd Ste 200
Dallas, TX 75244-4639, USA

Smith, Quincy (Baseball Player)
Cleveland Buckeyes
715 S 14th St
Terre Haute, IN 47807-4920, USA

Smith, Quinn (Actor)
1738 Whitley Ave
Hollywood, CA 90028-4809

Smith, Rachel (Beauty Pageant Winner)
c/o Steve Rohr *Lexicon Public Relations*
1049 Havenhurst Dr # 365
West Hollywood, CA 90046-6002, USA

Smith, Ralph (Cartoonist)
c/o Staff Member *King Features Syndication*
300 W 57th St Fl 15
New York, NY 10019-5238, USA

Smith, Ralph (Athlete, Football Player)
PO Box 1406
McComb, MS 39649-1406, USA

Smith, Randy (Baseball Player)
7941 E Via De Luna Dr
Scottsdale, AZ 85255-4113, USA

Smith, Ray (Athlete, Baseball Player)
163 Old Milligan Hwy
Johnson City, TN 37601-7024, USA

Smith, Ray E (Religious Leader)
Open Bible Standard Churches
2020 Bell Ave
Des Moines, IA 50315-1096, USA

Smith, RD (Race Car Driver)
Congdon Racing
4500 Turnberry Ct SW
Concord, NC 28027-0432, USA

Smith, Regan (Race Car Driver)
Furniture Row Racing
4000 Forest St
Denver, CO 80216-4537, USA

Smith, Reggie (Athlete, Baseball Player)
Reggie Smith Baseball Center
16161Ventura Blvd Ste 775
Encino, CA 91436-2522, USA

Smith, Reggie (Athlete, Basketball Player)
6975 Claywood Way
San Jose, CA 95120-2241, USA

Smith, Renee Felice (Actor)
c/o Hannah Roth *Buchwald*
5900 Wilshire Blvd Ste 3100
Los Angeles, CA 90036-5030, USA

Smith, Rex (Actor, Musician)
16986 Encino Hills Dr
Encino, CA 91436-4008, USA

Smith, Rick (Athlete, Hockey Player)
RR 1
Perth Road, ON KOH 2LO, Canada

Smith, Rickie (Race Car Driver)
Rt 3 Box 19
Kirby Rd
King, NC 27021, USA

Smith, Rico (Athlete, Football Player)
8976 Foothill Blvd Ste B7
Rancho Cucamonga, CA 91730-3400, USA

Smith, Riley (Actor)
c/o Siri Garber *Platform PR*
2666 N Beachwood Dr
Los Angeles, CA 90068-2308, USA

Smith, R Jackson (Swimmer)
122 Palmers Hill Rd Unit 3101
Stamford, CT 06902-2147, USA

Smith, Robert (Musician)
c/o Martin Hopewell *Primary Talent International (UK)*
10-11 Jockeys Fields
The Primary Bldg
London WC1R 4BN, UNITED KINGDOM

Smith, Robert (Athlete, Baseball Player)
1274 Norman Rd
Colton, CA 92324-1713, USA

Smith, Robert B (Athlete, Football Player)
1012 S Royal St
Bogalusa, LA 70427-5457, USA

Smith, Robert C (Bob) (Politician, Senator)
9012 Rocky Lake Ct
Sarasota, FL 34238-4008, USA

Smith, Robert L (Athlete, Football Player)
426 Cape Lookout Dr
Corpus Christi, TX 78412-2636, USA

Smith, Robert S (Athlete, Football Player)
5668 Harrison Ave
Maple Heights, OH 44137-3331, USA

Smith, Robin (Doctor, Writer)
226 W Rittenhouse Sq Apt 210
Philadelphia, PA 19103-5738, USA

Smith, Rod (Athlete, Football Player)
821 W 4th St
Charlotte, NC 28202-1103, USA

Smith, Roger Guenveur (Actor, Writer)
Luna Ray Films
2018 Vine St
Los Angeles, CA 90068-3915, USA

Smith, Rolland (Correspondent)
CBS-TV
524 W 57th St
News Dept
New York, NY 10019-2924, USA

Smith, Ron (Athlete, Football Player)
1804 Park Ave
Richmond, VA 23220-2821, USA

Smith, Ron (Athlete, Football Player)
266 York St
Trussville, AL 35173-3224, USA

Smith, Ron (Race Car Driver)
14933 175th Pl SE
Renton, WA 98059, USA

Smith, Roy (Athlete, Baseball Player)
472 Gramatan Ave Apt G2
Mount Vernon, NY 10552-2940, USA

Smith, Roy (Athlete, Baseball Player)
908 Woodbridge Ct
Safety Harbor, FL 34695-2951, USA

Smith, Russell (Musician)
LC Media
PO Box 965
Antioch, TN 37011-0965, USA

Smith, Sam (Musician)
c/o Kirk Sommer *WME/IMG*
9601 Wilshire Blvd
Beverly Hills, CA 90210-5213, USA

Smith, Sam (Athlete, Basketball Player)
5790 Cedar Bay Dr
Millington, TN 38053-8410, USA

Smith, Sarah Christine (Actor)
c/o Staff Member *Hervey/Grimes Talent Agency*
10561 Missouri Ave Apt 2
Los Angeles, CA 90025-5940, USA

Smith, Sean (Athlete, Football Player)
c/o Roger Green *WME/IMG*
9601 Wilshire Blvd
Beverly Hills, CA 90210-5213, USA

Smith, Seth (Athlete, Baseball Player)
101 Elizabeth Dr
Brandon, MS 39042-6501, USA

Smith, Shane (Business Person, Journalist, Television Host)
c/o Staff Member *Vice Media*
49 S 2nd St
Brooklyn, NY 11249-5119, USA

Smith, Shawnee (Actor)
c/o Brian Wilkins *LINK Entertainment*
11872 La Grange Ave
Los Angeles, CA 90025-5282, USA

Smith, Shelley (Actor)
4184 Colfax Ave
Studio City, CA 91604-2165, USA

Smith, Shelley (Athlete, Football Player)

Smith, Shepard (Television Host)
c/o Staff Member *Fox News*
1211 Avenue of the Americas Lowr C1
New York, NY 10036-8705, USA

Smith, Sherman (Athlete, Football Player)
1421 Primrose Ln
Franklin, TN 37064-9333, USA

Smith, Shevin (Athlete, Football Player)
10110 Farmingdale Pl
Tampa, FL 33624-5419, USA

Smith, Sid (Athlete, Football Player)
1939 Melody Ln
Richmond, TX 77406-2411, USA

Smith, Sinjin (Athlete, Volleyball Player)
Beach Volleyball Camps
PO Box 1714
Pacific Palisades, CA 90272-1714, USA

Smith, Skip (Race Car Driver)
2143C Statesville Blvd # 117
Salisbury, NC 28147-1411, USA

Smith, Sonny (Baseball Player)
Chicago American Giants
3549 N College Ave
Indianapolis, IN 46205-3733, USA

Smith, Stanley (Race Car Driver)
1740 Rd #39
Chelsea, AL 35043, USA

Smith, Stanley R (Stan) (Tennis Player)
ProServe
1101 Woodrow Wilson Blvd
#1800
Arlington, VA 22209, USA

Smith, Stephen A (Actor, Correspondent, Radio Personality)
c/o Staff Member *ESPN (Main)*
935 Middle St
Espn Plaza
Bristol, CT 06010-1000, USA

Smith, Steve (Athlete, Football Player)
c/o Ben Dogra *Relativity Sports*
2029 Century Park E Ste 1550
Century City, CA 90067-3000, USA

Smith, Steve (Athlete, Hockey Player)
Edmonton Oilers
11230 110 St NW
Edmonton, AB T5G 3H7, Canada

Smith, Steve (Race Car Driver)
c/o Staff Member *RacingWest*
1772 Los Arboles
Suite #J-186
Thousand Oaks, CA 91362, USA

Smith, Steve (Athlete, Baseball Player, Olympic Athlete)
PO Box 1253
San Clemente, CA 92674-1253, USA

Smith, Steve (Athlete, Football Player)
Steve Smith Foundation
PO Box 77401
Charlotte, NC 28271-7009, USA

Smith, Steve (Athlete, Olympic Athlete)
1305 Via Avila
San Clemente, CA 92672-2341, USA

Smith, Steve (Producer)
c/o Staff Member *Hall Webber*
1200 Bay St Suite 400
Toronto, ON M5R 2A5, Canada

Smith, Steven (Astronaut)
c/o Staff Member *NASA-JSC*
2101 Nasa Pkwy # 1
Astronaut Office - Mail Code Cb
Houston, TX 77058-3607, USA

Smith, Stevonne (Steve Sr) (Athlete, Football Player)
c/o Derrick Fox *Derrick Fox Management*
Prefers to be contacted by telephone
CA, USA

Smith, Taran (Actor)
Full Circle Mgmt
12665 Kling St
North Hollywood, CA 91604-1143, USA

Smith, Tasha (Actor)
c/o CeCe Yorke *True Public Relations*
3575 Cahuenga Blvd W Ste 360
Los Angeles, CA 90068-1361, USA

Smith, Taylor John (Actor)
c/o Annett Wolf *Wolf-Kasteler Public Relations*
6255 W Sunset Blvd Ste 1111
Los Angeles, CA 90028-7426, USA

Smith, Telvin (Athlete, Football Player)
c/o Adisa P Bakari *Kelley Drye & Warren LLP*
3050 K St NW Ste 400
Washington, DC 20007-5100, USA

Smith, Terry (Sportscaster)
12 Cleome St
Ladera Ranch, CA 92694-0858, USA

Smith, Thomas (Athlete, Football Player)
RR 1 Box 198
Gates, NC 27937, USA

Smith, Tiffany (Actor)
c/o Heather Weiss-Besignano *ICON PR*
8961 W Sunset Blvd Ste 1C
W Hollywood, CA 90069-1886, USA

Smith, Tommie (Athlete, Olympic Athlete, Track Athlete)
1800 Lilburn Stone Mountain Rd
Stone Mountain, GA 30087-1720, USA

Smith, Tommy (Athlete, Baseball Player)
1299 E Cannon Ave
Albemarle, NC 28001-4360, USA

Smith, Tony (Athlete, Basketball Player)
2645 N 40th St
Milwaukee, WI 53210-2505, USA

Smith, Tony (Athlete, Football Player)
PO Box 480234
Charlotte, NC 28269-5302, USA

Smith, Torrey (Athlete, Football Player)
c/o Deb Poquette *Prestige Lifestyle Management*
1300 Saint Michaels Rd
Mount Airy, MD 21771-3228, USA

Smith, Travian (Athlete, Football Player)
13941 County Road 2167D
Tatum, TX 75691-3214, USA

Smith, Travis (Athlete, Baseball Player)
2271 Deer Pointe Dr
Clarkston, WA 99403-5005, USA

Smith, Tre'Quan (Athlete, Football Player)
c/o Fred Lyles *NZone Sports Management Agency*
PO Box 251545
Plano, TX 75025-1500, USA

Smith, Troy (Athlete, Football Player, Heisman Trophy Winner)
c/o Staff Member *Baltimore Ravens*
6 Rod Cir
Middletown, MD 21769-7868, USA

Smith, Tyron (Football Player)
c/o Eric Metz *Lock Metz Milanovic LLC*
6900 E Camelback Rd Ste 600
Scottsdale, AZ 85251-8044, USA

Smith, Vern (Athlete, Hockey Player)
15 Meadowlark Dr
East Longmeadow, MA 01028-3173

Smith, Vernice (Athlete, Football Player)
4347 Arajo Ct
Belle Isle, FL 32812-2854, USA

Smith, Vince (Musician)
Process Talent Management
439 Wiley Ave
Franklin, PA 16323-2834, USA

Smith, Wallace B (Religious Leader)
Reorganized Church of Latter Day Saints
PO Box 1059
Independence, MO 64051-0559, USA

Smith, Wayne (Athlete, Football Player)
7730 S Bishop St Apt 1
Chicago, IL 60620-4127, USA

Smith, Wilbur (Writer)
Charles Pick Constituency
3 Bryanston Place
#3
London W1H 7FN, UNITED KINGDOM (UK)

Smith, Will (Actor, Musician, Producer)
c/o Meredith O'Sullivan Wasson *The Lede Company*
9701 Wilshire Blvd # 930
Beverly Hills, CA 90212-2020, USA

Smith, William (Actor)
3202 Anacapa St
Santa Barbara, CA 93105, USA

Smith, William A. (Athlete, Basketball Player)
4379 Tami Ln
Central Point, OR 97502-1040, USA

Smith, Willie (Athlete, Baseball Player)
1330 E 68th St
Savannah, GA 31404-5718, USA

Smith, Willie (Football Player)
Baltimore Ravens
Ravens Stadium
11001 Russell St
Baltimore, MD 21230, USA

Smith, Willow (Actor)
c/o Brian Nossokoff *United Talent Agency (UTA)*
9336 Civic Center Dr
Beverly Hills, CA 90210-3604, USA

Smith, W Lawrence (Athlete, Football Player)
5020 Bayshore Blvd Apt 305
Tampa, FL 33611-3855, USA

Smith, Wyatt (Athlete, Hockey Player)
17465 46th Ave N
Minneapolis, MN 55446-1957

Smith, Yandy (Actor)
c/o Janique Burke *M.Y.M. Management and Media*
Prefers to be contacted via email
n

Smith, Yeardley (Actor)
c/o Barry Krost *Barry Krost Management*
9220 W Sunset Blvd Ste 106
Los Angeles, CA 90069-3500, USA

Smith, Zadie (Writer)
Random House
1745 Broadway Frnt 3 # B1
New York, NY 10019-4343, USA

Smith, Zane (Athlete, Baseball Player)
420 Windship Pl
Atlanta, GA 30327-4967, USA

Smithberg, Roger (Athlete, Baseball Player)
988 Glenmore Ln
Elgin, IL 60124-2303, USA

Smith Court, Margaret (Tennis Player)
21 Lewanna Way
City Beach
Perth, WA 06010, AUSTRALIA

Smithereens, The (Music Group, Musician)
c/o Len Fico *Fuel Management Group*
Prefers to be contacted via telephone or email
CA, USA

Smitherman, Stephen (Athlete, Baseball Player)
HC 74 Box 240-10
Hartshorne, OK 74502-1890, USA

Smithers, Jan (Actor)
c/o Staff Member *Innovative Artists*
1505 10th St
Santa Monica, CA 90401-2805, USA

Smithers, William (Actor)
2202 Anacapa St
Santa Barbara, CA 93105-3506, USA

Smith Jr, John F (Jack) (Business Person)
General Motors Corp
100 Renaissance Ctr
Detroit, MI 48243-1114, USA

Smith Jr, Lonnie Liston (Musician)
Associated Booking Corp
1995 Broadway # 501
New York, NY 10023-5882, USA

Smith-McCulloch, Colleen (Athlete, Baseball Player)
228 20th Ave W
Vancouver, BC V5Y 2C6, CANADA

Smith-McPhee, Sianoa (Actor)
c/o Kenny Goodman *Goodmanagement*
9220 W Sunset Blvd Ste 106
W Hollywood, CA 90069-3500, USA

Smith Osborne, Madolyn (Actor)
United Talent Agency
9336 Civic Center Dr
Beverly Hills, CA 90210-3604, USA

Smith-Schuster, Juju (Athlete, Football Player)
c/o Kimblery Miale *Roc Nation*
1411 Broadway Fl 38
New York, NY 10018-3409, USA

Smithson, Carly (Musician)

Smithson, Mike (Athlete, Baseball Player)
2540 Swan Creek Rd
Centerville, TN 37033-4374, USA

Smithson, Ryan (Writer)
c/o Staff Member *HarperCollins Publishers*
195 Broadway Fl 2
New York, NY 10007-3132, USA

Smit-McPhee, Kodi (Actor)
c/o Kenny Goodman *Goodmanagement*
9220 W Sunset Blvd Ste 106
W Hollywood, CA 90069-3500, USA

Smitrovich, Bill (Actor)
c/o Pearl Wexler *The Kohner Agency*
9300 Wilshire Blvd Ste 555
Beverly Hills, CA 90212-3211, USA

Smits, Jimmy (Actor)
PO Box 49922
Barrington Station
Los Angeles, CA 90049-0922, USA

Smits, Rik (Athlete, Basketball Player)
38951 N School House Rd
Cave Creek, AZ 85331-8661, USA

Smolan, Rick (Artist, Photographer)
Workman Publishers
225 Varick St Fl 9
New York, NY 10014-4381, USA

Smolinski, Bryan (Athlete, Hockey Player)
4869 Stoneleigh Rd
Bloomfield Hills, MI 48302-2171

Smolinski, Mark (Athlete, Football Player)
3300 Country Club Rd
Petoskey, MI 49770-8211, USA

Smolka, James W (Misc)
7388 Mission Hills Dr
Las Vegas, NV 89113-1328, USA

Smollett, Jurnee (Actor)
c/o Meredith O'Sullivan Wasson *The Lede Company*
9701 Wilshire Blvd # 930
Beverly Hills, CA 90212-2020, USA

Smollett, Jussie (Actor, Musician)
c/o Craig Rubin *Sharp & Associates*
1516 N Fairfax Ave
Los Angeles, CA 90046-2608, USA

Smoltz, John (Athlete, Baseball Player)
1817 Leisure World
Mesa, AZ 85206-5304, USA

Smoot, Fred (Athlete, Football Player)
c/o Bus Cook *Bus Cook Sports, Inc*
1 Willow Bend Dr
Hattiesburg, MS 39402-8552, USA

Smoove, J.B. (Actor)
c/o Rick Dorfman *Authentic Talent and Literary Management (NY)*
20 Jay St Ste M17
Brooklyn, NY 11201-8300, USA

Smothers, Dick (Actor, Comedian)
c/o Staff Member *WME|IMG*
9601 Wilshire Blvd
Beverly Hills, CA 90210-5213, USA

Smothers, Tom (Actor, Comedian)
PO Box 759
Kenwood, CA 95452-0759, USA

Smothers Brothers, The (Comedian)
c/o Staff Member *WME|IMG*
9601 Wilshire Blvd
Beverly Hills, CA 90210-5213, USA

Smrek, Peter (Athlete, Hockey Player)
J Mazura 14/52
Martin 1, 036 01 Slovakia

Smrke, John (Athlete, Hockey Player)
4 Brooks Rd
Ajax, ON L1S 6G3, Canada

Smulders, Cobie (Actor)
c/o Will Ward *Fourward*
10250 Constellation Blvd Ste 2710
Los Angeles, CA 90067-6227, USA

Smurfit, Victoria (Actor)
c/o Richard Cook *WME|IMG*
9601 Wilshire Blvd
Beverly Hills, CA 90210-5213, USA

S. Murphy, Christopher (Congressman, Politician)
412 Cannon Hob
Washington, DC 20515-2509, USA

Smyl, Stan (Athlete, Hockey Player)
Vancouver Canucks
800 Griffiths Way
Vancouver, BC V6B 6G1, Canada

Smyl, Stan (Athlete, Hockey Player)
4730 The Glen
West Vancouver, BC V7S 3C3, Canada

Smyth, Charles P (Misc)
245 Prospect Ave
Princeton, NJ 08540-5303, USA

Smyth, Greg (Athlete, Hockey Player)
62 Carrick Dr
St. John's, NL A1A 4N7, Canada

Smyth, Joe (Music Group, Musician)
Sawyer Brown Inc
5200 Old Harding Rd
Franklin, TN 37064-9406, USA

Smyth, Kevin (Athlete, Hockey Player)
4881 Key St
Blaine, WA 98230-7000

Smyth, Patty (Musician)
23712 Malibu Colony Rd
Malibu, CA 90265-6629, USA

Smyth, Ryan (Athlete, Hockey Player)
Chance Restaurant
2550-10155 102 St NW
Edmonton, AB T5J 4G8, Canada

Smyth, Ryan (Athlete, Hockey Player)
52314th St
Manhattan Beach, CA 90266-4836

Smyth, Steve (Athlete, Baseball Player)
44005 Northgate Ave
Temecula, CA 92592-3000, USA

Smythe, Marcus (Actor)
c/o Bob Waters *Bob Waters Agency*
9301 Wilshire Blvd Ste 300
Beverly Hills, CA 90210-6119, USA

Snare, Ryan (Athlete, Baseball Player)
2671 Derby Walk NE
Brookhaven, GA 30319-3657, USA

Snarr, Trevor (Actor)
c/o Elizabeth Knight *KnightStar Multimedia*
PO Box 893
Lehi, UT 84043-1188, USA

Snead, Esix (Athlete, Baseball Player)
1332 42nd St
Orlando, FL 32839-1276, USA

Snead, Jesse Caryle (J C) (Golfer)
PO Box 782170
Wichita, KS 67278-2170, USA

Snead, Norm (Athlete, Football Player)
6311 Courthouse Rd
Providence Forge, VA 23140-2644, USA

Snead, W T Sr (Religious Leader)
Baptist Convention Missionary
1404 Firestone Blvd
Los Angeles, CA 90001-3827, USA

Sneaker Pimps (Music Group)
c/o Staff Member *Paradigm (Monterey)*
404 W Franklin St
Monterey, CA 93940-2303, USA

Snedden, Stephen (Actor)
c/o Don Carroll *The Green Room*
7080 Hollywood Blvd Ste 1100
Los Angeles, CA 90028-6938, USA

Sneddon, Bob (Athlete, Football Player)
901 E 1140 S
Ogden, UT 84404-6448, USA

Snedeker, Brandt (Athlete, Golfer)
2509 Iron Gate Ct
Franklin, TN 37069-7240, USA

Sneed, Ed (Golfer)
4155 Nottinghill Gate Rd
Columbus, OH 43220-3942, USA

Sneed, Floyd (Musician)
McKenzie Accountancy
5171 Caliente St Unit 134
Las Vegas, NV 89119-2198, USA

Snell, Chris (Athlete, Hockey Player)
883 Peggoty Cir
Oshawa, ON L1K 2G6, Canada

Snell, Esmond E (Misc)
819 Tempted Ways Dr
Longmont, CO 80504-8467, USA

Snell, Ian (Athlete, Baseball Player)
90 Beechwood Ave Trlr 9
Dover, DE 19901-5236, USA

Snell, Matthews (Matt) (Athlete, Football Player)
S C I Limited Inc
175 Clendenny Ave
Jersey City, NJ 07304-1201, USA

Snell, Nate (Athlete, Baseball Player)
7299 Old State Rd
Holly Hill, SC 29059-8514, USA

Snell, Peter (Athlete, Olympic Athlete, Track Athlete)
6452 Dunstan Ln
Dallas, TX 75214-2239, USA

Snell, Ray (Athlete, Football Player)
10306 Councils Way
Temple Terrace, FL 33617-4058, USA

Snelling, Chris (Athlete, Baseball Player)
18122 Rhodes Lake Rd E
Bonney Lake, WA 98391-8143, USA

Snelling, Jason (Athlete, Football Player)
c/o Scott Smith *XAM Sports*
3509 Ice Age Dr
Madison, WI 53719-5409, USA

Snepsts, Harold (Athlete, Hockey Player)
5623 Highfield Dr
Burnaby, BC V5B 1E4, Canada

Sneva, Jerry (Race Car Driver)
2652 E 35th Ave
Spokane, WA 99223-4678, USA

Sneva, Tom (Race Car Driver)
3301 E Valley Vista Ln
Paradise Valley, AZ 85253-3739, USA

Sniadecki, Jim (Athlete, Football Player)
3267 Congressional Cir
Fairfield, CA 94534-7869, USA

Snider, Dee (Musician)
c/o Phil Carson *Phil Carson Management*
4931 Coldwater Canyon Ave Apt 1
Sherman Oaks, CA 91423-2229, USA

Snider, George (Race Car Driver)
7404 Lucille Ave
Bakersfield, CA 93308-2725, USA

Snider, Mike (Musician)
PO Box 610
Gleason, TN 38229-0610, USA

Snider, Stacey (Business Person)
c/o Staff Member *Dreamworks Television*
100 Universal Plaza Bldg 5125
Universal City, CA 91608, USA

Snider, Todd (Music Group, Musician, Songwriter, Writer)
Al Bunneta Mgmt
33 Music Sq W Ste 102B
Nashville, TN 37203-6607, USA

Snider, Travis (Athlete, Baseball Player)
18511 31st Ave SE
Bothell, WA 98012-8822, USA

Snider, Van (Athlete, Baseball Player)
1615 Windsor Dr
Cleveland, OH 44124-3616, USA

Snipes, Wesley (Actor)
c/o Cindy Guagenti *Baker Winokur Ryder Public Relations*
9100 Wilshire Blvd
W Tower #500
Beverly Hills, CA 90212-3415, USA

Snipscheer, Fred (Athlete, Hockey Player)
13404 Macaw Pl
Carmel, IN 46033-8964, USA

Snitker, Brian (Athlete, Baseball Player)
3057 Moss Stone Ln
Marietta, GA 30064-6416, USA

Snitzier, Larry (Musician)
Lindy Martin Mgmt
5 Loblolly Ct
Pinehurst, NC 28374-9349, USA

Snodgrass, William (Writer)
3061 Hughes Rd
Erieville, NY 13061-4128, USA

Snodgrass, William D (Writer)
3061 Hughes Rd
Erieville, NY 13061-4128, USA

Snook, Frank (Athlete, Baseball Player)
2580 Elysium Ave
Eugene, OR 97401-7441, USA

Snopek, Chris (Athlete, Baseball Player)
103 Bradford Dr
Cynrhiana, KY 39110-8468, USA

Snow (Artist, Musician, Songwriter, Writer)
Hype Music
510-2076 Sherobee Rd
Mississauga, ON L5A 4C4, CANADA

Snow, Al (Athlete, Wrestler)
1227 Leland Ave
Lima, OH 45805-1935, USA

Snow, Brittany (Actor)
c/o Marcel Pariseau *True Public Relations*
3575 Cahuenga Blvd W Ste 360
Los Angeles, CA 90068-1361, USA

Snow, DeShawn (Reality Star)
c/o Abbey Sibucao-MacDonald *New Wave Entertainment (LA)*
2660 W Olive Ave
Burbank, CA 91505-4525, USA

Snow, Eric (Athlete, Basketball Player)
2229 Edgartown Ln SE
Smyrna, GA 30080-6501, USA

Snow, Garth (Athlete, Hockey Player)
New York Islanders
200 Merrick Ave
East Meadow, NY 11554-1596

Snow, Garth (Athlete, Hockey Player, Olympic Athlete)
4 Weeping Willow Ct
Glen Head, NY 11545-2420

Snow, Gene (Race Car Driver)
5719 Airport Fwy
Ft Worth, TX 76117-6007, USA

Snow, John (Politician)
122 Tempsford Ln
Richmond, VA 23226-2319, USA

Snow, Jon (Actor)
c/o Staff Member *Knight Ayton Management*
35 Great James St
London WC1N 3HB, UK

Snow, J T (Athlete, Baseball Player)
15 Bridle Ct
Hillsborough, CA 94010-7451, USA

Snow, Justin (Athlete, Football Player)
1826 Milford St
Carmel, IN 46032-7207, USA

Snow, Kate (Television Host)

Snow, Mark (Composer, Musician)
c/o Staff Member *Robert Urband & Associates*
1200 Esplanade Apt 222
Redondo Beach, CA 90277-4951, USA

Snow, Percy L (Athlete, Football Player)
2010 48th St NE
Canton, OH 44705-3082, USA

Snowden, Alison (Director, Writer)
c/o Melissa Myers *WME|IMG*
9601 Wilshire Blvd
Beverly Hills, CA 90210-5213, USA

Snowdon, Lisa (Actor, Model)
c/o Marki Costello *Creative Management Entertainment Group (CMEG)*
2050 S Bundy Dr Ste 280
Los Angeles, CA 90025-6128, USA

Snowe, Olympia (Politician)
101 E Kingsbridge Rd
Bronx, NY 10468-7510, USA

Snow Patrol (Music Group)
c/o John Peets *Q Prime (TN)*
131 S 11th St
Nashville, TN 37206-2954, USA

Snuggerud, Dave (Athlete, Hockey Player, Olympic Athlete)
968 Bavaria Hills Ter
Chaska, MN 55318-2722, USA

Snvder, Kyle (Athlete, Baseball Player)
1869 Upper Cove Ter
Sarasota, FL 34231-5437, USA

Snyder, Adam (Athlete, Football Player)
c/o David Dunn *Athletes First*
23091 Mill Creek Dr
Laguna Hills, CA 92653-1258, USA

Snyder, Ben (Comedian)
c/o Staff Member *Gersh*
9465 Wilshire Blvd Ste 600
Beverly Hills, CA 90212-2605, USA

Snyder, Bill (Coach, Football Coach)
Kansas State University
Athletic Dept
Manhattan, KS 66506, USA

Snyder, Brian (Athlete, Baseball Player)
405 Craig Dr
Stephens City, VA 22655-2316, USA

Snyder, Chris (Athlete, Baseball Player)
8800 Cumberland Ct
Waxhaw, NC 28173-6571, USA

Snyder, Cory (Athlete, Baseball Player, Olympic Athlete)
468 N Loafer Dr
Payson, UT 84651-4535, USA

Snyder, Daniel (Football Executive)
c/o Staff Member *Washington Redskins*
21300 Redskin Park Dr
Ashburn, VA 20147-6100, USA

Snyder, Dick (Athlete, Basketball Player)
4621 E Mockingbird Ln
Paradise Valley, AZ 85253-2420, USA

Snyder, Dylan Riley (Actor)
c/o Alexandra Heller *Advantage PR*
3900 W Alameda Ave Ste 1200
Burbank, CA 91505-4317, USA

Snyder, Earl (Athlete, Baseball Player)
58 Diamond Ave
Plainville, CT 06062-2904, USA

Snyder, Fonda (Actor)
c/o Staff Member *WME|IMG*
9601 Wilshire Blvd
Beverly Hills, CA 90210-5213, USA

Snyder, Gary (Writer)
18442 MacNab Cypress Rd
Nevada City, CA 95959-8504, USA

Snyder, Gary S (Writer)
18442 MacNab Cypress Rd
Nevada City, CA 95959-8504, USA

Snyder, James (Actor)
c/o Brad Schenck *ICM Partners*
10250 Constellation Blvd Fl 7
Los Angeles, CA 90067-6207, USA

Snyder, Jerry (Athlete, Baseball Player)
2553 Wild Oak Forest Ln
Seabrook, TX 77586-2632, USA

Snyder, Jim (Athlete, Baseball Player)
7516 Dunbridge Dr
Odessa, FL 33556-2270, USA

Snyder, Jim (Athlete, Baseball Player, Coach)
7516 Dunbridge Dr
Odessa, FL 33556-2270, USA

Snyder, John (Athlete, Baseball Player)
18241 W Cinnabar Ave
Waddell, AZ 85355-4351, USA

Snyder, Joshua (Actor)
c/o Staff Member *Main Title Entertainment*
8383 Wilshire Blvd Ste 408
Beverly Hills, CA 90211-2435, USA

Snyder, Kyle (Athlete, Baseball Player)
1869 Upper Cove Ter
Sarasota, FL 34231-5437, USA

Snyder, Liza (Actor)

Snyder, Loren (Athlete, Football Player)
12852 War Horse St
San Diego, CA 92129-2222, USA

Snyder, Russ (Athlete, Baseball Player)
PO Box 264
Nelson, NE 68961-0264, USA

Snyder, Suzanne (Actor)
Premiere Artists Agency
1875 Century Park E Ste 2250
Los Angeles, CA 90067-2563, USA

Snyder, Todd (Football Player)
Atlanta Falcons
850 S Valley Ln
Palatine, IL 60067-7185, USA

Snyder, Todd (Race Car Driver)
Brian Stewart Racing
PO Box 251
L.P.O.
Niagara Falls, NY 14304-0251, usa

Snyder, William (Journalist)
508 Young St
Dallas, TX 75202-4808, USA

Snyder, William D (Journalist, Photographer)
Dallas Morning News
Communivations Center
Editorial Dept
Dallas, TX 75265, USA

Snyder, Zack (Director, Writer)
c/o Staff Member *Believe Media*
1455 Gordon St
Los Angeles, CA 90028-8408, USA

Snyderman, Nancy (Doctor, Television Host)
c/o Staff Member *NBC News (NY)*
30 Rockefeller Plz
New York, NY 10112-0015, USA

So, David (Actor)
c/o Siri Garber *Platform PR*
2666 N Beachwood Dr
Los Angeles, CA 90068-2308, USA

So, Linda (Model)
6130 W Tropicana Ave # 280
Las Vegas, NV 89103-4604

Soares, Jr., John (Race Car Driver)
4004 Dyer Rd
Livermore, CA 94551-7489, USA

Sobchuk, Dennis (Athlete, Hockey Player)
37300 N Tom Darlington Dr N # N
Carefree, AZ 85377, USA

Sobchuk, Gene (Athlete, Hockey Player)
Farm
Milestone, SK SOG 3LO, Canada

Sobers, Rickey (Athlete, Basketball Player)
PO Box 50058
Henderson, NV 89016-0058, USA

Sobieski, Leelee (Actor)
c/o Bianca Bianconi *42West*
600 3rd Ave Fl 23
New York, NY 10016-1914, USA

Sobkowiak, Scott (Athlete, Baseball Player)
817 Symphony Dr
Aurora, IL 60504-5554, USA

Sobule, Jill (Musician, Songwriter)
Fleming Artists
PO Box 1568
Ann Arbor, MI 48106-1568, USA

Socha, Lauren (Actor)
c/o Nicola Van Gelder *Conway van Gelder Grant*
8-12 Broadwick St
London W1F 8HW, UNITED KINGDOM

Socha, Michael (Actor)
c/o Jordyn Palos *Persona Public Relations*
6255 W Sunset Blvd Ste 705
Hollywood, CA 90028-7408, USA

Sochor, James (Jim) (Coach, Football Coach)
1018 Kent Dr
Davis, CA 95616-0933, USA

Social Distortion (Music Group, Musician)
c/o Jim Guerinot *Rebel Waltz Inc*
PO Box 9215
Laguna Beach, CA 92652-7212, USA

Society, Honor (Music Group, Musician)
c/o Staff Member *Walt Disney Music*
500 S Buena Vista St
Burbank, CA 91521-0007, USA

Socolofsky, Shelley (Artist)
3285 Sumac Dr S
Salem, OR 97302-4080, USA

Sodano, Angelo Cardinal (Religious Leader)
Office of Secretary of State
Palazzo Apostolico
00120, VATICAN CITY

Soderbergh, Steven (Director, Producer)
c/o Michael Sugar *Anonymous Content*
3532 Hayden Ave
Culver City, CA 90232-2413, USA

Soderholm, Eric (Athlete, Baseball Player)
10S360 Hampshire Ln
Willowbrook, IL 60527-6018, USA

Soderstrom, Steve (Athlete, Baseball Player)
301 N Faith Home Rd
Turlock, CA 95380-9458, USA

Soderstrom, Tommy (Athlete, Hockey Player)
Oxelvagen 41
Alta, 13832 Sweden

Sodowsky, Client (Athlete, Baseball Player)
2801 Tropicana Ave
Norman, OK 73071-1711, USA

Soetaert, Doug (Athlete, Hockey Player)
13006 66th Ave SE
Snohomish, WA 98296-8997

Sofer, Rena (Actor)
c/o Nancy Iannios *Core Public PR*
1875 Century Park E Ste 930
Los Angeles, CA 90067-2540, USA

Soff, Ray (Athlete, Baseball Player)
146 Drew Ave
Deerfield, MI 49238-9787, USA

Soffer, Jesse Lee (Actor)
c/o Christina Gualazzi *Silver Lining Entertainment*
421 S Beverly Dr Fl 7
Beverly Hills, CA 90212-4408, USA

Sofield, Rick (Athlete, Baseball Player)
21 Blackstone River Rd
Bluffton, SC 29910-4462, USA

Sofie von Otter, Anne (Musician)
c/o Staff Member *ICM Partners*
10250 Constellation Blvd Fl 7
Los Angeles, CA 90067-6207, USA

Softley, Iain (Director)
32A Camaby St
London, W1V 1PA UNITED KINGDOM

Sogard, Eric (Athlete, Baseball Player)
15039 N 19th Way
Phoenix, AZ 85022-3904, USA

Sohn, Sonja (Actor)
c/o James Suskin *Suskin Management*
2 Charlton St Apt 5K
New York, NY 10014-4970, USA

Sohn Kee-Chung (Athlete, Track Athlete)
Korean Olympic Committee
International PO Box 1106
Seoul, SOUTH KOREA

Sojo, Luis (Athlete, Baseball Player)
17647 SW 20th St
Miramar, FL 33029-5238, USA

Sokol, Marilyn (Actor)
24 W 40th St # 1700
New York, NY 10018-3904, USA

Sokolinski, Stephanie (Soko) (Musician)
c/o Margrit Polak *Margrit Polak Management*
1920 Hillhurst Ave Ste 405
Los Angeles, CA 90027-2712, USA

Sokoloff, Marla (Actor)
c/o Marni Rosenzweig *The Rosenzweig Group*
8840 Wilshire Blvd # 111
Beverly Hills, CA 90211-2606, USA

Sokolosky, John (Football Player)
Detroit Lions
13240 Leech Dr
Sterling Heights, MI 48312-3253, USA

Sokolov, Grigory L (Musician)
Trawick Artists
1926 Broadway
New York, NY 10023-6915, USA

Sokomanu, A George (President)
Mele Village
PO Box 1319
Port Villa, VANUATU

Sokurov, Alexander N (Director)
Smolenskaya Nab 4 #222
Saint Petersburg 199048, RUSSIA

Solano, Jose (Actor)
c/o Staff Member *Stephany Hurkos Management*
5014 Whitsett Ave Unit 2
Valley Village, CA 91607-3078, USA

Solar, CJ (Musician)
c/o Barry Jeffrey *WME (Nashville)*
1201 Demonbreun St
Nashville, TN 37203-3140, USA

Solberg, Magnar (Athlete)
Stabellvn 60
Trondheim 07000, NORWAY

Solder, Nate (Football Player)
c/o David Dunn *Athletes First*
23091 Mill Creek Dr
Laguna Hills, CA 92653-1258, USA

Soleil, Stella (Music Group, Musician)
Kurfirst/Blackwell
350 W End Ave Apt 1A
New York, NY 10024-6818, USA

Soles, Pamela Jayne (PJ) (Actor)
c/o Bill Philputt *Re-Evolution*
Prefers to be contacted via telephone
Los Angeles Area, CA 90069, USA

Solet, Paul (Director)
c/o David Gardner *Artists First*
9465 Wilshire Blvd Ste 900
Beverly Hills, CA 90212-2608, USA

Solh, Rashid (Prime Minister)
Chambre of Deputes
Place de l'Etoile
Beirut, LABANON

Solheim, Ken (Athlete, Hockey Player)
44 Shaw Cres SE
Medicine Hat, AB T1B 3Y6, CANADA

Soliai, Paul (Athlete, Football Player)

Solich, Frank (Coach, Football Coach)
University of Nebraska
Athletic Dept
Lincoln, NE 68588, USA

Solis, Alex (Horse Racer)
2241 Redwood Dr
Glendora, CA 91741-6421, USA

Sollscher, Goran (Musician)
Kunstleragentur Raab & Bohm
Plankengasse 7
Vienna 01010, AUSTRIA

Solo, Hope (Athlete, Olympic Athlete, Soccer Player)
c/o Dan Levy *Wasserman Media Group (NC)*
4208 Six Forks Rd Ste 1020
Raleigh, NC 27609-5738, USA

Solo, Ksenia (Actor)
c/o Pamela Kohl *3 Arts Entertainment*
9460 Wilshire Blvd Fl 7
Beverly Hills, CA 90212-2713, USA

Soloman, Freddie (Athlete, Football Player)
803 Turtle River Ct
Plant City, FL 33567-2474, USA

Solomon, Ariel (Football Player)
Pittsburgh Steelers
3142 5th St
Boulder, CO 80304-2504, USA

Solomon, David (Director)
c/o Cori Wellins *WME/IMG*
9601 Wilshire Blvd
Beverly Hills, CA 90210-5213, USA

Solomon, Ed (Producer)
c/o Staff Member *Writers Co-Op*
4000 Warner Blvd Bldg 1
Burbank, CA 91522-0001, USA

Solomon, Edward I (Misc)
Stanford University
Chemistry Dept
Stanford, CA 94305, USA

Solomon, Harold (Tennis Player)
Int'l Mgmt Group
1 Erieview Plz
1360 E 9th St #1300
Cleveland, OH 44114-1738, USA

Solomon, Jesse (Athlete, Football Player)
Minnesota Vikings
205 W Bunker St
Madison, FL 32340-2309, USA

Solomon, Scott (Athlete, Football Player)
c/o W Vann McElroy *Select Sports Group*
2700 Post Oak Blvd Ste 1450
Houston, TX 77056-5785, USA

Solomon, Sophie (Musician)
c/o Staff Member *Paradigm (Monterey)*
404 W Franklin St
Monterey, CA 93940-2303, USA

Solomon, Stacey (Musician, Reality Star)
c/o Staff Member *Max Clifford Associates*
Moss House
15-16 Brooks Mews
Mayfair, London W1K 4DS, UNITED KINGDOM

Solomon, Susan (Misc)
National Oceanic & Atmospheric Admin
325 Broadway St
Boulder, CO 80305-3337, USA

Solomon, Yonty (Musician)
56 Canonbury Park N
London N1 2JT, UNITED KINGDOM (UK)

Solondz, Todd (Director, Writer)
Industry Entertainment
955 Carrillo Dr Ste 300
Los Angeles, CA 90048-5400, USA

Solovey, Sam (Actor)
c/o Staff Member *Ruth Webb Enterprises*
10580 Des Moines Ave
Northridge, CA 91326-2926, USA

Solovyev, Sergei A (Director, Writer)
Akademika Pilyugina Str 8
Korp 1 #330
Moscow 11393, RUSSIA

Soloway, Jill (Producer)
c/o Staff Member *ICM Partners*
10250 Constellation Blvd Fl 7
Los Angeles, CA 90067-6207, USA

Solt, Ron (Athlete, Football Player)
1200 Thornhurst Rd
Bear Creek Township, PA 18702-8212, USA

Soltau, Gordie (Athlete, Football Player)
1290 Sharon Park Dr Apt 50
Menlo Park, CA 94025-7038, USA

Soltau, Gordon (Gordy) (Football Player)
1290 Sharon Park Dr
Menlo Park, CA 94025-7052, USA

Soluna (Music Group)
c/o Staff Member *Creative Artists Agency (CAA)*
2000 Avenue of the Stars Ste 100
Los Angeles, CA 90067-4705, USA

Solvay, Jacques (Business Person)
Solvay Cie SA
Rue de Prince Albert 33
Brussels 01050, BELGIUM

Solymosi, Zoltan (Dancer)
Royal Ballet
Covent GArden
Bow St
London WC2E 9DD, UNITED KINGDOM (UK)

Solyom, Janos P (Musician)
Norr Malarstrand 54
VII
Stockholm 11220, SWEDEN

Solzhenitsyn, Ignat (Musician)
Columbia Artists Mgmt Inc
165 W 57th St
New York, NY 10019-2201, USA

Somare, Michael T (Prime Minister)
Assembly House
Karan
Murik Lakes
East Sepik, PAPUA NEW GUINEA

Sombrotto, Vincent R (Misc)
National Letter Carriers Assn
100 Indiana Ave NW Ste 709
Washington, DC 20001-2196, USA

Somerhalder, Ian (Actor)
630 Woodlawn Ave
Venice, CA 90291-4851, USA

Somers, Gwen (Actor, Model)
Alice Fries Agency
1927 Vista Del Mar St
Los Angeles, CA 90068-4004, USA

Somers, Suzanne (Actor)
252 Ridge Rd
Palm Springs, CA 92264-8940, USA

Somerset, Willie (Athlete, Basketball Player)
6441 Oak View Dr
Harrisburg, PA 17112-1889, USA

Somerville, Bonnie (Actor)
c/o Staff Member *McKeon-Myones Management*
3500 W Olive Ave Ste 770
Burbank, CA 91505-5527, USA

Somerville, Geraldine (Actor)
c/o Ciara Parkes *Public Eye Communications*
535 Kings Rd
#313 Plaza
London SW10 0SZ, UNITED KINGDOM

Something Corporate (Music Group)
c/o Staff Member *Agency for the Performing Arts (APA)*
405 S Beverly Dr Ste 500
Beverly Hills, CA 90212-4425, USA

Sommars, Julie (Actor)
7272 Outlook Cove Dr
Los Angeles, CA 90068, USA

Sommaruga, Cornelio (Misc)
International Red Cross
19 Ave de la Paix
Genoa 01202, SWITZERLAND

Sommer, Elke (Actor)
Atzelaberger Str 46
Marloffstein D-91080, GERMANY

Sommer, Rich (Actor)
c/o Staff Member *Davis Spylios Management*
244 W 54th St Ste 707
New York, NY 10019-5515, USA

Sommer, Roy (Athlete, Hockey Player)
Worcester Sharks
525 W Santa Clara St
San Jose, CA 95113-1520

Sommer, Roy (Athlete, Hockey Player)
PO Box 882
Kila, MT 59920-0882

Sommerfeld, Kent (Sportscaster)
Milwaukee Brewers
13935 W Maria Dr
New Berlin, WI 53151-6891, USA

Sommers, Denny (Athlete, Baseball Player)
210 W Bath St Apt 133
Hortonville, WI 54944-9425, USA

Sommers, Gordon L (Religious Leader)
Moravian Church Northem Province
1021 Center St
Bethlehem, PA 18018-2838, USA

Sommers, Joanie (Musician)
Xentel
900 SE 3rd Ave Ste 201
Fort Lauderdale, FL 33316-1118, USA

Sommers, Stephen (Director, Producer, Writer)
c/o Stuart Rosenthal *Bloom Hergott Diemer Rosenthal Laviolette Feldman Schenkman & Goodman*
150 S Rodeo Dr Fl 3
Beverly Hills, CA 90212-2410, USA

Sommore (Comedian)
c/o Staff Member *ICM Partners*
10250 Constellation Blvd Fl 7
Los Angeles, CA 90067-6207, USA

Somogyi, Jozsef (Artist)
Marton Utca 3/5
Budapest 01038, HUNGARY

Somorjai, Gabor A (Misc)
665 San Luis Rd
Berkeley, CA 94707-1725, USA

Sondheim, Stephen (Musician)
246 E 49th St
New York, NY 10017-1502, USA

Sondrini, Joe (Athlete, Baseball Player)
16712 Stockland Ct
Huntersville, NC 28078-6438, USA

Sonenclar, Carly Rose (Musician)
c/o Melissa Chusid *Hope Productions*
Prefers to be contacted by email or phone.
New York, NY NA, USA

Song, Brenda (Actor)
c/o Shannon Barr *Rogers & Cowan*
1840 Century Park E Fl 18
Los Angeles, CA 90067-2101, USA

Song, Xiaodong (Misc)
Columbia University
Lamont-Doherty Earth Observatory
New York, NY 10027, USA

Songaila, Darius (Athlete, Basketball Player)
141 S Longfellow Ln
Mooresville, NC 28117-7116, USA

Songin, Tom (Athlete, Hockey Player)
70 Cascade Ter
Walpole, MA 02081-3239, USA

Songz, Trey (Musician)
c/o Kevin Liles *KWL Management*
112 Madison Ave Fl 4
New York, NY 10016-7416, USA

Soni, Jimmy (Journalist, Writer)
c/o Staff Member *St Martins Press*
175 5th Ave
Publicity Dept
New York, NY 10010-7703, USA

Soni, Karan (Actor)
c/o Staff Member *3 Arts Entertainment (NY)*
49 W 27th St Fl 5
New York, NY 10001-6936, USA

Soni, Rebecca (Athlete, Swimmer)
1723 W Sunshine Dr
Flagstaff, AZ 86005-9025, USA

Sonja (Royalty)
Det Kongelige Slott
Drammensveien 1
Oslo 00010, NORWAY

Sonnanstine, Andy (Athlete, Baseball Player)
526 Reimer Rd
Wadsworth, OH 44281-9247, USA

Sonnenfeld, Barry (Director)
c/o Staff Member *Right Coast Productions*
289 Springs Fireplace Rd
East Hampton, NY 11937-4823, USA

Sonnenschein, Klaus (Actor)
Breisgauer Str. 15a
Berlin D-14129, Germany

Sonnier, Jo-El (Musician)
Entertainment Artists
2409 21st Ave S Ste 100
Nashville, TN 37212-5317, USA

Sons of the Desert (Music Group)
c/o Staff Member *WME (Nashville)*
1201 Demonbreun St
Nashville, TN 37203-3140, USA

Sonus Quartet (Music Group, Musician)
Prefers to be contacted via telephone or email

Sonzero, Jim (Writer)
c/o Andrew Cannava *United Talent Agency (UTA)*
9336 Civic Center Dr
Beverly Hills, CA 90210-3604, USA

Sood, Veena (Actor, Producer)
c/o Robyn Friedman *Artist Management Inc*
464 King St E
Toronto, ON M5A 1L7, CANADA

Soo Hoo, Hayward (Actor)
1411 Solar Dr
Monterey Park, CA 91754-4548, USA

Soomekh, Bahar (Actor)
c/o Paul Kohner *The Kohner Agency*
9300 Wilshire Blvd Ste 555
Beverly Hills, CA 90212-3211, USA

Sopel, Brent (Athlete, Hockey Player)
5905 Grand Ave
Downers Grove, IL 60516-2044, USA

Sophia (Royalty)
Palacio de la Zarzuela
Madrid 28071, SPAIN

Sopko, Michael D (Business Person)
Inco Ltd
145 King St W
Toronto, ON M5H 1J8, CANADA

Sopkovic, Kay (Athlete, Baseball Player)
6540 W Butler Dr Unit 62
Glendale, AZ 85302-4313, USA

Sorbo, Kevin (Actor)
c/o Sherry Marsh *Marsh Entertainment*
818 Warren Ave
Venice, CA 90291-2812, USA

Sorel, Edward (Artist)
156 Franklin St
New York, NY 10013-2908, USA

Sorel, Jean (Actor)
Cineart
36 Rue de Ponthieu
Paris 75008, FRANCE

Sorel, Louise (Actor)
10808 Lindbrook Dr
Los Angeles, CA 90024-3007, USA

Sorel, Ted (Actor)
c/o Staff Member *Kerin-Goldberg Associates*
155 E 55th St Ste 5D
New York, NY 10022-4038, USA

Sorensen, Jacki F (Misc)
Jacki's Inc
129 1/2 N Woodland Blvd Ste 5
Deland, FL 32720-4269, USA

Sorensen, Lary (Athlete, Baseball Player)
42515 Northville Place Dr Apt 406
Northville, MI 48167-3186, USA

Sorensen, Nick (Athlete, Football Player)
305 Grandview Dr
Blacksburg, VA 24060-6222, USA

Sorensen, Zach (Athlete, Baseball Player)
1322 S 2670 E
Saint George, UT 84790-6197, USA

Sorenson, Heidi (Actor, Model)
Shelly & Pierce
13775A Mono Way # 220
Sonora, CA 95370-8813, USA

Sorenson, Reed (Race Car Driver)
Richard Petty Motorsports
320 Aviation Dr
Statesville, NC 28677-2509, USA

Sorenson, Zach (Athlete, Baseball Player)
2690 E 1400 South Cir
Saint George, UT 84790-6198, USA

Sorenstam, Annika (Golfer)
c/o Staff Member *IMG (Cleveland)*
1360 E 9th St Ste 100
Cleveland, OH 44114-1730, USA

Sorenstam, Charlotta (Golfer)
c/o Patrick Levine
1411 W Whitman Ct
Anthem, AZ 85086-3927, USA

Sorey, Revie (Athlete, Football Player)
485 Saint Moritz Dr Apt 1C
Glen Ellyn, IL 60137-4320, USA

Sorgers, Jana (Athlete)
Potsdamer RG
An Der Pirschheide
Potsdam 14471, GERMANY

Sorgi, Jim (Athlete, Football Player)
72 Hollaway Blvd
Brownsburg, IN 46112-8355, USA

Soria, Oscar (Sportscaster)
3302 E Dry Creek Rd
Phoenix, AZ 85044-7021, USA

Soriano, Alfonso G (Baseball Player)
Texas Rangers
1000 Ballpark Way Ste 400
Arlington, TX 76011-5170, USA

Soriano, Rafael (Athlete, Baseball Player)
6820 81st Dr NE
Marysville, WA 98270-6598, USA

Sorkin, Aaron (Producer, Writer)
c/o Joy Fehily *PMK/BNC Public Relations*
1840 Century Park E Ste 1400
Los Angeles, CA 90067-2115, USA

Sorkin, Andrew Ross (Commentator)
c/o Matthew Snyder *Creative Artists Agency (CAA)*
2000 Avenue of the Stars Ste 100
Los Angeles, CA 90067-4705, USA

Sorkin, Arleen (Actor)
623 S Beverly Glen Blvd
Los Angeles, CA 90024-2531, USA

Soros, Alexander (Business Person)
Jewish Funds for Justice
330 7th Ave Ste 1902
New York, NY 10001-5241, USA

Soros, George (Business Person)
Open Society Foundations
224 W 57th St Frnt 2
New York, NY 10019-3268, USA

Sorrentino, Mike (The Situation) (Reality Star)
c/o Michael Schweiger *Central Entertainment Group*
250 W 40th St Fl 12
New York, NY 10018-4601, USA

Sorrento, Paul (Athlete, Baseball Player)
5918 Mont Blanc Pl NW
Issaquah, WA 98027-7859, USA

Sorrento, Paul A (Baseball Player)
5918 Mont Blanc Pl NW
Issaquah, WA 98027-7859, USA

Sorsa, T Kalevi (Prime Minister)
Hakaniemenranta 16D
Helsinki 00530, FINLAND

Sorte, Maria (Actor)
c/o Staff Member *Televisa*
Blvd Adolfo Lopez Mateos 232
Colonia San Angel INN
DF CP 01060, MEXICO

Sortun, Henrik (Athlete, Football Player)
6708 16th Ave NW
Seattle, WA 98117-5513, USA

Sorum, Matt (Musician)
c/o Todd Cameron *Abrams Artists Agency*
750 N San Vicente Blvd
E Tower Fl 11
Los Angeles, CA 90069-5788, USA

Sorvino, Mira (Actor)
c/o Lindsay Krug *ID Public Relations*
7060 Hollywood Blvd Fl 8th
Los Angeles, CA 90028-6021, USA

Sorvino, Paul (Actor)
c/o Kieran Maguire *The Arlook Group*
11663 Gorham Ave Apt 5
Los Angeles, CA 90049-4749, USA

Sosa, Elias (Athlete, Baseball Player)
3126 Summerfield Ridge Ln
Matthews, NC 28105-8509, USA

Sosa, Sammy (Athlete, Baseball Player)
Riverhead Homes
2900 N 24th Ave Apt 8104
Hollywood, FL 33020-1460, USA

Sosenka, Don (Race Car Driver)
Mr Magoo
PO Box 679
Spring Branch, TX 78070-0679, USA

So Solid Crew (Music Group)
c/o Staff Member *Mission Control Artists Agency*
Unit 3 City Business Centre
St Olav's Court, Lower Road
London SE16 2XB, UNITED KINGDOM (UK)

Sospiri, Vincenzo (Race Car Driver)
Dan Gurney's All American Racing
2334 S Broadway
Santa Ana, CA 92707-3250, USA

Sossamon, Lou (Athlete, Football Player)
6308 Exum Dr
West Columbia, SC 29169-7184, USA

Sossamon, Shannyn (Actor)
c/o Oren Segal *Management Production Entertainment (MPE)*
9229 W Sunset Blvd Ste 301
W Hollywood, CA 90069-3417, USA

Soter, Paul (Comedian)
c/o Staff Member *United Talent Agency (UTA)*
9336 Civic Center Dr
Beverly Hills, CA 90210-3604, USA

Sotillo, Nolan (Actor, Musician)
c/o Brian DePersia *WME|IMG*
9601 Wilshire Blvd
Beverly Hills, CA 90210-5213, USA

Soto, Blanca (Actor)
c/o Bryan Brucks *Luber Roklin Management*
5815 W Sunset Blvd Ste 208
Los Angeles, CA 90028-6481, USA

Soto, Gabriel (Actor)
c/o Staff Member *Televisa*
Blvd Adolfo Lopez Mateos 232
Colonia San Angel INN
DF CP 01060, MEXICO

Soto, Geovany (Athlete, Baseball Player)
6319 Perch Creek Dr
Houston, TX 77049-3447, USA

Soto, Mario M (Athlete, Baseball Player)
6319 Perch Creek Dr
Houston, TX 77049-3447, USA

Soto, Talisa (Actor)
c/o Peg Donegan *Framework Entertainment*
9057 Nemo St # C
W Hollywood, CA 90069-5511, USA

Sotomayor, Antonio (Artist)
3 Leroy Pl
San Francisco, CA 94109-4224, USA

Sotomayor Sanabria, Javier (Athlete, Track Athlete)
Int'l Mgmt Group
1 Erieview Plz
1360 E 9th St #1300
Cleveland, OH 44114-1738, USA

Sottsass Jr, Ettore (Designer)
Via Manzoni 14
Milan 20121, ITALY

Soucy, Christian (Athlete, Hockey Player)
274 Wildflower Cir
Williston, VT 05495-9391, USA

Souders, Cecil (Athlete, Football Player)
1803 Channingway Court E
Reynoldsburg, OH 43068, USA

Soul, David (Actor, Musician)
c/o Staff Member *Diamond Management*
31 Percy St
London W1T 2DD, UNITED KINGDOM

Soulages, Pierre (Artist)
18 Rue des Trois-Portes
Paris 75005, FRANCE

Soul Asylum (Music Group)
c/o Wesley Kidd *Red Light Management*
455 2nd St NE
#500
Charlottesville, VA 22902-5791, USA

SoulDecision (Music Group)
c/o Staff Member *Bruce Allen Talent*
425 Carrall St
Suite 400
Vancouver, BC V6B 6E3, CANADA

Soule, Samantha (Actor)
c/o Jessica Pierson *Vision PR*
2 Penn Plz Rm 2601
New York, NY 10121-0001, USA

Soul II Soul (Music Group)
c/o Staff Member *Profile Artists Agency*
Unit 10, J Block
Tower Bridge Business Complex, 110 Clements Road
London SE16 4DG, United Kingdom

Sound Tribe Sector 9 (Music Group)
c/o Staff Member *Paradigm (Monterey)*
404 W Franklin St
Monterey, CA 93940-2303, USA

Souray, Sheldon (Athlete, Hockey Player)
7006 S Nighthawk Ct
Harrison, ID 83833-6003, USA

Sousa, Mauricio de (Cartoonist)
Mauricio de Sousa Producoes
Rua do Curtume 745
Sao Paulo SP, BRAZIL

Soutendijk, Renee (Actor)
Marion Rosenberg
PO Box 69826
West Hollywood, CA 90069-0826, USA

Souter, David H (Attorney)
US Supreme Court
214 Hopkins Green Rd
Contoocook, NH 03229-2611, USA

Southam, James (Athlete, Olympic Athlete, Track Athlete)
18230 Norway Dr
Anchorage, AK 99516-6033, USA

Souther, JD (Musician, Songwriter)
c/o David Strunk *UTA Music/The Agency Group*
9336 Civic Center Dr
Beverly Hills, CA 90210-3604, USA

Southerland, Ron (Race Car Driver)
7416 E Palo Verde Dr
Scottsdale, AZ 85250-6030, USA

Southerland II, Steve (Congressman, Politician)
1229 Longworth Hob
Washington, DC 20515-1315, USA

Southern, Silas (Eddie) (Athlete, Track Athlete)
2006 Custer Pkwy
Richardson, TX 75080-3403, USA

Southward, Dezmen (Athlete, Football Player)

Southworth, Bill (Athlete, Baseball Player)
320 Dobbin Rd
Saint Louis, MO 63119-4515, USA

Southworth, Carrie (Actor)
c/o Van Johnson *Van Johnson Company*
9595 Wilshire Blvd Ste 900
Beverly Hills, CA 90212-2509, USA

Souza, Karla (Actor)
c/o Troy Nankin *Wishlab*
195 S Beverly Dr Ste 414
Beverly Hills, CA 90212-3044, USA

Souza, Mark (Athlete, Baseball Player)
10001 Woodcreek Oaks Blvd Unit 817
Roseville, CA 95747-5105, USA

Sovereign, Lady (Musician)
c/o Staff Member *Paradigm (Monterey)*
404 W Franklin St
Monterey, CA 93940-2303, USA

Sovey, William P (Business Person)
Newell Co
20 E Milwaukee St Ste 212
Janesville, WI 53545-3061, USA

Sovran, Gino (Athlete, Basketball Player)
7304 Forest Way
Brighton, MI 48116-7799, USA

Soward, R J (Athlete, Football Player)
7660 Chipwood Ln
Jacksonville, FL 32256-2338, USA

Sowell, Arnold (Arnie) (Athlete, Track Athlete)
1647 Waterstone Ln # 1
Charlotte, NC 28262-3176, USA

Sowell, Bradley (Athlete, Football Player)

Sowells, Rich (Athlete, Football Player)
2614 Teal Run Place Dr
Fresno, TX 77545-8824, USA

Sowers, Barbara (Athlete, Baseball Player)
5601 Duncan Rd Lot 199
Punta Gorda, FL 33982-4762, USA

Sowers, Jeremy (Athlete, Baseball Player)
43793 Apache Wells Ter
Leesburg, VA 20176-7423, USA

Soyer, David (Musician)
PO Box 307
Brattleboro, VT 05302-0307, USA

Spaak, Catherine (Actor)
Viale Parioli 59
Rome 00197, Italy

Spacek, Jaroslav (Athlete, Hockey Player)
4401 N Federal Hwy Ste 201
Boca Raton, FL 33431-5164, USA

Spacek, Sissy (Actor)
c/o Courtney Kivowitz *MGMT Entertainment (The Schiff Company)*
9220 W Sunset Blvd Ste 106
W Hollywood, CA 90069-3500, USA

Spacey, Kevin (Actor, Producer)
c/o Staff Member *Trigger Street Productions*
11766 Wilshire Blvd Ste 1610
Los Angeles, CA 90025-6565, USA

Spaddky, Boris V (Misc)
State Committee for Sports
Skatertny Pereulok 4
Moscow, RUSSIA

Spade, David (Actor, Comedian)
c/o Chelsea Thomas *The Lede Company*
9701 Wilshire Blvd # 930
Beverly Hills, CA 90212-2020, USA

Spader, James (Actor)
c/o Dar Rollins *ICM Partners*
10250 Constellation Blvd Fl 7
Los Angeles, CA 90067-6207, USA

Spaeny, Cailee (Actor, Musician)
c/o Katie Greenthal *The Lede Company*
9701 Wilshire Blvd # 930
Beverly Hills, CA 90212-2020, USA

Spagnardi, Darren (Athlete, Baseball Player)
2364 W Center Street Ext
Lexington, NC 27295-5943, USA

Spagnola, John S (Athlete, Football Player)
414 Hillbrook Rd
Bryn Mawr, PA 19010-3634, USA

Spahn, Ryan (Actor)
c/o Ann Kelly *Ann Kelly Management*
245 W 51st St Apt 411
New York, NY 10019-6281, USA

Spain, Douglas (Actor)
Innovative Artists
1505 10th St
Santa Monica, CA 90401-2805, USA

Spalding, Esperanza (Musician)
c/o Scott Southard *International Music Network (IMN)*
278 Main St
Gloucester, MA 01930-6022, USA

Spalding, Leslie (Athlete, Golfer)
1055 O Malley Dr
Billings, MT 59102-2524, USA

Spali, Timothy (Actor)
Markham & Froggatt
Julian House
4 Windmill St
London W1P 1HF, UNITED KINGDOM (UK)

Spall, Rafe (Actor)
c/o Laura Colman *Premier PR*
2-4 Bucknall St
London WC2H 8LA, UNITED KINGDOM

Spall, Timothy (Actor)
c/o Laura Berwick *Berwick & Kovacik*
6230 Wilshire Blvd
Los Angeles, CA 90048-5126, USA

Spanarkel, Jim (Athlete, Basketball Player)
436 Edgewood Pl
Rutherford, NJ 07070-2662, USA

Spanger, Amy (Actor)
c/o Maureen Taran *New Wave Entertainment (LA)*
2660 W Olive Ave
Burbank, CA 91505-4525, USA

Spangler, Al (Athlete, Baseball Player)
27202 Afton Way
Huffman, TX 77336-3601, USA

Spangler, Al (Athlete, Baseball Player)
18523 Triana Bend Ln
Humble, TX 77346-3980, USA

Spang-McCook, Laurette (Actor)
4154 Colbath Ave
Sherman Oaks, CA 91423-4208, USA

Spanhel, Martin (Athlete, Hockey Player)
1017 Starlight Ln
Westerville, OH 43082-7092, USA

Spani, Gary (Athlete, Football Player)
3920 NE Sequoia St
Lees Summit, MO 64064-1574, USA

Spanic, Gabriela (Actor)
c/o Staff Member *Televisa*
Blvd Adolfo Lopez Mateos 232
Colonia San Angel INN
DF CP 01060, MEXICO

Spanjers, Martin (Actor)
c/o Sommer Smith *Innovative Artists*
1505 10th St
Santa Monica, CA 90401-2805, USA

Spano, Joe (Actor)
EC Assoc
10315 Woodley Ave Ste 110
Granada Hills, CA 91344-6900, USA

Spano, Nick (Actor)
c/o Justin Evans *The Independent Group*
6363 Wilshire Blvd Ste 115
Los Angeles, CA 90048-5734, USA

Spano, Robert (Musician)
c/o Staff Member *ICM Partners*
10250 Constellation Blvd Fl 7
Los Angeles, CA 90067-6207, USA

Spano, Vincent (Actor)
c/o Jo Kincaid *Gilbertson Management*
1334 3rd Street Promenade Ste 201
Santa Monica, CA 90401-1320, USA

Spanos, Alex (Football Executive)
1533 W Lincoln Rd
Stockton, CA 95207-2447, USA

Spanoulis, Vassilis (Athlete, Basketball Player)
c/o Jeff Schwartz *Excel Sports Management*
1700 Broadway Fl 29
New York, NY 10019-6559, USA

Spanswick, Bill (Athlete, Baseball Player)
1200 Commonwealth Cir Apt 202
Naples, FL 34116-6631, USA

Sparks, Dana (Actor)
VOX
5670 Wilshire Blvd Ste 820
Los Angeles, CA 90036-5613, USA

Sparks, Daniel (Athlete, Basketball Player)
2396 N Bruceville Rd
Vincennes, IN 47591-9698, USA

Sparks, Hal (Actor, Comedian, Musician)
c/o Penny Vizcarra *PV Public Relations*
121 N Almont Dr Apt 203
Beverly Hills, CA 90211-1860, USA

Sparks, Jeff (Athlete, Baseball Player)
714 W 42nd St
Houston, TX 77018-4429, USA

Sparks, Joe (Athlete, Baseball Player)
3915 E Cholla St
Phoenix, AZ 85028-2116, USA

Sparks, Jordin (Musician)
3007 Lakeridge Dr
Los Angeles, CA 90068-1809, USA

Sparks, Kylie (Actor)
c/o Myrna Lieberman *Myrna Lieberman Management*
3001 Hollyridge Dr
Hollywood, CA 90068-1951, USA

Sparks, Nicholas (Writer)
c/o Theresa Park *Park Literary*
1 Exchange Plz Ste 1601
New York, NY 10006-3797, USA

Sparks, Phillippi (Athlete, Football Player)
3315 W Walter Way
Phoenix, AZ 85027-1084, USA

Sparks, Stephanie (Golfer)
48 Redwood Ln
Wheeling, WV 26003-4854, USA

Sparks, Steve (Athlete, Baseball Player)
3307 Oak Tree Ct
Sugar Land, TX 77479-2494, USA

Sparks, Steve (Athlete, Baseball Player)
23378 Wilson Dr
Loxley, AL 36551-8559, USA

Sparlis, Alexander (Al) (Athlete, Football Player)
HC 4 Box 243
Porterville, CA 93257-9706, USA

Sparrow, Guy (Athlete, Basketball Player)
1709 McCulloch Blvd S
Lake Havasu City, AZ 86406-8847, USA

Sparrow, Rory (Athlete, Basketball Player)
117 Avenue C
Haledon, NJ 07508-1027, USA

Sparv, Camilla (Actor)
1500 Ocean Dr Apt 602
Miami Beach, FL 33139-3179, USA

Sparxxx, Bubba (Musician)
c/o Staff Member *Paradigm (Monterey)*
404 W Franklin St
Monterey, CA 93940-2303, USA

Speake, Bob (Athlete, Baseball Player)
4742 SW Urish Rd
Topeka, KS 66610-9758, USA

Speakman, Jeff (Actor)
7868 Milliken Ave
Rancho Cucamonga, CA 91730-8401, USA

Speaks, Ruben L (Religious Leader)
African Methodist Episcopal Zion Church
PO Box 32843
Charlotte, NC 28232-2843, USA

Spearman, Alvin (Athlete, Baseball Player)
12924 S Aberdeen St
Calumet Park, IL 60827-6502, USA

Spearritt, Hannah (Actor, Musician)
c/o Jeb Brandon *Corner Booth Entertainment*
11872 La Grange Ave Fl 1
Los Angeles, CA 90025-5283, USA

Spears, Aries (Actor, Comedian)
11406 Santini Ln
Porter Ranch, CA 91326-4427, USA

Spears, Britney (Dancer, Musician)
c/o Jeff Raymond *Rogers & Cowan*
1840 Century Park E Fl 18
Los Angeles, CA 90067-2101, USA

Spears, Eddie (Actor)
c/o Jennie Saks *NASS Talent Management*
2212 Lea Ave
Bozeman, MT 59715-2264, USA

Spears, Ernest (Athlete, Football Player)
528 Clark Rd
Northfield, VT 05663-6182, USA

Spears, Jamie Lynn (Actor, Musician)
c/o Staff Member *Creative Artists Agency (CAA)*
2000 Avenue of the Stars Ste 100
Los Angeles, CA 90067-4705, USA

Spears, Marcus (Athlete, Football Player)
10402 Reading Rd
Richmond, TX 77469-7330, USA

Spears, Peter (Actor)
c/o Jaclyn Travers *Creative Artists Agency (CAA)*
2000 Avenue of the Stars Ste 100
Los Angeles, CA 90067-4705, USA

Spears, Randy (Adult Film Star)
c/o Staff Member *Wicked Pictures*
9040 Eton Ave
Canoga Park, CA 91304-1616, USA

Spears, William D (Football Player)
63 Waterbridge Pl
Ponte Vedra Beach, FL 32082-2323, USA

Specht, Greg (Athlete, Football Player)
8650 SW Woodside Dr
Portland, OR 97225-1742, USA

Speck, Cliff (Athlete, Baseball Player)
823 S Nueva Vista Dr
Palm Springs, CA 92264-3425, USA

Speck, Fred (Athlete, Hockey Player)

Specter, Rachel (Actor)
c/o Adam Griffin *LINK Entertainment*
11872 La Grange Ave
Los Angeles, CA 90025-5282, USA

Spector, Phil (Business Person, Songwriter)
686 S Arroyo Pkwy # PH175
Pasadena, CA 91105-3233, USA

Spector, Ronnie (Musician)
c/o Barry Dickins *International Talent Booking*
9 Kingsway
Fl 6
London WC2B 6XF, UNITED KINGDOM

Speech (Artist, Musician)
William Morris Agency
1325 Avenue of the Americas
New York, NY 10019-6026, USA

Speed, Grant (Artist)
139 S 400 E
Lindon, UT 84042-2120, USA

Speed, Horace (Athlete, Baseball Player)
6821 State Boulevard Ext
Meridian, MS 39305-8420, USA

Speed, Lake (Race Car Driver)
c/o Staff Member *NASCAR*
1801 W Speedway Blvd
Daytona Beach, FL 32114-1243, USA

Speed, Lizz (Producer)
c/o Staff Member *Jackoway Tyerman Wertheimer Austen Mandelbaum Morris & Klein*
1925 Century Park E Fl 22
Los Angeles, CA 90067-2701, USA

Speedman, Scott (Actor)
c/o Sandra Chang *Anonymous Content*
3532 Hayden Ave
Culver City, CA 90232-2413, USA

Speer, Bill (Athlete, Hockey Player)

Speer, Del (Athlete, Football Player)
17620 NW 40th Ave
Miami Gardens, FL 33055-3864, USA

Speer, Hugo (Actor)
c/o Fiona McLoughlin *Independent Talent Group*
40 Whitfield St
London W1T 2RH, UNITED KINGDOM

Speers, Ted (Athlete, Hockey Player)
61515 Brookway Dr
South Lyon, MI 48178-7056, USA

Spehr, Tim (Athlete, Baseball Player)
8524 Briargrove Dr
Woodway, TX 76712-2305, USA

Speier, Chris (Athlete, Baseball Player)
3102 N Manor Dr W
Phoenix, AZ 85014-5525, USA

Speier, Jackie (Congressman, Politician)
211 Cannon Hob
Washington, DC 20515-0549, USA

Speier, Justin (Athlete, Baseball Player)
9405 S 51st St
Phoenix, AZ 85044-5686, USA

Speier, Ryan (Athlete, Baseball Player)
15450 FM 1325 Apt 1724
Austin, TX 78728-2841, USA

Speight, Derrick (Producer)
c/o Staff Member *Screen Door Entertainment*
15223 Burbank Blvd
Sherman Oaks, CA 91411-3505, USA

Speight, Lester (Rasta) (Actor)
c/o Staff Member *WME|IMG*
9601 Wilshire Blvd
Beverly Hills, CA 90210-5213, USA

Speigner, Levale (Athlete, Baseball Player)
1041 Bond St
Thomasville, GA 31757-0221, USA

Speiser, Jerry (Musician)
TPA
PO Box 124
Round Corner, NSW, AUSTRALIA

Spektor, Regina (Actor, Musician)
c/o Tony Dimitriades *East End Management*
15260 Ventura Blvd Ste 2100
Sherman Oaks, CA 91403-5360, USA

Spelling, Candy (Actor)
c/o Kevin Sasaki *Kevin Sasaki Public Relations & Media Counsel*
8491 W Sunset Blvd Ste 224
Los Angeles, CA 90069-1911, USA

Spelling, Randy (Actor)
c/o Staff Member *Innovative Artists*
1505 10th St
Santa Monica, CA 90401-2805, USA

Spelling, Tori (Actor)
c/o Geordie Frey *GEF Entertainment*
533 N Las Palmas Ave
Los Angeles, CA 90004-1017, USA

Spellman, Alonzo R (Athlete, Football Player)
1300 Marigold Way
Pflugerville, TX 78660-4137, USA

Spelvin, Georgina (Actor)
3121 Ledgewood Dr
Hollywood, CA 90068-1913

Spence, Akeem (Athlete, Football Player)
c/o Mitchell Frankel *Impact Sports (FL)*
2799 NW 2nd Ave Ste 203
Boca Raton, FL 33431-6709, USA

Spence, Blake (Athlete, Football Player)
14005 SW Teal Blvd Apt D
Beaverton, OR 97008-4305, USA

Spence, Bob (Athlete, Baseball Player)
1426 Antioch Ave
Chula Vista, CA 91913-1477, USA

Spence, Bruce (Actor)
c/o Imogen Johnson *Johnson and Laird Management*
P.O. Box 78340
Grey Lynn Auckland 01245, NEW ZEALAND

Spence, Dave (Misc)
Horseshores Union
RR 2 Box 71C
Englishtown, NJ 07726, USA

Spence, Gerry (Attorney)
PO Box 548
Jackson, WY 83001-0548, USA

Spence, Sean (Athlete, Football Player)
c/o Drew Rosenhaus *Rosenhaus Sports Representation*
3921 Alton Rd # 440
Miami Beach, FL 33140-3852, USA

Spence, Sebastian (Actor)
c/o Lesa Kirk *Open Entertainment*
1051 Cole Ave
Los Angeles, CA 90038-2601, USA

Spencer, Abigail (Actor)
Innerlight Films
16030 Ventura Blvd Ste 380
Encino, CA 91436-2778, USA

Spencer, Andre (Athlete, Basketball Player)
1315 W Gage Ave
Los Angeles, CA 90044-2733, USA

Spencer, Anthony (Athlete, Football Player)
c/o Eugene Parker *Independent Sports & Entertainment (ISE-IN)*
6435 W Jefferson Blvd # 197
Fort Wayne, IN 46804-6203, USA

Spencer, Charlotte (Actor)
c/o Pandora Weldon *Public Eye Communications*
535 Kings Rd
#313 Plaza
London SW10 0SZ, UNITED KINGDOM

Spencer, Chaske (Actor)
c/o Staff Member *Josselyne Herman & Associates*
345 E 56th St Apt 3B
New York, NY 10022-3745, USA

Spencer, Chris (Actor)
c/o Julia Buchwald *Buchwald*
5900 Wilshire Blvd Ste 3100
Los Angeles, CA 90036-5030, USA

Spencer, Chris (Athlete, Football Player)
c/o Tom Condon *Creative Artists Agency (CAA)*
401 Commerce St PH
Nashville, TN 37219-2516, USA

Spencer, Danielle (Actor)
c/o Martin Bedford *Bedford & Pearce Management Martin Bedford*
2/263-269 Alfred St N
North Sydney NSW 2060, Australia

Spencer, Darryl (Athlete, Football Player)
1473 Beechfern Dr
Melbourne, FL 32935-5989, USA

Spencer, Daryl (Athlete, Baseball Player)
2740 S Larkin Dr
Wichita, KS 67216-1258, USA

Spencer, Elizabeth (Writer)
402 Longleaf Dr
Chapel Hill, NC 27517-3042, USA

Spencer, Elmore (Athlete, Basketball Player)
2770 Foxlair Trl
Atlanta, GA 30349-4436, USA

Spencer, Felton (Athlete, Basketball Player)
4102 Nicholas Roy Ct
Prospect, KY 40059-8209, USA

Spencer, Freddie (Race Car Driver)
Freddie Specer's
7055 Speedway Blvd # E-106
Las Vegas, NV 89115-1807, USA

Spencer, GC (Race Car Driver)
698 S Pickens Bridge Rd
Gray, TN 37615-4017, USA

Spencer, George (Athlete, Baseball Player)
8160 Hickory Ave
Galena, OH 43021-8508, USA

Spencer, Jesse (Actor)
c/o Kathryn Fleming *The Fleming Agency*
38 Driver Ave Bldg 19
Fox Studios Australia
Moore Park NSW 02021, AUSTRALIA

Spencer, Jimmy (Football Player)
5331 Talavero Pl
Parker, CO 80134-2799, USA

Spencer, Jimmy (Race Car Driver)
160 Gasoline Aly
Mooresville, NC 28117-6502, USA

Spencer, John (Athlete, Misc)
17 Knowles St
Radcliffe
Lancs M26 0DN, UNITED KINGDOM (UK)

Spencer, Lara (Television Host)
c/o Jonathan Rosen *WME|IMG (NY)*
11 Madison Ave Fl 18
New York, NY 10010-3669, USA

Spencer, Irv (Athlete, Hockey Player)

Spencer, Marc (Radio Personality)
c/o Staff Member *WPKX*
1331 Main St Ste 4
Springfield, MA 01103-1621, USA

Spencer, Maurice (Athlete, Football Player)
61 W 62nd St
New York, NY 10023-7015, USA

Spencer, Octavia (Actor)
c/o Melissa Kates *Viewpoint Inc*
8820 Wilshire Blvd Ste 220
Beverly Hills, CA 90211-2622, USA

Spencer, Sean (Athlete, Baseball Player)
3584 E Calistoga Ct
Port Orchard, WA 98366-4084, USA

Spencer, Shane (Athlete, Baseball Player)
13049 Laurel Canyon Rd
Lakeside, CA 92040-3519, USA

Spencer, Stan (Athlete, Baseball Player)
3100 NE 188th St
Ridgefield, WA 98642-9515, USA

Spencer, Timothy (Tim) (Athlete, Football Player)
1435 Sherborne Ln
Powell, OH 43065-7604, USA

Spencer, Tom (Athlete, Baseball Player)
2021 E Conner Stra
Tucson, AZ 85719-3206, USA

Spencer, Tracie (Musician)
Rogers & Cowan
6340 Breckenridge Run
Rex, GA 30273-1841, USA

Spencer, Willie (Athlete, Football Player)
1109 Johnson St SE
Massillon, OH 44646-8266, USA

Spencer-Devlin, Muffin (Golfer)
1278 Glenneyre St Apt 155
Laguna Beach, CA 92651-3103, USA

Spenn, Fred (Athlete, Baseball Player)
5201 Desoto Rd
Sarasota, FL 34235-3607, USA

Spergel, David (Misc)
Princeton University
Astrophysicist Dept
Princeton, NJ 08544-0001, USA

Sperring, Rob (Athlete, Baseball Player)
4655 County Road 194
Jonesboro, TX 76538-1241, USA

Spevack, Jason (Actor)
c/o Dana Fletcher *Coast to Coast Talent Group*
3350 Barham Blvd
Los Angeles, CA 90068-1404, USA

Speyrer, Cotton (Athlete, Football Player)
7905 San Felipe Blvd Apt 117
Austin, TX 78729-7638, USA

Spezza, Jason (Athlete, Hockey Player)
The Orr Hockey Group
PO Box 290836
Charlestown, MA 02129-0215, USA

Spheeris, Penelope (Director)
PO Box 1128
Studio City, CA 91614-0128, USA

Spice 1 (Artist, Musician)
JL Entertainment
18653 Ventura Blvd # 340
Tarzana, CA 91356-4103, USA

Spice Girls (Music Group)
35 Parkgate Rd. #32 Ransome Dock
London, ENGLAND SW11 4NP

Spicer, Bob (Athlete, Baseball Player)
423 McPhee Dr
Fayetteville, NC 28305-5129, USA

Spicer, Sean (Politician)
c/o Staff Member *White House, The*
1600 Pennsylvania Ave NW
Washington, DC 20500-0004, USA

SPider Loc (Musician)
c/o Staff Member *Interscope Records*
1755 Broadway Fl 6
New York, NY 10019-3768, USA

Spidia, Vladimir (Prime Minister)
Kancelar Presidenta Republiky
Hradecek
Prague 1 119 08, CZECH REPUBLIC

Spiegel, Evan (Business Person, Internet Star)
Snapchat Inc
579 Toyopa Dr
Pacific Palisades, CA 90272-4470, USA

Spiegelman, Art (Writer)
c/o Staff Member *Steven Barclay Agency*
12 Western Ave
Petaluma, CA 94952-2907, USA

Spieier, Patrick (Baseball Player)
6635 S 108th Ave
Omaha, NE 68137-4733, USA

Spielberg, David (Actor)
130 S Sepulveda Blvd Unit 108
Los Angeles, CA 90049-3150, USA

Spielberg, Steven (Director, Producer)
c/o Staff Member *Amblin Entertainment*
100 Universal Plaza
Bldg 477
Universal City, CA 91608, USA

Spieler, Patrick (Athlete, Baseball Player)
15963 Adams St
Omaha, NE 68135-6325, USA

Spielman, Chris (Athlete, Football Player, Sportscaster)
OSU 336 LLC
PO Box 342
Attn: Carry Billy
Powell, OH 43065-0342, USA

Spier, Peter E (Artist)
PO Box 566
Shoreham, NY 11786-0566, USA

Spiers, Bill (Athlete, Baseball Player)
9233 Old State Rd
Cameron, SC 29030-8129, USA

Spiers, Judi (Actor)
c/o Staff Member *Glen King PR & Marketing*
48 Queen St
Exeter EX4 3JR, UK

Spies, Joshua (Artist)
PO Box 90
Watertown, SD 57201-0090, USA

Spieth, Jordan (Athlete, Golfer)
c/o Staff Member *Pro Golfers Association (PGA)*
112 TPC Blvd
Ponte Vedra Beach, FL 32082, USA

Spiezio, Ed (Athlete, Baseball Player)
2027 Taller Rd
Morris, IL 60450-6831, USA

Spiezio, Scott (Athlete, Baseball Player)
2027 Taller Rd
Morris, IL 60450-6831, USA

Spikes, Brandon (Athlete, Football Player)
716 Hogart St
Raeford, NC 28376-7322, USA

Spikes, Cameron (Athlete, Football Player)
3001 Fraternity Row # 132
College Station, TX 77845-6504, USA

Spikes, Charlie (Athlete, Baseball Player)
531 N Border Dr
Bogalusa, LA 70427-3307, USA

Spikes, Jack E (Athlete, Football Player)
9537 Highland View Dr
Dallas, TX 75238-1025, USA

Spikes, Takeo (Athlete, Football Player)
5005 Heatherwood Ct
Roswell, GA 30075-2285, USA

Spilborghs, Ryan (Athlete, Baseball Player)
2220 Elise Way
Santa Barbara, CA 93109-1814, USA

Spilde, Jenna (Model, Reality Star)

Spiller, C.J. (Athlete, Football Player)

Spillman, C.J. (Athlete, Football Player)

Spillner, Dan (Athlete, Baseball Player)
18505 SE Newport Way Unit C113
Issaquah, WA 98027-9032, USA

Spilman, Harry (Athlete, Baseball Player)
4423 Saint Phillips Rd S
Mount Vernon, IN 47620-9629, USA

Spin Doctors, The (Music Group)
c/o Staff Member *Paradigm (Monterey)*
404 W Franklin St
Monterey, CA 93940-2303, USA

Spinella, Stephen (Actor)
c/o Staff Member *Innovative Artists*
1505 10th St
Santa Monica, CA 90401-2805, USA

Spinelli, Jerry (Writer)
331 Melvin Rd
Phoenixville, PA 19460, USA

Spiner, Brent (Actor)
c/o Steve Smith *Stagecoach Entertainment*
1990 S Bundy Dr Ste 645
Los Angeles, CA 90025-6365, USA

Spinetta, Jean-Cyril (Business Person)
Group Air France
45 Rue de Paris
Roissy CDG Cedex 95747, FRANCE

Spinks, Michael (Athlete, Boxer, Olympic Athlete)
Butch Lewis Productions
925 Centre Rd
Wilmington, DE 19807-2823, USA

Spinks, Scipio (Athlete, Baseball Player)
11422 Rock Bridge Ln
Sugar Land, TX 77498-0923, USA

Spinney, Caroll (Actor)
940 Brickyard Rd
Woodstock, CT 06281-1302, USA

Spinto Band, The (Music Group)
c/o Charlie Myatt *13 Artists (UK)*
11-14 Kensington St
Brighton BN1 4AJ, UNITED KINGDOM

Spires, Greg (Athlete, Football Player)
175 Centre St # 520
Quincy, MA 02169-8600, USA

Spiridakos, Tracy (Actor)
c/o Anne Woodward *Authentic Talent & Literary Management*
3615 Eastham Dr # 650
Culver City, CA 90232-2410, USA

Spiro, Jordana (Actor)
c/o Larry Taube *Principal Entertainment*
9255 W Sunset Blvd Ste 500
Los Angeles, CA 90069-3301, USA

Spiro, Lev L (Director)
c/o Staff Member *WME|IMG*
9601 Wilshire Blvd
Beverly Hills, CA 90210-5213, USA

Spirtas, Kevin (Actor)
c/o Robert Baird *Baird Artists Management*
PO Box 5016 Stn A
Station A
Toronto, ON M5W 1N4, Canada

Spitler, Austin (Athlete, Football Player)
c/o Joe Flanagan *BTI Sports Advisors*
615 South Blvd Apt C
Oak Park, IL 60302-4606, USA

Spittka, Marko (Athlete)
Judo Club 90
Zielona-Gora-Str 9
Frankfurt/Ober 15230, GERMANY

Spitz, Mark (Athlete, Olympic Athlete, Swimmer)
383 Dalehurst Ave
Los Angeles, CA 90024-2573, USA

Spitzer, Eliot (Commentator, Politician)
c/o Staff Member *Current TV (NY)*
435 Hudson Ave # 400
Albany, NY 12203-1211, USA

Spivakov, Vladmir T (Musician)
Vspolny Per 17
#14
Moscow, RUSSIA

Spivey, Junior (Athlete, Baseball Player)
4140 S Ambrosia Dr
Chandler, AZ 85248-4804, USA

Spivey, Sebron (Athlete, Football Player)
435 Capitol View Dr
Columbus, OH 43203-1037, USA

Splatt, Rachel (Race Car Driver)
12631 N Tatum Blvd
Phoenix, AZ 85032-7710, USA

Splatt, Rachelle (Race Car Driver)
12631 N Tatum Blvd
Phoenix, AZ 85032-7710, USA

Spoelstra, Erik (Basketball Coach)
3060 Matilda St
Miami, FL 33133-4546, USA

Spoliaric, Paul (Athlete, Baseball Player)
545 Gramiak Rd
KelownaBC V1X 1K4, BC V1X 1K4 Canada, USA

Spoljario, Paul (Baseball Player)
Toronto Blue Jays
13261 N 73rd Ave
Peoria, AZ 85381-6054, USA

Sponenburgh, Mark (Artist)
5562 NW Pacific Coast Hwy
Seal Rock, OR 97376-9619, USA

Spong, John S (Religious Leader)
514 Libbie Ave Apt 4
Richmond, VA 23226-2668, USA

Spooneybarger, Tim (Athlete, Baseball Player)
4109 Bamboo Dr
Pensacola, FL 32526-8425, USA

Spork, Shirley (Golfer)
73010 Somera Rd
Palm Desert, CA 92260-6032, USA

Sporleder, Gregory (Actor)
c/o Julia Buchwald *Buchwald*
5900 Wilshire Blvd Ste 3100
Los Angeles, CA 90036-5030, USA

Sposa, Mike (Golfer)
8317 Old Town Dr
Tampa, FL 33647-3335, USA

Spottiswoode, Roger (Director)
c/o Staff Member *ICM Partners*
10250 Constellation Blvd Fl 7
Los Angeles, CA 90067-6207, USA

Spottsville, Ray (Baseball Player)
Houston Eagles
PO Box 591
Colfax, LA 71417-0591, USA

Spound, Michael (Actor)
James/Levy/Jacobson
3500 W Olive Ave Ste 1470
Burbank, CA 91505-5514, USA

Spradlin, Danny (Athlete, Football Player)
1011 Laurie St
Maryville, TN 37803-6731, USA

Spradlin, Jerry (Athlete, Baseball Player)
2824 E Diana Ave
Anaheim, CA 92806-4412, USA

Spradling, Charlie (Actor)
c/o Staff Member *Buchwald (NY)*
10 E 44th St
New York, NY 10017-3601, USA

Spragan, Donnie (Athlete, Football Player)
312 Riviera Dr
Union City, CA 94587-3722, USA

Sprague, Ed (Athlete, Olympic Athlete, Swimmer)
4677 Pine Valley Cir
Stockton, CA 95219-1881, USA

Sprague, Ed (Athlete, Baseball Player)
19015 N Davis Rd
Lodi, CA 95242-9203, USA

Sprague, Jack (Race Car Driver)

Spratlan, Lewis (Composer)
Amherst College
Music Dept
Amherst, MA 01002, USA

Sprayberry, Dylan (Actor)
c/o Laura Pallas *Pallas Management*
4536 Greenbush Ave
Sherman Oaks, CA 91423-3112, US

Spreitler, Taylor (Actor)
c/o Cameron Curtis *Curtis Talent Management*
9607 Arby Dr
Beverly Hills, CA 90210-1202, USA

Sprewell, Latrell (Athlete, Basketball Player)
1918 E Lafayette Pl UNIT 309
Milwaukee, WI 53202-1396, USA

Spriggs, George (Athlete, Baseball Player)
77A W Bay Front Rd Apt A
Lothian, MD 20711-9711, USA

Spriggs, Larry (Athlete, Basketball Player)
2430 Thoreau St
Inglewood, CA 90303-2549, USA

Spring, Dan (Athlete, Hockey Player)
2005 Canyon St
Creston, BC V0B 1G5, Canada

Spring, Don (Athlete, Hockey Player)
Spring Fuel Distributors
2780 Acland Rd
Kelowna, BC V1X 7X1, Canada

Spring, Frank (Athlete, Hockey Player)
638 Upper Ottawa St
Hamilton, ON L8T 3T5, CANADA

Spring, Jack (Athlete, Baseball Player)
3006 W Mark Ct
Spokane, WA 99208-8822, USA

Spring, Sherwood C (Astronaut)
8244 Native Violet Dr
Lorton, VA 22079-5664, USA

Spring, Sherwood C Colonel (Astronaut)
2116 McDonough Ln
San Diego, CA 92106-6087, USA

Springer, Dennis (Athlete, Baseball Player)
537 Sherwood Ct
Hanford, CA 93230-6859, USA

Springer, Jerry (Talk Show Host, Television Host)
454 N Columbus Dr # 200
Chicago, IL 60611-5807, USA

Springer, Michael (Golfer)
1482 E Forest Oaks Dr
Fresno, CA 93730-3443, USA

Springer, Mike (Golfer)
1482 E Forest Oaks Dr
Fresno, CA 93730-3443, USA

Springer, Robert C (Astronaut)
202 Village Cir
Sheffield, AL 35660-5632, USA

Springer, Robert C Colonel (Astronaut)
202 Village Cir
Sheffield, AL 35660-5632, USA

Springer, Russ (Athlete, Baseball Player)
PO Box 185
4357 Highway 8
Pollock, LA 71467-0185, USA

Springer, Steve (Athlete, Baseball Player)
6962 Carla Cir
Huntington Beach, CA 92647-4315, USA

Springfield, Marty (Athlete, Baseball Player)
5164 Flicker Field Cir
Sarasota, FL 34231-3242, USA

Springfield, Rick (Actor, Musician)
PO Box 261640
Encino, CA 91426-1640, USA

Springgs, Marcus (Athlete, Football Player)
830 Regal St
Houston, TX 77034-1231, USA

Springs, Kirk (Athlete, Football Player)
4925 Paddock Rd
Cincinnati, OH 45237-5548, USA

Springs, Shawn (Football Player)
Washington Redskins
21300 Redskin Park Dr
Ashburn, VA 20147-6100, USA

Springsteen, Bruce (Musician, Songwriter)
Thrill Hill Recording
132 Muhlenbrink Rd
Colts Neck, NJ 07722-1508, USA

Springsteen, Pamela (Actor, Photographer)
c/o Caryn Weiss *Weiss Artists*
6121 W Sunset Blvd Ste 306
Los Angeles, CA 90028-6448, USA

Sproles, Darren (Athlete, Football Player)
c/o Jimmy Sexton *CAA (Memphis)*
6060 Poplar Ave Ste 470
Memphis, TN 38119-0910, USA

Sprotte, Jimmy (Athlete, Football Player)
2163 E Palmcroft Dr
Tempe, AZ 85282-3062, USA

Sprouse, Cole (Actor)
c/o Annick Oppenheim *Wolf-Kasteler Public Relations*
6255 W Sunset Blvd Ste 1111
Los Angeles, CA 90028-7426, USA

Sprouse, Dylan (Actor)
c/o Bonnie Liedtke *Authentic Talent & Literary Management*
3615 Eastham Dr # 650
Culver City, CA 90232-2410, USA

Sprout, Bob (Athlete, Baseball Player)
227 County Road 740
Enterprise, AL 36330-6827, USA

Sprowl, Bobby (Athlete, Baseball Player)
4711 Leeward Ave
Northport, AL 35473-1934, USA

Spruce, Andy (Athlete, Hockey Player)
12 Rathgar St
London, ON N5Z 1Y4, Canada

Spruill, Marquis (Athlete, Football Player)
c/o Joe Linta *JL Sports*
1204 Main St Ste 179
Branford, CT 06405-3787, USA

Spurgeon, Jay (Athlete, Baseball Player)
212 Hartsdale Rd
Rochester, NY 14622-2007, USA

Spurling, Chris (Athlete, Baseball Player)
27247 Copper Ridge Dr
Wesley Chapel, FL 33544-7331, USA

Spurlock, Morgan (Actor, Director, Producer)
c/o Richard Arlook *The Arlook Group*
11663 Gorham Ave Apt 5
Los Angeles, CA 90049-4749, USA

Spurrier, Steve (Athlete, Coach, Football Coach, Football Player, Heisman Trophy Winner)
17050 Silver Charm Pl
Leesburg, VA 20176-7152, USA

Square, Damion (Athlete, Football Player)
c/o Brian E. Overstreet *E.O. Sports Management*
1314 Texas St Ste 1212
Houston, TX 77002-3525, USA

Squerciati, Marina (Actor)
c/o Myrna Jacoby *MJ Management*
130 W 57th St Apt 11A
New York, NY 10019-3311, USA

Squibb, June (Actor)
c/o Martin Gage *BRS / Gage Talent Agency (LA)*
6300 Wilshire Blvd Ste 1430
Los Angeles, CA 90048-5216, USA

Squierek, Jack (Football Player)
4051 Vezber Dr
Seven Hills, OH 44131-6233, USA

Squirek, Jack (Athlete, Football Player)
4051 Vezber Dr
Seven Hills, OH 44131-6233, USA

Squires, Mike (Athlete, Baseball Player)
9548 Autumnwood Cir
Kalamazoo, MI 49009-9385, USA

Srb, Adrian M (Misc)
411 Cayuga Heights Rd
Ithaca, NY 14850-1401, USA

Sremmurd, Rae (Musician)
c/o Caroline Yim *Creative Artists Agency (CAA)*
2000 Avenue of the Stars Ste 100
Los Angeles, CA 90067-4705, USA

Sri Chinmoy (Religious Leader)
85-45 Sri Chinmoy St
Jamaica, NY 11432, USA

Staab, Rebecca (Actor)
Don Buchwald
5900 Wilshire Blvd Ste 3100
Los Angeles, CA 90036-5030, USA

Staal, Eric (Athlete, Hockey Player)
The Orr Hockey Group
PO Box 290836
Charlestown, MA 02129-0215, USA

Staal, Jordan (Athlete, Hockey Player)
c/o Rick Curran *The Orr Hockey Group (PA)*
411 Timber Ln
Devon, PA 19333-1232, USA

Staal, Marc (Athlete, Hockey Player)
Candy Mountain Dr RR 6
Thunder Bay, ON P7C 5N5, Canada

Staats, Dewavne (Sportscaster)
1170 Gulf Blvd Apt 1601
Clearwater Beach, FL 33767-2785, USA

Staats, Dewayne (Baseball Player, Sportscaster)
Tampa Bay Devil Rays
1170 Gulf Blvd Apt 1601
Clearwater Beach, FL 33767-2785, USA

Stabenow, Deborah (Politician)
238 9th St SE
Washington, DC 20003-2111, USA

Stablein, George (Athlete, Baseball Player)
2903 Penman
Tustin, CA 92782-3314, USA

Stables, Kelly (Actor)
c/o Kurt Patino *Patino Management Company*
10201 Riverside Dr Ste 207
Toluca Lake, CA 91602-2538, USA

Stacey, Caitlin (Actor)
21 Esmond Rd
London W4 1JG, UNITED KINGDOM

Stacey, Siran (Athlete, Football Player)
PO Box 131
Hartford, AL 36344-0131, USA

Stacey Q (Actor, Music Group, Musician)
641 S Palm St Ste D
La Habra, CA 90631-5758, USA

Stachel, Ari'el (Actor, Musician)
c/o Michael Gagliardo *PMK/BNC Public Relations*
622 3rd Ave Fl 8
New York, NY 10017-6707, USA

Stack, Brian (Writer)
c/o Staff Member *3 Arts Entertainment*
9460 Wilshire Blvd Fl 7
Beverly Hills, CA 90212-2713, USA

Stack, Rosemarie (Actor)
10375 Wilshire Blvd Apt 1B
Los Angeles, CA 90024-4712, USA

Stackhouse, Charles (Athlete, Football Player)
240 Shady Grove St
Marion, AR 72364-9412, USA

Stackhouse, Jerry (Athlete, Basketball Player)
5266 Settles Bridge Rd
Suwanee, GA 30024-7695, USA

Stackhouse, Ron (Athlete, Hockey Player)
RR 2
Haliburton, ON KOM 1SO, Canada

Stacom, Kevin (Athlete, Basketball Player)
14 Florida Ave
Jamestown, RI 02835-1548, USA

Stacy, Billy (Athlete, Football Player)
400 Colonial Cir
Starkville, MS 39759-4214, USA

Stacy, Hollis (Athlete, Golfer)
Endicott
PO Box 10850
Palm Desert, CA 92255-0850, USA

Stadlen, Lewis J. (Actor)
c/o Staff Member *Access Talent Voice Overs*
171 Madison Ave Ste 900
New York, NY 10016-5110, USA

Stadler, Craig (Golfer)
113 Elk Xing
Evergreen, CO 80439-4114, USA

Stadler, Sergei V (Musician)
Kaiserstr 43
Munich 80801, GERMANY

Stadtman, Earl R (Misc)
1502 Auburn Ave
Rockville, MD 20850-1120, USA

Stadtman, Thressa C (Misc)
1502 Auburn Ave
Rockville, MD 20850-1120, USA

Staehle, Marv (Athlete, Baseball Player)
19421 Cromwell Ct Apt 208
Fort Myers, FL 33912-0386, USA

Staffieri, Joe (Athlete, Football Player)
6825 Polo Fields Pkwy
Cumming, GA 30040-5731, USA

Stafford, Ben (Horse Racer)
22 Glen Dr
Voorhees, NJ 08043-1404, USA

Stafford, Daimion (Athlete, Football Player)

Stafford, Jim (Comedian, Musician)
9562 Hampton Reserve Dr
Brentwood, TN 37027-8491, USA

Stafford, John R (Business Person)
American Home Products
1901 Doolittle Dr
Bridgewater, NJ 08807-7032, USA

Stafford, Matthew (Athlete, Football Player)
c/o Tom Condon *Creative Artists Agency (CAA)*
401 Commerce St PH
Nashville, TN 37219-2516, USA

Stafford, Michelle (Actor)
c/o Marlan Willardson *MWPR*
10153 Riverside Dr # 157
Toluca Lake, CA 91602-2562, USA

Stafford, Nancy (Actor)
Nest Inc
2792 Lakeridge Ln
Westlake Vlg, CA 91361-3301, USA

Stafford, Steve (Actor)
Studio Wings, Inc.
855 Aviation Dr
Camarillo, CA 93010-8849, USA

Stageman-Roberts, Donna (Athlete, Baseball Player)
1831 Jerome Pl
Helena, MT 59601-4735, USA

Staggers, Jon (Athlete, Football Player)
3835 Oakes Dr
Hayward, CA 94542-1720, USA

Staggs, Jeff (Athlete, Football Player)
4641 Jeri Way
El Cajon, CA 92020-8329, USA

Staggs, Steve (Athlete, Baseball Player)
4021 Kent St
Norman, OK 73072-2222, USA

Stagus, Gus (Coach, Swimmer)
University of Michigan
Athletic Dept
Ann Arbor, MI 48104, USA

Stahl, Jerry (Actor, Writer)
c/o Staff Member *United Talent Agency (UTA)*
9336 Civic Center Dr
Beverly Hills, CA 90210-3604, USA

Stahl, Larry (Athlete, Baseball Player)
1506 E Main St # A
Belleville, IL 62221-5436, USA

Stahl, Lesley (Journalist)
c/o 60 Minutes *CBS News (NY)*
524 W 57th St Fl 8
New York, NY 10019-2930, USA

Stahl, Leslie (Actor)
c/o Staff Member *WME|IMG*
9601 Wilshire Blvd
Beverly Hills, CA 90210-5213, USA

Stahl, Lisa (Actor)
Don Buchwald
5900 Wilshire Blvd Ste 3100
Los Angeles, CA 90036-5030, USA

Stahl, Nick (Actor)
c/o Sean Fay *LINK Entertainment*
11872 La Grange Ave
Los Angeles, CA 90025-5282, USA

Stahl-David, Michael (Actor)
c/o Emily Rennert *Imprint PR*
375 Hudson St
New York, NY 10014-3658, USA

Stahley, Adele (Baseball Player)
3700 SE Jennings Rd Apt 214W
Port St Lucie, FL 34952-7701, USA

Stahoviak, Scott (Athlete, Baseball Player)
507 Balmoral Ct
Grayslake, IL 60030-9303, USA

Stai, Brendon (Athlete, Football Player)
1431 Teal Trce
Pittsburgh, PA 15237-3848, USA

Staib, David P (Astronaut)
6905 Vantage Dr
Alexandria, VA 22306-1245, USA

Staiger, Roy (Athlete, Baseball Player)
1233 Tyler Dr
Lebanon, MO 65536-4121, USA

Staind (Music Group)
c/o Staff Member *Mitch Schneider Organization (MSO)*
14724 Ventura Blvd Ste 410
Sherman Oaks, CA 91403-3537, USA

Staios, Steve (Athlete, Hockey Player)
1213 Newbridge Tree NE
Atlanta, GA 30319-4549, USA

Stairs, Matt (Athlete, Baseball Player)
76 Skyline Rd
Bangor, ME 04401-2156, USA

Staite, Jewel (Actor)
c/o Nicole Nassar *Nicole Nassar PR*
1111 10th St Unit 104
Santa Monica, CA 90403-5363, USA

Stajan, Matthew (Athlete, Hockey Player)
Newport Sports Management
400-201 City Centre Dr
Attn Don Meehan
Mississauga, ON L5B 2T4, Canada

Stalcup, Jerry (Athlete, Football Player)
960 N Mulford Rd Apt 206
Rockford, IL 61107-3875, USA

Staley, Alan "'Red"' (Athlete, Hockey Player)
600-337 6th Ave N
Saskatoon, SK S7K 2S4, Canada

Staley, Bill (Athlete, Football Player)
9210 Todd Rd
Potter Valley, CA 95469-9727, USA

Staley, Dawn (Athlete, Basketball Player, Olympic Athlete)
Dawn Staley Foundation
1224 Glenwood Rd
Columbia, SC 29204-3351, USA

Staley, Dawn M (Basketball Player, Coach)
1228 Callowhill St #603
Philadelphia, PA 19123, USA

Staley, Joan (Actor)
24431 Lyons Ave Apt 302
Newhall, CA 91321-2359, USA

Staley, Joe (Athlete, Football Player)
c/o Ryan Tollner *REP 1 Sports Group*
80 Technology Dr
Irvine, CA 92618-2301, USA

Staley, Lex (Radio Personality)
c/o Staff Member *The Lex & Terry Morning Radio Network*
11700 Central Pkwy
Jacksonville, FL 32224-2600, USA

Staley, Matthew R (Actor, Musician)
PO Box 590
New York, NY 10108-0590, USA

Stallard, Tracy (Athlete, Baseball Player)
10319 Abbott Rd
Manassas, VA 20110-6151, USA

Staller, Ilona (Cicciolina) (Adult Film Star, Politician)
Via Cassia 1818
Rome I-00123, ITALY

Stallings, Gene (Athlete, Football Coach, Football Player)
6508 County Road 43200
Powderly, TX 75473-5320, USA

Stallings, Larry (Athlete, Football Player)
13458 Kingscross Ln Apt 2
Saint Louis, MO 63141-7256, USA

Stallings, Matthew Davey (Race Car Driver)
632 Wears Valley Rd
Pigeon Forge, TN 37863-7752, USA

Stallone, Frank (Actor, Musician)
c/o Marina Anderson *Media Hound PR*
PO Box 261939
Encino, CA 91426-1939, USA

Stallone, Jackie (Actor)
PO Box 491550
Los Angeles, CA 90049-9550, USA

Stallone, Sistine Rose (Model)
c/o Carrie Gordon *The Lede Company*
401 Broadway Ste 206
New York, NY 10013-3033, USA

Stallone, Sylvester (Actor, Director, Producer)
Instone LLC
251 California St
Irvine, CA 92617, USA

Stalls, David (Athlete, Football Player)
2100 Stout St
Denver, CO 80205-2827, USA

Stallworth, Bud (Athlete, Basketball Player)
14 Westwood Rd
Lawrence, KS 66044-4560, USA

Stallworth, Donte (Athlete, Football Player)
6 Arvis Ct
Sacramento, CA 95835-1643, USA

Stallworth, Johnny L (John) (Athlete, Football Player)
302 Osman Dr
Madison, AL 35756-3499, USA

Stallworth, Ron (Athlete, Football Player)
1834 Parkview Dr S
Montgomery, AL 36117-7701, USA

Stam, Jessica (Model)
c/o Staff Member *IMG*
304 Park Ave S Fl 12
New York, NY 10010-4314, USA

Stam, Katie (Beauty Pageant Winner)
The Miss America Organization
PO Box 1919
Atlantic City, NJ 08404-1919, USA

Stamatopoulos, Dino (Writer)
c/o Greg Cavic *United Talent Agency (UTA)*
9336 Civic Center Dr
Beverly Hills, CA 90210-3604, USA

Stamberg, Josh (Actor)
c/o Ruth Bernstein *Viewpoint Inc*
8820 Wilshire Blvd Ste 220
Beverly Hills, CA 90211-2622, USA

Stamile, Lauren (Actor)
c/o Craig Schneider *Pinnacle Public Relations*
8721 Santa Monica Blvd # 133
W Hollywood, CA 90069-4507, USA

Stamkos, Steven (Athlete, Hockey Player)
Newport Sports Management
400-201 City Centre Dr
Attn Don Meehan
Mississauga, ON L5B 2T4, Canada

Stamler, Jonathan (Misc)
Duke University
Medical Center
Hematology Dept
Durham, NC 27708-0001, USA

Stamler, Lorne (Athlete, Hockey Player)
1011 Orca Ct
Holiday, FL 34691-9817, USA

Stamm, Michael (Mike) (Athlete, Swimmer)
2826 Birdsall Ave
Oakland, CA 94619-3302, USA

Stammen, Craig (Athlete, Baseball Player)
13219 State Route 127
Rossburg, OH 45362-9505, USA

Stamos, John (Actor, Musician)
c/o Staff Member *St Amos Productions*
3480 Barham Blvd
Los Angeles, CA 90068-1470, USA

Stamos, Theodoros (Artist)
37 W 83rd St
New York, NY 10024-5201, USA

Stamp, Terence (Actor)
c/o Beth Holden-Garland *Untitled Entertainment*
350 S Beverly Dr Ste 200
Beverly Hills, CA 90212-4819, USA

Stamps, Sylvester (Athlete, Football Player)
Atlanta Falcons
951 Royal Oak Dr
Jackson, MS 39209-6736, USA

Stams, Frank (Athlete, Football Player)
2870 Marcia Blvd
Cuyahoga Falls, OH 44223-1146, USA

Stan, Jason (Musician)
Visions Casting Agency Pty Ltd
Level 6/3 Bowen Crs
Victoria, Melbourne 03000, AUSTRALIA

Stan, Sebastian (Actor)
c/o Nicole Caruso *Relevant (NY)*
333 Hudson St Rm 502
New York, NY 10013-1033, USA

Stanback, Haskel (Athlete, Football Player)
1530 Kingston Dr
Kannapolis, NC 28083-9280, USA

Stanchfield, Darby (Actor)
c/o Marsha McManus *Principal Entertainment*
9255 W Sunset Blvd Ste 500
Los Angeles, CA 90069-3301, USA

Standen, Clive (Actor)
c/o Susan Patricola *Patricola Public Relations*
369 S Doheny Dr # 1408
Beverly Hills, CA 90211-3508, USA

Standhardt, Kenneth (Artist)
620 Elwood Dr
Eugene, OR 97401-6012, USA

Standing, George (Athlete, Hockey Player)
34 Cliff Ave
Huntsville, ON P1H 1G1, Canada

Standing, John (Actor)
International Creative Mgmt
76 Oxford St
London W1N 0AX, UNITED KINGDOM (UK)

Standly, Mike (Golfer)
2306 Columbia Cir
League City, TX 77573-7622, USA

Standridge, Jason (Athlete, Baseball Player)
6228 Cardinal Dr
Pinson, AL 35126-3492, USA

Stanek, Al (Athlete, Baseball Player)
96 Allyn St Apt 2
Holyoke, MA 01040-2549, USA

Stanfel, Richard (Dick) (Athlete, Coach, Football Player)
1104 Juniper Pkwy
Libertyville, IL 60048-3543, USA

Stanfield, Fred (Athlete, Hockey Player)
59 Cheshire Ln
East Amherst, NY 14051-2602, USA

Stanfield, Jack (Athlete, Hockey Player)
5100 San Felipe St Unit 381E
Houston, TX 77056-3621, United States

Stanfield, Keith (Lakeith) (Actor)
c/o Siri Garber *Platform PR*
2666 N Beachwood Dr
Los Angeles, CA 90068-2308, USA

Stanfield, Kevin (Athlete, Baseball Player)
7565 Newcomb St
San Bernardino, CA 92410-4333, USA

Stanfill, William T (Bill) (Athlete, Football Player)
3117 Wisteria Ct
Albany, GA 31721-2988, USA

Stanford, Aaron (Actor)
c/o Lainie Sorkin Becky *Management 360*
9111 Wilshire Blvd
Beverly Hills, CA 90210-5508, USA

Stanford, Angela (Golfer)
6225 Pecan Orchard Ct
Ft Worth, TX 76179-9290, USA

Stanford, Jason (Athlete, Baseball Player)
4505 W Mesquital Del Oro
Tucson, AZ 85742-9704, USA

Stang, Peter J (Misc)
University of Utah
Chemistry Dept
Salt Lake City, UT 84112, USA

Stangassinger, Thomas (Skier)
Hofgasse 19
Durenberg-Hallein 05422, AUSTRIA

Stange, Lee (Athlete, Baseball Player)
436 Dolphin St
Melbourne Beach, FL 32951-2916, USA

Stange, Maya (Actor)
c/o Lindy King *United Agents*
12-26 Lexington St
London W1F OLE, UNITED KINGDOM

Stangel, Eric (Producer, Writer)
c/o Staff Member *3 Arts Entertainment*
9460 Wilshire Blvd Fl 7
Beverly Hills, CA 90212-2713, USA

Stangel, Justin (Producer, Writer)
c/o Staff Member *3 Arts Entertainment*
9460 Wilshire Blvd Fl 7
Beverly Hills, CA 90212-2713, USA

Stanger, Patti (Business Person, Reality Star)
c/o Lance Klein *WME|IMG*
9601 Wilshire Blvd
Beverly Hills, CA 90210-5213, USA

Stanhope, Doug (Comedian)
c/o Brian Hennigan *Theatre Corporation*
1204 N Curson Ave
West Hollywood, CA 90046-5429, USA

Stanhouse, Don (Athlete, Baseball Player)
4 Creekmere Dr
Roanoke, TX 76262-9755, USA

Stanicek, Pete (Athlete, Baseball Player)
525 Wilson St
Downers Grove, IL 60515-3845, USA

Stanicek, Steve (Athlete, Baseball Player)
16354 W Lanfear Dr
Lockport, IL 60441-4747, USA

Stanich, George (Athlete, Baseball Player, Beauty Pageant Winner, Olympic Athlete)
15816 Marigold Ave
Gardena, CA 90249-4837, USA

Stanifer, Rob (Athlete, Baseball Player)
10618 Park Place Dr
Largo, FL 33778-3402, USA

Stanis, Bernadette (Actor)
Sheba Media Group
11152 Westheimer Rd # 299
C/O Vanessa Morman
Houston, TX 77042-3208, USA

Stanka, Joe (Athlete, Baseball Player)
5734 Village Green Dr
Katy, TX 77493-1247, USA

Stankavage, Scott (Athlete, Football Player)
3843 Somerset Dr
Durham, NC 27707-5016, USA

Stankiewicz, Andy (Athlete, Baseball Player)
9729 Wren Bluff Dr
San Diego, CA 92127-3462, USA

Stankiewicz, Myron (Athlete, Hockey Player)
53 Tynedale Ave
London, ON N6H 5P6, Canada

Stankovic, Borislav (Boris) (Athlete, Basketball Player)
P.O. Box 7005
Munich D-81479, Germany

Stankowski, Paul (Athlete, Golfer)
4713 Rangewood Dr
Flower Mound, TX 75028-1695, USA

Stanler, John W (Misc)
Coutts & Co
440 Strand
London SC2R 0QS, UNITED KINGDOM (UK)

Stanley, Bob (Athlete, Baseball Player)
PO Box 1146
Stratham, NH 03885-1146, USA

Stanley, Chad (Athlete, Football Player)
17496 US Highway 69 S
Tyler, TX 75703-8094, USA

Stanley, Christopher (Actor)
c/o Dan Baron *Agency for the Performing Arts (APA)*
405 S Beverly Dr Ste 500
Beverly Hills, CA 90212-4425, USA

Stanley, Daryl (Athlete, Hockey Player)
PO Box 164
Balmoral, MB R0C 0H0, Canada

Stanley, Fred (Athlete, Baseball Player)
2109 Winthrop Hill Rd
Argyle, TX 76226-2103, USA

Stanley, Israel (Athlete, Football Player)
3850 S Miner St
Milwaukee, WI 53221-1250, USA

Stanley, James (Producer)
c/o Staff Member *United Talent Agency (UTA)*
9336 Civic Center Dr
Beverly Hills, CA 90210-3604, USA

Stanley, Marianne Crawford (Coach)
New York Liberty
2 Penn Plz Fl 15
Madison Square Garden
New York, NY 10121-1700, USA

Stanley, Mark (Actor)
c/o Staff Member *Tavistock Wood Management*
45 Conduit St
London W1S 2YN, UNITED KINGDOM

Stanley, Marlanne Crawford (Basketball Player, Coach)
Washington Mystics
601 F St NW
Mcl Center
Washington, DC 20004-1605, USA

Stanley, Mickey (Athlete, Baseball Player)
6370 Cunningham Lake Rd
Brighton, MI 48116-5222, Brighton

Stanley, Mike (Athlete, Baseball Player)
7900 NW 6th St
Plantation, FL 33324-1405, USA

Stanley, Paul (Musician)
c/o Doc McGhee *McGhee Entertainment*
8730 W Sunset Blvd Ste 175
Los Angeles, CA 90069-2246, USA

Stanley, Richard (Athlete, Football Player)
4248 S FM 2869
Hawkins, TX 75765-5300, USA

Stanley, Sadie (Actor)
c/o Ruth Bernstein *Viewpoint Inc*
8820 Wilshire Blvd Ste 220
Beverly Hills, CA 90211-2622, USA

Stanley, Scott M (Writer)
University of Denver
2199 S University Blvd
Denver, CO 80210-4700, USA

Stanley, Steven M (Misc)
4308 Folly Quarter Rd
Ellicott City, MD 21042-1424, USA

Stanley, Walter (Athlete, Football Player)
23977 E Alamo Pl
Aurora, CO 80016-4247, USA

Stansberry, Craig (Athlete, Baseball Player)
804 S Coppell Rd
Coppell, TX 75019-4513, U S A

Stansbury, Terrace (Athlete, Basketball Player)
901 N Franklin St # 2
Wilmington, DE 19806-4529, USA

Stansfield, Lisa (Music Group, Musician, Songwriter, Writer)
PO Box 59
Ashwell
Herts SG7 5NG, UNITED KINGDOM (UK)

Stanton, Andrew (Animator, Director)
c/o Staff Member *Pixar Animation Studios*
1200 Park Ave
Emeryville, CA 94608-3677, USA

Stanton, Drew (Athlete, Football Player)
c/o Mark Bartelstein *Priority Sports & Entertainment (Chicago)*
325 N La Salle Dr Ste 650
Chicago, IL 60654-8182, USA

Stanton, Frank N (Misc)
25 W 52nd St
New York, NY 10019-6104, USA

Stanton, Giancarlo (Athlete, Baseball Player)
c/o Joel Wolfe *Wasserman Media Group*
10960 Wilshire Blvd Ste 1200
Los Angeles, CA 90024-3714, USA

Stanton, Jeff (Race Car Driver)
1137 Athens Rd
Sherwood, MI 49089-9721, USA

Stanton, Leroy (Athlete, Baseball Player)
1751 N Norwood Ln
Florence, SC 29506-6901, U S A

Stanton, Mike (Athlete, Baseball Player)
3801 E Van Buren St
Phoenix, AZ 98282-7090, USA

Stanton, Molly (Actor)
c/o Rick Kurtzman *Creative Artists Agency (CAA)*
2000 Avenue of the Stars Ste 100
Los Angeles, CA 90067-4705, USA

Stanton, Paul (Athlete, Hockey Player)
2150 Sheepshead Dr
Naples, FL 34102-1506, USA

Stapf, David (Business Person)
c/o Staff Member *CBS Paramount Network Television*
4024 Radford Ave
Cbs Studios
Studio City, CA 91604-2190, USA

Stapinski, Helene (Writer)
Saint Martin's Press
175 5th Ave Ste 400
New York, NY 10010-7848, USA

Staples, Karissa Lee (Actor)
c/o John Griffin *Agency for the Performing Arts (APA)*
405 S Beverly Dr Ste 500
Beverly Hills, CA 90212-4425, USA

Staples, Mavis (Music Group, Musician)
10960 Wilshire Blvd Fl 5
Los Angeles, CA 90024-3708, USA

Staples, Vince (Musician)
c/o Julie Colbert *WME|IMG*
9601 Wilshire Blvd
Beverly Hills, CA 90210-5213, USA

Stapleton, Chris (Musician)
c/o Jay Williams *WME (Nashville)*
1201 Demonbreun St
Nashville, TN 37203-3140, USA

Stapleton, Dave (Athlete, Baseball Player)
51 N Bayview St
Fairhope, AL 36532-2537, USA

Stapleton, Dave (Athlete, Baseball Player)
418 S Galaxy Dr
Chandler, AZ 85226-4644

Stapleton, Jacinta (Actor)
c/o Stacey Testro *Stacey Testro International*
8265 W Sunset Blvd Ste 102
West Hollywood, CA 90046-2433, USA

Stapleton, Kevin (Actor)
Gersh Agency
232 N Canon Dr
Beverly Hills, CA 90210-5302, USA

Stapleton, Mike (Athlete, Hockey Player)
PO Box 1896
Sault Sainte Marie, MI 49783-7896, USA

Stapleton, Pat (Athlete, Hockey Player)
623 Saulsbury St
Strathroy, ON N7G 3R4, Canada

Stapleton, Sullivan (Actor)
c/o Lindsay Galin *Rogers & Cowan*
909 3rd Ave Fl 9
New York, NY 10022-4752, USA

Stapp, Scott (Musician)
c/o John Branigan *WME|IMG*
9601 Wilshire Blvd
Beverly Hills, CA 90210-5213, USA

Star, Darren (Producer, Writer)
c/o Staff Member *Darren Star Productions*
9200 W Sunset Blvd Ste 430
Los Angeles, CA 90069-3506, USA

Star, Jeffree (Internet Star)
c/o Ash Avildsen *Sumerian Entertainment*
2811 Cahuenga Blvd W
Los Angeles, CA 90068-2106, USA

Star, Marilyn (Adult Film Star)
1521 Alton Rd # 369
Miami Beach, FL 33139-3301, USA

Star, Ryan (Musician)
c/o Dave Klein *Creative Artists Agency (CAA)*
2000 Avenue of the Stars Ste 100
Los Angeles, CA 90067-4705, USA

Starbird, Kate (Basketball Player)
Indiana Fever
125 S Pennsylvania St
Conseco Fieldhouse
Indianapolis, IN 46204-3610, USA

Starbuck, Jo Jo (Athlete, Figure Skater, Olympic Athlete)
33 Pomeroy Rd
Madison, NJ 07940-2638, USA

Starch, Ken (Athlete, Football Player)
603 E Hillcrest Dr
Verona, WI 53593-1517, USA

Starck, Philippe (Designer)
3 Rue Faisans
Shiltigheim 67300, FRANCE

Stargell, Tony (Athlete, Football Player)
131 Jenny Rd
Grantville, GA 30220-2134, USA

Starikov, Sergei (Athlete, Hockey Player)
209 Greenbrook Rd
Green Brook, NJ 08812-2205, USA

Stark, Chad (Athlete, Football Player)
3316 46th Ave S
Fargo, ND 58104-6655, USA

Stark, Collin (Actor)
c/o Peter Himberger *Impact Artists Group LLC*
42 Hamilton Ter
New York, NY 10031-6403, USA

Stark, Dennis (Athlete, Baseball Player)
213 N Elm St
Edgerton, OH 43517-9672, USA

Stark, Don (Actor)
c/o Richard Kerner *Kerner Management Associates*
311 N Robertson Blvd # 288
Beverly Hills, CA 90211-1705, USA

Stark, Graham (Actor)
International Creative Mgmt
76 Oxford St
London W1N 0AX, UNITED KINGDOM (UK)

Stark, Koo (Actor)
Rebecca Blond
52 Shaftesbury Ave
London W1V 7DE, UNITED KINGDOM (UK)

Stark, Matt (Athlete, Baseball Player)
721 Shirehampton Dr
Las Vegas, NV 89178-1233, USA

Stark, Melissa (Correspondent, Sportscaster)
NBC-TV
30 Rockefeller Plz
News Dept
New York, NY 10112-0015, USA

Stark, Rohn T (Athlete, Football Player)
PO Box 10067
Lahaina, HI 96761-0067, USA

Starke, Anthony (Actor)
c/o Staff Member *Paradigm*
8942 Wilshire Blvd
Beverly Hills, CA 90211-1908, USA

Starkey, Jason (Athlete, Football Player)
1525 Washington Ave # 1
Huntington, WV 25704-1520, USA

Starks, Duane (Athlete, Football Player)
811 NW 199th St
Miami, FL 33169-2847, USA

Starks, James (Athlete, Football Player)
c/o Dave Butz *Sportstars Inc*
1370 Avenue of the Americas Fl 19
New York, NY 10019-4602, USA

Starks, John (Athlete, Basketball Player)
PO Box 8146
Stamford, CT 06905-8146, USA

Starks, Max (Athlete, Football Player)
c/o Ashley Smith Becker *Relativity Sports*
2029 Century Park E Ste 1550
Century City, CA 90067-3000, USA

Starks, Randy (Athlete, Football Player)
c/o Tony Paige *Dream Point Sports*
1455 Pennsylvania Ave NW Ste 225
Washington, DC 20004-1026, USA

Starner, Shelby (Music Group, Musician)
Morebam Music
30 Hillcrest Ave
Morristown, NJ 07960-5090, USA

Starnes, John G (Athlete, Football Player)
8826 Shade Tree
San Antonio, TX 78254-6821, USA

Staroba, Paul (Athlete, Football Player)
9235 McWain Rd
Grand Blanc, MI 48439-8006, USA

Starr, Antony (Actor)
c/o Grahame Dunster *Auckland Actors*
PO Box 56-460
Dominion Road
Auckland 00003, NEW ZEALAND

Starr, Bart (Athlete, Football Coach, Football Player)
Healthcare Realty Services
2647 Rocky Ridge Ln
Vestavia Hills, AL 35216-4809, USA

Starr, Beau (Actor)
c/o Geneva Bray *GVA Talent Agency Inc*
193 N Robertson Blvd
Beverly Hills, CA 90211-2103, USA

Starr, Brenda K (Music Group, Musician)
Brothers Mgmt
141 Dunbar Ave
Fords, NJ 08863-1551, USA

Starr, David (Race Car Driver)
Boys Will Be Boys Racing
610 Performance Rd
Mooresville, NC 28115-9595, USA

Starr, Dick (Athlete, Baseball Player)
660 Woodward Ave
Kittanning, PA 16201-1220, USA

Starr, Fredro (Actor, Artist, Musician)
c/o Keith Brown *KBiz Entertainment*
6938 Laurel Canyon Blvd Unit 214
North Hollywood, CA 91605-6850, USA

Starr, Garrison (Musician)
c/o Staff Member *MCT Management*
520 8th Ave Rm 2205
New York, NY 10018-4160, USA

Starr, Keith (Athlete, Basketball Player)
1S83 Graystone Canyon Ave
Las Vegas, NV 89183-6309, USA

Starr, Ken (Judge)
Pepperdine Law School
24255 Pacific Coast Hwy # 3418
Malibu, CA 90263-3999, USA

Starr, Leonard (Cartoonist)
Tribune Media Services
319 Bayberry Ln
Westport, CT 06880-1314, USA

Starr, Martin (Actor)
c/o Ben Feigin *Anonymous Content*
3532 Hayden Ave
Culver City, CA 90232-2413, USA

Starr, Paul E (Misc)
Princeton University
Sociology Dept
Green Hall
Princeton, NJ 08544-0001, USA

Starr, Randy (Music Group, Musician, Songwriter, Writer)
DDS
230 Park Ave
New York, NY 10169-0005, USA

Starr, Ringo (Actor, Musician)
918 N Hillcrest Rd
Beverly Hills, CA 90210-2611, USA

Starr, Steve (Journalist, Photographer)
720 Arcadia Place
720 Arcadia Pl
Colorado Springs, CO 80903-2813, USA

Starr, Tyler (Athlete, Football Player)

Starrette, Herm (Athlete, Baseball Player)
103 Howard Pond Loop
Statesville, NC 28625-2280, USA

Starring, Stephen (Athlete, Football Player)
6120 W Tropicana Ave Ste A16
Las Vegas, NV 89103-4697, USA

Star Sailor (Musician)
c/o Staff Member *Solo Agency Ltd (UK)*
53-55 Fulham High St
Fl 2
London SW6 3JJ, UNITED KINGDOM

Starsailor (Music Group)
c/o Staff Member *Paradigm (Monterey)*
404 W Franklin St
Monterey, CA 93940-2303, USA

Start, Brix Smith (Musician, Television Host)
c/o Vivienne Clore *The Richard Stone Partnership*
3 De Walden Ct
85 New Cavendish Street
London W1W 6XD, UNITED KINGDOM

Starting Line (Music Group)
c/o Staff Member *Virgin Records (NY)*
150 5th Ave Fl 7
New York, NY 10011-4372, USA

Starzewski, Tomasz (Designer, Fashion Designer)
House of Tomasz Trarzewski
15-17 Pont St
London SW1X 9EH, UNITED KINGDOM (UK)

Stasey, Caitlin (Actor)
c/o Shelley Browning *Magnolia Entertainment*
9595 Wilshire Blvd Ste 601
Beverly Hills, CA 90212-2506, USA

Stashwick, Todd (Actor)
c/o Staff Member *Meghan Schumacher Management*
13351D Riverside Dr Ste 387
Sherman Oaks, CA 91423-2508, USA

Stasiuk, Vic (Athlete, Hockey Player)
7 Canyon Gdns W
Lethbridge, AB T1K 6V1, Canada

Stassforth, Bowen (Athlete, Olympic Athlete, Swimmer)
26203 Birchfield Ave
Rancho Palos Verdes, CA 90275-1719, USA

Stastny, Anton (Athlete, Hockey Player)
Rte De Broye 45
Prilly 01030, Switzerland

Stastny, Marian (Athlete, Hockey Player)
Club de Golf Marian Stastny
537 Rte Marie-Victorin
Levis, QC G7A 2X6, Canada

Stastny, Paul (Athlete, Hockey Player)
465 S Mason Rd
Saint Louis, MO 63141-8519, USA

Stastny, Peter (Athlete, Hockey Player)
465 S Mason Rd
Saint Louis, MO 63141-8519, USA

Stastny, Yan (Athlete, Hockey Player)
465 S Mason Rd
Saint Louis, MO 63141-8519, USA

Staszak, Ray (Athlete, Hockey Player)
8273 96th Ct S
Boynton Beach, FL 33472-4405, USA

Stata, Raymond S (Business Person)
Analog Devices Inc
1 Technology Way
Norwood, MA 02062-2666, USA

Staten, Vince (Writer)
9323 Loch Lea Ln
Louisville, KY 40291-1477, USA

Statham, Jason (Actor)
c/o Whitney Tancred *42West*
1840 Century Park E Ste 700
Los Angeles, CA 90067-2122, USA

Static, Wayne (Musician)
Andy Gould Mgmt
9100 Wilshire Blvd Ste 400W
Beverly Hills, CA 90212-3464, USA

Statler Brothers (Music Group)
The Statler Brothers, LLC
PO Box 2703
Staunton, VA 24402-2703, USA

Staton, Aaron (Actor)
4437 Farmdale Ave
Studio City, CA 91602-2001, USA

Staton, Candi (Musician)
c/o Bill Carpenter *Capital Entertainment*
217 Seaton Pl NE
Washington, DC 20002-1528, USA

Staton, Dave (Athlete, Baseball Player)
2175 Arnold Dr
Rocklin, CA 95765-5901, USA

Staton, Joe (Athlete, Baseball Player)
2929 76th Ave SE Apt 201
Mercer Island, WA 98040-2715, USA

Staton, Leroy (Athlete, Baseball Player)
1751 N Norwood Ln
Florence, SC 29506-6901, USA

Staton, Mike (Athlete, Baseball Player)
19602 Indigo Lake Dr
Magnolia, TX 77355-3158, USA

Status Quo (Music Group, Musician)
c/o Simon Porter *Duroc Media Ltd.*
Riverside House
10-12 Victoria Road
Uxbridge, Middlesex UB8 2TW, UK

Staub, Danielle (Reality Star)
c/o Steve Honig *Honig Company, The*
4804 Laurel Canyon Blvd # 828
Studio City, CA 91607-3717, USA

Staubach, Roger (Athlete, Football Player, Heisman Trophy Winner)
5242 Ravine Dr
Dallas, TX 75220-2260, USA

Staubach, Scott (Athlete, Football Player)
6701 Miwok Ct
Bakersfield, CA 93309-3436, USA

Stauber, Liz (Actor)
c/o Sally Ware *Gersh*
41 Madison Ave Ste 3301
New York, NY 10010-2210, USA

Stauber, Robb (Athlete, Hockey Player)
Stauber's Goal Crease
7401A Washington AveS
Minneapolis, MN 55439, USA

Stauffer, Tim (Athlete, Baseball Player)
1502 Uno Verde Ct
Solana Beach, CA 92075-2129, USA

Stauffer, William A (Bill) (Athlete, Basketball Player)
913 Shoalcreek Pl
Wilmington, NC 28405-5211, USA

Staunton, Imelda (Actor)
P F D
Drury House
34-43 Russell St
London WC2B 5HA, UNITED KINGDOM (UK)

Staurovsky, Jason (Athlete, Football Player)
4822 E 87th Pl
Tulsa, OK 74137-2825, USA

Stause, Chrishell (Actor)
c/o Staff Member *Rooster Films*
5225 Wilshire Blvd Ste 406
Los Angeles, CA 90036-4348, USA

Stautberg, Gerald (Athlete, Football Player)
3200 Park Rd
Monkton, MD 21111, USA

Stavinoha, Nick (Athlete, Baseball Player)
30606 N Holly Oaks Cir
Magnolia, TX 77355-5733, USA

Stavropoulos, William S (Business Person)
Dow Chemical
2030 Dow Ctr
Midland, MI 48674-2030, USA

Staysniak, Joseph A (Joe) (Athlete, Football Player)
4094 Forest Dr
Brownsburg, IN 46112-8672, USA

St. Clair, Jessica (Actor)
c/o Christie Smith *Rise Management*
6338 Wilshire Blvd
Los Angeles, CA 90048-5002, USA

St Clair, Mike (Athlete, Football Player)
1606 Birchwood Ave
Cincinnati, OH 45224-2002, USA

St Claire, Randy (Athlete, Baseball Player)
7117 State Route 8
Brant Lake, NY 12815-2234, USA

StClaire, Randy (Athlete, Baseball Player)
7117 State Route 8
Brant Lake, NY 12815-2234, USA

St. Croix, Rick (Athlete, Hockey Player)
27 Brigantine Bay
Winnipeg, MB R3P 1R1, CANADA

Steadman, Alison (Actor)
P F D
Drury House
34-43 Russell St
London WC2B 5HA, UNITED KINGDOM (UK)

Steadman, Mark (Writer)
450 Pin Du Lac Dr
Central, SC 29630-9435, USA

Steadman, Ralph I (Cartoonist)
Old Loose Court
Loose Valley Maidstone
Kent ME15 9SE, UNITED KINGDOM (UK)

Steall, Ben (Horse Racer)
1 Harts Run Ct
Towson, MD 21286-1661, USA

Steamboat, Ricky (Athlete, Wrestler)
PO Box 7859
Stamford, CT 06905, USA

Stearns, Cheryl (Misc)
613 Saddlebred Ln
Raeford, NC 28376-5535, USA

Stearns, Cliff (Congressman, Politician)
2306 Rayburn Hob
Washington, DC 20515-3516, USA

Stearns, John (Athlete, Baseball Player)
Columbus Clippers 1155 W Mound St
Columbus, OH 34986-3405, USA

Stebbins, Richard (Athlete, Olympic Athlete, Track Athlete)
10675 Gramercy Pl Unit 317
Columbia, MD 21044-3027, USA

Stecher, Renate Meissner- (Athlete, Track Athlete)
Haydnstr 11
#526/38
Jena 07749, GERMANY

Stechschulte, Gene (Athlete, Baseball Player)
206 Wellington Pl
Findlay, OH 45840-8303, USA

Steckel, David (Athlete, Hockey Player)
1516 Jefferson St
West Bend, WI 53090-1343, USA

Steckel, Les (Athlete, Football Coach, Football Player)
9152 Saddlebow Dr
Brentwood, TN 37027-6028, USA

Steckler, Ray Dennis (Director)
2375 E Tropicana Ave
Las Vegas, NV 89119-6564, USA

Steding, Katy (Athlete, Basketball Player, Olympic Athlete)
21625 SW 100th Dr
Tualatin, OR 97062-8581, USA

Steed, Joel (Athlete, Football Player)
2639 Holly St
Denver, CO 80207-3229, USA

Steedle, Meg Chambers (Actor)
c/o Maria Candida *Shelter PR*
5670 Wilshire Blvd Ste 1200
Los Angeles, CA 90036-5621, USA

Steel, Amy (Actor)
c/o Stephany Hurkos *Stephany Hurkos Management*
5014 Whitsett Ave Unit 2
Valley Village, CA 91607-3078, USA

Steel, Danielle (Writer)
PO Box 470130
San Francisco, CA 94147-0130, USA

Steel, John (Musician)
Lustig Talent
PO Box 770850
Orlando, FL 32877-0850, USA

Steele, Alex (Actor)
c/o Laura Ackerman *Advantage PR*
3900 W Alameda Ave Ste 1200
Burbank, CA 91505-4317, USA

Steele, Allan (Actor)
c/o Staff Member *Baumgarten Management*
11925 Wilshire Blvd Ste 310
Los Angeles, CA 90025-6649, USA

Steele, Amanda (Internet Star)
c/o Staff Member *WME|IMG*
9601 Wilshire Blvd
Beverly Hills, CA 90210-5213, USA

Steele, Barbara (Actor)
2460 Benedict Canyon Dr
Beverly Hills, CA 90210-1433, USA

Steele, Brian (Actor)
c/o Joan Vento-Hall *Law Offices of Joan Vento-Hall, The*
10250 Constellation Blvd Fl 19
Los Angeles, CA 90067-6219, USA

Steele, Cassie (Actor)
c/o Staff Member *Noble Caplan Abrams*
1260 Yonge St Fl 2
Toronto, ON M4T 1W5, CANADA

Steele, Dave (Race Car Driver)
Team Sabco
114 Meadow Hill Cir
Mooresville, NC 28117-8089, USA

Steele, Glen (Athlete, Football Player)
303 E 5th St
Ligonier, IN 46767-2205, USA

Steele, Joshua (Flux Pavilion) (DJ, Producer)
c/o Staff Member *Atlantic Records*
1290 Avenue of the Americas Fl 28
New York, NY 10104-0106, USA

Steele, Joyce (Athlete, Baseball Player)
91 Hospital Dr
Towanda, PA 18848-9702, USA

Steele, Larry (Athlete, Basketball Player)
27448 NW Saint Helens Rd Slip 470
Slip 25
Scappoose, OR 97056-3233, USA

Steele, Michael (Musician)
Bangles Mall
1341 W Fullerton Ave # 180
Chicago, IL 60614-2362, USA

Steele, Michael (Politician)
Republican National Committee
310 1st St SE
Washington, DC 20003-1885, USA

Steele, Riley (Actor, Adult Film Star, Model)
c/o Staff Member *Media Artists Group*
8222 Melrose Ave Ste 304
Los Angeles, CA 90046-6839, USA

Steele, Robert (Football Player)
3045 S Pioneer Way
Las Vegas, NV 89117-3244, USA

Steele, Shelby (Writer)
San Jose State University
English Dept
San Jose, CA 95192-0001, USA

Steele, Tim (Race Car Driver)
24th Avenue
Marne, MI 49435, USA

Steele, Tommy (Actor, Musician)
IMG
Media House
3 Burlington Lane
London W4 2TH, UNITED KINGDOM (UK)

Steel Magnolia (Music Group, Musician)
c/o Staff Member *Big Machine Records*
1219 16th Ave S
Nashville, TN 37212-2901, USA

Steels, Jim (Athlete, Baseball Player)
1654 Via Rico
Santa Maria, CA 93454-2609, USA

Steely Dan (Music Group)
c/o Irving Azoff *Azoff Music Management*
1100 Glendon Ave Ste 2000
Los Angeles, CA 90024-3524, USA

Steen, Alexander (Athlete, Hockey Player)
Vagsnasvagen 166
Dornsji 892 92, SWEDEN

Steen, Anders (Athlete, Hockey Player)
Farjestadsvagen 85
Karlstad S-65465, Sweden

Steen, Jessica (Actor)
c/o Tim Angle *Shelter Entertainment*
9255 W Sunset Blvd Ste 300
Los Angeles, CA 90069-3313, USA

Steen, Thomas (Athlete, Hockey Player)
Winnipeg City Council
510 Main St
Winnipeg, MB R3B 1B9, Canada

Steenburgen, Mary (Actor)
c/o Samantha Hill *Wolf-Kasteler Public Relations*
6255 W Sunset Blvd Ste 1111
Los Angeles, CA 90028-7426, USA

Steenstra, Ken (Athlete, Baseball Player)
1228 Pheasant Ct
Liberty, MO 64068-8464, USA

Steenstra, Kennie (Athlete, Baseball Player)
1228 Pheasant Ct
Liberty, MO 64068-8464, USA

Steeples, Eddie (Actor)
c/o Staff Member *LRB Publicity*
2206 Rockefeller Ln Unit 1
Redondo Beach, CA 90278-3723, USA

Steere, Richard (Athlete, Football Player)
440 Independence Pkwy Apt 2314
Plano, TX 75075-8043, USA

Steers, Burr (Director)
c/o Shawn Simon *Anonymous Content*
3532 Hayden Ave
Culver City, CA 90232-2413, USA

Steevens, Morrie (Athlete, Baseball Player)
14465 Cadillac Dr
San Antonio, TX 78248-1001, USA

Stefan, Greg (Athlete, Hockey Player)
37648 Baywood Dr Unit 33
Farmington Hills, MI 48335-3604, USA

Stefan, Patrik (Athlete, Hockey Player)
620 W Frank St
Birmingham, MI 48009-1409, USA

Stefani, Gwen (Musician, Songwriter)
c/o Irving Azoff *Azoff Music Management*
1100 Glendon Ave Ste 2000
Los Angeles, CA 90024-3524, USA

Stefanik, MIke (Race Car Driver)
106 Pierremount Ave
New Britain, CT 06053-2345, USA

Stefanski, Bud (Athlete, Hockey Player)
RR 1
Buckhorn, ON K0L 1J0, Canada

Stefanson, Leslie (Actor)
c/o Andy Cohen *Gersh*
9465 Wilshire Blvd Ste 600
Beverly Hills, CA 90212-2605, USA

Stefanyshyn-Piper, Heidemarie (Astronaut)

Stefero, John (Athlete, Baseball Player)
6239 Chestnut Oak Ln
Linthicum Heights, MD 21090-2148, USA

Steffen, Dave (Baseball Player)
30531 Maple View Ln
Flat Rock, MI 48134-2744, USA

Steffen, Jim (Athlete, Football Player)
1440 Westway
Arnold, MD 21012-2428, USA

Steffes, Kent (Athlete, Volleyball Player)
14675 Titus St
Panorama City, CA 91402-4922, USA

Stefy (Music Group)
Wind-up Records
72 Madison Ave Fl 8
New York, NY 10016-8731, USA

Stegall, Keith (Musician)
c/o Staff Member *Sony Music Nashville*
8 Music Sq W
Nashville, TN 37203-3204, USA

Stegall, Milt (Athlete, Football Player)
466 Sumer Ln N
Douglasville, GA 30134-4459, USA

Stegent, Larry (Athlete, Football Player)
1177 West Loop S Ste 525
Houston, TX 77027-9049, USA

Steger, Michael (Actor)
c/o Greg Mehlman *SMS Talent*
8383 Wilshire Blvd Ste 230
Beverly Hills, CA 90211-2436, USA

Steger, Will (Misc)
International Arctic Project
990 3rd St E
Saint Paul, MN 55106-5243, USA

Stegman, Dave (Athlete, Baseball Player)
3234 Simmons Dr
Grove City, OH 43123-1835, USA

Stegman, Millie (Actor)
c/o Staff Member *Telefe (Argentina)*
Pavon 2444
Buenos Aires C1248AAT, ARGENTINA

Stehlin, Savannah (Actor)
c/o Sharon Lane *Lane Management Group*
4370 Tujunga Ave Ste 130
Studio City, CA 91604-2769, USA

Stein, Ben (Actor, Comedian, Producer, Writer)
c/o Staff Member *Innovative Artists*
1505 10th St
Santa Monica, CA 90401-2805, USA

Stein, Bill (Athlete, Baseball Player)
13713 Tajamar St
Corpus Christi, TX 78418-6056, USA

Stein, Blake (Athlete, Baseball Player)
115 Formosa Dr
Brandon, MS 39047-7912, USA

Stein, Bob (Basketball Player, Misc)
Minnesota Timberwolves
600 1st Ave N
Target Center
Minneapolis, MN 55403-1400, USA

Stein, Chris (Musician)
Shore Fire Media
32 Court St Ste 1600
Brooklyn, NY 11201-4441, USA

Stein, Garth (Writer)
c/o Staff Member *HarperCollins Publishers*
195 Broadway Fl 2
New York, NY 10007-3132, USA

Stein, Gilbert (Gil) (Athlete, Hockey Player)
650 5th Ave Ste 3300
New York, NY 10019-6108, USA

Stein, Irving (Writer)
8708 Ridgeway Ave
Skokie, IL 60076-2214, USA

Stein, James (Business Person)
Fluor Corp
3353 Michelson Dr
Irvine, CA 92612-7622, USA

Stein, Jill (Politician)
PO Box 260197
Madison, WI 53726-0197, USA

Stein, Joel (Writer)
c/o Roger Green *WME/IMG*
9601 Wilshire Blvd Ste 240
Beverly Hills, CA 90210-5205, USA

Stein, Mark (Music Group, Musician)
Future Vision
280 Riverside Dr Apt 12L
New York, NY 10025-9032, USA

Steinauer, Orlondo (Athlete, Football Player)
2378 Highcroft Rd
Oakville, ON L6M 4Y6, Canada

Steinbach, Alice (Journalist)
Baltimore Sun
501 N Calvert St
Editorial Dept
Baltimore, MD 21278-1000, USA

Steinbach, Terry (Athlete, Baseball Player)
PO Box 181
Terry Steinbach Scholarship Fund
Hamel, MN 55340-0181, USA

Steinberg, K.J. (Actor)
c/o Ari Greenburg *WME/IMG*
9601 Wilshire Blvd
Beverly Hills, CA 90210-5213, USA

Steinberg, Paul (Cartoonist)
New Yorker Magazine
4 Times Sq
Editorial Dept
New York, NY 10036-6518, USA

Steinbrenner, Hal (Baseball Player)
4926 Andros Dr
Tampa, FL 33629-4802, USA

Steinbrenner, Hank (Baseball Player)
402 Saint Andrews Dr
Belleair, FL 33756-1935, USA

Steindorff, Scott (Producer)
c/o Staff Member *Stone Village Entertainment*
1925 Century Park E Ste 420
Los Angeles, CA 90067-1758, USA

Steinel, Laura (Actor)
c/o Staff Member *Artists First*
9465 Wilshire Blvd Ste 900
Beverly Hills, CA 90212-2608, USA

Steinem, Gloria (Journalist, Writer)
118 E 73rd St
New York, NY 10021-4238, USA

Steiner, Andre (Athlete)
Bismarckstr 4
Berlin 14109, GERMANY

Steiner, Charley (Commentator, Sportscaster)
767 S Bundy Dr
Los Angeles, CA 90049-5216, USA

Steiner, George (Writer)
32 Barrow Road
Cambridge, UNITED KINGDOM (UK)

Steiner, Mel (Baseball Player)
11296 Linda Way
Los Alamitos, CA 90720-3918, USA

Steiner, Paul (Cartoonist)
Washington Times
3600 New York Ave NE
Washington, DC 20002-1996, USA

Steiner, Peter (Cartoonist)
New Yorker Magazine
4 Times Sq
Editorial Dept
New York, NY 10036-6518, USA

Steiner, Rebel (Athlete, Football Player)
112 Aaronvale Cir
Birmingham, AL 35242-7353, USA

Steiner, Reed (Producer)
c/o Staff Member *WME/IMG*
9601 Wilshire Blvd
Beverly Hills, CA 90210-5213, USA

Steines, Mark (Television Host)

Steinfeld, Hailee (Actor)
c/o Doug Wald *Anonymous Content*
3532 Hayden Ave
Culver City, CA 90232-2413, USA

Steinfeld, Jake (Actor, Athlete, Fitness Expert)
622 Toyopa Dr
Pacific Palisades, CA 90272-4471, USA

Steinfort, Fred (Athlete, Football Player)
PO Box 24981
Denver, CO 80224-0981, USA

Steinhardt, Arnold (Musician)
Herbert Barrett
266 W 37th St # 2000
New York, NY 10018-6609, USA

Steinhauer, Sherri (Golfer)
5010 Hammersley Rd
Madison, WI 53711-2616, USA

Steinkraus, William (Athlete, Olympic Athlete)
PO B40 Great Is
Darien, CT 06820, USA

Steinkuhler, Dean (Athlete, Football Player)
PO Box 247
Syracuse, NE 68446-0247, USA

Steinman, Jim (Songwriter, Writer)
DAS Communications
83 Riverside Dr
New York, NY 10024-5713, USA

Steinmetz, Richard (Actor)
c/o Staff Member *Personal Management Company*
425 N Robertson Blvd
West Hollywood, CA 90048-1735, USA

Steinsaltz, Adin (Religious Leader)
Israel Talmudic Publications Institute
PO Box 1458
Jerusalem, ISRAEL

Steinseifer Bates, Carrie (Swimmer)
9309 Benzon Dr
Pleasanton, CA 94588-4767, USA

Steirer, Ricky (Athlete, Baseball Player)
1015 Haverhill Rd
Baltimore, MD 21229-5115, USA

Stela, Annie (Musician)
c/o Staff Member *Paradigm (Monterey)*
404 W Franklin St
Monterey, CA 93940-2303, USA

Stella, Frank (Artist)
17 Jones St
New York, NY 10014-4131, USA

Stella, Lennon (Actor, Musician)
c/o Jeff Frasco *Creative Artists Agency (CAA)*
2000 Avenue of the Stars Ste 100
Los Angeles, CA 90067-4705, USA

Stella, Maisy (Actor)
c/o Jeff Frasco *Creative Artists Agency (CAA)*
2000 Avenue of the Stars Ste 100
Los Angeles, CA 90067-4705, USA

Stella, Martina (Actor)
c/o Daniela di Santo *Moviement*
Via P Cavallini 24
Rome 00193, ITALY

Stelmaszek, Rick (Athlete, Baseball Player)
2734 E 97th St
Chicago, IL 60617-4928, USA

Stelter, Brian (Commentator, Journalist, Television Host)
c/o Staff Member *CNN (NY)*
10 Columbus Cir
Time Warner Center
New York, NY 10019-1158, USA

Stember, Jeff (Athlete, Baseball Player)
9517 E Altadena Ave
Scottsdale, AZ 85260-5865, USA

Stemie, Steve (Athlete, Baseball Player)
4011 Weatherby Way
New Albany, IN 47150-9676, USA

Stemkowski, Peter (Athlete, Hockey Player)
146 Albany Blvd Apt 21C
Atlantic Beach, NY 11509-1207, USA

Stemle, Steve (Athlete, Baseball Player)
714 Academy Dr Apt 19
New Albany, IN 47150-3294, USA

Stempel, Herbert (Misc)
10510 66th Ave Apt 3G
Forest Hills, NY 11375-2103, USA

Stempniak, Lee (Athlete, Hockey Player)
4469 Clinton St
Buffalo, NY 14224-1700, USA

Stemrick, Greg (Athlete, Football Player)
1012 Matthews Dr
Cincinnati, OH 45215-1804, USA

Stenberg, Amandla (Actor)
c/o Brett Ruttenberg *Imprint PR*
6121 W Sunset Blvd
Neuehouse
Los Angeles, CA 90028-6442, USA

Stenders, Kriv (Director)
c/o Staff Member *HLA Management*
PO Box 1536
Strawberry Hills 02012, AUSTRALIA

Stenger, Brian (Athlete, Football Player)
7921 Kellogg Creek Dr
Mentor, OH 44060-7111, USA

Stenhouse, Dave (Athlete, Baseball Player)
20 Hayward St
Cranston, RI 02910-2701, USA

Stenhouse, Gavin (Actor)
c/o Joanne Horowitz *Joanne Horowitz Management*
928 N Beverly Dr
Beverly Hills, CA 90210-2913, USA

Stenhouse, Mike (Athlete, Baseball Player)
70 Woodbury Rd
Cranston, RI 02905-3317, USA

Stenko, Paul (Athlete, Football Player)
414 Martzville Rd
Berwick, PA 18603-5642, USA

Stenlund, Vern (Athlete, Hockey Player)
1220 Cabana Rd W
Windsor, ON N9G 1B7, Canada

Stenmark, Ingemar (Skier)
Residence l'Annonciade
17 Av de l'Anncenciade
Monte Carlo 98000, MONACO

Stennett, Rennie (Athlete, Baseball Player)
6519 Boticelli Dr
Lake Worth, FL 33467-7037, USA

Stensrud, Mike (Athlete, Football Player)
304 S Winnebago St
Lake Mills, IA 50450-1637, USA

Stenstrom, Steve (Athlete, Football Player)
1845 Bay Laurel Dr
Menlo Park, CA 94025-5833, USA

Stepanova, Maria (Basketball Player)
Phoenix Mercury
201 E Jefferson St
American West Arena
Phoenix, AZ 85004-2412, USA

Stephanapoulous, Constantinos (Politician)
President of the Hellenic Rej:>ublic
Athens, Greece

Stephanie (Royalty)
Maison Clos St Martin
Saint Remy de Provence, FRANCE

Stephanopolous, Constantine (Costis) (President)
Presidential Palace
7 Vas Georgiou B
Odos Zalokosta 10
Athens, GREECE

Stephanopoulos, George (Journalist, Politician)
c/o Staff Member *ABC News*
77 W 66th St Fl 3
New York, NY 10023-6201, USA

Stephanson, Ken (Athlete, Hockey Player)
6 Heron Road Box 1491
Gimli, MB ROC 1BO, Canada

Stephen, Buzz (Athlete, Baseball Player)
15512 Sycamore St
Porterville, CA 93257-2594, USA

Stephen, Scott (Athlete, Football Player)
4132 Palm Tree Ct
La Mesa, CA 91941-7238, USA

Stephen, Shamar (Athlete, Football Player)
c/o Alan Herman *Sportstars Inc*
1370 Avenue of the Americas Fl 19
New York, NY 10019-4602, USA

Stephens, Darryl (Actor)

Stephens, Everette (Athlete, Basketball Player)
4012 Campion St
Lafayette, IN 47909-8214, USA

Stephens, Gene (Athlete, Baseball Player)
6504 Circo Dr
Granbury, TX 76049-5261, USA

Stephens, Hal (Athlete, Football Player)
221 W Virginia St
Rocky Mount, NC 27804-4940, USA

Stephens, Jamain (Athlete, Football Player)
105 W 6th St
Tabor City, NC 28463-1633, USA

Stephens, Janaya (Actor)
c/o Penny Noble *Noble Caplan Abrams*
1260 Yonge St Fl 2
Toronto, ON M4T 1W5, CANADA

Stephens, John (Athlete, Baseball Player)
1325 Oak Point Ct
Venice, FL 34292-1635, USA

Stephens, John (Athlete, Football Player)
PO Box 496
Shreveport, LA 71162-0496, USA

Stephens, Laraine (Actor)
10800 Chalon Rd
Los Angeles, CA 90077-3220, USA

Stephens, Ray (Athlete, Baseball Player)
1065 Council Rd NE
Charleston, TN 37310-6232, USA

Stephens, Robert (Business Person)
Adaptec Inc
691 S Milpitas Blvd
Milpitas, CA 95035-5476, USA

Stephens, Santo (Athlete, Football Player)
1205 Winding Meadows Rd
Rockledge, FL 32955-8404, USA

Stephens, Sloane (Athlete, Tennis Player)
c/o John Tobias *TLA Worldwide (FL)*
1245 S Alhambra Cir
Coral Gables, FL 33146-3104, USA

Stephens, Stanley (Politician)
20 Claremont St Apt 1001
Kalispell, MT 59901-3664, USA

Stephens, Toby (Actor)
c/o Simon Halls *Slate PR*
901 N Highland Ave
W Hollywood, CA 90038-2412, USA

Stephens, Tom (Athlete, Football Player)
4186 27th Ct SW APT 102
Naples, FL 34116-0924, USA

Stephenson, Bob (Athlete, Hockey Player)
8 Tufts Cres
Outlook, SK SOL 2ND, Canada

Stephenson, Donald (Athlete, Football Player)

Stephenson, Dwight E (Athlete, Football Player)
4785 Tree Fern Dr
Delray Beach, FL 33445-7025, USA

Stephenson, Earl (Athlete, Baseball Player)
4043 Zacks Mill Rd
Angier, NC 27501-7185, USA

Stephenson, Garrett (Athlete, Baseball Player)
947 W State St
Eagle, ID 83616-4807, USA

Stephenson, John (Athlete, Baseball Player)
7 Mauroner Dr
Hammond, LA 70401-1728, USA

Stephenson, Kay (Athlete, Football Player)
310 Plantation Hill Rd
Gulf Breeze, FL 32561-4818, USA

Stephenson, Pamela (Actor, Writer)
c/o Gavin Barker *Gavin Barker Assoc*
2D Wimpole St
London W1G 0EB, UNITED KINGDOM

Stephenson, Phil (Athlete, Baseball Player)
1307 Hancock St
Dodge City, KS 67801-3451, USA

Steppe, Brook (Athlete, Basketball Player)
3486 Clare Cottage Trce SW
Marietta, GA 30008-6075, USA

Steptoe, Jack (Athlete, Football Player)
41615 Morningside Ct # B
Rancho Mirage, CA 92270-4133, USA

Steranko, Jim (Cartoonist)
PO Box 974
Reading, PA 19603-0974, USA

Sterban, Richard (Musician)
125 Bluegrass Cir
Hendersonville, TN 37075-2726, USA

Stereo MC's (Music Group)
c/o Staff Member *Paradigm (Monterey)*
404 W Franklin St
Monterey, CA 93940-2303, USA

Stereophonics (Music Group)
c/o Staff Member *Nettwerk Management (Canada)*
1850 W Second Ave
Vancouver BC V6J 4R3, CANADA

Sterger, Jenn (Model, Television Host)
PO Box 2642
Lutz, FL 33548-2642, USA

Sterkel, Jill (Athlete, Olympic Athlete, Swimmer)
2206 Heritage Well Ln
Pflugerville, TX 78660-2968, USA

Sterling, Ashleigh (Actor)
10 Silkleaf
Irvine, CA 92614-5404, USA

Sterling, Donald (Business Person)
9441 Wilshire Blvd
Beverly Hills, CA 90212-2808, USA

Sterling, John (Sportscaster)
808 Alexander Way
Edgewater, NJ 07020-2507, USA

Sterling, Mindy (Actor)
7307 Melrose Ave
Los Angeles, CA 90046-7512, USA

Sterling, Nici (Adult Film Star)
c/o Staff Member *Atlas Multimedia Inc*
9005 Eton Ave Ste C
Canoga Park, CA 91304-6533, USA

Sterling, Rachel (Actor)
c/o Darren Trattner *Jackoway Tyerman Wertheimer Austen Mandelbaum Morris & Klein*
1925 Century Park E Fl 22
Los Angeles, CA 90067-2701, USA

Sterling, Raheem (Athlete, Soccer Player)

Sterling, Randy (Athlete, Baseball Player)
2516 Linda Ave
Key West, FL 33040-5114, USA

Sterling, Tisha (Actor)
PO Box 788
Ketchum, ID 83340-0781, USA

Stern, Adam (Athlete, Baseball Player)
40 Summit Ave
London, ON N6H 4S3 Ca, USA

Stern, Andrew L (Misc)
Service Employees International Union
1313 L St NW
Washington, DC 20005-4110, USA

Stern, Beth Ostrosky (Activist, Actor)
c/o Evelyn Alexander Wildlife Rescue Center
228 W Montauk Hwy
Hampton Bays, NY 11946-3510, USA

Stern, Daniel (Actor, Director)
Lost Men Productions
10960 Wilshire Blvd Ste 700
Los Angeles, CA 90024-3710, USA

Stern, David J (Basketball Player, Misc)
National Basketball Assn
122 E 55th St
Olympic Tower
New York, NY 10022-4535, USA

Stern, Dawn (Actor)
c/o Staff Member *McCabe Group*
3211 Cahuenga Blvd W Ste 104
Los Angeles, CA 90068-1372, USA

Stern, Gardner (Producer, Writer)
c/o Dave Brown *Echo Lake Management*
421 S Beverly Dr Fl 8
Beverly Hills, CA 90212-4408, USA

Stern, Howard (Radio Personality, Talk Show Host)
Howard Stern Production Company
10 E 44th St
New York, NY 10017-3601, USA

Stern, Joseph (Actor, Producer)
c/o Chris Simonian *Creative Artists Agency (CAA)*
2000 Avenue of the Stars Ste 100
Los Angeles, CA 90067-4705, USA

Stern, Michael (Mike) (Musician)
Tropix International
163 3rd Ave # 206
New York, NY 10003-2523, USA

Stern, Shoshannah (Actor)
c/o Paul Young *MAKE GOOD Content*
1800 Century Park E Ste 1000
Los Angeles, CA 90067-1513, USA

Sternberg, Stuart (Baseball Player)
85 Bellevue Ave
Rye, NY 10580-1840, USA

Sternberg, Thomas (Business Person)
Staples Inc
PO Box 9265
Framingham, MA 01701-9265, USA

Sternecky, Neal (Cartoonist)
52 Bluebird Ln
Naperville, IL 60565-1347, USA

Sterner, Ulf (Athlete, Hockey Player)
Grava-Rud 761
Karlstad 655 9', Sweden

Sternhagen, Frances (Actor)
152 Sutton Manor Rd
New Rochelle, NY 10801-5756, USA

Stetter, Mitch (Athlete, Baseball Player)
3120 N Marigold Dr
Phoenix, AZ 85018-6741, USA

Steuert-Armstrong, Beverly (Athlete, Baseball Player)
211 Cathi Ln
Kernersville, NC 27284-9363, USA

Steussie, Todd E (Athlete, Football Player)
34535 Emigrant Trl
Shingletown, CA 96088-9342, USA

Steve, Rehage (Athlete, Football Player)
2632 Montana Ave
Metairie, LA 70003-5246, USA

Steve Miller Band (Music Group)
Sailor Music
14 E 60th St Ste 704
New York, NY 10022-7174, USA

Stevens, Amber (Actor)
c/o Robert Enriquez *Red Baron Management*
1600 Rosecrans Ave
Manhattan Beach, CA 90266-3708, USA

Stevens, Andrew (Actor)
Irv Schechter
9300 Wilshire Blvd Ste 410
Beverly Hills, CA 90212-3228, USA

Stevens, April (Music Group, Musician)
19530 Superior St
Northridge, CA 91324-1648, USA

Stevens, Bob (Producer)
c/o Staff Member *United Talent Agency (UTA)*
9336 Civic Center Dr
Beverly Hills, CA 90210-3604, USA

Stevens, Brad (Basketball Coach)
c/o Jordan Cerf *WME/IMG*
9601 Wilshire Blvd
Beverly Hills, CA 90210-5213, USA

Stevens, Brinke (Actor, Athlete)
PO Box 7112
Van Nuys, CA 91409-7112, USA

Stevens, Cat (Musician)
c/o Staff Member *WME/IMG (UK)*
103 New Oxford St WMA
Centrepoint
London WC1A 1DD, UNITED KINGDOM

Stevens, Connie (Actor, Musician)
c/o Kevin Sasaki *Kevin Sasaki Public Relations & Media Counsel*
8491 W Sunset Blvd Ste 224
Los Angeles, CA 90069-1911, USA

Stevens, Courtenay J (Actor)
c/o Caldwell Jeffery
943 Queen St E Fl E2ND
Toronto, ON M4M 1J6, CANADA

Stevens, Craig (Athlete, Football Player)
c/o Ken Zuckerman *Priority Sports & Entertainment - (LA)*
15233 Ventura Blvd Ste 718
Sherman Oaks, CA 91403-2237, USA

Stevens, Dan (Actor)
c/o Victoria Belfrage *Julian Belfrage & Associates*
9 Argyll St Fl 3
London W1F 7TG, UNITED KINGDOM

Stevens, Dave (Athlete, Baseball Player)
2630 Candlewood Way
La Habra, CA 90631-6203, USA

Stevens, Dirk (Race Car Driver)
PO Box 1197
Huntersville, NC 28070-1197, USA

Stevens, Dodie (Musician)
c/o Jim Wagner *American Management*
19948 Mayall St
Chatsworth, CA 91311-3522, USA

Stevens, Eric Sheffer (Actor)
c/o Philip Adelman *BRS / Gage Talent Agency (NY)*
1650 Broadway Ste 1410
New York, NY 10019-6957, USA

Stevens, Fisher (Actor)
c/o Staff Member *Insurgent Media*
247 Centre St Fl 7
New York, NY 10013-3216, USA

Stevens, Gary (Horse Racer)
1308 Isleworth Dr
Louisville, KY 40245-5252, USA

Stevens, George Jr (Producer)
New Liberty Productions
John F Kennedy Center
Washington, DC 20566-0001, USA

Stevens, Howard (Athlete, Football Player)
834 Saint Catherines Dr
Wake Forest, NC 27587-6639, USA

Stevens, Jeremy (Actor, Producer, Writer)
c/o Staff Member *WME|IMG*
9601 Wilshire Blvd
Beverly Hills, CA 90210-5213, USA

Stevens, Jerramy (Athlete, Football Player)
10047 Main St Apt 515
Bellevue, WA 98004-5319, USA

Stevens, John (Athlete, Hockey Player)
Los Angeles Kings
1111 S Figueroa St Ste 3100
Attn Coaching Staff
Los Angeles, CA 90015-1333, USA

Stevens, John Paul (Attorney)
US Supreme Court
United States Supreme Court 11th St NE
Washington, DC 20543-0001, USA

Stevens, Katie (Musician)
c/o Simon Fuller *XIX Entertainment (UK)*
32/33 Ransomes Dock
London SW11 4NP, UNITED KINGDOM (UK)

Stevens, Kevin (Athlete, Hockey Player, Olympic Athlete)
70 Onion Hill Rd
Duxbury, MA 02332-3808, USA

Stevens, Lee (Athlete, Baseball Player)
9157 Buck Hill Dr
Highlands Ranch, CO 80126-5042, USA

Stevens, Michael (Internet Star)
c/o Avi Ghandi *WME|IMG*
9601 Wilshire Blvd
Beverly Hills, CA 90210-5213, USA

Stevens, Rachel (Actor, Musician)
c/o Staff Member *Artists Rights Group (ARG)*
4A Exmoor St
London W10 6BD, UNITED KINGDOM

Stevens, Ray (Musician, Songwriter)
4412 Chickering Ln
Nashville, TN 37215-4915, USA

Stevens, Richard (Athlete, Football Player)
4100 Cimmaron Trl
Granbury, TX 76049-5252, USA

Stevens, Richie (Race Car Driver)
Richie Stevens Fan Club
9600 Chef Menteur Hwy
New Orleans, LA 70127-4234, USA

Stevens, Robert J (Business Person)
Lockheed Martin Corp
6801 Rockledge Dr
Bethesda, MD 20817-1877, USA

Stevens, Rogers (Musician)
Shapiro Co
10990 Wilshire Blvd Fl 8
Los Angeles, CA 90024-3918, USA

Stevens, Ronnie (Actor)
Caroline Dawson
125 Gloucester Road
London SW7 4IE, UNITED KINGDOM (UK)

Stevens, Scott (Athlete, Hockey Player)
New Jersey Devils
165 Mulberry St
Attn Special Assignment Coach
Newark, NJ 07102-3607, USA

Stevens, Scott (Athlete, Hockey Player)
280 Spook Hollow Rd
Far Hills, NJ 07931-2707, USA

Stevens, Shadoe (Radio Personality)
2934 N Beverly Glen Cir # 399
Los Angeles, CA 90077-1724, USA

Stevens, Shakin' (Music Group, Musician)
c/o Ed Stringfellow *UTA Music/The Agency Group (UK)*
361-373 City Rd
London EC1V 1PQ, UNITED KINGDOM

Stevens, Shakin (Musician)
c/o Ed Stringfellow *UTA Music/The Agency Group (UK)*
361-373 City Rd
London EC1V 1PQ, UNITED KINGDOM

Stevens, Stella (Actor, Model)
5328 Alhama Dr
Woodland Hls, CA 91364-2013, USA

Stevens, Steve (Musician)

Stevens, Steven (Actor)
Stevens Group
3518 Cahuenga Blvd W
Los Angeles, CA 90068-1304, USA

Stevens, Sufjan (Musician)
c/o Phyllis Belezos *International Talent Booking*
9 Kingsway
Fl 6
London WC2B 6XF, UNITED KINGDOM

Stevens, Tony (Musician)
Lustig Talent
PO Box 770850
Orlando, FL 32877-0850, USA

Stevens, William S (Athlete, Football Player)
PO Box 221320
El Paso, TX 79913-4320, USA

Stevenson, Cynthia (Actor)
c/o Kelly Garner *Pop Art Management*
PO Box 55363
Sherman Oaks, CA 91413-0363, USA

Stevenson, DeShawn (Basketball Player)
Utah Jazz
1348 Lake Whitney Dr
301 W South Temple
Windermere, FL 34786-6072, USA

Stevenson, Jeremy (Athlete, Hockey Player)
7899 W 6 Mile Rd
Brimley, MI 49715-9281, USA

Stevenson, Juliet (Actor)
c/o Staff Member *Markham & Froggatt*
4 Windmill St
London W1T 1HZ, UNITED KINGDOM

Stevenson, Parker (Actor)
c/o Laina Cohn *Cohn / Torgan Management*
Prefers to be contacted by telephone or email
Los Angeles, CA, USA

Stevenson, Ray (Actor)
c/o Liz Nelson *Conway van Gelder Grant*
8-12 Broadwick St
London W1F 8HW, UNITED KINGDOM

Stevenson, Shayne (Athlete, Hockey Player)
33 Glendower Cres
Keswick, ON L4P 0A5, Canada

Stevenson, Turner (Athlete, Hockey Player)
5623 245th Ave NE
Redmond, WA 98053-2566, USA

Stevenson, Venetia (Actor)
3150 Howell Mill Rd NW
Atlanta, GA 30327-2108, USA

Steve-O (Actor, Comedian, Reality Star)
c/o Mike Liotta *True Public Relations*
3575 Cahuenga Blvd W Ste 360
Los Angeles, CA 90068-1361, USA

Steverson, Todd (Athlete, Baseball Player)
109 W Glenhaven Dr
Phoenix, AZ 85045-0717, USA

Steves, Rick (Television Host, Writer)
Rick Stevess Europe Inc
130 4th Ave N
Edmonds, WA 98020-3114, USA

Stewart, Al (Music Group, Musician, Songwriter, Writer)
Chapman & Co
14011 Ventura Blvd Ste 405
Sherman Oaks, CA 91423-5230, USA

Stewart, Alana (Actor)
c/o Arnold Robinson *Rogers & Cowan*
1840 Century Park E Fl 18
Los Angeles, CA 90067-2101, USA

Stewart, Amy (Actor)
c/o Lisa DiSante-Frank *DiSante Frank & Company*
10061 Riverside Dr Ste 377
Toluca Lake, CA 91602-2560, USA

Stewart, Andy (Athlete, Baseball Player)
641 Geddes St
Wilmington, DE 19805-3718, USA

Stewart, Bill (Musician)
Blue Note Records
6920 W Sunset Blvd
Los Angeles, CA 90028-7010, USA

Stewart, Bill (Athlete, Baseball Player)
44842 Aspen Ridge Dr
Northville, MI 48168-4435, USA

Stewart, Bill (Athlete, Hockey Player)
7175 McColl Dr
Niagara Falls, ON L2J 1G7, Canada

Stewart, Blair (Athlete, Hockey Player)
1604 Cottenham Ln
Virginia Beach, VA 23454-6406, USA

Stewart, Boo Boo (Actor)
c/o Staff Member *Osbrink Talent Agency*
4343 Lankershim Blvd # 100
North Hollywood, CA 91602-2705, USA

Stewart, BooBoo (Actor)
c/o Siri Garber *Platform PR*
2666 N Beachwood Dr
Los Angeles, CA 90068-2308, USA

Stewart, Cam (Athlete, Hockey Player)
2929 Buffalo Speedway Unit 218
Houston, TX 77098-1719, USA

Stewart, Cameron Deane (Actor)
c/o Pamela Fisher *Abrams Artists Agency*
750 N San Vicente Blvd
E Tower Fl 11
Los Angeles, CA 90069-5788, USA

Stewart, Catherine Mary (Actor)
c/o Philip Adelman *BRS / Gage Talent Agency (NY)*
1650 Broadway Ste 1410
New York, NY 10019-6957, USA

Stewart, Danica (Actor)
c/o Terrance Hines *Hines and Hunt Entertainment*
1213 W Magnolia Blvd
Burbank, CA 91506-1829, USA

Stewart, Darian (Athlete, Football Player)
c/o Dave Butz *Sportstars Inc*
1370 Avenue of the Americas Fl 19
New York, NY 10019-4602, USA

Stewart, Dave (Composer, Musician, Producer)
c/o Allison Elbl *ID Public Relations*
7060 Hollywood Blvd Fl 8th
Los Angeles, CA 90028-6021, USA

Stewart, Dave (Athlete, Baseball Player)
17762 Vineyard Ln
Poway, CA 92064-1061, USA

Stewart, David K (Dave) (Baseball Player)
Los Angeles Dodgers
17762 Vineyard Ln
Poway, CA 92064-1061, USA

Stewart, Fivel (Actor)
c/o Matt Jackson *Rebel Entertainment Partners*
5700 Wilshire Blvd Ste 470
Los Angeles, CA 90036-4379, USA

Stewart, French (Actor)
c/o JC Robbins *JC Robbins Management*
865 S Sherbourne Dr
Los Angeles, CA 90035-1809, USA

Stewart, Jackie (Race Car Driver)
The British Racing Drivers Club
24 Rte. de Divonne
Nyon 01260, SWITZERLAND

Stewart, James B (Journalist)
Wall Street Journal
200 Liberty St
Editorial Dept
New York, NY 10281-1003, USA

Stewart, Jim (Athlete, Hockey Player)
57 Lincoln St
Spencer, MA 01562-1623, USA

Stewart, Jimmy (Athlete, Baseball Player)
15644 Eastbourn Dr
Odessa, FL 33556-2850, USA

Stewart, John (Athlete, Hockey Player)
1085 Southlake Cv
Hoover, AL 35244-3283, USA

Stewart, John A (Athlete, Hockey Player)
16424 Grenwich Ter
Eden Prairie, MN 55346-1421, USA

Stewart, Jon (Actor, Comedian, Television Host)
c/o Staff Member *Busboy Productions*
375 Greenwich St
New York, NY 10013-2376, USA

Stewart, Jonathan (Athlete, Football Player)
c/o Ben Dogra *Relativity Sports*
2029 Century Park E Ste 1550
Century City, CA 90067-3000, USA

Stewart, Josh (Actor)
c/o Marcel Pariseau *True Public Relations*
3575 Cahuenga Blvd W Ste 360
Los Angeles, CA 90068-1361, USA

Stewart, Josh (Athlete, Baseball Player)
182 Stewart Ln
Ledbetter, KY 42058-9549, USA

Stewart, Kimberly (Actor, Model, Reality Star)
c/o Kenya Knight *Nous Model Management*
117 N Robertson Blvd
Los Angeles, CA 90048-3101, USA

Stewart, Kordell (Athlete, Football Player)
2045 Caladium Way
Roswell, GA 30075-2401, USA

Stewart, Kristen (Actor)
c/o Ruth Bernstein *Viewpoint Inc*
8820 Wilshire Blvd Ste 220
Beverly Hills, CA 90211-2622, USA

Stewart, lan (Athlete, Baseball Player)
12 Ocaso Dr
Asheville, NC 28806-8202, USA

Stewart, Lisa (Actor, Producer)
c/o Staff Member *Vinyl Films*
5555 Melrose Ave
Los Angeles, CA 90038-3989, USA

Stewart, Lisa (Musician)
1344 Lexington Ave
Friedman & Larosa
New York, NY 10128-1507, USA

Stewart, Martha (Business Person, Television Host)
Martha Stewart Living Omnimedia
601 W 26th St Rm 900
New York, NY 10001-1143, USA

Stewart, Maxine (Actor)
180 Comanche
Topanga, CA 90290-4426, USA

Stewart, Mel (Athlete, Olympic Athlete, Swimmer)
7308 Seneca Falls Loop
Austin, TX 78739-2216, USA

Stewart, Melvin Jr (Swimmer)
c/o Scott Karp *The Syndicate*
10203 Santa Monica Blvd Fl 5
Los Angeles, CA 90067-6416, USA

Stewart, Michael (Athlete, Football Player)
717 Palo Verde St
Bakersfield, CA 93309-1863, USA

Stewart, Natalie (Musician, Songwriter, Writer)
DreamWorks Records
9268 W 3rd St
Beverly Hills, CA 90210-3713, USA

Stewart, Norman (Athlete, Basketball Player)
University of Missouri
3201 Westcrest Circle
Columbia, MO 65203, USA

Stewart, Patrick (Actor, Director, Producer)
c/o Chris Kanarick *ID Public Relations (NY)*
40 Wall St Fl 51
New York, NY 10005-1385, USA

Stewart, Paul (Athlete, Hockey Player)
16 Bridgeview Cir
Walpole, MA 02081-3766, USA

Stewart, Paul Anthony (Actor)
c/o Paul Reisman *Abrams Artists Agency*
275 7th Ave Fl 26
New York, NY 10001-6708, USA

Stewart, Ralph (Athlete, Hockey Player)
175 Sherwood Dr
Thunder Bay, ON P7B 6L1, Canada

Stewart, Ray (Golfer)
2777 Dehavilland Dr
Abbotsford, BC V2T 5L3, CANADA

Stewart, Robert L Brig Gen (Astronaut)
815 Sun Valley Dr
Woodland Park, CO 80863-7729, USA

Stewart, Rod (Musician, Songwriter)
1435 S Ocean Blvd
Palm Beach, FL 33480-5005, USA

Stewart, Ryan (Athlete, Football Player)
2715 Owens Ave SW
Marietta, GA 30064-4253, USA

Stewart, Scott (Actor)
c/o Jeff Okin *Anonymous Content*
3532 Hayden Ave
Culver City, CA 90232-2413, USA

Stewart, Scott (Athlete, Baseball Player)
5243 Hickory Knoll Ln
Mount Holly, NC 28120-9344, USA

Stewart, Shannon (Athlete, Baseball Player)
14348 SW 156th Ave
Miami, FL 33196-6072, USA

Stewart, Shannon H (Athlete, Baseball Player)
14348 SW 156th Ave
Miami, FL 33196-6072, USA

Stewart, Steve (Athlete, Football Player)
1161 Jeans Ln
Amery, WI 54001-5109, USA

Stewart, Tonea (Actor)
Alabama State University
Theater Arts Dept
Montgomery, AL 36101, USA

Stewart, Tony (Race Car Driver)
Tony Stewart Racing
6001 Haas Way
Kannapolis, NC 28081-7730, USA

Stewart, Tyler (Musician)
Nettwerk Mgmt
8730 Wilshire Blvd # 304
Beverly Hills, CA 90211-2716, USA

Stewart, Will Foster (Actor)
8730 Santa Monica Blvd # 1
Los Angeles, CA 90069-4547, USA

Stewart-Hardway, Donna (Actor)
PO Box 777
Pinch, WV 25156-0777, USA

Steyn, Mark (Writer)
Mark Steyn Enterprises Inc
PO Box 30
Woodsville, NH 03785-0030, USA

Stezer, Philip (Musician)
I M G Artists
3 Burlington Lane
Chiswick
London W4 2TH, UNITED KINGDOM (UK)

Stich, Michael (Tennis Player)
Ernst-Barlach-Str 44
Elmshom 25336, GERMANY

Sticht, J Paul (Business Person)
11732 Lake House Ct
North Palm Beach, FL 33408-3320, USA

Stickle, Leon (Athlete, Hockey Player)
National Hockey League
SO Bay Street 11th Floor
Toronto, ON MSJ 2X8, Canada

Stickler, Alfons M Cardinal (Religious Leader)
Piazza del S Uffizio 11
Rome 00193, ITALY

Stickles, Montford (Monty) (Athlete, Football Player)
1363 3rd Ave
San Francisco, CA 94122-2718, USA

Stickles, Ted (Swimmer)
1142 Sharynwood Dr
Baton Rouge, LA 70808-6069, USA

Stidham, Howard (Athlete, Football Player)
185 Bell Dr W
Winchester, TN 37398-5401, USA

Stidham, Phil (Athlete, Baseball Player)
5025 Malabar Blvd
Melbourne Beach, FL 32951-3268, USA

Stieb, David (Dave) A (Athlete, Baseball Player)
9450 Stony Hill Rd
Reno, NV 89521-4447, USA

Stieber, Tamar (Journalist)
Albuquerque Journal
7777 Jefferson St NE
Editorial Dept
Albuquerque, NM 87109-4360, USA

Stiegler, Josef (Pepi) (Skier)
PO Box 290
Teton Village, WY 83025-0290, USA

Stiegler, Resi (Athlete, Olympic Athlete, Skier)
PO Box 1150
Wilson, WY 83014-1150, USA

Stienburg, Trevor (Athlete, Hockey Player)
2376 Connaught Ave
Halifax, NS B3L 2Z4, Canada

Stienke, Jim (Athlete, Football Player)
4707 Interlachen Ln
Austin, TX 78747-1457, USA

Stieve, Terry (Athlete, Football Player)
635 E Essex Ave
Saint Louis, MO 63122-3044, USA

Stigers, Curtis (Actor, Musician)
Shore Fire Media
32 Court St Fl 16
Brooklyn, NY 11201-4441, USA

Stigman, Dick (Athlete, Baseball Player)
12914 5th Ave S
Burnsville, MN 55337-3504, USA

Stiles, Darron (Athlete, Golfer)
130 Wild Turkey Run
Pinehurst, NC 28374-9658, USA

Stiles, Jackie (Athlete, Basketball Player)
Patrick J Stiles
115 E Hamilton St
Claflin, KS 67525-5200, USA

Stiles, Julia (Actor)
c/o Annick Muller *Wolf-Kasteler Public Relations*
40 Exchange Pl Ste 704
New York, NY 10005-2778, USA

Stiles, Ryan (Actor, Comedian)
c/o Kay Liberman *Liberman/Zerman Management*
252 N Larchmont Blvd Ste 200
Los Angeles, CA 90004-3754, USA

Stiles, Sarah (Actor)
c/o Bryan Leder *Authentic Talent & Literary Management*
3615 Eastham Dr # 650
Culver City, CA 90232-2410, USA

Stiles, Tony (Athlete, Hockey Player)
Calgary Police Service
133 6 Ave SE
Attn Tactical Unit
Calgary, AB T2G 4Z1, Canada

Stilgoe, Richard (Songwriter, Writer)
Noel Gray Artists
24 Denmark St
London WC2H 8NJ, UNITED KINGDOM (UK)

Still, Arthur B (Art) (Athlete, Football Player)
9813 Betsy Ross Ln
Liberty, MO 64068-8527, USA

Still, Bryan (Athlete, Football Player)
3812 Brennen Robert Pl
Glen Allen, VA 23060-2505, USA

Still, Devon (Athlete, Football Player)
c/o Drew Rosenhaus *Rosenhaus Sports Representation*
3921 Alton Rd # 440
Miami Beach, FL 33140-3852, USA

Still, Ken (Golfer)
1210 Princeton St
Fircrest, WA 98466-6035, USA

Still, William C Jr (Misc)
Columbia University
Chemistry Dept
New York, NY 10027, USA

Stiller, Ben (Actor, Comedian, Director)
c/o Staff Member *Red Hour Films*
629 N La Brea Ave
Los Angeles, CA 90036-2013, USA

Stiller, Jerry (Actor, Comedian)
c/o Paul Hilepo *PH Entertainment Group*
2728 Thomson Ave
Long Island City, NY 11101-2922, USA

Stiller, Stephen (Music Group, Musician)
17525 Ventura Blvd Ste 210
Encino, CA 91316-5111, USA

Still-Kilrain, Susan (Astronaut)
625 Cedar Ln
Virginia Bch, VA 23452-1805, USA

Stillman, Cory (Athlete, Hockey Player)
1 Panther Pkwy
Attn: Player Development Dept
Sunrise, FL 33323-5315, USA

Stillman, Royle (Athlete, Baseball Player)
580 Jb Ct
Glenwood Springs, CO 81601-8733, USA

Stillman, Whit (Director)
International Creative Mgmt
8942 Wilshire Blvd # 219
Beverly Hills, CA 90211-1908, USA

Stills, Chris (Musician)
Atlantic Records
9229 W Sunset Blvd Ste 900
Los Angeles, CA 90069-3410, USA

Stills, Ken (Athlete, Football Player)
647 Michael St
Oceanside, CA 92057-3505, USA

Stills, Kenny (Athlete, Football Player)

Stills, Stephen (Musician)
c/o Marsha Vlasic *Artist Group International (NY)*
150 E 58th St Fl 19
New York, NY 10155-1900, USA

Stills, The (Music Group)
c/o Staff Member *Paradigm (Monterey)*
404 W Franklin St
Monterey, CA 93940-2303, USA

Stillwagon, Jim (Athlete, Football Player)
890 Gatehouse Ln
Columbus, OH 43235-1734, United States

Stillwagon, Jim R (Athlete, Football Player)
3999 Parkway Ln
Hilliard, OH 43026-1252, USA

Stillwell, Kurt (Athlete, Baseball Player)
1105 Lassen View Dr
Westwood, CA 96137-9537, USA

Stillwell, Ron (Athlete, Baseball Player)
1105 Lassen View Dr
Westwood, CA 96137-9537, USA

Stilson, Jeff (Comedian, Producer)
c/o Bonnie Burns *Burns & Burns Management*
10523 Mars Ln
Los Angeles, CA 90077-3109, USA

Stilwell, Victoria (Television Host)

Stinchcomb, Matt (Athlete, Football Player)
3817 Sweet Bottom Dr
Duluth, GA 30096-3159, USA

Stincic, Thomas (Athlete, Football Player)
2121 E Oasis St
Mesa, AZ 85213-9743, USA

Stine, Richard (Cartoonist)
PO Box 348
Hansville, WA 98340-0348, USA

Stine, RL (Writer)
Scholastic Book Services
555 Broadway
New York, NY 10012-3919, USA

Stineman, Galadriel (Actor)
c/o Kurt Patino *Patino Management Company*
10201 Riverside Dr Ste 207
Toluca Lake, CA 91602-2538, USA

Sting (Musician)
PO Box 34902
London SW6 5WZ, UNITED KINGDOM

Sting, Charlotte (Athlete, Basketball Player)
333 E Trade St
Charlotte, NC 28202-2331, USA

Stinnett, Kelly (Athlete, Baseball Player)
6840 E Portia St
Mesa, AZ 85207-1558, USA

Stinson, Bob (Athlete, Baseball Player)
4107 Woodside Dr Apt 1
Coral Springs, FL 33065-1974, USA

Stinson, Ed (Athlete, Football Player)
c/o Drew Rosenhaus *Rosenhaus Sports Representation*
3921 Alton Rd # 440
Miami Beach, FL 33140-3852, USA

Stipanovich, Steve (Athlete, Basketball Player)
8060 Watkins Dr
Saint Louis, MO 63105-2566, USA

Stipe, Michael (Musician)
c/o Buck Williams *Progressive Global Agency*
PO Box 50294
Nashville, TN 37205-0294, USA

Stiritz, William P (Business Person)
Ralston Purina Co
Checkerboard Square
Saint Louis, MO 63164-0001, USA

Stirling, Lindsey (Musician)
c/o Sara Newkirk Simon *WME/IMG*
9601 Wilshire Blvd
Beverly Hills, CA 90210-5213, USA

Stirling, Rachel (Actor)
c/o Staff Member *Management Inc*
2032 Pinehurst Rd
Los Angeles, CA 90068-3732

Stirling, Steve (Athlete, Coach, Hockey Player)
118 Sassamon Ave
Milton, MA 02186-5828, USA

Stirvins, Alex (Athlete, Basketball Player)
11330 N Sundown Dr
Scottsdale, AZ 85260-5538, USA

Stith, Bryant (Athlete, Basketball Player)
20697 Governor Harrison Pkwy
Freeman, VA 23856-2451, USA

Stith, Samuel (Athlete, Basketball Player)
36 Madison St NE
Washington, DC 20011-2352, USA

Stith, Thomas (Athlete, Basketball Player)
105 Overlook Dr
Farmingville, NY 11738-3107, USA

Stivers, Steve (Congressman, Politician)
1007 Longworth Hob
Washington, DC 20515-0539, USa

St James, James (Jimmy) (Actor, Radio Personality)
The Real Jimmy Hollywood
7510 W Sunset Blvd # 333
Los Angeles, CA 90046-3408, USA

St. James, Lyn (Race Car Driver)
57 Gasoline Aly Ste D
Indianapolis, IN 46222-5932, USA

St. James, Rebecca (Musician)
c/o Staff Member *Smallbone Management*
PO Box 1524
Franklin, TN 37065-1524, USA

St Jean, Garry (Basketball Player, Coach)
Golden State Warriors
1001 Broadway
Oakland, CA 94607-4019, USA

St Jean, Len (Athlete, Football Player)
32 Ledgebrook Ave
Stoughton, MA 02072-1054, USA

St John, Andrew (Actor)
c/o Abby Bluestone *Innovative Artists*
1505 10th St
Santa Monica, CA 90401-2805, USA

St John, Gina (Actor, Television Host)
Howard Talent West
10657 Riverside Dr
Toluca Lake, CA 91602-2341, USA

St John, Jill (Actor)
115 Johnson Dr
Aspen, CO 81611-9719, USA

St John, Lara (Musician)
Columbia Artists Mgmt Inc
165 W 57th St
New York, NY 10019-2201, USA

St John, Mia (Boxer)
c/o Staff Member *Amsel, Eisenstadt & Frazier Talent Agency (AEF)*
5055 Wilshire Blvd Ste 860
Los Angeles, CA 90036-6108, USA

St Laurent, Andre (Athlete, Hockey Player)
947 Rue Riverview
Otterburn Park, QC J3H 1Z1, Canada

St Louis, Martin (Athlete, Hockey Player)
18145 Longwater Run Dr
Tampa, FL 33647-2212, USA

St. Marseille, Frank (Athlete, Hockey Player)
RR #4
Ashton, ON KOA 1BO, CANADA

Stoa, Ryan (Athlete, Hockey Player)
9634 12th Avenue Cir
Bloomington, MN 55425-2510, USA

Stobart, John (Artist)
613/4 Bat Club Dr
Fort Lauderdale, FL 33308, USA

Stock, Barbara (Actor)
22532 Margarita Dr
Woodland Hills, CA 91364-4030, USA

Stock, Mark (Athlete, Football Player)
9344 Crest Hill Rd
Marshall, VA 20115-3017, USA

Stock, Micah (Actor)
c/o Tony Lipp *Anonymous Content*
3532 Hayden Ave
Culver City, CA 90232-2413, USA

Stock, P J (Athlete, Hockey Player)
Team 990
1310 Greene Ave Suite 300
Montreal, QC H3Z 2BS, Canada

Stock, Wes (Athlete, Baseball Player)
8105 N Thorne Ln SW
Lakewood, WA 98498-2106, USA

Stockdale, Gretchen (Actor)
520 Washington Blvd
#248
Marina Del Rey, CA 90292, USA

Stockemer, Ralph (Athlete, Football Player)
4001 Madison Cir
Plano, TX 75023-5910, USA

Stocker, Kevin (Athlete, Baseball Player)
24839 E Ludlow Ave
Liberty Lake, WA 99019-9476, USA

Stocker, Luke (Athlete, Football Player)
c/o Jimmy Sexton *CAA (Memphis)*
6060 Poplar Ave Ste 470
Memphis, TN 38119-0910, USA

Stocker-Bottazzi, Jeanette (Athlete, Baseball Player)
1440 W Walnut St Apt 811
Allentown, PA 18102-4444, USA

Stockham, Benjamin (Actor)
c/o Matt Goldman *Silver Lining Entertainment*
421 S Beverly Dr Fl 7
Beverly Hills, CA 90212-4408, USA

Stocking, Hannah (Actor)
c/o Staff Member *WME/IMG*
9601 Wilshire Blvd
Beverly Hills, CA 90210-5213, USA

Stocklin, Erik (Actor)
c/o Gabrielle Krengel *Domain Talent*
1880 Century Park E Ste 1100
Los Angeles, CA 90067-1608, USA

Stockman, David (Politician)
Blackstone Group
150 Greenfield Rd
Winter Haven, FL 33884-1306, USA

Stockman, Phil (Athlete, Baseball Player)
2013 Red Oak Rd
Norcross, GA 30071-3819, USA

Stockman, Shawn (Musician)
c/o Joe Mulvihill *LiveWire Entertainment (FL)*
7575 Dr Phillips Blvd Ste 255
Orlando, FL 32819-7220, USA

Stockton, Dave (Athlete, Golfer)
PO Box 38
Dillon, CO 80435-0038, USA

Stockton, David (Golfer)
222 Escondido Dr
Redlands, CA 92373-7215, USA

Stockton, David Jr (Golfer)
4814 Nelson Ct
Carlsbad, CA 92010-5600, USA

Stockton, Dick (Sportscaster)
715 Stadium Dr
San Antonio, TX 78212-7201, USA

Stockton, John (Athlete, Basketball Player)

Stockwell, Dean (Actor)
95723 Highway 99 W
Junction City, OR 97448-9395, USA

Stockwell, Jeff (Writer)
c/o Staff Member *United Talent Agency (UTA)*
9336 Civic Center Dr
Beverly Hills, CA 90210-3604, USA

Stockwell, John (Actor)
c/o Michael McConnell *Zero Gravity Management (II)*
5660 Silver Valley Ave
Agoura Hills, CA 91301-4000, USA

Stoddard, Bob (Athlete, Baseball Player)
5766 Pony Express Trl Spc 15
Pollock Pines, CA 95726-9751, USA

Stoddard, Tim (Athlete, Baseball Player)
104 Hawthorn Dr
Twin Lakes, WI 53181-9564, USA

Stodden, Courtney (Actor, Reality Star)
c/o Charles Lago *DTLA Entertainment Group*
301 N Palm Canyon Dr Ste A
Palm Springs, CA 92262-5672, USA

Stofa, John (Athlete, Football Player)
7344 Jefferson Meadows Dr
Blacklick, OH 43004-9813, USA

Stoffer, Karen (Race Car Driver)
1408 Industrial Way Ste 16
Gardnerville, NV 89410-5719, USA

Stoitchkov, Hristo (Soccer Player)
DC United
14120 Newbrook Dr
Chantilly, VA 20151-2273, USA

Stojan, Maya (Actor)
c/o Susan Ferris *Bohemia Group*
1680 Vine St Ste 518
Los Angeles, CA 90028-8833, USA

Stojko, Elvis (Figure Skater)
Mentor Marketing
2 Saint Clair Ave E
Toronto, ON M4T 2T, CANADA

Stokes, Brian (Athlete, Baseball Player)
8310 140th St
Seminole, FL 33776-2904, USA

Stokes, Chris (Business Person, Director, Musician)
c/o Staff Member *Tobin & Associates PR*
4929 Wilshire Blvd Ste 245
Los Angeles, CA 90010-3859, USA

Stokes, Fred (Athlete, Football Player)
735 Mosleytown Rd
Tarrytown, GA 30470-4052, USA

Stokes, Greg (Athlete, Basketball Player)
2505 Plymouth St
Marion, IA 52302-5609, USA

Stokes, Jesse (Athlete, Football Player)
627 Butler Pt
San Antonio, TX 78251-4292, USA

Stokes, Sims (Athlete, Football Player)
2511 Wedglea Dr APT 1119
Dallas, TX 75211-2045, USA

Stokes of Leyland, Donald G (Business Person)
2 Branksome Cliff
Westminster Road Poole
Dorset BH13 6JW, UNITED KINGDOM (UK)

Stokkan, Bill (Race Car Driver)
Championship Auto Racing
5350 Lakeview Parkway South Dr
Indianapolis, IN 46268-5129, USA

Stokley, Brandon (Athlete, Football Player)
12479 Autumn Gate Way
Carmel, IN 46033-8284, USA

Stoklos, Randy (Athlete, Volleyball Player)
Beach Volleyball Camps
PO Box 1714
Pacific Palisades, CA 90272-1714, USA

Stole, Mink (Actor)
635 Colorado Ave Apt 3B
Baltimore, MD 21210-2135, USA

Stolhandske, Tom (Athlete, Football Player)
2531 Old Orchard Ln
San Antonio, TX 78230-4610, USA

Stolhanske, Erik (Comedian)
c/o Staff Member *United Talent Agency (UTA)*
9336 Civic Center Dr
Beverly Hills, CA 90210-3604, USA

Stoll, Corey (Actor)
c/o Ruth Bernstein *Viewpoint Inc*
8820 Wilshire Blvd Ste 220
Beverly Hills, CA 90211-2622, USA

Stoll, Jarret (Athlete, Hockey Player)
2021 Monterey Blvd
Hermosa Beach, CA 90254-2913, USA

Stolle, Frederick S (Tennis Player)
Turnberry Isle Yacht & Racquet Club
19735 Turnberry Way
Miami, FL 33180-2797, USA

Stoller, Mike (Composer)
Leiber/Stoller Entertainment
9000 W Sunset Blvd Ste 720
West Hollywood, CA 90069-5828, USA

Stoller, Nicholas (Director)

Stollery, David (Actor)
3203 Bern Ct
Laguna Beach, CA 92651-2007, USA

Stolojan, Theodor (Prime Minister)
World Bank
1818 H St NW
Washington, DC 20433-0002, USA

Stolper, Pinchas (Religious Leader)
Orthodox Jewish Congregations Union
11 Broadway
New York, NY 10004-1303, USA

Stolte, Christian (Actor)
c/o Staff Member *Grossman & Jack Talent*
33 W Grand Ave Ste 402
Chicago, IL 60654-6799, USA

Stoltenberg, Bryan (Athlete, Football Player)
3207 W Farmington Ln
Sugar Land, TX 77479-1883, USA

Stoltz, Eric (Actor, Director, Producer)
c/o Helen Sugland *Landmark Artists*
4116 W Magnolia Blvd Ste 101
Burbank, CA 91505-2700, USA

Stoltz, Roland (Athlete, Hockey Player)
Lillgatan 16
Skelleftea S-93154, Sweden

Stoltzfus, Levi (Horse Racer)
234A N Harvest Rd Apt C
Ronks, PA 17572-9727, USA

Stolze, Lena (Actor)
Agentur Carola Studlar
Neuroeder Str 1C
Planegg 82152, GERMANY

Stone, Albert L (Race Car Driver)
700 Central Ave
PO Box 8427
Louisville, KY 40208-1212, USA

Stone, Allen (Musician)
c/o Erin Cooney *The Fun Star*
8439 W Sunset Blvd Ste 2
Los Angeles, CA 90069-1925, USA

Stone, Andrew L (Director)
2132 Century Park Ln Apt 212
Los Angeles, CA 90067-3320, USA

Stone, Angie (Musician)
c/o Jonathan Clardy *CN Publicity*
9107 Wilshire Blvd Ste 450
Beverly Hills, CA 90210-5535, USA

Stone, Benjamin (Actor)
c/o Jordan McKirahan *Jordan McKirahan Talent Agency (LA)*
6303 Owensmouth Ave Fl 10
Woodland Hills, CA 91367-2262, USA

Stone, Biz (Business Person)
Twitter Inc
1355 Market St Ste 900
San Francisco, CA 94103-1337, USA

Stone, Curtis (Chef, Television Host)
3220 Tahoe Pl
Los Angeles, CA 90068-1657, USA

Stone, Dean (Athlete, Baseball Player)
213 13th St
Silvis, IL 61282-1267, USA

Stone, Dee Wallace (Actor)
23035 Cumorah Crest Dr
Woodland Hills, CA 91364-3709, USA

Stone, Doug (Musician)
PO Box 943
Springfield, TN 37172-0943

Stone, Eddie (Adult Film Star)
c/o Staff Member *Diva Central Inc*
7510 W Sunset Blvd # 1445
Los Angeles, CA 90046-3408, USA

Stone, Emma (Actor)
c/o Alexandra Crotin *The Lede Company*
9701 Wilshire Blvd # 930
Beverly Hills, CA 90212-2020, USA

Stone, Fred (Artist)
133 N Primrose Ave
Monrovia, CA 91016-2116, USA

Stone, Gene (Athlete, Baseball Player)
6897 Highway 262 SE
Othello, WA 99344-9761, USA

Stone, George H (Athlete, Baseball Player)
1304 Fairfield Dr
Ruston, LA 71270-3540, USA

Stone, Jack (Athlete, Football Player)
16125 Crestridge Ave
Sonora, CA 95370-8542, USA

Stone, Jack (Religious Leader)
Church of Nazarene
6401 Paseo Blvd
Kansas City, MO 64131-1213, USA

Stone, James (Athlete, Football Player)

Stone, Jeff (Athlete, Baseball Player)
911 S Swan Lake Dr
Hayti, MO 63851-1829, USA

Stone, Jennifer (Actor)
c/o Laura Ackerman *Advantage PR*
3900 W Alameda Ave Ste 1200
Burbank, CA 91505-4317, USA

Stone, Joss (Musician, Songwriter)
c/o Rob Light *Creative Artists Agency (CAA)*
2000 Avenue of the Stars Ste 100
Los Angeles, CA 90067-4705, USA

Stone, Ken (Athlete, Football Player)
1158 Jason Way
West Palm Beach, FL 33406-5255, USA

Stone, Lara (Model)
c/o Staff Member *IMG World*
200 5th Ave Fl 7
New York, NY 10010-3307, USA

Stone, Matt (Animator, Director, Producer, Writer)
2337 McKinley Ave
Venice, CA 90291-4623, USA

Stone, Melanie (Actor)
c/o Stephen Belden *More/Medavoy Management*
10203 Santa Monica Blvd # 400
Los Angeles, CA 90067-6405, USA

Stone, Michael (Athlete, Football Player)
c/o Eugene Parker *Independent Sports & Entertainment (ISE-IN)*
6435 W Jefferson Blvd # 197
Fort Wayne, IN 46804-6203, USA

Stone, Moses (Musician)
c/o Lee Runchey *Chrome PR*
9107 Wilshire Blvd Ste 450
Beverly Hills, CA 90210-5535, USA

Stone, Nicole (Athlete, Olympic Athlete, Skier)
5272 Heather Ln
Park City, UT 84098-5967, USA

Stone, Nikki (Skier)
Podium Enterprises
PO Box 680-332
Park City, UT 84068, USA

Stone, Oliver (Actor, Director, Producer)
c/o Staff Member *Ixtlan Corporation*
2001 Wilshire Blvd Ste 250
Santa Monica, CA 90403-5681, USA

Stone, Richard (Politician)
4508 Foxhall Cres NW
Washington, DC 20007-1055, USA

Stone, Ricky (Athlete, Baseball Player)
6494 Lakeview Ct
Fairfield Township, OH 45011-8139, USA

Stone, Robert (Director)
c/o Staff Member *Robert Stone Productions*
11 Morton Rd
Studio Building
Rhinebeck, NY 12572-2534, USA

Stone, Roger D (Business Person, Commentator, Politician)
34 W 88th St
New York, NY 10024-2558, USA

Stone, Ron (Athlete, Baseball Player)
11720 NW Lovejoy St
Portland, OR 97229-5028, USA

Stone, Sharon (Actor)
c/o Paul Nelson *Mosaic Media Group*
407 N Maple Dr # 100
Beverly Hills, CA 90210-3818, USA

Stone, Steve (Athlete, Baseball Player, Sportscaster)
9261 N 128th Way
Scottsdale, AZ 85259-6233, USA

Stone, William J (Athlete, Football Player)
618 Woodland Knolls Rd
Germantown Hills, IL 61548-9429, USA

Stone, Yael (Actor)
c/o Jason Gutman *Gersh*
41 Madison Ave Ste 3301
New York, NY 10010-2210, USA

Stonebreaker, Mike (Athlete, Football Player)
3300 Delaware Ave Apt A
Kenner, LA 70065-3689, USA

Stonecipher, Harry C (Business Person)
Boeing Co
PO Box 3707
Seattle, WA 98124-2207, USA

Stone Foxes, The (Music Group, Musician)
c/o Rob Weldon *Wingman Music*
Prefers to be contacted by email or telephone
CA, USA

Stone III, Charles (Actor, Director, Writer)
c/o Barbara Dreyfus *United Talent Agency (UTA)*
9336 Civic Center Dr
Beverly Hills, CA 90210-3604, USA

Stoneman, Bill (Athlete, Baseball Player)
2519 N San Miguel Dr
Orange, CA 92867-8604, USA

Stoner, Alyson (Musician)
c/o Cindy Osbrink *Osbrink Talent Agency*
4343 Lankershim Blvd # 100
North Hollywood, CA 91602-2705, USA

Stoner, Bob (Race Car Driver)
Vapor Racing
6100 W H Ave
Kalamazoo, MI 49009-8502, USA

Stoner, Sherri (Actor, Producer, Writer)
c/o Tom Strickler *WME|IMG*
9601 Wilshire Blvd
Beverly Hills, CA 90210-5213, USA

Stoner, Tobi (Athlete, Baseball Player)

Stone-Richards, Lucille (Athlete, Baseball Player)
17 Stonemeadow Dr
Bridgewater, MA 02324-1995, USA

Stones, Dwight E (Athlete, Olympic Athlete)
27472 Portola Pkwy Ste 205
Foothill Ranch, CA 92610-2853, USA

Stonesipher, Don (Athlete, Football Player)
1502 Canberry Court
Wheeling, IL 60090, USA

Stone Sour (Music Group)
c/o Michael Moses *Baker Winokur Ryder Public Relations*
9100 Wilshire Blvd
W Tower #500
Beverly Hills, CA 90212-3415, USA

Stonestreet, Eric (Actor)
c/o Steven Kavovit *Thruline Entertainment*
9250 Wilshire Blvd Fl Ground
Beverly Hills, CA 90212-3352, USA

Stone Temple Pilots (Music Group)
c/o Rod MacSween *International Talent Booking*
9 Kingsway
Fl 6
London WC2B 6XF, UNITED KINGDOM

Stookey, Paul (Music Group, Musician, Songwriter, Writer)
Newworld
RR 175
South Blue Hill Falls, ME 04615, USA

Stoops, Bob (Coach, Football Coach)
University of Oklahoma
108 W Brooks St
Athletic Dept
Norman, OK 73019-6000, USA

Stoops, Jim (Athlete, Baseball Player)
10472 S Monaco Way
Traverse City, MI 49684-6861, USA

Stoops, Mike (Coach, Football Coach)
Arizona State University
Athletic Dept
Tempe, AZ 85287-0001, USA

Stopanovich, Steve (Athlete, Basketball Player)
14 Ridgecreek
Saint Louis, MO 63141-8042, USA

Stopel, Terry (Athlete, Football Player)
804 Saddlebrook Dr S
Bedford, TX 76021-5360, USA

Stoppard, Tom (Writer)
P F D
Peters Fraser and Dunlop Group 504/506
The Chambers Chelsea
London SW10 OXF, England

Storch, Larry (Actor)
330 W End Ave # 17F
New York, NY 10023-8171, USA

Storch, Scott (Producer)
c/o David Weintraub *DWE Talent*
Prefers to be contacted by email or phone.
Los Angeles, CA 90069, USA

Storen, Drew (Athlete, Baseball Player)
c/o Staff Member *Cincinnati Reds*
100 Main St
Great American Ball Park
Cincinnati, OH 45202-5108, USA

Stori, Moneca (Actor)
c/o Elena Kirschner *Red Management*
415 Esplanade W Box 3
North Vancouver, BC V7M 1A6, CANADA

Stork, Jeff (Athlete, Coach, Volleyball Player)
California State University Northridge
Athletic Dept
18111 Nordhoff St
Northridge, CA 91330-0001, USA

Stork, Travis Lane (Doctor, Talk Show Host)
The Doctors
5555 Melrose Ave Fl Second
Los Angeles, CA 90038-3989, USA

Storke, Adam (Actor)
c/o Marc Epstein *Marc Epstein Entertainment*
108 Breeze Ave
Venice, CA 90291-3360, USA

Storm, Avery (Musician)
c/o Staff Member *Derrty Entertainment*
9648 Olive Blvd # 230
Saint Louis, MO 63132-3002, USA

Storm, Hannah (Correspondent, Sportscaster)
c/o Staff Member *ESPN (Main)*
935 Middle St
Espn Plaza
Bristol, CT 06010-1000, USA

Storm, Jim (Athlete, Hockey Player)
2609 Harvest Hill Dr
Brighton, MI 48114-8299, USA

Storm, Lance (Athlete, Wrestler)
PO Box 58013
Chaparral RPO, Calgary 72X 3V2, CANADA

Storm, Lauren (Actor)
c/o Staff Member *Aquarius Public Relations*
5320 Sylmar Ave
Sherman Oaks, CA 91401-5612, USA

Storm, Tempest (Dancer)
3907 Cambridge St Unit 1
Las Vegas, NV 89119-7403, USA

Stormare, Peter (Actor)
c/o Jeff Golenberg *Silver Lining Entertainment*
421 S Beverly Dr Fl 7
Beverly Hills, CA 90212-4408, USA

Storms, Kirsten (Actor)
c/o Nicole Nassar *Nicole Nassar PR*
1111 10th St Unit 104
Santa Monica, CA 90403-5363, USA

Storr, Jamie (Athlete, Hockey Player)
Jamie Storr Goalie School
650 N Sepulveda Blvd
Los Angeles, CA 90049-2108, USA

Story, Laura (Musician)
c/o David Breen *The Breen Agency*
25 Music Sq W
Nashville, TN 37203-3205, USA

Story, Tim (Director)
c/o Michael Sheresky *United Talent Agency (UTA)*
9336 Civic Center Dr
Beverly Hills, CA 90210-3604, USA

Story, Winston (Actor)
c/o Brian McCabe *Venture IAB*
3211 Cahuenga Blvd W Ste 104
Los Angeles, CA 90068-1372, USA

Storz, Erik (Athlete, Football Player)
114 Andrea Dr
Rockaway, NJ 07866-3702, USA

Stossel, John (Journalist)
211 Central Park W Apt 15-K
New York, NY 10024-6020, USA

Stott, Kathryn L (Musician)
Mire House
West Martor near Skipton
Yorks BD23 3UQ, UNITED KINGDOM (UK)

Stott, Ken (Actor)
c/o Kimberley Donovan *The Artists Partnership*
101 Finsbury Pavement
London EC2A 1RS, UNITED KINGDOM

Stott, Nicole P (Astronaut)
c/o Staff Member *NASA-JSC*
2101 Nasa Pkwy # 1
Astronaut Office - Mail Code Cb
Houston, TX 77058-3607, USA

Stottlemyre, Todd (Athlete, Baseball Player)
6918 E Bronco Dr
Paradise Valley, AZ 85253-3123, USA

Stotts, Terry (Athlete, Basketball Coach, Basketball Player, Coach)
3109 Douglas Cir
Lake Oswego, OR 97035-3550, USA

Stoudamire, Damon (Athlete, Basketball Player)
c/o Lon Rosen *Magic Johnson Enterprises Inc*
5335 Wisconsin Ave NW Ste 850
Washington, DC 20015-2052, USA

Stoudemire, Amare (Athlete, Basketball Player)
16800 Berkshire Ct
Southwest Ranches, FL 33331-1332, USA

Stouder, Sharon M (Swimmer)
144 Loucks Ave
Los Altos, CA 94022-1045, USA

Stoudt, Cliff (Athlete, Football Player)
5348 Drumcally Ln
Dublin, OH 43017-2438, USA

Stouffer, Kelly (Athlete, Football Player)
HC 81 Box 55
Rushville, NE 69360-9729, USA

Stoughton, Blaine (Athlete, Hockey Player)
8770 Ashbrook Dr
West Chester, OH 45069-3350, USA

Stovall, Da Rond (Athlete, Baseball Player)
1107 Goelz Dr
East Saint Louis, IL 62203-1917, USA

Stovall, Jerry L (Athlete, Football Player)
417 Highland Trace Dr # D
Baton Rouge, LA 70810-5062, USA

Stove, Betty (Tennis Player)
Advantage International
1025 Thomas Jefferson St NW # 450
Washington, DC 20007-5201, USA

Stover, George (Actor)
PO Box 10005
Baltimore, MD 21285-0005, USA

Stover, Irwin Russ Juno (Athlete, Swimmer)
512 Lanai Cir
Union City, CA 94587-4113, USA

Stover, Jeff (Athlete, Football Player)
260 Cohasset Rd Ste 190
Chico, CA 95926-2282, USA

Stover, Matt (Athlete, Football Player)
10024 Rustleleaf Dr
Dallas, TX 75238-2143, USA

Stover, Stewart (Athlete, Football Player)
9334 La Highway 82
Abbeville, LA 70510-2356, USA

Stowe, David H Jr (Business Person)
Deere Co
John Deere Road
Moline, IL 61265, USA

Stowe, Hal (Athlete, Baseball Player)
1361 Union New Hope Rd
Gastonia, NC 28056-8574, USA

Stowe, Madeleine (Actor)
c/o Cynthia Pett-Dante *Brillstein Entertainment Partners*
9150 Wilshire Blvd Ste 350
Beverly Hills, CA 90212-3453, USA

Stowe, Medeleine (Actor)
United Talent Agency
9336 Civic Center Dr
Beverly Hills, CA 90210-3604, USA

Stowe, Otto (Athlete, Football Player)
546 Mills Way
Goleta, CA 93117-4021, USA

Stowell, Austin (Actor)
c/o Will Ward *Fourward*
10250 Constellation Blvd Ste 2710
Los Angeles, CA 90067-6227, USA

Stowers, Chris (Athlete, Baseball Player)
3773 Wakefield Hall Sq SE
Smyrna, GA 30080-4917, USA

Stowers, Tommie (Athlete, Football Player)
2435 NW Valley View Dr
Lees Summit, MO 64081-1977, USA

Stoya (Actor, Adult Film Star, Model)
c/o Drew Elliot *Artist International*
333 E 43rd St Apt 115
New York, NY 10017-4822, USA

Stoyanov, Michael (Actor)
c/o Charles Riley *Charles Riley*
7122 Beverly Blvd Ste F
Los Angeles, CA 90036-2572, USA

Stoyanovich, Peter (Athlete, Football Player)
44836 Broadmoor Cir S
Northville, MI 48168-8642, USA

St Patrick, Mathew (Actor)
c/o Gary Ousdahl *Advanced Management*
8033 W Sunset Blvd # 935
Los Angeles, CA 90046-2401, USA

St. Pierre, Georges (Athlete)
c/o Staff Member *Creative Artists Agency (CAA)*
2000 Avenue of the Stars Ste 100
Los Angeles, CA 90067-4705, USA

Stracey, John (Boxer)
Van Laeken 4
Norsey Road Billericay
Essex CM11 2AD, UNITED KINGDOM (UK)

Strachan, Gordon (Politician)
PO Box 3747
Park City, UT 84060-3747, USA

Strachan, Mike (Athlete, Football Player)
PO Box 642007
Kenner, LA 70064-2007, USA

Strachan, Rod (Athlete, Olympic Athlete, Swimmer)
11632 Ranch Hl
Santa Ana, CA 92705-3130, USA

Strachan, Steve (Athlete, Football Player)
46 Crimson Rd
Billerica, MA 01821-5420, USA

Strachan, Tyaon (Athlete, Hockey Player)
5550 Flint Creek Ave
Dublin, OH 43016-9645, USA

Straczynski, J Michael (Actor)
c/o Chris Harbert *Creative Artists Agency (CAA)*
2000 Avenue of the Stars Ste 100
Los Angeles, CA 90067-4705, USA

Strader, Cam (Athlete, Race Car Driver)
10974 Heritage Green Dr
Cornelius, NC 28031-7407, USA

Stradlin, Izzy (Musician)
605 McAndrew Rd
Ojai, CA 93023-9313, USA

Strahan, Michael (Athlete, Football Player, Talk Show Host, Television Host)
c/o Staff Member *Good Morning America (GMA)*
44th St & Broadway
New York, NY 10112, USA

Strahler, Mike (Athlete, Baseball Player)
9932 Bella Vista St
Apple Valley, CA 92308-8524, USA

Strahovski, Yvonne (Actor)
c/o Laura Myones *McKeon-Myones Management*
3500 W Olive Ave Ste 770
Burbank, CA 91505-5527, USA

Straight, Bering (Music Group)
c/o Staff Member *Creative Artists Agency (CAA)*
401 Commerce St PH
Nashville, TN 37219-2516, USA

Strain, Joe (Athlete, Baseball Player)
8668 E Otero Cir
Centennial, CO 80112-3351, USA

Strain, Julie (Actor, Model)
Cooking with Mama
8491 W Sunset Blvd Ste 1850
West Hollywood, CA 90069-1911, USA

Strain, Sammy (Music Group, Musician)
Associated Booking Corp
1995 Broadway # 501
New York, NY 10023-5882, USA

Strait, Bob (Race Car Driver)
Carnes-Miller Motorsports
12515 Kenedo Cir
Elbert, CO 80106-8819, USA

Strait, George (Musician)
c/o Erv Woolsey *Erv Woolsey Agency*
1000 18th Ave S
Nashville, TN 37212-2184, USA

Strait, Steven (Actor)
c/o Chris Andrews *Creative Artists Agency (CAA)*
2000 Avenue of the Stars Ste 100
Los Angeles, CA 90067-4705, USA

Straka, Martin (Athlete, Hockey Player)
HC Plzen Stefanikovo namesti. 1
Pl zen 301 33, Czech Republic

Straker, Lee (Athlete, Baseball Player)
Philadelphia Phillies
1 Citizens Bank Way Ofc
Attn: Venezulan Baseball Academy
Philadelphia, PA 19148-5249, USA

Strampe, Bob (Athlete, Baseball Player)
19210 W Lance Hill Rd
Cheney, WA 99004-7907, USA

Strand, Robin (Actor)
4118 Elmer Ave
North Hollywood, CA 91602-3312, USA

Strang, Deborah (Actor)
Henderson/Hogan
8285 W Sunset Blvd Ste 1
West Hollywood, CA 90046-2420, USA

Strange, Doug (Athlete, Baseball Player)
104 Sorrento Dr
Greenville, SC 29609-3076, USA

Strange, Sarah (Actor)
c/o Elizabeth Hodgson *Elizabeth Hodgson Management Group*
405-1688 Cypress St
Vancouver, BC V6J 5J1, CANADA

Strange Boys, The (Music Group)
c/o Staff Member *Paradigm (Monterey)*
404 W Franklin St
Monterey, CA 93940-2303, USA

Strange-Hansen, Martin (Actor)
c/o Staff Member *Gersh*
9465 Wilshire Blvd Ste 600
Beverly Hills, CA 90212-2605, USA

Stransky, Bob (Athlete, Football Player)
5970 W Colgate Pl
Denver, CO 80227-3814, USA

Strasburg, Stephen (Athlete, Baseball Player)
1204 Suncast Ln Ste 2
El Dorado Hills, CA 95762-9665, USA

Strasser, Teresa (Comedian, Television Host)
c/o Anthony Mattero *Vigliano Associates*
405 Park Ave Ste 1700
New York, NY 10022-9402, USA

Strasser, Todd (Writer)
PO Box 859
Larchmont, NY 10538-0859, USA

Strathairn, David (Actor)
Ryan Entertainment
461 S Ogden Dr
C/O Madeline Ryan
Los Angeles, CA 90036-3119, USA

Stratham, Jason (Actor)
International Creative Mgmt
8942 Wilshire Blvd # 219
Beverly Hills, CA 90211-1908, USA

Strathiam, David (Actor)
United Talent Agency
9336 Civic Center Dr
Beverly Hills, CA 90210-3604, USA

Stratten, Louise (Actor, Producer)

Stratton, Frederick P Jr (Business Person)
Briggs & Stratton
PO Box 702
Milwaukee, WI 53201-0702, USA

Stratton, Mike (Athlete, Football Player)
2611 Shore Line Rd
Knoxville, TN 37932-1724, USA

Stratus, Trish (Wrestler)
c/o Michael Braverman *Braverman Bloom Company*
14320 Ventura Blvd Ste 632
Sherman Oaks, CA 91423-2717, USA

Straub, Peter (Writer)
360 Furman St Apt 719
Brooklyn, NY 11201-4716, USA

Straub, Peter F (Writer)
360 Furman St Apt 719
Brooklyn, NY 11201-4716, USA

Strauss, Neil (Journalist, Writer)
8491 W Sunset Blvd # 348
W Hollywood, CA 90069-1911, USA

Strauss, Peter (Actor)
Wolf/Kasteller
335 N Maple Dr Ste 351
Beverly Hills, CA 90210-5174, USA

Strauss-Schulson, Todd (Director)
c/o Christie Smith *Rise Management*
6338 Wilshire Blvd
Los Angeles, CA 90048-5002, USA

Straw, Syd (Musician)
c/o Staff Member *UTA/The Agency Group*
888 7th Ave Fl 7
New York, NY 10106-0700, USA

Strawberry, Darryl E (Athlete, Baseball Player)
Strawberry's Sports Grill
2 Bridal Oak Ct
O Fallon, MO 63366-1401, USA

Strawberry, D J (Athlete, Basketball Player)
943 Bellevue St
Cape Girardeau, MO 63701-5401, USA

Stray Cats (Music Group)
c/o Dave Kaplan *Dave Kaplan Management*
1126 S Coast Hwy Ste 101
Encinitas, CA 92024-5003, USA

Strayed, Cheryl (Writer)
c/o Janet Silver *Zachary Shuster Harmsworth Talent Agency*
19 W 21st St Rm 501
New York, NY 10010-6874, USA

Strayhorn, Les (Athlete, Football Player)
315 Seigel St Apt 113
Brooklyn, NY 11206-3835, USA

Streep, Meryl (Actor)
c/o Morgan Pesante *42West*
1840 Century Park E Ste 700
Los Angeles, CA 90067-2122, USA

Street, Devin (Athlete, Football Player)

Street, Huston (Athlete, Baseball Player)
8300 Big View Dr
Austin, TX 78730-1520, USA

Street, John (Politician)
Mayor's Office
City Hall
23 N Juniper St
Philadelphia, PA 19107, USA

Street, Picabo (Athlete, Olympic Athlete, Skier)
PO Box 2167
Hailey, ID 83333-2167, USA

Street, Rebecca (Actor)
19 W 69th St Apt 101
New York, NY 10023-4754, USA

Streeter, George (Athlete, Football Player)
35 Brentwood Pl
Fort Thomas, KY 41075-2446, USA

Streiber, Whitley (Writer)
c/o Paul Canterna *Seven Summits Pictures & Management*
8906 W Olympic Blvd
Beverly Hills, CA 90211-3550, USA

Streisand, Barbra (Actor, Director, Musician, Producer)
405 S Beverly Dr # 440
Beverly Hills, CA 90212-4416, USA

Streit, Clarence K (Journalist)
2853 Ontario Rd NW Apt 509
Washington, DC 20009-2238, USA

Streit, Mark (Athlete, Hockey Player)
C A A Sports
2000 Avenue of the Stars Fl 3
Los Angeles, CA 90067-4704, USA

Streitwieser Jr, Andrew (Misc)
University of California
Chemistry Dept
Berkeley, CA 94720-0001, USA

Stremme, David (Race Car Driver)
Penske Racing
200 Penske Way
Mooresville, NC 28115-8022, USA

Strenger, Rich (Athlete, Football Player)
1064 Arbroak Way
Lake Orion, MI 48362-2500, USA

Stretch, Gary (Actor)
c/o George Hayum *Hirsch Wallerstein Hayum Matlof & Fishman*
10100 Santa Monica Blvd Fl 23
Los Angeles, CA 90067-4003, USA

Streuli, Wait (Athlete, Baseball Player)
14 Sage Brush Ct
Greensboro, NC 27409-2707, USA

Streuli, Walt (Athlete, Baseball Player)
14 Sage Brush Ct
Greensboro, NC 27409-2707, USA

Stricker, Bill (Athlete, Basketball Player)
2930 Driftwood Pl Apt 70
Stockton, CA 95219-8027, USA

Stricker, Steve (Athlete, Golfer)
5804 N Sherman Ave
Madison, WI 53704-2147, USA

Strickland, Donald (Athlete, Football Player)
1110 Gilman Ave
San Francisco, CA 94124-3623, USA

Strickland, Gail (Actor)
14732 Oracle Pl
Pacific Palisades, CA 90272-2642, USA

Strickland, Jim (Athlete, Baseball Player)
2139 Equestrian Rd
Paso Robles, CA 93446-4149, USA

Strickland, KaDee (Actor)
c/o Erica Gray *Viewpoint Inc*
8820 Wilshire Blvd Ste 220
Beverly Hills, CA 90211-2622, USA

Strickland, Rod (Athlete, Basketball Player)
3120 Hemingway Ln
Lexington, KY 40513-1858, USA

Strickland, Scott (Athlete, Baseball Player)
415 Enchanted River Dr
Spring, TX 77388-5981, USA

Stricklin, Hut (Race Car Driver)
9990 Caldwell Rd
Mount Ulla, NC 28125-8704, USA

Strieber, Whitley (Writer)
c/o Staff Member *Gersh*
9465 Wilshire Blvd Ste 600
Beverly Hills, CA 90212-2605, USA

Strief, Zach (Athlete, Football Player)
5480 Carterway Dr
Milford, OH 45150-9624, USA

Striker, Jake (Athlete, Baseball Player)
1963 SE Gregory Dr
Dallas, OR 97338-2746, USA

Stringer, Howard (Business Person)
Sony Corporation of America
Sony Drive
Park Ridge, NJ 07656, USA

Stringer, Rob (Business Person)
c/o Staff Member *Epic Records Group*
550 Madison Ave Fl 22
New York, NY 10022-3211, USA

Stringer, Vivian (Athlete, Basketball Coach)
6 Lavender Dr
Princeton, NJ 08540-9448, USA

Stringert, Hal (Athlete, Football Player)
1711 Dole St Apt 603
Honolulu, HI 96822-4946, USA

Stringfield, Sherry (Actor)
c/o Leanne Coronel *Coronel Group*
1100 Glendon Ave Fl 17
Los Angeles, CA 90024-3588, USA

Strittmatter, Mark (Athlete, Baseball Player)
6533 Dutch Creek St
Highlands Ranch, CO 80130-3859, USA

Strobel, Eric (Athlete, Hockey Player, Olympic Athlete)
6617 129th St W
Saint Paul, MN 55124-7967, USA

Stroble, Bobby (Golfer)
524 5th Ave # B
Albany, GA 31701-1908, USA

Strock, Donald J (Don) (Athlete, Coach, Football Coach, Football Player)
1512 Passion Vine Cir
Weston, FL 33326-3656, USA

Strode, Lester (Athlete, Baseball Player)
2523 Trenton Sta
Saint Charles, MO 63303-2913, USA

Strohmayer, John (Athlete, Baseball Player)
1825 Crosby Ln
Redding, CA 96003-7754, USA

Strokes, The (Music Group)
c/o Marsha Vlasic *Artist Group International (NY)*
150 E 58th St Fl 19
New York, NY 10155-1900, USA

Strolz, Hubert (Skier)
6767 Warth 19
AUSTRIA

Strom, Brent (Athlete, Baseball Player)
2202 N Catalina Vista Loop
Tucson, AZ 85749-7908, USA

Strom, Brock T (Football Player)
4301 W 110th St
Leawood, KS 66211-1424, USA

Strom, Rick (Athlete, Football Player)
8905 Moor Park Run
Duluth, GA 30097-6622, USA

Stroma, Freddie (Actor)
c/o Daphne Waring *Waring and McKenna*
17 S Molton St
London W1K 5QT, UNITED KINGDOM

Stroman, Susan (Director)

Stromberg, Mike (Athlete, Football Player)
PO Box 1510
Shelter Island, NY 11964-1510, USA

Strominger, Jack L (Misc)
Dana Faber Cancer Institute
44 Binney St
Biochemistry Dept
Boston, MA 02115-6084, USA

Stronach, Belinda (Business Person)
Magna International
600 Wilshire Dr
Troy, MI 48084-1625, USA

Strong, Brenda (Actor)
c/o Kay Liberman *Liberman/Zerman Management*
252 N Larchmont Blvd Ste 200
Los Angeles, CA 90004-3754, USA

Strong, Charlie (Coach, Football Coach)
University Of Texas Athletics
405 E 23rd St
Austin, TX 78712, USA

Strong, Danny (Actor, Producer)
c/o Staff Member *Gotham Group*
1041 N Formosa Ave # 200
West Hollywood, CA 90046-6703, USA

Strong, Derek (Athlete, Basketball Player)
5434 Hillcrest Dr
Los Angeles, CA 90043-2323, USA

Strong, Jamal (Athlete, Baseball Player)
15016 W Windrose Dr
Surprise, AZ 85379-5972, USA

Strong, Jeremy (Actor)
c/o Paul Nelson *Mosaic Media Group*
407 N Maple Dr # 100
Beverly Hills, CA 90210-3818, USA

Strong, Jim (Athlete, Football Player)
25330 Richards Rd
Spring, TX 77386-1506, USA

Strong, Joe (Athlete, Baseball Player)
1340 Corcoran Ave
Vallejo, CA 94589-1878, USA

Strong, Johnny (Actor)
Strong/Morrone Ent
9100 Wilshire Blvd Ste 503E
Beverly Hills, CA 90212-3419

Strong, Ken (Athlete, Hockey Player)
1100 Birchview Ave
Oakville, ON L6J 6N3, Canada

Strong, Mack (Football Player)
c/o Staff Member *Maxx Sports & Entertainment*
546 5th Ave Fl 6
New York, NY 10036-5000, USA

Strong, Mark (Actor)
c/o Lisa Kasteler *Wolf-Kasteler Public Relations*
6255 W Sunset Blvd Ste 1111
Los Angeles, CA 90028-7426, USA

Strong, Rider (Actor)
c/o Ellen Meyer *Ellen Meyer Management*
315 S Beverly Dr Ste 202
Beverly Hills, CA 90212-4310, USA

Strong, Tara (Actor)
c/o Kathy Schmidt *Integrity Talent Agency*
11255 Yarmouth Ave
Granada Hills, CA 91344-4055, USA

Strossen, Nadine (Politician)
57 Worth St
New York, NY 10013-2926, USA

Stroud, Carlos (Misc)
Rockefeller University
Physics Dept
1230 York Ave
Cambridge, MA 02138, USA

Stroud, Don (Actor)
500 Lunalilo Home Rd Apt 16A
Honolulu, HI 96825-1718, USA

Stroud, Morris (Athlete, Football Player)
4661 Hiram Lithia Springs Rd
Powder Springs, GA 30127-3118, USA

Stroughter, Steve (Athlete, Baseball Player)
323 NE 2nd Ave
Visalia, CA 93291-3724, USA

Stroup, Jessica (Actor)
c/o Erica Tarin *ID Public Relations*
7060 Hollywood Blvd Fl 8th
Los Angeles, CA 90028-6021, USA

Strube, Juergen F (Business Person)
BASF Corp
Carl-Bosch Str 38
Ludwigshafen 67063, GERMANY

Struber, Larry (Producer)
c/o Staff Member *WME|IMG*
9601 Wilshire Blvd
Beverly Hills, CA 90210-5213, USA

Strudwick, Suzanne (Golfer)
5500 Crestwood Dr
Knoxville, TN 37914-5108, USA

Strug, Kerri (Athlete, Gymnast, Olympic Athlete)
2611 N Santa Lucia Dr
Tucson, AZ 85715-3137, USA

Strugnell, John (Misc)
Harvard University
45 Francis Ave
Divinity School
Cambridge, MA 02138-2115, USA

Strus, Lusia (Actor)
c/o Staff Member *Steve Himber Entertainment*
211 S Beverly Dr # 601
Beverly Hills, CA 90212-3807, USA

Struthers, Sally (Actor)
c/o Staff Member *Sharp & Associates*
1516 N Fairfax Ave
Los Angeles, CA 90046-2608, USA

Struycken, Carel (Actor)
1665 E Mountain St
Pasadena, CA 91104-3936, USA

Stryker, Bradley (Actor)
c/o Staff Member *The House of Representatives*
3118 Wilshire Blvd Ste D
Santa Monica, CA 90403-2345, USA

Strykert, Ron (Musician)
TPA
PO Box 124
Round Corner, NSW 02158, AUSTRALIA

Stuart, Brad (Athlete, Hockey Player)
C A A Sports
2000 Avenue of the Stars Fl 3
Los Angeles, CA 90067-4704, USA

Stuart, Eric (Actor, Musician)
330 Carroll St
Brooklyn, NY 11231-5008, USA

Stuart, Jason (Actor, Comedian)
c/o Bonny Dore *Bonny Dore Management*
8530 Wilshire Blvd # 499
Beverly Hills, CA 90211-3122, USA

Stuart, Katie (Actor)
c/o Russ Mortensen *Pacific Artists Management*
112 3rd Ave E Suite 210
Vancouver, BC V5T 1C8, CANADA

Stuart, Katie (Actor)

Stuart, Mark (Athlete, Hockey Player)
6320 Oak Meadow Ln NW
Rochester, MN 55901-8820, USA

Stuart, Marty (Musician, Songwriter)
c/o Staff Member *Paradigm (Monterey)*
404 W Franklin St
Monterey, CA 93940-2303, USA

Stuart, Roy (Athlete, Football Player)
6800 S Granite Ave Apt 339
Tulsa, OK 74136-7043, USA

Stubblefield, Dana W (Athlete, Football Player)
5226 Pisa Ct
San Jose, CA 95138-2122, USA

Stubblefield, Marga (Golfer)
PO Box 140
Kailua, HI 96734-0140, USA

Stubblefield, Mickey (Athlete, Baseball Player)
Kansas City Monarchs
4870 Seldon Way SE
Smyrna, GA 30080-9266, USA

Stubbs, Franklin (Athlete, Baseball Player)
13706 Mockingbird Dr
Prospect, KY 40059-9026, USA

Stubbs, Imogen (Actor)
c/o Roxane Vacca *Roxane Vacca Management*
61 Judd St
London WC1H 9QT, UNITED KINGDOM

Stubing, Larry (Moose) (Athlete, Baseball Player, Coach)
10821 Laconia Dr
Villa Park, CA 92861-6408, USA

Stuck, Hans-Joachim (Race Car Driver)
Harmstatt 3
Ellmau/Tirol 06352, AUSTRIA

Stuckey, Darrell (Athlete, Football Player)
c/o Adam Heller *Vantage Management Group*
518 Reamer Dr
Carnegie, PA 15106-1845, USA

Stuckey, Henry (Athlete, Football Player)
3615 Winchester Ave
Atlantic City, NJ 08401-3544, USA

Stuckey, James (Jim) (Athlete, Football Player)
1314 Headquarters Plantation Dr
Johns Island, SC 29455-3100, USA

Stuckey, Rodney (Athlete, Basketball Player)
c/o Steve Banks *Banks Sports Ventures*
1126 17th Ave
Seattle, WA 98122-4645, USA

Studaway, Mark (Athlete, Football Player)
4524 Saint Honore Dr
Memphis, TN 38116-2012, USA

Studdard, Ruben (Musician)
c/o Jocelyn Coleman *Favor PR*
5900 Wilshire Blvd Fl 26
Los Angeles, CA 90036-5013, USA

Studdard, Vern (Athlete, Football Player)
11449 Tara Blvd
Lovejoy, GA 30250, USA

Studebaker, Andy (Athlete, Football Player)

Studi, Wes (Actor)
c/o Nevin Dolcefino *Innovative Artists*
1505 10th St
Santa Monica, CA 90401-2805, USA

Studnicka-Caden, Mary Lou (Athlete, Baseball Player)
29 Mazarron Dr
Hot Springs Village, AR 71909-5827, USA

Studstill, Patrick L (Pat) (Athlete, Football Player)
2235 Linda Flora Dr
Los Angeles, CA 90077-1410, USA

Studt, Amy (Musician)

Studwell, Scott (Athlete, Football Player)
10415 Brown Farm Cir
Eden Prairie, MN 55347-4926, USA

Stuffel, Paul (Athlete, Baseball Player)
25786 Buttercup Ct
Bonita Springs, FL 34135-9407, USA

Stuhlbarg, Michael (Actor)
c/o Lisa Loosemore *Viking Entertainment*
445 W 23rd St Ste 1A
New York, NY 10011-1445, USA

Stuhr, Jerzy (Actor, Director)
Graffutu Ltd
Ul SW Gertrudy 5
Cracow 31-107, POLAND

Stuhr-Thompsen, Beverly (Athlete, Baseball Player)
6379 N Muscatel Ave
San Gabriel, CA 91775-1843, USA

Stuhr-Thompson, Beverly (Baseball Player)
6379 N Muscatel Ave
San Gabriel, CA 91775-1843, USA

Stukes, Charles (Athlete, Football Player)
2040 Bishop St
Petersburg, VA 23805-2220, USA

Stull, Everett (Athlete, Baseball Player)
1667 Fieldgreen Overlook
Stone Mountain, GA 30088-3112, USA

Stults, Eric (Athlete, Baseball Player)
11390 County Road 14
Middlebury, IN 46540-9604, USA

Stults, Geoff (Actor)
c/o Chris Kanarick *ID Public Relations (NY)*
40 Wall St Fl 51
New York, NY 10005-1385, USA

Stults, George (Actor)
c/o Liza Anderson *Anderson Group Public Relations*
8060 Melrose Ave Fl 4
Los Angeles, CA 90046-7038, USA

Stump, Gene (Athlete, Basketball Player)
1418 Coral Ave
Vero Beach, FL 32963-2338, USA

Stump, Jim (Athlete, Baseball Player)
7432 Creekside Dr
Lansing, MI 48917-9693, USA

Stump, Patrick (Musician)
c/o Staff Member *Fueled By Ramen*
PO Box 1803
Tampa, FL 33601-1803, USA

Stumpel, Jozef (Athlete, Hockey Player)
12057 NW 69th Ct
Parkland, FL 33076-3335, USA

Stumpf, Paul K (Misc)
1515 Shasta Dr Apt 2219
Davis, CA 95616-6683, USA

Stumps, Kathy (Actor)
c/o Staff Member *Gersh*
9465 Wilshire Blvd Ste 600
Beverly Hills, CA 90212-2605, USA

Stuper, John (Athlete, Baseball Player)
38 Lake St
Hamden, CT 06517-2315, USA

Sturckow, Frederick W (Rick) (Astronaut)
19585 Descanso St
Tehachapi, CA 93561-6208, USA

Sturgess, Jim (Actor)
c/o Clair Dobbs *CLD Communications*
4 Broadway Ct
The Broadway
London SW191RG, UNITED KINGDOM

Sturgess, Shannon (Actor)
1223 Wilshire Blvd # 577
Santa Monica, CA 90403-5406, USA

Sturgis, Caleb (Athlete, Football Player)

Sturm, Jerry (Athlete, Football Player)
3 Niblick Ln
Littleton, CO 80123-6621, USA

Sturm, John F (Misc)
Newspaper Assn of America
1921 Gallows Rd # 4
Vienna, VA 22182-3900, USA

Sturm, Yfke (Model)
c/o Staff Member *Storm Model Management*
5 Jubilee Pl
1st Floor
London SW3 3TD, UK

Sturman, Eugene (Artist)
1108 W Washington Blvd
Venice, CA 90291, USA

Sturmer, Christina (Musician)
Postfach 113
Wien A-1218, Austria

Sturr, Jimmy (Musician)
United Polka Artists
PO Box 1
Florida, NY 10921-0001, USA

Sturridge, Charles (Director)
PFD
Drury House
34-43 Russell St
London WC2B 5HA, UNITED KINGDOM (UK)

Sturridge, Tom (Actor)
c/o Ciara Parkes *Public Eye Communications*
535 Kings Rd
#313 Plaza
London SW10 0SZ, UNITED KINGDOM

Sturt, Fred (Athlete, Football Player)
120 N Berkey Southern Rd
Swanton, OH 43558-8907, USA

Sturtevant, Julian M (Misc)
14025 3rd Ave NW
NW
Seattle, WA 98177-3923, USA

Sturtze, Tanyon (Athlete, Baseball Player)
9141 Equus Cir
Boynton Beach, FL 33472-4315, USA

Sturza, Ion (Prime Minister)
Premier's Office
Piaca Maril Atuner Nacional
Chishinev 277033, MOLDOVA

Stutter, Jason (Director, Producer, Writer)
c/o Simon Millar *Rumble Media*
1620 Broadway Ste C
Santa Monica, CA 90404-2777, USA

Stutzman, Martin (Congressman, Politician)
1728 Longworth Hob
Washington, DC 20515-4307, USA

Styler, Kara (Actor)
PO Box 8002
Honolulu, HI 96830-0002

Styler, Trudie (Actor, Director, Producer)
c/o Staff Member *Maven Pictures*
148 Spring St Fl 4
New York, NY 10012-3898, USA

Styles, Harry (Musician)
c/o Staff Member *Modest! Management*
91A Peterborough Rd
London SW6 3BU, UNITED KINGDOM

Stynes, Chris (Athlete, Baseball Player)
1980 NE 7th St Apt 106
Deerfield Beach, FL 33441-3778, USA

Styx (Music Group)
Alliance Artists
6025 the Corners Pkwy Ste 202
Norcross, GA 30092-3328, USA

Suarez, Carlos (Actor)
c/o Staff Member *Televisa*
Blvd Adolfo Lopez Mateos 232
Colonia San Angel INN
DF CP 01060, MEXICO

Suarez, Cecilia (Actor)
c/o Adriana Ayub *Lolo & Company*
Alvaro Obreg??n 187 int 16
Col. Roma Norte
Ciudad de Mexico CDMX 06700, MEXICO

Suarez, Ken (Athlete, Baseball Player)
6000 Forest Ln
Fort Worth, TX 76112-1060, USA

Suarez Gomez, Hector (Actor)
c/o Gabriel Blanco *Gabriel Blanco Iglesias (Mexico)*
Rio Balsas 35-32
Colonia Cuauhtemoc
DF 06500, Mexico

Suazo, Chloe (Actor)
c/o Cindy Osbrink *Osbrink Talent Agency*
4343 Lankershim Blvd # 100
North Hollywood, CA 91602-2705, USA

Subban, PK (Athlete, Hockey Player)
c/o Donald Meehan *Newport Sports Management*
201 City Centre Dr
Suite 400
Mississauga, ON L58 2T4, CANADA

Subban, PK (Athlete, Hockey Player)
c/o Staff Member *WME/IMG*
9601 Wilshire Blvd
Beverly Hills, CA 90210-5213, USA

Sublime with Rome (Music Group)
c/o Jon Phillips *Silverback Professional Artist Management*
9469 Jefferson Blvd Ste 101
Culver City, CA 90232-2915, USA

Subotnick, Morton L (Composer)
25 Minetta Ln Apt 4B
New York, NY 10012-1253, USA

Subways, The (Music Group)
c/o Staff Member *Paradigm (Monterey)*
404 W Franklin St
Monterey, CA 93940-2303, USA

Succop, Ryan (Athlete, Football Player)

Such, Alec John (Musician)
Bon Jovi Mgmt
248 W 17th St Apt 501
New York, NY 10011-5319, USA

Such, Dick (Athlete, Baseball Player)
7614 Divot Dr
Sanford, NC 27332-8804, USA

Suchet, David (Actor, Producer)
Twickenham Film Studios
Barons, St Margaret's
Twickenham, MDDX TW1 2AW, UNITED KINGDOM

Suchocka, Hanna (Prime Minister)
Urzad Rady Ministrow
Al Ujazdowskie 1/3
Warsaw 00-567, POLAND

Suci, Robert (Athlete, Football Player)
2341 Morton Ave
Flint, MI 48507-4445, USA

Sucsy, Michael (Director)
c/o Amanda Lundberg *42West*
600 3rd Ave Fl 23
New York, NY 10016-1914, USA

Sudakis, Bill (Athlete, Baseball Player)
81150 Avenida Graneros
Indio, CA 92203-7894, USA

Sudano, Brooklyn (Actor)
c/o Alex Spieller *Baker Winokur Ryder Public Relations*
200 5th Ave Fl 5
New York, NY 10010-3307, USA

Sudduth, Jill (Athlete, Swimmer)
9917 Calabasas Ave
Las Vegas, NV 89117-7513, USA

Sudduth, Skipp (Actor)
c/o Heather Reynolds *One Entertainment (NY)*
347 5th Ave Rm 1404
New York, NY 10016-5034, USA

Sudduth-Smith, Jill (Athlete, Olympic Athlete, Swimmer)
7615 Kiva Dr
Austin, TX 78749-2915, USA

Sudeikis, Jason (Actor, Comedian)
405 Clinton Ave
Brooklyn, NY 11238-1601, USA

Sudfeld, Zach (Athlete, Football Player)
c/o Scott Smith *XAM Sports*
3509 Ice Age Dr
Madison, WI 53719-5409, USA

Sudol, Alison (Actor, Musician)
c/o Emma Lewis *Paradigm*
8942 Wilshire Blvd
Beverly Hills, CA 90211-1908, USA

Suess, Hans E (Misc)
University of California
Chemistry Dept
La Jolla, CA 92093-0001, USA

Sugar, Alan (Business Person, Reality Star)
Amstrad Plc
Brentwood House
169 Kings Rd
Brentwood, Essex CM14 4EF, UK

Sugar, Leo T (Athlete, Football Player)
7161 Golden Eagle Ct Apt 1012
Fort Myers, FL 33912-1708, USA

Sugarcult (Actor)
Kio Novina Management & Booking
545 N Rossmore Ave Apt 3
Los Angeles, CA 90004-2440

Sugarland (Music Group)
c/o Jason Owen *Sandbox Entertainment*
3810 Bedford Ave Ste 200
Nashville, TN 37215-2555, USA

Sugarman, Burt (Producer)
3688/3700 E. Lakeshore Dr
Whitefish, MT 59937, USA

Sugarman, Joseph (Joe) (Business Person, Writer)
Blublocker Corp
7020 W Warm Springs Rd Ste 160
Las Vegas, NV 89113-4468, USA

Sugg, Diana K (Journalist)
Baltimore Sun
501 N Calvert St
Editorial Dept
Baltimore, MD 21278-1000, USA

Sugg, Joe (Internet Star)
c/o Matthew Harvey *WME/IMG (UK)*
103 New Oxford St WMA
Centrepoint
London WC1A 1DD, UNITED KINGDOM

Suggs, Shafer (Athlete, Football Player)
371 Janes Ave UNIT 107
Bolingbrook, IL 60440-3194, USA

Suggs, Terrell (Athlete, Football Player)
c/o Denise White *EAG Sports Management*
909 N Pacific Coast Hwy Ste 360
El Segundo, CA 90245-3864, USA

Suggs, Walt (Athlete, Football Player)
11105 Bradyville Pike
Readyville, TN 37149-4513, USA

Sugihara, Anri (Actor)
c/o Staff Member *Fitone*
4-32-12-4F Jingumae
Shibuya
Tokyo 150-0001, Japan

Suh, Ndamukong (Athlete, Football Player)
c/o Roosevelt Barnes *Independent Sports & Entertainment (ISE-IN)*
6435 W Jefferson Blvd # 197
Fort Wayne, IN 46804-6203, USA

Suh, Ndamunkong (Athlete, Football Player)
c/o Jimmy Sexton *CAA (Memphis)*
6060 Poplar Ave Ste 470
Memphis, TN 38119-0910, USA

suharto, Mohammed (Politician)
8 Jalan Cendana
Jakarta, Indonesia

Suhey, Matthew J (Matt) (Athlete, Football Player)
550 Carriage Way
Deerfield, IL 60015-4535, USA

Suhonen, Alpo (Coach)
Chicago Blackhawks
1901 W Madison St
United Center
Chicago, IL 60612-2459, USA

Suits, Julia (Cartoonist)
Creators Syndicate
5777 W Century Blvd # 700
Los Angeles, CA 90045-5600, USA

Sukezane, Kiki (Actor)
c/o Cheryl McLean *Creative Public Relations*
3385 Oak Glen Dr
Los Angeles, CA 90068-1311, USA

Sukla, Ed (Athlete, Baseball Player)
2725 4th St Apt 1
Santa Monica, CA 90405-4231, USA

Sukova, Helena (Tennis Player)
1 Ave Grande Bretagne
Monte Carlo, MONACO

Sukowa, Barbara (Actor)
Artmedia
20 Ave Rapp
Paris 75007, FRANCE

Sukselainen, Vieno J (Prime Minister)
Palvattarenpolku 2
Tapiola 02100, FINALND

Sula, Jessica (Actor)
c/o Daphne Waring *Waring and McKenna*
17 S Molton St
London W1K 5QT, UNITED KINGDOM

Sulaiman, Jose (Misc)
World Boxing Council
Genova 33
Colonia Juarez
Cuahtetemoc 00660, MEXICO

Sularz, Guy (Athlete, Baseball Player)
10818 N 83rd St
Scottsdale, AZ 85260-6550, USa

Suleman, Nadya (Octomom) (Reality Star)
2051 Madonna Ln
La Habra, CA 90631-3344, USA

Suliman, Ali (Actor)
c/o Jack Kingsrud *Zero Gravity Management*
11110 Ohio Ave Ste 100
Los Angeles, CA 90025-3329, USA

Sulkin, Gregg (Actor)
c/o Danielle Allman-Del *D2 Management*
10351 Santa Monica Blvd Ste 210
Los Angeles, CA 90025-6937, USA

Sullenberger, Chelsey (Sully) (Misc)
c/o CeCe Yorke *True Public Relations*
3575 Cahuenga Blvd W Ste 360
Los Angeles, CA 90068-1361, USA

Sulliman, Doug (Athlete, Hockey Player)
117454 N 100th Pl
Scottsdale, AZ 85255, USA

Sullivan, Brian (Athlete, Hockey Player)
392 E Beach Rd
Charlestown, RI 02813-1311, USA

Sullivan, Charlotte (Actor)
c/o Dani De Lio *Creative Drive Artists*
20 Minowan Miikan Lane
Toronto, ON M6J 0E5, CANADA

Sullivan, Chip (Golfer)
49 Homestead Cir
Troutville, VA 24175-6995, USA

Sullivan, Chris (Actor)
c/o James Suskin *Suskin Management*
2 Charlton St Apt 5K
New York, NY 10014-4970, USA

Sullivan, CHris (Athlete, Football Player)
64 Wagon Wheel Rd
North Attleboro, MA 02760-3576, USA

Sullivan, Cory (Athlete, Baseball Player)
1214 S Ogden St
Denver, CO 80210-1713, USA

Sullivan, Dan (Athlete, Football Player)
25 Algonquin Ave
Andover, MA 01810-5527, USA

Sullivan, Daniel (Producer, Writer)
c/o Alan Wertheimer *Jackoway Tyerman Wertheimer Austen Mandelbaum Morris & Klein*
1925 Century Park E Fl 22
Los Angeles, CA 90067-2701, USA

Sullivan, Erik Per (Actor)
c/o Jodi Peikoff *Peikoff Mahan Law Office*
173-175 E Broadway
Suite C1
New York, NY 10002, USA

Sullivan, Frank (Athlete, Baseball Player)
PO Box 1873
Lihue, HI 96766-5873, USA

Sullivan, Franklin L (Frank) (Athlete, Baseball Player)
PO Box 1873
Lihue, HI 96766-5873, USA

Sullivan, George (Athlete, Football Player)
41 Howard St
Norwood, MA 02062-2323, USA

Sullivan, George ""Red"" (Athlete, Hockey Player)
RR 2
Indian River, ON KOL 2BO, Canada

Sullivan, Greg (Musician)
David Levin Mgmt
200 W 57th St Ste 308
New York, NY 10019-3211, USA

Sullivan, Jazmine (Musician)
c/o Daniel Kim *Creative Artists Agency (CAA)*
2000 Avenue of the Stars Ste 100
Los Angeles, CA 90067-4705, USA

Sullivan, John (Athlete, Football Player)
c/o David Dunn *Athletes First*
23091 Mill Creek Dr
Laguna Hills, CA 92653-1258, USA

Sullivan, John (Athlete, Baseball Player)
24 Highland Ave
Dansville, NY 14437-1648, USA

Sullivan, John (Congressman, Politician)
434 Cannon Hob
Washington, DC 20515-2004, USA

Sullivan, Kathleen (Journalist)
1025 N Kings Rd Apt 202
West Hollywood, CA 90069-6008, USA

Sullivan, Kathryn D (Astronaut)
795 Old Oak Trce
Columbus, OH 43235-1761, USA

Sullivan, Kathryn D Dr (Astronaut)
795 Old Oak Tree
Columbus, OH 43235-1761, USA

Sullivan, Kevin (Journalist)
Washington Post
Editorial Dept
1150 15th St NW
Washington, DC 20071-0001, USA

Sullivan, Kevin Rodney (Actor, Director, Producer, Writer)
c/o Arnold Robinson *Rogers & Cowan*
1840 Century Park E Fl 18
Los Angeles, CA 90067-2101, USA

Sullivan, Louis (Politician)
Morehouse College
5287 N Powers Ferry Rd
Atlanta, GA 30327-4666, USA

Sullivan, Marc (Athlete, Baseball Player)
2038 W 1st St Ste 100
Fort Myers, FL 33901-3109, USA

Sullivan, Michael J (Mike) (Politician)
Rothgerber, Johnson, & Lyons
1124 S Durbin St
Casper, WY 82601-4328, USA

Sullivan, Mike (Athlete, Football Player)
Cleveland Brown
76 Lou Groza Blvd
Attn: Coaching Staff
Berea, OH 44017-1269, USA

Sullivan, Mike (Athlete, Coach, Hockey Player)
275 Elm St
Duxbury, MA 02332-4820, USA

Sullivan, Nicole (Actor)
c/o Tom Drumm *Think Tank Management*
1416 N La Brea Ave
the Jim Henson Lot
Los Angeles, CA 90028-7506, USA

Sullivan, Pat (Coach, Football Coach, Football Player, Heisman Trophy Winner)
1717 Indian Creek Dr
Vestavia, AL 35243-1745, USA

Sullivan, Peter (Athlete, Hockey Player)
316 Fairway Rd
Regina, SK S4Y 1JS, Canada

Sullivan, Phil (Athlete, Football Player)
4113 Rollingwood Ct
Jacksonville, FL 32257-7665, USA

Sullivan, Russ (Athlete, Baseball Player)
1701 Hill N Dale St
Fredericksburg, VA 22405-2735, USA

Sullivan, Scott (Athlete, Baseball Player)
1649 Mayfair Ct
Auburn, AL 36830-2128, USA

Sullivan, Steve (Athlete, Hockey Player)
5536 Iron Gate Dr
Franklin, TN 37069-7238, USA

Sullivan, Susan (Actor)
15355 Mulholland Dr
Los Angeles, CA 90077-1622, USA

Sullivan, Tim (Director)
Agency for Performing Arts
9200 W Sunset Blvd Ste 900
Los Angeles, CA 90069-3604, USA

Sullivan, Tom (Actor)
c/o Ryan Saul *Metropolitan (MTA)*
4526 Wilshire Blvd
Los Angeles, CA 90010-3801, USA

Sultan, Altoon (Artist)
PO Box 2
Groton, VT 05046-0002, USA

Sultan, Donald K (Artist)
19 E 70th St
New York, NY 10021-4982, USA

Sultanov, Alexel (Musician)
Columbia Artists Mgmt Inc
165 W 57th St
New York, NY 10019-2201, USA

Sultan Salman, Abdulaziz Al-Saud (Astronaut)
PO Box 18368
Riyadh 11415, SAUDI ARABIA

Sultonov, Outkir T (Prime Minister)
Prime Minister's Office
Mustarilik 5
Tashkent 70008, UZBEKISTAN

Sum 41 (Music Group)
c/o Ron Laffitte *Red Light Management*
5800 Bristol Pkwy Ste 400
Culver City, CA 90230-6898, USA

Sumaye, Frederick T (Prime Minister)
Prime Minister's Office
PO Box 980
Dodoma, TANZANIA

Sumika, Aya (Actor)
c/o Jill Littman *Impression Entertainment*
9229 W Sunset Blvd Ste 700
Los Angeles, CA 90069-3407, USA

Sumino, Naoko (Astronaut)
NASDA
Tsukuba Space Center
2-1-1 Sengen Tukubashi
Ibaraka 00305, JAPAN

Summer, Cree (Actor)
Monterey Peninsula Artists
509 Hartnell St
Monterey, CA 93940-2825, USA

Summer-Francks, Cree (Actor)
PO Box 5617
Beverly Hills, CA 90209-5617

Summerhays, Bob (Athlete, Football Player)
12345 SE 91st Ave
Summerfield, FL 34491-8251, USA

Summerhays, Boyd (Athlete, Golfer)
297 Frontier Rd
Farmington, UT 84025-2616, USA

Summerleigh, George A (Pat) (Athlete, Football Player)
710 S White Chapel Blvd
Southlake, TX 76092-7319, USA

Summers, Andy (Musician)
1111 San Vicente Blvd
Santa Monica, CA 90402-2007, USA

Summers, Carol (Artist)
2817 Smith Grade
Santa Cruz, CA 95060-9764, USA

Summers, Champ (Athlete, Baseball Player)
13708 SW 111th Ave
Dunnellon, FL 34432-8797, USA

Summers, Dana (Cartoonist)
Orlando Sentinel
633 N Orange Ave Lbby
Editorial Dept
Orlando, FL 32801-1349, USA

Summers, Jerry (Musician)
American Promotions
2011 Ferry Ave Apt U19
Camden, NJ 08104-1900, USA

Summers, Lawrence (Politician)
Harvard University
5409 Falmouth Rd
Bethesda, MD 20816-2918, USA

Summers, Marc (Actor, Chef, Director, Producer, Television Host)
c/o Staff Member *Marc Summers Productions*
23705 Vanowen St Ste 105
Canoga Park, CA 91307-3030, USA

Summers, Tara (Actor)
c/o Lena Roklin *Luber Roklin Management*
5815 W Sunset Blvd Ste 208
Los Angeles, CA 90028-6481, USA

Summers, Wilbur (Athlete, Football Player)
PO Box 72734
Louisville, KY 40272-0734, USA

Sumner, Mickey (Actor)

Sumner, Peter (Actor)
15/71 Avenue Road
Mosman 02088, AUSTRALIA

Sumner, Walt (Athlete, Football Player)
PO Box 112
Ocilla, GA 31774-0112, USA

Sumners, Rosalynn (Athlete, Figure Skater, Olympic Athlete)
7815 115th Pl NE
Kirkland, WA 98033-6710, USA

Sumpter, Jeremy (Actor)
c/o Mark Robert *Mark Robert Management*
2208 Patricia Ave
Los Angeles, CA 90064-2318, USA

Sumpter, Tika (Actor)
c/o Emily Gerson Saines *Brookside Artists Management*
250 W 57th St Ste 1820
New York, NY 10107-1802, USA

Sumpter, Tony (Athlete, Football Player)
5503 E 109th St
Tulsa, OK 74137-7245, USA

Sun Dao Lin (Actor, Director)
Shanghai Film Studio
595 Tsao Hsi North Road
Shanghai 200030, CHINA

Sunday, Gabriel (Actor)
c/o Judy Savage *Savage Agency*
1041 N Formosa Ave
West Hollywood, CA 90046-6703, USA

Sundberg, Jim (Athlete, Baseball Player)
2308 Newforest Ct
Arlington, TX 76017-2638, USA

Sundberg, Nick (Athlete, Football Player)
c/o Ryan Tollner *REP 1 Sports Group*
80 Technology Dr
Irvine, CA 92618-2301, USA

Sunde, Milt (Athlete, Football Player)
6008 W 104th St
Bloomington, MN 55438-1826, USA

Sunderland, Zac (Athlete)
1710 N Moorpark Rd # 212
Thousand Oaks, CA 91360-5133, USA

Sundhage, Pia (Coach)
U.S. Soccer Federation
1801 S Prairie Ave
Women's National Team
Chicago, IL 60616-1356, USA

Sundin, Gordie (Athlete, Baseball Player)
28132 Goby Trl
Bonita Springs, FL 34135-8469, USA

Sundin, Mats (Athlete, Hockey Player)
C A A Hockey
204-822 11 Ave SW
Attn J P Barry
Calgary, AB T2R 0E5, Canada

Sundstrom, Peter (Athlete, Hockey Player)
Bygardesvagen 32
Malmo 21621, Sweden

Sundvold, Jon (Athlete, Basketball Player)
2700 Westbrook Way
Columbia, MO 65203-5221, USA

Sundwall, Mina (Actor)
c/o Jill Fritzo *Jill Fritzo Public Relations*
208 E 51st St # 305
New York, NY 10022-6557, USA

Sung, Elizabeth (Actor)
c/o Staff Member *GVA Talent Agency Inc*
193 N Robertson Blvd
Beverly Hills, CA 90211-2103, USA

Sunjata, Daniel (Actor)
c/o Meg Mortimer *Authentic Talent and Literary Management (NY)*
20 Jay St Ste M17
Brooklyn, NY 11201-8300, USA

Sunseri, Vinnie (Athlete, Football Player)

Sunshine, Caroline (Actor)
c/o Shannon Barr *Rogers & Cowan*
1840 Century Park E Fl 18
Los Angeles, CA 90067-2101, USA

Sunshine Underground, The (Music Group)
c/o Staff Member *Paradigm (Monterey)*
404 W Franklin St
Monterey, CA 93940-2303, USA

Sununu, John E (Politician)
49 Linden Rd
Hampton Falls, NH 03844-2035, USA

Suotamo, Joonas (Actor)

Superdrag (Music Group)
c/o Staff Member *Paradigm (Monterey)*
404 W Franklin St
Monterey, CA 93940-2303, USA

Supergrass (Music Group)
c/o Staff Member *Paradigm (Monterey)*
404 W Franklin St
Monterey, CA 93940-2303, USA

Supernaw, Kywin (Athlete, Football Player)
1123 Clairborne Ct
Indianapolis, IN 46280-1100, USA

Suplee, Ethan (Actor)
Don Buchwald
5900 Wilshire Blvd Ste 3100
Los Angeles, CA 90036-5030, USA

Suppan, Jeff (Athlete, Baseball Player)
25315 Prado De La Felicidad
Calabasas, CA 91302-3651, USA

Suquia Goicoechea, Angel Cardinal (Religious Leader)
El Cardenal Arxobispo
San Justo 2
Madrid 28074, SPAIN

Sura, Bob (Basketball Player)
Atlanta Hawks
190 Marietta St NW Ste 405
Atlanta, GA 30303-2717, USA

Sure, Al B (Musician)
c/o Staff Member *ICM Partners*
10250 Constellation Blvd Fl 7
Los Angeles, CA 90067-6207, USA

Surhoff, BJ (Athlete, Baseball Player, Olympic Athlete)
2205 Pine Hill Farms Ln
Cockeysville, MD 21030-1023, USA

Surhoff, Rick (Athlete, Baseball Player)
1839 White Oak Dr
Reading, PA 19608-9468, USA

Surin, Bruny (Athlete, Track Athlete)
PO Box 2 Succ Saint-Michel
Succ Saint Michel
Montreal, QC H2A 3L8, CANADA

Surkowski-Delmonico, Lee (Athlete, Baseball Player)
10 Via Las Colinas Apt 1
Rancho Mirage, CA 92270-6015, USA

Surkowski-Deyotte, Anne (Athlete, Baseball Player)
632 Southwind Dr
Kelowna, BC V1W 3G1, CANADA

Surma, Damian (Athlete, Hockey Player)
1057 Emmons Blvd
Lincoln Park, MI 48146-4240, USA

Surratt, Al (Baseball Player)
Kansas City Monarchs
3448 E 54th St
Kansas City, MO 64130-4027, USA

Sursok, Tammin (Actor)
c/o Julie Bloom *Art/Work Entertainment*
5670 Wilshire Blvd Ste 900
Los Angeles, CA 90036-5699, USA

Surtain, Patrick (Athlete, Football Player)
14557 Sherwood St
Overland Park, KS 66224-9807, USA

Susana, Marta (Actor)
c/o Staff Member *Univision*
605 3rd Ave Fl 12
New York, NY 10158-0034, USA

Susclick, Kenneth S (Misc)
University of Illinois
Chemistry Dept
Champaign, IL 61820, USA

Susco, Stephen (Producer, Writer)
c/o David Saunders *Agency for the Performing Arts (APA)*
405 S Beverly Dr Ste 500
Beverly Hills, CA 90212-4425, USA

Susman, Todd (Actor)
Pakula/King
9229 W Sunset Blvd Ste 315
Los Angeles, CA 90069-3403, USA

Sussman, Adam (Writer)
c/o Staff Member *McKuin Frankel Whitehead*
141 El Camino Dr Ste 100
Beverly Hills, CA 90212-2717, USA

Sussman, Kevin (Actor)
c/o Jill McGrath *Door24*
115 W 29th St Rm 1102
New York, NY 10001-5106, USA

Sutcliffe, David (Actor)
c/o Robert Stein *Robert Stein Management*
PO Box 3797
Beverly Hills, CA 90212-0797, USA

Sutcliffe, Richard L (Rick) (Athlete, Baseball Player)
616 NE Seabrook Ct
Lees Summit, MO 64064-1261, USA

Suter, Gary (Athlete, Hockey Player, Olympic Athlete)
2128 County Road D
Lac Du Flambeau, WI 54538-9726, USA

Suter, Ryan (Athlete, Hockey Player)
6604 Indian Hills Rd
Minneapolis, MN 55439-1009, USA

Sutherin, Don (Athlete, Football Player)
1043 Cayuga Trl SW
Hartville, OH 44632-9488, USA

Sutherland, Alyssa (Actor)
c/o Brett Ruttenberg *Imprint PR*
6121 W Sunset Blvd
Neuehouse
Los Angeles, CA 90028-6442, USA

Sutherland, Angus (Actor)
6369 Ivarene Ave
Los Angeles, CA 90068-2821, USA

Sutherland, Bill (Actor)
c/o Staff Member *Select Artists Ltd (CA-Westside Office)*
1138 12th St Apt 1
Santa Monica, CA 90403-5459, USA

Sutherland, Darrell (Athlete, Baseball Player)
1011 NW Jeffrey Pl
Beaverton, OR 97006-6335, USA

Sutherland, David (Golfer)
5431 Tree Side Dr
Carmichael, CA 95608-5958, USA

Sutherland, Donald (Actor, Musician, Producer)
c/o Catherine Olim *PMK/BNC Public Relations*
1840 Century Park E Ste 1400
Los Angeles, CA 90067-2115, USA

Sutherland, Doug (Athlete, Football Player)
511 Kenilworth Ave
Duluth, MN 55803-2113, USA

Sutherland, Gary (Athlete, Baseball Player)
338 Oakcliff Rd
Monrovia, CA 91016-1823, USA

Sutherland, Kevin (Golfer)
1230 Carter Rd
Sacramento, CA 95864-5328, USA

Sutherland, Kiefer (Actor)
c/o Annett Wolf *Wolf-Kasteler Public Relations*
6255 W Sunset Blvd Ste 1111
Los Angeles, CA 90028-7426, USA

Sutherland, Kristine (Actor)
c/o Staff Member *SMS Talent*
8383 Wilshire Blvd Ste 230
Beverly Hills, CA 90211-2436, USA

Sutherland, Leo (Athlete, Baseball Player)
12082 Nieta Dr
Garden Grove, CA 92840-3524, USA

Sutherland, Sarah (Actor)
c/o Scott Swiontek *Gersh*
41 Madison Ave Ste 3301
New York, NY 10010-2210, USA

Sutherland, Shirley (Athlete, Baseball Player)
9613 Ritter Dr
Machesney Park, IL 61115-1759, USA

Sutherland, Steve (Athlete, Hockey Player)
275 Av Wilfrid-Laurier
Quebec, QC G1R 2K8, Canada

Sutko, Glenn (Athlete, Baseball Player)
4475 Settles Bridge Rd
Suwanee, GA 30024-1981, USA

Sutor, George (Athlete, Basketball Player)
29840 State Highway 27
Holcombe, WI 54745-8798, USA

Sutter, Brent (Athlete, Hockey Player)
PO Box 1540 Stn M
Attn: Coaching Staff
Calgary, AB T2P 3B9, Canada

Sutter, Brent (Athlete, Coach, Hockey Player)
PO Box 545
Viking, AB T0B 4N0, Canada

Sutter, Brian (Athlete, Coach, Hockey Player)
PO Box 545
Viking, AB T0B 4N0, Canada

Sutter, Bruce (Athlete, Baseball Player)
59 Waterside Dr SE
Cartersville, GA 30121-6615, USA

Sutter, Darryl (Athlete, Coach, Hockey Player)
PO Box 1540 Stn M
Station M
Calgary, AB T2P 3B9, Canada

Sutter, Duane (Athlete, Hockey Player)
3703 High Pine Dr
Coral Springs, FL 33065-6014, USA

Sutter, Eddie (Athlete, Football Player)
5104 N Bevalon Pl
Peoria, IL 61614-4606, USA

Sutter, Kurt (Producer)
c/o Tom Monjack *Tom Monjack Celebrity Enterprises*
28650 Avenida Maravilla # A
Cathedral City, CA 92234-8115, USA

Sutter, Rich (Athlete, Hockey Player)
1920 17 St
SUTTER ICE
Coaldale, AB T1M 1M1, Canada

Sutter, Ron (Athlete, Hockey Player)
44 Chaparral Cove SE
Calgary, AB T2X 3L4, Canada

Sutter, Ryan (Athlete, Football Player)
9543 Cedarhurst Ln Unit C
Highlands Ranch, CO 80129-2565, USA

Sutter, Trista (Reality Star)
c/o Marissa Lerner *Evolution Management + Marketing*
14622 Ventura Blvd
Sherman Oaks, CA 91403-3600, USA

Sutterluty, Elizabeth (Actor)
Cineart
36 Rue de Ponthleu
Paris 75008, FRANCE

Suttle, Dane (Athlete, Basketball Player)
138 W 69th St
Los Angeles, CA 90003-1824, USA

Sutton, Andy (Athlete, Hockey Player)
491 Peachtree Battle Ave NW
Atlanta, GA 30305-4062, USA

Sutton, Courtland (Athlete, Football Player)
c/o Jake Presser *PFS Agency (NY)*
200 E 33rd St Apt 23E
New York, NY 10016-4830, USA

Sutton, Daron (Baseball Player)
9273 E Pershing Ave
Scottsdale, AZ 85260-7401, USA

Sutton, Don (Athlete, Baseball Player)
611 Riverlawn Ct
Atlanta, GA 30339-2993, USA

Sutton, Drew (Athlete, Baseball Player)
1600 Birchmont Ln
Keller, TX 76248-8221, USA

Sutton, Greg (Athlete, Basketball Player)
PO Box 1801
Edmond, OK 73083-1801, USA

Sutton, Hal (Golfer)
909 Trabue St
Shreveport, LA 71106-1114, USA

Sutton, John (Athlete, Baseball Player)
536 Blueberry Blvd
Dallas, TX 75217-4201, USA

Sutton, Kelly (Race Car Driver)
8410 Streamview Dr Apt G
Huntersville, NC 28078-6117, USA

Sutton, Ken (Athlete, Hockey Player)
223 Oakfern Way SW
Calgary, AB T2V 4K2, Canada

Sutton, Larry (Athlete, Baseball Player)
14209 Woodward St
Overland Park, KS 66223-2561, USA

Sutton, Michael (Actor)
Somers Teitelbaum David
8840 Wilshire Blvd # 200
Beverly Hills, CA 90211-2606, USA

Sutton, Percy E (Politician)
10 W 135th St
New York, NY 10037-2602, USA

Sutton, Ricky (Athlete, Football Player)
1112 To Lani Farm Rd
Stone Mountain, GA 30083-5364, USA

Sutton, Will (Athlete, Football Player)
c/o Bruce Tollner *REP 1 Sports Group*
80 Technology Dr
Irvine, CA 92618-2301, USA

Suvadova, Silvia (Actor)
c/o Michael Henderson *Heresun Management*
4119 W Burbank Blvd
Burbank, CA 91505-2122, USA

Suvari, Mena (Actor)
c/o Bianca Bianconi *42West*
600 3rd Ave Fl 23
New York, NY 10016-1914, USA

Suwa, Gen (Misc)
University of California
Human Evolutionary Science Lab # 303
Berkeley, CA 94720-0001, USA

Suwyn, Mark A (Business Person)
Louisiana-Pacific Corp
111 SW 5th Ave
Portland, OR 97204-3604, USA

Suzman, Janet (Actor)
Faircroft
11 Keats Grove
Hampstead
London NW3, UNITED KINGDOM (UK)

Suzor, Mark (Athlete, Hockey Player)
7 Beartooth Dr
Sheridan, WY 82801-9004, USA

Suzuki, Ichiro (Athlete, Baseball Player)
4101 185th Pl SE
Issaquah, WA 98027-9765, USA

Suzuki, Kurt (Athlete, Baseball Player)
5111 Steveann St
Torrance, CA 90503-5359, USA

Suzuki, Mac (Athlete, Baseball Player)
5122 E Shea Blvd Unit 1164
Scottsdale, AZ 85254-4677, USA

Suzy (Writer)
18 E 68th St # 1B
New York, NY 10065-5807, USA

Svankmajer, Jan (Director)
Ceminska 5
Prague 1 118 00, CZECH REPUBLIC

Svare, Harland (Athlete, Coach, Football Coach, Football Player)
6773 Turnstone Ave
Castle Rock, CO 80104-8745, USA

Svatos, Marek (Athlete, Hockey Player)
9310 E Winding Hill Ave
Lone Tree, CO 80124-8482, USA

Svehla, Robert (Athlete, Hockey Player)
Dukla Trencin Hockey Club Povaszka 34
Attn: President's Office
Trencin 91101, Slovakia

Svejkovsky, Jaroslav (Yogi) (Athlete, Hockey Player)
184 Kilarney Pl
Point Roberts, WA 98281-9518, USA

Svenden, Birgitta (Musician)
Ulf Tomqvist
Sankt Eriksgatan 100
Stockholm 113 31, SWEDEN

Sveningsson, Magnus (Musician)
Motor SE
Gotabergs Gatan 2
Gothenburg 400 14, SWEDEN

Svenson, Bo (Actor)
c/o Gerry Jordan *Jordan & Associates*
125-720 King St W
Toronto, ON M5V 3S5, CANADA

Svensson, Leif (Athlete, Hockey Player)
Lisselbyvagan 39
Leksand S-79333, Sweden

Svensson, Peter (Musician, Songwriter, Writer)
Motor SE
Gotabergs Gatan 2
Gothenburg 400 14, SWEDEN

Sverak, Jan (Director)
PO Box 33
Prague 515 155 00, CZECH REPUBLIC

Sveum, Dale (Athlete, Baseball Player)
13483 E Estrella Ave
Scottsdale, AZ 85259-5417, USA

Svihus, Bob (Athlete, Football Player)
23000 Guidotti Dr
Salinas, CA 93908-1022, USA

Svitov, Alexander (Athlete, Hockey Player)
Puckagency LLC
555 Pleasantville Rd Ste 210N
Attn Jay Grossman
Briarcliff Manor, NY 10510-1900, USA

Svoboda, Petr (Athlete, Hockey Player)
818 18th St Unit F
Santa Monica, CA 90403-1935, USA

Swaby, Donn (Actor)
c/o Staff Member *Artists & Representatives (Stone Manners Salners)*
6100 Wilshire Blvd Ste 1500
Los Angeles, CA 90048-5110, USA

Swaby, Donn (Actor)

Swagerty, Jane (Swimmer)
9128 N 70th St
Paradise Valley, AZ 85253-1960, USA

Swagerty, Keith (Athlete, Basketball Player)
22232 17th Ave SE Ste 205
Bothell, WA 98021-7411, USA

Swaggart, Jimmy L (Misc)
PO Box 262550
Baton Rouge, LA 70826-2550, USA

Swaggerty, Bill (Athlete, Baseball Player)
116 S Forney Ave
Hanover, PA 17331-3711, USA

Swail, Julie (Athlete, Coach)
University of California
Athletic Dept
Irvine, CA 92697-0001, USA

Swain, Brennan (Athlete)
c/o Jerry Shandrew *Shandrew Public Relations*
1050 S Stanley Ave
Los Angeles, CA 90019-6634, USA

Swain, Chelse (Actor)
c/o Staff Member *Identity Talent Agency (ID)*
9107 Wilshire Blvd Ste 500
Beverly Hills, CA 90210-5526, USA

Swain, Dominique (Actor)
c/o Luc Chaudhary *International Artists Management*
25-27 Heath St.
Hamstead NW3 6TR, UNITED KINGDOM

Swain, Garry (Athlete, Hockey Player)
PO Box 729
West Simsbury, CT 06092-0729, USA

Swain, John (Athlete, Football Player)
409 E 135th St
Burnsville, MN 55337-4019, USA

Swan, Billy (Musician, Songwriter, Writer)
Muirhead Mgmt
202 Fulham Road
Chelsea
London SW10 9PJ, UNITED KINGDOM (UK)

Swan, Charles W (Actor)
2043 Golf Course Rd
Halifax, VA 24558-3069, USA

Swan, Craig (Athlete, Baseball Player)
296 Sound Beach Ave
Old Greenwich, CT 06870-1626, USA

Swan, John W D (President)
Swan Building
26 Victoria St
Hamilton HM12, BERMUDA

Swan, Michael (Actor)
13576 Cheltenham Dr
Sherman Oaks, CA 91423-4818, USA

Swan, Serinda (Actor)
c/o Alex Cole *Elevate Entertainment*
6300 Wilshire Blvd # 807
Los Angeles, CA 90048-5204, USA

Swanagon, Mary Lou (Baseball Player)
2193 E Amarillo Way
Palm Springs, CA 92264-8637, USA

Swanepoel, Candice (Model)
c/o Liz Carpenter *IMG Models (NY)*
304 Park Ave S PH N
New York, NY 10010-4303, USA

Swank, Hilary (Actor)
400 W 12th St Apt 16A
New York, NY 10014-1861, USA

Swanke, Karl (Athlete, Football Player)
4 Butternut Ct
Essex Junction, VT 05452-3959, USA

Swann, Lynn C (Athlete, Football Player, Sportscaster)
506 Hegner Way # 2
Sewickley, PA 15143-1552, USA

Swann, Pedro (Athlete, Baseball Player)
9 Westbury Dr
New Castle, DE 19720-8812, USA

Swanson, Jackie (Actor)
15155 Albright St
Pacific Palisades, CA 90272-2511, USA

Swanson, John (Race Car Driver)
235-237 Main St.
Maynard, MA 01754, USA

Swanson, Judith (Actor)
Persona Mgmt
40 E 9th St
New York, NY 10003-6421, USA

Swanson, Kristy (Actor)
c/o David Shapira *David Shapira & Associates*
193 N Robertson Blvd
Beverly Hills, CA 90211-2103, USA

Swanson, Red (Athlete, Baseball Player)
1139 Chippenham Dr
Baton Rouge, LA 70808-5694, USA

Swanson, Stan (Athlete, Baseball Player)
688 Bass Ln
Corvallis, MT 59828-9739, USA

Swanson, Steven R (Astronaut)
2677 E Rhyolite Ct
Boise, ID 83712-8432, USA

Swanson, Travis (Athlete, Football Player)
c/o David Dunn *Athletes First*
23091 Mill Creek Dr
Laguna Hills, CA 92653-1258, USA

Swarbrick, George (Athlete, Hockey Player)
14918 Ridgeview Dr
Plattsmouth, NE 68048-8798, USA

Sward, Melinda (Actor)

Swardson, Nick (Actor, Musician)
c/o Tim Sarkes *Brillstein Entertainment Partners*
9150 Wilshire Blvd Ste 350
Beverly Hills, CA 90212-3453, USA

Swarn, George (Football Player)
442 Daisy St
Mansfield, OH 44903-1305, USA

Swarovski, Fiona (Business Person)
Unterhirzinger Hof
Kitzbuhel 06370, Austria

Swartwoudt, Gregg (Athlete, Football Player)
202 Anderson Rd
Esko, MN 55733-9413, USA

Swartz, Steven R (Business Person)
Hearst
300 W 57th St Fl 32
New York, NY 10019-3788, USA

Swartzbaugh, Dave (Athlete, Baseball Player)
113 Orchard St
Middletown, OH 45044-4920, USA

Swatek, Barret (Actor)
c/o Tammy Rosen *Sanders Armstrong Caserta*
4111 W Alameda Ave Ste 505
Burbank, CA 91505-4163, USA

Swatland, Richard (Athlete, Football Player)
107 Club Rd
Stamford, CT 06905-2121, USA

Sway (Television Host)
c/o Staff Member *MTV (NY)*
1515 Broadway
New York, NY 10036-8901, USA

Swayne, Harry (Football Player)
Tampa Bay Buccaneers
956 Cheswick Dr
Gurnee, IL 60031-5600, USA

Swayze, Don (Actor)
c/o Steve Rodriguez *McGowan Management*
170 S Beverly Dr Ste 304
Beverly Hills, CA 90212-3000, USA

Swearingen, John E Jr (Business Person)
1420 N Lake Shore Dr
Chicago, IL 60610-6657, USA

Swearinger, D.J. (Athlete, Football Player)
c/o Todd France *Creative Artists Agency (CAA) Sports*
3500 Lenox Rd NE
Atlanta, GA 30326-4228, USA

Sweat, Keith (Musician, Songwriter)
c/o Michael Irving *Emancipated Talent*
344 Grove St Ste 21
Jersey City, NJ 07302-5923, USA

Sweat, Lynn (Artist)
29 Bantry Rd
Simsbury, CT 06070-3192, USA

Swedberg, Heidi (Actor)
c/o Staff Member *Marathon Entertainment*
8060 Melrose Ave Ste 400
Los Angeles, CA 90046-7038

Swedish House Mafia (DJ, Music Group)

Swedlin, Rosalie (Producer)
c/o Staff Member *Jackoway Tyerman Wertheimer Austen Mandelbaum Morris & Klein*
1925 Century Park E Fl 22
Los Angeles, CA 90067-2701, USA

Sweeney, Alison (Actor)
c/o Carrie Simons *Triple 7 PR*
11693 San Vicente Blvd # 333
Los Angeles, CA 90049-5105, USA

Sweeney, Bob (Athlete, Hockey Player)
110 Brookview Dr
North Andover, MA 01845-3253, USA

Sweeney, Brian (Athlete, Baseball Player)
111 Old Coach Rd
Clifton Park, NY 12065-7618, USA

Sweeney, Calvin (Athlete, Football Player)
4120 Olympiad Dr
View Park, CA 90043-1632, USA

Sweeney, DB (Actor)
c/o Ashley Franklin *Thruline Entertainment*
9250 Wilshire Blvd Fl Ground
Beverly Hills, CA 90212-3352, USA

Sweeney, Don (Athlete, Hockey Player)
100 Legends Way Ste 250
Attn: Asst General Manager
Boston, MA 02114-1390, USA

Sweeney, Don (Athlete, Hockey Player)
10 Munroe Rd
Lexington, MA 02421-7812, USA

Sweeney, John J (Politician)
AFL-CIO
1750 New York Ave NW Ste 230
Washington, DC 20006-5306, USA

Sweeney, Julia (Actor, Comedian)
c/o Staff Member *WME|IMG*
9601 Wilshire Blvd
Beverly Hills, CA 90210-5213, USA

Sweeney, Kevin (Athlete, Football Player)
12401 N Via Tuscania Ave
Clovis, CA 93619-8382, USA

Sweeney, Mark (Athlete, Baseball Player)
10804 Heather Ridge Dr
San Diego, CA 92130-6941, USA

Sweeney, Michael J (Mike) (Athlete, Baseball Player)
2802 E Tam 0 Shanter Ct
Ontario, CA 91761-7423, USA

Sweeney, Ryan (Athlete, Baseball Player)
6941 Waterview Dr SW
Cedar Rapids, IA 52404-7749, USA

Sweeney, Sunny (Musician)
c/o Staff Member *WME (Nashville)*
1201 Demonbreun St
Nashville, TN 37203-3140, USA

Sweeney, Terry (Actor, Comedian, Writer)
c/o Staff Member *Creative Artists Agency (CAA)*
2000 Avenue of the Stars Ste 100
Los Angeles, CA 90067-4705, USA

Sweeney, Tim (Athlete, Hockey Player)
47 Ledgewood Dr
Hanover, MA 02339-1329, USA

Sweet, Don (Athlete, Football Player)
5-20751 87 Ave
Langley, BC V1M 2X3, Canada

Sweet, Joe (Athlete, Football Player)
1503 NE 89th Ct
Vancouver, WA 98664-6413, USA

Sweet, Matthew (Musician, Songwriter, Writer)
Russell Carter Artists Mgmt
315 W Ponce De Leon Ave Ste 755
Decatur, GA 30030-2497, USA

Sweet, Phillip (Musician)
809 Legends Glen Ct
Franklin, TN 37069-4600, USA

Sweet, Rachel (Producer)
c/o Staff Member *WME/IMG*
9601 Wilshire Blvd
Beverly Hills, CA 90210-5213, USA

Sweet, Rick (Athlete, Baseball Player)
2398 N Heritage St
Buckeye, AZ 85396-1624, USA

Sweet, Shay (Adult Film Star)
c/o Staff Member *Atlas Multimedia Inc*
9005 Eton Ave Ste C
Canoga Park, CA 91304-6533, USA

Sweeten, Madylin (Actor)
c/o Dino May *Dino May Management*
13223 Bloomfield St
Sherman Oaks, CA 91423-3207, USA

Sweetin, Jodie (Actor)
c/o Jessica Cohen *JCPR*
9903 Santa Monica Blvd # 983
Beverly Hills, CA 90212-1671, USA

Sweetney, Mike (Basketball Player)
New York Knicks
2 Penn Plz Fl 15
Madison Square Garden
New York, NY 10121-1700, USA

Swenson, Eliza (Actor, Musician)
Ad Astra Management
5118 Vineland Ave # 102
North Hollywood, CA 91601-3814, USA

Swenson, Inga (Actor, Musician)
3351 Halderman St
Los Angeles, CA 90066-1719, USA

Swenson, Robert C (Bob) (Athlete, Football Player)
910 Cypress Ln
Louisville, CO 80027-9428, USA

Swick, Mike (Athlete)
c/o Staff Member *Zinkin Entertainment & Sports Management*
5 E River Park Pl W Ste 203
Fresno, CA 93720-1557, USA

Swicord, Robin (Writer)
c/o Jenny Maryasis *United Talent Agency (UTA)*
9336 Civic Center Dr
Beverly Hills, CA 90210-3604, USA

Swider, Larry (Athlete, Football Player)
1903 W 93rd Ave
Crown Point, IN 46307-1809, USA

Swienton, Gregory T (Business Person)
Ryder System Inc
3600 NW 82nd Ave
Doral, FL 33166-6623, USA

Swierc, Carl (Athlete, Football Player)
Carl Swierc
Houston, TX 77018-1209, USA

Swift, Billy (Athlete, Baseball Player)
5880 E Sapphire Ln
Paradise Valley, AZ 85253-2200, USA

Swift, Clive (Actor)
Roxane Vacca Mgmt
8 Silver Place
London W1R 3LJ, UNITED KINGDOM (UK)

Swift, Doug (Athlete, Football Player)
265 S 25th St
Philadelphia, PA 19103-5551, USA

Swift, Graham C (Writer)
AP Watt
20 John St
London WC1N 2DR, UNITED KINGDOM (UK)

Swift, Harley (Athlete, Basketball Player)
357 Cliffside Dr
Kingsport, TN 37660-7103, USA

Swift, Stephanie (Adult Film Star)
PO Box 9864
Canoga Park, CA 91309-0864, USA

Swift, Stromile (Athlete, Basketball Player)
1111 Lincoln Rd Fl 4
Miami Beach, FL 33139-2439, USA

Swift, Taylor (Musician)
Taylor Swift Enterprises
242 W Main St # 412
Hendersonville, TN 37075-3318, USA

Swilley, Dennis (Athlete, Football Player)
1020 Gruene River Dr
New Braunfels, TX 78132-3298, USA

S. Wilson, Frederica (Congressman, Politician)
208 Cannon Hob
Washington, DC 20515-0107, USA

Swindell, Cole (Musician)
c/o Staff Member *WME (Nashville)*
1201 Demonbreun St
Nashville, TN 37203-3140, USA

Swindell, F Gregory (Greg) (Athlete, Baseball Player)
6213 Terwilliger Way
Houston, TX 77057-2803, USA

Swindell, Jeff (Race Car Driver)
TW Racing
1921 W 4th St
Marion, IN 46952-6200, USA

Swindell, Sammy (Race Car Driver)
7540 Bartlett Corporate Cv E
Bartlett, TN 38133-3963, USA

Swindells, William Jr (Business Person)
Williamette Industries
1300 SW 5th Ave
Portland, OR 97201-5667, USA

Swindle, RJ (Athlete, Baseball Player)
9382 Ayscough Rd
Summerville, SC 29485-8677, USA

Swindoll, Luci (Writer)
Thomas Nelson, Inc
PO Box 141000
Nashville, TN 37214-1000, USA

Swinford, Wayne (Athlete, Football Player)
100 Beacham Dr
Athens, GA 30606-4004, USA

Swingle, Paul (Athlete, Baseball Player)
6844 S Whetstone Pl
Chandler, AZ 85249-9149, USA

Swink, James E (Jim) (Athlete, Football Player)
723 Euclid Ave
Rusk, TX 75785-1919, USA

Swinney, Clovis (Athlete, Football Player)
611 Candis Dr
Jonesboro, AR 72404-9049, USA

Swinny, Wayne (Musician)
Helter Skelter Plaza
535 Kings Road
London SW10 0S, UNITED KINGDOM (UK)

Swinson, Aaron (Athlete, Basketball Player)
1004 Longley Cv
Heathrow, FL 32746-1921, USA

Swinton, Tilda (Actor)
c/o Christian Hodell *Hamilton Hodell Ltd*
20 Golden Sq
Fl 5
London W1F 9JL, UNITED KINGDOM

Swisher, Carl C (Misc)
Institute of Human Origins
1288 9th St
Berkeley, CA 94710-1501, USA

Swisher, Nick (Athlete, Baseball Player)
c/o Team Member *New York Yankees*
161st St & River Ave
Yankee Stadium
Bronx, NY 10451, USA

Swisher, Steve (Athlete, Baseball Player)
11237 Blacksmith Dr
Tampa, FL 33626-2675, USA

Swisshelm, Ann (Athlete, Olympic Athlete)
855 W Erie St Apt 106
Chicago, IL 60642-5948, USA

Swisten, Amanda (Actor)
c/o Cheryl McLean *Creative Public Relations*
3385 Oak Glen Dr
Los Angeles, CA 90068-1311, USA

Swistowicz, Mike (Athlete, Football Player)
2519 S Drake Ave
Chicago, IL 60623-3919, USA

Swit, Loretta (Actor)
c/o Robert Malcolm *The Artists Group*
1650 Broadway # 711
New York, NY 10019-6833, USA

Switchfoot (Music Group)
c/o Staff Member *Red Light Management*
5800 Bristol Pkwy Ste 400
Culver City, CA 90230-6898, USA

Switzer, Barry (Athlete, Coach, Football Coach, Football Player)
700 W Timberdell Rd
Norman, OK 73072-6323, USA

Switzer, Barry (Basketball Player)
PO Box 43021
Lubbock, TX 79409-3021, USA

Switzer, Jon (Athlete, Baseball Player)
3915 Oakmont Blvd
Austin, TX 78731-6048, USA

Switzer, Veryl (Athlete, Football Player)
1412 Wreath Ave
Manhattan, KS 66503-2402, USA

Swoboda, Ron (Athlete, Baseball Player)
315 Alonzo St
New Orleans, LA 70115-2119, USA

Swoopes, Sheryl (Athlete, Basketball Player, Olympic Athlete)
14110 Scarborough Fair St
Houston, TX 77077-1820, USA

Sword, Sam (Athlete, Football Player)
2781 San Leandro Blvd
San Leandro, CA 94578-2583, USA

Syal, Meera (Actor)
c/o Dallas Smith *United Agents*
12-26 Lexington St
London W1F OLE, UNITED KINGDOM

Syberberg, Hans-Jurgen (Director)
Genter Str 15A
Munich 80805, GERMANY

Sybil (Musician)
Mission Control
Business Center
Lower Road
London SE16 2XB, UNITED KINGDOM (UK)

Sydney, Harry (Athlete, Football Player)
2025 Argonne St
Green Bay, WI 54304-4007, USA

sydor, Darryl (Athlete, Hockey Player)
3358 Windmill Curv
Saint Paul, MN 55129-6708, USA

Sykes, Bob (Athlete, Baseball Player)
1451 County Road 900 E
Carmi, IL 62821, USA

Sykes, Ephraim (Actor)
c/o Christina Papadopoulos *Baker Winokur Ryder Public Relations*
200 5th Ave Fl 5
New York, NY 10010-3307, USA

Sykes, Eugene (Gene) (Athlete, Football Player)
8155 Jefferson Hwy Apt 903
Baton Rouge, LA 70809-1616, USA

Sykes, Melanie (Actor)
c/o Staff Member *Money Management*
22 Noel Street
London W1f 8GS, UNITED KINGDOM

Sykes, Nathan (Actor)
c/o Oliver Slinger *Independent Talent Group*
40 Whitfield St
London W1T 2RH, UNITED KINGDOM

Sykes, Peter (Director)
International Creative Mgmt
76 Oxford St
London W1N 0AX, UNITED KINGDOM (UK)

Sykes, Phil (Athlete, Hockey Player)
1486 Brooke Ct
Hastings, MN 55033-3266, USA

Sykes, Wanda (Actor, Comedian)
c/o Staff Member *Push It Productions*
121 W Lexington Dr # 635
Glendale, CA 91203-2203, USA

Sykora, Michal (Athlete, Hockey Player)
Tepleho 2034
Pardubice 530 02, Czech Republic

Sylbert, Anthea (Designer)
13949 Ventura Blvd # 309
Sherman Oaks, CA 91423-3584, USA

Sylver, Marshall (Misc)
1027 S Rainbow Blvd Ste 281
Las Vegas, NV 89145-6232, USA

Sylvester, Chuck (Horse Racer)
5340 Aragon Ave
De Leon Springs, FL 32130-3402, USA

Sylvester, Dean (Athlete, Hockey Player)
51 Upland Rd
Plympton, MA 02367-1602, USA

Sylvester, Harold (Actor)
International Creative Mgmt
8942 Wilshire Blvd # 219
Beverly Hills, CA 90211-1908, USA

Sylvester, Steven P (Athlete, Football Player)
10425 Londonderry Ct
Cincinnati, OH 45242-5029, USA

Sylvester, Stevenson (Athlete, Football Player)
c/o Peter Schaffer *Authentic Athletix*
400 S Steele St Unit 47
Denver, CO 80209-3535, USA

Sylvestri, Don (Athlete, Hockey Player)
327-1758 Lasalle Blvd
Sudbury, ON P3A 5W4, Canada

Sylvia (Musician)
So Much More Media
PO Box 120426
Nashville, TN 37212-0426, USA

Symington, Fife (Politician)
1700 W Washington St
Phoenix, AZ 85007-2812, USA

Symmonds, Nick (Athlete, Olympic Athlete, Track Athlete)
c/o Staff Member *Total Sports Management*
115 Beechnut St Apt D3
Johnson City, TN 37601-1540, USA

Symms, Steven (Politician)
43527 Butler Pl
Leesburg, VA 20176-7428, USA

Symon, Michael (Chef, Television Host)
c/o Jeff Googel *WME|IMG (NY)*
11 Madison Ave Fl 18
New York, NY 10010-3669, USA

Symone, Raven (Actor, Musician, Talk Show Host)
c/o Shannon Barr *Rogers & Cowan*
1840 Century Park E Fl 18
Los Angeles, CA 90067-2101, USA

Symonette, Josh (Athlete, Football Player)
4923 Forrest Run
Lithonia, GA 30038-2794, USA

Symons, Bill (Athlete, Football Player)
235 Wilton Dr
ATTN
Bolton, ON L7E 4W6, Canada

Syms, Sylvia (Actor)
Barry Brown
47 West Square
London SE11 4SP, UNITED KINGDOM (UK)

Syndergaard, Noah (Athlete, Baseball Player)
c/o Ron Hamill *Creative Artists Agency (CAA)*
2000 Avenue of the Stars Ste 100
Los Angeles, CA 90067-4705, USA

Sypek, Ryan (Actor)
c/o Nicole Nassar *Nicole Nassar PR*
1111 10th St Unit 104
Santa Monica, CA 90403-5363, USA

System of a Down (Music Group)
c/o David Benveniste *Velvet Hammer*
9014 Melrose Ave
Los Angeles, CA 90069-5610, USA

Sytsma, John F (Politician)
Locomotive Engineers Brotherhood
7061 E Pleasant Valley Rd
Independence, OH 44131-5543, USA

Syvret, Dave (Athlete, Hockey Player)
17 Binkly Cres
Waterdown, ON LOR 2HO, Canada

SZA (Musician)
c/o Caroline Yim *Creative Artists Agency (CAA)*
2000 Avenue of the Stars Ste 100
Los Angeles, CA 90067-4705, USA

Szabo, Istvan (Director)
Objektiy Fil Studio-MAFILM
Rona Utca 174
Budapest 01149, HUNGARY

Szajda, Pawel (Actor)
c/o Staff Member *Artists & Representatives (Stone Manners Salners)*
6100 Wilshire Blvd Ste 1500
Los Angeles, CA 90048-5110, USA

Szarabajka, Keith (Actor)
c/o Staff Member *Bauman Redanty & Shaul Agency*
5757 Wilshire Blvd
Suite 473
Beverly Hills, CA 90212, USA

Szczerbiak, Wally (Athlete, Basketball Player, Sportscaster)
c/o Jim Ornstein *WME|IMG (NY)*
11 Madison Ave Fl 18
New York, NY 10010-3669, USA

Szczerbiak, Walt (Wally) (Athlete, Basketball Player)
20 Peabody Rd
Cold Spring Harbor, NY 11724-1709, USA

Szegedy, Todd (Race Car Driver)
13 Mallory Hill Rd
Ridgefield, CT 06877-6302, USA

Szekely, Eva (Swimmer)
Szepvolgyi Utca 4/B
Budapest 01025, HUNGARY

Szep, Paul M (Cartoonist)
7286 Villa D Este Dr
Sarasota, FL 34238-5646, USA

Szeto, Hayden (Actor)
c/o Staff Member *Torque Entertainment*
401 Wilshire Blvd PH
Santa Monica, CA 90401-1416, USA

Szewczenki, Tanya (Figure Skater)
Niederbeerbacher Str 10
Muhital 64367, GERMANY

Szmanda, Eric (Actor)
c/o Richard Fisher *Abrams Artists Agency*
275 7th Ave Fl 26
New York, NY 10001-6708, USA

Szohr, Jessica (Actor)
c/o Brett Ruttenberg *Imprint PR*
6121 W Sunset Blvd
Neuehouse
Los Angeles, CA 90028-6442, USA

Szostak, Stephanie (Actor)
c/o Marla Farrell *Shelter PR*
928 Broadway Ste 505
New York, NY 10010-8143, USA

Szotkiewicz, Ken (Athlete, Baseball Player)
849 Dusky Sap Ct
Griffin, GA 30223-5994, USA

Szott, David (Athlete, Football Player)
11 Manor Dr
Morristown, NJ 07960-2600, USA

Szuminski, Jason (Athlete, Baseball Player)
1766 Jackson St
San Francisco, CA 94109-2918, USA

Szura, Joe (Athlete, Hockey Player)

Szymanski, Jim (Athlete, Football Player)
541 Riverwalk Dr
Mason, MI 48854-9361, USA

Szymanski, Richard (Dick) (Athlete, Football Player)
5270 Forest Edge Ct
Sanford, FL 32771-7160, USA

T

Ta'amu, Alameda (Athlete, Football Player)
c/o Bruce Tollner *REP 1 Sports Group*
80 Technology Dr
Irvine, CA 92618-2301, USA

Tabackin, Lewis B (Lew) (Musician)
38 W 94th St Apt 1
New York, NY 10025-7123, USA

Tabai, Ieremia T (President)
South Pacific Forum Secretariat
Ratu Su Kuna Rd
GPO Box 856
Suva, FIJI

Tabak, Zan (Athlete, Basketball Player)
Saint Joseph Girona Basketball Team
Av Josep Tarradellas 22-24
Girona 17007, SPAIN

Tabaka, Jeff (Athlete, Baseball Player)
1481 Norview Dr
New Franklin, OH 44216-8804, USA

Tabaksblat, Morris (Business Person)
Unilever NV
Weena 455
Rotterdam, DK 03000, NETHERLANDS

Tabaracci, Rick (Athlete, Hockey Player)
7771 N Westhills Trl
Park City, UT 84098-6262, USA

Tabb, Jerry (Athlete, Baseball Player)
7819 Gable Bridge Ln
Richmond, TX 77407-5586, USA

Taber, Catherine (Actor)
c/o Staff Member *Charles Riley*
7122 Beverly Blvd Ste F
Los Angeles, CA 90036-2572, USA

Tabitha, Masentle (Royalty)
Royal Palace
PO Box 524
Maseru, LESOTHO

Tabler, Pat (Athlete, Baseball Player, Sportscaster)
Toronto Blue Jays
1 Blue Jays Way Attn Br
Toronto, ON M5V 1J1, Canada

Tabone, Anton (President)
33 Carmel St
Slierna, MALTA

Tabor, Greg (Athlete, Baseball Player)
29317 Whalebone Way
Hayward, CA 94544-6427, USA

Tabor, Paul (Athlete, Football Player)
3308 Riverwalk Dr
Norman, OK 73072-4852, USA

Tabor, Phil (Athlete, Football Player)
806 Wood N Creek Rd
Ardmore, OK 73401-2940, USA

Tabori, Kristoffer (Actor)
International Artists
235 Regent St
London W1R 8AX, USA

Taccone, Jorma (Writer)
c/o Molly Kawachi *ID Public Relations (NY)*
40 Wall St Fl 51
New York, NY 10005-1385, USA

Tackett, Jeffrey (Jeff) (Athlete, Baseball Player)
1574 Frazier St
Camarillo, CA 93012-4431, USA

Taco (Musician)
8124 W 3rd St Ste 204
Los Angeles, CA 90048-4341, USA

Tada, Joni Eareckson (Writer)
Joni And Friends headquarters
PO Box 3333
Agoura Hills, CA 91376-3333, USA

Tadic, Boris (President)
President's Office
Nemanjina 11
Belgrade 11000, SERBIA

Taekman, Kristen (Model, Reality Star)
c/o Katie Mason Stern *Luber Roklin Management*
5815 W Sunset Blvd Ste 208
Los Angeles, CA 90028-6481, USA

Taffe, Jeff (Athlete, Hockey Player)
1455 Truax Cir
Hastings, MN 55033-2476, USA

Taffoni, Joe (Athlete, Football Player)
103 Pine Valley Dr
Medford, NJ 08055-9210, USA

Tafone, Phil (Horse Racer)
419 Star St
East Meadow, NY 11554-3308, USA

Tafoya, Michele (Sportscaster)
CBS-TV
51 W 52nd St
Sports Dept
New York, NY 10019-6119, USA

Tafoya, Michele (Sportscaster)
c/o Staff Member *ESPN (Main)*
935 Middle St
Espn Plaza
Bristol, CT 06010-1000, USA

Taft, Reed (Athlete, Football Player)
1101 Atlanta St
Hattiesburg, MS 39401-1454, USA

Taft, Robert (Politician)
2933 Lower Bellbrook Rd
Spring Valley, OH 45370-8761, USA

Taft, William Howard (Politician)
PO Box 227
Lorton, VA 22199-0227, USA

Tagawa, Cary-Hiroyuki (Actor)
c/o Penny Vizcarra *PV Public Relations*
121 N Almont Dr Apt 203
Beverly Hills, CA 90211-1860, USA

Tagge, Jerry (Athlete, Football Player)
3565 S 188th St
Omaha, NE 68130-6036, USA

Taghmaoui, Said (Actor)
c/o Staff Member *Markham & Froggatt*
4 Windmill St
London W1T 1HZ, UNITED KINGDOM

Tagliabue, Paul (Business Person, Football Executive)
4149 Parkglen Ct NW
Washington, DC 20007-2137, USA

Taglianetti, Peter (Athlete, Hockey Player)
67 Bayhill Dr
Bridgeville, PA 15017-1088, USA

Tagliani, Alex (Race Car Driver)
Players//Forsythe Racing
7321 Georgetown Rd.
Indianapolis, IN 46268, USA

Tagliavini, Gabriela (Director, Producer)
c/o Staff Member *Venus Films*
859 N Stanley Ave
West Hollywood, CA 90046-7427, USA

Taguchi, So (Athlete, Baseball Player)
12931 Twin Meadows Ct
Saint Louis, MO 63146-1803, USA

Tahir, Faran (Actor)

Tai, Kobe (Adult Film Star)
c/o Staff Member *Atlas Multimedia Inc*
9005 Eton Ave Ste C
Canoga Park, CA 91304-6533, USA

Tailor, Jade (Actor)
c/o Amanda Nesbitt *The Lede Company*
9701 Wilshire Blvd # 930
Beverly Hills, CA 90212-2020, USA

Taimak (Actor)
c/o Karen Riposo *KPA Management*
355 8th Ave Apt 7C
New York, NY 10001-4846, USA

Tait, John (Athlete, Football Player)
876 E Tyson Ct
Gilbert, AZ 85295-5456, USA

Tait, John E (Business Person)
Penn Mutual Life
Independence Square
Philadelphia, PA 19172-0001, USA

Tait, Tristan (Actor)
Paradigm Agency
10100 Santa Monica Blvd Ste 2500
Los Angeles, CA 90067-4116, USA

Takac, Robby (Musician)
c/o Staff Member *Atlas/Third Rail Entertainment*
9200 W Sunset Blvd Ste 10
Los Angeles, CA 90069-3608, USA

Takacs, Tibor (Director)
104 RICHVIEW AVE
IP
Toronto, ON M5P 3E9, CANADA

Takacs-Nagy, Gabor (Musician)
Case Postale 196
Collonge-Bellerive 01245, SWITZERLAND

Takagi, Tora (Race Car Driver)
Nakajima Planing
1-3-10 Higuishi
Shivuya-ku
Tokyo 150-0011, JAPAN

Takahashi, Alpha (Actor)
c/o Adam Park *Park Noack Agency*
10866 Wilshire Blvd Ste 400
Los Angeles, CA 90024-4338, USA

Takahashi, Daisuke (Athlete, Figure Skater)
Kansai University Skating Club
Kansai University
Ice Arena
Osaka, Japan

Take 6 (Music Group, Musician)
c/o Staff Member *Agency for the Performing Arts (APA)*
405 S Beverly Dr Ste 500
Beverly Hills, CA 90212-4425, USA

Takei, George (Actor)
c/o Michael Greenwald *Endorse Management Group*
9854 National Blvd # 454
Los Angeles, CA 90034-2713, USA

Takezawa, Kyoko (Musician)
I C M Artists
40 W 57th St
New York, NY 10019-4001, USA

Takko, Kari (Athlete, Hockey Player)
2601 Avenue of the Stars Ste 100
Attn Dir European Scouting
Frisco, TX 75034-9016, USA

Takle, Darien (Actor)
c/o Staff Member *Robert Bruce Agency*
218 Richmond Rd, Tobermory House
Grey Lynn
Auckland 01021, NEW ZEALAND

Takter, Jimmy (Horse Racer)
1079 Old York Rd
East Windsor, NJ 08520-4710, USA

Tal, Alona (Actor)
c/o Laura Myones *McKeon-Myones Management*
3500 W Olive Ave Ste 770
Burbank, CA 91505-5527, USA

Talafous, Dean (Athlete, Hockey Player)
2418 Foxglove Cir
Hudson, WI 54016-8251, USA

Talalay, Rachel (Director)
1047 Grant St
Santa Monica, CA 90405-1411, USA

Talamini, Robert (Athlete, Football Player)
8919 Summer Ash Ln
Sugar Land, TX 77479-5484, USA

Talancon, Ana Claudia (Actor)
c/o Carlos Carreras *Agency for the Performing Arts (APA)*
405 S Beverly Dr Ste 500
Beverly Hills, CA 90212-4425, USA

Talavera, Tracee (Athlete, Gymnast)
106 Mandala Ct
Walnut Creek, CA 94596-5830, USA

Talbert, Billy (Athlete)
194 Bellevue Ave
Newport, RI 02840-3515, USA

Talbert, Diron (Athlete, Football Player)
PO Box 388
Rosenberg, TX 77471-0388, USA

Talbert, Don (Athlete, Football Player)
PO Box 261
3027 Highway 123
Richmond, TX 77406-0007, USA

Talbot, Bob (Athlete, Baseball Player)
608 W Kaweah Ave
Visalia, CA 93277-2510, USA

Talbot, Diron V (Athlete, Football Player)
3803 B F Terry Blvd
Rosenberg, TX 77471-5657, USA

Talbot, Don (Coach, Swimmer)
Sports Federation
333 River Rd
Vanier
Ottawa, ON K1L 8B9, CANADA

Talbot, Fred (Athlete, Baseball Player)
7701 Lunceford Ln
Falls Church, VA 22043-1207, USA

Talbot, Joby (Composer, Musician)
c/o Catherine Manners *Manners McDade Artist Management*
46 Copperfield St
London SE1 0DY, UK

Talbot, Maxime (Athlete, Hockey Player)
111 Bellevue Ave
Pittsburgh, PA 15229-1705, USA

Talbot, Mitch (Athlete, Baseball Player)
1138 Brook St
Cedar City, UT 84721-6340, USA

Talbot, Nita (Actor)
3420 Merrimac Rd
Los Angeles, CA 90049-1034, USA

Talbot, Susan (Actor)
Media Artists Group
6300 Wilshire Blvd Ste 1470
Los Angeles, CA 90048-5200, USA

Talbott, Gloria (Actor)
2066 Montecito Dr
Glendale, CA 91208-1824, USA

Talbott, John R (Writer)
c/o Staff Member *St Martins Press*
175 5th Ave
Publicity Dept
New York, NY 10010-7703, USA

Talbott, Michael (Actor)
4553 N Eagle Pointe Pl
Star, ID 83669-5361, USA

Talbott, Strobe (Journalist)
State Department
2201 C St NW
Washington, DC 20520-0099, USA

Talent, James (Politician)
1470 Country Lake Estates Dr
Chesterfield, MO 63005-4347, USA

Talese, Gay (Writer)
154 E Atlantic Blvd
Ocean City, NJ 08226-4511, USA

Taliaferro, George (Athlete, Football Player)
5373 Merten Dr Apt 104
Mason, OH 45040-9521, USA

Taliaferro, Lorenzo (Athlete, Football Player)
c/o Joby Branion *Vanguard Sports Group*
23091 Mill Creek Dr
Laguna Hills, CA 92653-1258, USA

Taliaferro, Mike (Athlete, Football Player)
7332 Oakbluff Dr
Dallas, TX 75254-2739, USA

Talib, Aqib (Athlete, Football Player)
c/o Todd France *Creative Artists Agency (CAA) Sports*
3500 Lenox Rd NE
Atlanta, GA 30326-4228, USA

Talla (DJ)
c/o Staff Member *Diva Central Inc*
7510 W Sunset Blvd # 1445
Los Angeles, CA 90046-3408, USA

Tallackson, Barry (Athlete, Hockey Player)
10011 Colorado Ave N
Minneapolis, MN 55445-2363, USA

Tallas, George (Race Car Driver)
21st Century Racing
5245 Crooked Mountain Ct
Las Vegas, NV 89149-6462, USA

Tallas, Rob (Athlete, Hockey Player)
1844 Classic Drive
Coral Springs, FL 33071-7753, USA

Tallent, Garry (Musician)
534 Twin Bridges Rd
Whitefish, MT 59937-8314, USA

Tallet, Brian (Athlete, Baseball Player)
3167 McClendon Ct
Baton Rouge, LA 70810-8376, USA

Talley, Darryl V (Athlete, Football Player)
8713 Lake Tibet Ct
Orlando, FL 32836-5481, USA

Talley, Gary (Musician)
Horizon Mgmt
PO Box 8770
Endwell, NY 13762-8770, USA

Talley, Stan (Athlete, Football Player)
24241 Porto Cristo
Dana Point, CA 92629-4511, USA

Talley, Steve (Actor)
c/o Mary Ellen Mulcahy *Framework Entertainment*
9057 Nemo St # C
W Hollywood, CA 90069-5511, USA

Tallinder, Henrik (Athlete, Hockey Player)
40 Maple Ave
Madison, NJ 07940-2618, USA

Tallman, Patricia (Actor)
PMB 2161
1801 E Tropicana Ave Ste 9
Las Vegas, NV 89119-6559, USA

Tallon, Dale (Athlete, Hockey Player)
1480 Ocean Dr Apt 3H
Vero Beach, FL 32963-5345, USA

Tall Paul (Musician)
PO Box 771
Madison, TN 37116-0771, USA

Talton, Tim (Athlete, Baseball Player)
130 Hardy Talton Rd NW
Pikeville, NC 27863-8601, USA

Tam, Jeffrey (Jeff) (Athlete, Baseball Player)
3350 Davis Macaulay Pl
Melbourne, FL 32934-8387, USA

Tamahori, Lee W (Director)
International Creative Mgmt
8942 Wilshire Blvd # 219
Beverly Hills, CA 90211-1908, USA

Tamargo, John (Athlete, Baseball Player)
19018 Fern Meadow Loop
Lutz, FL 33558-4000, USA

Tamaro, Janet (Journalist)
c/o Rob Kenneally *Creative Artists Agency (CAA)*
2000 Avenue of the Stars Ste 100
Los Angeles, CA 90067-4705, USA

Tambellini, Roger (Athlete, Golfer)
32531 N Scottsdale Rd Ste 105
Scottsdale, AZ 85266-1519, USA

Tambellini, Steve (Athlete, Hockey Player)
11230 110 St NW
Edmonton Oilers Attn General Manager
Edmonton, AB T5G 3H7, Canada

Tambiah, Stanley J (Misc)
Harvard University
Anthropology Dept
Cambridge, MA 02138, USA

Tamblyn, Amber (Actor)
c/o Alla Plotkin *ID Public Relations (NY)*
40 Wall St Fl 51
New York, NY 10005-1385, USA

Tamblyn, Russ (Actor, Dancer)
2310 6th St Apt 2
Santa Monica, CA 90405-2443, USA

Tambor, Jeffrey (Actor)
c/o Joannie Burstein *Burstein Company*
15304 W Sunset Blvd Ste 208
Pacific Palisades, CA 90272-3656, USA

Tamburello, Ben (Athlete, Football Player)
4385 Milner Rd W
Birmingham, AL 35242-7355, USA

Tamer, Chris (Athlete, Hockey Player)
4215 Cornwell Ln
Whitmore Lake, MI 48189-9771, USA

Tamke, George W (Business Person)
Emerson Electric Co
PO Box 4100
Saint Louis, MO 63136-8506, USA

Tamm, Ralph (Athlete, Football Player)
1965 Grant Ave Apt 315
Ogden, UT 84401-0412, USA

Tammet, Daniel (Writer)
c/o Andrew Lownie *Andrew Lownie Literary Agency*
36 Great Smith St
London SW1P 3BU, UNITED KINGDOM

Tan, Amy (Writer)
c/o Staff Member *Steven Barclay Agency*
12 Western Ave
Petaluma, CA 94952-2907, USA

Tan, Dun (Composer)
Columbia University
Arts School
Dodge Hall
New York, NY 10027, USA

Tan, Elaine (Actor)
CAM
19 Denmark Street
London WC2H 8NA, UNITED KINGDOM (UK)

Tan, Melvyn (Musician)
Valerie Barber Mgmt
4 Winsley St
#305
London W1N 7AR, UNITED KINGDOM (UK)

Tan, Phillip (Actor)
c/o Michael Henderson *Heresun Management*
4119 W Burbank Blvd
Burbank, CA 91505-2122, USA

Tanabe, David (Athlete, Hockey Player)
2321 Fieldstone Curv
Saint Paul, MN 55129-6218, USA

Tanaev, Nikoly (Prime Minister)
Prime Minister's Office
Ul Perromayskaya 57
Bishkek, KYRGYZSTAN

Tanaka, Masahiro (Athlete, Baseball Player)
c/o Casey Close *Excel Sports Management*
1700 Broadway Fl 29
New York, NY 10019-6559, USA

Tanana, Frank (Athlete, Baseball Player)
28492 S Harwich Dr
Farmington Hills, MI 48334-4281, USA

Tancill, Chris (Athlete, Hockey Player)
14 Kingswood Cir
Verona, WI 53593-7921, USA

Tancredo, Tom (Politician)
15342 W Iliff Dr
Lakewood, CO 80228-6443, USA

Tandy, Keith (Athlete, Football Player)
c/o Adisa P Bakari *Kelley Drye & Warren LLP*
3050 K St NW Ste 400
Washington, DC 20007-5100, USA

Tandy, Meagan (Actor)
c/o Pamela Sharp *Sharp & Associates*
1516 N Fairfax Ave
Los Angeles, CA 90046-2608, USA

Tang, Felicia (Race Car Driver)
9461 Charleville Blvd # 352
Beverly Hills, CA 90212-3017, USA

Tango, Dave (Reality Star)
c/o Joe Rose *Abrams Artists Agency*
750 N San Vicente Blvd
E Tower Fl 11
Los Angeles, CA 90069-5788, USA

Tanguay, Alex (Athlete, Hockey Player)
Jandec Inc
803-3080 Le Carrefour Blvd
Attn Robert Sauve
Laval, QC H7T 2R5, Canada

Tani, Daniel M (Astronaut)
c/o Staff Member *NASA-JSC*
2101 Nasa Pkwy # 1
Astronaut Office - Mail Code Cb
Houston, TX 77058-3607, USA

Tank (Musician)
c/o Mitch Blackman *ICM Partners (NY)*
730 5th Ave
New York, NY 10019-4105, USA

Tanka, Aiko (Model)
PO Box 1025
Beverly Hills, CA 90213-1025, USA

Tankersley, Dennis (Athlete, Baseball Player)
1032 Pearview Dr
Saint Peters, MO 63376-2269, USA

Tankersley, Taylor (Athlete, Baseball Player)
853 Chartier Ct
Asheboro, NC 27205-0545, USA

Tankian, Serj (Musician)
c/o David Holmes *3D Management*
1901 Main St Fl 3
Santa Monica, CA 90405-1075, USA

Tannahill, Don (Athlete, Hockey Player)
10113 Lakeview Dr
Rancho Mirage, CA 92270-1474, USA

Tannehill, Ryan (Athlete, Football Player)
c/o Pat Dye Jr *SportsTrust Advisors*
3340 Peachtree Rd NE Fl 16
Atlanta, GA 30326-1000, USA

Tannen, Steve (Athlete, Football Player)
735 N Niagara St
Burbank, CA 91505-3006, USA

Tanner, Alain (Director)
Chemin Point-du-Jour 12
Geneva 01202, SWITZERLAND

Tanner, Antwon (Actor)
c/o Jeff Golenberg *Silver Lining Entertainment*
421 S Beverly Dr Fl 7
Beverly Hills, CA 90212-4408, USA

Tanner, Barron (Athlete, Football Player)
7556 W Oregon Ave
Glendale, AZ 85303-5685, USA

Tanner, Bruce (Athlete, Baseball Player)
7607 Whitebridge Gln
University Park, FL 34201-2243, USA

Tanner, John (Athlete, Hockey Player)
101-5150 Spectrum Way
HEWLETT PACKARD
Mississauga, ON L4W 5G2, Canada

Tanner, Joseph R (Astronaut)
PO Box 1166
Ridgway, CO 81432-1166, USA

Tantaros, Andrea (Television Host)

Tanti, Tony (Athlete, Hockey Player)
121-2323 Boundary Rd
TANTI INTERIORS
Vancouver, BC V5M 4V8, Canada

Taormina, Sheila (Athlete, Olympic Athlete, Swimmer)
5700 Midnight Pass Rd Ste 1
Sarasota, FL 34242-3083, USA

Tapani, Kevin (Athlete, Baseball Player)
781 Ferndale Rd N
Wayzata, MN 55391-1010, USA

Tapert, Robert (Director, Producer, Writer)
c/o Staff Member *Renaissance Pictures / Ghost House Pictures*
315 S Beverly Dr Ste 216
Beverly Hills, CA 90212-4310, USA

Tapes N Tapes (Music Group)
c/o Staff Member *Paradigm (Monterey)*
404 W Franklin St
Monterey, CA 93940-2303, USA

Tapia, Roberto (Musician)
c/o Staff Member *Universal Music Group*
100 Universal City Plz
Universal City, CA 91608-1002, USA

Tapp, Darryl (Athlete, Football Player)
c/o Fletcher Smith *Revolution Sports*
270 17th St NW Unit 3001
Atlanta, GA 30363-1261, USA

Tappan V, Alfredo (Director)
c/o Gabriel Blanco *Gabriel Blanco Iglesias (Mexico)*
Rio Balsas 35-32
Colonia Cuauhtemoc
DF 06500, Mexico

Tapper, Brad (Athlete, Hockey Player)
8132 Bibiana Way Apt 103
Fort Myers, FL 33912-9022, USA

Tapper, Brad (Athlete, Hockey Player)
Florida Everblades 11000 Everblades Pkwy
Attn: Coaching Staff
Louebec, QC GlG 3Z8, Canada

Tapper, Jake (Correspondent)
c/o Staff Member *N.S. Bienstock*
888 7th Ave Fl 7
New York, NY 10106-0700, USA

Tapping, Amanda (Actor)
c/o Vickie Petronio *Play Management*
220-807 Powell St
Vancouver, BC V6A 1H7, CANADA

Tapply, William G. (Writer)
c/o Staff Member *St Martins Press*
175 5th Ave
Publicity Dept
New York, NY 10010-7703, USA

Taproot (Music Group)
Velvet Hammer Music
9014 Melrose Ave
W Hollywood, CA 90069-5610, USA

Tarabay, Nick (Actor)
c/o Jordyn Palos *Persona Public Relations*
6255 W Sunset Blvd Ste 705
Hollywood, CA 90028-7408, USA

Tarand, Andres (Prime Minister)
Riigikogu
Lossi Plats 1A
New York, NY 10130-0001, ESTONIA

Tarango, Jeff (Athlete, Olympic Athlete, Tennis Player)
1166 Longfellow Dr
Manhattan Beach, CA 90266-6848, USA

Tarantina, Brian (Actor)
c/o Staff Member *Cunningham Escott Slevin & Doherty (CESD)*
10635 Santa Monica Blvd Ste 130
Los Angeles, CA 90025-8306, USA

Tarantino, Quentin (Actor, Director, Producer, Writer)
7471 Woodrow Wilson Dr
Los Angeles, CA 90046-1322, USA

Tarasco, Tony (Athlete, Baseball Player)
3528 Maplewood Ave
Los Angeles, CA 90066-3020, USA

Tarasova, Tatiana (Coach, Figure Skater)
Connecticut Skating Center
300 Alumni Rd
Newington, CT 06111-1868, USA

Tarasovic, George (Athlete, Football Player)
1503 Michael Dr
Pittsburgh, PA 15227-3958, USA

Tarbuck, Jimmy (Comedian)
c/o Staff Member *Talking Concepts*
74 Albert Promenade
Loughborough
Leicestershire WS13 6PW, UNITED KINGDOM

Tardif, Patrice (Athlete, Hockey Player)
1472 Rue Michel Louvain
Thetford Mines, QC G6G 7S8, Canada

Tardiff, Marc (Athlete, Hockey Player)
16070 Boul Henri-Bourassa
CHARLESBOURG TOYOTA
Quebec, QC G1G 3Z8, Canada

Tardits, Richard (Athlete, Football Player)
3590 Round Bottom Rd
Cincinnati, OH 45244-3026, USA

Tarkan (Musician)
c/o Staff Member *Hitt Produksiyon*
5. Gazeteciler Sitesi Soltas Evleri
Hare Sok G-12 No. 5 Akatlar
Besiktas/Istanbul 34335, Turkey

Tarkenton, Fran (Athlete, Business Person, Football Player)
3340 Peachtree Rd NE Ste 2570
Atlanta, GA 30326-1088, USA

Tarle, Jim (Athlete, Football Player)
2125 Willesdon Dr E
Jacksonville, FL 32246-0549, USA

Tarnas, Richard (Misc)
California Institute of Integral Studies
1453 Mission St Fl 4
San Francisco, CA 94103-2561, USA

Tarnasky, Nick (Athlete, Hockey Player)
6010 Interba¥' Blvd
Tampa, FL 33611-4745, USA

Tarpinian, Jeff (Athlete, Football Player)

Tarpley, Ron (Athlete, Basketball Player)
819 Foxridge Dr
Arlington, TX 76017-6451, USA

Tarpley, Roy (Athlete, Basketball Player)
819 Foxridge Dr
Arlington, TX 76017-6451, USA

Tarses, Matt (Producer)
c/o Staff Member *WME/IMG*
9601 Wilshire Blvd
Beverly Hills, CA 90210-5213, USA

Tartabull, Danilio (Dan) (Athlete, Baseball Player)
8200 Redlands St Apt 112
Playa Del Rey, CA 90293-6101, USA

Tartabull, Danny (Athlete, Baseball Player)
28990 Oak Creek Ln Apt 1611
Agoura Hills, CA 91301-6437, USA

Tartabull, Jose (Athlete, Baseball Player)
1658 W 72nd St
Hialeah, FL 33014-4443, USA

Tartaglia, John (Actor, Producer, Writer)
Shrek, The Musical
1681 Broadway
Broadway Theatre
New York, NY 10019-5827, USA

Tartakovsky, Genndy (Director, Producer, Writer)
c/o Staff Member *WME/IMG*
9601 Wilshire Blvd
Beverly Hills, CA 90210-5213, USA

Tarver, Antonio (Athlete, Boxer, Olympic Athlete)
3959 Van Dyke Rd
Lutz, FL 33558-8025, USA

Tarver, John (Athlete, Football Player)
PO Box 5419
Pine Mountain Club, CA 93222-5419, USA

Tarver, Katelyn (Musician)
c/o Marta Michaud *Cinematic Management*
249 1/2 E 13th St
New York, NY 10003-5602, USA

Tarver, Laschelle (Athlete, Baseball Player)
4410 N Emerson Ave
Fresno, CA 93705-1203, USA

Tarzier, Carol (Artist)
1217 32nd St
Oakland, CA 94608-4201, USA

Tasby, Willie (Athlete, Baseball Player)
1210 E Renfro St
Plant City, FL 33563-5850, USA

Taschner, Jack (Athlete, Baseball Player)
2170 Hidden Creek Rd
Neenah, WI 54956-8916, USA

Tash, Lola (Actor)
c/o Shari Quallenberg *AMI Artist Management*
464 King St E
Toronto, ON M5A 1L7, CANADA

Tasker, Steven J (Steve) (Athlete, Football Player, Sportscaster)
16 Gypsy Ln
East Aurora, NY 14052-2108, USA

Taslim, Joe (Actor)
c/o Jeff Barry *ICM Partners*
10250 Constellation Blvd Fl 7
Los Angeles, CA 90067-6207, USA

Tata, Joe E (Actor)
c/o Jeffrey Leavitt *Leavitt Talent Group*
11500 W Olympic Blvd Ste 400
Los Angeles, CA 90064-1525, USA

Tata, Jordan (Athlete, Baseball Player)
6529 Llano Stage Trl
Austin, TX 78738-6200, USA

Tata, Terry (Athlete, Baseball Player)
23 Stonegate Cir
Cheshire, CT 06410-3461, USA

Tatar, Jerome F (Business Person)
Mead Corp
Courthouse Plaza N
Dayton, OH 45463, USA

Tatarek, Bob (Athlete, Football Player)
951 Governors Cir
Lancaster, OH 43130-7740, USA

Tataryn, Dave (Athlete, Hockey Player)
27 Fairway Crt
Shanty Bay, ON L0L 2L0, Canada

Tataurangi, Phil (Golfer)
5204 Glen Heather Dr
Flower Mound, TX 75028-6035, USA

Tate, Ben (Athlete, Football Player)
c/o David Dunn *Athletes First*
23091 Mill Creek Dr
Laguna Hills, CA 92653-1258, USA

Tate, Brandon (Athlete, Football Player)
c/o Joel Segal *Lagardere Unlimited (NY)*
456 Washington St Apt 9L
New York, NY 10013-1555, USA

Tate, Bruce (Musician)
David Harris Enterprises
24210 E East Fork Rd Spc 9
Azusa, CA 91702-6249, USA

Tate, Catherine (Actor, Writer)
c/o Dawn Sedgwick *Dawn Sedgwick Management*
3 Goodwins Ct
Covent Garden
London WC2N 4LL, United Kingdom

Tate, David (Athlete, Football Player)
3481 S Blackhawk Way
Aurora, CO 80014-3984, USA

Tate, Frank (Boxer)
12731 Water Oak Dr
Missouri City, TX 77489-3903, USA

Tate, Golden (Athlete, Football Player)
c/o Todd France *Creative Artists Agency (CAA) Sports*
3500 Lenox Rd NE
Atlanta, GA 30326-4228, USA

Tate, Lahmard (Actor)
c/o Rob D'Avola *Rob DAvola & Associates*
9107 Wilshire Blvd # 405
Beverly Hills, CA 90210-5531, USA

Tate, Larenz (Actor)
c/o Lisa Perkins *Baker Winokur Ryder Public Relations*
9100 Wilshire Blvd
W Tower #500
Beverly Hills, CA 90212-3415, USA

Tate, Lee (Athlete, Baseball Player)
6905 Pratt St
Omaha, NE 68104-2528, USA

Tate, Miesha (Athlete, Wrestler)
c/o Josh Jones *KHI Management*
NA
NA NA, USA

Tate, Randy (Athlete, Baseball Player)
670 Old Highway 20
Tuscumbia, AL 35674-6086, USA

Tate, Randy (Politician)
Chrsitian Coalition
100 Centerville Tumpike
Virginia Beach, VA 23463-0001, USA

Tate, Stu (Athlete, Baseball Player)
1436 Nocoseka Trl Apt N1
Anniston, AL 36207-6739, USA

Tatlitug, Kivanc (Actor)
c/o Gaye Sokmen *Gaye Sökmen Talent Agency*
Karanfil Caddesi Yolal Sokak Ic
Levent No:3
Istanbul 34330, Turkey

Tatrai, Vilmos (Musician)
R Wallenberg Utca 4
Budapest XIII 01136, HUNGARY

TATU (Music Group)
c/o Robert Hayes *Sound Management*
1525 S Winchester Blvd
San Jose, CA 95128-4335, USA

Tatum, Channing (Actor)
16030 Ventura Blvd Ste 240
Encino, CA 91436-4487, USA

Tatum, Craig (Athlete, Baseball Player)
105 Morrell Cir
Hattiesburg, MS 39402-8142, USA

Tatum, Earl (Athlete, Basketball Player)
2300 W Skyline Rd
Milwaukee, WI 53209-2176, USA

Tatum, Jim (Athlete, Baseball Player)
7433 Indian Wells Cv
Lone Tree, CO 80124-4207, USA

Tatum, Ken (Athlete, Baseball Player)
19 Oakdale Dr
Montevallo, AL 35115-5435, USA

Tatum, Kinnon (Athlete, Football Player)
4109 Knollwood Dr
Fayetteville, NC 28304-5208, USA

Tatupu, Lofa (Athlete, Football Player)
5817 106th Ave NE
Kirkland, WA 98033-7410, USA

Taubensee, Ed (Athlete, Baseball Player)
2234 Fountain Key Cir
Windermere, FL 34786-5804, USA

Ta'ufo'ou, Will (Athlete, Football Player)
c/o Ryan Tollner *REP 1 Sports Group*
80 Technology Dr
Irvine, CA 92618-2301, USA

Taupin, Bernie (Musician, Songwriter, Writer)
2905 Roundup Rd
Santa Ynez, CA 93460-9558, USA

Taurasi, Diana (Athlete, Basketball Player)
c/o Lindsay Kagawa Colas *Wasserman Media Group*
10960 Wilshire Blvd Ste 1200
Los Angeles, CA 90024-3714, USA

Taurel, Sidney (Business Person)
Eli Lilly Co
Lilly Corporate Center
Indianapolis, IN 46285-0001, USA

Tausch, Terry (Athlete, Football Player)
2804 Ryder Ct
Plano, TX 75093-3426, USA

Tauscher, Hansjorg (Skier)
Schwand 7
Oberstdorf 87561, GERMANY

Tauscher, Mark (Athlete, Football Player)
2245 Red Tail Gin
De Pere, WI 54115, USA

Tauskey, Mary (Athlete, Horse Racer, Olympic Athlete)
6 Morris Rd
Ambler, PA 19002-5407, USA

Taussig, Don (Athlete, Baseball Player)
1111 Ocean Dunes Cir
Jupiter, FL 33477-9128, USA

Tautalatasi, Junior (Athlete, Football Player)
1032 Eagle Ave Apt A
Alameda, CA 94501-1111, USA

Tautolo, Terry (Athlete, Football Player)
5713 E Huntdale St
Long Beach, CA 90808-2717, USA

Tautou, Audrey (Actor)
c/o Claire Blondel *ArtMedia*
8 rue Danielle Casanova
Paris 75002, FRANCE

Tauziat, Nathalie (Tennis Player)
Federation de Tennis
1 Ave Gordon Bennett
Paris 75016, FRANCE

Tavard, Georges H (Misc)
330 Market St
Brighton, MA 02135-2131, USA

Tavare, Jay (Actor)
c/o Paul Greenstone *Paul Greenstone Entertainment*
1400 California Ave Apt 201
Santa Monica, CA 90403-4395, USA

Tavares, Alex (Athlete, Baseball Player)
Calle 7B #18
Reparto Perello Santiago, Dominican Republic

Tavares, Fernanda (Model)
c/o Scott Lipps *One Management*
42 Bond St Fl 2
New York, NY 10012-2768, USA

Tavares, John (Athlete, Hockey Player)
c/o Pat Brisson *Creative Artists Agency (CAA)*
2000 Avenue of the Stars Ste 100
Los Angeles, CA 90067-4705, USA

Tavarez, Christopher (Actor, Football Player)
c/o Staff Member *Ella Bee*
505 N Figueroa St Apt 400
Los Angeles, CA 90012-2190, USA

Tavarez, Julian (Athlete, Baseball Player)
1108 Fireside Trl
Broadview Heights, OH 44147-3625, USA

Taveras, Willy (Athlete, Baseball Player)
6014 Floyd St
Houston, TX 77007-5008, USA

Tavernier, Bertrand R M (Director)
Little Bear Productions
7-9 Rue Arthur Groussler
Paris 75010, FRANCE

Taviani, Paolo (Director)
Instituto Luce SPA
Via Tuscolana 1055
Rome 00173, ITALY

Taviani, Vittorio (Director)
Instituto Luce SPA
Via Tuscolana 1055
Rome 00173, ITALY

Tawfiq, Hisham (Actor)
c/o Penny Vizcarra *PV Public Relations*
121 N Almont Dr Apt 203
Beverly Hills, CA 90211-1860, USA

Taxier, Arthur (Actor)
Pakula/King
9229 W Sunset Blvd Ste 315
Los Angeles, CA 90069-3403, USA

Taya, Maawiya Ould Sid'Ahmed (President)
President's Office
Boite Postale 184
Nouakchott, MAURITANIA

Taylor, Aaron (Athlete, Baseball Player, Sportscaster)
c/o Jim Ornstein *WME|IMG (NY)*
11 Madison Ave Fl 18
New York, NY 10010-3669, USA

Taylor, Alphonso (Athlete, Football Player)
330 W Bridge St
Morrisville, PA 19067-2302, USA

Taylor, Andy (Musician)
DD Productions
93A Westbourne Park Villas
London W2 5ED, UNITED KINGDOM (UK)

Taylor, Anthony (Athlete, Basketball Player)
5300 Parkview Dr Apt 1093
Lake Oswego, OR 97035-8728, USA

Taylor, Ben (Football Player)

Taylor, Billy (Athlete, Baseball Player)
PO Box 6362
Thomasville, GA 31758-6362, USA

Taylor, Billy (Athlete, Football Player)
3 Greenwich Dr Apt 86
Jersey City, NJ 07305-1158, USA

Taylor, Bob (Athlete, Baseball Player)
27 Sunnybrook Rd
Springfield, MA 01119-2209, USA

Taylor, Bobby (The Chief) (Athlete, Hockey Player)
3912 Americana Dr
Tampa, FL 33634-7405, USA

Taylor, Brian (Athlete, Basketball Player)
16706 McCormick St
Encino, CA 91436-1020, USA

Taylor, Brien (Baseball Player)
147 Brien Taylor Ln
Beaufort, NC 28516-6664, USA

Taylor, Bruce (Athlete, Baseball Player)
8 Highland Park Rd
Rutland, MA 01543-1742, USA

Taylor, Bruce L. (Athlete, Football Player)
10324 Pontofino Cir
Trinity, FL 34655-7056, USA

Taylor, Buck (Actor)
1305 Clyde Dr
Marrero, LA 70072-3609, USA

Taylor, Carl (Athlete, Baseball Player)
2356 Riviera Dr
Sarasota, FL 34232-3522, USA

Taylor, Chad (Musician)
Freedman & Smith
1790 Broadway # 131
New York, NY 10019-1412, USA

Taylor, Charles R (Charley) (Athlete, Football Executive, Football Player)
12023 Canter Ln
Reston, VA 20191-2129, USA

Taylor, Chris (Athlete, Hockey Player)
Rochester Americans
1 War Memorial Sq Ste 228
Rochester, NY 14614-2192

Taylor, Chris (Athlete, Hockey Player)
24 W Ham Cir
North Chili, NY 14514-9762

Taylor, Christian (Actor)
c/o Steven Lafferty *Creative Artists Agency (CAA)*
2000 Avenue of the Stars Ste 100
Los Angeles, CA 90067-4705, USA

Taylor, Christine (Actor)
c/o Kimberlin Belloni *Artists First*
9465 Wilshire Blvd Ste 900
Beverly Hills, CA 90212-2608, USA

Taylor, Christy (Actor)
10990 Massachusetts Ave Apt 3
Los Angeles, CA 90024-5530, USA

Taylor, Christy (Race Car Driver)
10990 Massachusetts Ave Apt 3
Los Angeles, CA 90024-5530, USA

Taylor, Cindy (Actor)
c/o Allee Newhoff *DAS Model Management*
119 Washington Ave Ste 501
Miami Beach, FL 33139-7228, USA

Taylor, Clarice (Actor)
380 Elkwood Ter
Englewood, NJ 07631-1935, USA

Taylor, Cooper (Athlete, Football Player)
c/o Alan Herman *Sportstars Inc*
1370 Avenue of the Americas Fl 19
New York, NY 10019-4602, USA

Taylor, Cordell (Athlete, Football Player)
1825 Chasewood Park Dr
Marietta, GA 30066-4298, USA

Taylor, Corey (Musician)
c/o Staff Member *UTA Music/The Agency Group*
9336 Civic Center Dr
Beverly Hills, CA 90210-3604, USA

Taylor, Dana (Actor)
100 S Sunrise Way # 468
Palm Springs, CA 92262-6779, USA

Taylor, Dave (Athlete, Hockey Player)
18920 Pasadero Dr
Tarzana, CA 91356-5122, USA

Taylor, David (Writer)
c/o Author Mail *Bantam-Dell Publishing (NY)*
1745 Broadway
New York, NY 10019-4640, USA

Taylor, David (Athlete, Football Player)
82 Manchester St
Glen Rock, PA 17327-1302, USA

Taylor, Dennis (Race Car Driver)
5867 Springhill Dr NE
Albany, OR 97321-9160, USA

Taylor, Deon (Director, Producer)
c/o Staff Member *Hidden Empire Film Group*
PO Box 6931
Folsom, CA 95763-6931, USA

Taylor, Devin (Athlete, Football Player)

Taylor, Dorn (Athlete, Baseball Player)
405 Avenue D
Horsham, PA 19044-2020, USA

Taylor, Doug (Race Car Driver)
6630 Denver Industrial Park Rd
Denver, NC 28037-9795, USA

Taylor, Dwight (Athlete, Baseball Player)
5163 Queen Mary Ln
Jackson, MS 39209-3141, USA

Taylor, Ed (Athlete, Football Player)
2901 Clarke Rd
Memphis, TN 38115-2402, USA

Taylor, Eliza (Actor)
c/o John Powell *Active Artists Management*
43/38 Manchester Ln
Melbourne VIC 3000, AUSTRALIA

Taylor, Eric (Artist)
13 Tredgold Ave
Branhope near Leeds
West Yorkshire LS16 9BS, UNITED KINGDOM (UK)

Taylor, Eunice (Baseball Player)
955 Carroll Ln
Mount Dora, FL 32757-3726, USA

Taylor, Femi (Actor)
Paul Telford Mgmt
23 Noel St
London W1V 3RD, UNITED KINGDOM (UK)

Taylor, Fred (Athlete, Football Player)

Taylor, Gary (Athlete, Baseball Player)
816 N Werners Landing Dr
Bronson, MI 49028-8321, USA

Taylor, Glen (Basketball Player)
Minnesota Timberwolves
600 1st Ave N
Target Center
Minneapolis, MN 55403-1400, USA

Taylor, Graham (Athlete, Baseball Player)
2705 Vera Cruz Dr
Villa Hills, KY 41017-1070, USA

Taylor, Harry (Athlete, Baseball Player)
2125 Cooks Ln
Fort Worth, TX 76120-5301, USA

Taylor, Henry S (Writer)
83 Calimo Cir
Santa Fe, NM 87505-8917, USA

Taylor, Holland (Actor)
c/o Bob Gersh *Gersh*
9465 Wilshire Blvd Ste 600
Beverly Hills, CA 90212-2605, USA

Taylor, Holly (Actor)
c/o Jennifer Hebert *Brilliant Talent*
PO Box 58003
Sherman Oaks, CA 91413-3003, USA

Taylor, Hosea (Athlete, Football Player)
208 Bobby St
Longview, TX 75602-3804, USA

Taylor, Ike (Athlete, Football Player)
c/o Denise White *EAG Sports Management*
909 N Pacific Coast Hwy Ste 360
El Segundo, CA 90245-3864, USA

Taylor, Jamar (Athlete, Football Player)

Taylor, James (Musician, Songwriter)
2238 Dundas St W
PO Box 59039 Rpo Dundas St
Toronto, ON M6R 3B5, CANADA

Taylor, James Arnold (Actor)
c/o Pat Brady *Cunningham Escott Slevin & Doherty (CESD)*
10635 Santa Monica Blvd Ste 130
Los Angeles, CA 90025-8306, USA

Taylor, James (JT) (Musician)
c/o Carlos Keyes *Red Entertainment Agency*
3537 36th St Ste 2
Astoria, NY 11106-1347, USA

Taylor, Jason (Athlete, Football Player)
11042 Blue Palm St
Plantation, FL 33324-8236, USA

Taylor, Jason (Rugby Player)
Parramatta Eels
PO BOX 2666
North Parramatta, NSW 01750, AUSTRALIA

Taylor, Jay (Business Person)
Placer Dome Inc
1600-1055 Dunsmuir St
Vancouver, BC V7X 1P1, CANADA

Taylor, Jayceon Terrell (The Game) (Musician)
c/o Billy Terry Wood *WME|IMG (UK)*
103 New Oxford St WMA
Centrepoint
London WC1A 1DD, UNITED KINGDOM

Taylor, Jeff (Race Car Driver)
2017 E 5th St
Lumberton, NC 28358-6111, USA

Taylor, Jennifer Bini (Actor)
c/o Staff Member *Artists & Representatives (Stone Manners Salners)*
6100 Wilshire Blvd Ste 1500
Los Angeles, CA 90048-5110, USA

Taylor, Jeremy Ray (Actor)
c/o Jeremy Ray Taylor *JRT Management*
PO Box 3056
Bristol, TN 37625-3056, USA

Taylor, Jim (Producer)
c/o David Lubliner *United Talent Agency (UTA)*
9336 Civic Center Dr
Beverly Hills, CA 90210-3604, USA

Taylor, Jonathan (Producer)
c/o Staff Member *United Talent Agency (UTA)*
9336 Civic Center Dr
Beverly Hills, CA 90210-3604, USA

Taylor, Josh (Actor)
4151 Vanalden Ave
Tarzana, CA 91356-5527, USA

Taylor, Karen (Comedian)
c/o Staff Member *Avalon Management (UK)*
4A Exmoor St
London W10 6BD, UNITED KINGDOM

Taylor, Kerry (Athlete, Baseball Player)
1705 33 1/2 St S
Moorhead, MN 56560-3945, USA

Taylor, Kim (Musician)
c/o Staff Member *Paradigm (Monterey)*
404 W Franklin St
Monterey, CA 93940-2303, USA

Taylor, Kitrick L (Athlete, Football Player)
18215 Foothill Blvd Apt 94
Fontana, CA 92335-8512, USA

Taylor, Lawrence (Athlete, Football Player)
532 Enclave Cir E
Pembroke Pines, FL 33027-1214, USA

Taylor, Lili (Actor)
c/o Staff Member *Dontanville/Frattaroli (D/F)*
270 Lafayette St Ste 402
New York, NY 10012-3327, USA

Taylor, Lionel (Athlete, Coach, Football Coach, Football Player)
201 Pinnacle Dr SE Apt 3614
Rio Rancho, NM 87124-0458, USA

Taylor, Livingston (Musician)
Fat City Artists
1906 Chet Atkins Pl Apt 502
Nashville, TN 37212-2122, USA

Taylor, Mams (Musician)
12427 Kling St
Studio City, CA 91604-1215, USA

Taylor, Marianne (Actor)
Jack Scagnatti
5118 Vineland Ave # 102
North Hollywood, CA 91601-3814, USA

Taylor, Mark (Athlete, Hockey Player)
110-5620 152 St
Surrey, BC V3S 3K2, CANADA

Taylor, Mark L (Actor)
7919 Norton Ave
West Hollywood, CA 90046-5204, USA

Taylor, Maurice (Basketball Player)
Houston Rockets
2 Greenway Plz
Toyota Center
Houston, TX 77046-0297, USA

Taylor, Meldrick (Athlete, Boxer, Olympic Athlete)
2736 W Lehigh Ave
Philadelphia, PA 19132-3128, USA

Taylor, Michael (Athlete, Football Player)
5014 Crane St
Detroit, MI 48213-2917, USA

Taylor, Mick (Musician)
Jacobson & Colin
60 Madison Ave Ste 1026
New York, NY 10010-1666, USA

Taylor, Mike (Athlete, Football Player)
19632 Quiet Bay Ln
Huntington Beach, CA 92648-2614, USA

Taylor, Mya (Actor)
c/o Caitlin Hughes *Brigade Marketing*
116 W 23rd St Fl 5
New York, NY 10011-2599, USA

Taylor, Natascha (Actor)
c/o Staff Member *ICM Partners*
10250 Constellation Blvd Fl 7
Los Angeles, CA 90067-6207, USA

Taylor, Niki (Actor, Model)
c/o Lou Taylor *Tri Star Sports & Entertainment Group (TN)*
11 Music Cir S Ste 200
Nashville, TN 37203-4312, USA

Taylor, Noah (Actor)
June Cann Mgmt
110 Quenn St
Woolahra, NSW 02025, AUSTRALIA

Taylor, Ollie (Athlete, Basketball Player)
3125 Harkey Rd
Pearland, TX 77584-8367, USA

Taylor, Otis (Athlete, Football Player)
6608 Woodson Rd
Raytown, MO 64133-5400, USA

Taylor, Penny (Basketball Player)
Cleveland Rockers
1 Center Ct
Gund Arena
Cleveland, OH 44115-4001, USA

Taylor, Phil (Athlete, Football Player)
c/o Peter Schaffer *Authentic Athletix*
400 S Steele St Unit 47
Denver, CO 80209-3535, USA

Taylor, Priscilla Inga (Actor, Model)
c/o Staff Member *Heartrock Pictures*
260 Peachtree St NW Ste 2200
Atlanta, GA 30303-1292, USA

Taylor, Rachael (Actor)
c/o Rebecca Sides Capellan *ID Public Relations (NY)*
40 Wall St Fl 51
New York, NY 10005-1385, USA

Taylor, Reggie (Athlete, Baseball Player)
828 Havird St
Newberry, SC 29108-3727, USA

Taylor, Regina (Actor)
c/o Staff Member *Creative Artists Agency (CAA)*
2000 Avenue of the Stars Ste 100
Los Angeles, CA 90067-4705, USA

Taylor, Renee (Actor)
1 Lincoln Plz Apt 23K
New York, NY 10023-7150, USA

Taylor, Rip (Actor, Comedian)
1133 N Clark St Apt 301
Los Angeles, CA 90069-2075, USA

Taylor, Robin Lord (Actor)
c/o Samantha Stoller *Abrams Artists Agency*
275 7th Ave Fl 26
New York, NY 10001-6708, USA

Taylor, Roger (Musician)
c/o Staff Member *DD Productions*
122 Av. Des Champs-Élysées
Paris 75008, FRANCE

Taylor, Roger (Tennis Player)
39 Newstead Way
Wimbledon SW19, UNITED KINGDOM (UK)

Taylor, Roland (Athlete, Basketball Player)
3812 Homewood Ave
Ashtabula, OH 44004-5939, USA

Taylor, Ron (Athlete, Baseball Player)
SC Cooper Sports Medical Clinic
600 University Ave
Toronto, ON M5G 1X5, CANADA

Taylor, Roosevelt (Athlete, Football Player)
7331 Ebbtide Dr
New Orleans, LA 70126-2057, USA

Taylor, Ryan (Athlete, Football Player)
c/o Joby Branion *Vanguard Sports Group*
23091 Mill Creek Dr
Laguna Hills, CA 92653-1258, USA

Taylor, Sam (Sammy) (Athlete, Baseball Player)
248 N 74th St
East Saint Louis, IL 62203-2411, USA

Taylor, Sandra (Actor, Model)
c/o Craig Wyckoff *Epstein Wyckoff Corsa Ross (LA)*
11350 Ventura Blvd Ste 100
Studio City, CA 91604-3140, USA

Taylor, Scott (Athlete, Baseball Player)
1349 N Forestview Ct
Wichita, KS 67235-7033, USA

Taylor, Stepfan (Athlete, Football Player)
c/o Doug Hendrickson *Relativity Sports*
2029 Century Park E Ste 1550
Century City, CA 90067-3000, USA

Taylor, Stephen Monroe (Actor)
c/o Staff Member *Main Title Entertainment*
8383 Wilshire Blvd Ste 408
Beverly Hills, CA 90211-2435, USA

Taylor, Susan L (Producer)
c/o Staff Member *American Program Bureau*
1 Gateway Ctr Ste 751
Newton, MA 02458-2817, USA

Taylor, Tamara (Actor)
c/o Natasha Dubin-Collatos *Independent Public Relations*
9601 Wilshire Blvd Ste 750
Beverly Hills, CA 90210-5228, USA

Taylor, Tate (Director)
c/o John Norris *Artists and Directors Cooperative*
1041 N Formosa Ave
Writers Building Suite 8
West Hollywood, CA 90046-6703, USA

Taylor, Ted (Athlete, Hockey Player)
PO Box 244
Oak Lake, MB R0M 1P0, Canada

Taylor, Terry (Athlete, Baseball Player)
743 W Walnut Ave
Crestview, FL 32536-3919, USA

Taylor, Teyana (Musician)
c/o Miatta Johnson *MVD Inc*
8737 Venice Blvd Ste 100
Los Angeles, CA 90034-3259, USA

Taylor, Tommy (Athlete, Baseball Player)
Kansas City Monarchs
743 W Walnut Ave
Crestview, FL 32536-3919, USA

Taylor, Tony (Athlete, Baseball Player)
8415 NW 165th Ter
Miami Lakes, FL 33016-6137, USA

Taylor, TW (Race Car Driver)
22909 Airpark Dr
North Dinwiddie, VA 23803-6969, USA

Taylor, Tyrod (Athlete, Football Player)
c/o Adisa P Bakari *Kelley Drye & Warren LLP*
3050 K St NW Ste 400
Washington, DC 20007-5100, USA

Taylor, Tyshawn (Athlete, Basketball Player)
c/o Jeff Schwartz *Excel Sports Management*
1700 Broadway Fl 29
New York, NY 10019-6559, USA

Taylor, Vaughn (Golfer)
2536 Queens Ct
Grovetown, GA 30813-4520, USA

Taylor, Wade (Athlete, Baseball Player)
6 Sleepy Hollow Cv
Longwood, FL 32750-3845, USA

Taylor, Wayne (Race Car Driver)
501 N Orlando Ave Ste 313-189
Winter Park, FL 32789-7310, USA

Taylor, Wilson H (Business Person)
CIGNA Corp
1 Liberty Pl
1650 Market St
Philadelphia, PA 19103-4201, USA

Taylor-Compton, Scout (Actor)
c/o Jessica Katz *Katz Public Relations*
14527 Dickens St
Sherman Oaks, CA 91403-3756, USA

Taylor-Johnson, Aaron (Actor)
c/o Christine Tripicchio *Shelter PR*
5670 Wilshire Blvd Ste 1200
Los Angeles, CA 90036-5621, USA

Taylor-Joy, Anya (Actor, Model)
c/o Alexa Pearson *Beaumont Communications*
535 Kings Rd
Suite 313 Plaza
London SW10 0SZ, UNITED KINGDOM

Taylor-Taylor, Courtney (Musician)
Monqui Records
PO Box 5908
Portland, OR 97228-5908, USA

Taylor-Young, Leigh (Actor)
11300 W Olympic Blvd Ste 610
Los Angeles, CA 90064-1643, USA

Taymor, Julie (Director, Producer, Writer)
c/o Katherine Rowe *Rowe PR*
901 N Highland Ave Ste 915
West Hollywood, CA 90038-2412, USA

Tayor, Lane (Athlete, Football Player)

Tchaikovsky, Aleksandr V (Composer, Musician)
Leningradsky Prosp 14
#4
Moscow 125040, RUSSIA

Teaff, Grant (Coach, Football Coach)
8265 Forest Ridge Dr
Waco, TX 76712-2405, USA

Teagarden, Taylor (Baseball Player)
2007 Bluestem Ln
Carrollton, TX 75007-5313

Teagle, Terry (Athlete, Basketball Player)
2111 Heatherwood Dr
Missouri City, TX 77489-3277, USA

Teague, George (Athlete, Football Player)
6561 Meadow Lark Dr
Montgomery, AL 36116-4227, USA

Teague, Jeff (Athlete, Basketball Player)
c/o Andy Miller *ASM Sports*
450 Fashion Ave Ste 1700
New York, NY 10123-1700, USA

Teague, Kerry (Race Car Driver)
3110 Roberta Rd
Concord, NC 28027-9080, United States

Teague, Marshall (Actor)
c/o Andras Jones *Bohemia Group*
1680 Vine St Ste 518
Los Angeles, CA 90028-8833, USA

Teague, Owen (Actor)
c/o Traci Danielle *Brevard Talent Group*
100 S Eola Dr Ste 200
Orlando, FL 32801-6603, USA

Teahen, Mark (Athlete, Baseball Player)
8882 E Bronco Trl
Scottsdale, AZ 85255-3692, USA

Teal, Jeff (Athlete, Hockey Player)
1840 Wood Duck Ln
Excelsior, MN 55331-6507

Teal, Jim F (Athlete, Football Player)
38444 Kingsway Ct
Farmington Hills, MI 48331-1651, USA

Teal, Jimmy D (Athlete, Football Player)
2636 Spring Branch Rd
Mesquite, TX 75181-2668, USA

Teal, Willie (Athlete, Football Player)
1322 Westchester Dr
Baton Rouge, LA 70810-5234, USA

Tea Leaf Green (Music Group)
c/o Staff Member *Paradigm (Monterey)*
404 W Franklin St
Monterey, CA 93940-2303, USA

Teannaki, Teatao (President)
President's Office
PO Box 68
Bairiki
Tarawa Atoll, KIRBATI

Tearry, Larry (Athlete, Football Player)
1334 Kienast Dr
Fayetteville, NC 28314-5422, USA

Tears For Fears (Music Group)
c/o Staff Member *Creative Artists Agency (CAA)*
2000 Avenue of the Stars Ste 100
Los Angeles, CA 90067-4705, USA

Teasdale, Kathryn (Race Car Driver)
PO Box 4950
Pinehurst, NC 28374-4950, USA

Teasley, Nikki (Basketball Player)
Los Angeles Sparks
1111 S Figueroa St
Staples Center
Los Angeles, CA 90015-1300, USA

Teasley, Ron (Athlete, Baseball Player)
New York Cubans
19317 Coyle St
Detroit, MI 48235-2039, USA

Tebow, Tim (Athlete, Football Player, Heisman Trophy Winner)
Tim Tebow Foundation
2220 County Road 210 W Ste 108 PMB 317
Jacksonville, FL 32259-4060, USA

Techine, Andre J F (Director)
Artmedia
20 Ave Rapp
Paris 75007, FRANCE

Tedder, Ryan (Musician)
c/o Jeff Frasco *Creative Artists Agency (CAA)*
2000 Avenue of the Stars Ste 100
Los Angeles, CA 90067-4705, USA

Tedeschi, Susan (Musician)
Blue Sky Artists
761 Washington Ave N
Minneapolis, MN 55401-1101, USA

Tedford, Travis (Actor)
c/o Staff Member *Acme Talent & Literary*
4727 Wilshire Blvd Ste 333
Los Angeles, CA 90010-3874, USA

TedZed (Musician)
c/o Peter Price *WME/IMG (UK)*
103 New Oxford St WMA
Centrepoint
London WC1A 1DD, UNITED KINGDOM

Teegarden, Aimee (Actor)
c/o Robert Haas *Innovative Artists*
1505 10th St
Santa Monica, CA 90401-2805, USA

Teerlinck, John (Athlete, Football Player)
9713 Bay Hill Dr
Lone Tree, CO 80124-3182, USA

Teeter, Mike (Athlete, Football Player)
4393 E Mount Garfield Rd
Fruitport, MI 49415-9782, USA

Teevens, Buddy (Coach, Football Coach)
Stanford University
Athletic Dept
Stanford, CA 94395, USA

Tefkin, Blair (Actor)
Lucie Gamelon
8022 Sunset Blvd #4049
Los Angeles, CA 90046, USA

Tegan and Sara (Music Group)
c/o Todd Jordan *Paquin Entertainment Agency (Winnipeg)*
468 Stradbrook Ave
Winnipeg MB M6K 3J1, CANADA

Tegart Dalton, Judy (Tennis Player)
72 Grange Road
Toorak, VIC 03412, AUSTRALIA

Teglianetti, Peter (Athlete, Hockey Player)
67 Bayhill Dr
Bridgeville, PA 15017-1088, USA

Teichner, Helmut (Skier)
4250 N Marine Dr Apt 2101
Chicago, IL 60613-1733, USA

Teigen, Chrissy (Model)
c/o Luke Dillon *3 Arts Entertainment*
9460 Wilshire Blvd Fl 7
Beverly Hills, CA 90212-2713, USA

Teillet-Schick, Yolande (Baseball Player)
1016 Chevrier Blvd
FT GARRY
Winnipeg, MB R3T 1X9, CANADA

Teitel, Robert (Producer)
c/o Staff Member *Creative Artists Agency (CAA)*
2000 Avenue of the Stars Ste 100
Los Angeles, CA 90067-4705, USA

Teitler, William (Producer)
c/o Staff Member *ICM Partners*
10250 Constellation Blvd Fl 7
Los Angeles, CA 90067-6207, USA

Teixeira, Mark (Athlete, Baseball Player)
2220 King Fisher Dr
Westlake, TX 76262-4815, USA

Tejada, Miguel O M (Athlete, Baseball Player)
3013 NE 20th Ct # C
Ft Lauderdale, FL 33305-1807, USA

Tejada, Ruben (Athlete, Baseball Player)
c/o Peter Greenberg *TLA Worldwide (The Legacy Agency)*
1500 Broadway Ste 2501
New York, NY 10036-4082, USA

Tejeda, Robinson (Baseball Player)
45 Appletree Ln Apt D
Old Bridge, NJ 08857-4586

Tejera, Michael (Athlete, Baseball Player)
2459 SW 154th Ct
Miami, FL 33185-5766, USA

Tekulve, Kenton C (Kent) (Athlete, Baseball Player)
350 Fruitwood Dr
Bethel Park, PA 15102-1008, USA

Telemaco, Amaury (Athlete, Baseball Player)
830 S Webster Ave
Scranton, PA 18505-4384, USA

Telfer, Paul (Actor)

Telford, Anthony (Athlete, Baseball Player)
9109 Cypress Keep Ln
Odessa, FL 33556-3150, USA

Telford, Zoe (Actor)
c/o Sue Latimer *Artists Rights Group (ARG)*
4A Exmoor St
London W10 6BD, UNITED KINGDOM

Telgheder, David (Athlete, Baseball Player)
50 Orchard Crest Dr
Westtown, NY 10998-3425, USA

Tellem, Nancy (Business Person)
c/o Staff Member *CBS Paramount International Television*
7800 Beverly Blvd
Los Angeles, CA 90036-2112, USA

Teller (Actor, Comedian, Magician)
c/o Peter Golden *Golden Entertainment West*
5328 Alhama Dr
Woodland Hills, CA 91364-2013, USA

Teller, Miles (Actor)
c/o Susan Patricola *Patricola Public Relations*
369 S Doheny Dr # 1408
Beverly Hills, CA 90211-3508, USA

Telles, Rick (Director, Producer)
c/o Josh Levenbrown *Agency for the Performing Arts (APA)*
405 S Beverly Dr Ste 500
Beverly Hills, CA 90212-4425, USA

Tellez, Steve (Actor)
c/o Staff Member *Innovative Artists*
1505 10th St
Santa Monica, CA 90401-2805, USA

Tellman, Tom (Athlete, Baseball Player)
1021 Yankee Bush Rd
Warren, PA 16365-8536, USA

Tellmann, Tom (Baseball Player)
1021 Yankee Bush Rd
Warren, PA 16365-8536, USA

Tellqvist, Mikael (Athlete, Hockey Player)
7932 E Feathersong Ln
Scottsdale, AZ 85255-6418

Telnaes, Ann (Cartoonist)
Tribune Media Services
435 N Michigan Ave Ste 1500
Chicago, IL 60611-4012, USA

Teltscher, Eliot (Coach, Tennis Player)
Pepperdine University
Athletic Dept
Malibu, CA 90265, USA

Teltschik, John (Athlete, Football Player)
9624 Nathan Way
Plano, TX 75025-5896, USA

Telushkin, Rabbi Joseph (Writer)
2316 Delaware Ave Ste 266
Ste 4-B
Buffalo, NY 14216-2638, USA

Telymonde, Louis (Horse Racer)
8707 Valley Ranch Pkwy W Apt 357
Irving, TX 75063-9351, USA

Temchen, Sybil (Actor)
c/o Michael Greenwald *Endorse Management Group*
9854 National Blvd # 454
Los Angeles, CA 90034-2713, USA

Temesvari, Andrea (Tennis Player)
ProServe
1101 Woodrow Wilson Blvd
#1800
Arlington, VA 22209, USA

Temko, Allan B (Journalist)
San Francisco Chronicle
901 Mission St
Editorial Dept
San Francisco, CA 94103-2934, USA

Temp, Jim (Athlete, Football Player)
311 Roselawn Blvd
Green Bay, WI 54301-1305, USA

Tempero, Bill (Race Car Driver)
915 Turman Dr
Fort Collins, CO 80525-9312, USA

Temple, Collins (Athlete, Basketball Player)
2614 Dalrymple Dr
Baton Rouge, LA 70808-2038, USA

Temple, Collis (Athlete, Basketball Player)
1974 San Antonio Spurs
2614 Dalrvmole Drbaton Rouge, LA 70808-2038

Temple, Jordan (Comedian)
c/o Lisa Mierkle *Mosaic Media Group*
407 N Maple Dr # 100
Beverly Hills, CA 90210-3818, USA

Temple, Josh (Television Host)
c/o Steven Neibert *Imperium 7 Talent Agency*
5455 Wilshire Blvd Ste 1706
Los Angeles, CA 90036-4217, USA

Temple, Juno (Actor)
c/o Jessica Kolstad *Relevant*
400 S Beverly Dr Ste 220
Beverly Hills, CA 90212-4404, USA

Temple, Lew (Actor)
c/o Matt Luber *Luber Roklin Management*
5815 W Sunset Blvd Ste 208
Los Angeles, CA 90028-6481, USA

Templeman, Simon (Actor)
c/o Jeff Witjas *Agency for the Performing Arts (APA)*
405 S Beverly Dr Ste 500
Beverly Hills, CA 90212-4425, USA

Templeton, Ben (Cartoonist)
Tribune Media Services
435 N Michigan Ave Ste 1500
Chicago, IL 60611-4012, USA

Templeton, Garry L (Athlete, Baseball Player)
13552 Del Poniente Rd
Poway, CA 92064-2230, USA

Tempo, Nino (Actor)
9255 Doheny Rd Apt 2504
W Hollywood, CA 90069-3207

Temptations, The (Music Group)
c/o Steve Levine *ICM Partners*
10250 Constellation Blvd Fl 7
Los Angeles, CA 90067-6207, USA

Ten, Ana Mulvoy (Actor)
c/o Jason Shapiro *Silver Lining Entertainment*
421 S Beverly Dr Fl 7
Beverly Hills, CA 90212-4408, USA

Tena, Natalia (Actor)
c/o Sarah Spear *Curtis Brown Ltd*
28-29 Hay Market
Hay Market House
London SW1Y 4SP, UNITED KINGDOM

Tenace, F Gene (Athlete, Baseball Player, Coach)
2650 Cliff Hawk Ct
Redmond, OR 97756-7301, USA

Tenenbaum, Stephen (Producer)
c/o Staff Member *Morra Brezner Steinberg & Tenenbaum (MBST) Entertainment*
345 N Maple Dr Ste 200
Beverly Hills, CA 90210-5174, USA

Teng-Hui, Lee (President)
Chaehshou Hall Chung King South Rd.
Taipei 10728, TAIWAN

Tenison, Rosie (Actor)
The Tenison Group
171 Pier Ave # 403
Santa Monica, CA 90405-5311, USA

Tennant, Andy (Actor, Director, Writer)

Tennant, David (Actor)
c/o Billy Lazarus *United Talent Agency (UTA)*
9336 Civic Center Dr
Beverly Hills, CA 90210-3604, USA

Tennant, Emily (Actor)
c/o Tyman Stewart *Characters Talent Agency*
200-1505 2nd Ave W
Vancouver, BC V6H 3Y4, CANADA

Tennant, Stella (Model)
Select Model Mgmt
Archer House
43 King St
London WC2E 8RJ, UNITED KINGDOM (UK)

Tennant, Victoria (Actor)
PO Box 929
Beverly Hills, CA 90213-0929, USA

Ten Napel, Garth (Athlete, Football Player)
PO Box 26
Carmen, ID 83462-0026, USA

Tenney, Jon (Actor)
c/o Brian Wilkins *LINK Entertainment*
11872 La Grange Ave
Los Angeles, CA 90025-5282, USA

Tennille, Toni (Actor, Musician)
850 Cameron Pass
Prescott, AZ 86301-6660, USA

Tennison, Chalee (Musician)
Tanasi Entertainment
1204 17th Ave S
Nashville, TN 37212-2802, USA

Tennon, Julius (Actor)
c/o Staff Member *JuVee Productions*
3500 W Olive Ave Ste 1470
Burbank, CA 91505-5514, USA

Tennyson, Brian (Athlete, Golfer)
2775 Mesa Verde Dr E Apt P114
Costa Mesa, CA 92626-5008, USA

Tensi, Steve (Athlete, Football Player)
300 Flannery Fork Rd
Blowing Rock, NC 28605-9333, USA

Tension, Renee (Actor)
The Tenison Group
171 Pier Ave # 403
Santa Monica, CA 90405-5311, USA

Tenth Avenue North (Musician)
c/o Staff Member *Reunion Records*
741 Cool Springs Blvd
Provident Music Group / Sony Bmg
Franklin, TN 37067-2750, USA

Tenuta, Judy (Actor, Comedian)
c/o Brandon Kjar *Kjar and Associates*
10153 1/2 Riverside Dr
Toluca Lake, CA 91602-2561, USA

Te'o, Manti (Athlete, Football Player)
c/o Tom Condon *Creative Artists Agency (CAA)*
401 Commerce St PH
Nashville, TN 37219-2516, USA

Tepedino, Frank (Athlete, Baseball Player)
2 Pear Ct
Saint James, NY 11780-2143, USA

Tepper, David (Business Person)
Appaloosa Management
51 John F Kennedy Pkwy Ste 500
Short Hills, NJ 07078-2706, USA

Tepper, Lou (Coach, Football Coach)
University of Illinois
Assembly Hall
Champaign, IL 61820, USA

Tepper, Stephen (Athlete, Hockey Player)
35 Brook St
Shrewsbury, MA 01545-4804

Tequila Nguyen, Tila (Model, Reality Star)
8033 W Sunset Blvd # 1029
W Hollywood, CA 90046-2401, USA

Terai, Hidezo (Business Person)
World Co., Ltd
8-1, 6-Chome, Minatojima-Nakamachi, Chuo-ku
Kobe 650-8585, Japan

Teran, Arlet (Actor)
c/o Gabriel Blanco *Gabriel Blanco Iglesias (Mexico)*
Rio Balsas 35-32
Colonia Cuauhtemoc
DF 06500, Mexico

Teraoka, Masami (Artist)
41-048 Kaulu St
Waimanalo, HI 96795-1612, USA

TerBlanche, Esta (Actor)
c/o Chris Schmidt *Paradigm*
8942 Wilshire Blvd
Beverly Hills, CA 90211-1908, USA

Tereschenko, Sergei A (Prime Minister)
Prime Minister's Office
Dom Pravieelstra
Alma-Ata 148008, KAZAKHSTAN

Tereshinski, Joe (Athlete, Football Player)
6508 Millwood Rd
Bethesda, MD 20817-6056, USA

Tergesen, Lee (Actor)
c/o Bill Butler *Industry Entertainment Partners*
1133 Broadway Ste 630
New York, NY 10010-8072, USA

Terlecki, Bob (Athlete, Baseball Player)
113 Shady Brook Dr
Langhorne, PA 19047-8028, USA

Terlecky, Greg (Athlete, Baseball Player)
2130 Camino Laurel
San Clemente, CA 92673-5650, USA

Terlesky, John (Actor)
14229 Dickens St Apt 5
Sherman Oaks, CA 91423-4107, USA

Termeer, Henricus A (Business Person)
Genzyme Corp
1 Kendall Sq
Cambridge, MA 02139-1562, USA

Terminator X (Musician)
c/o Staff Member *WME/IMG*
9601 Wilshire Blvd
Beverly Hills, CA 90210-5213, USA

Ter-Petrosyan, Levon A (President)
Marshal Baghramjan Prospect 19
Memphis, TN 37501-0001, ARMENIA

Terpko, Jeff (Athlete, Baseball Player)
3546 Riverside Dr
Sayre, PA 18840-7864, USA

Terraciano, Andrew (Actor)
c/o Jaime Misher *Innovative Artists*
235 Park Ave S Fl 7
New York, NY 10003-1405, USA

Terraciano, Tony (Actor)
c/o Jaime Misher *Innovative Artists*
235 Park Ave S Fl 7
New York, NY 10003-1405, USA

Terranova, Joe (Musician)
Joe Taylor Mgmt
PO Box 279
Williamstown, NJ 08094-0279, USA

Terranova, Phil (Boxer)
30 Bogardus Pl
New York, NY 10040-2320, USA

Terrasson, Jacky (Musician)
Joel Chriss
300 Mercer St Apt 3J
New York, NY 10003-6732, USA

Terrazas Sandoval, Julio Cardinal (Religious Leader)
Arzobispado Casilla 25
Calle Ingavi 49
Santa Cruz, BOLIVIA

Terrell, David (Athlete, Football Player)
43628 Cather Ct
Ashburn, VA 20147-4789, USA

Terrell, Ira (Athlete, Basketball Player)
1327 Fernwood Ave
Dallas, TX 75216-1265, USA

Terrell, Jerry (Athlete, Baseball Player)
1301 NE Sunny Creek Ln
Blue Springs, MO 64014-2041, USA

Terrell, Walt (Athlete, Baseball Player)
1304 Oxley Ct
Union, KY 41091-7145, USA

Terreri, Chris (Athlete, Hockey Player, Olympic Athlete)
120 Lake Dr
Mountain Lakes, NJ 07046-1646, USA

Terrero, Jessy (Director, Producer)
c/o Darrell Miller *Fox Rothschild*
10250 Constellation Blvd Fl 9
Los Angeles, CA 90067-6209, USA

Terrion, Greg (Athlete, Hockey Player)
Terri on Esso Service Ltd
PO Box 428
Marmora, ON K0K 2M0, Canada

Terry, Chuck (Athlete, Basketball Player)
11 Ravenna
Irvine, CA 92614-5329, USA

Terry, Claude (Athlete, Basketball Player)
4621 Via Fiori
Modesto, CA 95357-0658, USA

Terry, Hilda (Cartoonist)
8 Henderson Pl
New York, NY 10028-7557, USA

Terry, Jason (Athlete, Basketball Player)
105 Kingston Mnr
Atlanta, GA 30342-2183, USA

Terry, John (Soccer Player)
The FA
25 Soho Square
London W1D 4FA, UNITED KINGDOM

Terry, Lee (Congressman, Politician)
2331 Rayburn Hob
Washington, DC 20515-3214, USA

Terry, Megan D (Writer)
2309 Hanscom Blvd
Omaha, NE 68105-3143, USA

Terry, Nat (Athlete, Football Player)
3003 W Palmetto St
Tampa, FL 33607-2936, USA

Terry, Nigel (Actor)
c/o Staff Member *BBC Artist Mail*
PO Box 1116
Belfast BT2 7AJ, United Kingdom

Terry, Ralph W (Athlete, Baseball Player)
801 Park St
Larned, KS 67550-2632, USA

Terry, Richard E (Business Person)
Peoples Energy Corp
130 E Randolph St
Chicago, IL 60601-6207, USA

Terry, Rick (Athlete, Football Player)
109 Highgate Ln
Lexington, NC 27292-5372, USA

Terry, Ruth (Actor, Musician)
622 Hospitality Dr
Rancho Mirage, CA 92270-1312, USA

Terry, Scott (Athlete, Baseball Player)
4943 Montford Dr
Saint Louis, MO 63128-3134, USA

Terwilliger, Wayne (Athlete, Baseball Player)
1909 Clear Creek Dr
Weatherford, TX 76087-3802, USA

Terzian, Jacques (Artist)
PO Box 883753
San Francisco, CA 94188-3753, USA

Tesh, John (Musician)
TeshMedia Group
13245 Riverside Dr Ste 305
Sherman Oaks, CA 91423-5608, USA

Tesher, Howard (Horse Racer)
525 E 72nd St Apt 22B
New York, NY 10021-9607, USA

Teske, Rachel (Golfer)
c/o Staff Member *Pro Golfers Association (PGA)*
112 TPC Blvd
Ponte Vedra Beach, FL 32082, USA

Tesori, Jeanine (Composer, Musician)
c/o John Buzzetti *WME/IMG (NY)*
11 Madison Ave Fl 18
New York, NY 10010-3669, USA

Tesori, Kathleen (Fitness Expert, Model)
2215 Country Oaks Dr
Layton, UT 84040-7862, USA

Tess, John (Business Person)
Oregon Cultural Trust
775 Summer St NE
Suite 200
Portland, OR 97209, USA

Tessier, Orval (Athlete, Hockey Player)
412 Fifth St E
Cornwall, ON K6H 2M2, Canada

Tessmer, Jay (Athlete, Baseball Player)
2359 Livingston Bridge Rd
Norman Park, GA 31771-4258, USA

Testa, Nick (Athlete, Baseball Player)
1 Consulate Dr Apt 2L
Tuckahoe, NY 10707-2432, USA

Testaverde, Vinny (Athlete, Football Player, Heisman Trophy Winner)
Jesuit High School of Tampa
4701 N Himes Ave
Attn: Boys Football Program Coach
Tampa, FL 33614-6694, USA

Testerman, Don (Athlete, Football Player)
3101 Bridges St
Morehead City, NC 28557-3365, USA

Testi, Fabio (Actor)
Via Francesco Siacci 38
Rome I-00197, Italy

Testone, Elise (Musician)
c/o Staff Member *19 Entertainment*
401 Wilshire Blvd Ste 1070
Santa Monica, CA 90401-1428, USA

Tetarenko, Joey (Athlete, Hockey Player)
5307 Chelsea Fair Ln
Spring, TX 77379-6244

Teteak, Deral (Athlete, Football Player)
9458 S County Road G
Suring, WI 54174, USA

Teter, Hannah (Athlete, Olympic Athlete, Snowboarder)
1554 Plumas Cir
South Lake Tahoe, CA 96150-4822, USA

Tetrault, Roger E (Business Person)
McDermott International
PO Box 61961
New Orleans, LA 70161-1961, USA

Tetro-Atkinson, Barbara (Athlete, Baseball Player)
7110 Cross Creek Blvd
Louisville, KY 40228-1305, USA

Tettamanzi, Dlonigi Cardinal (Religious Leader)
Arclvescovado
Plazza Matteotti 4
Genoa 16123, ITALY

Tettleton, Mickey (Athlete, Baseball Player)
346 W Franklin Rd
Norman, OK 73069-8105, USA

Tetzlaff, Christian (Musician)
Shuman Assoc
850 7th Ave Ste 1006
New York, NY 10019-0027, USA

Teufel, Tim (Athlete, Baseball Player)
PO Box 3517
Jupiter, FL 33469-1009, USA

Teut, Nate (Athlete, Baseball Player)
2010 Sugar Creek Dr # D
Waukee, IA 50263-8093, USA

Teutul Jr, Paul (Business Person, Reality Star)
Orange County Choppers
14 Crossroads Ct
Newburgh, NY 12550-5064, USA

Teutul Sr, Paul (Reality Star, Television Host)
c/o Sean Perry *WME/IMG*
9601 Wilshire Blvd
Beverly Hills, CA 90210-5213, USA

Tewell, Doug (Athlete, Golfer)
16377 Scotland Way
Edmond, OK 73013-3103, USA

Tewes, Lauren (Actor)
157 W 57th St # 604
New York, NY 10019-2205, USA

Tewkesbury, Joan F (Director, Writer)
c/o Staff Member *Creative Artists Agency (CAA)*
2000 Avenue of the Stars Ste 100
Los Angeles, CA 90067-4705, USA

Tewksbury, Bob (Athlete, Baseball Player)
55 Mount Vernon St
Somersworth, NH 03878-2642, USA

Tews, Andreas (Boxer)
Hamburger Allee 1
Schwerin 19063, GERMANY

Texada, Tia (Actor)
c/o Mike Wilson *Mavrick Artists Agency*
8447 Wilshire Blvd Ste 301
Beverly Hills, CA 90211-3206, USA

Texas Hippie Coalition (Music Group)

Thacker, Tom (Athlete, Basketball Player)
3655 Dogwood Ln
Cincinnati, OH 45213-2601, USA

Thackery, Jimmy (Musician)
Mongrel Music
743 Center Blvd
Fairfax, CA 94930-1764, USA

Thagard, Norman E Dr (Astronaut)
502 N Ride
Tallahassee, FL 32303-5127, USA

Thaksin, Shinawatra (Prime Minister)
Premier's Office
Govt House
Luke Road
Bangkok 10300/2, THAILAND

Thal, Eric (Actor)
c/o Phillip Carlson *Carlson Menashe Agency*
149 5th Ave Ste 1204
New York, NY 10010-6801

Thalia (Actor, Musician)
c/o Staff Member *WME/IMG*
9601 Wilshire Blvd
Beverly Hills, CA 90210-5213, USA

Thames, Marcus (Athlete, Baseball Player)
72 Overview Rd
Starkville, MS 39759-6489, USA

Thani, Sheikh Hamad bin Khalifa al (Royalty)
Royal Palace
PO Box 923
Dohar, QATAR

Thapa, Surya Bahadur (Prime Minister)
Tangal
Kathmandu, NEPAL

Tharp, Twyla (Dancer)
Twyla Tharp Productions
336 Central Park W Apt 17B
New York, NY 10025-7127, USA

Tharpe, Larry (Athlete, Football Player)
3665 Greenbriar Rd E
Macon, GA 31204-4228, USA

Thatcher, Joe (Athlete, Baseball Player)
310 Ruddell Dr
Kokomo, IN 46901-4249, USA

Thatcher, Roland (Golfer)
18 Flowertuft Ct
Spring, TX 77380-1529, USA

Thaxton, Galand (Athlete, Football Player)
1571 N 22nd St
Laramie, WY 82072-2387, USA

Thaxton, James (Athlete, Football Player)
4319 Deergrove Rd
Memphis, TN 38141-7021, USA

Thayer, Bill (Misc)
PO Box 233
Snohomish, WA 98291-0233, USA

Thayer, Brynn (Actor)
c/o Steven Neibert *Imperium 7 Talent Agency*
5455 Wilshire Blvd Ste 1706
Los Angeles, CA 90036-4217, USA

Thayer, Greg (Athlete, Baseball Player)
1000 3rd St N
Sauk Rapids, MN 56379-2417, USA

Thayer, Helen (Skier)
PO Box 233
Snohomish, WA 98291-0233, USA

Thayer, Maria (Actor)
c/o Barry McPherson *Agency for the Performing Arts*
135 W 50th St Fl 17
New York, NY 10020-1201, USA

Thayer, Tom (Athlete, Football Player)
330 W Diversey Pkwy Apt 2303
Chicago, IL 60657-6204, USA

Thayer, Tommy (Musician)
PO Box 7147
Thousand Oaks, CA 91359-7147, USA

The 1975 (Music Group)
c/o Staff Member *Universal Music Ltd (UK)*
22 St Peters Square
London W6 9NW, UNITED KINGDOM

The Academy Is (Music Group)
c/o Bob McLynn *Crush Music Management*
60-62 E 11th St
Fl 7
New York, NY 10003, USA

The Band Perry (Music Group)
Band Perry Live
2818 Azalea Pl
Nashville, TN 37204-3118, USA

The Beach Boys (Music Group)
c/o Elliott Lott *Boulder Creek Entertainment*
PO Box 91002
San Diego, CA 92169-3002, USA

Theberge, Greg (Athlete, Hockey Player)
31 Edgar
Sundridge, ON POA 1ZO, Canada

The Bronx (Music Group)
c/o Jonathan Daniel *Crush Music Management*
60-62 E 11th St
Fl 7
New York, NY 10003, USA

The Cable Guy, Larry (Comedian)
c/o Jason Heyman *United Talent Agency (UTA)*
9336 Civic Center Dr
Beverly Hills, CA 90210-3604, USA

The Color Fred (Music Group, Musician)
c/o Matt Galle *Paradigm*
140 Broadway Ste 2600
New York, NY 10005-1011, USA

The Darkness (Music Group)
c/o Sue Whitehouse *Whitehouse Management*
PO Box 43829
London NW6 3PJ, UNITED KINGDOM

The Dear & Departed (Music Group)
c/o Francesca Caldara *Equal Vision Records*
PO Box 38202
Albany, NY 12203-8202, USA

The Decemberists (Music Group)
c/o Ron Laffitte *Red Light Management*
5800 Bristol Pkwy Ste 400
Culver City, CA 90230-6898, USA

Thedford, Marcello (Actor)
c/o JC Robbins *JC Robbins Management*
865 S Sherbourne Dr
Los Angeles, CA 90035-1809, USA

The Expendables (Music Group, Musician)
c/o Jon Phillips *Silverback Professional Artist Management*
9469 Jefferson Blvd Ste 101
Culver City, CA 90232-2915, USA

The Fabulous Thunderbirds (Music Group)
c/o Patrick McAuliff *Monterey International (Chicago)*
72 W Adams St # 1000
Chicago, IL 60603-5107, USA

The Fall of Troy (Music Group)
c/o David Benveniste *Velvet Hammer*
9014 Melrose Ave
Los Angeles, CA 90069-5610, USA

The Fray (Music Group)
c/o Jonathan Adelman *Paradigm*
140 Broadway Ste 2600
New York, NY 10005-1011, USA

The Godfathers (Music Group)
c/o Matt Suhar *Tantrum Management*
457 N Virgil Ave
Los Angeles, CA 90004-2313, USA

The Good The Bad & The Queen (Music Group)
c/o Staff Member *Paradigm (Monterey)*
404 W Franklin St
Monterey, CA 93940-2303, USA

The Great Khali (Writer)
c/o Kerry Rodgerson *World Wrestling Entertainment (WWE)*
1241 E Main St
Stamford, CT 06902-3520, USA

Theile, David (Swimmer)
84 Woodville St
Hendea
Brisbane, QLD 04011, AUSTRALIA

The Imponderables (Music Group, Musician)
c/o Monique Moss *Integrated PR*
9025 Wilshire Blvd Ste 400
Beverly Hills, CA 90211-1828, USA

The Insult Comic Dog, Triumph (Actor, Comedian)
c/o Staff Member *Creative Artists Agency (CAA)*
2000 Avenue of the Stars Ste 100
Los Angeles, CA 90067-4705, USA

Theis, Dave (Athlete, Baseball Player)
7250 Lewis Ridge Pkwy Apt 206
Minneapolis, MN 55439-1938, USA

Theismann, Joe (Athlete, Football Player)
PO Box 186
Leesburg, VA 20178-0186, USA

Theiss, Duane (Athlete, Baseball Player)
66 Juniper Ave
Westerville, OH 43081-1700, USA

The Jets (Music Group)
c/o Staff Member *Lustig Talent Enterprises Inc*
PO Box 770850
Orlando, FL 32877-0850, USA

The Killers (Music Group)
c/o Jen Appel *Grandstand Media*
39 W 32nd St Rm 1603
New York, NY 10001-3839, USA

Thelan, Jodi (Actor)
8428 Melrose Pl Ste C
Los Angeles, CA 90069-5300, USA

Theler, Derek (Actor)
c/o Sean Elliott *Authentic Talent & Literary Management*
3615 Eastham Dr # 650
Culver City, CA 90232-2410, USA

The Lonely Island (Music Group)
c/o Staff Member *Silva Artist Management (SAM)*
722 Seward St
Los Angeles, CA 90038-3504, USA

The Lumineers (Music Group)
c/o Joe Atamian *Paradigm*
140 Broadway Ste 2600
New York, NY 10005-1011, USA

Thelven, Michael (Athlete, Hockey Player)
TSS AB PO Box 7296
Taby 18714, Sweden

The Maine (Music Group)
c/o Tim Kirch *8123 Management*
Prefers to be contacted by telephone or email
New York, NY, USA

Themmen, Paris (Actor)
2109 S Wilbur Ave
Walla Walla, WA 99362-9048, USA

The Moody Blues (Music Group, Musician)
c/o Ivy Stewart *Threshold Recording Co. Ltd.*
53 High St
Cobham KT11 3DP, UK

The National (Music Group)
c/o Dawn Berger *Post Hoc Management*
320 7th Ave # 145
Brooklyn, NY 11215-4194, USA

The Neptunes (Musician, Producer)
c/o Staff Member *Star Trak Entertainment*
1755 Broadway Frnt 3
New York, NY 10019-3743, USA

Theobald, Ron (Athlete, Baseball Player)
319 Jacaranda Pl
Fullerton, CA 92832-1434, USA

Theodorakis, Mikis (Composer)
Epifanous 1
Akropolis
Athens, GREECE

Theodore, Donna (Actor)
10000 Santa Monica Blvd PH 305
Los Angeles, CA 90067-7037, USA

Theodore, George (Athlete, Baseball Player)
1388 E Princeton Ave
Salt Lake City, UT 84105-1921, USA

Theodore, Jose (Athlete, Hockey Player)
Newport Sports Management
400-201 City Centre Dr
Attn Don Meehan
Mississauga, ON L5B 2T4, Canada

Theodorescu, Monica (Athlete)
Gestit Lindenhof
Sassenberg 48336, GERMANY

Theodosius, Primate Metropolitian (Religious Leader)
Orthodox Church in America
PO Box 675
Syosset, NY 11791-0675, USA

Theofiledes, Harry (Athlete, Football Player)
17806 Carrollwood Dr
Dallas, TX 75252-6357, USA

Theo Paphitis, Theo Paphitis (Business Person)
Ryman House , Savoy Rd
Crewe
Cheshire CW1 6NA, UK

The Pointer Sisters (Music Group, Musician)
c/o Konrad Leh *Creative Talent Group*
1900 Avenue of the Stars Ste 2475
Los Angeles, CA 90067-4512, USA

The Pretenders (Music Group)
c/o Staff Member *WME|IMG*
9601 Wilshire Blvd
Beverly Hills, CA 90210-5213, USA

The Priests (Music Group, Musician)
Bishop's House
Lisbreen, 73 Somerton Rd
Belfast BT15 4DE, Ireland

The Prize Fighter Inferno (Music Group, Musician)

The Rasmus (Music Group)
c/o Staff Member *Playground Music Scandinavia*
Box 3171
Malm?? s-200 22, SWEDEN

Therien, Chris (Athlete, Hockey Player)
Philadelphia Flyers
3601 S Broad St Ste 2
Philadelphia, PA 19148-5297

Therien, Chris (Athlete, Hockey Player)
15 Milford Dr
Marlton, NJ 08053-5408

Theriot, Ryan (Athlete, Baseball Player)
2935 Dakin Ave
Baton Rouge, LA 70820-4434, USA

Theron, Charlize (Actor, Model)
c/o Staff Member *Denver and Delilah Productions*
100 Universal City Plz
Universal City, CA 91608-1002, USA

Theroux, Justin (Actor)
c/o Aleen Keshishian *Lighthouse Management and Media*
9000 W Sunset Blvd Ste 1520
Los Angeles, CA 90069-5815, USA

Theroux, Louis (Television Host)
c/o Staff Member *BBC Artist Mail*
PO Box 1116
Belfast BT2 7AJ, United Kingdom

Theroux, Paul E (Writer)
35 Elsynge Road
London SW18 2NR, UNITED KINGDOM (UK)

Therrien, Gaston (Athlete, Hockey Player)
300-1755 Boul Rene-Levesque E
RDS
Montreal, QC H2K 4P6, Canada

Therrien, Michel (Athlete, Hockey Player)
3800 Hillcrest Dr Apt 1204
Hollywood, FL 33021-7940

The Saturdays (Music Group, Musician)
c/o Staff Member *Polydor Records*
364-366 Kensington High St
London W14 8NS, UK

The Saw Doctors (Music Group)
Saw Doctors Office
3 St Mary's Terrace
Galway, IRELAND

The Script (Music Group)
c/o Cindi Berger *PMK/BNC Public Relations*
622 3rd Ave Fl 8
New York, NY 10017-6707, USA

These New Puritans (Music Group)
c/o Frank Riley *High Road Touring*
751 Bridgeway Fl 2
Sausalito, CA 94965-2174, USA

The Snake The Cross The Crown (Music Group, Musician)
c/o Staff Member *Equal Vision Records*
PO Box 38202
Albany, NY 12203-8202, USA

The The (Music Group)
c/o Staff Member *Paradigm (Monterey)*
404 W Franklin St
Monterey, CA 93940-2303, USA

Theuriau, Melissa (Television Host)
Beaugard
4 Sente Des Robertines
Chanteloup-les-Vignes 78570, FRANCE

Theus, Reggie (Athlete, Basketball Player)
2364 Tuscan Hills Ln
Las Cruces, NM 88011-4105, USA

The Vaccines (Music Group, Musician)
c/o Staff Member *Paradigm*
140 Broadway Ste 2600
New York, NY 10005-1011, USA

The Veronicas (Music Group, Musician)
c/o Staff Member *Wilhelmina Dan Agency*
1503 Union Ave Ste 211
Kimbrough Office Tower
Memphis, TN 38104-3739, USA

The Wanted (Music Group)
c/o Scooter Braun *SB Management*
755 N Bonhill Rd
Los Angeles, CA 90049-2303, USA

The War on Drugs (Music Group)
c/o Adam Voith *WME (Nashville)*
1201 Demonbreun St
Nashville, TN 37203-3140, USA

The Weeknd (Musician)
c/o Beau Benton *Republic Records*
1755 Broadway Fl 6
New York, NY 10019-3768, USA

The Wiggles (Music Group, Musician)
The Wiggles Office
P.O. Box 7873
Baulkham Hills, BC NSW 2153, Australia

Thewlis, David (Actor)
c/o Staff Member *United Talent Agency (UTA)*
9336 Civic Center Dr
Beverly Hills, CA 90210-3604, USA

They Might Be Giants (Music Group)
c/o Jamie Kitman *The Hornblow Group*
PO Box 176
Palisades, NY 10964-0176, USA

Theys, Didier (Race Car Driver)
5773 N 78th Pl
Scottsdale, AZ 85250-6169, USA

Thiandoum, Hyacinthe Cardinal (Religious Leader)
Archeveche
Ave Jean XXIII
Dakar 01908, SENEGAL

Thibaud, Todd (Musician)
c/o Staff Member *Paradigm (Monterey)*
404 W Franklin St
Monterey, CA 93940-2303, USA

Thibaudet, Jean-Yves (Musician)
4466 Beck Ave
North Hollywood, CA 91602-1902, USA

Thibault, Jocelyn (Athlete, Hockey Player)
550 Ch du Domaine RR 5
Saint-Denis-De-Brompton, QC J0B 2P0, Canada

Thibeaux, Peter (Athlete, Basketball Player)
2036 Paradise Dr Apt 2
Belvedere Tiburon, CA 94920-1985, USA

Thibert, Jim (Athlete, Football Player)
1365 County Road L
Swanton, OH 43558-9791, USA

Thibiant, Aida (Designer, Fashion Designer)
Institut de Beaute
449 N Canon Dr
Beverly Hills, CA 90210-4819, USA

Thibodeau, Tom (Basketball Coach)
c/o Terry Prince *CAA Sports*
2000 Avenue of the Stars Ste 100
Los Angeles, CA 90067-4705, USA

Thibodeaux, Keith (Actor)
5372 Jamaica Dr
Jackson, MS 39211-4057, USA

Thicke, Robin (Musician)
c/o Staff Member *Roc Nation*
9348 Civic Center Dr
Beverly Hills, CA 90210-3624, USA

Thiebaud, Wayne (Artist)
1617 7th Ave
Sacramento, CA 95818-3803, USA

Thieben, Bill (Athlete, Basketball Player)
225 Jayne Ave
Patchogue, NY 11772-2628, USA

Thiedemann, Fritz (Misc)
Ostreherweg 28
Heide 25746, GERMANY

Thiel, Bert (Athlete, Baseball Player)
W11077 County Road D
Marion, WI 54950-9068, USA

Thiel, Peter (Business Person)
The Thiel Foundation
9200 W Sunset Blvd Ste 1110
West Hollywood, CA 90069-3616, USA

Thiele, Gerhard P J (Astronaut)
ESA/EAC
Linder Hohe
Cologne 51147, GERMANY

Thiele, Gerhard P J Dr (Astronaut)
European Space Policy Institute
Schwarzenbergplatz 6 Attn: Resident Fellow
Wien 01030, Austria

Thielemann, Ray C (R C) (Athlete, Football Player)
841 Vista Del Sol Ln
Panama City, FL 32404-2694, USA

Thielen, Adam (Athlete, Football Player)
1600 Warren St Apt 304
Mankato, MN 56001-7108, USA

Thielen, Gunter (Business Person)
Bertelsmann AG
Carl-Bertelsmann-Str 270
Guetersloh 33311, GERMANY

Thieme, Paul (Misc)
Tubingen University
Wilhelmstr 7
Tubingen 72074, GERMANY

Thieriot, Max (Actor)
c/o Ruth Bernstein *Viewpoint Inc*
8820 Wilshire Blvd Ste 220
Beverly Hills, CA 90211-2622, USA

Thierry, John F (Athlete, Football Player)
1431 Federal Rd
Opelousas, LA 70570-1172, USA

Thies, Dave (Baseball Player)
35737 Tympani Cir
Palm Desert, CA 92211-3067

Thies, Jake (Athlete, Baseball Player)
4 Cornflower Ct
Florissant, MO 63033-6530, USA

Thiessen, Tiffani (Actor)
c/o Diandra Escamilla *PMK/BNC Public Relations*
1840 Century Park E Ste 1400
Los Angeles, CA 90067-2115, USA

Thievery Corporation (Music Group, Musician)
c/o Staff Member *WME|IMG*
9601 Wilshire Blvd
Beverly Hills, CA 90210-5213, USA

Thigpen, Bobby (Athlete, Baseball Player)
926 Brookstown Ave
Winston Salem, NC 27101-3625, USA

Thigpen, Curtis (Athlete, Baseball Player)
345 Logan Ranch Rd
Georgetown, TX 78628-1208, USA

Thile, Chris (Actor, Musician)
c/o Staff Member *IMG World*
304 Park Ave S Fl 11
New York, NY 10010-4305, USA

Thimmesch, Nicholas (Journalist)
6301 Broad Branch Rd
Chevy Chase, MD 20815-3343, USA

Thinnes, Roy (Actor)
952 Peekskill Hollow Rd Apt A
Putnam Valley, NY 10579-1705, USA

Third Day (Music Group)
c/o Staff Member *Red Light Management*
5800 Bristol Pkwy Ste 400
Culver City, CA 90230-6898, USA

Third Eye Blind (Music Group)
c/o Eric Godtland *Eric Godtland Management*
1040 Mariposa St Ste 200
San Francisco, CA 94107-2520, USA

Third World (Music Group)
Lion Entertainment
PO Box 5231
Hollywood, FL 33083-5231, USA

Thirlby, Olivia (Actor)
c/o William Choi *Management 360*
9111 Wilshire Blvd
Beverly Hills, CA 90210-5508, USA

Thirsk, Robert (Astronaut)
Candian Institutes of Health Research
160 Elgin St Fl 9
Attn VP Public Government & Institute Affairs
Ottawa, ON K1A 0W9, CANADA

This Time Next Year (Music Group, Musician)
c/o Staff Member *Equal Vision Records*
PO Box 38202
Albany, NY 12203-8202, USA

Thobe, J J (Athlete, Baseball Player)
902 Grovemont St
Santa Ana, CA 92706-2046, USA

Thobe, Tom (Baseball Player)
17400 Modoc St Apt 15
Fountain Valley, CA 92708-4658

Thoenen, Dick (Athlete, Baseball Player)
862 Smith St
Harrisburg, OR 97446-9505, USA

Thom, Sandi (Musician)
c/o Staff Member *Paradigm (Monterey)*
404 W Franklin St
Monterey, CA 93940-2303, USA

Thoma, Dieter (Skier)
Am Rossleberg 35
Hinterzarten 79856, GERMANY

Thoma, Georg (Skier)
Bisten 6
Hinterzarten 79856, GERMANY

Thomas, Aaron (Athlete, Football Player)
2906 NW Golf Course Dr
Bend, OR 97703-5504, USA

Thomas, Adalius (Athlete, Football Player)
1 Willow Bend Dr
Hattiesburg, MS 39402-8552, USA

Thomas, Alex (Actor)
c/o Staff Member *Identity Talent Agency (ID)*
9107 Wilshire Blvd Ste 500
Beverly Hills, CA 90210-5526, USA

Thomas, Andy (Astronaut)
c/o Staff Member *NASA-JSC*
2101 Nasa Pkwy # 1
Astronaut Office - Mail Code Cb
Houston, TX 77058-3607, USA

Thomas, Aurelius (Athlete, Football Player)
PO Box 91157
Columbus, OH 43209-7157, USA

Thomas, Ben (Athlete, Football Player)
2155 Herndon St
Auburn, AL 36830-6603, USA

Thomas, Betty (Actor, Director, Producer)
c/o Bryan Lourd *Creative Artists Agency (CAA)*
2000 Avenue of the Stars Ste 100
Los Angeles, CA 90067-4705, USA

Thomas, BJ (Musician)
c/o Alec Vidmar *UTA Music*
209 10th Ave S Ste 511
Nashville, TN 37203-0795, USA

Thomas, Blair (Athlete, Football Player)
401 Gulph Ridge Dr
King Of Prussia, PA 19406-3213, USA

Thomas, Broderick (Athlete, Football Player)
14442 Junction Place Dr
Houston, TX 77045-6562, USA

Thomas, Bruce (Actor)
c/o Jerry Shandrew *Shandrew Public Relations*
1050 S Stanley Ave
Los Angeles, CA 90019-6634, USA

Thomas, Calvin (Athlete, Football Player)
908 Manchester Ave
Westchester, IL 60154-2719, USA

Thomas, Cam (Athlete, Football Player)

Thomas, Carl (Musician)
c/o Staff Member *Red Entertainment Agency*
3537 36th St Ste 2
Astoria, NY 11106-1347, USA

Thomas, Carl (Athlete, Baseball Player)
4349 N 70th St
Scottsdale, AZ 85251-2306, USA

Thomas, Charles (Athlete, Baseball Player)
137 Black Oak Dr
Asheville, NC 28804-1835, USA

Thomas, Chris (Musician)
Associated Booking Corp
1995 Broadway # 501
New York, NY 10023-5882, USA

Thomas, Chuck (Athlete, Football Player)
2201 Purple Majesty Ct
Las Vegas, NV 89117-2747, USA

Thomas, Clarence (Attorney)
US Supreme Court
United States Supreme Court 11th St NE
Washington, DC 20543-0001, USA

Thomas, Clendon (Athlete, Football Player)
7508 Rumsey Rd
Oklahoma City, OK 73132-5335, USA

Thomas, Clete (Athlete, Baseball Player)
802 Wyoming Ave
Lynn Haven, FL 32444-1963

Thomas, Craig (Producer)
c/o Matt Rice *United Talent Agency (UTA)*
9336 Civic Center Dr
Beverly Hills, CA 90210-3604, USA

Thomas, Dallas (Athlete, Football Player)
c/o Bill Johnson *SportsTrust Advisors*
3340 Peachtree Rd NE Fl 16
Atlanta, GA 30326-1000, USA

Thomas, Daniel (Athlete, Football Player)
c/o Mitchell Frankel *Impact Sports (FL)*
2799 NW 2nd Ave Ste 203
Boca Raton, FL 33431-6709, USA

Thomas, Dave (Comedian)
c/o Staff Member *Gersh*
9465 Wilshire Blvd Ste 600
Beverly Hills, CA 90212-2605, USA

Thomas, Dave G (Athlete, Football Player)
2127 Brickell Ave Apt 3404
Miami, FL 33129-2105, USA

Thomas, David (Athlete, Football Player)
c/o Staff Member *New England Patriots*
1 Patriot Pl
Foxboro, MA 02035-1388, USA

Thomas, David (Business Person)
Thomson Corp
1 Station Pl
Metro Center
Stamford, CT 06902-6800, USA

Thomas, David (Musician)
74 Hyde Vale
Greenwich
London SE10 8HP, UNITED KINGDOM (UK)

Thomas, De'Anthony (Athlete, Football Player)
c/o Joe Panos *Athletes First*
23091 Mill Creek Dr
Laguna Hills, CA 92653-1258, USA

Thomas, DeAnthony (Athlete, Football Player)
c/o David Dunn *Athletes First*
23091 Mill Creek Dr
Laguna Hills, CA 92653-1258, USA

Thomas, Debra J (Deb) (Figure Skater)
Mentor Mgmt
202 S Michigan St Ste 810
South Bend, IN 46601-2012, USA

Thomas, Demaryius (Athlete, Football Player)
c/o Todd France *Creative Artists Agency (CAA) Sports*
3500 Lenox Rd NE
Atlanta, GA 30326-4228, USA

Thomas, Dennis (DT) (Musician)
c/o Staff Member *Pyramid Entertainment Group*
377 Rector Pl Apt 21A
New York, NY 10280-1439, USA

Thomas, Derrel (Athlete, Baseball Player)
c/o Staff Member *JD Legends Promotions*
10808 Foothill Blvd Ste 160 PMB 454
Rancho Cucamonga, CA 91730-0601, USA

Thomas, Dominic R (Religious Leader)
Church of Jesus Christ
6th & Lincoln Sts
Monongahela, PA 15063, USA

Thomas, Donald (Athlete, Football Player)
c/o Drew Rosenhaus *Rosenhaus Sports Representation*
3921 Alton Rd # 440
Miami Beach, FL 33140-3852, USA

Thomas, Donald A (Astronaut)
1029 Hart Rd
Towson, MD 21286-1630, USA

Thomas, Donald A Dr (Astronaut)
1029 Hart Rd
Towson, MD 21286-1630, USA

Thomas, Doug (Athlete, Football Player)
11220 NE 53rd St
Kirkland, WA 98033-7505, USA

Thomas, Duane (Athlete, Football Player)
PO Box 862
Del Mar, CA 92014-0862, USA

Thomas, Earl (Athlete, Football Player)
1000 Farrah Ln Apt 825
Stafford, TX 77477-6046, USA

Thomas, Earlie (Athlete, Football Player)
PO Box 1445
Laporte, CO 80535-1445, USA

Thomas, Eddie Kaye (Actor)
c/o Jamie Harhay Skinner *Baker Winokur Ryder Public Relations*
9100 Wilshire Blvd
W Tower #500
Beverly Hills, CA 90212-3415, USA

Thomas, Elizabeth Marshall (Writer)
80 E Mountain Rd
Peterborough, NH 03458-2318, USA

Thomas, Emmitt (Athlete, Football Player)
1813 NE Parks Summit Blvd
Lees Summit, MO 64064-7949, USA

Thomas, Ernest (Actor)
Coast to Coast Talent
3350 Barham Blvd
Los Angeles, CA 90068-1404, USA

Thomas, Etan (Athlete, Basketball Player)
c/o Arn Tellem *Wasserman Media Group*
10960 Wilshire Blvd Ste 1200
Los Angeles, CA 90024-3714, USA

Thomas, Evan (Writer)
c/o Staff Member *Public Affairs Books*
1094 Flex Dr
Jackson, TN 38301-5070, USA

Thomas, Frank (Athlete, Baseball Player)
1515 Sunnyview Rd
Libertyville, IL 60048-5328, USA

Thomas, Frank J (Athlete, Baseball Player)
4202 Lenox Oval
Pittsburgh, PA 15237-1659, USA

Thomas, Gareth (Actor)
c/o Staff Member *Julian Belfrage & Associates*
9 Argyll St Fl 3
London W1F 7TG, UNITED KINGDOM

Thomas, George (Athlete, Baseball Player)
5804 Ivrea Dr
Sarasota, FL 34238-4730

Thomas, Gorman (Athlete, Baseball Player)
W331S5179 Hood Pkwy
North Prairie, WI 53153-9719, USA

Thomas, Heather (Actor)
1433 San Vicente Blvd
Santa Monica, CA 90402-2203, USA

Thomas, Heidi (Actor)

Thomas, Henry (Actor)
c/o Jennifer Craig *Gersh*
9465 Wilshire Blvd Ste 600
Beverly Hills, CA 90212-2605, USA

Thomas, Henry L Jr (Athlete, Football Player)
16811 Southern Oaks Dr
Houston, TX 77068-1509, USA

Thomas, Henry W (Writer)
3214 Warder St NW
Washington, DC 20010-2521, USA

Thomas, Hollis (Athlete, Football Player)
920 Yeadon Ave
Lansdowne, PA 19050-3713, USA

Thomas, Imogen (Actor, Model, Reality Star)
c/o Mark Thomas *TM Media*
45 Circus Rd
London NW8 9JH, UNITED KINGDOM

Thomas, Irma (Musician)
c/o Staff Member *Concerted Efforts*
PO Box 440326
Somerville, MA 02144-0004, USA

Thomas, Irving (Athlete, Basketball Player)
5117 Lakosee Ct
Orlando, FL 32818-8330, USA

Thomas, Isaac (Athlete, Football Player)
510 Grady Ln
Cedar Hill, TX 75104-4212, USA

Thomas, Jabe (Race Car Driver)
850 Mountain View Dr
Christiansburg, VA 24073-4330, USA

Thomas, Jake (Actor)
c/o Connie Tavel *Forward Entertainment*
1880 Century Park E Ste 1405
Los Angeles, CA 90067-1630, USA

Thomas, Jean (Artist)
1427 Summit Rd
Berkeley, CA 94708-2214, USA

Thomas, Jeremy (Producer)
c/o Staff Member *Hanway Films*
24 Hanway St
London W1T 1UH, UNITED KINGDOM

Thomas, Joe L (Musician)
c/o Staff Member *Kedar Entertainment*
21 W 39th St Fl 6
New York, NY 10018-0614, USA

Thomas, Joey (Athlete, Football Player)
c/o Eugene Parker *Independent Sports & Entertainment (ISE-IN)*
6435 W Jefferson Blvd # 197
Fort Wayne, IN 46804-6203, USA

Thomas, John (Basketball Player)
Toronto Raptors
40 Bay St
Air Canada Center
Toronto, ON M5J 2X2, CANADA

Thomas, John (Bud) (Athlete, Baseball Player)
2475 Woodland Dr
Sedalia, MO 65301-8915, USA

Thomas, Johnny (Athlete, Football Player)
1818 Darby Ln
Fresno, TX 77545-9233, USA

Thomas, Jonathan Taylor (Actor)
c/o Abby Bluestone *Innovative Artists*
1505 10th St
Santa Monica, CA 90401-2805, USA

Thomas, Josh (Athlete, Football Player)
c/o Alan Herman *Sportstars Inc*
1370 Avenue of the Americas Fl 19
New York, NY 10019-4602, USA

Thomas, J T (Athlete, Football Player)
408 Arden Dr
Monroeville, PA 15146-4855, USA

Thomas, J.T. (Athlete, Football Player)

Thomas, Julius (Athlete, Football Player)
c/o Frank Bauer *Sun West Sports*
7883 N Pershing Ave
Stockton, CA 95207-1749, USA

Thomas, Justin (Athlete, Golfer)
12300 Warner Dr
Goshen, KY 40026-9429, USA

Thomas, Khleo (Actor)
c/o Staff Member *Beverly Hecht Agency*
3500 W Olive Ave Ste 1180
Burbank, CA 91505-4651, USA

Thomas, Kleo (Musician)

Thomas, Kurt (Athlete, Gymnast, Olympic Athlete)
4421 Hidden Hill Rd
Norman, OK 73072-2899, USA

Thomas, Kurt (Athlete, Basketball Player)
1826 Brook Terrace Trl
Dallas, TX 75232-3708, USA

Thomas, Lamar (Athlete, Football Player)
2907 NW 9th Pl
Gainesville, FL 32605-5056, USA

Thomas, Larry (Actor)
c/o Jackie Lewis *LB Talent Agency*
3406 W Burbank Blvd
Burbank, CA 91505-2232, USA

Thomas, Larry (Athlete, Baseball Player)
3825 Graham Ln
Eight Mile, AL 36613-2306, USA

Thomas, LaToya (Basketball Player)
San Antonio Silver Stars
1 at and T Center Pkwy
San Antonio, TX 78219-3604, USA

Thomas, Lavale (Athlete, Football Player)
2626 Northwoods Lake Ct
Duluth, GA 30096-7997, USA

Thomas, Lee (Athlete, Baseball Player)
14260 Manderleigh Woods Dr
Chesterfield, MO 63017-8051, USA

Thomas, Logan (Athlete, Football Player)
c/o David Dunn *Athletes First*
23091 Mill Creek Dr
Laguna Hills, CA 92653-1258, USA

Thomas, Mark A (Athlete, Football Player)
556 Hillsboro St
Monticello, GA 31064-1046, USA

Thomas, Marlo (Actor)
420 E 54th St
22F
New York, NY 10022-5179, USA

Thomas, Mary (Musician)
Superstars Unlimited
PO Box 371371
Las Vegas, NV 89137-1371, USA

Thomas, Mike (Athlete, Baseball Player)
4808 Gregory Cv
Jonesboro, AR 72401-7943, USA

Thomas, Mike (Athlete, Football Player)
PO Box 446
Missouri City, TX 77459-0446, USA

Thomas, Norris (Athlete, Football Player)
4510 Chippewa Ave
Pascagoula, MS 39581-2501, USA

Thomas, Pamela (Business Person)
c/o Staff Member *CNBC (Main)*
900 Sylvan Ave
Englewood Cliffs, NJ 07632-3312, USA

Thomas, Pat (Athlete, Football Player)
612 Middle Cove Dr
Plano, TX 75023-4802, USA

Thomas, Philip Michael (Actor)
PO Box 23714
Brooklyn, NY 11202-3714, USA

Thomas, Pierre (Athlete, Football Player)
c/o Lamont Smith *All Pro Sports and Entertainment*
50 S Steele St Ste 480
Denver, CO 80209-2836, USA

Thomas, Pinklon (Athlete, Boxer)
c/o Staff Member *Chappell Entertainment Corp*
214 N Griffin Dr
Casselberry, FL 32707-2965, USA

Thomas, Ralph (Athlete, Football Player)
3270 Alum Creek Ct
Reno, NV 89509-7117, USA

Thomas, Randy (Athlete, Football Player)
2945 Jones St Apt 4
Atlanta, GA 30344-4130, USA

Thomas, Reg (Athlete, Hockey Player)
7245 Colonel Talbot Rd
London, ON N6L 1H9, Canada

Thomas, Richard (Actor)
c/o Emily Gerson Saines *Brookside Artists Management*
250 W 57th St Ste 1820
New York, NY 10107-1802, USA

Thomas, Ricky (Athlete, Football Player)
4621 Melbourne Rd
Indianapolis, IN 46228-2773, USA

Thomas, Rob (Director, Producer)
c/o Ari Greenburg *WME|IMG*
9601 Wilshire Blvd
Beverly Hills, CA 90210-5213, USA

Thomas, Rob (Musician, Songwriter)
PO Box 7149
San Francisco, CA 94120-7149, USA

Thomas, Robb (Athlete, Football Player)
179 NW Outlook Vista Dr
Bend, OR 97703-5472, USA

Thomas, Robert L (Athlete, Football Player)
2810 W Slauson Ave Apt 5
Los Angeles, CA 90043-2583, USA

Thomas, Robert R (Athlete, Football Player)
970 Ridgewood Dr
West Chicago, IL 60185-5007, USA

Thomas, Robin (Actor)
c/o Staff Member *Marshak/Zachary Company, The*
8840 Wilshire Blvd Fl 1
Beverly Hills, CA 90211-2606, USA

Thomas, Ross (Actor)
c/o Bryan Bukowski *Simmons & Scott Entertainment*
7942 Mulholland Dr
Los Angeles, CA 90046-1225, USA

Thomas, Roy (Athlete, Baseball Player)
3825 Tribute Cir E
Fife, WA 98424-3797, USA

Thomas, Scott (Athlete, Hockey Player)
143 Berryman Dr
Buffalo, NY 14226-4373

Thomas, Sean Patrick (Actor)
c/o Karen Samfilippo *IMPR*
1158 26th St # 548
Santa Monica, CA 90403-4698, USA

Thomas, Serena Scott (Actor)
c/o Andi Schecter *Jonas Public Relations*
1327 Ocean Ave Ste F
Santa Monica, CA 90401-1024, USA

Thomas, Shamarko (Athlete, Football Player)

Thomas, Stan (Athlete, Baseball Player)
90 Choice Loop
Sequim, WA 98382-8152, USA

Thomas, Stayve (Slim Thug) (Musician)
c/o Wes Stevens *Vox*
5670 Wilshire Blvd Ste 820
Los Angeles, CA 90036-5613, USA

Thomas, Steve (Athlete, Hockey Player)
Plain and Simple
289 Bering Ave
Toronto, ON M8Z 3A5, Canada

Thomas, Ted (Business Person)
C/O Jones & Trevor Marketing
234 Willard St Ste C
Cocoa, FL 32922-7984, USA

Thomas, Thurman L (Athlete, Football Player)
240 Pound Rd
Elma, NY 14059-9681, USA

Thomas, Tim (Athlete, Hockey Player)
c/o Staff Member *Acme World Sports LLC*
8770 W Bryn Mawr Ave Ste 1300
Chicago, IL 60631-3557, USA

Thomas, Tony (Actor, Producer)
Witt/Thomas/Harris Productions
11901 Santa Monica Blvd Ste 596
West Los Angeles, CA 90025-5188, USA

Thomas, Tra (Athlete, Football Player)
1 Novacare Way
Philadelphia, PA 19145-5900, USA

Thomas, Wayne (Athlete, Hockey Player)
525 W Santa Clara St
San Jose, CA 95113-1520

Thomas, William H Jr (Athlete, Football Player)
2401 Echo Dr
Amarillo, TX 79107-6405, USA

Thomas, William J (Athlete, Football Player)
16 Russell St Apt 2
Waltham, MA 02453-8505, USA

Thomas, Zach (Athlete, Football Player)
1051 NW 122nd Ave
Plantation, FL 33323-2529, USA

Thomaselli, Rich (Athlete, Football Player)
96A Seneca St
Weirton, WV 26062-2627, USA

Thomas III, Isiah L (Athlete, Basketball Player)
24 Carol Ct
Rye Brook, NY 10573-5414, USA

Thomas III, Leon (Actor)
c/o Bryan Leder *Authentic Talent & Literary Management*
3615 Eastham Dr # 650
Culver City, CA 90232-2410, USA

Thomas Jr, James (Athlete, Basketball Player)
4499 Willow Hill Rd
Portal, GA 30450-5344, USA

Thomason, Bob (Athlete, Football Player)
2645 Bucknell Ave
Charlotte, NC 28207-2649, USA

Thomason, CJ (Actor)
c/o Staff Member *Robert Stein Management*
PO Box 3797
Beverly Hills, CA 90212-0797, USA

Thomason, Erskine (Athlete, Baseball Player)
932 Dial Pl
Laurens, SC 29360-8850, USA

Thomason, Harry (Producer)
c/o Staff Member *Mozark Productions*
4024 Radford Ave Bldg 5
Studio City, CA 91604-2101, USA

Thomason, Marsha (Actor)
c/o Kesha Williams *KW Entertainment*
3727 W Magnolia Blvd Ste 430
Burbank, CA 91505-2818, USA

Thomassin, Florence (Actor)
c/o Elisabeth Tanner *Time-Art*
8 rue Danielle Casanova
Paris 75002, FRANCE

Thomasson, Gary (Athlete, Baseball Player)
8300 N 53rd St
Paradise Valley, AZ 85253-2512, USA

Thome, Jim (Athlete, Baseball Player)
c/o Ashley Smith Becker *Relativity Sports*
2029 Century Park E Ste 1550
Century City, CA 90067-3000, USA

Thomerson, Tim (Actor)
2635 28th St Apt 14
Santa Monica, CA 90405-2960, USA

Thomlinson, Dave (Athlete, Hockey Player)
52 Kenilworth Cres
St. Albert, AB T8N 7G3, Canada

Thomlinson, John (Baseball Player)
Negro Baseball Leagues
2351 Beach Way SW
Atlanta, GA 30310-1005, USA

Thomopoulos, Anthony (Business Person)
MTM
2877 Guardian Ln
Virginia Beach, VA 23452-7330, USA

Thompkins, Kenbrell (Athlete, Football Player)
c/o Drew Rosenhaus *Rosenhaus Sports Representation*
3921 Alton Rd # 440
Miami Beach, FL 33140-3852, USA

Thompson, Ahmir-Khalib (Questlove) (Musician)
c/o Carleen Donovan *Donovan Public Relations*
30 E 20th St Ste 2FE
New York, NY 10003-1310, USA

Thompson, Alana (Honey Boo Boo) (Reality Star)
338 Kentwood Springs Dr
Hampton, GA 30228-5937, USA

Thompson, Andrea (Actor)
Dayton Milrad Cho Management
8306 Wilshire Blvd # 56
Beverly Hills, CA 90211-2304, USA

Thompson, Andy (Athlete, Baseball Player)
1405 Bayshore Blvd
Tampa, FL 33606-3001, USA

Thompson, Anthony (Athlete, Coach, Football Coach, Football Player)
Athletic Dept
Bloomington, IN 47405, USA

Thompson, Arland (Athlete, Football Player)
6692 S Routt St
Littleton, CO 80127-4962, USA

Thompson, Aundra (Athlete, Football Player)
12060 Galva Dr
Dallas, TX 75243-3702, USA

Thompson, Barbara (Athlete, Baseball Player)
3347 Amelia Run Way
North Fort Myers, FL 33917-7165, USA

Thompson, Bennie (Athlete, Football Player)
Baltimore Ravens
11001 Russell St
Baltimore, MD 21230, USA

Thompson, Billy (Athlete, Basketball Player)
32 Lake Side Trl
Lake Placid, FL 33852-8413, USA

Thompson, Brandon (Athlete, Football Player)

Thompson, Brent (Athlete, Hockey Player)
Bridgeport Sound Tigers
600 Main St Ste 1
Bridgeport, CT 06604-5106

Thompson, Brooks (Athlete, Basketball Player)
29222 Oakview Rdg
Boerne, TX 78015-4457, USA

Thompson, Charissa (Actor, Sportscaster)
c/o Nick Khan *Creative Artists Agency (CAA)*
2000 Avenue of the Stars Ste 100
Los Angeles, CA 90067-4705, USA

Thompson, Cornelius (Athlete, Basketball Player)
207 Lamentation Dr
Berlin, CT 06037-3727, USA

Thompson, Craig (Athlete, Football Player)
913 C St
Hartsville, SC 29550-3166, USA

Thompson, Daley (Athlete)
1 Church Row Wandsworth Plain
London, ENGLAND SW18 1ES

Thompson, Darrell (Athlete, Football Player)
4220 Oakview Ln N
Plymouth, MN 55442-2773, USA

thompson, Deonte (Athlete, Football Player)

Thompson, Derek (Athlete, Baseball Player)
3212 Pine Shadow Dr
Land O Lakes, FL 34639-4516, USA

Thompson, Don (Business Person)
McDonald's Corp
1 Kroc Dr
McDonald's Plaza
Oak Brook, IL 60523-2275, USA

Thompson, Donnell (Athlete, Football Player)
1302 Village Crossing Dr
Chapel Hill, NC 27517-7572, USA

Thompson, Emma (Actor)
c/o Catherine Olim *PMK/BNC Public Relations*
1840 Century Park E Ste 1400
Los Angeles, CA 90067-2115, USA

Thompson, Errol (Athlete, Hockey Player)
20 Nevada Crt
Summerside, PEI C1N 6A8, Canada

Thompson, F M (Daley) (Athlete, Track Athlete)
Olympic Assn
1 Wadsworth Plain
London SW18 1EH, UNITED KINGDOM (UK)

Thompson, Gary (Basketball Player)
2531 Park Vista Cir
Ames, IA 50014-4568, USA

Thompson, Gary Scott (Producer, Writer)
c/o Phillip d'Amecourt *WME|IMG*
9601 Wilshire Blvd
Beverly Hills, CA 90210-5213, USA

Thompson, Georgie (Correspondent)
c/o Caroline Michel *Peters, Fraser And Dunlop*
Drury House
34-43 Russell St
London WC2B 5HA, UK

Thompson, Glenn (Congressman, Politician)
124 Cannon Hob
Washington, DC 20515-4401, USA

Thompson, G Ralph (Religious Leader)
Seventh-Day Adventists
12501 Old Columbia Pike
Silver Spring, MD 20904-6600, USA

Thompson, Ian (Actor)
44 Perryn Rd
London W3 7NA, UNITED KINGDOM

Thompson, Jack (Actor)
c/o Nathan Morris *Linsten Morris Management*
3 Gladstone St
Suite 301
Newtown, NSW 02042, AUSTRALIA

Thompson, Jack (Athlete, Football Player)
2507 29th Ave W
Seattle, WA 98199-3323, USA

Thompson, Jack E (Business Person)
Homestake Mining Co
650 California St
San Francisco, CA 94108-2702, USA

Thompson, Jason (Actor)
c/o Troy Nankin *Wishlab*
195 S Beverly Dr Ste 414
Beverly Hills, CA 90212-3044, USA

Thompson, Jason (Athlete, Baseball Player)
10535 Oak Terrace Ave
Las Vegas, NV 89149-1504, USA

Thompson, Jason D (Athlete, Baseball Player)
4056 Summerfield Dr
Troy, MI 48085-7033, USA

Thompson, Jenny (Athlete, Swimmer)
Maine Medical Center
22 Bramhall St
Anesthesiologist Dept
Portland, ME 04102-3175, USA

Thompson, Jill (Cartoonist)
DC Comics
2900 W Alameda Ave # 1
Burbank, CA 91505-4220, USA

Thompson, John (Athlete, Basketball Player, Olympic Athlete)
Basketball Hall of Fame
1000 Hall of Fame Ave Ste 100
Springfield, MA 01105-2545, USA

Thompson, Justin (Athlete, Baseball Player)
32807 Clearwater Ct
Magnolia, TX 77354-3233, USA

Thompson, Kenan (Actor)
c/o Michael Goldman *Michael Goldman Management*
7471 Melrose Ave Ste &11
Los Angeles, CA 90046-7551, USA

Thompson, Kevin (Athlete, Basketball Player)
9808 Westpark Dr
Benbrook, TX 76126-3125, USA

Thompson, Klay (Athlete, Basketball Player)
c/o Bill Duffy *BDA Sports Management*
700 Ygnacio Valley Rd Ste 330
Walnut Creek, CA 94596-3838, USA

Thompson, Lasalle (Athlete, Basketball Player)
111 W Main St Apt 2A
Carmel, IN 46032-2034, USA

Thompson, Lea (Actor)
c/o Gordon Gilbertson *Gilbertson Management*
1334 3rd Street Promenade Ste 201
Santa Monica, CA 90401-1320, USA

Thompson, Leonard (Athlete, Football Player)
5534 W Glenrosa Ave
Phoenix, AZ 85031-2220, USA

Thompson, Leonard (Golfer)
4300 S Beach Pkwy Apt 3224
Jacksonville Beach, FL 32250-8181, USA

Thompson, Leroy (Athlete, Football Player)
5005 Princess Ann Ct
Knoxville, TN 37918-9274, USA

Thompson, Linda (Musician)
6342 Sycamore Meadows Dr
Malibu, CA 90265-4439, USA

Thompson, Mark (Athlete, Baseball Player)
2600 Chandler Dr Apt 1311
Bowling Green, KY 42104-6235, USA

Thompson, Marty (Athlete, Football Player)
1290 Lone Star Ct
Calimesa, CA 92320-1501, USA

Thompson, Mike (Athlete, Baseball Player)
7565 Turner Dr
Denver, CO 80221-3432, USA

Thompson, Mike (Congressman, Politician)
231 Cannon Hob
Washington, DC 20515-3311, USA

Thompson, Milt (Athlete, Baseball Player)
PO Box 663
Williamstown, NJ 08094-0663, USA

Thompson, Morgan (Actor)
c/o Staff Member *Luber Roklin Management*
5815 W Sunset Blvd Ste 208
Los Angeles, CA 90028-6481, USA

Thompson, Mychal (Athlete, Basketball Player)
11 Paverstone Ln
Ladera Ranch, CA 92694-0454, USA

Thompson, Mychel (Athlete, Basketball Player)
c/o Bill Duffy *BDA Sports Management*
700 Ygnacio Valley Rd Ste 330
Walnut Creek, CA 94596-3838, USA

Thompson, Norm (Athlete, Football Player)
PO Box 4552
Hayward, CA 94540-4552, USA

Thompson, Obadele (Athlete, Track Athlete)
Amateur Athletics Assn
PO Box 46
Bridgetown, BARBADOS

Thompson, Paul (Athlete, Basketball Player)
3422 N 40th St
Milwaukee, WI 53216-3637, USA

Thompson, Ray (Athlete, Football Player)
1501 N Johnson St Apt A208
New Orleans, LA 70116-1757, USA

Thompson, Raynoch (Athlete, Football Player)
1739 2nd St
New Orleans, LA 70113-1657, USA

Thompson, Reece (Actor)
c/o Vickie Petronio *Play Management*
220-807 Powell St
Vancouver, BC V6A 1H7, CANADA

Thompson, Reyna (Athlete, Football Player)
1502 NW 183rd Ter
Pembroke Pines, FL 33029-3095, USA

Thompson, Rich (Athlete, Baseball Player)
7 Chambers Ct
Huntington Station, NY 11746-2620, USA

Thompson, Rich (Athlete, Baseball Player)
47 Murray St
Binghamton, NY 13905-4522, USA

Thompson, Richard (Musician, Songwriter, Writer)
Elizabeth Rush Agency
100 Park St Apt 4
Montclair, NJ 07042-2996, USA

Thompson, Richard K (Religious Leader)
African Methodist Episcopal Zion Church
PO Box 32843
Charlotte, NC 28232-2843, USA

Thompson, Ricky (Athlete, Football Player)
815 Woodland West Dr
Waco, TX 76712-3415, USA

Thompson, Robert (Athlete, Football Player)
Deerfield Beach High School
910 SW 15th St
Deerfield Beach, FL 33441-6299, USA

Thompson, Robert L (Athlete, Football Player)
10712 S 7th Ave
Inglewood, CA 90303-1510, USA

Thompson, Robert R (Robby) (Athlete, Baseball Player)
PO Box 4100
Seattle, WA 98194-0100, USA

Thompson, Rocky (Athlete, Hockey Player)
Oklahoma City Barons
501 N Walker Ave Ste 140
Oklahoma City, OK 73102-1233

Thompson, Ryan (Athlete, Baseball Player)
2153 Fullerton Dr
Indianapolis, IN 46214-2130, USA

Thompson, Sarah (Actor)
c/o Gerry Harrington *Brillstein Entertainment Partners*
9150 Wilshire Blvd Ste 350
Beverly Hills, CA 90212-3453, USA

Thompson, Scot (Athlete, Baseball Player)
6142 Penn Dr
Butler, PA 16002-0406, USA

Thompson, Scottie (Actor)
c/o Cheryl McLean *Creative Public Relations*
3385 Oak Glen Dr
Los Angeles, CA 90068-1311, USA

Thompson, Shaq (Athlete, Football Player)
c/o Doug Hendrickson *Relativity Sports*
2029 Century Park E Ste 1550
Century City, CA 90067-3000, USA

Thompson, Shaun (Dancer, Fitness Expert)
c/o Tom Estey *Tom Estey Publicity*
144 E 22nd St Apt 1B
New York, NY 10010-6333, USA

Thompson, Sophie (Actor)
Jonathan Altaras
13 Shorts Gardens
London WC2H 9AT, UNITED KINGDOM (UK)

Thompson, Steve M (Athlete, Football Player)
11115 Vernon Rd
Lake Stevens, WA 98258-8541, USA

Thompson, Sue (Musician)
Curb Entertainment
3907 W Alameda Ave Ste 200
Burbank, CA 91505-4359, USA

Thompson, Susanna (Actor)
PO Box 15717
Beverly Hills, CA 90209-1717, USA

Thompson, Tara (Actor)

Thompson, Taylor (Athlete, Football Player)
c/o W Vann McElroy *Select Sports Group*
2700 Post Oak Blvd Ste 1450
Houston, TX 77056-5785, USA

Thompson, Ted (Athlete, Football Player)
Green Bay Packers
PO Box 10628
Director of Player Personnel
Green Bay, WI 54307-0628, USA

Thompson, Tessa (Actor)
c/o Ashley Josephson *Mosaic Media Group*
407 N Maple Dr # 100
Beverly Hills, CA 90210-3818, USA

Thompson, Tim (Athlete, Baseball Player)
536 Summit Dr
Lewistown, PA 17044-1252, USA

Thompson, Tommy (Politician)
1313 Manassas Trl
Madison, WI 53718-8243, USA

Thompson, Trayce (Athlete, Basketball Player)
c/o Lenny Strelitz *Wasserman Media Group*
10960 Wilshire Blvd Ste 1200
Los Angeles, CA 90024-3714, USA

Thompson, Weegie (Athlete, Football Player)
14501 Felbridge Way
Midlothian, VA 23113-6721, USA

Thompson, William A (Athlete, Football Player)
14616 E Hawaii Pl
Aurora, CO 80012-5747, USA

Thompson, William P (Religious Leader)
World Council of Churches
475 Riverside Dr Ste 727
New York, NY 10115-0070, USA

Thompson Square (Music Group, Musician)
c/o Staff Member *WME (Nashville)*
1201 Demonbreun St
Nashville, TN 37203-3140, USA

Thoms, Art (Athlete, Football Player)
90 Goodfellow Dr
Moraga, CA 94556-1584, USA

Thoms, Tracie (Actor)
c/o Ted Schachter *Schachter Entertainment*
1157 S Beverly Dr Fl 2
Los Angeles, CA 90035-1119, USA

Thomsen, Cecilie (Actor)
c/o Staff Member *Special Artists Agency*
9200 W Sunset Blvd Ste 410
W Hollywood, CA 90069-3506, USA

Thomsen, Ulrich (Actor)
c/o Tammy Rosen *Sanders Armstrong Caserta*
4111 W Alameda Ave Ste 505
Burbank, CA 91505-4163, USA

Thomson, Anna (Actor)
Innovative Artists
1505 10th St
Santa Monica, CA 90401-2805, USA

Thomson, Brian E (Designer)
5 Little Dowling St
Paddington, NSW 02021, AUSTRALIA

Thomson, Cyndi (Musician)
The Firm
9100 Wilshire Blvd Ste 100W
Beverly Hills, CA 90212-3435, USA

Thomson, David (Business Person)
The Thomson Corporation
1 Station Pl
Metro Center
Stamford, CT 06902-6800, USA

Thomson, Floyd (Athlete, Hockey Player)
GD
Dunchurch, ON POA 1GO, Canada

Thomson, Gordon (Actor)
10620 Whipple St Unit 308
North Hollywood, CA 91602-2934, USA

Thomson, H C (Hank) (Misc)
PO Box 38
Mullett Lake, MI 49761-0038, USA

Thomson, Jim (Athlete, Hockey Player)
18 Blackbird Cres
Richmond Hill, ON L4E 4B3, Canada

Thomson, John (Athlete, Baseball Player)
1414 E Kent Dr
Sulphur, LA 70663-5017, USA

Thomson, June (Correspondent)
KNBC-TV
News Dept
3000 W Alameda Ave
Burbank, CA 91523-0001, USA

Thomson, Rob (Athlete, Baseball Player)
17428 Equestrian Trl
Odessa, FL 33556-1846, USA

Thomson, Scott (DJ)
c/o Staff Member *Sharp Talent*
117 N Orlando Ave
Los Angeles, CA 90048-3403, USA

Thon, Dickie (Athlete, Baseball Player)
C17 Calle Lirio Del Mar
Urb Dorado Del Mar
Dorado, PR 00646-2126, USA

Thoni, Gustav (Coach, Skier)
39026 Prato Allo
Stelvio-Prao, BZ, ITALY

Thor, Brad (Writer)
c/o Staff Member *Sanford J Greenburger Associates Inc*
55 5th Ave
New York, NY 10003-4301, USA

Thora (Actor)
CunninghamEscottDipene
10635 Santa Monica Blvd Ste 130
Los Angeles, CA 90025-8306, USA

Thorburn, Christine (Athlete, Cycler, Olympic Athlete)
141 Mimosa Way
Portola Valley, CA 94028-7429, USA

Thorell, Clarke (Actor)
614 Stratford Ave
South Pasadena, CA 91030-2803

Thoren, Skip (Athlete, Basketball Player)
330 Buckland Trce
Louisville, KY 40245-4272, USA

Thorin, Christopher (Musician)
Shapiro Co
10990 Wilshire Blvd Fl 8
Los Angeles, CA 90024-3918, USA

Thorman, Scott (Athlete, Baseball Player)
561 Trico Dr
Cambridge, ON N3H 5M8, Canada

Thormodsgard, Paul (Athlete, Baseball Player)
7752 E Rose Ln
Scottsdale, AZ 85250-4724, USA

Thorn, Gaston (Prime Minister)
1 Rue de la Forge
Luxembourg, LUXEMBOURG

Thorn, Paul (Musician)
c/o Staff Member *Paradigm (Monterey)*
404 W Franklin St
Monterey, CA 93940-2303, USA

Thorn, Rod (Athlete, Basketball Player)
20 Loewen Ct
Rye, NY 10580-2823, USA

Thorn, Tracey (Musician)
JFD Mgmt
Acklam Worshops
10 Acklam Road
London W10 5QZ, UNITED KINGDOM (UK)

Thornberry, Mac (Congressman, Politician)
2209 Rayburn Hob
Washington, DC 20515-3010, USA

Thornbladh, Robert (Athlete, Football Player)
3775 Bradford Square Dr
Ann Arbor, MI 48103-6317, USA

Thornburgh, Richard (Dick) (Politician)
315 Grandview Dr
Verona, PA 15147-3898, USA

Thornbury, Tom (Athlete, Hockey Player)
PO Box 262
Woodville, ON K0M 2T0, Canada

Thorne, Bella (Actor)
c/o Elan Ruspoli *Creative Artists Agency (CAA)*
2000 Avenue of the Stars Ste 100
Los Angeles, CA 90067-4705, USA

Thorne, Callie (Actor)
c/o Elise Konialian *Untitled Entertainment (NY)*
215 Park Ave S Fl 8
New York, NY 10003-1622, USA

Thorne, Dyanne (Actor)
5192 Placentia Pkwy
Las Vegas, NV 89118-1489, USA

Thorne, Frank (Cartoonist)
1967 Grenville Rd
Scotch Plains, NJ 07076-2907, USA

Thorne, Gary (Correspondent)
ABC-TV
77 W 66th St
Sports Dept
New York, NY 10023-6201, USA

Thorne, Remy (Actor)
c/o Adam Griffin *LINK Entertainment*
11872 La Grange Ave
Los Angeles, CA 90025-5282, USA

Thorne-Smith, Courtney (Actor, Model)
c/o Karen Samfilippo *IMPR*
1158 26th St # 548
Santa Monica, CA 90403-4698, USA

Thornhill, Josh (Athlete, Football Player)
1580 Haddon Hall Dr
Holt, MI 48842-8688, USA

Thornhill, Leeroy (Dancer)
Midi Mgmt
Jenkins Lane
Great Hallinsbury, Essex CM22 9QL, UNITED KINGDOM (UK)

Thornhill, Lisa (Actor)
208-11 Amin St
Bedford Nova
Bedford, NS B4A 4E3, CANADA

Thornton, Andre (Athlete, Baseball Player)
PO Box 395
Chagrin Falls, OH 44022-0395, USA

Thornton, Billy Bob (Actor, Director)
733 N Kings Rd Apt 209
W Hollywood, CA 90069-5948, USA

Thornton, Bob (Athlete, Basketball Player)
27865 Espinoza
Mission Viejo, CA 92692-2151, USA

Thornton, Bruce (Athlete, Football Player)
3117 Hazlewood Ct
Bedford, TX 76021-2953, USA

Thornton, Cedric (Athlete, Football Player)
c/o Pat Dye Jr *SportsTrust Advisors*
3340 Peachtree Rd NE Fl 16
Atlanta, GA 30326-1000, USA

Thornton, Dick (Athlete, Football Player)
5022 P Burgos Street Suite 11
Makati City, Metro Manila, USA

Thornton, George (Athlete, Football Player)
1495 Bon Terre Blvd
Pike Road, AL 36064-2674, USA

Thornton, Hugh (Athlete, Football Player)

Thornton, James (Athlete, Football Player)
1010 Fuller Rd
Gurnee, IL 60031-1834, USA

Thornton, Joe (Athlete, Hockey Player)
c/o Staff Member *San Jose Sharks*
525 W Santa Clara St
San Jose, CA 95113-1500, USA

Thornton, John (Athlete, Football Player)
6192 Otoole Ln
Mount Morris, MI 48458-2628, USA

Thornton, John (Athlete, Football Player)
7340 Indian Hill Rd
Cincinnati, OH 45243-4022, USA

Thornton, Kalen (Athlete, Football Player)
c/o Eugene Parker *Independent Sports & Entertainment (ISE-IN)*
6435 W Jefferson Blvd # 197
Fort Wayne, IN 46804-6203, USA

Thornton, Kathryn C (Astronaut)
100 Bedford Pl
Charlottesville, VA 22903-4622, USA

Thornton, Kathryn C Dr (Astronaut)
100 Bedford Pl
Charlottesville, VA 22903-4622, USA

Thornton, Lou (Athlete, Baseball Player)
725 Henderson Rd
Hope Hull, AL 36043-4429, USA

Thornton, Matt (Athlete, Baseball Player)
9820 W Eagle Talon Trl
Peoria, AZ 85383-2926, USA

Thornton, Melody (Musician)
JH Management
PO Box 1071
Rye, NY 10580-0871, USA

Thornton, Otis (Athlete, Baseball Player)
4312 Avenue L
Birmingham, AL 35208-1812, USA

Thornton, Scott (Athlete, Hockey Player)
23 Stewart Rd
LNDESTRI GVM
Collingwood, ON L9Y 4M7, Canada

Thornton, Shawn (Athlete, Hockey Player)
8630 Watercrest Cir W
Parkland, FL 33076-2682, USA

Thornton, Sidney (Athlete, Football Player)
748 Royal St
Natchitoches, LA 71457-5741, USA

Thornton, Sigrid (Actor)
International Casting Services
147 King St
Sydney, NSW 02000, AUSTRALIA

Thornton, Tiffany (Actor)
c/o Nikki Pederson *Nikki Pederson Talent*
Prefers to be contacted via telephone or email
The Woodlands, TX, USA

Thornton, William E (Astronaut)
7640 Pimlico Ln
Boerne, TX 78015-4820, USA

Thornton, William E Dr (Astronaut)
2501 Monterey St
Sarasota, FL 34231-5275, USA

Thornton, Zach (Soccer Player)
Chicago Fire
980 N Michigan Ave Ste 1998
Chicago, IL 60611-7504, USA

Thorogood, George (Musician)
c/o Staff Member *Monterey International*
72 W Adams St # 1000
Chicago, IL 60603-5107, USA

Thorp, Amanda (Actor)

Thorpe, Alexis (Actor)
c/o Marv Dauer *Marv Dauer Management*
11661 San Vicente Blvd Ste 104
Los Angeles, CA 90049-5150, USA

Thorpe, Ian (Athlete, Olympic Athlete, Swimmer)
PO Box 402
Worcester, MA 01613-0402, Australia

Thorpe, James (Director)
20 Loeffler Rd Apt T320
Bloomfield, CT 06002-2277, USA

Thorpe, Otis (Athlete, Basketball Player)
632 Casper Ave
West Palm Bch, FL 33413-1227, USA

Thorson, Celeste (Producer, Writer)

Thorson, Linda (Actor)
c/o Penny Noble *Noble Caplan Abrams*
1260 Yonge St Fl 2
Toronto, ON M4T 1W5, CANADA

Those, Tom (Athlete, Baseball Player)
740 E Mingus Ave Apt 1012
Cottonwood, AZ 86326-3780, USA

Thousand Foot Krutch (Music Group)
Tooth & Nail Records
PO Box 12698
Seattle, WA 98111-4698, USA

Thranhardt, Carlo (Athlete, Olympic Athlete, Track Athlete)
Brauweilerstr. 14
Koln D-50859, Germany

Thrash, James (Athlete, Football Player)
16005 Hampton Rd
Hamilton, VA 20158-3311, USA

Threadgill, Henry L (Composer, Musician)
Joel Chriss
300 Mercer St Apt 3J
New York, NY 10003-6732, USA

Threats, Jabbar (Athlete, Football Player)
2015 Miracle Mile
Springfield, OH 45503-2836, USA

Threatt, Sedale (Athlete, Basketball Player)
8400 E Dixileta Dr Unit 191
Scottsdale, AZ 85266-2270, USA

Three 6 Mafia (Music Group, Musician)
c/o Jennifer Wentzo (Wilson) *CodedPR*
54 W 39th St Fl 10
New York, NY 10018-2066, USA

Three Days Grace (Music Group)
c/o Cliff Burnstein *Q Prime (NY)*
729 7th Ave Fl 16
New York, NY 10019-6831, USA

Threets, Erick (Athlete, Baseball Player)
2080 Vintage Ln
Livermore, CA 94550-8202, USA

Threlfall, David (Actor)
c/o Staff Member *Independent Talent Group*
40 Whitfield St
London W1T 2RH, UNITED KINGDOM

Thrice (Music Group)
c/o Staff Member *Nick Ben-Meir CPA*
2850 Ocean Park Blvd Ste 300
Santa Monica, CA 90405-6216, USA

Thrift, Cliff (Athlete, Football Player)
705 Trisha Ln
Norman, OK 73072-3718, USA

Throop, George (Athlete, Baseball Player)
239 Windwood Ln
Sierra Madre, CA 91024-2677, USA

Thrower, Jim (Athlete, Football Player)
17421 Pontchartrain Blvd
Detroit, MI 48203-1720, USA

Throwing Muses (Composer, Musician)
c/o Staff Member *Concerted Efforts*
PO Box 440326
Somerville, MA 02144-0004, USA

Thug, Young (Musician)
c/o Cara Lewis *Cara Lewis Group*
7 W 18th St Fl 3
New York, NY 10011-4663, USA

Thurber, Rawson Marshall (Director)
c/o Dan Aloni *WME|IMG*
9601 Wilshire Blvd
Beverly Hills, CA 90210-5213, USA

Thurlby, Tom (Athlete, Hockey Player)
158 Welborne Ave
Kingston, ON K7M 4E9, Canada

Thurlow, Steve (Athlete, Football Player)
5105 Saint Andrews Island Dr
Vero Beach, FL 32967-7246, USA

Thurm, Maren (Actor)
ZBF Agentur
Ordensmeisterstr 15-16
Berlin 12099, GERMANY

Thurman, Annie (Actor)
c/o Tina Treadwell *Treadwell Entertainment*
1327 W Valleyheart Dr
Burbank, CA 91506-3035, USA

Thurman, Corey (Athlete, Baseball Player)
713 S Duke St
York, PA 17401-3113, USA

Thurman, Dennis L (Athlete, Football Player)
4501 Eli Dr Apt G
Owings Mills, MD 21117-3798, USA

Thurman, Gary (Athlete, Baseball Player)
225 W 32nd St
Indianapolis, IN 46208-4603, USA

Thurman, Mike (Athlete, Baseball Player)
1360 7th St
West Linn, OR 97068-4718, USA

Thurman, Uma (Actor, Producer)
c/o Lisa Kasteler *Wolf-Kasteler Public Relations*
6255 W Sunset Blvd Ste 1111
Los Angeles, CA 90028-7426, USA

Thurmond, Mark (Athlete, Baseball Player)
1614 Kings Castle Dr
Katy, TX 77450-4300, USA

Thurmond, Walter (Athlete, Football Player)
c/o Joel Segal *Lagardere Unlimited (NY)*
456 Washington St Apt 9L
New York, NY 10013-1555, USA

Thursday (Music Group)
c/o Staff Member *Island Records*
825 8th Ave Rm C2
New York, NY 10019-7472, USA

Thurston, Joe (Athlete, Baseball Player)
9024 Paso Robles Way
Elk Grove, CA 95758-6131, USA

Thwaites, Brenton (Actor)
c/o Natasha Harrison *United Management*
Marlborough House
Ste 45, Level 4, 61 Marlborough St
Surry HillsNSW 02010, AUSTRALIA

Thyer, Mario (Athlete, Hockey Player)
170 Silver Rd
Bangor, ME 04401-5829

Thyne, TJ (Actor)
c/o Alex Czuleger *The Green Room*
7080 Hollywood Blvd Ste 1100
Los Angeles, CA 90028-6938, USA

T.I. (Actor, Musician)
c/o Cortez Bryant *Maverick Management*
9350 Civic Center Dr Ste 100
Beverly Hills, CA 90210-3629, USA

Tiant, Luis (Athlete, Baseball Player)
392 Clubhouse Rd
Wells, ME 04090-7375, USA

Tibbetts, Billy (Athlete, Hockey Player)
79 Jericho Rd
Scituate, MA 02066-4809

Tibbs, Jay (Athlete, Baseball Player)
6723 McEachern Ln SE
Owens X Rds, AL 35763-8001, USA

Tice, John (Athlete, Football Player)
1004 Bartlett Loop Apt B
West Point, NY 10996-1201, USA

Tice, Michael P (Mike) (Athlete, Football Coach, Football Player)
2114 Gail Ave Apt A
Jacksonville Beach, FL 32250-6170, USA

Tichenor, Todd (Athlete, Baseball Player)
504 David Ave
Holcomb, KS 67851-9771, USA

Tichmarsh, Alan (Actor, Writer)
c/o Staff Member *Arlington Enterprises Ltd*
1-3 Charlotte St
London W1P 1HD, UNITED KINGDOM (UK)

Tichnor, Alan (Religious Leader)
United Synagogues of Conservative Judaism
155 5th Ave
New York, NY 10010-6858, USA

Tichy, Milan (Athlete, Hockey Player)
2413 NW 7th St
Boynton Beach, FL 33426-8783

Tickner, Charles (Athlete, Figure Skater, Olympic Athlete)
1826 Dolphin Ct
Discovery Bay, CA 94505-9362, USA

Ticotin, Rachel (Actor)
c/o Staff Member *Artists & Representatives (Stone Manners Salners)*
6100 Wilshire Blvd Ste 1500
Los Angeles, CA 90048-5110, USA

Tiddy, Kim (Actor)
Bosun House
1 Deer Park Rd
Merton
London SW19 9TL, ENGLAND

Tidey, Alec (Athlete, Hockey Player)
1877 Marine Dr
N-Vancouver, BC V7P 1V5, CANADA

Tidrow, Dick (Athlete, Baseball Player)
324 NE Warrington Ct
Lees Summit, MO 64064-1605, USA

Tiefenbach, Dov (Actor)
c/o Staff Member *Bauman Redanty & Shaul Agency*
5757 Wilshire Blvd
Suite 473
Beverly Hills, CA 90212, USA

Tiefenthaler, Verfe (Athlete, Baseball Player)
1852 Quint Ave
Carroll, IA 51401-3567, USA

Tiefenthaler, Verle (Athlete, Baseball Player)
1852 Quint Ave
Carroll, IA 51401-3567, USA

Tiegs, Cheryl (Model, Television Host)
c/o Chuck Binder *Binder & Associates*
1465 Lindacrest Dr
Beverly Hills, CA 90210-2519, USA

Tiernan, Andrew (Actor)
c/o Paula Rosenberg *ICA Talent Management*
1112 Montana Ave Ste 520
Santa Monica, CA 90403-7236, USA

Tierney, Maura (Actor)
c/o Christina Papadopoulos *Baker Winokur Ryder Public Relations*
200 5th Ave Fl 5
New York, NY 10010-3307, USA

Tiesto (DJ, Musician)
c/o Paul Morris *Paradigm*
140 Broadway Ste 2600
New York, NY 10005-1011, USA

Tiffany (Musician)
Tiffany's Boutique
301 Highway 76
White House, TN 37188-8194, USA

Tiffee, Terry (Athlete, Baseball Player)
510 Autumn Run
Midlothian, TX 76065-1372, USA

Tiffin, Pamela (Actor)
15 W 67th St
New York, NY 10023-6226, USA

Tighe, Kevin (Actor)
c/o Joannie Burstein *Burstein Company*
15304 W Sunset Blvd Ste 208
Pacific Palisades, CA 90272-3656, USA

Tikkanen, Esa (Athlete, Hockey Player)
Curtiusstr 2
Essen 45144, Germany

Tilford, Terrell (Actor)
c/o Staff Member *SMS Talent*
8383 Wilshire Blvd Ste 230
Beverly Hills, CA 90211-2436, USA

Tilker, Ewald (Athlete)
2767 40th Ave
San Francisco, CA 94116-2707, USA

Till, Brian (Race Car Driver)
13701 S Lake Dr
Plainfield, IL 60544-8113, USA

Till, Lucas (Actor)
c/o Jim Osborne *Agency for the Performing Arts (APA)*
405 S Beverly Dr Ste 500
Beverly Hills, CA 90212-4425, USA

Tilleman, Mike (Athlete, Football Player)
180 County Road 800 NW
Havre, MT 59501-5714, USA

Tiller, Chris (Athlete, Baseball Player)
604 Morningside
Bullard, TX 75757-5181, USA

Tiller, Joe (Coach, Football Coach)
Purdue University
Athletic Dept
W Lafayette, IN 47907, USA

Tiller, Nadja (Actor)
Via Tamporiva 26
Castagnola 06976, SWITZERLAND

Tilley, Patrick L (Pat) (Athlete, Coach, Football Coach, Football Player)
PO Box 4523
Shreveport, LA 71134-0523, USA

Tilley, Tom (Athlete, Hockey Player)
14724 Maple St
Overland Park, KS 66223-1216

Tillis, Pam (Musician, Songwriter)
c/o Brian Edwards *Enter Talking Client Relations*
645 W 9th St Ste 110
Los Angeles, CA 90015-1662, USA

Tillison, Ed (Athlete, Football Player)
38504 James Crosby Rd
Pearl River, LA 70452-3431, USA

Tillman, Andre (Athlete, Football Player)
PO Box 743204
Dallas, TX 75374-3204, USA

Tillman, Charles (Athlete, Football Player)
Charles Tillman Cornerstone Foundation
4 E Ogden Ave # 801
Westmont, IL 60559-3506, USA

Tillman, Kerry Rusty (Athlete, Baseball Player)
35119th St
Atlantic Beach, FL 32233-4540, USA

Tillman, Lewis (Athlete, Football Player)
PO Box 166
Madison, MS 39130-0166, USA

Tillman, Robert L (Business Person)
Lowe's Companies
1605 Curtis Bridge Rd
Wilkesboro, NC 28697-2263, USA

Tillman, Rusty (Athlete, Baseball Player)
8711 Newton Rd Apt 61
Jacksonville, FL 32216-4661, USA

Tillman Jr, George (Director, Producer, Writer)
State Street Pictures
10201 W Pico Blvd Bldg 52
Los Angeles, CA 90064-2606, USA

Tillotson, Johnny (Musician)
American Mgmt
19948 Mayall St
Chatsworth, CA 91311-3522, USA

Tilly, Jennifer (Actor)
c/o Whitney Tancred *42West*
1840 Century Park E Ste 700
Los Angeles, CA 90067-2122, USA

Tilly, Meg (Actor)
c/o Rich Caplan *Noble Caplan Abrams*
1260 Yonge St 2nd Fl
Toronto, ON M4T 1W5, CANADA

Tilly, Theresa (Actor)
c/o Michael Mogan *Mogan Entertainment*
1801 Century Park E Fl 24
Los Angeles, CA 90067-2302, USA

Tilson, Joseph (Joe) (Artist)
2 Brook Street Mansions
41 Davies St
London W1Y 1FJ, UNITED KINGDOM (UK)

Tilton, Charlene (Actor)
c/o Staff Member *Bohemia Group*
1680 Vine St Ste 518
Los Angeles, CA 90028-8833, USA

Tilton, Charline (Actor)
c/o Staff Member *Bohemia Group*
1680 Vine St Ste 518
Los Angeles, CA 90028-8833, USA

Tilton, Glenn F (Business Person)
UAL Corp
1200 E Algonquin Rd
Arlington Heights, IL 60005-4712, USA

Tilton, Robert (Misc)
Robert Tilton Ministries
PO Box 22066
Tulsa, OK 74121-2066, USA

Timberlake, Gary (Athlete, Baseball Player)
14016 Waters Edge Dr
Louisville, KY 40245-5250, USA

Timberlake, George (Athlete, Football Player)
13880 Canoe Brook Dr Apt 4D
Seal Beach, CA 90740-3856, USA

Timberlake, Justin (Actor, Musician)
c/o Rick Yorn *LBI Entertainment*
2000 Avenue of the Stars
N Tower Fl 3
Los Angeles, CA 90067-4700, USA

Timberlake, Robert W (Bob) (Athlete, Football Player)
2219 E Jarvis St
Milwaukee, WI 53211-2149, USA

Timchal, Cindy (Coach)
University of Maryland
Athletic Dept
College Park, MD 20742-0001, USA

Times, Ken (Athlete, Football Player)
2603 Sanford Ave
Sanford, FL 32773-5249, USA

Timken, William R Jr (Business Person)
Timken Co
1835 Dueber Ave SW
Canton, OH 44706-2798, USA

Timlin, Addison (Actor)
c/o Lindsay Porter *Gersh*
41 Madison Ave Ste 3301
New York, NY 10010-2210, USA

Timlin, Mike (Athlete, Baseball Player)
355 High Ridge Way
Castle Pines, CO 80108-3422, USA

Timmerman, Adam (Athlete, Football Player)
1635 585th St
Cherokee, IA 51012-7295, USA

Timmermann, Tom (Athlete, Baseball Player)
197 Coyote Ct
Pinckney, MI 48169-8022, USA

Timmermann, Ulf (Athlete, Track Athlete)
Conrad Blenkle Str 34
Berlin 01055, GERMANY

Timmins, Call (Actor)
The Agency
1800 Avenue of the Stars Ste 400
Los Angeles, CA 90067-4206, USA

Timmons, Jeff (Musician)
DAS Communications
83 Riverside Dr
New York, NY 10024-5713, USA

Timmons, Lawrence (Athlete, Football Player)
c/o Drew Rosenhaus *Rosenhaus Sports Representation*
3921 Alton Rd # 440
Miami Beach, FL 33140-3852, USA

Timmons, Margo (Musician)
Macklam Feldman Mgmt
200-1505 2nd Ave W
Vancouver, BC V6H 3Y4, CANADA

Timmons, Michael (Musician, Songwriter, Writer)
Macklam Feldman Mgmt
200-1505 2nd Ave W
Vancouver, BC V6H 3Y4, CANADA

Timmons, Ozzie (Athlete, Baseball Player)
4901 S 83rd St
Tampa, FL 33619-7101, USA

Timmons, Peter (Musician)
Macklam Feldman Mgmt
200-1505 2nd Ave W
Vancouver, BC V6H 3Y4, CANADA

Timmons, Tim (Athlete, Baseball Player)
5055 Johnstown Rd
New Albany, OH 43054-9578, USA

Timmons, Tim (Athlete, Baseball Player)
PO Box 574
New Albany, OH 43054-0574, USA

Timofeev, Valeri (Artist)
464 Blue Mountain Lake
East Stroudsburg, PA 18301, USA

Timonen, Kimmo (Athlete, Hockey Player)
125 Upland Way
Haddonfield, NJ 08033-3603, USA

Timpner, Clay (Athlete, Baseball Player)
3847 Shaftburv Pl
Oviedo, FL 32765-9311, USA

Timpson, Michael D (Athlete, Football Player)
PO Box 93234
Lakeland, FL 33804-3234, USA

Tinashe (Musician)
c/o Derek Sherron *The Chamber Group*
75 Broad St Rm 708
New York, NY 10004-3244, USA

Tindle, David (Astronaut)
Redfern Gallery
20 Cork St
London W1, UNITED KINGDOM (UK)

Ting, Rich (Actor)
c/o Nicole Miller *NMA PR*
7916 Melrose Ave Ste 1
Los Angeles, CA 90046-7160, USA

Tingelhoff, Mick (Athlete, Football Player)
20517 Kalmeadow Ct
Lakeville, MN 55044-6705, USA

Tingle, Scott D Cmdr (Astronaut)
2106 Bayou Cove Ln
League City, TX 77573-3248, USA

Tinglehoff, H Michael (Mick) (Athlete, Football Player)
19288 Judicial Rd
Prior Lake, MN 55372, USA

Tingley, Freya (Actor)
c/o Samira Higham *Independent Talent Group*
40 Whitfield St
London W1T 2RH, UNITED KINGDOM

Tingley, Leeann (Beauty Pageant Winner)
Miss Rhode Island Pageant
PO Box 3509
Cranston, RI 02910-0509, USA

Tingley, Ron (Athlete, Baseball Player)
349 Omni Dr
Sparks, NV 89441-7295, USA

Ting Tings, The (Music Group)

Tinker, Grant (Business Person)
531 Barnaby Rd
Los Angeles, CA 90077-3213, USA

Tinoco, Diego (Actor)
c/o Peter Kluge *Impact Artist Group LLC (LA)*
244 N California St
Fl 1
Burbank, CA 91505-3505, USA

Tinordi, Mark (Athlete, Hockey Player)
545 Devonshire Ct
Severna Park, MD 21146-1001, Canada

Tinsley, George (Athlete, Basketball Player)
The Tinsley Group
PO Box 469
Winter Haven, FL 33882-0469, USA

Tinsley, Jamaal (Basketball Player)
Indiana Pacers
125 S Pennsylvania St
Conseco Fieldhouse
Indianapolis, IN 46204-3610, USA

Tinsley, Lee (Athlete, Baseball Player)
237 Tenor St
Shelbyville, KY 40065-9255, USA

Tinsley, Scott (Athlete, Football Player)
26852 Sommerset Ln
Lake Forest, CA 92630-5800, USA

Tippet, Andre B (Athlete, Football Player)
17 Knob Hill St
Sharon, MA 02067-3119, USA

Tippett, Dave (Athlete, Hockey Player)
Phoenix Coyotes
6751 N Sunset Blvd Ste 200
Glendale, AZ 85305-3162

Tippett, Dave (Athlete, Coach, Hockey Player)
19468 N lOlst St
Scottsdale, AZ 85255-3779

Tippin, Aaron (Musician, Songwriter)
Tip Top Entertainment
PO Box 41689
Nashville, TN 37204-1689, USA

Tippins, Ken (Athlete, Football Player)
RR 2 Box 173
Adel, GA 31620, USA

Tipton, Analeigh (Actor)
c/o Sarah Yorke *Baker Winokur Ryder Public Relations*
200 5th Ave Fl 5
New York, NY 10010-3307, USA

Tipton, Daniel (Religious Leader)
Churches of Christ in Christian Union
PO Box 30
Circleville, OH 43113-0030, USA

Tipton, Dave L (Athlete, Football Player)
915 Bonneville Way
Sunnyvale, CA 94087-3038, USA

Tiriac, Ion (Coach, Tennis Player)
Blvd. D'Italie 44
Monte Carlo, MONACO

Tirico, Mike (Sportscaster)
ABC-TV
77 W 66th St
Sports Dept
New York, NY 10023-6201, USA

Tirimo, Martino (Musician)
1 Romeyn Road
London SW16 2NU, UNITED KINGDOM (UK)

Tisch, James S (Business Person)
Loews Corp
667 Madison Ave Fl 7
New York, NY 10065-8087, USA

Tisch, Steve (Writer)
1162 Tower Rd
Beverly Hills, CA 90210-2131, USA

Tischinski, Tom (Athlete, Baseball Player)
9905 N Donnelly Ave
Kansas City, MO 64157-7861, USA

Tischiski, Tom (Athlete, Baseball Player)
9905 N Donnelly Ave
Kansas City, MO 64157-7861, USA

Tisdale, Ashley (Actor)
c/o Staff Member *Blondie Girl Productions*
2500 Broadway Ste 125
Santa Monica, CA 90404-3080, USA

Tisdale, Jennifer (Actor)
c/o Staff Member *Gersh*
9465 Wilshire Blvd Ste 600
Beverly Hills, CA 90212-2605, USA

Tishby, Noa (Actor)
c/o Ben Dey *Creative Artists Agency (CAA)*
2000 Avenue of the Stars Ste 100
Los Angeles, CA 90067-4705, USA

Titanic, Morris (Athlete, Hockey Player)
120 Cambrook Row
Buffalo, NY 14221-5228

Titchmarsh, Alan (Television Host)
c/o Staff Member *Arlington Enterprises Ltd*
1-3 Charlotte St
London W1P 1HD, UNITED KINGDOM (UK)

Titensor, Glen (Athlete, Football Player)
729 Montrose Ct
Flower Mound, TX 75022-8000, USA

Tito, Dennis (Astronaut)
1800 Alta Mura Rd
Pacific Palisades, CA 90272-2700, USA

Tito, Teburoro (President)
President's Office
Tarawa, KIRIBATI

Titone, Jackie (Actor)
c/o Staff Member *WME/IMG*
9601 Wilshire Blvd
Beverly Hills, CA 90210-5213, USA

Titov, German (Athlete, Hockey Player)
246 Slopeview Dr SW
Calgary, AB T3H 4G5, Canada

Titov, Yuri E (Gymnast)
Kolokolnikov Per 6
#19
Moscow 103045, RUSSUA

Titus, Christopher (Comedian, Television Host)
c/o Jeff Abraham *Jonas Public Relations*
1327 Ocean Ave Ste F
Santa Monica, CA 90401-1024, USA

Titus-Carmel, Gerard (Artist)
La Grand Maison
Oulchy Le Chateau 02210, FRANCE

Tixby, Dexter (Musician)
David Harris Enterprises
24210 E East Fork Rd Spc 9
Azusa, CA 91702-6249, USA

Tiziani, Mario (Athlete, Golfer)
c/o Jim Lehrman *Medalist Management Inc*
36855 W Main St Ste 200
Purcellville, VA 20132-3561, USA

Tizon, Albert (Journalist)
Seattle Times
1120 John St
Editorial Dept
Seattle, WA 98109-5321, USA

Tizzio, Thomas R Sr (Business Person)
American Int'l Group
175 Water St
New York, NY 10038-4918, USA

Tkachuk, Keith (Athlete, Hockey Player, Olympic Athlete)
Pro-Athletes Management
2 Center Plz Ste 420
Boston, MA 02108-1909, USA

Tkaczuk, Daniel (Athlete, Hockey Player)
iHockey Trainer 172 Dunlop St W Unit A
Barrie, ON L4N 1B3, Canada

Tkaczuk, Ivan (Religious Leader)
Ukrainian Orthodox Church
3 Davenport Ave Apt 2A
New Rochelle, NY 10805-3438, USA

Tkaczuk, Walter R (Walt) (Athlete, Hockey Player)
River Valley Golf and Country Club RR 3
Lakeside, ON N0M 2G0, Canada

T. King, Peter (Congressman, Politician)
339 Cannon Hob
Washington, DC 20515-3003, USA

TLC (Music Group)
c/o Staff Member *Creative Artists Agency (CAA)*
2000 Avenue of the Stars Ste 100
Los Angeles, CA 90067-4705, USA

T. McCaul, Michael (Congressman, Politician)
131 Cannon Hob
Washington, DC 20515-2501, USA

TNA Wrestling (Wrestler)
c/o Staff Member *Paradigm (Monterey)*
404 W Franklin St
Monterey, CA 93940-2303, USA

To, Tony (Director, Producer)
c/o Staff Member *Walt Disney Co, The (Buena Vista Motion Picture Group)*
500 S Buena Vista St
Burbank, CA 91521-0007

Toale, Will (Actor)

Toback, James (Director)
11 E 87th St
New York, NY 10128-0527, USA

Tobeck, Robbie (Athlete, Football Player)
2018 Newport Way NW
Issaquah, WA 98027-5392, USA

Tober, Ronnie (Business Person)
C/O Jan Jochems
Tober Jochems VOF
Stadskade 258
Apeldoorn 7311 XV, NETHERLANDS

Tobey, James (Actor)
Paradigm Agency
10100 Santa Monica Blvd Ste 2500
Los Angeles, CA 90067-4116, USA

Tobias, Andrew (Business Person, Writer)
787 NE 71st St
Miami, FL 33138-5717, USA

Tobias, Oliver (Actor)
Gavin Barker Assoc
2D Wimpole St
London W1G 0EB, UNITED KINGDOM (UK)

Tobias, Randall L (Business Person)
Eli Lilly Co
Lilly Corporate Center
Indianapolis, IN 46285-0001, USA

Tobias, Robert M (Misc)
National Treasury Employees Union
901 E St NW
Washington, DC 20004-2037, USA

Tobias, Stephen C (Business Person)
Norfolk Southern Corp
3 Commercial Pl Ste 1A
Norfolk, VA 23510-2108, USA

Tobik, Dave (Athlete, Baseball Player)
11087 Gravois Rd Apt 101
Saint Louis, MO 63126-3642, USA

Tobin, Becca (Actor)
c/o Ricky Rollins *Hyphenate Creative Management*
8149 Santa Monica Blvd # 111
West Hollywood, CA 90046-4912, USA

Tobin, Don (Cartoonist)
12312 Ranchwood Rd
Santa Ana, CA 92705-3349, USA

Tobin, Matt (Athlete, Football Player)
c/o Joe Linta *JL Sports*
1204 Main St Ste 179
Branford, CT 06405-3787, USA

Tobin, Vince (Athlete, Coach, Football Coach, Football Player)
15997 W Monterey Way
Goodyear, AZ 85395-8054, USA

Tobolowsky, Stephen (Actor, Director)
c/o Steven Levy *Framework Entertainment*
9057 Nemo St # C
W Hollywood, CA 90069-5511, USA

Toboni, Jacqueline (Actor)
c/o Anne Woodward *Authentic Talent & Literary Management*
3615 Eastham Dr # 650
Culver City, CA 90232-2410, USA

Toburen, Nelson (Athlete, Football Player)
1007 Village Dr
Pittsburg, KS 66762-3552, USA

Tobymac (Musician)
c/o Staff Member *True Artist Management*
227 3rd Ave N
Franklin, TN 37064-2504, USa

Toca, Jorge (Athlete, Baseball Player)
7940 NW 167th Ter
Miami Lakes, FL 33016-3424, USA

Tocchet, Rick (Athlete, Hockey Player)
6835 E Camelback Rd Unit 1108
Scottsdale, AZ 85251-3162, USA

Tocker, Julian (Julz) (Dancer)
DanceSport Ireland, LTD
17 Bailis Manor
Navan, Co Mea
Athlumney, Ireland

Todd, Anne E (Actor)
2419 Oregon St
Berkeley, CA 94705-1113, USA

Todd, Chuck (Actor)
c/o Staff Member *NBC News (NY)*
30 Rockefeller Plz
New York, NY 10112-0015, USA

Todd, Eric (Actor)
c/o Vikram Dhawer *Authentic Talent and Literary Management (NY)*
20 Jay St Ste M17
Brooklyn, NY 11201-8300, USA

Todd, Hallie (Actor)
Ann Morgan Guilbert
550 Erskine Dr
Pacific Palisades, CA 90272-4247, USA

Todd, Jackson (Athlete, Baseball Player)
8958 E 76th St
Tulsa, OK 74133-4406, USA

Todd, James R (Jim) (Athlete, Baseball Player)
21639 Hill Gail Way
Parker, CO 80138-7249, USA

Todd, Josh (Musician)
The Firm
9100 Wilshire Blvd Ste 100W
Beverly Hills, CA 90212-3435, USA

Todd, Kate (Actor)
c/o Robert Lanni *Coalition Entertainment Management*
10271 Yonge St Suite 302
Richmond Hill, ON L4C 3B5, Canada

Todd, Kendra (Business Person, Reality Star)
C/O Eric Hanson
423 W 55th St Fl 2
New York, NY 10019-4460, USA

Todd, Kevin (Athlete, Hockey Player)
15 Narla Ln
Utica, NY 13501-5560

Todd, Mark (Horse Racer)
PO Box 507
Cambridge, NEW ZEALAND

Todd, Rachel (Actor)
6310 San Vicente Blvd Ste 520
Los Angeles, CA 90048-5421, USA

Todd, Richard (Football Player)
New York Jets
PO Box 471
Sheffield, AL 35660-0471, USA

Todd, Tony (Actor)
c/o Jeff Goldberg *Jeff Goldberg Management*
817 Monte Leon Dr
Beverly Hills, CA 90210-2629, USA

Todd, Trisha (Actor)
c/o Staff Member *Henry Downey Talent Management*
4045 Vineland Ave PH 538
Studio City, CA 91604-4481, USA

Todd, Virgil H (Religious Leader)
Memphis Theological
168 E Parkway S
Memphis, TN 38104-4340, USA

Todman, Jordan (Athlete, Football Player)
c/o David Dunn *Athletes First*
23091 Mill Creek Dr
Laguna Hills, CA 92653-1258, USA

Todorov, Stanko (Prime Minister)
Narodno Sobranie
Sofia, BULGARIA

Todorovsky, Piotr Y (Director)
Vernadskogo Prospect 70A
#23
Moscow 117454, RUSSIA

Todosey, Jordan (Actor)
c/o Amanda Rosenthal *Amanda Rosenthal Talent Agency*
315 Harbord St
Toronto, ON M6G 1G9, CANADA

Toerzs, Gregor (Actor)
c/o Richard Schwartz *Richard Schwartz Management*
2934 1/2 N Beverly Glen Cir # 107
Los Angeles, CA 90077-1724, USA

Toews, Jeffrey M (Jeff) (Athlete, Football Player)
11924 Silver Oak Dr
Davie, FL 33330-1911, USA

Toews, Jonathan (Athlete, Hockey Player)
c/o Pat Brisson *Creative Artists Agency (CAA)*
2000 Avenue of the Stars Ste 100
Los Angeles, CA 90067-4705, USA

Toews, Loren (Athlete, Football Player)
165 Hawthorne Ave
Los Altos, CA 94022-3704, USA

Tofani, Loretta A (Journalist)
Philadelphia Inquirer
400 N Broad St
Editorial Dept
Philadelphia, PA 19130-4015, USA

Tognini, Michel Brig Gen (Astronaut)
15 ter rue des Tourelles
L'Hay-les-Roses F-94240, France

Tognoni, Gina (Actor)
c/o Marnie Sparer *Power Entertainment Group*
1505 10th St
Santa Monica, CA 90401-2805, USA

Togo, Jonathan (Actor)
c/o Cynthia Shelton-Droke *Sweet Mud Group*
648 Broadway # 1002
New York, NY 10012-2348, USA

Togunde, Victor (Actor)
c/o Staff Member *GVA Talent Agency Inc*
193 N Robertson Blvd
Beverly Hills, CA 90211-2103, USA

Tohn, Jackie (Actor, Comedian)
c/o Joslyn Sifuentes *Shelter PR*
5670 Wilshire Blvd Ste 1200
Los Angeles, CA 90036-5621, USA

Toilolo, Levine (Athlete, Football Player)
c/o Frank Bauer *Sun West Sports*
7883 N Pershing Ave
Stockton, CA 95207-1749, USA

Tointon, Kara (Actor)
c/o Hayley Stubbs *Public Eye Communications*
535 Kings Rd
#313 Plaza
London SW10 0SZ, UNITED KINGDOM

Tokes, Laszlo (Politician, Religious Leader)
Calvin Str 1
Oradea 03700, ROMANIA

Tokio Hotel (Music Group, Musician)
c/o Staff Member *Universal Music Deutschland*
Stralauer Allee 1
Berlin 10245, Germany

Toksvig, Sandi (Actor, Producer)
c/o David Lazenby *The Richard Stone Partnership*
3 De Walden Ct
85 New Cavendish Street
London W1W 6XD, UNITED KINGDOM

Tolan, Bob (Athlete, Baseball Player)
2213 Signal Hill Dr
Pearland, TX 77584-1672, USA

Tolan, Peter (Actor, Director, Producer, Writer)

Tolar, Kevin (Athlete, Baseball Player)
3738 Greentree Cir
Panama City, FL 32405-6624, USA

Tolbert, Berlinda (Actor)
c/o Staff Member *Pallas Management*
4536 Greenbush Ave
Sherman Oaks, CA 91423-3112, US

Tolbert, Jim (Athlete, Football Player)
1811 Lemonadeberry Ln
Vista, CA 92084-7415, USA

Tolbert, Mike (Athlete, Football Player)

Tolbert, Ray (Athlete, Basketball Player)
11860 Gatwick View Dr
Fishers, IN 46037-4167, USA

Tolbert, Tom (Athlete, Basketball Player)
368 Creedon Cir
Alameda, CA 94502-7793, USA

Tolbert, Tony L (Athlete, Football Player)
704 Venice Ave
Southlake, TX 76092-8240, USA

Toldeo, Esteban (Golfer)
135 Spring Vly
Irvine, CA 92602-0919, USA

Toledo, Alejandro (President)
Palacio de Gobierno S/N
Plaza de Armas S/N
Lima 00001, PERU

Tolentino, Jose (Athlete, Baseball Player)
26711 Caceres Cir
Mission Viejo, CA 92691-5503, USA

Toler, Greg (Athlete, Football Player)
c/o Hadley Engelhard *Enter-Sports Management*
6000 Lake Forrest Dr Ste 370
Atlanta, GA 30328-5902, USA

Toler, Ken (Athlete, Football Player)
2064 Brecon Dr
Jackson, MS 39211-5838, USA

Toles, Alvin (Athlete, Football Player)
106 Todd Creek Pl
Forsyth, GA 31029, USA

Toles, Ted (Athlete, Baseball Player)
822 Braceville Robinson Rd SW
Newton Falls, OH 44444-9529, USA

Tolins, Jonathan (Writer)
c/o Cori Wellins *WME|IMG*
9601 Wilshire Blvd
Beverly Hills, CA 90210-5213, USA

Toliver, Freddie (Athlete, Baseball Player)
25401 Geddy Dr
Land O Lakes, FL 34639-5670, USA

Toliver, Jerry (Mad Man) (Race Car Driver)
7402 Mountjoy Dr Ste A
Huntington Beach, CA 92648-1238, USA

Tolkan, James (Actor)
Paradigm Agency
10100 Santa Monica Blvd Ste 2500
Los Angeles, CA 90067-4116, USA

Tollberg, Brian (Athlete, Baseball Player)
2104 39th St W
Bradenton, FL 34205-1334, USA

Tolle, Eckhart (Writer)
Eckhart Teachings
PO Box 93661 RPO Nelson Park
Vancouver, BC V6E 4L7, CANADA

Tollefsen, Ole-Kristian (Athlete, Hockey Player)
250 Daniel Burnham Sq Unit 702
Columbus, OH 43215-2697, USA

Tollerod, Siri (Model)
c/o Staff Member *Modelwerk Modelagentur GmbH*
Rothenbaum Chaussee 1
Hamburg 20148, Germany

Tolles, Tommy (Golfer)
c/o Staff Member *Pro Golfers Association (PGA)*
112 TPC Blvd
Ponte Vedra Beach, FL 32082, USA

Tolleson, Steve (Athlete, Baseball Player)
313 Mossycup Oak Ct
Spartanburg, SC 29306-6627, USA

Tolleson, Wayne (Athlete, Baseball Player)
313 Mossycup Oak Ct
Spartanburg, SC 29306-6627, USA

Tollin, Michael (Director, Producer, Writer)
c/o Staff Member *Tollin/Robbins Management*
4130 Cahuenga Blvd Ste 305
Toluca Lake, CA 91602-2847, USA

Tolliver, Billy Joe (Athlete, Football Player)
9837 Neesonwood Dr
Shreveport, LA 71106-7738, USA

Tolman, Allison (Actor)
c/o Naomi Odenkirk *Odenkirk Provissiero Entertainment*
1936 N Bronson Ave
Raleigh Studios
Los Angeles, CA 90068-5602, USA

Tolman, Tim (Athlete, Baseball Player)
11425 N Ingot Loop
Tucson, AZ 85737-9450, USA

Tolsky, Susan (Actor)
10815 Acama St
North Hollywood, CA 91602-3204, USA

Tolson, Byron (Athlete, Basketball Player)
4012 N Orchard St
Tacoma, WA 98407-4215, USA

Tolzien, Scott (Athlete, Football Player)
c/o Joe Panos *Athletes First*
23091 Mill Creek Dr
Laguna Hills, CA 92653-1258, USA

Tom, Braatz (Athlete, Football Player)
3131 NE 55th Ct
Fort Lauderdale, FL 33308-3428, USA

Tom, Dimmick (Athlete, Football Player)
204 Broadmoor Blvd
Lafayette, LA 70503-5114, USA

Tom, Duniven (Athlete, Football Player)
503 Seis Lagos Trl
Wylie, TX 75098-8228, USA

Tom, Heather (Actor)
c/o Staff Member *Michael Einfeld Management*
10630 Moorpark St Unit 101
Toluca Lake, CA 91602-2797, USA

Tom, Kiana (Actor, Fitness Expert)
KT Productions
555 N El Camino Real Ste A401
San Clemente, CA 92672-6740, USA

Tom, Lauren (Actor)
c/o Kelly Garner *Pop Art Management*
PO Box 55363
Sherman Oaks, CA 91413-0363, USA

Tom, Logan (Athlete, Olympic Athlete, Volleyball Player)
2001 E 21st St Unit 136
Signal Hill, CA 90755-5960, USA

Tom, Nicholle (Actor)
c/o Michael Einfeld *Michael Einfeld Management*
10630 Moorpark St Unit 101
Toluca Lake, CA 91602-2797, USA

Toma, David (Writer)
PO Box 854
Clark, NJ 07066-0854, USA

Tomaini, Amadeo (Athlete, Football Player)
3750 Oakhill Dr
Titusville, FL 32780-3521, USA

Tomaino, Jamie (The Jet) (Race Car Driver)
Impact Motorsports
6610 Hudspeth
Harrisburg, NC 28075, USA

Tomalty, Glenn (Athlete, Hockey Player)
GE Capital Rail Services
2100-530 8 Ave SW
Attn Senior Account Manager
Calgary, AB T2P 3S8, CANADA

Tomanek, Dick (Athlete, Baseball Player)
165 Duff Dr
Avon Lake, OH 44012-1234, USA

Tomas, Hildi Santo (Actor, Television Host)
741 Parkside Trl NW
Marietta, GA 30064-4714, USA

Tomasetti, Louis (Athlete, Football Player)
100 Powell St
Old Forge, PA 18518-1728, USA

Tomasik, Kathleen (Director)
c/o David Krintzman *Morris Yorn Barnes Levine Krintzman Rubenstein Kohner & Gellman*
2000 Avenue of the Stars Ste 300N
Tower N Fl 3
Los Angeles, CA 90067-4704, USA

Tomba, Alberto (Skier)
Castel dei Britti
Bologna 40100, ITALY

Tomberlin, Andy (Athlete, Baseball Player)
7411 Crooked Creek Church Rd
Monroe, NC 28110-8283, USA

Tomberlin, Pat (Athlete, Football Player)
891 Arthur Moore Dr
Green Cove Springs, FL 32043-9510, USA

Tombs, Tina (Golfer)
1916 E Medlock Dr
Phoenix, AZ 85016-4127, USA

Tomczak, Mike (Athlete, Football Player)
400 Broad St # 106
Sewickley, PA 15143-1500, USA

Tomei, Concetta (Actor)
765 Linda Flora Dr
Los Angeles, CA 90049-1626, USA

Tomei, Marisa (Actor)
1416 Havenhurst Dr Apt 2B
West Hollywood, CA 90046-3885, USA

Tomel, Marisa (Actor)
Three Arts Entertainment
9460 Wilshire Blvd Ste 700
Beverly Hills, CA 90212-2713, USA

Tomey, Dick (Coach, Football Coach)
San Francisco 49ers
4949 Marie P Debartolo Way
Santa Clara, CA 95054-1156, USA

Tomfohrde, Heinn F (Business Person)
GAF Corp
1361 Alps Rd
Wayne, NJ 07470-3687, USA

Tomich, Jared (Athlete, Football Player)
2525 W 800 N
Rensselaer, IN 47978-7559, USA

Tomita, Tamlyn (Actor)
c/o Nancy Moon-Broadstreet *Sovereign Talent Group*
1642 Westwood Blvd Ste 202
Los Angeles, CA 90024-5609, USA

Tomjanovich, Rudolph (Rudy) (Athlete, Basketball Player, Coach)
8555 Fair Oaks Xing Apt 558
Dallas, TX 75243-8089, USA

Tom Jr, Layne (Actor)
3838 Humboldt Dr
Huntington Beach, CA 92649-2156, USA

Tomkins, Calvin (Writer)
c/o Staff Member *Henry Holt & Company*
175 5th Ave Ste 400
New York, NY 10010-7726, USA

Tomko, Brett (Athlete, Baseball Player)
14008 Lake Poway Rd
Poway, CA 92064-1421, USA

Tomko, Jozef Cardinal (Religious Leader)
Villa Betania
Via Urbano VIII-16
Rome 00165, ITALY

Tomlak, Mike (Athlete, Hockey Player)
2200 Bordeaux Cres
Thunder Bay, ON P7K 1C2, Canada

Tomlin, Chris (Musician)
c/o Bryan Myers *Creative Artists Agency (CAA)*
401 Commerce St PH
Nashville, TN 37219-2516, USA

Tomlin, Dave (Athlete, Baseball Player)
2020 Clayton Pike
Manchester, OH 45144-9429, USA

Tomlin, Lily (Actor, Comedian)
c/o Jennifer Allen *Viewpoint Inc*
8820 Wilshire Blvd Ste 220
Beverly Hills, CA 90211-2622, USA

Tomlin, Mike (Athlete, Football Coach, Football Player)
1224 Shady Ave
Pittsburgh, PA 15232-2812, USA

Tomlin, Randy (Athlete, Baseball Player)
153 Ridgeview Ln
Madison Heights, VA 24572-6037, USA

Tomlinson, Charles (Writer)
Bristol University
English Dept
Bristol BS8 1TH, UNITED KINGDOM (UK)

Tomlinson, Dave (Athlete, Hockey Player)
Vancouver Canucks
800 Griffiths Way
Vancouver, BC V6B 6G1, Canada

Tomlinson, LaDainian (Athlete, Football Player)
c/o Tom Condon *Creative Artists Agency (CAA)*
401 Commerce St PH
Nashville, TN 37219-2516, USA

Tomlinson, Laken (Athlete, Football Player)
c/o Andrew Kessler *Athletes First*
23091 Mill Creek Dr
Laguna Hills, CA 92653-1258, USA

Tomlinson, Louis (Musician)
c/o Richard Griffiths *Modest! Management*
91A Peterborough Rd
London SW6 3BU, UNITED KINGDOM

Tomlinson, Taylor (Comedian)
c/o Judi Brown *Levity Entertainment Group (LEG)*
6701 Center Dr W Ste 300
Los Angeles, CA 90045-2482, USA

Tommy Tutone (Music Group)
c/o Craig Marquardo *Fathom Artist Management*
Prefers to be contacted by phone or email.
Portland, OR NA, USA

Tompkins, Allie (Baseball Player)
Pittsburgh Crawfords
931 1/2 Clarissa St
Pittsburgh, PA 15219-5770, USA

Tompkins, Angel (Actor)
Hurkos
11935 Kling St Apt 10
Valley Village, CA 91607-5406, USA

Tompkins, Barry (Sportscaster)
PO Box 8
Ross, CA 94957-0008, USA

Tompkins, Dariene (Actor)
15413 Hall Rd # 230
Macomb, MI 48044-3840, USA

Tompkins, Paul F (Writer)
3018 Gracia St
Los Angeles, CA 90039-2306, USA

Tompkins, Ron (Athlete, Baseball Player)
25072 Leucadia St Unit G
Laguna Niguel, CA 92677-7598, USA

Tompkins, Susie (Designer, Fashion Designer)
2500 Steiner St PH
San Francisco, CA 94115-1100, USA

Toms, David (Golfer)
6606 Gilbert Dr
Shreveport, LA 71106-2300, USA

Toms, Tommy (Athlete, Baseball Player)
126 Leadbetter Rd
Wayne, ME 04284-3144, USA

Tomsco, George (Musician)
Fireballs Entertainment
1224 Cottonwood St
Raton, NM 87740-3513, USA

Tomsic, Dubravka (Musician)
Trawick Artists
1926 Broadway
New York, NY 10023-6915, USA

Tomsic, Ronald (Athlete, Basketball Player, Olympic Athlete)
22 Twilight Blf
Newport Coast, CA 92657-2126, USA

Toneff, Robert (Bob) (Athlete, Football Player)
18 Dutch Valley Ln
San Anselmo, CA 94960-1016, USA

Tonelli, John (Athlete, Hockey Player)
4 Vincent Ln
Armonk, NY 10504-1245

Tone Loc (Musician)
c/o Bobby Bessone *Entertainment Artists*
2409 21st Ave S Ste 100
Nashville, TN 37212-5317, USA

Toner, Mike (Journalist)
Atlanta Journal-Constitution
72 Marietta St NW
Editorial Dept
Atlanta, GA 30303-2804, USA

Toner Jr, Ed (Athlete, Football Player)
12 Preston Ct
Swampscott, MA 01907-1650, USA

Toney, Andrew (Athlete, Basketball Player)
1044 Villa Rica Ct Apt A
Birmingham, AL 35215-6854, USA

Toney, Sedric (Athlete, Basketball Player)
3831 Sweetwater Dr
Brecksville, OH 44141-4102, USA

Tong, Jian (Figure Skater)
c/o Staff Member *Champions on Ice*
3500 American Blvd W Ste 190
Minneapolis, MN 55431-4431, USA

Tong, Pete (DJ, Musician)
c/o Joel Zimmerman *WME|IMG (NY)*
11 Madison Ave Fl 18
New York, NY 10010-3669, USA

Tong, Stanley (Director)
c/o Ramses Ishak *United Talent Agency (UTA)*
9336 Civic Center Dr
Beverly Hills, CA 90210-3604, USA

Tongue, Marco (Athlete, Football Player)
8051 Winding Wood Rd
Glen Burnie, MD 21061-5020, USA

Tonic (Music Group)
Tonic Tonic
2850 Ocean Park Blvd Ste 300
Santa Monica, CA 90405-6216

Tonini, Ersilio Cardinal (Religious Leader)
Via Santa Teresa 8
Ravenna 48100, ITALY

Tonioli, Bruno (Actor)
c/o Duncan Heath *Independent Talent Group*
40 Whitfield St
London W1T 2RH, UNITED KINGDOM

Tonis, Mike (Athlete, Baseball Player)
9231 Bella Vista Pl
Elk Grove, CA 95624-2152, USA

Tonkin, Phoebe (Actor)
c/o Matt Andrews *Marquee Management*
188 Oxford St Studio B
The Gatehouse
Paddington NSW 02021, AUSTRALIA

Tonko, Paul (Congressman, Politician)
422 Cannon Hob
Washington, DC 20515-3303, USA

Tonkovich, Andy (Athlete, Basketball Player)
2400 Forest Dr Apt 210
Inverness, FL 34453-3705, USA

Too, Slim (Musician)
New Frontier Mgmt
1921 Broadway
Nashville, TN 37203-2719, USA

Tookey, Tim (Athlete, Hockey Player)
21008 W Ridge Rd
Buckeye, AZ 85396-1590

Tool (Music Group)
Tool Dissectional
2311 W Empire Ave
Burbank, CA 91504-3318, USA

Toolson, Andy (Athlete, Basketball Player)
7904 NE 173rd Ave
Vancouver, WA 98682-1581, USA

Toomay, John (Athlete, Basketball Player)
7103 Primrose Way
Carlsbad, CA 92011-4834, USA

Toomay, Pat (Athlete, Football Player)
5603 Guadalupe Trl NW
Albuquerque, NM 87107-5423, USA

Toomer, Amani (Athlete, Football Player)
25 Regency Pl
Weehawken, NJ 07086-6600, USA

Toomer, Korey (Athlete, Football Player)

Toomey, Bill (Athlete, Decathlon Athlete, Olympic Athlete)
240 Pelton Ln
Incline Village, NV 89451-9304, USA

Toomey, Pat (Senator)
US Senate
Russell Office Bldg
Washington, DC 20510-0001, USA

Toomey, Sean (Athlete, Hockey Player)
1741 Saunders Ave
Saint Paul, MN 55116-2432

Toomey, Toomey (Cartoonist, Writer)
Andrews & McMeel
4520 Main St Ste 340
Kansas City, MO 64111-7705, USA

Toon, Al (Athlete, Football Player)
4915 Champions Run
Middleton, WI 53562-4078, USA

Toon, Nick (Athlete, Football Player)
c/o Jeff Sperbeck *The Novo Agency*
1537 Via Romero Ste 100
Alamo, CA 94507-1527, USA

Tootoo, Jardin (Athlete, Hockey Player)
2600 Hillsboro Pike Apt 359
Nashville, TN 37212-5666

Tootoosis, Gordon (Actor)
c/o Staff Member *Artist Representation Company, The*
1147 Big Island Rd S RR 1
Demorestville, ON K0K 1W0, CANADA

Toots & The Maytals (Music Group)
c/o Staff Member *WME|IMG (NY)*
11 Madison Ave Fl 18
New York, NY 10010-3669, USA

Top, Carrot (Actor, Comedian)
11 Isle of Sicily
Winter Park, FL 32789-1505, USA

Toploader (Music Group)
c/o Staff Member *Helter Skelter (UK)*
535 Kings Rd
The Plaza
London SW10 0SZ, UNITED KINGDOM (UK)

Topol, Chaim (Actor)
22 Vale Court Maidville
London W9 1RT, UNITED KINGDOM (UK)

Topor, Ted (Athlete, Football Player)
3525 Drivers Way
Chesterton, IN 46304-8849, USA

Toporowski, Shayne (Athlete, Hockey Player)
65 Roman Dr
Shrewsbury, MA 01545-5819

Topp, Robert (Athlete, Football Player)
10351 Douglas Ave
Plainwell, MI 49080-9664, USA

Topp, Shayne (Comedian, Internet Star)
c/o Ellen Marano *Marano Entertainment*
21650 Oxnard St Ste 350
Woodland Hills, CA 91367-7855, USA

Topper, John (Musician)
Monterey Peninsula Artists
509 Hartnell St
Monterey, CA 93940-2825, USA

Toppin, Rupe (Athlete, Baseball Player)
PO Box 25724
Miami, FL 33102-5724, USA

Topping, Marshall (Race Car Driver)
2950 Randolph Ave
Costa Mesa, CA 92626-4382, USA

Toradze, Alexander (Musician)
Columbia Artists Mgmt Inc
165 W 57th St
New York, NY 10019-2201, USA

Torborg, Jeff (Athlete, Baseball Player, Coach)
4757 S Atlantic Ave Unit 401
Port Orange, FL 32127-8130, USA

Torcato, Tony (Athlete, Baseball Player)
9934 SE Talbert St
Clackamas, OR 97015-9638, USA

Torchett, John (Athlete, Hockey Player)
14 Crows Nest Ln
Marshfield, MA 02050-3161

Torchetti, John (Athlete, Hockey Player)
Houston Aeros
5300 Memorial Dr
Houston, TX 77007-8200

Torczon, Laverne J (Athlete, Football Player)
6472 Country Club Dr
Columbus, NE 68601-8338, USA

Toregas, Wyatt (Athlete, Baseball Player)
420 Wyandotte Trl SW
Hartville, OH 44632-9419, USA

Torgeson, Lavern (Athlete, Football Player)
17672 Gainsford Ln
Huntington Beach, CA 92649-4723, USA

Torkelson, Eric (Athlete, Football Player)
1196 Pleasant Valley Dr
Oneida, WI 54155-8634, USA

Torme, Daisy (Actor)
c/o Steven Neibert *Imperium 7 Talent Agency*
5455 Wilshire Blvd Ste 1706
Los Angeles, CA 90036-4217, USA

Torme, Steve March (Actor, Musician)
c/o Mark Lourie *Skyline Music*
28 Union St
Whitefield, NH 03598-3503, USA

Tormohlen, Gene (Athlete, Basketball Player)
2248 Walker Dr
Lawrenceville, GA 30043-2472, USA

Torn, Rip (Actor)
c/o Alan Somers *Pure Arts Entertainment/ Rose Group*
9925 Jefferson Blvd
Culver City, CA 90232-3505, USA

Tornatore, Giuseppe (Director)
c/o Staff Member *Marco Patrizi*
Viale Giuseppe Mazzini, 11
Roma 00195, Italy

Torrance, Sam (Golfer)
Carnegie Sports
The Glassmill
Battersea Bridge Rd
London SW11 3BZ, UNITED KINGDOM (UK)

Torre, Joe (Athlete, Baseball Player, Coach)
c/o Maury Gostfrand *Vision Sports Group*
675 Thrd Ave
Suite 2500
New York, NY 10017, USA

Torre, Jose Maria (Actor)
c/o Staff Member *Televisa*
Blvd Adolfo Lopez Mateos 232
Colonia San Angel INN
DF CP 01060, MEXICO

Torre, Steve (Horse Racer)
240 Court Pl Apt B
Brick, NJ 08723, USA

Torrealba, Yorvit (Athlete, Baseball Player)
3801 S Ocean Dr Apt 15F
Hollywood, FL 33019-2901, USA

Torrence, Gwendolyn (Gwen) (Athlete, Track Athlete)
Gold Medal Mgmt
1750 14th St
Boulder, CO 80302-6332, USA

Torrens, David (Actor)
c/o Gabriel Blanco *Gabriel Blanco Iglesias (Mexico)*
Rio Balsas 35-32
Colonia Cuauhtemoc
DF 06500, Mexico

Torres, Dara (Athlete, Olympic Athlete, Swimmer)
c/o Staff Member *Premier Management Group (PMG Sports)*
700 Evanvale Ct
Cary, NC 27518-2806, USA

Torres, Dayanara (Actor, Model)
c/o Sheila Legette *Media Artists Group*
8222 Melrose Ave Ste 304
Los Angeles, CA 90046-6839, USA

Torres, Diego (Actor)
c/o Jon Simmons *Simmons & Scott Entertainment*
7942 Mulholland Dr
Los Angeles, CA 90046-1225, USA

Torres, Eve (Athlete, Wrestler)
c/o Ray Moheet *Mainstay Entertainment*
9250 Beverly Blvd Fl 3
Beverly Hills, CA 90210-3710, USA

Torres, Felix (Athlete, Baseball Player)
HC 1 Box 6424
Santa Isabel, PR 00757-9777, USA

Torres, Fernando (Athlete, Soccer Player)
c/o Staff Member *Chelsea Football Club*
Stamford Bridge
Fulham Road
London SW6 1HS, UNITED KINGDOM

Torres, Gina (Actor)
c/o Alyx Carr *42West*
600 3rd Ave Fl 23
New York, NY 10016-1914, USA

Torres, Harold (Musician)
Brothers Mgmt
141 Dunbar Ave
Fords, NJ 08863-1551, USA

Torres, Hector (Athlete, Baseball Player)
662 Lexington St
Dunedin, FL 34698-8405, USA

Torres, Jacques (Chef, Television Host)
c/o Staff Member *The Food Network.com*
1180 Avenue of the Americas Fl 14
New York, NY 10036-8401, USA

Torres, Jose (Boxer)
364B Greenwich St
#B
New York, NY 10013, USA

Torres, Oscar (Athlete, Basketball Player)
c/o Michael (Mike) Esola *WME|IMG*
9601 Wilshire Blvd
Beverly Hills, CA 90210-5213, USA

Torres, Raffi (Athlete, Hockey Player)
59 Eakin Mill Rd
Markham, ON L6E 1N9, Canada

Torres, Rusty (Athlete, Baseball Player)
51 Thorman Ave Unit 3
Hicksville, NY 11801-1352, USA

Torres, Salomon (Athlete, Baseball Player)
101 Crimson Dr
Pittsburgh, PA 15237-1069, USA

Torres, Tia Maria (Reality Star)
Villalobos Rescue Center
PO Box 1544
Canyon Country, CA 91386-1544, USA

Torres, Tico (Musician)
c/o Rob Light *Creative Artists Agency (CAA)*
2000 Avenue of the Stars Ste 100
Los Angeles, CA 90067-4705, USA

Torres, Tommy (Musician)
c/o Staff Member *Sony Music (Miami)*
404 Washington Ave Ste 700
Miami Beach, FL 33139-6615, USA

Torretta, Gino (Athlete, Football Player, Heisman Trophy Winner)
7322 SW 54th Ct
Miami, FL 33143-5702, USA

Torrey, Rich (Cartoonist)
c/o Staff Member *King Features Syndication*
300 W 57th St Fl 15
New York, NY 10019-5238, USA

Torrez, Mike (Athlete, Baseball Player)
7921 Tasso Ct
Seminole, FL 33777-4456, USA

Torricelli, Robert (Politician)
PO Box 229
Rosemont, NJ 08556-0229, USA

Torriero, Talan (Actor)
c/o Scott Karp *The Syndicate*
10203 Santa Monica Blvd Fl 5
Los Angeles, CA 90067-6416, USA

Torrijos, Martin (President)
Palaclo Presidencial
Valija 50
Panama City 00001, PANAMA

Torrini, Emiliana (Musician)
c/o Staff Member *Paradigm (Monterey)*
404 W Franklin St
Monterey, CA 93940-2303, USA

Torry, Guy (Actor, Comedian)
c/o Janean Glover *Screen Partners*
9663 Santa Monica Blvd # 639
Beverly Hills, CA 90210-4303, USA

Torry, Joe (Comedian)
c/o Staff Member *WME|IMG*
9601 Wilshire Blvd
Beverly Hills, CA 90210-5213, USA

Torteller, Yan Pascal (Musician)
MA de Valmalete
Building Gaceau
11 Ave Delcasse
Paris 75635, FRANCE

Torti, Robert (Actor)
388 Rushing Creek Ct
Henderson, NV 89014-4518, USA

Tortorella, John (Athlete, Coach, Hockey Player)
108 3rd Ave
St Pete Beach, FL 33706-4306, USA

Tortorella, Nico (Actor)
c/o Bianca Bianconi *42West*
600 3rd Ave Fl 23
New York, NY 10016-1914, USA

Torv, Anna (Actor)
c/o Christine Tripicchio *Shelter PR*
5670 Wilshire Blvd Ste 1200
Los Angeles, CA 90036-5621, USA

Torvaids, Linus (Designer)
Transmeta Corp
3990 Freedom Cir
Santa Clara, CA 95054-1204, USA

Torve, Kelvin (Athlete, Baseball Player)
902 Fulton St
Rapid City, SD 57701-3553, USA

Torvill, Jayne (Dancer)
Sue Young
PO Box 32
Heathfield, East Sussex TN21 0BW, UNITED KINGDOM (UK)

Tosca, Carlos (Athlete, Baseball Player, Coach)
PO Box 3623
Brandon, FL 33509-3623, USA

Toscano, Andrew (Horse Racer)
PO Box 34
Verbank, NY 12585-0034, USA

Toscano, Harry (Golfer)
3209 Mercer Rd
New Castle, PA 16105-5311, USA

Toscano, Linda (Horse Racer)
49 Euretta Ave
Freehold, NJ 07728-2631, USA

Toscano, Pia (Musician)
c/o Mark DiDia *Red Light Management*
5800 Bristol Pkwy Ste 400
Culver City, CA 90230-6898, USA

Tosh, Daniel (Actor, Comedian)
c/o Christie Smith *Rise Management*
6338 Wilshire Blvd
Los Angeles, CA 90048-5002, USA

Toski, Bob (Golfer)
20914 Hamaca Ct
Boca Raton, FL 33433-2716, USA

Totah, Josie (Actor)
c/o Brett Ruttenberg *Imprint PR*
6121 W Sunset Blvd
Neuehouse
Los Angeles, CA 90028-6442, USA

Totenberg, Nina (Correspondent)
National Public Radio
News Dept
615 Main Ave NW
Washington, DC 20024, USA

Toth, Tom (Athlete, Football Player)
13723 Lindsay Dr
Orland Park, IL 60462-7011, USA

Toth, Zollie (Athlete, Football Player)
1612 Hideaway Ct
Baton Rouge, LA 70806-7674, USA

Totmianina, Tatyana (Figure Skater)
c/o Staff Member *Champions on Ice*
3500 American Blvd W Ste 190
Minneapolis, MN 55431-4431, USA

Totten, Robert (Director)
PO Box 7180
Big Bear Lake, CA 92315-7180, USA

Totter, Audrey (Actor)
Motion Picture Country Home
23388 Mulholland Dr
Woodland Hills, CA 91364-2792, USA

Toub, Shaun (Actor)
c/o Dean Panaro *Abrams Artists Agency*
750 N San Vicente Blvd
E Tower Fl 11
Los Angeles, CA 90069-5788, USA

Toubia, Emeraude (Actor)
c/o Andres Budnik *Vision Entertainment*
119 Hurricane St
Marina Del Rey, CA 90292-5974, USA

Toure, Yaya (Athlete, Soccer Player)
c/o Staff Member *Manchester City FC*
City of Manchester Stadium
SportCity
Manchester M11 3FF, UK

Toure, Younoussi (Prime Minister)
Union Economique/Monetaire
01 BP 543
Quagadougou 01, Burkina Faso, MALI

Toussaint, Allen (Composer, Musician)
272 Abalon Ct
New Orleans, LA 70114-1374, USA

Toussaint, Beth (Actor)
c/o Staff Member *Buchwald*
5900 Wilshire Blvd Ste 3100
Los Angeles, CA 90036-5030, USA

Toussaint, Lorraine (Actor, Producer)
c/o Jonathan Howard *Innovative Artists*
1505 10th St
Santa Monica, CA 90401-2805, USA

Tovah, Mageina (Actor)
c/o Staff Member *Lemonlime*
3245 Casitas Ave Ste 107
Los Angeles, CA 90039-2269, USA

Tovar, Steve (Athlete, Football Player)
1026 Brower Rd
Lima, OH 45801-2316, USA

Tovey, Russell (Actor)
c/o Clair Dobbs *CLD Communications*
4 Broadway Ct
The Broadway
London SW191RG, UNITED KINGDOM

Towe, Monte (Athlete, Basketball Player, Coach)
3616 Dade St
Raleigh, NC 27612-4606, USA

Tower, Joan P (Composer)
Bard College
Music Dept
Annandale-On-Hudson, NY 12504, USA

Tower, Keith (Athlete, Basketball Player)
12530 Aldershot Ln
Windermere, FL 34786-6610, USA

Tower of Power (Music Group, Musician)
c/o Staff Member *CT Creative Talent GmbH*
Koepenicker Strasse 48/49
New York, NY 10179-0001, GERMANY

Towers, Constance (Actor)
c/o Staff Member *Artists & Representatives (Stone Manners Salners)*
6100 Wilshire Blvd Ste 1500
Los Angeles, CA 90048-5110, USA

Towers, Josh (Athlete, Baseball Player)
1033 Crescent Falls St
Henderson, NV 89011-2506, USA

Towers, Kevin (Baseball Player)
5580 La Jolla Blvd
La Jolla, CA 92037-7651, USA

Towery, Blackie (Athlete, Basketball Player)
314 W Carlisle St
Marion, KY 42064-1506, USA

Towle, Stephen R (Steve) (Athlete, Football Player)
609 NE Lake Pointe Dr
Lees Summit, MO 64064-1193, USA

Towles, J R (Athlete, Baseball Player)
27502 Decker Prairie Rosehl Rd
Magnolia, TX 77355-7904, USA

Towles, Tom (Actor)
c/o Craig Dorfman *Frontline Management*
5670 Wilshire Blvd Ste 1370
Los Angeles, CA 90036-5649, USA

Towne, Katharine (Actor)
c/o Mitch Clem *Mitch Clem Management*
7080 Hollywood Blvd Ste 1100
Hollywood, CA 90028-6938, USA

Towne, Robert (Writer)
c/o Carri McClure *McClure and Associates Public Relations*
10153 1/2 Riverside Dr # 686
Toluca Lake, CA 91602-2561, USA

Towner, Ralph N (Musician)
Ted Kurtland
173 Brighton Ave
Boston, MA 02134-2003, USA

Townes, Linton (Athlete, Basketball Player)
PO Box 254
Luray, VA 22835-0254, USA

Townes, Willie (Athlete, Football Player)
5714 Logancraft Dr
Dallas, TX 75227-2847, USA

Towns, Bobby (Athlete, Football Player)
1351 Jennings Mill Rd
Unit A
Bogart, GA 30622, USA

Towns, Edolphus (Congressman, Politician)
2232 Rayburn Hob
Washington, DC 20515-3210, USA

Towns, Karl-Anthony (Athlete, Basketball Player)
c/o Leon Rose *CAA Basketball*
405 Lexington Ave Fl 19
New York, NY 10174-1800, USA

Towns, Morris (Athlete, Football Player)
7102 Rustling Oaks Dr
Richmond, TX 77469-7338, USA

Townsell, Jo Jo (Athlete, Football Player)
1857 Borda Way
Gardnerville, NV 89410-6679, USA

Townsend, Andre (Athlete, Football Player)
6206 Providence Club Dr
Mableton, GA 30126-3697, USA

Townsend, Colleen (Actor)
645 E Champlain Dr Apt 150
Fresno, CA 93730-1295, USA

Townsend, Raymond (Athlete, Basketball Player)
5160 Caibari Knls
San Jose, CA 995135-132, USA

Townsend, Robert (Actor, Director, Producer, Writer)
c/o Jeff Witjas *Agency for the Performing Arts (APA)*
405 S Beverly Dr Ste 500
Beverly Hills, CA 90212-4425, USA

Townsend, Roscoe (Religious Leader)
Evangelical Friends
2018 W Maple St
Wichita, KS 67213-3314, USA

Townsend, Stuart (Actor)
c/o Vanessa Pereira *Artists Independent Management (LA)*
1522 2nd St
Santa Monica, CA 90401-2303, USA

Townsend, Tammy (Actor)
c/o Marni Goldman *Abrams Artists Agency*
750 N San Vicente Blvd
E Tower Fl 11
Los Angeles, CA 90069-5788, USA

Townsend, Wade (Athlete, Baseball Player)
Columbus Catfish
PO Box 2744
Columbus, GA 31902-2744, USA

Townshend, Graeme (Athlete, Hockey Player)
169 Bradley St
Saco, ME 04072-3101, USA

Townshend, Pete (Musician, Songwriter)
4 Friars Ln
Richmond, Surrey TW9 1NL, UNITED KINGDOM

Toya (Musician)

Toyoda, Akio (Business Person)
Toyota
1 Toyota-Cho
Toyota City
Aichi 471-8571, Japan

Tozzi, Tahyna (Actor)
c/o Flise Konialian *Untitled Entertainment (NY)*
215 Park Ave S Fl 8
New York, NY 10003-1622, USA

T Pain (Musician)
c/o Staff Member *Jive Records*
550 Madison Ave Frnt 1
New York, NY 10022-3211, USA

T-Pain (Musician)
c/o Michael Blumstein *Chase Entertainment*
7378 W Atlantic Blvd Ste 250
Margate, FL 33063-4214, USA

Traa (Musician)
East West America Records
75 Rockefeller Plz
New York, NY 10019-6908, USA

Traber, Billy (Athlete, Baseball Player)
836 Lomita St
El Segundo, CA 90245-2541, USA

Traber, Jim (Athlete, Baseball Player)
16232 Josiah Pl
Edmond, OK 73013-9774, USA

Trabert, Tony (Actor)
115 Knotty Pine Trl
Ponte Vedra, FL 32082-3024

Tracewski, Dick (Athlete, Baseball Player, Coach)
5 Flora Dr
Peckville, PA 18452-1004, USA

Trachsel, Stephen P (Steve) (Athlete, Baseball Player)
18750 Heritage Dr
Poway, CA 92064-6643, USA

Trachta, Jeff (Actor)
PO Box 124
Skyforest, CA 92385-0124, USA

Trachte, Don (Cartoonist)
c/o Staff Member *King Features Syndication*
300 W 57th St Fl 15
New York, NY 10019-5238, USA

Trachtenberg, Dan (Director)
c/o Benjamin Rowe *Oasis Media Group*
9100 Wilshire Blvd Ste 210W
Beverly Hills, CA 90212-3555, USA

Trachtenberg, Michelle (Actor)
c/o Peg Donegan *Framework Entertainment*
9057 Nemo St # C
W Hollywood, CA 90069-5511, USA

Tracy, Adrian (Athlete, Football Player)

Tracy, Andy (Athlete, Baseball Player)
2226 Park Cir
Lewis Center, OH 43035-6052, USA

Tracy, Brian (Business Person, Writer)
Brian Tracy International
462 Stevens Ave Ste 305
Solana Beach, CA 92075-2066, USA

Tracy, Chad (Athlete, Baseball Player)
9422 Sir Huon Ln
Waxhaw, NC 28173-0112, USA

Tracy, James E (Jim) (Athlete, Baseball Player, Coach)
9191 E Harvard Ave
Denver, CO 80231-3843, USA

Tracy, Jeanie (Musician)
c/o Staff Member *Diva Central Inc*
7510 W Sunset Blvd # 1445
Los Angeles, CA 90046-3408, USA

Tracy, Keegan Connor (Actor)
c/o Deb Dillistone *Red Management*
415 Esplanade W Box 3
North Vancouver, BC V7M 1A6, CANADA

Tracy, Michael C (Dancer, Director)
Pilobolus Dance Theater
PO Box 388
Washington Depot, CT 06794-0388, USA

Tracy, Paul (Race Car Driver)
Hogan Penske Racing
9700 Highridge Dr
Las Vegas, NV 89134-6723, USA

Trader, Larry (Athlete, Hockey Player)
105 Sufian St
Pembroke, ON K8A 6W6, Canada

Trafficant, James (Politician)
125 Market St
Youngstown, OH 44503-1780

Trafton, Stephanie Brown (Athlete, Track Athlete)
c/o Staff Member *USA Track & Field*
130 E Washington St Ste 800
Indianapolis, IN 46204-4619, USA

Trailer Park Boys (Music Group)
c/o Louis Thomas *Sonic Entertainment Group*
1674 Hollis St
Halifax, NS B3J 1V7, CANADA

Traill, Phil (Director)
c/o Rosalie Swedlin *Anonymous Content*
3532 Hayden Ave
Culver City, CA 90232-2413, USA

Train (Music Group)
c/o Jon Lullo *Crush Music Management*
60-62 E 11th St
Fl 7
New York, NY 10003, USA

Trainor, Jerry (Actor)
c/o Joannie Burstein *Burstein Company*
15304 W Sunset Blvd Ste 208
Pacific Palisades, CA 90272-3656, USA

Trainor, Meghan (Musician)
10500 Camarillo St
Toluca Lake, CA 91602-1528, USA

Trammell, Alan (Athlete, Baseball Player, Coach)
5852 Box Canyon Rd
La Jolla, CA 92037-7405, USA

Trammell, Sam (Actor)
c/o Jillian Roscoe *ID Public Relations*
7060 Hollywood Blvd Fl 8th
Los Angeles, CA 90028-6021, USA

Trammell, Thomas (Bubba) (Athlete, Baseball Player)
4672 NW 114th Ave Apt 310
Doral, FL 33178-4825, USA

Tran, Duc Luong (President)
President's Office
Hoang Hoa Tham St
St Hanoi, VIETNAM

Tran, Karrueche (Actor, Model)
c/o Jacob York *Electric Republic*
2870 Peachtree Rd NW # 976
Atlanta, GA 30305-2918, USA

Tran, Kelly Marie (Actor)
c/o Charlie Jennings *Creative Artists Agency (CAA)*
2000 Avenue of the Stars Ste 100
Los Angeles, CA 90067-4705, USA

Tranelli, Deborah (Actor, Musician)
c/o Staff Member *Image Entertainment*
20525 Nordhoff St Ste 200
Chatsworth, CA 91311-6104, USA

Traore, Rokia (Actor, Composer)
c/o Staff Member *Concerted Efforts*
PO Box 440326
Somerville, MA 02144-0004, USA

Trapp, John (Athlete, Basketball Player)
1836 Remembrance Hill St
Las Vegas, NV 89144-5420, USA

Trask, Stephen (Composer)
c/o Brice Gaeta *Broder Webb Chervin Silbermann Agency, The (BWCS)*
10250 Constellation Blvd
Los Angeles, CA 90067-6200, USA

Trask, Thomas E (Religious Leader)
Assemblies of God
1445 N Boonville Ave
Springfield, MO 65802-1894, USA

Traue, Antje (Actor)
c/o Staff Member *Anthem Entertainment*
9595 Wilshire Blvd Ste 900
Beverly Hills, CA 90212-2509, USA

Trauth, AJ (Actor)
c/o Felicia Sager *Sager Management*
260 S Beverly Dr Ste 205
Beverly Hills, CA 90212-3812, USA

Trautmann, Richard (Athlete)
Horemansstr 29
Munich 80636, GERMANY

Trautwein, John (Athlete, Baseball Player)
16225 On Par Blvd
Fort Myers, FL 33908-2832, USA

Trautwig, Al (Sportscaster)
ABC-TV
77 W 66th St
Sports Dept
New York, NY 10023-6201, USA

Travanti, Daniel J (Actor)
1077 Melody Rd
Lake Forest, IL 60045-1547, USA

Travers, Bill (Athlete, Baseball Player)
10 Shoreline Dr
Foxboro, MA 02035-1115, USA

Travers, Pat (Musician)
ARM
1257 Arcade St
Saint Paul, MN 55106-2022, USA

Travis (Music Group)
c/o Staff Member *MCT Management*
520 8th Ave Rm 2205
New York, NY 10018-4160, USA

Travis, Kylie (Actor, Model)
1196 Summit Dr
Beverly Hills, CA 90210-2248, USA

Travis, Mack (Athlete, Football Player)
605 Holland Ave
Las Vegas, NV 89106-2651, USA

Travis, Nancy (Actor, Producer)
c/o Teri Weigel *The Creative Group PR*
324 S Beverly Dr # 216
Beverly Hills, CA 90212-4801, USA

Travis, Randy (Musician, Songwriter)
c/o Zach Farnum *117 Management*
PO Box 22359
Nashville, TN 37202-2359, USA

Travis, Stacey (Actor)
c/o Donald Spradlin *Essential Talent Management*
7958 Beverly Blvd
Los Angeles, CA 90048-4511, USA

Travolta, Ellen (Actor)
6470 E Sunnyside Rd
Coeur D Alene, ID 83814-9503, USA

Travolta, Joey (Actor)
c/o Staff Member *Stephany Hurkos Management*
5014 Whitsett Ave Unit 2
Valley Village, CA 91607-3078, USA

Travolta, John (Actor)
PO Box 410
N Hollywood, CA 91603-0410, USA

Trayham, Jerry (Athlete, Football Player)
6606 S Tomaker Ln
Spokane, WA 99223-6202, USA

Traylor, B Keith (Athlete, Football Player)
1000 Football Dr
Lake Forest, IL 60045, USA

Traylor, Keith (Athlete, Football Player)
11043 S 4317
Chouteau, OK 74337-6063, USA

Traylor, Susan (Actor)
Propaganda Films Mgmt
1741 Ivar Ave
Los Angeles, CA 90028-5105, USA

Traynham, Wade (Athlete, Football Player)
PO Box 176
Wake, VA 23176-0176, USA

Traynor, Jay (Musician)
Jet Music
17 Pauline Ct
Rensselaer, NY 12144-9780, USA

Traynowicz, Mark (Athlete, Football Player)
8000 Alimark Ln
Lincoln, NE 68516-4095, USA

Treach (Musician)
International Creative Mgmt
8942 Wilshire Blvd # 219
Beverly Hills, CA 90211-1908, USA

Treacy, Philip (Designer, Fashion Designer)
Philip Treacy Ltd
69 Elizabeth St
London SW1W 9PJ, UNITED KINGDOM (UK)

Treadaway, John (Athlete, Football Player)
3140 N 83rd Ave
Phoenix, AZ 85033-4724, USA

Treadway, Edward A (Politician)
Elevator Constructors Union
5565 Sterrett Pl
Columbia, MD 21044-2665, USA

Treadway, Jeff (Athlete, Baseball Player)
8812 Estes Rd
Macon, GA 31220-5649, USA

Treadway, Nick (Athlete, Baseball Player)
1442 Bishop Dr
Troy, MO 63379-3336, USA

Treadway, Ty (Actor, Television Host)
c/o Ken Lindner *Ken Lindner & Associates*
1901 Avenue Of The Stars Ste 1010
Los Angeles, CA 90067-6012, USA

Treadwell, David (Athlete, Football Player)
5445 Dtc Pkey
Suite 800
Greenwood Village, CO 80111, USA

Treadwell, Laquon (Athlete, Football Player)
c/o Tory Dandy *Independent Sports & Entertainment (ISE-IN)*
6435 W Jefferson Blvd # 197
Fort Wayne, IN 46804-6203, USA

Treanor, Matt (Athlete, Baseball Player)
1440 Coral Ridge Dr
Coral Springs, FL 33071-5433, USA

Treat, Dr Casey (Religious Leader)
Christian Faith Center
33645 20th Ave S
Federal Way, WA 98003-7743, USA

Trebek, Alex (Game Show Host)
Jeopardy!
10202 Washington Blvd
Culver City, CA 90232-3119, USA

Trebelhorn, Thomas L (Tom) (Athlete, Baseball Player, Coach)
7753 E Montebello Ave
Scottsdale, AZ 85250-6165, USA

Trebi, Dan (Athlete, Hockey Player)
8551 Big Woods Ln
Eden Prairie, MN 55347-5361

Trebunskaya, Anna (Dancer, Reality Star)
c/o Harold Augenstein *Kazarian, Measures, Ruskin & Associates*
5200 Lankershim Blvd Ste 820
N Hollywood, CA 91601-3194, USA

Trejo, Danny (Actor)
15226 Lassen St
Mission Hills, CA 91345-3042, USA

Tremblay, Brent (Athlete, Hockey Player)
671 Ski Club Rd
North Bay, ON P1B 7R5, Canada

Tremblay, Mario (Athlete, Coach, Hockey Player)
RDS - Le Reseau des Sports
1755 Boul Rene Levesque-Est
Clifton, NJ Q7012-1867, CANADA

Tremblay, Michel (Writer)
5E-294 Rue du Square-Saint-Louis
Montreal, QC H2X 1A4, CANADA

Tremblay, Yannick (Athlete, Hockey Player)
9911 Carrington Ln
Alpharetta, GA 30022-8527

Trembley, Dave (Athlete, Baseball Player, Coach)
Baltimore Orioles
3145 S Atlantic Ave Apt 601
Daytona Beach Shores, FL 32118-6273, USA

Tremie, Chris (Athlete, Baseball Player)
484 Marion Ln
New Waverly, TX 77358-4504, USA

Tremlett, David R (Artist)
Broadlawns
Chipperfield Road
Bovingdon, Herts, UNITED KINGDOM (UK)

Tremont, Ray C (Religious Leader)
Volunteers of America
3939 N Causeway Blvd Ste 400
Metairie, LA 70002-1777, USA

Trenary, Jill (Athlete, Figure Skater, Olympic Athlete)
4115 Stone Manor Hts
Colorado Springs, CO 80906-5799, USA

Trendy, Bobby (Designer)
Bobby Trendy & Associates
369 S Doheny Dr
Beverly Hills, CA 90211-3508, USA

Trent, Buck (Musician)
Buck Trent Breakfast Theater
106 Hampshire Dr
Branson, MO 65616-3765, USA

Trent, Gary (Athlete, Basketball Player)
1150 Northwood Cir
New Albany, OH 43054-9056, USA

Trenyce (Reality Star)
c/o Staff Member *Diva Central Inc*
7510 W Sunset Blvd # 1445
Los Angeles, CA 90046-3408, USA

Trese, Adam (Actor)
c/o Staff Member *Robert Stein Management*
PO Box 3797
Beverly Hills, CA 90212-0797, USA

Tressel, Jim (Coach, Football Coach)
Ohio State University
Athletic Dept
Columbus, OH 43210, USA

Trestman, Marc (Football Player)
Minnesota Vikings
PO Box 888
Phoenix, AZ 85001-0888, USA

Tresvant, John (Athlete, Basketball Player)
14814 61st Dr SE
Snohomish, WA 98296-4221, USA

Tretiak, Vladislav (Athlete, Hockey Player)
1925 Birch Rd
Northbrook, IL 60062-5911

Tretlak, Vladislav (Athlete, Coach, Hockey Player)
94 Festival Dr
Toronto, ON M2R 3V1, Canada

Tretter, J.C. (Athlete, Football Player)

Treu, Adam (Athlete, Football Player)
556 Creedon Cir
Alameda, CA 94502-7794, USA

Treuel, Ralph (Athlete, Baseball Player)
15 Middleton Rd
Wolfeboro, NH 03894-4421, USA

Trevathan, Danny (Athlete, Football Player)
c/o Bus Cook *Bus Cook Sports, Inc*
1 Willow Bend Dr
Hattiesburg, MS 39402-8552, USA

Trevena-Brown, James (Actor)
c/o Gail Cowan *Gail Cowan Management*
7a Scanlan St
Grey Lynn
Auckland 01021, NEW ZEALAND

Trevi, Gloria (Musician)
Leisil Entertainment
Avenida Parque 67 Napoles
Mexico City, DF 03810, MEXICO

Trevino, Alex (Athlete, Baseball Player)
PO Box 288
Houston, TX 77001-0288, USA

Trevino, Lee (Athlete, Golfer)
4906 Park Ln
Dallas, TX 75220-2031, USA

Trevino, Michael (Actor)
c/o Lena Roklin *Luber Roklin Management*
5815 W Sunset Blvd Ste 208
Los Angeles, CA 90028-6481, USA

Trevino, Rick (Musician)
William Morris Agency
2100 W End Ave Ste 1000
Nashville, TN 37203-5240, USA

Trevor, Linden (Athlete, Hockey Player)
1362 23 St SE
Medicine Hat, AB T1A 2C9, Canada

Trevor, William (Writer)
P F D
Drury House
34-43 Russell St
London WC2B 5HA, UNITED KINGDOM (UK)

Triandos, C Gus (Athlete, Baseball Player)
PO Box 26385
San Jose, CA 95159-6385, USA

Trias, Jasmine (Musician)
c/o Stephen Ford *Diva Central Inc*
7510 W Sunset Blvd # 1445
Los Angeles, CA 90046-3408, USA

Tribbett, Tye (Musician)
c/o Jeff Epstein *M.A.G./Universal Attractions*
15 W 36th St Fl 8
New York, NY 10018-7927, USA

Tribe Called Quest, A (Music Group)
c/o Carleen Donovan *Donovan Public Relations*
30 E 20th St Ste 2FE
New York, NY 10003-1310, USA

Trice, Obie (Musician)
BME Recordings
2144 Hills Ave NW Ste D2
Atlanta, GA 30318-2805, USA

Trick Daddy (Musician)
16573 SW 19th St
Miramar, FL 33027-4466, USA

Trickett, Libby (Athlete, Swimmer)
c/o Staff Member *International Quarterback*
12 Ross St
Brisbane
Newstead QLD 4006, Australia

Trickle, Dick (Race Car Driver)
Donlavey Racing
5415 Vesuvius Furnace Rd
Iron Station, NC 28080-7729, USA

Triffle, Carol (Director)
Imago Theater
17 SE 8th Ave
Portland, OR 97214-1239, USA

Trigg, Alex (Baseball Player)
Detroit Stars
900 Turner Ln
Shreveport, LA 71106-4528, USA

Trigger, Sarah (Actor)
Paradigm Agency
10100 Santa Monica Blvd Ste 2500
Los Angeles, CA 90067-4116, USA

Trillo, Manny (Athlete, Baseball Player)
Calle 724 Ave 3AM Ed. Everest #14
Maracaibo, Venezuela

Trimble, Solomon (Actor)
c/o Kaili Canfield *Arthouse Talent and Literary*
8195 SW Nimbus Ave
Beaverton, OR 97008-6414, USA

Trimble, Vivian (Musician)
Metropolitan Entertainment
2 Penn Plz # 2600
New York, NY 10121-0101, USA

Trimper, Tim (Athlete, Hockey Player)
1028 Broughton Lane
Newmarket, ON L3X 2L7, Canada

Trina (Musician)
c/o Staff Member *Pyramid Entertainment Group*
377 Rector Pl Apt 21A
New York, NY 10280-1439, USA

Trinh, Eugene (Astronaut)
NASA Headquarters
300 E St SW
Washington, DC 20546-0005, USA

Trinh, Eugene H Dr (Astronaut)
3549 Kelton Ave
Los Angeles, CA 90034-5505, USA

Trinidad, Felix (Tito) (Boxer)
RR 6 Box 11479
Rio Piedras, PR 00926, USA

Trinneer, Connor (Actor)
c/o Gregg A Klein *AKA Talent Agency*
325 N Larchmont Blvd
Los Angeles, CA 90004-3011, USA

Trintignant, Jean-Louis (Actor)
Artmedia
20 Ave Rapp
Paris 75007, FRANCE

Triplett, Bill (Athlete, Football Player)
222 Beachwood Dr
Youngstown, OH 44505-4282, USA

Triplett, Kirk (Athlete, Golfer)
6631 E Maverick Rd
Paradise Valley, AZ 85253-2634, USA

Tripp, Jordan (Athlete, Football Player)

Tripp, Valerie (Writer)
Pleasant Company Publications
PO Box 620991
Middleton, WI 53562-0991, USA

Trippi, Charles L (Charlie) (Athlete, Football Player)
125 Riverhill Ct
Athens, GA 30606-4034, USA

Tripplehorn, Jeanne (Actor)
c/o Cynthia Pett-Dante *Brillstein Entertainment Partners*
9150 Wilshire Blvd Ste 350
Beverly Hills, CA 90212-3453, USA

Tripplett, Larry (Athlete, Football Player)
5324 Overdale Dr
Los Angeles, CA 90043-2023, USA

Triptow, Dick (Athlete, Basketball Player)
325 Birkdale Rd
Lake Bluff, IL 60044-2334, USA

Tripucka, Kelly (Athlete, Basketball Player)
14 Devon Rd
Boonton, NJ 07005-9305, USA

Tritt, Travis (Actor, Musician)
c/o Duke Cooper *Quantum Management*
5340 Forest Acres Dr
Nashville, TN 37220-2123, USA

Trivium (Music Group)
c/o Josh Kline *UTA/The Agency Group*
888 7th Ave Fl 7
New York, NY 10106-0700, USA

Trlicek, Rick (Athlete, Baseball Player)
PO Box 1109
La Grange, TX 78945-1109, USA

Troche, Rose (Actor, Director, Producer, Writer)
c/o Staff Member *Gersh*
41 Madison Ave Ste 3301
New York, NY 10010-2210, USA

Troedson, Rich (Athlete, Baseball Player)
899 Bowen Ave
San Jose, CA 95123-5303, USA

Troegel, Butch (Athlete, Football Player)
230 Norcross St
Bossier City, LA 71111-6046, USA

Troger, Christian-Alexander (Swimmer)
I Muncher SC
Josefstr 26
Deisenhofen 82941, GERMANY

Trohman, Joe (Musician)
4058 Woking Way
Los Angeles, CA 90027-1324, USA

Troisgros, Pierre E R (Business Person)
Place Jean Troisgros
Roanne 42300, FRANCE

Troliope, Joanna (Writer)
P F D
Drury House
34-43 Russell St
London WC2B 5HA, UNITED KINGDOM (UK)

Trombley, Mike (Athlete, Baseball Player)
2 Hilltop Park
Wilbraham, MA 01095-1753, USA

Trondheim, Lewis (Artist)
c/o Staff Member *Fantagraphics Books*
7563 Lake City Way NE
Seattle, WA 98115-4218, USA

Trone, Roland (Don) (Musician)
Mars Talent
27 L Ambiance Ct
Bardonia, NY 10954-1421, USA

Tropper, Jonathan (Director, Producer)
c/o Taylor Johnson *ID Public Relations*
7060 Hollywood Blvd Fl 8th
Los Angeles, CA 90028-6021, USA

Trosch, Gene (Athlete, Football Player)
6393 Oak Tree Dr
Mc Calla, AL 35111-3926, USA

Trosky, Hal (Athlete, Baseball Player)
1414 Curtis Bridge Rd NE
Swisher, IA 52338-9588, USA

Trotter, Deedee (Athlete, Olympic Athlete, Track Athlete)
Test Me I'm Clean
PO Box 31654
Knoxville, TN 37930-1654, USA

Trotter, Tariq (Black Thought) (Musician)
c/o Staff Member *Coolhunter Management*
1 Presidential Blvd
Bala Cynwyd, PA 19004-1017, USA

Trottier, Bryan J (Athlete, Coach, Hockey Player)
133 Highcroft Cir
Eighty Four, PA 15330-1003, USA

Trottier, Rocky (Athlete, Hockey Player)
9562 International Dr
Indianapolis, IN 46268-3267

Trotz, Barry (Athlete, Hockey Player)
Nashville Predators
61 Transverse Rd
Garden City, NY 11530-1821

Trotz, Barry (Athlete, Hockey Player)
61 Transverse Rd
Garden City, NY 11530-1821

Trouble, Valli (Musician)
Q Prime
729 7th Ave Ste 1600
New York, NY 10019-6880, USA

Troupe, Tom (Actor)
8829 Ashcroft Ave
West Hollywood, CA 90048-2401, USA

Trousdale, Chris (Actor, Musician)
c/o Staff Member *Adonis Productions*
175 Skillman St
Brooklyn, NY 11205-3537, USA

Trout, David (Athlete, Football Player)
408 Paddock Ct
Sewell, NJ 08080-2509, USA

Trout, Mike (Athlete, Baseball Player)
257 Cherry Ln
Millville, NJ 08332-4129, USA

Trout, Steve (Athlete, Baseball Player)
PO Box 1155
Tinley Park, IL 60477-7955, USA

Troutman, Jonnie (Athlete, Football Player)
c/o Scott Smith *XAM Sports*
3509 Ice Age Dr
Madison, WI 53719-5409, USA

Trova, Ernest T (Artist)
6 Layton Ter
Saint Louis, MO 63124-1893, USA

Trower, Robin (Musician)
Stardust Enterprises
4600 Franklin Ave
Los Angeles, CA 90027-4202, USA

Troxel, Melanie (Race Car Driver)
PO Box 637
Brownsburg, IN 46112-0637, USA

Troy, Cowboy (Musician)
919 Sam Johnson Rd
Columbia, TN 38401-7754, USA

Troy, Drake (Athlete, Football Player)
20103 Desert Forest Dr
Ashburn, VA 20147-3179, USA

Troy, Mike (Athlete, Olympic Athlete, Swimmer)
21187 E Alyssa Rd
Queen Creek, AZ 85142-6558, USA

Troyer, Maynard (Race Car Driver)
4555 Lyell Rd
Rochester, NY 14606-4316, United States

Troyer, Verne (Actor)
c/o Ray Hughes *Ray Hughes Management*
12400 Ventura Blvd Ste 630
Studio City, CA 91604-2406, USA

Truax, Billy (Athlete, Football Player)
49 Lakeside Dr
Kearney, NE 68845-7618, USA

Truax, Dalton (Athlete, Football Player)
77 Chateau Magdelaine Dr
Kenner, LA 70065-2026, USA

Truax, Mike (Athlete, Football Player)
5925 Cleveland Pl
Metairie, LA 70003-1047, USA

Trubisky, Mitchell (Athlete, Football Player)
c/o Bruce Tollner *REP 1 Sports Group*
80 Technology Dr
Irvine, CA 92618-2301, USA

Truby, Chris (Athlete, Baseball Player)
12244 Silverado Dr
Fishers, IN 46037-8328, USA

Trucco, Michael (Actor)
McKeon-Myones
3500 W Olive Ave Ste 710
Burbank, CA 91505-4686, USA

Trudeau, Garry (Cartoonist)
14 Governors Is
Branford, CT 06405, USA

Trudeau, Jack F (Athlete, Football Player)
9150 Timberwolf Ln
Zionsville, IN 46077-8320, USA

Trudeau, Margaret (Writer)
c/o Staff Member *HarperCollins Publishers*
195 Broadway Fl 2
New York, NY 10007-3132, USA

TRUE, Rachel (Actor)
c/o Ben Levine *LINK Entertainment*
11872 La Grange Ave
Los Angeles, CA 90025-5282, USA

Truesdale, William (Misc)
Central Ave Veterinary Hospital
455 Central Ave
Seekonk, MA 02771-3943, USA

Truesdale, Yanic (Actor)
c/o Danielle Allman-Del *D2 Management*
10351 Santa Monica Blvd Ste 210
Los Angeles, CA 90025-6937, USA

Truex Jr, Martin (Race Car Driver)
c/o Staff Member *Michael Waltrip Racing*
PO Box 70
Sherrills Ford, NC 28673-0070, USA

Trufant, Desmond (Athlete, Football Player)
c/o Doug Hendrickson *Relativity Sports*
2029 Century Park E Ste 1550
Century City, CA 90067-3000, USA

Trufant, Isaiah (Athlete, Football Player)
c/o Doug Hendrickson *Relativity Sports*
2029 Century Park E Ste 1550
Century City, CA 90067-3000, USA

Trufant, Marcus (Athlete, Football Player)
11220 NE 53rd St
Kirkland, WA 98033-7505, USA

Truhitte, Daniel (Actor)
4630 Sapp Rd
Concord, NC 28025-1567, USA

Truitt, Anne D (Artist)
29 Boutonville Rd
South Salem, NY 10590-1517, USA

Truitt, Ansley (Athlete, Basketball Player)
18601 Cairo Ave
Carson, CA 90746-1715, USA

Truitt, Olanda (Athlete, Football Player)
1901 16th Way N
Bessemer, AL 35020-3930, USA

Trujillo, J J (Athlete, Baseball Player)
1329 York Ave
Corpus Christi, TX 78415-4337, USA

Trujillo, Mike (Athlete, Baseball Player)
16373 6475 Rd
Montrose, CO 81403-8578, USA

Trujillo, Solomon D (Business Person)
US West Inc
1801 California St Ste 1600
Denver, CO 80202-2628, USA

Trull, Don (Athlete, Football Player)
16435 Elmwood Point Ln
Sugar Land, TX 77498-7134, USA

Trulli, Jarno (Race Car Driver)
Jordan Grand Prix
Buckingham Rd.
Silverstone
Norhants NN12 9TJ, UNITED KINGDOM (UK)

Truman, Dan (Musician)
Dreamcatcher Artists Mgmt
2908 Poston Ave
Nashville, TN 37203-1312, USA

Trumbo, Karen (Actor)
c/o Staff Member *Creative Artists Management (OR)*
909 SW Saint Clair Ave
Portland, OR 97205-1300, USA

Trumbo, Mark (Athlete, Baseball Player)
1801 E Katella Ave Apt 4131
Anaheim, CA 92805-6672, USA

Trumka, Richard L (Politician)
AFL-CIO
1750 New York Ave NW Ste 230
Washington, DC 20006-5306, USA

Trump, Donald (Business Person, Politician, President, Reality Star)
The White House
1600 Pennsylvania Ave NW
Washington, DC 20500-0004, USA

Trump, Eric (Business Person)
The Trump Organization
725 5th Ave Bsmt A
New York, NY 10022-2519, USA

Trump, Ivana (Business Person, Misc, Model)
PO Box 8104
West Palm Bch, FL 33407-0104, USA

Trump, Ivanka (Business Person, Model, Reality Star)
c/o Staff Member *The Trump Organization*
725 5th Ave Bsmt A
New York, NY 10022-2519, USA

Trump, Melania (Model)
The White House
1600 Pennsylvania Ave NW
Washington, DC 20500-0004, USA

Trump Jr, Donald (Business Person)
The Trump Organization
725 5th Ave Bsmt A
New York, NY 10022-2519, USA

Trumpy, Robert T (Bob) Jr (Athlete, Football Player, Sportscaster)
75 Oak St
Cincinnati, OH 45246-4437, USA

Trundy, Natalie (Actor)
2109 S Wilbur Ave
Walla Walla, WA 99362-9048, USA

Trunfio, Nicole (Model)
c/o Staff Member *Independent Management Company*
87-103 Epsom Rd
#15
Rosebery NSW 2018, AUSTRALIA

Truscott, Lucian K IV (Writer)
Avon/William Morrow
1350 Avenue of the Americas
New York, NY 10019-4702, USA

Trusnik, Jason (Athlete, Football Player)

Truth, Hurts (Actor, Songwriter, Writer)
Aftermath/Interscope Records
2220 Colorado Ave
Santa Monica, CA 90404-3506, USA

Truvillion, Eric (Athlete, Football Player)
10436 Saint Tropez Pl
Tampa, FL 33615-4213, USA

Truvillion, Tobias (Actor)
c/o Wink Woodall *Talent Connect*
1118 Bedford Ave # 1
Brooklyn, NY 11216-1303, USA

Tryba, Ted (Athlete, Golfer)
6321 Cheryl St
Orlando, FL 32819-7511, USA

Tryon, Ty (Golfer)
8713 the Esplanade Apt 1
Orlando, FL 32836-8784, USA

Tsai, Cheryl (Actor)
c/o Jason Solomon *Full Circle Management*
4932 Lankershim Blvd Ste 202
North Hollywood, CA 91601-4452, USA

Tsakalidis, Iakovos (Jake) (Basketball Player)
Memphis Grizzlies
175 Toyota Plz Ste 150
Memphis, TN 38103-6601, USA

Tsamis, George (Athlete, Baseball Player)
12 Sweetbriar Ct
Colchester, CT 06415-1887, USA

Tsamis, George (Athlete, Baseball Player)
St Paul Saints 1771 Energy Park Dr
Attn Managers Office
Saint Paul, MN 55108-2720

Tsang, Bion (Musician)
Columbia Artists Mgmt Inc
165 W 57th St
New York, NY 10019-2201, USA

Tsantiris, Len (Athlete, Football Player)
Athletic Dept
Storrs Mansfield, CT, USA

Tschechowa, Vera (Actor)
c/o Ute Nicolai *Agentur Ute Nicolai*
Gosslerstrasse 2
Berlin 12161, Germany

Tschetter, Kris (Athlete, Golfer)
13 Culpeper St
Warrenton, VA 20186-3319, USA

Tschida, Tim (Athlete, Baseball Player)
1440 Randolph Ave Apt 119
Saint Paul, MN 55105-2562, USA

Tschida, Tim (Baseball Player)
1440 Randolph Ave Apt 119
Saint Paul, MN 55105-2562, USA

T. Schilling, Robert (Congressman, Politician)
507 Cannon Hob
Washington, DC 20515-2703, USA

Tschogl, John (Athlete, Basketball Player)
295 Shirley St
Chula Vista, CA 91910-1101, USA

Tseng, Yani (Athlete, Golfer)
9138 Sloane St
Orlando, FL 32827, USA

Tsitouris, John (Athlete, Baseball Player)
5207 Austin Rd
Monroe, NC 28112-7948, USA

Tskitishvili, Nikoloz (Basketball Player)
Denver Nuggets
1000 Chopper Cir
Pepsi Center
Denver, CO 80204-5805, USA

Tsongas, Niki (Congressman, Politician)
1607 Longworth Hob
Washington, DC 20515-3009, USA

Tsu, Irene (Actor)
c/o Richard A. Castleberry *Castleberry Talent*
636 Acanto St Apt 205
Los Angeles, CA 90049-2128, USA

Tu, Francesca (Actor)
c/o Staff Member *Agentur Jovanovic*
Theresienstrasse 124
Munchen 80333, Germany

Tuaolo, Esera (Athlete, Football Player)
6520 Promontory Dr
Eden Prairie, MN 55346-1915, USA

Tubbs, Billy (Coach)
Lamar University
Athletic Dept
Beaumont, TX 77710, USA

Tubbs, Greg (Athlete, Baseball Player)
833 Clay Ave
Cookeville, TN 38501-2261, USA

Tubbs, Winfred (Athlete, Football Player)
RR 1 Box 800
Oakwood, TX 75855, USA

Tubert, Marcelo (Actor)
c/o Staff Member *Richard Schwartz Management*
2934 1/2 N Beverly Glen Cir # 107
Los Angeles, CA 90077-1724, USA

Tuberville, Tommy (Coach, Football Coach)
Aubum University
Athletic Dept
Auburn University, AL 36849-0001, USA

Tubiola, Nicole (Actor)
c/o Charlton Blackburne *Charlton Blackburne Management*
4022 Los Feliz Blvd
Los Angeles, CA 90027-2305, USA

Tucci, Michael (Actor)
1425 Irving Ave
Glendale, CA 91201-1274, USA

Tucci, Roberto Cardinal (Religious Leader)
Palazzo Pio
Piazza Pia 3
Rome 00193, ITALY

Tucci, Stanley (Actor, Director)
c/o Jennifer Plante *Slate PR (NY)*
307 7th Ave Rm 2401
New York, NY 10001-6019, USA

Tuck, Gary (Athlete, Baseball Player)
20819 79th Ave E
Bradenton, FL 34202-8216, USA

Tuck, Hillary (Actor)
c/o Justin Evans *The Independent Group*
6363 Wilshire Blvd Ste 115
Los Angeles, CA 90048-5734, USA

Tuck, Jessica (Actor)
Brett Adams
448 W 44th St
New York, NY 10036-5220, USA

Tuck, Justin (Athlete, Football Player)
c/o Doug Hendrickson *Relativity Sports*
2029 Century Park E Ste 1550
Century City, CA 90067-3000, USA

Tucker, Barbara (Musician)
c/o Staff Member *Diva Central Inc*
7510 W Sunset Blvd # 1445
Los Angeles, CA 90046-3408, USA

Tucker, Bill (Boxer)
PO Box 969
Higley, AZ 85236-0969, USA

Tucker, Bob (Athlete, Football Player)
8 Hunter Rd
Hazleton, PA 18201-6817, USA

Tucker, Brett (Actor)
c/o Tiffany Kuzon *Mosaic Media Group*
407 N Maple Dr # 100
Beverly Hills, CA 90210-3818, USA

Tucker, Chris (Actor, Comedian)
PO Box 1030
McDonough, GA 30253-1030, USA

Tucker, Corin (Musician)
Legends of 21st Century
7 Trinity Row
Florence, MA 01062-1931, USA

Tucker, Darcy (Athlete, Hockey Player)
Turning Point Sports Management
102 W Main St Ste 301
Auburn, WA 98001-4926, USA

Tucker, Eddie (Athlete, Baseball Player)
2216 Red Maple Ln
Dawsonville, GA 30534-8032, USA

Tucker, Jason (Athlete, Football Player)
620 Remington Park
Robinson, TX 76706-7255, USA

Tucker, Jerry (Actor)
PO Box 15
Farmingville, NY 11738-0015, USA

Tucker, Jim (Athlete, Basketball Player)
1781 Linden Cv
Saint Paul, MN 55110-6202

Tucker, John (Athlete, Hockey Player)
19833 Michigan Ave
Odessa, FL 33556-4237

Tucker, Jonathan (Actor)
8265 W Sunset Blvd Ste 201
West Hollywood, CA 90046-2470, USA

Tucker, Justin (Athlete, Football Player)
c/o Staff Member *Baltimore Ravens*
6 Rod Cir
Middletown, MD 21769-7868, USA

Tucker, Michael (Actor, Producer)
c/o Staff Member *Artists & Representatives (Stone Manners Salners)*
6100 Wilshire Blvd Ste 1500
Los Angeles, CA 90048-5110, USA

Tucker, Michael (Athlete, Baseball Player, Olympic Athlete)
407 Maple Ave N
Lehigh Acres, FL 33972-4001, USA

Tucker, Paul (Musician)
c/o Staff Member *Kitchenware Management*
The Stables
St. Thomas Street
Newcastle Upon Tyne NE1 4LE, UK

Tucker, Rex (Athlete, Football Player)
2300 Culpeper Dr
Midland, TX 79705-6314, USA

Tucker, Ryan (Athlete, Football Player)
c/o Team Member *Cleveland Browns*
76 Lou Groza Blvd
Berea, OH 44017-1269, USA

Tucker, Tanya (Musician)
Tanya Tucker Inc
5200 Maryland Way Ste 103
Brentwood, TN 37027-5072, USA

Tucker, T J (Athlete, Baseball Player)
6616 Ridge Top Dr
New Port Richey, FL 34655-5614, USA

Tucker, Tony (Boxer)
Club Prana
1619 E 7th Ave
Ybor City
Tampa, FL 33605-3705, USA

Tucker, Travis (Athlete, Football Player)
1568 Lee Terrace Dr
Wickliffe, OH 44092-1604, USA

Tucker, Trent (Athlete, Basketball Player)
433 River St
Minneapolis, MN 55401-2515, USA

Tucker, Wendell (Athlete, Football Player)
2042 E 171st Pl
South Holland, IL 60473-3718, USA

Tucker, Y Arnold (Athlete, Football Player)
P.O. Box 514
Hilbert, WI 54129, USA

Tudor, John (Athlete, Baseball Player)
1361 Summer Hollow Rd
Greensboro, GA 30642-3299, USA

Tudor, Rob (Athlete, Hockey Player)
2 Drake Landing Rd
Okotoks, AB T1S 2M2, Canada

Tudyk, Alan (Actor)
c/o Tom Spriggs *Coronel Group*
1100 Glendon Ave Fl 17
Los Angeles, CA 90024-3588, USA

Tuel, Jeff (Athlete, Football Player)

Tuero, Esteban (Race Car Driver)
Minardi Italia
via Spallanzani 21
Faenza 48081, ITALY

Tueting, Sarah (Athlete, Hockey Player, Olympic Athlete)
488 Ash St
Winnetka, IL 60093-2604, USA

Tufts, Bob (Athlete, Baseball Player)
6738 108th St Apt A27
Forest Hills, NY 11375-2358, USA

Tuggle, Anthony (Athlete, Football Player)
12345 Plymouth Dr
Baton Rouge, LA 70807-1961, USA

Tuggle, Jessie (Athlete, Football Player)
540 Avala Ct
Alpharetta, GA 30022-5576, USA

Tugnutt, Ron (Athlete, Hockey Player)
Peterborough Petes
151 Lansdowne St W
Peterborough, ON K9J 1Y4, Canada

Tugnutt, Ron (Athlete, Hockey Player)
2427 Julia's Creek Rd RR 2
Douro-Dummer, ON K0L 2H0, Canada

Tuiasosopo, Marques (Athlete, Football Player)
5569 Gold Creek Dr
Castro Valley, CA 94552-5442, USA

Tuiasosopo, Peter Navy (Actor)
c/o Harold Gray *Shirley Wilson Agency*
5410 Wilshire Blvd Ste 806
Los Angeles
Los Angeles, CA 90036-4267, USA

Tuilaepa, Sailele Maljelegaio (Prime Minister)
Prime Minister's Office
PO Box 193
Apia, SAMOA

Tuinei, Tom (Athlete, Football Player)
714 Kihapai Pl Apt B2
Kailua, HI 96734-2677, USA

Tuipala, Joe (Athlete, Football Player)
43845 Thornberry Sq Unit 103
Leesburg, VA 20176-3403, USA

Tuitt, Stephon (Athlete, Football Player)
c/o Jimmy Sexton *CAA (Memphis)*
6060 Poplar Ave Ste 470
Memphis, TN 38119-0910, USA

Tull, Thomas (Producer)
Legendary Pictures
4000 Warner Blvd Bldg 76
Burbank, CA 91522-0001, ISA

Tullis, Willie (Athlete, Football Player)
9296 S County Road 67
Midland City, AL 36350-4057, USA

Tulloch, Stephen (Athlete, Football Player)
c/o Drew Rosenhaus *Rosenhaus Sports Representation*
3921 Alton Rd # 440
Miami Beach, FL 33140-3852, USA

Tully, Susan (Actor, Director)
c/o Bryn Newton *Saraband Associates*
265 Liverpool Rd
London N1 1LX, UNITED KINGDOM (UK)

Tulowitzki, Troy (Athlete, Baseball Player)
2986 Taper Ave
Santa Clara, CA 95051-2343, USA

Tulving, Endel (Misc)
45 Baby Point Cres
York, ON M6S 2B7, CANADA

Tumi, Christian W Cardinal (Religious Leader)
Archveche
BP 179
Douala, CAMEROON

Tumpane, John (Athlete, Baseball Player)
9900 S 55th Court Apt 3M
Oak Lawn, IL 60453, USA

Tumulty, Tom (Athlete, Football Player)
167 Woodside Ln
Verona, PA 15147-3425, USA

Tune, Tommy (Actor, Dancer)
222 Park Ave S Apt 12C
New York, NY 10003-1508, USA

Tung, Chee-Hwa (Misc)
Asia Pacific Finance Tower
3 Garden Road
Hong Kong, CHINA

Tunie, Tamara (Actor)
c/o Jean-Pierre (JP) Henraux *Henraux Management*
Prefers to be contacted by telephone
CA, USA

Tunnell, Lee (Athlete, Baseball Player)
6000 Kingsbridge Dr
Oklahoma City, OK 73162-3208, USA

Tunney, Robin (Actor)
c/o Joan Hyler *Hyler Management*
20 Ocean Park Blvd Unit 25
Santa Monica, CA 90405-3590, USA

Tupa, Thomas J (Tom) (Athlete, Football Player)
5921 Fawn Ln
Brecksville, OH 44141-2849, USA

Tupman, Matt (Athlete, Baseball Player)
16 Prince St
Concord, NH 03301-4246, USA

Tupou, Christian (Athlete, Football Player)
c/o Jeff Sperbeck *The Novo Agency*
1537 Via Romero Ste 100
Alamo, CA 94507-1527, USA

Tupper, James (Actor)
c/o Alissa Vradenburg *Untitled Entertainment*
350 S Beverly Dr Ste 200
Beverly Hills, CA 90212-4819, USA

Tupper, Jeff (Athlete, Football Player)
32497 W 127th St
Olathe, KS 66061-8645, USA

Turang, Brian (Athlete, Baseball Player)
3014 McNab Ave
Long Beach, CA 90808-4002, USA

Turco, Marty (Athlete, Hockey Player)
3616 Wolcott Dr
Flower Mound, TX 75028-8712

Turco, Paige (Actor)
c/o Rhonda Price *Gersh*
41 Madison Ave Ste 3301
New York, NY 10010-2210, USA

Turcotte, Alfie (Athlete, Hockey Player)
711 River Oaks Ln
Island Lake, IL 60042-9662

Turcotte, Darren (Athlete, Hockey Player)
North Bay Skyhawks Hockey Club
100 Chippewa St W
North Bay, ON P1B 6G2, Canada

Turcotte, Mel (Horse Racer)
4260 NW 12th St
Coconut Creek, FL 33066-1506, USA

Tureaud, Laurence (Mr T) (Actor)
c/o Peter Young *Sovereign Talent Group*
1642 Westwood Blvd Ste 202
Los Angeles, CA 90024-5609, USA

Turek, Roman (Athlete, Hockey Player)
The Sports Corporation
10088 102 Ave NW Twr 2735
TO
Edmonton, AB T5J 2Z1, Canada

Turgeon, Pierre (Athlete, Hockey Player)
2930 E Iliff Ave
Denver, CO 80210-5507, USA

Turiaf, Ronny (Athlete, Basketball Player)
c/o Mark Bartelstein *Priority Sports & Entertainment (Chicago)*
325 N La Salle Dr Ste 650
Chicago, IL 60654-8182, USA

Turin Brakes (Music Group)
c/o Staff Member *Paradigm (Monterey)*
404 W Franklin St
Monterey, CA 93940-2303, USA

Turk, Brian (Actor)
c/o Staff Member *The House of Representatives*
3118 Wilshire Blvd Ste D
Santa Monica, CA 90403-2345, USA

Turk, Godwin (Athlete, Football Player)
1303 Magnolia Cir
Orange, TX 77632-8996, USA

Turk, Stephen (Cartoonist)
927 Westbourne Dr
Los Angeles, CA 90069-4113, USA

Turkel, Ann (Actor)
c/o Mark Baintree *Brian Baintree Agency*
4 W 58th St
New York, NY 10019-2515, USA

Turkoglu, Hidayet (Hedo) (Athlete, Basketball Player)
100 S Eola Dr Unit 1603
Orlando, FL 32801-6601, USA

Turkson, Peter K A Cardinal (Religious Leader)
Archdiocese
PO Box 112
Cape Coast, GHANA

Turley, Kyle (Athlete, Football Player)
Neuro Armour
121 S Tejon St
Colorado Springs, CO 80903-2216, USA

Turlik, Gordon (Athlete, Hockey Player)
3618 E Garnet Ave
Spokane, WA 99217-6916

Turlington, Christy (Model)
c/o Debra Duffy *Dan Klores Communications (DKC)*
261 5th Ave Fl 2
New York, NY 10016-7601, USA

Turman, Glynn (Actor, Director, Musician)
48421 3 Points Rd
Lake Hughes, CA 93532-1124, USA

Turnage, Mark-Anthony (Composer)
Schott Co
Great Marlborough St
London W1V 2BN, UNITED KINGDOM (UK)

Turnbow, Derrick (Athlete, Baseball Player)
2224 Brienz Valley Dr
Franklin, TN 37064-1401, USA

Turnbow, Scot (Baseball Player)
Anaheim Angels
404 Newbary Ct
Franklin, TN 37069-1848, USA

Turnbull, Kitana (Actor)
c/o Matt Sherman *Matt Sherman Management*
8840 Wilshire Blvd # 109
Beverly Hills, CA 90211-2606, USA

Turnbull, Ian (Athlete, Hockey Player)
23930 Ocean Ave Apt 154
Torrance, CA 90505-5880

Turnbull, Perry (Athlete, Hockey Player)
2186 Cedar Forest Ct
Chesterfield, MO 63017-7201

Turnbull, Wendy (Tennis Player)
5684 Regency Cir E
Boca Raton, FL 33496-2721, USA

Turner, Aiden (Actor)
c/o Marnie Sparer *Power Entertainment Group*
1505 10th St
Santa Monica, CA 90401-2805, USA

Turner, Bake (Athlete, Football Player)
PO Box 277
Alpine, TX 79831-0277, USA

Turner, Bree (Actor)
c/o Sarah Yorke *Baker Winokur Ryder Public Relations*
200 5th Ave Fl 5
New York, NY 10010-3307, USA

Turner, Callum (Actor)
c/o Clair Dobbs *CLD Communications*
4 Broadway Ct
The Broadway
London SW191RG, UNITED KINGDOM

Turner, Cathy (Speed Skater)
251 East Ave
Hilton, NY 14468-1333, USA

Turner, Cecil (Athlete, Football Player)
2717 Dog Leg Trl
McKinney, TX 75069-8043, USA

Turner, Chris (Athlete, Baseball Player)
28SS3 N Quarry Dr
Elberta, AL 36530-5792, USA

Turner, Dean (Athlete, Hockey Player)
26900 Captains Ln
Franklin, MI 48025-1717

Turner, Elston (Athlete, Basketball Player)
23 Commanders Cv
Missouri City, TX 77459-6517, USA

Turner, Evan (Athlete, Basketball Player)
c/o David Falk *F.A.M.E*
Prefers to be contacted via telephone
Washington, DC, USA

Turner, Floyd (Athlete, Football Player)
9626 Garden Row Dr
Sugar Land, TX 77498-1033, USA

Turner, Fred (Race Car Driver)
107 Brush Rd
Greensboro, NC 27409-9658, USA

Turner, Gideon (Actor)
c/o Staff Member *Ken McReddie Ltd*
101 Finsbury Pavement
London EC2A 1RS, UK

Turner, Glenn (Business Person)
PO Box 952608
Lake Mary, FL 32795-2608, USA

Turner, Guinevere (Actor)
Gersh Agency
41 Madison Ave Ste 3301
New York, NY 10010-2210, USA

Turner, Hamp (Athlete, Football Player)
430172 Milledge Ter
Athens, GA 30605, USA

Turner, Herschel (Athlete, Football Player)
16622 Equestrian Ln
Chesterfield, MO 63005-4880, USA

Turner, Hersh (Athlete, Basketball Player)
1706 Lamberton Creek Ct NE
Grand Rapids, MI 49505-7702, USA

Turner, James A (Jim) (Athlete, Football Player)
14155 W 59th Pl
Arvada, CO 80004-3724, USA

Turner, James Jr (Business Person)
General Dynamics
3190 Fairview Park Dr
Falls Church, VA 22042-4530, USA

Turner, Janine (Actor, Model)
c/o Steve Glick *Glick Agency*
1321 7th St Ste 203
Santa Monica, CA 90401-1631, USA

Turner, Jerry (Athlete, Baseball Player)
44626 Kurtallen Ct
Lancaster, CA 93535-1767, USA

Turner, John (Athlete, Football Player)
3217 Cedar Ave S
Minneapolis, MN 55407-3802, USA

Turner, John N (Prime Minister)
27 Dunloe Rd
Toronto, ON M4V 2W4, CANADA

Turner, Josh (Musician)
c/o Staff Member *Modern Management*
1625 Broadway Ste 600
Nashville, TN 37203-3141, USA

Turner, Karri (Actor)
Premiere Artists Agency
1875 Century Park E Ste 2250
Los Angeles, CA 90067-2563, USA

Turner, Kathleen (Actor)
c/o Jonathan Mason *Buchwald (NY)*
10 E 44th St
New York, NY 10017-3601, USA

Turner, Keena (Athlete, Coach, Football Coach, Football Player)
8200 W Erb Way
Tracy, CA 95304-8896, USA

Turner, Ken (Athlete, Baseball Player)
PO Box 252
San Marcos, CA 92079-0252, USA

Turner, Kenneth (Race Car Driver)
1081 S Trade St
Tryon, NC 28782-3790, USA

Turner, Kriss (Producer)
c/o Staff Member *WME|IMG*
9601 Wilshire Blvd
Beverly Hills, CA 90210-5213, USA

Turner, Kristopher (Actor)
c/o Shelley Browning *Magnolia Entertainment*
9595 Wilshire Blvd Ste 601
Beverly Hills, CA 90212-2506, USA

Turner, Lane (Musician)
c/o Staff Member *Paradigm (Monterey)*
404 W Franklin St
Monterey, CA 93940-2303, USA

Turner, Lowri (Actor)
c/o Staff Member *Noel Gay Artists*
2 Stephen St
London W1T 1AN, UNITED KINGDOM

Turner, Marcus (Athlete, Football Player)
5032 Meadow Wood Ave
Lakewood, CA 90712-2855, USA

Turner, Matt (Athlete, Baseball Player)
829 Della Dr
Lexington, KY 40504-2319, USA

Turner, Maurice (Athlete, Football Player)
3558 Tiffany Ln
Shoreview, MN 55126-3072, USA

Turner, Michael (Football Player)
c/o Staff Member *Atlanta Falcons*
4400 Falcon Pkwy
Flowery Branch, GA 30542-3176, USA

Turner, Norv (Athlete, Coach, Football Coach, Football Player)
1256 Rose Ln
Lafayette, CA 94549-3032, USA

Turner, Odessa (Athlete, Football Player)
1416 Perry Ave
Bastrop, LA 71220, USA

Turner, Richard (Athlete, Football Player)
408 Piney Oak Dr
Norman, OK 73072-4603, USA

Turner, Ryan (Baseball Player)
1221 Shafter St
San Mateo, CA 94402-2901, USA

Turner, Shane (Athlete, Baseball Player)
3032 Van Reed Rd
Reading, PA 19608-1037, USA

Turner, Sherri (Athlete, Golfer)
PO Box 26
Yale, OK 74085-0026, USA

Turner, Sophie (Actor, Model)
c/o Hayley Stubbs *Public Eye Communications*
535 Kings Rd
#313 Plaza
London SW10 0SZ, UNITED KINGDOM

Turner, Stacie (Business Person, Reality Star)
c/o Staff Member *Bravo TV (NY)*
30 Rockefeller Plz
New York, NY 10112-0015, USA

Turner, Ted (Business Person, Producer)
Turner Foundation
133 Luckie St NW Ste 200
Atlanta, GA 30303-2036, USA

Turner, Teddy (Politician)
Charleston Collegiate School
2024 Academy Rd
Johns Island, SC 29455-4437, USA

Turner, Thomas (Athlete, Baseball Player)
4140 Clayton Pike
Manchester, OH 45144-9404, USA

Turner, Tina (Musician)
Villa Chateau Algonquin
Seestrasse 180
Kusnacht ZH CH-8700, SWITZERLAND

Turner, Toby (Actor)
c/o Dan Weinstein *Collective Digital Studio*
8383 Wilshire Blvd Ste 1050
Beverly Hills, CA 90211-2415, USA

Turner, Trai (Athlete, Football Player)
c/o Peter Schaffer *Authentic Athletix*
400 S Steele St Unit 47
Denver, CO 80209-3535, USA

Turner, Tyrin (Actor)
c/o David Saunders *Agency for the Performing Arts (APA)*
405 S Beverly Dr Ste 500
Beverly Hills, CA 90212-4425, USA

Turner, Vernon (Athlete, Football Player)
86 Crosshill St
Staten Island, NY 10301-3308, USA

Turner, William (Athlete, Basketball Player)
3271 Wisteria Tree St
Las Vegas, NV 89135-1787, USA

Turnesa, Jim (Golfer)
1087 SW Balmoral Trce
Stuart, FL 34997-7188, USA

Turnesa, Mike (Golfer)
c/o Staff Member *Pro Golfers Association (PGA)*
112 TPC Blvd
Ponte Vedra Beach, FL 32082, USA

Turnesa, Willie (Golfer)
41 Sheraton Dr
Poughkeepsie, NY 12601-5629, USA

Turow, Scott (Writer)
c/o Robert (Bob) Bookman *Paradigm*
8942 Wilshire Blvd
Beverly Hills, CA 90211-1908, USA

Turpin, Miles (Athlete, Football Player)
8444 Wildflower Pl
Lone Tree, CO 80124-3022, USA

Turris, Kyle (Athlete, Hockey Player)
19820 N 84th St
Scottsdale, AZ 85255-3964

Turteltaub, Jon (Director)
Junction Entertainment
500 S Buena Vista St
Animation Building Ste 1B
Burbank, CA 91521-0001, USA

Turturro, Aida (Actor)
c/o Peg Donegan *Framework Entertainment*
9057 Nemo St # C
W Hollywood, CA 90069-5511, USA

Turturro, John (Actor)
c/o Joe Funicello *ICM Partners*
10250 Constellation Blvd Fl 7
Los Angeles, CA 90067-6207, USA

Turturro, Nicholas (Nick) (Actor)
c/o Joseph Le *Joseph Le Talent Agency*
3500 W Olive Ave Ste 300
Burbank, CA 91505-4647, USA

Tushingham, Rita (Actor)
c/o Michele Milburn *Milburn Browning Associates*
91, Brick Lane
The Old Truman Brewery
London E1 6QL, UNITED KINGDOM

Tuten, Rick (Athlete, Football Player)
1146 SE 15th St
Ocala, FL 34471-4514, USA

Tutera, David (Reality Star)
c/o Eda Kalkay *EKPR*
43 W Front St Ste 11
Red Bank, NJ 07701-1600, USA

Tutson, Tom (Athlete, Football Player)
6655 Poplar Grove Way
Stone Mountain, GA 30087-4791, USA

Tutt, Brian (Athlete, Hockey Player)
PO Box 306
Evansburg, AB T0E 0T0, Canada

Tuttle, Perry (Athlete, Football Player)
226 W John St
Matthews, NC 28105-5366, USA

Tuttle, Steve (Athlete, Hockey Player)
928 Belfair Rd
Bellevue, WA 98004-4013

Tutu, Desmond (Religious Leader)
PO Box 1092
Milnerton, Cape Town 07435, SOUTH AFRICA

Tuzzolino, Tony (Athlete, Hockey Player)
4466 Sunflower Cir Apt 39
Clarkston, MI 48346-4956

Tveit, Aaron (Actor)
c/o Elin McManus-Flack *Elin Flack Management*
435 W 57th St Apt 3M
New York, NY 10019-1724, USA

Tverdovsky, Oleg (Athlete, Hockey Player)
8850 E Garden View Dr
Anaheim, CA 92808-1677

Tvrdon, Roman (Athlete, Hockey Player)
Mierova 1435/53
Galanta, 924 01 Slovakia

Twain, Shania (Actor, Musician)
c/o Scott Rodger *Maverick*
9350 Civic Center Dr
Beverly Hills, CA 90210-3629, USA

Twardzik, Dave (Athlete, Basketball Player)
2139 Alaqua Lakes Blvd
Longwood, FL 32779-3206, USA

Tway, Bob (Athlete, Golfer)
6405 Oak Tree Cir
Edmond, OK 73025-2512, USA

Tweed, Shannon (Actor, Model, Reality Star)
2650 Benedict Canyon Dr
Beverly Hills, CA 90210-1023, USA

Tweeden, Leeann (Actor, Model, Sportscaster)
c/o Staff Member *ABC Television (LA)*
500 S Buena Vista St
Burbank, CA 91521-0001, USA

Tweet, Rodney (Athlete, Football Player)
2675 Via Caballero Del Norte
Santa Fe, NM 87505-6528, USA

Twenty One Pilots (Music Group)
Fueled by Ramen
1633 Broadway # 1000
New York, NY 10019-6708, USA

Twigg, Rebecca (Athlete, Cycler, Olympic Athlete)
7001 Old Redmond Rd Apt E318
Redmond, WA 98052-4293, USA

Twiggs, Greg (Golfer)
c/o Staff Member *Pro Golfers Association (PGA)*
112 TPC Blvd
Ponte Vedra Beach, FL 32082, USA

Twigs, FKA (Musician)
c/o Sam Kirby *WME|IMG (NY)*
11 Madison Ave Fl 18
New York, NY 10010-3669, USA

Twilight Singers (Music Group)
c/o Staff Member *Paradigm (Monterey)*
404 W Franklin St
Monterey, CA 93940-2303, USA

Twilley, Howard J Jr (Athlete, Football Player)
3109 S Columbia Cir
Tulsa, OK 74105-2329, USA

Twist, Tony (Athlete, Hockey Player)
63 Nordic Ln
Defiance, MO 63341-2332

Twista (Actor, Musician)
c/o Juliette Harris *It Girl Public Relations*
3763 Eddingham Ave
Calabasas, CA 91302-5835, USA

Twisted Wheel (Music Group)
c/o Angus Baskerville *13 Artists (UK)*
11-14 Kensington St
Brighton BN1 4AJ, UNITED KINGDOM

Twitty, Howard (Golfer)
8259 E Chino Dr
Scottsdale, AZ 85255-3922, USA

Twitty, Jeff (Athlete, Baseball Player)
812 Willow Cove Rd
Chapin, SC 29036-8733, USA

Twohy, David (Actor)
c/o John Burnham *ICM Partners*
10250 Constellation Blvd Fl 7
Los Angeles, CA 90067-6207, USA

Twohy, Mike (Cartoonist)
605 Beloit Ave
Kensington, CA 94708-1117, USA

Twohy, Robert (Cartoonist)
New Yorker Magazine
4 Times Sq
Editorial Dept
New York, NY 10036-6518, USA

Tyers, Kathy (Writer)
Martha Millard Agency
204 Park Ave
Madison, NJ 07940-1128, USA

Tyga (Musician)
c/o Tammy Brook *FYI Public Relations*
174 5th Ave Ste 404
New York, NY 10010-5964, USA

Tykwer, Tom (Actor, Composer, Director, Producer, Writer)
X-Filme Creative Pool
Kurfürstenstrasse 57
Berlin 10785, Germany

Tyler, Aisha (Actor, Comedian)
c/o Lisa Morbete *Morbete Publicity Group*
838 N Fairfax Ave
Los Angeles, CA 90046-7208, USA

Tyler, Anne (Writer)
c/o Joseph (Joe) Veltre *Gersh*
41 Madison Ave Ste 3301
New York, NY 10010-2210, USA

Tyler, Bonnie (Musician, Songwriter)
c/o Andrew Leighton *Leighton Pope Organization*
8 Glenthorpe Mews
115A Glenthorpe Road
London W6 0LJ, UNITED KINGDOM (UK)

Tyler, Brian (Race Car Driver)
4410 W Alva St
Tampa, FL 33614-7639, USA

Tyler, Brian (Composer, Musician)
7711 Flynn Ranch Rd
Los Angeles, CA 90046-1257, USA

Tyler, James Michael (Actor)
c/o Craig Mobbs *AKA Talent Agency*
325 N Larchmont Blvd
Los Angeles, CA 90004-3011, USA

Tyler, Jess (Radio Personality)
c/o Staff Member *WPKX*
1331 Main St Ste 4
Springfield, MA 01103-1621, USA

Tyler, Karmyn (Actor, Musician)
c/o Staff Member *BMI (LA)*
8730 W Sunset Blvd Fl 3
Los Angeles, CA 90069-2210

Tyler, Liv (Actor)
c/o Bianca Bianconi *42West*
600 3rd Ave Fl 23
New York, NY 10016-1914, USA

Tyler, Maurice (Athlete, Football Player)
7066 Whitfield Dr
Riverdale, GA 30296-2161, USA

Tyler, Mia (Actor)
c/o Staff Member *Core/Lapides Lear Entertainment*
16255 Ventura Blvd Ste 625
Encino, CA 91436-2307, USA

Tyler, Richard (Designer, Fashion Designer)
c/o Staff Member *Richard Tyler*
525 Mission St
S Pasadena, CA 91030-3035, USA

Tyler, Robert (Actor)
Innovative Artists
1505 10th St
Santa Monica, CA 90401-2805, USA

Tyler, Steven (Musician, Songwriter)
c/o Rebecca Lambrecht *Chicane Group*
6442 Santa Monica Blvd Ste 200B
Los Angeles, CA 90038-1530, USA

Tyler, Terry (Athlete, Basketball Player)
6500 Tauton Rd NW
Albuquerque, NM 87120-2061, USA

Tyler, Wendell A (Athlete, Football Player)
4083 W Avenue L Apt 294
Quartz Hill, CA 93536-4202, USA

Tylo, Michael (Actor)
11684 Ventura Blvd # 910
Studio City, CA 91604-2699, USA

Tylo, Noa (DJ)
c/o Len Evans *Project Publicity*
540 W 43rd St
New York, NY 10036, USA

Tylski, Richard (Athlete, Football Player)
5456 Tierra Verde Ln
Jacksonville, FL 32258-2281, USA

Tynan, Ronan (Musician)
c/o Daniel Strone *Trident Media Group LLC*
41 Madison Ave Fl 36
New York, NY 10010-2257, USA

Tyner, Charles (Actor)
Dade/Schultz
6442 Coldwater Canyon Ave Ste 206
Valley Glen, CA 91606-1174, USA

Tyner, Jason (Athlete, Baseball Player)
5535 Sul Ross Ln
Beaumont, TX 77706-3435, USA

Tyner, Tray (Athlete, Golfer)
208 Plantation Path
Boerne, TX 78006-3879, USA

Type O Negative (Music Group)
c/o Staff Member *Helter Skelter (UK)*
535 Kings Rd
The Plaza
London SW10 0SZ, UNITED KINGDOM (UK)

Tyree, David (Athlete, Football Player)
514 Boonton Ave
Boonton, NJ 07005-1510, USA

Tyrell, Steve (Musician)
c/o Staff Member *WME|IMG*
9601 Wilshire Blvd
Beverly Hills, CA 90210-5213, USA

Tyrone, Jim (Athlete, Baseball Player)
1115 Park Vista Dr Apt 703
Arlington, TX 76012-2349, USA

Tyrone, Wayne (Athlete, Baseball Player)
1808 Holm Oak St
Arlington, TX 76012-5608, USA

Tyrrell, Tim (Athlete, Football Player)
17 Fallstone Dr
Streamwood, IL 60107-1071, USA

Tysoe, Ronald W (Business Person)
Federated Department Stores
151 W 34th St
New York, NY 10001-2101, USA

Tyson, Cathy (Actor)
P F D Drury House
34-43 Russell St
London WC2B 5HA, UNITED KINGDOM (UK)

Tyson, Cicely (Actor)

Tyson, Deangelo (Athlete, Football Player)
c/o Anthony J. Agnone *Eastern Athletic Services*
11350 McCormick Rd
Suite 800 - Executive Plaza
Hunt Valley, MD 21031-1002, USA

Tyson, Dick (Athlete, Football Player)
3835 N 67th St
Kansas City, KS 66104-1023, USA

Tyson, Ian (Musician)
Richard Flohil Assoc
60 McGill St
Toronto, ON M5B 1H2, CANADA

Tyson, Laura D'Andrea (Politician)
1600 Pennsylvania Ave NW
Washington, DC 20500-0005, USA

Tyson, Mike (Athlete, Baseball Player)
479 Thunderhead Canyon Dr
Wildwood, MO 63011-1736, USA

Tyson, Mike (Athlete, Boxer)
1258 Imperia Dr
Henderson, NV 89052-4051, USA

Tyson, Richard (Actor)
c/o Staff Member *Cunningham Escott Slevin & Doherty (CESD)*
10635 Santa Monica Blvd Ste 130
Los Angeles, CA 90025-8306, USA

Tyus, Wyomia (Athlete, Olympic Athlete, Track Athlete)
1048 Keniston Ave
Los Angeles, CA 90019-1707, USA

Tyutin, Fedor (Athlete, Hockey Player)
7871 S Argonne St
Centennial, CO 80016-1801

U2 (Musician)
c/o Guy Oseary *Maverick Management*
9350 Civic Center Dr Ste 100
Beverly Hills, CA 90210-3629, USA

UB40 (Music Group)
c/o Lydia Kirschstein *Trinifold Management*
12 Oval Rd
Camden
London NW1 7DH, UNITED KINGDOM

Ubach, Alanna (Actor)
8863 Cynthia St
Los Angeles, CA 90069-4510, USA

Uberroth, Peter (Baseball Player)
Baseball Commissioner's Office
184 Emerald Bay
Laguna Beach, CA 92651-1209, USA

Ubriaco, Gene (Athlete, Hockey Player)
Chicago Wolves
2301 Ravine Way
Glenview, IL 60025-7627

Ubriaco, Gene (Athlete, Coach, Hockey Player)
Chicago Wolves
621 Winston Dr
Melrose Park, IL 60160-2350

Uchida, Mitsuko (Musician)
Arts Management Group
1133 Broadway Ste 1025
New York, NY 10010-7985, USA

Uchitel, Rachel (Reality Star)
c/o Gloria Allred *Allred, Maroko & Goldberg*
6300 Wilshire Blvd Ste 1500
Los Angeles, CA 90048-5217, USA

Udenio, Fabiana (Actor)

Uderzo, Albert (Director, Writer)
26 av. Victor Hugo
Paris F-75116, France

Udrih, Beno (Athlete, Basketball Player)
825 N Prospect Ave Unit 23E2
Milwaukee, WI 53202-3979

Udvar-Hazy, Steven (Business Person)
67 Beverly Park Ct
Beverly Hills, CA 90210-1543, USA

Udvati, Frank (Athlete, Hockey Player)
6 Willow St
Waterloo, ON N2J 4S3, CANADA

Udy, Helene (Actor)
Sterling/Winters
10877 Wilshire Blvd # 15
Los Angeles, CA 90024-4341, USA

Ueberroth, John A (Business Person)
Preferred Hotel Group
311 S Wacker Dr Ste 1900
Chicago, IL 60606-6676, USA

Ueberroth, Peter (Baseball Player)
184 Emerald Bay
Laguna Beach, CA 92651-1209

Ueberroth, Peter V (Misc)
Doubletree Hotels Corp
755 Crossover Ln
Memphis, TN 38117-4906, USA

Uecker, Bob (Athlete, Baseball Player, Sportscaster)
c/o Deborah Miller *Shelter Entertainment*
9255 W Sunset Blvd Ste 300
Los Angeles, CA 90069-3313, USA

Uecker, Gunther (Artist)
Dusseldorfer Str 29A
Dusseldorf 40545, GERMANY

Uecker, Keith (Athlete, Football Player)
1230 Sunset View Dr
Akron, OH 44313-7839, USA

Uehara, Koji (Athlete, Baseball Player)
c/o Staff Member *SFX Sports Management*
5335 Wisconsin Ave NW Ste 850
Washington, DC 20015-2052, USA

Uelses, John (Athlete, Track Athlete)
30660 Rolling Hills Dr
Valley Center, CA 92082-3351, USA

Ufland, Len (Actor, Director)
4400 Hillcrest Dr Apt 901
Hollywood, FL 33021-7979, USA

Uggams, Leslie (Actor, Musician)
9255 W Sunset Blvd Ste 404
W Hollywood, CA 90069-3302, USA

Uggla, Dan (Athlete, Baseball Player)
3325 Piedmont Rd NE Unit 3201
Atlanta, GA 30305-4821, USA

Ughi, Uto (Musician)
Cannareggio 4990/E
Venice 30121, ITALY

U-God (Artist)
Famous Artists Agency
250 W 57th St
New York, NY 10107-0001, USA

Ugueto, Luis (Athlete, Baseball Player)
21915 NE 85th St
Redmond, WA 98053-2204, USA

Uh Huh Her (Music Group)
c/o Staff Member *Paradigm (Monterey)*
404 W Franklin St
Monterey, CA 93940-2303, USA

Uhlenhake, Jeffrey (Athlete, Football Player)
1304 Normandy Dr
Newark, OH 43055-9201, USA

Uhlig, Anneliese (Actor)
1519 Escalona Dr
Santa Cruz, CA 95060-3311, USA

Uhry, Alfred (Writer)
Marshall Purdy
226 W 47th St Ste 900
New York, NY 10036-1413, USA

Ujdur, Jerry (Athlete, Baseball Player)
112 Riveness Rd
Duluth, MN 55811-2873, USA

Ulevich, Neal (Journalist, Photographer)
11954 Glencoe Dr
Thornton, CO 80233-1895, USA

Ulion, Gretchen (Athlete, Hockey Player)
22181 Toro Hills Dr
Salinas, CA 93908-1132, USA

Ulion-Silverman, Gretchen (Athlete, Hockey Player, Olympic Athlete)
505 Westledge Dr
Torrington, CT 06790-4490, USA

Ullger, Scott (Athlete, Baseball Player)
1 Twins Way
Minneapolis, MN 55403-1418, USA

Ulliel, Gaspard (Actor)
c/o Brinda Bhatt *Innovative Artists*
1505 10th St
Santa Monica, CA 90401-2805, USA

Ullman, Norman V A (Norm) (Athlete, Hockey Player)
819-25 Austin Dr
Markham, ON L3R 8H4, Canada

Ullman, Ricky (Actor)
c/o Terry Saperstein *Nani/Saperstein Management*
481 8th Ave # 1575
New York, NY 10001-1809, USA

Ullman, Tracey (Actor, Comedian)
c/o Ciara Parkes *Public Eye Communications*
535 Kings Rd
#313 Plaza
London SW10 0SZ, UNITED KINGDOM

Ullmann, Liv J (Actor)
Hafrsfjordgata 7
Oslo N-0273, Norway

Ulloa, Christina (Actor)
c/o Michael Greenwald *Endorse Management Group*
9854 National Blvd # 454
Los Angeles, CA 90034-2713, USA

Ullsten, Ola (Prime Minister)
Folkpartiet
PO Box 6508
Stockholm 11383, SWEDEN

Ulmar, Bin Hassan (Musician)
Agency Group
3 Columbus Cir Ste 2120
New York, NY 10019-8712, USA

Ulmer, Arthur (Athlete, Football Player)
1133 Lloyd Dr
Forest Park, GA 30297-1516, USA

Ulmer, John (Athlete, Football Player)
3050 Aries Pl
Burnaby, BC V3J 7E9, Canada

Ulmer, Kristen (Athlete)
3671 E Willow Canyon Dr
Salt Lake City, UT 84121-6184, USA

Ulmer, Layne (Athlete, Hockey Player)
2024 Foley Dr
North Battleford, SK S9A 3G9, Canada

Ulrich, Kim Johnston (Actor)
S D B Partners
1801 Ave of Stars
#902
Los Angeles, CA 90067, USA

Ulrich, Lars (Musician)
Q Prime Inc
729 7th Ave Ste 1600
New York, NY 10019-6880, USA

Ulrich, Skeet (Actor)
c/o Lena Roklin *Luber Roklin Management*
5815 W Sunset Blvd Ste 208
Los Angeles, CA 90028-6481, USA

Ulrich, Thomas (Boxer)
Brunsbutteler Damm 29
Berlin 13581, GERMANY

Ultra, Nate (Musician)
Peach Bisquit
451 Washington Ave Apt 5A
Brooklyn, NY 11238-1838, USA

Ultraista (Musician)
c/o Steve Martin *Nasty Little Man*
285 W Broadway Rm 310
New York, NY 10013-2257, USA

Ulufa'alu, Bartholomew (Prime Minister)
Premier's Office
Legakiki Ridge
Honiara
Guadacanal, SOLOMON ISLANDS

Ulvaeus, Bjorn (Composer, Musician)
Mono Music
Sodra Brobanken 41A
Skeppsholmen
Stockholm 11149, Sweden

Ulvang, Vegard (Skier)
Fiellveien 53
Kirkenes 09900, NORWAY

Umana, Christina (Actor)
c/o Staff Member *TV Caracol*
Calle 76 #11 - 35
Piso 10AA
Bogota DC 26484, COLOMBIA

Umansky, Mauricio (Business Person, Reality Star)
The Agency
331 Foothill Rd Ste 100
Beverly Hills, CA 90210-3667, USA

Umbach, Arnie (Athlete, Baseball Player)
760 Moores Mill Rd
Auburn, AL 36830-6032, USA

Umbarger, Jim (Athlete, Baseball Player)
10701 N 99th Ave Lot 161
Peoria, AZ 85345-5442, USA

Umberger, Andy (Actor)
c/o Claire Miller *Bauman Redanty & Shaul Agency*
5757 Wilshire Blvd
Suite 473
Beverly Hills, CA 90212, USA

Umberger, RJ (Athlete, Hockey Player)
1616 Woodland Hall Dr
Delaware, OH 43015-7109, USA

Umbers, Mark (Actor)
c/o Nick Frenkel *3 Arts Entertainment*
9460 Wilshire Blvd Fl 7
Beverly Hills, CA 90212-2713, USA

Umenyiora, Osi (Athlete, Football Player)
c/o Tom Condon *Creative Artists Agency (CAA)*
401 Commerce St PH
Nashville, TN 37219-2516, USA

Umphlett, Tommy (Athlete, Baseball Player)
104 Berkley Rd
Ahoskie, NC 27910-9575, USA

Umphrey's McGee (Music Group)
c/o Staff Member *Paradigm (Monterey)*
404 W Franklin St
Monterey, CA 93940-2303, USA

Unanue, Emil R (Misc)
Washington University
Medical School
Pathology Dept
Saint Louis, MO 63110, USA

Underhill, Barbara (Figure Skater)
c/o Staff Member *Guelph Storm Hockey Club*
55 Wyndham St N
Guelph, ON N1H 7T8, Canada

Underhill, Matt (Athlete, Hockey Player)
29 Draper St
Medford, MA 02155-1203, USA

Underwood, Blair (Actor)
c/o Ron West *Thruline Entertainment*
9250 Wilshire Blvd Fl Ground
Beverly Hills, CA 90212-3352, USA

Underwood, Brittany (Actor)
c/o Judith Lesley *Sinclair Management*
95 Christopher St Apt 6F
New York, NY 10014-6626, USA

Underwood, Carrie (Musician)
c/o Brad Cafarelli *PMK/BNC Public Relations*
1840 Century Park E Ste 1400
Los Angeles, CA 90067-2115, USA

Underwood, Cecil (Politician)
1578 Kanawha Blvd E Apt 1C
Charleston, WV 25311-2459, USA

Underwood, Jacob (Musician)
Trans Continental Records
7380 W Sand Lake Rd # 350
Orlando, FL 32819-5248, USA

Underwood, Jay (Actor)
6100 Wilshire Blvd Ste 1170
Los Angeles, CA 90048-5116, USA

Underwood, Matthew (Sportscaster)
c/o Glenn Hughes III *Gem Entertainment Group*
10920 Wilshire Blvd Ste 150
Los Angeles, CA 90024-3990, USA

Underwood, Olen (Athlete, Football Player)
302 N Main St
Conroe, TX 77301-2810, USA

Underwood, Pat (Athlete, Baseball Player)
708 Riverview Dr
Kokomo, IN 46901-7024, USA

Underwood, Ron (Director)
United Talent Agency
9336 Civic Center Dr
Beverly Hills, CA 90210-3604, USA

Underwood, Sam (Actor)
c/o Sarah Spear *Curtis Brown Ltd*
28-29 Hay Market
Hay Market House
London SW1Y 4SP, UNITED KINGDOM

Underwood, Scott (Musician)
Jon Landua
80 Mason St
Greenwich, CT 06830-5515, USA

Underwood, Sheryl (Actor)
c/o Staff Member *CBS Paramount Network Television*
4024 Radford Ave
Cbs Studios
Studio City, CA 91604-2190, USA

Ungaro, Emanuel M (Designer, Fashion Designer)
2 Ave du Montaigne
Paris 75008, FRANCE

Unger, Billy (Actor)
c/o Matt Luber *Luber Roklin Management*
5815 W Sunset Blvd Ste 208
Los Angeles, CA 90028-6481, USA

Unger, Brian (Actor)
5750 Wilshire Blvd
Los Angeles, CA 90036-3697, USA

Unger, Deborah Kara (Actor)
c/o Sarah Jackson *Seven Summits Pictures & Management*
8906 W Olympic Blvd
Beverly Hills, CA 90211-3550, USA

Unger, Garry D (Athlete, Hockey Player)
Banff Hockey Academy
PO Box 2242
Banff, AB T1L 1B9, Canada

Unger, Max (Athlete, Football Player)
c/o Don Yee *Yee & Dubin Sports, LLC*
725 S Figueroa St Ste 3085
Los Angeles, CA 90017-5430, USA

Union, Gabrielle (Actor)
c/o Staff Member *I'll Have Another*
10202 Washington Blvd
Culver City, CA 90232-3119, USA

Union, Sarah (Actor)
c/o Jason Barrett *Alchemy Entertainment*
7024 Melrose Ave Ste 420
Los Angeles, CA 90038-3394, USA

Unkefer, Ronald A (Business Person)
Good Guys Inc
1600 Harbor Bay Pkwy
Alameda, CA 94502-3085, USA

Uno, Osamu (Business Person)
1-46 Showacho
Hamadera Sakai
Osaka 00592, JAPAN

Unrein, Mitch (Athlete, Football Player)
c/o Frank Bauer *Sun West Sports*
7883 N Pershing Ave
Stockton, CA 95207-1749, USA

Unroe, Tim (Athlete, Baseball Player)
2719 S Joplin
Mesa, AZ 85209-2508, USA

Unruh, James A (Business Person)
5426 E Morrison Ln
Paradise Valley, AZ 85253-3017, USA

Unseld, Wes (Athlete, Basketball Player, Coach)
2210 Cedar Circle Dr
Catonsville, MD 21228-3747, USA

Unser, Al (Race Car Driver)
7625 Central Ave NW
Albuquerque, NM 87121-2115, USA

Unser, Bobby (Race Car Driver)
7700 Central Ave SW
Albuquerque, NM 87121-2113, USA

Unser, Del (Athlete, Baseball Player)
33516 N 79th Way
Scottsdale, AZ 85266-4244, USA

Unser Jr, Al (Race Car Driver)
PO Box 56696
Albuquerque, NM 87187-6696, USA

Unutoa, Morris (Athlete, Football Player)
821B Country Club Pkwy
Mount Laurel, NJ 08054-2714, USA

Upchurch, Rickie (Rick) (Athlete, Football Player)
463 Hagens Aly
Mesquite, NV 89027-5815, USA

Upham, John (Athlete, Baseball Player)
1502 Pierre Ave
Windsor, ON N8X 4P5, Canada

Upham, Misty (Actor)
c/o Richard Kerner *Kerner Management Associates*
311 N Robertson Blvd # 288
Beverly Hills, CA 90211-1705, USA

Uphoff-Becker, Nicole (Horse Racer)
Freiherr-von-Lanen-Str 15
Warendorf 48231, GERMANY

Upshaw, Courtney (Athlete, Football Player)

Upshaw, Marv (Athlete, Football Player)
209 Dyer Ave
Manteca, CA 95336-5951, USA

Upshaw, Regan (Athlete, Football Player)
21300 Redskin Park Dr
Ashburn, VA 20147-6100, USA

Upshaw, Willie (Athlete, Baseball Player)
500 Main St Attn Ofc
Bridgeport, CT 06604-5136, USA

Upton, Fred (Congressman, Politician)
2183 Rayburn Hob
Washington, DC 20515-1803, USA

Upton, Justin (Athlete, Baseball Player)
7275 N Scottsdale Rd Unit 1017
Scottsdale, AZ 85253-2616, USA

Upton, Kate (Model)
c/o Brad Cafarelli *PMK/BNC Public Relations*
1840 Century Park E Ste 1400
Los Angeles, CA 90067-2115, USA

Upton, Melvin ""B J"" (Athlete, Baseball Player)
10960 Wilshire Blvd FL 5
Los Angeles, CA 90024-3708, USA

Upton, Melvin (B J) (Athlete, Baseball Player)
10960 Wilshire Blvd FL 5
Los Angeles, CA 90024-3708, USA

Urb, Johann (Actor)
c/o Lena Roklin *Luber Roklin Management*
5815 W Sunset Blvd Ste 208
Los Angeles, CA 90028-6481, USA

Urban, Brent (Athlete, Football Player)
c/o Todd France *Creative Artists Agency (CAA) Sports*
3500 Lenox Rd NE
Atlanta, GA 30326-4228, USA

Urban, Karl (Actor)
c/o Alexandra Crotin *The Lede Company*
9701 Wilshire Blvd # 930
Beverly Hills, CA 90212-2020, USA

Urban, Keith (Musician)
PO Box 40725
Nashville, TN 37204-0725, USA

Urban, Thomas N (Business Person)
Pioneer Hi-Bred Int'l
400 Locust St
Capital Square
Des Moines, IA 50309-2331, USA

Urban, Tim (Musician)
c/o Simon Fuller *XIX Entertainment (UK)*
32/33 Ransomes Dock
London SW11 4NP, UNITED KINGDOM (UK)

Urbanchek, Jon (Coach)
University of Michigan
Athletic Dept
Ann Arbor, MI 48109, USA

Urbanek, Karel (President)
Kvetna 54
Brno, CZECHOSLOVAKIA

Urbani, Tom (Athlete, Baseball Player)
3347 Corinthian Ln
Auburn, CA 95603-9066, USA

Urbano, Mike (Musician)
c/o Staff Member *Creative Artists Agency (CAA)*
2000 Avenue of the Stars Ste 100
Los Angeles, CA 90067-4705, USA

Urbanski, Douglas (Actor, Producer, Writer)
Douglas Management Group (
9713 Little Santa Monica Blvd
Suite 218
Beverly Hills, CA 90210, USA

Urbik, Kraig (Athlete, Football Player)
c/o Joe Panos *Athletes First*
23091 Mill Creek Dr
Laguna Hills, CA 92653-1258, USA

Urch, Scott (Athlete, Football Player)
14 Elmo Dr
Macomb, IL 61455-9505, USA

Ure, Midge (Musician)
#8 Glenthome 115A Glenhome
Hammersm
London W6 0LJ, UNITED KINGDOM (UK)

Urenda, Herman (Athlete, Football Player)
225 Upton Pyne Dr
Brentwood, CA 94513-6425, USA

Uresti, Omar (Golfer)
2503 Pebble Beach Dr
Austin, TX 78747-1618, USA

Urguhart, Lawrence M (Business Person)
English China Clays
Business Park
Theale
Reading RG7 4SA, UNITED KINGDOM (UK)

Uribe, Diane (Actor)
23874 Via Jacara
Valencia, CA 91355-2520, USA

Uribe, Juan (Athlete, Baseball Player)
5740 SW 130th Ter
Pinecrest, FL 33156-6400, USA

Urich, Justin (Actor)
Talent Group
5670 Wilshire Blvd Ste 820
Los Angeles, CA 90036-5613, USA

Urie, Brendon (Musician)
c/o Staff Member *Fueled By Ramen*
PO Box 1803
Tampa, FL 33601-1803, USA

Urie, Michael (Actor)
c/o Staff Member *Ur-Mee Entertainment*
601 W 57th St Apt 7B
New York, NY 10019-1066, USA

Urkal, Oklay (Boxer)
Bautzener Str 4
Berlin 10829, GERMANY

Urlacher, Brian (Football Player)
7524 S McCormick Way
Queen Creek, AZ 85142-4565, USA

Urness, Ted (Athlete, Football Player)
PO Box 267
Rose Valley, SK S0E 1M0, Canada

Urrea, John (Athlete, Baseball Player)
75 E 24th St
Upland, CA 91784-8353, USA

Urschel, John (Athlete, Football Player)
c/o Jim Ivler *Sportstars Inc*
1370 Avenue of the Americas Fl 19
New York, NY 10019-4602, USA

Urseth, Bonnie (Actor)
c/o Staff Member *The Gage Group*
5757 Wilshire Blvd Ste 659
Los Angeles, CA 90036-3682, USA

Urshan, Nathaniel A (Religious Leader)
United Pentecostal Church International
8855 Dunn Rd
Hazelwood, MO 63042-2212, USA

Ursi, Corrado Cardinal (Religious Leader)
Via Capodimonte 13
Naples 80136, ITALY

Used, The (Music Group)
c/o John Reese *Freeze Management*
32941 Calle Perfecto # C
San Juan Capistrano, CA 92675-4705, USA

Usher, Bob (Athlete, Baseball Player)
1420 Curci Dr Unit 407
San Jose, CA 95126-3982, USA

Usher, Jessie T (Actor)
c/o Annick Oppenheim *Wolf-Kasteler Public Relations*
6255 W Sunset Blvd Ste 1111
Los Angeles, CA 90028-7426, USA

Usher, Paul (Actor)
c/o Staff Member *Qdos Entertainment*
8 King St
Covent Garden
London WC2 8HN, UNITED KINGDOM

Usher, Thomas J (Business Person)
USX Corp
600 Grant St Ste 431
Pittsburgh, PA 15219-2805, USA

Ushkowitz, Jenna (Actor)
c/o Jill Fritzo *Jill Fritzo Public Relations*
208 E 51st St # 305
New York, NY 10022-6557, USA

Uslan, Michael (Producer, Writer)
Branded Entertainment
333 Crestmont Rd
Cedar Grove, NJ 07009-1907, USA

Usova, Maya (Figure Skater)
Connecticut Skating Center
300 Alumni Rd
Newington, CT 06111-1868, USA

Ustorf, Stefan (Athlete, Hockey Player)
8502 Waynesboro Way
Waynesville, OH 45068-7720

Ustvolskaya, Galina I (Composer)
Prospect Gagarina 27
#72
Saint Petersburg 196135, RUSSIA

Utay, William (Actor)

Uteem, Cassam (President)
President's Office
Le Redult
Port Louis, MAURITIUS

Utley, Adrian (Musician)
Fruit
Saga Centre
326 Kensal Road
London W10 5BZ, UNITED KINGDOM (UK)

Utley, Chase (Athlete, Baseball Player)
21031 Ventura Blvd Ste 1000
Woodland Hills, CA 91364-2227, USA

Utley, Mike (Athlete, Football Player)
PO Box 349
Orondo, WA 98843-0349, USA

Utley, Stan (Golfer)
20701 N Scottsdale Rd Ste 107 PMB 619
Scottsdale, AZ 85255-6413, USA

Utt, Ben (Athlete, Football Player)
3378 Habersham Rd NW
Atlanta, GA 30305-1171, USA

Utterback, Sarah (Actor)
c/o Staff Member *Abrams Artists Agency*
750 N San Vicente Blvd
E Tower Fl 11
Los Angeles, CA 90069-5788, USA

Uwais, Iko (Actor)
c/o Dean Schnider *Management 360*
9111 Wilshire Blvd
Beverly Hills, CA 90210-5508, USA

Vaca, Joselito (Soccer Player)
Dallas Burn
14800 Quorum Dr Ste 300
Dallas, TX 75254-1408, USA

Vacariou, Nicolae (Prime Minister)
Romanian Senate
Piata Revolutiei
Bucharest 71243, ROMANIA

Vacariu, Alina (Model)
c/o Staff Member *Elite Model Management (LA)*
518 N La Cienega Blvd
West Hollywood, CA 90048-2002, USA

Vaccaro, Brenda (Actor)
c/o Stephen (Steve) LaManna *Innovative Artists*
1505 10th St
Santa Monica, CA 90401-2805, USA

Vaccaro, Kenny (Athlete, Football Player)
c/o Andrew Kessler *Athletes First*
23091 Mill Creek Dr
Laguna Hills, CA 92653-1258, USA

Vaccaro, Owen (Actor)
c/o Brandi George *Advantage PR*
3900 W Alameda Ave Ste 1200
Burbank, CA 91505-4317, USA

Vacendak, Steve (Athlete, Basketball Player)
608 Gaston St Ste 100
Raleigh, NC 27603-1258, USA

Vachon, Christine (Producer)
c/o Staff Member *Killer Films (US)*
526 W 26th St Rm 715
New York, NY 10001-5524, USA

Vachon, Louis-Albert Cardinal (Religious Leader)
Seminaire de Quebec
1 Rue des Remparts
Quebec, QC G1R 5L7, CANADA

Vachon, Nicholas (Athlete, Hockey Player)
1926 Curtis Ave Apt B
Redondo Beach, CA 90278-2313

Vachon, Paul (Wrestler)
RR 4
Mansonville, QC J0E 1X0, CANADA

Vachon, Rogatien R (Rogie) (Athlete, Coach, Hockey Player)
2228 Glyndon Ave
Venice, CA 90291-4043

Vachon, Rogie (Athlete, Hockey Player)
Los Angeles Kings
1111 S Figueroa St Ste 3100
Los Angeles, CA 90015-1333

Vack, Peter (Actor)
c/o Christina Papadopoulos *Baker Winokur Ryder Public Relations*
200 5th Ave Fl 5
New York, NY 10010-3307, USA

Vactor, Ted (Athlete, Football Player)
11504 Channing Dr
Wheaton, MD 20902-2908, USA

Vadsaria, Dilshad (Actor)
c/o Robbie Kass *Kass Management*
1011 Euclid St Unit B
Santa Monica, CA 90403-4296, USA

Vaea of Houma, Baron (Prime Minister)
Prime Minister's Office
Nuku'alofa, TONGA

Vaglica, Jim (Actor)
c/o Lisa Lobel *Boston Casting Inc*
129 Braintree St Ste 107
Boston, MA 02134-1613, USA

Vago, Constantin (Misc)
University of Sciences
Place Eugene Bataillon
Montpellier 34095, FRANCE

Vahi, Tiit (Prime Minister)
Coalition Party Eesti Koonderakond
Kuhlbarsi 1
Tallinn 00104, ESTONIA

Vai, Steve (Musician)
c/o Ruta Seopetys *Sepetys Entertainment Group*
5543 Edmondson Pike Ste 8A
Nashville, TN 37211-5808, USA

Vaic, Lubomir (Athlete, Hockey Player)
Jeronymova 37 I 577
Liberic 46007, Czech Republic

Vaidisova, Nicole (Tennis Player)
c/o Staff Member *IMG (Cleveland)*
1360 E 9th St Ste 100
Cleveland, OH 44114-1730, USA

Vaidya, Daya (Actor)
c/o Brady McKay *Haven Entertainment*
8111 Beverly Blvd Ste 201
Los Angeles, CA 90048-4531, USA

Vail, Eric (Athlete, Hockey Player)
10055 Piney Ridge Walk
Alpharetta, GA 30022-5065

Vail, Justina (Actor)
651 N Kilkea Dr
Los Angeles, CA 90048-2213, USA

Vail, Mike (Athlete, Baseball Player)
523 Winter Ct
Nampa, ID 83686-2907, USA

Vails, Nelson (Athlete, Cycler, Olympic Athlete)
7914 Tanager Ln
Indianapolis, IN 46256-1720, USA

Vaive, Rick (Athlete, Hockey Player)
574 Blenheim Cres
Oakville, ON L6J 6P6, Canada

Valabik, Boris (Athlete, Hockey Player)
13 South Ave SE
Atlanta, GA 30315, USA

Valance, Holly (Musician)
c/o Andrew Edwards *Zero Gravity Management*
11110 Ohio Ave Ste 100
Los Angeles, CA 90025-3329, USA

Valandrey, Charlotte (Actor)
c/o Francois-Xavier Molin *ArtMedia*
8 rue Danielle Casanova
Paris 75002, FRANCE

Valar, Paul (Skier)
34 Hubertus Ring
Franconia, NH 03580-5114, USA

Valastro, Buddy (Chef)
Carlos Bakery
95 Washington St Ste A
Hoboken, NJ 07030-4533, USA

Valbuena, Gary (Athlete, Football Player)
5040 Breckenridge Ave
Banning, CA 92220-7140, USA

Valderrama, Carlos (Soccer Player)
Colorado Rapids
555 17th St # 3350
Denver, CO 80202-3950, USA

Valderrama, Wilmer (Actor)
WV Enterprises
8687 Melrose Ave Ste G271
West Hollywood, CA 90069-5710, USA

Valdes, Carlos (Actor)
c/o Peter Kaiser *Talent House (NY)*
325 W 38th St Rm 605
New York, NY 10018-9642, USA

Valdes, Ismael (Athlete, Baseball Player)
13732 SW 285th St
Homestead, FL 33033-5708, USA

Valdes, Jesus (Chucho) (Musician)
IMN
278 Main St
Gloucester, MA 01930-6022, USA

Valdes, Marc (Athlete, Baseball Player)
PO Box 598
Binghamton, NY 13902-0598, USA

Valdes, Mark (Athlete, Baseball Player)
7519 Paula Dr
Tampa, FL 33615-4113, USA

Valdespino, Sandy (Athlete, Baseball Player)
434 SE 3rd St
Dania, FL 33004-4014, USA

Valdes-Rodriguez, Alisa (Writer)
c/o Staff Member *Greater Talent Network Inc*
437 5th Ave Ste 8A
New York, NY 10016-2205, USA

Valdez, Erik (Actor)
c/o Ray Hughes *Ray Hughes Management*
12400 Ventura Blvd Ste 630
Studio City, CA 91604-2406, USA

Valdez, Ismael (Athlete, Baseball Player)
4001 26th St
Vero Beach, FL 32960-1930, USA

Valdez, Luis (Writer)
El Teatro Capesino
705 4th St
San Juan Bautista, CA 95045, USA

Valdivielso, Jose (Athlete, Baseball Player)
14 Rita Dr
Mount Sinai, NY 11766-2215, USA

Vale, Angelica (Actor)
c/o Staff Member *Televisa*
Blvd Adolfo Lopez Mateos 232
Colonia San Angel INN
DF CP 01060, MEXICO

Vale, Tina (Musician)
DreamWorks Records
9268 W 3rd St
Beverly Hills, CA 90210-3713, USA

Valen, Nancy (Actor)
c/o Michael Livingston *Artists Agency Inc*
1180 S Beverly Dr Ste 301
Los Angeles, CA 90035-1154, USA

Valencia, Danny (Athlete, Baseball Player)
2289 NW 36th St
Boca Raton, FL 33431-5417, USA

Valensi, Nick (Musician)
12701 Hortense St
Studio City, CA 91604-1122, USA

Valent, Eric (Athlete, Baseball Player)
107 Lengle Ave
Wernersville, PA 19565-1331, USA

Valente, Catarina (Musician)
Villa Corallo Via Ai Ronci
Danbury, CT 06816-0001,
SWITZERLAND

Valente, Caterina (Musician)
ERAKI Entertainment
Casella Postale 91
6976 Castagnola
SWITZERLAND

Valentin, John (Athlete, Baseball Player)
1601 Avenida Cesar Chavez SE
Albuquerque, NM 87106-3930, USA

Valentin, Jose (Athlete, Baseball Player)
Fort Wayne Tincaps 1301 Ewing Street
Attn: Managers Office
Wayne, IN 46802, USA

Valentine, Bill (Athlete, Baseball Player)
15 Blue Ridge Cir
Little Rock, AR 72207-1901, USA

Valentine, Bill (Baseball Player)
15 Blue Ridge Cir
Little Rock, AR 72207-1901, USA

Valentine, Bobby (Athlete, Baseball Player, Coach)
71 Wynnewood Ln
Stamford, CT 06903-1931, USA

Valentine, Brooke (Musician)
c/o Staff Member *Virgin Records (NY)*
150 5th Ave Fl 7
New York, NY 10011-4372, USA

Valentine, Chris (Athlete, Hockey Player)
Freedom 55 Financial
1223 Michael St N Suite 300
Ottawa, ON K1J 7T2, Canada

Valentine, Dan (Business Person)
C-Cube Microsystems
1551 McCarthy Blvd
Milpitas, CA 95035-7437, USA

Valentine, Darnell (Athlete, Basketball Player, Olympic Athlete)
7546 SW Ashford St
Portland, OR 97224-7143, USA

Valentine, Donald T (Business Person)
Network Appliance Inc
495 E Java Dr
Sunnyvale, CA 94089-1125, USA

Valentine, Ellis (Athlete, Baseball Player)
2708 Bridgemarker Dr
Grand Prairie, TX 75054-7262, USA

Valentine, Fred (Athlete, Baseball Player)
4838 Blagden Ave NW
Washington, DC 20011-3716, USA

Valentine, Gary (Actor, Comedian)
c/o Melinda Morris Zanoni *Legacy Talent & Entertainment*
1300 Baxter St Ste 100A
Charlotte, NC 28204-3806, USA

Valentine, Greg (Hammer) (Athlete, Wrestler)
c/o Staff Member *Aries Entertainment*
PO Box 771
Harlan, KY 40831-0771, USA

Valentine, James (Musician)
c/o Staff Member *Creative Artists Agency (CAA)*
2000 Avenue of the Stars Ste 100
Los Angeles, CA 90067-4705, USA

Valentine, Joe (Athlete, Baseball Player)
4168 Chiffon Ln
North Port, FL 34287-3236, USA

Valentine, Karen (Actor)
PO Box 1410
Washington Depot, CT 06793-0410, USA

Valentine, Kym (Actor)
Julie Torrance Management
P O Box 463
Elwood, Victoria 03184, AUSTRALIA

Valentine, Raymond C (Misc)
University of California
Plant Growth Laboratory
Davis, CA 95616, USA

Valentine, Scott (Actor)
17465 Flanders St
Granada Hills, CA 91344-2211, USA

Valentine, Stacy (Adult Film Star)
200 W Houston St
New York, NY 10014-4828, USA

Valentine, Steve (Actor)
c/o Amanda Rosenthal *Amanda Rosenthal Talent Agency*
315 Harbord St
Toronto, ON M6G 1G9, CANADA

Valentine, Zack (Athlete, Football Player)
162 Harvest Rd
Swedesboro, NJ 08085-1427, USA

Valentinetti, Vito (Athlete, Baseball Player)
271 Summit Ave
Mount Vernon, NY 10552-3309, USA

Valentino, Bobby (Musician)
c/o Staff Member *Island Def Jam Group*
825 8th Ave Fl 28
New York, NY 10019-7416, USA

valenzuela, Benny (Athlete, Baseball Player)
Bahia San Esteban #267
Sur Los Mochis
Sinaloa, Mexico, USA

Valenzuela, Fernando (Athlete, Baseball Player)
2123 N Beachwood Dr
Los Angeles, CA 90068-3403, USA

Valera, Julio (Athlete, Baseball Player)
685 Urb Colinas
Verdes D4
San Sebastian, PR 00685, USA

Valicevic, Rob (Athlete, Hockey Player)
54666 Sassafras Dr
Shelby Township, MI 48315-6902

Valiquette, Jack (Athlete, Hockey Player)
28 Peacock Lane
Barrie, ON L4N 3R8, Canada

Valk, Garry (Athlete, Hockey Player)
681 Baycrest Dr
North Vancouver, BC V7G 1N7, Canada

Valladolid, Marcela (Chef)
c/o Staff Member *Fluent Media Group*
5230 Alton Rd
Miami Beach, FL 33140-2005, USA

Valle, Aurora (Actor)
c/o Staff Member *TV Azteca*
Periferico Sur 4121
Colonia Fuentes del Pedregal
DF CP 14141, Mexico

Valle, Dave (Athlete, Baseball Player)
2260 95th Ave NE
Clyde Hill, WA 98004-2516, USA

Valle, Hector (Athlete, Baseball Player)
HC 2 Box 19813
Cabo Rojo, PR 00623-9240, USA

Valle Costa, Filipe (Actor)
c/o Chinyere Anyanwu *Cooper Company*
1185 Avenue Of The Americas Fl 3
New York, NY 10036-2600, USA

Vallely, James (Jim) (Writer)
c/o Staff Member *Creative Artists Agency (CAA)*
2000 Avenue of the Stars Ste 100
Los Angeles, CA 90067-4705, USA

Vallely, John (Athlete, Basketball Player)
2042 Commodore Rd
Newport Beach, CA 92660-4306, USA

Valletta, Amber (Actor, Model)
c/o Nicole Perna *Imprint PR*
6121 W Sunset Blvd
Neuehouse
Los Angeles, CA 90028-6442, USA

Valley, Mark (Actor)
c/o Doug Fronk *Paradigm*
8942 Wilshire Blvd
Beverly Hills, CA 90211-1908, USA

Vallez, Emilio (Football Player)
Chicago Bears
General Delivery
Polvadera, NM 87828-9999, USA

Valli, Frankie (Musician)
c/o Victoria Varela *Varela Media*
45 Rockefeller Plz Fl 20
New York, NY 10111-3193, USA

Vallien, Bertil (Artist)
Roleks Vall
93 Visby
00621, SWEDEN

Valmon, Andrew (Athlete, Olympic Athlete, Track Athlete)
16403 Danforth Ct
Rockville, MD 20853-3278, USA

Valo, Ville (Musician)
HIM
P.O. Box 194
Helsinki FIN-00121, Finland

Valot, Daniel L (Business Person)
Total Petroleum
900 19th St
Denver, CO 80202, USA

Valverde, Jose (Athlete, Baseball Player)
773 W Raven Dr
Chandler, AZ 85286-4484, USA

Valverde, Rawley (Actor)
15207 Magnolia Blvd Unit 106
Sherman Oaks, CA 91403-1105, USA

Vampire Weekend (Music Group)
c/o Perri Cohen *Nasty Little Man*
285 W Broadway Rm 310
New York, NY 10013-2257, USA

Van, Allen (Athlete, Hockey Player)
4890 Ashley Ln Apt 206
Inver Grove Heights, MN 55077-1234, USA

Van Acker, Drew (Actor)
c/o Shepard Smith *Luber Roklin Management*
5815 W Sunset Blvd Ste 208
Los Angeles, CA 90028-6481, USA

Van Allsburg, Chris (Writer)
222 Berkeley St Ste 8
C/O Houghton Mifflin Children's Books
Boston, MA 02116-3753, USA

VanAlmsick, Franziska (Franzi) (Swimmer)
Eichhom
Bizetstr 1
Berlin 13088, GERMANY

VanAmerongen, Jerry (Cartoonist)
2533 Washburn Ave S
Minneapolis, MN 55416-4350, USA

Van Ark, Joan (Actor)
c/o Konrad Leh *Creative Talent Group*
1900 Avenue of the Stars Ste 2475
Los Angeles, CA 90067-4512, USA

VanArsdale, Dick (Athlete, Basketball Player)
6028 E Calle Tuberia
Scottsdale, AZ 85251-4229, USA

VanArsdale, Tom (Athlete, Basketball Player)
7510 N Eucalyptus Dr
Paradise Valley, AZ 85253-3319, USA

Vanasse, Karine (Actor)
c/o Annick Muller *Wolf-Kasteler Public Relations*
40 Exchange Pl Ste 704
New York, NY 10005-2778, USA

VanAuken, John A (Misc)
Canadian Tennis Technology
PO Box 1538 Stn A
Sydney, NS B1P 6R7, CANADA

Van Basten, Marco (Soccer Player)
AC Milan
Via Turati 3
Milan 20121, ITALY

Van Benschoten, John (Athlete, Baseball Player)
2937 Gateland Sq
Marietta, GA 30062-8358, USA

Vanbiesbrouck, John (Athlete, Hockey Player, Olympic Athlete)
67960 Campground Rd
Washington, MI 48095-1217, USA

Van Boxmeer, John (Athlete, Hockey Player)
8033 E Santa Cruz Ave
Orange, CA 92869-5652

Van Brabant, Ozzie (Athlete, Baseball Player)
7257 Mariposa Ave
Citrus Heights, CA 95610-3029, USA

Van Breda Kolff, Jan (Athlete, Basketball Player)
6510 Valen Way Apt 305
Naples, FL 34108-8274, USA

Van Buren, Ebert (Athlete, Football Player)
2100 Highway 165 S
Monroe, LA 71202-8219, USA

Van Buren, Jermaine (Athlete, Baseball Player)
557 Acree Ln
Columbus, OH 43228-8907, USA

Van Burkleo, Ty (Athlete, Baseball Player)
19681 Rabon Valley Rd
Grass Valley, CA 95949-8166, USA

Van Buuren, Armin (DJ)
c/o Carmen van der Werf *Armada Music B.V.*
PO Box 75247
Amsterdam 1070 AE, The Netherlands

VanCamp, Emily (Actor)
c/o Billy Lazarus *United Talent Agency (UTA)*
9336 Civic Center Dr
Beverly Hills, CA 90210-3604, USA

Vance, Cory (Athlete, Baseball Player)
1321 Surrey Rd
Vandalia, OH 45377-1646, USA

Vance, Courtney B (Actor, Producer)
c/o Staff Member *Bassett/Vance Productions*
1520 Ocean Park Blvd Apt C
Santa Monica, CA 90405-4853, USA

Vance, Ellis (Athlete, Basketball Player)
6 Carriage Way
Champaign, IL 61821-5119, USA

Vance, Eric (Athlete, Football Player)
924 Bentley Dr
Roanoke, TX 76262-7419, USA

Vance, Kenny (Musician)
PO Box 116
Fort Tilden, NY 11695, USA

Vance, Sandy (Athlete, Baseball Player)
5863 Chelton Dr
Oakland, CA 94611-2423, USA

VanClief, D G (Race Car Driver)
Breeders Cup Ltd
215 W Main St Ste 250
Lexington, KY 40507-1774, USA

VanCulin, Samuel (Religious Leader)
All Hallows Church
43 Trinity Square
London EC3N 4DJ, UNITED KINGDOM (UK)

Van Dam, Rob (Actor, Athlete, Wrestler)
2986 Knoll View Dr
Rancho Palos Verdes, CA 90276, USA

Van Damme, Jean-Claude (Actor)
c/o Francois Beghin *Franç Beghin*
Rue De Praetere
Brussels 01050, BELGIUM

Vande Berg, Ed (Athlete, Baseball Player)
4903 S Meadows Pl
Chandler, AZ 85248-5460, USA

Vande Hei, Mark T Ltcolonel (Astronaut)
1831 Raintree Cir
El Lago, TX 77586-5930, USA

Vande Hei, Mark T Lt Colonel (Astronaut)
1831 Raintree Cir
El Lago, TX 77586-5930, USA

VandenBerg, Lodewijk (Astronaut)
Constellation Technology Corp
7887 Bryan Dairy Rd Ste 100
Largo, FL 33777-1498, USA

Van Den Berg, Lodewijk Dr (Astronaut)
9658 Leeward Ave
Largo, FL 33773-4423, USA

VandenBergh, M A (Business Person)
Royal Dutch Petroleum
30 Van Bylandtlaan
Hague, HR 02596, NETHERLANDS

Vanden Bosch, Kyle (Athlete, Football Player)
13630 S Canyon Dr
Phoenix, AZ 85048-9081, USA

VandenBussche, Ryan (Athlete, Hockey Player)
Tri-County Pros Hockey School
150 Oak St Unit 14
Simcoe, ON N3Y 5M5, Canada

VanDenHoogenband, Pieter (Athlete, Swimmer)
PO Box 302
Amhem, AH 06800, NETHERLANDS

Vander, Jagt Guy (Misc)
Baker & Hostetler
1050 Connecticut Ave NW Ste 1100
Washington, DC 20036-5318, USA

Vander, Musetta (Actor)
c/o Jeff Goldberg *Jeff Goldberg Management*
817 Monte Leon Dr
Beverly Hills, CA 90210-2629, USA

Van Der Beek, James (Actor)
c/o Whitney Tancred *42West*
1840 Century Park E Ste 700
Los Angeles, CA 90067-2122, USA

Vanderbeek, Matt (Athlete, Football Player)
4 Monstad St
Aliso Viejo, CA 92656-6246, USA

Vanderberg Shaw, Helen (Coach)
Heaven's Fitness
301 14th St NW
Calgary, AB T2N 2A1, CANADA

Vanderbilt, Gloria (Writer)
c/o Staff Member *HarperCollins Publishers*
195 Broadway Fl 2
New York, NY 10007-3132, USA

Vanderbundt, Skip (Athlete, Football Player)
4225 Los Coches Way
Sacramento, CA 95864-5241, USA

Van Derbur, Marilyn (Actor)
195 S Dahlia St
Denver, CO 80246-1046, USA

Vanderbush, Carin Cone (Athlete, Olympic Athlete, Swimmer)
47 Rose Dr
Highland Falls, NY 10928-4310, USA

Vandergriff Jr, Bob (Race Car Driver)
845 McFarland Pkwy
Alpharetta, GA 30004-3365, USA

Vanderkaay, Peter (Athlete, Olympic Athlete, Swimmer)
292 W Woodland St
Ferndale, MI 48220-2706, USA

Vanderkelen, Ron (Athlete, Football Player)
5300 Vernon Ave S Apt 102
Edina, MN 55436-2328, USA

Vanderlip-Ozburn, Dolly (Athlete, Baseball Player)
W18878 US Highway 53 54 93
Galesville, WI 54630-2805, USA

Vanderloo, Mark (Model)
c/o Sean Patterson *SAM Worldwide*
92 Laight St Apt 9B
New York, NY 10013-2025, USA

Vandermeer, Jim (Athlete, Hockey Player)
17967 N 95th St
Scottsdale, AZ 85255-6086

Vandermeersch, Bernard (Misc)
University of Bordeaux
Anthropology Dept
Bordeaux, FRANCE

Van Der Perren, Kevin (Figure Skater)
Emily Bruines
Dr W Drees laan 35
Goes 4463 XE, NETHERLANDS

Van der Pol, Anneliese (Actor, Musician)
c/o Victoria Morris *Kazarian, Measures, Ruskin & Associates*
5200 Lankershim Blvd Ste 820
N Hollywood, CA 91601-3194, USA

Vanderpump, Lisa (Business Person, Reality Star)
Villa Blanca Restaurant
9601 Brighton Way
Beverly Hills, CA 90210-5109, USA

Vandersea, Phil (Athlete, Football Player)
34 Hunting Ave
Shrewsbury, MA 01545-3177, USA

Vanderveen, Loet (Artist)
Lime Creek 5
Big Sur, CA 93920, USA

VanDerveer, Tara (Athlete, Basketball Player, Olympic Athlete)
1036 Cascade Dr
Menlo Park, CA 94025-6629, USA

Vandervoort, Laura (Actor)
c/o Mona Loring *Status PR*
PO Box 6191
Westlake Village, CA 91359-6191, USA

VanderWaal, Grace (Musician)
c/o AnnMarie Thompson *Syco Entertainment*
9830 Wilshire Blvd Fl 3
Beverly Hills, CA 90212-1804, USA

Vander Wal, John (Athlete, Baseball Player)
5474 Highbury Dr SE
Ada, MI 49301-7736, USA

Vanderwoort, Laura (Actor, Musician)
c/o Norbert Abrams *Noble Caplan Abrams*
1260 Yonge St Fl 2
Toronto, ON M4T 1W5, CANADA

Van Devere, Trish (Actor)
7036 Grasswood Ave
Malibu, CA 90265-4247, USA

Vandeweghe, Coco (Athlete, Tennis Player)
c/o Staff Member *Women's Tennis Association (WTA (UK))*
Palliser House
Palliser Rd
London W149EB, UK

Vandeweghe, Kiki (Athlete, Basketball Player)
c/o Staff Member *Denver Nuggets*
1000 Chopper Cir
Denver, CO 80204-5805, USA

Van Dien, Casper (Actor)
c/o Wes Stevens *Vox*
5670 Wilshire Blvd Ste 820
Los Angeles, CA 90036-5613, USA

Van Doren, Mamie (Actor)
3419 Via Lido # 184
Newport Beach, CA 92663-3908, USA

Van Dusen, Fred (Athlete, Baseball Player)
319 N Rowan Ave
Los Angeles, CA 90063-2323, USA

VanDusen, Granville (Actor)
10974 Alta View Dr
Studio City, CA 91604-3903, USA

Van Dyk, Paul (DJ, Musician)
c/o Joel Zimmerman *WME|IMG (NY)*
11 Madison Ave Fl 18
New York, NY 10010-3669, USA

Van Dyke, Barry (Actor)
27800 Blythedale Rd
Agoura, CA 91301-1824, USA

Van Dyke, Bruce (Athlete, Football Player)
143 Lakeview Dr
Mc Murray, PA 15317-2747, USA

Van Dyke, Dick (Actor)
c/o Jeff Kolodny *Paradigm*
8942 Wilshire Blvd
Beverly Hills, CA 90211-1908, USA

Van Dyke, Leroy (Musician)
Rt. 1 Box 271
Smithton, MO 65350, USA

VanDyke, Philip (Actor)
1464 Madera Rd # 108N
Simi Valley, CA 93065-3077, USA

Van Eeghen, Mark (Athlete, Football Player)
90 Woodstock Ln
Cranston, RI 02920-4639, USA

Van Egmond, Tim (Athlete, Baseball Player)
8839 Callaway Rd
Gay, GA 30218-1817, USA

Vanek, Thomas (Athlete, Hockey Player)
2302 Nicolle Ave N
Stillwater, MN 55082-1782, USA

Van Ert, Sondra (Athlete, Olympic Athlete, Snowboarder)
PO Box 671
Northport, WA 99157-0671, USA

Van Every, Jonathan (Athlete, Baseball Player)
555 Dixton Dr
Brandon, MS 39047-8125, USA

Van Exel, Nick (Athlete, Basketball Player)
3102 Noble Lakes Ln
Houston, TX 77082-6809, USA

Van Galder, Don (Athlete, Football Player)
1611 Giles St
Austin, TX 78722-1242, USA

Vangelis (Musician)
c/o Staff Member *Robert Urband & Associates*
1200 Esplanade Apt 222
Redondo Beach, CA 90277-4951, USA

Vangen, Scott D (Astronaut)
2101 Nasa Pkwy Spc Centerbldg
Houston, TX 77058-3607, USA

Van Gorder, Dave (Athlete, Baseball Player)
212 Black Eagle Ave
Henderson, NV 89002-9234, USA

Van Gorkum, Harry (Actor)
2552 Dearborn Dr
Los Angeles, CA 90068-2240, USA

Vangsness, Kirsten (Actor)
137 N Larchmont Blvd # 234
Los Angeles, CA 90004-3704, USA

Van Gundy, Jeff (Sportscaster)
c/o Staff Member *WME/IMG*
9601 Wilshire Blvd
Beverly Hills, CA 90210-5213, USA

Van Gundy, Stan (Basketball Coach, Coach)
7500 Deer Park Trl
Clarkston, MI 48346-1221, USA

Van Halen (Music Group)
c/o Irving Azoff *Azoff Music Management*
1100 Glendon Ave Ste 2000
Los Angeles, CA 90024-3524, USA

Van Halen, Alex (Musician)
c/o Irving Azoff *Azoff Music Management*
1100 Glendon Ave Ste 2000
Los Angeles, CA 90024-3524, USA

Van Halen, Eddie (Musician)
c/o Irving Azoff *Azoff Music Management*
1100 Glendon Ave Ste 2000
Los Angeles, CA 90024-3524, USA

Van Hekken, Andy (Athlete, Baseball Player)
4742 64th St
Holland, MI 49423-8980, USA

Van Heusen, Billy (Athlete, Football Player)
835 Hudson St
Denver, CO 80220-4436, USA

Van Hoften, James D Dr (Astronaut)
131 Camelia Ln
Lafayette, CA 94549-2733, USA

Van Hollen, Chris (Congressman, Politician)
51 Monroe St Ste 507
Rockville, MD 20850-2406, USA

Van Hollen, Chris (Congressman, Politician)
1707 Longworth Hob
Washington, DC 20515-0523, USA

Van Holt, Brian (Actor)
c/o Carlos Carreras *Agency for the Performing Arts (APA)*
405 S Beverly Dr Ste 500
Beverly Hills, CA 90212-4425, USA

VanHorn, Buddy (Director)
4409 Ponca Ave
Toluca Lake, CA 91602-2513, USA

Van Horn, Doug (Athlete, Football Player)
149 Feronia Way
Rutherford, NJ 07070-2437, USA

Van Horn, Kelly (Producer, Writer)
c/o Staff Member *Mirisch Agency*
8840 Wilshire Blvd Ste 100
Beverly Hills, CA 90211-2606, USA

Van Horne, Dave (Sportscaster)
202 Bent Tree Dr
Palm Beach Gardens, FL 33418-3401, USA

Van Horne, Keith (Athlete, Football Player)
c/o Staff Member *Dallas Mavericks*
1333 N Stemmons Fwy Ste 105
Dallas, TX 75207-3722, USA

Van Houten, Carice (Actor)
c/o Kat Gosling *Troika*
10A Christina St.
London EC2A 4PA, UNITED KINGDOM

Van Impe, Ed (Athlete, Hockey Player)
Philadelphia Flyers Alumni Association
137 W 5th Ave Apt B9
Conshohocken, PA 19428-1646, USA

van Johnson, Rodney (Actor)
Passions

Van Kempen, Simon (Reality Star)
c/o Staff Member *Bravo TV (NY)*
30 Rockefeller Plz
New York, NY 10112-0015, USA

Van Keulen, Isabelle (Musician)
c/o Staff Member *Columbia Artists Mgmt Inc*
1790 Broadway Fl 6
New York, NY 10019-1537, USA

Van Landingham, William (Athlete, Baseball Player)
3023 Old Hillsboro Rd
Franklin, TN 37064-9544, USA

van Munster, Bertram (Producer)
c/o Staff Member *Earthview Inc*
200 Continental Blvd Fl 2
El Segundo, CA 90245-4510, USA

Vann, Marc (Actor)

Van Ness, Jonathan (Television Host)
c/o Jordyn Palos *Persona Public Relations*
6255 W Sunset Blvd Ste 705
Hollywood, CA 90028-7408, USA

van Nistelrooy, Ruud (Athlete, Soccer Player)
c/o Staff Member *Manchester United PLC*
Sir Matt Busby Way
Old Trafford
Manchester M160RA, UNITED KINGDOM

Van Note, Jeff (Athlete, Football Player)
345 Hollyberry Dr
Roswell, GA 30076-1215, USA

Van Noy, Kyle (Athlete, Football Player)
c/o David Dunn *Athletes First*
23091 Mill Creek Dr
Laguna Hills, CA 92653-1258, USA

Van Ornum, John (Athlete, Baseball Player)
PO Box 26808
Fresno, CA 93729-6808, USA

Vanous, Lucky (Actor, Model)
28345 La Calenta Mission
Vlejo, CA 92692, USA

Vanover, Larry (Athlete, Baseball Player)
3037 Sterling Ct
Owensboro, KY 42303-6393, USA

Vanover, Larry (Baseball Player)
801 Glenn Ct
Owensboro, KY 42303-0520, USA

Vanover, Tamarick (Athlete, Football Player)
703 NW Wilson St
Lake City, FL 32055-1863, USA

Vanoy, Vern (Athlete, Football Player)
3710 E 51st St Apt 409
Kansas City, MO 64130-3061, USA

Van Patten, Grace (Actor)
c/o Carrie Gordon *The Lede Company*
401 Broadway Ste 206
New York, NY 10013-3033, USA

Van Patten, Tim (Actor, Director, Producer, Writer)
c/o Chris Simonian *Creative Artists Agency (CAA)*
2000 Avenue of the Stars Ste 100
Los Angeles, CA 90067-4705, USA

Van Patten, Vincent (Actor)
13926 Magnolia Blvd
Sherman Oaks, CA 91423-1230, USA

Van Peebles, Mario (Actor, Director, Producer)
c/o Matt Luber *Luber Roklin Management*
5815 W Sunset Blvd Ste 208
Los Angeles, CA 90028-6481, USA

Van Peebles, Melvin (Writer)
10 Timber Trl
Rye, NY 10580-1935, USA

Van Pelt, Alex (Athlete, Football Player)
7209 Quaker Rd
Orchard Park, NY 14127-2008, USA

Van Pelt, Bo (Athlete, Golfer)
c/o Jim Lehrman *Medalist Management Inc*
36855 W Main St Ste 200
Purcellville, VA 20132-3561, USA

Van Pelt, Erika (Musician)
c/o Staff Member *19 Entertainment*
401 Wilshire Blvd Ste 1070
Santa Monica, CA 90401-1428, USA

Van Pelt, Scott (Sportscaster)
c/o Staff Member *ESPN (Main)*
935 Middle St
Espn Plaza
Bristol, CT 06010-1000, USA

Van Poppel, Todd (Athlete, Baseball Player)
340 Springfield Bnd
Argyle, TX 76226-6848, USA

Van Praagh, James (Actor, Producer, Writer)
Spiritual Horizons
PO Box 60517
Pasadena, CA 91116-6517, USA

Van Raaphorst, Dick (Athlete, Football Player)
720 Devon Ct
San Diego, CA 92109-8005, USA

Van Raschke, Baron (Athlete, Wrestler)
4600 Lacosta Dr
Albany, GA 31721-9475, USA

Van Riemsdyk, James (Athlete, Hockey Player)
54 Foxwood Run
Middletown, NJ 07748-2428, USA

Van Ryn, Ben (Athlete, Baseball Player)
8911 Saddle Trl Unit 1
San Antonio, TX 78255-2372, USA

Van Ryn, Mike (Athlete, Hockey Player)
Houston Aeros
5300 Memorial Dr
Houston, TX 77007-8200

Van Ryn, Mike (Athlete, Hockey Player)
17681 SW 54th St
Southwest Ranches, FL 33331-2308

Van Sant, Doug G (Director)
c/o Gabrielle (Gaby) Morgerman
WME/IMG
9601 Wilshire Blvd
Beverly Hills, CA 90210-5213, USA

Van Sant, Gus (Actor, Director, Producer, Writer)
c/o Gabrielle (Gaby) Morgerman
WME/IMG
9601 Wilshire Blvd
Beverly Hills, CA 90210-5213, USA

VanSanten, Shantel (Actor)
c/o Mia Hansen *Portrait PR*
5320 Sylmar Ave
Sherman Oaks, CA 91401-5612, USA

Van Sant-Machado, Helene (Baseball Player)
1221 Marion Ave
San Bernardino, CA 92407-1217, USA

Van Slyke, Andy (Athlete, Baseball Player)
710 S Price Rd
Saint Louis, MO 63124-1867, USA

Van Susteren, Greta (Television Host)
c/o Staff Member *Fox News*
1211 Avenue of the Americas Lowr C1
New York, NY 10036-8705, USA

Van Valkenberg, Pete (Athlete, Football Player)
3072 Ninebark Cir
Saint George, UT 84790-8226, USA

Van Valkenburgh, Deborah (Actor)
c/o Beth Stein *Beth Stein and Associates*
925 N La Brea Ave # 4
West Hollywood, CA 90038-2321, USA

Van Varenberg, Kristopher (Actor)
c/o Jack Gilardi *ICM Partners*
10250 Constellation Blvd Fl 7
Los Angeles, CA 90067-6207, USA

Van Vleet, Michael (Athlete, Baseball Player)
3995 Hollow Wood Dr
Portage, MI 49024-2005, USA

Van Vleet, Michael (Baseball Player)
118 Dreamfield Dr
Battle Creek, MI 49014-7846, USA

Van Wageningen, Yorick (Actor)
c/o Liz Nelson *Conway van Gelder Grant*
8-12 Broadwick St
London W1F 8HW, UNITED KINGDOM

Van Wagner, James (Athlete, Football Player)
5246 N Royal Dr
Traverse City, MI 49684-6984, USA

Van Wieren, Pete (Athlete, Baseball Player)
12260 Magnolia Cir
Alpharetta, GA 30005-7234, USA

Van Winkle, Travis (Actor)
c/o Scott Fish *Velocity Entertainment Partners*
5455 Wilshire Blvd Ste 1502
Los Angeles, CA 90036-4204, USA

Van Wormer, Steve (Actor)
c/o Staff Member *Innovative Artists*
1505 10th St
Santa Monica, CA 90401-2805, USA

Van Zandt, Caitlin (Actor)
Persona Management
40 E 9th St Apt 11J
New York, NY 10003-6426, USA

Van Zandt, Steven (Actor)
c/o Staff Member *Renegade Nation Holdings*
434 6th Ave Fl 6
New York, NY 10011-8411, USA

Van Zant, Donnie (Musician)
c/o Staff Member *Vector Management*
PO Box 120479
Nashville, TN 37212-0479, USA

Vanzant, Iyanla (Television Host, Writer)
Inner Visions Institute for Spiritual Development
PO Box 8517
Silver Spring, MD 20907-8517, USA

VanZant, Paige (Athlete)
c/o Liza Anderson *Anderson Group Public Relations*
8060 Melrose Ave Fl 4
Los Angeles, CA 90046-7038, USA

Van Zeeland, Kathy (Designer)
77 Beverly Park Ln
Beverly Hills, CA 90210-1571, USA

Varada, Vaclav (Athlete, Hockey Player)
9042 Stonebriar Dr.
Clarence Center, NY 14032

Varda, Agnes (Director)
Cine-Tamaris
86 Rue Daguerre
Paris 75014, FRANCE

Vardalos, Nia (Actor)
c/o Evan Hainey *Untitled Entertainment*
350 S Beverly Dr Ste 200
Beverly Hills, CA 90212-4819, USA

Vardell, Tommy (Athlete, Football Player)
2424 E Ruby Hill Dr
Pleasanton, CA 94566-5100, USA

Varela, Leonor (Actor)
c/o Adam Griffin *LINK Entertainment*
11872 La Grange Ave
Los Angeles, CA 90025-5282, USA

Varela, Matias (Actor)
c/o Jenny Planthaber *Agentfirman Planthaber/Kilden*
Drottninggatan 112
Stockholm 11360, SWEDEN

Varga, Imre (Artist)
Bartha Utca 1
Budapest XII, HUNGARY

Vargas, Elizabeth (Television Host)
c/o Alan Berger *Creative Artists Agency (CAA)*
2000 Avenue of the Stars Ste 100
Los Angeles, CA 90067-4705, USA

Vargas, Jacob (Actor)
c/o Ben Feigin *Anonymous Content*
3532 Hayden Ave
Culver City, CA 90232-2413, USA

Vargas, Jason (Athlete, Baseball Player)
14775 Keota Ln
Apple Valley, CA 92307-5137, USA

Vargas, Jose Antonio (Director, Journalist, Producer)
c/o Staff Member *United Talent Agency (UTA)*
9336 Civic Center Dr
Beverly Hills, CA 90210-3604, USA

Vargas, Valentina (Actor)
5 Rue Norvins
Paris 75018, FRANCE

Vargo, Ed (Athlete, Baseball Player)
J15 Forest Hts
Butler, PA 16001-3910, USA

Vargo, Larry (Athlete, Football Player)
23337 S Colonial Ct
Saint Clair Shores, MI 48080-2605, USA

Vargo, Tim (Business Person)
AutoZone Inc
123 S Front St
Memphis, TN 38103-3618, USA

Varitek, Jason (Athlete, Baseball Player)
c/o Scott Boras *Boras Corporation*
18 Corporate Plaza Dr
Newport Beach, CA 92660-7901, USA

Varkonyi, Robert (Misc)
6 Willow Ln
Great Neck, NY 11023-1139, USA

Varlamov, Sergei (Athlete, Hockey Player)
213 Germain St
Saint John, NB E2L 2G5, Canada

Varma, Indira (Actor)
c/o Tammy Rosen *Sanders Armstrong Caserta*
4111 W Alameda Ave Ste 505
Burbank, CA 91505-4163, USA

Varnado, Victor (Actor, Comedian)
c/o Staff Member *The Luedtke Agency*
4528 21st St # 2
Long Island City, NY 11101-5247, USA

Varney, Pete (Athlete, Baseball Player)
14 Juniper Ridge Rd
Acton, MA 01720-2213, USA

Varo, Marton (Artist)
Phillips Gallery
PO Box 5807
Carmel, CA 93921-5807, USA

Varone, Phil (Musician)
c/o Barbara Papageorge *Barbara Papageorge PR*
790 Amsterdam Ave Apt 4E
New York, NY 10025-5710, USA

Varoni, Miguel (Actor)

Varrichione, Frank (Athlete, Football Player)
300 W Farm Pond Rd Apt 335
Framingham, MA 01702-6251, USA

Varrichone, Frank (Athlete, Football Player)
RR 72 Box 319
Alton, NJ 03809, USA

Varsho, Gary (Athlete, Baseball Player, Coach)
11921 Starr Rd
Chili, WI 54420-9502, USA

Vartan, Michael (Actor)
c/o Nancy Iannios *Core Public PR*
1875 Century Park E Ste 930
Los Angeles, CA 90067-2540, USA

Vartan, Sylvie (Musician)
Scotti
706 N Beverly Dr
Beverly Hills, CA 90210-3322, USA

Varty, Keith (Designer, Fashion Designer)
Bosco di San Francesco #6
Sirolo, ITALY

Varvatos, John (Designer, Fashion Designer)
John Varvatos
315 Bowery Frnt 2
New York, NY 10003-7151, USA

Vasary, Tamas (Musician)
9 Village Road
London N3, UNITED KINGDOM (UK)

Vasile, Radu (Prime Minister)
Premier's Office
Piata Vicotriel 1
Bucharest 71201, ROMANIA

Vaske, Dennis (Athlete, Hockey Player)
9236 Dunmore Dr
Orland Park, IL 60462-1152

Vasquez, Junior (DJ, Musician)
Junior Vasquez Music
647 9th Ave
New York, NY 10036-3661, USA

Vasquez, Randy (Actor)
c/o Jasmin Espada *Espada PR*
925 N La Brea Ave Ste 14118
West Hollywood, CA 90038-2321, USA

Vasquez, Valerie (Adult Film Star)
c/o Liza Anderson *Anderson Group Public Relations*
8060 Melrose Ave Fl 4
Los Angeles, CA 90046-7038, USA

Vasquez, Virgil (Athlete, Baseball Player)
32 Saint Francis Way
Santa Barbara, CA 93105-2552, USA

Vass, Zita (Actor)
c/o Kim Matuka *Schuller Talent (LA)*
332 S Beverly Dr Ste 100
Beverly Hills, CA 90212-4812, USA

Vasser, Jimmy (Race Car Driver)
8605 Robinson Ridge Dr
Las Vegas, NV 89117-5807, USA

Vassey, Liz (Actor)
c/o Andy Cohen *Grade A Entertainment*
149 S Barrington Ave # 719
Los Angeles, CA 90049-3310, USA

Vassilieva, Sofia (Actor)
c/o Jason Trawick *WME|IMG*
9601 Wilshire Blvd
Beverly Hills, CA 90210-5213, USA

Vassillou, George V (President)
PO Box 874
21 Academiou Ave
Aglandjia, Nicosia, CYPRUS

Vasys, Arunas (Athlete, Football Player)
2525 Hanford Ln
Aurora, IL 60502-6971, USA

Vatcher, Jim (Athlete, Baseball Player)
16039 Northfield St
Pacific Palisades, CA 90272-4261, USA

Vatterott, Charles (Athlete, Football Player)
3708 W Pine Orchard Dr
Pearland, TX 77581-8814, USA

Vaughan, Charlie (Athlete, Baseball Player)
5717 Brazilwood Ct
Harlingen, TX 78552-2027, USA

Vaughan, Denis E (Musician)
c/o Staff Member *Schofer/Gold Agency*
51 Riverside Dr
New York, NY 10024, USA

Vaughan, Dustin (Athlete, Football Player)

Vaughan, Greg (Actor)
c/o Katie Mason Stern *Luber Roklin Management*
5815 W Sunset Blvd Ste 208
Los Angeles, CA 90028-6481, USA

Vaughan, Jimmie (Musician)
c/o Cory L Moore *The Luther Wolf Agency*
PO Box 162078
Austin, TX 78716-2078, USA

Vaughan, Stoll (Musician)
c/o Staff Member *Paradigm (Monterey)*
404 W Franklin St
Monterey, CA 93940-2303, USA

Vaughn, Bruce (Golfer)
5615 N Monroe St
Hutchinson, KS 67502-3251, USA

Vaughn, Cassius (Athlete, Football Player)

Vaughn, Charles (Athlete, Basketball Player)
PO Box 95
Cairo, IL 62914-0095, USA

Vaughn, Countess (Actor)
c/o Staff Member *Amsel, Eisenstadt & Frazier Talent Agency (AEF)*
5055 Wilshire Blvd Ste 860
Los Angeles, CA 90036-6108, USA

Vaughn, Damian (Athlete, Football Player)
423 Danvers Ct
Orrville, OH 44667-9579, USA

Vaughn, David (Basketball Player)
New Jersey Nets
390 Murray Hill Pkwy
East Rutherford, NJ 07073-2109, USA

Vaughn, Dewayne (Athlete, Baseball Player)
5501 NW 37th St
Warr Acres, OK 73122-2210, USA

Vaughn, Gregory L (Greg) (Athlete, Baseball Player)
10830 Sheldon Woods Way
Elk Grove, CA 95624-9630, USA

Vaughn, Jacque (Athlete, Basketball Player)
c/o Jeff Austin *Octagon Home Office*
7950 Jones Branch Dr # 700N
Mc Lean, VA 22107-0002, USA

Vaughn, Jimmie (Musician)
Mark I Mgmt
PO Box 29480
Austin, TX 78755-6480, USA

Vaughn, John H (Johnny) (Athlete, Coach, Football Player)
Highway 6 W
Oxford, MS 38655, USA

Vaughn, Jonathan S (Jon) (Athlete, Football Player)
224 N Highway 67 St
Florissant, MO 63031-5904, USA

Vaughn, Linda (Race Car Driver)
PO Box 352
Newville, PA 17241-0352, USA

Vaughn, Matthew (Actor, Director)
c/o Naren Desai *Brillstein Entertainment Partners*
9150 Wilshire Blvd Ste 350
Beverly Hills, CA 90212-3453, USA

Vaughn, Maurice (Mo) (Athlete, Baseball Player)
Omni New York LLC 1 Dag
Hammarskjold Plz Bsmt C
Newyork, NY 10017-2201, USA

Vaughn, Ned (Actor)
James/Levy/Jacobson
3500 W Olive Ave Ste 920
Burbank, CA 91505-5514, USA

Vaughn, Terri J (Actor)
c/o Sandra Siegal *Siegal Company, The*
9025 Wilshire Blvd Ste 400
Beverly Hills, CA 90211-1828, USA

Vaughn, Thomas R (Athlete, Football Player)
860 E Linda Ln
Gilbert, AZ 85234-5969, USA

Vaughn, Vince (Actor)
c/o Alan Nierob *Rogers & Cowan*
1840 Century Park E Fl 18
Los Angeles, CA 90067-2101, USA

Vaught, Loy (Athlete, Basketball Player)
1289 Perkins Ave NE
Grand Rapids, MI 49505-5625, USA

Vaugier, Emmanuelle (Actor)
c/o Murray Gibson *Red Management*
415 Esplanade W Box 3
North Vancouver, BC V7M 1A6, CANADA

Vavra, Joe (Athlete, Baseball Player)
E4640 483rd Ave
Menomonie, WI 54751-5481, USA

Vayda, Brandon Michael (Actor)
c/o Molly Fenton *Cohen & Gardner*
345 N Maple Dr Ste 181
Beverly Hills, CA 90210-5185, USA

Vaydik, Greg (Athlete, Hockey Player)
3211 Wessex Cir
Richardson, TX 75082-3113

Vaynerchuk, Gary (Business Person, Writer)
c/o Staff Member *Vaynermedia*
586 Morris Ave
Springfield, NJ 07081-1017, USA

Vayntrub, Milana (Actor)
c/o Lewis Kay *Kovert Creative*
506 Santa Monica Blvd Ste 400
Santa Monica, CA 90401-2412, USA

Vaziri, Khosrow (Wrestler)
c/o Eric Simms *ESS Promotions*
PO Box 52
Marlboro, NJ 07746-0052, USA

Vazquez, Armondo (Baseball Player)
Indianapolis Clowns
160 W 85th St Apt 1K
New York, NY 10024-4410, USA

Vazquez, Javier (Athlete, Baseball Player)
1441 S Prairie Ave
Chicago, IL 60605-2886, USA

Vazquez, LaLa (Actor)
c/o Shannon Barr *Rogers & Cowan*
1840 Century Park E Fl 18
Los Angeles, CA 90067-2101, USA

Vazquez, Yul (Actor)
c/o Jamie Harhay Skinner *Baker Winokur Ryder Public Relations*
9100 Wilshire Blvd
W Tower #500
Beverly Hills, CA 90212-3415, USA

Veal, Coot (Athlete, Baseball Player)
238 Stonegables Dr
Gray, GA 31032-5526, USA

Veal, Donnie (Athlete, Baseball Player)
2721 E Daniel Dr
Gilbert, AZ 85298-0572, USA

Veale, Robert A (Bob) (Athlete, Baseball Player)
2833 Bush Blvd
Birmingham, AL 35208-2227, USA

Veals, Elton (Athlete, Football Player)
2981 Joyce Dr
Baton Rouge, LA 70814-2568, USA

Vedder, Eddie (Musician)
7999 44th Ave SW
Seattle, WA 98136-2200, USA

Vega, Alexa (Actor, Musician)
c/o John Carrabino *John Carrabino Management*
5900 Wilshire Blvd Ste 740
Los Angeles, CA 90036-5032, USA

Vega, Makenzie (Actor)
c/o Ro Diamond *SDB Partners Inc*
315 S Beverly Dr Ste 411
Beverly Hills, CA 90212-4301, USA

Vega, Paz (Actor)
c/o Orson Salazar *Pro Aicos*
Cardena Marcelo Espinola
Madrid 28016, SPAIN

Vega, Suzanne (Musician)
c/o Staff Member *WME/IMG (NY)*
11 Madison Ave Fl 18
New York, NY 10010-3669, USA

Vega 4 (Music Group)
c/o Staff Member *Paradigm (Monterey)*
404 W Franklin St
Monterey, CA 93940-2303, USA

Vegas, Dirty (Music Group)
c/o Staff Member *Creative Artists Agency (CAA)*
2000 Avenue of the Stars Ste 100
Los Angeles, CA 90067-4705, USA

Vegas, Johnny (Actor)
c/o Nick Forgacs *Independent Talent Group*
40 Whitfield St
London W1T 2RH, UNITED KINGDOM

Veils, The (Music Group)
c/o Staff Member *Paradigm (Monterey)*
404 W Franklin St
Monterey, CA 93940-2303, USA

Veingrad, Alan (Athlete, Football Player)
614 SE 26th Ave
Fort Lauderdale, FL 33301-2708, USA

Veisor, Mike (Athlete, Hockey Player)
16091 W Lakepoint Ct
Prairieville, LA 70769-4980

Veitch, Darren (Athlete, Hockey Player)
11645 Aspen View Dr
San Diego, CA 92128-5274

Vejar, Chico (Boxer)
56 Glenbrook Road
#3214
Stamford, CT 06902, USA

Velaquez, Nydia M. (Congressman, Politician)
266 Broadway Ste 201
Brooklyn, NY 11211-6306, USA

Velarde, Randy (Athlete, Baseball Player)
4902 Thames Ct
Midland, TX 79705-1796, USA

Velasco, Fernando (Athlete, Football Player)

Velasquez, Cain (Athlete)
c/o Bob Cook *Zinkin Entertainment & Sports Management*
5 E River Park Pl W Ste 203
Fresno, CA 93720-1557, USA

Velasquez, Guillermo (Athlete, Baseball Player)
13842 Clear Trail Ln
Houston, TX 77034-2158, USA

Velasquez, Jaci (Musician)
Jaci Inc
PO Box 3568
Brentwood, TN 37024-3568, USA

Velasquez, Patricia (Actor, Model)
c/o Staff Member *Principal Entertainment*
9255 W Sunset Blvd Ste 500
Los Angeles, CA 90069-3301, USA

Velasquez, Regine (Actor)
c/o Marissa Nilon *Wasserman Media Group*
10960 Wilshire Blvd Ste 1200
Los Angeles, CA 90024-3714, USA

Velazquez, Freddie (Athlete, Baseball Player)
Jose Amado Soler No. 70
Santo Domingo, Dominican Republic

Velazquez, Freddie (Athlete, Baseball Player)
Dominican Republic
Jose Amado Soler No. 70
Santo Domingo, USA

Velazquez, Gil (Athlete, Baseball Player)
9424 Wakashan Ave
Las Vegas, NV 89149-0501, USA

Velazquez, Jamila (Actor, Musician)
c/o Bryan Brucks *Luber Roklin Management*
5815 W Sunset Blvd Ste 208
Los Angeles, CA 90028-6481, USA

Velazquez, John (Horse Racer)
133 Avon Pl
West Hempstead, NY 11552-1703, USA

Velazquez, Nadine (Actor, Model)
c/o Patricia Mora *Metro Public Relations*
8671 Wilshire Blvd # 208
Beverly Hills, CA 90211-2926, USA

Veldheer, Jared (Athlete, Football Player)

Velez, Eddie (Actor)
c/o Staff Member *Artists & Representatives (Stone Manners Salners)*
6100 Wilshire Blvd Ste 1500
Los Angeles, CA 90048-5110, USA

Velez, Fermin (Race Car Driver)
701 S Girls School Rd
Indianapolis, IN 46231-3132, USA

Velez, Gloria (Model)
c/o Mike Esterman *Esterman.Com, LLC*
Prefers to be contacted via email
Baltimore, MD XXXXX, USA

Velez, Lauren (Actor)
c/o Tina Thor *TMT Entertainment Group*
648 Broadway # 1002
New York, NY 10012-2348, USA

Velez, Lisa Lisa (Musician)
c/o JD Sobol *Almond Talent Management*
8217 Beverly Blvd Ste 8
W Hollywood, CA 90048-4534, USA

Velez, Luna Lauren (Actor)
c/o Estelle Lasher *Lasher Group*
1133 Avenue of the Americas Fl 27
New York, NY 10036-6710, USA

Velez, Otto (Baseball Player)
33 Villas de Cambalache
Rio Grande, PR 00966, USA

Velez-Mitchell, Jane (Actor, Correspondent)
c/o Staff Member *CNN (NY)*
10 Columbus Cir
Time Warner Center
New York, NY 10019-1158, USA

Velischek, Randy (Athlete, Hockey Player)
126 Ch du Lac Quenouville
Vai-Des-Lacs, QC JOT 2PO, Canada

VelJohnson, Reginald (Actor)
c/o Lori DeWaal *Lori DeWaal & Associates PR*
14724 Ventura Blvd Ste 507
Sherman Oaks, CA 91403-3515, USA

Vella, John (Athlete, Football Player)
1890 Saint George Rd
Danville, CA 94526-6253, USA

Vellano, Joe (Athlete, Football Player)

Vellucci, Mike (Athlete, Hockey Player)
17302 Cameron Dr
Northville, MI 48168-3212

Veloso, Caetano (Musician, Songwriter, Writer)
Natasha Records/Shows
Rua Marquis Sao Vincente
Rio de Janiero, BRAZIL

Velvet Revolver (Music Group)
c/o Carl Stubner *Sanctuary Music Management*
15301 Arizona Ave
Bldg B #400
Santa Monica, CA 91403, USA

Vemtrone, Raymond (Athlete, Hockey Player)
c/o Staff Member *Boston Bruins*
100 Legends Way Ste 250
Td Banknorth Garden
Boston, MA 02114-1389, USA

Venable, Mac (Athlete, Baseball Player)
4364 S Stargazer Pl
Boise, ID 83716-6652, USA

Venable, Max (Athlete, Baseball Player, Coach)
4364 S Stargazer Pl
Boise, ID 83716-6652, USA

Venable, Will (Athlete, Baseball Player)
4364 S Stargazer Pl
Boise, ID 83716-6652, USA

Venables, Terry F (Coach, Football Coach)
Terry Venables Holdings
213 Putney Bridge Road
London SW15 2NY, UNITED KINGDOM (UK)

Venafro, Mike (Athlete, Baseball Player)
15151 Whimbrel Ct
Fort Myers, FL 33908-8107, USA

Venasky, Vic (Athlete, Hockey Player)
4307 W 234th Pl # Pi
Torrance, CA 90505-4506

Vendt, Erik (Athlete, Olympic Athlete, Swimmer)
17 Amberwood Ct
Buzzards Bay, MA 02532-8324, USA

Veneruzzo, Gary (Athlete, Hockey Player)
185 Fans Haw St
Thunder Bay, ON P7C 5T7, Canada

Venet, Bernar (Artist)
533 Canal St
New York, NY 10013-1328, USA

Veneziale, Mike (Baseball Player)
110 Cloverdale Ln
Williamstown, NJ 08094-2341, USA

Vengerov, Maxim (Musician)
Lies Askonas
6 Henrietta St
London WC2E 8LA, UNITED KINGDOM (UK)

Venita, Carla (Musician)
3087 James Rd
Memphis, TN 38128-2921, USA

Venitucci, Michele (Actor)
Carol Levi Co
Vla Giuseppe Pisanelli
Rome 00196, ITALY

Venora, Diane (Actor)
c/o Pamela Wagner *Wagner Talent*
4526 Wilshire Blvd
Los Angeles, CA 90010-3801, USA

Ventimiglia, John (Actor)
c/o Stacy Abrams *Abrams Entertainment*
5225 Wilshire Blvd Ste 515
Los Angeles, CA 90036-4349, USA

Ventimiglia, Milo (Actor)
c/o Staff Member *Divide Pictures*
710 N El Centro Ave Fl 4
Los Angeles, CA 90038-4341, USA

Ventimilia, Jeffrey (Actor)
c/o Staff Member *ICM Partners*
10250 Constellation Blvd Fl 7
Los Angeles, CA 90067-6207, USA

Vento, Mike (Athlete, Baseball Player)
7142 Kendall Heath Way
Land O Lakes, FL 34637-7554, USA

Ventresca, Vincent (Actor)
Mindel/Donigan
9057 Nemo St # C
West Hollywood, CA 90069-5511, USA

Ventrone, Raymond (Athlete, Football Player)
c/o Staff Member *New England Patriots*
1 Patriot Pl
Foxboro, MA 02035-1388, USA

Ventura, Jesse (Athlete, Politician, Talk Show Host, Wrestler)
100 Apple Orchard Rd
Saint Paul, MN 55110-1241, USA

Ventura, Robin (Athlete, Baseball Player)
1088 Newsom Springs Rd
Arroyo Grande, CA 93420-3618, USA

Ventura, Robin M (Baseball Player)
106 Dingletown Rd
Greenwich, CT 06830-3540, USA

Venturella, Michelle (Athlete, Olympic Athlete, Softball Player)
219 Carver Hawkeye Arena
Iowa University Softball
Iowa City, IA 52242-1020, USA

Ventures, The (Music Group)
11761 E Speedway Blvd
Tucson, AZ 85748-2017, USA

Venturi, Rick (Athlete, Football Coach, Football Player)
1935 Sumter Ridge Ct
Chesterfield, MO 63017-8733, USA

Venturini, Bill (Race Car Driver)
7621 Texas Trl
Boca Raton, FL 33487-1423, USA

Venturini, Tisha (Athlete, Olympic Athlete, Soccer Player)
7101 Del Rio Dr
Modesto, CA 95356-9643, USA

Venus Hum (Music Group)
c/o Staff Member *Paradigm (Monterey)*
404 W Franklin St
Monterey, CA 93940-2303, USA

Vera, Audry (Actor)
c/o Staff Member *Televisa*
Blvd Adolfo Lopez Mateos 232
Colonia San Angel INN
DF CP 01060, MEXICO

Vera, Billy (Musician)
8730 W Sunset Blvd # Ph-W
W Hollywood, CA 90069-2210, USA

Veras, Quilvio (Athlete, Baseball Player)
7522 Wiles Rd Ste 206
Coral Springs, FL 33067-2056, USA

Verastegui, Eduardo (Producer)
c/o Staff Member *Rain Management Group*
11162 La Grange Ave
Los Angeles, CA 90025-5632, USA

Verba, Ross (Athlete, Football Player)
3066 Arden Pl
Saint Paul, MN 55129-5211, USA

Verbanic, Joe (Athlete, Baseball Player)
9722 Groffs Mill Dr
Mill Dr Ste 107
Owings Mills, MD 21117-6341, USA

Verbeek, Lotte (Actor)
c/o Lindsay Galin *Rogers & Cowan*
909 3rd Ave Fl 9
New York, NY 10022-4752, USA

Verbeek, Pat (Athlete, Hockey Player)
Tampa Bay Lightning
401 Channelside Dr
Tampa, FL 33602-5400

Verbeek, Pat (Athlete, Hockey Player)
Verbeek Farm RR 1
Wyoming, ON N0N 1T0, Canada

Verbinski, Gore (Director, Producer)
c/o Dave Morrison *Anonymous Content*
3532 Hayden Ave
Culver City, CA 90232-2413, USA

Verble, Gene (Athlete, Baseball Player)
1144 Asheford Green Ave NW
Concord, NC 28027-8185, USA

Verboom, Hanna (Actor)
c/o Greg Siegel *WME/IMG*
9601 Wilshire Blvd
Beverly Hills, CA 90210-5213, USA

Verchere, Graham (Actor)
c/o Melanie Turner *Pacific Artists Management*
112 3rd Ave E Suite 210
Vancouver, BC V5T 1C8, CANADA

Verchota, Phil (Athlete, Hockey Player, Olympic Athlete)
PO Box 1181
Bemidji, MN 56619-1181, USA

Verdi, Robert (Television Host)
c/o Jeff Googel *WME/IMG (NY)*
11 Madison Ave Fl 18
New York, NY 10010-3669, USA

Verdin, Clarence (Athlete, Football Player)
6221 Eastover Dr
New Orleans, LA 70128-3619, USA

Vereen, Ben (Actor, Dancer, Musician)
c/o Pamela Cooper *Cooper Company*
1185 Avenue Of The Americas Fl 3
New York, NY 10036-2600, USA

Vereen, Brock (Athlete, Football Player)

Vereen, Carl (Athlete, Football Player)
140 Connemara Rd
Roswell, GA 30075-4883, USA

Vereen, Shane (Athlete, Football Player)
c/o David Dunn *Athletes First*
23091 Mill Creek Dr
Laguna Hills, CA 92653-1258, USA

Veres, Dave (Athlete, Baseball Player)
12361 Montano Ct
Castle Pines, CO 80108-8131, USA

Veres, Randy (Athlete, Baseball Player)
10010 W Spur Dr
Peoria, AZ 85383-5398, USA

Vergara, Sandra (Actor)
c/o David (Dave) Fleming *Atlas Artists*
9220 W Sunset Blvd Ste 225
Los Angeles, CA 90069-3513, USA

Vergara, Sofia (Actor)
c/o Luis Balaguer *Latin World Entertainment (LA)*
9777 Wilshire Blvd Ste 915
Beverly Hills, CA 90212-1902, USA

Verhoeven, John (Athlete, Baseball Player)
20805 Paseo De La Rambla
Yorba Linda, CA 92887-2429, USA

Verhoeven, Paul (Director, Writer)
14980 Camarosa Dr
Pacific Palisades, CA 90272-4427, USA

Verhoeven, Peter (Athlete, Basketball Player)
12722 Fargo Ave
Hanford, CA 93230-9645, USA

Verica, Tom (Actor)

Veris, Garin (Athlete, Football Player)
23 Nichols Ave
Newmarket, NH 03857-1207, USA

Verlander, Justin (Athlete, Baseball Player)
1238 Hawkwell Dr
Maidens, VA 23102-2240, USA

Vermeil, Dick (Athlete, Coach, Football Coach, Football Player)
775 Fairview Rd
Coatesville, PA 19320-4453, USA

Vermette, Antoine (Athlete, Hockey Player)
2475 Sherwin Rd
Columbus, OH 43221-3621

Vermette, Mark (Athlete, Hockey Player)
235 Hammell Road
Red Lake, ON POV 2MO, Canada

Vermilyea, Jamie (Athlete, Baseball Player)
7051 E Calle Arandas
Tucson, AZ 85750-2563, USA

Vernarsky, Kris (Athlete, Hockey Player)
24323 Tallman Ave
Warren, MI 48089-1847, USA

Verner, Alterraun (Athlete, Football Player)
c/o Mark Bartelstein *Priority Sports & Entertainment (Chicago)*
325 N La Salle Dr Ste 650
Chicago, IL 60654-8182, USA

Vernon, Conrad (Actor)
c/o Ilan Breil *Mosaic Media Group*
407 N Maple Dr # 100
Beverly Hills, CA 90210-3818, USA

Vernon, Kate (Actor)
c/o Staff Member *Shelter Entertainment*
9255 W Sunset Blvd Ste 300
Los Angeles, CA 90069-3313, USA

Vernon, Olivier (Athlete, Football Player)
c/o Drew Rosenhaus *Rosenhaus Sports Representation*
3921 Alton Rd # 440
Miami Beach, FL 33140-3852, USA

Veroni, Craig (Actor)
c/o Staff Member *Muse Artists Management*
401-207 Hastings St W
Vancouver, BC V6B 1H7, Canada

Verplank, Scott (Athlete, Golfer)
1850 W Waterloo Rd
Edmond, OK 73025-1801, USA

Verraros, Jim (Musician)
PO Box 99
West Dundee, IL 60118-0099

Verreos, Nick (Fashion Designer)
NIKOLAKI DESIGN
530 Molino St Ste 108
Los Angeles, CA 90013-2275, USA

Verret, Claude (Athlete, Hockey Player)
Ligue Majeure de Hockey Olympique CP
88218 Succ Vai-Belair
Quebec, QC G3J 1Y9, Canada

Verrett, Jason (Athlete, Football Player)
c/o Doug Hendrickson *Relativity Sports*
2029 Century Park E Ste 1550
Century City, CA 90067-3000, USA

Versace, Donatella (Designer, Fashion Designer)
Gianni Versace SPA
Via Manzoni 38
Milan 20121, ITALY

Versace, Jay (Internet Star)
c/o Stephanie Piza *Select Management Group*
6100 Wilshire Blvd Ste 400
Los Angeles, CA 90048-5109, USA

Verser, David (Athlete, Football Player)
2600 SW Arvonia Pl
Topeka, KS 66614-5294, USA

Verstappen, Jos (Race Car Driver)
Arrows Grand Prix
Leafield Tech. Centre
Oakland Pl. OX8 5PF, UNITED KINGDOM (UK)

Versteeg, Kris (Athlete, Hockey Player)
Thunder Creek Management
453-230 22nd St E
Attn David Kaye
Saskatoon, SK S7K 0E9, Canada

Vert, Lil Uzi (Musician)
c/o Sydney Margetson *Atlantic Records*
1290 Avenue of the Americas Fl 28
New York, NY 10104-0106, USA

Vertical Horizon (Music Group)
c/o Andrew Buck *Agency for the Performing Arts (APA)*
405 S Beverly Dr Ste 500
Beverly Hills, CA 90212-4425, USA

Veruca Salt (Music Group)
Veruca Salt/Louise Post
PO Box 291105
Los Angeles, CA 90029-9105, USA

Verveen, Arie (Actor)
c/o Scott Karp *The Syndicate*
10203 Santa Monica Blvd Fl 5
Los Angeles, CA 90067-6416, USA

Verve Pipe, The (Music Group)
c/o Staff Member *Paradigm (Monterey)*
404 W Franklin St
Monterey, CA 93940-2303, USA

Ververgaert, Dennis (Athlete, Hockey Player)
34484 Stoneleigh Ave
Abbotsford, BC V2S 8N5, Canada

Verve, The (Music Group)
c/o Marty Diamond *Paradigm*
140 Broadway Ste 2600
New York, NY 10005-1011, USA

Verwey, Bob (Golfer)
I M G
1360 E 9th St Ste 100
Cleveland, OH 44114-1730, USA

Vesey, Jim (Athlete, Hockey Player)
11 Ellwood St
Charlestown, MA 02129-3809

Vessey, Tricia (Actor)
c/o Staff Member *Brillstein Entertainment Partners*
9150 Wilshire Blvd Ste 350
Beverly Hills, CA 90212-3453, USA

Vest, Jake (Cartoonist)
PO Box 350757
Grand Island, FL 32735-0757, USA

Vest, R Lamar (Religious Leader)
Church of God
PO Box 2430
Cleveland, TN 37320-2430, USA

Veters, Michael (Race Car Driver)
Black Stallion Racing
17137 Black Stallion Ln
Hagerstown, MD 21740-1891, USA

Vetri, Victoria (Actor)
7045 Hawthorn Ave Apt 206
Los Angeles, CA 90028-6942, USA

Vette, Vicky (Actor, Adult Film Star, Model)
101-1565 Victoria Ave
Saint-Lambert, QC J4R 1R6, CANADA

Vettel, Sebastian (Race Car Driver)
Postfach 1479
Heppenheim D-64632, Germany

Vetter, Jack (Athlete, Football Player)
312 N Grand St
McPherson, KS 67460-4428, USA

Vettori, Ernst (Skier)
Fohrenweg 1
Absam, Eichat 06060, AUSTRIA

Vettrus, Richard J (Religious Leader)
Church of Lutheran Brethren
707 Crestview Dr
West Union, IA 52175-1004, USA

Veysey, Sid (Athlete, Hockey Player)
178 Ridgevale Dr
Bedford, NS B4A 3S7, Canada

V. Gutterrez, Luis (Congressman, Politician)
2266 Rayburn Hob
Washington, DC 20515-0308, USA

Viaene, David (Athlete, Football Player)
W9859 School Rd
Hortonville, WI 54944-9630, USA

Vial, Dennis (Athlete, Hockey Player)
Aqua Valley Water Co Ltd
6998 Highway 1 Unit 4
Coldbrook, NS B4R 1C5, Canada

Viall, Nick (Reality Star)
c/o Brooks Butterfield *PMK/BNC Public Relations*
1840 Century Park E Ste 1400
Los Angeles, CA 90067-2115, USA

Viardo, Vladimir V (Musician)
457 Piermont Rd
Cresskill, NJ 07626-1524, USA

Viciedo, Dayan (Athlete, Baseball Player)
1001 Brickell Bay Dr Fl 9
Miami, FL 33131-4937, USA

Vicius, Nicole (Actor)
c/o Mimi DiTrani *MGMT Entertainment (The Schiff Company)*
9220 W Sunset Blvd Ste 106
W Hollywood, CA 90069-3500, USA

Vick, Michael (Athlete, Football Player)
c/o Alan Morell *The Creative Management Agency: Creative Management Partners*
433 N Camden Dr Fl 6
Beverly Hills, CA 90210-4416, USA

Vick, Roger (Athlete, Football Player)
12919 Windfern Rd Apt 1902
Houston, TX 77064-3068, USA

Vickaryous, Scott (Actor)
c/o Staff Member *Artists Only Management*
10203 Santa Monica Blvd
Los Angeles, CA 90067-6405, USA

Vickers, Brian (Race Car Driver)
BLV Motorsports
42 High Tech Blvd
Thomasville, NC 27360-5560, USA

Vickers, Kipp (Athlete, Football Player)
3224 Acacia Dr
Indianapolis, IN 46214-1934, USA

Vickers, Steve (Athlete, Hockey Player)
238 Zokol Dr
Aurora, ON L4G 0C2, Canada

Vickers, Steve (Athlete, Hockey Player)
209 Washington Ave
Batavia, NY 14020-2211, USA

Vickerson, Kevin (Athlete, Football Player)
c/o Drew Rosenhaus *Rosenhaus Sports Representation*
3921 Alton Rd # 440
Miami Beach, FL 33140-3852, USA

Victorino, Shane (Athlete, Baseball Player)
1997 Alcova Ridlle Dr
Las Vegas, NV 89135-1551, USA

Victorin (Ursache), Archbishop (Religious Leader)
Romanian Orthodox Church
19959 Riopelle St
Detroit, MI 48203-1249, USA

Vida Blue (Music Group)
c/o Staff Member *Paradigm (Monterey)*
404 W Franklin St
Monterey, CA 93940-2303, USA

Vidal, Christina (Actor)
c/o Bob McGowan *McGowan Management*
170 S Beverly Dr Ste 304
Beverly Hills, CA 90212-3000, USA

Vidal, Deborah (Golfer)
2033 Paramount Dr
Los Angeles, CA 90068-3120, USA

Vidal, Jean-Pierre (Skier)
Ski Federation
50 Rue de Marquisats
BP 51
Annecy Cedex 74011, FRANCE

Vidal, Lisa (Actor)
c/o Dannielle Thomas *Untitled Entertainment*
350 S Beverly Dr Ste 200
Beverly Hills, CA 90212-4819, USA

Vidal, Ricardo J Cardinal (Religious Leader)
PO Box 52
Chancery
Ansonia, CT 06401-0052, PHILIPINES

Vidal, Rodrigo (Actor)
c/o Staff Member *Televisa*
Blvd Adolfo Lopez Mateos 232
Colonia San Angel INN
DF CP 01060, MEXICO

Vidali, Lynn (Swimmer)
14750 Mosegard Ln
Morgan Hill, CA 95037-9604, USA

Vidmar, Peter (Athlete, Gymnast, Olympic Athlete)
c/o Peter Carlisle *Octagon Olympics & Action Sports*
7 Ocean St Ste 2
South Portland, ME 04106-2800, USA

Vidrine, David M (Astronaut)
1796 E Mulberry
Prescott Vly, AZ 86314-2012, USA

Vidro, Jose (Athlete, Baseball Player)
PO Box 385
Sabana Grande, PR 00637-0385, USA

Vie, Richard C (Business Person)
PO Box 191
Lake Forest, IL 60045-0191, USA

Vieillard, Roger (Artist)
7 Rue de l'Estrapade
Paris 75005, FRANCE

Vieira, Meredith (Game Show Host, Television Host)
Meredith Vieira Productions
65 E 55th St Fl 12
New York, NY 10022-3429, USA

Vieira, Patrick (Athlete, Soccer Player)
Juventus FC
Corso Galileo Ferraris 32
Turin 10128, ITALY

Vieluf, Vince (Actor)
c/o Tammy Rosen *Sanders Armstrong Caserta*
4111 W Alameda Ave Ste 505
Burbank, CA 91505-4163, USA

Viener, John (Actor)
c/o Kevin Crotty *ICM Partners*
10250 Constellation Blvd Fl 7
Los Angeles, CA 90067-6207, USA

Viereck, Peter (Writer)
1346 Murrell Ave
Columbus, OH 43212-3558, USA

Vieth, Michelle (Actor)
c/o Staff Member *Televisa*
Blvd Adolfo Lopez Mateos 232
Colonia San Angel INN
DF CP 01060, MEXICO

View, The (Music Group)
c/o Staff Member *Paradigm (Monterey)*
404 W Franklin St
Monterey, CA 93940-2303, USA

Vieyra, Veronica (Actor)
c/o Staff Member *Telefe (Argentina)*
Pavon 2444
Buenos Aires C1248AAT, ARGENTINA

Vig, Butch (Musician)
c/o Staff Member *Borman Entertainment (TN)*
4322 Harding Pike Ste 429
Nashville, TN 37205-2661, USA

Vigman, Gillian (Actor)
c/o Jeanne Newman *Hansen, Jacobson, Teller, Hoberman, Newman, Warren & Richman*
450 N Roxbury Dr Fl 8
Beverly Hills, CA 90210-4222, USA

Vigneault, Alain (Athlete, Coach, Hockey Player)
800 Griffiths Way
Attn: Coaching Staff Vancouver Canucks
Vancouver, BC V6B 6G1, Canada

Vigneron, Thierry (Athlete, Track Athlete)
Adidas USA
5675 N Blackstock Rd
Spartanburg, SC 29303-6329, USA

Vigorito, Tommy (Athlete, Football Player)
20 Hilltop Ter
Wayne, NJ 07470-5808, USA

Vikander, Alicia (Actor)
Vikarious Productions
45 Conduit St
London W1S 2YN, UNITED KINGDOM

Vila, Bob (Actor, Producer, Television Host)
Vila Media LLC
PO Box 835
West Barnstable, MA 02668-0835, USA

Vila, Rosalia (Actor, Musician)
c/o Daniel Molina Torres *WME|IMG*
9601 Wilshire Blvd
Beverly Hills, CA 90210-5213, USA

Vilanch, Bruce (Comedian, Writer)
c/o Joan Hyler *Hyler Management*
20 Ocean Park Blvd Unit 25
Santa Monica, CA 90405-3590, USA

Vilanich, Bruce (Comedian)
c/o Staff Member *WME|IMG*
9601 Wilshire Blvd
Beverly Hills, CA 90210-5213, USA

Vilar, Tracy (Actor)
c/o Doug Wald *Anonymous Content*
3532 Hayden Ave
Culver City, CA 90232-2413, USA

Vilasuso, Jordi (Actor)
c/o Siri Garber *Platform PR*
2666 N Beachwood Dr
Los Angeles, CA 90068-2308, USA

Vilasuso, Jordie (Actor)
c/o Staff Member *Innovative Artists*
1505 10th St
Santa Monica, CA 90401-2805, USA

Vilgraln, Claude (Athlete, Hockey Player)
85 Douglasdale Cres SE
PLAYWORKS
Calgary, AB T2Z 3B3, Canada

Villa, Aston (Athlete, Soccer Player)
Aston Villa FC
Villa Park
Birmingham B6 6HE, UK

Villacis, Eduardo (Athlete, Baseball Player, Coach)
Casper Rockies
PO Box 1293
Attn: Coaching Staff
Casper, WY 82602-1293, USA

Villa-Cryan, Marge (Athlete, Baseball Player)
16305 Summershade Dr
La Mirada, CA 90638-2742, USA

Villafuerte, Brandon (Athlete, Baseball Player)
PO Box 188
North Bridgton, ME 04057-0188, USA

Villalobos, Sebastian (Internet Star)
c/o Staff Member *Latin World Entertainment (FL)*
3470 NW 82nd Ave Ste 670
Doral, FL 33122-1026, USA

Villalon, Jade Valerie (Musician)
c/o Staff Member *Universal Records*
825 8th Ave
New York, NY 10019-7416, USA

Villano, Mike (Baseball Player)
Bowman
1041 South Dr
Mt Pleasant, MI 48858-2856, USA

Villanueva, Carlos (Athlete)
c/o Staff Member *SFX Sports Management*
5335 Wisconsin Ave NW Ste 850
Washington, DC 20015-2052, USA

Villanueva, Charlie (Athlete, Basketball Player)
c/o Jeff Schwartz *Excel Sports Management*
1700 Broadway Fl 29
New York, NY 10019-6559, USA

Villanueva, Danny (Athlete, Football Player)
PO Box 258
Somis, CA 93066-0258, USA

Villapiano, Phillip J (Phil) (Athlete, Football Player)
21 Riverside Dr
Rumson, NJ 07760-1026, USA

Villaraigosa, Antonio (Politician)
City of Los Angeles
200 N Spring St Ste 303
Los Angeles, CA 90012-3239, USA

Villari, Guy (Musician)
293 Airport Rd
Liberty, NY 12754-2613, USA

Villarrial, Chris (Athlete, Football Player)
254 Hidden Meadow Ln
Ebensburg, PA 15931-7511, USA

Villasenor, Melissa (Actor, Comedian)
c/o Tatiana Senor *Primary Wave Entertainment*
10850 Wilshire Blvd Fl 6
Los Angeles, CA 90024-4319, USA

Villegas, Camilo (Athlete, Golfer)
c/o Staff Member *IMG Miami*
150 Alhambra Cir Ste 825
Coral Gables, FL 33134-4539, USA

Villemure, Gilles (Athlete, Hockey Player)
38 Grey Ln
Levittown, NY 11756-4498, USA

Villeneuve, Denis (Director)
c/o Staff Member *Claude Girard Agency*
5228, Boul. Saint-Laurent
Montreal QC H2T 1S1, CANADA

Villeneuve, Jacques (Race Car Driver)
British American Racing
PO Box 5014
Brackley
Northamptonshire NN13 7YY, UNITED KINGDOM (UK)

Villepique, Jean (Actor)
c/o Hannah Roth *Buchwald*
5900 Wilshire Blvd Ste 3100
Los Angeles, CA 90036-5030, USA

Villiers, Christopher (Actor)
c/o Staff Member *Katie Threlfall Associates*
2A Gladstone Rd
London SW19 1QT, UNITED KINGDOM (UK)

Villone, Ron (Athlete, Baseball Player)
3 Schindler Ct
Upper Saddle River, NJ 07458-2363, USA

Vilma, Jonathan (Athlete, Football Player)
c/o Maury Gostfrand *Vision Sports Group*
675 Thrd Ave
Suite 2500
New York, NY 10017, USA

Viloria, Brian (Boxer)

Vilsack, Thomas (Politician)
2229 Bancroft Pl NW Apt 101
Washington, DC 20008-4026, USA

Viltz, Theo (Athlete, Football Player)
2729 E De Soto St
Long Beach, CA 90814-2337, USA

Vina, Fernando (Athlete, Baseball Player)
11703 Colony Rd
Galt, CA 95632-8547, USA

Vinaite, Bria (Actor, Model)
c/o Melissa Raubvogel *Imprint PR*
375 Hudson St
New York, NY 10014-3658, USA

Vinatieri, Adam (Athlete, Football Player)
11595 Ditch Rd
Carmel, IN 46032-8888, USA

Vince, Pruitt Taylor (Actor)
c/o Joannie Burstein *Burstein Company*
15304 W Sunset Blvd Ste 208
Pacific Palisades, CA 90272-3656, USA

Vince, Taylor (Misc)
20160 NW 9th Dr
Pembroke Pines, FL 33029-3422, USA

Vincelette, Dan (Athlete, Hockey Player)
1345 Rue Bernier RR 3
Acton Vale, QC J0H 1A0, Canada

Vincent, Brooke (Actor)

Vincent, Cerina (Actor)
c/o Adam Seid *Bohemia Group*
1680 Vine St Ste 518
Los Angeles, CA 90028-8833, USA

Vincent, Christian (Actor, Dancer)
c/o Danielle Bilodeau *Cue Agency*
196 3rd Ave W Suite 102
Vancouver, BC V5Y 1E9, Canada

Vincent, Fay (Athlete, Baseball Player)
290 Harbor Dr
Stamford, CT 06902-8700, USA

Vincent, Jay (Athlete, Basketball Player)
PO Box 27459
Lansing, MI 48909-0459, USA

Vincent, Rhonda (Musician)
PO Box 686
Sparta, TN 38583-0686, USA

Vincent, Richard F (Misc)
House of Lords
Westminster
London SW1A 0PW, UNITED KINGDOM (UK)

Vincent, Rick (Musician, Songwriter, Writer)
Carter Career Mgmt
1028 18th Ave S # B
Nashville, TN 37212-2105, USA

Vincent, Sam (Athlete, Basketball Player)
6727 Fairway Cove Dr
Orlando, FL 32835-5747, USA

Vincent, Troy (Athlete, Football Player)
18900 Longhouse Pl
Leesburg, VA 20176-6464, USA

Vinci, Charles (Athlete, Olympic Athlete, Weightlifter)
14508 Birchwood Ave
Cleveland, OH 44111-1314, USA

Vinci, Vince (Horse Racer)
9 Summit Dr
Denville, NJ 07834-2312, USA

Vincz, Melanie (Actor)
917 Medinah Dr
McKinney, TX 75069-1959, USA

Vines, C Jerry (Religious Leader)
First Baptist Church
124 W Ashley St
Jacksonville, FL 32202-3189, USA

Vines, Mark (Athlete, Hockey Player)
75 Hazelglen Dr
Kitchener, ON N2M 2E2, Canada

Vines, The (Music Group)
c/o Rick Roskin *Creative Artists Agency (CAA)*
2000 Avenue of the Stars Ste 100
Los Angeles, CA 90067-4705, USA

Vineyard, Dave (Athlete, Baseball Player)
1850 Tariff Rd
Left Hand, WV 25251-9542, USA

Vinge, Vernor (Writer)
Tom Doherty Associates, LLC
175 5th Ave
New York, NY 10010-7703, USA

Vining, Ken (Athlete, Baseball Player)
7123 Meyer Rd
Rd
Fort Mill, SC 29715-7843, USA

Vinnie (Artist, Music Group)
International Creative Mgmt
8942 Wilshire Blvd # 219
Beverly Hills, CA 90211-1908, USA

Vinson, Charlie (Athlete, Baseball Player)
3821 Walters Ln
District Heights, MD 20747-3943, USA

Vinson, Fernandus (Athlete, Football Player)
6572 Glenwood Ave Apt 221
Raleigh, NC 27612-7156, USA

Vinson, Fred (Athlete, Football Player)
11220 NE 53rd St
Kirkland, WA 98033-7505, USA

Vinson, Fred (Athlete, Basketball Player)
13701 Marina Pointe Dr Apt 304
Marina Del Rey, CA 90292-9242, USA

Vinson, Sharni (Actor)
c/o Craig McMahon *McMahon Management*
390 Clarendon St
S Melbourne VIC 3205, AUSTRALIA

Vint, Jesse Lee III (Actor)
Film Artists
13563 1/2 Ventura Blvd #200
Sherman Oaks, CA 91423, USA

Vinton, Bobby (Musician)
820 Manasota Key Rd
Englewood, FL 34223, USA

Viola, Bill (Artist)
282 Granada Ave Apt A
Long Beach, CA 90803-5520, USA

Viola, Frank (Athlete, Baseball Player)
1510 London Rd
Mooresville, NC 28115-7224, USA

Viola, Lisa (Dancer)
Paul Taylor Dance Co
552 Broadway
New York, NY 10012-3922, USA

Viola, Vincent (Business Person)
Virtu Financial
645 Madison Ave Fl 1200
New York, NY 10022-1010, USA

Violent Femmes (Music Group)
c/o Frank Riley *High Road Touring*
751 Bridgeway Fl 2
Sausalito, CA 94965-2174, USA

Violette, Chris (Actor)

Vipond, Pete (Athlete, Hockey Player)
69 Admiral Drive
Fenelon Falls, ON KOM INO, Canada

Virata, Cesar E (Prime Minister)
63 E Maya Dr
Quezon City, PHILIPPINES

Virden, Claude (Athlete, Basketball Player)
337 Fernwood Dr
Akron, OH 44320-2317, USA

Virdon, William C (Bill) (Athlete, Baseball Player, Coach)
1311 E River Rd
Springfield, MO 65804-7901, USA

Viren, Lasse (Athlete, Track Athlete)
Suomen Urhellulirto Ry
Box 25202
Helsinki 25 00250, FINLAND

Virgil Jr, Ozzie (Athlete, Baseball Player)
4316 W Mescal St
Glendale, AZ 85304-4132, USA

Virgil Sr, Ozzie (Athlete, Baseball Player)
5444 W Creedance Blvd
Glendale, AZ 85310-3724, Dominican Republic

Virgin, JJ (Fitness Expert)
JJ Virgin & Associates Inc
30 Lincoln Pl
Rancho Mirage, CA 92270-1970, USA

Virgins, The (Music Group)
c/o Staff Member *Paradigm (Monterey)*
404 W Franklin St
Monterey, CA 93940-2303, USA

Virts, Terry W Jr (Astronaut)
1904 Edgewater Dr
Friendswood, TX 77546-7845, USA

Virts, Terry W Major (Astronaut)
1904 Edgewater Dr
Friendswood, TX 77546-7845, USA

Virtue, Doreen (Writer)
Angel Therapy
PO Box 5100
Carlsbad, CA 92018-5100, USA

Virtue, Frank (Musician)
8309 Rising Sun Ave
Philadelphia, PA 19111, USA

Virtue, Thomas (Tom) (Actor)
c/o Staff Member *The Gage Group*
5757 Wilshire Blvd Ste 659
Los Angeles, CA 90036-3682, USA

Virzaladze, Elizo K (Music Group, Musician)
Moscow Conservatory
Bolshaya Nikitskaya Str 13
Moscow, RUSSIA

Vis, Anthony (Religious Leader)
Reformed Church in America
475 Riverside Dr Ste 1606
New York, NY 10115-0093, USA

Visclosky, Pete (Congressman, Politician)
7895 Broadway Ste A
Merrillville, IN 46410-5529, USA

Visconti, Tony (Musician, Producer)
Star Mangement Group
1311 Mamaroneck Ave Ste 220
White Plains, NY 10605-5222, USA

Viscuso, Sal (Actor)
6491 Ivarene Ave
Los Angeles, CA 90068-2823, USA

Vise, David A (Journalist)
Washington Post
Editorial Dept
1150 15th St NW
Washington, DC 20071-0001, USA

Vishnevski, Vitali (Athlete, Hockey Player)
International Sports Advisors
878 Ridge View Way
Franklin Lakes, NJ 07417-1524, USA

Visitor, Nana (Actor)
c/o Christopher Sherman *Rooster Films*
5225 Wilshire Blvd Ste 406
Los Angeles, CA 90036-4348, USA

Visnjic, Goran (Actor)
c/o Gabriel Cohen *Management 360*
9111 Wilshire Blvd
Beverly Hills, CA 90210-5508, USA

Visnovsky, Lubomir (Athlete, Hockey Player)
15319th St
Manhattan Beach, CA 90266-6126, USA

Viso, Michel (Misc)
7 Domaine Chateau-Gaillard
Maison-d' Alfort 94700, FRANCE

Visser, Lesley (Sportscaster)
c/o Staff Member *CBS Television*
51 W 52nd St
New York, NY 10019-6119, USA

Viswanathan, Padma (Writer)
213 N Summit Ave
Fayetteville, AR 72701-1312, USA

Vitale, Dick (Athlete, Basketball Player, Coach, Sportscaster)
7810 Mathern Ct
Lakewood Ranch, FL 34202-2592, USA

Vitale, Joe (Business Person, Writer)
The Vitale Estate
121 Canyon Gap Rd
Wimberley, TX 78676-6314, USA

Vitale, Tony (Actor, Director, Writer)
c/o Staff Member *Hansen, Jacobson, Teller, Hoberman, Newman, Warren & Richman*
450 N Roxbury Dr Fl 8
Beverly Hills, CA 90210-4222, USA

Vitamin-C (Actor, Musician)
c/o Carter Cohn *ICM Partners*
10250 Constellation Blvd Fl 7
Los Angeles, CA 90067-6207, USA

Vitez, Michael (Journalist)
Philadelphia Inquirer
400 N Broad St
Editorial Dept
Philadelphia, PA 19130-4015, USA

Vitiello, Joe (Athlete, Baseball Player)
13615 Old El Camino Real
San Diego, CA 92130-3088, USA

Vitiello, Sandro (Athlete, Football Player)
9 Dwight Cir
Commack, NY 11725-3313, USA

Vitko, Joe (Athlete, Baseball Player)
1853 Frankstown Rd Apt 1
Johnstown, PA 15902-4504, USA

Vito, Don (Producer)
606 Treecrest Pkwy
Decatur, GA 30035-3564, USA

Vitolo, Dennis (Race Car Driver)
Payton-Coyne Racing
13400 S Budler Rd
Plainfield, IL 60544-9493, USA

Vitrano, Bob (Horse Racer)
16 Farnworth Close
Freehold, NJ 07728-3852, USA

Vitti, Monica (Actor)
IPC
Via F Siacci 38
Rome 00197, ITALY

Vittori, Roberto (Astronaut)
Europe Astronaut Center
520 N Iowa Ave
League City, TX 77573-2356, Italy

Vitukhnovskaya, Alina A (Writer)
Leningradskoye Shosse 80 #89
Moscow 125565, RUSSIA

Vivas, Juan Carlos (Actor)
c/o Gabriel Blanco *Gabriel Blanco Iglesias (Mexico)*
Rio Balsas 35-32
Colonia Cuauhtemoc
DF 06500, Mexico

Viviano, Joseph P (Business Person)
Hershey Foods Corp
100 Crystal A Dr Unit 8
Hershey, PA 17033-9702, USA

Vizcaino, Jose (Athlete, Baseball Player)
5976 Germaine Ln
La Jolla, CA 92037-7430, USA

Vizquel, Omar E (Athlete, Baseball Player)
2704 212th Ave SE
Sammamish, WA 98075-7167, USA

V. Johnson, Timothy (Congressman, Politician)
8426 Porter Ln
Alexandria, VA 22308-2139, USA

Vlacil, Frantisek (Director)
Cinska 5
Prague 6 160 00, CZECH REPUBLIC

Vladimir, Potanin (Business Person, Politician)
Interros
40 Bolshaya Yakimanka St
Moscow 119049, Russia

Vlady, Marina (Actor)
10 Ave de Marivaux
Mission Lafitte 78800, FRANCE

Vlardo, Vladimir V (Musician)
457 Piermont Rd
Cresskill, NJ 07626-1524, USA

Vlasak, Tomas (Athlete, Hockey Player)
Stefanikovo nam. 1
Pi zen 30133, Czech Republic

Vlasic, Mark (Athlete, Football Player)
12809 Catalina St
Leawood, KS 66209-3327, USA

Vlk, Miloslav Cardinal (Religious Leader)
Arcibiskupstvi
Hradcanske Nam 16/56
Prague 1 119 02, CZECH REPUBLIC

Voce, Gary (Athlete, Basketball Player)
25912 147th Ave
Rosedale, NY 11422-3321, USA

Vodianova, Natalia (Model)
c/o Staff Member *DNA Model Management*
555 W 25th St Fl 6
New York, NY 10001-5542, USA

Voelkel, Riley (Actor)
c/o Mara Santino *Luber Roklin Management*
5815 W Sunset Blvd Ste 208
Los Angeles, CA 90028-6481, USA

Vogel, Bob (Athlete, Football Player)
2065 N Galena Rd
Sunbury, OH 43074-9588, USA

Vogel, Dariene (Actor)
Michael Slessinger
8730 W Sunset Blvd Ste 220W
Los Angeles, CA 90069-2275, USA

Vogel, Darlene (Actor)

Vogel, Frank (Basketball Coach)
c/o Lonnie Cooper *Career Sports and Entertainment*
600 Galleria Pkwy SE Ste 1900
Atlanta, GA 30339-5990, USA

Vogel, Mark (Composer, Musician)
c/o Staff Member *Gorfaine/Schwartz Agency Inc*
4111 W Alameda Ave Ste 509
Burbank, CA 91505-4171, USA

Vogel, Matt (Athlete, Olympic Athlete, Swimmer)
209 Wingood Rd
Windsor, ME 04363-3708, USA

Vogel, Mike (Actor)
c/o Ruth Bernstein *Viewpoint Inc*
8820 Wilshire Blvd Ste 220
Beverly Hills, CA 90211-2622, USA

Vogelsong, Ryan (Athlete, Baseball Player)

Vogler, Tim (Athlete, Football Player)
6710 Woodland Dr
Hamburg, NY 14075-6521, USA

Vogt, Lars (Musician)
c/o Staff Member *ICM Partners (NY)*
730 5th Ave
New York, NY 10019-4105, USA

Vogt, Paul (Actor)
c/o Judy Coppage *Coppage Company, The*
5411 Camellia Ave
North Hollywood, CA 91601-2615, USA

Vogtli, Jillian (Athlete, Olympic Athlete, Skier)
PO Box 683153
Park City, UT 84068-3153, USA

Vogt-Roberts, Jordan (Director)
c/o Joy Fehily *PMK/BNC Public Relations*
1840 Century Park E Ste 1400
Los Angeles, CA 90067-2115, USA

Voight, Jon (Actor, Producer)
c/o Staff Member *Jon Voight Entertainment*
10203 Santa Monica Blvd
Los Angeles, CA 90067-6405, USA

Voight, Karen (Fitness Expert)
Entertaining Fitness, Inc
827 Chautauqua Blvd
Pacific Palisades, CA 90272-3802, USA

Voight, Stu (Athlete, Football Player)
8832 Hunters Way
Apple Valley, MN 55124-9478, USA

Voigt, Cynthia (Writer)
866 3rd Ave
New York, NY 10022-6221, USA

Voigt, Jack (Athlete, Baseball Player)
1759 Bayshore Rd
Nokomis, FL 34275-1413, USA

Voisard, Mark (Baseball Player)
222 Meadowlane Dr
Sidney, OH 45365-7000, USA

Vokoun, Tomas (Athlete, Hockey Player)
6685 NW 122nd Ave
Parkland, FL 33076-3325, USA

Volbeat (Music Group)
c/o Staff Member *Artist Group International (NY)*
150 E 58th St Fl 19
New York, NY 10155-1900, USA

Volcan, Mickey (Athlete, Hockey Player)
10716 69 St NW
Edmonton, AB T6A 2T1, Canada

Volchenkov, Anton (Athlete, Hockey Player)
Puckagency LLC
555 Pleasantville Rd Ste 210N
Attn Jay Grossman
Briarcliff Manor, NY 10510-1900, USA

Volcker, Paul (Politician)
151 E 79th St Fl 7
New York, NY 10075-0564, USA

Voldstad, John (Actor)
24812 Van Owen St
West Hills, CA 91300, USA

Volek, Billy (Athlete, Football Player)
14544 Millards Rd
Poway, CA 92064-5036, USA

Volek, David (Athlete, Hockey Player)
5 Blue Sky Ct
Huntington, NY 11743-2901, USA

Volibracht, Michaele (Artist, Designer, Fashion Designer)
General Delivery
Safety Harbor, FL 34695, USA

Volk, Igor P (Misc)
Potchta Kosmonavtov
Moskovskoi Oblasti
Syvisdny Goroduk 141160, RUSSIA

Volk, Patricia (Writer)
Gloria Loomis
101 N Spring Garden Ave
Nutley, NJ 07110-1529, USA

Volk, Phil (Musician)
Paradise Artists
108 E Matilija St
Ojai, CA 93023-2639, USA

Volk, Richard R (Rick) (Athlete, Football Player)
15860 Irish Ave
Monkton, MD 21111-2120, USA

Volker, Sandra (Swimmer)
DESG
Mensingen Str 68
Munich 80992, GERMANY

Volkert, Stephan (Athlete)
Semmelweisstr 42
Cologne 51061, GERMANY

Volkov, Aleksandr A (Misc)
Potchta Kosmonavtov
Moskovskoi Oblasti
Syvisdny Goroduk 141160, RUSSIA

Volkov, Alexander (Athlete, Basketball Player)
1413 Waterford Green Dr
Marietta, GA 30068-2910, USA

Voll, Rich (Actor)

Vollenweider, Andreas (Musician)
Sempacher Str 16
Zurich 08032, SWITZERLAND

Vollmer, Dana (Athlete, Olympic Athlete, Swimmer)
573 Camino Caballo
Nipomo, CA 93444-9558, USA

Vollmer, Sebastian (Athlete, Football Player)
c/o Ben Dogra *Relativity Sports*
2029 Century Park E Ste 1550
Century City, CA 90067-3000, USA

Volodos, Arcadl (Musician)
Columbia Artists Mgmt Inc
165 W 57th St
New York, NY 10019-2201, USA

Volstad, Chris (Athlete, Baseball Player)
11774 Hemlock St
Palm Beach Gardens, FL 33410-2637, USA

Volstad, John (Actor)
c/o Brandon Pender *Ithaca Entertainment Media Group*
PO Box 1880
Studio City, CA 91614-0880, USA

VOltaggio, Vic (Athlete, Baseball Player)
1049 Florian Way
Spring Hill, FL 34609-9021, USA

Voltaggio, Vic (Baseball Player)
1049 Florian Way
Spring Hill, FL 34609-9021, USA

Volynov, Boris V (Misc)
Potchta Kosmonavtov
Moskovskoi Oblasti
Syvisdny Goroduk 141160, RUSSIA

Volz, Wolfgang (Actor)
Konstanzer Strasse 8
Berlin D-10707, Germany

Von, Theo (Comedian)
c/o Arlene Thornton *Arlene Thornton & Associates*
12711 Ventura Blvd Ste 490
Studio City, CA 91604-2477, USA

Von Daniken, Eric (Writer)
Chalet Aelpli
Portsmouth, NH 03803-0001, Switzerland

von Detten, Erik (Actor)
c/o Elissa Leeds-Fickman *Reel Talent Management*
PO Box 491035
Los Angeles, CA 90049-9035, USA

von Dohlen, Lenny (Actor)
c/o Martin Gage *BRS / Gage Talent Agency (LA)*
6300 Wilshire Blvd Ste 1430
Los Angeles, CA 90048-5216, USA

Von Drachenberg, Katherine (Artist, Reality Star)
High Voltage Tattoo
1259 N La Brea Ave
West Hollywood, CA 90038-1023, USA

Von Erich, Jaret (Actor, Musician)
c/o Linda Kordek *UTA Music/The Agency Group*
9336 Civic Center Dr
Beverly Hills, CA 90210-3604, USA

VonErich, Waldo (Wrestler)
Columbia Sports Med Center
9-145 Columbia W
Waterloo, ON N2L 3L2, CANADA

Von Franckenstein, Clement (Actor)
c/o Sharon Nixon Kelly *American Artists Group Management*
13321 Ventura Blvd Ste C
Sherman Oaks, CA 91423-6214, USA

Von Furstenberg, Diane (Fashion Designer)
DVF
874 Washington St
New York, NY 10014-1102, USA

VonFurstenberg, Egon (Designer, Fashion Designer)
50 E 72nd St
New York, NY 10021-4246, USA

VonGarnier, Katja (Director, Writer)
c/o John Campisi *Creative Artists Agency (CAA)*
2000 Avenue of the Stars Ste 100
Los Angeles, CA 90067-4705, USA

Vongerichten, Jean-Georges (Chef)
Jean-Georges Management
11 Prince St Fl 2
New York, NY 10012-3578, USA

VonGrunigen, Michael (Skier)
Chalet Sunneblick
Schonried 03778, SWITZERLAND

VonHippel, Peter H (Misc)
1900 Crest Dr
Eugene, OR 97405-1753, USA

Von Hoff, Bruce (Athlete, Baseball Player)
5289 6th PlS
Gulfoort, FL 33707-2501, USA

Von Moger, Calum (Fitness Expert)
c/o Edwin Mejia Jr *The Vladar Company*
134 W 29th St Rm 902
New York, NY 10001-5797, USA

Vonn, Lindsey (Athlete, Skier)
PO Box 4758
Vail, CO 81658-4758, USA

Vonnegut Jr, Kurt (Writer)
Seven Stories Press
140 Watts St
New York, NY 10013-1738, USA

Von Nieda, Whitey (Athlete, Basketball Player)
1105 James Buchanan Dr
Elizabethtown, PA 17022-3169, USA

Vonoelhoffen, Kimo (Athlete, Football Player)
1503 Scarlet Oak Dr
Wexford, PA 15090-6931, USA

Von Ohlen, Dave (Athlete, Baseball Player)
653 Windmill Ave
West Babylon, NY 11704-4403, USA

Vonohlen, Dave (Baseball Player)
St Louis Cardinals
74 Elizabeth St
Floral Park, NY 11001-2129, USA

Von Oy, Jenna (Actor)
913 Battlefield Dr
Nashville, TN 37204-3017, USA

von Pfetten, Stefanie (Actor)
c/o Marina D'Amico *Precision Entertainment*
6338 Wilshire Blvd
Los Angeles, CA 90048-5002, USA

VonPierer, Heinrich (Business Person)
Seimens AG
Wittelsbacherplatz 2
Munich 80333, GERMANY

VonQuast, Veronika (Actor)
ZBF Agentur
Leopoldstr 19
Munich 80802, GERMANY

Von Rittberg, Alicia (Actor)
c/o Marie-Louise Schmidt *Die Agenten*
Motzstraße 60
Berlin 10777, GERMANY

VonRunkle, Theodora (Designer, Fashion Designer)
8805 Lookout Mountain Ave
Los Angeles, CA 90046-1819, USA

VonSaltza Olmstead, S Christine (Chris) (Swimmer)
7060 Fairway Pl
Carmel, CA 93923-9586, USA

Von Schamann, Uwe (Athlete, Football Player)
PO Box 5562
Norman, OK 73070-5562, USA

Von Scherler Mayer, Daisy (Director)
c/o Keith Addis *Industry Entertainment Partners*
955 Carrillo Dr Ste 300
Los Angeles, CA 90048-5400, USA

Vonsonn, Andrew (Athlete, Football Player)
PO Box 791538
Paia, HI 96779-1538, USA

VonStrateen, Frans (Artist)
Samuel Muller Plein 17C
Rotterdam 03023, DENMARK

Von Sydow, Max (Actor)
c/o Staff Member *United Talent Agency (UTA)*
9336 Civic Center Dr
Beverly Hills, CA 90210-3604, USA

Von Teese, Dita (Dancer, Model)
7095 Hollywood Blvd Ste 715
Los Angeles, CA 90028-8912, USA

von Trier, Lars (Director)
c/o Staff Member *Zentropa Entertainment*
Filmbyen 22
Hvidovre 02650, DENMARK

von Wietersheim, Sharon (Director)
Leopoldstr. 19
Munich D-80802, Germany

Voog, Ana (Music Group, Musician, Songwriter, Writer)
MCA Records
1755 Broadway Fl 6
New York, NY 10019-3793, USA

Voorhies, Lark (Actor)
10635 Santa Monica Blvd Ste 130
Los Angeles, CA 90025-8306, USA

Voorman, Klaus (Artist)
K & K Galleries Grindelalla 182
Hamburg D-20144, Germany

Vopat, Jan (Athlete, Hockey Player)
Skalni 426
Litvinov 3 436 01, Czech Republic

Vorgan, Gigi (Actor)
3637 Stone Canyon
Sherman Oaks, CA 91403, USA

Vorhies, Lark (Actor)
c/o Geoff Cheddy *Brillstein Entertainment Partners*
9150 Wilshire Blvd Ste 350
Beverly Hills, CA 90212-3453, USA

Voris, Roy M (Butch) (Misc)
14563 Fruitvale Ave
Saratoga, CA 95070-6152, USA

Voronin, Vladimir (President)
President's Office
23 Nicolae Iorge Str
Chishinev 277033, MOLDOVA

Voronina, Irina (Model)
7119 W Sunset Blvd # 293
Los Angeles, CA 90046-4411, USA

Vos, Rich (Actor, Comedian)
c/o Jason Steinberg *Steinberg Talent Management Group*
165 W 46th St Ste 405
New York, NY 10036-2522, USA

Vosberg, Ed (Athlete, Baseball Player)
11057 E Carved Tree Ct
Tucson, AZ 85749-5707, USA

Voser, Peter (Business Person)
Shell U.K. Limited
Shell Centre
London SE1 7NA, UK

Vosloo, Arnold (Actor)
c/o James (Jim) Gosnell *Agency for the Performing Arts (APA)*
405 S Beverly Dr Ste 500
Beverly Hills, CA 90212-4425, USA

Voss, Bill (Athlete, Baseball Player)
10625 E Oak Creek Trl
Cornville, AZ 86325-5824, USA

Votaw, Ty (Golfer)
Ladies Pro Golf Assn
100 International Golf Dr
Daytona Beach, FL 32124-1082, USA

Voth, Julia (Actor)
c/o Alex Fox *Nu Talent*
10635 Santa Monica Blvd Ste 130
Los Angeles, CA 90025-8306, USA

Votto, Joey (Athlete, Baseball Player)
4 Nantucket Cres
Brampton, ON L6S 3X5, CANADA

Vouyer, Vince (Adult Film Star)
Vouyer Media Inc
9020 Eton Ave Ste G
Canoga Park, CA 91304-6514, USA

Vowell, Sarah (Actor, Writer)
c/o Staff Member *Steven Barclay Agency*
12 Western Ave
Petaluma, CA 94952-2907, USA

Voyce, Inez (Athlete, Baseball Player)
9630 Sombra Valley Dr
Sunland, CA 91040-1524, USA

Voyles, Brad (Athlete, Baseball Player)
314 East Ave
Casco, WI 54205-9647, USA

Voytek, Edward (Athlete, Football Player)
2111 NW 13th St
Blue Springs, MO 64015-7734, USA

Vrabel, Mike (Athlete, Football Player)
4723 Linden St
Bellaire, TX 77401-4430, USA

Vranes, Danny (Athlete, Basketball Player, Olympic Athlete)
6480 S Canyon Ranch Rd
Salt Lake City, UT 84121-6366, USA

Vranes, Slavko (Basketball Player)
c/o Staff Member *Portland Trail Blazers*
1 N Center Court St Ste 200
Portland, OR 97227-2103, USA

Vranitzky, Franz (Actor)
Ballhausplatz 2
Vienna 01015, Austria

Vreeland, Caroline (Actor, Musician)
c/o Chris Manno *Next Model Management (LA)*
8447 Wilshire Blvd PH
Beverly Hills, CA 90211-1683, USA

Vuckovich, Peter D (Pete) (Athlete, Baseball Player)
86 Leonard St
Johnstown, PA 15902-1234, USA

Vujicic, Nick (Activist)
Life Without Limbs
PO Box 2430
Agoura Hills, CA 91376-2430, USA

Vujtek, Vladimir (Athlete, Hockey Player)
Mexico- 813
Vresina 74285, Czech Republic

Vukota, Mick (Athlete, Hockey Player)
PO Box 3213
7 PEASES POINT RD
Edgartown, MA 02539-3213, USA

Vukovich, George (Athlete, Baseball Player)
305 W Calle Gota
Sahuarita, AZ 85629-7845, USA

Vulcano, Sal (Actor, Producer)
c/o Dexter Scott *Vector Management*
276 5th Ave Rm 604
New York, NY 10001-4527, USA

Vulkovich, Frances (Athlete, Baseball Player)
258 W 28th St
Holland, MI 49423-4939, USA

Vullo, Maria T (Attorney)
1285 Avenue of the Americas
New York, NY 10019-6031, USA

Vyent, Louise (Model)
Pauline's Talent Corp
379 W Broadway # 502
New York, NY 10012-5121, USA

W, Kristine (Musician)
8585 La Cienega St
Las Vegas, NV 89123-1648, USA

Waadataar, Paar (Musician)
Banada Mgmt
11 Elvaston Place #300
London SW 7 5QC, UNITED KINGDOM (UK)

Waalkes, Otto (Actor)
Papenhuder Str. 61
Hamburg D-22087, Germany

Wachowski, Andy (Director, Producer)
c/o Lawrence Mattis *Circle of Confusion (NY)*
270 Lafayette St Ste 402
New York, NY 10012-3327, USA

Wachowski, Lana (Director)
c/o Lawrence Mattis *Circle of Confusion (NY)*
270 Lafayette St Ste 402
New York, NY 10012-3327, USA

Wachowski, Larry (Director, Producer, Writer)
2309 Ocean Front Walk
Venice, CA 90291-4317, USA

Wachs, Caitlin (Actor)
c/o Staff Member *ICM Partners*
10250 Constellation Blvd Fl 7
Los Angeles, CA 90067-6207, USA

Wachsberger, Patrick (Producer)
c/o Staff Member *Summit Entertainment*
1630 Stewart St Ste 120
Santa Monica, CA 90404-4020, USA

Wachtel, Christine (Athlete, Track Athlete)
Rostock Sports Club
Rostock
Mecklenburg-Vorpommoem, GERMANY

Wachter, Anita (Skier)
Gantschierstr 579
Schruns 06780, AUSTRIA

Waddell, Charles (Athlete, Football Player)
202 Glendevon Way
Columbia, SC 29229-8109, USA

Waddell, Don (Athlete, Hockey Player)
2554 Thurleston Ln
Duluth, GA 30097-7474, USA

Waddell, Ernest (Actor)
c/o Bob McGowan *McGowan Management*
170 S Beverly Dr Ste 304
Beverly Hills, CA 90212-3000, USA

Waddell, Jason (Athlete, Baseball Player)
3574 Gwinnett Dr
Riverside, CA 92503-5013, USA

Waddell, John Henry (Artist)
Star Route 2273
Oak Creek Village Road
Cornville, AZ 86325, USA

Waddell, Justine (Actor)
International Creative Mgmt
8942 Wilshire Blvd # 219
Beverly Hills, CA 90211-1908, USA

Waddell, Tom (Athlete, Baseball Player)
10171 E Achi St
Tucson, AZ 85748-1803, USA

Waddell-Wyatt, Helen (Athlete, Baseball Player)
7714 Deerfield Rd
Loves Park, IL 61111-3218, USA

Waddington, Steven (Actor)
Julian Belfrage Associates
Adam House
14 New Burlington Street
London W1S 3BQ, UNITED KINGDOM (UK)

Waddle, Tom (Athlete, Football Player)
315 Chuniloti Cir
Loudon, TN 37774-2608, USA

Waddy, Billy (Athlete, Football Player)
2838 Highway 88
Minneapolis, MN 55418-3243, USA

Wade, Abdoulaye (President)
President's Office
Ave Roume
Dakar BPI 168, SENEGAL

Wade, Adam (Musician)
118 E 25th St # 600
New York, NY 10010-2915, USA

Wade, Charlie (Athlete, Football Player)
3109 E Raines Rd
Memphis, TN 38118-6756, USA

Wade, Cory (Athlete, Baseball Player)
c/o Staff Member *Los Angeles Dodgers*
1000 Elysian Park Ave
Los Angeles, CA 90012, USA

Wade, Dwyane (Athlete, Basketball Player)
c/o Leon Rose *CAA Basketball*
308 Harper Dr Ste 210
Moorestown, NJ 08057-3245, USA

Wade, Ed (Actor)
436 SW 50th Ave
Pratt, KS 67124-7731, USA

Wade, Ed (Athlete, Baseball Player)
169 Pitman Downer Rd
Sewell, NJ 08080-1878, USA

Wade, Edgar L (Religious Leader)
4466 Elvis Presley Blvd Ste 222
Memphis, TN 38116-7100, USA

Wade, Gale (Athlete, Baseball Player)
4809 Granada Blvd
Sebring, FL 33872-1531, USA

Wade, Jason (Musician)
849 Forest Acres Dr
Nashville, TN 37220-1804, USA

Wade, Jenny (Actor)
c/o Courtney Kivowitz *MGMT Entertainment (The Schiff Company)*
9220 W Sunset Blvd Ste 106
W Hollywood, CA 90069-3500, USA

Wade, Joivan (Actor)
c/o David Marsden *Sainow Agency*
10-11 Lower John St.
Golden Square
London W1F 9EB, UNITED KINGDOM

Wade, Kevin (Writer)
c/o David Lonner *Oasis Media Group*
9100 Wilshire Blvd Ste 210W
Beverly Hills, CA 90212-3555, USA

Wade, Mark (Athlete, Basketball Player)
2245 Barbour Ct
San Pedro, CA 90731-5927, USA

Wade, Sonny (Athlete, Football Player)
943 Jones Ridge Rd
Axton, VA 24054-2888, USA

Wade, Terrell (Athlete, Baseball Player)
6380 Dinkins Mill Rd
Rembert, SC 29128-9789, USA

Wade, Todd (Athlete, Football Player)
217 Hendricks Isle Apt 302
Fort Lauderdale, FL 33301-5753, USA

Wade, Tom (Athlete, Football Player)
3309 Oak Knoll Dr
Tyler, TX 75707-1619, USA

Wade, Virginia (Tennis Player)
Sharstead Court
Sittingbourne
Kent, UNITED KINGDOM (UK)

Wadkins, Bobby (Golfer)
204 Kinloch Rd
Manakin Sabot, VA 23103-2911, USA

Wadkins, Lanny (Athlete, Golfer)
5200 Keller Springs Rd Apt 1217
Dallas, TX 75248-2751, USA

Wadsworth, Andre (Athlete, Football Player)
14003 N 99th Way
Scottsdale, AZ 85260-8851, USA

Wadsworth, Charles W (Musician)
PO Box 157
Charleston, SC 29402-0157, USA

Wadsworth, Fred (Golfer)
823 Bryon Rd
Columbia, SC 29209-2303, USA

Waechter, Doug (Athlete, Baseball Player)
4590 13th WayNE
Saint Petersburg, FL 33703-5324, USA

Wafer, Von (Athlete, Basketball Player)
2503 Dallas St
Houston, TX 77003-3605, USA

Wages, Harmon (Athlete, Football Player)
1846 Margaret St Apt 3C
Jacksonville, FL 32204-4423, USA

Wages, Robert E (Misc)
Oil Chemical Atomic Workers International Union
PO Box 2812
Denver, CO 80201-2812, USA

Waggoner, Lyle (Actor)
1409 Marine Way
Oxnard, CA 93035, USA

Waggoner, Paul E (Misc)
314 Vineyard Point Rd
Guilford, CT 06437-3255, USA

Wagner, Alex (Journalist)
c/o Staff Member *MSNBC*
30 Rockefeller Plz Fl 2
New York, NY 10112-0043, USA

Wagner, Allison (Athlete, Olympic Athlete, Swimmer)
912 NW 45th Ter
Gainesville, FL 32605-4590

Wagner, Bret (Baseball Player)
US Olympic Team Bowman
489 Ridge Rd
Lewisberry, PA 17339-9308, USA

Wagner, Brett (Actor, Television Host)
1487 Queens Rd
Los Angeles, CA 90069-1914, USA

Wagner, Bruce (Writer)
United Talent Agency
9336 Civic Center Dr
Beverly Hills, CA 90210-3604, USA

Wagner, Bryan (Athlete, Football Player)
PO Box 222
Westfield Center, OH 44251-0222, USA

Wagner, Chuck (Actor, Musician)
1200 Maldonado Dr
Pensacola Beach, FL 32561-2244, USA

Wagner, Dajuan (Basketball Player)
Cleveland Cavaliers
1 Center Ct
Gund Arena
Cleveland, OH 44115-4001, USA

Wagner, Fred (Cartoonist)
c/o Staff Member *King Features Syndication*
300 W 57th St Fl 15
New York, NY 10019-5238, USA

Wagner, Gary (Athlete, Baseball Player)
1707 Northbrook Ct
Seymour, IN 47274-4801, USA

Wagner, Harold A (Business Person)
Air Products & Chemicals
7201 Hamilton Blvd
Allentown, PA 18195-9642, USA

Wagner, Jack (Actor, Musician)
314 Waverly Place Ct
Chesterfield, MO 63017-7819, USA

Wagner, Jane (Actor)
PO Box 27700
Los Angeles, CA 90027-0700, USA

Wagner, Jill (Actor)
c/o Staff Member *United Talent Agency (UTA)*
9336 Civic Center Dr
Beverly Hills, CA 90210-3604, USA

Wagner, John (Cartoonist)
Hallmark Cards
101 McDonald Dr
Shoebox Division
Lawrence, KS 66044-1056, USA

Wagner, Katey (Actor)
1500 Old Oak Rd
Los Angeles, CA 90049-2504, USA

Wagner, Katie (Actor, Television Host)

Wagner, Lindsay (Actor)
c/o Sanford Brokaw *Brokaw Company*
PO Box 462
Culver City, CA 90232-0462, USA

Wagner, Lou (Actor)
21224 Celtic St
Chatsworth, CA 91311-1468, USA

Wagner, Maggie (Actor)
Stephany Hurkos Management
400 W 43rd St Apt 35O
New York, NY 10036-6359, USA

Wagner, Mark (Athlete, Baseball Player)
3506 Ninevah Rd
Ashtabula, OH 44004-8610, USA

Wagner, Matt (Cartoonist)
DC Comics
2900 W Alameda Ave # 1
Burbank, CA 91505-4220, USA

Wagner, Matt (Athlete, Baseball Player)
1112 Lilac Ln
Cedar Falls, IA 50613-5342, USA

Wagner, Melinda (Composer)
Theodore Presser
588 N Gulph Rd Ste B
King Of Prussia, PA 19406-2831, USA

Wagner, Michael R (Mike) (Athlete, Football Player)
203 East Cherry Dr
Mars, PA 16046, USA

Wagner, Mike (Athlete, Football Player)
874 Bayou View Dr
Brandon, FL 33510-2018, USA

Wagner, Natasha Gregson (Actor)
c/o Amy Guenther *Gateway Management Company Inc*
860 Via De La Paz Ste F10
Pacific Palisades, CA 90272-3631, USA

Wagner, Paul (Athlete, Baseball Player)
N1960 State Road 67
Neosho, WI 53059-9723, USA

Wagner, Paula (Producer)
Chestnut Ridge Productions
3000 Olympic Blvd Bldg 2515
Santa Monica, CA 90404-5073, USA

Wagner, Phillip (Athlete, Basketball Player)
328 Glenloch Ln
Stockbridge, GA 30281-5920, USA

Wagner, Ricky (Athlete, Football Player)
c/o Joe Panos *Athletes First*
23091 Mill Creek Dr
Laguna Hills, CA 92653-1258, USA

Wagner, Robert (Actor)
c/o Chuck Binder *Binder & Associates*
1465 Lindacrest Dr
Beverly Hills, CA 90210-2519, USA

Wagner, Robin S A (Designer)
Robin Wagner Studio
890 Broadway Fl 6
New York, NY 10003-1211, USA

Wagner, Roy H (Actor, Director)
c/o Lisa Helsing Lenhoff *Lenhoff & Lenhoff*
324 S Beverly Dr
Beverly Hills, CA 90212-4801

Wagner, Ryan (Athlete, Baseball Player)
59 County Road 311
Yoakum, TX 77995-6014, USA

Wagner, William E (Billy) (Athlete, Baseball Player)
5066 Jones Mill Rd
Crozet, VA 22932-2610, USA

Wagoner, Dan (Athlete, Football Player)
714 Carriage Hill Rd
Simpsonville, SC 29681-5281, USA

Wagoner, David R (Writer)
5416 154th Pl SW
Edmonds, WA 98026-4348, USA

Wagoner, Richard (Rick) (Business Person)
General Motors Corp
100 Renaissance Ctr
Detroit, MI 48243-1114, USA

Wahl, Ken (Actor)
c/o Susan Balistocky *Law Offices of Sysan Balistocky*
1901 Avenue of the Stars Ste 1900
Los Angeles, CA 90067-6020, USA

Wahlberg, Donnie (Actor, Musician)
c/o Jonathan Baruch *Rain Management Group*
11162 La Grange Ave
Los Angeles, CA 90025-5632, USA

Wahlberg, Mark (Actor, Model, Musician)
c/o Staff Member *Closest to the Hole Productions*
3030 Pennsylvania Ave
Santa Monica, CA 90404-4112, USA

Wahle, Mike (Athlete, Football Player)
914 Laurie Dr
Madison, WI 53711-2417, USA

Wahler, Jason (Actor, Reality Star)
c/o Ashley Moore *Rogers & Cowan*
1840 Century Park E Fl 18
Los Angeles, CA 90067-2101, USA

Wahlquist, Heather (Actor)

Wahlstrom, Becky (Actor)
c/o Rob D'Avola *Rob DAvola & Associates*
9107 Wilshire Blvd # 405
Beverly Hills, CA 90210-5531, USA

Wahlstrom, Jarl H (Religious Leader)
Borgstrominkuja 1A10
Helsinki 84 00840, FINLAND

Waihee, John D III (Politician)
733 Ulumaika St
Honolulu, HI 96816-5109, USA

Wainhouse, Dave (Athlete, Baseball Player)
6101 85th Pl SE
Mercer Island, WA 98040-4916, USA

Wainscott, Loyd (Athlete, Football Player)
401 Tarpey Rd
Texas City, TX 77591-3159, USA

Wainwright, Adam (Athlete, Baseball Player)
60 E Rio Salado Pkwy Ste 1012
Tempe, AZ 85281-9501, USA

Wainwright, James (Actor)
Lew Sherrell
937 N Sinova
Mesa, AZ 85205-5438, USA

Wainwright, Loudon (Actor)
c/o Harriet Sternberg *Harriet Sternberg Management*
4530 Gloria Ave
Encino, CA 91436-2718, USA

Wainwright, Loudon III (Musician, Songwriter, Writer)
Teddy Wainwright
521 SW Halpatiokee St
Stuart, FL 34994-2815, USA

Wainwright, Marcus (Designer)
Rag & Bone
425 W 13th St Fl 3
New York, NY 10014-1123, USA

Wainwright, Rufus (Musician)
c/o Bianca Bianconi *42West*
600 3rd Ave Fl 23
New York, NY 10016-1914, USA

Wainwright, Rupert (Director)
1756 N. Sierra Bonita Ave
Los Angeles, CA 90046, USA

Waite, Jimmy (Athlete, Hockey Player)
Chicoutimi Sagueneens
643 Rue Begin Suite
Staff Coaching
Chicoutimi, QC G7H 4N7, Canada

Waite, John (Musician, Songwriter)
1018 4th St Unit 301
Santa Monica, CA 90403-6128, USA

Waite, Terence H (Terry) (Religious Leader)
Wheelrights Green Harvest
Bury Saint Demunds
Suffolk IP29 4DH, UNITED KINGDOM (UK)

Waite, Terry (Politician)
Wheelrights The Green Hartest Burv St Edmunds
Suffolk IP29 4DH, England

Waiters, Granville (Athlete, Basketball Player)
481 Oakwood Ave
Columbus, OH 43205-1935, USA

Waiters, Van (Athlete, Football Player)
6021 NW 201st Ln
Hialeah, FL 33015-4865, USA

Waithe, Lena (Actor)
c/o Andrew Coles *Mission Entertainment*
642 N Laurel Ave
Los Angeles, CA 90048-2321, USA

Waitley, Denis (Business Person)
The Waitley Institute
PO Box 197
Rancho Santa Fe, CA 92067-0197, USA

Waitley, Denis (Writer)
The Waitley Institute
PO Box 197
Rancho Santa Fe, CA 92067-0197, USA

Waits, Cy (Business Person)
2020 Doral Ct
Henderson, NV 89074-1074, USA

Waits, Rick (Athlete, Baseball Player)
PO Box 1001
Patagonia, AZ 85624-1001, USA

Waits, Tom (Musician)
c/o Adam Isaacs *MGMT Entertainment (The Schiff Company)*
9220 W Sunset Blvd Ste 106
W Hollywood, CA 90069-3500, USA

Waitt, Theodore W (Ted) (Business Person)
Gateway Inc
7565 Irvine Center Dr Ste 150
Irvine, CA 92618-4933, USA

Wakaluk, Darcy (Athlete, Hockey Player)
Calgary Hitmen
PO Box 1540 Stn M
Attn: Coaching Staff
Calgary, AB T2P 3B9, Canada

Wakamatsu, Don (Athlete, Baseball Player)
8740 Ramblewood Ct
Keller, TX 76248-0361, USA

Wakata, Koichi (Astronaut)
Japanese Aerospace Exploration Agency
2-1-1- Sengen
Tsukaba-shi, Ibaraki 305-8505, JAPAN

Wake, Cameron (Athlete, Football Player)

Wakefield, Abbey-May (Actor)
c/o Simon Millar *Rumble Media*
1620 Broadway Ste C
Santa Monica, CA 90404-2777, USA

Wakefield, Andre (Athlete, Basketball Player)
320 Wisconsin Ave Apt 519
Oak Park, IL 60302-3459, USA

Wakefield, Bill (Athlete, Baseball Player)
1 Baypoint Village Dr
San Rafael, CA 94901-8409, USA

Wakefield, Cameron (Actor)
c/o Simon Millar *Rumble Media*
1620 Broadway Ste C
Santa Monica, CA 90404-2777, USA

Wakefield, Rhys (Actor)
c/o Sandra Chang *Anonymous Content*
3532 Hayden Ave
Culver City, CA 90232-2413, USA

Wakefield, Tim (Athlete, Baseball Player)
241 Lansing Island Dr
Indian Harbour Beach, FL 32937-5102, USA

Wakeland, Chris (Athlete, Baseball Player)
PO Box 1701
Saint Helens, OR 97051-1735, USA

Wakeley, Amanda (Designer, Fashion Designer)
79-91 New Kings Road
London SW6 4SQ, UNITED KINGDOM (UK)

Wakely, Ernie (Athlete, Hockey Player)
11052 E Roundup Dr
Dewey, AZ 86327-5411, USA

Wakeman, Rick (Musician, Songwriter, Writer)
Bajonor House
2 Bridge St Peel
Isle of Man, UNITED KINGDOM (UK)

Wako, Gabriel Zubeir Cardinal (Religious Leader)
Archdiocese
PO Box 49
Khartoum, SUDAN

Wakoski, Diane (Writer)
607 Division St
East Lansing, MI 48823-3428, USA

Walackas, Augie (Race Car Driver)
255 Plymouth St
Whitman, MA 02382-1626, USA

Walbeck, Matt (Athlete, Baseball Player)
8216 Olive Ave
Fair Oaks, CA 95628-7623, USA

Walberg, Mark L. (Actor, Television Host)
c/o Staff Member *WME|IMG*
9601 Wilshire Blvd
Beverly Hills, CA 90210-5213, USA

Walberg, Tim (Congressman, Politician)
418 Cannon Hob
Washington, DC 20515-0301, USA

Walby, Chris (Athlete, Football Player)
22 Serenity Cove
Winnipeg, MB R2G 2P7, CANADA

Walcott, Jennifer (Model)
4400 N Scottsdale Rd Ste 9
Scottsdale, AZ 85251-3331, USA

Walcott, Theo (Athlete)
c/o Staff Member *Key Sports Management Ltd*
35 Soho Square
1st Floor
London W1D 3QX, UK

Walczak, Mark (Athlete, Football Player)
PO Box 372
Scottsdale, AZ 85252-0372, USA

Wald, Jeff (Producer)
c/o Staff Member *Jeff Wald Entertainment*
12855 Runway Rd Apt 1550
Playa Vista, CA 90094-2680, USA

Waldemore, Stan (Athlete, Football Player)
PO Box 611
New Vernon, NJ 07976-0611, USA

Walden, Erik (Athlete, Football Player)
c/o Ashley Smith Becker *Relativity Sports*
2029 Century Park E Ste 1550
Century City, CA 90067-3000, USA

Walden, Greg (Congressman, Politician)
2182 Rayburn Hob
Washington, DC 20515-3310, USA

Walden, Robert (Actor)
415 E 54th St # 24C
New York, NY 10022-5116, USA

Walden, Robert E (Bobby) (Athlete, Football Player)
1403 Douglas Dr
Bainbridge, GA 39819-5176, USA

Walden, Ronnie (Athlete, Baseball Player)
1007 Autumn Way
Blanchard, OK 73010-8961, USA

Walder, Katie (Actor)
c/o Stephanie Nese *Levity Entertainment Group (LEG)*
6701 Center Dr W Ste 300
Los Angeles, CA 90045-2482, USA

Waldheim, Kurt (President)
1 Lobkowitz Platz
Vienna 01010, AUSTRIA

Waldhorn, Gary (Actor)
London Mgmt
2-4 Noel St
London W1V 3RB, UNITED KINGDOM (UK)

Waldie, Marc (Athlete, Volleyball Player)
Murray Lampert Construction
3545 Camino Del Rio S Ste C
San Diego, CA 92108-4025, USA

Waldman, Suzyn (Sportscaster)
8 Foster Ct
Croton On Hudson, NY 10520-3303, USA

Waldner, Jan-Ove (Athlete, Tennis Player)
Banda
Skiulstagatan 1O
Eskilstuna 632 29, SWEDEN

Waldorf, Duffy (Golfer)
17100 Halsted St
Northridge, CA 91325-1960, USA

Wale (Musician)
c/o Brent Smith *WME|IMG*
9601 Wilshire Blvd
Beverly Hills, CA 90210-5213, USA

Wales, Jimmy (Business Person)
Wikimedia Foundation
PO Box 78350
San Francisco, CA 94107-8350, USA

Wales, Ross (Swimmer)
2730 Walsh Rd
Cincinnati, OH 45208-3425, USA

Walesa, Lech (Politician)
Polskistr 53
Gdansk-Oiiwa, POLAND

Waletrs, David (Politician)
RR 2
Watts, OK 74964, USA

Walewander, Jim (Athlete, Baseball Player)
19056 Crimson Clover Ter
Leesburg, VA 20176-8457, USA

Walger, Sonya (Actor)
c/o Jon Rubinstein *Authentic Talent and Literary Management (NY)*
20 Jay St Ste M17
Brooklyn, NY 11201-8300, USA

Walheim, Rex J (Astronaut)
142 Hidden Lake Dr
League City, TX 77573-6976, USA

Walheim, Rex J Lt Colonel (Astronaut)
142 Hidden Lake Dr
League City, TX 77573-6976, USA

Walik, Billy (Athlete, Football Player)
PO Box 10712
Bainbridge Island, WA 98110-0712, USA

Walk, Bob (Athlete, Baseball Player)
2494 Shadowbrook Dr
Wexford, PA 15090-7982, USA

Walken, Christopher (Actor)
142 Cedar Rd
Wilton, CT 06897-3631, USA

Walker, Adam (Athlete, Football Player)
915 Brookline Way
Alpharetta, GA 30022-3745, USA

Walker, Alan (Misc)
Johns Hopkins
Medical School
Cell Biology/Anatomy Dept
Baltimore, MD 21205, USA

Walker, Alice (Writer)
PO Box 378
Philo, CA 95466, USA

Walker, Ally (Actor)
c/o Erik Bright *Prodigy Public Relations*
2601 Ocean Park Blvd Ste 300
Santa Monica, CA 90405-5274, USA

Walker, Andrew (Actor)
c/o Amanda Rosenthal *Amanda Rosenthal Talent Agency*
315 Harbord St
Toronto, ON M6G 1G9, CANADA

Walker, Ann (Actor)
c/o Pam Ellis *Ellis Talent Group*
4705 Laurel Canyon Blvd Ste 300
Valley Village, CA 91607-5901, USA

Walker, Antoine (Athlete, Basketball Player)
6 Athena Ct
Tinley Park, IL 60477-4815, USA

Walker, Arnetia (Actor)
19551 Turtle Ridge Ln
Northridge, CA 91326-3808, USA

Walker, Benjamin (Actor)
c/o Cara Tripicchio *Shelter PR*
5670 Wilshire Blvd Ste 1200
Los Angeles, CA 90036-5621, USA

Walker, Bree (Actor)
3347 Tareco Dr
Los Angeles, CA 90068-1527, USA

Walker, Brian (Cartoonist)
c/o Staff Member *King Features Syndication*
300 W 57th St Fl 15
New York, NY 10019-5238, USA

Walker, Bruce (Athlete, Football Player)
279 Eastlawn St
Detroit, MI 48215-3072, USA

Walker, Butch (Musician)
c/o Jonathan Daniel *Crush Music Management*
60-62 E 11th St
Fl 7
New York, NY 10003, USA

Walker, Caroline (Actor)
c/o Staff Member *Badgley-Connor-King*
9229 W Sunset Blvd Ste 311
Los Angeles, CA 90069-3403, USA

Walker, Case (Musician)
c/o Staff Member *Authentic Talent & Literary Management*
3615 Eastham Dr # 650
Culver City, CA 90232-2410, USA

Walker, Charles D (Astronaut)
Boeing Co
13884 N Placita Meseta De Oro
Oro Valley, AZ 85755-8658, USA

Walker, Chet (Athlete, Basketball Player)
4225 Via Marina Apt 201
Marina Del Rey, CA 90292-4536, USA

Walker, Chico (Athlete, Baseball Player)
6 Athena Ct
Tinley Park, IL 60477-4815, USA

Walker, Chris (Actor)
Roll Kruger
121 Gloucester Place
London W1H 3PJ, UNITED KINGDOM (UK)

Walker, Chuck (Athlete, Football Player)
1613 Tradd Ct
Chesterfield, MO 63017-5627, USA

Walker, Clarence "Foots (Athlete, Basketball Player)
4629 S Eastland Center Dr Apt 1524
Independence, MO 64055-7808, USA

Walker, Clay (Musician)
4294 Skelley Rd
Santa Fe, TN 38482-3003, USA

Walker, Cleo (Athlete, Football Player)
1504 Anna Ln
Louisville, KY 40216-5444, USA

Walker, Cody (Actor)
c/o Staff Member *Luber Roklin Management*
5815 W Sunset Blvd Ste 208
Los Angeles, CA 90028-6481, USA

Walker, Darnell (Athlete, Football Player)
2636 Columbus St
Muskogee, OK 74401-5129, USA

Walker, Darrell (Athlete, Basketball Player, Coach)
16122 Patriot Dr
Little Rock, AR 72212-2669, USA

Walker, Delanie (Athlete, Football Player)

Walker, Denard (Athlete, Football Player)
17214 Lechlade Ln
Dallas, TX 75252-4208, USA

Walker, Derrick (Race Car Driver)
Walker Racing
147 Midland Rd Royston
Bamsley
S York S71 4B1, UNITED KINGDOM (UK)

Walker, Dewayne (Athlete, Football Player)
2364 Tuscan Hills Ln
Las Cruces, NM 88011-4105, USA

Walker, Django (Musician)
c/o Jon Folk *Red 11 Music (Nashville)*
Prefers to be contacted via telephone or email
Nashville, TN, USA

Walker, Dreama (Actor)
c/o Randi Goldstein *Gersh*
41 Madison Ave Ste 3301
New York, NY 10010-2210, USA

Walker, Duane (Athlete, Baseball Player)
2509 Georgia Ave
Deer Park, TX 77536-4732, USA

Walker, Dwight (Athlete, Football Player)
221 N Laurel St Apt B
Metairie, LA 70003-6268, USA

Walker, Eamonn (Actor)
c/o Scott Schachter *United Talent Agency (UTA)*
9336 Civic Center Dr
Beverly Hills, CA 90210-3604, USA

Walker, Fiona (Writer)
c/o Susan Fletcher *Hodder & Stoughton Limited*
338 Euston Rd
London NW1 3BH, UK

Walker, Glen (Athlete, Football Player)
PO Box 3427
Cypress, CA 90630-7427, USA

Walker, Greg (Cartoonist)
c/o Staff Member *King Features Syndication*
300 W 57th St Fl 15
New York, NY 10019-5238, USA

Walker, Greg (Athlete, Baseball Player)
530 N Lake Shore Dr Apt 1009
Chicago, IL 60611-7426, USA

Walker, Herschel (Athlete, Football Player, Heisman Trophy Winner)
2210 King Fisher Dr
Westlake, TX 76262-4815, USA

Walker, Hezekiah (Musician)
c/o Staff Member *The Alliance Agency*
1035 Bates Ct
Hendersonville, TN 37075-8864, USA

Walker, Howard (Athlete, Hockey Player)
PO Box 254
Wembley, AB T0H 3S0, Canada

Walker, Hugh (Baseball Player)
Bowman
24 Georgeann Dr
Jacksonville, AR 72076-5352, USA

Walker, Jackie (Athlete, Football Player)
13014 N Dale Mabry Hwy # 120
Tampa, FL 33618-2808, USA

Walker, James L (Jimmy) (Misc)
Fireman & Oilers Brotherhood
1100 Circle 75 Pkwy SE
Atlanta, GA 30339-3064, USA

Walker, Jamie (Athlete, Baseball Player)
11450 W 187th St
Spring Hill, KS 66083-7593, USA

Walker, Javon (Athlete, Football Player)
7375 Talon Trl
Parker, CO 80138-7956, USA

Walker, Jeff (Athlete, Football Player)
3712 Ringgold Rd Apt 204
Chattanooga, TN 37412-1638, USA

Walker, Jerry (Athlete, Baseball Player)
2015 Collins Blvd
Ada, OK 74820-7015, USA

Walker, Jerry Jeff (Musician, Songwriter)
Tried & True Music
PO Box 39
Austin, TX 78767-0039, USA

Walker, Jimmie (Actor, Comedian)
c/o Roger Paul *Roger Paul Talent*
1650 Broadway Ste 304A
New York, NY 10019-6833, USA

Walker, Joe Louis (Musician)
Rick Bates Mgmt
714 Brookside Ln
Sierra Madre, CA 91024-1426, USA

Walker, John (Athlete, Track Athlete)
Jeffs Road
RD Papatoetoe, NEW ZEALAND

Walker, Johnny (Athlete, Baseball Player)
Raleigh Tigers
718 Franklin St SE
Grand Rapids, MI 49507-1307, USA

Walker, Kenny (Athlete, Basketball Player)
7235 Darsena
Grand Prairie, TX 75054-6508, USA

Walker, Kenyatta (Athlete, Football Player)
14813 Tudor Chase Dr
Tampa, FL 33626-3353, USA

Walker, Kevin (Athlete, Baseball Player)
759 Chestnut Ave
Holtville, CA 92250-1410, USA

Walker, Kurt (Athlete, Hockey Player)
9390 Martin Rd
Roswell, GA 30076-3022, USA

Walker, Larry (Athlete, Baseball Player)
1667 Flagler Pkwy
West Palm Beach, FL 33411-1874, USA

Walker, Luke (Athlete, Baseball Player)
316 Loma Linda St
Wake Village, TX 75501-8638, USA

Walker, Malcolm (Athlete, Football Player)
7140 Winterwood Ln
Dallas, TX 75248-5246, USA

Walker, Marquis (Athlete, Football Player)
17576 Cherrylawn St
Detroit, MI 48221-2508, USA

Walker, Mickey (Athlete, Football Player)
1319 Saint Clair Blvd
Algonac, MI 48001-1436, USA

Walker, Mike (Athlete, Baseball Player)
23195 Tankersley Rd
Brooksville, FL 34601-4818, USA

Walker, Mike (Athlete, Baseball Player)
24616 Marks Rd
Splendora, TX 77372-3407, USA

Walker, Pete (Athlete, Baseball Player)
2 White Oak Ln
Quaker Hill, CT 06375-1045, USA

Walker, Peter (Director)
23 Bentick St
London W1, UNITED KINGDOM (UK)

Walker, Phillip (Athlete, Basketball Player)
720 E Phil Ellena St
Philadelphia, PA 19119-1531, USA

Walker, Polly (Actor)
c/o Christian Hodell *Hamilton Hodell Ltd*
20 Golden Sq
Fl 5
London W1F 9JL, UNITED KINGDOM

Walker, Rick (Athlete, Football Player)
906 Winstead St
Great Falls, VA 22066-2546, USA

Walker, Sammy (Athlete, Football Player)
1031 Kings Row
Mc Kinney, TX 75069-6207, USA

Walker, Scott (Director)
c/o BeBe Lerner *ID Public Relations*
7060 Hollywood Blvd Fl 8th
Los Angeles, CA 90028-6021, USA

Walker, Shannon Dr (Astronaut)
2421 Clopper St
Seabrook, TX 77586-3738, USA

Walker, Summer (Actor)
c/o Brittany Myers *WME|IMG*
9601 Wilshire Blvd
Beverly Hills, CA 90210-5213, USA

Walker, Suzie (Reality Star)
c/o Staff Member *Celeb Agents*
77 Oxford St
London ON W1D 2ES, UNITED KINGDOM (UK)

Walker, Todd (Athlete, Baseball Player)
212 Madonna Dr
Benton, LA 71006-4217, USA

Walker, Tom (Athlete, Baseball Player)
817 Whippoorwill Hill Rd
Gibsonia, PA 15044-8985, USA

Walker, Tony (Athlete, Baseball Player)
2030 Goldenrod Ln
San Ramon, CA 94582-5543, USA

Walker, Tyler (Race Car Driver)
222 Raceway Dr
Mooresville, NC 28117-6510, United States

Walker, Tyler (Athlete, Baseball Player)
400 Sansome St
San Francisco, CA 94111-3353, USA

Walker, Tyrunn (Athlete, Football Player)
c/o Sean Kiernan *Impact Sports (LA)*
12429 Ventura Ct
Studio City, CA 91604-2417, USA

Walker, Val Joe (Athlete, Football Player)
3857 S Versailles Ave
Dallas, TX 75209-5927, USA

Walker, Vance (Athlete, Football Player)

Walker, Wally (Athlete, Basketball Player)
154 Lombard St Apt 58
San Francisco, CA 94111-1125, USA

Walker, Wayne (Athlete, Football Player)
2033 S White Pine Ln
Boise, ID 83706-4048, USA

Walker, Wesley D (Athlete, Football Player)
PO Box 20438
Huntington Station, NY 11746-0857, USA

Walker, William D (Business Person)
Tektronix Inc
26600 Sourtwest Parkway
Wilsonville, OR 97070, USA

Walkom, Stephen (Athlete, Hockey Player)
1709 Wheatland Ct
Coraopolis, PA 15108-9208, USA

Walk the Moon (Music Group)
c/o Michael McDonald *Mick Management*
35 Washington St
Brooklyn, NY 11201-1028, USA

Wall, Bob (Athlete, Hockey Player)
1203 Canuck Trail RR 5
Minden, ON K0M 2A1, Canada

Wall, Brian A (Artist)
306 Lombard St
San Francisco, CA 94133-2415, USA

Wall, Donne (Athlete, Baseball Player)
116 River Breeze Way
Saint Louis, MO 63129-4855, USA

Wall, Frederick T (Athlete, Football Player)
2044 Kerwood Ave
Los Angeles, CA 90025-6007, USA

Wall, John (Athlete, Basketball Player)
c/o Dan Fegan *Relativity Sports*
2029 Century Park E Ste 1550
Century City, CA 90067-3000, USA

Wall, Lindsay (Hockey Player)
University of Minnesota
Athletic Dept
Minneapolis, MN 55455, USA

Wall, Paul (Musician)
c/o Drew Elliot *Artist International*
333 E 43rd St Apt 115
New York, NY 10017-4822, USA

Wall, Shana (Actor)
c/o Elizabeth Much *East 2 West Collective*
11022 Santa Monica Blvd Ste 350
Los Angeles, CA 90025-7532, USA

Wall, Stan (Athlete, Baseball Player)
9907 E 80th St
Raytown, MO 64138-1929, USA

Wall, Travis (Dancer)
c/o Liza Anderson *Anderson Group Public Relations*
8060 Melrose Ave Fl 4
Los Angeles, CA 90046-7038, USA

Wallace, Aaron (Athlete, Football Player)
612 Gardenia St
Desoto, TX 75115-1449, USA

Wallace, Andy (Race Car Driver)
Childress-Howard Motorsports
PO Box 889
Denver, 28037 USA, USA

Wallace, Anthony F C (Misc)
University of Pennsylvania
Anthropology Dept
Philadelphia, PA 19014, USA

Wallace, Aria (Actor)
c/o DebraLynn Findon *Discover Management (LA)*
11425 Moorpark St
Studio City, CA 91602-2009, USA

Wallace, Barron Steven (Steve) (Athlete, Football Player)
305 Heards Ferry Rd
Atlanta, GA 30328-4716, USA

Wallace, Ben (Basketball Player)
c/o Staff Member *Chicago Bulls*
1901 W Madison St
Chicago, IL 60612-2459, USA

Wallace, B J (Athlete, Baseball Player, Olympic Athlete)
12775 River Creek Dr
Fairhope, AL 36532-6501, USA

Wallace, Bob (Athlete, Football Player)
44111 N 43rd Dr
New River, AZ 85087-5956, USA

Wallace, Chris (Correspondent)
2439 Wyoming Ave NW
Washington, DC 20008-1644, USA

Wallace, Cody (Athlete, Football Player)

Wallace, Cooper (Athlete, Football Player)
c/o Chad Speck *Allegiant Athletic Agency*
35 Market Sq Ste 201
Knoxville, TN 37902-1420, USA

Wallace, Dave (Athlete, Baseball Player)
29 Meetinghouse Rd
Norfolk, MA 02056-1793, USA

Wallace, Derek (Athlete, Baseball Player)
6723 SE Silverbell Ave
Stuart, FL 34997-2248, USA

Wallace, Don (Actor)
c/o Staff Member *SMS Talent*
8383 Wilshire Blvd Ste 230
Beverly Hills, CA 90211-2436, USA

Wallace, Don (Athlete, Baseball Player)
23 Kris Ln
Manitou Springs, CO 80829-2709, USA

Wallace, George (Musician)
c/o Staff Member *Paradigm (Monterey)*
404 W Franklin St
Monterey, CA 93940-2303, USA

Wallace, Gerald (Athlete, Basketball Player)
8381 Providence Rd
Charlotte, NC 28277-9753, USA

Wallace, Jeff (Athlete, Baseball Player)
235 Crawford St
Beckley, WV 25801-5633, USA

Wallace, Julie T (Actor)
Annette Stone
9 Newburgh St
London W1V 1LH, UNITED KINGDOM (UK)

Wallace, Kenny (Race Car Driver)
4806 Old Lemay Ferry Rd
Imperial, MO 63052-1306, USA

Wallace, Laurie (Actor)
PO Box 3023
Guttenberg, NJ 07093-6023, USA

Wallace, Mike (Race Car Driver)
Morgan-McClure Racing
26502 Newbanks Rd
Abingdon, VA 24210-7500, USA

Wallace, Mike (Athlete, Baseball Player)
12483 Elk Run Rd
Midland, VA 22728-2316, USA

Wallace, Mike (Athlete, Football Player)

Wallace, Nicolle (Journalist, Television Host)
c/o Lawrence Stuart *ICM Partners (NY)*
730 5th Ave
New York, NY 10019-4105, USA

Wallace, Randall (Actor, Director, Producer, Writer)
c/o Staff Member *Wheelhouse, The*
15464 Ventura Blvd
Sherman Oaks, CA 91403-3002

Wallace, Rasheed (Athlete, Basketball Player)
27506 Shores Ct
Spring, TX 77386-3826, USA

Wallace, Ray (Athlete, Football Player)
2480 Port Kembla Dr
Mount Juliet, TN 37122-7512, USA

Wallace, Rheagan (Actor)
c/o Linda McAlister *Linda McAlister Talent*
30 N Raymond Ave Ste 213
Pasadena, CA 91103-3997, USA

Wallace, Rick (Director, Producer)
29033 Grayfox St
Malibu, CA 90265-4256, USA

Wallace, Rodney (Athlete, Football Player)
20566 E Maplewood Pl
Centennial, CO 80016-1264, USA

Wallace, Roger (Athlete, Football Player)
408 N Oakland St
Urbana, OH 43078-1521, USA

Wallace, Rusty (Race Car Driver)
c/o Lou Oppenheim *ICM Partners (NY)*
730 5th Ave
New York, NY 10019-4105, USA

Wallace, Steve (Race Car Driver)
c/o Staff Member *Rusty Wallace Racing, LLC*
149 Knob Hill Rd
Mooresville, NC 28117-6847, USA

Wallace, Tommy Lee (Director)
Innovative Artists
1505 10th St
Santa Monica, CA 90401-2805, USA

Wallace, Will (Director)
c/o Staff Member *Cutler Management*
12424 Wilshire Blvd Ste 9
Los Angeles, CA 90025-1071, USA

Wallach, Tim (Athlete, Baseball Player)
21750 Deveron Cv
Yorba Linda, CA 92887-2662, USA

Wallechinsky, David (Writer)
c/o Staff Member *HarperCollins Publishers*
195 Broadway Fl 2
New York, NY 10007-3132, USA

Wallem, Linda (Actor, Producer)
c/o Staff Member *Creative Artists Agency (CAA)*
2000 Avenue of the Stars Ste 100
Los Angeles, CA 90067-4705, USA

Waller, Dwight (Athlete, Basketball Player)
1038 S Brookside Dr
Gallatin, TN 37066-5612, USA

Waller, Jamie (Athlete, Basketball Player)
904 Owens Ave
South Boston, VA 24592-3728, USA

Waller, Ron (Athlete, Football Player)
900 Concord Rd
Seaford, DE 19973, USA

Waller, Ty (Athlete, Baseball Player)
16963 Silver Crest Dr
San Diego, CA 92127-2816, USA

Waller, Tye (Athlete, Baseball Player)
16963 Silver Crest Dr
San Diego, CA 92127-2816, USA

Waller-Bridge, Phoebe (Actor)
c/o Aileen McEwan *Hatton McEwan Penford*
The Leathermarket Weston St
Weston St
London SE1 3ER, UNITED KINGDOM

Wallerstein, Ralph G (Misc)
3447 Clay St
San Francisco, CA 94118-2008, USA

Wallflowers, The (Music Group)
c/o Rick Roskin *Creative Artists Agency (CAA)*
2000 Avenue of the Stars Ste 100
Los Angeles, CA 90067-4705, USA

Wallin, Niclas (Athlete, Hockey Player)
244 Johnson Ave
Los Gatos, CA 95030-6218, USA

Walling, Camryn (Actor)
c/o Staff Member *Abrams Artists Agency*
750 N San Vicente Blvd
E Tower Fl 11
Los Angeles, CA 90069-5788, USA

Walling, Denny (Athlete, Baseball Player)
PO Box 1312
Waynesboro, VA 22980-0902, USA

Wallis, Annabelle (Actor)
c/o Pippa Beng *Premier PR*
2-4 Bucknall St
London WC2H 8LA, UNITED KINGDOM

Wallis, Joe (Athlete, Baseball Player)
PO Box 2284
Saint Louis, MO 63109-0284, USA

Wallis, Kevin (Horse Racer)
2874 NE 33rd St
Lighthouse Point, FL 33064-8551, USA

Wallis, Quvenzhane (Actor)
c/o Chris Chambers *The Chamber Group*
75 Broad St Rm 708
New York, NY 10004-3244, USA

Wallis, Shani (Actor)
PO Box 3604
Dana Point, CA 92629-8604, USA

Walliser, Maria (Skier)
Selfwingert
Malans 07208, SWITZERLAND

Wallnau, Lance (Writer)
Lance Learning Group
550 Reserve St Ste 190
Southlake, TX 76092-1575, USA

Wallner, Hakan (Horse Racer)
PO Box 3153
Pompano Beach, FL 33072-3153, USA

Walls, Denise (Nee-C) (Musician, Songwriter, Writer)
2113 South Ave
Youngstown, OH 44502-2255, USA

Walls, Everson C (Athlete, Football Player)
1925 Antwerp Ave
Plano, TX 75025-3320, USA

Walls, Herkie (Athlete, Football Player)
1002 Cherrywood Dr
Garland, TX 75040-7437, USA

Walls, Jeannette (Writer)
c/o Jennifer Rudolph Walsh *WME/IMG (NY)*
11 Madison Ave Fl 18
New York, NY 10010-3669, USA

Walls, Lenny (Athlete, Football Player)
2800 Bush St
San Francisco, CA 94115-2905, USA

Walls, Sinqua (Actor)
c/o Alyx Carr *42West*
600 3rd Ave Fl 23
New York, NY 10016-1914, USA

Walls, Wesley (Athlete, Football Player)
8711 Lake Challis Ln
Charlotte, NC 28226-2666, USA

Wallstrom, Martin (Actor)
c/o Staff Member *United Talent Agency (UTA)*
9336 Civic Center Dr
Beverly Hills, CA 90210-3604, USA

Walmsley, Jon (Actor)
c/o Staff Member *Howard Talent West*
PO Box 5403
Chatsworth, CA 91313-5403, USA

Walpot, Heike (Astronaut)
DLR
Abt Raumflugbetrieb
Cologne 51170, GERMANY

Walrond, Les (Athlete, Baseball Player)
5170 Hickory Hollow Pkwy Unit 262
Antioch, TN 37013-3062, USA

Walser, Derrick (Athlete, Hockey Player)
592 Lorne St
New Glasgow, NS B2H 4L3, Canada

Walser, Don (Musician, Songwriter, Writer)
Nancy Fly Agency
6618 Wolfcreek Pass
Austin, TX 78749-1744, USA

Walsh, Addie (Writer)
c/o Staff Member *WME/IMG*
9601 Wilshire Blvd
Beverly Hills, CA 90210-5213, USA

Walsh, Amanda (Actor)
c/o Laina Cohn *Cohn / Torgan Management*
Prefers to be contacted by telephone or email
Los Angeles, CA, USA

Walsh, Blair (Athlete, Football Player)

Walsh, Bradley (Actor)
c/o Debi Allen *DAA Management*
66-67 Wells St
Welbeck House
London WIT 3PY, UNITED KINGDOM

Walsh, Chris (Athlete, Football Player)
4834 N 74th St
Scottsdale, AZ 85251-1306, USA

Walsh, Dave (Athlete, Baseball Player)
832 1/2 NW 37th St
Oklahoma City, OK 73118-7131, USA

Walsh, Don (Athlete, Swimmer)
International Maritime Inc
14758 Sitkum Ln
Myrtle Point, OR 97458-9692, USA

Walsh, Donnie (Basketball Coach, Coach)
5625 Audubon Ridge Ln
Indianapolis, IN 46250-2320, USA

Walsh, Dylan (Actor)
c/o Lori Jonas *Jonas Public Relations*
1327 Ocean Ave Ste F
Santa Monica, CA 90401-1024, USA

Walsh, Frances (Fran) (Producer, Writer)
c/o Staff Member *WingNut Films*
PO Box 15-208
Miramar
Wellington 06003, NEW ZEALAND

Walsh, Gwynyth (Actor)
c/o Staff Member *Characters Talent Agency*
200-1505 2nd Ave W
Vancouver, BC V6H 3Y4, CANADA

Walsh, JD (Actor)
4404 Henley Ct
Westlake Vlg, CA 91361-4305, USA

Walsh, Joe (Musician, Songwriter)
c/o Irving Azoff *Azoff Music Management*
1100 Glendon Ave Ste 2000
Los Angeles, CA 90024-3524, USA

Walsh, Joe (Congressman, Politician)
432 Cannon Hob
Washington, DC 20515-4004, USA

Walsh, John (Television Host)
Silver Spring Studios
699 Prince St
Alexandria, VA 22314-3117, USA

Walsh, Kate (Actor)
PO Box 261067
Encino, CA 91426-1067, USA

Walsh, Kerri (Athlete, Volleyball Player)
c/o Brandon Swibel *TLA Worldwide (The Legacy Agency)*
1500 Broadway Ste 2501
New York, NY 10036-4082, USA

Walsh, Kimberley (Actor, Musician)
c/o Staff Member *Artists Rights Group (ARG)*
4A Exmoor St
London W10 6BD, UNITED KINGDOM

Walsh, Louis (Actor)
c/o Staff Member *Hackford Jones PR*
19 Nassau St
London W1W 7AF, UK

Walsh, Maiara (Actor)
c/o Staff Member *Mattie Management*
1438 N Gower St Ste 57
Los Angeles, CA 90028-8358, USA

Walsh, Martin (Misc)
National Organization on Disability
910 16th St NW
Washington, DC 20006-2903, USA

Walsh, Matt (Actor, Comedian)
c/o Antonio D'Alessandro *AntonioPaulPR*
PO Box 801651
Santa Clarita, CA 91380-1651, USA

Walsh, M Emmet (Actor)
c/o Cynthia Snyder *Cynthia Snyder Public Relations*
5739 Colfax Ave
N Hollywood, CA 91601-1636, USA

Walsh, Morgan (Actor)
c/o Glenn Salners *Artists & Representatives (Stone Manners Salners)*
6100 Wilshire Blvd Ste 1500
Los Angeles, CA 90048-5110, USA

Walsh, Peter (Designer)
Peter Walsh Design
15030 Ventura Blvd Ste 19
Sherman Oaks, CA 91403-2444, USA

Walsh, Sheila (Musician, Writer)
PO Box 150783
Nashville, TN 37215-0783, USA

Walsh, Shelia (Musician, Writer)
PO Box 1516
Celina, TX 75009-1516, USA

Walsh, Stephen J (Steve) (Athlete, Football Player)
339 Flamingo Dr
West Palm Beach, FL 33401-7721, USA

Walsh, Sydney (Actor)
Innovative Artists
1505 10th St
Santa Monica, CA 90401-2805, USA

Walsh, Tom (Artist)
PO Box 133
Philomath, OR 97370-0133, USA

Walsh, Ward (Athlete, Football Player)
1658 W Carson St Ste C
Torrance, CA 90501-2897, USA

Walshe, Tommy (Actor, Television Host)
c/o Staff Member *Arlington Enterprises Ltd*
1-3 Charlotte St
London W1P 1HD, UNITED KINGDOM (UK)

Walske, Steven (Business Person)
Parametric Technology
140 Kendrick St Ste C120
Needham Heights, MA 02494-2743, USA

Walsman, Leanna (Actor)
c/o Chris Andrews *Creative Artists Agency (CAA)*
2000 Avenue of the Stars Ste 100
Los Angeles, CA 90067-4705, USA

Walte, Grant (Golfer)
9380 S Magnolia Ave
Ocala, FL 34476-7535, USA

Walter, Dr Ulrich (Astronaut)
IBM Deutschland Entwicklung Abtig 8515
Schonaicherstrasse 220
Boblingen D-71032, Germany

Walter, Gene (Athlete, Baseball Player)
1901 Fairway Dr
La Grange, KY 40031-9697, USA

Walter, Harriet (Actor)
c/o Jeremy Conway *Conway van Gelder Grant*
8-12 Broadwick St
London W1F 8HW, UNITED KINGDOM

Walter, Jessica (Actor)
c/o Teri Weigel *The Creative Group PR*
324 S Beverly Dr # 216
Beverly Hills, CA 90212-4801, USA

Walter, Joe (Athlete, Football Player)
4136 Binley Dr
Richardson, TX 75082-3723, USA

Walter, Lisa Ann (Actor)
c/o Mel McKeon *McKeon-Myones Management*
3500 W Olive Ave Ste 770
Burbank, CA 91505-5527, USA

Walter, Michael (Athlete, Football Player)
32229 SW Boones Bend Rd
Wilsonville, OR 97070-6416, USA

Walter, Mike (Athlete, Football Player)
32229 SW Boones Bend Rd
Wilsonville, OR 97070-6416, USA

Walter, Paul H L (Misc)
3 Benedictine Retreat
Savannah, GA 31411-1624, USA

Walter, Robert D (Business Person)
Cardinal Health
7000 Cardinal Pl
Dublin, OH 43017-1091, USA

Walter, Ryan (Athlete, Hockey Player)
19633 8 Av
Langley, BC V2Z 1W1, Canada

Walter, Tracey (Actor)
257 N Rexford Dr
Beverly Hills, CA 90210-4907, USA

Walter, Ulrich (Astronaut)
IBM Germany
Schonaicherstr 220
Boblingen 71032, GERMANY

Walters, Anthony (Athlete, Football Player)

Walters, Barbara (Journalist, Talk Show Host)
c/o Staff Member *Barwall Productions*
320 W 66th St # 200
New York, NY 10023-6304, USA

Walters, Charles (Director)
23922 De Ville Way Apt A
Malibu, CA 90265-4844, USA

Walters, Charlie (Athlete, Baseball Player)
906 S Highview Cir
Saint Paul, MN 55118-3686, USA

Walters, Dan (Athlete, Baseball Player)
Physically Unable To Sign Autographs

Walters, David (Politician)
RR 2
Watts, OK 74964, USA

Walters, Hugh (Actor)
15 Christchurch Ave
London, ENGLAND NW6 7QP

Walters, Jamie (Actor, Musician)
4702 Ethel Ave
Sherman Oaks, CA 91423-3315, USA

Walters, Julie (Actor)
c/o Tom Burke *ICM Partners*
10250 Constellation Blvd Fl 7
Los Angeles, CA 90067-6207, USA

Walters, Lisa (Athlete, Golfer)
302 N Clearview Ave
Tampa, FL 33609-1312, USA

Walters, Melora (Actor)
c/o Staff Member *Platform PR*
2666 N Beachwood Dr
Los Angeles, CA 90068-2308, USA

Walters, Mike (Athlete, Baseball Player)
79070 Desert Stream Dr
La Quinta, CA 92253-4295, USA

Walters, Peter I (Business Person)
22 Hill St
London W1X 7FU, UNITED KINGDOM (UK)

Walters, Phil (Race Car Driver)
23 Sycamore
Homosassa, FL 32646, USA

Walters, PJ (Athlete, Baseball Player)
29476 Oakstone Dr E
Daphne, AL 36526-5602, USA

Walters, Rex (Athlete, Basketball Player)
21602 W 99th St
Lenexa, KS 66220-2678, USA

Walters, Scot (Race Car Driver)
Brewco Motorsports
PO Box 37
321 W. Reservoir
Central City, KY 42330-0037, USA

Walters, Stan (Athlete, Football Player)
10 Icklingham Wood
Sewell, NJ 08080, USA

Walters, Susan (Actor)
c/o Gabrielle Krengel *Domain Talent*
1880 Century Park E Ste 1100
Los Angeles, CA 90067-1608, USA

Walters, Tom (Athlete, Football Player)
8 Heritage Ln
Magnolia, TX 77354-1337, USA

Walterschield, Len (Athlete, Football Player)
2312 I Rd
Grand Junction, CO 81505-9646, USA

Walther, Paul (Athlete, Basketball Player)
6555 Riverside Dr
Atlanta, GA 30328-2705, USA

Waltman, Sean (X-Pac) (Athlete, Wrestler)
c/o Staff Member *World Wrestling Entertainment (WWE)*
1241 E Main St
Stamford, CT 06902-3520, USA

Walton, Alice (Business Person)
Wal-Mart Stores
702 SW 8th St
Bentonville, AR 72716-6299, USA

Walton, Ann (Business Person)
1807 W Nifong Blvd
Columbia, MO 65203-5913, USA

Walton, Anna (Actor)
c/o Rupert Fowler *ID Public Relations (UK)*
Pall Mall Deposit 124-128 Barlby Rd
Unit 27A
London W10 6BL, UNITED KINGDOM

Walton, Anthony J (Tony) (Designer)
International Creative Mgmt
40 W 57th St Ste 1800
New York, NY 10019-4033, USA

Walton, Bennie (Baseball Player)
188 S Palm Villas Way
Palm Springs, FL 33461-1084, USA

Walton, Bill (Athlete, Basketball Player, Sportscaster)
1010 Myrtle Way
San Diego, CA 92103-5123, USA

Walton, Bruce (Athlete, Baseball Player)
10704 Sunset Canyon Dr
Bakersfield, CA 93311-2746, USA

Walton, Christy (Business Person)
Wal-Mart Stores
702 SW 8th St
Bentonville, AR 72712-6209, USA

Walton, Danny (Athlete, Baseball Player)
PO Box 296
Huntsville, UT 84317-0296, USA

Walton, David (Actor)
c/o Nick Collins *Gersh*
9465 Wilshire Blvd Ste 600
Beverly Hills, CA 90212-2605, USA

Walton, J.D. (Athlete, Football Player)
c/o Bill Johnson *SportsTrust Advisors*
3340 Peachtree Rd NE Fl 16
Atlanta, GA 30326-1000, USA

Walton, Jerome (Athlete, Baseball Player)
4500 Shannon Blvd Apt 8C
Union City, GA 30291-1534, USA

Walton, Jess (Actor)
4033 Weslin Ave
Sherman Oaks, CA 91423-4658, USA

Walton, Jim (Business Person)
The Walton Family Foundation
PO Box 2030
Bentonville, AR 72712-2030, USA

Walton, John (Athlete, Football Player)
401 New York Ave
Elizabeth City, NC 27909-5939, USA

Walton, Joseph (Joe) (Athlete, Coach, Football Coach, Football Player)
8 Windycrest Dr
Beaver Falls, PA 15010-3041, USA

Walton, Lawrence (Athlete, Football Player)
8636 N 96th Ln
Peoria, AZ 85345-7759, USA

Walton, Luke (Athlete, Basketball Player)
1240 5th St
Manhattan Beach, CA 90266-6001, USA

Walton, Mike (Athlete, Hockey Player)
RE/MAX Realty
102B-45 Bramalea Rd
Brampton, ON L6T 2W4, Canada

Walton, Reggie (Athlete, Baseball Player)
1142 S Curson Ave
Los Angeles, CA 90019-6611, USA

Walton, Robin (Golfer)
8404 SW 50th Ln
Gainesville, FL 32608-4307, USA

Walton, S Robson (Business Person)
Wal-Mart Stores
702 SW 8th St
Bentonville, AR 72716-6299, USA

Walton, Whip (Athlete, Football Player)
5662 Weatherstone Ct
San Diego, CA 92130-4826, USA

Walton Laurie, Nancy (Business Person)
1186 MacDonald Ranch Dr
Henderson, NV 89012-7272, USA

Waltrip, Darrell (Race Car Driver)
110 Deerfield
Franklin, TN 37064, USA

Waltrip, Michael (Race Car Driver)
Mark Martin Museum & Gift Shop
1601 Batesville Blvd
Batesville, AR 72501-8372, USA

Waltrip, Robert L (Business Person)
Service Corp International
1929 Allen Pkwy
Houston, TX 77019-2506, USA

Waltz, Christoph (Actor)
c/o Lisa Kasteler *Wolf-Kasteler Public Relations*
6255 W Sunset Blvd Ste 1111
Los Angeles, CA 90028-7426, USA

Waltz, Lisa (Actor)
c/o Donald Spradlin *Essential Talent Management*
7958 Beverly Blvd
Los Angeles, CA 90048-4511, USA

Waltz, Rich (Sportscaster)
1429 NW 127th Ave
Coral Springs, FL 33071-5447, USA

Walz, Carl E (Astronaut)
129 Lake Point Dr
League City, TX 77573-6973, USA

Walz, Carl E Col (Astronaut)
1507 McGuire Rd
League City, TX 77573-7777, USA

Walz, Wes (Athlete, Hockey Player)
2377 Fieldstone Curv
Saint Paul, MN 55129-6218, USA

Walz, Zach (Athlete, Football Player)
6270 E Wilshire Dr
Scottsdale, AZ 85257-1114, USA

Wambach, Abby (Athlete, Olympic Athlete, Soccer Player)
Powerplay Consultants
1600 Parkwood Cir SE Ste 600
Atlanta, GA 30339-2147, USA

Wambaugh, Joseph (Writer)
30 Linda Isle
Newport Beach, CA 92660-7206, USA

Wambold, Richard L (Business Person)
Pactiv Corp
1900 W Field Ct
Lake Forest, IL 60045-4828, USA

Wamsley, Rick (Athlete, Hockey Player)
1171 Wildhorse Meadows Dr
Chesterfield, MO 63005-1349, USA

Wan, James (Director)
755 Stradella Rd
Los Angeles, CA 90077-3307, USA

Wanamaker, Zoe (Actor)
Conway Van Gelder Robinson
18-21 Jermyn St
London SW1Y 6NB, UNITED KINGDOM (UK)

Wang, Alexander (Designer, Fashion Designer)
Alexander Wang Inc
386 Broadway Fl 3
New York, NY 10013-6021, USA

Wang, Garrett (Actor)
501 E Del Mar Blvd Apt 310
Pasadena, CA 91101-3613, USA

Wang, Jida (Artist)
7612 35th Ave Apt 3E
Jackson Heights, NY 11372-4612, USA

Wang, Junxia (Athlete, Track Athlete)
Athletic Assn
9 Tlyuguan Road
Chongwen District
Beijing 10061, CHINA

Wang, Leehom (Actor)
c/o Jason Newman *Untitled Entertainment*
350 S Beverly Dr Ste 200
Beverly Hills, CA 90212-4819, USA

Wang, Tian-Ren (Artist)
Shaanxi Sculpture Institute
Longshoucun
Xi'am
Shaanxi 710016, CHINA

Wang, Vera (Designer, Fashion Designer)
610 Cole Pl
Beverly Hills, CA 90210-1918, USA

Wang, Wayne (Director)
1888 Century Park E Ste 1888
Los Angeles, CA 90067-1722, USA

Wang Zhl Zhi (Basketball Player)
Miami Heat
601 Biscayne Blvd
American Airlines Arena
Miami, FL 33132-1801, USA

Wanner, H Eric (Misc)
Russell Sage Foundation
112 E 64th St
New York, NY 10065-7383, USA

Wannsdedt, David R (Dave) (Coach, Football Coach)
12600 N Stonebrook Cir
Davie, FL 33330-1288, USA

Wannstedt, David R (Dave) (Athlete, Coach, Football Coach, Football Player)
151 Rock Haven Ln
Pittsburgh, PA 15228-1879, USA

Wansel, Dexter (Musician)
Walt Reeder Productions
PO Box 27641
Philadelphia, PA 19118-0641, USA

Wap, Fetty (Musician)
c/o April King *ICM Partners*
10250 Constellation Blvd Fl 7
Los Angeles, CA 90067-6207, USA

Waples, Keith (Horse Racer)
PO Box 632
Durham, ON N0G 1R0, CANADA

Waples, Ron (Horse Racer)
7 Mill Run W
Hightstown, NJ 08520-3021, USA

Wapnick, Steve (Athlete, Baseball Player)
7518 Plateau Rd
Greeley, CO 80634-9388, USA

Wappel, Gord (Athlete, Hockey Player)
5544 Kartusch Pl
Regina, SK S4X 4Kl, Canada

Warbeck, Stephen (Composer)
c/o Staff Member *Soundtrack Music Assoc*
1460 4th St Ste 308
Santa Monica, CA 90401-3483, USA

Warburton, Patrick (Actor)
c/o Liza Anderson *Anderson Group Public Relations*
8060 Melrose Ave Fl 4
Los Angeles, CA 90046-7038, USA

Ward, Aaron (Athlete, Hockey Player)
2478 Terrmini Dr
Apex, NC 27502-9673, USA

Ward, Andre (Athlete, Boxer)
c/o James Prince *Prince Boxing Enterprises*
3030 Jensen Dr
Houston, TX 77026-5511, USA

Ward, Anita (Musician)
c/o Staff Member *Diva Central Inc*
7510 W Sunset Blvd # 1445
Los Angeles, CA 90046-3408, USA

Ward, Bert (Actor)
c/o Wes Stevens *Vox*
5670 Wilshire Blvd Ste 820
Los Angeles, CA 90036-5613, USA

Ward, Bryan (Athlete, Baseball Player)
140 Bannock Ct
East Dundee, IL 60118-1626, USA

Ward, Burt (Actor)
c/o Roger Neal *Neal Public Relations & Management*
3042 N Keystone St
Burbank, CA 91504-1621, USA

Ward, Cam (Athlete, Hockey Player)
501 Regency Dr
Sherwood Park, AB T8A 5N2, Canada

Ward, Charlie (Athlete, Basketball Player, Football Player, Heisman Trophy Winner)
3768 Longfellow Rd
Tallahassee, FL 32311-3708, USA

Ward, Chris (Athlete, Baseball Player)
PO Box 840561
Houston, TX 77284-0561, USA

Ward, Chris (Athlete, Football Player)
1920 Sylvan Ridge Dr SW
Atlanta, GA 30310-4945, USA

Ward, Christopher L (Chris) (Athlete, Football Player)
PO Box 1365
Inglewood, CA 90308-1365, USA

Ward, Colby (Athlete, Baseball Player)
1508 Hobble Creek Dr
Springville, UT 84663-2890, USA

Ward, Colin (Athlete, Baseball Player)
1220 E Commerce Ave
Gilbert, AZ 85234-4856, USA

Ward, Dale (Musician)
A Crosse the World
PO Box 23066
London W11 3FR, UNITED KINGDOM (UK)

Ward, Daryle (Athlete, Baseball Player)
18073 Granite Ave
Riverside, CA 92508-9777, USA

Ward, Dedric (Athlete, Football Player)
3435 N 45th St
Phoenix, AZ 85018-6028, USA

Ward, Dixon (Athlete, Hockey Player)
Okanagan Hockey School
201-853 Eckhardt Ave W
Attn: Vice President's Office
Penticton, BC V2A 9C4, Canada

Ward, Ed (Athlete, Hockey Player)
9150 Weathervane Trl
Galesburg, MI 49053-9777, USA

Ward, Fred (Actor)
1214 Cabrillo Ave
Venice, CA 90291-3704, USA

Ward, Gary (Athlete, Baseball Player)
18073 Granite Ave
Riverside, CA 92508-9777, USA

Ward, Gemma (Actor, Model)
c/o Ann Churchill-Brown *Shanahan Management*
Level 3 Berman House
Surry Hills 02010, AUSTRALIA

Ward, Gerry (Athlete, Basketball Player)
14 Comstock Ct
Ridgefield, CT 06877-5826, USA

Ward, Hines (Athlete, Football Player)
6215 Riverside Dr
Sandy Springs, GA 30328-3623, USA

Ward, Jason (Athlete, Hockey Player)
133 Emerald Hill Way
Valrico, FL 33594-5027

Ward, Jeff (Actor)
c/o Jessica Katz *Katz Public Relations*
14527 Dickens St
Sherman Oaks, CA 91403-3756, USA

Ward, Jeff (Race Car Driver)
AJ Foyt Racing
6415 Toledo St.
Houston, TX 77008, USA

Ward, Joe (Athlete, Hockey Player)
2218 199th St SW
Lynnwood, WA 98036-7014, USA

Ward, Joel (Athlete, Hockey Player)
Cooney Management
220 Boylston St Apt 1202
Boston, MA 02116-3950, USA

Ward, John (Athlete, Football Player)
9501 Silver Lake Dr
Oklahoma City, OK 73162-7547, USA

Ward, John F (Business Person)
Russell Corp
755 Lee St
Alexander City, AL 35010-2638, USA

Ward, Jonathan (Actor)
Auckland Actors
Po Box 56460
Dominion Road
Auckland 01030, NEW ZELAND

Ward, Jon P (Business Person)
RR Donnelley & Sons
77 W Wacker Dr
Chicago, IL 60601-1604, USA

Ward, Kevin (Athlete, Baseball Player)
160 F Ave
Coronado, CA 92118-1212, USA

Ward, Lala (Actor)
London Mgmt
2-4 Noel St
London W1V 3RB, UNITED KINGDOM (UK)

Ward, Mary (Actor)
Melbourne Artists
643 Saint Kilda Road
Melbourne, VIC 03004, AUSTRALIA

Ward, Mary B (Actor)
Innovative Artists
1505 10th St
Santa Monica, CA 90401-2805, USA

Ward, Mateus (Actor)
c/o Nicole Miller *NMA PR*
7916 Melrose Ave Ste 1
Los Angeles, CA 90046-7160, USA

Ward, Megan (Actor)
PO Box 481219
Los Angeles, CA 90036, USA

Ward, Micky (Athlete, Boxer)
c/o Nick Cordasco *Prince Marketing Group*
18 Seneca Trl
Sparta, NJ 07871-1514, USA

Ward, Pete (Athlete, Baseball Player)
575 G Ave
Lake Oswego, OR 97034-2272, USA

Ward, Preston (Athlete, Baseball Player)
4371 De Silva Pl
Las Vegas, NV 89121-5347, USA

Ward, Rachel (Actor)
c/o Kate Richter *HLA Management*
PO Box 1536
Strawberry Hills 02012, AUSTRALIA

Ward, R Duane (Athlete, Baseball Player)
PO Box 312
361 S CAMINO DEL RIO
Durango, CO 81302-0312, USA

Ward, Robert R (Bob) (Athlete, Football Player)
PO Box 535
Riva, MD 21140-0535, USA

Ward, Ronald L (Ron) (Athlete, Hockey Player)
3178 W 140th St
Cleveland, OH 44111-1442, USA

Ward, Sela (Actor)
c/o Karen Samfilippo *IMPR*
1158 26th St # 548
Santa Monica, CA 90403-4698, USA

Ward, Sterling (Religious Leader)
Brethren Church
27 High St
Ashland, OH 44805-8705, USA

Ward, Susan (Actor)
c/o Staff Member *UTA Music/The Agency Group*
9336 Civic Center Dr
Beverly Hills, CA 90210-3604, USA

Ward, T.J. (Athlete, Football Player)

Ward, Tony (Designer, Model, Photographer)
c/o Siri Garber *Platform PR*
2666 N Beachwood Dr
Los Angeles, CA 90068-2308, USA

Ward, Turner M (Athlete, Baseball Player)
232 Autumn Dr
Saraland, AL 36571-2619, USA

Ward, Vincent (Director)
PO Box 423
Kings Cross
Sydney, NSW 02011, AUSTRALIA

Ward, Vincent M (Actor)
c/o Lesa Kirk *Open Entertainment*
1051 Cole Ave
Los Angeles, CA 90038-2601, USA

Ward, Wendy (Golfer)
12845 Sassin Station Rd N
Edwall, WA 99008-9564, USA

Ward, Zach (Actor)
c/o Emilio Salituro *Lucas Talent Inc*
1238 Homer St Suite 6
Vancouver, BC V6B 2Y5, CANADA

Ward, ZZ (Musician)
c/o Carleen Donovan *Donovan Public Relations*
30 E 20th St Ste 2FE
New York, NY 10003-1310, USA

Warden, Jon (Athlete, Baseball Player)
6575 Oasis Dr
Loveland, OH 45140-5817, USA

Wardle, Curt (Athlete, Baseball Player)
13900 Pheasant Knoll Ln
Moreno Valley, CA 92553-5330, USA

Wardle, Graham (Actor)
c/o Candace Fulton *Kirk Talent Agencies Inc*
196 3rd Ave W Suite 102
Vancouver, BC V5Y 1E9, CANADA

Ware, Andre (Athlete, Football Player, Heisman Trophy Winner)
3910 Wood Park
Sugar Land, TX 77479-2838, USA

Ware, Chris (Artist)
c/o Staff Member *Fantagraphics Books*
7563 Lake City Way NE
Seattle, WA 98115-4218, USA

Ware, DeMarcus (Athlete, Football Player)
c/o Pat Dye Jr *SportsTrust Advisors*
3340 Peachtree Rd NE Fl 16
Atlanta, GA 30326-1000, USA

Ware, Derek (Athlete, Football Player)
4426 E Desert Willow Rd
Phoenix, AZ 85044-6064, USA

Ware, Hannah (Actor)
c/o Annick Oppenheim *Wolf-Kasteler Public Relations*
6255 W Sunset Blvd Ste 1111
Los Angeles, CA 90028-7426, USA

Ware, Jeff (Athlete, Baseball Player)
4467 Fallbrook Blvd
Palm Harbor, FL 34685-2653, USA

Warfield, Eric (Athlete, Football Player)
718 Meadows Rd
Texarkana, AR 71854-8341, USA

Warfield, Paul D (Athlete, Football Player)
16 Normandy Way
Rancho Mirage, CA 92270-1635, USA

Warford, Larry (Athlete, Football Player)
c/o Neil Schwartz *Schwartz & Feinsod*
4 Hillandale Rd
Rye Brook, NY 10573-1705, USA

Wargo, Tom (Athlete, Golfer)
2801 Putter Dr
Centralia, IL 62801-6183, USA

Warhola, James (Writer)
56 Walkers Hl
Tivoli, NY 12583-5806, USA

Warhols, James (Writer)
PO Box 748
Rhinebeck, NY 12572-0748, USA

Warhop, George (Athlete, Football Coach, Football Player)
4767 Hill Top View Pl
San Jose, CA 95138-2708, USA

Wariner, Steve (Musician, Songwriter)
Steve Wariner Productions
PO Box 1647
Franklin, TN 37065-1647, USA

Waring, Todd (Actor)
Artists Agency
1180 S Beverly Dr Ste 301
Los Angeles, CA 90035-1154, USA

Wark, Robert R (Misc)
Huntington Library & Art Gallery
1151 Oxford Rd
San Marino, CA 91108-1299, USA

Warlick, Ernie (Athlete, Football Player)
121 Presidents Walk
Buffalo, NY 14221-2447, USA

Warlock, Billy (Actor)
c/o Staff Member *Peter Strain & Associates Inc (LA)*
10901 Whipple St Apt 322
N Hollywood, CA 91602-3245, USA

Warmack, Chance (Athlete, Football Player)
c/o Ashley Smith Becker *Relativity Sports*
2029 Century Park E Ste 1550
Century City, CA 90067-3000, USA

Warmenhoven, Daniel (Business Person)
Network Appliance Inc
495 E Java Dr
Sunnyvale, CA 94089-1125, USA

Warne, Jim (Athlete, Football Player)
5850 Hardy Ave
Apt 112
San Diego, CA 92115, USA

Warnecke, Mark (Swimmer)
Am Schichtmeister 100
Witten 58453, GERMANY

Warner, Amelia (Actor)
c/o Jon Rubinstein *Authentic Talent and Literary Management (NY)*
20 Jay St Ste M17
Brooklyn, NY 11201-8300, USA

Warner, Charley (Athlete, Football Player)
1890 Rena St
Beaumont, TX 77705-4729, USA

Warner, Chris (Cartoonist)
Dark House Publishing
10956 SE Main St
Milwaukie, OR 97222-7644, USA

Warner, Cornell (Athlete, Basketball Player)
2479 Glen Meadow Ln
Escondido, CA 92027-2810, USA

Warner, Dan (Actor)
c/o Staff Member *Players Talent Agency*
7700 W Sunset Blvd # 1
Los Angeles, CA 90046-3913, USA

Warner, David (Actor)
Julian Belfarge
46 Albermarle St
London W1X 4PP, UNITED KINGDOM (UK)

Warner, Jack (Athlete, Baseball Player)
5938 W Calle Lejos
Glendale, AZ 85310-3505, USA

Warner, Jackie (Fitness Expert, Reality Star)
c/o Jean Kwolek *Artist & Brand Management*
9320 Wilshire Blvd Ste 212
Beverly Hills, CA 90212-3217, USA

Warner, Jackie (Athlete, Baseball Player)
19136 US Highway 18
Apple Valley, CA 92307-2507, USA

Warner, John (Politician)
2011 Fort Dr
Alexandria, VA 22307-1133, USA

Warner, Julie (Actor, Director, Producer)
333 S Roxbury Dr
Beverly Hills, CA 90212-3710, USA

Warner, Kirk (Athlete, Football Player)
PO Box 463
Cochran, GA 31014-0463, USA

Warner, Kurt (Athlete, Football Player)
c/o Michael McCartney *Priority Sports & Entertainment (Chicago)*
325 N La Salle Dr Ste 650
Chicago, IL 60654-8182, USA

Warner, Malcolm-Jamal (Actor)
c/o Jordyn Palos *Persona Public Relations*
6255 W Sunset Blvd Ste 705
Hollywood, CA 90028-7408, USA

Warner, Margaret (Correspondent)
News Hour Show
2700 S Quincy St Ste 250
Arlington, VA 22206-2222, USA

Warner, Mark (Politician)
1227 King St
Alexandria, VA 22314, USA

Warner, T C (Actor)
S D B Partners
1801 Ave of Stars #902
Los Angeles, CA 90067, USA

Warner, Todd (Artist)
8799 Boyne City Rd
Charlevoix, MI 49720-9102, USA

Warner, Tom (Producer)
Carsey-Warner Productions
4024 Radford Ave Bldg 3
Studio City, CA 91604-2101, USA

Warner, Ty (Designer)
Ty Inc
PO Box 5377
Oak Brook, IL 60522-5377, USA

Warner, William W (Writer)
2243 47th St NW
Washington, DC 20007-1034, USA

Warnes, Jennifer (Musician, Songwriter, Writer)
Donald Miller
12746 Kling St
Studio City, CA 91604-1125, USA

Warnock, John (Business Person)
Adobe Systems
345 Park Ave
San Jose, CA 95110-2704, USA

Warren, Cash (Producer)
1913 N Beverly Dr
Beverly Hills, CA 90210-1612, USA

Warren, Chris (Athlete, Football Player)
Seattle Seahawks
13707 Black Spruce Way
Chantilly, VA 20151-2346, USA

Warren, Cicero (Athlete, Baseball Player)
Homestead Grays
119 Brookwood St
East Orange, NJ 07018-2317, USA

Warren, Diane (Musician, Songwriter)
Realsongs
6363 W Sunset Blvd Ste 810
Los Angeles, CA 90028-7317, USA

Warren, Don (Athlete, Football Player)
Centerville High School
6001 Union Mill Rd
Attn: Athletic Dept
Clifton, VA 20124-1131, USA

Warren, Elizabeth (Politician)
15 New Sudbury St Rm 2400
2400 Jfk Federal Bldg
Boston, MA 02203-0093, USA

Warren, Estella (Actor, Model)
c/o Steven Jensen *FORM.B entertainment*
1516 N Fairfax Ave
Los Angeles, CA 90046-2608, USA

Warren, Frank (Internet Star)
27652 Country Lane Rd
Laguna Niguel, CA 92677-3804, USA

Warren, Gerard (Football Player)
c/o Staff Member *Denver Broncos*
13655 Broncos Pkwy
Englewood, CO 80112-4151, USA

Warren, Gloria (Actor, Musician)
16872 Bosque Dr
Encino, CA 91436-3531, USA

Warren, Jennifer (Actor)
1675 Old Oak Rd
Los Angeles, CA 90049-2505, USA

Warren, Karle (Actor)
c/o Justine Hunt *Hines and Hunt Entertainment*
1213 W Magnolia Blvd
Burbank, CA 91506-1829, USA

Warren, Kiersten (Actor)
2458 N Beachwood Dr
Los Angeles, CA 90068-3005, USA

Warren, Lesley Ann (Actor)
Radius Entertainment
9229 W Sunset Blvd Ste 301
West Hollywood, CA 90069-3417, USA

Warren, Michael (Mike) (Actor, Basketball Player)
21216 Escondido St
Woodland Hills, CA 91364-5905, USA

Warren, Mike (Athlete, Baseball Player)
12281 Diane St
Garden Grove, CA 92840-3224, USA

Warren, Rick (Religious Leader, Writer)
Saddleback Church
1 Saddleback Pkwy
Lake Forest, CA 92630-8700, USA

Warren, Robert (Athlete, Basketball Player)
989 Hardin Wadesboro Rd
Hardin, KY 42048-9034, USA

Warren, Ron (Athlete, Baseball Player)
Detroit Stars
4025 Paddock Rd Apt 401
Cincinnati, OH 45229-1635, USA

Warren, Sahron (Actor)
c/o Kathryn Boole *Studio Talent Group*
1328 12th St
Santa Monica, CA 90401-2051, United states

Warren, Thomas L (Misc)
National Wildlife Federation
11100 Wildlife Center Dr
Reston, VA 20190-5362, USA

Warren, TJ (Athlete, Basketball Player)
c/o Henry Thomas *CAA Sports*
2000 Avenue of the Stars Ste 100
Los Angeles, CA 90067-4705, USA

Warren, Tom (Athlete)
2393 La Marque St
San Diego, CA 92109-2342, USA

Warren, Ty (Athlete, Football Player)
c/o Staff Member *New England Patriots*
1 Patriot Pl
Foxboro, MA 02035-1388, USA

Warren Brothers, The (Music Group)
c/o Staff Member *Creative Artists Agency (CAA)*
401 Commerce St PH
Nashville, TN 37219-2516, USA

Warrener, Rhett (Athlete, Hockey Player)
761 W Ferry St
Buffalo, NY 14222-1618, USA

Warren Jr, Chris (Athlete, Football Player)
c/o Genevieve Penn *Luber Roklin Management*
5815 W Sunset Blvd Ste 208
Los Angeles, CA 90028-6481, USA

Warrick, Peter (Athlete, Football Player)
4305 17th St E
Ellenton, FL 34222-2688, USA

Warriner, Todd (Athlete, Hockey Player)
Blenheim Blades
PO Box 1775
Attn: Coaching Staff
Blenheim, ON N0P 1A0, Canada

Warrington, Clint (Horse Racer)
69 Oakcrest Ln
Westampton, NJ 08060-5729, USA

Warrington, Steve (Horse Racer)
31926 Lambson Forest Rd
Galena, MD 21635-1523, USA

Warrington, Walter (Horse Racer)
31930 Lambson Forest Rd
Galena, MD 21635-1523, USA

Warthen, Dan (Athlete, Baseball Player)
3933 SW Wapato Ave
Portland, OR 97239-1412, USA

Warwick, Carl (Athlete, Baseball Player)
14102 Bonney Brier Dr
Houston, TX 77069-1324, USA

Warwick, Dionne (Musician)
3849 Crestway Dr
View Park, CA 90043-1738, USA

Warwick, Ken (Producer)
1149 Calle Vista Dr
Beverly Hills, CA 90210-2507, USA

Warwick, Lonnie (Athlete, Football Player)
828 Main St
Mount Hope, WV 25880-1321, USA

Warzeka, Ron (Athlete, Football Player)
424 McEwen Dr
Belgrade, MT 59714-3125, USA

Was, Don (Composer, Musician)
c/o Alia Fahlborg *Nettwerk Management (LA)*
1545 Wilcox Ace
Suite 200
Los Angeles, CA 90028, USA

Wasdin, John (Athlete, Baseball Player)
2676 Riverport Dr S
Jacksonville, FL 32223-7115, USA

Wash, Martha (Musician)
c/o Stephen Ford *Diva Central Inc*
7510 W Sunset Blvd # 1445
Los Angeles, CA 90046-3408, USA

Washbrook, Johnny (Actor)
66 RR 1
Edgartown, MA 02539, USA

Washburn, Abigail (Musician)
c/o Staff Member *Paradigm (Monterey)*
404 W Franklin St
Monterey, CA 93940-2303, USA

Washburn, Barbara (Misc)
1010 Waltham St Apt D327
Lexington, MA 02421-8044, USA

Washburn, Beverly (Actor)
2561 Olivia Heights Ave
Henderson, NV 89052-7130, USA

Washburn, Greg (Athlete, Baseball Player)
724 Trotter Dr
Coal City, IL 60416-2463, USA

Washburn, Jarrod M (Athlete, Baseball Player)
10003 Olinger Rd
Webster, WI 54893-7435, USA

Washburn, Ray C (Athlete, Baseball Player)
1103 N 49th St
Seattle, WA 98103-6630, USA

Washburn Jr, H Bradford (Misc)
1010 Waltham St Apt D237
Lexington, MA 02421-8044, USA

Washington, Algernod Lanier (Plies) (Musician)
c/o Cara Donatto *Atlantic Records*
3400 W Olive Ave Fl 2
Burbank, CA 91505-5538, USA

Washington, Alonzo (Cartoonist)
Omega 7
PO Box 171046
Kansas City, KS 66117-0046, USA

Washington, Baby (Musician)
Headline Talent
1650 Broadway Ste 508
New York, NY 10019-6833, USA

Washington, Chris (Athlete, Football Player)
2823 Lloyd St
San Diego, CA 92117-6029, USA

Washington, Claudell (Athlete, Baseball Player)
4081 Clayton Rd Apt 227
Concord, CA 94521-2615, USA

Washington, Corey (Athlete, Football Player)

Washington, Cornelius (Athlete, Football Player)
c/o Anthony J. Agnone *Eastern Athletic Services*
11350 McCormick Rd
Suite 800 - Executive Plaza
Hunt Valley, MD 21031-1002, USA

Washington, Daryl (Athlete, Football Player)
c/o Jordan Woy *Willis & Woy Management*
4890 Alpha Rd Ste 200
Dallas, TX 75244-4639, USA

Washington, Denzel (Actor)
PO Box 27623
Los Angeles, CA 90027-0623, USA

Washington, Dewayne (Athlete, Football Player)
6205 Rocky Creek Way
Wake Forest, NC 27587-6267, USA

Washington, Eugene (Gene) (Athlete, Football Player)
3330 Edinborough Way Apt 1602
Minneapolis, MN 55435-5919, USA

Washington, Evelyn Ashford (Athlete, Olympic Athlete, Track Athlete)
Rascoff/Zysblat Organization
250 W 57th St Ste 814
New York, NY 10107-0807, USA

Washington, Gene A (Athlete, Football Player)
10521 Bellagio Rd
Los Angeles, CA 90077-3820, USA

Washington, Hayma (Producer)
c/o Lindsay Williams *Gotham Group*
1041 N Formosa Ave # 200
West Hollywood, CA 90046-6703, USA

Washington, Herb (Athlete, Baseball Player)
640 Saddlebrook Dr
Youngstown, OH 44512-4781, USA

Washington, Isaiah (Actor)
1888 Century Park E # 550
Los Angeles, CA 90067-1702, USA

Washington, Jascha (Actor)
c/o Staff Member *The House of Representatives*
3118 Wilshire Blvd Ste D
Santa Monica, CA 90403-2345, USA

Washington, Jim (Athlete, Basketball Player)
1108 Cardinal Way SW
Atlanta, GA 30311-2417, USA

Washington, Joe (Athlete, Football Player)
434 E 42nd Pl Apt 1
Chicago, IL 60653-2916, USA

Washington, Joe (Athlete, Football Player)
4 Treadwell Ct
Lutherville Timonium, MD 21093-3716, USA

Washington, Joe D (Athlete, Football Player)
2350 W Joppa Rd
Lutherville, MD 21093-4616, USA

Washington, John David (Actor)
c/o Andrew Finkelstein *WME|IMG*
9601 Wilshire Blvd
Beverly Hills, CA 90210-5213, USA

Washington, Keith (Athlete, Football Player)
548 Parkview Dr
Grand Prairie, TX 75052-3168, USA

Washington, Kelley (Athlete, Football Player)
c/o Chad Speck *Allegiant Athletic Agency*
35 Market Sq Ste 201
Knoxville, TN 37902-1420, USA

Washington, Kelly Lynn (Actor)
c/o Cindy Schultzel-Ambers *Art/Work Entertainment*
5670 Wilshire Blvd Ste 900
Los Angeles, CA 90036-5699, USA

Washington, Kermit (Athlete, Basketball Player)
7208 NE Hazel Dell Ave
Vancouver, WA 98665-8341, USA

Washington, Kerry (Actor)
c/o Katie Greenthal *The Lede Company*
9701 Wilshire Blvd # 930
Beverly Hills, CA 90212-2020, USA

Washington, Larue (Athlete, Baseball Player)
3315 Sturbridge Ave
Easton, PA 18045-8139, USA

Washington, Leon (Athlete, Football Player)

Washington, Lionel (Athlete, Football Player)
1873 Horseshoe Ln
De Pere, WI 54115-7943, USA

Washington, MaliVai (Tennis Player)
5 S Roscoe Blvd
Ponte Vedra Beach, FL 32082-3813, USA

Washington, Marcus (Athlete, Football Player)
19276 Summit Ash Ct
Leesburg, VA 20175-8710, USA

Washington, Mickey (Athlete, Football Player)
9420 Riggs St
Beaumont, TX 77707-1164, USA

Washington, Mike L (Athlete, Football Player)
3235 Hernon Rd
Montgomery, AL 36106, USA

Washington, Richard (Athlete, Basketball Player)
4606 SE Logus Rd
Portland, OR 97222-5150, USA

Washington, Rico (Athlete, Baseball Player)
911 Golf Valley Dr
Apopka, FL 32712-4074, USA

Washington, Ron (Athlete, Baseball Player)
2406 Copper Ridge Rd
Arlington, TX 76006-2726, USA

Washington, Ron (Athlete, Baseball Player, Coach)
7365 Perth St
New Orleans, LA 70126-1753, USA

Washington, Ronnie (Athlete, Football Player)
2204 Burg Jones Ln
Monroe, LA 71202-4411, USA

Washington, Russ (Athlete, Football Player)
9060 Gramercy Dr
San Diego, CA 92123-2395, USA

Washington, Sam (Athlete, Football Player)
7111 Cumberland Pl
Tampa, FL 33617-8423, USA

Washington, Ted (Athlete, Football Player)
PO Box 434
Waxhaw, NC 28173-1047, USA

Washington, Theodore (Ted) (Athlete, Football Player)
3522 E 26th Ave
Tampa, FL 33605-1602, USA

Washington, U L (Athlete, Baseball Player)
PO Box 164
Stringtown, OK 74569-0164, USA

Washington, Wilson (Athlete, Basketball Player)
2625 Mapleton Ave
Norfolk, VA 23504-3717, USA

Wasikowska, Mia (Actor)
c/o Christine Tripicchio *Shelter PR*
5670 Wilshire Blvd Ste 1200
Los Angeles, CA 90036-5621, USA

Wasinger, Mark (Athlete, Baseball Player)
324 N Chautauqua Ave
Wichita, KS 67214-4723, USA

Waskiewicz, Jim (Athlete, Football Player)
4360 Nelson Dr
Broomfield, CO 80023-9598, USA

Waslewski, Gary (Athlete, Baseball Player)
1799 E Terrestrial Pl
Tucson, AZ 85737-3469, USA

Wasmeier, Markus (Athlete, Skier)
D&F Academy
Shanghaiallee 9
Hamburg D-20457, Germany

Wass, Ted (Actor)
3825 Longridge Ave
Sherman Oaks, CA 91423-4921, USA

Wasserman, Allan (Actor)
c/o Judy Orbach *Judy O Productions*
6136 Glen Holly St
Hollywood, CA 90068-2338, USA

Wasserman, Dale (Writer)
Casa Blanca Estates
#37
Paradise Valley, AZ 95253, USA

Wasserman, Kevin (Noodles) (Musician)
c/o Staff Member *Sugaroo! LLC*
3650 Helms Ave
Culver City, CA 90232-2417, USA

Wasserman Schultz, Debbie (Congressman, Politician)
118 Cannon Hob
Washington, DC 20515-4403, USA

Wasserstein, Wendy (Writer)
c/o Robert (Bob) Bookman *Paradigm*
8942 Wilshire Blvd
Beverly Hills, CA 90211-1908, USA

Wasson, Erin (Model)
c/o Bianca Bianconi *42West*
600 3rd Ave Fl 23
New York, NY 10016-1914, USA

Waszgis, BJ (Athlete, Baseball Player)
2708 Dover Ln
Albany, GA 31721-1583, USA

Waszgis, B J (Athlete, Baseball Player)
2708 Dover Ln
Albany, GA 31721-1583, USA

Watanabe, Ken (Actor)
2-7-10-5F
Higashi
Shibuya, Tokyo 150-0011, JAPAN

Watanabe, Sadao (Musician)
International Music Network
278 Main St # 400
Gloucester, MA 01930-6022, USA

Waterbury, Steve (Athlete, Baseball Player)
710 N Garfield St
Marion, IL 62959-3429, USA

Waterhouse, Matthew (Actor)
Boyce
1 Kingsway House
Albion Rd
London N16 0TA, UNITED KINGDOM (UK)

Waterhouse, Suki (Actor)
c/o Oliver Azis *Independent Talent Group*
40 Whitfield St
London W1T 2RH, UNITED KINGDOM

Waterman, Felicity (Actor)
PO Box 536
Mendocino, CA 95460-0536, USA

Waters, Alice (Chef)
Chez Panisse
1517 Shattuck Ave
Berkeley, CA 94709-1598, USA

Waters, Brian (Athlete, Football Player)
1417 Wolf Dr
Desoto, TX 75115-1736, USA

Waters, Charles T (Charlie) (Athlete, Coach, Football Coach, Football Player)
9305 Moss Trl
Dallas, TX 75231-1409, USA

Waters, Crystal (Musician)
c/o Stephen Ford *Diva Central Inc*
7510 W Sunset Blvd # 1445
Los Angeles, CA 90046-3408, USA

Waters, Derek (Actor)
c/o Naomi Odenkirk *Odenkirk Provissiero Entertainment*
1936 N Bronson Ave
Raleigh Studios
Los Angeles, CA 90068-5602, USA

Waters, Drew (Actor, Producer)
Argentum Entertainment
207 Wind Ship Ln
Woodstock, GA 30189-5286, USA

Waters, Frank (Muddy) (Coach, Football Coach)
4850 Gratiot Rd
No. 2D
Saginaw, MI 48638-6202, USA

Waters, John (Director)
c/o Steve Rabineau *WME|IMG*
9601 Wilshire Blvd
Beverly Hills, CA 90210-5213, USA

Waters, Lou (Correspondent)
Cable News Network
1050 Techwood Dr NW
News Dept
Atlanta, GA 30318-5695, USA

Waters, Mark (Director)
c/o Jay Baker *Creative Artists Agency (CAA)*
2000 Avenue of the Stars Ste 100
Los Angeles, CA 90067-4705, USA

Waters, Maxine (Congressman, Politician)
2344 Rayburn Hob
Washington, DC 20515-0535, USA

Waters, Roger (Musician)
157 E 61st St # 5
New York, NY 10065-8112, USA

Waterston, James (Actor)
c/o Beth Colt *Gateway Management Company Inc*
860 Via De La Paz Ste F10
Pacific Palisades, CA 90272-3631, USA

Waterston, Katherine (Actor)
c/o Jason Shapiro *Silver Lining Entertainment*
421 S Beverly Dr Fl 7
Beverly Hills, CA 90212-4408, USA

Waterston, Sam (Actor)
92 Great Hollow Rd
West Cornwall, CT 06796-1806, USA

Watford, Earl (Athlete, Football Player)
c/o Anthony J. Agnone *Eastern Athletic Services*
11350 McCormick Rd
Suite 800 - Executive Plaza
Hunt Valley, MD 21031-1002, USA

Wathan, Dusty (Athlete, Baseball Player)
725 Amanda Dr
Matthews, NC 28104-9397, USA

Wathan, John D (Athlete, Baseball Player, Coach)
1354 NE Todd George Rd
Lees Summit, MO 64086-5337, USA

Watkins, Ben (Producer)
c/o Ashley Holland *WME|IMG*
9601 Wilshire Blvd
Beverly Hills, CA 90210-5213, USA

Watkins, Bob (Athlete, Baseball Player)
4417 W 58th Pl
Los Angeles, CA 90043-3409, USA

Watkins, Bobby (Athlete, Football Player)
110 Northbrook Dr
Waxahachie, TX 75165-0008, USA

Watkins, Carlene (Actor)
104 Fremont Pl
Los Angeles, CA 90005-3867, USA

Watkins, Danny (Football Player)
c/o Joe Panos *Athletes First*
23091 Mill Creek Dr
Laguna Hills, CA 92653-1258, USA

Watkins, Dave (Athlete, Baseball Player)
506 Ridgewood Rd
Louisville, KY 40207-1325, USA

Watkins, Jaylen (Athlete, Football Player)

Watkins, Michaela (Actor, Comedian)
c/o Amy Slomovits *Haven Entertainment*
8111 Beverly Blvd Ste 201
Los Angeles, CA 90048-4531, USA

Watkins, Michelle (Actor)
Capital Artists
6404 Wilshire Blvd Ste 950
Los Angeles, CA 90048-5529, USA

Watkins, Pat (Athlete, Baseball Player)
10301 Falls Mill Dr Apt 104
Raleigh, NC 27614-6432, USA

Watkins, Robert A (Athlete, Football Player)
6 White Alder Way
South Dartmouth, MA 02748-1429, USA

Watkins, Sammy (Athlete, Football Player)
c/o Eugene Parker *Independent Sports & Entertainment (ISE-IN)*
6435 W Jefferson Blvd # 197
Fort Wayne, IN 46804-6203, USA

Watkins, Scott (Athlete, Baseball Player)
14660 W 18th St S
Sand Springs, OK 74063-4405, USA

Watkins, Steve (Athlete, Baseball Player)
3408 Evanston Ave
Lubbock, TX 79407-4039, USA

Watkins, Tionne (T-Boz) (Artist, Musician)
Diggit Entertainment
6 W 18th St # 800
New York, NY 10011-4608, USA

Watkins, Tommy (Athlete, Baseball Player)
Beloit Snappers
PO Box 855
Attn: Coaching Staff Beloit
Beloit, WI 53512-0855, USA

Watkins, Tuc (Actor)
c/o Karen Forman *Karen Forman Management*
17547 Ventura Blvd Ste 102
Encino, CA 91316-5164, USA

Watkins, William D (Business Person)
Seagate Technology
920 Disc Dr
Scotts Valley, CA 95066-4544, USA

Watley, Jody (Musician)
c/o Bill Coleman *Peace Bisquit*
963 Kent Ave Bldg E
Brooklyn, NY 11205-4461, USA

Watling, Leonor (Actor)
c/o Staff Member *WME|IMG*
9601 Wilshire Blvd
Beverly Hills, CA 90210-5213, USA

Watlington, Neal (Athlete, Baseball Player)
PO Box 418
Yanceyville, NC 27379-0418, USA

Watney, Heidi (Baseball Player)
160 Boylston St Apt 2362
Chestnut Hill, MA 02467-2017, U S A

Watney, Nick (Athlete, Golfer)
c/o Staff Member *Gaylord Sports Management*
13845 N Northsight Blvd Ste 200
Scottsdale, AZ 85260-3609, USA

Watrin, Ray (Athlete, Football Player)
5 Downey Bay
Okotoks, AB T1S 1H7, Canada

Watros, Cynthia (Actor)
c/o Marsha McManus *Principal Entertainment*
9255 W Sunset Blvd Ste 500
Los Angeles, CA 90069-3301, USA

Watrous, Cynthia (Actor)
c/o Staff Member *Innovative Artists*
1505 10th St
Santa Monica, CA 90401-2805, USA

Watson, Alberta (Actor)
c/o Staff Member *Cathy Atkinson*
2629 Main St PMB 129
Santa Monica, CA 90405-4001, USA

Watson, Allen (Athlete, Baseball Player)
6144 65th St
Middle Village, NY 11379-1027, USA

Watson, Angela (Actor)
c/o Tom Chasin *Chasin Agency, The*
8281 Melrose Ave Ste 202
Los Angeles, CA 90046-6890, USA

Watson, Barry (Actor)
c/o Ruth Bernstein *Viewpoint Inc*
8820 Wilshire Blvd Ste 220
Beverly Hills, CA 90211-2622, USA

Watson, Benjamin (Athlete, Football Player)
c/o Staff Member *New England Patriots*
1 Patriot Pl
Foxboro, MA 02035-1388, USA

Watson, Bill (Athlete, Hockey Player)
1725 Vermilion Rd
Duluth, MN 55803-2508, USA

Watson, Bob (Athlete, Baseball Player)
9319 Montridge Dr
Houston, TX 77080-5429, USA

Watson, Brandon (Athlete, Baseball Player)
22121 Germain St
Chatsworth, CA 91311-2009, USA

Watson, Bryan (Athlete, Hockey Player)
24663 Long Haul Rd
St Michaels, MD 21663, USA

Watson, Bubba (Athlete, Golfer)
c/o Jens Beck *Pro-Sport Management*
6157 E Indian School Rd
Scottsdale, AZ 85251-5441, USA

Watson, Dale (Musician)
Crowley Artist Mgmt
602 Wayside Dr
Wimberley, TX 78676-0020, USA

Watson, Dave (Athlete, Hockey Player)
195 Pembrooke Ridge Ct
Advance, NC 27006-9597, USA

Watson, Dekoda (Athlete, Football Player)
c/o Peter Schaffer *Authentic Athletix*
400 S Steele St Unit 47
Denver, CO 80209-3535, USA

Watson, Denis (Athlete, Golfer)
14209 Evans Rd
Pacific Palisades, CA 90272, USA

Watson, Deshaun (Athlete, Football Player)
c/o David Mulugheta *Athletes First (TX)*
1139 Hidden Ridge Dr
Mesquite, TX 75181-4260, USA

Watson, Emily (Actor)
c/o George Freeman *WME|IMG*
9601 Wilshire Blvd
Beverly Hills, CA 90210-5213, USA

Watson, Emma (Actor)
c/o Jason Weinberg *Untitled Entertainment*
350 S Beverly Dr Ste 200
Beverly Hills, CA 90212-4819, USA

Watson, Gene (Musician)
Bobby Roberts
909 Meadowlark Ln
Goodlettsville, TN 37072-2309, USA

Watson, Jamie (Athlete, Basketball Player)
PO Box 761
Elm City, NC 27822-0761, USA

Watson, Jim (Athlete, Hockey Player)
8190 W Deer Valley Rd Ste 104
Peoria, AZ 85382-2126, USA

Watson, Jim (Athlete, Hockey Player)
1702 Coventry Ln
Glen Mills, PA 19342-9426, USA

Watson, Joe (Athlete, Hockey Player)
220 Park Pl
Media, PA 19063-2045, USA

Watson, Mark (Athlete, Baseball Player)
2750 Manor Bridge Dr
Alpharetta, GA 30004-2836, USA

Watson, Martha (Athlete, Olympic Athlete)
5509 Royal Vista Ln
Las Vegas, NV 89149-6644, USA

Watson, Matt (Athlete, Baseball Player)
636 Quail Crk
Manheim, PA 17545-8770, USA

Watson, Max P Jr (Business Person)
BMC Software
2103 Citywest Blvd Ste 2100
Houston, TX 77042-2857, USA

Watson, Menelik (Athlete, Football Player)
c/o Pat Dye Jr *SportsTrust Advisors*
3340 Peachtree Rd NE Fl 16
Atlanta, GA 30326-1000, USA

Watson, Mills (Actor)
PO Box 600
Talent, OR 97540-0600, USA

Watson, Paul (Journalist, Photographer)
Toronto Star
Editorial Dept
1 Yonge St
Toronto, ON M5E 1E6, CANADA

Watson, Paul (Misc)
Sea Shepherd Conservation Society
PO Box 2616
Friday Harbor, WA 98250-2616, USA

Watson, Polly Jo (Misc)
Washington University
Anthropology Dept
Saint Louis, MO 63130, USA

Watson, Robert (Athlete, Basketball Player)
1625 Sherwood Dr
Owensboro, KY 42301-3578, USA

Watson, Robert M (Bobby) Jr (Musician)
Split Second Timing
11 Ridge Rd
Chappaqua, NY 10514-2508, USA

Watson, Russell (Musician)
Box 806
Manchester M60 2XS, UNITED KINGDOM (UK)

Watson, Steve (Athlete, Football Player)

Watson, Susan Kelechi (Actor)
c/o Brett Ruttenberg *Imprint PR*
6121 W Sunset Blvd
Neuehouse
Los Angeles, CA 90028-6442, USA

Watson, Tim (Athlete, Football Player)
113 Crestwood Dr
RR 13
Fort Valley, GA 31030-6738, USA

Watson, Tom (Athlete, Golfer)
Assured Management Company
7301 Mission Rd Ste 154
Prairie Village, KS 66208-3023, USA

Watson, Wayne (Musician)
TBA Artist Mgmt
300 10th Ave S
Nashville, TN 37203-4125, USA

Watson, Whit (Sportscaster)
810 N Phelps Ave
Winter Park, FL 32789-2759, USA

Watson-Johnson, Vernee (Actor)
Gage Group
14724 Ventura Blvd Ste 505
Sherman Oaks, CA 91403-3505, USA

Watson Richardson, Lillian (Pockey) (Swimmer)
4960 Maunalani Cir
Honolulu, HI 96816-4016, USA

Watt, Ben (Musician, Songwriter, Writer)
JFD Mgmt
Acklam Workshops
10 Acklam Road
London W10 5QZ, UNITED KINGDOM (UK)

Watt, Chris (Athlete, Football Player)
c/o Michael McCartney *Priority Sports & Entertainment (Chicago)*
325 N La Salle Dr Ste 650
Chicago, IL 60654-8182, USA

Watt, Eddie (Athlete, Baseball Player)
940 Locust St
North Bend, NE 68649-4543, USA

Watt, James (Politician)
1558 Calle Encantado
Wickenburg, AZ 85390-3132, USA

Watt, Jim (Athlete, Hockey Player)
52 Amy Ln
Esko, MN 55733-9566, USA

Watt, JJ (Athlete, Football Player)
c/o Tom Condon *Creative Artists Agency (CAA)*
401 Commerce St PH
Nashville, TN 37219-2516, USA

Watt, Mike (Musician)
c/o Staff Member *UTA/The Agency Group*
888 7th Ave Fl 7
New York, NY 10106-0700, USA

Watt, Mike (Athlete, Hockey Player)
N84W27677 Twin Pines Cir
Hartland, WI 53029-8572, USA

Watt, Tom (Athlete, Coach, Hockey Player)
PO Box 1540 Stn M
Station M
Calgary, AB T2P 3B9, Canada

Wattelet, Frank (Athlete, Football Player)
4 Deer Run Dr
Joplin, MO 64804-5832, USA

Watters, Bill (Correspondent)
c/o Staff Member *Landmark Sport Group*
1 City Centre Dr Suite 605
Mississauga, ON L5B 1M2, Canada

Watters, Richard J (Rickie) (Athlete, Football Player)
11100 NE 8th St Ste 600
Bellevue, WA 98004-4402, USA

Watters, Ricky (Athlete, Football Player)
8815 Conroy Windermere Rd # 332
Orlando, FL 32835-3129, USA

Watters, Tim (Athlete, Hockey Player)
219 E Oregon Ave
Phoenix, AZ 85012-1435, USA

Watterson, John B (Brett) (Astronaut)
2508 Via Anacapa
Palos Verdes Estates, CA 90274-4333, USA

Wattle, Dave (Athlete, Olympic Athlete, Track Athlete)
9245 Forest Hill Ln
Germantown, TN 38139-7906, USA

Wattles, Stan (Race Car Driver)
2391 Old Dixie Hwy
Riviera Beach, FL 33404-5456, USA

Watts, Andre (Musician)
205 W 57th St
New York, NY 10019-2105, USA

Watts, Brandon (Athlete, Football Player)
c/o Joe Linta *JL Sports*
1204 Main St Ste 179
Branford, CT 06405-3787, USA

Watts, Brian (Athlete, Golfer)
1701 Wisteria Way
Westlake, TX 76262-9083, USA

Watts, Brian (Athlete, Hockey Player)
6417 Vista Pacifica
Rancho Palos Verdes, CA 90275-5896, USA

Watts, Charles R (Charlie) (Musician)
Halsdon Farm
Dolton Winkleigh
Devon EX19 8RF, UK

Watts, D Henry (Business Person)
Norfolk Southern Corp
3 Commercial Pl Ste 1A
Norfolk, VA 23510-2108, USA

Watts, Donald (Athlete, Basketball Player)
51315 256th Ave NE
Redmond, WA 981353-851, USA

Watts, Ernest J (Ernie) (Musician)
DeLeon Artists
4031 Panama Ct
Piedmont, CA 94611-4930, USA

Watts, Ernie (Designer, Director)
International Creative Mgmt
40 W 57th St Ste 1800
New York, NY 10019-4033, USA

Watts, JC (Athlete, Football Player)
921 Siena Springs Dr
Norman, OK 73071-5509, USA

Watts, J C (Politician)
600 13th St NW Ste 790
Washington, DC 20005-3021, USA

Watts, Kristi (Religious Leader, Television Host)
c/o 700 Club *Christian Broadcasting Network (CBN)*
977 Centerville Tpke
Virginia Beach, VA 23463-1001, USA

Watts, Naomi (Actor)
12307 7th Helena Dr
Los Angeles, CA 90049-3932, USA

Watts, Quincy (Athlete, Track Athlete)
First Team Marketing
PO Box 67581
Los Angeles, CA 90067, USA

Watts, Reggie (Musician)
c/o Rob Greenwald *Rogers & Cowan*
1840 Century Park E Fl 18
Los Angeles, CA 90067-2101, USA

Watts, Robert (Athlete, Football Player)
99 Villa Dr
San Pablo, CA 94806-3736, USA

Watts, Rolonda (Actor, Musician)
6002/6010 Graciosa Dr
Los Angeles, CA 90068, USA

Watts, Ronald (Athlete, Basketball Player)
11800 Sunset Hills Rd Unit 908
Reston, VA 20190-4787, USA

Waugh, John S (Misc)
Massachusetts Institute of Technology
Chemistry Dept
Cambridge, MA 02139, USA

Waugh, Seth (Athlete, Business Person, Golfer)
11418 Turtle Beach Rd
North Palm Beach, FL 33408-3343, USA

Wawrinka, Stan (Athlete, Tennis Player)
c/o Staff Member *Lagardere Unlimited (DC)*
5335 Wisconsin Ave NW Ste 850
Washington, DC 20015-2052, USA

Wawryshyn-Moroz, Evelyn (Athlete, Baseball Player)
139 Royal Ave
Winnipeg, MB R2V 1H5, CANADA

Wax, Ruby (Actor, Comedian)
c/o Nicola Richardson *QVoice*
161 Drury Ln, Covent Garden
3rd Floor
London WC2B 5PN, UK

Waxman, Henry (Congressman, Politician)
2204 Rayburn Hob
Washington, DC 20515-0530, USA

Waxman, Keoni (Director, Writer)
c/o Jeff Okin *Anonymous Content*
3532 Hayden Ave
Culver City, CA 90232-2413, USA

Way, Benjamin (Business Person)
cloudSMART Ltd
Synergy House
Manchester Science Park
Manchester M15 6SY, UK

Way, Gerard (Musician)
3820 San Rafael Ave
Los Angeles, CA 90065-3225, USA

Way, Tony (Actor)
c/o Helen Robinson *United Agents*
12-26 Lexington St
London W1F OLE, UNITED KINGDOM

Wayans, Damien Dante (Actor, Director, Producer)
c/o Jessica Cohen *JCPR*
9903 Santa Monica Blvd # 983
Beverly Hills, CA 90212-1671, USA

Wayans, Damon (Actor)
c/o Staff Member *Wayans/Alvarez Productions*
100 Universal City Plz
Bungalow 5186
Universal City, CA 91608-1002, USA

Wayans, Keenen Ivory (Actor, Director, Producer)
c/o Staff Member *Wayans/Alvarez Productions*
100 Universal City Plz
Bungalow 5186
Universal City, CA 91608-1002, USA

Wayans, Kim (Actor)
c/o Staff Member *Wayans/Alvarez Productions*
100 Universal City Plz
Bungalow 5186
Universal City, CA 91608-1002, USA

Wayans, Marlon (Actor, Comedian, Producer)
c/o Staff Member *Wayans/Alvarez Productions*
100 Universal City Plz
Bungalow 5186
Universal City, CA 91608-1002, USA

Wayans, Shawn (Actor, Comedian, DJ, Producer)
c/o Karynne Tencer *Tencer and Associates*
411 N Oakhurst Dr
Beverly Hills, CA 90210-4037, USA

Wayans Jr, Damon (Actor)
c/o Staff Member *Wayans/Alvarez Productions*
100 Universal City Plz
Bungalow 5186
Universal City, CA 91608-1002, USA

Wayne, Gary (Athlete, Baseball Player)
8354 S Holland Way Unit 102
Littleton, CO 80128-9258, USA

Wayne, Jeff (Actor, Comedian)
c/o Gail Parenteau *Parenteau Guidance*
132 E 35th St # J
New York, NY 10016-3892, USA

Wayne, Jimmy (Musician)
Big Machine Music
1219 16th Ave S
Nashville, TN 37212-2901, USA

Wayne, Justin (Athlete, Baseball Player)
302 Muirfield Ct
Jupiter, FL 33458-8060, USA

Wayne, Nathaniel (Athlete, Football Player)
2878 Grey Moss Pass
Duluth, GA 30097-5226, USA

Wayne, Patrick (Actor)
PO Box 2476
Toluca Lake, CA 91610-0476, USA

Wayne, Reggie (Athlete, Football Player)
16850 Stratford Ct
Southwest Ranches, FL 33331-1359, USA

Waynes, Trae (Athlete, Football Player)
c/o Joe Panos *Athletes First*
23091 Mill Creek Dr
Laguna Hills, CA 92653-1258, USA

Wayt, Russell (Athlete, Football Player)
600 E Tuttle Rd
White Oak, TX 75693-1354, USA

Wazed, Sheik Hasina (Prime Minister)
Sere-e Bangla Nagar
Gono Bhaban
Sher-e-Banglanagar
Dakar, BANGLADESH

W. Boustany Jr., Charles (Congressman, Politician)
1431 Longworth Hob
Washington, DC 20515-4802, USA

W. Dent, Charles (Congressman, Politician)
1009 Longworth Hob
Washington, DC 20515-3511, USA

Weah, George (Soccer Player)
AC Milan
Via Turati 3
Washington, DC 20221-0001, ITALY

Wearstler, Kelly (Writer)
c/o Staff Member *HarperCollins Publishers*
195 Broadway Fl 2
New York, NY 10007-3132, USA

Weary, Jake (Actor)
c/o Marianna Shafran *Shafran PR*
195 S Beverly Dr Ste 414
Beverly Hills, CA 90212-3044, USA

Weatherford, Steve (Athlete, Football Player)
c/o Drew Rosenhaus *Rosenhaus Sports Representation*
3921 Alton Rd # 440
Miami Beach, FL 33140-3852, USA

Weatherholtz, Walter (Trey) (Reality Star)
c/o Mike Esterman *Esterman.Com, LLC*
Prefers to be contacted via email
Baltimore, MD XXXXX, USA

Weatherly, Gerald (Athlete, Football Player)
506 1/2 E Clayton St
Cuero, TX 77954-2820, USA

Weatherly, Jim (Athlete, Football Player)
23679 Calabasas Rd Apt 558
Calabasas, CA 91302-1502, USA

Weatherly, Michael (Actor)
Solar Drive Productions
4024 Radford Ave
R&D Bldg
Studio City, CA 91604-2101, USA

Weatherly, Shwan (Actor, Beauty Pageant Winner)
135 N Westgate Ave
Los Angeles, CA 90049-2916, USA

Weathers, Carl (Actor, Athlete, Football Player)
c/o Paul Alan Smith *Equitable Stewardship for Artists (ESA)*
6363 Wilshire Blvd Ste 650
Los Angeles, CA 90048-5725, USA

Weathers, Dave (Athlete, Baseball Player)
979 Lexington Hwy
Loretto, TN 38469-2732, USA

Weatherspoon, Cephus (Athlete, Football Player)
5322 W Henderson Pl
Santa Ana, CA 92704-1036, USA

Weatherspoon, Clarence (Athlete, Basketball Player)
PO Box 117
Crawford, MS 39743-0117, USA

Weatherspoon, Sean (Athlete, Football Player)
c/o David Dunn *Athletes First*
23091 Mill Creek Dr
Laguna Hills, CA 92653-1258, USA

Weatherspoon, Teresa G (Basketball Player)
Los Angeles Sparks
1111 S Figueroa St
Staples Center
Los Angeles, CA 90015-1300, USA

Weaver, Blayne (Actor)
c/o Paul Greenstone *Paul Greenstone Entertainment*
1400 California Ave Apt 201
Santa Monica, CA 90403-4395, USA

Weaver, Dewitt (Athlete, Golfer)
2860 Thistle Trl
Suwanee, GA 30024-1035, USA

Weaver, Eric (Athlete, Baseball Player)
2641 Weaver Rd
Illiopolis, IL 62539-3640, USA

Weaver, Gary (Athlete, Football Player)
3496 Arden Rd
Hayward, CA 94545-3906, USA

Weaver, Herman (Athlete, Football Player)
1675 Eversedge Dr
Alpharetta, GA 30009-7133, USA

Weaver, Jacki (Actor)
c/o Alex Cole *Elevate Entertainment*
6300 Wilshire Blvd # 807
Los Angeles, CA 90048-5204, USA

Weaver, James (Race Car Driver)
165 Smith St
Poughkeepsie, NY 12601-2100, United States

Weaver, Jason (Actor)

Weaver, Jed (Athlete, Football Player)
696 E 16th Ave
Eugene, OR 97401, USA

Weaver, Jeff (Athlete, Baseball Player, Olympic Athlete)
1740 Classic Rose Ct
Westlake Village, CA 91362-5134, USA

Weaver, Jered (Athlete, Baseball Player)
c/o Staff Member *Los Angeles Dodgers*
1000 Elysian Park Ave
Los Angeles, CA 90012, USA

Weaver, Jim (Athlete, Baseball Player)
6916 8th Ave W
Bradenton, FL 34209-3416, USA

Weaver, Jim (Athlete, Baseball Player)
626 Prince George Dr
Lancaster, PA 17601-8802, USA

Weaver, John (Athlete, Football Player)
105 Carrol Gate Rd
Wheaton, IL 60189-1811, USA

Weaver, John (Race Car Driver)
Dream Weaver Family Racing
9246 Lacey Blvd
Hanford, CA 93230-4733, USA

Weaver, Michael (Actor)
1076 Nowita Pl
Venice, CA 90291-3519, USA

Weaver, Patty (Actor)
7281 Pierpoint Dr
Huntingtn Bch, CA 92648-3022, USA

Weaver, Reg (Misc)
National Education Assn
1201 16th St NW
Washington, DC 20036-3290, USA

Weaver, Roger (Athlete, Baseball Player)
65 Moyer St
Canajoharie, NY 13317-1430, USA

Weaver, Sigourney (Actor)
Goat Cay Productions
PO Box 38
New York, NY 10150-0038, USA

Weaver, Warren E (Misc)
7607 Horsepen Road
Richmond, VA 23229, USA

Weaver, Wayne (Business Person, Football Executive)
6120 San Jose Blvd W
Jacksonville, FL 32217-2345, USA

Weaving, Hugo (Actor)
c/o Ann Churchill-Brown *Shanahan Management*
Level 3 Berman House
Surry Hills 02010, AUSTRALIA

Weaving, Samara (Actor)
c/o Kimberly Christman *42West*
1840 Century Park E Ste 700
Los Angeles, CA 90067-2122, USA

Webb, Brandon (Athlete, Baseball Player)
8750 Tipton Ross Rd
Ashland, KY 41102-8920, USA

Webb, Bresha (Actor, Musician)
c/o Alyx Carr *42West*
600 3rd Ave Fl 23
New York, NY 10016-1914, USA

Webb, B.W. (Athlete, Football Player)

Webb, Casey (Actor, Reality Star, Television Host)
c/o Adam Nettler *Creative Artists Agency (CAA)*
405 Lexington Ave Fl 19
New York, NY 10174-1800, USA

Webb, Charley (Actor)

Webb, Chloe (Actor)
PO Box 2824
Venice, CA 90294-2824, USA

Webb, Christiaan (Musician, Songwriter, Writer)
SuperVision Mgmt
109B Regents Park Road
London NW1 8UR, UNITED KINGDOM (UK)

Webb, Hank (Athlete, Baseball Player)
4527 Lake Valencia Blvd W
Palm Harbor, FL 34684-3920, USA

Webb, James R (Jimmy) (Athlete, Football Player)
1319 S Prairie Flower Rd
Turlock, CA 95380-9367, USA

Webb, Jeff (Athlete, Basketball Player)
4037 Northview Ln
Dallas, TX 75229-2855, USA

Webb, Jim (Politician)
PO Box 284
Burke, VA 22009-0284, USA

Webb, Joe (Athlete, Football Player)
c/o Pat Dye Jr *SportsTrust Advisors*
3340 Peachtree Rd NE Fl 16
Atlanta, GA 30326-1000, USA

Webb, Justin (Musician, Songwriter, Writer)
SuperVision Mgmt
109B Regents Park Road
London NW1 8UR, UNITED KINGDOM (UK)

Webb, Karrie (Athlete, Golfer)
725 Presidential Dr
Boynton Beach, FL 33435-2431, USA

Webb, Katherine (Beauty Pageant Winner, Model)
c/o Alexander Shekarchian *ASManagement*
9440 Santa Monica Blvd Ste 700
Beverly Hills, CA 90210-4609, USA

Webb, Lardarius (Athlete, Football Player)

Webb, Lee (Religious Leader, Television Host)
c/o 700 Club *Christian Broadcasting Network (CBN)*
977 Centerville Tpke
Virginia Beach, VA 23463-1001, USA

Webb, Lucy (Actor, Comedian)
1360 N Crescent Heights Blvd # 38
West Hollywood, CA 90046-4553, USA

Webb, Marc (Director)
c/o Michael Sugar *Anonymous Content*
3532 Hayden Ave
Culver City, CA 90232-2413, USA

Webb, Morgan (Actor)
c/o Andrea Ross *Creative Artists Agency (CAA)*
2000 Avenue of the Stars Ste 100
Los Angeles, CA 90067-4705, USA

Webb, Richmond J (Athlete, Football Player)
4120 Humphrey Dr
Dallas, TX 75216-4908, USA

Webb, Robert (Actor)
c/o Michele Milburn *Milburn Browning Associates*
91, Brick Lane
The Old Truman Brewery
London E1 6QL, UNITED KINGDOM

Webb, Russell (Athlete)
611 Knob Hill Ave
Redondo Beach, CA 90277-4255, USA

Webb, Sonny (Baseball Player)
Negro Baseball Leagues
3194 Jordan Rd
Pleasant Plain, OH 45162-9238, USA

Webb, Spud (Athlete, Basketball Player)
1453 Mosslake Dr
Desoto, TX 75115-7709, USA

Webb, Steve (Athlete, Hockey Player)
35 Blackberry Ln
Center Moriches, NY 11934-1412, USA

Webb, Tamilee (Athlete)
7031 Calle Portone
Rancho Santa Fe, CA 92091-0262, USA

Webb, Veronica (Actor, Model)
c/o Rae Ruff *Buchwald (NY)*
10 E 44th St
New York, NY 10017-3601, USA

Webb, Wellington E (Misc)
Mayor's Office
1437 Bannock St Rm 350
City-County Building
Denver, CO 80202-5376, USA

Webb, William H (Business Person)
Altria Group
120 Park Ave
New York, NY 10017-5577, USA

Webber, Andrew Lloyd (Composer, Musician, Producer)
c/o Staff Member *The Really Useful Group*
17 Slingsby Pl
London WC2E 9AB, UNITED KINGDOM (UK)

Webber, Blake (Comedian, Internet Star)
c/o Staff Member *Gersh*
9465 Wilshire Blvd Ste 600
Beverly Hills, CA 90212-2605, USA

Webber, Chris (Sportscaster)
c/o Andy Elkin *Creative Artists Agency (CAA)*
2000 Avenue of the Stars Ste 100
Los Angeles, CA 90067-4705, USA

Webber, Julian Lloyd (Musician)
Columbia Artists Mgmt Inc
165 W 57th St
New York, NY 10019-2201, USA

Webber, Mark (Actor, Producer)
c/o Nicole Perna *Imprint PR*
6121 W Sunset Blvd
Neuehouse
Los Angeles, CA 90028-6442, USA

Webber, Mayce (Athlete, Basketball Player)
21731 Ventura Blvd Ste 31313
Woodland Hills, CA 91364-1845, USA

Webber, Tristan (Designer, Fashion Designer)
Brower Lewis
74 Gloucester Place
London W1H 3HN, UNITED KINGDOM (UK)

Webby, Chris (Musician)
c/o Jesse Kirschbaum *New Universal Entertainment Agency*
150 5th Ave
New York, NY 10011-4311, USA

Weber, Amy (Actor, Model, Musician)
c/o Staff Member *Select Artists Ltd (CA-Westside Office)*
1138 12th St Apt 1
Santa Monica, CA 90403-5459, USA

Weber, Ben (Actor)
c/o Amy Guenther *Gateway Management Company Inc*
860 Via De La Paz Ste F10
Pacific Palisades, CA 90272-3631, USA

Weber, Ben (Athlete, Baseball Player)
5550 Baird St
Groves, TX 77619-3231, USA

Weber, Bruce (Coach)
University of Illinois
Athletic Dept
Assembly Hall
Champaign, IL 61820, USA

Weber, Charlie (Actor)
c/o Jamie Harhay Skinner *Baker Winokur Ryder Public Relations*
9100 Wilshire Blvd
W Tower #500
Beverly Hills, CA 90212-3415, USA

Weber, Chuck (Athlete, Football Player)
12740 Cobblestone Creek Rd
Poway, CA 92064-5348, USA

Weber, George B (Misc)
Chemin Moise-Duboule 19
Geneva 01209, SWITZERLAND

Weber, Jack (Actor)
Gersh Agency
232 N Canon Dr
Beverly Hills, CA 90210-5302, USA

Weber, Jake (Actor)
c/o Kimberly Hines *Framework Entertainment*
9057 Nemo St # C
W Hollywood, CA 90069-5511, USA

Weber, Mary E (Astronaut)
14 Hawkview St
Portola Valley, CA 94028-8037, USA

Weber, Mary Ellen Dr (Astronaut)
14 Hawkview St
Portola Valley, CA 94028-8037, USA

Weber, Neil (Athlete, Baseball Player)
1 Morning Vw
Irvine, CA 92603-3716, USA

Weber, Shea (Athlete, Hockey Player)
4527 Yancey Dr
Nashville, TN 37215-4115, USA

Weber, Steven (Actor)
c/o Daniel (Danny) Sussman *Brillstein Entertainment Partners*
9150 Wilshire Blvd Ste 350
Beverly Hills, CA 90212-3453, USA

Weber, Vin (Misc)
Empower America
1776 I St NW
Washington, DC 20006-3700, USA

Weber Jr, Bob (Cartoonist)
c/o Staff Member *King Features Syndication*
300 W 57th St Fl 15
New York, NY 10019-5238, USA

Webster, Ben (Horse Racer)
452 Oak Haven Dr
Altamonte Springs, FL 32701-6318, USA

Webster, Chick (Athlete, Football Player)
PO Box 124
Mattawa, ON P0H 1V0, CANADA

Webster, Corey (Athlete, Football Player)
c/o Jimmy Sexton *CAA (Memphis)*
6060 Poplar Ave Ste 470
Memphis, TN 38119-0910, USA

Webster, Cornell (Athlete, Football Player)
4575 Palm Ave Apt H
Riverside, CA 92501-3966, USA

Webster, Daniel (Congressman, Politician)
1039 Longworth Hob
Washington, DC 20515-0917, USA

Webster, Jason (Athlete, Football Player)
c/o Staff Member *New England Patriots*
1 Patriot Pl
Foxboro, MA 02035-1388, USA

Webster, Jeff (Athlete, Basketball Player)
10405 SE 15th St
Oklahoma City, OK 73130-5714, USA

Webster, Kayvon (Athlete, Football Player)
c/o Drew Rosenhaus *Rosenhaus Sports Representation*
3921 Alton Rd # 440
Miami Beach, FL 33140-3852, USA

Webster, Larry (Athlete, Football Player)
12 Oakridge Ct
Elkton, MD 21921-3928, USA

Webster, Lenny (Athlete, Baseball Player)
6211 Bridgeport Dr
Charlotte, NC 28215-2319, USA

Webster, Mitch (Athlete, Baseball Player)
3120 NE 91st Ter
Kansas City, MO 64156-1071, USA

Webster, Ramon (Athlete, Baseball Player)
PO Box 6-5790
ElDorado, Panama, USA

Webster, Ray (Athlete, Baseball Player)
311 5th St
Marysville, CA 95901-5714, USA

Webster, Robert D (Bob) (Athlete, Swimmer)
269 Hacienda Carmel
Carmel, CA 93923-7947, USA

Webster, Tom (Athlete, Coach, Hockey Player)
1750 Longfellow Dr
Canton, MI 48187-2995, USA

Webster, Victor (Actor)
c/o Michelle Gauvin *Performers Management*
5-636 Clyde Ave
West Vancouver, BC V7T 1E1, CANADA

We Came As Romans (Music Group, Musician)
c/o Matthew Stewart *Outerloop Management*
2200 Clarendon Blvd Ste 1400
Arlington, VA 22201-3331, USA

Wechsler, Nick (Actor)
c/o Gordon Gilbertson *Gilbertson Management*
1334 3rd Street Promenade Ste 201
Santa Monica, CA 90401-1320, USA

Wecker, Andreas (Gymnast)
Am Dorfplatz 1
Klein-Ziethen 16766, GERMANY

Weddington, Mike (Athlete, Football Player)
8644 Iron Horse Dr
Irving, TX 75063-3922, USA

Weddington, Sarah R (Attorney)
709 W 14th St
Austin, TX 78701-1707, USA

Weddle, Eric (Athlete, Football Player)

Weddle-Hines, Mary (Athlete, Baseball Player)
329 Park Hills Rd
Corbin, KY 40701-2583, USA

Wedeen, Kelsey (Actor)
c/o Staff Member *Select Artists Ltd (CA-Westside Office)*
1138 12th St Apt 1
Santa Monica, CA 90403-5459, USA

Wedel, Dieter (Director)
Tonndorfer Strand 2
Hamburg 22045, GERMANY

Weder, Gustav (Athlete)
Haltenstr 2
Stachen/TG, SWITZERLAND

Wedge, Chris (Actor, Director, Writer)
c/o Staff Member *Blue Sky Studios*
1 American Ln Ste 210
Greenwich, CT 06831-2563, USA

Wedge, Eric M (Athlete, Baseball Player, Coach)
8285 SE 82nd St
Mercer Island, WA 98040-5653, USA

Wedman, Scott (Athlete, Basketball Player)
7912 NW Scenic Dr
Kansas City, MO 64152-1645, USA

Weed, Kent (Director, Producer)
c/o Staff Member *A Smith & Co Productions*
4130 Cahuenga Blvd Ste 315
Toluca Lake, CA 91602-2849, USA

Weed, Maurice James (Composer, Musician)
308 Overlook Rd # 55
Asheville, NC 28803-3319, USA

Weeden, Brandon (Athlete, Football Player)
c/o Sean Howard *Octagon Football*
600 Battery St Fl 2
San Francisco, CA 94111-1820, USA

Weekend Players (Music Group)
c/o Staff Member *Paradigm (Monterey)*
404 W Franklin St
Monterey, CA 93940-2303, USA

Weekes, Kevin (Athlete, Hockey Player)
251 Yonge St Suite 8 887
Richmond Hill, ON L4C 9T3, Canada

Weekley, Thomas (Boo) (Athlete, Golfer)
2555 New York St
Jay, FL 32565-2956, USA

Weeks, Ed (Actor)
c/o Hilary Hansen *Vision PR*
2 Penn Plz Rm 2601
New York, NY 10121-0001, USA

Weeks, John D (Misc)
15301 Watergate Rd
Silver Spring, MD 20905-5779, USA

Weeks, Rickie (Athlete, Baseball Player)
353 Woldunn Cir
Lake Mary, FL 32746-3942, USA

Weeks, Steve (Athlete, Hockey Player)
8210 Woodiron Dr
Duluth, GA 30097-3753, USA

Weezer (Music Group)
c/o Jen Appel *Grandstand Media*
39 W 32nd St Rm 1603
New York, NY 10001-3839, USA

Wegener, Mike (Athlete, Baseball Player)
1507 Bennett Rd
Madison, OH 44057-1415, USA

Weger, Mike (Athlete, Football Player)
2044 Earl Rd
Fort Myers, FL 33901-8000, USA

Wegman, Bill (Athlete, Baseball Player)
20521 Heather Ct
Lawrenceburg, IN 47025-9396, USA

Wegman, Marie (Baseball Player)
4158 Westwood Northern Blvd
Cincinnati, OH 45211-2444, USA

Wegman, William G (Artist, Photographer)
239 W 18th St Fl 2
New York, NY 10011-4502, USA

Wegner, Hans J (Designer)
Tinglevej 17
Gentoftte 02820, DENMARK

Wegner, Mark (Athlete, Baseball Player)
2607 Lakeview Way
Plant City, FL 33566-6774, USA

Wegner, Mark (Baseball Player)
3215 Stevenson St
Plant City, FL 33566-9517, USA

Wehling, Ulrich (Athlete)
Skiverband
Hubertusstr 1
Munich 81477, GERMANY

Wehner, John (Athlete, Baseball Player)
135 N Green Ln
Zelienople, PA 16063-1106, USA

Wehr, Dick (Athlete, Basketball Player)
4425 Thomas Dr Unit 813A
Panama City, FL 32408-8320, USA

Wehrli, Roger R (Athlete, Football Player)
46 Fox Meadows Ct
Saint Charles, MO 63303-1701, USA

Wehrmeister, Dave (Athlete, Baseball Player)
4216 Dubhe Ct
Concord, CA 94521-1820, USA

Wei, Dan-Wen (Musician)
Columbia Artists Mgmt Inc
165 W 57th St
New York, NY 10019-2201, USA

Weibring, D A (Athlete, Golfer)
5865 Versailles Ave
Frisco, TX 75034-5957, USA

Weich, Gillian (Musician)
DS Mgmt
1017 16th Ave S
Nashville, TN 37212-2324, USA

Weickgenannt, Bob (Race Car Driver)
B&B Racing
8835 Columbia 100 Pkwy Ste M
Columbia, MD 21045-2147, USA

Weide, Bob (Director)
Wahyaduck Productions
4804 Laurel Canyon Blvd PMB 502
North Hollywood, CA 91607-3717, USA

Weide, Robert B (Director, Producer)
c/o Jonathan Brandstein *Morra Brezner Steinberg & Tenenbaum (MBST) Entertainment*
345 N Maple Dr Ste 200
Beverly Hills, CA 90210-5174, USA

Weidemann, Jakob (Artist)
Ringsveen
Lillehammer 02600, NORWAY

Weider, Betty (Actor)
131 S Hudson Ave
Los Angeles, CA 90004-1033, USA

Weidner, Bert (Athlete, Football Player)
517 NW 106th Ave
Plantation, FL 33324-1629, USA

Weidner, Brant (Athlete, Basketball Player)
1111 Colfax St
Evanston, IL 60201-2610, USA

Weigel, Teri (Actor, Adult Film Star, Model)
Web It Promotions
33221 287th St
Dallas, SD 57529-6303, USA

Weigert, Robin (Actor)
c/o Staff Member *Frontline Management*
5670 Wilshire Blvd Ste 1370
Los Angeles, CA 90036-5649, USA

Weight, Doug (Athlete, Hockey Player, Olympic Athlete)
72 Feeks Ln
Locust Valley, NY 11560-2022, USA

Weikel, M Keith (Business Person)
Manor Care Inc
333 N Summit St
Toledo, OH 43604-1531, USA

Weil, Andrew (Doctor, Writer)
c/o Richard S. Pine *Inkwell Management*
521 5th Ave
New York, NY 10175-0003, USA

Weil, Cynthia (Musician, Songwriter)
c/o Staff Member *Gorfaine/Schwartz Agency Inc*
4111 W Alameda Ave Ste 509
Burbank, CA 91505-4171, USA

Weil, Frank A (Misc)
Smithsonian Institution
900 Jefferson Dr SW
Washington, DC 20560-0005, USA

Weil, Jeri (Actor)
11564 Kling St # N
North Hollywood, CA 91602-1054, USA

Weil, Liza (Actor)
c/o Marsha McManus *Principal Entertainment*
9255 W Sunset Blvd Ste 500
Los Angeles, CA 90069-3301, USA

Weiland, Paul (Director)
c/o Jenne Casarotto *Casarotto Ramsay & Associates Ltd (UK)*
Waverley House
7-12 Noel St
London W1F 8GQ, UNITED KINGDOM

Weill, Claudia B (Director)
2800 Seattle Dr
Los Angeles, CA 90046-1209, USA

Weill, Dave (Athlete, Olympic Athlete)
120 Mountain Spring Ave
San Francisco, CA 94114-2120, USA

Weill, Sanford I (Sandy) (Business Person)
Citigroup Inc
399 Park Ave
New York, NY 10022-4614, USA

Weinbach, Arthur F (Business Person)
Automatic Data Processing
1 Adp Blvd Ste 1
Roseland, NJ 07068-1728, USA

Weinbach, Lawrence A (Business Person)
Unisys Corp
Unisys Way
Blue Bell, PA 19424-0001, USA

Weinberg, Max (Musician)
2/36 Bayside Dr
Atlantic Highlands, NJ 07716, USA

Weinberg, Mike (Actor)
c/o Elissa Leeds-Fickman *Reel Talent Management*
PO Box 491035
Los Angeles, CA 90049-9035, USA

Weinbrecht, Donna (Athlete, Olympic Athlete, Skier)
177 High Crest Dr
West Milford, NJ 07480-3707, USA

Weiner, Anthony (Politician)

Weiner, Eric (Producer, Writer)
c/o Staff Member *ICM Partners*
10250 Constellation Blvd Fl 7
Los Angeles, CA 90067-6207, USA

Weiner, Jennifer (Writer)
c/o Jake Weiner *Good Fear Film + Management*
6255 W Sunset Blvd Ste 800
Los Angeles, CA 90028-7409, USA

Weiner, Marc (Comedian)
102 West Ln
Stamford, CT 06905-3955, USA

Weiner, Matthew (Producer)
159 S Alta Vista Blvd
Los Angeles, CA 90036-2823, USA

Weiner, Timothy E (Tim) (Journalist, Writer)
c/o Staff Member *Creative Artists Agency (CAA)*
2000 Avenue of the Stars Ste 100
Los Angeles, CA 90067-4705, USA

Weiner-Davis, Michele (Writer)
c/o Staff Member *21st Century Speakers*
1352 Lake Ave
Gouldsboro, PA 18424, USA

Weinhandl, Mattias (Athlete, Hockey Player)
Puckagency LLC
555 Pleasantville Rd Ste 210N
Attn Jay Grossman
Briarcliff Manor, NY 10510-1900, USA

Weinke, Chris (Athlete, Football Player, Heisman Trophy Winner)
John Madden Football Academy
5500 34th St W
Attn: Directors Office
Bradenton, FL 34210-3506, USA

Weinman, Roz (Producer)
c/o Staff Member *Wolf Films Inc (LA)*
260 S Los Robles Ave Ste 309
Pasadena, CA 91101-2897, USA

Weinrich, Eric (Athlete, Hockey Player, Olympic Athlete)
337 Sea Meadows Ln
Yarmouth, ME 04096-5556, USA

Weinstein, Bob (Business Person, Producer)
Miramax Films
1995 Broadway
New York, NY 10023-5882, USA

Weinstein, Harvey (Business Person, Producer)
c/o Benjamin Brafman *Brafman & Associates*
767 3rd Ave Fl 26
New York, NY 10017-9002, USA

Weir, Amanda (Athlete, Olympic Athlete, Swimmer)
765 Barongate Dr
Lawrenceville, GA 30044-6079, USA

Weir, Arabella (Actor)
c/o Staff Member *Lip Service Casting Ltd*
60-66 Wardour St
London W1F 0TA, UK

Weir, Bill (Correspondent)

Weir, Bob (Musician)
PO Box 1566
Montclair, NJ 07042-1566, USA

Weir, Gillian C (Musician)
78 Robin Way
Tilehurst
Berks RG3 5SW, UNITED KINGDOM (UK)

Weir, Glen (Athlete, Football Player)
40 Maxwell Cres
London, ON N5X 1Z1, Canada

Weir, Johnny (Athlete, Figure Skater, Olympic Athlete)
c/o Laina Cohn *Cohn / Torgan Management*
Prefers to be contacted by telephone or email
Los Angeles, CA, USA

Weir, Judith (Composer)
Chester Music
8/9 Frith St
London W1V 5TZ, UNITED KINGDOM (UK)

Weir, Mike (Athlete, Golfer)
Taboo Muskoka Sands
Muskoka Beach Rd
Gravenhurst, ON P1P 1R1, CANADA

Weir, Peter (Director)
Salt Pan Films
PO Box 29
Boston, MA 02133-0029, AUSTRALIA

Weir, Stephnie (Actor)
1484 N Chester Ave
Pasadena, CA 91104-2540, USA

Weir, Wally (Athlete, Hockey Player)
448 Lakeshore Rd
Beaconsfield, QC H9W 4J5, Canada

Weirs, Peter (Director)
c/o Staff Member *Anonymous Content*
3532 Hayden Ave
Culver City, CA 90232-2413, USA

Weis, Al (Athlete, Baseball Player)
902 S Poplar Ave
Elmhurst, IL 60126-4547, USA

Weis, Charlie (Athlete, Coach, Football Coach, Football Player)
11878 Hawk Holw
Rail # T-5
Lake Worth, FL 33449-8403, USA

Weis, Scott (Race Car Driver)
Wiseguys/Weis Racing
5401 Lakeside Ave
Richmond, VA 23228-6009, USA

Weisacosky, Ed (Athlete, Football Player)
15321 Lawrence 2090
Mount Vernon, MO 65712-7281, USA

Weisberg, Ruth (Artist)
11452 W Washington Blvd
Los Angeles, CA 90066-6013, USA

Weisberg, Tim (Musician)
c/o Staff Member *Pyramid Entertainment Group*
377 Rector Pl Apt 21A
New York, NY 10280-1439, USA

Weisburg, Alyssa (Producer)
c/o Staff Member *Casting Society of America*
606 N Larchmont Blvd Ste 4B
Los Angeles, CA 90004-1309, USA

Weishoff, Paula (Athlete, Olympic Athlete, Volleyball Player)
3 Mayer Ct
Irvine, CA 92617-4113, USA

Weishuhn, Clayton (Athlete, Football Player)
4521 Krupala Rd
San Angelo, TX 76905-7412, USA

Weisman, Annie (Comedian)
c/o Staff Member *Gersh*
9465 Wilshire Blvd Ste 600
Beverly Hills, CA 90212-2605, USA

Weisman, Kevin (Actor)
c/o Andi Schecter *Jonas Public Relations*
1327 Ocean Ave Ste F
Santa Monica, CA 90401-1024, USA

Weisman, Sam (Actor, Director)
United Talent Agency
9336 Civic Center Dr
Beverly Hills, CA 90210-3604, USA

Weiss, Barry (Reality Star)
Storage Wars
308 W Verdugo Ave
C/O Original Production
Burbank, CA 91502-2340, USA

Weiss, Brian L (Writer)
c/o Staff Member *WME|IMG*
9601 Wilshire Blvd
Beverly Hills, CA 90210-5213, USA

Weiss, Daniel B (DB) (Producer, Writer)
c/o Guymon Casady *Management 360*
9111 Wilshire Blvd
Beverly Hills, CA 90210-5508, USA

Weiss, Frank (Athlete, Football Player)
729 Fairfax Dr
Salinas, CA 93901-1250, USA

Weiss, Gary (Athlete, Baseball Player)
1700 Weiss Ln
Brenham, TX 77833-7063, USA

Weiss, Glenn (Director, Producer, Writer)

Weiss, Janet (Musician)
Legends of 21st Century
7 Trinity Row
Florence, MA 01062-1931, USA

Weiss, Julie (Designer)
International Creative Mgmt
8942 Wilshire Blvd # 219
Beverly Hills, CA 90211-1908, USA

Weiss, Karen (Athlete, Golfer)
1135 Raymond Ave
Saint Paul, MN 55108-1922, USA

Weiss, Margaret (Writer)
TSR
PO Box 707
Renton, WA 98057-0707, USA

Weiss, Michael (Figure Skater, Olympic Athlete)
The Michael Weiss Foundation
1098 Mill Rdg
Mc Lean, VA 22102-2145, USA

Weiss, Michael T (Actor, Director)
2616 Strongs Dr
Venice, CA 90291-4434, USA

Weiss, Morry (Business Person)
American Greetings Corp
1 American Rd
Cleveland, OH 44144-2354, USA

Weiss, Roberta (Actor)
Sarnoff Co
3500 W Olive Ave Ste 300
Burbank, CA 91505-4647, USA

Weiss, Robert W (Bob) (Athlete, Basketball Player, Coach)
1600 Windermere Dr E
Seattle, WA 98112-3738, USA

Weiss, Shaun (Actor)
c/o Don Gibble *Don Gibble & Associates*
8945 Canby Ave
Northridge, CA 91325-2702, USA

Weiss, Stephen (Athlete, Hockey Player)
899 NW 123rd Dr
Coral Springs, FL 33071-5039, USA

Weiss, Walter W (Walt) (Athlete, Baseball Player)
1275 Castle Pointe Dr
Castle Rock, CO 80104-3258, USA

Weissenhofer, Ron (Athlete, Football Player)
16156 Seneca Lake Cir
Crest Hill, IL 60403-1500, USA

Weisser, Morgan (Actor)
1030 Superba Ave
Venice, CA 90291-3940, USA

Weisser, Norbert (Actor)
1030 Superba Ave
Venice, CA 90291-3940, USA

Weissflog, Jens (Skier)
Markt 2
Kurort Oberweisenthal 09484, GERMANY

Weissman, Malina (Actor)
c/o Lindsey Ludwig-Rahm *Viewpoint Inc*
89 5th Ave Ste 402
New York, NY 10003-3020, USA

Weissman, Robert (Business Person)
IMS Health Inc
1499 Post Rd
Fairfield, CT 06824-5940, USA

Weissman, Steven (Artist)
c/o Staff Member *Fantagraphics Books*
7563 Lake City Way NE
Seattle, WA 98115-4218, USA

Weisz, Martin (Director)
c/o Doreen Wilcox Little *Anonymous Content*
3532 Hayden Ave
Culver City, CA 90232-2413, USA

Weisz, Rachel (Actor)
c/o Rebecca Sides Capellan *ID Public Relations (NY)*
40 Wall St Fl 51
New York, NY 10005-1385, USA

Weithaas, Antje (Musician)
Harrison/Parrott
12 Penzance Place
London W11 4PA, UNITED KINGDOM (UK)

Weithorn, Michael (Director, Writer)
363 18th St
Santa Monica, CA 90402-2405, USA

Weitz, Bruce (Actor)
18826 Erwin St
Tarzana, CA 91335-6827, USA

Weitz, Chris (Actor, Producer)
c/o Staff Member *Depth of Field*
1724 Whitley Ave
Los Angeles, CA 90028-4809, USA

Weitz, Paul (Director, Writer)
c/o George Freeman *WME|IMG*
9601 Wilshire Blvd
Beverly Hills, CA 90210-5213, USA

Weitzenberg, Charles B (Athlete, Olympic Athlete, Water Polo Player)
5153 Oak Meadow Dr
Santa Rosa, CA 95401-5518, USA

Weitzman, Rick (Athlete, Basketball Player)
4206 Woodbridge Rd
Peabody, MA 01960-4763, USA

Weiwei, Ai (Activist, Artist)

Weixler, Jess (Actor)
c/o Rhonda Price *Gersh*
41 Madison Ave Ste 3301
New York, NY 10010-2210, USA

Wejbe, Jolean (Actor)
c/o Bob McGowan *McGowan Management*
170 S Beverly Dr Ste 304
Beverly Hills, CA 90212-3000, USA

Wek, Alek (Model)
c/o Staff Member *IMG*
304 Park Ave S Fl 12
New York, NY 10010-4314, USA

Welbourn, John (Athlete, Football Player)
3301 Palos Verdes Dr N
Palos Verdes Estates, CA 90274-1030, USA

Welbring, D A (Golfer)
c/o Staff Member *Pro Golfers Association (PGA)*
112 TPC Blvd
Ponte Vedra Beach, FL 32082, USA

Welch, Brian (Head) (Musician)
4025 E Chandler Blvd Ste 70
Phoenix, AZ 85048-8833, USA

Welch, Claxton (Athlete, Football Player)
9721 SE Ankeny St
Portland, OR 97216-2311, USA

Welch, Florence (Musician)
c/o Mairead Nash *LuvLuvLuv Management*
106 Leonard St Fl 1
London EC2A 4RH, UNITED KINGDOM (UK)

Welch, Gillian (Musician)
c/o Cliff Burnstein *Q Prime (NY)*
729 7th Ave Fl 16
New York, NY 10019-6831, USA

Welch, Herb (Athlete, Football Player)
999 La Senda
Santa Barbara, CA 93105-4512, USA

Welch, Jack (Business Person)
Jack Welch Management Institute
2303 Dulles Station Blvd # 6C
Strayer University Office of the General Counsel
Herndon, VA 20171-6353, USA

Welch, Justin (Musician)
CMO Mgmt
Ransomes Dock
35037 Parkgate Road
London SW11 4NP, UNITED KINGDOM (UK)

Welch, Lenny (Musician)
Brothers Mgmt
141 Dunbar Ave
Fords, NJ 08863-1551, USA

Welch, Michael (Actor)
c/o Susan Curtis *Curtis Talent Management*
9607 Arby Dr
Beverly Hills, CA 90210-1202, USA

Welch, Mike (Athlete, Baseball Player)
3 Inca Dr
Nashua, NH 03063-3544, USA

Welch, Milt (Athlete, Baseball Player)
4725 Village Plaza Loop Ste 200
Eugene, OR 97401-6677, USA

Welch, Raquel (Actor)
9903 Santa Monica Blvd Ste 514
Beverly Hills, CA 90212-1671, USA

Welch, Tahnee (Actor, Model)
PO Box 823
Beverly Hills, CA 90213-0823, USA

Welchel, Don (Athlete, Baseball Player)
21518 Patton Ave
Lago Vista, TX 78645-6770, USA

Welch Jr, John F (Business Person)
General Electric Co
3135 Easton Tpke
Fairfield, CT 06828-0001, USA

Weld, Tuesday (Actor)
c/o Alexa Pagonas *Michael Black Management*
9701 Wilshire Blvd Fl 10
Beverly Hills, CA 90212-2010, USA

Weldon, Ann (Actor)
c/o Staff Member *Sutton Barth & Vennari Inc*
5900 Wilshire Blvd Ste 700
Los Angeles, CA 90036-5009, USA

Weldon, Fay (Writer)
Casorotto Ramsay
National House
62/66 Wardour
London W1V 3HP, UNITED KINGDOM (UK)

Weldon, Joan (Actor)
67 E 78th St
New York, NY 10075-0273, USA

Weldon, W Casey (Athlete, Football Player)
8829 Roberts Rd
Odessa, FL 33556-1920, USA

Welk, Lawrence (Actor)
841 N Saint Elena St
Gilbert, AZ 85234-3586, USA

Welk, Tanya (Actor)
9633 La Tuna Canyon Rd
Sun Valley, CA 91352-2233, USA

Welke, Tim (Athlete, Baseball Player)
7790 Doubletree Ct
Kalamazoo, MI 49009-9771, USA

Welke, William (Bill) (Athlete, Baseball Player)
16285 13 Mile Rd
Battle Creek, MI 49014-7939, USA

Welker, Frank (Actor)
c/o Staff Member *Cunningham Escott Slevin & Doherty (CESD)*
10635 Santa Monica Blvd Ste 130
Los Angeles, CA 90025-8306, USA

Welker, Wes (Athlete, Football Player)
2006 North Blvd
Houston, TX 77098-5353, USA

Welland, Colin (Actor, Writer)
Peter Charlesworth
68 Old Brompton Road
London SW7 3LQ, UNITED KINGDOM (UK)

Wellborn, Joe (Athlete, Football Player)
803 Paulus St
Schulenburg, TX 78956-1424, USA

Wellemeyer, Todd (Athlete, Baseball Player)
8402 Westover Dr
Prospect, KY 40059-9497, USA

Wellens, Jesse (Internet Star)
Cohen & Silver
227 Pine St
Philadelphia, PA 19106-4326, USA

Weller, Paul (Musician)
c/o Staff Member *Variety Artists International Inc*
1111 Riverside Ave Ste 501
Paso Robles, CA 93446-2683, USA

Weller, Peter (Actor)
c/o Craig Baumgarten *Zero Gravity Management*
11110 Ohio Ave Ste 100
Los Angeles, CA 90025-3329, USA

Weller, Rene (Boxer)
Hirsauerstrasse 50
Pforzheim D-75180, Germany

Weller, Robb (Television Host)
4249 Beck Ave
Studio City, CA 91604-2913, USA

Weller, Watter (Musician)
Doblinger Hauptstr 40
Vienna 01190, AUSTRIA

Welles, Tori (Actor, Adult Film Star, Model)
c/o Staff Member *Sirius/XM Satellite Radio*
1221 Avenue of the Americas Fl 19
New York, NY 10020-1001, USA

Welling, Tom (Actor)
Tom Welling Productions
16000 Ventura Blvd Ste 900
Encino, CA 91436-2760, USA

Wellman, Brad (Athlete, Baseball Player)
333 Wild Horse Cir
Boulder, CO 80304-0489, USA

Wellman, Gary (Athlete, Football Player)
1638 Wellington Pl
Westlake Village, CA 91361-1535, USA

Wellman Jr, William (Actor)
15935 Meadowcrest Rd
Sherman Oaks, CA 91403-4715, USA

Wells, Annie (Journalist, Photographer)
Press Democrat
427 Mendocino Ave
Editorial Dept
Santa Rosa, CA 95401-6385, USA

Wells, Bob (Athlete, Baseball Player)
154 Wilcox Rd
Cowiche, WA 98923-9775, USA

Wells, Carole (Actor)
c/o Staff Member *Burton Moss*
10533 Strathmore Dr
Los Angeles, CA 90024-2540, USA

Wells, Casper (Athlete, Baseball Player)
252 Guy Park Ave
Amsterdam, NY 12010-2333, USA

Wells, Charles (Athlete, Baseball Player)
Philadelphia Stars
1035 Beaver Creek Dr
Duncanville, TX 75137-3731, USA

Wells, Chris (Athlete, Hockey Player)
PO Box 880883
Boca Raton, FL 33488-0883, USA

Wells, Claudia (Actor)
Armani Wells
16950 Sherman Way
Van Nuys, CA 91406-3613, USA

Wells, Dan (Actor)
c/o Jon Simmons *Simmons & Scott Entertainment*
7942 Mulholland Dr
Los Angeles, CA 90046-1225, USA

Wells, David (Athlete, Baseball Player)
PO Box 8107
Rancho Santa Fe, CA 92067-8107, USA

Wells, Dawn (Actor)
11684 Ventura Blvd # 965
Studio City, CA 91604-2699, USA

Wells, Dean (Athlete, Football Player)
1146 Copperfield Dr
Georgetown, IN 47122-9082, USA

Wells, Gawen D (Bonzi) (Basketball Player)
c/o Staff Member *Sacramento Kings*
1 Sports Pkwy
Sacramento, CA 95834-2301, USA

Wells, Greg (Athlete, Baseball Player)
1 Sterling Ct
Cartersville, GA 30120-6469, USA

Wells, Harold (Athlete, Football Player)
4110 Henline Dr
Raleigh, NC 27604-4200, USA

Wells, Jane (Correspondent)
c/o Staff Member *CNBC (Main)*
900 Sylvan Ave
Englewood Cliffs, NJ 07632-3312, USA

Wells, Jay (Athlete, Hockey Player)
990 Keg Lane
Paris, ON N3L 3E2, Canada

Wells, Jay (Athlete, Hockey Player)
555 Bayview Dr
Attn Coaching Staff Barrie Colts
Barrie, ON L4N 8Y2, Canada

Wells, Joel (Athlete, Football Player)
11 Flicker Pt
Greenville, SC 29609-6646, USA

Wells, John (Producer)
c/o Staff Member *John Wells Productions*
4000 Warner Blvd Bldg 1
Burbank, CA 91522-0001, USA

Wells, Kip (Athlete, Baseball Player)
12891 Westbrook Dr
Tyler, TX 75704-2460, USA

Wells, LLewellyn (Producer)
c/o Wayne Fitterman *United Talent Agency (UTA)*
9336 Civic Center Dr
Beverly Hills, CA 90210-3604, USA

Wells, Mark (Athlete, Hockey Player, Olympic Athlete)
451 SW South River Dr Apt 104
Stuart, FL 34997-3228, USA

Wells, Noel (Actor)
c/o Rachael Wesolowski *Independent Public Relations*
9601 Wilshire Blvd Ste 750
Beverly Hills, CA 90210-5228, USA

Wells, Norman (Athlete, Football Player)
600 Lakes Edge Dr
Oxford, MI 48371-5229, USA

Wells, Patricia (Journalist)
Harper Collins Publishers
10 E 53rd St
New York, NY 10022-5244, USA

Wells, Scott (Athlete, Football Player)
291 Jones Pkwy
Brentwood, TN 37027-4458, USA

Wells, Terry (Athlete, Baseball Player)
110 Seymour Creek Dr
Cary, NC 27519-5870, USA

Wells, Terry (Athlete, Football Player)
25036 Polktown Rd
Lucedale, MS 39452, USA

Wells, Thelma (Writer)
1934 Lanark Ave
Dallas, TX 75203-4523, USA

Wells, Theodore V (Attorney)
Paul, Weiss, Rifkind, Warton & Garrison, LLC 1285 Avenue ofthe Americas
New York, NY 10019-6031, USA

Wells, Vernon (Athlete, Baseball Player)
1400 Fountain Grass Ct
Westlake, TX 76262-9032, USA

Wells, Wayne (Athlete, Olympic Athlete, Wrestler)
PO Box 69
Arcadia, OK 73007-0069, USA

Wells-Hawkes, Sharlene (Beauty Pageant Winner)
77 W Lund Ln
Centerville, UT 84014-2710, USA

Welp, Christian (Athlete, Basketball Player)
149 NW Tupelo Way
Poulsbo, WA 98370-8378, USA

Welsh, Chris (Athlete, Baseball Player)
12640 Huey Ln
Walton, KY 41094-9511, USA

Welsh, Dave (Musician)
2417 W 32nd Ave Unit 7
Denver, CO 80211-3374, USA

Welsh, Irvine (Writer)
c/o Laura Hassan *Random House Group Limited*
The Book Service Limited
20 Vauxhall Bridge Road
London SW1V 2SA, United Kingdom

Welsh, Moray M (Musician)
28 Somerfield Ave
Queens Park
London NW6 6JY, UNITED KINGDOM (UK)

Welsh, Stephanie (Journalist, Photographer)
PO Box 277
Wayne, ME 04284-0277, USA

Welsom, Elleen (Journalist)
Albuquerque Tribune
7777 Jefferson St NE
Editorial Dept
Albuquerque, NM 87109-4360, USA

Welsome-Martin, Eileen (Journalist, Photographer)
2040 Locust St
Denver, CO 80207-3941, USA

Welti, Lisa (Actor)
c/o Staff Member *Select Artists Ltd (CA-Westside Office)*
1138 12th St Apt 1
Santa Monica, CA 90403-5459, USA

Wen, Jinbao (Prime Minister)
Premier's Office
Zhonganahai
Beijing, CHINA

Wen, Ming-Na (Actor)
c/o Erik Kritzer *LINK Entertainment*
11872 La Grange Ave
Los Angeles, CA 90025-5282, USA

Wendeii-Pohl, Krissy (Athlete, Hockey Player, Olympic Athlete)
10812 Falling Water Ln Unit G
Saint Paul, MN 55129-5267, USA

Wendell, Krissy (Hockey Player)
University of Minnesota
Athletic Dept
Minneapolis, MN 55455, USA

Wendell, Ryan (Athlete, Football Player)
c/o Staff Member *New England Patriots*
1 Patriot Pl
Foxboro, MA 02035-1388, USA

Wendell, Steven ""Turk"" (Athlete, Baseball Player)
9258 Ironwood Dr
West Des Moines, IA 50266-8901, USA

Wendelstedt, Hunter (Athlete, Baseball Player)
101 Hawthorne Hollow Dr
Madisonville, LA 70447-9340, USA

Wenden, Michael (Swimmer)
Palm Beach Currmbin Center
Thrower Dr
Palm Beach Queens, AUSTRALIA

Wenders, Wim (Director)
c/o Staff Member *Neue Road Movies*
Saarbr??cker Straße 24
Berlin 10405, GERMANY

Wendkos, Gina (Writer)
c/o Staff Member *Industry Entertainment Partners*
955 Carrillo Dr Ste 300
Los Angeles, CA 90048-5400, USA

Wendt, George (Actor)
3856 Vantage Ave
Studio City, CA 91604-3636, USA

Wenge, Ralph (Correspondent)
Cable News Network
1050 Techwood Dr NW
News Dept
Atlanta, GA 30318-5695, USA

Wenger, Arsene (Coach)
Arsenal Football Club
Highbury House
75 Drayton Park
London N5 1BU, UNITED KINGDOM

Wengert, Don (Athlete, Baseball Player)
3240 Terrace Dr
Des Moines, IA 50312-4537, USA

Wenglikowski, Alan (Athlete, Football Player)
422 Lake Ave
Franklin, OH 45005-3521, USA

Wengren, Mike (Musician)
c/o Staff Member *Mitch Schneider Organization (MSO)*
14724 Ventura Blvd Ste 410
Sherman Oaks, CA 91403-3537, USA

Wenham, David (Actor, Producer)
c/o Julie Curran *Shanahan Management*
Level 3 Berman House
Surry Hills 02010, AUSTRALIA

Wenner, Jann S (Business Person)
Wenner Media
1290 Avenue of the Americas Fl 2
New York, NY 10104-0295, USA

Wenning, Keith (Athlete, Football Player)

Wennington, Bill (Athlete, Basketball Player)
1085 Oak Grove Ln
Lake Forest, IL 60045-1629, USA

Wensink, John (Athlete, Hockey Player)
29311 Bidwell Creek Rd
Fredericktown, MO 63645-8900, USA

Wenstrom, Matt (Athlete, Basketball Player)
15714 Blanco Trails Ln
Cypress, TX 77429-4618, USA

Wente, Jean R (Business Person)
California State Automobile Assn
PO Box 422940
San Francisco, CA 94142, USA

Wente, Jr., Bob (Race Car Driver)
59 Windam Place Dr
Saint Charles, MO 63304-7417, USA

Wentworth, Ali (Actor, Comedian)
20 Dunemere Ln
East Hampton, NY 11937-2706, USA

Wentz, Carson (Athlete, Football Player)
c/o Ryan Tollner *REP 1 Sports Group*
80 Technology Dr
Irvine, CA 92618-2301, USA

Wentz, Pete (Musician)
c/o Raj Raghavan *Creative Artists Agency (CAA)*
2000 Avenue of the Stars Ste 100
Los Angeles, CA 90067-4705, USA

Wenz, Fred (Athlete, Baseball Player)
1 Circle Dr
Branchburg, NJ 08876-3905, USA

Wenzel, Andreas (Athlete, Skier)
Oberhul 151
Liechtenstein-Gamprin, LIECHENSTEIN

Wenzel, Hanni Weirather- (Skier)
Fanalwegle 4
Schaan 09494, LIECHENSTEIN

Wenzell, Marge (Baseball Player)
78287 Brookhaven Ln
Palm Desert, CA 92211-2735, USA

Wepner, Chuck (Boxer)
153 Avenue E
Bayonne, NJ 07002-4434, USA

Wepper, Fritz (Actor)

Werb, Mike (Director, Producer)
9270 Sierra Mar Dr
Los Angeles, CA 90069-1735, USA

Werbach, Adam (Misc)
Sierra Club
85 2nd St Ste 200
San Francisco, CA 94105-3488, USA

Werbowy, Daria (Model)
c/o Vanessa Gringer *IMG Models (NY)*
304 Park Ave S PH N
New York, NY 10010-4303, USA

Werdann, Robert (Athlete, Basketball Player)
4739 40th St Apt 5F
Sunnyside, NY 11104-4035, USA

Werhas, Johnny (Athlete, Baseball Player)
23705 Via Del Rio
Yorba Linda, CA 92887-2717, USA

Werkheiser, Devon (Actor)
c/o Susan Curtis *Curtis Talent Management*
9607 Arby Dr
Beverly Hills, CA 90210-1202, USA

Werner, Anna (Correspondent)
KHOU
PO Box 131069
News Department
Houston, TX 77219-1069, USA

Werner, Bjoern (Athlete, Football Player)
c/o Ben Dogra *Relativity Sports*
2029 Century Park E Ste 1550
Century City, CA 90067-3000, USA

Werner, Clyde (Athlete, Football Player)
3009 Islandview Ct
Gig Harbor, WA 98335-1258, USA

Werner, Don (Athlete, Baseball Player)
2204 Briarwood Blvd
Arlington, TX 76013-3316, USA

Werner, Marianne (Athlete, Track Athlete)
Gauseland 2A
Dortmund 44227, GERMANY

Werner, Michael (Misc)
Michael Werner Ltd
21 E 67th St
New York, NY 10065-5817, USA

Werner, Roger L Jr (Television Host)
Prime Sports Ventures
10000 Santa Monica Blvd
Los Angeles, CA 90067-7000, USA

Werner, Tom (Producer)
c/o Staff Member *Carsey-Werner Company*
16027 Ventura Blvd Ste 600
Encino, CA 91436-2798, USA

Wersching, Annie (Actor)
c/o Craig Schneider *Pinnacle Public Relations*
8721 Santa Monica Blvd # 133
W Hollywood, CA 90069-4507, USA

Wersching, Raimund (Ray) (Athlete, Football Player)
18 Buttercup Ln
San Carlos, CA 94070-1528, USA

Wert, Don (Athlete, Baseball Player)
c/o Staff Member *Athlete Connection LLC*
PO Box 380135
Clinton Township, MI 48038-0060, USA

Werth, Dennis (Athlete, Baseball Player)
2505 Tartan Way
Springfield, IL 62711-6755, USA

Werth, Isabell (Horse Racer)
Winterswicker Feld 4
Rheinberg 47495, USA

Werth, Jayson (Athlete, Baseball Player)
2713 Tartan Way
Springfield, IL 62711-6717, USA

Wertheim, Jorge (Misc)
UNESCO
Director's Office
UN Plaza
New York, NY 10017, USA

Wertheimer, Fredric M (Misc)
3502 Macomb St NW
Washington, DC 20016-3162, USA

Wertheimer, Linda (Correspondent)
National Public Radio
2025 M St NW
News Dept
Washington, DC 20036-3309, USA

Wertmuller, Lina (Director)
Piazza Clotilde
Rome 00196, ITALY

Wertz, Bill (Athlete, Baseball Player)
5430 Bayside Ridge Ct
Galena, OH 43021-8535, USA

Wesley, Blake (Athlete, Hockey Player)
Okanagan Hockey Schools
201-853 Eckhardt Ave W
Attn Senior Director of Hockey Operations
Penticton, BC V2A 9C4, Canada

Wesley, Dante (Athlete, Football Player)
104 Fawn Cv
White Hall, AR 71602-4774, USA

Wesley, David (Athlete, Basketball Player)
2S06 Baywater Canyon Dr
Pearland, TX 77S84-4310, USA

Wesley, Glen (Athlete, Hockey Player)
2891 Westview Trl
Park City, UT 84098-6251, USA

Wesley, James (Musician)
c/o Staff Member *Broken Bow Records*
209 10th Ave S Ste 230
Cummins Station
Nashville, TN 37203-0722, USA

Wesley, Norman (Business Person)
Fortune Brands Inc
300 Tower Pkwy
Lincolnshire, IL 60069-3640, USA

Wesley, Paul (Actor)
c/o Susan Calogerakis *SC Management*
9465 Wilshire Blvd Fl 7
Beverly Hills, CA 90212-2606, USA

Wesley, Rutina (Actor)
c/o Iris Grossman *Echo Lake Management*
421 S Beverly Dr Fl 8
Beverly Hills, CA 90212-4408, USA

Wesley, Walt (Athlete, Basketball Player)
6417 Scott Ln
Fort Myers, FL 33966-4713, USA

WesleySmith, Michael (Actor)
c/o Staff Member *Sharon Power Management*
Pope Street
Camborne, Wellington, New Zealand

Wessinger, Jim (Athlete, Baseball Player)
4275 Altair Crse
Liverpool, NY 13090-2230, USA

Wessling, John (Actor, Comedian)
c/o Nick Nuciforo *United Talent Agency (UTA)*
9336 Civic Center Dr
Beverly Hills, CA 90210-3604, USA

Wesson, Barry (Athlete, Baseball Player)
36 Shore Dr NE
Brookhaven, MS 39601-8756, USA

West, Andrew J (Actor)
c/o Mia Hansen *Portrait PR*
5320 Sylmar Ave
Sherman Oaks, CA 91401-5612, USA

West, Billy (Actor)
c/o Glenn Schwartz *Glenn Schwartz Company*
4046 Declaration Ave
Calabasas, CA 91302-5741, USA

West, Bob (Athlete, Football Player)
3915 Boston Ave
San Diego, CA 92113-3318, USA

West, Cornel (Business Person, Doctor)
Princeton University
African American Studies Program
Princeton, NJ 08544-0001, USA

West, David (Athlete, Baseball Player)
1242 SW Seahawk Way
Palm City, FL 34990-4246, USA

West, David (Basketball Player)
New Orleans Hornets
1501 Girod St
New Orleans Arena
New Orleans, LA 70113-3124, USA

West, David (Athlete, Baseball Player)
1242 SW Seahawk Way
Palm City, FL 34990-4246, USA

West, Delonte (Athlete, Basketball Player)
c/o Aaron Goodwin *Goodwin Sports Management*
121 Lakeside Ave Ste B
Seattle, WA 98122-6599, USA

West, Dominic (Actor, Director)
c/o Angharad Wood *Tavistock Wood Management*
45 Conduit St
London W1S 2YN, UNITED KINGDOM

West, Doug (Athlete, Basketball Player)
Villanova University see E Lancaster Ave
Attn Basketball Coaching Staff
Villanova, PA 1908S-1478, USA

West, Ed (Athlete, Football Player)
1930 Ma Lee Dr
Moody, AL 35004-2813, USA

West, Jake (Misc)
International Assn of Iron Workers
1750 New York Ave NW Ste 400
Washington, DC 20006-5315, USA

West, Jeff (Athlete, Football Player)
21613 162nd Dr SE
Monroe, WA 98272-4520, USA

West, Jerry (Athlete, Basketball Player, Olympic Athlete)
Golden State Warriors
1011 Broadway
Attn: Executive Board
Oakland, CA 94607-4027, USA

West, Joe (Athlete, Baseball Player)
13788 Hartle Groves Pl APT 209
Clermont, FL 34711-8787, USA

West, Joel (Model)
William Morris Agency
1325 Avenue of the Americas
New York, NY 10019-6026, USA

West, Kanye (Designer, Musician)
Roc-a-Fella Records
160 Varick St # 1200
New York, NY 10013-1220, USA

West, Leslie (Musician)
James Faith Entertainment
318 Wynn Ln Ste 14
Port Jefferson, NY 11777-1699, USA

West, Lizzie (Musician)
Warner Bors Records
3300 Warner Blvd
Burbank, CA 91505-4694, USA

West, Lori (Golfer)
2110 Augusta Dr SE
Marietta, GA 30067-8215, USA

West, Lyle (Athlete, Football Player)
719 1st St SE
Moultrie, GA 31768-5509, USA

West, Mario (Athlete, Basketball Player)
390 Vine Mountain Way
Mableton, GA 30126-7255, USA

West, Mark (Athlete, Basketball Player)
644 Old Wagner Rd
Petersburg, VA 23805-9319, USA

West, Matthew (Musician)
c/o Lori Mahon *Merge PR*
PO Box 1271
Franklin, TN 37065-1271, USA

West, Maura (Actor)
c/o Marnie Sparer *Power Entertainment Group*
1505 10th St
Santa Monica, CA 90401-2805, USA

West, Nathan (Actor)
c/o Jason Egenberg *Authentic Talent & Literary Management*
3615 Eastham Dr # 650
Culver City, CA 90232-2410, USA

West, Paula (Musician)
PO Box 2142
San Francisco, CA 94126-2142, USA

West, Price (Athlete, Baseball Player)
Raleigh Tigers
3540 Mill Point Dr SE
Grand Rapids, MI 49512-9337, USA

West, Red (Actor)
c/o David Shapira *David Shapira & Associates*
193 N Robertson Blvd
Beverly Hills, CA 90211-2103, USA

West, Roland (Athlete, Basketball Player)
7464 Shaker Run Ln
West Chester, OH 45069-6301, USA

West, Ronnie (Athlete, Football Player)
PO Box 110
Pineview, GA 31071-0110, USA

West, Samuel (Actor)
P F D
Drury House
34-43 Russell St
London WC2B 5HA, UNITED KINGDOM (UK)

West, Shane (Actor)
c/o Evelyn O'Neill *Management 360*
9111 Wilshire Blvd
Beverly Hills, CA 90210-5508, USA

West, Simon (Director)
c/o Staff Member *Simon West Productions*
5555 Melrose Ave
Dressing Room Building 109
Los Angeles, CA 90038-3989, USA

West, Timothy L (Actor)
Gavin Barker Assoc
2D Wimpote St
London W1G 0EB, UNITED KINGDOM (UK)

West, Troy (Athlete, Football Player)
725 N Greenberry Ave
West Covina, CA 91790-1331, USA

West, Willie (Athlete, Football Player)
PO Box 50430
Eugene, OR 97405-0980, USA

Westbrook, Brian (Athlete, Football Player)
c/o Deb Poquette *Prestige Lifestyle Management*
1300 Saint Michaels Rd
Mount Airy, MD 21771-3228, USA

Westbrook, Brian (Athlete, Football Player)

Westbrook, Bryant (Athlete, Football Player)
310 S 4th St Unit 1710
Phoenix, AZ 85004-2472, USA

Westbrook, Erinn (Actor)
c/o Tina Treadwell *Treadwell Entertainment*
1327 W Valleyheart Dr
Burbank, CA 91506-3035, USA

Westbrook, Jake (Athlete, Baseball Player)
PO Box 574
Danielsville, GA 30633-0574, USA

Westbrook, Jimi (Musician)
56 Annandale
Nashville, TN 37215-5819, USA

Westbrook, Marie (Actor)

Westbrook, Michael (Athlete, Football Player)
1585 Oregon Trl
Elk Grove Village, IL 60007-2853, USA

Westbrook, Nicole (Musician)
c/o Siri Garber *Platform PR*
2666 N Beachwood Dr
Los Angeles, CA 90068-2308, USA

Westbrook, Russell (Athlete, Basketball Player)
c/o Arn Tellem *Wasserman Media Group*
10960 Wilshire Blvd Ste 1200
Los Angeles, CA 90024-3714, USA

Westbrooks, Greg (Athlete, Football Player)
3832 10th Avenue Pl
Moline, IL 61265-2429, USA

West Coast, Chanel (Musician)
c/o Josh Klein *Talentgroup*
215 W 6th St # PH5
Los Angeles, CA 90014-1865, USA

Westcott, Seth (Athlete, Snowboarder)
c/o Staff Member *US Ski And Snowboard Association*
1 Victory Ln # 100
Park City, UT 84060-7463, USA

Westenhoefer, Suzanne (Actor, Comedian)
100 South 4th Street
Los Angeles, CA 90046

Westenra, Hayley (Actor)
c/o Staff Member *Decca Music Group Limited*
Beaumont House
Avonmore Road
London W14 8TS, UK

Wester, Travis (Actor)
c/o Abby Bluestone *Innovative Artists*
1505 10th St
Santa Monica, CA 90401-2805, USA

Westerberg, Paul (Musician, Songwriter)
4107 W 42nd St
Edina, MN 55416-5005, USA

Westerfeld, Scott (Writer)
c/o Matthew Snyder *Creative Artists Agency (CAA)*
2000 Avenue of the Stars Ste 100
Los Angeles, CA 90067-4705, USA

Westerman-Austin, Helen (Baseball Player)
1837 Stonehenge Rd
Springfield, IL 62702-3244, USA

Western, Johnny (Musician)
19 E 16th Ave
Hutchinson, KS 67501-5533, USA

Western Underground (Music Group)
c/o Staff Member *Paradigm (Monterey)*
404 W Franklin St
Monterey, CA 93940-2303, USA

Westfall, Ed (Athlete, Hockey Player)
PO Box 39
Locust Valley, NY 11560-0039

Westfall, V Edward (Ed) (Athlete, Hockey Player)
699 Hillside Ave
New Hyde Park, NY 11040-2512, USA

Westfeldt, Jennifer (Actor)
2035 N Catalina St
Los Angeles, CA 90027-1825, USA

Westfield, Ernest (Athlete, Baseball Player)
PO Box 7091
Champaign, IL 61826-7091, USA

Westhead, Barb (Golfer)
9820 E Thompson Peak Pkwy
Pkwy Unit 707
Scottsdale, AZ 85255-6614, USA

Westhead, Paul (Athlete, Basketball Coach, Basketball Player, Coach)
2217 Via Alamitos
Palos Verdes Estates, CA 90274-1652, USA

Westheimer, Ruth (Doctor, Writer)
7 Wildwood Ln
Putnam Valley, NY 10579-2243, USA

Westheimer, Ruth (Writer)
900 W 190th St Apt 100
New York, NY 10040-3633, USA

Westlake, Wally (Athlete, Baseball Player)
1050 Piedmont Dr
Sacramento, CA 95822-1704, USA

Westlife (Music Group)
c/o Staff Member *Solo Agency Ltd (UK)*
53-55 Fulham High St
Fl 2
London SW6 3JJ, UNITED KINGDOM

Westmore, McKenzie (Actor)
3904 Laurel Canyon Blvd
#766
Studio City, CA 91604, USA

Westmoreland, Dick (Athlete, Football Player)
5601 Sea Reef Pl
San Diego, CA 92154, USA

Westmoreland, James (Actor)
8019 1/2 Norton Ave
West Hollywood, CA 90046-5002, USA

Westmoreland, Lynn (Congressman, Politician)
2433 Rayburn Hob
Washington, DC 20515-1602, USA

Weston, Celia (Actor)
c/o Staff Member *Innovative Artists*
1505 10th St
Santa Monica, CA 90401-2805, USA

Weston, David (Actor)
123-A Grosvenor Rd
London SW1, UNITED KINGDOM

Weston, Jeff (Athlete, Football Player)
7235 Alakoko St
Honolulu, HI 96825-2712, USA

Weston, Jonny (Actor)
c/o Sarah Shyn *3 Arts Entertainment*
9460 Wilshire Blvd Fl 7
Beverly Hills, CA 90212-2713, USA

Weston, Kim (Musician)
Powerplay
5434 W Sample Rd PMB 533
Margate, FL 33073-3453, USA

Weston, Mickey (Athlete, Baseball Player)
2713 White Pine Cir
Valparaiso, IN 46383-3957, USA

Weston-Jones, Tom (Actor)
c/o Esther Chang *WME|IMG*
9601 Wilshire Blvd
Beverly Hills, CA 90210-5213, USA

Westphal, Paul D (Athlete, Basketball Player, Coach)
8433 E Camino Real
Scottsdale, AZ 85255-3505, USA

Westwick, Ed (Actor)
c/o Melanie Greene *Affirmative Entertainment*
6525 W Sunset Blvd # 7
Los Angeles, CA 90028-7212, USA

Westwood, Lee (Athlete, Golfer)
c/o Andrew ""Chubby"" Chandler *International Sports Management Ltd (ISM UK)*
Cherry Tree Farm
Cherry Tree Lane
Rostherne, Cheshire WA14 3RZ, UNITED KINGDOM

Westwood, Vivienne (Designer, Fashion Designer)
Westwood Studios
9-15 Elcho St
London SW11 4AU, UNITED KINGDOM (UK)

We The Kings (Musician)
c/o Staff Member *Ozone Entertainment*
60-62 E. 11th St
7th Floor
New York, NY 10003, USA

Wetherbee, James D (Astronaut)
710 Huntercrest St
El Lago, TX 77586-5933, USA

Wetherbee, James D Captain (Astronaut)
61649 Hosmer Lake Dr
Bend, OR 97702-3671, USA

Wetherby, Jeff (Athlete, Baseball Player)
4644 Rolling Green Dr
Wesley Chapel, FL 33543-6886, USA

Wetnight, Ryan S (Athlete, Football Player)
3156 Griffon Ct
Simi Valley, CA 93065-0500, USA

Wetoska, Robert (Athlete, Football Player)
1875 Old Willow Rd Unit 113
Northfield, IL 60093-2953, USA

Wetteland, John (Athlete, Baseball Player)
1229 Kentucky Derby Dr
Argyle, TX 76226-7005, USA

Wetter, Friedrich Cardinal (Religious Leader)
Kardinal-Faulhaber-Str 7
Munich 80333, GERMANY

Wetterich, Brett (Athlete, Golfer)
2696 Devils Backbone Rd
Cincinnati, OH 45233-4421, USA

Wetterlund, Alice (Actor, Comedian)
c/o Hillary Robbie *WME|IMG (NY)*
11 Madison Ave Fl 18
New York, NY 10010-3669, USA

Wettig, Patricia (Actor)
c/o Jonathan Howard *Innovative Artists*
1505 10th St
Santa Monica, CA 90401-2805, USA

Wetzel, Carl (Athlete, Hockey Player)
609 4th St # 477
Gaylord, MN 55334-4465, USA

Wetzel, John (Athlete, Basketball Player, Coach)
13011 N Sunrise Canyon Ln
Marana, AZ 85658-4035, USA

Wever, Stefan (Athlete, Baseball Player)
7 Corte Los Sombras
Greenbrae, CA 94904-1149, USA

Wexner, Leslie H (Business Person)
Limited Inc
3 Limited Pkwy
PO Box 16000
Columbus, OH 43230-1467, USA

Weyerhaeuser, George (Business Person)
Weyerhaeuser Co
33663 32nd Ave S
Federal Ave, WA 98023, USA

Whalen, Jim (Athlete, Football Player)
9 Wauketa Rd
Gloucester, MA 01930-1423, USA

Whalen, Lindsay (Basketball Player)
Connecticut Sun
Mohegan Sun Arena
Uncasville, CT 06382, USA

Whalen, Sara (Athlete, Olympic Athlete, Soccer Player)
10 Francis Dr
Greenlawn, NY 11740-2504, USA

Whaley, Frank (Actor)
c/o Staff Member *Shelter Entertainment*
9255 W Sunset Blvd Ste 300
Los Angeles, CA 90069-3313, USA

Whaley, Joanne (Actor)
c/o Staff Member *Creative Artists Agency (CAA)*
2000 Avenue of the Stars Ste 100
Los Angeles, CA 90067-4705, USA

Whalin, Justin (Actor)
c/o Deborah Miller *Shelter Entertainment*
9255 W Sunset Blvd Ste 300
Los Angeles, CA 90069-3313, USA

Whalley, Joanne (Actor)
1435 Lindacrest Dr
Beverly Hills, CA 90210-2519, USA

Whalum, Kirk (Musician)
Cole Classic Mgmt
PO Box 231
Canoga Park, CA 91305-0231, USA

Whang, Suzanne (Actor)
c/o Staff Member *Kragen & Company*
2103 Ridge Dr
Los Angeles, CA 90049-1153, USA

Whannell, Leigh (Actor, Writer)
c/o Stacey Testro *Stacey Testro International*
8265 W Sunset Blvd Ste 102
West Hollywood, CA 90046-2433, USA

W. Hanorable, Colleen (Congressman, Politician)
238 Cannon Hob
Washington, DC 20515-3502, USA

Whatley, Ennis (Athlete, Basketball Player)
PO Box 43
Highland, MD 20777-0043, USA

Wheatley, Terrence (Athlete, Football Player)
c/o Staff Member *New England Patriots*
1 Patriot Pl
Foxboro, MA 02035-1388, USA

Wheatley, Tyrone (Athlete, Football Player)
20730 Westhampton St
Oak Park, MI 48237-2710, USA

Wheaton, David (Tennis Player)
20045 Cottagewood Ave
Excelsior, MN 55331-9239, USA

Wheaton, Kenny (Athlete, Football Player)
6427 S 21st Pl
Phoenix, AZ 85042-4652, USA

Wheaton, Markus (Athlete, Football Player)
c/o Jamie Fritz *Fritz Martin Management*
8550 W Charleston Blvd Ste 102 PMB 335
Las Vegas, NV 89117-9086, USA

Wheaton, Wil (Actor)
c/o Christopher Black *Opus Entertainment*
5225 Wilshire Blvd Ste 905
Los Angeles, CA 90036-4353, USA

Wheatus (Music Group)
c/o Robert Hollingsworth *So Called Management*
1006-1055 Homer St
Vancouver, BC V6B 1G3, CANADA

Whedon, Joss (Director, Producer, Writer)
c/o Chris Harbert *Creative Artists Agency (CAA)*
2000 Avenue of the Stars Ste 100
Los Angeles, CA 90067-4705, USA

Wheeler, Blake (Athlete, Hockey Player)
c/o Staff Member *Boston Bruins*
100 Legends Way Ste 250
Td Banknorth Garden
Boston, MA 02114-1389, USA

Wheeler, Cheryl (Musician, Songwriter, Writer)
Morningstar Mgmt
PO Box 1770
Hendersonville, TN 37077-1770, USA

Wheeler, Chris (Sportscaster)
302 Saint Andrews Pl
Blue Bell, PA 19422-1290, USA

Wheeler, Clinton (Athlete, Basketball Player)
199 Scenic View Ln
Stone Mountain, GA 30087-6222, USA

Wheeler, Daniel (Dan) (Athlete, Baseball Player)
215 Harrison Ave
Belleair Beach, FL 33786-3619, USA

Wheeler, Dwight (Athlete, Football Player)
2124 Blair Blvd
Nashville, TN 37212-4902, USA

Wheeler, Ellen (Actor)
13576 Cheltenham Dr
Sherman Oaks, CA 91423-4818, USA

Wheeler, John (Actor)
Levin Agency
8484 Wilshire Blvd Ste 745
Beverly Hills, CA 90211-3235, USA

Wheeler, Maggie (Actor)
c/o Kesha Williams *KW Entertainment*
3727 W Magnolia Blvd Ste 430
Burbank, CA 91505-2818, USA

Wheeler, Mark (Athlete, Football Player)
101 Meadowridge Cv
San Marcos, TX 78666-2251, USA

Wheelock, Douglas H Lt Colonel (Astronaut)
PO Box 580408
Houston, TX 77258-0408, USA

Wheelock, Gary (Athlete, Baseball Player)
3724 N Springfield St
Buckeye, AZ 85396-3537, USA

Whelan, Bill (Composer)
Sony Records
2100 Colorado Ave
Santa Monica, CA 90404-3504, USA

Whelan, Jill (Actor)
c/o Staff Member *Scott Stander & Associates*
4533 Van Nuys Blvd Ste 401
Sherman Oaks, CA 91403-2950, USA

Whelan, Julia (Actor)

Whelan, Nicky (Actor)
c/o Lena Roklin *Luber Roklin Management*
5815 W Sunset Blvd Ste 208
Los Angeles, CA 90028-6481, USA

Whelchel, Lisa (Actor)
Mom Time Ministries
PO Box 271739
Flower Mound, TX 75027-1739, USA

Whelpley, John (Actor)
c/o Staff Member *Lenhoff & Lenhoff*
324 S Beverly Dr
Beverly Hills, CA 90212-4801

Whibley, Deryck (Musician)
16000 Ventura Blvd Ste 600
Encino, CA 91436-2753, USA

Whicker, Alan D (Correspondent)
Le Gallais Chambers
Saint Helier
Jersey, UNITED KINGDOM (UK)

Whigham, Larry (Athlete, Football Player)
6110 Midway Rd
Raymond, MS 39154-8357, USA

Whigham, Shea (Actor)
c/o Larry Taube *Principal Entertainment*
9255 W Sunset Blvd Ste 500
Los Angeles, CA 90069-3301, USA

Whillock, Jack (Athlete, Baseball Player)
2118 River Ridge Rd
Arlington, TX 76017-2758, USA

Whinnery, Barbara (Actor)
Baier/Kleinman
3575 Cahuenga Blvd W Ste 500
Los Angeles, CA 90068-1344, USA

Whipple Jr, Allen (Race Car Driver)
GAS Motorsports
Route 11 & 103 Newport Rd.
Claremont, NH 03743, USA

Whirry, Shannon (Actor)
Shapiro-Lichtman
8827 Beverly Blvd
Los Angeles, CA 90048-2405, USA

Whisenant, Matt (Athlete, Baseball Player)
4670 Galendo St
Woodland Hills, CA 91364-5312, USA

Whisenhunt, Ken (Athlete, Football Player)
1511 W Grand Canyon Dr
Chandler, AZ 85248-4816, USA

Whisenton, Larry (Athlete, Baseball Player)
524 Main St
Canton, MS 39046-3208, USA

Whishaw, Anthony (Artist)
7A Albert Place
Victoria Road
London W8 5PD, UNITED KINGDOM (UK)

Whishaw, Ben (Actor)
c/o Clair Dobbs *CLD Communications*
4 Broadway Ct
The Broadway
London SW191RG, UNITED KINGDOM

Whiskey Myers (Music Group)
c/o Staff Member *AristoPR*
PO Box 22765
Nashville, TN 37202-2765, USA

Whisler, J Steven (Business Person)
Phelps Dodge Corp
1 N Central Ave
Phoenix, AZ 85004-4414, USA

Whisler, Randy (Athlete, Baseball Player)
6920 Hilyard Ct
Klamath Falls, OR 97603-9620, USA

Whisler, Wes (Athlete, Baseball Player)
15029 Midland Ln
Noblesville, IN 46062-4637, USA

Whisman, Greg (Athlete, Golfer)
1908 129th Pl SE
Everett, WA 98208-7121, USA

Whistle, Rob (Athlete, Hockey Player)
154 King Lane
Hampton, ON L0B 1J0, Canada

Whiston, Don (Athlete, Hockey Player, Olympic Athlete)
2 Jeffreys Neck Rd
Ipswich, MA 01938-1328, USA

Whitacre, Edward E Jr (Business Person)
SBC Communications
175 E Houston St
San Antonio, TX 78205-2255, USA

Whitaker, Alaina (Musician)
PO Box 703165
Tulsa, OK 74170-3165, USA

Whitaker, Denzel (Actor)
c/o Brad Slater *WME/IMG*
9601 Wilshire Blvd
Beverly Hills, CA 90210-5213, USA

Whitaker, Ed (Race Car Driver)
923 Wagner Rd
Bristol, VA 24201-2436, USA

Whitaker, Forest (Actor, Director, Producer)
c/o Staff Member *Spirit Dance Entertainment*
1023 N Orange Dr
Los Angeles, CA 90038-2317, USA

Whitaker, Jack (Sportscaster)
225 Broadway Fl 20
New York, NY 10007-3001, USA

Whitaker, Johnny (Actor)
PO Box 93162
Los Angeles, CA 90093-0162, USA

Whitaker, Louis R (Lou) Jr (Athlete, Baseball Player)
17 Brownstone Ln
Greensboro, NC 27410-5145, USA

Whitaker, Pernell (Athlete, Boxer, Olympic Athlete)
3808 Cranberry Ct
Virginia Beach, VA 23456-8109, USA

Whitaker, Steve (Athlete, Baseball Player)
900 SE 6th Ct
Fort Lauderdale, FL 33301-3018, USA

Whitaker, William (Athlete, Football Player)
Lake Road 135
Gravois Mills, MO 65037, USA

Whitbank, Ben (Baseball Player)
203 E Apollo Ln
Milton, DE 19968-9781, USA

Whitbread, Fatima (Athlete, Track Athlete)
Chafford Information Ctr
Elozabeth Road
Grays
Essex RM16 6QZ, UNITED KINGDOM (UK)

Whitby, Bill (Athlete, Baseball Player)
13926 Huntersville Concord Rd
Huntersville, NC 28078-6262, USA

Whitcomb, Bob (Race Car Driver)
Whitcomb Racing
9201 Garrison Road
Charlotte, NC 28278, USA

Whitcomb, Ian (Musician, Songwriter, Writer)
PO Box 451
Altadena, CA 91003-0451, USA

White, Adrian (Athlete, Football Player)
686 Allen Ln
Orange Park, FL 32073-3986, USA

White, Alan (Musician)
Ignition Mgmt
54 Linhope St
London NW1 6HL, UNITED KINGDOM (UK)

White, Albert (Baseball Player)
St Louis Browns
32 Jessana Hts
Colorado Springs, CO 80906-7902, USA

White, Andre (Athlete, Football Player)
225 S Poplar St APT 2714
Charlotte, NC 28202-0120, USA

White, Ben (Horse Racer)
452 Oak Haven Dr
Altamonte Springs, FL 32701-6318, USA

White, Betty (Actor, Comedian)
PO Box 491965
Los Angeles, CA 90049-8965, USA

White, Bob W (Athlete, Football Player)
763D Espada Dr
El Paso, TX 79912-1913, USA

White, Brain (Athlete, Hockey Player)
3 Godlclc Rd
Burltnaton, MA 01803-1007, USA

White, Brian (Actor)
c/o Shannon Barr *Rogers & Cowan*
1840 Century Park E Fl 18
Los Angeles, CA 90067-2101, USA

White, Brooke (Musician)
c/o Rick Canny *Favor the Artist Management*
8750 Wilshire Blvd Ste 200
Beverly Hills, CA 90211-2707, USA

White, Bryan (Musician, Songwriter)
Loudmouth Public Relations
PO Box 128192
Nashville, TN 37212-8192, USA

White, Charles (Athlete, Football Player, Heisman Trophy Winner)
31841 Via Faisan
Trabuco Canyon, CA 92679-4182, USA

White, Charlie (Figure Skater, Olympic Athlete)
US Figure Skating
20 1st St
Colorado Springs, CO 80906-3697, USA

White, Cheryl (Musician)
Hallmark Direction
713 18th Ave S
Nashville, TN 37203-3214, USA

White, Chris (Athlete, Football Player)
c/o Bus Cook *Bus Cook Sports, Inc*
1 Willow Bend Dr
Hattiesburg, MS 39402-8552, USA

White, Chris (Musician)
Lustig Talent
PO Box 770850
Orlando, FL 32877-0850, USA

White, Cody (Athlete, Football Player)
c/o David Dunn *Athletes First*
23091 Mill Creek Dr
Laguna Hills, CA 92653-1258, USA

White, Colin (Athlete, Hockey Player)
1221 Crosstns Way
Wayne, NJ 07470-4738, USA

White, Corey (Athlete, Football Player)
c/o Dave Butz *Sportstars Inc*
1370 Avenue of the Americas Fl 19
New York, NY 10019-4602, USA

White, Dana (Business Person)
Zuffa LLC
2960 W Sahara Ave Ste 200
Las Vegas, NV 89102-1709, USA

White, Danny (Athlete, Coach, Football Player)
111 Saint Joseph St S
South Bend, IN 46601-1939, USA

White, David AR (Producer)
c/o Ben Laurro *Pure Publicity*
188 Front St Ste 116 PMB 6
Franklin, TN 37064-5089, USA

White, Dean (Producer)
c/o Sean Freidin *ICM Partners*
10250 Constellation Blvd Fl 7
Los Angeles, CA 90067-6207, USA

White, Derrick (Athlete, Baseball Player)
3524 Derby Shire Cir
Windsor Mill, MD 21244-3624, USA

White, Devon M (Athlete, Baseball Player)
6440 E Sierra Vista Dr
Paradise Valley, AZ 85253-4351, USA

White, Diamond (Musician)
c/o Mitchell Gossett *Industry Entertainment Partners*
955 Carrillo Dr Ste 300
Los Angeles, CA 90048-5400, USA

White, Diz (Actor)
203 N Plymouth Blvd
Los Angeles, CA 90004-3833, USA

White, Donna (Athlete, Golfer)
200 Caribe Ct
Greenacres, FL 33413-2150, USA

White, Dwayne (Athlete, Football Player)
1916 Dickinson St
Philadelphia, PA 19146-4662, USA

White, Ed (Athlete, Football Player)
PO Box 1437
Julian, CA 92036-1437, USA

White, Edmund (Writer)
185 Nassau St Rm 224
Princeton, NJ 08544-2003, USA

White, Edward A (Ed) (Athlete, Football Player)
PO Box 1437
Julian, CA 92036-1437, USA

White, Eric (Athlete, Basketball Player)
1945 Bush St Apt K
San Francisco, CA 94115-3226, USA

White, Eugene (Baseball Player)
Chicago American Giants
4166 Lockhart Dr N
Jacksonville, FL 32209-1928, USA

White, Frank (Athlete, Baseball Player)
PO Box 573
Blue Springs, MO 64013-0573, USA

White, Gabe (Athlete, Baseball Player)
708 Rustin Lake Rd
Butler, GA 31006-5922, USA

White, Gerald (Athlete, Football Player)
Halo Creative Concepts
1501 Halo Dr
Troy, MI 48084, USA

White, Gilbert F (Misc)
624 Pearl St Apt 302
Boulder, CO 80302-5072, USA

White, Glodean (Musician)
8000 Oceanus Dr
Los Angeles, CA 90046-2047, USA

White, Hubie (Athlete, Basketball Player)
101 E Gowen Ave
Philadelphia, PA 19119-1613, USA

White, Jack (Musician)
c/o Ken Weinstein *Big Hassle Media*
40 Exchange Pl Ste 1900
New York, NY 10005-2714, USA

White, Jahidi (Athlete, Basketball Player)
c/o Staff Member *Washington Wizards*
601 F St NW
Washington, DC 20004-1605, USA

White, Jaleel (Actor)
1440 Via Anita
Pacific Palisades, CA 90272-2357, USA

White, James C (Athlete, Football Player)
14430 Andrea Way Ln
Houston, TX 77083-7712, USA

White, James (Whirlwind) (Misc)
c/o Staff Member *Peller Artistes Limited*
39 Princes Ave
London N3 2DA, UK

White, Jamie (Radio Personality)
c/o Staff Member *Star 98.7 FM*
3400 W Olive Ave Ste 550
Burbank, CA 91505-5544, USA

White, Jan (Athlete, Football Player)
6507 Burkwood Dr
Clayton, OH 45315-9602, USA

White, Jason (Musician)
c/o Brian Bumbery *BB Gun Press*
9229 W Sunset Blvd Ste 305
Los Angeles, CA 90069-3403, USA

White, Jason (Athlete, Football Player, Heisman Trophy Winner)
3203 Stone Dr
Tuttle, OK 73089-7972, USA

White, Jeremy Allen (Actor)
c/o Jillian Roscoe *ID Public Relations*
7060 Hollywood Blvd Fl 8th
Los Angeles, CA 90028-6021, USA

White, Jeris (Athlete, Football Player)
PO Box 3031
Frederick, MD 21705-3031, USA

White, Jerry (Athlete, Baseball Player)
581 Glen Dr
San Leandro, CA 94577-2900, USA

White, Jessica (Model)
c/o Staff Member *IMG*
304 Park Ave S Fl 12
New York, NY 10010-4314, USA

White, Jonah (Business Person)
Billy Bob Teeth, Inc.
PO Box 389
Hardin, IL 62047-0389, USA

White, Joy Lynn (Musician)
Buddy Lee
665 Whyte Ave
Roseville, CA 95661-5240, USA

White, Julie (Actor)
c/o Alex Spieller *Baker Winokur Ryder Public Relations*
200 5th Ave Fl 5
New York, NY 10010-3307, USA

White, Karyn (Musician)
1556 Hascall Dr SW
Marietta, GA 30064-4820, USA

White, Kevin (Athlete, Football Player)
c/o Tory Dandy *Independent Sports & Entertainment (ISE-IN)*
6435 W Jefferson Blvd # 197
Fort Wayne, IN 46804-6203, USA

White, Lan (Athlete, Hockey Player)
310 Cedar Cres
Steinbach, MB R5G 0K5, Canada

White, Larri (Musician, Songwriter, Writer)
Carter Career Mgmt
1028 18th Ave S # B
Nashville, TN 37212-2105, USA

White, Larry (Athlete, Baseball Player)
PO Box 54455
Phoenix, AZ 85078, USA

White, Lee (Athlete, Football Player)
600 Langtry Dr
Las Vegas, NV 89107-2019, USA

White, Leon (Athlete, Football Player)
11033 Paseo Castanada
La Mesa, CA 91941-7330, USA

White, Lorenzo (Athlete, Football Player)
3450 NW 7th St
Lauderhill, FL 33311-6505, USA

White, Marco P (Chef)
The Restaurant
66 Knightsbridge
London SW1X 7LA, UNITED KINGDOM (UK)

White, Marilyn (Athlete, Track Athlete)
9605 S 6th Ave
Inglewood, CA 90305-3207, USA

White, Mark (Musician)
DAS Communications
84 Riverside Dr
New York, NY 10024-5723, USA

White, Marsh (Athlete, Football Player)
104 S Wood Ave
Denison, TX 75020-3555, USA

White, Matt (Athlete, Baseball Player)
1853 Old Route 9
Windsor, MA 01270-9397, USA

White, Meg (Music Group, Musician)
Jack White Productions
Muenchner Str 45
Unterfoehring 85774, GERMANY

White, Melvin (Athlete, Football Player)

White, Michael Jai (Actor)
c/o Staff Member *Goliath Entertainment*
28203 Infinity Cir
Santa Clarita, CA 91390-5230, USA

White, Mike (Actor)
c/o Staff Member *Black and White Productions*
100 Universal City Plz Bldg 4113
Universal City, CA 91608-1002, USA

White, Mike (Athlete, Baseball Player)
26438 S Jardin Dr
Sun Lakes, AZ 85248-7114, USA

White, Mike (Athlete, Coach, Football Coach, Football Player)
115 Grand Canal
Newport Beach, CA 92662-1329, USA

White, Miles D (Business Person)
Abbott Laboratories
100 Abbott Park Rd
Abbott Park, IL 60064-3500, USA

White, Myron (Athlete, Baseball Player)
3201 S Deegan Dr
Santa Ana, CA 92704-6614, USA

White, Paula (Religious Leader, Television Host, Writer)
Paula White Ministries
PO Box 25151
Tampa, FL 33622-5151, USA

White, Persia (Actor)
c/o Gwenn Pepper *Defining Artists Agency*
8721 W Sunset Blvd Ste 209
W Hollywood, CA 90069-2272, USA

White, Persia (Actor)
c/o Dede Binder-Goldsmith *Defining Artists Agency*
8721 W Sunset Blvd Ste 209
W Hollywood, CA 90069-2272, USA

White, Peter (Actor)
S M S Talant
8730 W Sunset Blvd Ste 440
Los Angeles, CA 90069-2277, USA

White, Randy L (Athlete, Football Player)
Randy White's HOF BBQ
9225 Preston Rd
Frisco, TX 75033-3916, USA

White, Reggie (Athlete, Football Player)
3631 Washington Ave
Baltimore, MD 21244-3776, USA

White, Rex (Race Car Driver)
187 Rivers Rd Lot 222
Fayetteville, GA 30214-3250, USA

White, Richard (Actor)
c/o Staff Member *Professional Artists Agency*
630 9th Ave Ste 207
New York, NY 10036-4752, USA

White, Rick (Athlete, Baseball Player)
2860 Windy Ridge Dr
Springfield, OH 45502-7230, USA

White, Roddy (Athlete, Football Player)
c/o Neil Schwartz *Schwartz & Feinsod*
4 Hillandale Rd
Rye Brook, NY 10573-1705, USA

White, Rodney (Basketball Player)
Denver Nuggets
1000 Chopper Cir
Pepsi Center
Denver, CO 80204-5805, USA

White, Ron (Actor, Comedian)
c/o Matthew Blake *Creative Artists Agency (CAA)*
2000 Avenue of the Stars Ste 100
Los Angeles, CA 90067-4705, USA

White, Rondell (Athlete, Baseball Player)
11111 Pine Lodge Trl
Davie, FL 33328-7317, USA

White, Rory (Athlete, Basketball Player)
S303 32nd St S
Fargo, NO S8104-6743, USA

White, Roy (Athlete, Baseball Player)
M D M Sports Marketing
218 Washington Ave Apt C14
Attn:David Ratner
Cedarhurst, NY 11516-1510, USA

White, Roy H (Baseball Player)
1001 2nd St
Sacramento, CA 95814-3201, USA

White, Russell (Athlete, Football Player)
17450 Vanowen St Unit 4
Van Nuys, CA 91406-4312, USA

White, Sammy (Athlete, Football Player)
102 Margaret Dr
Monroe, LA 71203-9588, USA

White, Santi (Santigold) (Musician)
c/o Larry Webman *Paradigm*
140 Broadway Ste 2600
New York, NY 10005-1011, USA

White, Shaun (Athlete, Snowboarder)
c/o Christopher Hart *United Talent Agency (UTA)*
9336 Civic Center Dr
Beverly Hills, CA 90210-3604, USA

White, Sheldon (Athlete, Football Player)
PO Box 622
Novi, MI 48376-0622, USA

White, Sherman (Athlete, Football Player)
2710 Summerland Rd
Aromas, CA 95004-9117, USA

White, Shernan E (Sherm) (Athlete, Football Player)
PO Box 1856
Pebble Beach, CA 93953-1856, USA

White, Stan (Athlete, Football Player)
10716 Pot Spring Rd
Cockeysville, MD 21030-3021, USA

White, Stephen (Writer)
Penguin Books
375 Hudson St Bsmt 3
New York, NY 10014-3672, USA

White, Steve (Athlete, Football Player)
11928 Middlebury Dr
Tampa, FL 33626-2520, USA

White, Timothy D (Misc)
University of California
Hiuman Evolutionary Studies Lab # 26
Berkeley, CA 94720-0001, USA

White, Todd (Athlete, Hockey Player)
16 Charlesworth Crt
Kanata, ON K2K 3L5, CANADA

White, Tony (Athlete, Basketball Player)
3006 Brooksview Rd
Lenoir City, TN 37772-4523, USA

White, Tony L (Business Person)
PE Corp
710 Bridgeport Ave
Shelton, CT 06484-4750, USA

White, Vanna (Model, Television Host)
c/o Staff Member *PAT Productions*
10202 Washington Blvd
Robert Young Bldg, Suite 2000
Culver City, CA 90232-3119, USA

White, Verdine (Musician)
c/o Staff Member *Atlas/Third Rail Entertainment*
9200 W Sunset Blvd Ste 10
Los Angeles, CA 90069-3608, USA

White, Walter (Athlete, Football Player)
504 NW 44th Ter
Kansas City, MO 64116-1580, USA

White, Wilford (Athlete, Football Player)
30A S Macdonald
Mesa, AZ 85210, USA

White, William (Athlete, Football Player)
4619 Sandwich Ct
Dublin, OH 43016-8292, USA

White, William B (Bill) (Athlete, Baseball Player)
PO Box 199
Upper Black Eddy, PA 18972-0199, USA

Whited, Ed (Athlete, Baseball Player)
1482 Esprit Dr
Carmel, IN 46074-8946, USA

Whitefield, A D (Athlete, Football Player)
807 Tangle Way Ct
Cedar Hill, TX 75104-7817, USA

Whitehead, Barb (Athlete, Golfer)
18539 N 97th Way
Scottsdale, AZ 85255-9238, USA

Whitehead, Bud (Athlete, Football Player)
5438 N Brooks Ave
Fresno, CA 93711-2913, USA

Whitehead, Fionn (Actor)
c/o Sophie Holden *Curtis Brown Ltd*
28-29 Hay Market
Hay Market House
London SW1Y 4SP, UNITED KINGDOM

Whitehead, Jerome (Athlete, Basketball Player)
1543 Merritt Dr
El Cajon, CA 92020-7847, USA

Whitehead, Kimberly (Race Car Driver)
Miss Dirt Motorsports
PO Box 206
Sussex, NJ 07461-0206, USA

Whitehead, Paxton (Actor)
c/o Robert Attermann *Abrams Artists Agency*
275 7th Ave Fl 26
New York, NY 10001-6708, USA

Whitehead, Tahir (Athlete, Football Player)
c/o Chad Wiestling *Integrated Sports Management*
2120 Texas St Apt 2204
Houston, TX 77003-3054, USA

Whitehouse, Josh (Actor)
c/o Daniela Agnello *Premier PR*
2-4 Bucknall St
London WC2H 8LA, UNITED KINGDOM

Whitehouse, Len (Athlete, Baseball Player)
300 Shore Rd
Burlington, VT 05408-2632, USA

Whitehurst, C David (Athlete, Football Player)
11010 Linbrook Ln
Duluth, GA 30097-1772, USA

Whitehurst, Charlie (Athlete, Football Player)
c/o Pat Dye Jr *SportsTrust Advisors*
3340 Peachtree Rd NE Fl 16
Atlanta, GA 30326-1000, USA

White Jr, Josh (Musician)
30759 Crest Frst
Farmington Hills, MI 48331-1072, USA

Whitemore, Hugh (Writer)
c/o Staff Member *Creative Artists Agency (CAA)*
2000 Avenue of the Stars Ste 100
Los Angeles, CA 90067-4705, USA

Whiten, Mark (Athlete, Baseball Player)
5810 Jefferson Park Dr
Tampa, FL 33625-3313, USA

Whiten, Richard (Actor)
247 S Beverly Dr # 102
Beverly Hills, CA 90212-3830, USA

Whiteread, Rachel (Artist)
Anthony d'Offay
22 Dering St
London W1R 9AA, UNITED KINGDOM (UK)

Whitesell, Emily (Producer, Writer)
c/o Staff Member *WME|IMG*
9601 Wilshire Blvd
Beverly Hills, CA 90210-5213, USA

Whitesell, Josh (Athlete, Baseball Player)
1719 Deanna Way
Redlands, CA 92374-4716, USA

Whiteside, Eli (Athlete, Baseball Player)
414 S Central Ave
New Albany, MS 38652-3701, USA

Whiteside, Matt (Athlete, Baseball Player)
255 Palisades Ridge Ct
Eureka, MO 63025-3706, USA

Whiteside, Sean (Athlete, Baseball Player)
3506 N Hills Dr
Haleyville, AL 35565-6746, USA

Whiteside, Sean (Athlete, Baseball Player)
654 W Olymoic Pl APt 501
Seattle, WA 98119-3698, USA

Whitesides, George M (Misc)
124 Grasmere St
Newton, MA 02458-2235, USA

Whitesnake (Music Group)
c/o Rod MacSween *International Talent Booking*
9 Kingsway
Fl 6
London WC2B 6XF, UNITED KINGDOM

White Stripes, The (Music Group)
c/o Ian Montone *Monotone Inc.*
820 Seward St
Los Angeles, CA 90038-3602, USA

Whitfield, Annelie (Actor)
c/o Catriona Ribon *The Rights House (UK)*
Drury House
34-43 Russell St
London WC2B 5HA, UNITED KINGDOM

Whitfield, Dondre T (Actor)
c/o Jonathan Baruch *Rain Management Group*
11162 La Grange Ave
Los Angeles, CA 90025-5632, USA

Whitfield, Ed (Congressman, Politician)
2368 Rayburn Hob
Washington, DC 20515-0105, USA

Whitfield, Fred (Athlete, Baseball Player)
2532 Fairview Rd
Gadsden, AL 35904-3102, USA

Whitfield, Fredricka (Correspondent)
c/o Staff Member *CNN (Atlanta)*
1 Cnn Ctr NW
PO Box 105366
Atlanta, GA 30303-2762, USA

Whitfield, Lynn (Actor)
c/o Peter Larsen *Sharp & Associates*
1516 N Fairfax Ave
Los Angeles, CA 90046-2608, USA

Whitfield, Sheree (Designer, Reality Star)
c/o Staff Member *People Store*
645 Lambert Dr NE
Atlanta, GA 30324-4125, USA

Whitfield, Terry (Athlete, Baseball Player)
849 Clearfield Dr
Millbrae, CA 94030-2148, USA

Whitfield, Trent (Athlete, Hockey Player)
5 Bryant Ln
Kennebunkport, ME 04046-7242, USA

Whitford, Brad (Musician)
12811 Ninebark Trl
Charlotte, NC 28278-6837, USA

Whitford, Bradley (Actor)
c/o Melissa Kates *Viewpoint Inc*
8820 Wilshire Blvd Ste 220
Beverly Hills, CA 90211-2622, USA

Whiting, Leonard (Actor)
7 Leicester Pl.
London, England WC2H 7BP, UNITED KINGDOM

Whitley, Kim E (Actor, Producer)
c/o Judy Apperson *Morra Brezner Steinberg & Tenenbaum (MBST) Entertainment*
345 N Maple Dr Ste 200
Beverly Hills, CA 90210-5174, USA

Whitley, Kym (Actor, Producer)
19320 Hatteras St
Tarzana, CA 91356-1118, USA

Whitlock, Bod (Athlete, Hockey Player)
Whitlock Insurance Services
1403 Bay Ave
Trail, BC V1R 4A9, Canada

Whitlow, Bob (Athlete, Football Player)
315 W Gordon Pike
Bloomington, IN 47403-4570, USA

Whitman, Kari (Actor, Model)
1155 N La Cienega Blvd Apt 104
West Hollywood, CA 90069-2430, USA

Whitman, Mae (Actor)
c/o Meredith Wechter *WME/IMG*
9601 Wilshire Blvd
Beverly Hills, CA 90210-5213, USA

Whitman, Meg (Business Person)
HP
1140 Enterprise Way
Sunnyvale, CA 94089-1412, USA

Whitman, Stuart (Actor)
749 San Ysidro Rd
Santa Barbara, CA 93108-1328, USA

Whitmer, Dan (Athlete, Baseball Player)
232 Priscilla Way
Redlands, CA 92373-6176, USA

Whitmire, Steve (Actor)

Whitmore, Darrell (Athlete, Baseball Player)
301 E 15th St
Front Royal, VA 22630-4112, USA

Whitmore, Kay (Athlete, Hockey Player)
National Hockey League
50 Bay St 11th Fl
Attn: Director of Goaltender Eauioment
Toronto, ON M5J 3A5, Canada

Whitmyer, Nat (Athlete, Football Player)
5305 W Goldenwood Dr
Inglewood, CA 90302-1037, USA

Whitney, Ashley (Athlete, Olympic Athlete, Swimmer)
124 Hearthstone Manor Cir
Brentwood, TN 37027-4344, USA

Whitney, CeCe (Actor)
1145 E Barham Dr Spc 217
San Marcos, CA 92078-4547, USA

Whitney, David (Athlete, Baseball Player)
Kansas City Monarchs
2178 Popps Ferry Rd
Biloxi, MS 39532-4233, USA

Whitney, Ray (Athlete, Hockey Player)
2908 Spaldwick Ct
Raleigh, NC 27613-5471, USA

Whitney, Russ (Business Person, Misc)
Whitney Education Group Inc
1612 Cape Coral Pkwy E
Cape Coral, FL 33904-9618, USA

Whitney, Ryan (Athlete, Hockey Player)
179 Edward Foster Rd
Scituate, MA 02066-4342, USA

Whitney-Dearfield, Norma (Athlete, Baseball Player)
1803 Delaware Ave
White Oak, PA 15131-1660, USA

Whitsett, Vivicca (Actor)
c/o Karin Olsen *Amazon PR*
269 S Beverly Dr # 750
Beverly Hills, CA 90212-3851, USA

Whitson, Ed (Athlete, Baseball Player)
10473 MacKenzie Way
Dublin, OH 43017-8775, USA

Whitson, Peggy (Astronaut)
207 Quail Run Ct
Spicewood, TX 78669-3171, USA

Whitt, Ernie (Athlete, Baseball Player)
37370 Moravian Dr
Clinton Township, MI 48036-3604, USA

Whittaker, Roger (Musician, Songwriter, Writer)
BML Mgmt
426 Marsh Point Cir
Saint Augustine, FL 32080-5863, USA

Whitted, Alvis (Athlete, Football Player)
6107 Bent Oak Dr
Durham, NC 27705-9115, USA

Whittington, Art (Athlete, Football Player)
6709 La Tijera Blvd Apt 190
Los Angeles, CA 90045-2017, USA

Whittington, Bill (Race Car Driver)
1881 W State Road 84
Ft Lauderdale, FL 33315-2208, USA

Whittington, C L (Athlete, Football Player)
2332 Galilee Rd Apt 121
Hallsville, TX 75650-6189, USA

Whittington, Dale (Race Car Driver)
1881 W State Road 84
Ft Lauderdale, FL 33315-2208, USA

Whittington, Don (Race Car Driver)
1881 W State Road 84
Ft Lauderdale, FL 33315-2208, USA

Whittington, Michael S (Athlete, Football Player)
4246 Turtle Mound Rd
Melbourne, FL 32934-8505, USA

Whittle, Ricky (Athlete, Football Player)
c/o Naisha Arnold *Untitled Entertainment*
350 S Beverly Dr Ste 200
Beverly Hills, CA 90212-4819, USA

Whitwam, David R (Business Person)
Whirlpool Corp
2000 N State St
RR 63
Benton Harbor, MI 49022, USA

Whitwell, Mike (Athlete, Football Player)
PO Box 6
Cotulla, TX 78014-0006, USA

Whitworth, Andrew (Athlete, Football Player)
c/o Pat Dye Jr *SportsTrust Advisors*
3340 Peachtree Rd NE Fl 16
Atlanta, GA 30326-1000, USA

Whitworth, Johnny (Actor)
c/o Lena Roklin *Luber Roklin Management*
5815 W Sunset Blvd Ste 208
Los Angeles, CA 90028-6481, USA

Whitworth, Kathy (Athlete, Golfer)
1735 Mistletoe Dr
Flower Mound, TX 75022-5316, USA

Wholey, Dennis (Television Host)
Dennis Wholey Enterprises
1333 H St NW
Washington, DC 20005-4707, USA

Who (Newham), Betty (Jessica Ann) (Musician)

Whoppers, Wendy (Actor)
c/o Staff Member *Wow Entertainment Inc*
8362 Pines Blvd # 296
Pembroke Pines, FL 33024-6600, USA

Who, The (Music Group)
c/o Lydia Kirschstein *Trinifold Management*
12 Oval Rd
Camden
London NW1 7DH, UNITED KINGDOM

Whyte, Sandra (Athlete, Hockey Player, Olympic Athlete)
81 Golden Hills Rd
Saugus, MA 01906-4010, USA

Whyte, Sean (Athlete, Hockey Player)
600 W Grove Pkwy #1026
Mesa, AZ 85283, USA

WI, Charlie (Athlete, Golfer)
9400 Burnet Ave Unit 109
North Hills, CA 91343-7907, USA

Wiberg, Kenneth B (Misc)
160 Carmalt Rd
Hamden, CT 06517-1904, USA

Wiberg, Pernilla (Skier)
Katterunsvagen 32
Norrkopping 60 210, SWEDEN

Wick, Douglas (Producer)
c/o David O'Connor *Creative Artists Agency (CAA)*
2000 Avenue of the Stars Ste 100
Los Angeles, CA 90067-4705, USA

Wickander, Kevin (Athlete, Baseball Player)
4319 W Banff Ln
Glendale, AZ 85306-3601, USA

Wicker, Floyd (Athlete, Baseball Player)
1758 W Greensboro Chapel Hill Rd
Snow Camp, NC 27349-9544, USA

Wicker, tom (Writer)
PO Box 361
Rochester, VT 05767-0361

Wickersham, Dave (Athlete, Baseball Player)
25340 Quivira Rd
Louisburg, KS 66053-5204, USA

Wickert, Tom (Athlete, Football Player)
3717 Beach Dr SW Apt 306
Seattle, WA 98116-3055, USA

Wickham, Daniel (Athlete, Baseball Player)
3221 E Mountain Vista Dr
Phoenix, AZ 85048-5802, USA

Wickman, Robert J (Bob) (Athlete, Baseball Player)
6568 Cheyenne Dr
Abrams, WI 54101-9434, USA

Wicks, Chuck (Musician)

Wicks, Sidney (Athlete, Basketball Player)
112 Great Oak Dr
Hampstead, NC 28443-2142, USA

Wicks, Sue (Basketball Player)
New York Liberty
2 Penn Plz Fl 15
Madison Square Garden
New York, NY 10121-1700, USA

Wicoff, Erika (Athlete, Golfer)
4094 Basswood Dr
Danville, IN 46122-5523, USA

Widby, G Ronald (Ron) (Athlete, Basketball Player, Football Player)
542 Mahler Rd
Wichita Falls, TX 76310-0326, USA

Widdoes, Kathleen (Actor)
24 E 11th St
New York, NY 10003-4402, USA

Widdrington, Peter N T (Business Person)
Laidlaw Inc
3221 N Service Road
Burlington, ON L7R 3Y8, CANADA

Widell, Dave (Athlete, Football Player)
111 Rimini Ct
Jacksonville, FL 32225-8001, USA

Widell, Doug (Athlete, Football Player)
870 21st St
Vero Beach, FL 32960-5314, USA

Wideman, Dennis (Athlete, Hockey Player)
26 Stillman St Apt 5-2
Boston, MA 02113-1695, USA

Wideman, John Edgar (Writer)
University of Massachusetts
Englesh Dept
Amherst, MA 01003, USA

Widenhouse, Bill (Race Car Driver)
PO Box 34
Highway 601
Midland, NC 28107-0034, USA

Widenhouse, Dink (Race Car Driver)
693 Warren St NE
Concord, NC 28025-3120, USA

Widestrom, Jennifer (Fitness Expert)
c/o Amy Malin *Trueheart Management*
20732 Wells Dr
Woodland Hills, CA 91364-3437, USA

Widger, Chris (Athlete, Baseball Player)
95 Fort Mott Rd
Pennsville, NJ 08070-2839, USA

Widman, Herbert (Herb) (Athlete, Swimmer)
844 Monarch Cir
San Jose, CA 95138-1343, USA

Widmer, Corey (Athlete, Football Player)
2640 Lake Shore Dr Unit 2508
Riviera Beach, FL 33404-4674, USA

Widmer, Jason (Athlete, Hockey Player)
PO Box 55289
Lexington, KY 40555-5289, USA

Widom, Benjamin (Misc)
1006 Savage Farm Dr
Ithaca, NY 14850-6529, USA

Wie, Michelle (Athlete, Golfer)
189 Bears Club Dr
Jupiter, FL 33477-4201, USA

Wieand, Ted (Athlete, Baseball Player)
216 S Walnut St
Slatington, PA 18080-2026, USA

Wiebe, Mark (Athlete, Golfer)
1856 McDaniel Ave
San Jose, CA 95126-1924, USA

Wiebe, Susanne (Designer, Fashion Designer)
Amalienstr 39
Munich 80799, GERMANY

Wieber, Jordyn (Athlete, Gymnast, Olympic Athlete)
Twistars Gymnastics
9410 Davis Hwy
Dimondale, MI 48821-9439, USA

Wiedenbauer, Tom (Athlete, Baseball Player)
1460 Kilrush Dr
Ormond Beach, FL 32174-2882, USA

Wiedlin, Jane (Musician)
724 Wainaku St APT B
Hilo, HI 96720, USA

Wiegart, Zach (Athlete, Football Player)
3747 Saltmeadow Ct S
Jacksonville, FL 32224-9652, USA

Wiegert, Zach (Athlete, Football Player)
919 N 264th St
Waterloo, NE 68069-6207, USA

Wieghaus, Tom (Athlete, Baseball Player)
9724 E 8000N Rd
Grant Park, IL 60940-5364, USA

Wiegmann, Casey (Athlete, Football Player)
30051 N Waukegan Rd
North Chicago, IL 60064, USA

Wiehl, Christopher (Actor)
c/o Dan Baron *Agency for the Performing Arts (APA)*
405 S Beverly Dr Ste 500
Beverly Hills, CA 90212-4425, USA

Wiemer, Jason (Athlete, Hockey Player)
428-5201 Dalhousie Dr NW
Calgary, AB T3A 5Y7, CANADA

Wier, Murray (Athlete, Basketball Player, Coach)
118 Goodwater St
Georgetown, TX 78633-4505, USA

Wiesen, Bernard (Director)
Weisgerberstr 2
Munich 80805, GERMANY

Wiesenhahn, Robert (Athlete, Basketball Player)
3315 Hickorycreek Dr
Cincinnati, OH 45244-2533, USA

Wiesler, Bob (Athlete, Baseball Player)
3655 Viembra Dr
Florissant, MO 63034-2372, USA

Wiesner, Kenneth (Athlete, Olympic Athlete)
8670 Parkview Rd
Minocqua, WI 54548-9325, USA

Wiest, Dianne (Actor)
670 W End Ave APT 12E
New York, NY 10025-7328, USA

Wieters, Matt (Athlete, Baseball Player)
4703 Hunters Run
Sarasota, FL 34241-9200, USA

Wiggin, Paul (Athlete, Coach, Football Coach, Football Player)
5013 Ridge Rd
Edina, MN 55436-1013, USA

Wiggins, Al (Athlete, Olympic Athlete, Swimmer)
167 Chancery Ln
Ligonier, PA 15658-1286, USA

Wiggins, Andres (Athlete, Basketball Player)
c/o Staff Member *Minnesota Vikings*
2600 Vikings Cir
Saint Paul, MN 55121-1000, USA

Wiggins, Andrew (Athlete, Basketball Player)
c/o Bill Duffy *BDA Sports Management*
700 Ygnacio Valley Rd Ste 330
Walnut Creek, CA 94596-3838, USA

Wiggins, Audrey (Musician)
William Morris Agency
2100 W End Ave Ste 1000
Nashville, TN 37203-5240, USA

Wiggins, Candice (Athlete, Basketball Player)
BDA Sports Management
700 Ygnacio Valley Rd Ste 330
Walnut Creek, CA 94596-3838, USA

Wiggins, Jermaine (Athlete, Football Player)
403 Overlook Dr
Beckley, WV 25801-9255, USA

Wiggins, John (Musician)
William Morris Agency
2100 W End Ave Ste 1000
Nashville, TN 37203-5240, USA

Wiggins, Mitchell (Athlete, Basketball Player)
PO Box 5072
Kinston, NC 28503-5072, USA

Wiggins, Scott (Athlete, Baseball Player)
17 N Crescent Ave
Fort Thomas, KY 41075-2109, USA

Wigginton, Ty (Athlete, Baseball Player)
120 Manitoba Ln
Mooresville, NC 28117-5822, USA

Wigglesworth, Marian McKean (Skier)
General Delivery
Wilson, WY 83014, USA

Wight, Paul (Big Show) (Athlete, Wrestler)
c/o Staff Member *World Wrestling Entertainment (WWE)*
1241 E Main St
Stamford, CT 06902-3520, USA

Wightman, Donald E (Misc)
Utility Workers Union
815 16th St NW
Washington, DC 20006-4101, USA

Wihtol, Sandy (Athlete, Baseball Player)
496 1st St Ste 200
Los Altos, CA 94022-3678, USA

Wiig, Kristen (Actor)
c/o Nicole Caruso *Relevant (NY)*
333 Hudson St Rm 502
New York, NY 10013-1033, USA

Wiik, Sven (Skier)
PO Box 774484
Steamboat Springs, CO 80477-4484, USA

Wijdenbosch, Jules A (President)
Presidential Palace
Onafhankelikheidsplein 1
Paramaribo, SURINAME

Wilander, Mats (Athlete, Tennis Player)
104 Cove Creek Rd
Hailey, ID 83333-5100, USA

Wilber, Doreen V H (Athlete)
1401 W Lincoln Way
Jefferson, IA 50129-1675, USA

Wilber, Kyle (Athlete, Football Player)
c/o Andy Ross *Select Sports Group*
2700 Post Oak Blvd Ste 1450
Houston, TX 77056-5785, USA

Wilborn, Ted (Athlete, Baseball Player)
6671 Pocket Rd
Sacramento, CA 95831-1904, USA

Wilburn, J R (Athlete, Football Player)
2211 Chalkwell Dr
Midlothian, VA 23113-3897, USA

Wilburn, Ken (Athlete, Basketball Player)
17 E Meyran Ave
Somers Point, NJ 08244-2720, USA

Wilby, James (Actor)
William Morris Agency
52/53 Poland Place
London W1F 7KX, UNITED KINGDOM (UK)

Wilcher, Mary (Actor)
c/o Staff Member *Levine Management*
8549 Wilshire Blvd # 212
Beverly Hills, CA 90211-3104, USA

Wilcox, Barry (Athlete, Hockey Player)
18859 86 Ave
Surrey, BC V4N 6E3, Canada

Wilcox, Chris (Athlete, Basketball Player)
c/o Jeff Schwartz *Excel Sports Management*
1700 Broadway Fl 29
New York, NY 10019-6559, USA

Wilcox, David (Composer, Music Group, Musician, Songwriter, Writer)
c/o Staff Member *Concerted Efforts*
PO Box 440326
Somerville, MA 02144-0004, USA

Wilcox, Davie (Dave) (Athlete, Football Player)
94471 Willamette Dr
Junction City, OR 97448-9606, USA

Wilcox, J.J. (Athlete, Football Player)
c/o Anthony J. Agnone *Eastern Athletic Services*
11350 McCormick Rd
Suite 800 - Executive Plaza
Hunt Valley, MD 21031-1002, USA

Wilcox, John (Athlete, Football Player)
82038 S Fork Walla Walla River Rd
Milton Freewater, OR 97862-7025, USA

Wilcox, Larry (Actor)
10 Appaloosa Ln
Bell Canyon, CA 91307-1002, USA

Wilcox, Lisa (Actor)
c/o Kate Ward *Ward Agency*
1617 N El Centro Ave Ste 15
Hollywood, CA 90028-6429, USA

Wilcox, Milt (Athlete, Baseball Player)
10064 Vernon Ave
Huntington Woods, MI 48070-1522, USA

Wilcox, Shannon (Actor)
1753 Centinela Ave Apt A
Santa Monica, CA 90404-4204, USA

Wilcutt, Terence W (Terry) (Astronaut)
1216 Red Wing Dr
Friendswood, TX 77546-5888, USA

Wilcutt, Terrence W Colonel (Astronaut)
1216 Red Wing Dr
Friendswood, TX 77546-5888, USA

Wilde, Kim (Musician, Songwriter, Writer)
Dance Crazy Mgmt
294-296 Nether St
Finchley
Lake Forest N31 RJ, UNITED KINGDOM (UK)

Wilde, Olivia (Actor)
c/o Maria Herrera *PMK/BNC Public Relations*
1840 Century Park E Ste 1400
Los Angeles, CA 90067-2115, USA

Wilder, Alan (Musician)
Reach Media
295 Greenwich St # 109
New York, NY 10007-1049, USA

Wilder, Bert (Athlete, Football Player)
501 Willow View Dr
Greensboro, NC 27455-1379, USA

Wilder, Deontay (Athlete, Boxer)
2907 Meadowlake Ave
Northport, AL 35473-8071, USA

Wilder, Don (Cartoonist)
North American Syndicate
235 E 45th St
New York, NY 10017-3305, USA

Wilder, James (Actor)
Stone Manners
6500 Wilshire Blvd # 550
Los Angeles, CA 90048-4920, USA

Wilder, L Douglas (Politician)
2805 E Weyburn Rd
Richmond, VA 23235-3257, USA

Wilder, Sharon (Athlete, Golfer)
73340 Indian Creek Way
Palm Desert, CA 92260-1169, USA

Wilder, Yvonne (Actor)
11836 Hesby St
Valley Village, CA 91607-3218, USA

Wilding, Anna (Actor)
c/o Staff Member *Carpe Diem Films LLC*
9663 Santa Monica Blvd # 557
Beverly Hills, CA 90210-4303, USA

Wildman, George (Cartoonist)
1640 Shepard Ave
Hamden, CT 06518-2036, USA

Wildman, Valerie (Actor)
110 Hurricane St Apt 305
Marina Del Rey, CA 90292-5935, USA

Wild Orchid (Music Group)
c/o Staff Member *Diva Central Inc*
7510 W Sunset Blvd # 1445
Los Angeles, CA 90046-3408, USA

Wilds, Tristan (Actor)
c/o Elise Koseff *MKSD Talent Management (NY)*
15 W 28th St Fl 9
New York, NY 10001-6430, USA

Wiles, Jason (Actor)
c/o David Roberson *Roberson Public Relations*
7200 Franklin Ave Apt 501
Los Angeles, CA 90046-3085, USA

Wiles, Randy (Athlete, Baseball Player)
3716 Lake Catherine Dr
Harvey, LA 70058-5509, USA

Wiley, Enloe Steve (Baseball Player)
Negro Baseball Leagues
1222 Cedar St
Clarksville, TN 37040-3515, USA

Wiley, Lee (Musician)
Country Crossroads
7787 Monterey St
Gilroy, CA 95020-5217, USA

Wiley, Marcellus (Athlete, Football Player)
5132 S Garth Ave
Los Angeles, CA 90056-1110, USA

Wiley, Marcus D. (Actor)
3550 Main St Apt 6211
Houston, TX 77002-9593, USA

Wiley, Mark (Athlete, Baseball Player)
10750 Mobberley Cir
Orlando, FL 32832-6988, USA

Wiley, Michael (Athlete, Basketball Player)
2461 Elm Ave Apt 2
Long Beach, CA 90806-3142, USA

Wiley, Michael E (Business Person)
Atlantic Richfield Co
333 S Hope St
Los Angeles, CA 90071-1406, USA

Wiley, Morlan (Athlete, Basketball Player)
2S21 Fallview Ln
Carrollton, TX 75007-1934, USA

Wiley, Morlon (Athlete, Basketball Player)
1967 Legacy Cove Dr
Maitland, FL 32751-7524, USA

Wiley, Samira (Actor)
c/o Scott Boute *Serge PR*
339 W 12th St
New York, NY 10014-1721, USA

Wiley, William T (Artist)
640 Santana Rd
Novato, CA 94945-1531, USA

Wilfong, Rob (Athlete, Baseball Player)
126 Maverick Dr
San Dimas, CA 91773-1127, USA

Wilford, John Noble Jr (Journalist)
67 S Howells Point Rd
Bellport, NY 11713-2621, USA

Wilfork, Vince (Athlete, Football Player)
c/o Staff Member *New England Patriots*
1 Patriot Pl
Foxboro, MA 02035-1388, USA

Wilheim, Jim (Athlete, Baseball Player)
3 Burdell Ct
Novato, CA 94949-6607, USA

Wilhelm, Erik (Athlete, Football Player)
6452 SE Division St
Portland, OR 97206-1278, USA

Wilhelm, Jim (Athlete, Baseball Player)
3 Burdell Ct
Novato, CA 94949-6607, USA

Wilhelm, John W (Misc)
Hotel & Restaurant Employees Union
1219 28th St NW
Washington, DC 20007-3362, USA

Wilhelm, Kati (Athlete)
SC Motor Zella-Mehlis
Bierbachstr 68
Zella-Mehlis 98544, USA

Wilhite, Jonathan (Athlete, Football Player)
c/o Staff Member *New England Patriots*
1 Patriot Pl
Foxboro, MA 02035-1388, USA

Wilhoite, Kathleen (Actor)
PO Box 5617
Beverly Hills, CA 90209-5617, USA

Wilhoite, Michael (Athlete, Football Player)

Wilk, Brad (Musician)
c/o Rod MacSween *International Talent Booking*
9 Kingsway
Fl 6
London WC2B 6XF, UNITED KINGDOM

Wilk, Vic (Athlete, Golfer)
1350 N Town Center Dr Unit 2082
Las Vegas, NV 89144-0587, USA

Wilkens, Lenny (Athlete, Basketball Coach, Basketball Player, Coach)
3429 Evergreen Point Rd
Medina, WA 98039-1022, USA

Wilkerson, Bob (Bobby) (Athlete, Basketball Player)
PO Box 74S3
Upper Marlboro, MD 20792-74S3, USA

Wilkerson, Brad (Athlete, Baseball Player, Olympic Athlete)
5975 Whirlaway Rd
Palm Beach Gardens, FL 33418-7740, USA

Wilkerson, Bruce (Athlete, Football Player)
2013 Breakers Pt
Knoxville, TN 37922-5676, USA

Wilkerson, Curtis (Athlete, Baseball Player)
PO Box 182993
Arlington, TX 76096-2993, USA

Wilkerson, Doug (Athlete, Football Player)
PO Box 7090
Rancho Santa Fe, CA 92067-7090, USA

Wilkerson, Muhammad (Football Player)
c/o Chad Wiestling *Integrated Sports Management*
2120 Texas St Apt 2204
Houston, TX 77003-3054, USA

Wilkerson, Tim (Race Car Driver)
Demand Flow Racing
2901 Adlai Stevenson Dr
Springfield, IL 62703-4551, USA

Wilkes, Glenn (Basketball Player, Coach)
Stetson University
Athletic Dept
Campus Box 8359
Deland, FL 32720, USA

Wilkes, Jamal (Athlete, Basketball Player)
7846 W 81st St
Playa Del Rey, CA 90293-7911, USA

Wilkes, Jimmy (Baseball Player)
Newark Eagles
26-C Oakhill Drive
Brantford, ON N3T 1R1, CANADA

Wilkes, Reggie (Athlete, Football Player)
6912 Wissahickon Ave
Philadelphia, PA 19119-3728, USA

Wilkie, Bob (Athlete, Hockey Player)
303 S Forge Rd
Palmyra, PA 17078-2613, USA

Wilkie, Chris (Musician)
Primary Talent Int'l
2-12 Petonville Road
London N1 9PL, UNITED KINGDOM (UK)

Wilkie, David (Athlete, Hockey Player)
9008 N 155th St
Bennington, NE 68007-8090, USA

Wilkie, David (Swimmer)
Oaklands Queens Hill
Ascot
Berkshire, UNITED KINGDOM (UK)

Wilkin, Richard E (Religious Leader)
Winebrenner Theological Seminary
950 N Main St
Findlay, OH 45840-3652, USA

Wilkins, Dean (Athlete, Baseball Player)
10974 Tobago Rd
San Diego, CA 92126-2040, USA

Wilkins, Dominique (Athlete, Basketball Player)
4415 Felix Way SE
Smyrna, GA 30082-4700, USA

Wilkins, Donna (Athlete, Golfer)
3617 Bancroft Main NW
Kennesaw, GA 30144-6011, USA

Wilkins, Eddie Lee (Athlete, Basketball Player)
304S Mockingbird Ln
Atlanta, GA 30344-S679, USA

Wilkins, Eric (Athlete, Baseball Player)
830 115th St SW Unit A
Everett, WA 98204-5967, USA

Wilkins, Laisha (Actor)
c/o Staff Member *Televisa*
Blvd Adolfo Lopez Mateos 232
Colonia San Angel INN
DF CP 01060, MEXICO

Wilkins, Mac (Athlete, Olympic Athlete, Track Athlete)
2127 Olympic Pkwy Ste 1006 # 332
Chula Vista, CA 91915-1361, USA

Wilkins, Marc (Athlete, Baseball Player)
505 Stockton Rdg
Cranberry Twp, PA 16066-2280, USA

Wilkins, Mardell (Athlete, Golfer)
26982 Durango Ln
Mission Viejo, CA 92691-4431, USA

Wilkins, Rick (Athlete, Baseball Player)
12766 Longview Dr W
Jacksonville, FL 32223-2620, USA

Wilkins Myrick, Sue (Congressman, Politician)
230 Cannon Hob
Washington, DC 20515-3309, USA

Wilkinson, Adrienne (Actor)
c/o Ryan Hayden *Ideal Talent Agency (I.T.A.)*
10806 Ventura Blvd Ste 2
Studio City, CA 91604-3300, USA

Wilkinson, Amanda (Music Group, Musician)
Fitzgerald-Hartley
1908 Wedgewood Ave
Nashville, TN 37212-3733, USA

Wilkinson, Bill (Athlete, Baseball Player)
3738 Yuhas Ave
Helena, MT 59602-7404, USA

Wilkinson, Dale (Athlete, Basketball Player)
2168 E 3100 N
Layton, UT 84040-8479, USA

Wilkinson, Dan (Athlete, Football Player)
222 Republic Dr
Allen Park, MI 48101-3650, USA

Wilkinson, Jonathan (Jonny) (Athlete, Soccer Player)
c/o Staff Member *Newcastle Falcons RFC*
Kingston Park
Brunton Rd, Kenton Bank Foot
Newcastle NE138AF, UK

Wilkinson, June (Actor, Model)
4060 E Grenora Way
Long Beach, CA 90815-2613, USA

Wilkinson, Kendra (Model, Reality Star)
c/o Troy Nankin *Wishlab*
195 S Beverly Dr Ste 414
Beverly Hills, CA 90212-3044, USA

Wilkinson, Steve (Musician)
Fitzgerald Hartley
1908 Wedgewood Ave
Nashville, TN 37212-3733, USA

Wilkinson, Tom (Actor)
c/o Larry Taube *Principal Entertainment*
9255 W Sunset Blvd Ste 500
Los Angeles, CA 90069-3301, USA

Wilkinson, Tyler (Musician)
Fritzgerald Hartley
1908 Wedgewood Ave
Nashville, TN 37212-3733, USA

Wilkos, Steve (Television Host)
311 Noroton Ave
Darien, CT 06820-3317, USA

Wilks, Jim (Athlete, Football Player)
4314 Leaflock Ln
Katy, TX 77450-8251, USA

Will, George (Journalist)
9 Grafton St
Chevy Chase, MD 20815-3427, USA

Will, George (Writer)
9 Grafton St
Chevy Chase, MD 20815-3427, USA

Willard, Fred (Actor, Comedian)
5056 Woodley Ave
Encino, CA 91436-1411, USA

Willard, Jerry (Athlete, Baseball Player)
1421 Kumquat Pl
Oxnard, CA 93036-6219, USA

Willard, Kenneth H (Ken) (Athlete, Football Player)
3071 Viewpoint Rd
Midlothian, VA 23113, USA

Willard, Rod (Athlete, Hockey Player)
7736 Arboretum Dr Apt 108
Charlotte, NC 28270-0348

Willcocks, David V (Musician)
13 Grange Road
Cambridge CB3 9AS, UNITED KINGDOM (UK)

Willcox, Toyah (Actor)
c/o Staff Member *Roseman Organisation, The*
51 Queen Anne St
London W1G 9HS, UK

Willebrands, Johannes Cardinal (Religious Leader)
Council for Promoting Christian Unity
Via dell'Erba I
Rome 00120, ITALY

Willerton, Amy (Actor, Beauty Pageant Winner, Model, Reality Star)
c/o Lion Shirdan *UPRISE Management*
2317 Mount Olympus Dr
Los Angeles, CA 90046-1639, USA

Willet, E Crosby (Artist)
Willet Stained Glass Studios
811 E Cayuga St
Philadelphia, PA 19124-3815, USA

Willets, Kathy (Actor)
3251 Spanish River Dr
Pompano Beach, FL 33062-6809

Willett, Malcolm (Cartoonist)
Universal Press Syndicate
4520 Main St Ste 340
Kansas City, MO 64111-7705, USA

Willey, Cary (Athlete, Baseball Player)
PO Box 64
Cherryfield, ME 04622-0064, USA

Will-Halpin, Maggie (Athlete, Golfer)
12423 Carnoustie Ln
North Chesterfield, VA 23236-4172, USA

Willhite, Gerald (Athlete, Football Player)
516 Fisher Cir
Folsom, CA 95630-9540, USA

Willhite, Kevin (Athlete, Football Player)
9784 W Taron Dr
Elk Grove, CA 95757-8193, USA

Will.I.Am (Musician)
1965 De Mille Dr
Los Angeles, CA 90027-1705, USA

William, Edward (Religious Leader)
Bible Way Church
5118 Clarendon Rd
Brooklyn, NY 11203-5329, USA

William, Prince (Royalty)
St James Palace
London SW1A 1BS, UNITED KINGDOM

Williams, Aaron (Athlete, Football Player)
c/o Tom Condon *Creative Artists Agency (CAA)*
401 Commerce St PH
Nashville, TN 37219-2516, USA

Williams, Adrian (Basketball Player)
Phoenix Mercury
201 E Jefferson St
American West Arena
Phoenix, AZ 85004-2412, USA

Williams, Aeneas D (Athlete, Football Player)
746 High Hampton Rd
Saint Louis, MO 63124-1018, USA

Williams, Al (Athlete, Baseball Player)
3428 E Shore Rd
Miramar, FL 33023-4978, USA

Williams, Al (Athlete, Basketball Player)
2809 S 36th St
Fort Smith, AR 72903-4501, USA

Williams, Alfred H (Athlete, Football Player)
Sportsradio 950 The Fan
7800 E Orchard Rd Ste 400
Greenwood Village, CO 80111-2599, USA

Williams, Allison (Actor, Musician)
c/o Lindsay Galin *Rogers & Cowan*
909 3rd Ave Fl 9
New York, NY 10022-4752, USA

Williams, Alvin (Basketball Player)
Toronto Raptors
40 Bay St
Air Canada Center
Toronto, ON M5J 2X2, CANADA

Williams, Andre (Athlete, Football Player)
c/o Erik Burkhardt *Select Sports Group*
2700 Post Oak Blvd Ste 1450
Houston, TX 77056-5785, USA

Williams, Anson (Actor)
811 Foothill Ln
Ojai, CA 93023-1714, USA

Williams, Anthony A (Politician)
Mayor's Office
District Building
14th & E Sts NW
Washington, DC 20004, USA

Williams, Ashley (Actor)
c/o Lena Roklin *Luber Roklin Management*
5815 W Sunset Blvd Ste 208
Los Angeles, CA 90028-6481, USA

Williams, Barbara (Actor)
Innovative Artists
1505 10th St
Santa Monica, CA 90401-2805, USA

Williams, Barry (Actor, Musician)
c/o Anthony Anzaldo *Good Guy Entertainment*
555 Esplanade Apt 316
Redondo Beach, CA 90277-4085, USA

Williams, Bernard (Athlete, Football Player)
1570 Waverly Ave
Memphis, TN 38106-2424, USA

Williams, Bernie (Athlete, Baseball Player, Musician)
PO Box 203
Vega Alta, PR 00692-0203, USA

Williams, Billy (Athlete, Baseball Player)
3227 Randolph Ave
Oakland, CA 94602-1539, USA

Williams, Billy (Athlete, Baseball Player)
586 Prince Edward Rd
Glen Ellyn, IL 60137-6711, USA

Williams, Billy Dee (Actor)
c/o Derek Maki *Coolwaters Productions*
10061 Riverside Dr # 531
Toluca Lake, CA 91602-2560, USA

Williams, Branden (Actor)
c/o Staff Member *Edward Horowitz*
1155 N La Cienega Blvd Apt 203
West Hollywood, CA 90069-2430, USA

Williams, Brandon (Athlete, Football Player)
c/o Pat Dye Jr *SportsTrust Advisors*
3340 Peachtree Rd NE Fl 16
Atlanta, GA 30326-1000, USA

Williams, Brandon (Athlete, Football Player)

Williams, Brian (Athlete, Baseball Player)
2409 Colt Ln
Crowley, TX 76036-4703, USA

Williams, Brian (Athlete, Football Player)
343 Lakeview Terrace Blvd
Waconia, MN 55387-9692, USA

Williams, Brian (Athlete, Football Player)
5319 Lyoncrest Ct
Dallas, TX 75287-5500, USA

Williams, Brian (Correspondent, Journalist, Television Host)
151 E 58th St Apt 34D
New York, NY 10022-1347, USA

Williams, Brooke (Actor)
c/o Staff Member *United Talent Agency (UTA)*
9336 Civic Center Dr
Beverly Hills, CA 90210-3604, USA

Williams, Bryan (Baby) (Musician)
c/o Staff Member *Universal Music Group*
100 Universal City Plz
Universal City, CA 91608-1002, USA

Williams, Bryan (Birdman) (Musician)
c/o Staff Member *Young Money Cash Money*
1755 Broadway Fl 7
New York, NY 10019-3743, USA

Williams, Buck (Athlete, Basketball Player)
9219 Fox Meadow Ln
Potomac, MD 20854-4619, USA

Williams, Calvin (Athlete, Football Player)
5032 Yellowwood Ave
Baltimore, MD 21209-4602, USA

Williams, Cara (Actor)
Dann
9903 Santa Monica Blvd # 606
Beverly Hills, CA 90212-1671, USA

Williams, Carlton (Athlete, Football Player)
5 Pinegate Ct
Peachtree City, GA 30269-1144, USA

Williams, Carnell (Cadillac) (Football Player)
c/o Jim Steiner *CAA (St. Louis)*
222 S Central Ave Ste 1008
Saint Louis, MO 63105-3509, USA

Williams, Cary (Athlete, Football Player)
c/o Harold C Lewis *National Sports Agency*
12181 Prichard Farm Rd
Maryland Heights, MO 63043-4203, USA

Williams, Charlie (Athlete, Basketball Player)
4229 Augusta Ter E
Bradenton, FL 34203-4016, USA

Williams, Charlie (Athlete, Football Player)
2607 Encina
Irving, TX 75038-5559, USA

Williams, Chris (Actor)
c/o Carolyn Govers *Anonymous Content*
3532 Hayden Ave
Culver City, CA 90232-2413, USA

Williams, Chris (Athlete, Football Player)
c/o Bill Johnson *SportsTrust Advisors*
3340 Peachtree Rd NE Fl 16
Atlanta, GA 30326-1000, USA

Williams, Chris A (Athlete, Football Player)
2800 Christopher Blvd
Hamburg, NY 14075-3456, USA

Williams, Christopher (Musician)
c/o Ken Maldonado *Zia Artists*
506 Fort Washington Ave Apt 1H
New York, NY 10033-2081, USA

Williams, Cindy (Actor)
Cindy Williams Productions
499 N Canon Dr # 216
Beverly Hills, CA 90210-4887, USA

Williams, C K (Writer)
Princeton University
English Dept
Princeton, NJ 08544-0001, USA

Williams, Clarence (Journalist)
Los Angeles Times
2300 E Imperial Hwy
El Segundo, CA 90245-2813, USA

Williams, Cliff (Musician)
417 E Charlton St
Savannah, GA 31401-4609, USA

Williams, Clyde (Athlete, Football Player)
9754 Highway 79
Bethany, LA 71007, USA

Williams, Clyde (Baseball Player)
Cleveland Buckeyes
17135 San Juan Dr
Detroit, MI 48221-2622, USA

Williams, Colleen (Correspondent)
KNBC-TV
News Dept
3000 W Alameda Ave
Burbank, CA 91523-0001, USA

Williams, Cress (Actor)
c/o Staff Member *Sinclair Entertainment Group*
6709 La Tijera Blvd # 382
Los Angeles, CA 90045-2017, USA

Williams, Curtis (Actor)
c/o Sharyn Berg *Sharyn Talent Management*
PO Box 18033
Encino, CA 91416-8033, USA

Williams, Cynda (Actor)
Innovative Artists
1505 10th St
Santa Monica, CA 90401-2805, USA

Williams, Dallas (Athlete, Baseball Player)
7638 Allenwood Cir
Indianapolis, IN 46268-4738, USA

Williams, Dan (Athlete, Football Player)
c/o Joel Segal *Lagardere Unlimited (NY)*
456 Washington St Apt 9L
New York, NY 10013-1555, USA

Williams, Dana (Musician)
Dreamcatcher Artists Mgmt
2908 Poston Ave
Nashville, TN 37203-1312, USA

Williams, Dana (Athlete, Baseball Player)
121 Arlene Ave
North Versailles, PA 15137-2432, USA

Williams, Danny (Boxer)
c/o Frank Warren *Sports Network*
Centurion House
Bircherley Green
Hertford HERTS SG14 1AP, UNITED KINGDOM

Williams, Darnell (Actor)
Stone Manners
6500 Wilshire Blvd # 550
Los Angeles, CA 90048-4920, USA

Williams, Darryl (Athlete, Football Player)
7351 Peppertree Cir S
Davie, FL 33314-6922, USA

Williams, Dave (Athlete, Baseball Player)
157 Carter Ln
Camden, DE 19934-1212, USA

Williams, David (Producer, Writer)
c/o Jane Cameron *Cameron Creswell Agency*
61 Marlborough St
Fl 7
Surry Hills, NSW 02010, AUSTRALIA

Williams, David (Actor, Producer, Writer)
c/o Kevin McLaughlin *Main Stage Public Relations*
Prefers to be contacted by email or phone.
New York, NY NA, USA

Williams, David (Athlete, Football Player)
30201 Redtree Dr
Leesburg, FL 34748-9584, USA

Williams, David (Athlete, Football Player)
30826 Tanoa Rd
Evergreen, CO 80439-7963, USA

Williams, David (Athlete, Football Player)
109 E Oxford St
Valley Stream, NY 11580-4622, USA

Williams, David (Athlete, Hockey Player)
5 Barn Swallow Ln
Duxbury, MA 02332-3628, USA

Williams, Davida (Actor)
c/o Marvet Britto *Britto Agency PR*
277 Broadway Ste 110
New York, NY 10007-2072, USA

Williams, David W (Athlete, Football Player)
108 E Oxford St
Valley Stream, NY 11580, USA

Williams, DeAngelo (Athlete, Football Player)
c/o Jimmy Sexton *CAA (Memphis)*
6060 Poplar Ave Ste 470
Memphis, TN 38119-0910, USA

Williams, Delvin (Athlete, Football Player)
173 Sierra Vista Ave Apt 11
Mountain View, CA 94043-4468, USA

Williams, Deniece (Musician)
Green Light Talent Agency
24024 Saint Moritz Dr
Valencia, CA 91355-2033, USA

Williams, Deren (Athlete, Basketball Player)
4347 W Northwest Hwy Ste 130
Dallas, TX 75220-3866, USA

Williams, Deron (Athlete, Basketball Player)
c/o Bob McClaren *McClaren Sports*
16200 Park Row Ste 195
Houston, TX 77084-7654, USA

Williams, Derwin (Athlete, Football Player)
2150 White Dahlia Dr
Apopka, FL 32712-6070, USA

Williams, D.J. (Athlete, Football Player)
c/o Mitchell Frankel *Impact Sports (FL)*
2799 NW 2nd Ave Ste 203
Boca Raton, FL 33431-6709, USA

Williams, D.J. (Athlete, Football Player)

Williams, Don (Athlete, Baseball Player)
5597 Greene 125 Rd
Paragould, AR 72450-9020, USA

Williams, Don (Athlete, Basketball Player)
6109 Rosedale Dr
Hyattsville, MD 20782-2296, USA

Williams, Donald E (Astronaut)
Science Applications Int'l
2200 Space Park Dr Ste 200
Houston, TX 77058-3678, USA

Williams, Donald E Captain (Astronaut)
16430 Larkfield Dr
Houston, TX 77059-5415, USA

Williams, Donald '"Spin"' (Athlete, Baseball Player)
240 Shoute Division
El Dorado, AR 71730-8984, USA

Williams, Doug (Comedian)
c/o James Kellem *JKA Talent*
4324 Troost Ave Unit 206
Studio City, CA 91604-2886, USA

Williams, Douglas L (Doug) (Athlete, Coach, Football Coach, Football Player)
10120 Lemon Rd
Zachary, LA 70791-6407, USA

Williams, Duke (Athlete, Football Player)
c/o Adisa P Bakari *Kelley Drye & Warren LLP*
3050 K St NW Ste 400
Washington, DC 20007-5100, USA

Williams, Easy (Actor)
Judy Schoen
606 N Larchmont Blvd Ste 309
Los Angeles, CA 90004-1309, USA

Williams, Eboni (Journalist, Television Host)
c/o Staff Member *Fox News*
1211 Avenue of the Americas Lowr C1
New York, NY 10036-8705, USA

Williams, Ed (Athlete, Football Player)
521 Royal Ave
Oklahoma City, OK 73130-2719, USA

Williams, Eddie (Athlete, Baseball Player)
22809 Boxwood Ln
Santa Clarita, CA 91390-4155, USA

Williams, Edy (Actor, Model)
PO Box 6325
Woodland Hills, CA 91365-6325, USA

Williams, Eli (Baseball Player)
St Louis Stars
214 Thomas Ct NW
Fort Walton Beach, FL 32548-4139, USA

Williams, Ellery (Athlete, Football Player)
1987 Wimbledon Pl
Los Altos, CA 94024-7062, USA

Williams, Elmo (Director, Producer)
1249 Iris St
Brookings, OR 97415-9643, USA

Williams, Eric (Basketball Player)
c/o Staff Member *Toronto Raptors*
400-40 Bay St
Toronto, ON M5J 2X2, CANADA

Williams, Eric (Football Player)
c/o Staff Member *Pittsburgh Steelers*
3400 S Water St
Pittsburgh, PA 15203-2358, USA

Williams, Eric (Football Player)
c/o Staff Member *St Louis Cardinals*
700 Clark Ave
Saint Louis, MO 63102-1727, USA

Williams, Eric M (Athlete, Football Player)
13330 Noel Rd Apt 825
Dallas, TX 75240-5092, USA

Williams, Erik (Athlete, Football Player)
1 Wortham Ct
Bear, DE 19701-2060, USA

Williams, Ernie (Athlete, Football Player)
45 Oakwood Dr
Chapel Hill, NC 27517-5650, USA

Williams, Erwin (Athlete, Football Player)
33 Manly St
Portsmouth, VA 23702-1019, USA

Williams, Frank (Basketball Player)
New York Knicks
2 Penn Plz Fl 15
Madison Square Garden
New York, NY 10121-1700, USA

Williams, Freeman (Athlete, Basketball Player)
450 W 41st Pl
Los Angeles, CA 90037-2119, USA

Williams, Gary (Basketball Player, Coach)
University of Maryland
Athletic Dept
College Park, MD 20742-0001, USA

Williams, Gary Anthony (Actor)
4178 Dixie Canyon Ave
Sherman Oaks, CA 91423-4338, USA

Williams, George (Athlete, Baseball Player)
N5250 County Road M
West Salem, WI 54669-9202, USA

Williams, Gerald (Athlete, Baseball Player)
17011 Candeleda De Avila
Tampa, FL 33613-5213, USA

Williams, Gerald (Athlete, Football Player)
9613 Callis Ct
Harrisburg, NC 28075-9619, USA

Williams, Gluyas (Cartoonist)
New Yorker Magazine
4 Times Sq
Editorial Dept
New York, NY 10036-6518, USA

Williams, Greg (Actor)
1680 Vine St Ste 604
Los Angeles, CA 90028-8833, USA

Williams, Gregg (Athlete, Coach, Football Coach, Football Player)
16897 Bold Venture Dr
Leesburg, VA 20176-7162, USA

Williams, Gregory Alan (Actor)
c/o Staff Member *Pakula/King & Associates*
9229 W Sunset Blvd Ste 315
Los Angeles, CA 90069-3403, USA

Williams, Gus (Athlete, Basketball Player)
PO Box 262
Mount Vernon, NY 10552-0262, USA

Williams, Hal (Actor)
Marter
PO Box 14227
Palm Desert, CA 92255-4227, USA

Williams, Harland (Actor)
c/o Evan Miller *Abrams Artists Agency*
750 N San Vicente Blvd
E Tower Fl 11
Los Angeles, CA 90069-5788, USA

Williams, Harold M (Misc)
J Paul Getty Museum
1200 Getty Center Dr
Getty Center
Los Angeles, CA 90049-1657, USA

Williams, Hayley (Musician)
c/o Louisa Spring *Louisa Spring Management*
404 Carroll Canal
Venice, CA 90291-4682, USA

Williams, Herb (Athlete, Basketball Coach, Basketball Player, Coach)
67 Revonah Cir
Stamford, CT 06905-4026, USA

Williams, Howard L (Howie) (Athlete, Football Player)
4731 Proctor Ave
Oakland, CA 94618-2540, USA

Williams, Howie (Athlete, Basketball Player)
1940 Hamilton Ln
Carmel, IN 46032-3521, USA

Williams, Hype (Actor, Director, Producer)
c/o Staff Member *Creative Artists Agency (CAA)*
2000 Avenue of the Stars Ste 100
Los Angeles, CA 90067-4705, USA

Williams, Ian (Athlete, Football Player)
c/o Drew Rosenhaus *Rosenhaus Sports Representation*
3921 Alton Rd # 440
Miami Beach, FL 33140-3852, USA

Williams, Inka (Actor)
c/o Claire Dickens *IMG (London)*
McCormack House
Burlington Lane
London W4 2TH, UNITED KINGDOM

Williams, Ivy (Writer)
Mediachase
834 N Harper Ave
Los Angeles, CA 90046-6804, USA

Williams, Jacquian (Athlete, Football Player)
c/o Drew Rosenhaus *Rosenhaus Sports Representation*
3921 Alton Rd # 440
Miami Beach, FL 33140-3852, USA

Williams, Jaimie (Actor)
1019 Kane Concourse Ste 202
Bay Harbor Islands, FL 33154-2138, USA

Williams, Jamal (Athlete, Football Player)
4020 Murphy Canyon Rd
San Diego, CA 92123-4407, USA

Williams, James A (Froggy) (Athlete, Football Player)
296 Sugarberry Cir
Houston, TX 77024-7248, USA

Williams, James F (Jimy) (Athlete, Baseball Player, Coach)
1506 S Evergreen Ave
Clearwater, FL 33756-2263, USA

Williams, James (Fly) (Athlete, Basketball Player)
672 Ralph Ave Apt 4A
Brooklyn, NY 11212-3852, USA

Williams, James O (Athlete, Football Player)
1111 S Waukegan Rd Unit 4
Lake Forest, IL 60045-3758, USA

Williams, Jason (Athlete, Football Player)
c/o Dave Butz *Sportstars Inc*
1370 Avenue of the Americas Fl 19
New York, NY 10019-4602, USA

Williams, Jason (Athlete, Hockey Player)
Newport Sports Management
400-201 City Centre Dr
Attn Wade Arnott
Mississauga, ON L5B 2T4, Canada

Williams, Jason (Athlete, Basketball Player)
6103 Louise Cove Dr
Windermere, FL 34786-8939, USA

Williams, Jay (Basketball Player)
Chicago Bulls
1901 W Madison St
United Center
Chicago, IL 60612-2459, USA

Williams, Jay (Athlete, Football Player)
1503 Alydar Ct
Waxhaw, NC 28173-6672, USA

Williams, Jayson (Basketball Player, Sportscaster)
NBC-TV
30 Rockefeller Plz
Sports Dept
New York, NY 10112-0015, USA

Williams, Jeff (Athlete, Football Player)
9710 15th Ave NW
Seattle, WA 98117-2314, USA

Williams, Jeffrey N (Astronaut)
4918 Cross Creek Ln
League City, TX 77573-6267, USA

Williams, Jeffrey N Colonel (Astronaut)
4918 Cross Creek Ln
League City, TX 77573-6267, USA

Williams, Jennifer (Fitness Expert, Reality Star)
Flirty Girl Fitness
PO Box 8349
Van Nuys, CA 91409-8349, USA

Williams, Jerome (Athlete, Basketball Player)
c/o Staff Member *Toronto Raptors*
400-40 Bay St
Toronto, ON M5J 2X2, CANADA

Williams, Jerrol (Athlete, Football Player)
601 Azure Banks Ave
North Las Vegas, NV 89031-1753, USA

Williams, Jesse (Actor)
c/o Alyx Carr *42West*
600 3rd Ave Fl 23
New York, NY 10016-1914, USA

Williams, Jessica (Musician)
c/o Staff Member *Diva Central Inc*
7510 W Sunset Blvd # 1445
Los Angeles, CA 90046-3408, USA

Williams, Jim (Athlete, Baseball Player)
16 Stone Pne
Aliso Viejo, CA 92656-2132, USA

Williams, Jimmy (Athlete, Baseball Player, Coach)
4 Old Sound Rd
Joppa, MD 21085-4525, USA

Williams, JoBeth (Actor)
c/o Lori Jonas *Jonas Public Relations*
1327 Ocean Ave Ste F
Santa Monica, CA 90401-1024, USA

Williams, Joel (Athlete, Football Player)
1515 Penn Ave Apt 305
Wilkinsburg, PA 15221-2659, USA

Williams, John (Actor, Composer)
c/o Staff Member *Gorfaine/Schwartz Agency Inc*
4111 W Alameda Ave Ste 509
Burbank, CA 91505-4171, USA

Williams, John (Composer, Musician)
333 Loring Ave
Los Angeles, CA 90024-2640, USA

Williams, Juan (Correspondent)
c/o 21st Century Speakers
Box 1422
Gouldsboro, PA 18424, USA

Williams, Justin (Athlete, Hockey Player)
103 Rutherglen Dr
Cary, NC 27511-6430, USA

Williams, Kameelah (Musician)
c/o Staff Member *Creative Artists Agency (CAA)*
2000 Avenue of the Stars Ste 100
Los Angeles, CA 90067-4705, USA

Williams, Karen (Comedian)
HaHA Institute
PO Box 32147
Cleveland, OH 44132-0147, USA

Williams, Karl (Athlete, Football Player)
6502 Falcon St
Rowlett, TX 75089-8260, USA

Williams, Katt (Actor, Comedian)
c/o Janice Lee *Rogers & Cowan*
1840 Century Park E Fl 18
Los Angeles, CA 90067-2101, USA

Williams, Keith (Athlete, Baseball Player)
1756 N Avignon Ln
Clovis, CA 93619-3799, USA

Williams, Kelli (Actor, Musician)
c/o John Carrabino *John Carrabino Management*
5900 Wilshire Blvd Ste 740
Los Angeles, CA 90036-5032, USA

Williams, Ken (Athlete, Baseball Player)
6430 E Sierra Vista Dr
Paradise Valley, AZ 85253-4351, USA

Williams, Kevin (Athlete, Football Player)
c/o Tom Condon *Creative Artists Agency (CAA)*
401 Commerce St PH
Nashville, TN 37219-2516, USA

Williams, Kevin (Athlete, Basketball Player)
1102 Blake Ave # 2
Brooklyn, NY 11208-3634, USA

Williams, Kevin (Athlete, Football Player)
2201 Wembley Downs Dr
Arlington, TX 76017-4548, USA

Williams, Kiely Alexis (Actor, Director, Musician)
c/o Laurie Pozmantier *WME|IMG*
9601 Wilshire Blvd
Beverly Hills, CA 90210-5213, USA

Williams, Kim (Athlete, Golfer)
34350 Tuscany Ave
Sorrento, FL 32776-6921, USA

Williams, Kimberly Kevon (Actor)
c/o TJ Stein *Stein Entertainment Group*
1351 N Crescent Heights Blvd Apt 312
West Hollywood, CA 90046-4549, USA

Williams, Kyle (Athlete, Football Player)

Williams, Lauryn (Athlete, Track Athlete)
PO Box 8008
Gray, TN 37615-0008, USA

Williams, Lee E (Athlete, Football Player)
11651 NW 4th St
Plantation, FL 33325-2509, USA

Williams, Leona (Musician)
Leona Williams Enterprises
PO Box 744
Gallatin, TN 37066-0744, USA

Williams, Leonard (Athlete, Football Player)
c/o Eugene Parker *Independent Sports & Entertainment (ISE-IN)*
6435 W Jefferson Blvd # 197
Fort Wayne, IN 46804-6203, USA

Williams, Lucinda (Musician, Songwriter)
11487 Laurelcrest Dr
Studio City, CA 91604-3873, USA

Williams, Madieu (Athlete, Football Player)
PO Box 96503
Washington, DC 20090-6503, USA

Williams, Maisie (Actor)
c/o Staff Member *Louise Johnston Management*
Cheltenham Film Studios
Arle Court
Cheltenham, Gloucestershire GL51 6PN, UK

Williams, Maiya (Producer)
c/o Staff Member *Principal Entertainment*
9255 W Sunset Blvd Ste 500
Los Angeles, CA 90069-3301, USA

Williams, Malinda (Actor)
c/o Staff Member *Leverage Management*
3030 Pennsylvania Ave
Santa Monica, CA 90404-4112, USA

Williams, Mario (Athlete, Football Player)
c/o Jim Steiner *CAA (St. Louis)*
222 S Central Ave Ste 1008
Saint Louis, MO 63105-3509, USA

Williams, Mark (Athlete, Baseball Player)
1453 Trumansburg Rd
Ithaca, NY 14850-9530, USA

Williams, Mary Alice (Correspondent)
c/o Staff Member *CBS News (NY)*
524 W 57th St Fl 8
New York, NY 10019-2930, USA

Williams, Mason (Composer, Musician)
13479 SE Lost Lake Dr
Prineville, OR 97754-8487, USA

Williams, Matt (Athlete, Baseball Player)
205 Tearose Ln
Lake Jackson, TX 77566-6043, USA

Williams, Matt (Athlete, Baseball Player)
4400 N Scottsdale Rd Ste 381
Scottsdale, AZ 85251-3331, USA

Williams, Matt (Writer)
c/o Staff Member *Wind Dancer Productions*
38 Commerce St
New York, NY 10014-3755, USA

Williams, Maurice (Musician)
Willis Blume Agency, The
PO Box 509
Orangeburg, SC 29116-0509, USA

Williams, Maurice J (Misc)
Overseas Development Council
1875 Connecticut Ave NW
Washington, DC 20009-5728, USA

Williams, Merriwether (Producer)
c/o Bruce Gellman *Felker, Toczek, Gellman, Suddleson*
10880 Wilshire Blvd Ste 2080
Los Angeles, CA 90024-4120, USA

Williams, Michael (Athlete, Basketball Player)
1005 Lakeridge Ct
Colleyville, TX 76034-2825, USA

Williams, Michael D (Mike) (Athlete, Baseball Player)
302 Horseshoe Farm Rd
Pembroke, VA 24136-3478, USA

Williams, Michael Kenneth (Actor)
c/o Matt Goldman *Silver Lining Entertainment*
421 S Beverly Dr Fl 7
Beverly Hills, CA 90212-4408, USA

Williams, Michael L (Actor)
Julian Belfarge
46 Albermarle St
London W1X 4PP, UNITED KINGDOM (UK)

Williams, Micheal (Basketball Player)
1415 Reynoldston Ln
Dallas, TX 75232-2411, USA

Williams, Michelle (Actor)
c/o Mara Buxbaum *ID Public Relations*
7060 Hollywood Blvd Fl 8th
Los Angeles, CA 90028-6021, USA

Williams, Michelle (Musician)
c/o Staff Member *Agency for the Performing Arts (APA)*
405 S Beverly Dr Ste 500
Beverly Hills, CA 90212-4425, USA

Williams, Mike (Athlete, Football Player)
c/o Hadley Engelhard *Enter-Sports Management*
6000 Lake Forrest Dr Ste 370
Atlanta, GA 30328-5902, USA

Williams, Mike (Athlete, Football Player)
c/o Mitchell Frankel *Impact Sports (FL)*
2799 NW 2nd Ave Ste 203
Boca Raton, FL 33431-6709, USA

Williams, Mikell (Athlete, Football Player)
222 W Edwards St
Covington, LA 70433-1626, USA

Williams, Mitch (Athlete, Baseball Player)
1005 Antelope Trl
Stephenville, TX 76401-6087, USA

Williams, Montel (Actor, Producer, Talk Show Host)
c/o Staff Member *Montel Media Group*
31 W 34th St Fl 7
New York, NY 10001-3031, USA

Williams, Natalie (Basketball Player)
Indiana Fever
125 S Pennsylvania St
Conseco Fieldhouse
Indianapolis, IN 46204-3610, USA

Williams, Natashia (Actor)
c/o Teresa Valente *Beverly Hecht Agency*
3500 W Olive Ave Ste 1180
Burbank, CA 91505-4651, USA

Williams, Nate (Athlete, Basketball Player)
132 Stanmore Cir
Vallejo, CA 94591-6859, USA

Williams, Nicholas (Trinidad James) (Musician)
c/o Joshua Dick *UTA/The Agency Group*
888 7th Ave Fl 7
New York, NY 10106-0700, USA

Williams, Nick (Athlete, Football Player)
21760 Parklane St
Farmington Hills, MI 48335-4221, USA

Williams, O L (Religious Leader)
United Free Will Baptist Church
1101 University St
Kinston, NC 28501, USA

Williams, Oliver (Athlete, Football Player)
11924 Daleside Ave
Hawthorne, CA 90250-1925, USA

Williams, Olivia (Actor)
c/o Hildy Gottlieb *ICM Partners*
10250 Constellation Blvd Fl 7
Los Angeles, CA 90067-6207, USA

Williams, Parker (Adult Film Star)
c/o Staff Member *Diva Central Inc*
7510 W Sunset Blvd # 1445
Los Angeles, CA 90046-3408, USA

Williams, Pat (Football Player)
DVA Brand Communications
1968 W Adams Blvd Ste 205
C/O Danielle Gibbs
Los Angeles, CA 90018-3515, USA

Williams, Paul H (Actor)
c/o Chris Fenton *DMG Entertainment*
9290 Civic Center Dr # E
Beverly Hills, CA 90210-3714, USA

Williams, Perry (Athlete, Football Player)
273 Old Laurinburg Rd
Hamlet, NC 28345-8069, USA

Williams, Perry (Athlete, Football Player)
480 Canyon Oaks Dr Apt A
Oakland, CA 94605-3858, USA

Williams, Pete (Journalist)
c/o Chris Fenton *DMG Entertainment*
9290 Civic Center Dr # E
Beverly Hills, CA 90210-3714, USA

Williams, Pharrell (Actor, Composer, Musician)
c/o Caron Veazy *Maverick*
9350 Civic Center Dr
Beverly Hills, CA 90210-3629, USA

Williams, Porsha (Stewart) (Reality Star, Television Host)
Hosea Helps
8 E Lake Dr NE
Atlanta, GA 30317-2808, USA

Williams, Prince Charles (Boxer)
Boxing Ministry
3675 Polley Dr
Austintown, OH 44515-3349, USA

Williams, Randy (Athlete, Baseball Player)
610 Reynaldo St
Dickinson, TX 77539-6123, USA

Williams, Randy (Athlete, Track Athlete)
5655 N Marty Ave Apt 204
Fresno, CA 93711-1575, USA

Williams, Reggie (Athlete, Baseball Player)
9300 Clearstone Cv
Collierville, TN 38017-9414, USA

Williams, Reggie (Athlete, Baseball Player)
4313 Whitney Dr
North Charleston, SC 29405-6831, USA

Williams, Reggie (Athlete, Basketball Player)
2016 Callaway St
Temple Hills, MD 20748-4354, USA

Williams, Reginald (Reggie) (Athlete, Football Player)
503 Jennifer Ln
Windermere, FL 34786-8400, USA

Williams, Reuben (Baseball Player)
Chicago American Giants
PO Box 3982
Winter Haven, FL 33885-3982, USA

Williams, Richard (Cartoonist)
138 Royal College Street
London, NWI OTA, England

Williams, Rick (Athlete, Baseball Player, Coach)
1217 Wessmith Way
Madera, CA 93638-1854, USA

Williams, Robbie (Musician)
c/o Josie Cliff *ie Music Ltd*
111 Frithville Gardens
Shepherds Bush
London W12 7JQ, UNITED KINGDOM (UK)

Williams, Robert (Artist)
c/o Staff Member *Fantagraphics Books*
7563 Lake City Way NE
Seattle, WA 98115-4218, USA

Williams, Robert (Baseball Player)
Newark Eagles
6233 Delancey St
Philadelphia, PA 19143-1019, USA

Williams, Robert A (Athlete, Football Player)
602 Stone Barn Rd
Towson, MD 21286-1418, USA

Williams, Robert C (Athlete, Football Player)
347 Walnut Grove Ln
Coppell, TX 75019-5342, USA

Williams, Robert J (Ben) (Athlete, Football Player)
5961 Huntview Dr
Jackson, MS 39206-2128, USA

Williams, Rodney (Athlete, Football Player)
44520 15th St E Unit 3
Lancaster, CA 93535-6321, USA

Williams, Roland (Athlete, Football Player)
5671 Wrenwyck Pl
Weldon Spring, MO 63304-1240, USA

Williams, Rosel (Athlete, Baseball Player)
Birmingham Black Barons
PO Box 442
Ninety Six, SC 29666-0442, USA

Williams, Roshumba (Model)
c/o Gail Parenteau *Parenteau Guidance*
132 E 35th St # J
New York, NY 10016-3892, USA

Williams, Rowan (Religious Leader)
Lambert Palace
London SE1 9JU, UNITED KINGDOM (UK)

Williams, Roy (Athlete, Football Player)
1 Cowboys Pkwy
Irving, TX 75063-4924, USA

Williams, Sam (Athlete, Basketball Player)
9751 W Teresa Ln
Milwaukee, WI 53224-4651, USA

Williams, Sam (Athlete, Football Player)
28960 Westfield St
Livonia, MI 48150-3137, USA

Williams, Samuel (Athlete, Basketball Player)
6116 S Verdun Ave
Los Angeles, CA 90043-3632, USA

Williams, Scott (Athlete, Football Player)
284 Heathrow Dr
Riverdale, GA 30274-2729, USA

Williams, Scott (Basketball Player)
Phoenix Suns
8217 N Coconino Rd
Paradise Valley, AZ 85253-8104, USA

Williams, Serena (Athlete, Olympic Athlete, Tennis Player)
6231 Pga Blvd Ste 104
Palm Beach Gardens, FL 33418-4033, USA

Williams, Shad (Athlete, Baseball Player)
4682 E Cornell Ave
Fresno, CA 93703-1607, USA

Williams, Shammond (Athlete, Basketball Player)
200 Gardner Cir
Chapel Hill, NC 27516-8373, USA

Williams, Shaun (Athlete, Football Player)
11738 Gruen St
Lake View Terrace, CA 91342-6117, USA

Williams, Shawn (Athlete, Football Player)
c/o Anthony J. Agnone *Eastern Athletic Services*
11350 McCormick Rd
Suite 800 - Executive Plaza
Hunt Valley, MD 21031-1002, USA

Williams, Shawne (Athlete, Basketball Player)
c/o Travis King *Relativity Sports*
2029 Century Park E Ste 1550
Century City, CA 90067-3000, USA

Williams, Sherman (Athlete, Football Player)
119 Patricia Ave
Prichard, AL 36610-2114, USA

Williams, Sidney (Athlete, Football Player)
1044 W 82nd St
Los Angeles, CA 90044-3518, USA

Williams, Simon (Actor)
Rebecca Blond Assoc
69A Kings Road
London SW3 4NX, UNITED KINGDOM (UK)

Williams, Stanley W (Stan) (Athlete, Baseball Player)
4702 Hayter Ave
Lakewood, CA 90712-3509, USA

Williams, Stepfret (Athlete, Football Player)
913 S Talton St
Minden, LA 71055-5448, USA

Williams, Stephanie E (Actor)
S M S Talent
8730 W Sunset Blvd Ste 440
Los Angeles, CA 90069-2277, USA

Williams, Stephen (Misc)
1017 Foothills Trl
Santa Fe, NM 87505-4537, USA

Williams, Steven (Actor)
c/o Richard Kerner *Kerner Management Associates*
311 N Robertson Blvd # 288
Beverly Hills, CA 90211-1705, USA

Williams, Sun ita L Cdr (Astronaut)
1522 Festival Dr
Houston, TX 77062-4526, USA

Williams, Sylvester (Athlete, Football Player)
c/o Todd France *Creative Artists Agency (CAA) Sports*
3500 Lenox Rd NE
Atlanta, GA 30326-4228, USA

Williams, Tamika (Basketball Player)
Minnesota Lunx
600 1st Ave N Ste Sky
Target Center
Minneapolis, MN 55403-1400, USA

Williams, Tank (Athlete, Football Player)
c/o Staff Member *New England Patriots*
1 Patriot Pl
Foxboro, MA 02035-1388, USA

Williams, Tavares (Monty) (Athlete, Basketball Coach, Basketball Player, Coach)
c/o Steve Kauffman *Kauffman Sports Management Group*
Prefers to be contacted by telephone
Malibu, CA, USA

Williams, Terrance (Athlete, Football Player)
c/o W Vann McElroy *Select Sports Group*
2700 Post Oak Blvd Ste 1450
Houston, TX 77056-5785, USA

Williams, Terry (Musician)
Damage Mgmt
16 Lambton Place
London W11 2SH, UNITED KINGDOM (UK)

Williams, Thomas S Cardinal (Religious Leader)
Viard
21 Eccleston Hill Po Box 198
Wellington 00001, NEW ZELAND

Williams, Todd (Actor)
c/o Scott Manners *Artists & Representatives (Stone Manners Salners)*
6100 Wilshire Blvd Ste 1500
Los Angeles, CA 90048-5110, USA

Williams, Todd (Athlete, Baseball Player)
16707 Whispering Glen Dr
Lutz, FL 33558-4960, USA

Williams, Tom (Athlete, Hockey Player)
2411 Princess Ave
Windsor, ON N8T 1V2, Canada

Williams, Tony (Athlete, Football Player)
1321 W Liberty Dr
Wheaton, IL 60187-4740, USA

Williams, Tonya Lee (Actor)
c/o Sheila Legette *Media Artists Group*
8222 Melrose Ave Ste 304
Los Angeles, CA 90046-6839, USA

Williams, Tourek (Athlete, Football Player)

Williams, Tramon (Athlete, Football Player)

Williams, Treat (Actor)
2554 Silver Cloud Ct
Park City, UT 84060-7068, USA

Williams, Trent (Athlete, Football Player)
c/o Ben Dogra *Relativity Sports*
2029 Century Park E Ste 1550
Century City, CA 90067-3000, USA

Williams, Tyler James (Actor)
c/o Staff Member *Osbrink Talent Agency*
4343 Lankershim Blvd # 100
North Hollywood, CA 91602-2705, USA

Williams, Tyrone (Athlete, Football Player)
9516 Valley Ranch Pkwy E Apt 1024
Irving, TX 75063-7851, USA

Williams, Ulis (Athlete, Track Athlete)
2511 29th St
Santa Monica, CA 90405-2913, USA

Williams, Van (Athlete, Football Player)
1804 Parkwood Ln Apt 26
Johnson City, TN 37604-7784, USA

Williams, Vanessa (Actor, Musician)
c/o Brad Cafarelli *PMK/BNC Public Relations*
1840 Century Park E Ste 1400
Los Angeles, CA 90067-2115, USA

Williams, Vanessa Lynn (Actor)
c/o Linda Jones *The Mass Appeal*
11607 Burbank Blvd Ste A
N Hollywood, CA 91601-2345, USA

Williams, Venus (Athlete, Olympic Athlete, Tennis Player)
6231 Pga Blvd Ste 104
Palm Beach Gardens, FL 33418-4033, USA

Williams, Victoria (Musician, Songwriter, Writer)
PO Box 342
Joshua Tree, CA 92252-0342, USA

Williams, Victor L (Actor, Musician)

Williams, Vince (Athlete, Football Player)
c/o Ashley Smith Becker *Relativity Sports*
2029 Century Park E Ste 1550
Century City, CA 90067-3000, USA

Williams, Virginia (Actor)
c/o Kelsey Hertel *S/W PR Shop*
584 N Larchmont Blvd # B
Los Angeles, CA 90004-1306, USA

Williams, Wade (Actor)
5445 Buffalo Ave
Sherman Oaks, CA 91401-5224, USA

Williams, Walt (Athlete, Basketball Player)
3240 Beaumont St
Temple Hills, MD 20748-4541, USA

Williams, Walter (Musician)
Associated Booking Corp
1995 Broadway # 501
New York, NY 10023-5882, USA

Williams, Warren Milton (Butch) (Athlete, Hockey Player)
518 N 15th Ave E
Duluth, MN 55812-1237, USA

Williams, W Clyde (Religious Leader)
Christian Methodist Episcopal Church
4466 Elvis Presley Blvd
Memphis, TN 38116-7180, USA

Williams, Wendy (Radio Personality, Talk Show Host)
The Wendy Williams Show
221 W 26th St
New York, NY 10001-6703, USA

Williams, Wendy Lian (Athlete, Swimmer)
Advantage International
1025 Thomas Jefferson St NW # 450
Washington, DC 20007-5201, USA

Williams, William A (Astronaut)
Environmental Protection Agency
200 SW 35th St
Corvallis, OR 97333-4902, USA

Williams, Willie (Athlete, Football Player)
4928 Country Club Dr
Mesquite, TX 75150-1169, USA

Williams, Willie (Athlete, Football Player)
1402 Forest Edge Ct
Wexford, PA 15090-9598, USA

Williams, Willie (Baseball Player)
Newark Eagles
2729 20th St
Sarasota, FL 34234-7807, USA

Williams, Woody (Athlete, Baseball Player)
5110 Newpoint Dr
Fresno, TX 77545-9212, USA

Williams, Zelda (Actor)
c/o Allison Band *Gersh*
9465 Wilshire Blvd Ste 600
Beverly Hills, CA 90212-2605, USA

Williams Brothers (Music Group, Musician)
c/o Staff Member *M.A.G./Universal Attractions*
15 W 36th St Fl 8
New York, NY 10018-7927, USA

Williams III, Clarance (Actor)
c/o Staff Member *Abrams Artists Agency*
750 N San Vicente Blvd
E Tower Fl 11
Los Angeles, CA 90069-5788, USA

Williams III, James (Fly) (Actor)
c/o Margaret Matuka *Schuller Talent (NY)*
276 5th Ave Rm 206
New York, NY 10001-4509, USA

Williams III, Shelton Hank (Musician)
c/o Mitch Schneider *Mitch Schneider Organization (MSO)*
14724 Ventura Blvd Ste 410
Sherman Oaks, CA 91403-3537, USA

Williams Jr, Ernest H (Writer)
c/o Staff Member *Oxford University Press*
Great Clarendon Street
Oxford OX2 6DP, UNITED KINGDOM

Williams Jr, Hank (Actor, Musician, Songwriter)
c/o Ken Levitan *Vector Management*
PO Box 120479
Nashville, TN 37212-0479, USA

Williams Jr, Warren (Athlete, Football Player)
1935 Pauldo St
Fort Myers, FL 33916-4122, USA

Williamson, Antone (Athlete, Baseball Player)
9419 S Stanley Pl
Tempe, AZ 85284-4109, USA

Williamson, Avery (Athlete, Football Player)
c/o Neil Cornrich *NC Sports, LLC*
best to contact via email
Columbus, OH 43201, USA

Williamson, Corliss (Basketball Player)
c/o Staff Member *Sacramento Kings*
1 Sports Pkwy
Sacramento, CA 95834-2301, USA

Williamson, Cris (Musician)
Bird Ankles Music
PO Box 30067
Seattle, WA 98113-2067, USA

Williamson, Fred (Actor, Athlete, Football Player)
c/o David Levy Martin *Momentum Talent and Literary Agency*
3500 W Olive Ave Ste 300
Burbank, CA 91505-4647, USA

Williamson, Jay (Athlete, Golfer)
24 Clermont Ln
Saint Louis, MO 63124-1346, USA

Williamson, Joanne S (Writer)
c/o Staff Member *Bethlehem Books*
10194 Garfield St S
Bathgate, ND 58216-4031, USA

Williamson, Joe (Actor)
c/o Sharon Paz *Abrams Artists Agency*
750 N San Vicente Blvd
E Tower Fl 11
Los Angeles, CA 90069-5788, USA

Williamson, Kerry (Writer)
c/o Staff Member *Gersh*
9465 Wilshire Blvd Ste 600
Beverly Hills, CA 90212-2605, USA

Williamson, Kevin (Director, Producer, Writer)
326 S Windsor Blvd
Los Angeles, CA 90020-4712, USA

Williamson, Marianne (Writer)
Los Angeles Center for Living
8265 W Sunset Blvd
West Hollywood, CA 90046-2429, USA

Williamson, Mark (Athlete, Baseball Player)
1260 Hidden Mountain Dr
El Cajon, CA 92019-3639, USA

Williamson, Michael (Journalist)
Washington Post
18334 Streamside Dr APT 301
Gaithersburg, MD 20879-5234, USA

Williamson, Michael (Writer)
18334 Streamside Dr APT 301
Gaithersburg, MD 20879-5234, USA

Williamson, Mykelti (Actor)
c/o Michael Geiser *Jill Fritzo Public Relations*
208 E 51st St # 305
New York, NY 10022-6557, USA

Williamson, Richard (Athlete, Football Coach, Football Player)
3412 Oak Grove Cir
Montgomery, AL 36116-1183, USA

Williamson, Scott (Athlete, Baseball Player)
21563 Fox Rd
Guilford, IN 47022-9706, USA

Williamson, Shaun (Actor)
McIntosh Rae Management
Thornton House
Thornton Road
London SW19 4NG, ENGLAND

Williams-Paisley, Kimberly (Actor, Producer)
c/o Brian Wilkins *LINK Entertainment*
11872 La Grange Ave
Los Angeles, CA 90025-5282, USA

Williford, Duncan (Athlete, Basketball Player)
3703 Westfield St
High Point, NC 27265-2113, USA

Williford, Vann (Athlete, Basketball Player)
4455 Fair Oaks Ln
High Point, NC 27265-8705, USA

Willig, Matt (Actor, Athlete, Football Player)
c/o Lee Wallman *Wallman Public Relations*
3859 Goldwyn Ter
Culver City, CA 90232-3103, USA

Willimon, Beau (Producer, Writer)
c/o Staff Member *PMK/BNC Public Relations*
1840 Century Park E Ste 1400
Los Angeles, CA 90067-2115, USA

Willingham, Josh (Athlete, Baseball Player)
108 Cascade Dr
Florence, AL 35633-7621, USA

Willingham, Larry (Athlete, Football Player)
983 W Lagoon Ave
Gulf Shores, AL 36542-6301, USA

Willingham, Tyrone (Coach, Football Coach)
University of Washington
Athletic Dept
Seattle, WA 98195-0001, USA

Willis, Bruce (Actor)
PO Box 2343
Hailey, ID 83333-2343, USA

Willis, Carl (Athlete, Baseball Player)
6811 Lipscomb Dr
Durham, NC 27712-9292, USA

Willis, Connie (Writer)
c/o Staff Member *Random House Publicity*
1745 Broadway Frnt 3
New York, NY 10019-4343, USA

Willis, Dale (Athlete, Baseball Player)
3415 Hayes Bayou Dr
Ruskin, FL 33570-6157, USA

Willis, Dave (Writer)
c/o Staff Member *WME/IMG*
9601 Wilshire Blvd
Beverly Hills, CA 90210-5213, USA

Willis, Dontrelle (Athlete, Baseball Player)
9820 E Thompson Peak Pkwv Unit 726
Scottsdale, AZ 85255-6657, USA

Willis, Fred (Athlete, Football Player)
31 Blithewood Ave Apt 601
Worcester, MA 01604-3558, USA

Willis, Garrett (Athlete, Golfer)
628 Mountain Pass Ln
Knoxville, TN 37923-5725, USA

Williams, Natashia (Actor)
c/o Teresa Valente *Beverly Hecht Agency*
3500 W Olive Ave Ste 1180
Burbank, CA 91505-4651, USA

Williams, Nate (Athlete, Basketball Player)
132 Stanmore Cir
Vallejo, CA 94591-6859, USA

Williams, Nicholas (Trinidad James) (Musician)
c/o Joshua Dick *UTA/The Agency Group*
888 7th Ave Fl 7
New York, NY 10106-0700, USA

Williams, Nick (Athlete, Football Player)
21760 Parklane St
Farmington Hills, MI 48335-4221, USA

Williams, O L (Religious Leader)
United Free Will Baptist Church
1101 University St
Kinston, NC 28501, USA

Williams, Oliver (Athlete, Football Player)
11924 Daleside Ave
Hawthorne, CA 90250-1925, USA

Williams, Olivia (Actor)
c/o Hildy Gottlieb *ICM Partners*
10250 Constellation Blvd Fl 7
Los Angeles, CA 90067-6207, USA

Williams, Parker (Adult Film Star)
c/o Staff Member *Diva Central Inc*
7510 W Sunset Blvd # 1445
Los Angeles, CA 90046-3408, USA

Williams, Pat (Football Player)
DVA Brand Communications
1968 W Adams Blvd Ste 205
C/O Danielle Gibbs
Los Angeles, CA 90018-3515, USA

Williams, Paul H (Actor)
c/o Chris Fenton *DMG Entertainment*
9290 Civic Center Dr # E
Beverly Hills, CA 90210-3714, USA

Williams, Perry (Athlete, Football Player)
273 Old Laurinburg Rd
Hamlet, NC 28345-8069, USA

Williams, Perry (Athlete, Football Player)
480 Canyon Oaks Dr Apt A
Oakland, CA 94605-3858, USA

Williams, Pete (Journalist)
c/o Chris Fenton *DMG Entertainment*
9290 Civic Center Dr # E
Beverly Hills, CA 90210-3714, USA

Williams, Pharrell (Actor, Composer, Musician)
c/o Caron Veazy *Maverick*
9350 Civic Center Dr
Beverly Hills, CA 90210-3629, USA

Williams, Porsha (Stewart) (Reality Star, Television Host)
Hosea Helps
8 E Lake Dr NE
Atlanta, GA 30317-2808, USA

Williams, Prince Charles (Boxer)
Boxing Ministry
3675 Polley Dr
Austintown, OH 44515-3349, USA

Williams, Randy (Athlete, Baseball Player)
610 Reynaldo St
Dickinson, TX 77539-6123, USA

Williams, Randy (Athlete, Track Athlete)
5655 N Marty Ave Apt 204
Fresno, CA 93711-1575, USA

Williams, Reggie (Athlete, Baseball Player)
9300 Clearstone Cv
Collierville, TN 38017-9414, USA

Williams, Reggie (Athlete, Baseball Player)
4313 Whitney Dr
North Charleston, SC 29405-6831, USA

Williams, Reggie (Athlete, Basketball Player)
2016 Callaway St
Temple Hills, MD 20748-4354, USA

Williams, Reginald (Reggie) (Athlete, Football Player)
503 Jennifer Ln
Windermere, FL 34786-8400, USA

Williams, Reuben (Baseball Player)
Chicago American Giants
PO Box 3982
Winter Haven, FL 33885-3982, USA

Williams, Richard (Cartoonist)
138 Royal College Street
London, NWI OTA, England

Williams, Rick (Athlete, Baseball Player, Coach)
1217 Wessmith Way
Madera, CA 93638-1854, USA

Williams, Robbie (Musician)
c/o Josie Cliff *ie Music Ltd*
111 Frithville Gardens
Shepherds Bush
London W12 7JQ, UNITED KINGDOM (UK)

Williams, Robert (Artist)
c/o Staff Member *Fantagraphics Books*
7563 Lake City Way NE
Seattle, WA 98115-4218, USA

Williams, Robert (Baseball Player)
Newark Eagles
6233 Delancey St
Philadelphia, PA 19143-1019, USA

Williams, Robert A (Athlete, Football Player)
602 Stone Barn Rd
Towson, MD 21286-1418, USA

Williams, Robert C (Athlete, Football Player)
347 Walnut Grove Ln
Coppell, TX 75019-5342, USA

Williams, Robert J (Ben) (Athlete, Football Player)
5961 Huntview Dr
Jackson, MS 39206-2128, USA

Williams, Rodney (Athlete, Football Player)
44520 15th St E Unit 3
Lancaster, CA 93535-6321, USA

Williams, Roland (Athlete, Football Player)
5671 Wrenwyck Pl
Weldon Spring, MO 63304-1240, USA

Williams, Rosel (Athlete, Baseball Player)
Birmingham Black Barons
PO Box 442
Ninety Six, SC 29666-0442, USA

Williams, Roshumba (Model)
c/o Gail Parenteau *Parenteau Guidance*
132 E 35th St # J
New York, NY 10016-3892, USA

Williams, Rowan (Religious Leader)
Lambert Palace
London SE1 9JU, UNITED KINGDOM (UK)

Williams, Roy (Athlete, Football Player)
1 Cowboys Pkwy
Irving, TX 75063-4924, USA

Williams, Sam (Athlete, Basketball Player)
9751 W Teresa Ln
Milwaukee, WI 53224-4651, USA

Williams, Sam (Athlete, Football Player)
28960 Westfield St
Livonia, MI 48150-3137, USA

Williams, Samuel (Athlete, Basketball Player)
6116 S Verdun Ave
Los Angeles, CA 90043-3632, USA

Williams, Scott (Athlete, Football Player)
284 Heathrow Dr
Riverdale, GA 30274-2729, USA

Williams, Scott (Basketball Player)
Phoenix Suns
8217 N Coconino Rd
Paradise Valley, AZ 85253-8104, USA

Williams, Serena (Athlete, Olympic Athlete, Tennis Player)
6231 Pga Blvd Ste 104
Palm Beach Gardens, FL 33418-4033, USA

Williams, Shad (Athlete, Baseball Player)
4682 E Cornell Ave
Fresno, CA 93703-1607, USA

Williams, Shammond (Athlete, Basketball Player)
200 Gardner Cir
Chapel Hill, NC 27516-8373, USA

Williams, Shaun (Athlete, Football Player)
11738 Gruen St
Lake View Terrace, CA 91342-6117, USA

Williams, Shawn (Athlete, Football Player)
c/o Anthony J. Agnone *Eastern Athletic Services*
11350 McCormick Rd
Suite 800 - Executive Plaza
Hunt Valley, MD 21031-1002, USA

Williams, Shawne (Athlete, Basketball Player)
c/o Travis King *Relativity Sports*
2029 Century Park E Ste 1550
Century City, CA 90067-3000, USA

Williams, Sherman (Athlete, Football Player)
119 Patricia Ave
Prichard, AL 36610-2114, USA

Williams, Sidney (Athlete, Football Player)
1044 W 82nd St
Los Angeles, CA 90044-3518, USA

Williams, Simon (Actor)
Rebecca Blond Assoc
69A Kings Road
London SW3 4NX, UNITED KINGDOM (UK)

Williams, Stanley W (Stan) (Athlete, Baseball Player)
4702 Hayter Ave
Lakewood, CA 90712-3509, USA

Williams, Stepfret (Athlete, Football Player)
913 S Talton St
Minden, LA 71055-5448, USA

Williams, Stephanie E (Actor)
S M S Talent
8730 W Sunset Blvd Ste 440
Los Angeles, CA 90069-2277, USA

Williams, Stephen (Misc)
1017 Foothills Trl
Santa Fe, NM 87505-4537, USA

Williams, Steven (Actor)
c/o Richard Kerner *Kerner Management Associates*
311 N Robertson Blvd # 288
Beverly Hills, CA 90211-1705, USA

Williams, Sun ita L Cdr (Astronaut)
1522 Festival Dr
Houston, TX 77062-4526, USA

Williams, Sylvester (Athlete, Football Player)
c/o Todd France *Creative Artists Agency (CAA) Sports*
3500 Lenox Rd NE
Atlanta, GA 30326-4228, USA

Williams, Tamika (Basketball Player)
Minnesota Lunx
600 1st Ave N Ste Sky
Target Center
Minneapolis, MN 55403-1400, USA

Williams, Tank (Athlete, Football Player)
c/o Staff Member *New England Patriots*
1 Patriot Pl
Foxboro, MA 02035-1388, USA

Williams, Tavares (Monty) (Athlete, Basketball Coach, Basketball Player, Coach)
c/o Steve Kauffman *Kauffman Sports Management Group*
Prefers to be contacted by telephone
Malibu, CA, USA

Williams, Terrance (Athlete, Football Player)
c/o W Vann McElroy *Select Sports Group*
2700 Post Oak Blvd Ste 1450
Houston, TX 77056-5785, USA

Williams, Terry (Musician)
Damage Mgmt
16 Lambton Place
London W11 2SH, UNITED KINGDOM (UK)

Williams, Thomas S Cardinal (Religious Leader)
Viard
21 Eccleston Hill Po Box 198
Wellington 00001, NEW ZELAND

Williams, Todd (Actor)
c/o Scott Manners *Artists & Representatives (Stone Manners Salners)*
6100 Wilshire Blvd Ste 1500
Los Angeles, CA 90048-5110, USA

Williams, Todd (Athlete, Baseball Player)
16707 Whispering Glen Dr
Lutz, FL 33558-4960, USA

Williams, Tom (Athlete, Hockey Player)
2411 Princess Ave
Windsor, ON N8T 1V2, Canada

Williams, Tony (Athlete, Football Player)
1321 W Liberty Dr
Wheaton, IL 60187-4740, USA

Williams, Tonya Lee (Actor)
c/o Sheila Legette *Media Artists Group*
8222 Melrose Ave Ste 304
Los Angeles, CA 90046-6839, USA

Williams, Tourek (Athlete, Football Player)

Williams, Tramon (Athlete, Football Player)

Williams, Treat (Actor)
2554 Silver Cloud Ct
Park City, UT 84060-7068, USA

Williams, Trent (Athlete, Football Player)
c/o Ben Dogra *Relativity Sports*
2029 Century Park E Ste 1550
Century City, CA 90067-3000, USA

Williams, Tyler James (Actor)
c/o Staff Member *Osbrink Talent Agency*
4343 Lankershim Blvd # 100
North Hollywood, CA 91602-2705, USA

Williams, Tyrone (Athlete, Football Player)
9516 Valley Ranch Pkwy E Apt 1024
Irving, TX 75063-7851, USA

Williams, Ulis (Athlete, Track Athlete)
2511 29th St
Santa Monica, CA 90405-2913, USA

Williams, Van (Athlete, Football Player)
1804 Parkwood Ln Apt 26
Johnson City, TN 37604-7784, USA

Williams, Vanessa (Actor, Musician)
c/o Brad Cafarelli *PMK/BNC Public Relations*
1840 Century Park E Ste 1400
Los Angeles, CA 90067-2115, USA

Williams, Vanessa Lynn (Actor)
c/o Linda Jones *The Mass Appeal*
11607 Burbank Blvd Ste A
N Hollywood, CA 91601-2345, USA

Williams, Venus (Athlete, Olympic Athlete, Tennis Player)
6231 Pga Blvd Ste 104
Palm Beach Gardens, FL 33418-4033, USA

Williams, Victoria (Musician, Songwriter, Writer)
PO Box 342
Joshua Tree, CA 92252-0342, USA

Williams, Victor L (Actor, Musician)

Williams, Vince (Athlete, Football Player)
c/o Ashley Smith Becker *Relativity Sports*
2029 Century Park E Ste 1550
Century City, CA 90067-3000, USA

Williams, Virginia (Actor)
c/o Kelsey Hertel *S/W PR Shop*
584 N Larchmont Blvd # B
Los Angeles, CA 90004-1306, USA

Williams, Wade (Actor)
5445 Buffalo Ave
Sherman Oaks, CA 91401-5224, USA

Williams, Walt (Athlete, Basketball Player)
3240 Beaumont St
Temple Hills, MD 20748-4541, USA

Williams, Walter (Musician)
Associated Booking Corp
1995 Broadway # 501
New York, NY 10023-5882, USA

Williams, Warren Milton (Butch) (Athlete, Hockey Player)
518 N 15th Ave E
Duluth, MN 55812-1237, USA

Williams, W Clyde (Religious Leader)
Christian Methodist Episcopal Church
4466 Elvis Presley Blvd
Memphis, TN 38116-7180, USA

Williams, Wendy (Radio Personality, Talk Show Host)
The Wendy Williams Show
221 W 26th St
New York, NY 10001-6703, USA

Williams, Wendy Lian (Athlete, Swimmer)
Advantage International
1025 Thomas Jefferson St NW # 450
Washington, DC 20007-5201, USA

Williams, William A (Astronaut)
Environmental Protection Agency
200 SW 35th St
Corvallis, OR 97333-4902, USA

Williams, Willie (Athlete, Football Player)
4928 Country Club Dr
Mesquite, TX 75150-1169, USA

Williams, Willie (Athlete, Football Player)
1402 Forest Edge Ct
Wexford, PA 15090-9598, USA

Williams, Willie (Baseball Player)
Newark Eagles
2729 20th St
Sarasota, FL 34234-7807, USA

Williams, Woody (Athlete, Baseball Player)
5110 Newpoint Dr
Fresno, TX 77545-9212, USA

Williams, Zelda (Actor)
c/o Allison Band *Gersh*
9465 Wilshire Blvd Ste 600
Beverly Hills, CA 90212-2605, USA

Williams Brothers (Music Group, Musician)
c/o Staff Member *M.A.G./Universal Attractions*
15 W 36th St Fl 8
New York, NY 10018-7927, USA

Williams III, Clarance (Actor)
c/o Staff Member *Abrams Artists Agency*
750 N San Vicente Blvd
E Tower Fl 11
Los Angeles, CA 90069-5788, USA

Williams III, James (Fly) (Actor)
c/o Margaret Matuka *Schuller Talent (NY)*
276 5th Ave Rm 206
New York, NY 10001-4509, USA

Williams III, Shelton Hank (Musician)
c/o Mitch Schneider *Mitch Schneider Organization (MSO)*
14724 Ventura Blvd Ste 410
Sherman Oaks, CA 91403-3537, USA

Williams Jr, Ernest H (Writer)
c/o Staff Member *Oxford University Press*
Great Clarendon Street
Oxford OX2 6DP, UNITED KINGDOM

Williams Jr, Hank (Actor, Musician, Songwriter)
c/o Ken Levitan *Vector Management*
PO Box 120479
Nashville, TN 37212-0479, USA

Williams Jr, Warren (Athlete, Football Player)
1935 Pauldo St
Fort Myers, FL 33916-4122, USA

Williamson, Antone (Athlete, Baseball Player)
9419 S Stanley Pl
Tempe, AZ 85284-4109, USA

Williamson, Avery (Athlete, Football Player)
c/o Neil Cornrich *NC Sports, LLC*
best to contact via email
Columbus, OH 43201, USA

Williamson, Corliss (Basketball Player)
c/o Staff Member *Sacramento Kings*
1 Sports Pkwy
Sacramento, CA 95834-2301, USA

Williamson, Cris (Musician)
Bird Ankles Music
PO Box 30067
Seattle, WA 98113-2067, USA

Williamson, Fred (Actor, Athlete, Football Player)
c/o David Levy Martin *Momentum Talent and Literary Agency*
3500 W Olive Ave Ste 300
Burbank, CA 91505-4647, USA

Williamson, Jay (Athlete, Golfer)
24 Clermont Ln
Saint Louis, MO 63124-1346, USA

Williamson, Joanne S (Writer)
c/o Staff Member *Bethlehem Books*
10194 Garfield St S
Bathgate, ND 58216-4031, USA

Williamson, Joe (Actor)
c/o Sharon Paz *Abrams Artists Agency*
750 N San Vicente Blvd
E Tower Fl 11
Los Angeles, CA 90069-5788, USA

Williamson, Kerry (Writer)
c/o Staff Member *Gersh*
9465 Wilshire Blvd Ste 600
Beverly Hills, CA 90212-2605, USA

Williamson, Kevin (Director, Producer, Writer)
326 S Windsor Blvd
Los Angeles, CA 90020-4712, USA

Williamson, Marianne (Writer)
Los Angeles Center for Living
8265 W Sunset Blvd
West Hollywood, CA 90046-2429, USA

Williamson, Mark (Athlete, Baseball Player)
1260 Hidden Mountain Dr
El Cajon, CA 92019-3639, USA

Williamson, Michael (Journalist)
Washington Post
18334 Streamside Dr APT 301
Gaithersburg, MD 20879-5234, USA

Williamson, Michael (Writer)
18334 Streamside Dr APT 301
Gaithersburg, MD 20879-5234, USA

Williamson, Mykelti (Actor)
c/o Michael Geiser *Jill Fritzo Public Relations*
208 E 51st St # 305
New York, NY 10022-6557, USA

Williamson, Richard (Athlete, Football Coach, Football Player)
3412 Oak Grove Cir
Montgomery, AL 36116-1183, USA

Williamson, Scott (Athlete, Baseball Player)
21563 Fox Rd
Guilford, IN 47022-9706, USA

Williamson, Shaun (Actor)
McIntosh Rae Management
Thornton House
Thornton Road
London SW19 4NG, ENGLAND

Williams-Paisley, Kimberly (Actor, Producer)
c/o Brian Wilkins *LINK Entertainment*
11872 La Grange Ave
Los Angeles, CA 90025-5282, USA

Williford, Duncan (Athlete, Basketball Player)
3703 Westfield St
High Point, NC 27265-2113, USA

Williford, Vann (Athlete, Basketball Player)
4455 Fair Oaks Ln
High Point, NC 27265-8705, USA

Willig, Matt (Actor, Athlete, Football Player)
c/o Lee Wallman *Wallman Public Relations*
3859 Goldwyn Ter
Culver City, CA 90232-3103, USA

Willimon, Beau (Producer, Writer)
c/o Staff Member *PMK/BNC Public Relations*
1840 Century Park E Ste 1400
Los Angeles, CA 90067-2115, USA

Willingham, Josh (Athlete, Baseball Player)
108 Cascade Dr
Florence, AL 35633-7621, USA

Willingham, Larry (Athlete, Football Player)
983 W Lagoon Ave
Gulf Shores, AL 36542-6301, USA

Willingham, Tyrone (Coach, Football Coach)
University of Washington
Athletic Dept
Seattle, WA 98195-0001, USA

Willis, Bruce (Actor)
PO Box 2343
Hailey, ID 83333-2343, USA

Willis, Carl (Athlete, Baseball Player)
6811 Lipscomb Dr
Durham, NC 27712-9292, USA

Willis, Connie (Writer)
c/o Staff Member *Random House Publicity*
1745 Broadway Frnt 3
New York, NY 10019-4343, USA

Willis, Dale (Athlete, Baseball Player)
3415 Hayes Bayou Dr
Ruskin, FL 33570-6157, USA

Willis, Dave (Writer)
c/o Staff Member *WME|IMG*
9601 Wilshire Blvd
Beverly Hills, CA 90210-5213, USA

Willis, Dontrelle (Athlete, Baseball Player)
9820 E Thompson Peak Pkwv Unit 726
Scottsdale, AZ 85255-6657, USA

Willis, Fred (Athlete, Football Player)
31 Blithewood Ave Apt 601
Worcester, MA 01604-3558, USA

Willis, Garrett (Athlete, Golfer)
628 Mountain Pass Ln
Knoxville, TN 37923-5725, USA

Willis, Jim (Artist)
5323 SW 53rd Ct
Portland, OR 97221-1937, USA

Willis, Jim (Athlete, Baseball Player)
PO Box 35
Boyce, LA 71409-0035, USA

Willis, Katherine (Actor)

Willis, Keith (Athlete, Football Player)
114 Birdo Point Way
Garner, NC 27529-6649, USA

Willis, Kelly (Musician)
c/o Staff Member *Davis McLarty Agency*
708 S Lamar Blvd Ste D
Austin, TX 78704-1541, USA

Willis, Kevin A (Athlete, Basketball Player)
1481 Jones Rd
Roswell, GA 30075-2723, USA

Willis, Mark (Musician)
c/o Staff Member *WME (Nashville)*
1201 Demonbreun St
Nashville, TN 37203-3140, USA

Willis, Mike (Athlete, Baseball Player)
6234 Taggart St
Houston, TX 77007-2051, USA

Willis, Mitch (Athlete, Football Player)
1398 Fairhaven Dr
Mansfield, TX 76063-3765, USA

Willis, Nadine (Model)
c/o Staff Member *New York Model Management*
71 W 23rd St Ste 301
New York, NY 10010-3519, USA

Willis, Patrick (Athlete, Football Player)
c/o Denise White *EAG Sports Management*
909 N Pacific Coast Hwy Ste 360
El Segundo, CA 90245-3864, USA

Willis, Pete (Musician)
Q Prime Mgmt
729 7th Ave Ste 1400
New York, NY 10019-6889, USA

Willis, Peter Tom (Athlete, Football Player)
PO Box 237
Morris, AL 35116-0237, USA

Willis, Rumer (Actor)
c/o Jennifer Merlino *Untitled Entertainment*
350 S Beverly Dr Ste 200
Beverly Hills, CA 90212-4819, USA

Willison, Mike (Musician)
Metropolitan Entertainment Group
2 Penn Plz Rm 1549
New York, NY 10121-1704, USA

Willman, David (Journalist)
Los Angeles Times
2300 E Imperial Hwy
Editorial Dept
El Segundo, CA 90245-2813, USA

Willman, Justin (Actor, Magician)
c/o Rob Greenwald *Rogers & Cowan*
1840 Century Park E Fl 18
Los Angeles, CA 90067-2101, USA

Willmon, Trent (Musician)
Hallmark Direction Company
713 18th Ave S
C/O Shelia Shipley Biddy
Nashville, TN 37203-3214, USA

Willms, Andre (Athlete)
Rennebogen 94
Magdeburg 39130, GERMANY

Willoch, Kare I (Prime Minister)
Fr Nansens V 17
Lysaker 01324, NORWAY

Willoughby, Bill (Basketball Player)
350 W Englewood Ave
Englewood, NJ 07631-3239, USA

Willoughby, Holly (Television Host)
This Morning
LTS
London SE1 9LT, UNITED KINGDOM

Willoughby, Jim (Athlete, Baseball Player)
PO Box 707
Eufaula, OK 74432-0707, USA

Wills, Dave (Sportscaster)
PO Box 4057
Eatonton, GA 31024-4057, U S A

Wills, Elliott (Bump) (Athlete, Baseball Player)
1124 S Robinhood St
Spokane Valley, WA 99206-6951, USA

Wills, Maurice M (Maury) (Athlete, Baseball Player, Coach)
M & R Sports Marketing
5 Dalton Valley Dr
Saint Peters, MO 63376-7720, USA

Wills, Rick (Musician)
Hard to Handle Mgmt
16501 Ventura Blvd Ste 602
Encino, CA 91436-2072, USA

Wills, Ted (Athlete, Baseball Player)
10585 E Duckpoint Way
Clovis, CA 93619-4629, USA

Willson, Don (Athlete, Hockey Player)
1303 Rendezvous Dr
Windsor, ON N8P 1K7, Canada

Willson, John (Business Person)
Placer Dome Inc
1600-1055 Dunsmuir St
Vancouver, BC V7X 1P1, CANADA

Will to Power (Music Group)
c/o Staff Member *Diva Central Inc*
7510 W Sunset Blvd # 1445
Los Angeles, CA 90046-3408, USA

Wilmarth, Dick (Misc)
1111 F St
Anchorage, AK 99501-4344, USA

Wilmer, Douglas (Actor)
Julian Belfarge
46 Albermarle St
London W1X 4PP, UNITED KINGDOM (UK)

Wilmes, Gary (Actor)
c/o Ruthanne Secunda *ICM Partners*
10250 Constellation Blvd Fl 7
Los Angeles, CA 90067-6207, USA

Wilmet, Paul (Athlete, Baseball Player)
716 4th St
De Pere, WI 54115-1928, USA

Wilmore, Barry E (Astronaut)
3002 Bryant Ln
Webster, TX 77598-6011, USA

Wilmore, Barry E Cdr (Astronaut)
3002 Bryant Ln
Webster, TX 77598-6011, USA

Wilmore, Larry (Actor, Producer)
c/o Lewis Kay *Kovert Creative*
506 Santa Monica Blvd Ste 400
Santa Monica, CA 90401-2412, USA

Wilmsmeyer, Klaus (Athlete, Football Player)
1509 Bellingham Ct
Louisville, KY 40245-4488, USA

Wilmut, Ian (Misc)
Roslin Institute
Roslin Bio Centre
Midlothian EH25 9PS, SCOTLAND

Wilpon, Fred (Baseball Player)
New York Mets
100 Sheep Ln
Locust Valley, NY 11560-1115, USA

Wilson, Adrian (Athlete, Football Player)
c/o Eugene Parker *Independent Sports & Entertainment (ISE-IN)*
6435 W Jefferson Blvd # 197
Fort Wayne, IN 46804-6203, USA

Wilson, Al (Athlete, Football Player)
3445 Stratford Rd NE Apt 3901
Atlanta, GA 30326-1728, USA

Wilson, Alexandra (Actor)
c/o Staff Member *GVA Talent Agency Inc*
193 N Robertson Blvd
Beverly Hills, CA 90211-2103, USA

Wilson, A N (Writer)
21 Arlington Road
London NW1 7ER, UNITED KINGDOM (UK)

Wilson, Ann (Actor, Musician)
2410 Boyer Ave E Apt 108
Seattle, WA 98112-2140, USA

Wilson, Behn (Athlete, Hockey Player)
955 Bolender Dr
Delray Beach, FL 33483-4970, USA

Wilson, Ben (Athlete, Football Player)
702 Maple St
Crossett, AR 71635-3520, USA

Wilson, Bill (Athlete, Baseball Player)
132 Wickenby Ct
Roseville, CA 95661-4044, USA

Wilson, Blaine (Athlete, Gymnast, Olympic Athlete)
7441 Murrayfield Dr
Columbus, OH 43085-1739, USA

Wilson, Bob (Athlete, Baseball Player)
8301 Old Sauk Rd APT 201
Middleton, WI 53562-4392, USA

Wilson, Brian (Musician, Songwriter)
c/o Jean Sievers *Beachwood Entertainment Collective*
2271 Cheremoya Ave
Los Angeles, CA 90068-3006, USA

Wilson, Brian (Athlete, Baseball Player)
741 S Banning Cir
Mesa, AZ 85206-4104, USA

Wilson, Brian (Athlete, Basketball Player)
1201 Hummingbird Hill Rd
Chapel Hill, NC 27517-7791, USA

Wilson, Brian Anthony (Actor)
Bernard Liebhaber
352 7th Ave
New York, NY 10001-5012, USA

Wilson, Carey (Athlete, Hockey Player)
85 Jean Louis Rd
Winnipeg, MB R2N 4A9, CANADA

Wilson, Carnie (Musician)
c/o Terry Anzaldo *Good Guy Entertainment*
555 Esplanade Apt 316
Redondo Beach, CA 90277-4085, USA

Wilson, Casey (Actor)
c/o Staff Member *Odenkirk Provissiero Entertainment*
1936 N Bronson Ave
Raleigh Studios
Los Angeles, CA 90068-5602, USA

Wilson, Cassandra (Musician)
Dream Street Mgmt
4346 Redwood Ave Unit 307
Marina Del Rey, CA 90292-6495, USA

Wilson, Chandra (Actor)
c/o Edie Robb *Station3 (NY)*
300 W 55th St Apt 5L
New York, NY 10019-5163, USA

Wilson, Charles (Athlete, Football Player)
5444 Calder Dr
Tallahassee, FL 32317-1429, USA

Wilson, Charlie (Musician)
c/o Michael Paran *P Music Group*
11511 Vimy Rd
Granada Hills, CA 91344-2138, USA

Wilson, Cherilyn (Actor)
c/o Jon Simmons *Simmons & Scott Entertainment*
7942 Mulholland Dr
Los Angeles, CA 90046-1225, USA

Wilson, Chris (Musician)
c/o Staff Member *Fein Music*
81 Pondfield Rd Ste 236
Bronxville, NY 10708-3818, USA

Wilson, Cindy (Musician)
5343 Vernon Lake Dr
Atlanta, GA 30338-3526, USA

Wilson, C.J. (Athlete, Football Player)
c/o Pat Dye Jr *SportsTrust Advisors*
3340 Peachtree Rd NE Fl 16
Atlanta, GA 30326-1000, USA

Wilson, Craig (Athlete, Baseball Player)
461 S Brent St
Ventura, CA 93003-4706, USA

Wilson, Dan (Musician, Songwriter, Writer)
Monterey Peninsula Artists
509 Hartnell St
Monterey, CA 93940-2825, USA

Wilson, Daniel A (Dan) (Athlete, Baseball Player)
1150 18th Ave E
Seattle, WA 98112-3319, USA

Wilson, Daniel H (Writer)
c/o Linda Chester *Linda Chester Literary Agency*
630 Fifth Ave Ste 2036
Rockefeller Center
New York, NY 10111-2901, USA

Wilson, Dave (Athlete, Football Player)
4301 San Rufino Cir
Yorba Linda, CA 92886-2351, USA

Wilson, David (Athlete, Football Player)
c/o Joel Segal *Lagardere Unlimited (NY)*
456 Washington St Apt 9L
New York, NY 10013-1555, USA

Wilson, Dean (Athlete, Golfer)
10914 Iris Canyon Ln
Las Vegas, NV 89135-1719, USA

Wilson, De'Angelo (Actor)

Wilson, Debra (Actor)
c/o Charles Riley *Charles Riley*
7122 Beverly Blvd Ste F
Los Angeles, CA 90036-2572, USA

Wilson, Desi (Athlete, Baseball Player)
8 Janet Ln
Glen Cove, NY 11542-2809, USA

Wilson, Desire (Race Car Driver)
4197 Serenade Rd
Castle Rock, CO 80104-7716, USA

Wilson, Dorien (Actor)
c/o Penny Vizcarra *PV Public Relations*
121 N Almont Dr Apt 203
Beverly Hills, CA 90211-1860, USA

Wilson, Doug (Athlete, Hockey Player)
San Jose Sharks
525 W Santa Clara St
Attn: General Manager
San Jose, CA 95113-1500, USA

Wilson, Doug (Athlete, Hockey Player)
9444 E Legacy Cove Cir
Scottsdale, AZ 85255-6556, USA

Wilson, Duane (Athlete, Baseball Player)
1945 N Porter Ave Apt A54
Wichita, KS 67203-2293, USA

Wilson, Dune (Athlete, Hockey Player)
PO Box 28
Rossland, BC V0G 1Y0, Canada

Wilson, Earl (Athlete, Football Player)
1510 W Riverside Dr
Atlantic City, NJ 08401-1643, USA

Wilson, Earle L (Religious Leader)
Wesleyan Church
PO Box 50434
Indianapolis, IN 46250-0434, USA

Wilson, Edward O (Writer)
Harvard University
Department of Organismic and
Evolutionary Biology
Cambridge, MA 02138, USA

Wilson, F Paul (Writer)
1933 State Route 35 Ste 337
Wall Township, NJ 07719-3502, USA

Wilson, Frank (Race Car Driver)
North Carlonia Motor Speedway
PO Box 500
Rockingham, NC 28380, USA

Wilson, Gahan (Cartoonist)
New Yorker Magazine
PO Box 1558
Sag Harbor, NY 11963-0057, USA

Wilson, Gale (Race Car Driver)
203 Nortbmont Dr.
Statesville, NC 28677, USA

Wilson, Gary (Athlete, Baseball Player)
327 40th St
Sacramento, CA 95819-2027, USA

Wilson, Gary (Athlete, Baseball Player)
713 Ouachita 64
Camden, AR 71701-9616, USA

Wilson, George (Athlete, Football Player)
c/o Todd France *Creative Artists Agency (CAA) Sports*
3500 Lenox Rd NE
Atlanta, GA 30326-4228, USA

Wilson, George (Athlete, Basketball Player, Olympic Athlete)
151 Twin Lakes Dr
Fairfield, OH 45014-5257, USA

Wilson, Georges (Director)
Moulin de Vilgris
Rambouillet 78120, FRANCE

Wilson, Glenn (Athlete, Baseball Player)
300 Tara Park
Conroe, TX 77302-3756, USA

wilson, Gord (Athlete, Hockey Player)
Ottawa Senators
110-1000 Palladium Dr
Attn: Broadcast Dept
Ottawa, ON K2V 1A5, Canada

Wilson, Gretchen (Musician)
c/o Dale Morris *Morris Artists Management*
2001 Blair Blvd
Nashville, TN 37212-5007, USA

Wilson, Harry (Athlete, Football Player)
3010 N Bonsall St
Philadelphia, PA 19132-1402, USA

Wilson, Harry C (Religious Leader)
Wesleyan Church Int'l Center
6060 Castleway West Dr
Indianapolis, IN 46250-1906, USA

Wilson, Jack (Athlete, Baseball Player)
365 E Avenida De Los Arboles
Thousand Oaks, CA 91360-2975, USA

Wilson, James (Athlete, Football Player)
877 NW Charlie Horse Dr
Lake City, FL 32055-9294, USA

Wilson, J C (Athlete, Football Player)
4785 Young Rd
Waldorf, MD 20601-4483, USA

Wilson, J C (Athlete, Football Player)
13410 Buchanan Dr
Fort Washington, MD 20744-2931, USA

Wilson, Jeannie (Actor)
General Delivery
Ketchum, ID 83340-9999, USA

Wilson, Jerry (Athlete, Football Player)
2117 Mountain View Dr
Vestavia Hills, AL 35216-2023, USA

Wilson, Jerry (Athlete, Football Player)
4272 Ironwood Ct
Weston, FL 33331-3827, USA

Wilson, Jim (Athlete, Baseball Player)
8112 NW Bacon Rd
Vancouver, WA 98665-6634, USA

Wilson, Jimmy (Athlete, Football Player)
c/o Drew Rosenhaus *Rosenhaus Sports Representation*
3921 Alton Rd # 440
Miami Beach, FL 33140-3852, USA

Wilson, Joe (Athlete, Football Player)
323 Carlton Dr
Milton, DE 19968-1368, USA

Wilson, Joe (Congressman, Politician)
2229 Rayburn Hob
Washington, DC 20515-2105, USA

Wilson, Josh (Athlete, Baseball Player)
2304 Cramden Rd
Pittsburgh, PA 15241-2438, USA

Wilson, J Tylee (Business Person)
PO Box 2057
Ponte Vedra Beach, FL 32004-2057, USA

Wilson, Justin (Musician)
David Levin Mgmt
200 W 57th St Ste 308
New York, NY 10019-3211, USA

Wilson, Kim (Musician)
Ricci Assoc
28205 Agoura Rd Ste A
Agoura Hills, CA 91301-2431, USA

Wilson, Kris (Athlete, Baseball Player)
PO Box 15
Chillicothe, MO 64601-0015, USA

Wilson, Kristen (Actor)
c/o Rick Genow *Stone, Meyer, Genow, Smelkinson and Binder*
9665 Wilshire Blvd Ste 500
Beverly Hills, CA 90212-2312, USA

Wilson, Kyle (Athlete, Football Player)
c/o Patricia Mora *Metro Public Relations*
8671 Wilshire Blvd # 208
Beverly Hills, CA 90211-2926, USA

Wilson, Lambert (Actor)
91 rue Saint-Honore
Paris 75001, FRANCE

Wilson, Landon (Athlete, Hockey Player)
127 Tennyson Pl
Coppell, TX 75019-5364

Wilson, Lawrence F (Larry) (Athlete, Football Player)
11834 N Blackheath Rd
Scottsdale, AZ 85254-4809, USA

Wilson, Luke (Actor)
615 San Lorenzo St
Santa Monica, CA 90402-1321, USA

Wilson, Lulu (Actor)
c/o Joshua Pasch *Authentic Talent & Literary Management*
3615 Eastham Dr # 650
Culver City, CA 90232-2410, USA

Wilson, Mara (Actor, Writer)
c/o Hannah Tenenbaum *Paradigm*
8942 Wilshire Blvd
Beverly Hills, CA 90211-1908, USA

Wilson, Marc (Athlete, Football Player)
4200 N Seasons View Dr Apt D3040
Lehi, UT 84043-6219, USA

Wilson, Marc D (Athlete, Football Player)
113113 Mount Wallace Ct
Alta Loma, CA 91737, USA

Wilson, Mark (Athlete, Golfer)
N41W27751 Ishnala Trl
Pewaukee, WI 53072-2140, USA

Wilson, Marquess (Athlete, Football Player)

Wilson, Marty (Musician)
c/o Staff Member *VocalPoint*
25 Denmark St Fl 1
London WC2H 8NJ, UNITED KINGDOM (UK)

Wilson, Mary (Musician)
21 Hassayampa Trl
Henderson, NV 89052-6668, USA

Wilson, Max (Race Car Driver)
Minardi Team Spa
Via Spallanzani 21
Faenza 48018, ITALY

Wilson, Melanie (Actor)
Irv Schechter
9300 Wilshire Blvd Ste 410
Beverly Hills, CA 90212-3228, USA

Wilson, Michael G (Producer)
c/o Staff Member *Danjag*
2400 Colorado Ave
Suite 310
Santa Monica, CA 90404, USA

Wilson, Michael (Tack) (Athlete, Baseball Player)
1089 Olde Hinge Way
Snellville, GA 30078-7716, USA

Wilson, Mike (Athlete, Hockey Player)
4647 Lake Charles Dr
Independence, OH 44131-6062, USA

Wilson, Mike D (Athlete, Football Player)
1967 Litchfield Ave
Dayton, OH 45406-3811, USA

Wilson, Mike R (Athlete, Football Player)
2908 N Poinsettia Ave
Manhattan Beach, CA 90266-2405, USA

wilson, Mitch (Athlete, Hockey Player)
PO Box 343
Brinnon, WA 98320-0343, USA

Wilson, Mookie (Athlete, Baseball Player)
1111 Heyward Wilson Rd
Eastover, SC 29044-9627, USA

wilson, Murray (Athlete, Hockey Player)
Wilson Consulting
432-410 Bank St
Ottawa, ON K2P 1Y8, Canada

Wilson, Neal C (Religious Leader)
Seventh-Day Adventists
12501 Old Columbia Pike
Silver Spring, MD 20904-6600, USA

Wilson, Neil (Athlete, Baseball Player)
4300 Highway 412 W
Lexington, TN 38351-5423, USA

Wilson, Nemiah (Athlete, Football Player)
11000 E Idaho Pl
Aurora, CO 80012-4118, USA

Wilson, Nigel (Athlete, Baseball Player)
35 Sabbe Cres
Ajax, ON L1T 4E3, Canada

Wilson, Othell (Athlete, Basketball Player)
3413 Caledonia Cir
Woodbridge, VA 22192-1069, USA

Wilson, Otis (Athlete, Football Player)
7B W 15th St
Chicago, IL 60605-2723, USA

Wilson, Owen (Actor)
c/o Ina Treciokas *Slate PR*
901 N Highland Ave
W Hollywood, CA 90038-2412, USA

Wilson, Patrick (Actor, Musician)
2532 Luciernaga St
Carlsbad, CA 92009-5819, USA

Wilson, Paul (Athlete, Baseball Player)
949 Lenmore Ct
Orlando, FL 32812-1980, USA

Wilson, Peta (Actor)
c/o Julia Verdin *Rough Diamond Management*
1424 N Kings Rd
West Hollywood, CA 90069-1908, USA

Wilson, Preston (Athlete, Baseball Player)
136 Paloma Dr
Coral Gables, FL 33143-6545, USA

Wilson, Rachel (Actor)
c/o Dani De Lio *Creative Drive Artists*
20 Minowan Miikan Lane
Toronto, ON M6J 0E5, CANADA

Wilson, Rainn (Actor)
5683 Colodny Dr
Agoura Hills, CA 91301-2217, USA

Wilson, Rebel (Actor)
c/o Staff Member *Weiner Media Group*
1155 N La Cienega Blvd Apt 611
W Hollywood, CA 90069-2440, USA

Wilson, Reinard (Athlete, Football Player)
2595 NW 49th Ave Apt 108
Lauderdale Lakes, FL 33313-3354, USA

Wilson, Rick (Athlete, Basketball Player)
535 E Ormsby Ave
Louisville, KY 40203-2620, USA

Wilson, Rick (Athlete, Coach, Hockey Player)
1624 Reno Run
Lewisville, TX 75077-7522, USA

Wilson, Rick (Race Car Driver)
PO Box 304
Mulberry, FL 33860-0304, USA

Wilson, Ricky (Athlete, Basketball Player)
3014 NW Chapin Dr
Portland, OR 97229-8070, USA

Wilson, Rik (Athlete, Hockey Player)
345 Lakewood Dr
Ballwin, MO 63011-2410, USA

Wilson, Rita (Actor)
c/o Heidi Schaeffer *PMK/BNC Public Relations*
1840 Century Park E Ste 1400
Los Angeles, CA 90067-2115, USA

Wilson, Robert E (Bobby) (Athlete, Football Player)
1034 Liberty Park Dr Apt 408R
Austin, TX 78746-6854, USA

Wilson, Robert M (Actor)
RW Work
131 Varick St Ste 908
New York, NY 10013-1444, USA

Wilson, Robert Scott (Actor)
c/o Matt Vioral *Gersh*
9465 Wilshire Blvd Ste 600
Beverly Hills, CA 90212-2605, USA

Wilson, Roger (Actor)
c/o Staff Member *Joel Stevens Entertainment*
5627 Allott Ave
Van Nuys, CA 91401-4502, USA

Wilson, Ron (Athlete, Hockey Player)
400-40 Bay St
Attn: Coaching Staff Toronto Maple Leafs
Toronto, ON M5J 2X2, Canada

Wilson, Ron (Athlete, Coach, Hockey Player)
20 Strandhill Ave
Bluffton, SC 29910-7821, USA

Wilson, Russell (Athlete, Football Player)
c/o Chantal Artur *Sunshine Sachs*
720 Cole Ave
Los Angeles, CA 90038-3606, USA

Wilson, Ruth (Actor)
c/o Jessica Kolstad *Relevant*
400 S Beverly Dr Ste 220
Beverly Hills, CA 90212-4404, USA

Wilson, Ryan (Actor)
c/o Cindy Osbrink *Osbrink Talent Agency*
4343 Lankershim Blvd # 100
North Hollywood, CA 91602-2705, USA

Wilson, Sherlee (Actor)
c/o Staff Member *Cunningham Escott Slevin & Doherty (CESD)*
10635 Santa Monica Blvd Ste 130
Los Angeles, CA 90025-8306, USA

Wilson, Stephanie D (Astronaut)
14910 Hollydale Dr
Houston, TX 77062-2907, USA

Wilson, Stephen (Athlete, Basketball Player)
71 S Jones Creek Ln
Pine, CO 80470-9675, USA

Wilson, Steve (Athlete, Baseball Player)
23-1041 Comox St
Vancouver, BC V6E 1K1, Canada

Wilson, Steve (Athlete, Football Player)
3503 Brymore Ct
Pearland, TX 77584, USA

Wilson, Steven (Musician)
c/o Kim Estlund *Baker Winokur Ryder Public Relations*
9100 Wilshire Blvd Ste 700E
W Tower #500
Beverly Hills, CA 90212-3423, USA

Wilson, Stuart (Actor)

Wilson, Tavon (Athlete, Football Player)
c/o Chad Wiestling *Integrated Sports Management*
2120 Texas St Apt 2204
Houston, TX 77003-3054, USA

Wilson, Thomas L (Athlete, Football Player)
4342 Oakdale Pl
Pittsburg, CA 94565-6256, USA

Wilson, Thomas (Tom) F (Actor)
c/o Alex Murray *Brillstein Entertainment Partners*
9150 Wilshire Blvd Ste 350
Beverly Hills, CA 90212-3453, USA

Wilson, TJ (Tyson Kidd) (Athlete, Wrestler)
6617 Marina Pt Vlg Ct Apt 305
Tampa, FL 33635-9034, USA

Wilson, Tom (Athlete, Baseball Player)
1833 E Troon Dr
Lake Havasu City, AZ 86404-5970, USA

Wilson, Torrie (Model, Wrestler)
525 Woods Landing Trl
Oldsmar, FL 34677-4220, USA

Wilson, Trevor (Athlete, Baseball Player)
11857 White Ln
Oregon City, OR 97045-5716, USA

Wilson, Trevor (Athlete, Basketball Player)
824 15th St
Hermosa Beach, CA 90254-3202, USA

Wilson, Troy (Athlete, Football Player)
14213 W 138th Pl
Olathe, KS 66062-5877, USA

Wilson, Vance (Athlete, Baseball Player)
6368 Elizabeth Ave
Springdale, AR 72762-4234, USA

Wilson, Wayne (Athlete, Football Player)
5430 Lynx Ln Apt 152
Columbia, MD 21044-2301, USA

Wilson, Wendy (Musician)
4316 Bellaire Ave
Studio City, CA 91604-1526, USA

Wilson, William (Athlete, Basketball Player)
130 Belmont St
Englewood, NJ 07631-1502, USA

Wilson, Willie (Athlete, Baseball Player)
15328 W Surrey Dr
Surprise, AZ 85379-8165, USA

Wilson, Woody (Cartoonist)
c/o Staff Member *King Features Syndication*
300 W 57th St Fl 15
New York, NY 10019-5238, USA

Wilson David, Mackenzie (Director)
Lifeboat House
Castletown
Isle of Man IM9 1LD, UNITED KINGDOM (UK)

Wilson Phillips (Music Group)

Wilson-Sampras, Bridgette (Actor)
c/o Andrea Pett-Joseph *Brillstein Entertainment Partners*
9150 Wilshire Blvd Ste 350
Beverly Hills, CA 90212-3453, USA

Wiltsie, Brian (Athlete, Hockey Player)
45 Meadowbrook Rd
Randolph, NJ 07869-3862, USA

Wilzig, Ivan (Musician)
1874 Deerfield Rd
Water Mill, NY 11976-2109, USA

Wimbley, Kamerion (Athlete, Football Player)
c/o Denise White *EAG Sports Management*
909 N Pacific Coast Hwy Ste 360
El Segundo, CA 90245-3864, USA

Wimmer, Brian (Actor)
c/o Jean-Pierre (JP) Henraux *Henraux Management*
Prefers to be contacted by telephone
CA, USA

Wimmer, Chris (Athlete, Baseball Player, Olympic Athlete)
4027 E Countryside Plz
Wichita, KS 67218-4103, USA

Wimmer, Kurt (Actor, Director, Producer, Writer)
c/o Tom Strickler *WME/IMG*
9601 Wilshire Blvd Ste 250
Beverly Hills, CA 90210-5230, USA

Wimmer, Scott (Race Car Driver)
Richard Childress Racing
425 Industrial Dr.
Welcome, NC 27374, USA

Winans, BeBe (Musician)
c/o Jeff Epstein *M.A.G./Universal Attractions*
15 W 36th St Fl 8
New York, NY 10018-7927, USA

Winans, CeCe (Musician)
47 Annandale
Nashville, TN 37215-5821, USA

Winans, Jeff (Athlete, Football Player)
175 21st Ave SE
Saint Petersburg, FL 33705-2826, USA

Winans, Mario (Musician)
c/o Staff Member *Combs Enterprises*
1440 Broadway Frnt 3
New York, NY 10018-2301, USA

Winans, Matthew (Matt) (Athlete, Baseball Player)
136 Grove St
Scituate, MA 02066-3625, USA

Winans, Tydus (Athlete, Football Player)
92 W Rall Ave
Clovis, CA 93612-4308, USA

Winans, Vickie (Musician)
c/o Staff Member *Covenant Agency, The*
123 California Ave Apt 116
Santa Monica, CA 90403-3560, USA

Winborne, Jamie (Athlete, Football Player)
195 Roscoe Lee Cir
Wetumpka, AL 36092-3681, USA

Winbush, Angela (Musician, Songwriter, Writer)
Joyce Agency
370 Harrison Ave
Harrison, NY 10528-2714, USA

Winbush, Camille (Actor)
c/o Judy Landis *Judy Landis Management*
Prefers to be contacted by telephone or email
Westlake Village, CA 91362, USA

Winbush, Troy (Actor)
c/o Staff Member *Paradigm*
8942 Wilshire Blvd
Beverly Hills, CA 90211-1908, USA

Winceniak, Ed (Athlete, Baseball Player)
21536 Wolf Rd Unit 3000
Mokena, IL 60448-2148, USA

Wincer, Simon (Director, Producer)
c/o Adam Kanter *Paradigm*
8942 Wilshire Blvd
Beverly Hills, CA 90211-1908, USA

Wincer, Simon G (Director)
PO Box 241
Toorak, VIC 03142, AUSTRALIA

Winchester, Brad (Athlete, Hockey Player)
15920 Sandalwood Creek Dr
Wildwood, MO 63011-5517, USA

Winchester, Philip (Actor)
c/o Jane Epstein *Independent Talent Group*
40 Whitfield St
London W1T 2RH, UNITED KINGDOM

Winchester, Scott (Athlete, Baseball Player)
4705 Oakridge Dr
Midland, MI 48640-7409, USA

Wincott, Jeff P (Actor)
Judy Shane & Associates
606 N Larchmont Blvd
Los Angeles, CA 90004-1321

Winder, Sammy (Athlete, Football Player)
Winder Construction
4823 Greens Crossing Rd
Ridgeland, MS 39157-5042, USA

Winders, Wim (Director)
Paul Kohner
9300 Wilshire Blvd Ste 555
Beverly Hills, CA 90212-3211, USA

Windhorn, Gordie (Athlete, Baseball Player)
145 Bent Creek Rd
Danville, VA 24540-5213, USA

Windis, Tony (Athlete, Basketball Player)
404 1st St
Rawlins, WY 82301-5502, USA

Windle, William F (Misc)
229 Cherry St
Granville, OH 43023-1195, USA

Windsor, Barbara (Actor, Comedian)
104 Crouch Hill
London NB 9EA, UNITED KINGDOM (UK)

Windsor, Jason Windsor (Athlete, Baseball Player)
23972 Dublin St
Lake Forest, CA 92630-2927, USA

Windsor, Robert E (Athlete, Football Player)
2625 Legends Way
Ellicott City, MD 21042-2257, USA

Windsor-Smith, Barry (Artist)
c/o Staff Member *Fantagraphics Books*
7563 Lake City Way NE
Seattle, WA 98115-4218, USA

Wine, Bobby (Athlete, Baseball Player, Coach)
2614 Woodland Ave
Norristown, PA 19403-1636, USA

Wine, David M (Religious Leader)
Church of Brethren
1451 Dundee Ave
Elgin, IL 60120-1694, USA

Wine, Robbie (Athlete, Baseball Player)
240 Bryce Jordan Ctr
University Park, PA 16802-7102, USA

Winegardner, Mark (Writer)
Random House
1745 Broadway Frnt 3
New York, NY 10019-4343, USA

Winer, Jason (Director)
c/o Michael Lasker *Mosaic Media Group*
407 N Maple Dr # 100
Beverly Hills, CA 90210-3818, USA

Winfield, Antoine (Athlete, Football Player)
10451 White Tail Xing
Eden Prairie, MN 55347-5026, USA

Winfield, David (Dave) (Athlete, Baseball Player)
2235 Stratford Cir
Los Angeles, CA 90077-1316, USA

Winfield, Earl (Athlete, Football Player)
716 Inlet Quay Apt C
Chesapeake, VA 23320-9298, USA

Winfield, Peter (Actor)
3725 Goodland Ave
Studio City, CA 91604-2313, USA

Winfrey, Oprah (Actor, Business Person, Producer, Talk Show Host)
c/o Ari Emanuel *WME|IMG*
9601 Wilshire Blvd
Beverly Hills, CA 90210-5213, USA

Winfrey, Travis (Actor)
c/o Peter Kluge *Impact Artist Group LLC (LA)*
244 N California St
Fl 1
Burbank, CA 91505-3505, USA

Winfrey, W C (Bill) (Misc)
7802 Sierra Trail
Spring Lake, NC 28390, USA

Wing, Murray (Athlete, Hockey Player)
RR 5
Sta. F.
Thunder Bay, ON P7C SM9, CANADA

Wing, Ted (Horse Racer)
3 Rehobeth Rd
Flanders, NJ 07836-9447, USA

Wingate, David (Athlete, Basketball Player)
11404 Glaetzer Ln
Charlotte, NC 28270-1574, USA

Wingate, Elmer (Athlete, Football Player)
807 Wellington Rd
Baltimore, MD 21212-1931, USA

Wingate, J W (Athlete, Baseball Player)
Kansas City Monarchs
3215 Case St
Beaumont, TX 77703-3607, USA

Winger, Debra (Actor)
300 W 109th St Apt 2JK
New York, NY 10025-2110, USA

Winger, Kip (Musician)
2001 Galbraith Dr # A
Nashville, TN 37215-3406, USA

Winget, Larry (Business Person, Writer)
6929 N Hayden Rd Ste C4-619
Scottsdale, AZ 85250-7282, USA

Wingfield, Dantonio (Athlete, Basketball Player)
1602 Gadsden Dr
Albany, GA 31701-3566, USA

Wingfield, Dontonio (Athlete, Basketball Player)
1602 Gadsden Dr
Albany, GA 31701-3566, USA

Wingle, Blake (Athlete, Football Player)
8200 Stockdale Hwy Apt 10
Bakersfield, CA 93311-1091, USA

Wingo, Harthorne (Athlete, Basketball Player)
862 Macon St Apt 2B
Brooklyn, NY 11233-5405, USA

Wingrove-Earl, Elsie (Baseball Player)
PO Box 61
North Portal, SK S0C 1W0, CANADA

Winiger, Melanie (Actor, Model)
Rindlisbacher
ch Carmenstr 32
Zurich 08032, SWITZERLAND

Winings, Meagan (Beauty Pageant Winner)
PO Box 21
Atkinson, NE 68713-0021, USA

Winkelsas, Joe (Athlete, Baseball Player)
213 Virgil Ave
Buffalo, NY 14216-1836, USA

Winkleman, Sophie (Actor)
c/o Gabriel Cohen *Management 360*
9111 Wilshire Blvd
Beverly Hills, CA 90210-5508, USA

Winkler, David (Director)
Rigberg Roberts Rugoto
1180 S Beverly Dr Ste 604
Los Angeles, CA 90035-1158, USA

Winkler, Francis M (Athlete, Football Player)
8223 Creekside Cir S # 0
Apt 10
Cordova, TN 38016-5117, USA

Winkler, Henry (Actor, Producer)
c/o Staff Member *Fair Dinkum Productions*
PO Box 49914
Los Angeles, CA 90049-0914, USA

Winkler, Irwin (Director, Producer)
c/o Staff Member *Winkler Films*
190 N Canon Dr Ste 302
Beverly Hills, CA 90210-5314, USA

Winkler, Marvin (Athlete, Basketball Player)
1304 Hidalgo Blvd
Zapata, TX 78076-3596, USA

Winkles, Bobby B (Athlete, Baseball Player, Coach)
3470 Summersorin11s Dr
Las Ve11as, NV 89129-6391, USA

Winklevoss, Cameron (Business Person)
Winklevoss Capital
30 W 24th St Fl 4
New York, NY 10010-3558, USA

Winklevoss, Tyler (Business Person)
Winklevoss Capital
30 W 24th St Fl 4
New York, NY 10010-3558, USA

Winn, Billy (Athlete, Football Player)
c/o Jeff Sperbeck *The Novo Agency*
1537 Via Romero Ste 100
Alamo, CA 94507-1527, USA

Winn, Jim (Athlete, Baseball Player)
3440 S Delaware Ave Apt 123
Springfield, MO 65804-6447, USA

Winn, Randy (Athlete, Baseball Player)
12221 Broadwater Loop
Thonotosassa, FL 33592-3954, USA

Winner, Charley (Athlete, Football Coach, Football Player)
10100 Cypress Cove Dr Apt 371
Fort Myers, FL 33908-7667, USA

Winnes, Chris (Athlete, Hockey Player)
22 Ambrose Dr
Bristol, RI 02809-2913, USA

Winnick, Katheryn (Actor)
c/o Jason Barrett *Alchemy Entertainment*
7024 Melrose Ave Ste 420
Los Angeles, CA 90038-3394, USA

Winningham, Herm (Athlete, Baseball Player)
1542 Belleville Rd
Orangeburg, SC 29115-3702, USA

Winningham, Mare (Actor)
c/o Christy Hall *Paradigm*
8942 Wilshire Blvd
Beverly Hills, CA 90211-1908, USA

Winokur, Marissa Jaret (Actor)
c/o Michael Valeo *Valeo Entertainment*
8581 Santa Monica Blvd Ste 570
West Hollywood, CA 90069-4120, USA

Winslet, Kate (Actor)
c/o Dallas Smith *United Agents*
12-26 Lexington St
London W1F OLE, UNITED KINGDOM

Winslow, Dan (Musician)
3807 114th Ln NE
Minneapolis, MN 55449-7031, USA

Winslow, Don (Writer)
The Story Factory
141 S Barrington Ave Ste E
Los Angeles, CA 90049-3314, USA

Winslow, Ernest (Race Car Driver)
Randy Dixon Motorsports
955 Riverside Rd
Grifton, 28530 NC, USA

Winslow, George (Athlete, Football Player)
14 Daisy Ln
Maple Glen, PA 19002-2326, USA

Winslow, Michael (Actor, Comedian)
c/o Lora Huntington *Classic Talent Agency*
2190 Brandon Trl # 8
Alpharetta, GA 30004-8457, USA

Winslow Jr, Kellen (Athlete, Football Player)
2431 Cornerstone
Westlake, OH 44145-4111, USA

Winsor, Jackie (Artist)
Paula Cooper Gallery
526 W 26th St
New York, NY 10001-5517, USA

Winspear, Jacqueline (Writer)
c/o Amy Rennert *The Amy Rennert Agency*
98 Main St Ste 302
Tiburon, CA 94920-2517, USA

Winstead, Mary Elizabeth (Actor)
c/o Nicole Perna *Imprint PR*
6121 W Sunset Blvd
Neuehouse
Los Angeles, CA 90028-6442, USA

Winston, Dennis (Athlete, Football Player)
150 Chesterfield Ln Apt 8
Maumee, OH 43537-3881, USA

Winston, George (Composer, Musician)
c/o Staff Member *High Road Touring*
751 Bridgeway Fl 2
Sausalito, CA 94965-2174, USA

Winston, Hattie (Actor)
c/o Cheryl Kagan *Cheryl Kagan Public Relations*
100 N Crescent Dr Ste 100
Beverly Hills, CA 90210-5447, USA

Winston, Jameis (Athlete, Football Player)
c/o Greg Genske *The Legacy Agency*
500 Newport Center Dr Ste 800
Newport Beach, CA 92660-7008, USA

Winston, Roy C (Athlete, Football Player)
708 Highway 401
Napoleonville, LA 70390-3205, USA

Winstone, Ray (Actor)
c/o Donna Mills *Premier PR*
2-4 Bucknall St
London WC2H 8LA, UNITED KINGDOM

Winter, Alex (Actor)
c/o John Sloss *Sloss Eckhouse LawCo*
555 W 25th St Fl 4
New York, NY 10001-5542, USA

Winter, Ariel (Actor)
c/o Jeffrey Chassen *Imprint PR*
6121 W Sunset Blvd
Neuehouse
Los Angeles, CA 90028-6442, USA

Winter, Blaise (Athlete, Football Player)
17943 Camargo Ln
Orlando, FL 32820-2725, USA

Winter, Edgar (Musician)
9233 Burton Way Unit 402
Beverly Hills, CA 90210-3718, USA

Winter, Eric (Actor)
c/o Colton Gramm *Brillstein Entertainment Partners*
9150 Wilshire Blvd Ste 350
Beverly Hills, CA 90212-3453, USA

Winter, Fred (Tex) (Coach)
Los Angeles Lakers
1111 S Figueroa St
Staples Center
Los Angeles, CA 90015-1300, USA

Winter, Judy (Actor)
c/o Staff Member *Agentur Stimmgerecht*
Soorstr. 14
Berlin 14050, Germany

Winter, Katia (Actor)
c/o Brantley Brown *Authentic Talent & Literary Management*
3615 Eastham Dr # 650
Culver City, CA 90232-2410, USA

Winter, Mark Leonard (Actor)
c/o Lisa Mann *Lisa Mann Creative Management*
19-25 Cope St
Redfern NSW 02016, AUSTRALIA

Winter, Morice '"Tex"' (Athlete, Basketball Player)
Brian Winter
1117 Village Dr
Manhattan, KS 66503-2566, USA

Winter, Olaf (Athlete)
An der Pirschheide 28
Potsdam 14471, GERMANY

Winter, Paul T (Musician)
Living Music Records
PO Box 72
Litchfield, CT 06759-0072, USA

Winter, Ralph (Producer)
c/o Richard Caleel *Worldwide Production Agency (WPA)*
144 N Robertson Blvd Fl 2
West Hollywood, CA 90048-3131, USA

Winter, Terence (Producer)
c/o Staff Member *Creative Artists Agency (CAA)*
2000 Avenue of the Stars Ste 100
Los Angeles, CA 90067-4705, USA

Winter, Terrence (Producer, Writer)
c/o Staff Member *Jackoway Tyerman Wertheimer Austen Mandelbaum Morris & Klein*
1925 Century Park E Fl 22
Los Angeles, CA 90067-2701, USA

Winterbottom, Michael (Director, Producer, Writer)
c/o Staff Member *Revolution Films*
9A Dallington St
London EC1V 0BQ, UNITED KINGDOM (UK)

Winters, Anne (Actor)
c/o Jordyn Palos *Persona Public Relations*
6255 W Sunset Blvd Ste 705
Hollywood, CA 90028-7408, USA

Winters, Brian (Athlete, Football Player)
c/o Joel Segal *Lagardere Unlimited (NY)*
456 Washington St Apt 9L
New York, NY 10013-1555, USA

Winters, Brian (Athlete, Basketball Player)
6144 S Moline Way
Englewood, CO 80111-5845, USA

Winters, Chris (Actor, Model)
933 Backspin Ct
Newport News, VA 23602-9428, USA

Winters, Dean (Actor)
c/o Sandra Chang *Anonymous Content*
3532 Hayden Ave
Culver City, CA 90232-2413, USA

Winters, Frank (Football Player)
Cleveland Browns
820 17th St
Union City, NJ 07087-1928, USA

Winters, Matt (Athlete, Baseball Player)
1201 Foxfire Dr
Greensboro, NC 27410-3253, USA

Winters, Mike (Athlete, Baseball Player)
13644 Boquita Dr
Del Mar, CA 92014-3408, USA

Winters, Scott William (Actor)
c/o Staff Member *Artists & Representatives (Stone Manners Salners)*
6100 Wilshire Blvd Ste 1500
Los Angeles, CA 90048-5110, USA

Winters, Voise (Athlete, Basketball Player)
7305 S Rockwell St
Chicago, IL 60629-2037, USA

Winther, Richard (Athlete, Football Player)
1620 6th Way NW
Center Point, AL 35215-5374, USA

Wintour, Anna (Business Person)
Vogue Magazine / Conde Nast
1 World Trade Ctr Fl 20
New York, NY 10007-0090, USA

Winwood, Steve (Musician)
700 12th Ave S Unit 203
Nashville, TN 37203-3329, USA

Wire II, William S (Business Person)
706 Overton Park
Nashville, TN 37215-2452, USA

Wirgowski, Dennis (Athlete, Football Player)
1127 Brissette Beach Rd
Kawkawlin, MI 48631-9454, USA

Wirth, Alan (Athlete, Baseball Player)
2858 E Jasmine St
Mesa, AZ 85213-3123, USA

Wirth, Billy (Actor, Director)
c/o Katie Mason Stern *Luber Roklin Management*
5815 W Sunset Blvd Ste 208
Los Angeles, CA 90028-6481, USA

Wirth, Timothy E (Politician, Senator)
United Nations Foundation
2201 Est NW
Washington, DC 20521-0001, USA

Wisdom, Robert (Actor)
c/o Nicole Nassar *Nicole Nassar PR*
1111 10th St Unit 104
Santa Monica, CA 90403-5363, USA

Wise, Dewanda (Actor)
c/o Shannon Barr *Rogers & Cowan*
1840 Century Park E Fl 18
Los Angeles, CA 90067-2101, USA

Wise, Dewayne (Athlete, Baseball Player)
709 Old Lexington Hwy
Chapin, SC 29036-7980, USA

Wise, Madeline (Actor)
c/o Matthew Lesher *Insight*
5358 Melrose Ave # 200W
Los Angeles, CA 90038-5117, USA

Wise, Matt (Athlete, Baseball Player)
11627 E Twilight Ct
Chandler, AZ 85249-4546, USA

Wise, Ray (Actor)
c/o Brady McKay *Haven Entertainment*
8111 Beverly Blvd Ste 201
Los Angeles, CA 90048-4531, USA

wise, Richard C (Rick) (Athlete, Baseball Player)
8235 SW 184th Ave
Beaverton, OR 97007-5764, USA

Wise, William A (Business Person)
El Paso Energy Corp
1001 Louisiana St
Houston, TX 77002-5083, USA

Wise, Willie (Athlete, Basketball Player)
2320 185th Pl NE
Redmond, WA 98052-6019, USA

Wiseman, Brian (Athlete, Hockey Player)
2960 Walnut Ridge Dr
Ann Arbor, MI 48103-2189, USA

Wiseman, Frederick (Producer)
Zipporah Films
1 Richdale Ave Unit 4
Cambridge, MA 02140-2610, USA

Wiseman, Gregory Reid Ltcmdr (Astronaut)
2436 Mountain Falls Ct
Friendswood, TX 77546-5590, USA

Wiseman, Len (Director)
c/o Heidi Lopata *Narrative*
1601 Vine St Fl 6
Los Angeles, CA 90028-8802, USA

Wisener, Gary (Athlete, Football Player)
10 Encantado Way
Hot Springs Village, AR 71909-7405, USA

Wish Bone (Actor, Composer, Musician)
c/o Staff Member *Creative Artists Agency (CAA)*
2000 Avenue of the Stars Ste 100
Los Angeles, CA 90067-4705, USA

Wisin and Yandel (Musician)
c/o Staff Member *Universal Music Publishing Group (Latin)*
420 Lincoln Rd Ste 200
Miami Beach, FL 33139-3014, USA

Wiska, Jeffrey R (Athlete, Football Player)
18579 Fox Hollow Ct
Northville, MI 48168-8848, USA

Wismann, Pete (Athlete, Football Player)
3312 Saint Michael Dr
Palo Alto, CA 94306-3057, USA

Wisniewski, Andreas (Actor)
Gage Group
14724 Ventura Blvd Ste 505
Sherman Oaks, CA 91403-3505, USA

Wisniewski, Leo (Athlete, Football Player)
8036 Woodcreek Dr
Bridgeville, PA 15017-3610, USA

Wisniewski, Stefen (Athlete, Football Player)
c/o Anthony J. Agnone *Eastern Athletic Services*
11350 McCormick Rd
Suite 800 - Executive Plaza
Hunt Valley, MD 21031-1002, USA

Wisniewski, Stephen A (Steve) (Athlete, Football Player)
36 El Alamo Ct
Danville, CA 94526-1455, USA

Wisoff, Jeff Dr (Astronaut)
4268 Brindisi Pl
Pleasanton, CA 94566-2238, USA

Wisoff, Peter J K (Jeff) (Astronaut)
4268 Brindisi Pl
Pleasanton, CA 94566-2238, USA

Wissel, Sharon (Athlete, Figure Skater)
c/o Staff Member *Bobby Ball Talent Agency*
4342 Lankershim Blvd
Universal City, CA 91602, USA

Wissman, Dave (Athlete, Baseball Player)
PO Box 38
Derby, VT 05829-0038, USA

Wistrom, Grant (Athlete, Football Player)
5769 S Fox Hollow Ave
Springfield, MO 65810-2326, USA

Witasick, Jay (Athlete, Baseball Player)
200 Wellin11ton Ct
Bel Air, MD 21014-3100, USA

Withem, Shannon (Athlete, Baseball Player)
39668 Dorchester Cir
Canton, MI 48188-5016, USA

Withers, Bill (Musician, Songwriter)
Mattie Music Group
PO Box 16698
Beverly Hills, CA 90209-2698, USA

Withers, Jane (Actor)
c/o Staff Member *Keller & Vanderneth Inc*
1133 Broadway Ste 911
New York, NY 10010-8029, USA

Withers, Pick (Musician)
Damage Mgmt
16 Lambton Place
London W11 2SH, UNITED KINGDOM (UK)

Witherspoon, John (Actor, Comedian)
c/o Alex Goodman *Levity Entertainment Group (LEG)*
6701 Center Dr W Ste 300
Los Angeles, CA 90045-2482, USA

Witherspoon, Reese (Actor, Producer)
c/o Chelsea Thomas *The Lede Company*
9701 Wilshire Blvd # 930
Beverly Hills, CA 90212-2020, USA

Withrow, Phil (Athlete, Football Player)
730 Oakland Hills Cir Apt 106
Lake Mary, FL 32746-5833, USA

Withrow, Ray (Athlete, Baseball Player)
3842 Bordeaux Loop S
Owensboro, KY 42303-2550, USA

with Spencer Davis, Strawberry Alarm Clock (Music Group)
c/o Geoffrey Blumenauer *Geoffrey Blumenauer Artists*
PO Box 343
Burbank, CA 91503-0343, USA

Witiuk, Steve (Athlete, Hockey Player)
11821 N Hemlock St
Spokane, WA 99218-2718, CANADA

Witkin, Isaac (Artist)
Bennington College
Art Dept
Bennington, VT 05201, USA

Witkop, Bernhard (Misc)
3807 Montrose Dr
Chevy Chase, MD 20815-4701, USA

Witman, Jon (Athlete, Football Player)
568 Woodsview Ln
Hellam, PA 17406-9344, USA

Witmeyer, Ron (Athlete, Baseball Player)
PO Box 763
Rancho Santa Fe, CA 92067-0763, USA

Witt, Alexander (Director)
c/o Ann Murtha *Murtha Agency*
1025 Colorado Ave Ste B
Santa Monica, CA 90401-2847, USA

Witt, Alicia (Actor)
c/o Daniel (Danny) Sussman *Brillstein Entertainment Partners*
9150 Wilshire Blvd Ste 350
Beverly Hills, CA 90212-3453, USA

Witt, Bobby (Athlete, Baseball Player, Olympic Athlete)
4601 Winewood Ct
Colleyville, TX 76034-4887, USA

Witt, Brendan (Athlete, Hockey Player)
6461 Surfside Ln
Carlsbad, CA 92011-3208, USA

Witt, George (Athlete, Baseball Player)
2209 Catalina
Laguna Beach, CA 92651-3607, USA

Witt, Katarina (Athlete, Figure Skater, Olympic Athlete)
c/o Gail Parenteau *Parenteau Guidance*
132 E 35th St # J
New York, NY 10016-3892, USA

Witt, Kevin (Athlete, Baseball Player)
6350 Concho Bay Dr
Houston, TX 77041-6171, USA

Witt, Michael A (Mike) (Athlete, Baseball Player)
37 Poppy Hills Rd
Laguna Niguel, CA 92677-1010, USA

Witte, Luke (Athlete, Basketball Player)
3223 Arbor Pointe Dr
Charlotte, NC 28210-7994, USA

Witten, Jason (Athlete, Football Player)
2001 Navasota Cv
Westlake, TX 76262-4801, USA

Wittma, Randy (Athlete, Basketball Coach, Basketball Player, Coach)
c/o Lonnie Cooper *Career Sports and Entertainment*
600 Galleria Pkwy SE Ste 1900
Atlanta, GA 30339-5990, USA

Wittrock, Finn (Actor)
c/o Nicole Caruso *Relevant (NY)*
333 Hudson St Rm 502
New York, NY 10013-1033, USA

Wittwer, Linda Jezek (Athlete, Olympic Athlete, Swimmer)
673 Oak Park Way
Emerald Hills, CA 94062-4041, USA

Witty, Chris (Athlete, Olympic Athlete, Speed Skater)
2644 E 2940 S
Salt Lake City, UT 84109-2527, USA

Witucki, Casimir (Athlete, Football Player)
3909 Spring Ter
Temple Hills, MD 20748-3439, USA

Witwer, Sam (Actor)
c/o Gordon Gilbertson *Gilbertson Management*
1334 3rd Street Promenade Ste 201
Santa Monica, CA 90401-1320, USA

Wizbicki, Alex (Athlete, Football Player)
10B Hayes Ct
Superior, WI 54880-2939, USA

Wlasiuk, Gene (Athlete, Football Player)
816 Shannon Rd
Regina, SK S4S 5K2, Canada

Wlcek, James (Actor)
c/o Terrie Marroquin *Tlynn Talent Management*
10153 Riverside Dr Ste 566
Toluca Lake, CA 91602-2562, USA

W. Meeks, Gregory (Congressman, Politician)
2234 Rayburn Hob
Washington, DC 20515-2202, USA

Wockenfuss, Anett (Model)
c/o Chadwick model management
Private Bag 38
Darlinghurst NSW 2010, AUSTRALIA

Wockenfuss, John (Athlete, Baseball Player)
2265 Kristina Park
Watertown, NY 13601-9340, USA

Wocket-Eckert, Barbel (Athlete)
Im Bangert 61
Lutzelbach 64750, GERMANY

Woebcken, Charlie (Producer)
c/o Staff Member *Babelsberg Film*
August-Bebelstr. 26-53
Potsdam 14482, Germany

Woerner, Scott (Athlete, Football Player)
11268 Turner Rd
Hampton, GA 30228-1534, USA

Wofford, Harris (Politician, Senator)
955 26th St NW Apt 501
Washington, DC 20037-2040, USA

Wofford, James (Athlete, Horse Racer, Olympic Athlete)
22145 Greengarden Rd
Upperville, VA 20184-3105, USA

Wogan, Gerald N (Misc)
Massachusetts Institute of Technology
Toxicology Div
Cambridge, MA 02139, USA

Woggon, Bill (Cartoonist)
2724 Cabot Ct
Thousand Oaks, CA 91360-1640, USA

Wohl, Dave (Athlete, Basketball Player, Coach)
137 Morley Cir
Melville, NY 11747-4843, USA

Wohlers, Mark E (Athlete, Baseball Player)
302 Whistle Wood Ln
Woodstock, GA 30188-2037, USA

Wohlford, Jim (Athlete, Baseball Player)
24186 Lomitas Dr
Woodlake, CA 93286-9505, USA

Wohlhuter, Richard (Athlete, Olympic Athlete, Track Athlete)
5605 Passion Flower Way
The Villages, FL 32163-0369, USA

Wohlwender-Fricker, Marian (Athlete, Baseball Player)
14006 Castle Hill Way
Fort Myers, FL 33919-7369, USA

Woiwode, Larry (Writer)
State University of New York
English Dept
Binghamton, NY 13901, USA

Wojciechowski, John (Athlete, Football Player)
13317 Clyde Rd
Holly, MI 48442-9010, USA

Wojciechowski, Steve (Athlete, Baseball Player)
4646 Thornberry Hill Ct NE
Grand Rapids, MI 49525-9489, USA

Wojcik, John (Athlete, Baseball Player)
8303 Salford Way
Louisville, KY 40222-5529, USA

Wojna, Ed (Athlete, Baseball Player)
225 Sussex Pl
Carson City, NV 89703-5372, USA

Wojtowicz, R P (Misc)
Railway Carmen Union
3 Research Pl
Rockville, MD 20850-3279, USA

Wolanin, Craig (Athlete, Hockey Player)
4891 Gallagher Rd
Rochester, MI 48306-1508, USA

Wolcott, Bob (Athlete, Baseball Player)
3323 Bryson Way
Medford, OR 97504-5811, USA

Wolf, David A (Astronaut)
1714 Neptune Ln
Houston, TX 77062-6108, USA

Wolf, David A Dr (Astronaut)
1714 Neptune Ln
Houston, TX 77062-6108, USA

Wolf, Dick (Producer)
c/o Staff Member *Wolf Films Inc (LA)*
260 S Los Robles Ave Ste 309
Pasadena, CA 91101-2897, USA

Wolf, Jim (Athlete, Baseball Player)
8054 Royer Ave
West Hills, CA 91304-3535, USA

Wolf, Joe (Athlete, Football Player)
2826 Kingsbridge Ln
Allentown, PA 18103-9251, USA

Wolf, Michelle (Comedian, Talk Show Host, Television Host)
c/o Lewis Kay *Kovert Creative*
506 Santa Monica Blvd Ste 400
Santa Monica, CA 90401-2412, USA

Wolf, Naomi (Writer)
Random House
1745 Broadway Frnt 3 # B1
New York, NY 10019-4343, USA

Wolf, Randy (Athlete, Baseball Player)
18580 Corte Fresco
Rancho Santa Fe, CA 92091-0227, USA

Wolf, Ross (Athlete, Baseball Player)
15524 N 400th St
Wheeler, IL 62479-2300, USA

Wolf, Scott (Actor)
c/o Heather Lylis *Sunshine Sachs*
136 Madison Ave Fl 17
New York, NY 10016-6734, USA

Wolf, Sigrid (Skier)
Elbigenalp 45 A
06652, AUSTRIA

Wolf, Wally (Athlete, Baseball Player)
18580 Corte Fresco
Rancho Santa Fe, CA 92091-0227, USA

Wolfe, Bernie (Athlete, Hockey Player)
8012 Glenbrook Rd
Bethesda, MD 20814-2608, USA

Wolfe, Bob (Athlete, Football Player)
13165 Emiline Cir
Omaha, NE 68138-6132, USA

Wolfe, Brian (Athlete, Baseball Player)
39398 Calle Anita
Temecula, CA 92592-8213, USA

Wolfe, David (Writer)
1259 N Crescent Heights Blvd Apt D
C/O Angela Hartman
West Hollywood, CA 90046-5018, USA

Wolfe, Derek (Athlete, Football Player)
c/o Joe Panos *Athletes First*
23091 Mill Creek Dr
Laguna Hills, CA 92653-1258, USA

Wolfe, George C (Director)
Shakespeare Festival
425 Lafayette St
New York, NY 10003-7087, USA

Wolfe, Jenna (Actor, Correspondent)
c/o Staff Member *IF Management, Inc.*
152 W 57th St Fl 19
New York, NY 10019-3310, USA

Wolfe, Kenneth L (Business Person)
Hershey Foods Corp
100 Crystal A Dr Unit 8
Hershey, PA 17033-9702, USA

Wolfe, Larry (Athlete, Baseball Player)
5200 Blossomwood Ct
Fair Oaks, CA 95628-3836, USA

Wolfe, Michael (Producer)
c/o Rosanna Bilow *Creative Artists Agency (CAA)*
2000 Avenue of the Stars Ste 100
Los Angeles, CA 90067-4705, USA

Wolfe, Mike (Reality Star)
Antique Archaeology
1300 Clinton St Ste 130
Nashville, TN 37203-7014, USA

Wolfe, Paul (Race Car Driver)
Baldwin Racing
182 Raceway Dr # B
Mooresville, NC 28117-6509, USA

Wolfe, Sterling (Actor)
2609 W Wyoming Ave Ste A
Burbank, CA 91505-1950, USA

Wolfe, Tom (Composer, Musician)
c/o Staff Member *Aperture Music*
PO Box 90010
Pasadena, CA 91109-5010, USA

Wolfe, Traci (Actor)
c/o Staff Member *Cunningham Escott Slevin & Doherty (CESD)*
10635 Santa Monica Blvd Ste 130
Los Angeles, CA 90025-8306, USA

Wolfermann, Klaus (Athlete, Track Athlete)
Fasenenweg 13A
Herzogenaurach 91074, GERMANY

Wolff, Alex (Actor, Musician)
c/o Lindsay Galin *Rogers & Cowan*
909 3rd Ave Fl 9
New York, NY 10022-4752, USA

Wolff, Christian (Composer, Musician)
Zinnkopfstr. 6
Aschau/Chiemsee D-83229, GERMANY

Wolff, Earl (Athlete, Football Player)
c/o Tony Paige *Dream Point Sports*
1455 Pennsylvania Ave NW Ste 225
Washington, DC 20004-1026, USA

Wolff, Jon A (Misc)
1122 University Bay Dr
Madison, WI 53705-2252, USA

Wolff, Jonathan (Composer, Musician)
c/o Steve Winogradsky *Winogradsky Co, The*
11240 Magnolia Blvd Ste 104
N Hollywood, CA 91601-3790, USA

Wolff, Nat (Actor, Musician)
Naked Brothers Band/Yovia
1909 3rd St N
Jacksonville Beach, FL 32250-7427, USA

Wolff, Sanford I (Misc)
8141 Broadway
New York, NY 10023, USA

Wolff, Toblas J A (Writer)
Stanford University
English Dept
Stanford, CA 94305, USA

Wolfhard, Finn (Actor)
c/o Jill Fritzo *Jill Fritzo Public Relations*
208 E 51st St # 305
New York, NY 10022-6557, USA

Wolfley, Craig (Athlete, Football Player)
1767 Robson Dr
Pittsburgh, PA 15241-2617, USA

Wolford, Will (Athlete, Football Player)
205 Waterleaf Way
Louisville, KY 40207-5720, USA

Wolfson, Louis E (Business Person)
10205 Collins Ave
Bal Harbour, FL 33154-1403, USA

Wolk, James (Actor)
c/o Melissa Kates *Viewpoint Inc*
8820 Wilshire Blvd Ste 220
Beverly Hills, CA 90211-2622, USA

Wolken, Jonathan (Artist, Dancer, Director)
Pilobolus Dance Theater
PO Box 388
Washington Depot, CT 06794-0388, USA

Woll, Deborah Ann (Actor)
923 Hauser Blvd
Los Angeles, CA 90036-4723, USA

Wolov, Julia Lea (Actor, Writer)
c/o Jonathan Brandstein *Morra Brezner Steinberg & Tenenbaum (MBST) Entertainment*
345 N Maple Dr Ste 200
Beverly Hills, CA 90210-5174, USA

Wolpe, Lenny (Actor)
c/o Staff Member *The Gage Group*
5757 Wilshire Blvd Ste 659
Los Angeles, CA 90036-3682, USA

Wolski, Dariusz (Director)
The Mack Agency
4705 Laurel Canyon Blvd Ste 204
Valley Village, CA 91607-3998, USA

Wolter, Sherilyn (Actor)
128 Old Topanga Canyon Rd
Topanga, CA 90290-3807

Wolters, Kara (Basketball Player)
137 Westfield Dr
Holliston, MA 01746-1256, USA

W. Olver, John (Congressman, Politician)
1111 Longworth Hob
Washington, DC 20515-3229, USA

Womack, Bruce L (Athlete, Football Player)
2206 Pomeran Dr
Houston, TX 77080-5112, USA

Womack, Dooley (Athlete, Baseball Player)
209 Weeping Cherry Ln
Columbia, SC 29212-8617, USA

Womack, Floyd (Athlete, Football Player)
c/o Eugene Parker *Independent Sports & Entertainment (ISE-IN)*
6435 W Jefferson Blvd # 197
Fort Wayne, IN 46804-6203, USA

Womack, Lee Ann (Actor, Musician)
c/o Erv Woolsey *Erv Woolsey Agency*
1000 18th Ave S
Nashville, TN 37212-2184, USA

Womack, Steve (Congressman, Politician)
1508 Longworth Hob
Washington, DC 20515-3804, USA

Womack, Tony (Athlete, Baseball Player)
8434 Darcy Hopkins Dr
Charlotte, NC 28277-0227, USA

Wombats, The (Music Group)
c/o Staff Member *Paradigm (Monterey)*
404 W Franklin St
Monterey, CA 93940-2303, USA

Womble, Royce (Athlete, Football Player)
6172 River Forest Dr
Manassas, VA 20112-3045, USA

Wonder, Stevie (Musician, Songwriter)
Steveland Morris Music
4616 W Magnolia Blvd
Burbank, CA 91505-2731, USA

Wong, Ali (Comedian)
c/o Josh Lieberman *3 Arts Entertainment*
9460 Wilshire Blvd Fl 7
Beverly Hills, CA 90212-2713, USA

Wong, BD (Actor)
c/o John Domingos *Paradigm*
140 Broadway Ste 2600
New York, NY 10005-1011, USA

Wong, Kailee (Athlete, Football Player)
5003 Mimosa Dr
Bellaire, TX 77401-5736, USA

Wong, Mike (Athlete, Hockey Player)
16081 Hyland Ave
Lakeville, MN 55044-6221, USA

Wong, Russell (Actor)
c/o Chris Lee *Authentic Talent & Literary Management*
3615 Eastham Dr # 650
Culver City, CA 90232-2410, USA

Wong, Wesley (Actor)
c/o Amy Brownstein *PRStudio USA*
1875 Century Park E Ste 930
Los Angeles, CA 90067-2540, USA

Wonsley, George (Athlete, Football Player)
6418 Amblewood Pl
Jackson, MS 39213-7803, USA

Woo, John (Director, Producer)
30 Gale Pl
Santa Monica, CA 90402-2202, USA

Wood, Anna (Actor)
c/o Lenore Zerman *Liberman/Zerman Management*
252 N Larchmont Blvd Ste 200
Los Angeles, CA 90004-3754, USA

Wood, Bebe (Actor)
c/o Diandra Escamilla *PMK/BNC Public Relations*
1840 Century Park E Ste 1400
Los Angeles, CA 90067-2115, USA

Wood, Brandon (Athlete, Baseball Player)
5936 E Saint John Rd
Scottsdale, AZ 85254-5961, USA

Wood, Brenton (Musician)
PO Box 4127
Inglewood, CA 90309-4127, USA

Wood, Carolyn (Swimmer)
4380 SW 86th Ave
Portland, OR 97225-2428, USA

Wood, Carri (Athlete, Golfer)
2001 Sabal Ridge Ct Apt H
Palm Beach Gardens, FL 33418-8922, USA

Wood, Charles G (Writer)
London Mgmt
2-4 Noel St
London W1V 3RB, UNITED KINGDOM (UK)

Wood, Chris (Actor)
c/o Rebecca Taylor *PMK/BNC Public Relations*
1840 Century Park E Ste 1400
Los Angeles, CA 90067-2115, USA

Wood, Cierre (Athlete, Football Player)

Wood, Danny (Musician)
c/o Erica Gerard *PMK/BNC Public Relations*
622 3rd Ave Fl 8
New York, NY 10017-6707, USA

Wood, Darin '"Dody"' (Athlete, Hockey Player)
4941 S Woodside Ave
Independence, MO 64055-5738, USA

Wood, David (Athlete, Basketball Player)
5915 Crescent Moon Ct
Reno, NV 89511-4357, USA

Wood, Dick (Athlete, Football Player)
41 Audubon Pl
Newnan, GA 30265-2003, USA

Wood, Duane (Athlete, Football Player)
407 W Caddo Ave
Wilburton, OK 74578-3431, USA

Wood, Eddie (Race Car Driver)
21 Performance Dr
Koute 2 Box 77
Stuart, VA 24171-4000, USA

Wood, Eden (Beauty Pageant Winner, Reality Star)
c/o Staff Member *VH1 Television*
1515 Broadway
New York, NY 10036-8901, USA

Wood, Elijah (Actor)
608 W Mary St
Austin, TX 78704-4136, USA

Wood, Eric (Athlete, Football Player)
c/o Joby Branion *Vanguard Sports Group*
23091 Mill Creek Dr
Laguna Hills, CA 92653-1258, USA

Wood, Evan Rachel (Actor)
c/o Amanda Silverman *The Lede Company*
401 Broadway Ste 206
New York, NY 10013-3033, USA

Wood, Jake (Athlete, Baseball Player)
9129 Daytona Dr
Pensacola, FL 32506-2904, USA

Wood, James N (Director)
Art Institute of Chicago
111 S Michigan Ave
Chicago, IL 60603-6488, USA

Wood, Janet (Actor)
Acme Talent
4727 Wilshire Blvd Ste 333
Los Angeles, CA 90010-3874, USA

Wood, Jason (Athlete, Baseball Player)
9899 N Cascade Dr
Fresno, CA 93730-0864, USA

Wood, Jeff (Race Car Driver)
821 N Linden Ct
Wichita, KS 67206-4005, USA

Wood, John (Actor)
Royal Shakespeare Co
Stratford-on-Avon
Warwickshire CV37 6BB, UNITED KINGDOM (UK)

Wood, Jon (Race Car Driver)
137 High Hills Dr
Mooresville, NC 28117-9000, USA

Wood, Kerry (Athlete, Baseball Player)
6838 E Cheney Dr
Paradise Valley, AZ 85253-3525, USA

Wood, Lana (Actor)
7008 Wilbur Ave
Reseda, CA 91335-3937, USA

Wood, Len (Race Car Driver)
21 Performance Dr
Route 2 Box 77
Stuart, VA 24171-4000, USA

Wood, Leon (Athlete, Basketball Player, Olympic Athlete)
2227 Archway
Irvine, CA 92618-8823, USA

Wood, Martin '"Al"' (Athlete, Basketball Player)
411 Belvedere Ln
Waxhaw, NC 28173-6581, USA

Wood, Mike (Athlete, Baseball Player)
1199 Cherlynn Ter
West Palm Beach, FL 33406-5272, USA

Wood, Mike (Athlete, Football Player)
630 N Geyer Rd
Saint Louis, MO 63122-2756, USA

Wood, Rachel Hurd (Actor)
c/o Michael Lazo *Untitled Entertainment*
350 S Beverly Dr Ste 200
Beverly Hills, CA 90212-4819, USA

Wood, Randy (Athlete, Hockey Player)
2 Bridge St
Manchester, MA 01944-1474, USA

Wood, Richard (Athlete, Football Player)
5413 Windbrush Dr
Tampa, FL 33625-4051, USA

Wood, Robert (Athlete, Basketball Player)
12930 Echo Dr
Rockton, IL 61072-2816, USA

Wood, Robert J (Astronaut)
McDonnell Douglas Corp
PO Box 516
Saint Louis, MO 63166-0516, USA

Wood, Ronnie (Musician)
c/o Christopher Dalston *Creative Artists Agency (CAA)*
2000 Avenue of the Stars Ste 100
Los Angeles, CA 90067-4705, USA

Wood, Sharon (Misc)
PO Box 1482
Canmore, AB T0L 0M0, CANADA

Wood, Ted (Athlete, Baseball Player)
1810 Beckley Pl NW
Kennesaw, GA 30152-4265, USA

Wood, Ted (Athlete, Baseball Player, Olympic Athlete)
1810 Beckley Pl NW
Kennesaw, GA 30152-4265, USA

Wood, Ted (Athlete, Baseball Player)
1810 Becklev Pl NW
Kennesaw, GA 30152-4265, USA

Wood, Ted (Athlete, Baseball Player, Olympic Athlete)
1810 Beckley Pl NW
Kennesaw, GA 30152-4265, USA

Wood, Wilbur F (Athlete, Baseball Player)
3 Elmbrook Rd
Bedford, MA 01730-1810, USA

Wood, William V (Athlete, Football Player)
7941 16th St NW
Washington, DC 20012-1230, USA

Wood, William V (Willie) (Athlete, Football Player)
Willie Wood Mechanical Systems
7941 16th St NW
Washington, DC 20012-1230, USA

Wood, Willie (Athlete, Golfer)
6120 Stonegate Pl
Edmond, OK 73025-2526, USA

Woodall, Al (Athlete, Football Player)
131 Field Crest Rd
New Canaan, CT 06840-6331, USA

Woodall, Brad (Athlete, Baseball Player)
6508 Whittlesey Rd
Middleton, WI 53562-1171, USA

Woodall, Rob (Congressman, Politician)
1725 Longworth Hob
Washington, DC 20515-0532, USA

Woodard, Alfre (Actor)
602 Bay St
Santa Monica, CA 90405-1215, USA

Woodard, Bob (Writer)
2907 Q St NW
Washington, DC 20007-3010, USA

Woodard, Charlayne (Actor)
c/o Tim Angle *Shelter Entertainment*
9255 W Sunset Blvd Ste 300
Los Angeles, CA 90069-3313, USA

Woodard, Darrell (Athlete, Baseball Player)
1227 E 69th St
Los Angeles, CA 90001-1657, USA

Woodard, Lynette (Athlete, Basketball Player, Olympic Athlete)
4206 Quail Pointe Ter
Lawrence, KS 66047-1902, USA

Woodard, Mike (Athlete, Baseball Player)
PO Box 35
Maywood, IL 60153-0035, USA

Woodard, Ray (Athlete, Football Player)
1917 FM 352
Corrigan, TX 75939-6822, USA

Woodard, Rickey (Musician)
JVC Music
3800 Barham Blvd Ste 409
Los Angeles, CA 90068-1042, USA

Woodard, Steven L (Steve) (Athlete, Baseball Player)
800 Frost Ct SW
Hartselle, AL 35640-2714, USA

Woodbine, Bokeem (Actor)
c/o Carlos Augusto Gonzalez *Gersh*
9465 Wilshire Blvd Ste 600
Beverly Hills, CA 90212-2605, USA

Woodbridge, Todd (Tennis Player)
Advantage International
PO Box 3297
North Burnley, VIC 03121, AUSTRALIA

Wood Brothers, The (Music Group)
c/o Staff Member *Paradigm (Monterey)*
404 W Franklin St
Monterey, CA 93940-2303, USA

Woodburn, Danny (Actor)
7250 Franklin Ave Unit 808
Los Angeles, CA 90046-3043, USA

Wooden, Shawn (Athlete, Football Player)
17741 SW 12th St
Pembroke Pines, FL 33029-4811, USA

Woodeshivk, Tom (Athlete, Football Player)
PO Box 716
Blakeslee, PA 18610-0716, USA

Woodforde, Mark (Athlete, Tennis Player)
c/o Staff Member *Octagon (VA)*
7100 Forest Ave Ste 201
Richmond, VA 23226-3742, USA

Woodhead, Cynthia (Swimmer)
PO Box 1193
Riverside, CA 92502-1193, USA

Wooding, Michelle (Athlete, Golfer)
3825 E Camelback Rd Unit 148
Phoenix, AZ 85018-2645, USA

Wood Jr, Roy (Comedian, Correspondent)
c/o Derek Van Pelt *Mainstay Entertainment*
9250 Beverly Blvd Fl 3
Beverly Hills, CA 90210-3710, USA

Woodland, Rich (Race Car Driver)
Rich Woodland Racing
2000 Pitts School Rd
Concord, NC 28027, USA

Woodley, LaMarr (Athlete, Football Player)
52960 Trailwood Dr
South Lyon, MI 48178-8303, USA

Woodley, Shailene (Actor)
c/o Cara Tripicchio *Shelter PR*
5670 Wilshire Blvd Ste 1200
Los Angeles, CA 90036-5621, USA

Woodlief, Doug (Athlete, Football Player)
7928 Wilkinson Ave
N Hollywood, CA 91605-2209, USA

Woodring, Jim (Artist)
c/o Staff Member *Fantagraphics Books*
7563 Lake City Way NE
Seattle, WA 98115-4218, USA

Woodring, Wendell P (Misc)
6647 El Colegio Rd
Goleta, CA 93117-4203, USA

Woodruff, Billie (Actor)
c/o Joe Gatta *Gersh*
41 Madison Ave Ste 3301
New York, NY 10010-2210, USA

Woodruff, Blake (Actor)
c/o Justine Hunt *Hines and Hunt Entertainment*
1213 W Magnolia Blvd
Burbank, CA 91506-1829, USA

Woodruff, Bob (Journalist)
c/o Staff Member *ABC News*
77 W 66th St Fl 3
New York, NY 10023-6201, USA

Woodruff, Dwayne (Athlete, Football Player)
10382 Grubbs Rd
Wexford, PA 15090-9420, USA

Woodruff, Judy C (Correspondent, Television Host)
Cable News Network
820 1st St NE Ste 1000
News Dept
Washington, DC 20002-4363, USA

Woods, Al (Athlete, Baseball Player)
2600 San Leandro Blvd Apt 1004
Blvd Act 1004
San Leandro, CA 94578-5032, USA

Woods, Al (Athlete, Football Player)
c/o Pat Dye Jr *SportsTrust Advisors*
3340 Peachtree Rd NE Fl 16
Atlanta, GA 30326-1000, USA

Woods, Al (Athlete, Baseball Player)
1315 148th Ave
San Leandro, CA 94578-2901, USA

Woods, Barbara Alyn (Actor)
Honey Prod
22611 Federalist Rd
Calabasas, CA 91302-4807, USA

Woods, Chris (Athlete, Football Player)
PO Box 2971
Birmingham, AL 35202-3805, USA

Woods, Christine (Actor)
c/o Justin Grey Stone *Management 360*
9111 Wilshire Blvd
Beverly Hills, CA 90210-5508, USA

Woods, Dan (Actor)
The Core Group Talent Agencies
89 Bloor St W 3rd Fl
Toronto, ON M5S 1M1, CANADA

Woods, Della (Race Car Driver)
302 Bellevue Ave
Lake Orion, MI 48362-2708, USA

Woods, Don (Athlete, Football Player)
10415 Johncock Ave SW
Albuquerque, NM 87121-9414, USA

Woods, Gary (Athlete, Baseball Player)
PO Box 151
Solvang, CA 93464-0151, USA

Woods, George (Athlete, Track Athlete)
7631 Green Hedge Rd
Edwardsville, IL 62025-6135, USA

Woods, Ickey (Athlete, Football Player)
505 E Sharon Rd # A
Cincinnati, OH 45246-4726, USA

Woods, Jake (Athlete, Baseball Player)
1405 Mehlert St
Kingsburg, CA 93631-2423, USA

Woods, James (Actor)
c/o Nina Nisenholtz *N2N Entertainment*
610 Harbor St Apt 3
Venice, CA 90291-5516, USA

Woods, Jerome (Athlete, Football Player)
1 Arrowhead Dr
Kansas City, MO 64129-1651, USA

Woods, Jerry L (Athlete, Football Player)
8976 Stratford Ct
Minneapolis, MN 55443-2976, USA

Woods, Jim (Athlete, Baseball Player)
4509 Gardenia Ave
Keyes, CA 95328-9701, USA

Woods, Michael (Actor)
c/o Staff Member *GVA Talent Agency Inc*
193 N Robertson Blvd
Beverly Hills, CA 90211-2103, USA

Woods, Paul (Athlete, Hockey Player)
600 Civic Center Dr
Attn Broadcast Dept
Detroit, MI 48226-4408, USA

Woods, Paul (Athlete, Hockey Player)
4276 S Shore St
Waterford, MI 48328-1157, USA

Woods, Pierre (Athlete, Football Player)
c/o Staff Member *New England Patriots*
1 Patriot Pl
Foxboro, MA 02035-1388, USA

Woods, Qyntel (Basketball Player)
Portland Trail Blazers
1 N Center Court St Ste 200
Rose Garden
Portland, OR 97227-2103, USA

Woods, Rick (Athlete, Football Player)
713 Baldwin St
Meadville, PA 16335-1959, USA

Woods, Robert E (Athlete, Football Player)
c/o Andrew Kessler *Athletes First*
23091 Mill Creek Dr
Laguna Hills, CA 92653-1258, USA

Woods, Robert S (Actor)
ITA
227 Central Park W Apt 5A
New York, NY 10024-6057, USA

Woods, Ron (Athlete, Baseball Player)
5209 Desert Star Dr
Las Vegas, NV 89130-0159, USA

Woods, Simon (Actor)
c/o Staff Member *ICM Partners*
10250 Constellation Blvd Fl 7
Los Angeles, CA 90067-6207, USA

Woods, Stuart (Writer)
Harper Collins Publishers
10 E 53rd St
New York, NY 10022-5244, USA

Woods, Tiger (Athlete, Golfer)
Tiger Woods Foundation
1 Tiger Woods Way
Anaheim, CA 92801-5039, USA

Woods, Zach (Actor)
c/o Alexandra Crotin *The Lede Company*
9701 Wilshire Blvd # 930
Beverly Hills, CA 90212-2020, USA

Woodside, DB (Actor)
c/o Myrna Jacoby *MJ Management*
130 W 57th St Apt 11A
New York, NY 10019-3311, USA

Woodson, Alli (Musician)
Superstars Unlimited
PO Box 371371
Las Vegas, NV 89137-1371, USA

Woodson, Charles (Athlete, Football Player, Heisman Trophy Winner)
9080 Great Heron Cir
Orlando, FL 32836-5483, USA

Woodson, Darren (Athlete, Football Player)
6821 Memorial Dr
Frisco, TX 75034-7295, USA

Woodson, Dick (Athlete, Baseball Player)
27879 Panorama Hills Dr
Menifee, CA 92584-7401, USA

Woodson, Kerry (Athlete, Baseball Player)
19392 La Serena Dr
Estero, FL 33967-0525, USA

Woodson, Michael (Mike) (Athlete, Basketball Coach, Basketball Player)
6951 S Centinela Ave
Playa Vista, CA 90094-2532, USA

Woodson, Rod (Athlete, Football Player)
c/o Eugene Parker *Independent Sports & Entertainment (ISE-IN)*
6435 W Jefferson Blvd # 197
Fort Wayne, IN 46804-6203, USA

Woodson, Sean (Athlete, Football Player)
1135 Ellis Ave
Jackson, MS 39209-7325, USA

Woodson, Tracy (Athlete, Baseball Player)
9027 Fascine Ct
Mechanicsville, VA 23116-6570, USA

Woodson, Warren V (Coach, Football Coach)
12680 Hillcrest Rd Apt 1106
Dallas, TX 75230-2019, USA

Woodville, Kate (Actor)
PO Box 6613
Malibu, CA 90264-6613, USA

Woodward, Bob (Journalist)
3305 Old Point Rd
Edgewater, MD 21037-3110, USA

Woodward, Chris (Athlete, Baseball Player)
1423 Ribolla Dr
Palm Harbor, FL 34683-4012, USA

Woodward, Joanne (Actor)
270/274 North Ave
Westport, CT 06880, USA

Woodward, Kirsten (Designer, Fashion Designer)
Kirsten Woodward Hats
26 Portobello Green Arcade
London W10, UNITED KINGDOM (UK)

Woodward, Morgan (Actor)
2111 Rockledge Rd
Los Angeles, CA 90068-3135, USA

Woodward, Neil W Cdr (Astronaut)
1935 Edgemont Pl W
Seattle, WA 98199-3914, USA

Woodward, Peter (Actor)
c/o Anna Liza Recto *Bold Management & Production*
8228 W Sunset Blvd # 106
West Hollywood, CA 90046-2414, USA

Woodward, Rob (Athlete, Baseball Player)
58 Eastman Hill Rd
Lebanon, NH 03766-2103, USA

Woodward, Shannon (Actor)
6961 La Presa Dr
Los Angeles, CA 90068-3102, USA

Woodward, Woody (Athlete, Baseball Player)
10 San Marco Ct
Palm Coast, FL 32137-2104, USA

Woodward III, Neil W (Astronaut)
5701 Ridgefield Rd
Bethesda, MD 20816-1250, USA

Woody, Damien (Football Player)
New England Patriots
12170 Ashland Heights Rd
Ashland, VA 23005-7634, USA

Woody, Paul (Misc)
New Frontier Mgmt
1921 Broadway
Nashville, TN 37203-2719, USA

Woody, Woody (Athlete, Football Player)
9122 Weymouth Dr
Houston, TX 77031-3034, USA

Woodyard, Wesley (Athlete, Football Player)
c/o Tony Fleming *Impact Sports (LA)*
12429 Ventura Ct
Studio City, CA 91604-2417, USA

Woog, Doug (Athlete, Hockey Player)
2738 96th St E
Inver Grove Heights, MN 55077-4938, USA

Woogon, Bill (Cartoonist)
2724 Cabot Ct
Thousand Oaks, CA 91360-1640, USA

Wool, Breeda (Actor)
c/o Michael Kaleda *Bold Management & Production*
8228 W Sunset Blvd # 106
West Hollywood, CA 90046-2414, USA

Wool, Christopher (Artist)
Luhring Augustine Gallery
531 W 24th St
New York, NY 10011-1104, USA

Wooldridge, Dean E (Business Person)
355 S Grand Ave Ste 2600
Los Angeles, CA 90071-1505, USA

Woolery, Chuck (Actor, Television Host)
Western Creative
26135 Plymouth Rd Ste 200
Redford, MI 48239-2173, USA

Woolfolk, Andre (Athlete, Football Player)
460 Great Circle Rd
Nashville, TN 37228-1404, USA

Woolfolk, Harold (Butch) (Football Player)
New York Giants
4519 Magnolia Ln
Sugar Land, TX 77478-5457, USA

Woolford, Donnell (Athlete, Football Player)
2925 Spur Ave
Fayetteville, NC 28306-8387, USA

Woolford, Gary (Athlete, Football Player)
3914 E Aquarius Pl
Chandler, AZ 85249-5896, USA

Woollard, Bob (Athlete, Basketball Player)
166 Barnard Mill Rd
Hamptonville, NC 27020-7377, USA

Woolley, Catherine (Writer)
PO Box 67
Higgins Hollow Road
Orleans, MA 02653-0067, USA

Woolley, Jason (Athlete, Hockey Player)
4019 Quarton Rd
Bloomfield Hills, MI 48302-4061, USA

Woolley, Jordan (Actor)
c/o Suzanne Bennett-Harrison *Diverse Talent Group*
1875 Century Park E Ste 2250
Los Angeles, CA 90067-2563, USA

Woolridge, Susan (Actor)
c/o Sally Long-Innes *Independent Talent Group*
40 Whitfield St
London W1T 2RH, UNITED KINGDOM

Woolsey, Roland (Football Player)
Dallas Cowboys
10499 W Sultana Ln
Boise, ID 83714-3661, USA

Woolsey, William Tripp (Athlete, Olympic Athlete, Swimmer)
1032 Seascape Cir
Rodeo, CA 94572-1815, USA

Woolstenhume Jr, Rick (Musician)
23345 Hamlin St
West Hills, CA 91307-3316, USA

Woolwine, Chris (Race Car Driver)
Woolwine Motorsports
2705 6lst St. #107
Galveston, TX 77551, USA

Woomble, Roddy (Musician)
Agency Group Ltd
370 City Road
London EC1V 2QA, UNITED KINGDOM (UK)

Woosnam, Ian H (Athlete, Golfer)
I M G
1360 E 9th St Ste 100
Cleveland, OH 44114-1730, USA

Wooten, Hubert (Daddy) (Athlete, Baseball Player)
120 Sandy Dr
Goldsboro, NC 27534-8803, USA

Wooten, Jim (Correspondent)
ABC-TV
5010 Creston St
News Dept
Hyattsville, MD 20781-1216, USA

Wooten, John (Athlete, Football Player)
505 Boronia Rd
Arlington, TX 76002-4515, USA

Wooten, Morgan (Coach)
De Matha High School
Athletic Dept
Hyattsville, MD 20781, USA

Wooten, Nicholas (Producer)
c/o Staff Member *WME|IMG*
9601 Wilshire Blvd
Beverly Hills, CA 90210-5213, USA

Wooten, Ron (Football Player)
New England Patriots
2401 Lewis Grove Ln
Raleigh, NC 27608-1380, USA

Wooten, Shawn (Athlete, Baseball Player)
17535 49th Ave N
Minneapolis, MN 55446-1741, USA

Wooten, Victor (Musician)
1020 Yellow Hammer Dr
Kingston Springs, TN 37082-5233, USA

Wooton, John (Football Player)
Cleveland Browns
13520 Darley Ave
Cleveland, OH 44110-2122, USA

Wootten, Morgan (Athlete, Basketball Player)
6912 Wells Pkwy
University Park, MD 20782-1051, USA

Wootton, Corey (Athlete, Football Player)
c/o Michael McCartney *Priority Sports & Entertainment (Chicago)*
325 N La Salle Dr Ste 650
Chicago, IL 60654-8182, USA

Wopat, Tom (Actor, Musician)
c/o Sanford Brokaw *Brokaw Company*
PO Box 462
Culver City, CA 90232-0462, USA

Word, Barry (Athlete, Football Player)
5746 Janneys Mill Cir
Haymarket, VA 20169-6196, USA

Word, Roscoe (Football Player)
New York Jets
175 Richardson Rd
Ridgeland, MS 39157-9781, USA

Worden, Alfred (Astronaut)

Worden, Neil (Football Player)
Philadelphia Eagles
2 Indian Camp Trl
Portage, IN 46368-1001, USA

Worilds, Jason (Athlete, Football Player)
c/o Scott Smith *XAM Sports*
3509 Ice Age Dr
Madison, WI 53719-5409, USA

Working Title, The (Music Group)
c/o Staff Member *Paradigm (Monterey)*
404 W Franklin St
Monterey, CA 93940-2303, USA

Workman, Hank (Athlete, Baseball Player)
307 19th St
Santa Monica, CA 90402-2409, USA

Workman, Haywoode (Athlete, Basketball Player)
8350 Savannah Trace Cir Apt 208
Tampa, FL 33615-5513, USA

Workman, Shanelle (Actor)
12954 Magnolia Blvd
Sherman Oaks, CA 91423-1619, USA

Workman, Tom (Athlete, Basketball Player)
422 NE Roth St
Portland, OR 97211-1084, USA

Workman, Vincent (Vince) (Athlete, Football Player)
1265 Brookwood Dr
Green Bay, WI 54304-4043, USA

World Party (Music Group)
c/o Staff Member *Paradigm (Monterey)*
404 W Franklin St
Monterey, CA 93940-2303, USA

Worley, Darryl (Musician)
Darryl Worley Foundation
325 Main St
Savannah, TN 38372-2056, USA

Worley, Jo Anne (Actor)
4714 Arcola Ave
Toluca Lake, CA 91602-1522, USA

Worley, Tim (Athlete, Football Player)
531 Sydnor Ave
Ridgecrest, CA 93555-3143, USA

Wormald, Kenny (Actor)
c/o Melissa Kates *Viewpoint Inc*
8820 Wilshire Blvd Ste 220
Beverly Hills, CA 90211-2622, USA

Worndl, Frank (Skier)
Burgsiedlung 19C
Sonthofen 87527, GERMANY

Woronov, Mary (Actor)
4350 1/4 Beverly Blvd
Los Angeles, CA 90004, USA

Worrell, Mark (Athlete, Baseball Player)
300 Scotia Dr Apt 103
Hypoluxo, FL 33462-7002, USA

Worrell, Peter (Athlete, Hockey Player)
3707 Coral Tree Cir
Coconut Creek, FL 33073-4418, USA

Worrell, Tim (Athlete, Baseball Player)
4719 W El Cortez Pl
Phoenix, AZ 85083-2206, USA

Worrell, Todd (Athlete, Baseball Player)
810 Simmons Ave
Saint Louis, MO 63122-2754, USA

Worrilow, Paul (Athlete, Football Player)

Worth, Jody (Actor, Producer)
c/o Jeff Jacobs *Creative Artists Agency (CAA)*
2000 Avenue of the Stars Ste 100
Los Angeles, CA 90067-4705, USA

Wortham, Barron (Athlete, Football Player)
8608 Busch Gardens Dr
Fort Worth, TX 76123-1445, USA

Wortham, Rich (Athlete, Baseball Player)
10247 Missel Thrush Dr
Austin, TX 78750-2136, USA

Worthen, Sam (Athlete, Basketball Player)
Harlem Wizards
311 E Park St Ste 2
Moonachie, NJ 07074-1143, USA

Worthington, Al (Athlete, Baseball Player)
12070 Highwav 55
Sterrett, AL 35147-9601, USA

Worthington, Al (Athlete, Baseball Player)
12070 Highway 55
Sterrett, AL 35147-9601, USA

Worthington, Craig (Athlete, Baseball Player)
10019 Mattock Ave
Downey, CA 90240-3528, USA

Worthington, Melvin L (Religious Leader)
Free Will Baptists
PO Box 5002
Antioch, TN 37011-5002, USA

Worthington, Sam (Actor)
c/o Ann Churchill-Brown *Shanahan Management*
Level 3 Berman House
Surry Hills 02010, AUSTRALIA

Worthy, Calum (Actor)
c/o Brooks Butterfield *PMK/BNC Public Relations*
1840 Century Park E Ste 1400
Los Angeles, CA 90067-2115, USA

Worthy, James (Athlete, Basketball Player, Sportscaster)
5750 Corbett St
Los Angeles, CA 90016-4545, USA

Worthy, Rick (Actor)
c/o Siri Garber *Platform PR*
2666 N Beachwood Dr
Los Angeles, CA 90068-2308, USA

Wortman, Keith (Football Player)
Green Bay Packers
240 Big Sky Dr
Saint Charles, MO 63304-7170, USA

Wortman, Kevin (Athlete, Hockey Player)
42 David Dr
Saugus, MA 01906-1214, USA

Wosniak, Stephen (Actor, Writer)
c/o Staff Member *Inevitable Film Group*
8484 Wilshire Blvd Ste 465
Beverly Hills, CA 90211-3233, USA

Wosniak, Steve (Business Person)
c/o Bob Thomas *Worldwide Speakers Group, LLC*
99 Canal Center Plz Ste 100
Alexandria, VA 22314-1588, USA

Wottie, David J (Dave) (Athlete, Track Athlete)
9245 Forest Hill Ln
Germantown, TN 38139-7906, USA

Wottle, Dave (Athlete, Olympic Athlete, Track Athlete)
9245 Forest Hill Ln
Germantown, TN 38139-7906, USA

Wotton, Mark (Athlete, Hockey Player)
113-276 Midpark Gdns SE
Attn Art Breeze Pro Rep Entertainment Consulting
Calgary, AB T2X 1T3, Canada

Wotus, Ron (Athlete, Baseball Player)
6 Monteira Ln
Martinez, CA 94553-9768, USA

Wouk, Herman (Writer)
3763 Serenity Trl
Palm Springs, CA 92262-9774, USA

Wow, Bow (Actor, Musician)
2838 Grey Moss Pass
Duluth, GA 30097-5226, USA

Woytowicz-Rudnicka, Stefania (Musician)
Al Przyiaciol 2 m
Warsaw 00-565, POLAND

Woywitka, Jeff (Athlete, Hockey Player)
RR 1
Mannville, AB T0B 2W0, Canada

Wozniacki, Caroline (Athlete, Tennis Player)
c/o Staff Member *Women's Tennis Association (WTA-US)*
1 Progress Plz Ste 1500
St Petersburg, FL 33701-4335, USA

Wozniak, Steve (Business Person)
16400 Blackberry Hill Rd
Los Gatos, CA 95030-7513, USA

Wozniewski, Andy (Athlete, Hockey Player)
7448 Coulter Lake Rd
Frisco, TX 75036-5069, USA

Wragg, John (Artist)
6 Castle Lane
Devizes
Wilts, SN10 1HJ, UNITED KINGDOM (UK)

Wregget, Ken (Athlete, Hockey Player)
1778 McMillan Rd
Pittsburgh, PA 15241-2654, USA

Wreh-Wilson, Blidi (Athlete, Football Player)
c/o Alan Herman *Sportstars Inc*
1370 Avenue of the Americas Fl 19
New York, NY 10019-4602, USA

Wren, Darryl (Football Player)
New England Patriots
1418 Skipjack Dr
Fort Washington, MD 20744-4216, USA

Wren, Frank (Baseball Player)
500 Tuxedo Ln
Peachtree City, GA 30269-4070, USA

Wrenn, Peter (Horse Racer)
5215 Wren Ct
Carmel, IN 46033-9646, USA

Wrenn, Robert (Bob) (Athlete, Golfer)
8911 Alendale Rd
Richmond, VA 23229-7701, USA

Wright, Alexander (Athlete, Football Player)
501 S Mississippi St
Amarillo, TX 79106-8735, USA

Wright, Ben (Sportscaster)
CBS-TV
51 W 52nd St
Sports Dept
New York, NY 10019-6119, USA

Wright, Betty (Musician)
Rodgers Redding
1048 Tattnall St
Macon, GA 31201-1537, USA

Wright, Bonnie (Actor)
c/o Ruth Young *United Agents*
12-26 Lexington St
London W1F OLE, UNITED KINGDOM

Wright, Bracey (Basketball Player)
c/o Staff Member *Minnesota Timberwolves*
600 1st Ave N
Minneapolis, MN 55403-1400, USA

Wright, Brad (Athlete, Basketball Player)
5057 Orrville Ave
Woodland Hills, CA 91367-5747, USA

Wright, Charles (Football Player)
St Louis Cardinals
2698 Wakefield Ln
Westlake, OH 44145-3837, USA

Wright, Chase (Athlete, Baseball Player)
6703 Kit Carson Trl
Wichita Falls, TX 76310-2708, USA

Wright, Chely (Musician)
PO Box 122332
Goodlettsville, TN 37212, USA

Wright, Clyde (Athlete, Baseball Player)
528 S Jeanine St
Anaheim, CA 92806-4415, USA

Wright, Dan (Athlete, Baseball Player)
310 Vernon Dr
Batesville, AR 72501-4112, USA

Wright, David (Athlete, Baseball Player)
1105 Hillston Ct
Chesapeake, VA 23322-9534, USA

Wright, Dick (Cartoonist)
Columbus Dispatch
34 S 3rd St
Editorial Dept
Columbus, OH 43215-4241, USA

Wright, Donald C (Don) (Cartoonist)
PO Box 1176
Palm Beach, FL 33480-1176, USA

Wright, Dorell (Athlete, Basketball Player)
158 Twin Peaks Dr
Walnut Creek, CA 94595-1728, USA

Wright, Doug (Writer)
c/o Staff Member *ICM Partners (NY)*
730 5th Ave
New York, NY 10019-4105, USA

Wright, Edgar (Director)
c/o Staff Member *Big Talk Productions*
26 Nassau St.
London W1W 7AQ, UNITED KINGDOM

Wright, Elmo (Football Player)
Kansas City Chiefs
11419 Olympia Dr
Houston, TX 77077-6419, USA

Wright, Eric (Athlete, Football Player)
c/o Tony Fleming *Impact Sports (LA)*
12429 Ventura Ct
Studio City, CA 91604-2417, USA

Wright, Evan (Writer)
c/o Richie Kern *WME/IMG (NY)*
11 Madison Ave Fl 18
New York, NY 10010-3669, USA

Wright, Felix (Football Player)
Cleveland Browns
2698 Wakefield Ln
Westlake, OH 44145-3837, USA

Wright, Felix E (Business Person)
Leggett & Platt Inc
1 Leggett Rd
Carthage, MO 64836-9649, USA

Wright, Geoffrey (Actor)
Innovative Artists
1505 10th St
Santa Monica, CA 90401-2805, USA

Wright, George (Athlete, Baseball Player)
3306 Tranquility Dr
Arlington, TX 76016-2057, USA

Wright, George (Football Player)
Baltimore Colts
10627 Seaford Dr
Houston, TX 77089-1425, USA

Wright, Gerald (Director)
Guthrie Theatre
725 Vineland Pl
Minneapolis, MN 55403-1139, USA

Wright, Howard (Athlete, Basketball Player)
3019 Kingswood Way
Louisville, KY 40216-4914, USA

Wright, Hugh (Musician)
William Morris Agency
2100 W End Ave Ste 1000
Nashville, TN 37203-5240, USA

Wright, Ian (Television Host)
c/o Staff Member *Arena Entertainment Consultants*
Regent's Court
39 Harrogate Rd
Leeds LS7 3PD, UK

Wright, Jamey (Athlete, Baseball Player)
4325 Fairfax Ave
Dallas, TX 75205-3026, USA

Wright, Jaret (Athlete, Baseball Player)
23 Calle Viviana
San Clemente, CA 92673-7049, USA

Wright, Jarius (Athlete, Football Player)
c/o Ryan Morgan *MAG Sports Agency*
8222 Melrose Ave Fl 2
Los Angeles, CA 90046-6825, USA

Wright, Jay (Writer)
General Delivery
Piermont, NH 03779, USA

Wright, Jeff (Athlete, Football Player)
23426 N 21st Pl
Phoenix, AZ 85024-8631, USA

Wright, Jeff (Football Player)
Minnesota Vikings
6341 Rolf Ave
Edina, MN 55439-1434, USA

Wright, Jeffrey S (Actor)
c/o Charlotte Burke *ID Public Relations (NY)*
40 Wall St Fl 51
New York, NY 10005-1385, USA

Wright, Jim (Athlete, Baseball Player)
6526 N Saint Marys Rd
Peoria, IL 61614-2830, USA

Wright, Jim (Athlete, Baseball Player)
549 E Randall St
Coopersville, MI 49404-9649, USA

Wright, Joby (Athlete, Basketball Player)
University of Wyoming
P.O. Box 3434
Athletic Dept
Laramie, WY 82071, USA

Wright, John (Athlete, Hockey Player)
116 Hillsdale Ave W
Toronto, ON M5P 1G5, Canada

Wright, Johnny (Producer)
Wright Entertainment Group
7680 Universal Blvd Ste 500
Orlando, FL 32819-8998, USA

Wright, Joseph ""Joby"" (Athlete, Basketball Player)
5608 Woodworth Way
Indianapolis, IN 46237-3168, USA

Wright, Judith A (Writer)
17 Devonport St
#1
Lyons, ACT 02060, AUSTRALIA

Wright, Julian (Athlete, Basketball Player)
212 Forest Oaks Dr
New Orleans, LA 70131-3376, USA

Wright, Keith (Athlete, Football Player)
17750 County Road 605
Farmersville, TX 75442-6895, USA

Wright, Keith (Athlete, Hockey Player)
78 Malvern Ave
Toronto, ON M4E 3E5, Canada

Wright, Ken (Athlete, Baseball Player)
1651 Ora Dr
Pensacola, FL 32506-8250, USA

Wright, Kendall (Athlete, Football Player)
c/o W Vann McElroy *Select Sports Group*
2700 Post Oak Blvd Ste 1450
Houston, TX 77056-5785, USA

Wright, K.J. (Athlete, Football Player)
c/o Bus Cook *Bus Cook Sports, Inc*
1 Willow Bend Dr
Hattiesburg, MS 39402-8552, USA

Wright, Larry (Athlete, Basketball Player)
17 Yester Oaks Dr
West Monroe, LA 71291-7812, USA

Wright, Larry (Athlete, Hockey Player)
PO Box 1790 Stn Main
Regina, SK S4P 3C8, Canada

Wright, Letitia (Actor)
c/o Femi Oguns *Identity Agency Group (UK)*
95 Grays Inn Rd
London WC1X 8TX, UNITED KINGDOM

Wright, Louie (Football Player)
Denver Broncos
2263 S Quentin Way # 301
Aurora, CO 80014-7316, USA

Wright, Louis D (Athlete, Football Player)
Seismic Corp
3140 S Peoria St #K274
Aurora, CO 80014, USA

Wright, Major (Athlete, Football Player)
c/o Sean Kiernan *Impact Sports (LA)*
12429 Ventura Ct
Studio City, CA 91604-2417, USA

Wright, Max (Actor)
241 Valley Dr
Hermosa Beach, CA 90254-4660, USA

Wright, Michael (Actor)
c/o Steven Arcieri *Arcieri & Associates Inc*
60 E 42nd St Ste 2315
New York, NY 10165-5015, USA

Wright, Michael W (Business Person)
Super Valu Inc
11840 Valley View Rd
Eden Prairie, MN 55344-3691, USA

Wright, Michelle (Musician)
Savannah Music
205 Powell Pl # 214
Brentwood, TN 37027-7522, USA

Wright, Mickey (Athlete, Golfer)
2972 SE Treasure Island Rd
Port Saint Lucie, FL 34952-5773, USA

Wright, Mike (Athlete, Football Player)
c/o Staff Member *New England Patriots*
1 Patriot Pl
Foxboro, MA 02035-1388, USA

Wright, Nathaniel (Nate) (Football Player)
Atlanta Falcons
2398 Leafdale Cir
Castle Rock, CO 80109-3755, USA

Wright, N'Bushe (Actor)
c/o Staff Member *Innovative Artists*
1505 10th St
Santa Monica, CA 90401-2805, USA

Wright, Pamela (Athlete, Golfer)
11333 N 92nd St Unit 2006
Scottsdale, AZ 85260-6154, USA

Wright, Pat (Musician)
Superstars Unlimited
PO Box 371371
Las Vegas, NV 89137-1371, USA

Wright, Petra (Actor)
c/o Bob Glennon *Authentic Talent and Literary Management (NY)*
20 Jay St Ste M17
Brooklyn, NY 11201-8300, USA

Wright, Randy (Football Player)
Green Bay Packers
3591 Richie Rd
Verona, WI 53593-9649, USA

Wright, Rick (Musician)
Agency Group
370 City Road
London EC1V 2QA, UNITED KINGDOM (UK)

Wright, Ricky (Athlete, Baseball Player)
7760 Farm Road 195
Paris, TX 75462-1729, USA

Wright, Robin (Actor, Producer)
c/o Cheryl Maisel *PMK/BNC Public Relations*
1840 Century Park E Ste 1400
Los Angeles, CA 90067-2115, USA

Wright, Ron (Athlete, Baseball Player)
509 S Five Sisters Dr
Saint George, UT 84790-4027, USA

Wright, Ronald (Winkie) (Boxer)
c/o James Prince *Prince Boxing Enterprises*
3030 Jensen Dr
Houston, TX 77026-5511, USA

Wright, Roy (Athlete, Baseball Player)
331 Pinehurst Cir
Chickamauga, GA 30707-1459, USA

Wright, Samuel E (Actor)
c/o Marvin Josephson *Marvin A Josephson Management*
16 W 22nd St
New York, NY 10010-5803, USA

Wright, Sarah (Actor)
c/o Ellen Meyer *Ellen Meyer Management*
315 S Beverly Dr Ste 202
Beverly Hills, CA 90212-4310, USA

Wright, Shareece (Athlete, Football Player)

Wright, Sharone (Athlete, Basketball Player)
6080 Lakeview Rd Apt 3504
Warner Robins, GA 31088-9157, USA

Wright, Stephen T (Athlete, Football Player)
14 Conifer Sq
Augusta, GA 30909-4505, USA

Wright, Steve (Athlete, Football Player)
15 Camel Point Dr
Laguna Beach, CA 92651-6988, USA

Wright, Steven (Actor, Comedian)
c/o Tim Sarkes *Brillstein Entertainment Partners*
9150 Wilshire Blvd Ste 350
Beverly Hills, CA 90212-3453, USA

Wright, Tim (Athlete, Football Player)
c/o Joe Flanagan *BTI Sports Advisors*
615 South Blvd Apt C
Oak Park, IL 60302-4606, USA

Wright, Tom (Actor)
c/o Steven Siebert *Lighthouse Entertainment Group*
9229 W Sunset Blvd Ste 630
W Hollywood, CA 90069-3419, USA

Wright, Tom (Athlete, Baseball Player)
1116 Poplar Springs Church Rd
Shelby, NC 28152-8071, USA

Wright, Trevor (Actor)
c/o Justin Deanda *ICM Partners*
10250 Constellation Blvd Fl 7
Los Angeles, CA 90067-6207, USA

Wright, Tyler (Athlete, Hockey Player)
200 W Nationwide Blvd Unit 1
Attn Coaching Staff
Columbus, OH 43215-2561, USA

Wright, Van Earl (Actor)
c/o Jill Smoller *WME|IMG*
9601 Wilshire Blvd
Beverly Hills, CA 90210-5213, USA

Wright, Weldon (Athlete, Football Player)
701 E Bluff St Apt 6406
Fort Worth, TX 76102-2372, USA

Wright, Wesley (Athlete, Baseball Player)
9661 Colleton Pl
Montgomery, AL 36117-8458, USA

Wright, Willie (Athlete, Football Player)
13456 Dry Gulch Rd
Paonia, CO 81428-7119, USA

Wright, Winky (Athlete, Boxer)
3021 59th Ave S
St Petersburg, FL 33712-5202, USA

Wright Jr, Charles P (Writer)
940 Locust Ave
Charlottesville, VA 22901-4030, USA

Wrightman, Tim (Football Player)
Chicago Bears
3505 S Denison Ave
San Pedro, CA 90731-6803, USA

Wrona, Rick (Athlete, Baseball Player)
2946 E 57th St
Tulsa, OK 74105-7404, USA

Wszola, Jacek (Athlete, Track Athlete)
Ul Chrzanowskiego 7 m 70
Warsaw 04-381, POLAND

Wu, Alice (Writer)
c/o Staff Member *Creative Artists Agency (CAA)*
2000 Avenue of the Stars Ste 100
Los Angeles, CA 90067-4705, USA

Wu, Constance (Actor)
c/o Marsha McManus *Principal Entertainment*
9255 W Sunset Blvd Ste 500
Los Angeles, CA 90069-3301, USA

Wu, Daniel (Actor)
Diversion Pictures
906 Westlands Centre
20 Westlands Rd
Quarry Bay, HONG KONG

Wu, David (Congressman, Politician)
2338 Rayburn Hob
Washington, DC 20515-0546, USA

Wu, Gordon Y S (Business Person)
Hopewell Holdings
Hopewell Center
183 Queen Road East
Hong Kong, CHINA

Wu, Jason (Designer)
Jason Wu
240 W 35th St Fl 11
New York, NY 10001-2506, USA

Wu, Kristy (Actor)
c/o Craig Dorfman *Frontline Management*
5670 Wilshire Blvd Ste 1370
Los Angeles, CA 90036-5649, USA

Wu, Lisa (Reality Star)
c/o Staff Member *Bravo TV (NY)*
30 Rockefeller Plz
New York, NY 10112-0015, USA

Wu, Vivian (Actor)
McKeon-Myones Management
9100 Wilshire Blvd Ste 350W
C/O Laura Myones
Beverly Hills, CA 90212-3437, USA

Wudunn, Sheryl (Journalist)
35 W 89th St Apt 1A
New York, NY 10024-2016, USA

Wuerffel, Danny (Athlete, Football Player, Heisman Trophy Winner)
424 Mimosa Dr
Decatur, GA 30030-3736, USA

Wuertz, Michael (Athlete, Baseball Player)
15029 N Thompson
Peak Pkwy Ste B111
Scottsdale, AZ 85260-2223, USA

Wuhl, Robert (Actor)
Sophie K Entertainment
262 W 38th St Rm 1604
New York, NY 10018-1134, USA

Wuhrer, Kari (Actor, Musician)
PO Box 69188
Los Angeles, CA 90069-0188, USA

Wunderlich, Paul (Artist)
Haynstr 2
Hamburg 20949, GERMANY

Wunsch, Jerry (Football Player)
Tampa Bay Buccaneers
2601 Red Maple Rd
Wausau, WI 54401-9151, USA

Wunsch, Kelly (Athlete, Baseball Player)
11613 Hunters Green Trl
Austin, TX 78732-2055, USA

Wuorinen, Charles P (Composer)
Howard Stokar Mgmt
870 W End Ave
New York, NY 10025-4918, USA

Wurtzel, Elizabeth (Actor, Writer)

Wurz, Alexander (Race Car Driver)
McLaren Int'l Working Park
Albert Dr
Woking
Surrey GU21 5JY, UNITED KINGDOM (UK)

Wu-Tang Clan (Music Group)
PO Box 405
Asbury Park, NJ 07712-0405, USA

Wuycik, Dennis (Athlete, Basketball Player)
31 Rogerson Dr
Chapel Hill, NC 27517-4037, USA

Wu Yigong (Director)
52 Yong Fu Road
Shanghai, CHINA

Wyant, Fred (Football Player)
Washington Redskins
516 Westwood Ave
Morgantown, WV 26505-2125, USA

Wyatt, Alvin (Football Player)
Oakland Raiders
PO Box 244
Daytona Beach, FL 32115-0244, USA

Wyatt, Doug (Athlete, Football Player)
23 Andante Trail Pl
Shenandoah, TX 77381-2775, USA

Wyatt, Jennifer (Golfer)
Carolina Group
2321 Devine St Ste A
Columbia, SC 29205-2428, USA

Wyatt, Keke (Musician)
Universal Attractions
145 W 57th St # 1500
New York, NY 10019-2220, USA

Wyatt, Shannon (Actor)
8949 Falling Creek Ct
Annandale, VA 22003-4108, USA

Wyatt, Sharon (Actor)
16830 Ventura Blvd Ste 300
Encino, CA 91436-1715, USA

Wyatt, Summer (Beauty Pageant Winner)
2015 Unity Rd
Princeton, WV 24739-8587, USA

Wyatt Jr, Oscar S (Business Person)
Coastal Corp
6955 S Union Park Ctr Ste 540
Midvale, UT 84047-6520, USA

Wyche, Samuel D (Sam) (Athlete, Coach, Football Coach, Football Player, Sportscaster)
PO Box 1570
Pickens, SC 29671-1570, USA

Wycheck, Frank (Athlete, Football Player)
4674 Sunrise Ave
Bensalem, PA 19020-1112, USA

Wycinsky, Craig (Football Player)
Cleveland Browns
6890 E Sunrise Dr Ste 120
Tucson, AZ 85750-0739, USA

Wycoff, Brooks (Athlete)
1 Mohegan Sun Blvd
Uncasville, CT 06382-1355

Wyden, Ron (Politician)
312 A St NE
Washington, DC 20002-5938, USA

Wyeth, James Browning '''Jamie''' (Artist)
Jamie Wyeths Editions
701 Smiths Bridge Rd
Wilmington, DE 19807-1325, USA

Wygal, Terry (Business Person)
Express Home Solutions Ltd
3005 Woodland Hills Dr
Kingwood, TX 77339-1403, USA

Wylde, Chris (Actor, Comedian)
3313 1/2 Barham Blvd
Los Angeles, CA 90068-1450, USA

Wylde, Peter (Athlete, Horse Racer, Olympic Athlete)
247 Wood Dale Dr
Wellington, FL 33414-4719, USA

Wylde, Zakk (Musician)
c/o Bob Ringe *Survival Management*
30765 Pacific Coast Hwy Ste 325
Malibu, CA 90265-3643, USA

Wylde Bunch, The (Music Group)
c/o Staff Member *Paradigm (Monterey)*
404 W Franklin St
Monterey, CA 93940-2303, USA

Wyle, Noah (Actor, Director, Producer)
PO Box 1798
Santa Ynez, CA 93460-1798, USA

Wylie, Adam (Actor)
14011 Ventura Blvd Ste 202
Sherman Oaks, CA 91423-3594, USA

Wylie, Joe (Athlete, Football Player)
8312 Bucknell Dr
Tyler, TX 75703-5103, USA

Wylie, Paul (Athlete, Figure Skater, Olympic Athlete)
2046 Kilmonack Ln
Charlotte, NC 28270-9780, USA

Wyludda, Ilke (Athlete, Track Athlete)
LAC Chemnitz
Relchengainer Str 154
Chemnitz 09125, GERMANY

Wyman, Bill (Actor, Composer, Musician)
Ripple Productions
344 Kings Road
London SW3 5UR, United Kingdom

Wyman, David (Football Player)
20918 NE Redmond Fall City Rd
Redmond, WA 98053, USA

Wyman, Joel (Producer, Writer)
c/o Staff Member *Creative Artists Agency (CAA)*
2000 Avenue of the Stars Ste 100
Los Angeles, CA 90067-4705, USA

Wynalda, Eric (Soccer Player)
710 Triunfo Canyon Rd
Westlake Village, CA 91361-1842, USA

Wyn-Davies, Geraint (Actor)
438 Queen St E
Oscars Abrams Zimel
Toronto, ON M5A 1T4, CANADA

Wynder, A J (Athlete, Basketball Player)
1 Cardenti Ct
Newark, DE 19702-6833, USA

Wynegar, Butch (Athlete, Baseball Player)
PO Box 915811
Longwood, FL 32791-5811, USA

Wyner, George (Actor)
3450 Laurie Pl
Studio City, CA 91604-3881, USA

Wynn, Bob (Athlete, Golfer)
78455 Calle Orense
La Quinta, CA 92253-2370, USA

Wynn, Elaine (Business Person)
Elaine Wynn Family Foundation
3800 Howard Hughes Pkwy Ste 960
Las Vegas, NV 89169-6018, USA

Wynn, Jarius (Athlete, Football Player)

Wynn, Jimmy (Athlete, Baseball Player)
5507 Sandy Field Ct
Rosharon, TX 77583-2040, USA

Wynn, Kerry (Athlete, Football Player)

Wynn, Renaldo (Football Player)
Jacksonville Jaguars
19805 Rothschild Ct
Ashburn, VA 20147-4124, USA

Wynn, Spergon (Football Player)
Cleveland Browns
614 32nd St
Galveston, TX 77550-1325, USA

Wynn, Stephen (Misc)
PO Box 93598
Las Vegas, NV 89193-3598, USA

Wynn, Stephen A (Business Person)
Wynn Las Vegas
3131 Las Vegas Blvd S
Las Vegas, NV 89109-1967, USA

Wynn, Steve (Business Person)
Wynn Las Vegas
3131 Las Vegas Blvd S
Las Vegas, NV 89109-1967, USA

Wynne, Billy (Athlete, Baseball Player)
7722 Greenwich Ct W
Jacksonville, FL 32277-0924, USA

Wynne, Marvell (Athlete, Baseball Player)
39640 Del Val Dr
Murrieta, CA 92562-4038, USA

Wynorski, Jim (Director, Producer)
19653 Schoenborn St
Northridge, CA 91324-4144, USA

Wynter, Sarah (Actor)
c/o David (Dave) Fleming *Atlas Artists*
9220 W Sunset Blvd Ste 225
Los Angeles, CA 90069-3513, USA

Wyrozub, Randy (Athlete, Hockey Player)
6717 Westminster Dr
East Amherst, NY 14051-2805, USA

Wysocki, Ben (Musician)
4500 W 30th Ave
Denver, CO 80212-3019, USA

Wyss, Amanda (Actor)
c/o Staff Member *Badgley-Connor-King*
9229 W Sunset Blvd Ste 311
Los Angeles, CA 90069-3403, USA

Xan, Lil (Musician)
c/o Josh Rittenhouse *Agency for the Performing Arts (APA)*
405 S Beverly Dr Ste 500
Beverly Hills, CA 90212-4425, USA

Xie, Fiona (Actor)
c/o Jaeson Ma *East West Artists*
5200 W Century Blvd # 701
Los Angeles, CA 90045-5928, USA

Xie Bingxin (Writer)
Central Nationalities Institute
Residential Qtrs
Beijing 100081, CHINA

Xie Jin (Director)
Shanghai Film Studio
595 Caoxi Beilu
Shanghai, CHINA

Xscape (Musician)
c/o Staff Member *So So Def Recordings Inc*
1350 Spring St NW Ste 750
Atlanta, GA 30309-2870, USA

Xu Bing (Artist)
540 Metropolitan Ave
Brooklyn, NY 11211-8445, USA

Xuereb, Emanuel (Actor)
c/o Staff Member *Pantheon Talent*
1801 Century Park E Ste 1910
Los Angeles, CA 90067-2321, USA

Xuereb, Salvator (Actor)
4118 Warner Blvd APT D
Burbank, CA 91505-4127, USA

Xue Wei (Musician)
134 Sheaveshill Ave
London NW9, UNITED KINGDOM (UK)

Xu Shuyang (Artist)
Zheijang Academy of Fine Arts
PO Box 169
Hangzhou, CHINA

Xzibit (Musician)
c/o Eric Skinner *Open Bar Entertainment*
16000 Ventura Blvd Ste 600
Encino, CA 91436-2753, USA

Yabians, Frank (Producer)
88 Bull Path
East Hampton, NY 11937-4622, USA

Yablonski, Jeremy (Athlete, Hockey Player)
2615 Maverick Way
Celina, TX 75009-1420, USA

Yabu, Keiichi (Athlete, Baseball Player)
c/o Team Member *San Francisco Giants*
24 Willie Mays Plz
Sbc Park
San Francisco, CA 94107-2199, USA

Yachmenev, Vitali (Athlete, Hockey Player)
1485 Gulf of Mexico Dr Unit 104
Longboat Key, FL 34228-3472, USA

Yachty, Lil (Musician)
c/o Pierre Thomas *Quality Control Music*
1479 Metropolitan Pkwy SW
Atlanta, GA 30310-4453, USA

Yaeger, Andrea (Tennis Player)
1490 S Ute Ave
Aspen, CO 81611-2814, USA

Yager, Rick (Cartoonist)
North American Syndicate
235 E 45th St
New York, NY 10017-3305, USA

Yagher, Jeff (Actor)
15057 Sherview Pl
Sherman Oaks, CA 91403-5037, USA

Yago, Gideon (Journalist, Television Host)
c/o Staff Member *MTV (NY)*
1515 Broadway
New York, NY 10036-8901, USA

Yaguda, Stan (Musician)
Joyce Agency
370 Harrison Ave
Harrison, NY 10528-2714, USA

Yagudin, Alexei (Figure Skater)
Connecticut Skating Center
300 Alumni Rd
Newington, CT 06111-1868, USA

Yahr, Betty (Athlete, Baseball Player)
10360 Timber Ridge Dr
Milan, MI 48160-8929, USA

Yakavonis, Ray (Athlete, Football Player)
8 Strand St
Hanover Township, PA 18706-4011, USA

Yake, Terry (Athlete, Hockey Player)
7827 Wind Hill Dr
O Fallon, MO 63368-4135, USA

Yale, Brian (Musician)
2616 Bayview Dr
Ft Lauderdale, FL 33306-1766, USA

Yaleborough, Cale (Race Car Driver)
2723 W Palmetto St Unit B
Florence, SC 29501-5929, USA

Yallop, Frank (Coach)
San Jose Earthquakes
3550 Stevens Creek Blvd Ste 200
San Jose, CA 95117-1031, USA

Yamagata, Hiro (Artist)
1080 Ave D
Redondo Beach, CA 90277, USA

Yamagata, Rachel (Musician)
c/o Staff Member *Paradigm (Monterey)*
404 W Franklin St
Monterey, CA 93940-2303, USA

Yamaguchi, Kristi (Athlete, Figure Skater, Olympic Athlete)
c/o Yuki Saegusa *IMG Models (NY)*
304 Park Ave S PH N
New York, NY 10010-4303, USA

Yamaguchi, Roy (Business Person)
Roy's Restaurant
6600 Kalanianaole Hwy Ste 110
Kai Corporate Plaza
Honolulu, HI 96825-1282, USA

Yamame, Marlene Mitsuko (Actor)
Herb Tannen
10801 National Blvd Ste 101
Los Angeles, CA 90064-4140, USA

Yamamoto, Takuma (Business Person)
Fujitsu Ltd
1-6-1 Marunouchi
Chiyodaku
Tokyo 00100, JAPAN

Yamamoto, Yohji (Designer, Fashion Designer)
14-15 Conduit St
London W1R 9TG, UNITED KINGDOM (UK)

Yamanaka, Tsuyoshi (Swimmer)
6-10-33-212 Akasaka
Minatoku
Tokyo, JAPAN

Yamaoka, Seigen H (Religious Leader)
Buddhist Churches of America
1710 Octavia St
San Francisco, CA 94109-4341, USA

Yamasaki, Lindsey (Athlete, Basketball Player)
767 Union St
San Francisco, CA 94133-2723, USA

Yamasaki, Taro M (Journalist)
People Magazine Editorial Dept
Time-Life Building
New York, NY 10020, USA

Yamazaki, Naoko (Astronaut)
Japanese Aerospace Exploration Agency
2-1-1- Sengen
Tsukuba-shi
Ibaraki 305 8505, JAPAN

Yamin, Elliott (Actor, Musician)
c/o Carlos Keyes *Red Entertainment Agency*
3537 36th St Ste 2
Astoria, NY 11106-1347, USA

Yan, Esteban (Athlete, Baseball Player)
851 60th Ave S
St Petersburg, FL 33705-5533, USA

Yanchar, William (Athlete, Football Player)
PO Box 460141
Aurora, CO 80046-0141, USA

Yancy, Emily (Actor)
Henderson/Hogan
8285 W Sunset Blvd Ste 1
West Hollywood, CA 90046-2420, USA

Yancy, Hugh (Athlete, Baseball Player)
1708 Marilyn Ave
Bradenton, FL 34207-4633, USA

Yanda, Marshal (Athlete, Football Player)
c/o Neil Cornrich *NC Sports, LLC*
best to contact via email
Columbus, OH 43201, USA

Yandle, Keith (Athlete, Hockey Player)
646 Canton Ave
Milton, MA 02186-3133, USA

Yanez, Eduardo (Actor)
c/o Thomas Richards *Corsa Agency, The*
11849 W Olympic Blvd Ste 100
Los Angeles, CA 90064-1164, USA

Yang, Janet (Producer)
Manifest Film Company
PO Box 832
Santa Monica, CA 90406-0832, USA

Yang, Jerry (Business Person)
455B Portage Ave
Palo Alto, CA 94306-2213, USA

Yang, Jimmy O (Actor, Comedian)
c/o Bryan Walsh *Artists First*
9465 Wilshire Blvd Ste 900
Beverly Hills, CA 90212-2608, USA

Yang, Liwei (Misc)
Satellite Launch Center
Jiuquan
Gansu Province, CHINA

Yang, Young A (Athlete, Golfer)
4805 Lyons View Pike Apt 302
Knoxville, TN 37919-6487, USA

Yankee, Daddy (Musician)
c/o Staff Member *Relentless Agency*
261 E 134th St Fl 2
Bronx, NY 10454-4405, USA

Yankey, David (Athlete, Football Player)
c/o Michael McCartney *Priority Sports & Entertainment (Chicago)*
325 N La Salle Dr Ste 650
Chicago, IL 60654-8182, USA

Yankovic, Al (Weird Al) (Comedian, Musician)
1631 Magnetic Ter
Los Angeles, CA 90069-1149, USA

Yankowski, Ron (Athlete, Football Player)
686 Bell Rd
Wright City, MO 63390-2102, USA

Yanni (Musician, Songwriter)
PO Box 107
8983 Okeechobee Blvd #202
West Palm Beach, FL 33402-0107, USA

Yaralian, Zaven (Athlete, Football Player)
PO Box 1080
Summerland, CA 93067-1080, USA

Yarber, Eric (Athlete, Football Player)
Oregon State University
325 Valley Football Ctr
Attn: Football Program
Corvallis, OR 97331-8544, USA

Yarborough, W Caleb (Cale) (Race Car Driver)
Yarborough Racing
2723 W Palmetto St
Florence, SC 29501-5929, USA

Yarbrough, Cedric (Actor)
c/o Adri Palmieri *Baker Winokur Ryder Public Relations*
9100 Wilshire Blvd
W Tower #500
Beverly Hills, CA 90212-3415, USA

Yarbrough, Curtis (Religious Leader)
General Baptists Assn
100 Stinson Dr
Poplar Bluff, MO 63901-8746, USA

Yarbrough, Jim (Athlete, Football Player)
720 N Phelps Ave
Winter Park, FL 32789-2757, USA

Yarbrough, Jim (Athlete, Football Player)
440 Capricorn St
Cedar Hill, TX 75104-8106, USA

Yardbirds, The (Music Group)
PO Box 1821
Ojai, CA 93024-1821, USA

Yared, Gabriel (Composer)
c/o Staff Member *Evolution Music Partners*
1680 Vine St Ste 500
Hollywood, CA 90028-8800, USA

Yaremchuk, Gary (Athlete, Hockey Player)
408 Crimson Dr
Sherwood Park, AB T8H 0H2, Canada

Yarkin, Cori (Musician)
GreeneHouse Management
PO Box 151234
C/O Allan Greene
Altamonte Springs, FL 32715-1234, USA

Yarlett, Claire (Actor)
c/o Lorraine Berglund *Lorraine Berglund Management*
11537 Hesby St
North Hollywood, CA 91601-3618, USA

Yarmuth, Jobn (Congressman, Politician)
435 Cannon Hob
Washington, DC 20515-4312, USA

Yarmuth, John A (Congressman, Politician)
600 Dr Martin Luther King Pl Ste 216
Romano Mazzoli Federal Building
Louisville, KY 40202-2285, USA

Yarnall, Ed (Athlete, Baseball Player)
9837 Vouvray Dr
Baton Rouge, LA 70817-7646, USA

Yarnell, Ed (Athlete, Baseball Player)
9837 Vouvray Dr
Baton Rouge, LA 70817-7646, USA

Yarno, George (Athlete, Football Player)
1529 18th St
Lewiston, ID 83501-3657, USA

Yarno, John (Athlete, Football Player)
10535 158th Ave NE
Redmond, WA 98052-2659, USA

Yarrow, Peter (Musician, Songwriter, Writer)
27 W 67th St # 5E
New York, NY 10023-6258, USA

Yary, Ron (Athlete, Football Player)

Yasbeck, Amy (Actor)
1100 Alta Loma Rd OFC
West Hollywood, CA 90069-2436, USA

Yashin, Alexei (Athlete, Hockey Player)
6 Polo Dr
Old Westbury, NY 11568-1043, USA

Yastrzemski, Carl (Athlete, Baseball Player)
22 Lakeshore Rd
Boxford, MA 01921-1115, USA

Yasukawa, Roger (Race Car Driver)
2801 Sepulveda Blvd UNIT 4
Torrance, CA 90505-2802, USA

Yasutake, Patti (Actor)
145 S Fairfax Ave Ste 310
Los Angeles, CA 90036-2176, USA

Yates, Bill (Cartoonist)
c/o Staff Member *King Features Syndication*
300 W 57th St Fl 15
New York, NY 10019-5238, USA

Yates, Billy (Athlete, Football Player)
c/o Staff Member *New England Patriots*
1 Patriot Pl
Foxboro, MA 02035-1388, USA

Yates, Bob (Athlete, Football Player)
391 Bentwood Dr
Spring Branch, TX 78070-6016, USA

Yates, Doug (Race Car Driver)
Doug Yates Racing
112 Byers Creek Rd
Mooresville, NC 28117-4376, USA

Yates, Jim (Race Car Driver)
Commonwealth Service & Supply
4740 Eisenhower Ave
Alexandria, VA 22304-4806, USA

Yates, T.J. (Athlete, Football Player)

Yates, Tyler (Athlete, Baseball Player)
c/o Pat Rooney *SFX Baseball*
676 N Michigan Ave Ste 3000
Chicago, IL 60611-2860, USA

Yates, Wayne (Athlete, Basketball Player)
210 Yates Rd
Robeline, LA 71469, USA

Yates, Yvette (Producer)
c/o Erik Bright *Prodigy Public Relations*
2601 Ocean Park Blvd Ste 300
Santa Monica, CA 90405-5274, USA

Yavari, Leila (Actor)
c/o Staff Member *Cunningham Escott Slevin & Doherty (CESD)*
10635 Santa Monica Blvd Ste 130
Los Angeles, CA 90025-8306, USA

Yawney, Trent (Athlete, Hockey Player)
7750 E Appaloosa Trl
Orange, CA 92869-2407, USA

Yayo, Tony (Musician)
c/o Staff Member *Interscope Records*
1755 Broadway Fl 6
New York, NY 10019-3768, USA

Yazpik, Jose Maria (Actor)
c/o Carlos Carreras *Agency for the Performing Arts (APA)*
405 S Beverly Dr Ste 500
Beverly Hills, CA 90212-4425, USA

Yeager, Charles (Chuck) (Misc)
PO Box 579
Penn Valley, CA 95946-0579, USA

Yeager, Jeana (Misc)
3695 Highway 50
Campbell, TX 75422, USA

Yeager, Steve (Athlete, Baseball Player)
JD Legends Promotions
9639 Sagebrush Ave
Chatsworth, CA 91311-4764, USA

Yeagley, Jerry (Coach)
1418 S Sare Rd
Bloomington, IN 47401-4431, USA

Yeah Yeah Yeahs (Music Group)
c/o Tony Cuilla *Ciulla Management*
1509 N Crescent Heights Blvd Ste 4
West Hollywood, CA 90046-2425, USA

Yeakel, Scott (Astronaut)
23372 Mersey Rd
Middleburg, VA 20117-3522, USA

Yearley, Douglas C (Business Person)
Phelps Dodge Corp
1 N Central Ave
Phoenix, AZ 85004-4414, USA

Yearwood, Trisha (Musician)
PO Box 120895
Nashville, TN 37212-0895, USA

Yeates, Jeff (Athlete, Football Player)
3793 Club Dr NE
Atlanta, GA 30319-1107, USA

Yeatman, Will (Athlete, Football Player)

Yeats, Matthew (Athlete, Hockey Player)
7221 35th St E
Sarasota, FL 34243-3327, USA

Yelding, Eric (Athlete, Baseball Player)
PO Box 325
Montrose, AL 36559-0325, USA

Yeley, JJ (Race Car Driver)
Mayfield Motorsports
2220 Hwy. 49 N
Harrisburg, NC 28075, USA

Yelle, Stephane (Athlete, Hockey Player)
212 Maplehurst Pt
Highlands Ranch, CO 80126-5613, USA

Yellen, Larry (Athlete, Baseball Player)
3886 Toccoa Falls Dr
Duluth, GA 30097-8105, USA

Yellen, Linda B (Director, Producer)
3 Sheridan Sq Apt 17B
New York, NY 10014-6834, USA

Yellowcard (Musician)
Capitol Records
1750 Vine St # T-06
Hollywood, CA 90028-5274, USA

Yelvington, Richard J (Athlete, Football Player)
2105 Barbe St
Lake Charles, LA 70601-9017, USA

Yen, Donnie (Actor)
c/o Staff Member *Bullet Films Productions*
16/F Sun Hing Industrial Bldg
46 Wong Chuk Hang Rd
Aberdeen NIL NIL HKSAR, HONG KONG

Yeo, Gwendoline (Actor)
c/o Liza Anderson *Anderson Group Public Relations*
8060 Melrose Ave Fl 4
Los Angeles, CA 90046-7038, USA

Yeo, Mike (Athlete, Hockey Player)
317 Washington St
Attn Coaching Staff
Saint Paul, MN 55102-1609, USA

Yeoh, Michelle (Actor)
c/o David Unger *Artist International Group*
8439 W Sunset Blvd Ste 309
W Hollywood, CA 90069-1926, USA

Yeoman, Owain (Actor)
3170 Durand Dr
Los Angeles, CA 90068-1614, USA

Yeoman, William F (Bill) (Athlete, Coach, Football Coach, Football Player)
607 Bendwood Dr
Houston, TX 77024-4027, USA

Yerman, Jack (Athlete, Olympic Athlete, Track Athlete)
PO Box 4125
Chico, CA 95927-4125, USA

Yes (Music Group)
c/o Staff Member *10th Street Entertainment*
700 N San Vicente Blvd # G410
W Hollywood, CA 90069-5060, USA

Yeston, Maury (Composer)
Yale University
Music Dept
New Haven, CT 06520, USA

Yett, Rich (Athlete, Baseball Player)
5840 E Fairbrook Cir
Mesa, AZ 85205-5559, USA

Yeun, Steven (Actor)
c/o Peter McHugh *Gotham Group*
1041 N Formosa Ave # 200
West Hollywood, CA 90046-6703, USA

Yewchyn, Darren (Athlete, Football Player)
184 Oakview Ave
Winnipeg, MB R2K 0R8, Canada

Yewcic, Thomas (Tom) (Athlete, Baseball Player, Football Player)
21 Crescent St Apt 332
Wakefield, MA 01880-2458, USA

Yi, Charlyne (Actor, Producer, Writer)
c/o Christie Smith *Rise Management*
6338 Wilshire Blvd
Los Angeles, CA 90048-5002, USA

Yilmaz, A Mesut (Prime Minister)
Basbakanlik
Bakanliklar
Ankara, TURKEY

Yimou, Zhang (Actor, Director, Producer, Writer)
c/o William (Bill) Kong *Edko Films*
1212 Tower 2
Admiralty Centre
Hong Kong, CHINA

Ying Yang Twins (Music Group)
TVT Records
23 E 4th St Fl 3
New York, NY 10003-7023, USA

Yip, David (Actor)
15 Golden Square #315
London, ENGLAND W1R 3AG, UNITED KINGDOM

Yip, Francoise (Actor)
Infinite Artists
10-206 East 6th Ave
Vancouver, BC V5T 1J8, CANADA

Yip, Vern (Designer, Television Host)
24 Wakefield Dr NE
Atlanta, GA 30309-1515, USA

Ylonen, Juha (Athlete, Hockey Player)
1000 Palladium Dr
Kanata, ON K2V 1A4, Canada

Ylonen, Lauri Johannes (Musician)
c/o Staff Member *Rasmus, The*
Playground Music Scandinavia
Box 3171
Malm?? s-200 22, SWEDEN

Yoakam, Dwight (Musician, Songwriter)
Bluebird House
10153 1/2 Riverside Dr Ste 419
Toluca Lake, CA 91602-2561, USA

Yoba, Malik (Actor)
c/o Matt Luber *Luber Roklin Management*
5815 W Sunset Blvd Ste 208
Los Angeles, CA 90028-6481, USA

Yochim, Len (Athlete, Baseball Player)
316 Nelson Dr
New Orleans, LA 70123-1958, USA

Yochum, Dan (Athlete, Football Player)
88 Doges Promenade
Lindenhurst, NY 11757-6408, USA

Yocum, Matt (Race Car Driver)
9910 Devonshire Dr
Huntersville, NC 28078-5965, USA

Yoder, Kevin (Congressman, Politician)
214 Cannon Hob
Washington, DC 20515-3007, USA

Yodoyman, Joseph (Prime Minister)
Prime Minister's Office
N'Djamena, CHAD

Yo Gotti (Musician)
c/o Jennifer Williams *J Sharpe Agency PR*
304 Park Ave S
New York, NY 10010-4301, USA

Yohn, John (Athlete, Football Player)
12 Riverview Dr
Middletown, PA 17057-3433, USA

Yoho, Mack (Athlete, Football Player)
2205 Sacramento St Apt 304
San Francisco, CA 94115-2394, USA

Yoken, Mel B (Writer)
261 Carroll St
New Bedford, MA 02740-1412, USA

Yonakor, Rich (Athlete, Basketball Player)
38140 Tamarac Blvd Apt 106
Willoughby, OH 44094-3448, USA

Yonder Mountain String Band (Music Group)
c/o Staff Member *Paradigm (Monterey)*
404 W Franklin St
Monterey, CA 93940-2303, USA

Yoo, Aaron (Actor)
c/o Tony Cloer *Blue Ridge Entertainment*
3 Columbus Cir Fl 15
New York, NY 10019-8716, USA

Yoo, Paula (Writer)
c/o Nancy Etz *ICM Partners*
10250 Constellation Blvd Fl 7
Los Angeles, CA 90067-6207, USA

Yore, Jim (Athlete, Football Player)
1084 Westlake Woods Dr
Springfield, MI 49037-7665, USA

York, Francine (Actor)
6430 W Sunset Blvd Ste 1205
Los Angeles, CA 90028-8002, USA

York, Jason (Athlete, Hockey Player)
1403 Sherruby Way
Kanata, ON K2W 1B1, Canada

York, Jim (Athlete, Baseball Player)
31262 Via Del Verde
San Juan Capistrano, CA 92675-6315, USA

York, John J (Actor)
4846 Agnes Ave
Valley Village, CA 91607-3703, USA

York, Kathleen (Bird) (Actor)
2235 Alcyona Dr
Los Angeles, CA 90068-2804, USA

York, Michael (Actor)
c/o Lori DeWaal *Lori DeWaal & Associates PR*
14724 Ventura Blvd Ste 507
Sherman Oaks, CA 91403-3515, USA

York, Michael M (Journalist)
Lexington Herald-Leader
Editorial Dept
Main & Midland
Lexington, KY 40507, USA

York, Mike (Athlete, Baseball Player)
8001 S 84th Ct
Justice, IL 60458-1420, USA

York, Mike (Athlete, Hockey Player, Olympic Athlete)
3335 Sherman Park Dr
Sault Sainte Marie, MI 49783-1119, USA

York, Morgan (Actor)
c/o Meredith Fine *Coast to Coast Talent Group*
3350 Barham Blvd
Los Angeles, CA 90068-1404, USA

York, Taylor (Musician)
c/o Randy Dease *Fly South Music Group*
37 N Orange Ave Ste 790
Orlando, FL 32801-2450, USA

Yorke, Helene (Actor)
c/o Russell Gregory *Regarding Entertainment*
341 Eastern Pkwy Apt 7A
Brooklyn, NY 11216-4860, USA

Yorke, Thom (Musician)
c/o Staff Member *Creative Artists Agency (CAA)*
2000 Avenue of the Stars Ste 100
Los Angeles, CA 90067-4705, USA

Yorkin, Peg (Politician)
Fund for Feminist Majority
1600 Wilson Blvd Ste 704
Arlington, VA 22209-2505, USA

Yorn, Peter (Musician, Songwriter, Writer)
c/o Rick Yorn *LBI Entertainment*
2000 Avenue of the Stars
N Tower Fl 3
Los Angeles, CA 90067-4700, USA

Yoseliani, Otar D (Director)
Mitskewitch 1 Korp
1 #38
Tbilisi 380060, GEORGIA

Yoshiki (Musician)
c/o Staff Member *WME|IMG*
9601 Wilshire Blvd
Beverly Hills, CA 90210-5213, USA

Yost, David (Actor)
8837 Cortina Cir
Roseville, CA 95678-2940, USA

Yost, Elvy (Actor)
c/o Alyx Carr *42West*
600 3rd Ave Fl 23
New York, NY 10016-1914, USA

Yost, Ned (Athlete, Baseball Player, Coach)
Milwaukee Brewers
108 Victoria Dr
Lagrange, GA 30240-6338, USA

Yothers, Tina (Actor, Musician)
1834 S Helen Ave
Ontario, CA 91762-6023, USA

Youel, Jim (Athlete, Football Player)
1102 Avenue F
Fort Madison, IA 52627-2743, USA

Youkilis, Kevin (Athlete, Baseball Player)
19475 N Grayhawk Dr Unit 1083
Scottsdale, AZ 85255-7420, USA

Youmans, Floyd (Athlete, Baseball Player)
2716 Water Ln
Nolensville, TN 37135-5017, USA

Youmans, Maury (Athlete, Football Player)
300 Beach Dr NE Apt 2104
Saint Petersburg, FL 33701-3461, USA

You Me at Six (Music Group)
c/o Mike Hayes *ICM Partners*
10250 Constellation Blvd Fl 7
Los Angeles, CA 90067-6207, USA

Young, Ace (Musician)
c/o Stephen Ford *Diva Central Inc*
7510 W Sunset Blvd # 1445
Los Angeles, CA 90046-3408, USA

Young, Aden (Actor)
c/o Ann Churchill-Brown *Shanahan Management*
Level 3 Berman House
Surry Hills 02010, AUSTRALIA

Young, Adrian (Musician)
4220 Lakewood Dr
Lakewood, CA 90712-3839, USA

Young, Al (Athlete, Football Player)
PO Box 7641
North Augusta, SC 29861-7641, USA

Young, Almon (Athlete, Football Player)
PO Box 983
Mc Crory, AR 72101-0983, USA

Young, Andrew (Politician)
National Council of Churches
523 Spring Oaks Blvd
Altamonte Springs, FL 32714-2314, USA

Young, Angus (Musician)
c/o Christopher Dalston *Creative Artists Agency (CAA)*
2000 Avenue of the Stars Ste 100
Los Angeles, CA 90067-4705, USA

Young, Anthony (Athlete, Football Player)
914 Colonial Ct
Coatesville, PA 19320-1685, USA

Young, Archie (Athlete, Baseball Player)
Birmingham Black Barons
1804 Ethel Ave SW
Birmingham, AL 35211-4914, USA

Young, Barbara (Actor)
23-B Deodar Rd.
London, ENGLAND SWl5- 2NP, UNITED KINGDOM

Young, Bellamy (Actor)
c/o Alex Spieller *Baker Winokur Ryder Public Relations*
200 5th Ave Fl 5
New York, NY 10010-3307, USA

Young, Bob (Cartoonist)
c/o Staff Member *King Features Syndication*
300 W 57th St Fl 15
New York, NY 10019-5238, USA

Young, Boyd (Misc)
United Paperworkers Union
60 Blvd Of The Allies Ste 902
Pittsburgh, PA 15222-1258, USA

Young, Brian (Musician)
MOB Agency
6404 Wilshire Blvd Ste 505
Los Angeles, CA 90048-5507, USA

Young, Brian (Athlete, Hockey Player)
PO Box 835
Jasper, AB T0E 1E0, Canada

Young, Bryant C (Athlete, Football Player)
5802 Country Club Pkwy
San Jose, CA 95138-2223, USA

Young, Burt (Actor)
Higgins Harte International
11 W Pioneer Blvd Bldg 4
Mesquite, NV 89027-3510, USA

Young, Charle E (Athlete, Football Player)
16035 Mink Rd NE
Woodinville, WA 98077-9460, USA

Young, Charles E (Athlete, Football Player)
16035 Mink Rd NE
Woodinville, WA 98077-9460, USA

Young, Charles L (Athlete, Football Player)
2120 Daufuskie Dr
Raleigh, NC 27604-2074, USA

Young, Chris (Athlete, Baseball Player)
c/o Staff Member *Arizona Diamondbacks*
PO Box 2095
Phoenix, AZ 85001-2095, USA

Young, Chris (Musician)
c/o Ron Shapiro *Shapiro Sher Guinot & Sandler*
36 S Charles St Ste 2000
Baltimore, MD 21201-3104, USA

Young, CJ (Athlete, Hockey Player, Olympic Athlete)
130 Hoover Rd
Needham, MA 02494-1548, USA

Young, Curt (Athlete, Baseball Player)
10800 E Cactus Rd Unit 2
Scottsdale, AZ 85259-2503, USA

Young, Danny (Athlete, Baseball Player)
1841 Lascassas Pike Apt J153
Murfreesboro, TN 37130-0609, USA

Young, Darrel (Athlete, Football Player)

Young, Dean (Cartoonist)
c/o Staff Member *King Features Syndication*
300 W 57th St Fl 15
New York, NY 10019-5238, USA

Young, Delmon (Athlete, Baseball Player)
5904 Pelican Bay Plz S
Gulfport, FL 33707-3943, USA

young, Delwyn (Athlete, Baseball Player)
2212 Radcourt Dr
Hacienda Heights, CA 91745-5716, USA

Young, Dmitri (Athlete, Baseball Player)
26 SE lOth Ave
Fort Lauderdale, FL 33301-2054, USA

Young, Don (Athlete, Baseball Player)
4122 E Milton Dr
Cave Creek, AZ 85331-5843, USA

Young, Don (Congressman, Politician)
2314 Rayburn Hob
Washington, DC 20515-4907, USA

Young, Duane (Athlete, Football Player)
2255 River Run Dr
San Diego, CA 92108-5888, USA

Young, Earl (Athlete, Track Athlete)
4344 Livingston Ave
Dallas, TX 75205-2608, USA

Young, Eric O (Athlete, Baseball Player)
120 Brewster Ave
Piscataway, NJ 08854-2205, USA

Young, Ernie (Athlete, Baseball Player, Olympic Athlete)
8995 E Palm Ridge Dr
Scottsdale, AZ 85260-7533, USA

Young, Fred (Musician)
Mitchell Fox Mgmt
212 3rd Ave N
#301
Nashville, TN 37201-1604, USA

Young, Fredd (Athlete, Football Player)
4200 Real Del Sur
Las Cruces, NM 88011-7204, USA

Young, George (Athlete, Olympic Athlete)
8926 N Cox Rd
Casa Grande, AZ 85194-7230, USA

Young, Gerald (Athlete, Baseball Player)
10014 Rain Cloud Dr
Houston, TX 77095-2442, USA

Young, Guard (Athlete, Gymnast, Olympic Athlete)
1715 E 130 N
Spanish Fork, UT 84660-5789, USA

Young, H Edwin (Religious Leader)
Southern Baptist Convention
901 Commerce St Ste 400
Nashville, TN 37203-3628, USA

Young, Jacob (Actor)
c/o Alex D'Andrea *Edmonds Management*
1635 N Cahuenga Blvd Fl 5
Los Angeles, CA 90028-6201, USA

Young, James (Athlete, Football Player)
9630 Hillis St
Houston, TX 77078-2825, USA

Young, Jason (Athlete, Baseball Player)
1021 Washington St
San Francisco, CA 94108-1107, USA

Young, Jesse Colin (Musician, Songwriter, Writer)
Skyline Music
PO Box 31
Lancaster, NH 03584-0031, USA

Young, Jewell L (Basketball Player)
4480 Fairways Blvd Apt 203
Bradenton, FL 34209-8027, USA

Young, Jim (Coach, Football Coach)
US Military Academy
Athletic Dept
West Point, NY 10966, USA

Young, Joe (Athlete, Football Player)
33261 Windtree Ave
Wildomar, CA 92595-8235, USA

Young, John A (Business Person)
Norvell Inc
122 E 1700 S
Provo, UT 84606-6194, USA

Young, John Lloyd (Actor)
c/o Staff Member *Dona R Miller*
8391 Beverly Blvd
3378
Los Angeles, CA 90048-2633, USA

Young, Judith Knight (Actor)
Ann Steel
330 W 42nd St # 1800
New York, NY 10036-6902, USA

Young, Kathryn (Athlete, Golfer)
323 Date Ave
Imperial Beach, CA 91932-1915, USA

Young, Kathy (Musician)
Cape Entertainment
1161 NW 76th Ave
Plantation, FL 33322-5120, USA

Young, Keone (Actor)
Gage Group
14724 Ventura Blvd Ste 505
Sherman Oaks, CA 91403-3505, USA

Young, Kevin (Athlete, Baseball Player)
4793 E Charles Dr
Paradise Valley, AZ 85253-2427, USA

Young, Kevin (Athlete, Track Athlete)
8860 Corbin Ave
Northridge, CA 91324-3309, USA

Young, Kip (Athlete, Baseball Player)
1290 S Taylorsville Rd
Hillsboro, OH 45133-6729, USA

Young, Larry (Athlete, Baseball Player)
PO Box 255
Roscoe, IL 61073-0255, USA

Young, Laurence Retman (Astronaut)
PO Box 217
Waterville Valley, NH 03215-0217, USA

Young, Laurence R Prof (Astronaut)
PO Box 217
Waterville Valley, NH 03215-0217, USA

Young, Lonnie (Athlete, Football Player)
Express Personnel Services
6437 S Cedar St
Lansing, MI 48911-5960, USA

Young, M Adrian (Athlete, Football Player)
10300 4th St Ste 100
Rancho Cucamonga, CA 91730-5808, USA

Young, Mark L (Actor)
c/o Mia Hansen *Portrait PR*
5320 Sylmar Ave
Sherman Oaks, CA 91401-5612, USA

Young, Martin D (Misc)
1110 Marshall Rd # 2007
Greenwood, SC 29646-4216, USA

Young, Matt (Athlete, Baseball Player)

Young, Melissa (Actor)
Badgley Connor Talent
9229 W Sunset Blvd Ste 311
Los Angeles, CA 90069-3403, USA

Young, Michael (Athlete, Basketball Player)
6707 Broad Oaks Dr
Dr
Richmond, TX 77406-7629, USA

Young, Michael (Athlete, Baseball Player)
5038 Deloache Ave
Dallas, TX 75220-2004, USA

Young, Mighty Joe (Musician)
Jay Reil
3430 Bayberry Dr
Northbrook, IL 60062-2217, USA

Young, Mike (Athlete, Football Player)
20 Cherry Hills Farm Dr
Englewood, CO 80113-7165, USA

Young, Mike (Athlete, Baseball Player)
1166 Rockspring Way
Antioch, CA 94531-8308, USA

Young, Neil (Musician)
c/o Elliot Roberts *Lookout Management*
1460 4th St Ste 300
Santa Monica, CA 90401-3415, USA

Young, Nick (Athlete, Basketball Player)
c/o Mark Bartelstein *Priority Sports & Entertainment (Chicago)*
325 N La Salle Dr Ste 650
Chicago, IL 60654-8182, USA

Young, Nina (Actor)
c/o Staff Member *BBC Television Centre*
Incoming Mail
Wood Lane
London W12 7RJ, UNITED KINGDOM

Young, Parker (Actor)
c/o Mona Loring *Status PR*
PO Box 6191
Westlake Village, CA 91359-6191, USA

Young, Paul (Musician)
What Mgmt
PO Box 1463
Culver City, CA 90232-1463, USA

Young, Pete (Athlete, Baseball Player)
PO Box 95
Summit, MS 39666-0095, USA

Young, Peter (Misc)
1902 Coldwater Canyon Dr
Beverly Hills, CA 90210-1731, USA

Young, Ric (Actor)
c/o Staff Member *Coast to Coast Talent Group*
3350 Barham Blvd
Los Angeles, CA 90068-1404, USA

Young, Richard (Actor)
1275 Westwood Blvd
Los Angeles, CA 90024-4811, USA

Young, Rickey (Athlete, Football Player)
1768 Pinehurst Ave
Saint Paul, MN 55116-2117, USA

Young, Robert (Athlete, Football Player)
RR 7 Box 306
Carthage, MS 39051, USA

Young, Roynell (Athlete, Football Player)
11823 Beinhorn Dr
Houston, TX 77065-1607, USA

Young, Sam (Athlete, Football Player)
c/o Drew Rosenhaus *Rosenhaus Sports Representation*
3921 Alton Rd # 440
Miami Beach, FL 33140-3852, USA

Young, Scott (Athlete, Hockey Player, Olympic Athlete)
17 Sandy Ridge Rd
Sterling, MA 01564-2361, USA

Young, Sean (Actor)
c/o David Shapira *David Shapira & Associates*
193 N Robertson Blvd
Beverly Hills, CA 90211-2103, USA

Young, Shelby (Actor)
c/o Katie Mason Stern *Luber Roklin Management*
5815 W Sunset Blvd Ste 208
Los Angeles, CA 90028-6481, USA

Young, Steve (Athlete, Football Player, Sportscaster)
245 Southwood Dr
Palo Alto, CA 94301-3137, USA

Young, Tim (Athlete, Baseball Player, Olympic Athlete)
20730 SE Sherry Ave
Blountstown, FL 32424-2265, USA

Young, Tim (Athlete, Hockey Player)
15808 Park Terrace Dr
Eden Prairie, MN 55346-2433, USA

Young, Tom (Coach)
Washington Wizards
601 F St NW
Washington, DC 20004-1605, USA

Young, Tyler (Actor)
c/o Bryan Leder *Authentic Talent & Literary Management*
3615 Eastham Dr # 650
Culver City, CA 90232-2410, USA

Young, Ulysses (Athlete, Baseball Player)
4023 W 60th St
Los Angeles, CA 90043-3636, USA

Young, Usama (Athlete, Football Player)

Young, Vince (Athlete, Football Player)
c/o Denise White *EAG Sports Management*
909 N Pacific Coast Hwy Ste 360
El Segundo, CA 90245-3864, USA

Young, Vincent (Actor)
Don Buchwald
5900 Wilshire Blvd Ste 3100
Los Angeles, CA 90036-5030, USA

Young, Walter (Athlete, Baseball Player)
134 Center St
Purvis, MS 39475-4540, USA

Young, Warren (Athlete, Hockey Player)
5960 Murray Ave
Bethel Park, PA 15102-3489, USA

Young, Wayne (Athlete, Gymnast, Olympic Athlete)
1136 E Mahogany Ln
Pleasant Grove, UT 84062-2069, USA

Young, Wendell (Athlete, Hockey Player)
2301 Ravine Way
Attn: General Manager
Glenview, IL 60025-7627, USA

Young, Wendell (Athlete, Hockey Player)
1616 E Campbell St
Arlington Heights, IL 60004-6550, USA

Young, Wilbur (Athlete, Football Player)
121 W Bannister Rd
Kansas City, MO 64114-4010, USA

Young, Wiliam Paul (Writer)
Wind Rumors Inc
PO Box 2107
Oregon City, OR 97045-0107, USA

Young, Will (Musician)
c/o Simon Fuller *XIX Entertainment (UK)*
32/33 Ransomes Dock
London SW11 4NP, UNITED KINGDOM (UK)

Young, William Allen (Actor)
c/o Staff Member *Artists & Representatives (Stone Manners Salners)*
6100 Wilshire Blvd Ste 1500
Los Angeles, CA 90048-5110, USA

Young, Willie (Athlete, Football Player)

Youngberg, Renae (Athlete, Baseball Player)
PO Box 217
Eden, WI 53019, USA

Youngblood, George (Athlete, Football Player)
16429 Lazare Ln
Huntington Beach, CA 92649-1862, USA

Youngblood, H Jackson (Jack) (Athlete, Football Player, Sportscaster)
4377 Steed Ter
Winter Park, FL 32792-7630, USA

Youngblood, Jimmy L (Jim) (Athlete, Football Player)
322 Allendale Rd
Oxford, AL 36203-9738, USA

Youngblood, Joel (Athlete, Baseball Player)
4446 E Camelback Rd Unit 113
Phoenix, AZ 85018-2837, USA

Youngblood, Rob (Actor)
1604 N Vista St
Los Angeles, CA 90046-2818, USA

Youngblood, Sydney (Musician)
Postfach 20 13 43
Hamburg D-29243, GERMANY

Youngblood Brass Band (Music Group)
c/o Andy Duggan *Primary Talent International (UK)*
10-11 Jockeys Fields
The Primary Bldg
London WC1R 4BN, UNITED KINGDOM

Youngen, Lois (Athlete, Baseball Player)
45 Prall Ln
Eugene, OR 97405-3335, USA

Younger, Ben (Director, Writer)
c/o Joseph Cohen *Creative Artists Agency (CAA)*
2000 Avenue of the Stars Ste 100
Los Angeles, CA 90067-4705, USA

Youngerman, Jack (Artist)
PO Box 508
Bridgehampton, NY 11932-0508, USA

Youngfellow, Barrie (Actor)
c/o Staff Member *The Gage Group*
5757 Wilshire Blvd Ste 659
Los Angeles, CA 90036-3682, USA

Young Gunz (Musician)
c/o Staff Member *Roc-A-Fella Records*
825 8th Ave Fl 23
New York, NY 10019-7472, USA

Younghans, Tom (Athlete, Hockey Player)
6133 Sheridan Ave S
Minneapolis, MN 55410-2917, USA

Young Jeezy (Musician)
Corporate Thugs Entertainment
2221 Peachtree Rd NE Ste D602
Atlanta, GA 30309-1148, USA

Young Jr, Walter R (Business Person)
Champion Enterprises
2710 University Dr
Auburn Hills, MI 48326, USA

Young Knives, The (Music Group)
c/o Staff Member *Paradigm (Monterey)*
404 W Franklin St
Monterey, CA 93940-2303, USA

Young MC (Musician)
Universal Attractions
145 W 57th St # 1500
New York, NY 10019-2220, USA

Young Turks (Internet Star)
c/o Pete Axtman *Sunshine Sachs*
720 Cole Ave
Los Angeles, CA 90038-3606, USA

Yount, Larry (Athlete, Baseball Player)
5701 E Mockingbird Ln
Paradise Valley, AZ 85253-2221, USA

Yount, Robin (Athlete, Baseball Player)
5040 E Shea Blvd Ste 254
Scottsdale, AZ 85254-4687, USA

Yount, Robin R (Athlete, Baseball Player)
5040 E Shea Blvd Ste 254
Scottsdale, AZ 85254-4687, USA

Yousafzai, Malala (Activist)
c/o Karolina Sutton *Curtis Brown Ltd*
28-29 Hay Market
Hay Market House
London SW1Y 4SP, UNITED KINGDOM

Youso, Frank (Athlete, Football Player)
1931 2nd Ave
International Falls, MN 56649-3452, USA

Youssef, Bassem (Comedian)
c/o Matt Sadeghian *Avalon Management*
9171 Wilshire Blvd Ste 320
Beverly Hills, CA 90210-5516, USA

Youssoufi, Abdderrahmane El (Prime Minister)
Prime Minister's Office
Rabat, MOROCCO

Yowarsky, Walt (Athlete, Football Player)
395 Dogwood Pl NW
Cleveland, TN 37312-4414, USA

Yo-Yo (Musician)
William Morris Agency
1325 Avenue of the Americas
New York, NY 10019-6026, USA

Y. Schwartz, Allyson (Congressman, Politician)
1227 Longworth Hob
Washington, DC 20515-1403, USA

Ysebaert, Paul (Athlete, Hockey Player)
865 St Clair Pkwy RR 1
Mooretown, ON N0N 1M0, CANADA

Yu, Ronnie (Director, Producer)
c/o Richard Arlook *The Arlook Group*
11663 Gorham Ave Apt 5
Los Angeles, CA 90049-4749, USA

Yuan, Ron (Actor)
c/o Staff Member *MiniFlix Films*
5440 Tujunga Ave Apt 514
N Hollywood, CA 91601-4968, USA

Yuasa, Joji (Composer, Musician)
1517 Shields Ave
Encinitas, CA 92024-2911, USA

Yue Jingyu (Swimmer)
Physical Culture/Sports Bureau
9 Tiyuguan Road
Beijing, CHINA

Yuen, Corey (Actor, Director)
c/o Steve Chasman *Current Entertainment*
9378 Wilshire Blvd Ste 210
Beverly Hills, CA 90212-3167, USA

Yuh Nelson, Jennifer (Actor)
c/o Tanya Cohen *WME/IMG*
9601 Wilshire Blvd
Beverly Hills, CA 90210-5213, USA

Yulin, Harris (Actor)
40 W 86th St # 5C
New York, NY 10024-3605, USA

Yune, Johnny (Actor, Comedian)
1921 Scenic Sunrise Dr
Las Vegas, NV 89117-7237, USA

Yune, Rick (Actor)
c/o David Gardner *Artists First*
9465 Wilshire Blvd Ste 900
Beverly Hills, CA 90212-2608, USA

Yun-Fat, Chow (Actor)
c/o Samantha Mast *Rogers & Cowan*
1840 Century Park E Fl 18
Los Angeles, CA 90067-2101, USA

Yung, Elodie (Actor)
c/o Elizabeth Simpson *Agence Elizabeth Simpson*
59 Rue De Richelieu
Paris 75002, FRANCE

Yunis, Jorge J (Misc)
Thomas Jefferson University
Jefferson Medical College
Philadelphia, PA 19107, USA

Yun Lee, Will (Actor)
c/o Sam Maydew *Silver Lining Entertainment*
421 S Beverly Dr Fl 7
Beverly Hills, CA 90212-4408, USA

Yurak, Jeff (Athlete, Baseball Player)
PO Box 1931
Sumner, WA 98390-0420, USA

Yushchenko, Victor (President)
President's Office
Bankova Str 11
Kiev 01220, UKRAINE

Yushkevich, Dmitri (Athlete, Hockey Player)
878 Ridge View Way
Franklin Lakes, NJ 07417-1524, USA

Yusuke, Yamamoto (Actor)
c/o Staff Member *Ever Green Entertainment*
3-12-7-1009 Kita Aoyama
Minato
Tokyo, Japan

Ywecic, Tom (Athlete, Football Player)
21 Crescent St APT 332
Wakefield, MA 01880-2458, USA

Yzerman, Steve (Athlete, Hockey Player)
401 Channelside Dr
Attn: General Manager
Tampa, FL 33602-5400, USA

Zaa, Charlie (Musician)
c/o Staff Member *Sony Music (Miami)*
404 Washington Ave Ste 700
Miami Beach, FL 33139-6615, USA

Zabaleta, Nicanor (Musician)
Villa Izar
Aldapeta
San Sebasatian 20009, SPAIN

Zabarain, Ines (Actor)
c/o Staff Member *TV Caracol*
Calle 76 #11 - 35
Piso 10AA
Bogota DC 26484, COLOMBIA

Zabel, Mark (Athlete)
Grosse Fischerei 18A
Calbe/Saale 39240, GERMANY

Zabel, Steven G (Steve) (Athlete, Football Player)
6000 Oak Tree Rd
Edmond, OK 73025-2625, USA

Zabiela, James (DJ, Musician)
c/o Joel Zimmerman *WME/IMG (NY)*
11 Madison Ave Fl 18
New York, NY 10010-3669, USA

Zabka, William (Actor)
c/o Gary Ousdahl *Advanced Management*
8033 W Sunset Blvd # 935
Los Angeles, CA 90046-2401, USA

Zaborowski, Robert R J M (Religious Leader)
Mariavite Old Catholic Church
2803 10th St
Wyandotte, MI 48192-4994, USA

Zabransky, Libor (Athlete, Hockey Player)
Rybarska specialka Zabransky Koliste 59
Brno 602 00, Czech Republic

Zabriski, Bruce (Athlete, Golfer)
6228 Winding Lake Dr
Jupiter, FL 33458-3787, USA

Zabriskie, Grace (Actor)
1536 Murray Dr
Los Angeles, CA 90026-1646, USA

Zac Brown Band (Music Group)
c/o John Huie *Creative Artists Agency (CAA)*
401 Commerce St PH
Nashville, TN 37219-2516, USA

Zachar, Jacob (Actor)
c/o Jamie Freed *Paris Hilton Entertainment*
2934 1/2 N Beverly Glen Cir # 383
Los Angeles, CA 90077-1724, USA

Zachara, Jan (Boxer)
Sladkovicova 13
Nova Dubnica 01851, CZECH REPUBLIC

Zachary, Ken (Football Player)
San Diego Chargers
General Delivery
Newalla, OK 74857-9999, USA

Zachry, Pat (Athlete, Baseball Player)
3102 Barton Point Dr
Austin, TX 78733-6318, USA

Zackham, Justin (Director, Producer)
8489 Crescent Dr
Los Angeles, CA 90046-1802, USA

Zadegan, Necar (Actor)
c/o Liza Anderson *Anderson Group Public Relations*
8060 Melrose Ave Fl 4
Los Angeles, CA 90046-7038, USA

Zadel, C William (Business Person)
Millipore Corp
80 Ashby Rd
Bedford, MA 01730-2200, USA

Zadora, Pia (Actor)
69 Hawk Ridge Dr
Las Vegas, NV 89135-7864, USA

Zafferani, Rosa (Misc)
Co-Regent's Office
Government Palace
47031, SAN MARINO

Zagar, Jeremiah (Director)
c/o Dan Janvey *Untitled Entertainment (NY)*
215 Park Ave S Fl 8
New York, NY 10003-1622, USA

Zagaria, Anita (Actor)
Carol Levi Co
Via Giuseppe Pisanelli
Rome 00196, ITALY

Zaglmann-Willinger, Cornelia (Director)
Siegfriedstr 9
Munich 80802, GERMANY

Zagurski, Mike (Athlete, Baseball Player)
2723 Via Capri Unit 819
Clearwater, FL 33764-3991, USA

Zaharko, Miles (Athlete, Hockey Player)
GD
Two Hills, AB T0B 4K0, Canada

Zahn, Geoff (Athlete, Baseball Player)
6536 Walsh Rd
Dexter, MI 48130-9656, USA

Zahn, Paula (Journalist)
188 E 76th St Apt 26A
New York, NY 10021-2856, USA

Zahn, Steve (Actor)
c/o Marsha McManus *Principal Entertainment*
9255 W Sunset Blvd Ste 500
Los Angeles, CA 90069-3301, USA

Zahn, Timothy (Writer)
PO Box 1755
Coos Bay, OR 97420-0340, USA

Zaillian, Steve (Director, Producer)
30918 Broad Beach Rd
Malibu, CA 90265-2664, USA

Zaine, Rod (Athlete, Hockey Player)
64 Drouin Ave
Ottawa, ON K1K 2A7, Canada

Zajac, Travis (Athlete, Hockey Player)
1016 Smith Manor Blvd
West Orange, NJ 07052-4227, USA

Zakaria, Fareed (Commentator, Television Host)
c/o Staff Member *CNN (NY)*
10 Columbus Cir
Time Warner Center
New York, NY 10019-1158, USA

Zakarian, Geoffrey (Chef)
c/o Jaret Keller *Key Group Worldwide*
300 E 71st St Apt 11K
New York, NY 10021-5248, USA

Zaki, Zeeko (Actor)
c/o Susan Tolar Walters *STW Talent*
PO Box 16675
Wilmington, NC 28408-6675, USA

Zaklinsky, Konstantin (Dancer)
Mariinsky Theater
Teatralnaya Square 1
Saint Petersburg 190000, RUSSIA

Zaks, Jerry (Director)
c/o Susan Weaving *WME/IMG (NY)*
11 Madison Ave Fl 18
New York, NY 10010-3669, USA

Zal, Roxana (Actor)
c/o Staff Member *Main Title Entertainment*
8383 Wilshire Blvd Ste 408
Beverly Hills, CA 90211-2435, USA

Zalapski, Zarley (Athlete, Hockey Player)
Eishockey Club
Olten AG Postfach 523
Olten, PA CH-4601, USA

Zale, Richard N (Misc)
724 Santa Ynez St
Stanford, CA 94305-8441, USA

Zall, Alexis G (Actor)
c/o Maggie Haskins *Artists First*
9465 Wilshire Blvd Ste 900
Beverly Hills, CA 90212-2608, USA

Zalnasky, Mitch (Athlete, Football Player)
18 Scalena Pl
Winnipeg, MB R3K 1Y2, Canada

Zaloom, Paul (Actor, Writer)
c/o Wayne Alexander *Alexander, Nau, Lawrence, Frumes & Labowitz*
1925 Century Park E Ste 850
Los Angeles, CA 90067-2709, USA

Zamba, Frieda (Misc)
2706 S Central Ave
Flagler Beach, FL 32136-4037, USA

Zambrano, Carlos (Athlete, Baseball Player)
c/o Staff Member *Chicago Cubs Spring Training*
HoHoKam Stadium
1235 N St
Mesa, AZ 85201, USA

Zambri, Chris (Athlete, Golfer)
1329 La Culebra Cit
Camarillo, CA 93012-5551, USA

Zamka, George D (Astronaut)
1936 Mandy Ln
League City, TX 77573-3991, USA

Zamora, Oscar (Athlete, Baseball Player)
5301 SW 98th Ct
Miami, FL 33165-7244, USA

Zamora, Tye (Musician)
1215 Pamplona Dr
Riverside, CA 92508-8731, USA

Zampini, Carina (Actor)
c/o Staff Member *Telefe (Argentina)*
Pavon 2444
Buenos Aires C1248AAT, ARGENTINA

Zamprogna, Dominic (Actor)

Zamuner, Rob (Athlete, Hockey Player)
4317 Beau Rivage Cir
Lutz, FL 33558-5353, USA

Zander, Carl (Athlete, Football Player)
2536 W Palomino Dr
Chandler, AZ 85224-1639, USA

Zander, Robin (Musician)
2106 Scarlet Oaks St
Clearwater, FL 33759-1608, USA

Zander, Thomas (Wrestler)
Grundfeldstr 23
Aalen 73432, GERMANY

Zanders, Emanuel (Athlete, Football Player)
11015 Goodwood Blvd
Baton Rouge, LA 70815-5222, USA

Zane, Billy (Actor)
c/o Chris Dennis *Underground Management*
1180 S Beverly Dr Ste 509
Los Angeles, CA 90035-1157, USA

Zane, Frank (Fitness Expert)
PO Box 1964
La Mesa, CA 91944-1964, USA

Zane, Lisa (Actor)
505 N Lake Shore Dr Apt 2812
Chicago, IL 60611-6420, USA

Zanes, Dan (Musician, Songwriter, Writer)
c/o Harriet Sternberg *Harriet Sternberg Management*
4530 Gloria Ave
Encino, CA 91436-2718, USA

Zanetti, Eugenio (Actor, Director)
c/o Frank Wuliger *Gersh*
9465 Wilshire Blvd Ste 600
Beverly Hills, CA 90212-2605, USA

Zang, Nat (Actor)
c/o Nick Campbell *Velocity Entertainment Partners*
5455 Wilshire Blvd Ste 1502
Los Angeles, CA 90036-4204, USA

Zanier, Mike (Athlete, Hockey Player)
306 Rossland Ave
Trail, BC V1R 3M8, Canada

Zanni, Dom (Athlete, Baseball Player)
7 Sussex Ave
Massapequa, NY 11758-2434, USA

Zano, Nick (Actor)
c/o John Carrabino *John Carrabino Management*
5900 Wilshire Blvd Ste 740
Los Angeles, CA 90036-5032, USA

Zanon, Greg (Athlete, Hockey Player)
11839 58th St N
Lake Elmo, MN 55042-6106, USA

Zanotto, Kendra (Athlete, Olympic Athlete, Swimmer)
18834 Lakeview Ct
Los Gatos, CA 95033-9593, USA

Zanuck, Lili Fini (Director, Producer)
Zanuck Co
1131 Miradero Rd
Beverly Hills, CA 90210-2531, USA

Zanuck, Ron (Athlete, Hockey Player)
1135 Trailwood N
Hopkins, MN 55343-7914, USA

Zanussi, Joe (Athlete, Hockey Player)
1192 Shutek Dr
Trail, BC V1R 4R2, Canada

Zanussi, Krzysztof (Director)
Ul Kaniowska 114
Warsaw 01-529, POLAND

Zanussi, Ron (Athlete, Hockey Player)
PO Box 11326
Saint Paul, MN 55111-0326, USA

Zapalac, Willie (Athlete, Football Player)
1400 Shannon Oaks Trl
Austin, TX 78746-7345, USA

Zapata, Laura (Actor)
c/o Staff Member *Televisa*
Blvd Adolfo Lopez Mateos 232
Colonia San Angel INN
DF CP 01060, MEXICO

Zapiec, Chuck (Athlete, Football Player)
PO Box 6055
Hilton Head Island, SC 29938-6055, USA

Zapp, Jim (Athlete, Baseball Player)
Baltimore Elite Giants
820 Youngs Ln
Nashville, TN 37207-4828, USA

Zappa, Ahmet (Actor, Producer, Writer)
114 N McCadden Pl
Los Angeles, CA 90004-1022, USA

Zappa, Dweezil (Actor, Musician)
10508 Woodbridge St
Toluca Lake, CA 91602-2825, USA

Zappa, Moon (Musician)
PO Box 5265
N Hollywood, CA 91616-5265, USA

Zara, Lucy (Actor, Model)

Zarate, Carlos (Boxer)
Gene Aguilera
PO Box 113
Montebello, CA 90640-0113, USA

Zardon, Jose (Athlete, Baseball Player)
8209 NW 58th Pl
Tamarac, FL 33321-4522, USA

Zarin, Jill (Reality Star)
c/o Darren Bettencourt *The Representatives*
Prefers to be contacted by phone/email.
New York, NY NA, USA

Zarley, Kermit (Athlete, Golfer)
16600 N Thompson Peak Pkwy Unit 2081
Scottsdale, AZ 85260-2185, USA

Zarnas, August C (Gust) (Athlete, Football Player)
850 Jennings St
Bethlehem, PA 18017-7010, USA

Zaske, Jeff (Athlete, Baseball Player)
2404 185th Pl SE
Bothell, WA 98012-6999, USA

Zastudil, Dave (Athlete, Football Player)
c/o Neil Cornrich *NC Sports, LLC*
best to contact via email
Columbus, OH 43201, USA

Zatkoff, Roger (Athlete, Football Player)
5726 Woodwind Dr
Bloomfield Hills, MI 48301-1068, USA

Zatopkova, Dana (Athlete, Track Athlete)
Nad Kazankov 3
Prague 7 171 00, CZECH REPUBLIC

Zaun, Gregg (Athlete, Baseball Player)
2613 Grand Lakeside Dr
Palm Harbor, FL 34684-1028, USA

Zaunbrecher, Godfrey (Athlete, Football Player)
532 Pacific St
Elkhorn, NE 68022, USA

Zavada, Clay (Athlete, Baseball Player)
1113 N 1850th Rd
Streator, IL 61364-9327, USA

Zavaleta, Cara (Actor, Model)
c/o Staff Member *Gersh*
9465 Wilshire Blvd Ste 600
Beverly Hills, CA 90212-2605, USA

Zavaras, Clint (Athlete, Baseball Player)
9675 S Thimbleberry Way
Parker, CO 80134-8860, USA

Zavisha, Brad (Athlete, Hockey Player)
GD
Hines Creek, AB T0H 2A0, Canada

Zawadzkas, Gerald (Athlete, Football Player)
2712 Alcazar St NE
Albuquerque, NM 87110-3514, USA

zawadzki, lance (Athlete, Baseball Player)
259 Cordaville Rd
Southborough, MA 01772-2085, USA

Zayas, David (Actor)
c/o Andrew Tetenbaum *ATA Management (NY)*
85 Broad St Fl 18
New York, NY 10004-2783, USA

Z. Bordallo, Madeleine (Congressman, Politician)
2441 Rayburn Hob
Washington, DC 20515-1604, USA

Zdeb, Joe (Athlete, Baseball Player)
5225 Rosehill Rd
Shawnee, KS 66216-1465, USA

Zduriencik, Jack (Baseball Player)
1012 Old Orchard Dr
Gibsonia, PA 15044-6080, USA

Zea, Natalie (Actor)
c/o Robert Semon *True Management*
8964 W 25th St
Los Angeles, CA 90034-2012, USA

Zeal, Meredith (Actor)
c/o Marv Dauer *Marv Dauer Management*
11661 San Vicente Blvd Ste 104
Los Angeles, CA 90049-5150, USA

Zeber, George (Athlete, Baseball Player)
13101 Barrett Hill Cir
Santa Ana, CA 92705-6301, USA

Zecher, Rich (Athlete, Football Player)
PO Box 1859
Eureka, MT 59917-1859, USA

Zedd (DJ, Musician)
c/o Clayton Blaha *Biz 3 Publicity*
1321 N Milwaukee Ave # 452
Chicago, IL 60622-9151, USA

Zedillo Ponce de Leon, Ernesto (Politician, President)
Institutional Revolutionary
Insurges N 61
Mexico City, DF 06350, MEXICO

Zedlitz, Jean (Athlete, Golfer)
4587 Gatetree Cir
Pleasanton, CA 94566-6031, USA

Zednik, Richard (Athlete, Hockey Player)
4401 N Federal Hwy
Boca Raton, FL 33431-5164, USA

Zee, Joe (Designer, Journalist, Reality Star)
c/o Ennis Kamcili *United Talent Agency (UTA)*
9336 Civic Center Dr
Beverly Hills, CA 90210-3604, USA

Zee, Ona (Adult Film Star)
2523A Folsom St
San Francisco, CA 94110-2621, USA

Zegen, Michael (Actor)
c/o Jennifer Sims *Imprint PR*
375 Hudson St
New York, NY 10014-3658, USA

Zegers, Kevin (Actor)
12841 Woodbridge St Unit 12
Studio City, CA 91604-1503, USA

Zegler, Rachel (Actor)
c/o Alyx Carr *42West*
600 3rd Ave Fl 23
New York, NY 10016-1914, USA

Zeh, Geoffrey N (Misc)
Maintenance of Way Employees Brotherhood
12050 Woodward Ave
Detroit, MI 48203-3578, USA

Zehetner, Nora (Actor)
c/o Staff Member *Anonymous Content*
3532 Hayden Ave
Culver City, CA 90232-2413, USA

Zeier, Eric (Athlete, Football Player)
PO Box 327
Nashville, GA 31639-0327, USA

Zeigler, Alma (Athlete, Baseball Player)
403 Gold St
Auburn, CA 95603-5521, USA

Zeigler, Dusty (Athlete, Football Player)
440 Hodgeville Rd
Guyton, GA 31312-7103, USA

Zeigler, Heidi (Actor)
c/o Staff Member *Mary Grady Agency (MGA)*
4400 Coldwater Canyon Ave Ste 135
the Landmark Bldg
Studio City, CA 91604-5038, USA

Zeigler, Marie (Athlete, Baseball Player)
3037 N 24th Dr
Phoenix, AZ 85015-5681, USA

Zeile, Todd E (Actor, Athlete, Baseball Player, Producer)
5445 Via Nicola
Newbury Park, CA 91320-6884, USA

Zeilic, Mauricio (Actor)
c/o Staff Member *Telemundo*
2470 W 8th Ave
Hialeah, FL 33010-2000, USA

Zeitler, Kevin (Athlete, Football Player)
c/o Joe Panos *Athletes First*
23091 Mill Creek Dr
Laguna Hills, CA 92653-1258, USA

Zelezny, Jan (Athlete, Track Athlete)
Rue Armady 683
Boleslav, CZECH REPUBLIC

Zell, Samuel (Business Person)
Itel Corp
2 N Riverside Plz
Chicago, IL 60606-2600, USA

Zellars, Ray (Athlete, Football Player)
1327 Island Ave
Pittsburgh, PA 15212-2845, USA

Zeller, Bart (Athlete, Baseball Player)
13885 E Lupine Ave
Scottsdale, AZ 85259-3719, USA

Zeller, David (Athlete, Basketball Player)
406 N Parkway Dr
Piqua, OH 45356-4424, USA

Zellner, Peppi (Athlete, Football Player)
31 Dew Pl
Forsyth, GA 31029-3302, USA

Zellweger, Renee (Actor, Musician, Producer)
c/o Dominique Appel *Imprint PR*
6121 W Sunset Blvd
Neuehouse
Los Angeles, CA 90028-6442, USA

Zelman, Aaron (Writer)
c/o Alan Rautbourt *Circle of Confusion*
8931 Ellis Ave
Los Angeles, CA 90034-3336, USA

Zelmani, Sophie (Musician)
United Stage Artists
PO Box 11029
Stockholm 100 61, SWEDEN

Zeman, Ed (Athlete, Football Player)
3002 Jeffrey Dr Apt C
Costa Mesa, CA 92626-6945, USA

Zeman, E Robert (Athlete, Football Player)
PO Box 132907
Big Bear Lake, CA 92315-8998, USA

Zeman, Jacklyn (Actor)
STone Manners
6500 Wilshire Blvd # 550
Los Angeles, CA 90048-4920, USA

Zeman, Milos (Prime Minister)
Premier's Office
Nabrezi E Benese 4
Prague 1 118 01, CZECH REPUBLIC

Zemanova, Veronica (Model)
Veronica Zemanova Management
G Noodtstr 12 SW
Nijmegen 06511, NETHERLANDS

Zembriski, Walter (Athlete, Golfer)
6507 Doubletrace Ln
Orlando, FL 32819-4653, USA

Zemeckis, Robert (Director, Producer)
c/o Staff Member *ImageMovers*
100 Universal City Plz Ste 484
Universal City, CA 91608-1002, USA

Zemlak, Richard (Athlete, Hockey Player)
20681 Keystone Ave
Lakeville, MN 55044-6123, USA

Zemlin, Matt (Actor)
c/o Staff Member *Independent Talent Group*
40 Whitfield St
London W1T 2RH, UNITED KINGDOM

Zendaya (Actor, Musician)
c/o Jessie Greene *Monster Talent Management*
6333 W 3rd St Ste 912
Los Angeles, CA 90036-3176, USA

Zendejas, Luis (Athlete, Football Player)
6609 S 47th Pl
Phoenix, AZ 85042-5352, USA

Zender, Hans (Composer)
Am Rosenheck
Bad Soden 65812, GERMANY

Zender, Stuart (Musician)
Searles
Chapel
26A Munster St
London SW6 4EN, UNITED KINGDOM (UK)

Zennstrom, Niklas (Business Person)
Atomico
50 New Bond St
London W1S 1BJ, UK

Zeno, Lance (Athlete, Football Player)
530 Landfair Ave
Los Angeles, CA 90024-2104, USA

Zeno, Tony (Athlete, Basketball Player)
4419 Fulton Ave Apt 30
Sherman Oaks, CA 91423-5116, USA

Zent, Jason (Athlete, Hockey Player)
271 Dartmouth St Apt 4G
Boston, MA 02116-2827, USA

Zentmyer Jr, George A (Misc)
955 S El Camino Real # 216
San Mateo, CA 94402-2346, USA

Zepeda, David (Actor)
c/o Raul Xumalin *MAFAE Artist Management*
Amatlan 101B Int 103
Hipodromo Condesa
Mexico City 06170, MEXICO

Zephaniah, Benjamin (Actor, Writer)
18 Fountain Street
Ulverston LA12 7EQ, UNITED KINGDOM

Zepp, Bill (Athlete, Baseball Player)
15000 Farmbrook Dr
Plymouth, MI 48170-2748, USA

Zeppelin, Dread (Musician)
The M.O.B Agency
6404 Wilshire Blvd Ste 700
Los Angeles, CA 90048-5509

Zeppelin, Led (Music Group, Musician)
c/o Seth Rappaport *UTA/The Agency Group*
888 7th Ave Fl 7
New York, NY 10106-0700, USA

Zerbe, Anthony (Actor)
411 W 115th St Apt 51
New York, NY 10025-1730, USA

Zerbe, Chad (Athlete, Baseball Player)
7248 Palomino St
Highland, CA 92346-5032, USA

Zereoue, Amos (Athlete, Football Player)
116 Tanglewood Dr
Wexford, PA 15090-8692, USA

Zero, Mark (Musician)
PO Box 656507
Fresh Meadows, NY 11365-6507, USA

Zeta-Jones, Catherine (Actor)
c/o CeCe Yorke *True Public Relations*
3575 Cahuenga Blvd W Ste 360
Los Angeles, CA 90068-1361, USA

Zetsche, Dieter (Business Person)
Daimler-Chrysler AG
Plieningstr
Stuggart 70546, GERMANY

Zetterberg, Henrik (Athlete, Hockey Player)
1300 Division Rd Ste 202
Attn: Marc Levine
West Warwick, RI 02893-7558, USA

Zetterstrom, Lars (Athlete, Hockey Player)
Vikengatan 17C
Karlstad 65228, Sweden

Zettler, Rob (Athlete, Hockey Player)
Toronto Maple Leafs 400-40 Bay St
Attn: Coaching Staff
Toronto, ON M5J 2X2, Canada

Zgonina, Jeff (Athlete, Football Player)
4949 Marie P Debartolo Way
Santa Clara, CA 95054-1156, USA

Zhamnov, Alexei (Athlete, Hockey Player)
9601 Collins Ave Apt 509
Bal Harbour, FL 33154-2211, USA

Zhang, Xianliang (Writer)
Ningxia Writers Assn
Yinchuan City, CHINA

Zhang, Ziyi (Actor)
c/o Staff Member *Flying Box Co Ltd*
4F Parkside House
2 Ichibancho
Chiyoda-ku Tokyo 102-0082, JAPAN

Zherdev, Nikolai (Athlete, Hockey Player)
251 Daniel Burnham Sq # 253
Columbus, OH 43215-2681, USA

Zhe-Xi Lo (Misc)
Camegie Natural History Museum
4400 Forbes Ave
Pittsburgh, PA 15213-4007, USA

Zhislin, Grigory Y (Musician)
25 Whiteball Gardens
London W3 9RD, UNITED KINGDOM (UK)

Zhitnik, Alexei (Athlete, Hockey Player)
8 Boxwood Way
Manhasset, NY 11030-3938

Zhitnik, Alexel (Athlete, Hockey Player)
1 Seymour St
Buffalo, NY 14210, USA

Zhou Long (Composer)
University of Missouri
Music Dept
Kansas City, MO 64110, USA

Zhvanetsky, Mikhail M (Actor, Writer)
Lesnaya Str 4
#63
Moscow 125047, RUSSIA

Zia, B Khaleda (Prime Minister)
Sere-e Bangla Nagar
Gono
Bhaban Sher-e-Banglanagar
Dakah, BANGLADESH

Zicherman, Stu (Director)
c/o Staff Member *WME|IMG*
9601 Wilshire Blvd
Beverly Hills, CA 90210-5213, USA

Zick, Bob (Athlete, Baseball Player)
5228 W Diana Ave
Glendale, AZ 85302-4939, USA

Zickel, Mather (Actor)
c/o Marni Rosenzweig *The Rosenzweig Group*
8840 Wilshire Blvd # 111
Beverly Hills, CA 90211-2606, USA

Zidane, Zinedine (Athlete, Soccer Player)
Avenida De Concha Espina, 1
Estadio Santiago Bernabeu
Madrid E-28 036, Spain

Zidek, George (Athlete, Basketball Player)
551 Landfair Ave
Los Angeles, CA 90024-2172, USA

Zidlicky, Marek (Athlete, Hockey Player)
2006 Sweetbriar Ave
Nashville, TN 37212-5412, USA

Ziegelmeyer, Nicole (Athlete, Olympic Athlete, Speed Skater)
5908 Mastodon Pines Dr
Imperial, MO 63052-2175, USA

Ziegler, Alicia (Actor)
c/o Peter Himberger *Impact Artists Group LLC*
42 Hamilton Ter
New York, NY 10031-6403, USA

Ziegler, Brad (Athlete, Baseball Player)
14650 Cedar St
Overland Park, KS 66224-7800, USA

Ziegler, Larry (Athlete, Golfer)
10315 Luton Ct
Orlando, FL 32836-3733, USA

Ziegler, Mackenzie (Actor, Musician)
c/o Morgan Pesante *42West*
1840 Century Park E Ste 700
Los Angeles, CA 90067-2122, USA

Ziegler, Maddie (Actor)
c/o Katie Greenthal *The Lede Company*
9701 Wilshire Blvd # 930
Beverly Hills, CA 90212-2020, USA

Ziem, Steve (Athlete, Baseball Player)
79885 Fiesta Dr
La Quinta, CA 92253-4308, USA

Ziemann, Sonia (Actor)
Via del Alp Dorf
Saint Moritz 07500, SWITZERLAND

Zien, Chip (Actor)
c/o Staff Member *Gersh*
9465 Wilshire Blvd Ste 600
Beverly Hills, CA 90212-2605, USA

Zien, Sam (Chef, Producer, Television Host, Writer)
c/o Staff Member *Wiley John & Sons Incorporated*
111 River St Ste 2000
Author's Mail (Publicity)
Hoboken, NJ 07030-5790, USA

Ziering, Ian (Actor)
2700 Jalmia Dr
Los Angeles, CA 90046-1720, USA

Ziering, Nikki (Actor)
c/o Jerry Shandrew *Shandrew Public Relations*
1050 S Stanley Ave
Los Angeles, CA 90019-6634, USA

Zigomanis, Mike (Athlete, Hockey Player)
39 Jimston Dr
Markham, ON L3R 6R6, Canada

Zikarsky, Bengt (Swimmer)
SV Wurzburg 05
Oberer Bogenweg 1
Wurzburg 97074, GERMANY

Zikarsky, Bjorn (Swimmer)
555 California St Ste 2600
San Francisco, CA 94104-1602, USA

Zilinskas, Annette (Actor, Musician)
c/o Staff Member *Creative Artists Agency (CAA)*
2000 Avenue of the Stars Ste 100
Los Angeles, CA 90067-4705, USA

Zima, Madeline (Actor)
c/o John Carrabino *John Carrabino Management*
5900 Wilshire Blvd Ste 740
Los Angeles, CA 90036-5032, USA

Zima, Yvonne (Actor)
c/o Danny Mancini *Inspire Entertainment (LA)*
2332 Cotner Ave Ste 302
Los Angeles, CA 90064-1848, USA

Zimbalist, Stephanie (Actor, Writer)
c/o Staff Member *AMT Artists*
15260 Ventura Blvd Ste 1200
Sherman Oaks, CA 91403-5347, USA

Zimerman, Krystian (Musician)
Columbia Artists Mgmt Inc
165 W 57th St
New York, NY 10019-2201, USA

Zimm, Bruno H (Misc)
2522 Horizon Way
La Jolla, CA 92037-1122, USA

Zimmer, Constance (Actor)
c/o David Sweeney *Sweeney Entertainment*
1601 Vine St # 6
Los Angeles, CA 90028-8802, USA

Zimmer, Dawn (Politician)
59 Madison St Apt 2
Hoboken, NJ 07030-1805, USA

Zimmer, Hans (Composer, Musician)
6825 Zumirez Dr
Malibu, CA 90265-4316, USA

Zimmer, Norma (Actor)
661 Wood Lake Dr
Brea, CA 92821-2828

Zimmer, Tom (Athlete, Baseball Player)
7296 Marathon Dr Apt 602
Seminole, FL 33777-3837, USA

Zimmerer, Wolfgang (Athlete)
Schwaigangerstr 22
Mumau 82418, GERMANY

Zimmerlink, Geno (Athlete, Football Player)
318 Crestwood Dr
Milltown, NJ 08850-1849, USA

Zimmerman, Denny (Race Car Driver)
15 Downing Way
Suffield, CT 06078-2071, USA

Zimmerman, Don (Athlete, Football Player)
107 Coretta St
Monroe, LA 71202-6901, USA

Zimmerman, Gary W (Athlete, Football Player)
17450 Skyliners Rd
Bend, OR 97703-5203, USA

Zimmerman, H Leroy (Athlete, Football Player)
808 Willis Ace
Madera, CA 93637, USA

Zimmerman, Howard E (Misc)
7813 Westchester Dr
Middleton, WI 53562-3671, USA

Zimmerman, James M (Business Person)
Federated Department Stores
151 W 34th St
New York, NY 10001-2101, USA

Zimmerman, Jeff (Athlete, Baseball Player)
2416 Chippendale Rd
West Vancouver, BC V7S 3J2, Canada

Zimmerman, Jordan (Athlete, Baseball Player)
15436 W Alexandria Way
Surprise, AZ 85379-8107, USA

Zimmerman, Mary Beth (Athlete, Golfer)
2403 Bonshaw Ln
Marietta, GA 30064-5756, USA

Zimmerman, Philip (Phil) (Designer)
Network Assoc
4677 Old Ironsides Dr
Santa Clara, CA 95054-1809, USA

Zimmerman, Ryan (Athlete, Baseball Player)
524 Innsbruck Ave
Great Falls, VA 22066-2632, USA

Zimmermann, Egon (Skier)
Hotel Krisberg
Am Arlberg 67644, AUSTRIA

Zimmermann, Frank P (Musician)
Riaskoff Mgmt
Concertgebouwplein 15
Amsterdam 1071 LL, NETHERLANDS

Zimmermann, Markus (Athlete)
Waldhauserstr 51-33
Schonau am Konigsee 83471, GERMANY

Zimmermann, Udo (Composer)
Operhaus Leipzig
Augustusptatz
Leipzig 04109, GERMANY

Zimmern, Andrew (Chef, Television Host)
c/o Rebecca Brooks *Brooks Group*
10 W 37th St Fl 5
New York, NY 10018-7396, USA

Zim Zum (Musician)
c/o Staff Member *Mitch Schneider Organization (MSO)*
14724 Ventura Blvd Ste 410
Sherman Oaks, CA 91403-3537, USA

Zinczenko, David (Writer)
Rodale
33 E Minor St
Emmaus, PA 18098-0001, USA

Zink, Charlie (Athlete, Baseball Player)
893 Queen Victoria Ct
El Dorado Hills, CA 95762-4100, USA

Zinke, Olaf (Speed Skater)
Johannes Bobrowski Str 22
Berlin 12627, GERMANY

Zinner, Nick (Musician)
Yeah Yeah Yeahs
249 Metropolitan Ave
Brooklyn, NY 11211-4009, USA

Zinter, Alan (Athlete, Baseball Player)
3064 E Trigger Way
Gilbert, AZ 85297-6038, USA

Zipaladelli, Greg (Race Car Driver)
114 Whaling Ln
Mooresville, NC 28117-6034, USA

Zipfel, Bud (Athlete, Baseball Player)
57 Whiteside Dr
Belleville, IL 62221-2542, USA

Zippel, David (Musician)
Kraft-Benjamin-Engel
15233 Ventura Blvd Ste 200
Sherman Oaks, CA 91403-2244, USA

Zirinsky, Susan (Producer)
c/o Staff Member *CBS Television*
51 W 52nd St
New York, NY 10019-6119, USA

Zisk, Randall (Director, Producer)
1823 Old Ranch Rd
Los Angeles, CA 90049-2206, USA

Zisk, Richard W (Richie) (Athlete, Baseball Player)
4231 NE 26th Ter
Lighthouse Point, FL 33064-8053, USA

Zito, Barry (Athlete, Baseball Player)
9270 Kinglet Dr
Los Angeles, CA 90069-1114, USA

Zito, Chuck (Actor, Boxer)
c/o Darren Prince *Prince Marketing Group*
18 Seneca Trl
Sparta, NJ 07871-1514, USA

Zivkovic, Zoran (Prime Minister)
Prime Minister's Office
Nemanjina 11
Belgrade 11000, SERBIA

Zlotoff, Lee David (Director, Producer)
c/o Wendi Niad *Niad Management*
15021 Ventura Blvd Ste 860
Sherman Oaks, CA 91403-2442, USA

Zmed, Adrian (Actor)
3600 Redwood St
Las Vegas, NV 89103-1054, USA

Zmeskal, Kim (Gymnast)
Cincinnati Gymnastics Academy
3635 Woodridge Blvd
Fairfield, OH 45014-8521, USA

Zmievskaya Petrenko, Galina (Nina) (Coach)
International Skating Center
PO Box 577
Simsbury, CT 06070-0577, USA

Zmolek, Doug (Athlete, Hockey Player)
537 Frederichs Dr NW
Rochester, MN 55901-3840, USA

Zo, Edward (Actor)
c/o Eric Pan *Asian Cinema Entertainment*
8564 Hillside Ave
Los Angeles, CA 90069-1507, USA

Zobrist, Ben (Athlete, Baseball Player)
545 Overview Ln
Franklin, TN 37064-5557, USA

Zoccolillo, Pete (Athlete, Baseball Player)
11 Triumph Ct
Flanders, NJ 07836-4404, USA

Zoe, Deborah (Actor)
c/o Kim Matuka *Schuller Talent (LA)*
332 S Beverly Dr Ste 100
Beverly Hills, CA 90212-4812, USA

Zoe, Rachel (Reality Star, Talk Show Host, Television Host)
c/o Staff Member *ID Public Relations*
7060 Hollywood Blvd Fl 8th
Los Angeles, CA 90028-6021, USA

ZoeGirl (Music Group)
EMI Christian Music Group
101 Winners Cir N
Brentwood, TN 37027-5352, USA

Zoeller, Fuzzy (Athlete, Golfer)
418 Deer Run Trce
Floyds Knobs, IN 47119-8505

Zofko, Mickey (Athlete, Football Player)
321 W Fern Ave
Foley, AL 36535-2128, USA

Zokol, Richard (Athlete, Golfer)
Contemporary Communications
1663 7th Ave W
Vancouver, BC V6J 1S4, CANADA

Zolak, Scott (Athlete, Football Player)
40 Comstock Dr
Wrentham, MA 02093-1852, USA

Zolciak-Biermann, Kim (Reality Star)
c/o Staff Member *Bravo TV (NY)*
30 Rockefeller Plz
New York, NY 10112-0015, USA

Zolot, Natassia (Kreayshawn) (Musician)
c/o Matt Galle *Paradigm*
140 Broadway Ste 2600
New York, NY 10005-1011, USA

Zomalt, Eric (Athlete, Football Player)
25387 Delphinium Ave
Moreno Valley, CA 92553-7153, USA

Zombie, Rob (Musician)
Zombie HQ
8491 W Sunset Blvd Ste 215
West Hollywood, CA 90069-1911, USA

Zombie, Sheri Moon (Actor)
8491 W Sunset Blvd # 215
West Hollywood, CA 90069-1911, USA

Zombo, Frank (Athlete, Football Player)
c/o Joe Flanagan *BTI Sports Advisors*
615 South Blvd Apt C
Oak Park, IL 60302-4606, USA

Zombo, Rick (Athlete, Hockey Player)
2918 Ossenfort Rd
Glencoe, MO 63038-1718, USA

Zook, John E (Athlete, Football Player)
2951 N Governeour St APT 202
Wichita, KS 67226-1764, USA

Zook, Ron (Coach, Football Coach)
University of Illinois
Athletic Dept
Champaign, IL 61820, USA

Zopf, Bill (Athlete, Basketball Player)
351 Wealdstone Rd
Cranberry Township, PA 16066-8310, USA

Zophres, Mary (Designer)
c/o Staff Member *United Talent Agency (UTA)*
9336 Civic Center Dr
Beverly Hills, CA 90210-3604, USA

Zordich, Mike (Athlete, Football Player)
373 S Hazelwood Ave
Youngstown, OH 44509-2228, USA

Zorich, Christopher R (Chris) (Athlete, Football Player)
47 W Polk St Ste 100
Chicago, IL 60605-2085, USA

Zorn, James A (Jim) (Coach, Football Coach)
c/o Staff Member *Washington Redskins*
21300 Redskin Park Dr
Ashburn, VA 20147-6100, USA

Zorn, Jim (Athlete, Football Player)
2130 Brookwood Rd
Mission Hills, KS 66208-1225, USA

Zorrilla, Alberto (Swimmer)
580 Park Ave
New York, NY 10065-7313, USA

Zorrilla, China (Actor)
c/o Staff Member *Telefe (Argentina)*
Pavon 2444
Buenos Aires C1248AAT, ARGENTINA

Zosky, Eddie (Athlete, Baseball Player)
27471 Sky Harbour Rd
Friant, CA 93626-9767, USA

Zovatto, Daniel (Actor)
c/o Lena Roklin *Luber Roklin Management*
5815 W Sunset Blvd Ste 208
Los Angeles, CA 90028-6481, USA

Zubak, Kresimir (President)
Presidency
Marsala Titz 7A
Sarajevo 71000, BOSNIA-HERZEGOVINA

Zuber, Jon (Athlete, Baseball Player)
197 Fernwood Dr
Moraga, CA 94556-2315, USA

Zubov, Sergei (Athlete, Hockey Player)
3 Carriage Hill Rd
White Plains, NY 10604-1525, USA

Zubrus, Dainius (Athlete, Hockey Player)
9920 Bay Leaf Ct
Parkland, FL 33076-4444, USA

Zubrus, Dainus (Athlete, Hockey Player)
9920 Bay Leaf Ct
Parkland, FL 33076-4444, USA

Zucco, Victor (Athlete, Football Player)
2276 Wulfert Rd
Sanibel, FL 33957-2209, USA

Zucker, Arianne (Actor, Model)
4213 Beeman Ave
Studio City, CA 91604-1519, USA

Zucker, David (Director, Producer)
c/o Staff Member *Scott Free Productions*
42-44 Beak St
London W1F 9RH, UNITED KINGDOM

Zucker, Jeff (Business Person)
211 E 70th St Apt 21A
New York, NY 10021-5209, USA

Zucker, Jerry (Director, Producer)
c/o Staff Member *Zucker Productions*
1250 6th St Ste 201
Santa Monica, CA 90401-1637, USA

Zuckerberg, Mark (Business Person, Internet Star)
Facebook
1 Hacker Way Bldg 10
Menlo Park, CA 94025-1456, USA

Zuckerberg, Randi (Business Person)
c/o Stephanie Jones *Jonesworks*
211 E 43rd St Rm 1502
New York, NY 10017-4746, USA

Zuckerman, Andrew (Director, Producer)
c/o Jon Rubinstein *Authentic Talent and Literary Management (NY)*
20 Jay St Ste M17
Brooklyn, NY 11201-8300, USA

Zuckerman, Eugenia (Musician)
Brooklyn College of Music
Bedford & H Aves
Brooklyn, NY 11210, USA

Zuckerman, Josh (Actor)
c/o Anne Woodward *Authentic Talent & Literary Management*
3615 Eastham Dr # 650
Culver City, CA 90232-2410, USA

Zuckoff, Mitchell (Writer)
c/o Richard Abate *3 Arts Entertainment*
9460 Wilshire Blvd Fl 7
Beverly Hills, CA 90212-2713, USA

Zuger, Joe (Athlete, Football Player)
37 Fairgreen Close
Cambridge, ON N1T 1T7, Canada

Zugsmith, Albert (Director)
23388 Mulholland Dr
Woodland Hills, CA 91364-2733, USA

Zuiker, Anthony (Producer)
27033 Sea Vista Dr
Malibu, CA 90265-4434, USA

Zukav, Gary (Writer)
Fireside/Simon & Schuster
1230 Avenue of the Americas Fl CONC1
New York, NY 10020-1586, USA

Zuke, Mike (Athlete, Hockey Player)
430 Norman Gate Dr
Ballwin, MO 63011-2440, USA

Zuker, Danny (Producer, Writer)
c/o Keith Addis *Industry Entertainment Partners*
955 Carrillo Dr Ste 300
Los Angeles, CA 90048-5400, USA

Zukerman, Ashley (Actor)
c/o Lisa Mann *Lisa Mann Creative Management*
19-25 Cope St
Redfern NSW 02016, AUSTRALIA

Zukerman, Eugenia (Musician)
Brooklyn College of Music
Bedford & H Aves
Brooklyn, NY 11210, USA

Zuleta, Julio (Athlete, Baseball Player)
18251 Parkridge Ct
Fort Myers, FL 33908-4665, USA

Zullo, Alan (Cartoonist)
Tribune Media Services
435 N Michigan Ave Ste 1500
Chicago, IL 60611-4012, USA

Zuma, Jacob (Politician, President)
President's Office
Union Buildings
Pretoria 00001, SOUTH AFRICA

Zumann, Lucas Jade (Actor)
c/o Mark Modesitt *MODE Public Relations*
3450 Cahuenga Blvd W Apt 907
Los Angeles, CA 90068-1594, USA

Zumaya, Joel (Athlete, Baseball Player)
801 Auburn Ave
Chula Vista, CA 91913-2604, USA

Zumwalt, Jordan (Athlete, Football Player)
c/o Bruce Tollner *REP 1 Sports Group*
80 Technology Dr
Irvine, CA 92618-2301, USA

Zuniga, Daphne (Actor)
c/o Jonathan Baruch *Rain Management Group*
11162 La Grange Ave
Los Angeles, CA 90025-5632, USA

Zuniga, Jose (Actor)
c/o Laura Myones *McKeon-Myones Management*
3500 W Olive Ave Ste 770
Burbank, CA 91505-5527, USA

Zuniga, Markos Moulitsas (Writer)
c/o Staff Member *Puffin Publicity, Penguin Books (UK)*
80 Strand
London WC2R 0LR, UNITED KINGDOM

Zuniga, Miles (Musician)
c/o Staff Member *Russell Carter Artist Management*
567 Ralph McGill Blvd NE
Atlanta, GA 30312-1110, USA

Zupcic, Bob (Athlete, Baseball Player)
4309 Overbecks Ln
Waxhaw, NC 28173-7085, USA

Zupko, Ramon (Composer, Musician)
Western Michigan University
Music Dept
Kalamazoo, MI 49008, USA

Zurbriggen, Pirmin (Athlete, Skier)
Hotel Larchenhof
3905 Saas-Almagell
SWITZERLAND

Zurer, Ayelet (Actor)
c/o David Lillard *Industry Entertainment Partners*
955 Carrillo Dr Ste 300
Los Angeles, CA 90048-5400, USA

Zurkowski-Holmes, Agnes (Athlete, Baseball Player)
206-2339 Lorne St
Regina, SK S4P 2N2, CANADA

Zurrer, Emily (Athlete, Olympic Athlete, Soccer Player)
c/o Staff Member *Canadian Soccer*
237 Metcalfe St
Soccer Canada
Ottawa, ON K2P 1R2, CANADA

Zusi, Graham (Athlete, Soccer Player)
Sporting Kansas City
210 W 19th Ter Ste 200
Kansas City, MO 64108-2046, USA

Zuttah, Jeremy (Athlete, Football Player)

Zuvella, Paul (Athlete, Baseball Player)
2040 Canyon Crest Ave
San Ramon, CA 94582-4841, USA

Zuverink, George (Athlete, Baseball Player)
1027 E McNair Dr
Tempe, AZ 85283-4733, USA

Zvereva, Natasha (Athlete, Tennis Player)
c/o Staff Member *Women's Tennis Association (WTA-US)*
1 Progress Plz Ste 1500
St Petersburg, FL 33701-4335, USA

Zvonareva, Vera (Athlete, Tennis Player)
c/o Staff Member *SFX Sports (Miami)*
846 Lincoln Rd # 500
Miami Beach, FL 33139-2878, USA

Zwart, Harald (Director)
c/o Staff Member *Zwart Arbeid*
1158 26th St Ste 587
Santa Monica, CA 90403-4698, USA

Zweibel, Alan (Writer)
c/o Lee Kernis *Brillstein Entertainment Partners*
9150 Wilshire Blvd Ste 350
Beverly Hills, CA 90212-3453, USA

Zweig, Ivan (Athlete, Baseball Player)
6502 Duffield Dr
Dallas, TX 75248-1314, USA

Zwerling, Darrell (Actor)
c/o Staff Member *CLInc Talent*
843 N Sycamore Ave
Los Angeles, CA 90038-3316, USA

Zwick, Alyse (Actor, Model)
c/o Staff Member *OmniPop Talent Group*
4605 Lankershim Blvd Ste 201
Toluca Lake, CA 91602-1874, USA

Zwick, Edward (Actor, Director, Producer)
c/o Staff Member *Bedford Falls Company, The*
409 Santa Monica Blvd PH
Santa Monica, CA 90401-2232, USA

Zwick, Joel (Director)
c/o Brian Wilkins *LINK Entertainment*
11872 La Grange Ave
Los Angeles, CA 90025-5282, USA

Zwigoff, Terry (Director)
c/o Tracey Jacobs *United Talent Agency (UTA)*
9336 Civic Center Dr
Beverly Hills, CA 90210-3604, USA

Zwilich, Ellen Taaffe (Composer, Musician)
c/o Staff Member *Music Association of America*
224 King St
Englewood, NJ 07631-3026, USA

Zwilling, David (Athlete, Skier)
Hotel Zwilling Resort
Waldhof 64
5441 Rotenau/Voglau
AUSTRIA

Zydeco, Buckwheat (Musician)
c/o Staff Member *Concerted Efforts*
PO Box 440326
Somerville, MA 02144-0004, USA

Zyglis, Adam (Artist, Cartoonist)
Buffalo News
PO Box 100
Editorial Dept
Buffalo, NY 14220-0100, USA

Zylberstein, Elsa (Actor)
c/o Cecile Felsenberg *UBBA*
6 rue de Braque
Paris 75003, FRANCE

Zylka, Chris (Actor)
c/o Simon Halls *Slate PR*
901 N Highland Ave
W Hollywood, CA 90038-2412, USA

Zyman, Sergio (Business Person)
c/o Staff Member *BigSpeak*
23 S Hope Ave Ste E
Santa Barbara, CA 93105-5114, USA

Zyrus, Jake (Charice) (Musician)
c/o Edward Shapiro *Reed Smith*
599 Lexington Ave Fl 26
New York, NY 10022-7684, USA

Zyuzin, Andrei (Athlete, Hockey Player)
2426 Westgate Ave
San Jose, CA 95125-4039, USA

ZZ Top (Music Group)
Tower Top Tours Inc
PO Box 3238
Sugar Land, TX 77487-3238, USA

CPSIA information can be obtained
at www.ICGtesting.com
Printed in the USA
BVHW010726290719
554557BV00015B/323/P

9 781604 870176